PETERSON'S

GRADUATE PROGRAMS IN THE PHYSICAL SCIENCES, MATHEMATICS, AGRICULTURAL SCIENCES, THE ENVIRONMENT & NATURAL RESOURCES

2000

THIRTY-FOURTH EDITION

BOOK 4

Peterson's
Thomson Learning™

Australia • Canada • Denmark • Japan • Mexico • New Zealand • Philippines
Puerto Rico • Singapore • Spain • United Kingdom • United States

About Peterson's

Peterson's is the country's largest educational information/communications company, providing the academic, consumer, and professional communities with books, software, and online services in support of lifelong education access and career choice. Well-known references include Peterson's annual guides to private schools, summer programs, colleges and universities, graduate and professional programs, financial aid, international study, adult learning, and career guidance. Peterson's Web site at petersons.com is the only comprehensive—and most heavily traveled—education resource on the Internet. The site carries all of Peterson's fully searchable major databases and includes financial aid sources, test-prep help, job postings, direct inquiry and application features, and specially created Virtual Campuses for every accredited academic institution and summer program in the U.S. and Canada that offers in-depth narratives, announcements, and multimedia features.

The colleges and universities represented in this book recognize that federal laws, where applicable, require compliance with Title IX (Education Amendments of 1972), Title VII (Civil Rights Act of 1964), and Section 504 of the Rehabilitation Act of 1973 as amended, prohibiting discrimination on the basis of sex, race, color, handicap, or national or ethnic origin in their educational programs and activities, including admissions and employment.

Editorial inquiries concerning this book should be addressed to:
Editor, Peterson's, P.O. Box 2123, Princeton, New Jersey 08543-2123

ISSN 1093-8443
ISBN 0-7689-0270-3

Composition and design by Peterson's

Printed in the United States of America

10 9 8 7 6 5 4 3 2 1

Contents

Introduction

How to Use These Guides

OVERVIEW

The six volumes of Peterson's Annual Guides to Graduate Study, the only annually updated reference work of its kind, provide wide-ranging information on the graduate and professional programs offered by accredited colleges and universities in the United States and U.S. territories and by those institutions in Canada, Mexico, Europe, and Africa that are accredited by U.S. accrediting bodies. More than 37,000 individual academic and professional programs at more than 1,700 institutions are listed. Peterson's Annual Guides to Graduate Study have been used for more than thirty years by prospective graduate and professional students, placement counselors, faculty advisers, and all others interested in postbaccalaureate education.

- Book 1, *Graduate & Professional Programs: An Overview*, contains information on institutions as a whole, while Books 2 through 6 are devoted to specific academic and professional fields.
- Book 2—*Graduate Programs in the Humanities, Arts & Social Sciences*
- Book 3—*Graduate Programs in the Biological Sciences*
- Book 4—*Graduate Programs in the Physical Sciences, Mathematics, Agricultural Sciences, the Environment & Natural Resources*
- Book 5—*Graduate Programs in Engineering & Applied Sciences*
- Book 6—*Graduate Programs in Business, Education, Health, Information Studies, Law & Social Work*

The books may be used individually or as a set. For example, if you have chosen a field of study but do not know what institution you want to attend or if you have a college or university in mind but have not chosen an academic field of study, the best place to begin is Book 1.

Book 1 presents several directories to help you identify programs of study that might interest you; you can then research those programs further in Books 2 through 6. The Directory of Graduate and Professional Programs by Field lists the 397 fields for which there are program directories in Books 2 through 6 and gives the names of those institutions that offer graduate degree programs in each.

For geographical or financial reasons, you may be interested in attending a particular institution and will want to know what it has to offer. You should turn to the Directory of Institutions and Their Offerings, which lists the degree programs available at each institution, again, in the 397 academic and professional fields for which Books 2 through 6 have program directories. As in the Graduate and Professional Programs by Field directory, the level of degrees offered is also indicated.

Finally, the Directory of Combined-Degree Programs lists the areas in which two graduate degrees may be earned concurrently and the schools that offer them.

CLASSIFICATION OF PROGRAMS

After you identify the particular programs and institutions that interest you, use both Book 1 and the specialized volumes to obtain detailed information—Book 1 for information on the institutions overall and Books 2 through 6 for details about the individual graduate units and their degree programs.

Books 2 through 6 are divided into sections that contain one or more directories devoted to programs in a particular field. If you do not find a directory devoted to your field of interest in a specific book, consult the Index of Directories and Subject Areas in Books 2–6; this index appears at the end of each book. After you have identified the correct book, consult the Index of Directories and Subject Areas in This Book, which shows (as does the more general directory) what directories cover subjects not specifically named in a directory or section title. This index in Book 2, for example, will tell you that if you are interested in sculpture, you should see the directory entitled Art/Fine Arts. The Art/Fine Arts entry will direct you to the proper page.

Books 2 through 6 have a number of general directories. These directories have entries for the largest unit at an institution granting graduate degrees in that field. For example, the general Engineering and Applied Sciences directory in Book 5 consists of profiles for colleges, schools, and departments of engineering and applied sciences.

General directories are followed by other directories, or sections, in Books 2, 3, 5, and 6 that give more detailed information about programs in particular areas of the general field that has been covered. The general Engineering and Applied Sciences directory, in the example above, is followed by nineteen sections in specific areas of engineering, such as Chemical Engineering, Industrial Engineering, and Mechanical Engineering.

Because of the broad nature of many fields, any system of organization is bound to involve a certain amount of overlap. Environmental studies, for example, is a field whose various aspects are studied in several types of departments and schools. Readers interested in such studies will find information on relevant programs in Book 3 under Ecology and Environmental Biology; in Book 4 under Environmental Policy and Resource Management and Natural Resources; in Book 5 under Energy Management and Policy and Environmental Engineering; and in Book 6 under Environmental and Occupational Health. To help you find all of the programs of interest to you, the introduction to each section of Books 2 through 6 includes, if applicable, a paragraph suggesting other sections and directories with information on related areas of study to consult.

In addition, this book contains listings of academic centers and institutes, including information about the graduate students served, affiliated faculty members, and research budgets. This information can be found in the Research and Training Opportunities section in this volume.

SCHOOL AND PROGRAM INFORMATION

In all of the books, information is presented in three forms: profiles—capsule summaries of basic information—and the short announcements and in-depth descriptions written by graduate school and program administrators. The format of the profiles is constant, making it easy to compare one institution with another and one program with another. A description of the information in the profiles in Books 2 through 6 may be found below; the Book 1 profile description is found immediately preceding the profiles in Book 1. A number of graduate school and program administrators have attached brief announcements to the end of their profile listings. In them you will find information that an institution or program wants to emphasize. The in-depth descriptions are by their very nature more expansive and flexible than the profiles, and the administrators who have written them may emphasize different aspects of their programs. All of these in-depth descriptions are organized in the same way, and in each one you will find information on the same basic topics, such as programs of study, research facilities, tuition and fees, financial aid, and application procedures. If an institution or program has submitted an in-depth description, a boldface cross-reference appears below its profile. As with the profile announcements, all of the in-depth descriptions in the guides have been submitted by choice of administrators; the absence of an announcement or in-depth description does not reflect any type of editorial judgment on the part of Peterson's.

Interdisciplinary Programs

In addition to the regular directories that present profiles of programs in each field of study, many sections in Books 2 through 6 contain special notices under the heading Cross-Discipline Announcements. Appearing at the end of the profiles in many sections, these Cross-Discipline Announcements inform you about programs that you may find of interest described in a different section. A biochemistry department, for example, may place a notice under Cross-Discipline Announcements in the Chemistry section (Book 4) to alert chemistry students to their current description in the Biochemistry section of Book 3. Cross-discipline announcements, also written by administrators to highlight their programs, will be helpful to you not only in finding out about programs in fields related to your own but also in locating departments that are actively recruiting students with a specific undergraduate major.

Profiles of Graduate Units (Books 2–6)

The profiles found in the 397 directories in Books 2 through 6 provide basic data about the graduate units in capsule form for quick reference. To make these directories as useful as possible, profiles are generally listed for an institution's smallest academic unit within a subject area. In other words, if an institution has a College of Liberal Arts that administers many related programs, the profile for the individual program (e.g., Program in History), not the entire College, appears in the directory.

There are some programs that do not fit into any current directory and are not given individual profiles. The directory structure is reviewed annually in order to keep this number to a minimum and to accommodate major trends in graduate education.

The following outline describes the profile information found in the guides and explains how best to use that information. Any item that does not apply to or was not provided by a graduate unit is omitted from its listing.

Identifying Information. The institution's name, in boldface type, is followed by a complete listing of the administrative structure for that field of study. (For example, **University of Akron,** Buchtel College of Arts and Sciences, Department of Mathematical Sciences and Statistics, Program in Mathematics.) The last unit listed is the one to which all information in the profile pertains. The institution's address follows.

Offerings. Each field of study offered by the unit is listed with all postbaccalaureate degrees awarded. Degrees that are not preceded by a specific concentration are awarded in the general field listed in the unit name. Frequently, fields of study are broken down into subspecializations, and those appear following the degrees awarded; for example, "Offerings in secondary education (M Ed), including English education, mathematics education, science education." Students enrolled in the M.Ed. program would be able to specialize in any of the three fields mentioned.

Professional Accreditation. Profiles indicate whether a program is professionally accredited. Specific information on the accreditation status of a unit is obtained directly from the accreditation agency's most current listing at the time of publication. However, because it is possible for a program to receive or lose professional accreditation at any time, students entering fields in which accreditation is important to a career should verify the status of programs by contacting either the chairperson or the appropriate accrediting association (see Accreditation and Accrediting Agencies in each book).

Jointly Offered Degrees. Explanatory statements concerning programs that are offered in cooperation with other institutions are included in the list of degrees offered. This occurs most commonly on a regional basis (for example, two state universities offering a cooperative Ph.D. in special education) or where the specialized nature of the institutions encourages joint efforts (a J.D./M.B.A. offered by a law school at an institution with no formal business programs and an institution with a business school but lacking a law school). Only programs that are truly cooperative are listed; those involving only limited course work at another institution are not. Interested students should contact the heads of such units for further information.

Part-Time and Evening/Weekend Programs. When information regarding the availability of part-time or evening/weekend study appears in the profile, it means that students are able to earn a degree exclusively through such study.

Postbaccalaureate Distance Learning Degrees. A postbaccalaureate distance learning degree program signifies that course requirements can be fulfilled with minimal or no on-campus study. If these programs require minimal on-campus study or no on-campus study it may be indicated here.

Faculty. Figures on the number of faculty members actively involved with graduate students through teaching or research are separated into full-and part-time as well as men and women whenever the information has been supplied.

Matriculated Students. Figures for the number of students enrolled in graduate and professional programs pertain to the semester of highest enrollment from the 1998–99 academic year. These figures are broken down into full- and part-time and men and women whenever the data have been supplied. Information on the number of matriculated students enrolled in the unit who are members of a minority group or are international students appears here. The average age of the matriculated students is followed by the number of applicants and the percentage accepted for fall 1998.

Degrees Awarded. In addition to the number of degrees awarded in the 1998 calendar year, this section contains information on the percentages of students who have gone on to continue full-time study, entered university research or teaching, or chosen other work related to their field and information on the average amount of time required to earn the degree for full-time and part-time students. Many doctoral programs offer a terminal master's degree if students leave the program after completing only part of the requirements for a doctoral degree; that is indicated here. All degrees are classified into one of four types: master's, doctoral, first professional, and other advanced degrees. A unit may award one or several degrees at a given level; however, the data are only collected by type and may therefore represent several different degree programs.

Degree Requirements. The information in this section is also broken down by type of degree, and all information for a degree level pertains to all degrees of that type unless otherwise specified. Degree requirements are collected in a simplified form to provide some very basic information on the nature of the program and on foreign language, computer language, and thesis or dissertation requirements. Many units also provide a short list of additional requirements, such as fieldwork or an internship. No information is listed on the number of courses or credits required for completion or whether a minimum or maximum number of years or semesters is needed. For complete information on graduation requirements, contact the graduate school or program directly.

Entrance Requirements. Entrance requirements are broken down into the four degree levels of master's, doctoral, first professional, and other advanced degrees. Within each level, information may be provided in two basic categories, entrance exams and other requirements. The entrance exams use the standard acronyms used by the testing agencies, unless they are not well known. Additional information on each of the common tests is provided in the section Tests Required of Applicants. The usual format in this part of the profile is a test name followed by a minimum score. When a minimum or average combined score is given for the GRE General Test, it is for the verbal and quantitative sections combined (without the analytical section) unless otherwise specified. More information on the scale and other aspects of the test may be obtained directly from the testing agency. Other entrance requirements are quite varied, but they often contain an undergraduate or graduate grade point average (GPA). Unless otherwise stated, the GPA is calculated on a 4.0 scale and is listed as a minimum required for admission. The standard application deadlines, any nonrefundable application fee, and whether electronic applications are accepted may be listed here. Note that the deadline should be used for reference only; these dates are subject to change, and students interested in applying should contact the graduate unit directly about application procedures and deadlines.

Expenses. The typical cost of study for the 1999–2000 academic year is given in two basic categories, tuition and fees. It is not possible to represent the complete tuition and fees schedule for each graduate unit, so a simplified version of the cost of studying in that unit is provided. In general, the costs of both full- and part-time study are listed if the unit allows for both types of programs and lists separate costs. For public institutions, the tuition and fees are listed for both state residents and nonresidents. Cost of study may be quite complex at a graduate institution. There are often sliding scales for part-time study, a different cost for first-year students, and other variables that make it impossible to completely cover the cost of study for each graduate program. To provide the most usable information, figures are given for full-time study for a full year where available and for part-time study in terms of a per-unit rate (per credit, per semester hour, etc.). Occasionally, variances may be noted in tuition and fees for reasons such as the type of program, whether courses are taken during the day or evening, whether courses are at the master's or doctoral level, or other institution-specific reasons. Expenses are usually subject to change; for exact costs at any given time, contact your chosen schools and programs directly. Keep in mind that the tuition of Canadian institutions is usually given in Canadian dollars.

Financial Aid. This section contains data on the number of awards that are administered by the institution and were given to graduate students during the 1998–99 academic year. The first figure given represents the total number of students receiving financial aid enrolled in that unit. If the unit has provided information on graduate appointments, these are broken down into three major categories: *fellowships* give money to graduate students to cover the cost of study and living expenses and are not based on a work obligation or research commitment, *research assistantships* provide stipends to graduate students for assistance in a formal research project with a faculty member, and *teaching assistantships* provide stipends to graduate students for teaching or for assisting faculty members in teaching undergraduate classes. Within each category, figures are given for the total number of awards, the average yearly amount per award, and whether full or partial tuition reimbursements are awarded.

In addition to graduate appointments, the availability of several other financial aid sources is covered in this section. *Tuition waivers* are routinely part of a graduate appointment, but units sometimes waive part or all of a student's tuition even if a graduate appointment is not available. *Federal Work-Study* is made available to students who demonstrate need and meet the federal guidelines; this form of aid normally includes 10 or more hours of work per week in an office of the institution. *Institutionally sponsored loans* are low-interest loans available to graduate students to cover both educational and living expenses. *Career-related internships* or *fieldwork* offer money to students who are participating in a formal off-campus research project or practicum. Grants, scholarships, traineeships, unspecified assistantships, and other awards may also be noted. The availability of financial aid to part-time students is also indicated here. Some programs list the financial aid application deadline and the forms that need to be completed for students to be eligible for financial aid. There are two forms: FAFSA, the Free Application for Federal Student Aid, which is required for federal aid; and the CSS Financial Aid PROFILE, if required.

Faculty Research. Each unit has the opportunity to list several keyword phrases describing the current research involving faculty members and graduate students. Space limitations prevent the unit from listing complete information on all research programs. The total expenditure for funded research from the previous academic year may also be included.

Unit Head and Application Contact. The head of the graduate program for each unit is listed with the academic title and telephone, fax, and e-mail numbers if available. In addition to the unit head, many graduate programs list separate contacts for application and admis-

sion information, which follows the listing for the unit head. If no unit head or application contact is given, you should contact the overall institution for information on graduate admissions.

Data Collection and Editorial Procedures

DIRECTORIES AND PROFILES

The information published in the directories and profiles of all the books is collected through Peterson's Annual Survey of Graduate Institutions. The survey is sent each spring to more than 1,700 institutions offering postbaccalaureate degree programs, including accredited institutions in the United States and U.S. territories and those institutions in Canada, Mexico, Europe, and Africa that are accredited by U.S. accrediting bodies. Deans and other administrators complete these surveys, providing information on programs in the 397 academic and professional fields covered in the guides as well as overall institutional information. Peterson's staff then goes over each returned survey carefully and verifies or revises responses after further research and discussion with administrators at the institutions. Extensive files on past responses are kept from year to year.

While every effort has been made to ensure the accuracy and completeness of the data, information is sometimes unavailable or changes occur after publication deadlines. All usable information received in time for publication has been included. The omission of any particular item from a directory or profile signifies either that the item is not applicable to the institution or program or that information was not available. Profiles of programs scheduled to begin during the 1999–2000 academic year cannot, obviously, include statistics on enrollment or, in many cases, the number of faculty members. If no usable data were submitted by an institution, its name, address, and program name where appropriate nonetheless appear in order to indicate the existence of graduate work.

ANNOUNCEMENTS AND IN-DEPTH DESCRIPTIONS

The announcements and in-depth descriptions are supplementary insertions submitted by deans, chairs, and other administrators who wish to make an additional, more individualized statement to readers. Those who have chosen to write these insertions are responsible for the accuracy of the content, but Peterson's editors have reserved the right to delete irrelevant material or questionable self-appraisals and to edit for style. Statements regarding a university's objectives and accomplishments are a reflection of its own beliefs and are not the opinions of the editors. Since inclusion of announcements and descriptions is by choice, their presence or absence in the guides should not be taken as an indication of status, quality, or approval.

The Graduate Adviser

This section consists of two essays and information about admissions tests and accreditation. The first essay, Applying to Graduate and Professional Schools, was written by Jane E. Levy of Cornell University and Elinor R. Workman. It covers topics of interest to students considering post-baccalaureate work, including types of degrees, choosing a specialization, researching programs, applying, and some issues for returning, part-time, and international students. The second essay is Financing Your Graduate and Professional Education, by Patricia McWade of Georgetown University. It covers determining your need for financial aid, the types of aid available, and how and when to apply for aid as it relates to degree programs in the physical sciences, mathematics, agricultural sciences, the environment, and natural resources. Both essays appear in each of the six Graduate Guides. Tests Required of Applicants lists all standardized admissions tests relevant to programs in the physical sciences, mathematics, agricultural sciences, the environment, and natural resources. Accreditation and Accrediting Agencies gives information on accreditation and its purpose and lists first institutional accrediting agencies and then specialized accrediting agencies relevant to the physical sciences, mathematics, agricultural sciences, the environment, and natural resources. This section is filled with crucial information for all students; it is addressed to the reader who is still in college but also contains information specifically for returning, part-time, and international students.

Applying to Graduate and Professional Schools

The decision to attend graduate school and the choice of an institution and degree program require serious consideration. The time, money, and energy you will expend doing graduate work are significant, and you will want to analyze your options carefully. Before you begin filing applications, you should evaluate your interests and goals, know what programs are available, and be clear about your reasons for pursuing a particular degree.

There are two excellent reasons for attending graduate school, and if your decision is based on one of these, you probably have made the right choice. There are careers such as medicine, law, and college and university teaching that require specialized training and, therefore, necessitate advanced education. Another motivation is to specialize in a subject that you have decided is of great importance, either for career goals or for personal satisfaction.

Degrees

Traditionally, graduate education has involved acquiring and communicating knowledge gained through original research in a particular academic field. The highest earned academic degree, which requires the pursuit of original research, is the Doctor of Philosophy (Ph.D.). In contrast, professional training stresses the practical application of knowledge and skills; this is true, for example, in the fields of business, law, and medicine. At the doctoral level, degrees in these areas include the Doctor of Business Administration (D.B.A.), Juris Doctor (J.D.), and the Doctor of Medicine (M.D.).

Master's degrees are offered in most fields and may also be academic or professional in orientation. In many fields, the master's degree may be the only professional degree needed for employment. This is the case, for example, in fine arts (M.F.A.), library science (M.L.S.), and social work (M.S.W.). (For a list of the graduate and professional degrees currently being offered in the United States and Canada, readers may refer to the appendix of degree abbreviations.)

Some people decide to earn a master's degree at one institution and then select a different university or a somewhat different program of study for doctoral work. This can be a way of acquiring a broad background: you can choose a master's program with one emphasis or orientation and a doctoral program with another. The total period of graduate study may be somewhat lengthened by proceeding this way, but probably not by much.

In recent years, the distinctions between traditional academic programs and professional programs have become blurred. The course of graduate education has changed direction in the last thirty years, and many programs have redefined their shape and focus. There are centers and institutes for research, many graduate programs are now interdepartmental and interdisciplinary, off-campus graduate programs have multiplied, and part-time graduate programs have increased. Colleges and universities have also established combined-degree programs, in many cases in order to enable students to combine academic and professional studies. As a result of such changes, you now have considerable freedom in determining the program best suited to your current needs as well as your long-term goals.

Choosing a Specialization and Researching Programs

There are several sources of information you should make use of in choosing a specialization and a program. A good way to begin is to consult the appropriate directories in these guides, which will tell you what programs exist in the field or fields you are interested in and, for each one, will give you information on degrees, research facilities, the faculty, financial aid resources, tuition and other costs, application requirements, and so on.

Talk with your college adviser and professors about your areas of interest and ask for their advice about the best programs to research. Besides being very well informed themselves, these faculty members may have colleagues at institutions you are investigating, and they can give you inside information about individual programs and the kind of background they seek in candidates for admission.

The valuable perspective of educators should not be overlooked. If the faculty members you know through your courses are not involved in your field of interest, do not hesitate to contact other appropriate professors at your institution or neighboring institutions to ask for advice on programs that might suit your goals. In addition, talk to graduate students studying in your field of interest; their advice can be valuable also.

Your decision about a field of study may be determined by your research interests or, if you choose to enter a professional school, by the appeal of a particular career. In either case, as you attempt to limit the number of institutions you will apply to, you will want to familiarize yourself with publications describing current research in your discipline. Find related professional journals and note who is publishing in the areas of specialization that interest you, as well as where they are teaching. Take note of the institutions represented on the publications' editorial boards (they are usually listed on the inside cover); such representation usually reflects strength in the discipline.

Being aware of who the top people are and where they are will pay off in a number of ways. A graduate department's reputation rests heavily on the reputation of its faculty, and in some disciplines it is more important to study under someone of note than it is to study at a college or university with a prestigious name. In addition, in certain fields graduate funds are often tied to a particular research project and, as a result, to the faculty member directing that project. Finally, most Ph.D. candidates (and nonprofessional master's degree candidates) must pick an adviser and one or more other faculty members who form a committee that directs and approves their work. Many times this choice must be made during the first semester, so it is important to learn as much as you can about faculty members before you begin your studies. As you research the faculties of various departments, keep in mind the following questions: What is their academic training? What are their research activities? What kind of concern do they have for teaching and student development?

There are other important factors to consider in judging the educational quality of a program. First, what kind of students enroll in the program? What are their academic abilities, achievements, skills, geographic representation, and level of professional success upon completion of the program? Second, what are the program's resources? What kind of financial support does it have? How complete is the library? What laboratory equipment and computer facilities are available? And third, what does the program have to offer in terms of both curriculum and services? What are its purposes, its course offerings, and its job placement and student advisement services? What is the student-faculty ratio, and what kind of interaction is there between students and professors? What internships, assistantships, and other experiential education opportunities are available?

When evaluating a particular institution's reputation in a given field, you may also want to look at published graduate program ratings. There is no single rating that is universally accepted, so you would be well advised to read several and not place too much importance on any one. Most consist of what are known as "peer ratings"; that is, they are the results of polls of respected scholars who are asked to rate graduate departments in their field of expertise. Many academicians feel that these ratings are too heavily based upon traditional concepts of what constitutes quality—such as the publications of the faculty—and that they perpetuate the notion of a research-oriented department as the only model of excellence in graduate education. Depending on whether your own goals are research-oriented, you may want to attribute more or less importance to this type of rating.

If possible, visit the institutions that interest you and talk with faculty members and currently enrolled students. Be sure, however, to write or call the admissions office a week in advance to give the person in charge a chance to set up appointments for you with faculty members and students.

The Application Process

TIMETABLE

It is important to start gathering information early to be able to complete your applications on time. Most people should start the process a full year and a half before their anticipated date of matriculation. There are, however, some exceptions to this rule. The time frame will be different if you are applying for national scholarships or if your undergraduate institution has an evaluation committee through which you are applying, for example, to a health-care program. In such a situation, you may have to begin the process two years before your date of matriculation in order to take your graduate admission test and arrange for letters of recommendation early enough to meet deadlines.

Application deadlines may range from August (a year prior to matriculation) for early decision programs at medical schools using the American Medical College Application Service (AMCAS) to late spring or summer (when beginning graduate school in the fall) for a few programs with rolling admissions. Most deadlines for entry in the fall are between January and March. You should in all cases plan to meet formal deadlines; beyond this, you should be aware of the fact that many schools with rolling admissions encourage and act upon early applications. Applying early to a school with rolling admissions is usually advantageous, as it shows your enthusiasm for the program and gives admissions committees more time to evaluate the subjective components of your application, rather than just the "numbers." Applicants are not rejected early unless they are clearly below an institution's standards.

The timetable that appears below represents the ideal for most applicants.

Six months prior to applying
- Research areas of interest, institutions, and programs.
- Talk to advisers about application requirements.
- Register and prepare for appropriate graduate admission tests.
- Investigate national scholarships.
- If appropriate, obtain letters of recommendation.

Three months prior to applying
- Take required graduate admission tests.
- Write for application materials or request them online.
- Write your application essay.
- Check on application deadlines and rolling admissions policies.
- For medical, dental, osteopathy, podiatry, or law school, you may need to register for the national application or data assembly service most programs use.

Fall, a year before matriculating
- Obtain letters of recommendation.
- Take graduate admission tests if you haven't already.
- Send in completed applications.

Winter, before matriculating in the fall
- Complete the Free Application for Federal Student Aid (FAFSA) and Financial Aid PROFILE, if required.

Spring, before matriculating in the fall
- Check with all institutions before their deadlines to make sure your file is complete.
- Visit institutions that accept you.
- Send a deposit to your institution of choice.
- Notify other colleges and universities that accepted you of your decision so that they can admit students on their waiting list.
- Send thank-you notes to people who wrote your recommendation letters, informing them of your success.

You may not be able to adhere to this timetable if your application deadlines are very early, as is the case with medical schools, or if you decide to attend graduate school at the last minute. In any case, keep in mind the various application requirements and be sure to meet all deadlines. If deadlines are impossible to meet, call the institution to see if a late application will be considered.

OBTAINING AAPPLICATION FORMS AND INFORMATION

To obtain the materials you need, send a neatly typed or handwritten postcard requesting an application, a bulletin, and financial aid information to the address provided in this Guide. However, you may want to request an application by writing a formal letter directly to the department chair in which you briefly describe your training, experience, and specialized research interests. If you want to write to a particular faculty member about your background and interests in order to explore the possibility of an assistantship, you should also feel free to do so. However, do not ask a faculty member for an application, as this may cause a significant delay in your receipt of the forms.

NATIONAL APPLICATION SERVICES

In a few professional fields, there are national services that provide assistance with some part of the application process. These services are the Law School Data Assembly Service (LSDAS), American Medical College Application Service (AMCAS), American Association of Colleges of Osteopathic Medicine Application Service (AACOMAS), American Association of Colleges of Podiatric Medicine Application Service (AACPMAS), and American Association of Dental Schools Application Service (AADSAS). Many programs require applicants to use these services because they simplify the application process for both the professional programs' admissions committees and the applicant. The role these services play varies from one field to another. The LSDAS, for example, analyzes your transcript(s) and submits the analysis to the law schools to which you are applying, while the other services provide a more complete application service. More information and applications for these services can be obtained from your undergraduate institution.

MEETING APPLICATION REQUIREMENTS

Requirements vary from one field to another and from one institution to another. Read each program's requirements carefully; the importance of this cannot be overemphasized.

Graduate Admission Tests

Colleges and universities usually require a specific graduate admission test, and departments sometimes have their own requirements as well. Scores are used in evaluating the likelihood of your success in a particular program (based upon the success rate of past students with similar scores). Most programs will not accept scores more than three to five years old. The various tests are described a little later in this book.

Transcripts

Admissions committees require official transcripts of your grades to evaluate your academic preparation for graduate study. Grade point averages are important but are not examined in isolation; the rigor of the courses you have taken, your course load, and the reputation of the undergraduate institution you have attended are also scrutinized. To have your college transcript sent to graduate institutions, contact your college registrar.

Letters of Recommendation

Choosing people to write recommendations can be difficult, and most graduate schools require two or three letters. While recommendations from faculty members are essential for academically oriented programs, professional programs may seriously consider nonacademic recommendations from professionals in the field. Indeed, often these nonacademic recommendations are as respected as those from faculty members.

To begin the process of choosing references, identify likely candidates from among those you know through your classes, extracurricular activities, and jobs. A good reference will meet several of the following criteria: he or she has a high opinion of you, knows you well in more than one area of your life, is familiar with the institutions to which you are applying as well as the kind of study you are pursuing, has taught or worked with a large number of students and can make a favorable comparison of you with your peers, is known by the admissions committee and is regarded as someone whose judgment should be given weight, and has good written communication skills. No one person is likely to satisfy all these criteria, so choose those people who come closest to the ideal.

Once you have decided whom to ask for letters, you may wonder how to approach them. Ask them if they think they know you well enough to write a meaningful letter. Be aware that the later in the semester you ask, the more likely they are to hesitate because of time constraints; ask early in the fall semester of your senior year. Once those you ask to write letters agree in a suitably enthusiastic manner, make an appointment to talk with them. Go to the appointment with recommendation forms in hand, being sure to include addressed, stamped envelopes for their convenience. In addition, give them other supporting materials that will assist them in writing a good, detailed letter on your behalf. Such documents as transcripts, a résumé, a copy of your application essay, and a copy of a research paper can help them write a thorough recommendation.

On the recommendation form, you will be asked to indicate whether you wish to waive or retain the right to see the recommendation. Before you decide, discuss the confidentiality of the letter with each writer. Many faculty members will not write a letter unless it is confidential. This does not necessarily mean that they will write a negative letter but, rather, that they believe it will carry more weight as part of your application if it is confidential. Waiving the right to see a letter does, in fact, usually increase its validity.

If you will not be applying to graduate school as a senior but you plan to pursue further education in the future, open a credentials file if your college or university offers this service. Letters of recommendation can be kept on file for you until you begin the application process. If you are returning to school after working for several years and did not establish a credentials file, it may be difficult to obtain letters of recommendation from professors at your undergraduate institution. In this case, contact the graduate schools you are applying to and ask what their policies are regarding your situation. They may waive the requirement of recommendation letters, allow you to substitute letters from employment supervisors, or suggest you enroll in relevant courses at a nearby institution and obtain letters from professors upon completion of the course work. Program policies vary considerably, so it is best to check with each school.

Application Essays

Writing an essay, or personal statement, is often the most difficult part of the application process. Requirements vary widely in this regard. Some programs request only one or two paragraphs about why you want to pursue graduate study, while others require five or six separate essays in which you are expected to write at length about your motivation for graduate study, your strengths and weaknesses, your greatest achievements, and solutions to hypothetical problems. Business schools are notorious for requiring several time-consuming essays.

An essay or personal statement for an application should be essentially a statement of your ideas and goals. Usually it includes a certain amount of personal history, but, unless an institution specifically requests autobiographical information, you do not have to supply any. Even when the requirement is a "personal statement," the possibilities are almost unlimited. There is no set formula to follow, and, if you do write an autobiographical piece, it does not have to be arranged chronologically. Your aim should be a clear, succinct statement showing that you have a definite sense of what you want to do and enthusiasm for the field of study you have chosen. Your essay should reflect your writing abilities; more important, it should reveal the clarity, the focus, and the depth of your thinking.

Before writing anything, stop and consider what your reader might be looking for; the general directions or other parts of the application may give you an indication of this. Admissions committees may be trying to evaluate a number of things from your statement, including the following things about you:

• Motivation and commitment to a field of study
• Expectations with regard to the program and career opportunities

• Writing ability
• Major areas of interest
• Research or work experience
• Educational background
• Immediate and long-term goals
• Reasons for deciding to pursue graduate education in a particular field and at a particular institution
• Maturity
• Personal uniqueness—what you would add to the diversity of the entering class

There are two main approaches to organizing an essay. You can outline the points you want to cover and then expand on them, or you can put your ideas down on paper as they come to you, going over them, eliminating certain sentences, and moving others around until you achieve a logical sequence. Making an outline will probably lead to a well-organized essay, whereas writing spontaneously may yield a more inspired piece of writing. Use the approach you feel most comfortable with. Whichever approach you use, you will want someone to critique your essay. Your adviser and those who write your letters of recommendation may be very helpful to you in this regard. If they are in the field you plan to pursue, they will be able to tell you what things to stress and what things to keep brief. Do not be surprised, however, if you get differing opinions on the content of your essay. In the end, only you can decide on the best way of presenting yourself.

If there is information in your application that might reflect badly on you, such as poor grades or a low admission test score, it is better not to deal with it in your essay unless you are asked to. Keep your essay positive. You will need to explain anything that could be construed as negative in your application, however, as failure to do so may eliminate you from consideration. You can do this on a separate sheet entitled "Addendum," which you attach to the application, or in a cover letter that you enclose. In either form, your explanation should be short and to the point, avoiding long, tedious excuses. In addition to supplying your own explanation, you may find it appropriate to ask one or more of your recommenders to address the issue in their recommendation letter. Ask them to do this only if they are already familiar with your problem and could talk about it from a positive perspective.

In every case, essays should be word processed or typed. It is usually acceptable to attach pages to your application if the space provided is insufficient. Neatness, spelling, and grammar are important.

Interviews, Portfolios, and Auditions

Some graduate programs will require you to appear for an interview. In certain fields, you will have to submit a portfolio of your work or schedule an audition.

Interviews. Interviews are usually required by medical schools and are often required or suggested by business schools and other programs. An interview can be a very important opportunity for you to persuade an institution's admissions officer or committee that you would be an excellent doctor, dentist, manager, etc. Interviewers will be interested in the way you think and approach problems and will probably concentrate on questions that enable them to assess your thinking skills, rather than questions that call upon your grasp of technical knowledge. Some interviewers will ask controversial questions, such as "What is your viewpoint on abortion?" or give you a hypothetical situation and ask how you would handle it. Bear in mind that the interviewer is more interested in how you think than in what you think. As in your essay, you may be asked to address such topics as your motivation for graduate study, personal philosophy, career goals, related research and work experience, and areas of interest.

You should prepare for a graduate school interview as you would for a job interview. Think about the questions you are likely to be asked and practice verbalizing your answers. Think too about what you want interviewers to know about you so that you can present this information when the opportunity is given. Dress as you would for an employment interview.

Portfolios. Many graduate programs in art, architecture, journalism, environmental design, and other fields involving visual creativity may require a portfolio as part of the application. The function of the portfolio is to show your skills and ability to do further work in a particular field, and it should reflect the scope of your cumulative training and experience. If you are applying to a program in graphic design, you may be required to submit a portfolio showing advertisements, posters, pamphlets, and illustrations you have prepared. In fine arts, applicants must submit a portfolio with pieces related to their proposed major. Individual programs have very specific requirements regarding what your portfolio should contain and how it should be arranged and labeled. Many programs request an interview and ask you to present your portfolio at that time. They may not want you to send the portfolio in advance or leave it with them after the interview, as they are not insured against its loss. If you do send it, you usually do so at your own risk, and you should label all pieces with your name and address.

Auditions. Like a portfolio, the audition is a demonstration of your skills and talent, and it is often required by programs in music, theater, and dance. Although all programs require a reasonable level of proficiency, standards vary according to the field of study. In a nonperformance area like music education, you need only show that you have attained the level of proficiency normally acquired through an undergraduate program in that field. For a performance major, however, the audition is the most important element of the graduate application. Programs set specific requirements as to what material is appropriate, how long the performance should be, whether it should be memorized, and so on. The audition may be live or taped, but a live performance is usually preferred. In the case of performance students, a committee of professional musicians will view the audition and evaluate it according to prescribed standards.

SUBMITTING COMPLETED APPLICATIONS

Graduate schools have established a wide variety of procedures for filing applications, so read each institution's instructions carefully. Some may request that you send all application materials in one package (including letters of recommendation). Others—medical schools, for example—may have a two-step application process. This system requires the applicant to file a preliminary application; if this is reviewed favorably, he or she submits a second set of documents and a second application fee. Pay close attention to each school's instructions.

Graduate schools generally require an application fee. Sometimes this fee may be waived if you meet certain financial criteria. Check with your undergraduate financial aid office and the graduate schools to which you are applying to see if you qualify.

ADMISSION DECISIONS

At most institutions, once the graduate school office has received all of your application materials, your file is sent directly to the academic department. A faculty committee (or the department chairperson) then makes a recommendation to the chief graduate school officer (usually a graduate dean or vice president), who is responsible for the final admission decision. Professional schools at most institutions act independently of the graduate school office; applications are submitted to them directly, and they make their own admission decisions.

Usually a student's grade point average, letters of recommendation, and graduate admission test scores are the primary factors considered by admissions committees. The appropriateness of the undergraduate degree, an interview, and evidence of creative talent may also be taken into account. Normally the student's total record is examined closely, and the weight assigned to specific factors fluctuates from program to program. Few, if any, institutions base their decisions purely on numbers, that is, admission test scores and grade point average. A study by the Graduate Record Examinations Board found that grades and recommendations by known faculty members were considered to be somewhat more important than GRE General Test scores and that GRE Subject Test scores were rated as relatively unimportant (Oltman and Hartnett, 1984). This indicates that some graduate admission test scores may be of less importance than is commonly believed, but this will of course differ from program to program.

Some of the common reasons applicants are rejected for admission to graduate schools are inappropriate undergraduate curriculum; poor grades or lack of academic prerequisites; low admission test scores; weak or ineffective recommendation letters; a poor interview, portfolio, or audition; and lack of extracurricular activities, volunteer experience, or research activities. To give yourself the best chances of being admitted where you apply, try to make a realistic assessment of an institution's admission standards and your own qualifications. Remember, too, that missing deadlines and filing an incomplete application can also be a cause for rejection; be sure that your transcripts and recommendation letters are received on time.

Returning Students

Many graduate programs not only accept the older, returning student but actually prefer these "seasoned" candidates. Programs in business administration, social work, and other professional fields value mature applicants with work experience, for they have found that these students often show a higher level of motivation and commitment and work harder than 21-year-olds. Many programs also seek the diversity older students bring to the student body, as differences in perspective and experience make for interesting—and often intense—class discussions. Nonprofessional programs also view older students favorably if their academic and experiential preparation is recent enough and sufficient for the proposed fields of study.

Many institutions have programs designed to make the transition to academic life easier for the returning student. Such programs include low-cost child-care centers, emotional support programs for both the returning student and his or her spouse, and review courses of various kinds.

Other than making the necessary changes in their life-style, older students report that the most difficult aspect of returning to school is recovering, or developing, appropriate study habits. Initially, older students often feel at a disadvantage compared to students fresh out of an undergraduate program who are accustomed to preparing research papers and taking tests. This feeling can be overcome by taking advantage of noncredit courses in study skills and time management and review courses in math and writing, as well as by taking a tour of the library and becoming thoroughly familiar with it. By the end of the graduate program, most returning students feel that their life experience gave them an edge, because they could use concrete experiences to help them understand academic theory.

If you choose to go back to school, you are not alone. A significant number of adults are currently enrolled in some kind of educational program in order to make their lives or careers more rewarding.

Part-Time Students

As graduate education has changed over the past thirty years, the number of part-time graduate programs has increased. Traditionally, graduate programs were completed by full-time students. Graduate schools instituted residence requirements, demanding that students take a full course load for a certain number of consecutive semesters. It was felt that total immersion in the field of study and extensive interaction with the faculty were necessary to achieve mastery of an academic area.

In most academic Ph.D. programs as well as many health-care fields, this is still the only approach. However, many other programs now admit part-time students or allow a portion of the requirements to be completed on a part-time basis. Professional schools are more likely to allow part-time study because many students work full-time in the field and pursue their degree in order to enhance their career credentials. Other applicants choose part-time study because of financial considerations. By continuing to work full-time while attending school, they take fewer economic risks.

Part-time programs vary considerably in quality and admissions standards. When evaluating a part-time program, use the same criteria you would use in judging the reputation of any graduate program. Some schools use more adjunct faculty members with weaker academic training for their night and weekend courses, and this could lower the quality of the program; however, adjunct lecturers often have excellent experiential knowledge. Admissions standards may be lower for a part-time program than for an equivalent full-time program at the same school, but, again, your fellow students in the part-time program may be practicing in the field and may have much to add to class discussions. Another concern is placement opportunities upon completion of the program. Some schools may not offer placement services to part-time students, and many employers do not value part-time training as highly as a full-time education. However, if a part-time program is the best option for you, do not hesitate to enroll after carefully researching available programs.

International Students

If you are an international student, you will follow the same application procedures as other graduate school applicants. However, you will have to meet additional requirements.

Since your success as a graduate student will depend on your ability to understand, write, read, and speak English, if English is not your native language, you will be required to take the Test of English as a Foreign Language (TOEFL), or a similar test. Some schools will waive the language test requirement, however, if you have a degree from a college or university in a country where the native language is English or if you have studied two or more years in an undergraduate or graduate program in a country where the native language is English. As for all other tests, score requirements vary, but some schools admit students with lower scores on the condition that they enroll in an intensive English program before or during their graduate study. You should ask each school or department about its policies.

In addition to scores on your English test, or proof of competence in English, your formal application must be accompanied by a certified English translation of your academic transcripts. You may also be required to submit records of immunization and certain health certificates as well as documented evidence of financial support at the time of application. However, since you may apply for financial assistance from graduate schools as well as other sources, some institutions require evidence of financial support only as the last step in your formal admittance and may grant you conditional acceptance first.

Once you have been formally admitted into a graduate program and have submitted evidence of your source or sources of financial support, the school will send you Form I-20 or Form IAP-66, Certificate of Eligibility for Non-Immigrant Status. You must present this document, along with a passport from your own government, and evidence of financial support (some schools will require evidence of support for the entire course of study, while others require evidence of support only for the first year of study, if there is also documentation to show reasonable expectation of continued support) to a U.S. embassy or consulate to obtain an international student visa (F-1 with the Form I-20 or J-1 with the Form IAP-66).

Your own government may have other requirements you must meet to study in the United States. Be sure to investigate those requirements as well.

Once all the paperwork has been completed and approved, you are ready to make your travel arrangements. If your port of entry into the United States will be New York's Kennedy Airport, you can arrange, for a fee, to be met and assisted by a representative of the YMCA Arrivals Program. This person will help you through customs and assist you in making travel connections. He or she can also help you find temporary overnight accommodations, if needed. To inquire about fees for this service, contact the Arrivals Program by phone (212-727-8800 Ext. 130), fax (212-727-8814), or e-mail (jholt@ymcanyc.org). If you decide to take advantage of this assistance, you must provide the Arrivals Program with the following information: your name, age, sex, date and time of arrival, airline and flight number, college or university you will be attending, sponsoring agency (if any), and connecting flight information. Include a photo to help identify you, and note if you need overnight accommodations in New York. This information should be sent well in advance to YMCA Arrivals Program, 71 West 23rd Street, Suite 1904, New York, New York 10010.

When you arrive on your American college campus, you will want to contact the international student adviser. This person's job is to help international students in their academic and social adjustment. The adviser often coordinates special orientation programs for new students, which may consist of lectures on American culture, intensive language instruction, campus tours, academic placement examinations, and visits to places of cultural interest in the community. This adviser will also help you with travel and employment questions as well as financial concerns and will keep copies of your visa documents on file, which is required by U.S. immigration law.

A number of nonprofit educational organizations are available throughout the world to assist international students in planning graduate study in the United States. To learn how to get in touch with these organizations for detailed information, contact the U.S. embassy in your country.

Jane E. Levy
Senior Associate Director
University Career Center
Cornell University
and
Elinor R. Workman

Financing Your Graduate and Professional Education

If you're considering attending graduate school but fear you don't have enough money, don't despair. Financial support for graduate study does exist, although, admittedly, the information about support sources can be difficult to find.

Support for graduate study can take many forms, depending upon the field of study and program you pursue. For example, some 60 percent of doctoral students receive support in the form of either grants/fellowships or assistantships, whereas most students in master's programs rely on loans to pay for their graduate study. In addition, doctoral candidates are more likely to receive grants/fellowships and assistantships than master's degree students, and students in the sciences are more likely to receive aid than those in the arts and humanities.

For those of you who have experience with financial aid as an undergraduate, you will notice right away that aid to graduate students is different. For one, aid to undergraduates is based primarily on need (although the number of colleges that now offer undergraduate merit-based aid is increasing). But graduate aid is often based on academic merit, especially in the arts and sciences. Second, as a graduate student, you are automatically "independent" for federal financial aid purposes, meaning your parents' income and asset information is not required in assessing your need for federal aid. And third, at some graduate schools, the awarding of aid may be administered by the academic departments or the graduate school itself, not the financial aid office. This means that at some schools, you may be involved with as many as three offices: a central financial aid office, the graduate school, *and* your academic department.

FINANCIAL AID MYTHS

- **Financial aid is just for poor people.**
- **Financial aid is just for smart people.**
- **Financial aid is mainly for minority students.**
- **I have a job, so I must not be eligible for aid.**
- **If I apply for aid, it will affect whether or not I'm admitted.**
- **Loans are not financial aid.**

Be Prepared

Being prepared for graduate school means you should put together a financial plan. So, before you enter graduate school, you should have answers to these questions:

- What should I be doing now to prepare for the cost of my graduate education?
- What can I do to minimize my costs once I arrive on campus?
- What financial aid programs are available at each of the schools to which I am applying?
- What financial aid programs are available outside the university, at the federal, state, or private level?
- What financing options do I have if I cannot pay the full cost from my own resources and those of my family?
- What should I know about the loans I am being offered?
- What impact will these loans have on me when I complete my program?

You'll find your answers in three guiding principles: think ahead, live within your means, and keep your head above water.

Think Ahead

The first step to putting together your financial plan comes from thinking about the future: the loss of your income while you're attending school, your projected income after you graduate, the annual rate of inflation, additional expenses you will incur as a student and after you graduate, and any loss of income you may experience later on from unintentional periods of unemployment, pregnancy, or disability. The cornerstone of thinking ahead is following a step-by-step process.

1. *Set your goals.* Decide what and where you want to study, whether you will attend full- or part-time, whether you'll work while attending, and what an appropriate level of debt would be. Consider whether you would attend full-time if you had enough financial aid or whether keeping your full-time job is an important priority in your life. Keep in mind that some employers have tuition reimbursement plans for full-time employees.
2. *Take inventory.* Collect your financial information and add up your assets—bank accounts, stocks, bonds, real estate, business and personal property. Then subtract your liabilities—money owed on your assets including credit card debt and car loans—to yield your net worth.
3. *Calculate your need.* Compare your net worth with the costs at the schools you are considering to get a rough estimate of how much of your assets you will need to use for your schooling.
4. *Create an action plan.* Determine how much you'll earn while in school, how much you think you will receive in grants and scholarships, and how much you plan to borrow. Don't forget to consider inflation and possible life changes that could affect your overall financial plan.
5. *Review your plan regularly.* Measure the progress of your plan every year and make adjustments for such things as increases in salary or other changes in your goals or circumstances.

Live Within Your Means

The second step in being prepared is knowing how much you spend now so you can determine how much you'll spend when you're in school. Use the standard cost of attendance budget published by your school as a guide. But don't be surprised if your estimated budget is higher than the one the school provides, especially if you've been out of school for a while. Once you've figured out your budget, see if you can pare down your current costs and financial obligations so the lean years of graduate school don't come as too large a shock.

Keep Your Head Above Water

Finally, the third step is managing the debt you'll accrue as a graduate student. Debt is manageable only when considered in terms of five things:

1. Your future income
2. The amount of time it takes to repay the loan
3. The interest rate you are being charged
4. Your personal lifestyle and expenses after graduation
5. Unexpected circumstances that change your income or your ability to repay what you owe

To make sure your educational debt is manageable, you should borrow an amount that requires payments of between 8 and 15 percent of your starting salary.

The approximate monthly installments for repaying borrowed principal at 5, 8–10, and 12 percent are indicated on page 8.

Estimated Loan Repayment Schedule
Monthly Payments for Every $1000 Borrowed

Rate	5 years	10 years	15 years	20 years	25 years
5%	$18.87	$10.61	$ 7.91	$ 6.60	$ 5.85
8%	20.28	12.13	9.56	8.36	7.72
9%	20.76	12.67	10.14	9.00	8.39
10%	21.74	13.77	10.75	9.65	9.09
12%	22.24	14.35	12.00	11.01	10.53

You can use this table to estimate your monthly payments on a loan for any of the five repayment periods (5, 10, 15, 20, and 25 years). The amounts listed are the monthly payments for a $1000 loan for each of the interest rates. To estimate your monthly payment, choose the closest interest rate and multiply the amount of the payment listed by the total amount of your loan and then divide by 1,000. For example, for a total loan of $15,000 at 9 percent to be paid back over 10 years, multiply $12.67 times 15,000 (190,050) divided by 1,000. This yields $190.05 per month.

If you're wondering just how much of a loan payment you can afford monthly without running into payment problems, consult the chart below.

HOW MUCH CAN YOU AFFORD TO REPAY?

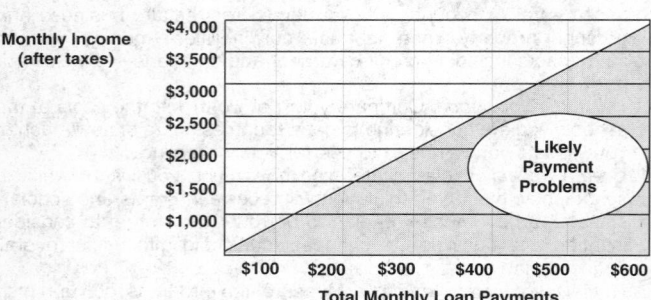

This graph shows the monthly cash-flow outlook based on your total monthly loan payments in comparison with your monthly income earned after taxes. Ideally, to eliminate likely payment problems, your monthly loan payment should be less than 15 percent of your monthly income.

Of course, the best way to manage your debt is to borrow less. While cutting your personal budget may be one option, there are a few others you may want to consider:

• *Ask Your Family for Help:* Although the federal government considers you "independent," your parents and family may still be willing and able to help pay for your graduate education. If your family is not open to just giving you money, they may be open to making a low-interest (or deferred-interest) loan. Family loans usually have more attractive interest rates and repayment terms than commercial loans. They may also have tax consequences, so you may want to check with a tax adviser.

• *Push to Graduate Early:* It's possible to reduce your total indebtedness by completing your program ahead of schedule. You can either take more courses per semester or during the summer. Keep in mind, though, that these options reduce the time you have available to work.

• *Work More, Attend Less:* Another alternative is to enroll part-time, leaving more time to work. Remember, though, to qualify for aid, you must be enrolled at least half time, which is usually considered six credits per term. And if you're enrolled less than half time, you'll have to start repaying your loans once the grace period has expired.

Roll Your Loans into One

There's a good chance that as a graduate student you will have two or more loans included in your aid package, plus any money you borrowed as an undergraduate. That means when you start repaying, you could be making loan payments to several different lenders. Not only can the recordkeeping be a nightmare, but with each loan having a minimum payment, your total monthly payments may be more than you can handle. If that is the case, you may want to consider consolidating your federal loans.

There is no minimum or maximum on the amount of loans you must have in order to consolidate. Also, there is no consolidation fee. The interest rate varies annually, is adjusted every July 1, and is capped at 8.25 percent. Your repayment can also be extended to up to thirty years, depending on the total amount you borrow, which will make your monthly payments lower (of course, you'll also be paying more total interest). With a consolidated loan, some lenders offer graduated or income-sensitive repayment options. Consult with your lender or the U.S. Department of Education about the types of consolidation provisions offered.

Plastic Mania

Any section on managing debt would be incomplete if it didn't mention the responsible use of credit cards. Most graduate students hold one or more credit cards, and many students find themselves in financial difficulties because of them. Here are two suggestions: use credit cards only for convenience, never for extended credit; and, if you have more than one credit card, keep only the one that has the lowest finance charge and the lowest limit.

Credit: Don't Let Your Past Haunt You

Many schools will check your credit history before they process any private educational loans for you. To make sure your credit rating is accurate, you may want to request a copy of your credit report before you start graduate school. You can get a copy of your report by sending a signed, written request to one of the four national credit reporting agencies at the address listed below. Include your full name, social security number, current address (and proof of current address such as a driver's license or utility bill), any previous addresses for the past five years, date of birth, and daytime phone number. Call the agency before you request your report so you know whether there is a fee for this report. Note that you are entitled to a free copy of your credit report if you have been denied credit within the last sixty days. In addition, Experian currently provides complimentary credit reports once every twelve months.

Credit criteria used to review and approve student loans can include the following:

• Absence of negative credit
• No bankruptcies, foreclosures, repossessions, charge-offs, or open judgments
• No prior educational loan defaults, unless paid in full or making satisfactory repayments
• Absence of excessive past due accounts; that is, no 30-, 60-, or 90-day delinquencies on consumer loans or revolving charge accounts within the past two years

CREDIT REPORTING AGENCIES

Experian
P.O. Box 2104
Allen, Texas 75013-2104
888-397-3742

Equifax
P.O. Box 105873
Atlanta, Georgia 30348
800-685-1111

CSC Credit Services
Consumer Assistance Center
P.O. Box 674402
Houston, Texas 77267-4402
800-759-5979

Trans Union Corporation
P.O. Box 390
Springfield, Pennsylvania 19064-0390
800-888-4213

Types of Aid Available

There are three types of aid: money given to you (grants, scholarships, and fellowships), money you earn through work, and loans.

GRANTS, SCHOLARSHIPS, AND FELLOWSHIPS

Most grants, scholarships, and fellowships are outright awards that require no service in return. Often they provide the cost of tuition and fees plus a stipend to cover living expenses. Some are based exclusively on financial need, some exclusively on academic merit, and some on a combination of need and merit. As a rule, grants are awarded to those with financial need, although they may require the recipient to have expertise in a certain field. Fellowships and scholarships often connote selectivity based on ability—financial need is usually not a factor.

Federal Support

Several federal agencies fund fellowship and trainee programs for graduate and professional students. The amounts and types of assistance offered vary considerably by field of study. The following are programs available for those studying in the areas of physical sciences, mathematics, agricultural sciences, the environment, and natural resources:

Graduate Assistantships in Areas of National Need. This program was designed to offer fellowships to outstanding doctoral candidates of superior ability. It is designed to offer financial assistance to students enrolled in specific programs for which there is both a national need and lack of qualified personnel. The definition of national need is determined by the Secretary of Education. Current areas include chemistry, engineering, mathematics, physics, and area studies. Funds are awarded to schools who then select their recipients, based on academic merit. Awardees must also demonstrate financial need. Awards include tuition plus a living expense stipend. Awards are not to exceed four years. Contact the graduate dean's office or academic department to see whether the school participates in this program.

National Science Foundation. Graduate Research Program Fellowships include tuition and fees plus a $15,000 stipend for three years of graduate study in engineering, mathematics, the natural sciences, the social sciences, and the history and philosophy of science. The application deadline is in early November. For more information, write to the National Science Foundation at Oak Ridge Associated Universities, P.O. Box 3010, Oak Ridge, Tennessee 37831-3010, call 423-241-4300, or visit their Web site at http://www.orau.org/nsf/nsffel.htm.

National Institutes of Health (NIH). NIH sponsors many different fellowship opportunities. For example, it offers training grants administered through schools' research departments. Training grants provide tuition plus a twelve-month stipend of $11,496. For more information, call 301-435-0714 or e-mail grantsinfo@nih.gov.

Veterans' Benefits. Veterans may use their educational benefits for training at the graduate and professional levels. Contact your regional office of the Veterans Administration for more details.

State Support

Some states offer grants for graduate study, with California, Michigan, New York, North Carolina, Texas, and Virginia offering the largest programs. States grant approximately $2.9 billion per year to graduate students. Due to fiscal constraints, however, some states have had to reduce or eliminate their financial aid programs for graduate study. To qualify for a particular state's aid you must be a resident of that state. Residency is established in most states after you have lived there for at least twelve consecutive months prior to enrolling in school. Many states provide funds for in-state students only; that is, funds are not transferable out of state. Contact your state scholarship office to determine what aid it offers.

Institutional Aid

Educational institutions using their own funds provide more than $3 billion in graduate assistance in the form of fellowships, tuition waivers, and assistantships. Consult each school's catalog for information about aid programs.

Corporate Aid

Some corporations provide graduate student support as part of the employee benefits package. Most employees who receive aid study at the master's level or take courses without enrolling in a particular degree program.

Aid from Foundations

Most foundations provide support in areas of interest to them. For example, for those studying for the Ph.D., the Howard Hughes Institute funds students in the biomedical sciences, while the Spencer Foundation funds dissertation research in the field of education.

The Foundation Center of New York City publishes several reference books on foundation support for graduate study. For more information, call 212-620-4230 or access their Web site at http://www.fdncenter.org.

Financial Aid for Minorities and Women

Bureau of Indian Affairs. The Bureau of Indian Affairs (BIA) offers aid to students who are at least one quarter American Indian or native Alaskan and from a federally recognized tribe. Contact your tribal education officer, BIA area office, or call the Bureau of Indian Affairs at 202-208-3710.

The Ford Foundation Doctoral Fellowship for Minorities. Provides three-year doctoral fellowships and one-year dissertation fellowships. Predoctoral fellowships include an annual stipend of $14,000 to the fellow and an annual institutional grant of $7500 to the fellowship institution in lieu of tuition and fees. Dissertation fellows receive a stipend of $21,500 for a twelve-month period. Applications are due in November. For more information, contact the Fellowship Office, National Research Council at 202-334-2872 or visit their Web site at http://www2.nas.edu/fo/.

National Consortium for Graduate Degrees in Engineering and Science (GEM). GEM was founded in 1976 to help minority men and women pursue graduate study in engineering by helping them obtain practical experience through summer internships at consortium worksites and finance graduate study toward a master's or Ph.D. degree. For more information, contact GEM, Box 537, Notre Dame, Indiana 46556, call 219-631-7771, or visit their Web site at http://www.nd.edu/~gem/.

National Physical Sciences Consortium. Graduate fellowships are available in astronomy, chemistry, computer science, geology, materials science, mathematics, and physics for women and Black, Hispanic, and Native American students. These fellowships are available only at member universities. Awards may vary by year in school and the application deadline is November 1. Fellows receive tuition plus a stipend of between $12,500 and $15,000. Contact National Physical Sciences Consortium, MSC 3NPS, New Mexico State University, P.O. Box 30001, Las Cruces, New Mexico 88033-8001, call 800-952-4118, or visit their Web site at http://www.npsc.org. In addition, below are some books available that describe financial aid opportunities for women and minorities.

The Directory of Financial Aids for Women by Gail Ann Schlachter (Reference Service Press, 1998) lists sources of support and identifies foundations and other organizations interested in helping women secure funding for graduate study.

The Association for Women in Science publishes *Grants-at-a-Glance,* a booklet highlighting fellowships for women in science. It can be ordered by calling 202-326-8940 or by visiting their Web site at http://www.awis.org.

Books such as *Financial Aid for Minorities* (Garrett Park, MD: Garrett Park Press, 1998) describe financial aid opportunities for minority students. For more information, call 301-946-2553.

Reference Service Press also publishes four directories specifically for minorities: *Financial Aid for African Americans, Financial Aid for Asian Americans, Financial Aid for Hispanic Americans,* and *Financial Aid for Native Americans.*

Also, see the Minority On-Line Information Service (MOLIS) Web site at http://web.fie.com/web/mol/.

Disabled students are eligible to receive aid from a number of organizations. *Financial Aid for the Disabled and Their Families, 1998–2000* by Gail Ann Schlachter and David R. Weber (Reference Service Press) lists aid opportunities for disabled students. The Vocational Rehabilitation Services in your home state can also provide information.

Researching Grants and Fellowships

The books listed below are good sources of information on grant and fellowship support for graduate education and should be consulted before you resort to borrowing. Keep in mind that grant support varies dramatically from field to field.

Annual Register of Grant Support: A Directory of Funding Sources, Wilmette, Illinois: National Register Publishing Co. This is a comprehensive guide to grants and awards from government agencies, foundations, and business and professional organizations.

Corporate Foundation Profiles, 10th ed. New York: Foundation Center, 1998. This is an in-depth, analytical profile of 250 of the largest company-sponsored foundations in the United States. Brief descriptions of all 700 company-sponsored foundations are also included. There is an index of subjects, types of support, and geographical locations.

The Foundation Directory. Edited by Stan Olsen. New York: Foundation Center, 1998. This directory, with a supplement, gives detailed information on U.S. foundations with brief descriptions of the purpose and activities of each.

The Grants Register 1999, 17th ed. Edited by Lisa Williams. New York: St. Martin's, 1999. This lists grant agencies alphabetically and gives information on awards available to graduate students, young professionals, and scholars for study and research.

Peterson's Grants for Graduate & Postdoctoral Study, 5th ed. Princeton: Peterson's, 1998. This book includes information on 1,400 grants, scholarships, awards, fellowships, and prizes. Originally compiled by the Office of Research Affairs at the Graduate School of the University of Massachusetts at Amherst, this guide is updated periodically by Peterson's.

Graduate schools sometimes publish listings of support sources in their catalogs, and some provide separate publications, such as the *Graduate Guide to Grants,* compiled by the Harvard Graduate School of Arts and Sciences. For more information, call 617-495-1814.

THE INTERNET AS A SOURCE OF FUNDING INFORMATION

If you have not explored the financial resources on the World Wide Web (the Web, for short), your research is not complete. Now available on the Web is a wealth of information ranging from loan and entrance applications to minority grants and scholarships.

University-Specific Information on the Web

Most university financial aid offices have Web sites. Florida, Virginia Tech, Massachusetts, Emory, and Georgetown are just a few. Admission applications can now be downloaded from the Web to start the graduate process. After that, detailed information can be obtained on financial aid processes, forms, and deadlines. University-specific grant

and scholarship information can also be found, and more may be learned about financing information by using the Web than by an actual visit. Questions can be answered on line.

Scholarships on the Web

Many benefactors and other scholarship donors have Web sites. You can reach this information through a variety of methods. For example, you can find a directory listing minority scholarships, quickly look at the information online, decide if it applies to you, and then move on. New scholarship pages are being added to the Web daily. Library and Web resources are productive—and free.

The Web also lists many services that will look for scholarships for you. Some of these services cost money and advertise more scholarships per dollar than any other service. While some of these might be helpful, beware. Check references to make sure a bona fide service is being offered. Your best bet initially is to surf the Web and use the traditional library resources on available scholarships.

Bank and Loan Information on the Web

Banks and loan servicing centers have pages on the Web, making it easier to access loan information on the Web. Having the information on screen in front of you instantaneously is more convenient than being put on hold on the phone. Any loan information such as interest rate variations, descriptions of loans, loan consolidation programs, and repayment charts can all be found on the Web. Also, many lenders now allow you to fill out loan applications online.

WORK PROGRAMS

Certain types of support, such as teaching, research, and administrative assistantships, require recipients to provide service to the university in exchange for a salary or stipend; sometimes tuition is also provided or waived.

Teaching Assistantships

If your field of study is taught at the undergraduate level, you stand a good chance of securing a teaching assistantship. These positions usually involve conducting small classes, delivering lectures, correcting class work, grading papers, counseling students, and supervising laboratory groups. Usually about 20 hours of work is required each week.

Teaching assistantships provide excellent educational experience as well as financial support. TAs generally receive a salary (now considered taxable income). Sometimes tuition is provided or waived as well. In addition, at some schools, TAs can be declared state residents, qualifying them for the in-state tuition rates. Appointments are based on academic qualifications and are subject to the availability of funds within a department. If you are interested in a teaching assistantship, contact the academic department. Ordinarily you are not considered for such positions until you have been admitted to the graduate school.

Research Assistantships

Research Assistantships usually require that you assist in the research activities of a faculty member. Appointments are ordinarily made for the academic year. They are rarely offered to first-year students. Contact the academic department, describing your particular research interests. As is the case with teaching assistantships, research assistantships provide excellent academic training as well as practical experience and financial support.

Administrative Assistantships

These positions usually require 10 to 20 hours of work each week in an administrative office of the university. For example, those seeking a graduate degree in education may work in the admissions, financial aid, student affairs, or placement office of the school they are attending. Some administrative assistantships provide a tuition waiver, others a salary. Details concerning these positions can be found in the school catalog or by contacting the academic department directly.

Federal Work-Study Program (FWS)

This federally funded program provides eligible students with employment opportunities, usually in public and private nonprofit organizations. Federal funds pay up to 75 percent of the wages, with the remainder paid by the employing agency. FWS is available to graduate students who demonstrate financial need. Not all schools have these funds, and some only award undergraduates. Each school sets its application deadline and work-study earnings limits. Wages vary and are related to the type of work done.

Additional Employment Opportunities

Many schools provide on-campus employment opportunities that do not require demonstrated financial need. The student employment office on most campuses assists students in securing jobs both on and off the campus.

LOANS

Most needy graduate students, except those pursuing Ph.D.'s in certain fields, borrow to finance their graduate programs. There are basically two sources of student loans–the federal government and private loan programs. You should read and understand the terms of these loan programs before submitting your loan application.

Federal Loans

Federal Stafford Loans. The Federal Stafford Loan Program offers government-sponsored, low-interest loans to students through a private lender such as a bank, credit union, or savings and loan association. There are two components of the Federal Stafford Loan program. Under the *subsidized* component of the program, the federal government pays the interest accruing on the loan while you are enrolled in graduate school on at least a half-time basis. Under the *unsubsidized* component of the program, you pay the interest on the loan from the day proceeds are issued. Eligibility for the federal subsidy is based on demonstrated financial need as determined by the financial aid office from the information you provide on the Free Application for Federal Student Aid (FAFSA). A cosigner is not required, since the loan is not based on creditworthiness.

Although Unsubsidized Federal Stafford Loans may not be as desirable as Subsidized Federal Stafford Loans from the consumer's perspective, they are a useful source of support for those who may not qualify for the subsidized loans or who need additional financial assistance.

Graduate students may borrow up to $18,500 per year through the Stafford Loan Program, up to a maximum of $138,500, including undergraduate borrowing. This may include up to $8500 in Subsidized Stafford Loans, depending on eligibility, up to a maximum of $65,000, including undergradutate borrowing. The amount of the loan borrowed through the Unsubsidized Stafford Program equals the total amount of the loan (as much as $18,500) minus your eligibility for a Subsidized Stafford Loan (as much as $8500). You may borrow up to the cost of the school in which you are enrolled or will attend, minus estimated financial assistance from other federal, state, and private sources, up to a maximum of $18,500.

The interest rate for the Federal Stafford Loans varies annually and is set every July. The rate during in-school, grace, and deferment periods is based on the 91-Day U.S. Treasury Bill rate plus 2.5 percent, capped at 8.25 percent. The rate in repayment is based on the 91-Day U.S. Treasury Bill rate plus 3.1 percent, capped at 8.25 percent.

Two fees are deducted from the loan proceeds upon disbursement: a guarantee fee of up to 1 percent, which is deposited in an insurance pool to ensure repayment to the lender if the borrower defaults, and a federally mandated 3 percent origination fee, which is used to offset the administrative cost of the Federal Stafford Loan Program.

Under the *subsidized* Federal Loan Program, repayment begins six months after your last enrollment on at least a half-time basis. Under the *unsubsidized* program, repayment of interest begins within thirty days from disbursement of the loan proceeds, and repayment of the principal begins six months after your last enrollment on at least a half-time basis. Some lenders may require that some payments be made even while you are in school, although most lenders will allow you to defer payments and will add the accrued interest to the loan balance. Under both components of the program repayment may extend over a maximum of ten years with no prepayment penalty.

Federal Direct Loans. Some schools are participating in the Department of Education's Direct Lending Program instead of offering Federal Stafford Loans. The two programs are essentially the same except

that with the Direct Loans, schools themselves originate the loans with funds provided from the federal government. Terms and interest rates are virtually the same except that there are a few more repayment options with Federal Direct Loans.

Federal Perkins Loans. The Federal Perkins Loan is a long-term loan available to students demonstrating financial need and is administered directly by the school. Not all schools have these funds, and some may award them to undergraduates only. Eligibility is determined from the information you provide on the FAFSA. The school will notify you of your eligibility. Eligible graduate students may borrow up to $5000 per year, up to a maximum of $30,000, including undergraduate borrowing (even if your previous Perkins Loans have been repaid.) The interest rate for Federal Perkins Loans is 5 percent, and no interest accrues while you remain in school at least half-time. There are no guarantee, loan, or disbursement fees. Repayment begins nine months after your last enrollment on at least a half-time basis and may extend over a maximum of ten years with no prepayment penalty.

Deferring Your Federal Loan Repayments. If you borrowed under the Federal Stafford Loan Program or the Federal Perkins Loan Program for previous undergraduate or graduate study, some of your repayments may be deferred (i.e., suspended) when you return to graduate school, depending on when you borrowed and under which program. There are other deferment options available if you are temporarily unable to repay your loan. Information about these deferments is provided at your entrance and exit interviews. If you believe you are eligible for a deferment of your loan repayments, you must contact your lender to complete a deferment form. The deferment must be filed prior to the time your repayment is due, and it must be refiled when it expires if you remain eligible for deferment at that time.

Supplemental Loans

Many lending institutions offer supplemental loan programs and other financing plans, such as the ones described below, to students seeking assistance in meeting their expected contribution toward educational expenses.

If you are considering borrowing through a supplemental loan program, you should carefully consider the terms of the program and be sure to "read the fine print." Check with the program sponsor for the most current terms that will be applicable to the amounts you intend to borrow for graduate study. Most supplemental loan programs for graduate study offer unsubsidized, credit-based loans. In general, a credit-ready borrower is one who has a satisfactory credit history or no credit history at all. A creditworthy borrower generally must pass a credit test to be eligible to borrow or act as a cosigner for the loan funds.

Many supplemental loan programs have a minimum annual loan limit and a maximum annual loan limit. Some offer amounts equal to the cost of attendance minus any other aid you will receive for graduate study. If you are planning to borrow for several years of graduate study, consider whether there is a cumulative or aggregate limit on the amount you may borrow. Often this cumulative or aggregate limit will include any amounts you borrowed and have not repaid for undergraduate or previous graduate study.

The combination of the annual interest rate, loan fees, and the repayment terms you choose will determine how much the amount is that you will repay over time. Compare these features in combination before you decide which loan program to use. Some loans offer interest rates that are adjusted monthly, some quarterly, some annually. Some offer interest rates that are lower during the in-school, grace, and deferment periods, and then increase when you begin repayment. Most programs include a loan "origination" fee, which is usually deducted from the principal amount you receive when the loan is disbursed, and must be repaid along with the interest and other principal when you graduate, withdraw from school, or drop below half-time study. Sometimes the loan fees are reduced if you borrow with a qualified cosigner. Some programs allow you to defer interest and/or principal payments while you are enrolled in graduate school. Many programs allow you to capitalize your interest payments; the interest due on your loan is added to the outstanding balance of your loan, so you don't have to repay immediately, but this increases the amount you owe. Other programs allow you to pay the interest as you go, which will reduce the amount you later have to repay.

For more information about supplemental loan programs, visit http://www.estudentloans.com. This Web site has the most up-to-date information about supplemental loans.

International Education and Study Abroad

A variety of funding sources are offered for study abroad and for foreign nationals studying in the United States. The Institute of International Education in New York assists students in locating such aid. It publishes *Funding for U.S. Study—A Guide for International Students and Professionals* and *Financial Resources for International Study,* a guide to organizations offering awards for overseas study. Both books can be ordered on line at http://www.iiebooks.org.

The Council on International Educational Exchange in New York publishes the *Student Travel Catalogue,* which lists fellowship sources and explains the council's services both for United States students traveling abroad and for foreign students coming to the United States. For more information, see their Web site at http://www.ciee.org.

The U.S. Department of Education administers programs that support fellowships related to international education. Foreign Language and Area Studies Fellowships and Fulbright-Hays Doctoral Dissertation Awards were established to promote knowledge and understanding of other countries and cultures. They offer support to graduate students interested in foreign languages and international relations. Discuss these and other foreign study opportunities with the financial aid officer or someone in the graduate school dean's office at the school you will attend.

How to Apply

All applicants for federal aid must complete the Free Application for Federal Student Aid (FAFSA). This application must be submitted *after* January 1 preceding enrollment in the fall. It is a good idea to submit the FAFSA as soon as possible after this date. You can fill out the paper form, or you can apply online at http://www.fafsa.ed.gov. On this form you report your income and asset information for the preceding calendar year and specify which schools will receive the data. Two to four weeks later you'll receive an acknowledgment, the Student Aid Report (SAR), on which you can make any corrections. The schools you've designated will also receive the information and may begin asking you to send them documents, usually your U.S. income tax return, verifying what you reported.

In addition to the FAFSA, some graduate schools want additional information and will ask you to complete the CSS Financial Aid PROFILE. If your school requires this form, it will be listed in the PROFILE registration form available in college financial aid offices. Other schools use their own supplemental application. Check with your financial aid office to confirm which forms they require.

If you have already filed your federal income tax for the year, it will be much easier for you to complete these forms. If not, use estimates, but be certain to notify the financial aid office if your estimated figures differ from the actual ones once you have calculated them.

APPLICATION DEADLINES

Application deadlines vary. Some schools require you to apply for aid when applying for admission; others require that you be admitted before applying for aid. Aid application instructions and deadlines should be clearly stated in each school's application material. The FAFSA must be filed after January 1 of the year you are applying for aid but the Financial Aid PROFILE should be completed earlier, in October or November.

Determining Financial Need

Eligibility for need-based financial aid is based on your income during the calendar year prior to the academic year in which you apply for aid. Prior-year income is used because it is a good predictor of current-year income and is verifiable. If you have a significant reduction in income or assets after your aid application is completed, consult a financial aid counselor. If, for example, you are returning to school after working, you should let the financial aid counselor know your projected income for the year you will be in school. Aid counselors may use their "professional judgment" to revise your financial need, based on the actual income you will earn while you are in graduate school.

Need is determined by examining the difference between the cost of attendance at a given institution and the financial resources you bring to the table. Eligibility for aid is calculated by subtracting your resources from the total cost of attendance budget. These standard student budgets are generally on the low side of the norm. So if your expenses are higher because of medical bills, higher research travel, or more costly books, for example, a financial aid counselor can make an adjustment. Of course, you'll have to document any unusual expenses. Also, keep in mind that with limited grant and scholarship aid, a higher budget will probably mean either more loan or more working hours for you.

Tax Issues

Since the passage of the Tax Reform Act of 1986, grants, scholarships, and fellowships may be considered taxable income. That portion of the grant used for payment of tuition and course-required fees, books, supplies, and equipment is excludable from taxable income. Grant support for living expenses is taxable. A good rule of thumb for determining the tax liability for grants and scholarships is to view anything that exceeds the actual cost of tuition, required fees, books, supplies related to courses, and required equipment as taxable.

- If you are employed by an educational institution or other organization that gives tuition reimbursement, you must pay tax on the value that exceeds $5250.
- If your tuition is waived in exchange for working at the institution, the tuition waiver is taxable. This includes waivers that come with teaching or research assistantships.
- Other student support, such as stipends and wages paid to research assistants and teaching assistants, is also taxable income. Student loans, however, are not taxable.
- If you are an international student you may or may not owe taxes depending upon the agreement the U.S. has negotiated with your home country. The United States has tax treaties with more than forty countries. You are responsible for making sure that the school you attend follows the terms of the tax treaty. If your country does not have a tax treaty with the U.S., you may have as much as 30 percent withheld from your paycheck.

A Final Note

While amounts and eligibility criteria vary from field to field as well as from year to year, with thorough research you can uncover many opportunities for graduate financial assistance. If you are interested in graduate study, discuss your plans with faculty members and advisers. Explore all options. Plan ahead, complete forms on time, and be tenacious in your search for support. No matter what your financial situation, if you are academically qualified and knowledgeable about the different sources of aid, you should be able to attend the graduate school of your choice.

Patricia McWade
Dean of Student Financial Services
Georgetown University

Tests Required of Applicants

Many graduate schools require that applicants submit scores on one or more standardized tests, often the Graduate Record Examinations (GRE) or the Miller Analogies Test (MAT). Professional schools usually require that applicants take a specific admission test. Virtually all graduate and professional schools ask students whose native language is not English to take the Test of English as a Foreign Language (TOEFL), and some also ask for TOEFL's Test of Written English (TWE) or the Test of Spoken English (TSE).

Brief descriptions of these tests and the addresses to write to for additional information are given below.

GRADUATE RECORD EXAMINATIONS

The GRE General Test and Subject Tests are designed to assess academic knowledge and skills relevant to graduate study. The General Test measures verbal, quantitative, and analytical reasoning skills, and the Subject Tests measure achievement in particular fields of study. The GRE tests are administered worldwide by Educational Testing Service (ETS) of Princeton, New Jersey, under policies established by the Graduate Record Examinations Board, an independent board affiliated with the Association of Graduate Schools and the Council of Graduate Schools.

Subject Tests, offered only as paper-based tests, are available in fourteen areas: biochemistry, cell and molecular biology; biology; chemistry; computer science; economics; engineering; geology; history; literature in English; mathematics; music; physics; psychology; and sociology.

The CAT (Computer Adaptive Test) General Test is offered year-round at more than 600 test centers around the world. The CAT offers convenient scheduling, immediate viewing of unofficial scores, and faster score reporting. To schedule an appointment in the U.S., U.S. Territories, or Canada, call 800-GRE-CALL. For international testing, refer to the 1999–2000 *GRE Information and Registration Bulletin* or the GRE Web site (http://www.gre.org) for a list of the regional registration centers. The *GRE Bulletin* contains registration and program services information.

The 1999–2000 GRE Subject Test dates are November 6, December 11, and April 8; the economics, geology, history, music, and sociology tests will not be offered on the November test date. The General Test is offered on the November and April test dates only.

Fees for the General Test and Subject Tests are $96 for testing in the U.S. and U.S. Territories and $120 in all other locations. Fees are subject to change.

Nonstandard testing accommodations are available for test takers with disabilities through the testing programs. Students who cannot test on Saturdays for religious reasons may request a Monday paper-based administration immediately following a regular Saturday test date. Refer to the *GRE Bulletin* for more information.

Test takers can register by phone, fax, mail, or online. Test takers should consider admission deadlines and register early to get their preferred test dates.

Further information on registration is available from the GRE Web site or by writing to GRE-ETS, P.O. Box 6000, Princeton, New Jersey 08541-6000 or by calling 609-771-7670.

Peterson's offers *GRE Success*, a complete guide to the GRE. Visit your local bookstore or contact Peterson's at 800-225-0261.

MILLER ANALOGIES TEST

The MAT is published and administered by The Psychological Corporation, a division of Harcourt Brace & Company. The MAT is a high-level mental ability test that requires the solution of 100 problems stated in the form of analogies. The MAT is accepted by more than 2,300 graduate school programs as part of their admission process. The test items use different types of analogies to sample general information and a variety of fields, such as fine arts, literature, mathematics, natural science, and social science. Examinees are allowed 50 minutes to complete the test.

The MAT is offered at more than 600 test centers in the United States and Canada. For examinee convenience, the test is given on an as-needed basis at most test centers. Fees are also determined by each test center.

Additional information about the MAT, including preparatory materials and test center locations, is available from The Psychological Corporation, 555 Academic Court, San Antonio, Texas 78204. Telephone: 210-299-1061 or 800-622-3231 (7 a.m. to 7 p.m., Monday through Friday, Central time).

TEST OF ENGLISH AS A FOREIGN LANGUAGE

The purpose of the TOEFL is to evaluate the English proficiency of people whose native language is not English.

The TOEFL is administered as a computer-based test throughout most of the world. The computer-based TOEFL is available year-round by appointment only. It is not necessary to have previous computer experience to take the test. Examinees will be given all the instructions and practice needed to perform the necessary computer tasks before the actual test begins. The test consists of four sections—listening, reading, structure, and writing. Total testing time is approximately 4 hours. The fee for the computer-based TOEFL is $100, which must be paid in U.S. dollars. The *Information Bulletin for Computer-Based Testing* contains information about the new testing format, registration procedures, and testing sites.

TOEFL will remain paper-based in Bangladesh, Bhutan, Cambodia, Hong Kong, India, Japan, Korea, Laos, Macau, Pakistan, People's Republic of China, Taiwan, Thailand, and Vietnam. For 1999–2000, in these countries tests will be offered on December 17, March 17, and June 9.

The paper-based TOEFL consists of three sections—listening comprehension, structure and written expression, and reading comprehension. Testing time is approximately 3 hours. In December, February, and May, the Test of Written English (TWE) will also be given. TWE is a 30-minute essay that measures the examinee's ability to compose in English. Examinees receive a TWE score separate from their TOEFL score. The fee for the paper-based TOEFL is $75, which must be paid in U.S. dollars. There is no additional charge for TWE. The *Information Bulletin* contains information on local fees and registration procedures.

The TOEFL is given at many test centers throughout the world and is administered by Educational Testing Service (ETS) under the general direction of a policy council established by the College Board and the Graduate Record Examinations Board.

Additional information and registration material is available from the TOEFL Program Office, P.O. Box 6151, Princeton, New Jersey 08541-6151. Telephone: 609-771-7100. E-mail: toefl@ets.org. World Wide Web: http://www.toefl.org.

Peterson's offers *TOEFL Success*, a complete guide to the TOEFL. Visit your local bookstore or contact Peterson's at 800-225-0261.

TEST OF SPOKEN ENGLISH

The major purpose of the TSE is to evaluate the spoken English proficiency of people whose native language is not English. The test, which takes about 30 minutes, requires examinees to demonstrate their ability to speak English by answering a variety of questions presented in printed and recorded form. All the answers to test questions are recorded on tape; no writing is required. TSE is given at selected TOEFL test centers worldwide. The test is administered by Educational Testing Service (ETS) under the general direction of a policy council established by the College Board and the Graduate Record Examinations Board.

The 1999–2000 test dates are November 20, January 15, February 26, April 15, and May 13. The registration fee is $125, which must be paid in U.S. dollars.

Additional information and registration material can be found in the *Information Bulletin for the Test of Spoken English*, available from the TOEFL Program Office, P.O. Box 6151, Princeton, New Jersey 08541-6151, U.S.A. Telephone: 609-771-7100.

Accreditation and Accrediting Agencies

Colleges and universities in the United States, and their individual academic and professional programs, are accredited by nongovernmental agencies concerned with monitoring the quality of education in this country. Agencies with both regional and national jurisdictions grant accreditation to institutions as a whole, while specialized bodies acting on a nationwide basis—often national professional associations—grant accreditation to departments and programs in specific fields.

Institutional and specialized accrediting agencies share the same basic concerns: the purpose an academic unit—whether university or program—has set for itself and how well it fulfills that purpose, the adequacy of its financial and other resources, the quality of its academic offerings, and the level of services it provides. Agencies that grant institutional accreditation take a broader view, of course, and examine universitywide or collegewide services that a specialized agency may not concern itself with.

Both types of agencies follow the same general procedures when considering an application for accreditation. The academic unit prepares a self-evaluation, focusing on the concerns mentioned above and usually including an assessment of both its strengths and weaknesses; a team of representatives of the accrediting body reviews this evaluation, visits the campus, and makes its own report; and finally, the accrediting body makes a decision on the application. Often, even when accreditation is granted, the agency makes a recommendation regarding how the institution or program can improve. All institutions and programs are also reviewed every few years to determine whether they continue to meet established standards; if they do not, they may lose their accreditation.

Accrediting agencies themselves are reviewed and evaluated periodically by the U.S. Department of Education and the Council for Higher Education Accreditation (CHEA). Agencies recognized adhere to certain standards and practices, and their authority in matters of accreditation is widely accepted in the educational community.

This does not mean, however, that accreditation is a simple matter, either for schools wishing to become accredited or for students deciding where to apply. Indeed, in certain fields the very meaning and methods of accreditation are the subject of a good deal of debate. For their part, those applying to graduate school should be aware of the safeguards provided by regional accreditation, especially in terms of degree acceptance and institutional longevity. Beyond this, applicants should understand the role that specialized accreditation plays in their field, as this varies considerably from one discipline to another. In certain professional fields, it is necessary to have graduated from a program that is accredited in order to be eligible for a license to practice, and in some fields the federal government also makes this a hiring requirement. In other disciplines, however, accreditation is not as essential, and there can be excellent programs that are not accredited. In fact, some programs choose not to seek accreditation, although most do.

Institutions and programs that present themselves for accreditation are sometimes granted the status of candidate for accreditation, or what is known as "preaccreditation." This may happen, for example, when an academic unit is too new to have met all the requirements for accreditation. Such status signifies initial recognition and indicates that the school or program in question is working to fulfill all requirements; it does not, however, guarantee that accreditation will be granted.

Readers are advised to contact agencies directly for answers to their questions about accreditation. The names and addresses of all agencies recognized by the U.S. Department of Education and the Council for Higher Education Accreditation are listed below.

Institutional Accrediting Agencies—Regional

MIDDLE STATES ASSOCIATION OF COLLEGES AND SCHOOLS
Accredits institutions in Delaware, District of Columbia, Maryland, New Jersey, New York, Pennsylvania, Puerto Rico, and the Virgin Islands.
Jean Avnet Morse, Executive Director
Commission on Higher Education
3624 Market Street
Philadelphia, Pennsylvania 19104-2680
Telephone: 215-662-5606
Fax: 215-662-5950
E-mail: jamorse@msache.org

NEW ENGLAND ASSOCIATION OF SCHOOLS AND COLLEGES
Accredits institutions in Connecticut, Maine, Massachusetts, New Hampshire, Rhode Island, and Vermont.
Charles M. Cook, Director
Commission on Institutions of Higher Education
209 Burlington Road
Bedford, Massachusetts 01730-1433
Telephone: 781-271-0022
Fax: 781-271-0950
E-mail: ccook@neasc.org

NORTH CENTRAL ASSOCIATION OF COLLEGES AND SCHOOLS
Accredits institutions in Arizona, Arkansas, Colorado, Illinois, Indiana, Iowa, Kansas, Michigan, Minnesota, Missouri, Nebraska, New Mexico, North Dakota, Ohio, Oklahoma, South Dakota, West Virginia, Wisconsin, and Wyoming.
Steve Crow, Executive Director
Commission on Institutions of Higher Education
30 North LaSalle, Suite 2400
Chicago, Illinois 60602-2504
Telephone: 312-263-0456
Fax: 312-263-7462
E-mail: crow@ncacihe.org

NORTHWEST ASSOCIATION OF SCHOOLS AND COLLEGES
Accredits institutions in Alaska, Idaho, Montana, Nevada, Oregon, Utah, and Washington.
Sandra E. Elman, Executive Director
Commission on Colleges
11130 Northeast 33rd Place, Suite 120
Seattle, Washington 98004
Telephone: 425-827-2005
Fax: 425-827-3395
E-mail: selman@u.washington.edu

SOUTHERN ASSOCIATION OF COLLEGES AND SCHOOLS
Accredits institutions in Alabama, Florida, Georgia, Kentucky, Louisiana, Mississippi, North Carolina, South Carolina, Tennessee, Texas, and Virginia.
James T. Rogers, Executive Director
Commission on Colleges
1866 Southern Lane
Decatur, Georgia 30033-4097
Telephone: 404-679-4500
Fax: 404-679-4558
E-mail: jrogers@sacscoc.org

WESTERN ASSOCIATION OF SCHOOLS AND COLLEGES
Accredits institutions in California, Guam, and Hawaii.
Ralph A. Wolff, Executive Director
Accrediting Commission for Senior Colleges and Universities
Mills College
P.O. Box 9990
Oakland, California 94613-0990
Telephone: 510-632-5000
Fax: 510-632-8361
E-mail: rwolff@wasc.mills.edu

Institutional Accrediting Agencies—Other

ACCREDITING COUNCIL FOR INDEPENDENT COLLEGES AND SCHOOLS
Stephen D. Parker, Executive Director
750 First Street, NE, Suite 980
Washington, D.C. 20002-4241
Telephone: 202-336-6780
Fax: 202-842-2593
E-mail: acics@digex.net
World Wide Web: www.acics.org

DISTANCE EDUCATION AND TRAINING COUNCIL
Michael P. Lambert, Executive Secretary
1601 Eighteenth Street, NW
Washington, D.C. 20009-2529
Telephone: 202-234-5100
Fax: 202-332-1386
E-mail: detc@detc.org
World Wide Web: www.detc.org

Specialized Accrediting Agencies
[Only Book 1 of Peterson's Annual Guides to Graduate Study includes the complete list of specialized accrediting groups recognized by the U.S. Department of Education and the Council on Higher Education Accreditation (CHEA). The lists in Books 2, 4, 5, and 6 are abridged, and there are no such recognized specialized accrediting bodies for the programs in Book 3.]

FORESTRY
P. Gregory Smith, Director, Science and Education
Committee on Education
Society of American Foresters
5400 Grosvenor Lane
Bethesda, Maryland 20814-2198
Telephone: 301-897-8720 Ext. 119
Fax: 301-897-3690
E-mail: smithg@safnet.org
World Wide Web: www.safnet.org

Directory of Institutions with Programs in the Physical Sciences, Mathematics, Agricultural Sciences, the Environment, and Natural Resources

This directory lists institutions in alphabetical order and includes beneath each name the academic fields in the phyical sciences, mathematics, agricultural sciences, the environment, and natural resources in which each institution offers graduate programs. The degree level in each field is also indicated, provided that the institution has supplied that information in response to Peterson's Annual Survey of Graduate Institutions. An *M* indicates that a master's degree program is offered; a *D* indicates that a doctoral degree program is offered; a *P* indicates that the first professional degree is offered; an *O* signifies that other advanced degrees (e.g., certificates or specialist degrees) are offered; and an * (asterisk) indicates that an in-depth description and/or announcement is located in this volume. See the index for the page number of the in-depth description and/or announcement.

ACADIA UNIVERSITY
Chemistry — M
Geology — M

ADELPHI UNIVERSITY
Environmental Policy and
   Resource Management — M,O
Geosciences — M,O
Mathematics — M,D
Physics — M

AIR FORCE INSTITUTE OF TECHNOLOGY
Applied Mathematics — M,D
Environmental Policy and
   Resource Management — M
Meteorology — M,D

ALABAMA AGRICULTURAL AND MECHANICAL UNIVERSITY
Agricultural Sciences—General — M,D
Agronomy and Soil Sciences — M,D
Animal Sciences — M,D
Applied Physics — M,D
Environmental Sciences — M,D
Food Science and Technology — M,D
Optical Sciences — M,D
Physics — M,D

ALABAMA STATE UNIVERSITY
Mathematics — M,O

ALASKA PACIFIC UNIVERSITY
Environmental Sciences — M

ALCORN STATE UNIVERSITY
Agricultural Sciences—General — M
Agronomy and Soil Sciences — M
Animal Sciences — M

AMERICAN UNIVERSITY
Applied Mathematics — M
Chemistry — M,D*
Environmental Policy and
   Resource Management — M,D,O
Environmental Sciences — M*
Mathematics — M*
Physics — M*
Statistics — M,D,O

ANDREWS UNIVERSITY
Mathematics — M
Physics — M

ANGELO STATE UNIVERSITY
Animal Sciences — M
Mathematics — M

ANTIOCH NEW ENGLAND GRADUATE SCHOOL
Environmental Policy and
   Resource Management — M*
Environmental Sciences — D*

ANTIOCH UNIVERSITY SEATTLE
Environmental Policy and
   Resource Management — M

APPALACHIAN STATE UNIVERSITY
Applied Physics — M
Mathematics — M

ARIZONA STATE UNIVERSITY
Applied Mathematics — M,D
Astronomy — M,D
Chemistry — M,D*
Mathematics — M,D*
Physics — M,D
Statistics — M,D

ARKANSAS STATE UNIVERSITY
Agricultural Sciences—General — M,O
Chemistry — M,O
Environmental Sciences — M,D,O
Mathematics — M

AUBURN UNIVERSITY
Agricultural Sciences—General — M,D
Agronomy and Soil Sciences — M,D
Animal Sciences — M,D
Applied Mathematics — M,D
Aquaculture — M,D
Chemistry — M,D
Fish, Game, and Wildlife
   Management — M,D
Food Science and Technology — M,D
Forestry — M,D
Geology — M*
Horticulture — M,D
Hydrology — M,D
Mathematics — M,D
Physics — M,D
Statistics — M,D

BALL STATE UNIVERSITY
Chemistry — M
Geology — M
Geosciences — M
Mathematics — M
Natural Resources — M
Physics — M
Statistics — M

BARD COLLEGE
Environmental Policy and
   Resource Management — M
Environmental Sciences — M*
Natural Resources — M

BARUCH COLLEGE OF THE CITY UNIVERSITY OF NEW YORK
Statistics — M

BAYLOR UNIVERSITY
Chemistry — M,D
Environmental Policy and
   Resource Management — M
Geology — M,D
Geosciences — M,D
Limnology — M,D
Mathematics — M
Physics — M,D
Statistics — M,D

BEMIDJI STATE UNIVERSITY
Environmental Policy and
   Resource Management — M

BOISE STATE UNIVERSITY
Environmental Policy and
   Resource Management — M
Geology — M
Geophysics — M

BOSTON COLLEGE
Analytical Chemistry — M,D
Chemistry — M,D*
Geology — M
Geophysics — M
Inorganic Chemistry — M,D
Mathematics — M
Organic Chemistry — M,D
Physical Chemistry — M,D
Physics — M,D

BOSTON UNIVERSITY
Astronomy — M,D
Biostatistics — M,D
Chemistry — M,D
Environmental Policy and
   Resource Management — M,O
Geosciences — M,D
Inorganic Chemistry — M,D
Mathematics — M,D
Organic Chemistry — M,D
Physical Chemistry — M,D
Physics — M,D*
Statistics — M,D
Theoretical Chemistry — M,D

BOWLING GREEN STATE UNIVERSITY
Astronomy — M
Chemistry — M,D
Geology — M
Mathematics — M,D,O*
Physics — M
Statistics — M,D,O

BRADLEY UNIVERSITY
Chemistry — M

BRANDEIS UNIVERSITY
Chemistry — M,D
Inorganic Chemistry — M,D
Mathematics — D*
Organic Chemistry — M,D
Physical Chemistry — M,D
Physics — M,D

BRIGHAM YOUNG UNIVERSITY
Agricultural Sciences—General — M,D
Agronomy and Soil Sciences — M,D
Analytical Chemistry — M,D
Animal Sciences — M
Astronomy — M,D
Chemistry — M,D*
Fish, Game, and Wildlife
   Management — M,D
Food Science and Technology — M
Geology — M
Horticulture — M
Inorganic Chemistry — M,D
Mathematics — M,D
Organic Chemistry — M,D
Physical Chemistry — M,D
Physics — M,D
Range Science — M,D
Statistics — M

BROCK UNIVERSITY
Chemistry — M
Geosciences — M
Physics — M

BROOKLYN COLLEGE OF THE CITY UNIVERSITY OF NEW YORK
Applied Physics — M,D
Chemistry — M,D
Geology — M,D
Mathematics — M,D
Physics — M,D*

BROWN UNIVERSITY
Applied Mathematics — M,D*
Biostatistics — M,D*
Chemistry — M,D
Environmental Policy and
   Resource Management — M
Geosciences — M,D
Mathematics — M,D
Physics — M,D*

BRYN MAWR COLLEGE
Chemistry — M,D
Geology — M,D
Mathematics — M,D
Physics — M,D

BUCKNELL UNIVERSITY
Chemistry — M
Mathematics — M

BUTLER UNIVERSITY
Chemistry — M

CALIFORNIA INSTITUTE OF TECHNOLOGY
Applied Mathematics — D*
Applied Physics — M,D
Astronomy — D
Chemistry — D
Computational Sciences — M,D
Geochemistry — M,D
Geology — M,D
Geophysics — M,D
Mathematics — D
Physics — D*
Planetary and Space Sciences — M,D
Plasma Physics — M,D

CALIFORNIA POLYTECHNIC STATE UNIVERSITY, SAN LUIS OBISPO
Agricultural Sciences—General — M
Mathematics — M

CALIFORNIA STATE POLYTECHNIC UNIVERSITY, POMONA
Agricultural Sciences—General — M
Animal Sciences — M
Applied Mathematics — M
Chemistry — M
Food Science and Technology — M
Mathematics — M

CALIFORNIA STATE UNIVERSITY, BAKERSFIELD
Geology — M
Hydrology — M

CALIFORNIA STATE UNIVERSITY, CHICO
Agricultural Sciences—General — M
Geosciences — M
Hydrology — M

CALIFORNIA STATE UNIVERSITY, FRESNO
Agricultural Sciences—General — M
Animal Sciences — M
Chemistry — M
Food Science and Technology — M
Geology — M
Marine Sciences — M
Mathematics — M*
Physics — M*

CALIFORNIA STATE UNIVERSITY, FULLERTON
Analytical Chemistry — M
Applied Mathematics — M
Chemistry — M
Environmental Policy and
   Resource Management — M
Environmental Sciences — M
Geochemistry — M
Inorganic Chemistry — M
Mathematics — M
Organic Chemistry — M
Physical Chemistry — M
Physics — M
Statistics — M

CALIFORNIA STATE UNIVERSITY, HAYWARD
Chemistry — M

CALIFORNIA STATE UNIVERSITY, LONG BEACH *(continued top)*
Geology — M
Marine Sciences — M
Mathematics — M
Statistics — M

CALIFORNIA STATE UNIVERSITY, LONG BEACH
Applied Mathematics — M
Chemistry — M
Geology — M
Mathematics — M
Physics — M

CALIFORNIA STATE UNIVERSITY, LOS ANGELES
Analytical Chemistry — M
Applied Mathematics — M
Chemistry — M
Geology — M
Inorganic Chemistry — M
Mathematics — M
Organic Chemistry — M
Physical Chemistry — M
Physics — M

CALIFORNIA STATE UNIVERSITY, NORTHRIDGE
Chemistry — M
Geology — M
Mathematics — M
Physics — M

CALIFORNIA STATE UNIVERSITY, SACRAMENTO
Chemistry — M
Marine Sciences — M
Mathematics — M
Statistics — M

CALIFORNIA STATE UNIVERSITY, SAN BERNARDINO
Mathematics — M

CALIFORNIA STATE UNIVERSITY, SAN MARCOS
Mathematics — M

CALIFORNIA UNIVERSITY OF PENNSYLVANIA
Geosciences — M

CARLETON UNIVERSITY
Chemistry — M,D
Environmental Policy and
   Resource Management — M,D
Geosciences — M,D
Mathematics — M,D
Physics — M,D

CARNEGIE MELLON UNIVERSITY
Applied Physics — M,D
Chemistry — M,D*
Computational Sciences — D
Mathematics — M,D*
Physics — M,D*
Statistics — M,D*

CASE WESTERN RESERVE UNIVERSITY
Analytical Chemistry — M,D
Applied Mathematics — M,D
Astronomy — M,D
Biostatistics — M,D
Chemistry — M,D
Geology — M,D
Geosciences — M,D
Inorganic Chemistry — M,D
Mathematics — M,D
Organic Chemistry — M,D
Physical Chemistry — M,D
Physics — M,D
Statistics — M,D

THE CATHOLIC UNIVERSITY OF AMERICA
Acoustics — M,D
Chemistry — M,D
Physics — M,D

CENTRAL CONNECTICUT STATE UNIVERSITY
Chemistry — M
Geosciences — M
Mathematics — M
Physics — M

CENTRAL MICHIGAN UNIVERSITY
Chemistry — M
Mathematics — M,D
Physics — M

CENTRAL MISSOURI STATE UNIVERSITY
Agricultural Sciences—General — M
Mathematics — M

CENTRAL WASHINGTON UNIVERSITY

Chemistry	M
Environmental Policy and Resource Management	M
Geology	M
Mathematics	M

CHAPMAN UNIVERSITY

Food Science and Technology	M

CHICAGO STATE UNIVERSITY

Mathematics	M

CHRISTOPHER NEWPORT UNIVERSITY

Applied Physics	M
Environmental Sciences	M

CITY COLLEGE OF THE CITY UNIVERSITY OF NEW YORK

Atmospheric Sciences	M,D
Chemistry	M,D
Environmental Sciences	M,D
Geosciences	M,D
Mathematics	M,D
Physics	M,D*

CLAREMONT GRADUATE UNIVERSITY

Applied Mathematics	M,D
Mathematics	M,D*
Statistics	M,D

CLARK ATLANTA UNIVERSITY

Applied Mathematics	M
Chemistry	M,D
Inorganic Chemistry	M,D
Organic Chemistry	M,D
Physical Chemistry	M,D
Physics	M

CLARKSON UNIVERSITY

Analytical Chemistry	M,D
Chemistry	M,D
Inorganic Chemistry	M,D
Mathematics	M,D*
Organic Chemistry	M,D
Physical Chemistry	M,D
Physics	M,D

CLARK UNIVERSITY

Chemistry	M,D*
Environmental Policy and Resource Management	M
Physics	M,D

CLEMSON UNIVERSITY

Agricultural Sciences—General	M,D*
Agronomy and Soil Sciences	M,D
Animal Sciences	M,D
Applied Mathematics	M,D
Aquaculture	M
Astronomy	M,D
Astrophysics	M,D
Atmospheric Sciences	M,D
Chemistry	M,D
Computational Sciences	M,D
Environmental Sciences	M,D
Fish, Game, and Wildlife Management	M
Food Science and Technology	M,D
Forestry	M,D
Horticulture	M,D
Hydrology	M
Mathematics	M,D
Physics	M,D*
Statistics	M,D

CLEVELAND STATE UNIVERSITY

Analytical Chemistry	M,D
Applied Mathematics	M
Chemistry	M,D
Environmental Sciences	M,D
Geology	M,D
Inorganic Chemistry	M,D
Mathematics	M
Optical Sciences	M
Organic Chemistry	M,D
Physical Chemistry	M,D
Physics	M

COLGATE UNIVERSITY

Geology	M

COLLEGE OF STATEN ISLAND OF THE CITY UNIVERSITY OF NEW YORK

Chemistry	D
Environmental Sciences	M

COLLEGE OF THE ATLANTIC

Environmental Policy and Resource Management	M

COLLEGE OF WILLIAM AND MARY

Chemistry	M
Computational Sciences	M*
Marine Sciences	M,D*
Physics	M,D

COLORADO SCHOOL OF MINES

Applied Physics	M,D
Chemistry	M,D
Environmental Sciences	M,D
Geochemistry	M,D,O
Geology	M,D
Geophysics	M,D,O
Geosciences	M,D,O
Hydrology	M,D,O
Mathematics	M,D
Physics	M,D

COLORADO STATE UNIVERSITY

Agricultural Sciences—General	M,D
Agronomy and Soil Sciences	M,D
Animal Sciences	M,D
Atmospheric Sciences	M,D
Chemistry	M,D
Environmental Policy and Resource Management	M,D
Environmental Sciences	M,D
Fish, Game, and Wildlife Management	M,D
Food Science and Technology	M,D
Forestry	M,D
Geology	M
Geosciences	M,D
Horticulture	M,D
Hydrology	M,D
Mathematics	M,D*
Physics	M,D
Range Science	M,D
Statistics	M,D
Water Resources	M,D

COLUMBIA UNIVERSITY

Applied Mathematics	M,D
Applied Physics	M,D*
Astronomy	M,D
Atmospheric Sciences	M,D*
Biostatistics	M,D
Chemistry	M,D
Geochemistry	M,D
Geodetic Sciences	M,D
Geophysics	M,D
Geosciences	M,D
Inorganic Chemistry	M,D
Mathematics	M,D*
Oceanography	M,D
Organic Chemistry	M,D
Physical Chemistry	M,D
Physics	M,D
Planetary and Space Sciences	M,D
Plasma Physics	M,D
Statistics	M,D

COLUMBUS STATE UNIVERSITY

Environmental Sciences	M

CONCORDIA UNIVERSITY (CANADA)

Chemistry	M,D
Mathematics	M,D,O
Physics	M,D
Statistics	M,D,O

CORNELL UNIVERSITY

Agronomy and Soil Sciences	M,D*
Analytical Chemistry	D
Animal Sciences	M,D
Applied Mathematics	M,D*
Applied Physics	M,D
Astronomy	D
Astrophysics	D
Atmospheric Sciences	M,D
Biometrics	M,D
Chemistry	D*
Computational Sciences	M,D
Environmental Policy and Resource Management	M,D
Fish, Game, and Wildlife Management	M,D
Food Science and Technology	M,D
Forestry	M,D
Geochemistry	M,D
Geology	M,D*
Geophysics	M,D
Geosciences	M,D
Horticulture	M,D
Hydrology	M,D
Inorganic Chemistry	D
Limnology	D
Mathematics	D
Natural Resources	M,D
Oceanography	D
Organic Chemistry	D
Physical Chemistry	D
Physics	D
Planetary and Space Sciences	D
Statistics	M,D
Theoretical Chemistry	D
Theoretical Physics	M,D

CREIGHTON UNIVERSITY

Atmospheric Sciences	M
Mathematics	M
Physics	M
Statistics	M

DALHOUSIE UNIVERSITY

Agricultural Sciences—General	M
Applied Mathematics	M,D
Chemistry	M,D
Environmental Policy and Resource Management	M
Food Science and Technology	M,D
Geosciences	M,D
Mathematics	M,D
Oceanography	M,D*
Physics	M,D
Statistics	M,D

DARTMOUTH COLLEGE

Astronomy	M,D*
Chemistry	D
Geosciences	M,D
Mathematics	D*
Physics	M,D*

DELAWARE STATE UNIVERSITY

Chemistry	M
Physics	M

DEPAUL UNIVERSITY

Applied Mathematics	M
Applied Physics	M
Chemistry	M
Physics	M

DREXEL UNIVERSITY

Atmospheric Sciences	M,D
Biostatistics	M,D
Chemistry	M,D*
Environmental Sciences	M,D*
Food Science and Technology	M,D
Mathematics	M,D*
Physics	M,D

DUKE UNIVERSITY

Chemistry	D
Environmental Policy and Resource Management	M,D*
Environmental Sciences	M,D
Forestry	M,D
Geology	M,D*
Marine Sciences	M,D*
Mathematics	D
Natural Resources	M,D*
Physics	D*
Statistics	D
Water Resources	M,D*

DUQUESNE UNIVERSITY

Chemistry	M,D*
Environmental Policy and Resource Management	M,O
Environmental Sciences	M,O*

EAST CAROLINA UNIVERSITY

Applied Mathematics	M
Chemistry	M
Geology	M
Mathematics	M
Physics	M,D*

EASTERN ILLINOIS UNIVERSITY

Chemistry	M*
Mathematics	M

EASTERN KENTUCKY UNIVERSITY

Chemistry	M
Geology	M,D
Mathematics	M

EASTERN MICHIGAN UNIVERSITY

Chemistry	M*
Mathematics	M
Physics	M

EASTERN NEW MEXICO UNIVERSITY

Chemistry	M
Mathematics	M

EASTERN WASHINGTON UNIVERSITY

Geology	M
Mathematics	M

EAST TENNESSEE STATE UNIVERSITY

Chemistry	M,D
Mathematics	M

ÉCOLE POLYTECHNIQUE DE MONTRÉAL

Applied Mathematics	M,D
Mathematics	M,D
Optical Sciences	M,D,O

EMBRY-RIDDLE AERONAUTICAL UNIVERSITY

Computational Sciences	M*

EMORY UNIVERSITY

Biostatistics	M,D*
Chemistry	D
Mathematics	M,D*

Physics	D*

EMPORIA STATE UNIVERSITY

Chemistry	M
Geosciences	M
Mathematics	M
Physics	M

THE EVERGREEN STATE COLLEGE

Environmental Policy and Resource Management	M*

FAIRLEIGH DICKINSON UNIVERSITY, FLORHAM-MADISON CAMPUS

Chemistry	M
Mathematics	M

FAIRLEIGH DICKINSON UNIVERSITY, TEANECK–HACKENSACK CAMPUS

Chemistry	M
Environmental Policy and Resource Management	M
Mathematics	M
Physics	M

FAYETTEVILLE STATE UNIVERSITY

Mathematics	M

FISK UNIVERSITY

Chemistry	M
Physics	M

FLORIDA AGRICULTURAL AND MECHANICAL UNIVERSITY

Chemistry	M
Physics	M

FLORIDA ATLANTIC UNIVERSITY

Chemistry	M
Environmental Sciences	M
Geology	M
Mathematics	M,D
Physics	M,D

FLORIDA INSTITUTE OF TECHNOLOGY

Applied Mathematics	M,D
Chemistry	M,D
Environmental Policy and Resource Management	M
Environmental Sciences	M,D*
Marine Sciences	M,D*
Oceanography	M,D*
Physics	M,D*
Planetary and Space Sciences	M

FLORIDA INTERNATIONAL UNIVERSITY

Chemistry	M,D*
Environmental Policy and Resource Management	M
Environmental Sciences	M*
Geology	M,D
Mathematics	M
Physics	M,D

FLORIDA STATE UNIVERSITY

Analytical Chemistry	M,D
Applied Mathematics	M,D
Chemistry	M,D*
Food Science and Technology	M,D
Geology	M,D
Geophysics	D
Inorganic Chemistry	M,D
Mathematics	M,D
Meteorology	M,D
Oceanography	M,D*
Organic Chemistry	M,D
Physical Chemistry	M,D
Physics	M,D*
Statistics	M,D

FORT HAYS STATE UNIVERSITY

Geology	M

FRAMINGHAM STATE COLLEGE

Food Science and Technology	M*

FRIENDS UNIVERSITY

Environmental Policy and Resource Management	M

FROSTBURG STATE UNIVERSITY

Fish, Game, and Wildlife Management	M

FURMAN UNIVERSITY

Chemistry	M

GEORGE MASON UNIVERSITY

Applied Physics	M
Chemistry	M
Computational Sciences	D*
Environmental Policy and Resource Management	M,D
Environmental Sciences	M
Mathematics	M
Statistics	M

20

Peterson's Graduate Programs in the Physical Sciences, Mathematics, Agricultural Sciences, the Environment & Natural Resources 2000

GEORGETOWN UNIVERSITY

Analytical Chemistry	M,D
Biostatistics	M
Chemistry	M,D*
Inorganic Chemistry	M,D
Organic Chemistry	M,D
Physical Chemistry	M,D
Theoretical Chemistry	M,D

THE GEORGE WASHINGTON UNIVERSITY

Analytical Chemistry	M,D
Applied Mathematics	M
Biostatistics	M,D
Chemistry	M,D
Computational Sciences	M
Environmental Policy and Resource Management	M
Geochemistry	M
Geology	M,D
Inorganic Chemistry	M,D
Mathematics	M,D*
Organic Chemistry	M,D
Physical Chemistry	M,D
Physics	D
Statistics	M,D*

GEORGIA INSTITUTE OF TECHNOLOGY

Applied Mathematics	M,D
Applied Physics	M,D
Atmospheric Sciences	M,D*
Chemistry	M,D*
Geochemistry	M,D
Geophysics	M,D
Geosciences	M,D*
Mathematics	M,D
Physics	M,D*
Statistics	M,D

GEORGIAN COURT COLLEGE

Mathematics	M

GEORGIA SOUTHERN UNIVERSITY

Mathematics	M

GEORGIA STATE UNIVERSITY

Astronomy	D*
Chemistry	M,D*
Geology	M*
Mathematics	M*
Physics	M,D*

GOVERNORS STATE UNIVERSITY

Analytical Chemistry	M

GRADUATE SCHOOL AND UNIVERSITY CENTER OF THE CITY UNIVERSITY OF NEW YORK

Chemistry	D
Environmental Sciences	D
Geosciences	D
Mathematics	D
Physics	D

HAMPTON UNIVERSITY

Applied Mathematics	M
Chemistry	M
Physics	M,D

HARDIN-SIMMONS UNIVERSITY

Environmental Policy and Resource Management	M

HARVARD UNIVERSITY

Applied Mathematics	M,D
Applied Physics	M,D
Astronomy	M,D*
Astrophysics	M,D
Biostatistics	M,D*
Chemistry	M,D
Environmental Sciences	M
Forestry	M,D*
Geosciences	M,D
Inorganic Chemistry	M,D
Mathematics	M,D
Organic Chemistry	M,D
Physical Chemistry	M,D*
Physics	M,D
Planetary and Space Sciences	M,D*
Statistics	M,D
Theoretical Physics	M,D

HOFSTRA UNIVERSITY

Applied Mathematics	M

HOWARD UNIVERSITY

Analytical Chemistry	M,D
Applied Mathematics	M,D
Atmospheric Sciences	M,D
Chemistry	M,D
Inorganic Chemistry	M,D
Mathematics	M,D
Organic Chemistry	M,D
Physical Chemistry	M,D
Physics	M,D
Theoretical Chemistry	M,D

HUMBOLDT STATE UNIVERSITY

Environmental Sciences	M
Natural Resources	M

HUNTER COLLEGE OF THE CITY UNIVERSITY OF NEW YORK

Applied Mathematics	M
Mathematics	M
Physics	M,D

ICR GRADUATE SCHOOL

Astrophysics	M
Geology	M
Geophysics	M

IDAHO STATE UNIVERSITY

Chemistry	M
Geology	M
Geophysics	M
Hydrology	M
Mathematics	M,D
Physics	M

ILLINOIS INSTITUTE OF TECHNOLOGY

Analytical Chemistry	M,D
Chemistry	M,D*
Environmental Policy and Resource Management	M*
Food Science and Technology	M,D
Inorganic Chemistry	M,D
Organic Chemistry	M,D
Physical Chemistry	M,D
Physics	M,D
Theoretical Chemistry	M,D

ILLINOIS STATE UNIVERSITY

Agricultural Sciences—General	M
Chemistry	M
Hydrology	M
Mathematics	M

INDIANA STATE UNIVERSITY

Chemistry	M
Geosciences	M,D
Mathematics	M
Physics	M

INDIANA UNIVERSITY BLOOMINGTON

Analytical Chemistry	M,D
Applied Mathematics	M,D
Astronomy	M,D
Astrophysics	D
Chemistry	M,D
Environmental Sciences	M,D*
Geochemistry	M,D
Geology	M,D*
Geophysics	M,D
Geosciences	M,D
Inorganic Chemistry	M,D
Mathematics	M,D
Optical Sciences	M,D
Physical Chemistry	M,D
Physics	M,D*
Statistics	M,D

INDIANA UNIVERSITY OF PENNSYLVANIA

Applied Mathematics	M
Chemistry	M
Mathematics	M
Physics	M

INDIANA UNIVERSITY–PURDUE UNIVERSITY FORT WAYNE

Applied Mathematics	M
Chemistry	M
Mathematics	M

INDIANA UNIVERSITY–PURDUE UNIVERSITY INDIANAPOLIS

Applied Mathematics	M,D
Chemistry	M,D
Geology	M
Mathematics	M,D
Physics	M,D
Statistics	M,D

INSTITUTE OF PAPER SCIENCE AND TECHNOLOGY

Chemistry	M,D*
Mathematics	M,D
Physics	M,D

INSTITUTO TECNOLÓGICO Y DE ESTUDIOS SUPERIORES DE MONTERREY, CAMPUS MONTERREY

Agricultural Sciences—General	M,D
Chemistry	M,D
Organic Chemistry	M,D
Statistics	M,D

IOWA STATE UNIVERSITY OF SCIENCE AND TECHNOLOGY

Agricultural Sciences—General	M,D
Agronomy and Soil Sciences	M,D
Animal Sciences	M,D
Applied Mathematics	M,D
Astronomy	M,D
Chemistry	M,D
Fish, Game, and Wildlife Management	M,D
Food Science and Technology	M,D*
Forestry	M,D
Geology	M,D*
Geosciences	M,D
Horticulture	M,D
Mathematics	M,D*
Meteorology	M,D
Physics	M,D
Statistics	M,D
Water Resources	M,D

JACKSON STATE UNIVERSITY

Chemistry	M,D
Environmental Sciences	M,D
Mathematics	M

JACKSONVILLE STATE UNIVERSITY

Mathematics	M

JOHN CARROLL UNIVERSITY

Chemistry	M
Mathematics	M
Physics	M

JOHNS HOPKINS UNIVERSITY

Astronomy	D
Biostatistics	M,D
Chemistry	M,D*
Geochemistry	M,D
Geology	M,D
Geophysics	M,D
Mathematics	M,D*
Oceanography	M,D
Physics	D*
Planetary and Space Sciences	M,D
Water Resources	M,D

KANSAS STATE UNIVERSITY

Agricultural Sciences—General	M,D
Agronomy and Soil Sciences	M,D
Analytical Chemistry	M,D
Animal Sciences	M,D
Chemistry	M,D*
Environmental Policy and Resource Management	M,D*
Food Science and Technology	M
Geology	M,D
Horticulture	M,D
Inorganic Chemistry	M,D
Organic Chemistry	M,D
Physical Chemistry	M,D
Physics	M,D
Range Science	M,D
Statistics	M,D

KENT STATE UNIVERSITY

Analytical Chemistry	M,D
Applied Mathematics	M,D
Chemistry	M,D*
Geology	M,D
Inorganic Chemistry	M,D
Mathematics	M,D*
Organic Chemistry	M,D
Physical Chemistry	M,D*
Physics	M,D*

KUTZTOWN UNIVERSITY OF PENNSYLVANIA

Mathematics	M

LAKEHEAD UNIVERSITY

Chemistry	M
Forestry	M
Geology	M
Mathematics	M
Physics	M
Statistics	M

LAMAR UNIVERSITY

Chemistry	M
Environmental Policy and Resource Management	M
Mathematics	M

LAURENTIAN UNIVERSITY

Applied Physics	M
Chemistry	M
Geology	M

LEHIGH UNIVERSITY

Analytical Chemistry	M,D
Applied Mathematics	M,D
Chemistry	M,D
Environmental Sciences	M,D
Geology	M,D
Geosciences	M,D*
Inorganic Chemistry	M,D
Mathematics	M,D
Organic Chemistry	M,D

LEHMAN COLLEGE OF THE CITY UNIVERSITY OF NEW YORK

Mathematics	M

LESLEY COLLEGE

Environmental Policy and Resource Management	M,O

LOMA LINDA UNIVERSITY

Biostatistics	M
Geology	M

LONG ISLAND UNIVERSITY, BROOKLYN CAMPUS

Chemistry	M*

LONG ISLAND UNIVERSITY, C.W. POST CAMPUS

Applied Mathematics	M
Environmental Policy and Resource Management	M
Environmental Sciences	M
Mathematics	M

LONGWOOD COLLEGE

Environmental Policy and Resource Management	M

LOUISIANA STATE UNIVERSITY AND AGRICULTURAL AND MECHANICAL COLLEGE

Agricultural Sciences—General	M,D
Agronomy and Soil Sciences	M,D
Animal Sciences	M,D
Astronomy	M,D
Astrophysics	M,D
Chemistry	M,D
Environmental Policy and Resource Management	M
Environmental Sciences	M,D
Fish, Game, and Wildlife Management	M,D
Food Science and Technology	M,D
Forestry	M,D
Geology	M,D
Geophysics	M,D
Horticulture	M,D
Mathematics	M,D
Oceanography	M,D
Physics	M,D*
Statistics	M

LOUISIANA STATE UNIVERSITY HEALTH SCIENCE CENTER

Biometrics	M,D

LOUISIANA TECH UNIVERSITY

Chemistry	M
Computational Sciences	M,D
Mathematics	M
Physics	M,D
Statistics	M

LOYOLA MARYMOUNT UNIVERSITY

Environmental Sciences	M

LOYOLA UNIVERSITY CHICAGO

Chemistry	M,D
Mathematics	M*

LOYOLA UNIVERSITY NEW ORLEANS

Mathematics	M

MAHARISHI UNIVERSITY OF MANAGEMENT

Mathematics	M
Physics	M,D

MARQUETTE UNIVERSITY

Analytical Chemistry	M,D
Chemistry	M,D
Inorganic Chemistry	M,D
Mathematics	M,D
Organic Chemistry	M,D
Physical Chemistry	M,D
Statistics	M,D

MARSHALL UNIVERSITY

Chemistry	M
Environmental Sciences	M
Mathematics	M
Physics	M

MASSACHUSETTS COLLEGE OF PHARMACY AND HEALTH SCIENCES

Chemistry	M,D

MASSACHUSETTS INSTITUTE OF TECHNOLOGY

Atmospheric Sciences	M,D

Massachusetts Institute of Technology (continued)

Chemistry	M,D
Computational Sciences	D
Geochemistry	M,D
Geology	M,D
Geophysics	M,D
Geosciences	M,D*
Inorganic Chemistry	D
Mathematics	D
Meteorology	M,D
Oceanography	M,D,O*
Organic Chemistry	D
Physical Chemistry	D
Physics	M,D
Planetary and Space Sciences	M,D

MCGILL UNIVERSITY

Agricultural Sciences—General	M,D,O
Agronomy and Soil Sciences	M,D
Animal Sciences	M,D
Atmospheric Sciences	M,D
Biostatistics	M,D,O
Chemistry	M,D
Fish, Game, and Wildlife Management	M,D
Food Science and Technology	M,D
Forestry	M,D
Geosciences	M,D,O
Mathematics	M,D
Meteorology	M,D
Natural Resources	M,D
Oceanography	M,D
Physics	M,D
Planetary and Space Sciences	M,D,O
Water Resources	M,D

MCMASTER UNIVERSITY

Analytical Chemistry	M,D
Astrophysics	M,D
Chemistry	M,D
Geochemistry	M,D
Geology	M,D
Geosciences	M,D*
Inorganic Chemistry	M,D
Mathematics	M,D
Organic Chemistry	M,D
Physical Chemistry	M,D
Physics	M,D
Statistics	M,D

MCNEESE STATE UNIVERSITY

Chemistry	M
Environmental Sciences	M
Mathematics	M
Statistics	M

MEDICAL COLLEGE OF WISCONSIN

Biostatistics	D*

MEDICAL UNIVERSITY OF SOUTH CAROLINA

Biometrics	M,D
Biostatistics	M,D
Environmental Sciences	M

MEMORIAL UNIVERSITY OF NEWFOUNDLAND

Aquaculture	M
Chemistry	M,D
Computational Sciences	M
Environmental Sciences	M
Fish, Game, and Wildlife Management	M
Food Science and Technology	M,D
Geology	M,D
Geophysics	M,D
Geosciences	M,D
Marine Sciences	M
Mathematics	M,D
Oceanography	M,D
Physics	M,D
Statistics	M,D

MIAMI UNIVERSITY

Chemistry	M,D*
Environmental Sciences	M
Geology	M,D
Mathematics	M
Physics	M
Statistics	M

MICHIGAN STATE UNIVERSITY

Agricultural Sciences—General	M,D
Agronomy and Soil Sciences	M,D
Analytical Chemistry	M,D
Animal Sciences	M,D
Applied Mathematics	M,D
Astrophysics	M,D
Chemistry	M,D
Computational Sciences	M,D
Environmental Policy and Resource Management	M,D
Environmental Sciences	M,D
Fish, Game, and Wildlife Management	M,D
Food Science and Technology	M,D
Forestry	M,D
Geology	M,D

Geosciences	M,D
Horticulture	M,D
Inorganic Chemistry	M,D
Mathematics	M,D
Organic Chemistry	M,D
Physical Chemistry	M,D
Physics	M,D*
Statistics	M,D*

MICHIGAN TECHNOLOGICAL UNIVERSITY

Applied Physics	M,D
Chemistry	M,D
Computational Sciences	M,D
Environmental Policy and Resource Management	M
Forestry	M,D
Geology	M,D
Geophysics	M
Mathematics	M,D
Physics	M,D*

MIDDLE TENNESSEE STATE UNIVERSITY

Chemistry	M,D
Mathematics	M

MINNESOTA STATE UNIVERSITY, MANKATO

Astronomy	M
Chemistry	M
Environmental Sciences	M
Mathematics	M
Physics	M
Statistics	M

MISSISSIPPI COLLEGE

Chemistry	M
Mathematics	M

MISSISSIPPI STATE UNIVERSITY

Agricultural Sciences—General	M,D
Agronomy and Soil Sciences	M,D
Animal Sciences	M,D
Chemistry	M,D
Computational Sciences	M,D*
Fish, Game, and Wildlife Management	M,D
Food Science and Technology	M,D
Forestry	M
Geosciences	M
Mathematics	M,D
Physics	M*
Statistics	M,D

MONTANA STATE UNIVERSITY–BOZEMAN

Agricultural Sciences—General	M,D
Animal Sciences	M
Chemistry	M,D
Environmental Sciences	M,D
Fish, Game, and Wildlife Management	M,D
Geosciences	M
Mathematics	M,D
Natural Resources	M,D
Physics	M,D
Range Science	M
Statistics	M,D

MONTANA TECH OF THE UNIVERSITY OF MONTANA

Geochemistry	M
Geology	M
Geosciences	M
Hydrology	M

MONTCLAIR STATE UNIVERSITY

Applied Mathematics	M
Chemistry	M
Environmental Policy and Resource Management	M
Environmental Sciences	M
Geosciences	M
Mathematics	M
Statistics	M

MONTEREY INSTITUTE OF INTERNATIONAL STUDIES

Environmental Policy and Resource Management	M*

MORGAN STATE UNIVERSITY

Mathematics	M

MOUNT ALLISON UNIVERSITY

Chemistry	M

MOUNT SINAI SCHOOL OF MEDICINE OF NEW YORK UNIVERSITY

Biometrics	D*

MURRAY STATE UNIVERSITY

Agricultural Sciences—General	M
Chemistry	M
Marine Sciences	M
Mathematics	M
Physics	M

THE NAROPA UNIVERSITY

Environmental Policy and Resource Management	M

NATIONAL UNIVERSITY

Environmental Policy and Resource Management	M

NAVAL POSTGRADUATE SCHOOL

Acoustics	M,D
Mathematics	M,D
Meteorology	M,D
Oceanography	M,D
Physics	M,D

NEW JERSEY INSTITUTE OF TECHNOLOGY

Applied Mathematics	M,D
Applied Physics	M,D
Chemistry	M,D
Environmental Policy and Resource Management	M,D
Environmental Sciences	M,D
Mathematics	M,D

NEW MEXICO HIGHLANDS UNIVERSITY

Chemistry	M
Environmental Policy and Resource Management	M
Environmental Sciences	M

NEW MEXICO INSTITUTE OF MINING AND TECHNOLOGY

Astrophysics	M,D
Atmospheric Sciences	M,D
Chemistry	M,D
Environmental Sciences	M,D
Geochemistry	M,D
Geology	M,D
Geophysics	M,D
Geosciences	M,D
Hydrology	M,D
Mathematical Physics	M,D
Mathematics	M
Physics	M,D

NEW MEXICO STATE UNIVERSITY

Agricultural Sciences—General	M,D
Agronomy and Soil Sciences	M,D
Animal Sciences	M,D
Astronomy	M,D*
Chemistry	M,D
Fish, Game, and Wildlife Management	M
Geology	M
Horticulture	M,D
Mathematics	M,D
Physics	M,D
Range Science	M,D
Statistics	M

NEW YORK INSTITUTE OF TECHNOLOGY

Environmental Policy and Resource Management	M,O

NEW YORK MEDICAL COLLEGE

Biostatistics	M

NEW YORK UNIVERSITY

Biostatistics	M,D
Chemistry	M,D*
Mathematics	M,D*
Physics	M,D
Statistics	M,D,O

NICHOLLS STATE UNIVERSITY

Applied Mathematics	M
Mathematics	M

NORTH CAROLINA AGRICULTURAL AND TECHNICAL STATE UNIVERSITY

Agricultural Sciences—General	M
Chemistry	M

NORTH CAROLINA CENTRAL UNIVERSITY

Chemistry	M
Geosciences	M
Mathematics	M

NORTH CAROLINA STATE UNIVERSITY

Agricultural Sciences—General	M,D*
Agronomy and Soil Sciences	M,D
Animal Sciences	M,D
Applied Mathematics	M,D
Atmospheric Sciences	M,D
Biometrics	M,D*
Chemistry	M,D
Environmental Policy and Resource Management	M
Fish, Game, and Wildlife Management	M
Food Science and Technology	M,D
Forestry	M,D
Geology	M,D
Geophysics	M,D
Geosciences	M,D*

Horticulture	M,D
Marine Sciences	M,D
Mathematics	M,D*
Meteorology	M,D
Natural Resources	M,D
Oceanography	M,D
Physics	M,D
Statistics	M,D*

NORTH DAKOTA STATE UNIVERSITY

Agricultural Sciences—General	M,D
Agronomy and Soil Sciences	M,D
Animal Sciences	M,D
Applied Mathematics	M,D
Chemistry	M,D
Environmental Policy and Resource Management	M
Food Science and Technology	M
Horticulture	M
Mathematics	M,D
Physics	M
Range Science	M,D
Statistics	M,D

NORTHEASTERN ILLINOIS UNIVERSITY

Chemistry	M
Environmental Policy and Resource Management	M
Geosciences	M
Mathematics	M

NORTHEASTERN UNIVERSITY

Analytical Chemistry	M,D
Chemistry	M,D
Inorganic Chemistry	M,D
Mathematics	M,D
Organic Chemistry	M,D
Physical Chemistry	M,D
Physics	M,D*

NORTHEAST LOUISIANA UNIVERSITY

Chemistry	M
Geosciences	M

NORTHERN ARIZONA UNIVERSITY

Chemistry	M
Forestry	M,D
Geology	M
Geosciences	M
Mathematics	M
Statistics	M

NORTHERN ILLINOIS UNIVERSITY

Chemistry	M,D
Geology	M,D
Mathematics	M,D
Physics	M
Statistics	M

NORTHERN MICHIGAN UNIVERSITY

Chemistry	M

NORTHWESTERN UNIVERSITY

Applied Mathematics	M,D*
Astronomy	D
Astrophysics	D
Chemistry	D
Geology	D
Geosciences	M,D
Mathematics	D*
Physics	D
Statistics	M,D

NORTHWEST MISSOURI STATE UNIVERSITY

Agricultural Sciences—General	M

NOVA SCOTIA AGRICULTURAL COLLEGE

Agricultural Sciences—General	M
Agronomy and Soil Sciences	M
Animal Sciences	M
Environmental Policy and Resource Management	M
Food Science and Technology	M
Geology	M

NOVA SOUTHEASTERN UNIVERSITY

Environmental Sciences	M,D
Marine Sciences	M,D
Oceanography	M,D*

OAKLAND UNIVERSITY

Applied Mathematics	M
Chemistry	M,D
Environmental Sciences	M
Mathematics	M,D,O
Physics	M,D
Statistics	M,D,O

THE OHIO STATE UNIVERSITY

Agricultural Sciences—General	M,D
Agronomy and Soil Sciences	M,D
Astronomy	M,D
Atmospheric Sciences	M,D
Biostatistics	M,D
Chemistry	M,D
Environmental Sciences	M,D

Food Science and Technology	M,D
Geodetic Sciences	M,D
Geology	M,D
Horticulture	M,D
Mathematics	M,D*
Natural Resources	M
Optical Sciences	M,D
Physical Chemistry	M,D
Physics	M,D
Statistics	M,D*

OHIO UNIVERSITY

Environmental Policy and Resource Management	M
Geology	M
Mathematics	M,D*
Physics	M,D*

OKLAHOMA STATE UNIVERSITY

Agricultural Sciences—General	M,D
Agronomy and Soil Sciences	M,D
Animal Sciences	M,D
Applied Mathematics	M,D
Chemistry	M,D
Environmental Sciences	M,D
Food Science and Technology	M,D
Forestry	M
Geology	M
Horticulture	M
Mathematics	M,D*
Physics	M,D
Statistics	M,D

OLD DOMINION UNIVERSITY

Analytical Chemistry	M,D
Applied Mathematics	M,D
Chemistry	M,D
Geology	M
Mathematics	M,D*
Oceanography	M,D
Organic Chemistry	M,D
Physical Chemistry	M,D
Physics	M,D
Statistics	M,D

OREGON GRADUATE INSTITUTE OF SCIENCE AND TECHNOLOGY

Environmental Policy and Resource Management	M,D
Environmental Sciences	M,D*

OREGON HEALTH SCIENCES UNIVERSITY

Biostatistics	M

OREGON STATE UNIVERSITY

Agricultural Sciences—General	M,D*
Agronomy and Soil Sciences	M,D
Analytical Chemistry	M,D
Animal Sciences	M,D
Atmospheric Sciences	M,D
Biometrics	M,D
Chemistry	M,D
Environmental Policy and Resource Management	M*
Fish, Game, and Wildlife Management	M,D
Food Science and Technology	M,D*
Forestry	M,D*
Geology	M,D
Geophysics	M,D
Horticulture	M,D
Inorganic Chemistry	M
Marine Sciences	M,D
Mathematics	M,D*
Oceanography	M,D
Organic Chemistry	M,D
Physical Chemistry	M,D
Physics	M,D*
Range Science	M,D
Statistics	M,D*

PACE UNIVERSITY

Environmental Sciences	M*

PENNSYLVANIA STATE UNIVERSITY GREAT VALLEY SCHOOL OF GRADUATE PROFESSIONAL STUDIES

Environmental Sciences	M

PENNSYLVANIA STATE UNIVERSITY HARRISBURG CAMPUS OF THE CAPITAL COLLEGE

Environmental Sciences	M

PENNSYLVANIA STATE UNIVERSITY UNIVERSITY PARK CAMPUS

Acoustics	M,D
Agricultural Sciences—General	M,D*
Agronomy and Soil Sciences	M,D
Animal Sciences	M,D
Applied Mathematics	M,D
Astronomy	M,D
Astrophysics	M,D
Chemistry	M,D
Environmental Policy and Resource Management	M,D

Environmental Sciences	M
Fish, Game, and Wildlife Management	M,D
Food Science and Technology	M,D
Forestry	M,D
Geochemistry	M,D*
Geology	M,D*
Geophysics	M,D*
Geosciences	M,D*
Horticulture	M,D
Mathematics	M,D*
Meteorology	M,D*
Physics	M,D*
Statistics	M,D

PITTSBURG STATE UNIVERSITY

Applied Physics	M
Chemistry	M
Mathematics	M
Physics	M

POLYTECHNIC UNIVERSITY, BROOKLYN CAMPUS

Chemistry	M,D*
Environmental Sciences	M
Mathematics	M,D
Physics	M,D

POLYTECHNIC UNIVERSITY, FARMINGDALE CAMPUS

Chemistry	M,D
Mathematics	M,D
Physics	M,D

POLYTECHNIC UNIVERSITY, WESTCHESTER GRADUATE CENTER

Chemistry	M

PONTIFICAL CATHOLIC UNIVERSITY OF PUERTO RICO

Chemistry	M

PORTLAND STATE UNIVERSITY

Chemistry	M,D
Environmental Policy and Resource Management	M,D
Environmental Sciences	M,D*
Geology	M,D
Mathematics	M,D
Physics	M,D

PRAIRIE VIEW A&M UNIVERSITY

Agricultural Sciences—General	M
Agronomy and Soil Sciences	M
Animal Sciences	M
Chemistry	M
Mathematics	M

PRESCOTT COLLEGE

Environmental Policy and Resource Management	M

PRINCETON UNIVERSITY

Applied Mathematics	M,D*
Applied Physics	M,D
Astrophysics	D
Atmospheric Sciences	M,D*
Chemistry	D
Computational Sciences	D
Environmental Policy and Resource Management	M,D
Geology	D
Geophysics	D
Geosciences	D
Mathematical Physics	D
Mathematics	D
Oceanography	M,D
Physical Chemistry	D
Physics	D
Plasma Physics	D
Statistics	M,D

PURDUE UNIVERSITY

Agricultural Sciences—General	M,D
Agronomy and Soil Sciences	M,D
Analytical Chemistry	M,D
Animal Sciences	M,D
Atmospheric Sciences	M,D
Chemistry	M,D
Food Science and Technology	M,D*
Forestry	M,D
Geosciences	M,D
Horticulture	M,D
Inorganic Chemistry	M,D*
Mathematics	M,D*
Natural Resources	M,D
Organic Chemistry	M,D
Physical Chemistry	M,D
Physics	M,D
Statistics	M,D*

PURDUE UNIVERSITY CALUMET

Applied Mathematics	M

QUEENS COLLEGE OF THE CITY UNIVERSITY OF NEW YORK

Chemistry	M
Geology	M
Mathematics	M
Physics	M

QUEEN'S UNIVERSITY AT KINGSTON

Biostatistics	M
Chemistry	M,D
Geology	M,D
Mathematics	M,D
Physics	M,D
Statistics	M,D

RADFORD UNIVERSITY

Computational Sciences	M
Geosciences	M

RENSSELAER AT HARTFORD

Environmental Policy and Resource Management	M

RENSSELAER POLYTECHNIC INSTITUTE

Analytical Chemistry	M,D
Applied Mathematics	M*
Applied Physics	M,D
Astrophysics	M,D*
Chemistry	M,D
Environmental Policy and Resource Management	M,D*
Environmental Sciences	M,D
Geochemistry	M,D
Geology	M,D
Geophysics	M,D
Geosciences	M,D*
Hydrology	M
Inorganic Chemistry	M,D
Mathematics	M,D*
Organic Chemistry	M,D
Physical Chemistry	M,D
Physics	M,D*
Planetary and Space Sciences	M,D
Plasma Physics	M,D
Statistics	M*

RHODE ISLAND COLLEGE

Mathematics	M,O

RICE UNIVERSITY

Applied Mathematics	M,D
Applied Physics	M,D*
Astronomy	M,D
Astrophysics	M,D
Chemistry	M,D
Computational Sciences	M,D
Environmental Sciences	M,D
Geology	M,D
Geophysics	M,D
Mathematics	M,D
Physics	M,D
Statistics	M,D

ROCHESTER INSTITUTE OF TECHNOLOGY

Applied Mathematics	M
Chemistry	M
Environmental Policy and Resource Management	M
Optical Sciences	M,D*
Statistics	M,O

ROOSEVELT UNIVERSITY

Chemistry	M
Mathematics	M

ROSE-HULMAN INSTITUTE OF TECHNOLOGY

Optical Sciences	M

ROWAN UNIVERSITY

Mathematics	M

RUTGERS, THE STATE UNIVERSITY OF NEW JERSEY, CAMDEN

Chemistry	M
Mathematics	M

RUTGERS, THE STATE UNIVERSITY OF NEW JERSEY, NEWARK

Analytical Chemistry	M,D
Chemistry	M,D*
Geology	M
Inorganic Chemistry	M,D
Mathematics	D
Organic Chemistry	M,D
Physical Chemistry	M,D

RUTGERS, THE STATE UNIVERSITY OF NEW JERSEY, NEW BRUNSWICK

Analytical Chemistry	M,D
Animal Sciences	M,D
Applied Mathematics	M,D
Chemistry	M,D*
Environmental Sciences	M,D*

Food Science and Technology	M,D*
Geology	M,D
Horticulture	M,D
Inorganic Chemistry	M,D
Mathematics	M,D
Oceanography	M,D*
Organic Chemistry	M,D
Physical Chemistry	M,D*
Physics	M,D
Statistics	M,D
Theoretical Physics	M,D
Water Resources	M,D

SACRED HEART UNIVERSITY

Chemistry	M

ST. CLOUD STATE UNIVERSITY

Environmental Policy and Resource Management	M
Mathematics	M

ST. FRANCIS XAVIER UNIVERSITY

Chemistry	M
Geology	M
Physics	M

ST. JOHN'S UNIVERSITY (NY)

Applied Mathematics	M
Chemistry	M
Mathematics	M
Statistics	M

SAINT JOSEPH COLLEGE

Chemistry	M,O

SAINT JOSEPH'S UNIVERSITY

Chemistry	M
Environmental Policy and Resource Management	M

SAINT LOUIS UNIVERSITY

Atmospheric Sciences	M,D
Chemistry	M
Geosciences	M,D
Mathematics	M,D

SAINT MARY-OF-THE-WOODS COLLEGE

Environmental Policy and Resource Management	M

SAINT MARY'S UNIVERSITY

Astronomy	M

SALEM STATE COLLEGE

Mathematics	M

SAMFORD UNIVERSITY

Environmental Policy and Resource Management	M

SAM HOUSTON STATE UNIVERSITY

Agricultural Sciences—General	M
Chemistry	M
Mathematics	M
Physics	M

SAN DIEGO STATE UNIVERSITY

Applied Mathematics	M
Astronomy	M
Biostatistics	M,D
Chemistry	M,D
Geology	M
Mathematics	M,D
Physics	M
Statistics	M

SAN FRANCISCO STATE UNIVERSITY

Astrophysics	M
Chemistry	M
Environmental Policy and Resource Management	M
Geosciences	M
Mathematics	M
Physics	M

SAN JOSE STATE UNIVERSITY

Analytical Chemistry	M
Chemistry	M
Environmental Policy and Resource Management	M
Geology	M
Inorganic Chemistry	M
Marine Sciences	M
Mathematics	M
Meteorology	M
Organic Chemistry	M
Physical Chemistry	M
Physics	M

SANTA CLARA UNIVERSITY

Applied Mathematics	M

THE SCRIPPS RESEARCH INSTITUTE

Chemistry	D

SETON HALL UNIVERSITY

Analytical Chemistry	M,D
Chemistry	M,D*
Inorganic Chemistry	M,D
Organic Chemistry	M,D
Physical Chemistry	M,D

SHIPPENSBURG UNIVERSITY OF PENNSYLVANIA

Environmental Policy and Resource Management	M
Mathematics	M

SIMON FRASER UNIVERSITY

Applied Mathematics	M,D
Chemistry	M,D
Environmental Policy and Resource Management	M,D
Geosciences	M
Mathematics	M,D
Physical Chemistry	M,D
Physics	M,D
Statistics	M,D

SLIPPERY ROCK UNIVERSITY OF PENNSYLVANIA

Environmental Policy and Resource Management	M
Natural Resources	M

SMITH COLLEGE

Chemistry	M

SOUTH DAKOTA SCHOOL OF MINES AND TECHNOLOGY

Atmospheric Sciences	M,D*
Chemistry	M,D
Environmental Sciences	D
Geology	M
Physics	M,D
Water Resources	D

SOUTH DAKOTA STATE UNIVERSITY

Agricultural Sciences—General	M,D
Agronomy and Soil Sciences	M,D
Analytical Chemistry	M,D
Animal Sciences	M,D
Atmospheric Sciences	D*
Chemistry	M,D
Environmental Sciences	D
Fish, Game, and Wildlife Management	M,D
Inorganic Chemistry	M,D
Mathematics	M
Organic Chemistry	M,D
Physical Chemistry	M,D
Physics	M
Water Resources	D

SOUTHEAST MISSOURI STATE UNIVERSITY

Chemistry	M
Geosciences	M
Mathematics	M

SOUTHERN CONNECTICUT STATE UNIVERSITY

Chemistry	M
Mathematics	M

SOUTHERN ILLINOIS UNIVERSITY CARBONDALE

Agricultural Sciences—General	M
Agronomy and Soil Sciences	M
Animal Sciences	M
Chemistry	M,D
Forestry	M
Geology	M,D*
Horticulture	M
Mathematics	M,D
Physics	M
Statistics	M,D

SOUTHERN ILLINOIS UNIVERSITY EDWARDSVILLE

Chemistry	M
Environmental Sciences	M
Mathematics	M
Physics	M
Statistics	M

SOUTHERN METHODIST UNIVERSITY

Applied Mathematics	M,D
Chemistry	M,D
Geology	M,D
Geophysics	M,D
Mathematics	M,D*
Physics	M,D
Statistics	M,D*

SOUTHERN OREGON UNIVERSITY

Mathematics	M

SOUTHERN UNIVERSITY AND AGRICULTURAL AND MECHANICAL COLLEGE

Agricultural Sciences—General	M

Analytical Chemistry	M
Chemistry	M
Environmental Sciences	M
Forestry	M
Inorganic Chemistry	M
Mathematics	M
Organic Chemistry	M
Physical Chemistry	M
Physics	M

SOUTHWEST MISSOURI STATE UNIVERSITY

Chemistry	M
Environmental Policy and Resource Management	M
Mathematics	M

SOUTHWEST TEXAS STATE UNIVERSITY

Chemistry	M
Environmental Policy and Resource Management	M
Mathematics	M
Physics	M

STANFORD UNIVERSITY

Applied Physics	M,D
Chemistry	D*
Computational Sciences	M,D
Environmental Policy and Resource Management	M
Environmental Sciences	M,D,O
Geophysics	M,D
Geosciences	M,D,O
Mathematics	M,D
Physics	M,D
Statistics	M,D

STATE UNIVERSITY OF NEW YORK AT ALBANY

Atmospheric Sciences	M,D*
Biometrics	M,D
Chemistry	M,D
Environmental Policy and Resource Management	M
Geology	M,D
Geosciences	M,D
Mathematics	M,D
Physics	M,D
Statistics	M,D

STATE UNIVERSITY OF NEW YORK AT BINGHAMTON

Analytical Chemistry	M,D
Applied Physics	M
Chemistry	M,D
Geology	M,D
Inorganic Chemistry	M,D
Mathematics	M,D
Organic Chemistry	M,D
Physical Chemistry	M,D
Physics	M,D
Statistics	M,D

STATE UNIVERSITY OF NEW YORK AT BUFFALO

Biometrics	M
Chemistry	M,D
Geology	M,D
Mathematics	M,D
Physics	M,D
Statistics	M,D

STATE UNIVERSITY OF NEW YORK AT NEW PALTZ

Chemistry	M
Geology	M
Mathematics	M

STATE UNIVERSITY OF NEW YORK AT OSWEGO

Chemistry	M

STATE UNIVERSITY OF NEW YORK AT STONY BROOK

Applied Mathematics	M,D
Atmospheric Sciences	M,D*
Chemistry	M,D
Environmental Sciences	M
Geosciences	M,D
Marine Sciences	M
Mathematics	M,D
Oceanography	D
Physics	M,D
Planetary and Space Sciences	M,D
Statistics	M,D

STATE UNIVERSITY OF NEW YORK COLLEGE AT BROCKPORT

Mathematics	M*

STATE UNIVERSITY OF NEW YORK COLLEGE AT BUFFALO

Chemistry	M

STATE UNIVERSITY OF NEW YORK COLLEGE AT FREDONIA

Chemistry	M

STATE UNIVERSITY OF NEW YORK COLLEGE AT ONEONTA

Geosciences	M

STATE UNIVERSITY OF NEW YORK COLLEGE AT POTSDAM

Mathematics	M

STATE UNIVERSITY OF NEW YORK COLLEGE OF ENVIRONMENTAL SCIENCE AND FORESTRY

Chemistry	M,D*
Environmental Policy and Resource Management	M,D
Environmental Sciences	M,D*
Forestry	M,D*

STEPHEN F. AUSTIN STATE UNIVERSITY

Chemistry	M
Environmental Sciences	M
Forestry	M,D
Geology	M
Mathematics	M
Physics	M
Statistics	M

STEVENS INSTITUTE OF TECHNOLOGY

Analytical Chemistry	M,D,O
Applied Mathematics	M,D
Chemistry	M,D,O
Mathematics	M,D
Organic Chemistry	M,D,O
Physical Chemistry	M,D,O
Physics	M,D,O
Statistics	M,O

SUL ROSS STATE UNIVERSITY

Animal Sciences	M
Chemistry	M
Fish, Game, and Wildlife Management	M
Geology	M*
Range Science	M

SYRACUSE UNIVERSITY

Chemistry	M,D
Geology	M,D
Hydrology	M,D
Mathematics	M,D
Physics	M,D
Statistics	M

TARLETON STATE UNIVERSITY

Agricultural Sciences—General	M
Environmental Sciences	M
Mathematics	M

TEMPLE UNIVERSITY

Applied Mathematics	M,D
Chemistry	M,D
Computational Sciences	M,D
Geology	M*
Mathematics	M,D*
Physics	M,D*
Statistics	M,D

TENNESSEE STATE UNIVERSITY

Agricultural Sciences—General	M
Chemistry	M
Mathematics	M

TENNESSEE TECHNOLOGICAL UNIVERSITY

Chemistry	M
Environmental Sciences	D
Fish, Game, and Wildlife Management	M
Mathematics	M

TEXAS A&M INTERNATIONAL UNIVERSITY

Mathematics	M

TEXAS A&M UNIVERSITY

Agricultural Sciences—General	M,D
Agronomy and Soil Sciences	M,D
Animal Sciences	M,D
Chemistry	M,D*
Fish, Game, and Wildlife Management	M,D
Food Science and Technology	M,D
Forestry	M,D
Geology	M,D
Geophysics	M,D
Horticulture	M,D
Hydrology	M,D
Mathematics	M,D*
Meteorology	M,D
Natural Resources	M,D
Oceanography	M,D
Physics	M,D*
Range Science	M,D
Statistics	M,D

TEXAS A&M UNIVERSITY–COMMERCE

Agricultural Sciences—General	M
Chemistry	M

Geosciences	M
Mathematics	M
Physics	M

TEXAS A&M UNIVERSITY–CORPUS CHRISTI

Environmental Sciences	M
Mathematics	M

TEXAS A&M UNIVERSITY–KINGSVILLE

Agricultural Sciences—General	M,D
Agronomy and Soil Sciences	M
Animal Sciences	M
Chemistry	M
Fish, Game, and Wildlife Management	M,D
Geology	M
Mathematics	M
Range Science	M

TEXAS CHRISTIAN UNIVERSITY

Chemistry	M,D
Environmental Sciences	M
Geology	M
Physics	M,D

TEXAS SOUTHERN UNIVERSITY

Chemistry	M
Mathematics	M

TEXAS TECH UNIVERSITY

Agricultural Sciences—General	M,D
Agronomy and Soil Sciences	M,D
Animal Sciences	M,D
Applied Physics	M,D
Atmospheric Sciences	M,D
Chemistry	M,D
Environmental Policy and Resource Management	D
Fish, Game, and Wildlife Management	M,D
Food Science and Technology	M,D
Geosciences	M,D
Horticulture	M,D
Mathematics	M,D
Physics	M,D
Range Science	M,D
Statistics	M,D

TEXAS WOMAN'S UNIVERSITY

Chemistry	M
Food Science and Technology	M,D
Mathematics	M

TOWSON UNIVERSITY

Applied Mathematics	M

TRENT UNIVERSITY

Chemistry	M
Environmental Policy and Resource Management	M,D
Physics	M

TROY STATE UNIVERSITY

Environmental Policy and Resource Management	M

TRUMAN STATE UNIVERSITY

Mathematics	M

TUFTS UNIVERSITY

Analytical Chemistry	M,D
Chemistry	M,D*
Environmental Policy and Resource Management	M,D,O
Environmental Sciences	M,D
Inorganic Chemistry	M,D
Mathematics	M,D
Optical Sciences	O
Organic Chemistry	M,D
Physical Chemistry	M,D
Physics	M,D*

TULANE UNIVERSITY

Applied Mathematics	M,D
Biostatistics	M,D
Chemistry	M,D*
Geology	M,D*
Mathematics	M,D
Physics	M,D
Statistics	M,D

TUSKEGEE UNIVERSITY

Agricultural Sciences—General	M
Agronomy and Soil Sciences	M
Animal Sciences	M
Chemistry	M
Environmental Sciences	M
Food Science and Technology	M

UNIVERSIDAD DE LAS AMÉRICAS–PUEBLA

Food Science and Technology	M

UNIVERSIDAD DEL TURABO

Environmental Policy and Resource Management	M

UNIVERSIDAD METROPOLITANA
Environmental Policy and
  Resource Management — M

UNIVERSITÉ DE MONCTON
Chemistry — M
Food Science and Technology — M
Mathematics — M
Physics — M

UNIVERSITÉ DE MONTRÉAL
Chemistry — M,D
Environmental Policy and
  Resource Management — O
Geology — M,D
Mathematics — M,D
Physics — M,D
Statistics — M,D

UNIVERSITÉ DE SHERBROOKE
Chemistry — M,D
Environmental Sciences — M,O
Mathematics — M,D
Physics — M,D

UNIVERSITÉ DU QUÉBEC À CHICOUTIMI
Environmental Policy and
  Resource Management — M
Geosciences — M

UNIVERSITÉ DU QUÉBEC À MONTRÉAL
Atmospheric Sciences — M,D,O
Chemistry — M
Environmental Sciences — M,D
Geosciences — M
Mathematics — M,D
Meteorology — M,D,O

UNIVERSITÉ DU QUÉBEC À RIMOUSKI
Environmental Policy and
  Resource Management — M
Fish, Game, and Wildlife
  Management — M,O
Oceanography — M,D

UNIVERSITÉ DU QUÉBEC À TROIS-RIVIÈRES
Chemistry — M
Environmental Sciences — M
Mathematics — M

UNIVERSITÉ DU QUÉBEC, INSTITUT NATIONAL DE LA RECHERCHE SCIENTIFIQUE
Geosciences — M,D
Water Resources — M,D

UNIVERSITÉ LAVAL
Agricultural Sciences—General — M,D,O
Agronomy and Soil Sciences — M,D
Animal Sciences — M,D
Chemistry — M,D
Food Science and Technology — M,D
Forestry — M,D
Geodetic Sciences — M,D
Geology — M,D
Geosciences — M,D
Mathematics — M,D
Physics — M,D
Statistics — M

THE UNIVERSITY OF AKRON
Analytical Chemistry — M,D
Applied Mathematics — M,D
Chemistry — M,D
Environmental Sciences — M
Food Science and Technology — M
Geology — M
Geophysics — M
Geosciences — M
Inorganic Chemistry — M,D
Mathematics — M
Organic Chemistry — M,D
Physical Chemistry — M,D
Physics — M
Statistics — M

THE UNIVERSITY OF ALABAMA
Applied Mathematics — M,D
Chemistry — M,D
Geology — M,D
Mathematics — M,D
Physics — M,D
Statistics — M,D

THE UNIVERSITY OF ALABAMA AT BIRMINGHAM
Applied Mathematics — M,D
Biometrics — M,D
Biostatistics — M,D*
Chemistry — M,D
Mathematics — M,D
Physics — M,D

THE UNIVERSITY OF ALABAMA IN HUNTSVILLE
Applied Mathematics — M,D
Atmospheric Sciences — M,D
Chemistry — M
Environmental Sciences — M,D
Mathematics — M,D
Optical Sciences — D
Physics — M,D

UNIVERSITY OF ALASKA ANCHORAGE
Environmental Sciences — M

UNIVERSITY OF ALASKA FAIRBANKS
Astrophysics — M,D
Atmospheric Sciences — M,D
Chemistry — M,D
Environmental Policy and
  Resource Management — M
Environmental Sciences — M
Fish, Game, and Wildlife
  Management — M,D
Geology — M,D
Geophysics — M,D
Limnology — M,D
Marine Sciences — M,D
Mathematics — M,D
Oceanography — M,D
Physics — M,D

UNIVERSITY OF ALBERTA
Agricultural Sciences—General — M,D
Agronomy and Soil Sciences — M,D
Applied Mathematics — M,D,O
Astrophysics — M,D
Chemistry — M,D
Environmental Policy and
  Resource Management — M,D
Environmental Sciences — M,D
Geophysics — M,D
Geosciences — M,D
Mathematical Physics — M,D,O
Mathematics — M,D,O
Natural Resources — M,D
Optical Sciences — M,D
Physics — M,D
Plasma Physics — M,D
Statistics — M,D,O

THE UNIVERSITY OF ARIZONA
Agricultural Sciences—General — M,D*
Agronomy and Soil Sciences — M,D
Animal Sciences — M,D
Applied Mathematics — M,D*
Astronomy — M,D
Atmospheric Sciences — M,D
Chemistry — M,D
Environmental Policy and
  Resource Management — M,D
Environmental Sciences — M
Fish, Game, and Wildlife
  Management — M,D
Forestry — M,D
Geosciences — M,D*
Hydrology — M,D
Mathematics — M,D
Natural Resources — M,D
Optical Sciences — M,D
Physics — M,D
Planetary and Space Sciences — M,D*
Range Science — M,D
Statistics — M,D
Water Resources — M,D

UNIVERSITY OF ARKANSAS
Agricultural Sciences—General — M,D
Agronomy and Soil Sciences — M,D
Animal Sciences — M,D
Chemistry — M,D
Food Science and Technology — M,D
Geology — M
Horticulture — M
Mathematics — M
Physics — M,D
Statistics — M

UNIVERSITY OF ARKANSAS AT LITTLE ROCK
Applied Mathematics — M
Chemistry — M
Statistics — M

UNIVERSITY OF ARKANSAS AT MONTICELLO
Forestry — M
Natural Resources — M

UNIVERSITY OF BRITISH COLUMBIA
Agricultural Sciences—General — M,D
Agronomy and Soil Sciences — M,D
Animal Sciences — M,D
Applied Mathematics — M,D
Astronomy — M,D
Atmospheric Sciences — M,D
Chemistry — M,D
Environmental Policy and
  Resource Management — M,D

Food Science and Technology — M,D
Forestry — M,D
Geology — M,D
Geophysics — M,D
Hydrology — D
Mathematics — M,D
Oceanography — M,D
Physics — M,D
Statistics — M,D

UNIVERSITY OF CALGARY
Analytical Chemistry — M,D
Astronomy — M,D
Chemistry — M,D
Environmental Policy and
  Resource Management — M,D
Geology — M,D
Geophysics — M,D
Inorganic Chemistry — M,D
Mathematics — M,D
Organic Chemistry — M,D
Physical Chemistry — M,D
Physics — M,D
Statistics — M,D
Theoretical Chemistry — M,D

UNIVERSITY OF CALIFORNIA, BERKELEY
Applied Mathematics — D
Astrophysics — D
Biostatistics — M,D
Chemistry — M,D
Environmental Policy and
  Resource Management — M,D*
Environmental Sciences — M,D
Forestry — M,D
Geology — M,D
Geophysics — M,D
Mathematics — M,D,O
Physics — M,D
Range Science — M,D
Statistics — M,D

UNIVERSITY OF CALIFORNIA, DAVIS
Agricultural Sciences—General — M
Agronomy and Soil Sciences — M,D
Animal Sciences — M
Applied Mathematics — M,D
Atmospheric Sciences — M,D*
Chemistry — M,D*
Environmental Sciences — M,D*
Food Science and Technology — M,D
Geology — M,D
Horticulture — M
Hydrology — M,D
Mathematics — M,D
Physics — M,D
Statistics — M,D

UNIVERSITY OF CALIFORNIA, IRVINE
Chemistry — M,D
Environmental Policy and
  Resource Management — M,D
Geosciences — M,D
Mathematics — M,D
Physics — M,D

UNIVERSITY OF CALIFORNIA, LOS ANGELES
Astronomy — M,D
Astrophysics — M,D
Atmospheric Sciences — M,D
Biometrics — M,D*
Biostatistics — M,D
Chemistry — M,D
Environmental Sciences — D
Geochemistry — M,D
Geology — M,D
Geophysics — M,D
Geosciences — M,D
Mathematics — M,D
Physics — M,D*
Planetary and Space Sciences — M,D

UNIVERSITY OF CALIFORNIA, RIVERSIDE
Agronomy and Soil Sciences — M,D
Chemistry — M,D
Environmental Sciences — M,D
Geology — M,D*
Geosciences — M,D
Mathematics — M,D
Physics — M,D
Statistics — M,D

UNIVERSITY OF CALIFORNIA, SAN DIEGO
Applied Mathematics — M,D
Applied Physics — M,D
Chemistry — D*
Geology — M,D
Marine Sciences — M,D
Mathematics — M,D
Oceanography — M,D
Physics — M,D*
Statistics — M,D

UNIVERSITY OF CALIFORNIA, SANTA BARBARA
Applied Mathematics — M
Chemistry — M,D
Environmental Policy and
  Resource Management — M
Environmental Sciences — M*
Geology — M,D
Geophysics — M,D
Marine Sciences — M,D*
Mathematics — M,D
Physics — D
Statistics — M,D

UNIVERSITY OF CALIFORNIA, SANTA CRUZ
Applied Mathematics — M,D
Astronomy — D
Astrophysics — D
Chemistry — M,D
Environmental Policy and
  Resource Management — D
Geosciences — M,D
Marine Sciences — M,D
Mathematics — M,D
Physics — M,D

UNIVERSITY OF CENTRAL ARKANSAS
Mathematics — M

UNIVERSITY OF CENTRAL FLORIDA
Chemistry — M
Mathematics — M,D*
Optical Sciences — M,D*
Physics — M,D
Statistics — M

UNIVERSITY OF CENTRAL OKLAHOMA
Applied Mathematics — M
Applied Physics — M
Mathematics — M
Statistics — M

UNIVERSITY OF CHARLESTON, SOUTH CAROLINA
Environmental Sciences — M
Mathematics — M

UNIVERSITY OF CHICAGO
Applied Mathematics — M,D
Astronomy — M,D
Astrophysics — M,D
Atmospheric Sciences — M,D
Chemistry — M,D
Environmental Policy and
  Resource Management — M,D
Environmental Sciences — M,D
Geophysics — M,D
Geosciences — M,D
Mathematics — M
Physics — M,D
Planetary and Space Sciences — M,D
Statistics — M,D

UNIVERSITY OF CINCINNATI
Analytical Chemistry — M,D
Applied Mathematics — M,D
Biostatistics — M,D
Chemistry — M,D
Environmental Sciences — M,D
Geology — M,D
Inorganic Chemistry — M,D
Mathematics — M,D
Organic Chemistry — M,D
Physical Chemistry — M,D
Physics — M,D
Statistics — M,D

UNIVERSITY OF COLORADO AT BOULDER
Applied Mathematics — M,D
Astrophysics — M,D
Atmospheric Sciences — M,D
Chemistry — M,D
Geology — M,D
Geophysics — M,D
Mathematical Physics — M,D
Mathematics — M,D
Physics — M,D
Plasma Physics — M,D

UNIVERSITY OF COLORADO AT COLORADO SPRINGS
Applied Mathematics — M
Physics — M

UNIVERSITY OF COLORADO AT DENVER
Applied Mathematics — M,D
Chemistry — M
Environmental Sciences — M

UNIVERSITY OF CONNECTICUT
Agricultural Sciences—General — M,D
Agronomy and Soil Sciences — M,D
Animal Sciences — M,D

Peterson's Graduate Programs in the Physical Sciences, Mathematics, Agricultural Sciences, the Environment & Natural Resources 2000

25

University of Connecticut (continued)

Chemistry	M,D
Environmental Policy and Resource Management	M
Geology	M,D
Geophysics	M,D
Marine Sciences	M,D
Mathematics	M,D
Natural Resources	M
Oceanography	M,D
Physics	M,D*
Statistics	M,D

UNIVERSITY OF DAYTON

Applied Mathematics	M
Optical Sciences	M,D

UNIVERSITY OF DELAWARE

Agricultural Sciences—General	M,D
Agronomy and Soil Sciences	M,D
Applied Mathematics	M,D
Astronomy	M,D
Atmospheric Sciences	D
Chemistry	M,D
Environmental Policy and Resource Management	M,D*
Food Science and Technology	M,D
Geology	M,D*
Horticulture	M
Marine Sciences	M,D
Mathematics	M,D*
Physics	M,D

UNIVERSITY OF DENVER

Applied Mathematics	M,D
Chemistry	M,D
Environmental Policy and Resource Management	M
Mathematics	M,D
Physics	M,D*

UNIVERSITY OF DETROIT MERCY

Chemistry	M,D*
Mathematics	M

THE UNIVERSITY OF FINDLAY

Environmental Policy and Resource Management	M

UNIVERSITY OF FLORIDA

Agricultural Sciences—General	M,D,O
Agronomy and Soil Sciences	M,D
Animal Sciences	M,D
Applied Mathematics	M,D
Aquaculture	M,D
Astronomy	M,D
Chemistry	M,D
Fish, Game, and Wildlife Management	M,D
Food Science and Technology	M,D*
Forestry	M,D
Geology	M,D
Horticulture	M,D
Limnology	M,D
Marine Sciences	M,D
Mathematics	M,D
Physics	M,D*
Statistics	M,D
Water Resources	M,D

UNIVERSITY OF GEORGIA

Agricultural Sciences—General	M,D
Agronomy and Soil Sciences	M,D
Analytical Chemistry	M,D
Animal Sciences	M,D
Applied Mathematics	M
Chemistry	M,D
Food Science and Technology	M,D*
Forestry	M,D
Geochemistry	M,D
Geophysics	M,D
Horticulture	M,D
Inorganic Chemistry	M,D
Marine Sciences	M,D*
Mathematics	M,D
Natural Resources	M,D
Oceanography	M,D
Organic Chemistry	M,D
Physical Chemistry	M,D
Physics	M,D
Statistics	M,D*

UNIVERSITY OF GUAM

Environmental Sciences	M

UNIVERSITY OF GUELPH

Agricultural Sciences—General	M,D
Agronomy and Soil Sciences	M,D
Animal Sciences	M,D
Applied Mathematics	M,D
Aquaculture	M
Atmospheric Sciences	M,D
Chemistry	M,D
Environmental Policy and Resource Management	M,D
Food Science and Technology	M,D
Horticulture	M,D

Mathematics	M,D
Physics	M,D
Statistics	M,D

UNIVERSITY OF HAWAII AT MANOA

Agricultural Sciences—General	M,D*
Agronomy and Soil Sciences	M,D
Animal Sciences	M
Astronomy	M,D
Biostatistics	M,D
Chemistry	M,D
Environmental Policy and Resource Management	M
Food Science and Technology	M
Geochemistry	M,D
Geology	M,D
Geophysics	M,D
Horticulture	M,D
Hydrology	M,D
Mathematics	M,D
Meteorology	M,D
Oceanography	M,D
Physics	M,D
Planetary and Space Sciences	M,D

UNIVERSITY OF HOUSTON

Applied Mathematics	M,D
Chemistry	M,D
Geology	M,D
Geophysics	M,D
Mathematics	M,D*
Physics	M,D*
Statistics	M,D

UNIVERSITY OF HOUSTON–CLEAR LAKE

Chemistry	M
Environmental Policy and Resource Management	M
Environmental Sciences	M
Mathematics	M
Statistics	M

UNIVERSITY OF IDAHO

Agricultural Sciences—General	M,D
Agronomy and Soil Sciences	M,D
Animal Sciences	M,D
Chemistry	M,D
Environmental Policy and Resource Management	M,D
Environmental Sciences	M
Fish, Game, and Wildlife Management	M,D
Food Science and Technology	M
Forestry	M,D
Geology	M,D
Geophysics	M
Hydrology	M
Mathematics	M,D
Physics	M,D
Range Science	M,D
Statistics	M

UNIVERSITY OF ILLINOIS AT CHICAGO

Applied Mathematics	M,D
Biostatistics	M,D
Chemistry	M,D*
Geochemistry	M,D
Geology	M,D*
Geophysics	M,D
Geosciences	M,D
Hydrology	M,D
Mathematics	M,D*
Physics	M,D*
Statistics	M,D
Water Resources	M,D

UNIVERSITY OF ILLINOIS AT SPRINGFIELD

Environmental Policy and Resource Management	M

UNIVERSITY OF ILLINOIS AT URBANA–CHAMPAIGN

Agricultural Sciences—General	M,D
Agronomy and Soil Sciences	M,D
Animal Sciences	M,D
Applied Mathematics	M,D
Astronomy	M,D
Atmospheric Sciences	M,D
Chemistry	M,D
Environmental Sciences	M,D
Food Science and Technology	M,D*
Geochemistry	M,D
Geology	M,D
Geophysics	M,D
Geosciences	M,D
Mathematics	M,D*
Natural Resources	M,D
Physics	M,D
Statistics	M,D

THE UNIVERSITY OF IOWA

Applied Mathematics	D
Astronomy	M
Biostatistics	M,D
Chemistry	M,D
Computational Sciences	D
Geology	M,D

Mathematics	M,D
Physics	M,D
Statistics	M,D

UNIVERSITY OF KANSAS

Applied Mathematics	M,D
Astronomy	M,D
Chemistry	M,D
Environmental Sciences	M,D
Geology	M,D
Mathematics	M,D
Physics	M,D*
Statistics	M,D
Water Resources	M,D

UNIVERSITY OF KENTUCKY

Agricultural Sciences—General	M,D
Agronomy and Soil Sciences	M,D
Animal Sciences	M,D
Astronomy	M,D
Chemistry	M,D
Food Science and Technology	M
Forestry	M
Geology	M,D
Mathematics	M,D
Physics	M,D
Statistics	M,D

UNIVERSITY OF LOUISVILLE

Analytical Chemistry	M,D
Chemistry	M,D*
Inorganic Chemistry	M,D
Mathematics	M
Organic Chemistry	M,D
Physical Chemistry	M,D
Physics	M

UNIVERSITY OF MAINE

Agricultural Sciences—General	M,D
Agronomy and Soil Sciences	M,D
Animal Sciences	M
Chemistry	M,D
Environmental Policy and Resource Management	M
Environmental Sciences	M,D
Fish, Game, and Wildlife Management	M,D
Food Science and Technology	M,D
Forestry	M,D
Geology	M,D
Geosciences	M,D
Horticulture	M
Marine Sciences	M
Mathematics	M
Natural Resources	M,D
Oceanography	M,D
Physics	M,D

UNIVERSITY OF MANITOBA

Agricultural Sciences—General	M,D
Agronomy and Soil Sciences	M,D
Animal Sciences	M,D
Applied Mathematics	M
Chemistry	M,D
Environmental Policy and Resource Management	M
Food Science and Technology	M
Geology	M,D
Geophysics	M,D
Horticulture	M,D
Mathematics	M,D
Physics	M,D
Statistics	M,D

UNIVERSITY OF MARYLAND

Environmental Sciences	M,D
Marine Sciences	M,D

UNIVERSITY OF MARYLAND, BALTIMORE COUNTY

Applied Mathematics	M,D
Applied Physics	M,D*
Atmospheric Sciences	M,D
Chemistry	D*
Environmental Sciences	M,D
Marine Sciences	M,D
Optical Sciences	M,D
Physics	M,D
Statistics	M,D

UNIVERSITY OF MARYLAND, COLLEGE PARK

Agricultural Sciences—General	M,D
Agronomy and Soil Sciences	M,D
Analytical Chemistry	M,D
Animal Sciences	M,D
Applied Mathematics	M,D
Astronomy	M,D
Chemistry	M,D
Environmental Policy and Resource Management	M
Environmental Sciences	M,D
Food Science and Technology	M,D
Geology	M,D*
Horticulture	M,D
Inorganic Chemistry	M,D
Marine Sciences	M,D*
Mathematics	M,D
Meteorology	M,D*

Organic Chemistry	M,D
Physical Chemistry	M,D
Physics	M,D*
Statistics	M,D

UNIVERSITY OF MARYLAND UNIVERSITY COLLEGE

Environmental Policy and Resource Management	M

UNIVERSITY OF MASSACHUSETTS AMHERST

Agronomy and Soil Sciences	M,D
Animal Sciences	M,D
Applied Mathematics	M
Astronomy	M,D
Chemistry	M,D*
Fish, Game, and Wildlife Management	M,D
Food Science and Technology	M,D
Forestry	M,D
Geology	M,D
Geosciences	D
Mathematics	M,D
Physics	M,D
Statistics	M,D

UNIVERSITY OF MASSACHUSETTS BOSTON

Applied Physics	M
Chemistry	M
Environmental Sciences	M,D
Marine Sciences	D

UNIVERSITY OF MASSACHUSETTS DARTMOUTH

Chemistry	M
Physics	M*

UNIVERSITY OF MASSACHUSETTS LOWELL

Applied Mathematics	M
Applied Physics	M,D
Chemistry	M,D
Environmental Sciences	M,D
Mathematics	M
Optical Sciences	M,D
Physics	M,D*

THE UNIVERSITY OF MEMPHIS

Applied Mathematics	M,D
Chemistry	M,D
Geology	M,D
Geophysics	M,D
Mathematics	M,D
Physics	M
Statistics	M,D

UNIVERSITY OF MIAMI

Atmospheric Sciences	M,D
Chemistry	M,D
Fish, Game, and Wildlife Management	M,D
Geology	M,D
Geophysics	M,D
Inorganic Chemistry	M,D
Marine Sciences	M,D
Mathematics	M,D
Meteorology	M,D*
Oceanography	M,D*
Organic Chemistry	M,D
Physical Chemistry	M,D
Physics	M,D*

UNIVERSITY OF MICHIGAN

Analytical Chemistry	D
Applied Physics	D
Astronomy	M,D
Atmospheric Sciences	M,D
Biostatistics	M,D
Chemistry	D
Environmental Policy and Resource Management	D
Forestry	M,D*
Geochemistry	M,D
Geology	M,D
Geosciences	M,D
Inorganic Chemistry	D
Mathematics	M,D
Natural Resources	M,D*
Oceanography	M,D
Organic Chemistry	D
Physical Chemistry	D
Physics	M,D*
Planetary and Space Sciences	M,D
Statistics	M,D

UNIVERSITY OF MINNESOTA, DULUTH

Applied Mathematics	M*
Chemistry	M
Computational Sciences	M
Geology	M*
Physics	M*

UNIVERSITY OF MINNESOTA, TWIN CITIES CAMPUS

Agricultural Sciences—General	M,D
Agronomy and Soil Sciences	M,D
Animal Sciences	M,D

Astronomy	M,D
Astrophysics	M,D
Biostatistics	M,D
Chemistry	M,D*
Computational Sciences	M,D
Environmental Policy and Resource Management	M
Fish, Game, and Wildlife Management	M,D
Food Science and Technology	M,D
Forestry	M,D*
Geology	M,D
Geophysics	M,D
Horticulture	M,D
Mathematics	M,D
Physics	M,D
Statistics	M,D
Water Resources	M,D

UNIVERSITY OF MISSISSIPPI

Chemistry	M,D
Computational Sciences	M,D
Mathematics	M,D
Physics	M,D

UNIVERSITY OF MISSOURI–COLUMBIA

Agricultural Sciences—General	M,D
Agronomy and Soil Sciences	M,D
Analytical Chemistry	M,D
Animal Sciences	M,D
Applied Mathematics	M
Atmospheric Sciences	M,D
Chemistry	M,D
Fish, Game, and Wildlife Management	M,D
Food Science and Technology	M,D
Forestry	M,D
Geology	M,D
Horticulture	M,D
Inorganic Chemistry	M,D
Mathematics	M,D
Organic Chemistry	M,D
Physical Chemistry	M,D
Physics	M,D
Statistics	M,D

UNIVERSITY OF MISSOURI–KANSAS CITY

Analytical Chemistry	M,D
Chemistry	M,D*
Geology	M,D
Geosciences	M,D*
Inorganic Chemistry	M,D
Mathematics	M,D
Organic Chemistry	M,D
Physical Chemistry	M,D
Physics	M,D
Statistics	M,D

UNIVERSITY OF MISSOURI–ROLLA

Applied Mathematics	M
Chemistry	M,D
Geochemistry	M,D
Geology	M,D
Geophysics	M,D
Hydrology	M,D
Mathematics	M,D
Physics	M,D
Water Resources	M,D

UNIVERSITY OF MISSOURI–ST. LOUIS

Applied Mathematics	M,D
Applied Physics	M,D
Astrophysics	M,D
Chemistry	M,D
Environmental Policy and Resource Management	M,D,O
Inorganic Chemistry	M,D
Mathematics	M,D
Organic Chemistry	M,D
Physical Chemistry	M,D
Physics	M,D

THE UNIVERSITY OF MONTANA–MISSOULA

Applied Mathematics	M,D
Chemistry	M,D
Environmental Policy and Resource Management	M*
Environmental Sciences	M
Fish, Game, and Wildlife Management	M,D
Forestry	M,D
Geology	M,D
Inorganic Chemistry	M,D
Mathematics	M,D*
Natural Resources	M
Organic Chemistry	M,D
Physical Chemistry	M,D
Statistics	M,D

UNIVERSITY OF NEBRASKA AT OMAHA

Mathematics	M

UNIVERSITY OF NEBRASKA–LINCOLN

Agricultural Sciences—General	M,D
Agronomy and Soil Sciences	M,D

Analytical Chemistry	M,D
Animal Sciences	M,D
Astronomy	M,D
Biometrics	M
Chemistry	M,D
Food Science and Technology	M,D
Forestry	D
Geosciences	M,D
Horticulture	M,D
Inorganic Chemistry	M,D
Mathematics	M,D*
Natural Resources	M
Organic Chemistry	M,D
Physical Chemistry	M,D
Physics	M,D
Statistics	M,D

UNIVERSITY OF NEVADA, LAS VEGAS

Analytical Chemistry	M
Applied Mathematics	M
Chemistry	M
Environmental Sciences	M
Geosciences	M,D
Mathematics	M
Physics	M,D
Statistics	M
Water Resources	M

UNIVERSITY OF NEVADA, RENO

Agricultural Sciences—General	M,D
Animal Sciences	M,D
Atmospheric Sciences	M,D
Chemistry	M,D
Environmental Policy and Resource Management	M
Environmental Sciences	M,D
Geochemistry	M,D,O
Geology	M,D,O
Geophysics	M,D,O
Hydrology	M,D
Mathematics	M
Physics	M,D
Statistics	M

UNIVERSITY OF NEW BRUNSWICK

Chemistry	M,D
Forestry	M,D
Geodetic Sciences	M,D,O
Geology	M,D
Hydrology	M,D
Mathematics	M,D
Physics	M,D
Statistics	M,D
Water Resources	M,D

UNIVERSITY OF NEW HAMPSHIRE

Agricultural Sciences—General	M,D
Agronomy and Soil Sciences	M,D
Animal Sciences	M,D
Applied Mathematics	M,D
Chemistry	M,D
Environmental Policy and Resource Management	M,D
Fish, Game, and Wildlife Management	M,D
Forestry	M,D
Geochemistry	M,D
Geology	M,D
Geosciences	M,D
Hydrology	M
Mathematics	M,D*
Natural Resources	M,D
Oceanography	M,D
Physics	M,D
Water Resources	M,D

UNIVERSITY OF NEW HAVEN

Environmental Sciences	M

UNIVERSITY OF NEW MEXICO

Chemistry	M,D
Geosciences	M,D
Mathematics	M,D
Optical Sciences	M,D
Physics	M,D*
Planetary and Space Sciences	M,D
Statistics	M,D
Water Resources	M

UNIVERSITY OF NEW ORLEANS

Applied Physics	M
Chemistry	M,D
Geology	M
Geophysics	M
Mathematics	M
Physics	M

THE UNIVERSITY OF NORTH CAROLINA AT CHAPEL HILL

Astronomy	M,D
Astrophysics	M,D
Biostatistics	M,D
Chemistry	M,D
Environmental Sciences	M,D
Geology	M,D
Marine Sciences	M,D
Mathematics	M,D*

Statistics	M,D

UNIVERSITY OF NORTH CAROLINA AT CHARLOTTE

Applied Mathematics	M,D
Applied Physics	M
Chemistry	M
Geosciences	M
Mathematics	M,D*
Statistics	M,D

UNIVERSITY OF NORTH CAROLINA AT GREENSBORO

Chemistry	M
Mathematics	M

UNIVERSITY OF NORTH CAROLINA AT WILMINGTON

Chemistry	M
Geology	M
Mathematics	M

UNIVERSITY OF NORTH DAKOTA

Atmospheric Sciences	M
Chemistry	M,D
Fish, Game, and Wildlife Management	M,D
Geology	M,D
Mathematics	M
Physics	M,D
Planetary and Space Sciences	M*

UNIVERSITY OF NORTHERN COLORADO

Chemistry	M,D
Geosciences	M
Mathematics	M,D

UNIVERSITY OF NORTHERN IOWA

Chemistry	M
Environmental Sciences	M
Mathematics	M

UNIVERSITY OF NORTH FLORIDA

Mathematics	M
Statistics	M

UNIVERSITY OF NORTH TEXAS

Chemistry	M,D
Environmental Sciences	M,D
Mathematics	M,D
Physics	M,D*

UNIVERSITY OF NOTRE DAME

Chemistry	M,D*
Geosciences	M,D
Inorganic Chemistry	M,D*
Mathematics	M,D*
Organic Chemistry	M,D
Physical Chemistry	M,D
Physics	D*

UNIVERSITY OF OKLAHOMA

Astrophysics	M,D
Chemistry	M,D
Environmental Sciences	M,D
Geology	M,D
Geophysics	M
Mathematics	M,D*
Meteorology	M,D
Physics	M,D
Water Resources	M,D

UNIVERSITY OF OKLAHOMA HEALTH SCIENCES CENTER

Biostatistics	M,D

UNIVERSITY OF OREGON

Chemistry	M,D
Environmental Policy and Resource Management	M*
Geology	M,D
Mathematics	M,D
Physics	M,D*

UNIVERSITY OF OTTAWA

Chemistry	M,D
Geosciences	M,D
Mathematics	M,D
Physics	M,D
Statistics	M,D

UNIVERSITY OF PENNSYLVANIA

Astrophysics	D
Chemistry	M,D
Geology	M,D
Mathematics	M,D
Physics	D*
Statistics	M,D

UNIVERSITY OF PITTSBURGH

Applied Mathematics	M
Astronomy	M,D
Biostatistics	M,D
Chemistry	M,D*
Geology	M,D

Mathematics	M,D*
Physics	M,D*
Planetary and Space Sciences	M,D
Statistics	M,D

UNIVERSITY OF PUERTO RICO, MAYAGÜEZ CAMPUS

Agricultural Sciences—General	M
Agronomy and Soil Sciences	M
Animal Sciences	M
Applied Mathematics	M
Chemistry	M
Computational Sciences	M
Food Science and Technology	M
Geology	M*
Horticulture	M
Marine Sciences	M,D*
Mathematics	M
Oceanography	M,D
Physics	M
Statistics	M

UNIVERSITY OF PUERTO RICO, MEDICAL SCIENCES CAMPUS

Biostatistics	M

UNIVERSITY OF PUERTO RICO, RÍO PIEDRAS

Applied Physics	M,D
Chemistry	M,D*
Mathematics	M
Physical Chemistry	M,D
Physics	M,D*

UNIVERSITY OF REGINA

Analytical Chemistry	M,D
Chemistry	M,D
Geology	M
Inorganic Chemistry	M,D
Mathematics	M,D
Organic Chemistry	M,D
Physical Chemistry	M,D
Physics	M,D
Statistics	M,D

UNIVERSITY OF RHODE ISLAND

Animal Sciences	M
Applied Mathematics	M,D
Aquaculture	M
Chemistry	M,D
Environmental Policy and Resource Management	M,D*
Fish, Game, and Wildlife Management	M
Food Science and Technology	M,D
Geology	M
Mathematics	M,D
Natural Resources	M,D
Oceanography	M,D
Physics	M,D
Statistics	M,D

UNIVERSITY OF ROCHESTER

Astronomy	M,D
Biostatistics	M,D
Chemistry	M,D
Environmental Sciences	M
Geology	M,D
Mathematics	M,D
Optical Sciences	M,D*
Physics	M,D*
Statistics	M,D*

UNIVERSITY OF ST. THOMAS (MN)

Environmental Policy and Resource Management	M,O

UNIVERSITY OF SAN DIEGO

Environmental Policy and Resource Management	M
Marine Sciences	M

UNIVERSITY OF SAN FRANCISCO

Chemistry	M*
Environmental Policy and Resource Management	M

UNIVERSITY OF SASKATCHEWAN

Agricultural Sciences—General	M,D
Agronomy and Soil Sciences	M,D
Animal Sciences	M,D
Chemistry	M,D
Computational Sciences	M,D
Food Science and Technology	M,D
Geology	M,D
Horticulture	M,D
Mathematics	M,D
Physics	M,D

THE UNIVERSITY OF SCRANTON

Chemistry	M

UNIVERSITY OF SOUTH ALABAMA

Marine Sciences	M,D
Mathematics	M

UNIVERSITY OF SOUTH CAROLINA

Astronomy	M,D
Biostatistics	M,D
Chemistry	M,D
Environmental Policy and Resource Management	M
Geology	M,D*
Geosciences	M,D
Marine Sciences	M,D
Mathematics	M,D
Physics	M,D*
Statistics	M,D

UNIVERSITY OF SOUTH DAKOTA

Chemistry	M
Mathematics	M

UNIVERSITY OF SOUTHERN CALIFORNIA

Applied Mathematics	M,D
Biometrics	M,D*
Chemistry	M,D*
Geosciences	M,D
Marine Sciences	M,D
Mathematics	M,D*
Oceanography	M,D
Physical Chemistry	D
Physics	M,D
Statistics	M

UNIVERSITY OF SOUTHERN MISSISSIPPI

Analytical Chemistry	M,D
Astronomy	M
Chemistry	M,D
Geology	M
Inorganic Chemistry	M,D
Marine Sciences	M,D
Mathematics	M
Organic Chemistry	M,D
Physical Chemistry	M,D
Physics	M

UNIVERSITY OF SOUTH FLORIDA

Analytical Chemistry	M,D
Applied Mathematics	M,D
Applied Physics	M,D
Biostatistics	M,D
Chemistry	M,D
Geology	M,D,O
Hydrology	M,D,O
Inorganic Chemistry	M,D
Marine Sciences	M,D*
Mathematics	M,D
Oceanography	M,D
Organic Chemistry	M,D
Physical Chemistry	M,D
Physics	M,D

UNIVERSITY OF SOUTHWESTERN LOUISIANA

Applied Physics	M
Geology	M
Mathematics	M,D
Physics	M

UNIVERSITY OF TENNESSEE AT CHATTANOOGA

Environmental Sciences	M

THE UNIVERSITY OF TENNESSEE AT MARTIN

Food Science and Technology	M

UNIVERSITY OF TENNESSEE, KNOXVILLE

Agricultural Sciences—General	M,D
Agronomy and Soil Sciences	M,D
Analytical Chemistry	M,D
Animal Sciences	M,D
Applied Mathematics	M,D
Chemistry	M,D
Environmental Policy and Resource Management	M,D
Fish, Game, and Wildlife Management	M
Food Science and Technology	M,D
Forestry	M,D
Geology	M,D
Horticulture	M
Inorganic Chemistry	M,D
Mathematics	M,D
Organic Chemistry	M,D
Physical Chemistry	M,D
Physics	M,D*
Statistics	M,D
Theoretical Chemistry	M,D

UNIVERSITY OF TENNESSEE SPACE INSTITUTE

Applied Mathematics	M
Physics	M,D

THE UNIVERSITY OF TEXAS AT ARLINGTON

Chemistry	M,D*
Environmental Sciences	M
Geology	M
Mathematics	M,D

Physics	M,D

THE UNIVERSITY OF TEXAS AT AUSTIN

Analytical Chemistry	M,D
Applied Mathematics	M,D
Astronomy	M,D
Chemistry	M,D
Computational Sciences	M,D
Geology	M,D
Geosciences	M,D
Inorganic Chemistry	M,D
Marine Sciences	M,D*
Mathematics	M,D
Organic Chemistry	M,D
Physical Chemistry	M,D
Physics	M,D*
Statistics	M,D

THE UNIVERSITY OF TEXAS AT DALLAS

Applied Mathematics	M,D
Chemistry	M,D
Geosciences	M,D
Mathematics	M,D*
Physics	M,D
Statistics	M,D

THE UNIVERSITY OF TEXAS AT EL PASO

Chemistry	M
Environmental Sciences	D
Geology	M
Geophysics	M
Mathematics	M
Physics	M
Statistics	M

THE UNIVERSITY OF TEXAS AT SAN ANTONIO

Chemistry	M
Environmental Sciences	M*
Geology	M
Mathematics	M
Statistics	M

THE UNIVERSITY OF TEXAS AT TYLER

Chemistry	M
Mathematics	M
Physics	M

THE UNIVERSITY OF TEXAS—HOUSTON HEALTH SCIENCE CENTER

Biometrics	M,D

THE UNIVERSITY OF TEXAS OF THE PERMIAN BASIN

Geology	M

THE UNIVERSITY OF TEXAS—PAN AMERICAN

Mathematics	M

UNIVERSITY OF THE DISTRICT OF COLUMBIA

Mathematics	M

UNIVERSITY OF THE INCARNATE WORD

Mathematics	M,D

UNIVERSITY OF THE PACIFIC

Chemistry	M,D

UNIVERSITY OF TOLEDO

Analytical Chemistry	M,D
Applied Mathematics	M,D
Chemistry	M,D
Geology	M
Inorganic Chemistry	M,D
Mathematics	M,D
Organic Chemistry	M,D
Physical Chemistry	M,D
Physics	M,D
Statistics	M,D

UNIVERSITY OF TORONTO

Astronomy	M,D
Chemistry	M,D
Environmental Policy and Resource Management	M
Environmental Sciences	M
Forestry	M
Geology	M,D
Mathematics	M,D
Physics	M,D
Statistics	M,D

UNIVERSITY OF TULSA

Chemistry	M
Geology	M
Geosciences	M,D
Mathematics	M

UNIVERSITY OF UTAH

Biostatistics	M
Chemistry	M,D
Geology	M,D
Geophysics	M,D
Mathematics	M,D*

UNIVERSITY OF VERMONT

Agricultural Sciences—General	M,D
Agronomy and Soil Sciences	M,D
Animal Sciences	M,D
Biostatistics	M
Chemistry	M,D
Environmental Policy and Resource Management	M,D
Fish, Game, and Wildlife Management	M
Forestry	M
Geology	M
Mathematics	M,D
Physics	M
Statistics	M
Water Resources	M

UNIVERSITY OF VICTORIA

Applied Mathematics	M,D
Astronomy	M,D
Astrophysics	M,D
Chemistry	M,D
Geochemistry	M,D
Geology	M,D
Geophysics	M,D
Geosciences	M,D
Mathematics	M,D
Oceanography	M,D
Physics	M,D
Statistics	M,D
Theoretical Physics	M,D

UNIVERSITY OF VIRGINIA

Astronomy	M,D
Chemistry	M,D
Environmental Sciences	M,D*
Mathematics	M,D
Physics	M,D*
Statistics	M,D

UNIVERSITY OF WASHINGTON

Applied Mathematics	M,D
Applied Physics	M,D
Astronomy	M,D
Atmospheric Sciences	M,D*
Biostatistics	M,D
Chemistry	M,D
Environmental Policy and Resource Management	M,D*
Fish, Game, and Wildlife Management	M,D
Forestry	M,D*
Geology	M,D
Geophysics	M,D*
Horticulture	M,D
Hydrology	M,D
Marine Sciences	M
Mathematics	M,D
Oceanography	M,D
Physics	M,D
Statistics	M,D

UNIVERSITY OF WATERLOO

Applied Mathematics	M,D
Biostatistics	M,D
Chemistry	M,D
Environmental Policy and Resource Management	M
Geosciences	M,D*
Mathematics	M,D
Physics	M,D
Statistics	M,D

THE UNIVERSITY OF WESTERN ONTARIO

Applied Mathematics	M,D
Astronomy	M,D
Biostatistics	M,D
Chemistry	M,D
Environmental Sciences	M,D
Geosciences	M,D
Mathematics	M,D
Physics	M,D
Statistics	M,D

UNIVERSITY OF WEST FLORIDA

Environmental Policy and Resource Management	M
Mathematics	M
Statistics	M

UNIVERSITY OF WINDSOR

Chemistry	M,D
Geology	M
Mathematics	M,D
Physics	M,D
Statistics	M,D

UNIVERSITY OF WISCONSIN—GREEN BAY

Environmental Policy and Resource Management	M
Environmental Sciences	M

UNIVERSITY OF WISCONSIN—MADISON

Agricultural Sciences—General	M,D
Agronomy and Soil Sciences	M,D
Animal Sciences	M,D
Astronomy	D
Atmospheric Sciences	M,D
Biometrics	M
Chemistry	M,D
Environmental Policy and Resource Management	M,D
Environmental Sciences	M,D
Food Science and Technology	M,D
Forestry	M,D
Geology	M,D
Geophysics	M,D
Horticulture	M,D
Limnology	M,D
Marine Sciences	M,D
Mathematics	M,D
Oceanography	M,D
Physics	M,D
Statistics	M,D
Water Resources	M

UNIVERSITY OF WISCONSIN—MILWAUKEE

Chemistry	M,D
Geology	M,D
Mathematics	M,D
Physics	M,D

UNIVERSITY OF WISCONSIN—OSHKOSH

Physics	M

UNIVERSITY OF WISCONSIN—PLATTEVILLE

Agricultural Sciences—General	M

UNIVERSITY OF WISCONSIN—RIVER FALLS

Agricultural Sciences—General	M

UNIVERSITY OF WISCONSIN—STEVENS POINT

Natural Resources	M

UNIVERSITY OF WISCONSIN—STOUT

Food Science and Technology	M

UNIVERSITY OF WYOMING

Agricultural Sciences—General	M,D
Agronomy and Soil Sciences	M,D
Animal Sciences	M,D
Astronomy	M,D
Atmospheric Sciences	M,D
Chemistry	M,D
Food Science and Technology	M
Geology	M,D
Geophysics	M,D
Mathematics	M,D
Natural Resources	M
Physics	M,D
Range Science	M,D
Statistics	M,D

UTAH STATE UNIVERSITY

Agricultural Sciences—General	M,D
Agronomy and Soil Sciences	M,D
Animal Sciences	M,D
Chemistry	M,D
Fish, Game, and Wildlife Management	M,D
Food Science and Technology	M,D
Forestry	M,D
Geology	M
Mathematics	M,D
Natural Resources	M
Physics	M,D
Range Science	M,D
Statistics	M
Water Resources	M,D

VANDERBILT UNIVERSITY

Astronomy	M
Chemistry	M,D
Geology	M
Mathematics	M,D
Physics	M,D

VASSAR COLLEGE

Chemistry	M

VERMONT LAW SCHOOL

Environmental Policy and Resource Management	M

VILLANOVA UNIVERSITY

Chemistry	M,D
Mathematics	M
Statistics	M

VIRGINIA COMMONWEALTH UNIVERSITY

Applied Mathematics	M
Applied Physics	M
Biostatistics	M,D
Chemistry	M,D,O

Environmental Policy and Resource Management	M
Environmental Sciences	M
Mathematics	M,O
Physics	M
Statistics	M,O

VIRGINIA POLYTECHNIC INSTITUTE AND STATE UNIVERSITY

Agricultural Sciences—General	M,D
Agronomy and Soil Sciences	M,D
Animal Sciences	M,D
Applied Mathematics	M,D
Aquaculture	M,D
Chemistry	M,D
Environmental Sciences	M,D
Fish, Game, and Wildlife Management	M,D
Food Science and Technology	M,D*
Forestry	M,D
Geology	M,D*
Geophysics	M,D
Horticulture	M,D
Mathematical Physics	M,D
Mathematics	M,D*
Natural Resources	M,D*
Physics	M,D
Statistics	M,D*

VIRGINIA STATE UNIVERSITY

Mathematics	M
Physics	M

WAKE FOREST UNIVERSITY

Analytical Chemistry	M,D
Chemistry	M,D*
Inorganic Chemistry	M,D
Mathematics	M
Organic Chemistry	M,D
Physical Chemistry	M,D
Physics	M,D

WASHINGTON STATE UNIVERSITY

Agricultural Sciences—General	M,D
Agronomy and Soil Sciences	M,D
Analytical Chemistry	M,D
Animal Sciences	M,D
Applied Mathematics	M,D
Chemistry	M,D
Environmental Sciences	M,D*
Food Science and Technology	M,D
Geology	M,D
Horticulture	M,D
Inorganic Chemistry	M,D
Mathematics	M,D*
Natural Resources	M,D
Organic Chemistry	M,D
Physical Chemistry	M,D
Physics	M,D

WASHINGTON UNIVERSITY IN ST. LOUIS

Chemistry	M,D

Environmental Sciences	M
Geochemistry	M,D
Geology	M,D
Geophysics	M,D
Geosciences	M,D
Mathematics	M,D
Organic Chemistry	D*
Physics	M,D*
Planetary and Space Sciences	M,D
Statistics	M,D

WAYNE STATE UNIVERSITY

Applied Mathematics	M,D
Chemistry	M,D
Food Science and Technology	M,D
Geology	M
Mathematics	M,D
Physics	M,D
Statistics	M,D

WEBSTER UNIVERSITY

Environmental Policy and Resource Management	M

WESLEYAN UNIVERSITY

Astronomy	M
Chemistry	M,D*
Geosciences	M
Inorganic Chemistry	M,D
Mathematics	M,D*
Organic Chemistry	M,D
Physical Chemistry	M,D
Physics	M,D
Theoretical Chemistry	M,D

WEST CHESTER UNIVERSITY OF PENNSYLVANIA

Astronomy	M
Chemistry	M
Geology	M
Mathematics	M

WESTERN CAROLINA UNIVERSITY

Chemistry	M
Mathematics	M
Physics	M

WESTERN CONNECTICUT STATE UNIVERSITY

Environmental Sciences	M
Geosciences	M
Mathematics	M
Planetary and Space Sciences	M

WESTERN ILLINOIS UNIVERSITY

Chemistry	M
Mathematics	M

Physics	M

WESTERN KENTUCKY UNIVERSITY

Agricultural Sciences—General	M
Chemistry	M
Mathematics	M

WESTERN MICHIGAN UNIVERSITY

Applied Mathematics	M
Biostatistics	M
Chemistry	M
Computational Sciences	M
Geology	M,D
Geosciences	M
Mathematics	M,D
Physics	M,D
Statistics	M,D

WESTERN WASHINGTON UNIVERSITY

Chemistry	M
Environmental Sciences	M
Geology	M
Mathematics	M

WEST TEXAS A&M UNIVERSITY

Agricultural Sciences—General	M
Animal Sciences	M
Chemistry	M
Environmental Sciences	M
Mathematics	M

WEST VIRGINIA UNIVERSITY

Agricultural Sciences—General	M,D
Agronomy and Soil Sciences	M,D
Animal Sciences	M,D
Chemistry	M,D*
Environmental Policy and Resource Management	D*
Fish, Game, and Wildlife Management	M
Food Science and Technology	D
Forestry	M,D
Geology	M,D
Mathematics	M,D
Natural Resources	D
Physics	M,D
Statistics	M

WICHITA STATE UNIVERSITY

Applied Mathematics	M,D
Chemistry	M,D
Environmental Sciences	M
Geology	M
Mathematics	M,D
Physics	M
Statistics	M,D

WILKES UNIVERSITY

Mathematics	M
Physics	M

WILLIAM PATERSON UNIVERSITY OF NEW JERSEY

Limnology	M

WINTHROP UNIVERSITY

Mathematics	M

WORCESTER POLYTECHNIC INSTITUTE

Applied Mathematics	M,D,O
Chemistry	M,D
Mathematics	M,D,O
Physics	M,D
Statistics	M,D,O

WRIGHT STATE UNIVERSITY

Applied Mathematics	M
Chemistry	M
Environmental Sciences	M
Geology	M
Geophysics	M
Hydrology	M
Mathematics	M
Physics	M*
Statistics	M

YALE UNIVERSITY

Applied Mathematics	M,D*
Applied Physics	M,D*
Astronomy	M,D
Biostatistics	M,D
Chemistry	D*
Environmental Sciences	M,D
Forestry	M,D*
Geochemistry	D
Geology	D*
Geophysics	D
Geosciences	D
Inorganic Chemistry	D
Mathematics	M,D
Meteorology	D
Oceanography	D
Organic Chemistry	D
Physical Chemistry	D
Physics	D*
Statistics	M,D

YORK UNIVERSITY

Astronomy	M,D
Chemistry	M,D
Environmental Policy and Resource Management	M,D*
Geosciences	M,D
Mathematics	M,D
Physics	M,D
Planetary and Space Sciences	M,D
Statistics	M,D

YOUNGSTOWN STATE UNIVERSITY

Chemistry	M
Mathematics	M

Academic and Professional Programs in the Physical Sciences

This part of Book 4 consists of six sections covering the physical sciences. Each section has a table of contents (listing the program directories, announcements, and in-depth descriptions); program directories, which consist of brief profiles of programs in the relevant fields (and 50-word or 100-word announcements following the profiles, if programs have chosen to include them); Cross-Discipline Announcements, if any programs have chosen to submit such entries; and in-depth descriptions, which are more individualized statements, if programs have chosen to submit them.

Section 1
Astronomy and Astrophysics

This section contains a directory of institutions offering graduate work in astronomy and astrophysics, followed by in-depth entries submitted by institutions that chose to prepare detailed program descriptions. Additional information about programs listed in the directory but not augmented by an in-depth entry may be obtained by writing directly to the dean of a graduate school or chair of a department at the address given in the directory.

For programs offering related work, see also in this book Geosciences, Meteorology and Atmospheric Sciences, and Physics. In Book 3, see Biological and Biomedical Sciences and Biophysics; and in Book 5, see Aerospace/Aeronautical Engineering, Engineering and Applied Sciences, Mechanical Engineering and Mechanics, and Energy and Power Engineering (Nuclear Engineering).

CONTENTS

Astronomy

Arizona State University, Graduate College, College of Liberal Arts and Sciences, Department of Physics and Astronomy, Tempe, AZ 85287. Offers MNS, MS, PhD. *Faculty:* 44 full-time (5 women). *Students:* 59 full-time (14 women), 11 part-time (2 women); includes 3 minority (all Hispanic Americans), 26 international. Average age 29. 83 applicants, 51% accepted. In 1998, 10 master's, 10 doctorates awarded. *Degree requirements:* For master's, thesis, oral and written exams required; for doctorate, dissertation required. *Entrance requirements:* For master's and doctorate, GRE. Application fee: $45. *Faculty research:* Electromagnetic interaction of hadrons, investigation of tripartition fission, and beta activity of various elements formed in fission processes; phase transitions in solids. *Unit head:* Dr. Howard G. Voss, Chair, 480-965-3561. *Application contact:* Dr. Kevin Schmidt, 480-965-4702.

Boston University, Graduate School of Arts and Sciences, Department of Astronomy, Boston, MA 02215. Offers MA, PhD. *Faculty:* 22 full-time (3 women), 3 part-time (2 women). *Students:* 26 full-time (8 women), 1 part-time, 9 international. Average age 26. 53 applicants, 26% accepted. In 1998, 3 master's, 4 doctorates awarded. Terminal master's awarded for partial completion of doctoral program. *Degree requirements:* For master's, one foreign language, thesis or alternative, comprehensive exam required; for doctorate, one foreign language, dissertation, comprehensive/qualifying exam required. *Entrance requirements:* For master's and doctorate, GRE General Test, GRE Subject Test, TOEFL (minimum score of 550 required). *Average time to degree:* Master's–2 years full-time; doctorate–5 years full-time. *Application deadline:* For fall admission, 4/1. Applications are processed on a rolling basis. Application fee: $50. Tuition: Full-time $23,770; part-time $743 per credit. Required fees: $220. Tuition and fees vary according to class time, course level, campus/location and program. *Financial aid:* In 1998–99, 25 students received aid, including 1 fellowship, 18 research assistantships, 7 teaching assistantships; Federal Work-Study and unspecified assistantships also available. Aid available to part-time students. Financial aid application deadline: 1/15; financial aid applicants required to submit FAFSA. *Faculty research:* Galactic and extragalactic astrophysics, dynamics of the Earth's magnetosphere and ionosphere, theoretical astrophysics and cosmology. *Unit head:* W. Jeffrey Hughes, Chairman, 617-353-2471, Fax: 617-353-5704, E-mail: hughes@buasta.bu.edu. *Application contact:* Tereasa Brainerd, Assistant Professor, 617-353-6646, Fax: 617-353-5704, E-mail: brainerd@bu.edu.

Bowling Green State University, Graduate College, College of Arts and Sciences, Department of Physics and Astronomy, Bowling Green, OH 43403. Offers physics (MAT, MS); physics and astronomy (MAT). *Faculty:* 5 full-time (0 women). *Students:* 8 full-time (1 woman), 1 part-time, (all international). 28 applicants, 61% accepted. In 1998, 3 degrees awarded. *Degree requirements:* For master's, thesis or alternative required, foreign language not required. *Entrance requirements:* For master's, GRE General Test, TOEFL (minimum score of 550 required). Application fee: $30. Electronic applications accepted. *Financial aid:* Research assistantships with full tuition reimbursements, teaching assistantships with full tuition reimbursements, career-related internships or fieldwork, institutionally-sponsored loans, and unspecified assistantships available. Financial aid applicants required to submit FAFSA. *Faculty research:* Computational physics, solid-state physics, materials science, theoretical physics. *Unit head:* Dr. Robert I. Boughton, Chair, 419-372-2421. *Application contact:* Dr. Lewis Fulcher, Graduate Coordinator, 419-372-2635.

Brigham Young University, Graduate Studies, College of Physical and Mathematical Sciences, Department of Physics and Astronomy, Provo, UT 84602-1001. Offers physics (MS, PhD); physics and astronomy (PhD). Part-time programs available. *Faculty:* 30 full-time (0 women), 2 part-time (1 woman). *Students:* 21 full-time (2 women), 4 part-time; includes 1 minority (Hispanic American), 11 international. Average age 28. 28 applicants, 29% accepted. In 1998, 5 master's awarded (40% found work related to degree, 40% continued full-time study); 3 doctorates awarded (100% entered university research/teaching). Terminal master's awarded for partial completion of doctoral program. *Degree requirements:* For master's, thesis required; for doctorate, dissertation required, dissertation required. *Entrance requirements:* For master's and doctorate, GRE Subject Test, minimum GPA of 3.0 in last 60 hours. *Average time to degree:* Master's–2.5 years full-time, 4.7 years part-time; doctorate–6.8 years full-time. *Application deadline:* For fall admission, 2/1. Application fee: $30. Electronic applications accepted. Tuition: Full-time $3,330; part-time $185 per credit hour. Tuition and fees vary according to program and student's religious affiliation. *Financial aid:* In 1998–99, 19 students received aid, including 2 research assistantships with tuition reimbursements available (averaging $4,160 per year), 17 teaching assistantships with tuition reimbursements available (averaging $4,289 per year); fellowships with tuition reimbursements available, career-related internships or fieldwork, institutionally-sponsored loans, and tuition waivers (partial) also available. Aid available to part-time students. Financial aid application deadline: 2/1. *Faculty research:* Acoustics; astrophysics; atomic, molecular, and optical physics; plasma; theoretical and mathematical physics; condensed matter. *Unit head:* Dr. Dorian M. Hatch, Chair, 801-378-4361, Fax: 801-378-2265, E-mail: hatchd@wigner.byu.edu. *Application contact:* Dr. Jean-Francois S. Van Huele, Graduate Coordinator, 801-378-4481, Fax: 801-378-2265, E-mail: graduatep_physics@byu.edu.

California Institute of Technology, Division of Physics, Mathematics and Astronomy, Department of Astronomy, Pasadena, CA 91125-0001. Offers PhD. *Faculty:* 11. *Students:* 21 full-time (3 women), 3 international. Average age 25. 67 applicants, 19% accepted. In 1998, 2 degrees awarded. *Degree requirements:* For doctorate, dissertation, candidacy and final exams required. *Entrance requirements:* For doctorate, GRE General Test, GRE Subject Test, TOEFL. *Application deadline:* For fall admission, 1/15. Application fee: $0. *Financial aid:* In 1998–99, 21 students received aid, including 2 fellowships with full tuition reimbursements available (averaging $15,900 per year), 13 research assistantships with full tuition reimbursements available (averaging $18,300 per year), 10 teaching assistantships with full tuition reimbursements available (averaging $11,754 per year); Federal Work-Study, institutionally-sponsored loans, and outside awards also available. Financial aid application deadline: 1/15. *Faculty research:* Observational and theoretical astrophysics, cosmology, radio astronomy, solar physics. *Unit head:* Dr. Shrinivas Kulkarni, Executive Officer, 626-395-4010. *Application contact:* Sterl Phinney, Option Representative, 626-395-4308.

Case Western Reserve University, School of Graduate Studies, Department of Astronomy, Cleveland, OH 44106. Offers MS, PhD. Part-time programs available. *Degree requirements:* For doctorate, dissertation required. *Entrance requirements:* For master's and doctorate, GRE General Test, GRE Subject Test (physics), TOEFL (minimum score of 550 required). *Faculty research:* Ground-based optical astronomy, high- and low-dispersion spectroscopy, theoretical astrophysics, galactic structure.

Clemson University, Graduate School, College of Engineering and Science, Department of Physics and Astronomy, Clemson, SC 29634. Offers physics (MS, PhD), including astronomy and astrophysics, atmospheric physics, biophysics. Part-time programs available. *Students:* 33 full-time (8 women), 4 part-time; includes 1 minority (African American), 11 international. Terminal master's awarded for partial completion of doctoral program. *Degree requirements:* For master's, thesis or alternative required, foreign language not required; for doctorate, dissertation required, foreign language not required. *Entrance requirements:* For master's and doctorate, GRE General Test, TOEFL. *Application deadline:* For fall admission, 2/15 (priority date). Applications are processed on a rolling basis. Application fee: $35. *Unit head:* Dr. Peter J. McNulty, Chair, 864-656-3419, Fax: 864-656-0805, E-mail: mpeter@clemson.edu. *Application contact:* Dr. Miguel F. Larsen, Graduate Coordinator, 864-656-5309, Fax: 864-656-0805, E-mail: mlarson@clemson.edu.

Columbia University, Graduate School of Arts and Sciences, Division of Natural Sciences, Department of Astronomy, New York, NY 10027. Offers M Phil, MA, PhD. Part-time programs available. *Degree requirements:* For master's, foreign language and thesis not required; for doctorate, dissertation, M Phil required, foreign language not required. *Entrance requirements:* For master's and doctorate, GRE General Test, TOEFL, major in astronomy or physics. *Faculty research:* Theoretical astrophysics, x-ray astronomy, radio astronomy.

Cornell University, Graduate School, Graduate Fields of Arts and Sciences, Field of Astronomy and Space Sciences, Ithaca, NY 14853-0001. Offers astronomy (PhD); astrophysics (PhD); general space sciences (PhD); infrared astronomy (PhD); planetary studies (PhD); radio astronomy (PhD); radiophysics (PhD); theoretical astrophysics (PhD). *Faculty:* 26 full-time. *Students:* 23 full-time (9 women); includes 3 minority (2 Asian Americans or Pacific Islanders, 1 Hispanic American), 8 international. 88 applicants, 27% accepted. In 1998, 6 doctorates awarded. *Degree requirements:* For doctorate, dissertation required, foreign language not required. *Entrance requirements:* For doctorate, GRE General Test, GRE Subject Test, TOEFL (minimum score of 600 required). *Application deadline:* For fall admission, 1/15. Application fee: $65. Electronic applications accepted. *Financial aid:* In 1998–99, 22 students received aid, including 6 fellowships with full tuition reimbursements available, 8 research assistantships with full tuition reimbursements available, 8 teaching assistantships with full tuition reimbursements available; institutionally-sponsored loans, scholarships, tuition waivers (full and partial), and unspecified assistantships also available. Financial aid applicants required to submit FAFSA. *Faculty research:* High energy astrophysics, cosmology, star formation. *Unit head:* Director of Graduate Studies, 607-255-4341, Fax: 607-255-5907. *Application contact:* Graduate Field Assistant, 607-255-4341, E-mail: oconnor@astrosun.tn.cornell.edu.

Dartmouth College, School of Arts and Sciences, Department of Physics and Astronomy, Hanover, NH 03755. Offers MS, PhD. *Faculty:* 18 full-time (1 woman), 4 part-time (0 women). *Students:* 30 full-time (12 women); includes 1 minority (African American), 7 international. 184 applicants, 16% accepted. In 1998, 2 master's awarded (100% found work related to degree); 5 doctorates awarded (20% entered university research/teaching, 80% found other work related to degree). Terminal master's awarded for partial completion of doctoral program. *Degree requirements:* For master's and doctorate, thesis/dissertation required. *Entrance requirements:* For master's and doctorate, GRE General Test, GRE Subject Test. *Application deadline:* For fall admission, 2/28 (priority date). Application fee: $15. *Financial aid:* In 1998–99, 30 students received aid, including 10 research assistantships with full tuition reimbursements available; fellowships with full tuition reimbursements available, grants, institutionally-sponsored loans, scholarships, and tuition waivers (full) also available. *Unit head:* Dr. Mary Hudson, Chair, 603-646-2359. *Application contact:* Judy Lowell, Administrative Assistant, 603-646-2359.

Announcement: Graduate studies in observational astronomy and cosmology. Research takes advantage of Dartmouth's 2.4- and 1.3-meter telescopes on Kitt Peak, as well as Hubble Space Telescope and other national facilities and includes large-scale structure of the universe, galactic velocities, supernovae, cataclysmic binaries, and phase transitions in the early universe.

Georgia State University, College of Arts and Sciences, Department of Physics and Astronomy, Program in Astronomy, Atlanta, GA 30303-3083. Offers PhD. *Students:* 6 full-time (3 women), 2 part-time; includes 1 minority (Asian American or Pacific Islander), 2 international. Average age 26. 17 applicants, 71% accepted. In 1998, 4 doctorates awarded (100% entered university research/teaching). *Degree requirements:* For doctorate, 2 foreign languages (computer language can substitute for one), dissertation required. *Entrance requirements:* For doctorate, GRE General Test, GRE Subject Test, TOEFL (minimum score of 550 required), minimum GPA of 3.0. *Average time to degree:* Doctorate–5 years full-time. Application fee: $25. Tuition, state resident: full-time $2,896; part-time $121 per credit hour. Tuition, nonresident: full-time $11,584; part-time $483 per credit hour. Required fees: $468. Tuition and fees vary according to program. *Financial aid:* Fellowships, research assistantships, teaching assistantships, Federal Work-Study, institutionally-sponsored loans, and tuition waivers (full and partial) available. Financial aid application deadline: 5/1. *Faculty research:* Extragalactic photometry, theoretical astrophysics, young stellar objects. Total annual research expenditures: $1.3 million. *Unit head:* Robert P. Lowell, Graduate Coordinator, 404-894-9472, Fax: 404-894-5638. *Application contact:* Dr. Paul Wiita, Director of Graduate Studies, 404-651-1367, Fax: 404-651-1389, E-mail: wiita@chara.gsu.edu.

Announcement: The Department of Physics and Astronomy offers the PhD in astronomy with 14 astronomy faculty and staff members. Research areas include optical/IR interferometry, binary star speckle interferometry, spectroscopy of hot stars, IR studies of star-forming regions, photometric studies of active galaxies, and theory of AGN phenomena.

Harvard University, Graduate School of Arts and Sciences, Department of Astronomy, Cambridge, MA 02138. Offers astronomy (AM, PhD); astrophysics (AM, PhD). *Students:* 36 full-time (6 women). 72 applicants, 18% accepted. In 1998, 10 master's, 5 doctorates awarded. *Degree requirements:* For doctorate, dissertation, paper, research project required, foreign language not required. *Entrance requirements:* For master's, GRE General Test, TOEFL (minimum score of 550 required); for doctorate, GRE General Test, GRE Subject Test (physics), TOEFL (minimum score of 550 required). *Application deadline:* For fall admission, 12/14. Application fee: $60. *Financial aid:* Fellowships, research assistantships, teaching assistantships, career-related internships or fieldwork, Federal Work-Study, and institutionally-sponsored loans available. Financial aid application deadline: 12/30. *Faculty research:* Atomic and molecular physics, electromagnetism, solar physics, nuclear physics, fluid dynamics. *Unit head:* Dr. Ramesh Narayan, Chairman, 617-495-3752. *Application contact:* Office of Admissions and Financial Aid, 617-495-5315.

See in-depth description on page 41.

Indiana University Bloomington, Graduate School, College of Arts and Sciences, Department of Astronomy, Bloomington, IN 47405. Offers astronomy (MA, PhD); astrophysics (PhD). PhD offered through the University Graduate School. Part-time programs available. *Faculty:* 7 full-time (1 woman). *Students:* 7 full-time (1 woman), 5 part-time, 2 international. In 1998, 2 degrees awarded. Terminal master's awarded for partial completion of doctoral program. *Degree requirements:* For master's, thesis, oral exam required, foreign language not required; for doctorate, dissertation, written qualifying exam required, foreign language not required. *Entrance requirements:* For master's and doctorate, GRE General Test, GRE Subject Test (physics), TOEFL, BA or BS in a science. *Average time to degree:* Doctorate–4 years full-time. *Application deadline:* For fall admission, 1/15 (priority date); for spring admission, 9/1 (priority date). Applications are processed on a rolling basis. Application fee: $40. Electronic applications accepted. Tuition, state resident: part-time $161 per credit hour. Tuition, nonresident: part-time $468 per credit hour. Required fees: $360 per year. Tuition and fees vary according to course load and program. *Financial aid:* In 1998–99, 2 fellowships, 2 research assistantships (averaging $12,000 per year), 7 teaching assistantships (averaging $11,000 per year) were awarded.; Federal Work-Study and tuition waivers (full and partial) also available. Aid available to part-time students. Financial aid application deadline: 5/2. *Faculty research:* Galaxies and cosmology, stellar astronomy, cataclysmic variables, high-energy astrophysics, globular clusters. *Unit head:* Dr. R. Kent Honeycutt, Chair, 812-855-6912, Fax: 812-855-8725, E-mail: honey@astro.indiana.edu. *Application contact:* Brenda Records, Secretary, 812-855-6912, Fax: 812-855-8725, E-mail: brecords@indiana.edu.

Iowa State University of Science and Technology, Graduate College, College of Liberal Arts and Sciences, Department of Physics and Astronomy, Ames, IA 50011. Offers MS, PhD. Part-time programs available. *Faculty:* 51 full-time, 3 part-time. *Students:* 83 full-time (12 women), 5 part-time; includes 2 minority (1 Asian American or Pacific Islander, 1 Hispanic American), 44 international. 102 applicants, 58% accepted. In 1998, 7 master's, 15 doctorates awarded. Terminal master's awarded for partial completion of doctoral program. *Degree requirements:* For master's, thesis or alternative required; for doctorate, dissertation required. *Entrance requirements:* For master's and doctorate, GRE General Test, GRE Subject Test (physics), TOEFL (minimum score of 550 required). *Application deadline:* For fall admission, 2/15 (priority date). Applications are processed on a rolling basis. Application fee: $20 ($50 for international students). Electronic applications accepted. Tuition, state resident: full-time $3,308. Tuition, nonresident: full-time $9,744. Part-time tuition and fees vary according to course load, campus/location and program. *Financial aid:* In 1998–99, 37 research assistantships with partial tuition reimbursements (averaging $12,241 per year), 43 teaching assistantships with partial tuition reimbursements (averaging $11,646 per year) were awarded.; fellowships, Federal Work-Study, institutionally-sponsored loans, and scholarships also available. Aid available to part-time students. Financial aid application deadline: 2/15. *Faculty research:* Condensed-matter physics, including superconductivity and new materials; high-energy and nuclear physics; astronomy and astrophysics; atmospheric and environmental physics. Total annual research expenditures: $8.8 million. *Unit head:* Dr. Douglas K. Finnemore, Chair, 515-294-5441, Fax: 515-294-6027, E-mail: phys_astro@iastate.edu.

Johns Hopkins University, Zanvyl Krieger School of Arts and Sciences, Department of Physics and Astronomy, Baltimore, MD 21218-2699. Offers astronomy (PhD); physics (PhD). *Faculty:* 32 full-time (2 women), 8 part-time (1 woman). *Students:* 79 full-time (16 women); includes 5 minority (2 African Americans, 3 Asian Americans or Pacific Islanders), 39 international. Average age 25. 259 applicants, 21% accepted. In 1998, 17 doctorates awarded. *Degree requirements:* For doctorate, dissertation, comprehensive exam required, foreign language not required. *Entrance requirements:* For doctorate, GRE General Test, GRE Subject Test, TOEFL. *Average time to degree:* Doctorate–6.5 years full-time. *Application deadline:* For fall admission, 1/15 (priority date). Application fee: $55. Tuition: Full-time $23,660. Tuition and fees vary according to program. *Financial aid:* In 1998–99, 1 fellowship, 34 research assistantships, 33 teaching assistantships were awarded.; career-related internships or fieldwork, Federal Work-Study, institutionally-sponsored loans, and tuition waivers (full and partial) also available. Financial aid application deadline: 3/14; financial aid applicants required to submit FAFSA. *Faculty research:* High-energy physics, condensed-matter astrophysics, particle and experimental physics, physics theory. Total annual research expenditures: $34.7 million. *Unit head:* Dr. Paul D. Feldman, Chair, 410-516-7346, Fax: 410-516-7239. *Application contact:* Janet Krupsaw, Academic Program Coordinator, 410-516-7344, Fax: 410-516-7239, E-mail: krupsaw@pha.jhu.edu.

Louisiana State University and Agricultural and Mechanical College, Graduate School, College of Basic Sciences, Department of Physics and Astronomy, Baton Rouge, LA 70803. Offers astronomy (PhD); astrophysics (PhD); physics (MS, PhD). *Faculty:* 32 full-time (0 women). *Students:* 58 full-time (10 women), 4 part-time; includes 3 minority (all African Americans), 30 international. Average age 29. 39 applicants, 51% accepted. In 1998, 5 master's, 9 doctorates awarded. Terminal master's awarded for partial completion of doctoral program. *Degree requirements:* For master's, thesis or alternative required, foreign language not required; for doctorate, dissertation required, foreign language not required. *Entrance requirements:* For master's, GRE General Test, TOEFL (minimum score of 550 required for admission, 560 required for assistantships), minimum GPA of 3.0; for doctorate, GRE General Test, TOEFL (minimum score of 550 required), minimum GPA of 3.0. *Average time to degree:* Master's–2.9 years full-time; doctorate–6.6 years full-time. *Application deadline:* For fall admission, 1/25 (priority date). Applications are processed on a rolling basis. Application fee: $25. *Financial aid:* In 1998–99, 9 fellowships, 16 research assistantships with partial tuition reimbursements, 31 teaching assistantships with partial tuition reimbursements were awarded.; institutionally-sponsored loans and unspecified assistantships also available. Financial aid application deadline: 3/15. *Faculty research:* Experimental and theoretical atomic, nuclear, particle, cosmic-ray, low-temperature, and condensed-matter physics. *Unit head:* Dr. William Metcalf, Chair, 225-388-2261, Fax: 225-388-5855, E-mail: metcalf@phzeus.phys.lsu.edu. *Application contact:* Dr. Philip Adams, Chair, Assistantship Committee, 225-388-1194, Fax: 225-388-5855, E-mail: phadan@lsuvm.sncc.lsu.edu.

Minnesota State University, Mankato, College of Graduate Studies, College of Science, Engineering and Technology, Department of Physics and Astronomy, Mankato, MN 56002-8400. Offers MS, MT. *Faculty:* 10 full-time (2 women). *Students:* 1 full-time (0 women), 1 part-time. Average age 34. *Degree requirements:* For master's, thesis or alternative, comprehensive exam required. *Entrance requirements:* For master's, minimum GPA of 3.0 during previous 2 years. *Application deadline:* For fall admission, 7/9 (priority date); for spring admission, 11/27. Applications are processed on a rolling basis. Application fee: $20. *Financial aid:* Teaching assistantships with partial tuition reimbursements, Federal Work-Study available. Aid available to part-time students. Financial aid application deadline: 3/15; financial aid applicants required to submit FAFSA. *Unit head:* Dr. Sandford Schuster, Chairperson, 507-389-5743. *Application contact:* Joni Roberts, Admissions Coordinator, 507-389-2321, Fax: 507-389-5974, E-mail: grad@mankato.msus.edu.

New Mexico State University, Graduate School, College of Arts and Sciences, Department of Astronomy, Las Cruces, NM 88003-8001. Offers MS, PhD. Part-time programs available. *Faculty:* 6 full-time (1 woman), 1 part-time (0 women). *Students:* 23 full-time (9 women), 4 part-time (1 woman); includes 1 minority (Hispanic American), 4 international. Average age 26. 35 applicants, 26% accepted. In 1998, 3 master's, 2 doctorates awarded. Terminal master's awarded for partial completion of doctoral program. *Degree requirements:* For master's and doctorate, thesis/dissertation required, foreign language not required. *Entrance requirements:* For master's and doctorate, GRE General Test, GRE Subject Test (advanced physics). *Application deadline:* For fall admission, 2/15 (priority date). Applications are processed on a rolling basis. Application fee: $15 ($35 for international students). Electronic applications accepted. Tuition, state resident: full-time $2,682; part-time $112 per credit. Tuition, nonresident: full-time $8,376; part-time $349 per credit. Tuition and fees vary according to course load. *Financial aid:* Fellowships, research assistantships, teaching assistantships available. Financial aid application deadline: 3/1. *Faculty research:* Planetary systems, accreting binary stars. *Unit head:* Dr. Reinirus Walterbos, Head, 505-646-4438, Fax: 505-646-1602, E-mail: rwalterb@nmsu.edu.

Announcement: Graduate research in planetary atmospheres and interiors, solar system space exploration, extra-solar planets, X-ray binaries, interstellar medium, stellar populations, active galaxies, galaxy clusters, and cosmology. Access to supercomputers and APO Observatory, with operational 3.5-m ARC telescope and NMSU 1-m imaging telescope. WWW: http://charon.nmsu.edu.

Northwestern University, The Graduate School, Judd A. and Marjorie Weinberg College of Arts and Sciences, Department of Physics and Astronomy, Evanston, IL 60208. Offers astronomy (PhD); astrophysics (PhD); physics (PhD). Admissions and degrees offered through The Graduate School. *Faculty:* 27 full-time (3 women). *Students:* 74 full-time (13 women); includes 6 minority (5 Asian Americans or Pacific Islanders, 1 Hispanic American), 51 international. 87 applicants, 59% accepted. In 1998, 5 doctorates awarded. *Degree requirements:* For doctorate, dissertation, qualifying exam required, foreign language not required. *Entrance requirements:* For doctorate, GRE General Test, GRE Subject Test, TOEFL (minimum score of 600 required; average 630). Application fee: $50 ($55 for international students). *Financial aid:* In 1998–99, 12 fellowships with full tuition reimbursements (averaging $11,673 per year), 27 research assistantships with partial tuition reimbursements (averaging $17,016 per year), 19 teaching assistantships with full tuition reimbursements (averaging $12,042 per year) were awarded.; career-related internships or fieldwork, Federal Work-Study, and institutionally-sponsored loans also available. Financial aid application deadline: 1/15; financial aid applicants required to submit FAFSA. *Faculty research:* Nuclear and particle physics, condensed-matter physics, nonlinear physics, astrophysics. Total annual research expenditures: $5.2 million. *Unit head:* David E. Buchholz, Chair, 847-491-3644, Fax: 847-491-9982, E-mail: physics-astronomy@nwu.edu. *Application contact:* Mary Rosenthal, Admission Contact, 847-491-3644, Fax: 847-491-9982, E-mail: physics-astronomy@nwu.edu.

The Ohio State University, Graduate School, College of Mathematical and Physical Sciences, Department of Astronomy, Columbus, OH 43210. Offers MS, PhD. *Faculty:* 14 full-time, 5 part-time. *Students:* 18 full-time (3 women), 11 international. 55 applicants, 31% accepted. In 1998, 3 master's, 5 doctorates awarded. *Degree requirements:* For master's, thesis, comprehensive exam required; for doctorate, dissertation, oral and written comprehensive exams required. *Entrance requirements:* For master's and doctorate, GRE General Test, TOEFL (minimum score of 550 required), minimum GPA of 2.7. *Application deadline:* For fall admission, 8/15. Applications are processed on a rolling basis. Application fee: $30 ($40 for international students). *Financial aid:* Fellowships, research assistantships, teaching assistantships, Federal Work-Study and institutionally-sponsored loans available. Aid available to part-time students. *Unit head:* Patrick S. Osmer, Chairman, 614-292-1773, Fax: 614-292-2928, E-mail: osmer.1@osu.edu.

Pennsylvania State University University Park Campus, Graduate School, Eberly College of Science, Department of Astronomy and Astrophysics, State College, University Park, PA 16802-1503. Offers MS, PhD. *Students:* 17 full-time (7 women), 1 part-time. *Entrance requirements:* For master's and doctorate, GRE General Test. Application fee: $50. *Unit head:* Dr. Peter I. Meszaros, Head, 814-865-0418.

Rice University, Graduate Programs, Wiess School of Natural Sciences, Department of Space Physics and Astronomy, Houston, TX 77251-1892. Offers MS, PhD. *Degree requirements:* For master's and doctorate, thesis/dissertation required, foreign language not required. *Entrance requirements:* For master's, GRE General Test, TOEFL (minimum score of 550 required), minimum GPA of 3.0; for doctorate, GRE General Test (score in 70th percentile or higher required), minimum GPA of 3.0. *Faculty research:* Magnetospheric physics, planetary atmospheres, astrophysics.

Saint Mary's University, Faculty of Science, Department of Astronomy, Halifax, NS B3H 3C3, Canada. Offers M Sc. Part-time programs available. *Faculty:* 5 full-time (0 women). *Students:* 3 full-time (1 woman), 3 part-time (1 woman). Average age 33. 8 applicants, 38% accepted. In 1998, 2 degrees awarded. *Degree requirements:* For master's, thesis required, foreign language not required. *Entrance requirements:* For master's, TOEFL (minimum score of 550 required), honors degree. *Application deadline:* For fall admission, 3/31. Application fee: $35. *Financial aid:* Fellowships, research assistantships, teaching assistantships, career-related internships or fieldwork, institutionally-sponsored loans, and scholarships available. Aid available to part-time students. Financial aid application deadline: 5/1. *Faculty research:* Young stellar objects, interstellar medium, star clusters, galactic structure, early-type galaxies. *Unit head:* Dr. Gary Welch, Chairman, 902-420-5637.

San Diego State University, Graduate and Research Affairs, College of Sciences, Department of Astronomy, San Diego, CA 92182. Offers MS. *Students:* 1 full-time (0 women), 10 part-time (2 women); includes 2 minority (both Asian Americans or Pacific Islanders) Average age 30. 11 applicants, 27% accepted. In 1998, 2 degrees awarded. *Degree requirements:* For master's, thesis required, foreign language not required. *Entrance requirements:* For master's, GRE General Test (minimum combined score of 950 required), TOEFL (minimum score of 550 required). *Application deadline:* For fall admission, 7/1 (priority date); for spring admission, 12/1. Applications are processed on a rolling basis. Application fee: $55. *Financial aid:* In 1998–99, 2 research assistantships, 7 teaching assistantships were awarded. *Faculty research:* CCD, classical and dwarf novae, photometry, interactive binaries. Total annual research expenditures: $365,000. *Unit head:* Ronald J. Angione, Chair, 619-594-6182, Fax: 619-594-1413, E-mail: angione@mintaka.sdsu.edu. *Application contact:* C. T. Daub, Graduate Coordinator, 619-594-1414, Fax: 619-594-1413, E-mail: daub@mintaka.sdsu.edu.

The University of Arizona, Graduate College, College of Science, Department of Astronomy, Tucson, AZ 85721. Offers MS, PhD. *Faculty:* 32. *Students:* 27 full-time (11 women), 1 part-time; includes 1 minority (Asian American or Pacific Islander), 9 international. Average age 29. 73 applicants, 7% accepted. In 1998, 2 master's, 5 doctorates awarded. *Degree requirements:* For master's, foreign language and thesis not required; for doctorate, dissertation required, foreign language not required. *Entrance requirements:* For master's and doctorate, GRE General Test, GRE Subject Test, TOEFL (minimum score of 550 required). *Application deadline:* For fall admission, 2/7. Applications are processed on a rolling basis. Application fee: $35. *Financial aid:* Fellowships, research assistantships, teaching assistantships, scholarships available. *Faculty research:* Astrophysics, submillimeter astronomy, infrared astronomy, SIRTE, NICMOS. *Unit head:* Dr. Peter A. Strittmatter, Head Director, Astronomy/Steward Observatory, 520-621-6524. *Application contact:* Helen Bluestein, Administrative Assistant, 520-621-2289, Fax: 520-621-1532.

University of British Columbia, Faculty of Graduate Studies, Faculty of Science, Department of Geophysics and Astronomy, Vancouver, BC V6T 1Z2, Canada. Offers astronomy (M Sc, MA Sc, PhD); geophysics (M Sc, MA Sc, PhD). *Degree requirements:* For master's, thesis required; for doctorate, dissertation, comprehensive exam required. *Entrance requirements:* For master's and doctorate, TOEFL. *Faculty research:* Stellar astronomy, cosmology, crustal and earthquake seismology, geophysical inverse theory, glacier and ice sheet physics.

University of Calgary, Faculty of Graduate Studies, Faculty of Science, Department of Physics and Astronomy, Calgary, AB T2N 1N4, Canada. Offers M Sc, PhD. Part-time programs available. *Faculty:* 18 full-time (1 woman), 1 part-time (0 women). *Students:* 17 full-time (7 women). Average age 28. 25 applicants, 16% accepted. In 1998, 3 master's awarded (67% found work related to degree, 33% continued full-time study); 1 doctorate awarded (100% found work related to degree). *Degree requirements:* For master's, thesis required; for doctorate, dissertation, oral candidacy exam, written qualifying exam required. *Entrance requirements:* For master's and doctorate, GRE General Test, GRE Subject Test, TOEFL (minimum score of 550 required). *Application deadline:* For fall admission, 3/1. Applications are processed on a rolling basis. Application fee: $60. *Financial aid:* Fellowships, research assistantships, teaching assistantships, institutionally-sponsored loans available. Financial aid application deadline: 5/31. *Faculty research:* Astronomy and astrophysics, mass spectrometry, atmospheric physics, space physics, condensed–matter physics, medical physics. Total annual research expenditures: $3.3 million. *Unit head:* Dr. J. S. Murphree, Head, 403-220-5385, Fax: 403-289-3331, E-mail: murphree@phys.ucalgary.ca. *Application contact:* Dr. S. Kwok, Chairman, Graduate Affairs, 403-220-5414, Fax: 403-289-3331, E-mail: kwok@acs.ucalgary.ca.

University of California, Los Angeles, Graduate Division, College of Letters and Science, Department of Physics and Astronomy, Program in Astronomy, Los Angeles, CA 90095. Offers MAT, MS, PhD. *Students:* 26 full-time (9 women); includes 3 minority (all Asian Americans or Pacific Islanders), 3 international. 45 applicants, 24% accepted. *Degree requirements:* For doctorate, dissertation, oral and written qualifying exams required, foreign language not required. *Entrance requirements:* For master's, GRE General Test, GRE Subject Test (physics), minimum GPA of 3.0; for doctorate, GRE General Test, GRE Subject Test (physics), minimum undergraduate GPA of 3.0. *Application deadline:* For fall admission, 12/15. Application fee: $40. Electronic applications accepted. *Financial aid:* In 1998–99, 24 students received aid, including 24 fellowships, 16 teaching assistantships; research assistantships, Federal Work-Study, institutionally-sponsored loans, scholarships, and tuition waivers (full and partial) also available. Financial aid application deadline: 3/1. *Unit head:* Jaime Albano, Graduate Affairs Officer, 949-824-4261, Fax: 949-824-8571. *Application contact:* Departmental Office, 310-825-2307, E-mail: apply@physics.ucla.edu.

University of California, Santa Cruz, Graduate Division, Division of Natural Sciences, Program in Astronomy and Astrophysics, Santa Cruz, CA 95064. Offers PhD. *Faculty:* 9 full-time. *Students:* 32 full-time (13 women); includes 5 minority (1 African American, 4 Asian Americans or Pacific Islanders), 3 international. 71 applicants, 32% accepted. In 1998, 3 doctorates awarded. *Degree requirements:* For doctorate, one foreign language (computer language can substitute), dissertation, qualifying exam required. *Entrance requirements:* For doctorate, GRE General Test, GRE Subject Test. *Application deadline:* For fall admission, 1/15. Application fee: $40. *Financial aid:* Fellowships, research assistantships, teaching assistantships, Federal Work-Study and institutionally-sponsored loans available. Financial aid application deadline: 1/15. *Faculty research:* Stellar structure and evolution, stellar spectroscopy, the interstellar medium, galactic structure, external galaxies and quasars. *Unit head:* Dr. Stan

Astronomy

University of California, Santa Cruz (continued)
Woosley, Chairperson, 831-459-2976, E-mail: woosley@ucolick.org. *Application contact:* Graduate Admissions, 831-459-2301.

University of Chicago, Division of the Physical Sciences, Department of Astronomy and Astrophysics, Chicago, IL 60637-1513. Offers SM, PhD. Terminal master's awarded for partial completion of doctoral program. *Degree requirements:* For master's, candidacy exam required, foreign language and thesis not required; for doctorate, dissertation for publication required. *Entrance requirements:* For doctorate, GRE General Test, GRE Subject Test (physics), TOEFL, minimum GPA of 3.0. *Faculty research:* Adaptive optics, quasi-stellar object absorption lines, fluid dynamics, interstellar matter, particle physics.

University of Delaware, College of Arts and Science, Joint Graduate Program of Department of Physics and Astronomy and Bartol Research Institute, Newark, DE 19716. Offers MS, PhD. Part-time programs available. *Faculty:* 22 full-time (1 woman), 5 part-time (1 woman). *Students:* 43 full-time (4 women), 2 part-time; includes 8 minority (1 African American, 7 Asian Americans or Pacific Islanders), 16 international. 180 applicants, 29% accepted. In 1998, 2 master's awarded (100% entered university research/teaching); 9 doctorates awarded (67% entered university research/teaching, 33% found other work related to degree). Terminal master's awarded for partial completion of doctoral program. *Degree requirements:* For master's and doctorate, thesis/dissertation required, foreign language not required. *Entrance requirements:* For master's and doctorate, GRE General Test, GRE Subject Test. *Application deadline:* For fall admission, 7/1. Application fee: $45. *Financial aid:* In 1998–99, 41 students received aid, including 5 fellowships, 9 research assistantships, 26 teaching assistantships; career-related internships or fieldwork, Federal Work-Study, institutionally-sponsored loans, and corporate sponsorship also available. *Faculty research:* Magnetoresistance and magnetic materials, ultrafast optical phenomena, superfluidity, elementary particle physics, stellar atmospheres. Total annual research expenditures: $1.4 million. *Unit head:* Dr. Henry R. Glyde, Chair, 302-831-3361. *Application contact:* Dr. S. B. Woo, 302-831-1995, Fax: 302-831-1637, E-mail: grad.physics@udel.edu.

University of Florida, Graduate School, College of Liberal Arts and Sciences, Department of Astronomy, Gainesville, FL 32611. Offers MS, MST, PhD. *Faculty:* 25. *Students:* 27 full-time (10 women), 2 part-time (1 woman); includes 2 minority (both Asian Americans or Pacific Islanders), 4 international. 17 applicants, 53% accepted. In 1998, 3 master's, 1 doctorate awarded. Terminal master's awarded for partial completion of doctoral program. *Degree requirements:* For master's, thesis (terminal MS) required; for doctorate, dissertation required. *Entrance requirements:* For master's and doctorate, GRE General Test (minimum combined score of 1200 required), minimum GPA of 3.0. *Application deadline:* For fall admission, 6/1. Applications are processed on a rolling basis. Application fee: $20. Electronic applications accepted. *Financial aid:* In 1998–99, 25 students received aid, including 12 fellowships, 12 research assistantships, 10 teaching assistantships; unspecified assistantships also available. Financial aid application deadline: 1/31. *Faculty research:* Cosmology, photometry, variable and binary stars, dynamical solar system astronomy, infrared. Total annual research expenditures: $550,000. *Unit head:* Dr. Stanley F. Dermott, Chairman, 352-392-2052, Fax: 352-392-5089, E-mail: dermott@astro.ufl.edu. *Application contact:* Dr. Robert Leacock, Graduate Coordinator, 352-392-2052, Fax: 352-392-5089, E-mail: leacock@astro.ufl.edu.

University of Hawaii at Manoa, Graduate Division, College of Arts and Sciences, College of Natural Sciences, Department of Physics and Astronomy, Honolulu, HI 96822. Offers MS, PhD. *Faculty:* 58 full-time (5 women). *Students:* 32 full-time (8 women), 1 (woman) part-time. 54 applicants, 20% accepted. In 1998, 6 master's, 7 doctorates awarded. *Degree requirements:* For master's, qualifying exam or thesis required; for doctorate, dissertation, oral comprehensive and qualifying exams required. *Entrance requirements:* For master's and doctorate, GRE General Test, GRE Subject Test. *Application deadline:* For fall admission, 2/1 (priority date). Application fee: $25 ($50 for international students). *Financial aid:* In 1998–99, 27 research assistantships (averaging $17,641 per year), 18 teaching assistantships (averaging $14,829 per year) were awarded. *Unit head:* Dr. James R. Gaines, Chairperson, 808-956-7087, E-mail: gaines@uhhepg.phys.hawaii.edu. *Application contact:* Dr. Gareth Wynn-Williams, Graduate Chair, 808-956-8807, E-mail: wynnwill@ifa.hawaii.edu.

University of Illinois at Urbana–Champaign, Graduate College, College of Liberal Arts and Sciences, Department of Astronomy, Urbana, IL 61801. Offers MS, PhD. *Faculty:* 17 full-time (2 women). *Students:* 22 full-time (6 women); includes 1 minority (Asian American or Pacific Islander), 10 international. 37 applicants, 14% accepted. In 1998, 2 master's, 4 doctorates awarded. *Degree requirements:* For master's, foreign language and thesis not required; for doctorate, dissertation required, foreign language not required. *Entrance requirements:* For master's and doctorate, GRE General Test, GRE Subject Test. *Application deadline:* Applications are processed on a rolling basis. Application fee: $40 ($50 for international students). Tuition, state resident: full-time $4,040. Tuition, nonresident: full-time $11,192. Full-time tuition and fees vary according to program. *Financial aid:* In 1998–99, 1 fellowship, 13 research assistantships, 7 teaching assistantships were awarded. Financial aid application deadline: 2/15. *Unit head:* Richard M. Crutcher, Chair, 217-333-3090. *Application contact:* Margaret Meixner, Director of Graduate Studies, 217-333-9380, Fax: 217-244-7638, E-mail: meixner@astro.uiuc.edu.

The University of Iowa, Graduate College, College of Liberal Arts, Department of Physics and Astronomy, Program in Astronomy, Iowa City, IA 52242-1316. Offers MS. *Students:* 3 full-time (0 women), 1 part-time; includes 1 minority (Asian American or Pacific Islander) 3 applicants, 100% accepted. In 1998, 1 degree awarded. *Degree requirements:* For master's, thesis optional. *Entrance requirements:* For master's, GRE General Test, GRE Subject Test. *Application deadline:* For fall admission, 1/1. Applications are processed on a rolling basis. Application fee: $30 ($50 for international students). *Financial aid:* In 1998–99, 4 teaching assistantships were awarded.; fellowships, research assistantships Financial aid applicants required to submit FAFSA. *Unit head:* Wayne N. Polyzou, Chair, Department of Physics and Astronomy, 319-335-1688, Fax: 319-335-1753.

University of Kansas, Graduate School, College of Liberal Arts and Sciences, Department of Physics and Astronomy, Lawrence, KS 66045. Offers computational physics and astronomy (MS); physics (MS, PhD). *Faculty:* 24 full-time. *Students:* 16 full-time (5 women), 24 part-time (4 women); includes 1 minority (Hispanic American), 23 international. In 1998, 7 master's, 8 doctorates awarded. *Degree requirements:* For master's, foreign language and thesis not required; for doctorate, computer language, dissertation required. *Entrance requirements:* For master's and doctorate, TOEFL (minimum score of 570 required). *Financial aid:* Fellowships, research assistantships, teaching assistantships available. *Faculty research:* Condensed-matter and chaos cosmology, elementary particles, nuclear physics, space physics. *Unit head:* Dr. Raymond G. Ammar, Chair, 785-864-4626. *Application contact:* Douglas McKay, Graduate Director.

University of Kentucky, Graduate School, Graduate School Programs from the College of Arts and Sciences, Program in Physics and Astronomy, Lexington, KY 40506-0032. Offers MS, PhD. *Degree requirements:* For master's, comprehensive exam required, thesis optional, foreign language not required; for doctorate, dissertation, comprehensive exam required, foreign language not required. *Entrance requirements:* For master's, GRE General Test, minimum undergraduate GPA of 2.5; for doctorate, GRE General Test, minimum graduate GPA of 3.0. *Faculty research:* Astrophysics, active galactic nuclei, interstellar masses, and radio astronomy; atomic physics, Rydbert atoms, and electron scattering; TOF neutron and (n, n'o) spectroscopy, hyperon interactions and muons; solid-state, STM, charge-density waves, fulleneues, and 1-dimensional systems; particle theory, lattice gauge theory, quark, and skyrmion models.

University of Maryland, College Park, Graduate School, College of Computer, Mathematical and Physical Sciences, Department of Astronomy, College Park, MD 20742-5045. Offers MS, PhD. *Faculty:* 62 full-time (9 women), 5 part-time (1 woman). *Students:* 23 full-time (6 women), 7 part-time (2 women); includes 3 minority (1 Asian American or Pacific Islander, 2 Hispanic Americans), 11 international. 48 applicants, 46% accepted. In 1998, 8 master's, 2 doctorates awarded. *Degree requirements:* For master's, thesis or alternative, written exam required, foreign language not required; for doctorate, dissertation, research project required. *Entrance requirements:* For master's, GRE Subject Test, minimum GPA of 3.0; for doctorate, GRE Subject Test. *Application deadline:* Applications are processed on a rolling basis. Application fee: $50 ($70 for international students). Tuition, state resident: part-time $272 per credit hour. Tuition, nonresident: part-time $475 per credit hour. Required fees: $632; $379 per year. *Financial aid:* In 1998–99, 3 fellowships with full tuition reimbursements (averaging $14,000 per year), 21 research assistantships with tuition reimbursements (averaging $16,438 per year), 13 teaching assistantships with tuition reimbursements (averaging $11,894 per year) were awarded.; career-related internships or fieldwork, Federal Work-Study, grants, and scholarships also available. Aid available to part-time students. Financial aid applicants required to submit FAFSA. *Faculty research:* Solar radio astronomy, plasma and high-energy astrophysics, galactic and extragalactic astronomy. Total annual research expenditures: $5.4 million. *Unit head:* Dr. Marvin Levanthal, Chair, 301-405-1508, Fax: 301-314-9067. *Application contact:* Trudy Lindsey, Director, Graduate Admission and Records, 301-405-4198, Fax: 301-314-9305, E-mail: grschool@deans.umd.edu.

University of Massachusetts Amherst, Graduate School, College of Natural Sciences and Mathematics, Department of Physics and Astronomy, Program in Astronomy, Amherst, MA 01003. Offers MS, PhD. Part-time programs available. *Faculty:* 21 full-time (4 women). *Students:* 4 full-time (1 woman), 15 part-time (5 women); includes 1 minority (Hispanic American), 5 international. Average age 28. 47 applicants, 34% accepted. In 1998, 1 doctorate awarded. Terminal master's awarded for partial completion of doctoral program. *Degree requirements:* For master's, foreign language and thesis not required; for doctorate, dissertation required, foreign language not required. *Entrance requirements:* For master's and doctorate, GRE General Test, GRE Subject Test. *Application deadline:* For fall admission, 2/1 (priority date); for spring admission, 10/1. Applications are processed on a rolling basis. Application fee: $40. Tuition, state resident: full-time $2,640; part-time $165 per credit. Tuition, nonresident: full-time $9,756; part-time $407 per credit. Required fees: $1,221 per term. One-time fee: $110. Full-time tuition and fees vary according to course load, campus/location and reciprocity agreements. *Financial aid:* Fellowships with full tuition reimbursements, research assistantships with full tuition reimbursements, teaching assistantships with full tuition reimbursements, career-related internships or fieldwork, Federal Work-Study, grants, scholarships, traineeships, and unspecified assistantships available. Aid available to part-time students. Financial aid application deadline: 2/1. *Unit head:* Dr. William Gerace, Director, 413-545-2548, Fax: 413-545-0648, E-mail: gerace@phast.umass.edu. *Application contact:* Dr. Donald Candela, Chair, Admissions Committee, 413-545-2407, E-mail: candela@phast.umass.edu.

University of Michigan, Horace H. Rackham School of Graduate Studies, College of Literature, Science, and the Arts, Department of Astronomy, Ann Arbor, MI 48109. Offers MS, PhD. *Faculty:* 9 full-time, 2 part-time. *Students:* 17 full-time (8 women); includes 3 minority (2 African Americans, 1 Hispanic American), 1 international. Average age 25. 50 applicants, 6% accepted. In 1998, 3 master's awarded (0% continued full-time study); 2 doctorates awarded (50% entered university research/teaching, 50% found other work related to degree). *Degree requirements:* For master's, foreign language and thesis not required; for doctorate, dissertation, oral defense of dissertation, preliminary exam required, foreign language not required. *Entrance requirements:* For master's and doctorate, GRE General Test, GRE Subject Test. *Average time to degree:* Doctorate–6 years full-time. *Application deadline:* For fall admission, 2/1. Applications are processed on a rolling basis. Application fee: $55. Electronic applications accepted. *Financial aid:* In 1998–99, 2 research assistantships with full tuition reimbursements (averaging $11,328 per year), 1 teaching assistantship with full tuition reimbursement (averaging $11,328 per year) were awarded.; fellowships with full tuition reimbursements, institutionally-sponsored loans also available. Financial aid application deadline: 2/1. *Faculty research:* Radio astronomy, interstellar medium, stellar evolution, dynamics of stellar systems, gravitational lensing. Total annual research expenditures: $1 million. *Unit head:* Dr. Hugh D. Aller, Chair, 734-764-3440, Fax: 734-763-6317, E-mail: haller@umich.edu. *Application contact:* Christina M. Arabadjis, Department Secretary, 734-764-3440, Fax: 734-763-6317, E-mail: cdrews@umich.edu.

University of Minnesota, Twin Cities Campus, Graduate School, Institute of Technology, School of Physics and Astronomy, Department of Astronomy, Minneapolis, MN 55455-0213. Offers astrophysics (MS, PhD). *Faculty:* 10 full-time (1 woman). *Students:* 15 full-time (5 women), 2 international. Average age 22. 28 applicants, 18% accepted. In 1998, 4 master's awarded (50% entered university research/teaching, 50% found other work related to degree); 2 doctorates awarded (100% entered university research/teaching). Terminal master's awarded for partial completion of doctoral program. *Degree requirements:* For master's, thesis optional; for doctorate, dissertation required. *Entrance requirements:* For master's and doctorate, GRE General Test, GRE Subject Test. *Average time to degree:* Master's–4 years full-time; doctorate–5 years full-time. *Application deadline:* For fall admission, 7/15. Applications are processed on a rolling basis. Application fee: $50 ($55 for international students). *Financial aid:* In 1998–99, 15 students received aid, including 1 fellowship with full tuition reimbursement available (averaging $12,000 per year), 5 research assistantships with full tuition reimbursements available (averaging $11,700 per year), 8 teaching assistantships with full tuition reimbursements available (averaging $11,700 per year); Federal Work-Study and institutionally-sponsored loans also available. Financial aid application deadline: 1/15. *Faculty research:* Evolution of stars and galaxies; the interstellar medium; cosmology; observational, optical, infrared, and radio astronomy; computational astrophysics. Total annual research expenditures: $2.5 million. *Unit head:* Evan Skillman, Director of Graduate Studies, 612-624-9523, Fax: 612-626-2029, E-mail: skillman@astro.spa.umn.edu.

University of Nebraska–Lincoln, Graduate College, College of Arts and Sciences, Department of Physics and Astronomy, Lincoln, NE 68588. Offers astronomy (MS, PhD); physics (MS, PhD). *Faculty:* 24 full-time (1 woman), 2 part-time (0 women). *Students:* 40 full-time (6 women), 6 part-time (1 woman); includes 3 minority (1 African American, 2 Asian Americans or Pacific Islanders), 25 international. Average age 30. 72 applicants, 33% accepted. In 1998, 10 master's, 10 doctorates awarded. *Degree requirements:* For master's, thesis optional, foreign language not required; for doctorate, dissertation, comprehensive exams required. *Entrance requirements:* For master's and doctorate, GRE General Test, TOEFL (minimum score of 550 required). *Average time to degree:* Doctorate–4 years full-time. *Application deadline:* For fall admission, 2/1 (priority date). Applications are processed on a rolling basis. Application fee: $35. Electronic applications accepted. *Financial aid:* In 1998–99, 4 fellowships, 28 research assistantships, 23 teaching assistantships were awarded.; Federal Work-Study also available. Aid available to part-time students. Financial aid application deadline: 2/15. *Faculty research:* Electromagnetics of solids and thin films, photoionization, ion collisions with atoms, molecules and surfaces, search for top quark. *Unit head:* Dr. Roger Kirby, Chair, 402-472-2784.

The University of North Carolina at Chapel Hill, Graduate School, College of Arts and Sciences, Department of Physics and Astronomy, Chapel Hill, NC 27599. Offers astronomy and astrophysics (MS, PhD). *Degree requirements:* For master's, comprehensive exam required; for doctorate, dissertation, comprehensive exam required. *Entrance requirements:* For master's and doctorate, GRE General Test (minimum combined score of 1000 required), minimum GPA of 3.0.

University of Pittsburgh, Faculty of Arts and Sciences, Department of Physics and Astronomy, Pittsburgh, PA 15260. Offers astronomy (MS, PhD); physics (MS, PhD). Part-time programs available. *Faculty:* 39 full-time (4 women). *Students:* 69 full-time (5 women), 2 part-time (1 woman); includes 5 minority (2 African Americans, 2 Asian Americans or Pacific Islanders, 1 Hispanic American), 41 international. 173 applicants, 26% accepted. In 1998, 13 master's, 3 doctorates awarded. Terminal master's awarded for partial completion of doctoral program. *Degree requirements:* For master's, thesis optional, foreign language not required; for doctorate, dissertation required, foreign language not required. *Entrance requirements:* For master's and doctorate, GRE General Test, GRE Subject Test, TOEFL (minimum score of 575 required), minimum QPA of 3.0. *Average time to degree:* Master's–2 years full-time, 3.5 years part-time; doctorate–5.5 years full-time. *Application deadline:* For fall admission, 1/31 (priority date). Applications are processed on a rolling basis. Application fee: $30 ($40 for international students). Electronic applications accepted. *Financial aid:* In 1998–99, 7 fellowships with full tuition reimbursements (averaging $15,150 per year), 31 research assistantships with full tuition reimbursements (averaging $10,600 per year), 32 teaching assistantships with full tuition reimbursements (averaging $10,815 per year) were awarded.; scholarships also available. Financial aid application deadline: 1/31; financial aid applicants required to submit FAFSA. *Faculty research:* Astrophysics, general relativity and condensed-matter physics, atomic physics, particle physics, nuclear physics. Total annual research expenditures: $4 million. *Unit head:* Dr. Frank Tabakin, Chairman, 412-624-6381, Fax: 412-624-9163, E-mail: frankt@tabakin.phyast.pitt.edu. *Application contact:* Peter M. Koehler, Admissions, 412-624-9000, Fax: 412-624-9163.

University of Rochester, The College, Arts and Sciences, Department of Physics and Astronomy, Rochester, NY 14627-0250. Offers physics (MA, MS, PhD); physics and astronomy (PhD). Part-time programs available. *Faculty:* 28. *Students:* 89 full-time (12 women); includes 1 minority (Hispanic American), 36 international. 273 applicants, 30% accepted. In 1998, 13 master's, 16 doctorates awarded. Terminal master's awarded for partial completion of doctoral program. *Degree requirements:* For master's, thesis (for some programs), comprehensive exam required, foreign language not required; for doctorate, dissertation, comprehensive exam, qualifying exam required, foreign language not required. *Entrance requirements:* For master's, GRE General Test; for doctorate, GRE General Test, TOEFL. *Application deadline:* For fall admission, 2/1 (priority date). Application fee: $25. *Financial aid:* Fellowships, research assistantships, teaching assistantships, tuition waivers (full and partial) available. Financial aid application deadline: 2/1. *Unit head:* Arie Bodek, Chair, 716-275-4351. *Application contact:* Barbara Warren, Graduate Program Secretary, 716-275-4351.

University of South Carolina, Graduate School, College of Science and Mathematics, Department of Physics and Astronomy, Columbia, SC 29208. Offers IMA, MAT, MS, PhD. IMA and MAT offered in cooperation with the College of Education. Part-time programs available. *Faculty:* 23 full-time (0 women), 2 part-time (0 women). *Students:* 26 full-time (2 women), 4 part-time (1 woman); includes 1 minority (Asian American or Pacific Islander), 18 international. Average age 30. 28 applicants, 18% accepted. In 1998, 1 master's awarded (0% continued full-time study); 2 doctorates awarded (100% entered university research/teaching). Terminal master's awarded for partial completion of doctoral program. *Degree requirements:* For master's, thesis required, foreign language not required; for doctorate, one foreign language, dissertation required. *Entrance requirements:* For master's and doctorate, GRE General Test, GRE Subject Test. *Application deadline:* For fall admission, 8/1 (priority date). Applications are processed on a rolling basis. Application fee: $35. Electronic applications accepted. Tuition, state resident: full-time $4,014; part-time $202 per credit hour. Tuition, nonresident: full-time $8,528; part-time $428 per credit hour. Required fees: $100; $4 per credit hour. Tuition and fees vary according to program. *Financial aid:* Fellowships, research assistantships, teaching assistantships, Federal Work-Study available. Aid available to part-time students. *Faculty research:* Mechanics, electron-spin resonance, foundations of quantum magnetism, intermediate-energy nuclear physics, high-energy physics. Total annual research expenditures: $2.2 million. *Unit head:* Dr. James M. Knight, Chair, 803-777-4121, Fax: 803-777-3065, E-mail: knight@sc.edu. *Application contact:* Dr. Milind V. Purohit, Director of Graduate Studies, 803-777-6996, Fax: 803-777-3065, E-mail: purohit@charm.psc.sc.edu.

University of Southern Mississippi, Graduate School, College of Science and Technology, School of Mathematical Sciences, Department of Physics and Astronomy, Hattiesburg, MS 39406-5167. Offers MS. *Faculty:* 7 full-time (0 women), 1 part-time (0 women). *Students:* 4 full-time (0 women). Average age 27. 18 applicants, 17% accepted. In 1998, 1 degree awarded. *Degree requirements:* For master's, thesis, oral/written comprehensive exam required, foreign language not required. *Entrance requirements:* For master's, GRE General Test (minimum combined score of 1000 required), TOEFL (minimum score of 580 required), minimum GPA of 2.75. *Application deadline:* For fall admission, 8/6 (priority date). Applications are processed on a rolling basis. Application fee: $0 ($25 for international students). Tuition, state resident: full-time $2,250; part-time $137 per semester hour. Tuition, nonresident: full-time $3,102; part-time $172 per semester hour. Required fees: $602. *Financial aid:* Teaching assistantships, Federal Work-Study available. Financial aid application deadline: 3/15. *Faculty research:* Polymers, atomic physics, fluid mechanics, liquid crystals, refractory materials. Total annual research expenditures: $80,000. *Unit head:* Dr. William E. Hughes, Chairman, 601-266-4934, Fax: 601-266-5149.

The University of Texas at Austin, Graduate School, College of Natural Sciences, Department of Astronomy, Austin, TX 78712-1111. Offers MA, PhD. *Faculty:* 21 full-time (1 woman). *Students:* 30 full-time (7 women), 11 international. 72 applicants, 28% accepted. In 1998, 3 master's, 3 doctorates awarded. *Entrance requirements:* For master's and doctorate, GRE General Test, GRE Subject Test (physics). *Average time to degree:* Doctorate–6.4 years full-time. *Application deadline:* For fall admission, 1/15 (priority date). Application fee: $50 ($75 for international students). Electronic applications accepted. *Financial aid:* In 1998–99, 15 research assistantships, 15 teaching assistantships were awarded.; fellowships Financial aid application deadline: 2/1. *Faculty research:* Stars, interstellar medium, galaxies, planetary astronomy. *Unit head:* Christopher Sneden, Chair, 512-471-3302. *Application contact:* Edward L. Robinson, Graduate Adviser, 512-471-3350, Fax: 512-471-6016, E-mail: studentinfo@astro.as.utexas.edu.

University of Toronto, School of Graduate Studies, Physical Sciences Division, Department of Astronomy, Toronto, ON M5S 1A1, Canada. Offers M Sc, PhD. Part-time programs available. *Degree requirements:* For master's, thesis not required; for doctorate, dissertation required.

University of Victoria, Faculty of Graduate Studies, Faculty of Science, Department of Physics and Astronomy, Victoria, BC V8W 2Y2, Canada. Offers astronomy and astrophysics (M Sc, PhD); condensed matter physics (M Sc, PhD); geophysics (M Sc, PhD); medical physics (PhD); nuclear and particle studies (M Sc, PhD); theoretical physics (M Sc, PhD). *Faculty:* 20 full-time (0 women), 22 part-time (1 woman). *Students:* 28 full-time (7 women). Average age 25. 56 applicants, 16% accepted. In 1998, 5 master's, 2 doctorates awarded. *Degree requirements:* For master's and doctorate, thesis/dissertation required, foreign language not required. *Average time to degree:* Master's–3.06 years full-time; doctorate–4.33 years full-time. *Application deadline:* For fall admission, 5/31 (priority date); for spring admission, 10/31. Applications are processed on a rolling basis. Application fee: $50. *Financial aid:* Fellowships, research assistantships, teaching assistantships, career-related internships or fieldwork and institutionally-sponsored loans available. Financial aid application deadline: 2/15. *Faculty research:* Old stellar populations in globular clusters; observational cosmology and large scale structure; muonium-antimuonium conversion; kaon rare decay modes; geomagnetism, seismology, and space physics. *Unit head:* Dr. C. E. Picciotto, Chair, 250-721-7698, E-mail: pic@uvic.ca. *Application contact:* Dr. A. Watton, Graduate Adviser, 250-721-7703, Fax: 250-721-7715, E-mail: awatt@uvvm.uvic.ca.

University of Virginia, College and Graduate School of Arts and Sciences, Department of Astronomy, Charlottesville, VA 22903. Offers MA, PhD. *Faculty:* 14 full-time (1 woman), 2 part-time (1 woman). *Students:* 15 full-time (2 women), 2 part-time (1 woman), 4 international. Average age 26. 32 applicants, 56% accepted. In 1998, 1 master's, 1 doctorate awarded. *Degree requirements:* For master's, thesis required; for doctorate, dissertation required. *Entrance requirements:* For master's and doctorate, GRE General Test, GRE Subject Test. *Application deadline:* For fall admission, 7/15; for spring admission, 2/1. Applications are processed on a rolling basis. Application fee: $60. *Financial aid:* Application deadline: 2/1. *Unit head:* Robert W. O'Connell, Chairman, 804-924-7494. *Application contact:* Duane J. Osheim, Associate Dean, 804-924-7184, E-mail: grad-a-s@virginia.edu.

University of Washington, Graduate School, College of Arts and Sciences, Department of Astronomy, Seattle, WA 98195. Offers MS, PhD. *Faculty:* 13 full-time (2 women), 1 part-time (0 women). *Students:* 22 full-time (3 women). Average age 29. 150 applicants, 1% accepted. In 1998, 4 master's awarded (100% entered university research/teaching); 2 doctorates awarded (100% entered university research/teaching). Terminal master's awarded for partial completion of doctoral program. *Degree requirements:* For master's, foreign language and thesis not required; for doctorate, dissertation required, foreign language not required. *Entrance requirements:* For master's and doctorate, GRE General Test, GRE Subject Test, TOEFL (minimum score of 500 required), minimum GPA of 3.0. *Application deadline:* For fall admission, 2/1. Application fee: $50. Tuition, state resident: full-time $5,196; part-time $475 per credit. Tuition, nonresident: full-time $13,485; part-time $1,285 per credit. Required fees: $387; $38 per credit. Tuition and fees vary according to course load. *Financial aid:* In 1998–99, 7 research assistantships, 10 teaching assistantships were awarded.; fellowships, Federal Work-Study and traineeships also available. *Faculty research:* Solar system dust, space astronomy, high-energy astrophysics, galactic and extragalactic astronomy, stellar astrophysics. *Unit head:* Dr. Craig J. Hogan, Chair, 206-685-2112, Fax: 206-685-0403. *Application contact:* K. L. Fisher, Program Assistant, 206-543-2888, Fax: 206-685-0403, E-mail: office@astro.washington.edu.

The University of Western Ontario, Faculty of Graduate Studies, Physical Sciences Division, Department of Physics and Astronomy, Program in Astronomy, London, ON N6A 5B8, Canada. Offers M Sc, PhD. *Degree requirements:* For master's, written comprehensive exam required, thesis optional, foreign language not required; for doctorate, dissertation, oral and written comprehensive exams required, foreign language not required. *Entrance requirements:* For master's, minimum B average; for doctorate, minimum B average or M Sc. *Faculty research:* Observational and theoretical astrophysics spectroscopy, photometry, spectro-polarimetry, variable stars, cosmology.

University of Wisconsin–Madison, Graduate School, College of Letters and Science, Department of Astronomy, Madison, WI 53706-1380. Offers PhD. *Faculty:* 12 full-time (1 woman), 1 part-time (0 women). *Students:* 19 full-time (4 women); includes 2 minority (1 Hispanic American, 1 Native American), 2 international. Average age 24. 37 applicants, 24% accepted. In 1998, 1 degree awarded (100% entered university research/teaching). *Degree requirements:* For doctorate, dissertation, comprehensive exam required, foreign language not required. *Entrance requirements:* For doctorate, GRE General Test, GRE Subject Test (physics), TOEFL (minimum score of 625 required), bachelor's degree in related field. *Average time to degree:* Doctorate–5 years full-time. *Application deadline:* For fall admission, 1/5. Application fee: $38. Electronic applications accepted. *Financial aid:* In 1998–99, 1 fellowship with full tuition reimbursement (averaging $16,560 per year), 5 research assistantships with full tuition reimbursements (averaging $10,375 per year), 6 teaching assistantships with full tuition reimbursements (averaging $22,315 per year) were awarded. *Faculty research:* Kinematics, evolution of galaxies, cosmic distance, scale and large scale structures, interstellar intergalactic medium, star formation and evolution, solar system chemistry and dynamics. Total annual research expenditures: $6 million. *Unit head:* Dr. Christopher M. Anderson, Chair, 608-262-3071, Fax: 608-263-6386, E-mail: anderson@astro.wisc.edu. *Application contact:* Sicrid Gerhardt, Graduate coordinator, 608-262-8544, Fax: 608-263-6386, E-mail: gerhardt@astro.wisc.edu.

University of Wyoming, Graduate School, College of Arts and Sciences, Department of Physics and Astronomy, Laramie, WY 82071. Offers MS, MST, PhD. *Faculty:* 17. *Students:* 14 full-time (7 women), 5 part-time, 5 international. 9 applicants, 67% accepted. In 1998, 4 doctorates awarded. *Degree requirements:* For doctorate, dissertation required, foreign language not required, foreign language not required. *Entrance requirements:* For master's and doctorate, GRE General Test, GRE Subject Test, minimum GPA of 3.0. *Application deadline:* For fall admission, 6/1 (priority date). Applications are processed on a rolling basis. Application fee: $40. Tuition, state resident: full-time $2,520; part-time $140 per credit hour. Tuition, nonresident: full-time $7,790; part-time $433 per credit hour. Required fees: $400; $7 per credit hour. Full-time tuition and fees vary according to course load and program. *Financial aid:* In 1998–99, 6 research assistantships, 15 teaching assistantships were awarded.; institutionally-sponsored loans also available. Financial aid application deadline: 3/1. *Faculty research:* Astrophysics; atomic, molecular, and optic physics; atmospheric physics; medium-energy, nuclear, and particle physics. *Unit head:* Dr. Paul Johnson, Head, 307-766-6150.

Vanderbilt University, Graduate School, Department of Physics and Astronomy, Program in Astronomy, Nashville, TN 37240-1001. Offers MS. *Faculty:* 3 full-time (0 women). *Students:* 1 full-time (0 women). 3 applicants, 33% accepted. *Degree requirements:* For master's, thesis, comprehensive exam required, foreign language not required. *Entrance requirements:* For master's, GRE General Test. *Application deadline:* For fall admission, 1/15. Application fee: $40. *Financial aid:* In 1998–99, 1 student received aid, including 1 research assistantship with full tuition reimbursement available (averaging $13,000 per year); teaching assistantships, career-related internships or fieldwork, Federal Work-Study, and institutionally-sponsored loans also available. Financial aid application deadline: 1/15. *Faculty research:* Binary and variable stars, protostars. *Unit head:* Douglas S. Hall, Director, 615-373-4897, Fax: 615-343-7263, E-mail: e.waters@ctrvax.vanderbilt.edu. *Application contact:* Royal G. Albridge, Director of Graduate Studies, 615-322-2774, Fax: 615-343-7263, E-mail: albridrg@ctrvax.vanderbilt.edu.

Wesleyan University, Graduate Programs, Department of Astronomy, Middletown, CT 06459-0260. Offers MA. Part-time programs available. *Degree requirements:* For master's, thesis required, foreign language not required. *Entrance requirements:* For master's, GRE General Test, GRE Subject Test. *Faculty research:* Observational-theoretical astronomy andastrophysics.

West Chester University of Pennsylvania, Graduate Studies, College of Arts and Sciences, Department of Geology and Astronomy, West Chester, PA 19383. Offers physical science (MA). Part-time and evening/weekend programs available. *Faculty:* 4 part-time. *Students:* 26. Average age 32. *Degree requirements:* For master's, comprehensive exam required, foreign language and thesis not required. *Application deadline:* For fall admission, 4/15 (priority date); for spring admission, 10/15. Applications are processed on a rolling basis. Application fee: $25. Tuition, state resident: full-time $3,780; part-time $210 per credit. Tuition, nonresident: full-time $6,610; part-time $367 per credit. Required fees: $684; $39 per credit. Tuition and fees vary according to course load. *Financial aid:* In 1998–99, 1 research assistantship with full tuition reimbursement (averaging $5,000 per year) was awarded. Aid available to part-time students. Financial aid application deadline: 2/15. *Unit head:* Dr. Gil Wiswall, Chair, 610-436-2570. *Application contact:* Dr. Steven Good, Graduate Coordinator, 610-436-2203, E-mail: sgood@wcupa.edu.

Yale University, Graduate School of Arts and Sciences, Department of Astronomy, New Haven, CT 06520. Offers MS, PhD. *Faculty:* 13 full-time (0 women). *Students:* 12 full-time (4 women), 6 international. 28 applicants, 36% accepted. In 1998, 2 doctorates awarded. *Degree requirements:* For doctorate, dissertation required, foreign language not required. *Entrance requirements:* For doctorate, GRE General Test, GRE Subject Test (physics). *Average time to degree:* Doctorate–6.4 years full-time. *Application deadline:* For fall admission, 1/4. Application fee: $65. *Financial aid:* Fellowships, research assistantships, teaching assistantships, Federal Work-Study and institutionally-sponsored loans available. Aid available to part-time students. *Unit head:* Chair, 203-432-3011. *Application contact:* Admissions Information, 203-432-2770.

York University, Faculty of Graduate Studies, Faculty of Science, Program in Physics and Astronomy, Toronto, ON M3J 1P3, Canada. Offers M Sc, PhD. Part-time and evening/weekend programs available. *Degree requirements:* For master's, thesis optional, foreign language not required; for doctorate, dissertation required, foreign language not required.

Astrophysics

Clemson University, Graduate School, College of Engineering and Science, Department of Physics and Astronomy, Clemson, SC 29634. Offers physics (MS, PhD), including astronomy and astrophysics, atmospheric physics, biophysics. Part-time programs available. *Students:* 33 full-time (8 women), 4 part-time; includes 1 minority (African American), 11 international. Terminal master's awarded for partial completion of doctoral program. *Degree requirements:* For master's, thesis or alternative required, foreign language not required; for doctorate, dissertation required, foreign language not required. *Entrance requirements:* For master's and doctorate, GRE General Test, TOEFL. *Application deadline:* For fall admission, 2/15 (priority date). Applications are processed on a rolling basis. Application fee: $35. *Unit head:* Dr. Peter J. McNulty, Chair, 864-656-3419, Fax: 864-656-0805, E-mail: mpeter@clemson.edu. *Application contact:* Dr. Miguel F. Larsen, Graduate Coordinator, 864-656-5309, Fax: 864-656-0805, E-mail: mlarson@clemson.edu.

Cornell University, Graduate School, Graduate Fields of Arts and Sciences, Field of Astronomy and Space Sciences, Ithaca, NY 14853-0001. Offers astronomy (PhD); astrophysics (PhD); general space sciences (PhD); infrared astronomy (PhD); planetary studies (PhD); radio astronomy (PhD); radiophysics (PhD); theoretical astrophysics (PhD). *Faculty:* 26 full-time. *Students:* 23 full-time (9 women); includes 3 minority (2 Asian Americans or Pacific Islanders, 1 Hispanic American), 8 international. *Degree requirements:* For doctorate, dissertation required, foreign language not required. *Entrance requirements:* For doctorate, GRE General Test, GRE Subject Test, TOEFL (minimum score of 600 required). *Application deadline:* For fall admission, 1/15. Application fee: $65. Electronic applications accepted. *Unit head:* Director of Graduate Studies, 607-255-4341, Fax: 607-255-5907. *Application contact:* Graduate Field Assistant, 607-255-4341, E-mail: oconnor@astrosun.tn.cornell.edu.

Harvard University, Graduate School of Arts and Sciences, Department of Astronomy, Cambridge, MA 02138. Offers astronomy (AM, PhD); astrophysics (AM, PhD). *Students:* 36 full-time (6 women). *Degree requirements:* For doctorate, dissertation, paper, research project required, foreign language not required. *Entrance requirements:* For master's, GRE General Test, TOEFL (minimum score of 550 required); for doctorate, GRE General Test, GRE Subject Test (physics), TOEFL (minimum score of 550 required). *Application deadline:* For fall admission, 12/14. Application fee: $60. *Unit head:* Dr. Ramesh Narayan, Chairman, 617-495-3752. *Application contact:* Office of Admissions and Financial Aid, 617-495-5315.

See in-depth description on page 41.

ICR Graduate School, Graduate Programs, Santee, CA 92071. Offers astro/geophysics (MS); biology (MS); geology (MS); science education (MS). Part-time programs available. *Faculty:* 4 full-time (0 women), 6 part-time (0 women). *Students:* 13 full-time (5 women), 23 part-time (9 women). *Degree requirements:* For master's, thesis required (for some programs), foreign language not required. *Entrance requirements:* For master's, BS degree in field of graduate study. *Application deadline:* Applications are processed on a rolling basis. Application fee: $30. *Unit head:* Kenneth B. Cumming, Dean, 619-448-0900, Fax: 619-448-3469. *Application contact:* Dr. Jack Kriege, Registrar, 619-448-0900, Fax: 619-448-3469.

Indiana University Bloomington, Graduate School, College of Arts and Sciences, Department of Astronomy, Program in Astrophysics, Bloomington, IN 47405. Offers PhD. PhD offered jointly with the Department of Physics through the University Graduate School. *Students:* 1 (woman) full-time; minority (Asian American or Pacific Islander) *Degree requirements:* For doctorate, dissertation, written qualifying exam required, foreign language not required. *Entrance requirements:* For doctorate, GRE General Test, GRE Subject Test (physics), TOEFL, BA or BS in a science. *Average time to degree:* Doctorate–4 years full-time. *Application deadline:* For fall admission, 1/15 (priority date); for spring admission, 9/1 (priority date). Applications are processed on a rolling basis. Application fee: $40. Electronic applications accepted. Tuition, state resident: part-time $161 per credit hour. Tuition, nonresident: part-time $468 per credit hour. Required fees: $360 per year. Tuition and fees vary according to course load and program. *Financial aid:* In 1998–99, research assistantships (averaging $12,000 per year), teaching assistantships (averaging $11,000 per year) were awarded. Financial aid application deadline: 5/2. *Faculty research:* Nuclear astrophysics, cosmic-ray physics, astrophysical fluid dynamics, active galactic nuclei, high-energy astrophysics. *Application contact:* Brenda Records, Secretary, 812-855-6912, Fax: 812-855-8725, E-mail: brecords@indiana.edu.

Louisiana State University and Agricultural and Mechanical College, Graduate School, College of Basic Sciences, Department of Physics and Astronomy, Baton Rouge, LA 70803. Offers astronomy (PhD); astrophysics (PhD); physics (MS, PhD). *Faculty:* 32 full-time (0 women). *Students:* 58 full-time (10 women), 4 part-time; includes 3 minority (all African Americans), 30 international. Terminal master's awarded for partial completion of doctoral program. *Degree requirements:* For master's, thesis or alternative required, foreign language not required; for doctorate, dissertation required, foreign language not required. *Entrance requirements:* For master's, GRE General Test, TOEFL (minimum score of 550 required for admission, 560 required for assistantships), minimum GPA of 3.0; for doctorate, GRE General Test, TOEFL (minimum score of 550 required), minimum GPA of 3.0. *Application deadline:* For fall admission, 1/25 (priority date). Applications are processed on a rolling basis. Application fee: $25. *Unit head:* Dr. William Metcalf, Chair, 225-388-2261, Fax: 225-388-5855, E-mail: metcalf@phzeus.phys.lsu.edu. *Application contact:* Dr. Philip Adams, Chair, Assistantship Committee, 225-388-1194, Fax: 225-388-5855, E-mail: phadan@lsuvm.sncc.lsu.edu.

McMaster University, School of Graduate Studies, Faculty of Science, Department of Physics and Astronomy, Hamilton, ON L8S 4M2, Canada. Offers astrophysics (PhD); chemical physics (M Sc, PhD); health and radiation physics (M Sc); physics (PhD). Part-time programs available. *Degree requirements:* For master's, thesis or alternative required, foreign language not required; for doctorate, dissertation, comprehensive exam required, foreign language not required. *Entrance requirements:* For master's and doctorate, minimum B+ average. *Faculty research:* Condensed matter, astrophysics, nuclear, medical, nonlinear dynamics.

Michigan State University, Graduate School, College of Natural Science, Department of Physics and Astronomy, East Lansing, MI 48824-1020. Offers astrophysics (MS, PhD); chemical physics (MS); physics (MAT, MS, PhD). *Faculty:* 57. *Students:* 111 full-time (22 women), 12 part-time (2 women); includes 8 minority (3 African Americans, 5 Asian Americans or Pacific Islanders), 53 international. Terminal master's awarded for partial completion of doctoral program. *Degree requirements:* For master's, thesis or alternative required, foreign language not required; for doctorate, dissertation required, foreign language not required. *Entrance requirements:* For master's, GRE. *Application deadline:* For fall admission, 3/15. Applications are processed on a rolling basis. Application fee: $30 ($40 for international students). *Unit head:* Dr. Raymond Brock, Chairperson, 517-353-5286, Fax: 517-353-4500.

New Mexico Institute of Mining and Technology, Graduate Studies, Department of Physics, Socorro, NM 87801. Offers astrophysics (MS, PhD); atmospheric physics (MS, PhD); instrumentation (MS); mathematical physics (PhD). *Faculty:* 11 full-time (1 woman), 5 part-time (0 women). *Students:* 26 full-time (6 women), 8 international. *Degree requirements:* For master's and doctorate, thesis/dissertation required, foreign language not required. *Entrance requirements:* For master's, GRE General Test, TOEFL (minimum score of 540 required); for doctorate, GRE General Test, GRE Subject Test, TOEFL (minimum score of 540 required). *Application deadline:* For fall admission, 3/1 (priority date); for spring admission, 6/1. Applications are processed on a rolling basis. Application fee: $16. *Unit head:* Dr. Alan Blyth, Chairman, 505-835-5744, Fax: 505-835-5707, E-mail: blyth@kestrel.nmt.edu. *Application contact:* Dr. David B. Johnson, Dean of Graduate Studies, 505-835-5513, Fax: 505-835-5476, E-mail: graduate@nmt.edu.

Northwestern University, The Graduate School, Judd A. and Marjorie Weinberg College of Arts and Sciences, Department of Physics and Astronomy, Evanston, IL 60208. Offers astronomy (PhD); astrophysics (PhD); physics (PhD). Admissions and degrees offered through The Graduate School. *Faculty:* 27 full-time (3 women). *Students:* 74 full-time (13 women); includes 6 minority (5 Asian Americans or Pacific Islanders, 1 Hispanic American), 51 international. *Degree requirements:* For doctorate, dissertation, qualifying exam required, foreign language not required. *Entrance requirements:* For doctorate, GRE General Test, GRE Subject Test, TOEFL (minimum score of 600 required; average 630). Application fee: $50 ($55 for international students). *Unit head:* David E. Buchholz, Chair, 847-491-3644, Fax: 847-491-9982, E-mail: physics-astronomy@nwu.edu. *Application contact:* Mary Rosenthal, Admission Contact, 847-491-3644, Fax: 847-491-9982, E-mail: physics-astronomy@nwu.edu.

Pennsylvania State University University Park Campus, Graduate School, Eberly College of Science, Department of Astronomy and Astrophysics, State College, University Park, PA 16802-1503. Offers MS, PhD. *Students:* 17 full-time (7 women), 1 part-time. *Entrance requirements:* For master's and doctorate, GRE General Test. Application fee: $50. *Unit head:* Dr. Peter I. Meszaros, Head, 814-865-0418.

Princeton University, Graduate School, Department of Astrophysical Sciences, Princeton, NJ 08544-1019. Offers astrophysical sciences (PhD); plasma physics (PhD). *Degree requirements:* For doctorate, dissertation required. *Entrance requirements:* For doctorate, GRE General Test, GRE Subject Test. *Faculty research:* Theoretical astrophysics, cosmology, galaxy formation, galactic dynamics, interstellar and intergalactic matter.

Rensselaer Polytechnic Institute, Graduate School, School of Science, Department of Physics, Applied Physics and Astronomy, Troy, NY 12180-3590. Offers physics (MS, PhD). Part-time programs available. *Faculty:* 19 full-time (1 woman), 2 part-time (0 women). *Students:* 53 full-time (13 women), 6 part-time; includes 2 minority (1 Asian American or Pacific Islander, 1 Hispanic American), 26 international. 87 applicants, 55% accepted. In 1998, 6 master's, 6 doctorates awarded. Terminal master's awarded for partial completion of doctoral program. *Degree requirements:* For doctorate, dissertation required, foreign language not required, foreign language not required. *Entrance requirements:* For master's and doctorate, GRE General Test, GRE Subject Test, TOEFL (minimum score of 575 required). *Application deadline:* For fall admission, 2/1 (priority date). Applications are processed on a rolling basis. Application fee: $35. *Financial aid:* In 1998–99, 56 students received aid, including 9 fellowships (averaging $11,800 per year), 22 research assistantships (averaging $11,800 per year), 25 teaching assistantships (averaging $11,800 per year); career-related internships or fieldwork and institutionally-sponsored loans also available. Financial aid application deadline: 2/1. *Faculty research:* Astrophysics, condensed matter, nuclear physics, optics, physics education. Total annual research expenditures: $2 million. *Unit head:* Dr. Leo Schowalter, Chair, 518-276-6435, Fax: 518-276-6680. *Application contact:* Dr. Gary Adams, Chair, Graduate Recruitment Committee, 518-276-8391, Fax: 518-276-6680, E-mail: fanchj@rpi.edu.

Rice University, Graduate Programs, Wiess School of Natural Sciences, Department of Space Physics and Astronomy, Houston, TX 77251-1892. Offers MS, PhD. *Degree requirements:* For master's and doctorate, thesis/dissertation required, foreign language not required. *Entrance requirements:* For master's, GRE General Test, TOEFL (minimum score of 550 required), minimum GPA of 3.0; for doctorate, GRE General Test (score in 70th percentile or higher required), minimum GPA of 3.0. *Faculty research:* Magnetospheric physics, planetary atmospheres, astrophysics.

San Francisco State University, Graduate Division, College of Science and Engineering, Department of Physics and Astronomy, San Francisco, CA 94132-1722. Offers physics and astrophysics (MS). *Students:* 56 full-time (12 women). In 1998, 11 degrees awarded. *Degree requirements:* For master's, computer language, thesis required. *Entrance requirements:* For master's, minimum GPA of 2.5 in last 60 units. *Average time to degree:* Master's–2.5 years full-time. *Application deadline:* For fall admission, 11/30 (priority date). Applications are processed on a rolling basis. Application fee: $55. *Financial aid:* In 1998–99, 35 students received aid; research assistantships, teaching assistantships, career-related internships or fieldwork, Federal Work-Study, institutionally-sponsored loans, and tuition waivers (partial) available. Financial aid application deadline: 3/1. *Faculty research:* Quark search, thin-films, dark matter detection, search for planetary systems, low temperature. Total annual research expenditures: $705,000. *Unit head:* Dr. Robert Rogers, Chair, 415-338-1659, E-mail: rrogers@stars.sfsu.edu. *Application contact:* Dr. Susan Lea, Graduate Coordinator, 415-338-1691, E-mail: lea@stars.sfsu.edu.

University of Alaska Fairbanks, Graduate School, College of Science, Engineering and Mathematics, Department of Physics, Fairbanks, AK 99775-7480. Offers atmospheric science (MS, PhD); physics (MS, PhD); space physics (MS, PhD). Part-time programs available. *Faculty:* 19 full-time (1 woman). *Students:* 24 full-time (8 women), 2 part-time; includes 2 minority (1 African American, 1 Hispanic American) Terminal master's awarded for partial completion of doctoral program. *Degree requirements:* For master's, thesis, comprehensive exam required, foreign language not required; for doctorate, one foreign language (computer language can substitute), dissertation, comprehensive exam required. *Entrance requirements:* For master's and doctorate, GRE General Test, GRE Subject Test, TOEFL (minimum score of 550 required). *Application deadline:* For fall admission, 2/15. Application fee: $35. *Unit head:* Dr. Brenton Watkins, Head, 907-474-7339. *Application contact:* Dr. Brenton Watkins, Head, 907-474-7339.

University of Alberta, Faculty of Graduate Studies and Research, Department of Physics, Edmonton, AB T6G 2E1, Canada. Offers astrophysics (M Sc, PhD); condensed matter (M Sc, PhD); geophysics (M Sc, PhD); medical physics (M Sc, PhD); nuclear physics (M Sc, PhD); subatomic physics (M Sc, PhD). *Degree requirements:* For master's and doctorate, thesis/dissertation required. *Entrance requirements:* For master's and doctorate, TOEFL (minimum score of 550 required), minimum GPA of 7.0 on a 9.0 scale. *Faculty research:* Cosmology, astro-particle physics, high-intermediate energy, magnetism, superconductivity, electron microscopy, low-temperature physics, seismology, geodynamics, MRI.

University of California, Berkeley, Graduate Division, College of Letters and Science, Department of Astronomy, Berkeley, CA 94720-1500. Offers astrophysics (PhD). *Students:* 29 full-time (7 women); includes 2 minority (1 Asian American or Pacific Islander, 1 Hispanic American), 7 international. 84 applicants, 17% accepted. In 1998, 8 degrees awarded. *Degree requirements:* For doctorate, dissertation, qualifying exam required. *Entrance requirements:* For doctorate, GRE General Test, GRE Subject Test (physics), minimum GPA of 3.0. *Application deadline:* For fall admission, 1/5. Application fee: $40. *Financial aid:* Fellowships available. Financial aid application deadline: 12/19. *Unit head:* Dr. Jonathan Arons, Chair, 510-642-4730, E-mail: jarons@astro.berkeley.edu. *Application contact:* Juliane Monroe, Academic Assistant, 510-642-8520, Fax: 510-642-3411, E-mail: jmonroe@astron.berkeley.edu.

University of California, Los Angeles, Graduate Division, College of Letters and Science, Department of Earth and Space Sciences, Program in Geophysics and Space Physics, Los Angeles, CA 90095. Offers MS, PhD. *Students:* 26 full-time (9 women); includes 2 minority (both Asian Americans or Pacific Islanders), 9 international. 35 applicants, 40% accepted. *Degree requirements:* For master's, comprehensive exams or thesis required; for doctorate, dissertation, oral and written qualifying exams required, foreign language not required. *Entrance requirements:* For master's, GRE General Test, minimum GPA of 3.0; for doctorate, GRE General Test, minimum undergraduate GPA of 3.0. *Application deadline:* For fall admission, 12/15. Application fee: $40. Electronic applications accepted. *Financial aid:* In 1998–99, 18 fellowships, 7 teaching assistantships were awarded.; research assistantships, Federal Work-Study, institutionally-sponsored loans, scholarships, and tuition waivers (full and partial) also available. Financial aid application deadline: 3/1. *Unit head:* Departmental Office, 310-825-

2307, E-mail: apply@physics.ucla.edu. *Application contact:* Departmental Office, 888-377-8252, E-mail: verity@ess.ucla.edu.

University of California, Santa Cruz, Graduate Division, Division of Natural Sciences, Program in Astronomy and Astrophysics, Santa Cruz, CA 95064. Offers PhD. *Faculty:* 9 full-time. *Students:* 32 full-time (13 women); includes 5 minority (1 African American, 4 Asian Americans or Pacific Islanders), 3 international. 71 applicants, 32% accepted. In 1998, 3 doctorates awarded. *Degree requirements:* For doctorate, one foreign language (computer language can substitute), dissertation, qualifying exam required. *Entrance requirements:* For doctorate, GRE General Test, GRE Subject Test. *Application deadline:* For fall admission, 1/15. Application fee: $40. *Financial aid:* Fellowships, research assistantships, teaching assistantships, Federal Work-Study and institutionally-sponsored loans available. Financial aid application deadline: 1/15. *Faculty research:* Stellar structure and evolution, stellar spectroscopy, the interstellar medium, galactic structure, external galaxies and quasars. *Unit head:* Dr. Stan Woosley, Chairperson, 831-459-2976, E-mail: woosley@ucolick.org. *Application contact:* Graduate Admissions, 831-459-2301.

University of Chicago, Division of the Physical Sciences, Department of Astronomy and Astrophysics, Chicago, IL 60637-1513. Offers SM, PhD. Terminal master's awarded for partial completion of doctoral program. *Degree requirements:* For master's, candidacy exam required, foreign language and thesis not required; for doctorate, dissertation for publication required. *Entrance requirements:* For doctorate, GRE General Test, GRE Subject Test (physics), TOEFL, minimum GPA of 3.0. *Faculty research:* Adaptive optics, quasi-stellar object absorption lines, fluid dynamics, interstellar matter, particle physics.

University of Colorado at Boulder, Graduate School, College of Arts and Sciences, Department of Astrophysical, Planetary, and Atmospheric Sciences, Boulder, CO 80309. Offers astrophysical and geophysical fluid dynamics (MS, PhD); astrophysics (MS, PhD); plasma physics (MS, PhD). Terminal master's awarded for partial completion of doctoral program. *Degree requirements:* For master's, thesis or alternative, comprehensive exam required, foreign language not required; for doctorate, dissertation required. *Entrance requirements:* For master's and doctorate, GRE General Test, GRE Subject Test.

University of Minnesota, Twin Cities Campus, Graduate School, Institute of Technology, School of Physics and Astronomy, Department of Astronomy, Minneapolis, MN 55455-0213. Offers astrophysics (MS, PhD). *Faculty:* 10 full-time (1 woman). *Students:* 15 full-time (5 women), 2 international. Average age 22. 28 applicants, 18% accepted. In 1998, 4 master's awarded (50% entered university research/teaching, 50% found other work related to degree); 2 doctorates awarded (100% entered university research/teaching). Terminal master's awarded for partial completion of doctoral program. *Degree requirements:* For master's, thesis optional; for doctorate, dissertation required. *Entrance requirements:* For master's and doctorate, GRE General Test, GRE Subject Test. *Average time to degree:* Master's–4 years full-time; doctorate–5 years full-time. *Application deadline:* For fall admission, 7/15. Applications are processed on a rolling basis. Application fee: $50 ($55 for international students). *Financial aid:* In 1998–99, 15 students received aid, including 1 fellowship with full tuition reimbursement available (averaging $12,000 per year), 5 research assistantships with full tuition reimbursements available (averaging $11,700 per year), 8 teaching assistantships with full tuition reimbursements available (averaging $11,700 per year); Federal Work-Study and institutionally-sponsored loans also available. Financial aid application deadline: 1/15. *Faculty research:* Evolution of stars and galaxies; the interstellar medium; cosmology; observational, optical, infrared, and radio astronomy; computational astrophysics. Total annual research expenditures: $2.5 million. *Unit head:* Evan Skillman, Director of Graduate Studies, 612-624-9523, Fax: 612-626-2029, E-mail: skillman@astro.spa.umn.edu.

University of Missouri–St. Louis, Graduate School, College of Arts and Sciences, Department of Physics and Astronomy, St. Louis, MO 63121-4499. Offers applied physics (MS); astro physics (MS); physics (PhD). Part-time and evening/weekend programs available. *Faculty:* 11. *Students:* 7 full-time (0 women), 6 part-time (1 woman); includes 1 minority (Asian American or Pacific Islander), 6 international. Terminal master's awarded for partial completion of doctoral program. *Degree requirements:* For master's, thesis optional, foreign language not required; for doctorate, dissertation required, foreign language not required. *Entrance requirements:* For master's and doctorate, GRE General Test. *Application deadline:* For fall admission, 4/1 (priority date); for spring admission, 12/1 (priority date). Applications are processed on a rolling basis. Application fee: $24 ($40 for international students). Electronic applications accepted. *Unit head:* Dr. Bruce Wilking, Director of Graduate Studies, 314-516-5023, Fax: 314-516-6152, E-mail: graduate@newton.umsl.edu. *Application contact:* Graduate Admissions, 314-516-5458, Fax: 314-516-6759, E-mail: gradadm@umsl.edu.

The University of North Carolina at Chapel Hill, Graduate School, College of Arts and Sciences, Department of Physics and Astronomy, Chapel Hill, NC 27599. Offers astronomy and astrophysics (MS, PhD). *Degree requirements:* For master's, comprehensive exam required; for doctorate, dissertation, comprehensive exam required. *Entrance requirements:* For master's and doctorate, GRE General Test (minimum combined score of 1000 required), minimum GPA of 3.0.

University of Oklahoma, Graduate College, College of Arts and Sciences, Department of Physics and Astronomy, Program in Astrophysics, Norman, OK 73019-0390. Offers M Nat Sci, MS, PhD. *Degree requirements:* For master's, thesis or alternative, departmental qualifying exam required, foreign language not required; for doctorate, dissertation, comprehensive, departmental qualifying, oral, and written exams required, foreign language not required. *Entrance requirements:* For master's and doctorate, GRE General Test, GRE Subject Test, TOEFL (minimum score of 600 required), previous course work in physics. *Application deadline:* For fall admission, 3/1. Application fee: $25. Tuition, state resident: part-time $86 per credit hour. Tuition, nonresident: part-time $275 per credit hour. Tuition and fees vary according to course level, course load and program. *Financial aid:* Application deadline: 3/1. *Application contact:* Dr. Mark Keil, Chair, Graduate Selection Committee, 800-522-0772 Ext. 3961, E-mail: bondy@phyast.nhn.uokhsc.edu.

University of Pennsylvania, School of Arts and Sciences, Graduate Group in Physics and Astronomy, Philadelphia, PA 19104. Offers physics (PhD). Part-time programs available. *Degree requirements:* For doctorate, dissertation, oral, preliminary and final exams required, foreign language not required. *Entrance requirements:* For doctorate, GRE General Test, GRE Subject Test, TOEFL, TSE (recommended). Electronic applications accepted. *Faculty research:* Astrophysics, condensed matter experiment, condensed matter theory, particle experiment, particle theory.

University of Victoria, Faculty of Graduate Studies, Faculty of Science, Department of Physics and Astronomy, Victoria, BC V8W 2Y2, Canada. Offers astronomy and astrophysics (M Sc, PhD); condensed matter physics (M Sc, PhD); geophysics (M Sc, PhD); medical physics (PhD); nuclear and particle studies (M Sc, PhD); theoretical physics (M Sc, PhD). *Faculty:* 20 full-time (0 women), 22 part-time (1 woman). *Students:* 28 full-time (7 women). *Degree requirements:* For master's and doctorate, thesis/dissertation required, foreign language not required. *Application deadline:* For fall admission, 5/31 (priority date); for spring admission, 10/31. Applications are processed on a rolling basis. Application fee: $50. *Unit head:* Dr. C. E. Picciotto, Chair, 250-721-7698, E-mail: pic@uvic.ca. *Application contact:* Dr. A. Watton, Graduate Adviser, 250-721-7703, Fax: 250-721-7715, E-mail: awatt@uvvm.uvic.ca.

Cross-Discipline Announcement

Michigan Technological University, Graduate School, College of Sciences and Arts, Department of Physics, Houghton, MI 49931-1295.

The physics department at Michigan Technological University offers multidisciplinary programs in astrophysics and remote sensing. Research areas include observational and theoretical astrophysics, particularly of close binary star systems, planetary atmospheres, extra-solar planets, gravitational lensing, hyperspectral imaging, and wave propagation in random media. Teaching and research assistantships and fellowships are available. For more information, contact Michigan Technological University, Department of Physics, 1400 Townsend Drive, Houghton, MI 49931. For online information, visit the University's Web site at http://www.phy.mtu.edu.

HARVARD UNIVERSITY

Department of Astronomy

Programs of Study

The Department of Astronomy offers a rich and varied program of theoretical, observational and experimental graduate work leading to the Ph.D. in astronomy. Entering students should have a strong background in physics and mathematics. They need not have majored in astronomy as an undergraduate; however, they are expected to pass an oral examination based on topics in Frank Shu's *The Physical Universe* before the end of their first term. The first two years of study are normally devoted to taking courses and working on a research project that must be completed before beginning work on a thesis. The topic may be in the area of intended thesis work, although research in another area is encouraged. After completing the project, students embark on their thesis research, which normally takes two to three years to complete. Progress is monitored by a thesis advisory committee consisting of the student's adviser and 3 other faculty members.

Research Facilities

Research is carried out at the Harvard College Observatory, which shares buildings and general facilities with the Smithsonian Astrophysical Observatory. Together, the two observatories constitute the Harvard-Smithsonian Center for Astrophysics, a large and diverse research institute that provides opportunities in nearly every branch of astrophysical work, from atomic physics to cosmology, using the full range of techniques from gamma-ray detectors through radio antennas. More than 150 Ph.D. scientists are engaged in work at the Center for Astrophysics (CfA), providing students with an unusually wide choice of thesis topics and opportunities for learning through courses and seminars. Students involved in research in optical or infrared astronomy have access to the Multiple Mirror Telescope (4.5-meter-equivalent aperture, being upgraded to a single 6.5-meter mirror) and to Whipple Observatory's 1.5-meter and 1.2-meter telescopes, all located on Mt. Hopkins, near Tucson, Arizona. Students also use Kitt Peak National Observatory in Arizona and Cerro Tololo Inter-American Observatory in Chile. Harvard is a participant in the Magellan Project, an enterprise to build two 6.5-meter telescopes at Las Campanas, Chile. Facilities for radio astronomy students are available at Haystack Observatory in Westford, Massachusetts, Arecibo in Puerto Rico, and the National Radio Astronomy Observatory's VLA. A 1.2-meter telescope for CO observations operates from the roof of the observatory in Cambridge.

High-energy astrophysics facilities include the entire Einstein X-ray Observatory database, rocket (solar X-rays) and balloon (hard X-ray imaging of cosmic sources) experiments, and X-ray astronomy satellites. Data from the X-ray telescope ROSAT are processed at the Center for Astrophysics. Facilities for laboratory astrophysics include spectrographs and an ion-beam facility. Students in theoretical astrophysics have access to a wide variety of talent at the Center for Astrophysics to carry out investigations ranging from atomic processes through exploding stars to the origin of the universe. Computational facilities at the Center for Astrophysics include a large network of more than sixty Sun and DEC workstations and two Convex parallel-processing machines. All graduate student offices are equipped with graphics terminals that connect to virtually all CfA computers via an Ethernet link.

Financial Aid

The Department of Astronomy plans to support all students who are accepted for graduate study. The support may be in the form of a national or University fellowship, a teaching fellowship, or a research assistantship. The normal pattern of student support is a combination of all three. Students gain teaching experience during their graduate career as part-time teaching fellows during two terms.

Cost of Study

Tuition and fees are provided for all graduate students as described above.

Living and Housing Costs

There are a wide variety of dormitory rooms for single students, with costs that range from $3280 (for a small single room) to $5260 (for a two-room suite) per academic year. These figures do not include meals.

Married students and single graduate students may apply for apartments in graduate student housing or other University-owned apartments. The monthly cost is $718–$976 for a one-room studio apartment, $876–$1265 for a one-bedroom apartment, $1113–$1708 for a two-bedroom apartment, and $1583 and up for a three-bedroom apartment. There are also many privately owned accommodations within commuting distance.

Student Group

The Graduate School of Arts and Sciences has an enrollment of 3,065. Thirty-five men and women are currently pursuing Ph.D. research in the Astronomy Department. Of these, 9 are from other nations.

Location

The Astronomy Department is housed within the several buildings that make up the CfA on its own grounds on Observatory Hill in Cambridge. This area is a 10-minute walk from the main Harvard Campus. Cambridge and nearby Boston provide a wealth of cultural resources. Harvard Square is adjacent to the main campus, with numerous shops, bookstores, theaters, and restaurants. Boston is home to several museums, musical organizations (including the Boston Symphony Orchestra), and professional sports teams.

The University and the Department

Harvard College was established in 1636, and its charter, which still guides the University, was granted in 1650. Today, Harvard University, with its network of graduate schools, occupies a noteworthy position in the academic world, and the Department of Astronomy offers an educational program in keeping with the University's long-standing record of achievement.

Applying

Prospective graduate students should write to the Admissions Office of the Graduate School of Arts and Sciences for application material and to the Department of Astronomy for full information on the program. Applicants should have a bachelor's degree and a substantial background in physics and mathematics. The GRE General Test and the Subject Test in physics are required of all applicants, and students from non-English-speaking countries must take the TOEFL. Completed application forms and all supporting material should be returned to the Admissions Office by December 15.

Correspondence and Information

For information on the program:
Department Administrator
Astronomy Department
Harvard University
60 Garden Street
Cambridge, Massachusetts 02138
Telephone: 617-495-3752
E-mail: department@cfa.harvard.edu

For applications for admission:
Admissions Office
Graduate School of Arts and Sciences
Harvard University
8 Garden Street, 2nd Floor
Cambridge, Massachusetts 02138

Harvard University

THE FACULTY AND THEIR RESEARCH

Alexander Dalgarno, Phillips Professor of Astronomy. Theoretical studies of atomic, molecular, chemical, and dynamical processes in astrophysical and atmospheric environments; development and application of quantum mechanical methods to atomic and molecular physics and chemistry.

Margaret J. Geller, Professor of Astronomy. Large-scale galaxy distribution, formation, and evolution of clusters of galaxies and the relationship between the characteristics of individual cluster members and the cluster environment; cosmology.

Owen J. Gingerich, Professor of Astronomy and of the History of Science. Historical topics, including Nicolaus Copernicus, Johannes Kepler, and Harlow Shapley; early astronomical books and instruments.

Alyssa A. Goodman, Associate Professor of Astronomy. Studies of the interstellar medium, interstellar dust and star formation, including single-dish and interferometric spectral-line mapping, polarimetry, Zeeman observations, infrared photometry, stellar spectroscopy, satellite observations, and theoretical investigations.

Jonathan E. Grindlay, Professor of Astronomy. Compact binaries in globular clusters; X-ray binaries containing white dwarfs, neutron stars, and black holes; nonthermal phenomena and AGN; development of hard X-ray imaging detectors and telescopes.

Lars Hernquist, Professor of Astronomy. Theoretical studies of dynamical processes in cosmology and galaxy formation/galaxy evolution; numerical simulations of stellar dynamical and hydrodynamical systems; investigations of the physics of compact objects, particularly neutron stars and the interplay between thermal and magnetic processes in strongly magnetized neutron stars.

John P. Huchra, Professor of Astronomy. Observational cosmology, particularly the distribution and dynamics of matter in the universe and the formation of structure in the universe; active galactic nuclei; X-ray sources; globular clusters around galaxies; star formation in galaxies.

Robert P. Kirshner, Professor of Astronomy. Supernovae, supernova remnants, galaxy dynamics and evolution, clusters, and galaxy distributions on very large scales using KPNO, CTIO, Las Campanas, IUE, Whipple Observatory, HST, and the MMT.

Abraham Loeb, Professor of Astronomy. Theoretical cosmology, particularly the early formation of structure in the universe; the microwave background; gravitational lensing by stars and galaxies; gamma-ray bursts.

James M. Moran, Professor of Astronomy. High angular resolution studies of radio sources, conducted with the VLA and various VLBI networks, including H_2O, OH, and SiO masers in late-type stars and newly formed stars, compact H II regions, and quasars.

Ramesh Narayan, Professor of Astronomy and Chairman. Gravitational lensing: accretion disks around black holes, neutron stars, and white dwarfs; origin and evolution of radio pulsars and X-ray binaries; scattering and scintillation; gamma-ray bursts.

Robert W. Noyes, Professor of Astronomy. Understanding solar and stellar internal structure and magnetic activity; spectroscopic observations of the sun and similar stars from ground-based observatories and spacecraft, aimed at measuring solar and stellar magnetic fields, spot cycles, global oscillations, and chromospheric and coronal phenomena.

William H. Press, Professor of Astronomy and of Physics. Aspects of the evolution of the very early universe, cosmic strings, N-body dynamics, evolution of large-scale structure in the universe, practical numerical methods, hydrodynamics, gravitating systems, statistical methods of signal processing.

George B. Rybicki, Professor of the Practice of Astronomy. Radiation processes, radiation transfer, spectral distortions in the CMB, reverberation mapping of AGNs, statistical analysis of time series.

Dimitar D. Sasselov, Assistant Professor of Astronomy and Head Tutor. Dynamic stellar atmospheres, chromospheric heating, and mass loss through coupled hydrodynamics and radiative transfer; galactic stellar populations and nucleosynthesis; submillimeter studies of star formation.

Irwin I. Shapiro, Timken University Professor and Professor of Physics. Applications of radio and radar techniques to astrometry, astrophysics, geophysics, planetary physics, and tests of theories of gravitation.

Patrick Thaddeus, Professor of Astronomy and Applied Physics. Radio astronomy: molecules in the interstellar gas, structure of molecular clouds and their distribution in the Milky Way and nearby galaxies, laboratory spectroscopy in the millimeter-wave band of reactive molecules.

Martin J. White, Assistant Professor of Astronomy. Cosmology, including the cosmic microwave background and structure formation; neutrino astrophysics and the early universe.

Section 2
Chemistry

This section contains a directory of institutions offering graduate work in chemistry, followed by in-depth entries submitted by institutions that chose to prepare detailed program descriptions. Additional information about programs listed in the directory but not augmented by an in-depth entry may be obtained by writing directly to the dean of a graduate school or chair of a department at the address given in the directory.

For programs offering related work, see also in this book Geosciences and Physics. In Book 3, see Biological and Biomedical Sciences, Biochemistry, Biophysics, Nutrition, and Pharmacology and Toxicology; in Book 5, see Engineering and Applied Sciences; Agricultural Engineering; Chemical Engineering; Geological, Mineral/Mining, and Petroleum Engineering; and Materials Sciences and Engineering; and in Book 6, see Pharmacy and Pharmaceutical Sciences.

CONTENTS

Peterson's Graduate Programs in the Physical Sciences, Mathematics, Agricultural Sciences, the Environment & Natural Resources 2000

43

CONTENTS

Analytical Chemistry

Boston College, Graduate School of Arts and Sciences, Department of Chemistry, Chestnut Hill, MA 02467-3800. Offers analytical chemistry (MS, PhD); biochemistry (MS, PhD); chemistry (MS); inorganic chemistry (MS, PhD); organic chemistry (MS, PhD); physical chemistry (MS, PhD). Part-time programs available. *Faculty:* 20 full-time (2 women). *Students:* 25 full-time (11 women), 75 part-time (29 women); includes 12 minority (1 African American, 8 Asian Americans or Pacific Islanders, 2 Hispanic Americans, 1 Native American), 28 international. Terminal master's awarded for partial completion of doctoral program. *Degree requirements:* For master's, thesis required; for doctorate, dissertation, qualifying exam required. *Entrance requirements:* For master's and doctorate, GRE General Test, GRE Subject Test. *Application deadline:* For fall admission, 2/1. Application fee: $40. *Unit head:* Dr. Larry McLaughlin, Chairperson, 617-552-3605, E-mail: larry.mclaughlin@bc.edu. *Application contact:* Dr. Mary Roberts, Graduate Program Director, 617-552-3616, E-mail: mary.roberts@bc.edu.

See in-depth description on page 93.

Brigham Young University, Graduate Studies, College of Physical and Mathematical Sciences, Department of Chemistry and Biochemistry, Provo, UT 84602-1001. Offers analytical chemistry (MS, PhD); biochemistry (MS, PhD); inorganic chemistry (MS, PhD); organic chemistry (MS, PhD); physical chemistry (MS, PhD). *Faculty:* 33 full-time (1 woman), 3 part-time (0 women). *Students:* 70 full-time (24 women); includes 1 minority (Asian American or Pacific Islander), 39 international. *Degree requirements:* For master's and doctorate, thesis/dissertation required, foreign language not required. *Entrance requirements:* For master's and doctorate, minimum GPA of 3.0 in last 60 hours. *Application deadline:* For fall admission, 2/1 (priority date). Applications are processed on a rolling basis. Application fee: $30. Tuition: Full-time $3,330; part-time $185 per credit hour. Tuition and fees vary according to program and student's religious affiliation. *Unit head:* Dr. Francis R. Nordmeyer, Chair, 801-378-3667, Fax: 801-378-5474, E-mail: fran_nordmeyer@byu.edu. *Application contact:* N. Kent Dalley, Coordinator, Graduate Admissions, 801-378-3434, Fax: 801-378-5474, E-mail: chemgrad@byu.edu.

See in-depth description on page 97.

California State University, Fullerton, Graduate Studies, School of Natural Science and Mathematics, Department of Chemistry and Biochemistry, Fullerton, CA 92834-9480. Offers analytical chemistry (MS); biochemistry (MS); geochemistry (MS); inorganic chemistry (MS); organic chemistry (MS); physical chemistry (MS). Part-time programs available. *Faculty:* 18 full-time, 14 part-time. *Students:* 8 full-time (3 women), 32 part-time (14 women); includes 19 minority (14 Asian Americans or Pacific Islanders, 5 Hispanic Americans), 6 international. *Degree requirements:* For master's, thesis, departmental qualifying exam required, foreign language not required. *Entrance requirements:* For master's, minimum GPA of 2.5 in last 60 units, major in chemistry or related field. Application fee: $55. Tuition, nonresident: part-time $264 per unit. *Unit head:* Dr. Bruce Weber, Chair, 714-278-3621. *Application contact:* Dr. Gregory Williams, Adviser, 714-278-2170.

California State University, Los Angeles, Graduate Studies, School of Natural and Social Sciences, Department of Chemistry and Biochemistry, Los Angeles, CA 90032-8530. Offers analytical chemistry (MS); biochemistry (MS); chemistry (MS); inorganic chemistry (MS); organic chemistry (MS); physical chemistry (MS). Part-time and evening/weekend programs available. *Faculty:* 14 full-time, 20 part-time. *Students:* 13 full-time (6 women), 11 part-time (4 women); includes 16 minority (1 African American, 12 Asian Americans or Pacific Islanders, 3 Hispanic Americans), 3 international. *Degree requirements:* For master's, one foreign language (computer language can substitute), comprehensive exam or thesis required. *Entrance requirements:* For master's, TOEFL (minimum score of 550 required). *Application deadline:* For fall admission, 6/30; for spring admission, 2/1. Applications are processed on a rolling basis. Application fee: $55. *Unit head:* Dr. Scott Grover, Acting Chair, 323-343-2300.

Case Western Reserve University, School of Graduate Studies, Department of Chemistry, Cleveland, OH 44106. Offers analytical chemistry (MS, PhD); inorganic chemistry (MS, PhD); organic chemistry (MS, PhD); physical chemistry (MS, PhD). Part-time programs available. Terminal master's awarded for partial completion of doctoral program. *Degree requirements:* For master's, thesis not required; for doctorate, dissertation required. *Entrance requirements:* For master's and doctorate, GRE General Test, GRE Subject Test, TOEFL (minimum score of 550 required). *Faculty research:* Electrochemistry, synthetic chemistry, chemistry of life process, spectroscopy, kinetics.

Clarkson University, Graduate School, School of Science, Department of Chemistry, Potsdam, NY 13699. Offers analytical chemistry (MS, PhD); inorganic chemistry (MS, PhD); organic chemistry (MS, PhD); physical chemistry (MS, PhD). *Faculty:* 9 full-time (0 women). *Students:* 25 full-time (13 women); includes 1 minority (African American), 15 international. *Degree requirements:* For master's, foreign language and thesis not required; for doctorate, dissertation, departmental qualifying exam required, foreign language not required. *Entrance requirements:* For master's, GRE, TOEFL. *Application deadline:* For fall admission, 5/15 (priority date); for spring admission, 10/15 (priority date). Applications are processed on a rolling basis. Application fee: $25 ($35 for international students). Tuition: Part-time $661 per credit hour. Required fees: $215 per semester. *Unit head:* Dr. Stig Friberg, Chair, 315-268-6500, Fax: 315-268-6610, E-mail: fbg@clarkson.edu.

Cleveland State University, College of Graduate Studies, College of Arts and Sciences, Department of Chemistry, Cleveland, OH 44115-2440. Offers analytical chemistry (MS, PhD); clinical chemistry (MS, PhD); inorganic chemistry (MS); organic chemistry (MS); physical chemistry (MS); structural analysis (MS, PhD). Part-time and evening/weekend programs available. *Faculty:* 13 full-time (1 woman). *Students:* 1 full-time (0 women), 53 part-time (22 women); includes 5 minority (1 African American, 3 Asian Americans or Pacific Islanders, 1 Hispanic American), 25 international. *Degree requirements:* For master's, thesis required (for some programs), foreign language not required; for doctorate, dissertation required, foreign language not required. *Entrance requirements:* For master's and doctorate, GRE General Test, GRE Subject Test, TOEFL (minimum score of 525 required). *Application deadline:* For fall admission, 7/15 (priority date). Applications are processed on a rolling basis. Application fee: $25. *Unit head:* Dr. Stan Duraj, Interim Chair, 216-523-7312, Fax: 216-687-9298.

Cornell University, Graduate School, Graduate Fields of Arts and Sciences, Field of Chemistry, Ithaca, NY 14853-0001. Offers analytical chemistry (PhD); bio-organic chemistry (PhD); biophysical chemistry (PhD); chemical physics (PhD); inorganic chemistry (PhD); material chemistry (PhD); organic chemistry (PhD); physical chemistry (PhD); polymer chemistry (PhD); theoretical chemistry (PhD). *Faculty:* 38 full-time. *Students:* 139 full-time (44 women); includes 10 minority (1 African American, 4 Asian Americans or Pacific Islanders, 4 Hispanic Americans, 1 Native American), 51 international. *Degree requirements:* For doctorate, dissertation required, foreign language not required. *Entrance requirements:* For doctorate, GRE General Test, GRE Subject Test, TOEFL (minimum score of 600 required). *Application deadline:* For fall admission, 1/15. Application fee: $65. Electronic applications accepted. *Unit head:* Director of Graduate Studies, 607-255-4139. *Application contact:* Graduate Field Assistant, 607-255-4139, E-mail: chemgrad@cornell.edu.

See in-depth description on page 109.

Florida State University, Graduate Studies, College of Arts and Sciences, Department of Chemistry, Tallahassee, FL 32306. Offers analytical chemistry (MS, PhD); biochemistry (MS, PhD); chemical physics (MS, PhD); inorganic chemistry (MS, PhD); organic chemistry (MS, PhD); physical chemistry (MS, PhD). Part-time programs available. *Faculty:* 38 full-time (4 women). *Students:* 87 full-time (27 women), 8 part-time (2 women). Terminal master's awarded for partial completion of doctoral program. *Degree requirements:* For master's, cumulative and diagnostic exams required; for doctorate, dissertation, cumulative and diagnostic exams required, foreign language not required. *Entrance requirements:* For master's and doctorate, GRE General Test, minimum B average in undergraduate course work. *Application deadline:* Applications are processed on a rolling basis. Application fee: $20. Tuition, state resident: part-time $139 per credit hour. Tuition, nonresident: part-time $482 per credit hour. Tuition and fees vary according to program. *Unit head:* Dr. John G. Dorsey, Chairman, 850-644-9625, Fax: 850-644-8281. *Application contact:* Dr. Naresh Dalal, Chair, Graduate Admissions Committee, 850-644-3398, Fax: 850-644-8281, E-mail: gradinfo@chem.fsu.edu.

See in-depth description on page 123.

Georgetown University, Graduate School, Department of Chemistry, Washington, DC 20057. Offers analytical chemistry (MS, PhD); biochemistry (MS, PhD); chemical physics (MS, PhD); inorganic chemistry (MS, PhD); organic chemistry (MS, PhD); physical chemistry (MS, PhD); theoretical chemistry (MS, PhD). Terminal master's awarded for partial completion of doctoral program. *Degree requirements:* For master's, thesis (for some programs), qualifying exam required, foreign language not required; for doctorate, dissertation, comprehensive exam required. *Entrance requirements:* For master's and doctorate, GRE General Test, TOEFL (minimum score of 550 required, 600 for teaching assistants).

See in-depth description on page 125.

The George Washington University, Columbian School of Arts and Sciences, Department of Chemistry, Washington, DC 20052. Offers analytical chemistry (MS, PhD); inorganic chemistry (MS, PhD); materials science (MS, PhD); organic chemistry (MS, PhD); physical chemistry (MS, PhD). Part-time and evening/weekend programs available. *Faculty:* 5 full-time (0 women). *Students:* 19 full-time (14 women), 7 part-time (4 women); includes 6 minority (1 African American, 3 Asian Americans or Pacific Islanders, 2 Hispanic Americans), 6 international. Terminal master's awarded for partial completion of doctoral program. *Degree requirements:* For master's, computer language, thesis or alternative, comprehensive exam required; for doctorate, computer language, dissertation, general exam required. *Entrance requirements:* For master's and doctorate, GRE General Test, interview, minimum GPA of 3.0. Application fee: $55. Tuition: Full-time $17,328; part-time $722 per credit hour. Required fees: $828; $35 per credit hour. Tuition and fees vary according to campus/location and program. *Unit head:* Dr. Michael King, Chair, 202-994-6121.

Governors State University, College of Arts and Sciences, Division of Science, Program in Analytical Chemistry, University Park, IL 60466. Offers MS. Part-time and evening/weekend programs available. *Faculty:* 6 full-time (2 women), 1 part-time (0 women). *Students:* 2 full-time, 20 part-time; includes 4 African Americans, 1 Asian American or Pacific Islander In 1998, 2 degrees awarded. *Degree requirements:* For master's, computer language, thesis or alternative required, foreign language not required. *Application deadline:* For fall admission, 7/15 (priority date); for spring admission, 11/10. Applications are processed on a rolling basis. Application fee: $0. *Financial aid:* Research assistantships, career-related internships or fieldwork, Federal Work-Study, institutionally-sponsored loans, and scholarships available. Aid available to part-time students. Financial aid application deadline: 5/1. *Faculty research:* Electrochemistry, photochemistry, spectrochemistry, biochemistry. *Unit head:* Dr. Edwin Cehelnik, Chairperson, Division of Science, 708-534-4520.

Howard University, Graduate School of Arts and Sciences, Department of Chemistry, Washington, DC 20059-0002. Offers analytical chemistry (MS, PhD); biochemistry (MS, PhD); inorganic chemistry (MS, PhD); organic chemistry (MS, PhD); physical chemistry (MS, PhD); polymer chemistry (MS, PhD); theoretical chemistry (MS, PhD). Part-time programs available. Terminal master's awarded for partial completion of doctoral program. *Degree requirements:* For master's, one foreign language (computer language can substitute), thesis, comprehensive exam, teaching experience required; for doctorate, 2 foreign languages (computer language can substitute for one), dissertation, comprehensive exam, teaching experience required. *Entrance requirements:* For master's, GRE General Test, minimum GPA of 2.7; for doctorate, GRE General Test, minimum GPA of 3.0. *Faculty research:* Stratospheric aerosols, liquid crystals, polymer coatings, terrestrial and extraterrestrial atmospheres, amidogen reaction.

Illinois Institute of Technology, Graduate College, Armour College of Engineering and Sciences, Department of Biological, Chemical and Physical Sciences, Chemistry Division, Chicago, IL 60616-3793. Offers analytical chemistry (MAC, MS, PhD); chemistry (M Chem); inorganic chemistry (MS, PhD); organic chemistry (MS, PhD); physical chemistry (MS, PhD); polymer chemistry (MS, PhD); theoretical chemistry (MS, PhD). Part-time and evening/weekend programs available. *Faculty:* 8 full-time (0 women), 2 part-time (0 women). *Students:* 14 full-time (7 women), 70 part-time (27 women); includes 19 minority (10 African Americans, 9 Asian Americans or Pacific Islanders), 16 international. Terminal master's awarded for partial completion of doctoral program. *Degree requirements:* For master's, thesis (for some programs), comprehensive exam required, foreign language not required; for doctorate, dissertation, comprehensive exam required, foreign language not required. *Entrance requirements:* For master's and doctorate, GRE (minimum score of 1200 required), TOEFL (minimum score of 550 required), undergraduate GPA of 3.0 required. *Application deadline:* For fall admission, 7/1; for spring admission, 11/1. Applications are processed on a rolling basis. Application fee: $30. Electronic applications accepted. *Unit head:* Dr. Carlo Segre, Associate Chair, 312-567-3480, Fax: 312-567-3494, E-mail: segre@iit.edu. *Application contact:* Dr. S. Mohammad Shahidehpour, Dean of Graduate College, 312-567-3024, Fax: 312-567-7517, E-mail: grad@minna.cns.iit.edu.

See in-depth description on page 135.

Indiana University Bloomington, Graduate School, College of Arts and Sciences, Department of Chemistry, Bloomington, IN 47405. Offers analytical chemistry (PhD); biological chemistry (PhD); chemistry (MAT, MS); inorganic chemistry (PhD); physical chemistry (PhD). PhD offered through the University Graduate School. *Faculty:* 28 full-time (1 woman), 1 (woman) part-time. *Students:* 96 full-time (32 women), 65 part-time (10 women); includes 12 minority (1 African American, 9 Asian Americans or Pacific Islanders, 2 Hispanic Americans), 42 international. Terminal master's awarded for partial completion of doctoral program. *Degree requirements:* For master's and doctorate, thesis/dissertation required, foreign language not required. *Entrance requirements:* For master's and doctorate, GRE General Test, GRE Subject Test, TOEFL. *Application deadline:* For fall admission, 1/15 (priority date); for spring admission, 9/1 (priority date). Applications are processed on a rolling basis. Application fee: $40. Tuition, state resident: part-time $161 per credit hour. Tuition, nonresident: part-time $468 per credit hour. Required fees: $360 per year. Tuition and fees vary according to course load and program. *Unit head:* Dr. Gary M. Hieftje, Chairperson, 812-855-6239, Fax: 812-855-8300, E-mail: cemchair@indiana.edu. *Application contact:* Dr. Jack K. Crandall, Chairperson of Admissions, 812-855-2068, Fax: 812-855-8300, E-mail: chemgrad@indiana.edu.

Kansas State University, Graduate School, College of Arts and Sciences, Department of Chemistry, Manhattan, KS 66506. Offers analytical chemistry (MS); chemistry (PhD); inorganic chemistry (MS); organic chemistry (MS); physical chemistry (MS). *Faculty:* 16 full-time (1 woman). *Students:* 43 full-time (12 women), 2 part-time (1 woman); includes 2 minority (both Asian Americans or Pacific Islanders), 25 international. Terminal master's awarded for partial completion of doctoral program. *Degree requirements:* For master's and doctorate, thesis/dissertation required, foreign language not required. *Entrance requirements:* For master's and doctorate, GRE, minimum GPA of 3.0. *Application deadline:* For fall admission, 6/1 (priority date); for spring admission, 12/1. Applications are processed on a rolling basis. Application fee: $0 ($25 for international students). *Unit head:* Peter M. A. Sherwood, Head, 785-532-6665, Fax: 785-532-6666, E-mail: escashem@ksu.edu. *Application contact:* Christer B. Aakeroy, Graduate Coordinator, 785-532-1468, Fax: 785-532-6666.

See in-depth description on page 143.

Analytical Chemistry

Kent State University, College of Arts and Sciences, Department of Chemistry, Kent, OH 44242-0001. Offers analytical chemistry (MS, PhD); biochemistry (PhD); chemistry (MA, MS, PhD); inorganic chemistry (MS, PhD); organic chemistry (MS, PhD); physical chemistry (MS, PhD). *Faculty:* 23 full-time. *Students:* 36 full-time (20 women), 2 part-time (both women); includes 1 minority (African American), 19 international. *Degree requirements:* For master's and doctorate, thesis/dissertation required, foreign language not required. *Entrance requirements:* For master's, minimum GPA of 2.75; for doctorate, minimum GPA of 3.0. *Application deadline:* For fall admission, 7/12; for spring admission, 11/29. Applications are processed on a rolling basis. Application fee: $30. *Unit head:* Dr. Rathindra N. Bose, Chairman, 330-672-2032, Fax: 330-672-3816.

See in-depth description on page 147.

Lehigh University, College of Arts and Sciences, Department of Chemistry, Bethlehem, PA 18015-3094. Offers biochemistry and analytical chemistry (MS, PhD); chemistry (DA); clinical chemistry (MS); inorganic chemistry (MS, PhD); organic chemistry (MS, PhD); pharmaceutical chemistry (PhD); physical chemistry (MS, PhD). Part-time programs available. Postbaccalaureate distance learning degree programs offered (no on-campus study). *Students:* 30 full-time (14 women), 92 part-time (46 women); includes 10 minority (7 Asian Americans or Pacific Islanders, 3 Hispanic Americans), 10 international. Terminal master's awarded for partial completion of doctoral program. *Degree requirements:* For master's, foreign language and thesis not required; for doctorate, dissertation required. *Entrance requirements:* For master's and doctorate, GRE General Test, TSE (minimum score of 230 required). *Application deadline:* For fall admission, 7/15; for spring admission, 12/1. Applications are processed on a rolling basis. Application fee: $40. *Unit head:* Dr. Keith J. Schray, Chairman, 610-758-3474, Fax: 610-758-6536, E-mail: kjs0@lehigh.edu. *Application contact:* Dr. James E. Roberts, Graduate Coordinator, 610-758-4847, Fax: 610-758-6536, E-mail: jer1@lehigh.edu.

Marquette University, Graduate School, College of Arts and Sciences, Department of Chemistry, Milwaukee, WI 53201-1881. Offers analytical chemistry (MS, PhD); bioanalytical chemistry (MS, PhD); biophysical chemistry (MS, PhD); chemical physics (MS, PhD); inorganic chemistry (MS, PhD); organic chemistry (MS, PhD); physical chemistry (MS, PhD). Part-time programs available. *Faculty:* 15 full-time (2 women), 1 part-time (0 women). *Students:* 33 full-time (12 women), 6 part-time (1 woman); includes 5 minority (2 African Americans, 3 Asian Americans or Pacific Islanders), 30 international. Terminal master's awarded for partial completion of doctoral program. *Degree requirements:* For master's, comprehensive exam required; for doctorate, dissertation, cumulative exams required, foreign language not required. *Entrance requirements:* For master's and doctorate, TOEFL (minimum score of 550 required), GRE Subject Test. Application fee: $40. Tuition: Part-time $510 per credit hour. Tuition and fees vary according to program. *Unit head:* Dr. Charles Wilkie, Chairman, 414-288-7065, Fax: 414-288-7066. *Application contact:* Dr. Mark Steinmetz, Director of Graduate Studies, 414-288-3535, Fax: 414-288-7066.

McMaster University, School of Graduate Studies, Faculty of Science, Department of Chemistry, Hamilton, ON L8S 4M2, Canada. Offers analytical chemistry (M Sc, PhD); chemical physics (M Sc, PhD); chemistry (M Sc, PhD); inorganic chemistry (M Sc, PhD); organic chemistry (M Sc, PhD); physical chemistry (M Sc, PhD); polymer chemistry (M Sc, PhD). Part-time programs available. *Faculty:* 21 full-time (2 women), 4 part-time (0 women). *Students:* 67 full-time (23 women), 1 part-time, 1 international. Terminal master's awarded for partial completion of doctoral program. *Degree requirements:* For master's, thesis required, foreign language not required; for doctorate, dissertation, comprehensive exam required, foreign language not required. *Entrance requirements:* For master's, minimum B+ average. *Application deadline:* For fall admission, 4/30; for spring admission, 3/15. Applications are processed on a rolling basis. Application fee: $50. *Unit head:* Dr. M. J. McGlinchey, Chair, 905-525-9140 Ext. 24504, Fax: 905-522-2509, E-mail: mcglinchey@mcmail.cis.mcmaster.ca. *Application contact:* Carol Dada, Administrator, 905-525-9140 Ext. 23487, Fax: 905-522-2509, E-mail: dada@mcmail.cis.mcmaster.ca.

Michigan State University, Graduate School, College of Natural Science, Department of Chemistry, East Lansing, MI 48824-1020. Offers analytical chemistry (MS, PhD); chemistry (MAT, MS, PhD); chemistry-environmental toxicology (PhD); environmental toxicology (PhD); inorganic chemistry (MS, PhD); organic chemistry (MS, PhD); physical chemistry (PhD). *Faculty:* 36 full-time (4 women). *Students:* 149 full-time (46 women), 18 part-time (9 women); includes 12 minority (6 African Americans, 3 Asian Americans or Pacific Islanders, 2 Hispanic Americans, 1 Native American), 80 international. Terminal master's awarded for partial completion of doctoral program. *Degree requirements:* For master's, thesis required (for some programs), foreign language not required; for doctorate, dissertation required, foreign language not required. *Entrance requirements:* For master's and doctorate, GRE, TOEFL. *Application deadline:* Applications are processed on a rolling basis. Application fee: $30 ($40 for international students). *Unit head:* Dr. Katharine C. Hunt, Chairperson, 517-355-9715, Fax: 517-353-1793, E-mail: chemdept@cem.msu.edu. *Application contact:* Dr. Richard Schwendeman, Associate Chair, Graduate Program, 517-355-9715 Ext. 344, Fax: 517-353-1793, E-mail: gradoff@cem.msu.edu.

Northeastern University, College of Arts and Sciences, Department of Chemistry, Boston, MA 02115-5096. Offers analytical chemistry (PhD); chemistry (MAT, MS, PhD); inorganic chemistry (PhD); organic chemistry (PhD); physical chemistry (PhD). Part-time and evening/weekend programs available. *Faculty:* 20 full-time (3 women), 1 part-time (0 women). *Students:* 59 full-time (25 women), 23 part-time (9 women). Terminal master's awarded for partial completion of doctoral program. *Degree requirements:* For master's, thesis required (for some programs); for doctorate, dissertation, qualifying exam in specialty area required, foreign language not required. *Entrance requirements:* For master's and doctorate, TOEFL (minimum score of 580 required). *Application deadline:* For fall admission, 4/15. Applications are processed on a rolling basis. Application fee: $50. Electronic applications accepted. *Unit head:* Dr. David A. Forsyth, Chairman, 617-373-2822, Fax: 617-373-8795, E-mail: chemistry-grad-info@neu.edu. *Application contact:* Dr. Philip W. LeQuesne, Chair, Graduate Admissions Committee, 617-373-2383, Fax: 617-373-8795.

Old Dominion University, College of Sciences, Department of Chemistry and Biochemistry, Norfolk, VA 23529. Offers analytical chemistry (MS); biochemistry (MS); biomedical sciences (PhD); clinical chemistry (MS); environmental chemistry (MS); organic chemistry (MS); physical chemistry (MS). Part-time and evening/weekend programs available. *Faculty:* 16 full-time (4 women). *Students:* 20 full-time (13 women), 12 part-time (8 women); includes 3 minority (1 African American, 2 Asian Americans or Pacific Islanders), 4 international. Terminal master's awarded for partial completion of doctoral program. *Degree requirements:* For master's and doctorate, thesis/dissertation, comprehensive exam required, foreign language not required. *Entrance requirements:* For master's, GRE General Test, TOEFL, minimum GPA of 3.0 in major, 2.5 overall; for doctorate, GRE General Test (minimum combined score of 1000 required), GRE Subject Test (minimum score of 600 required), TOEFL. *Application deadline:* For fall admission, 7/1; for spring admission, 11/1. Applications are processed on a rolling basis. Application fee: $30. *Unit head:* Dr. John R. Donet, Chair, 757-683-4078, E-mail: jdonet@odu.edu. *Application contact:* Dr. John R. Donet, Chair, 757-683-4078, E-mail: jdonet@odu.edu.

Oregon State University, Graduate School, College of Science, Department of Chemistry, Corvallis, OR 97331. Offers analytical chemistry (MS, PhD); chemistry (MA, MAIS); inorganic chemistry (MS, PhD); nuclear and radiation chemistry (MS, PhD); organic chemistry (MS, PhD); physical chemistry (MS, PhD). Part-time programs available. *Faculty:* 25 full-time (3 women), 5 part-time (2 women). *Students:* 68 full-time (24 women), 2 part-time; includes 4 minority (all Asian Americans or Pacific Islanders), 30 international. Terminal master's awarded for partial completion of doctoral program. *Degree requirements:* For master's and doctorate, one foreign language, thesis/dissertation required. *Entrance requirements:* For master's and doctorate, TOEFL (minimum score of 620 required), minimum GPA of 3.0 in last 90 hours. *Application deadline:* For fall admission, 3/1 (priority date). Applications are processed on a rolling basis. Application fee: $50. *Unit head:* Dr. John Westall, Chair, 541-737-6700, Fax: 541-737-2062, E-mail: john.westall@orst.edu. *Application contact:* Carolyn Brumley, Graduate Secretary, 541-737-6707, Fax: 541-737-2062, E-mail: carolyn.brumley@orst.edu.

Purdue University, Graduate School, School of Science, Department of Chemistry, West Lafayette, IN 47907. Offers analytical chemistry (MS, PhD); biochemistry (MS, PhD); chemical education (MS, PhD); inorganic chemistry (MS, PhD); organic chemistry (MS, PhD); physical chemistry (MS, PhD). *Accreditation:* NCATE (one or more programs are accredited). *Faculty:* 46 full-time, 1 part-time. *Students:* 246 full-time (83 women), 59 part-time (20 women); includes 36 minority (14 African Americans, 7 Asian Americans or Pacific Islanders, 14 Hispanic Americans, 1 Native American), 100 international. Terminal master's awarded for partial completion of doctoral program. *Degree requirements:* For master's and doctorate, thesis/dissertation required, foreign language not required. *Entrance requirements:* For master's and doctorate, TOEFL (minimum score of 550 required). Application fee: $30. Electronic applications accepted. *Unit head:* Dr. R. A. Walton, Head, 765-494-5203. *Application contact:* R. E. Wild, Chairman, Graduate Admissions, 765-494-5200, E-mail: wild@purdue.edu.

Purdue University, School of Pharmacy and Pharmacal Sciences, Graduate Programs in Pharmacy and Pharmacal Sciences, Department of Medicinal Chemistry and Molecular Pharmacology, West Lafayette, IN 47907. Offers analytical medicinal chemistry (PhD); computational and biophysical medicinal chemistry (PhD); medicinal and bioorganic chemistry (PhD); medicinal biochemistry and molecular biology (PhD); molecular pharmacology and toxicology (PhD); natural products and pharmacognosy (PhD); nuclear pharmacy (MS); radiopharmaceutical chemistry and nuclear pharmacy (PhD). *Faculty:* 26 full-time (2 women). *Students:* 48 full-time (22 women), 4 part-time (3 women); includes 5 minority (1 Asian American or Pacific Islander, 4 Hispanic Americans), 16 international. Terminal master's awarded for partial completion of doctoral program. *Degree requirements:* For master's and doctorate, thesis/dissertation required, foreign language not required. *Entrance requirements:* For master's, GRE General Test, TOEFL, minimum B average; BS in biology, chemistry, or pharmacy; for doctorate, GRE General Test, TOEFL, minimum B average; BS in biology, chemistry, or pharmacology. *Application deadline:* Applications are processed on a rolling basis. Application fee: $30. Electronic applications accepted. *Unit head:* Dr. R. F. Borch, Head of the Graduate Program, 765-494-1403. *Application contact:* Dr. D. E. Bergstrom, Graduate Committee, 765-494-6275.

Rensselaer Polytechnic Institute, Graduate School, School of Science, Department of Chemistry, Troy, NY 12180-3590. Offers analytical chemistry (MS, PhD); biochemistry (MS, PhD); inorganic chemistry (MS, PhD); organic chemistry (MS, PhD); physical chemistry (MS, PhD); polymer chemistry (MS, PhD). Part-time and evening/weekend programs available. *Faculty:* 17 full-time (2 women), 1 part-time (0 women). *Students:* 52 full-time (18 women), 3 part-time (1 woman); includes 4 minority (3 Asian Americans or Pacific Islanders, 1 Hispanic American), 30 international. *Degree requirements:* For master's, thesis required (for some programs), foreign language not required; for doctorate, dissertation required, foreign language not required. *Entrance requirements:* For master's and doctorate, GRE General Test, TOEFL (minimum score of 550 required). *Application deadline:* For fall admission, 2/1 (priority date). Applications are processed on a rolling basis. Application fee: $35. *Unit head:* Dr. Thomas Apple, Chair, 518-276-6344. *Application contact:* Dr. Wilfredo Colon, Chair, Graduate Committee, 518-276-6340, Fax: 518-276-6434, E-mail: colonw@rpi.edu.

See in-depth description on page 167.

Rutgers, The State University of New Jersey, Newark, Graduate School, Department of Chemistry, Newark, NJ 07102-3192. Offers analytical chemistry (MS, PhD); biochemistry (MS, PhD); inorganic chemistry (MS, PhD); organic chemistry (MS, PhD); physical chemistry (MS, PhD). Part-time and evening/weekend programs available. *Faculty:* 22 full-time (4 women). *Students:* 28 full-time (11 women), 39 part-time (19 women); includes 29 minority (1 African American, 24 Asian Americans or Pacific Islanders, 4 Hispanic Americans) Terminal master's awarded for partial completion of doctoral program. *Degree requirements:* For master's, cumulative exams required, thesis optional, foreign language not required; for doctorate, dissertation, exams, research proposal required, foreign language not required. *Entrance requirements:* For master's and doctorate, GRE General Test, TOEFL (minimum score of 550 required; 590 for financial aid), minimum undergraduate B average. *Application deadline:* For fall admission, 7/1 (priority date); for spring admission, 12/1. Applications are processed on a rolling basis. Application fee: $40. *Unit head:* Prof. Hugh W. Thompson, Coordinator, 973-353-5173, Fax: 973-353-1264.

See in-depth description on page 169.

Rutgers, The State University of New Jersey, New Brunswick, Graduate School, Program in Chemistry, New Brunswick, NJ 08903. Offers analytical chemistry (MS, PhD); biological chemistry (PhD); chemistry education (MST); inorganic chemistry (MS, PhD); organic chemistry (MS, PhD); physical chemistry (MS, PhD). Part-time and evening/weekend programs available. *Faculty:* 44 full-time (9 women), 4 part-time (2 women). *Students:* 100 full-time (35 women), 69 part-time (29 women); includes 27 minority (2 African Americans, 24 Asian Americans or Pacific Islanders, 1 Hispanic American), 79 international. Terminal master's awarded for partial completion of doctoral program. *Degree requirements:* For master's, exam required, thesis optional, foreign language not required; for doctorate, dissertation, cumulative exams required, foreign language not required. *Entrance requirements:* For master's, GRE General Test, GRE Subject Test, TOEFL; for doctorate, GRE General Test, GRE Subject Test, TOEFL (minimum score of 575 required). *Application deadline:* For fall admission, 4/15 (priority date); for spring admission, 11/1. Applications are processed on a rolling basis. Application fee: $50. *Unit head:* Dr. Martha A. Cotter, Director, 732-445-2259, Fax: 732-445-5312, E-mail: gradexec@rutchem.rutgers.edu.

See in-depth description on page 173.

San Jose State University, Graduate Studies, College of Science, Department of Chemistry, San Jose, CA 95192-0001. Offers analytical chemistry (MS); biochemistry (MS); chemistry (MA); inorganic chemistry (MS); organic chemistry (MS); physical chemistry (MS); polymer chemistry (MS); radiochemistry (MS). Part-time and evening/weekend programs available. *Faculty:* 24 full-time (3 women), 5 part-time (2 women). *Students:* 7 full-time (5 women), 30 part-time (17 women); includes 24 minority (2 African Americans, 21 Asian Americans or Pacific Islanders, 1 Hispanic American), 4 international. *Degree requirements:* For master's, thesis or alternative required, foreign language not required. *Entrance requirements:* For master's, GRE, minimum B average. *Application deadline:* For fall admission, 6/1. Applications are processed on a rolling basis. Application fee: $59. Tuition, nonresident: part-time $246 per unit. Required fees: $1,939; $1,309 per year. *Unit head:* Dr. Pamela Stacks, Chair, 408-924-5000, Fax: 408-924-4945. *Application contact:* Dr. Roger Biringer, Graduate Adviser, 408-924-4961.

Seton Hall University, College of Arts and Sciences, Department of Chemistry, South Orange, NJ 07079-2694. Offers analytical chemistry (MS, PhD); biochemistry (MS, PhD); chemistry (MS); inorganic chemistry (MS, PhD); organic chemistry (MS, PhD); physical chemistry (MS, PhD). Part-time and evening/weekend programs available. Terminal master's awarded for partial completion of doctoral program. *Degree requirements:* For master's, formal seminar required, thesis optional; for doctorate, dissertation, comprehensive exams, annual seminars required. *Entrance requirements:* For master's, TOEFL, undergraduate major in chemistry or related field with a minimum of 30 credits in chemistry, including 2 semesters of physical chemistry; for doctorate, oral matriculation exam based on proposed doctoral research, minimum GPA of 3.0 in course distribution requirements, formal seminar. *Faculty research:* DNA metal reactions; chromatography; bioinorganic, biophysical, organometallic, and polymer chemistry; heterogeneous catalysis.

South Dakota State University, Graduate School, College of Arts and Science, Department of Chemistry, Brookings, SD 57007. Offers analytical chemistry (MS, PhD); biochemistry (MS, PhD); chemistry (MS, PhD); inorganic chemistry (MS, PhD); organic chemistry (MS, PhD); physical chemistry (MS, PhD). *Degree requirements:* For master's, thesis, oral exam required, foreign language not required; for doctorate, dissertation, preliminary oral and written exams, research tool required. *Entrance requirements:* For master's, TOEFL (minimum score of 580 required), bachelor's degree in chemistry or equivalent; for doctorate, TOEFL (minimum score of 580 required). *Faculty research:* Environmental chemistry, computational chemistry, organic synthesis and photochemistry, novel material development and characterization.

Southern University and Agricultural and Mechanical College, Graduate School, College of Sciences, Department of Chemistry, Baton Rouge, LA 70813. Offers analytical chemistry (MS); biochemistry (MS); environmental sciences (MS); inorganic chemistry (MS); organic chemistry (MS); physical chemistry (MS). *Faculty:* 9 full-time (2 women), 3 part-time (2 women). *Students:* 4 full-time (3 women), 20 part-time (12 women); includes 19 minority (all African Americans), 4 international. *Degree requirements:* For master's, thesis required, foreign language not required. *Entrance requirements:* For master's, GMAT or GRE General Test, TOEFL. *Application deadline:* For fall admission, 6/1 (priority date); for spring admission, 11/1. Applications are processed on a rolling basis. Application fee: $5. *Unit head:* Dr. Robert Harvey Miller, Chairman, 225-771-3990, Fax: 225-771-3992.

State University of New York at Binghamton, Graduate School, School of Arts and Sciences, Department of Chemistry, Binghamton, NY 13902-6000. Offers analytical chemistry (PhD); chemistry (MA, MS); inorganic chemistry (PhD); organic chemistry (PhD); physical chemistry (PhD). *Faculty:* 13 full-time, 7 part-time. *Students:* 48 full-time (11 women), 7 part-time (2 women); includes 2 minority (1 African American, 1 Hispanic American), 30 international. Terminal master's awarded for partial completion of doctoral program. *Degree requirements:* For master's, thesis or alternative, oral exam, seminar presentation required, foreign language not required; for doctorate, dissertation, cumulative exams required, foreign language not required. *Entrance requirements:* For master's and doctorate, GRE General Test, GRE Subject Test, TOEFL. *Application deadline:* For fall admission, 4/15 (priority date); for spring admission, 11/1. Applications are processed on a rolling basis. Application fee: $50. Electronic applications accepted. Tuition, state resident: full-time $5,100; part-time $213 per credit. Tuition, nonresident: full-time $8,416; part-time $351 per credit. Required fees: $77 per credit. Part-time tuition and fees vary according to course load. *Unit head:* Dr. Alistair J. Lees, Chairperson, 607-777-2362.

Stevens Institute of Technology, Graduate School, School of Applied Sciences and Liberal Arts, Department of Chemistry and Chemical Biology, Hoboken, NJ 07030. Offers chemistry (MS, PhD, Certificate), including analytical chemistry, chemical biology, chemical physiology (Certificate), instrumental analysis (Certificate), organic chemistry (MS, PhD), physical chemistry (MS, PhD), polymer chemistry. Part-time and evening/weekend programs available. Terminal master's awarded for partial completion of doctoral program. *Degree requirements:* For master's, thesis or alternative required, foreign language not required; for doctorate, one foreign language, dissertation required; for Certificate, computer language, project or thesis required. *Entrance requirements:* For master's and doctorate, TOEFL (minimum score of 550 required). Electronic applications accepted.

Tufts University, Division of Graduate and Continuing Studies and Research, Graduate School of Arts and Sciences, Department of Chemistry, Medford, MA 02155. Offers analytical chemistry (MS, PhD); bioorganic chemistry (MS, PhD); environmental chemistry (MS, PhD); inorganic chemistry (MS, PhD); organic chemistry (MS, PhD); physical chemistry (MS, PhD). *Faculty:* 13 full-time, 1 part-time. *Students:* 52 (27 women); includes 5 minority (1 African American, 3 Asian Americans or Pacific Islanders, 1 Hispanic American) 14 international. Terminal master's awarded for partial completion of doctoral program. *Degree requirements:* For master's and doctorate, thesis/dissertation required, foreign language not required. *Entrance requirements:* For master's and doctorate, GRE General Test, GRE Subject Test, TOEFL (minimum score of 600 required). *Application deadline:* For fall admission, 2/15; for spring admission, 10/15. Applications are processed on a rolling basis. Application fee: $50. *Unit head:* Marc d'Alarco, Chair, 617-627-3441, Fax: 617-627-3443. *Application contact:* Samuel Kounaves, 617-627-3124, Fax: 617-627-3443.

See in-depth description on page 181.

The University of Akron, Graduate School, Buchtel College of Arts and Sciences, Department of Chemistry, Akron, OH 44325-0001. Offers analytical chemistry (MS, PhD); biochemistry (MS, PhD); chemistry (MS, PhD); inorganic chemistry (MS, PhD); organic chemistry (MS, PhD); physical chemistry (MS, PhD). Part-time and evening/weekend programs available. *Faculty:* 17 full-time, 1 part-time. *Students:* 63 full-time (25 women), 9 part-time (6 women); includes 8 minority (6 African Americans, 2 Hispanic Americans), 31 international. Terminal master's awarded for partial completion of doctoral program. *Degree requirements:* For master's, one foreign language (computer language can substitute), thesis, seminar presentation required; for doctorate, 2 foreign languages (computer language can substitute for one), dissertation, cumulative exams required. *Entrance requirements:* For master's, TOEFL, minimum GPA of 2.75; for doctorate, TOEFL. *Application deadline:* For fall admission, 3/1. Applications are processed on a rolling basis. Application fee: $25 ($50 for international students). Tuition, state resident: part-time $189 per credit. Tuition, nonresident: part-time $353 per credit. Required fees: $7.3 per credit. *Unit head:* Dr. Gerald Koser, Chair, 330-972-7372, E-mail: koser@uakron.edu.

University of Calgary, Faculty of Graduate Studies, Faculty of Science, Department of Chemistry, Calgary, AB T2N 1N4, Canada. Offers analytical chemistry (M Sc, PhD); applied chemistry (M Sc, PhD); inorganic chemistry (M Sc, PhD); organic chemistry (M Sc, PhD); physical chemistry (M Sc, PhD); polymer chemistry (M Sc, PhD); theoretical chemistry (M Sc, PhD). *Faculty:* 29 full-time (4 women), 1 part-time (0 women). *Students:* 60 full-time (25 women). *Degree requirements:* For master's, thesis required, foreign language not required; for doctorate, dissertation, candidacy exam required, foreign language not required. *Entrance requirements:* For master's and doctorate, TOEFL (minimum score of 580 required). *Application deadline:* For fall admission, 12/1 (priority date). Applications are processed on a rolling basis. Application fee: $60. *Unit head:* Dr. R. A. Kydd, Head, 403-220-5340. *Application contact:* Greta Prihodko, Graduate Program Administrator, 403-220-6252, E-mail: gradinfo@chem.ucalgary.ca.

University of Cincinnati, Division of Research and Advanced Studies, McMicken College of Arts and Sciences, Department of Chemistry, Cincinnati, OH 45221-0091. Offers analytical chemistry (MS, PhD); biochemistry (MS, PhD); inorganic chemistry (MS, PhD); organic chemistry (MS, PhD); physical chemistry (MS, PhD); polymer chemistry (MS, PhD). Part-time and evening/weekend programs available. *Faculty:* 25 full-time. *Students:* 87 full-time (26 women), 26 part-time (3 women); includes 12 minority (1 African American, 11 Asian Americans or Pacific Islanders), 34 international. Terminal master's awarded for partial completion of doctoral program. *Degree requirements:* For master's, thesis optional, foreign language not required; for doctorate, dissertation required, foreign language not required. *Entrance requirements:* For master's and doctorate, GRE General Test, GRE Subject Test. *Application deadline:* For fall admission, 2/1. Application fee: $30. *Unit head:* Dr. Marshall Wilson, Head, 513-556-9200, Fax: 513-556-9239, E-mail: marshall.wilson@uc.edu. *Application contact:* Thomas Ridgway, Graduate Program Director, 513-556-9200, Fax: 513-556-9239, E-mail: thomas.ridgway@uc.edu.

University of Georgia, Graduate School, College of Arts and Sciences, Department of Chemistry, Athens, GA 30602. Offers analytical chemistry (MS, PhD); inorganic chemistry (MS, PhD); organic chemistry (MS, PhD); physical chemistry (MS, PhD). *Faculty:* 23 full-time (1 woman). *Students:* 107 full-time (26 women), 11 part-time (4 women). *Degree requirements:* For master's, thesis required, foreign language not required; for doctorate, one foreign language (computer language can substitute), dissertation required. *Entrance requirements:* For master's and doctorate, GRE General Test. *Application deadline:* For fall admission, 7/1 (priority date); for spring admission, 11/15. Application fee: $30. Electronic applications accepted. *Unit head:* Dr. I. Jonathan Amster, Graduate Coordinator, 706-542-1936, Fax: 706-542-9454, E-mail: mauldin@sunchem.chem.uga.edu.

University of Louisville, Graduate School, College of Arts and Sciences, Department of Chemistry, Louisville, KY 40292-0001. Offers analytical chemistry (MS, PhD); chemical physics (PhD); inorganic chemistry (MS, PhD); organic chemistry (MS, PhD); physical chemistry (MS, PhD). *Faculty:* 20 full-time (3 women), 1 part-time (0 women). *Students:* 52 full-time (20 women), 4 part-time (2 women); includes 2 minority (both Hispanic Americans), 30 international. *Degree requirements:* For master's, thesis required; for doctorate, dissertation required. *Entrance requirements:* For master's and doctorate, GRE General Test, TOEFL (minimum score of 550 required). *Application deadline:* Applications are processed on a rolling basis. Application fee: $25. *Unit head:* Dr. George R. Pack, Chair, 502-852-6798, Fax: 502-852-8149, E-mail: george.pack@louisville.edu.

See in-depth description on page 199.

University of Maryland, College Park, Graduate School, College of Life Sciences, Department of Chemistry and Biochemistry, Chemistry Program, College Park, MD 20742-5045. Offers analytical chemistry (MS, PhD); inorganic chemistry (MS, PhD); organic chemistry (MS, PhD); physical chemistry (MS, PhD). *Students:* 76 full-time (34 women), 16 part-time (6 women); includes 8 minority (2 African Americans, 4 Asian Americans or Pacific Islanders, 1 Hispanic American, 1 Native American), 36 international. *Degree requirements:* For master's, thesis optional, foreign language not required; for doctorate, dissertation, 2 seminar presentations, oral exam required. *Entrance requirements:* For master's, GRE General Test, minimum GPA of 3.1; for doctorate, GRE General Test. *Application deadline:* Applications are processed on a rolling basis. Application fee: $50 ($70 for international students). Tuition, state resident: part-time $272 per credit hour. Tuition, nonresident: part-time $475 per credit hour. Required fees: $632; $379 per year. *Unit head:* Marlin Harmony, Graduate Director, 785-864-4670, Fax: 785-864-5396. *Application contact:* Trudy Lindsey, Director, Graduate Admission and Records, 301-405-4198, Fax: 301-314-9305, E-mail: grschool@deans.umd.edu.

University of Michigan, Horace H. Rackham School of Graduate Studies, College of Literature, Science, and the Arts, Department of Chemistry, Ann Arbor, MI 48109. Offers analytical chemistry (PhD); chemical biology (PhD); inorganic chemistry (PhD); organic chemistry (PhD); physical chemistry (PhD). *Faculty:* 43 full-time (7 women). *Students:* 161 full-time (60 women); includes 5 minority (2 African Americans, 2 Asian Americans or Pacific Islanders, 1 Hispanic American), 43 international. *Degree requirements:* For doctorate, dissertation, oral defense of dissertation, preliminary exam, organic cumulative proficiency exams required, foreign language not required. *Entrance requirements:* For doctorate, GRE General Test, GRE Subject Test (recommended), statement of prior research. *Application deadline:* For fall admission, 2/15 (priority date). Applications are processed on a rolling basis. Application fee: $55. *Unit head:* Dr. Joseph P. Marino, Chair, 734-763-9681, Fax: 734-647-4847, E-mail: jpmarino@umich.edu. *Application contact:* Warren Noone, Assistant Director of Graduate Studies, 734-764-7278, Fax: 734-747-4865, E-mail: nooner@umich.edu.

University of Missouri–Columbia, Graduate School, College of Arts and Sciences, Department of Chemistry, Columbia, MO 65211. Offers analytical chemistry (MS, PhD); inorganic chemistry (MS, PhD); organic chemistry (MS, PhD); physical chemistry (MS, PhD). *Faculty:* 23 full-time (3 women). *Students:* 68 full-time (23 women), 24 part-time (7 women); includes 6 minority (1 African American, 2 Asian Americans or Pacific Islanders, 2 Hispanic Americans, 1 Native American), 47 international. *Degree requirements:* For master's, thesis required, foreign language not required; for doctorate, dissertation required. *Entrance requirements:* For master's and doctorate, GRE General Test, minimum GPA of 3.0. *Application deadline:* For fall admission, 7/1 (priority date). Applications are processed on a rolling basis. Application fee: $30 ($50 for international students). *Unit head:* Dr. Richard Thompson, Director of Graduate Studies, 573-882-7356.

University of Missouri–Kansas City, College of Arts and Sciences, Department of Chemistry, Kansas City, MO 64110-2499. Offers analytical chemistry (MS, PhD); inorganic chemistry (MS, PhD); organic chemistry (MS, PhD); physical chemistry (MS, PhD); polymer chemistry (MS, PhD). PhD offered through the School of Graduate Studies. Part-time programs available. *Faculty:* 12 full-time (2 women), 2 part-time (0 women). *Students:* 25 full-time (7 women), 7 part-time (2 women), 18 international. *Degree requirements:* For master's, thesis required (for some programs), foreign language not required; for doctorate, dissertation required, foreign language not required. *Entrance requirements:* For master's, TOEFL (minimum score of 550 required); for doctorate, GRE General Test (minimum combined score of 1500 on three sections required), TOEFL (minimum score of 550 required), TWE (minimum score of 4 required). *Application deadline:* For fall and spring admission, 2/1 (priority date); for winter admission, 9/1 (priority date). Applications are processed on a rolling basis. Application fee: $25. *Unit head:* Dr. Jerry Jean, Interim Chairperson, 816-235-2280, Fax: 816-235-5502, E-mail: jean@cctr.umkc.edu.

See in-depth description on page 211.

University of Nebraska–Lincoln, Graduate College, College of Arts and Sciences, Department of Chemistry, Lincoln, NE 68588. Offers analytical chemistry (PhD); chemistry (MS); inorganic chemistry (PhD); organic chemistry (PhD); physical chemistry (PhD). *Faculty:* 23 full-time (2 women), 1 part-time (0 women). *Students:* 79 full-time (15 women), 23 part-time (2 women); includes 6 minority (1 African American, 2 Asian Americans or Pacific Islanders, 2 Hispanic Americans, 1 Native American), 47 international. *Degree requirements:* For master's, departmental qualifying exam required, thesis optional; for doctorate, dissertation, comprehensive and departmental qualifying exams required. *Entrance requirements:* For master's and doctorate, GRE Subject Test, TOEFL (minimum score of 550 required). *Application deadline:* For fall admission, 3/1 (priority date). Applications are processed on a rolling basis. Application fee: $35. Electronic applications accepted. *Unit head:* Dr. Lawrence Parkhurst, Chair, 402-472-3501, Fax: 402-472-9402.

University of Nevada, Las Vegas, Graduate College, College of Science, Department of Chemistry, Las Vegas, NV 89154-9900. Offers environmental analytical chemistry (MS); general chemistry (MS). *Faculty:* 18 full-time (5 women). *Students:* 10 full-time (7 women), 6 part-time (5 women); includes 2 minority (1 Asian American or Pacific Islander, 1 Hispanic American), 7 international. *Degree requirements:* For master's, thesis required, foreign language not required. *Entrance requirements:* For master's, GRE General Test, minimum GPA of 2.75. *Application deadline:* For fall admission, 6/15 (priority date); for spring admission, 11/15. Applications are processed on a rolling basis. Application fee: $40 ($95 for international students). *Unit head:* Dr. Brian Spangelo, Chair, 702-895-3510. *Application contact:* Graduate Coordinator, 702-895-3753.

University of Regina, Faculty of Graduate Studies and Research, Faculty of Science, Department of Chemistry, Regina, SK S4S 0A2, Canada. Offers analytical chemistry (M Sc, PhD); biochemistry (M Sc, PhD); clinical biochemistry (M Sc, PhD); inorganic chemistry (M Sc, PhD); organic chemistry (M Sc, PhD); physical chemistry (M Sc, PhD); x-ray crystallography (M Sc, PhD). Part-time programs available. *Faculty:* 10 full-time (1 woman), 3 part-time (0 women). *Students:* 9 full-time (5 women), 6 part-time (3 women). *Degree requirements:* For master's, thesis, departmental qualifying exam required, foreign language not required; for doctorate, variable foreign language requirement, dissertation, departmental qualifying exam required. *Entrance requirements:* For master's, TOEFL (minimum score of 580 required); for doctorate, TOEFL. *Application deadline:* Applications are processed on a rolling basis. Application fee: $0. *Expenses:* Tuition and fees charges are reported in Canadian dollars. Tuition, state resident: full-time $1,688 Canadian dollars; part-time $94 Canadian dollars per credit hour. International tuition: $3,375 Canadian dollars full-time. Required fees: $65 Canadian dollars per course. Tuition and fees vary according to course load and program. *Unit head:* Dr. K. Johnson, Head, 306-585-4146, Fax: 306-585-4894, E-mail: chem@max.cc.uregina.ca.

University of Southern Mississippi, Graduate School, College of Science and Technology, Department of Chemistry and Biochemistry, Hattiesburg, MS 39406-5167. Offers analytical chemistry (MS, PhD); biochemistry (MS, PhD); inorganic chemistry (MS, PhD); organic chemistry (MS, PhD); physical chemistry (MS, PhD). *Faculty:* 16 full-time (2 women), 1 part-time (0

Analytical Chemistry–Chemistry

University of Southern Mississippi (continued)
women). *Students:* 25 full-time (10 women); includes 8 minority (3 African Americans, 4 Asian Americans or Pacific Islanders, 1 Hispanic American) *Degree requirements:* For master's, thesis required, foreign language not required; for doctorate, 2 foreign languages (computer language can substitute for one), dissertation required. *Entrance requirements:* For master's, GRE General Test, TOEFL, minimum GPA of 2.75; for doctorate, GRE General Test, TOEFL, minimum GPA of 3.5. *Application deadline:* For fall admission, 8/6 (priority date). Applications are processed on a rolling basis. Application fee: $0 ($25 for international students). Tuition, state resident: full-time $2,250; part-time $137 per semester hour. Tuition, nonresident: full-time $3,102; part-time $172 per semester hour. Required fees: $602. *Unit head:* Dr. Stella Elakovich, Chair, 601-266-4701. *Application contact:* Dr. Gordon Cannon, 601-266-4702.

University of South Florida, Graduate School, College of Arts and Sciences, Department of Chemistry, Tampa, FL 33620-9951. Offers analytical chemistry (MS, PhD); biochemistry (MS, PhD); inorganic chemistry (MS, PhD); organic chemistry (MS, PhD); physical chemistry (MS, PhD). Part-time programs available. *Faculty:* 23 full-time (3 women), 3 part-time (1 woman). *Students:* 44 full-time (14 women), 10 part-time (1 woman); includes 2 African Americans, 3 Hispanic Americans Terminal master's awarded for partial completion of doctoral program. *Degree requirements:* For master's, thesis required; for doctorate, 2 foreign languages (computer language can substitute for one), dissertation, colloquium required. *Entrance requirements:* For master's and doctorate, GRE General Test (minimum combined score of 1000 required), minimum GPA of 3.0 in last 30 hours of chemistry course work. *Application deadline:* For fall admission, 6/5 (priority date); for spring admission, 10/23 (priority date). Applications are processed on a rolling basis. Application fee: $20. Electronic applications accepted. Tuition, state resident: part-time $148 per credit hour. Tuition, nonresident: part-time $509 per credit hour. *Unit head:* Dr. Robert Potter, Chairperson, 813-974-4129, Fax: 813-974-1731, E-mail: potter@chuma1.cas.usf.edu. *Application contact:* Andy Zekter, Graduate Director, 813-974-9666, Fax: 813-974-3203, E-mail: zekter@chuma1.cas.usf.edu.

University of Tennessee, Knoxville, Graduate School, College of Arts and Sciences, Department of Chemistry, Knoxville, TN 37996. Offers analytical chemistry (MS, PhD); chemical physics (PhD); environmental chemistry (MS, PhD); inorganic chemistry (MS, PhD); organic chemistry (MS, PhD); physical chemistry (MS, PhD); polymer chemistry (MS, PhD); theoretical chemistry (PhD). Part-time programs available. *Faculty:* 31 full-time (1 woman), 1 (woman) part-time. *Students:* 55 full-time (15 women), 44 part-time (11 women); includes 1 minority (Asian American or Pacific Islander), 23 international. Terminal master's awarded for partial completion of doctoral program. *Degree requirements:* For master's and doctorate, thesis/dissertation required, foreign language not required. *Entrance requirements:* For master's and doctorate, GRE General Test, TOEFL (minimum score of 550 required), minimum GPA of 2.7. *Application deadline:* For fall admission, 2/1 (priority date). Applications are processed on a rolling basis. Application fee: $35. Electronic applications accepted. *Unit head:* Dr. Michael Sepaniak, Head, 423-974-3141, Fax: 423-974-3454, E-mail: msepaniak@utk.edu. *Application contact:* Dr. Charles Feigerle, Graduate Representative, E-mail: cfeigerle@utk.edu.

The University of Texas at Austin, Graduate School, College of Natural Sciences, Department of Chemistry and Biochemistry, Austin, TX 78712-1111. Offers analytical chemistry (MA, PhD); biochemistry (MA, PhD); inorganic chemistry (MA, PhD); organic chemistry (MA, PhD); physical chemistry (MA, PhD). *Students:* 278 (94 women); includes 28 minority (3 African Americans, 11 Asian Americans or Pacific Islanders, 13 Hispanic Americans, 1 Native American) 61 international. *Entrance requirements:* For master's and doctorate, GRE General Test. Application fee: $50 ($75 for international students). *Unit head:* Dr. Marvin L. Hackert, Chairman, 512-471-3949. *Application contact:* Dr. Jennifer Brodbelt, Graduate Adviser, 512-471-0028.

University of Toledo, Graduate School, College of Arts and Sciences, Department of Chemistry, Toledo, OH 43606-3398. Offers analytical chemistry (MS, MS Ed, PhD); biological chemistry (MS, MS Ed, PhD); inorganic chemistry (MS, MS Ed, PhD); organic chemistry (MS, MS Ed, PhD); physical chemistry (MS, MS Ed, PhD). Part-time programs available. *Degree requirements:* For master's and doctorate, thesis/dissertation required, foreign language not required. *Entrance requirements:* For master's and doctorate, GRE General Test, GRE Subject Test, TOEFL. Electronic applications accepted. *Faculty research:* Enzymology, materials chemistry, crystallography, theoretical chemistry.

Wake Forest University, Graduate School, Department of Chemistry, Winston-Salem, NC 27109. Offers analytical chemistry (MS, PhD); inorganic chemistry (MS, PhD); organic chemistry (MS, PhD); physical chemistry (MS, PhD). Part-time programs available. *Faculty:* 14 full-time (1 woman). *Students:* 22 full-time (11 women), 2 part-time; includes 5 minority (2 African Americans, 3 Asian Americans or Pacific Islanders) *Degree requirements:* For master's, one foreign language (computer language can substitute), thesis required; for doctorate, 2 foreign languages (computer language can substitute for one), dissertation required. *Entrance requirements:* For master's and doctorate, GRE General Test, GRE Subject Test. *Application deadline:* For fall admission, 2/15. Application fee: $25. *Unit head:* Dr. Jim Fishbein, Director, 336-758-6139, E-mail: fishbein@wfu.edu.

See in-depth description on page 227.

Washington State University, Graduate School, College of Sciences, Department of Chemistry, Pullman, WA 99164. Offers analytical chemistry (MS, PhD); inorganic chemistry (MS, PhD); nuclear chemistry (MS, PhD); organic chemistry (MS, PhD); physical chemistry (MS, PhD). *Faculty:* 28 full-time (4 women). *Students:* 39 full-time (14 women), 3 part-time (2 women); includes 4 minority (2 Asian Americans or Pacific Islanders, 1 Hispanic American, 1 Native American), 8 international. Terminal master's awarded for partial completion of doctoral program. *Degree requirements:* For master's, oral exam, teaching experience required, thesis optional, foreign language not required; for doctorate, dissertation, oral exam, teaching experience required, foreign language not required. *Entrance requirements:* For master's and doctorate, GRE General Test, minimum GPA of 3.0. *Application deadline:* For fall admission, 3/1 (priority date). Applications are processed on a rolling basis. Application fee: $35. *Unit head:* Dr. Ralph Yount, Chair, 509-335-1516. *Application contact:* James O. Schenk, Chair, Admissions Committee, 509-335-8866, E-mail: carrie@wsu.edu.

Chemistry

Acadia University, Faculty of Pure and Applied Science, Department of Chemistry, Wolfville, NS B0P 1X0, Canada. Offers M Sc. *Faculty:* 8 full-time (1 woman). *Students:* 3 full-time (0 women). Average age 26. 20 applicants, 5% accepted. *Degree requirements:* For master's, thesis required. *Application deadline:* For fall admission, 2/1. Application fee: $25. *Expenses:* Tuition and fees charges are reported in Canadian dollars. Tuition, state resident: full-time $4,361 Canadian dollars. International tuition: $8,722 Canadian dollars full-time. Required fees: $147 Canadian dollars. Full-time tuition and fees vary according to program and student level. *Financial aid:* Teaching assistantships available. Financial aid application deadline: 2/1. *Faculty research:* Analytical studies of nonmetals, fungal metabolic studies, kinetics of gas-phase reactions, chemistry of thiols and thiolates, inhibitions of fruit ripening processes by flavonoids. *Unit head:* Dr. Sharon G. Roscoe, Head, 902-585-1172, E-mail: sharon.roscoe@acadiau.ca. *Application contact:* Avril Bird, Secretary, 902-585-1242, Fax: 902-585-1114, E-mail: avril.bird@acadiau.ca.

American University, College of Arts and Sciences, Department of Chemistry, Program in Chemistry, Washington, DC 20016-8001. Offers MS, PhD. *Faculty:* 8 full-time (3 women), 7 part-time (2 women). *Students:* 16 full-time (9 women), 28 part-time (12 women); includes 11 minority (7 African Americans, 4 Asian Americans or Pacific Islanders), 16 international. 32 applicants, 69% accepted. In 1998, 2 master's, 6 doctorates awarded. *Degree requirements:* For master's, comprehensive exam required; for doctorate, one foreign language (computer language can substitute), dissertation, comprehensive exams required. *Entrance requirements:* For master's and doctorate, minimum GPA of 3.0. *Application deadline:* For fall admission, 2/1 (priority date); for spring admission, 10/1 (priority date). Applications are processed on a rolling basis. Application fee: $50. *Financial aid:* In 1998–99, 28 students received aid, including 10 fellowships with full tuition reimbursements available (averaging $14,500 per year), 4 research assistantships with full tuition reimbursements available (averaging $8,500 per year), 5 teaching assistantships with full tuition reimbursements available (averaging $8,500 per year); career-related internships or fieldwork, Federal Work-Study, grants, and traineeships also available. Financial aid application deadline: 2/1. *Unit head:* Dr. Nina Roscher, Chair, Department of Chemistry, 202-885-1750, Fax: 202-885-1752, E-mail: nrosche@american.edu.

See in-depth description on page 89.

Arizona State University, Graduate College, College of Liberal Arts and Sciences, Department of Chemistry and Biochemistry, Tempe, AZ 85287. Offers MNS, MS, PhD. *Faculty:* 38 full-time (7 women), 4 part-time (1 woman). *Students:* 95 full-time (30 women), 12 part-time (4 women); includes 9 minority (2 African Americans, 5 Asian Americans or Pacific Islanders, 2 Hispanic Americans), 29 international. Average age 27. 75 applicants, 84% accepted. In 1998, 6 master's, 9 doctorates awarded. *Degree requirements:* For master's, thesis required, foreign language not required; for doctorate, one foreign language, dissertation required. *Entrance requirements:* For master's and doctorate, GRE, TOEFL (minimum score of 580 required), TSE (minimum score of 230 required). *Application deadline:* For fall admission, 2/1 (priority date). Application fee: $45. *Financial aid:* Research assistantships, teaching assistantships, tuition waivers (full) available. *Faculty research:* Meteorite chemistry, structure of biopolymers, electron microprobe analysis of air pollutants, x-ray crystallography. *Unit head:* Dr. J. Devens Gust, Chair, 480-965-3461. *Application contact:* Dr. Ana Moore, Director of Graduate Studies, 480-965-4664, Fax: 480-965-2747, E-mail: chmgrad@asu.edu.

See in-depth description on page 91.

Arkansas State University, Graduate School, College of Arts and Sciences, Department of Chemistry and Physics, Jonesboro, State University, AR 72467. Offers chemistry (MS); chemistry education (MSE, SCCT). *Accreditation:* NCATE (one or more programs are accredited). Part-time programs available. *Faculty:* 12 full-time (0 women). Average age 27. In 1998, 3 master's awarded. *Degree requirements:* For master's, thesis or alternative, comprehensive exam required; for SCCT, comprehensive exam required, foreign language and thesis not required. *Entrance requirements:* For master's, GRE General Test or MAT, appropriate bachelor's degree; for SCCT, GRE General Test or MAT, interview, master's degree. *Application deadline:* For fall admission, 7/1 (priority date); for spring admission, 11/15 (priority date). Applications are processed on a rolling basis. Application fee: $15 ($25 for international students). *Financial aid:* Teaching assistantships available. Aid available to part-time students. Financial aid application deadline: 7/1; financial aid applicants required to submit FAFSA. *Unit head:* Dr. Paul Nave, Chairman, 870-972-3086, Fax: 870-972-3089, E-mail: pnave@navajo.astate.edu.

Auburn University, Graduate School, College of Sciences and Mathematics, Department of Chemistry, Auburn, Auburn University, AL 36849-0002. Offers MACT, MS, PhD. Part-time programs available. *Faculty:* 22 full-time (1 woman). *Students:* 26 full-time (8 women), 41 part-time (12 women); includes 5 minority (4 African Americans, 1 Hispanic American), 37 international. 39 applicants, 62% accepted. In 1998, 3 master's, 6 doctorates awarded. *Degree requirements:* For master's, thesis (MS) required; for doctorate, dissertation, oral and written exams required, foreign language not required. *Entrance requirements:* For master's and doctorate, GRE General Test. *Application deadline:* For fall admission, 9/1; for spring admission, 3/1. Applications are processed on a rolling basis. Application fee: $25 ($50 for international students). Tuition, state resident: full-time $2,760; part-time $76 per credit hour. Tuition, nonresident: full-time $8,280; part-time $228 per credit hour. *Financial aid:* Fellowships, research assistantships, teaching assistantships available. Financial aid application deadline: 3/15. *Unit head:* Dr. J. Howard Hargis, Head, 334-844-4043, Fax: 334-844-4043, E-mail: hargijh@mail.auburn.edu.

Ball State University, Graduate School, College of Sciences and Humanities, Department of Chemistry, Muncie, IN 47306-1099. Offers MA, MS. *Faculty:* 9. *Students:* 3 full-time (2 women), 5 part-time (3 women). Average age 27. 7 applicants, 43% accepted. In 1998, 3 degrees awarded. *Degree requirements:* Foreign language not required. Application fee: $15 ($25 for international students). *Financial aid:* Research assistantships available. *Faculty research:* Synthetic and analytical chemistry, biochemistry, theoretical chemistry. *Unit head:* Dr. Lynn Sousa, Chair, 765-285-8060, E-mail: lsousa@bsu.edu.

Baylor University, Graduate School, College of Arts and Sciences, Department of Chemistry, Waco, TX 76798. Offers MS, PhD. Part-time programs available. *Faculty:* 14 full-time (2 women). *Students:* 8 full-time (4 women), 22 part-time (8 women); includes 1 minority (Asian American or Pacific Islander), 18 international. In 1998, 4 master's awarded. Terminal master's awarded for partial completion of doctoral program. *Degree requirements:* For master's, thesis required, foreign language not required; for doctorate, dissertation, comprehensive exam required, foreign language not required. *Entrance requirements:* For master's and doctorate, GRE General Test, GRE Subject Test, TOEFL (minimum score of 550 required), minimum GPA of 3.0. *Average time to degree:* Master's–3 years full-time. *Application deadline:* For fall admission, 8/1. Applications are processed on a rolling basis. Application fee: $25. *Financial aid:* In 1998–99, 20 students received aid; fellowships, research assistantships, teaching assistantships, Federal Work-Study, institutionally-sponsored loans, and tuition waivers (full) available. Aid available to part-time students. *Unit head:* Dr. Marianna Busch, Chair, 254-710-3311, Fax: 254-710-2403, E-mail: marianna_busch@baylor.edu. *Application contact:* Dr. Carlos Manzanares, Director of Graduate Studies, 254-710-4247, Fax: 254-710-2403, E-mail: carlos_manzanares@baylor.edu.

Boston College, Graduate School of Arts and Sciences, Department of Chemistry, Chestnut Hill, MA 02467-3800. Offers analytical chemistry (MS, PhD); biochemistry (MS, PhD); chemistry (MS); inorganic chemistry (MS, PhD); organic chemistry (MS, PhD); physical chemistry (MS, PhD). Part-time programs available. *Faculty:* 20 full-time (2 women). *Students:* 25 full-time (11 women), 75 part-time (29 women); includes 12 minority (1 African American, 8 Asian Americans or Pacific Islanders, 2 Hispanic Americans, 1 Native American), 28 international. 202 applicants, 28% accepted. In 1998, 10 master's, 4 doctorates awarded. Terminal master's awarded for partial completion of doctoral program. *Degree requirements:* For master's, thesis required; for doctorate, dissertation, qualifying exam required. *Entrance requirements:* For master's and doctorate, GRE General Test, GRE Subject Test. *Application deadline:* For fall admission, 2/1. Application fee: $40. *Financial aid:* Fellowships with full tuition reimbursements, research assistantships with full tuition reimbursements, teaching assistantships with full tuition reimbursements, Federal Work-Study available. Aid available to part-time students. Financial aid application deadline: 3/15; financial aid applicants required to submit FAFSA. *Unit head:* Dr. Larry McLaughlin, Chairperson, 617-552-3605, E-mail: larry.mclaughlin@bc.edu. *Application contact:* Dr. Mary Roberts, Graduate Program Director, 617-552-3616, E-mail: mary.roberts@bc.edu.

See in-depth description on page 93.

Boston University, Graduate School of Arts and Sciences, Department of Chemistry, Boston, MA 02215. Offers biochemistry (MA, PhD); chemical physics (MA, PhD); inorganic chemistry (MA, PhD); organic chemistry (MA, PhD); photochemistry (MA, PhD); physical chemistry (MA, PhD); theoretical chemistry (MA, PhD). *Faculty:* 21 full-time (1 woman). *Students:* 81 full-time (26 women), 1 (woman) part-time; includes 4 minority (2 African Americans, 2 Asian Americans or Pacific Islanders), 58 international. Average age 28. 199 applicants, 37% accepted. In 1998, 13 master's, 12 doctorates awarded. Terminal master's awarded for partial completion of doctoral program. *Degree requirements:* For master's, one foreign language, thesis not required; for doctorate, one foreign language, dissertation, exams required. *Entrance requirements:* For master's and doctorate, GRE General Test, GRE Subject Test (recommended), TOEFL (minimum score of 550 required). *Average time to degree:* Master's–3 years full-time; doctorate–5 years full-time. *Application deadline:* For fall admission, 7/1. Applications are processed on a rolling basis. Application fee: $50. Tuition: Full-time $23,770; part-time $743 per credit. Required fees: $220. Tuition and fees vary according to class time, course level, campus/location and program. *Financial aid:* In 1998–99, 67 students received aid, including 2 fellowships with tuition reimbursements available (averaging $12,500 per year), 18 research assistantships with tuition reimbursements available (averaging $12,500 per year), 43 teaching assistantships with tuition reimbursements available (averaging $12,500 per year); Federal Work-Study, scholarships, and tuition waivers (full) also available. Aid available to part-time students. Financial aid application deadline: 1/15; financial aid applicants required to submit FAFSA. *Unit head:* Thomas D. Tullius, Chairman, 617-353-4277, Fax: 617-353-6466, E-mail: tullius@chem.bu.edu. *Application contact:* Kevin Burgoyne, Academic Administrator, 617-353-2503, Fax: 617-353-6466, E-mail: burgoyne@chem.bu.edu.

Bowling Green State University, Graduate College, College of Arts and Sciences, Center for Photochemical Sciences, Bowling Green, OH 43403. Offers PhD. *Faculty:* 9 full-time (1 woman). *Students:* 34 full-time (14 women), 2 part-time, 32 international. 64 applicants, 22% accepted. In 1998, 9 degrees awarded. *Degree requirements:* For doctorate, dissertation, comprehensive exam required, foreign language not required. *Entrance requirements:* For doctorate, GRE General Test, TOEFL (minimum score of 620 required). *Application deadline:* For fall admission, 1/1 (priority date). Application fee: $30. *Financial aid:* Research assistantships with full tuition reimbursements, teaching assistantships with full tuition reimbursements, Federal Work-Study, tuition waivers (full), and unspecified assistantships available. Financial aid applicants required to submit FAFSA. *Faculty research:* Laser-initiated photopolymerization, spectroscopic and kinetic studies, optoelectronics of semiconductor multiple quantum wells, electron transfer processes, carotenoid pigments. *Unit head:* Dr. Douglas C. Neckers, Executive Director, 419-372-2033. *Application contact:* Patricia Green, Graduate Coordinator, 419-372-2033, E-mail: pgreen@bgnet.bgsu.edu.

Bowling Green State University, Graduate College, College of Arts and Sciences, Department of Chemistry, Bowling Green, OH 43403. Offers chemistry (MAT, MS). Part-time programs available. *Faculty:* 13 full-time (1 woman). *Students:* 14 full-time (7 women); includes 3 minority (2 African Americans, 1 Hispanic American), 5 international. 30 applicants, 33% accepted. In 1998, 7 degrees awarded. *Degree requirements:* For master's, thesis or alternative required, foreign language not required. *Entrance requirements:* For master's, GRE General Test, TOEFL (minimum score of 600 required). *Application deadline:* Applications are processed on a rolling basis. Application fee: $30. Electronic applications accepted. *Financial aid:* Research assistantships with full tuition reimbursements, teaching assistantships with full tuition reimbursements, Federal Work-Study, tuition waivers (full), and unspecified assistantships available. Financial aid applicants required to submit FAFSA. *Faculty research:* Organic, inorganic, physical, and analytical chemistry; biochemistry; surface science. *Unit head:* Dr. Deanne Snavely, Chair, 419-372-2033. *Application contact:* Dr. Tom Kinstle, Graduate Coordinator, 419-372-2658.

Bradley University, Graduate School, College of Liberal Arts and Sciences, Department of Chemistry, Peoria, IL 61625-0002. Offers MS. Part-time and evening/weekend programs available. *Degree requirements:* For master's, thesis, comprehensive exam required, foreign language not required. *Entrance requirements:* For master's, TOEFL (minimum score of 500 required).

Brandeis University, Graduate School of Arts and Sciences, Program in Chemistry, Waltham, MA 02454-9110. Offers inorganic chemistry (MS, PhD); organic chemistry (MS, PhD); physical chemistry (MS, PhD). *Faculty:* 16 full-time (2 women). *Students:* 44 full-time (22 women); includes 1 minority (African American), 26 international. Average age 25. 74 applicants, 39% accepted. In 1998, 4 master's, 4 doctorates awarded (50% entered university research/teaching, 50% found other work related to degree). Terminal master's awarded for partial completion of doctoral program. *Degree requirements:* For master's, 1 year of residency required, foreign language and thesis not required; for doctorate, one foreign language (computer language can substitute), dissertation, 3 years of residency, 2 seminars, qualifying exams required. *Entrance requirements:* For master's and doctorate, GRE General Test. *Application deadline:* For fall admission, 1/15 (priority date). Applications are processed on a rolling basis. Application fee: $60. *Financial aid:* In 1998–99, 44 students received aid, including 17 fellowships (averaging $15,200 per year), 19 research assistantships (averaging $15,200 per year), 8 teaching assistantships (averaging $15,200 per year); institutionally-sponsored loans and scholarships also available. Financial aid application deadline: 4/15; financial aid applicants required to submit CSS PROFILE or FAFSA. *Faculty research:* Oscillating chemical reactions, molecular recognition systems, protein crystallography, synthesis of natural product spectroscopy and magnetic resonance. Total annual research expenditures: $1.1 million. *Unit head:* Dr. I. Y. Chan, Chair, 781-736-2554, Fax: 781-736-2516. *Application contact:* Charlotte Haygazian, Secretary, 781-736-2500, Fax: 781-736-2516, E-mail: chemadm@brandeis.edu.

Brigham Young University, Graduate Studies, College of Physical and Mathematical Sciences, Department of Chemistry and Biochemistry, Provo, UT 84602-1001. Offers analytical chemistry (MS, PhD); biochemistry (MS, PhD); inorganic chemistry (MS, PhD); organic chemistry (MS, PhD); physical chemistry (MS, PhD). *Faculty:* 33 full-time (1 woman), 3 part-time (0 women). *Students:* 70 full-time (24 women); includes 1 minority (Asian American or Pacific Islander), 39 international. Average age 29. 281 applicants, 14% accepted. In 1998, 10 master's awarded (10% entered university research/teaching, 10% found other work related to degree, 70% continued full-time study); 7 doctorates awarded (70% entered university research/teaching, 15% found other work related to degree, 15% continued full-time study). *Degree requirements:* For master's and doctorate, thesis/dissertation required, foreign language not required. *Entrance requirements:* For master's and doctorate, minimum GPA of 3.0 in last 60 hours. *Average time to degree:* Master's–2.3 years full-time; doctorate–4.3 years full-time. *Application deadline:* For fall admission, 2/1 (priority date). Applications are processed on a rolling basis. Application fee: $30. Tuition: Full-time $3,330; part-time $185 per credit hour. Tuition and fees vary according to program and student's religious affiliation. *Financial aid:* In 1998–99, 70 students received aid, including 10 fellowships, 28 research assistantships, 32 teaching assistantships; institutionally-sponsored loans, scholarships, and tuition waivers (full) also available. Financial aid application deadline: 2/1. *Faculty research:* Separation science, molecular recognition, organic synthesis and biomedical application, biochemistry and molecular biology, molecular spectroscopy. Total annual research expenditures: $3.6 million. *Unit head:* Dr. Francis R. Nordmeyer, Chair, 801-378-3667, Fax: 801-378-5474, E-mail: fran_nordmeyer@byu.edu. *Application contact:* N. Kent Dalley, Coordinator, Graduate Admissions, 801-378-3434, Fax: 801-378-5474, E-mail: chemgrad@byu.edu.

See in-depth description on page 97.

Brock University, Graduate Studies and Research, Faculty of Mathematics and Science, Department of Chemistry, St. Catharines, ON L2S 3A1, Canada. Offers M Sc. Part-time programs available. *Faculty:* 11 full-time (1 woman), 1 part-time (0 women). *Students:* 12 full-time (4 women), 5 international. Average age 24. 65 applicants, 18% accepted. In 1998, 5 degrees awarded. *Degree requirements:* For master's, thesis required, foreign language not required. *Entrance requirements:* For master's, TOEFL (minimum score of 550 required), honors B Sc in chemistry. *Average time to degree:* Master's–2 years full-time, 4 years part-time. *Application deadline:* For fall admission, 3/1 (priority date). Applications are processed on a rolling basis. Application fee: $35. *Financial aid:* Fellowships, research assistantships, teaching assistantships, career-related internships or fieldwork, grants, scholarships, and unspecified assistantships available. Aid available to part-time students. *Faculty research:* Inorganic, organic, analytical, theoretical, and physical chemistry. *Unit head:* Dr. Jack Miller, Chair, 905-688-5550 Ext. 3400, Fax: 905-688-9020, E-mail: jmiller@cosc.ac.brocku.ca. *Application contact:* Dr. Herbert Holland, Graduate Officer, 905-688-5550 Ext. 3403, Fax: 905-682-9020, E-mail: holland@chemiris.labs.brocku. ca.

Brooklyn College of the City University of New York, Division of Graduate Studies, Department of Chemistry, Brooklyn, NY 11210-2889. Offers applied chemistry (MA); chemistry (MA, PhD). Part-time programs available. *Faculty:* 3 full-time (0 women). In 1998, 2 degrees awarded. *Degree requirements:* For master's, one foreign language (computer language can substitute), thesis or alternative required. *Entrance requirements:* For master's, TOEFL (minimum score of 500 required). *Application deadline:* For fall admission, 3/1; for spring admission, 11/1. Application fee: $40. *Financial aid:* Federal Work-Study, institutionally-sponsored loans, and scholarships available. Aid available to part-time students. Financial aid application deadline: 5/1; financial aid applicants required to submit FAFSA. *Unit head:* Dr. Dominick Labianca, Chairperson, 718-951-5458. *Application contact:* Dr. Darryl G. Howery, Graduate Deputy, 718-951-5458.

Brown University, Graduate School, Department of Chemistry, Providence, RI 02912. Offers biochemistry (PhD); chemistry (Sc M, PhD). *Degree requirements:* For master's, thesis required, foreign language not required; for doctorate, dissertation, cumulative exam required.

Bryn Mawr College, Graduate School of Arts and Sciences, Department of Chemistry, Bryn Mawr, PA 19010-2899. Offers biochemistry (MA, PhD); chemistry (MA, PhD). *Faculty:* 10. *Students:* 4 full-time (1 woman), 6 part-time (2 women), 3 international. 12 applicants, 75% accepted. In 1998, 3 master's awarded. *Degree requirements:* For master's, thesis required; for doctorate, dissertation required. *Entrance requirements:* For master's and doctorate, GRE General Test, GRE Subject Test. *Application deadline:* For fall admission, 6/30; for spring admission, 12/7. Application fee: $40. *Financial aid:* In 1998–99, 1 research assistantship, 7 teaching assistantships were awarded.; fellowships, Federal Work-Study and institutionally-sponsored loans also available. Aid available to part-time students. Financial aid application deadline: 1/2. *Unit head:* Dr. Sharon Burgmayer, Chairman, 610-526-5104. *Application contact:* Graduate School of Arts and Sciences, 610-526-5072.

Bucknell University, Graduate Studies, College of Arts and Sciences, Department of Chemistry, Lewisburg, PA 17837. Offers MA, MS. *Faculty:* 11 full-time. *Students:* 6 (1 woman). *Degree requirements:* For master's, thesis required, foreign language not required. *Entrance requirements:* For master's, GRE General Test (minimum combined score of 1000 required), GRE Subject Test, TOEFL (minimum score of 550 required), minimum GPA of 2.8. *Application deadline:* For fall admission, 6/1 (priority date); for spring admission, 12/1 (priority date). Applications are processed on a rolling basis. Application fee: $25. Tuition: Part-time $2,600 per course. Tuition and fees vary according to course load. *Financial aid:* Unspecified assistantships available. Financial aid application deadline: 3/1. *Unit head:* Dr. Charles Clapp, Head, 570-577-3258.

Butler University, College of Liberal Arts and Sciences, Department of Chemistry, Indianapolis, IN 46208-3485. Offers MS. Part-time and evening/weekend programs available. *Faculty:* 6 full-time (2 women), 1 part-time (0 women). In 1998, 3 degrees awarded. *Degree requirements:* For master's, thesis required (for some programs), foreign language not required. *Application deadline:* For fall admission, 8/15 (priority date). Applications are processed on a rolling basis. Application fee: $25. *Financial aid:* Career-related internships or fieldwork available. Financial aid applicants required to submit FAFSA. *Unit head:* Dr. Joseph Kirsch, Head, 317-940-9400.

California Institute of Technology, Division of Chemistry and Chemical Engineering, Department of Chemistry, Pasadena, CA 91125-0001. Offers PhD. *Degree requirements:* For doctorate, dissertation required, foreign language not required. *Faculty research:* Genetic structure and gene expression, organic synthesis, reagents and mechanisms, homogeneous and electrochemical catalysis.

California State Polytechnic University, Pomona, Graduate Studies, College of Science, Program in Chemistry, Pomona, CA 91768-2557. Offers MS. Part-time programs available. *Students:* 3 full-time (1 woman), 20 part-time (10 women); includes 11 minority (1 African American, 8 Asian Americans or Pacific Islanders, 2 Hispanic Americans), 5 international. Average age 28. 19 applicants, 74% accepted. In 1998, 3 degrees awarded. *Degree requirements:* For master's, thesis required, thesis required. *Entrance requirements:* For master's, GRE General Test. *Application deadline:* Applications are processed on a rolling basis. Application fee: $55. Tuition, nonresident: part-time $164 per unit. *Financial aid:* In 1998–99, 6 students received aid. Career-related internships or fieldwork, Federal Work-Study, and institutionally-sponsored loans available. Aid available to part-time students. Financial aid application deadline: 3/2; financial aid applicants required to submit FAFSA. *Unit head:* Dr. Michael L. Keith, Coordinator, 909-869-3662, E-mail: mlkeith@csupomona.edu.

California State University, Fresno, Division of Graduate Studies, School of Natural Sciences, Department of Chemistry, Fresno, CA 93740-0057. Offers MS. Part-time programs available. *Faculty:* 18 full-time (2 women). *Students:* 8 full-time (1 woman), 12 part-time (6 women); includes 7 minority (6 Asian Americans or Pacific Islanders, 1 Hispanic American), 3 international. Average age 31. 16 applicants, 81% accepted. In 1998, 2 degrees awarded. *Degree requirements:* For master's, thesis or alternative required, foreign language not required. *Entrance requirements:* For master's, GRE General Test, TOEFL (minimum score of 550 required), minimum GPA of 2.5. *Average time to degree:* Master's–3.5 years full-time. *Application deadline:* For fall admission, 8/1 (priority date); for spring admission, 12/1. Applications are processed on a rolling basis. Application fee: $55. Electronic applications accepted. Tuition, nonresident: part-time $246 per unit. Required fees: $1,906; $620 per semester. *Financial aid:* In 1998–99, 1 research assistantship, 16 teaching assistantships were awarded.; fellowships, career-related internships or fieldwork, Federal Work-Study, scholarships, and unspecified assistantships also available. Financial aid application deadline: 3/1; financial aid applicants required to submit FAFSA. *Faculty research:* Genetics, viticulture, DNA, soils, molecular modeling. *Unit head:* Dr. Joseph Gandler, Chair, 559-278-2103, Fax: 559-278-7139, E-mail: joseph_gandler@csufresno.edu. *Application contact:* Dr. Ronald Marhenke, Graduate Coordinator, 559-278-2103, Fax: 559-278-7139, E-mail: ronald_marhenke@csufresno.edu.

California State University, Fullerton, Graduate Studies, School of Natural Science and Mathematics, Department of Chemistry and Biochemistry, Fullerton, CA 92834-9480. Offers analytical chemistry (MS); biochemistry (MS); geochemistry (MS); inorganic chemistry (MS); organic chemistry (MS); physical chemistry (MS). Part-time programs available. *Faculty:* 18 full-time, 14 part-time. *Students:* 8 full-time (3 women), 32 part-time (14 women); includes 19 minority (14 Asian Americans or Pacific Islanders, 5 Hispanic Americans), 6 international. Average age 28. 38 applicants, 74% accepted. In 1998, 9 degrees awarded. *Degree requirements:* For master's, thesis, departmental qualifying exam required, foreign language not required. *Entrance requirements:* For master's, minimum GPA of 2.5 in last 60 units, major in chemistry or related field. Application fee: $55. Tuition, nonresident: part-time $264 per unit. *Financial aid:* Teaching assistantships, career-related internships or fieldwork, Federal Work-Study, grants, and institutionally-sponsored loans available. Aid available to part-time students. Financial aid application deadline: 3/1. *Unit head:* Dr. Bruce Weber, Chair, 714-278-3621. *Application contact:* Dr. Gregory Williams, Adviser, 714-278-2170.

Chemistry

California State University, Hayward, Graduate Programs, School of Science, Department of Chemistry, Hayward, CA 94542-3000. Offers biochemistry (MS); chemistry (MS). *Faculty:* 11 full-time (2 women). *Students:* 3 full-time (all women), 12 part-time (5 women); includes 10 minority (2 African Americans, 7 Asian Americans or Pacific Islanders, 1 Hispanic American), 1 international. 9 applicants, 100% accepted. In 1998, 7 degrees awarded. *Degree requirements:* For master's, comprehensive exam or thesis required. *Entrance requirements:* For master's, minimum GPA of 2.5 in field during previous 2 years. Application fee: $55. Tuition, nonresident: part-time $164 per unit. Required fees: $587 per quarter. *Financial aid:* Career-related internships or fieldwork, Federal Work-Study, and institutionally-sponsored loans available. Aid available to part-time students. Financial aid application deadline: 3/1. *Unit head:* Dr. Leroy Chauffe, Chair, 510-885-3452. *Application contact:* Jennifer Rice, Graduate Program Assistant, 510-885-3286, Fax: 510-885-4795, E-mail: gradprograms@csuhayward.edu.

California State University, Long Beach, Graduate Studies, College of Natural Sciences, Department of Chemistry and Biochemistry, Long Beach, CA 90840. Offers biochemistry (MS); chemistry (MS). Part-time programs available. *Students:* 8 full-time (1 woman), 12 part-time (4 women); includes 9 minority (all Asian Americans or Pacific Islanders), 2 international. Average age 29. 42 applicants, 26% accepted. In 1998, 5 degrees awarded. *Degree requirements:* For master's, thesis, departmental qualifying exam required, foreign language not required. *Application deadline:* For fall admission, 8/1; for spring admission, 12/1. Applications are processed on a rolling basis. Application fee: $55. Electronic applications accepted. Tuition, nonresident: part-time $246 per unit. Required fees: $569 per semester. Tuition and fees vary according to course load. *Financial aid:* Research assistantships, teaching assistantships, Federal Work-Study, grants, institutionally-sponsored loans, and unspecified assistantships available. Financial aid application deadline: 3/2. *Faculty research:* Enzymology, organic synthesis, molecular modeling, environmental chemistry, reaction kinetics. *Unit head:* Dr. Nail Senozan, Chair, 562-985-4941, Fax: 562-985-2315. *Application contact:* Dr. Henry Po, Graduate Coordinator, 562-985-4953, Fax: 562-985-2315, E-mail: hpo@csulb.edu.

California State University, Los Angeles, Graduate Studies, School of Natural and Social Sciences, Department of Chemistry and Biochemistry, Major in Chemistry, Los Angeles, CA 90032-8530. Offers MS. *Students:* 11 full-time (6 women), 11 part-time (4 women); includes 15 minority (1 African American, 11 Asian Americans or Pacific Islanders, 3 Hispanic Americans), 2 international. In 1998, 7 degrees awarded. *Degree requirements:* For master's, one foreign language (computer language can substitute), comprehensive exam or thesis required. *Entrance requirements:* For master's, TOEFL (minimum score of 550 required). *Application deadline:* For fall admission, 6/30; for spring admission, 2/1. Applications are processed on a rolling basis. Application fee: $55. *Financial aid:* In 1998–99, 10 students received aid. Application deadline: 3/1. *Faculty research:* Transition-metal chemistry, electrochemistry, chromatography, computer modeling of reactions. *Unit head:* Dr. Scott Grover, Acting Chair, Department of Chemistry and Biochemistry, 323-343-2300.

California State University, Northridge, Graduate Studies, College of Science and Mathematics, Department of Chemistry, Northridge, CA 91330. Offers MS. *Faculty:* 29 full-time, 8 part-time. *Students:* 4 full-time (all women), 15 part-time (7 women); includes 6 minority (5 Asian Americans or Pacific Islanders, 1 Hispanic American), 5 international. Average age 31. 28 applicants, 68% accepted. In 1998, 1 degree awarded. *Degree requirements:* For master's, thesis required, foreign language not required. *Entrance requirements:* For master's, TOEFL, GRE General Test or minimum GPA of 2.5. *Application deadline:* For fall admission, 11/30. Application fee: $55. Tuition, nonresident: part-time $246 per unit. International tuition: $7,874 full-time. Required fees: $1,970. Tuition and fees vary according to course load. *Financial aid:* Teaching assistantships available. Aid available to part-time students. Financial aid application deadline: 3/1. *Unit head:* Dr. Sandor Reichman, Chair, 818-677-3381. *Application contact:* Dr. Francis L. Harris, Graduate Coordinator, 818-677-3371.

California State University, Sacramento, Graduate Studies, School of Natural Sciences and Mathematics, Department of Chemistry, Sacramento, CA 95819-6048. Offers MS. Part-time programs available. *Degree requirements:* For master's, thesis or alternative, departmental qualifying exam, writing proficiency exam required, foreign language not required. *Entrance requirements:* For master's, TOEFL (minimum score of 550 required), minimum GPA of 2.5 during previous 2 years, BA in chemistry or equivalent. *Application deadline:* For fall admission, 4/15; for spring admission, 11/1. Application fee: $55. *Financial aid:* Career-related internships or fieldwork and Federal Work-Study available. Aid available to part-time students. Financial aid application deadline: 3/1. *Unit head:* Dr. James Hill, Chair, 916-278-6684.

Carleton University, Faculty of Graduate Studies, Faculty of Science, Department of Chemistry, Ottawa, ON K1S 5B6, Canada. Offers M Sc, PhD. *Faculty:* 14 full-time (1 woman). *Students:* 39 full-time (14 women), 1 (woman) part-time. Average age 28. In 1998, 3 master's, 7 doctorates awarded. *Degree requirements:* For master's, thesis required; for doctorate, dissertation, comprehensive exam required. *Entrance requirements:* For master's, TOEFL (minimum score of 550 required), honors degree; for doctorate, TOEFL (minimum score of 550 required), M Sc. *Average time to degree:* Master's–2 years full-time; doctorate–3.9 years full-time. *Application deadline:* For fall admission, 3/1 (priority date). Applications are processed on a rolling basis. Application fee: $35. *Financial aid:* Application deadline: 3/1. *Faculty research:* Bioorganic chemistry, analytical toxicology, theoretical and physical chemistry, inorganic chemistry. Total annual research expenditures: $926,000. *Unit head:* R. J. Crutchley, Associate Director, 613-520-2600 Ext. 3848, Fax: 613-520-3749, E-mail: robert_crutchley@carleton.ca.

Carnegie Mellon University, Mellon College of Science, Department of Chemistry, Pittsburgh, PA 15213-3891. Offers chemical instrumentation (MS); chemistry (MS, PhD); colloids, polymers and surfaces (MS); polymer science (MS). Part-time programs available. *Faculty:* 40 full-time (7 women), 1 part-time (0 women). *Students:* 58 full-time (22 women), 3 part-time; includes 1 minority (Asian American or Pacific Islander), 29 international. Average age 27. In 1998, 6 master's, 4 doctorates awarded. Terminal master's awarded for partial completion of doctoral program. *Degree requirements:* For doctorate, dissertation, departmental qualifying and oral exams, teaching experience required, foreign language not required, foreign language not required. *Entrance requirements:* For master's, GRE General Test; for doctorate, GRE General Test, GRE Subject Test, TOEFL. *Average time to degree:* Master's–2 years full-time; doctorate–6 years full-time. *Application deadline:* For fall admission, 1/15 (priority date). Applications are processed on a rolling basis. Application fee: $0. Electronic applications accepted. *Financial aid:* In 1998–99, 1 fellowship, 20 research assistantships, 34 teaching assistantships were awarded. *Faculty research:* Physical and theoretical chemistry, chemical synthesis, biophysical/bioinorganic chemistry. Total annual research expenditures: $2.7 million. *Unit head:* Krzystof Matyjaszewski, Head, 412-268-3209. *Application contact:* Valerie Bridge, Student Specialist, 412-268-3150, Fax: 412-268-1061, E-mail: vbog@andrew.cmu.edu.

See in-depth description on page 101.

Case Western Reserve University, School of Graduate Studies, Department of Chemistry, Cleveland, OH 44106. Offers analytical chemistry (MS, PhD); inorganic chemistry (MS, PhD); organic chemistry (MS, PhD); physical chemistry (MS, PhD). Part-time programs available. Terminal master's awarded for partial completion of doctoral program. *Degree requirements:* For master's, thesis not required; for doctorate, dissertation required. *Entrance requirements:* For master's and doctorate, GRE General Test, GRE Subject Test, TOEFL (minimum score of 550 required). *Faculty research:* Electrochemistry, synthetic chemistry, chemistry of life process, spectroscopy, kinetics.

The Catholic University of America, School of Arts and Sciences, Department of Chemistry, Washington, DC 20064. Offers MS, PhD. Part-time programs available. *Faculty:* 8 full-time (3 women), 2 part-time (both women). *Students:* 3 full-time (1 woman), 15 part-time (6 women); includes 1 minority (African American), 15 international. Average age 33. 79 applicants, 57% accepted. In 1998, 4 master's, 1 doctorate awarded. Terminal master's awarded for partial completion of doctoral program. *Degree requirements:* For master's, one foreign language (computer language can substitute), thesis or alternative, comprehensive exam required; for doctorate, one foreign language (computer language can substitute), dissertation, comprehensive exam required. *Entrance requirements:* For master's, GRE General Test, GRE Subject Test, TOEFL; for doctorate, GRE General Test, GRE Subject Test. *Application deadline:* For fall admission, 8/1 (priority date); for spring admission, 12/1. Applications are processed on a rolling basis. Application fee: $50. *Financial aid:* Fellowships, research assistantships, teaching assistantships, career-related internships or fieldwork, Federal Work-Study, institutionally-sponsored loans, scholarships, and tuition waivers (full and partial) available. Aid available to part-time students. Financial aid application deadline: 2/1. *Faculty research:* Theoretical chemistry; bioinorganic chemistry; chemical kinetics; synthetic organic chemistry; inorganic, bioorganic, and physical organic chemistry. Total annual research expenditures: $610,617. *Unit head:* Dr. Greg Brewer, Chair, 202-319-5385. *Application contact:* Dr. Ying Nan Chiu, Graduate Admissions Chairman, 202-319-5399, Fax: 202-319-5381.

Central Connecticut State University, School of Graduate Studies, School of Arts and Sciences, Department of Chemistry, New Britain, CT 06050-4010. Offers MS. Part-time and evening/weekend programs available. *Faculty:* 7 full-time (0 women), 5 part-time (1 woman). *Students:* 1 (woman) full-time. Average age 37. 13 applicants, 8% accepted. *Degree requirements:* For master's, thesis or alternative, comprehensive exam required, foreign language not required. *Entrance requirements:* For master's, TOEFL (minimum score of 550 required), minimum GPA of 2.7. *Application deadline:* For fall admission, 6/1 (priority date); for spring admission, 12/1. Applications are processed on a rolling basis. Application fee: $40. *Financial aid:* In 1998–99, 1 research assistantship (averaging $4,800 per year) was awarded.; teaching assistantships, Federal Work-Study also available. Financial aid application deadline: 3/15; financial aid applicants required to submit FAFSA. *Unit head:* Dr. John Mantzaris, Chair, 860-832-2681.

Central Michigan University, College of Graduate Studies, College of Science and Technology, Department of Chemistry, Mount Pleasant, MI 48859. Offers chemistry (MS); teaching chemistry (MA). *Accreditation:* NCATE (one or more programs are accredited). *Faculty:* 25 full-time (2 women). *Students:* 6 full-time (3 women), 16 part-time (9 women); includes 4 minority (2 African Americans, 1 Asian American or Pacific Islander, 1 Hispanic American), 7 international. Average age 28. In 1998, 9 degrees awarded. *Degree requirements:* For master's, thesis or alternative required, foreign language not required. *Application deadline:* Applications are processed on a rolling basis. Application fee: $30. Tuition, state resident: part-time $144 per credit hour. Tuition, nonresident: part-time $285 per credit hour. Required fees: $240 per semester. Tuition and fees vary according to degree level and program. *Financial aid:* In 1998–99, 5 research assistantships with tuition reimbursements, 9 teaching assistantships with tuition reimbursements were awarded.; fellowships with tuition reimbursements, career-related internships or fieldwork and Federal Work-Study also available. Financial aid application deadline: 3/7. *Faculty research:* Biochemistry, analytical and organic-inorganic chemistry, polymer chemistry. *Unit head:* Dr. Karl Lindfors, Chairperson, 517-774-3981, Fax: 517-774-7106, E-mail: karl.r.lindfors@cmich.edu.

Central Washington University, Graduate Studies and Research, College of the Sciences, Department of Chemistry, Ellensburg, WA 98926. Offers MS. *Faculty:* 8 full-time (3 women). *Students:* 1 full-time (0 women), 1 (woman) part-time, 1 international. 3 applicants, 67% accepted. *Degree requirements:* For master's, thesis required. *Entrance requirements:* For master's, GRE General Test, GRE Subject Test, minimum GPA of 3.0. *Application deadline:* For fall admission, 4/1; for winter admission, 10/1; for spring admission, 1/1. Applications are processed on a rolling basis. Application fee: $35. Tuition, state resident: full-time $4,389; part-time $146 per credit. Tuition, nonresident: full-time $13,365; part-time $446 per credit. Tuition and fees vary according to course load. *Financial aid:* In 1998–99, 1 teaching assistantship with partial tuition reimbursement (averaging $6,470 per year) was awarded.; research assistantships, career-related internships or fieldwork and Federal Work-Study also available. Financial aid application deadline: 2/15; financial aid applicants required to submit FAFSA. *Unit head:* Dr. Joanne DeLuca, Chair, 509-963-2811, Fax: 509-963-1050. *Application contact:* Christie A. Fevergeon, Program Coordinator, Graduate Studies and Research, 509-963-3103, Fax: 509-963-1799, E-mail: masters@cwu.edu.

City College of the City University of New York, Graduate School, College of Liberal Arts and Science, Division of Science, Department of Chemistry, Program in Chemistry, New York, NY 10031-9198. Offers MA, PhD. PhD offered through the Graduate School and University Center of the City University of New York. Terminal master's awarded for partial completion of doctoral program. *Degree requirements:* For master's, foreign language and thesis not required; for doctorate, one foreign language, dissertation required. *Entrance requirements:* For master's, TOEFL (minimum score of 500 required); for doctorate, GRE, TOEFL. *Faculty research:* Laser spectroscopy, bioorganic chemistry, polymer chemistry and crystallography, electroanalytical chemistry, ESR of metal clusters.

Clark Atlanta University, School of Arts and Sciences, Department of Chemistry, Atlanta, GA 30314. Offers inorganic chemistry (MS, PhD); organic chemistry (MS, PhD); physical chemistry (MS, PhD); science education (DA). Part-time programs available. *Students:* 17 full-time (11 women), 20 part-time (11 women); includes 33 minority (28 African Americans, 2 Asian Americans or Pacific Islanders, 3 Hispanic Americans), 3 international. In 1998, 11 master's, 1 doctorate awarded. *Degree requirements:* For master's, one foreign language (computer language can substitute), thesis, comprehensive exam required; for doctorate, 2 foreign languages (computer language can substitute for one), dissertation, cumulative exam required. *Entrance requirements:* For master's, GRE General Test, minimum GPA of 2.5; for doctorate, GRE General Test, GRE Subject Test, minimum graduate GPA of 3.0. *Application deadline:* For fall admission, 4/1; for spring admission, 11/1. Applications are processed on a rolling basis. Application fee: $40. *Financial aid:* Fellowships, research assistantships, career-related internships or fieldwork available. Financial aid application deadline: 4/30. *Unit head:* Dr. Reynold Verrett, Chairperson, 404-880-8154. *Application contact:* Michelle Clark-Davis, Graduate Program Assistant, 404-880-8709.

Clarkson University, Graduate School, School of Science, Department of Chemistry, Potsdam, NY 13699. Offers analytical chemistry (MS, PhD); inorganic chemistry (MS, PhD); organic chemistry (MS, PhD); physical chemistry (MS, PhD). *Faculty:* 9 full-time (0 women). *Students:* 25 full-time (13 women); includes 1 minority (African American), 15 international. Average age 24. 109 applicants, 28% accepted. In 1998, 2 master's, 10 doctorates awarded. *Degree requirements:* For master's, foreign language and thesis not required; for doctorate, dissertation, departmental qualifying exam required, foreign language not required. *Entrance requirements:* For master's, GRE, TOEFL. *Application deadline:* For fall admission, 5/15 (priority date); for spring admission, 10/15 (priority date). Applications are processed on a rolling basis. Application fee: $25 ($35 for international students). Tuition: Part-time $661 per credit hour. Required fees: $215 per semester. *Financial aid:* In 1998–99, 7 research assistantships, 14 teaching assistantships were awarded.; fellowships *Faculty research:* Particle adhesion phenomena, airborne radon, ceramic materials, materials processing, chemical kinetics. Total annual research expenditures: $708,831. *Unit head:* Dr. Stig Friberg, Chair, 315-268-6500, Fax: 315-268-6610, E-mail: fbg@clarkson.edu.

Clark University, Graduate School, Department of Chemistry, Worcester, MA 01610-1477. Offers MA, PhD. *Students:* 20 (9 women). 46 applicants, 30% accepted. In 1998, 6 master's, 2 doctorates awarded. Terminal master's awarded for partial completion of doctoral program. *Degree requirements:* For master's, thesis or alternative required, foreign language not required; for doctorate, dissertation required. *Entrance requirements:* For master's and doctorate, GRE General Test, TOEFL (minimum score of 575 required). *Application deadline:* For fall admission, 2/15 (priority date). Applications are processed on a rolling basis. Application fee: $40. *Financial aid:* Research assistantships, teaching assistantships available. *Faculty research:* Nuclear chemistry, molecular biology. *Unit head:* Dr. Alan Jones, Chair, 508-793-7116.

See in-depth description on page 105.

Clemson University, Graduate School, College of Engineering and Science, Department of Chemistry, Clemson, SC 29634. Offers MS, PhD. *Students:* 67 full-time (20 women), 5 part-time (1 woman); includes 3 minority (2 African Americans, 1 Asian American or Pacific Islander), 28 international. Average age 25. 88 applicants, 28% accepted. In 1998, 6 master's, 10 doctorates awarded. *Degree requirements:* For master's and doctorate, one foreign language (computer language can substitute), thesis/dissertation required. *Entrance requirements:* For master's and doctorate, GRE General Test, TOEFL. *Application deadline:* For fall admission, 6/1. Application fee: $35. *Financial aid:* Fellowships, research assistantships, teaching assistantships, unspecified assistantships available. Financial aid applicants required to submit FAFSA. *Faculty research:* Fluorine chemistry, organic synthetic methods and natural products, metal and non-metal clusters, analytical spectroscopies, polymers. *Unit head:* Dr. Adolf Beyerlein, Chair, 864-656-3065, Fax: 864-656-6613, E-mail: albrl@clemson.edu. *Application contact:* Dr. D. D. Des Marteau, Graduate Coordinator, 864-656-4705, Fax: 864-656-6613, E-mail: flourin@clemson.edu.

Cleveland State University, College of Graduate Studies, College of Arts and Sciences, Department of Chemistry, Cleveland, OH 44115-2440. Offers analytical chemistry (MS, PhD); clinical chemistry (MS, PhD); inorganic chemistry (MS); organic chemistry (MS); physical chemistry (MS); structural analysis (MS, PhD). Part-time and evening/weekend programs available. *Faculty:* 13 full-time (1 woman). *Students:* 1 full-time (0 women), 53 part-time (22 women); includes 5 minority (1 African American, 3 Asian Americans or Pacific Islanders, 1 Hispanic American), 25 international. Average age 33. 23 applicants, 61% accepted. In 1998, 11 master's, 7 doctorates awarded. *Degree requirements:* For master's, thesis required (for some programs), foreign language not required; for doctorate, dissertation required, foreign language not required. *Entrance requirements:* For master's and doctorate, GRE General Test, GRE Subject Test, TOEFL (minimum score of 525 required). *Application deadline:* For fall admission, 7/15 (priority date). Applications are processed on a rolling basis. Application fee: $25. *Financial aid:* In 1998–99, 1 fellowship, 1 research assistantship, 25 teaching assistantships were awarded.; Federal Work-Study and unspecified assistantships also available. *Faculty research:* Trace metal analysis in biological systems, application of HPLC/LPCC to clinical systems, synthetic organic and inorganic chemistry, molecular structure determinations. *Unit head:* Dr. Stan Duraj, Interim Chair, 216-523-7312, Fax: 216-687-9298.

College of Staten Island of the City University of New York, Graduate Programs, Program in Polymer Chemistry, Staten Island, NY 10314-6600. Offers PhD. *Faculty:* 6 full-time (1 woman). *Students:* 14 full-time (3 women), (all international). 12 applicants, 25% accepted. In 1998, 3 degrees awarded (100% found work related to degree). *Degree requirements:* For doctorate, one foreign language, dissertation required. *Entrance requirements:* For doctorate, GRE. *Average time to degree:* Doctorate–5 years full-time. *Application deadline:* For fall admission, 12/1 (priority date). Applications are processed on a rolling basis. Application fee: $40. Tuition, state resident: full-time $4,350; part-time $185 per credit. Tuition, nonresident: full-time $7,600; part-time $320 per credit. Required fees: $53; $27 per term. *Financial aid:* In 1998–99, 2 fellowships with partial tuition reimbursements (averaging $15,000 per year), 2 research assistantships with partial tuition reimbursements (averaging $15,000 per year), 10 teaching assistantships with partial tuition reimbursements (averaging $15,000 per year) were awarded.; tuition waivers (partial) also available. *Faculty research:* Polymer synthesis, characterization, and properties. *Unit head:* Dr. George Odian, Coordinator, 718-982-3895, Fax: 718-982-3910, E-mail: odian@postbox.csi.cuny.edu.

College of William and Mary, Faculty of Arts and Sciences, Department of Chemistry, Williamsburg, VA 23187-8795. Offers MA, MS. *Faculty:* 16 full-time (3 women), 1 (woman) part-time. *Students:* 7 full-time (2 women); includes 2 minority (both Asian Americans or Pacific Islanders), 1 international. Average age 22. 34 applicants, 21% accepted. In 1998, 9 degrees awarded. *Degree requirements:* For master's, thesis, comprehensive exam required, foreign language not required. *Entrance requirements:* For master's, GRE General Test (minimum combined score of 1200 on three sections required; average 1600), minimum GPA of 2.5. *Average time to degree:* Master's–1.3 years full-time, 3 years part-time. *Application deadline:* For fall admission, 5/1 (priority date). Applications are processed on a rolling basis. Application fee: $30. *Financial aid:* In 1998–99, teaching assistantships with tuition reimbursements (averaging $9,300 per year) Financial aid application deadline: 5/1; financial aid applicants required to submit FAFSA. *Faculty research:* Organic, inorganic, physical, and analytic chemistry; biochemistry. Total annual research expenditures: $300,000. *Unit head:* Dr. Richard L. Kiefer, Chair, 757-221-2540. *Application contact:* Dr. Christopher Abelt, Graduate Director, 757-221-2551.

Colorado School of Mines, Graduate School, Department of Chemistry and Geochemistry, Program in Chemistry, Golden, CO 80401-1887. Offers MS, PhD. Part-time programs available. *Students:* 17 full-time (5 women), 10 part-time (2 women); includes 4 minority (2 Asian Americans or Pacific Islanders, 2 Hispanic Americans), 5 international. In 1998, 2 doctorates awarded (100% found work related to degree). *Degree requirements:* For master's, thesis required, foreign language not required; for doctorate, dissertation, comprehensive exam required, foreign language not required. *Entrance requirements:* For master's and doctorate, GRE General Test, minimum GPA of 3.0. *Application deadline:* Applications are processed on a rolling basis. Application fee: $40. *Financial aid:* In 1998–99, 27 students received aid, including 1 fellowship, 9 research assistantships, 10 teaching assistantships; unspecified assistantships also available. Aid available to part-time students. Financial aid applicants required to submit FAFSA. *Application contact:* Pat MacCarthy, Professor, 303-273-3629, Fax: 303-273-3629, E-mail: pmaccart@mines.edu.

Colorado State University, Graduate School, College of Natural Sciences, Department of Chemistry, Fort Collins, CO 80523-0015. Offers MS, PhD. Part-time programs available. *Faculty:* 27 full-time (4 women). *Students:* 59 full-time (18 women), 48 part-time (12 women); includes 5 minority (4 Asian Americans or Pacific Islanders, 1 Hispanic American), 10 international. Average age 31. 201 applicants, 16% accepted. In 1998, 7 master's, 20 doctorates awarded. Terminal master's awarded for partial completion of doctoral program. *Degree requirements:* For master's and doctorate, thesis/dissertation required, foreign language not required. *Entrance requirements:* For master's and doctorate, GRE General Test, GRE Subject Test, TOEFL, minimum GPA of 3.0. *Application deadline:* For fall admission, 2/1 (priority date); for spring admission, 9/15. Applications are processed on a rolling basis. Application fee: $30. Electronic applications accepted. *Financial aid:* In 1998–99, 2 fellowships, 61 research assistantships, 29 teaching assistantships were awarded.; traineeships also available. *Faculty research:* Synthetic organic chemistry, organometallic electrochemistry, spectroscopy, inorganic chemistry, materials chemistry. Total annual research expenditures: $6 million. *Unit head:* Oren P. Anderson, Chairman, 970-491-5391, Fax: 970-491-1801. *Application contact:* Louis Hegedus, Chairman, Graduate Admissions Committee, 970-491-6376, Fax: 970-491-1801, E-mail: bjwilson@lamar.colostate.edu.

Columbia University, Graduate School of Arts and Sciences, Division of Natural Sciences, Department of Chemistry, New York, NY 10027. Offers chemical physics (M Phil, PhD); inorganic chemistry (M Phil, MS, PhD); organic chemistry (M Phil, MS, PhD). *Degree requirements:* For master's, comprehensive exams (MS); 1 foreign language, teaching experience, oral and written exams (M Phil) required, thesis not required; for doctorate, one foreign language, dissertation, M Phil required. *Entrance requirements:* For master's and doctorate, GRE General Test, GRE Subject Test, TOEFL. *Faculty research:* Biophysics.

Concordia University, School of Graduate Studies, Faculty of Arts and Science, Department of Chemistry and Biochemistry, Montréal, PQ H3G 1M8, Canada. Offers chemistry (M Sc, PhD). *Students:* 47 full-time (24 women), 6 part-time. *Degree requirements:* For master's and doctorate, thesis/dissertation required. *Entrance requirements:* For master's, honors degree in chemistry; for doctorate, M Sc in biochemistry, biology, or chemistry. *Application deadline:* For fall admission, 3/31 (priority date). Application fee: $50. *Financial aid:* Teaching assistantships available. *Faculty research:* Bioanalytical, bio-organic, and inorganic chemistry; materi-

als and solid-state chemistry. *Unit head:* Dr. J. A. Capobianco, Chair, 514-848-3355, Fax: 514-848-2868. *Application contact:* Dr. Ann English, Director, 514-848-3356, Fax: 514-848-2868.

Cornell University, Graduate School, Graduate Fields of Arts and Sciences, Field of Chemistry, Ithaca, NY 14853-0001. Offers analytical chemistry (PhD); bio-organic chemistry (PhD); biophysical chemistry (PhD); chemical physics (PhD); inorganic chemistry (PhD); material chemistry (PhD); organic chemistry (PhD); physical chemistry (PhD); polymer chemistry (PhD); theoretical chemistry (PhD). *Faculty:* 38 full-time. *Students:* 139 full-time (44 women); includes 10 minority (1 African American, 4 Asian Americans or Pacific Islanders, 4 Hispanic Americans, 1 Native American), 51 international. 254 applicants, 46% accepted. In 1998, 25 doctorates awarded. *Degree requirements:* For doctorate, dissertation required, foreign language not required. *Entrance requirements:* For doctorate, GRE General Test, GRE Subject Test, TOEFL (minimum score of 600 required). *Application deadline:* For fall admission, 1/15. Application fee: $65. Electronic applications accepted. *Financial aid:* In 1998–99, 139 students received aid, including 21 fellowships with full tuition reimbursements available, 66 research assistantships with full tuition reimbursements available, 52 teaching assistantships with full tuition reimbursements available; institutionally-sponsored loans, scholarships, tuition waivers (full and partial), and unspecified assistantships also available. Financial aid applicants required to submit FAFSA. *Unit head:* Director of Graduate Studies, 607-255-4139. *Application contact:* Graduate Field Assistant, 607-255-4139, E-mail: chemgrad@cornell.edu.

See in-depth description on page 109.

Dalhousie University, Faculty of Graduate Studies, College of Arts and Science, Faculty of Science, Department of Chemistry, Halifax, NS B3H 3J5, Canada. Offers M Sc, PhD. Part-time programs available. *Faculty:* 28 full-time (2 women), 5 part-time (0 women). *Students:* 40 full-time (17 women); includes 5 minority (2 Asian Americans or Pacific Islanders, 3 Hispanic Americans), 9 international. Average age 25. 128 applicants, 13% accepted. In 1998, 10 master's awarded (70% found work related to degree, 30% continued full-time study); 8 doctorates awarded (12% entered university research/teaching, 25% found other work related to degree, 63% continued full-time study). Terminal master's awarded for partial completion of doctoral program. *Degree requirements:* For master's and doctorate, thesis/dissertation required, foreign language not required. *Entrance requirements:* For master's and doctorate, GRE Subject Test (for non-U.S. or Canadian), TOEFL (minimum score of 580 required). *Average time to degree:* Master's–2 years full-time; doctorate–4 years full-time. *Application deadline:* For fall admission, 4/15 (priority date); for winter admission, 10/31 (priority date); for spring admission, 2/28 (priority date). Applications are processed on a rolling basis. Application fee: $55. *Financial aid:* In 1998–99, 39 students received aid, including 39 fellowships with full tuition reimbursements available (averaging $10,730 Canadian dollars per year), 39 teaching assistantships (averaging $2,520 Canadian dollars per year); scholarships also available. Financial aid application deadline: 4/15. *Faculty research:* Analytical, inorganic, organic, physical, and theoretical chemistry. Total annual research expenditures: $1.7 million. *Unit head:* Dr. R. J. Boyd, Chair, 902-494-3707, Fax: 902-494-1310, E-mail: russell.boyd@dal.ca. *Application contact:* Graduate Coordinator, 902-494-3306, Fax: 902-494-1310, E-mail: dalchem@is.dal.ca.

Dartmouth College, School of Arts and Sciences, Department of Chemistry, Hanover, NH 03755. Offers PhD. *Faculty:* 17 full-time (1 woman), 7 part-time (0 women). *Students:* 35 full-time (15 women), 19 international. 176 applicants, 16% accepted. In 1998, 10 doctorates awarded. *Degree requirements:* For doctorate, dissertation, departmental qualifying exam required. *Entrance requirements:* For doctorate, GRE General Test, GRE Subject Test. *Application deadline:* For fall admission, 2/15 (priority date). Application fee: $25 ($35 for international students). *Financial aid:* In 1998–99, 35 students received aid, including 11 research assistantships; fellowships, Federal Work-Study, grants, institutionally-sponsored loans, scholarships, traineeships, tuition waivers (full), and unspecified assistantships also available. *Unit head:* Joe BelBruno, Chairman, 603-646-2501. *Application contact:* Deb Carr, Administrative Assistant, 603-646-2501.

Delaware State University, Graduate Programs, Department of Chemistry, Dover, DE 19901-2277. Offers applied chemistry (MS); chemistry (MS). Part-time and evening/weekend programs available. *Degree requirements:* Foreign language not required. *Entrance requirements:* For master's, GRE, minimum GPA of 3.0 in major, 2.75 overall. *Faculty research:* Chemiluminescence, environmental chemistry, forensic chemistry, heteropoly anions anti-cancer and antiviral agents, low temperature infrared studies of lithium salts.

DePaul University, College of Liberal Arts and Sciences, Department of Chemistry, Chicago, IL 60604-2287. Offers MS. *Faculty:* 7 full-time (3 women), 5 part-time (3 women). *Students:* 13 full-time (7 women), 20 part-time (5 women); includes 6 minority (3 African Americans, 3 Asian Americans or Pacific Islanders) Average age 30. In 1998, 6 degrees awarded. *Degree requirements:* For master's, thesis (for some programs), oral exam required, foreign language not required. *Entrance requirements:* For master's, BS in chemistry or equivalent. *Application deadline:* Applications are processed on a rolling basis. Application fee: $25. *Financial aid:* In 1998–99, 6 teaching assistantships with tuition reimbursements (averaging $5,000 per year) were awarded. Financial aid application deadline: 4/1. *Faculty research:* Polymers, DNA sequencing, computationalchemistry, water pollution, diffusion kinetics, electrochemistry, geochemistry, airchemistry. *Unit head:* Dr. Wendy Sue Wolbach, Chair, 773-325-7420, Fax: 773-325-7421, E-mail: wwolbach@wppost.depaul.edu. *Application contact:* Director of Graduate Admissions, 773-362-8880.

Drexel University, Graduate School, College of Arts and Sciences, Department of Chemistry, Philadelphia, PA 19104-2875. Offers MS, PhD. Part-time programs available. *Faculty:* 14 full-time (1 woman), 1 part-time (0 women). *Students:* 27 full-time (12 women), 27 part-time (8 women); includes 12 minority (6 African Americans, 5 Asian Americans or Pacific Islanders, 1 Hispanic American), 16 international. Average age 30. 192 applicants, 41% accepted. In 1998, 15 master's, 3 doctorates awarded. Terminal master's awarded for partial completion of doctoral program. *Degree requirements:* For master's, thesis optional, foreign language not required; for doctorate, one foreign language, dissertation required. *Entrance requirements:* For master's, GRE, TOEFL (minimum score of 570 required), TSE (for teaching assistants); for doctorate, GRE, TOEFL (minimum score of 570 required). *Application deadline:* For fall admission, 8/21. Applications are processed on a rolling basis. Application fee: $35. Tuition: Full-time $15,795; part-time $585 per credit. Required fees: $375; $67 per term. Tuition and fees vary according to program. *Financial aid:* In 1998–99, 4 research assistantships, 21 teaching assistantships were awarded.; career-related internships or fieldwork, Federal Work-Study, institutionally-sponsored loans, tuition waivers (partial), and unspecified assistantships also available. Financial aid application deadline: 2/1. *Faculty research:* Inorganic, analytical, organic, physical, and atmospheric polymer chemistry. *Unit head:* Dr. Robert O. Hutchins, Head, 215-895-2638, Fax: 215-895-2639. *Application contact:* Director of Graduate Admissions, 215-895-6700, Fax: 215-895-5939.

See in-depth description on page 113.

Duke University, Graduate School, Department of Chemistry, Durham, NC 27708-0586. Offers PhD. *Faculty:* 20 full-time, 11 part-time. *Students:* 75 full-time (26 women), 28 international. 207 applicants, 39% accepted. In 1998, 17 doctorates awarded. *Degree requirements:* For doctorate, dissertation required. *Entrance requirements:* For doctorate, GRE General Test, GRE Subject Test (recommended). *Application deadline:* For fall admission, 12/31. Application fee: $75. *Financial aid:* Fellowships, research assistantships, teaching assistantships available. Financial aid application deadline: 12/31. *Unit head:* Eric J. Toone, Director of Graduate Studies, 919-681-1546, Fax: 919-660-1607, E-mail: dgs@biochem.duke.edu.

Duquesne University, Bayer School of Natural and Environmental Sciences, Department of Chemistry and Biochemistry, Pittsburgh, PA 15282-0001. Offers biochemistry (MS, PhD); chemistry (MS, PhD). Part-time programs available. *Faculty:* 15 full-time (0 women), 6 part-time (1 woman). *Students:* 35 full-time (10 women), 2 part-time (1 woman), 15 international.

Chemistry

Duquesne University (continued)
Average age 30. 170 applicants, 8% accepted. In 1998, 6 master's awarded (67% found work related to degree, 33% continued full-time study). Terminal master's awarded for partial completion of doctoral program. *Degree requirements:* For master's, thesis required (for some programs), foreign language not required; for doctorate, dissertation required, foreign language not required. *Entrance requirements:* For master's and doctorate, GRE General Test, TOEFL (minimum score of 620 required), TSE (for international students seeking assistantships). *Average time to degree:* Master's–3.2 years full-time, 6 years part-time. *Application deadline:* For fall admission, 1/31 (priority date); for spring admission, 9/30. Applications are processed on a rolling basis. Application fee: $40. Tuition: Part-time $511 per credit. Required fees: $46 per credit. $50 per year. One-time fee: $125 part-time. Tuition and fees vary according to program. *Financial aid:* In 1998–99, 1 fellowship with full tuition reimbursement (averaging $18,000 per year), 5 research assistantships with full tuition reimbursements (averaging $15,000 per year), 25 teaching assistantships with full tuition reimbursements (averaging $15,000 per year) were awarded.; scholarships and tuition waivers (partial) also available. Financial aid application deadline: 5/15; financial aid applicants required to submit FAFSA. *Faculty research:* Computational physical chemistry, bioinorganic chemistry, analytical chemistry, biophysics, synthetic organic chemistry. Total annual research expenditures: $800,000. *Unit head:* Dr. Thomas L. Isenhour, Chair, 412-396-6341, Fax: 412-396-5683, E-mail: isenhour@duq3.cc.duq.edu. *Application contact:* Amy Johnson, Assistant to the Dean, Graduate Student Administrator, 412-396-6339, Fax: 412-396-4881, E-mail: gradinfo@duq.edu.

See in-depth description on page 115.

East Carolina University, Graduate School, College of Arts and Sciences, Department of Chemistry, Greenville, NC 27858-4353. Offers MS. Part-time programs available. *Faculty:* 14 full-time (1 woman). *Students:* 10 full-time (2 women), 5 part-time (3 women); includes 2 minority (1 African American, 1 Asian American or Pacific Islander), 6 international. Average age 26. 19 applicants, 37% accepted. In 1998, 4 degrees awarded. *Degree requirements:* For master's, one foreign language (computer language can substitute), thesis, comprehensive exams required. *Entrance requirements:* For master's, GRE General Test, TOEFL. *Application deadline:* For fall admission, 6/1 (priority date); for spring admission, 10/15. Applications are processed on a rolling basis. Application fee: $40. Tuition, state resident: full-time $1,012. Tuition, nonresident: full-time $8,578. Required fees: $1,006. Part-time tuition and fees vary according to course load. *Financial aid:* Teaching assistantships, Federal Work-Study available. Financial aid application deadline: 6/1. *Faculty research:* Organometallic, natural-product syntheses; chemometrics; electroanalytical method development; microcomputer adaptations for handicapped students. *Unit head:* Dr. Paul Gemperline, Director of Graduate Studies, 252-328-6767, Fax: 252-328-6210, E-mail: gemperlinep@mail.ecu.edu. *Application contact:* Dr. Paul D. Tschetter, Senior Associate Dean, 252-328-6012, Fax: 252-328-6071, E-mail: grad@mail.ecu.edu.

Eastern Illinois University, Graduate School, College of Sciences, Department of Chemistry, Charleston, IL 61920-3099. Offers MS. *Degree requirements:* For master's, thesis required, foreign language not required. *Entrance requirements:* For master's, GRE General Test.

Announcement: The Department of Chemistry offers a rigorous, research-based program leading to the MS degree. Specializations in analytical, biochemical, environmental, inorganic, organic, and physical chemistry prepare students for PhD programs or for direct employment in industry, government, or academia. Environment features close student-faculty interaction. Modern research equipment includes 300-MHz FT-NMR, FTIR, GC/MS, and UV-VIS instruments; several chromatography units; and computing facilities. World Wide Web: http://www.eiu.edu/~~eiuchem/.

Eastern Kentucky University, The Graduate School, College of Natural and Mathematical Sciences, Department of Chemistry, Richmond, KY 40475-3101. Offers MS. Part-time and evening/weekend programs available. *Students:* 7. In 1998, 3 degrees awarded. *Degree requirements:* For master's, computer language required, thesis not required. *Entrance requirements:* For master's, GRE General Test, minimum GPA of 2.5. Application fee: $0. *Financial aid:* Research assistantships, teaching assistantships, Federal Work-Study available. Aid available to part-time students. *Faculty research:* Organic synthesis, surface chemistry, inorganic chemistry, analytical chemistry. *Unit head:* Dr. John Zahrt, Chair, 606-622-1457.

Eastern Michigan University, Graduate School, College of Arts and Sciences, Department of Chemistry, Ypsilanti, MI 48197. Offers MS, MS/PhD. Evening/weekend programs available. *Faculty:* 21 full-time (5 women). *Students:* 14 full-time (6 women), 10 part-time (4 women); includes 1 African American, 3 Asian Americans or Pacific Islanders, 1 Native American, 13 international. Average age 24. 22 applicants, 86% accepted. In 1998, 11 degrees awarded. *Degree requirements:* For master's, thesis required, foreign language not required. *Entrance requirements:* For master's, GRE General Test, TOEFL (minimum score of 500 required). *Application deadline:* For fall admission, 5/15. Applications are processed on a rolling basis. Application fee: $30. *Financial aid:* In 1998–99, 12 teaching assistantships were awarded.; career-related internships or fieldwork, Federal Work-Study, and institutionally-sponsored loans also available. Aid available to part-time students. Financial aid application deadline: 3/15; financial aid applicants required to submit FAFSA. *Unit head:* Dr. Wade Tornquist, Head, 734-487-0106. *Application contact:* Dr. Krish Rengan, Coordinator, 734-487-0106.

Announcement: The Department of Chemistry offers comprehensive programs leading to a professional MS degree. Specializations include analytical, biochemical, inorganic, organic, physical, radiochemical, and toxicological areas. The professional MS degree prepares students for work as industrial chemists and for doctoral study. The department is housed in the 6-story Jefferson Science Complex. Major equipment includes research-quality FT-IR, UV, and visible spectrophotometers; Bruker 250-MHz superconducting FT-NMR spectrometer; gas chromatograph–mass spectrometer; preparative and analytical gas chromatographs; analytical HPLC; ultracentrifuge; fluorometer; DTA-TGA-DSC titration microcalorimeter; thermal analysis system; high-speed membrane osmometer; autoviscometer; and liquid scintillation counters, gamma counters, and multichannel analyzer.

Eastern New Mexico University, Graduate School, College of Liberal Arts and Sciences, Department of Physical Sciences, Portales, NM 88130. Offers chemistry (MS). Part-time programs available. *Faculty:* 4 full-time (0 women). *Students:* 1 full-time (0 women), 4 part-time (2 women); includes 1 minority (African American), 2 international. Average age 34. 4 applicants, 100% accepted. In 1998, 3 degrees awarded. *Degree requirements:* For master's, field exam required, thesis optional, foreign language not required. *Entrance requirements:* For master's, minimum GPA of 2.5. *Application deadline:* Applications are processed on a rolling basis. Application fee: $10. *Financial aid:* In 1998–99, 5 teaching assistantships (averaging $6,580 per year) were awarded.; fellowships, research assistantships, career-related internships or fieldwork and Federal Work-Study also available. Aid available to part-time students. Financial aid application deadline: 4/1. *Faculty research:* Synfuel, electrochemistry, protein chemistry. *Unit head:* Dr. Don Averill, Graduate Coordinator, 505-562-2494, E-mail: donald.averill@enmu.edu.

East Tennessee State University, James H. Quillen College of Medicine, Biomedical Science Graduate Program, Johnson City, TN 37614-0734. Offers anatomy and cell biology (MS, PhD); biochemistry and molecular biology (MS, PhD); biological sciences (MS); chemistry (MS); microbiology (MS, PhD); pharmacology (MS, PhD); physiology (MS, PhD). Part-time programs available. Terminal master's awarded for partial completion of doctoral program. *Degree requirements:* For master's, one foreign language (computer language can substitute), thesis, comprehensive qualifying exam required; for doctorate, 2 foreign languages (computer language can substitute for one), dissertation required. *Entrance requirements:* For master's, GRE General Test, minimum GPA of 3.0, bachelor's degree in biological or related science; for doctorate, GRE General Test, GRE Subject Test.

East Tennessee State University, School of Graduate Studies, College of Arts and Sciences, Department of Chemistry, Johnson City, TN 37614-0734. Offers MS. Part-time and evening/weekend programs available. *Degree requirements:* For master's, thesis, comprehensive exam required, foreign language not required. *Entrance requirements:* For master's, TOEFL (minimum score of 550 required), bachelor's degree in ACS-approved curriculum. *Faculty research:* Reaction mechanism, organic super conductor, organometallic crystal growth, computational chemistry.

Emory University, Graduate School of Arts and Sciences, Department of Chemistry, Atlanta, GA 30322-1100. Offers PhD. *Faculty:* 20 full-time (1 woman). *Students:* 107 full-time (45 women); includes 11 minority (4 African Americans, 6 Asian Americans or Pacific Islanders, 1 Hispanic American), 39 international. 154 applicants, 45% accepted. In 1998, 4 doctorates awarded. *Degree requirements:* For doctorate, dissertation, comprehensive exam required, foreign language not required. *Entrance requirements:* For doctorate, GRE General Test, TOEFL. *Application deadline:* For fall admission, 1/20 (priority date). Applications are processed on a rolling basis. Application fee: $45. *Financial aid:* In 1998–99, 80 fellowships were awarded.; research assistantships, teaching assistantships, Federal Work-Study, institutionally-sponsored loans, and scholarships also available. Financial aid application deadline: 1/20; financial aid applicants required to submit FAFSA. *Faculty research:* Organometallic synthesis and catalysis, synthesis of natural products, x-ray crystallography, mass spectrometry, analytical neurochemistry, laser spectroscopy, synthesis of polymers, *abinitio* molecular orbital theory and calculations, heterocyclic chemistry, polyoxometalate redox chemistry, application of transition metal complexes to organic synthesis. Total annual research expenditures: $5.1 million. *Unit head:* Dr. Lanny S. Liebeskind, Chairman, 404-727-6585. *Application contact:* Dr. Karl Hagaw, Director of Graduate Studies, 404-727-6585, Fax: 404-727-6586, E-mail: gradchem@emory.edu.

Emporia State University, School of Graduate Studies, College of Liberal Arts and Sciences, Division of Physical Sciences, Emporia, KS 66801-5087. Offers chemistry (MS); earth science (MS); physics (MS). *Faculty:* 18 full-time (1 woman), 3 part-time (0 women). *Students:* 10 full-time (4 women), 11 part-time (3 women); includes 1 minority (Native American), 8 international. *Degree requirements:* For master's, comprehensive exam or thesis required. *Entrance requirements:* For master's, TOEFL (minimum score of 550 required), written exam. *Application deadline:* For fall admission, 8/15 (priority date). Applications are processed on a rolling basis. Application fee: $30 ($75 for international students). Electronic applications accepted. Tuition, state resident: full-time $2,356; part-time $106 per credit hour. Tuition, nonresident: full-time $6,158; part-time $264 per credit hour. *Unit head:* Dr. DeWayne Backhus, Chair, 316-341-5330, E-mail: backhusd@emporia.edu.

Fairleigh Dickinson University, Florham-Madison Campus, Maxwell Becton College of Arts and Sciences, Department of Chemistry, Madison, NJ 07940-1099. Offers MS. *Faculty:* 5 full-time (0 women). *Degree requirements:* For master's, thesis optional, foreign language not required. *Entrance requirements:* For master's, GRE General Test. *Application deadline:* Applications are processed on a rolling basis. Application fee: $35. Tuition: Full-time $9,396; part-time $522 per credit. Required fees: $69 per semester. *Unit head:* Dr. Ronald Strange, Chairperson, 973-443-8779.

Fairleigh Dickinson University, Teaneck–Hackensack Campus, University College: Arts, Sciences, and Professional Studies, School of Natural Sciences, Department of Chemistry, Teaneck, NJ 07666-1914. Offers MS. *Degree requirements:* For master's, thesis or alternative required, foreign language not required. *Entrance requirements:* For master's, GRE General Test. *Faculty research:* Aquatic ecology, toxicology, desalination, lightwave technology, neuroendocrinology.

Fisk University, Graduate Programs, Department of Chemistry, Nashville, TN 37208-3051. Offers MA. *Faculty:* 5 full-time (1 woman). *Students:* 5 full-time (3 women); includes 4 minority (all African Americans) Average age 25. In 1998, 1 degree awarded (0% continued full-time study). *Degree requirements:* For master's, thesis, comprehensive exam required, foreign language not required. *Entrance requirements:* For master's, GRE General Test, GRE Subject Test, minimum GPA of 3.0. *Application deadline:* For fall admission, 6/15 (priority date). Applications are processed on a rolling basis. Application fee: $25. Tuition: Full-time $8,480; part-time $471 per semester hour. Required fees: $540; $270 per semester. *Financial aid:* In 1998–99, 2 research assistantships with full tuition reimbursements (averaging $8,000 per year) were awarded.; fellowships *Faculty research:* General organic chemistry, general kinetics. *Unit head:* Dr. Princilla S. Evans, Chair, 615-329-8628. *Application contact:* Anthony Jones, Director of Admissions, 615-329-8665, Fax: 615-329-8774, E-mail: ajones@dubois_fisk.edu.

Florida Agricultural and Mechanical University, Division of Graduate Studies, Research, and Continuing Education, College of Arts and Sciences, Department of Chemistry, Tallahassee, FL 32307-3200. Offers MS. *Students:* 1; minority (African American) *Degree requirements:* For master's, thesis required. *Entrance requirements:* For master's, GRE General Test (minimum combined score of 1000 required), minimum GPA of 3.0. *Application deadline:* For fall admission, 5/13. Application fee: $20. *Unit head:* Dr. Ralph Turner, Chairperson, 850-599-3638, Fax: 850-561-2388.

Florida Atlantic University, Charles E. Schmidt College of Science, Department of Chemistry and Biochemistry, Boca Raton, FL 33431-0991. Offers MS, MST. Part-time programs available. *Faculty:* 13 full-time (2 women). *Students:* 32 full-time (11 women), 5 part-time; includes 8 minority (4 African Americans, 1 Asian American or Pacific Islander, 3 Hispanic Americans), 12 international. Average age 30. 42 applicants, 62% accepted. In 1998, 9 degrees awarded. *Degree requirements:* For master's, thesis required, foreign language not required. *Entrance requirements:* For master's, GRE General Test (minimum combined score of 1000 required; average 1100), minimum GPA of 3.0. *Application deadline:* For fall admission, 6/1. Application fee: $20. Tuition, state resident: part-time $148 per credit hour. Tuition, nonresident: part-time $509 per credit hour. *Financial aid:* In 1998–99, 24 teaching assistantships were awarded.; fellowships, research assistantships, Federal Work-Study also available. *Faculty research:* Polymer synthesis and characterization, spectroscopy, geochemistry, environmental chemistry, biomedical chemistry. Total annual research expenditures: $50,000. *Unit head:* Dr. Donald Baird, Chair, 561-297-3390. *Application contact:* Dr. Earl Baker, Professor, 561-297-3308, Fax: 561-297-2759, E-mail: baker@acc.fau.edu.

Florida Institute of Technology, Graduate School, College of Science and Liberal Arts, Department of Chemistry, Melbourne, FL 32901-6975. Offers MS, PhD. Part-time programs available. *Faculty:* 9 full-time (1 woman), 1 part-time (0 women). *Students:* 7 full-time (4 women), 7 part-time (4 women); includes 2 minority (both Asian Americans or Pacific Islanders) Average age 29. 56 applicants, 59% accepted. Terminal master's awarded for partial completion of doctoral program. *Degree requirements:* For master's, thesis required, foreign language not required; for doctorate, one foreign language (computer language can substitute), dissertation, comprehensive exam, oral defense of dissertation required. *Entrance requirements:* For master's, minimum GPA of 3.0; for doctorate, minimum GPA of 3.2. *Application deadline:* Applications are processed on a rolling basis. Application fee: $50. Electronic applications accepted. Tuition: Part-time $575 per credit hour. Required fees: $100. Tuition and fees vary according to campus/location and program. *Financial aid:* In 1998–99, 12 students received aid, including 1 research assistantship (averaging $11,692 per year), 11 teaching assistantships (averaging $3,158 per year); tuition remissions also available. Financial aid application deadline: 3/1; financial aid applicants required to submit FAFSA. *Faculty research:* Energy storage applications, marine and organic chemistry, stereochemistry, materials chemistry, medicinal chemistry. Total annual research expenditures: $453,000. *Unit head:* Dr. Michael W. Babich, Head, 407-674-8046, Fax: 407-674-8951, E-mail: babich@fit.edu. *Application contact:* Carolyn P. Farrior, Associate Dean of Graduate Admissions, 407-674-7118, Fax: 407-723-9468, E-mail: cfarrior@fit.edu.

Florida International University, College of Arts and Sciences, Department of Chemistry, Miami, FL 33199. Offers MS, PhD. Part-time and evening/weekend programs available. *Faculty:* 15 full-time (3 women), 5 part-time (1 woman). *Students:* 18 full-time (8 women), 9 part-time (5 women); includes 9 minority (1 African American, 1 Asian American or Pacific Islander, 7 Hispanic Americans), 11 international. Average age 31. 31 applicants, 61% accepted. In 1998, 11 degrees awarded. *Degree requirements:* For master's and doctorate, one foreign language, thesis/dissertation required. *Entrance requirements:* For master's and doctorate, GRE General Test (minimum combined score of 1000 required), TOEFL (minimum score of 550 required). *Application deadline:* For fall admission, 4/1 (priority date); for spring admission, 10/1. Applications are processed on a rolling basis. Application fee: $20. Tuition, state resident: part-time $145 per credit hour. Tuition, nonresident: part-time $506 per credit hour. Required fees: $158; $158 per year. *Financial aid:* Research assistantships, teaching assistantships, Federal Work-Study, institutionally-sponsored loans, and tuition waivers (full and partial) available. Aid available to part-time students. Financial aid application deadline: 4/1. *Faculty research:* Organic synthesis and reaction catalysis, environmental chemistry, molecular beam studies, organic geochemistry, bioinorganic and organometallic chemistry. *Unit head:* Dr. Kenneth G. Furton, Chairperson, 305-348-2606, Fax: 305-348-3772, E-mail: furton@fiu.edu.

See in-depth description on page 119.

Florida State University, Graduate Studies, College of Arts and Sciences, Department of Chemistry, Tallahassee, FL 32306. Offers analytical chemistry (MS, PhD); biochemistry (MS, PhD); chemical physics (MS, PhD); inorganic chemistry (MS, PhD); organic chemistry (MS, PhD); physical chemistry (MS, PhD). Part-time programs available. *Faculty:* 38 full-time (4 women). *Students:* 87 full-time (27 women), 8 part-time (2 women). Average age 25. 149 applicants, 53% accepted. In 1998, 9 master's, 15 doctorates awarded. Terminal master's awarded for partial completion of doctoral program. *Degree requirements:* For master's, cumulative and diagnostic exams required; for doctorate, dissertation, cumulative and diagnostic exams required, foreign language not required. *Entrance requirements:* For master's and doctorate, GRE General Test, minimum B average in undergraduate course work. *Average time to degree:* Master's–3 years full-time; doctorate–4.6 years full-time, 8.3 years part-time. *Application deadline:* Applications are processed on a rolling basis. Application fee: $20. Tuition, state resident: part-time $139 per credit hour. Tuition, nonresident: part-time $482 per credit hour. Tuition and fees vary according to program. *Financial aid:* In 1998–99, 3 fellowships (averaging $12,000 per year), 34 research assistantships (averaging $15,000 per year), 50 teaching assistantships (averaging $15,000 per year) were awarded.; career-related internships or fieldwork, Federal Work-Study, and institutionally-sponsored loans also available. Financial aid application deadline: 2/15; financial aid applicants required to submit FAFSA. *Faculty research:* Spectroscopy, computational chemistry, nuclear chemistry, separations, synthesis. Total annual research expenditures: $7.1 million. *Unit head:* Dr. John G. Dorsey, Chairman, 850-644-9625, Fax: 850-644-8281. *Application contact:* Dr. Naresh Dalal, Chair, Graduate Admissions Committee, 850-644-3398, Fax: 850-644-8281, E-mail: gradinfo@chem.fsu.edu.

See in-depth description on page 123.

Furman University, Graduate Division, Department of Chemistry, Greenville, SC 29613. Offers MS. *Faculty:* 7. *Students:* 8 full-time (4 women). *Degree requirements:* For master's, thesis required. *Entrance requirements:* For master's, GRE General Test, GRE Subject Test. *Application deadline:* Applications are processed on a rolling basis. Application fee: $25. *Unit head:* Dr. Lon Knight, Graduate Director.

George Mason University, College of Arts and Sciences, Department of Chemistry, Fairfax, VA 22030-4444. Offers MS. *Faculty:* 14 full-time (2 women), 5 part-time (2 women). *Students:* 2 full-time (1 woman), 14 part-time (6 women); includes 8 minority (1 African American, 6 Asian Americans or Pacific Islanders, 1 Hispanic American) Average age 31. 13 applicants, 77% accepted. In 1998, 9 degrees awarded. *Degree requirements:* For master's, thesis or alternative required, foreign language not required. *Entrance requirements:* For master's, GRE General Test, minimum GPA of 3.0 in last 60 hours. *Application deadline:* For fall admission, 5/1; for spring admission, 11/1. Application fee: $30. Electronic applications accepted. Tuition, state resident: full-time $4,416; part-time $184 per credit hour. Tuition, nonresident: full-time $12,516; part-time $522 per credit hour. Tuition and fees vary according to program. *Financial aid:* Research assistantships available. Aid available to part-time students. Financial aid application deadline: 3/1; financial aid applicants required to submit FAFSA. *Unit head:* Dr. George Mushrush, Chairman, 703-993-1080, Fax: 703-993-1070, E-mail: gmushrus@osf1.gmu.edu.

Georgetown University, Graduate School, Department of Chemistry, Washington, DC 20057. Offers analytical chemistry (MS, PhD); biochemistry (MS, PhD); chemical physics (MS, PhD); inorganic chemistry (MS, PhD); organic chemistry (MS, PhD); physical chemistry (MS, PhD); theoretical chemistry (MS, PhD). Terminal master's awarded for partial completion of doctoral program. *Degree requirements:* For master's, thesis (for some programs), qualifying exam required, foreign language not required; for doctorate, dissertation, comprehensive exam required. *Entrance requirements:* For master's and doctorate, GRE General Test, TOEFL (minimum score of 550 required, 600 for teaching assistants).

See in-depth description on page 125.

The George Washington University, Columbian School of Arts and Sciences, Department of Chemistry, Washington, DC 20052. Offers analytical chemistry (MS, PhD); inorganic chemistry (MS, PhD); materials science (MS, PhD); organic chemistry (MS, PhD); physical chemistry (MS, PhD). Part-time and evening/weekend programs available. *Faculty:* 5 full-time (0 women). *Students:* 19 full-time (14 women), 7 part-time (4 women); includes 6 minority (1 African American, 3 Asian Americans or Pacific Islanders, 2 Hispanic Americans), 6 international. Average age 27. 52 applicants, 79% accepted. In 1998, 8 master's, 3 doctorates awarded. Terminal master's awarded for partial completion of doctoral program. *Degree requirements:* For master's, computer language, thesis or alternative, comprehensive exam required; for doctorate, computer language, dissertation, general exam required. *Entrance requirements:* For master's and doctorate, GRE General Test, interview, minimum GPA of 3.0. Application fee: $55. Tuition: Full-time $17,328; part-time $722 per credit hour. Required fees: $828; $35 per credit hour. Tuition and fees vary according to campus/location and program. *Financial aid:* In 1998–99, 15 students received aid, including 12 fellowships, 10 teaching assistantships; research assistantships, Federal Work-Study also available. Financial aid application deadline: 2/1. *Unit head:* Dr. Michael King, Chair, 202-994-6121.

Georgia Institute of Technology, Graduate Studies and Research, College of Sciences, School of Chemistry and Biochemistry, Atlanta, GA 30332-0001. Offers MS, MS Chem, PhD. Terminal master's awarded for partial completion of doctoral program. *Degree requirements:* For master's, thesis required (for some programs), foreign language not required; for doctorate, dissertation required, foreign language not required. *Entrance requirements:* For master's and doctorate, GRE General Test, GRE Subject Test, TOEFL (minimum score of 550 required), minimum GPA of 2.7. Electronic applications accepted. *Faculty research:* Inorganic, organic, physical, and analytical chemistry.

See in-depth description on page 129.

Georgia State University, College of Arts and Sciences, Department of Chemistry, Atlanta, GA 30303-3083. Offers MS, PhD. Part-time programs available. *Faculty:* 18 full-time (4 women). *Students:* 46 full-time (24 women), 8 part-time (4 women); includes 15 minority (6 African Americans, 9 Asian Americans or Pacific Islanders), 23 international. Average age 29. 45 applicants, 56% accepted. In 1998, 16 master's, 9 doctorates awarded. Terminal master's awarded for partial completion of doctoral program. *Degree requirements:* For master's, one foreign language (computer language can substitute), thesis required; for doctorate, 2 foreign languages (computer language can substitute for one), dissertation required. *Entrance requirements:* For master's, GRE General Test, GRE Subject Test, TOEFL (minimum score of 550 required), minimum GPA of 3.0; for doctorate, GRE General Test, TOEFL (minimum score of 550 required), minimum GPA of 3.0. *Average time to degree:* Master's–2.5 years full-time, 5 years part-time; doctorate–5 years full-time, 9 years part-time. Application fee: $25. Tuition, state resident: full-time $2,896; part-time $121 per credit hour. Tuition, nonresident: full-time $11,584; part-time $483 per credit hour. Required fees: $468. Tuition and fees vary according to program. *Financial aid:* Fellowships, research assistantships, teaching assistantships, career-related internships or fieldwork, Federal Work-Study, institutionally-sponsored loans, tuition waivers (partial), and unspecified assistantships available. Aid available to part-time students. *Faculty research:* DNA, AIDS, drug design, biothermodynamics, biological electron transfer and NMR applied to biochemical systems. Total annual research expenditures: $2.4 million. *Unit head:* Dr. Alfons Baumstark, Chair, 404-651-1716, Fax: 404-651-1416, E-mail: chealb@panther.gsu.edu. *Application contact:* Alpa Patel, Graduate Coordinator, 404-651-3120, Fax: 404-651-1416, E-mail: cheaup@panther.gsu.edu.

See in-depth description on page 131.

Graduate School and University Center of the City University of New York, Graduate Studies, Program in Chemistry, New York, NY 10036-8099. Offers PhD. *Faculty:* 64 full-time (5 women). *Students:* 99 full-time (31 women); includes 10 minority (6 African Americans, 1 Asian American or Pacific Islander, 2 Hispanic Americans, 1 Native American) Average age 33. 135 applicants, 20% accepted. In 1998, 16 degrees awarded. *Degree requirements:* For doctorate, dissertation required. *Entrance requirements:* For doctorate, GRE General Test, GRE Subject Test. *Application deadline:* For fall admission, 4/15. Application fee: $40. *Financial aid:* In 1998–99, 74 students received aid, including 68 fellowships; research assistantships, teaching assistantships, career-related internships or fieldwork, Federal Work-Study, institutionally-sponsored loans, and tuition waivers (full and partial) also available. Financial aid application deadline: 2/1; financial aid applicants required to submit FAFSA. *Unit head:* Dr. Gerald Koeppl, Executive Officer, 212-642-2451.

Hampton University, Graduate College, Department of Chemistry, Hampton, VA 23668. Offers MS. Part-time and evening/weekend programs available. *Faculty:* 9 full-time (2 women). *Students:* 7 full-time (2 women), 1 (woman) part-time; includes 7 minority (all African Americans), 1 international. In 1998, 4 degrees awarded. *Degree requirements:* For master's, thesis required, foreign language not required. *Entrance requirements:* For master's, GRE General Test (minimum score of 450 on verbal section required). *Application deadline:* For fall admission, 6/1 (priority date); for spring admission, 11/1. Applications are processed on a rolling basis. Application fee: $25. Tuition: Full-time $9,490; part-time $230 per semester hour. Required fees: $60; $35 per semester. Tuition and fees vary according to course load. *Financial aid:* Fellowships, research assistantships, teaching assistantships, career-related internships or fieldwork, Federal Work-Study, institutionally-sponsored loans, and scholarships available. Aid available to part-time students. Financial aid application deadline: 5/1; financial aid applicants required to submit FAFSA. *Unit head:* Dr. Isai Urasa, Chairman, 757-727-5396. *Application contact:* Erika Henderson, Director, Graduate Programs, 757-727-5454, Fax: 757-727-5084.

Harvard University, Graduate School of Arts and Sciences, Committee on Chemical Physics, Cambridge, MA 02138. Offers chemical physics (PhD); chemistry (AM); physics (AM). *Students:* 2 full-time (0 women); includes 1 minority (Hispanic American) *Degree requirements:* For doctorate, dissertation, cumulative exams required. *Entrance requirements:* For master's, GRE General Test, TOEFL (minimum score of 550 required); for doctorate, GRE General Test, GRE Subject Test, TOEFL (minimum score of 550 required). *Application deadline:* For fall admission, 1/1. Application fee: $60. *Unit head:* Dr. William Klemperer, Director of Graduate Studies, 617-495-4094. *Application contact:* Department of Chemistry and Chemical Biology, 617-496-3208.

Harvard University, Graduate School of Arts and Sciences, Department of Chemistry and Chemical Biology, Cambridge, MA 02138. Offers biochemical chemistry (AM, PhD); inorganic chemistry (AM, PhD); organic chemistry (AM, PhD); physical chemistry (AM, PhD). *Students:* 188 full-time (36 women). 346 applicants, 24% accepted. In 1998, 20 master's, 33 doctorates awarded. *Degree requirements:* For doctorate, dissertation, cumulative exams required, foreign language not required. *Entrance requirements:* For master's, GRE General Test, TOEFL (minimum score of 550 required); for doctorate, GRE General Test, GRE Subject Test, TOEFL (minimum score of 550 required). *Application deadline:* For fall admission, 12/31. Application fee: $60. *Financial aid:* Fellowships, research assistantships, teaching assistantships, career-related internships or fieldwork, Federal Work-Study, and institutionally-sponsored loans available. Financial aid application deadline: 12/30. *Unit head:* Dr. David Evans, Chair, 617-495-2948. *Application contact:* Graduate Admissions Office, 617-496-3208.

See in-depth description on page 133.

Howard University, Graduate School of Arts and Sciences, Department of Chemistry, Washington, DC 20059-0002. Offers analytical chemistry (MS, PhD); biochemistry (MS, PhD); inorganic chemistry (MS, PhD); organic chemistry (MS, PhD); physical chemistry (MS, PhD); polymer chemistry (MS, PhD); theoretical chemistry (MS, PhD). Part-time programs available. Terminal master's awarded for partial completion of doctoral program. *Degree requirements:* For master's, one foreign language (computer language can substitute), thesis, comprehensive exam, teaching experience required; for doctorate, 2 foreign languages (computer language can substitute for one), dissertation, comprehensive exam, teaching experience required. *Entrance requirements:* For master's, GRE General Test, minimum GPA of 2.7; for doctorate, GRE General Test, minimum GPA of 3.0. *Faculty research:* Stratospheric aerosols, liquid crystals, polymer coatings, terrestrial and extraterrestrial atmospheres, amidogen reaction.

Idaho State University, Graduate School, College of Arts and Sciences, Department of Chemistry, Pocatello, ID 83209. Offers MNS, MS. MS students must enter as undergraduates. *Degree requirements:* Foreign language not required. *Entrance requirements:* For master's, GRE General Test. *Faculty research:* Natural product synthesis, solar energy devices, low temperature plasma, chemometrics.

Illinois Institute of Technology, Graduate College, Armour College of Engineering and Sciences, Department of Biological, Chemical and Physical Sciences, Chemistry Division, Chicago, IL 60616-3793. Offers analytical chemistry (MAC, MS, PhD); chemistry (M Chem); inorganic chemistry (MS, PhD); organic chemistry (MS, PhD); physical chemistry (MS, PhD); polymer chemistry (MS, PhD); theoretical chemistry (MS, PhD). Part-time and evening/weekend programs available. *Faculty:* 8 full-time (0 women), 2 part-time (0 women). *Students:* 14 full-time (7 women), 70 part-time (27 women); includes 19 minority (10 African Americans, 9 Asian Americans or Pacific Islanders), 16 international. 115 applicants, 31% accepted. In 1998, 1 master's, 2 doctorates awarded. Terminal master's awarded for partial completion of doctoral program. *Degree requirements:* For master's, thesis (for some programs), comprehensive exam required, foreign language not required; for doctorate, dissertation, comprehensive exam required, foreign language not required. *Entrance requirements:* For master's and doctorate, GRE (minimum score of 1200 required), TOEFL (minimum score of 550 required), undergraduate GPA of 3.0 required. *Application deadline:* For fall admission, 7/1; for spring admission, 11/1. Applications are processed on a rolling basis. Application fee: $30. Electronic applications accepted. *Financial aid:* In 1998–99, 2 fellowships, 2 research assistantships, 9 teaching assistantships were awarded.; institutionally-sponsored loans and scholarships also available. Financial aid application deadline: 3/1. *Faculty research:* Molecular chemistry, chemical synthesis. *Unit head:* Dr. Carlo Segre, Associate Chair, 312-567-3480, Fax: 312-567-3494, E-mail: segre@iit.edu. *Application contact:* Dr. S. Mohammad Shahidehpour, Dean of Graduate College, 312-567-3024, Fax: 312-567-7517, E-mail: grad@minna.cns.iit.edu.

See in-depth description on page 135.

Illinois State University, Graduate School, College of Arts and Sciences, Department of Chemistry, Normal, IL 61790-2200. Offers MS. *Faculty:* 17 full-time (5 women). *Students:* 36 full-time (10 women), 14 part-time (5 women); includes 5 minority (3 African Americans, 2

Chemistry

Illinois State University (continued)
Asian Americans or Pacific Islanders), 8 international. 25 applicants, 72% accepted. In 1998, 14 degrees awarded. *Degree requirements:* For master's, thesis required. *Entrance requirements:* For master's, GRE General Test, minimum GPA of 2.6 in last 60 hours. *Application deadline:* Applications are processed on a rolling basis. Application fee: $0. Tuition, state resident: full-time $2,526; part-time $105 per credit hour. Tuition, nonresident: full-time $7,578; part-time $316 per credit hour. Required fees: $1,082; $38 per credit hour. Tuition and fees vary according to course load and program. *Financial aid:* In 1998–99, 33 research assistantships were awarded.; teaching assistantships, tuition waivers (full) and unspecified assistantships also available. Financial aid application deadline: 4/1. *Faculty research:* Synthesis of novel porphyrinoids by the "3 + 1" approach, binuclear thiosemicarbazone complexes. Total annual research expenditures: $228,180. *Unit head:* Dr. Michael Kurz, Chairperson, 309-438-7661.

Indiana State University, School of Graduate Studies, College of Arts and Sciences, Department of Chemistry, Terre Haute, IN 47809-1401. Offers MS. Part-time programs available. *Faculty:* 6 full-time (0 women). *Students:* 3 full-time (all women), 1 (woman) part-time, 3 international. Average age 28. 20 applicants, 55% accepted. *Degree requirements:* For master's, thesis (for some programs), 2 research seminars required, foreign language not required. *Average time to degree:* Master's–2 years full-time, 5 years part-time. *Application deadline:* For fall admission, 7/1 (priority date); for spring admission, 11/1 (priority date). Applications are processed on a rolling basis. Application fee: $20. Electronic applications accepted. *Financial aid:* Research assistantships with partial tuition reimbursements, teaching assistantships with partial tuition reimbursements available. Financial aid application deadline: 3/1; financial aid applicants required to submit FAFSA. *Faculty research:* Water pollution, enzymes, quantum chemistry, organometallics, forensics. *Unit head:* Dr. Arthur M. Halpern, Chairperson, 812-237-2240.

Indiana University Bloomington, Graduate School, College of Arts and Sciences, Department of Chemistry, Bloomington, IN 47405. Offers analytical chemistry (PhD); biological chemistry (PhD); chemistry (MAT, MS); inorganic chemistry (PhD); physical chemistry (PhD). PhD offered through the University Graduate School. *Faculty:* 28 full-time (1 woman), 1 (woman) part-time. *Students:* 96 full-time (32 women), 65 part-time (10 women); includes 12 minority (1 African American, 9 Asian Americans or Pacific Islanders, 2 Hispanic Americans), 42 international. 309 applicants, 41% accepted. In 1998, 14 master's, 24 doctorates awarded. Terminal master's awarded for partial completion of doctoral program. *Degree requirements:* For master's and doctorate, thesis/dissertation required, foreign language not required. *Entrance requirements:* For master's and doctorate, GRE General Test, GRE Subject Test, TOEFL. *Average time to degree:* Master's–2.2 years full-time; doctorate–5.8 years full-time. *Application deadline:* For fall admission, 1/15 (priority date); for spring admission, 9/1 (priority date). Applications are processed on a rolling basis. Application fee: $40. Tuition, state resident: part-time $161 per credit hour. Tuition, nonresident: part-time $468 per credit hour. Required fees: $360 per year. Tuition and fees vary according to course load and program. *Financial aid:* In 1998–99, 23 fellowships with full tuition reimbursements (averaging $15,091 per year), 57 research assistantships with full tuition reimbursements (averaging $14,844 per year), 78 teaching assistantships with full tuition reimbursements (averaging $15,588 per year) were awarded.; Federal Work-Study and institutionally-sponsored loans also available. *Faculty research:* Synthesis of complex natural products, organic reaction mechanisms, organic electrochemistry, transitive-metal chemistry, solid-state and surface chemistry. Total annual research expenditures: $7.7 million. *Unit head:* Dr. Gary M. Hieftje, Chairperson, 812-855-6239, Fax: 812-855-8300, E-mail: cemchair@indiana.edu. *Application contact:* Dr. Jack K. Crandall, Chairperson of Admissions, 812-855-2068, Fax: 812-855-8300, E-mail: chemgrad@indiana.edu.

Indiana University of Pennsylvania, Graduate School, College of Natural Sciences and Mathematics, Department of Chemistry, Indiana, PA 15705-1087. Offers MA, MS. Part-time programs available. *Students:* 8 full-time (4 women), 3 part-time (1 woman); includes 1 minority (Asian American or Pacific Islander), 8 international. Average age 25. 13 applicants, 69% accepted. In 1998, 6 degrees awarded. *Degree requirements:* For master's, thesis required (for some programs), foreign language not required. *Entrance requirements:* For master's, TOEFL (minimum score of 500 required). *Application deadline:* For fall admission, 7/1 (priority date); for spring admission, 11/1. Applications are processed on a rolling basis. Application fee: $30. *Financial aid:* Research assistantships, Federal Work-Study available. Aid available to part-time students. Financial aid application deadline: 3/15. *Unit head:* Dr. Pothen Varughese, Chairperson, 724-357-2361, E-mail: pvarugh@grove.iup.edu. *Application contact:* Dr. John Woolcock, Graduate Coordinator, 724-357-4828, E-mail: woolcock@grove.iup.edu.

Indiana University–Purdue University Fort Wayne, School of Arts and Sciences, Department of Chemistry, Fort Wayne, IN 46805-1499. Offers MS. Part-time and evening/weekend programs available. *Faculty:* 2 full-time (0 women), 1 part-time (0 women). Average age 31. 5 applicants, 80% accepted. *Degree requirements:* For master's, foreign language and thesis not required. *Entrance requirements:* For master's, minimum GPA of 3.0, major in chemistry. *Average time to degree:* Master's–5 years part-time. *Application deadline:* For fall admission, 8/1 (priority date); for spring admission, 12/1. Applications are processed on a rolling basis. Application fee: $30. *Financial aid:* Federal Work-Study available. Financial aid application deadline: 3/1. *Faculty research:* Photochemistry, organic and inorganic chemistry, chemical dynamics, advanced analytical techniques. Total annual research expenditures: $60,000. *Unit head:* Kenneth L. Stevenson, Chairperson, 219-481-6297, Fax: 219-481-6070, E-mail: stevenso@ipfw.edu.

Indiana University–Purdue University Indianapolis, School of Science, Department of Chemistry, Indianapolis, IN 46202-2896. Offers MS, PhD, MD/PhD. Part-time and evening/weekend programs available. *Students:* 4 full-time (2 women), 22 part-time (6 women); includes 2 minority (1 African American, 1 Asian American or Pacific Islander) Average age 25. In 1998, 11 master's, 5 doctorates awarded. Terminal master's awarded for partial completion of doctoral program. *Degree requirements:* For master's, thesis required (for some programs), foreign language not required; for doctorate, dissertation required, foreign language not required. *Entrance requirements:* For master's and doctorate, GRE (international applicants), TOEFL (minimum score of 630 required), minimum GPA of 3.0. *Average time to degree:* Master's–2 years full-time, 5 years part-time; doctorate–5 years full-time. *Application deadline:* Applications are processed on a rolling basis. Application fee: $25 ($50 for international students). Tuition, state resident: part-time $158 per credit hour. Tuition, nonresident: part-time $455 per credit hour. Required fees: $121 per year. Tuition and fees vary according to course load and degree level. *Financial aid:* In 1998–99, 2 fellowships with partial tuition reimbursements (averaging $16,200 per year), 9 research assistantships with partial tuition reimbursements (averaging $16,200 per year), 16 teaching assistantships with partial tuition reimbursements (averaging $16,200 per year) were awarded.; career-related internships or fieldwork, institutionally-sponsored loans, tuition waivers (partial), and co-op position also available. Financial aid application deadline: 3/1. *Faculty research:* Analytical, biological, inorganic, organic, and physical chemistry. Total annual research expenditures: $1.6 million. *Unit head:* Dr. David J. Malik, Chair, 317-274-6872, Fax: 317-274-4701, E-mail: malik@chem.iupui.edu. *Application contact:* Eric Long, 317-274-6888, Fax: 317-274-4701, E-mail: long@chem.iupui.edu.

Institute of Paper Science and Technology, Graduate Programs, Program in Chemistry, Atlanta, GA 30318-5794. Offers MS, PhD. Part-time programs available. Terminal master's awarded for partial completion of doctoral program. *Degree requirements:* For master's, industrial experience, research project required, foreign language and thesis not required; for doctorate, dissertation required, foreign language not required. *Entrance requirements:* For master's and doctorate, GRE (score in 50th percentile or higher required), minimum GPA of 3.0. *Application deadline:* For fall admission, 3/1 (priority date). Application fee: $0. *Financial aid:* Fellowships, career-related internships or fieldwork and institutionally-sponsored loans available. Financial aid applicants required to submit FAFSA. *Unit head:* Dr. Earl W. Malcolm, Director, Chemical and Biological Sciences Division, 404-894-9708, Fax: 404-894-4778. *Application contact:* Dana Carter, Student Development Counselor, 404-894-5745, Fax: 404-894-4778, E-mail: dana.carter@ipst.edu.

See in-depth description on page 137.

Instituto Tecnológico y de Estudios Superiores de Monterrey, Campus Monterrey, Graduate and Research Division, Program in Natural and Social Sciences, Monterrey, 64849, Mexico. Offers biotechnology (MS); chemistry (MS, PhD); communications (MS); education (MA). Part-time programs available. *Degree requirements:* For master's and doctorate, thesis/dissertation required. *Entrance requirements:* For master's, PAEG, TOEFL; for doctorate, PAEG, TOEFL, master's in related field. *Faculty research:* Cultural industries, mineral substances, bioremediation, food processing, CQ in industrial chemical processing.

Iowa State University of Science and Technology, Graduate College, College of Liberal Arts and Sciences, Department of Chemistry, Ames, IA 50011. Offers MS, PhD. *Faculty:* 32 full-time. *Students:* 192 full-time (43 women), 10 part-time (2 women); includes 5 minority (4 Asian Americans or Pacific Islanders, 1 Hispanic American), 100 international. 103 applicants, 37% accepted. In 1998, 11 master's, 31 doctorates awarded. *Degree requirements:* For master's and doctorate, thesis/dissertation required. *Entrance requirements:* For master's and doctorate, GRE General Test (international students), TOEFL (minimum score of 570 required). *Application deadline:* For fall admission, 2/1 (priority date). Applications are processed on a rolling basis. Application fee: $20 ($50 for international students). Electronic applications accepted. Tuition, state resident: full-time $3,308. Tuition, nonresident: full-time $9,744. Part-time tuition and fees vary according to course load, campus/location and program. *Financial aid:* In 1998–99, 114 research assistantships with partial tuition reimbursements (averaging $12,645 per year), 50 teaching assistantships with partial tuition reimbursements (averaging $13,222 per year) were awarded.; fellowships, scholarships also available. *Unit head:* Dr. George A. Kraus, Chair, 515-294-6342, Fax: 515-294-0105, E-mail: chemgrad@iastate.edu.

Jackson State University, Graduate School, School of Science and Technology, Department of Chemistry, Jackson, MS 39217. Offers MS, PhD. Part-time and evening/weekend programs available. *Faculty:* 13 full-time (2 women). *Students:* 4 full-time (2 women), 4 part-time (2 women); includes 5 minority (all African Americans), 3 international. In 1998, 1 degree awarded. *Degree requirements:* For master's and doctorate, thesis/dissertation, comprehensive exam required. *Entrance requirements:* For master's, GRE General Test (minimum combined score of 1000 required), TOEFL (minimum score of 550 required); for doctorate, MAT (minimum score of 45 required). *Application deadline:* For fall admission, 3/1 (priority date); for spring admission, 10/1. Applications are processed on a rolling basis. Application fee: $20. *Financial aid:* In 1998–99, 2 students received aid. Career-related internships or fieldwork, Federal Work-Study, scholarships, and unspecified assistantships available. Aid available to part-time students. Financial aid application deadline: 3/1; financial aid applicants required to submit FAFSA. *Faculty research:* Electrochemical and spectroscopic studies on charge transfer and energy transfer processes, spectroscopy of trapped molecular ions, respirable mine dust. *Unit head:* Dr. Richard Sullivan, Chair, 601-968-2171, Fax: 601-973-3730, E-mail: sullivan@tiger.jsums.edu. *Application contact:* Curtis Gore, Admissions Coordinator, 601-974-5841, Fax: 601-974-6196, E-mail: cgore@ccaix.jsums.edu.

John Carroll University, Graduate School, Department of Chemistry, University Heights, OH 44118-4581. Offers MS. Part-time and evening/weekend programs available. *Faculty:* 9 full-time (2 women), 1 part-time (0 women). *Students:* 4 full-time (0 women), 8 part-time (5 women); includes 1 minority (African American) Average age 28. 3 applicants, 67% accepted. In 1998, 2 degrees awarded (100% found work related to degree). *Degree requirements:* For master's, comprehensive exam, research essay or thesis required. *Entrance requirements:* For master's, bachelor's degree in chemistry. *Average time to degree:* Master's–2.5 years full-time, 6 years part-time. *Application deadline:* For fall admission, 8/1; for spring admission, 12/15. Applications are processed on a rolling basis. Application fee: $25 ($35 for international students). *Financial aid:* In 1998–99, 5 students received aid, including 5 teaching assistantships with tuition reimbursements available (averaging $8,500 per year); institutionally-sponsored loans, tuition waivers (partial), and summer research support also available. *Faculty research:* Protein–nucleic acid interactions, catalysis, butyllithium compounds, vanadium-sulfur compounds, copper proteins. Total annual research expenditures: $40,000. *Unit head:* Dr. David W. Ewing, Chairperson, 216-397-4241, Fax: 216-397-3033, E-mail: ewing@jcu.edu.

Johns Hopkins University, Zanvyl Krieger School of Arts and Sciences, Department of Chemistry, Baltimore, MD 21218-2699. Offers MA, PhD. *Faculty:* 17 full-time (1 woman). *Students:* 76 full-time (24 women); includes 1 minority (Hispanic American), 24 international. Average age 25. 209 applicants, 29% accepted. In 1998, 14 master's, 10 doctorates awarded. Terminal master's awarded for partial completion of doctoral program. *Degree requirements:* For master's, oral exam required; for doctorate, dissertation, oral exams required, foreign language not required. *Entrance requirements:* For master's and doctorate, GRE General Test, GRE Subject Test. *Average time to degree:* Master's–2 years full-time; doctorate–6 years full-time. *Application deadline:* For fall admission, 1/15 (priority date); for spring admission, 11/15. Applications are processed on a rolling basis. Application fee: $55. Tuition: Full-time $23,660. Tuition and fees vary according to program. *Financial aid:* In 1998–99, 3 fellowships, 37 research assistantships were awarded.; teaching assistantships, Federal Work-Study and institutionally-sponsored loans also available. Financial aid application deadline: 3/14; financial aid applicants required to submit FAFSA. Total annual research expenditures: $3.7 million. *Unit head:* Dr. Paul J. Dagdigian, Chair, 410-516-7444, Fax: 410-516-8420. *Application contact:* Anne B. Aschemeier, Academic Program Coordinator, 410-516-7427, Fax: 410-516-8420, E-mail: chem.grad.adm@jhu.edu.

See in-depth description on page 139.

Kansas State University, Graduate School, College of Arts and Sciences, Department of Chemistry, Manhattan, KS 66506. Offers analytical chemistry (MS); chemistry (PhD); inorganic chemistry (MS); organic chemistry (MS); physical chemistry (MS). *Faculty:* 16 full-time (1 woman). *Students:* 43 full-time (12 women), 2 part-time (1 woman); includes 2 minority (both Asian Americans or Pacific Islanders), 25 international. 32 applicants, 100% accepted. In 1998, 6 master's, 3 doctorates awarded. Terminal master's awarded for partial completion of doctoral program. *Degree requirements:* For master's and doctorate, thesis/dissertation required, foreign language not required. *Entrance requirements:* For master's and doctorate, GRE, minimum GPA of 3.0. *Average time to degree:* Master's–2.9 years full-time; doctorate–4.6 years full-time. *Application deadline:* For fall admission, 6/1 (priority date); for spring admission, 12/1. Applications are processed on a rolling basis. Application fee: $0 ($25 for international students). *Financial aid:* In 1998–99, 14 research assistantships, 29 teaching assistantships with full tuition reimbursements were awarded.; fellowships Financial aid application deadline: 8/1. Total annual research expenditures: $2 million. *Unit head:* Peter M. A. Sherwood, Head, 785-532-6665, Fax: 785-532-6666, E-mail: escashem@ksu.edu. *Application contact:* Christer B. Aakeroy, Graduate Coordinator, 785-532-1468, Fax: 785-532-6666.

See in-depth description on page 143.

Kent State University, College of Arts and Sciences, Department of Chemistry, Kent, OH 44242-0001. Offers analytical chemistry (MS, PhD); biochemistry (PhD); chemistry (MA, MS, PhD); inorganic chemistry (MS, PhD); organic chemistry (MS, PhD); physical chemistry (MS, PhD). *Faculty:* 23 full-time. *Students:* 36 full-time (20 women), 2 part-time (both women); includes 1 minority (African American), 19 international. 160 applicants, 60% accepted. In 1998, 5 master's, 4 doctorates awarded. *Degree requirements:* For master's and doctorate, thesis/dissertation required, foreign language not required. *Entrance requirements:* For master's, minimum GPA of 2.75; for doctorate, minimum GPA of 3.0. *Application deadline:* For fall admission, 7/12; for spring admission, 11/29. Applications are processed on a rolling basis. Application fee: $30.

Financial aid: Fellowships, research assistantships, teaching assistantships, Federal Work-Study, institutionally-sponsored loans, and tuition waivers (full) available. Financial aid application deadline: 2/1. *Unit head:* Dr. Rathindra N. Bose, Chairman, 330-672-2032, Fax: 330-672-3816.

See in-depth description on page 147.

Lakehead University, Graduate Studies and Research, Faculty of Arts and Science, Department of Chemistry, Thunder Bay, ON P7B 5E1, Canada. Offers M Sc. Part-time and evening/weekend programs available. *Degree requirements:* For master's, thesis required, foreign language not required. *Entrance requirements:* For master's, TOEFL (minimum score of 550 required), minimum B+ average. *Faculty research:* Physical inorganic chemistry, photochemistry, physical chemistry.

Lamar University, College of Graduate Studies, College of Arts and Sciences, Department of Chemistry, Beaumont, TX 77710. Offers MS. Part-time programs available. *Faculty:* 7 full-time (0 women). *Students:* 7 full-time (4 women), 7 part-time (4 women); includes 2 minority (1 African American, 1 Asian American or Pacific Islander), 9 international. Average age 27. In 1998, 5 degrees awarded. *Degree requirements:* For master's, computer language, thesis, practicum required, foreign language not required. *Entrance requirements:* For master's, GRE General Test (minimum combined score of 1000 required), TOEFL (minimum score of 550 required), minimum GPA of 2.5 in last 60 hours. *Application deadline:* For fall admission, 8/1; for spring admission, 12/1. Applications are processed on a rolling basis. Application fee: $0. *Financial aid:* In 1998–99, 7 teaching assistantships were awarded.; unspecified assistantships also available. Financial aid application deadline: 4/1. *Faculty research:* Environmental chemistry, surface chemistry, polymer chemistry, organic synthesis. *Unit head:* Dr. Shawn B. Allin, Interim Chair, 409-880-8267, Fax: 409-880-8270, E-mail: chemistry@hal.lamar.edu. *Application contact:* Dr. David L. Cocke, Gill Chair of Analytical Chemistry, 409-880-8372, Fax: 409-880-8270, E-mail: cocked@hal.lamar.edu.

Laurentian University, School of Graduate Studies and Research, Programme in Chemistry and Biochemistry, Sudbury, ON P3E 2C6, Canada. Offers M Sc. Part-time programs available. *Faculty:* 11 full-time (2 women), 5 part-time (0 women). *Students:* 7 full-time (2 women), 5 part-time (2 women), 1 international. 19 applicants, 21% accepted. In 1998, 3 degrees awarded. *Degree requirements:* For master's, thesis or alternative required, foreign language not required. *Entrance requirements:* For master's, honors degree with second class or better. *Application deadline:* For fall admission, 9/1 (priority date). Application fee: $50. *Financial aid:* In 1998–99, 3 fellowships (averaging $2,000 per year), 5 teaching assistantships (averaging $6,500 per year) were awarded.; research assistantships, institutionally-sponsored loans and scholarships also available. *Faculty research:* Computer simulation and characterization of both molecular structure and shape dynamics in large interacting systems, molecular control of apoptosis in mammalian cells, metal-atom mediated chemical transformations, functionalized nanoporous oxides, using kinetic isotope effect to model the SN2 transition state. Total annual research expenditures: $393,458. *Unit head:* Dr. Werner Rank, Chairman, 705-675-1151 Ext. 2101, Fax: 705-675-4844. *Application contact:* 705-675-1151 Ext. 3909, Fax: 705-675-4843.

Lehigh University, College of Arts and Sciences, Department of Chemistry, Bethlehem, PA 18015-3094. Offers biochemistry and analytical chemistry (MS, PhD); chemistry (DA); clinical chemistry (MS); inorganic chemistry (MS, PhD); organic chemistry (MS, PhD); pharmaceutical chemistry (PhD); physical chemistry (MS, PhD). Part-time programs available. Postbaccalaureate distance learning degree programs offered (no on-campus study). *Students:* 30 full-time (14 women), 92 part-time (46 women); includes 10 minority (7 Asian Americans or Pacific Islanders, 3 Hispanic Americans), 10 international. 42 applicants, 93% accepted. In 1998, 18 master's, 3 doctorates awarded. Terminal master's awarded for partial completion of doctoral program. *Degree requirements:* For master's, foreign language and thesis not required; for doctorate, dissertation required. *Entrance requirements:* For master's and doctorate, GRE General Test, TSE (minimum score of 230 required). *Average time to degree:* Master's–2.5 years full-time, 4 years part-time; doctorate–6 years full-time. *Application deadline:* For fall admission, 7/15; for spring admission, 12/1. Applications are processed on a rolling basis. Application fee: $40. *Financial aid:* In 1998–99, 26 students received aid, including 4 fellowships, 3 research assistantships, 16 teaching assistantships; career-related internships or fieldwork and institutionally-sponsored loans also available. Financial aid application deadline: 1/15. *Unit head:* Dr. Keith J. Schray, Chairman, 610-758-3474, Fax: 610-758-6536, E-mail: kjs0@lehigh.edu. *Application contact:* Dr. James E. Roberts, Graduate Coordinator, 610-758-4847, Fax: 610-758-6536, E-mail: jer1@lehigh.edu.

Long Island University, Brooklyn Campus, Richard L. Conolly College of Liberal Arts and Sciences, Department of Chemistry, Brooklyn, NY 11201-8423. Offers MS. Part-time and evening/weekend programs available. *Faculty:* 10 full-time. *Students:* 13 full-time (6 women), 13 part-time (5 women); includes 16 minority (7 African Americans, 7 Asian Americans or Pacific Islanders, 2 Hispanic Americans) 21 applicants, 76% accepted. In 1998, 10 degrees awarded. *Degree requirements:* For master's, thesis or alternative required, foreign language not required. *Application deadline:* Applications are processed on a rolling basis. Application fee: $30. Electronic applications accepted. *Financial aid:* In 1998–99, 17 teaching assistantships with full tuition reimbursements (averaging $7,000 per year) were awarded.; fellowships, scholarships also available. Aid available to part-time students. Financial aid application deadline: 8/1; financial aid applicants required to submit FAFSA. *Faculty research:* Clinical chemistry, free radicals, heats of hydrogenation. *Unit head:* Dr. Albert L. Hirschberg, Chair, 718-488-1208. *Application contact:* Bernard W. Sullivan, Associate Director of Admissions, 718-488-1011, Fax: 718-797-2399, E-mail: attend@liu.edu.

See in-depth description on page 151.

Louisiana State University and Agricultural and Mechanical College, Graduate School, College of Basic Sciences, Department of Chemistry, Baton Rouge, LA 70803. Offers MS, PhD. Part-time programs available. *Faculty:* 27 full-time (0 women), 2 part-time (0 women). *Students:* 111 full-time (47 women), 11 part-time (4 women); includes 36 minority (30 African Americans, 1 Asian American or Pacific Islander, 2 Hispanic Americans, 3 Native Americans), 37 international. Average age 29. 38 applicants, 55% accepted. In 1998, 4 master's, 6 doctorates awarded. Terminal master's awarded for partial completion of doctoral program. *Degree requirements:* For master's, thesis required (for some programs), foreign language not required; for doctorate, dissertation, general exam required, foreign language not required. *Entrance requirements:* For master's and doctorate, GRE General Test, TOEFL, minimum GPA of 3.0. *Average time to degree:* Doctorate–5.3 years full-time. *Application deadline:* For fall admission, 3/1 (priority date); for spring admission, 8/1. Applications are processed on a rolling basis. Application fee: $25. *Financial aid:* In 1998–99, 13 fellowships, 40 research assistantships with partial tuition reimbursements, 54 teaching assistantships with partial tuition reimbursements were awarded.; unspecified assistantships also available. Financial aid application deadline: 7/1. *Faculty research:* Free radicals, bioinorganic chemistry, polymers, synthesis, spectroscopy. Total annual research expenditures: $3 million. *Unit head:* Dr. Brian Hales, Chair, 225-388-3361, Fax: 225-388-3458, E-mail: brian.hales@chemgate.chem.lsu.edu. *Application contact:* Dr. Steven Watkins, Director of Graduate Studies, 225-388-3467, E-mail: steve.watkins@chem.lsu.edu.

Louisiana Tech University, Graduate School, College of Engineering and Science, Department of Chemistry, Ruston, LA 71272. Offers MS. Part-time programs available. *Degree requirements:* For master's, computer language, thesis required, foreign language not required. *Entrance requirements:* For master's, GRE General Test (minimum combined score of 1070 required; average 1245), TOEFL (minimum score of 550 required), minimum GPA of 3.0 in last 60 hours. *Faculty research:* Vibrational spectroscopy, quantum studies of chemical reactions, enzyme kinetics, synthesis of transition metal compounds, NMR spectrometry.

Loyola University Chicago, Graduate School, Department of Chemistry, Chicago, IL 60611-2196. Offers MS, PhD. *Degree requirements:* For master's and doctorate, thesis/dissertation required, foreign language not required. *Entrance requirements:* For master's and doctorate, GRE General Test, GRE Subject Test, TOEFL. *Faculty research:* Magnetic resonance of membrane/protein systems, organometallic catalysis, novel synthesis of natural products.

Marquette University, Graduate School, College of Arts and Sciences, Department of Chemistry, Milwaukee, WI 53201-1881. Offers analytical chemistry (MS, PhD); bioanalytical chemistry (MS, PhD); biophysical chemistry (MS, PhD); chemical physics (MS, PhD); inorganic chemistry (MS, PhD); organic chemistry (MS, PhD); physical chemistry (MS, PhD). Part-time programs available. *Faculty:* 15 full-time (2 women), 1 part-time (0 women). *Students:* 33 full-time (12 women), 6 part-time (1 woman); includes 5 minority (2 African Americans, 3 Asian Americans or Pacific Islanders), 30 international. Average age 32. In 1998, 3 master's, 7 doctorates awarded. Terminal master's awarded for partial completion of doctoral program. *Degree requirements:* For master's, comprehensive exam required; for doctorate, dissertation, cumulative exams required, foreign language not required. *Entrance requirements:* For master's and doctorate, TOEFL (minimum score of 550 required), GRE Subject Test. Application fee: $40. Tuition: Part-time $510 per credit hour. Tuition and fees vary according to program. *Financial aid:* In 1998–99, 3 research assistantships, 27 teaching assistantships were awarded.; fellowships, Federal Work-Study, institutionally-sponsored loans, scholarships, and tuition waivers (full and partial) also available. Aid available to part-time students. Financial aid application deadline: 2/15. *Faculty research:* Inorganic complexes, laser Raman spectroscopy, organic synthesis, chemical dynamics, biophysiology. Total annual research expenditures: $496,000. *Unit head:* Dr. Charles Wilkie, Chairman, 414-288-7065, Fax: 414-288-7066. *Application contact:* Dr. Mark Steinmetz, Director of Graduate Studies, 414-288-3535, Fax: 414-288-7066.

Marshall University, Graduate College, College of Science, Department of Chemistry, Huntington, WV 25755-2020. Offers MS. *Faculty:* 10 full-time (1 woman). *Students:* 10 full-time (5 women), 9 part-time (6 women), 2 international. In 1998, 2 degrees awarded. *Degree requirements:* For master's, thesis required, foreign language not required. *Entrance requirements:* For master's, GRE General Test. *Financial aid:* Career-related internships or fieldwork available. *Unit head:* Dr. Daniel Babb, Chairperson, 304-696-2430, E-mail: babb@marshall.edu. *Application contact:* Ken O'Neal, Assistant Vice President, Adult Student Services, 304-746-2500 Ext. 1907, Fax: 304-746-1902, E-mail: oneal@marshall.edu.

Massachusetts College of Pharmacy and Health Sciences, Graduate Studies, Program in Chemistry, Boston, MA 02115-5896. Offers MS, PhD. *Faculty:* 7 full-time (0 women). *Students:* 11 full-time (6 women), 2 part-time (1 woman); includes 2 minority (both Asian Americans or Pacific Islanders), 11 international. Average age 24. 12 applicants, 67% accepted. Terminal master's awarded for partial completion of doctoral program. *Degree requirements:* For master's, oral defense of thesis required; for doctorate, one foreign language (computer language can substitute), oral defense of dissertation, qualifying exam required. *Entrance requirements:* For master's and doctorate, GRE General Test (minimum combined score of 1650 on three sections required), TOEFL (minimum score of 550 required), minimum QPA of 3.0. *Average time to degree:* Master's–3 years full-time; doctorate–5 years full-time. *Application deadline:* For fall admission, 2/1 (priority date). Application fee: $60. *Financial aid:* In 1998–99, 8 students received aid, including 8 teaching assistantships with full tuition reimbursements available (averaging $11,000 per year); fellowships with partial tuition reimbursements available, research assistantships with partial tuition reimbursements available, tuition waivers (partial) and unspecified assistantships also available. Financial aid application deadline: 2/1. *Faculty research:* Organic synthesis, analytical medicinal chemistry, medicinal chemistry, bioanalytical chemistry, nucleoside chemistry. Total annual research expenditures: $30,000. *Unit head:* Dr. Stephen Kerr, Head, 617-732-2093, Fax: 617-732-2801, E-mail: skerr@mcp.edu. *Application contact:* Lovie Condrick, Coordinator of Graduate Admissions, 617-732-2986, Fax: 617-732-2801, E-mail: admissions@mcp.edu.

Massachusetts Institute of Technology, School of Science, Department of Chemistry, Cambridge, MA 02139-4307. Offers biochemistry (PhD); biological chemistry (PhD, Sc D); inorganic chemistry (PhD, Sc D); organic chemistry (PhD, Sc D); physical chemistry (PhD, Sc D). *Faculty:* 27 full-time (2 women). *Students:* 172 full-time (51 women); includes 19 minority (3 African Americans, 6 Asian Americans or Pacific Islanders, 9 Hispanic Americans, 1 Native American), 53 international. Average age 26. 397 applicants, 35% accepted. In 1998, 44 doctorates awarded. *Degree requirements:* For doctorate, dissertation, comprehensive oral exam, oral presentation, written exams required, foreign language not required. *Average time to degree:* Doctorate–5 years full-time. *Application deadline:* For fall admission, 1/15. Application fee: $55. *Financial aid:* In 1998–99, 22 fellowships with full tuition reimbursements (averaging $15,940 per year), 94 research assistantships with full tuition reimbursements (averaging $17,100 per year), 48 teaching assistantships with full tuition reimbursements (averaging $18,405 per year) were awarded.; career-related internships or fieldwork and traineeships also available. Financial aid application deadline: 1/14. *Faculty research:* Synthetic organic chemistry, enzymatic reaction mechanisms, inorganic and organometallic spectroscopy, high resolution NMR spectroscopy. Total annual research expenditures: $11.1 million. *Unit head:* Dr. Stephen J. Lippard, Chairman, 617-253-1845. *Application contact:* Susan Brighton, Graduate Administrator, 617-253-1845, Fax: 617-258-0241, E-mail: brighton@mit.edu.

Massachusetts Institute of Technology, School of Science, Department of Earth, Atmospheric, and Planetary Sciences, Program in Atmospheric Chemistry, Cambridge, MA 02139-4307. Offers SM, PhD, Sc D. *Faculty:* 2 full-time (0 women). *Degree requirements:* For master's, thesis required, foreign language not required; for doctorate, dissertation, general exam required, foreign language not required. *Entrance requirements:* For master's and doctorate, GRE General Test, GRE Subject Test. *Application deadline:* For fall admission, 1/15; for spring admission, 11/1. Application fee: $55. *Financial aid:* Application deadline: 1/15. *Unit head:* Anastasia Frangos, Administrative Assistant, 617-253-3381, Fax: 617-253-8298, E-mail: eapsinfo@mit.edu. *Application contact:* Anastasia Frangos, Administrative Assistant, 617-253-3381, Fax: 617-253-8298, E-mail: eapsinfo@mit.edu.

McGill University, Faculty of Graduate Studies and Research, Faculty of Science, Department of Chemistry, Montréal, PQ H3A 2T5, Canada. Offers M Sc, PhD. *Faculty:* 30 full-time (4 women), 5 part-time (1 woman). *Students:* 108 full-time (40 women), 2 part-time. In 1998, 13 master's, 20 doctorates awarded. *Degree requirements:* For master's and doctorate, thesis/dissertation required. *Entrance requirements:* For master's, TOEFL (minimum score of 575 required), minimum GPA of 3.0; for doctorate, TOEFL (minimum score of 575 required). *Application deadline:* For fall admission, 3/1 (priority date). Applications are processed on a rolling basis. Application fee: $60. *Financial aid:* Stipends available. *Unit head:* R. B. Lennox, Director of Graduate Studies, 514-398-6941, Fax: 514-398-3797, E-mail: renee@omc.lan.mcgill.ca.

McMaster University, School of Graduate Studies, Faculty of Science, Department of Chemistry, Hamilton, ON L8S 4M2, Canada. Offers analytical chemistry (M Sc, PhD); chemical physics (M Sc, PhD); chemistry (M Sc, PhD); inorganic chemistry (M Sc, PhD); organic chemistry (M Sc, PhD); physical chemistry (M Sc, PhD); polymer chemistry (M Sc, PhD). Part-time programs available. *Faculty:* 21 full-time (2 women), 4 part-time (0 women). *Students:* 67 full-time (23 women), 1 part-time, 1 international. Average age 24. In 1998, 2 master's, 4 doctorates awarded. Terminal master's awarded for partial completion of doctoral program. *Degree requirements:* For master's, thesis required, foreign language not required; for doctorate, dissertation, comprehensive exam required, foreign language not required. *Entrance requirements:* For master's, minimum B+ average. *Average time to degree:* Master's–2 years full-time; doctorate–4.5 years full-time. *Application deadline:* For fall admission, 4/30; for spring admission, 3/15. Applications are processed on a rolling basis. Application fee: $50. *Financial aid:* Teaching assistantships available. *Unit head:* Dr. M. J. McGlinchey, Chair, 905-525-9140 Ext. 24504, Fax: 905-522-2509, E-mail: mcglinchey@mcmail.cis.mcmaster.ca. *Application contact:* Carol Dada, Administrator, 905-525-9140 Ext. 23487, Fax: 905-522-2509, E-mail: dada@mcmail.cis.mcmaster.ca.

McNeese State University, Graduate School, College of Science, Department of Chemistry, Lake Charles, LA 70609-2495. Offers MS. Evening/weekend programs available. *Faculty:* 13 full-time (3 women). *Students:* 2 full-time (0 women), 8 part-time (2 women). In 1998, 3

Chemistry

McNeese State University (continued)
degrees awarded. *Degree requirements:* For master's, one foreign language (computer language can substitute), thesis or alternative required. *Entrance requirements:* For master's, GRE General Test. *Application deadline:* For fall admission, 7/15 (priority date). Applications are processed on a rolling basis. Application fee: $10 ($25 for international students). *Financial aid:* Teaching assistantships available. Financial aid application deadline: 5/1. *Faculty research:* Environmental studies, carotenoids, polymers, chemical education. *Unit head:* Dr. Russell Ham, Head, 318-475-5776.

Memorial University of Newfoundland, School of Graduate Studies, Department of Chemistry, St. John's, NF A1C 5S7, Canada. Offers M Sc, PhD. *Students:* 41 full-time (10 women), 4 part-time (2 women), 14 international. 47 applicants, 9% accepted. In 1998, 7 master's, 6 doctorates awarded. *Degree requirements:* For master's and doctorate, thesis/dissertation required. *Entrance requirements:* For master's, B Sc or honors degree in chemistry (preferred); for doctorate, American Chemical Society placement test, Master's degree in chemistry or honors bachelor's degree. *Application deadline:* For fall admission, 4/30 (priority date). Applications are processed on a rolling basis. Application fee: $40. *Financial aid:* Fellowships, research assistantships, teaching assistantships available. *Faculty research:* Analytical/environmental chemistry; medicinal electrochemistry; inorganic, marine, organic, physical, and theoretical/computational chemistry. *Unit head:* Dr. Robert Lucas, Head, 709-737-8772, Fax: 709-737-3702, E-mail: rlucas@morgan.ucs.mun.ca. *Application contact:* Dr. R. A. Poirier, Graduate Officer, 709-737-8609, Fax: 709-737-3702, E-mail: rpoirier@morgan.ucs.mun.ca.

Miami University, Graduate School, College of Arts and Sciences, Department of Chemistry and Biochemistry, Oxford, OH 45056. Offers biochemistry (MS, PhD); chemistry (MS, PhD). Part-time programs available. *Faculty:* 30. *Students:* 52 full-time (21 women), 3 part-time (1 woman); includes 3 minority (2 Asian Americans or Pacific Islanders, 1 Hispanic American), 15 international. 26 applicants, 81% accepted. In 1998, 4 master's, 7 doctorates awarded. *Degree requirements:* For master's, thesis, final exam required; for doctorate, dissertation, comprehensive and final exams required. *Entrance requirements:* For master's, minimum undergraduate GPA of 3.0 during previous 2 years or 2.75 overall; for doctorate, minimum undergraduate GPA of 2.75, 3.0 graduate. *Application deadline:* For fall admission, 3/1. Application fee: $35. *Financial aid:* Fellowships, research assistantships, teaching assistantships, Federal Work-Study and tuition waivers (full) available. Financial aid application deadline: 3/1. *Unit head:* Dr. Michael Novak, Chair, 513-529-2813. *Application contact:* Dr. Chris Makaroff, Director of Graduate Studies, 513-529-1659.

See in-depth description on page 155.

Michigan State University, Graduate School, College of Natural Science, Department of Chemistry, East Lansing, MI 48824-1020. Offers analytical chemistry (MS, PhD); chemistry (MAT, MS, PhD); chemistry-environmental toxicology (PhD); environmental toxicology (PhD); inorganic chemistry (MS, PhD); organic chemistry (MS, PhD); physical chemistry (PhD). *Faculty:* 36 full-time (4 women). *Students:* 149 full-time (46 women), 18 part-time (9 women); includes 12 minority (6 African Americans, 3 Asian Americans or Pacific Islanders, 2 Hispanic Americans, 1 Native American), 80 international. Average age 28. 199 applicants, 49% accepted. In 1998, 3 master's, 30 doctorates awarded. Terminal master's awarded for partial completion of doctoral program. *Degree requirements:* For master's, thesis required (for some programs), foreign language not required; for doctorate, dissertation required, foreign language not required. *Entrance requirements:* For master's and doctorate, GRE, TOEFL. *Application deadline:* Applications are processed on a rolling basis. Application fee: $30 ($40 for international students). *Financial aid:* In 1998–99, 53 research assistantships (averaging $12,265 per year), 13 teaching assistantships (averaging $12,075 per year) were awarded.; fellowships Financial aid applicants required to submit FAFSA. *Faculty research:* Analytical instrumentation, laser spectroscopy, fundamental materials, theoretical chemistry, biophysical and biorganic chemistry. Total annual research expenditures: $4.8 million. *Unit head:* Dr. Katharine C. Hunt, Chairperson, 517-355-9715, Fax: 517-353-1793, E-mail: chemdept@cem.msu.edu. *Application contact:* Dr. Richard Schwendeman, Associate Chair, Graduate Program, 517-355-9715 Ext. 344, Fax: 517-353-1793, E-mail: gradoff@cem.msu.edu.

Michigan Technological University, Graduate School, College of Sciences and Arts, Department of Chemistry, Houghton, MI 49931-1295. Offers MS, PhD. Part-time programs available. *Faculty:* 19 full-time (4 women). *Students:* 34 full-time (13 women), 24 international. Average age 28. 59 applicants, 51% accepted. In 1998, 6 master's, 2 doctorates awarded. *Degree requirements:* For master's and doctorate, thesis/dissertation required, foreign language not required. *Entrance requirements:* For master's and doctorate, TOEFL (minimum score of 600 required). *Average time to degree:* Master's–3.7 years full-time; doctorate–4.7 years full-time. *Application deadline:* For fall admission, 3/15 (priority date). Applications are processed on a rolling basis. Application fee: $30 ($35 for international students). Tuition, state resident: full-time $4,377. Tuition, nonresident: full-time $9,108. Required fees: $126. Tuition and fees vary according to course load. *Financial aid:* In 1998–99, 4 fellowships (averaging $3,156 per year), 3 research assistantships (averaging $10,095 per year), 20 teaching assistantships (averaging $9,315 per year) were awarded.; career-related internships or fieldwork, Federal Work-Study, institutionally-sponsored loans, and unspecified assistantships also available. Aid available to part-time students. Financial aid application deadline: 3/1; financial aid applicants required to submit FAFSA. *Faculty research:* Physical chemistry, inorganic chemistry, organic chemistry, polymer chemistry, analytical chemistry. Total annual research expenditures:$491,756. *Unit head:* Dr. James P. Riehl, Chair, 906-487-2048, Fax: 906-482-2061, E-mail: jpriehl@mtu.edu.

Middle Tennessee State University, College of Graduate Studies, College of Basic and Applied Sciences, Department of Chemistry, Murfreesboro, TN 37132. Offers chemistry (MS, DA); natural science (MS). *Faculty:* 23 full-time (7 women), 2 part-time (0 women). *Students:* 10 full-time (6 women), 21 part-time (6 women); includes 9 minority (5 African Americans, 4 Asian Americans or Pacific Islanders), 2 international. Average age 34. 14 applicants, 29% accepted. In 1998, 9 master's, 3 doctorates awarded. *Degree requirements:* For master's, one foreign language, thesis, comprehensive exams required; for doctorate, dissertation, comprehensive exams required, foreign language not required. *Entrance requirements:* For master's, GRE, MAT; for doctorate, GRE. *Application deadline:* For fall admission, 8/1 (priority date). Applications are processed on a rolling basis. Application fee: $25. Electronic applications accepted. *Financial aid:* Teaching assistantships, institutionally-sponsored loans available. Aid available to part-time students. Financial aid application deadline: 5/1; financial aid applicants required to submit FAFSA. Total annual research expenditures: $21,622. *Unit head:* Dr. Earl F. Pearson, Chair, 615-898-2956, Fax: 615-898-5182, E-mail: epearson@mtsu.edu.

Minnesota State University, Mankato, College of Graduate Studies, College of Science, Engineering and Technology, Department of Chemistry and Geology, Mankato, MN 56002-8400. Offers chemistry (MA, MS). *Faculty:* 8 full-time (2 women). *Students:* 1 full-time (0 women), 3 part-time (2 women); includes 2 minority (both Asian Americans or Pacific Islanders) Average age 27. *Degree requirements:* For master's, one foreign language, thesis or alternative, comprehensive exam, departmental qualifying exam required. *Entrance requirements:* For master's, minimum GPA of 3.0 during previous 2 years. *Application deadline:* For fall admission, 7/9 (priority date); for spring admission, 11/27. Applications are processed on a rolling basis. Application fee: $20. *Financial aid:* Teaching assistantships with partial tuition reimbursements, career-related internships or fieldwork, Federal Work-Study, and institutionally-sponsored loans available. Aid available to part-time students. Financial aid application deadline: 3/15; financial aid applicants required to submit FAFSA. *Unit head:* Jeff Pribyl, Chairperson, 507-389-1963. *Application contact:* Joni Roberts, Admissions Coordinator, 507-389-2321, Fax: 507-389-5974, E-mail: grad@mankato.msus.edu.

Mississippi College, Graduate School, College of Arts and Sciences, Program in Combined Sciences, Clinton, MS 39058. Offers biology (MCS); chemistry (MCS); mathematics (MCS). *Faculty:* 25 full-time (7 women), 16 part-time (7 women). *Degree requirements:* For master's, thesis or alternative, comprehensive exam required, foreign language not required. *Entrance requirements:* For master's, GRE General Test (minimum combined score of 850 required), minimum GPA of 2.5. *Application deadline:* For fall admission, 8/15 (priority date). Applications are processed on a rolling basis. Application fee: $25 ($75 for international students). *Unit head:* Dr. Ron Howard, Dean, College of Arts and Sciences, 601-925-3327, Fax: 601-925-3499.

Mississippi State University, College of Arts and Sciences, Department of Chemistry, Mississippi State, MS 39762. Offers MS, PhD. *Students:* 47 full-time (18 women), 4 part-time (1 woman); includes 30 minority (4 African Americans, 26 Asian Americans or Pacific Islanders), 2 international. Average age 31. 42 applicants, 38% accepted. In 1998, 3 master's, 5 doctorates awarded. Terminal master's awarded for partial completion of doctoral program. *Degree requirements:* For master's and doctorate, thesis/dissertation, comprehensive oral or written exam required, foreign language not required. *Entrance requirements:* For master's, TOEFL, minimum GPA of 2.75; for doctorate, TOEFL. *Application deadline:* For fall admission, 7/1; for spring admission, 11/1. Applications are processed on a rolling basis. Application fee: $25 for international students. *Financial aid:* Research assistantships with full tuition reimbursements, teaching assistantships with full tuition reimbursements, Federal Work-Study, institutionally-sponsored loans, and unspecified assistantships available. Financial aid applicants required to submit FAFSA. *Faculty research:* Spectroscopy, fluorometry, NMR, organic and inorganic synthesis, electrochemistry. Total annual research expenditures: $2.3 million. *Unit head:* Dr. Philip B. Oldham, Head, 662-325-3584, Fax: 662-325-1618, E-mail: pbo1@ra.msstate.edu. *Application contact:* Jerry B. Inmon, Director of Admissions, 662-325-2224, Fax: 662-325-7360, E-mail: admit@admissions.msstate.edu.

Montana State University–Bozeman, College of Graduate Studies, College of Letters and Science, Department of Chemistry, Bozeman, MT 59717. Offers biochemistry (MS, PhD); chemistry (MS, PhD). Part-time programs available. *Students:* 35 full-time (9 women), 31 part-time (7 women); includes 1 minority (Native American) Average age 29. 29 applicants, 86% accepted. In 1998, 5 master's, 7 doctorates awarded. *Degree requirements:* For master's, thesis or alternative required, foreign language not required; for doctorate, dissertation required, foreign language not required. *Entrance requirements:* For master's and doctorate, GRE General Test (minimum score of 420 on verbal section required), TOEFL (minimum score of 570 required). *Application deadline:* For fall admission, 6/1 (priority date); for spring admission, 11/1. Applications are processed on a rolling basis. Application fee: $50. *Financial aid:* Research assistantships, teaching assistantships, career-related internships or fieldwork, Federal Work-Study, and scholarships available. Financial aid application deadline: 3/1; financial aid applicants required to submit FAFSA. *Faculty research:* Analytical, physical, organic, and inorganic chemistry. Total annual research expenditures: $2.6 million. *Unit head:* Dr. Paul Grieco, Head, 406-994-4801, Fax: 406-994-5407, E-mail: pgrieco@montana.edu.

Montclair State University, Office of Graduate Studies, College of Science and Mathematics, Department of Chemistry and Biochemistry, Upper Montclair, NJ 07043-1624. Offers chemistry (MS). Part-time and evening/weekend programs available. *Degree requirements:* For master's, comprehensive exam required, foreign language and thesis not required. *Entrance requirements:* For master's, GRE General Test.

Mount Allison University, Faculty of Science, Department of Chemistry, Sackville, NB E4L 1E4, Canada. Offers M Sc. *Degree requirements:* For master's, thesis required, foreign language not required. *Entrance requirements:* For master's, honors degree in chemistry. *Faculty research:* Biophysical chemistry of model biomembranes, organic synthesis, fast-reaction kinetics, physical chemistry of micelles.

Murray State University, College of Science, Department of Chemistry, Murray, KY 42071-0009. Offers MAT, MS. Part-time programs available. *Students:* 3 full-time (1 woman), 7 part-time (2 women), 5 international. 2 applicants, 100% accepted. *Degree requirements:* For master's, thesis required (for some programs), foreign language not required. *Entrance requirements:* For master's, GRE General Test, TOEFL (minimum score of 500 required). *Application deadline:* Applications are processed on a rolling basis. Application fee: $20. *Financial aid:* Research assistantships, teaching assistantships, Federal Work-Study available. Financial aid application deadline: 4/1. *Unit head:* Dr. Oliver Muscio, Graduate Coordinator, 502-762-6597, Fax: 502-762-6474, E-mail: oliver.muscio@murraystate.edu.

New Jersey Institute of Technology, Office of Graduate Studies, Department of Chemical Engineering, Chemistry and Environmental Science, Program in Applied Chemistry, Newark, NJ 07102-1982. Offers applied chemistry (MS); chemistry (PhD). PhD offered jointly with Rutgers, The State University of New Jersey, Newark. *Degree requirements:* For doctorate, dissertation, residency required, foreign language not required, foreign language not required. *Entrance requirements:* For master's, GRE General Test (minimum score of 450 on verbal section, 600 on quantitative, 550 on analytical required); for doctorate, GRE General Test (minimum score of 450 on verbal section, 600 on quantitative, 550 on analytical required), minimum graduate GPA of 3.5.

New Mexico Highlands University, Graduate Office, College of Arts and Sciences, Department of Physical Sciences, Las Vegas, NM 87701. Offers applied chemistry (MS). Part-time programs available. *Faculty:* 8 full-time (1 woman). *Students:* 10 full-time (3 women), 1 part-time; includes 1 minority (Hispanic American), 9 international. Average age 30. *Degree requirements:* For master's, thesis or alternative required, foreign language not required. *Entrance requirements:* For master's, minimum undergraduate GPA of 3.0. *Application deadline:* For fall admission, 8/1 (priority date). Applications are processed on a rolling basis. Application fee: $15. Tuition, state resident: full-time $1,988; part-time $83 per credit hour. Tuition, nonresident: full-time $8,034; part-time $83 per credit hour. Tuition and fees vary according to course load. *Financial aid:* Federal Work-Study available. Financial aid application deadline: 3/1. *Unit head:* Dr. Larry Sveum, Director, 505-454-3204, Fax: 505-454-3103, E-mail: lksueum@merlin.nmhu.edu. *Application contact:* Dr. Glen W. Davidson, Provost, 505-454-3311, Fax: 505-454-3558, E-mail: glendavidson@venus.nmhu.edu.

New Mexico Institute of Mining and Technology, Graduate Studies, Department of Chemistry, Socorro, NM 87801. Offers biochemistry (MS); chemistry (MS); environmental chemistry (PhD); explosives technology and atmospheric chemistry (PhD). *Faculty:* 7 full-time (1 woman). *Students:* 13 full-time (3 women); includes 1 minority (Hispanic American), 7 international. Average age 30. 61 applicants, 20% accepted. In 1998, 8 master's awarded. *Degree requirements:* For master's and doctorate, thesis/dissertation required, foreign language not required. *Entrance requirements:* For master's, GRE General Test, TOEFL (minimum score of 540 required); for doctorate, GRE General Test, GRE Subject Test, TOEFL (minimum score of 540 required). *Average time to degree:* Master's–4 years full-time; doctorate–7 years full-time. *Application deadline:* For fall admission, 3/1 (priority date); for spring admission, 6/1. Applications are processed on a rolling basis. Application fee: $16. *Financial aid:* In 1998–99, 4 research assistantships (averaging $9,670 per year), 8 teaching assistantships (averaging $9,670 per year) were awarded.; fellowships, Federal Work-Study and institutionally-sponsored loans also available. Financial aid application deadline: 3/1; financial aid applicants required to submit CSS PROFILE or FAFSA. *Faculty research:* Organic, analytical, environmental, and explosives chemistry. *Unit head:* Dr. Lawrence Werbelow, Chairman, 505-835-5263, Fax: 505-835-5364, E-mail: werbelow@jupiter.nmt.edu. *Application contact:* Dr. David B. Johnson, Dean of Graduate Studies, 505-835-5513, Fax: 505-835-5476, E-mail: graduate@nmt.edu.

New Mexico State University, Graduate School, College of Arts and Sciences, Department of Chemistry and Biochemistry, Las Cruces, NM 88003-8001. Offers MS, PhD. Part-time programs available. *Faculty:* 19 full-time (1 woman). *Students:* 39 full-time (8 women), 6 part-time (3 women); includes 5 minority (4 Hispanic Americans, 1 Native American), 20 international. Average age 30. 49 applicants, 37% accepted. In 1998, 5 master's, 12 doctorates awarded. *Degree requirements:* For master's and doctorate, thesis/dissertation required, foreign language not required. *Entrance requirements:* For master's and doctorate, GRE, TOEFL, BS in chemistry or biochemistry, minimum GPA of 3.0. *Application deadline:* For fall admission, 7/1 (priority date); for spring admission, 11/1. Applications are processed on a rolling basis. Application fee: $15 ($35 for international students). Tuition, state resident: full-time $2,682; part-time $112 per credit. Tuition, nonresident: full-time $8,376; part-time $349 per credit. Tuition and fees vary according to course load. *Financial aid:* Fellowships, research assistantships, teaching assistantships, career-related internships or fieldwork and Federal Work-Study available. Aid available to part-time students. Financial aid application deadline: 3/1. *Faculty research:* Clays, surfaces, and water structure; electroanalytical and environmental chemistry; organometallic synthesis and organobiomimetics; molecular genetics and enzymology of stress; spectroscopy and reaction kinetics. *Unit head:* Dr. Wolfgang Mueller, Head, 505-646-5877, Fax: 505-646-2649, E-mail: wmueller@nmsu.edu. *Application contact:* Dr. Jeff Arterburn, Assistant Professor, Chemistry, 505-646-2738, Fax: 505-646-2649.

New York University, Graduate School of Arts and Science, Department of Chemistry, New York, NY 10012-1019. Offers MS, PhD. *Faculty:* 25 full-time (3 women), 3 part-time. *Students:* 95 full-time (30 women), 4 part-time (3 women); includes 7 minority (1 African American, 5 Asian Americans or Pacific Islanders, 1 Hispanic American), 79 international. Average age 26. 215 applicants, 20% accepted. In 1998, 19 master's, 13 doctorates awarded. *Degree requirements:* For master's, thesis or alternative required, foreign language not required; for doctorate, one foreign language, dissertation required. *Entrance requirements:* For master's and doctorate, GRE General Test, GRE Subject Test, TOEFL, TSE. *Application deadline:* For fall admission, 1/4. Application fee: $60. Tuition: Full-time $17,880; part-time $745 per credit. Required fees: $1,140; $35 per credit. Tuition and fees vary according to course load and program. *Financial aid:* Fellowships, research assistantships, teaching assistantships, Federal Work-Study, institutionally-sponsored loans, tuition waivers (full and partial), and teaching fellowships available. Financial aid application deadline: 1/4; financial aid applicants required to submit FAFSA. *Faculty research:* Biomolecular chemistry, organic/inorganic chemistry, theoretical and experimental physical chemistry. *Unit head:* Jules Moskowitz, Chairman, 212-998-8400. *Application contact:* Nadrian Seeman, Director of Graduate Studies, 212-998-8400, Fax: 212-260-7905, E-mail: gradchem@nyu.edu.

See in-depth description on page 157.

North Carolina Agricultural and Technical State University, Graduate School, College of Arts and Sciences, Department of Chemistry, Greensboro, NC 27411. Offers MS. Part-time and evening/weekend programs available. *Faculty:* 11 full-time (3 women). *Students:* 6 full-time (5 women), 7 part-time (3 women); includes 11 minority (10 African Americans, 1 Asian American or Pacific Islander), 2 international. Average age 28. 14 applicants, 64% accepted. *Degree requirements:* For master's, thesis or alternative, comprehensive exam, qualifying exam required, foreign language not required. *Entrance requirements:* For master's, GRE General Test, minimum GPA of 3.0. *Application deadline:* For fall admission, 6/1 (priority date); for spring admission, 12/1. Applications are processed on a rolling basis. Application fee: $35. *Financial aid:* Fellowships, research assistantships, teaching assistantships, career-related internships or fieldwork available. Financial aid application deadline: 6/1. *Faculty research:* Tobacco pesticides. *Unit head:* Alex Williamson, Chairperson, 336-334-7601, E-mail: alex@garfield.ncat.edu.

North Carolina Central University, Division of Academic Affairs, College of Arts and Sciences, Department of Chemistry, Durham, NC 27707-3129. Offers MS. *Faculty:* 8 full-time (1 woman), 1 part-time (0 women). *Students:* 2 full-time (1 woman), 6 part-time (3 women); all minorities (7 African Americans, 1 Asian American or Pacific Islander) Average age 30. 1 applicants, 100% accepted. In 1998, 1 degree awarded. *Degree requirements:* For master's, one foreign language, computer language, thesis, comprehensive exam required. *Entrance requirements:* For master's, minimum GPA of 3.0 in major, 2.5 overall. *Application deadline:* For fall admission, 8/1. Application fee: $30. *Financial aid:* Career-related internships or fieldwork, Federal Work-Study, and institutionally-sponsored loans available. Aid available to part-time students. Financial aid application deadline: 5/1. *Unit head:* Dr. Wendell W. Wilkerson, Chairperson, 919-560-6351. *Application contact:* Dr. Bernice D. Johnson, Dean, College of Arts and Sciences, 919-560-6368.

North Carolina State University, Graduate School, College of Physical and Mathematical Sciences, Department of Chemistry, Raleigh, NC 27695. Offers MCH, MS, PhD. Part-time programs available. *Faculty:* 31 full-time (3 women), 8 part-time (1 woman). *Students:* 82 full-time (28 women), 19 part-time (9 women); includes 10 minority (5 African Americans, 3 Asian Americans or Pacific Islanders, 1 Hispanic American, 1 Native American), 17 international. Average age 28. 175 applicants, 35% accepted. In 1998, 10 master's, 14 doctorates awarded. Terminal master's awarded for partial completion of doctoral program. *Degree requirements:* For master's and doctorate, thesis/dissertation required, foreign language not required. *Entrance requirements:* For master's and doctorate, GRE General Test, minimum GPA of 3.0. *Application deadline:* For fall admission, 4/15 (priority date); for spring admission, 9/1. Applications are processed on a rolling basis. Application fee: $45. *Financial aid:* In 1998–99, 2 fellowships (averaging $6,065 per year), 79 research assistantships (averaging $5,858 per year) were awarded.; teaching assistantships, career-related internships or fieldwork also available. Financial aid application deadline: 3/1. *Faculty research:* Biological chemistry, electrochemistry, organic/inorganic materials, natural products, organometallics, photocatalysis, polymers, synthesis, zeolites. Total annual research expenditures: $4.3 million. *Unit head:* Dr. Bruce M. Novak, Head, 919-515-4563, Fax: 919-515-5079, E-mail: bruce_novak@ncsu.edu. *Application contact:* Dr. Russell J. Linderman, Director of Graduate Programs, 919-515-3616, Fax: 919-515-5079, E-mail: russell_linderman@ncsu.edu.

North Dakota State University, Graduate Studies and Research, College of Science and Mathematics, Department of Chemistry, Fargo, ND 58105. Offers MS, PhD. *Faculty:* 14 full-time (0 women). *Students:* 34 full-time (10 women); includes 1 minority (African American), 14 international. Average age 24. 20 applicants, 50% accepted. In 1998, 3 master's awarded (33% found work related to degree, 67% continued full-time study); 4 doctorates awarded (25% entered university research/teaching, 70% found other work related to degree). Terminal master's awarded for partial completion of doctoral program. *Degree requirements:* For master's and doctorate, thesis/dissertation required, foreign language not required. *Entrance requirements:* For master's and doctorate, TOEFL. *Application deadline:* For fall admission, 6/1 (priority date). Applications are processed on a rolling basis. Application fee: $25. *Financial aid:* In 1998–99, 34 students received aid, including 2 fellowships with tuition reimbursements available (averaging $18,000 per year), 16 research assistantships with tuition reimbursements available (averaging $13,450 per year), 16 teaching assistantships with tuition reimbursements available (averaging $13,950 per year); Federal Work-Study, institutionally-sponsored loans, and scholarships also available. Financial aid application deadline: 4/15. *Faculty research:* Analytical, syntheticorganic, inorganic, physical, and theoretical chemistry. Total annual research expenditures: $2.2 million. *Unit head:* Dr. Gregory J. McCarthy, Chair, 701-231-7193, Fax: 701-231-8831, E-mail: gmccarth@prairie.nodak.edu. *Application contact:* Dr. Mukund S. Sibi, Chair, Graduate Admissions.

Northeastern Illinois University, Graduate College, College of Arts and Sciences, Department of Chemistry, Program in Chemistry, Chicago, IL 60625-4699. Offers MS. Part-time and evening/weekend programs available. *Faculty:* 5 full-time (2 women), 3 part-time (0 women). *Students:* 2 full-time (0 women), 20 part-time (9 women); includes 6 minority (all Asian Americans or Pacific Islanders), 1 international. Average age 35. 2 applicants, 100% accepted. In 1998, 2 degrees awarded. *Degree requirements:* For master's, final exam or thesis required. *Entrance requirements:* For master's, minimum B average in 2 semesters of chemistry; 2 semesters of course work in calculus, organic chemistry, physical chemistry, and physics; 1 semester of course work in analytic chemistry; minimum GPA of 2.75. *Application deadline:* For fall admission, 3/31 (priority date); for spring admission, 9/30. Applications are processed on a rolling basis. Application fee: $0. *Financial aid:* In 1998–99, 9 students received aid, including 2 research assistantships; career-related internships or fieldwork, Federal Work-Study, institutionally-sponsored loans, and tuition waivers (full and partial) also available. Aid available to part-time students. Financial aid applicants required to submit FAFSA. *Faculty research:* Liquid chromatographic separation of pharmaceuticals, Diels-Alder reaction products, organogermanium chemistry, mass spectroscopy. *Unit head:* Dr. V. Curtis-Palmer, Graduate Adviser, 773-794-2558. *Application contact:* Dr. Mohan K. Sood, Dean of Graduate College, 773-583-4050 Ext. 6143, Fax: 773-794-6670, E-mail: m-sood@neiu.edu.

Northeastern University, College of Arts and Sciences, Department of Chemistry, Boston, MA 02115-5096. Offers analytical chemistry (PhD); chemistry (MAT, MS, PhD); inorganic chemistry (PhD); organic chemistry (PhD); physical chemistry (PhD). Part-time and evening/weekend programs available. *Faculty:* 20 full-time (3 women), 1 part-time (0 women). *Students:* 59 full-time (25 women), 23 part-time (9 women). Average age 25. 135 applicants, 20% accepted. In 1998, 5 master's awarded (100% found work related to degree); 10 doctorates awarded. Terminal master's awarded for partial completion of doctoral program. *Degree requirements:* For master's, thesis required (for some programs); for doctorate, dissertation, qualifying exam in specialty area required, foreign language not required. *Entrance requirements:* For master's and doctorate, TOEFL (minimum score of 580 required). *Average time to degree:* Master's–2 years full-time; doctorate–5 years full-time. *Application deadline:* For fall admission, 4/15. Applications are processed on a rolling basis. Application fee: $50. Electronic applications accepted. *Financial aid:* In 1998–99, 56 students received aid, including 12 fellowships with tuition reimbursements available, 21 research assistantships with tuition reimbursements available, 23 teaching assistantships with tuition reimbursements available; career-related internships or fieldwork, tuition waivers (partial), and unspecified assistantships also available. Financial aid application deadline: 4/15; financial aid applicants required to submit FAFSA. *Faculty research:* Electron transfer, theoretical chemical physics, analytical biotechnology, mass spectrometry, materials chemistry. Total annual research expenditures: $250,000. *Unit head:* Dr. David A. Forsyth, Chairman, 617-373-2822, Fax: 617-373-8795, E-mail: chemistry-grad-info@neu.edu. *Application contact:* Dr. Philip W. LeQuesne, Chair, Graduate Admissions Committee, 617-373-2383, Fax: 617-373-8795.

Northeast Louisiana University, Graduate Studies and Research, College of Pure and Applied Sciences, Department of Chemistry, Monroe, LA 71209-0001. Offers MS. *Faculty:* 11 full-time (1 woman). *Students:* 12 full-time (6 women), 2 part-time (both women), 13 international. Average age 28. In 1998, 6 degrees awarded. *Degree requirements:* For master's, one foreign language (computer language can substitute), thesis required. *Entrance requirements:* For master's, GRE General Test, minimum GPA of 2.8, 3.0 in last 24 hours of chemistry. *Application deadline:* For fall admission, 7/1 (priority date); for spring admission, 11/1. Applications are processed on a rolling basis. Application fee: $15 ($25 for international students). Tuition, state resident: full-time $1,650. Tuition, nonresident: full-time $7,608. Required fees: $378. *Financial aid:* Research assistantships, teaching assistantships, career-related internships or fieldwork, Federal Work-Study, and unspecified assistantships available. Financial aid application deadline: 7/1. *Faculty research:* Organic synthesis, pesticides, equine ovulation, smog analysis, PAH's, VUV photophysics, protein crystallography, evolving factor analysis. *Unit head:* Dr. Fred H. Watson, Head, 318-342-1825, E-mail: chwatson@alpha.nlu.edu.

Northern Arizona University, Graduate College, College of Arts and Sciences, Department of Chemistry, Flagstaff, AZ 86011. Offers MS. Part-time programs available. *Faculty:* 17 full-time (4 women). *Students:* 16 full-time (5 women), 4 part-time; includes 1 Asian American or Pacific Islander, 1 Hispanic American, 1 Native American, 1 international. Average age 26. 11 applicants, 100% accepted. In 1998, 8 degrees awarded. *Degree requirements:* For master's, thesis required, foreign language not required. *Application deadline:* For fall admission, 3/15 (priority date). Applications are processed on a rolling basis. Application fee: $45. *Financial aid:* In 1998–99, 13 research assistantships, 13 teaching assistantships were awarded.; fellowships, Federal Work-Study and tuition waivers (full and partial) also available. *Faculty research:* Biochemistry of exercise, organic and inorganic mechanism studies, inhibition of ice mutation, polymer separation. Total annual research expenditures: $261,191. *Unit head:* Dr. Wayne Hildebrandt, Chairman, 520-523-3008. *Application contact:* Dr. John MacDonald, 520-523-8893, E-mail: john.macdonald@nau.edu.

Northern Illinois University, Graduate School, College of Liberal Arts and Sciences, Department of Chemistry and Biochemistry, De Kalb, IL 60115-2854. Offers MS, PhD. Part-time programs available. *Faculty:* 17 full-time (2 women), 2 part-time (0 women). *Students:* 37 full-time (20 women), 10 part-time (2 women); includes 2 minority (1 African American, 1 Hispanic American), 7 international. Average age 31. 35 applicants, 46% accepted. In 1998, 4 master's, 4 doctorates awarded. Terminal master's awarded for partial completion of doctoral program. *Degree requirements:* For master's, comprehensive exam, research seminar required, thesis optional, foreign language not required; for doctorate, one foreign language (computer language can substitute), candidacy exam, dissertation defense, research seminar required. *Entrance requirements:* For master's, GRE General Test, TOEFL (minimum score of 550 required; 213 for computer-based), bachelor's degree in mathematics or science, minimum GPA of 2.75; for doctorate, GRE General Test, TOEFL (minimum score of 550 required; 213 for computer-based), bachelor's degree in mathematics or science, minimum GPA of 2.75 (undergraduate), 3.2 (graduate). *Application deadline:* For fall admission, 6/1; for spring admission, 11/1. Applications are processed on a rolling basis. Application fee: $30. *Financial aid:* In 1998–99, 3 research assistantships, 32 teaching assistantships were awarded.; fellowships, career-related internships or fieldwork, Federal Work-Study, tuition waivers (full), and unspecified assistantships also available. Aid available to part-time students. *Unit head:* Dr. James Erman, Chair, 815-753-1181. *Application contact:* Dr. Jon Carnahan, Director, Graduate Studies, 815-753-6879.

Northern Michigan University, College of Graduate Studies, College of Arts and Sciences, Department of Chemistry, Marquette, MI 49855-5301. Offers MS. Part-time programs available. *Faculty:* 7 full-time (2 women), 2 part-time (1 woman). *Students:* 5 full-time (2 women), 5 part-time (2 women). 3 applicants, 100% accepted. In 1998, 3 degrees awarded. *Degree requirements:* For master's, thesis required, foreign language not required. *Entrance requirements:* For master's, GRE General Test, minimum GPA of 2.75. *Application deadline:* For fall admission, 7/1 (priority date); for spring admission, 11/1. Applications are processed on a rolling basis. Application fee: $25. *Financial aid:* Career-related internships or fieldwork, Federal Work-Study, institutionally-sponsored loans, and unspecified assistantships available. Aid available to part-time students. Financial aid application deadline: 3/1. *Unit head:* Dr. Jerome Roth, Head, 906-227-2911.

Northwestern University, The Graduate School, Judd A. and Marjorie Weinberg College of Arts and Sciences, Department of Chemistry, Evanston, IL 60208. Offers PhD. Admissions and degrees offered through The Graduate School. *Faculty:* 22 full-time (1 woman), 1 part-time (0 women). *Students:* 134 full-time (48 women); includes 9 minority (3 African Americans, 3 Asian Americans or Pacific Islanders, 3 Hispanic Americans), 40 international. 263 applicants, 53% accepted. In 1998, 18 doctorates awarded. *Degree requirements:* For doctorate, dissertation required, foreign language not required. *Entrance requirements:* For doctorate, GRE General Test, TOEFL (minimum score of 560 required). Application fee: $50 ($55 for international students). *Financial aid:* In 1998–99, 17 fellowships with full tuition reimbursements (averaging $11,673 per year), 68 research assistantships with partial tuition reimbursements (averaging $12,342 per year), 36 teaching assistantships with full tuition reimbursements (averaging $12,042 per year) were awarded.; institutionally-sponsored loans, scholarships, and tuition waivers (full and partial) also available. Financial aid application deadline: 1/15; financial aid applicants required to submit FAFSA. *Faculty research:* Inorganic, organic, physical, bio-organic biophysical, and theoretical chemistry. Total annual research expenditures: $6.4 million. *Unit head:* James Ibers, Chair, 847-491-2968. *Application contact:* Susan Arden, Admission Contact, 847-491-2968, E-mail: chemdept@chem.nwu.edu.

Oakland University, Graduate Studies, College of Arts and Sciences, Department of Chemistry, Rochester, MI 48309-4401. Offers chemistry (MS, PhD); health and environmental chemistry (PhD). *Faculty:* 15 full-time. *Students:* 8 full-time (5 women), 5 part-time (2 women); includes 2

Chemistry

Oakland University (continued)
minority (both Asian Americans or Pacific Islanders), 5 international. Average age 32. 11 applicants, 36% accepted. In 1998, 4 master's, 1 doctorate awarded. *Degree requirements:* For master's and doctorate, thesis/dissertation required, foreign language not required. *Entrance requirements:* For master's, minimum GPA of 3.0 for unconditional admission; for doctorate, GRE Subject Test, minimum GPA of 3.0 for unconditional admission. *Application deadline:* For fall admission, 7/15; for spring admission, 3/15. Application fee: $30. Tuition, state resident: part-time $221 per credit hour. Tuition, nonresident: part-time $488 per credit hour. Required fees: $214 per semester. Part-time tuition and fees vary according to program. *Financial aid:* Federal Work-Study, institutionally-sponsored loans, and tuition waivers (full) available. Financial aid application deadline: 3/1; financial aid applicants required to submit FAFSA. *Unit head:* Dr. Michael Sevilla, Chair, 248-370-2328. *Application contact:* Dr. Arthur W. Bull, Coordinator, 248-370-2320.

The Ohio State University, Graduate School, College of Mathematical and Physical Sciences, Department of Chemistry, Columbus, OH 43210. Offers MS, PhD. *Faculty:* 38 full-time, 7 part-time. *Students:* 200 full-time (67 women), 6 part-time (1 woman); includes 18 minority (6 African Americans, 9 Asian Americans or Pacific Islanders, 3 Hispanic Americans), 89 international. 380 applicants, 20% accepted. In 1998, 15 master's, 33 doctorates awarded. *Degree requirements:* For master's, thesis optional, foreign language not required; for doctorate, dissertation required, foreign language not required. *Entrance requirements:* For master's, GRE General Test, GRE Subject Test. *Application deadline:* For fall admission, 8/15. Applications are processed on a rolling basis. Application fee: $30 ($40 for international students). *Financial aid:* Fellowships, research assistantships, teaching assistantships, Federal Work-Study and institutionally-sponsored loans available. Aid available to part-time students. *Unit head:* Matthew S. Platz, Chairman, 614-292-2251, Fax: 614-292-1685, E-mail: platz.1@osu.edu. *Application contact:* Larry B. Anderson, Vice Chair for Graduate Studies, 614-292-8917.

Oklahoma State University, Graduate College, College of Arts and Sciences, Department of Chemistry, Stillwater, OK 74078. Offers MS, PhD. *Faculty:* 16 full-time (3 women), 2 part-time (0 women). *Students:* 22 full-time (4 women), 30 part-time (11 women); includes 9 minority (1 African American, 1 Hispanic American, 7 Native Americans), 20 international. Average age 28. In 1998, 4 master's, 3 doctorates awarded. *Degree requirements:* For master's and doctorate, thesis/dissertation required, foreign language not required. *Entrance requirements:* For master's and doctorate, TOEFL (minimum score of 550 required). *Application deadline:* For fall admission, 6/1 (priority date). Application fee: $25. *Financial aid:* In 1998–99, 47 students received aid, including 19 research assistantships (averaging $14,582 per year), 28 teaching assistantships (averaging $16,375 per year); fellowships, Federal Work-Study and tuition waivers (partial) also available. Aid available to part-time students. Financial aid application deadline: 3/1. *Faculty research:* Materials science, surface chemistry, and nanoparticles; theoretical physical chemistry; synthetic and medicinal chemistry; bioanalytical chemistry; electromagnetic (UV, VIS, IR, Raman), mass, and x-ray spectroscopes. *Unit head:* Dr. Neil Purdie, Head, 405-744-5920.

Old Dominion University, College of Sciences, Department of Chemistry and Biochemistry, Norfolk, VA 23529. Offers analytical chemistry (MS); biochemistry (MS); biomedical sciences (PhD); clinical chemistry (MS); environmental chemistry (MS); organic chemistry (MS); physical chemistry (MS). Part-time and evening/weekend programs available. *Faculty:* 16 full-time (4 women). *Students:* 20 full-time (13 women), 12 part-time (8 women); includes 3 minority (1 African American, 2 Asian Americans or Pacific Islanders), 4 international. Average age 27. In 1998, 7 master's, 3 doctorates awarded. Terminal master's awarded for partial completion of doctoral program. *Degree requirements:* For master's and doctorate, thesis/dissertation, comprehensive exam required, foreign language not required. *Entrance requirements:* For master's, GRE General Test, TOEFL, minimum GPA of 3.0 in major, 2.5 overall; for doctorate, GRE General Test (minimum combined score of 1000 required), GRE Subject Test (minimum score of 600 required), TOEFL. *Application deadline:* For fall admission, 7/1; for spring admission, 11/1. Applications are processed on a rolling basis. Application fee: $30. *Financial aid:* In 1998–99, 32 students received aid, including 13 research assistantships (averaging $13,497 per year), 6 teaching assistantships (averaging $7,702 per year); fellowships, career-related internships or fieldwork and grants also available. Financial aid application deadline: 2/15; financial aid applicants required to submit FAFSA. *Faculty research:* Electroanalytical chemistry, clinical applications of trace element analysis, environmental-atmospheric chemistry, cancer biochemistry, drug chemistry. Total annual research expenditures: $1.1 million. *Unit head:* Dr. John R. Donet, Chair, 757-683-4078, E-mail: jdonet@odu.edu. *Application contact:* Dr. John R. Donet, Chair, 757-683-4078, E-mail: jdonet@odu.edu.

Oregon State University, Graduate School, College of Science, Department of Chemistry, Corvallis, OR 97331. Offers analytical chemistry (MS, PhD); chemistry (MA, MAIS); inorganic chemistry (MS, PhD); nuclear and radiation chemistry (MS, PhD); organic chemistry (MS, PhD); physical chemistry (MS, PhD). Part-time programs available. *Faculty:* 25 full-time (3 women), 5 part-time (2 women). *Students:* 68 full-time (24 women), 2 part-time; includes 4 minority (all Asian Americans or Pacific Islanders), 30 international. Average age 27. In 1998, 6 master's, 11 doctorates awarded. Terminal master's awarded for partial completion of doctoral program. *Degree requirements:* For master's and doctorate, one foreign language, thesis/dissertation required. *Entrance requirements:* For master's and doctorate, TOEFL (minimum score of 620 required), minimum GPA of 3.0 in last 90 hours. *Application deadline:* For fall admission, 3/1 (priority date). Applications are processed on a rolling basis. Application fee: $50. *Financial aid:* Fellowships, research assistantships, teaching assistantships, institutionally-sponsored loans available. Aid available to part-time students. Financial aid application deadline: 2/1. *Faculty research:* Solid state chemistry, enzyme reaction mechanisms, structure and dynamics of gas molecules, chemiluminescence, nonlinear optical spectroscopy. *Unit head:* Dr. John Westall, Chair, 541-737-6700, Fax: 541-737-2062, E-mail: john.westall@orst.edu. *Application contact:* Carolyn Brumley, Graduate Secretary, 541-737-6707, Fax: 541-737-2062, E-mail: carolyn.brumley@orst.edu.

Pennsylvania State University University Park Campus, Graduate School, Eberly College of Science, Department of Chemistry, State College, University Park, PA 16802-1503. Offers MS, PhD. *Students:* 187 full-time (60 women), 4 part-time (2 women). In 1998, 16 master's, 31 doctorates awarded. *Entrance requirements:* For master's and doctorate, GRE General Test. Application fee: $50. *Unit head:* Dr. Peter Jurs, Interim Head, 814-865-6553. *Application contact:* Dr. Thomas Mallouk, Chair, 814-863-8461.

Pittsburg State University, Graduate School, College of Arts and Sciences, Department of Chemistry, Pittsburg, KS 66762-5880. Offers MS. *Students:* 5 full-time, 4 part-time, 3 international. In 1998, 5 degrees awarded. *Degree requirements:* For master's, thesis or alternative required, foreign language not required. Application fee: $0 ($40 for international students). Tuition, state resident: full-time $2,466; part-time $105 per credit hour. Tuition, nonresident: full-time $6,268; part-time $264 per credit hour. *Financial aid:* Research assistantships, teaching assistantships, career-related internships or fieldwork and Federal Work-Study available. *Unit head:* Dr. Gerald Caple, Chairperson, 316-235-4747. *Application contact:* Marvene Darraugh, Administrative Officer, 316-235-4220, Fax: 316-235-4219, E-mail: mdarraug@pittstate.edu.

Polytechnic University, Brooklyn Campus, Department of Chemical Engineering, Chemistry and Materials Science, Major in Chemistry, Brooklyn, NY 11201-2990. Offers MS, PhD. Part-time and evening/weekend programs available. *Faculty:* 21. *Students:* 10 full-time (3 women), 20 part-time (5 women); includes 2 minority (1 African American, 1 Asian American or Pacific Islander), 18 international. Average age 33. 26 applicants, 31% accepted. In 1998, 4 master's, 3 doctorates awarded. Terminal master's awarded for partial completion of doctoral program. *Degree requirements:* For master's, thesis or alternative required; for doctorate, dissertation required. *Entrance requirements:* For master's and doctorate, GRE General Test, GRE Subject Test. *Application deadline:* Applications are processed on a rolling basis. Application fee: $45. Electronic applications accepted. *Financial aid:* Fellowships, research assistantships, teaching assistantships, institutionally-sponsored loans available. Aid available to part-time students. Financial aid applicants required to submit FAFSA. *Faculty research:* Optical rotation of light by plastic films, supramolecular chemistry, unusual stereochemical opportunities, polyaniline copolymers. Total annual research expenditures: $752,970. *Unit head:* Dr. Lee Kump, Associate Head, 814-865-7394. *Application contact:* John S. Kerge, Dean of Admissions, 718-260-3200, Fax: 718-260-3446, E-mail: admitme@poly.edu.

See in-depth description on page 161.

Polytechnic University, Brooklyn Campus, Department of Chemical Engineering, Chemistry and Materials Science, Major in Materials Chemistry, Brooklyn, NY 11201-2990. Offers PhD. Part-time and evening/weekend programs available. *Degree requirements:* For doctorate, dissertation required. *Application deadline:* Applications are processed on a rolling basis. Application fee: $45. Electronic applications accepted. *Financial aid:* Fellowships, research assistantships, teaching assistantships, institutionally-sponsored loans available. Aid available to part-time students. Financial aid applicants required to submit FAFSA. *Unit head:* John S. Kerge, Dean of Admissions, 718-260-3200, Fax: 718-260-3446, E-mail: admitme@poly.edu. *Application contact:* John S. Kerge, Dean of Admissions, 718-260-3200, Fax: 718-260-3446, E-mail: admitme@poly.edu.

Polytechnic University, Farmingdale Campus, Graduate Programs, Department of Chemical Engineering, Chemistry and Material Science, Major in Chemistry, Farmingdale, NY 11735-3995. Offers MS, PhD. Average age 33. *Degree requirements:* For doctorate, dissertation required. Application fee: $45. *Unit head:* John S. Kerge, Dean of Admissions, 718-260-3200, Fax: 718-260-3446, E-mail: admitme@poly.edu. *Application contact:* John S. Kerge, Dean of Admissions, 718-260-3200, Fax: 718-260-3446, E-mail: admitme@poly.edu.

Polytechnic University, Westchester Graduate Center, Graduate Programs, Department of Chemical Engineering, Chemistry, and Materials Science, Major in Chemistry, Hawthorne, NY 10532-1507. Offers MS. Average age 33. 2 applicants, 50% accepted. *Degree requirements:* For master's, computer language required. *Application deadline:* Applications are processed on a rolling basis. Application fee: $45. Electronic applications accepted. *Unit head:* Prof. Jing Li, Executive Officer, 856-225-6160, Fax: 856-225-6506, E-mail: jingli@camden.rutgers.edu. *Application contact:* John S. Kerge, Dean of Admissions, 718-260-3200, Fax: 718-260-3446, E-mail: admitme@poly.edu.

Pontifical Catholic University of Puerto Rico, College of Sciences, Department of Chemistry, Ponce, PR 00717-0777. Offers MS. Part-time and evening/weekend programs available. *Faculty:* 4 full-time (all women), 1 (woman) part-time. Average age 32. 5 applicants, 80% accepted. *Degree requirements:* For master's, thesis required, foreign language not required. *Entrance requirements:* For master's, GRE General Test, minimum GPA of 3.0, minimum 37 credits in chemistry. *Application deadline:* For fall admission, 4/30 (priority date). Applications are processed on a rolling basis. Application fee: $15. Electronic applications accepted. *Financial aid:* Fellowships, Federal Work-Study and tuition waivers (partial) available. Aid available to part-time students. Financial aid application deadline: 7/15. *Unit head:* Dr. Gladys Rodriguez, Director, 787-841-2000 Ext. 1537. *Application contact:* Ana O. Bonilla, Director of Admissions, 787-841-2000 Ext. 1000, Fax: 787-840-4295.

Portland State University, Graduate Studies, College of Liberal Arts and Sciences, Department of Chemistry, Portland, OR 97207-0751. Offers MA, MS, PhD. Part-time programs available. *Faculty:* 10 full-time (2 women), 4 part-time (1 woman). *Students:* 7 full-time (6 women), 1 (woman) part-time, 4 international. Average age 26. 5 applicants, 40% accepted. In 1998, 2 degrees awarded. *Degree requirements:* For master's, one foreign language, thesis required; for doctorate, one foreign language, dissertation, cumulative exams, seminar presentations required. *Entrance requirements:* For master's, TOEFL (minimum score of 550 required), minimum GPA of 3.0 in upper-division course work or 2.75 overall. *Application deadline:* For fall admission, 5/1 (priority date); for spring admission, 11/1. Applications are processed on a rolling basis. Application fee: $50. *Financial aid:* In 1998–99, 4 research assistantships were awarded.; teaching assistantships, career-related internships or fieldwork, Federal Work-Study, and institutionally-sponsored loans also available. Aid available to part-time students. Financial aid application deadline: 3/1; financial aid applicants required to submit FAFSA. *Faculty research:* Synthetic inorganic chemistry, atmospheric chemistry, organic photochemistry, enzymology, analytical chemistry. Total annual research expenditures: $405,841. *Unit head:* Dr. David Peyton, Head, 503-725-3811, Fax: 503-725-3888, E-mail: peytond@pdx.edu. *Application contact:* Raymond Lutz, Coordinator, 503-725-3811, Fax: 503-725-3888, E-mail: lutzr@pdx.edu.

Prairie View A&M University, Graduate School, College of Arts and Sciences, Department of Chemistry, Prairie View, TX 77446-0188. Offers MS. *Faculty:* 2 full-time (1 woman). *Students:* 4 full-time (3 women), 4 part-time (2 women); includes 5 minority (4 African Americans, 1 Hispanic American), 3 international. Average age 27. *Degree requirements:* For master's, one foreign language, thesis required. *Entrance requirements:* For master's, GRE General Test. *Average time to degree:* Master's–2.5 years full-time, 4 years part-time. *Application deadline:* For fall admission, 7/1 (priority date); for spring admission, 11/1. Applications are processed on a rolling basis. Application fee: $10. *Financial aid:* Federal Work-Study and institutionally-sponsored loans available. Aid available to part-time students. Financial aid application deadline: 8/1. *Unit head:* Dr. John Williams, Head, 409-857-3910, Fax: 409-857-2095, E-mail: john_r_william@pvamu.edu.

Princeton University, Graduate School, Department of Chemistry, Princeton, NJ 08544-1019. Offers chemistry (PhD); industrial chemistry (MS); physics and chemical physics (PhD); polymer sciences and materials (MSE, PhD). PhD (polymer sciences and materials) offered in conjunction with the Department of Chemical Engineering. *Degree requirements:* For doctorate, dissertation, cumulative and general exams required. *Entrance requirements:* For master's, GRE General Test; for doctorate, GRE General Test, GRE Subject Test. *Faculty research:* Chemistry of interfaces, organic synthesis, organometallic chemistry, inorganic reactions, biostructural chemistry.

See in-depth description on page 163.

Purdue University, Graduate School, School of Science, Department of Chemistry, West Lafayette, IN 47907. Offers analytical chemistry (MS, PhD); biochemistry (MS, PhD); chemical education (MS, PhD); inorganic chemistry (MS, PhD); organic chemistry (MS, PhD); physical chemistry (MS, PhD). *Accreditation:* NCATE (one or more programs are accredited). *Faculty:* 46 full-time, 1 part-time. *Students:* 246 full-time (83 women), 59 part-time (20 women); includes 36 minority (14 African Americans, 7 Asian Americans or Pacific Islanders, 14 Hispanic Americans, 1 Native American), 100 international. 237 applicants, 36% accepted. In 1998, 13 master's, 49 doctorates awarded. Terminal master's awarded for partial completion of doctoral program. *Degree requirements:* For master's and doctorate, thesis/dissertation required, foreign language not required. *Entrance requirements:* For master's and doctorate, TOEFL (minimum score of 550 required). Application fee: $30. Electronic applications accepted. *Financial aid:* In 1998–99, 2 fellowships with partial tuition reimbursements (averaging $18,000 per year), 55 teaching assistantships with partial tuition reimbursements (averaging $17,400 per year) were awarded.; research assistantships with partial tuition reimbursements, tuition waivers (partial) also available. Aid available to part-time students. Financial aid applicants required to submit FAFSA. Total annual research expenditures: $9 million. *Unit head:* Dr. R. A. Walton, Head, 765-494-5203. *Application contact:* R. E. Wild, Chairman, Graduate Admissions, 765-494-5200, E-mail: wild@purdue.edu.

Queens College of the City University of New York, Division of Graduate Studies, Mathematics and Natural Sciences Division, Department of Chemistry, Flushing, NY 11367-1597. Offers biochemistry (MA); chemistry (MA). Part-time and evening/weekend programs available. *Faculty:* 16 full-time (2 women). *Students:* 4 full-time (1 woman), 3 part-time (2 women); includes 3 minority (1 African American, 2 Asian Americans or Pacific Islanders), 2 international. 22 applicants, 86% accepted. In 1998, 8 degrees awarded. *Degree requirements:* For master's, comprehensive exam required, foreign language and thesis not required. *Entrance requirements:* For master's, GRE, TOEFL (minimum score of 500 required), previous course work in calculus and physics, minimum GPA of 3.0. *Application deadline:* For fall admission, 4/1; for spring admission, 11/1. Applications are processed on a rolling basis. Application fee: $40. Tuition, state resident: full-time $4,350; part-time $185 per credit. Tuition, nonresident: full-time $7,600; part-time $320 per credit. Required fees: $114; $57 per semester. Tuition and fees vary according to course load and program. *Financial aid:* Career-related internships or fieldwork, Federal Work-Study, institutionally-sponsored loans, tuition waivers (partial), and adjunct lectureships available. Aid available to part-time students. Financial aid application deadline: 4/1; financial aid applicants required to submit FAFSA. *Unit head:* Dr. Thomas C. Strekas, Chairperson, 718-997-4100. *Application contact:* Graduate Adviser, 718-997-4100.

Queen's University at Kingston, School of Graduate Studies and Research, Faculty of Arts and Sciences, Department of Chemistry, Kingston, ON K7L 3N6, Canada. Offers M Sc, PhD. Part-time programs available. *Students:* 79 full-time (23 women), 2 part-time (1 woman). In 1998, 7 master's, 14 doctorates awarded. *Degree requirements:* For master's, thesis optional, foreign language not required; for doctorate, dissertation, comprehensive exam required, foreign language not required. *Entrance requirements:* For master's and doctorate, TOEFL (minimum score of 580 required). *Application deadline:* For fall admission, 2/28 (priority date). Application fee: $60. Electronic applications accepted. *Financial aid:* Fellowships, research assistantships, teaching assistantships, institutionally-sponsored loans available. Financial aid application deadline: 3/1. *Unit head:* Dr. R. S. Brown, Head, 613-533-2624. *Application contact:* Dr. D. Macartney, Graduate Coordinator, 613-533-2617.

Rensselaer Polytechnic Institute, Graduate School, School of Science, Department of Chemistry, Troy, NY 12180-3590. Offers analytical chemistry (MS, PhD); biochemistry (MS, PhD); inorganic chemistry (MS, PhD); organic chemistry (MS, PhD); physical chemistry (MS, PhD); polymer chemistry (MS, PhD). Part-time and evening/weekend programs available. *Faculty:* 17 full-time (2 women), 1 part-time (0 women). *Students:* 52 full-time (18 women), 3 part-time (1 woman); includes 4 minority (3 Asian Americans or Pacific Islanders, 1 Hispanic American), 30 international. 143 applicants, 22% accepted. In 1998, 6 master's, 5 doctorates awarded. *Degree requirements:* For master's, thesis required (for some programs), foreign language not required; for doctorate, dissertation required, foreign language not required. *Entrance requirements:* For master's and doctorate, GRE General Test, TOEFL (minimum score of 550 required). *Application deadline:* For fall admission, 2/1 (priority date). Applications are processed on a rolling basis. Application fee: $35. *Financial aid:* In 1998–99, 24 research assistantships with full tuition reimbursements (averaging $13,000 per year), 32 teaching assistantships with full tuition reimbursements (averaging $13,000 per year) were awarded.; fellowships with full tuition reimbursements, institutionally-sponsored loans and tuition waivers (full and partial) also available. Financial aid application deadline: 2/1. *Faculty research:* Biophysics, materials chemistry, environmental science. Total annual research expenditures: $3 million. *Unit head:* Dr. Thomas Apple, Chair, 518-276-6344. *Application contact:* Dr. Wilfredo Colon, Chair, Graduate Committee, 518-276-6340, Fax: 518-276-6434, E-mail: colonw@rpi.edu.

See in-depth description on page 167.

Rensselaer Polytechnic Institute, Graduate School, School of Science, Department of Earth and Environmental Sciences, Troy, NY 12180-3590. Offers environmental chemistry (MS, PhD); geochemistry (MS, PhD); geology (MS, PhD); geophysics (MS, PhD); hydrogeology (MS); petrology (MS, PhD); planetary geology (MS, PhD); tectonics (MS, PhD). Part-time programs available. *Faculty:* 7 full-time (0 women), 2 part-time (0 women). *Students:* 19 full-time (8 women), 1 (woman) part-time; includes 2 minority (1 African American, 1 Native American) *Degree requirements:* For master's, thesis required (for some programs); for doctorate, dissertation required. *Entrance requirements:* For master's and doctorate, GRE General Test, TOEFL (minimum score of 550 required). *Application deadline:* For fall admission, 2/1 (priority date). Applications are processed on a rolling basis. Application fee: $35. *Unit head:* Dr. Robert McCaffrey, Chair, 518-276-6474, Fax: 518-276-6680, E-mail: ees@rpi.edu. *Application contact:* Dr. Steven Roecker, Associate Professor, 518-276-6474, Fax: 518-276-6680, E-mail: ees@rpi.edu.

Rice University, Graduate Programs, Wiess School of Natural Sciences, Department of Chemistry, Houston, TX 77251-1892. Offers MA, PhD. Terminal master's awarded for partial completion of doctoral program. *Degree requirements:* For master's and doctorate, thesis/dissertation required, foreign language not required. *Entrance requirements:* For master's, GRE General Test, TOEFL (minimum score of 550 required), minimum GPA of 3.0; for doctorate, GRE General Test (score in 70th percentile or higher required), minimum GPA of 3.0. *Faculty research:* NMR spectroscopy, organic synthesis, photochemistry, fluorine chemistry, transition-metal complexes.

Rochester Institute of Technology, Part-time and Graduate Admissions, College of Science, Department of Allied Health Sciences, Rochester, NY 14623-5604. Offers clinical chemistry (MS). *Students:* 5 full-time (1 woman), 3 part-time (2 women); includes 2 minority (both African Americans), 3 international. 7 applicants, 57% accepted. In 1998, 2 degrees awarded. *Entrance requirements:* For master's, minimum GPA of 3.0. *Application deadline:* For fall admission, 3/1 (priority date). Applications are processed on a rolling basis. Application fee: $40. *Financial aid:* Teaching assistantships available. *Unit head:* John Waud, Head, 716-475-2978, E-mail: jmwscl@rit.edu.

Rochester Institute of Technology, Part-time and Graduate Admissions, College of Science, Department of Chemistry, Rochester, NY 14623-5604. Offers MS. Part-time and evening/weekend programs available. *Students:* 11 full-time (8 women), 11 part-time (5 women); includes 1 minority (Asian American or Pacific Islander), 7 international. 37 applicants, 73% accepted. In 1998, 4 degrees awarded. *Entrance requirements:* For master's, American Chemical Society Exam, GRE, TOEFL, minimum GPA of 3.0. *Application deadline:* For fall admission, 3/1 (priority date). Applications are processed on a rolling basis. Application fee: $40. *Financial aid:* Teaching assistantships, career-related internships or fieldwork, Federal Work-Study, institutionally-sponsored loans, and tuition waivers (full and partial) available. Aid available to part-time students. *Faculty research:* Organic polymer chemistry, magnetic resonance and imaging, inorganic coordination polymers, biophysical chemistry, physical polymer chemistry. *Unit head:* Dr. Gerald Takacs, Head, 716-475-2497, E-mail: gatsch@rit.edu.

Roosevelt University, Graduate Division, College of Arts and Sciences, School of Science and Mathematics, Program in Chemistry, Chicago, IL 60605-1394. Offers MS. Part-time and evening/weekend programs available. *Faculty:* 4 full-time (1 woman), 4 part-time (0 women). *Students:* 2 full-time (1 woman), 12 part-time (4 women); includes 8 minority (2 African Americans, 5 Asian Americans or Pacific Islanders, 1 Hispanic American), 1 international. Average age 28. 6 applicants, 67% accepted. In 1998, 4 degrees awarded (100% found work related to degree). *Degree requirements:* For master's, thesis optional, foreign language not required. *Entrance requirements:* For master's, minimum GPA of 2.7, basic undergraduate science and mathematics course work. *Average time to degree:* Master's–2.5 years full-time, 4 years part-time. *Application deadline:* For fall admission, 6/1 (priority date); for spring admission, 11/1. Applications are processed on a rolling basis. Application fee: $25 ($35 for international students). *Financial aid:* In 1998–99, 1 student received aid, including 1 teaching assistantship; tuition waivers (partial) also available. Aid available to part-time students. Financial aid application deadline: 2/15. *Faculty research:* Phase-transfer catalysts, bioinorganic chemistry, long chain dicarboxylic acids, organosilicon compounds, spectroscopic studies. Total annual research expenditures: $1,000. *Unit head:* Joshua Telser, Graduate Adviser, 312-341-3687. *Application contact:* Joanne Canyon-Heller, Coordinator of Graduate Admissions, 312-341-3612, Fax: 312-341-3523, E-mail: applyru@roosevelt.edu.

Rutgers, The State University of New Jersey, Camden, Graduate School, Program in Chemistry, Camden, NJ 08102-1401. Offers MS. *Faculty:* 6 full-time (3 women). *Students:* 4 full-time (0 women), 11 part-time (3 women); includes 3 minority (2 African Americans, 1 Asian American or Pacific Islander), 2 international. Average age 25. 20 applicants, 75% accepted. *Degree requirements:* For master's, thesis required, foreign language not required. *Application deadline:* For fall admission, 9/1 (priority date); for spring admission, 12/31 (priority date). Applications are processed on a rolling basis. Application fee: $50. Electronic applications accepted. *Financial aid:* In 1998–99, 1 research assistantship with tuition reimbursement (averaging $12,000 per year), 3 teaching assistantships with tuition reimbursements (averaging $12,000 per year) were awarded.; unspecified assistantships and summer research assistantships also available. Financial aid applicants required to submit FAFSA. *Faculty research:* Organic and inorganic synthesis, enzyme biochemistry, trace metal analysis, theoretical and molecular modeling. Total annual research expenditures: $500,000. *Unit head:* Prof. Luke A. Burke, Department Chair, 856-225-6142, E-mail: burke@camden.rutgers.edu. *Application contact:* Prof. Jing Li, Executive Officer, 856-225-6160, Fax: 856-225-6506, E-mail: jingli@camden.rutgers.edu.

Rutgers, The State University of New Jersey, Newark, Graduate School, Department of Chemistry, Newark, NJ 07102-3192. Offers analytical chemistry (MS, PhD); biochemistry (MS, PhD); inorganic chemistry (MS, PhD); organic chemistry (MS, PhD); physical chemistry (MS, PhD). Part-time and evening/weekend programs available. *Faculty:* 22 full-time (4 women). *Students:* 28 full-time (11 women), 39 part-time (19 women); includes 29 minority (1 African American, 24 Asian Americans or Pacific Islanders, 4 Hispanic Americans) 126 applicants, 31% accepted. In 1998, 9 master's, 3 doctorates awarded. Terminal master's awarded for partial completion of doctoral program. *Degree requirements:* For master's, cumulative exams required, thesis optional, foreign language not required; for doctorate, dissertation, exams, research proposal required, foreign language not required. *Entrance requirements:* For master's and doctorate, GRE General Test, TOEFL (minimum score of 550 required; 590 for financial aid), minimum undergraduate B average. *Application deadline:* For fall admission, 7/1 (priority date); for spring admission, 12/1. Applications are processed on a rolling basis. Application fee: $40. *Financial aid:* In 1998–99, 35 students received aid, including 9 fellowships with full tuition reimbursements available (averaging $12,000 per year), 3 research assistantships, 18 teaching assistantships with full tuition reimbursements available (averaging $12,136 per year); Federal Work-Study and institutionally-sponsored loans also available. Financial aid application deadline: 3/1. *Faculty research:* Medicinal chemistry, natural products, isotope effects, biophysics and biorganic approaches to enzyme mechanisms, organic and organometallic synthesis. *Unit head:* Prof. Hugh W. Thompson, Coordinator, 973-353-5173, Fax: 973-353-1264.

See in-depth description on page 169.

Rutgers, The State University of New Jersey, New Brunswick, Graduate School, Program in Chemistry, New Brunswick, NJ 08903. Offers analytical chemistry (MS, PhD); biological chemistry (PhD); chemistry education (MST); inorganic chemistry (MS, PhD); organic chemistry (MS, PhD); physical chemistry (MS, PhD). Part-time and evening/weekend programs available. *Faculty:* 44 full-time (9 women), 4 part-time (2 women). *Students:* 100 full-time (35 women), 69 part-time (29 women); includes 27 minority (2 African Americans, 24 Asian Americans or Pacific Islanders, 1 Hispanic American), 79 international. Average age 25. 187 applicants, 38% accepted. In 1998, 18 master's, 15 doctorates awarded (47% entered university research/teaching, 53% found other work related to degree). Terminal master's awarded for partial completion of doctoral program. *Degree requirements:* For master's, exam required, thesis optional, foreign language not required; for doctorate, dissertation, cumulative exams required, foreign language not required. *Entrance requirements:* For master's, GRE General Test, GRE Subject Test, TOEFL; for doctorate, GRE General Test, GRE Subject Test, TOEFL (minimum score of 575 required). *Average time to degree:* Master's–3 years full-time, 5 years part-time; doctorate–5 years full-time, 8 years part-time. *Application deadline:* For fall admission, 4/15 (priority date); for spring admission, 11/1. Applications are processed on a rolling basis. Application fee: $50. *Financial aid:* In 1998–99, 86 students received aid, including 4 research assistantships with full tuition reimbursements available, 74 teaching assistantships with full tuition reimbursements available; fellowships, Federal Work-Study also available. Financial aid application deadline: 3/1; financial aid applicants required to submit FAFSA. *Faculty research:* Biophysical organic/bioorganic, inorganic/bioinorganic, theoretical, and solid-state/surface chemistry. Total annual research expenditures: $6.5 million. *Unit head:* Dr. Martha A. Cotter, Director, 732-445-2259, Fax: 732-445-5312, E-mail: gradexec@rutchem.rutgers.edu.

See in-depth description on page 173.

Rutgers, The State University of New Jersey, New Brunswick, Graduate School, Program in Environmental Sciences, New Brunswick, NJ 08903. Offers air resources (MS, PhD); aquatic biology (MS, PhD); aquatic chemistry (MS, PhD); chemistry and physics of aerosol and hydrosol systems (MS, PhD); environmental chemistry (MS, PhD); environmental microbiology (MS, PhD); environmental toxicology (MS, PhD); exposure assessment (PhD); water and wastewater treatment (MS, PhD); water resources (MS, PhD). Part-time and evening/weekend programs available. *Faculty:* 33 full-time (7 women), 36 part-time (6 women). *Students:* 42 full-time (16 women), 92 part-time (30 women); includes 22 minority (17 Asian Americans or Pacific Islanders, 5 Hispanic Americans), 31 international. Terminal master's awarded for partial completion of doctoral program. *Degree requirements:* For master's, thesis or alternative, oral final exam required, foreign language not required; for doctorate, dissertation, thesis defense, qualifying exam required, foreign language not required. *Entrance requirements:* For master's and doctorate, GRE General Test (minimum score of 500 on verbal section, 600 on quantitative required), TOEFL (minimum score of 590 required). *Application deadline:* For fall admission, 3/1; for spring admission, 11/1. Applications are processed on a rolling basis. Application fee: $50. *Unit head:* Dr. Peter F. Strom, Director, 732-932-8078, Fax: 732-932-8644, E-mail: strom@aesop.rutgers.edu. *Application contact:* Paul J. Lioy, Graduate Admissions Committee, 732-932-0150, Fax: 732-445-0116, E-mail: plioy@eohsi.rutgers.edu.

Sacred Heart University, Graduate Studies, College of Arts and Sciences, Faculty of Chemistry, Fairfield, CT 06432-1000. Offers MS. Part-time and evening/weekend programs available. *Faculty:* 8 full-time (4 women), 4 part-time (0 women). *Students:* 2 full-time (both women), 16 part-time (6 women); includes 3 minority (1 African American, 1 Asian American or Pacific Islander, 1 Native American) Average age 30. 15 applicants, 80% accepted. In 1998, 2 degrees awarded. *Degree requirements:* For master's, thesis optional. *Entrance requirements:* For master's, bachelor's degree in related area, minimum GPA of 2.75. *Application deadline:* Applications are processed on a rolling basis. Application fee: $40 ($100 for international students). Tuition: Part-time $375 per credit. Required fees: $83 per term. Tuition and fees vary according to campus/location and program. *Financial aid:* Career-related internships or fieldwork available. Financial aid applicants required to submit FAFSA. *Unit head:* Dr. Babu George, Chair, 203-371-7793, E-mail: gradstudies@sacredheart.edu. *Application contact:* Mike Kennedy, Graduate Admissions Counselor, 203-365-7619, Fax: 203-365-4732, E-mail: gradstudies@sacredheart.edu.

St. Francis Xavier University, Graduate Studies, Program in Chemistry, Antigonish, NS B2G 2W5, Canada. Offers M Sc. *Faculty:* 6 full-time (1 woman). *Students:* 2 full-time (1 woman). 5 applicants, 40% accepted. In 1998, 2 degrees awarded (100% entered university research/teaching). *Degree requirements:* For master's, thesis required, foreign language not required. *Entrance requirements:* For master's, minimum undergraduate B average, undergraduate major in chemistry or related field. *Average time to degree:* Master's–4 years full-time. *Application deadline:* For fall admission, 9/1 (priority date). Applications are processed on a rolling basis. Application fee: $30. *Faculty research:* Photoelectron spectroscopy, synthesis and properties of surfactants, nucleic acid synthesis, transition metal chemistry. Total annual research expenditures: $150,000. *Unit head:* Dr. John Beck, Chair, 902-867-2192, Fax: 902-867-2414, E-mail: jbeck@stfx.ca. *Application contact:* Admissions Office, 902-867-2219, Fax: 902-867-2329, E-mail: admit@stfx.ca.

St. John's University, Graduate School of Arts and Sciences, Department of Chemistry, Jamaica, NY 11439. Offers MS. Part-time and evening/weekend programs available. *Faculty:*

Chemistry

St. John's University (continued)
8 full-time (1 woman), 16 part-time (1 woman). *Students:* 7 full-time (4 women), 13 part-time (3 women); includes 5 minority (2 African Americans, 2 Asian Americans or Pacific Islanders, 1 Hispanic American), 4 international. Average age 29. 17 applicants, 94% accepted. In 1998, 4 degrees awarded. *Degree requirements:* For master's, one foreign language (computer language can substitute), comprehensive exam required, thesis optional. *Entrance requirements:* For master's, minimum GPA of 3.0. *Application deadline:* Applications are processed on a rolling basis. Application fee: $40. Tuition: Full-time $13,200; part-time $500 per credit. Required fees: $150; $75 per term. Tuition and fees vary according to degree level and program. *Financial aid:* In 1998–99, 5 research assistantships were awarded.; scholarships also available. Aid available to part-time students. Financial aid application deadline: 3/1; financial aid applicants required to submit FAFSA. *Faculty research:* Organic chemistry, photochemistry, Lewis-based acid reactions, solution thermodynamics, synthesis and reactivity of heterocyclic systems, synthesis of OC-lactoma, potential anti-cancer agents. *Unit head:* Dr. Neil D. Jespersen, Chairman, 718-990-6927, E-mail: jespersn@stjohns.edu. *Application contact:* Patricia G. Armstrong, Director, Office of Admission, 718-990-2028, Fax: 718-990-2096, E-mail: armstrop@stjohns.edu.

Saint Joseph College, Graduate Division, Field of Natural Sciences, Department of Chemistry, West Hartford, CT 06117-2700. Offers chemistry (Certificate); chemistry and biological chemistry (MS). Part-time and evening/weekend programs available. *Faculty:* 5 full-time (1 woman). *Students:* 15 (7 women). Average age 30. In 1998, 2 degrees awarded. *Degree requirements:* For master's, thesis or alternative required, foreign language not required. *Entrance requirements:* For master's, GRE or MAT. *Application deadline:* Applications are processed on a rolling basis. Application fee: $25. *Financial aid:* Application deadline: 8/1; *Unit head:* Harold T. McKone, Chair, 860-232-4571 Ext. 241, Fax: 860-233-5695.

Saint Joseph's University, College of Arts and Sciences, Department of Chemistry, Philadelphia, PA 19131-1395. Offers MS. Evening/weekend programs available. *Students:* 19 (3 women); includes 7 minority (1 African American, 6 Asian Americans or Pacific Islanders) 2 international. Average age 31. In 1998, 8 degrees awarded. *Degree requirements:* For master's, thesis optional. *Entrance requirements:* For master's, TOEFL. *Application deadline:* For fall admission, 7/15. Application fee: $30. *Financial aid:* Fellowships, unspecified assistantships available. *Unit head:* Dr. Roger Murray, Chairman, 610-660-1780.

Saint Louis University, Graduate School, College of Arts and Sciences, Department of Chemistry, St. Louis, MO 63103-2097. Offers MS, MS(R). Part-time programs available. *Faculty:* 13 full-time (2 women), 1 part-time (0 women). *Students:* 8 full-time (4 women), 3 part-time (1 woman); includes 4 minority (1 African American, 3 Asian Americans or Pacific Islanders), 2 international. Average age 28. 9 applicants, 56% accepted. In 1998, 6 degrees awarded. *Degree requirements:* For master's, comprehensive oral exam, thesis for MS(R) required. *Entrance requirements:* For master's, GRE General Test. *Application deadline:* For fall admission, 7/1; for spring admission, 11/1. Applications are processed on a rolling basis. Application fee: $40. Tuition: Full-time $20,520; part-time $507 per credit hour. Required fees: $38 per term. Tuition and fees vary according to program. *Financial aid:* In 1998–99, 10 students received aid, including 1 fellowship, 2 research assistantships, 5 teaching assistantships Financial aid application deadline: 4/1; financial aid applicants required to submit FAFSA. *Faculty research:* Chemistry of organotransition metal complexes, NMR studies of lanthanide complexes, electro-organic chemistry, ESR studies of molecular motion. *Unit head:* Dr. Vincent Spaziano, Chairman, 314-977-2850, Fax: 314-977-2521. *Application contact:* Dr. Marcia Buresch, Assistant Dean of the Graduate School, 314-977-2240, Fax: 314-977-3943, E-mail: bureschm@slu.edu.

Sam Houston State University, College of Arts and Sciences, Chemistry Department, Huntsville, TX 77341. Offers M Ed, MS. Part-time programs available. *Students:* 4 full-time (2 women), 3 part-time (1 woman), 4 international. Average age 29. In 1998, 2 degrees awarded. *Degree requirements:* For master's, thesis required (for some programs). *Entrance requirements:* For master's, GRE General Test (minimum combined score of 1000 required), TOEFL (minimum score of 550 required). *Application deadline:* For fall admission, 8/15 (priority date). Applications are processed on a rolling basis. Application fee: $15. *Financial aid:* Research assistantships, teaching assistantships, Federal Work-Study, institutionally-sponsored loans, and tuition waivers (partial) available. Aid available to part-time students. Financial aid application deadline: 8/15. *Faculty research:* Analytical, biochemical, inorganic, organic, physical, and environmental chemistry. *Unit head:* Dr. Mary Plishker, Chair, 409-294-1526, Fax: 409-299-1585. *Application contact:* Dr. Tom Chasteen, Graduate Adviser, 409-294-1533, Fax: 409-299-1585.

San Diego State University, Graduate and Research Affairs, College of Sciences, Department of Chemistry, San Diego, CA 92182. Offers chemistry (MA, MS, PhD). *Students:* 7 full-time (1 woman), 41 part-time (16 women); includes 13 minority (1 African American, 8 Asian Americans or Pacific Islanders, 3 Hispanic Americans, 1 Native American), 9 international. Average age 30. In 1998, 11 master's, 1 doctorate awarded. Terminal master's awarded for partial completion of doctoral program. *Degree requirements:* For master's, foreign language and thesis not required; for doctorate, dissertation required, foreign language not required. *Entrance requirements:* For master's, GRE General Test, TOEFL (minimum score of 550 required), bachelor's degree in related field; for doctorate, GRE General Test, GRE Subject Test. *Application deadline:* For fall admission, 7/1 (priority date); for spring admission, 12/1. Applications are processed on a rolling basis. Application fee: $55. *Financial aid:* Fellowships, research assistantships, teaching assistantships available. *Faculty research:* Nonlinear, laser, and electrochemistry;surface reaction dynamics; catalysis, synthesis, and organometallics;proteins, enzymology, and gene expression regulation. Total annual research expenditures: $900,000. *Unit head:* Dale Chatfield, Chair, 619-594-4418, Fax: 619-594-4634, E-mail: dchatfield@sciences.sdsu.edu. *Application contact:* Karen Peterson, Graduate Adviser, 619-594-4507, Fax: 619-594-4634, E-mail: kpeterso@chemistry.sdsu.edu.

San Francisco State University, Graduate Division, College of Science and Engineering, Department of Chemistry and Biochemistry, San Francisco, CA 94132-1722. Offers chemistry (MS). Part-time programs available. *Faculty:* 14 full-time (3 women), 1 part-time (0 women). *Students:* 8 (5 women). In 1998, 8 degrees awarded (50% found work related to degree, 50% continued full-time study). *Degree requirements:* For master's, thesis, ACS exams in 3 chemical disciplines (including physical chemistry), essay test required, foreign language not required. *Entrance requirements:* For master's, TOEFL (minimum score of 550 required), minimum GPA of 2.5 in last 60 units. *Application deadline:* For fall admission, 11/30 (priority date). Applications are processed on a rolling basis. Application fee: $55. *Financial aid:* Fellowships, research assistantships, teaching assistantships, Federal Work-Study available. Financial aid application deadline: 3/1. *Faculty research:* Physical chemistry of macromolecules, physical and synthetic organic chemistry, membrane and enzyme biochemistry, organometallic chemistry. Total annual research expenditures: $750,000. *Unit head:* Dr. James Orenberg, Chair, 415-338-1288, Fax: 415-338-2384, E-mail: orenberg@sfsu.edu. *Application contact:* Dr. James Keeffe, Graduate Coordinator, 415-338-1117, Fax: 415-338-2384, E-mail: keeffe@sfsu.edu.

San Jose State University, Graduate Studies, College of Science, Department of Chemistry, San Jose, CA 95192-0001. Offers analytical chemistry (MS); biochemistry (MS); chemistry (MA); inorganic chemistry (MS); organic chemistry (MS); physical chemistry (MS); polymer chemistry (MS); radiochemistry (MS). Part-time and evening/weekend programs available. *Faculty:* 24 full-time (3 women), 5 part-time (2 women). *Students:* 7 full-time (5 women), 30 part-time (17 women); includes 24 minority (2 African Americans, 21 Asian Americans or Pacific Islanders, 1 Hispanic American), 4 international. Average age 31. 22 applicants, 32% accepted. In 1998, 20 degrees awarded. *Degree requirements:* For master's, thesis or alternative required, foreign language not required. *Entrance requirements:* For master's, GRE, minimum B average. *Application deadline:* For fall admission, 6/1. Applications are processed on a rolling basis. Application fee: $59. Tuition, nonresident: part-time $246 per unit. Required fees: $1,939; $1,309 per year. *Financial aid:* In 1998–99, 8 teaching assistantships were awarded.; career-related internships or fieldwork, Federal Work-Study, and institutionally-sponsored loans also available. Aid available to part-time students. Financial aid application deadline: 6/5. *Faculty research:* Intercalated compounds, organic/biochemical reaction mechanisms, complexing agents in biochemistry, DNA repair, metabolic inhibitors. *Unit head:* Dr. Pamela Stacks, Chair, 408-924-5000, Fax: 408-924-4945. *Application contact:* Dr. Roger Biringer, Graduate Adviser, 408-924-4961.

The Scripps Research Institute, Office of Graduate Studies, Chemistry Graduate Program, La Jolla, CA 92037. Offers PhD. *Faculty:* 17 full-time (0 women). *Students:* 61 full-time (11 women). Average age 22. 143 applicants, 20% accepted. In 1998, 9 degrees awarded. *Degree requirements:* For doctorate, dissertation required, foreign language not required. *Entrance requirements:* For doctorate, GRE General Test (average 83rd percentile), GRE Subject Test (average 78th percentile), TOEFL. *Average time to degree:* Doctorate–5 years full-time. *Application deadline:* For fall admission, 1/1. Application fee: $0. *Financial aid:* Institutionally-sponsored loans and stipends available. *Faculty research:* Synthetic organic chemistry and natural product synthesis, bioorganic chemistry and molecular design, biocatalysis and protein design, chemical biology. *Application contact:* Marylyn Rinaldi, Graduate Program Administrator, 619-784-8469, Fax: 619-784-2802, E-mail: mrinaldi@scripps.edu.

Seton Hall University, College of Arts and Sciences, Department of Chemistry, South Orange, NJ 07079-2694. Offers analytical chemistry (MS, PhD); biochemistry (MS, PhD); chemistry (MS); inorganic chemistry (MS, PhD); organic chemistry (MS, PhD); physical chemistry (MS, PhD). Part-time and evening/weekend programs available. Terminal master's awarded for partial completion of doctoral program. *Degree requirements:* For master's, formal seminar required, thesis optional; for doctorate, dissertation, comprehensive exams, annual seminars required. *Entrance requirements:* For master's, TOEFL, undergraduate major in chemistry or related field with a minimum of 30 credits in chemistry, including 2 semesters of physical chemistry; for doctorate, oral matriculation exam based on proposed doctoral research, minimum GPA of 3.0 in course distribution requirements, formal seminar. *Faculty research:* DNA metal reactions; chromatography; bioinorganic, biophysical, organometallic, and polymer chemistry; heterogeneous catalysis.

Announcement: Strong associations with local chemical industry. Industrial Advisory Committee composed of industrial chemists who aid in program development. Full-time and part-time MS and PhD (1-year residency required) programs with all graduate courses taught in the evenings and weekends. Research and nonresearch MS tracks including a minor in business.

Simon Fraser University, Graduate Studies, Faculty of Science, Department of Chemistry, Burnaby, BC V5A 1S6, Canada. Offers chemical physics (M Sc, PhD); chemistry (M Sc, PhD). *Faculty:* 29 full-time (2 women). *Students:* 59 full-time (20 women), 1 (woman) part-time. Average age 30. In 1998, 3 master's, 5 doctorates awarded. *Degree requirements:* For master's and doctorate, thesis/dissertation required. *Entrance requirements:* For master's, TOEFL (minimum score of 570 required), TWE (minimum score of 5 required), or International English Language Test (minimum score of 7.5 required), minimum GPA of 3.0; for doctorate, TOEFL (minimum score of 570 required), TWE (minimum score of 5 required), or International English Language Test (minimum score of 7.5 required), minimum GPA of 3.5. Application fee: $55. *Financial aid:* In 1998–99, 18 fellowships were awarded.; research assistantships, teaching assistantships *Faculty research:* Biochemistry, nuclear chemistry, physical chemistry, inorganic chemistry, theoretical chemistry. *Unit head:* R. Korteling, Chair, 604-291-3590, Fax: 604-291-3765. *Application contact:* Graduate Secretary, 604-291-3345, Fax: 604-291-3765, E-mail: gradappl@bohr.chem.sfu.ca.

Smith College, Graduate Studies, Department of Chemistry, Northampton, MA 01063. Offers MAT. Part-time programs available. *Degree requirements:* For master's, thesis required. *Entrance requirements:* For master's, GRE General Test, GRE Subject Test.

South Dakota School of Mines and Technology, Graduate Division, Division of Material Engineering and Science, Doctoral Program in Materials Engineering and Science, Rapid City, SD 57701-3995. Offers chemical engineering (PhD); chemistry (PhD); civil engineering (PhD); electrical engineering (PhD); mechanical engineering (PhD); metallurgical engineering (PhD); physics (PhD). Part-time programs available. *Students:* 14 full-time (2 women), 9 international. *Degree requirements:* For doctorate, dissertation required, foreign language not required. *Entrance requirements:* For doctorate, TOEFL (minimum score of 520 required), TWE, minimum graduate GPA of 3.0. *Application deadline:* For fall admission, 6/15 (priority date); for spring admission, 10/15. Applications are processed on a rolling basis. Application fee: $15. Electronic applications accepted. Tuition, state resident: part-time $89 per hour. Tuition, nonresident: part-time $261 per hour. Part-time tuition and fees vary according to program. *Unit head:* Dr. Chris Jenkins, Coordinator, 605-394-2406. *Application contact:* Brenda Brown, Secretary, 800-454-8162 Ext. 2493, Fax: 605-394-5360, E-mail: graduate_admissions@silver.sdmt.edu.

South Dakota School of Mines and Technology, Graduate Division, Division of Material Engineering and Science, Master's Program in Materials Engineering and Science, Rapid City, SD 57701-3995. Offers chemistry (MS); metallurgical engineering (MS); physics (MS). *Students:* 17. *Degree requirements:* Foreign language not required. *Entrance requirements:* For master's, TOEFL (minimum score of 520 required), TWE. *Application deadline:* For fall admission, 6/15 (priority date); for spring admission, 10/15. Applications are processed on a rolling basis. Application fee: $15. Electronic applications accepted. Tuition, state resident: part-time $89 per hour. Tuition, nonresident: part-time $261 per hour. Part-time tuition and fees vary according to program. *Unit head:* James W. Smolka, Coordinator, 805-258-5936. *Application contact:* Brenda Brown, Secretary, 800-454-8162 Ext. 2493, Fax: 605-394-5360, E-mail: graduate_admissions@silver.sdmt.edu.

South Dakota State University, Graduate School, College of Arts and Science, Department of Chemistry, Brookings, SD 57007. Offers analytical chemistry (MS, PhD); biochemistry (MS, PhD); chemistry (MS, PhD); inorganic chemistry (MS, PhD); organic chemistry (MS, PhD); physical chemistry (MS, PhD). *Degree requirements:* For master's, thesis, oral exam required, foreign language not required; for doctorate, dissertation, preliminary oral and written exams, research tool required. *Entrance requirements:* For master's, TOEFL (minimum score of 580 required), bachelor's degree in chemistry or equivalent; for doctorate, TOEFL (minimum score of 580 required). *Faculty research:* Environmental chemistry, computational chemistry, organic synthesis and photochemistry, novel material development and characterization.

Southeast Missouri State University, Graduate School, Department of Chemistry, Cape Girardeau, MO 63701-4799. Offers MNS. *Degree requirements:* Foreign language not required.

Southern Connecticut State University, School of Graduate Studies, School of Arts and Sciences, Department of Chemistry, New Haven, CT 06515-1355. Offers chemistry (MS). Part-time and evening/weekend programs available. *Faculty:* 5 full-time. *Students:* 1 (woman) full-time, 11 part-time (7 women); includes 2 minority (1 African American, 1 Asian American or Pacific Islander) 17 applicants, 24% accepted. In 1998, 3 degrees awarded. *Degree requirements:* For master's, thesis or alternative required, foreign language not required. *Entrance requirements:* For master's, interview. *Application deadline:* For fall admission, 7/15 (priority date). Applications are processed on a rolling basis. Application fee: $40. *Financial aid:* Teaching assistantships available. Financial aid application deadline: 4/15; financial aid applicants required to submit FAFSA. *Unit head:* Dr. James Barrante, Chairman, 203-392-6267, Fax: 203-392-6396, E-mail: barrante@scsu.ctstateu.edu. *Application contact:* Dr. Robert Snyder, Graduate Coordinator, 203-392-6263, Fax: 203-392-6396, E-mail: snyder_r@scsu.ctstateu.edu.

Southern Illinois University Carbondale, Graduate School, College of Science, Department of Chemistry and Biochemistry, Carbondale, IL 62901-6806. Offers MS, PhD. Part-time programs available. *Faculty:* 10 full-time (1 woman). *Students:* 31 full-time (18 women), 4 part-time (2 women); includes 2 minority (both African Americans), 16 international. Average age 25. 28 applicants, 46% accepted. In 1998, 3 master's, 5 doctorates awarded. Terminal master's awarded for partial completion of doctoral program. *Degree requirements:* For master's, one foreign language, thesis required; for doctorate, variable foreign language requirement, dissertation required. *Entrance requirements:* For master's, TOEFL, minimum GPA of 2.7; for doctorate, GRE General Test, TOEFL (minimum score of 550 required), minimum GPA of 3.25. *Average time to degree:* Master's–5 years full-time; doctorate–3 years full-time. *Application deadline:* Applications are processed on a rolling basis. Application fee: $0. *Financial aid:* In 1998–99, 32 students received aid; fellowships with full tuition reimbursements available, research assistantships with full tuition reimbursements available, teaching assistantships with full tuition reimbursements available, Federal Work-Study, institutionally-sponsored loans, and tuition waivers (full) available. Aid available to part-time students. *Faculty research:* Materials, separations, computational chemistry, synthetics. *Unit head:* John Phillips, Chair, 618-453-6475, Fax: 618-453-6408, E-mail: phillips@chem.siu.edu. *Application contact:* Steve Scheiner, Chair, Graduate Admissions Committee, 618-453-6476, Fax: 618-453-6408, E-mail: scheiner@chem.siu.edu.

Southern Illinois University Edwardsville, Graduate Studies and Research, College of Arts and Sciences, Department of Chemistry, Edwardsville, IL 62026-0001. Offers MS. Part-time programs available. *Students:* 11 full-time (4 women), 10 part-time (5 women); includes 2 minority (both African Americans), 5 international. 10 applicants, 70% accepted. In 1998, 8 degrees awarded. *Degree requirements:* For master's, one foreign language, thesis or alternative, final exam required. *Entrance requirements:* For master's, TOEFL (minimum score of 550 required). *Application deadline:* For fall admission, 7/24. Application fee: $25. *Financial aid:* In 1998–99, 1 research assistantship with full tuition reimbursement, 15 teaching assistantships with full tuition reimbursements were awarded.; fellowships with full tuition reimbursements, Federal Work-Study, institutionally-sponsored loans, and unspecified assistantships also available. Aid available to part-time students. *Unit head:* Dr. James Eilers, Chair, 618-650-3559, E-mail: jeilers@siue.edu.

Southern Methodist University, Dedman College, Department of Chemistry, Dallas, TX 75275. Offers MS. *Faculty:* 11 full-time (1 woman). *Students:* 1 full-time (0 women), 2 part-time; includes 1 minority (African American), 2 international. Average age 31. 5 applicants, 20% accepted. *Degree requirements:* For master's, thesis required, foreign language not required. *Entrance requirements:* For master's, GRE General Test, TOEFL (minimum score of 550 required), bachelor's degree in chemistry, minimum GPA of 3.0. *Application deadline:* For fall admission, 6/30; for spring admission, 11/30. Application fee: $50. Tuition: Part-time $686 per credit hour. Required fees: $88 per credit hour. Part-time tuition and fees vary according to course load and program. *Financial aid:* Fellowships, tuition waivers (full and partial) available. Financial aid applicants required to submit FAFSA. *Faculty research:* Organic and inorganic synthesis, theoretical chemistry, organometallic chemistry, inorganic polymer chemistry, fundamental quantum chemistry. *Unit head:* Dr. Edward R. Biehl, Chairman, 214-768-1280, Fax: 214-768-4089. *Application contact:* Dr. Mark Schell, Graduate Adviser, 214-768-2478, Fax: 214-768-4089.

Southern University and Agricultural and Mechanical College, Graduate School, College of Sciences, Department of Chemistry, Baton Rouge, LA 70813. Offers analytical chemistry (MS); biochemistry (MS); environmental sciences (MS); inorganic chemistry (MS); organic chemistry (MS); physical chemistry (MS). *Faculty:* 9 full-time (2 women), 3 part-time (2 women). *Students:* 4 full-time (3 women), 20 part-time (12 women); includes 19 minority (all African Americans), 4 international. Average age 23. In 1998, 1 degree awarded. *Degree requirements:* For master's, thesis required, foreign language not required. *Entrance requirements:* For master's, GMAT or GRE General Test, TOEFL. *Average time to degree:* Master's–2 years full-time, 4 years part-time. *Application deadline:* For fall admission, 6/1 (priority date); for spring admission, 11/1. Applications are processed on a rolling basis. Application fee: $5. *Financial aid:* In 1998–99, 3 research assistantships (averaging $7,000 per year) were awarded. Financial aid application deadline: 4/15. *Faculty research:* Synthesis of macrocyclic ligands, latex accelerators, anticancer drugs, biosensors, absorption isotheums, isolation of specific enzymes from plants. Total annual research expenditures: $400,000. *Unit head:* Dr. Robert Harvey Miller, Chairman, 225-771-3990, Fax: 225-771-3992.

Southwest Missouri State University, Graduate College, College of Natural and Applied Sciences, Department of Chemistry, Springfield, MO 65804-0094. Offers MS. Part-time programs available. *Faculty:* 16 full-time (2 women). *Students:* 12 full-time (4 women), 2 part-time; includes 1 minority (Hispanic American), 1 international. Average age 24. 9 applicants, 67% accepted. In 1998, 1 degree awarded. *Degree requirements:* For master's, thesis, comprehensive exam required, foreign language not required. *Entrance requirements:* For master's, GRE General Test, minimum undergraduate GPA of 3.0. *Application deadline:* For fall admission, 8/7 (priority date); for spring admission, 12/17 (priority date). Applications are processed on a rolling basis. Application fee: $25. Electronic applications accepted. *Financial aid:* In 1998–99, research assistantships with tuition reimbursements (averaging $6,000 per year), teaching assistantships with tuition reimbursements (averaging $6,000 per year) were awarded.; Federal Work-Study, scholarships, and unspecified assistantships also available. *Faculty research:* Chemistry of environmental systems, mechanisms of organic and organometallic reactions, enzymatic activity inlipid and protein reactions, computational chemistry, polymer properties. Total annual research expenditures: $80,000. *Unit head:* Dr. Tamera Jahnke, Head, 417-836-5506, Fax: 417-836-6934, E-mail: tsj118f@mail.smsu.edu.

Southwest Texas State University, Graduate School, School of Science, Department of Chemistry, San Marcos, TX 78666. Offers M Ed, MA, MS. *Faculty:* 8 full-time (1 woman). *Students:* 8 full-time (2 women), 7 part-time (2 women); includes 4 minority (1 Asian American or Pacific Islander, 2 Hispanic Americans, 1 Native American), 1 international. Average age 29. In 1998, 4 degrees awarded. *Degree requirements:* For master's, thesis (for some programs), comprehensive exam required, foreign language not required. *Entrance requirements:* For master's, GRE General Test (minimum combined score of 950 required), TOEFL (minimum score of 550 required), minimum GPA of 2.75 in last 60 hours. *Application deadline:* For fall admission, 6/15 (priority date); for spring admission, 10/15 (priority date). Applications are processed on a rolling basis. Application fee: $25 ($50 for international students). Tuition, state resident: full-time $684; part-time $38 per semester hour. Tuition, nonresident: full-time $4,572; part-time $254 per semester hour. *Financial aid:* Research assistantships, teaching assistantships, career-related internships or fieldwork, Federal Work-Study, and institutionally-sponsored loans available. Aid available to part-time students. Financial aid application deadline: 4/1; financial aid applicants required to submit FAFSA. *Faculty research:* Metal ions in biological systems, cancer chemotherapy, absorption of pesticides on solid surfaces, polymer chemistry, biochemistry of nucleic acids. *Unit head:* Dr. Carl Carrano, Chair, 512-245-3117, Fax: 512-245-2374, E-mail: cc05@swt.edu. *Application contact:* Dr. J. Michael Willoughby, Dean of the Graduate School, 512-245-2581, Fax: 512-245-8365, E-mail: jw02@swt.edu.

Stanford University, School of Humanities and Sciences, Department of Chemistry, Stanford, CA 94305-9991. Offers PhD. *Faculty:* 21 full-time (1 woman). *Students:* 145 full-time (41 women), 35 part-time (9 women); includes 21 minority (1 African American, 16 Asian Americans or Pacific Islanders, 3 Hispanic Americans, 1 Native American), 48 international. Average age 26. 369 applicants, 29% accepted. In 1998, 40 doctorates awarded. *Degree requirements:* For doctorate, 2 foreign languages, dissertation required. *Entrance requirements:* For doctorate, GRE General Test, GRE Subject Test, TOEFL. *Application deadline:* For fall admission, 1/1. Application fee: $65 ($80 for international students). Electronic applications accepted. Tuition: Full-time $23,058. Required fees: $152. Part-time tuition and fees vary according to course load. *Financial aid:* Fellowships, research assistantships, teaching assistantships, institutionally-sponsored loans available. *Unit head:* Barry M. Trost, Chair, 650-723-3385, Fax: 650-725-0259, E-mail: bmtrost@leland.stanford.edu. *Application contact:* Graduate Admissions Committee, 650-723-1525.

See in-depth description on page 175.

State University of New York at Albany, College of Arts and Sciences, Department of Chemistry, Albany, NY 12222-0001. Offers MS, PhD. Evening/weekend programs available. *Faculty:* 14 full-time (0 women), 1 (woman) part-time. *Students:* 37 full-time (13 women); includes 1 minority (African American), 31 international. Average age 26. 42 applicants, 38% accepted. In 1998, 2 master's, 6 doctorates awarded. *Degree requirements:* For master's, one foreign language (computer language can substitute), thesis, major field exam required; for doctorate, 2 foreign languages (computer language can substitute for one), dissertation, cumulative exams, oral proposition required. *Entrance requirements:* For doctorate, GRE. Application fee: $50. Tuition, state resident: full-time $5,100; part-time $213 per credit. Tuition, nonresident: full-time $8,416; part-time $351 per credit. Required fees: $31 per credit. *Financial aid:* Research assistantships, teaching assistantships, minority assistantships available. *Faculty research:* Synthetic, organic, and inorganic chemistry; polymer chemistry; ESR and NMR spectroscopy; theoretical chemistry; physical biochemistry. *Unit head:* Dr. John Welch, Chair, 518-442-4400.

State University of New York at Binghamton, Graduate School, School of Arts and Sciences, Department of Chemistry, Binghamton, NY 13902-6000. Offers analytical chemistry (PhD); chemistry (MA, MS); inorganic chemistry (PhD); organic chemistry (PhD); physical chemistry (PhD). *Faculty:* 13 full-time, 7 part-time. *Students:* 48 full-time (11 women), 7 part-time (2 women); includes 2 minority (1 African American, 1 Hispanic American), 30 international. Average age 30. 34 applicants, 76% accepted. In 1998, 4 master's, 6 doctorates awarded. Terminal master's awarded for partial completion of doctoral program. *Degree requirements:* For master's, thesis or alternative, oral exam, seminar presentation required, foreign language not required; for doctorate, dissertation, cumulative exams required, foreign language not required. *Entrance requirements:* For master's and doctorate, GRE General Test, GRE Subject Test, TOEFL. *Application deadline:* For fall admission, 4/15 (priority date); for spring admission, 11/1. Applications are processed on a rolling basis. Application fee: $50. Electronic applications accepted. Tuition, state resident: full-time $5,100; part-time $213 per credit. Tuition, nonresident: full-time $8,416; part-time $351 per credit. Required fees: $77 per credit. Part-time tuition and fees vary according to course load. *Financial aid:* In 1998–99, 44 students received aid, including 2 fellowships with full tuition reimbursements available (averaging $9,793 per year), 9 research assistantships with full tuition reimbursements available (averaging $8,528 per year), 30 teaching assistantships with full tuition reimbursements available (averaging $7,953 per year); career-related internships or fieldwork, Federal Work-Study, institutionally-sponsored loans, and unspecified assistantships also available. Aid available to part-time students. Financial aid application deadline: 2/15. *Unit head:* Dr. Alistair J. Lees, Chairperson, 607-777-2362.

State University of New York at Buffalo, Graduate School, College of Arts and Sciences, Department of Chemistry, Buffalo, NY 14260. Offers MA, PhD. Part-time programs available. *Faculty:* 27 full-time (1 woman), 6 part-time (1 woman). *Students:* 54 full-time (18 women), 66 part-time (19 women); includes 9 minority (2 African Americans, 3 Asian Americans or Pacific Islanders, 4 Hispanic Americans), 41 international. Average age 24. 121 applicants, 23% accepted. In 1998, 7 master's, 12 doctorates awarded. Terminal master's awarded for partial completion of doctoral program. *Degree requirements:* For master's, thesis or alternative, project required, foreign language not required; for doctorate, dissertation required, foreign language not required. *Entrance requirements:* For master's and doctorate, GRE General Test, GRE Subject Test, TOEFL (minimum score of 600 required). *Average time to degree:* Master's–2 years full-time; doctorate–5 years full-time. *Application deadline:* For fall admission, 5/15 (priority date). Applications are processed on a rolling basis. Application fee: $35. Tuition, state resident: full-time $5,100; part-time $213 per credit hour. Tuition, nonresident: full-time $8,416; part-time $351 per credit hour. Required fees: $870; $75 per semester. Tuition and fees vary according to course load and program. *Financial aid:* In 1998–99, 6 fellowships with full tuition reimbursements, 62 research assistantships with full tuition reimbursements, 50 teaching assistantships with full tuition reimbursements were awarded.; Federal Work-Study, institutionally-sponsored loans, and unspecified assistantships also available. Financial aid application deadline: 6/15; financial aid applicants required to submit FAFSA. Total annual research expenditures: $4.7 million. *Unit head:* Dr. Jim D. Atwood, Chairman, 716-645-6800 Ext. 2015, Fax: 716-645-6963, E-mail: chechair@acsu.buffalo.edu. *Application contact:* Dr. Huw M.L. Davies, Director of Graduate Studies, 716-645-6800 Ext. 2030, Fax: 716-645-6963.

State University of New York at Buffalo, Graduate School, Graduate Programs in Biomedical Sciences at Roswell Park Cancer Institute, Program in Interdisciplinary Natural and Biomedical Sciences at Roswell Park Cancer Institute, Buffalo, NY 14260. Offers biochemistry (MS); biometry (MS); biophysics (MS); cellular molecular biology (MS); chemistry (MS); epidemiology (MS); immunology (MS); pathology (MS); pharmacology (MS); physiology (MS). Part-time programs available. *Faculty:* 11 full-time (2 women). *Students:* 43 full-time (15 women), 35 part-time (17 women); includes 14 minority (4 African Americans, 8 Asian Americans or Pacific Islanders, 2 Hispanic Americans), 5 international. *Degree requirements:* For master's, thesis, defense of thesis, research project required. *Entrance requirements:* For master's, GRE General Test, TOEFL, TSE (minimum score of 50 required), TWE (minimum score of 4.0 required). *Application deadline:* For fall admission, 6/1 (priority date). Applications are processed on a rolling basis. Application fee: $35. Electronic applications accepted. Tuition, state resident: full-time $5,100; part-time $213 per credit hour. Tuition, nonresident: full-time $8,416; part-time $351 per credit hour. Required fees: $870; $75 per semester. Tuition and fees vary according to course load and program. *Unit head:* Dr. Robert Gregory, Graduate Director, 214-768-3075, Fax: 214-768-2701, E-mail: bgregory@mail.smu.edu. *Application contact:* Craig R. Johnson, Director of Graduate Studies, 716-845-2339, Fax: 716-845-8178, E-mail: rpgradapp@sc3103.med.buffalo.edu.

State University of New York at New Paltz, Graduate School, Faculty of Liberal Arts and Sciences, Department of Chemistry, New Paltz, NY 12561. Offers MA, MAT, MS Ed. *Degree requirements:* For master's, thesis required. *Entrance requirements:* For master's, GRE General Test, minimum GPA of 3.0. *Application deadline:* For fall admission, 3/15 (priority date). Applications are processed on a rolling basis. Application fee: $50. *Financial aid:* Research assistantships, teaching assistantships, Federal Work-Study and institutionally-sponsored loans available. *Unit head:* Dr. Richard Tofte, Chairman, 914-257-3790.

State University of New York at Oswego, Graduate Studies, Division of Arts and Sciences, Department of Chemistry, Oswego, NY 13126. Offers MS. Part-time programs available. *Faculty:* 4 full-time. *Students:* 5 full-time (1 woman), 5 part-time (3 women); includes 1 minority (Hispanic American) Average age 25. 4 applicants, 100% accepted. In 1998, 1 degree awarded. *Degree requirements:* For master's, one foreign language (computer language can substitute), thesis, written comprehensive exams required. *Entrance requirements:* For master's, GRE General Test, GRE Subject Test, BA or BS in chemistry. *Application deadline:* For fall admission, 7/1; for spring admission, 10/1. Applications are processed on a rolling basis. Application fee: $50. Tuition, state resident: full-time $5,100; part-time $213 per credit. Tuition, nonresident: full-time $8,416; part-time $351 per credit. *Financial aid:* In 1998–99, 7 teaching assistantships were awarded.; career-related internships or fieldwork, Federal Work-Study, institutionally-sponsored loans, and tuition waivers (partial) also available. Aid available to part-time students. Financial aid application deadline: 4/1; financial aid applicants required to submit FAFSA. *Unit head:* Dr. Augustine Silveira, Chair, 315-341-3048. *Application contact:* Dr. Raymond O'Donnell, Graduate Coordinator, 315-341-3048.

State University of New York at Stony Brook, Graduate School, College of Arts and Sciences, Department of Chemistry, Stony Brook, NY 11794. Offers MAT, MS, PhD. MAT offered through the School of Professional Development and Continuing Studies. *Faculty:* 29 full-time (5 women), 5 part-time (1 woman). *Students:* 99 full-time (36 women), 32 part-time (8 women); includes 11 minority (1 African American, 9 Asian Americans or Pacific Islanders, 1 Hispanic American), 85 international. Average age 27. 168 applicants, 38% accepted. In 1998, 10 master's, 18 doctorates awarded. Terminal master's awarded for partial completion of doctoral program. *Degree requirements:* For master's, thesis required, foreign language not required; for doctorate, dissertation required. *Entrance requirements:* For master's and doctorate, GRE General Test, TOEFL. *Application deadline:* For fall admission, 1/15. Application fee: $50. *Financial aid:* In 1998–99, 1 fellowship, 57 research assistantships, 57 teaching assistant-

Chemistry

State University of New York at Stony Brook (continued)
ships were awarded. Total annual research expenditures: $5 million. *Unit head:* Dr. Iwao Ojima, Chairman, 516-632-7880, Fax: 516-632-7960. *Application contact:* Dr. Scott Sieburth, Director, 516-632-7851, Fax: 516-632-7960, E-mail: ssieburth@notes.cc.sunysb.edu.

State University of New York College at Buffalo, Graduate Studies and Research, Faculty of Natural and Social Sciences, Department of Chemistry, Buffalo, NY 14222-1095. Offers chemistry (MA); secondary education (MS Ed), including chemistry. *Accreditation:* NCATE (one or more programs are accredited). Part-time and evening/weekend programs available. *Faculty:* 7 full-time (2 women). Average age 27. 11 applicants, 64% accepted. In 1998, 3 degrees awarded. *Degree requirements:* For master's, thesis required (for some programs), foreign language not required. *Entrance requirements:* For master's, minimum GPA of 2.6 in last 60 hours, New York teaching certificate (MS Ed). *Application deadline:* For fall admission, 5/1 (priority date); for spring admission, 10/1 (priority date). Applications are processed on a rolling basis. Application fee: $50. *Financial aid:* In 1998–99, 1 fellowship with full tuition reimbursement (averaging $7,000 per year), 4 research assistantships with partial tuition reimbursements were awarded.; career-related internships or fieldwork, Federal Work-Study, and unspecified assistantships also available. Aid available to part-time students. Financial aid application deadline: 3/1. *Unit head:* Dr. Gregory Ebert, Chairperson, 716-878-5204, Fax: 716-878-4028, E-mail: ebertgw@buffalostate.edu.

State University of New York College at Fredonia, Graduate Studies, Department of Chemistry, Fredonia, NY 14063. Offers MS, MS Ed. Part-time and evening/weekend programs available. *Faculty:* 2 full-time (0 women), 1 part-time (0 women). 2 applicants, 100% accepted. In 1998, 2 degrees awarded. *Degree requirements:* For master's, thesis required, foreign language not required. *Application deadline:* For fall admission, 7/5. Application fee: $50. Tuition, state resident: full-time $5,100; part-time $213 per credit hour. Tuition, nonresident: full-time $8,416; part-time $351 per credit hour. Required fees: $775; $32 per credit hour. *Financial aid:* In 1998–99, 2 teaching assistantships with partial tuition reimbursements were awarded.; research assistantships, tuition waivers (full and partial) also available. Aid available to part-time students. Financial aid application deadline: 3/15. *Faculty research:* Gas chromatography, organometallic synthesis, polymer chemistry. *Unit head:* Dr. Thomas Janik, Chairman, 716-673-3281.

State University of New York College of Environmental Science and Forestry, Faculty of Chemistry, Syracuse, NY 13210-2779. Offers environmental and forest chemistry (MS, PhD). *Faculty:* 14 full-time (0 women). *Students:* 27 full-time (11 women), 2 part-time (both women); includes 1 minority (Asian American or Pacific Islander), 15 international. Average age 29. 63 applicants, 70% accepted. In 1998, 1 master's, 1 doctorate awarded. Terminal master's awarded for partial completion of doctoral program. *Degree requirements:* For master's, thesis or alternative required, foreign language not required; for doctorate, dissertation required. *Entrance requirements:* For master's and doctorate, GRE General Test (minimum combined score of 1800 on three sections required), GRE Subject Test (minimum score of 600 required), minimum GPA of 3.0. *Application deadline:* For fall admission, 4/15 (priority date); for spring admission, 11/15. Applications are processed on a rolling basis. Application fee: $50. *Financial aid:* In 1998–99, 20 research assistantships, 9 teaching assistantships were awarded.; fellowships, career-related internships or fieldwork and Federal Work-Study also available. *Faculty research:* Polymer chemistry, biochemistry. Total annual research expenditures: $2 million. *Unit head:* Dr. John P. Hassett, Chairperson, 315-470-6827, Fax: 315-470-6856, E-mail: jhassett@mailbox.syr.edu.. *Application contact:* Dr. Robert H. Frey, Dean, Instruction and Graduate Studies, 315-470-6599, Fax: 315-470-6978, E-mail: esfgrad@esf.edu.

See in-depth description on page 177.

Stephen F. Austin State University, Graduate School, College of Sciences and Mathematics, Department of Chemistry, Program in Chemistry, Nacogdoches, TX 75962. Offers MS. *Students:* 4 full-time (1 woman), 1 part-time, 1 international. Average age 25. 4 applicants, 100% accepted. In 1998, 2 degrees awarded. *Degree requirements:* For master's, comprehensive exam required, foreign language and thesis not required. *Entrance requirements:* For master's, GRE General Test (minimum combined score of 1000 required), TOEFL, minimum GPA of 2.8 in last 60 hours, 2.5 overall. *Application deadline:* For fall admission, 8/1 (priority date); for spring admission, 12/15. Applications are processed on a rolling basis. Application fee: $0 ($50 for international students). Tuition, state resident: full-time $1,792. Tuition, nonresident: full-time $6,880. *Financial aid:* In 1998–99, teaching assistantships (averaging $6,750 per year) Financial aid application deadline: 3/1. *Unit head:* Dr. Wayne Boring, Chair, Department of Chemistry, 409-468-3606.

Stevens Institute of Technology, Graduate School, School of Applied Sciences and Liberal Arts, Department of Chemistry and Chemical Biology, Hoboken, NJ 07030. Offers chemistry (MS, PhD, Certificate), including analytical chemistry, chemical biology, chemical physiology (Certificate), instrumental analysis (Certificate), organic chemistry (MS, PhD), physical chemistry (MS, PhD), polymer chemistry. Part-time and evening/weekend programs available. Terminal master's awarded for partial completion of doctoral program. *Degree requirements:* For master's, thesis or alternative required, foreign language not required; for doctorate, one foreign language, dissertation required; for Certificate, computer language, project or thesis required. *Entrance requirements:* For master's and doctorate, TOEFL (minimum score of 550 required). Electronic applications accepted.

Sul Ross State University, School of Arts and Sciences, Department of Geology and Chemistry, Alpine, TX 79832. Offers MS. Part-time programs available. *Degree requirements:* For master's, thesis optional, foreign language not required. *Entrance requirements:* For master's, GRE General Test (minimum combined score of 850 required), minimum GPA of 2.5 in last 60 hours of undergraduate work.

Syracuse University, Graduate School, College of Arts and Sciences, Department of Chemistry, Syracuse, NY 13244-0003. Offers MS, PhD. *Faculty:* 17. *Students:* 60 full-time (14 women), 2 part-time (1 woman); includes 5 minority (2 African Americans, 2 Asian Americans or Pacific Islanders, 1 Hispanic American), 15 international. Average age 28. 143 applicants, 29% accepted. In 1998, 3 master's, 6 doctorates awarded. *Degree requirements:* For master's, one foreign language required; for doctorate, dissertation required. *Entrance requirements:* For master's and doctorate, GRE General Test, GRE Subject Test. *Application deadline:* Applications are processed on a rolling basis. Application fee: $40. Tuition: Full-time $13,992; part-time $583 per credit hour. *Financial aid:* Fellowships, research assistantships, teaching assistantships, Federal Work-Study and tuition waivers (partial) available. Financial aid application deadline: 3/1. *Unit head:* Laurence Nafie, Chair, 315-443-4109.

Temple University, Graduate School, College of Science and Technology, Department of Chemistry, Philadelphia, PA 19122-6096. Offers MA, PhD. Evening/weekend programs available. *Faculty:* 16 full-time (2 women). *Students:* 58 (24 women); includes 30 minority (5 African Americans, 25 Asian Americans or Pacific Islanders) 8 international. 4 applicants, 75% accepted. In 1998, 4 master's, 8 doctorates awarded. Terminal master's awarded for partial completion of doctoral program. *Degree requirements:* For master's, thesis required (for some programs), foreign language not required; for doctorate, dissertation, teaching experience required, foreign language not required. *Entrance requirements:* For master's and doctorate, GRE General Test (minimum combined score of 1650 on three sections required), GRE Subject Test, minimum GPA of 3.0 during previous 2 years, 2.8 overall. *Application deadline:* For fall admission, 7/1. Application fee: $40. Electronic applications accepted. *Financial aid:* Fellowships, research assistantships, teaching assistantships available. Financial aid application deadline: 7/1. *Faculty research:* Polymers, nonlinear optics, natural products, materials science, enantioselective synthesis. *Unit head:* Dr. Robert Solomon, Chair, 215-204-5772, Fax: 215-204-1532, E-mail: v5515@vm.temple.edu. *Application contact:* Franklin Davis, Admissions Coordinator, 215-204-1980, Fax: 215-204-1532, E-mail: chemgrad@blue.vm.temple.edu.

Tennessee State University, Graduate School, College of Arts and Sciences, Department of Chemistry, Nashville, TN 37209-1561. Offers MS. *Faculty:* 5 full-time (0 women). *Students:* 2 full-time (1 woman), 6 part-time (3 women); includes 2 minority (1 African American, 1 Asian American or Pacific Islander), 3 international. Average age 28. 2 applicants, 100% accepted. In 1998, 3 degrees awarded. *Degree requirements:* For master's, thesis required, foreign language not required. *Entrance requirements:* For master's, GRE General Test (minimum combined score of 870 required), GRE Subject Test, minimum GPA of 3.0, BS in engineering or science. *Application deadline:* Applications are processed on a rolling basis. Application fee: $15. Tuition, state resident: full-time $2,962; part-time $182 per credit hour. Tuition, nonresident: full-time $7,788; part-time $393 per credit hour. *Financial aid:* In 1998–99, 6 teaching assistantships (averaging $17,772 per year) were awarded.; research assistantships, unspecified assistantships also available. Financial aid application deadline: 5/1. *Faculty research:* Binding benzol pyrenemetabolites to DNA. *Unit head:* Dr. Carlos L. Lee, Interim Head, 615-963-5004.

Tennessee Technological University, Graduate School, College of Arts and Sciences, Department of Chemistry, Cookeville, TN 38505. Offers MS. Part-time programs available. *Faculty:* 16 full-time (1 woman). *Students:* 8 full-time (4 women), 2 part-time; includes 6 minority (all Asian Americans or Pacific Islanders) Average age 28. 22 applicants, 45% accepted. In 1998, 2 degrees awarded. *Degree requirements:* For master's, thesis required, foreign language not required. *Entrance requirements:* For master's, GRE General Test, TOEFL (minimum score of 525 required). *Application deadline:* For fall admission, 3/1 (priority date); for spring admission, 8/1. Application fee: $25 ($30 for international students). Tuition, state resident: part-time $137 per hour. Tuition, nonresident: part-time $361 per hour. Required fees: $17 per hour. Tuition and fees vary according to course load. *Financial aid:* In 1998–99, 8 students received aid, including 4 teaching assistantships (averaging $6,080 per year); research assistantships, career-related internships or fieldwork also available. Financial aid application deadline: 4/1. *Unit head:* Dr. Scott Northrup, Interim Chairperson, 931-372-3421, Fax: 931-372-3434, E-mail: snorthrup@tntech.edu. *Application contact:* Dr. Rebecca F. Quattlebaum, Dean of the Graduate School, 931-372-3233, Fax: 931-372-3497, E-mail: rquattlebaum@tntech.edu.

Texas A&M University, College of Science, Department of Chemistry, College Station, TX 77843. Offers MS, PhD. *Faculty:* 54 full-time (3 women). *Students:* 211 full-time (70 women); includes 20 minority (6 African Americans, 7 Asian Americans or Pacific Islanders, 7 Hispanic Americans), 76 international. Average age 28. 468 applicants, 25% accepted. In 1998, 10 master's, 44 doctorates awarded. *Degree requirements:* For master's and doctorate, thesis/dissertation required, foreign language not required. *Entrance requirements:* For master's and doctorate, GRE General Test, TOEFL. *Average time to degree:* Master's–4 years full-time; doctorate–5.5 years full-time. *Application deadline:* For fall admission, 3/1 (priority date). Applications are processed on a rolling basis. Application fee: $50 ($75 for international students). Electronic applications accepted. *Financial aid:* In 1998–99, fellowships with partial tuition reimbursements (averaging $18,000 per year), research assistantships with partial tuition reimbursements (averaging $15,960 per year), teaching assistantships with partial tuition reimbursements (averaging $18,000 per year) were awarded. Financial aid application deadline: 3/1; financial aid applicants required to submit FAFSA. *Faculty research:* Analytical biological, inorganic, organic, and physical chemistry. Total annual research expenditures: $10.9 million. *Unit head:* Dr. Emile A. Schweikert, Head, 409-845-2011, Fax: 409-845-4719. *Application contact:* Dr. Frank M. Ranshel, Graduate Adviser, 409-845-5345, Fax: 409-845-5211, E-mail: gradmail@mail.chem.tamu.edu.

See in-depth description on page 179.

Texas A&M University–Commerce, Graduate School, College of Arts and Sciences, Department of Chemistry, Commerce, TX 75429-3011. Offers M Ed, MS. Part-time programs available. *Faculty:* 3 full-time (0 women). *Students:* 5 full-time (2 women), 5 part-time; includes 1 minority (African American), 5 international. Average age 36. In 1998, 2 degrees awarded. *Degree requirements:* For master's, thesis (for some programs), comprehensive exam required. *Entrance requirements:* For master's, GRE General Test (minimum combined score of 850 required). *Application deadline:* For fall admission, 6/1 (priority date); for spring admission, 11/1 (priority date). Applications are processed on a rolling basis. Application fee: $0 ($25 for international students). Electronic applications accepted. *Financial aid:* In 1998–99, research assistantships (averaging $7,750 per year), teaching assistantships (averaging $7,750 per year) were awarded.; Federal Work-Study, institutionally-sponsored loans, and scholarships also available. Financial aid application deadline: 5/1; financial aid applicants required to submit FAFSA. *Unit head:* Dr. Kenneth Ashley, Head, 903-886-5392. *Application contact:* Betty Hunt, Graduate Admissions Adviser, 903-886-5167, Fax: 903-886-5165, E-mail: betty_hunt@tamu_commerce.edu.

Texas A&M University–Kingsville, College of Graduate Studies, College of Arts and Sciences, Department of Chemistry, Kingsville, TX 78363. Offers MS. Part-time programs available. *Faculty:* 6 full-time (0 women). *Students:* 1 full-time (0 women), 4 part-time (2 women). *Degree requirements:* For master's, thesis or alternative, comprehensive exam required, foreign language not required. *Entrance requirements:* For master's, GRE General Test (minimum combined score of 800 required), TOEFL (minimum score of 500 required), minimum GPA of 3.0. *Application deadline:* For fall admission, 6/1; for spring admission, 11/15. Applications are processed on a rolling basis. Application fee: $15 ($25 for international students). Tuition, state resident: full-time $2,062. Tuition, nonresident: full-time $7,246. *Financial aid:* Fellowships, research assistantships, teaching assistantships, institutionally-sponsored loans and tuition waivers (partial) available. Financial aid application deadline: 5/15. *Faculty research:* Organic heterocycles, amino alcohol complexes, rare earth arsine complexes. Total annual research expenditures: $30,000. *Unit head:* Dr. Mauro Castro, Graduate Coordinator, 361-593-2914.

Texas Christian University, Add Ran College of Arts and Sciences, Department of Chemistry, Fort Worth, TX 76129-0002. Offers MA, MS, PhD. Part-time and evening/weekend programs available. *Students:* 24 (11 women); includes 1 minority (Hispanic American) 15 international. 92 applicants, 9% accepted. In 1998, 1 master's, 5 doctorates awarded. *Degree requirements:* For master's, one foreign language required, thesis optional; for doctorate, dissertation, cumulative exams required. *Entrance requirements:* For master's, GRE General Test (minimum combined score of 1000 required), TOEFL (minimum score of 550 required); for doctorate, GRE General Test, TOEFL (minimum score of 550 required). *Application deadline:* For fall admission, 3/1; for spring admission, 12/1. Applications are processed on a rolling basis. Application fee: $0. *Financial aid:* Fellowships, teaching assistantships, unspecified assistantships available. Financial aid application deadline: 3/1. *Unit head:* Dr. Robert H. Neilson, Chairperson, 817-257-7195.

Texas Southern University, Graduate School, College of Arts and Sciences, Department of Chemistry, Houston, TX 77004-4584. Offers MS. *Degree requirements:* For master's, one foreign language (computer language can substitute), thesis, comprehensive exam required. *Entrance requirements:* For master's, GRE General Test, TOEFL, minimum GPA of 2.5. *Faculty research:* Analytical and physical chemistry, geochemistry, inorganic chemistry, biochemistry, organic chemistry.

Texas Tech University, Graduate School, College of Arts and Sciences, Department of Chemistry and Biochemistry, Lubbock, TX 79409. Offers chemistry (MS, PhD). Part-time programs available. *Faculty:* 21 full-time (1 woman), 1 part-time (0 women). *Students:* 57 full-time (17 women), 5 part-time; includes 4 minority (2 African Americans, 1 Asian American or Pacific Islander, 1 Hispanic American), 34 international. Average age 28. 51 applicants, 53% accepted. In 1998, 9 master's, 15 doctorates awarded. *Degree requirements:* For master's and doctorate, thesis/dissertation required. *Entrance requirements:* For master's, GRE General Test (combined average 1147); for doctorate, GRE General Test. *Application deadline:* For fall admission, 4/15 (priority date); for spring admission, 11/1 (priority date). Applications are processed on a rolling basis. Application fee: $25 ($50 for international students). Electronic applications accepted. *Financial aid:* In 1998–99, 42 research assistantships (averaging $11,414 per year), 25 teaching assistantships (averaging $11,613 per year) were awarded.; fellowships, career-related internships or fieldwork, Federal Work-Study, and institutionally-sponsored loans also available. Aid available to part-time students. Financial aid application deadline: 5/15; financial aid applicants required to submit FAFSA. *Faculty research:* Continuous termination of gas and aerosol phase acidity, separation of metal ions and neural molecules by special complexing agents. Total annual research expenditures: $2.8 million. *Unit head:* Dr. David M. Roundhill, Chairman, 806-742-3067, Fax: 806-742-1289.

Texas Woman's University, Graduate School, College of Arts and Sciences, Department of Chemistry and Physics, Denton, TX 76204. Offers chemistry (MS). Part-time programs available. *Faculty:* 6 full-time (1 woman). *Students:* 8 full-time (6 women), 31 part-time (29 women); includes 9 minority (1 African American, 4 Asian Americans or Pacific Islanders, 3 Hispanic Americans, 1 Native American), 1 international. Average age 39. 9 applicants, 22% accepted. In 1998, 17 degrees awarded (100% found work related to degree). *Degree requirements:* For master's, thesis required, foreign language not required. *Entrance requirements:* For master's, GRE General Test (minimum combined score of 700 required), minimum GPA of 3.0. *Average time to degree:* Master's–2 years full-time. Application fee: $30. *Financial aid:* In 1998–99, 8 students received aid, including 3 research assistantships, 5 teaching assistantships; career-related internships or fieldwork, Federal Work-Study, and institutionally-sponsored loans also available. Aid available to part-time students. Financial aid application deadline: 4/1. *Faculty research:* Mechanisms of organic reactions, leucotrienes, science education, coordination chemistry, protein chemistry. Total annual research expenditures: $35,000. *Unit head:* Dr. Carlton Wendel, Chair, 940-898-2550, Fax: 940-898-2548, E-mail: d_wendel@twu.edu.

Trent University, Graduate Studies, Program in Applications of Modelling in the Natural and Social Sciences, Department of Chemistry, Peterborough, ON K9J 7B8, Canada. Offers M Sc. Part-time programs available. *Degree requirements:* For master's, thesis required, foreign language not required. *Entrance requirements:* For master's, honours degree. *Application deadline:* For fall admission, 2/1 (priority date). Applications are processed on a rolling basis. Application fee: $45. *Financial aid:* Research assistantships, teaching assistantships available. *Faculty research:* Synthetic-organic chemistry, mass spectrometry and ion storage. *Unit head:* Dr. M. Berrill, Chair, 705-748-1298, E-mail: mberrill@trentu.ca. *Application contact:* Graduate Studies Officer, 705-748-1245, Fax: 705-748-1625.

Tufts University, Division of Graduate and Continuing Studies and Research, Graduate School of Arts and Sciences, Department of Chemistry, Medford, MA 02155. Offers analytical chemistry (MS, PhD); bioorganic chemistry (MS, PhD); environmental chemistry (MS, PhD); inorganic chemistry (MS, PhD); organic chemistry (MS, PhD); physical chemistry (MS, PhD). *Faculty:* 13 full-time, 1 part-time. *Students:* 52 (27 women); includes 5 minority (1 African American, 3 Asian Americans or Pacific Islanders, 1 Hispanic American) 14 international. 86 applicants, 41% accepted. In 1998, 4 master's, 3 doctorates awarded. Terminal master's awarded for partial completion of doctoral program. *Degree requirements:* For master's and doctorate, thesis/dissertation required, foreign language not required. *Entrance requirements:* For master's and doctorate, GRE General Test, GRE Subject Test, TOEFL (minimum score of 600 required). *Application deadline:* For fall admission, 2/15; for spring admission, 10/15. Applications are processed on a rolling basis. Application fee: $50. *Financial aid:* Research assistantships with full and partial tuition reimbursements, teaching assistantships with full and partial tuition reimbursements, Federal Work-Study, scholarships, and tuition waivers (partial) available. Financial aid application deadline: 2/15; financial aid applicants required to submit FAFSA. *Unit head:* Marc d'Alarco, Chair, 617-627-3441, Fax: 617-627-3443. *Application contact:* Samuel Kounaves, 617-627-3124, Fax: 617-627-3443.

See in-depth description on page 181.

Tulane University, Graduate School, Department of Chemistry, New Orleans, LA 70118-5669. Offers MS, PhD. *Students:* 61 full-time (16 women), 1 part-time; includes 5 minority (all African Americans), 37 international. 103 applicants, 31% accepted. In 1998, 6 master's, 3 doctorates awarded. Terminal master's awarded for partial completion of doctoral program. *Degree requirements:* For master's and doctorate, thesis/dissertation required, foreign language not required. *Entrance requirements:* For master's, GRE General Test (minimum combined score of 1000 required; average 1200), TOEFL (minimum score of 600 required), TSE (minimum score of 220 required), minimum B average in undergraduate course work; for doctorate, GRE General Test (minimum combined score of 1000 required; average 1200), TOEFL (minimum score of 600 required), TSE (minimum score of 220 required). *Average time to degree:* Master's–3 years full-time; doctorate–4.5 years full-time. *Application deadline:* For fall admission, 2/1. Application fee: $45. Electronic applications accepted. *Financial aid:* Fellowships, research assistantships, teaching assistantships, career-related internships or fieldwork, Federal Work-Study, and institutionally-sponsored loans available. Financial aid application deadline: 2/1. *Faculty research:* Enzyme mechanisms, organic synthesis, photochemistry, theory of polymer dynamics. Total annual research expenditures: $2.8 million. *Unit head:* Dr. William L. Alworth, Chair, 504-865-5573.

See in-depth description on page 183.

Tuskegee University, Graduate Programs, College of Agricultural, Environmental and Natural Sciences, Department of Chemistry, Tuskegee, AL 36088. Offers MS. *Faculty:* 6 full-time (1 woman). *Students:* 6 full-time (1 woman), 3 part-time (1 woman); includes 7 minority (6 African Americans, 1 Asian American or Pacific Islander), 2 international. Average age 24. In 1998, 1 degree awarded. *Degree requirements:* For master's, computer language, thesis required, foreign language not required. *Entrance requirements:* For master's, GRE General Test. *Application deadline:* For fall admission, 7/15. Applications are processed on a rolling basis. Application fee: $25 ($35 for international students). *Financial aid:* Fellowships, teaching assistantships, Federal Work-Study and institutionally-sponsored loans available. Aid available to part-time students. Financial aid application deadline: 4/15. *Unit head:* Dr. Adriane Ludwick, Head, 334-727-8833.

Université de Moncton, Faculty of Science, Department of Chemistry and Biochemistry, Moncton, NB E1A 3E9, Canada. Offers biochemistry (M Sc); chemistry (M Sc). *Faculty:* 7 full-time (1 woman). *Students:* 11 full-time (3 women); includes 1 minority (African American), 1 international. Average age 25. *Degree requirements:* For master's, one foreign language, thesis required. *Entrance requirements:* For master's, minimum GPA of 3.0. *Average time to degree:* Master's–2 years full-time. *Application deadline:* For fall admission, 6/1 (priority date); for winter admission, 11/15 (priority date). Applications are processed on a rolling basis. Application fee: $50. Electronic applications accepted. *Financial aid:* In 1998–99, 5 teaching assistantships were awarded. *Faculty research:* Environmental contaminants, cytoskeleton structure, mitochondrial DNA, protein and hormones, oxidation of alkaloids. *Unit head:* Dr. Charles Bourque, Director, 506-858-4331, Fax: 506-858-4541, E-mail: bourquch@umoncton.ca.

Université de Montréal, Faculty of Graduate Studies, Faculty of Arts and Sciences, Department of Chemistry, Montréal, PQ H3C 3J7, Canada. Offers M Sc, PhD. *Faculty:* 33 full-time (1 woman), 1 part-time (0 women). *Students:* 135 full-time (46 women). 37 applicants, 35% accepted. In 1998, 20 master's, 19 doctorates awarded. *Degree requirements:* For doctorate, dissertation, general exam required. *Entrance requirements:* For doctorate, M Sc in chemistry or related field. Application fee: $30. *Faculty research:* Analytical, inorganic, physical, and organic chemistry. *Unit head:* Marius D'Amboise, Graduate Chairman, 514-343-7604. *Application contact:* Andre Beauchamp, Professor, 514-343-6446.

Université de Sherbrooke, Faculty of Sciences, Department of Chemistry, Sherbrooke, PQ J1K 2R1, Canada. Offers M Sc, PhD. *Degree requirements:* For master's and doctorate, thesis/dissertation required, foreign language not required. *Entrance requirements:* For doctorate, master's degree. *Faculty research:* Organic, electro-, theoretical, and physical chemistry.

Université du Québec à Montréal, Graduate Programs, Program in Chemistry, Montréal, PQ H3C 3P8, Canada. Offers M Sc. Offered jointly with the Université du Québec à Trois-Rivières. Part-time programs available. *Degree requirements:* For master's, thesis required. *Entrance requirements:* For master's, appropriate bachelor's degree or equivalent and proficiency in French.

Université du Québec à Trois-Rivières, Graduate Programs, Program in Chemistry, Trois-Rivières, PQ G9A 5H7, Canada. Offers M Sc. Part-time programs available. *Students:* 4 full-time (2 women). 5 applicants, 0% accepted. *Degree requirements:* For master's, thesis required. *Entrance requirements:* For master's, appropriate bachelor's degree, proficiency in French. *Application deadline:* For fall admission, 2/1. Application fee: $30. *Financial aid:* Fellowships, research assistantships, teaching assistantships available. *Unit head:* René LaSage, Director, 819-376-5053 Ext. 3356, Fax: 819-376-5012, E-mail: rene_lesage@uqtr.uquebec.ca. *Application contact:* Suzanne Camirand, Admissions Officer, 819-376-5045 Ext. 2591, Fax: 819-376-5210, E-mail: suzanne_camirand@uqtr.uquebec.ca.

Université Laval, Faculty of Graduate Studies, Faculty of Sciences and Engineering, Department of Chemistry, Sainte-Foy, PQ G1K 7P4, Canada. Offers M Sc, PhD. *Students:* 78 full-time (24 women), 2 part-time (1 woman). 31 applicants, 55% accepted. In 1998, 8 master's, 6 doctorates awarded. *Application deadline:* For fall admission, 3/1. Application fee: $30. *Unit head:* Michel Pézolet, Director, 418-656-2131 Ext. 2481, Fax: 418-656-7916, E-mail: michel.pezolet@chm.ulaval.ca.

The University of Akron, Graduate School, Buchtel College of Arts and Sciences, Department of Chemistry, Akron, OH 44325-0001. Offers analytical chemistry (MS, PhD); biochemistry (MS, PhD); chemistry (MS, PhD); inorganic chemistry (MS, PhD); organic chemistry (MS, PhD); physical chemistry (MS, PhD). Part-time and evening/weekend programs available. *Faculty:* 17 full-time, 1 part-time. *Students:* 63 full-time (25 women), 9 part-time (6 women); includes 8 minority (6 African Americans, 2 Hispanic Americans), 31 international. Average age 30. In 1998, 6 master's, 7 doctorates awarded. Terminal master's awarded for partial completion of doctoral program. *Degree requirements:* For master's, one foreign language (computer language can substitute), thesis, seminar presentation required; for doctorate, 2 foreign languages (computer language can substitute for one), dissertation, cumulative exams required. *Entrance requirements:* For master's, TOEFL, minimum GPA of 2.75; for doctorate, TOEFL. *Average time to degree:* Master's–2 years full-time, 4 years part-time; doctorate–4 years full-time. *Application deadline:* For fall admission, 3/1. Applications are processed on a rolling basis. Application fee: $25 ($50 for international students). Tuition, state resident: part-time $189 per credit. Tuition, nonresident: part-time $353 per credit. Required fees: $7.3 per credit. *Financial aid:* In 1998–99, 59 students received aid, including 5 fellowships with full tuition reimbursements available, 13 research assistantships with full tuition reimbursements available, 37 teaching assistantships with full tuition reimbursements available; tuition waivers (full) also available. Aid available to part-time students. *Faculty research:* NMR studies, catalyzing organic reactions, free radical chemistry, natural product synthesis, laser spectroscopy. *Unit head:* Dr. Gerald Koser, Chair, 330-972-7372, E-mail: koser@uakron.edu.

The University of Alabama, Graduate School, College of Arts and Sciences, Department of Chemistry, Tuscaloosa, AL 35487. Offers MS, PhD. Postbaccalaureate distance learning degree programs offered (minimal on-campus study). *Degree requirements:* For doctorate, one foreign language, dissertation required. *Entrance requirements:* For master's and doctorate, American Chemical Society Exam, GRE General Test (minimum combined score of 1500 on three sections required), MAT, minimum GPA of 3.0. Electronic applications accepted. *Faculty research:* Synthetic chemistry, environmental chemistry and green manufacturing, materials science and information technology, biological chemistry and biomolecular products.

The University of Alabama at Birmingham, Graduate School, School of Natural Sciences and Mathematics, Department of Chemistry, Birmingham, AL 35294. Offers MS, PhD. *Faculty:* 15 full-time, 6 part-time. *Students:* 22 full-time (5 women), 5 part-time (1 woman), 10 international. 40 applicants, 20% accepted. In 1998, 3 master's, 2 doctorates awarded. *Degree requirements:* For master's and doctorate, thesis/dissertation required, foreign language not required. *Entrance requirements:* For master's, GRE General Test (minimum combined score of 1000 required), TOEFL (minimum score of 550 required); for doctorate, GRE General Test (minimum combined score of 1100 required), TOEFL (minimum score of 550 required). *Application deadline:* Applications are processed on a rolling basis. Application fee: $30 ($60 for international students). *Financial aid:* In 1998–99, 10 fellowships with full tuition reimbursements (averaging $13,500 per year), 6 research assistantships with full tuition reimbursements (averaging $13,500 per year), 4 teaching assistantships with full tuition reimbursements (averaging $13,500 per year) were awarded.; career-related internships or fieldwork, Federal Work-Study, institutionally-sponsored loans, tuition waivers (full and partial), and unspecified assistantships also available. Aid available to part-time students. Financial aid application deadline: 5/1; financial aid applicants required to submit FAFSA. *Faculty research:* General and biochemical synthesis; spectroscopic studies of chemical systems; analysis using chromatography, GC/MS, and designed electrode system. *Unit head:* Dr. Larry K. Krannich, Chairman, 205-934-8017, Fax: 205-934-2543, E-mail: krannich@uab.edu.

The University of Alabama in Huntsville, School of Graduate Studies, College of Science, Department of Chemistry, Huntsville, AL 35899. Offers MS. Part-time and evening/weekend programs available. *Faculty:* 16 full-time (1 woman). *Students:* 11 full-time (7 women), 4 part-time (2 women); includes 4 minority (all African Americans), 4 international. Average age 31. 6 applicants, 100% accepted. In 1998, 5 degrees awarded. *Degree requirements:* For master's, oral and written exams required, thesis optional, foreign language not required. *Entrance requirements:* For master's, GRE General Test (minimum combined score of 1500 on three sections required), minimum GPA of 3.0. *Application deadline:* For fall admission, 7/24 (priority date); for spring admission, 11/15 (priority date). Applications are processed on a rolling basis. Application fee: $20. Tuition and fees vary according to course load. *Financial aid:* In 1998–99, 14 students received aid, including 6 research assistantships with full and partial tuition reimbursements available (averaging $9,368 per year), 8 teaching assistantships with full and partial tuition reimbursements available (averaging $7,180 per year); fellowships with full and partial tuition reimbursements available, career-related internships or fieldwork, Federal Work-Study, grants, institutionally-sponsored loans, scholarships, and tuition waivers (full and partial) also available. Aid available to part-time students. Financial aid application deadline: 4/1; financial aid applicants required to submit FAFSA. *Faculty research:* Kinetics and bonding, organic nonlinear optical materials, x-ray crystallography, crystal growth in space, polymers, Raman spectroscopy. Total annual research expenditures: $862,487. *Unit head:* Dr. Clyde Riley, Chair, 256-890-6153, Fax: 256-890-6349, E-mail: criley@matsci.uah.edu.

University of Alaska Fairbanks, Graduate School, College of Science, Engineering and Mathematics, Department of Chemistry, Fairbanks, AK 99775-7480. Offers biochemistry (MS, PhD); chemistry (MA, MAT, MS). *Faculty:* 10 full-time (2 women), 2 part-time (1 woman). *Students:* 15 full-time (7 women), 3 part-time; includes 1 minority (Hispanic American), 3 international. Average age 31. 8 applicants, 75% accepted. In 1998, 2 master's awarded (0% continued full-time study); 1 doctorate awarded. *Degree requirements:* For master's, thesis, comprehensive exam required, foreign language not required; for doctorate, one foreign language (computer language can substitute), dissertation, comprehensive exam required. *Entrance requirements:* For master's, GRE General Test, TOEFL (minimum score of 550 required); for doctorate, GRE General Test, GRE Subject Test (biology or chemistry), TOEFL (minimum score of 550 required). *Application deadline:* For fall admission, 3/1. Application fee: $35. *Financial aid:* Research assistantships, teaching assistantships available. Financial aid application deadline: 3/1. *Faculty research:* Chemical ecology, spectroscopy, chemometrics. *Unit head:* Dr. Larry Duffy, Head, 907-474-7525.

University of Alberta, Faculty of Graduate Studies and Research, Department of Chemistry, Edmonton, AB T6G 2E1, Canada. Offers M Sc, PhD. *Degree requirements:* For master's and doctorate, thesis/dissertation required, foreign language not required. *Faculty research:* DNA sequencing, microinstrumentation, computational studies of structure and reactivity of molecules, carbohydrate chemistry.

Chemistry

The University of Arizona, Graduate College, College of Science, Department of Chemistry, Tucson, AZ 85721. Offers MA, MS, PhD. *Faculty:* 40. *Students:* 124 full-time (40 women), 18 part-time (5 women); includes 13 minority (2 African Americans, 4 Asian Americans or Pacific Islanders, 7 Hispanic Americans), 30 international. Average age 27. 44 applicants, 86% accepted. In 1998, 22 master's, 21 doctorates awarded. Terminal master's awarded for partial completion of doctoral program. *Degree requirements:* For master's, thesis required, foreign language not required; for doctorate, dissertation required. *Entrance requirements:* For master's, GRE, TOEFL (minimum score of 550 required), SPEAK test or TSE (minimum score of 230 required); for doctorate, TOEFL (minimum score of 550 required), SPEAK test or TSE (minimum score of 230 required). *Application deadline:* For fall admission, 2/1 (priority date). Applications are processed on a rolling basis. Application fee: $35. *Financial aid:* Fellowships, research assistantships, teaching assistantships, institutionally-sponsored loans, scholarships, and tuition waivers (partial) available. *Faculty research:* Analytical, inorganic, organic, and physical chemistry. *Unit head:* Dr. Dennis Lichtenberger, Head, 520-621-6354. *Application contact:* Penny Davis, Senior Office Specialist, 520-621-1362, Fax: 520-621-8407.

University of Arkansas, Graduate School, J. William Fulbright College of Arts and Sciences, Department of Chemistry and Biochemistry, Fayetteville, AR 72701-1201. Offers chemistry (MS, PhD). *Faculty:* 22 full-time (0 women). *Students:* 43 full-time (17 women), 3 part-time (2 women); includes 6 minority (4 African Americans, 1 Asian American or Pacific Islander, 1 Native American), 16 international. 56 applicants, 20% accepted. In 1998, 3 master's, 8 doctorates awarded. *Degree requirements:* For master's and doctorate, one foreign language, thesis/dissertation required. Application fee: $40 ($50 for international students). Tuition, state resident: full-time $3,186. Tuition, nonresident: full-time $7,560. Required fees: $378. *Financial aid:* In 1998–99, 12 research assistantships, 38 teaching assistantships were awarded.; career-related internships or fieldwork and Federal Work-Study also available. Aid available to part-time students. Financial aid application deadline: 4/1; financial aid applicants required to submit FAFSA. *Unit head:* Dr. Don Bobbitt, Chair, 501-575-4601, E-mail: dchem@comp.uark.edu.

University of Arkansas at Little Rock, Graduate School, College of Sciences and Engineering Technology, Department of Chemistry, Little Rock, AR 72204-1099. Offers MA, MS. Part-time and evening/weekend programs available. *Degree requirements:* For master's, thesis (MS) required. *Entrance requirements:* For master's, minimum GPA of 2.7.

University of British Columbia, Faculty of Graduate Studies, Faculty of Science, Department of Chemistry, Vancouver, BC V6T 1Z2, Canada. Offers M Sc, PhD. Terminal master's awarded for partial completion of doctoral program. *Degree requirements:* For master's, thesis required, foreign language not required; for doctorate, dissertation, comprehensive exam required, foreign language not required. *Entrance requirements:* For master's and doctorate, GRE General Test, GRE Subject Test, TOEFL. *Faculty research:* Organic, physical, analytical, inorganic, and bio-chemical projects.

University of Calgary, Faculty of Graduate Studies, Faculty of Science, Department of Chemistry, Calgary, AB T2N 1N4, Canada. Offers analytical chemistry (M Sc, PhD); applied chemistry (M Sc, PhD); inorganic chemistry (M Sc, PhD); organic chemistry (M Sc, PhD); physical chemistry (M Sc, PhD); polymer chemistry (M Sc, PhD); theoretical chemistry (M Sc, PhD). *Faculty:* 29 full-time (4 women), 1 part-time (0 women). *Students:* 60 full-time (25 women). Average age 25. 105 applicants, 21% accepted. In 1998, 9 master's, 13 doctorates awarded. *Degree requirements:* For master's, thesis required, foreign language not required; for doctorate, dissertation, candidacy exam required, foreign language not required. *Entrance requirements:* For master's and doctorate, TOEFL (minimum score of 580 required). *Average time to degree:* Master's–3 years full-time; doctorate–5 years full-time. *Application deadline:* For fall admission, 12/1 (priority date). Applications are processed on a rolling basis. Application fee: $60. *Financial aid:* In 1998–99, research assistantships (averaging $5,500 per year), teaching assistantships (averaging $10,688 per year) were awarded.; fellowships Financial aid application deadline: 12/1. *Faculty research:* Chemical analysis, chemical dynamics, synthesis theory, polymer, applied chemistry. *Unit head:* Dr. R. A. Kydd, Head, 403-220-5340. *Application contact:* Greta Prihodko, Graduate Program Administrator, 403-220-6252, E-mail: gradinfo@chem.ucalgary.ca.

University of California, Berkeley, Graduate Division, College of Chemistry, Department of Chemistry, Berkeley, CA 94720-1500. Offers PhD. *Students:* 358 full-time (115 women); includes 67 minority (5 African Americans, 48 Asian Americans or Pacific Islanders, 13 Hispanic Americans, 1 Native American), 49 international. 484 applicants, 38% accepted. In 1998, 56 degrees awarded. *Degree requirements:* For doctorate, dissertation, qualifying exam required. *Entrance requirements:* For doctorate, GRE General Test, GRE Subject Test, minimum GPA of 3.0. *Application deadline:* For fall admission, 1/15. Application fee: $40. *Financial aid:* Fellowships, research assistantships, teaching assistantships available. Financial aid application deadline: 12/15. *Unit head:* Dr. Paul A. Bartlett, Chair, 510-643-0573. *Application contact:* Graduate Assistant for Admission, 510-642-5882, Fax: 510-642-9675, E-mail: chemgrad@cchem.berkeley.edu.

University of California, Berkeley, Graduate Division, College of Natural Resources, Group in Agricultural and Environmental Chemistry, Berkeley, CA 94720-1500. Offers MS, PhD. *Students:* 11 full-time (7 women). 3 applicants, 33% accepted. Terminal master's awarded for partial completion of doctoral program. *Degree requirements:* For master's, exam or thesis required; for doctorate, dissertation, qualifying exam, seminar presentation required. *Entrance requirements:* For master's and doctorate, GRE General Test, minimum GPA of 3.0. *Application deadline:* For fall admission, 1/5. Application fee: $40. *Financial aid:* Research assistantships, Federal Work-Study and institutionally-sponsored loans available. Financial aid application deadline: 1/5. *Unit head:* Dr. Isao Kubo, Chair, 510-642-5167. *Application contact:* Jennifer Vorih, Graduate Assistant for Admission, 510-642-5167, Fax: 510-642-4995, E-mail: pmb.stud@nature.berkeley.edu.

University of California, Davis, Graduate Studies, Program in Agriculture and Environmental Chemistry, Davis, CA 95616. Offers MS, PhD. *Students:* 40 full-time (16 women); includes 1 minority (Asian American or Pacific Islander), 15 international. 32 applicants, 75% accepted. In 1998, 2 master's, 8 doctorates awarded. *Degree requirements:* For master's and doctorate, thesis/dissertation required. *Entrance requirements:* For master's and doctorate, GRE General Test, minimum GPA of 3.0. *Application deadline:* For fall admission, 1/15. Application fee: $40. Electronic applications accepted. *Financial aid:* In 1998–99, 12 fellowships with full and partial tuition reimbursements, 15 research assistantships with full and partial tuition reimbursements, 6 teaching assistantships with full and partial tuition reimbursements were awarded. Financial aid application deadline: 1/15; financial aid applicants required to submit FAFSA. *Unit head:* David S. Reid, Graduate Adviser, 530-752-1415.

University of California, Davis, Graduate Studies, Program in Chemistry, Davis, CA 95616. Offers MS, PhD. *Faculty:* 31 full-time (4 women). *Students:* 137 full-time (56 women); includes 27 minority (3 African Americans, 21 Asian Americans or Pacific Islanders, 3 Hispanic Americans), 34 international. Average age 25. 195 applicants, 58% accepted. In 1998, 10 master's awarded (100% found work related to degree); 19 doctorates awarded. *Degree requirements:* For master's and doctorate, thesis/dissertation required. *Entrance requirements:* For master's, minimum GPA of 3.0; for doctorate, GRE, minimum GPA of 3.0. *Application deadline:* For fall admission, 4/1. Applications are processed on a rolling basis. Application fee: $40. Electronic applications accepted. *Financial aid:* In 1998–99, 95 fellowships with full and partial tuition reimbursements, 50 research assistantships with full and partial tuition reimbursements, 59 teaching assistantships with full and partial tuition reimbursements were awarded. Financial aid application deadline: 1/15; financial aid applicants required to submit FAFSA. *Faculty research:* Analytical, biological, organic, inorganic, and theoretical chemistry. *Unit head:* Alan Balch, Graduate Adviser, 530-752-0953, Fax: 530-752-8995. *Application contact:* Dee Kindelt, Graduate Program Staff, 530-752-0953.

See in-depth description on page 187.

University of California, Irvine, Office of Research and Graduate Studies, School of Physical Sciences, Department of Chemistry, Irvine, CA 92697. Offers MS, PhD. *Faculty:* 38 full-time. *Students:* 157 full-time (39 women), 1 part-time; includes 31 minority (1 African American, 24 Asian Americans or Pacific Islanders, 6 Hispanic Americans), 21 international. 210 applicants, 56% accepted. In 1998, 23 master's, 27 doctorates awarded. Terminal master's awarded for partial completion of doctoral program. *Degree requirements:* For master's, thesis or alternative required, foreign language not required; for doctorate, computer language, dissertation required, foreign language not required. *Entrance requirements:* For master's, GRE General Test, GRE Subject Test, minimum GPA of 3.0; for doctorate, GRE General Test, GRE Subject Test. *Application deadline:* For fall admission, 1/15 (priority date). Applications are processed on a rolling basis. Application fee: $40. Electronic applications accepted. *Financial aid:* Fellowships, research assistantships, teaching assistantships, institutionally-sponsored loans and tuition waivers (full and partial) available. Financial aid application deadline: 3/2; financial aid applicants required to submit FAFSA. *Faculty research:* Analytical, organic, inorganic, physical, and atmospheric chemistry; biogeochemistry and climate; synthetic chemistry; chemical and materials physics. *Unit head:* Dr. Keith Woerpel, Graduate Admissions Committee Chair, 949-824-8509. *Application contact:* Jaime Albano, Graduate Affairs Officer, 949-824-4261, Fax: 949-824-8571.

University of California, Los Angeles, Graduate Division, College of Letters and Science, Department of Chemistry and Biochemistry, Program in Chemistry, Los Angeles, CA 90095. Offers MS, PhD. *Students:* 182 full-time (65 women); includes 53 minority (2 African Americans, 33 Asian Americans or Pacific Islanders, 16 Hispanic Americans, 2 Native Americans), 47 international. 275 applicants, 36% accepted. *Entrance requirements:* For master's, GRE General Test, GRE Subject Test, minimum GPA of 3.0; for doctorate, GRE General Test, GRE Subject Test, minimum undergraduate GPA of 3.0. *Application deadline:* For fall admission, 1/15. Application fee: $40. Electronic applications accepted. *Financial aid:* In 1998–99, 139 fellowships, 161 teaching assistantships were awarded.; research assistantships, scholarships also available. *Unit head:* Mei Griebenow, Graduate Assistant for Admission, 510-642-5574, Fax: 510-643-9980, E-mail: meig@seismo.berkeley.edu. *Application contact:* Departmental Office, 310-825-3150, E-mail: grad@chem.ucla.edu.

University of California, Riverside, Graduate Division, College of Natural and Agricultural Sciences, Department of Chemistry, Riverside, CA 92521-0102. Offers MS, PhD. *Faculty:* 19 full-time (2 women). *Students:* 66 full-time (13 women), 1 (woman) part-time; includes 9 minority (1 African American, 8 Asian Americans or Pacific Islanders), 10 international. Average age 28. In 1998, 7 master's, 8 doctorates awarded. Terminal master's awarded for partial completion of doctoral program. *Degree requirements:* For master's, comprehensive exams or thesis required; for doctorate, dissertation, qualifying exams, 3 quarters of teaching experience, research proposition required, foreign language not required. *Entrance requirements:* For master's and doctorate, GRE General Test (minimum combined score of 1100 required), TOEFL (minimum score of 550 required), minimum GPA of 3.2. *Average time to degree:* Master's–1.6 years full-time; doctorate–5.3 years full-time. *Application deadline:* For fall admission, 5/1; for winter admission, 9/1; for spring admission, 12/1. Applications are processed on a rolling basis. Application fee: $40. Electronic applications accepted. *Financial aid:* In 1998–99, 10 fellowships with full tuition reimbursements (averaging $25,000 per year), 30 research assistantships with full tuition reimbursements (averaging $18,049 per year), 36 teaching assistantships with full tuition reimbursements (averaging $20,101 per year) were awarded.; career-related internships or fieldwork, Federal Work-Study, institutionally-sponsored loans, and tuition waivers (full and partial) also available. Financial aid application deadline: 2/1; financial aid applicants required to submit FAFSA. *Faculty research:* Analytical, inorganic, organic, and physical chemistry; chemical physics. Total annual research expenditures: $4 million. *Unit head:* Prof. Dallas L. Rabenstein, Graduate Adviser, 909-787-3520, Fax: 909-787-4713, E-mail: dallas.rabenstein@ucr.edu. *Application contact:* Prof. David F. Bocian, Graduate Adviser, 909-787-3520, Fax: 909-787-4713, E-mail: david.bocian@ucr.edu.

University of California, San Diego, Graduate Studies and Research, Department of Chemistry and Biochemistry, La Jolla, CA 92093-5003. Offers chemistry (PhD). *Faculty:* 52. *Students:* 158 (58 women). 383 applicants, 44% accepted. In 1998, 30 doctorates awarded. *Degree requirements:* For doctorate, dissertation required. *Entrance requirements:* For doctorate, GRE General Test, GRE Subject Test. Application fee: $40. *Unit head:* Mark Thiemens, Chair. *Application contact:* Applications Coordinator, 619-534-6871.

See in-depth description on page 191.

University of California, Santa Barbara, Graduate Division, College of Letters and Science, Division of Math, Life and Physical Science, Department of Chemistry, Santa Barbara, CA 93106. Offers MA, MS, PhD. *Faculty:* 32 full-time (4 women), 1 part-time (0 women). *Students:* 91 full-time (33 women); includes 27 minority (3 African Americans, 16 Asian Americans or Pacific Islanders, 8 Hispanic Americans), 8 international. Average age 25. 146 applicants, 47% accepted. In 1998, 5 master's, 19 doctorates awarded. Terminal master's awarded for partial completion of doctoral program. *Degree requirements:* For master's, thesis or alternative required, foreign language not required; for doctorate, dissertation required, foreign language not required. *Entrance requirements:* For master's and doctorate, GRE, TOEFL (minimum score of 550 required). *Average time to degree:* Master's–2 years full-time; doctorate–5 years full-time. *Application deadline:* For fall admission, 5/1; for spring admission, 1/1. Applications are processed on a rolling basis. Application fee: $40. Electronic applications accepted. *Financial aid:* In 1998–99, 91 students received aid, including 10 fellowships, 31 research assistantships, 50 teaching assistantships; career-related internships or fieldwork, Federal Work-Study, institutionally-sponsored loans, and tuition waivers (full and partial) also available. Financial aid application deadline: 1/15; financial aid applicants required to submit FAFSA. *Faculty research:* Organic, biological, inorganic, physical, and materials chemistry. Total annual research expenditures: $4.6 million. *Unit head:* Dr. Dan Little, Chair, 805-893-2056. *Application contact:* Deedrea Edgar, Graduate Program Coordinator, 805-893-2638, E-mail: edgar@chem.ucsb.edu.

University of California, Santa Cruz, Graduate Division, Division of Natural Sciences, Department of Chemistry, Santa Cruz, CA 95064. Offers MS, PhD. *Faculty:* 21 full-time. *Students:* 76 full-time (29 women); includes 9 minority (4 Asian Americans or Pacific Islanders, 5 Hispanic Americans), 10 international. 101 applicants, 57% accepted. In 1998, 2 master's, 9 doctorates awarded. *Degree requirements:* For doctorate, one foreign language (computer language can substitute), dissertation, qualifying exam required. *Entrance requirements:* For master's and doctorate, GRE General Test, GRE Subject Test. *Application deadline:* For fall admission, 1/15. Application fee: $40. *Financial aid:* Fellowships, research assistantships, teaching assistantships, Federal Work-Study and institutionally-sponsored loans available. Financial aid application deadline: 1/15. *Faculty research:* Marine chemistry; biochemistry; inorganic, organic, and physical chemistry. *Unit head:* Dr. Thomas Schleich, Chairperson, 831-459-2067. *Application contact:* Evie Alloy, Department Assistant, 831-459-2023, E-mail: gradinfo@chemistry.ucsc.edu.

University of Central Florida, College of Arts and Sciences, Program in Industrial Chemistry, Orlando, FL 32816. Offers MS. Part-time and evening/weekend programs available. *Faculty:* 16 full-time, 5 part-time. *Students:* 15 full-time (11 women), 10 part-time (4 women); includes 6 minority (1 African American, 4 Asian Americans or Pacific Islanders, 1 Hispanic American), 8 international. Average age 31. 26 applicants, 27% accepted. In 1998, 9 degrees awarded. *Degree requirements:* For master's, thesis, final examination required, foreign language not required. *Entrance requirements:* For master's, GRE General Test (minimum combined score of 1000 required), TOEFL (minimum score of 500 required; 173 computer-based), minimum GPA of 3.0 in last 60 hours. *Application deadline:* For fall admission, 7/15; for spring admission, 12/15. Application fee: $20. Tuition, state resident: full-time $2,054; part-time $137 per credit. Tuition, nonresident: full-time $7,207; part-time $480 per credit. Required fees: $47 per term. *Financial aid:* In 1998–99, 20 students received aid, including 1 fellowship with partial tuition reimbursement available (averaging $2,303 per year), 17 research assistantships with partial tuition reimbursements available (averaging $3,423 per year), teaching assistantships with partial tuition reimbursements available (averaging $4,695 per year); career-related internships or fieldwork, Federal Work-Study, institutionally-sponsored loans, tuition waivers (partial), and unspecified assistantships also available. Financial aid application deadline: 3/1; financial aid applicants required to submit FAFSA. *Faculty research:* Physical and synthetic organic chemistry, lasers, polymers, biochemical action of pesticides, environmental analysis. Total annual research expenditures: $645,000. *Unit head:* Dr. Glenn N. Cunningham, Chair, 407-823-5451, Fax: 407-823-2252, E-mail: gcunning@pegasus.cc.ucf.edu. *Application contact:* Dr. Howard Miles, Coordinator, 407-823-2246, Fax: 407-823-2252, E-mail: hmiles@pegasus.cc.ucf.edu.

University of Chicago, Division of the Physical Sciences, Department of Chemistry, Chicago, IL 60637-1513. Offers SM, PhD. Terminal master's awarded for partial completion of doctoral program. *Degree requirements:* For master's, foreign language and thesis not required; for doctorate, dissertation required, foreign language not required. *Entrance requirements:* For master's and doctorate, GRE General Test, GRE Subject Test, TOEFL.

University of Cincinnati, Division of Research and Advanced Studies, McMicken College of Arts and Sciences, Department of Chemistry, Cincinnati, OH 45221-0091. Offers analytical chemistry (MS, PhD); biochemistry (MS, PhD); inorganic chemistry (MS, PhD); organic chemistry (MS, PhD); physical chemistry (MS, PhD); polymer chemistry (MS, PhD). Part-time and evening/weekend programs available. *Faculty:* 25 full-time. *Students:* 87 full-time (26 women), 26 part-time (3 women); includes 12 minority (1 African American, 11 Asian Americans or Pacific Islanders), 34 international. 91 applicants, 25% accepted. In 1998, 13 master's, 15 doctorates awarded. Terminal master's awarded for partial completion of doctoral program. *Degree requirements:* For master's, thesis optional, foreign language not required; for doctorate, dissertation required, foreign language not required. *Entrance requirements:* For master's and doctorate, GRE General Test, GRE Subject Test. *Average time to degree:* Master's–3.4 years full-time; doctorate–6.3 years full-time. *Application deadline:* For fall admission, 2/1. Application fee: $30. *Financial aid:* Fellowships, tuition waivers (full) and unspecified assistantships available. Aid available to part-time students. Financial aid application deadline: 5/1. *Faculty research:* Biomedical chemistry, laser chemistry, surface science, chemical sensors, synthesis. Total annual research expenditures: $669,373. *Unit head:* Dr. Marshall Wilson, Head, 513-556-9200, Fax: 513-556-9239, E-mail: marshall.wilson@uc.edu. *Application contact:* Thomas Ridgway, Graduate Program Director, 513-556-9200, Fax: 513-556-9239, E-mail: thomas.ridgway@uc.edu.

University of Colorado at Boulder, Graduate School, College of Arts and Sciences, Department of Chemistry and Biochemistry, Boulder, CO 80309. Offers biochemistry (PhD); chemistry (MS, PhD). Terminal master's awarded for partial completion of doctoral program. *Degree requirements:* For master's, thesis or alternative, comprehensive exam required; for doctorate, dissertation required. *Entrance requirements:* For master's and doctorate, GRE General Test.

University of Colorado at Denver, Graduate School, College of Liberal Arts and Sciences, Program in Chemistry, Denver, CO 80217-3364. Offers MS. Part-time programs available. *Faculty:* 10. *Students:* 9 full-time (5 women), 29 part-time (14 women); includes 6 minority (3 Asian Americans or Pacific Islanders, 3 Hispanic Americans), 9 international. Average age 27. 9 applicants, 78% accepted. In 1998, 4 degrees awarded. *Degree requirements:* For master's, thesis or alternative required. *Entrance requirements:* For master's, GRE, undergraduate degree in chemistry. *Application deadline:* For fall admission, 6/1; for spring admission, 11/1. Applications are processed on a rolling basis. Application fee: $50 ($60 for international students). Electronic applications accepted. Tuition, state resident: part-time $185 per credit hour. Tuition, nonresident: part-time $735 per credit hour. Required fees: $3 per credit hour. $130 per year. One-time fee: $25 part-time. Tuition and fees vary according to program. *Financial aid:* Research assistantships, teaching assistantships, Federal Work-Study available. Financial aid application deadline: 3/1; financial aid applicants required to submit FAFSA. Total annual research expenditures: $176,050. *Unit head:* Doug Dyckes, Chair, 303-556-3204, Fax: 303-556-4776. *Application contact:* Bonita Mays, Administrative Assistant, 303-556-4885, Fax: 303-556-4776.

University of Connecticut, Graduate School, College of Liberal Arts and Sciences, Field of Chemistry, Storrs, CT 06269. Offers MS, PhD. *Degree requirements:* For doctorate, dissertation required. *Entrance requirements:* For master's and doctorate, GRE General Test, GRE Subject Test.

University of Delaware, College of Arts and Science, Department of Chemistry and Biochemistry, Newark, DE 19716. Offers biochemistry (MA, MS, PhD); chemistry (MA, MS, PhD). Part-time programs available. *Faculty:* 31 full-time (4 women). *Students:* 96 full-time (33 women), 8 part-time (4 women); includes 7 minority (2 African Americans, 3 Asian Americans or Pacific Islanders, 2 Hispanic Americans), 32 international. Average age 25. 169 applicants, 35% accepted. In 1998, 9 master's awarded (33% found work related to degree, 66% continued full-time study); 15 doctorates awarded (47% entered university research/teaching, 53% found other work related to degree). Terminal master's awarded for partial completion of doctoral program. *Degree requirements:* For master's, one foreign language, thesis required (for some programs); for doctorate, one foreign language, dissertation, comprehensive exams required. *Entrance requirements:* For master's and doctorate, GRE General Test, GRE Subject Test, TOEFL, TSE. *Average time to degree:* Master's–5.5 years full-time; doctorate–2.2 years full-time. *Application deadline:* For fall admission, 3/31 (priority date). Applications are processed on a rolling basis. Application fee: $45. Electronic applications accepted. *Financial aid:* In 1998–99, 2 fellowships, 36 research assistantships with full tuition reimbursements (averaging $16,200 per year), 50 teaching assistantships with full tuition reimbursements (averaging $16,200 per year) were awarded. Financial aid application deadline: 3/31. *Faculty research:* Protein studies; mechanism of enzymes; synthesis, electronic structure, and bonding of inorganic and organometallic compounds; spectroscopy studies. Total annual research expenditures: $3.5 million. *Unit head:* Dr. Steven D. Brown, Chairman, 302-831-1247, Fax: 302-831-6335, E-mail: sdb@udel.edu. *Application contact:* Elizabeth Painter, Executive Secretary, 302-831-1247, Fax: 302-831-6335, E-mail: elizabeth.painter@mvs.udel.edu.

University of Denver, Graduate Studies, Faculty of Natural Sciences, Mathematics and Engineering, Department of Chemistry, Denver, CO 80208. Offers MA, MS, PhD. Part-time programs available. *Faculty:* 12. *Students:* 16 (7 women); includes 1 minority (Hispanic American) 7 international. 23 applicants, 57% accepted. In 1998, 3 master's, 2 doctorates awarded. Terminal master's awarded for partial completion of doctoral program. *Degree requirements:* For master's and doctorate, thesis/dissertation required, foreign language not required. *Entrance requirements:* For master's and doctorate, GRE General Test, TOEFL (minimum score of 570 required), TSE (minimum score of 230 required). *Application deadline:* Applications are processed on a rolling basis. Application fee: $40 ($45 for international students). *Financial aid:* In 1998–99, 16 students received aid, including 3 fellowships with full and partial tuition reimbursements available (averaging $4,000 per year), 3 research assistantships with full and partial tuition reimbursements available (averaging $20,244 per year), 10 teaching assistantships with full and partial tuition reimbursements available (averaging $13,644 per year); career-related internships or fieldwork, Federal Work-Study, institutionally-sponsored loans, and scholarships also available. Aid available to part-time students. Financial aid application deadline: 3/1; financial aid applicants required to submit FAFSA. *Faculty research:* Atmospheric chemistry, magnetic resonance, molecular spectroscopy, laser photolysis, biophysical chemistry. Total annual research expenditures: $1.4 million. *Unit head:* Dr. T. Gregory Dewey, Chairperson, 303-871-2436. *Application contact:* Dr. Juliana Gilbert, Chair, Graduate Committee, 303-871-2993.

University of Detroit Mercy, College of Engineering and Science, Department of Chemistry and Biochemistry, Detroit, MI 48219-0900. Offers economic aspects of chemistry (MSEC); macromolecular chemistry (MS, PhD). Evening/weekend programs available. *Degree requirements:* For master's and doctorate, thesis/dissertation required, foreign language not required. *Entrance requirements:* For master's, GRE General Test, minimum GPA of 3.0; for doctorate, GRE Subject Test, minimum GPA of 3.0. *Faculty research:* Polymer and physical chemistry, industrial aspects of chemistry.

See in-depth description on page 193.

University of Florida, College of Medicine, Interdisciplinary Program in Biomedical Sciences, Department of Pathology, Gainesville, FL 32611. Offers clinical chemistry (MS); immunology and molecular pathology (PhD). Terminal master's awarded for partial completion of doctoral program. *Degree requirements:* For master's and doctorate, thesis/dissertation required, foreign language not required. *Entrance requirements:* For master's, GRE General Test (minimum combined score of 1000 required), TOEFL (minimum score of 550 required), minimum GPA of 3.0; for doctorate, GRE General Test (minimum combined score of 1000 required), TOEFL (minimum score of 600 required), minimum GPA of 3.0. Electronic applications accepted. *Faculty research:* Molecular immunology, autoimmunity and transplantation, tumor biology, oncogenic viruses, human immunodeficiency viruses.

University of Florida, Graduate School, College of Liberal Arts and Sciences, Department of Chemistry, Gainesville, FL 32611. Offers MS, MST, PhD. *Faculty:* 56. *Students:* 180 full-time (50 women), 10 part-time (5 women); includes 19 minority (4 African Americans, 10 Asian Americans or Pacific Islanders, 5 Hispanic Americans), 55 international. 200 applicants, 23% accepted. In 1998, 5 master's, 36 doctorates awarded. *Degree requirements:* For master's, thesis required, foreign language not required; for doctorate, dissertation required. *Entrance requirements:* For master's, GRE General Test, minimum GPA of 3.0; for doctorate, GRE General Test, TSE (minimum score of 220 required), minimum GPA of 3.0. *Application deadline:* For fall admission, 6/1 (priority date). Applications are processed on a rolling basis. Application fee: $20. Electronic applications accepted. *Financial aid:* In 1998–99, 180 students received aid, including 1 fellowship, 91 research assistantships, 85 teaching assistantships; institutionally-sponsored loans and unspecified assistantships also available. *Faculty research:* Organic, analytical, physical, inorganic, and biological chemistry. *Unit head:* Dr. John R. Eyler, Chair, 352-392-5266, Fax: 352-392-8758, E-mail: eyeler@chem.ufl.edu. *Application contact:* Dr. J. Deyrup, Graduate Coordinator, 352-392-0256, Fax: 352-392-8758, E-mail: deyrup@chem.ufl.edu.

University of Georgia, Graduate School, College of Arts and Sciences, Department of Chemistry, Athens, GA 30602. Offers analytical chemistry (MS, PhD); inorganic chemistry (MS, PhD); organic chemistry (MS, PhD); physical chemistry (MS, PhD). *Faculty:* 23 full-time (1 woman). *Students:* 107 full-time (26 women), 11 part-time (4 women). 102 applicants, 52% accepted. In 1998, 16 master's, 14 doctorates awarded. *Degree requirements:* For master's, thesis required, foreign language not required; for doctorate, one foreign language (computer language can substitute), dissertation required. *Entrance requirements:* For master's and doctorate, GRE General Test. *Application deadline:* For fall admission, 7/1 (priority date); for spring admission, 11/15. Application fee: $30. Electronic applications accepted. *Financial aid:* Fellowships, research assistantships, teaching assistantships, unspecified assistantships available. *Unit head:* Dr. I. Jonathan Amster, Graduate Coordinator, 706-542-1936, Fax: 706-542-9454, E-mail: mauldin@sunchem.chem.uga.edu.

University of Guelph, Faculty of Graduate Studies, College of Physical and Engineering Science, Guelph-Waterloo Centre for Graduate Work in Chemistry and Biochemistry, Guelph, ON N1G 2W1, Canada. Offers biochemistry (M Sc, PhD); chemistry (M Sc, PhD). Part-time programs available. *Faculty:* 59 full-time (7 women), 6 part-time (0 women). *Students:* 140 full-time (52 women), 6 part-time (4 women). In 1998, 33 master's, 17 doctorates awarded. *Degree requirements:* For master's and doctorate, thesis/dissertation required. *Average time to degree:* Master's–2 years full-time, 4 years part-time; doctorate–4 years full-time, 6 years part-time. Application fee: $60. *Expenses:* Tuition and fees charges are reported in Canadian dollars. Tuition, area resident: Full-time $4,725 Canadian dollars; part-time $1,055 Canadian dollars per term. International tuition: $6,999 Canadian dollars full-time. Required fees: $295 Canadian dollars per term. *Financial aid:* Fellowships, research assistantships, teaching assistantships available. *Faculty research:* Inorganic, analytical, biological, physical/theoretical, polymer, and organic chemistry. *Unit head:* Dr. R. J. Balahura, Director, 519-824-4120 Ext. 3848, Fax: 519-766-9220, E-mail: gwc@uoguelph.ca. *Application contact:* A. Wetmore, Administrative Assistant, 519-824-4120 Ext. 3848, Fax: 519-766-9220, E-mail: gwc@uoguelph.ca.

University of Hawaii at Manoa, Graduate Division, College of Arts and Sciences, College of Natural Sciences, Department of Chemistry, Honolulu, HI 96822. Offers MS, PhD. *Faculty:* 18 full-time (1 woman). *Students:* 13 full-time (5 women), 26 part-time (9 women); includes 4 Asian Americans or Pacific Islanders 136 applicants, 18% accepted. In 1998, 3 master's, 5 doctorates awarded. *Degree requirements:* For master's and doctorate, thesis/dissertation required, foreign language not required. *Entrance requirements:* For master's and doctorate, GRE General Test, GRE Subject Test. *Average time to degree:* Master's–3 years full-time; doctorate–5.5 years full-time. *Application deadline:* For fall admission, 3/1; for spring admission, 9/1. Applications are processed on a rolling basis. Application fee: $25 ($50 for international students). *Financial aid:* In 1998–99, 8 research assistantships (averaging $15,635 per year), 25 teaching assistantships (averaging $13,308 per year) were awarded. Aid available to part-time students. *Faculty research:* Marine natural products, biophysical spectroscopy, zeolites, organometallic hydrides, new visual pigments, theory of surfaces. Total annual research expenditures: $2.1 million. *Unit head:* Edgar F. Kiefer, Chair, 808-956-7480, Fax: 808-956-5908, E-mail: kiefer@gold.chem.hawaii.edu. *Application contact:* John Head, Graduate Admissions Chair, 808-956-7480, E-mail: johnh@hawaii.edu.

University of Houston, College of Natural Sciences and Mathematics, Department of Chemistry, Houston, TX 77004. Offers MS, PhD. Part-time programs available. *Faculty:* 26 full-time (2 women). *Students:* 115 full-time (46 women), 8 part-time (3 women); includes 12 minority (2 African Americans, 6 Asian Americans or Pacific Islanders, 4 Hispanic Americans), 95 international. Average age 29. 215 applicants, 17% accepted. In 1998, 6 master's awarded (100% found work related to degree); 13 doctorates awarded. Terminal master's awarded for partial completion of doctoral program. *Degree requirements:* For master's, thesis required, foreign language not required; for doctorate, dissertation, oral presentation required, foreign language not required. *Entrance requirements:* For master's, GRE General Test (combined average 1770 on three sections), TOEFL (minimum score of 600 required), TSE (minimum score of 45 required); for doctorate, GRE General Test (combined average 1770 on three sections), TOEFL (average 572). *Average time to degree:* Master's–3 years full-time; doctorate–4.5 years full-time. *Application deadline:* For fall admission, 7/20 (priority date); for spring admission, 11/20. Applications are processed on a rolling basis. Application fee: $0 ($75 for international students). Electronic applications accepted. *Financial aid:* Fellowships, research assistantships, teaching assistantships, career-related internships or fieldwork, Federal Work-Study, institutionally-sponsored loans, scholarships, and tuition waivers (partial) available. Financial aid application deadline: 4/1. Total annual research expenditures: $8.1 million. *Unit head:* Dr. Montgomery Pettitt, Chairman, 713-743-3263, Fax: 713-743-2709. *Application contact:* Dr. Thomas Albright, Chair, Graduate Committee, 713-743-3270, Fax: 713-743-2709, E-mail: albright@uh.edu.

University of Houston–Clear Lake, School of Natural and Applied Sciences, Program in Chemistry, Houston, TX 77058-1098. Offers MS. *Faculty:* 5 full-time (0 women), 3 part-time (1 woman). *Students:* 1 (woman) full-time, 12 part-time (3 women); includes 5 minority (1 African American, 3 Asian Americans or Pacific Islanders, 1 Hispanic American) Average age 32. *Degree requirements:* Foreign language not required. *Entrance requirements:* For master's, GRE General Test. *Application deadline:* Applications are processed on a rolling basis. Application fee: $30 ($70 for international students). *Financial aid:* Research assistantships, teaching assistantships available. Financial aid application deadline: 5/1. *Unit head:* Dr. Ramiro Sanchez, Chair, 281-283-3770, Fax: 281-283-3707, E-mail: sanchez@uhcl4.cl.uh.edu. *Application contact:* Dr. Robert Ferebee, Associate Dean, 281-283-3700, Fax: 281-283-3707, E-mail: ferebee@uhcl4.cl.uh.edu.

Chemistry

University of Idaho, College of Graduate Studies, College of Letters and Science, Department of Chemistry, Moscow, ID 83844-4140. Offers chemistry (MS, PhD); chemistry education (MAT). *Accreditation:* NCATE (one or more programs are accredited). *Faculty:* 16 full-time (3 women), 1 part-time (0 women). *Students:* 41 full-time (8 women), 12 part-time (3 women); includes 1 minority (Hispanic American), 19 international. In 1998, 7 master's, 11 doctorates awarded. *Degree requirements:* For master's, thesis or alternative required, foreign language not required; for doctorate, dissertation required. *Entrance requirements:* For master's, minimum GPA of 2.8; for doctorate, minimum undergraduate GPA of 2.8, 3.0 graduate. *Application deadline:* For fall admission, 8/1; for spring admission, 12/15. Application fee: $35 ($45 for international students). *Financial aid:* In 1998–99, 11 research assistantships (averaging $12,887 per year), 24 teaching assistantships (averaging $13,580 per year) were awarded.; fellowships Financial aid application deadline: 2/15. *Unit head:* Dr. Chien M. Wai, Head, 208-885-6552.

University of Illinois at Chicago, College of Pharmacy, Graduate Programs in Pharmacy, Chicago, IL 60607-7128. Offers forensic science (MS); medicinal chemistry (MS, PhD); pharmaceutics (MS, PhD); pharmacodynamics (MS, PhD); pharmacognosy (MS, PhD); pharmacy administration (MS, PhD). *Faculty:* 42 full-time (4 women). *Students:* 98 full-time (49 women), 20 part-time (10 women); includes 11 minority (5 African Americans, 4 Asian Americans or Pacific Islanders, 2 Hispanic Americans), 72 international. Terminal master's awarded for partial completion of doctoral program. *Degree requirements:* For master's and doctorate, variable foreign language requirement, thesis/dissertation required. *Entrance requirements:* For master's and doctorate, GRE General Test, TOEFL. *Application deadline:* For fall admission, 7/3; for spring admission, 11/8. Application fee: $40 ($50 for international students). *Unit head:* Dr. Michael E. Johnson, Associate Dean, Research and Graduate Education, 312-996-0796.

University of Illinois at Chicago, Graduate College, College of Liberal Arts and Sciences, Department of Chemistry, Chicago, IL 60607-7128. Offers MS, PhD. Part-time programs available. *Faculty:* 29 full-time (2 women). *Students:* 128 full-time (49 women), 6 part-time (2 women); includes 17 minority (3 African Americans, 11 Asian Americans or Pacific Islanders, 3 Hispanic Americans), 79 international. Average age 28. 116 applicants, 55% accepted. In 1998, 23 master's, 18 doctorates awarded. Terminal master's awarded for partial completion of doctoral program. *Degree requirements:* For master's, thesis or cumulative exam required; for doctorate, one foreign language, dissertation, cumulative exams required. *Entrance requirements:* For master's and doctorate, GRE Subject Test, TOEFL (minimum score of 580 required), minimum GPA of 4.0 on a 5.0 scale. *Application deadline:* For fall admission, 7/3; for spring admission, 11/8. Application fee: $40 ($50 for international students). *Financial aid:* In 1998–99, 106 students received aid; fellowships, research assistantships, teaching assistantships, Federal Work-Study, institutionally-sponsored loans, and tuition waivers (full) available. *Unit head:* Eric Gislason, Head, 312-996-3179. *Application contact:* Patricia Ratajczyk, Graduate Secretary, 312-996-5121.

See in-depth description on page 195.

University of Illinois at Urbana–Champaign, Graduate College, College of Liberal Arts and Sciences, School of Chemical Sciences, Department of Chemistry, Urbana, IL 61801. Offers MS, PhD. *Faculty:* 37 full-time (3 women). *Students:* 275 full-time (91 women); includes 27 minority (3 African Americans, 18 Asian Americans or Pacific Islanders, 6 Hispanic Americans), 47 international. 145 applicants, 32% accepted. In 1998, 31 master's, 35 doctorates awarded. *Degree requirements:* For master's, foreign language and thesis not required; for doctorate, dissertation required. *Application deadline:* Applications are processed on a rolling basis. Application fee: $40 ($50 for international students). Tuition, state resident: full-time $4,616. Tuition, nonresident: full-time $11,768. Full-time tuition and fees vary according to course load. *Financial aid:* In 1998–99, 3 fellowships, 123 research assistantships, 144 teaching assistantships were awarded. Financial aid application deadline: 2/15. *Unit head:* Paul W. Bohn, Head, 217-333-0711, Fax: 217-244-8068, E-mail: bohn@aries.scs.uiuc.edu.

The University of Iowa, Graduate College, College of Liberal Arts, Department of Chemistry, Iowa City, IA 52242-1316. Offers MS, PhD. *Faculty:* 31 full-time, 1 part-time. *Students:* 51 full-time (15 women), 38 part-time (10 women); includes 6 minority (3 African Americans, 3 Asian Americans or Pacific Islanders), 40 international. 256 applicants, 15% accepted. In 1998, 6 master's, 14 doctorates awarded. *Degree requirements:* For master's, thesis optional; for doctorate, dissertation, comprehensive exam required. *Entrance requirements:* For master's and doctorate, GRE General Test. *Application deadline:* Applications are processed on a rolling basis. Application fee: $30 ($50 for international students). *Financial aid:* In 1998–99, 4 fellowships, 25 research assistantships, 55 teaching assistantships were awarded. Financial aid applicants required to submit FAFSA. *Unit head:* Darrell P. Eyman, Chair, 319-335-1350, Fax: 319-335-1270.

University of Kansas, Graduate School, College of Liberal Arts and Sciences, Department of Chemistry, Lawrence, KS 66045. Offers MS, PhD. *Faculty:* 23 full-time. *Students:* 100 full-time (43 women), 19 part-time (9 women); includes 9 minority (3 African Americans, 4 Asian Americans or Pacific Islanders, 1 Hispanic American, 1 Native American), 33 international. In 1998, 3 master's, 9 doctorates awarded. *Degree requirements:* For master's, thesis required, foreign language not required; for doctorate, dissertation required. *Entrance requirements:* For master's and doctorate, GRE General Test, GRE Subject Test, TOEFL (minimum score of 570 required), TSE (minimum score of 50 required). Application fee: $25. *Financial aid:* Fellowships, research assistantships, teaching assistantships available. *Unit head:* Kristin Bowman-James, Chair, 785-864-4673, Fax: 785-864-5396, E-mail: kbowmanjames@caco3.chem.ukans.edu. *Application contact:* Marlin Harmony, Graduate Director, 785-864-4670, Fax: 785-864-5396.

University of Kentucky, Graduate School, Graduate School Programs from the College of Arts and Sciences, Program in Chemistry, Lexington, KY 40506-0032. Offers MS, PhD. Part-time programs available. Terminal master's awarded for partial completion of doctoral program. *Degree requirements:* For master's, comprehensive exam required, thesis optional, foreign language not required; for doctorate, dissertation, comprehensive exam required, foreign language not required. *Entrance requirements:* For master's, GRE General Test, minimum undergraduate GPA of 2.5; for doctorate, GRE General Test, minimum graduate GPA of 3.0. *Faculty research:* Analytical, inorganic, organic, and physical chemistry; biological chemistry; nuclear chemistry; radiochemistry; materials chemistry.

University of Louisville, Graduate School, College of Arts and Sciences, Department of Chemistry, Louisville, KY 40292-0001. Offers analytical chemistry (MS, PhD); chemical physics (PhD); inorganic chemistry (MS, PhD); organic chemistry (MS, PhD); physical chemistry (MS, PhD). *Faculty:* 20 full-time (3 women), 1 part-time (0 women). *Students:* 52 full-time (20 women), 4 part-time (2 women); includes 2 minority (both Hispanic Americans), 30 international. Average age 30. In 1998, 3 master's, 9 doctorates awarded. *Degree requirements:* For master's, thesis required; for doctorate, dissertation required. *Entrance requirements:* For master's and doctorate, GRE General Test, TOEFL (minimum score of 550 required). *Application deadline:* Applications are processed on a rolling basis. Application fee: $25. *Financial aid:* Fellowships, research assistantships, teaching assistantships available. *Unit head:* Dr. George R. Pack, Chair, 502-852-6798, Fax: 502-852-8149, E-mail: george.pack@louisville.edu.

See in-depth description on page 199.

University of Maine, Graduate School, College of Liberal Arts and Sciences, Department of Chemistry, Orono, ME 04469. Offers MS, PhD. *Faculty:* 12 full-time (2 women). *Students:* 17 full-time (4 women), 7 part-time (3 women), 18 international. 73 applicants, 16% accepted. In 1998, 4 master's awarded. Terminal master's awarded for partial completion of doctoral program. *Degree requirements:* For master's, thesis required, foreign language not required; for doctorate, dissertation, oral exam required, foreign language not required. *Entrance requirements:* For master's and doctorate, GRE General Test, GRE Subject Test, TOEFL (minimum score of 550 required). *Application deadline:* For fall admission, 2/1 (priority date); for spring admission, 10/15. Applications are processed on a rolling basis. Application fee: $50. *Financial aid:* In 1998–99, 3 research assistantships with tuition reimbursements (averaging $10,650 per year), 16 teaching assistantships with tuition reimbursements (averaging $7,898 per year) were awarded.; tuition waivers (full and partial) also available. Financial aid application deadline: 3/1. *Faculty research:* Quantum mechanics, insect chemistry, organic synthesis. *Unit head:* Dr. Francois Amar, Interim Chair, 207-581-1169, Fax: 207-581-1191. *Application contact:* Scott G. Delcourt, Director of the Graduate School, 207-581-3218, Fax: 207-581-3232, E-mail: graduate@maine.edu.

University of Manitoba, Faculty of Graduate Studies, Faculty of Science, Department of Chemistry, Winnipeg, MB R3T 2N2, Canada. Offers M Sc, PhD. *Degree requirements:* For master's, thesis required, foreign language not required; for doctorate, dissertation required. *Unit head:* Dr. J. C. Jamieson, Head.

University of Maryland, Baltimore County, Graduate School, Department of Chemistry and Biochemistry, Program in Chemistry, Baltimore, MD 21250-5398. Offers PhD. Part-time and evening/weekend programs available. *Students:* 37 full-time (15 women), 8 part-time (1 woman); includes 8 minority (3 African Americans, 5 Asian Americans or Pacific Islanders), 20 international. 120 applicants, 20% accepted. In 1998, 4 degrees awarded. *Degree requirements:* For doctorate, dissertation, comprehensive exams required, foreign language not required. *Entrance requirements:* For doctorate, GRE General Test, GRE Subject Test, TOEFL, minimum GPA of 3.0. *Application deadline:* For fall admission, 7/1. Applications are processed on a rolling basis. Application fee: $45. *Faculty research:* Bio-organic chemistry and enzyme catalysis, protein-nucleic acid interactions. *Unit head:* Dr. Richard L. Karpel, Director, Graduate Program, 410-455-2510. *Application contact:* Dr. Richard L. Karpel, Director, Graduate Program, 410-455-2510.

See in-depth description on page 201.

University of Maryland, College Park, Graduate School, College of Life Sciences, Department of Chemistry and Biochemistry, Chemistry Program, College Park, MD 20742-5045. Offers analytical chemistry (MS, PhD); inorganic chemistry (MS, PhD); organic chemistry (MS, PhD); physical chemistry (MS, PhD). *Students:* 76 full-time (34 women), 16 part-time (6 women); includes 8 minority (2 African Americans, 4 Asian Americans or Pacific Islanders, 1 Hispanic American, 1 Native American), 36 international. 234 applicants, 18% accepted. In 1998, 12 master's, 19 doctorates awarded. *Degree requirements:* For master's, thesis optional, foreign language not required; for doctorate, dissertation, 2 seminar presentations, oral exam required. *Entrance requirements:* For master's, GRE General Test, minimum GPA of 3.1; for doctorate, GRE General Test. *Application deadline:* Applications are processed on a rolling basis. Application fee: $50 ($70 for international students). Tuition, state resident: part-time $272 per credit hour. Tuition, nonresident: part-time $475 per credit hour. Required fees: $632; $379 per year. *Financial aid:* Fellowships, research assistantships, teaching assistantships with partial tuition reimbursements available. Financial aid applicants required to submit FAFSA. *Faculty research:* Environmental chemistry, nuclear chemistry, lunar and environmental analysis, x-ray crystallograph. *Unit head:* Marlin Harmony, Graduate Director, 785-864-4670, Fax: 785-864-5396. *Application contact:* Trudy Lindsey, Director, Graduate Admission and Records, 301-405-4198, Fax: 301-314-9305, E-mail: grschool@deans.umd.edu.

University of Massachusetts Amherst, Graduate School, College of Natural Sciences and Mathematics, Department of Chemistry, Amherst, MA 01003. Offers MS, PhD. Part-time programs available. *Faculty:* 30 full-time (5 women). *Students:* 42 full-time (12 women), 68 part-time (22 women); includes 3 minority (2 Asian Americans or Pacific Islanders, 1 Hispanic American), 74 international. Average age 28. 266 applicants, 22% accepted. In 1998, 11 master's, 14 doctorates awarded. Terminal master's awarded for partial completion of doctoral program. *Degree requirements:* For master's, thesis required, foreign language not required; for doctorate, one foreign language, dissertation required. *Application deadline:* For fall admission, 2/1 (priority date); for spring admission, 10/1. Applications are processed on a rolling basis. Application fee: $40. Tuition, state resident: full-time $2,640; part-time $165 per credit. Tuition, nonresident: full-time $9,756; part-time $407 per credit. Required fees: $1,221 per term. One-time fee: $110. Full-time tuition and fees vary according to course load, campus/location and reciprocity agreements. *Financial aid:* In 1998–99, 15 fellowships with full tuition reimbursements (averaging $1,835 per year), 88 research assistantships with full tuition reimbursements (averaging $8,599 per year), 53 teaching assistantships with full tuition reimbursements (averaging $9,802 per year) were awarded.; career-related internships or fieldwork, Federal Work-Study, grants, scholarships, traineeships, and unspecified assistantships also available. Aid available to part-time students. Financial aid application deadline: 2/1. *Unit head:* Dr. Lila M. Gierasch, Director, 413-545-2318, Fax: 413-545-4490, E-mail: gierasch@chem.umass.edu.

See in-depth description on page 205.

University of Massachusetts Boston, Graduate Studies, College of Arts and Sciences, Faculty of Sciences, Program in Chemistry, Boston, MA 02125-3393. Offers MS. *Degree requirements:* For master's, thesis, comprehensive exams required, foreign language not required. *Entrance requirements:* For master's, minimum GPA of 2.75.

University of Massachusetts Dartmouth, Graduate School, College of Arts and Sciences, Department of Chemistry, North Dartmouth, MA 02747-2300. Offers MS. Part-time programs available. *Faculty:* 20 full-time (4 women), 1 (woman) part-time. *Students:* 6 full-time (1 woman), 6 part-time (2 women), 7 international. Average age 30. 14 applicants, 64% accepted. In 1998, 5 degrees awarded. *Degree requirements:* For master's, thesis or alternative required, foreign language not required. *Entrance requirements:* For master's, TOEFL. *Application deadline:* For fall admission, 4/20 (priority date); for spring admission, 11/15 (priority date). Application fee: $40 for international students. Tuition, area resident: Full-time $3,107; part-time $129 per credit. Tuition, state resident: full-time $2,071; part-time $86 per credit. Tuition, nonresident: full-time $7,845; part-time $327 per credit. Required fees: $2,888. Full-time tuition and fees vary according to program and reciprocity agreements. Part-time tuition and fees vary according to course load and reciprocity agreements. *Financial aid:* In 1998–99, 3 research assistantships with full tuition reimbursements (averaging $10,000 per year), 11 teaching assistantships with full tuition reimbursements (averaging $9,600 per year) were awarded.; Federal Work-Study and unspecified assistantships also available. Aid available to part-time students. Financial aid application deadline: 3/15; financial aid applicants required to submit FAFSA. *Faculty research:* Raman spectroscopy, physical and theoretical organic chemistry, transition-metal chemistry, biochemistry of phospholipids, analytical radiochemistry. Total annual research expenditures: $504,000. *Unit head:* Dr. Timothy Su, Director, 508-999-8244, Fax: 508-999-9167, E-mail: tsu@umassd.edu. *Application contact:* Carol A. Novo, Graduate Admissions Office, 508-999-8026, Fax: 508-999-8183, E-mail: graduate@umassd.edu.

University of Massachusetts Lowell, Graduate School, College of Arts and Sciences, Department of Chemistry, Lowell, MA 01854-2881. Offers biochemistry (PhD); chemistry (MS, PhD); environmental studies (PhD); polymer sciences (MS, PhD). PhD (biochemistry) offered jointly with the Department of Biological Sciences. *Faculty:* 24 full-time (2 women). *Students:* 36 full-time (11 women), 35 part-time (23 women); includes 12 minority (all Asian Americans or Pacific Islanders), 32 international. 80 applicants, 45% accepted. In 1998, 11 master's, 8 doctorates awarded. Terminal master's awarded for partial completion of doctoral program. *Degree requirements:* For master's, thesis required, foreign language not required; for doctorate, 2 foreign languages, computer language, dissertation required. *Entrance requirements:* For master's and doctorate, GRE General Test. *Application deadline:* For fall admission, 4/1 (priority date); for spring admission, 10/1. Applications are processed on a rolling basis. Application fee: $20 ($35 for international students). *Financial aid:* In 1998–99, 13 fellowships, 13 research assistantships, 30 teaching assistantships were awarded.; career-related internships or fieldwork also available. Financial aid application deadline: 4/1. *Unit head:* Dr. Edwin

Johngen, Chair, 978-934-3663. *Application contact:* Dr. Melissa McDonald, Coordinator, 978-934-3683, E-mail: melissa_mcdonald@woods.uml.edu.

The University of Memphis, Graduate School, College of Arts and Sciences, Department of Chemistry, Memphis, TN 38152. Offers MS, PhD. *Faculty:* 14 full-time (0 women), 3 part-time (0 women). *Students:* 25 full-time (10 women), 3 part-time; includes 1 minority (African American), 20 international. Average age 31. 44 applicants, 27% accepted. In 1998, 1 master's, 2 doctorates awarded. *Degree requirements:* For master's, thesis, oral comprehensive exam required; for doctorate, dissertation, oral comprehensive exam required, foreign language not required. *Entrance requirements:* For master's, GRE General Test, GRE Subject Test, 32 undergraduate hours in chemistry; for doctorate, GRE General Test, GRE Subject Test, MS in chemistry. *Application deadline:* For fall admission, 8/1; for spring admission, 12/1. Applications are processed on a rolling basis. Application fee: $25 ($50 for international students). Tuition, state resident: full-time $3,410; part-time $178 per credit hour. Tuition, nonresident: full-time $8,670; part-time $408 per credit hour. Tuition and fees vary according to program. *Financial aid:* In 1998–99, 26 students received aid, including 6 research assistantships, 17 teaching assistantships *Faculty research:* Computational chemistry, molecular spectroscopy, heterocyclic compounds, nonlinear optical properties of molecules. Total annual research expenditures: $200,000. *Unit head:* Dr. Peter K. Bridson, Chairman, 901-678-4414, Fax: 901-678-3447, E-mail: pbridson@memphis.edu. *Application contact:* Dr. Roger V. Lloyd, Coordinator of Graduate Studies, 901-678-2632, Fax: 901-678-3447, E-mail: rvlloyd@memphis.edu.

University of Miami, Graduate School, College of Arts and Sciences, Department of Chemistry, Coral Gables, FL 33124. Offers chemistry (MS); inorganic chemistry (PhD); organic chemistry (PhD); physical chemistry (PhD). *Faculty:* 11 full-time (1 woman). *Students:* 40 full-time (18 women); includes 6 minority (1 African American, 1 Asian American or Pacific Islander, 4 Hispanic Americans), 33 international. Average age 28. 250 applicants, 4% accepted. In 1998, 2 master's, 5 doctorates awarded. Terminal master's awarded for partial completion of doctoral program. *Degree requirements:* For master's, foreign language and thesis not required; for doctorate, dissertation required, foreign language not required. *Entrance requirements:* For master's and doctorate, GRE General Test (minimum combined score of 1000 required), TOEFL (minimum score of 550 required). *Average time to degree:* Master's–2 years full-time; doctorate–5 years full-time. *Application deadline:* For fall admission, 1/15. Application fee: $35. Electronic applications accepted. Tuition: Full-time $15,336; part-time $852 per credit. Required fees: $174. Tuition and fees vary according to program. *Financial aid:* In 1998–99, 32 students received aid, including 4 fellowships with full tuition reimbursements available, 28 teaching assistantships with full tuition reimbursements available; research assistantships with full tuition reimbursements available, tuition waivers (full) also available. Financial aid application deadline: 5/1. *Faculty research:* Synthetic and mechanistic chemistry, supramolecular chemistry, high-pressure chemistry, thermochemistry, theoretical chemistry. *Unit head:* Dr. Roger LeBlanc, Chairman, 305-284-2174, Fax: 305-284-4571. *Application contact:* Dr. Luis Echogoyen, Graduate Adviser, 305-661-2847, Fax: 305-284-4571, E-mail: ldookie@umiami.ir.miami.edu.

University of Miami, Graduate School, Rosenstiel School of Marine and Atmospheric Science, Division of Marine and Atmospheric Chemistry, Coral Gables, FL 33124. Offers MA, MS, PhD. *Faculty:* 14 full-time (2 women). *Students:* 10 full-time (4 women), 5 international. Average age 25. 21 applicants, 29% accepted. In 1998, 3 master's, 2 doctorates awarded. Terminal master's awarded for partial completion of doctoral program. *Degree requirements:* For master's and doctorate, thesis/dissertation required. *Entrance requirements:* For master's and doctorate, GRE General Test, TOEFL (minimum score of 550 required). *Average time to degree:* Master's–3 years full-time; doctorate–6 years full-time. *Application deadline:* For fall admission, 2/1 (priority date). Applications are processed on a rolling basis. Application fee: $35. Electronic applications accepted. Tuition: Full-time $15,336; part-time $852 per credit. Required fees: $174. Tuition and fees vary according to program. *Financial aid:* In 1998–99, 8 students received aid, including 1 fellowship with tuition reimbursement available, 7 research assistantships with tuition reimbursements available (averaging $17,000 per year), teaching assistantships with tuition reimbursements available (averaging $17,000 per year); institutionally-sponsored loans also available. Financial aid application deadline: 2/1. *Faculty research:* Global change issues, chemistry of marine waters and marine atmosphere. Total annual research expenditures: $4 million. *Unit head:* Dr. Rod Zika, Chairperson, 305-361-4722, Fax: 305-361-4689. *Application contact:* Dr. Frank Millero, Associate Dean, 305-361-4155, Fax: 305-361-4771, E-mail: gso@rsmas.miami.edu.

University of Michigan, Horace H. Rackham School of Graduate Studies, College of Literature, Science, and the Arts, Department of Chemistry, Ann Arbor, MI 48109. Offers analytical chemistry (PhD); chemical biology (PhD); inorganic chemistry (PhD); organic chemistry (PhD); physical chemistry (PhD). *Faculty:* 43 full-time (7 women). *Students:* 161 full-time (60 women); includes 5 minority (2 African Americans, 2 Asian Americans or Pacific Islanders, 1 Hispanic American), 43 international. Average age 26. 326 applicants, 42% accepted. In 1998, 36 degrees awarded. *Degree requirements:* For doctorate, dissertation, oral defense of dissertation, preliminary exam, organic cumulative proficiency exams required, foreign language not required. *Entrance requirements:* For doctorate, GRE General Test, GRE Subject Test (recommended), statement of prior research. *Average time to degree:* Doctorate–5 years full-time. *Application deadline:* For fall admission, 2/15 (priority date). Applications are processed on a rolling basis. Application fee: $55. *Financial aid:* In 1998–99, 10 fellowships with tuition reimbursements (averaging $17,750 per year), 64 research assistantships with tuition reimbursements (averaging $15,500 per year), 110 teaching assistantships with tuition reimbursements (averaging $15,500 per year) were awarded. Financial aid applicants required to submit FAFSA. Total annual research expenditures: $6.8 million. *Unit head:* Dr. Joseph P. Marino, Chair, 734-763-9681, Fax: 734-647-4847, E-mail: jpmarino@umich.edu. *Application contact:* Warren Noone, Assistant Director of Graduate Studies, 734-764-7278, Fax: 734-747-4865, E-mail: nooner@umich.edu.

University of Minnesota, Duluth, Graduate School, College of Science and Engineering, Department of Chemistry, Duluth, MN 55812-2496. Offers MS. Part-time programs available. *Faculty:* 21 full-time (3 women), 1 part-time (0 women). *Students:* 11 full-time (4 women); includes 1 minority (Asian American or Pacific Islander), 5 international. 23 applicants, 48% accepted. In 1998, 11 degrees awarded (45% found work related to degree, 55% continued full-time study). *Degree requirements:* For master's, thesis required (for some programs), foreign language not required. *Entrance requirements:* For master's, bachelor's degree in chemistry, minimum GPA of 3.0. *Average time to degree:* Master's–2 years full-time, 4 years part-time. *Application deadline:* For fall admission, 7/15; for spring admission, 1/15. Applications are processed on a rolling basis. Application fee: $50 ($55 for international students). *Financial aid:* In 1998–99, research assistantships with full tuition reimbursements (averaging $10,460 per year), teaching assistantships with full tuition reimbursements (averaging $10,460 per year) were awarded.; fellowships with full tuition reimbursements, Federal Work-Study and institutionally-sponsored loans also available. Financial aid application deadline: 3/15. *Faculty research:* Physical, inorganic, organic, and analytical chemistry; biochemistry and molecular biology. Total annual research expenditures: $500,000. *Unit head:* Dr. Donald P. Poe, Director of Graduate Studies, 218-726-7217, Fax: 218-726-7394, E-mail: grad@d.umn.edu.

University of Minnesota, Twin Cities Campus, Graduate School, Institute of Technology, Department of Chemistry, Minneapolis, MN 55455-0213. Offers MS, PhD. Part-time programs available. *Faculty:* 42 full-time (2 women), 7 part-time (1 woman). *Students:* 197 full-time (60 women), 2 part-time; includes 5 minority (3 African Americans, 1 Hispanic American, 1 Native American), 48 international. 600 applicants, 21% accepted. In 1998, 9 master's, 43 doctorates awarded. Terminal master's awarded for partial completion of doctoral program. *Degree requirements:* For master's, thesis or alternative required; for doctorate, dissertation, preliminary candidacy exams required. *Entrance requirements:* For master's and doctorate, GRE General Test, TOEFL. *Average time to degree:* Master's–2 years full-time, 3 years part-time; doctorate–5 years full-time. *Application deadline:* For fall admission, 1/1 (priority date). Applications are

processed on a rolling basis. Application fee: $50 ($55 for international students). *Financial aid:* In 1998–99, 192 students received aid; fellowships, research assistantships, teaching assistantships, career-related internships or fieldwork, Federal Work-Study, and institutionally-sponsored loans available. *Faculty research:* Analytical, biological, inorganic, organic, and physical chemistry. Total annual research expenditures: $7 million. *Unit head:* Wayne L. Gladfelter, Chairman, 612-624-6000. *Application contact:* Susan Page, Assistant to Director of Graduate Studies, 612-626-7444, Fax: 612-626-7541, E-mail: inquiry@chem.umn.edu.

See in-depth description on page 209.

University of Minnesota, Twin Cities Campus, School of Public Health, Division of Environmental and Occupational Health, Area in Environmental Chemistry, Minneapolis, MN 55455-0213. Offers MS, PhD. *Degree requirements:* For doctorate, dissertation required, foreign language not required, foreign language not required. *Entrance requirements:* For master's and doctorate, GRE General Test (minimum combined score of 1500 on three sections required), minimum GPA of 3.0. *Application deadline:* For fall admission, 3/1 (priority date). Applications are processed on a rolling basis. Application fee: $50 ($75 for international students). *Financial aid:* Fellowships, research assistantships available. Financial aid application deadline: 3/1. *Application contact:* Kathy Soupir, Student Coordinator, 612-625-0622, Fax: 612-626-4837, E-mail: ksoupir@mail.eoh.umn.edu.

University of Mississippi, Graduate School, College of Liberal Arts, Department of Chemistry, Oxford, University, MS 38677-9702. Offers MS, DA, PhD. *Faculty:* 14 full-time (1 woman). *Students:* 24 full-time (13 women), 1 part-time; includes 6 minority (5 African Americans, 1 Asian American or Pacific Islander), 13 international. In 1998, 2 master's, 6 doctorates awarded. *Degree requirements:* For master's, thesis required, foreign language not required; for doctorate, one foreign language, dissertation required. *Entrance requirements:* For master's, GRE General Test, TOEFL, minimum GPA of 3.0; for doctorate, GRE General Test, TOEFL. *Application deadline:* For fall admission, 8/1. Applications are processed on a rolling basis. Application fee: $0 ($25 for international students). Tuition, state resident: full-time $3,053; part-time $170 per credit hour. Tuition, nonresident: full-time $6,155; part-time $342 per credit hour. Tuition and fees vary according to program. *Financial aid:* Application deadline: 3/1. *Unit head:* Dr. Charles Hussey, Chairman, 601-232-7301, Fax: 601-232-7300, E-mail: chclh@chem1.olemiss.edu.

University of Missouri–Columbia, Graduate School, College of Arts and Sciences, Department of Chemistry, Columbia, MO 65211. Offers analytical chemistry (MS, PhD); inorganic chemistry (MS, PhD); organic chemistry (MS, PhD); physical chemistry (MS, PhD). *Faculty:* 23 full-time (3 women). *Students:* 68 full-time (23 women), 24 part-time (7 women); includes 6 minority (1 African American, 2 Asian Americans or Pacific Islanders, 2 Hispanic Americans, 1 Native American), 47 international. 33 applicants, 58% accepted. In 1998, 5 master's, 6 doctorates awarded. *Degree requirements:* For master's, thesis required, foreign language not required; for doctorate, dissertation required. *Entrance requirements:* For master's and doctorate, GRE General Test, minimum GPA of 3.0. *Application deadline:* For fall admission, 7/1 (priority date). Applications are processed on a rolling basis. Application fee: $30 ($50 for international students). *Financial aid:* Research assistantships, teaching assistantships, institutionally-sponsored loans available. *Unit head:* Dr. Richard Thompson, Director of Graduate Studies, 573-882-7356.

University of Missouri–Kansas City, College of Arts and Sciences, Department of Chemistry, Kansas City, MO 64110-2499. Offers analytical chemistry (MS, PhD); inorganic chemistry (MS, PhD); organic chemistry (MS, PhD); physical chemistry (MS, PhD); polymer chemistry (MS, PhD). PhD offered through the School of Graduate Studies. Part-time programs available. *Faculty:* 12 full-time (2 women), 2 part-time (0 women). *Students:* 25 full-time (7 women), 7 part-time (2 women), 18 international. Average age 29. 87 applicants, 47% accepted. In 1998, 3 master's awarded. *Degree requirements:* For master's, thesis required (for some programs), foreign language not required; for doctorate, dissertation required, foreign language not required. *Entrance requirements:* For master's, TOEFL (minimum score of 550 required); for doctorate, GRE General Test (minimum combined score of 1500 on three sections required), TOEFL (minimum score of 550 required), TWE (minimum score of 4 required). *Application deadline:* For fall and spring admission, 2/1 (priority date); for winter admission, 9/1 (priority date). Applications are processed on a rolling basis. Application fee: $25. *Financial aid:* In 1998–99, 1 fellowship with partial tuition reimbursement (averaging $11,000 per year), 11 research assistantships with partial tuition reimbursements (averaging $12,000 per year), 14 teaching assistantships with partial tuition reimbursements (averaging $11,235 per year) were awarded.; Federal Work-Study and institutionally-sponsored loans also available. Aid available to part-time students. Financial aid application deadline: 2/15. *Faculty research:* Molecular spectroscopy, characterization and synthesis of materials and compounds, computational chemistry. Total annual research expenditures: $238,280. *Unit head:* Dr. Jerry Jean, Interim Chairperson, 816-235-2280, Fax: 816-235-5502, E-mail: jean@cctr.umkc.edu.

See in-depth description on page 211.

University of Missouri–Rolla, Graduate School, College of Arts and Sciences, Department of Chemistry, Rolla, MO 65409-0910. Offers chemistry (MS, PhD); chemistry education (MST). *Faculty:* 20 full-time (2 women), 2 part-time (0 women). *Students:* 68 full-time (23 women); includes 6 minority (3 African Americans, 2 Asian Americans or Pacific Islanders, 1 Hispanic American), 37 international. Average age 30. 98 applicants, 89% accepted. In 1998, 4 master's awarded (75% found work related to degree, 25% continued full-time study); 12 doctorates awarded. Terminal master's awarded for partial completion of doctoral program. *Degree requirements:* For master's, foreign language and thesis not required; for doctorate, one foreign language, dissertation required. *Entrance requirements:* For master's and doctorate, minimum GPA of 3.0. *Average time to degree:* Master's–3 years full-time; doctorate–6 years full-time. *Application deadline:* For fall admission, 7/1. Applications are processed on a rolling basis. Application fee: $25. Electronic applications accepted. *Financial aid:* In 1998–99, 2 fellowships (averaging $2,000 per year), 25 research assistantships with full and partial tuition reimbursements (averaging $12,532 per year), 37 teaching assistantships with full and partial tuition reimbursements (averaging $12,267 per year) were awarded.; institutionally-sponsored loans also available. *Faculty research:* Structure and properties of materials; bioanalytical, environmental, and polymer chemistry. Total annual research expenditures: $1.6 million. *Unit head:* Dr. Harvest L. Collier, Interim Chairman, 573-341-4420, Fax: 573-341-6033, E-mail: hcollier@umr.edu.

University of Missouri–St. Louis, Graduate School, College of Arts and Sciences, Department of Chemistry, St. Louis, MO 63121-4499. Offers chemistry (MS, PhD), including biochemistry, inorganic chemistry, organic chemistry, physical chemistry. Part-time and evening/weekend programs available. *Faculty:* 20. *Students:* 33 full-time (10 women), 26 part-time (9 women); includes 7 minority (2 African Americans, 4 Asian Americans or Pacific Islanders, 1 Hispanic American), 21 international. In 1998, 7 master's, 3 doctorates awarded. Terminal master's awarded for partial completion of doctoral program. *Degree requirements:* For master's, thesis optional, foreign language not required; for doctorate, dissertation required, foreign language not required. *Entrance requirements:* For doctorate, GRE General Test, GRE Subject Test. *Application deadline:* For fall admission, 7/1 (priority date); for spring admission, 12/7 (priority date). Applications are processed on a rolling basis. Application fee: $25 ($40 for international students). Electronic applications accepted. *Financial aid:* In 1998–99, 1 fellowship with partial tuition reimbursement (averaging $12,000 per year), 14 research assistantships with partial tuition reimbursements (averaging $12,400 per year), 15 teaching assistantships with partial tuition reimbursements (averaging $12,400 per year) were awarded. *Faculty research:* Metallaborane chemistry, serum transferrin chemistry, natural products chemistry, organic synthesis. Total annual research expenditures: $903,252. *Unit head:* Dr. R. E. K. Winter, Director of Graduate Studies, 314-516-5337, Fax: 314-516-5342, E-mail: chejjoll@jinx.umsl.edu. *Application contact:* Graduate Admissions, 314-516-5458, Fax: 314-516-6759, E-mail: gradadm@umsl.edu.

Chemistry

The University of Montana–Missoula, Graduate School, College of Arts and Sciences, Department of Chemistry, Missoula, MT 59812-0002. Offers chemistry (MS, PhD); chemistry teaching (MST); environmental chemistry (PhD); inorganic chemistry (PhD); organic chemistry (PhD); physical chemistry (PhD). Part-time programs available. *Faculty:* 14 full-time (3 women), 1 part-time (0 women). *Students:* 15 full-time (3 women), 3 part-time; includes 3 minority (all Asian Americans or Pacific Islanders) 6 applicants, 100% accepted. In 1998, 1 master's, 1 doctorate awarded (100% entered university research/teaching). Terminal master's awarded for partial completion of doctoral program. *Degree requirements:* For master's, thesis required (for some programs); for doctorate, dissertation required. *Entrance requirements:* For master's, GRE General Test; for doctorate, GRE General Test, GRE Subject Test. *Application deadline:* For fall admission, 3/15 (priority date); for spring admission, 10/15. Applications are processed on a rolling basis. Application fee: $45. *Financial aid:* Research assistantships, teaching assistantships, Federal Work-Study available. Financial aid application deadline: 3/1. *Faculty research:* Reaction mechanisms and kinetics, inorganic and organic synthesis, analytical chemistry, natural products. *Unit head:* Dr. Michael D. DeGrandpre, Graduate Coordinator, 403-243-4022, Fax: 406-243-4227.

University of Nebraska–Lincoln, Graduate College, College of Arts and Sciences, Department of Chemistry, Lincoln, NE 68588. Offers analytical chemistry (PhD); chemistry (MS); inorganic chemistry (PhD); organic chemistry (PhD); physical chemistry (PhD). *Faculty:* 23 full-time (2 women), 1 part-time (0 women). *Students:* 79 full-time (15 women), 23 part-time (2 women); includes 6 minority (1 African American, 2 Asian Americans or Pacific Islanders, 2 Hispanic Americans, 1 Native American), 47 international. Average age 28. 105 applicants, 52% accepted. In 1998, 7 master's, 15 doctorates awarded. *Degree requirements:* For master's, departmental qualifying exam required, thesis optional; for doctorate, dissertation, comprehensive and departmental qualifying exams required. *Entrance requirements:* For master's and doctorate, GRE Subject Test, TOEFL (minimum score of 550 required). *Average time to degree:* Doctorate–5.3 years full-time. *Application deadline:* For fall admission, 3/1 (priority date). Applications are processed on a rolling basis. Application fee: $35. Electronic applications accepted. *Financial aid:* In 1998–99, 10 fellowships, 50 research assistantships, 51 teaching assistantships were awarded.; Federal Work-Study also available. Aid available to part-time students. Financial aid application deadline: 2/15. *Faculty research:* Bioorganic and bioinorganic chemistry, biophysical and bioanalytical chemistry, structure-function of DNA and proteins, organometallics, mass spectrometry. *Unit head:* Dr. Lawrence Parkhurst, Chair, 402-472-3501, Fax: 402-472-9402.

University of Nevada, Las Vegas, Graduate College, College of Science, Department of Chemistry, Las Vegas, NV 89154-9900. Offers environmental analytical chemistry (MS); general chemistry (MS). *Faculty:* 18 full-time (5 women). *Students:* 10 full-time (7 women), 6 part-time (5 women); includes 2 minority (1 Asian American or Pacific Islander, 1 Hispanic American), 7 international. 11 applicants, 45% accepted. In 1998, 3 degrees awarded. *Degree requirements:* For master's, thesis required, foreign language not required. *Entrance requirements:* For master's, GRE General Test, minimum GPA of 2.75. *Application deadline:* For fall admission, 6/15 (priority date); for spring admission, 11/15. Applications are processed on a rolling basis. Application fee: $40 ($95 for international students). *Financial aid:* In 1998–99, 2 research assistantships with partial tuition reimbursements (averaging $8,500 per year), 8 teaching assistantships with partial tuition reimbursements (averaging $8,500 per year) were awarded. Financial aid application deadline: 3/1. *Unit head:* Dr. Brian Spangelo, Chair, 702-895-3510. *Application contact:* Graduate Coordinator, 702-895-3753.

University of Nevada, Reno, Graduate School, College of Arts and Science, Department of Chemistry, Reno, NV 89557. Offers MS, PhD. Terminal master's awarded for partial completion of doctoral program. *Degree requirements:* For master's, thesis required, foreign language not required; for doctorate, one foreign language (computer language can substitute), dissertation required. *Entrance requirements:* For master's, GRE, TOEFL (minimum score of 500 required), minimum GPA of 2.75; for doctorate, GRE, TOEFL (minimum score of 500 required), minimum GPA of 3.0.

University of New Brunswick, School of Graduate Studies, Faculty of Science, Department of Chemistry, Fredericton, NB E3B 5A3, Canada. Offers M Sc, PhD. Part-time programs available. *Degree requirements:* For master's and doctorate, thesis/dissertation required. *Entrance requirements:* For master's and doctorate, TOEFL, TWE, minimum GPA of 3.0.

University of New Hampshire, Graduate School, College of Engineering and Physical Sciences, Department of Chemistry, Durham, NH 03824. Offers MS, MST, PhD. *Faculty:* 18 full-time. *Students:* 31 full-time (13 women), 24 part-time (9 women); includes 4 minority (3 African Americans, 1 Asian American or Pacific Islander), 17 international. Average age 26. 62 applicants, 47% accepted. In 1998, 3 master's, 3 doctorates awarded. Terminal master's awarded for partial completion of doctoral program. *Degree requirements:* For master's, thesis required, foreign language not required; for doctorate, one foreign language (computer language can substitute), dissertation required. *Application deadline:* For fall admission, 4/1 (priority date). Applications are processed on a rolling basis. Application fee: $50. Tuition, area resident: Full-time $5,750; part-time $319 per credit. Tuition, state resident: full-time $8,625. Tuition, nonresident: full-time $14,640; part-time $598 per credit. Required fees: $224 per semester. Tuition and fees vary according to course load, degree level and program. *Financial aid:* In 1998–99, 2 fellowships, 6 research assistantships, 33 teaching assistantships were awarded.; Federal Work-Study, scholarships, and tuition waivers (full and partial) also available. Aid available to part-time students. Financial aid application deadline: 2/15. *Faculty research:* Analytical, physical, organic, and inorganic chemistry. *Unit head:* Dr. Rudy Seitz, Chairperson, 603-862-2358. *Application contact:* Dr. N. Dennis Chasteen, Graduate Coordinator, 603-862-2520.

University of New Mexico, Graduate School, College of Arts and Sciences, Department of Chemistry, Albuquerque, NM 87131-2039. Offers MS, PhD. Part-time programs available. *Faculty:* 33 full-time (5 women), 1 part-time (0 women). *Students:* 47 full-time (16 women), 14 part-time (6 women); includes 4 minority (3 Asian Americans or Pacific Islanders, 1 Hispanic American), 32 international. Average age 30. 22 applicants, 45% accepted. In 1998, 9 master's, 6 doctorates awarded. Terminal master's awarded for partial completion of doctoral program. *Degree requirements:* For master's, thesis optional, foreign language not required; for doctorate, dissertation required, foreign language not required. *Entrance requirements:* For master's, TOEFL (minimum score of 520 required). Application fee: $25. *Financial aid:* In 1998–99, 2 fellowships (averaging $265 per year), 38 research assistantships with tuition reimbursements (averaging $5,102 per year), 17 teaching assistantships with tuition reimbursements (averaging $13,180 per year) were awarded. *Faculty research:* Analytical, inorganic, organic, and physical chemistry; biochemistry. Total annual research expenditures: $2 million. *Unit head:* Fritz S. Allen, Chair, 505-277-6655, Fax: 505-277-2609, E-mail: fallen@unm.edu. *Application contact:* Cary J. Morrow, Professor, 505-277-3159, Fax: 505-277-2609, E-mail: cmorrow@unm.edu.

University of New Orleans, Graduate School, College of Sciences, Department of Chemistry, New Orleans, LA 70148. Offers MS, PhD. *Faculty:* 20 full-time (0 women). *Students:* 39 full-time (16 women), 4 part-time; includes 5 minority (4 African Americans, 1 Asian American or Pacific Islander), 22 international. Average age 31. 32 applicants, 59% accepted. In 1998, 1 master's, 6 doctorates awarded. *Degree requirements:* For master's and doctorate, thesis/dissertation, departmental qualifying exam required. *Entrance requirements:* For master's and doctorate, GRE General Test. *Application deadline:* For fall admission, 7/1 (priority date); for spring admission, 11/15. Applications are processed on a rolling basis. Application fee: $20. Tuition, state resident: full-time $2,362. Tuition, nonresident: full-time $7,888. Part-time tuition and fees vary according to course load. *Faculty research:* Synthesis and reactions of novel compounds, high-temperature kinetics, calculations of molecular electrostatic potentials, structures and reactions of metal complexes. *Unit head:* Dr. Jack Timberlake, Chairman, 504-280-6855, Fax: 504-280-6860, E-mail: jwtcm@uno.edu. *Application contact:* Dr. Mark Trudell, Graduate Coordinator, 504-280-7337, Fax: 504-280-6860, E-mail: mltcm@uno.edu.

The University of North Carolina at Chapel Hill, Graduate School, College of Arts and Sciences, Department of Chemistry, Chapel Hill, NC 27599. Offers MA, MS, PhD. *Degree requirements:* For master's, thesis (for some programs), comprehensive exam required, foreign language not required; for doctorate, dissertation, comprehensive exam required, foreign language not required. *Entrance requirements:* For master's and doctorate, GRE General Test (minimum combined score of 1000 required), GRE Subject Test, minimum GPA of 3.0.

University of North Carolina at Charlotte, Graduate School, College of Arts and Sciences, Department of Chemistry, Charlotte, NC 28223-0001. Offers MS. Part-time programs available. *Faculty:* 17 full-time (2 women). *Students:* 3 full-time (0 women), 14 part-time (6 women); includes 3 minority (1 African American, 2 Asian Americans or Pacific Islanders), 1 international. Average age 31. 13 applicants, 85% accepted. In 1998, 9 degrees awarded. *Degree requirements:* For master's, thesis required. *Entrance requirements:* For master's, GRE General Test or MAT, minimum GPA of 3.0 in undergraduate major, 2.75 overall. *Application deadline:* For fall admission, 7/15; for spring admission, 11/15. Applications are processed on a rolling basis. Application fee: $35. Electronic applications accepted. *Financial aid:* In 1998–99, 13 teaching assistantships were awarded.; career-related internships or fieldwork and Federal Work-Study also available. Financial aid application deadline: 4/1. *Faculty research:* Inorganic chemistry, analytical chemistry, biotechnology. *Unit head:* Dr. Arthur Greenburg, Chair, 704-547-4765, Fax: 704-547-3151, E-mail: agreebe@email.uncc.edu. *Application contact:* Kathy Barringer, Assistant Director of Graduate Admissions, 704-547-3366, Fax: 704-547-3279, E-mail: gradadm@email.uncc.edu.

University of North Carolina at Greensboro, Graduate School, College of Arts and Sciences, Department of Chemistry, Greensboro, NC 27412-5001. Offers M Ed, MS. *Faculty:* 11 full-time (1 woman), 2 part-time (0 women). *Students:* 3 full-time (all women), 20 part-time (12 women); includes 5 minority (3 African Americans, 1 Asian American or Pacific Islander, 1 Native American), 2 international. 20 applicants, 60% accepted. In 1998, 4 degrees awarded. *Degree requirements:* For master's, one foreign language (computer language can substitute), thesis required. *Entrance requirements:* For master's, GRE General Test, TOEFL. *Application deadline:* Applications are processed on a rolling basis. Application fee: $35. *Financial aid:* In 1998–99, 11 research assistantships were awarded. *Faculty research:* Synthesis of novel cyclopentadienes, molybdenum hydroxylase-cata ladder polymers, vinyl silicones. *Unit head:* Dr. Terance Nile, Head, 336-334-5714, Fax: 336-334-5402, E-mail: terry-nile@uncg.edu. *Application contact:* Dr. James Lynch, Director of Graduate Recruitment, 336-334-4881, Fax: 336-334-4424, E-mail: jmlynch@office.uncg.edu.

University of North Carolina at Wilmington, College of Arts and Sciences, Department of Chemistry, Wilmington, NC 28403-3201. Offers MS. Part-time programs available. *Faculty:* 6 full-time (2 women). *Students:* 5 full-time (1 woman), 21 part-time (12 women); includes 1 minority (Asian American or Pacific Islander) Average age 29. 18 applicants, 28% accepted. In 1998, 5 degrees awarded. *Degree requirements:* For master's, computer language, thesis, oral and written comprehensive exams required. *Entrance requirements:* For master's, GRE General Test, minimum B average in undergraduate major. *Application deadline:* For fall admission, 6/1. Applications are processed on a rolling basis. Application fee: $35. *Financial aid:* In 1998–99, 11 teaching assistantships were awarded.; career-related internships or fieldwork and Federal Work-Study also available. Aid available to part-time students. Financial aid application deadline: 3/15. *Unit head:* Dr. William J. Cooper, Chairman, 910-962-3450. *Application contact:* Neil F. Hadley, Dean, Graduate School, 910-962-4117, Fax: 910-962-3787, E-mail: hadleyn@uncwil.edu.

University of North Dakota, Graduate School, College of Arts and Sciences, Department of Chemistry, Grand Forks, ND 58202. Offers MS, PhD. *Faculty:* 12 full-time (3 women). *Students:* 26 full-time (7 women). 11 applicants, 91% accepted. In 1998, 3 master's, 2 doctorates awarded. Terminal master's awarded for partial completion of doctoral program. *Degree requirements:* For master's, thesis required; for doctorate, one foreign language, dissertation required. *Entrance requirements:* For master's, GRE General Test, GRE Subject Test, TOEFL (minimum score of 550 required), minimum GPA of 3.0; for doctorate, GRE General Test, GRE Subject Test, TOEFL (minimum score of 550 required), minimum GPA of 3.5. *Application deadline:* For fall admission, 3/1 (priority date). Applications are processed on a rolling basis. Application fee: $20. *Financial aid:* In 1998–99, 23 students received aid, including 7 research assistantships, 16 teaching assistantships; fellowships, Federal Work-Study, institutionally-sponsored loans, and tuition waivers (full and partial) also available. Financial aid application deadline: 3/15. *Unit head:* Dr. Harmon Abrahamson, Chairperson, 701-777-4427, Fax: 701-777-2331, E-mail: habraham@plains.nodak.edu .und.nodak.edu.

University of Northern Colorado, Graduate School, College of Arts and Sciences, Department of Chemistry, Greeley, CO 80639. Offers chemical education (MA, PhD); chemical research (MA). *Accreditation:* NCATE (one or more programs are accredited). *Faculty:* 9 full-time (1 woman). *Students:* 15 full-time (8 women), 3 part-time (2 women); includes 1 minority (Hispanic American), 1 international. Average age 29. 18 applicants, 56% accepted. In 1998, 5 master's, 1 doctorate awarded. *Degree requirements:* For master's, thesis or alternative, comprehensive exams required; for doctorate, dissertation, comprehensive exams required. *Entrance requirements:* For doctorate, GRE General Test. *Application deadline:* Applications are processed on a rolling basis. Application fee: $35. *Financial aid:* In 1998–99, 17 students received aid, including 4 fellowships, 7 research assistantships, 6 teaching assistantships; unspecified assistantships also available. Financial aid application deadline: 3/1. *Unit head:* Dr. David Pringle, Chairperson, 970-351-2559.

University of Northern Iowa, Graduate College, College of Natural Sciences, Department of Chemistry, Cedar Falls, IA 50614. Offers MA. Part-time programs available. *Faculty:* 7 full-time (0 women). *Students:* 5 full-time (all women), 1 part-time; includes 1 minority (African American), 1 international. Average age 33. 3 applicants, 100% accepted. In 1998, 1 degree awarded. *Degree requirements:* For master's, thesis or alternative required, foreign language not required. *Entrance requirements:* For master's, GRE. *Application deadline:* For fall admission, 8/1 (priority date). Applications are processed on a rolling basis. Application fee: $20 ($30 for international students). Tuition, state resident: full-time $3,308; part-time $184 per hour. Tuition, nonresident: full-time $8,156; part-time $454 per hour. Required fees: $202; $88 per semester. Tuition and fees vary according to course load. *Financial aid:* Career-related internships or fieldwork, Federal Work-Study, scholarships, and tuition waivers (full and partial) available. Aid available to part-time students. Financial aid application deadline: 3/1. *Unit head:* Dr. Duane E. Bartak, Head, 319-273-2437, Fax: 319-273-7127, E-mail: duane.bartak@uni.edu.

University of North Texas, Robert B. Toulouse School of Graduate Studies, College of Arts and Sciences, Department of Chemistry, Denton, TX 76203. Offers MS, PhD. Part-time and evening/weekend programs available. *Faculty:* 19 full-time (2 women), 1 part-time (0 women). *Students:* 58 full-time (20 women), 11 part-time (7 women); includes 8 minority (2 African Americans, 2 Asian Americans or Pacific Islanders, 3 Hispanic Americans, 1 Native American), 41 international. Average age 27. In 1998, 11 master's, 6 doctorates awarded. Terminal master's awarded for partial completion of doctoral program. *Degree requirements:* For master's, thesis (for some programs), comprehensive exam required, foreign language not required; for doctorate, one foreign language (computer language can substitute), dissertation, comprehensive exams required. *Entrance requirements:* For master's, GRE General Test (minimum combined score of 950 required); for doctorate, GRE General Test (minimum combined score of 1000 required). *Application deadline:* For fall admission, 7/17. Application fee: $25 ($50 for international students). *Financial aid:* Fellowships, research assistantships, teaching assistantships, career-related internships or fieldwork, Federal Work-Study, and institutionally-sponsored loans available. Financial aid application deadline: 4/1. *Faculty research:* Analytical, inorganic, physical, and organic chemistry and materials. Total annual research expenditures: $2 million. *Unit head:* Dr. Ruthanne Thomas, Chair, 940-565-3515, Fax: 940-565-4318, E-mail: rthomas@unt.edu. *Application contact:* Dr. Martin Schwartz, Graduate Adviser, 940-565-3542, Fax: 940-565-4318, E-mail: mshwart@cas.unt.edu.

University of Notre Dame, Graduate School, College of Science, Department of Chemistry and Biochemistry, Notre Dame, IN 46556. Offers biochemistry (MS, PhD); inorganic chemistry (MS, PhD); organic chemistry (MS, PhD); physical chemistry (MS, PhD). *Faculty:* 32 full-time (3 women). *Students:* 110 full-time (38 women), 1 part-time; includes 3 minority (2 African Americans, 1 Asian American or Pacific Islander), 57 international. 177 applicants, 32% accepted. In 1998, 8 master's, 12 doctorates awarded. Terminal master's awarded for partial completion of doctoral program. *Degree requirements:* For master's, thesis, comprehensive exam required, foreign language not required; for doctorate, dissertation, qualifying exam required, foreign language not required. *Entrance requirements:* For master's, GRE General Test, GRE General Subject Test (strongly recommended), TOEFL (minimum score of 600 required; 250 for computer-based); for doctorate, GRE General Test, GRE Subject Test (strongly recommended), TOEFL (minimum score of 600 required; 250 for computer-based). *Average time to degree:* Master's–3.3 years full-time; doctorate–5.8 years full-time. *Application deadline:* For fall admission, 2/1 (priority date). Applications are processed on a rolling basis. Application fee: $40. *Financial aid:* In 1998–99, 109 students received aid, including 25 fellowships with full tuition reimbursements available (averaging $16,000 per year), 42 research assistantships with full tuition reimbursements available (averaging $13,500 per year), 42 teaching assistantships with full tuition reimbursements available (averaging $13,500 per year); tuition waivers (full) also available. Financial aid application deadline: 2/1. *Faculty research:* Protein, carbohydrate and lipid metabolism, structure and function; synthesis, structure, and reactivity of organometallic and cluster complexes; synthesis and structure determination of novel compounds. Total annual research expenditures: $8.7 million. *Unit head:* Dr. A. Graham Lappin, Chairman, 219-631-7058, Fax: 219-631-6652, E-mail: lappin.1@nd.edu. *Application contact:* Dr. Terrence J. Akai, Director of Graduate Admissions, 219-631-7706, Fax: 219-631-4183, E-mail: gradad@nd.edu.

See in-depth description on page 215.

University of Oklahoma, Graduate College, College of Arts and Sciences, Department of Chemistry and Biochemistry, Norman, OK 73019-0390. Offers MS, PhD. Part-time programs available. *Faculty:* 32 full-time (7 women), 2 part-time (1 woman). *Students:* 18 full-time (6 women), 75 part-time (30 women); includes 7 minority (2 African Americans, 1 Asian American or Pacific Islander, 2 Hispanic Americans, 2 Native Americans), 38 international. Average age 29. 53 applicants, 47% accepted. In 1998, 20 master's, 13 doctorates awarded. Terminal master's awarded for partial completion of doctoral program. *Degree requirements:* For master's, thesis optional; for doctorate, dissertation required. *Entrance requirements:* For master's, GRE, TOEFL (minimum score of 550 required), BS in chemistry; for doctorate, GRE, TOEFL (minimum score of 550 required). *Application deadline:* For fall admission, 4/1 (priority date); for spring admission, 9/1 (priority date). Applications are processed on a rolling basis. Application fee: $25. Tuition, state resident: part-time $86 per credit hour. Tuition, nonresident: part-time $275 per credit hour. Tuition and fees vary according to course level, course load and program. *Financial aid:* In 1998–99, 26 research assistantships, 41 teaching assistantships were awarded.; fellowships, Federal Work-Study, institutionally-sponsored loans, and tuition waivers (partial) also available. Financial aid application deadline: 4/1. *Faculty research:* Analytic, organic, physical, and inorganic chemistry. *Unit head:* Dr. Glenn Dryhurst, Chair, 405-325-4811. *Application contact:* Dr. Stan Neely, Chair, Graduate Committee, 405-325-2946, Fax: 405-325-6111.

University of Oregon, Graduate School, College of Arts and Sciences, Department of Chemistry, Eugene, OR 97403. Offers biochemistry (MA, MS, PhD); chemistry (MA, MS, PhD). *Faculty:* 29 full-time (5 women), 11 part-time (5 women). *Students:* 76 full-time (31 women), 5 part-time (2 women); includes 4 minority (2 Asian Americans or Pacific Islanders, 2 Hispanic Americans), 8 international. 20 applicants, 100% accepted. In 1998, 12 master's awarded (100% found work related to degree); 10 doctorates awarded. Terminal master's awarded for partial completion of doctoral program. *Degree requirements:* For master's, foreign language and thesis not required; for doctorate, dissertation required, foreign language not required. *Entrance requirements:* For master's and doctorate, GRE General Test, TOEFL (minimum score of 620 required). *Application deadline:* For fall admission, 1/10 (priority date). Applications are processed on a rolling basis. Application fee: $50. *Financial aid:* In 1998–99, 57 teaching assistantships were awarded.; Federal Work-Study and institutionally-sponsored loans also available. Financial aid application deadline: 4/15. *Faculty research:* Organic chemistry, organometallic chemistry, inorganic chemistry, physical chemistry, materials science, biochemistry, chemical physics, molecular or cell biology. *Unit head:* Mark Lonergan, Head, 541-346-4601. *Application contact:* Lynde Ritzow, Graduate Recruiting Coordinator, 800-782-4713.

University of Ottawa, School of Graduate Studies and Research, Faculty of Science, Ottawa-Carleton Chemistry Institute, Ottawa, ON K1N 6N5, Canada. Offers M Sc, PhD. *Faculty:* 45 full-time, 1 part-time. *Students:* 112 full-time (46 women), 4 part-time (3 women), 24 international. Average age 30. In 1998, 10 master's, 17 doctorates awarded. *Degree requirements:* For master's and doctorate, thesis/dissertation required, foreign language not required. *Entrance requirements:* For master's, honors degree or equivalent, minimum B average; for doctorate, minimum B+ average. *Application deadline:* For fall admission, 3/1 (priority date). Applications are processed on a rolling basis. Application fee: $35. *Financial aid:* Fellowships, research assistantships, teaching assistantships, Federal Work-Study available. *Unit head:* René Roy, Director, 613-562-5800 Ext. 6055, Fax: 613-562-5170. *Application contact:* Lise Maisonneuve, Administrative Assistant, 613-562-5800 Ext. 6050, Fax: 613-562-5170, E-mail: lise@science.uottawa.ca.

University of Pennsylvania, School of Arts and Sciences, Graduate Group in Chemistry, Philadelphia, PA 19104. Offers MS, PhD. *Degree requirements:* For doctorate, dissertation required, foreign language not required. *Entrance requirements:* For doctorate, GRE General Test (combined average 1944 on three sections), GRE Subject Test, TOEFL, previous graduate course work in organic, inorganic, and physical chemistry each with a lab; differential and integral calculus; and general physics with a lab.

University of Pittsburgh, Faculty of Arts and Sciences, Department of Chemistry, Pittsburgh, PA 15260. Offers MS, PhD. Part-time and evening/weekend programs available. *Faculty:* 39 full-time (3 women), 2 part-time (1 woman). *Students:* 168 full-time (58 women), 10 part-time (6 women); includes 13 minority (3 African Americans, 9 Asian Americans or Pacific Islanders, 1 Hispanic American), 91 international. 543 applicants, 15% accepted. In 1998, 14 master's, 23 doctorates awarded. Terminal master's awarded for partial completion of doctoral program. *Degree requirements:* For master's and doctorate, thesis/dissertation required, foreign language not required. *Entrance requirements:* For master's, GRE General Test, GRE Subject Test, TOEFL; for doctorate, GRE General Test, GRE Subject Test, TOEFL (minimum score of 600 required). *Average time to degree:* Master's–2 years full-time, 7 years part-time; doctorate–5 years full-time, 10 years part-time. *Application deadline:* For fall admission, 2/1 (priority date). Applications are processed on a rolling basis. Application fee: $30 ($40 for international students). *Financial aid:* In 1998–99, 163 students received aid, including 6 fellowships (averaging $14,000 per year), 85 research assistantships (averaging $14,832 per year), 72 teaching assistantships (averaging $16,222 per year); Federal Work-Study and grants also available. Financial aid application deadline: 2/1. *Faculty research:* Analytical, inorganic, organic, physical, and surface chemistry. Total annual research expenditures: $6.5 million. *Unit head:* Dr. Craig S. Wilcox, Chairman, 412-624-8200, Fax: 412-624-8611, E-mail: daylite+@pitt.edu. *Application contact:* Nancy Sattler, Administrative Assistant, 412-624-8501, Fax: 412-624-8611, E-mail: nsattler@vms.cis.pitt.edu.

See in-depth description on page 219.

University of Puerto Rico, Mayagüez Campus, Graduate Studies, College of Arts and Sciences, Department of Chemistry, Mayagüez, PR 00681-5000. Offers MS. *Degree requirements:* For master's, one foreign language, thesis, comprehensive exam required. *Faculty research:* Biochemistry, spectroscopy, food chemistry, physical chemistry, electrochemistry.

University of Puerto Rico, Río Piedras, Faculty of Natural Sciences, Department of Chemistry, San Juan, PR 00931. Offers MS, PhD. Part-time and evening/weekend programs available. *Students:* 84 full-time (37 women), 28 part-time (16 women); includes 91 minority (all Hispanic Americans), 21 international. Average age 29. 34 applicants, 59% accepted. In 1998, 10 master's, 2 doctorates awarded. *Degree requirements:* For master's and doctorate, one foreign language, thesis/dissertation, comprehensive exam required. *Entrance requirements:* For master's, GRE General Test, GRE Subject Test, TOEFL, interview, minimum GPA of 3.0; for doctorate, GRE General Test, GRE Subject Test, TOEFL, minimum GPA of 3.0. *Average time to degree:* Master's–6 years full-time; doctorate–8 years full-time. *Application deadline:* For fall admission, 2/1. Application fee: $17. *Financial aid:* Fellowships, research assistantships, teaching assistantships, Federal Work-Study, institutionally-sponsored loans, and tuition waivers (partial) available. Financial aid application deadline: 5/31. *Faculty research:* Organometallic synthesis, transition metal chemistry, organic air pollutants, acylmetalloids. *Unit head:* Dr. Nestor Car, Coordinator, 787-764-0000 Ext. 4817, Fax: 787-756-8242, E-mail: aguadal@upracd.upr.clu.edu.

See in-depth description on page 221.

University of Regina, Faculty of Graduate Studies and Research, Faculty of Science, Department of Chemistry, Regina, SK S4S 0A2, Canada. Offers analytical chemistry (M Sc, PhD); biochemistry (M Sc, PhD); clinical biochemistry (M Sc, PhD); inorganic chemistry (M Sc, PhD); organic chemistry (M Sc, PhD); physical chemistry (M Sc, PhD); x-ray crystallography (M Sc, PhD). Part-time programs available. *Faculty:* 10 full-time (1 woman), 3 part-time (0 women). *Students:* 9 full-time (5 women), 6 part-time (3 women). 29 applicants, 21% accepted. In 1998, 2 master's, 2 doctorates awarded. *Degree requirements:* For master's, thesis, departmental qualifying exam required, foreign language not required; for doctorate, variable foreign language requirement, dissertation, departmental qualifying exam required. *Entrance requirements:* For master's, TOEFL (minimum score of 580 required); for doctorate, TOEFL. *Application deadline:* Applications are processed on a rolling basis. Application fee: $0. *Expenses:* Tuition and fees charges are reported in Canadian dollars. Tuition, state resident: full-time $1,688 Canadian dollars; part-time $94 Canadian dollars per credit hour. International tuition: $3,375 Canadian dollars full-time. Required fees: $65 Canadian dollars per course. Tuition and fees vary according to course load and program. *Financial aid:* In 1998–99, 7 research assistantships, 4 teaching assistantships were awarded.; fellowships, scholarships also available. Financial aid application deadline: 6/15. *Faculty research:* Analytical biochemistry, cancer. *Unit head:* Dr. K. Johnson, Head, 306-585-4146, Fax: 306-585-4894, E-mail: chem@max.cc.uregina.ca.

University of Rhode Island, Graduate School, College of Arts and Sciences, Department of Chemistry, Kingston, RI 02881. Offers MS, PhD.

University of Rochester, The College, Arts and Sciences, Department of Chemistry, Rochester, NY 14627-0250. Offers MS, PhD. *Faculty:* 19. *Students:* 78 full-time (30 women); includes 7 minority (2 African Americans, 4 Asian Americans or Pacific Islanders, 1 Hispanic American), 17 international. 62 applicants, 79% accepted. In 1998, 28 master's, 12 doctorates awarded. Terminal master's awarded for partial completion of doctoral program. *Degree requirements:* For master's, thesis not required; for doctorate, dissertation, qualifying exam required, foreign language not required. *Entrance requirements:* For master's, GRE General Test; for doctorate, GRE General Test, GRE Subject Test, TOEFL. *Application deadline:* For fall admission, 2/1 (priority date). Application fee: $25. *Financial aid:* Fellowships, research assistantships, teaching assistantships available. Financial aid application deadline: 2/1. *Unit head:* James Farrar, Chair, 716-275-4231. *Application contact:* Mary Fisher, Graduate Program Secretary, 716-275-0635.

University of San Francisco, College of Arts and Sciences, Department of Chemistry, San Francisco, CA 94117-1080. Offers MS. Part-time and evening/weekend programs available. *Faculty:* 7 full-time (2 women). *Students:* 11 full-time (8 women), 1 (woman) part-time; includes 4 minority (3 Asian Americans or Pacific Islanders, 1 Hispanic American), 7 international. Average age 29. 32 applicants, 72% accepted. In 1998, 5 degrees awarded. *Degree requirements:* For master's, thesis required, foreign language not required. *Entrance requirements:* For master's, GRE General Test, GRE Subject Test, BS in chemistry or related field. *Application deadline:* Applications are processed on a rolling basis. Application fee: $40 ($50 for international students). Tuition: Full-time $12,618; part-time $701 per unit. Tuition and fees vary according to course load, degree level, campus/location and program. *Financial aid:* In 1998–99, 10 students received aid; fellowships, research assistantships, teaching assistantships, career-related internships or fieldwork, Federal Work-Study, institutionally-sponsored loans, and tuition waivers (partial) available. Aid available to part-time students. Financial aid application deadline: 3/2. *Faculty research:* Organic photochemistry, genetics of chromatic adaptation, electron transfer processes in solution, metabolism of protein hormones. Total annual research expenditures: $75,000. *Unit head:* Dr. Jeff Curtis, Chairman, 415-422-6391, Fax: 415-422-2346, E-mail: curtis@alm.admin.usfca.edu.

See in-depth description on page 223.

University of Saskatchewan, College of Graduate Studies and Research, College of Arts and Sciences, Department of Chemistry, Saskatoon, SK S7N 5A2, Canada. Offers M Sc, PhD. *Degree requirements:* For master's and doctorate, thesis/dissertation required. *Entrance requirements:* For master's, CANTEST (minimum score of 4.5 required) or International English Language Testing System (minimum score of 6 required) or Michigan English Language Assessment Battery (minimum score of 80 required), orTOEFL (minimum score of 550 required; average 560); for doctorate, TOEFL.

The University of Scranton, Graduate School, Department of Chemistry, Program in Chemistry, Scranton, PA 18510. Offers MA, MS. Part-time and evening/weekend programs available. *Faculty:* 11 full-time (4 women), 1 part-time (0 women). *Students:* 4 full-time (1 woman), 3 part-time (1 woman), 3 international. Average age 24. 4 applicants, 100% accepted. In 1998, 2 degrees awarded. *Degree requirements:* For master's, thesis (for some programs), capstone experience required, foreign language not required. *Entrance requirements:* For master's, TOEFL (minimum score of 500 required), minimum GPA of 2.75. *Application deadline:* Applications are processed on a rolling basis. Application fee: $35. Tuition: Part-time $490 per credit. Required fees: $25 per semester. Tuition and fees vary according to program. *Financial aid:* Teaching assistantships, career-related internships or fieldwork, Federal Work-Study, and teaching fellowships available. Aid available to part-time students. Financial aid application deadline: 3/1. *Application contact:* Dr. Christopher A. Baumann, Director, 570-941-6389, Fax: 570-941-7510, E-mail: cab@tiger.uofs.edu.

The University of Scranton, Graduate School, Department of Chemistry, Program in Clinical Chemistry, Scranton, PA 18510. Offers MA, MS. Part-time and evening/weekend programs available. *Faculty:* 11 full-time (4 women), 1 part-time (0 women). Average age 28. 4 applicants, 100% accepted. In 1998, 5 degrees awarded. *Degree requirements:* For master's, thesis (for some programs), capstone experience required, foreign language not required. *Entrance requirements:* For master's, TOEFL (minimum score of 500 required), minimum GPA of 2.75. *Application deadline:* Applications are processed on a rolling basis. Application fee: $35. Tuition: Part-time $490 per credit. Required fees: $25 per semester. Tuition and fees vary according to program. *Financial aid:* Teaching assistantships, career-related internships or fieldwork, Federal Work-Study, and teaching fellowships available. Aid available to part-time students. Financial aid application deadline: 3/1. *Unit head:* Mary Jane Tiernan, Director of Graduate Admissions, 619-260-4524, Fax: 619-260-4158, E-mail: grads@acusd.edu. *Application contact:* Dr. Christopher A. Baumann, Director, 570-941-6389, Fax: 570-941-7510, E-mail: cab@tiger.uofs.edu.

University of South Carolina, Graduate School, College of Science and Mathematics, Department of Chemistry and Biochemistry, Columbia, SC 29208. Offers IMA, MAT, MS, PhD. IMA and MAT offered in cooperation with the College of Education. Part-time programs available. *Faculty:* 28 full-time (5 women). *Students:* 117 full-time (51 women), 9 part-time (4 women); includes 14 minority (7 African Americans, 5 Asian Americans or Pacific Islanders, 2 Hispanic Americans), 31 international. Average age 27. 376 applicants, 18% accepted. In 1998, 9

Chemistry

University of South Carolina (continued)
master's, 16 doctorates awarded. Terminal master's awarded for partial completion of doctoral program. *Degree requirements:* For master's and doctorate, thesis/dissertation required, foreign language not required. *Entrance requirements:* For master's and doctorate, GRE General Test. *Application deadline:* For fall admission, 4/15. Applications are processed on a rolling basis. Application fee: $35. Electronic applications accepted. Tuition, state resident: full-time $4,014; part-time $202 per credit hour. Tuition, nonresident: full-time $8,528; part-time $428 per credit hour. Required fees: $100; $4 per credit hour. Tuition and fees vary according to program. *Financial aid:* In 1998–99, 13 fellowships, 54 teaching assistantships were awarded.; Federal Work-Study, institutionally-sponsored loans, and tuition waivers (full) also available. Financial aid application deadline: 4/15. *Faculty research:* Spectroscopy, crystallography, organic and organometallic synthesis, analytical chemistry, materials, optical sensing. *Unit head:* Dr. R. Bruce Dunlap, Chair, 803-777-5264, Fax: 803-777-9521. *Application contact:* Dr. John Dawson, Chairman, Graduate Admissions, 803-777-7234.

University of South Dakota, Graduate School, College of Arts and Sciences, Department of Chemistry, Vermillion, SD 57069-2390. Offers MA, MNS. *Faculty:* 6 full-time (0 women), 1 part-time (0 women). *Students:* 8 full-time (3 women), 5 international. 16 applicants, 50% accepted. In 1998, 5 degrees awarded. *Degree requirements:* For master's, thesis, oral and written comprehensive exams required, foreign language not required. *Entrance requirements:* For master's, GRE. *Application deadline:* Applications are processed on a rolling basis. Application fee: $15. *Financial aid:* Research assistantships, teaching assistantships available. Aid available to part-time students. *Faculty research:* Electrochemistry, photochemistry, inorganic synthesis, environmental and solid-state chemistry. *Unit head:* Dr. Miles Kopang, Chair, 605-677-5487.

University of Southern California, Graduate School, College of Letters, Arts and Sciences, Department of Chemistry, Program in Chemistry, Los Angeles, CA 90089. Offers MA, MS, PhD. *Students:* 110 full-time (29 women); includes 20 minority (1 African American, 17 Asian Americans or Pacific Islanders, 2 Hispanic Americans), 49 international. Average age 26. 822 applicants, 3% accepted. In 1998, 4 master's, 11 doctorates awarded. *Degree requirements:* For master's and doctorate, thesis/dissertation, qualifying exam required. *Entrance requirements:* For master's and doctorate, GRE General Test. *Application deadline:* For fall admission, 4/1 (priority date). Application fee: $0. Tuition: Full-time $22,198; part-time $748 per unit. Required fees: $406. Tuition and fees vary according to program. *Financial aid:* In 1998–99, 92 students received aid, including 23 fellowships with tuition reimbursements available (averaging $18,660 per year), 18 research assistantships with tuition reimbursements available (averaging $18,660 per year), 52 teaching assistantships with tuition reimbursements available (averaging $18,660 per year); Federal Work-Study and institutionally-sponsored loans also available. Financial aid application deadline: 3/1. *Application contact:* Paul Langford, Coordinator, 213-740-7036, Fax: 213-740-2701, E-mail: chemmail@cheml.usc.edu.

Announcement: The Department of Chemistry offers excellent opportunities for graduate research in organic, biological, inorganic, polymer, physical, and theoretical chemistries; chemical physics; and surface science. USC is the home for the Hydrocarbon Research Institute and the Center for the Study of Fast Transient Processes, which are on the cutting edge of research in hydrocarbon chemistry and chemical dynamics, respectively. The department is well equipped with instruments, including NMR, EPR, X-ray, SQUID, GC/MS, and a variety of lasers and excellent computing facilities, including a molecular modeling facility. For further inquiries, e-mail at chemmail@cheml.usc.edu or fax 213-740-2701. Web site: http://www.usc.edu/dept/chemistry.

University of Southern Mississippi, Graduate School, College of Science and Technology, Department of Chemistry and Biochemistry, Hattiesburg, MS 39406-5167. Offers analytical chemistry (MS, PhD); biochemistry (MS, PhD); inorganic chemistry (MS, PhD); organic chemistry (MS, PhD); physical chemistry (MS, PhD). *Faculty:* 16 full-time (2 women), 1 part-time (0 women). *Students:* 25 full-time (10 women); includes 8 minority (3 African Americans, 4 Asian Americans or Pacific Islanders, 1 Hispanic American) Average age 28. 44 applicants, 23% accepted. In 1998, 3 master's, 4 doctorates awarded. *Degree requirements:* For master's, thesis required, foreign language not required; for doctorate, 2 foreign languages (computer language can substitute for one), dissertation required. *Entrance requirements:* For master's, GRE General Test, TOEFL, minimum GPA of 2.75; for doctorate, GRE General Test, TOEFL, minimum GPA of 3.5. *Application deadline:* For fall admission, 8/6 (priority date). Applications are processed on a rolling basis. Application fee: $0 ($25 for international students). Tuition, state resident: full-time $2,250; part-time $137 per semester hour. Tuition, nonresident: full-time $3,102; part-time $172 per semester hour. Required fees: $602. *Financial aid:* Fellowships, research assistantships, teaching assistantships, Federal Work-Study and institutionally-sponsored loans available. Aid available to part-time students. Financial aid application deadline: 3/15. *Faculty research:* Plant biochemistry, photo chemistry, polymer chemistry, x-ray analysis, enzyme chemistry. *Unit head:* Dr. Stella Elakovich, Chair, 601-266-4701. *Application contact:* Dr. Gordon Cannon, 601-266-4702.

University of South Florida, Graduate School, College of Arts and Sciences, Department of Chemistry, Tampa, FL 33620-9951. Offers analytical chemistry (MS, PhD); biochemistry (MS, PhD); inorganic chemistry (MS, PhD); organic chemistry (MS, PhD); physical chemistry (MS, PhD). Part-time programs available. *Faculty:* 23 full-time (3 women), 3 part-time (1 woman). *Students:* 44 full-time (14 women), 10 part-time (1 woman); includes 2 African Americans, 3 Hispanic Americans Average age 30. 36 applicants, 67% accepted. In 1998, 4 master's, 4 doctorates awarded. Terminal master's awarded for partial completion of doctoral program. *Degree requirements:* For master's, thesis required; for doctorate, 2 foreign languages (computer language can substitute for one), dissertation, colloquium required. *Entrance requirements:* For master's and doctorate, GRE General Test (minimum combined score of 1000 required), minimum GPA of 3.0 in last 30 hours of chemistry course work. *Average time to degree:* Master's–2.5 years full-time, 5 years part-time; doctorate–5 years full-time, 8 years part-time. *Application deadline:* For fall admission, 6/5 (priority date); for spring admission, 10/23 (priority date). Applications are processed on a rolling basis. Application fee: $20. Electronic applications accepted. Tuition, state resident: part-time $148 per credit hour. Tuition, nonresident: part-time $509 per credit hour. *Financial aid:* In 1998–99, 48 students received aid, including 1 fellowship, 11 research assistantships with tuition reimbursements available (averaging $15,000 per year), 44 teaching assistantships with tuition reimbursements available (averaging $13,300 per year); Federal Work-Study and institutionally-sponsored loans also available. Aid available to part-time students. Financial aid applicants required to submit FAFSA. *Faculty research:* Synthesis, bioorganic chemistry, bioinorganic chemistry, environmental chemistry, NMR. Total annual research expenditures: $600,000. *Unit head:* Dr. Robert Potter, Chairperson, 813-974-4129, Fax: 813-974-1731, E-mail: potter@chuma1.cas.usf.edu. *Application contact:* Andy Zekter, Graduate Director, 813-974-9666, Fax: 813-974-3203, E-mail: zekter@chuma1.cas.usf.edu.

University of Tennessee, Knoxville, Graduate School, College of Arts and Sciences, Department of Chemistry, Knoxville, TN 37996. Offers analytical chemistry (MS, PhD); chemical physics (PhD); environmental chemistry (MS, PhD); inorganic chemistry (MS, PhD); organic chemistry (MS, PhD); physical chemistry (MS, PhD); polymer chemistry (MS, PhD); theoretical chemistry (PhD). Part-time programs available. *Faculty:* 31 full-time (1 woman), 1 (woman) part-time. *Students:* 55 full-time (15 women), 44 part-time (11 women); includes 1 minority (Asian American or Pacific Islander), 23 international. 105 applicants, 45% accepted. In 1998, 10 master's, 10 doctorates awarded. Terminal master's awarded for partial completion of doctoral program. *Degree requirements:* For master's and doctorate, thesis/dissertation required, foreign language not required. *Entrance requirements:* For master's and doctorate, GRE General Test, TOEFL (minimum score of 550 required), minimum GPA of 2.7. *Application deadline:* For fall admission, 2/1 (priority date). Applications are processed on a rolling basis. Application fee: $35. Electronic applications accepted. *Financial aid:* In 1998–99, 9 fellowships, 62 research assistantships, 73 teaching assistantships were awarded.; Federal Work-Study and institutionally-sponsored loans also available. Financial aid application deadline: 2/1; financial aid applicants required to submit FAFSA. *Unit head:* Dr. Michael Sepaniak, Head, 423-974-3141, Fax: 423-974-3454, E-mail: msepaniak@utk.edu. *Application contact:* Dr. Charles Feigerle, Graduate Representative, E-mail: cfeigerle@utk.edu.

The University of Texas at Arlington, Graduate School, College of Science, Department of Chemistry and Biochemistry, Arlington, TX 76019. Offers applied chemistry (PhD); chemistry (MS, PhD). *Faculty:* 14 full-time (0 women). *Students:* 28 full-time (11 women), 6 part-time (1 woman); includes 2 minority (both Asian Americans or Pacific Islanders), 22 international. 63 applicants, 25% accepted. In 1998, 4 doctorates awarded. *Degree requirements:* For master's, thesis required (for some programs), foreign language not required; for doctorate, computer language, internship, oral defense of dissertation required. *Entrance requirements:* For master's and doctorate, GRE General Test (minimum combined score of 1100 required). *Application deadline:* Applications are processed on a rolling basis. Application fee: $25 ($50 for international students). Tuition, state resident: full-time $1,368; part-time $76 per semester hour. Tuition, nonresident: full-time $5,454; part-time $303 per semester hour. Required fees: $66 per semester hour. $86 per term. Tuition and fees vary according to course load. *Financial aid:* Fellowships, research assistantships, teaching assistantships, career-related internships or fieldwork, Federal Work-Study, institutionally-sponsored loans, and tuition waivers (partial) available. *Unit head:* Dr. Ronald L. Elsenbaumer, Chairman, 817-272-3171, Fax: 817-272-3808, E-mail: elsenbaumer@uta.edu. *Application contact:* Dr. Richard B. Timmons, Graduate Adviser, 817-272-3171, Fax: 817-272-3808, E-mail: timmons@uta.edu.

Announcement: The Department of Chemistry and Biochemistry offers a program leading to the PhD in applied chemistry. In addition to the traditional PhD curriculum and dissertation, this program offers a paid industrial internship at a major US corporation and a series of survey courses in various aspects of applied chemistry. Graduates from this program have been 100% successful in obtaining employment after completion of this degree. The program is ideally suited for students interested in a career in chemical industry or in academics. The department is active in a wide range of modern chemical/biochemical/materials research areas. Visit the department's Web site at http://utachem.uta.edu.

The University of Texas at Austin, Graduate School, College of Natural Sciences, Department of Chemistry and Biochemistry, Austin, TX 78712-1111. Offers analytical chemistry (MA, PhD); biochemistry (MA, PhD); inorganic chemistry (MA, PhD); organic chemistry (MA, PhD); physical chemistry (MA, PhD). *Students:* 278 (94 women); includes 28 minority (3 African Americans, 11 Asian Americans or Pacific Islanders, 13 Hispanic Americans, 1 Native American) 61 international. 228 applicants, 43% accepted. In 1998, 18 master's, 32 doctorates awarded. *Entrance requirements:* For master's and doctorate, GRE General Test. Application fee: $50 ($75 for international students). *Financial aid:* Fellowships, research assistantships, teaching assistantships, scholarships available. Financial aid application deadline: 2/1. *Unit head:* Dr. Marvin L. Hackert, Chairman, 512-471-3949. *Application contact:* Dr. Jennifer Brodbelt, Graduate Adviser, 512-471-0028.

The University of Texas at Dallas, School of Natural Sciences and Mathematics, Programs in Chemistry, Richardson, TX 75083-0688. Offers chemistry (MS); industrial chemistry (D Chem). Part-time and evening/weekend programs available. *Students:* 52 full-time (21 women), 5 part-time (2 women); includes 11 minority (2 African Americans, 7 Asian Americans or Pacific Islanders, 2 Hispanic Americans), 24 international. Average age 28. In 1998, 12 master's, 5 doctorates awarded. *Degree requirements:* For master's, thesis (for some programs), thesis or internship required, foreign language not required; for doctorate, research practicums required, foreign language and thesis not required. *Entrance requirements:* For master's, GRE General Test (minimum combined score of 1100 required), TOEFL (minimum score of 660 required), minimum GPA of 3.0 in upper-level course work in field; for doctorate, GRE General Test (minimum combined score of 1100 required), TOEFL (minimum score of 600 required), minimum GPA of 3.0 in upper-level course work in field. *Application deadline:* For fall admission, 7/15; for spring admission, 11/15. Applications are processed on a rolling basis. Application fee: $25 ($75 for international students). *Financial aid:* Fellowships, research assistantships, teaching assistantships, career-related internships or fieldwork, Federal Work-Study, grants, institutionally-sponsored loans, and scholarships available. Aid available to part-time students. Financial aid application deadline: 4/30; financial aid applicants required to submit FAFSA. *Faculty research:* Organic photochemistry, bioinorganic chemistry, organic solid-state and polymer chemistry, environmental chemistry, scanning probe microscopy. *Unit head:* Dr. John Ferraris, Head, 972-883-2901, Fax: 972-883-2925, E-mail: ferraris@utdallas.edu. *Application contact:* Janie Jury, Graduate Student Adviser, 972-883-2902, Fax: 972-883-2925, E-mail: jjury@utdallas.edu.

The University of Texas at El Paso, Graduate School, College of Science, Department of Chemistry, El Paso, TX 79968-0001. Offers MS. Part-time programs available. *Faculty:* 11 full-time (0 women), 3 part-time (0 women). *Students:* 20 full-time (7 women), 3 part-time (1 woman); includes 6 minority (1 Asian American or Pacific Islander, 5 Hispanic Americans), 15 international. Average age 29. 25 applicants, 44% accepted. In 1998, 10 degrees awarded. *Degree requirements:* For master's, thesis required, foreign language not required. *Entrance requirements:* For master's, GRE General Test, TOEFL (minimum score of 550 required), minimum GPA of 3.0. *Application deadline:* Applications are processed on a rolling basis. Application fee: $15 ($65 for international students). Electronic applications accepted. Tuition, state resident: full-time $2,118. Tuition, nonresident: full-time $7,230. Tuition and fees vary according to program. *Financial aid:* In 1998–99, 6 fellowships, 6 research assistantships, 11 teaching assistantships were awarded.; Federal Work-Study and tuition waivers (partial) also available. Financial aid applicants required to submit FAFSA. *Faculty research:* Advanced materials, environmental chemistry, organometallic chemistry, organic synthesis, physical chemistry. Total annual research expenditures: $619,156. *Unit head:* Russell Chianelli, Chairperson, 915-747-5701. *Application contact:* Susan Jordan, Director, Graduate Student Services, 915-747-5491, Fax: 915-747-5788, E-mail: sjordan@utep.edu.

The University of Texas at San Antonio, College of Sciences and Engineering, Division of Earth and Physical Sciences, San Antonio, TX 78249-0617. Offers chemistry (MS); environmental sciences (MS); geology (MS). *Faculty:* 22 full-time (1 woman), 27 part-time (6 women). *Students:* 22 full-time (11 women), 83 part-time (29 women); includes 27 minority (2 African Americans, 6 Asian Americans or Pacific Islanders, 19 Hispanic Americans), 6 international. *Entrance requirements:* For master's, GRE General Test. *Application deadline:* For fall admission, 7/1. Applications are processed on a rolling basis. Application fee: $25. *Unit head:* Dr. Weldon Hammond, Interim Director, 210-458-4455.

The University of Texas at Tyler, Graduate Studies, College of Sciences and Mathematics, Department of Chemistry, Tyler, TX 75799-0001. Offers interdisciplinary studies (MS). *Faculty:* 4 full-time (0 women). *Degree requirements:* For master's, foreign language and thesis not required. *Entrance requirements:* For master's, GRE General Test (minimum combined score of 1000 required), BS in chemistry, minimum GPA of 2.5 in last 60 hours. Application fee: $0. *Financial aid:* Application deadline: 7/1. *Faculty research:* Bioremediation, development of smart polymers, organic synthesis. Total annual research expenditures: $9,000. *Unit head:* Dr. Don McClaugherty, Chair, 903-566-7196, Fax: 903-566-7189, E-mail: dmcclaug@mail.uttyl.edu. *Application contact:* Martha D. Wheat, Director of Admissions and Student Records, 903-566-7201, Fax: 903-566-7068.

University of the Pacific, Graduate School, Department of Chemistry, Stockton, CA 95211-0197. Offers biochemistry (MS, PhD); chemistry (MS, PhD). *Faculty:* 10 full-time (0 women). *Students:* 6 full-time (1 woman), 10 part-time (5 women), 14 international. In 1998, 4 master's awarded. Terminal master's awarded for partial completion of doctoral program. *Degree requirements:* For master's, thesis required, foreign language not required; for doctorate, one foreign language (computer language can substitute), dissertation required. *Entrance requirements:* For master's and doctorate, GRE General Test, GRE Subject Test. *Application deadline:* For fall admission, 3/1 (priority date); for spring admission, 10/15. Applications are processed on a rolling basis. Application fee: $50. *Financial aid:* Teaching assistantships, institutionally-sponsored loans available. Aid available to part-time students. Financial aid application deadline: 3/1. *Unit head:* Dr. Pat Jones, Chairman, 209-946-2241, E-mail: pjones@uop.edu.

University of Toledo, Graduate School, College of Arts and Sciences, Department of Chemistry, Toledo, OH 43606-3398. Offers analytical chemistry (MS, MS Ed, PhD); biological chemistry (MS, MS Ed, PhD); inorganic chemistry (MS, MS Ed, PhD); organic chemistry (MS, MS Ed, PhD); physical chemistry (MS, MS Ed, PhD). Part-time programs available. *Degree requirements:* For master's and doctorate, thesis/dissertation required, foreign language not required. *Entrance requirements:* For master's and doctorate, GRE General Test, GRE Subject Test, TOEFL. Electronic applications accepted. *Faculty research:* Enzymology, materials chemistry, crystallography, theoretical chemistry.

University of Toronto, School of Graduate Studies, Physical Sciences Division, Department of Chemistry, Toronto, ON M5S 1A1, Canada. Offers M Sc, PhD. *Degree requirements:* For master's and doctorate, thesis/dissertation required.

University of Tulsa, Graduate School, College of Engineering and Applied Sciences, Department of Chemistry, Tulsa, OK 74104-3189. Offers MS. *Faculty:* 8 full-time (0 women). 1 applicants, 100% accepted. *Degree requirements:* Foreign language not required. *Entrance requirements:* For master's, GRE General Test, TOEFL, bachelor's degree with 32 hours of undergraduate chemistry, minimum GPA of 3.0. *Application deadline:* Applications are processed on a rolling basis. Application fee: $30. Electronic applications accepted. Tuition: Full-time $8,640; part-time $480 per hour. Required fees: $3 per hour. One-time fee: $200 full-time. Tuition and fees vary according to program. *Financial aid:* In 1998–99, 1 student received aid, including 1 research assistantship with full and partial tuition reimbursement available (averaging $8,000 per year); career-related internships or fieldwork, Federal Work-Study, and tuition waivers (partial) also available. Aid available to part-time students. Financial aid application deadline: 2/1. *Unit head:* Dr. Dale C. Teeters, Chairperson, 918-631-3147, Fax: 918-631-3404, E-mail: dale_teeters@utulsa.edu.

University of Utah, Graduate School, College of Science, Department of Chemistry, Salt Lake City, UT 84112-1107. Offers chemical physics (PhD); chemistry (M Phil, MA, MS, PhD); science teacher education (MS). *Faculty:* 29 full-time (2 women), 27 part-time (2 women). *Students:* 136 full-time (38 women), 14 part-time (3 women); includes 12 minority (1 African American, 6 Asian Americans or Pacific Islanders, 2 Hispanic Americans, 3 Native Americans), 26 international. Average age 27. In 1998, 9 master's, 19 doctorates awarded. Terminal master's awarded for partial completion of doctoral program. *Degree requirements:* For master's, thesis or alternative required; for doctorate, dissertation, exams required, foreign language not required. *Entrance requirements:* For master's and doctorate, TOEFL (minimum score of 500 required). *Application deadline:* For fall admission, 7/1. Application fee: $30 ($50 for international students). *Financial aid:* In 1998–99, 53 teaching assistantships were awarded. *Faculty research:* Theoretical, inorganic, organic, and physical-analytical chemistry. *Unit head:* C. Dale Poulter, Chair, 801-581-6685, Fax: 801-581-4391. *Application contact:* Charles A. Wight, Director of Graduate Studies, 801-581-8796.

University of Vermont, Graduate College, College of Arts and Sciences, Department of Chemistry, Burlington, VT 05405-0160. Offers chemistry (MS, MST, PhD); chemistry education (MAT). *Accreditation:* NCATE (one or more programs are accredited). *Degree requirements:* For master's, one foreign language (computer language can substitute), thesis required; for doctorate, 2 foreign languages (computer language can substitute for one), dissertation required. *Entrance requirements:* For master's and doctorate, GRE General Test, TOEFL (minimum score of 550 required).

University of Victoria, Faculty of Graduate Studies, Faculty of Science, Department of Chemistry, Victoria, BC V8W 2Y2, Canada. Offers M Sc, PhD. *Faculty:* 17 full-time (2 women), 1 part-time. *Students:* 32 full-time (10 women), 10 international. Average age 26. 19 applicants, 53% accepted. In 1998, 1 master's, 10 doctorates awarded. *Degree requirements:* For master's and doctorate, thesis/dissertation required, foreign language not required. *Entrance requirements:* For master's and doctorate, GRE Subject Test (score in 85th percentile or higher required), TOEFL (minimum score of 575 required). *Average time to degree:* Master's–2.96 years full-time; doctorate–5.06 years full-time. *Application deadline:* For fall admission, 5/31 (priority date). Applications are processed on a rolling basis. Application fee: $50. *Financial aid:* In 1998–99, 8 fellowships were awarded.; research assistantships, teaching assistantships, career-related internships or fieldwork, institutionally-sponsored loans, and awards also available. Financial aid application deadline: 2/15. *Faculty research:* Laser spectroscopy and dynamics; inorganic, organic, and organometallic synthesis; electro and surface chemistry. Total annual research expenditures: $900,000. *Unit head:* Dr. P. C. Wan, Chair, 250-721-7150. *Application contact:* Dr. W. J. Balfour, Graduate Adviser, 250-721-7168, Fax: 250-721-7147, E-mail: chemoff@uvic.ca.

University of Virginia, College and Graduate School of Arts and Sciences, Department of Chemistry, Charlottesville, VA 22903. Offers chemistry (MA, MS, PhD); chemistry education (MAT). *Accreditation:* NCATE (one or more programs are accredited). *Faculty:* 26 full-time (2 women), 1 (woman) part-time. *Students:* 118 full-time (40 women); includes 8 minority (3 African Americans, 4 Asian Americans or Pacific Islanders, 1 Hispanic American), 14 international. Average age 26. 79 applicants, 92% accepted. In 1998, 15 master's, 16 doctorates awarded. *Degree requirements:* For master's and doctorate, thesis/dissertation required, foreign language not required. *Entrance requirements:* For master's and doctorate, GRE General Test, GRE Subject Test. *Application deadline:* For fall admission, 7/15; for spring admission, 12/1. Applications are processed on a rolling basis. Application fee: $60. *Financial aid:* Application deadline: 2/1. *Unit head:* Timothy L. MacDonald, Chairman, 804-924-3344. *Application contact:* Duane J. Osheim, Associate Dean, 804-924-7184, E-mail: grad-a-s@virginia.edu.

University of Washington, Graduate School, College of Arts and Sciences, Department of Chemistry, Seattle, WA 98195. Offers MS, PhD. Terminal master's awarded for partial completion of doctoral program. *Degree requirements:* For master's, thesis required (for some programs), foreign language not required; for doctorate, dissertation required, foreign language not required. *Entrance requirements:* For master's and doctorate, GRE General Test, TOEFL (minimum score of 580 required), TSE (minimum score of 55 required), minimum GPA of 3.0. Tuition, state resident: full-time $5,196; part-time $475 per credit. Tuition, nonresident: full-time $13,485; part-time $1,285 per credit. Required fees: $387; $38 per credit. Tuition and fees vary according to course load. *Faculty research:* Biopolymers, spectroscopy, reaction mechanisms, catalysis, synthesis, instrumental analysis.

University of Waterloo, Graduate Studies, Guelph-Waterloo Centre for Graduate Work in Chemistry and Biochemistry, Waterloo, ON N2L 3G1, Canada. Offers chemistry (M Sc, PhD). Part-time programs available. *Faculty:* 29 full-time (4 women), 25 part-time (1 woman). *Students:* 86 full-time (30 women), 3 part-time (2 women). In 1998, 16 master's, 7 doctorates awarded. *Degree requirements:* For master's; for doctorate, dissertation required. *Entrance requirements:* For master's, TOEFL (minimum score of 580 required), honors degree, minimum B average; for doctorate, TOEFL (minimum score of 580 required), master's degree. Application fee: $60. *Expenses:* Tuition and fees charges are reported in Canadian dollars. Tuition, state resident: full-time $3,168 Canadian dollars; part-time $792 Canadian dollars per term. Tuition, nonresident: full-time $8,000 Canadian dollars; part-time $2,000 Canadian dollars. Required fees: $45 Canadian dollars per term. Tuition and fees vary according to program. *Financial aid:* Research assistantships, teaching assistantships available. *Faculty research:* Analytical, polymer, physical, inorganic, organic, and theoretical chemistry. *Unit head:* Dr. R. J. Balahura, Director, 519-824-4120 Ext. 3848, Fax: 519-766-9220. *Application contact:* A. Wetmore, Administrative Assistant, 519-824-4120 Ext. 3848, Fax: 519-766-9220, E-mail: gwc@uoguelph.ca.

The University of Western Ontario, Faculty of Graduate Studies, Physical Sciences Division, Department of Chemistry, London, ON N6A 5B8, Canada. Offers M Sc, PhD. *Degree requirements:* For master's and doctorate, thesis/dissertation required. *Entrance requirements:* For master's, minimum B+ average, honors B Sc; for doctorate, M Sc or equivalent. Electronic applications accepted. *Faculty research:* Analytical, inorganic, organic, physical and theoretical chemistry.

University of Windsor, College of Graduate Studies and Research, Faculty of Science, Department of Chemistry and Biochemistry, Windsor, ON N9B 3P4, Canada. Offers biochemistry (M Sc, PhD); chemistry (M Sc, PhD); clinical chemistry (M Sc, PhD). Part-time programs available. *Degree requirements:* For master's and doctorate, thesis/dissertation required. *Entrance requirements:* For master's, TOEFL (minimum score of 550 required), minimum B average; for doctorate, TOEFL (minimum score of 550 required), master's degree. *Faculty research:* Analytical chemistry, organic chemistry, toxicology.

University of Wisconsin–Madison, Graduate School, College of Engineering, Water Chemistry Program, Madison, WI 53706-1380. Offers MS, PhD. Part-time programs available. *Faculty:* 2 full-time (0 women), 2 part-time (0 women). *Students:* 8 full-time (3 women), 2 international. 5 applicants, 40% accepted. In 1998, 2 doctorates awarded (100% found work related to degree). Terminal master's awarded for partial completion of doctoral program. *Degree requirements:* For master's, thesis or alternative required, foreign language not required; for doctorate, dissertation required, foreign language not required. *Entrance requirements:* For master's and doctorate, GRE General Test. *Application deadline:* For fall admission, 1/1 (priority date). Application fee: $45. Electronic applications accepted. *Financial aid:* Fellowships, research assistantships, Federal Work-Study and institutionally-sponsored loans available. Financial aid application deadline: 1/1. *Faculty research:* Chemical limnology, chemical remediation, geochemistry, photocatalysis, water quality. *Unit head:* Dr. David E. Armstrong, Chair, 608-263-3264, E-mail: armstron@engr.wisc.edu. *Application contact:* Ann McLain, Student Services Coordinator, 608-263-3264, Fax: 608-265-2340, E-mail: asmclain@facstaff.wisc.edu.

University of Wisconsin–Madison, Graduate School, College of Letters and Science, Department of Chemistry, Madison, WI 53706-1380. Offers MS, PhD. Part-time programs available. *Faculty:* 39 full-time (2 women), 5 part-time (2 women). *Students:* 202 full-time (61 women), 1 part-time; includes 9 minority (6 Asian Americans or Pacific Islanders, 3 Hispanic Americans), 58 international. Average age 24. 356 applicants, 46% accepted. In 1998, 21 master's, 41 doctorates awarded. Terminal master's awarded for partial completion of doctoral program. *Degree requirements:* For master's, thesis required (for some programs), foreign language not required; for doctorate, dissertation, cumulative exams, research proposal, seminar required, foreign language not required. *Average time to degree:* Master's–1.5 years full-time; doctorate–5.5 years full-time. *Application deadline:* For fall admission, 2/15 (priority date). Applications are processed on a rolling basis. Application fee: $45. *Financial aid:* In 1998–99, 203 students received aid, including 7 fellowships with full tuition reimbursements available (averaging $15,690 per year), 113 research assistantships with full tuition reimbursements available (averaging $15,525 per year), 78 teaching assistantships with full tuition reimbursements available (averaging $15,000 per year); traineeships also available. *Faculty research:* Analytical, inorganic, organic, physical, and macromolecular chemistry. Total annual research expenditures: $9.1 million. *Unit head:* Charles P. Casey, Chair, 608-262-1483, Fax: 608-262-3160, E-mail: chemdept@chem.wisc.edu. *Application contact:* Mary Kay Sorenson, Admissions Secretary, 800-442-6690, Fax: 608-262-3160, E-mail: sorenson@chem.wisc.edu.

University of Wisconsin–Milwaukee, Graduate School, College of Letters and Sciences, Department of Chemistry, Milwaukee, WI 53201-0413. Offers MS, PhD. *Faculty:* 21 full-time (2 women). *Students:* 57 full-time (27 women), 11 part-time (1 woman); includes 3 minority (1 African American, 2 Asian Americans or Pacific Islanders), 41 international. 82 applicants, 29% accepted. In 1998, 3 master's, 7 doctorates awarded. *Degree requirements:* For master's, thesis or alternative required, foreign language not required; for doctorate, dissertation required, foreign language not required. *Application deadline:* For fall admission, 1/1 (priority date); for spring admission, 9/1. Applications are processed on a rolling basis. Application fee: $45 ($75 for international students). *Financial aid:* In 1998–99, 3 fellowships, 16 research assistantships, 40 teaching assistantships were awarded.; career-related internships or fieldwork and unspecified assistantships also available. Aid available to part-time students. Financial aid application deadline: 4/15. *Unit head:* James Cook, Chair, 414-229-4098.

University of Wyoming, Graduate School, College of Arts and Sciences, Department of Chemistry, Laramie, WY 82071. Offers MS, MST, PhD. *Faculty:* 14 full-time (2 women), 4 part-time (0 women). *Students:* 37 full-time (11 women), 16 part-time (5 women); includes 3 minority (1 African American, 2 Asian Americans or Pacific Islanders), 8 international. 12 applicants, 58% accepted. In 1998, 2 master's, 7 doctorates awarded. *Degree requirements:* For master's and doctorate, thesis/dissertation required, foreign language not required. *Entrance requirements:* For master's and doctorate, GRE General Test, minimum GPA of 3.0. *Average time to degree:* Master's–2 years full-time; doctorate–4.5 years full-time. *Application deadline:* For fall admission, 4/15 (priority date). Applications are processed on a rolling basis. Application fee: $40. Electronic applications accepted. Tuition, state resident: full-time $2,520; part-time $140 per credit hour. Tuition, nonresident: full-time $7,790; part-time $433 per credit hour. Required fees: $400; $7 per credit hour. Full-time tuition and fees vary according to course load and program. *Financial aid:* In 1998–99, 2 fellowships, 26 research assistantships, 21 teaching assistantships were awarded.; traineeships and tuition waivers (full and partial) also available. Financial aid application deadline: 3/1. *Unit head:* Dr. Edward L. Clennan, Head, 307-766-2434, Fax: 307-766-2807. *Application contact:* Robert C. Corcoran, Graduate Admissions Committee, 307-766-4363, Fax: 307-766-2807, E-mail: rcc@uwyo.edu.

Utah State University, School of Graduate Studies, College of Science, Department of Chemistry and Biochemistry, Logan, UT 84322. Offers biochemistry (MS, PhD); chemistry (MS, PhD). Part-time programs available. *Faculty:* 19 full-time (2 women), 3 part-time (0 women). *Students:* 39 full-time (11 women), 14 part-time (5 women), 22 international. Average age 28. 48 applicants, 44% accepted. In 1998, 7 master's, 5 doctorates awarded. Terminal master's awarded for partial completion of doctoral program. *Degree requirements:* For master's and doctorate, thesis/dissertation, oral and written exams required, foreign language not required. *Entrance requirements:* For master's and doctorate, GRE General Test (score in 40th percentile or higher required), TOEFL (minimum score of 550 required), minimum GPA of 3.0. *Application deadline:* For fall admission, 4/15 (priority date); for spring admission, 10/15. Applications are processed on a rolling basis. Application fee: $40. Tuition, state resident: full-time $1,492. Tuition, nonresident: full-time $5,232. Required fees: $434. Tuition and fees vary according to course load. *Financial aid:* In 1998–99, 30 research assistantships with partial tuition reimbursements, 37 teaching assistantships with partial tuition reimbursements were awarded.; fellowships, Federal Work-Study, institutionally-sponsored loans, and tuition waivers (partial) also available. Aid available to part-time students. Financial aid application deadline: 4/15. *Faculty research:* Analytical, inorganic, organic, and physical chemistry. *Unit head:* Dr. Vernon Parker, Head, 435-797-1619, Fax: 435-797-3390. *Application contact:* Dr. Brad S. Davidson, Admissions Chair, 435-797-1628, Fax: 435-797-3390.

Vanderbilt University, Graduate School, Department of Chemistry, Nashville, TN 37240-1001. Offers MA, MAT, MS, PhD. *Faculty:* 20 full-time (2 women), 4 part-time (0 women). *Students:* 59 full-time (22 women); includes 3 minority (1 African American, 2 Asian Americans or Pacific Islanders), 18 international. Average age 26. 108 applicants, 41% accepted. In 1998, 5 master's, 9 doctorates awarded. *Degree requirements:* For master's, thesis or alternative required, foreign language not required; for doctorate, dissertation, area, qualifying, and final exams required, foreign language not required. *Entrance requirements:* For master's and doctorate, GRE General Test, GRE Subject Test (recommended). *Application deadline:* For fall admission, 1/15. Application fee: $40. *Financial aid:* In 1998–99, 53 students received aid, including research assistantships with full tuition reimbursements available (averaging $14,750 per year), 35 teaching assistantships with full tuition reimbursements available (averaging $14,750 per year); fellowships, Federal Work-Study, institutionally-sponsored loans, and traineeships also available. Financial aid application deadline: 1/15. *Faculty research:* Chemical synthesis; mechanistic, theoretical, bioorganic, analytical, and spectroscopic chemistry. *Unit head:* David M. Hercules, Chair, 615-322-2861, Fax: 615-322-4936, E-mail: hercules@ctrvax.

Chemistry

Vanderbilt University (continued)

vanderbilt.edu. *Application contact:* Charles M. Lukehart, Director of Graduate Studies, 615-322-2861, Fax: 615-322-4936, E-mail: lukehacm@ctrvax.vanderbilt.edu.

Vassar College, Graduate Programs, Department of Chemistry, Poughkeepsie, NY 12604. Offers MS. *Degree requirements:* For master's, one foreign language, thesis required. *Entrance requirements:* For master's, GRE General Test, bachelor's degree in related field. *Application deadline:* For fall admission, 1/1. Application fee: $60. *Unit head:* Marianne Begemann, Chair, 914-437-5730.

Villanova University, Graduate School of Liberal Arts and Sciences, Department of Chemistry, Villanova, PA 19085-1699. Offers MA, MS, PhD. Part-time and evening/weekend programs available. *Students:* 34 full-time (11 women), 9 part-time (4 women); includes 3 minority (all Asian Americans or Pacific Islanders), 8 international. Average age 31. 27 applicants, 78% accepted. In 1998, 12 master's, 6 doctorates awarded. Terminal master's awarded for partial completion of doctoral program. *Degree requirements:* For master's and doctorate, thesis/dissertation required, foreign language not required. *Entrance requirements:* For master's, GRE General Test, GRE Subject Test, minimum GPA of 3.0; for doctorate, minimum GPA of 3.0. *Application deadline:* For fall admission, 8/1 (priority date); for spring admission, 12/1. Application fee: $40. *Financial aid:* Research assistantships, Federal Work-Study available. Financial aid application deadline: 4/1; financial aid applicants required to submit FAFSA. *Unit head:* Dr. Robert Giuliano, Chair, 610-519-4840.

Virginia Commonwealth University, School of Graduate Studies, College of Humanities and Sciences, Department of Chemistry, Richmond, VA 23284-9005. Offers MS, PhD. Part-time programs available. *Faculty:* 16. *Students:* 33 full-time (12 women), 20 part-time (7 women); includes 14 minority (7 African Americans, 5 Asian Americans or Pacific Islanders, 1 Hispanic American, 1 Native American) In 1998, 2 master's, 4 doctorates awarded. Terminal master's awarded for partial completion of doctoral program. *Degree requirements:* For master's, thesis required, foreign language not required; for doctorate, dissertation, comprehensive cumulative exams, research proposal required. *Entrance requirements:* For master's and doctorate, GRE General Test, GRE Subject Test. *Application deadline:* For fall admission, 3/15 (priority date); for spring admission, 11/15. Applications are processed on a rolling basis. Application fee: $30. Tuition, state resident: full-time $4,031; part-time $224 per credit hour. Tuition, nonresident: full-time $11,946; part-time $664 per credit hour. Required fees: $1,081; $40 per credit hour. Tuition and fees vary according to campus/location and program. *Financial aid:* Fellowships, research assistantships, teaching assistantships, career-related internships or fieldwork and institutionally-sponsored loans available. Aid available to part-time students. Financial aid application deadline: 7/1. *Faculty research:* Physical, organic, inorganic, analytical, and polymer chemistry. *Unit head:* Dr. Fred M. Hawkridge, Chair, 804-828-7505, Fax: 804-828-8599, E-mail: fmhawkri@saturn.vcu.edu. *Application contact:* Dr. M. Sammy El-Shall, Graduate Program Director, 804-828-1298, Fax: 804-828-8599, E-mail: mselshal@vcu.edu.

Virginia Commonwealth University, School of Graduate Studies, School of Medicine Graduate Programs, Department of Biochemistry and Molecular Biophysics, Richmond, VA 23284-9005. Offers biochemistry and molecular biophysics (MS, CBHS); chemistry (PhD); molecular biology and genetics (PhD); neurosciences (PhD). *Students:* 21 full-time (7 women), 3 part-time (2 women); includes 11 minority (10 Asian Americans or Pacific Islanders, 1 Native American) *Degree requirements:* For master's, thesis required, foreign language not required; for doctorate, dissertation, comprehensive oral and written exams required, foreign language not required. *Entrance requirements:* For master's and doctorate, GRE General Test. *Application deadline:* For fall admission, 5/1. Application fee: $30. Tuition, state resident: full-time $4,031; part-time $224 per credit hour. Tuition, nonresident: full-time $11,946; part-time $664 per credit hour. Required fees: $1,081; $40 per credit hour. Tuition and fees vary according to campus/location and program. *Unit head:* Dr. Robert K. Yu, Chair, 804-828-9762, Fax: 804-828-1473. *Application contact:* Dr. Zendra E. Zehner, Program Director, 804-828-8753, Fax: 804-828-1473, E-mail: zezehner@vcu.edu.

Virginia Polytechnic Institute and State University, Graduate School, College of Arts and Sciences, Department of Chemistry, Blacksburg, VA 24061. Offers MS, PhD. Part-time programs available. *Faculty:* 26 full-time (0 women). *Students:* 95 full-time (35 women), 7 part-time (2 women); includes 17 minority (11 African Americans, 2 Asian Americans or Pacific Islanders, 4 Hispanic Americans), 32 international. Average age 25. 137 applicants, 50% accepted. In 1998, 7 master's, 14 doctorates awarded. Terminal master's awarded for partial completion of doctoral program. *Degree requirements:* For master's, thesis required (for some programs), foreign language not required; for doctorate, dissertation required, foreign language not required. *Entrance requirements:* For master's and doctorate, GRE General Test, GRE Subject Test, TOEFL (minimum score of 600 required). *Application deadline:* For fall admission, 12/1 (priority date). Applications are processed on a rolling basis. Application fee: $25. *Financial aid:* Fellowships, research assistantships, teaching assistantships, career-related internships or fieldwork, Federal Work-Study, institutionally-sponsored loans, and unspecified assistantships available. Aid available to part-time students. Financial aid application deadline: 4/1. *Faculty research:* Analytical, inorganic, organic, physical, and polymer chemistry. *Unit head:* Dr. Larry T. Taylor, Head, 540-231-5391, E-mail: betaylo3@vt.edu.

Wake Forest University, Graduate School, Department of Chemistry, Winston-Salem, NC 27109. Offers analytical chemistry (MS, PhD); inorganic chemistry (MS, PhD); organic chemistry (MS, PhD); physical chemistry (MS, PhD). Part-time programs available. *Faculty:* 14 full-time (1 woman). *Students:* 22 full-time (11 women), 2 part-time; includes 5 minority (2 African Americans, 3 Asian Americans or Pacific Islanders) Average age 28. 60 applicants, 22% accepted. In 1998, 1 master's awarded (100% found work related to degree); 3 doctorates awarded (100% found work related to degree). *Degree requirements:* For master's, one foreign language (computer language can substitute), thesis required; for doctorate, 2 foreign languages (computer language can substitute for one), dissertation required. *Entrance requirements:* For master's and doctorate, GRE General Test, GRE Subject Test. *Application deadline:* For fall admission, 2/15. Application fee: $25. *Financial aid:* In 1998–99, 13 research assistantships, 16 teaching assistantships were awarded.; scholarships also available. Aid available to part-time students. Financial aid application deadline: 2/15; financial aid applicants required to submit FAFSA. *Unit head:* Dr. Jim Fishbein, Director, 336-758-6139, E-mail: fishbein@wfu.edu.

See in-depth description on page 227.

Washington State University, Graduate School, College of Sciences, Department of Chemistry, Pullman, WA 99164. Offers analytical chemistry (MS, PhD); inorganic chemistry (MS, PhD); nuclear chemistry (MS, PhD); organic chemistry (MS, PhD); physical chemistry (MS, PhD). *Faculty:* 28 full-time (4 women). *Students:* 39 full-time (14 women), 3 part-time (2 women); includes 4 minority (2 Asian Americans or Pacific Islanders, 1 Hispanic American, 1 Native American), 8 international. Average age 25. In 1998, 5 master's, 7 doctorates awarded. Terminal master's awarded for partial completion of doctoral program. *Degree requirements:* For master's, oral exam, teaching experience required, thesis optional, foreign language not required; for doctorate, dissertation, oral exam, teaching experience required, foreign language not required. *Entrance requirements:* For master's and doctorate, GRE General Test, minimum GPA of 3.0. *Average time to degree:* Master's–2 years full-time; doctorate–4 years full-time. *Application deadline:* For fall admission, 3/1 (priority date). Applications are processed on a rolling basis. Application fee: $35. *Financial aid:* In 1998–99, 15 research assistantships, 25 teaching assistantships were awarded.; fellowships, Federal Work-Study, institutionally-sponsored loans, tuition waivers (partial), and teaching associateships also available. Financial aid application deadline: 4/1; financial aid applicants required to submit FAFSA. Total annual research expenditures: $1.9 million. *Unit head:* Dr. Ralph Yount, Chair, 509-335-1516. *Application contact:* James O. Schenk, Chair, Admissions Committee, 509-335-8866, E-mail: carrie@wsu.edu.

Washington University in St. Louis, Graduate School of Arts and Sciences, Department of Chemistry, St. Louis, MO 63130-4899. Offers MA, PhD. *Students:* 74 full-time (28 women); includes 4 minority (3 African Americans, 1 Asian American or Pacific Islander), 36 international. 142 applicants, 37% accepted. In 1998, 15 master's, 23 doctorates awarded. Terminal master's awarded for partial completion of doctoral program. *Degree requirements:* For master's, thesis or alternative required; for doctorate, dissertation required. *Entrance requirements:* For master's and doctorate, GRE General Test, GRE Subject Test. *Application deadline:* For fall admission, 1/15 (priority date). Applications are processed on a rolling basis. Application fee: $35. *Financial aid:* Fellowships, research assistantships, teaching assistantships, Federal Work-Study, institutionally-sponsored loans, and tuition waivers (full and partial) available. Financial aid application deadline: 1/15. *Unit head:* Dr. Joseph J. H. Ackerman, Chairman, 314-935-6593.

Wayne State University, Graduate School, College of Science, Department of Chemistry, Detroit, MI 48202. Offers MA, MS, PhD. *Degree requirements:* For master's, thesis required (for some programs); for doctorate, dissertation required. *Faculty research:* Natural products synthesis, coordination chemistry, molecular biology, chromatography, molecular mechanics calculations.

Wesleyan University, Graduate Programs, Department of Chemistry, Middletown, CT 06459-0260. Offers biochemistry (MA, PhD); chemical physics (MA, PhD); inorganic chemistry (MA, PhD); organic chemistry (MA, PhD); physical chemistry (MA, PhD); theoretical chemistry (MA, PhD). Terminal master's awarded for partial completion of doctoral program. *Degree requirements:* For master's and doctorate, one foreign language (computer language can substitute), thesis/dissertation required. *Entrance requirements:* For master's, GRE General Test, GRE Subject Test; for doctorate, GRE Subject Test.

See in-depth description on page 233.

West Chester University of Pennsylvania, Graduate Studies, College of Arts and Sciences, Department of Chemistry, West Chester, PA 19383. Offers chemistry (MS); clinical chemistry (MS). *Faculty:* 10 part-time. *Students:* 24. Average age 30. *Degree requirements:* For master's, one foreign language (computer language can substitute), comprehensive exam required, thesis optional. *Entrance requirements:* For master's, GRE General Test (recommended). *Application deadline:* For fall admission, 4/15 (priority date); for spring admission, 10/15. Applications are processed on a rolling basis. Application fee: $25. Tuition, state resident: full-time $3,780; part-time $210 per credit. Tuition, nonresident: full-time $6,610; part-time $367 per credit. Required fees: $684; $39 per credit. Tuition and fees vary according to course load. *Financial aid:* In 1998–99, 2 research assistantships with full tuition reimbursements (averaging $5,000 per year) were awarded. Aid available to part-time students. Financial aid application deadline: 2/15. *Unit head:* Dr. Jamal Ghoroghchian, Chair, 610-436-2631. *Application contact:* Dr. Naseer Ahmad, Graduate Coordinator, 610-436-2476, E-mail: anaseer@wcupa.edu.

Western Carolina University, Graduate School, College of Arts and Sciences, Department of Chemistry and Physics, Cullowhee, NC 28723. Offers MAT, MS. Part-time and evening/weekend programs available. *Faculty:* 13. *Students:* 6 full-time (3 women), 2 part-time (1 woman); includes 1 minority (African American) 12 applicants, 58% accepted. In 1998, 7 degrees awarded. *Degree requirements:* For master's, variable foreign language requirement, thesis, comprehensive exam required. *Entrance requirements:* For master's, GRE General Test. *Application deadline:* For fall admission, 5/1 (priority date); for spring admission, 10/1 (priority date). Applications are processed on a rolling basis. Application fee: $35. Tuition, state resident: full-time $918. Tuition, nonresident: full-time $8,188. Required fees: $881. *Financial aid:* In 1998–99, 7 students received aid, including 1 research assistantship with full and partial tuition reimbursement available (averaging $7,000 per year), 6 teaching assistantships with full and partial tuition reimbursements available (averaging $7,583 per year); fellowships, Federal Work-Study, grants, and institutionally-sponsored loans also available. Financial aid application deadline: 3/15; financial aid applicants required to submit FAFSA. *Unit head:* Paul Brandt, Head, 828-227-7260. *Application contact:* Kathleen Owen, Assistant to the Dean, 828-227-7398, Fax: 828-227-7480, E-mail: kowen@wcu.edu.

Western Illinois University, School of Graduate Studies, College of Arts and Sciences, Department of Chemistry, Macomb, IL 61455-1390. Offers MS. Part-time programs available. *Faculty:* 7 full-time (1 woman). *Students:* 7 full-time (2 women), 1 (woman) part-time; includes 1 minority (Asian American or Pacific Islander), 3 international. Average age 32. 5 applicants, 80% accepted. In 1998, 7 degrees awarded. *Degree requirements:* For master's, thesis or alternative required, foreign language not required. *Application deadline:* Applications are processed on a rolling basis. Application fee: $0 ($25 for international students). *Financial aid:* In 1998–99, 7 students received aid, including 7 research assistantships with full tuition reimbursements available (averaging $4,880 per year) Financial aid applicants required to submit FAFSA. *Faculty research:* Water quality, blood coagulation, biochemistry, organic chemistry, photoconversion. *Unit head:* Dr. N. Made Gowda, Chairperson, 309-298-1538. *Application contact:* Barbara Baily, Director of Graduate Studies, 309-298-1806, Fax: 309-298-2245, E-mail: barb_baily@ccmail.wiu.edu.

Western Kentucky University, Graduate Studies, Ogden College of Science, Technology, and Health, Department of Chemistry, Bowling Green, KY 42101-3576. Offers chemistry (MA Ed, MS). *Accreditation:* NCATE (one or more programs are accredited). Part-time programs available. *Faculty:* 14 full-time (0 women). *Students:* 10 full-time (2 women), 5 part-time (2 women); includes 2 minority (both Asian Americans or Pacific Islanders), 6 international. Average age 27. 17 applicants, 71% accepted. In 1998, 9 degrees awarded. *Degree requirements:* For master's, one foreign language (computer language can substitute), thesis, comprehensive exam required. *Entrance requirements:* For master's, GRE General Test, previous course work in chemistry (MS). *Average time to degree:* Master's–2 years full-time, 3 years part-time. *Application deadline:* For fall admission, 8/1 (priority date); for spring admission, 12/1. Applications are processed on a rolling basis. Application fee: $30. Tuition, state resident: full-time $2,590; part-time $140 per hour. Tuition, nonresident: full-time $6,430; part-time $387 per hour. Required fees: $370. *Financial aid:* In 1998–99, 5 research assistantships with partial tuition reimbursements (averaging $3,000 per year), 8 teaching assistantships with partial tuition reimbursements (averaging $3,000 per year) were awarded.; Federal Work-Study, institutionally-sponsored loans, and service awards also available. Aid available to part-time students. Financial aid application deadline: 4/1; financial aid applicants required to submit FAFSA. *Faculty research:* Coal chemistry. *Unit head:* Dr. Lowell Shank, Head, 270-745-4986, Fax: 270-745-5361, E-mail: lowell.shank@wku.edu. *Application contact:* Wei-Ping Pan, Professor, 270-745-5322, Fax: 270-745-5361, E-mail: wei-ping.pan@wku.edu.

Western Michigan University, Graduate College, College of Arts and Sciences, Department of Chemistry, Kalamazoo, MI 49008. Offers MA. *Students:* 4 full-time (1 woman), 18 part-time (7 women); includes 1 minority (Asian American or Pacific Islander), 16 international. 25 applicants, 56% accepted. In 1998, 3 degrees awarded. *Degree requirements:* For master's, thesis, departmental qualifying and oral exams required, foreign language not required. *Application deadline:* For fall admission, 2/15 (priority date). Applications are processed on a rolling basis. Application fee: $25. *Financial aid:* Fellowships, research assistantships, teaching assistantships, Federal Work-Study available. Financial aid application deadline: 2/15; financial aid applicants required to submit FAFSA. *Unit head:* Dr. Jay C. Means, Chairperson, 616-387-2923. *Application contact:* Paula J. Boodt, Coordinator, Graduate Admissions and Recruitment, 616-387-2000, Fax: 616-387-2355, E-mail: paula.boodt@wmich.edu.

Western Washington University, Graduate School, College of Arts and Sciences, Department of Chemistry, Bellingham, WA 98225-5996. Offers MS. Part-time programs available. *Faculty:* 17. *Students:* 5 full-time (1 woman), 1 part-time, 1 international. 5 applicants, 100% accepted. In 1998, 2 degrees awarded. *Degree requirements:* For master's, thesis required (for some programs), foreign language not required. *Entrance requirements:* For master's, GRE General Test, TOEFL, minimum GPA of 3.0 in last 60 semester hours or last 90 quarter hours. *Application deadline:* For fall admission, 6/1; for winter admission, 10/1; for spring admission, 2/1. Applications are processed on a rolling basis. Application fee: $35. Tuition, state resident: full-time $3,247; part-time $146 per credit hour. Tuition, nonresident: full-time $13,364; part-time $445 per credit hour. Required fees: $254; $85 per quarter. *Financial aid:* In 1998–99, 1 research assistantship with partial tuition reimbursement (averaging $7,563 per year), 2 teaching assistantships with partial tuition reimbursements (averaging $7,563 per year) were awarded.; career-related internships or fieldwork, Federal Work-Study, institutionally-sponsored loans, scholarships, and tuition waivers (partial) also available. Aid available to part-time students. Financial aid application deadline: 2/15; financial aid applicants required to submit FAFSA. *Unit head:* Dr. Mark Wicholas, Chair, 360-650-3071. *Application contact:* Dr. David Patrick, Graduate Adviser, 360-650-3128.

West Texas A&M University, College of Agriculture, Nursing, and Natural Sciences, Department of Mathematics, Physical Sciences and Engineering Technology, Program in Chemistry, Canyon, TX 79016-0001. Offers MS. Part-time programs available. *Faculty:* 4 full-time (0 women), 2 part-time (0 women). *Students:* 9 full-time (2 women), 4 part-time (1 woman), 4 international. Average age 34. 4 applicants, 25% accepted. In 1998, 4 degrees awarded. *Degree requirements:* For master's, comprehensive exam required, thesis optional, foreign language not required. *Entrance requirements:* For master's, GRE General Test (combined average 964). *Average time to degree:* Master's–3 years full-time, 6 years part-time. *Application deadline:* Applications are processed on a rolling basis. Application fee: $0 ($50 for international students). Electronic applications accepted. Tuition, state resident: full-time $1,152; part-time $48 per credit. Tuition, nonresident: full-time $6,336; part-time $264 per credit. Required fees: $1,063; $531 per semester. *Financial aid:* In 1998–99, 4 research assistantships (averaging $6,500 per year), 3 teaching assistantships (averaging $6,500 per year) were awarded.; career-related internships or fieldwork, Federal Work-Study, grants, institutionally-sponsored loans, scholarships, and tuition waivers (partial) also available. Aid available to part-time students. Financial aid applicants required to submit FAFSA. *Faculty research:* Biochemistry; inorganic, organic, and physical chemistry; vibrational spectroscopy; magnetic susceptibilities; carbene chemistry. *Unit head:* Dr. Chris Suczek, Graduate Adviser, 360-650-3590. *Application contact:* Dr. Gene Carlisle, Graduate Adviser, 806-651-2282, E-mail: gcarlisle.mail.wtamu.edu.

West Virginia University, Eberly College of Arts and Sciences, Department of Chemistry, Morgantown, WV 26506. Offers MS, PhD. Part-time and evening/weekend programs available. Postbaccalaureate distance learning degree programs offered (no on-campus study). Terminal master's awarded for partial completion of doctoral program. *Degree requirements:* For master's, thesis required, foreign language not required; for doctorate, dissertation, comprehensive exam required, foreign language not required. *Entrance requirements:* For master's, GRE General Test, GRE Subject Test, TOEFL (minimum score of 600 required), minimum GPA of 2.5; for doctorate, GRE General Test, GRE Subject Test, TOEFL (minimum score of 600 required), minimum GPA of 3.0. *Faculty research:* Analytical, inorganic, organic, and physical chemistry; polymers; material science.

See in-depth description on page 237.

Wichita State University, Graduate School, Fairmount College of Liberal Arts and Sciences, Department of Chemistry, Wichita, KS 67260. Offers MS, PhD. *Faculty:* 12 full-time (0 women), 1 part-time (0 women). *Students:* 13 full-time (0 women), 16 part-time (7 women); includes 1 minority (Asian American or Pacific Islander), 22 international. Average age 28. 34 applicants, 41% accepted. In 1998, 3 master's, 5 doctorates awarded. *Degree requirements:* For master's, variable foreign language requirement, thesis required; for doctorate, computer language, dissertation, comprehensive exam required. *Entrance requirements:* For master's and doctorate, GRE, TOEFL (minimum score of 570 required). *Application deadline:* For fall admission, 7/1 (priority date); for spring admission, 1/1. Applications are processed on a rolling basis. Application fee: $25 ($40 for international students). Electronic applications accepted. *Financial aid:* In 1998–99, 8 research assistantships (averaging $6,000 per year), 12 teaching assistantships with full tuition reimbursements (averaging $10,000 per year) were awarded.; fellowships, Federal Work-Study and institutionally-sponsored loans also available. Financial aid application deadline: 4/1; financial aid applicants required to submit FAFSA. *Faculty research:* Biochemistry; analytic, inorganic, organic, and polymer chemistry. Total annual research expenditures: $716,084. *Unit head:* Dr. Paul Rillema, Chairperson, 316-978-3120, Fax: 316-978-3431, E-mail: rillema@twsuvm.uc.twsu.edu. *Application contact:* Dr. Dennis Burns, Graduate Coordinator, 316-978-3120, Fax: 316-978-3431, E-mail: burns@twsuvm.uc.twsu.edu.

Worcester Polytechnic Institute, Graduate Studies, Department of Chemistry and Biochemistry, Worcester, MA 01609-2280. Offers biochemistry (MS, PhD); chemistry (MS, PhD). *Faculty:* 11 full-time (1 woman). *Students:* 21 full-time (7 women), 1 (woman) part-time; includes 2 minority (1 Asian American or Pacific Islander, 1 Hispanic American), 12 international. 91 applicants, 37% accepted. In 1998, 3 master's awarded. *Degree requirements:* For master's and doctorate, thesis/dissertation required, foreign language not required. *Entrance requirements:* For master's and doctorate, GRE General Test (combined average 1899 on three sections), TOEFL (minimum score of 550 required; average 619). *Average time to degree:* Master's–2 years full-time; doctorate–5 years full-time. *Application deadline:* For fall admission, 2/15 (priority date); for spring admission, 10/15 (priority date). Applications are processed on a rolling basis. Application fee: $50. Electronic applications accepted. *Financial aid:* In 1998–99, 18 students received aid, including 5 research assistantships with full tuition reimbursements available (averaging $15,000 per year), 13 teaching assistantships with full tuition reimbursements available (averaging $11,970 per year); career-related internships or fieldwork, grants, institutionally-sponsored loans, and scholarships also available. Financial aid application deadline: 2/15; financial aid applicants required to submit FAFSA. *Faculty research:* Biomembrane studies, computational photochemistry, laser flash, photolysis, organic photochemistry, alkaloid synthesis. Total annual research expenditures: $531,351. *Unit head:* Dr. James P. Dittami, Head, 508-831-5149, Fax: 508-831-5933, E-mail: jdittami@wpi.edu. *Application contact:* W. Grant McGimpsey, Graduate Coordinator, 508-831-5486, Fax: 508-831-5933, E-mail: wgm@wpi.edu.

Wright State University, School of Graduate Studies, College of Science and Mathematics, Department of Chemistry, Dayton, OH 45435. Offers chemistry (MS); environmental sciences (MS). Part-time and evening/weekend programs available. *Students:* 22 full-time (14 women), 5 part-time (1 woman); includes 1 minority (Hispanic American), 6 international. Average age 28. 16 applicants, 63% accepted. In 1998, 16 degrees awarded. *Degree requirements:* For master's, oral defense of thesis, seminar required. *Entrance requirements:* For master's, TOEFL (minimum score of 600 required). *Application deadline:* For fall admission, 6/1 (priority date). Applications are processed on a rolling basis. Application fee: $25. *Financial aid:* Fellowships, research assistantships, teaching assistantships, unspecified assistantships available. Aid available to part-time students. Financial aid applicants required to submit FAFSA. *Faculty research:* Polymer synthesis and characterization, laser kinetics, organic and inorganic synthesis, analytical and environmental chemistry. Total annual research expenditures: $60,000. *Unit head:* Dr. M. Paul Servé, Chair, 937-775-2855, Fax: 937-775-2717. *Application contact:* Dr. Paul G. Seybold, Chair, Graduate Studies Committee, 937-775-2407, Fax: 937-775-2717.

Yale University, Graduate School of Arts and Sciences, Department of Chemistry, New Haven, CT 06520. Offers biophysical chemistry (PhD); inorganic chemistry (PhD); organic chemistry (PhD); physical chemistry (PhD). *Faculty:* 61 full-time (14 women). *Students:* 139 full-time (62 women); includes 11 minority (8 Asian Americans or Pacific Islanders, 3 Hispanic Americans), 53 international. 163 applicants, 51% accepted. In 1998, 26 degrees awarded. *Degree requirements:* For doctorate, dissertation required. *Entrance requirements:* For doctorate, GRE General Test, GRE Subject Test, TOEFL. *Average time to degree:* Doctorate–5.5 years full-time. *Application deadline:* For fall admission, 1/4. Application fee: $65. *Financial aid:* Fellowships, research assistantships, teaching assistantships, Federal Work-Study and institutionally-sponsored loans available. Aid available to part-time students. *Unit head:* Chair, 203-432-3912. *Application contact:* Admissions Information, 203-432-2770.

See in-depth description on page 241.

York University, Faculty of Graduate Studies, Faculty of Science, Program in Chemistry, Toronto, ON M3J 1P3, Canada. Offers M Sc, PhD. Part-time and evening/weekend programs available. *Degree requirements:* For master's, thesis optional, foreign language not required; for doctorate, dissertation required, foreign language not required.

Youngstown State University, Graduate School, College of Arts and Sciences, Department of Chemistry, Youngstown, OH 44555-0001. Offers MS. Part-time programs available. *Faculty:* 15 full-time (3 women). *Students:* 11 full-time (2 women), 6 part-time (3 women); includes 3 minority (2 African Americans, 1 Asian American or Pacific Islander), 1 international. 9 applicants, 89% accepted. In 1998, 12 degrees awarded. *Degree requirements:* For master's, thesis required, foreign language not required. *Entrance requirements:* For master's, TOEFL (minimum score of 550 required), bachelor's degree in chemistry, minimum GPA of 2.7. *Application deadline:* For fall admission, 8/15 (priority date); for winter admission, 11/15 (priority date); for spring admission, 2/15 (priority date). Applications are processed on a rolling basis. Application fee: $30 ($75 for international students). Tuition, state resident: part-time $97 per credit hour. Tuition, nonresident: part-time $219 per credit hour. Required fees: $21 per credit hour. $41 per quarter. *Financial aid:* In 1998–99, 9 research assistantships with full tuition reimbursements (averaging $7,500 per year), 9 teaching assistantships with full tuition reimbursements (averaging $7,500 per year) were awarded.; Federal Work-Study, institutionally-sponsored loans, and scholarships also available. Aid available to part-time students. Financial aid application deadline: 3/1. *Faculty research:* Analysis of antioxidants, chromotography, defects and disorder in crystalline oxides, hydrogen bonding, novel organic and organometallic materials. *Unit head:* Dr. Daryl W. Mincey, Chair, 330-742-3663, Fax: 330-742-1579. *Application contact:* Dr. Peter J. Kasvinsky, Dean of Graduate Studies, 330-742-3091, Fax: 330-742-1580, E-mail: amgrad03@ysub.ysu.edu.

Inorganic Chemistry

Boston College, Graduate School of Arts and Sciences, Department of Chemistry, Chestnut Hill, MA 02467-3800. Offers analytical chemistry (MS, PhD); biochemistry (MS, PhD); chemistry (MS); inorganic chemistry (MS, PhD); organic chemistry (MS, PhD); physical chemistry (MS, PhD). Part-time programs available. *Faculty:* 20 full-time (2 women). *Students:* 25 full-time (11 women), 75 part-time (29 women); includes 12 minority (1 African American, 8 Asian Americans or Pacific Islanders, 2 Hispanic Americans, 1 Native American), 28 international. Terminal master's awarded for partial completion of doctoral program. *Degree requirements:* For master's, thesis required; for doctorate, dissertation, qualifying exam required. *Entrance requirements:* For master's and doctorate, GRE General Test, GRE Subject Test. *Application deadline:* For fall admission, 2/1. Application fee: $40. *Unit head:* Dr. Larry McLaughlin, Chairperson, 617-552-3605, E-mail: larry.mclaughlin@bc.edu. *Application contact:* Dr. Mary Roberts, Graduate Program Director, 617-552-3616, E-mail: mary.roberts@bc.edu.

See in-depth description on page 93.

Boston University, Graduate School of Arts and Sciences, Department of Chemistry, Boston, MA 02215. Offers biochemistry (MA, PhD); chemical physics (MA, PhD); inorganic chemistry (MA, PhD); organic chemistry (MA, PhD); photochemistry (MA, PhD); physical chemistry (MA, PhD); theoretical chemistry (MA, PhD). *Faculty:* 21 full-time (1 woman). *Students:* 81 full-time (26 women), 1 (woman) part-time; includes 4 minority (2 African Americans, 2 Asian Americans or Pacific Islanders), 58 international. Terminal master's awarded for partial completion of doctoral program. *Degree requirements:* For master's, one foreign language, thesis not required; for doctorate, one foreign language, dissertation, exams required. *Entrance requirements:* For master's and doctorate, GRE General Test, GRE Subject Test (recommended), TOEFL (minimum score of 550 required). *Application deadline:* For fall admission, 7/1. Applications are processed on a rolling basis. Application fee: $50. Tuition: Full-time $23,770; part-time $743 per credit. Required fees: $220. Tuition and fees vary according to class time, course level, campus/location and program. *Unit head:* Thomas D. Tullius, Chairman, 617-353-4277, Fax: 617-353-6466, E-mail: tullius@chem.bu.edu. *Application contact:* Kevin Burgoyne, Academic Administrator, 617-353-2503, Fax: 617-353-6466, E-mail: burgoyne@chem.bu.edu.

Brandeis University, Graduate School of Arts and Sciences, Program in Chemistry, Waltham, MA 02454-9110. Offers inorganic chemistry (MS, PhD); organic chemistry (MS, PhD); physical chemistry (MS, PhD). *Faculty:* 16 full-time (2 women). *Students:* 44 full-time (22 women); includes 1 minority (African American), 26 international. Terminal master's awarded for partial completion of doctoral program. *Degree requirements:* For master's, 1 year of residency required, foreign language and thesis not required; for doctorate, one foreign language (computer language can substitute), dissertation, 3 years of residency, 2 seminars, qualifying exams required. *Entrance requirements:* For master's and doctorate, GRE General Test. *Application deadline:* For fall admission, 1/15 (priority date). Applications are processed on a rolling basis. Application fee: $60. *Unit head:* Dr. I. Y. Chan, Chair, 781-736-2554, Fax: 781-736-2516. *Application contact:* Charlotte Haygazian, Secretary, 781-736-2500, Fax: 781-736-2516, E-mail: chemadm@brandeis.edu.

Brigham Young University, Graduate Studies, College of Physical and Mathematical Sciences, Department of Chemistry and Biochemistry, Provo, UT 84602-1001. Offers analytical chemistry (MS, PhD); biochemistry (MS, PhD); inorganic chemistry (MS, PhD); organic chemistry (MS, PhD); physical chemistry (MS, PhD). *Faculty:* 33 full-time (1 woman), 3 part-time (0 women). *Students:* 70 full-time (24 women); includes 1 minority (Asian American or Pacific Islander), 39 international. *Degree requirements:* For master's and doctorate, thesis/dissertation required, foreign language not required. *Entrance requirements:* For master's and doctorate, minimum GPA of 3.0 in last 60 hours. *Application deadline:* For fall admission, 2/1 (priority date). Applications are processed on a rolling basis. Application fee: $30. Tuition: Full-time $3,330; part-time $185 per credit hour. Tuition and fees vary according to program and student's religious affiliation. *Unit head:* Dr. Francis R. Nordmeyer, Chair, 801-378-3667, Fax: 801-378-5474, E-mail: fran_nordmeyer@byu.edu. *Application contact:* N. Kent Dalley, Coordinator, Graduate Admissions, 801-378-3434, Fax: 801-378-5474, E-mail: chemgrad@byu.edu.

See in-depth description on page 97.

California State University, Fullerton, Graduate Studies, School of Natural Science and Mathematics, Department of Chemistry and Biochemistry, Fullerton, CA 92834-9480. Offers analytical chemistry (MS); biochemistry (MS); geochemistry (MS); inorganic chemistry (MS);

Inorganic Chemistry

California State University, Fullerton (continued)
organic chemistry (MS); physical chemistry (MS). Part-time programs available. *Faculty:* 18 full-time, 14 part-time. *Students:* 8 full-time (3 women), 32 part-time (14 women); includes 19 minority (14 Asian Americans or Pacific Islanders, 5 Hispanic Americans), 6 international. *Degree requirements:* For master's, thesis, departmental qualifying exam required, foreign language not required. *Entrance requirements:* For master's, minimum GPA of 2.5 in last 60 units, major in chemistry or related field. Application fee: $55. Tuition, nonresident: part-time $264 per unit. *Unit head:* Dr. Bruce Weber, Chair, 714-278-3621. *Application contact:* Dr. Gregory Williams, Adviser, 714-278-2170.

California State University, Los Angeles, Graduate Studies, School of Natural and Social Sciences, Department of Chemistry and Biochemistry, Los Angeles, CA 90032-8530. Offers analytical chemistry (MS); biochemistry (MS); chemistry (MS); inorganic chemistry (MS); organic chemistry (MS); physical chemistry (MS). Part-time and evening/weekend programs available. *Faculty:* 14 full-time, 20 part-time. *Students:* 13 full-time (6 women), 11 part-time (4 women); includes 16 minority (1 African American, 12 Asian Americans or Pacific Islanders, 3 Hispanic Americans), 3 international. *Degree requirements:* For master's, one foreign language (computer language can substitute), comprehensive exam or thesis required. *Entrance requirements:* For master's, TOEFL (minimum score of 550 required). *Application deadline:* For fall admission, 6/30; for spring admission, 2/1. Applications are processed on a rolling basis. Application fee: $55. *Unit head:* Dr. Scott Grover, Acting Chair, 323-343-2300.

Case Western Reserve University, School of Graduate Studies, Department of Chemistry, Cleveland, OH 44106. Offers analytical chemistry (MS, PhD); inorganic chemistry (MS, PhD); organic chemistry (MS, PhD); physical chemistry (MS, PhD). Part-time programs available. Terminal master's awarded for partial completion of doctoral program. *Degree requirements:* For master's, thesis not required; for doctorate, dissertation required. *Entrance requirements:* For master's and doctorate, GRE General Test, GRE Subject Test, TOEFL (minimum score of 550 required). *Faculty research:* Electrochemistry, synthetic chemistry, chemistry of life process, spectroscopy, kinetics.

Clark Atlanta University, School of Arts and Sciences, Department of Chemistry, Atlanta, GA 30314. Offers inorganic chemistry (MS, PhD); organic chemistry (MS, PhD); physical chemistry (MS, PhD); science education (DA). Part-time programs available. *Students:* 17 full-time (11 women), 20 part-time (11 women); includes 33 minority (28 African Americans, 2 Asian Americans or Pacific Islanders, 3 Hispanic Americans), 3 international. *Degree requirements:* For master's, one foreign language (computer language can substitute), thesis, comprehensive exam required; for doctorate, 2 foreign languages (computer language can substitute for one), dissertation, cumulative exam required. *Entrance requirements:* For master's, GRE General Test, minimum GPA of 2.5; for doctorate, GRE General Test, GRE Subject Test, minimum graduate GPA of 3.0. *Application deadline:* For fall admission, 4/1; for spring admission, 11/1. Applications are processed on a rolling basis. Application fee: $40. *Unit head:* Dr. Reynold Verrett, Chairperson, 404-880-8154. *Application contact:* Michelle Clark-Davis, Graduate Program Assistant, 404-880-8709.

Clarkson University, Graduate School, School of Science, Department of Chemistry, Potsdam, NY 13699. Offers analytical chemistry (MS, PhD); inorganic chemistry (MS, PhD); organic chemistry (MS, PhD); physical chemistry (MS, PhD). *Faculty:* 9 full-time (0 women). *Students:* 25 full-time (13 women); includes 1 minority (African American), 15 international. *Degree requirements:* For master's, foreign language and thesis not required; for doctorate, dissertation, departmental qualifying exam required, foreign language not required. *Entrance requirements:* For master's, GRE, TOEFL. *Application deadline:* For fall admission, 5/15 (priority date); for spring admission, 10/15 (priority date). Applications are processed on a rolling basis. Application fee: $25 ($35 for international students). Tuition: Part-time $661 per credit hour. Required fees: $215 per semester. *Unit head:* Dr. Stig Friberg, Chair, 315-268-6500, Fax: 315-268-6610, E-mail: fbg@clarkson.edu.

Cleveland State University, College of Graduate Studies, College of Arts and Sciences, Department of Chemistry, Cleveland, OH 44115-2440. Offers analytical chemistry (MS, PhD); clinical chemistry (MS, PhD); inorganic chemistry (MS); organic chemistry (MS); physical chemistry (MS); structural analysis (MS, PhD). Part-time and evening/weekend programs available. *Faculty:* 13 full-time (1 woman). *Students:* 1 full-time (0 women), 53 part-time (22 women); includes 5 minority (1 African American, 3 Asian Americans or Pacific Islanders, 1 Hispanic American), 25 international. *Degree requirements:* For master's, thesis required (for some programs), foreign language not required; for doctorate, dissertation required, foreign language not required. *Entrance requirements:* For master's and doctorate, GRE General Test, GRE Subject Test, TOEFL (minimum score of 525 required). *Application deadline:* For fall admission, 7/15 (priority date). Applications are processed on a rolling basis. Application fee: $25. *Unit head:* Dr. Stan Duraj, Interim Chair, 216-523-7312, Fax: 216-687-9298.

Columbia University, Graduate School of Arts and Sciences, Division of Natural Sciences, Department of Chemistry, New York, NY 10027. Offers chemical physics (M Phil, PhD); inorganic chemistry (M Phil, MS, PhD); organic chemistry (M Phil, MS, PhD). *Degree requirements:* For master's, comprehensive exams (MS); 1 foreign language, teaching experience, oral and written exams (M Phil) required, thesis not required; for doctorate, one foreign language, dissertation, M Phil required. *Entrance requirements:* For master's and doctorate, GRE General Test, GRE Subject Test, TOEFL. *Faculty research:* Biophysics.

Cornell University, Graduate School, Graduate Fields of Arts and Sciences, Field of Chemistry, Ithaca, NY 14853-0001. Offers analytical chemistry (PhD); bio-organic chemistry (PhD); biophysical chemistry (PhD); chemical physics (PhD); inorganic chemistry (PhD); material chemistry (PhD); organic chemistry (PhD); physical chemistry (PhD); polymer chemistry (PhD); theoretical chemistry (PhD). *Faculty:* 38 full-time. *Students:* 139 full-time (44 women); includes 10 minority (1 African American, 4 Asian Americans or Pacific Islanders, 4 Hispanic Americans, 1 Native American), 51 international. *Degree requirements:* For doctorate, dissertation required, foreign language not required. *Entrance requirements:* For doctorate, GRE General Test, GRE Subject Test, TOEFL (minimum score of 600 required). *Application deadline:* For fall admission, 1/15. Application fee: $65. Electronic applications accepted. *Unit head:* Director of Graduate Studies, 607-255-4139. *Application contact:* Graduate Field Assistant, 607-255-4139, E-mail: chemgrad@cornell.edu.

See in-depth description on page 109.

Florida State University, Graduate Studies, College of Arts and Sciences, Department of Chemistry, Tallahassee, FL 32306. Offers analytical chemistry (MS, PhD); biochemistry (MS, PhD); chemical physics (MS, PhD); inorganic chemistry (MS, PhD); organic chemistry (MS, PhD); physical chemistry (MS, PhD). Part-time programs available. *Faculty:* 38 full-time (4 women). *Students:* 87 full-time (27 women), 8 part-time (2 women). Terminal master's awarded for partial completion of doctoral program. *Degree requirements:* For master's, cumulative and diagnostic exams required; for doctorate, dissertation, cumulative and diagnostic exams required, foreign language not required. *Entrance requirements:* For master's and doctorate, GRE General Test, minimum B average in undergraduate course work. *Application deadline:* Applications are processed on a rolling basis. Application fee: $20. Tuition, state resident: part-time $139 per credit hour. Tuition, nonresident: part-time $482 per credit hour. Tuition and fees vary according to program. *Unit head:* Dr. John G. Dorsey, Chairman, 850-644-9625, Fax: 850-644-8281. *Application contact:* Dr. Naresh Dalal, Chair, Graduate Admissions Committee, 850-644-3398, Fax: 850-644-8281, E-mail: gradinfo@chem.fsu.edu.

See in-depth description on page 123.

Georgetown University, Graduate School, Department of Chemistry, Washington, DC 20057. Offers analytical chemistry (MS, PhD); biochemistry (MS, PhD); chemical physics (MS, PhD); inorganic chemistry (MS, PhD); organic chemistry (MS, PhD); physical chemistry (MS, PhD); theoretical chemistry (MS, PhD). Terminal master's awarded for partial completion of doctoral program. *Degree requirements:* For master's, thesis (for some programs), qualifying exam required, foreign language not required; for doctorate, dissertation, comprehensive exam required. *Entrance requirements:* For master's and doctorate, GRE General Test, TOEFL (minimum score of 550 required, 600 for teaching assistants).

See in-depth description on page 125.

The George Washington University, Columbian School of Arts and Sciences, Department of Chemistry, Washington, DC 20052. Offers analytical chemistry (MS, PhD); inorganic chemistry (MS, PhD); materials science (MS, PhD); organic chemistry (MS, PhD); physical chemistry (MS, PhD). Part-time and evening/weekend programs available. *Faculty:* 5 full-time (0 women). *Students:* 19 full-time (14 women), 7 part-time (4 women); includes 6 minority (1 African American, 3 Asian Americans or Pacific Islanders, 2 Hispanic Americans), 6 international. Terminal master's awarded for partial completion of doctoral program. *Degree requirements:* For master's, computer language, thesis or alternative, comprehensive exam required; for doctorate, computer language, dissertation, general exam required. *Entrance requirements:* For master's and doctorate, GRE General Test, interview, minimum GPA of 3.0. Application fee: $55. Tuition: Full-time $17,328; part-time $722 per credit hour. Required fees: $828; $35 per credit hour. Tuition and fees vary according to campus/location and program. *Unit head:* Dr. Michael King, Chair, 202-994-6121.

Harvard University, Graduate School of Arts and Sciences, Department of Chemistry and Chemical Biology, Cambridge, MA 02138. Offers biochemical chemistry (AM, PhD); inorganic chemistry (AM, PhD); organic chemistry (AM, PhD); physical chemistry (AM, PhD). *Students:* 188 full-time (36 women). *Degree requirements:* For doctorate, dissertation, cumulative exams required, foreign language not required. *Entrance requirements:* For master's, GRE General Test, TOEFL (minimum score of 550 required); for doctorate, GRE General Test, GRE Subject Test, TOEFL (minimum score of 550 required). *Application deadline:* For fall admission, 12/31. Application fee: $60. *Unit head:* Dr. David Evans, Chair, 617-495-2948. *Application contact:* Graduate Admissions Office, 617-496-3208.

See in-depth description on page 133.

Howard University, Graduate School of Arts and Sciences, Department of Chemistry, Washington, DC 20059-0002. Offers analytical chemistry (MS, PhD); biochemistry (MS, PhD); inorganic chemistry (MS, PhD); organic chemistry (MS, PhD); physical chemistry (MS, PhD); polymer chemistry (MS, PhD); theoretical chemistry (MS, PhD). Part-time programs available. Terminal master's awarded for partial completion of doctoral program. *Degree requirements:* For master's, one foreign language (computer language can substitute), thesis, comprehensive exam, teaching experience required; for doctorate, 2 foreign languages (computer language can substitute for one), dissertation, comprehensive exam, teaching experience required. *Entrance requirements:* For master's, GRE General Test, minimum GPA of 2.7; for doctorate, GRE General Test, minimum GPA of 3.0. *Faculty research:* Stratospheric aerosols, liquid crystals, polymer coatings, terrestrial and extraterrestrial atmospheres, amidogen reaction.

Illinois Institute of Technology, Graduate College, Armour College of Engineering and Sciences, Department of Biological, Chemical and Physical Sciences, Chemistry Division, Chicago, IL 60616-3793. Offers analytical chemistry (MAC, MS, PhD); chemistry (M Chem); inorganic chemistry (MS, PhD); organic chemistry (MS, PhD); physical chemistry (MS, PhD); polymer chemistry (MS, PhD); theoretical chemistry (MS, PhD). Part-time and evening/weekend programs available. *Faculty:* 8 full-time (0 women), 2 part-time (0 women). *Students:* 14 full-time (7 women), 70 part-time (27 women); includes 19 minority (10 African Americans, 9 Asian Americans or Pacific Islanders), 16 international. Terminal master's awarded for partial completion of doctoral program. *Degree requirements:* For master's, thesis (for some programs), comprehensive exam required, foreign language not required; for doctorate, dissertation, comprehensive exam required, foreign language not required. *Entrance requirements:* For master's and doctorate, GRE (minimum score of 1200 required), TOEFL (minimum score of 550 required), undergraduate GPA of 3.0 required. *Application deadline:* For fall admission, 7/1; for spring admission, 11/1. Applications are processed on a rolling basis. Application fee: $30. Electronic applications accepted. *Unit head:* Dr. Carlo Segre, Associate Chair, 312-567-3480, Fax: 312-567-3494, E-mail: segre@iit.edu. *Application contact:* Dr. S. Mohammad Shahidehpour, Dean of Graduate College, 312-567-3024, Fax: 312-567-7517, E-mail: grad@minna.cns.iit.edu.

See in-depth description on page 135.

Indiana University Bloomington, Graduate School, College of Arts and Sciences, Department of Chemistry, Bloomington, IN 47405. Offers analytical chemistry (PhD); biological chemistry (PhD); chemistry (MAT, MS); inorganic chemistry (PhD); physical chemistry (PhD). PhD offered through the University Graduate School. *Faculty:* 28 full-time (1 woman), 1 (woman) part-time. *Students:* 96 full-time (32 women), 65 part-time (10 women); includes 12 minority (1 African American, 9 Asian Americans or Pacific Islanders, 2 Hispanic Americans), 42 international. Terminal master's awarded for partial completion of doctoral program. *Degree requirements:* For master's and doctorate, thesis/dissertation required, foreign language not required. *Entrance requirements:* For master's and doctorate, GRE General Test, GRE Subject Test, TOEFL. *Application deadline:* For fall admission, 1/15 (priority date); for spring admission, 9/1 (priority date). Applications are processed on a rolling basis. Application fee: $40. Tuition, state resident: part-time $161 per credit hour. Tuition, nonresident: part-time $468 per credit hour. Required fees: $360 per year. Tuition and fees vary according to course load and program. *Unit head:* Dr. Gary M. Hieftje, Chairperson, 812-855-6239, Fax: 812-855-8300, E-mail: cemchair@indiana.edu. *Application contact:* Dr. Jack K. Crandall, Chairperson of Admissions, 812-855-2068, Fax: 812-855-8300, E-mail: chemgrad@indiana.edu.

Kansas State University, Graduate School, College of Arts and Sciences, Department of Chemistry, Manhattan, KS 66506. Offers analytical chemistry (MS); chemistry (PhD); inorganic chemistry (MS); organic chemistry (MS); physical chemistry (MS). *Faculty:* 16 full-time (1 woman). *Students:* 43 full-time (12 women), 2 part-time (1 woman); includes 2 minority (both Asian Americans or Pacific Islanders), 25 international. Terminal master's awarded for partial completion of doctoral program. *Degree requirements:* For master's and doctorate, thesis/dissertation required, foreign language not required. *Entrance requirements:* For master's and doctorate, GRE, minimum GPA of 3.0. *Application deadline:* For fall admission, 6/1 (priority date); for spring admission, 12/1. Applications are processed on a rolling basis. Application fee: $0 ($25 for international students). *Unit head:* Peter M. A. Sherwood, Head, 785-532-6665, Fax: 785-532-6666, E-mail: escashem@ksu.edu. *Application contact:* Christer B. Aakeroy, Graduate Coordinator, 785-532-1468, Fax: 785-532-6666.

See in-depth description on page 143.

Kent State University, College of Arts and Sciences, Department of Chemistry, Kent, OH 44242-0001. Offers analytical chemistry (MS, PhD); biochemistry (PhD); chemistry (MA, MS, PhD); inorganic chemistry (MS, PhD); organic chemistry (MS, PhD); physical chemistry (MS, PhD). *Faculty:* 23 full-time. *Students:* 36 full-time (20 women), 2 part-time (both women); includes 1 minority (African American), 19 international. *Degree requirements:* For master's and doctorate, thesis/dissertation required, foreign language not required. *Entrance requirements:* For master's, minimum GPA of 2.75; for doctorate, minimum GPA of 3.0. *Application deadline:* For fall admission, 7/12; for spring admission, 11/29. Applications are processed on a rolling basis. Application fee: $30. *Unit head:* Dr. Rathindra N. Bose, Chairman, 330-672-2032, Fax: 330-672-3816.

See in-depth description on page 147.

Lehigh University, College of Arts and Sciences, Department of Chemistry, Bethlehem, PA 18015-3094. Offers biochemistry and analytical chemistry (MS, PhD); chemistry (DA); clinical chemistry (MS); inorganic chemistry (MS, PhD); organic chemistry (MS, PhD); pharmaceutical chemistry (PhD); physical chemistry (MS, PhD). Part-time programs available. Postbaccalaureate distance learning degree programs offered (no on-campus study). *Students:*

30 full-time (14 women), 92 part-time (46 women); includes 10 minority (7 Asian Americans or Pacific Islanders, 3 Hispanic Americans), 10 international. Terminal master's awarded for partial completion of doctoral program. *Degree requirements:* For master's, foreign language and thesis not required; for doctorate, dissertation required. *Entrance requirements:* For master's and doctorate, GRE General Test, TSE (minimum score of 230 required). *Application deadline:* For fall admission, 7/15; for spring admission, 12/1. Applications are processed on a rolling basis. Application fee: $40. *Unit head:* Dr. Keith J. Schray, Chairman, 610-758-3474, Fax: 610-758-6536, E-mail: kjs0@lehigh.edu. *Application contact:* Dr. James E. Roberts, Graduate Coordinator, 610-758-4847, Fax: 610-758-6536, E-mail: jer1@lehigh.edu.

Marquette University, Graduate School, College of Arts and Sciences, Department of Chemistry, Milwaukee, WI 53201-1881. Offers analytical chemistry (MS, PhD); bioanalytical chemistry (MS, PhD); biophysical chemistry (MS, PhD); chemical physics (MS, PhD); inorganic chemistry (MS, PhD); organic chemistry (MS, PhD); physical chemistry (MS, PhD). Part-time programs available. *Faculty:* 15 full-time (2 women), 1 part-time (0 women). *Students:* 33 full-time (12 women), 6 part-time (1 woman); includes 5 minority (2 African Americans, 3 Asian Americans or Pacific Islanders), 30 international. Terminal master's awarded for partial completion of doctoral program. *Degree requirements:* For master's, comprehensive exam required; for doctorate, dissertation, cumulative exams required, foreign language not required. *Entrance requirements:* For master's and doctorate, TOEFL (minimum score of 550 required), GRE Subject Test. Application fee: $40. Tuition: Part-time $510 per credit hour. Tuition and fees vary according to program. *Unit head:* Dr. Charles Wilkie, Chairman, 414-288-7065, Fax: 414-288-7066. *Application contact:* Dr. Mark Steinmetz, Director of Graduate Studies, 414-288-3535, Fax: 414-288-7066.

Massachusetts Institute of Technology, School of Science, Department of Chemistry, Cambridge, MA 02139-4307. Offers biochemistry (PhD); biological chemistry (PhD, Sc D); inorganic chemistry (PhD, Sc D); organic chemistry (PhD, Sc D); physical chemistry (PhD, Sc D). *Faculty:* 27 full-time (2 women). *Students:* 172 full-time (51 women); includes 19 minority (3 African Americans, 6 Asian Americans or Pacific Islanders, 9 Hispanic Americans, 1 Native American), 53 international. *Degree requirements:* For doctorate, dissertation, comprehensive oral exam, oral presentation, written exams required, foreign language not required. *Application deadline:* For fall admission, 1/15. Application fee: $55. *Unit head:* Dr. Stephen J. Lippard, Chairman, 617-253-1845. *Application contact:* Susan Brighton, Graduate Administrator, 617-253-1845, Fax: 617-258-0241, E-mail: brighton@mit.edu.

McMaster University, School of Graduate Studies, Faculty of Science, Department of Chemistry, Hamilton, ON L8S 4M2, Canada. Offers analytical chemistry (M Sc, PhD); chemical physics (M Sc, PhD); chemistry (M Sc, PhD); inorganic chemistry (M Sc, PhD); organic chemistry (M Sc, PhD); physical chemistry (M Sc, PhD); polymer chemistry (M Sc, PhD). Part-time programs available. *Faculty:* 21 full-time (2 women), 4 part-time (0 women). *Students:* 67 full-time (23 women), 1 part-time, 1 international. Terminal master's awarded for partial completion of doctoral program. *Degree requirements:* For master's, thesis required, foreign language not required; for doctorate, dissertation, comprehensive exam required, foreign language not required. *Entrance requirements:* For master's, minimum B+ average. *Application deadline:* For fall admission, 4/30; for spring admission, 3/15. Applications are processed on a rolling basis. Application fee: $50. *Unit head:* Dr. M. J. McGlinchey, Chair, 905-525-9140 Ext. 24504, Fax: 905-522-2509, E-mail: mcglinchey@mcmail.cis.mcmaster.ca. *Application contact:* Carol Dada, Administrator, 905-525-9140 Ext. 23487, Fax: 905-522-2509, E-mail: dada@mcmail.cis.mcmaster.ca.

Michigan State University, Graduate School, College of Natural Science, Department of Chemistry, East Lansing, MI 48824-1020. Offers analytical chemistry (MS, PhD); chemistry (MAT, MS, PhD); chemistry-environmental toxicology (PhD); environmental toxicology (PhD); inorganic chemistry (MS, PhD); organic chemistry (MS, PhD); physical chemistry (PhD). *Faculty:* 36 full-time (4 women). *Students:* 149 full-time (46 women), 18 part-time (9 women); includes 12 minority (6 African Americans, 3 Asian Americans or Pacific Islanders, 2 Hispanic Americans, 1 Native American), 80 international. Terminal master's awarded for partial completion of doctoral program. *Degree requirements:* For master's, thesis required (for some programs), foreign language not required; for doctorate, dissertation required, foreign language not required. *Entrance requirements:* For master's and doctorate, GRE, TOEFL. *Application deadline:* Applications are processed on a rolling basis. Application fee: $30 ($40 for international students). *Unit head:* Dr. Katharine C. Hunt, Chairperson, 517-355-9715, Fax: 517-353-1793, E-mail: chemdept@cem.msu.edu. *Application contact:* Dr. Richard Schwendeman, Associate Chair, Graduate Program, 517-355-9715 Ext. 344, Fax: 517-353-1793, E-mail: gradoff@cem.msu.edu.

Northeastern University, College of Arts and Sciences, Department of Chemistry, Boston, MA 02115-5096. Offers analytical chemistry (PhD); chemistry (MAT, MS, PhD); inorganic chemistry (PhD); organic chemistry (PhD); physical chemistry (PhD). Part-time and evening/weekend programs available. *Faculty:* 20 full-time (3 women), 1 part-time (0 women). *Students:* 59 full-time (25 women), 23 part-time (9 women). Terminal master's awarded for partial completion of doctoral program. *Degree requirements:* For master's, thesis required (for some programs); for doctorate, dissertation, qualifying exam in specialty area required, foreign language not required. *Entrance requirements:* For master's and doctorate, TOEFL (minimum score of 580 required). *Application deadline:* For fall admission, 4/15. Applications are processed on a rolling basis. Application fee: $50. Electronic applications accepted. *Unit head:* Dr. David A. Forsyth, Chairman, 617-373-2822, Fax: 617-373-8795, E-mail: chemistry-grad-info@neu.edu. *Application contact:* Dr. Philip W. LeQuesne, Chair, Graduate Admissions Committee, 617-373-2383, Fax: 617-373-8795.

Oregon State University, Graduate School, College of Science, Department of Chemistry, Corvallis, OR 97331. Offers analytical chemistry (MS, PhD); chemistry (MA, MAIS); inorganic chemistry (MS, PhD); nuclear and radiation chemistry (MS, PhD); organic chemistry (MS, PhD); physical chemistry (MS, PhD). Part-time programs available. *Faculty:* 25 full-time (3 women), 5 part-time (2 women). *Students:* 68 full-time (24 women), 2 part-time; includes 4 minority (all Asian Americans or Pacific Islanders), 30 international. Terminal master's awarded for partial completion of doctoral program. *Degree requirements:* For master's and doctorate, one foreign language, thesis/dissertation required. *Entrance requirements:* For master's and doctorate, TOEFL (minimum score of 620 required), minimum GPA of 3.0 in last 90 hours. *Application deadline:* For fall admission, 3/1 (priority date). Applications are processed on a rolling basis. Application fee: $50. *Unit head:* Dr. John Westall, Chair, 541-737-6700, Fax: 541-737-2062, E-mail: john.westall@orst.edu. *Application contact:* Carolyn Brumley, Graduate Secretary, 541-737-6707, Fax: 541-737-2062, E-mail: carolyn.brumley@orst.edu.

Purdue University, Graduate School, School of Science, Department of Chemistry, West Lafayette, IN 47907. Offers analytical chemistry (MS, PhD); biochemistry (MS, PhD); chemical education (MS, PhD); inorganic chemistry (MS, PhD); organic chemistry (MS, PhD); physical chemistry (MS, PhD). *Accreditation:* NCATE (one or more programs are accredited). *Faculty:* 46 full-time, 1 part-time. *Students:* 246 full-time (83 women), 59 part-time (20 women); includes 36 minority (14 African Americans, 7 Asian Americans or Pacific Islanders, 14 Hispanic Americans, 1 Native American), 100 international. Terminal master's awarded for partial completion of doctoral program. *Degree requirements:* For master's and doctorate, thesis/dissertation required, foreign language not required. *Entrance requirements:* For master's and doctorate, TOEFL (minimum score of 550 required). Application fee: $30. Electronic applications accepted. *Unit head:* Dr. R. A. Walton, Head, 765-494-5203. *Application contact:* R. E. Wild, Chairman, Graduate Admissions, 765-494-5200, E-mail: wild@purdue.edu.

Rensselaer Polytechnic Institute, Graduate School, School of Science, Department of Chemistry, Troy, NY 12180-3590. Offers analytical chemistry (MS, PhD); biochemistry (MS, PhD); inorganic chemistry (MS, PhD); organic chemistry (MS, PhD); physical chemistry (MS, PhD); polymer chemistry (MS, PhD). Part-time and evening/weekend programs available. *Faculty:* 17 full-time (2 women), 1 part-time (0 women). *Students:* 52 full-time (18 women), 3 part-time (1 woman); includes 4 minority (3 Asian Americans or Pacific Islanders, 1 Hispanic American), 30 international. *Degree requirements:* For master's, thesis required (for some programs), foreign language not required; for doctorate, dissertation required, foreign language not required. *Entrance requirements:* For master's and doctorate, GRE General Test, TOEFL (minimum score of 550 required). *Application deadline:* For fall admission, 2/1 (priority date). Applications are processed on a rolling basis. Application fee: $35. *Unit head:* Dr. Thomas Apple, Chair, 518-276-6344. *Application contact:* Dr. Wilfredo Colon, Chair, Graduate Committee, 518-276-6340, Fax: 518-276-6434, E-mail: colonw@rpi.edu.

See in-depth description on page 167.

Rutgers, The State University of New Jersey, Newark, Graduate School, Department of Chemistry, Newark, NJ 07102-3192. Offers analytical chemistry (MS, PhD); biochemistry (MS, PhD); inorganic chemistry (MS, PhD); organic chemistry (MS, PhD); physical chemistry (MS, PhD). Part-time and evening/weekend programs available. *Faculty:* 22 full-time (4 women). *Students:* 28 full-time (11 women), 39 part-time (19 women); includes 29 minority (1 African American, 24 Asian Americans or Pacific Islanders, 4 Hispanic Americans) Terminal master's awarded for partial completion of doctoral program. *Degree requirements:* For master's, cumulative exams required, thesis optional, foreign language not required; for doctorate, dissertation, exams, research proposal required, foreign language not required. *Entrance requirements:* For master's and doctorate, GRE General Test, TOEFL (minimum score of 550 required; 590 for financial aid), minimum undergraduate B average. *Application deadline:* For fall admission, 7/1 (priority date); for spring admission, 12/1. Applications are processed on a rolling basis. Application fee: $40. *Unit head:* Prof. Hugh W. Thompson, Coordinator, 973-353-5173, Fax: 973-353-1264.

See in-depth description on page 169.

Rutgers, The State University of New Jersey, New Brunswick, Graduate School, Program in Chemistry, New Brunswick, NJ 08903. Offers analytical chemistry (MS, PhD); biological chemistry (PhD); chemistry education (MST); inorganic chemistry (MS, PhD); organic chemistry (MS, PhD); physical chemistry (MS, PhD). Part-time and evening/weekend programs available. *Faculty:* 44 full-time (9 women), 4 part-time (2 women). *Students:* 100 full-time (35 women), 69 part-time (29 women); includes 27 minority (2 African Americans, 24 Asian Americans or Pacific Islanders, 1 Hispanic American), 79 international. Terminal master's awarded for partial completion of doctoral program. *Degree requirements:* For master's, exam required, thesis optional, foreign language not required; for doctorate, dissertation, cumulative exams required, foreign language not required. *Entrance requirements:* For master's, GRE General Test, GRE Subject Test, TOEFL; for doctorate, GRE General Test, GRE Subject Test, TOEFL (minimum score of 575 required). *Application deadline:* For fall admission, 4/15 (priority date); for spring admission, 11/1. Applications are processed on a rolling basis. Application fee: $50. *Unit head:* Dr. Martha A. Cotter, Director, 732-445-2259, Fax: 732-445-5312, E-mail: gradexec@rutchem.rutgers.edu.

See in-depth description on page 173.

San Jose State University, Graduate Studies, College of Science, Department of Chemistry, San Jose, CA 95192-0001. Offers analytical chemistry (MS); biochemistry (MS); chemistry (MA); inorganic chemistry (MS); organic chemistry (MS); physical chemistry (MS); polymer chemistry (MS); radiochemistry (MS). Part-time and evening/weekend programs available. *Faculty:* 24 full-time (3 women), 5 part-time (2 women). *Students:* 7 full-time (5 women), 30 part-time (17 women); includes 24 minority (2 African Americans, 21 Asian Americans or Pacific Islanders, 1 Hispanic American), 4 international. *Degree requirements:* For master's, thesis or alternative required, foreign language not required. *Entrance requirements:* For master's, GRE, minimum B average. *Application deadline:* For fall admission, 6/1. Applications are processed on a rolling basis. Application fee: $59. Tuition, nonresident: part-time $246 per unit. Required fees: $1,939; $1,309 per year. *Unit head:* Dr. Pamela Stacks, Chair, 408-924-5000, Fax: 408-924-4945. *Application contact:* Dr. Roger Biringer, Graduate Adviser, 408-924-4961.

Seton Hall University, College of Arts and Sciences, Department of Chemistry, South Orange, NJ 07079-2694. Offers analytical chemistry (MS, PhD); biochemistry (MS, PhD); chemistry (MS); inorganic chemistry (MS, PhD); organic chemistry (MS, PhD); physical chemistry (MS, PhD). Part-time and evening/weekend programs available. Terminal master's awarded for partial completion of doctoral program. *Degree requirements:* For master's, formal seminar required, thesis optional; for doctorate, dissertation, comprehensive exams, annual seminars required. *Entrance requirements:* For master's, TOEFL, undergraduate major in chemistry or related field with a minimum of 30 credits in chemistry, including 2 semesters of physical chemistry; for doctorate, oral matriculation exam based on proposed doctoral research, minimum GPA of 3.0 in course distribution requirements, formal seminar. *Faculty research:* DNA metal reactions; chromatography; bioinorganic, biophysical, organometallic, and polymer chemistry; heterogeneous catalysis.

South Dakota State University, Graduate School, College of Arts and Science, Department of Chemistry, Brookings, SD 57007. Offers analytical chemistry (MS, PhD); biochemistry (MS, PhD); chemistry (MS, PhD); inorganic chemistry (MS, PhD); organic chemistry (MS, PhD); physical chemistry (MS, PhD). *Degree requirements:* For master's, thesis, oral exam required, foreign language not required; for doctorate, dissertation, preliminary oral and written exams, research tool required. *Entrance requirements:* For master's, TOEFL (minimum score of 580 required), bachelor's degree in chemistry or equivalent; for doctorate, TOEFL (minimum score of 580 required). *Faculty research:* Environmental chemistry, computational chemistry, organic synthesis and photochemistry, novel material development and characterization.

Southern University and Agricultural and Mechanical College, Graduate School, College of Sciences, Department of Chemistry, Baton Rouge, LA 70813. Offers analytical chemistry (MS); biochemistry (MS); environmental sciences (MS); inorganic chemistry (MS); organic chemistry (MS); physical chemistry (MS). *Faculty:* 9 full-time (2 women), 3 part-time (2 women). *Students:* 4 full-time (3 women), 20 part-time (12 women); includes 19 minority (all African Americans), 4 international. *Degree requirements:* For master's, thesis required, foreign language not required. *Entrance requirements:* For master's, GMAT or GRE General Test, TOEFL. *Application deadline:* For fall admission, 6/1 (priority date); for spring admission, 11/1. Applications are processed on a rolling basis. Application fee: $5. *Unit head:* Dr. Robert Harvey Miller, Chairman, 225-771-3990, Fax: 225-771-3992.

State University of New York at Binghamton, Graduate School, School of Arts and Sciences, Department of Chemistry, Binghamton, NY 13902-6000. Offers analytical chemistry (PhD); chemistry (MA, MS); inorganic chemistry (PhD); organic chemistry (PhD); physical chemistry (PhD). *Faculty:* 13 full-time, 7 part-time. *Students:* 48 full-time (11 women), 7 part-time (2 women); includes 2 minority (1 African American, 1 Hispanic American), 30 international. Terminal master's awarded for partial completion of doctoral program. *Degree requirements:* For master's, thesis or alternative, oral exam, seminar presentation required, foreign language not required; for doctorate, dissertation, cumulative exams required, foreign language not required. *Entrance requirements:* For master's and doctorate, GRE General Test, GRE Subject Test, TOEFL. *Application deadline:* For fall admission, 4/15 (priority date); for spring admission, 11/1. Applications are processed on a rolling basis. Application fee: $50. Electronic applications accepted. Tuition, state resident: full-time $5,100; part-time $213 per credit. Tuition, nonresident: full-time $8,416; part-time $351 per credit. Required fees: $77 per credit. Part-time tuition and fees vary according to course load. *Unit head:* Dr. Alistair J. Lees, Chairperson, 607-777-2362.

Tufts University, Division of Graduate and Continuing Studies and Research, Graduate School of Arts and Sciences, Department of Chemistry, Medford, MA 02155. Offers analytical chemistry (MS, PhD); bioorganic chemistry (MS, PhD); environmental chemistry (MS, PhD); inorganic chemistry (MS, PhD); organic chemistry (MS, PhD); physical chemistry (MS, PhD). *Faculty:* 13 full-time, 1 part-time. *Students:* 52 (27 women); includes 5 minority (1 African American, 3 Asian Americans or Pacific Islanders, 1 Hispanic American) 14 international.

Inorganic Chemistry

Tufts University (continued)
Terminal master's awarded for partial completion of doctoral program. *Degree requirements:* For master's and doctorate, thesis/dissertation required, foreign language not required. *Entrance requirements:* For master's and doctorate, GRE General Test, GRE Subject Test, TOEFL (minimum score of 600 required). *Application deadline:* For fall admission, 2/15; for spring admission, 10/15. Applications are processed on a rolling basis. Application fee: $50. *Unit head:* Marc d'Alarco, Chair, 617-627-3441, Fax: 617-627-3443. *Application contact:* Samuel Kounaves, 617-627-3124, Fax: 617-627-3443.

See in-depth description on page 181.

The University of Akron, Graduate School, Buchtel College of Arts and Sciences, Department of Chemistry, Akron, OH 44325-0001. Offers analytical chemistry (MS, PhD); biochemistry (MS, PhD); chemistry (MS, PhD); inorganic chemistry (MS, PhD); organic chemistry (MS, PhD); physical chemistry (MS, PhD). Part-time and evening/weekend programs available. *Faculty:* 17 full-time, 1 part-time. *Students:* 63 full-time (25 women), 9 part-time (6 women); includes 8 minority (6 African Americans, 2 Hispanic Americans), 31 international. Terminal master's awarded for partial completion of doctoral program. *Degree requirements:* For master's, one foreign language (computer language can substitute), thesis, seminar presentation required; for doctorate, 2 foreign languages (computer language can substitute for one), dissertation, cumulative exams required. *Entrance requirements:* For master's, TOEFL, minimum GPA of 2.75; for doctorate, TOEFL. *Application deadline:* For fall admission, 3/1. Applications are processed on a rolling basis. Application fee: $25 ($50 for international students). Tuition, state resident: part-time $189 per credit. Tuition, nonresident: part-time $353 per credit. Required fees: $7.3 per credit. *Unit head:* Dr. Gerald Koser, Chair, 330-972-7372, E-mail: koser@uakron.edu.

University of Calgary, Faculty of Graduate Studies, Faculty of Science, Department of Chemistry, Calgary, AB T2N 1N4, Canada. Offers analytical chemistry (M Sc, PhD); applied chemistry (M Sc, PhD); inorganic chemistry (M Sc, PhD); organic chemistry (M Sc, PhD); physical chemistry (M Sc, PhD); polymer chemistry (M Sc, PhD); theoretical chemistry (M Sc, PhD). *Faculty:* 29 full-time (4 women), 1 part-time (0 women). *Students:* 60 full-time (25 women). *Degree requirements:* For master's, thesis required, foreign language not required; for doctorate, dissertation, candidacy exam required, foreign language not required. *Entrance requirements:* For master's and doctorate, TOEFL (minimum score of 580 required). *Application deadline:* For fall admission, 12/1 (priority date). Applications are processed on a rolling basis. Application fee: $60. *Unit head:* Dr. R. A. Kydd, Head, 403-220-5340. *Application contact:* Greta Prihodko, Graduate Program Administrator, 403-220-6252, E-mail: gradinfo@chem.ucalgary.ca.

University of Cincinnati, Division of Research and Advanced Studies, McMicken College of Arts and Sciences, Department of Chemistry, Cincinnati, OH 45221-0091. Offers analytical chemistry (MS, PhD); biochemistry (MS, PhD); inorganic chemistry (MS, PhD); organic chemistry (MS, PhD); physical chemistry (MS, PhD); polymer chemistry (MS, PhD). Part-time and evening/weekend programs available. *Faculty:* 25 full-time. *Students:* 87 full-time (26 women), 26 part-time (3 women); includes 12 minority (1 African American, 11 Asian Americans or Pacific Islanders), 34 international. Terminal master's awarded for partial completion of doctoral program. *Degree requirements:* For master's, thesis optional, foreign language not required; for doctorate, dissertation required, foreign language not required. *Entrance requirements:* For master's and doctorate, GRE General Test, GRE Subject Test. *Application deadline:* For fall admission, 2/1. Application fee: $30. *Unit head:* Dr. Marshall Wilson, Head, 513-556-9200, Fax: 513-556-9239, E-mail: marshall.wilson@uc.edu. *Application contact:* Thomas Ridgway, Graduate Program Director, 513-556-9200, Fax: 513-556-9239, E-mail: thomas.ridgway@uc.edu.

University of Georgia, Graduate School, College of Arts and Sciences, Department of Chemistry, Athens, GA 30602. Offers analytical chemistry (MS, PhD); inorganic chemistry (MS, PhD); organic chemistry (MS, PhD); physical chemistry (MS, PhD). *Faculty:* 23 full-time (1 woman). *Students:* 107 full-time (26 women), 11 part-time (4 women). *Degree requirements:* For master's, thesis required, foreign language not required; for doctorate, one foreign language (computer language can substitute), dissertation required. *Entrance requirements:* For master's and doctorate, GRE General Test. *Application deadline:* For fall admission, 7/1 (priority date); for spring admission, 11/15. Application fee: $30. Electronic applications accepted. *Unit head:* Dr. I. Jonathan Amster, Graduate Coordinator, 706-542-1936, Fax: 706-542-9454, E-mail: mauldin@sunchem.chem.uga.edu.

University of Louisville, Graduate School, College of Arts and Sciences, Department of Chemistry, Louisville, KY 40292-0001. Offers analytical chemistry (MS, PhD); chemical physics (PhD); inorganic chemistry (MS, PhD); organic chemistry (MS, PhD); physical chemistry (MS, PhD). *Faculty:* 20 full-time (3 women), 1 part-time (0 women). *Students:* 52 full-time (20 women), 4 part-time (2 women); includes 2 minority (both Hispanic Americans), 30 international. *Degree requirements:* For master's, thesis required; for doctorate, dissertation required. *Entrance requirements:* For master's and doctorate, GRE General Test, TOEFL (minimum score of 550 required). *Application deadline:* Applications are processed on a rolling basis. Application fee: $25. *Unit head:* Dr. George R. Pack, Chair, 502-852-6798, Fax: 502-852-8149, E-mail: george.pack@louisville.edu.

See in-depth description on page 199.

University of Maryland, College Park, Graduate School, College of Life Sciences, Department of Chemistry and Biochemistry, Chemistry Program, College Park, MD 20742-5045. Offers analytical chemistry (MS, PhD); inorganic chemistry (MS, PhD); organic chemistry (MS, PhD); physical chemistry (MS, PhD). *Students:* 76 full-time (34 women), 16 part-time (6 women); includes 8 minority (2 African Americans, 4 Asian Americans or Pacific Islanders, 1 Hispanic American, 1 Native American), 36 international. *Degree requirements:* For master's, thesis optional, foreign language not required; for doctorate, dissertation, 2 seminar presentations, oral exam required. *Entrance requirements:* For master's, GRE General Test, minimum GPA of 3.1; for doctorate, GRE General Test. *Application deadline:* Applications are processed on a rolling basis. Application fee: $50 ($70 for international students). Tuition, state resident: part-time $272 per credit hour. Tuition, nonresident: part-time $475 per credit hour. Required fees: $632; $379 per year. *Unit head:* Marlin Harmony, Graduate Director, 785-864-4670, Fax: 785-864-5396. *Application contact:* Trudy Lindsey, Director, Graduate Admission and Records, 301-405-4198, Fax: 301-314-9305, E-mail: grschool@deans.umd.edu.

University of Miami, Graduate School, College of Arts and Sciences, Department of Chemistry, Coral Gables, FL 33124. Offers chemistry (MS); inorganic chemistry (PhD); organic chemistry (PhD); physical chemistry (PhD). *Faculty:* 11 full-time (1 woman). *Students:* 40 full-time (18 women); includes 6 minority (1 African American, 1 Asian American or Pacific Islander, 4 Hispanic Americans), 33 international. Terminal master's awarded for partial completion of doctoral program. *Degree requirements:* For master's, foreign language and thesis not required; for doctorate, dissertation required, foreign language not required. *Entrance requirements:* For master's and doctorate, GRE General Test (minimum combined score of 1000 required), TOEFL (minimum score of 550 required). *Application deadline:* For fall admission, 1/15. Application fee: $35. Electronic applications accepted. Tuition: Full-time $15,336; part-time $852 per credit. Required fees: $174. Tuition and fees vary according to program. *Unit head:* Dr. Roger LeBlanc, Chairman, 305-284-2174, Fax: 305-284-4571. *Application contact:* Dr. Luis Echogoyen, Graduate Adviser, 305-661-2847, Fax: 305-284-4571, E-mail: ldookie@umiami.ir.miami.edu.

University of Michigan, Horace H. Rackham School of Graduate Studies, College of Literature, Science, and the Arts, Department of Chemistry, Ann Arbor, MI 48109. Offers analytical chemistry (PhD); chemical biology (PhD); inorganic chemistry (PhD); organic chemistry (PhD); physical chemistry (PhD). *Faculty:* 43 full-time (7 women). *Students:* 161 full-time (60 women); includes 5 minority (2 African Americans, 2 Asian Americans or Pacific Islanders, 1 Hispanic American), 43 international. *Degree requirements:* For doctorate, dissertation, oral defense of dissertation, preliminary exam, organic cumulative proficiency exams required, foreign language not required. *Entrance requirements:* For doctorate, GRE General Test, GRE Subject Test (recommended), statement of prior research. *Application deadline:* For fall admission, 2/15 (priority date). Applications are processed on a rolling basis. Application fee: $55. *Unit head:* Dr. Joseph P. Marino, Chair, 734-763-9681, Fax: 734-647-4847, E-mail: jpmarino@umich.edu. *Application contact:* Warren Noone, Assistant Director of Graduate Studies, 734-764-7278, Fax: 734-747-4865, E-mail: nooner@umich.edu.

University of Missouri–Columbia, Graduate School, College of Arts and Sciences, Department of Chemistry, Columbia, MO 65211. Offers analytical chemistry (MS, PhD); inorganic chemistry (MS, PhD); organic chemistry (MS, PhD); physical chemistry (MS, PhD). *Faculty:* 23 full-time (3 women). *Students:* 68 full-time (23 women), 24 part-time (7 women); includes 6 minority (1 African American, 2 Asian Americans or Pacific Islanders, 2 Hispanic Americans, 1 Native American), 47 international. *Degree requirements:* For master's, thesis required, foreign language not required; for doctorate, dissertation required. *Entrance requirements:* For master's and doctorate, GRE General Test, minimum GPA of 3.0. *Application deadline:* For fall admission, 7/1 (priority date). Applications are processed on a rolling basis. Application fee: $30 ($50 for international students). *Unit head:* Dr. Richard Thompson, Director of Graduate Studies, 573-882-7356.

University of Missouri–Kansas City, College of Arts and Sciences, Department of Chemistry, Kansas City, MO 64110-2499. Offers analytical chemistry (MS, PhD); inorganic chemistry (MS, PhD); organic chemistry (MS, PhD); physical chemistry (MS, PhD); polymer chemistry (MS, PhD). PhD offered through the School of Graduate Studies. Part-time programs available. *Faculty:* 12 full-time (2 women), 2 part-time (0 women). *Students:* 25 full-time (7 women), 7 part-time (2 women), 18 international. *Degree requirements:* For master's, thesis required (for some programs), foreign language not required; for doctorate, dissertation required, foreign language not required. *Entrance requirements:* For master's, TOEFL (minimum score of 550 required); for doctorate, GRE General Test (minimum combined score of 1500 on three sections required), TOEFL (minimum score of 550 required), TWE (minimum score of 4 required). *Application deadline:* For fall and spring admission, 2/1 (priority date); for winter admission, 9/1 (priority date). Applications are processed on a rolling basis. Application fee: $25. *Unit head:* Dr. Jerry Jean, Interim Chairperson, 816-235-2280, Fax: 816-235-5502, E-mail: jean@cctr.umkc.edu.

See in-depth description on page 211.

University of Missouri–St. Louis, Graduate School, College of Arts and Sciences, Department of Chemistry, St. Louis, MO 63121-4499. Offers chemistry (MS, PhD), including biochemistry, inorganic chemistry, organic chemistry, physical chemistry. Part-time and evening/weekend programs available. *Faculty:* 20. *Students:* 33 full-time (10 women), 26 part-time (9 women); includes 7 minority (2 African Americans, 4 Asian Americans or Pacific Islanders, 1 Hispanic American), 21 international. Terminal master's awarded for partial completion of doctoral program. *Degree requirements:* For master's, thesis optional, foreign language not required; for doctorate, dissertation required, foreign language not required. *Entrance requirements:* For doctorate, GRE General Test, GRE Subject Test. *Application deadline:* For fall admission, 7/1 (priority date); for spring admission, 12/7 (priority date). Applications are processed on a rolling basis. Application fee: $25 ($40 for international students). Electronic applications accepted. *Unit head:* Dr. R. E. K. Winter, Director of Graduate Studies, 314-516-5337, Fax: 314-516-5342, E-mail: chejjoll@jinx.umsl.edu. *Application contact:* Graduate Admissions, 314-516-5458, Fax: 314-516-6759, E-mail: gradadm@umsl.edu.

The University of Montana–Missoula, Graduate School, College of Arts and Sciences, Department of Chemistry, Missoula, MT 59812-0002. Offers chemistry (MS, PhD); chemistry teaching (MST); environmental chemistry (PhD); inorganic chemistry (PhD); organic chemistry (PhD); physical chemistry (PhD). Part-time programs available. *Faculty:* 14 full-time (3 women), 1 part-time (0 women). *Students:* 15 full-time (3 women), 3 part-time; includes 3 minority (all Asian Americans or Pacific Islanders) Terminal master's awarded for partial completion of doctoral program. *Degree requirements:* For master's, thesis required (for some programs); for doctorate, dissertation required. *Entrance requirements:* For master's, GRE General Test; for doctorate, GRE General Test, GRE Subject Test. *Application deadline:* For fall admission, 3/15 (priority date); for spring admission, 10/15. Applications are processed on a rolling basis. Application fee: $45. *Unit head:* Dr. Michael D. DeGrandpre, Graduate Coordinator, 403-243-4022, Fax: 406-243-4227.

University of Nebraska–Lincoln, Graduate College, College of Arts and Sciences, Department of Chemistry, Lincoln, NE 68588. Offers analytical chemistry (PhD); chemistry (MS); inorganic chemistry (PhD); organic chemistry (PhD); physical chemistry (PhD). *Faculty:* 23 full-time (2 women), 1 part-time (0 women). *Students:* 79 full-time (15 women), 23 part-time (2 women); includes 6 minority (1 African American, 2 Asian Americans or Pacific Islanders, 2 Hispanic Americans, 1 Native American), 47 international. *Degree requirements:* For master's, departmental qualifying exam required, thesis optional; for doctorate, dissertation, comprehensive and departmental qualifying exams required. *Entrance requirements:* For master's and doctorate, GRE Subject Test, TOEFL (minimum score of 550 required). *Application deadline:* For fall admission, 3/1 (priority date). Applications are processed on a rolling basis. Application fee: $35. Electronic applications accepted. *Unit head:* Dr. Lawrence Parkhurst, Chair, 402-472-3501, Fax: 402-472-9402.

University of Notre Dame, Graduate School, College of Science, Department of Chemistry and Biochemistry, Notre Dame, IN 46556. Offers biochemistry (MS, PhD); inorganic chemistry (MS, PhD); organic chemistry (MS, PhD); physical chemistry (MS, PhD). *Faculty:* 32 full-time (3 women). *Students:* 110 full-time (38 women), 1 part-time; includes 3 minority (2 African Americans, 1 Asian American or Pacific Islander), 57 international. Terminal master's awarded for partial completion of doctoral program. *Degree requirements:* For master's, thesis, comprehensive exam required, foreign language not required; for doctorate, dissertation, qualifying exam required, foreign language not required. *Entrance requirements:* For master's, GRE General Test, GRE General Subject Test (strongly recommended), TOEFL (minimum score of 600 required; 250 for computer-based); for doctorate, GRE General Test, GRE Subject Test (strongly recommended), TOEFL (minimum score of 600 required; 250 for computer-based). *Application deadline:* For fall admission, 2/1 (priority date). Applications are processed on a rolling basis. Application fee: $40. *Unit head:* Dr. A. Graham Lappin, Chairman, 219-631-7058, Fax: 219-631-6652, E-mail: lappin.1@nd.edu. *Application contact:* Dr. Terrence J. Akai, Director of Graduate Admissions, 219-631-7706, Fax: 219-631-4183, E-mail: gradad@nd.edu.

See in-depth description on page 215.

University of Regina, Faculty of Graduate Studies and Research, Faculty of Science, Department of Chemistry, Regina, SK S4S 0A2, Canada. Offers analytical chemistry (M Sc, PhD); biochemistry (M Sc, PhD); clinical biochemistry (M Sc, PhD); inorganic chemistry (M Sc, PhD); organic chemistry (M Sc, PhD); physical chemistry (M Sc, PhD); x-ray crystallography (M Sc, PhD). Part-time programs available. *Faculty:* 10 full-time (1 woman), 3 part-time (0 women). *Students:* 9 full-time (5 women), 6 part-time (3 women). *Degree requirements:* For master's, thesis, departmental qualifying exam required, foreign language not required; for doctorate, variable foreign language requirement, dissertation, departmental qualifying exam required. *Entrance requirements:* For master's, TOEFL (minimum score of 580 required); for doctorate, TOEFL. *Application deadline:* Applications are processed on a rolling basis. Application fee: $0. *Expenses:* Tuition and fees charges are reported in Canadian dollars. Tuition, state resident: full-time $1,688 Canadian dollars; part-time $94 Canadian dollars per credit hour. International tuition: $3,375 Canadian dollars full-time. Required fees: $65 Canadian dollars per course. Tuition and fees vary according to course load and program. *Unit head:* Dr. K. Johnson, Head, 306-585-4146, Fax: 306-585-4894, E-mail: chem@max.cc.uregina.ca.

University of Southern Mississippi, Graduate School, College of Science and Technology, Department of Chemistry and Biochemistry, Hattiesburg, MS 39406-5167. Offers analytical chemistry (MS, PhD); biochemistry (MS, PhD); inorganic chemistry (MS, PhD); organic chemistry (MS, PhD); physical chemistry (MS, PhD). *Faculty:* 16 full-time (2 women), 1 part-time (0 women). *Students:* 25 full-time (10 women); includes 8 minority (3 African Americans, 4 Asian Americans or Pacific Islanders, 1 Hispanic American) *Degree requirements:* For master's, thesis required, foreign language not required; for doctorate, 2 foreign languages (computer language can substitute for one), dissertation required. *Entrance requirements:* For master's, GRE General Test, TOEFL, minimum GPA of 2.75; for doctorate, GRE General Test, TOEFL, minimum GPA of 3.5. *Application deadline:* For fall admission, 8/6 (priority date). Applications are processed on a rolling basis. Application fee: $0 ($25 for international students). Tuition, state resident: full-time $2,250; part-time $137 per semester hour. Tuition, nonresident: full-time $3,102; part-time $172 per semester hour. Required fees: $602. *Unit head:* Dr. Stella Elakovich, Chair, 601-266-4701. *Application contact:* Dr. Gordon Cannon, 601-266-4702.

University of South Florida, Graduate School, College of Arts and Sciences, Department of Chemistry, Tampa, FL 33620-9951. Offers analytical chemistry (MS, PhD); biochemistry (MS, PhD); inorganic chemistry (MS, PhD); organic chemistry (MS, PhD); physical chemistry (MS, PhD). Part-time programs available. *Faculty:* 23 full-time (3 women), 3 part-time (1 woman). *Students:* 44 full-time (14 women), 10 part-time (1 woman); includes 2 African Americans, 3 Hispanic Americans Terminal master's awarded for partial completion of doctoral program. *Degree requirements:* For master's, thesis required; for doctorate, 2 foreign languages (computer language can substitute for one), dissertation, colloquium required. *Entrance requirements:* For master's and doctorate, GRE General Test (minimum combined score of 1000 required), minimum GPA of 3.0 in last 30 hours of chemistry course work. *Application deadline:* For fall admission, 6/5 (priority date); for spring admission, 10/23 (priority date). Applications are processed on a rolling basis. Application fee: $20. Electronic applications accepted. Tuition, state resident: part-time $148 per credit hour. Tuition, nonresident: part-time $509 per credit hour. *Unit head:* Dr. Robert Potter, Chairperson, 813-974-4129, Fax: 813-974-1731, E-mail: potter@chuma1.cas.usf.edu. *Application contact:* Andy Zekter, Graduate Director, 813-974-9666, Fax: 813-974-3203, E-mail: zekter@chuma1.cas.usf.edu.

University of Tennessee, Knoxville, Graduate School, College of Arts and Sciences, Department of Chemistry, Knoxville, TN 37996. Offers analytical chemistry (MS, PhD); chemical physics (PhD); environmental chemistry (MS, PhD); inorganic chemistry (MS, PhD); organic chemistry (MS, PhD); physical chemistry (MS, PhD); polymer chemistry (MS, PhD); theoretical chemistry (PhD). Part-time programs available. *Faculty:* 31 full-time (1 woman), 1 (woman) part-time. *Students:* 55 full-time (15 women), 44 part-time (11 women); includes 1 minority (Asian American or Pacific Islander), 23 international. Terminal master's awarded for partial completion of doctoral program. *Degree requirements:* For master's and doctorate, thesis/dissertation required, foreign language not required. *Entrance requirements:* For master's and doctorate, GRE General Test, TOEFL (minimum score of 550 required), minimum GPA of 2.7. *Application deadline:* For fall admission, 2/1 (priority date). Applications are processed on a rolling basis. Application fee: $35. Electronic applications accepted. *Unit head:* Dr. Michael Sepaniak, Head, 423-974-3141, Fax: 423-974-3454, E-mail: msepaniak@utk.edu. *Application contact:* Dr. Charles Feigerle, Graduate Representative, E-mail: cfeigerle@utk.edu.

The University of Texas at Austin, Graduate School, College of Natural Sciences, Department of Chemistry and Biochemistry, Austin, TX 78712-1111. Offers analytical chemistry (MA, PhD); biochemistry (MA, PhD); inorganic chemistry (MA, PhD); organic chemistry (MA, PhD); physical chemistry (MA, PhD). *Students:* 278 (94 women); includes 28 minority (3 African Americans, 11 Asian Americans or Pacific Islanders, 13 Hispanic Americans, 1 Native American) 61 international. *Entrance requirements:* For master's and doctorate, GRE General Test. Application fee: $50 ($75 for international students). *Unit head:* Dr. Marvin L. Hackert, Chairman, 512-471-3949. *Application contact:* Dr. Jennifer Brodbelt, Graduate Adviser, 512-471-0028.

University of Toledo, Graduate School, College of Arts and Sciences, Department of Chemistry, Toledo, OH 43606-3398. Offers analytical chemistry (MS, MS Ed, PhD); biological chemistry (MS, MS Ed, PhD); inorganic chemistry (MS, MS Ed, PhD); organic chemistry (MS, MS Ed, PhD); physical chemistry (MS, MS Ed, PhD). Part-time programs available. *Degree requirements:* For master's and doctorate, thesis/dissertation required, foreign language not required. *Entrance requirements:* For master's and doctorate, GRE General Test, GRE Subject Test, TOEFL. Electronic applications accepted. *Faculty research:* Enzymology, materials chemistry, crystallography, theoretical chemistry.

Wake Forest University, Graduate School, Department of Chemistry, Winston-Salem, NC 27109. Offers analytical chemistry (MS, PhD); inorganic chemistry (MS, PhD); organic chemistry (MS, PhD); physical chemistry (MS, PhD). Part-time programs available. *Faculty:* 14 full-time (1 woman). *Students:* 22 full-time (11 women), 2 part-time; includes 5 minority (2 African Americans, 3 Asian Americans or Pacific Islanders) *Degree requirements:* For master's, one foreign language (computer language can substitute), thesis required; for doctorate, 2 foreign languages (computer language can substitute for one), dissertation required. *Entrance requirements:* For master's and doctorate, GRE General Test, GRE Subject Test. *Application deadline:* For fall admission, 2/15. Application fee: $25. *Unit head:* Dr. Jim Fishbein, Director, 336-758-6139, E-mail: fishbein@wfu.edu.

See in-depth description on page 227.

Washington State University, Graduate School, College of Sciences, Department of Chemistry, Pullman, WA 99164. Offers analytical chemistry (MS, PhD); inorganic chemistry (MS, PhD); nuclear chemistry (MS, PhD); organic chemistry (MS, PhD); physical chemistry (MS, PhD). *Faculty:* 28 full-time (4 women). *Students:* 39 full-time (14 women), 3 part-time (2 women); includes 4 minority (2 Asian Americans or Pacific Islanders, 1 Hispanic American, 1 Native American), 8 international. Terminal master's awarded for partial completion of doctoral program. *Degree requirements:* For master's, oral exam, teaching experience required, thesis optional, foreign language not required; for doctorate, dissertation, oral exam, teaching experience required, foreign language not required. *Entrance requirements:* For master's and doctorate, GRE General Test, minimum GPA of 3.0. *Application deadline:* For fall admission, 3/1 (priority date). Applications are processed on a rolling basis. Application fee: $35. *Unit head:* Dr. Ralph Yount, Chair, 509-335-1516. *Application contact:* James O. Schenk, Chair, Admissions Committee, 509-335-8866, E-mail: carrie@wsu.edu.

Wesleyan University, Graduate Programs, Department of Chemistry, Middletown, CT 06459-0260. Offers biochemistry (MA, PhD); chemical physics (MA, PhD); inorganic chemistry (MA, PhD); organic chemistry (MA, PhD); physical chemistry (MA, PhD); theoretical chemistry (MA, PhD). Terminal master's awarded for partial completion of doctoral program. *Degree requirements:* For master's and doctorate, one foreign language (computer language can substitute), thesis/dissertation required. *Entrance requirements:* For master's, GRE General Test, GRE Subject Test; for doctorate, GRE Subject Test.

See in-depth description on page 233.

Yale University, Graduate School of Arts and Sciences, Department of Chemistry, New Haven, CT 06520. Offers biophysical chemistry (PhD); inorganic chemistry (PhD); organic chemistry (PhD); physical chemistry (PhD). *Faculty:* 61 full-time (14 women). *Students:* 139 full-time (62 women); includes 11 minority (8 Asian Americans or Pacific Islanders, 3 Hispanic Americans), 53 international. *Degree requirements:* For doctorate, dissertation required. *Entrance requirements:* For doctorate, GRE General Test, GRE Subject Test, TOEFL. *Application deadline:* For fall admission, 1/4. Application fee: $65. *Unit head:* Chair, 203-432-3912. *Application contact:* Admissions Information, 203-432-2770.

See in-depth description on page 241.

Organic Chemistry

Boston College, Graduate School of Arts and Sciences, Department of Chemistry, Chestnut Hill, MA 02467-3800. Offers analytical chemistry (MS, PhD); biochemistry (MS, PhD); chemistry (MS); inorganic chemistry (MS, PhD); organic chemistry (MS, PhD); physical chemistry (MS, PhD). Part-time programs available. *Faculty:* 20 full-time (2 women). *Students:* 25 full-time (11 women), 75 part-time (29 women); includes 12 minority (1 African American, 8 Asian Americans or Pacific Islanders, 2 Hispanic Americans, 1 Native American), 28 international. Terminal master's awarded for partial completion of doctoral program. *Degree requirements:* For master's, thesis required; for doctorate, dissertation, qualifying exam required. *Entrance requirements:* For master's and doctorate, GRE General Test, GRE Subject Test. *Application deadline:* For fall admission, 2/1. Application fee: $40. *Unit head:* Dr. Larry McLaughlin, Chairperson, 617-552-3605, E-mail: larry.mclaughlin@bc.edu. *Application contact:* Dr. Mary Roberts, Graduate Program Director, 617-552-3616, E-mail: mary.roberts@bc.edu.

See in-depth description on page 93.

Boston University, Graduate School of Arts and Sciences, Department of Chemistry, Boston, MA 02215. Offers biochemistry (MA, PhD); chemical physics (MA, PhD); inorganic chemistry (MA, PhD); organic chemistry (MA, PhD); photochemistry (MA, PhD); physical chemistry (MA, PhD); theoretical chemistry (MA, PhD). *Faculty:* 21 full-time (1 woman). *Students:* 81 full-time (26 women), 1 (woman) part-time; includes 4 minority (2 African Americans, 2 Asian Americans or Pacific Islanders), 58 international. Terminal master's awarded for partial completion of doctoral program. *Degree requirements:* For master's, one foreign language, thesis not required; for doctorate, one foreign language, dissertation, exams required. *Entrance requirements:* For master's and doctorate, GRE General Test, GRE Subject Test (recommended), TOEFL (minimum score of 550 required). *Application deadline:* For fall admission, 7/1. Applications are processed on a rolling basis. Application fee: $50. Tuition: Full-time $23,770; part-time $743 per credit. Required fees: $220. Tuition and fees vary according to class time, course level, campus/location and program. *Unit head:* Thomas D. Tullius, Chairman, 617-353-4277, Fax: 617-353-6466, E-mail: tullius@chem.bu.edu. *Application contact:* Kevin Burgoyne, Academic Administrator, 617-353-2503, Fax: 617-353-6466, E-mail: burgoyne@chem.bu.edu.

Brandeis University, Graduate School of Arts and Sciences, Program in Chemistry, Waltham, MA 02454-9110. Offers inorganic chemistry (MS, PhD); organic chemistry (MS, PhD); physical chemistry (MS, PhD). *Faculty:* 16 full-time (2 women). *Students:* 44 full-time (22 women); includes 1 minority (African American), 26 international. Terminal master's awarded for partial completion of doctoral program. *Degree requirements:* For master's, 1 year of residency required, foreign language and thesis not required; for doctorate, one foreign language (computer language can substitute), dissertation, 3 years of residency, 2 seminars, qualifying exams required. *Entrance requirements:* For master's and doctorate, GRE General Test. *Application deadline:* For fall admission, 1/15 (priority date). Applications are processed on a rolling basis. Application fee: $60. *Unit head:* Dr. I. Y. Chan, Chair, 781-736-2554, Fax: 781-736-2516. *Application contact:* Charlotte Haygazian, Secretary, 781-736-2500, Fax: 781-736-2516, E-mail: chemadm@brandeis.edu.

Brigham Young University, Graduate Studies, College of Physical and Mathematical Sciences, Department of Chemistry and Biochemistry, Provo, UT 84602-1001. Offers analytical chemistry (MS, PhD); biochemistry (MS, PhD); inorganic chemistry (MS, PhD); organic chemistry (MS, PhD); physical chemistry (MS, PhD). *Faculty:* 33 full-time (1 woman), 3 part-time (0 women). *Students:* 70 full-time (24 women); includes 1 minority (Asian American or Pacific Islander), 39 international. *Degree requirements:* For master's and doctorate, thesis/dissertation required, foreign language not required. *Entrance requirements:* For master's and doctorate, minimum GPA of 3.0 in last 60 hours. *Application deadline:* For fall admission, 2/1 (priority date). Applications are processed on a rolling basis. Application fee: $30. Tuition: Full-time $3,330; part-time $185 per credit hour. Tuition and fees vary according to program and student's religious affiliation. *Unit head:* Dr. Francis R. Nordmeyer, Chair, 801-378-3667, Fax: 801-378-5474, E-mail: fran_nordmeyer@byu.edu. *Application contact:* N. Kent Dalley, Coordinator, Graduate Admissions, 801-378-3434, Fax: 801-378-5474, E-mail: chemgrad@byu.edu.

See in-depth description on page 97.

California State University, Fullerton, Graduate Studies, School of Natural Science and Mathematics, Department of Chemistry and Biochemistry, Fullerton, CA 92834-9480. Offers analytical chemistry (MS); biochemistry (MS); geochemistry (MS); inorganic chemistry (MS); organic chemistry (MS); physical chemistry (MS). Part-time programs available. *Faculty:* 18 full-time, 14 part-time. *Students:* 8 full-time (3 women), 32 part-time (14 women); includes 19 minority (14 Asian Americans or Pacific Islanders, 5 Hispanic Americans), 6 international. *Degree requirements:* For master's, thesis, departmental qualifying exam required, foreign language not required. *Entrance requirements:* For master's, minimum GPA of 2.5 in last 60 units, major in chemistry or related field. Application fee: $55. Tuition, nonresident: part-time $264 per unit. *Unit head:* Dr. Bruce Weber, Chair, 714-278-3621. *Application contact:* Dr. Gregory Williams, Adviser, 714-278-2170.

California State University, Los Angeles, Graduate Studies, School of Natural and Social Sciences, Department of Chemistry and Biochemistry, Los Angeles, CA 90032-8530. Offers analytical chemistry (MS); biochemistry (MS); chemistry (MS); inorganic chemistry (MS); organic chemistry (MS); physical chemistry (MS). Part-time and evening/weekend programs available. *Faculty:* 14 full-time, 20 part-time. *Students:* 13 full-time (6 women), 11 part-time (4 women); includes 16 minority (1 African American, 12 Asian Americans or Pacific Islanders, 3 Hispanic Americans), 3 international. *Degree requirements:* For master's, one foreign language (computer language can substitute), comprehensive exam or thesis required. *Entrance requirements:* For master's, TOEFL (minimum score of 550 required). *Application deadline:* For fall admission, 6/30; for spring admission, 2/1. Applications are processed on a rolling basis. Application fee: $55. *Unit head:* Dr. Scott Grover, Acting Chair, 323-343-2300.

Case Western Reserve University, School of Graduate Studies, Department of Chemistry, Cleveland, OH 44106. Offers analytical chemistry (MS, PhD); inorganic chemistry (MS, PhD); organic chemistry (MS, PhD); physical chemistry (MS, PhD). Part-time programs available. Terminal master's awarded for partial completion of doctoral program. *Degree requirements:* For master's, thesis not required; for doctorate, dissertation required. *Entrance requirements:* For master's and doctorate, GRE General Test, GRE Subject Test, TOEFL (minimum score of 550 required). *Faculty research:* Electrochemistry, synthetic chemistry, chemistry of life process, spectroscopy, kinetics.

Clark Atlanta University, School of Arts and Sciences, Department of Chemistry, Atlanta, GA 30314. Offers inorganic chemistry (MS, PhD); organic chemistry (MS, PhD); physical chemistry (MS, PhD); science education (DA). Part-time programs available. *Students:* 17 full-time (11

Organic Chemistry

Clark Atlanta University *(continued)*
women), 20 part-time (11 women); includes 33 minority (28 African Americans, 2 Asian Americans or Pacific Islanders, 3 Hispanic Americans), 3 international. *Degree requirements:* For master's, one foreign language (computer language can substitute), thesis, comprehensive exam required; for doctorate, 2 foreign languages (computer language can substitute for one), dissertation, cumulative exam required. *Entrance requirements:* For master's, GRE General Test, minimum GPA of 2.5; for doctorate, GRE General Test, GRE Subject Test, minimum graduate GPA of 3.0. *Application deadline:* For fall admission, 4/1; for spring admission, 11/1. Applications are processed on a rolling basis. Application fee: $40. *Unit head:* Dr. Reynold Verrett, Chairperson, 404-880-8154. *Application contact:* Michelle Clark-Davis, Graduate Program Assistant, 404-880-8709.

Clarkson University, Graduate School, School of Science, Department of Chemistry, Potsdam, NY 13699. Offers analytical chemistry (MS, PhD); inorganic chemistry (MS, PhD); organic chemistry (MS, PhD); physical chemistry (MS, PhD). *Faculty:* 9 full-time (0 women). *Students:* 25 full-time (13 women); includes 1 minority (African American), 15 international. *Degree requirements:* For master's, foreign language and thesis not required; for doctorate, dissertation, departmental qualifying exam required, foreign language not required. *Entrance requirements:* For master's, GRE, TOEFL. *Application deadline:* For fall admission, 5/15 (priority date); for spring admission, 10/15 (priority date). Applications are processed on a rolling basis. Application fee: $25 ($35 for international students). Tuition: Part-time $661 per credit hour. Required fees: $215 per semester. *Unit head:* Dr. Stig Friberg, Chair, 315-268-6500, Fax: 315-268-6610, E-mail: fbg@clarkson.edu.

Cleveland State University, College of Graduate Studies, College of Arts and Sciences, Department of Chemistry, Cleveland, OH 44115-2440. Offers analytical chemistry (MS, PhD); clinical chemistry (MS, PhD); inorganic chemistry (MS); organic chemistry (MS); structural analysis (MS, PhD). Part-time and evening/weekend programs available. *Faculty:* 13 full-time (1 woman). *Students:* 1 full-time (0 women), 53 part-time (22 women); includes 5 minority (1 African American, 3 Asian Americans or Pacific Islanders, 1 Hispanic American), 25 international. *Degree requirements:* For master's, thesis required (for some programs), foreign language not required; for doctorate, dissertation required, foreign language not required. *Entrance requirements:* For master's and doctorate, GRE General Test, GRE Subject Test, TOEFL (minimum score of 525 required). *Application deadline:* For fall admission, 7/15 (priority date). Applications are processed on a rolling basis. Application fee: $25. *Unit head:* Dr. Stan Duraj, Interim Chair, 216-523-7312, Fax: 216-687-9298.

Columbia University, Graduate School of Arts and Sciences, Division of Natural Sciences, Department of Chemistry, New York, NY 10027. Offers chemical physics (M Phil, PhD); inorganic chemistry (M Phil, MS, PhD); organic chemistry (M Phil, MS, PhD). *Degree requirements:* For master's, comprehensive exams (MS); 1 foreign language, teaching experience, oral and written exams (M Phil) required, thesis not required; for doctorate, one foreign language, dissertation, M Phil required. *Entrance requirements:* For master's and doctorate, GRE General Test, GRE Subject Test, TOEFL. *Faculty research:* Biophysics.

Cornell University, Graduate School, Graduate Fields of Arts and Sciences, Field of Chemistry, Ithaca, NY 14853-0001. Offers analytical chemistry (PhD); bio-organic chemistry (PhD); biophysical chemistry (PhD); chemical physics (PhD); inorganic chemistry (PhD); material chemistry (PhD); organic chemistry (PhD); physical chemistry (PhD); theoretical chemistry (PhD). *Faculty:* 38 full-time. *Students:* 139 full-time (44 women); includes 10 minority (1 African American, 4 Asian Americans or Pacific Islanders, 4 Hispanic Americans, 1 Native American), 51 international. *Degree requirements:* For doctorate, dissertation required, foreign language not required. *Entrance requirements:* For doctorate, GRE General Test, GRE Subject Test, TOEFL (minimum score of 600 required). *Application deadline:* For fall admission, 1/15. Application fee: $65. Electronic applications accepted. *Unit head:* Director of Graduate Studies, 607-255-4139. *Application contact:* Graduate Field Assistant, 607-255-4139, E-mail: chemgrad@cornell.edu.

See in-depth description on page 109.

Florida State University, Graduate Studies, College of Arts and Sciences, Department of Chemistry, Tallahassee, FL 32306. Offers analytical chemistry (MS, PhD); biochemistry (MS, PhD); chemical physics (MS, PhD); inorganic chemistry (MS, PhD); organic chemistry (MS, PhD); physical chemistry (MS, PhD). Part-time programs available. *Faculty:* 38 full-time (4 women). *Students:* 87 full-time (27 women), 8 part-time (2 women). Terminal master's awarded for partial completion of doctoral program. *Degree requirements:* For master's, cumulative and diagnostic exams required; for doctorate, dissertation, cumulative and diagnostic exams required, foreign language not required. *Entrance requirements:* For master's and doctorate, GRE General Test, minimum B average in undergraduate course work. *Application deadline:* Applications are processed on a rolling basis. Application fee: $20. Tuition, state resident: part-time $139 per credit hour. Tuition, nonresident: part-time $482 per credit hour. Tuition and fees vary according to program. *Unit head:* Dr. John G. Dorsey, Chairman, 850-644-9625, Fax: 850-644-8281. *Application contact:* Dr. Naresh Dalal, Chair, Graduate Admissions Committee, 850-644-3398, Fax: 850-644-8281, E-mail: gradinfo@chem.fsu.edu.

See in-depth description on page 123.

Georgetown University, Graduate School, Department of Chemistry, Washington, DC 20057. Offers analytical chemistry (MS, PhD); biochemistry (MS, PhD); chemical physics (MS, PhD); inorganic chemistry (MS, PhD); organic chemistry (MS, PhD); physical chemistry (MS, PhD); theoretical chemistry (MS, PhD). Terminal master's awarded for partial completion of doctoral program. *Degree requirements:* For master's, thesis (for some programs), qualifying exam required, foreign language not required; for doctorate, dissertation, comprehensive exam required. *Entrance requirements:* For master's and doctorate, GRE General Test, TOEFL (minimum score of 550 required, 600 for teaching assistants).

See in-depth description on page 125.

The George Washington University, Columbian School of Arts and Sciences, Department of Chemistry, Washington, DC 20052. Offers analytical chemistry (MS, PhD); inorganic chemistry (MS, PhD); materials science (MS, PhD); organic chemistry (MS, PhD); physical chemistry (MS, PhD). Part-time and evening/weekend programs available. *Faculty:* 5 full-time (0 women), 7 part-time (4 women); includes 6 minority (1 African American, 3 Asian Americans or Pacific Islanders, 2 Hispanic Americans), 6 international. Terminal master's awarded for partial completion of doctoral program. *Degree requirements:* For master's, computer language, thesis or alternative, comprehensive exam required; for doctorate, computer language, dissertation, general exam required. *Entrance requirements:* For master's and doctorate, GRE General Test, interview, minimum GPA of 3.0. Application fee: $55. Tuition: Full-time $17,328; part-time $722 per credit hour. Required fees: $828; $35 per credit hour. Tuition and fees vary according to campus/location and program. *Unit head:* Dr. Michael King, Chair, 202-994-6121.

Harvard University, Graduate School of Arts and Sciences, Department of Chemistry and Chemical Biology, Cambridge, MA 02138. Offers biochemical chemistry (AM, PhD); inorganic chemistry (AM, PhD); organic chemistry (AM, PhD); physical chemistry (AM, PhD). *Students:* 188 full-time (36 women). *Degree requirements:* For doctorate, dissertation, cumulative exams required, foreign language not required. *Entrance requirements:* For master's, GRE General Test, TOEFL (minimum score of 550 required); for doctorate, GRE General Test, GRE Subject Test, TOEFL (minimum score of 550 required). *Application deadline:* For fall admission, 12/31. Application fee: $60. *Unit head:* Dr. David Evans, Chair, 617-495-2948. *Application contact:* Graduate Admissions Office, 617-496-3208.

See in-depth description on page 133.

Howard University, Graduate School of Arts and Sciences, Department of Chemistry, Washington, DC 20059-0002. Offers analytical chemistry (MS, PhD); biochemistry (MS, PhD); inorganic chemistry (MS, PhD); organic chemistry (MS, PhD); physical chemistry (MS, PhD); polymer chemistry (MS, PhD); theoretical chemistry (MS, PhD). Part-time programs available. Terminal master's awarded for partial completion of doctoral program. *Degree requirements:* For master's, one foreign language (computer language can substitute), thesis, comprehensive exam, teaching experience required; for doctorate, 2 foreign languages (computer language can substitute for one), dissertation, comprehensive exam, teaching experience required. *Entrance requirements:* For master's, GRE General Test, GRE General Test, minimum GPA of 3.0. *Faculty research:* Stratospheric aerosols, liquid crystals, polymer coatings, terrestrial and extraterrestrial atmospheres, amidogen reaction.

Illinois Institute of Technology, Graduate College, Armour College of Engineering and Sciences, Department of Biological, Chemical and Physical Sciences, Chemistry Division, Chicago, IL 60616-3793. Offers chemistry (MAC, MS, PhD); chemistry (M Chem); inorganic chemistry (MS, PhD); organic chemistry (MS, PhD); physical chemistry (MS, PhD); polymer chemistry (MS, PhD); theoretical chemistry (MS, PhD). Part-time and evening/weekend programs available. *Faculty:* 8 full-time (0 women), 14 full-time (7 women), 70 part-time (27 women); includes 19 minority (10 African Americans, 9 Asian Americans or Pacific Islanders), 16 international. Terminal master's awarded for partial completion of doctoral program. *Degree requirements:* For master's, thesis (for some programs), comprehensive exam, foreign language not required; for doctorate, dissertation, comprehensive exam required, foreign language not required. *Entrance requirements:* For master's and doctorate, GRE (minimum score of 1200 required), TOEFL (minimum score of 550 required), undergraduate GPA of 3.0 required. *Application deadline:* For fall admission, 7/1; for spring admission, 11/1. Applications are processed on a rolling basis. Application fee: $30. Electronic applications accepted. *Unit head:* Dr. Carlo Segre, Associate Chair, 312-567-3480, Fax: 312-567-3494, E-mail: segre@iit.edu. *Application contact:* Dr. S. Mohammad Shahidehpour, Dean of Graduate College, 312-567-3024, Fax: 312-567-7517, E-mail: grad@minna.cns.iit.edu.

See in-depth description on page 135.

Instituto Tecnológico y de Estudios Superiores de Monterrey, Campus Monterrey, Graduate and Research Division, Program in Natural and Social Sciences, Monterrey, 64849, Mexico. Offers biotechnology (MS); chemistry (MS, PhD); communications (MS); education (MA). Part-time programs available. *Degree requirements:* For master's and doctorate, thesis/dissertation required. *Entrance requirements:* For master's, PAEG, TOEFL; for doctorate, PAEG, TOEFL, master's in related field. *Faculty research:* Cultural industries, mineral substances, bioremediation, food processing, CQ in industrial chemical processing.

Kansas State University, Graduate School, College of Arts and Sciences, Department of Chemistry, Manhattan, KS 66506. Offers inorganic chemistry (MS); chemistry (PhD); inorganic chemistry (MS); organic chemistry (MS); physical chemistry (MS). *Faculty:* 16 full-time (1 woman). *Students:* 43 full-time (12 women), 2 part-time (1 woman); includes 2 minority (both Asian Americans or Pacific Islanders), 25 international. Terminal master's awarded for partial completion of doctoral program. *Degree requirements:* For master's and doctorate, thesis/dissertation required, foreign language not required. *Entrance requirements:* For master's and doctorate, GRE, minimum GPA of 3.0. *Application deadline:* For fall admission, 6/1 (priority date); for spring admission, 12/1. Applications are processed on a rolling basis. Application fee: $0 ($25 for international students). *Unit head:* Peter M. A. Sherwood, Head, 785-532-6665, Fax: 785-532-6666, E-mail: escashem@ksu.edu. *Application contact:* Christer B. Aakeroy, Graduate Coordinator, 785-532-1468, Fax: 785-532-6666.

See in-depth description on page 143.

Kent State University, College of Arts and Sciences, Department of Chemistry, Kent, OH 44242-0001. Offers analytical chemistry (MS, PhD); biochemistry (PhD); chemistry (MA, MS, PhD); inorganic chemistry (MS, PhD); organic chemistry (MS, PhD); physical chemistry (MS, PhD). *Faculty:* 23 full-time. *Students:* 36 full-time (20 women), 2 part-time (both women); includes 1 minority (African American), 19 international. *Degree requirements:* For master's and doctorate, thesis/dissertation required, foreign language not required. *Entrance requirements:* For master's, minimum GPA of 2.75; for doctorate, minimum GPA of 3.0. *Application deadline:* For fall admission, 7/12; for spring admission, 11/29. Applications are processed on a rolling basis. Application fee: $30. *Unit head:* Dr. Rathindra N. Bose, Chairman, 330-672-2032, Fax: 330-672-3816.

See in-depth description on page 147.

Lehigh University, College of Arts and Sciences, Department of Chemistry, Bethlehem, PA 18015-3094. Offers biochemistry and analytical chemistry (MS, PhD); chemistry (DA); clinical chemistry (MS); inorganic chemistry (MS, PhD); organic chemistry (MS, PhD); pharmaceutical chemistry (PhD); physical chemistry (MS, PhD). Part-time programs available. Postbaccalaureate distance learning degree programs offered (no on-campus study). *Students:* 30 full-time (14 women), 92 part-time (46 women); includes 10 minority (7 Asian Americans or Pacific Islanders, 3 Hispanic Americans), 10 international. Terminal master's awarded for partial completion of doctoral program. *Degree requirements:* For master's, foreign language and thesis not required; for doctorate, dissertation required. *Entrance requirements:* For master's and doctorate, GRE General Test, TSE (minimum score of 230 required). *Application deadline:* For fall admission, 7/15; for spring admission, 12/1. Applications are processed on a rolling basis. Application fee: $40. *Unit head:* Dr. Keith J. Schray, Chairman, 610-758-3474, Fax: 610-758-6536, E-mail: kjs0@lehigh.edu. *Application contact:* Dr. James E. Roberts, Graduate Coordinator, 610-758-4847, Fax: 610-758-6536, E-mail: jer1@lehigh.edu.

Marquette University, Graduate School, College of Arts and Sciences, Department of Chemistry, Milwaukee, WI 53201-1881. Offers analytical chemistry (MS, PhD); bioanalytical chemistry (MS, PhD); biophysical chemistry (MS, PhD); chemical physics (MS, PhD); inorganic chemistry (MS, PhD); organic chemistry (MS, PhD); physical chemistry (MS, PhD). Part-time programs available. *Faculty:* 15 full-time (2 women), 1 part-time (0 women). *Students:* 33 full-time (12 women), 6 part-time (1 woman); includes 5 minority (2 African Americans, 3 Asian Americans or Pacific Islanders), 30 international. Terminal master's awarded for partial completion of doctoral program. *Degree requirements:* For master's, comprehensive exam required; for doctorate, dissertation, cumulative exams required, foreign language not required. *Entrance requirements:* For master's and doctorate, TOEFL (minimum score of 550 required), GRE Subject Test. Application fee: $40. Tuition: Part-time $510 per credit hour. Tuition and fees vary according to program. *Unit head:* Dr. Charles Wilkie, Chairman, 414-288-7065, Fax: 414-288-7066. *Application contact:* Dr. Mark Steinmetz, Director of Graduate Studies, 414-288-3535, Fax: 414-288-7066.

Massachusetts Institute of Technology, School of Science, Department of Chemistry, Cambridge, MA 02139-4307. Offers biochemistry (PhD); biological chemistry (PhD, Sc D); inorganic chemistry (PhD, Sc D); organic chemistry (PhD, Sc D); physical chemistry (PhD, Sc D). *Faculty:* 27 full-time (2 women). *Students:* 172 full-time (51 women); includes 19 minority (3 African Americans, 6 Asian Americans or Pacific Islanders, 9 Hispanic Americans, 1 Native American), 53 international. *Degree requirements:* For doctorate, dissertation, comprehensive oral exam, oral presentation, written exams required, foreign language not required. *Application deadline:* For fall admission, 1/15. Application fee: $55. *Unit head:* Dr. Stephen J. Lippard, Chairman, 617-253-1845. *Application contact:* Susan Brighton, Graduate Administrator, 617-253-1845, Fax: 617-258-0241, E-mail: brighton@mit.edu.

McMaster University, School of Graduate Studies, Faculty of Science, Department of Chemistry, Hamilton, ON L8S 4M2, Canada. Offers analytical chemistry (M Sc, PhD); chemical physics (M Sc, PhD); chemistry (M Sc, PhD); inorganic chemistry (M Sc, PhD); organic chemistry (M Sc, PhD); physical chemistry (M Sc, PhD); polymer chemistry (M Sc, PhD). Part-time programs available. *Faculty:* 21 full-time (2 women), 4 part-time (0 women). *Students:* 67

full-time (23 women), 1 part-time, 1 international. Terminal master's awarded for partial completion of doctoral program. *Degree requirements:* For master's, thesis required, foreign language not required; for doctorate, dissertation, comprehensive exam required, foreign language not required. *Entrance requirements:* For master's, minimum B+ average. *Application deadline:* For fall admission, 4/30; for spring admission, 3/15. Applications are processed on a rolling basis. Application fee: $50. *Unit head:* Dr. M. J. McGlinchey, Chair, 905-525-9140 Ext. 24504, Fax: 905-522-2509, E-mail: mcglinchey@mcmail.cis.mcmaster.ca. *Application contact:* Carol Dada, Administrator, 905-525-9140 Ext. 23487, Fax: 905-522-2509, E-mail: dada@mcmail.cis.mcmaster.ca.

Michigan State University, Graduate School, College of Natural Science, Department of Chemistry, East Lansing, MI 48824-1020. Offers analytical chemistry (MS, PhD); chemistry (MAT, MS, PhD); chemistry-environmental toxicology (PhD); environmental toxicology (PhD); inorganic chemistry (MS, PhD); organic chemistry (MS, PhD); physical chemistry (PhD). *Faculty:* 36 full-time (4 women). *Students:* 149 full-time (46 women), 18 part-time (9 women); includes 12 minority (6 African Americans, 3 Asian Americans or Pacific Islanders, 2 Hispanic Americans, 1 Native American), 80 international. Terminal master's awarded for partial completion of doctoral program. *Degree requirements:* For master's, thesis required (for some programs), foreign language not required; for doctorate, dissertation required, foreign language not required. *Entrance requirements:* For master's and doctorate, GRE, TOEFL. *Application deadline:* Applications are processed on a rolling basis. Application fee: $30 ($40 for international students). *Unit head:* Dr. Katharine C. Hunt, Chairperson, 517-355-9715, Fax: 517-353-1793, E-mail: chemdept@cem.msu.edu. *Application contact:* Dr. Richard Schwendeman, Associate Chair, Graduate Program, 517-355-9715 Ext. 344, Fax: 517-353-1793, E-mail: gradoff@cem.msu.edu.

Northeastern University, College of Arts and Sciences, Department of Chemistry, Boston, MA 02115-5096. Offers analytical chemistry (PhD); chemistry (MAT, MS, PhD); inorganic chemistry (PhD); organic chemistry (PhD); physical chemistry (PhD). Part-time and evening/weekend programs available. *Faculty:* 20 full-time (3 women), 1 part-time (0 women). *Students:* 59 full-time (25 women), 23 part-time (9 women). Terminal master's awarded for partial completion of doctoral program. *Degree requirements:* For master's, thesis required (for some programs); for doctorate, dissertation, qualifying exam in specialty area required, foreign language not required. *Entrance requirements:* For master's and doctorate, TOEFL (minimum score of 580 required). *Application deadline:* For fall admission, 4/15. Applications are processed on a rolling basis. Application fee: $50. Electronic applications accepted. *Unit head:* Dr. David A. Forsyth, Chairman, 617-373-2822, Fax: 617-373-8795, E-mail: chemistry-grad-info@neu.edu. *Application contact:* Dr. Philip W. LeQuesne, Chair, Graduate Admissions Committee, 617-373-2383, Fax: 617-373-8795.

Old Dominion University, College of Sciences, Department of Chemistry and Biochemistry, Norfolk, VA 23529. Offers analytical chemistry (MS); biochemistry (MS); biomedical sciences (PhD); clinical chemistry (MS); environmental chemistry (MS); organic chemistry (MS); physical chemistry (MS). Part-time and evening/weekend programs available. *Faculty:* 16 full-time (4 women). *Students:* 20 full-time (13 women), 12 part-time (8 women); includes 3 minority (1 African American, 2 Asian Americans or Pacific Islanders), 4 international. Terminal master's awarded for partial completion of doctoral program. *Degree requirements:* For master's and doctorate, thesis/dissertation, comprehensive exam required, foreign language not required. *Entrance requirements:* For master's, GRE General Test, TOEFL, minimum GPA of 3.0 in major, 2.5 overall; for doctorate, GRE General Test (minimum combined score of 1000 required), GRE Subject Test (minimum score of 600 required), TOEFL. *Application deadline:* For fall admission, 7/1; for spring admission, 11/1. Applications are processed on a rolling basis. Application fee: $30. *Unit head:* Dr. John R. Donet, Chair, 757-683-4078, E-mail: jdonet@odu.edu. *Application contact:* Dr. John R. Donet, Chair, 757-683-4078, E-mail: jdonet@odu.edu.

Oregon State University, Graduate School, College of Science, Department of Chemistry, Corvallis, OR 97331. Offers analytical chemistry (MS, PhD); chemistry (MA, MAIS); inorganic chemistry (MS, PhD); nuclear and radiation chemistry (MS, PhD); organic chemistry (MS, PhD); physical chemistry (MS, PhD). Part-time programs available. *Faculty:* 25 full-time (3 women), 5 part-time (2 women). *Students:* 68 full-time (24 women), 2 part-time; includes 4 minority (all Asian Americans or Pacific Islanders), 30 international. Terminal master's awarded for partial completion of doctoral program. *Degree requirements:* For master's and doctorate, one foreign language, thesis/dissertation required. *Entrance requirements:* For master's and doctorate, TOEFL (minimum score of 620 required), minimum GPA of 3.0 in last 90 hours. *Application deadline:* For fall admission, 3/1 (priority date). Applications are processed on a rolling basis. Application fee: $50. *Unit head:* Dr. John Westall, Chair, 541-737-6700, Fax: 541-737-2062, E-mail: john.westall@orst.edu. *Application contact:* Carolyn Brumley, Graduate Secretary, 541-737-6707, Fax: 541-737-2062, E-mail: carolyn.brumley@orst.edu.

Purdue University, Graduate School, School of Science, Department of Chemistry, West Lafayette, IN 47907. Offers analytical chemistry (MS, PhD); biochemistry (MS, PhD); chemical education (MS, PhD); inorganic chemistry (MS, PhD); organic chemistry (MS, PhD); physical chemistry (MS, PhD). *Accreditation:* NCATE (one or more programs are accredited). *Faculty:* 46 full-time, 1 part-time. *Students:* 246 full-time (83 women), 59 part-time (20 women); includes 36 minority (14 African Americans, 7 Asian Americans or Pacific Islanders, 14 Hispanic Americans, 1 Native American), 100 international. Terminal master's awarded for partial completion of doctoral program. *Degree requirements:* For master's and doctorate, thesis/dissertation required, foreign language not required. *Entrance requirements:* For master's and doctorate, TOEFL (minimum score of 550 required). Application fee: $30. Electronic applications accepted. *Unit head:* Dr. R. A. Walton, Head, 765-494-5203. *Application contact:* R. E. Wild, Chairman, Graduate Admissions, 765-494-5200, E-mail: wild@purdue.edu.

Rensselaer Polytechnic Institute, Graduate School, School of Science, Department of Chemistry, Troy, NY 12180-3590. Offers analytical chemistry (MS, PhD); biochemistry (MS, PhD); inorganic chemistry (MS, PhD); organic chemistry (MS, PhD); physical chemistry (MS, PhD); polymer chemistry (MS, PhD). Part-time and evening/weekend programs available. *Faculty:* 17 full-time (2 women), 1 part-time (0 women). *Students:* 52 full-time (18 women), 3 part-time (1 woman); includes 4 minority (3 Asian Americans or Pacific Islanders, 1 Hispanic American), 30 international. *Degree requirements:* For master's, thesis required (for some programs), foreign language not required; for doctorate, dissertation required, foreign language not required. *Entrance requirements:* For master's and doctorate, GRE General Test, TOEFL (minimum score of 550 required). *Application deadline:* For fall admission, 2/1 (priority date). Applications are processed on a rolling basis. Application fee: $35. *Unit head:* Dr. Thomas Apple, Chair, 518-276-6344. *Application contact:* Dr. Wilfredo Colon, Chair, Graduate Committee, 518-276-6340, Fax: 518-276-6434, E-mail: colonw@rpi.edu.

See in-depth description on page 167.

Rutgers, The State University of New Jersey, Newark, Graduate School, Department of Chemistry, Newark, NJ 07102-3192. Offers analytical chemistry (MS, PhD); biochemistry (MS, PhD); inorganic chemistry (MS, PhD); organic chemistry (MS, PhD); physical chemistry (MS, PhD). Part-time and evening/weekend programs available. *Faculty:* 22 full-time (4 women). *Students:* 28 full-time (11 women), 39 part-time (19 women); includes 29 minority (1 African American, 24 Asian Americans or Pacific Islanders, 4 Hispanic Americans) Terminal master's awarded for partial completion of doctoral program. *Degree requirements:* For master's, cumulative exams required, thesis optional, foreign language not required; for doctorate, dissertation, exams, research proposal required, foreign language not required. *Entrance requirements:* For master's and doctorate, GRE General Test, TOEFL (minimum score of 550 required; 590 for financial aid), minimum undergraduate B average. *Application deadline:* For fall admission, 7/1 (priority date); for spring admission, 12/1. Applications are processed on a rolling basis. Application fee: $40. *Unit head:* Prof. Hugh W. Thompson, Coordinator, 973-353-5173, Fax: 973-353-1264.

See in-depth description on page 169.

Rutgers, The State University of New Jersey, New Brunswick, Graduate School, Program in Chemistry, New Brunswick, NJ 08903. Offers analytical chemistry (MS, PhD); biological chemistry (PhD); chemistry education (MST); inorganic chemistry (MS, PhD); organic chemistry (MS, PhD); physical chemistry (MS, PhD). Part-time and evening/weekend programs available. *Faculty:* 44 full-time (9 women), 4 part-time (2 women). *Students:* 100 full-time (35 women), 69 part-time (29 women); includes 27 minority (2 African Americans, 24 Asian Americans or Pacific Islanders, 1 Hispanic American), 79 international. Terminal master's awarded for partial completion of doctoral program. *Degree requirements:* For master's, exam required, thesis optional, foreign language not required; for doctorate, dissertation, cumulative exams required, foreign language not required. *Entrance requirements:* For master's, GRE General Test, GRE Subject Test, TOEFL; for doctorate, GRE General Test, GRE Subject Test, TOEFL (minimum score of 575 required). *Application deadline:* For fall admission, 4/15 (priority date); for spring admission, 11/1. Applications are processed on a rolling basis. Application fee: $50. *Unit head:* Dr. Martha A. Cotter, Director, 732-445-2259, Fax: 732-445-5312, E-mail: gradexec@rutchem.rutgers.edu.

See in-depth description on page 173.

San Jose State University, Graduate Studies, College of Science, Department of Chemistry, San Jose, CA 95192-0001. Offers analytical chemistry (MS); biochemistry (MS); chemistry (MA); inorganic chemistry (MS); organic chemistry (MS); physical chemistry (MS); polymer chemistry (MS); radiochemistry (MS). Part-time and evening/weekend programs available. *Faculty:* 24 full-time (3 women), 5 part-time (2 women). *Students:* 7 full-time (5 women), 30 part-time (17 women); includes 24 minority (2 African Americans, 21 Asian Americans or Pacific Islanders, 1 Hispanic American), 4 international. *Degree requirements:* For master's, thesis or alternative required, foreign language not required. *Entrance requirements:* For master's, GRE, minimum B average. *Application deadline:* For fall admission, 6/1. Applications are processed on a rolling basis. Application fee: $59. Tuition, nonresident: part-time $246 per unit. Required fees: $1,939; $1,309 per year. *Unit head:* Dr. Pamela Stacks, Chair, 408-924-5000, Fax: 408-924-4945. *Application contact:* Dr. Roger Biringer, Graduate Adviser, 408-924-4961.

Seton Hall University, College of Arts and Sciences, Department of Chemistry, South Orange, NJ 07079-2694. Offers analytical chemistry (MS, PhD); biochemistry (MS, PhD); chemistry (MS); inorganic chemistry (MS, PhD); organic chemistry (MS, PhD); physical chemistry (MS, PhD). Part-time and evening/weekend programs available. Terminal master's awarded for partial completion of doctoral program. *Degree requirements:* For master's, formal seminar required, thesis optional; for doctorate, dissertation, comprehensive exams, annual seminars required. *Entrance requirements:* For master's, TOEFL, undergraduate major in chemistry or related field with a minimum of 30 credits in chemistry, including 2 semesters of physical chemistry; for doctorate, oral matriculation exam based on proposed doctoral research, minimum GPA of 3.0 in course distribution requirements, formal seminar. *Faculty research:* DNA metal reactions; chromatography; bioinorganic, biophysical, organometallic, and polymer chemistry; heterogeneous catalysis.

South Dakota State University, Graduate School, College of Arts and Science, Department of Chemistry, Brookings, SD 57007. Offers analytical chemistry (MS, PhD); biochemistry (MS, PhD); chemistry (MS, PhD); inorganic chemistry (MS, PhD); organic chemistry (MS, PhD); physical chemistry (MS, PhD). *Degree requirements:* For master's, thesis, oral exam required, foreign language not required; for doctorate, dissertation, preliminary oral and written exams, research tool required. *Entrance requirements:* For master's, TOEFL (minimum score of 580 required), bachelor's degree in chemistry or equivalent; for doctorate, TOEFL (minimum score of 580 required). *Faculty research:* Environmental chemistry, computational chemistry, organic synthesis and photochemistry, novel material development and characterization.

Southern University and Agricultural and Mechanical College, Graduate School, College of Sciences, Department of Chemistry, Baton Rouge, LA 70813. Offers analytical chemistry (MS); biochemistry (MS); environmental sciences (MS); inorganic chemistry (MS); organic chemistry (MS); physical chemistry (MS). *Faculty:* 9 full-time (2 women), 3 part-time (2 women). *Students:* 4 full-time (3 women), 20 part-time (12 women); includes 19 minority (all African Americans), 4 international. *Degree requirements:* For master's, thesis required, foreign language not required. *Entrance requirements:* For master's, GMAT or GRE General Test, TOEFL. *Application deadline:* For fall admission, 6/1 (priority date); for spring admission, 11/1. Applications are processed on a rolling basis. Application fee: $5. *Unit head:* Dr. Robert Harvey Miller, Chairman, 225-771-3990, Fax: 225-771-3992.

State University of New York at Binghamton, Graduate School, School of Arts and Sciences, Department of Chemistry, Binghamton, NY 13902-6000. Offers analytical chemistry (PhD); chemistry (MA, MS); inorganic chemistry (PhD); organic chemistry (PhD); physical chemistry (PhD). *Faculty:* 13 full-time, 7 part-time. *Students:* 48 full-time (11 women), 7 part-time (2 women); includes 2 minority (1 African American, 1 Hispanic American), 30 international. Terminal master's awarded for partial completion of doctoral program. *Degree requirements:* For master's, thesis or alternative, oral exam, seminar presentation required, foreign language not required; for doctorate, dissertation, cumulative exams required, foreign language not required. *Entrance requirements:* For master's and doctorate, GRE General Test, GRE Subject Test, TOEFL. *Application deadline:* For fall admission, 4/15 (priority date); for spring admission, 11/1. Applications are processed on a rolling basis. Application fee: $50. Electronic applications accepted. Tuition, state resident: full-time $5,100; part-time $213 per credit. Tuition, nonresident: full-time $8,416; part-time $351 per credit. Required fees: $77 per credit. Part-time tuition and fees vary according to course load. *Unit head:* Dr. Alistair J. Lees, Chairperson, 607-777-2362.

Stevens Institute of Technology, Graduate School, School of Applied Sciences and Liberal Arts, Department of Chemistry and Chemical Biology, Hoboken, NJ 07030. Offers chemistry (MS, PhD, Certificate), including analytical chemistry, chemical biology, chemical physiology (Certificate), instrumental analysis (Certificate), organic chemistry (MS, PhD), physical chemistry (MS, PhD), polymer chemistry. Part-time and evening/weekend programs available. Terminal master's awarded for partial completion of doctoral program. *Degree requirements:* For master's, thesis or alternative required, foreign language not required; for doctorate, one foreign language, dissertation required; for Certificate, computer language, project or thesis required. *Entrance requirements:* For master's and doctorate, TOEFL (minimum score of 550 required). Electronic applications accepted.

Tufts University, Division of Graduate and Continuing Studies and Research, Graduate School of Arts and Sciences, Department of Chemistry, Medford, MA 02155. Offers analytical chemistry (MS, PhD); bioorganic chemistry (MS, PhD); environmental chemistry (MS, PhD); inorganic chemistry (MS, PhD); organic chemistry (MS, PhD); physical chemistry (MS, PhD). *Faculty:* 13 full-time, 1 part-time. *Students:* 52 (27 women); includes 5 minority (1 African American, 3 Asian Americans or Pacific Islanders, 1 Hispanic American) 14 international. Terminal master's awarded for partial completion of doctoral program. *Degree requirements:* For master's and doctorate, thesis/dissertation required, foreign language not required. *Entrance requirements:* For master's and doctorate, GRE General Test, GRE Subject Test, TOEFL (minimum score of 600 required). *Application deadline:* For fall admission, 2/15; for spring admission, 10/15. Applications are processed on a rolling basis. Application fee: $50. *Unit head:* Marc d'Alarco, Chair, 617-627-3441, Fax: 617-627-3443. *Application contact:* Samuel Kounaves, 617-627-3124, Fax: 617-627-3443.

See in-depth description on page 181.

The University of Akron, Graduate School, Buchtel College of Arts and Sciences, Department of Chemistry, Akron, OH 44325-0001. Offers analytical chemistry (MS, PhD); biochemistry (MS, PhD); chemistry (MS, PhD); inorganic chemistry (MS, PhD); organic chemistry (MS, PhD); physical chemistry (MS, PhD). Part-time and evening/weekend programs available. *Faculty:* 17 full-time, 1 part-time. *Students:* 63 full-time (25 women), 9 part-time (6 women); includes 8 minority (6 African Americans, 2 Hispanic Americans), 31 international. Terminal

Organic Chemistry

The University of Akron (continued)
master's awarded for partial completion of doctoral program. *Degree requirements:* For master's, one foreign language (computer language can substitute), thesis, seminar presentation required; for doctorate, 2 foreign languages (computer language can substitute for one), dissertation, cumulative exams required. *Entrance requirements:* For master's, TOEFL, minimum GPA of 2.75; for doctorate, TOEFL. *Application deadline:* For fall admission, 3/1. Applications are processed on a rolling basis. Application fee: $25 ($50 for international students). Tuition, state resident: part-time $189 per credit. Tuition, nonresident: part-time $353 per credit. Required fees: $7.3 per credit. *Unit head:* Dr. Gerald Koser, Chair, 330-972-7372, E-mail: koser@uakron.edu.

University of Calgary, Faculty of Graduate Studies, Faculty of Science, Department of Chemistry, Calgary, AB T2N 1N4, Canada. Offers analytical chemistry (M Sc, PhD); applied chemistry (M Sc, PhD); inorganic chemistry (M Sc, PhD); organic chemistry (M Sc, PhD); physical chemistry (M Sc, PhD); polymer chemistry (M Sc, PhD); theoretical chemistry (M Sc, PhD). *Faculty:* 29 full-time (4 women), 1 part-time (0 women). *Students:* 60 full-time (25 women). *Degree requirements:* For master's, thesis required, foreign language not required; for doctorate, dissertation, candidacy exam required, foreign language not required. *Entrance requirements:* For master's and doctorate, TOEFL (minimum score of 580 required). *Application deadline:* For fall admission, 12/1 (priority date). Applications are processed on a rolling basis. Application fee: $60. *Unit head:* Dr. R. A. Kydd, Head, 403-220-5340. *Application contact:* Greta Prihodko, Graduate Program Administrator, 403-220-6252, E-mail: gradinfo@chem.ucalgary.ca.

University of Cincinnati, Division of Research and Advanced Studies, McMicken College of Arts and Sciences, Department of Chemistry, Cincinnati, OH 45221-0091. Offers analytical chemistry (MS, PhD); biochemistry (MS, PhD); inorganic chemistry (MS, PhD); organic chemistry (MS, PhD); physical chemistry (MS, PhD); polymer chemistry (MS, PhD). Part-time and evening/weekend programs available. *Faculty:* 25 full-time. *Students:* 87 full-time (26 women), 26 part-time (3 women); includes 12 minority (1 African American, 11 Asian Americans or Pacific Islanders), 34 international. Terminal master's awarded for partial completion of doctoral program. *Degree requirements:* For master's, thesis optional, foreign language not required; for doctorate, dissertation required, foreign language not required. *Entrance requirements:* For master's and doctorate, GRE General Test, GRE Subject Test. *Application deadline:* For fall admission, 2/1. Application fee: $30. *Unit head:* Dr. Marshall Wilson, Head, 513-556-9200, Fax: 513-556-9239, E-mail: marshall.wilson@uc.edu. *Application contact:* Thomas Ridgway, Graduate Program Director, 513-556-9200, Fax: 513-556-9239, E-mail: thomas.ridgway@uc.edu.

University of Georgia, Graduate School, College of Arts and Sciences, Department of Chemistry, Athens, GA 30602. Offers analytical chemistry (MS, PhD); inorganic chemistry (MS, PhD); organic chemistry (MS, PhD); physical chemistry (MS, PhD). *Faculty:* 23 full-time (1 woman). *Students:* 107 full-time (26 women), 11 part-time (4 women). *Degree requirements:* For master's, thesis required, foreign language not required; for doctorate, one foreign language (computer language can substitute), dissertation required. *Entrance requirements:* For master's and doctorate, GRE General Test. *Application deadline:* For fall admission, 7/1 (priority date); for spring admission, 11/15. Application fee: $30. Electronic applications accepted. *Unit head:* Dr. I. Jonathan Amster, Graduate Coordinator, 706-542-1936, Fax: 706-542-9454, E-mail: mauldin@sunchem.chem.uga.edu.

University of Louisville, Graduate School, College of Arts and Sciences, Department of Chemistry, Louisville, KY 40292-0001. Offers analytical chemistry (MS, PhD); chemical physics (PhD); inorganic chemistry (MS, PhD); organic chemistry (MS, PhD); physical chemistry (MS, PhD). *Faculty:* 20 full-time (3 women), 1 part-time (0 women). *Students:* 52 full-time (20 women), 4 part-time (2 women); includes 2 minority (both Hispanic Americans), 30 international. *Degree requirements:* For master's, thesis required; for doctorate, dissertation required. *Entrance requirements:* For master's and doctorate, GRE General Test, TOEFL (minimum score of 550 required). *Application deadline:* Applications are processed on a rolling basis. Application fee: $25. *Unit head:* Dr. George R. Pack, Chair, 502-852-6798, Fax: 502-852-8149, E-mail: george.pack@louisville.edu.

See in-depth description on page 199.

University of Maryland, College Park, Graduate School, College of Life Sciences, Department of Chemistry and Biochemistry, Chemistry Program, College Park, MD 20742-5045. Offers analytical chemistry (MS, PhD); inorganic chemistry (MS, PhD); organic chemistry (MS, PhD); physical chemistry (MS, PhD). *Students:* 76 full-time (34 women), 16 part-time (6 women); includes 8 minority (2 African Americans, 4 Asian Americans or Pacific Islanders, 1 Hispanic American, 1 Native American), 36 international. *Degree requirements:* For master's, thesis optional, foreign language not required; for doctorate, dissertation, 2 seminar presentations, oral exam required. *Entrance requirements:* For master's, GRE General Test, minimum GPA of 3.1; for doctorate, GRE General Test. *Application deadline:* Applications are processed on a rolling basis. Application fee: $50 ($70 for international students). Tuition, state resident: part-time $272 per credit hour. Tuition, nonresident: part-time $475 per credit hour. Required fees: $632; $379 per year. *Unit head:* Marlin Harmony, Graduate Director, 785-864-4670, Fax: 785-864-5396. *Application contact:* Trudy Lindsey, Director, Graduate Admission and Records, 301-405-4198, Fax: 301-314-9305, E-mail: grschool@deans.umd.edu.

University of Miami, Graduate School, College of Arts and Sciences, Department of Chemistry, Coral Gables, FL 33124. Offers chemistry (MS); inorganic chemistry (PhD); organic chemistry (PhD); physical chemistry (PhD). *Faculty:* 11 full-time (1 woman). *Students:* 40 full-time (18 women); includes 6 minority (1 African American, 1 Asian American or Pacific Islander, 4 Hispanic Americans), 33 international. Terminal master's awarded for partial completion of doctoral program. *Degree requirements:* For master's, foreign language and thesis not required; for doctorate, dissertation required, foreign language not required. *Entrance requirements:* For master's and doctorate, GRE General Test (minimum combined score of 1000 required), TOEFL (minimum score of 550 required). *Application deadline:* For fall admission, 1/15. Application fee: $35. Electronic applications accepted. Tuition: Full-time $15,336; part-time $852 per credit. Required fees: $174. Tuition and fees vary according to program. *Unit head:* Dr. Roger LeBlanc, Chairman, 305-284-2174, Fax: 305-284-4571. *Application contact:* Dr. Luis Echogoyen, Graduate Adviser, 305-661-2847, Fax: 305-284-4571, E-mail: ldookie@umiami.ir.miami.edu.

University of Michigan, Horace H. Rackham School of Graduate Studies, College of Literature, Science, and the Arts, Department of Chemistry, Ann Arbor, MI 48109. Offers analytical chemistry (PhD); chemical biology (PhD); inorganic chemistry (PhD); organic chemistry (PhD); physical chemistry (PhD). *Faculty:* 43 full-time (7 women). *Students:* 161 full-time (60 women); includes 5 minority (2 African Americans, 2 Asian Americans or Pacific Islanders, 1 Hispanic American), 43 international. *Degree requirements:* For doctorate, dissertation, oral defense of dissertation, preliminary exam, organic cumulative proficiency exams required, foreign language not required. *Entrance requirements:* For doctorate, GRE General Test, GRE Subject Test (recommended), statement of prior research. *Application deadline:* For fall admission, 2/15 (priority date). Applications are processed on a rolling basis. Application fee: $55. *Unit head:* Dr. Joseph P. Marino, Chair, 734-763-9681, Fax: 734-647-4847, E-mail: jpmarino@umich.edu. *Application contact:* Warren Noone, Assistant Director of Graduate Studies, 734-764-7278, Fax: 734-747-4865, E-mail: nooner@umich.edu.

University of Missouri–Columbia, Graduate School, College of Arts and Sciences, Department of Chemistry, Columbia, MO 65211. Offers analytical chemistry (MS, PhD); inorganic chemistry (MS, PhD); organic chemistry (MS, PhD); physical chemistry (MS, PhD). *Faculty:* 23 full-time (3 women). *Students:* 68 full-time (23 women), 24 part-time (7 women); includes 6 minority (1 African American, 2 Asian Americans or Pacific Islanders, 2 Hispanic Americans, 1 Native American), 47 international. *Degree requirements:* For master's, thesis required, foreign language not required; for doctorate, dissertation required. *Entrance requirements:* For master's and doctorate, GRE General Test, minimum GPA of 3.0. *Application deadline:* For fall admission, 7/1 (priority date). Applications are processed on a rolling basis. Application fee: $30 ($50 for international students). *Unit head:* Dr. Richard Thompson, Director of Graduate Studies, 573-882-7356.

University of Missouri–Kansas City, College of Arts and Sciences, Department of Chemistry, Kansas City, MO 64110-2499. Offers analytical chemistry (MS, PhD); inorganic chemistry (MS, PhD); organic chemistry (MS, PhD); physical chemistry (MS, PhD); polymer chemistry (MS, PhD). PhD offered through the School of Graduate Studies. Part-time programs available. *Faculty:* 12 full-time (2 women), 2 part-time (0 women). *Students:* 25 full-time (7 women), 7 part-time (2 women), 18 international. *Degree requirements:* For master's, thesis required (for some programs), foreign language not required; for doctorate, dissertation required, foreign language not required. *Entrance requirements:* For master's, TOEFL (minimum score of 550 required); for doctorate, GRE General Test (minimum combined score of 1500 on three sections required), TOEFL (minimum score of 550 required), TWE (minimum score of 4 required). *Application deadline:* For fall and spring admission, 2/1 (priority date); for winter admission, 9/1 (priority date). Applications are processed on a rolling basis. Application fee: $25. *Unit head:* Dr. Jerry Jean, Interim Chairperson, 816-235-2280, Fax: 816-235-5502, E-mail: jean@cctr.umkc.edu.

See in-depth description on page 211.

University of Missouri–St. Louis, Graduate School, College of Arts and Sciences, Department of Chemistry, St. Louis, MO 63121-4499. Offers chemistry (MS, PhD), including biochemistry, inorganic chemistry, organic chemistry, physical chemistry. Part-time and evening/weekend programs available. *Faculty:* 20. *Students:* 33 full-time (10 women), 26 part-time (9 women); includes 7 minority (2 African Americans, 4 Asian Americans or Pacific Islanders, 1 Hispanic American), 21 international. Terminal master's awarded for partial completion of doctoral program. *Degree requirements:* For master's, thesis optional, foreign language not required; for doctorate, dissertation required, foreign language not required. *Entrance requirements:* For doctorate, GRE General Test, GRE Subject Test. *Application deadline:* For fall admission, 7/1 (priority date); for spring admission, 12/7 (priority date). Applications are processed on a rolling basis. Application fee: $25 ($40 for international students). Electronic applications accepted. *Unit head:* Dr. R. E. K. Winter, Director of Graduate Studies, 314-516-5337, Fax: 314-516-5342, E-mail: chejjoll@jinx.umsl.edu. *Application contact:* Graduate Admissions, 314-516-5458, Fax: 314-516-6759, E-mail: gradadm@umsl.edu.

The University of Montana–Missoula, Graduate School, College of Arts and Sciences, Department of Chemistry, Missoula, MT 59812-0002. Offers chemistry (MS, PhD); chemistry teaching (MST); environmental chemistry (PhD); inorganic chemistry (PhD); organic chemistry (PhD); physical chemistry (PhD). Part-time programs available. *Faculty:* 14 full-time (3 women), 1 part-time (0 women). *Students:* 15 full-time (3 women), 3 part-time; includes 3 minority (all Asian Americans or Pacific Islanders) Terminal master's awarded for partial completion of doctoral program. *Degree requirements:* For master's, thesis required (for some programs); for doctorate, dissertation required. *Entrance requirements:* For master's, GRE General Test; for doctorate, GRE General Test, GRE Subject Test. *Application deadline:* For fall admission, 3/15 (priority date); for spring admission, 10/15. Applications are processed on a rolling basis. Application fee: $45. *Unit head:* Dr. Michael D. DeGrandpre, Graduate Coordinator, 403-243-4022, Fax: 406-243-4227.

University of Nebraska–Lincoln, Graduate College, College of Arts and Sciences, Department of Chemistry, Lincoln, NE 68588. Offers analytical chemistry (PhD); chemistry (MS); inorganic chemistry (PhD); organic chemistry (PhD); physical chemistry (PhD). *Faculty:* 23 full-time (2 women), 1 part-time (0 women). *Students:* 79 full-time (15 women), 23 part-time (2 women); includes 6 minority (1 African American, 2 Asian Americans or Pacific Islanders, 2 Hispanic Americans, 1 Native American), 47 international. *Degree requirements:* For master's, departmental qualifying exam required, thesis optional; for doctorate, dissertation, comprehensive and departmental qualifying exams required. *Entrance requirements:* For master's and doctorate, GRE Subject Test, TOEFL (minimum score of 550 required). *Application deadline:* For fall admission, 3/1 (priority date). Applications are processed on a rolling basis. Application fee: $35. Electronic applications accepted. *Unit head:* Dr. Lawrence Parkhurst, Chair, 402-472-3501, Fax: 402-472-9402.

University of Notre Dame, Graduate School, College of Science, Department of Chemistry and Biochemistry, Notre Dame, IN 46556. Offers biochemistry (MS, PhD); inorganic chemistry (MS, PhD); organic chemistry (MS, PhD); physical chemistry (MS, PhD). *Faculty:* 32 full-time (3 women). *Students:* 110 full-time (38 women), 1 part-time; includes 3 minority (2 African Americans, 1 Asian American or Pacific Islander), 57 international. Terminal master's awarded for partial completion of doctoral program. *Degree requirements:* For master's, thesis, comprehensive exam required, foreign language not required; for doctorate, dissertation, qualifying exam required, foreign language not required. *Entrance requirements:* For master's, GRE General Test, GRE General Subject Test (strongly recommended), TOEFL (minimum score of 600 required; 250 for computer-based); for doctorate, GRE General Test, GRE Subject Test (strongly recommended), TOEFL (minimum score of 600 required; 250 for computer-based). *Application deadline:* For fall admission, 2/1 (priority date). Applications are processed on a rolling basis. Application fee: $40. *Unit head:* Dr. A. Graham Lappin, Chairman, 219-631-7058, Fax: 219-631-6652, E-mail: lappin.1@nd.edu. *Application contact:* Dr. Terrence J. Akai, Director of Graduate Admissions, 219-631-7706, Fax: 219-631-4183, E-mail: gradad@nd.edu.

See in-depth description on page 215.

University of Regina, Faculty of Graduate Studies and Research, Faculty of Science, Department of Chemistry, Regina, SK S4S 0A2, Canada. Offers analytical chemistry (M Sc, PhD); biochemistry (M Sc, PhD); clinical biochemistry (M Sc, PhD); inorganic chemistry (M Sc, PhD); organic chemistry (M Sc, PhD); physical chemistry (M Sc, PhD); x-ray crystallography (M Sc, PhD). Part-time programs available. *Faculty:* 10 full-time (1 woman), 3 part-time (0 women). *Students:* 9 full-time (5 women), 6 part-time (3 women). *Degree requirements:* For master's, thesis, departmental qualifying exam required, foreign language not required; for doctorate, variable foreign language requirement, dissertation, departmental qualifying exam required. *Entrance requirements:* For master's, TOEFL (minimum score of 580 required); for doctorate, TOEFL. *Application deadline:* Applications are processed on a rolling basis. Application fee: $0. *Expenses:* Tuition and fees charges are reported in Canadian dollars. Tuition, state resident: full-time $1,688 Canadian dollars; part-time $94 Canadian dollars per credit hour. International tuition: $3,375 Canadian dollars full-time. Required fees: $65 Canadian dollars per course. Tuition and fees vary according to course load and program. *Unit head:* Dr. K. Johnson, Head, 306-585-4146, Fax: 306-585-4894, E-mail: chem@max.cc.uregina.ca.

University of Southern Mississippi, Graduate School, College of Science and Technology, Department of Chemistry and Biochemistry, Hattiesburg, MS 39406-5167. Offers analytical chemistry (MS, PhD); biochemistry (MS, PhD); inorganic chemistry (MS, PhD); organic chemistry (MS, PhD); physical chemistry (MS, PhD). *Faculty:* 16 full-time (2 women), 1 part-time (0 women). *Students:* 25 full-time (10 women); includes 8 minority (3 African Americans, 4 Asian Americans or Pacific Islanders, 1 Hispanic American) *Degree requirements:* For master's, thesis required, foreign language not required; for doctorate, 2 foreign languages (computer language can substitute for one), dissertation required. *Entrance requirements:* For master's, GRE General Test, TOEFL, minimum GPA of 2.75; for doctorate, GRE General Test, TOEFL, minimum GPA of 3.5. *Application deadline:* For fall admission, 8/6 (priority date). Applications are processed on a rolling basis. Application fee: $0 ($25 for international students). Tuition, state resident: full-time $2,250; part-time $137 per semester hour. Tuition, nonresident: full-time $3,102; part-time $172 per semester hour. Required fees: $602. *Unit head:* Dr. Stella Elakovich, Chair, 601-266-4701. *Application contact:* Dr. Gordon Cannon, 601-266-4702.

University of South Florida, Graduate School, College of Arts and Sciences, Department of Chemistry, Tampa, FL 33620-9951. Offers analytical chemistry (MS, PhD); biochemistry (MS, PhD); inorganic chemistry (MS, PhD); organic chemistry (MS, PhD); physical chemistry (MS,

PhD). Part-time programs available. *Faculty:* 23 full-time (3 women), 3 part-time (1 woman). *Students:* 44 full-time (14 women), 10 part-time (1 woman); includes 2 African Americans, 3 Hispanic Americans Terminal master's awarded for partial completion of doctoral program. *Degree requirements:* For master's, thesis required; for doctorate, 2 foreign languages (computer language can substitute for one), dissertation, colloquium required. *Entrance requirements:* For master's and doctorate, GRE General Test (minimum combined score of 1000 required), minimum GPA of 3.0 in last 30 hours of chemistry course work. *Application deadline:* For fall admission, 6/5 (priority date); for spring admission, 10/23 (priority date). Applications are processed on a rolling basis. Application fee: $20. Electronic applications accepted. Tuition, state resident: part-time $148 per credit hour. Tuition, nonresident: part-time $509 per credit hour. *Unit head:* Dr. Robert Potter, Chairperson, 813-974-4129, Fax: 813-974-1731, E-mail: potter@chuma1.cas.usf.edu. *Application contact:* Andy Zekter, Graduate Director, 813-974-9666, Fax: 813-974-3203, E-mail: zekter@chuma1.cas.usf.edu.

University of Tennessee, Knoxville, Graduate School, College of Arts and Sciences, Department of Chemistry, Knoxville, TN 37996. Offers analytical chemistry (MS, PhD); chemical physics (PhD); environmental chemistry (MS, PhD); inorganic chemistry (MS, PhD); organic chemistry (MS, PhD); physical chemistry (MS, PhD); polymer chemistry (MS, PhD); theoretical chemistry (PhD). Part-time programs available. *Faculty:* 31 full-time (1 woman), 1 (woman) part-time. *Students:* 55 full-time (15 women), 44 part-time (11 women); includes 1 minority (Asian American or Pacific Islander), 23 international. Terminal master's awarded for partial completion of doctoral program. *Degree requirements:* For master's and doctorate, thesis/dissertation required, foreign language not required. *Entrance requirements:* For master's and doctorate, GRE General Test, TOEFL (minimum score of 550 required), minimum GPA of 2.7. *Application deadline:* For fall admission, 2/1 (priority date). Applications are processed on a rolling basis. Application fee: $35. Electronic applications accepted. *Unit head:* Dr. Michael Sepaniak, Head, 423-974-3141, Fax: 423-974-3454, E-mail: msepaniak@utk.edu. *Application contact:* Dr. Charles Feigerle, Graduate Representative, E-mail: cfeigerle@utk.edu.

The University of Texas at Austin, Graduate School, College of Natural Sciences, Department of Chemistry and Biochemistry, Austin, TX 78712-1111. Offers analytical chemistry (MA, PhD); biochemistry (MA, PhD); inorganic chemistry (MA, PhD); organic chemistry (MA, PhD); physical chemistry (MA, PhD). *Students:* 278 (94 women); includes 28 minority (3 African Americans, 11 Asian Americans or Pacific Islanders, 13 Hispanic Americans, 1 Native American) 61 international. *Entrance requirements:* For master's and doctorate, GRE General Test. Application fee: $50 ($75 for international students). *Unit head:* Dr. Marvin L. Hackert, Chairman, 512-471-3949. *Application contact:* Dr. Jennifer Brodbelt, Graduate Adviser, 512-471-0028.

University of Toledo, Graduate School, College of Arts and Sciences, Department of Chemistry, Toledo, OH 43606-3398. Offers analytical chemistry (MS, MS Ed, PhD); biological chemistry (MS, MS Ed, PhD); inorganic chemistry (MS, MS Ed, PhD); organic chemistry (MS, MS Ed, PhD); physical chemistry (MS, MS Ed, PhD). Part-time programs available. *Degree requirements:* For master's and doctorate, thesis/dissertation required, foreign language not required. *Entrance requirements:* For master's and doctorate, GRE General Test, GRE Subject Test, TOEFL. Electronic applications accepted. *Faculty research:* Enzymology, materials chemistry, crystallography, theoretical chemistry.

Wake Forest University, Graduate School, Department of Chemistry, Winston-Salem, NC 27109. Offers analytical chemistry (MS, PhD); inorganic chemistry (MS, PhD); organic chemistry (MS, PhD); physical chemistry (MS, PhD). Part-time programs available. *Faculty:* 14 full-time (1 woman). *Students:* 22 full-time (11 women), 2 part-time; includes 5 minority (2 African Americans, 3 Asian Americans or Pacific Islanders) *Degree requirements:* For master's, one foreign language (computer language can substitute), thesis required; for doctorate, 2 foreign languages (computer language can substitute for one), dissertation required. *Entrance requirements:* For master's and doctorate, GRE General Test, GRE Subject Test. *Application deadline:* For fall admission, 2/15. Application fee: $25. *Unit head:* Dr. Jim Fishbein, Director, 336-758-6139, E-mail: fishbein@wfu.edu.

See in-depth description on page 227.

Washington State University, Graduate School, College of Sciences, Department of Chemistry, Pullman, WA 99164. Offers analytical chemistry (MS, PhD); inorganic chemistry (MS, PhD); nuclear chemistry (MS, PhD); organic chemistry (MS, PhD); physical chemistry (MS, PhD). *Faculty:* 28 full-time (4 women). *Students:* 39 full-time (14 women), 3 part-time (2 women); includes 4 minority (2 Asian Americans or Pacific Islanders, 1 Hispanic American, 1 Native American), 8 international. Terminal master's awarded for partial completion of doctoral program. *Degree requirements:* For master's, oral exam, teaching experience required, thesis optional, foreign language not required; for doctorate, dissertation, oral exam, teaching experience required, foreign language not required. *Entrance requirements:* For master's and doctorate, GRE General Test, minimum GPA of 3.0. *Application deadline:* For fall admission, 3/1 (priority date). Applications are processed on a rolling basis. Application fee: $35. *Unit head:* Dr. Ralph Yount, Chair, 509-335-1516. *Application contact:* James O. Schenk, Chair, Admissions Committee, 509-335-8866, E-mail: carrie@wsu.edu.

Washington University in St. Louis, Graduate School of Arts and Sciences, Division of Biology and Biomedical Sciences, Program in Bioorganic Chemistry, St. Louis, MO 63130-4899. Offers PhD. *Degree requirements:* For doctorate, dissertation required, foreign language not required. *Entrance requirements:* For doctorate, GRE General Test, GRE Subject Test. *Application deadline:* For fall admission, 1/1 (priority date). Applications are processed on a rolling basis. Application fee: $0. *Unit head:* Dr. George Gokel, Coordinator. *Application contact:* Rosemary Garagneni, Director of Admissions, 800-852-9074, E-mail: admissions@dbbs.wustl.edu.

See in-depth description on page 231.

Wesleyan University, Graduate Programs, Department of Chemistry, Middletown, CT 06459-0260. Offers biochemistry (MA, PhD); chemical physics (MA, PhD); inorganic chemistry (MA, PhD); organic chemistry (MA, PhD); physical chemistry (MA, PhD); theoretical chemistry (MA, PhD). Terminal master's awarded for partial completion of doctoral program. *Degree requirements:* For master's and doctorate, one foreign language (computer language can substitute), thesis/dissertation required. *Entrance requirements:* For master's, GRE General Test, GRE Subject Test; for doctorate, GRE Subject Test.

See in-depth description on page 233.

Yale University, Graduate School of Arts and Sciences, Department of Chemistry, New Haven, CT 06520. Offers biophysical chemistry (PhD); inorganic chemistry (PhD); organic chemistry (PhD); physical chemistry (PhD). *Faculty:* 61 full-time (14 women). *Students:* 139 full-time (62 women); includes 11 minority (8 Asian Americans or Pacific Islanders, 3 Hispanic Americans), 53 international. *Degree requirements:* For doctorate, dissertation required. *Entrance requirements:* For doctorate, GRE General Test, GRE Subject Test, TOEFL. *Application deadline:* For fall admission, 1/4. Application fee: $65. *Unit head:* Chair, 203-432-3912. *Application contact:* Admissions Information, 203-432-2770.

See in-depth description on page 241.

Physical Chemistry

Boston College, Graduate School of Arts and Sciences, Department of Chemistry, Chestnut Hill, MA 02467-3800. Offers analytical chemistry (MS, PhD); biochemistry (MS, PhD); chemistry (MS); inorganic chemistry (MS, PhD); organic chemistry (MS, PhD); physical chemistry (MS, PhD). Part-time programs available. *Faculty:* 20 full-time (2 women). *Students:* 25 full-time (11 women), 75 part-time (29 women); includes 12 minority (1 African American, 8 Asian Americans or Pacific Islanders, 2 Hispanic Americans, 1 Native American), 28 international. Terminal master's awarded for partial completion of doctoral program. *Degree requirements:* For master's, thesis required; for doctorate, dissertation, qualifying exam required. *Entrance requirements:* For master's and doctorate, GRE General Test, GRE Subject Test. *Application deadline:* For fall admission, 2/1. Application fee: $40. *Unit head:* Dr. Larry McLaughlin, Chairperson, 617-552-3605, E-mail: larry.mclaughlin@bc.edu. *Application contact:* Dr. Mary Roberts, Graduate Program Director, 617-552-3616, E-mail: mary.roberts@bc.edu.

See in-depth description on page 93.

Boston University, Graduate School of Arts and Sciences, Department of Chemistry, Boston, MA 02215. Offers biochemistry (MA, PhD); chemical physics (MA, PhD); inorganic chemistry (MA, PhD); organic chemistry (MA, PhD); photochemistry (MA, PhD); physical chemistry (MA, PhD); theoretical chemistry (MA, PhD). *Faculty:* 21 full-time (1 woman). *Students:* 81 full-time (26 women), 1 (woman) part-time; includes 4 minority (2 African Americans, 2 Asian Americans or Pacific Islanders), 58 international. Terminal master's awarded for partial completion of doctoral program. *Degree requirements:* For master's, one foreign language, thesis not required; for doctorate, one foreign language, dissertation, exams required. *Entrance requirements:* For master's and doctorate, GRE General Test, GRE Subject Test (recommended), TOEFL (minimum score of 550 required). *Application deadline:* For fall admission, 7/1. Applications are processed on a rolling basis. Application fee: $50. Tuition: Full-time $23,770; part-time $743 per credit. Required fees: $220. Tuition and fees vary according to class time, course level, campus/location and program. *Unit head:* Thomas D. Tullius, Chairman, 617-353-4277, Fax: 617-353-6466, E-mail: tullius@chem.bu.edu. *Application contact:* Kevin Burgoyne, Academic Administrator, 617-353-2503, Fax: 617-353-6466, E-mail: burgoyne@chem.bu.edu.

Brandeis University, Graduate School of Arts and Sciences, Program in Chemistry, Waltham, MA 02454-9110. Offers inorganic chemistry (MS, PhD); organic chemistry (MS, PhD); physical chemistry (MS, PhD). *Faculty:* 16 full-time (2 women). *Students:* 44 full-time (22 women); includes 1 minority (African American), 26 international. Terminal master's awarded for partial completion of doctoral program. *Degree requirements:* For master's, 1 year of residency required, foreign language and thesis not required; for doctorate, one foreign language (computer language can substitute), dissertation, 3 years of residency, 2 seminars, qualifying exams required. *Entrance requirements:* For master's and doctorate, GRE General Test. *Application deadline:* For fall admission, 1/15 (priority date). Applications are processed on a rolling basis. Application fee: $60. *Unit head:* Dr. I. Y. Chan, Chair, 781-736-2554, Fax: 781-736-2516. *Application contact:* Charlotte Haygazian, Secretary, 781-736-2500, Fax: 781-736-2516, E-mail: chemadm@brandeis.edu.

Brigham Young University, Graduate Studies, College of Physical and Mathematical Sciences, Department of Chemistry and Biochemistry, Provo, UT 84602-1001. Offers analytical chemistry (MS, PhD); biochemistry (MS, PhD); inorganic chemistry (MS, PhD); organic chemistry (MS, PhD); physical chemistry (MS, PhD). *Faculty:* 33 full-time (1 woman), 3 part-time (0 women). *Students:* 70 full-time (24 women); includes 1 minority (Asian American or Pacific Islander), 39 international. *Degree requirements:* For master's and doctorate, thesis/dissertation required, foreign language not required. *Entrance requirements:* For master's and doctorate, minimum GPA of 3.0 in last 60 hours. *Application deadline:* For fall admission, 2/1 (priority date). Applications are processed on a rolling basis. Application fee: $30. Tuition: Full-time $3,330; part-time $185 per credit hour. Tuition and fees vary according to program and student's religious affiliation. *Unit head:* Dr. Francis R. Nordmeyer, Chair, 801-378-3667, Fax: 801-378-5474, E-mail: fran_nordmeyer@byu.edu. *Application contact:* N. Kent Dalley, Coordinator, Graduate Admissions, 801-378-3434, Fax: 801-378-5474, E-mail: chemgrad@byu.edu.

See in-depth description on page 97.

California State University, Fullerton, Graduate Studies, School of Natural Science and Mathematics, Department of Chemistry and Biochemistry, Fullerton, CA 92834-9480. Offers analytical chemistry (MS); biochemistry (MS); geochemistry (MS); inorganic chemistry (MS); organic chemistry (MS); physical chemistry (MS). Part-time programs available. *Faculty:* 18 full-time, 14 part-time. *Students:* 8 full-time (3 women), 32 part-time (14 women); includes 19 minority (14 Asian Americans or Pacific Islanders, 5 Hispanic Americans), 6 international. *Degree requirements:* For master's, thesis, departmental qualifying exam required, foreign language not required. *Entrance requirements:* For master's, minimum GPA of 2.5 in last 60 units, major in chemistry or related field. Application fee: $55. Tuition, nonresident: part-time $264 per unit. *Unit head:* Dr. Bruce Weber, Chair, 714-278-3621. *Application contact:* Dr. Gregory Williams, Adviser, 714-278-2170.

California State University, Los Angeles, Graduate Studies, School of Natural and Social Sciences, Department of Chemistry and Biochemistry, Los Angeles, CA 90032-8530. Offers analytical chemistry (MS); biochemistry (MS); chemistry (MS); inorganic chemistry (MS); organic chemistry (MS); physical chemistry (MS). Part-time and evening/weekend programs available. *Faculty:* 14 full-time, 20 part-time. *Students:* 13 full-time (6 women), 11 part-time (4 women); includes 16 minority (1 African American, 12 Asian Americans or Pacific Islanders, 3 Hispanic Americans), 3 international. *Degree requirements:* For master's, one foreign language (computer language can substitute), comprehensive exam or thesis required. *Entrance requirements:* For master's, TOEFL (minimum score of 550 required). *Application deadline:* For fall admission, 6/30; for spring admission, 2/1. Applications are processed on a rolling basis. Application fee: $55. *Unit head:* Dr. Scott Grover, Acting Chair, 323-343-2300.

Case Western Reserve University, School of Graduate Studies, Department of Chemistry, Cleveland, OH 44106. Offers analytical chemistry (MS, PhD); inorganic chemistry (MS, PhD); organic chemistry (MS, PhD); physical chemistry (MS, PhD). Part-time programs available. Terminal master's awarded for partial completion of doctoral program. *Degree requirements:* For master's, thesis not required; for doctorate, dissertation required. *Entrance requirements:* For master's and doctorate, GRE General Test, GRE Subject Test, TOEFL (minimum score of 550 required). *Faculty research:* Electrochemistry, synthetic chemistry, chemistry of life process, spectroscopy, kinetics.

Clark Atlanta University, School of Arts and Sciences, Department of Chemistry, Atlanta, GA 30314. Offers inorganic chemistry (MS, PhD); organic chemistry (MS, PhD); physical chemistry (MS, PhD); science education (DA). Part-time programs available. *Students:* 17 full-time (11 women), 20 part-time (11 women); includes 33 minority (28 African Americans, 2 Asian Americans or Pacific Islanders, 3 Hispanic Americans), 3 international. *Degree requirements:* For master's, one foreign language (computer language can substitute), thesis, comprehensive exam required; for doctorate, 2 foreign languages (computer language can substitute for one), dissertation, cumulative exam required. *Entrance requirements:* For master's, GRE General

Physical Chemistry

Clark Atlanta University (continued)
Test, minimum GPA of 2.5; for doctorate, GRE General Test, GRE Subject Test, minimum graduate GPA of 3.0. *Application deadline:* For fall admission, 4/1; for spring admission, 11/1. Applications are processed on a rolling basis. Application fee: $40. *Unit head:* Dr. Reynold Verrett, Chairperson, 404-880-8154. *Application contact:* Michelle Clark-Davis, Graduate Program Assistant, 404-880-8709.

Clarkson University, Graduate School, School of Science, Department of Chemistry, Potsdam, NY 13699. Offers analytical chemistry (MS, PhD); inorganic chemistry (MS, PhD); organic chemistry (MS, PhD); physical chemistry (MS, PhD). *Faculty:* 9 full-time (0 women). *Students:* 25 full-time (13 women); includes 1 minority (African American), 15 international. *Degree requirements:* For master's, foreign language and thesis not required; for doctorate, dissertation, departmental qualifying exam required, foreign language not required. *Entrance requirements:* For master's, GRE, TOEFL. *Application deadline:* For fall admission, 5/15 (priority date); for spring admission, 10/15 (priority date). Applications are processed on a rolling basis. Application fee: $25 ($35 for international students). Tuition: Part-time $661 per credit hour. Required fees: $215 per semester. *Unit head:* Dr. Stig Friberg, Chair, 315-268-6500, Fax: 315-268-6610, E-mail: fbg@clarkson.edu.

Cleveland State University, College of Graduate Studies, College of Arts and Sciences, Department of Chemistry, Cleveland, OH 44115-2440. Offers analytical chemistry (MS, PhD); clinical chemistry (MS, PhD); inorganic chemistry (MS); organic chemistry (MS); physical chemistry (MS); structural analysis (MS, PhD). Part-time and evening/weekend programs available. *Faculty:* 13 full-time (1 woman). *Students:* 1 full-time (0 women), 53 part-time (22 women); includes 5 minority (1 African American, 3 Asian Americans or Pacific Islanders, 1 Hispanic American), 25 international. *Degree requirements:* For master's, thesis required (for some programs), foreign language not required; for doctorate, dissertation required, foreign language not required. *Entrance requirements:* For master's and doctorate, GRE General Test, GRE Subject Test, TOEFL (minimum score of 525 required). *Application deadline:* For fall admission, 7/15 (priority date). Applications are processed on a rolling basis. Application fee: $25. *Unit head:* Dr. Stan Duraj, Interim Chair, 216-523-7312, Fax: 216-687-9298.

Columbia University, Graduate School of Arts and Sciences, Division of Natural Sciences, Department of Chemistry, Program in Chemical Physics, New York, NY 10027. Offers M Phil, PhD. *Entrance requirements:* For master's, GRE General Test, GRE Subject Test, TOEFL.

Cornell University, Graduate School, Graduate Fields of Arts and Sciences, Field of Chemistry, Ithaca, NY 14853-0001. Offers analytical chemistry (PhD); bio-organic chemistry (PhD); biophysical chemistry (PhD); chemical physics (PhD); inorganic chemistry (PhD); material chemistry (PhD); organic chemistry (PhD); physical chemistry (PhD); polymer chemistry (PhD); theoretical chemistry (PhD). *Faculty:* 38 full-time. *Students:* 139 full-time (44 women); includes 10 minority (1 African American, 4 Asian Americans or Pacific Islanders, 4 Hispanic Americans, 1 Native American), 51 international. *Degree requirements:* For doctorate, dissertation required, foreign language not required. *Entrance requirements:* For doctorate, GRE General Test, GRE Subject Test, TOEFL (minimum score of 600 required). *Application deadline:* For fall admission, 1/15. Application fee: $65. Electronic applications accepted. *Unit head:* Director of Graduate Studies, 607-255-4139. *Application contact:* Graduate Field Assistant, 607-255-4139, E-mail: chemgrad@cornell.edu.

See in-depth description on page 109.

Florida State University, Graduate Studies, College of Arts and Sciences, Department of Chemistry, Program in Chemical Physics, Tallahassee, FL 32306. Offers MS, PhD. *Faculty:* 25 full-time (1 woman). *Students:* 4 full-time (0 women). Average age 24. *Degree requirements:* For master's, cumulative and diagnostic exams required; for doctorate, dissertation, cumulative and diagnostic exams required, foreign language not required. *Entrance requirements:* For master's and doctorate, GRE General Test (minimum combined score of 1100 required), minimum B average in undergraduate course work. *Application deadline:* For fall admission, 4/15. Applications are processed on a rolling basis. Application fee: $20. Tuition, state resident: part-time $139 per credit hour. Tuition, nonresident: part-time $482 per credit hour. Tuition and fees vary according to program. *Financial aid:* In 1998–99, 2 research assistantships, 2 teaching assistantships were awarded. Financial aid application deadline: 2/15; financial aid applicants required to submit FAFSA. *Faculty research:* Theoretical and experimental research in molecular and solid-state physics and chemistry, statistical mechanics. *Application contact:* Dr. Naresh Dalal, Chair, Graduate Admissions Committee, 850-644-3398, Fax: 850-644-8281.

Florida State University, Graduate Studies, College of Arts and Sciences, Department of Physics, Tallahassee, FL 32306. Offers chemical physics (MS, PhD); physics (MS, PhD). *Faculty:* 42 full-time (3 women). *Students:* 65 full-time (9 women), 4 part-time (1 woman); includes 4 minority (1 African American, 1 Asian American or Pacific Islander, 2 Hispanic Americans) Terminal master's awarded for partial completion of doctoral program. *Degree requirements:* For master's, thesis required (for some programs), foreign language not required; for doctorate, dissertation required, foreign language not required. *Entrance requirements:* For master's and doctorate, GRE General Test (minimum combined score of 1100 required), minimum GPA of 3.0. *Application deadline:* Applications are processed on a rolling basis. Application fee: $20. Electronic applications accepted. Tuition, state resident: part-time $139 per credit hour. Tuition, nonresident: part-time $482 per credit hour. Tuition and fees vary according to program. *Unit head:* Dr. Kirby W. Kemper, Chairman, 850-644-2867, Fax: 850-644-2338, E-mail: kirby@phy.fsu.edu.

Georgetown University, Graduate School, Department of Chemistry, Washington, DC 20057. Offers analytical chemistry (MS, PhD); biochemistry (MS, PhD); chemical physics (MS, PhD); inorganic chemistry (MS, PhD); organic chemistry (MS, PhD); physical chemistry (MS, PhD); theoretical chemistry (MS, PhD). Terminal master's awarded for partial completion of doctoral program. *Degree requirements:* For master's, thesis (for some programs), qualifying exam required, foreign language not required; for doctorate, dissertation, comprehensive exam required. *Entrance requirements:* For master's and doctorate, GRE General Test, TOEFL (minimum score of 550 required, 600 for teaching assistants).

See in-depth description on page 125.

The George Washington University, Columbian School of Arts and Sciences, Department of Chemistry, Washington, DC 20052. Offers analytical chemistry (MS, PhD); inorganic chemistry (MS, PhD); materials science (MS, PhD); organic chemistry (MS, PhD); physical chemistry (MS, PhD). Part-time and evening/weekend programs available. *Faculty:* 5 full-time (0 women). *Students:* 19 full-time (14 women), 7 part-time (4 women); includes 6 minority (1 African American, 3 Asian Americans or Pacific Islanders, 2 Hispanic Americans), 6 international. Terminal master's awarded for partial completion of doctoral program. *Degree requirements:* For master's, computer language, thesis or alternative, comprehensive exam required; for doctorate, computer language, dissertation, general exam required. *Entrance requirements:* For master's and doctorate, GRE General Test, interview, minimum GPA of 3.0. Application fee: $55. Tuition: Full-time $17,328; part-time $722 per credit hour. Required fees: $828; $35 per credit hour. Tuition and fees vary according to campus/location and program. *Unit head:* Dr. Michael King, Chair, 202-994-6121.

Harvard University, Graduate School of Arts and Sciences, Committee on Chemical Physics, Cambridge, MA 02138. Offers chemical physics (PhD); chemistry (AM); physics (AM). *Students:* 2 full-time (0 women); includes 1 minority (Hispanic American) *Degree requirements:* For doctorate, dissertation, cumulative exams required. *Entrance requirements:* For master's, GRE General Test, TOEFL (minimum score of 550 required); for doctorate, GRE General Test, GRE Subject Test, TOEFL (minimum score of 550 required). *Application deadline:* For fall admission, 1/1. Application fee: $60. *Financial aid:* Fellowships, research assistantships, teaching assistantships, career-related internships or fieldwork, Federal Work-Study, and institutionally-sponsored loans available. Financial aid application deadline: 12/30. *Unit head:* Dr. William Klemperer, Director of Graduate Studies, 617-495-4094. *Application contact:* Department of Chemistry and Chemical Biology, 617-496-3208.

Harvard University, Graduate School of Arts and Sciences, Department of Chemistry and Chemical Biology, Cambridge, MA 02138. Offers biochemical chemistry (AM, PhD); inorganic chemistry (AM, PhD); organic chemistry (AM, PhD); physical chemistry (AM, PhD). *Students:* 188 full-time (36 women). *Degree requirements:* For doctorate, dissertation, cumulative exams required, foreign language not required. *Entrance requirements:* For master's, GRE General Test, TOEFL (minimum score of 550 required); for doctorate, GRE General Test, GRE Subject Test, TOEFL (minimum score of 550 required). *Application deadline:* For fall admission, 12/31. Application fee: $60. *Unit head:* Dr. David Evans, Chair, 617-495-2948. *Application contact:* Graduate Admissions Office, 617-496-3208.

See in-depth description on page 133.

Howard University, Graduate School of Arts and Sciences, Department of Chemistry, Washington, DC 20059-0002. Offers analytical chemistry (MS, PhD); biochemistry (MS, PhD); inorganic chemistry (MS, PhD); organic chemistry (MS, PhD); physical chemistry (MS, PhD); polymer chemistry (MS, PhD); theoretical chemistry (MS, PhD). Part-time programs available. Terminal master's awarded for partial completion of doctoral program. *Degree requirements:* For master's, one foreign language (computer language can substitute), thesis, comprehensive exam, teaching experience required; for doctorate, 2 foreign languages (computer language can substitute for one), dissertation, comprehensive exam, teaching experience required. *Entrance requirements:* For master's, GRE General Test, minimum GPA of 2.7; for doctorate, GRE General Test, minimum GPA of 3.0. *Faculty research:* Stratospheric aerosols, liquid crystals, polymer coatings, terrestrial and extraterrestrial atmospheres, amidogen reaction.

Illinois Institute of Technology, Graduate College, Armour College of Engineering and Sciences, Department of Biological, Chemical and Physical Sciences, Chemistry Division, Chicago, IL 60616-3793. Offers analytical chemistry (MAC, MS, PhD); chemistry (M Chem); inorganic chemistry (MS, PhD); organic chemistry (MS, PhD); physical chemistry (MS, PhD); polymer chemistry (MS, PhD); theoretical chemistry (MS, PhD). Part-time and evening/weekend programs available. *Faculty:* 8 full-time (0 women), 2 part-time (0 women). *Students:* 14 full-time (7 women), 70 part-time (27 women); includes 19 minority (10 African Americans, 9 Asian Americans or Pacific Islanders), 16 international. Terminal master's awarded for partial completion of doctoral program. *Degree requirements:* For master's, thesis (for some programs), comprehensive exam required, foreign language not required; for doctorate, dissertation, comprehensive exam required, foreign language not required. *Entrance requirements:* For master's and doctorate, GRE (minimum score of 1200 required), TOEFL (minimum score of 550 required), undergraduate GPA of 3.0 required. *Application deadline:* For fall admission, 7/1; for spring admission, 11/1. Applications are processed on a rolling basis. Application fee: $30. Electronic applications accepted. *Unit head:* Dr. Carlo Segre, Associate Chair, 312-567-3480, Fax: 312-567-3494, E-mail: segre@iit.edu. *Application contact:* Dr. S. Mohammad Shahidehpour, Dean of Graduate College, 312-567-3024, Fax: 312-567-7517, E-mail: grad@minna.cns.iit.edu.

See in-depth description on page 135.

Indiana University Bloomington, Graduate School, College of Arts and Sciences, Department of Chemistry, Bloomington, IN 47405. Offers analytical chemistry (PhD); biological chemistry (PhD); chemistry (MAT, MS); inorganic chemistry (PhD); physical chemistry (PhD). PhD offered through the University Graduate School. *Faculty:* 28 full-time (1 woman), 1 (woman) part-time. *Students:* 96 full-time (32 women), 65 part-time (10 women); includes 12 minority (1 African American, 9 Asian Americans or Pacific Islanders, 2 Hispanic Americans), 42 international. Terminal master's awarded for partial completion of doctoral program. *Degree requirements:* For master's and doctorate, thesis/dissertation required, foreign language not required. *Entrance requirements:* For master's and doctorate, GRE General Test, GRE Subject Test, TOEFL. *Application deadline:* For fall admission, 1/15 (priority date); for spring admission, 9/1 (priority date). Applications are processed on a rolling basis. Application fee: $40. Tuition, state resident: part-time $161 per credit hour. Tuition, nonresident: part-time $468 per credit hour. Required fees: $360 per year. Tuition and fees vary according to course load and program. *Unit head:* Dr. Gary M. Hieftje, Chairperson, 812-855-6239, Fax: 812-855-8300, E-mail: cemchair@indiana.edu. *Application contact:* Dr. Jack K. Crandall, Chairperson of Admissions, 812-855-2068, Fax: 812-855-8300, E-mail: chemgrad@indiana.edu.

Kansas State University, Graduate School, College of Arts and Sciences, Department of Chemistry, Manhattan, KS 66506. Offers analytical chemistry (MS); chemistry (PhD); inorganic chemistry (MS); organic chemistry (MS); physical chemistry (MS). *Faculty:* 16 full-time (1 woman). *Students:* 43 full-time (12 women), 2 part-time (1 woman); includes 2 minority (both Asian Americans or Pacific Islanders), 25 international. Terminal master's awarded for partial completion of doctoral program. *Degree requirements:* For master's and doctorate, thesis/dissertation required, foreign language not required. *Entrance requirements:* For master's and doctorate, GRE, minimum GPA of 3.0. *Application deadline:* For fall admission, 6/1 (priority date); for spring admission, 12/1. Applications are processed on a rolling basis. Application fee: $0 ($25 for international students). *Unit head:* Peter M. A. Sherwood, Head, 785-532-6665, Fax: 785-532-6666, E-mail: escashem@ksu.edu. *Application contact:* Christer B. Aakeroy, Graduate Coordinator, 785-532-1468, Fax: 785-532-6666.

See in-depth description on page 143.

Kent State University, College of Arts and Sciences, Chemical Physics Interdisciplinary Program, Kent, OH 44242-0001. Offers MS, PhD. Offered in cooperation with the Departments of Chemistry, Mathematics and Computer Science, and Physics and the Liquid Crystal Institute. *Students:* 28 full-time (2 women), 1 part-time; includes 1 minority (Hispanic American), 22 international. 10 applicants, 90% accepted. *Degree requirements:* For master's, computer language, thesis required; for doctorate, computer language, dissertation, candidacy exam required. *Application deadline:* For fall admission, 1/31. Application fee: $30. *Unit head:* Dr. John L. West, Director, 330-672-2654. *Application contact:* P. Palffy-Muhoray, Graduate Coordinator, 330-672-2604, Fax: 330-672-2796, E-mail: mpalffy@cpip.kent.edu.

See in-depth description on page 145.

Kent State University, College of Arts and Sciences, Department of Chemistry, Kent, OH 44242-0001. Offers analytical chemistry (MS, PhD); biochemistry (PhD); chemistry (MA, MS, PhD); inorganic chemistry (MS, PhD); organic chemistry (MS, PhD); physical chemistry (MS, PhD). *Faculty:* 23 full-time. *Students:* 36 full-time (20 women), 2 part-time (both women); includes 1 minority (African American), 19 international. *Degree requirements:* For master's and doctorate, thesis/dissertation required, foreign language not required. *Entrance requirements:* For master's, minimum GPA of 2.75; for doctorate, minimum GPA of 3.0. *Application deadline:* For fall admission, 7/12; for spring admission, 11/29. Applications are processed on a rolling basis. Application fee: $30. *Unit head:* Dr. Rathindra N. Bose, Chairman, 330-672-2032, Fax: 330-672-3816.

See in-depth description on page 147.

Lehigh University, College of Arts and Sciences, Department of Chemistry, Bethlehem, PA 18015-3094. Offers biochemistry and analytical chemistry (MS, PhD); chemistry (DA); clinical chemistry (MS); inorganic chemistry (MS, PhD); organic chemistry (MS, PhD); pharmaceutical chemistry (PhD); physical chemistry (MS, PhD). Part-time programs available. Postbaccalaureate distance learning degree programs offered (no on-campus study). *Students:* 30 full-time (14 women), 92 part-time (46 women); includes 10 minority (7 Asian Americans or Pacific Islanders, 3 Hispanic Americans), 10 international. Terminal master's awarded for partial completion of doctoral program. *Degree requirements:* For master's, foreign language and thesis not required; for doctorate, dissertation required. *Entrance requirements:* For master's and doctorate, GRE General Test, TSE (minimum score of 230 required). *Application deadline:* For fall admission, 7/15; for spring admission, 12/1. Applications are processed on a rolling basis. Application fee: $40. *Unit head:* Dr. Keith J. Schray, Chairman, 610-758-3474, Fax: 610-758-6536, E-mail: kjs0@lehigh.edu. *Application contact:* Dr. James E. Roberts, Graduate Coordinator, 610-758-4847, Fax: 610-758-6536, E-mail: jer1@lehigh.edu.

Marquette University, Graduate School, College of Arts and Sciences, Department of Chemistry, Milwaukee, WI 53201-1881. Offers analytical chemistry (MS, PhD); bioanalytical chemistry (MS, PhD); biophysical chemistry (MS, PhD); chemical physics (MS, PhD); inorganic chemistry (MS, PhD); organic chemistry (MS, PhD); physical chemistry (MS, PhD). Part-time programs available. *Faculty:* 15 full-time (2 women), 1 part-time (0 women). *Students:* 33 full-time (12 women), 6 part-time (1 woman); includes 5 minority (2 African Americans, 3 Asian Americans or Pacific Islanders), 30 international. Terminal master's awarded for partial completion of doctoral program. *Degree requirements:* For master's, comprehensive exam required; for doctorate, dissertation, cumulative exams required, foreign language not required. *Entrance requirements:* For master's and doctorate, TOEFL (minimum score of 550 required), GRE Subject Test. Application fee: $40. Tuition: Part-time $510 per credit hour. Tuition and fees vary according to program. *Unit head:* Dr. Charles Wilkie, Chairman, 414-288-7065, Fax: 414-288-7066. *Application contact:* Dr. Mark Steinmetz, Director of Graduate Studies, 414-288-3535, Fax: 414-288-7066.

Massachusetts Institute of Technology, School of Science, Department of Chemistry, Cambridge, MA 02139-4307. Offers biochemistry (PhD); biological chemistry (PhD, Sc D); inorganic chemistry (PhD, Sc D); organic chemistry (PhD, Sc D); physical chemistry (PhD, Sc D). *Faculty:* 27 full-time (2 women). *Students:* 172 full-time (51 women); includes 19 minority (3 African Americans, 6 Asian Americans or Pacific Islanders, 9 Hispanic Americans, 1 Native American), 53 international. *Degree requirements:* For doctorate, dissertation, comprehensive oral exam, oral presentation, written exams required, foreign language not required. *Application deadline:* For fall admission, 1/15. Application fee: $55. *Unit head:* Dr. Stephen J. Lippard, Chairman, 617-253-1845. *Application contact:* Susan Brighton, Graduate Administrator, 617-253-1845, Fax: 617-258-0241, E-mail: brighton@mit.edu.

McMaster University, School of Graduate Studies, Faculty of Science, Department of Chemistry, Hamilton, ON L8S 4M2, Canada. Offers analytical chemistry (M Sc, PhD); chemical physics (M Sc, PhD); chemistry (M Sc, PhD); inorganic chemistry (M Sc, PhD); organic chemistry (M Sc, PhD); physical chemistry (M Sc, PhD); polymer chemistry (M Sc, PhD). Part-time programs available. *Faculty:* 21 full-time (2 women), 4 part-time (0 women). *Students:* 67 full-time (23 women), 1 part-time, 1 international. Terminal master's awarded for partial completion of doctoral program. *Degree requirements:* For master's, thesis required, foreign language not required; for doctorate, dissertation, comprehensive exam required, foreign language not required. *Entrance requirements:* For master's, minimum B+ average. *Application deadline:* For fall admission, 4/30; for spring admission, 3/15. Applications are processed on a rolling basis. Application fee: $50. *Unit head:* Dr. M. J. McGlinchey, Chair, 905-525-9140 Ext. 24504, Fax: 905-522-2509, E-mail: mcglinchey@mcmail.cis.mcmaster.ca. *Application contact:* Carol Dada, Administrator, 905-525-9140 Ext. 23487, Fax: 905-522-2509, E-mail: dada@mcmail.cis.mcmaster.ca.

McMaster University, School of Graduate Studies, Faculty of Science, Department of Physics and Astronomy, Program in Chemical Physics, Hamilton, ON L8S 4M2, Canada. Offers M Sc, PhD. *Degree requirements:* For master's, thesis or alternative required, foreign language not required; for doctorate, dissertation, comprehensive exam required, foreign language not required. *Entrance requirements:* For master's and doctorate, minimum B+ average.

Michigan State University, Graduate School, College of Natural Science, Department of Chemistry, East Lansing, MI 48824-1020. Offers analytical chemistry (MS, PhD); chemistry (MAT, MS, PhD); chemistry-environmental toxicology (PhD); environmental toxicology (PhD); inorganic chemistry (MS, PhD); organic chemistry (MS, PhD); physical chemistry (PhD). *Faculty:* 36 full-time (4 women). *Students:* 149 full-time (46 women), 18 part-time (9 women); includes 12 minority (6 African Americans, 3 Asian Americans or Pacific Islanders, 2 Hispanic Americans, 1 Native American), 80 international. Terminal master's awarded for partial completion of doctoral program. *Degree requirements:* For master's, thesis required (for some programs), foreign language not required; for doctorate, dissertation required, foreign language not required. *Entrance requirements:* For master's and doctorate, GRE, TOEFL. *Application deadline:* Applications are processed on a rolling basis. Application fee: $30 ($40 for international students). *Unit head:* Dr. Katharine C. Hunt, Chairperson, 517-355-9715, Fax: 517-353-1793, E-mail: chemdept@cem.msu.edu. *Application contact:* Dr. Richard Schwendeman, Associate Chair, Graduate Program, 517-355-9715 Ext. 344, Fax: 517-353-1793, E-mail: gradoff@cem.msu.edu.

Michigan State University, Graduate School, College of Natural Science, Program in Chemical Physics, East Lansing, MI 48824-1020. Offers MS. *Students:* 1. *Application deadline:* Applications are processed on a rolling basis. Application fee: $30 ($40 for international students). *Unit head:* Dr. James Harrison, Director, 517-355-9715 Ext. 295.

Northeastern University, College of Arts and Sciences, Department of Chemistry, Boston, MA 02115-5096. Offers analytical chemistry (PhD); chemistry (MAT, MS, PhD); inorganic chemistry (PhD); organic chemistry (PhD); physical chemistry (PhD). Part-time and evening/weekend programs available. *Faculty:* 20 full-time (3 women), 1 part-time (0 women). *Students:* 59 full-time (25 women), 23 part-time (9 women). Terminal master's awarded for partial completion of doctoral program. *Degree requirements:* For master's, thesis required (for some programs); for doctorate, dissertation, qualifying exam in specialty area required, foreign language not required. *Entrance requirements:* For master's and doctorate, TOEFL (minimum score of 580 required). *Application deadline:* For fall admission, 4/15. Applications are processed on a rolling basis. Application fee: $50. Electronic applications accepted. *Unit head:* Dr. David A. Forsyth, Chairman, 617-373-2822, Fax: 617-373-8795, E-mail: chemistry-grad-info@neu.edu. *Application contact:* Dr. Philip W. LeQuesne, Chair, Graduate Admissions Committee, 617-373-2383, Fax: 617-373-8795.

The Ohio State University, Graduate School, College of Mathematical and Physical Sciences, Program in Chemical Physics, Columbus, OH 43210. Offers MS, PhD. *Faculty:* 37 full-time. *Students:* 24 full-time (5 women), 17 international. 31 applicants, 35% accepted. In 1998, 4 master's, 2 doctorates awarded. *Degree requirements:* For master's, thesis optional; for doctorate, dissertation required. *Entrance requirements:* For master's and doctorate, GRE General Test, GRE Subject Test. *Application deadline:* For fall admission, 8/15. Applications are processed on a rolling basis. Application fee: $30 ($40 for international students). *Financial aid:* Fellowships, research assistantships, teaching assistantships, Federal Work-Study and institutionally-sponsored loans available. Aid available to part-time students. *Unit head:* Terry Miller, Graduate Studies Committee Chair, 614-292-2569, Fax: 614-292-1948, E-mail: miller.104@osu.edu.

Old Dominion University, College of Sciences, Department of Chemistry and Biochemistry, Norfolk, VA 23529. Offers analytical chemistry (MS); biochemistry (MS); biomedical sciences (PhD); clinical chemistry (MS); environmental chemistry (MS); organic chemistry (MS); physical chemistry (MS). Part-time and evening/weekend programs available. *Faculty:* 16 full-time (4 women). *Students:* 20 full-time (13 women), 12 part-time (8 women); includes 3 minority (1 African American, 2 Asian Americans or Pacific Islanders), 4 international. Terminal master's awarded for partial completion of doctoral program. *Degree requirements:* For master's and doctorate, thesis/dissertation, comprehensive exam required, foreign language not required. *Entrance requirements:* For master's, GRE General Test, TOEFL, minimum GPA of 3.0 in major, 2.5 overall; for doctorate, GRE General Test (minimum combined score of 1000 required), GRE Subject Test (minimum score of 600 required), TOEFL. *Application deadline:* For fall admission, 7/1; for spring admission, 11/1. Applications are processed on a rolling basis. Application fee: $30. *Unit head:* Dr. John R. Donet, Chair, 757-683-4078, E-mail: jdonet@odu.edu. *Application contact:* Dr. John R. Donet, Chair, 757-683-4078, E-mail: jdonet@odu.edu.

Oregon State University, Graduate School, College of Science, Department of Chemistry, Corvallis, OR 97331. Offers analytical chemistry (MS, PhD); chemistry (MA, MAIS); inorganic chemistry (MS, PhD); nuclear and radiation chemistry (MS, PhD); organic chemistry (MS, PhD); physical chemistry (MS, PhD). Part-time programs available. *Faculty:* 25 full-time (3 women), 5 part-time (2 women). *Students:* 68 full-time (24 women), 2 part-time; includes 4 minority (all Asian Americans or Pacific Islanders), 30 international. Terminal master's awarded for partial completion of doctoral program. *Degree requirements:* For master's and doctorate, one foreign language, thesis/dissertation required. *Entrance requirements:* For master's and doctorate, TOEFL (minimum score of 620 required), minimum GPA of 3.0 in last 90 hours. *Application deadline:* For fall admission, 3/1 (priority date). Applications are processed on a rolling basis. Application fee: $50. *Unit head:* Dr. John Westall, Chair, 541-737-6700, Fax: 541-737-2062, E-mail: john.westall@orst.edu. *Application contact:* Carolyn Brumley, Graduate Secretary, 541-737-6707, Fax: 541-737-2062, E-mail: carolyn.brumley@orst.edu.

Princeton University, Graduate School, Department of Chemistry, Princeton, NJ 08544-1019. Offers chemistry (PhD); industrial chemistry (MS); physics and chemical physics (PhD); polymer sciences and materials (MSE, PhD). PhD (polymer sciences and materials) offered in conjunction with the Department of Chemical Engineering. *Degree requirements:* For doctorate, dissertation, cumulative and general exams required. *Entrance requirements:* For master's, GRE General Test; for doctorate, GRE General Test, GRE Subject Test. *Faculty research:* Chemistry of interfaces, organic synthesis, organometallic chemistry, inorganic reactions, biostructural chemistry.

See in-depth description on page 163.

Princeton University, Graduate School, Department of Physics, Program in Physics and Chemical Physics, Princeton, NJ 08544-1019. Offers PhD. *Degree requirements:* For doctorate, dissertation required. *Entrance requirements:* For doctorate, GRE General Test, GRE Subject Test.

Purdue University, Graduate School, School of Science, Department of Chemistry, West Lafayette, IN 47907. Offers analytical chemistry (MS, PhD); biochemistry (MS, PhD); chemical education (MS, PhD); inorganic chemistry (MS, PhD); organic chemistry (MS, PhD); physical chemistry (MS, PhD). *Accreditation:* NCATE (one or more programs are accredited). *Faculty:* 46 full-time, 1 part-time. *Students:* 246 full-time (83 women), 59 part-time (20 women); includes 36 minority (14 African Americans, 7 Asian Americans or Pacific Islanders, 14 Hispanic Americans, 1 Native American), 100 international. Terminal master's awarded for partial completion of doctoral program. *Degree requirements:* For master's and doctorate, thesis/dissertation required, foreign language not required. *Entrance requirements:* For master's and doctorate, TOEFL (minimum score of 550 required). Application fee: $30. Electronic applications accepted. *Unit head:* Dr. R. A. Walton, Head, 765-494-5203. *Application contact:* R. E. Wild, Chairman, Graduate Admissions, 765-494-5200, E-mail: wild@purdue.edu.

Rensselaer Polytechnic Institute, Graduate School, School of Science, Department of Chemistry, Troy, NY 12180-3590. Offers analytical chemistry (MS, PhD); biochemistry (MS, PhD); inorganic chemistry (MS, PhD); organic chemistry (MS, PhD); physical chemistry (MS, PhD); polymer chemistry (MS, PhD). Part-time and evening/weekend programs available. *Faculty:* 17 full-time (2 women), 1 part-time (0 women). *Students:* 52 full-time (18 women), 3 part-time (1 woman); includes 4 minority (3 Asian Americans or Pacific Islanders, 1 Hispanic American), 30 international. *Degree requirements:* For master's, thesis required (for some programs), foreign language not required; for doctorate, dissertation required, foreign language not required. *Entrance requirements:* For master's and doctorate, GRE General Test, TOEFL (minimum score of 550 required). *Application deadline:* For fall admission, 2/1 (priority date). Applications are processed on a rolling basis. Application fee: $35. *Unit head:* Dr. Thomas Apple, Chair, 518-276-6344. *Application contact:* Dr. Wilfredo Colon, Chair, Graduate Committee, 518-276-6340, Fax: 518-276-6434, E-mail: colonw@rpi.edu.

See in-depth description on page 167.

Rutgers, The State University of New Jersey, Newark, Graduate School, Department of Chemistry, Newark, NJ 07102-3192. Offers analytical chemistry (MS, PhD); biochemistry (MS, PhD); inorganic chemistry (MS, PhD); organic chemistry (MS, PhD); physical chemistry (MS, PhD). Part-time and evening/weekend programs available. *Faculty:* 22 full-time (4 women). *Students:* 28 full-time (11 women), 39 part-time (19 women); includes 29 minority (1 African American, 24 Asian Americans or Pacific Islanders, 4 Hispanic Americans) Terminal master's awarded for partial completion of doctoral program. *Degree requirements:* For master's, cumulative exams required, thesis optional, foreign language not required; for doctorate, dissertation, exams, research proposal required, foreign language not required. *Entrance requirements:* For master's and doctorate, GRE General Test, TOEFL (minimum score of 550 required; 590 for financial aid), minimum undergraduate B average. *Application deadline:* For fall admission, 7/1 (priority date); for spring admission, 12/1. Applications are processed on a rolling basis. Application fee: $40. *Unit head:* Prof. Hugh W. Thompson, Coordinator, 973-353-5173, Fax: 973-353-1264.

See in-depth description on page 169.

Rutgers, The State University of New Jersey, New Brunswick, Graduate School, Program in Chemistry, New Brunswick, NJ 08903. Offers analytical chemistry (MS, PhD); biological chemistry (PhD); chemistry education (MST); inorganic chemistry (MS, PhD); organic chemistry (MS, PhD); physical chemistry (MS, PhD). Part-time and evening/weekend programs available. *Faculty:* 44 full-time (9 women), 4 part-time (2 women). *Students:* 100 full-time (35 women), 69 part-time (29 women); includes 27 minority (2 African Americans, 24 Asian Americans or Pacific Islanders, 1 Hispanic American), 79 international. Terminal master's awarded for partial completion of doctoral program. *Degree requirements:* For master's, exam required, thesis optional, foreign language not required; for doctorate, dissertation, cumulative exams required, foreign language not required. *Entrance requirements:* For master's, GRE General Test, GRE Subject Test, TOEFL; for doctorate, GRE General Test, GRE Subject Test, TOEFL (minimum score of 575 required). *Application deadline:* For fall admission, 4/15 (priority date); for spring admission, 11/1. Applications are processed on a rolling basis. Application fee: $50. *Unit head:* Dr. Martha A. Cotter, Director, 732-445-2259, Fax: 732-445-5312, E-mail: gradexec@rutchem.rutgers.edu.

See in-depth description on page 173.

San Jose State University, Graduate Studies, College of Science, Department of Chemistry, San Jose, CA 95192-0001. Offers analytical chemistry (MS); biochemistry (MS); chemistry (MA); inorganic chemistry (MS); organic chemistry (MS); physical chemistry (MS); polymer chemistry (MS); radiochemistry (MS). Part-time and evening/weekend programs available. *Faculty:* 24 full-time (3 women), 5 part-time (2 women). *Students:* 7 full-time (5 women), 30 part-time (17 women); includes 24 minority (2 African Americans, 21 Asian Americans or Pacific Islanders, 1 Hispanic American), 4 international. *Degree requirements:* For master's, thesis or alternative required, foreign language not required. *Entrance requirements:* For master's, GRE, minimum B average. *Application deadline:* For fall admission, 6/1. Applications are processed on a rolling basis. Application fee: $59. Tuition, nonresident: part-time $246 per unit. Required fees: $1,939; $1,309 per year. *Unit head:* Dr. Pamela Stacks, Chair, 408-924-5000, Fax: 408-924-4945. *Application contact:* Dr. Roger Biringer, Graduate Adviser, 408-924-4961.

Seton Hall University, College of Arts and Sciences, Department of Chemistry, South Orange, NJ 07079-2694. Offers analytical chemistry (MS, PhD); biochemistry (MS, PhD); chemistry (MS); inorganic chemistry (MS, PhD); organic chemistry (MS, PhD); physical chemistry (MS, PhD). Part-time and evening/weekend programs available. Terminal master's awarded for partial completion of doctoral program. *Degree requirements:* For master's, formal seminar required, thesis optional; for doctorate, dissertation, comprehensive exams, annual seminars required. *Entrance requirements:* For master's, TOEFL, undergraduate major in chemistry or related field with a minimum of 30 credits in chemistry, including 2 semesters of

Physical Chemistry

Seton Hall University (continued)
physical chemistry; for doctorate, oral matriculation exam based on proposed doctoral research, minimum GPA of 3.0 in course distribution requirements, formal seminar. *Faculty research:* DNA metal reactions; chromatography; bioinorganic, biophysical, organometallic, and polymer chemistry; heterogeneous catalysis.

Simon Fraser University, Graduate Studies, Faculty of Science, Department of Chemistry, Burnaby, BC V5A 1S6, Canada. Offers chemical physics (M Sc, PhD); chemistry (M Sc, PhD). *Faculty:* 29 full-time (2 women). *Students:* 59 full-time (20 women), 1 (woman) part-time. *Degree requirements:* For master's and doctorate, thesis/dissertation required. *Entrance requirements:* For master's, TOEFL (minimum score of 570 required), TWE (minimum score of 5 required), or International English Language Test (minimum score of 7.5 required), minimum GPA of 3.0; for doctorate, TOEFL (minimum score of 570 required), TWE (minimum score of 5 required), or International English Language Test (minimum score of 7.5 required), minimum GPA of 3.5. Application fee: $55. *Unit head:* R. Korteling, Chair, 604-291-3590, Fax: 604-291-3765. *Application contact:* Graduate Secretary, 604-291-3345, Fax: 604-291-3765, E-mail: gradappl@bohr.chem.sfu.ca.

Simon Fraser University, Graduate Studies, Faculty of Science, Department of Physics, Burnaby, BC V5A 1S6, Canada. Offers biophysics (M Sc, PhD); chemical physics (M Sc, PhD); physics (M Sc, PhD). *Faculty:* 23 full-time (2 women). *Students:* 51 full-time (5 women). *Degree requirements:* For master's and doctorate, thesis/dissertation required, foreign language not required. *Entrance requirements:* For master's, TOEFL (minimum score of 570 required), TWE (minimum score of 5 required), or International English Language Test (minimum score of 7.5 required), minimum GPA of 3.0; for doctorate, TOEFL (minimum score of 570 required), TWE (minimum score of 5 required), or International English Language Test (minimum score of 7.5 required), minimum GPA of 3.5. Application fee: $55. *Unit head:* R. F. Frindt, Chair, 604-291-4465, Fax: 604-291-3592. *Application contact:* Graduate Secretary, 604-291-4465, Fax: 604-291-3592, E-mail: physics_grad_office@sfu.ca.

South Dakota State University, Graduate School, College of Arts and Science, Department of Chemistry, Brookings, SD 57007. Offers analytical chemistry (MS, PhD); biochemistry (MS, PhD); chemistry (MS, PhD); inorganic chemistry (MS, PhD); organic chemistry (MS, PhD); physical chemistry (MS, PhD). *Degree requirements:* For master's, thesis, oral exam required, foreign language not required; for doctorate, dissertation, preliminary oral and written exams, research tool required. *Entrance requirements:* For master's, TOEFL (minimum score of 580 required), bachelor's degree in chemistry or equivalent; for doctorate, TOEFL (minimum score of 580 required). *Faculty research:* Environmental chemistry, computational chemistry, organic synthesis and photochemistry, novel material development and characterization.

Southern University and Agricultural and Mechanical College, Graduate School, College of Sciences, Department of Chemistry, Baton Rouge, LA 70813. Offers analytical chemistry (MS); biochemistry (MS); environmental sciences (MS); inorganic chemistry (MS); organic chemistry (MS); physical chemistry (MS). *Faculty:* 9 full-time (2 women), 3 part-time (2 women). *Students:* 4 full-time (3 women), 20 part-time (12 women); includes 19 minority (all African Americans), 4 international. *Degree requirements:* For master's, thesis required, foreign language not required. *Entrance requirements:* For master's, GMAT or GRE General Test, TOEFL. *Application deadline:* For fall admission, 6/1 (priority date); for spring admission, 11/1. Applications are processed on a rolling basis. Application fee: $5. *Unit head:* Dr. Robert Harvey Miller, Chairman, 225-771-3990, Fax: 225-771-3992.

State University of New York at Binghamton, Graduate School, School of Arts and Sciences, Department of Chemistry, Binghamton, NY 13902-6000. Offers analytical chemistry (PhD); chemistry (MA, MS); inorganic chemistry (PhD); organic chemistry (PhD); physical chemistry (PhD). *Faculty:* 13 full-time, 7 part-time. *Students:* 48 full-time (11 women), 7 part-time (2 women); includes 2 minority (1 African American, 1 Hispanic American), 30 international. Terminal master's awarded for partial completion of doctoral program. *Degree requirements:* For master's, thesis or alternative, oral exam, seminar presentation required, foreign language not required; for doctorate, dissertation, cumulative exams required, foreign language not required. *Entrance requirements:* For master's and doctorate, GRE General Test, GRE Subject Test, TOEFL. *Application deadline:* For fall admission, 4/15 (priority date); for spring admission, 11/1. Applications are processed on a rolling basis. Application fee: $50. Electronic applications accepted. Tuition, state resident: full-time $5,100; part-time $213 per credit. Tuition, nonresident: full-time $8,416; part-time $351 per credit. Required fees: $77 per credit. Part-time tuition and fees vary according to course load. *Unit head:* Dr. Alistair J. Lees, Chairperson, 607-777-2362.

Stevens Institute of Technology, Graduate School, School of Applied Sciences and Liberal Arts, Department of Chemistry and Chemical Biology, Hoboken, NJ 07030. Offers chemistry (MS, PhD, Certificate), including analytical chemistry, chemical biology, chemical physiology (Certificate), instrumental analysis (Certificate), organic chemistry (MS, PhD), physical chemistry (MS, PhD), polymer chemistry. Part-time and evening/weekend programs available. Terminal master's awarded for partial completion of doctoral program. *Degree requirements:* For master's, thesis or alternative required, foreign language not required; for doctorate, one foreign language, dissertation required; for Certificate, computer language, project or thesis required. *Entrance requirements:* For master's and doctorate, TOEFL (minimum score of 550 required). Electronic applications accepted.

Tufts University, Division of Graduate and Continuing Studies and Research, Graduate School of Arts and Sciences, Department of Chemistry, Medford, MA 02155. Offers analytical chemistry (MS, PhD); bioorganic chemistry (MS, PhD); environmental chemistry (MS, PhD); inorganic chemistry (MS, PhD); organic chemistry (MS, PhD); physical chemistry (MS, PhD). *Faculty:* 13 full-time, 1 part-time. *Students:* 52 (27 women); includes 5 minority (1 African American, 3 Asian Americans or Pacific Islanders, 1 Hispanic American) 14 international. Terminal master's awarded for partial completion of doctoral program. *Degree requirements:* For master's and doctorate, thesis/dissertation required, foreign language not required. *Entrance requirements:* For master's and doctorate, GRE General Test, GRE Subject Test, TOEFL (minimum score of 600 required). *Application deadline:* For fall admission, 2/15; for spring admission, 10/15. Applications are processed on a rolling basis. Application fee: $50. *Unit head:* Marc d'Alarco, Chair, 617-627-3441, Fax: 617-627-3443. *Application contact:* Samuel Kounaves, 617-627-3124, Fax: 617-627-3443.

See in-depth description on page 181.

The University of Akron, Graduate School, Buchtel College of Arts and Sciences, Department of Chemistry, Akron, OH 44325-0001. Offers analytical chemistry (MS, PhD); biochemistry (MS, PhD); chemistry (MS, PhD); inorganic chemistry (MS, PhD); organic chemistry (MS, PhD); physical chemistry (MS, PhD). Part-time and evening/weekend programs available. *Faculty:* 17 full-time, 1 part-time. *Students:* 63 full-time (25 women), 9 part-time (6 women); includes 8 minority (6 African Americans, 2 Hispanic Americans), 31 international. Terminal master's awarded for partial completion of doctoral program. *Degree requirements:* For master's, one foreign language (computer language can substitute), thesis, seminar presentation required; for doctorate, 2 foreign languages (computer language can substitute for one), dissertation, cumulative exams required. *Entrance requirements:* For master's, TOEFL, minimum GPA of 2.75; for doctorate, TOEFL. *Application deadline:* For fall admission, 3/1. Applications are processed on a rolling basis. Application fee: $25 ($50 for international students). Tuition, state resident: part-time $189 per credit. Tuition, nonresident: part-time $353 per credit. Required fees: $7.3 per credit. *Unit head:* Dr. Gerald Koser, Chair, 330-972-7372, E-mail: koser@uakron.edu.

Iniversity of Calgary, Faculty of Graduate Studies, Faculty of Science, Department of Chemistry, Calgary, AB T2N 1N4, Canada. Offers analytical chemistry (M Sc, PhD); applied ...mistry (M Sc, PhD); inorganic chemistry (M Sc, PhD); organic chemistry (M Sc, PhD); ...ical chemistry (M Sc, PhD); polymer chemistry (M Sc, PhD); theoretical chemistry (M Sc, PhD). *Faculty:* 29 full-time (4 women), 1 part-time (0 women). *Students:* 60 full-time (25 women). *Degree requirements:* For master's, thesis required, foreign language not required; for doctorate, dissertation, candidacy exam required, foreign language not required. *Entrance requirements:* For master's and doctorate, TOEFL (minimum score of 580 required). *Application deadline:* For fall admission, 12/1 (priority date). Applications are processed on a rolling basis. Application fee: $60. *Unit head:* Dr. R. A. Kydd, Head, 403-220-5340. *Application contact:* Greta Prihodko, Graduate Program Administrator, 403-220-6252, E-mail: gradinfo@chem.ucalgary.ca.

University of Cincinnati, Division of Research and Advanced Studies, McMicken College of Arts and Sciences, Department of Chemistry, Cincinnati, OH 45221-0091. Offers analytical chemistry (MS, PhD); biochemistry (MS, PhD); inorganic chemistry (MS, PhD); organic chemistry (MS, PhD); physical chemistry (MS, PhD); polymer chemistry (MS, PhD). Part-time and evening/weekend programs available. *Faculty:* 25 full-time. *Students:* 87 full-time (26 women), 26 part-time (3 women); includes 12 minority (1 African American, 11 Asian Americans or Pacific Islanders), 34 international. Terminal master's awarded for partial completion of doctoral program. *Degree requirements:* For master's, thesis optional, foreign language not required; for doctorate, dissertation required, foreign language not required. *Entrance requirements:* For master's and doctorate, GRE General Test, GRE Subject Test. *Application deadline:* For fall admission, 2/1. Application fee: $30. *Unit head:* Dr. Marshall Wilson, Head, 513-556-9200, Fax: 513-556-9239, E-mail: marshall.wilson@uc.edu. *Application contact:* Thomas Ridgway, Graduate Program Director, 513-556-9200, Fax: 513-556-9239, E-mail: thomas.ridgway@uc.edu.

University of Georgia, Graduate School, College of Arts and Sciences, Department of Chemistry, Athens, GA 30602. Offers analytical chemistry (MS, PhD); inorganic chemistry (MS, PhD); organic chemistry (MS, PhD); physical chemistry (MS, PhD). *Faculty:* 23 full-time (1 woman). *Students:* 107 full-time (26 women), 11 part-time (4 women). *Degree requirements:* For master's, thesis required, foreign language not required; for doctorate, one foreign language (computer language can substitute), dissertation required. *Entrance requirements:* For master's and doctorate, GRE General Test. *Application deadline:* For fall admission, 7/1 (priority date); for spring admission, 11/15. Application fee: $30. Electronic applications accepted. *Unit head:* Dr. I. Jonathan Amster, Graduate Coordinator, 706-542-1936, Fax: 706-542-9454, E-mail: mauldin@sunchem.chem.uga.edu.

University of Louisville, Graduate School, College of Arts and Sciences, Department of Chemistry, Louisville, KY 40292-0001. Offers analytical chemistry (MS, PhD); chemical physics (PhD); inorganic chemistry (MS, PhD); organic chemistry (MS, PhD); physical chemistry (MS, PhD). *Faculty:* 20 full-time (3 women), 1 part-time (0 women). *Students:* 52 full-time (20 women), 4 part-time (2 women); includes 2 minority (both Hispanic Americans), 30 international. *Degree requirements:* For master's, thesis required; for doctorate, dissertation required. *Entrance requirements:* For master's and doctorate, GRE General Test, TOEFL (minimum score of 550 required). *Application deadline:* Applications are processed on a rolling basis. Application fee: $25. *Unit head:* Dr. George R. Pack, Chair, 502-852-6798, Fax: 502-852-8149, E-mail: george.pack@louisville.edu.

See in-depth description on page 199.

University of Maryland, College Park, Graduate School, College of Computer, Mathematical and Physical Sciences, Program in Chemical Physics, College Park, MD 20742-5045. Offers MS, PhD. *Students:* 20 full-time (5 women), 9 part-time (3 women); includes 3 minority (1 African American, 2 Hispanic Americans), 19 international. 30 applicants, 43% accepted. *Degree requirements:* For master's, paper, qualifying exam required, thesis not required; for doctorate, dissertation, seminars required. *Entrance requirements:* For master's, GRE Subject Test, minimum GPA of 3.3; for doctorate, GRE Subject Test. *Application deadline:* Applications are processed on a rolling basis. Application fee: $50 ($70 for international students). Tuition, state resident: part-time $272 per credit hour. Tuition, nonresident: part-time $475 per credit hour. Required fees: $632; $379 per year. *Financial aid:* Fellowships, research assistantships, teaching assistantships, Federal Work-Study and grants available. Financial aid applicants required to submit FAFSA. *Faculty research:* Discrete molecules and gases; dynamic phenomena; thermodynamics, statistical mechanical theory and quantum mechanical theory; atmospheric physics; biophysics. *Unit head:* Dr. Michael Coplan, Director, 301-405-4780. *Application contact:* Trudy Lindsey, Director, Graduate Admission and Records, 301-405-4198, Fax: 301-314-9305, E-mail: grschool@deans.umd.edu.

University of Maryland, College Park, Graduate School, College of Life Sciences, Department of Chemistry and Biochemistry, Chemistry Program, College Park, MD 20742-5045. Offers analytical chemistry (MS, PhD); inorganic chemistry (MS, PhD); organic chemistry (MS, PhD); physical chemistry (MS, PhD). *Students:* 76 full-time (34 women), 16 part-time (6 women); includes 8 minority (2 African Americans, 4 Asian Americans or Pacific Islanders, 1 Hispanic American, 1 Native American), 36 international. *Degree requirements:* For master's, thesis optional, foreign language not required; for doctorate, dissertation, 2 seminar presentations, oral exam required. *Entrance requirements:* For master's, GRE General Test, minimum GPA of 3.1; for doctorate, GRE General Test. *Application deadline:* Applications are processed on a rolling basis. Application fee: $50 ($70 for international students). Tuition, state resident: part-time $272 per credit hour. Tuition, nonresident: part-time $475 per credit hour. Required fees: $632; $379 per year. *Unit head:* Marlin Harmony, Graduate Director, 785-864-4670, Fax: 785-864-5396. *Application contact:* Trudy Lindsey, Director, Graduate Admission and Records, 301-405-4198, Fax: 301-314-9305, E-mail: grschool@deans.umd.edu.

University of Miami, Graduate School, College of Arts and Sciences, Department of Chemistry, Coral Gables, FL 33124. Offers chemistry (MS); inorganic chemistry (PhD); organic chemistry (PhD); physical chemistry (PhD). *Faculty:* 11 full-time (1 woman). *Students:* 40 full-time (18 women); includes 6 minority (1 African American, 1 Asian American or Pacific Islander, 4 Hispanic Americans), 33 international. Terminal master's awarded for partial completion of doctoral program. *Degree requirements:* For master's, foreign language and thesis not required; for doctorate, dissertation required, foreign language not required. *Entrance requirements:* For master's and doctorate, GRE General Test (minimum combined score of 1000 required), TOEFL (minimum score of 550 required). *Application deadline:* For fall admission, 1/15. Application fee: $35. Electronic applications accepted. Tuition: Full-time $15,336; part-time $852 per credit. Required fees: $174. Tuition and fees vary according to program. *Unit head:* Dr. Roger LeBlanc, Chairman, 305-284-2174, Fax: 305-284-4571. *Application contact:* Dr. Luis Echogoyen, Graduate Adviser, 305-661-2847, Fax: 305-284-4571, E-mail: ldookie@umiami.ir.miami.edu.

University of Michigan, Horace H. Rackham School of Graduate Studies, College of Literature, Science, and the Arts, Department of Chemistry, Ann Arbor, MI 48109. Offers analytical chemistry (PhD); chemical biology (PhD); inorganic chemistry (PhD); organic chemistry (PhD); physical chemistry (PhD). *Faculty:* 43 full-time (7 women). *Students:* 161 full-time (60 women); includes 5 minority (2 African Americans, 2 Asian Americans or Pacific Islanders, 1 Hispanic American), 43 international. *Degree requirements:* For doctorate, dissertation, oral defense of dissertation, preliminary exam, organic cumulative proficiency exams required, foreign language not required. *Entrance requirements:* For doctorate, GRE General Test, GRE Subject Test (recommended), statement of prior research. *Application deadline:* For fall admission, 2/15 (priority date). Applications are processed on a rolling basis. Application fee: $55. *Unit head:* Dr. Joseph P. Marino, Chair, 734-763-9681, Fax: 734-647-4847, E-mail: jpmarino@umich.edu. *Application contact:* Warren Noone, Assistant Director of Graduate Studies, 734-764-7278, Fax: 734-747-4865, E-mail: nooner@umich.edu.

University of Missouri–Columbia, Graduate School, College of Arts and Sciences, Department of Chemistry, Columbia, MO 65211. Offers analytical chemistry (MS, PhD); inorganic chemistry (MS, PhD); organic chemistry (MS, PhD); physical chemistry (MS, PhD). *Faculty:* 23 full-time (3 women). *Students:* 68 full-time (23 women), 24 part-time (7 women); includes 6 minority (1 African American, 2 Asian Americans or Pacific Islanders, 2 Hispanic Americans, 1

Native American), 47 international. *Degree requirements:* For master's, thesis required, foreign language not required; for doctorate, dissertation required. *Entrance requirements:* For master's and doctorate, GRE General Test, minimum GPA of 3.0. *Application deadline:* For fall admission, 7/1 (priority date). Applications are processed on a rolling basis. Application fee: $30 ($50 for international students). *Unit head:* Dr. Richard Thompson, Director of Graduate Studies, 573-882-7356.

University of Missouri–Kansas City, College of Arts and Sciences, Department of Chemistry, Kansas City, MO 64110-2499. Offers analytical chemistry (MS, PhD); inorganic chemistry (MS, PhD); organic chemistry (MS, PhD); physical chemistry (MS, PhD); polymer chemistry (MS, PhD). PhD offered through the School of Graduate Studies. Part-time programs available. *Faculty:* 12 full-time (2 women), 2 part-time (0 women). *Students:* 25 full-time (7 women), 7 part-time (2 women), 18 international. *Degree requirements:* For master's, thesis required (for some programs), foreign language not required; for doctorate, dissertation required, foreign language not required. *Entrance requirements:* For master's, TOEFL (minimum score of 550 required); for doctorate, GRE General Test (minimum combined score of 1500 on three sections required), TOEFL (minimum score of 550 required), TWE (minimum score of 4 required). *Application deadline:* For fall and spring admission, 2/1 (priority date); for winter admission, 9/1 (priority date). Applications are processed on a rolling basis. Application fee: $25. *Unit head:* Dr. Jerry Jean, Interim Chairperson, 816-235-2280, Fax: 816-235-5502, E-mail: jean@cctr.umkc.edu.

See in-depth description on page 211.

University of Missouri–St. Louis, Graduate School, College of Arts and Sciences, Department of Chemistry, St. Louis, MO 63121-4499. Offers chemistry (MS, PhD), including biochemistry, inorganic chemistry, organic chemistry, physical chemistry. Part-time and evening/weekend programs available. *Faculty:* 20. *Students:* 33 full-time (10 women), 26 part-time (9 women); includes 7 minority (2 African Americans, 4 Asian Americans or Pacific Islanders, 1 Hispanic American), 21 international. Terminal master's awarded for partial completion of doctoral program. *Degree requirements:* For master's, thesis optional, foreign language not required; for doctorate, dissertation required, foreign language not required. *Entrance requirements:* For doctorate, GRE General Test, GRE Subject Test. *Application deadline:* For fall admission, 7/1 (priority date); for spring admission, 12/7 (priority date). Applications are processed on a rolling basis. Application fee: $25 ($40 for international students). Electronic applications accepted. *Unit head:* Dr. R. E. K. Winter, Director of Graduate Studies, 314-516-5337, Fax: 314-516-5342, E-mail: chejjoll@jinx.umsl.edu. *Application contact:* Graduate Admissions, 314-516-5458, Fax: 314-516-6759, E-mail: gradadm@umsl.edu.

The University of Montana–Missoula, Graduate School, College of Arts and Sciences, Department of Chemistry, Missoula, MT 59812-0002. Offers chemistry (MS, PhD); chemistry teaching (MST); environmental chemistry (PhD); inorganic chemistry (PhD); organic chemistry (PhD); physical chemistry (PhD). Part-time programs available. *Faculty:* 14 full-time (3 women), 1 part-time (0 women). *Students:* 15 full-time (3 women), 3 part-time; includes 3 minority (all Asian Americans or Pacific Islanders) Terminal master's awarded for partial completion of doctoral program. *Degree requirements:* For master's, thesis required (for some programs); for doctorate, dissertation required. *Entrance requirements:* For master's, GRE General Test; for doctorate, GRE General Test, GRE Subject Test. *Application deadline:* For fall admission, 3/15 (priority date); for spring admission, 10/15. Applications are processed on a rolling basis. Application fee: $45. *Unit head:* Dr. Michael D. DeGrandpre, Graduate Coordinator, 403-243-4022, Fax: 406-243-4227.

University of Nebraska–Lincoln, Graduate College, College of Arts and Sciences, Department of Chemistry, Lincoln, NE 68588. Offers analytical chemistry (PhD); chemistry (MS); inorganic chemistry (PhD); organic chemistry (PhD); physical chemistry (PhD). *Faculty:* 23 full-time (2 women), 1 part-time (0 women). *Students:* 79 full-time (15 women), 23 part-time (2 women); includes 6 minority (1 African American, 2 Asian Americans or Pacific Islanders, 2 Hispanic Americans, 1 Native American), 47 international. *Degree requirements:* For master's, departmental qualifying exam required, thesis optional; for doctorate, dissertation, comprehensive and departmental qualifying exams required. *Entrance requirements:* For master's and doctorate, GRE Subject Test, TOEFL (minimum score of 550 required). *Application deadline:* For fall admission, 3/1 (priority date). Applications are processed on a rolling basis. Application fee: $35. Electronic applications accepted. *Unit head:* Dr. Lawrence Parkhurst, Chair, 402-472-3501, Fax: 402-472-9402.

University of Notre Dame, Graduate School, College of Science, Department of Chemistry and Biochemistry, Notre Dame, IN 46556. Offers biochemistry (MS, PhD); inorganic chemistry (MS, PhD); organic chemistry (MS, PhD); physical chemistry (MS, PhD). *Faculty:* 32 full-time (3 women). *Students:* 110 full-time (38 women), 1 part-time; includes 3 minority (2 African Americans, 1 Asian American or Pacific Islander), 57 international. Terminal master's awarded for partial completion of doctoral program. *Degree requirements:* For master's, thesis, comprehensive exam required, foreign language not required; for doctorate, dissertation, qualifying exam required, foreign language not required. *Entrance requirements:* For master's, GRE General Test, GRE General Subject Test (strongly recommended), TOEFL (minimum score of 600 required; 250 for computer-based); for doctorate, GRE General Test, GRE Subject Test (strongly recommended), TOEFL (minimum score of 600 required; 250 for computer-based). *Application deadline:* For fall admission, 2/1 (priority date). Applications are processed on a rolling basis. Application fee: $40. *Unit head:* Dr. A. Graham Lappin, Chairman, 219-631-7058, Fax: 219-631-6652, E-mail: lappin.1@nd.edu. *Application contact:* Dr. Terrence J. Akai, Director of Graduate Admissions, 219-631-7706, Fax: 219-631-4183, E-mail: gradad@nd.edu.

See in-depth description on page 215.

University of Puerto Rico, Río Piedras, Faculty of Natural Sciences, Department of Physics, San Juan, PR 00931. Offers applied physics (MS); physics (MS); physics-chemical (PhD). Part-time and evening/weekend programs available. *Faculty:* 19. *Students:* 19 full-time (4 women), 13 part-time (2 women); includes 19 minority (all Hispanic Americans), 13 international. *Degree requirements:* For master's and doctorate, one foreign language, thesis/dissertation, comprehensive exam required. *Entrance requirements:* For master's, GRE, TOEFL, interview, minimum GPA of 3.0; for doctorate, GRE, master's degree, minimum GPA of 3.0. *Application deadline:* For fall admission, 2/1. Application fee: $17. *Unit head:* Dr. Luftul Bari Bhuiyan, Coordinator of Master Program, 787-764-0000 Ext. 2307, Fax: 787-764-4063. *Application contact:* Luis F. Fonseca, Coordinator of Doctoral Program, 787-764-0000 Ext. 4773, Fax: 787-764-4063.

University of Regina, Faculty of Graduate Studies and Research, Faculty of Science, Department of Chemistry, Regina, SK S4S 0A2, Canada. Offers analytical chemistry (M Sc, PhD); biochemistry (M Sc, PhD); clinical biochemistry (M Sc, PhD); inorganic chemistry (M Sc, PhD); organic chemistry (M Sc, PhD); physical chemistry (M Sc, PhD); x-ray crystallography (M Sc, PhD). Part-time programs available. *Faculty:* 10 full-time (1 woman), 3 part-time (0 women). *Students:* 9 full-time (5 women), 6 part-time (3 women). *Degree requirements:* For master's, thesis, departmental qualifying exam required, foreign language not required; for doctorate, variable foreign language requirement, dissertation, departmental qualifying exam required. *Entrance requirements:* For master's, TOEFL (minimum score of 580 required); for doctorate, TOEFL. *Application deadline:* Applications are processed on a rolling basis. Application fee: $0. *Expenses:* Tuition and fees charges are reported in Canadian dollars. Tuition, state resident: full-time $1,688 Canadian dollars; part-time $94 Canadian dollars per credit hour. International tuition: $3,375 Canadian dollars full-time. Required fees: $65 Canadian dollars per course. Tuition and fees vary according to course load and program. *Unit head:* Dr. K. Johnson, Head, 306-585-4146, Fax: 306-585-4894, E-mail: chem@max.cc.uregina.ca.

University of Southern California, Graduate School, College of Letters, Arts and Sciences, Department of Chemistry, Program in Chemical Physics, Los Angeles, CA 90089. Offers PhD. *Students:* 2 full-time (1 woman). Average age 27. In 1998, 2 degrees awarded (100% entered university research/teaching). *Degree requirements:* For doctorate, dissertation, qualifying

exam required. *Entrance requirements:* For doctorate, GRE General Test. *Average time to degree:* Doctorate–4.5 years full-time. *Application deadline:* For fall admission, 4/1 (priority date). Application fee: $0. Tuition: Full-time $22,198; part-time $748 per unit. Required fees: $406. Tuition and fees vary according to program. *Financial aid:* In 1998–99, 2 research assistantships with tuition reimbursements (averaging $18,660 per year) were awarded.; fellowships, teaching assistantships, Federal Work-Study and institutionally-sponsored loans also available. Financial aid application deadline: 3/1. *Unit head:* Kathy Lutz, Graduate Program Secretary, 716-275-5713. *Application contact:* Paul Langford, Coordinator, 213-740-7036, Fax: 213-740-2701, E-mail: chemmail@chem1.usc.edu.

University of Southern Mississippi, Graduate School, College of Science and Technology, Department of Chemistry and Biochemistry, Hattiesburg, MS 39406-5167. Offers analytical chemistry (MS, PhD); biochemistry (MS, PhD); inorganic chemistry (MS, PhD); organic chemistry (MS, PhD); physical chemistry (MS, PhD). *Faculty:* 16 full-time (2 women), 1 part-time (0 women). *Students:* 25 full-time (10 women); includes 8 minority (3 African Americans, 4 Asian Americans or Pacific Islanders, 1 Hispanic American) *Degree requirements:* For master's, thesis required, foreign language not required; for doctorate, 2 foreign languages (computer language can substitute for one), dissertation required. *Entrance requirements:* For master's, GRE General Test, TOEFL, minimum GPA of 2.75; for doctorate, GRE General Test, TOEFL, minimum GPA of 3.5. *Application deadline:* For fall admission, 8/6 (priority date). Applications are processed on a rolling basis. Application fee: $0 ($25 for international students). Tuition, state resident: full-time $2,250; part-time $137 per semester hour. Tuition, nonresident: full-time $3,102; part-time $172 per semester hour. Required fees: $602. *Unit head:* Dr. Stella Elakovich, Chair, 601-266-4701. *Application contact:* Dr. Gordon Cannon, 601-266-4702.

University of South Florida, Graduate School, College of Arts and Sciences, Department of Chemistry, Tampa, FL 33620-9951. Offers analytical chemistry (MS, PhD); biochemistry (MS, PhD); inorganic chemistry (MS, PhD); organic chemistry (MS, PhD); physical chemistry (MS, PhD). Part-time programs available. *Faculty:* 23 full-time (3 women), 3 part-time (1 woman). *Students:* 44 full-time (14 women), 10 part-time (1 woman); includes 2 African Americans, 3 Hispanic Americans Terminal master's awarded for partial completion of doctoral program. *Degree requirements:* For master's, thesis required; for doctorate, 2 foreign languages (computer language can substitute for one), dissertation, colloquium required. *Entrance requirements:* For master's and doctorate, GRE General Test (minimum combined score of 1000 required), minimum GPA of 3.0 in last 30 hours of chemistry course work. *Application deadline:* For fall admission, 6/5 (priority date); for spring admission, 10/23 (priority date). Applications are processed on a rolling basis. Application fee: $20. Electronic applications accepted. Tuition, state resident: part-time $148 per credit hour. Tuition, nonresident: part-time $509 per credit hour. *Unit head:* Dr. Robert Potter, Chairperson, 813-974-4129, Fax: 813-974-1731, E-mail: potter@chuma1.cas.usf.edu. *Application contact:* Andy Zekter, Graduate Director, 813-974-9666, Fax: 813-974-3203, E-mail: zekter@chuma1.cas.usf.edu.

University of Tennessee, Knoxville, Graduate School, College of Arts and Sciences, Department of Chemistry, Knoxville, TN 37996. Offers analytical chemistry (MS, PhD); chemical physics (PhD); environmental chemistry (MS, PhD); inorganic chemistry (MS, PhD); organic chemistry (MS, PhD); physical chemistry (MS, PhD); polymer chemistry (MS, PhD); theoretical chemistry (PhD). Part-time programs available. *Faculty:* 31 full-time (1 woman), 1 (woman) part-time. *Students:* 55 full-time (15 women), 44 part-time (11 women); includes 1 minority (Asian American or Pacific Islander), 23 international. Terminal master's awarded for partial completion of doctoral program. *Degree requirements:* For master's and doctorate, thesis/dissertation required, foreign language not required. *Entrance requirements:* For master's and doctorate, GRE General Test, TOEFL (minimum score of 550 required), minimum GPA of 2.7. *Application deadline:* For fall admission, 2/1 (priority date). Applications are processed on a rolling basis. Application fee: $35. Electronic applications accepted. *Unit head:* Dr. Michael Sepaniak, Head, 423-974-3141, Fax: 423-974-3454, E-mail: msepaniak@utk.edu. *Application contact:* Dr. Charles Feigerle, Graduate Representative, E-mail: cfeigerle@utk.edu.

The University of Texas at Austin, Graduate School, College of Natural Sciences, Department of Chemistry and Biochemistry, Austin, TX 78712-1111. Offers analytical chemistry (MA, PhD); biochemistry (MA, PhD); inorganic chemistry (MA, PhD); organic chemistry (MA, PhD); physical chemistry (MA, PhD). *Students:* 278 (94 women); includes 28 minority (3 African Americans, 11 Asian Americans or Pacific Islanders, 13 Hispanic Americans, 1 Native American) 61 international. *Entrance requirements:* For master's and doctorate, GRE General Test. Application fee: $50 ($75 for international students). *Unit head:* Dr. Marvin L. Hackert, Chairman, 512-471-3949. *Application contact:* Dr. Jennifer Brodbelt, Graduate Adviser, 512-471-0028.

University of Toledo, Graduate School, College of Arts and Sciences, Department of Chemistry, Toledo, OH 43606-3398. Offers analytical chemistry (MS, MS Ed, PhD); biological chemistry (MS, MS Ed, PhD); inorganic chemistry (MS, MS Ed, PhD); organic chemistry (MS, MS Ed, PhD); physical chemistry (MS, MS Ed, PhD). Part-time programs available. *Degree requirements:* For master's and doctorate, thesis/dissertation required, foreign language not required. *Entrance requirements:* For master's and doctorate, GRE General Test, GRE Subject Test, TOEFL. Electronic applications accepted. *Faculty research:* Enzymology, materials chemistry, crystallography, theoretical chemistry.

University of Utah, Graduate School, College of Science, Department of Chemistry, Salt Lake City, UT 84112-1107. Offers chemical physics (PhD); chemistry (M Phil, MA, MS, PhD); science teacher education (MS). *Faculty:* 29 full-time (2 women), 27 part-time (2 women). *Students:* 136 full-time (38 women), 14 part-time (3 women); includes 12 minority (1 African American, 6 Asian Americans or Pacific Islanders, 2 Hispanic Americans, 3 Native Americans), 26 international. Terminal master's awarded for partial completion of doctoral program. *Degree requirements:* For master's, thesis or alternative required; for doctorate, dissertation, exams required, foreign language not required. *Entrance requirements:* For master's and doctorate, TOEFL (minimum score of 500 required). *Application deadline:* For fall admission, 7/1. Application fee: $30 ($50 for international students). *Unit head:* C. Dale Poulter, Chair, 801-581-6685, Fax: 801-581-4391. *Application contact:* Charles A. Wight, Director of Graduate Studies, 801-581-8796.

Wake Forest University, Graduate School, Department of Chemistry, Winston-Salem, NC 27109. Offers analytical chemistry (MS, PhD); inorganic chemistry (MS, PhD); organic chemistry (MS, PhD); physical chemistry (MS, PhD). Part-time programs available. *Faculty:* 14 full-time (1 woman). *Students:* 22 full-time (11 women), 2 part-time; includes 5 minority (2 African Americans, 3 Asian Americans or Pacific Islanders) *Degree requirements:* For master's, one foreign language (computer language can substitute), thesis required; for doctorate, 2 foreign languages (computer language can substitute for one), dissertation required. *Entrance requirements:* For master's and doctorate, GRE General Test, GRE Subject Test. *Application deadline:* For fall admission, 2/15. Application fee: $25. *Unit head:* Dr. Jim Fishbein, Director, 336-758-6139, E-mail: fishbein@wfu.edu.

See in-depth description on page 227.

Washington State University, Graduate School, College of Sciences, Department of Chemistry, Pullman, WA 99164. Offers analytical chemistry (MS, PhD); inorganic chemistry (MS, PhD); nuclear chemistry (MS, PhD); organic chemistry (MS, PhD); physical chemistry (MS, PhD). *Faculty:* 28 full-time (4 women). *Students:* 39 full-time (14 women), 3 part-time (2 women); includes 4 minority (2 Asian Americans or Pacific Islanders, 1 Hispanic American, 1 Native American), 8 international. Terminal master's awarded for partial completion of doctoral program. *Degree requirements:* For master's, oral exam, teaching experience required, thesis optional, foreign language not required; for doctorate, dissertation, oral exam, teaching experience required, foreign language not required. *Entrance requirements:* For master's and doctorate, GRE General Test, minimum GPA of 3.0. *Application deadline:* For fall admission, 3/1 (priority date). Applications are processed on a rolling basis. Application fee: $35. *Unit head:* Dr. Ralph

Physical Chemistry–Cross-Discipline Announcements

Washington State University (continued)

Yount, Chair, 509-335-1516. *Application contact:* James O. Schenk, Chair, Admissions Committee, 509-335-8866, E-mail: carrie@wsu.edu.

Washington State University, Graduate School, College of Sciences, Department of Physics, Pullman, WA 99164. Offers chemical physics (PhD); material science (MS, PhD); physics (MS, PhD). *Faculty:* 20 full-time (1 woman). *Students:* 31 full-time (2 women), 5 part-time (1 woman); includes 3 minority (1 African American, 1 Asian American or Pacific Islander, 1 Hispanic American), 12 international. *Degree requirements:* For master's, thesis (for some programs), oral exam required; for doctorate, dissertation, oral exam required. *Entrance requirements:* For master's and doctorate, GRE General Test, GRE Subject Test, minimum GPA of 3.0. *Application deadline:* For fall admission, 3/1 (priority date). Applications are processed on a rolling basis. Application fee: $35. *Unit head:* Dr. Miles Dresser, Chair, 509-335-1698, Fax: 509-335-7816, E-mail: physics@wsu.edu. *Application contact:* Dr. Y. Gupta, 509-335-3140.

Wesleyan University, Graduate Programs, Department of Chemistry, Program in Chemical Physics, Middletown, CT 06459-0260. Offers MA, PhD. Terminal master's awarded for partial completion of doctoral program. *Degree requirements:* For master's, one foreign language (computer language can substitute), thesis required; for doctorate, one foreign language (computer language can substitute), dissertation, exams required. *Entrance requirements:* For master's, GRE General Test, GRE Subject Test; for doctorate, GRE Subject Test, BA or BS in chemistry or physics. *Faculty research:* Spectroscopy, photochemistry, reactive collisions, surface physics, quantum theory.

Yale University, Graduate School of Arts and Sciences, Department of Chemistry, New Haven, CT 06520. Offers biophysical chemistry (PhD); inorganic chemistry (PhD); organic chemistry (PhD); physical chemistry (PhD). *Faculty:* 61 full-time (14 women). *Students:* 139 full-time (62 women); includes 11 minority (8 Asian Americans or Pacific Islanders, 3 Hispanic Americans), 53 international. *Degree requirements:* For doctorate, dissertation required. *Entrance requirements:* For doctorate, GRE General Test, GRE Subject Test, TOEFL. *Application deadline:* For fall admission, 1/4. Application fee: $65. *Unit head:* Chair, 203-432-3912. *Application contact:* Admissions Information, 203-432-2770.

See in-depth description on page 241.

Theoretical Chemistry

Boston University, Graduate School of Arts and Sciences, Department of Chemistry, Boston, MA 02215. Offers biochemistry (MA, PhD); chemical physics (MA, PhD); inorganic chemistry (MA, PhD); organic chemistry (MA, PhD); photochemistry (MA, PhD); physical chemistry (MA, PhD); theoretical chemistry (MA, PhD). *Faculty:* 21 full-time (1 woman). *Students:* 81 full-time (26 women), 1 (woman) part-time; includes 4 minority (2 African Americans, 2 Asian Americans or Pacific Islanders), 58 international. Terminal master's awarded for partial completion of doctoral program. *Degree requirements:* For master's, one foreign language, thesis not required; for doctorate, one foreign language, dissertation, exams required. *Entrance requirements:* For master's and doctorate, GRE General Test, GRE Subject Test (recommended), TOEFL (minimum score of 550 required). *Application deadline:* For fall admission, 7/1. Applications are processed on a rolling basis. Application fee: $50. Tuition: Full-time $23,770; part-time $743 per credit. Required fees: $220. Tuition and fees vary according to class time, course level, campus/location and program. *Unit head:* Thomas D. Tullius, Chairman, 617-353-4277, Fax: 617-353-6466, E-mail: tullius@chem.bu.edu. *Application contact:* Kevin Burgoyne, Academic Administrator, 617-353-2503, Fax: 617-353-6466, E-mail: burgoyne@chem.bu.edu.

Cornell University, Graduate School, Graduate Fields of Arts and Sciences, Field of Chemistry, Ithaca, NY 14853-0001. Offers analytical chemistry (PhD); bio-organic chemistry (PhD); biophysical chemistry (PhD); chemical physics (PhD); inorganic chemistry (PhD); material chemistry (PhD); organic chemistry (PhD); physical chemistry (PhD); polymer chemistry (PhD); theoretical chemistry (PhD). *Faculty:* 38 full-time. *Students:* 139 full-time (44 women); includes 10 minority (1 African American, 4 Asian Americans or Pacific Islanders, 4 Hispanic Americans, 1 Native American), 51 international. *Degree requirements:* For doctorate, dissertation required, foreign language not required. *Entrance requirements:* For doctorate, GRE General Test, GRE Subject Test, TOEFL (minimum score of 600 required). *Application deadline:* For fall admission, 1/15. Application fee: $65. Electronic applications accepted. *Unit head:* Director of Graduate Studies, 607-255-4139. *Application contact:* Graduate Field Assistant, 607-255-4139, E-mail: chemgrad@cornell.edu.

See in-depth description on page 109.

Georgetown University, Graduate School, Department of Chemistry, Washington, DC 20057. Offers analytical chemistry (MS, PhD); biochemistry (MS, PhD); chemical physics (MS, PhD); inorganic chemistry (MS, PhD); organic chemistry (MS, PhD); physical chemistry (MS, PhD); theoretical chemistry (MS, PhD). Terminal master's awarded for partial completion of doctoral program. *Degree requirements:* For master's, thesis (for some programs), qualifying exam required, foreign language not required; for doctorate, dissertation, comprehensive exam required. *Entrance requirements:* For master's and doctorate, GRE General Test, TOEFL (minimum score of 550 required, 600 for teaching assistants).

See in-depth description on page 125.

Howard University, Graduate School of Arts and Sciences, Department of Chemistry, Washington, DC 20059-0002. Offers analytical chemistry (MS, PhD); biochemistry (MS, PhD); inorganic chemistry (MS, PhD); organic chemistry (MS, PhD); physical chemistry (MS, PhD); polymer chemistry (MS, PhD); theoretical chemistry (MS, PhD). Part-time programs available. Terminal master's awarded for partial completion of doctoral program. *Degree requirements:* For master's, one foreign language (computer language can substitute), thesis, comprehensive exam, teaching experience required; for doctorate, 2 foreign languages (computer language can substitute for one), dissertation, comprehensive exam, teaching experience required. *Entrance requirements:* For master's, GRE General Test, minimum GPA of 2.7; for doctorate, GRE General Test, minimum GPA of 3.0. *Faculty research:* Stratospheric aerosols, liquid crystals, polymer coatings, terrestrial and extraterrestrial atmospheres, amidogen reaction.

Illinois Institute of Technology, Graduate College, Armour College of Engineering and Sciences, Department of Biological, Chemical and Physical Sciences, Chemistry Division, Chicago, IL 60616-3793. Offers analytical chemistry (MAC, MS, PhD); chemistry (M Chem); inorganic chemistry (MS, PhD); organic chemistry (MS, PhD); physical chemistry (MS, PhD); polymer chemistry (MS, PhD); theoretical chemistry (MS, PhD). Part-time and evening/weekend programs available. *Faculty:* 8 full-time (0 women), 2 part-time (0 women). *Students:* 14 full-time (7 women), 70 part-time (27 women); includes 19 minority (10 African Americans, 9 Asian Americans or Pacific Islanders), 16 international. Terminal master's awarded for partial completion of doctoral program. *Degree requirements:* For master's, thesis (for some programs), comprehensive exam required, foreign language not required; for doctorate, dissertation, comprehensive exam required, foreign language not required. *Entrance requirements:* For master's and doctorate, GRE (minimum score of 1200 required), TOEFL (minimum score of 550 required), undergraduate GPA of 3.0 required. *Application deadline:* For fall admission, 7/1; for spring admission, 11/1. Applications are processed on a rolling basis. Application fee: $30. Electronic applications accepted. *Unit head:* Dr. Carlo Segre, Associate Chair, 312-567-3480, Fax: 312-567-3494, E-mail: segre@iit.edu. *Application contact:* Dr. S. Mohammad Shahidehpour, Dean of Graduate College, 312-567-3024, Fax: 312-567-7517, E-mail: grad@minna.cns.iit.edu.

See in-depth description on page 135.

University of Calgary, Faculty of Graduate Studies, Faculty of Science, Department of Chemistry, Calgary, AB T2N 1N4, Canada. Offers analytical chemistry (M Sc, PhD); applied chemistry (M Sc, PhD); inorganic chemistry (M Sc, PhD); organic chemistry (M Sc, PhD); physical chemistry (M Sc, PhD); polymer chemistry (M Sc, PhD); theoretical chemistry (M Sc, PhD). *Faculty:* 29 full-time (4 women), 1 part-time (0 women). *Students:* 60 full-time (25 women). *Degree requirements:* For master's, thesis required, foreign language not required; for doctorate, dissertation, candidacy exam required, foreign language not required. *Entrance requirements:* For master's and doctorate, TOEFL (minimum score of 580 required). *Application deadline:* For fall admission, 12/1 (priority date). Applications are processed on a rolling basis. Application fee: $60. *Unit head:* Dr. R. A. Kydd, Head, 403-220-5340. *Application contact:* Greta Prihodko, Graduate Program Administrator, 403-220-6252, E-mail: gradinfo@chem.ucalgary.ca.

University of Tennessee, Knoxville, Graduate School, College of Arts and Sciences, Department of Chemistry, Knoxville, TN 37996. Offers analytical chemistry (MS, PhD); chemical physics (PhD); environmental chemistry (MS, PhD); inorganic chemistry (MS, PhD); organic chemistry (MS, PhD); physical chemistry (MS, PhD); polymer chemistry (MS, PhD); theoretical chemistry (PhD). Part-time programs available. *Faculty:* 31 full-time (1 woman), 1 (woman) part-time. *Students:* 55 full-time (15 women), 44 part-time (11 women); includes 1 minority (Asian American or Pacific Islander), 23 international. Terminal master's awarded for partial completion of doctoral program. *Degree requirements:* For master's and doctorate, thesis/dissertation required, foreign language not required. *Entrance requirements:* For master's and doctorate, GRE General Test, TOEFL (minimum score of 550 required), minimum GPA of 2.7. *Application deadline:* For fall admission, 2/1 (priority date). Applications are processed on a rolling basis. Application fee: $35. Electronic applications accepted. *Unit head:* Dr. Michael Sepaniak, Head, 423-974-3141, Fax: 423-974-3454, E-mail: msepaniak@utk.edu. *Application contact:* Dr. Charles Feigerle, Graduate Representative, E-mail: cfeigerle@utk.edu.

Wesleyan University, Graduate Programs, Department of Chemistry, Middletown, CT 06459-0260. Offers biochemistry (MA, PhD); chemical physics (MA, PhD); inorganic chemistry (MA, PhD); organic chemistry (MA, PhD); physical chemistry (MA, PhD); theoretical chemistry (MA, PhD). Terminal master's awarded for partial completion of doctoral program. *Degree requirements:* For master's and doctorate, one foreign language (computer language can substitute), thesis/dissertation required. *Entrance requirements:* For master's, GRE General Test, GRE Subject Test; for doctorate, GRE Subject Test.

See in-depth description on page 233.

Cross-Discipline Announcements

Colorado State University, Graduate School, College of Engineering, Department of Atmospheric Science, Fort Collins, CO 80523-0015.

The Department of Atmospheric Science offers MS and PhD degrees with a specialization in atmospheric chemistry. Research areas include modeling, laboratory, and field experiment programs in aerosol physics, water chemistry, cloud physics, climate change, and air pollution. Students with backgrounds in chemistry, engineering, and physics are encouraged to apply.

Duke University, Graduate School, Department of Pharmacology, Durham, NC 27708-0586.

Pharmacology is a multidisciplinary science that utilizes the diverse strategies of chemistry, hysiology, cell/molecular biology, and genetics to explore the action of drugs. Pharmacology es drugs as tools to study cell function. It also explores therapeutic and toxic actions of ablished agents and facilitates the design of novel agents.

Hunter College of the City University of New York, Hunter Center for Gene Structure and Function, New York, NY 10021-5085.

The Center was founded in 1985 with a grant from the Research Centers in Minority Institutions Program of the National Institutes of Health. The Center provides educational and research opportunities in biomedical sciences. Participating faculty consists of more than 30 investigators in the biological sciences, chemistry, biopsychology, and biophysics programs who study the structure and functioning of genes with emphasis on oncogenes, signal transduction, immunology, and neuroscience. The goal of the program is to provide students with a strong interdisciplinary foundation and the latest technology in biomedical science research. For more information call212-772-5532. E-mail: admissions@genectr.hunter.cuny.edu; WWW: http://sonhouse.hunter.cuny.edu/genecenter.

Iowa State University of Science and Technology, Graduate College, College of Agriculture, Department of Biochemistry, Biophysics, and Molecular Biology, Ames, IA 50011.

Department offers graduate degree programs in biochemistry; biophysics; genetics; molecular, cellular, and developmental biology; plant physiology; immunobiology; and toxicology. The design of the molecular biology building enhances the opportunities for collaboration among faculty members in the life sciences. Students with degrees in chemistry are strongly encouraged to apply. See the Biochemistry section in Book 3 of this series for detailed descriptions of the program.

Johns Hopkins University, Intercampus Program in Molecular Biophysics, Baltimore, MD 21218-2699.

The Intercampus Program in Molecular Biophysics (IPMB) is staffed by about 40 faculty members with interests in molecular biophysics. It offers special opportunities to applicants trained in the physical sciences or mathematics for graduate study in areas such as protein crystallography, NMR and ESR, thermodynamics, statistical mechanics, computer modeling, biophysical chemistry, and biochemistry. It emphasizes studies on macromolecules, or on interacting assemblies of macromolecules, for which a combination of approaches—molecular genetics and structural studies, for example—may be necessary for real progress. Collaborative projects between faculty members are encouraged. For information, contact IPMB Office, 410-516-5197, fax: 410-516-5199, e-mail: ipmb@jhu.edu, World Wide Web: http://www.jhu.edu/~ipmb/

Massachusetts Institute of Technology, School of Engineering, Division of Bioengineering and Environmental Health, Cambridge, MA 02139-4307.

Program provides opportunities for specialization in molecular toxicology, including studies in environmental carcinogenesis; metabolism of foreign compounds; molecular dosimetry; genetic toxicology; molecular aspects of interactions of mutagens, carcinogens, and anticancer drugs with nucleic acids and proteins; and pathogenesis and molecular aspects of infectious disease. See program's in-depth description in the Pharmacology and Toxicology section in the Biological Sciences volume of this series.

The Ohio State University, College of Pharmacy, Graduate Programs in Pharmacy, Division of Medicinal Chemistry and Pharmacognosy, Columbus, OH 43210.

Graduate programs in the Division provide opportunities for studies in drug design, biochemistry, synthetic and natural products chemistry, spectroscopy, and bioanalytical chemistry preparatory for careers in design, synthesis, and isolation of drug molecules. Research laboratories provide access to NMR, mass, IR, and optical spectrometers; liquid chromatographs; and molecular modeling workstations.

Oregon State University, Graduate School, College of Oceanic and Atmospheric Sciences, Corvallis, OR 97331.

The College invites students with chemistry degrees to apply for graduate study in chemical oceanography, interdisciplinary oceanography, and atmospheric chemistry. Research areas include ocean and sediment geochemistry, biogeochemical cycles, organic geochemistry, trace metals, radiochemistry, petroleum geochemistry, modeling, cloud and rain chemistry, and aerosols. See program description under Marine Sciences and Oceanography in this volume.

Pennsylvania State University University Park Campus, Graduate School, Intercollege Graduate Programs, Intercollege Graduate Program in Integrative Biosciences, State College, University Park, PA 16802-1503.

The Life Sciences Consortium is especially interested in attracting graduate students for the integrative biosciences graduate program who have backgrounds in chemistry, physics, and math and plan to pursue research opportunities at the interface between the physical and biological sciences. See in-depth description in Book 3.

Princeton University, Graduate School, Princeton Materials Institute, Princeton, NJ 08540-5211.

The Princeton Materials Institute welcomes students interested in cross-disciplinary research involving any aspect of materials science and engineering. Faculty members from 8 academic departments collaborate in a remarkably broad range of programs, supported by outstanding facilities. Some fellowships are available. See the in-depth description in Book 5, Section 21.

Purdue University, School of Pharmacy and Pharmacal Sciences, Graduate Programs in Pharmacy and Pharmacal Sciences, West Lafayette, IN 47907.

The School of Pharmacy offers graduate programs in medicinal chemistry and natural products, pharmaceutics and industrial pharmacy, and molecular pharmacology. Applicants who have a desire to pursue pharmaceutical research and who have backgrounds in the chemical or biological sciences or chemical engineering are encouraged to apply. See in-depth description in Book 3, Section 16, and Book 6, Section 38.

Purdue University, Graduate School, Interdisciplinary Biochemistry and Molecular Biology Program, West Lafayette, IN 47907.

The Purdue University Biochemistry and Molecular Biology (BMB) Program—an integrated PhD program administered by more than 60 faculty members primarily from the Departments of Biochemistry, Biology, Chemistry, and Medicinal Chemistry and Molecular Pharmacology—offers a core of basic biochemistry courses, highly individualized advanced courses, and faculty-guided research designed to develop the capacity for independent, creative research. See program's in-depth description in the Biochemistry section of Book 3 in this series.

Rush University, Graduate College, Division of Biochemistry, Chicago, IL 60612-3832.

The PhD program emphasizes basic research in human health and disease. Research areas include biochemistry of connective tissue, tumor invasion, membrane lipids, metalloelements, regulation of gene expression, and development of clinical tests. Financial assistance available. Contact Dr. A. Bezkorovainy, 312-942-5429.

Rutgers, The State University of New Jersey, New Brunswick, Graduate School, Program in Food Science, New Brunswick, NJ 08903.

Food science applies basic knowledge of chemistry, biology, and engineering to complex food systems. Modern research facilities in a 122,000-square-foot complex, young energetic faculty members, substantial external support for graduate students, exciting NYC-Philadelphia metro area, and excellent job opportunities and salaries for MS and PhD graduates. See in-depth description in Section 8 of this volume.

University of California, San Francisco, School of Pharmacy, Department of Pharmaceutical Chemistry, San Francisco, CA 94143.

The PhD degree program in pharmaceutical chemistry is directed toward research at the interface between chemistry and biology. The program offers research in areas of bioorganic chemistry, macromolecular structure and function, computer-aided drug design, medicinal chemistry, drug metabolism and biochemical toxicology, drug delivery, molecular parasitology, molecular pharmacology, and pharmacokinetics/pharmacodynamics.

University of Connecticut, Graduate School, School of Pharmacy, Department of Pharmaceutical Sciences, Storrs, CT 06269.

The Department of Pharmaceutical Sciences offers graduate programs in pharmaceutics, medicinal chemistry, and natural products chemistry. Located at the center of campus, the School of Pharmacy has 30 faculty members and 50 graduate students in a variety of pharmacy-related disciplines. See in-depth description in Book 6 under the Pharmacy and Pharmaceutical Sciences section.

University of Michigan, Horace H. Rackham School of Graduate Studies, College of Engineering, Department of Materials Science and Engineering, Ann Arbor, MI 48109.

Interdisciplinary curriculum leads to master's and PhD degrees in materials science and engineering for chemistry students interested in solid-state chemistry, metals, ceramics, polymers, composites, and other engineering materials. Research assistantships and fellowships available on a competitive basis. See in-depth description of the department in the Engineering and Applied Sciences volume of this series.

University of Tennessee, Knoxville, Graduate School, College of Human Ecology, Department of Consumer and Industry Services Management, Knoxville, TN 37996.

Students specializing in textile science enter a research-oriented area strongly based in mathematics, chemistry, physics, and engineering. Emphasis is placed on textile structural characterization, properties of textile materials, and textile processing. New textile materials such as nonwoven webs and composites that expand the use of textiles are emphasized.

University of Virginia, College and Graduate School of Arts and Sciences, Interdisciplinary Program in Biophysics, Charlottesville, VA 22903.

The Interdisciplinary Program in Biophysics at the University of Virginia offers training and research opportunities with more than 35 faculty members in the Schools of Graduate Arts and Sciences, Engineering, and Medicine. Macromolecular structure and physical biochemistry, membrane biophysics, and radiological physics are areas of specific research strength. All students are financially supported.

University of Washington, School of Medicine, Graduate Programs in Medicine, Biomolecular Structure and Design Program, Seattle, WA 98195.

Innovative program prepares students from varied backgrounds to enter exciting, growing fields of structure determination of biomolecular structures, computational studies of structure/function relationships of biomacromolecules, structure prediction, and structure-based design and synthesis of new molecules. State-of-the-art structure determination (X-ray crystallography, NMR spectroscopy), bioorganic chemistry, and molecular biological, biophysical, and computational techniques.

University of Wisconsin–Madison, Graduate School, Training Program in Biotechnology, Madison, WI 53706-1380.

The University of Wisconsin–Madison offers a predoctoral training program in biotechnology. Trainees receive PhDs in their major field (for example, chemistry) while receiving extensive cross-disciplinary training through the minor degree. Trainees participate in industrial internships and a weekly student seminar series with other program participants. These experiences reinforce the cross-disciplinary nature of the program. Students choose a major and a minor professor from a list of more than 110 faculty members in 40 different departments who do research related to biotechnology. See in-depth description in the Biochemical Engineering, Bioengineering, and Biotechnology section of the Engineering and Applied Sciences volume of this series.

University of Wisconsin–Madison, School of Pharmacy, Madison, WI 53706-1380.

The characteristic feature of graduate study and research in the pharmaceutical sciences at Wisconsin is its fundamental approach at the chemistry/biology interface, with emphasis on underlying mechanisms at the molecular level and their quantitative description. The pharmaceutical sciences provide an interdisciplinary training program and research directed toward understanding fundamental aspects of drug delivery and targeting, developing new strategies in drug discovery and design, and elucidating mechanisms of drug action and toxicities.

AMERICAN UNIVERSITY

Department of Chemistry

Programs of Study
Accredited by the American Chemical Society, the Department of Chemistry serves the University and the region as a center for study and research. It offers advanced degrees to both full-time and part-time graduate students, with master's and doctoral programs that provide a blend of theoretical and applied chemistry. The Ph.D. degree provides a solid foundation for all aspects of a career in chemistry, whether in academia, government, or industry. The primary focus of the doctoral degree is independent research, and many Ph.D. chemists' initial positions are in research. Students in the M.S. in chemistry program may design a course of study that allows them to upgrade current skills or to explore a new facet. This degree prepares graduate students for careers in various areas of research, development, education, and administration or study at the doctoral level. The thesis requirement expands laboratory skills to give students better preparation for entry into the job market. The M.S. in toxicology is an interdisciplinary degree offered jointly by the Department of Chemistry and the Department of Biology. This degree prepares graduate students for careers in various areas of research, development, and administration. There is no thesis requirement.

Research Facilities
The Bender Library and Learning Resources Center houses more than 700,000 volumes, 3,000 periodical titles, extensive microform collections, and a nonprint media center. More than fourteen indexes in compact disc format are searchable using library microcomputers. Graduate students have unlimited borrowing privileges at six other university libraries in the Washington Research Library Consortium. All are accessible through the online catalog. Microcomputer resources can be used 24 hours a day at various campus locations. The Beeghly Chemistry Building houses 32,000 square feet of laboratories and workshops, as well as an animal room, a cold room, and a stockroom. Students may use spectrometers covering the ultraviolet and visible region, as well as Fourier transform infrared, 400 megahertz nuclear magnetic resonance, and fluorescence spectrometers; gas and high-pressure liquid chromatographs; a supercritical fluid chromatograph; light-scattering equipment; a differential scanning calorimeter; an atomic absorption spectrometer; and biochemical facilities. The University also offers special research opportunities with noted professionals in private and government laboratories. The department's computer room has a number of IBM personal computers equipped with up-to-date software and connection to chemical literature databases as well as connection to the Internet and the World Wide Web.

Financial Aid
Fellowships, scholarships, and graduate assistantships are available to full-time students. Special opportunity grants for minority group members parallel the regular honor awards. Research and teaching fellowships provide stipends plus tuition. Graduate assistantships provide up to 18 credit hours of tuition remission per year. The department has a number of graduate awards that are available to U.S. citizens and permanent residents, including the National Science Foundation Traineeships in Environmental Chemometrics, graduate assistantships in areas of national need, and several departmental research and teaching assistantships and fellowships. For international graduate students, American offers the Hall of Nations Scholarship, which is awarded to top international students, and the Department of Chemistry offers research and teaching assistantships and fellowships to some international students upon completion of their first year.

Cost of Study
For the 1999–2000 academic year, tuition is $721 per credit hour.

Living and Housing Costs
Although many graduate students live off campus, the University provides graduate dormitory rooms and apartments. The Off-Campus Housing Office maintains a referral file of rooms and apartments. Housing costs in Washington, D.C., are comparable to those in other major metropolitan areas.

Student Group
The 60 graduate students in the Department of Chemistry form a cosmopolitan, international group. Almost half are women; many are minority students, and there is a mix of international students. A total of twenty-seven doctoral and twenty-eight master's degrees have been awarded over the last five years.

Student Outcomes
Graduates of the master's and doctoral programs in chemistry have successful professional careers in major corporations, such as Hewlett-Packard, Pitney Bowes, Nestlé, Johnson & Johnson, Gillette, and Biotechnology Labs, Inc. They have also been employed by government laboratories such as the Food and Drug Administration, National Institutes of Health, National Institute of Standards and Technology, Naval Research Laboratory, Department of Engraving and Printing, U.S. Geological Survey, and Environmental Protection Agency.

Location
The national capital area offers students opportunities for practical applications of theoretical studies through research, internships, cooperative educational placements, and part-time jobs. Local bus and rail transportation from the campus provides easy access to sites in the greater metropolitan area.

The University and The Department
The University was founded as a Methodist institution, chartered by Congress in 1893 and originally intended for graduate study only. The University is located on an 84-acre site in a residential area of northwest Washington, D.C. As a member of the Consortium of Universities of the Washington Area, AU can offer its degree candidates the option of taking courses at other consortium universities for residence credit.

The Department of Chemistry provides a personal, congenial environment where students can develop and pursue a flexible program of study designed to fulfill individual interests and needs.

Applying
Applications for admission should be submitted prior to February 1 if the student is also applying for financial aid. Deadlines vary for different fields of study, but early application is always encouraged. The application fee is $50.

Correspondence and Information
To contact faculty members:
Department of Chemistry
College of Arts and Sciences
American University
4400 Massachusetts Avenue, NW
Washington, D.C. 20016-8014
Telephone: 202-885-1750
E-mail: chem@american.edu
World Wide Web: http://www.american.
   edu/academic.depts/cas/

For an application and information:
Office of Graduate Admissions
American University
4400 Massachusetts Avenue, NW
Washington, D.C. 20016-8001
Telephone: 202-885-6000
E-mail: afa@american.edu

American University

THE FACULTY AND THEIR RESEARCH

Frederick W. Carson, Associate Professor; Ph.D., Chicago (e-mail: fcarson@american.edu). Modeling of proteins that are AIDS vaccine candidates or drug targets using molecular mechanics.
Theoretical studies of relaxation of a monomeric subunit of HIV-1 protease in water using molecular dynamics. *Proteins: Struct., Funct., Genet.* 15:374–84, 1993. With Venable and Brooks.

Albert M. Cheh, Professor; Ph.D., Berkeley (e-mail: acheh@american.edu). DNA damage by polycyclic aromatic hydrocarbons and water chlorination products; the relationship between chemical structure DNA sequence and DNA damage.
Stereospecific differences in repair by human cell extracts of synthesized oligonucleotides containing transopened 7,8,9,10-tetrahydrobenzo[a]pyrene 7,8-Diol 9, 10-epoxide N^2-dG adduct stereoisomers located within the human k-*ras* codon 12 sequence. *Biochem.* 38 (2):569–81, 1999. With Mazur et al.

Kelley Donaghy, Assistant Professor; Ph.D., Pennsylvania (e-mail: kdonaghy@american.edu). Boron hydride chemistry and solid state materials.
Reactions of 1,1'-bis(diphenylphosphino)ferrocene with boranes, thiaboranes, and carboranes. *Inorg. Chem.* 36:547–53, 1997. With Carroll and Sneddon.

Hassan S. El Khadem, Isbell Professor (Emeritus); D.Sc., London. Carbohydrate and medicinal chemistry.
The reaction of phenylhydrazine with squaric acid: A model for carbohydrate osazone formation. *Carbohydr. Res.* 239:85–93, 1993. With Shalaby, Coxon, and Fatiadi.

James E. Girard, Professor; Ph.D., Penn State (e-mail: jgirard@american.edu). Separations: HPLC, ion chromatography, supercritical fluid chromatography, capillary electrophoresis; environmental analysis: mass spectrometry and LC-MS; DNA analysis: MALDI-TOF, MS, PNA probes.
Spectral measurements of intercalated PCR-amplified short tandem repeat alleles. *Anal. Chem.* 70 (21):4514–9, 1998. With Devaney, Davis, and Smith.

Derek Horton, Isbell Professor; Ph.D., D.Sc., Birmingham (England); Fellow of the Royal Institute of Chemistry, London (e-mail: carbchm@american.edu).
Stereocontrolled allylation of 2-amino-2-deoxy sugars by a free-radical procedure. *Carbohydr. Res.* 309:319-30, 1998. With Cui.

Lou (LaVelma) Thompson Hughes, Research Professor; Ph.D., Cornell (e-mail: luhug@speck.niddh.nih.gov). Biophysical studies of the structure and function of DNA/metal complexes, antibiotics, peptide hormones, and proteins. Nitric oxide cheletropic traps (NOCTs) with improved thermal stability and water solubility. *J. Am. Chem. Soc.* 116:2767–77, 1994. With Korth et al.

Jan Kutina, Research Professor; C.Sc., Karlova (Prague) (e-mail: jkutina@american.edu). Locating possible ore deposits; nature of chemical processes of ore deposits, ore microscopy.
A major structural intersection in the basement of the Okavango Basin, NE of Tsumeb, Namibia, indicated by satellite magnetometry and other data. *Global Tectonics Metallogeny* 6(3–4):205–13, 1998.

Anh Le, Associate Research Professor; Ph.D., American (e-mail: lea@oasys.dt.navy.mil). Physical and organic chemistry.
A comparative corrosion study of titanium and copper-nickel alloys. *Proceedings of Tri-Service Conference*, Atlantic City, NJ, 1989. With Dust.

Sharlyn J. Mazur, Assistant Research Professor; Ph.D., Wisconsin–Madison; Postdoctoral Fellow, Johns Hopkins. The interaction of DNA repair proteins and damaged DNA.
Stereospecific differences in repair of human cell extracts of synthesized oligonucleotides containing transopened 7,8,9,10-tetrahydrobenzo[a]pyrene 7,8-Diol 9, 10-epoxide N^2-dG adduct stereoisomers located within the human k-*ras* codon 12 sequence. *Biochem.* 38 (2):569–81, 1999. With Cheh et al.

Charles D. Pibel, Assistant Professor; Ph.D., Berkeley (e-mail: cpibel@american.edu). Photochemistry and spectroscopy of electronically excited atoms and molecules.
The vinyl radical (A^2A"←X^2A') spectrum between 530 and 415 nm measured by cavity ring-down spectroscopy. *J. Chem. Phys.* 110(4):1841–43, 1999. With McIllroy, Taatjes, Alfred, Patrick, and Halpern.

Nina M. Roscher, Professor and Department Chair; Ph.D., Purdue (e-mail: nrosche@american.edu). Reaction of alcohols with bromine and silver salts, photochemistry of hypobromites, organic synthesis; role of women in chemistry.
Photodecomposition of several compounds commonly used as sunscreen agents. *J. Photochem. Photobiol.* A 80:417–21, 1994. With Lindemann, Kong, Cho, and Jiang.

Paul F. Waters, Professor Emeritus; Ph.D., Rutgers. Polymer chemistry/physical chemistry, polymers applied to environmental problems, drag reduction and fuels efficiency.

Herman Ziffer, Research Professor; Ph.D., Oregon. Organic and biological chemistry structure and synthesis, stereochemistry, microbial synthesis, artemisinin and its derivatives.
Artemisinin: An endoperoxidic antimalarial from Artemisia annua L. *Progress in the Chemistry of Organic Natural Products,* vol. 72, pp. 121–214. Vienna: Springer-Verlag, 1997. With Highet and Klayman.

ARIZONA STATE UNIVERSITY

College of Arts and Sciences
Department of Chemistry and Biochemistry

Programs of Study

Arizona State University offers both M.S. and Ph.D. degree programs in chemistry and biochemistry. These are viewed as research degrees, and graduate students are encouraged to identify their field of interest early in their career. A wide range of active research programs from synthetic and structural organic and inorganic chemistry and analytical techniques to studies of the function of biological molecules and high-level theoretical chemistry are under way in the department, including a number of interdisciplinary programs. The M.S. degree is not a prerequisite for the Ph.D. program.

Research Facilities

Chemistry is housed in several wings of the Bateman Center for Physical Sciences, along with the Departments of Mathematics, Physics, and Geology; the Center for Solid State Science; and the Goldwater Center for Science and Engineering. The proximity of these gives a special opportunity for interdisciplinary research and fosters creative exchange between the sciences. Chemistry is well equipped for modern research, with extensive instrumentation for electronic vibrational and magnetic resonance spectroscopies and laboratories for crystal growth and materials characterization, electron- and ion-beam microanalysis, and a variety of experiments in laser photochemistry and spectroscopy using pulsed and tunable lasers. The department also has a variety of personal computers, workstations, and network servers and has access to the Universities Research UNIX Cluster, Visualization Center, and IBM MVS/TSO mainframe. Finally, the physical sciences center is the home of the internationally recognized Center for High Resolution Electron Microscopy, with the world's largest collection of electron microscopes offering resolution down to the atomic scale.

Financial Aid

Graduate teaching assistantships are offered to qualified students at a rate of $14,550 for the academic year. In addition, summer support is provided in the form of teaching and research assistantships. Students are guaranteed five years of support as either a teaching or a research assistant contingent upon satisfactory progress in the program. In-state tuition waivers are available on a competitive basis. Select applicants are guests of the department for a weekend visit in the spring.

Cost of Study

Graduate assistantships provide a waiver of out-of-state tuition. Registration fees are approximately $1030 per semester.

Living and Housing Costs

University housing in the Mariposa Graduate Residence Center and regular dormitories is available for single graduate students only. Requests for information should be addressed directly to the Housing Office of Arizona State University. A wide range of apartment housing is available within several blocks of the campus and throughout Tempe and the surrounding communities.

Student Group

The University attracts more than 45,000 students each year, including a graduate enrollment of 12,000. Chemistry has approximately 110 students pursuing graduate degrees and 30 new students registering each year.

Student Outcomes

Many graduate students have received employment offers from companies such as NIST, FDA, Shell, DuPont, Clorox, Motorola, and Dial Corporation. Graduate students who chose to accept postdoctoral positions have received offers from such prestigious universities as California, Davis; Pennsylvania; MIT; and Cornell.

Location

Arizona State University is located in the city of Tempe, part of the metropolitan area of Phoenix. The recent economic development in the Valley of the Sun has transformed Phoenix into a major center for the electronics and aerospace industries. The atmosphere of intense change and dynamic growth is reflected at Arizona State, as the University realizes its potential as a major research institution and assumes its responsibility as the cultural and intellectual center of central Arizona.

The University

Arizona State University began as a training college for teachers in the Southwest more than a century ago and has developed into a vigorous research university with a variety of creative and challenging programs. The original college buildings still stand, now surrounded by the modern architecture of the current University departments. The 566-acre campus provides a pleasant shady oasis in the sunny desert environment.

Applying

Applicants requesting fall admission should apply by February 1, but later applications will also be given due consideration. International students are required to demonstrate English proficiency by submitting a minimum score of 237 on the TOEFL and 55 on the TSE.

Correspondence and Information

Graduate Studies Office
Department of Chemistry and Biochemistry
Box 871604
Arizona State University
Tempe, Arizona 85287-1604
Telephone: 602-965-4664
Fax: 602-965-2747
E-mail: chmgrad@asu.edu
World Wide Web: http://www.asu.edu/clas/chemistry

Arizona State University

THE FACULTY AND THEIR RESEARCH

James Allen, Associate Professor; Ph.D., Illinois, 1982. Biochemistry: biophysical studies of photosynthetic systems, crystallography of membrane proteins.

Austen Angell, Professor; Ph.D., London, 1961. Physical and solid-state chemistry: molecular and ionic dynamics in liquids and glasses, glass transition, liquids under tension and spinodal collapse phenomena, geochemical fluids.

Allan L. Bieber, Professor; Ph.D., Oregon State, 1961. Biochemistry: protein structure, dependence of function of toxins and enzymes on structure.

James P. Birk, Professor; Ph.D., Iowa State, 1967. Chemical education: kinetics and mechanisms of inorganic reactions, transition-metal and oxy-anion oxidation-reduction reactions, catalyzed substitution reactions, linkage isomerisms, chemical education.

Robert E. Blankenship, Professor; Ph.D., Berkeley, 1975. Biochemistry: biophysics of photosynthesis, biological electron transfer reactions, evolution of energy-conserving systems.

Linda Bloom, Assistant Professor; Ph.D., Florida, 1990. Biochemistry: dynamic protein DNA interactions and mechanisms of enzymes involved in the replication and repair of DNA.

Karl Booksh, Assistant Professor; Ph.D., Washington (Seattle), 1994. Analytical chemistry: environmental sensor design: excitation emission fluorescence, surface plasmon resonance; chemometrics; multivariate/multiway calibration, automated diagnostics; theoretical analytical chemistry.

Theodore M. Brown, Professor; Ph.D., Iowa State, 1963. Inorganic chemistry: structure, kinetics, and properties of heavy transition-metal halide compounds (primarily groups IV, V, and VI).

Peter R. Buseck, Regents' Professor; Ph.D., Columbia, 1961. Geochemistry: high-resolution electron microscopy and electron diffraction of minerals, electron probe microanalysis, mineralogy and geochemistry of meteorites, ore genesis and process of deposition, air pollutant analysis.

Tyler Caudle, Assistant Professor; Ph.D., Duke, 1993. Metal-catalyzed CO_2 transfer reactions as photosynthesis models, novel metal-containing supramolecular motifs for molecular recognition and catalysis.

William S. Glaunsinger, Professor; Ph.D., Cornell, 1972. Physical and solid-state chemistry: chemical sensors for environmental analysis and process control, environmental applications of scanning tunneling microscopy, intercalation chemistry.

Ian Gould, Assistant Professor; Ph.D., Manchester (England), 1980. Organic chemistry, photochemistry, single electron transfer reactions, reactions of radical ions, organic photophysics, time-resolved laser methods.

J. Devens Gust, Professor; Ph.D., Princeton, 1974. Organic chemistry: design, synthesis, and spectroscopic studies of model systems for photosynthesis, synthesis, and NMR investigations of polyarylbenzenes.

Mark Hayes, Assistant Professor; Ph.D., Penn State, 1993. Analytical chemistry: design and construction of bioanalytical chemical probes; ultramicrosampling techniques, microseparations, and novel sensitive detection schemes and their use of in vivo analysis.

John R. Holloway, Professor; Ph.D., Penn State, 1970. Geochemistry: experimental investigations of silicate systems and interactions of silicates with volatile species (H_2O, CO_2, HF) at high pressures (to 10,000 atmospheres) and high temperatures (to 1500°C); thermodynamics of multicomponent, multiphase systems at high pressures and temperatures.

John Kouvetakis, Assistant Professor; Ph.D., Berkeley, 1988. Solid-state inorganic chemistry with particular emphasis on the design and synthesis of new materials with novel electronic, optical, and mechanical properties.

Dennis E. Lohr, Professor; Ph.D., North Carolina, 1972. Biochemistry: coordinating relations between transcription and the structural organization of chromatin.

Paul F. McMillan, Professor; Ph.D., Arizona State, 1981. Inorganic chemistry: micro-Raman and infrared spectroscopy in structural studies of amorphous and crystalline aluminosilicates; applications in solid state, materials science, and geochemistry.

Ana L. Moore, Professor; Ph.D., Texas Tech, 1972. Organic chemistry: organic synthesis and photophysics of carotenoids.

Carleton B. Moore, Regents' Professor; Ph.D., Caltech, 1960. Geochemistry: chemical investigation of meteorites, lunar samples, and terrestrial rocks; geochemistry; cosmochemistry, environmental chemistry.

Thomas A. Moore, Professor; Ph.D., Texas Tech, 1975. Biochemistry: photobiology; biomimetic chemistry, artificial photosynthesis, photoacoustic spectroscopy.

Morton E. Munk, Professor; Ph.D., Wayne State, 1957. Organic chemistry: computer-assisted structure elucidation of biologically interesting natural products, cycloaddition, and cycloreversion reactions; conformational analysis; photochemical and electron-impact reactions.

Michael O'Keeffe, Professor; Ph.D., Bristol (England), 1958. Physical and solid-state chemistry: crystal chemistry, phase transitions, reactivity of solids.

George R. Pettit, Professor; Ph.D., Wayne State, 1956. Organic chemistry: chemistry of natural products (nucleotides, peptides, steroids, and triterpenes), cancer chemotherapy, general organic synthesis.

William T. Petuskey, Professor; Sc.D., MIT, 1977. Physical and solid-state chemistry: synthesis chemistry and properties of oxides, carbides, and nitrides; ceramic chemistry; polycrystalline structures; atom transport; solid- and liquid-state electrochemistry.

Seth D. Rose, Professor; Ph.D., California, San Diego, 1974. Organic chemistry: developing suitable stains for electron microscopy of chromosome ultrastructure, photochemical damage to nucleic acids.

Edward B. Skibo, Professor; Ph.D., California, San Francisco, 1980. Organic chemistry: reductive alkylation (quinones and purines), design of alkylating agents.

Timothy C. Steimle, Professor; Ph.D., California, Santa Barbara, 1978. Physical and solid-state chemistry: high-resolution laser spectroscopy of nonequilibrium gas-phase chemical systems, nonlinear optical techniques and microwave techniques.

Peter Williams, Professor; Ph.D., London, 1966. Analytical chemistry: mass spectrometry of involatile materials; laser ablation TOF mass spectrometry of DNA and proteins, ion microscopy; sputtering, ion, and electron-stimulated desorption.

George H. Wolf, Associate Professor; Ph.D., Berkeley, 1981. Physical and solid-state chemistry: synthesis and study of materials at extreme conditions of pressure and temperature involving applications of diamond anvil cells, Raman and Brillouin scattering and X-ray diffraction.

Neal Woodbury, Associate Professor; Ph.D., Washington (Seattle), 1987. Biochemistry: specific mutagenesis of bacterial reaction centers, photosynthesis, studies of ultrafast electron transfer reactions using subpicosecond resolution pulsed laser spectroscopy.

Omar Yaghi, Assistant Professor; Ph.D., Illinois, 1990. Synthesis, physical properties, and reactivities of new inorganic, solid-state materials and large-cage and cluster molecules.

BOSTON COLLEGE

Department of Chemistry

Program of Study

Boston College offers a program of study leading to the Ph.D. and M.S. degrees with concentrations in physical, inorganic, and organic chemistry and biochemistry. The Master of Science in Teaching (M.S.T.) is offered through the School of Education to students interested in secondary school teaching.

The Ph.D. dissertation, accounting a well-organized and original research project, is the core of the Ph.D. program. An advanced chemistry curriculum, usually satisfied in two semesters, is offered to give the student breadth in the major branches of chemistry. Formal courses may be waived in whole or in part if the student demonstrates a mastery of the subject matter in placement examinations. An oral exam on research progress is required at the end of the second year. Cumulative exams are also given.

A graduate student–faculty ratio of 7:1 ensures a close working arrangement between the student and the research director throughout the study program. Frequent colloquia within the department and at neighboring institutions feature eminent scientists from university, industrial, and government laboratories.

Research Facilities

The department is located in the Eugene F. Merkert Chemistry Center, designed and built specifically for the study of chemistry. It contains research laboratories that are well equipped with modern instrumentation for NMR, ESR, IR, UV-VIS, atomic absorption, and mass spectrometry; laser spectroscopy; GC and HPLC; and facilities for studies in magnetic susceptibility, electrochemistry, fermentation, and DNA sequencing. Instrumentation for X-ray diffraction (including an area detector) as well as several computers and workstations with molecular graphics capabilities are available in the department. The Boston College campus is completely networked. The science section of the O'Neill Central Research Library contains an excellent and accessible collection of journals, monographs, and reference texts.

Financial Aid

Essentially all Ph.D. students receive financial support as teaching or research assistants. Graduate teaching assistantships carry ten-month stipends beginning at $13,800 plus tuition remission for the 1999–2000 academic year. Teaching or research assistantship support during the summer provides an additional $2000–$3000. Research assistantships carry stipends of $16,000 for the twelve months. Highly qualified students are awarded fellowships.

Cost of Study

The tuition costs for 1999–2000 are $1968 per course, with six courses typically taken in the first year. Scholarships provide tuition remission for teaching and research assistants and for fellowship holders.

Living and Housing Costs

Students usually share apartments in the Boston area or rent private rooms in the beautiful residential area surrounding the campus. The College provides assistance in locating suitable accommodations.

Student Group

The enrollment at Boston College is about 14,000, including 3,800 graduate students. The student body is drawn from all parts of the United States and from many other countries. The chemistry department has approximately 110 graduate students and 30 postdoctoral fellows. Forty percent of the graduate students are women.

Student Outcomes

Recent Ph.D. recipients have gone on to postdoctoral positions at a wide range of institutions (including Harvard, MIT, and Cornell) and obtained positions in biotechnology and pharmaceutical firms (primarily, though not exclusively, on the East Coast) or within government agencies (notably the NIH and the FDA). Several graduates have also opted for teaching positions at undergraduate institutions and Ph.D.-granting universities.

Location

As a recreational, cultural, and scientific center, Boston is unsurpassed. The Boston Symphony Orchestra, live theater performances, opera, ballet, art and science museums, and a rich historic past coexist with a modern city. The proximity of several universities and colleges and the establishment of many industrial research laboratories in the Boston area make this region the scientific center of the eastern United States. In addition, the renowned professional sports teams of Boston provide year-round spectator entertainment.

The College and The Department

Boston College, founded by the Jesuit order in 1863, is a university of ten colleges and schools dedicated to excellence in education. Faculty members and students are recruited internationally, regardless of religion, race, or color. Situated in an attractive residential area on a hill overlooking Boston, the main campus is 6 miles west of the State House and downtown district.

The motto of Boston College is "ever to excel," and in no department is this commitment taken more seriously than in the Department of Chemistry. The faculty members, who receive more than $4 million in external research support annually, are internationally renowned and have won numerous prestigious awards. However, the ultimate measure of the success and excellence of the department lies with the students. Faculty members take an active interest in all aspects of the education of every graduate student in the department from the classroom to the laboratory. The graduate students at Boston College are of an exceptional caliber, as is evidenced by the number of prestigious doctoral and postdoctoral fellowships they have garnered in recent years, as well as by the top academic and industrial positions occupied by recent graduates.

Applying

A preliminary assessment of admission prospects may be obtained by submitting the application form, an unofficial transcript, and one letter of reference (no application fee required). Formal applications for admission in September are evaluated under a rolling admission policy beginning early in January. The deadline for applications is February 15. Thus, early submission is recommended. Students are strongly urged to take the Graduate Record Examinations (the General Test and the Subject Test in chemistry). International students must submit TOEFL scores and the GRE Subject Test score.

Correspondence and Information

Graduate Admissions Committee
Department of Chemistry
Eugene F. Merkert Chemistry Center
Boston College
Chestnut Hill, Massachusetts 02167
Telephone: 617-552-3605
World Wide Web: http://chemserv.bc.edu/GradForm.html

Boston College

THE FACULTY AND THEIR RESEARCH

William H. Armstrong, Associate Professor of Inorganic Chemistry; Ph.D., Stanford, 1982. Bioinorganic chemistry, coordination chemistry, multielectron oxidations and reductions.

E. Joseph Billo Jr., Associate Professor of Inorganic and Analytical Chemistry; Ph.D., McMaster, 1967. Structural, thermodynamic, and kinetic studies of transition-metal complexes; macrocyclic complexes; solution equilibria.

Michael J. Clarke, Professor of Inorganic Chemistry; Ph.D., Stanford, 1974. Bioinorganic chemistry: interaction of transition-metal ions with nucleotides, nucleic acids, and coenzymes; radiopharmaceuticals and metal-containing anticancer drugs; electron transfer between metal ions and biologically important electron carriers; electrochemistry at solid electrodes.

Paul Davidovits, Professor of Physical Chemistry; Ph.D., Columbia, 1964. Study of gas molecules with liquid surfaces, using laser and mass spectrometry, with applications to atmospheric chemistry.

John T. Fourkas, Assistant Professor of Physical Chemistry; Ph.D., Stanford, 1991. Ultrafast nonlinear spectroscopy of bulk liquids, microconfined liquids, and stretched liquids; theory of light-matter interactions.

Amir H. Hoveyda, Professor of Organic Chemistry; Ph.D., Yale, 1986. Development of new reactions and methods for chemical synthesis, design and synthesis of substances of medicinal and biological significance, organometallic chemistry.

Evan R. Kantrowitz, Professor of Biochemistry; Ph.D., Harvard, 1976. Structure and function of proteins, the mechanism of cooperativity and use of recombinant DNA techniques to study proteins.

T. Ross Kelly, Professor of Organic Chemistry; Ph.D., Berkeley, 1968. Organic synthesis, natural products, cancer chemotherapy, medicinal chemistry, bioorganic chemistry, design of organic catalysts.

David L. McFadden, Professor of Physical Chemistry; Ph.D., MIT, 1972. Gas phase fast-reaction kinetics and dynamics, electron spin resonance and photoionization mass spectrometry applied to the study of elementary reactions of polyatomic free radicals and of electron capture reactions at high temperature.

Larry W. McLaughlin, Professor of Bioorganic Chemistry; Ph.D., Alberta, 1979. Chemistry and biochemistry of nucleic acids, sequence-dependent nucleic-acid recognition by proteins, synthesis and modification of oligonucleotides and nucleic acids.

Scott J. Miller, Assistant Professor of Organic Chemistry; Ph.D., Harvard, 1994. Organic synthesis, discovery of new reactions for complex molecule synthesis, asymmetric catalysis, organometallic chemistry.

Udayan Mohanty, Associate Professor of Theoretical Chemistry; Ph.D., Brown, 1981. Physical chemistry, supercooled and glassy states, polyelectrolytes, electrophoyetic mobility of A-tracts in gel.

Robert F. O'Malley, Emeritus Professor of Inorganic Chemistry; Ph.D., MIT, 1961. Electron transfer mechanism of halogenation of aromatic hydrocarbons.

Yuh'kang Pan, Professor of Theoretical Chemistry; Ph.D., Michigan State, 1966. Quantum theory of chemical reactivity, calculation of lifetimes of singlet and triplet states by perturbation theory, applications of Lie algebra to chemical dynamics and the theory of vibrational-rotational spectra, ab inito calculations of weakly bonded systems.

Mary F. Roberts, Professor of Biochemistry and Biophysical Chemistry; Ph.D., Stanford, 1974. Biological NMR, model biomembranes, cell metabolic pathways, studies of archaebacteria.

Dennis J. Sardella, Professor of Organic Chemistry; Ph.D., IIT, 1967. NMR spectroscopy, aromaticity; transmission of electronic effects in π-systems; chemical carcinogenesis; theoretical organic chemistry.

Lawrence T. Scott, Professor of Organic Chemistry; Ph.D., Harvard, 1970. Synthesis of unusual organic molecules, cyclic polyacetylenes and nonplanar aromatic hydrocarbons, thermal rearrangements of aromatic compounds.

Marc L. Snapper, Assistant Professor of Organic Chemistry; Ph.D., Stanford, 1991. Development of new synthetic methods for the construction of biologically interesting compounds; use of new synthetic molecules to probe the structure, function, and regulation of biological systems.

Martha M. Teeter, Associate Professor of Biochemistry; Ph.D., Penn State, 1973. Protein crystallography, biophysical chemistry, water-protein interactions, homology modeling.

SELECTED PUBLICATIONS

Pierce, D. T., T. L. Hatfield, **E. J. Billo,** and Y. Ping. Oxidatively induced isomerization of square-planar [Ni(1,4,8,11-tetraazacyclotetradecane)](ClO$_4$)$_2$. *Inorg. Chem.* 36:2950, 1997.

Billo, E. J. *Excel for Chemists: A Comprehensive Guide.* New York: John Wiley & Sons, 1997.

Billo, E. J., et al. Conformational characterization of square planar nickel(II) tetraaza macrocyclic complexes. Crystal structure of Ni(13aneN$_4$)ZnCl$_4$. *Inorg. Chim. Acta* 230:19, 1995.

Zhao, M., and **M. J. Clarke.** *Trans*-pyridine tetraammine complexes of Ru^{II} and Ru^{III} with N7-coordinated purine nucleosides. *J. Biol. Inorg. Chem.,* in press.

Zhao, M., and **M. J. Clarke.** Effects of *trans*-pyridine ligands on the binding and reactivity of Ru^{II} and Ru^{III} ammine complexes coordinated to guanine^{K7} on DNA. *J. Biol. Inorg. Chem.,* in press.

Clarke, M. J., F. Zhu, and D. Frasca. Non-platinum antitumor agents. *Chem. Rev.,* in press.

Clarke, M. J. Ruthenium in biology: DNA interactions. In *Electron Transfer Reactions, ACS Symposium Series,* Ch. 21, pp. 349–65, ed. S. Isied, 1997.

Rodriguez-Bailey, V. M., K. J. LaChance-Galang, P. E. Doan, and **M. J. Clarke.** ^{1}H and ^{31}P NMR and EPR of pentaammineruthenium(III) complexes of endocyclically coordinated nucleotides, nucleosides and related heterocyclic bases. Autoxidation of [(Guanosine$_K^{N7}$)(NH$_3$)$_5$Ru^{III}]. Crystal structure of [7MeGua$_K^{N9}$(NH$_3$)$_5$Ru]Cl$_3$•3H$_2$O. *Inorg. Chem.* 36:1873–83, 1997.

Rodriguez-Bailey, V. M., P. E. Doan, and **M. J. Clarke.** ^{1}H and ^{31}P NMR of pentaammineruthenium(III) complexes of exocyclically-coordinated adenine and cytosine ligands. Evidence for rotamers with distinct acidities. *Inorg. Chem.* 36:1611–8, 1997.

Frasca, D., et al. **(M. J. Clarke).** Effects of hypoxia and transferrin on toxicity and DNA binding of ruthenium antitumor agents in HeLa cells. *Metal-Based Drugs* 3:197–209, 1996.

LaChance-Galang, K. J., M. Zhao, and **M. J. Clarke.** Disproportionation of [(py)(NH$_3$)$_4$Ru^{III}] at the N7 of guanine nucleosides severs the N-glycosidic bond. *Inorg. Chem.* 36:4896–906, 1996.

Clarke, M. J., et al. ^{1}H NMR, EPR, UV-visible and electrochemical studies of imidazole complexes of Ru(III). Crystal structures of *cis*-[(Im)$_2$(NH$_3$)$_4$Ru^{III}]Br$_3$ and [(1MeIm)$_6$Ru^{II}]Cl$_2$•2H$_2$O. *Inorg. Chem.* 35:4896–903, 1996.

Clarke, M. J., and M. Stubbs. Interactions of metallopharmaceuticals with DNA. *Metal Ions Biol. Syst.* 32:727–80, 1996.

LaChance-Galang, K. J., et al. **(M. J. Clarke).** EPR and NMR spectra as probes of spin-density distributions in heterocyclic ligands coordinated in *trans*-[L(Im)(NH$_3$)$_4$Ru^{III}]: Implications for long range electron transfer. Crystal structure of *trans*-[(Im)$_2$(NH$_3$)$_4$Ru]Cl$_3$•H$_2$O. *J. Am. Chem. Soc.* 117:3529–38, 1995.

Loughnane, B. J., and **J. T. Fourkas.** Geometric effects in the dynamics of a nonwetting liquid in microconfinement: An optical Kerr effect study of methyl iodide in nanoporous glasses. *J. Phys. Chem. B* 102:10288, 1998.

Li, W.-X., T. Keyes, R. L. Murry, and **J. T. Fourkas.** Non-Cartesian coordinates for instantaneous normal mode (INM) theory of atomic liquids. *J. Chem. Phys.* 109:9096, 1998.

Murry, R. L., **J. T. Fourkas,** and T. Keyes. Nonresonant intermolecular spectroscopy beyond the Placzek approximation. II. Fifth-order spectroscopy. *J. Chem. Phys.* 109:7913, 1998.

Fourkas, J. T. Science in a state of transition. *Chem. Industry* 16:644, 1998.

Murry, R. L., **J. T. Fourkas,** and T. Keyes. Nonresonant intermolecular spectroscopy beyond the Placzek approximation. I. Third-order spectroscopy. *J. Chem. Phys.* 109:2814, 1998.

Loughnane, B. J., R. A. Farrer, and **J. T. Fourkas.** Evidence for the direct observation of molecular exchange of a liquid at the solid/liquid interface. *J. Phys. Chem. B* 102:5409, 1998.

Deschenes, L. A., et al. **(J. T. Fourkas** and **U. Mohanty).** Inhibition of bubble coalescence in aqueous solutions. I. Electrolytes. *J. Phys. Chem. B* 102:5115, 1998.

Deschenes, L. A., et al. **(J. T. Fourkas** and **U. Mohanty).** Quantitative measure of hydrophobicity: Experiment and theory. *J. Phys. Chem. B* 101:5777–9, 1997.

Harrity, J. P. A., et al. **(A. H. Hoveyda).** Metal-catalyzed rearrangement of styrenyl ethers to chromenes. Mechanism and utility in synthesis. *J. Am. Chem. Soc.* 120:2343, 1998.

Gomez-Bengoa, E., et al. **(A. H. Hoveyda).** Enantioselective Ni-catalyzed addition of Grignard reagents to cyclic allylic acetals. Phosphine-induced accelerated catalysis. *J. Am. Chem. Soc.* 120:7649, 1998.

Alexander, J. B., et al. **(A. H. Hoveyda).** Catalytic enantioselective ring-closing metathesis by a chiral biphen-Mo complex. *J. Am. Chem. Soc.* 120:4041, 1998.

Xu, Z., et al. **(A. H. Hoveyda).** Applications of Zr-catalyzed carbomagnesation and Mo-catalyzed macrocyclic ring closing metathesis in asymmetric synthesis. Enantioselective total synthesis of Sch 38516 (Fluvirucin B1). *J. Am. Chem. Soc.* 119:10302–16, 1997.

Xu, Z., C. W. Johannes, S. S. Salman, and **A. H. Hoveyda.** Enantioselective total synthesis of antifungal agent Sch 38516. *J. Am. Chem. Soc.* 118:10926, 1996.

Holtz, K. M., B. Stec, and **E. R. Kantrowitz.** A model of the transition state in the alkaline phosphatase reaction. *J. Biol. Chem.* 274:8351–4, 1999.

Stec, B., et al. **(E. R. Kantrowitz).** Kinetic and X-ray structural studies of three mutant *E. coli* alkaline phosphatases: Insights into the catalytic mechanism without the nucleophile Ser-102. *J. Mol. Biol.* 277:647–62, 1998.

Tsuruta, H., P. Vachette, and **E. R. Kantrowitz.** Direct observation of an altered quaternary structural transition in a mutant aspartate transcarbamoylase. *Proteins: Struct. Funct. Genet.* 31:383–90, 1998.

Williams, M. K., B. Stec, and **E. R. Kantrowitz.** A single mutation in the regulatory chain of *Escherichia coli* aspartate transcarbamoylase is an extreme T-state structure. *J. Mol. Biol.* 281:121–34, 1998.

Kelly, T. R., Y. Fu, and R. L. Xie. Structure revision of the APHEs through synthesis. *Tetrahedron Lett.* 40:1857, 1999.

Kelly, T. R., S. Chamberland, and R. A. Silva. Synthesis of luotonin A. *Tetrahedron Lett.* 40:2723, 1999.

Kelly, T. R., et al. A convergent total synthesis of the michellamines. *J. Org. Chem.* 63:1090, 1998.

Kelly, T. R., J. P. Sestelo, and I. Tellitu. New molecular devices: In search of a molecular ratchet. *J. Org. Chem.* 63:3655, 1998.

Kelly, T. R., R. L. Xie, C. K. Weinreb, and T. Bregant. A molecular vernier. *Tetrahedron Lett.* 39:3675, 1998.

Kuimelis, R. G., and **L. W. McLaughlin.** Mechanisms of ribozyme-mediated cleavage. *Chem. Rev.* 98:1027–44, 1998.

Bevers, S., T. O'Dea, and **L. W. McLaughlin.** Perylene- and naphthalene-based linkers for duplex and triplex stabilization. *J. Am. Chem. Soc.* 120:11004–5, 1998.

Robles, J., and **L. W. McLaughlin.** DNA triplex stabilization using a tethered minor-groove binding Hoechst 33258 analogue. *J. Am. Chem. Soc.* 119:6014–21, 1997.

Smith, S. A., and **L. W. McLaughlin.** Probing contacts to the DNA backbone in the trp repressor-operator sequence-specific protein-nucleic acid complex using diastereomeric methyl phosphonate analogues. *Biochemistry* 36:6046–58, 1997.

Miller, S. J., et al. Kinetic resolution of alcohols catalyzed by tripeptides containing the N-alkylimidazole substructure. *J. Am. Chem. Soc.* 120:1629–30, 1998.

Copeland, G. T., E. R. Jarvo, and **S. J. Miller.** Minimal acylase-like peptides. Conformational control over absolute stereospecificity. *J. Org. Chem.* 63:6784–5, 1998.

Miller, S. J., and C. D. Bayne. Diastereoselective enolsilane coupling reactions. *J. Org. Chem.* 62:5680–1, 1997.

Diezmann, G., **U. Mohanty,** and I. Oppenheim. Slow secondary relaxation in a free-energy landscape model for relaxation in glass-forming liquids. *Phys. Rev. E* 59:2067–83, 1999.

Mohanty, U., and N. Stellwagen. Free solution mobility of oligomeric DNA. *Biopolymers* 49:209–14, 1998.

Mohanty, U., T. Searls, and **L. W. McLaughlin.** Anomalous migration of short sequences of nucleic acids in polyacrylamide gels: Prediction and experiment. *J. Am. Chem. Soc.* 120:8275–6, 1998.

Mohanty, U. Polarization of counterions in a strongly coupled coulombic system: DNA. In *Proceedings of Strongly Coupled Coulomb Systems,* ed. G. Kalman. Plenum Press, 1998.

Mohanty, U. Entropic approach to relaxation behavior in glass-forming liquids. In *Supercooled Liquids: Advances and Novel Applications,* eds. **J. T. Fourkas** et al. ACS Symposium Series, 1997.

Boston College

Selected Publications (continued)

Manning, G. S., and **U. Mohanty.** Counterion condensation on ionic oligomers. *Physica* A247:196–204, 1997.

Gao, D., and **Y. K. Pan.** A QM/MM Monte Carlo simulation study of solvent effect on the decarboxylation reaction of N-carboxy-2-imidazolidinone anion in aqueous solution. *J. Org. Chem.* 64:1151–9, 1999.

Li, Z. R., F. M. Tao, and **Y. K. Pan.** Counterpoise procedure and equilibrium geometry of He-H2O complex. *Acta Chim. Sin.* 56:308–11, 1998.

Gao, D., and **Y. K. Pan** et al. Theoretical evidence for a concerted mechanism of oxirane cleavage and A-ring formation in oxidosqualene cyclization. *J. Am. Chem. Soc.* 120:4045–6, 1998.

Huff, W. R. A., et al. **(Y. K. Pan).** Structure determination of chemisorbed C (2X2) P/Fe (100) using angle-resolved photoemission extended fine structure and self-consistent-field Xa scattered-wave calculation: Comparison with C (2X2) S/Fe (100). *Phys. Rev.* 55B:10830–40, 1997.

Gao, D., et al. **(Y. K. Pan).** An ab initio study of the intermolecular potential surfaces of He-CH4 and Ne-CH4. *Chem. Phys. Lett.* 277:483–9, 1997.

Zhou, C., D. Horstman, G. Carpenter, and **M. F. Roberts.** Action of phosphatidylinositol-specific phospholipase Cγ1 on soluble and micellar substrates: Separating effects on catalysis from modulation of the surface. *J. Biol. Chem.* 274:2786–93, 1999.

Zhou, C., and **M. F. Roberts.** Non-essential activation and competitive inhibition of bacterial phosphatidylinositol-specific phospholipase C by short-chain phospholipids and analogs. *Biochemistry* 37:16430–9, 1998.

Chen, L., E. T. Spiliotis, and **M. F. Roberts.** Biosynthesis of di-*myo*-inositol-1,1'-phosphate, a novel osmolyte in archaea. *J. Bacteriol.* 180:3785–92, 1998.

Geng, D., J. Chura, and **M. F. Roberts.** Activation of phospholipase D by phosphatidic acid: Enhanced vesicle binding, phosphatidic acid-Ca^{2+} interaction, or an allosteric effect? *J. Biol. Chem.* 273:12195–202, 1998.

Tan, T. A., and **M. F. Roberts.** Engineering of the non-specific phospholipase C from *Bacillus cereus:* Replacement of glutamic acid-4 by alanine results in loss of interfacial catalysis and enhanced phosphomonoesterase activity. *Biochemistry* 37:4275–9, 1998.

Markman, O., C. Roh, **M. F. Roberts,** and **M. M. Teeter.** Designed additives for controlled growth of crystals of phospholipid interacting proteins *J. Cryst. Growth* 160:382–8, 1996.

Weitz, A., et al. **(L. T. Scott).** Dianions and tetraanions of two bowl-shaped fullerene fragments: Dibenzo[*a,g*]corannulene and dibenzo[*a,g*]cyclopenta[*kl*]corannulene. *Chem. Eur. J.* 4:234–9, 1998.

Chen, G., et al. **(L. T. Scott).** Electron affinities and C$_{60}$ anion clusters of certain bowl-shaped polycyclic aromatic hydrocarbons. *J. Mass Spectrom.* 32:1305–9, 1998.

Lafleur, A. L., et al. **(L. T. Scott).** Identification of some novel cyclopenta-fused polycyclic aromatic hydrocarbons in ethylene flames. *Polycyclic Aromat. Compd.* 12:223–37, 1998.

Shabtai, E., et al. **(L. T. Scott).** ^{3}He NMR of He@C$_{60}$$^{6-}$ and He@C$_{70}$$^{6-}$. New records for the most shielded and the most deshielded ^{3}He inside a fullerene. *J. Am. Chem. Soc.* 120:6389–93, 1998.

Hoffman, R. E., et al. **(L. T. Scott).** Self-diffusion measurements of polycyclic aromatic hydrocarbon alkali metal salts. *J. Chem. Soc., Perkin Trans.* 2:1659–64, 1998.

Stec, B., R. Troxler, and **M. M. Teeter.** Crystal structure of C-phycocyanin from C. Caldarium at 1.6$\approx$. *Biophys. J.,* in press.

Wilcox, R. E., et al. **(M. M. Teeter).** CoMFA-based prediction of agonist affinities at recombinant D1 vs. D2 dopamine receptors. *J. Med. Chem.* 41:4385–99, 1998.

Yamano, A., N. H. Heo, and **M. M. Teeter.** Crambin crystal structure of the Ser22/Ile25 form confirms solvent, side chain substate correlations. *J. Biol. Chem.* 272:9597–600, 1997.

Teeter, M. M., M. Froimowitz, B. Stec, and C. J. DuRand. Homology modeling of the dopamine D2 receptor and its testing by docking of agonists and tricyclic antagonists. *J. Med. Chem.* 37:2874–88, 1994.

BRIGHAM YOUNG UNIVERSITY

Department of Chemistry and Biochemistry

Programs of Study

The Department of Chemistry and Biochemistry at Brigham Young University (BYU) offers courses of study leading to Ph.D. and M.S. degrees in the areas of analytical, inorganic, organic, and physical chemistry and biochemistry. The research experience is the major element of the graduate programs. Most students complete their Ph.D. research in four years. Research groups often include cross-disciplinary collaboration with faculty members and students in biology, engineering, and physics as well as with other areas within chemistry and biochemistry. Department faculty members are highly involved in each student's progress and foster a strong tradition of mentoring. All students must pass entrance exams demonstrating competence at the undergraduate level in at least four subject areas by the end of their first year. An individualized schedule of graduate courses is established for each student based on his or her needs and interests. Most of this course work is taken during the first year, with the remainder completed in the second year. Depending on the area of study chosen by the student, either a written comprehensive examination or several periodic cumulative examinations are required. Also, all students present annual reviews and a research proposal to their faculty advisory committee. An active seminar schedule provides exposure to recent developments worldwide. Successful defense of a dissertation or thesis completes a student's training.

Research Facilities

Research activities occupy more than 50 percent of a 192,000-square-foot building. The University library, where the science collection includes more than 500,000 volumes and about 9,000 journal subscriptions, is located about 100 yards away. In addition to instruments and facilities used by individual research groups, special research facilities used by the entire department include NMR (200 and 500 MHz), mass spectrometry (high-resolution, quadrupole, and ion cyclotron resonance), X-ray diffraction (powder and single crystal), spectrophotometry (IR, visible, UV, X-ray, and γ-ray), lasers (YAG, excimer, dye), environmental analysis (PIXE; PIGE; trace gases; X-ray fluorescence; chromatography, including capillary column GC/MS, ion, and supercritical fluid; particle size analyzers; environmental chambers; ICP; and capillary electrophoresis), thermodynamics (calorimeters of all types, including temperature and pressure scanning, titration, flow, heat conduction, power compensation, combustion, and metabolic), and molecular biology (DNA synthesizer and sequencer, phosphorimager, tissue culture facility, recombinant DNA facility, and ultracentrifuges). All computing facilities are fully networked, including computational chemistry and laboratory workstations as well as office personal computers, with convenient connection to supercomputing facilities and the Internet. Fully staffed shops for glassblowing, machining, and electronics also serve research needs.

Financial Aid

The department provides full financial assistance to all students through teaching and research assistantships, fellowships, and tuition scholarships. The twelve-month stipend for beginning students for the 2000–01 year is $15,180 (taxable). The amount of the stipend is adjusted annually.

Cost of Study

Full-tuition scholarships are provided to all graduate students making normal progress. Books average about $100 per semester.

Living and Housing Costs

The University Housing Office assists students in locating accommodations for on- and off-campus housing. Monthly rent and utilities range from $180 to $300 for a single student and from $400 to $600 for families. Other expenses range from $200 to $400 for single students and from $300 to $800 for families.

Student Group

BYU has about 30,500 full-time students, with about 3,000 full-time graduate students. Students come from various academic and ethnic backgrounds and many geographic areas. The department averages 65 graduate students. Thirty percent are women; 55 percent are international students.

Student Outcomes

BYU graduate degrees lead to a wide range of independent careers, with former students serving in academia, government, and industrial positions. About half of recent Ph.D.'s have continued their training in postdoctoral positions at leading research institutions, with the remainder finding employment directly with regional or national firms, in academia, or at government labs.

Location

BYU's beautiful 536-acre campus, with all the cultural and sports programs of a major university, is located in Provo, Utah (population 95,000), a semiurban area at the foot of Utah Valley's Wasatch Mountains. Outdoor recreational areas for skiing (snow and water), hiking, and camping are nearby, including nine spectacular national parks, six beautiful national monuments, fourteen major ski resorts, and forty-five diverse state parks. In Salt Lake City, 45 miles to the north, are the Utah Symphony, Ballet West, Pioneer Theater Company, and the Utah Jazz basketball team.

The University

Brigham Young University is one of the largest privately owned universities in the United States. Established in 1875 as Brigham Young Academy and sponsored by the Church of Jesus Christ of Latter-day Saints, BYU has a tradition of high standards in moral integrity and academic scholarship. Along with extensive undergraduate programs, BYU offers graduate degrees in a variety of disciplines through fifty-five graduate departments, including the Marriott School of Management and the J. Reuben Clark Law School. The Department of Chemistry and Biochemistry is one of the leading research departments at BYU.

Applying

Applicants should submit transcripts, letters of recommendation, a $30 application fee, and the application form. International students must pass the Test of English as a Foreign Language (TOEFL) with a score of 550 or higher, although preference is given to students with scores of 600 or higher. GRE General and Subject tests in chemistry or biochemistry are required and should be taken in September or December of the senior year. All application materials should be received by the Office of Graduate Studies no later than February 1 to be considered for admission the following fall. Applicants are not discriminated against on the basis of race, color, national origin, religion, gender, or handicap.

Correspondence and Information

Dr. N. Kent Dalley
Coordinator, Graduate Admissions
C101 BNSN (Benson Science Building)
Brigham Young University
Provo, Utah 84602

Fax: 801-378-5474
E-mail: chemgrad@byu.edu
World Wide Web: http://chemwww.byu.edu/welcome.html

Brigham Young University

THE FACULTY AND THEIR RESEARCH

Merritt B. Andrus, Assistant Professor; Ph.D., Utah, 1991; postdoctoral study at Harvard. Organic chemistry: synthetic organic chemistry that includes asymmetric catalytic methods, natural product synthesis, and combinatorial libraries.

David A. Berges, Associate Professor; Ph.D., Indiana, 1967. CNRS Fellowship, 1967, Institut de Chimie des Substances Naturelles, Gif-sur-Yvette, France. Organic chemistry: synthetic organic and bioorganic chemistry; applications to enzymology, cellular biochemistry, cancer, and infectious diseases; mechanism-based enzyme inhibition.

Juliana Boerio-Goates, Professor; Ph.D., Michigan, 1979; postdoctoral study at Michigan. Physical chemistry: structural and thermodynamic studies of phase transitions in molecular and ionic crystals, thermodynamics of biological materials.

Jerald S. Bradshaw, Reed M. Izatt Professor; Ph.D., UCLA, 1963; postdoctoral study at Caltech. Organic chemistry: synthesis and complexation properties of macrocyclic multidentate compounds; chemistry of polysiloxanes, particularly as applied to cross-linked stationary phases for chromatography.

N. Kent Dalley, Professor; Ph.D., Texas at Austin, 1968; postdoctoral study at Argonne National Laboratory. X-ray crystallography: crystal structures of macrocyclic compounds and complexes and of nucleosides.

David V. Dearden, Assistant Professor; Ph.D., Caltech, 1989. NRC Fellowship, 1989, U.S. National Institute of Standards and Technology. Analytical/physical chemistry: host-guest molecular recognition in ion-molecule reactions, Fourier transform ion cyclotron resonance mass spectrometry with electrospray and laser ionization.

Delbert J. Eatough, Professor; Ph.D., Brigham Young, 1967. Physical chemistry: environmental atmospheric chemistry of SO_x, NO_x, and organics; environmental analytical techniques; tracers and source apportionment of atmospheric pollutants; indoor atmospheric chemistry.

Terry S. Elton, Associate Professor; Ph.D., Washington State, 1986; postdoctoral study at Washington State. NIH Fellowship, 1988, Alabama at Birmingham. Biochemistry: angiotensin II receptor gene regulation and signal transduction.

Paul B. Farnsworth, Professor; Ph.D., Wisconsin, 1981; postdoctoral study at Indiana. Analytical chemistry: fundamental and applied measurements on inductively coupled plasmas, element-specific detectors for chromatography, elemental mass spectrometry.

Steven A. Fleming, Associate Professor; Ph.D., Wisconsin, 1984. NIH Fellowship, 1984–86, Colorado State. Organic chemistry: photochemistry of aromatic compounds, rearrangements of small ring heterocycles, synthesis of natural products and novel compounds, determination of mechanisms of thermal rearrangements and photorearrangements.

Steven R. Goates, Professor; Ph.D., Michigan, 1981; postdoctoral study at Columbia. Analytical chemistry: analysis of complex samples by optical and especially laser-based methods, supersonic jet spectroscopy, spectroscopy of solid-state phenomena, investigation of chromatographic processes.

David M. Grant, Professor; Ph.D., Utah, 1957; postdoctoral study at Illinois. Physical chemistry: carbon-13 magnetic resonance; chemical shift theory and electronic structure of molecules; nuclear relaxation and molecular dynamics in liquids; high-resolution NMR in solids; application of carbon-13 magnetic resonance to fossil fuels, chemistry, and molecular biology.

Steven W. Graves, Associate Professor; Ph.D., Yale, 1978; postdoctoral fellow, Tufts University School of Medicine, 1978–81; clinical chemistry fellow, Washington University School of Medicine, 1981–83. Biochemistry and bioanalytical/clinical chemistry and physiology: mechanisms of hypertensive complications of pregnancy, Na^+ pump regulation in disease, clinical assay development.

Lee D. Hansen, Professor; Ph.D., Brigham Young, 1965. NIH Career Development Award, 1969–72. Physical chemistry: calorimetry, thermodynamics of batteries, kinetics of very slow processes, productivity and stress response of green plants.

Roger G. Harrison, Assistant Professor; Ph.D., Utah, 1993; postdoctoral study at Minnesota. Inorganic chemistry: metalloprotein active site understanding, catalytic enzyme model complexes, mechanism of alkane oxidation.

Douglas J. Henderson, Research Professor; Ph.D., Utah, 1961. Physical chemistry: statistical mechanics; intermolecular forces and their effects on the structure of liquids, interfaces, and colloids.

Roger L. Kaspar, Assistant Professor; Ph.D., Washington (Seattle), 1991; postdoctoral study at MIT. NIH Fellowship, 1995, Stanford Medical School. Biochemistry: role of mammalian mRNA untranslated regions in regulating gene expression, particularly at the level of mRNA translation.

John D. Lamb, Professor; Ph.D., Brigham Young, 1978. Program Manager, Separations and Analysis, Office of Basic Energy Sciences, U.S. D.O.E., 1982–84. Inorganic chemistry: macrocyclic ligand chemistry, liquid membrane separations, ion chromatography, calorimetry.

Milton L. Lee, H. Tracy Hall Professor; Ph.D., Indiana, 1975; postdoctoral study at MIT. Analytical chemistry: microcolumn chromatography, capillary column technology, capillary column gas chromatography, capillary column supercritical fluid chromatography, capillary electrophoresis, analytical mass spectrometry, high-resolution chromatography of coal-derived materials.

Nolan F. Mangelson, Professor; Ph.D., Berkeley, 1968. Research Associate, 1967–69, Washington (Seattle). Nuclear chemistry: multielement analysis by nuclear techniques such as proton induced X-ray and gamma-ray emission, EXAFS, and RBS applied to problems of environmental and biological interest.

Francis R. Nordmeyer, Professor; Ph.D., Stanford, 1967. Inorganic chemistry: electron transfer reactions, ion chromatography.

Noel L. Owen, Professor; Ph.D., Cambridge, 1963; postdoctoral study at Harvard. Physical chemistry: FTIR and NMR spectroscopy, structure and confirmation of novel and unstable compounds, bonding between wood and various reagents, molecular structure of wood polymers and other natural products, matrix isolation infrared spectroscopy, NMR studies of medicinally important compounds.

Matt A. Peterson, Assistant Professor; Ph.D., Arizona, 1992. NIH Fellowship, 1993, Colorado State. Organic chemistry: stereoselective synthesis, transition metal-mediated asymmetric catalysis, synthesis of glycosphingolipids, combinatorial peptide libraries and antisense oligonucleotides.

Morris J. Robins, J. Rex Goates Professor; Ph.D., Arizona State, 1965. Cancer Research Fellowship, 1965–66, Roswell Park Memorial Institute. Organic chemistry: chemistry of nucleic acid components, nucleoside analogues, and related biomolecules; transformations of natural product nucleosides; design of mechanism-based enzyme inhibitors; development of anticancer and antiviral agents.

Paul B. Savage, Assistant Professor; Ph.D., Wisconsin, 1993. NIH Fellowship, 1994–95, Ohio State. Organic chemistry: development of new receptors for small molecules, elucidation of the roles of noncovalent interactions in intermolecular association.

Randall B. Shirts, Associate Professor; Ph.D., Harvard, 1979; postdoctoral study at Joint Institute for Laboratory Astrophysics and University of Colorado. Physical chemistry: theoretical chemistry, nonlinear dynamics, semiclassical quantization, vibration-rotation dynamics, laser-molecule interaction, quantum-classical correspondence, molecular modeling of molecular recognition.

Daniel L. Simmons, Associate Professor; Ph.D., Wisconsin, 1986. NIH and Leukemia Society Fellowships, 1986–89, Harvard. Biochemistry: molecular mechanisms of neoplastic transformation by Rous sarcoma virus, messenger RNA splicing and translation mechanisms, prostaglandins and signal transduction.

James M. Thorne, Professor; Ph.D., Berkeley, 1966. Physical chemistry: cancer photoradiation therapy, X-ray diagnostics for laser fusion.

Gerald D. Watt, Professor; Ph.D., Brigham Young, 1968. NIH Fellowship, 1968, Yale. Biochemistry: nitrogenase, ferritins, metalloproteins.

Barry M. Willardson, Assistant Professor; Ph.D., Purdue, 1990; postdoctoral study at Los Alamos National Laboratory. Biochemistry: regulation of G-protein-mediated signal transduction.

Brian F. Woodfield, Assistant Professor; Ph.D., Berkeley, 1994; postdoctoral study at Naval Research Laboratory, Material Physics Branch, Washington, D.C. Physical chemistry: high temperature superconductors and material exhibiting "colossal" magneto resistance.

Earl M. Woolley, Professor; Ph.D., Brigham Young, 1969. NRC Canada Fellowship, 1969–70, Lethbridge. Physical chemistry: thermodynamics of reactions in mixed aqueous-organic solvents, intermolecular hydrogen bonding reactions, electrolyte solutions, and of ionic and nonionic reactions in solution including surfactants; calorimetric methods.

S. Scott Zimmerman, Associate Professor; Ph.D., Florida State, 1973. NIH Fellowship, 1973–77, Cornell. Biochemistry: molecular modeling and computational chemistry of biologically important molecules.

SELECTED PUBLICATIONS

Andrus, M. B., and S. D. Lepore. Asymmetric additions to dichlorophenyl dioxanes: new chiral acetal. *Tetrahedron Lett.* 36:9149–52, 1995.

Andrus, M. B., A. B. Argade, X. Chen, and M. G. Pamment. The asymmetric kharasch reaction. Catalytic enantioselective allylic acyloxylation of olefins with chiral copper (I) complexes and *tert*-butyl perbenzoate. *Tetrahedron Lett.* 36:2945–8, 1995.

Johnson, D.A., et al. **(M. B. Andrus).** Synthesis, structure, and mechanism in immunophilin research. *Synlett.* 381–92, 1994.

Xie, M., **D. A. Berges,** and **M. J. Robins.** Efficient 'dehomologation' of Di-O-Isopropylidenehexofuranose derivatives to give O-Isopropylidenepentofuranoses by sequential treatment with periodic acid in ethyl acetate and sodium borohydride. *J. Org. Chem.* 61:5157, 1996.

Wilkinson, K. D., et al. **(D. A. Berges).** Specific inhibitor of the ubiquitin activating enzyme: synthesis and characterization of adenosyl-phospho-ubiquitinol, a nonhydrolyzable ubiquitin adenylate analogue. *Biochemistry* 29:7373, 1990.

Hurtubise, R. J., S. M. Ramasamy, **J. Boerio-Goates,** and R. Putnam. A model for the loss of nonradiative energy from the triplet state of phosphors in solid matrices based on solid-state properties of the matrices. *J. Luminescence* 68:55–68, 1996.

Campbell, B. J., H. T. Stokes, and **J. Boerio-Goates.** NMR study of ammonium magnesium langbeinite. *Phys. Rev. B* 51:11315–8, 1995.

Pastushok, V. N., et al. **(J. S. Bradshaw).** Einhorn reaction for the synthesis of aromatic building blocks for macrocyclization. *J. Org. Chem.* 62:212–5, 1997.

Krakowiak, K. E., G. -L. Yi, and **J. S. Bradshaw.** Preparation of triazamacrocycles containing only secondary amine functions using both tosyl and BOC protecting groups. *J. Heterocyclic Chem.* 33:2013–7, 1996.

Bordunov, A.V., **J. S. Bradshaw,** V. N. Pastushok, and R. M. Izatt. Application of the Mannich reaction for the synthesis of Azamacroheterocycles. *Synlett.* 10:933–48, 1996.

Zhang, X. X., et al. **(J. S. Bradshaw** and **N. K. Dalley).** A new highly selective macrocycle for K$^+$ and Ba^{2+}: Effect of formation of a second ring through complexation. *J. Am. Chem. Soc.* 117:11507–11, 1995.

Dalley, N. K., X. Kou, C. J. O'Connor, and R. A. Holwerda. Magnetic susceptibility trends in oxo-bridged, dinuclear chromium (III) complexes. Crystal structure of [(tmpa)Cr(µ-O)(µ-CO$_3$)Cr(tmpa)] (ClO$_4$)$_2$·2H$_2$O]. *Inorg. Chem.* 35:2196–201, 1996.

Dearden, D. V., et al. **(J. S. Bradshaw).** Intrinsic contributions to chiral recognition: discrimination between enantiomeric amines by Dimethyldiketopyridino-18-crown-6 in the gas phase. *J. Am. Chem. Soc.* 119:353–9, 1997.

Chen, Q., K. Cannell, J. Nicoll, and **D. V. Dearden.** The macrobicyclic cryptate effect in the gas phase. *J. Am. Chem. Soc.* 118:6335–44,1996.

Chu, I.-H. and **D. V. Dearden.** Effects of alkyl substitution on the multidentate attachment of alkali metal cations by ligands in the gas phase: kinetics and thermochemistry of cation binding by isomers of dicyclohexano-18-crown-6. *J. Am Chem. Soc.* 117:8197–203,1995.

Eatough, D. J., H. Tang, W. Cui, and J. Machir. Determination of the size distribution and chemical composition of fine particulate semi-volatile organic material in urban environments using diffusion denuder technology. *Inhal. Toxicol.* 7(5):691–710, 1997.

Eatough, D. J., D. A. Eatough, L. Lewis, and E. A. Lewis. Fine particulate chemical composition and light extinction at Canyonlands National Park using organic particulate material concentrations obtained with a multisystem, multichannel diffusion denuder sampler. *J. Geophys. Res.* 101(D14):19515–31, 1996.

Eatough, D. J., M. Eatough, and N. L. Eatough. Apportionment of sulfur oxides at Canyonlands during the winter of 1990. III. Source apportionment of SO$_x$ and sulfate and the conversion of SO$_2$ to sulfate in the Green River Basin. *Atmos. Env.* 30(2):295–308,1996.

Randzio, S. L., **D. J. Eatough,** E. A. Lewis, and L. D. Hansen. Thermophysical properties of quinoline as a function of temperature (303–503K) and pressure (.1–400MPa). *Int. J. Thermophys.* 17(2):405–22, 1996.

Randzio, S. L., E. A. Lewis, **D. J. Eatough,** and L. D. Hansen. Thermophysical properties of *m*-Cresol as a function of temperature (303–503K) and pressure (.1–400MPa). *Int. J. Thermophys.* 16(4):883–900, 1995.

Su, B., M. M. Martin, and **T. S. Elton.** Human AT$_1$ receptor gene regulation. In *Recent Advances in Cellular and Molecular Aspects of Angiotensin Receptors.* pp. 11–22, eds. M. K. Raizada, M. I. Phillips, and C. Sumners. New York: Plenum Publishing, 1996.

Su, B., M. M. Martin, and **T. S. Elton.** The sequence and genomic organization of the human type 2 angiotension II receptor gene. *Biochem. Biophys. Res. Commun.* 209:554–62, 1995.

Martin, M. M., et al. **(T. S. Elton).** A functional comparison of the rat type-1 angiotensin II receptor (AT$_{1A}$R and AT$_{1B}$R) *Reg. Peptides* 60:135–47, 1995.

Farnsworth, P. B. Efficiency calculations for spectroscopic collection optics. *Spectrochim. Acta* 50B:1159–61, 1995.

Farnsworth, P. B., M. Wu, M. Tacquard, and M. L. Lee. Background correction device for enhanced element selective gas chromatographic detection by atomic emission spectroscopy. *Appl. Spectroscopy* 48:742–6, 1994.

Farnsworth, P. B., and N. Omenetto. The kinetics of charge exchange between argon and magnesium in the inductively coupled plasma. *Spectrochim. Acta* 48B:809–16, 1993.

Fleming, S. A., A. W. Jensen, and M. B. Ridges. Synthesis of non-steroidal antiinflammatory drug analogues for selective studies on the COX-II Enzyme. *J. Labeled Compounds Radiopharm.* 38:13–8, 1996.

Bradford, C. L., **S. A. Fleming,** and S. C. Ward. Regio-controlled Ene-Yne photochemical [2+2] cycloaddition using silicon as a tether. *Tetrahedron Lett.* 36:4189–92, 1995.

Fleming, S. A. Chemical reagents in photoaffinity labeling. *Tetrahedron* 51:12479–520, 1995.

Zhang, G., W. G. Pitt, **S. R. Goates,** and N. L. Owen. Studies on oxidative photodegradation of epoxy resins by IR-ATR spectroscopy. *J. Appl. Polymer Sci.* 54:419–27, 1994.

Page, S. H., H. Yun, M. L. Lee, and **S. R. Goates.** Rapid method for the determination of phase behavior of fluid mixtures employed in supercritical fluid experiments. *Anal. Chem.* 65:1493–5, 1993.

Sin, C. H., M. R. Linford, and **S. R. Goates.** Supercritical fluid/supersonic jet spectroscopy with a sheath-flow nozzle. *Anal. Chem.* 64:233–8, 1992.

Fontana, A. J., et al. **(L.D. Hansen).** Calorespirometric analysis of plant tissue metabolism using calorimetry and pressure measurement. *Thermochim. Acta* 258:1–15, 1995.

Kim J., **R. G. Harrison,** C. Kim, and L. Que Jr. Fe(TPA)-catalyzed alkane hydroxylation. Metal-based oxidation vs. radical chain autoxidation. *J. Am. Chem. Soc.* 118:4373–9, 1996.

Bennett, B. K., **R. G. Harrison,** and T. G. Richmond. Cobalticinium fluoride: A novel source of "naked" fluoride formed by carbon-fluorine bond activation in a saturated perfluorocarbon. *J. Am. Chem. Soc.* 116:11165, 1994.

Harrison, R. G., and T. G. Richmond. Reductive defluorination of saturated perfluorocarbons by organometallic nucleophiles. *J. Am. Chem. Soc.* 115:5303, 1993.

Henderson, D., and S. Sokolowski. Bridge function of a Lennard-Jones fluid calculated from a second order Percus-Yevick equation. *J. Chem. Phys.* 104:2971–5, 1996.

Duh, D.-M., and **D. Henderson.** Integral equation theory for Lennard-Jones fluids. The bridge function and applications to pure fluids and to mixtures. *J. Chem. Phys.* 104:6742–54, 1996.

Rousseau, D., et al. **(R. Kaspar).** Translation initiation of ornithine decarboxylase and nucleocytoplasmic transport of cyclin D1 mRNA are increased in cells overexpressing eukaryotic initiation factor 4E. *Proc. Natl. Acad. Sci. U.S.A.* 93:1065–70, 1996.

Rousseau, D., et al. **(R. Kaspar).** Eukaryotic translation initiation factor 4E regulates expression of cyclin D1 at transcriptional levels. *J. Biol. Chem.* 270:21176–80, 1995.

Kaspar, R. L., and L. Gehrke. PBMC stimulated with C5a or LPS to synthesize equivalent levels of IL-1β mRNA show unequal IL-1β protein accumalation but similar polyribosome profiles. *J. Immunol.* 153:277–86, 1994.

Lamb, J. D., and R. G. Smith. The application of macrocyclic ligands to high performance ion analysis. In *Comprehensive Supramolecular Chemistry*, vol. 10, pp. 79–112, ed. D. N. Reinhoudt. New York: Elsevier Science Ltd., 1996.

Lamb, J. D., and A. J. Schow. Polymer inclusion membranes containing macrocyclic carriers for use in cation separations. *J. Member Sci.* 111:291–5, 1996.

Lamb, J. D. Chem tutor CD-ROM and workbook. Massachusetts: Jones and Bartlett, 1996.

Chen, G., and **M. L. Lee.** Hydrophilic polymethylmethacrylate hollow fibers for capillary electrophoresis of bimolecules. *J. Microcolumn Separations* 9(2):57–62, 1997.

Brigham Young University

Selected Publications (continued)

Lazar, I. M., **M. L. Lee.** Design and optimization of a corona discharge ion source for supercritical fluid chromatography time-of-flight mass spectrometry. *Anal. Chem.* 68:1924, 1996.

Shen Y., J. S. Bradshaw, and **M. L. Lee.** Packed capillary column supercritical fluid chromatography of fat-soluble vitamins using liquid crystal polysiloxane coated particles. *Chromatographia* 43:53–8, 1996.

Du, Y., **N. F. Mangelson,** L. B. Rees, and R. T. Matheny. PIXE elemental analysis of South American mummy hair. *Nucl. Instrum. Meth. Phys. Res. B.* 109(110):673–6, 1996.

Williams, R. N., et al. **(N. F. Mangelson).** Elemental analysis of lichens from the intermountain western U.S.A. using PIXE. *Nucl. Instrum. Meth. Phys. Res. B.* 109(110):336–40, 1996.

Turner, D. C., **N. F. Mangelson,** and L. B. Rees. Determination of aluminum oxide stopping cross sections for protons and deuterons by backscattering from thin targets. *Nucl. Instrum. Meth. Phys. Res. B.* 103:28–32, 1995.

Hansen, L. D., et al. **(F. R. Nordmeyer).** Teaching concepts in beginning chemistry with simple exploratory experiments. *J. Chem. Ed.* 73(9):840, 1996.

Cheng, K., **F. R. Nordmeyer,** and **J. D. Lamb.** A novel buffer system for separation of metal cations by capillary electrophoresis with indirect UV detection. *J. Cap. Elec.* 002.6:279–85, 1995.

Sohlberg, K., S. P. Leary, **N. L. Owen,** and B. A. Trofimov. The infrared spectrum and conformation of acetone oxime vinyl ether. *Vibrational Spectroscopy* 13:227–34, 1997.

Li, Z., et al. **(N. L. Owen).** Structure determination of a new chromone glycoside by 2D INADEQUATE NMR and molecular modeling. *Magn. Reson. Chem.* 34:512–7, 1996.

Li, D., and **N. L. Owen.** Structure determination using the NMR INADEQUATE technique. In *Advances in Molecular Structure,* vol. 2, pp. 191–211, eds. M. and I. Hargittai. Connecticut: Jai Press, 1996.

Peterson, M. A., and **N. K. Dalley.** Highly stereoselective synthesis of a C_2-Symmetric 2,2'-Bipyridine derived from glucose. *Synthetic Comm.* 26(11):2223–8, 1996.

Peterson, M. A., and R. Polt. N-Diphenylmethylene-ProtectedGlycosyl Acceptors. Selective β-O-Glycosylation to form Lactosyl-*threo*-Ceramides. *J. Org. Chem.* 58:4309, 1993.

Robins, M. J., et al. **(M. A. Peterson).** Synthesis of 2', 3'-fused (3.3.0) γ-butyrolactone-nucleosides and coupling with amino nucleosides to give amide-linked nucleotide-dimer analogues. *Tetrahedron Lett.* 37:3921–4, 1996.

Robins, M. J., S. Sarker, V. Samano, and S. F. Wnuk. Nucleic acid related compounds. 94. Remarkably high steroselective reductions of 2'- and 3' ketonucleoside derivatives to give arabino, ribo, and xylofuranosyl nucleosides with hydrogen istopes at C2' and C3'. *Tetrahedron* 3:447–56, 1997.

Robins, M. J., Z. Guo, M. C. Samano, and S. F. Wnuk. Biomimetic modeling of the decomposition of 2'-chloro-2'-deoxynucleotides by ribonucleotide reductases to give 3(2H)-furanones which can effect mechanism-based inactivation by Michael-type alkylation. *J. Am. Chem. Soc.* 118:11317–8, 1996.

Robins, M. J., S. F. Wnuk, A. E. Hernández-Thirring, and M. C. Samano. Nucleic acid related compounds. 91. Biomimetic reactions are in harmony with loss of 2'-substituents as free radicals (not anions) during mechanism-based inactivation of ribonucleotide reductases. Differential interactions of azide, halogen, and alkylthio groups with tributylstannane and triphenylsilane. *J. Am. Chem. Soc.* 118:11341–8, 1996.

Paquette, L. A., L.-Q. Sun, D. Friedrich, and **P. B. Savage.** Highly enantioselective total synthesis of natural epoxydictymene. An alkoxy-directed cyclization route to highly strained *trans*-oxabicyclo [3.3.0] octanes. *Tetrahedron Lett.* 38:195, 1997.

Savage, P. B., S. K. Holmgren, and S. H. Gellman. Anion and ion pair complexation by a macrocyclic phosphine oxide disulfoxide. *J. Am. Chem. Soc.* 116:4069, 1994.

Savage, P. B., and S. H. Gellman. Complexation of ammonium hexoses: evidence for contributions from OH—OH hydrogen bonds in a hydroxylic medium. *J. Am. Chem. Soc.* 115:10448, 1993.

Sohlberg K., and **R. B. Shirts.** The symmetry of approximate Hamiltonians generated in Birkhoff-Gustavson normal form. *Phys. Rev. A* 54:416, 1996.

Shirts, R. B., and L. D. Stolworthy. Conformational sensitivity of polyether macrocycles to electrostatic potential: partial atomic charges, molecular mechanics and conformational prediction. *J. Incl. Phenom.* 20:297, 1995.

Sohlberg, K., and **R. B. Shirts.** Semiclassical quantization of nonintegrable system: pushing the Fourier method into the chaotic regime. *J. Chem. Phys.* 101:7763, 1994.

Ballif, B. A., et al. **(D. L. Simmons).** Interaction of cyclooxygenases with an apoptosis- and autoimmunity-associated protein. *Proc. Natl. Acad. Sci. U.S.A.* 93:5544–9, 1996.

Lu, X., et al. **(D. L. Simmons).** Nonsteroidal anti-inflammatory drugs cause apoptosis and induce cyclooxygenases in chicken embryo fibroblasts. *Proc. Natl. Acad. Sci. U.S.A.* 92:7961–5, 1995.

Xie, W., et al. **(D. L. Simmons).** Expression of a mitogen-responsive gene encoding protaglandin synthase is regulated by mRNA splicing. *Proc. Natl. Acad. Sci. U.S.A.* 88:2692–6, 1991.

Jones, J. E., et al. **(L. D. Hansen** and **J. M. Thorne).** Faradaic efficiencies less than 100% during electrolysis of water can account for reports of excess heat in "cold fusion" cells. *J. Phys. Chem.* 99:6973–9, 1995.

Thorne, J. M., J. K. Shurtleff, D. D. Allred, and R. T. Perkins. X-ray wave diffraction optics constructed by atomic layer epitaxy. Canadian Patent No. 1,333,426, December 6, 1994.

Johnson, J. L., A. M. Tolley, J. A. Erickson, and **G. D. Watt.** Steady state kinetic studies of dithionite utilization, component protein interaction, and the formation of an oxidized iron protein intermediate during *azotobacter vinelandii* nitrogenase catalysis. *Biochemistry* 35:11336–42, 1996.

Jacobs, D., D. Mitchell, and **G. D. Watt.** The concentration of cellular nitrogenase proteins in *azotobacter vinelandii* whole cells as determined by activity measurements and electron paramagnetic resonances. Spectroscopy. *Arch. Biochem. Biophys.* 324:317–24, 1995.

Watt, G. D., and K. R. N. Reddy. Formation of an all ferrous Fe_4S_4 cluster in the iron protein component of *azotobacter vinelandii* nitrogenase. *J. Inorg. Biochem.* 53:281–94, 1994.

Wilkins, J. F., M. W. Bitensky, and **B. M. Willardson.** Regulation of the kinetics of phosducin phosphorylation in retinal rods. *J. Biol. Chem.* 271:19232–7, 1996.

Willardson, B. M., J. F. Wilkins, T. Yoshida, and M. W. Bitenshky. Regulation of phosducin phosphorylation in retinal rods by Ca2+/calmodulin-dependent adenylyl cyclase. *Proc. Natl. Acad. Sci. U.S.A.* 93:1475–9, 1996.

Willardson, B. M., et al. The phosphorylation state of phosducin determines its ability to block transducin subunit interactions and inhibit transducin binding to activiated rhodopsin. *J. Biol. Chem.* 269:24050–7, 1994.

Fisher, R. A., et al. **(B. F. Woodfield).** The effects of variations in the oxygen content on the specific heat of $YBa_2Cu_3O_{7-δ}$. *Bull. Am. Phys. Soc.* 41:68/B10–1, 1996.

Fisher, R. A., et al. **(B. F. Woodfield).** Magnetic field dependence of the low-temperature specific heat of some high-T_c cooper-oxide superconductors: evidence for an $H^{1/2}T$ contribution in the mixed state. *Physica C* 252:237, 1995.

Emerson, J.P., et al. **(B. F. Woodfield).** The specific heat of oxygen depleted $BaCuO_{2-x}$ in O and 7 T. *Bull. Am. Phys. Soc.* 40:372/H34–109, 1995.

Dearden, L.V., and **E. M. Woolley.** Osmotic coefficients and enthalpies of dilution of aqueous sodium *n*-alkane-1-sulphonates at the temperatures (298.15, 313.15, 328.15, and 343.15) K. *J. Chem. Thermodynamics* 28:1283–301, 1996.

Woolley, E. M., and M. T. Bashford. Enthalpies of dilution of aqueous decyl-, dodecyl-, tetradecyl-, and hexadecyl-trimethylammonium bromide + sodium bromide solutions at 10°, 25°, 40°, and 55°C. *J. Phys. Chem.* 90:3038–46, 1986.

Black, D. R., C. G. Parker, **S. S. Zimmerman,** and M. L. Lee. Enantioselective binding of α-pinene and of some cyclohexanetriol derivatives by cyclodextrin hosts: a molecular modeling study. *J. Comput. Chem.* 17:931–9, 1996.

Lee, C. H., and **S. S. Zimmerman.** Calculations of the φ-ψ conformational contour maps for n-acetyl alanine n'-methyl amide and of the characteristic ratios of poly-l-alanine using various molecular mechanics forcefields. *J. Biomolec. Struct. Dyn.* 13:201–18, 1995.

CARNEGIE MELLON UNIVERSITY

Mellon College of Science
Department of Chemistry

Programs of Study

The Department of Chemistry offers programs leading to the M.S. and Ph.D. degrees. Most students are admitted to the Ph.D. program, but terminal master's programs in polymer science and in colloids, polymers, and surfaces are offered. The graduate program is highly individualized to allow exploration of interdisciplinary interests. Research is carried out in biochemistry and biophysics, bioorganic chemistry, chemical instrumentation, chemical physics, chemical synthesis, inorganic chemistry, nuclear chemistry and radiochemistry, NMR spectroscopy, organic chemistry, physical chemistry, polymer science, structural chemistry, theoretical chemistry, materials science, and environmental chemistry.

To be admitted to the Ph.D. program, students must pass attainment examinations in inorganic, organic, and physical chemistry. These are given just before the beginning of the fall semester and in the spring semester. The student then chooses a research supervisor and commences thesis research. Students are expected to pass at least four advanced courses in science with an average grade of B, present a seminar during the second year, write and defend orally a formal research proposal on a topic different from the thesis research, prepare a dissertation plan summary, and assist in undergraduate teaching for two semesters. The student must write and publicly defend a doctoral dissertation. The thesis must embody the results of extended research and constitute an original contribution to knowledge that is worthy of publication.

The graduate program at Carnegie Mellon University (CMU) emphasizes close interaction with all the faculty members. There are excellent opportunities for interdisciplinary programs with the Departments of Biological Sciences, Chemical Engineering, Materials Science, and Physics, along with the Biotechnology Program and the Center for Fluorescence Research in Biomedical Sciences.

Research Facilities

The Department of Chemistry is located in the Mellon Institute Building, a spacious and dramatic eight-story structure located near the main campus of CMU and directly adjacent to the University of Pittsburgh campus. The department has the most modern instrumentation, to which students have hands-on access. This includes the Center for Molecular Analysis, with LC-Q electrospray/ion-trap and MALDI/TOF mass spectrometry and access to high-field NMR (one 500-MHz and two 300-MHz), as well as major laser spectroscopy and chemical synthesis laboratories. Nuclear chemistry research is carried out at major facilities in the U.S. and abroad. Extensive computational facilities are readily available. These include state-of-the-art computers at the Pittsburgh Supercomputing Center, which is housed in the Mellon Institute Building along with the Department of Biological Sciences and the Center for Fluorescence Research in Biomedical Sciences. The library of the Mellon Institute is especially strong.

Financial Aid

All U.S. doctoral degree students are guaranteed financial aid for the first academic year, usually as teaching assistants, with a stipend of $1375 per month and a tuition scholarship. In addition, competitive fellowships are available, which pay an additional $2000–$4000 per year. Research assistantships are also available for succeeding years. International students may be admitted without being granted financial aid.

Cost of Study

Tuition is $22,100 for the 1999–2000 academic year.

Living and Housing Costs

Pittsburgh provides an attractive and reasonably priced living environment. On-campus housing is limited, but the Off-Campus Housing Office assists students in finding suitable accommodations. Most graduate students prefer to live in nearby rooms and apartments, which are readily available.

Student Group

Graduate enrollment at CMU totals 3,013 and includes students from all parts of the United States and many other countries. All students in the Department of Chemistry are receiving financial aid. Upon completing the Ph.D., a few students (15 percent) go directly into academic positions, but most continue as postdoctoral fellows (40 percent) or take industrial jobs (45 percent).

Location

Pittsburgh is in a large metropolitan area of 2.3 million people. The city is the headquarters for twelve Fortune 500 corporations, and there is a large concentration of research laboratories in the area. Carnegie Mellon is located in the Oakland neighborhood, the cultural and civic center of Pittsburgh. The campus covers 90 acres and adjoins Schenley Park, the largest city park. The city's cultural and recreational opportunities are truly outstanding.

The University

Carnegie Mellon was first established in 1900 as the Carnegie Technical School through a gift from Andrew Carnegie. In 1912, the name was changed to Carnegie Institute of Technology. The Mellon Institute was founded by A. W. and R. B. Mellon; it carried out both pure research and applied research in cooperation with local industry. In 1967, the two entities merged to form Carnegie-Mellon University. Four colleges—the Carnegie Institute of Technology, the Mellon College of Science, the College of Fine Arts, and the College of Humanities and Social Sciences—offer both undergraduate and graduate programs. The Graduate School of Industrial Administration and the School of Urban and Public Affairs offer graduate programs only. The University has assets in excess of $900 million, a total enrollment of 8,185, and 1,257 faculty members.

Applying

Completed applications and credentials for graduate study in chemistry should be submitted by January 15 for decision by mid-April. However, admission decisions are made on a continuous basis, and applications are considered at any time. In addition to the application form, transcripts from all college-level institutions attended, three letters of recommendation, and an official report of the applicant's scores on the General Test and the Subject Test in chemistry of the Graduate Record Examinations are required. An official report of the score from the Test of English as a Foreign Language (TOEFL) is required for international students. A full description of procedures and programs is given in the booklet *Graduate Studies in Chemistry,* which will be sent on request.

Correspondence and Information

Committee for Graduate Admissions
Department of Chemistry
Carnegie Mellon University
4400 Fifth Avenue
Pittsburgh, Pennsylvania 15213

Telephone: 412-268-3150
Fax: 412-268-1061
E-mail: vb0g@andrew.cmu.edu
World Wide Web: http://www.chem.cmu.edu

Carnegie Mellon University

THE FACULTY AND THEIR RESEARCH

Bruce A. Armitage, Assistant Professor; Ph.D., Arizona, 1993. Bioorganic and supramolecular chemistry: design and synthesis of functional DNA/RNA analogs, nucleic acid chemistry, photochemistry in supramolecular assemblies of molecules, development of probes for RNA structure and function, sensors for hybridization of nucleic acid probes.

Guy C. Berry, Professor; Ph.D., Michigan, 1960. Physical chemistry and polymer science, physical chemistry of macromolecules: photon correlation and integrated intensity light scattering, solution properties of flexible and rodlike polymers, rheology of polymers, properties of liquid crystalline polymers.

Terrence J. Collins, Professor; Ph.D., Auckland (New Zealand), 1978. Inorganic chemistry, green chemistry, the design of green oxidants, alternative chemistry for oxidation processes that produce persistent pollutants, bioinorganic chemistry of high-oxidation–state transition metal species, preparation of multinuclear transition metal ions with predetermined magnetic exchange coupling properties.

Susan T. Graul, Assistant Professor; Ph.D., Purdue, 1989. Physical organic chemistry. Gas-phase ion chemistry: reaction mechanisms and dynamics, cluster ions and highly charged ions, photoinduced and collisionally activated dissociation processes, statistical theory and molecular orbital calculations.

Michael P. Hendrich, Assistant Professor; Ph.D., Illinois, 1988. Biophysical and bioinorganic chemistry, transition metals associated with fundamental processes of living systems, electronic structure, high-frequency electron paramagnetic resonance, magnetochemistry.

Colin Horwitz, Senior Research Scientist; Ph.D., Northwestern, 1986. Inorganic and bioinorganic chemistry: synthesis and characterization of coordination complexes, oxidation chemistry.

Morton Kaplan, Professor; Ph.D., MIT, 1960. Nuclear chemistry, nuclear physics, and chemical physics: nuclear reactions of heavy ions and high-energy projectiles, ultrarelativistic nuclear collisions, recoil properties of radioactive products, Mössbauer resonance, perturbed angular correlations of gamma rays, statistical theory of nuclear reactions and light-particle emission.

Paul J. Karol, Professor; Ph.D., Columbia, 1967. Nuclear chemistry and physical chemistry: high-energy nuclear reactions; chemical separations, especially column chromatography.

Hyung J. Kim, Associate Professor; Ph.D., SUNY at Stony Brook, 1988. Theoretical chemistry, equilibrium and nonequilibrium statistical mechanics, chemical reaction dynamics and spectroscopy in condensed phases, molecular dynamics computer simulations and quantum chemistry in solution.

Miguel Llinás, Professor; Ph.D., Berkeley, 1971. Molecular biophysics:structural dynamics and functional studies of proteins in solution by NMR spectroscopy, plasminogen and blood coagulation proteins.

Krzysztof Matyjaszewski, Professor; Ph.D., Polish Academy of Sciences, 1976. Polymer organic chemistry: kinetics and thermodynamics of ionic reactions, cationic polymerization, radical polymerization, ring-opening polymerization, living polymers, inorganic and organometallic polymers, electronic materials.

Richard D. McCullough, Professor and Head; Ph.D., Johns Hopkins, 1988. Organic and materials chemistry: Self-assembly and synthesis of highly conductive organic polymers and oligomers; conjugated polymer sensors, nanoelectronic assembly, and nanowires; synthesis and development of organic-inorganic hybrid magnetic and electronic materials; crystal engineering and self-assembly.

Eckard Münck, Professor; Ph.D., Darmstadt Technical (Germany), 1967. Active sites of metalloproteins, in particular sites containing iron-sulfur clusters or oxo-bridged iron dimers; study of synthetic clusters which mimic structures in proteins; magnetochemistry: Heisenberg and double-exchange; Mössbauer spectroscopy and electron paramagnetic resonance.

Gary D. Patterson, Professor; Ph.D., Stanford, 1972. Chemical physics and polymer science: application of light-scattering spectroscopy to problems of structure and dynamics in amorphous materials, physics and chemistry of liquids and solutions, conformational statistics and molecular dynamics of polymers, nature and dynamics of the glass transition, structure and dynamics of biopolymers.

Linda A. Peteanu, Assistant Professor; Ph.D., Chicago, 1989. Physical chemistry; biophysical chemistry; laser spectroscopy; application of resonance Raman and Stark effect-based spectroscopies to the study of ultrafast photochemical and biological reactions: proton transfer, electron transfer, charge transfer, and cis-trans isomerizations; effect of solvent environment on reactive excited states.

Stuart W. Staley, Professor; Ph.D., Yale, 1964. Physical organic chemistry: synthesis, dynamic NMR studies of electron transfer systems and theoretically interesting molecules, X-ray diffraction and NMR studies of organic crystals, electronic structure calculations of molecular geometries and properties.

Robert F. Stewart, Professor; Ph.D., Caltech, 1962. Physical and theoretical chemistry: X-ray diffraction, high-energy electron-scattering calculations.

Charles H. Van Dyke, Associate Professor; Ph.D., Pennsylvania, 1964. Synthetic inorganic chemistry and chemical education.

David Yaron, Associate Professor; Ph.D., Harvard, 1990. Theoretical chemistry, electronic structure of conducting polymers and nonlinear optical materials, theoretical description of large-amplitude vibrational motions.

SELECTED PUBLICATIONS

Armitage, B. Photocleavage of nucleic acids. *Chem. Rev.* 98:1171–200, 1998.

Armitage, B., et al. Peptide nucleic acid (PNA)–DNA hybrid duplexes: Intercalation by an internally linked anthraquinone. *Nucleic Acids Res.* 26:715–20, 1998.

Armitage, B., et al. Peptide nucleic acid–anthraquinone conjugates: Strand invasion and photoinduced cleavage of duplex DNA. *Nucleic Acids Res.* 25:4674–8, 1997.

Armitage, B., et al. Peptide nucleic acid–DNA duplexes: Long-range hole migration from an internally linked anthraquinone. *Proc. Natl. Acad. Sci. U.S.A.* 94:12320–5, 1997.

Berry, G. C., and P. M. Cotts. Static and dynamic light scattering. In *Experimental Methods in Polymer Characterization,* eds. R. A. Pethrick and R. S. Stein. Sussex, UK: John Wiley & Sons Ltd., in press.

Berry, G. C., and D. J. Plazek. On the use of stretched-exponential functions for both linear viscoelastic creep and stress relaxation. *Rheol. Acta* 36:320–9, 1997.

Diao, B., and **G. C. Berry.** Studies on the texture of nematic solutions of a rodlike polymer. 1. Distortion of the director field in a magnetic field. *Liq. Cryst.* 22:225–38, 1997.

Berry, G. C. Crossover behavior in the viscosity of semiflexible polymers: Intermolecular interactions as a function of concentration and molecular weight. *J. Rheol.* 40:1129–54, 1996.

Mattoussi, H., **G. C. Berry,** and **G. D. Patterson.** The effects of surface layers on third harmonic generation from solutions of a nematogenic polymer. *J. Polym. Sci. Part B Polym. Phys.* 34:925–38, 1996.

Collins, T. J., et al. The design of green oxidants. In *Green Chemistry: Frontiers in Benign Chemical Synthese and Processes,* pp. 46–71, eds. P. T. Anastas and T. C. Williamson. Oxford: Oxford University Press, 1998.

Miller, C. G., et al. **(T. J. Collins).** A method for driving O-atom transfer: Secondary ion binding to a tetraamide macrocyclic ligand. *J. Am. Chem. Soc.* 120:11540–1, 1998.

Gordon-Wylie, S. W., et al. **(T. J. Collins).** New magnetically-coupled bimetallic complexes as potential building blocks for magnetic materials. *Chem. Eur. J.* 4:2173–81, 1998.

Graul, S. T., et al. Internal excitation in the products of nucleophilic substitution from the dissociation of metastable ion complexes. *J. Am. Chem. Soc.,* in press.

Graul, S. T., et al. Guided-ion beam measurements of X++NO (X=Ar, N2) reactions. *J. Am. Chem. Soc.* 100:7348–59, 1994.

Graul, S. T., and M. T. Bowers. Vibrational excitation in products of nucleophilic substitution: The dissociation of metastable X-(CH_3Y) in the gas phase. *J. Am. Chem. Soc.* 116:3875–83, 1994.

Dressler, R. A., et al. **(S. T. Graul).** Guided-ion beam measurements of the Kr++NO charge-transfer reaction. *Chem. Phys. Lett.* 215:656–61, 1993.

Yoo, S., et al. **(M. P. Hendrich** and **E. Münck).** Mössbauer and integer spin EPR studies and spin coupling analysis of the [4Fe-4S]0 cluster of the Fe protein from Azotobacter vinelandii nitrogenase. *J. Am. Chem. Soc.,* in press.

Petasis, D., and **M. P. Hendrich.** A new Q-band EPR spectrometer for quantitative studies of even electron metalloproteins. *J. Magn. Reson.* 136:200–6, 1999.

Hendrich, M. P., and P. G. Debrunner. EPR of non-Kramers systems in biology. In *Foundations of Modern EPR,* eds. Eaton, Eaton, and Salikhov. World Scientific, 1998.

Arciero, D. M., A. Golombek, **M. P. Hendrich,** and A. B. Hooper. Correlation of optical and EPR signals with the P460 heme of hydroxylamine oxidoreductase from nitrosomonas europaea. *Biochemistry* 37:523–9, 1998.

Patterson, R. E., et al. **(C. P. Horwitz).** Electron-transfer oxidation by phase separating reagents. *Inorg. Chem.* 37:4748–50, 1998.

Horwitz, C. P., et al. **(T. J. Collins).** Ligand design approach for securing robust oxidation catalysts. *J. Am. Chem. Soc.* 120:4867–8, 1998.

Kaplan, M., et al. Neutral strange particle production and flow at AGS energies. *J. Phys.* G25:225, 1999.

Kaplan, M., et al. Collective flow and particle spectra in relativistic heavy ion collisions. *Nucl. Phys. A* 630:549c, 1998.

Kaplan, M., et al. The E895 π correlation analysis—A status report. In *Advances in Nuclear Dynamics 4,* pp. 183–92, eds. W. Bauer and H.-G. Ritter. New York: Plenum Press, 1998.

Kaplan, M. Search for a short-lived dibaryon in Au + Au collisions: Status of AGS experiment E896. In *Advances in Nuclear Dynamics 3,* pp. 205–14. New York: Plenum Press, 1997.

Kaplan, M., et al. **(P. J. Karol).** Probing the degrees of freedom in hot composite nuclei: Systematics of charged particle evaporation. In *ACS Award Symposium in Nuclear Chemistry,* 1995.

Karol, P. J. Radioanalytical methods. In *Compendium of Analytical Nomenclature,* 3rd edition, chap. 16, eds. J. Inczédy, T. Lengyel, and A. Ure. Oxford: Blackwell, 1998.

Harris, J. W., et al. **(P. J. Karol).** The STAR experiment at the relativistic heavy ion collider. *Nucl. Phys. A* 566:277c, 1994.

Kolsky, K. L., and **P. J. Karol.** Deep spallation of medium mass isotopes by protons. *Phys. Rev. C* 48:236, 1993.

Bursulaya, B. D., and **H. J. Kim.** A molecular dynamics simulation study of water near critical conditions. II. Dynamics and spectroscopy. *J. Chem. Phys.* 110:9656–65, 1999.

Bursulaya, B. D., and **H. J. Kim.** Generalized molecular mechanics including quantum electronic structure variation of polar solvents. I. Theoretical formulation via a truncated adiabatic basis set description. *J. Chem. Phys.* 108:3277–85, 1998.

Jeon, J., and **H. J. Kim.** Electrostriction effects on electron transfer reactions in solution. I. Adiabatic regime. *J. Chem. Phys.* 106:5979–89, 1997.

Kim, H. J., and J. T. Hynes. Excited state intramolecular charge transfer rates for DMABN in solution. *J. Photochem. Photobiol. A Chem.* 105:337–43, 1997.

Cao, Y., et al. **(M. Llinás).** Kringle 5 of plasminogen: A novel inhibitor of endothelial cell growth. *J. Biol. Chem.* 272:22924–8, 1997.

Marti, D. N., et al. **(M. Llinás).** Ligand preference of kringle 2 and homologous domains of human plasminogen: Canvassing intermediate and high affinity binding sites by ^{1}H-NMR. *Biochemistry* 36:11591–604, 1997.

Cao, Y., et al. **(M. Llinás).** Kringle domains of human angiostatin: Characterization of the anti-proliferative activity on endothelial cells. *J. Biol. Chem.* 271:29461–7, 1996.

Söhndel, S., et al. **(M. Llinás).** Recombinant gene expression and ^{1}H-NMR characteristics of the Kringle (2+3) super-module: Spectroscopic/functional individuality of plasminogen Kringle domains. *Biochemistry* 35:2357–64, 1996.

Matyjaszewski, K. Mechanistic aspects of atom transfer radical polymerization. *ACS Symp. Ser.* 685:258, 1998.

Matyjaszewski, K., and S. G. Gaynor. How to make polymer chains of various shapes, compositions, and functionalities by Atom Transfer Radical Polymerization (ATRP). *ACS Symp. Ser.* 685:396, 1998.

Matyjaszewski, K., J.-L. Wang, T. Grimaud, and D. Shipp. Controlled/~living~ radical polymerization of methyl methacrylate by atom transfer radical polymerization using various initiation systems. *Macromolecules* 31:1527, 1998.

Coca, S., C. B. Jasieczek, K. L. Beers, and **K. Matyjaszewski.** Polymerization of acrylates by atom transfer radical polymerization. Homopolymerization of 2-hydroxethyl acrylate. *J. Polym. Sci. Polym. Chem.* 36:1417, 1998.

McCullough, R. D., P. C. Ewbank, and R. S. Loewe. Self-assembly and disassembly of regioregular, water soluble polythiophenes: Chemoselective ionchromatic sensing in water. *J. Am. Chem. Soc.* 119:631–2, 1997.

Angove, H. C., S. J. Yoo, B. K. Burgess, and **E. Münck.** Mössbauer and EPR evidence for an all-ferrous Fe_4S_4 cluster with S=4 in the Fe protein of Azotobacter vinelandi. *J. Am. Chem. Soc.* 119:8730–1, 1997.

Xia, J., et al. **(E. Münck).** Mössbauer and EPR study of Ni-activated α subunit of carbon monoxide dehydrogenase from *Clostridium pasteruianum. Am. Chem. Soc.* 119:8301–12, 1997.

Shu, L., et al. **(E. Münck).** An $Fe(IV)_2O_2$ core diamond core for the key intermediate Q of methane monooxygenase. *Science* 275:515–8, 1997.

Bominaar, E. L., et al. **(E. Münck).** Analysis of exchange interaction and electron delocalization as intramolecular determinants of intermolecular electron-transfer kinetics. *Inorg. Chem.* 36:3689–701, 1997.

Hwang, Y., **G. D. Patterson,** and J. R. Stevens. Photon correlation spectroscopy of bulk poly(n-hexyl methacylate) near the glass transition. *J. Polym. Sci. Part B Polym. Phys.* 34:2291–305, 1996.

Fishman, D. M., and **G. D. Patterson.** Light scattering studies of supercoiled and nicked DNA. *Biopolymers* 38:535–52, 1996.

Patterson, G. D., P. K. Jue, D. J. Ramsay, and J. R. Steven. Photon

Carnegie Mellon University

Selected Publications (continued)

correlation spectroscopy of syndiotactic poly(n-butylmethacrylate) near the glass transition. *J. Polym. Sci. Part B Polym. Phys.* 32:1137, 1994.

Locknar, S. A., **L. A. Peteanu,** Z. Shuai. Calculations of ground and excited-state polarizabilities of unsubstituted and donor/acceptor polyenes: A comparison of the finite-field and sum-over-states methods. *J. Phys. Chem. B* 103A:2197, 1999.

Premvardhan, L., and **L. A. Peteanu.** Electroabsorption measurements and ab initio calculations of the dipolar properties of 2-(2'-hydroxyphenyl)-benzothiazole and -benzoxazole: Two photostabilizers that undergo excited-state proton transfer. *Chem. Phys. Lett.* 298:521, 1998.

Locknar, S., and **L. A. Peteanu.** An investigation of the relationship between dipolar properties and *cis-trans* configuration in retinal polyenes: A stark spectroscopy study. *J. Phys. Chem. B* 102:4240–6, 1998.

Peteanu, L. A., and S. Locknar. Stark spectroscopy of an excited-state proton-transfer molecule: Comparison of experimental and computational results for *o*-hydroxyacetophenone. *Chem. Phys. Lett.* 274:79, 1997.

Staley, S. W., et al. Steric and electronic control of dynamic processes in aryl-bridged dicyclooctatetraenes and their dianions. *J. Am. Chem. Soc.,* in press.

Boman, P., et al. **(S. W. Staley).** Kinetics of bond shift and charge transfer in dialkynylphenylene-bridged dicyclooctatetraenes and their dianions. *J. Am. Chem. Soc.* 121:1558, 1999.

Staley, S. W., R. A. Grimm, and R. A. Sablosky. Influence of carbon group substituents on bond shift and electrochemical reduction of cyclooctaatetraene. *J. Am. Chem. Soc.* 120:3671, 1998.

Staley, S. W., R. A. Grimm, G. S. Martin, and R. A. Sablosky. Energetics of bond shift in monohalogen-substituted cyclooctatetraenes. *Tetrahedron* 53:10093, 1997.

Swaminathan S., B. M. Craven, M. A. Spackman, and **R. F. Stewart.** Theoretical and experimental studies of the charge density in urea. *Acta Cryst. Sec. B Struct. Sci.* B40:398, 1984.

Van der Wal, R. J., and **R. F. Stewart.** Shell population and l refinements with canonical and density-localized scattering factors in analytical form. *Acta. Cryst. Sec. A Found. Cryst.* A40:587, 1984.

Kirfel, A., F. Will, and **R. F. Stewart.** The chemical bonding in lithium metaborate $LiBo_2$, charge densities and electrostatic properties. *Acta Cryst.* B39:175, 1983.

Van der Wal, R. J., and **R. F. Stewart.** A cusp-constrained scattering factor for bonded hydrogen atoms. *Acta Cryst.* A39:422, 1983.

Yaron, D., E. Moore, Z. Shuai, and J.-L. Bredas. Comparison of density matrix renormalization group calculations with electron-hole models of exciton binding in conjugated polymers. *J. Chem. Phys.* 108:7451–8, 1998.

Moore, E., and **D. Yaron.** Models of coulomb screening and exciton binding in conjugated polymers. *Synth. Met.* 85:1023–4, 1997.

Moore, E., B. Gherman, and **D. Yaron.** Coulomb screening and exciton binding energies in conjugated polymers. *J. Chem. Phys.* 106:4216–27, 1997.

Yaron, D. Nonlinear optical response of conjugated polymers: Essential excitations and scattering. *Phys. Rev. B* 54:4609–20, 1996.

CLARK UNIVERSITY

Department of Chemistry and Biochemistry

Programs of Study

The Department of Chemistry and Biochemistry offers programs leading to the M.A. and Ph.D. degrees, with strong emphasis on the Ph.D. program. Areas of specialization include analytical, inorganic, organic, physical, and polymer chemistry and biochemistry and molecular biology. Most graduate research projects span more than one of these areas. Currently, two areas are receiving special attention: (1) biochemistry and molecular biology—NMR and EPR analysis of ligand binding and conformational changes in proteins, analysis of peptide and protein dynamics by both experimental NMR and molecular dynamics simulation techniques, recombinant DNA approaches to nucleic acid–protein interaction, and cloning and sequencing of structural genes (from archaebacteria, computer-aided drug design) and (2) polymer chemistry—structure and chain dynamics as probed by NMR and solution and solid-state studies and their relation to macroscopic properties. Following entrance exams, which are given to ascertain their proficiency in all areas of chemistry, students begin a program of core and advanced courses designed to meet their specific needs. Course programs are generally completed by the end of the second year. Students typically select a research adviser and begin research before the end of the first academic year. Ph.D. candidates take two consecutive qualifying exams, which are typically completed by the end of the second year. The first of these exams is written and tests the student's general knowledge in his or her chosen field of study. The second exam entails the writing of an original research proposal on a topic not directly related to the student's research project together with an oral defense of the proposal. The student must also demonstrate the ability to read the scientific literature in one foreign language. Finally, Ph.D. candidates must complete a research project, submit a dissertation, and successfully defend the dissertation in an oral exam.

Research Facilities

The Department of Chemistry and Biochemistry is housed in the Arthur M. Sackler Sciences Center, which includes the Jeppson Chemistry Laboratory and the biophysics building in addition to a recently completed $8-million shared research and teaching facility that includes a three-science (physics, biology, and chemistry) library. The Worcester Consortium NMR Facility, located in the Department of Chemistry and Biochemistry, consists of a Bruker AC/200 and MSL/300 NMR spectrometer (fully equipped for wide-line and magic angle spinning for solids) and a Varian Unity 500 NMR spectrometer (fully equipped for triple-resonance, high-resolution experiments). Other research-grade instruments include a Bruker EMX-EPR spectrometer, flame and furnace atomic absorption spectrometers, UV-visible absorption and FT-IR spectrophotometers, a differential scanning calorimeter, a polarimeter, HPLCs, an Amplitron II Thermolyne instrument for PCR, a Packard Tri-Carb liquid scintillation analyzer, a Beckman L8-70M ultracentrifuge, a GC mass spectrometer, and other specialized equipment. The department has modern microcomputer facilities for data analysis, including several Silicon Graphics Indy workstations and a Silicon Graphics Power Challenge workstation with four R8000 processors. There are also terminals in Jeppson that provide access to the University's VAX computers. Additional mass spectral facilities are available locally, and reactor facilities are available to the department. Students also have access to instrumentation at the Worcester Foundation for Biomedical Research and the University of Massachusetts Medical School and may choose to work toward a Clark degree with affiliate faculty members at these institutions.

Financial Aid

Students with good academic records are eligible for several kinds of financial aid, including tuition scholarships, teaching assistantships, research assistantships, and research fellowships from both private foundations and federal agencies such as the Department of Education and the National Science Foundation. First-year graduate students normally receive full tuition remission and are supported by teaching assistantships. Currently, a teaching assistantship for a twelve-month period, which covers the current academic year and the subsequent summer months, is for a minimum of $12,000. Graduate stipends range from $12,000 to $18,500.

Cost of Study

Tuition for the current academic year is $22,400. Special fees include optional health insurance, a diploma fee of $100 for the master's degree and $150 for the doctorate, and a fee of $200 per semester for students who have completed all formal University and departmental residence requirements.

Living and Housing Costs

Living accommodations for both married and single graduate students are available a short distance from the campus at various costs.

Student Group

Clark University has a total enrollment of about 2,500 students, about 15 percent of whom are graduate students. In the Department of Chemistry and Biochemistry, there are currently 30 full-time graduate students. It is the policy of Clark University that each individual, regardless of race, color, sex, religion, national origin, age, or handicap, shall have equal opportunity in education, employment, or services of the University. The University encourages minorities, women, Vietnam veterans, qualified handicapped individuals, and persons over 40 to apply.

Location

Worcester, a city of diversified industry located in central Massachusetts, is a rapidly emerging educational and cultural center. It has ten schools of higher learning with more than 10,000 students, as well as a modern medical school. Major cultural attractions include the Worcester Art Museum, Higgins Armory Museum, Worcester Historical Society, Worcester Public Library, and American Antiquarian Society. Worcester's civic center, the Centrum, offers a wide variety of popular performing artists and athletic events. The Worcester Music Festival presents an annual series of performances by internationally renowned artists. Boston and Cambridge are less than an hour's drive away.

The University

Clark University was founded as a graduate institution in 1887 and awarded its first doctorate in 1891. Undergraduate liberal arts education was established at Clark in 1902. The University has twenty-seven major buildings situated on a 35-acre campus. The Robert Hutchings Goddard Library opened in 1969 and is nationally known for its design as well as its holdings. It was named in honor of the father of the space age, who was a Clark alumnus and professor of physics at Clark from 1914 until 1942.

Applying

Applications should be received by February 15 for the fall term. However, late applications are periodically considered. Students are encouraged to take the Graduate Record Examinations General Test and Subject Test in chemistry. International students must also submit TOEFL scores. An application fee of $40 is charged.

Correspondence and Information

Coordinator of Graduate Admissions
Department of Chemistry and Biochemistry
Clark University
950 Main Street
Worcester, Massachusetts 01610-1477
Telephone: 508-793-7116
Fax: 508-793-8861
E-mail: chemistry@clarku.edu
World Wide Web: http://www.clarku.edu/~chem/

Clark University

THE FACULTY AND THEIR RESEARCH

Daeg S. Brenner, Professor; Ph.D., MIT, 1964. Nuclear chemistry, characterization of neutron-rich nuclei.

Rafael Brüschweiler, Carlson Chair; Ph.D., ETH Zurich, 1991. Biochemistry, biopolymer structure and dynamics by NMR.

Karen L. Erickson, Professor; Ph.D., Purdue, 1964. Natural products chemistry, metabolites from marine algae.

Frederick T. Greenaway, Professor; Ph.D., Canterbury, 1973. Bioinorganic chemistry, role of transition metals in proteins and drug action.

Alan A. Jones, University Professor and Chairman, Users' Group, NMR Facility; Ph.D., Wisconsin–Madison, 1972. Physical chemistry, study of polymer dynamics by NMR.

Donald J. Nelson, Professor; Ph.D., North Carolina at Chapel Hill, 1972. Physical biochemistry, conformational aspects of ligand binding to proteins.

David L. Thurlow, Associate Professor; Ph.D., Massachusetts, 1981. Biochemistry and molecular biology, molecular basis of protein-RNA interactions.

Edward N. Trachtenberg, Emeritus; Ph.D., Harvard, 1953. Organic chemistry, 1,3-dipolar addition reactions.

Mark M. Turnbull, Associate Professor and Chairman; Ph.D., Brandeis, 1986. Organic and organometallic chemistry, magnetochemistry and transition metal–phosphine complexes.

Wen-Yang Wen, Professor; Ph.D., Pittsburgh, 1957. Physical chemistry, coal chemistry and coal conversion.

Research, Adjunct, and Affiliate Faculty

Halina S. Brown, Professor (adjunct, Clark University Environmental Science and Policy Program); Ph.D., NYU, 1976. Toxicology, environmental policy on environmental policies.

Paul T. Inglefield, Professor, Research Associate, and Director, NMR Facility; Ph.D., British Columbia, 1967. Physical chemistry, NMR characterization of solids.

David Kupfer, Professor (affiliate, Worcester Foundation for Biomedical Research); Ph.D., UCLA, 1958. Biochemistry, role of cytochrome P-450 in prostaglandin hydroxylation.

Christopher P. Landee, Professor (adjunct, Clark University Physics Department); Ph.D., Michigan, 1975. Chemical physics, magnetic behavior of inorganic crystals.

David B. Ludlum, Professor (affiliate, University of Massachusetts Medical School); Ph.D., Wisconsin, 1954; M.D., NYU, 1962. Chemistry of DNA modifications by therapeutic and environmental agents, repair of DNA modifications and detection of low levels of DNA modification.

Timothy A. Lyerla, Professor (adjunct, Clark University Biology Department); Ph.D., Penn State, 1970. Developmental genetics.

William E. Royer Jr., Assistant Professor (affiliate, University of Massachusetts Medical School); Ph.D., Johns Hopkins, 1984. Biophysics, X-ray crystallographic studies of the structural principles governing the assembly of protein molecules.

George E. Wright, Professor (affiliate, University of Massachusetts Medical School); Ph.D., Illinois at Chicago, 1967. Organic and medicinal chemistry, inhibitors of DNA polymerases as chemotherapeutic agents.

The Arthur M. Sackler Sciences Center.

SELECTED PUBLICATIONS

Foy, B. D., et al. **(D. S. Brenner).** Mass measurements of proton-rich medium mass nuclides. *Phys. Rev. C* 58:749–53, 1998.

Uusitalo, J., et al. **(D. S. Brenner).** Decay of the odd-odd N=Z nuclide [78]Y. *Phys. Rev. C* 57:2259–63, 1998.

Barton, C. J., et al. **(D. S. Brenner).** Coulomb excitation of radioactive nuclear beams in inverse kinematics. *Nucl. Instrum. Methods* A391:289–300, 1997.

Brenner, D. S., N. V. Zamfir, and R. F. Casten. Reply to a comment "Shell closure at N=164: Spherical or deformed?" *Phys. Rev. C* 55:974–5, 1997.

Streletz, G., et al. **(D. S. Brenner).** Valence correlation scheme for single nucleon separation energies. *Phys. Rev. C* 54:R2815–9, 1996.

Van Isacker, P., D. D. Warner, and **D. S. Brenner.** A test of Wigner's spin-isospin symmetry from double binding energy differences. *Phys. Rev. Lett.* 74:4607–10, 1995.

Scheurer, C., et al. **(R. Brüschweiler).** Effects of dynamics and environment on 15N chemical shielding anisotropy in proteins. A combination of density functional theory, molecular dynamics simulation and NMR relaxation. *J. Am. Chem. Soc.,* in press.

Màdi, Z. L., **R. Brüschweiler,** and R. R. Ernst. One- and two-dimensional ensemble quantum computing in spin liouville space. *J. Chem. Phys.* 109:10603–11, 1998.

Lienin, S. F., et al. **(R. Brüschweiler).** Anisotropic intramolecular backbone dynamics of ubiquitin characterized by NMR relaxation and MD computer simulation. *J. Am. Chem. Soc.* 120:9870–9, 1998.

Fel'dman, E. B., **R. Brüschweiler,** and R. R. Ernst. From regular to erratic quantum dynamics in long spin ½ chain with an XY Hamiltonian. *Chem. Phys. Lett.* 294:297–304, 1998.

Skrynnikov, N. R., S. F. Lienin, **R. Brüschweiler,** and R. R. Ernst. Efficient scalar spin relaxation in the rotating for matched radio-frequency fields. *J. Chem. Phys.* 108:7662–9, 1998.

Lienin, S. F., **R. Brüschweiler,** and R. R. Ernst. Rotational motion of a solute molecule in a highly viscous liquid studied by 13C NMR: 1, 3-dibromoadamantane in polymeric chlorotrifluoroethene. *J. Magn. Reson.* 131:184–90, 1998.

Brüschweiler, R. Dipolar averaging in NMR spectroscopy: From polarization transfer to cross relaxation. *Prog. NMR Spectroscopy* 32:1–19, 1998.

Brutscher, B., et al. **(R. Brüschweiler).** Quantitative investigation of dipole-CSA cross-correlated relaxation by ZQ/DQ spectroscopy. *J. Magn. Reson.* 130:346–51, 1998.

Brutscher, B., **R. Brüschweiler,** and R. R. Ernst. Backbone dynamics and structural characterization of the partially folded A state of ubiquitin by ^{1}H, ^{13}C and ^{15}N NMR. *Biochemistry* 36:13043–53, 1997.

Du, Z., M. J. Haglund, L. A. Pratt, and **K. L. Erickson.** Carbanionic rearrangements of halomethylenecyclobutanes. The role of the halogen. *J. Org. Chem.* 63:8880, 1998.

Erickson, K. L., J. A. Beutler, J. H. Cardellina II, and M. R. Boyd. Salicylihalamides A and B, novel cytotoxic macrolides from the marine sponge *Haliclona sp. J. Org. Chem.* 62:8188, 1997.

Pettit, G. R., et al. **(K. L. Erickson).** Isolation and crystal structure of stylopeptide 1, a new marine porifera cycloheptapeptide. *J. Org. Chem.* 60:8257, 1995.

Erickson, K. L., J. A. Beutler, J. H. Cardellina II, and M. R. Boyd. Rottnestol, a new hemiketal from the marine sponge *Haliclona. Tetrahedron* 51:11953, 1995.

Erickson, K. L., et al. Majapolene-A, a cytotoxic sesquiterpenoid peroxide and related sesquiterpenoids from the red alga *Laurencia majuscula. J. Nat. Prod.* 58:1848, 1995.

Erickson, K. L., et al. A novel phorbol ester from *Exoecaria agallocha. J. Nat. Prod.* 58:769, 1995.

Greenaway, F. T., J. J. Hahn, N. Xi, and J. R. J. Sorenson. Interaction of copper (II) 3,5-diisopropylsalicylate with human serum albumin—an evaluation of spectroscopic data. *BioMetals* 11:21–6, 1998.

He, Z., D. Nadkarni, L. M. Sayre, and **F. T. Greenaway.** Mechanism-based inactivation of porcine kidney diamine oxidase by 1,4-diamino-2-butene. *Biochem. Biophys. Acta* 1253:117–27, 1995.

He, Z., Y. Zou, and **F. T. Greenaway.** Cyanide inhibition of porcine kidney diamine oxidase and bovine plasma amine oxidase: Evidence for multiple interaction sites. *Arch. Biochem. Biophys.* 319:185–95, 1995.

Greenaway, F. T. Structural aspects of metal ion-drug interactions. In *Handbook on Metal-Ligand Interactions in Biological Fluids. Bioinorganic Chemistry,* vol. 2, pp. 888–98, ed. G. Berthon. Marcel Dekker, 1995.

Castellano, F., Z. He, and **F. T. Greenaway.** Hydroxyl radical production in the reactions of copper-containing amine oxidases with substrates. *Biochim. Biophys. Acta* 1157:162, 1993.

Inglefield, P. T., C. Yang, **W.-Y. Wen,** and **A. A. Jones.** ^{129}Xe NMR of an ionomeric polymer blend system. *Polym. Mater. Sci. Eng. Prepr. (Am. Chem. Soc.)* 78:133, 1998.

English, A. D., **P. T. Inglefield, A. A. Jones,** and Y. Zhu. Polymer segmental dynamics and entanglement constrains. *Polymer* 39:309, 1998.

Inglefield, P. T., C. Yang, **W. -Y. Wen,** and **A. A. Jones.** 129Xe NMR of an ionomeric polymer blend system. *Polym. Mater. Sci. Prepr. (Am. Chem. Soc.)* 78:133–4, 1998.

English, A. D., **P. T. Inglefield, A. A. Jones,** and Y. Zhu. Polymer segmental dynamics and entanglement constrains. *Polym. Prepr. (Am. Chem. Soc., Div. Polym. Chem.)* 38(1):848–9, 1997.

Inglefield, P. T., A. A. Jones, J. M. Koons, and G. E. Pavlovskaya. Spin diffusion in methods for the determination of structure in polymer blends: Zero quantum correlation spectroscopy. *Polym. Prepr. (Am. Chem. Soc., Div. Polym. Chem.)* 38(1):878–9, 1997.

Shi, J.-F, **P. T. Inglefield, A. A. Jones,** and M. D. Meadows. Sub-glass transition motions in linear and crosslinked bisphenol type epoxy resins by deuterium line shape NMR. *Polym. Mater. Sci. Eng. Prepr. (Am. Chem. Soc.)* 74:96–7, 1996.

Zhao, J., **A. A. Jones, P. T. Inglefield,** and J. T. Bendler. A dynamic NMR study of dissolved and solid cyclohexyl polycarbonate. *Polymer* 39:1339, 1998.

Koons, J. M., G. E. Pavlovskaya, **A. A. Jones,** and **P. T. Inglefield.** Determination of interatomic distances by zero-quantum correlation spectroscopy under rotational-resonance conditions. *J. Mag. Res.* 124:499, 1997.

Revett, S. P., G. King, D. F. Hunt, and **D. J. Nelson.** Characterization of a helix-loop-helix (EF hand) motif of silver hake parvalbumin isoform (SHPV-B). *Protein Sci.* 6:2397–408, 1997.

Wang, X.-G., C. Trindle, R. B. Martin, and **D. J. Nelson.** Experimental and theoretical analysis of Al (III) complexation with ADP and ATP. *J. Inorg. Biochem.* 68:7–15, 1997.

Mari, F., et al. **(D. J. Nelson** and **G. E. Wright).** Structural studies by ^{1}H NMR of a prototypic alpha-helical peptide (LYQELQKTQTLK) and homologs in trifluoroethanol/water and on sodium dodecyl sulfate micelles. *J. Peptide Res.* 50:122–31, 1997.

Laney, E. L., et al. **(D. J. Nelson).** The isolation of parvalbumin isoforms from the tail muscle of the American alligator (*Alligator Mississipiensis*). *J. Inorg. Biochem.* 66:67–76, 1997.

Mari, F., X.-J. Xie, J. H. Simpson, and **D. J. Nelson.** Multidimensional NMR investigation of the neurotoxic peptide mastoparan in the absence and presence of calmodulin. In *Biological NMR Spectroscopy,* pp. 169–82, eds. J. L. Markley and S. J. Opella. Oxford University Press, 1997.

Nelson, D. J. Aluminum complexation with nucleoside di- and tri-phosphates and implication in nucleoside binding proteins. *Coord. Chem. Rev.* 149:95–111, 1996.

Rivera, D. T., G. M. Langford, D. G. Weiss, and **D. J. Nelson.** Calmodulin regulates fast axonal transport of squid axoplasm organelles. *Brain Res. Bull.* 37:47–52, 1995.

Wang, X.-G., J. H. Simpson, and **D. J. Nelson.** ^{1}H and ^{31}P NMR study of speciation in systems containing ADP, Al^{3+} and fluoride. *J. Inorg. Biochem.* 58:29–47, 1995.

Zhang, C.-Y., et al. **(D. J. Nelson).** Interaction of spin-labeled silver hake parvalbumin with metal ions and model membranes. *J. Inorg. Biochem.* 52:209–25, 1993.

Clark University

Selected Publications (continued)

Goldshmidt, T. G., et al. **(D. J. Nelson)**. Adsorption and helical coiling of amphipathic peptides on lipid vesicles leads to negligible protection from cathepsin B and cathepsin D. *Immun. Invest.* 22:25–40, 1993.

Li, Z., Y. Sun, and **D. L. Thurlow**. RNA minihelices as model substrates for ATP/CTP:tRNA nucleotidyltransferase. *Biochem. J.* 327:847–51, 1997.

Thurlow, D. L., G. M. Pulido, and K. J. Millar. Unidentified open reading frames in the genome of *Methanococcus jannaschii* are similar in sequence to an archaebacterial gene for tRNA nucleotidyltransferase. *J. Mol. Evol.* 44:686–9, 1997.

Li, Z., et al. **(D. L. Thurlow)**. Effects of nucleotide substitutions within the T-loop of precursor tRNAs on interaction with ATP/CTP:tRNA nucleotidyltransferases from *Escherichia coli* and yeast. *Biochem. J.* 314:49–53, 1996.

Karaoglu, D., and **D. L. Thurlow**. A chemical interference study on the interaction of ribosomal protein L11 from *Escherichia coli* with RNA molecules containing its binding site from 23S rRNA. *Nucleic Acids Res.* 19:5293–300, 1991.

Thurlow, D. L., D. Shilowski, and T. L. Marsh. Nucleotides in precursor tRNAs that are required intact for catalysis by RNase P RNAs. *Nucleic Acids Res.* 19:885–91, 1991.

Hegg, L. A., and **D. L. Thurlow**. Cytidines in tRNAs that are required intact by nucleotidyltransferases from *Escherichia coli* and *Saccharomyces cerevisiae*. *Nucleic Acids Res.* 18:5975–9, 1990.

Hammar, P. R., et al. **(M. M. Turnbull)**. Characterization of a quasi-one-dimensional spin-½ magnet which is gapless and paramagnetic for $g\mu_B H \leq J$ and $k_B T \ll J$. *Phys. Rev. B* 59:1008–15, 1999.

Francisco, M. E. Y., **M. M. Turnbull**, and **K. L. Erickson**. Cartilagineol, the fourth lineage of *Laurencia*-derived polyhalogenated chamigrene. *Tetrahedron Lett.* 39:5289, 1998.

Curtis, N. F., O. P. Gladkikh, and **M. M. Turnbull**. Copper (II) compounds with amine imine ligands; structures of (2,4,6,9,11-pentamethyl-5,8-diazadodeca-4,8-diene-2, 11-diamine) copper (II) perchlorate and (2,4-dimethyl-5,8,11-triazatridec-4-ene-2,13-diamine) copper(II) perchlorate. *Aust. J. Chem.* 51:631–6, 1998.

Prince, B. J., and **M. M. Turnbull**. Synthesis and structure of (2-amino-5-bromopyrimidine)bromocopper(I). *J. Coord. Chem.* 41: 339–45, 1997.

Albrecht, A. S., C. P. Landee, Z. Slanic, and **M. M. Turnbull**. New squares S=½ Heisenberg antiferromagnetic lattices: Pyridinium tetrahalocuprates and bispyrazinecopper(II) tetrafluoroborate. *Mol. Cryst. Liq. Cryst.* 305:333–40, 1997.

Zhang, W., et al. **(M. M. Turnbull)**. Synthesis, X-ray structures and magnetic properties of linear chain 4-cyanopyridine compounds: $[Cu(4\text{-}CNpy)_4(H_2O)](ClO_4)_2$ and $M(4\text{-}CNpy)_2Cl_2$, M=Mn, Fe, Co, Ni and Cu. *Inorg. Chim. Acta* 256:183–98, 1997.

Turnbull, M. M., T. Sugimoto, and L. K. Thompson, eds. *Molecule-Based Magnetic Materials: Theory, Techniques and Applications*. ACS Symposium Series 644. Washington, D.C.: American Chemical Society, 1996.

Koons, J. M., **W.-Y. Wen, P. T. Inglefield**, and **A. A. Jones**. Xenon-129 NMR as a probe of solid polymer sorption and transport. *Polym. Mater. Sci. Eng. Prepr. (Am. Chem. Soc.)* 76:433–4, 1997.

Simpson, J. H., et al. **(W.-Y. Wen, A. A. Jones**, and **P. T. Inglefield)**. Diffusion coefficients of xenon in polystyrene determined by xenon-129 NMR spectroscopy. *Macromolecules* 29:2138–42, 1996.

Simpson, J. H., et al. **(W.-Y. Wen, A. A. Jones**, and **P. T. Inglefield)**. Measurement of diffusion coefficients in polystyrene using xenon-129 NMR. *Appl. Magn. Reson.* 8:349–460, 1995.

Bandis, A., et al. **(W.-Y. Wen, A. A. Jones**, and **P. T. Inglefield)**. NMR study of segmental motion in polyisobutylene and the relationship to translational diffusion of sorbed CO_2. *Am. Chem. Soc., Div. Polym. Chem. Polym. Prep.* 35:427–8, 1994.

Wen, W.-Y. Motion of sorbed gases in polymers. *Chem. Soc. Rev.* 22:117–26, 1993.

CORNELL UNIVERSITY

Field of Chemistry

Program of Study

The diverse research specialties of the graduate faculty include both traditional areas and interdisciplinary expertise in biotechnology, chemical communication, polymer science, and molecular engineering. Cornell's graduate program is designed to provide broad training in the fundamentals of chemistry and research methods and to culminate in the award of the doctorate. In a 1995 survey, the National Research Council of the National Academy of Sciences ranked Cornell's graduate chemistry program sixth among such programs at leading research universities in the country. Several nationally renowned research centers and facilities at Cornell foster inquiry in traditional areas of the discipline and at the interface between chemistry and other physical and biological sciences, engineering, materials science, and mathematics. Graduate students enrolled in the field of chemistry select a major research concentration in one of the following subfields: analytical, bioorganic, biophysical, inorganic, materials, organic, organometallic, physical/chemical physics, polymer, or theoretical. Students also choose a minor concentration from these subfields or a related graduate field, such as materials science or biochemistry. Once major and minor concentrations have been selected, students choose permanent special committees consisting of the research adviser and 2 additional faculty members. First-year graduate students take proficiency examinations in inorganic, organic, and physical chemistry; a level of instruction suited to the student's background and future objectives is then recommended. The number of formal courses required depends on a student's previous preparation, chosen concentration, and the advice of the special committee. Students concentrating in organic chemistry prepare and defend a research proposal. Every student takes an admission-to-candidacy examination within the first two years of study. The Ph.D. is awarded upon completion of an original research project (directed by the chair of the special committee) and successful defense of the thesis.

Research Facilities

Research in the Department of Chemistry and Chemical Biology is supported by several departmental facilities, including the Nuclear Magnetic Resonance Facility, the X-Ray Diffraction Facility, Mass Spectrometry Facility, and Glass Shop. Additional related facilities at Cornell include the Center for High Energy Synchrotron Studies, the Center for Theory and Simulation, the Biotechnology Program in the New York State Center for Advanced Technology, and the Cornell Nanofabrication Facility.

Financial Aid

Fellowships, scholarships, loans, and teaching and research assistantships are available. Nearly all Ph.D. students have assistantship or fellowship support sufficient to cover tuition, fees, and living expenses. Fellowships and scholarships are also offered by state and national government agencies, foundations, and private corporations.

Cost of Study

Tuition and fees for students attending Cornell during the 1998–99 academic year were $22,780. Some increase for 1999–2000 is anticipated.

Living and Housing Costs

Living expenses for the academic year are typically $10,200 to $13,800 for single students. Additional expenses may include travel and medical and dental costs. The University maintains married student housing and graduate dormitory accommodations on and near the campus. Privately owned accommodations are available nearby.

Student Group

There are 126 graduate students currently enrolled in the Ph.D. program in the Department of Chemistry and Chemical Biology.

Location

Ithaca, a city of about 30,000 people, is located on Cayuga Lake in the beautiful Finger Lakes region of central New York State. The home of both Ithaca College and Cornell, the city is one of the country's great educational communities, offering cultural advantages that rival those of many large cities. Recreational activities, including hiking, cycling, boating, and skiing, abound. Light industry and technical and consulting firms are active in the area.

The University and The Department

Cornell University, founded in 1865 by Ezra Cornell, is composed of fourteen colleges and schools. Several of these schools and colleges were established under the land-grant college system and are part of the State University of New York; others, are privately endowed. The Department of Chemistry and Chemical Biology occupies more than 300,000 square feet of space in the recently renovated Baker Laboratory and the adjacent S. T. Olin Laboratory.

Applying

Only students who expect to complete a doctoral program (Ph.D.) should apply. Application to the graduate field of chemistry at Cornell is accepted for fall admission only. Early submission of applications is strongly encouraged, with applications being evaluated as early as December 1. Completed applications received before January 15 may also serve as applications for Cornell fellowships. Transcripts of all grades (whether or not a degree was conferred) and three letters of recommendation are required. Applications must include GRE General Test scores and one GRE Subject Test score in chemistry. International applicants must demonstrate proficiency in English, usually by submitting scores on the TOEFL. Minimum scores of 600, with at least a score of 60 in each of the three categories, are required for application consideration.

Correspondence and Information

Graduate Coordinator
Field of Chemistry
Baker Laboratory
Cornell University
Ithaca, New York 14853-1301
Telephone: 607-255-4139
Fax: 607-255-4137
E-mail: chemgrad@cornell.edu
World Wide Web: http://www.chem.cornell.edu

Cornell University

FACULTY

H. D. Abruña, Ph.D., North Carolina. Electrochemistry, chemically modified electrodes, biosensor, underpotential deposition of metals, X-ray–based techniques.

A. C. Albrecht, Ph.D. Washington (Seattle). Nonlinear spectroscopies with biophysical applications: theory and experiment.

B. A. Baird, Ph.D., Cornell. Structures and signal transduction mechanisms of cell surface receptors involved in immunological responses.

S. H. Bauer, Ph.D. Chicago. Kinetics of very fast gas phase reactions, shock tube pyrolysis, mechanisms of cluster production from supersaturated vapors, oxidation of boron hydrides.

T. P. Begley, Ph.D., Caltech. Bioorganic chemistry, enzymatic reaction mechanisms, DNA photochemistry, prolyl-4-hydroxylase, thiamine biosynthesis.

J. T. Brenna, Ph.D., Cornell. High-precision gas isotope ratio mass spectrometry, interfaces and data processing, ^{13}C and D labeled tracers, mammalian unsaturated fatty acid metabolism.

J. M. Burlitch, Ph.D., MIT. Inorganic chemistry of materials, synthesis, ceramics, nanocomposites, metal-to-ceramic adhesion.

B. K. Carpenter, Ph.D., University College (London). Mechanisms and dynamics of organic reactions, structures and properties of reactive intermediates, combustion reactions, neurochemistry.

R. A. Cerione, Ph.D., Rutgers. Structure and function of small molecular G proteins, cellular signal transduction.

J. C. Clardy, Ph.D., Harvard. Studies of biologically important compounds.

G. W. Coates, Ph.D., Stanford. Stereoselective catalysis, organic and polymer synthesis, reaction mechanisms.

D. B. Collum, Ph.D., Columbia. Organotransition metal and organolithium reaction mechanism, development of organometallic chemistry for organic synthesis.

H. F. Davis, Ph.D., Berkeley. Chemical reaction dynamics using laser and molecular beam techniques.

F. J. DiSalvo, Ph.D., Stanford. Solid-state chemistry, synthesis and structure, electrical and magnetic properties.

S. E. Ealick, Ph.D., Oklahoma. X-ray crystallography of macromolecules, applications of synchrotron radiation, enzymes of nucleotide metabolism, enzyme mechanism, structure-based drug design.

G. S. Ezra, Ph.D., Oxford. Theoretical chemical physics, intramolecular dynamics, semiclassical mechanics, electron correlation.

R. C. Fay, Ph.D., Illinois. Inorganic stereochemistry, kinetics and mechanism of molecular rearrangements.

J. H. Freed, Ph.D., Columbia. Theoretical and experimental studies of molecular dynamics and structure by magnetic resonance spectroscopy.

B. Ganem, Ph.D., Columbia. Synthetic organic and bioorganic chemistry, methods and reactions for the synthesis of rare natural products and biologically active compounds.

E. P. Giannelis, Ph.D., Michigan State. Materials chemistry, polymer nanocomposites, self-assembling systems.

G. P. Hess, Ph.D., Berkeley. Reaction mechanisms on cell surfaces, transient kinetics and laser-pulse photolysis.

M. A. Hines, Ph.D., Stanford. Reaction mechanisms in semiconductor surface chemistry, scanning tunneling microscopy.

R. Hoffmann, Ph.D., Harvard. Electronic structure of organic, organometallic, and inorganic molecules and extended structures, transition states and reaction intermediates.

P. L. Houston, Ph.D., MIT. Chemical kinetics and reaction dynamics.

S. Lee, Ph.D., Chicago. Materials chemistry, synthesis structure and electronic structure of entended solids.

R. F. Loring, Ph.D., Stanford. Theoretical chemical physics, polymer dynamics, nonequilibrium statistical mechanics.

J. A. Marohn, Ph.D., Caltech. Scanned-probe microscopy investigations of novel magnetic and electronic materials.

F. W. McLafferty, Ph.D., Cornell. Mass spectrometry, characterization of large (~100 kDa) biomolecules.

J. E. McMurry, Ph.D., Columbia. Textbook author.

J. Meinwald, Ph.D., Harvard. Organic chemistry; insect chemical ecology; characterization, biosynthesis, and synthesis of natural products.

G. H. Morrison, Ph.D., Princeton. Trace and microanalysis, ion microscopy, ion microprobe, mass spectrometry of solids.

C. K. Ober, Ph.D., Massachusetts. Polymer synthesis, self-assembling materials, microlithography, liquid crystalline polymers.

T. N. Rhodin, Ph.D., Princeton. Solid-state physical chemistry applications of molecular phenomena at surfaces.

H. A. Scheraga, Ph.D., Duke. Physical chemical studies of proteins and aqueous solutions.

D. Y. Sogah, Ph.D., UCLA. Supramolecular chemistry, polypeptide and carbohydrate-based polymers, group transfer polymerization; living free-radical polymerization; hyperbranched and helical polymers; organic-inorganic nanocomposites.

D. A. Usher, Ph.D., Cambridge. Polynucleotide analogs, template reactions, chemical evolution.

B. Widom, Ph.D., Cornell. Statistical mechanics of phase transitions, critical phenomena, and interfaces.

C. F. Wilcox, Ph.D. UCLA. Elucidation of the relationship between molecular structure and energy by theoretical analysis and synthesis of selected novel molecules.

P. T. Wolczanski, Ph.D., Caltech. Synthesis and reactivity of transition metal complexes, materials preparation.

D. B. Zax, Ph.D., Berkeley. NMR studies of novel polymeric materials and unusual irradiation sequences.

Analytical Chemistry
H. D. Abruña, J. T. Brenna, R. A. Cerione, J. A. Marohn, F. W. McLafferty, G. H. Morrison, D. B. Zax

Bioorganic Chemistry
T. P. Begley, J. C. Clardy, G. W. Coates, B. Ganem, F. W. McLafferty, J. E. McMurry, J. Meinwald, D. Y. Sogah, D. A. Usher

Biophysical Chemistry
B. A. Baird, J. C. Clardy, S. E. Ealick, J. H. Freed, G. P. Hess, H. A. Scheraga

Inorganic Chemistry
H. D. Abruña, J. M. Burlitch, G. W. Coates, D. B. Collum, F. J. DiSalvo, R. C. Fay, R. Hoffmann, S. Lee, P. T. Wolczanski, D. B. Zax

Materials Chemistry
H. D. Abruña, J. M. Burlitch, G. W. Coates, F. J. DiSalvo, E. P. Giannelis, M. A. Hines, R. Hoffmann, P. L. Houston, S. Lee, C. K. Ober, D. Y. Sogah, P. T. Wolczanski, D. B. Zax

Organic Chemistry
T. P. Begley, B. K. Carpenter, J. C. Clardy, G. W. Coates, D. B. Collum, B. Ganem, F. W. McLafferty, J. E. McMurry, J. Meinwald, D. Y. Sogah, D. A. Usher, C. F. Wilcox, P. T. Wolczanski

Organometallic Chemistry
G. W. Coates, D. B. Collum, P. T. Wolczanski

Physical/Chemical Physics Chemistry
H. D. Abruña, A. C. Albrecht, B. A. Baird, S. H. Bauer, H. F. Davis, F. J. DiSalvo, G. S. Ezra, J. H. Freed, M. A. Hines, R. Hoffmann, P. L. Houston, R. F. Loring, J. A. Marohn, T. N. Rhodin, H. A. Scheraga, B. Widom, D. B. Zax

Polymer Chemistry
G. W. Coates, E. P. Giannelis, R. Hoffmann, R. F. Loring, C. K. Ober, H. A. Scheraga, D. Y. Sogah

Theoretical Chemistry
A. C. Albrecht, G. S. Ezra, J. H. Freed, R. Hoffmann, S. Lee, R. F. Loring, H. A. Scheraga, B. Widom, C. F. Wilcox

SELECTED PUBLICATIONS

Pang, D.-W., and **H. D. Abruña.** Micromethod for investigation of the interactions between DNA and redox-active molecules. *Anal. Chem.* 70:3162, 1998.

Lorenzo, E., et al. **(H. D. Abruña).** Analytical strategies for amperometric biosensors based on chemically modified electrodes. *Biosensors Bioelect.* 13:319, 1998.

Albrecht, A. C., J. C. Kirkwood, D. J. Ulness, and M. J. Stimson. Coherent raman scattering with incoherent light for a multiply resonant mixture: Theory. *Phys. Rev. A* 57:1417, 1998.

Albrecht, A. C., J. C. Kirkwood, and D. J. Ulness. Electronically nonresonant coherent raman scattering using incoherent light: Two Brownian oscillator approaches. *J. Chem. Phys.* 108:9425, 1998.

Xu, K., B. Goldstein, D. Holowka, and **B. A. Baird.** Kinetics of multivalent antigen DNP-BSA binding to IgE-FcεRI in relationship to stimulated tyrosine phosphorylation of FcεRI. *J. Immunol.* 160:3225, 1998.

Pierini, L. M., N. T. Harris, D. Holowka, and **B. A. Baird.** Evidence supporting a role for microfilaments in regulating the coupling between aggregated FcεRI and downstream signaling pathways. *Biochemistry* 36:7447, 1997.

Yu, C.-L., and **S. H. Bauer.** The thermochemistry of the boranes. *J. Phys. Chem. Ref. Data,* in press.

Zhang, Y.-X., C.-L. Yu, and **S. H. Bauer.** The pyrolysis of azetidine: A shock-tube kinetics investigation. *Int. J. Chem. Kin.* 30:185, 1998.

Compobasso, N., et al. **(T. P. Begley).** The structure of thiaminase I from *Bacillus thiaminolyticus.* Accepted for publication in *Biochemistry.*

Taylor, S., et al. **(T. P. Begley).** Thiamin biosynthesis in *E.coli.:* Identification of ThiS thiocarboxylate as the immediate sulfur donor in the thiazole formation. *J. Biol. Chem.* 273:16555, 1998.

Brenna, J. T., T. N. Corso, H. J. Tobias, and R. J. Caimi. High precision continuous flow isotope ratio mass spectrometry. *Mass Spec. Rev.* 16:227, 1997.

Brenna, J. T. The use of stable isotopes to study fatty acid and lipoprotein metabolism in man. *Prostaglandins, Leukotrienes Essent. Fatty Acids* 57(4 and 5):467, 1997.

Agladze, N. I., et al. **(J. M. Burlitch).** Laboratory results on millimeter-wave absorption in silicate grain materials at cryogenic temperatures. *Astrophys. J.* 462:1026, 1996.

Jones, S. A., and **J. M. Burlitch.** Nickel-alumina composites: In situ synthesis by a displacement reaction, and mechanical properties. *Mater. Res. Soc. Symp. Proc.* 365:53, 1995.

Reyes, M. B., and **B. K. Carpenter.** Evidence for interception of nonstatistical reactive trajectories for a singlet biradical in supercritical propane. *J. Am. Chem. Soc.* 120:1641, 1998.

Jones, G. A., **B. K. Carpenter,** and M. N. Paddon-Row. Application of surface-hopping trajectories to the study of intramolecular electron transfer in polyatomic organic systems. *J. Am. Chem. Soc.* 120:5499, 1998.

Sandler, B., M. Murakami, and **J. C. Clardy.** Atomic structure of the trypsin-aeruginosin 98-B complex. *J. Am. Chem. Soc.* 120:595, 1998.

Schultz, L. W., and **J. C. Clardy.** Chemical inducers of dimerization: The atomic structure of FKBP12-FK1012A-FKBP12. *Bioorg. Med. Chem. Lett.* 8:1, 1998.

Grubbs, R. H., and **G. W. Coates.** α-Agostic interactions and olefin insertion in metallocene polymerization catalysts. *Acc. Chem. Res.* 29:85, 1996.

Coates, G. W., and R. M. Waymouth. Oscillating stereocontrol: A strategy for the synthesis of thermoplastic elastomeric polypropylene. *Science* 267:222, 1995.

Thompson, A., et al. **(D. B. Collum).** Lithium ephedrate-mediated 1,2-addition of a lithium acetylide to a ketone: Solution structures and relative reactivities of mixed aggregates underlying the high enantioselectivities. *J. Am. Chem. Soc.* 120:2028, 1998.

Remenar, J. F., and **D. B. Collum.** Lithium diisopropylamide-mediated dehydro-bromination: Evidence of competitive monomer- and open dimer-based pathways. *J. Am. Chem. Soc.* 120:4081, 1998.

Willis, P. A., R. Z. Hinrichs, H. U. Stauffer, and **H. F. Davis.** Rotatable source crossed beams apparatus with pulsed VUV photoionization detection. Submitted to *Rev. Sci. Instrum.*

Willis, P. A., R. Z. Hinrichs, H. U. Stauffer, and **H. F. Davis.** The reaction dynamics of Zr and Nb with ethylene. Submitted to *J. Chem. Phys.*

Niewa, R., et al. **(F. J. DiSalvo).** Unusual bonding in ternary nitrides: Preparation, structure and properties of Ce_2MnN_3. *Z. Naturforsh.* 53b:63, 1998.

Gelabert, M. C., et al. **(F. J. DiSalvo).** Structure and properties of $Ba_6Ni_{25}S_{27}$. *Chem.: Eur. J.* 3:1884, 1997.

Deacon, A. M., C. M. Weeks, R. Miller, and **S. E. Ealick.** The shake-and-bake structure determination of triclinic lysozyme. *Proc. Natl. Acad. Sci. U.S.A.* 95:9284, 1998.

Pugmire, M. J., et al. **(S. E. Ealick).** Structural and theoretical studies suggest domain movement produce an active conformation of thymidine phosphorylase. *J. Mol. Biol.* 281:285, 1998.

Ezra, G. S. Classical trajectory studies of intramolecular dynamics: Local mode dynamics, rotation-vibration interaction and the structure of multidimensional phase space. In *Intramolecular Dynamics and Nonlinear Dynamics,* ed. W. L. Hase. Greenwich, Connecticut: JAI Press, 1992.

Ezra, G. S., K. Richter, G. Tanner, and D. Wintgen. Semiclassical cycle expansion for the helium atom. *J. Phys. B* 24:L413, 1991.

Weir, J. R., and **R. C. Fay.** Stereochemistry and metal-centered rearrangements of eight-coordinate niobium(V) and tantalum(V) dithiocarbamates and monothiocarbamates. *Inorg. Chem.* 25:2969, 1986.

Lindmark, A. F., and **R. C. Fay.** Nuclear magnetic resonance studies of inversion and diketonate R-group exchange in dialkoxybis(β-diketonato)titanium(IV) complexes. Evidence for a twist mechanism. *J. Am. Chem. Soc.* 105:2118, 1983.

Patyal, B., R. H. Crepeau, and **J. H. Freed.** Lipid-gramicidin interactions using two-dimensional fourier-transform electron spin resonance. *Biophys. J.* 73:2201, 1997.

Barnes, J. P., and **J. H. Freed.** Dynamics and ordering in mixed model membranes of DMPC and DMPS: A 250 GHz ESR study. *Biophys. J.* 75, 1998.

Schoenfield, R. C., and **B. Ganem.** Synthesis of ceratinamine and moloka'iamine: Antifouling agents from the marine sponge *Pseudoceratina purpurea. Tetrahedron Lett.* 39:4147, 1998.

Lang, F., D. J. Kassab, and **B. Ganem.** Neighboring group effects in the regioselective cyclization of vicinal trans-1,2-bromohydrins to epoxides. *Tetrahedron Lett.* 39:5903, 1998.

Vaia, R. H., and **E. P. Giannelis.** Lattice model of polymer melt intercalation in organically-modified layerd silicates. *Macromolecules* 30:7990, 1997.

Vaia, R. A., B. B. Sauer, O. K. Tse, and **E. P. Giannelis.** Relaxations of confined chains in polymer nanocomposites: Glass transition properties of poly(ethylene oxide) intercalated in montmorillonite. *J. Poly. Sci. B: Poly. Phys.* 35:59, 1997.

Ulrich, H., et al. **(G. P. Hess).** In vitro selection of RNA molecules that displace cocaine from the membrane-bound nicotinic receptor. *Proc. Natl. Acad. Sci. U.S.A.,* in press.

Li, H., L. Avery, W. Denk, and **G. P. Hess.** Identification of chemical synapses in the pharynx of *Caenorhabiditis elegans. Proc. Natl. Acad. Sci. U.S.A.* 94:5912, 1997.

Flidr, J., Y.-C. Huang, T. A. Newton, and **M. A. Hines.** Extracting site-specific reaction rates from steady state surface morphologies: Kinetic Monte Carlo simulations of aqueous Si(111) etching. *J. Chem. Phys.* 108:5542, 1998.

Hines, M. A., Y. J. Chabal, T. D. Harris, and A. L. Harris. Raman studies of steric hindrance and surface relaxation on stepped H-terminated silicon surfaces. *Phys. Rev. Lett.* 71:2280, 1993.

Hoffmann, R. A. Qualitative thinking in the age of modern computational chemistry. *J. Mol. Struct. (Theochem.)* 424:1, 1998.

Liu, Q., N. Goldberg, and **R. A. Hoffmann.** 2,3-connected tellurium net and the Cs_3Te_{22} phase. *Chem. Eur. J.* 390, 1996.

Miller, R. L., et al. **(P. L. Houston).** The "ozone deficit" problem:

Cornell University

Selected Publications (continued)

Observation of an $O_2(X\upsilon\text{-}26) + O(^3P)$ channel in the 226-nm photodissociation of ozone. *Science* 265:1831, 1994.

Houston, P. L. Correlated photochemistry: The legacy of Johann Christian Doppler. *Acc. Chem. Res.* 22:309, 1989.

DiMasi, E., et al. **(S. Lee).** Chemical pressure and charge density waves in rare earth polytellurides. *Phys. Rev. B* 52:404, 1995.

Venkataraman, D., **S. Lee,** J. Zhang, and J. S. Moore. An organic solid with wide channels based on hydrogen bonding between macrocycles. *Nature* 371:591, 1994.

Spencer, C. F., and **R. F. Loring.** Dephasing of a solvated two-level system: A semiclassical approach for parallel computing. *J. Chem. Phys.* 105:6596, 1996.

Schvaneveldt, S. J., and **R. F. Loring.** Vibrational dephasing of a polar solute in a fused salt. *J. Phys. Chem.* 100:10355, 1996.

Marohn, J. A., R. Fainchtein, and D. S. Smith. An optimal magnetic tip configuration for magnetic resonance force microscopy of microscale buried features. *Appl. Phys. Lett.* 73(25):3778–80, 1998.

Marohn, J. A., et al. Optical larmor beat detection of high-resolution nuclear magnetic resonance in a semiconductor heterostructure. *Phys. Rev. Lett.* 75:1364–7, 1995.

Zubarev, R. A., N. L. Kelleher, and **F. W. McLafferty.** Electron capture dissociation of multiply charged protein cations. *J. Am. Chem. Soc.* 120:3265, 1998.

McLafferty, F. W., et al. Gaseous conformers of cytochrome *c. J. Am. Chem. Soc.* 120:4732, 1998.

McMurry, J. E., and M. Castellion. *Fundamentals of General, Organic, and Biological Chemistry,* 3rd Ed. Upper Saddle River, New Jersey: Prentice-Hall, 1999.

McMurry, J. E. *Organic Chemistry,* 4th Ed. Pacific Grove, Calif.: Brooks/Cole, 1996.

Eisner, T., et al. **(J. Meinwald).** Firefly "femmes fatales" acquire defensive steroids (Lucibufagins) from their firefly prey. *Proc. Natl. Acad. Sci. U.S.A.* 94:9723, 1997.

Eisner, T., and **J. Meinwald** (eds.). *Chemical Ecology: The Chemistry of Biotic Interaction.* Washington, D.C.: National Academy Press, 1995.

Chandra, S., and **G. H. Morrison.** Imaging ion and molecular transport at subcellular resolution by secondary ion mass spectrometry. *Int. J. Mass Spect. Ion Pro.* 143:161, 1995.

Chandra, S., et al. **(G. H. Morrison).** Imaging of total intracellular calcium and calcium influx and efflux in individual resting and stimulated tumor mast cells using ion microscopy. *J. Biol. Chem.* 269:15186, 1994.

Körner, H., A. Shiota, **C. K. Ober,** and T. Bunning. Orientation-on-demand thin films: Curing of liquid crystalline networks in AC electric fields. *Science* 272:252, 1996.

Chen, J. T., E. L. Thomas, **C. K. Ober,** and G.-P. Mao. Novel self-assembled smectic phases in rod-coil block copolymers. *Science* 273:343, 1996.

Rhodin, T. N., and C. Paulsen-Boaz. Overview on surface microstructuring by photodesorption etching of chlorinated silicon. *Prog. Surface Sci.* 54(3/4):287, 1997.

Rhodin, T. N. Mechanisms and models for photodesorption from semiconductor surfaces (review). *Prog. Surface Sci.* 50:131, 1995.

Wawak, R. J., et al. **(H. A. Scheraga).** Diffusion equation and distance scaling methods of global optimization: Applications to crystal structure prediction. *J. Phys. Chem.* 102:2904, 1998.

Maurer, M. C., et al. **(H. A. Scheraga).** Structural examination of the influence of phosphorylation on the binding of fibrin-opeptide A to bovine thrombin. *Biochemistry* 37:5888, 1998.

Puts, R. D., and **D. Y. Sogah.** Cationic ring-opening cyclopolymerization of bis(oxazolines). Synthesis of chiral polymers containing pendent heteromacrocycles. *Macromolecules* 30:6826, 1997.

Zheng, S., and **D. Y. Sogah.** Highly isotactic optically active methacrylate polymers by free radical cyclopolymerization. *Tetrahedron* 53:15469, 1997.

Harris, M., and **D. A. Usher.** A new amide-linked polynucleotide analog. *Origins Life Evol. Biosphere* 26:398, 1996.

Usher, D. A. Before antisense. *Antisense Nucl. Acid Drug Dev.* 7:445, 1997.

van Giessen, A. E., D. J. Bukman, and **B. Widom.** Contact angles of liquid drops on low-energy solid surfaces. *J. Coll. Interf. Sci.* 192:257, 1997.

Bukman, D. J., and **B. Widom.** Fluctuations in the structure of three-phase lines. *Physica A* 251:27, 1998.

Wilcox, C. F., and E. N. Farley. Dicyclooctyl[1,2,3,4-def:1'2'3'4'-jkl]-biphenylene: Benzenoid atropism in a highly antiaromatic polycycle. *J. Am. Chem. Soc.* 105:7191, 1983.

Wilcox, C. F. A topological definition of resonance energy. *Croat. Chim. Acta* 47:87, 1975.

Schafer II, D. F., and **P. T. Wolczanski.** d^0 Alkane complexes $(^tBu_3SiN=)_3$ W(RH) precede C-H activation and formation of $(^tBu_3SiN=)_2(^tBuSiNH)$ WR/R'. *J. Am. Chem. Soc.* 120:4881, 1998.

Vaid, T. P., et al. **(P. T. Wolcanski).** A structural dichotomy in 6-coordinate d^0 complexes: Trigonal prismatic $(^tBu_3SiC\!-\!C)_6Ta^-$ and octahedral $(^tBu_3SiC\!-\!C)_6M^{2-}$ (M=Zr, Hf). *J. Am. Chem. Soc.* 120:10067, 1998.

Yang, D.-K., J. E. Atkins, C. C. Lester, and **D. B. Zax.** New developments in NMR using noise spectroscopy. *Mol. Phys.,* in press.

Yang, D.-K., and **D. B. Zax.** Bandwidth extension in noise spectroscopy, submitted.

DREXEL UNIVERSITY

College of Arts and Sciences
Department of Chemistry

Programs of Study

The Department of Chemistry at Drexel offers both M.S. and Ph.D. degrees in chemistry. These degrees can be earned full-time or part-time. The M.S. degree is awarded to students who show sufficient competence at the advanced level in all areas of chemistry. Two options, thesis and nonthesis, are available.

The Ph.D. degree is conferred in recognition of breadth of scholarship and scientific attainment plus demonstrated ability to investigate scientific problems independently and efficiently. Areas of concentration include analytical, inorganic, organic, physical, and polymer chemistry and chemical education. Requirements of the program include course work, candidacy exams, and successful completion of a publishable Ph.D. thesis. The candidacy exams consist of written cumulative exams (five out of fifteen must be passed) and an original research proposal.

Research Facilities

Research is conducted in two chemical laboratories, Disque and Stratton Halls. The department provides a wide variety of state-of-the-art instruments. Instrumentation includes several mass spectrometers (with GC, exact mass, FAB, and MALTI capability), two FT-NMRs (90- and 250-MHz), ESR, CD, AA, Mössbauer, fluorescence, several FT-IRs, and several UV-visible spectrophotometers. A variety of lasers (nitrogen, rare gas excimer, and tunable dye), photolysis equipment, a DSC, a differential refractometer, and a recording polarimeter are available. Chromatographs include several HPLC and numerous GC instruments. Numerous microcomputers are available, many of which are interfaced with research instruments. An extensive campus computer network exists.

Financial Aid

Most full-time graduate students in the department hold teaching or research assistantships. Stipends range from $9775 to $11,200 per calendar year, and these assistantships typically include full tuition remission. Only a very select group of applicants is awarded assistantships. Information on loans and other forms of aid is provided by the Financial Aid Office.

Cost of Study

Tuition in the Department of Chemistry is $585 per credit hour in 1999–2000; there are 45 required credits for the M.S. and 90 credits for the Ph.D. The University general fee is $125 per term for full-time students and $67 per term for part-time students.

Living and Housing Costs

Ample housing is available in the University City neighborhood and environs. Living expenses for a single student are estimated at $11,450 per year.

Student Group

The department currently enrolls 62 students in its graduate programs. With 13 tenure-track faculty members, the student-faculty ratio is excellent. The majority of graduates from the chemistry program are employed in the chemical or pharmaceutical industries, in government research laboratories conducting a wide variety of basic research, and in academic settings.

Location

A city of more than 2 million, Philadelphia is a center of science, industry, and culture. With some forty colleges and universities in the metropolitan area, it is the second-largest community of institutions of higher education in the country. The University, easily reached from all parts of the area by bus, subway, railroad, and auto, is only a few minutes' walk from the heart of a city steeped in history. The city's flourishing cultural life is based in its museums and centers for theater, opera, symphony concerts, and ballet. Philadelphia also supports a number of major sports, including professional football, ice hockey, baseball, and basketball. Facilities for a variety of intramural sports are available at colleges and universities throughout the city.

The University

Drexel, founded in 1891 by Anthony J. Drexel, Philadelphia financier and philanthropist, was originally the Drexel Institute of Art, Science and Industry. For many years designated the Drexel Institute of Technology, Drexel formally became a university in the 1969–70 academic year. It now comprises five coeducational units: the Colleges of Arts and Sciences, Design Arts, Engineering, Business and Administration, and Information Studies.

Applying

Students are normally admitted for the fall quarter, which begins in late September, but they may enter the program at the beginning of any quarter. A bachelor's degree or its equivalent from an accredited university is a prerequisite. Applicants who wish to be considered for assistantships must submit their application by February 1. Application forms and additional information may be obtained from the address below.

Correspondence and Information

Office of Graduate Admissions, Box P
Drexel University
Philadelphia, Pennsylvania 19104
Telephone: 215-895-6700
E-mail: admissions-grad@post.drexel.edu

Drexel University

THE FACULTY AND THEIR RESEARCH

A. W. Addison, Ph.D., Kent at Canterbury. Inorganic and biophysical chemistry: molecular architecture of oxygen-binding and electron-transfer metalloproteins, synthesis and chemistry of biomimetic inorganic complexes, electrochemistry of small molecules, ESR spectroscopy of copper(II) compounds, spectroscopy of metalloproteins.

A. R. Bandy, Ph.D., Florida. Atmospheric and analytical chemistry: chemistry of trace reduced sulfur and hydrocarbon compounds in the atmosphere, relationship between naturally emitted hydrocarbons and photochemical oxidation.

J. P. Friend, Ph.D., Columbia. Atmospheric chemistry: atmospheric photochemistry, atmospheric transport of reacting species, global cycles of atmospheric trace constituents, formation of atmospheric nuclei, chemistry of atmospheric pollutants, atmospheric turbulent diffusion, modeling of atmospheric transport phenomena.

R. O. Hutchins, Ph.D., Purdue. Organic chemistry: conformational analysis and stereochemistry; new selective synthetic techniques, including asymmetric synthesis; neighboring group participation in bicyclic systems; phosphorus chemistry.

J.G. Kay, Ph.D., Kansas. Atmospheric, inorganic, and physical chemistry: radon, radon progeny, and other radiotracers in the atmosphere; fully automated instrumentation for detection and analysis of trace levels of radon in air; gas transport across air-water interfaces; single-atom laser studies of radon in air; matrix isolation with UV, visible, and IR spectroscopic studies of ruthenium oxides; electronic and molecular structures of small molecules evaporated from refractory metal oxides.

F. R. Longo, Ph.D., Pennsylvania. Physical chemistry and biochemistry:spectral and catalytic properties of porphyrins; structure of and reactions in microemulsions, including light scattering luminescence quenching, and catalytic hydrolysis of esters.

A. Nath, Ph.D., Moscow. Physical chemistry: isotopic exchange in the solid state; charge injection, electrons and holes; auger aftereffects; chemistry of vitamin B12; study of high temperature superconductors using emission Mössbauer spectroscopy.

K. G. Owens, Ph.D., Indiana. Analytical/physical chemistry: laser desorption/laser ionization time-of-flight mass spectrometry, supersonic jet spectroscopy, application of computers and chemometrics in new areas of chemistry.

C. M. Rosenthal, Ph.D., Harvard. Chemical physics: application of space-filling curves and line integral representations to scattering problems.

A. L. Smith, Ph.D., MIT. Physical chemistry: thermodynamic and spectroscopic properties of the fullerenes; laser spectroscopy, thermodynamics, and kinetics of the molecular species of elemental sulfur; computers in chemical research and education.

S. D. Solomon, Ph.D., Pennsylvania. Chemical education: courseware development, including highly interactive microcomputer applications, innovative lecture demonstrations, and project-oriented laboratory experiments; effective integration of principles with applications in textbook authoring.

P. A. Wade, Ph.D., Purdue. Organic chemistry: natural product synthesis, especially aminosugars and related compounds; heterocycles as synthetic intermediates; the chemistry of novel strained-ring nitro compounds; reactive intermediates; stereoselective processes; new synthetic methods.

Y. Wei, Ph.D., CUNY. Polymer and materials chemistry: electrically conductive polymers; stereochemistry and mechanism of polymerization; organic-inorganic molecular composites; high-temperature superconductors; solid-state organic chemistry.

DUQUESNE UNIVERSITY

School of Natural and Environmental Sciences
Department of Chemistry and Biochemistry

Program of Study

The Department of Chemistry and Biochemistry offers a program of graduate study in chemistry and biochemistry leading to the Ph.D. and M.S. degrees.

Graduate students begin laboratory research during their first semester in residence and participate in two semester-long research rotations in the laboratories of two different investigators during their first year. First-year students enroll in several short, intensive courses that emphasize applied research skills. Students typically do not enroll in any other courses during the first year, allowing complete focus upon research during this period. At the end of the first year, students are advanced to Ph.D. candidacy based upon successful completion and defense of their research rotation projects. Academic requirements during the second and subsequent years are determined by the student's dissertation committee and are designed on an individual basis. Candidates for the Ph.D. degree are required to submit and defend an original research proposal in an area unrelated to their dissertation research. The department sponsors a weekly research colloquium series that features speakers from academia, industry, and government.

For the M.S. degree, a minimum of 30 semester hours of combined course and research credits are required.

Research Facilities

The Department of Chemistry and Biochemistry is housed in the Richard King Mellon Hall of Science, an award-winning laboratory designed by Mies van der Rohe. Spectroscopic capability within the department includes multinuclear 500- and 300-MHz NMRs, GC/MS, laser Raman, FT-IR, UV/visible, fluorescence, and atomic absorption spectroscopies. Separations instrumentation includes ultra-high-speed and high-speed centrifuges, gas chromatographs, an ion chromatographic system, capillary electrophoresis, and HPLCs. An electrochemical instrumentation laboratory, a robotics and automation facility, a computer-controlled chemical microwave system, a clean laboratory facility, a single-crystal X-ray diffraction facility, and ICP-MS capabilities are available for research.

Financial Aid

A number of teaching and research assistantships are available for Ph.D students. Annual stipends are $15,500, plus tuition remission, for 1999–2000.

Cost of Study

Tuition and fees in 1999–2000 are $557 per credit. Scholarships provide tuition remission for teaching and research assistants as described above.

Living and Housing Costs

Off-campus housing is available within easy walking or commuting distance of the University. Living costs for off-campus housing are very reasonable compared with those in other urban areas of the United States.

Student Group

Duquesne University has a total enrollment of more than 9,500 students in its ten schools. With 176 graduate students and 36 faculty members in the graduate programs in the Bayer School of Natural and Environmental Sciences, the University offers students a highly personalized learning and advisement environment.

Location

Duquesne University is located on a bluff overlooking the city of Pittsburgh. This location offers ready access to the many cultural, social, and entertainment attractions of the city. Within walking distance of the campus are Heinz Hall for the Performing Arts (home of the symphony, opera, ballet, theater, and other musical and cultural institutions), the Civic Arena (center for indoor sporting events and various exhibitions, concerts, and conventions), Three Rivers Stadium (for outdoor sporting events), and Market Square (entertainment and nightlife center). The libraries, museums, art galleries, and music hall of the Carnegie Institute in the Oakland area are easily accessible by public transportation (routes pass immediately adjacent to the campus) or by private automobile. As the third-largest center for corporate headquarters and one of the twenty largest metropolitan areas in the United States, Pittsburgh also offers many professional career opportunities for its residents.

The University

Founded in 1878 by the Fathers and Brothers of the Congregation of the Holy Ghost, Duquesne University has provided the opportunity for an education to students from many backgrounds, without regard to sex, race, creed, color, or national or ethnic origins. In the past twenty-five years, the University has undergone a dramatic physical transformation, from a makeshift physical plant occupying approximately 12 acres to a modern, highly functional educational facility that is located on its own 40-acre hilltop overlooking downtown Pittsburgh.

Applying

Applications for admission to graduate study with financial aid should be submitted no later than February 1 for the academic year beginning in the following September. Applications for admission without financial aid may be made up to one month prior to the beginning of the term in which the student desires to begin graduate work. All applications require official transcripts of previous undergraduate and graduate work and three letters of recommendation from faculty members who are familiar with the applicant's past academic progress. Application forms are available by writing to or calling the office of the Department of Chemistry and Biochemistry.

Correspondence and Information

Graduate Programs
Bayer School of Natural and Environmental Sciences
100 Mellon Hall
Duquesne University
Pittsburgh, Pennsylvania 15282
Telephone: 412-396-4900
Fax: 412-396-4881
E-mail: gradinfo@duq.edu
World Wide Web: http://science.duq.edu

Duquesne University

THE FACULTY

Partha Basu, Assistant Professor; Ph.D., Jadavpur (India), 1991. Inorganic chemistry: synthesis, structure, reactivity, and magnetic interactions of biological and model molecules.

Bruce D. Beaver, Associate Professor; Ph.D., Massachusetts, 1984. Organic chemistry: oxygenation of organic molecules, development of new antioxidants, oxidative degradation of petroleum products, chemistry of wine making.

Fraser F. Fleming, Associate Professor; Ph.D., British Columbia, 1990. Organic chemistry: application of the chemistry of α,β-unsaturated nitriles to the synthesis of anti-AIDS and anticancer drugs; synthesis of natural products.

Thomas L. Isenhour, Professor and Chair; Ph.D., Cornell, 1965. Analytical chemistry: mass spectrometry of polychlorinated hydrocarbons, rapid remote sensing of environmental contaminants by passive infrared spectroscopy, development of natural-language processing for incorporation of standard analytical methods into automated systems.

Mitchell E. Johnson, Assistant Professor; Ph.D., Massachusetts, 1993. Analytical chemistry: trace analysis of molecular species, fluorescence spectroscopy, high-speed separations, biochemical analysis.

Shahed Khan, Associate Professor; Ph.D., Flinders (Australia), 1977. Physical chemistry: electrochemistry, photoelectrochemistry, solar energy conversion by thin-film organic and inorganic semiconductors, electrocatalytic biosensors, electrosynthesis of conducting polymers, electrochemical surface modification, theory of electron transfer reactions in condensed medium, effect of solvent dynamics on electrochemical electron transfer reactions.

H. M. Kingston, Professor; Ph.D., American, 1978. Analytical and environmental chemistry: microwave chemistry application, environmental methods and instrument development, speciated analysis, ICP-MS clean-room chemistry, chromatography, laboratory automation.

Jeffry D. Madura, Associate Professor; Ph.D., Purdue, 1985. Theoretical physical chemistry: computational chemistry and biophysics, classical simulations of biomolecules, Poisson-Boltzmann electrostatics coupled to molecular dynamics, simulation of proteins at ice/water interface, simulation of biomolecular diffusion-controlled rate constants, quantum mechanical calculation of small molecules.

David J. Merkler, Associate Professor; Ph.D., Penn State, 1985. Biochemistry: enzymology of peptidylglycine α-amidating enzyme, enzyme mechanisms involved in posttranslational modification of mammalian hormones.

David W. Seybert, Professor; Ph.D., Cornell, 1978. Biochemistry: lipid peroxidation in biomembranes and lipoproteins, antioxidants and inhibition of LDL oxidation, mechanism and regulation of cytochrome P450 catalyzed steroid hydroxylations.

Brian Space, Assistant Professor; Ph.D., Boston University, 1992. Theoretical physical chemistry: computer simulation of condensed phase classical and mixed quantum classical systems, instantaneous normal mode theory of fluids, spectroscopy of liquids.

Omar W. Steward, Professor; Ph.D., Penn State, 1957. Inorganic chemistry: synthesis and structural studies of carboxylato metal complexes by X-ray diffraction; magneto-structural studies of transition metal complexes with organosilicon ligands; organosilicon and organogermanium compounds; structure-reactivity studies.

Julian Talbot, Associate Professor; Ph.D., Southampton (England), 1985. Theoretical physical chemistry: statistical mechanics, Monte Carlo and molecular dynamic simulation of classical systems, theory of adsorption kinetics and equilibria, biomolecules at interfaces, gases in porous solids.

Theodore J. Weismann, Adjunct Professor; Ph.D., Duquesne, 1956. Physical chemistry: mass spectrometry, ion optics, free radical reactions, organoboron chemistry, geochemistry, stable isotope MS, petroleum source and characterization.

David W. Wright, Assistant Professor; Ph.D., MIT, 1994. Inorganic chemistry: malaria, biomineralization, biomaterial design and structure, biosynthesis and assembly of active sites within metalloproteins, self-assembly processes.

Richard King Mellon Hall of Science, which houses the Department of Chemistry and Biochemistry.

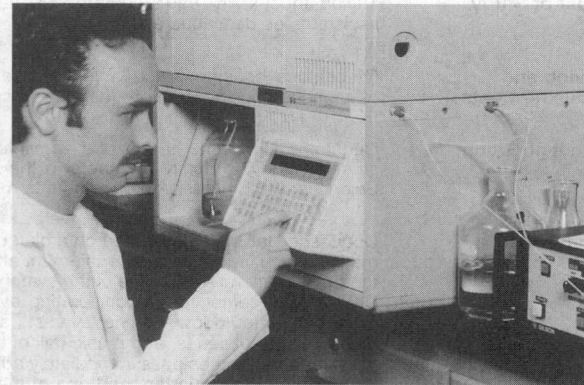

Research laboratory in Mellon Hall.

Professor H. M. "Skip" Kingston and an ICP–mass spectrometer.

SELECTED PUBLICATIONS

Wall, M. H. and **P. Basu**, et al. Photoinduced electron transfer in covalently linked oxo-molybdenum(V) porphyrin systems. *Inorg. Chem.* 36:5676–7, 1997.

Basu, P., and J. H. Enemark. A paramagnetic complex possessing two oxo-mo(V) centers. *Inorg. Chim. Acta* 263:81–6, 1997.

Basu, P., A. M. Raitsimring, J. H. Enemark, and F. A. Walker. Oxomolybdenum(V)/iron(III) porphyrinate complexes: The effect of axial ligand plane orientation on complex stability, reduction potential, NMR and EPR spectra. *Inorg. Chem.* 36:1088–94, 1997.

Pacheco, A., and **P. Basu**, et al. Multi-frequency ESEEM spectroscopy of sulfite oxidase in phosphate buffer: Direct evidence for coordinated phosphate. *Inorg. Chem.* 35:7001–8, 1996.

Raitsimring, A. M., **P. Basu**, N. V. Shokhirev, and J. H. Enemark. EPR studies on spin coupled oxo-molybdenum(V) and iron(III) porphyrin centers. *Appl. Magn. Res.* 9:173–93, 1995.

Basu, P., N. V. Shokhirev, F. Ann Walker, and J. H. Enemark. NMR studies of hindered ligand rotation, magnetic anisotropy, Curie behavior, proton spin relaxation and ligand exchange in some novel oxomolybdenum(V)/iron (III) porphyrinate complexes. *J. Am. Chem. Soc.* 117:9042–55, 1995.

Kurshev, V. V., L. Kevan, **P. Basu**, and J. H. Enemark. Measurement of the dipolar interaction between an oxomolybdenum center and a phosphorus nucleus in models for the molybdenum cofactor of enzymes by pulsed electron spin resources at S-band. *J. Phys. Chem.* 99:11288–91, 1995.

Basu, P., et al. Molecular structure and electronic properties of oxomolybdenum(V) catecholate complexes. *Inorg. Chem.* 34:405–7, 1995.

Beaver, B., et al. Structural effects on the reactivity of substituted arylphosphines as potential oxygen-scavenging additives for future jet fuels. *Heteroatom Chem.* 9(2):133–8, 1998.

Beaver, B., et al. Model studies directed at the development of new thermal oxidative stability enhancing additives for future jet fuels. *Energy Fuels* 11:396–401, 1997.

Fleming, F. F., and T. Jiang. Unsaturated nitriles: Optimized coupling of the chloroprene Grignard reagent with ω-bromonitriles. *J. Org. Chem.* 62:7890–1, 1997.

Fleming, F. F., Y. Pu, and F. Tercek. Unsaturated nitriles: Conjugate addition-silylation with Grignard reagents. *J. Org. Chem.* 62:4883–5, 1997.

Fleming, F. F., A. Huang, Y. Pu, and V. A. Sharief. α,β-Unsaturated nitriles: A domino ozonolysis-aldol synthesis of highly reactive oxonitriles. *J. Org. Chem.* 62:3036–7, 1997.

Fleming, F. F., Z. Hussain, R. E. Norman, and D. Weaver. α,β-Unsaturated nitriles: Stereoselective conjugate addition reactions. *J. Org. Chem.* 62:1305–9, 1997.

Ingling, L., and **T. L. Isenhour**. Quantitative open path-FTIR using isotopic standards. *Environ. Sci. Technol.*, in press.

Wright, C., D. E. Booth, **T. L. Isenhour**, and K. N. Berk. A joint estimation approach to monitoring the quality of automobile emissions. *J. Chem. Inf. Comput. Sci.*, in press.

Zhou, T., **T. L. Isenhour**, and J. C. Marshall. Object oriented programming applied to laboratory automation: III. The standard robot interface protocol for the analytical director. *J. Chem. Inf. Comput. Sci.* 34(2):558, 1994.

Feng, L., and **M. E. Johnson**. Selective fluorescence derivation and capillary electrophoretic separation of amidated amino acids. *J. Chromatogr.*, in press.

Johnson, M. E. Fluorescence spectroscopy for environmental analysis. In *Encyclopedia of Environmental Analysis and Remediation*, pp. 1757–86, ed. R. A. Meyers. New York: Wiley and Sons, 1998.

Gallaher, D. L., and **M. E. Johnson**. Characterization of a rugged, open-gap flowcell for confocal laser-induced fluorescence detection in capillary electrophoresis. *Appl. Spectroscopy* 52:292–7, 1998.

Petty, J. T., et al. **(M. E. Johnson)**. Characterization of DNA size determination of small fragments by flow cytometry. *Anal. Chem.* 67:1755–61, 1995.

Khan, S. U. M., and J. Akikusa. Stability and photoresponse of nanocrystalline n-TiO$_2$ and n-TiO$_2$/Mn$_2$O$_3$ thin film electrodes during water-spitting reactions. *J. Electrochem. Soc.* 145:89, 1998.

Khan, S. U. M. Electron transfer reaction in condensed media at electrodes. *Trends Chem. Phys.* 5:45, 1997.

Khan, S. U. M. Quantum mechanical treatments in electrode kinetics. In *Modern Aspects of Electrochemistry*, vol. 31, eds. J. O'M Bockris, B. E. Conway, and R. E. White. New York: Plenum, 1997.

Akikusa, J., and **S. U. M. Khan**. Stability of nanocrystalline n-TiO$_2$ and n-TiO$_2$/Mn$_2$O$_3$ films during photelectrolysis of water. In the *Chemical Society Proceedings on Quantum Confinement IV: Nanoscale Materials, Devices and Systems.*, vol. 97-11, pp. 65–78, eds. M. Cahay, J. P. Leburton, D. J. Lockwood, and S. Bandypadhyay. Pennington, 1997.

Khan, S. U. M. Quantum aspects of electrochemistry. *Royal Society of Chemistry, Book C.* London, 1996.

Khan, S. U. M., and S. Zhang. Photoresponse of electrochemically and spray pyrolytically deposited CdTe thin film electrodes. *J. Electrochem. Soc.* 142:2539–44, 1995.

Akikusa, J., and **S. U. M. Khan**. Photoresponse and stability of pyrolytically prepared n-TiO2 semiconductor films. In *Nanostructured Materials in Electrochemistry*, ed. P. C. Pearson and G. J. Mayer. Pennington, N.J.: Electrochemistry Society, 1995.

Kingston, H. M. "Skip", D. Huo, and Y. Lu. Accuracy in species analysis: Speciated isotope dilution mass spectrometry (SIDMS) exemplified by the evaluation of chromium species. *Spectrochem. Acta* Part B 53:299–309, 1998.

Huo, D., **H. M. Kingston**, and Y. Lu. Determination and correction of analytical biases and study on chemical mechanisms in the analysis of Cr (VI) in soil samples using EPA protocols. *Environ. Sci. Technol.* 32:3418–23, 1998.

Kingston, H. M., D. D. Link, and P. J. Walter. Development and validation of the new EPA microwave-assisted leach method 3051A. *Environ. Sci. Technol.* 32:3628–32, 1998.

Kingston, H. M., and P. J. Walter. The art and science of microwave sample preparation for trace and ultra-trace elemental analysis. In *Inductively Coupled Plasma Mass Spectrometry: From A to Z*, ed. A. Montaser. New York: Wiley-VCH, 1998.

Kingston, H. M., and P. J. Walter. The art and science of microwave sample preparation for trace and ultra-trace elemental analysis. In *Inductively Coupled Plasma Mass Spectrometry: From A to Z*, ed. A. Montaser. VCH, 1998.

Haswell, S., and **H. M. Kingston**, eds. *Microwave Enhanced Chemistry: Fundamentals, Sample Preparation, and Applications*. ACS Professional Reference Book Series. Washington, D.C.: American Chemical Society, 1997.

Kingston, H. M. "Skip", and S. Haswell, eds. *Microwave Enhanced Chemistry: Fundamentals, Sample Preparation, and Applications*, ACS Professional Reference Book Series. Washington, D.C.: American Chemical Society, 1997.

Chalk, S. J., W. Jiang, and **H. M. Kingston**. Ozone degradation of residual carbon in biological samples using microwave irradiation. *Analyst* 122:211–5, 1997.

Chalk, S., **H. M. Kingston**, E. Lorentzen, and P. J. Walter. A review of overview of microwave-assisted sample preparation. In *Microwave Enhanced Chemistry: Fundamentals, Sample Preparation, and Applications*. ACS Professional Reference Book Series, Chap. 2. Washington, D.C.: American Chemical Society, 1997.

Chalk, S., and **H. M. Kingston** et al. Environmental microwave sample preparation: Fundamentals, methods and applications. In *Microwave Enhanced Chemistry: Fundamentals, Sample Preparation, and Applications*. ACS Professional Reference Book Series, Chap. 3. Washington, D.C.: American Chemical Society, 1997.

Brown, J., S. Chalk, **H. M. Kingston**, and K. McQullin. SamplePrep Web: The analytical sample preparation and microwave chemistry research center. In *Microwave Enhanced Chemistry: Fundamentals, Sample Preparation, and Applications*. ACS Professional Reference Book Series, Chap. 15. Washington, D.C.: American Chemical Society, 1997.

Engelhart, G. W., **H. M. Kingston**, P. J. Parsons, and P. J. Walter. Chemical laboratory microwave safety. In *Microwave Enhanced Chemistry: Fundamentals, Sample Preparation, and Applications*. ACS Professional Reference Book Series, Chap. 16. Washington, D.C.: American Chemical Society, 1997.

Kingston, H. M. "Skip", et al. Environmental microwave sample preparation: Fundamentals, methods and application. In *Microwave Enhanced Chemistry: Fundamentals, Sample Preparation and Applications*, ACS Professional Reference Book Series. Washington D.C.: American Chemical Society, 1997.

Kingston, H. M., and S. J. Haswell, eds. *Microwave Enhanced Chemistry, ACS Professional Reference Book.* Washington, D.C.: American Chemical Society, 1997.

Collins, L. W., S. J. Chalk, and **H. M. "Skip" Kingston**. Atmospheric pressure microwave sample preparation procedure for the combined analysis of total phosphorus and kjeldahl nitrogen. *Anal. Chem.* 68:2610–4, 1996.

Franke, M., **H. M. Kingston**, and C. L. Winek. Extraction of selected drugs from serum using microwave irradiation. *Forensic Sci. Int.* 81:51–9, 1996.

Lorentzen, Elke M. L., and **H. M. "Skip" Kingston**. Comparison of microwave-assisted and conventional leaching using EPA method 3050B. *Anal. Chem.* 68(24):4316–20, 1996.

Taylor, D. B., and **H. M. Kingston**, et al. On-line solid-phase chelation for the determination of eight metals in environmental waters by ICP-MS. *JAAS* 11:187–91, March 1996.

Briggs, J. M., R. R. Gabdoulline, **J. D. Madura**, and R. C. Wade. Brownian dynamics. In *Encyclopedia of Computational Chemistry*, Vol. 2, pp. 141–54, eds. P. V. R. Schleyer et al. Chichester, UK: John Wiley & Sons, 1998.

Duquesne University

Selected Publications (continued)

Madura, J. D., et al. Physical and structural properties of taurine and taurine analogues. *Amino Acids* 13:131–9, 1997.

Aronson, N. N., C. J. Blanchard, and **J. D. Madura.** Homology modeling of glycosyl hydrolase family 18 enzymes and proteins. *J. Chem. Inf. Comput. Sci.* 37:999–1005, 1997.

Wierzbicki, A., **J. D. Madura,** C. Salmon, and F. Sönnichsen. Modeling studies of sea raven type II antifreeze protein to ice. *J. Chem. Inf. Comput. Sci.* 37:1006–10, 1997.

Madura, J. D., et al. The dynamics and binding of a type III antifreeze protein in water and on ice. *THEOCHEM* 388:65–77,1996.

Merkler, D. J., R. Kulathila, and D. E. Ash. The interactivation of bifunctional peptidyglycine α-amidating enzyme; evidence that the two enzyme-bound copper atoms are non-equivalent. *Arch. Biochem. Biophys.* 317:93–102, 1995.

Kulathila, R., et al. **(D. J. Merkler).** Bifunctional peptidyglycine α-amidating enzyme requires two copper atoms for maximum activity. *Arch. Biochem. Biophys.* 311:191–5, 1994.

Owens, J. W., M. B. Perry, and **D. W. Seybert.** Reactions of nitric oxide with cobaltous tetraphenylporphyrin and phthalocyanines. *Inorg. Chim. Acta* 277:1–7, 1998.

Hanlon, M. C., and **D. W. Seybert.** The pH dependence of lipid peroxidation using water-soluble azo initiators. *Free Radical Biol. Med.* 23:712–9, 1997.

Warburton, R. J., and **D. W. Seybert.** Structural and functional characterization of bovine adrenodoxin reductase by limited proteolysis. *Biochim. Biophys. Acta* 1246:39–46, 1995.

Ahlborn, H., X. Ji, P. B. Moore, and **B. Space.** An instantaneous normal mode theory of condensed phase absorption: The vibrational spectrum of condensed CS_2 from boiling to freezing. *Chem. Phys. Lett.* 296:259–65, 1998.

Space, B., and F. Bowen. The effective mass of excess electrons in condensed xenon: Toward methods for modeling metal-dielectric interfaces. *J. Chem. Phys.* 107:1922, 1997.

Moore, P., and **B. Space.** An instantaneous normal mode theory of condensed phase absorption: The collision-induced absorption spectra of liquid CO_2 *J. Chem. Phys.* 107:5635, 1997.

Space, B., H. Rabitz, A. Lorinez, and P. Moore. Feasibility of using photophoresis to create a concentration gradient of solvated molecules. *J. Chem. Phys.* 105:9515–21, 1996.

Space, B., H. Rabitz, and A. Askar. The subspace method for long time scale molecular dynamics. *J. Phys. Chem.* 99:7338–9, 1995.

Yaukey, T. S., **O. W. Steward,** and S.-C. Chang. Manganese(II) triphenylacetate hydratrate. A manganese(II) complex with a chain structure. *Acta Crystallog.* C54:1081–3, 1998.

Muto, Y., et al. **(O. W. Steward).** Characterization of dimeric copper(II) trichoroacetate complexes by electron spin resonance, infrared, and electronic reflectance spectra. Correlation of spectral parameters with molecular geometry. *Bull. Chem Soc. Jpn.* 70:1573, 1997.

Steward, O. W., et al. Structural and magnetic studies of dimeric copper(II) 2,2-diphenylpropanoato and triphenylacetato complexes with oxygen donor ligands. The cage geometry of dimeric α-phenyl substituted copper(II) carboxylates. *Bull. Chem. Soc. Jpn.* 69:34123–7, 1996.

Viot, P., P. R. Tassel, and **J. Talbot.** Nearest-neighbor functions in a one-dimensional generalized ballistic deposition model. *Phys. Rev. E,* in press.

Talbot, J. Analysis of adsorption selectively in a one-dimensional model system. *AIChE J.* 43:2471–8, 1997.

Van Tassel, P. R., **J. Talbot,** G. Tarjus, and P. Viot. A distribution function analysis of the structure of depleted particle configurations. *Phys. Rev. E* 56:1299R, 1997.

Choi, H. S., and **J. Talbot.** Effect of diffusion and convection on the flux of depositing particles near preadsorbed particle. *Korean J. Chem. Eng.,* 14:117–24, 1997.

Talbot, J. Molecular thermodynamics of binary mixture adsorption. *J. Chem. Phys.* 196:4696–706, 1997.

Van Tassel, P., **J. Talbot,** G. Tarjus, and P. Viot. The kinetics of irreversible adsorption with particle conformational change. *Phys. Rev. E* 53:785, 1996.

Talbot, J. Time-dependent desorption: A memory function approach. *Adsorption* 2:89, 1996.

Chang, R. T., **D. W. Wright,** and J. Ziegler. Multiple-antigenic peptides (MAPs) of histidine-rich protein II of *plasmodium falciparum:* A novel family of peptide dendrimers with protein-like activity. *J. Am. Chem. Soc.,* in press.

Armstrong, W. H., et al. **(D. W. Wright).** Characterization of the Mn oxidation states in photosystem II by Kβ X-ray fluorescence spectroscopy. *J. Chem. Phys. B* 102:8350–2, 1998.

Armstrong, W. H., et al. **(D. W. Wright).** Tetranuclear manganese-oxo aggregates relevant to the photosynthetic water oxidation center. *J. Am. Chem. Soc.* 120:3704–16, 1998.

Armstrong, W. H., C. E. Dube, H. J. Mok, and **D. W. Wright.** Implications for the solution state structure of dinuclear manganese-oxo aggregates: A ^1H NMR study with magnetic correlations. *Inorg. Chem.* 37:3714–8, 1998.

Armstrong, W. H., C. E. Dube, and **D. W. Wright.** Multiple reversible protonations of the adamantane-shaped $\{Mn_4O_6\}^{4+}$ core: Detection of protonation stereoisomers at the $\{Mn_4O_4(OH)_2\}^{6+}$ level. *J. Am. Chem. Soc.* 118:10910, 1996.

Armstrong, W. H., et al. **(D. W. Wright).** A novel vanadium (V) homocitrate complex: Synthesis, structure, and biological relevance of $[K_2(H_2O)_6][(VO)_2(R,S\text{-Homocitrate})_2]\cdot H_2O$. *J. Biol. Inorg. Chem.* 1:143, 1996.

Davis, W. M., P. A. Humiston, W. H. Orme-Johnson, and **D. W. Wright.** A unique coordination mode for citrate to a transition metal: $K_2[V(O)_2(C_6H_6O_7)]_2 4H_2O$. *Inorg. Chem.* 34:4194, 1994.

FLORIDA INTERNATIONAL UNIVERSITY

Department of Chemistry
Ph.D. Program

Program of Study

The Department of Chemistry offers a program of study leading to the degree of Doctor of Philosophy. Research programs are offered in the areas of analytical, environmental, forensic, inorganic, organic, and physical chemistry and in biochemistry. The chemistry department has strong affiliations with the Southeast Environmental Research Center and the International Forensic Research Institute, offering students a multidisciplinary approach to several research areas.

Upon entering the Ph.D. program, students are given proficiency exams in organic and physical chemistry. Students are expected to demonstrate proficiency in these two areas of chemistry by the end of their first semester, either by passing the proficiency exams or by the successful completion of specified courses. Student progress is also evaluated by cumulative exams, which are given five times per year. Students begin taking cumulative exams during their second semester and must pass four cumulative exams during the following two years. In the first two years, students must also successfully complete at least 18 credit hours of classes at the graduate level (at least 9 hours of which must satisfy the distribution requirements for course work), submit and defend a satisfactory original research proposal, and pass a pre–oral examination to be admitted to candidacy for the doctoral degree. The doctoral degree is awarded upon the approval of the student's dissertation committee after the student completes and publicly defends a research dissertation. The normal length of the Ph.D. program is four years.

A Master of Science degree is also offered.

Research Facilities

Research is conducted in the Chemistry and Physics Building, which was completed in 1991. Research facilities include a high-field 400-MHz NMR, LC/UV/MS, ICP/MS, Pyrolysis/GC/MS, GC-AED, Headspace-GC, Headspace-GC/MS, FT-IR, GC/MS, SPME/GC/MS/MS, capillary electrophoresis, supercritical fluid extractors, calorimeters, UV-visible and Raman spectrophotometers, and other specialized instrumentation in individual research groups. The University library, recently renovated and expanded, maintains an extensive collection of scientific journals, books, monographs, and reference literature and provides rapid automated search capabilities through several retrieval networks, including online searching.

Financial Aid

Financial aid is available in the form of teaching assistantships. The 1999–2000 stipend is $15,000 per year and includes a tuition waiver. Six contact hours and 12 hours of preparation and grading are required per week for the teaching assistantship. Research assistantships are also available at a comparable level of support. Assistantships are awarded on a competitive basis and are generally continued for a period of four years. Student loans are also available.

Cost of Study

The estimated cost of tuition for a full-time student during the 1998–99 academic year (9 credit hours during the fall and spring semesters, 6 credit hours during the summer semester) was $3110 for a Florida resident and $10,440 for a nonresident. Additional costs, which include the student health fee, the athletic fee, and textbooks, are estimated at $1000 per year.

Living and Housing Costs

Student housing is available in on-campus dormitories and apartments. On-campus housing costs for the 1998–99 academic year ranged from $3360 to $7280. Accommodations are also available in the surrounding community. A variety of meal plans are available to students. Estimated costs for food, housing, transportation, and entertainment for 1998–99 was $10,500 per year.

Student Group

There are approximately 30 students enrolled in the graduate program in chemistry. A wide range of academic, ethnic, and national backgrounds are represented.

Location

The main campus, University Park, is located on 342 acres in suburban Miami-Dade County, approximately 10 miles west of downtown Miami. The city of Miami, with its subtropical climate, cultural diversity, and strategic location, provides students with all of the advantages of attending a university in a major urban environment. The greater Miami area is home to a number of nationally recognized cultural and tourist attractions, beautiful beaches, the Florida Everglades, an active night life, and four major professional sports teams. Students can take advantage of Miami's hospitable climate, with an average annual temperature of 77°F and more than 300 days of sunshine per year.

The University

Florida International University (FIU), a member of the State University System of Florida, was established by the State Legislature on June 22, 1965. Classes were first offered on September 19, 1972. The University currently offers more than 200 degree programs at the undergraduate and graduate levels and has an enrollment of approximately 30,000 students.

Applying

Florida International University uses a common institutional application form for all graduate programs. Applications can be requested from the Graduate Admissions Office, CP 140, Florida International University, Miami, Florida 33199. Online registration is also available at the FIU Web site (http://www.fiu.edu/orgs/admiss). A $20 nonrefundable application fee, made payable to Florida International University, must accompany the application form.

Admissions requirements include a B.S. degree in chemistry that is comparable to the ACS-certified degree offered at FIU. Students can make up deficiencies in their background by taking undergraduate courses, but they are not fully admitted into the graduate program until all deficiencies are satisfied. Also, applicants are required to have an undergraduate grade point average of 3.0 (on a 4.0 scale) or submit a score of at least 1000 on the standard aptitude portion of the Graduate Record Examinations (GRE). All students are required to take the GRE regardless of their grade point average. International students whose native language is not English are required to submit a score of at least 550 on the Test of English as a Foreign Language (TOEFL).

Correspondence and Information

Graduate Program Director
Department of Chemistry
Florida International University
Miami, Florida 33199
World Wide Web: http://www.fiu.edu/orgs/chemistry

Florida International University

THE FACULTY AND THEIR RESEARCH

Jose R. Almirall. Analytical and forensic chemistry: novel extraction methodologies for ultrace analysis, hyphenated separation and identification techniques, forensic evaluation of materials.

David A. Becker. Organic chemistry: spin trapping, azulenyl nitrones, free radical chemistry and biology.

Yong Cai. Analytical and environmental chemistry: analytical methods for speciation of trace metals and organometallic compounds, biogeochemical cycling of environmentally important elements.

David C. Chatfield. Theoretical physical chemistry: molecular dynamics simulations of proteins, theoretical models for enzyme mechanisms, characterization of protein dynamics.

Yiwei Deng. Environmental and analytical chemistry: cycling of trace elements in aquatic and atmospheric environments, development of analytical methods for environmental applications.

Kenneth G. Furton. Analytical and forensic chemistry: supercritical fluid extraction and solid-phase microextraction as applied to environmental and forensic samples, canine scent selectivity and sensitivity.

Piero R. Gardinali. Analytical and environmental chemistry: analytical chemistry of persistent organic contaminants, source and fate of xenobiotics in the environment, trace organic analytical methods.

Gary G. Hoffman. Theoretical physical chemistry: electronic distributions and their effects on molecular properties and interactions, computational technique development.

Rudolf Jaffe. Analytical and environmental chemistry: organic geochemistry of the atmosphere, water, soil, and sediments; fate and transport of organic pollutants.

Jeffrey A. Joens. Physical chemistry: experimental and theoretical studies of the electronic spectra of small molecules, physical properties of molecular complexes.

Leonard S. Keller. Organic chemistry: organic synthesis and development of new synthetic methods, use of organometallics in the activation of arene ring systems.

John T. Landrum. Carotenoid chemistry: studies on the macular pigments in the human retina, analysis of carotenoids in biological samples.

Ramon Lopez de la Vega. Inorganic chemistry: kinetic and thermodynamic studies of inorganic reactions, investigation of ligand binding and ligand exchange reactions.

Kevin E. O'Shea. Organic chemistry: intermediates and mechanisms of organic reactions, photooxidation and photolysis of organic compounds.

J. Martin E. Quirke. Organic chemistry: porphyrin and metalloporphyrin chemistry; synthesis, isolation, and characterization of geoporphyrins.

Kathleen S. Rein. Marine biochemistry: bioactive marine natural products and their pharmacological properties, characterization of membrane receptors.

Stephen Winkle. Biochemistry: structure and function of DNA by spectroscopic studies and enzymatic and chemical probes, interaction of carcinogens with DNA.

Stanislaw F. Wnuk. Organic chemistry: organic chemistry of nucleosides and nucleotides with application to anticancer and antiviral medicine, synthesis of nucleoside analogues.

Florida International University

SELECTED PUBLICATIONS

Almirall, J. R., M. Cole, K. G. Furton, and G. Gettinby. Discrimination of glass sources using elemental composition and refractive index: Development of predictive models. *Sci. Justice* 38:93, 1998.

Curran, J., et al. (J. R. Almirall). The interpretation of elemental composition measurements from forensic glass. *Sci. Justice* 37:241, 1997.

Almirall, J. R., J. Bruna, and K. G. Furton. The recovery of accelerants in aqueous samples from fire debris using solid-phase microextraction. *Sci. Justice* 36:283, 1996.

Becker, D. A., R. Natero, L. Echegoyen, and R. C. Lawson. Redox behavior of azulenyl nitrones. Fully reversible one-electron oxidation by cyclic voltammetry at potentials in the range of biological antioxidants. *J. Chem. Soc. Perkins* 2:1289, 1998.

Klivenyi, P., et al. (D. A. Becker). Azulenyl nitrone spin traps protect against MPTP neurotoxicity. *Exp. Neurol.* 152:163, 1998.

Becker, D. A. Highly sensitive calorimetric detection and facile isolation of diamagnetic free radical adducts of novel chromotropic nitrone spin trapping agents readily derived from guaiazulene. *J. Am. Chem. Soc.* 118:905, 1996.

Cai, Y., et al. (K. G. Furton and R. Jaffé). Determination of methylmercury in fish and aqueous samples using solid-phase microextraction followed by gas chromatography–atomic fluorescence spectrometry. *Appl. Organometal. Chem.* 12:565, 1998.

Cai, Y., R. Jaffé, and R. D. Jones. Ethylmercury in the soils and sediments of the Florida Everglades. *Environ. Sci. Technol.* 31:302, 1997.

Cai, Y., R. Jaffé, A. Alli, and R. D. Jones. Determination of organomercury compounds in natural waters by solid-phase extraction with sulfhydryl cotton fiber and capillary gas chromatography–atomic fluorescence spectrometry. *Anal. Chim. Acta* 334:251, 1996.

Chatfield, D. C., A. Szabo, and B. R. Brooks. Molecular dynamics of staphylococcal nuclease: Comparison of simulation with ^{15}N and ^{13}C NMR relaxation data. *J. Am. Chem. Soc.* 120:5301, 1998.

Chatfield, D. C., K. P. Eurenius, and B. R. Brooks. HIV-1 protease cleavage mechanism: A theoretical investigation based on a classical MD simulation and reaction path calculations using a hybrid QM/MM potential. *Theochemistry* 423:79, 1998.

Deng, Y. Determination of major inorganic anions in rainwater by capillary electrophoresis. *Water Res.* 32:2249, 1998.

Deng, Y. Effect of pH on the reductive dissolution rates of iron (III) hydroxide by ascorbate. *Langmuir* 13:1835, 1997.

Deng, Y. Formation of iron (III) hydroxides from homogeneous solutions. *Water Res.* 31:1347, 1997.

Furton, K. G., J. Bruna, and J. R. Almirall. A simple, inexpensive, sensitive, and solventless technique for the analysis of accelerants in fire debris based on SPME. *J. High Res. Chromatogr.: HRC* 18:625, 1995.

Wade, T. L., T. J. Jackson, P. R. Gardinali, and L. Chambers. PCDD/PCDF sediment concentration distribution, Casco Bay, Maine, U.S.A. *Chemosphere* 34:1359, 1997.

Willett, K. L., P. R. Gardinali et al. Characterization of the H4IIE rat hepatoma cell bioassay for evaluation of environmental samples containing polynuclear aromatic hydrocarbons (PAHs). *Arch. Environ. Contam. Toxicol.* 32:1, 1997.

Gardinali, P. R., T. L. Wade, L. Chambers, and J. Brooks. A complete method for the quantitative analysis of planar, mono, and di-ortho PCBs, polychlorinated dibenzo-p-dioxins, and furans in environmental samples. *Chemosphere* 32:1, 1996.

Hoffman, G. G. The rotational partition function for linear molecules. *J. Math. Chem.* 21:115, 1997.

Hoffman, G. G. An integral for second order multiple scattering perturbation theory. *J. Comp. Phys.* 130:129, 1997.

Hoffman, G. G. Atom-centered functions in the optimized Thomas-Fremi theory. *J. Comp. Phys.* 116:154, 1995.

Jaffe, R., et al. (P. R. Gardinali). Baseline study on the levels of organic pollutants and heavy metals in bivalves of Morrocoy National Park, Venezuela. *Mar. Pollut. Bull.* 36:925–9, 1998.

Alvarado, J., and R. Jaffé. Determination of lead by atomic absorption spectrometry using tube in flame atomization and solid sampling. *J. Anal. Atomic Spectrom.* 13(11):1297, 1998.

Jaffé, R., A. Cabrera, N. Hajje, and H. Carvajal-Chitty. Organic biogeochemistry of a hypereutrophic tropical freshwater lake. Part 1: Particle associated and dissolved lipids. *Org. Geochem.* 25:227, 1997.

Jaffé, R., Y. Cai et al. On the occurrence of methylmercury in Lake Valencia, Venezuela. *Environ. Contam. Toxicol.* 59:99, 1997.

Jaffé, R., et al. (K. G. Furton). Hydrocarbon speciation in ancient sediments studied by stepwise high temperature supercritical carbon dioxide extraction. *Org. Geochem.* 26:59, 1997.

Jaffé, R., Y. Gong, and K. G. Furton. Temperature effects on supercritical carbon dioxide extractions of hydrocarbons from geological samples. *J. High Res. Chromatogr.* 20:586, 1997.

Pagan, M., W. J. Cooper, and J. A. Joens. Kinetic studies of the homogeneous abiotic reactions of several chlorinated aliphatic compounds in aqueous solution. *Appl. Geochem.* 13:779, 1998.

Casero, J. C., and J. A. Joens. Thermochemistry of the gasphase molecular complex of benzene with oxygen. *J. Phys. Chem.* 101:2607, 1997.

Joens, J. A. Alternative assignment for the vibrational structure of the $^3B_1$ - X^1A_1 band system of SO_2. *Chem. Phys. Lett.* 261:659, 1996.

Landrum, J. T., R. A. Bone, L. L. Moore, and C. Gomez. Analysis of zeaxanthin in individual human retinas. *Methods Enzymol.* 299:457, 1999.

Landrum, J. T., et al. A one-year study of the macular pigment: The effect of 140 days of a lutein supplement. *Exp. Eye Res.* 65:57, 1997.

Landrum, J. T., et al. A preliminary study of the stereochemistry of human lens zeaxanthin. *Invest. Ophthal. Vis. Sci.* 38:4785, 1997.

Stanley, K. D., L. Luo, R. Lopez de la Vega, and J. M. E. Quirke. Correlation of X-ray crystallographic data and spectroscopic properties of divalent metal complexes of octaethylporphyrin. *Inorg. Chem.* 32:1233, 1993.

O'Shea, K. E., A. Aguila, K. Vinodgopal, and P. V. Kamat. Reaction pathways and kinetic parameters of sonolytically induced oxidation of dimethyl-phosphonate in air-saturated aqueous solutions. *Res. Chem. Intermed.* 24:695, 1998.

O'Shea, K. E., et al. Photocatalytic decomposition of organophosphonates in irradiated TiO_2 suspensions. *J. Photochem. Photobiol. A: Chem.* 107:221, 1997.

Saltiel, J., et al. (K. E. O'Shea). Resolution of trans-1-(2-naphthyl)-2-phenylene fluorescence in the presence of tri-n-butylamine into pairs of monomer and exciplex spectra. Selectivity in conformer quenching. *J. Am. Chem. Soc.* 118:7478, 1996.

VanBerkel, G. J., J. M. E. Quirke et al. Derivatization for electrospray-ionization mass-spectrometry. 3. Electrochemically ionizable derivatives. *Anal. Chem.* 70:1544, 1998.

Lemke, C., et al. (J. M. E. Quirke). The effect of meso-nitro substitution on nickel (II) porphyrins. *Biophys. J.* 74:A83, 1998.

Laycock, J. D., et al. (J. M. E. Quirke). Electron ionization mass spectroscometric analysis of 5-nitro octaethylporphyrin: Evidence for scission of the porphyrin macrocycle. *J. Mass Spectrom.* 32:978, 1997.

Brousseau, J. L., et al. (K. S. Rein). UV-visible and inelastic electron-tunneling spectroscopies of brevetoxins. *Appl. Spectrosc.* 52:523, 1998.

Jeglitsch, J., K. S. Rein, D. G. Baden, and D. J. Adams. Brevetoxin-3 (PBTX-3) and its derivatives modulate single tetrodotoxin-sensitive sodium channels in rat sensory neurons. *J. Pharmacol. Exp. Ther.* 284:516, 1998.

Washburn, B. S., K. S. Rein et al. Brevetoxin-6 (PBTX-6), a nonaromatic marine neurotoxin, is a ligand of the aryl-hydrocarbon receptor. *Arch. Biochem. Biophys.* 343:149, 1997.

Winkle, S. A., et al. The interface between an alternating CG motif and a random sequence motif displays altered nuclease activity. *J. Biomol. Struct. Dynamics* 10:389, 1992.

Florida International University

Selected Publications (continued)

Combates, N. J., and **S. A. Winkle.** Using lambda exonuclease inhibition assays to map carcinogen binding sites. *J. Biomol. Struct. Dynamics* 10:63, 1992.

Wnuk, S. F., et al. Discovery of type II (covalent) interaction of S-adenosyl-L-homocysteine hydrolase. Synthesis and evaluation of dihalohomovinyl nucleoside analogues derived from adenosine. *J. Med. Chem.* 41:3078, 1998.

Robins, M. J., et al. **(S. F. Wnuk).** Nucleic acid related compounds. 101. S-adenosyl-L-homocysteine hydrolase does not hydrate (5'-fluoro) vinyl or (6'-halo) homovinyl analogues derived from 3'-deoxyadenosine or 3'-(chloro or fluoro)-3'deoxyadenosine. *J. Org. Chem.* 63:1205, 1998.

Robins, M. J., S. Sarker, and **S. F. Wnuk.** What are the practical limits for detection of minor (nucleoside) reaction products with HPLC(UV), ¹H NMR, and TLC? *Nucleosides Nucleotides* 17:785, 1998.

FLORIDA STATE UNIVERSITY

Department of Chemistry

Programs of Study

Graduate education in the Department of Chemistry, leading to the M.S. and Ph.D. degrees, can be pursued in both traditional and contemporary fields. Five areas—biochemistry and analytical, inorganic, organic, and physical chemistry—provide fundamental curricula in their disciplines, and a variety of research-oriented programs are available in each of these traditional areas. In addition, opportunities for chemical research at the interfaces with physics, biology, and materials science are available in research groups participating in the Materials Research and Technology Center, the Institute of Molecular Biophysics, the Supercomputer Computations Research Institute, and the National High Magnetic Field Laboratory. Interdisciplinary programs leading to advanced degrees in chemical physics and in molecular biophysics are offered in cooperation with the Department of Physics and the Department of Biological Science. A list of chemistry faculty members and their research interests is given on the back of this page.

Ph.D. candidates who perform satisfactorily on entrance examinations may immediately begin advanced course work and research. Although Ph.D. programs of study are structured to meet individual needs and vary among the divisions, most programs incorporate seven to twelve 1-semester courses at the graduate level. Mastery of the material in the area of interest is demonstrated by passing either cumulative examinations or comprehensive examinations, depending on the area of specialization. A thesis or dissertation is required in all but the courses-only option of the master's degree program. The presence of about 40 postdoctoral and visiting faculty researchers, in addition to the low faculty-student ratio, permits a high level of student-scientist interaction.

Research Facilities

Chemistry department research operations are housed mainly in the interconnected Dittmer Laboratory of Chemistry building and Institute of Molecular Biophysics building. Several adjacent structures serve other departmental teaching functions. Major items of research equipment include a variety of spectrometers and lasers for ultraviolet, visible, infrared, and Raman experiments; an ORD/CD spectrometer; an EPR spectrometer with cryogenic accessories; several high- and medium-resolution mass spectrometers with GC, EI, and CI capabilities; 150-, 200-, 270-, 300-, 400-, and 500-MHz NMR spectrometers; a metal-organic chemical vapor deposition (MOCVD) facility; an automated four-circle X-ray diffractometer with complete in-house solution and refinement capabilities; and a bioanalytical facility containing automated DNA synthesis, peptide synthesis, and protein sequencing equipment. The department has excellently staffed glassworking, machine, electronics, photographic/computer graphics, and woodworking shops in support of the teaching and research programs.

The departmental computing needs are met by a variety of workstations and microcomputers that are linked with the Internet. Several members of the chemistry faculty are members of the Supercomputer Computations Research Institute (SCRI) and have access to two Silicon Graphics Power Challenge supercomputers on the Florida State University (FSU) campus as well as to several supercomputers around the world. SCRI maintains two high-performance computer environments—a Connection Machine CM-2 and a large cluster of super workstations providing more than 8.2 gigaflops of computing power and more than 460 gigabytes of disk storage. The department is a sponsoring academic unit for the National High Magnetic Field Laboratory (NHMFL) and has access to the facilities and instrumentation of the NHMFL.

The University's Strozier Library, which includes the Dirac Science Library, houses 1.2 million volumes and maintains 12,650 active journal subscriptions. The Dirac Science Library is located adjacent to the Dittmer Laboratory of Chemistry.

Financial Aid

In addition to providing teaching and research assistantships, the department offers several special fellowships on a competitive basis. Nearly all graduate students are supported by one of these programs. Twelve-month teaching assistantships with stipends of $16,000 can be augmented by special fellowships ranging up to $3000. Competitive fellowships on the University and College levels are also available.

Cost of Study

Tuition for in-state residents was $1666 per semester and for out-of-state residents was $5597 per semester in 1998–99. These tuition costs are normally waived for teaching and research assistants, but the number of waivers available each year is determined in part by legislative appropriation. Nonwaivable fees, including the cost of health insurance ($42 per month), were approximately $310–$497 per semester in addition to the above tuition.

Living and Housing Costs

Single students sharing a 2-person room in graduate apartment housing paid $265 per month in 1998–99, in addition to utilities and telephone service. The University also operates an apartment complex of 795 units for single and married students. Rents ranged from $260 to $520 per month plus utilities for furnished one- to three-bedroom apartments. Off-campus accommodations began at about $400 per month.

Student Group

Graduate enrollment in chemistry is approximately 110 students. Although students come from all parts of the United States and numerous other countries, many are native to the eastern half of the United States.

Location

Metropolitan Tallahassee has a population of about 300,000 and is recognized for the scenic beauty of its rolling hills, abundant trees and flowers, and seasonal changes. As the capital of Florida, the city is host to many cultural affairs, including symphony, theater, and dance groups. Its location 30 minutes from the Gulf Coast, the area's many lakes, and an average annual temperature of 68°F make the region eminently suitable for a variety of year-round outdoor activities.

The University

Florida State University was founded in 1857 and is one of nine members of the State University System of Florida. Currently, enrollment is 30,519, including 5,800 graduate students. The University's rapid climb to prominence began with the adoption of an emphasis on graduate studies in 1947. The first doctoral degree was conferred in 1952. In addition to the College of Arts and Sciences, the University is composed of the Colleges of Business, Communication, Education, Engineering, Human Sciences, Law, and Social Sciences and the Schools of Criminology, Library and Information Studies, Music, Social Work, Theatre, and Visual Arts. Several departments, including chemistry, enjoy international recognition.

Applying

Application for admission may be made at any time; however, initial inquiries concerning assistantships, especially fellowships, should be made nine to twelve months prior to the anticipated enrollment date. Later requests are considered as funds are available for the following fall semester. Requests for forms, detailed requirements, and other information should be directed to the address below.

Correspondence and Information

Director of Graduate Admissions
Department of Chemistry
Florida State University
Tallahassee, Florida 32306-4390
Telephone: 850-644-1897
　　　　　888-525-9286 (toll-free in the United States)
Fax: 850-644-0465
E-mail: gradinfo@chem.fsu.edu
World Wide Web: http://www.chem.fsu.edu (Department of Chemistry)
　　　　　　　　http://admissions.fsu.edu (the University)

Florida State University

THE FACULTY AND THEIR RESEARCH

Susan D. Allen, Professor and Vice President for Research; Ph.D., USC, 1971. Effects, especially of technological significance, of laser irradiation on surfaces and interfaces, e.g., deposition, desorption, cleaning, annealing, and etching and micromachining of materials and devices.

Michael Blaber, Assistant Professor; Ph.D., California, Irvine, 1990. Analysis of protein stability, structure, and function using X-ray crystallography and microcalorimetry; analysis of serine protease structure and function.

Michael S. Chapman, Associate Professor; Ph.D., UCLA, 1987. Structural characterization of viral proteins using X-ray crystallography.

Gregory R. Choppin, Professor; Ph.D., Texas at Austin, 1953. Chemical properties of organic and inorganic complexes of lanthanide and transuranic actinide elements, separation methods for actinides, environmental chemistry of actinides.

Jerzy Cioslowski, Professor; Ph.D., Georgetown, 1987. Computational quantum chemistry, ab initio electronic structure calculations, development of algorithms for supercomputers.

Ronald J. Clark, Professor; Ph.D., Kansas, 1958. Synthesis and characterization of superconducting materials, ceramics, metal carbonyl trifluorophosphine chemistry.

William T. Cooper, Associate Professor; Ph.D., Indiana, 1981. Chromatography, environmental geochemistry of organic compounds in natural waters, surface chemistry of minerals, organic geochemistry of recent sediments.

Timothy A. Cross, Professor and Director, National High Magnetic Field Laboratory NMR Program; Ph.D., Pennsylvania, 1981. Structure and dynamics of membrane-bound polypeptides by solid-state nuclear magnetic resonance.

Klaus-Hermann Dahmen, Associate Professor; Ph.D., ETH-Zurich (Switzerland), 1986. Synthesis and characterization of precursors for metal-organic chemical vapor deposition (MOCVD) of thin films; MOCVD; growth kinetics; applications in microelectronics, optics, and sensors.

Naresh Dalal, Professor; Ph.D., British Columbia, 1971. Nuclear and electron magnetic resonance: technique development and applications in solid-state chemistry, synthesis and characterization of magnetic and ferroelectric compounds, high-temperature superconductivity, scanning probe microscopy, free radical and metal-ion reactivity and environmental chemistry.

John G. Dorsey, Professor and Chairperson; Ph.D., Cincinnati, 1979. Analytical separations, especially liquid chromatography and capillary electrophoresis; stationary phase synthesis; quantitative structure-retention relationships; flow injection analysis; analytical applications of organized media.

Ralph C. Dougherty, Professor; Ph.D., Chicago, 1963. Ion-molecule collisions and reactions, tunneling in chemical reactions, mesoscale (10 km) atmospheric chemical modeling, mass spectrometry and ion cyclotron resonance.

Robert L. Fulton, Professor; Ph.D., Harvard, 1964. Theories of linear and nonlinear dielectric properties and their relation to molecular motion, theories of solvent effects on spectral properties, theories of relaxation, development of methods for interpreting electronic wave functions.

Penny J. Gilmer, Professor; Ph.D., Berkeley, 1972. Biochemistry, immunochemistry, biochemical nature of cell-cell recognition, lysosomal processing, science education.

Kenneth A. Goldsby, Associate Professor and Associate Chairperson; Ph.D., North Carolina at Chapel Hill, 1983. Redox reactions of transition-metal complexes, directed electron transfer, mixed-valence complexes, electrochemistry.

Nancy L. Greenbaum, Assistant Professor; Ph.D., Pennsylvania, 1984. Determination of RNA structure by homonuclear and heteronuclear multidimensional NMR spectroscopy; role of RNA structural elements, RNA-RNA and RNA-protein interactions in pre-mRNA splicing reactions.

Edwin F. Hilinski, Associate Professor; Ph.D., Yale, 1982. Mechanistic studies of photochemical and thermal reactions of organic compounds in solution, picosecond laser spectroscopy, photoinduced phenomena in solids.

Robert A. Holton, Professor; Ph.D., Florida State, 1971. Synthetic organic, organometallic, and bioorganic chemistry; total synthesis of natural products.

Michael Kasha, University Professor; Ph.D., Berkeley, 1945. Molecular electronic spectroscopy, intermolecular electronic phenomena, theoretical photochemistry, molecular biophysics, singlet oxygen studies, laser studies of proton transfer.

Marie E. Krafft, Professor; Ph.D., Virginia Tech, 1983. Synthetic organic and organometallic chemistry, natural products synthesis.

Robley J. Light, Professor; Ph.D., Duke, 1960. Secondary metabolism in fungi and plants, lipid metabolism and function.

Timothy M. Logan, Assistant Professor; Ph.D., Chicago, 1991. Structural and dynamic studies of proteins and protein-ligand complexes and of protein folding pathways using multidimensional NMR spectroscopy.

Charles K. Mann, Professor; Ph.D., Virginia, 1955. Quantitative analysis by Raman spectroscopy, numerical methods for resolution of spectroscopic interferences.

Alan G. Marshall, Professor and Director, National High Magnetic Field Laboratory ICR Program; Ph.D., Stanford, 1970. Fourier transform ion cyclotron resonance mass spectrometry: theory, technique development, and experimental applications; mass-selected ion molecule reactions for synthesis, reactivity, spectroscopy, and structural analysis of new species.

William C. Rhodes, Professor; Ph.D., Johns Hopkins, 1958. Quantum theory of molecular excitation and relaxation; dynamic and thermodynamic properties of coupled molecular systems, especially biological macromolecules.

Randolph L. Rill, Professor; Ph.D., Northwestern, 1971. Physical biochemistry: chromatin and DNA structure and function, DNA–small molecule interactions, biochemical applications of NMR spectroscopy.

Sanford A. Safron, Professor; Ph.D., Harvard, 1969. Dynamics of chemical reactions, models of chemical reactions, dynamics of crystal surfaces, He atom-surface scattering experiments.

Jack Saltiel, Professor; Ph.D., Caltech, 1964. Photochemistry of organic molecules, elucidation of the mechanisms of photochemical reactions by chemical and spectroscopic means.

QingXiang Amy Sang, Assistant Professor; Ph.D., Georgetown, 1990. Protein chemistry, enzymology, molecular biology, and biochemistry of metalloproteinases; biochemical basis of angiogenesis; molecular carcinogenesis and mechanisms of cancer metastasis.

Joseph B. Schlenoff, Professor and Associate Director, MARTECH Program; Ph.D., Massachusetts Amherst, 1987. Synthesis and characterization of electrically conductive polymers and ceramics, electrochemical polymerization, properties of superconducting oxides.

Martin A. Schwartz, Professor; Ph.D., Stanford, 1965. Organic synthesis: biogenetic-type syntheses of natural products, synthesis of enzyme inhibitors.

Raymond K. Sheline, Professor; Ph.D., Berkeley, 1949. Nuclear spectroscopy and structure, decay schemes and nuclear reaction studies, experimental tests of nuclear models—recent emphasis on octupole shapes.

Oliver Steinbock, Assistant Professor; Ph.D., Göttingen (Germany), 1993. Kinetics, experimental and theoretical studies of nonequilibrium systems, chemical self-organization.

Albert E. Stiegman, Assistant Professor; Ph.D., Columbia, 1984. Synthesis of inorganic and hybrid organic/inorganic materials and nanocomposite structures; optical, dielectric, catalytic, and photochemical processes in solids; spectroscopy and photophysics of reactive metal centers in glasses.

Thomas J. Vickers, Professor; Ph.D., Florida, 1964. Spectrochemical analysis, Raman spectroscopy.

GEORGETOWN UNIVERSITY

Department of Chemistry

Programs of Study

Georgetown's Department of Chemistry offers a program leading to the Doctor of Philosophy (Ph.D.) degree, which prepares graduates for a variety of careers in college teaching, in university research and teaching, and in industry or government. Students may also earn a master's degree as an intermediate step on the way to the Ph.D. Entering graduate students take placement examinations in physical and organic chemistry and two of the three other fundamental areas of chemistry. Students normally take approximately three semesters of graduate courses in chemistry, although students with graduate-level credit from other institutions may be excused from some requirements. Students are expected to maintain a B average or better in order to continue working toward the Ph.D. The graduate program is designed to prepare and encourage students to move into research activity as soon as it is appropriate; all students are so engaged by the end of their second semester. New students participate in a weekly seminar series in which faculty members discuss their research programs in order to help students select a field of research from among the subdisciplines of analytical, inorganic, organic, and physical chemistry and biochemistry. Once a student has selected a research director (by the end of the first semester), an educational program consisting of research, course work, seminars, and self-study is tailored to fit his or her needs and interests. Research groups are relatively small and ensure close personal attention.

During the second or third year of graduate studies, students present an oral defense of an original research proposal and a defense of their plan for research. The final step is the preparation and defense of a written doctoral dissertation, demonstrating the student's important contribution to a field of human knowledge, before a faculty committee.

Research Facilities

The Department of Chemistry is located on Georgetown University's Main Campus, in the Reiss Science Center, with laboratories and offices in the adjacent White-Gravenor Hall. The department has more than $5 million worth of modern chemical instrumentation, including two 300-MHz and one 500-MHz NMR spectrometers, a Siemens SMART-CCD (charge-coupled device) X-ray diffractometer, a Fisons Instruments MD800/GC 8000 GC-mass spectrometer, a JASCO J-710 spectropolarimeter for circular and linear dichroism spectroscopy, and Nanoscope II atomic force and scanning tunneling microscopes for surface analysis. Other routine instrumentation includes FT-IR, UV-VIS, and a variety of chromatographic (GC, HPLC) instruments, mostly located in professors' laboratories. All of the instrumentation is readily available for use by graduate student researchers. In addition, the Department of Chemistry has ample computational and network resources, including modern molecular modeling facilities.

The department maintains a full-time technical staff, including an instrumentation specialist, an electronics engineer, and a master glassblower; a machine shop is also available. The Blommer Science Library is conveniently located in the Reiss Science Center and maintains subscriptions to leading scientific journals. It also provides electronic access to a variety of CD-ROM databases and offers assistance with Chemical Abstracts Service on-line searching of chemical literature.

Financial Aid

Nearly all full-time graduate students in good standing are offered full support by Graduate School assistantship awards or department teaching or research assistantships. Fellowship support is not normally available for students aiming at a terminal master's degree. Support includes graduate tuition and a generous stipend ($16,920 over twelve months for the 1999–2000 academic year) and is taxable. Most graduate students serve as teaching assistants for about two years, usually leading laboratory or recitation sections in the undergraduate general or organic chemistry courses. In subsequent years, many graduate students are supported as research assistants.

Cost of Study

For information about the cost of study, students should consult the financial aid section above.

Living and Housing Costs

Most graduate students live either a short walk away in apartments or houses in the District of Columbia or in the nearby suburbs of Virginia; on-campus housing is not available. Rental prices, generally for shared housing, range from $400 to $600 per month, depending on type and location; food and entertainment costs vary considerably.

Student Group

Of the current 45 graduate students working toward the Ph.D. (29 men and 16 women), 98 percent are full-time, and 69 percent are international students. The department also includes 12 postdoctoral research fellows and visiting scientists. The Department of Chemistry looks for graduate students with outstanding undergraduate records and laboratory research experience.

Student Outcomes

About 40 percent of Georgetown's chemistry Ph.D. graduates eventually pursue careers in higher education; recent alumni hold tenure-track positions at institutions such as Florida State University, Canisius College, and Emory University. Approximately one third go into government research laboratories (e.g., the Department of Energy, the National Institute of Science and Technology (NIST), and the Food and Drug Administration); the remainder work in industry (e.g., DuPont and Merck) or other fields.

Location

Washington, D.C., the nation's capital, is a major metropolitan area with cultural amenities such as the Smithsonian Institution, the Kennedy Center for the Performing Arts, Wolf Trap Farm Park, and many other museums and theaters. Several national parks and forests, including Shenandoah National Park and Assateague National Seashore, are within easy driving distance. The Chesapeake and Ohio National Park adjoins the Georgetown Campus. Washington is also an important scientific city, with government laboratories (such as NIH, NIST, and NRL) and almost 300 libraries, including the Library of Congress and the National Medical Library, nearby.

The University

Georgetown University, founded in 1789, is the oldest institution of learning in its geographical region. The University was founded before the area was selected for the new federal capital. The original port of Georgetown, now completely embedded in Washington, D.C., has retained an old-world character in the modern federal city. A highly selective private institution with a total enrollment of about 12,000 students, Georgetown University retains the intimate contact between students and staff members that is conducive to high quality in original research and scholarship. The University actively participates in the cultural and scientific life of Washington and of the nation.

Applying

Application forms are available by request from the Department of Chemistry; there is no application fee if the form is sent directly to the department. While GRE scores are not required, applicants are encouraged to forward them if they have taken the exam. International students must submit TOEFL scores (a minimum score of 600 (paper-based) or 250 (computer-based) is required for a full fellowship) and are strongly advised to submit GRE scores as well. Applicants from China should hold or be ready to receive the M.S. degree. There is no application deadline; students may begin studies in either January or August.

Correspondence and Information

Director of Graduate Admissions
Department of Chemistry
Georgetown University
Box 571227
Washington, D.C. 20057-1227
Telephone: 202-687-6073
Fax: 202-687-6209
E-mail: chemad@gusun.georgetown.edu
World Wide Web: http://www.georgetown.edu/departments/chemistry/chemistry.html

Georgetown University

THE FACULTY AND THEIR RESEARCH

Research interests of the Department of Chemistry faculty members cover all of the major areas of modern chemistry: physical, inorganic, organic, and analytical chemistry and biochemistry. In addition, most faculty members are involved in specialized or interdisciplinary research at the boundaries of the traditional areas, including structural crystallography, theoretical chemistry, organometallic chemistry, surface and materials science, and polymer chemistry. All faculty members are active in research.

Robert E. Bachman, Assistant Professor; Ph.D., Rice, 1994. Inorganic and materials chemistry: synthetic and structural inorganic chemistry; X-ray crystallography; physical effects of intermolecular interactions in materials; optical and electrical behavior of inorganic and organometallic materials.

Richard D. Bates Jr., Professor; Ph.D., Columbia, 1971. Experimental chemical physics: studies of molecular dynamics by laser and spectroscopic methods; laser-induced fluorescence studies of vibrational energy transfer processes; role of sensitizers in laser-stimulated chemical reactions; solvent-solute interactions studied by magnetic resonance techniques; dynamics of transient complexation.

DeLanson R. Crist, Associate Professor; Ph.D., MIT, 1967. Physical organic chemistry: organic mechanisms; complexes of polyfunctional organic donors with metal ions; electrochemical correlations, structure and reactivity of nitrones in unusually high oxidation states.

Angel C. de Dios, Assistant Professor; Ph.D., Illinois at Chicago, 1992. Physical and biophysical chemistry: theoretical and experimental studies in nuclear magnetic resonance (NMR) spectroscopy; structural elucidation of small peptides; ab initio interpretation of NMR chemical shifts in biological systems and catalysts.

Robert de Levie, Visiting Research Professor; Ph.D., Amsterdam, 1963. Electrochemistry and analytical chemistry: electrode kinetics, double layer structure, stochastic processes, electroanalysis, instrumentation; nucleation and growth processes; formation and properties of monolayer films; theory of analytical titrations.

Joseph E. Earley, Professor Emeritus and Research Professor; Ph.D., Brown, 1957. Dynamics of inorganic reactions in aqueous solutions: redox reactions of ruthenium and titanium complexes, catalytic antibodies; process philosophy: significance of recent developments in chemistry for philosophy and for evolutionary theory.

Colby A. Foss Jr., Assistant Professor; Ph.D., California, Davis, 1991. Analytical and materials chemistry: nanoengineered materials for surface enhanced spectroscopy and electroanalytical chemistry; solvent effects in electron transfer and optical absorption processes in nanoscopic cavities; optical and electrical properties of composite materials.

Janice M. Hicks, Associate Professor; Ph.D., Columbia, 1986. Physical chemistry: laser probes of the structure and dynamics of chemical environments such as liquids and surfaces using ultrafast and nonlinear optical techniques; adsorption phenomena; circular dichroism effects at interfaces.

Kennan V. Kellaris, Assistant Professor; Ph.D., California, San Diego, 1989. Biochemistry: mechanism of protein translocation across cellular membrane; protein structure.

Miklos Kertesz, Professor; Dr.R.N., Budapest, 1978; C.Sc., Hungarian Academy of Sciences, 1978. Applied quantum chemistry: conducting polymers, solid-state transformations, Jahn-Teller distortions, local perturbations.

Daniel E. Martire, Professor and Chair; Ph.D., Stevens, 1963. Thermodynamics and statistical mechanics: gas, liquid and supercritical-fluid chromatographic separations; nonaqueous and aqueous, nonelectrolytic liquid mixtures; hydrogen-bonded and charge-transfer molecular complexes; solvent properties of and phase transitions in liquid-crystalline systems; absorption on surfaces and at interfaces.

Michael T. Pope, Professor; D.Phil. Oxford, 1957. Inorganic and organometallic chemistry: polynuclear transition metal oxoanions (heteropolyanions), mixed valence chemistry, small molecule activation and catalysis.

Paul D. Roepe, Assistant Professor; Ph.D., Boston University, 1987. Biochemistry: molecular mechanisms of biological membrane transport; biochemical mechanisms of drug resistance; recombinant DNA approaches to identification of genes that are alternatively expressed upon exposure to toxic compounds; cellular ion transport physiology.

Jennifer A. Swift, Assistant Professor; Ph.D., Yale, 1997. Physical organic and materials chemistry: crystal growth mechanisms; scanning probe microscopy; supramolecular synthesis; molecular recognition at surfaces; X-ray crystallography.

Timothy H. Warren, Assistant Professor; Ph.D., MIT, 1997. Organometallic and inorganic chemistry: design, synthesis, and mechanistic study of homogeneous catalysts for alkane oxidation, olefin hydroamination, alpha-olefin polymerization; metal-ligand structure-reactivity relationships; low-coordinate first-row metal-oxo complexes.

Richard G. Weiss, Professor; Ph.D., Connecticut, 1969. Physical organic chemistry and organic photochemistry: reaction rates and mechanisms; anisotropic solvent effects on reaction mechanisms; liquid crystals as mechanistic probes; properties of thermally reversible gels.

David C.-H. Yang, Professor; Ph.D., Yale, 1973. Biochemistry: nucleic acid-protein interactions; structure and function of enzyme complexes.

SELECTED PUBLICATIONS

Tschinkl, M., **R. E. Bachman,** and F. P. Gabbai. Preparation of mercury-anthracene derivative. π-π-stacking, Hg···Cl and Hg···π interactions in the X-ray crystal structure of polymeric 9-chloromercurioanthracene. *J. Organomet. Chem.,* in press.

Bachman, R. E., A. Fiseha, and S. K. Pollack. The structure and attempted topochemical polymerization of single crystalline 1,1,4,4-bis(pentamethylene)-1,2,3-butatriene. *J. Chem. Crystallogr.,* in press.

Wei, X., **R. E. Bachman,** and **M. T. Pope.** Rhodium derivatives of lacunary heteropolytungstates illustrate metalloporphyrin analogies. Reductive dimerization to Rh_2-linked Keggin moieties. *J. Am. Chem. Soc.* 120:10248–53, 1998.

Bachman, R. E., and D. F. Andretta. Metal-ligand bonding in coinage metal-phosphine complexes: The synthesis and characterization of some low-coordinate silver(I)-phosphine complexes. *Inorg. Chem.* 37:5657–63, 1998.

Whitmire, K. H., et al. **(R. E. Bachman).** Main-group-transition metal carbonyl complexes. *Inorg. Synth.* 31:220, 1997.

Villamena, F. A., and **D. R. Crist.** Metal-nitrone complexes: Spin trapping and solution characterization. *J. Chem. Soc., Dalton Trans.* 4055–62, 1998.

Villamena, F. A., M. H. Dickman, and **D. R. Crist.** Nitrones as ligands in complexes of Cu(II), Mn(II), Co(II), Ni(II), Fe(II), and Fe(III) with N-t-butyl-α-(2-pyridyl)nitrone and 2,5,5-trimethyl-1-pyrroline-N-oxide. *Inorg. Chem.* 37:1446–53, 1998.

Villamena, F. A., M. H. Dickman, and **D. R. Crist.** Stabilization of a nitroxide with a β-hydrogen by metals: Structure and magnetic properties of adducts of N-oxy-N-tert-butyl(2-pyridyl)phenylmethanamine with Mn(II), Ni(II), and CO(II) hexafluoroacetylacetonates. *Inorg. Chem.* 37:1454–7, 1998.

Dickman, M. H., J. P. Ward, F. A. Villamena, and **D. R. Crist.** Bis μ-(N-[(methylthio)phenylmethylene]methanamine-N-oxide-O) bis (1,1,1,5,5,5,-hexafluoropentane-2,4-dionato-O,O')nickel(II). *Acta Crystallogr.* C54:929–30, 1998.

deDios, A. C., and J. L. Roach. ^{15}N shielding of the nitrosyl ligand in Co(NO)(TPP). *J. Phys. Chem.,* in press.

McMahon, M., and **A. C. deDios** et al. An experimental and quantum chemical investigation of CO binding to heme proteins and model systems: A unified model based on ^{13}C, ^{17}O, ^{57}Fe nuclear magnetic resonance, ^{57}Fe Mossbauer and infrared spectroscopy. *J. Am. Chem. Soc.* 120:4784–97, 1998.

Walling, A. E., R. E. Pargas, and **A. C. deDios.** Chemical shift tensors in peptides: A quantum mechanical study. *J. Phys. Chem. A* 101:7299–303, 1997.

deDios, A. C., and E. M. Earle. ^{13}C and ^{17}O chemical shifts and CO stretching frequency of carbon monoxide bound to Fe^{2+}. *J. Phys. Chem. A* 101:8132–4, 1997.

deDios, A. C., and C. J. Jameson. ^{129}Xe shielding with N_2 and CO as collision partners. *J. Phys. Chem.* 107:4253–70, 1997.

Havlin, R. H., et al. **(A. C. deDios).** An *ab initio* quantum chemical investigation of carbon-13 NMR shielding tensors in glycine, alanine, valine, isoleucine, serine and threonine: Comparisons between helical and sheet tensors, and the effects of χ_1 on shielding. *J. Am. Chem. Soc.* 119:11951–8, 1997.

de Levie, R. Gouy, Debye-Hüeckel, and Fick: Understanding a differential equation without solving it. *J. Chem. Educ.* 76:129–32, 1999.

Roudolph, M., M. Hromadova, and **R. de Levie.** Demystifying an electrochemical oscillator. *J. Phys. Chem.* 102:4405–10, 1998.

de Levie, R., T. Moisio, and M. Heikonen. Computer fitting of entire data sets, as exemplified by acid-base titrations. *Kemia-Kemi.* 25:121–3, 1998.

Wandlowski, T., M. Hromadova, and **R. de Levie.** On the kinetics of adsorption of lauryl sulfate at the mercury-water interface. *Langmuir* 13:2766–72, 1997.

de Levie, R. The pH in grapH. *Crit. Rev. Anal. Chem.* 27:51–76, 1997.

Sandrock, M. L., F. M. Pibel, F. M. Geiger, and **C. A. Foss Jr.** Synthesis and second-harmonic generation studies of non-centrosymmetric gold nanostructures. *J. Phys. Chem. B,* in press.

Ali, A. H., and **C. A. Foss Jr.** Electrochemically-induced shifts in the plasmon resonance bands of nanoscopic gold particles adsorbed on transparent electrodes. *J. Electrochem. Soc.* 146:628–36, 1999.

Al-Rawashdeh, N., M. L. Sandrock, C. J. Seugling, and **C. A. Foss**

Jr. Visible region polarization spectroscopic studies of template-synthesized gold particles oriented in polyethylene. *J. Phys. Chem. B* 102:361–71, 1998.

El-Kouedi, M., M. L. Sandrock, C. J. Seugling, and **C. A. Foss Jr.** Electrochemical synthesis of asymmetric gold-silver iodide nanoparticle composite films. *Chem. Mater.* 10:3287–9, 1998.

Al-Rawashdeh, N., and **C. A. Foss Jr.** UV/visible and infrared spectra of polyethylene/nanoscopic gold rod composite films: Effects of gold particle size, shape and orientation. *Nanostructured Mater.* 9:383–6, 1997.

Ali, A. H., R. J. Luther, **C. A. Foss Jr.,** and G. B. Chapman. Optical properties of nanoscopic gold particles adsorbed at electrode surfaces: The effect of applied potential on plasmon resonance absorption. *Nanostructured Mater.* 9:559–62, 1997.

Lu, A. H., G. H. Lu, A. M. Kessinger, and **C. A. Foss Jr.** Dichroic thin layer films prepared from alkanethiol-coated gold nanoparticles in friction-oriented poly(tetrafluoroethylene) matrices. *J. Phys. Chem. B* 101:9139–42, 1997.

Hicks, J. M., and T. Petralli-Mallow. Nonlinear optics of chiral surface systems. *Appl. Phys.,* in press.

Hicks, J. M., and N. Scherer (eds.). *Laser Techniques for Condensed Phase and Biological Systems, SPIE Conference Proceedings,* Vol. 3273. Bellingham, Wash.: Int. Soc. Opt. Eng., 1998.

Geiger, F. M., **J. M. Hicks,** and **A. C. deDios.** Ab initio study of HOCl, HCl, H_2O, and Cl_2 interacting with four water molecules. *J. Phys. Chem. A* 102:1514–22, 1998.

Geiger, F. M., and **J. M. Hicks.** Stratospheric ozone chemistry on ice surfaces. In *Laser Techniques for Surface Science II, SPIE Conference Proceedings,* 3272:296–305. Bellingham, Wash.: Int. Soc. Opt. Eng., 1998.

Hicks, J. M., W. Ho, and H. L. Dai (eds.). *Laser Techniques for Surface Science II, SPIE Conference Proceedings,* Vol. 2547. Bellingham, Wash.: Int. Soc. Eng., 1995.

Choi, C. H., **M. Kertesz,** S. Dobrin, and J. Michl. Argon-matrix–isolation Raman spectra and density functional study of 1,3-butadiene conformers. *Theor. Chem. Accounts,* in press.

Choi, C. H., and **M. Kertesz** et al. Conformational fingerprints in the IR and Raman spectra of oligoanilines: A combined theoretical and experimental study. *Chem. Mater.,* in press.

Choi, C. H., and **M. Kertesz.** Is a 1.9 A bond length in polymeric fullerides possible? *Chem. Phys. Lett.* 282:318–24, 1998.

Choi, C. H., and **M. Kertesz.** Bond length alternation and aromaticity in large annulenes. *J. Chem. Phys.* 108:6681–8, 1998.

Choi, C. H., and **M. Kertesz.** A new interpretation of the valence tautomerism of 1,6-methano[10]annulene and its derivatives. *J. Phys. Chem. A* 102:3429–37, 1998.

Karpfen, A., C. H. Choi, and **M. Kertesz.** Single bond torsional potentials in conjugated systems: A comparison of *ab initio* and density functional results. *J. Phys. Chem. A* 101:7426–33, 1997.

Choi, C. H., **M. Kertesz,** and A. Karpfen. Do localized structures of [14] and [18] annulenes exist? *J. Am. Chem. Soc.* 119:11994–5, 1997.

Frapper, G., et al. **(M. Kertesz).** Can CO polymerize? A theoretical investigation of polymeric carbon monoxide. *Chem. Commun.* 2011–2, 1997.

Boehm, R. E., and **D. E. Martire.** Theory of liquid chromatographic retention and solute transfer thermodynamics using the Bethe-Guggenheim quasi-chemical approach. *J. Phys. Chem.* 98:1317–27, 1994.

Boehm, R. E., and **D. E. Martire.** Theory of homopolymer retention in the weak adsorption limit. *J. Liq. Chromatogr.* 17:3145–77, 1994.

Alvarex-Zepeda, A., B. N. Barman, and **D. E. Martire.** A thermodynamic study of marked differences between acetonitrile + water and methanol + water mobile-phase systems in reversed-phase liquid chromatography. *Anal. Chem.* 64:1978–84, 1992.

Yan, C., and **D. E. Martire.** Determination and theoretical analysis of supercritical fluid chromatographic retention of PAHs in a polymeric smectic phase. *J. Phys. Chem.* 96:3505–12, 1992.

Müller, A., F. Peters, **M. T. Pope,** and D. Gatteschi. Polyoxometalates: Very large structures—nanoscale magnets. *Chem. Rev.* 98:239–71, 1998.

Pope, M. T., X. Wei, K. Wassermann, and M. H. Dickman. New

Georgetown University

Selected Publications (continued)

developments in the chemistry of heteropolytungstates of rhodium and cerium. *C. R. Acad. Sci. Paris* 1, Ser. IIc:297–304, 1998.

Wei, X., M. H. Dickman, and **M. T. Pope**. Rhodium-carbon bond formation in aqueous solution. Synthesis, structure, and reactivity of the functionalized heteropolytungstates, $[XW_{11}O_{39}RhCH_2COOH]^{5,6-}$ (X=P, Si). *J. Am. Chem. Soc.* 120:10254–5, 1998.

Wei, X., M. H. Dickman, and **M. T. Pope**. New routes for multiple derivatization of polyoxometalates. Diacetato-dirhodium-11-tungstophosphate, $[(PO_4)W_{11}O_{35}\{Rh_2(OAc)_2\}]^{5-}$. *Inorg. Chem.* 36: 130–1, 1997.

Ortéga, F., **M. T. Pope,** and H. T. Evans Jr. Tungstorhenate heteropolyanions. 2. Synthesis and characterization of enneatungstorhenates (V), -(VI), and -(VII). *Inorg. Chem.* 36:2166–9, 1997.

Wassermann, K., M. H. Dickman, and **M. T. Pope**. Self-assembly of supramolecular polyoxometalates. The compact, water-soluble heteropolytungstate anion $[As^{III}_{12}Ce^{III}_{16}(H_2O)_{36}W_{148}O_{524}]^{76-}$. *Angew. Chem. Int. Ed. Engl.* 36:1445–8, 1997.

Weisburg, J. H., **P. D. Roepe**, S. Dzekunov, and D. A. Scheinberg. Intracellular pH and complement: pH_i regulation of complement mediated cytotoxicity of nucleated human cells. *J. Biol. Chem.,* in press.

Fritz, F., E. M. Howard, M. M. Hoffman, and **P. D. Roepe**. Evidence for altered ion transport in *S. cerevisiae* overexpressing human MDR 1 protein. *Biochemistry,* in press.

Santai, C. T., J. Fritz, and **P. D. Roepe**. Effects of ion gradients on H+ transport mediated by human MDR 1 protein. *Biochemistry,* in press.

Roepe, P. D., and J. A. Martiney. Are ion exchange processes central to understanding drug resistance phenomena? *Trends Pharmacol. Sci.* 20:62–6, 1999.

Robinson, L. J., et al. **(P. D. Roepe)**. Human MDR 1 protein delays the apoptotic cascade in Chinese hamster ovary fibroblasts. *Biochemistry* 36:11169–78, 1997.

Hoffman, M. M., and **P. D. Roepe**. Analysis of ion transport perturbations caused by human MDR 1 protein overexpression. *Biochemistry* 36:11153–68, 1997.

Wei, L. Y., M. M. Hoffman, and **P. D. Roepe**. Altered pH_i regulation in CFTR transfectants with various levels of chemotherapeutic drug resistance. *Am. J. Physiol.* 272:C1642–53, 1997.

Swift, J. A., A. M. Pivovar, A. M. Reynolds, and M. D. Ward. Template directed architectural isomerism of open molecular frameworks: Engineering of crystalline clathrates. *J. Am. Chem. Soc.* 120:5887–94, 1998.

Swift, J. A., A. M. Reynolds, and M. D. Ward. Cooperative host-guest recognition in crystalline clathrates: Steric guest ordering by molecular gears. *Chem. Mater.* 10:4159–68, 1998.

Swift, J. A., R. Pal, and J. M. McBride. Using hydrogen-bonds and herringbone packing to design interfaces of 4,4'-disubstituted *meso*-hydrobenzoin crystals. The importance of unfavorable packing motifs. *J. Am. Chem. Soc.* 120:96–104, 1998.

Swift, J. A., V. A. Russell, and M. D. Ward. Organoporous hosts with adjustable molecular environments. *Adv. Mater.* 9:1183–6, 1997.

Warren, T. H., R. R. Schrock, and W. M. Davis. α-Hydrogen migration reactions in tungsten(VI) cyclopentadienyl alkylidyne complexes. *J. Organomet. Chem.* 569:125–37, 1998.

Warren, T. H., R. R. Schrock, and W. M. Davis. Neutral and cationic group 4 complexes containing bis(borylamide)$[R_2BNCH_2CH_2NBR_2]^{2-}$ ligands, (R=2,4,6-i-$Pr_3C_6H_2$, M=Zr; R=cyclohexyl, M=Ti,Zr,Hf). *Organometallics* 17:308–21, 1998.

Warren, T. H., R. R. Schrock, and W. M. Davis. Synthesis of group 4 organometallic complexes that contain the bis(borylamide) ligand $[Mes_2BNCH_2CH_2NBMes_2]^{2-}$. *Organometallics* 15:562–9, 1996.

Phillips, G. S., et al. **(R. G. Weiss)**. Observation of radiation effects on three-dimensional optical random access-memory materials for use in radiation dosimetry. *Appl. Radiat. Isot.* 50:875–81, 1999.

Zimerman, O. E., and **R. G. Weiss**. Static and dynamic fluorescence from α,ω-di(1-pyrenyl)alkanes as probes of poluethylene microstructure. *J. Phys. Chem.* 102:5364–74, 1998.

Lu, L., et al. **(R. G. Weiss)**. Solute induced liquid-crystalline behavior of a quaternary ammonium salt and its application to structure determination. *Liq. Cryst.* 25:295–300, 1998.

Khetrapal, C. L., and **R. G. Weiss**. NMR of oriented systems—Future hopes! *NMR Newslett.* 1998.

Talhavini, M., T. D. Z. Atvars, O. Schurr, and **R. G. Weiss**. Translocation of fluorescent probes upon stretching low-density polyethylene films. Comparison between "free" and covalently-attached anthryl groups. *Polymer* 39:3221–32, 1998.

Taraszka, J. A., and **R. G. Weiss**. Comparison of diffusion of N,N-dimethylaniline and N,N-dioctadecylaniline in a low-density polyethylene film. Activation energies and detection of two diffusion pathways. *Macromolecules* 30:2467–73, 1997.

Gu, W., L. Lu, G. B. Chapman, and **R. G. Weiss**. Polymerized gels and "reverse aerogels" from methyl methacrylate or styrene and tetraoctadecylammonium bromide as gelator. *Chem. Commun.* 543–4, 1997.

Quina, F. H., and **R. G. Weiss**. Time-resolved techniques in photochemistry, photophysics and photobiology. Introduction. *Photochem. Photobiol.* 65:2–3, 1997.

Terech, P., and **R. G. Weiss**. Low-molecular mass gelators of organic liquids and the properties of their gels. *Chem. Rev.* 97:3133–60, 1997.

Yang, D. C. H. Mammalian aminoacyl-tRNA synthetases. *Curr. Top. Cell. Regul.* 34:101–36, 1996.

Hermida, L., P. B. Chock, T. Curran, and **D. C. H. Yang**. Ubiquitination of transcription factors c-jun and c-fos using reconstituted ubiquitination enzymes: Isozyme specificity and proteolysis. *J. Biol. Chem.* 271:4530–6, 1996.

Vilalta, A., Z. Y. Yan, and **D. C. H. Yang**. Two human valyl-tRNA synthetases encoding cDNA sequences deposited in GeneBank bank display extensive differences. *Gene* 170:291, 1996.

GEORGIA INSTITUTE OF TECHNOLOGY
A Unit of the University System of Georgia

School of Chemistry and Biochemistry

Programs of Study

The School of Chemistry and Biochemistry offers programs leading to the degrees of Master of Science (M.S.) and Doctor of Philosophy (Ph.D.). The requirements for the M.S. degree in chemistry are 30 credit hours of approved course work and an approved M.S. thesis. The Ph.D. requires completion of 12 credit hours of a curriculum in a specific area (e.g., analytical, inorganic, organic, physical, or polymer chemistry or biochemistry), 9 credit hours outside of the major area, and approval of an original research thesis by a faculty committee. Students must maintain a minimum grade point average of 3.0/4.0 in graduate chemistry courses. Candidacy to the Ph.D. program is normally achieved at the end of the second year by successful completion of course work, literature examinations, an original research proposal, and a research seminar. Completion of the Ph.D. requirements, including the research thesis, takes four to five years.

Research Facilities

Research laboratories are located in the Boggs Chemistry Building, completed in 1976, and in the Institute of Bioengineering and Bioscience (IBB), completed in 1999. These buildings are located near the center of the Georgia Tech campus, with convenient access to the central library and student services buildings. In addition to individual research labs, the department houses state-of-the-art research instrumentation. Nuclear magnetic resonance spectroscopic facilities include 300-, 400-, and 500-MHz solution and 300- and 400-MHz solid-state instruments. Quadrupole and sector mass spectrometers interfaced to gas and liquid chromatography, as well as ESMS, MS/MS and ICP/MS facilities, are available. Powder-and single-crystal CCD X-ray diffractometers are available and have sophisticated programs for data analysis. Other research facilities within the department include scanning tunneling microscopes (STM), atomic force microscopes (AFM), a complete range of electrochemical equipment, spectrometers (UV-015, Cr-IR, NIR, UV/vis, CD/ORD, MCD atomic absorption, ESR, fluorimeters), SQUID magnetometers, equipment to study fast kinetics, thermal analysis equipment (DSC, TGA), peptide synthesizers, DNA synthesizers, capillary electrophoresis equipment, and a wide array of gas, liquid, and ion chromatographs. Computer terminals connected to the Institute network are located throughout the department. The Laser Dynamic Laboratory has state-of-the-art lasers and spectroscopic equipment for time-resolved optical, FTIR, and Raman studies in the time domain from femtosecond to millisecond time scales. The School maintains a stockroom and glass, and electronics shops to support research and teaching.

Financial Aid

Graduate students are supported through teaching and research assistantships. All graduate students in good standing pursuing Ph.D. and master's thesis degrees receive support for the duration of their studies. Students entering in fall 1999 receive stipends of $16,000. Supplemental awards of $1000 to $5500 are available to exceptionally well-qualified applicants. Competitive fellowships and scholarships are available for superior performance in teaching and research.

Cost of Study

All research and teaching assistants receive a waiver of tuition. Graduate students pay fees of $380 per semester.

Living and Housing Costs

Graduate student dormitories and married student apartments are available on campus. A diverse array of rental property is available in Atlanta.

Student Group

There are approximately 130 graduate students in the School of Chemistry and Biochemistry. The total enrollment at Georgia Tech is approximately 13,000.

Location

Georgia Institute of Technology is situated a few blocks from downtown Atlanta, a modern, vibrant city with a tradition of civic pride and diversity and widely recognized as the nation's southeastern hub of culture, science, technology, medicine, education, and commerce. The campus is pleasantly landscaped beneath a towering skyline that houses the headquarters of some of the nation's largest corporations. Atlanta is home to the Carter Presidential Center; the Martin Luther King, Jr. Center for Nonviolent Social Change; the Woodruff Memorial Arts Center; High Museum of Art; Fox Theater; a symphony; a zoo; and botanical gardens. Sports teams include the Braves, Falcons, and Hawks, and major venues include the Georgia Dome and the 1996 Olympic Stadium. Atlanta is served by a subway system, an extensive highway system, and Hartsfield International Airport, which has direct flights to worldwide destinations. The north Georgia mountains and Lake Lanier are each approximately 45 minutes from Georgia Tech.

The Institute

Georgia Institute of Technology, a unit of the University System of Georgia, was founded in 1885. Georgia Tech has long been recognized for its world-class research and in the education of both undergraduate and graduate students. Georgia Tech was the site of the 1996 Olympic village and athletic events.

Applying

Applications for admission to the Graduate School are accepted throughout the year. Most students begin study in the fall semester; admission for winter or summer semester may also be requested. Applicants are encouraged to submit GRE scores for the advanced test in chemistry. International student applications must be accompanied by a TOEFL score. Most applications are received between November and February. Competition for fellowships and stipend supplements is intense, and well-qualified students are encouraged to apply early. Applications can be obtained from the School of Chemistry and Biochemistry.

Correspondence and Information

Graduate Coordinator
School of Chemistry and Biochemistry
Georgia Institute of Technology
Atlanta, Georgia 30332-0400.

Telephone: 404-894-8227
Fax: 404-894-7452
E-mail: grad.info@chemistry.gatech.edu
World Wide Web: http://www.chemistry.gatech.edu

Georgia Institute of Technology

THE FACULTY AND THEIR RESEARCH INTERESTS

E. K. Barefield, Professor and Associate Dean; Ph.D., Ohio State, 1969. Synthesis of macrocyclic ligands, synthetic applications and reactions of coordinated ligands, organometallic chemistry of α-heteroatom substituted metal alkyls, thermal mechanisms of gas generation in nuclear waste.

H. W. Beckham, Assistant Professor in Textiles (adjunct with Chemistry); Ph.D., MIT, 1991. Polymer chemistry and physics, molecular-mobility-directed polymer synthesis, multidimensional solid-state NMR, NMR imaging.

R. F. Borkman, Professor; Ph.D., California, Riverside, 1966. Experimental studies in photobiology and protein photochemistry, ab initio calculations of ion-molecule reactions and ion clusters.

L. A. Bottomley, Professor; Ph.D., Houston, 1980. Electroanalytical chemistry, scanning tunneling and atomic force microscopy, nitrogen atom transfer chemistry.

R. F. Browner, Regents' Professor; Ph.D., Imperial College (London), 1970. Atomic, molecular, and mass spectrometry; interfacing for liquid and supercritical fluid chromatography coupled to organic and inorganic mass spectrometry; inductively coupled rf and microwave plasma and Fourier-transform infrared detection.

E. M. Burgess, Professor; Ph.D., MIT, 1962. Organic synthesis, drug design, new methods for drug structure-activity relationships, theoretical aspects of drug-protein interaction.

K. L. Busch, Professor; Ph.D., North Carolina, 1979. Mixture analysis by mass spectrometry, mass spectral interpretation, MS/MS ionization mechanisms, cluster and adduct ions of metal-containing compounds, instrument design, electrospray ionization.

D. M. Collard, Associate Professor and Graduate Coordinator; Ph.D., Massachusetts, 1989. Organic and polymer self-assembly, electronically conductive polymers, liquid crystals, self-assembled monolayers, organic electrochemistry, new functional polyesters.

R. M. Dickson, Assistant Professor; Ph.D., Chicago, 1996. Biophysical chemistry, development and utilization of single molecule optical techniques to elucidate biological mechanisms.

C. A. Eckert, Institute Professor in Chemical Engineering (adjunct with Chemistry); Ph.D., Berkeley, 1964. Supercritical fluid processing, separations, homogenous catalysis, chemical kinetics, phase equilibria, solution chemistry, and molecular thermodynamics.

M. A. El-Sayed, Julius Brown Professor; Ph.D., Florida State, 1959. Rate of energy redistribution in the transition state, nanocrystals, molecular mechanism(s) of solar-to-electric energy conversion in photosynthetic systems in nature.

C. J. Fahrni, Assistant Professor; Ph.D., Basel (Switzerland), 1995. Bioinorganic chemistry; bioorganometallic chemistry; protein engineering; molecular aspects of metal transport, storage, and homeostasis in cells; mechanistic aspects of metalloprotein catalysis; transition metal catalysis.

S. L. Gordon, Professor; Ph.D., Columbia, 1962. Structure and molecular motions in biologically interesting molecules using nuclear magnetic resonance relaxation techniques.

R. Hernandez, Assistant Professor; Ph.D., Berkeley, 1993. Theoretical physical chemistry and polymer reaction dynamics, semi-classical and mixed-classical dynamics in multidimensional gas and condensed phase systems.

N. V. Hud, Assistant Professor; Ph.D., California, Davis, 1992. Biophysical chemistry, NMR spectroscopy, investigations of nucleic acid structure, function, cation binding, and self-assembly.

J. Janata, Professor; Ph.D., Charles (Prague), 1965. Electroanalytical chemistry and chemical sensors, electrochemical synthesis and characterization of organic semiconductors, chemical electronics, tunneling microscopy at liquid-liquid interphase.

C. L. Liotta, Regents' Professor and Vice Provost for Research and Graduate Studies; Ph.D., Maryland, 1963. Use of macrocyclic polydentate ligands in developing new and useful regioselective and stereoselective reagents in organic synthesis, synthesis and characterization of new organic electrically conducting polymers, new nonlinear optical materials, reactions in supercritical fluids, synthesis of biocompatible materials.

L. A. Lyon, Assistant Professor; Ph.D., Northwestern, 1996. Bioanalytical and materials chemistry; intelligent polymer nanoparticles and interfaces; biosensors and assays based on optical, electrical, and microgravimetric transduction; bacterial adhesion chemistry.

S. W. May, Regents' Professor; Ph.D., Chicago, 1970. Molecular neurochemistry; neuropeptides and neuropeptide processing enzymes; rational design and evaluation of novel neurochemical effectors; biochemical oxidations and mechanisms of oxygenase enzymes; biotechnology, especially enzyme technology and biomaterials.

T. F. Moran, Professor; Ph.D., Notre Dame, 1962. Mass spectrometry, structure and reactivity of multiply charged molecular ions, cluster ion formation from fast-atom bombardment of condensed phase molecules.

J. C. Powers, Regents' Professor; Ph.D., MIT, 1963. Design and synthesis of protease inhibitors, mechanism-based and transition-state analog protease inhibitors, blood coagulation and cytotoxic lymphocyte enzymes, proteases involved in neurodegeneration.

S. Quirk, Assistant Professor; Ph.D., Johns Hopkins, 1991. Structural biochemistry of nucleotide metabolizing enzymes, protein X-ray crystallography, development of biosensors for the detection of enteropathogenic bacteria.

W. S. Rees Jr., Professor and Director, Molecular Design Institute; Ph.D., UCLA, 1986. Main-group and transition-metal organometallic and inorganic synthetic, mechanistic, and structural investigations directed at chemical vapor deposition of electronic materials, e.g., superconductors, conductors, semiconductors, and insulators; optical materials and structural materials.

G. B. Schuster, Professor and Dean; Ph.D., Rochester, 1971. Photochemistry and laser spectroscopy of DNA-photocleaving systems, investigation of chiroptical triggers for liquid-crystal spatial light modulators, electron transfer reactions of generated ion pairs.

R. E. Schwerzel, Adjunct Professor and Principal Research Scientist, Georgia Tech Research Institute; Ph.D., Florida State, 1970. Design and characterization of advanced photonic materials for nonlinear optical and integrated-optic waveguide devices, nanocomposites derived from polymers and colloidal semiconductor particles, photochromic materials.

K. L. Seley, Assistant Professor; Ph.D., Auburn, 1996. Medicinal/synthetic bioorganic chemistry; design and synthesis of nucleoside/nucleotide analogues as medicinal agents and as dimensional probes for the structural determination of enzyme-active sites; investigations into antisense/oligonucleotide therapy.

C. D. Sherrill, Assistant Professor; Ph.D., Georgia, 1996. Development and application of electronic structure theory to structure, bonding, and energetics of highly reactive species and prototype organic systems.

S. B. Shuker, Assistant Professor; Ph.D., Stanford, 1995. Bioorganic chemistry, synthesis of biologically active molecules, structure determination of protein–small molecule complexes using NMR spectroscopy, molecular recognition, application of host-guest chemistry to catalyst development, combinatorial chemistry.

L. M. Tolbert, Professor and Chair; Ph.D., Wisconsin, 1975. Organic photochemistry, thermal and photorearrangements of carbanions, chemistry of radical ions, electroactive polymers, theoretical organic chemistry.

R. L. Whetten, Professor in Physics (adjunct with Chemistry); Ph.D., Cornell, 1984. Materials chemistry; spectroscopic analysis, high resolution microscopy, and processing of nanometer scale crystallites.

A. P. Wilkinson, Assistant Professor; D.Phil., Oxford, 1992. Zeolites, aluminophosphates and chiral solids, sol-gel processed ferroelectrics, structural characterization using neutrons and synchrotron radiation.

L. D. Williams, Associate Professor; Ph.D., Duke, 1985. Structural, dynamic, and thermodynamic characterization of nucleic acid and protein complexes; 3-D structures of drugs and metals bound to DNA; 3-D structures of inhibitors bound to serine proteases.

P. H. Wine, Professor; Ph.D., Florida State, 1974. Chemical kinetics, gas- and condensed-phase atmospheric chemistry, photochemistry, reaction dynamics, combustion chemistry, free-radical thermochemistry.

L. H. Zalkow, Vasser-Wolley Institute and Regents' Professor; Ph.D., Georgia Tech, 1956. Structure elucidation and synthesis of antitumor agents, polyanionic chemical barriers to HIV-1 binding in CD4-expressing cells.

Z. John Zhang, Assistant Professor; Ph.D., Wisconsin, 1993. Materials chemistry, chemistry on the nanometer scale, magnetism and magnetic nanoparticles, superparamagnetism, high-density memory, magnetic carrier for detection and treatment of cancer.

GEORGIA STATE UNIVERSITY

College of Arts and Sciences
Department of Chemistry

Programs of Study

The Department of Chemistry offers programs leading to a Master of Science (M.S.) degree and, through the Laboratory of Biological and Chemical Sciences, the Doctor of Philosophy (Ph.D.) degree. Both a thesis and a nonthesis M.S. are available. Areas of specialization in the Ph.D. program include analytical, biophysical, and organic chemistry and biochemistry.

A wide range of research projects are currently being studied by chemistry faculty members, staff members, and students. They include immunochemistry, small molecule–macromolecule interactions, electron transfer kinetics, DNA and protein thermodynamics, enzyme modeling, computer simulation of macromolecular dynamics, oxidation reactions—unusual hydroperoxides, structural studies of capsular polysaccharides, potential sensitive molecular probes of membranes, design and synthesis of anti-HIV and anticancer drugs and amplifiers, synthesis and characterization of DNA-based supramolecules, picosecond spectroscopic studies of inorganic photoprocesses, C-H bond activation by organometallic catalysts, and capillary electrophoresis.

Research Facilities

Major equipment includes a wide array of optical instruments, including ultraviolet-visible spectrometers, fluorimeters, NMRs (CW and FT), IR spectrometers, stopped-flow/rapid mixing devices, a spectropolarimeter, laser-based kinetic equipment, and a static/dynamic light-scattering spectrometer. Other departmental equipment consists of chromatography systems, centrifuges, and high-sensitivity microcalorimeters. A transmission electron microscope is also available. Personal computer workstations, such as Silicon Graphics IRISes and Indigos, are linked via Ethernet to the University-wide mainframe network. Numerous IBM-compatible and Macintosh PCs are available, and some are connected to the University mainframe.

Financial Aid

Teaching and research assistantships are available for both M.S. and Ph.D. students. Students working on specific research programs may also be supported, in part or in full, by extramural funds. Full- and part-time employment in the department is frequently available.

Cost of Study

For current figures, students should visit the University's Web site (http://www.gsu.edu).

Living and Housing Costs

Georgia State University has a nonresidential campus located in downtown Atlanta at the center of a network of highways and rapid-transit services that extend throughout the greater metropolitan area. This transportation network makes it possible to live anywhere in the metropolitan area and get to downtown easily. The cost of living in Atlanta is moderate compared with that in other centers in the United States. Dormitory housing is available at the Georgia State Village, a short distance from Georgia State's downtown campus.

Student Group

Georgia State University is a public institution with more than 24,000 students. The graduate student population of more than 7,000 is one of the largest in the Southeast. The average age of graduate students is 33. Students from 113 countries and all fifty states attend the University.

Location

The University is located in the heart of Atlanta's central business district. The city is a rapidly growing metropolitan area characterized by a spectacular skyline and a culturally diverse population. Atlanta's Hartsfield International Airport is the world's largest and busiest, making the city easily accessible from anywhere in the world. The climate is moderate, with a mean July temperature of 23°C and a mean January temperature of 10°C. Atlanta is located in the foothills of the southern Appalachian Mountain range and is close to the Great Smokey Mountains and the Atlantic and Gulf coasts.

The University

Georgia State University is responsive to students' career goals and provides educational and research programs that are relevant to the practical needs of both the students and the community. The University offers nearly fifty undergraduate and graduate degree programs covering some 200 fields of study through its five colleges–Arts and Sciences, Business Administration, Education, Health and Human Sciences, and Law–and the School of Policy Studies.

Applying

Application materials can be obtained from the department or from the Office of Graduate Studies of the College of Arts and Sciences. Applicants must submit the application for graduate study and the University information forms, the $25 application fee, official copies of transcripts from each institution attended, and Graduate Record Examinations General Test scores. Applicants to the Ph.D. degree program must also submit three letters of recommendation and a statement of education and career goals. Applicants to the M.S. degree program must submit a list of references and the departmental supplemental form. Applicants may obtain additional information about the Department of Chemistry by contacting the director of graduate studies or by visiting the Web site, listed below.

Correspondence and Information

Chemistry Graduate Coordinator
Department of Chemistry
Georgia State University
University Plaza
Atlanta, Georgia 30303-3083
Telephone: 404-651-1664
Fax: 404-651-1416
E-mail: cheavp@panther.gsu.edu/
World Wide Web: http://heme.gsu.edu/

Georgia State University

THE FACULTY AND THEIR RESEARCH

Stuart A. Allison, Ph.D., Washington (Seattle), 1980. Dynamics and conformation of biological macromolecules.

Alfons L. Baumstark, Ph.D., Harvard, 1974. Chemistry of oxygen-containing organic compounds, synthesis of hydroperoxides and peroxides, oxidation reactions of unusual hydroperoxides and dioxiranes, dioxolane and a-azo hydroperoxide chemistry, reaction mechanisms, chemiluminescence dioxetanes, 17-O NMR spectroscopy.

David W. Boykin, Ph.D., Virginia, 1965. Synthesis of heterocyclic compounds and oxygen-17 NMR.

Robert Cherniak, Emeritus; Ph.D., Duke, 1964. Structural studies of capsular polysaccharides.

Dabney W. Dixon, Ph.D., MIT, 1976. Electron transfer of cytochromes and synthesis and spectroscopy of porphyrins.

Kathryn Grant, Ph.D., Columbia, 1994. Metal-promoted cleavage of peptides and proteins, artificial nucleases, synthesis of quinonoid drugs, dopamine receptors.

Henry F. Henneike, Ph.D., Illinois, 1967. Lewis acid–base interactions in inorganic chemistry, computers in chemistry.

Donald G. Hicks, Ph.D., Tennessee, 1965. Atomic absorption/emission and molecular spectroscopic methods.

Harry P. Hopkins, Emeritus; Ph.D., Carnegie Mellon, 1965. Thermodynamic studies on assembly phenomena, attachment of small molecules and ions to larger systems.

Ronald G. Jones, Ph.D., Georgia Tech, 1961. Applications of NMR in LFER and in carbohydrate studies.

G. Davon Kennedy, Ph.D., Emory, 1983. Higher-order dipolar cycloaddition in organic chemistry.

Thomas L. Netzel, Ph.D., Yale, 1972. Physical organometallic studies, picosecond spectroscopic studies of inorganic and intramolecular electron-transfer photoprocesses.

Gabor Patonay, Ph.D., Budapest Technical, 1979. Near-infrared spectroscopy, instrument development and optimization, application of laser diodes in analytical chemistry.

Curtis Sears, Ph.D., North Carolina, 1966. Effects of phosphine ligands on the structures and reactivity of complexes of transition metals.

Shahab Shamsi, Ph.D., Miami, 1995. Analytical separations, in particular liquid chromatography (LC), capillary electrophoresis (CE), and capillary electrochromatography (CEC); applications of polymerized micelles in molecular recognition and quantitative-structure activity-retention studies; analysis of combinatorial libraries by LC and CE coupled to mass spectrometry.

Jerry C. Smith, Ph.D., North Carolina, 1971. Anti-HIV and anti–*Pneumocystis carinii* drug candidate interactions with membranes, transit peptide interactions with model phospholipid bilayers.

Lucjan Strekowski, Ph.D., Institute of Organic Chemistry (Warsaw), 1972. Heterocyclic chemistry, new synthetic methods, interactions of chiral molecules with DNA.

W. David Wilson, Ph.D., Purdue, 1970. Biophysical chemistry of nucleic acids and their complexes; investigation of nucleic acids and the mechanisms of drug actions that target nucleic acids through a range of thermodynamic, kinetic, spectroscopic, and molecular modeling methods; therapeutic agents, from small organic cations to antisense (duplex) and antigene (triplex) agents.

Jenny Yang, Ph.D., Florida State, 1992. Elucidation of the relationship between the function of cell adhesion molecules and their structures, design of proteins with biological functions toward the development of medical drugs.

HARVARD UNIVERSITY

Department of Chemistry and Chemical Biology

Program of Study

The Department of Chemistry and Chemical Biology offers a program of study that leads to the degree of Doctor of Philosophy in chemistry in the special fields of biological, inorganic, organic, and physical chemistry. An interdepartmental Ph.D. program in chemical physics is also available. Upon entering the program, students formulate a plan of study in consultation with the Graduate Advisory Committee. Students must obtain honor grades in four advanced half-courses (five for chemical physics). The course work is usually expected to be completed by the end of the second term of residence. For students studying organic and physical chemistry, written examinations are given on a monthly basis from the time the student starts research until a specified number have been passed. Inorganic chemistry students must present and defend a research proposal in their second year of residence. Although the curriculum for the Ph.D. degree includes the course and cumulative examination requirements, the majority of the graduate student's time and energy is devoted to original investigations in a chosen field of research. Students are expected to join a research group in their second term of residence, but no later than the third. The Ph.D. dissertation is based on independent scholarly research, which, upon conclusion, is defended in an oral examination before a Ph.D. committee. The preparation of a satisfactory thesis normally requires at least four years of full-time research.

Research Facilities

The facilities of the Department of Chemistry and Chemical Biology are housed in four buildings, with the adjacent Science Center providing extensive undergraduate lecture and laboratory areas. An Instrument Center provides a central location for the following research instruments: one Varian 600-MHz NMR; two Bruker 500-MHz NMRs; two Bruker 400-MHz NMRs; two Bruker 300-MHz NMRs; one Bruker 250-MHz NMR; one Bruker ESP 300 EPR spectrometer; JEOL-AX505H and JEOL-SX102A mass spectrometers; a Micromass Platform II mass spectrometer equipped with electrospray ionization; and two PerSeptive Biosystems time-of-flight mass spectrometers, of which one is equipped for electrospray ionization and LC/MS and the other for matrix-assisted laser desorption ionization; two Siemens X-ray diffractometers, both with SMART area detection systems; and a Nicolet 7000 Fourier transform infrared spectrometer. Computing in the department is done mostly on workstations in individual research groups, with more than 200 devices linked by a department-wide network. The department, along with the Materials Research Laboratories at Harvard and MIT, operates and manages a Surface Sciences Center.

Financial Aid

The Department of Chemistry and Chemical Biology meets the financial needs of its graduate students through department fellowships, full-tuition grants, teaching fellowships, and research assistantships. Financial support is awarded on a twelve-month basis, enabling students to pursue their research throughout the year. Tuition is afforded all graduate students in good standing for the tenure of the Ph.D. program.

Cost of Study

As stated above, tuition is waived for all Ph.D. students in good standing.

Living and Housing Costs

Dormitory rooms for single students are available, with costs (excluding meals) ranging from $3180 for a single room to $5100 for a two-room suite. Married and single students may apply for apartments managed by Harvard Planning and Real Estate. The monthly costs are: studio apartment, $577–$931; one-bedroom apartment, $783–$1204; two-bedroom apartment, $1014–$1658; and three-bedroom apartment, $1208–$2065. There are also many privately owned apartments nearby and within commuting distance.

Student Group

The Graduate School of Arts and Sciences has an enrollment of 3,089 graduate students. There are 169 students in the Department of Chemistry and Chemical Biology, 54 of whom are international students.

Student Outcomes

In 1998, 11 percent of the Ph.D. recipients entered positions in academia, and 57 percent accepted positions in industry; 32 percent of the graduates will conduct postdoctoral research before accepting permanent positions in academia or industry.

Location

Cambridge, a city of 96,000, is just minutes away from Boston. It is a scientific and intellectual center, teeming with activities in all areas of creativity and study. The Cambridge/Boston area is a major cultural center with its many public and university museums, theaters, symphony, and numerous private, special interest, and historical collections and performances. New England abounds in possibilities for recreational pursuits, from camping, hiking, and skiing in the mountains of New Hampshire and Vermont to swimming and sailing on the seashores of Cape Cod and Maine.

The University

Harvard College was established in 1636, and its charter, which still guides the University, was granted in 1650. An early brochure, published in 1643, justified the College's existence: "To advance Learning and perpetuate it to Posterity...." Today, Harvard University, with its network of graduate and professional schools, occupies a noteworthy position in the academic world, and the Department of Chemistry and Chemical Biology offers an educational program in keeping with the University's long-standing record of achievement.

Applying

Applications for admission to study for the Ph.D. degree in chemistry are accepted from students who have received a bachelor's degree or equivalent. The application process should begin during the summer or fall of the year preceding desired entrance. Completed application forms and supporting materials should be returned to the Admissions Office by December 16.

Correspondence and Information

Graduate Admissions Office
Department of Chemistry and Chemical Biology
Harvard University
12 Oxford Street
Cambridge, Massachusetts 02138
Telephone: 617-496-3208
E-mail: admissions@chemistry.harvard.edu

Harvard University

THE FACULTY AND THEIR RESEARCH

James G. Anderson, Professor of Chemistry; Ph.D. (physical chemistry), Colorado, 1970. Chemical reactivity of radical-molecule systems, molecular orbital analysis of barrier height control, photochemistry of planetary atmospheres, in situ detection of radicals in troposphere and stratosphere, coupling of chemistry and dynamics in the climate system.

David A. Evans, Professor; Ph.D. (organic chemistry), Caltech, 1967. Organic synthesis, organometallic chemistry, asymmetric synthesis.

Cynthia M. Friend, Professor; Ph.D. (physical chemistry), Berkeley, 1981. Physical chemistry of surface phenomena, materials chemistry and catalysis, electron spectroscopies and chemical techniques applied to the understanding of complex surface reactions, relating chemical processes to electronic structure on surfaces.

Roy Gerald Gordon, Professor; Ph.D. (physical chemistry), Harvard, 1964. Intermolecular forces, transport processes and molecular motion, theory of crystal structures and phase transitions, kinetics of crystal growth, solar energy, chemical vapor deposition, synthesis of inorganic precursors to new materials, thin films and their applications to microelectronics and solar cells.

Eric J. Heller, Professor of Physics; Ph.D. (physical chemistry), Harvard, 1973. Theoretical atomic, molecular, and optical physics; scattering theory; ultracold collisions; molecular spectroscopy; quantum chaos; tunneling phenomena.

Dudley Robert Herschbach, Professor; Ph.D. (physical chemistry), Harvard, 1958. Molecular dynamics of chemical reactions, molecular alignment and trapping in intense laser fields, solvation of biomolecules, electronic structure from dimensional continuation.

Richard H. Holm, Professor; Ph.D. (inorganic and bioinorganic chemistry), MIT, 1959. Synthetic, structural, electronic, and reactivity properties of transition-element compounds; structure and function of metallobiomolecules.

Eric N. Jacobsen, Professor; Ph.D. (organic chemistry), Berkeley, 1986. Selective catalysis, new synthetic methods based on organometallic and coordination complexes, mechanistic studies of reactivity and recognition phenomena in homogeneous catalysis.

William Klemperer, Professor; Ph.D. (physical chemistry), Berkeley, 1954. Molecular and electronic structure, energy transfer, interstellar processes.

Charles Michael Lieber, Professor; Ph.D. (physical chemistry), Stanford, 1985. Chemistry and physics of materials; relationships between atomic structure and physical properties in low-dimensional and nanoscale materials; rational synthesis of new materials and nanostructured solids; chemical force microscopy and determination of intermolecular interactions in inorganic, organic, and biological systems.

David Liu, Assistant Professor; Ph.D. (organic chemistry and chemical biology), Berkeley, 1999. Design and synthesis of amplifiable and evolvable unnatural molecules; artificial in vivo and in vitro evolution of novel proteins and nucleic acids; bioorganic chemistry, enzymology, and protein engineering.

Andrew G. Myers, Professor; Ph.D. (organic chemistry), Harvard, 1985. Synthesis and study of complex organic molecules of importance in biology and human medicine.

Hongkun Park, Assistant Professor; Ph.D. (physical chemistry), Stanford, 1996. Physical chemistry and chemical physics of nanostructured materials; synthesis and characterization of complex oxide nanocrystals, phase transition of individual nanocrystals, scanning-probe microscopic and spectroscopic investigation of nanostructured solids.

David Robert Reichman, Assistant Professor; Ph.D. (physical chemistry), MIT, 1997. Theory of dynamical phenomena in condensed phases; charge transfer, energy transfer, and spectroscopy; theory of dynamics in glassy media.

Stuart L. Schreiber, Professor; Ph.D. (chemical biology), Harvard, 1981. Chemical genetics: synthesis of natural product-like compounds that alter the cellular functions of proteins in order to understand and control those functions and the discovery of such compounds using split-pool asymmetric synthesis, molecular cell biology, and miniaturization science.

Matthew D. Shair, Assistant Professor; Ph.D. (synthetic chemistry and chemical biology), Columbia, 1995. Development and implementation of new methods for the synthesis of complex natural and nonnatural molecules of biological importance, utilization of organic synthesis to probe biological processes.

Eugene I. Shakhnovich, Associate Professor; Ph.D. (physical chemistry), Moscow, 1984. Theory of protein folding; polymer theory, including branched polymers and networks; polymer dynamics; disordered systems; rational ligand design; protein-ligand interactions; experimental studies of protein folding.

Gregory L. Verdine, Professor; Ph.D. (chemical biology), Columbia, 1986. DNA repair; transcriptional control, chemistry for the conversion of peptides to ligands having cellular activity.

George M. Whitesides, Mallinckrodt Professor of Chemistry; Ph.D. (organic chemistry), Caltech, 1964. Biochemistry, materials science, surface science, optics.

X. Sunney Xie, Professor; Ph.D. (physical chemistry), California, San Diego, 1990. Biophysical chemistry, single-molecule spectroscopy and dynamics, developments of new approaches for molecular and cellular imaging.

Affiliate Members of the Department of Chemistry and Chemical Biology

Stephen C. Harrison, Professor of Biochemistry and Molecular Biology; Ph.D., Harvard, 1968. Chemical biology: macromolecular assembly, virus structure, transcriptional regulation, signal transduction.

David R. Nelson, Mallinckrodt Professor of Physics and Professor of Applied Physics; Ph.D., Cornell, 1975. Statistical mechanics and dynamics in condensed-matter and chemical physics; superfluids and superconductors, polymers, liquid crystals, and glasses.

Don C. Wiley, Professor of Biochemistry and Biophysics; Ph.D., Harvard, 1971. Structure of viral and cellular surface glycoproteins; mechanisms of membrane activities; antigenic variation, membrane fusion, receptor binding, and histocompatibility-restricted recognition; X-ray diffraction.

ILLINOIS INSTITUTE OF TECHNOLOGY

Department of Biological, Chemical and Physical Sciences

Programs of Study

The Department of Biological, Chemical and Physical Sciences offers M.S. and Ph.D. degrees in the fields of physics, chemistry, and biology. In addition, the department offers several professional master's and related certificate programs for part-time students, both locally and through distance learning. Within the department there are many opportunities for interdisciplinary education and research, and students in any of the disciplines have easy access to the expertise the full faculty brings. All students in the M.S. and Ph.D. programs are required to pass the written M.S. comprehensive/Ph.D. qualifying examination by the end of their fourth semester of study. Part-time students must pass this examination by a comparable stage of their program. A total of 32 credit hours of instruction is required for the master's degree, including up to 12 hours of thesis work. The professional master's programs do not require a thesis. A minimum of 96 credit hours, the passing of the Ph.D. comprehensive examination, and the oral thesis defense are required for the Ph.D.

Chemistry degree programs include the Master of Science, the Doctor of Philosophy, three professional master's programs, the Master of Chemistry, the Master of Analytical Chemistry, and the Master of Materials and Chemical Synthesis. Research specializations include analytical, inorganic, organic, polymer, and physical chemistry.

Physics degree programs include the Master of Science, the Doctor of Philosophy, and the professional master's program in health physics. Research specializations include experimental and theoretical condensed-matter physics, experimental and theoretical elementary particle physics, synchrotron radiation physics, structural and computational biophysics, magnetism, and electrodynamics.

The department also offers M.S. and Ph.D. degree programs in the areas of biochemistry, biotechnology, cell and molecular biology, and microbiology. For additional information on graduate programs in biology, students should see the Institute's description in Book 3 or access the Peterson's Education Center Web site and look at Biological and Biomedical Sciences. More information on graduate degree programs is also available online at the address listed below.

Research Facilities

State-of-the-art computer and laboratory equipment is available to both chemistry and physics students. Facilities are available for nuclear magnetic resonance, X-ray diffraction, polymer synthesis and characterization, and experimental research in biophysics, low-temperature solid-state physics, thin films, and particle physics. Also available are XPS/Auger spectrometers, atomic-force and scanning tunneling microscopes, Fourier-transform infrared spectrometers, mass spectrometers, and facilities for high-pressure liquid chromatography and gas chromatography. The department participates in interdisciplinary research with the Department of Chemical and Environmental Engineering Center for Electrochemical Technology, and collaborative programs are carried on with Fermi National Accelerator Laboratory, Argonne National Laboratory, and the Advanced Photon Source.

Financial Aid

Financial assistance is available through fellowships, teaching assistantships, and research assistantships that include varying stipends and full or partial tuition and through scholarships that provide all or a portion of tuition. Loans for eligible students may be arranged through the Financial Aid Office. Primary consideration for graduate financial aid is given to applicants whose applications are received before March 1.

Cost of Study

In 1999–2000, tuition is $590 per credit hour. Students must register for a minimum of 1 credit hour. International students are required to register for a minimum of 9 credits or the equivalent per semester.

Living and Housing Costs

Housing is available for graduate students in IIT residence halls. The 1999–2000 cost of room and board ranges from $5155 to $6880. Unfurnished IIT apartments are available for graduate students at costs ranging from $458 to $927 per month, including utilities. Early application for apartments is recommended. Several off-campus apartment complexes are located within 1 mile of the Main Campus.

Student Group

IIT's total enrollment in 1998–99 was approximately 5,900. Of this number, 946 were enrolled as full-time graduate students and 1,979 as part-time graduate students. Total undergraduate enrollment was 1,718. The remainder were law students. The Department of Biological, Chemical and Physical Sciences had an enrollment of 263 full- and part-time students graduate students.

Location

IIT's Main Campus is located near the heart of Chicago, just 3 miles from the Loop and central to the greater Chicago area's thriving technological community of business, industry, and research institutions. Internationally known for its architecture, museums, symphony, and theater; its beautiful lakefront on the western shore of Lake Michigan; and the unusually rich variety of its ethnic communities, Chicago offers a vast array of recreational and cultural opportunities. The Main Campus, designed by Ludwig Mies van der Rohe and regarded internationally as a landmark of twentieth-century architecture, occupies fifty buildings on a 120-acre site and includes research institutes, libraries, laboratories, residence halls, a sports center, and other facilities. Among its immediate neighbors are Comiskey Park, home of the Chicago White Sox; two major medical centers; and the McCormick Place Exposition Center. The Downtown Campus is in the Loop near the city's financial trading, banking, and legal centers. The Rice Campus is in suburban Wheaton, convenient to the Interstate 88 research and technology corridor west of the city. The Moffett Campus is in southwest suburban Summit-Argo.

The Institute

Illinois Institute of Technology was formed in 1940 by the merger of Armour Institute of Technology (founded in 1890) and Lewis Institute (founded 1896). IIT offers programs of study in engineering and the sciences, architecture, design, psychology, business, and law. IIT is a member of the prestigious Association of Independent Technological Universities (AITU).

Applying

Applications and supporting documents, including transcripts, test scores, and letters of recommendation, should be received by the Office of Graduate Admission, (3300 South Federal, Room 301A, Chicago, Illinois 60616) no later than June 1 for fall matriculation and November 1 for spring matriculation. The application deadline for the summer session is May 1. Applications that include requests for financial aid should be submitted by the March 1 deadline. Application forms and additional information are available online at the Web site (http://www.grad.iit.edu)

Correspondence and Information

Department of Biological, Chemical and Physical Sciences
Illinois Institute of Technology
3101 South Dearborn Street
Chicago, Illinois 60616

Telephone: 312-567-3480
E-mail: frugoli@charlie.cns.iit.edu
World Wide Web: http://www.iit.edu/departments/bcps

Illinois Institute of Technology

THE FACULTY AND THEIR RESEARCH

CHEMISTRY

Russell A. Bonham, Research Professor; Ph.D., Iowa State. Chemical physics and physical chemistry, X-ray and electron scattering from gases, electron correlation in atoms and molecules, development of laboratory experiments in physical chemistry.

Walter C. Eisenberg, Professor; Ph.D., Buffalo. Organic, oxidant, and singlet oxygen chemistry; biochemistry; air pollution; polycyclic aromatic hydrocarbon transformation; analytical methods development; professional graduate education.

Peter Y. Johnson, Professor; Ph.D., MIT. Organic chemistry, synthesis and reactions of biologically important compounds, computer-generated synthesis, expert systems, organic databases, undergraduate science and engineering education.

M. Ishaque Khan, Assistant Professor; Ph.D., Indian Institute of Technology. Inorganic chemistry; transition metal–oxide based advanced materials; zeolitic and layered solids, metal clusters, and intercalation compounds, materials for solid oxide fuel cells and rechargeable lithium batteries; host-guest chemistry and supramolecular structures; coordination chemistry of polyoxometalates, thiometalates, transition metal–mitrosyl and thionitrosyl compounds.

Peter Lykos, Professor; Ph.D., Carnegie Tech. Physical chemistry: teaching undergraduate and graduate physical chemistry, standards for undergraduate chemistry and chemistry curricula, combination theoretical (Hartree Fock) and experimental (synchrotron radiation) determination of correlation energy, semiempirical methods in quantum chemistry, computer applications in chemistry.

Braja K. Mandal, Associate Professor; Ph.D., Indian Institute of Technology. Polymer science and engineering electroactive polymers, macrocyclic compounds, heterocyclic compounds, solid polymer electrolytes.

Kenneth R. Schug, Professor; Ph.D., USC. Chemical education; coordination compounds of transition metals, with emphasis on chemical reactivity of ligands; enhancement programs for K–12 teachers; minority medical student programs; research opportunities for high school students.

Kenneth W. Stagliano, Assistant Professor; Ph.D., Temple. Organic chemistry; development of new chemical reactions for solving regiochemical and steroechemical problems for the total synthesis of biologically active natural products; medicinal chemistry, chemistry of the quinonoid compounds, new synthetic methods.

Eugene S. Smotkin, Associate Professor; Ph.D., Texas at Austin. Analytical chemistry: fuel cells, development of new electrochemical technology.

Joseph R. Stetter, Associate Professor; Ph.D., SUNY at Buffalo. Electroanalytical chemistry, environmental analytical chemistry, chemical sensors, detectors, development of new analytical methods.

PHYSICS

Grant Bunker, Associate Professor and Director of the Biophysics Collaborative Access Team; Ph.D., Washington (Seattle). X-ray absorption spectroscopy, biophysics, synchrotron radiation research, computational physics/chemistry.

Ray A. Burnstein, Professor; Ph.D., Michigan. Experimental elementary particle physics, interactive teaching and technology.

Dean Chapman, Associate Professor and Director of the Center for Synchrotron Radiation Research; Ph.D., Purdue. Physics of imaging, X-ray optics, biophysics.

Liam Coffey, Associate Professor; Ph.D., Chicago. Condensed-matter theory.

Thomas Erber, Professor; Ph.D., Chicago. Electrodynamics, magnetism, fatigue, complex systems.

Porter W. Johnson, Professor; Ph.D., Princeton. Elementary particle theory, science education.

John Kallend, Professor and Dean of the Undergraduate College; Ph.D., Cambridge. Computational methods of crystallography in texture analysis, properties of polycrystalline aggregates.

Daniel Kaplan, Associate Professor; Ph.D., SUNY at Stony Brook. Experimental high-energy physics, especially symmetry violation and rare decays of hyperons and charm and beauty hadrons; electronics for high-speed triggering and data acquisition.

James Karagiannes, Research Assistant Professor; Ph.D., IIT. Biophysics.

Leon Lederman, Pritzker Professor of Science and 1988 Nobel Laureate in Physics; Ph.D., Columbia. Experimental elementary particle physics.

James Longworth, Associate Professor; Ph.D., Sheffield (United Kingdom). Biophysics.

Timothy Morrison, Associate Professor of Physics and Chair of the Department; Ph.D., Illinois at Urbana-Champaign. Solid-state physics, catalysts, X-ray absorption, X-ray optics.

Eli Port, Research Associate Professor; M.S., Northwestern. Radiological health physics.

Howard A. Rubin, Professor; Ph.D., Maryland. Experimental elementary particle physics.

Carlo U. Segre, Associate Professor and Associate Chair of the Department; Ph.D., California, San Diego. Solid-state physics, experimental solid-state physics.

Harold N. Spector, Professor; Ph.D., Chicago. Solid-state theory, electronic and optical processes in semiconducting nanostructures.

Christopher White, Research Assistant Professor; Ph.D., Minnesota. Experimental elementary particle physics.

John Zasadzinski, Professor; Ph.D., Iowa State. Solid-state physics.

RESEARCH AREAS

High-Energy Physics

Theoretical: Analysis of unified electro-weak theory and quantum chromodynamics; exploring the features of new particles and new interactions at high energies; accelerator physics.

Experimental: Investigation of the properties of the electro-weak force as revealed in high-energy neutrino-nucleon interactions; detector development at Fermilab.

Condensed-Matter Physics

Theoretical: Transport properties of semiconducting heterostructures and superlattices; transport in semiconductors in strong electric and magnetic fields, high-temperature superconductivity.

Experimental: High-temperature superconductivity; magnetism, valence phenomena; synchrotron radiation studies of materials; thermal and electrical properties of solids; amorphous alloys; EXAFS and XANES of materials; radiation damage at low temperatures; growth and properties of thin films.

Biological Physics

Experimental: Protein structural biophysics using synchrotron sources; photophysics and photobiology at the molecular level.

Quantum Theory

Quantum mechanics of single atoms; electrodynamics; high-energy processes in intense magnetic fields; pseudo-random processes and deterministic chaos; hysteresis in magnetic and mechanical systems.

INSTITUTE OF PAPER SCIENCE AND TECHNOLOGY

A Multidisciplinary Program

Program of Study

The Institute of Paper Science and Technology (IPST), an independent graduate school in alliance with the Georgia Institute of Technology, offers graduate study in chemistry and chemical engineering through a broad academic program in engineering and the sciences. The educational philosophy of the Institute, particularly at the master's degree level, is to develop scientific generalists who are well versed in several disciplines within the sciences and who can range across the boundaries of disciplines in their pursuit of knowledge and insight. The Institute awards the Master of Science and Doctor of Philosophy degrees in pulp and paper science with specializations in organic and physical chemistry as well as in chemical engineering, mechanical engineering, physics, and biology.

In the master's program, the first year involves advanced work in engineering, chemistry, physics, and biology, and students who have not previously studied chemical engineering complete foundation courses in this field. In the second year, emphasis is placed upon the interrelationships among fields and the integration of disciplines, and each student carries out an individual research program.

Research Facilities

Research studies at the Institute cover a wide spectrum from the fundamental to the applied or developmental project. Well-equipped laboratories, modern instrumentation, sophisticated specialized equipment, and state-of-the-art computing facilities are available for studies in the physical and biological sciences and in engineering and technology. Areas of research interest for which equipment is available include chemical reaction mechanisms; kinetics; polymer sciences; wood, carbohydrate, lignin, and extractive chemistry; surface and colloid science; thermodynamics; heat, mass, and momentum transfer, particularly in porous media and fibrous structures; fluid mechanics and fluid dynamics; process dynamics, simulation, and control; mathematical modeling; increased efficiency in energy utilization; mechanical, electrical, and optical properties of fibers and fibrous materials; pulping, bleaching, and chemical recovery technology; corrosion processes and control technology; chemical reactions of molten salts; system engineering; applied mechanics of containers; two-phase flow and laser anemometry; forest genetics; plant tissue culture; and molecular biology.

Financial Aid

The Institute of Paper Science and Technology awards a fellowship and tuition scholarship, both of which are renewable, to each matriculated, degree-seeking student who is a citizen of the United States, Canada, or Mexico or a permenant resident of the United States. No services are required in return, but the student is expected to devote full time to graduate study. Fellowships are granted to M.S. and Ph.D. students in the amounts of $16,500 and $18,500 per year, respectively. In addition, scholarships to cover the cost of tuition are granted to M.S. and Ph.D. students in the amounts of $15,000 and $20,000 per year, respectively.

Cost of Study

Tuition costs are provided for by the arrangements explained above.

Living and Housing Costs

Housing facilities are available through the Georgia Institute of Technology Housing Office, Atlanta, Georgia 30332 (telephone: 404-894-2470).

Student Group

Fall term enrollment is approximately 100 students, including an entering class of about 35. Students have matriculated from more than 300 colleges and universities in the United States. Several countries are represented in the student body as well.

Location

The Institute of Paper Science and Technology is located on the Georgia Institute of Technology campus in Atlanta, Georgia. The Institute has established an alliance with Georgia Tech that involves a sharing of resources, thus enhancing the education opportunities available to students from both institutions who are interested in the pulp and paper industry and providing numerous opportunities for joint ventures in education and research.

The Institute

The Institute of Paper Science and Technology, formerly known as the Institute of Paper Chemistry, is a small graduate research institution that has programs oriented to the science and technology of the pulp and paper industry.

The Institute of Paper Science and Technology is the premier graduate education, research, and information services organization for an industry that employs about 800 technical graduates each year. The Institute supplies about one third of the technical manpower at the graduate level required by this dynamic industry. A large percentage of upper management positions in the pulp and paper industry are filled by IPST alumni.

In general, classes are small, and the atmosphere is one in which close student-faculty cooperation is maintained. Graduates are sought for responsible positions in research, development, technical service, sales, production, and management in many areas of the pulp and paper industry and in related industries. Some have entered the teaching profession, and several of the pulp and paper science programs in American colleges and universities are headed by IPST graduates.

Applying

Students normally are admitted in August, and applications should be submitted by March 1. Applicants must rank in the fiftieth percentile or higher on the Graduate Record Examinations and have a minimum GPA of 3.0. Successful applicants usually have completed courses in organic and physical chemistry, physics, and calculus.

Correspondence and Information

Office of Academic Affairs
Institute of Paper Science and Technology
500 10th Street NW
Atlanta, Georgia 30318
Telephone: 404-894-5700
World Wide Web: http://www.ipst.edu

Institute of Paper Science and Technology

THE FACULTY AND THEIR RESEARCH

Frederick W. Ahrens, Professor of Engineering; Ph.D., Wisconsin, 1971. Papermaking processes, transport phenomena in porous media, modeling.

Cyrus K. Aidun, Professor of Engineering; Ph.D., Clarkson, 1985. Fundamentals of coating systems, hydrodynamic instability, computational fluid dynamics.

Sujit Banerjee, Professor of Chemistry; Ph.D., Concordia, 1974. Analytical, environmental, and organic chemistry.

Gary A. Baum, Professor of Physics; Ph.D., Oklahoma State, 1969. Quality management, research effectiveness, materials science, fiber and paper physics, paper properties related to process variables, end-use performance.

Pierre H. Brodeur, Associate Professor of Physics; Ph.D., Montreal, 1984. Ultrasonics, optics, instrumentation, fiber and paper physics.

John Cairney, Assistant Professor of Biology; Ph.D., Dundee (Scotland), 1986. Plant molecular biology, gene expression, plant development.

Douglas W. Coffin, Assistant Professor of Engineering; Ph.D., Delaware, 1994. Dimensional stability, paper mechanics, composite materials, structural stability.

Barry W. Crouse, Professor of Chemistry; Ph.D., Duke, 1972. Material science, paper chemistry, wet-end chemistry, composite papers, fiber modification.

Yulin Deng, Assistant Professor of Polymer Chemistry; Ph.D., Manchester (England), 1992. Wet-end chemistry, colloid and surface chemistry, polymer synthetic chemistry.

Donald R. Dimmel, Professor of Chemistry; Ph.D., Purdue, 1966. Organic chemistry, mechanisms of the delignification of wood and pulps, carbohydrate chemistry, wood extractives, mass spectroscopy.

Jeff H. Empie, Professor of Engineering; Ph.D., Minnesota, 1969. Black liquor recovery, smelt crystallization.

James L. Ferris, Professor of Engineering and Management; Ph.D., Lawrence (IPC), 1974.

Wm. James Frederick, Professor of Chemical Engineering; Ph.D., Maine, 1973. Kraft recovery, mill closure.

Charles C. Habeger, Professor of Physics; Ph.D., Oklahoma, 1971. Ultrasonics, paper physics, instrumentation.

Theodore J. Heindel, Assistant Professor of Engineering; Ph.D., Purdue, 1994. Fluid mechanics, heat transfer, multiphase systems, energy utilization, recycling.

M. Kristiina Iisa, Assistant Professor of Chemical Engineering; Ph.D., Åbo Akademi (Finland), 1993. Kraft recovery.

Seppo Karrila, Associate Professor of Engineering; Ph.D., Wisconsin. Flow in compressible porous media, with a view to applications in forming and dewatering.

Jian Li, Associate Professor of Chemical Engineering; Ph.D., McGill, 1989. Gasification of black liquor, chemical pulping.

Lucian Lucia, Assistant Professor of Chemistry; Ph.D., Florida, 1996. Studies of reactive intermediates in pulping and bleaching.

Earl W. Malcolm, Professor of Chemistry; Ph.D., Lawrence (IPC), 1964. Pulping and bleaching, nonwovens, chemistry.

Thomas J. McDonough, Professor of Engineering; Ph.D., Toronto, 1972. Pulping and bleaching, reaction engineering, chemical kinetics, wood chemistry, pulp and paper properties, statistical methods.

Hiroki Nanko, Associate Professor of Fiber Physics; Ph.D., Kyoto (Japan), 1979. Ultrastructure of wood, fiber physics, dimensional stability of cellulose.

David I. Orloff, Professor of Engineering; Ph.D., Drexel, 1974. Heat transfer, combustion, web forming and consolidation.

Martin Ostoja-Starzewski, Associate Professor of Materials Engineering; Ph.D., McGill, 1983. Micromechanics, materials science and engineering, applied mechanics, computational methods.

Derek H. Page, Distinguished Professor of Physics; Ph.D., Cambridge, 1951. Paper and fiber physics.

Gary Peter, Assistant Professor of Biology; Ph.D., UCLA, 1988. Development of vascular tissues, biochemistry, cell biology, molecular biology.

Peter H. Pfromm, Associate Professor of Chemical Engineering; Ph.D., Texas at Austin, 1994. Polymer science, membrane separations, pulping chemical recovery.

Gerald S. Pullman, Professor of Biology; Ph.D., California, Davis, 1979. Plant cell and tissue culture, clonal propagation through in vitro techniques, somatic embryogenesis of conifers, fundamentals of natural embryo development, forest plant pathology, paper microbiology.

Arthur J. Ragauskas, Professor of Chemistry; Ph.D., Western Ontario, 1984. Bleaching chemistry, fundamentals of brightness, carbohydrate chemistry, spectroscopy.

Wayne B. Robbins, Associate Professor of Chemistry; Ph.D., Cincinnati, 1978. Papermaking and converting, paper properties related to fiber sourcing and related process variables.

Alan W. Rudie, Associate Professor of Chemistry; Ph.D., MIT, 1978. Transition metal chemistry, pulping, bleaching.

Preet M. Singh, Assistant Professor of Engineering; Ph.D., Newcastle (England), 1989. Corrosion, environment-sensitive fracture (stress corrosion cracking, corrosion fatigue, hydrogen embrittlement), mechanical properties of materials, failure analysis.

Xiaodong Wang, Assistant Professor of Engineering; Ph.D., MIT, 1995. Applied mechanics, finite-element analysis, fluid mechanics, computational fluid dynamics.

Junyong Zhu, Assistant Professor of Engineering; Ph.D., California, Irvine, 1991. Environmental air emissions, spray systems and combustion, particle/bubble/froth dynamics, pulp suspensions and multiphase flow, optical and analytical methods.

The Paper Tricentennial Building houses the Institute's laboratories and classrooms.

JOHNS HOPKINS UNIVERSITY

Department of Chemistry

Programs of Study

The department offers a broad program of graduate and postdoctoral study but maintains special strengths in experimental and theoretical chemical physics, biological chemistry, organic chemistry, inorganic chemistry, and materials science. The usual course of study leads to the Ph.D. degree. Individual programs are flexibly tailored to the student's background and interests but must include eight 1-semester graduate courses in chemistry and related subjects. Exceptionally well prepared students may petition for a reduction of this requirement. Most students finish their formal course work within two semesters.

Further requirements for the Ph.D. degree include a research dissertation suitable for publication; a broad fundamental knowledge of chemistry and related sciences, demonstrated in an oral examination; and participation in undergraduate teaching for at least one year.

Research Facilities

The Department of Chemistry occupies two large connected buildings—Remsen Hall and Dunning Hall. These buildings contain about 100,000 square feet of research space as well as classrooms, stockrooms, service laboratories, and the department's own machine and electronics shops. The chemistry buildings are directly adjacent to the University's central library, whose holdings include a consolidated science collection of more than 500,000 volumes and 2,600 technical journals. Specialized equipment is purchased or built according to the needs of the individual experimental research programs. In addition, the department owns and maintains a variety of instruments for general use, e.g., 300-, 400-, and 500-MHz NMRs, EPR, CG-MS, and X-ray instruments. Access to additional facilities is available through arrangements with the School of Medicine, the Applied Physics Laboratory, the Ballistics Research Laboratory, the School of Engineering, and the Departments of Biology, Biophysics, Geology, and Physics.

Financial Aid

All graduate students in the department currently receive full tuition in addition to stipends paid through fellowships, teaching assistantships, and/or faculty research grants and contracts. The nine-month first-year student stipend for 1999–2000 is $11,400. Financial support is normally available at the same rate for June, July, and August for an annual total of $15,200 ($38,860 including the tuition fellowship). The stipend is increased annually. Successful applicants are considered for both departmental fellowships and special University fellowship programs. In the latter instance, outstanding students are awarded an additional stipend for at least one year up to a maximum of four years of graduate study. Spouses of graduate students usually find opportunity for employment in the Baltimore area. Placement bureaus are available.

Cost of Study

The annual tuition of $23,660 is fully paid by a merit award fellowship as described above.

Living and Housing Costs

The overall cost of living in Baltimore is among the lowest in major East Coast cities. Many apartments are available in the surrounding residential area. A campus housing office helps students to locate suitable quarters.

Student Group

Johns Hopkins has always maintained a small, select student body and a low student-faculty ratio. The Department of Chemistry subscribes to this philosophy and normally enrolls no more than 15 to 20 new graduate students per year. The total number of graduate students in the department is about 90, and there are about 35 postdoctoral fellows. Hence, most formal classes are quite small, and working relationships between students and their research advisers are usually close.

Location

The department is located on the wooded 140-acre Homewood campus in northern Baltimore, adjacent to one of the nicest residential areas in the city. A variety of shops and restaurants are close by. During recent years, the historic port city of Baltimore (population of about 800,000) has been undergoing a dramatic physical, commercial, and cultural revitalization. Within convenient distances from the campus are a thriving downtown area, centered about an Inner Harbor that is now devoted largely to recreational facilities, parkland, museums, and outdoor entertainment and festivals; many excellent ethnic and seafood restaurants; theaters presenting touring, pre-Broadway, and local productions; two major art museums and several smaller galleries; the renowned Peabody Conservatory of Music, now affiliated with the University; the Meyerhoff Symphony Hall that houses the city's symphony orchestra; the Lyric Theater, which houses the opera company; Oriole Park at Camden Yards, home of the professional baseball team, the Orioles; and Pimlico race track, site of the Preakness. Baltimore's NFL team, the Ravens, started their 1998 season in a new stadium near the Inner Harbor.

Maryland's topography ranges from the Allegheny Mountains to the Chesapeake Bay and the Atlantic shore, and a corresponding variety of recreational facilities are offered.

The University

Secular and privately endowed, Johns Hopkins University was founded in 1876 as the first institution in the United States offering graduate education in the modern sense. Its tradition of independent inquiry and creative scholarship continues today. Johns Hopkins has remained unusual in its fusion of the intimacy of a deliberately small academic community with the intellectual and cultural resources of a great university.

Applying

No formal degree is required for admission, although most entering students hold bachelor's or master's degrees in chemistry or related sciences. Among the information weighed most heavily in evaluating applications are transcripts of previous academic work, letters of recommendation, students' individual statements of purpose, and, where possible, informal personal interviews. Scores on the GRE are required.

Application materials may be obtained from the address below. The department cannot guarantee that it will consider applications completed after January 15, but it will make every effort to do so. First-year students normally join the department in September, although it is possible to begin formally in January or informally in June.

Correspondence and Information

Academic Program Coordinator
Department of Chemistry
Johns Hopkins University
3400 North Charles Street
Baltimore, Maryland 21218-2685
Telephone: 410-516-7427
Fax: 410-516-8420
E-mail: chem.grad.adm@jhu.edu

Johns Hopkins University

THE FACULTY AND THEIR RESEARCH

Kit H. Bowen, Professor; Ph.D., Harvard, 1978. Experimental chemical physics: photoelectron spectroscopy of negative ions and negative cluster ions, structure and dynamics of gas-phase weakly bound molecular clusters, nanocluster materials.

Paul J. Dagdigian, Professor and Chair of the Department; Ph.D., Chicago, 1972. Experimental chemical physics: dynamics of gas-phase chemical reactions, collisional energy transfer, molecular structure and spectroscopy, free radicals, weakly bound complexes.

John P. Doering, Professor; Ph.D., Berkeley, 1961. Experimental chemical physics: electronic and ionic collision phenomena, electron energy loss spectroscopy, ionization, geophysics, planetary atmospheres.

David E. Draper, Professor; Ph.D., Oregon, 1977. Physical biochemistry: protein–nucleic acid interactions, ribosomal RNA structure, RNA folding.

D. Howard Fairbrother, Assistant Professor; Ph.D., Northwestern, 1994. Experimental surface chemistry/materials performance: surface chemistry of plasma-based polymer modification processes, radical source development, iron surface chemistry/environmental interfaces, in situ infrared surface spectroscopy.

David P. Goldberg, Assistant Professor; Ph.D., MIT, 1995. Inorganic/bioinorganic chemistry: structure-function relationships in heme proteins, artificial metalloproteins, biomimetic molybdenum and tungsten coordination compounds, metallohydrolase model compounds, ligand design, synthesis of tetrapyrrolic macrocycles for small-molecule activation and materials applications.

Kenneth D. Karlin, Professor; Ph.D., Columbia, 1975. Inorganic/bioinorganic chemistry: mimics for copper and heme-iron/copper enzymes involved in O_2-reactions; metal-dioxygen adducts, peroxides, oxidation chemistry; metal nitrogen-oxide (NO_x) reactions; metal cluster (i) interactions with DNA and proteins and (ii) ester and amide hydrolysis reactions.

Thomas Lectka, Assistant Professor; Ph.D., Cornell, 1991. Synthetic and physical organic chemistry, bioorganic chemistry: nonnatural products synthesis, synthetic methodology, asymmetric catalysis, synthetic amide rotamases, fluorine-containing carbocations.

Gerald J. Meyer, Assistant Professor; Ph.D., Wisconsin–Madison, 1989. Inorganic chemistry: electron and energy transfer processes in inorganic coordination compounds and materials, artificial photosynthesis.

Anne-Frances Miller, Assistant Professor; Ph.D., Yale. Biophysical chemistry: nuclear magnetic resonance spectroscopy of redox-active enzymes; structure, mechanism, enzyme engineering, and enzymatic detoxification.

Douglas Poland, Professor; Ph.D., Cornell, 1967. Theoretical chemistry: statistical mechanics, dynamics of cooperative phenomena, models for biological systems, phase transitions.

Gary H. Posner, Professor; Ph.D., Harvard, 1968. Medicinal, organic, and organometallic chemistry: new asymmetric synthetic methods, synthesis of natural products having pharmacological (e.g., antitumor, antimalarial, anti-psoriasis) activity, organocopper chemistry, organic reactions on metal oxide surfaces.

Harris J. Silverstone, Professor; Ph.D., Caltech, 1964. Theoretical chemistry: application of quantum mechanics to chemical problems, high-order perturbation theory, LoSurdo-Stark and Zeeman effects, hyperasymptotics, photoionization, semiclassical quantum mechanics, simulation of electronic and electron magnetic resonance spectra.

John P. Toscano, Assistant Professor; Ph.D., Yale, 1993. Physical organic chemistry: characterization of reactive intermediates and excited-state species, time-resolved IR spectroscopy, photochemistry and photobiology.

Craig A. Townsend, Professor; Ph.D., Yale, 1974. Organic and bioorganic chemistry: biosynthesis of natural products and biomimetic synthesis; protein isolation, mechanistic enzymology, and molecular biology of secondary metabolism; study of, design, and synthesis of sequence-specific DNA-cleaving agents.

Emil H. White, Professor; Ph.D., Purdue, 1950. Organic and bioorganic chemistry: chemiluminescence and bioluminescence, chemical production of excited states, deamination of amines, chemical modification of enzymes and active site mapping.

David R. Yarkony, Professor; Ph.D., Berkeley, 1975. Theoretical chemical physics: electronic structure of atoms and molecules, chemistry of electronically excited species, spin-forbidden processes.

SELECTED PUBLICATIONS

Thomas, O. C., S.-J., Xu, T. P. Lippa, and **K. H. Bowen.** Mass spectrometric and photoelectron spectroscopic studies of zirconium oxide molecular and cluster anions. *J. Cluster Sci.,* in press.

Lippa, T. P., et al. **(K. H. Bowen).** Photoelectron spectroscopy of As-, As_2^-, As_3^-, As_4^-, and As_5^-. *J. Chem. Phys.* 109:10727–31, 1998.

Lippa, T. P., S.-J. Xu, S. A. Lyapustina, and **K. H. Bowen.** Negative ion photoelectron spectroscopy of AsO^-. *J. Chem. Phys.* 109:9263–5, 1998.

Fancher, C. A., et al. **(K. H. Bowen).** Zinc oxide and its anion: A negative ion photoelectron spectroscopic study. *J. Chem. Phys.* 109:8426–9, 1998.

Gerasimov, I., X. Yang, and **P. J. Dagdigian.** Laser fluorescence excitation spectra of the AlNC and AlCN isomers. *J. Chem. Phys.* 110:220–8, 1999.

Lambert, H. M., and **P. J. Dagdigian.** Photodissociation of CH stretch overtone excited CH_3Cl and CHD_2Cl (v_{CH}=5): Cl spin-orbit branching and atomic fragment yields. *J. Chem. Phys.* 109:7810–20, 1998.

Yang, X., I. Gerasimov, and **P. J. Dagdigian.** Electronic spectroscopy and excited state dynamics of the $Al-N_2$ complex. *Chem. Phys.* 239:207–21, 1998.

Yang, X., and **P. J. Dagdigian.** Selective rotational energy transfer from individual Λ-doublet levels of highly rotationally excited $CN(A^2\Pi)$. *Chem. Phys. Lett.* 297:506–14, 1998.

Ford, M. J., et al. **(J. P. Doering).** Electron-impact double ionization of magnesium. *Phys. Rev. A* 57:325–30, 1998.

Goembel, L., et al. **(J. P. Doering).** Atmospheric O/N_2 ratios from photoelectron spectra. *J. Geophys. Res.* 102:7411–9, 1997.

Doering, J. P., and J. Yang. Comparison of the electron impact cross section for the N_{2+} first negative (O,O) band (λ3914Å) measured by optical fluorescence, coincidence electron impact, and photoionization experiments. *J. Geophys. Res.* 101:19723–8, 1996.

Yang, J., and **J. P. Doering.** Absolute differential and integral electron excitation cross sections for atomic nitrogen 3. The $^4S° \to {}^2D(\lambda5200Å)$ transition from 5 to 30 eV. *J. Geophys. Res.* 101:21765–8, 1996.

GuhaThakurta, D., and **D. E. Draper.** Protein-RNA sequence covariation in a ribosomal protein-rRNA complex. *Biochemistry,* in press.

Draper, D. E., and L. Reynaldo. RNA binding strategies of ribosomal proteins. *Nucl. Acids Res.* 27:381–8, 1999.

Markus, M. A., R. B. Gerstner, **D. E. Draper,** and D. A. Torchia. The solution structure of ribosomal protein S4Δ41 reveals two subdomains and a positively charged surface that may interact with RNA. *EMBO J.* 17:4559–71, 1998.

Conn, G. L., R. R. Gutell, and **D. E. Draper.** A functional ribosomal RNA tertiary structure involves a base triple interaction. *Biochemistry* 34:11980–8, 1998.

Fairbrother, D. H., J. G. Roberts, S. Rizzi, and G. A. Somorjai. Growth and structural characterization of magnesium chloride thin films on Pd(111). *Langmuir* 13:2090–6, 1997.

Fairbrother, D. H., et al. Resonance enhanced multiphoton ionization/time-of-flight measurements of the velocity and internal energy content of thermal and photochemical methyl radical sources. *Rev. Sci. Instrum.* 68:2031–7, 1997.

Fairbrother, D. H., K. A. Briggman, P. C. Stair, and E. Weitz. The role of adsorbate structure in the photodissociation dynamics of adsorbed species: Methyl iodide/MgO(100). *J. Chem. Phys.* 102:7267–76, 1995.

Fairbrother, D. H., X. D. Peng, P. C. Stair, and M. Trenary. Surface chemistry of methyl groups adsorbed on Pt(111). *Faraday Trans.* 91:3619–25, 1995.

Goldberg, D. P., et al. Metal ion binding to octakis(dimethylamino) porphyrazine: Core coordination of Mn(III) and peripheral coordination of Pd(II). *Inorg. Chem.* 37:2873–9, 1998.

Goldberg, D. P., et al. Molybdocene porphyrazines: A peripheral dithiolene metallacycle fused to a porphyrinic core. *Inorg. Chem.* 37:2100–1, 1998.

Goldberg, D. P., et al. EPR spectra from EPR-silent species: High-field EPR spectroscopy of manganese(III) porphyrins. *J. Am. Chem. Soc.* 119:8722–3, 1997.

Goldberg, D. P., D. Koulougliotis, G. W. Brudvig, and S. J. Lippard. A (μ-oxo)bis(μ-carboxylato)diiron(III) complex with a tethered phenoxyl radical as a model for the active site of the R2 protein of ribonucleotide reductase. *J. Am. Chem. Soc.* 117:3134–44, 1995.

Pidcock, E., et al. **(K. D. Karlin).** Spectroscopic and theoretical studies of oxygenated dicopper(I) complexes containing hydrocarbon-linked Bis[2-(2-pyridyl)ethyl]amine units: Investigation of a butterfly $[Cu_2-\mu-\eta^2:\eta^2)(O_2)]^{2+}$ core. *J. Am. Chem. Soc.* 121:1299–308, 1999.

Obias, H. V., et al. **(K. D. Karlin).** Heterobinucleating ligand induced structural and chemical variations in $[(L)Fe^{III}-O-Cu^{II}]^+\mu$-Oxo complexes. *J. Am. Chem. Soc.* 120:9696–9697, 1998.

Obias, H. V., et al. **(K. D. Karlin).** Peroxo-, oxo- and hydroxo-bridged dicopper complexes: Observation of exogenous hydrocarbon substrate oxidation. *J. Am. Chem. Soc.* 120:12960–1, 1998.

Karlin, K. D., S. Kaderli, and A. D. Zuberbühler. Kinetics and thermodynamics of copper(I)/dioxygen interaction. *Acc. Chem. Res.* 30:139–47, 1997.

Ferraris, D., et al. **(T. Lectka).** Catalytic, enantioselective alkylations of N,O-acetals. *J. Org. Chem.,* in press.

Cox, C., H. Wack, and **T. Lectka.** Strong hydrogen bonding to an amide nitrogen in an "amide protonsponge": Consequences for structure and reactivity. *Angew. Chem. Int. Educ. Eng.* 111:0000, 1999.

Drury, W. J. III, et al. **(T. Lectka).** A novel synthesis of amino acids through catalytic, enantioselective ene reactions of imino esters. *J. Am. Chem. Soc.* 120:11006–7, 1998.

Cox, C., and **T. Lectka.** Intramolecular catalysis of amide isomerization: The 5-N-H—Na interaction in prolyl peptides. *J. Am. Chem. Soc.* 120:10660–8, 1998.

Thompson, D. W., C. A. Kelly, F. Farzad, and **G. J. Meyer.** Sensitization of nanocrystalline TiO_2 initiated by reductive quenching of molecular excited states. *Langmuir* 15:650–3, 1999.

Argazzi, R., C. A. Bignozzi, G. M. Hasselmann, and **G. J. Meyer.** Efficient light-to-electrical energy conversion with dithiocarbamate-rutheniumpolypyridyl sensitizers. *Inorg. Chem.* 37:4533–7, 1998.

Castellano, F. N., and **G. J. Meyer.** Light induced processes in molecular gel materials. *Prog. Inorg. Chem.* 44:167–209, 1997.

Ruthkosky, M., C. A. Kelly, M. Zaros, and **G. J. Meyer.** Long-lived charge separated states following light excitation of Cu(I) donor-acceptor compounds. *J. Am. Chem. Soc.* 119:12004–5, 1997.

Vance, C. K., and **A.-F. Miller.** A simple proposal that can explain the inactivity of metal-substituted superoxide dismutases. *J. Am. Chem. Soc.* 120(3):461–7, 1998.

Sorkin, D. L., D. K. Duong, and **A.-F. Miller.** Mutation of tyrosine 34 to phenylalanine eliminates the active site pK of reduced Fe-SOD. *Biochemistry* 36:8202–8, 1997.

Sorkin, D. L., and **A.-F. Miller.** Observation of a long-predicted active site pK in Fe-superoxide dismutase from *E. coli. Biochemistry* 36(16):4916–24, 1997.

Vance, C. K., Y. M. Kang, and **A.-F. Miller.** Selective labeling and

Johns Hopkins University

Selected Publications (continued)

direct observation by NMR of the active site glutamine of Fe-containing superoxide dismutase. *J. Biomol. NMR* 9:201–6, 1997.

Poland, D. Kinetics of sequential adsorption from equilibrium statistical mechanics; comparison with exact series. *J. Chem. Phys.,* in press.

Poland, D. Generalized Bethe approximation. *Phys. Rev. E,* in press.

Poland, D. Planar lattice gas with gas, liquid, and solid phases. *Phys. Rev. E,* in press.

Poland, D. Summation of series in statistical mechanics by continued exponentials. *Physica A* 250:394–422, 1998.

Posner, G. H., et al. Non-calcemic, antiproliferative, transcriptionally active, 24-fluorinated hybrid analogs of the hormone 1a,25-dihydroxyvitamin D_3 synthesis and preliminary biological evaluation. *J. Med. Chem.* 41:3008–14, 1998.

Posner, G. H., et al. Antimalarial cyclic peroxy ketals. *J. Med. Chem.* 41:2164–7, 1998.

Posner, G. H., et al. Antimalarial sulfone trioxanes. *Tetrahedron Lett.* 39:2273–6, 1998.

Posner, G. H., et al. Orally active antimalarial 3-substituted trioxanes: New synthetic methodology and biological evaluation. *J. Med. Chem.* 41:940–51, 1998.

Gaffney, B. J., and **H. J. Silverstone.** Simulation methods for looping transitions. *J. Magn. Reson.* 134:57–66, 1998.

Silverstone, H. J. Exact expansion methods for atomic hydrogen in an external electrostatic field: divergent perturbation series, Borel summability, semiclassical approximation, and expansion of photoionization cross-section over resonance eigenvalues. In *Modern Electronic Structure Theory,* ch. 10, ed. D. R. Yarkony. Singapore: World Scientific Publishing, Co., 1995.

Alvarez, G., and **H. J. Silverstone.** Large-field behavior of the LoSurdo-Stark resonances in atomic hydrogen. *Phys. Rev. A* 50:4679–99, 1994.

Alvarez, G., R. J. Damburg, and **H. J. Silverstone.** Photoionization of atomic hydrogen in an electric field. *Phys. Rev. A* 44:3060–82, 1991.

Wang, Y., T. Yuzawa, H. Hamaguchi, **J. P. Toscano.** Time-resolved IR studies of 2-naphthylcarbomethoxycarbene: Reactivity and direct experimental estimate of the singlet/triplet energy gap. *J. Am. Chem. Soc.,* in press.

Nigam, M., et al. **(J. P. Toscano).** Generation and study of benzylchlorocarbene from a phenanthridene precursor. *J. Am. Chem. Soc.* 120:8055–9, 1998.

Srivastava, S., E. Yourd, and **J. P. Toscano.** Structural differences between $\pi\pi^*$ and $n\pi^*$ acetophenone triplet excited states as revealed by time-resolved IR spectroscopy. *J. Am. Chem. Soc.* 120:6173–4, 1998.

Srivastava, S., **J. P. Toscano,** R. J. Moran, and D. E. Falvey. Experimental confirmation of the iminocyclohexadienyl cation-like structure of arylnitrenium ions: Time-resolved IR studies of diphenylnitrenium ion. *J. Am. Chem. Soc.* 119:11552–3, 1997.

Zhou, J., et al. **(C. A. Townsend).** Substrate binding to the α-ketoglutarate-dependent non-heme iron enzyme clavaminate synthase 2: Coupling mechanism of oxidative decarboxylation and hydroxylation. *J. Am. Chem. Soc.* 120:13539–40, 1998.

Bachmann, B. O., R. F. Li, and **C. A. Townsend.** β-Lactam synthetase: A new biosynthetic enzyme. *Proc. Natl. Acad. Sci. U.S.A.* 95:9082–6, 1998.

Reeve, A. McE., S. D. Breazeale, and **C. A. Townsend.** Purification, characterization and cloning of an S-adenosylmethionine-dependent 3-amino-3-carboxypropyl transferase in nocardicin biosynthesis. *J. Biol. Chem.* 273:30695–703, 1998.

Watanabe, C. M. H., and **C. A. Townsend.** The in vitro conversion of norsolorinic acid to aflatoxin B_1. An improved method of cell-free enzyme preparation and stabilization. *J. Am. Chem. Soc.* 120:6231–9, 1998.

White, E. H., and D. F. Roswell. On the apparent lack of oxygen quenching of triplet excited states. *Photochem. Photobiol.* 67(4):404–6, 1998.

Darbeau, R. W., and **E. H. White.** The direct alkylation of π-rich, acid sensitive heterocyclic compounds via essentially free carbocations. *J. Org. Chem.* 62:8091–4, 1997.

White, E. H. An application of the reactivity-selectivity principle to the electrophilic substitution of aromatic compounds. *Tetrahedron Lett.* 38(44):7649–52, 1997.

White, E. H., et al. A new look at the Friedel-Crafts alkylation reaction. *J. Org. Chem.* 61(23):7986–7, 1996.

Yarkony, D. R. Determining the molecular Aharonov-Bohm phase angle: A rigorous approach employing a molecular properties based adiabatic to diabatic states transformation. *J. Chem. Phys.* 110:701–5, 1999.

Sadygov, R. G., and **D. R. Yarkony.** Unusual conical intersections in the Jahn-Teller Effect: The electronically excited states of Li_3. *J. Chem. Phys.* 110:3639–42, 1999.

Yarkony, D. R. Conical intersections diabolical and often misunderstood. *Acc. Chem. Res.* 31:511–8, 1998.

Yarkony, D. R. On the construction of diabatic bases using molecular properties. Rigorous results in the vicinity of a conical intersection. *J. Phys. Chem. A* 102:8073–7, 1998.

KANSAS STATE UNIVERSITY

Department of Chemistry

Programs of Study

The Department of Chemistry offers programs leading to the M.S. and Ph.D. degrees in analytical, biological, inorganic, materials, organic, and physical chemistry, as well as a Ph.D. in chemistry with emphasis on college teaching. Interdisciplinary programs at the Ph.D. level are also offered through the Center for Materials, which includes faculty members from the Departments of Chemistry and Physics and the College of Engineering. The course work requirements are typically 30 hours for the Ph.D. and 22 hours for the M.S. The student's program of study, which is developed by the student with the assistance of his or her dissertation or thesis adviser, normally includes at least one graduate-level course from each of the four general areas of chemistry plus additional courses in the area in which the student chooses to specialize. Many students also include supporting courses in biochemistry, physics, engineering, and mathematics in their programs of study.

Research, which constitutes the major portion of an advanced degree program in chemistry, normally involves 60 semester hours for the Ph.D. and 10–15 semester hours for the M.S. degree. The Ph.D. program is usually completed in four to five years; the normal time for the M.S. degree is two to two and a half years.

Research Facilities

The research and instructional activities of the chemistry department are conducted in modern, well-equipped laboratories and are supported by electronics, machine, glassblowing, and library staffs. Shared instrumentation includes Varian 500-MHz and 400-MHz multinuclear NMR spectrometers, mass spectrometers, an ESR spectrometer, and workstations for data processing and computation. Specialized instrumentation and facilities include XPS, SIMS, Auger, STM/AFM, X-ray, and electron microprobe; Fourier and Hadamard transform spectrometers for monitoring of environmental pollutants; a laser and spectroscopy laboratory for gas-phase kinetics studies; gas-phase ion-molecule kinetics using flowing afterglow and flowing afterglow selected ion flow tube methods; and a high-resolution Echelle multichannel plasma emission spectrometer for automated multielement analysis. Numerous liquid and gas chromatographs; ultraviolet, visible, and infrared spectrometers; and potentiostats for electrochemical studies are also available.

Financial Aid

Financial aid is available to all graduate students who are in good academic standing. Stipends for graduate teaching assistants (GTAs) for the 1999–2000 fiscal year range from $14,300 to $17,600, depending upon qualifications. For particularly well qualified students, stipends may be supplemented by Graduate School and other special fellowships in amounts up to $6000. Positions as graduate research assistants (GRAs) are also available and are normally awarded to those students who are conducting full-time research during the regular academic year and/or the summer session.

Cost of Study

The University waives all tuition for graduate teaching assistants (GTA). Graduate research assistants (GRA) pay resident fees per credit hour. Campus privilege fees for GTAs and GRAs for 1998–99 were estimated at $250 per semester.

Living and Housing Costs

University residence hall costs are $1975 per semester for room and board (20 meals per week); for married student housing, the monthly rental for a two-bedroom furnished apartment is $326 per month. A variety of off-campus housing is also available at moderate cost. Food, clothing, medical services, transportation, and other living expenses are generally below the national average.

Student Group

Approximately 80 graduate students, postdoctoral fellows, and visiting scientists are engaged in chemical research. The department has an excellent record of placing its graduates in industry, government, and academe.

Location

Manhattan, a progressive city of more than 40,000, is located near the nation's geographic center in the Flint Hills region of northeast Kansas. Thirty-mile-long Tuttle Creek Reservoir lies just north of the city and is a major recreational area for water and other outdoor sports. Four miles south of the city one finds the beauty and serenity of the 8,600-acre Konza Prairie, which is an important site for ecological research and is the last large native tall grass preserve in the United States. A wide variety of urban attractions and professional sports activities may be found in Kansas City, which is approximately a 2-hour drive to the east.

The University

Kansas State University has a long tradition of excellence in higher education. It was established in 1863 as one of the nation's first land-grant universities and has been awarding graduate degrees for more than 100 years. The 664-acre campus is beautifully landscaped and features a variety of striking architectural designs in its native limestone buildings. More than 21,000 students are enrolled in the University's colleges, the School of Veterinary Medicine, and the Graduate School. The general campus atmosphere reflects traditional Kansas friendliness and values; it is stimulating, open, and honest. The University provides a wide array of cultural, recreational, and athletic activities.

Applying

Applications for admission and financial assistance should be submitted by May 15 for admission beginning with the fall term. For international students the deadline is March 1. A B.S. degree in chemistry or a closely related curriculum is required. GRE scores, including those from the Subject Test in Chemistry, are strongly recommended for all applicants and are required of all applicants from institutions that are not within the United States. International applicants whose first language is not English must also submit TOEFL and TSE scores.

Correspondence and Information

Chair, Graduate Assistantship Committee
Department of Chemistry
Kansas State University
Manhattan, Kansas 66506-3701
Telephone: 785-532-6665
Fax: 785-532-6666

Kansas State University

THE FACULTY AND THEIR RESEARCH

Christer B. Aakeröy, Assistant Professor; D.Phil., Sussex (England), 1990. Supramolecular chemistry: design of hydrogen-bonded architectures for crystal engineering, polymorphism and cocrystals, molecular recognition, NLO materials, X-ray crystallography and computational chemistry.

Paul W. Baures, Assistant Professor; Ph.D., Minnesota, 1995. Bioorganic chemistry: synthesis of conformationally constrained small molecules for medicinal purposes, protein-protein interactions, hydrogen bonding in biological systems.

Keith R. Buszek, Associate Professor; Ph.D., UCLA, 1987. Organic chemistry: development of new synthetic methodologies and strategies, total synthesis of a wide range of architecturally complex natural products of biological interest, organometallic chemistry.

Maryanne M. Collinson, Assistant Professor; Ph.D., North Carolina State, 1992. Analytical chemistry: development and characterization of new materials for advanced analytical applications, sol-gel chemistry, zeolite chemistry, electrochemistry.

Robert M. Hammaker, Professor; Ph.D., Northwestern, 1960. Physical and environmental chemistry: molecular spectroscopy (IR and Raman), development of Hadamard transform spectroscopy, detection of volatile organic compounds using Fourier transform infrared spectroscopy.

M. Dale Hawley, Professor; Ph.D., Kansas, 1965. Analytical chemistry: electroanalytical chemistry, application of electrochemical methods to the study of electrode processes.

Daniel A. Higgins, Assistant Professor; Ph.D., Wisconsin-Madison, 1993. Analytical chemistry: microscopy and spectroscopy of mesostructured organic and inorganic semiconducting films, near field scanning optical microscopy, surface and thin-film science, nonlinear spectroscopy.

Mark D. Hollingsworth, Associate Professor; Ph.D., Yale, 1986. Solid-state organic chemistry: ferroelectric and ferroelastic domain switching of organic inclusion compounds, crystal engineering, molecular recognition in crystals, solid-state NMR, X-ray diffraction, crystal growth mechanisms, optical microscopy, EPR of radical pairs.

Duy H. Hua, Professor; Ph.D., Southern Illinois, 1979. Organic chemistry: asymmetric synthesis of biologically active natural products; synthesis of drugs for congestive heart failure, lowering of cholesterol levels, anti-cancer, anti-AIDS, and diabetes (cataracts and retinopathy).

Anne Myers Kelley, Professor; Ph.D., Berkeley, 1984. Physical chemistry: chemical physics; resonance Raman, experimental and theory; molecular dynamics of photoisomerization, photodissociation, electron transfer and spectral broadening in solution and amorphous solid phases; single-molecule spectroscopy.

David F. Kelley, Professor; Ph.D., Washington (Seattle), 1976. Physical chemistry: excited state dynamics of semiconductor nanoclusters, solvation effects on excited state proton transfer and electron transfer reactions, vibrational dynamics of gas phase van der Waals molecules.

Kenneth J. Klabunde, University Distinguished Professor; Ph.D., Iowa, 1969. Inorganic chemistry: synthesis and properties of clusters and nanoscale particles (magnetic, adsorption, catalytic, and optical properties), organometallic synthesis, metal-atom chemistry, colloidal metal particles, activated metal oxides, arene-metal complexes.

Eric A. Maatta, Professor; Ph.D., Indiana, 1980. Inorganic chemistry: synthetic inorganic and organometallic chemistry, multiply bonded nitrogenous ligands, catalysis, polyoxometalate clusters, multinuclear NMR spectroscopy, design and construction of extended molecular arrays.

Pedro L. Muiño, Assistant Professor; Ph.D., Montana State, 1993. Physical chemistry: laser spectroscopy of van der Waals clusters, molecular beams, spectroscopy of biologically relevant molecules, solvent effects, quantum mechanics, molecular modeling, molecular dynamics.

J. Vincent Ortiz, Professor; Ph.D., Florida, 1981. Theoretical chemistry: derivation, programming and application of propagator methods for calculating and interpreting molecular properties; qualitative molecular orbital theory.

Donald W. Setser, University Distinguished Professor; Ph.D., Washington (Seattle), 1961. Physical chemistry: molecular energy transfer, chemiluminescence, state-to-state reactions, spectroscopy of small molecules, laser-induced processes.

Peter M. A. Sherwood, University Distinguished Professor and Head; Ph.D., 1970, Sc.D., 1995, Cambridge. Analytical chemistry: surface science studies of corrosion and oxidation, application of surface science to carbon fibers with a view to understanding and enhancing their performance in composite materials.

Ralf Warmuth, Assistant Professor; Ph.D., Goethe Universität Frankfurt, 1992. Organic chemistry: reactive intermediates in molecular container compounds, design of molecular container compounds, inner-phase photochemistry, unnatural peptide helices.

The department's principal facilities: Chemistry/Biochemistry building in the foreground; King Hall in the background.

Windsurfing on nearby Tuttle Creek Reservoir.

KENT STATE UNIVERSITY

Chemical Physics Interdisciplinary Program

Program of Study

The Chemical Physics Interdisciplinary Program (CPIP) offers graduate courses and research leading to the Master of Science and Doctor of Philosophy degrees in chemical physics. The program involves the participation of the Departments of Chemistry, Physics, and Mathematics and Computer Science and the Liquid Crystal Institute and offers concentrations in optoelectronics, physical properties of liquid crystals, liquid-crystal synthesis and molecular design, lyotropic liquid crystals and membranes, and general chemical physics.

CPIP is designed to provide an opportunity for concentrated study of liquid crystalline materials and complex fluids with an emphasis on optics and display applications at the Liquid Crystal Institute at Kent State University. Research ranges from basic studies to optics and display applications. Students typically take core courses during the first two years of study. The M.S. degree requires 32 semester hours of courses and a thesis. The Ph.D. degree requires 90 semester hours of courses, seminars, and research beyond the bachelor's degree or 60 semester hours beyond the master's degree. Doctoral students are required to pass the candidacy examination before the start of their third year. Proficiency in a computer language is required.

Research Facilities

The program is housed in the Liquid Crystal Institute at Kent State University. The institute is a strong academic center of liquid-crystal and soft condensed-matter research and is the only institute of its kind in the United States. In 1991, the National Science Foundation established the Science and Technology Center on Advanced Liquid Crystalline Optical Materials (ALCOM), with the Liquid Crystal Institute as its hub. CPIP students have access to the expertise and research equipment of ALCOM and the Liquid Crystal Institute. Facilities for condensed matter research include state-of-the-art equipment for NMR, microcalorimetry, optical, scanning-tunneling, atomic-force, and scanning-electron microscopy; image analysis; high-resolution X-ray and light scattering; dielectric, magnetic, surface, and optical studies; and nonlinear optics. The Institute houses clean rooms for display device prototyping, as well as laser facilities and materials synthesis and characterization laboratories.

Financial Aid

In 1998–99, graduate appointments for the nine-month academic year carried a stipend of $12,600 plus a full tuition scholarship. Students receive comparable additional support during the summer. A limited number of fellowships from sponsoring industries are also available.

Cost of Study

In 1998–99, annual full-time tuition was $6460 for in-state residents and $12,286 for out-of-state residents.

Living and Housing Costs

Rooms are available for single graduate students in campus dormitories; current costs per month are $320 for single rooms, $297 for double rooms, and $385 for a deluxe single accommodation. Furnished apartments for married students in the University-owned Allerton Apartments currently cost $415 per month for one bedroom and $440 per month for two bedrooms. A variety of reasonably priced rental housing can be found in the Kent area. The Campus Bus Service provides a transportation network for the Kent campus and links the campus with shopping centers and residential neighborhoods in nearby communities; this service is free to all Kent students.

Student Group

The approximately 21,000 students on the Kent campus include 4,746 graduate students. The Chemical Physics Interdisciplinary Program, now in its fourth year, has 31 graduate students who represent eight countries. Approximately 20 out of a total of 50 graduate students from physics are also involved in liquid crystal–related research.

Student Outcomes

More than 100 Ph.D. degrees have been awarded by Kent State University in the field of liquid crystals. Graduates are employed in industry (Allied Signal, Phillips, Xerox, 3M, Tektronix, Westinghouse, and Samsung) and at universities (Calgary, Stanford, Southern Mississippi, Brown, and Calabria). Current employment prospects are excellent for graduates of the program, both in the rapidly growing flat panel display industry and in the soft condensed-matter materials/optics areas.

Location

Kent is a city of about 30,000 people and is located in northeastern Ohio. The Appalachian foothills to the east and Lake Erie to the north are within 1 hour's drive. The Akron-Canton, Cleveland, and Youngstown metropolitan areas are less than 1 hour's drive and provide a variety of cultural, entertainment, and sports attractions and employment opportunities.

The University and The Program

The Chemical Physics Interdisciplinary Program is housed in a new modern building for the Liquid Crystal Institute.

The Chemical Physics Interdisciplinary Program has 12 faculty members, with 6 having appointments in CPIP and 6 having joint appointments in chemistry, physics, and mathematics and computer science. Research funding per year to CPIP faculty members is in excess of $2.5 million from federal and state agencies, which also provide research assistantship support.

Applying

Application forms for admission and financial assistance may be obtained by writing to the Chemical Physics Interdisciplinary Program. Completed applications should be received before January 31 for fall admission. Due to strong competition for limited enrollment, early application is encouraged.

Correspondence and Information

Jack R. Kelly, Graduate Coordinator
Chemical Physics Interdisciplinary Program
Liquid Crystal Institute
Kent State University
Kent, Ohio 44242
Telephone: 330-672-2633
Fax: 330-672-2796
E-mail: jkelly@scorpio.kent.edu
World Wide Web: http://www.lci.kent.edu/cpip.html

Kent State University

THE FACULTY AND THEIR RESEARCH

David A. Allender, Professor (physics); Ph.D., Illinois, 1975. Theoretical physics of condensed matter, superconductivity theory, liquid crystals and membrane models.

Philip J. Bos, Associate Professor; Ph.D., Kent State, 1979. Electrooptics, liquid-crystal displays.

L.C. Chien, Associate Professor; Ph.D., Southern Mississippi, 1988. Polymers, polymeric liquid crystals, polymer-stabilized liquid crystals.

J. William Doane, Emeritus Professor; Ph.D., Missouri, 1965. Nuclear magnetic resonance of liquid crystals.

Julia Fulghum, Associate Professor (chemistry); Ph.D., North Carolina, 1987. Surface interactions, photoelectron emission spectroscopy, surface anchoring.

E.C. Gartland, Professor (mathematics and computer science); Ph.D., Purdue, 1980. Numerical modeling and computation of liquid-crystal systems.

Jack R. Kelly, Associate Professor; Ph.D., Clarkson, 1979. Electrooptic and dielectric properties of liquid crystals.

Satyendra Kumar, Professor (physics); Ph.D., Illinois at Urbana-Champaign, 1981. Liquid-crystal structure and phase transitions, liquid-crystal electrooptic effects.

Oleg Lavrentovich, Associate Professor; Ph.D., 1984, D.Sc., 1990, Ukrainian Academy of Sciences. Defects in liquid crystals, electrooptics of liquid crystals.

Peter Palffy-Muhoray, Professor; Ph.D., British Columbia, 1977. Nonlinear optics, pattern formation in liquid crystals.

Deng-Ke Yang, Assistant Professor; Ph.D., Hawaii, 1989. Electrooptics, polymer-stabilized liquid crystals.

ACTIVE RESEARCH TOPICS

Modeling of fluctuations, structural instabilities, and transitions.
Liquid crystals in porous media.
Optical information storage.
Pattern formation in liquid crystals.
Phase separation dynamics in polymer–liquid-crystal systems.
Switching phenomena in polymer-stabilized materials.
Modeling the optical response of nematic displays.
Ferroelectric liquid-crystal displays.
Phase transitions in confined liquid crystals.
Finite-element methods in free-energy minimization.
NMR of confined liquid crystals.
Optical field–induced instabilities.
Surface-anchoring measurements.
Dynamic light scattering and photon localization.
High-resolution X-ray and small-angle neutron scattering from complex fluids.
Ferroelectric displays.
Surface analysis and treatment.
Photoalignment.
Modeling reaction-diffusion systems.
Nematodynamics and the effects of shear.
Defect structure and dynamics.
Design and synthesis of liquid crystalline materials having new structures and effects.

KENT STATE UNIVERSITY

Department of Chemistry

Programs of Study	The Department of Chemistry offers programs leading to the Master of Science (M.S.)and Doctor of Philosophy (Ph.D.) degrees in the divisions of analytical, inorganic, organic, and physical chemistry and biochemistry. The doctoral program emphasizes research in the broadly defined areas of liquid crystals and separation and surface science. Also available are interdisciplinary doctoral programs in chemical physics and molecular and cellular biology.

Graduate students are required to complete a program of core courses in their area of specialization and at least one (for M.S. candidates) or two (for Ph.D. candidates) courses in other areas of chemistry. In addition to these courses, students may choose from a wide variety of electives. The program thus gives students considerable flexibility in curriculum design. At the end of the second year, doctoral candidates must pass a written examination in their field of specialization and present and subsequently defend an original research proposal on a topic different from their dissertation research. Students normally complete their doctoral program after four years. |
Research Facilities	Research laboratories are located primarily in Williams Hall and the adjoining Science Research Laboratory. In addition, facilities in the Liquid Crystal Institute, housed in the Materials Science Building, are available to chemistry students. Williams Hall houses two large lecture halls, classrooms, undergraduate and research laboratories, the research laboratories of the Separation Science Consortium, the Chemistry-Physics Library, chemical stockrooms, and glass and electronics shops. A machine shop, which is jointly operated with the physics department, is located in nearby Smith Hall. Spectrometers include 500-MHz and 300-MHz high-resolution and solids NMR instruments, several FT-IR spectrometers, photon-counting fluorometer, circular dichroism, UV/VIS, a GC-MS, and AA/AE equipment. The X-ray facility includes a Siemens D5000 Powder diffractometer and a Bruker AXS CCD instrument for single crystal structural elucidation that also operates at a low temperature (-110°C). Equipment available in specialty areas includes Kratos Axis Ultra Imaging XPS, stopped-flow spectrophotometers, a microwave spectrometer, a positron annihilation lifetime spectrometer, a liquid scintillation counter, various preparative centrifuges, and PCR and DNA sequencing facilities. Additional equipment available to the Separation Science Consortium includes a 400-MHz high-resolution and solids multinuclear NMR spectrometer, thermal analysis and gas adsorption equipment, and a variety of HPLC and GC instruments as well as an IBM RS 6000-590 computer. There are a wide range of computer facilities available at Kent State, from microcomputers to supercomputers. Individual research groups in the Department of Chemistry maintain a variety of computer systems, including PCs, SGI Indigo2 and O2 workstations, and IBM RS 6000 workstations. In addition, there are two computer labs that house microcomputers and IBM RS 6000 workstations. The department has advanced molecular modeling facilities, including Cerius, Felix, Hyperchem, InsightII/Discover, Macromodel, and Spartan packages for modeling surfaces and interfaces, polymers, proteins, and nucleic acids, as well as facilities for performing ab initio calculations of molecular properties and molecular dynamics studies and for the analysis of multidimensional NMR spectra. University Computer Services maintains a number of microcomputer labs on campus as well as an IBM 4381-R24 mainframe computer that runs the VM/CMS operating system. High-performance computing is available at the Ohio Supercomputer Center, which maintains Cray T94, Cray T3E, IBM SP2, and SGI Origin 2000 supercomputers. The abstracting and indexing service maintains an extensive collection of books in chemistry and physics. There is also online access to a variety of chemical databases, including the Chemical Abstracts Service.
Financial Aid	Graduate students are supported through teaching and research assistantships and University fellowships. Students in good academic standing are guaranteed appointments for periods of 4½ years (Ph.D. candidates) or 2½ years (M.S. candidates). Stipends for 1999–2000 range from $12,000 to $14,000 for a twelve-month appointment.
Cost of Study	Graduate tuition and fees for the 1999–2000 academic year are $4568, for which a tuition scholarship is provided to students in good academic standing.
Living and Housing Costs	Rooms in the graduate hall of residence are $1278 to $1538 per semester; married students' apartments may be rented for $403 to $550 per month. Information concerning off-campus housing may be obtained from the University Housing office. Costs vary widely, but apartments typically rent for $450 to $550 per month.
Student Group	Graduate students in chemistry currently number about 40. There are approximately 20,000 students enrolled at the main campus of Kent State University; 8,000 additional students attend the seven regional campuses.
Location	Kent, a city of about 28,000, is located 35 miles southeast of Cleveland and 12 miles east of Akron in a peaceful suburban setting. Kent offers the cultural advantages of a major metropolitan complex as well as the relaxed pace of semirural living. There are a number of theater and art groups at the University and in the community. Blossom Music Center, the summer home of the Cleveland Orchestra and the site of Kent State's cooperative programs in art, music, and theater, is only 15 miles from the main campus. The Akron and Cleveland art museums are also within easy reach of the campus. There are a wide variety of recreational facilities available on the campus and within the local area, including West Branch State Park and the Cuyahoga Valley National Recreation Area. Opportunities for outdoor activities such as summer sports, ice-skating, swimming, and downhill and cross-country skiing abound.
The University	Established in 1910, Kent State University is one of Ohio's largest state universities. The campus contains 820 acres of wooded hillsides plus an airport and an eighteen-hole golf course. There are approximately 100 buildings on the main campus. Bachelor's, master's, and doctoral degrees are offered in more than thirty subject areas. The faculty numbers approximately 800.
Applying	Forms for admission to the graduate programs are available on request from the address below. There is no formal deadline for admission, but graduate assistantships are normally awarded by May for the following fall. Applicants requesting assistantships should apply by March 1.
Correspondence and Information	Graduate Coordinator Department of Chemistry Kent State University Kent, Ohio 44242 Telephone: 330-672-2032

Kent State University

THE FACULTY AND THEIR RESEARCH

Rathindra N. Bose, Professor and Chairman; Ph.D., Georgetown, 1982. Bioinorganic chemistry: separations and characterization of nucleic acids and proteins by capillary electrophoresis and HPLC, structure of DNA Polymerase-α by 2D and 3D NMR spectroscopy, mechanisms of interaction of metal drugs with nucelosides and nucleotides, metal ion catalysis of phosphate hydrolysis reactions, electrochemistry of hypervalent metal complexes.

Stephen E. Cabaniss, Associate Professor; Ph.D., North Carolina, 1986. Analytical chemistry: environmental analysis and modeling, molecular fluorescence spectroscopy, metal binding to macromolecules and colloids, low-temperature aqueous geochemistry, aqueous FTIR.

Julia E. Fulghum, Associate Professor; Ph.D., North Carolina, 1987. Analytical chemistry: surface and microbeam analysis, X-ray photoelectron spectroscopy, time-of-flight secondary ion mass spectrometry, development of surface analysis methods for chemical analysis, quantitative surface analysis, with an emphasis on polymers, composite materials, and liquid crystals.

Edwin S. Gould, University Professor; Ph.D., UCLA, 1950. Inorganic chemistry: mechanisms of inorganic redox reactions; catalysis of redox reactions by organic species; electron-transfer reactions of flavin-related systems; reactions of cobalt, chromium, vanadium, titanium, europium, uranium, ruthenium, indium, peroxynitrous acid, and trioxodinitrate; reactions of water-soluble radical species.

Roger B. Gregory, Professor; Ph.D., Sheffield (England), 1980. Biochemistry: protein conformational dynamics, the characterization of dynamically distinct substructures in proteins, protein hydration, protein glass transition behavior and its role in protein stability and folding, solid-state NMR studies of proteins, positron annihilation lifetime spectroscopy of proteins, polymers and porous media, the characterization of protein-ligand matrix coprecipitates and their application in protein separations.

Lisa Ann Holland, Assistant Professor; Ph.D., North Carolina, 1996. Analytical chemistry: bioanalytical separations and sampling of peptides and other biomarkers of disease, including microcolumn liquid chromatography, capillary electrophoresis, and microdialysis.

Songping D. Huang, Assistant Professor; Ph.D., Michigan State, 1993. Inorganic chemistry: molecule-based magnetic and nonlinear optical materials, organic conductors and superconductors, novel microporous and mesoporous materials, synthesis and crystal growth of metal oxides and chalcogenides.

Mietek Jaroniec, Professor; Ph.D., Lublin (Poland), 1976. Physical/analytical chemistry: thermodynamics of adsorption and chromatography at the gas/solid and liquid/solid interfaces; studies of surface phenomena on heterogeneous and nanoporous solids, such as microporous carbonaceous adsorbents, chemically modified silicas, inorganic porous oxides, mesoporous ordered molecular sieves, and nanostructured solids; synthesis, modification, and characterization of adsorbents, chromatographic packings, and catalysts by using adsorption, chromatography, and thermal analysis; gas and liquid chromatographic separations.

M. Thomas Jones, Professor and Vice Provost and Dean for Research and Graduate Studies; Ph.D., Washington (St. Louis), 1961. Physical chemistry: synthesis, physical and chemical characterization of organic and organometallic synthetic metals and their application; the properties of interest include electrical and magnetic properties; chemical and physical properties related to molecular and electronic structure; ESR studies of free radical solids; fullerene anion radicals.

Kenneth K. Laali, Professor; Ph.D., Manchester (England), 1977. Organic chemistry, mechanistic organic (organometallic) chemistry, and synthetic applications: generation and NMR studies of persistent carbocations of fused polycyclic aromatics (mechanistic carcinogenesis), superacid chemistry and heterogeneous catalysis, new organic conducting materials (incorporation into polymers and liquid crystals), new fluorinating agents for aromatics and liquid crystals, organophosphorus chemistry, host-guest chemistry.

Hitoshi Masui, Assistant Professor; Ph.D., York (Ontario), 1994. Analytical chemistry: electrochemistry and electronic spectroscopy of inorganic materials and their applications to electronic devices and sensors.

R. Scott Prosser, Assistant Professor; Ph.D. Guelph (Canada), 1992. Physical chemistry: solid state and high-resolution NMR and low angle diffraction studies of lyotropic liquid crystals, membranes, and membrane-associated proteins; protein structural and dynamical properties, technique development in solid state NMR, and antibacterial peptides.

Thomas I. Pynadath, Professor; Ph.D., Georgetown, 1963. Biochemistry: effects of hormones and drugs on serum levels of lipoproteins and lipoprotein metabolism, induction of serum lipoproteins by drugs, effects of drugs on the synthesis of thromboxane and prostacyclin, effects and mechanism of action of drugs on platelet aggregation and thrombosis.

Casey C. Raymond, Assistant Professor; Ph.D., Colorado State, 1996. Inorganic/materials chemistry: synthesis of new layered oxide and phosphonate materials for coordination of metals; investigation of structure, optical, magnetic, catalytic, and metal complexation properties.

Paul Sampson, Associate Professor; Ph.D., Birmingham (England), 1983. Synthetic organic chemistry: development of new synthetic methods; new approaches for the construction of medium-sized and macrocyclic rings, with applications to the synthesis of analogs of the anticancer agent taxol; synthetic (stereoselective) organofluorine chemistry, with applications to the synthesis of fluorinated liquid crystals and carbohydrate analogs.

Alexander J. Seed, Assistant Professor; Ph.D., Hull (England), 1995. Organic chemistry: design, synthesis, and characterization of novel liquid crystalline materials, including chiral ferroelectric and antiferroelectric materials, and materials useful in optical switching devices; heterocyclic chemistry.

Chun-che Tsai, Professor; Ph.D., Indiana, 1968. Biochemistry: interaction of drugs with nucleic acids, structure and activity of anticancer drugs, antiviral agents and interferon inducers, structure and biological function relationships, X-ray diffraction and quantitative structure-activity relationships (QSAR).

Michael J. Tubergen, Assistant Professor; Ph.D., Chicago, 1991. Physical chemistry: high-resolution microwave spectroscopy for molecular structure determination of hydrogen-bonded complexes and biological molecules.

Robert J. Twieg, Associate Professor; Ph.D., Berkeley, 1976. Organic chemistry: development of organic and polymeric materials with novel electronic and optoelectronic properties, including nonlinear optical chromophores, photorefractive chromophores, transport agents and passive dielectrics, and liquid crystals, with emphasis on applications and durability issues.

Frederick G. Walz, Professor; Ph.D., SUNY Downstate Medical Center, 1966. Biochemistry: characterization of several sexually dimorphic xenobiotic and steroid reductases in the endoplasmic reticulum membrane of rat liver cells, using purification and sequencing; ribonuclease T_1 using site-directed and random mutagenesis methods; protein engineering of substrate specificity at the active site, the catalytic mechanism and its alteration by subsite interactions, and the effects of specific mutations on protein stability and dynamics.

John L. West, Professor and Director, Liquid Crystal Institute; Ph.D., Carnegie Mellon, 1980. Materials science: liquid crystal polymer formulations for display applications, basic studies of liquid crystal alignment.

SELECTED PUBLICATIONS

Bhowmik, P. K., et al. **(R. N. Bose).** Lyotropic liquid crystalline main-chain viologen polymers: Homopolymer of 4,4'-bipyridyl with the ditosylate of trans-1,4-cyclohexanedimethanol and its copolymers with the ditosylate of 1,8-octanediol. *Macromolecules* 31:621–30, 1998.

Bose, R. N., B. S. Fonkeng, S. Moghaddas, and D. Stroup. Mechanism of DNA damage by chromium(V) carcinogens. *Nucleic Acids. Res.* 26:1588–96, 1998.

Bose, R. N., et al. Micellar electrokinetic and high-performance chromatographic separations of platinum-DNA antitumor adducts and DNA metabolites formed by chromium carcinogens. *Adv. Chromatogr. Electrophoresis Related Separation Methods* 1:25–37, 1998.

Fonkeng, B. S., S. Moghaddas, and **R. N. Bose.** Electron paramagnetic resonance, kinetics of formation and decomposition studies of (bis(hydroxyethyl)amino-tris(hydroxymethyl)-methane)oxo-chromate(V): A model chromium(V) complex for DNA damage studies. *J. Inorg. Biochem.* 72:163–71, 1998.

Bose, R. N., S. K. Ghosh, and S. Moghaddas. Kinetic analysis of the cis-diamminedichloroplatinum(II)-cysteine reaction: Implications to the extent of platinum-DNA binding. *J. Inorg. Biochem.* 65:199–205, 1997.

Cabaniss, S.E., J. A. Leenheer, and I. F. McVey. Aqueous infrared carboxylate absorbances: Aliphatic di-acids. *Spectrochim. Acta* 54A:449–58, 1998.

Sutheimer, S. H., and **S. E. Cabaniss.** Aluminum binding to humic substances determined by high performance cation exchange chromatography. *Geochim. Cosmochim. Acta* 61:1–11, 1997.

Cabaniss, S. E. Propagation of uncertainty in aqueous equilibrium calculations: Non-gaussian output distributions. *Anal. Chem.* 69:3658–64, 1997.

Pullin, M. J., and **S. E. Cabaniss.** Rank analysis of the pH dependent synchronous fluorescence spectra of six standard humic substances. *Environ. Sci. Technol.* 29:1460–7, 1995.

Sutheimer, S. H., and **S. E. Cabaniss.** Aqueous Al(III) speciation by high performance cation exchange chromatography with fluorescence detection of the lumogallion complex. *Anal. Chem.* 67:2342–9, 1995.

Thomas, E. T., and **J. E. Fulghum.** Quantitative uses of the valence band region in the analysis of polymer blends. *J. Vac. Sci. Technol. A* 16:1106–11, 1998.

Tielsch, B. J., and **J. E. Fulghum.** Differential charging in XPS. Part III. A comparison of charging in thin polymer overlayers on conducting and non-conducting substrates. *Surf. Interface Anal.* 25:904–12, 1997.

Tielsch, B., and **J. E. Fulghum.** Differential charging in XPS. Part I: Demonstration of lateral charging in a bulk insulator using imaging XPS. *Surface Interface Anal.* 24:422, 1996.

Tielsch, B., and **J. E. Fulghum.** Application of angle-resolved XPS algorithms to overlayers and concentration gradients. *Surf. Interface Anal.* 21:621–30, 1994.

Al-Ajlouni, A. M., P. C. Paul, and **E. S. Gould.** Electron transfer. 136. The decomposition of peroxynitrite as catalyzed by sulfito-bound cobalt(III). *Inorg. Chem.* 37:1434, 1998.

Chandra, S. K., P. C. Paul, and **E. S. Gould.** Electron transfer. 135. Pendant groups in the mediation of the reactions of indium(I) with bound ruthenium(III). *Inorg. Chem.* 36:4684, 1997.

Chandra, S. K., and **E. S. Gould.** Electron transfer. 134. Reduction, by indium(I), of bound ruthenium(III). *Inorg. Chem.* 36:3485, 1997.

Al-Ajlouni, A. M., and **E. S. Gould.** Electron transfer. 133. Copper catalysis in the sulfite reduction of peroxynitrite. *Inorg. Chem.* 36:362, 1997.

Gregory, R. B. Protein hydration and glass transitions. In *The Role of Water in Foods,* pp. 55–99, ed. D. Reid. New York: Chapman-Hall, 1997.

Gregory, R. B. Protein hydration and glass transition behavior. In *Protein-Solvent Interactions,* pp. 191–264, ed. R. B. Gregory. New York: Marcel Dekker, Inc., 1995.

Gregory, R. B., and K.-J. Chai. A positron annihilation lifetime study of protein hydration—evidence for a glass transition. *J. Physique* 3:305–10, 1993.

Gregory, R. B., M. Gangoda, R. K. Gilpin, and W. Su. Influence of hydration on the conformation of lysozyme studied by solid-state ^{13}C-NMR spectroscopy. *Biopolymers* 33:513–19, 1993.

Gregory, R. B. Free-volume and pore size distributions determined by numerical Laplace inversion of positron annihilation lifetime data. *J. Appl. Phys.* 70:4665–70, 1991.

Holland, L. A., and S. M. Lunte. Post column reaction detection for capillary electrophoresis-electrochemistry employing dual electrode detection and electrogenerated bromine. *Anal. Chem.* 71:407, 1999.

Holland, L. A., and S. M. Lunte. Capillary electrophoresis coupled with electrochemical detection, a review of recent advances. *Anal. Commun.* 35:1H, 1998.

Holland, L. A., N. P. Chetwyn, M. D. Perkins, and S. M. Lunte. Capillary electrophoresis in pharmaceutical analysis. *Pharm. Res.* 14:372, 1997.

Holland, L. A., and J. W. Jorgenson. Separation of nanoliter samples of biological amines by a comprehensive two-dimensional microcolumn liquid chromatography system. *Anal. Chem.* 34:3275, 1995.

Huang, S. D., and Y. Shan. NH_4V_3O8: A novel sinusoidal layered compound formed by the cation templating effective. *J. Chem. Soc. Chem. Comm.* 669-70, 1998.

Restrepo, G. F., et al. **(S. D. Huang).** cis-diamminechloro(2,5-dimethyl-benzoxazol-N1)platinum(II) nitrate. *Acta Crystallogr.* C54:15–6, 1998.

Bacelo, D. E., **S. D. Huang,** and Y. Ishikawa. The Au(I)-Au(I) interaction: Hartree-Fock and Miller-Plesset second order perturbation theory calculations on $[Se_5Au_2]^{2-}$ and $[Se_6Au_2]^{2-}$ complexes. *Chem. Phys. Lett.* 277:215–22, 1997.

Huang, S. D., C. P. Lai, and C. L. Barnes. Organometallic chemistry under the hydro(solvo) thermal conditions: Synthesis and X-ray structure of $(Ph_4P)_2[Mn_3(CO)_9(S_2)_2(SH)](Ph_4P)[Mn_2(CO)_6(SH)_3]$ and $(Ph_4P)_2[Mn_4(CO)_{13}(Te_2)_3]$. *Agnew. Chem. Int. Engl.* 36:1854–6, 1997.

Huang, S. D., and R.-G. Xiong. Molecular recognition of organic chromophores by coordination polymers: Design and construction of nonlinear optical supramolecular assemblies. *Polyhedron* 16:3929–39, 1997.

Kruk, M., **M. Jaroniec,** and K. P. Gadkaree. Determination of the specific surface area and the pore size of microporous carbons from adsorption potential distribution. *Langmuir* 15:1442–8, 1999.

Kruk, M., **M. Jaroniec,** and A. Sayari. Relations between pore structure and their implications for characterization of MCM-41 using gas adsorption and X-ray diffraction. *Chem. Mater.* 11:492–500, 1999.

Jaroniec, C. P., M. Kruk, **M. Jaroniec,** and A. Sayari. Tailoring surface and structural properties of MCM-41 silicas by bonding organosilanes. *J. Phys. Chem.* B102:5503–10, 1998.

Sayari, A., M. Kruk, **M. Jaroniec,** and I. L. Moudrakovski. New approaches to pore size engineering of mesoporous silicates. *Adv. Mater.* 10:1376–9, 1998.

Bereznitski, Y., and **M. Jaroniec.** Characterization of silica-based octyl phases of different bonding density. I. Thermal stability studies. *J. Chromatogr.* A828:51–8, 1998.

Boulas, P. L., and **M. T. Jones** et al. Electrochemical and ESR characterization of C_{84} and its anions in aprotic solvents. *J. Phys. Chem.* 100:7573–9, 1996.

Subramanian, R., et al. **(M. T. Jones).** Chemical generation of C_{60}^{2-} and electron transfer mechanism for the reactions with alkyl bromides. *J. Phys. Chem.* 100:16327–35, 1996.

Boulas, P. L., R. Subramanian, **M. T. Jones,** and K. M. Kadish. ESR studies of alkylammonium, pyridinium and arsonium solid salts of C_{60}. *Appl. Magn. Res.* 11:239–51, 1996.

Boulas, P., **M. T. Jones** et al. ESR characterization singly-, doubly-, and triply-reduced C_{84} isomers. *J. Am. Chem. Soc.* 116:9393–94, 1994.

Laali, K. K., S. Hollenstein, P. E. Hansen, and R. J. Harvey. Stable ion studies of the chrysene skeleton: Protonation of chrysene, 6-halochrysenes (F, Cl, Br), 6-acetylchrysene and 4H-cyclo-penta[def]chrysene; NMR studies of charge distribution in chrysenium cations and AM1 calculations. *J. Org. Chem.* 62:4023–8, 1997.

Laali, K. K., W. Fiedler, and M. Regitz. Reaction of phosphaacetylenses tBuCP and 1-AdCP with $(PhSe)_2/XeF_2$: First examples of vicinal bis-selenenylation (at P and C) to form novel phosphaalkenes. *J. Chem. Soc. Chem. Commun.* 1641–2, 1997.

Laali, K. K., M. Tanaka, and S. Hollenstein. Persistent α-CF_3 substituted 1-pyrenyl(methyl)-, 1-pyrenyl(phenyl)-, 4-pyrenyl(methyl)- and 9-phenanthrenyl(methyl)-methylcarbenium ions: Enhancing PAH arenium ion character by increasing electron demand at carbocation. *J. Org. Chem.* 62:7752–7, 1997.

Laali, K. K. Stable ion studies of protonation and oxidation of polycyclic arenes. *Chem. Rev.* 96:1873–906, 1996.

Laali, K. K., et al. Generation of the first persistent phosphirenylium cation. *J. Am. Chem. Soc.* 116:9407, 1994.

Masui, H., et al. Effect of positive charge concentration on Tg in completely amorphous salt-polyether solutions. *Solid State Ionics,* accepted.

Masui, H., and R. W. Murray. Molten forms of ruthenium tris(bipyridine). *Inorg. Chem.* 36:5118, 1997.

Maness, K. M., **H. Masui,** R. M. Wightman, and R. W. Murray. Solid state electrochemically generated luminescence based on serial frozen concentration gradients of Ru(III/II) and Ru(II/I) couples in a molten ruthenium 2,2'-bipyridine complex. *J. Am. Chem. Soc.* 119:3987, 1997.

Masui, H., and A. B. P. Lever. Correlations between the ligand electrochemical parameter E(L) and the Hammett substituent parameter, sigma. *Inorg. Chem.* 32:2199, 1993.

Kent State University

Selected Publications (continued)

Prosser, R. S., V. B. Volkov, and I. V. Shiyanovskaya. Solid-state NMR studies of magnetically aligned phospholipid membranes: Taming lanthanides for membrane protein studies. *Biochem. Cell. Biol.* 76:443–51, 1998.

Prosser, R. S., J. A. Losonczi, and I. V. Shiyanovskaya. Use of a novel aqueous liquid crystalline medium for high-resolution NMR of macromolecules in solution. *J. Am. Chem. Soc.* 120(42):11010–1, 1998.

Prosser, R. S., V. B. Volkov, and I. V. Shiyanovskaya. Novel chelate-induced magnetic alignment of biological membranes. *Biophys. J.* 75(5):2163–9, 1998.

Sanders, C. R., and **R. S. Prosser.** Bicelles: A model membrane system for all seasons? *Structure* 6(10):1227–34, 1998.

Prosser, R. S., J. S. Hwang, and R. R. Vold. Magnetically aligned phospholipid bilayers with positive ordering: A new model membrane system. *Biophys. J.* 74(5):2405–18, 1998.

Pynadath, T. I. Inhibition of thromboxane A$_2$ synthesis in rats treated with phenobarbital. *Prostaglandins Leukotrienes Med.* 28:267, 1987.

Haghighi, A. Z., and **T. I. Pynadath.** Stimulation of prostacyclin synthesis in rats treated with phenobarbital. *Prostaglandins Leukotrienes Med.* 28:267–75, 1987.

Pynadath, T. I. A pathway for the formation of increased levels of cholesterol oleate in atherosclerosis. *Fed. Proc.* 42:2231, 1983.

Pynadath, T. I., A. H. Zendedel, and B. P. Maloney. Changes in liver plasma membrane composition of cholesterol-fed rats. *Fed. Proc.* 41:1613, 1982.

Eveland, R. W., **C. C. Raymond,** T. E. Albrecht-Schmitt, and D. F. Shriver. New SO$_2$ iron containing cluster compounds [PPN]$_2$[Fe$_3$(CO)$_9$(μ_3-η^2-SO$_2$)], [PPN]$_2$[Fe$_3$(CO)$_8$(μ_3-S], [PPN]$_2$[Fe$_3$(CO)$_8$(μ-SO$_2$)(μ_3-CCO)], and [PPN]$_2$[Fe$_2$(CO)$_6$(μ-SO$_2$)$_2$] from heterometal precursors. *Inorg. Chem.* 38:1282–7, 1998.

Eveland, R. W., **C. C. Raymond,** and D. F. Shriver. [PPN][Fe$_3$(CO)(C≡CH)] and [Fe$_3$(CO)$_9$(C≡COTi(THF)$_4$Cl] from the reaction of low-valent titanium with [Fe$_3$(CO)$_9$(CCO)]$^{2-}$. *Organometallics* 18:534–9, 1998.

Raymond, C. C., and P. K. Dorhout. One hundred and seventy five years of polychalcogenides: Speciation in aqueous solution—the myths and the magic. *Chemtracts* 10:861–73, 1997.

Raymond, C. C., and P. K. Dorhout. Electrospray mass spectrometry of aqueous polyselenide solutions. *Inorg. Chem.* 36:2678–81, 1997.

Lorenz, B., et al. **(C. C. Raymond).** High pressure absorption, luminescence, and Raman scattering study of Cs$_2$MoS$_4$. *Phys. Rev. B* 55:2800–7, 1997.

Dudones, J. D., and **P. Sampson.** Preparation of a C-1 oxygenated taxane A ring via a highly efficient Diels-Alder strategy utilizing an α-(aroyloxy) enone captodative dienophile. *J. Org. Chem.* 62:7508–11, 1997.

Janini, T. E., and **P. Sampson.** Cyclopropanation/reduction of a 3,4-disubstituted 2(5H)-furanone: A model for C-8 methylation at the taxane BC ring juncture. *J. Org. Chem.* 62:5069–73, 1997.

Chai, K.-B., and **P. Sampson.** Macrolactonization–transannular aldol condensation approach to the taxane AB ring system. *J. Org. Chem.* 58:6807–13, 1993.

Krishnan, G., and **P. Sampson.** Synthesis of β-fluoro-α,β-unsaturated esters and nitriles via a fluoro-Pummerer rearrangement. *Tetrahedron Lett.* 31:5609–12, 1990.

Panarin, Yu. P., et al. **(A. J. Seed).** Investigation of the field induced ferrielectric subphases in antiferroelectric liquid crystals. *Mol. Mat.* 6:69, 1996.

Robinson, W. K., et al. **(A. J. Seed).** The influence of sulfur on phenyl propiolates for ferroelectric applications. *Ferroelectrics* 180:291, 1996.

Robinson, W. K., et al. **(A. J. Seed).** The synthesis, mesomorphic behaviour and physical properties of a chiral liquid crystal exhibiting an antiferroelectric smectic I phase. *Ferroelectrics* 178:249, 1996.

Panarin, Yu. P., et al. **(A. J. Seed).** An investigation of the field-induced ferrielectric subphases in antiferroelectric liquid crystals. *J. Phys. Condens. Matter* 7:L351, 1995.

Seed, A. J., K. J. Toyne, J. W. Goodby, and D. G. McDonnell. Synthesis, optical anisotropies, polarisabilities and order parameters of 4-cyanophenyl and 4-isothiocyanatophenyl 4'-butylsulfanylbenzoates with oxygen and sulfur substitution in the ester linkage. *J. Mater. Chem.* 5:1–11, 1995.

Parakulam, R. R., M. L. Lesniewski, K. J. Taylor-McCabe, and **C.-c. Tsai.** QSAR studies of antiviral agents using molecular similarity analysis and structure-activity maps. *SAR QSAR Environ. Res.* 10:1–32, 1999.

Lesniewski, M. L., et al. **(C.-c. Tsai).** QSAR studies of antiviral agents using structure-activity maps. *Internet J. Chem.* 2(7):59, 1999.

Gifford, E. M., M. A. Johnson, D. A. Smith, and **C.-c. Tsai.** Structure-reactivity maps as a tool for visualizing xenobiotic structure-reactivity realtionships. *Network Sci.* 2(2):33 pp., February 1996.

Gifford, E. M., M. A. Johnson, D. G. Kaiser, and **C.-c. Tsai.** Modeling the relative metabolic occurrence of alkyl-nitrogen bond cleavage using strucure-reactivity maps. *Xenobiotica* 25:825–46, 1995.

Gifford, E. M., M. A. Johnson, D. G. Kaiser, and **C.-c. Tsai.** An analysis of the relative occurrence of N-demethylation and N-oxidation in xenobiotic metabolism using structure-reactivity maps. *SAR QSAR Environ. Res.* 2:105–27, 1994.

Kuhls, K. A., C. A. Centrone, and **M. J. Tubergen.** Microwave spectroscopy of the twist C$^\beta$-exo/C$^\gamma$-endo conformation of prolinamide. *J. Am. Chem. Soc.* 120:10194–8, 1998.

Tubergen, M. J., Flad, J. E., and DelBene, J. E. Microwave spectroscopic and ab initio studies of the hydrogen-bonded trimethylamine-hydrogen sulfide complex. *J. Chem. Phys.* 107:2227–31, 1997.

Tubergen, M. J., and R. L. Kuczkowski. Hydrogen bonding to dimethylamine: The microwave spectrum and structure of the dimethylamine-water complex. *J. Mol. Struct.* 352/353:335–44, 1995.

Tubergen, M. J., and R. L. Kuczkowski. Microwave spectrum and structure of the dimethylamine dimer: Evidence for a cyclic structure. *J. Chem. Phys.* 100:3377–83, 1994.

Tubergen, M. J., A. M. Andrews, and R. L. Kuczkowski. The microwave spectrum and structure of a hydrogen bonded pyrrole-water complex. *J. Phys. Chem.* 97:7451–57, 1993.

Lundquist, P. M., et al. **(R. J. Twieg).** Organic glasses—A new class of photorefractive materials. *Science* 274:1182, 1996.

Gorria, P., H. T. Nguyen, **R. J. Twieg,** K. Betterton, and G. Sigaud. Influence of structure on smectic A—smectic A phase separation. *Liq. Cryst.* 21:523, 1996.

Srinivasan, S., **R. J. Twieg,** J. L. Hedrick, and C. J. Hawker. Heterocycle-activated aromatic nucleophilic substitution of AB$_2$ poly(aryl ether phenylquinoxaline) monomers, 3^{11}. *Macromol.* 29:8543, 1996.

Hedrick, J. L., **R. J. Twieg,** and T. Matray. Poly(aryl ether benzimidazoles). *Macromol.* 29:7335, 1996.

Wortmann, R., et al. **(R. J. Twieg).** A novel sensitized photochromic organic glass for holographic optical storage. *Appl. Phys. Lett.* 69:1657, 1996.

Arni, R. K., et al. **(F. G. Walz Jr.).** Three-dimensional structure of ribonuclease T$_1$ complexed with an isosteric analogue of GpU: Alternate substrate binding modes and catalysis. *Biochemistry* 38:2452–61, 1999.

Walz, F. G., Jr. Upstream subsite interactions for oglionucleotide binding with ribonuclease T$_1$. *Biochim. Biophys. Acta* 1350:183–8, 1997.

Apanovitch, D., and **F. G. Walz, Jr.** S-warfarin (11S-OH) and progesterone (20β-OH) keto-reductases in rat hepatic microsomes are not identical. *Biochim. Biophys. Acta* 1291:16–26, 1996.

Kitareewan, S., and **F. G. Walz, Jr.** Genetic and developmental diversity of hepatic cytochromes P450: warfarin and progesterone metabolism by hepatic microsomes from four inbred strains of rat. *Drug Metab. Dispos.* 22:607–15, 1994.

West, J. L. ALCOM, the National Science Foundation Science and Technology Center for Advanced Liquid Crystalline Optical Materials. *Ekisho, J. Jpn. Liq. Cryst. Soc.* 2:57–61, 1998.

Yoshida, H., Y. Takizawa, T. M. Martin, and **J. L. West.** Reflective display with photoconductive layer and bistable reflective cholesteric mixture. *J. SID* 5/3:269–74. 1997.

Ji, Y., J. J. Francl, and **J. L. West.** The mechanism for the formation of polymer wall in higher polymer content cholesteric liquid crystal mixture. *Mol. Cryst. Liq. Cryst.* 299:395–400, 1997.

Wang, X., and **J. L. West.** The mechanism of pretilt generation on polarized ultraviolet light aligned polyimide film. *Proc. 1997 IDRC,* pp. 5–8, September 1997.

Seo, D. S., et al. **(J. L. West).** A study of hysteresis and bistability in a polymer stabilized nematic liquid crystal using paramagnetic resonance and electro-optical studies. *Mol. Cryst. Liq. Cryst.* 287:101–7, 1996.

LONG ISLAND UNIVERSITY, BROOKLYN CAMPUS

Department of Chemistry

Programs of Study

The Department of Chemistry offers programs of study leading to the M.S. degree. Course offerings and research topics are available in the areas of inorganic, organic, polymer, analytical, physical, and computational chemistry as well as biochemistry. The programs generally require two years to complete and involve the preparation of a research thesis. Thirty graduate credits are required for the degree. A 32-credit nonthesis program is also available.

Graduate classes meet in the late afternoon and evening during the week and during the day on weekends. A year-round schedule, including two 6-week summer sessions, is offered.

Research Facilities

The department is housed on three floors of the main building of the Brooklyn Campus. Most modern instrumentation is available, including a 400-MHz NMR apparatus, a GC–mass spectrometer, and a powder X-ray diffractometer. A variety of smaller research instruments may also be used, including FT-IR and UV spectrometers, gas chromatography units, a spectropolarimeter, a high-pressure liquid chromatograph, scintillation counters, and other common supporting pieces of equipment. The Science Division has recently acquired its own Silicon Graphics 200 processor with R10000 processor capability.

The Brooklyn Campus is part of a University-wide, electronically linked library/resource network of 2.4 million volumes that subscribes to leading chemical journals and 14,486 periodicals.

The Academic Computing Center supports teaching, research, and student computer needs. Staff are available to support the microcomputing environment and to help with connections to the wide-area network LIUNET, the CLSI library system, and the Internet. LIUNET consists of DEC Alpha computer systems, IBM RS 6000 UNIX systems, and hundreds of PCs (IBM and Apple). On campus, there are eighteen computer labs, including special labs for writing, science, and other disciplines, as well as general-access labs utilizing the latest in Macintosh and IBM technology. There is a wide range of software packages, including MM, for semi-empirical and *ab initio* calculations, interfacing hardware, and utilities for all systems.

Financial Aid

Teaching fellowships are available; these appointments require some service to the institution and carry full tuition remission. Free residence hall accommodations may be provided for students willing to serve as residence hall counselors. New York State residents are eligible for Tuition Assistance Program awards.

Cost of Study

Tuition was $480 per credit in 1998–99. The initial application fee is $30, and the University fees range from $65 to $300 per semester for student activities and specific programs.

Living and Housing Costs

Residence Hall accommodations were available at $2470 to $5430 per year for a residence hall room in 1998–99. Apartments are available at $4600 to $5620 per year. Meal plans cost between $1200 and $2530 per year. Meal plans are required for all resident students occupying a residence hall room. Meal plans are optional for residents occupying an apartment. There are apartments in the residence hall and other University houses, as well as in private apartment houses within easy commuting distance of the campus.

Student Group

There are more than 2,000 graduate students at the Brooklyn Campus. There are approximately 50 undergraduate and 25 graduate students in the department, about one half of whom receive University support.

Location

The campus occupies an 11-acre site in the downtown area of Brooklyn at the foot of the Brooklyn and Manhattan bridges, across the East River from Wall Street and the financial district. It may be reached quickly and conveniently by rapid transit lines and by commuter railroad.

The cultural and entertainment attractions of New York City are only a few minutes' traveling time from the Brooklyn Campus.

The Department

The Brooklyn Campus of Long Island University is the original unit of the multicampus institution. The department prides itself on its informality and the accessibility of all faculty members to students. The main thrust of the department's efforts is to give students a fundamental understanding of the basics of chemistry as well as to introduce them to the newest ideas and developments in chemistry. Thus, graduate and undergraduate students alike are capable of going on for further academic work or taking their places in the chemical industry and related fields. The Department of Chemistry's programs are approved by the American Chemical Society.

Applying

Applicants must supply complete transcripts of all graduate and undergraduate courses taken. Candidates for fellowships should apply for financial aid at the time they apply for admission. Students are admitted in June, September, and February.

Correspondence and Information

For program information:
Department of Chemistry
Long Island University, Brooklyn Campus
1 University Plaza
Brooklyn, New York 11201
Telephone: 718-488-1208
Fax: 718-488-1465
E-mail: rburton@phoenix.liu.edu

For admissions information:
Admissions Office
Long Island University, Brooklyn Campus
1 University Plaza
Brooklyn, New York 11201
Telephone: 718-488-1011
Fax: 718-797-2399
E-mail: attend@liu.edu

Long Island University, Brooklyn Campus

THE FACULTY AND THEIR RESEARCH

Azzedine Bensalem, Associate Professor and Chairman; Ph.D., Nantes (France), 1987. Solid-state synthesis of low-dimensional conductors and low-temperature synthesis of transition metal sulfides.

Ishwar D. Chawla, Professor; Ph.D., Kansas State, 1962. Thermodynamics and spectral studies of coordination compounds.

Denise L. Chung, Associate Professor; Ph.D., NYU, 1992. Study of the mechanistic action of potential inhibitors of oncogenic *ras*-encoded p21 protein.

Fernando Commodari, Ph.D., McGill, 1992. Multidimensional NMR and molecular modeling in drug design and biomedical NMR.

Edward J. Donahue, Assistant Professor; Ph.D., Polytechnic of Brooklyn, 1991. Synthesis of organometallic molecules and their use in the chemical vapor deposition of ferroelectric and ferromagnetic thin films.

Becky Gee, Assistant Professor; Ph.D., California, Santa Barbara, 1996. Physical and solid-state chemistry.

Albert I. Hirschberg, Professor; Ph.D., Polytechnic of Brooklyn, 1960. Nitrogen mustards derived from pyrazine.

Surat Kumar, Assistant Professor; Ph.D., Lucknow (India), 1986. 2-D NMR studies on DNA and related biomolecules.

Glen D. Lawrence, Professor; Ph.D., Utah State, 1976. Transition metal catalyzed redox reactions in biological systems.

Hannia Lujan-Upton, Assistant Professor; Ph.D., Polytechnic of Brooklyn, 1995. Luminescence of terbium (II) complexes of tactic polymethacrylic acids.

Margaret Mandziuk, Assistant Professor; Ph.D., NYU, 1994. Computational approaches to molecular modeling and dynamics.

Nikita Matsunaga, Ph.D., Iowa State, 1995. Computational calculations of thermodynamic properties and reaction coordinates.

Aderemi R. Oki, Assistant Professor; Ph.D., Wyoming, 1990. Synthesis, characterization, and catalytic properties of transition metal complexes derived from tripod ligands.

Donald W. Rogers, Professor; Ph.D., North Carolina at Chapel Hill, 1960. Computational and thermochemical studies of organic molecules.

Alexander M. Shedrinsky, Professor; Ph.D., NYU, 1986. Application of analytical pyrolsis gas chromatography to problems in art and archaeology.

John K. Tseng, Professor; Ph.D., North Dakota, 1967. Pathways for intercellular UMP synthesis in animal tissue.

Samuel Watson, Assistant Professor; Ph.D., Princeton, 1995. Synthesis and study of peptidominetics as specific enzyme inhibitors.

Andreas Zavitsas, Professor; Ph.D., Columbia, 1962. Free radical reactions, kinetics, semiempirical calculations, electrochemical gas sensors.

Long Island University, Brooklyn Campus

SELECTED PUBLICATIONS

Bensalem, A., G. Iyer, and S. Amar. Synthesis of layered MgHPO$_4$.1.2H$_2$O under ambient conditions. *Mater. Res. Bull.* 30:1471–9, 1995.

Bensalem, A., and T. V. Vijayaraghaven. Hydroxyapatite (HA) coating by electrodeposition on alpha and alpha-beta titanium alloys. *J. Dent. Res.* Abstract 589(74): 474, 1995.

Bensalem, A., and T. V. Vijayaraghavan. Electrodeposition of apatite coating on pure titanium and titanium alloys. *J. Mater. Sci. Lett.* 13:1782–5, 1995.

Bensalem, A., and G. Iyer. Ambient pressure and temperature synthesis of new layered magnesium phosphate MgHPO$_4$.0.78H$_2$O. *J. Solid State Chem.,* p. 114, 1994.

Bensalem, A., and D. M. Schleich. Low temperature synthesis of vanadium sulfides. *Inorg. Chem.* 30:9, 1991.

Monaco, R., et al. **(D. Chung).** Comparison of the computed three-dimensional structures of oncogenic forms (bound to GDP) of the RAS-gene-encoded p21 protein with the structure of the normal (non-transforming) wild-type protein. *J. Protein Chem.,* in press.

Monaco, R., et al. **(D. Chung).** Structural effects of the binding of GTP to the wild-type and oncogenic forms of the RAS-gene-encoded p21 proteins. *J. Protein Chem.,* in press.

Haspel, J., et al. **(D. Chung).** Raf induced kinases may be necessary but are not sufficient for RAS-p-21 protein induction of oocyte maturation. *Med. Sci. Res.* 23:455–7, 1995.

Chung, D., et al. Evidence that the ras oncogene-encoded p21 protein induces oocyte maturation via activation of protein kinase C. *Proc. Natl. Acad. Sci. U.S.A.* 89:1993–6, 1992.

Chung, D., et al. Evidence that oocyte maturation induced by an oncogenic ras p21 protein and insulin is mediated by overlapping yet distinct mechanisms. *Exp. Cell Res.* 203:329–35, 1992.

Donahue, E., et al. Synthesis and characterization of microcystalline titanium disulfide for use in cathodes. *Mater. Res. Soc. Symp. Proc.* 293:69–74, 1993.

Gee, B., C. R. Horne, E. J. Cairns, and J. A. Reimer. Supertransferred hyperfine interactions at ^{7}Li: Variable temperature ^{7}Li NMR studies of LiMn$_2$O$_4$–based spinels. *J. Phys. Chem. B* 102:10142–9, 1998.

Gee, B., and H. Eckert. Cation distribution in mixed alkali silicate glasses. NMR studies ^{23}N$_2$-{^{7}Li} and ^{23}N$_2$-{^{6}Li} spin echo double resonance. *J. Phys. Chem.* 100:3705–12, 1996.

Gee, B., and H. Eckert. Cation ordering scenarios in mixed alkali silicate glasses. Experimental constraints from ^{23}N$_2$-{^{6}Li} spin echo double resonance NMR. *Ber. Bunsen-Ges. Phys. Chem.* 100:1610–16, 1996.

Gee, B., and H. Eckert. ^{23}N$_2$ NMR spin echo decay spectroscopy of sodium silicate glasses and crystalline model compounds. *Solid State NMR* 5:113–22, 1995.

Lehr, G. J., S. M. Yuen, and **G. D. Lawrence.** Determination of atropine in nerve gas antidotes and other dosage forms by high performance liquid chromatography. *J. Assoc. Off. Anal.,* in press.

Goudie, J., M. Chandra, **G. D. Lawrence,** and P. Williams. Assessment of the possible role of Fe and Cu in cisplatin-induced nephroxicity in the rat. *Res. Commun. Chem. Pathol. Pharmacol.* 83:33–49, 1994.

Gardner, L. K., and **G. D. Lawrence.** Benzene production from decarboxylation of benzoic acid in the presence of ascorbic acid and a transition metal catalyst. *J. Agric. Food Chem.* 40:693–5, 1993; *Chem. Ed.* 70:156–7, 1993.

Ellis, R., and **G. D. Lawrence.** Quantitative measurements of biogenic amines and their metabolites in the brain of fish and amphibians. *Microchem. J.* 47:55–9, 1993.

Lujan-Upton, H., and Y. Okamoto. An electrochemically controlled drug delivery system based on a disulfide containing polymer. *Drug Deliv. Agents: J. Deliv. Target. Ther. Drugs,* in press.

Lujan-Upton, H., and Y. Okamoto. The effect of taciticy on the luminescence intensity and lifetimes of terbium (III) complexes of polymethacrylic acids. *J. Polym. Sci.,* in press.

Lujan-Upton, H., and Y. Okamoto. Investigation of the conformational behavior of Kemp's triacid and its isomer using trivalent terbium as a fluorescent probe. *J. Org. Chem.,* in press.

Okamoto, Y., and **H. Lujan-Upton.** *Metal containing polymeric materials,* pp. 369–82, eds. C. U. Pittman et al. New York: Plenum Publishing, 1995.

Okamoto, Y., **H. Lujan-Upton,** and M. Cho. Polymer preprints, polymeric materials for science and engineering, vol. 71, p. 23. *Proc. ACS Meeting,* Washington, D.C., August 1994.

Matsunaga, N., and D. R. Yarkony. Energies and derivative couplings in the vicinity of a conical intersection. II. CH$_2$(2 3A", 3 3A") and H$_2$S(1 1A", 2 1A"), unexpected results in an ostensibly standard case. *J. Chem. Phys.* 107:7825–38, 1997.

Parry, C. S., B. R. Brooks, **N. Matsunaga,** and L. M. Amzel. Structures of some substituted nitrophenois determined by ab initio computation. On the origin of heterocliticity in anti-nitropenol antibodies. *Theochemistry* 398:555–63, 1997.

Oki, A. R., J. Sanchez, A. Roxburgh, and T. Lester. Preparation and characterization of Co(II) complexes derived from hexadentate 'tripod' ligand and their potentials as epoxidation catalyst. *Synth. React. Inorg. Metal-Org. Chem.* 26:1–9, 1996.

Oki, A. R., J. Sanchez, R. J. Morgan, and L. Ngai. Monomeric copper (II) and nickel (II) complexes of N,N,N',N' -tetrakis (2-benzimidazoyl) -1,2-cyclohexanediamine: A chelating ligand containing imidazole groups. *Transition Met. Chem.* 21:43–8, 1996.

Hosmane, N. S., et al. **(A. R. Oki).** Chemistry of c-trimethylisilyl–substituted heterocarbons. 19. Synthetic and structural studies on trinuclear Ln(III)-carborane cluster-part 1. (In(III)=Sm,Gd,Tb,Dy, and Ho): Conversion to sandwiched manganese (II) and cobalt (III) carbon complexes. *Organometallics* 15:626–38, 1996.

Oki, A. R., P. R. Bommarreddy, H. Zhang, and N. S. Hosmane. Maganese (II) complex of the 'tripod' ligand tris (2-benzimidazolylmethyl) amine. Five coordinate and six coordinate Mn(II) in the crystal structure. *Inorg. Chim. Acta* 231:109–14, 1995.

Zhang, H., et al. **(A. R. Oki).** The first trinuclear terbium (III) carborane cluster (C$_{61}$H$_{159}$B$_{24}$Li$_6$O$_5$Si$_{12}$Tb$_3$)C$_6$H$_6$) *Acta Crystallogr. C* 51:635–8, 1995.

Rogers, D. W., and F. J. McLafferty. G2 ab initio calculations of enthalpies of formation of C3 hydrocarbons. *J. Phys. Chem.* 99:1375, 1995.

Abboud, J.-L. M., et al. **(D. W. Rogers).** Interrelations of the energetics of amides and alkenes. *J. Phys. Org. Chem.* 8:15, 1995.

Rogers, D. W., and F. J. McLafferty. G2 ab initio calculations of the enthalpy of formation of hydrazoic acid, methyl azide, ethyl azide, methyl amine and ethyl amine. *J. Chem. Phys.* 103:8302, 1995.

Rogers, D. W. *Computational Chemistry Using the Personal Computer,* 2nd ed. New York: VCH Publishers, Inc., 1994.

Wayne, G. S., G. J. Snyder, and **D. W. Rogers.** Measurement of the strain of a transient bridgehead imine, 4-azahomoadamant-3-ene, by photoacoustic calorimetry. *J. Am. Chem. Soc.* 115:9860, 1993.

Eglinton, M. A., J. J. Goni, and **A. M. Shedrinsky.** Molecular-level ^{13}C and ^{14}C analyses of fatty acids from Egyptian oil sample of archaeological interest. *Proc. 209th Am. Chem. Soc. Nat. Meet.,* Chicago, 1995.

Shedrinsky, A. M., and N. S. Baer. The application of analytical pyrolysis to the study of cultural materials. In *Handbook on Analytical Pyrolysis,* pp. 125–55. Marcel Dekker, Inc., 1995.

Shedrinsky, A. M. The application of conservation science in the examination and conservation of cultural property. In *Proceedings of the International Symposium on the Conservation and Preservation of Cultural Artifacts,* pp. 1–20. Taipei, May, 1995.

Grimaldi, D., **A. M. Shedrinsky,** A. Ross, and N. S. Baer. Forgeries of fossils in amber: History, identification and case studies. *Am. Mus. Nat. Hist.* 37(4):251–74, 1994.

Shedrinsky, A. M., D. Grimaldi, J. J. Boon, and N. S. Baer. Applications of Py-GC and Py-GC-MS for unmasking of faked ambers. *J. Anal. Appl. Pyrolysis* 25:77–95, 1993.

Tseng, L., et al **(J. K. Tseng).** Decidualization of human endometrial stromal cells in vitro. *Serono Symp. Publ. Raven Press* 96:213–24, 1993.

Taylor, E. C., **S. E. Watson,** and R. Chaudhari. Silicon-containing antifolates. *J. Org. Chem.,* in press.

Tay, E. C., and **S. E. Watson.** Conformationally unrestricted analogs of 5,10-methylene-tetrahydrofolate as thyymidylate synthase inhibitors and potential antitumor agents. *J. Org. Chem.,* in press.

Taylor, E. C., **S. E. Watson,** and H. Patel. Novel 2-amino-3 carboethoxyfuran synthesis. *Heterocycles,* in press.

Taylor, E. C., and **S. E. Watson.** Novel pyrrolo (2,3-d) pyrimidine ring forming methodology; applications to the synthesis of thymidylate synthase inhibitors. *Heterocycles,* in press.

Long Island University, Brooklyn Campus

Selected Publications (continued)

Zavitsas, A. A. Factors controlling reactivity in hydrogen abstractions by free radicals. *J. Chem. Soc.* (Perkins translation) 2:391–3, 1996.

Zavitsas, A. A., and C. Chatgilialoglu. Energies of activation; the paradigm of hydrogen abstractions by radicals. *J. Am. Chem. Soc.* 117:10654, 1995.

Beckwith, A. L. J., and **A. A. Zavitsas.** Accurate calculations of reactivities and disasterioselectivities in complex molecules: An AM1 study of 1,3-dioxolan-4-ones and related oxygen heterocycles. *J. Am. Chem. Soc.* 117:607–14, 1995.

Zavitsas, A. A. The energy distance relationship in chemical bonding; accurate calculation of potential energy curves. *J. Am. Chem. Soc.* 113:4755–67, 1991.

Zavitsas, A. A., and A. L. J. Beckwith. New potential energy function for bond extensions. *J. Phys. Chem.* 93:5419–26, 1989.

Zavitsas, A. A. Quantitative relationship between bond dissolution energies, infrared stretching frequencies, and force constants in polyatomic molecules. *J. Phys. Chem.* 91:5573–7, 1987.

MIAMI UNIVERSITY

Department of Chemistry and Biochemistry

Programs of Study
The Department of Chemistry and Biochemistry offers the Master of Science (M.S.) and Doctor of Philosophy (Ph.D.) degrees in the areas of analytical, inorganic, organic, physical, and theoretical chemistry; chemical education and biochemistry; and molecular biology. The program is designed to give students both an in-depth knowledge of their chosen area and a strong background in other areas of chemistry. During their first semester, students interview with faculty members to discuss potential research projects. Based on these interviews, students choose a research adviser by the start of the second semester.

The M.S. program normally requires two years to complete. The student must pass a preliminary oral exam, write a thesis based on original research he or she has conducted, and present an oral defense of the thesis. At least two courses in the chemistry field of specialization are required. In addition, three chemistry graduate courses of at least 6 hours must be taken outside the major field of specialization.

The Ph.D. program normally requires four to five years of post-baccalaureate work and generally includes course work, seminars, written and oral exams, and original research. Typically, most course work is finished in the first two years, with cumulative or comprehensive exams in the second and third years. The Ph.D. oral exam that follows is based on an original research proposal developed by the student. At least two courses in the major field of specialization and four courses outside this major area are required. Well-prepared students can skip the M.S. degree and proceed directly toward the Ph.D. degree.

Research Facilities
The Department of Chemistry and Biochemistry contains all the major research instrumentation needed to conduct experiments in modern chemistry and biochemistry. Major instrumentation includes 200-MHz and 300-MHz NMR's, GC-MS, an FTMS-equipped FAB source, TOF equipped with a laser desorption source, and EPR. The department also houses a fully automated X-ray diffractometer, as well as atomic absorption, atomic emission equipped with an ICP, luminescence, UV-visible, Fourier transform infrared, and Raman spectrophotometers. Electrochemical instrumentation includes four computer-interfaced potentiostats and power supplies for preparative electrolysis. All of the instrumentation necessary to perform a wide range of modern molecular and biochemical techniques is also available. A wide variety of chromatographic apparatus are available, representing all types of liquid and gas chromatography, including supercritical fluid techniques. The department is fully networked to provide University-wide and Internet access to all laboratories and offices. The department also houses several Silicon Graphics workstations (Indy, Indigo II, and Power Indigo II) specifically to support theoretical chemistry and computational chemistry.

Financial Aid
All graduate students in good standing are supported through teaching and research assistantships and fellowships. The graduate stipend for the 1998–99 academic year ranged from $13,200 to $14,300 for a twelve-month appointment. In addition, tuition waivers and partial health benefits are provided to all assistantship holders. Exceptionally well qualified students are considered for a supplemental Graduate School Academic Achievement Assistantship or departmental scholarships.

Cost of Study
Graduate tuition and fees for the 1998–99 academic year were $7112 and $13,212 for Ohio residents and nonresidents, respectively. The cost of tuition is waived for students in good standing.

Living and Housing Costs
Living costs are moderate in Oxford. Typical rents for off-campus apartments are approximately $350 per month for one bedroom and $480 per month for two bedrooms. A limited amount of University housing is available at costs that range from $390 to $430 per month.

Student Group
The department currently has approximately 55 graduate students and several postdoctoral fellows from throughout the United States and several other countries. Essentially all of the graduate students are full-time students.

Location
Miami University is located in Oxford, a town with a population of about 9,000 (excluding students) that offers a relaxed atmosphere for graduate study. It is 35 miles north of Cincinnati and 45 miles southwest of Dayton. Such proximity offers graduate students the opportunity to enjoy the diversity of city life and the beauty and serenity of a residential location.

The University
Miami University is a state-assisted liberal education university located in the rolling country of southwestern Ohio. The University was established in 1809 and is the second-oldest institution of higher learning in Ohio. The 1,100-acre main campus is considered by many to be one of the most beautiful campuses in the Midwest. Miami is renowned for its academic excellence and its commitment to the liberal arts. About 1,500 graduate students and 15,600 undergraduates are on the Oxford campus.

Applying
Consideration is given to applicants who have completed a bachelor's degree in chemistry or biochemistry from an accredited college or university. There is no formal deadline for admission, but graduate assistantships are normally awarded by May for the following fall. A limited number of assistantships are typically available for January admission. The General Test of the Graduate Records Examinations is recommended but not required. TOEFL and TWE scores are required for all international applicants.

Correspondence and Information
Director of Graduate Studies
Department of Chemistry and Biochemistry
Miami University
701 East High Street
Oxford, Ohio 45056
Telephone: 513-529-1659 or 2813
Fax: 513-529-2715
E-mail: cleveljm@muohio.edu
World Wide Web: http://miavx1.muohio.edu/~CHMCWIS/

Miami University

THE FACULTY AND THEIR RESEARCH

Each faculty member's area of specialization is listed in parentheses.

Carolyn J. Cassady, Associate Professor; Ph.D., Purdue, 1984 (analytical chemistry). Fundamental and analytical applications of Fourier transform ion cyclotron resonance mass spectrometry, fast-atom bombardment mass spectrometry, ion-molecule reactions, gas-phase metal ion cluster chemistry. (E-mail: cassadcj@muohio.edu)

James A. Cox, Professor; Ph.D., Illinois, 1967 (analytical chemistry). Trace analysis, electro-analytical methods, modified electrodes, environmental chemistry, metal speciation, membrane-based sample introduction methods for atomic spectroscopy and ion chromatography. (E-mail: coxja@muohio.edu)

Michael W. Crowder, Assistant Professor; Ph.D., Virginia, 1993 (bioinorganic chemistry). Metalloprotein characterization, antibiotic resistance mechanisms. (E-mail: crowdemw@muohio.edu)

S. Mark Cybulski, Assistant Professor; Ph.D., Southern Illinois, 1989 (theoretical chemistry). Computational chemistry, investigation of intermolecular forces. (E-mail: cybulssm@muohio.edu)

Neil D. Danielson, Professor; Ph.D., Georgia, 1978 (analytical chemistry). Ion chromatography; luminescence, high-performance liquid chromatography. (E-mail: danielnd@muohio.edu)

Gilbert Gordon, Professor; Ph.D., Michigan State, 1956 (inorganic chemistry). Mechanism of inorganic substitution and redox reactions by means of fast kinetics techniques; dynamics of chemical reaction; analytical chemistry of ozone, chlorine dioxide, and oxyhalogen species in water purification processes. (E-mail: gordong@muohio.edu)

Charles C. Griffin, Associate Professor; Ph.D., Johns Hopkins, 1969 (biochemistry). Mechanisms of regulatory enzymes; enzyme kinetics; protein-small molecule interactions: carbohydrate metabolism; membrane transport. (E-mail: grifficc@muohio.edu)

John R. Grunwell, Professor; Ph.D., MIT, 1967 (organic chemistry). Synthesis of natural products, synthetic methods, photochemistry. (E-mail: grunwejr@muohio.edu)

Benjamin W. Gung, Associate Professor; Ph.D., Kansas State, 1987 (organic chemistry). Diastereofacial ion asymmetrically substituted unsaturated organic compounds, synthesis and mechanism. (E-mail: gungbw@muohio.edu)

Ann E. Hagerman, Professor; Ph.D., Purdue, 1980 (biochemistry). Regulation of plant secondary product metabolism, especially phenolic metabolism; biochemical mechanisms of disease resistance; biological activity of lignin, tannin, and other plant polyphenolics. (E-mail: hagermae@muohio.edu)

James W. Hershberger, Associate Professor; Ph.D., Iowa State, 1981 (organic chemistry). Electrontransfer catalysis in the substitution and ligand exchange reactions of organic and organometallic compounds, reagents of organic synthesis, mechanistic and preparative electrochemistry. (E-mail: hershbjw@muohio.edu)

Alan D. Isaacson, Associate Professor; Ph.D., Berkeley, 1978 (physical chemistry). Quantum and classical theories of reactive and nonreactive atom-atom and atom-molecule scattering; quantum mechanics of interaction potentials and chemi-ionization, electron-atom and electron-molecule scattering, including resonances. (E-mail: isaacsad@muohio.edu)

Jan G. Jaworski, Professor; Ph.D., Purdue, 1972 (biochemistry). Fatty acid and lipid biosynthesis and metabolism of long chain fatty acids in cyanobacteria and plants. (E-mail: jaworsjg@muohio.edu)

Gary A. Lorigan, Assistant Professor; Ph.D., California, Davis, 1996 (physical chemistry). Magnetic resonance structural and dynamic studies of membrane proteins and lipid bilayers. (E-mail: lorigaga@muohio.edu)

Christopher A. Makaroff, Professor; Ph.D., Purdue, 1986 (biochemistry). Coordinate regulation of nuclear and mitochondrial gene expression, developmental regulation of pollen formation and factors controlling meiosis. (E-mail: makaroca@muohio.edu)

Robert E. Minto, Assistant Professor; Ph.D., Berkeley, 1994 (bioorganic chemistry). Mechanisms of biosynthesis, enzyme mechanism and regulation. (E-mail: mintore@muohio.edu)

Michael Novak, Professor and Chair; Ph.D., Cornell, 1976 (organic chemistry). Mechanistic investigations of reactions of molecules that have been implicated as chemical carcinogens, physical organic studies of toxic metabolites of common analgesics, enol phosphate chemistry. (E-mail: novakm@muohio.edu)

Gilbert E. Pacey, Professor; Ph.D., Loyola Chicago, 1979 (analytical chemistry). Flow injection analysis, analytical applications of chromogenic crown ethers, and remote sensors. (E-mail: paceyge@muohio.edu)

Thomas L. Riechel, Associate Professor; Ph.D., California, Riverside, 1976 (analytical chemistry). Electrochemical and spectroscopic studies of transition metal complexes as models for metal-centers in biological systems, development of mediators and chemically modified electrodes for the determination of biologically important species. (E-mail: riechetl@muohio.edu)

Jerry L. Sarquis, Professor; Ph.D., Texas A&M, 1974 (chemical education). Demonstrations that can be used to illustrate chemical phenomena, activities that can be used at the pre-high school level to introduce younger students to the science of chemistry to spark their interest in science. (E-mail: sarquijl@muohio.edu)

John F. Sebastian, Professor; Ph.D., California, Riverside, 1965 (biochemistry and organic chemistry). Structure and chemistry of carbanions; nuclear magnetic resonance spectroscopy; applications of molecular orbital theory; organometallic chemistry; mechanisms of action, inhibition, and activation of enzyme-catalyzed reaction: protein-DNA interactions. (E-mail: sebastjf@muohio.edu)

Andre J. Sommer, Assistant Professor; Ph.D., Lehigh, 1985 (analytical chemistry). Molecular microspectroscopy (infrared and Raman), instrumentation and methods development. (E-mail: sommeraj@muohio.edu)

Robert P. Stewart Jr., Professor; Ph.D., Berkeley, 1966 (inorganic chemistry). Synthesis and spectroscopic studies; transition metal organometallic chemistry; metal carbonyls, metal nitrosyls; homogeneous catalysis. (E-mail: stewarrp@muohio.edu)

Richard T. Taylor, Associate Professor; Ph.D., Ohio State, 1977 (organic chemistry). Synthetic organosilicon chemistry; synthesis and reactivity of strained hydrocarbons, polymeric reagents. (E-mail: taylorrt@muohio.edu)

NEW YORK UNIVERSITY

Department of Chemistry

Program of Study

The Department of Chemistry offers the Ph.D. degree. The chemistry of the components of living systems is a major focus of the department; faculty members and students in all subdisciplines of chemistry at NYU work on problems relevant to the molecules of life. Spectroscopy, materials, catalysis, organic mechanisms, and quantum calculations are additional areas of active research in which a student can pursue a degree.

The program is designed to train independent research scientists who can assume positions in teaching and research settings. These include universities; colleges; the chemical, pharmaceutical, and biotechnology industries; and public and private research institutions. A student participates in the seminars and journal clubs of one of three groups in the department: biomolecular chemistry (biophysical or bioorganic), organic chemistry, or physical chemistry (experimental, theoretical, or materials). The first year of study is typically spent in course work and in rotation through several research laboratories. Competence in the major field is established by satisfactory performance in first-year course work and a presentation based on first-year research experiences, after which dissertation research is normally begun.

Research Facilities

The major equipment in the chemistry department includes a rotating anode X-ray diffractometer, a scanning tunneling microscope with a high-vacuum specimen-coating device, a state-of-the-art laser laboratory for fast time-resolved studies of chemical processes, an electrospray mass spectrometer, and a computational center. The Department of Chemistry currently maintains a suite of Varian NMRs managed by a professional spectroscopist and serviced by experts in the department. A 200-MHz Gemini system handles routine measurements for both instructional classes and organic chemists. A 300-MHz Gemini is used for longer-term acquisition and variable temperature work. Finally, a 500-MHz Unity system is used for multidimensional experiments involving protein and nucleic acid samples. The department also has peptide and DNA synthesizers, a CD spectropolarimeter, three FT-IR spectrometers, photoacoustic and photothermal beam deflection spectrometers, microcalorimeters, and equipment for UV, ESR, fluorescence, and IR spectrometry. The W. M. Keck Laboratories for Biomolecular Imaging within the department have been completed recently.

The Academic Computing Center has, among other machines, high-end VAX's, ALPHAs, and a 4-processor Silicon Graphics machine. The Scientific Visualization Center houses a number of Silicon Graphics workstations with an extensive array of molecular modeling software. Within the department there are a large number of scientific workstations and IBM RISC 6000s. Bobst Library is one of the largest open-stack research libraries in the nation.

Financial Aid

All students admitted to the Ph.D. program receive financial support in the form of teaching assistantships, research assistantships, or University fellowships. Students usually receive support for the duration of their studies. The basic stipend for the 1999–2000 nine-month academic year is $14,500. Summer appointments as research or teaching assistants are available at comparable rates.

Cost of Study

Research and teaching appointments carry a waiver of tuition, which amounted to $17,160 for the 1998–99 academic year, and of registration fees, which are estimated at $1048 per academic year.

Living and Housing Costs

The standard budget for a single student for the academic year 1998–99 (exclusive of tuition) was approximately $13,000. This includes room and board, books, fees, and personal expenses. University, as well as privately owned, housing is available.

Student Group

The Graduate School of Arts and Science has an enrollment of 4,000 graduate students; about 85 are pursuing advanced degrees in chemistry. They represent a wide diversity of ethnic and national groups; more than a third are women. Upon receiving their Ph.D.'s, about 10 percent of recent graduates entered positions in academia, and the others were approximately equally divided between those who accepted industrial employment and those who elected to gain postdoctoral research experience before accepting permanent positions.

Location

Greenwich Village, the home of the University, has long been famous for its contributions to the fine arts, literature, and drama and for its personalized, smaller-scale, European style of living. It is one of the most desirable places to live in the city. New York City is the business, cultural, artistic, and financial center of the nation, and its extraordinary resources enrich both the academic programs and the experience of living at NYU.

The University

New York University, a private university, awarded its first doctorate in chemistry in 1866. Ten years later, the American Chemical Society was founded in the original University building, and the head of the chemistry department, John W. Draper, assumed the presidency.

Applying

Application forms may be obtained by writing to the address below. Students beginning graduate study are accepted only for September admission. Applicants are expected to submit scores on the GRE General Test and the Subject Test in chemistry or a related discipline. Students whose native language is not English must submit a score on the Test of English as a Foreign Language (TOEFL). Application deadlines are January 4, 2000. Applicants are invited to visit the University but are advised to contact the department beforehand to arrange an appointment.

Correspondence and Information

Director of Graduate Programs
Department of Chemistry
New York University
New York, New York 10003
Telephone: 212-998-8400
Fax: 212-260-7905
E-mail: chem.web@nyu.edu
World Wide Web: http://www.nyu.edu/pages/chemistry/

New York University

THE FACULTY AND THEIR RESEARCH

Zlatko Bačić, Professor; Ph.D., Utah, 1982. Theoretical chemistry: spectra and dynamics of highly vibrationally excited floppy molecules, dissociation dynamics of rare-gas clusters in collisions with solid surfaces.

Henry C. Brenner, Associate Professor; Ph.D., Chicago, 1972. Physical chemistry: effects of high pressure on energy transfer and luminescence, optically detected magnetic resonance of molecular crystals and biological systems.

James W. Canary, Associate Professor; Ph.D., UCLA, 1988. Organic and bioorganic chemistry: synthetic receptors for complexation and catalysis, metalloprotein mimics, biomimetic molecular devices.

John S. Evans, Assistant Professor; Ph.D., Caltech, 1993. Biomolecular materials: solution and solid-state NMR structure and dynamics of biomineralization and structural proteins, computational and molecular modeling of proteins and biomaterials.

Paul J. Gans, Professor; Ph.D., Case Tech, 1959. Theoretical chemistry: determination of conformational and thermodynamic properties of macromolecules by Monte Carlo simulation.

Nicholas E. Geacintov, Professor; Ph.D., Syracuse, 1961. Physical and biophysical chemistry: interaction of polycyclic aromatic carcinogens with nucleic acids, laser studies of fluorescence mechanisms and photoinduced electron transfer.

Neville R. Kallenbach, Professor; Ph.D., Yale, 1961. Biophysical chemistry of proteins and nucleic acids: structure, sequence, and site selectivity in DNA-drug interactions, protein folding, model helix and beta sheet structures.

Edward J. McNelis, Professor; Ph.D., Columbia, 1960. Organic chemistry: oxidation as a route to synthetically useful substances, novel organometallic catalysts.

Jules W. Moskowitz, Professor; Ph.D., MIT, 1961. Theoretical chemistry: Monte Carlo methods applied to quantum chemistry.

Yorke E. Rhodes, Associate Professor; Ph.D., Illinois, 1964. Organic chemistry: alkyl group migrations and rearrangement mechanisms, interaction of cyclopropane with neighboring cationic centers, organic astrochemistry.

Tamar Schlick, Professor; Ph.D., NYU, 1987. Molecular mechanics and dynamics, DNA supercoiling, polypeptide dynamics.

David I. Schuster, Professor; Ph.D., Caltech, 1961. Organic and bioorganic chemistry: photochemistry of enones, effects of paramagnetic reagents on photocycloadditions, time-resolved photoacoustic calorimetry, photoaffinity labeling of neuroreceptors.

David C. Schwartz, Associate Professor; Ph.D., Columbia, 1985. Physics and biology of large single DNA molecules, with applications to genomic analysis.

Nadrian C. Seeman, Professor; Ph.D., Pittsburgh, 1970. Biophysical chemistry: structural chemistry of recombination; design of nanometer-scale geometrical objects and devices from branched DNA; catenated and knotted DNA topologies; crystallography.

Robert Shapiro, Professor; Ph.D., Harvard, 1959. Organic and bioorganic chemistry: effects of mutagens on the structure and function of nucleic acids.

Mark Tuckerman, Assistant Professor; Ph.D., Columbia, 1993. Theoretical chemistry: ab initio molecular dynamic simulations and statistical mechanics.

Graham R. Underwood, Associate Professor; Ph.D., Melbourne, 1966. Organic and bioorganic chemistry: synthesis and study of carcinogen-DNA adducts, reactions at centers other than carbon.

Alexander Vologodskii, Research Professor; Ph.D., Moscow Physical Technical Institute, 1975. Statistical mechanical properties of DNA; supercoiling, catenanes, knots; effect of supercoiling on DNA-protein interaction.

Marc A. Walters, Associate Professor; Ph.D., Princeton, 1981. Inorganic chemistry: kinetics and energetics of metal thiolate and selenolate formation, synthesis of complexes for the uptake of many-electron equivalents.

Stephen Wilson, Professor; Ph.D., Rice, 1972. Organic chemistry: total synthesis of natural products, new synthetic methodology, synthesis of enzyme mimics.

John Z. H. Zhang, Professor; Ph.D., Houston, 1987. Theory: study of molecular collision dynamics and chemical reactions in the gas phase and on surfaces.

SELECTED PUBLICATIONS

Sabo, D., **Z. Bačić**, S. Graf, and S. Leutwyler. Four-dimensional model calculations of torsional levels of cyclic water tetramer. *J. Chem. Phys.* 109:5404–19, 1998.

Bačić, Z., and Y. Qiu. Vibration-rotation-tunneling dynamics of $(HF)_2$ and $(HCl)_2$ from full-dimensional quantum bound state calculations. In *Advances in Molecular Vibrations and Collision Dynamics,* Vol. III, pp. 183–204, eds. J. M. Bowman and **Z. Bačić.** Greenwich, Conn.: JAI Press Inc., 1998.

Niyaz, P., **Z. Bačić, J. W. Moskowitz,** and K. E. Schmidt. Ar_nHF (n=1-4) van der Waals clusters: A quantum Monte Carlo study of ground state energies, structures and HF vibrational frequency shifts. *Chem. Phys. Lett.* 252:23, 1996.

Schroeder, T., et al. **(Z. Bačić** and **J. W. Moskowitz).** Photodissociation of HF in Ar_nHF(n=1, 14, 54). In *Femtochemistry,* pp. 277–80, ed. M. Chergui. Singapore: World Scientific, 1996.

Liu, S., **Z. Bačić, J. W. Moskowitz,** and K. E. Schmidt. Isomer dependence of HF vibrational frequency shift for Ar_nHF (n=4-14) van der Waals clusters: Quantum five-dimensional bound state calculations. *J. Chem. Phys.* 103:1829, 1995.

Tringali, A. E., S. K. Kim, and **H. C. Brenner.** ODMR and fluorescence studies of pyrene solubilized in anionic and cationic micelles. *J. Luminescence* 81:85–100, 1999.

Tringali, A. E., and **H. C. Brenner.** Spin-lattice relaxation and ODMR line narrowing of the photoexcited triplet state of pyrene in polycrystalline Shpol'skii hosts and glassy matrices. *Chem. Phys.* 226:187–200, 1998.

Tringali, A. E., S. F. A. Pearce, E. Hawrot, and **H. C. Brenner.** Phosphorescence and ODMR study of the binding interactions of acetylcholine receptor alpha subunit peptides with alpha-cobratoxin. *FEBS Lett.* 308:225–8, 1992.

Xu, X., A. R. Lajmi, and **J. W. Canary.** Acetaldehyde hydration by zinc-hydroxo complexes: Coordination number expansion during catalysis. *Chem. Commun.* 24:2701, 1998.

Canary, J. W., et al. Solid state and solution characterization of chiral, conformationally mobile tripodal ligands. *Inorg. Chem.* 37:6255, 1998.

Zahn, S., and **J. W. Canary.** Redox-switched exciton-coupled circular dichroism: A novel strategy for binary molecular switching. *Angew. Chem. Int. Ed. Engl.* 37:305–7, 1998.

Xu, G., and **J. S. Evans.** Model peptide studies of sequence repeats derived from the intracrystalline biomineralization protein, SM50. I. GVGGR and GMGGQ repeats. *Biopolymers,* in press.

Xu, G., B. Zhang, and **J. S. Evans.** PFG- 1-filtered TOCSY experiments for the determination of long-range heteronuclear and coupling constants, and estimation of J-coupling "crosstalk" artifacts in 2-D 1-filtered "E. COSY-style" spectra. *J. Magn. Reson.,* in press.

Evans, D. A., and **J. S. Evans.** Host-guest interactions influence stability of the Rebek "tennis ball" dimer complex. *J. Org. Chem.* 63:8027–30, 1998.

Lyu, P. C., **P. J. Gans,** and **N. R. Kallenbach.** Energetic contribution of solvent-exposed ion pairs to alpha-helix structure. *J. Mol. Biol.* 223:343–50, 1992.

Gans, P. J., et al. **(N. R. Kallenbach).** The helix-coil transition in heterogeneous peptides with specific side-chain interactions: Theory and comparison with CD spectral data. *Biopolymers* 31:1605–14, 1991.

Ginsberg, D. M., and **P. J. Gans.** Statistical theory of thin film growth. *Thin Solid Films* 29:L17, 1975.

Xu, R., B. Mao, S. Amin, and **N. E. Geacintov.** Bending and circularization of site-specific and stereoisomeric carcinogen-DNA adducts. *Biochemistry* 37:769–78, 1998.

Geacintov, N. E., et al. NMR solution structures of stereoisomeric polycyclic aromatic carcinogen-DNA adducts: Principles, patterns and diversity (a review). *Chem. Res. Toxicol.* 10:111–46, 1997.

Hess, T. M., et al. **(N. E. Geacintov).** Base pair conformation-dependent excision of benzo[a]pyrene diol epoxide-guanine adducts by human nucleotide excision repair. *Mol. Cell. Biol.* 17:7069–76, 1997.

Kallenbach, N. R., P. Lyu, and H. Zhou. CD spectroscopy and the helix-coil transition in peptides and polypeptides. *Circ. Dichroism Conform. Anal. Biomol.* 201–59, 1996.

Zhao, Y., et al. **(N. R. Kallenbach).** HMG box proteins interact with multiple tandemly repeated $(GCC)_n$*$(GGC)_m$ DNA sequences. *J. Biomol. Struct. Dynamics* 14:235–8, 1996.

Berger, J. S., et al. **(N. R. Kallenbach).** Stabilization of helical peptides by mixed spaced salt bridges. *J. Biomol. Struct. Dynamics* 14:285–91.

Herault, X., and **E. McNelis.** Solvent effects on the rearrangements of tertiary alcohols. *New J. Chem.* 21:377–82, 1997.

Herault, X., and **E. McNelis.** Ring expansions of 1-haloethynyl-2-methylcyclopentanols. *Tetrahedron* 52:10267–78, 1996.

Djuardi, E., and **E. McNelis.** Comparison of iodonium-producing reagents in the shift reaction of a bromopropynol alcohol. *Synth. Commun.* 26:4091–6, 1996.

Rhodes, Y. E. Potential chemical relationships of polycyclic aromatic hydrocarbons and c-C_3H_2. In *Five College Radio Astronomy Observatory Proceedings.* New York: Springer-Verlag, 1988.

Jacobson, E. N., et al. **(Y. E. Rhodes).** Steric effects on the titanium tetrachloride-promoted dimerization of silyl ketene acetals. *Synth. Commun.* 15:301–6, 1985.

Takakis, I. M., and **Y. E. Rhodes.** Acetolysis and formolysis of (R)- and (S)-1-deuterio-2-cyclopropylethyl tosylate. *Tetrahedron Lett.* 4959–62, 1983.

Schlick, T., et al. Algorithmic challenges in computational molecular biophysics. *J. Comp. Phys.,* in press.

Jian, H., **T. Schlick,** and **A. Vologodskii.** Internal motion of supercoiled DNA: Brownian dynamics simulations of site juxtaposition. *J. Mol. Biol.* 284:287–96, 1998.

Barth, E., and **T. Schlick.** I. Overcoming stability limitations in biomolecular dynamics: Combining force splitting via extrapolation with Langevin dynamics in LN. *J. Chem. Phys.* 109:1617–32, 1998.

Cheng, P., **S. R. Wilson,** and **D. I. Schuster.** A novel parachute-shaped C_{60}-porphyrin hybrid. *Chem. Commun.* 89–90, 1999.

Schuster, D. I., et al. **(S. R. Wilson).** The role of singlet oxygen in the photochemical formation of $C_{60}O$. *Chem. Commun.* 2493–4, 1998.

Baran, P. S., et al. **(D. I. Schuster** and **S. R. Wilson).** Synthesis and cation-mediated electronic interactions of two novel classes of porphyrin-fullerene hybrids. *J. Am. Chem. Soc.* 119:8363–4, 1997.

Cai, W., et al. **(D. C. Schwartz).** Ordered restriction endonuclease maps of yeast artificial chromosomes created by optical mapping on surfaces. *Genetics* 92:5164–8, 1995.

Meng, X., et al. **(D. C. Schwartz).** Optical mapping of lambda bacteriophage clones using restriction endonucleases. *Nature Genet.* 9:432, 1995.

Schwartz, D. C., et al. Ordered restriction maps of *Saccharomyces cerevisiae* chromosomes constructed by optical mapping. *Science* 262:110–4, 1993.

Winfree, E., F. Liu, S. A. Wenzler, and **N. C. Seeman.** Design and self-assembly of two-dimensional DNA crystals. *Nature* 394:539–44, 1998.

Seeman, N. C. DNA nanotechnology: Novel DNA constructions. *Ann. Rev. Biophys. Biomol. Struct.* 27:225–48, 1998.

Sun, W., C. Mao, F. Liu, and **N. C. Seeman.** Sequence dependence of branch migratory minima. *J. Mol. Biol.* 282:59–70, 1998.

Shapiro, R. *Planetary Dreams. The Quest to Discover Life Beyond Earth.* New York: John Wiley & Sons, in press.

Shapiro, R., S. Ellis, B. E. Hingerty, and S. Broyde. Effect of ring size on conformations of aromatic amine-DNA adducts: The aniline-C8 guanine adduct resides in the B-DNA major groove. *Chem. Res. Toxicol.* 11:335–41, 1998.

Roy, D., B. E. Hingerty, **R. Shapiro,** and S. Broyde. A slipped replication intermediate model is stabilized by the syn orientation of N-2-(acetyl)aminofluorene-modified guanine at a mutational hotspot. *Chem. Res. Toxicol.* 11:1301–11, 1998.

Jacobson, M., and **R. Shapiro** et al. **(G. Underwood).** Synthesis and conformation of a dinucleotide monophosphate modified by aniline. *Chem. Res. Toxicol.* 1:152–9, 1988.

Tuckerman, M. E., C. J. Mundy, and G. J. Martyna. On the classical statistical mechanics of non-Hamiltonian systems. *Europhys. Lett.* 45:149, 1999.

Marx, D., **M. E. Tuckerman,** and M. Parrinello. The nature of the hydrated excess proton in water. *Nature* 397:601, 1999.

Martyna, G. J., and **M. E. Tuckerman.** A reciprocal space based method for treating long range forces in force-field based and *ab initio* calculations in clusters. *J. Chem. Phys.* 110:2810, 1999.

Constantinos, N., and **G. Underwood.** The solvolysis of N-acetoxy-4-acetaminostilbene: Irreversible formation of nitrenium ions. *Tetrahedron Lett.* 1479–82, 1989.

New York University

Selected Publications (continued)

Underwood, G., M. Price, and **R. Shapiro.** A new synthetic route to nucleotide adducts derived from N-acetylated and unacetylated 4-aminobiphenyl. *Carcinogenesis* 9:1817–21, 1988.

Vologodskii, A. V., X. Yang, and **N. C. Seeman.** Non-complementary DNA helical structure induced by positive torsional stress. *Nucleic Acids Res.* 26:1503–8, 1998.

Rybenkov, V. V., C. Ullsperger, **A. V. Vologodskii,** and N. R. Cozzarelli. Simplification of DNA topology below equilibrium values by type II topoisomerases. *Science* 277:690–3, 1997.

Bose, K., et al. **(M. A. Walters).** Evidence for charge-dipole effects in the rubredoxin model compound $[(CH_3)_4N]_2[SCH_2CON(CH_3)_2]_4$. *Inorg. Chem.* 36:4596–9, 1997.

Leung, Y., and **M. A. Walters** et al. Determination of the mineral phases and structure of the bone-implant interface using Raman spectroscopy. *J. Biomed. Mater. Res.* 29:591–4, 1995.

Huang, J., R. L. Ostrander, A. L. Rheingold, and **M. A. Walters.** The synthesis and electrochemistry of $Mo[HB(Me_2pz)_3](NO)[S(CH_2)_2CONH(CH_2)_2S]$ as a probe of the effects of N-H...S hydrogen bonding on redox potentials. *Inorg. Chem.* 34:1090–3, 1995.

Wilson, S. R. Biological aspects of fullerenes. In *The Fullerene Handbook.*, eds. K. Kadish and R. Ruoff. New York: John Wiley & Sons, 1999.

Erlanger, B. F., D. J. Coughlin, M. Das, and **S. R. Wilson.** Antigenicity of fullerenes: Antibodies specific for fullerenes and their characteristics. *Proc. Natl. Acad. Sci. U.S.A.* 95(18):10809–13, 1998.

Wilson, S. R., and A. W. Czarnick, eds. *Combinatorial Chemistry: Synthesis and Application.* New York: John Wiley & Sons, 1997.

Wang, D. Y., T. Peng, and **J. Z. H. Zhang.** Quantum dynamics from *ab initio* points. *Phys. Chem. Chem. Phys.* 1:1067, 1999.

Qiu, Y., **J. Z. H. Zhang,** and **Z. Bačić.** Six-dimensional quantum calculations of vibration-rotation-tunneling levels of v_1 and v_2 HCl-stretching excited $(HCl)_2$. *J. Chem. Phys.* 108:4804–16, 1998.

Wang, D. Y., and **J. Z. H. Zhang.** Correction of repulsive potential energy surface for photodissociation of H_2O in the A state. *J. Chem. Phys.* 108:10027, 1998.

Peng, T., W. Zhu, D. Y. Wang, and **J. Z. H. Zhang.** The reactant-product decoupling approach to state-to-state dynamics calculation for bimolecular reaction and unimolecular fragmentation. *Faraday Discuss.* 110:159, 1998.

"Brooklyn Poly"®

POLYTECHNIC UNIVERSITY, BROOKLYN CAMPUS

Department of Chemical Engineering, Chemistry and Materials Science

Programs of Study

The department offers programs leading to the Doctor of Philosophy degree in chemical engineering, materials chemistry, and materials science. The graduate programs emphasize research, particularly in the area of polymers, in which Polytechnic University has been consistently ranked as one of the top universities in the world. Polytechnic has had a distinguished history of academic excellence in the field of polymers, which began with the establishment of the first program in polymers in 1942 by Dr. Herman F. Mark, the father of polymer science, and has continued ever since.

Research Facilities

The professors in the Department of Chemical Engineering, Chemistry and Materials Science are all researchers at the leading edge of their fields. International symposia are organized at Polytechnic University on specific topics, and worldwide recognition is based on the enthusiastic activity of the faculty. Research fields include both government and industrial cooperation, with annual meetings to optimize recruiting, interaction, and information exchange. The faculty specializes in advanced characterization methods, using the University's Surface Analysis, Scattering, HOP-Chromatography, Molecular Modeling, X-Ray Scattering, Spectroscopy, and Microscopy (STEM, STM, and OM) Labs and the Lab for Electrical and Optical Properties of Materials. The wide variety of areas in research include chiral polymers and their importance in pharmaceutical industry and information technology and complex polymer fluids, which respond to external conditions such as temperature, pressure, and stress. Compositive materials and polymer blends involve research in which the desired properties are tailor-made for various structural applications. Electrical and optical properties of materials have brought fundamental science closer to applications and electroactive materials.

Financial Aid

A full range of financial packages is available. The recipients of fellowships in the 1998–99 academic year received stipends of $15,000 and a tuition waiver. Fellowships are available based on a competitive and academic background.

Cost of Study

The 1998–99 cost for graduate study based on 12 credits was $16,800 per academic year, including fees. Each additional credit over 12 was $675. The cost for books and supplies was $690.

Living and Housing Costs

The cost for room and board is $5500. Room costs are based on a double room. For a single room, costs are higher. Food costs vary depending upon the meal plan offered through Polytechnic-sponsored residence programs. Students interested in off-campus housing may take advantage of off-campus housing postings on bulletin boards at each campus.

Student Group

The total number of graduate students in the department is currently more than 150. A wide variety of academic, ethnic, and national backgrounds are represented among students.

Location

Polytechnic's main campus is located in downtown Brooklyn inside Metro Tech, the 16-acre, $1-billion academic/research/industrial complex, just 5 minutes from Wall Street and lower Manhattan. For the Polytechnic student, New York City provides access to one of the largest and most exciting "campuses" in the world. It is rich in cultural, educational, recreational, and social resources. New York City is one of the world's major crossroads and has a high level of diversity.

The University and The Department

Polytechnic is the leading technological university in the New York metropolitan area. Founded in 1854 and known for many years as Brooklyn Poly, the University was renamed Polytechnic University in 1985, a name that more accurately describes the range and quality of Polytechnic's programs and research.

Traditionally, Polytechnic has been strong in chemistry and chemical engineering. Building on that strength and in order to promote interdisciplinary cooperation and innovation, the departments of chemical engineering, chemistry, and materials science and engineering were combined in 1995 into an academic unit: the Department of Chemical Engineering, Chemistry and Materials Science.

Applying

Application to programs in the Department of Chemical Engineering, Chemistry and Materials Science must be made on a form available from the admissions office. For an admissions package and the departmental brochure, with detailed descriptions of faculty members and programs, students should contact the department (telephone: 718-260-3525 or 3470; fax: 718-260-3125) or e-mail (klevon@poly.edu).

Correspondence and Information

Prospective students should address all written correspondence about the chemical engineering, chemistry, and materials science programs to:

Dr. Kalle Levon, Department Head
Rogers Hall, Room 801
Polytechnic University
Six Metrotech Center
Brooklyn, New York 11201
Telephone: 718-260-3470
Fax: 718-260-3125
E-mail: klevon@duke.poly.edu
World Wide Web: http://www.poly.edu

Polytechnic University, Brooklyn Campus

THE FACULTY AND THEIR RESEARCH

Nitash P. Balsara, Professor of Chemical Engineering; Ph.D., Rensselaer. Microstructured polymer materials, thermodynamics and phase transitions, small-angle neutron scattering, dynamic light scattering.

Mary K. Cowman, Associate Professor of Biochemistry; Ph.D., Case Western Reserve. Polysaccharide roles in tissue organization and homeostasis, development of novel methods for purification and characterization of complex carbohydrate biopolymers, analysis of solution conformation and interactions of connective tissue polysaccharides, connective tissue network formation, biometics.

Bruce A. Garetz, Associate Professor of Chemistry; Ph.D., MIT. Laser spectroscopy, nonlinear optics and multiphoton processes, molecular dynamics.

Mark M. Green, Professor of Organic Chemistry; Ph.D., Princeton. Stereochemistry of reactive intermediates, macromolecular stereochemistry, isolation of bioactive plant substances.

Richard Gross, Herman F. Mark Professor; Ph.D., Polytechnic. Biocatalytic routes for polymer design, use of biocatalysts to perform various polymer-related transformations, use of whole cells and in-vitro enzyme systems, structural analysis of complex products derived from natural building blocks, preparation and evaluation of biobased surfactants and emulsifiers, studies on the biodegradability of polymers and complex natural products, design of bioactive glycolipids and matrices for specific cellular responses.

Kalle Levon, Professor of Chemistry, Department Head, and Director of the Polymer Research Institute; Dr.Agr., Tokyo. Competition between liquid-liquid phase separation and crystallization in polymer solutions and blends, one of the major factors determining the final property-morphology relationship.

Jovan Mijovic, Professor of Chemical Engineering; Ph.D., Wisconsin. In-situ time monitoring and modeling of processing of polymers and composites, impedance spectroscopy of polymers, structural relaxations in polymeric glasses.

Shirley M. Motzkin, Professor of Chemistry; Ph.D., NYU. Interactive mechanisms fields in living and model systems, basic concepts of ecology in industrial applications, normal and pathologic in-vivo and in-vitro bone formation and calcification, teratologic effects of chemical and physical insults on development.

Allan S. Myerson, Joseph J. and Violet J. Jacobs Professor of Chemical Engineering; Ph.D., Virginia. Crystallization from solution, nucleation, diffusion in polymers, molecular modeling.

Eli M. Pearce, University Professor; Ph.D., Polytechnic Institute of Brooklyn. Polymer synthesis and degradation, polymer compatibility, polymer structure-property relationships.

Yitzhak Shnidman, Assistant Professor of Chemistry; Ph.D., Weizmann (Israel). Statistical mechanics of interfaces and complex fluids; statics and dynamics of wetting, absorption, and adhesion; structure and rheology of complex fluids, colloids, and polymers.

Leonard I. Stiel, Associate Professor of Chemical Engineering; Ph.D., Northwestern. Thermodynamic and transport properties of fluids and mixtures, energy conversion.

Iwao Teraoka, Assistant Professor of Chemistry; Dr.Eng., Tokyo. Separation of polymer, polymer solutions and porous materials, dynamic light scattering.

Nancy M. Tooney, Associate Professor of Biochemistry and Assistant Provost for Academic Affairs; Ph.D., Brandeis. Structure and function of proteins and other biopolymers, blood-clotting system, fibronectin structure and function, environmental chemistry.

Abraham Ulman, Alstadt-Lord-Mark Professor of Chemistry; Ph.D., Weizmann (Israel). Self-assembled and Langmuir-Blodgett monolayers, surface engineering and surface phenomena, organic nonlinear optical materials, porphyrin-based advanced materials and catalysts, polymers for extreme conditions, especially poly(aryl sulfones).

Edward Ziegler, Associate of Chemical Engineering; Ph.D., Northwestern. Air pollution control engineering, reactor design, fluidization.

Walter P. Zurawsky, Associate Professor of Chemical Engineering; Ph.D., Illinois. Plasma polymerization, mass transfer in membranes.

PRINCETON UNIVERSITY

Department of Chemistry

Programs of Study

The Department of Chemistry offers a program of study leading to the degree of Doctor of Philosophy. Upon entering, students take qualifying examinations in the fields of biochemistry, inorganic and organic chemistry, chemical physics, and physical chemistry and are expected to demonstrate a satisfactory level of proficiency in three of these areas by the end of the first year of study. The graduate program emphasizes research, and students enter a research group by the end of the first semester. There are no formal course requirements. However, students are expected to take six graduate courses in chemistry and allied areas early in their graduate program and to participate throughout their graduate career in the active lecture and seminar programs.

To help evaluate the progress of graduate study, monthly cumulative examinations are given during the first two academic years. Each student must pass five of these exams. Early in the second year, the student takes a general examination that consists of an oral defense of a thesis-related subject. Upon satisfactory performance in the cumulative and general examinations, the student is readmitted for study toward the degree of Doctor of Philosophy in chemistry. The degree is awarded primarily on the basis of a thesis describing original research in one of the areas of chemistry. The normal length of the entire Ph.D. program is four years.

In cooperation with the physics department, a program of graduate study in the field of chemical physics leading to a joint Ph.D. in physics and chemical physics is also offered. A program in biostructural chemistry is also offered.

Research Facilities

Research is conducted in Frick Chemical Laboratory and the adjoining Hoyt Laboratory. Extensive renovation and modernization of the laboratory has recently been completed. NMR, IR, ESR, FT-IR, atomic absorption, UV-visible, and vacuum UV spectrometers and departmental computers are available to students. In addition, high-resolution FT-NMR spectrometers and mass spectrometers are run by operators for any research group. There is a wide variety of equipment in individual research groups, including lasers of many kinds, high-resolution spectrographs, molecular beam instrumentation, a microwave spectrometer, computers, gas chromatographs, and ultrahigh-vacuum systems for surface studies. The department has an electronics shop, a machine shop, a student machine shop, and a glassblower for designing and building equipment. Extensive shop facilities are available on campus, and there is a large supercomputing center.

Financial Aid

Appointments as assistants in instruction (compensation taxable) are normally available to all entering students. The 1999–2000 stipend is $15,000 for ten months (6 contact hours and 12–14 hours of preparation per week). Most entering students are also awarded a full tuition fellowship. Summer research stipends (also taxable) are also provided for the summer following the first year. Assistantships in research, fellowships, and student loans are available; they generally include support for the summer period.

Cost of Study

See Financial Aid section above.

Living and Housing Costs

Rooms at the Graduate College cost from $2442 to $3799 for the 1998–99 academic year of thirty-five weeks. Several meal plans were available, priced from $2479 to $3565. University apartments for married students currently rent for $453 to $1226 a month. Accommodations are also available in the surrounding community.

Student Group

The total number of graduate students in chemistry is currently about 130. Postdoctoral students number about 70. A wide variety of academic, ethnic, and national backgrounds are represented among these students.

Location

Princeton University and the surrounding community together provide an ideal environment for learning and research. From the point of view of a chemist in the University, the engineering, physics, mathematics, and molecular biology departments, as well as the Forrestal campus, provide valuable associates, supplementary facilities, and sources of special knowledge. Many corporations have located their research laboratories near Princeton, and interactions with them have been fruitful.

Because of the nature of the institutions located here, the small community of Princeton has a very high proportion of professional people. To satisfy the needs of this unusual community, the intellectual and cultural activities approach the number and variety ordinarily found only in large cities, but with the advantage that everything is within walking distance. There are many film series, a resident repertory theater, orchestras, ballet, and chamber music and choral groups. Scientific seminars and other symposia bring prominent visitors from every field of endeavor. Princeton's picturesque and rural countryside provides a pleasant area for work and recreation, yet New York City and Philadelphia are each only about an hour away.

The University

Princeton University was founded in 1746 as the College of New Jersey. At its 150th anniversary in 1896, the trustees changed the name to Princeton University. The Graduate School was organized in 1901 and has since won international recognition in mathematics, the natural sciences, philosophy, and the humanities.

Applying

Applications, specifying the chemistry department, must be made on a form available on request from the Admissions Office, Princeton Graduate School, Box 270. A nonrefundable fee of $70 for U.S. residents and international students must accompany each application. Consideration is given to applications received before January 3. All assistantships and fellowships for entering students are awarded to applicants at this time. Applications received after January 3 are normally not considered. Admission consideration is open to all qualified candidates without regard to race, color, national origin, religion, sex, or handicap.

Because the financial aid offered to chemistry students is in the form of assistantships, it is not necessary for students to submit a GAPSFAS form unless they are requesting a loan.

Correspondence and Information

Director of Graduate Studies
Department of Chemistry
Princeton University
Princeton, New Jersey 08544

Princeton University

THE FACULTY AND THEIR RESEARCH

Although all major areas of chemistry are represented by the faculty members, the department is small and housed in Frick Chemical Laboratory and the adjoining Hoyt Laboratory, so that fruitful collaborations develop. The following list briefly indicates the areas of interest of each faculty professor.

L. C. Allen. Theoretical chemistry: electronic structure theory; applications to physical, inorganic, organic, and biochemical problems.

S. L. Bernasek. Chemical physics of surfaces: basic studies of chemisorption and reaction on well-characterized transition-metal surfaces, using electron diffraction and electron spectroscopy; surface reaction dynamics; heterogeneous catalysis; electronic materials.

A. B. Bocarsly. Inorganic photochemistry, photoelectrochemistry, chemically modified electrodes, electrocatalysis, sensors, applications to solar energy conversion.

J. Carey. Biochemistry: protein and nucleic acid structure, function, and interactions; protein folding and stability.

R. Cava. Synthesis, solid-state chemistry, crystallography, stoichiometry and phase equilibria of transition metal oxides, chalcogenides, and pnictides and their relation to physical properties.

G. C. Dismukes. Molecular spectroscopy of biological molecules and mechanisms of their activity, photosynthetic electron transfer reactions, metalloenzyme electronic structure, synthetic models of metalloenzymes, magnetic resonance spectroscopy.

J. T. Groves. Organic and inorganic chemistry: synthetic and mechanistic studies of reactions of biological interest, metalloenzymes, transition-metal redox catalysis.

M. Hecht. Biochemistry: sequence determinants of protein structure and design of novel proteins.

M. Jones Jr. Reactions and spin states of carbenes, arynes, twisted π systems, and other reactive intermediates; carborane chemistry.

D. Kahne. Organic chemistry: synthetic methods, with an emphasis on the construction of oligosaccharides; studies on carbohydrate structure and function in biological molecules.

S. Lee. Coordination chemistry, synthesis of novel metal clusters, bioinorganic model complexes for nitrogen fixation.

K. K. Lehmann. High-resolution molecular spectroscopy, intramolecular energy redistribution, determination of potential energy surfaces, ultrasensitive methods of spectroscopic detection.

G. L. McLendon. Metallobiochemistry, protein electron transfer reactions, photochemistry, RNA-binding proteins, macromolecular structure.

M. Nooijen. Development of new computational and theoretical methods in electronic structure theory; applications to excited states, photochemical reactions, hydrogen bonded systems.

R. A. Pascal Jr. Catalytic mechanisms of redox enzymes, enzyme inhibitor design and synthesis, bioorganic chemistry, biochemistry of parasitic organisms, chemistry of distorted aromatic hydrocarbons.

H. Rabitz. Physical chemistry: atomic and molecular collisions, theory of chemical reactions and chemical kinetics, time- and space-dependent relaxation processes, heterogeneous phenomena, control of molecular motion.

C. E. Schutt. Structural biology: structure and function of proteins and cellular organelles, X-ray crystallography.

J. Schwartz. Applications of organometallic chemistry to organic synthesis, organozirconium chemistry, organometallic reaction mechanisms, surface organometallic chemistry.

G. Scoles. Chemical physics: laser spectroscopy, chemical dynamics and cluster studies with molecular beams; structure, dynamics, and spectroscopic properties of overlayers adsorbed on crystal surfaces.

M. F. Semmelhack. Organometallic and electrogenerated intermediates in organic synthesis, synthesis of unusual ring systems in natural and unnatural molecules.

K. Shokat. Structural biochemistry: chemical approaches to the study of contemporary problems in biological systems.

Z. G. Soos. Chemical physics: electronic states of π-molecular crystals and conjugated polymers, paramagnetic and charge-transfer excitons, linear chain crystals, energy transfer.

T. G. Spiro. Biological structure and dynamics from spectroscopic probes; role of metals in biology; metalloporphyrins in photocatalysis; chemically modified electrodes.

S. Walker. Structural biochemistry: DNA recognition.

W. S. Warren. Laser spectroscopy in gaseous and solid phases, coherence effects, multiphoton processes, nuclear magnetic resonance.

Associated Faculty

F. Hughson, Department of Molecular Biology. X-ray crystallography, membrane fusion proteins, protein folding.

F. M. M. Morel, Department of Geological and Geophysical Sciences. Environmental chemistry, trace metal geochemistry, metals-biota interactions.

J. Stock, Department of Biology. Structure and function of membrane receptors and signal transduction proteins.

Frick Chemical Laboratory.

SELECTED PUBLICATIONS

Allen, L. C., and J. F. Capitani. What is the metallic bond? *J. Am. Chem. Soc.* 116:8810, 1994.

Allen, L. C. Chemistry and electronegativity. *Int. J. Quant. Chem.* 49:253, 1994.

Allen, L. C., J. F. Capitani, G. A. Kolks, and G. D. Sproul. Van Arkel–Ketelaar triangles. *J. Mol. Struct.* 300:647, 1993.

Allen, L. C. Extension and completion of the periodic table. *J. Am. Chem. Soc.* 114:1510, 1992.

Cheng, L. C., **A. B. Bocarsly, S. L. Bernasek**, and T. A. Ramanarayanan. Adsorption and reaction of thiophene on the Fe(100) surface: Selective dehydrogenation and polymerization. *Surface Sci.* 374:357, 1997.

Bald, D., R. Kunkel, and **S. L. Bernasek**. Diode laser absorption study of internal energies of CO_2 produced from catalytic CO oxidation. *J. Chem. Phys.* 104:7719, 1996.

Aronoff, Y. G., et al. (**J. Schwartz** and **S. L. Bernasek**). Stabilization of self-assembled monolayers of carboxylic acids on native oxides of metals. *J. Am. Chem. Soc.* 119:259, 1996.

Hayward, M. J., et al. (**S. L. Bernasek**). Examination of sputtered ion mechanisms leading to the formation of C_7H_7 during surface induced dissociation (SID) tandem mass spectrometry (MS/MS) of benzene molecular cations. *J. Am. Chem. Soc.* 118:8375, 1996.

Chang, C. C., Y. Wu, E. P. Vicenzy, and **A. B. Bocarsly**. Inorganic photolithography: Interfacial, multicomponent pattern generation. *J. Chem. Ed.* 74:663, 1997.

Heibel, M., et al. (**A. B. Bocarsly**). Use of sol-gel chemistry for the preparation of cyanogels as ceramic and alloy precursors. *Chem. Mater.* 8:1504, 1996.

Kelly, M. T., J. K. M. Chun, and **A. B. Bocarsly**. A silicon sensor for SO_2. *Nature* 382:214, 1996.

Wu, Y., B. W. Pfennig, E. P. Vicenzi, and **A. B. Bocarsly**. Development of redox-active optical mesostructures at chemically modified electrode interfaces. *Inorg. Chem.* 34:4262, 1995.

Szwajkajzer, D., and **J. Carey**. Molecular and biological constraints on ligand-binding affinity and specificity. *Nucleic Acid Sci.* 44:181–98, 1997.

Sunnerhagen, M. S., M. Nilges, G. Otting, and **J. Carey**. Solution structure of the DNA-binding domain and model for the complex of multifunctional, hexameric arginine repressor with DNA. *Nature Struct. Biol.* 4:819–25, 1997.

Yang, J., et al. (**J. Carey**). In vivo and in vitro studies of TrpR-DNA interactions. *J. Mol. Biol.* 258:37–52, 1996.

Grandori, R., et al. (**J. Carey**). The DNA-binding domain of the hexameric arginine repressor. *J. Mol. Biol.* 254:150–62, 1995.

Cava, R. J., et al. Crystal structure and elementary physical properties of $La_5Cu_{19}P_{12}$ and $Ce_5Cu_{19}P_{12}$. *J. Solid State Chem.* 121:55, 1996.

Carter, S. A., and **R. J. Cava**, et al. Hole doping of the CuO_2 chains in $(La,Sr,Ca)_{14}Cu_{24}O_{41}$. *Phys. Rev. Lett.* 77:1378, 1996.

Cava, R. J., W. F. Peck Jr., and J. J. Krajewski. Enhancement of the dielectric constant of Ta_2O_5 through doping with TiO_2. *Nature* 377:215, 1995.

Cava, R. J., et al. Superconductivity in lanthanum nickel boro-nitride. *Nature* 372:759, 1994.

Ruttinger, W., and **G. C. Dismukes**. Synthetic water oxidation catalysts for artificial photosynthetic water oxidation. *Chem. Rev.*, in press.

Zheng, M., and **G. C. Dismukes**. Orbital configuration of the valence electrons, ligand field symmetry and manganese oxidation states of the photosynthetic water oxidizing complex: Analysis of the S2 state multiline EPR signals. *Inorg. Chem.* 35:3307–19, 1996.

Ananyev, G. M., and **G. C. Dismukes**. High-resolution kinetic studies of the reassembly of the Tetra-Mn cluster of photosynthetic water oxidation: Proton equilibrium, cations and electrostatics. *Biochemistry* 35:14608–17, 1996.

Dismukes, G. C. Manganese enzymes with binuclear active sites. *Chem. Rev.* 96:2909–26, 1996.

Lahiri, J., G. D. Fate, S. B. Ungashe, and **J. T. Groves**. Multi-heme self-assembly in phospholipid vesicles. *J. Am. Chem. Soc.* 118:2347, 1996.

Groves, J. T., M. Bonchio, T. Carofiglio, and K. Shalyaev. Rapid catalytic oxygenation of hydrocarbons by Ruthenium pentafluorophenylporphyrin complexes: Evidence for the involvement of a Ru(III) intermediate. *J. Am. Chem. Soc.* 118:8961, 1996.

Groves, J. T., and J. S. Roman. Nitrous oxide activation by a ruthenium porphyrin. *J. Am. Chem. Soc.* 117:5594, 1995.

Groves, J. T., and S. Marla. Peroxynitrite-induced DNA strand scission mediated by a manganese porphyrin. *J. Am. Chem. Soc.* 117:9578, 1995.

Roy S., et al. (**G. McLendon** and **M. H. Hecht**). A protein designed by binary patterning of polar and nonpolar amino acids displays native-like properties. *J. Am. Chem. Soc.* 119:5302–6, 1997.

Rojas, N. R., et al. (**T. G. Spiro** and **M. H. Hecht**). De novo heme proteins from designed combinatorial libraries. *Protein Sci.* 6:2512–24, 1997.

Xiong, H., B. L. Buckwalter, H. M. Shieh, and **M. H. Hecht**. Periodicity of polar and non-polar amino acids is the major determinant of secondary structure in self-assembling oligomeric peptides. *Proc. Natl. Acad. Sci. U.S.A.* 92:6349–53, 1995.

Kamtekar, S., et al. (**M. H. Hecht**). Protein design by binary patterning of polar and non-polar amino acids. *Science* 262:1680–5, 1993.

Hughson, F. M. Structural characterization of viral fusion proteins. *Curr. Biol.* 5:265, 1995.

Bullough, P. A., **F. M. Hughson**, et al. Structure of influenza haemagglutinin at the pH of membrane fusion. *Nature* 371:37, 1994.

Barrick, D., **F. M. Hughson**, and R. L. Baldwin. Molecular mechanisms of acid denaturation: The role of histidine residues in the partial unfolding of apomyoglobin. *J. Mol. Biol.* 237:588, 1994.

Wu, G., **M. Jones Jr.**, W. E. von Doering, and L. H. Knox. The non-reaction of methylene with the carbon-carbon bond. *Tetrahedron* 53:9913, 1997.

Thamattoor, D. M., **M. Jones Jr.**, W. Pan, and P. B. Shevlin. Cyclopropylmethylcarbene. *Tetrahedron Lett.* 37:8333, 1996.

Barnett-Thamattoor, L., et al. (**M. Jones Jr.**). Reaction of 1,2-dehydro-*o*-carborane with thiophenes. Cycloadditions and an easy synthesis of "Benzo-*o*-carboranes." *Inorg. Chem.* 35:7311, 1996.

Barnett-Thamattoor, L., J. J. Wu, D. M. Ho, and **M. Jones Jr.** Carboranophanes. *Tetrahedron Lett.* 37:7221, 1996.

Liang, R., et al. (**D. Kahne**). Parallel synthesis and screening of a solid phase carbohydrate library. *Science* 274:1520, 1996.

Yan, L., and **D. Kahne**. Generalizing glycosylation: Synthesis of the blood group antigens Le^a, Le^b, and Le^x using a standard set of reaction conditions. *J. Am. Chem. Soc.* 118:9239, 1996.

Lee, S. C., et al. Cyanide poisoning: An analogue to the binuclear site of oxidized cyanide-inhibited cytochrome *c* oxidase. *J. Am. Chem. Soc.* 116:401, 1994.

Scott, M. J., **S. C. Lee**, and R. H. Holm. Synthesis and structural characterization of unsupported [Fe^{III}-CN-Cu^{II}] bridges related to that in cyanide-inactivated cytochrome *c* oxidase. *Inorg. Chem.* 33:4651, 1994.

Lee, S. C., and R. H. Holm. Fluoride-bridged dimers: Binuclear copper(II) complexes and iron(III)-copper(II) assemblies. *Inorg. Chem.* 32:4745, 1993.

Lee, S. C., and R. H. Holm. Synthesis and characterization of an asymmetric bridged assembly containing the unsupported [Fe^{III}-O-Cu^{II}] bridge: An analogue of the binuclear site in oxidized cytochrome *c* oxidase. *J. Am. Chem. Soc.* 115:11789, 1993.

Higgins, J., et al. (**K. K. Lehmann** and **G. Scoles**). Photoinduced chemical dynamics of high-spin alkali trimers. *Science* 273:629–31, 1996.

Lehmann, K. K., and D. Romanini. The superposition principle and cavity ring-down spectroscopy. *J. Chem. Phys.* 105:10263–77, 1996.

Lehmann, K. K., B. H. Pate, and **G. Scoles**. Intramolecular dynamics from eigenstate-resolved infrared spectra. *Ann. Rev. Phys. Chem.* 45:241–74, 1994.

Romanini, D., and **K. K. Lehmann**. Ring-down absorption spectroscopy of the very weak HCN overtone bands with six, seven, and eight stretching quanta. *J. Chem. Phys.* 99:6287–301, 1993.

Komar-Panicucci, S., F. Sherman, and **G. McLendon**. Modulated growth of saccharomyces by altering the driving force of cytochrome c: Does Marcus theory apply in vivo? *Biochemistry* 35:4878–85, 1996.

Qiao, T., R. T. Witkowski, and **G. McLendon**. Kinetic studies of the hemoglobin: Hemoglobin reductase (cytochrome b_5) reaction. *J. Biol. Inorg. Chem.* 1:432, 1996.

Rehm, J., et al. (**G. McLendon**). Femtosecond electron-transfer dynamics at a sensitizing dye-semiconductor (TiO_2). *J. Phys. Chem.* 100:9577, 1996.

Mutz, M., et al. (**G. McLendon**). Electron transfer across self-assembled triple helix peptides. *Proc. Natl. Acad. Sci. U.S.A.* 93:9521, 1996.

Lee, J. G., S. R. Roberts, and **F. M. M. Morel**. Cadmium: A nutrient for the marine diatom *Thalassiosira weissflogii*. *Limnol. Oceanogr.* 40:1056–63, 1995.

Morel, F. M. M., et al. Carbon colimitation of marine phytoplankton. *Nature* 369:740–2, 1994.

Ahman, D., A. L. Roberts, L. R. Krumholz, and **F. M. M. Morel**. Microbial growth by arsenate reduction. *Nature* 371:750, 1994.

Princeton University

Selected Publications (continued)

Ahner, B. A., N. M. Price, and **F. M. M. Morel.** Phytochelatin production by marine phytoplankton and low free metal ion concentrations: Lab studies and field data for Massachusetts Bay. *Proc. Natl. Acad. Sci. U.S.A.* 91:8433–6, 1994.

Nooijen, M., and R. J. Bartlett. A new method for excited states: Similarity transformed equation of motion theory (STEOM). *J. Chem. Phys.* 106:6441, 1997.

Nooijen, M., and R. J. Bartlett. Similarity transformed equation of motion coupled cluster study of ionized, attached and excited states of free base porphin. *J. Chem. Phys.* 106:6449, 1997.

Nooijen, M., and R. J. Bartlett. Similarity transformed equation-of-motion theory: Details, examples, comparisons. *J. Chem. Phys.* 107(17):6812–30, 1997.

Nooijen, M. On many-body similarity transformations in fock space generated by normal ordered exponential operators. *J. Chem. Phys.* 104:2638–51, 1996.

Qiao, X., et al. (**C. E. Schutt** and **R. A. Pascal Jr.**). Octaphenylnaphthalene and decaphenylanthracene. *J. Am. Chem. Soc.* 118:741, 1996.

Shibata, K., A. A. Kulkarni, D. M. Ho, and **R. A. Pascal Jr.** The pursuit of perchlorotriphenylene. *J. Org. Chem.* 60:428, 1995.

Xu, K., D. M. Ho, and **R. A. Pascal Jr.** Azaaromatic chlorides: A prescription for crystal structures with extensive nitrogen-chlorine donor-acceptor interactions. *J. Am. Chem. Soc.* 116:105, 1994.

Pascal, R. A., Jr. and D. M. Ho. Molecular structure of Rebek's diacid-quinoxaline: Confirmation of two-point binding. *J. Am. Chem. Soc.* 115:8507, 1993.

Mazziotti, D. A., and **H. Rabitz.** Determining quantum bound-state eigenvalues and eigenvectors as functions of parameters in the Hamiltonian: An efficient evolutionary approach. *Mol. Phys.* 89:171, 1996.

Wang, N., **H. Rabitz,** A. S. Manka, and C. M. Bowden. Optimal control of piezophotonic and magnetiphotonic switching in a dense medium of three-level atoms. *Phys. Rev. A* 53:R2940, 1996.

Ho, T.-S., **H. Rabitz,** S. E. Choi, and M. I. Lester. Application of an inverse method to the determination of a two-dimensional intermolecular potential energy surface for the Ar-OH($A^2\Sigma^+$,v - 0) complex from rovibrational spectra. *J. Chem. Phys.* 104:1187, 1996.

Rojnuckarin, A., C. A. Floudas, **H. Rabitz,** and R. A. Yetter. Methane conversion to ethylene and acetylene: Optimal control with chlorine, oxygen and heat flux. *Ind. Eng. Chem. Res.* 35:683, 1996.

Thorn, K. S., et al. (**C. E. Schutt**). The crystal structure of *Arabidopsis* profilin I at 1.6 Å. *Structure* 5:19–32, 1997.

Chik, J. K., U. Lindberg, and **C. E. Schutt.** The structure of an open state of β-actin at 2.65 Å resolution. *J. Mol. Biol.* 263:607–23, 1996.

Schutt, C. E., M. D. Rozycki, J. C. Myslik, and U. Lindberg. A discourse on modeling F-actin. *J. Structural Biol.* 115:186–98, 1995.

VanderKam, S. K., G. Lu, **S. L. Bernasek,** and **J. Schwartz.** Ligand metathesis in surface-bound alkoxyzirconium complexes. *J. Am. Chem. Soc.* 119:11639, 1997.

Aronoff, Y. G., et al. (**J. Schwartz**). Stabilization of self-assembled monolayers of carboxylic acids on native oxides of metals. *J. Am. Chem. Soc.* 119:259, 1997.

Barden, M. C., and **J. Schwartz.** Stereoselective pinacol coupling in aqueous media. *J. Am. Chem. Soc.* 118:5484, 1996.

Spencer, R. P., and **J. Schwartz.** Variously substituted glycals are readily prepared from glycosyl bromides using $(Cp_2TiCl)_2$. *Tetrahedron Lett.* 37:4357, 1996.

Callegari, A., et al. (**K. K. Lehmann** and **G. Scoles**). Eigenstate resolved infrared-infrared double resonance study of intramolecular vibrational relaxation in benzene: First overtone of the CH stretch. *J. Chem. Phys.* 106(1):432–5, 1997.

Higgins, J., et al. (**K. K. Lehmann** and **G. Scoles**). Photoinduced chemical dynamics of high spin alkali trimers. *Science* 273:629–31, 1996.

Higgins, J., et al. (**K. K. Lehmann** and **G. Scoles**). Spin polarized alkali clusters: Observation of quartet states of the sodium trimer. *Phys. Rev. Lett.* 77:4532, 1996.

Camillone, N., III, et al. (**G. Scoles**). Chain length dependence of the striped phases of alkanethiol monolayers self-assembled on Au(111). *Langmuir* 12:2737–46, 1996.

Semmelhack, M. F., et al. The effect of DNA cleavage potency of tethering a simple cyclic enediyne to a netropsin analog. *J. Org. Chem.* 59:4357, 1994.

Semmelhack, M. F., T. Neu, and F. Foubelo. Arene 1,4-diradical formation from *o*-dialkynylarenes. *J. Org. Chem.* 59:5038, 1994.

Semmelhack, M. F., et al. Metal-catalyzed cyclopropene rearrangements for benzannulation: Evaluation of an anthraquinone synthesis pathway and reevaluation of the parallel approach via carbene-chromium complexes. *J. Am. Chem. Soc.* 116:7108, 1994.

Semmelhack, M. F., et al. Palladium-promoted synthesis of ionophore antibiotics. Strategy and assembly of the homochiral tetrahydrofuran and tetrahydropyran portions of tetronomycin. *J. Am. Chem. Soc.* 116:7455, 1994.

Shah, K., Y. Liu, and **K. M. Shokat.** Rational design of an orthogonal nucleotide substrate for v-Src: Tagging direct kinase substrates. *Proc. Natl. Acad. Sci. U.S.A.,* in press.

Shokat, K. M. Tyrosine kinases: Modular signaling enzymes with tunable specificities. *Chem. Biol.* 2:509–13, 1995.

Shokat, K. M., and C. C. Goodnow. Antigen-induced B cell death and elimination during germinal center immune responses. *Nature (London)* 375:334–8, 1995.

Shokat, K. M., T. Uno, and P. G. Schultz. Mechanistic studies of an antibody-catalyzed elimination reaction. *J. Am. Chem. Soc.* 116:2261–70, 1994.

Soos, Z. G., A. Painelli, A. Girlando, and D. Mukhopadhyay. Electron models of conjugated polymers: Vibrational and nonlinear optical spectra. In *Handbook of Conducting Polymers*, pp. 165–96, eds. T. A. Skotheim, R. Elsenbaumer, and T. Allen. New York: Marcel Dekker, 1997.

Soos, Z. G., M. H. Hennessy, and D. Mukhopadhyay. Correlations in conjugated polymers. In *Conjugated Polymers: Molecular Exciton versus Semiconductor Band Model*, pp. 1–28, ed. N. S. Sariciftci. Singapore: World Scientific, 1997.

Mukhopadhyay, D., and **Z. G. Soos.** Nonlinear optical and electroabsorption spectra of polydiacetylene crystals and films. *J. Chem. Phys.* 104:1600–10, 1996.

Soos, Z. G., and J. S. Schmidt. Equilibration with intrinsic traps in molecularly doped polymers. *Chem. Phys. Lett.* 265:427–33, 1996.

Qiu, D., M. Kumar, S. W. Ragsdale, and **T. G. Spiro.** Raman and infrared spectroscopy of cyanide-inhibited CO dehydrogenase/acetyl-COA synthase from *Clostridium thermoaceticum:* Evidence for bimetallic CO oxidation. *J. Am. Chem. Soc.* 118:10429–35, 1996.

Dong, S., R. Padmakumar, R. Banerjee, and **T. G. Spiro.** Resonance Raman Co-C stretching frequencies reflect bond strength changes in alkyl cobalamins, but are unaffected by trans-ligand substitution. *J. Am. Chem. Soc.* 118:9182–3, 1996.

Thomas, V. M., and **T. G. Spiro.** The U.S. dioxin inventory: Are there missing sources? *Environ. Sci. Technol.* 30(2):82A–85A, 1996.

Hu, X., H. Frei, and **T. G. Spiro.** Nanosecond step-scan FTIR spectroscopy of hemoglobin: Ligand recombination and protein conformational changes. *Biochemistry* 35:13001–5, 1996.

Surette, M. G., et al. (**J. B. Stock**). Dimerization Is required for the activity of the protein histidine kinase CheA that mediates signal transduction in bacterial chemotaxis. *J. Biol Chem.* 271:939–45, 1996.

Volker C., M. H. Pillinger, M. R. Philips, and **J. B. Stock.** Uses of prenylcysteine analogs to study the function of carboxyl methylation in signal transduction. *Meth. Enzymol.* 250, 216–25, 1995.

Philips, M. R., et al. (**J. B. Stock**). Activation-dependent carboxyl methylation of neutrophil G-protein γ-subunit. *Proc. Natl. Acad. Sci. U.S.A.* 92:2283–7, 1995.

Stock, J., and M. G. Surette. Chemotaxis in *Escherichia coli* and *Salmonella typhimurium.* In *Cellular and Molecular Biology,* 2nd Edition, ed. J. L. Ingraham, American Society of Microbiology, Washington, D.C., 1995.

Walker, S., J. Murnick, and **D. Kahne.** Structural characterization of a calicheamicin-DNA complex by NMR. *J. Am. Chem. Soc.* 115:7954, 1993.

Walker, S., et. al. Cationic facial amphiphiles: A promising class of transfection agents. *Proc. Natl. Acad. Sci. U.S.A.* 93:1585, 1996.

Tull, J. X., M. A. Dugan, and **W. S. Warren.** High resolution, ultrafast laser pulse shaping and its applications. *Adv. Magn. Opt. Reson.,* in press.

Lee, S., W. Richter, S. Vathyam, and **W. S. Warren.** Quantum treatment of the effects of dipole-dipole interactions in liquid NMR. *J. Chem. Phys.* 105:874, 1996.

Dugan, M., J. X. Tull, and **W. S. Warren.** High-resolution ultrafast laser pulse shaping for quantum control and terabit per second communications. *Ultrafast Phenomena X*, pp. 26–7, eds. P. F. Barbara, J. G. Fujimoto, W. H. Knox, and W. Zinth. Berlin: Springer, 1996.

Vathyam, S., S. Lee, and **W. S. Warren.** Homogeneous NMR spectra in inhomogeneous fields. *Science* 272:92, 1996.

Melinger, J. S., D. McMorrow, C. Hillegas, and **W. S. Warren.** Selective excitation of vibrational overtones in an anharmonic potential. *Phys. Rev.* A51:3366, 1995.

RENSSELAER POLYTECHNIC INSTITUTE

Department of Chemistry

Programs of Study

The Department of Chemistry faculty members work closely with each student to develop his or her interest in one of Rensselaer's very strong traditional research programs or in one of the numerous innovative cross-disciplinary areas. The Master of Science and Doctor of Philosophy degrees are offered with courses and research in biochemistry and biophysics, organic and bioorganic chemistry, natural products synthesis, medicinal chemistry, materials chemistry, polymer chemistry (synthesis and physical properties), analytical chemistry, inorganic chemistry, electrochemistry, coordination and organometallic chemistry, nuclear chemistry and radiochemistry, photochemistry (including laser techniques), physical chemistry, physical organic chemistry, solid-state chemistry and crystal growth, spectroscopy (laser, microwave, NMR, ESR, vibrational, fluorescence, and in situ environmental probes), and surface science. Courses and research are available for interdisciplinary programs.

For the degree of Doctor of Philosophy, a candidate must complete a minimum of 90 credit hours beyond the bachelor's degree, satisfy preliminary examination requirements, pass the candidacy examination, and complete the research thesis and final thesis defense. The degree of Master of Science is based upon 30 credits of courses and research and a research thesis; the residence requirement is at least two terms.

Research Facilities

Shared departmental research equipment is based in the Major Instrumentation Center, which is operated by professional staff and available to all research students. Instrumentation includes state-of-the-art solution and solid-state NMR spectrometer equipment and FT-IR, GC/MS, and single-crystal X-ray diffraction equipment. Individual laboratories contain a wide variety of GC, HPLC, IR, Vis-UV, electrochemical, laser, ESR, and thermal analysis equipment and other instruments. The Molecular Modeling Center has up-to-date computer hardware and software for molecular modeling and quantum mechanical calculations. The department's newest addition, the Center for Polymer Synthesis, provides students and faculty members with opportunities for industrial collaboration.

Research is also supported by such state-of-the-art facilities as the Rensselaer Libraries, whose electronic information systems provide access to collections, databases, and Internet resources from campus and remote terminals; the Rensselaer Computing System, which permeates the campus with a coherent array of advanced workstations, a shared toolkit of applications for interactive learning and research, and high-speed Internet connectivity; a visualization laboratory for scientific computation; and a high-performance computing facility that includes a 36-node SP2 parallel computer.

Financial Aid

Financial aid is available in the form of fellowships, research or teaching assistantships, and scholarships. The stipend for assistantships ranges up to $16,000 for a nine-month academic year. In addition, full tuition remission is granted. Stipends for the summer months are $1800 or more. Outstanding students may qualify for industry- and university-supported Rensselaer Scholar Fellowships, which carry a stipend of $15,000 and a full tuition scholarship. Low-interest, deferred-repayment graduate loans are also available to U.S. citizens with demonstrated need.

Cost of Study

Tuition for 1999–2000 is $665 per credit hour. Other fees amount to approximately $535 per semester. Books and supplies cost about $1700 per year.

Living and Housing Costs

The cost of rooms for single students in residence halls or apartments ranges from $3356 to $5298 for the 1999–2000 academic year. Family student housing, with monthly rents ranging from $592 to $720, is available.

Student Group

There are about 4,300 undergraduates and 1,750 graduate students representing all fifty states and more than eighty countries at Rensselaer. In the fall of 1998, there were 60 graduate students in the department.

Student Outcomes

Eighty-eight percent of Rensselaer's 1998 graduating students were hired after graduation, with starting salaries that averaged $56,259 for master's degree recipients and $57,000–$75,000 for doctoral degree recipients.

Location

Rensselaer is situated on a scenic 260-acre hillside campus in Troy, New York, across the Hudson River from the state capital of Albany. Troy's central Northeast location provides students with a supportive, active, medium-sized community in which to live; an easy commute to Boston, New York, and Montreal; and some of the country's finest outdoor recreation sites, including Lake George, Lake Placid, and the Adirondack, Catskill, Berkshire, and Green Mountains. The Capital Region has one of the largest concentrations of academic institutions in the United States. Sixty thousand students attend fourteen area colleges and benefit from shared activities and courses.

The University

Founded in 1824 and the first American college to award degrees in engineering and science, Rensselaer Polytechnic Institute today is accredited by the Middle States Association of Colleges and Schools and is a private, nonsectarian, coeducational university. Rensselaer has five schools—Architecture, Engineering, Management, Science, and Humanities and Social Sciences—that offer a total of ninety-eight graduate degrees in forty-seven fields.

Applying

Admissions applications and all supporting credentials should be submitted well in advance of the preferred semester of entry to allow sufficient time for departmental review and processing. The application fee is $35. Since the first departmental awards are made in February and March for the next full academic year, applicants requesting financial aid are encouraged to submit all required credentials by February 1 to ensure that they will receive consideration. GRE General Test scores are required.

Correspondence and Information

For written information about graduate work:
Department of Chemistry
Graduate Admissions Coordinator
Rensselaer Polytechnic Institute
110 8th Street
Troy, New York 12180-3590
Telephone: 518-276-2839
World Wide Web: http://www.rpi.edu

For applications and admissions information:
Director of Graduate Academic and Enrollment
   Services, Graduate Center
Rensselaer Polytechnic Institute
110 8th Street
Troy, New York 12180-3590
Telephone: 518-276-6789
E-mail: grad-services@rpi.edu
World Wide Web: http://www.rpi.edu

Rensselaer Polytechnic Institute

THE FACULTY AND THEIR RESEARCH

T. M. Apple, Professor and Chair; Ph.D., Delaware. Physical-analytical chemistry: solid-state NMR, zeolite and polymer materials.

R. A. Bailey, Professor; Ph.D., McGill. Inorganic chemistry: inorganic coordination complexes, electrochemistry and spectroscopy of metal ions in fused salt solutions, chemical reactions in molten salts.

B. C. Benicewicz, Professor and Director of the NYS Center for Polymer Synthesis; Ph.D., Connecticut. Polymer chemistry: polymer synthesis, characterization and properties, liquid crystalline polymers, electrically conducting polymers, biodegradable polymers.

C. M. Breneman, Associate Professor; Ph.D., California, Santa Barbara. Physical organic chemistry: structure activity relationships, molecular modeling, quantum chemistry, drug design.

W. Colón, Assistant Professor; Ph.D., Texas A&M. Biochemistry and biophysics; studies of molecular recognition in protein folding, oligomerization, and aggregation using protein engineering, optical spectroscopy, and stopped-flow techniques; special interest in protein misfolding and the mechanism of amyloid fibril formation.

J. V. Crivello, Professor; Ph.D., Notre Dame. Organic chemistry: organic nitrations, oxidations and arylations, polyimides, silicones, epoxides, and new photo-, thermal-, and transition metal initiators for cationic polymerizations.

A. R. Cutler, Professor; Ph.D., Brandeis. Organometallic chemistry: synthetic and mechanistic inorganic and transition organometallic chemistry, homogeneous catalysis, metallobiochemical processes, metal-containing oligomers and polymeric materials.

G. D. Daves Jr., Professor; Ph.D., MIT. Organic chemistry: organopalladium chemistry, C-glycoside synthesis, applications of mass and nuclear magnetic resonance spectrometries.

J. P. Ferris, Research Professor; Ph.D., Indiana. Biochemistry, organic chemistry, and photochemistry: astrobiology, chemistry of the origins of life, mineral catalysis of RNA formation, photochemistry of planetary atmospheres.

C. W. Gillies, Associate Professor; Ph.D., Michigan. Physical chemistry: pulsed-beam Fourier transform microwave spectroscopy applied to weakly bound molecular complexes and to aluminum sulfur and phosphorous compounds.

L. V. Interrante, Professor and Editor, *Chemistry of Materials;* Ph.D., Illinois at Urbana-Champaign. Materials chemistry: synthesis and study of organosilicon polymers, metal-organic precursors to ceramics and electronic materials, ceramic composites.

G. M. Korenowski, Professor; Ph.D., Cornell. Physical-analytical chemistry: interfacial science, linear and nonlinear spectroscopy and its applications.

S. Krause, Professor; Ph.D., Berkeley. Physical chemistry: solution properties of polymers; polymer compatibility; interfaces between semicrystalline polymers, polymer suspensions, and alloys in electric fields; electromechanical actuators; light, X-ray, and neutron scattering from polymer systems.

J. A. Moore, Professor; Ph.D., Polytechnic of Brooklyn. Organic polymer chemistry: preparation and chemical (photochemical) transformations of synthetic polymers and biopolymers, structure-property relationships in polymers, synthesis of novel materials for use in microelectronics, composites and protein separation.

A. G. Schultz, Professor; Ph.D., Rochester. Organic chemistry: asymmetric synthesis, synthesis of natural products, synthetic and mechanistic organic photochemistry, development of new organic synthetic methods.

J. A. Stenken, Assistant Professor; Ph.D., Kansas. Analytical chemistry: bioanalysis, in vivo sampling, membrane separations, drug metabolism.

S. C. Wait Jr., Professor and Associate Dean of the School of Science; Ph.D., Rensselaer. Physical chemistry: spectroscopy, vibrational analysis, simple and polyatomic systems.

J. T. Warden, Professor; Ph.D., Minnesota. Biophysical chemistry: physicochemical studies in photosynthesis, applications of ESR to biological electron transport, structure and function of hemoproteins, flash photolysis–ESR spectroscopy, photophysics, solar energy.

M. Wentland, Professor; Ph.D., Rice. Medicinal/organic chemistry: identification and optimization of lead structures applicable to the treatment of human disease caused by cocaine addiction and cancer; organic synthesis of novel hetero- and macrocyclic systems.

H. Wiedemeier, Research Professor; D.Sc., Muenster (Germany). Solid-state and high temperature chemistry: vapor phase crystal growth of electronic materials, thermodynamics and kinetics of solid-gas phase reactions, structural and phase transformations.

RUTGERS, THE STATE UNIVERSITY OF NEW JERSEY, NEWARK

Department of Chemistry

Programs of Study

The Department of Chemistry at Rutgers in Newark offers programs leading to the degrees of Master of Science and Doctor of Philosophy. (Separate M.S. and Ph.D. programs in chemistry are also offered at the New Brunswick campus. The description on this page refers only to the programs at Newark.)

All students must pass a core of required courses with grades of at least B and must pass written examinations that are cumulative in nature. In addition, students enrolled in the Ph.D. program must satisfactorily present a departmental seminar on a current research topic and must orally present and defend a research proposal. Thirty hours of course and research credit are required for the master's degree; 72 hours of course and research credit are required for the Ph.D.

Many fields of specialization are represented—biophysical and bioorganic approaches to enzyme mechanisms, molecular modeling and drug design, ultrafast spectroscopy, organic synthesis, biological membranes, and X-ray crystallography, among others.

Cooperative graduate program arrangements with the neighboring New Jersey Institute of Technology allow cross-registration for courses.

Research Facilities

Research in chemistry is conducted in the Carl A. Olson Memorial Chemistry Laboratories, a modern facility that houses state-of-the-art instrumentation. Major equipment includes 400- and 500-MHz multinuclear NMR spectrometers; GC–mass spectrometers; a wide selection of modern spectrophotometers for UV-vis, IR, fluorescence, phosphorescence, and circular dichroism; an X-ray diffractometer; a fast-reaction laboratory with stopped-flow capability; several HPLC instruments; electrochemistry units; a femtosecond laser for ultrafast spectroscopy; a picosecond resonance–Raman spectrometer; a time-correlated single-photon-counting instrument; an automated solid-phase peptide synthesizer; ultracentrifuges; and a pilot-scale fermenter. In addition, equipment available to researchers throughout the campus includes a DNA synthesizer, a transmission electron microscope, and a supercomputer.

Graduate students in the Department of Chemistry have access to numerous PCs and Macs, plus six computer workstations (SGI and IBM), including a multi-CPU supercomputer, for molecular modeling and computational chemistry. Commercial software packages available on the workstations include Sybyl, Gaussian, Spartan, and Biosym.

Financial Aid

In 1999–2000, graduate teaching assistantships provide $12,136 (plus remission of tuition) for the first academic year, with merit increases for subsequent years. Fellowships providing $12,000 per year for two years (plus tuition remission) are also available. More advanced students often receive research assistantships under the supervision of their research directors. Most students receive an additional $1800 summer stipend as either a teaching or research assistant. Thirty-three full-time students are supported by teaching or research assistantships or fellowships.

Cost of Study

In 1999–2000, tuition for full-time study is approximately $3388 per term for New Jersey state residents and $4968 per term for nonresidents. Part-time study costs are approximately $280 per credit for state residents and $412 per credit for nonresidents. Tuition is excused for assistantship and fellowship recipients. Fees are approximately $480 per semester for full-time students and correspondingly lower for part-time students.

Living and Housing Costs

Graduate student housing, consisting of suites of apartments, each with a kitchen, is available to full-time students at approximately $5000 for twelve months. Rooms and apartments are also available in the immediate urban and surrounding suburban areas.

Student Group

During the past academic year, more than 10,000 students were enrolled in all programs on the Newark campus. There are about 1,100 full-time graduate students enrolled at Newark. Each program selects graduate students from among applicants from the New York metropolitan area, various parts of the United States, and abroad. Many students have strong liberal arts backgrounds, and some already hold master's degrees. Many of the students in the graduate program in chemistry are already working in the vast chemical industry of northern New Jersey.

The Department of Chemistry has, in addition to 35 full-time graduate students, about 30 part-time students who work during the day and attend classes in the evening.

Location

Newark is New Jersey's largest city and, although located 30 minutes by road and rail from midtown Manhattan, is a major commercial center in its own right. Surrounded by communities that become increasingly suburban and rural with distance, Newark also lies at the center of the nation's largest concentration of chemical and pharmaceutical industries. Many Rutgers chemistry graduates find employment in the area.

The University

Rutgers University has several academic units on the Newark campus, including the Graduate School, the School of Law, the Graduate School of Management, the undergraduate Newark College of Arts and Sciences, the College of Nursing, and University College. The Newark units are part of a complex of higher education that includes Essex County College, New Jersey Institute of Technology, and the University of Medicine and Dentistry of New Jersey.

Applying

Applications for the fall semester should normally be submitted before August 1 and those requesting financial support by March 1. All forms, as well as a booklet describing the Department of Chemistry, may be obtained from the address given below. The nonrefundable application fee is $50.

Correspondence and Information

Graduate Program Coordinator
Department of Chemistry
Rutgers University
Newark, New Jersey 07102
Telephone: 973-353-5318 or 5173
World Wide Web: http://newark.rutgers.edu/~cheminfo/

Rutgers, The State University of New Jersey, Newark

THE FACULTY AND THEIR RESEARCH

Ramy S. Farid, Assistant Professor; Ph.D., Caltech. Bioinorganic chemistry, protein-mediated electron-transfer studies, peptide synthesis, porphyrin and transition metal complex binding to synthetic proteins, synthetic hyperthermophilic enzymes.

R. Ian Fryer, Professor; Ph.D., Manchester (England). Heterocyclic/medicinal chemistry, design and synthesis of novel benzodiazepines and other heterocycles, molecular modeling and drug design.

Elena Galoppini, Assistant Professor; Ph.D., Chicago. Organic chemistry, synthesis and properties of novel hydrocarbon cage compounds and rigid, extended 3-D organic networks.

Stan S. Hall, Professor; Ph.D., MIT. Synthetic methods, total synthesis, tandem reactions, (η^3-allyl)palladium chemistry.

W. Phillip Huskey, Associate Professor; Ph.D., Kansas. Physical organic chemistry, mechanistic enzymology, isotope effects.

Frank Jordan, Professor; Ph.D., Pennsylvania. Structure, mechanism, folding, and chemical models of thiamin-diphosphate-dependent 2-oxoacid decarboxylases and serine proteases.

Rudolph W. Kluiber, Professor; Ph.D., Wisconsin–Madison. Application of technology to undergraduate laboratory teaching.

Roger A. Lalancette, Professor; Ph.D., Fordham. X-ray diffraction and the structure of solids, synthesis and characterization of nitrogen and sulfur complexes, hydrogen bonding in keto-carboxylic acids.

Richard Mendelsohn, Professor; Ph.D., MIT. Biophysical chemistry, lipid-protein interactions in biological membranes, phospholipid phase transitions, IR reflection-absorption and Brewster-angle microscopy of aqueous monolayer structures, biomedical applications of IR spectroscopic imaging.

Ernst U. Monse, Professor; Ph.D., Max Planck Institute (Mainz). Isotope effects and their applications to theoretical chemistry, chemical dynamics in hydrogen-bonded systems.

Piotr Piotrowiak, Associate Professor and Graduate Program Coordinator; Ph.D., Chicago. Photoinduced charge and excitation transfer in organic and organometallic model systems, excited-state dynamics, ultrafast laser spectroscopy.

Susanne Raynor, Associate Professor; Ph.D., Georgetown. Quantum mechanics of molecular solids and clusters, collision dynamics.

James M. Schlegel, Professor; Ph.D., Iowa State. Electroanalytical chemistry, kinetics and mechanism of electrode reactions.

John B. Sheridan, Associate Professor; Ph.D., Bristol (England). Inorganic and organometallic chemistry; synthesis of inorganic polymers and application of transition-metal organometallic chemistry to organic synthesis.

Hugh W. Thompson, Professor; Ph.D., MIT. Mechanisms and stereochemical courses of organic reactions, compounds of unusual symmetry and stereochemistry, impacted-orbital systems, solid-state H-bonding patterns.

The Carl A. Olson Memorial Chemistry Laboratories.

Entrance to the campus.

The campus plaza.

Rutgers, The State University of New Jersey, Newark

SELECTED PUBLICATIONS

Guo, F., et al. (**R. S. Farid** and **F. Jordan**). Is a hydrophobic amino acid required to maintain the reactive V conformation of thiamin at the active center of thiamin diphosphate requiring enzymes? Experimental and computational studies of isoleucine-415 of yeast pyruvate decarboxylase. *Biochemistry* 37:13379–91, 1998.

Pilloud, L., et al. (**R. S. Farid**). Self-assembled monolayers of synthetic hemoproteins on silanized quartz. *J. Phys. Chem. B* 102:1926–37, 1998.

Greenfield, N. J., G. T. Montelione, **R. S. Farid,** and S. E. Hitchcock-DeGregori. The structure of the N-terminus of striated muscle α-tropomyosin in a chimeric peptide: Solution nuclear magnetic resonance structure and circular dichroism studies. *Biochemistry* 37:7834–43, 1998.

Wang, C. G., et al. (**R. I. Fryer**). Computer-aided molecular modeling, synthesis, and biological evaluation of 8-(benzyloxy)-2-phenylpyrazolo[4,3-c]quinoline as a novel benzodiazepine receptor agonist ligand. *J. Med. Chem.* 38:950–7, 1995.

Fryer, R. I., et al. Benzodiazepine-receptor (BZR) ligands: The conformational fit of agonist β-carbolines to an imidazobenzodiazepine template. *Med. Chem. Res.* 5:296–307, 1995.

Fryer, R. I., Z. Q. Gu, and L. Todaro. Nitration products of substituted 1,3-dihydro-5-phenyl-2H-1,4-benzodiazepin-2-ones. *J. Heterocyclic Chem.* 28:1203–8, 1991.

Fryer, R. I., Z. Q. Gu, and C. G. Wang. Synthesis of novel, substituted 4H-imidazo[1,5-a][1,4]benzodiazepines. *J. Heteroylic Chem.* 28:1661–9, 1991.

Fryer, R. I., et al. Addition of glycinate enolate equivalents to 1,4-benzodiazepine imino phosphates. Preparation of synthetically useful 2-(ethyl glycinat-α-yl-idene)-1,4-benzodiazepines and related derivatives. *J. Org. Chem.* 56:3715–9, 1991.

Walser, A., and **R. I. Fryer**. Hetero ring [e][1,4] diazepines. *Chem. Heterocyclic Compd.* 50:947–1052, 1991.

Galoppini, E., and R. Gilardi. Weak hydrogen bonding between acetylenic groups: The formation of diamondoid nets in the crystal structure of tetrakis(4-ethynylphenyl)methane. *Chem. Comm.* 173, 1999.

Galoppini, E., and M. A. Fox. Electric field effects on electron transfer rates in dichromophoric peptides: The effect of helix unfolding. *J. Am. Chem. Soc.* 119:5277, 1997.

Knorr, A., E. Galoppini, and M. A. Fox. Photoinduced electron transfer in dichromophore-appended α-helical peptides: Spectroscopic properties and preferred conformations. *J. Phys. Org. Chem.* 10:475, 1997.

Whitesell, J. K., et al. (**E. Galoppini**). Anisotropic energy and electron migration in multichromophore-laden polymers on metal surfaces. *Pure Appl. Chem.* 68:1469, 1996.

Galoppini, E., and M. A. Fox. Effect of the electric field generated by the helix dipole on photoinduced intramolecular electron transfer in dichromophoric α-helical peptides. *J. Am. Chem. Soc.* 118:2299, 1996.

Eaton, P. E., E. Galoppini, and R. Gilardi. Alkynylcubanes as precursors of rigid-rod molecules and alkynylcyclooctatetraenes. *J. Am. Chem. Soc.* 116:7588, 1994.

Flisak, J. R., and **S. S. Hall**. 4-alkenyl-1-methoxy-1,4-cyclohexadienes by tandem addition–multistep reduction of alkenyl aldehydes and ketones. Synthesis of 4-alkenyl-3-cyclohexen-1-ones by subsequent hydrolysis. *J. Am. Chem. Soc.* 112:7299–305, 1990.

Söderberg, B. C., B. Åkermark, Y.-H. Chen, and **S. S. Hall**. *trans*-bis(5-acetoxy-1,2,3-η³-cyclohexenyl)-palladium complexes by palladium(II)-promoted addition of acetate to 1,4-cyclohexadienes. *J. Org. Chem.* 55:1344–9, 1990.

Åkermark, B., B. C. Söderberg, and **S. S. Hall**. *trans*-bis(5-alkoxy and 5-hydroxy-1-3-η³-cyclohexenyl)-palladium complexes by palladium(II)-promoted addition of alcohols and water to 1,2-dialkyl-1,4-cyclohexadienes. *J. Org. Chem.* 54:1110–6, 1989.

Söderberg, B. C., B. Åkermark, and **S. S. Hall**. *trans*-bis(5-methoxy-1-3-η³-cyclohexenyl)palladium complexes by palladium(II)-promoted addition of methanol to 1,4-cyclohexadienes. Synthesis of methyl *trans*-5-methoxy-2-cyclohexene-1-carboxylates by subsequent methoxycarbonylation. *J. Org. Chem.* 53:2925–37, 1988.

Bao, D., **W. P. Huskey**, C. A. Kettner, and **F. Jordan**. Distinguished hydrogen bonding to active-site histidine in peptidyl boronic acid inhibitor complexes of chymotrypsin and subtilisin: Proton magnetic resonance assignments and H/D fractionation. *J. Am. Chem. Soc.*, in press.

Barletta, G. L., Y. Zou, **W. P. Huskey**, and **F. Jordan**. Kinetics of C(2α)-proton abstraction from 2-benzylthiazolium salts leading to enamines relevant to catalysis by thiamin-dependent enzymes. *J. Am. Chem. Soc.* 119:2356–62, 1997.

Hao, X., X. Wu, and **W. P. Huskey**. Carbon isotope effects on K_{cat} for formate dehydrogenase determined using a continuous-flow stirred-tank reactor. *J. Am. Chem. Soc.* 118:5804–5, 1996.

Melandri, F., et al. (**W. P. Huskey**). Kinetic studies on the inhibition of isopeptidase T by ubiquitin aldehyde. *Biochemistry* 35:12893–900, 1996.

Huskey, W. P. Model calculations of isotope effects using structures containing low-barrier hydrogen bonds. *J. Am. Chem. Soc.* 118:1663–8, 1996.

Rao, M., et al. (**W. P. Huskey**). Nitrogen isotope effects on acetylcholinesterase-catalyzed hydrolysis of o-nitroacetanilide. *J. Am. Chem. Soc.* 115:11676–81, 1993.

Casamassina, T. E., and **W. P. Huskey**. Solvation changes accompanying a proton transfer from a carbon acid to alkoxide bases as revealed by kinetic isotope effects. *J. Am. Chem. Soc.* 115:14–20, 1993.

Liu, L., and **W. P. Huskey**. Progress in establishing the rate-limiting features and kinetic mechanism for the glyceraldehyde-3-phosphate dehydrogenase reaction. *Biochemistry* 31:6898–903, 1992.

Huskey, W. P. Origins and interpretations of heavy-atom isotope effects. In *Enzyme Mechanism from Isotope Effects*, pp. 37–72, ed. P. F. Cook. Boca Raton, Fla.: CRC Press, 1991.

Jordan, F., et al. Regulation of thiamin diphosphate-dependent 2-oxoacid decarboxylases by substrate and thiamin diphosphate. Mg(II)-evidence for tertiary and quaternary interactions. *Biochim. Biophys. Acta* 1385:287–306, 1998.

Furey, W., et al. (**F. Jordan**). Structure-function relationships and flexible tetramer assembly in pyruvate decarboxylase revealed by analysis of crystal structures. *Biochim. Biophys. Acta* 1385:253–70, 151, 1998.

Bao, D., J.-T. Cheng, C. Kettner, and **F. Jordan**. Assignment of the $N^{ε2}H$ and $N^{δ1}H$ resonances at the active center histidine in chymotrypsin and subtilisin complexed to peptideboronic acids without specific N-15 labeling. *J. Am. Chem. Soc.* 120:3485–9, 1998.

Brunskill, A. P. J., **R. A. Lalancette**, and **H. W. Thompson**. (+)-3-oxo-5α-cholanic acid: Catemeric hydrogen bonding in a steroidal keto acid. *Acta Crystallogr.* C55:419–22, 1999.

Miller, A. J., A. P. J. Brunskill, **R. A. Lalancette**, and **H. W. Thompson**. (±)-10α-carboxy-1,8,10,10a-tetrahydrophenanthren-3(2H)-one: Catemeric hydrogen bonding in a δ-keto acid. *Acta Crystallogr.* C55:563–6, 1999.

Lalancette, R. A., A. P. J. Brunskill, and **H. W. Thompson**. (±)-1-indanone-2-acetic and -2-propionic acids: Catemeric versus dimeric hydrogen bonding in homologous γ- and δ-keto acids. *Acta Crystallogr.* C55:568–72, 1999.

Zewge, D., A. P. J. Brunskill, **R. A. Lalancette**, and **H. W. Thompson**. (±)-cis-10-carboxymethyl-2-decalone: Catemeric hydrogen bonding in an ε-keto acid. *Acta Crystallogr.* C54:1651–3, 1998.

Barcon, A., A. P. J. Brunskill, **R. A. Lalancette**, and **H. W. Thompson**. 3-oxo-1-cyclohexene-1-carboxylic acid: Hydrogen bonding and flexional ring disorder in a γ-keto acid. *Acta Crystallogr.* C54:1282–5, 1998.

Mendelsohn, R., et al. Infrared microspectroscopic imaging of biomineralized tissues using a mercury-cadmium-telluride focal-plane array detector. *Cell. Mol. Biol.* 44:109–15, 1998.

Mendelsohn, R., et al. Domain structure and molecular conformation in aqueous monolayers of annexin V/dimyristoylphosphatidic acid/Ca^{2+} complexes. A Brewster angle microscopy/IR reflection-absorption spectroscopy study. *Biophys. J.* 74:3273–81, 1998.

Mendelsohn, R., et al. (**R. S. Farid**). Propensity for helix formation in the hydrophobic peptides $K_2(LA)_x$ amide (x=6,8,10,12). In monolayer,

Rutgers, The State University of New Jersey, Newark

Selected Publications (continued)

bulk and lipid-containing phases. FT-IR, IRRAS and CD studies. *J. Am. Chem. Soc.* 120:792–9, 1998.

Piotrowiak, P. Photoinduced electron transfer in molecular systems: Recent developments. *Chem. Soc. Rev.* 28:143, 1999.

Siegel, A. M., **P. Piotrowiak**, S. M. Boue, and R. B. Cole. Polarizability and inductive effect contributions to solvent-cation binding observed in electrospray ionization mass spectrometry. *J. Am. Soc. Mass Spectrom.* 10:254, 1999.

Yip, W. T., D. H. Levy, R. Kobetic, and **P. Piotrowiak.** Energy transfer in bichromophoric molecules: The effect of symmetry and donor/acceptor energy gap. *J. Phys. Chem. A* 103:10, 1999.

Place, I., A. Farran, K. Deshayes, and **P. Piotrowiak.** Triplet energy transfer through the walls of hemicarcerands: Temperature dependence and the role of internal reorganization energy. *J. Am. Chem. Soc.* 120:12626, 1998.

Piotrowiak, P. Electrolyte effects in intramolecular excitation transfer. In *Photochemistry and Radiation Chemistry: Complementary Methods for the Study of Electron Transfer; Advances in Chemistry Series*, 254, p. 219, eds. J. F. Wishart and D. G. Nocera. 1998.

Raynor, S. Avoiding truncation errors in Hartree-Fock theories of periodic systems. *J. Chem. Phys.* 94:2940, 1991.

Raynor, S. Novel ab initio self-consistent-field approach to molecular solids under pressure: IV. MP3 and MP4 correlation corrections. *J. Chem. Phys.* 93:1834, 1990.

Raynor, S. Novel ab initio self-consistent-field approach to molecular solids under pressure: III. Second-order Møller-Plesset correlation corrections. *J. Chem. Phys.* 91:3577, 1989.

Raynor, S. Importance of high-order many-body interactions in models of molecular solids at high pressure. *J. Chem. Phys.* 91:7018, 1989.

Raynor, S. Novel ab initio self-consistent-field approach to molecular solids under pressure: I. Theory. *J. Chem. Phys.* 87:2790, 1987.

Schlegel, J. M., and R. F. Paretti. An electrochemical oscillator: The mercury/chloropentammine cobalt (III) oscillator. *J. Electroanal. Chem.* 335:67–74, 1992.

Temple, K., A. J. Lough, **J. B. Sheridan,** and I. Manners. Insertion of a Pt(0)-fragment into the strained silicon-carbon bond of a silicon-bridged [1]ferrocenophane: Synthesis, alkyne insertion chemistry, and catalytic reactivity of the [2]platinasilaferrocenophane Fe(η^5-C_5H_4)$_2$Pt(PEt$_3$)$_2$SiMe$_2$. *J. Chem. Soc., Dalton Trans.* 2799–805, 1998.

Ni, Y., I. Manners, **J. B. Sheridan,** and R. T. Oakley. Synthesis of a ferrocene-based polymer via ring-opening polymerization. *J. Chem. Educ.* 75:766–8, 1998.

Brunskill, A. P. J., **H. W. Thompson,** and **R. A. Lalancette.** Santonic acid: Catemeric hydrogen bonding in a γ,ϵ-diketocarboxylic acid. *Acta Crystallogr.* C55:566–8, 1999.

Thompson, H. W., A. P. J. Brunskill, and **R. A. Lalancette.** ($\pm$)-3-indanone-1-acetic acid: Heterochiral catemeric hydrogen-bonding in a δ-keto acid. *Acta Crystallogr.* C54:829–31, 1998.

Thompson, H. W., R. A. Lalancette, and A. P. J. Brunskill. ($\pm$)-4-oxo-1,2,3,4-tetrahydronaphthalene-1-carboxylic acid: Hydrogen-bonding and carboxyl disordering in a δ-keto acid. *Acta Crystallogr.* C54:1180–2, 1998.

RUTGERS, THE STATE UNIVERSITY OF NEW JERSEY, NEW BRUNSWICK

Graduate Program in Chemistry

Programs of Study

The Graduate Program in Chemistry at Rutgers in New Brunswick offers programs leading to the degrees of Master of Science, Master of Science for Teachers, and Doctor of Philosophy.

The principal requirement for the Ph.D. degree is the completion and successful oral defense of a thesis based on original research. A wide variety of research specializations are available in the traditional areas of chemistry—analytical, inorganic, organic, and physical—as well as in related areas and subdisciplines, including biological, bioinorganic, bioorganic, and biophysical chemistry; chemical physics; theoretical chemistry; and solid-state and surface chemistry.

The M.S. degree may be taken with or without a research thesis. The principal requirements are completion of 30 credits of graduate courses, a passing grade on the master's examination, and a master's essay or thesis. When the thesis option is chosen, 6 of the 30 credits may be in research.

Research Facilities

The research facilities of the program, located in the Wright and Rieman chemistry laboratories on the Busch campus, include a comprehensive chemistry library and glassworking, electronics, and machine shops. Research instruments of particular note include 600-, 500-, 400-, 300-, and 200-MHz NMR spectrometers with 2-D, 3-D, and solid-state capabilities; ESR spectrometers; single-crystal and powder X-ray diffractometers; a multiwire area detector for macromolecular structure determination; laser flash photolysis systems; a temperature-programmable ORD-CD spectropolarimeter; automated peptide and DNA synthesizers; a SQUID magnetometer; ultrahigh-vacuum surface analysis systems; scanning tunneling and atomic force microscopes; a helium-atom scattering apparatus; molecular beam and supersonic jet apparatuses; GC/quadrupole and ICP mass spectrometers; and extensive laser instrumentation, crystal-growing facilities, and calorimetric equipment. Computing facilities in the Wright-Rieman Laboratories include four multiprocessor servers, more than thirty-five graphics workstations, a forty-eight-processor cluster of PC-based workstations, a presenter system, video animation equipment, an assortment of approximately 100 personal computers and X-terminals, and an array of laser and color printers.

Financial Aid

Full-time Ph.D. students receive financial assistance in the form of fellowships, research assistantships, teaching assistantships, or a combination of these. Financial assistance for entering students ranges from approximately $13,000 to $16,000 plus tuition remission for a calendar-year appointment. This includes the J. R. L. Morgan fellowships awarded annually to outstanding applicants.

Cost of Study

In 1998–99, the full-time tuition (remitted for assistantship and fellowship recipients) was $3246 per semester for New Jersey residents and $4760 per semester for out-of-state residents. There is a fee for full-time students of $400 per semester. All of these fees are subject to change for the next academic year.

Living and Housing Costs

A furnished double room in the University residence halls or apartments rented for $3614 to $4088 per person for the 1998–99 academic year. Married student apartments rented for $563 to $716 per month. Current information may be obtained from the Department of Housing (732-445-2215), which also has information on private housing in the New Brunswick area.

Student Group

Total University enrollment is more than 47,000. Graduate and professional enrollment is approximately 13,500, of whom about 8,500 are in the Graduate School. Enrollment of graduate students in chemistry totals 140. Of these, about three fourths are full-time students. Students come from all parts of the United States as well as from other countries. In addition, there are approximately 50 postdoctoral research associates in residence.

Location

New Brunswick, with a population of about 42,000, is located in central New Jersey, roughly midway between New York City and Philadelphia. The cultural facilities of these two cities are easily accessible by automobile or regularly scheduled bus and train service. Within a 1½ hour drive of New Brunswick are the recreational areas of the Pocono Mountains of Pennsylvania and the beaches of the New Jersey shore. The University also offers a rich program of cultural, recreational, and social activities.

The University

Graduate instruction and research in chemistry are conducted on the University's Busch campus, which has a predominantly rural environment and is a few minutes' drive from downtown New Brunswick. On the same campus, within walking distance, are the Hill Center for the Mathematical Sciences (home of the University's computer center), the Library of Science and Medicine, the physics and biology laboratories, the Waksman Institute of Microbiology, the Robert Wood Johnson Medical School, the Center for Advanced Biotechnology and Medicine, and the College of Engineering. The University provides a free shuttle-bus service between the Busch and New Brunswick campuses.

Applying

Applications for assistantships and fellowships should be made at the same time as applications to the Graduate School. All forms, as well as a booklet describing the current research programs, may be obtained from the address given below. Admission consideration is open to all qualified candidates without regard to race, color, national origin, religion, sex, or handicap.

Correspondence and Information

Executive Officer
Graduate Program in Chemistry at New Brunswick
Wright-Rieman Laboratories
Rutgers, The State University of New Jersey
610 Taylor Road
Piscataway, New Jersey 08854-8087
Telephone: 732-445-3223
E-mail: gradexec@rutchem.rutgers.edu
World Wide Web: http://rutchem.rutgers.edu

Rutgers, The State University of New Jersey, New Brunswick

THE FACULTY AND THEIR RESEARCH

William H. Adams, Professor. Fundamental problems in the quantum theory of intermolecular interactions, particularly problems arising from electron indistinguishability in perturbation theory.

Stephen Anderson, Associate Professor. Alzheimer's disease, protein engineering, protein folding, molecular recognition, and structural genomics.

Georgia A. Arbuckle, Associate Professor. Synthesis and properties of conducting polymers, quartz crystal microbalance study of electroactive surfaces, spectroelectrochemical/QCM measurements.

Edward Arnold, Professor. Crystallographic studies of human viruses and viral proteins; molecular design, including drugs and vaccines; polymerase structure.

Jean Baum, Associate Professor. Biophysical chemistry, NMR, protein folding.

Helen Berman, Professor. X-ray crystallographic and molecular modeling studies of biological molecules.

Robert S. Boikess, Professor. Chemical education.

John G. Brennan, Associate Professor. Molecular and solid-state inorganic chemistry, lanthanide chalcogenides and pnictides, molecular approaches to semiconductor thin films and nanometer-sized clusters.

Kenneth J. Breslauer, Linus C. Pauling Professor. Characterization of the molecular interactions that control biopolymer structure and stability; drug-binding affinity and specificity; relating biophysical properties to biological function; correlating structure and energetics.

Edward Castner Jr., Associate Professor. Ultrafast photo-induced reactions in solution, molecular dynamics in condensed phases, time-resolved laser spectroscopy.

Kuang-Yu Chen, Professor. Biochemistry and function of polyamines and hypusine, transcription factors and cell senescence, nutrients and selective gene expression, molecular mechanism of tumor differentiation.

Martha A. Cotter, Professor and Executive Officer, Graduate Program. Theoretical investigations of liquid crystals and micellar solutions, phase transitions in simple model systems, theory of liquids.

Richard H. Ebright, Professor. Protein-DNA interaction; protein-protein interaction; structure, function, and regulation of transcription initiation complexes.

Eric L. Garfunkel, Professor. Surface science, adsorption and thin-film growth, materials for microelectronic devices.

Millie M. Georgiadis, Assistant Professor. Macromolecular crystallographic and related biochemical studies.

Alan S. Goldman, Associate Professor. Organometallic chemistry: homogeneous catalysis, reactions, and mechanisms; catalytic functionalization of hydrocarbons.

Lionel Goodman, Professor. Laser spectroscopy, particularly involving multiphoton excitation in supersonic jets; theoretical calculation and understanding of internal rotation potential surfaces for key molecules; application to biomolecules.

Martha Greenblatt, Professor. Solid-state inorganic chemistry, transition-metal oxides and chalcogenides, superionic conductors, intercalation compounds, high-T_c superconductors, low-dimensional solids.

Gene S. Hall, Associate Professor. Applied analytical chemistry, trace-element analysis of biological and environmental samples.

Gregory F. Herzog, Professor. Origin and evolution of meteorites, cosmogenic radioisotopes by accelerator mass spectrometry; stable isotopes by conventional forms of mass spectrometry.

Jane Hinch, Associate Professor. Molecular beam–surface interactions, surface diffractive techniques, scanning tunneling microscopy.

Stephen S. Isied, Professor. Bioinorganic and physical inorganic chemistry, photoinduced electron transfer in proteins, electron mediation by peptides with secondary structures, hydrogen bonding and other molecular recognition sites.

Leslie S. Jimenez, Associate Professor. Synthesis and characterization of analogs of antitumor antibiotics, total synthesis of natural products.

Roger A. Jones, Professor and Chair. Nucleic acid synthesis and NMR, ligand–nucleic acid interactions.

Spencer Knapp, Professor. Total synthesis of natural products; design and synthesis of enzyme models and inhibitors and of complex ligands, new synthetic methods.

Joachim Kohn, Professor. Development of structurally new polymers as biomaterials for medical applications, tissue engineering, drug delivery, studies on the interactions of cells with artificial surfaces.

John Krenos, Associate Professor. Chemical physics, energy transfer in hyperthermal collisions and collisions involving electronically excited reactants.

Karsten Krogh-Jespersen, Professor. Computational studies of molecular electronic structure, excited electronic states, solvation effects on photophysical properties, computational inorganic chemistry.

Jeehiun Katherine Lee, Assistant Professor. Biological and organic reactivity, recognition, and catalysis; computational chemistry; mass spectrometry.

Ronald M. Levy, Professor. Biophysical chemistry, chemical physics of liquids, protein structure, dynamics and protein folding.

Jing Li, Associate Professor. Experimental and theoretical studies of solid-state inorganic and inorganic-organic hybrid materials; synthesis, structure characterization, optical and thermal properties, and electronic band calculations.

Frederick H. Long, Assistant Professor. Laser spectroscopy of advanced materials and interfaces.

Richard D. Ludescher, Associate Professor. Food science: protein structure, dynamics, and function; luminescence spectroscopy; muscle biophysics.

Theodore E. Madey, State of New Jersey Professor of Surface Science. Structure and reactivity of surfaces and ultrathin films, electron-and photon-induced surface processes.

Gerald S. Manning, Professor. Physics and physical chemistry of polymers, ionic and elastic effects on biopolymer structure and configuration.

Gaetano T. Montelione, Associate Professor. Structure and dynamics of protein-protein and protein–nucleic acid complexes.

Robert A. Moss, Louis P. Hammett Professor. Biomimetic chemistry, destruction of toxic phosphates and phosphonates, organic chemistry in aggregates, physical organic chemistry of reactive intermediates, fast kinetics.

Wilma K. Olson, Mary I. Bunting Professor. Theoretical and computational studies of nucleic acid conformation, properties, and interactions.

Joseph A. Potenza, Professor. Molecular structure, X-ray diffraction, magnetic resonance.

Laurence S. Romsted, Professor. Theory of micellar effects on reaction rates and equilibria, ion binding at aqueous interfaces, organic reaction mechanisms, dediazoniation chemistry.

Heinz D. Roth, Professor. Electron transfer induced chemistry, physical organic chemistry of reactive intermediates, nuclear spin polarization, electron spin resonance, zeolite-induced chemistry.

Ronald R. Sauers, Professor. Computational chemistry, molecular modeling.

Harvey J. Schugar, Professor. Inorganic and bioinorganic chemistry, modeling of metalloprotein active sites, long-range electron transfer, modeling of photoreaction center special pairs.

Stanley Stein, Adjunct Professor. Methods development in protein analysis, synthesis of biologically active peptides and oligonucleotides.

John W. Taylor, Associate Professor. Bioactive peptide design and synthesis, multicyclic peptides, peptide conformation, protein engineering, peptide ligand-receptor interactions.

Irwin Tobias, Professor. Theoretical chemical physics, particularly the theory of the phenomena associated with the interaction of light with molecules; topology of biological molecules.

Sidney Toby, Professor. Chemical kinetics, photochemistry, and chemiluminescence, particularly of ozone reactions.

Kathryn E. Uhrich, Assistant Professor. Polymer synthesis, novel polymer architectures, biomedical polymers, micropatterning polymer surfaces.

STANFORD UNIVERSITY

Department of Chemistry

Program of Study

The Department of Chemistry strives for excellence in education and research. Only candidates for the Ph.D. degree are accepted. The department has a relatively small faculty, which promotes outstanding interactions between faculty, students, and staff. The faculty has achieved broad national and international recognition for its outstanding research contributions, and more than a third of its members belong to the National Academy of Sciences. The graduate program is based strongly on research, and students enter a research group by the end of the winter quarter of their first year. Students are also expected to complete a rigorous set of core courses in various areas of chemistry in their first year and to complement these courses later by studying upper-level subjects of their choice. Qualifying examinations are administered early in the fall quarter of the first year in inorganic, organic, physical, and biophysical chemistry and chemical physics. Students with deficiencies in undergraduate training in these areas are identified and work with the faculty to make them up. No other departmental examinations or orals are required of students progressing toward the Ph.D. degree. Much of the department's instruction is informal and includes diverse and active seminar programs, group meetings, and discussions with visiting scholars and with colleagues in other departments of the University. Stanford Ph.D. recipients are particularly well prepared for advanced scientific and technological study, and chemistry graduates typically accept positions on highly regarded university faculties or enter a wide variety of positions in industry.

Research Facilities

The department occupies five buildings with about 165,000 square feet. The department has a strong commitment to obtaining and maintaining state-of-the-art instrumentation for analysis and spectroscopy. Equipment available includes 200-, 300-, 400-, and 500-MHz NMR spectrometers; two FT-IR spectrometers; X-ray crystallography facilities; ultrafast absorption and fluorescence spectroscopy facilities; ultrahigh-resolution laser spectroscopy facilities; ion cyclotron resonance facilities; dynamic light-scattering spectroscopy facilities; tissue culture facilities; electrochemical systems; ultrahigh-vacuum facilities for surface analysis, including ESCA, Auger, EELS, LEED, and UPS; laser-Raman facilities; a superconducting magnetometer; and a Varian E-11 EPR spectrometer. Extensive computing capabilities are available in all research groups, and these are supplemented by a department computer network and the campus's IBM mainframe computers. Additional major instrumentation and expertise are available in the Center for Materials Research, the Stanford Synchrotron Radiation Laboratory, and the Stanford Magnetic Resonance Laboratory.

Financial Aid

Financial support of graduate students is provided in the form of teaching assistantships, research assistantships, and fellowships. All graduate students in good standing receive full financial support (tuition and stipend) for the duration of their graduate studies. The stipend for incoming first-year graduate students is $19,314; the amount of the stipend is adjusted annually to allow for inflation. Typical appointments involve teaching assistantships in the first year and research assistantships in subsequent years. Supplements are provided to holders of outside fellowships.

Cost of Study

Holders of teaching assistantships or research assistantships pay no academic tuition. In 1999–2000, nine-unit tuition is $19,128 for the year (four quarters).

Living and Housing Costs

Both University-owned and privately owned housing accommodations are available. Due to the residential nature of the surrounding area, it is not uncommon for several graduate students to share in a house rental. Escondido Village, an apartment development on campus, provides one- to three-bedroom apartments for married students and single parents. A survey of all graduate students in the department indicated that the median monthly expenditure for rent and utilities was $450 to $600.

Student Group

The total enrollment at Stanford University is 14,444, and there are 7,055 graduate students. The Department of Chemistry has 200 graduate students in its Ph.D. program.

Location

Stanford University is located in Palo Alto, a community of 60,000 about 35 miles south of San Francisco. Extensive cultural and recreational opportunities are available at the University and in surrounding areas, as well as in San Francisco. To the west lie the Santa Cruz Mountains and the Pacific Ocean, and to the east, the Sierra Nevada range with its many national parks, hiking and skiing trails, and redwood forests.

The University

Stanford is a private university founded in 1885 and ranked in the top few for academic excellence in physical and natural sciences, liberal arts, humanities, and engineering. The campus occupies 8,800 acres of land, of which 5,200 acres are in general academic use. In all disciplines, the University has a primary commitment to excellence in education and research.

Applying

Admission to the chemistry department is by competitive application. Application forms are available from the Graduate Admissions Office and should be filed before January 1 for admission in the fall quarter. All applicants are required to submit GRE scores from the verbal, quantitative, and analytical tests and the Subject Test in chemistry, as well as transcripts and three letters of recommendation. Applicants are notified of admission decisions before March 15. In unusual circumstances, late applications or a deferred enrollment will be considered.

Correspondence and Information

Graduate Admissions Committee
Department of Chemistry
Stanford University
Stanford, California 94305-5080
Telephone: 650-723-1525
E-mail: chem.admissions@forsythe.stanford.edu

Stanford University

THE FACULTY AND THEIR RESEARCH

Hans C. Andersen, Professor; Ph.D., MIT, 1966. Physical chemistry: statistical mechanics, theories of structure and properties of liquids, computer simulation methods, glass transition, water, exciton migration in random solids and polymers, phase transitions in lipid bilayer membranes, nonlinear spectroscopy.

Steven G. Boxer, Professor; Ph.D., Chicago, 1976. Physical and biophysical chemistry: structure, function, dynamics, and electrostatics in proteins and membranes; spectroscopy; photosynthesis; GFP; heme proteins; interface between living and nonliving surfaces.

John I. Brauman, Professor; Ph.D., Berkeley, 1963. Organic and physical chemistry: structure and reactivity of ions in the gas phase, photochemistry and spectroscopy of gas phase ions, electron photodetachment spectroscopy, electron affinities, reaction mechanisms.

Christopher E. D. Chidsey, Associate Professor; Ph.D., Stanford, 1983. Physical chemistry: electrochemical scanning tunneling microscopy, interfacial electron transfer, monomolecular films on metal and semiconductor surfaces.

James P. Collman, Professor; Ph.D., Illinois, 1958. Inorganic, organic, and organometallic chemistry: synthetic analogues of the active sites in hemoproteins, homogeneous catalysis, multielectron redox catalysts, multiple metal-metal bonds.

Hongjie Dai, Assistant Professor; Ph.D., Harvard, 1994. Physical and materials chemistry: synthesis, characterization, and applications of novel nanostructured materials; physics in well-defined low dimensional systems; processing of nanowires and their integration into quantum electronics; manipulation of nanowires for probe tips for atomic force microscopy studies of soft condensed systems.

Carl Djerassi, Professor; Ph.D., Wisconsin–Madison, 1945. Organic chemistry: chemistry of steroids, terpenes, and alkaloids with major emphasis on marine sources, application of chiroptical methods—especially circular dichroism and magnetic circular dichroism—to organic and biochemical problems, organic chemical applications of mass spectrometry, use of computer artificial-intelligence techniques in structure elucidation of organic compounds. Author of novels in genre of science-in-fiction and of science-in-theater plays.

Justin DuBois, Assistant Professor; Ph.D., Caltech, 1997. Organic chemistry: synthetic organic chemistry, transition metal catalysis, metalloenzyme modeling, molecular recognition.

Michael D. Fayer, Professor; Ph.D., Berkeley, 1974. Physical chemistry and chemical physics: dynamics in molecular condensed phases; laser spectroscopy; ultrafast nonlinear techniques; visible and infrared studies of dynamics and intermolecular interactions in liquids, supercritical fluids, glasses, proteins, and polymers.

Keith O. Hodgson, Professor; Ph.D., Berkeley, 1972. Inorganic, biophysical, and structural chemistry: chemistry and structure of metal sites in biomolecules, molecular and crystal structure analysis, protein crystallography, extended X-ray absorption fine-structure spectroscopy.

Wray H. Huestis, Professor; Ph.D., Caltech, 1972. Biophysical chemistry: chemistry of cell-surface receptors, membrane-mediated control mechanisms, biochemical studies of membrane protein complexes in situ, magnetic resonance studies of conformation and function in soluble proteins and protein-lipid complexes, viral fusion mechanisms, drug delivery.

Chaitan Khosla, Associate Professor; Ph.D., Caltech, 1990. Biological chemistry: structure, function, and engineering of multienzyme systems derived from natural product biosynthetic pathways; use of "unnatural" natural products to probe biological and biochemical phenomena.

Harden M. McConnell, Professor; Ph.D., Caltech, 1951. Physical chemistry, biophysics, immunology: membrane biophysics and immunology, cell-surface recognition, spin labels, surface diffraction of X rays, membrane phase transitions.

W. E. Moerner, Professor; Ph.D., Cornell, 1982. Physical chemistry: individual molecules in solids, liquids, and proteins probed by far-field and near-field optical spectroscopy; organic nonlinear optical materials; mechanisms of photorefractivity and photoconductivity in polymers; chemistry of optical materials.

Harry S. Mosher, Professor Emeritus; Ph.D., Penn State, 1942. Organic chemistry: stereochemistry, asymmetric organic reactions, Grignard reaction mechanisms, animal toxins.

Vijay Pande, Assistant Professor; Ph.D., MIT, 1995. Physical chemistry and biophysics: theoretical models and computer simulations to examine the equilibrium and nonequilibrium statistical mechanics of biological molecules, thermodynamics and kinetics of protein folding, polymer statistical mechanics and electron transfer.

Robert Pecora, Professor; Ph.D., Columbia, 1962. Physical chemistry:statistical mechanics of fluids and macromolecules, molecular motions in fluids, light-scattering spectroscopy of liquids, macromolecules and biological systems.

John Ross, Professor; Ph.D., MIT, 1951. Physical chemistry: experimental and theoretical studies of chemical kinetics, chemical instabilities, oscillatory reactions, strategies of determining complex reaction mechanisms, chemical computations, thermodynamics and fluctuations of systems far from equilibrium.

Edward I. Solomon, Professor; Ph.D., Princeton, 1972. Physical, inorganic, and bioinorganic chemistry: inorganic spectroscopy and ligand field theory, active sites, spectral and magnetic studies on bioinorganic systems directed toward understanding the structural origins of their activity, photoelectron spectroscopic studies on surfaces and heterogeneous catalysts.

T. Daniel P. Stack, Associate Professor; Ph.D., Harvard, 1988. Inorganic and bioinorganic chemistry: coordination chemistry of transition-metal complexes relevant to active sites in biological systems.

Henry Taube, Professor Emeritus; Ph.D., Berkeley, 1940. Inorganic chemistry: mechanisms of inorganic reactions and reactivity of inorganic substances, new aquo ions, dinitrogen as ligand, back-bonding as affecting properties including reactivity of ligands, mixed-valence molecules.

Barry M. Trost, Professor; Ph.D., MIT, 1965. Organic, organometallic, and bioorganic chemistry: new synthetic methods, natural product synthesis and structure determinations, insect chemistry, potentially antiaromatic unsaturated hydrocarbons, chemistry of ylides.

Thomas J. Wandless, Assistant Professor; Ph.D., Harvard, 1993. Organic and bioorganic chemistry: synthesis of natural and nonnatural products; study of their interactions with components of the cytoskeleton.

Robert M. Waymouth, Professor; Ph.D., Caltech, 1987. Inorganic, organometallic, and polymer chemistry: mechanistic and synthetic chemistry of the early transition elements, mechanisms of olefin polymerization, design of new polymerization catalysts.

Paul A. Wender, Professor; Ph.D., Yale, 1973. Organic, organometallic, bioorganic, and medicinal chemistry: synthesis of biologically active compounds, synthetic methods, biomacromolecular recognition, computer design, drug mechanisms.

Richard N. Zare, Professor; Ph.D., Harvard, 1964. Physical and analytical chemistry, chemical physics: application of lasers to chemical problems, molecular structure and molecular reaction dynamics.

Courtesy Faculty

Stacey F. Bent, Assistant Professor; Ph.D., Stanford, 1992. Semiconductor processing and surface reactivity; chemical vapor deposition, etching, and lithography; surface photochemistry; laser spectroscopy.

Karlene Cimprich, Assistant Professor; Ph.D., Harvard, 1994. Use of chemical and biochemical approaches to understand and control the DNA damage-induced cell cycle checkpoints and signal transduction cascades that allow the cell to detect and respond to DNA damage.

Curtis W. Frank, Professor; Ph.D., Illinois, 1972. Polymer physics: dependence of polymer chain configuration on interactions with its environment.

Alice P. Gast, Professor; Ph.D., Princeton, 1984. Complex and supermolecular fluids: adsorption, association, and concentrated suspension dynamics.

Daniel Herschlag, Associate Professor; Ph.D., Brandeis, 1988. Biological, bioorganic, and biophysical chemistry: chemical and physical principles of biological catalysis elucidated through study of reactions catalyzed by proteins and RNA and in model systems; RNA folding; mechanistic analysis of complex biological processes, including translation initiation and RNA processing.

Robert J. Madix, Professor; Ph.D., Berkeley, 1964. Surface and interface science: relationships between surface composition structure and heterogeneous reactivity of metal and metalloid surfaces, catalysis, organometallic surface chemistry, electrochemistry and corrosion, reaction dynamics.

STATE UNIVERSITY OF NEW YORK COLLEGE OF ENVIRONMENTAL SCIENCE AND FORESTRY

Faculty of Chemistry

Programs of Study

The Faculty of Chemistry offers programs in chemistry leading to the degrees of Master of Science and Doctor of Philosophy. The student makes an appropriate selection of courses and chooses a research problem in consultation with his or her major professor within general guidelines established by the Faculty. The course work requirements are a minimum of 30 credits for the Ph.D. and 18 credits for the M.S. In addition, a significant research effort, resulting in a written thesis, is required in both programs. Courses are chosen from those offered by the chemistry and other faculties at the College as well as from offerings of the physical and biological science departments of Syracuse University, whose campus adjoins that of the College. Optional interdisciplinary programs in chemical ecology, biotechnology, and environmental systems science are available and recommended.

Major research areas of the Faculty are in synthetic and natural polymers, membrane science, organic materials science, environmental chemistry, natural products, ecological chemistry, and biochemistry. The fields of specialization are biochemistry and analytical, organic, and physical chemistry. The usual fundamental courses in physics, mathematics, biology, and advanced chemistry appropriate for chemists and biochemists are required of all students and are available at the College and at Syracuse University. Specialized courses in polymer chemistry, membrane science, wood and natural products chemistry, environmental chemistry, spectrometric identification, and biochemistry are also available.

Research Facilities

The Faculty of Chemistry is located in the new E. C. Jahn Chemistry Laboratory, a 70,000-square-foot state-of-the-art chemistry building. Research equipment and facilities available at this laboratory include the most modern instrumentation necessary for conducting research in organic, physical, polymer, and environmental chemistry as well as biochemistry. Extensive computing resources are also available and easily accessible. The Cellulose Research Institute and the Polymer Research Institute are associated with the Faculty's programs.

Financial Aid

Essentially all M.S. and Ph.D. candidates in the Faculty are financially supported by fellowships, teaching assistantships, or government, industrial, or other research grants. Stipends vary from $9500 to $12,000 per year, in some cases with additional allowance for dependents. Tuition for fellows and assistants is waived. Teaching requirements are light.

Cost of Study

The tuition for 1998–99 was $2550 per semester for state residents and $4208 for out-of-state residents. Rates are subject to change for 1999–2000.

Living and Housing Costs

Syracuse University dormitories are available for single students. The University also operates rental units for married students with or without children. Rooms and apartments can be found in the neighborhood of the College. Meal tickets are available from the University.

Student Group

The student body at Syracuse University currently numbers 21,000. The number of graduate students in the department is approximately 45. In addition, there are more than 10 postdoctoral fellows and visiting scientists.

Student Outcomes

Graduates have been employed by various industrial and academic institutions such as Pfizer; Amoco; the University of Southern California; Biological Research Labs; Gas Tech, Inc.; Ford Motor Co.; International Paper Co.; Dow Corning Corp.; Parke-Davis; the University of Rochester; the University of Rochester Medical School; St. Vincent College; Acurex; Weyerhaeuser; Texaco; Xerox; Bristol-Myers Squibb; and Montgomery Watson, among others.

Location

The city of Syracuse is the center of an urban region with a population of about 500,000. In addition to the State University College of Environmental Science and Forestry and Syracuse University, the State University Health Sciences Center at Syracuse, LeMoyne College, and Onondaga Community College are located in Syracuse. Both the city of Syracuse and Syracuse University offer a great variety of cultural and recreational opportunities. Situated on hills, near several lakes, the city offers good facilities for both summer and winter sports. The attractive Finger Lakes region is less than 20 miles away, the Thousand Islands are 90 miles, and the Adirondack and Catskill mountains and Niagara Falls are all within 150 miles. Travel time to New York City by car is 5 hours.

The College

The College of Environmental Science and Forestry is part of the State University of New York, which is, with its 230,000 students and seventy units, the largest university system in the United States. The College, founded in 1911, at present has 1,000 undergraduates, about 500 graduate students, and 100 faculty members. The campus has six major buildings. The Faculty of Chemistry was founded in 1919 and has awarded more than 80 M.S. degrees and 100 Ph.D. degrees in chemistry during the past twenty years.

Applying

The usual requirement for entrance is a bachelor's degree in chemistry, biochemistry, or chemical engineering at the level of the American Chemical Society Accredited Curriculum, but deficiencies can be made up later. All applicants must take the Graduate Record Examinations. Typically, a student should have taken general chemistry, qualitative and quantitative analysis, instrumental analysis, organic chemistry, physical chemistry, at least a year of physics, and preferably a year and a half of calculus. There are no specific deadlines for applications. It is desirable, however, if admission is to be in September, that applications be submitted during the first few months of the year.

Correspondence and Information

Graduate Admissions
SUNY College of Environmental Science and Forestry
Syracuse, New York 13210
Telephone: 315-470-6599

State University of New York College of Environmental Science and Forestry

THE FACULTY AND THEIR RESEARCH

Gregory L. Boyer, Associate Professor of Biochemistry; Ph.D., Wisconsin–Madison, 1980. Harmful algal blooms, including techniques for the analysis of marine and freshwater toxins; iron, siderophores, and heavy-metal interactions in bacteria, fungi, and algae.

Israel Cabasso, Professor of Polymer Chemistry and Director of the Polymer Research Institute; Ph.D., Weizmann (Israel), 1973. Polymer membranes and processes, polymer blends, diffusion and transport in polymer matrices, batteries, fuel cells and electrochemical processes, ion-exchange polymers, inorganic polymers (Si, S, P), conductive polymers, carbonized polymers, radiopaque polymers.

Paul M. Caluwe, Professor of Polymer Chemistry; Ph.D., Leuven (Belgium), 1967. Synthesis of highly functionalized molecules, cellulose chemistry, heterocyclic chemistry, polycyclic aromatic hydrocarbons, organic chemistry computer software.

Theodore S. Dibble, Assistant Professor of Environmental Chemistry; Ph.D., Michigan, 1992. Atmospheric kinetics and photochemistry, radical chemistry, applications of lasers and quantum calculations to chemistry.

José-L. Giner, Assistant Professor of Organic Chemistry; Ph.D., Stanford, 1991. Bioorganic chemistry; biosynthesis of natural products, especially sterols of marine origin; mechanism and stereochemistry in enzyme reactions; new synthetic reactions; natural products of medical and agricultural significance.

Ivan Gitsov, Associate Professor of Polymer Chemistry; Ph.D., Sofia (Bulgaria), 1986. Synthesis and characterization of polymers with novel architectures that incorporate dendritic, hyperbranched, star-like, or cyclic fragments; amphiphilic copolymers; self-assembly and supramolecular chemistry.

John P. Hassett, Professor of Environmental Chemistry and Chair of the Faculty; Ph.D., Wisconsin–Madison, 1978. Behavior and analysis of natural and anthropogenic organic compounds in aquatic and soil environments.

David L. Johnson, Professor of Environmental Chemistry; Ph.D., Rhode Island, 1973. Analytical methods development, automated SEM/Image analysis, computerized individual particle characterizations, heavy-metal speciation, lead in soils and dusts, exposure models, bioavailability studies.

David J. Kieber, Associate Professor of Environmental Chemistry; Ph.D., Miami (Florida), 1988. Environmental organic chemistry, aquatic photochemistry, analytical methods development, chemical oceanography, oxidation of organic matter by manganese oxides/iron oxides, Antarctic research.

Robert T. LaLonde, Professor of Chemistry; Ph.D., Colorado, 1957. Chemical transformations of abundant natural products for industrial utilization, oxidative conversions of lignans, structure/activity relationships, modes of action and inactivation of aquatic mutagens.

Neil P. J. Price, Assistant Professor of Biochemistry; Ph.D., London (England), 1990. Oligosaccharide signals involved in symbiotic recognition; synthesis of fluorescent and photoactive oligosaccharides; lipopolysaccharide biochemistry; structure, function, and biosynthesis of biologically active oligosaccharides.

Arthur J. Stipanovic, Senior Research Associate and Director, Analytical and Technical Services; Ph.D., SUNY College of Environmental Science and Forestry, 1979. Characterization and application of polysaccharides, including the use of gels for the controlled release of biologically active compounds; polymer rheology and stimuli-responsive fluids; energy-conserving and biodegradable lubricants.

Francis X. Webster, Associate Professor of Ecological Chemistry; Ph.D., SUNY-ESF, 1986. Isolation, identification, and synthesis of insect, mammalian, and plant semiochemicals; discovery and development of methods for stereoselective and stereospecific reactions for the total synthesis of natural products.

William T. Winter, Professor of Polymer Chemistry and Director, Cellulose Research Institute; Ph.D., SUNY at Syracuse, 1974. Polymer morphology and conformation, diffraction and NMR studies of biopolymers, microbial polysaccharides, biopolymer-based nanocomposites, plant gums, molecular modeling, computational chemistry.

Adjunct Faculty

Terry L. Bluhm, Ph.D. Xerox Research and Development.
John L. Dillon, Ph.D. Bristol-Meyers Squibb Company.
F. W. Gordon Fearon, Ph.D. Dow Corning Company.
Harry L. Frisch, Distinguished Professor of Physics and Chemistry, Ph.D. SUNY at Albany.
D. Graiver, Ph.D. Dow Corning Company.
Donald E. Nettleton, Ph.D. Bristol-Myers Squibb Company.
Richard Zepp, Ph.D. USEPA, Environmental Research Lab.

TEXAS A&M UNIVERSITY

Department of Chemistry

Programs of Study

The Department of Chemistry offers M.S. and Ph.D. degrees in the traditional areas of chemistry as well as in chemical physics and biological, catalytic, electrochemical, environmental, nuclear, polymer, solid-state, spectroscopic, structural, and theoretical aspects of chemistry.

The M.S. research degree requires 18 semester hours and the Ph.D. approximately 15–20 semester hours of lecture course work. Requirements for the Ph.D. usually include a preliminary examination and a final thesis defense.

Graduate students usually select a research supervisor during the first semester of study. The results of the research investigation must be summarized in a dissertation suitable for later publication. There is no language requirement. The average period required to complete the Ph.D. degree is four to five years. Students interested in obtaining a Ph.D. degree are encouraged to work directly toward it without obtaining an intermediate M.S. degree.

Work is supervised by a faculty that has achieved broad national and international recognition for its outstanding research contributions; the faculty includes a National Medal of Science awardee, holders of international medals in a variety of chemistry subdisciplines, and members of both the National Academy of Sciences and Royal Society. The department has a graduate faculty of 53, whose efforts are supported by more than 100 postdoctoral and visiting faculty researchers and a graduate student body of nearly 250. The medium-sized research groups provide an intensive, personalized learning environment.

Research Facilities

The chemistry complex has 224,000 square feet of new or recently renovated space for teaching and research in four contiguous buildings, with major institutes housed in three other buildings. It maintains professionally staffed laboratories for high-resolution mass spectrometry, solution NMR, solid-state NMR, single-crystal and powder X-ray diffractions, and departmental computing. Departmental instrumentation includes ESCA, SIMS, Auger, and other surface-science instruments; a PerSeptive Biosystems, high-performance MALDI-TOF, two Extrel FTMS 2001 systems, a completely upgraded Kratos (AE1) MS-902S used for EB/R-TOF; and a variety of EPR, ENDOR infrared, Raman, UV-visible, fluorescence, atomic absorption, gamma-ray, and photoelectron spectrometers. Other campus facilities include the Nuclear Science Center (1-MW reactor) and the Cyclotron Institute, which includes a new superconducting cyclotron. In addition, there are a number of specialized facilities, including the Center for Biological Nuclear Magnetic Resonance, the Laboratory for Molecular Structure and Bonding, the Center for Chemical Characterization and Analysis, the Laboratory for Biological Mass Spectrometry, the Laboratory for Protein Chemistry, the Laboratory for Molecular Simulation, and the Center for Catalysis and Surface Science.

A major addition was recently added to the Evans Library, which houses 1.6 million volumes and maintains subscriptions to approximately 8,000 scientific and technical journals.

Financial Aid

Graduate students in good standing receive full financial support for the duration of their studies. Teaching assistantships are available to all qualified students. The 1998–99 stipend for nine-month teaching assistantships was $13,500. Teaching or research assistantship support during the summer provided an additional $4000. Research assistantship stipends averaged $15,960 per year. Prestigious twelve-month fellowships are available for outstanding applicants. For the 1999–2000 academic year, Texas A&M University offers the highest average stipend package to first-year students of any public institution in the United States. After deductions of all taxes, tuition, fees, and costs for high-quality medical insurance, the average monthly take-home stipend is $1315.41.

Cost of Study

In 1998–99, tuition and fees for graduate students were $1250 per semester (9 credit hours) for Texas residents. Students on assistantships and fellowships are considered in-state students for tuition purposes.

Living and Housing Costs

University apartments are available, although applications for University housing should be made early. Private rooms, apartments, and houses are available close to campus, and the cost of living is very low. In 1998–99, University apartments for students rented for as low as $211 per month, while private apartments ranged from $350 to $600 per month.

Student Body

The student body consists of more than 43,000 resident students enrolled in more than a dozen colleges and schools. Approximately 15 percent of the students are enrolled in the many programs of the Graduate College. All fifty states and numerous other countries are normally represented in the chemistry graduate student body. The percentages of members of minority groups and women have increased significantly in recent years. The Department of Chemistry has about 250 graduate students.

Location

As a university town, College Station has a high proportion of professional people and enjoys many of the advantages of a cosmopolitan center without the disadvantages of a congested urban environment. The crime rate is very low, and students feel safe on campus. There are many film series, a symphony, chamber music, and choral groups. College Station is situated in the middle of a triangle formed by Dallas, Houston, and Austin, and the symphonies, ballets, sporting events, museums, and concerts of these cities are within easy day-trip distance.

Mild, sunny winters make the region eminently suitable for year-round activities, from fishing and hiking in the beautiful piney woods of eastern Texas to boating, bicycling, and camping in the Texas hill country. There are more than 100 state parks within a day's drive of College Station.

The University and The Department

Founded in 1876, Texas A&M University is the state's oldest institution of higher education. Vigorous research programs in engineering, physics, mathematics, biochemistry, veterinary medicine, and medicine provide the chemist with supplementary facilities and intellectual resources.

An active faculty of 53 members generated approximately 450 publications and nearly $11.5 million in external grant funding in 1998. In 1996, the most recent year for which data are available, the American Chemical Society reported that Texas A&M ranked ninth in the nation in spending on chemical research and development and seventh in spending for research and development overall. Among United States colleges and universities, Texas A&M graduated the second-highest number of doctoral students in 1996. The department is generally considered to be one of the top fifteen in the country.

Applying

Inquiries regarding admission to the University, as well as information about facilities for advanced studies, research, and requirements for graduate work in chemistry, should be addressed to the Department of Chemistry. Application for admission should be filed no later than six weeks prior to the opening of the semester, but applications received prior to March 1 receive preferential treatment. Applications for assistantships and fellowships are accepted for both regular semesters and the summer session. Awards are made as long as funds are available, but early application is advised.

Correspondence and Information

Graduate Advisor
Graduate Student Office
Chemistry Department
Texas A&M University
P.O. Box 30012
College Station, Texas 77842-3012
Telephone: 409-845-5345
        800-334-1082 (toll-free)
Fax: 409-845-5211
E-mail: gradmail@mail.chem.tamu.edu
World Wide Web: http://www.chem.tamu.edu

Texas A&M University

THE FACULTY AND THEIR RESEARCH

Thomas O. Baldwin, Professor; Ph.D., Texas at Austin, 1971. Protein chemistry.
Hagan Bayley, Professor and Head of Medical Biochemistry and Genetics; Ph.D., Harvard, 1979. Medical biochemistry.
David Bergbreiter, Professor; Ph.D., MIT, 1974. Organic chemistry.
John Bevan, Professor; Ph.D., London, 1975. Physical chemistry.
Kevin Burgess, Professor; Ph.D., Cambridge, 1983. Organic chemistry.
Abraham Clearfield, Professor; Ph.D., Rutgers, 1954. Inorganic chemistry.
Dwight Conway, Professor; Ph.D., Chicago, 1956. Physical chemistry.
F. Albert Cotton, Distinguished Professor and Doherty-Welch Chair; Ph.D., Harvard, 1955. Inorganic chemistry.
Paul Cremer, Assistant Professor; Ph.D., Berkeley, 1996. Surface science.
Richard M. Crooks, Professor; Ph.D., Texas at Austin, 1987. Analytical and materials chemistry.
Donald J. Darensbourg, Professor; Ph.D., Illinois at Urbana-Champaign, 1968. Organometallic chemistry.
Marcetta Y. Darensbourg, Professor; Ph.D., Illinois at Urbana-Champaign, 1967. Organometallic chemistry.
Victoria J. DeRose, Assistant Professor; Ph.D., Berkeley, 1990. Biophysical chemistry.
Kim R. Dunbar, Professor; Ph.D., Purdue, 1984. Inorganic chemistry.
John P. Fackler Jr., Distinguished Professor; Ph.D., MIT, 1960. Inorganic chemistry.
Paul F. Fitzpatrick, Professor; Ph.D., Michigan, 1981. Biochemistry.
Francois Gabbai, Assistant Professor; Ph.D., Texas at Austin, 1994. Inorganic chemistry.
Karl A. Gingerich, Professor; Ph.D., Freiburg (Germany), 1957. Physical chemistry.
D. Wayne Goodman, Robert A. Welch Professor; Ph.D., Texas at Austin, 1974. Physical chemistry.
Michael B. Hall, Professor; Ph.D., Wisconsin–Madison, 1971. Inorganic chemistry.
Kenn E. Harding, Professor; Ph.D., Stanford, 1968. Organic chemistry.
Aaron Harper, Assistant Professor; Ph.D., USC, 1996. Organic chemistry.
James W. Haw, Professor; Ph.D., Virginia Tech, 1982. Analytical chemistry.
John L. Hogg, Professor; Ph.D., Kansas, 1974. Bioorganic chemistry.
Timothy Hughbanks, Professor; Ph.D., Cornell, 1983. Inorganic chemistry.
Arthur Johnson, Professor and Wehner-Welch Chair; Ph.D., Oregon, 1973. Biochemistry.
Jaan Laane, Professor; Ph.D., MIT, 1967. Physical chemistry.
Paul Lindahl, Associate Professor; Ph.D., MIT, 1985. Inorganic chemistry.
Robert R. Lucchese, Professor; Ph.D., Caltech, 1982. Theoretical chemistry.
Jack H. Lunsford, Professor; Ph.D., Rice, 1962. Physical chemistry.
Ronald D. Macfarlane, Professor; Ph.D., Carnegie Tech, 1959. Nuclear and physical chemistry.
Arthur E. Martell, Distinguished Professor; Ph.D., NYU, 1941. Inorganic chemistry.
Joseph B. Natowitz, Professor; Ph.D., Pittsburgh, 1965. Nuclear chemistry.
Simon North, Assistant Professor; Ph.D., Berkeley, 1995. Physical chemistry.
Frank M. Raushel, Professor; Ph.D., Wisconsin–Madison, 1976. Biochemistry.
Daniel Romo, Assistant Professor; Ph.D., Colorado State, 1991. Organic chemistry.
Michael P. Rosynek, Professor and Associate Head; Ph.D., Rice, 1972. Physical chemistry.
Marvin W. Rowe, Professor; Ph.D., Arkansas, 1966. Analytical cosmochemistry.
David H. Russell, Professor; Ph.D., Nebraska–Lincoln, 1978. Analytical chemistry.
James C. Sacchettini, Professor; Ph.D., Washington (St. Louis), 1987. Biochemistry.
Richard P. Schmitt, Professor; Ph.D., Berkeley, 1978. Nuclear chemistry.
Emile A. Schweikert, Professor and Head; Ph.D., Paris IV (Sorbonne), 1964. Activation analysis and analytical chemistry.
A. Ian Scott, Distinguished Professor; Ph.D., Glasgow, 1952. Organic chemistry, biochemistry.
Eric E. Simanek, Assistant Professor; Ph.D., Harvard, 1996. Organic chemistry.
Daniel A. Singleton, Professor; Ph.D., Minnesota, 1986. Organic chemistry.
Manual P. Soriaga, Professor; Ph.D., Hawaii, 1978. Analytical chemistry.
Robert F. Standaert, Assistant Professor; Ph.D., Harvard, 1992. Biological and organic chemistry.
Gary Sulikowski, Associate Professor; Ph.D., Pennsylvania, 1989. Organic chemistry.
Gyula Vigh, Associate Professor; Ph.D., Veszperm (Hungary), 1975. Analytical chemistry.
Rand L. Watson, Professor; Ph.D., Berkeley, 1966. Nuclear chemistry.
Robert D. Wells, Professor; Ph.D., Pittsburgh, 1964. Biochemistry.
Danny L. Yeager, Professor; Ph.D., Caltech, 1975. Theoretical chemistry.
Sherry J. Yennello, Associate Professor; Ph.D., Indiana, 1990. Nuclear chemistry.

TUFTS UNIVERSITY

Department of Chemistry

Programs of Study

The Department of Chemistry offers graduate programs leading to the degrees of Master of Science and Doctor of Philosophy in the fields of analytical, inorganic, organic, and physical chemistry and in the subdisciplinary areas of bioorganic, environmental, and materials science and chemistry-biotechnology. Programs of study may involve collaborations in related science departments or in the Sackler School of Graduate Biomedical Sciences, the Tufts–New England Medical Center, or Tufts Science and Technology Center.

Entering graduate students meet with the Graduate Committee to plan an academic course schedule best suited to the student's background and career goals. New students must complete four graduate courses, one course in each of the four chemistry disciplines (analytical, inorganic, organic, and physical) by the end of the third academic semester. This is to ensure that by the end of the third semester each student has a firm foundation in the fundamentals of chemistry. A research advisory committee, consisting of the thesis adviser and two other faculty members, then directs the student's course and research program.

A Ph.D. candidate must complete a minimum of six formal courses (exclusive of research) and present a departmental seminar. The student must also present an additional independent study topic, successfully defend a research proposal, and complete a dissertation reporting significant research of publishable quality. Additional course work may be required at the discretion of the research adviser.

The master's program is very flexible in order to accommodate individual goals. Each student must pass eight graduate-level courses, at least six of which must be formal classroom instruction. Up to half of the courses may be taken outside the Department of Chemistry in related fields. A thesis may or may not be required, depending on the importance of a thesis for the candidate's career plans.

Research Facilities

Research is carried out in the Pearson and Michael laboratories, combined facilities of 120,000 square feet. A wide array of modern instrumentation necessary for cutting-edge research in chemistry is available for general use by graduate students, including FT-NMR, FT-IR, UV-Vis, AA, AES, and fluorescence spectrometers; scanning probe (STM, AFM) and scanning electron microscopes; GC-MS and MALDI-TOF mass spectrometers; analytical and preparative gas and liquid chromotography equipment; pulsed and CW laser systems for analytical and physical measurement; computerized electrochemical instrumentation; UHV surface analysis equipment; a fermentor, incubator, and coldroom; and professionally staffed electronics and machine shops. Complementary instrumentation is available at other Tufts facilities, including the Sackler School of Graduate Biomedical Sciences, the Tufts–New England Medical Center, the Science and Technology Center, and the School of Nutrition. A departmental computer laboratory provides Macintosh and IBM computers for word processing, data analysis, and graphics preparation and for direct access to the University's mainframe computers, the Internet, and STN.

Financial Aid

To help students whose records indicate scholarly promise, a variety of financial awards and work opportunities are available. All Ph.D. candidates receive twelve months of financial support, which is guaranteed for five years. Students must remain in good academic standing, and make steady progress toward the Ph.D. degree. The current twelve-month minimum stipend is $16,000 and is derived from teaching or research assistantships. Graduate students are exempt from teaching during the first summer of graduate research and are supported by fellowships from the Dupont Foundation and Bristol-Meyers Squibb. Supplemental fellowship awards are also available for outstanding students. Stipends are reviewed annually.

Cost of Study

Most M.S. and all Ph.D. candidates receive tuition scholarships.

Living and Housing Costs

Most graduate students attending Tufts University live off campus in moderately priced apartments in the surrounding metropolitan area. Meal plans are available.

Student Group

At present the total enrollment in all divisions is about 7,000 students, including approximately 2,000 graduate and professional students.

Location

The Boston area offers an excellent environment for the pursuit of academic interests. Due to the high density of world famous institutions, many distinguished chemists visit the Boston area to present seminars and to confer with colleagues. All graduate students may obtain Boston library consortium privileges, enabling them to use the library facilities of other local universities. Researchers at Tufts have been able to take advantage of various facilities available at other local universities such as MIT and Harvard. The cultural offerings of the Boston area are some of the finest in the world, including the Boston Symphony, the Museum of Fine Arts, the Museum of Science, and the New England Aquarium, as well as innumerable chamber groups, performing groups, and theaters showing first-run and major international films.

The University

Since its designation as Tufts College in 1852, Tufts University has grown to include seven primary divisions: Arts and Sciences; the Fletcher School of Law and Diplomacy; the Schools of Medicine, Dental Medicine, and Veterinary Medicine; the Sackler School of Graduate Biomedical Sciences; and the School of Nutrition.

Applying

Application materials should be submitted directly to the Graduate School Office by February 15 for September enrollment and by October 15 for January enrollment. Applications received after these dates will be considered on a space-available basis. All U.S. applicants must submit their test scores on the General Test of the Graduate Record Examinations (GRE) and are strongly encouraged to take the Subject Test in chemistry. International students must submit scores on both the General Test and Subject Test in chemistry and the results of the Test of English as a Foreign Language (TOEFL). Applicants are urged to take the appropriate tests in October or December. Application forms for admission and support may be obtained directly from the Graduate School of Arts and Sciences or the chemistry department. Applicants are encouraged to visit the University; an appointment can be arranged with the department beforehand. Tufts University is an equal opportunity institution.

Correspondence and Information

Graduate Committee Chair
Department of Chemistry
Tufts University
Medford, Massachusetts 02155
Telephone: 617-627-3441
Fax: 617-627-3443
World Wide Web: http://chem.tufts.edu

Tufts University

THE FACULTY AND THEIR RESEARCH

Marc d'Alarcao, Ph.D., Illinois. Synthesis and evaluation of compounds of biological interest, especially inositol phosphates, nucleosides, and fatty acids; enzyme mechanisms.

Robert R. Dewald, Ph.D., Michigan State. Mechanistic studies of metal-ammonia reductions, chemistry of metal metalides and nonaqueous solvents.

Terry E. Haas, Ph.D., MIT. Physical inorganic chemistry; structure and electronic structure and optical, electronic, and transport properties of thin films, solids, and thin-film devices; synthesis and characterization of thin films; X-ray crystallography.

Karl H. Illinger, Ph.D., Princeton. Intermolecular forces and collisional perturbation of molecular spectra; experimental infrared spectroscopy, with applications in environmental chemistry; experimental measurement of absolute infrared intensities and structural correlations of this and other molecular properties employing ab initio quantum-mechanical calculations; infrared radiative properties of atmospheric gases.

Jonathan E. Kenny, Ph.D., Chicago. In situ detection of contaminants in soil and groundwater using laser-induced fluorescence and fiber optics, ab initio calculations of IR frequencies and intensities for estimation of global warming potential, conformational analysis of alkylated aromatic molecules, electronic and vibrational structure of nonbenzenoid aromatics, radiationless transitions of excited electronic states.

Samuel P. Kounaves, Ph.D., Geneva (Switzerland). Computerized electrochemical techniques with applications in environmental analysis and material science, development of IC-based ultramicroelectrodes and enzyme-based biosensors, environmental electroanalytical chemistry, nucleation studies, electrodeposition of alloys.

Krishna Kumar, Ph.D., Brown. Organic and bioorganic chemistry, materials science, autocatalytic reaction mechanisms, self-assembly, artificial enzymes and nanochemistry.

Clemens Richert, Ph.D. (human biology), Munich (Germany); Ph.D. (chemistry), ETH, Zurich (Switzerland). Synthesis, structural characterization, and in vitro testing of biologically interesting molecules, with an emphasis on analogues of natural biomolecules and applications in antisense inhibition of gene expression and photodynamic therapy.

Albert Robbat Jr., Ph.D., Penn State. Development of analytical methods for hazardous-waste site field investigations—gas, liquid, and supercritical chromatographies and a mobile mass spectrometer; PCBs in marine life, ocean water, and sediment; PAHs in hazardous-waste incinerator and coal combustion emissions; volatile and semivolatile organics in soil, ground, and surface water; electron transfer mechanisms and rate measurements in biological systems.

Elena V. Rybak-Akimova, Ph.D., Kiev (Ukraine). Coordination, supramolecular, and bioinorganic chemistry; synthetic macrocyclic transition metal complexes; molecular tweezers; redox catalysis and enzyme mimics; dioxygen binding and activation; spatiotemporal self-organization (oscillating reactions and pattern formation) in chemical reactions; molecular modeling of macrocyclic supramolecular aggregates.

Mary J. Shultz, Ph.D., MIT. Development of methods for probing liquid surfaces, either gas/liquid or solid/liquid; probing dynamical processes at liquid surfaces; mechanism of heterogeneous photochemistry of transition metal oxides; heterogeneous processes in atmospheric chemistry, including ozone depletion and photochemistry.

Robert D. Stolow, Ph.D., Illinois. NMR and computational studies of conformational equilibria in solution and in the gas phase; the influence of electrostatic interactions among polar groups upon conformational energies; computer-assisted synthetic analysis.

Arthur L. Utz, Ph.D., Wisconsin. Gas-surface reactions relevant to materials, environmental, and catalytic chemistry; supersonic molecular beam, laser excitation, and ultrahigh vacuum techniques; laser-induced chemistry at surfaces; mechanisms for heterogeneous catalysis; vibrational and translational energy as synthetic tools in materials chemistry.

David R. Walt, Ph.D., SUNY at Stony Brook. Fiber-optic chemical sensors, immunochemistry, neuroscience, microfabrication.

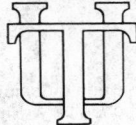

TULANE UNIVERSITY

Department of Chemistry

Program of Study

Tulane's graduate program in chemistry offers a balance between course work and research. The training that students receive prepares them for careers in industrial and/or academic settings. During the first two semesters, in addition to starting courses, students meet with individual faculty members and select a dissertation research adviser and dissertation committee. After the first year, the emphasis shifts toward research. Completion of the Ph.D. degree has the following requirements: four core courses and two additional courses, presentation of a literature seminar and seminar attendance, a dissertation research prospectus, successful completion of six cumulative examinations, sufficient progress in research, a final departmental seminar based on the dissertation research, and an oral defense of the dissertation research. Research groups tend to be of moderate size, fostering a close working relationship between the faculty member and the students in his/her group. Students, after receiving the appropriate training, have daily access to all departmental research facilities.

Research Facilities

The department maintains a wide range of instrumentation for the characterization of molecular systems. All major equipment in the department is available for use by graduate students. In addition to the equipment listed below, a large amount of specialized equipment is housed in individual research groups. Major departmental equipment includes a 200-MHz multinuclear NMR, a 400-MHz multinuclear NMR, a 300-MHz solids NMR, two GC/quadrupole mass spectrometers; a cluster of IBM RISC workstation computers (IBM), Silicon Graphics workstation computers, an automated X-ray diffractometer, a scanning AUGER spectrometer (GE), and an X-band ESR spectrometer. The University also manages a Coordinated Instrumentation Facility (CIF), housed in Boggs Hall, neighboring the chemistry department. Equipment run by the technical staff of the facility includes a 500-MHz NMR spectrometer (GE), a high-resolution mass spectrometer (Kratos), a scanning electron microscope, X-ray powder diffractometers, a GS/mass spectrometer (HP), elemental analysis equipment, graphite furnace atomic absorption, and an ICP spectrometer. Graduate students are allowed to use equipment in the CIF following training sessions offered by the technical staff. A large amount of laser spectroscopic and photochemical equipment is located in the Center for Photoinduced Processes, housed in the chemistry department. The Center supports major efforts in experimental physical chemistry, inorganic spectroscopy, and organic photochemisty. The laser facilities are designed to study the spectroscopy of excited molecules on the millisecond to femtosecond time scales. Laser facilities include nine excimer lasers (ns), nine dye lasers (ns), three Nd:YAG lasers, two nitrogen lasers (ns), two Argon ion laser systems (cw), one ring dye laser, one mode locked Argon ion laser (Ps), and a Ti sappheir laser.

Financial Aid

The department provides students with income in the form of research assistantships, teaching assistantships, or Board of Regents fellowships. For the 1999–2000 academic year, the nine-month assistantship stipend is $12,000. In addition, virtually all students receive summer support that typically ranges from $1000 to $3500 depending on the associated duties. During the academic year, teaching duties involve six to eight hours per week with assignments in laboratory instruction for general, organic, physical, or analytical chemistry. Each year the department awards two to four Board of Regents Fellowships to incoming students. These fellowships include four years of stipend support at $17,000 per calendar year. Qualified applicants to the graduate program are automatically considered for these fellowships. Once a student obtains financial assistance, either at admission or later, and maintains good academic performance, it is customary to continue that funding or increase it.

Cost of Study

Most graduate students receive full tuition scholarships. Students are required to pay a university fee of $300 per semester.

Living and Housing Costs

Graduate students generally find reasonably priced housing in the pleasant residential neighborhoods adjacent to the Tulane campus. On-campus housing is also available to graduate students on a first-come, first-served basis.

Student Group

The total number of graduate students in chemistry is currently about 60. Postdoctoral students number about 15. A wide variety of academic, ethnic, and national backgrounds are represented among these students.

Student Outcomes

An advanced degree in chemistry can provide access to many different career possibilities. Chemists in fields as diverse as biotechnology and semiconductors work in positions as different as bench chemist and information manager. Over the past few years graduates have established careers at places such as Abbott Labs, Du Pont, Ciba Geigy Pharmaceuticals, University of Arkansas, Johnson Matthey, Calgon Carbide, SmithKline Beecham, Loyola University, International Paper, University of Wisconsin–Oshkosh, Tuskeegee University, Southern University of Louisiana, Xavier University, Aldrich Chemical, and the Los Alamos National Laboratory. In addition, many recent Tulane graduates have continued in research with postdoctoral appointments at locations such as Caltech, MIT, Los Alamos National Laboratory, Sandia National Laboratory, Northwestern University, Oak Ridge National Laboratory, Carnegie Mellon Institute, University of Michigan, University of Chicago, Naval Research Laboratories, NASA, and NIST. Furthermore, several graduates have been awarded prestigious national fellowships to pursue their postdoctoral research.

Location

Tulane University is located in a pleasant residential area of New Orleans. This location provides both a college environment and convenient access to the multitude of activities available in this exciting city. With its unique history of French, Spanish, and African origins and two centuries to develop its own traditions, New Orleans has perfected the technique of having fun. Mardi Gras is celebrated each year, when as many as a million people have a virtual street party along the parade routes. In early May, New Orleans also holds a very special music festival, the Jazz and Heritage Festival. It is two weekends of the famous and best of jazz, including many of New Orleans' own exciting new and traditional groups. In addition to the many cultural events sponsored by Tulane, the city offers a symphony orchestra, opera, theaters, museums, a zoo, a world-class aquarium, and a lively local tradition of jazz and rhythm and blues clubs.

The University

Tulane University, which was funded in 1834, comprises 11 academic divisions with 6,500 undergraduates and 3,800 graduate students. The College of Arts and Sciences and Newcomb College are liberal arts colleges for men and women, respectively. Schools of Architecture, Business, and Engineering offer both undergraduate and graduate programs. Other divisions include the Graduate School and Schools of Law, Medicine, Public Health and Tropical Medicine, and Social Work. The juxtaposition of so many disciplines on one campus creates a lively academic atmosphere. At the same time, the relatively small size of the individual schools and colleges preserves an identity and intimacy for students that is more typical of a small college than a large university.

Applying

Application forms and information can be requested by writing to Karen Bowers, Department of Chemistry, Tulane University, New Orleans, Louisiana 70118. While applications are accepted throughout the year, applicants are encouraged to apply as early as possible for admission in the fall semester. In addition to the completed application form, college transcripts, three letters of recommendation, and GRE scores should be sent to the chemistry department. International students are also required to submit TOEFL scores.

Correspondence and Information

Karen Bowers
Department of Chemistry
Tulane University
New Orleans, Louisiana 70118
World Wide Web: http://www.tulane.edu/~chemstry

Tulane University

THE FACULTY AND THEIR RESEARCH

The Department of Chemistry offers a broad range of research opportunities to its graduate students. Faculty research interest include organic chemistry, inorganic chemistry, physical chemistry, biochemistry, environmental chemistry, materials chemistry, and theoretical chemistry.

William L. Alworth, Ph.D., 1965, Berkeley. Bio-organic chemistry: design, synthesis, and testing of compounds containing appropriate chemical functionality to serve as selective inhibitors of the cytochrome P450 isozymes involved in the metabolic activation of chemical carcinogens.

Larry Byers, Ph.D., 1972, Princeton. Biochemistry: mechanisms of enzyme action using structure reactivity relationships, kinetic isotope effects, and transition state analog inhibitors.

Harry Ensley, Ph.D., 1975, Harvard. Synthetic organic chemistry and the synthesis of biologically active natural products, the development of new synthetic reagents and procedures, study of the mechanism of ene reactions with electron-deficient olefins.

Mark J. Fink, Ph.D., 1983, Wisconsin. Synthetic inorganic chemistry: synthetic, mechanistic, and structural aspects of main group organometallic chemistry, with emphasis on the chemistry of reactive intermediates and compounds with novel structures; the chemistry of the metal-silicon bond as applied to the platinum group metals.

Michael F. Herman, Ph.D., 1980, Chicago. Theoretical chemistry: the development of semiclassical methods for the evolution of quantum mechanical systems, development of methods for the evaluation of energy relaxation rates of molecules in condensed phases, dynamics and viscoelastic response of concentrated polymer systems.

Brent Koplitz, Ph.D., 1985, Princeton. Physical chemistry: molecular dynamics, photochemistry, and laser spectroscopy; gas-phase, site-specific photochemistry; photochemistry of compounds relevant to atmospheric chemistry; laser-induced, gas-phase photochemistry of molecules used to grow III-V semiconductor materials.

Melvyn Levy, Ph.D., 1971, Indiana. Theoretical chemistry: the development and understanding of density functional theory concepts and methods for quantum mechanical electronic structure calculations.

Chao-Jun Li, Ph.D., 1992, McGill. Synthetic organic chemistry: synthesis of advanced materials for electronic, magnetic, and biological applications; development of more efficient methods for the synthesis of biologically active organic compounds; study of environmentally benign organic reactions, such as aqueous organic reactions.

Gary McPherson, Ph.D., 1969, Illinois. Inorganic chemistry: use of modern spectroscopic techniques to characterize chemically interesting systems, including high symmetry crystals containing pairs and extended arrays of metal ions; organogels; nanoparticle/polymer composites; water/soil/sediment samples from environmental field studies.

Joel T. Mague, Ph.D., 1965, MIT. Inorganic chemistry: synthetic organotransition metal chemistry and X-ray crystallography.

V. Ramamurthy, Ph.D., 1974, Hawaii. Organic chemistry: photochemistry and photophysics of organic molecules incorporated within organized assemblies: zeolites, cyclodextrins, and crystals; solid-state photochemistry; correlation of photochemical reactivity with crystal packing; enantioselective photoreactions.

Russell H. Schmehl, Ph.D., 1981, North Carolina. Inorganic chemistry: synthesis of molecular systems that can serve as light harvesting arrays for solar energy conversion, characterization of these systems using electroanalytical methods and time-resolved laser spectroscopy, development of methods for preparing light harvesting arrays on surfaces.

Daniel K. Schwartz, Ph.D (physics), 1991, Harvard. Physical chemistry: study of structural and statistical mechanical properties of ultra-thin films by atomic force microscopy; systems, including Langmuir monolayers, Langmuir-Blodgett films and self-assembled monolayers; study of phase transitions and hydrodynamic flow in these systems.

Mark Sulkes, Ph.D., 1978, Cornell. Physical chemistry: spectroscopic studies of chemically and biologically important chromophores in supersonic free jet or molecular beam systems using a variety of laser techniques.

Pernilla Wittung-Stafshede, Ph.D., Chalmers (Sweden). Biophysical chemistry: spectroscopic studies of protein stability and folding kinetics, with focus on pleated-sheet structures and cofactor-containing proteins; membrane-transport properties of DNA-like genetic drugs.

SELECTED PUBLICATIONS

Foroozesh, M. K., et al. (**W. L. Alworth**). Aryl acetylenes as mechanism-based inhibitors of cytochrome P450-dependent monooxygenase enzymes. *Chem. Res. Toxicol.* 10:91–102, 1997.

Beebe, L. E., et al. (**W. L. Alworth**). Mechanism-based inhibition of mouse P450 2b-10 by selected arylalkynes. *Biochem. Pharmacol.* 52:1507–13, 1996.

Roberts, E. S., S. Pernecky, **W. L. Alworth**, and P. F. Hollenberg. A role for threonine 302 in the mechanism-based inactivation of P450 2B4 by 2-ethynylnaphthalene. *Arch. Biochem. Biophys.* 331:170–6, 1996.

Beebe, L. E., et al. (**W. L. Alworth**). Effect of dietary aroclor 1254 exposure on lung and kidney cytochromes P450 in female rats: Evidence for P450 1A2 expression in kidney. *Chemico-Biol. Interact.* 97:215–27, 1995.

Roberts, E. S., et al. (**W. L. Alworth**). Mechanism-based inactivation of cytochrome P450 2B1 by 9-ethynylphenanthrene. *Arch. Biochem Biophys.* 323:295–302, 1995.

Roberts, E. S., et al. (**W. L. Alworth**). Mechanistic studies of 9-ethynylphenanthrene-inactivated cytochrome P450 2B1. *Arch. Biochem Biophys.* 323:303–12, 1995.

Roberts, E. S., et al. (**W. L. Alworth**). Identification of active-site peptides from ^{3}H-labeled 2-ethynylnaphthalene-inactivated P450 2B1 and 2B4 using amino acid sequencing and mass spectrometry. *Biochemistry* 33:3766–71, 1994.

De, D., **L. D. Byers**, and D. J. Krogstad. Antimalarials: Synthesis of 4-aminoquinolines that circumvent drug resistance in malaria parasites. *J. Heterocycl. Chem.* 34:315–20, 1997.

Veress, L., et al. (**L. D. Byers**). The role of his-176 in the chemical mechanism and thermal stability of glyceraldehyde-3-phosphate dehydrogenase. *FASEB J.* 10:1385, 1996.

De, D., et al. (**L. D. Byers** and **J. T. Mague**). Synthesis of (E)-2-(4,7-dichloroquinolines). *Tetrahedron Lett.* 36:205, 1995.

Gollapudi, S., et al. (**L. D. Byers** and **H. E. Ensley**). Isolation of a previously unidentified polysaccharide (MAR-10) from Hyssop officinalis that exhibits strong activity against human immunodeficiency virus type 1. *Biochem. Biophys. Res. Commun.* 210:145–51, 1995.

Li, Y. K., and **L. D. Byers**. Intramolecular nucleophilic attack by phosphonates. *J. Chem. Res.* 26, 1993.

Li, Y. K., and **L. D. Byers**. Phosphonate inhibitors of GPD and phosphoglycerate kinase. *Biochem. Biophys. Acta* 1164:17–21, 1993.

Mueller, A., et al. (**H. E. Ensley**). The application of various protic acids in the extraction of (1→3)-β-D-glucan from *Saccharomyces cerevisiae. Carboyhdr. Res.* 299:203–8, 1997.

Mueller, A., et al. (**H. E. Ensley**). Receptor binding and internalization of a water-soluble (1→3)-β-D-glucan biologic response modifier in two monocyte/macrophage cell lines. *J. Immunol.* 154:3418–25, 1996.

Baba, A. I., **H. E. Ensley**, and **R. H. Schmehl**. Influences of bridging ligand unsaturation on excited state behavior in mono and bimetallic Ru(II) diimine complexes. *Inorg. Chem.* 34:1198, 1995.

Ensley, H. E., et al. NMR analysis of a water-insoluble (1→3)-β-D-glucan isolated from *Saccharomyces cerevisiae. Carbohydr. Res.* 258:307–11, 1994.

Ensley, H. E., J. T. Barber, M. A. Polito, and A. I. Oliver. Toxicity and metabolism of 2,4-dichlorophenol by the aquatic angiosperm, *Lemna gibba. Environ. Toxocol. Chem.* 13:325–31, 1994.

Fink, M. J., and D. B. Puranik. The structure of 1-tris(trimethylsilyl)silyl–3,4,5,6-tetrakis(trimethylsilyl)cyclohex-1-ene. *J. Chem. Cryst.* 24:293–9, 1994.

Herman, M. F. Improving the accuracy of semiclassical wavepacket propagation using integral conditioning techniques. *Chem. Phys. Lett.* 245:445–52, 1997.

Herman, M. F., B. Panajotova, and K. T. Lorenz. A quantitative theory of linear chain polymer dynamics in the melt: I. General scaling behavior. *J. Chem. Phys.* 105:1153, 1996.

Herman, M. F., B. Panajotova, and K. T. Lorenz. A quantitative theory of linear chain polymer dynamics in the melt: II. Comparison with simulation data. *J. Chem. Phys.* 105:1162, 1996.

Lorenz, K. T., et al. (**M. F. Herman** and **B. Koplitz**). Understanding the role of stark effects when probing the nuclear hyperfine states of atomic hydrogen. *Chem. Phys. Lett.* 261:145–54, 1996.

Herman, M. F. The role of correlated many chain motions in linear chain polymer melts. *J. Chem. Phys.* 103:4324, 1995.

Tong, P., and **M. F. Herman**. Viscoelastic response of bidisperse melts in the lateral motion model. *J. Chem. Phys.* 102:7700, 1995.

Herman, M. F. Dynamics by semiclassical methods. *Ann. Rev. of Phys. Chem.* 45:83, 1994.

Arce, J. C., and **M. F. Herman**. Semiclassical surface-hopping approximations for the calculation of solvent-induced vibrational-relaxation rate constants. *J. Chem. Phys.* 101:7520, 1994.

Panayotov, V., et al. (**B. Koplitz**). Thin film deposition via laser ablation. *Mater. Res. Soc. Proc.* 441, 1996.

Wang, Z., M. G. Mathews, and **B. Koplitz**. Direct evidence for preferential β C-H bond cleavage resulting from 248 nm photolysis of the η-propyl radical using selectively-deuterated 1-bromopropane precursors. *J. Phys. Chem.* 99:6913–6, 1995.

Panayotov, V., et al. (**B. Koplitz**). Selective removal of potassium from $K_4In_4Sb_6$ via laser ablation/ionization. *App. Phys. Lett.* 66:2242–3, 1995.

Yen, Y.-F., Z. Wang, B. Xue, and **B. Koplitz**. Site propensities for HCl and DCl formation in the reaction of Cl with selectively-deuterated propanes. *J. Phys. Chem.* 98:4–7, 1994.

Levy, M., and N. H. March. Line-integral formulas for exchange and correlation separately. *Phys. Rev. A* 55:1885, 1997.

Görling, A., and **M. Levy**. Hybrid schemes combining the Hartree-Fock Method and Density-Functional Theory: Underlying formalism and properties of correlation functionals. *J. Chem. Phys.* 106:2675, 1997.

Levy, M. Additive density functional correlation corrections to single particle theories. *Int. J. Quantum Chem.* 61:281, 1997.

Levy, M., N. H. March, and N. C. Handy. On the adiabatic connection method, and scaling of electron interactions in the Thomas-Fermi Limit. *J. Chem. Phys.* 104:1989, 1996.

Levy, M. Excitation energies from density functional orbital energies. *Phys. Rev. A* 52:R4313, 1995. *(Rapid Communication)*

Levy, M., and A. Görling. Correlation-energy density-functional formulas from correlating first-order density matrices. *Phys. Rev. A* 52:R1808, 1995. *(Rapid Communication)*

Levy, M., and J. P. Perdew. Density functionals for exchange and correlation energies: Exact conditions and comparison of approximations. *Int. J. Quantum Chem.* 49:539–48, 1994.

Li, C. J., et al. Palladium catalyzed polymerization of acetylene gas with aryl diiodides: Novel synthesis of poly(areneethylenes) oligomers and polymers. *J. Chem. Soc. Chem. Commun.* 1569, 1997.

Yi, X. H., Y. Meng, and **C. J. Li**. Indium reactions in water: Efficient synthesis of beta-hydroxyl esters. *Tetrahedron Lett.* 38:4731, 1997.

Li, C. J., and T. H. Chan. *Organic Reactions in Aqueous Media.* New York: John Wiley & Sons, Inc., 1997.

Li, C. J., D. Wang, and W. T. Slaven IV. Synthesis of a bis-binaphthol. *Tetrahedron Lett.* 37:4459, 1996.

Li, C. J., et al. (**J. T. Mague**). Novel carbocyle englargement in aqueous medium. *J. Am. Chem. Soc.* 118:4216, 1996.

Li, C. J. Barbier-Grignard type of reactions in aqueous media: Scope, mechanism and synthetic applications. *Tetrahedron Rep.* 396(52):5643–68, 1996.

Mague, J. T. Heterobimetallic complexes derived from cyclopentadienylcyano(η[1]-bis(diphenylphosphino)methane)nickel. The crystal and molecular structure of cyclopentadienylnickel(μ-bis(diphenylphosphino)methane)cyano(triphenylphosphine)platinum. *J. Coord. Chem.* 41:327, 1997.

Apblett, A. W., G. D. Georgieva, and **J. T. Mague**. Synthesis, spectroscopic and thermal decomposition studies of alkali metal salts of 2-oximinopropionate. *Inorg. Chem.* 36:2656, 1997.

Copeland, E. P., I. A. Kahwa, **J. T. Mague**, and **G. L. McPherson**. Novel mixed-valence vanadium (IV/V) molecule exhibiting unusual electron transfer delocalization over the $[V_2O_3]^{3+}$ core. *J. Chem. Soc. Dalton Trans.* 2849–52, 1997.

Mague, J. T. Conformational diversity in the solid state structures of $[Rh_2$ $(\mu$-$CH_3N(P(OCH_3)_2)_2)_2)(CH_3N(P(OCH_3)_2)_2)_2)]X_2(X=O_3SCF_3$, $B(C_6H_5)_4)$. *Inorg. Chim. Acta* 229:17, 1995.

Mague, J. T., and Z. Lin. Rhenium(I) complexes of bis (difluorophosphino)methylamine. The crystal and molecular structure of hexacarbonyldi-μ-bromo-μ-bis(difluorophosphine) methylamine-dirhenium(I). *J. Coord. Chem.* 34:45, 1995.

Mague, J. T., and Z. Lin. A cationic rhenium/platinum complex:

Tulane University

Selected Publications (continued)

fac-tricarbonylrheniumbis(μ-methylaminobis(difluorophosphine) triphenylphosphineplatinumtrifluoromethane-sulfonate. *Acta Crystallogr.* C51:2508, 1995.

Mague, J. T. 'Short-Bite' ligands in cluster synthesis. *J. Cluster Sci.* 6:217, 1995.

Landtiser, R., et al. (**J. T. Mague** and **M. J. Fink**). Cleavage of bis(ithiophosphinyl) disulfanes, $R_2P(S)SSP(S)R_2$ (R = Et, Ph) by a novel low valent palladium dimer. *Inorg. Chem.* 34:6141–4, 1995.

Mague, J. T., C. A. Recatto, and **M. J. Fink**. Solid state structure of oxalato(bis(dicyclohexylphosphino)ethane)platinum(II)-acetonitile solvate''. *J. Chem. Cryst.* 24:191–3, 1994.

Mague, J. T. The structure of *fac*-bromotricarbonyl(bis(dimethyl-phosphino)methane)manganese(I) and -rhenium (I). *Acta Crystallogr.* C50:1391, 1994.

Premchandran, R., et al. (**G. L. McPherson**). Enzyme catalyzed synthesis of thiol-containing polymers for the preparation of polymer-CdS nanocomposites. *Chem. Mater.* 9:1342, 1997.

O'Connor, C. J., et al. (**G. L. McPherson**). Ferrite synthesis in microstructured media: Template effects and magnetic properties. *J. Appl. Phys.* 81:8, 1997.

Gharavi, A. R., and **G. L. McPherson**. UV emissions from Gd^{3+} ions excited by energy transfer from pairs of photoexcited Er^{3+} ions: Up-conversion luminescence from $CsMgCl_3$ crystals doped with Gd^{3+} and Er^{3+}. *J. Opt. Soc. Am. B* (Special Issue) 11:913, 1994.

O'Connor, C. J., et al. (**G. L. McPherson**). Superparamagnetism of ferrite particles dispersed in spherical polymeric particles. *IEEE Trans. Magnetism Magn. Mater.* 30:4954, 1994.

Tata, M., V. T. John, Y. Y. Waguespack, and **G. L. McPherson**. Intercalation in novel organogels with a "stacked" phenol microstructure. *J. Am. Chem. Soc.* 116:9464, 1994.

Pitchumani, K., et al. (**V. Ramamurthy**). Generation, entrapment and reactivity of long lived organic carbocations and cation radicals within a supramolecular assembly: Ca Y zeolite. *J. Chem. Soc. Chem. Commun.* 181, 1997.

Robbins, R., and **V. Ramamurthy**. Generation and reactivity of singlet oxygen within zeolites: Remarkable control of hydroperoxidation of alkenes. *J. Chem. Soc. Chem. Commun.* 1071, 1997.

Pitcumani, K., A. Joy, N. Prevost, and **V. Ramamurthy**. Zeolite as a reagent and as a catalyst: Reduction and isomerization of stilbenes by Ca Y. *J. Chem. Soc. Chem. Commun.* 127, 1997.

Li, X., and **V. Ramamurthy**. Selective oxidation of olefins within organic cation exchanged zeolites. *J. Am. Chem. Soc.* 118:10666, 1996.

Pitcumani, K., M. Warrier, and **V. Ramamurthy**. Remarkable product selectivity during photo-fries and photo-claisen rearrangements within zeolites. *J. Am. Chem. Soc.* 118:9428, 1996.

Ramamurthy, V. Excited state chemistry of organic molecules included within zeolites. In *Surface Photochemistry*, p. 65, ed. M. Anpo. Chichester: John Wiley, 1996.

Leibovitch, M., et al. (**V. Ramamurthy**). Asymmetric induction in photochemical reactions conducted in zeolites and in the crystalline state. *J. Am. Chem. Soc.* 118:1219, 1996.

Ramamurthy, V., and N. J. Turro. Photochemistry of organic molecules within zeolites: Role of cations. In *Inclusion Chemistry within Zeolites: Nanoscale Materials by Design*, pp. 239–82; eds. N. Herron and D. R. Corbin. Holland: Kluwer Academic Press, 1995.

Simon, J. A., et al. (**R. H. Schmehl**). Intramolecular electronic energy transfer in a conformationally locked Ru(II) diimine donor-pyrene acceptor complex: Weak electronic coupling through a single σ bond. *J. Am. Chem. Soc.* 119:11012, 1997.

Sauppe, J., et al. (**R. H. Schmehl**). Photochemistry with Pt doped, dye sensitized niobium titanate colloidal semiconductors. *J. Phys. Chem.* 101:2508, 1997.

Nasr, C., et al. (**R. H. Schmehl**). Photosensitization of composite semiconductor thin films. Photoelectrochemical behavior of SnO_2/CdS coupled nanocrystallites with a ruthenium polypyridyl complex. *J. Phys. Chem.* 101:7480, 1997.

Taffarel, E., et al. (**R. H. Schmehl**). Coexistence of ligand localized and MLCT excited states in a 2-(pyridyl)benzoquinoline complex of Ru(II). *Inorg. Chem.* 35:2127, 1996.

Liang, Y., A. I. Baba, and **R. H. Schmehl**. Intramolecular exchange energy transfer in a bridged bimetallic transition metal complex: Calculation of rate constants using emission spectral fitting parameters. *J. Phys. Chem.* 100:18408, 1996.

Shaw, J. R., et al. (**R. H. Schmehl**). Toward the development of supramolecular metal complex light harvesting arrays: Factors affecting photoinduced energy transfer in bimetallic complexes. *New J. Chem.* 20:749, 1996.

Liang, Y., and **R. H. Schmehl**. Coordination chemistry at a surface: Polymetallic complexes prepared on quartz by alternate deposition of Fe(II) and Ru(II) centres. *J. Chem. Soc. Chem. Commun.* 1007, 1995.

Kurnaz, M. L., and **D. K. Schwartz**. A technique for direct observation of particles under shear in a Langmuir monolayer. *J. Rheol.* 41:1173, 1997.

Sikes, H. D., J. T. Woodward IV, and **D. K. Schwartz**. Pattern formation in a substrate-induced phase transition during Langmuir-Blodgett transfer. *J. Phys. Chem.* 100:9093, 1996.

Kurnaz, M. L., and **D. K. Schwartz**. Morphology of micro-phase separation in arachide acid/cadmium arachidate Langmuir Blodgett multilayers. *J. Phys. Chem.* 100:11113, 1996.

Woodward, J. T., and **D. K. Schwartz**. In situ observation of self-assembled monolayer growth. *J. Am. Chem. Soc.* 118:7861, 1996.

Viswanathan, R., L. L. Madsen, J. A. N. Zasadzinski, and **D. K. Schwartz**. Liquid to hexatic to crystalline transition in Langmuir-Blodgett films. *Science* 269:51, 1995.

Schwartz, D. K., C. M. Knobler, and R. Bruinsma. Direct observations of Langmuir monolayer flow through a channel. *Phys. Rev. Let.* 73:2841, 1994.

Zasadzinski, J. A., et al. (**D. K. Schwartz**). Langmuir-Blodgett films. *Science* 263:1726, 1994.

Huang, Y., S. Arnold, and **M. Sulkes**. Spectroscopy and fluorescence lifetimes of jet cooled 7-azaindole: Electronic states and solvent complex geometry. *J. Phys. Chem.* 100:4734, 1996.

Huang, Y., and **M. Sulkes**. Anomalously short fluorescence lifetimes in jet-cooled 4-hydroxyindole: Evidence for excited state tautomerism and proton transfer in clusters. *Chem. Phys. Lett.* 254:242, 1996.

Huang, Y., and **M. Sulkes**. Jet-cooled solvent complexes with indoles. *J. Phys. Chem.* 100:16479, 1996.

Sulkes, M. Conformational analysis of jet cooled tryptophan analogs and histamine using the MM3(94) force field: Comparison with experiment. *J. Comput. Chem.* 16:973, 1995.

Huang, Y., **M. Sulkes**, and **M. J. Fink**. Photolysis of some organosilylene precursors in a molecular beam. *J. Organomet. Chem.* 499:1–5, 1995.

Arnold, S., L. Tong, and **M. Sulkes**. Fluorescence lifetimes of substituted indoles in solution and in free jets: Evidence for intramolecules charge transfer quenching. *J. Phys. Chem.* 98:2325, 1994.

Wittung-Stafshede, P., B. G. Malmstrom, J. R. Winkler, and H. B. Gray. Folding of deoxy myoglobin triggered by electron transfer. *J. Phys. Chem.* 102:5599–601, 1998.

Telford, J., **P. Wittung-Stafshede**, H. B. Gray, and J. R. Winkler. Protein folding triggered by electron transfer. *Acc. Chem. Res.* 31:755–63, 1998.

Wittung-Stafshede, P. Genetic drugs—when will it come to the drugstore? *Science* 281:657–8, 1998.

Wittung-Stafshede, P., P. Nielsen, B. NordÉn. Extended DNA-recognition repertoire of PNA. *Biochemistry* 36:7973–9, 1997.

Wittung-Stafshede, P., H. B. Gray, and J. R. Winkler. Rapid formation of a four helix bundle. Cytochrome b562 folding triggered by electron transfer. *J. Am. Chem. Soc.* 119:9562–3, 1997.

Wittung-Stafshede, P., et al. DNA-like double helix formed by peptide nucleic acid. *Nature* 368:561–3, 1994.

UNIVERSITY OF CALIFORNIA, DAVIS

Department of Chemistry

Programs of Study

The Department of Chemistry offers graduate curricula that lead to the Doctor of Philosophy degree or the Master of Science degree. Upon entering, students take four of five placement examinations in the fields of analytical, inorganic, organic, and physical chemistry and biochemistry. Students select their research director near the end of the first quarter. Because of the diverse research interests of the 34 faculty members, students can expect to find a wide selection of challenging research topics. Requirements for the Ph.D. degree include serving the equivalent of three academic quarters as a quarter-time teaching assistant; satisfying specific core/elective course requirements in the student's field of interest; taking an oral qualifying examination during the fifth quarter in residence, which examines the student's mastery of the dissertation research field, with an additional presentation and defense of a research proposal outside the immediate area of research; presenting a seminar during the third year of residence; and pursuing full-time research during the fourth year in preparation for a written dissertation. The normal length of the entire Ph.D. program is four years.

Research Facilities

Graduate students have the opportunity to use state-of-the-art instrumentation in their research. Research groups in the department routinely use sophisticated molecular graphics, lasers, high-field NMR, mass spectrometry, EPR, and HPLC equipment. The department maintains a variety of microcomputer and workstation computer systems that students are encouraged to use. Research within the department is supported by well-equipped shop facilities with machinists, electronics technicians, a glassblower, and a stockroom staff that is readily available for design, assembly, and consultation services. Campus facilities include the Center for Structural Biology, the Nuclear Magnetic Resonance Facility, the Institute for Theoretical Dynamics, the campus Facility for Advanced Instrumentation, the Protein Structure Laboratory, the Image Processing Facility, the Crocker Cyclotron, the Bodega Marine Lab, the Institute for Marine Resources, and the California Regional Primate Center. The University and medical school libraries are comprehensive and well stocked.

Financial Aid

Most first-year graduate students hold teaching assistantships at approximately $13,329 per academic year. This income is usually supplemented by research assistantships during the summer months (up to $3200). The Department of Chemistry also offers several Borge Scholarships to entering students. Awards are based on grades, research experience, and letters of recommendation. Support for continuing students is available with teaching or research assistantships and intramural fellowships. Various agencies that support research include the National Science Foundation, the National Institutes of Health, the Department of Energy, NATO, the Sloan Foundation, and the American Chemical Society.

Cost of Study

Student fees are $4483 per year. If a student is appointed as a teaching assistant, a partial fee remission reduces the fees to $1800 per year. If a student is appointed as a research assistant, the fees are paid by the research grant. If a student is a non-California resident, the tuition of $10,322 is waived for qualified first-year domestic students.

Living and Housing Costs

Accommodations that range from private rooms to studio apartments to townhouse apartments and individual houses are available for rent. The University maintains 180 rooms in the graduate residence hall for single students and 476 one- and two-bedroom apartments for student family housing. For additional housing information, students can visit the Web site at http://www.housing.ucdavis.edu.

Student Group

The total number of students is approximately 23,000, with more than 5,500 students in graduate and professional curricula. The total number of graduate students in chemistry is approximately 140.

Location

The campus, composed of about 5,500 acres and surrounded by rich agricultural fields, includes a formal arboretum intertwined by a 2-mile footpath. Davis lies in the Sacramento Valley, close to the state capital. The Pacific Ocean, Lake Tahoe, and the Sierra Nevada are within a 2-hour drive of the campus; San Francisco and Napa Valley are within a 1½-hour drive.

The University

Unique within the University of California system, the University of California, Davis offers a full range of undergraduate and graduate programs as well as professional school curricula in law, management, medicine, and veterinary medicine. Davis is renowned for its use of bicycles as a mode of transportation, with more than 50 miles of bike paths on campus and in the city. It is the largest of the nine campuses in acreage, second largest in budget, and third largest in enrollment.

Applying

Students are normally admitted in the fall. A bachelor's degree from a qualified college or university is required. Applications are obtained and processed directly through the Department of Chemistry. GRE scores are required of students who are applying for scholarships and/or fellowships. The deadline for the receipt of all application materials is May 15 or until the program is full.

Correspondence and Information

Dee Kindelt, Graduate Affairs Assistant
Department of Chemistry
University of California, Davis
One Shields Avenue
Davis, California 95616
Telephone: 530-752-0953
Fax: 530-752-8995
E-mail: kindelt@chem.ucdavis.edu
World Wide Web: http://www-chem.ucdavis.edu/

University of California, Davis

THE FACULTY AND THEIR RESEARCH

M. P. Augustine. Physical and biophysical chemistry: NMR and optical spectroscopy, protein and nucleic acid structure, nucleic acid binding, molecular excited states, time-dependent quantum mechanics.

A. L. Balch. Inorganic chemistry: bioinorganic chemistry, dioxygen activation, metalloprophyrin chemistry, heme degradation, fullerene chemistry, metal-metal bonding, luminescence properties, supramolecular chemistry.

E. Baldwin. Biological chemistry/structural biology: X-ray crystallography, protein engineering, enzyme mechanisms, biochemistry of DNA recombination enzymes and DNA-binding proteins, thermophillic proteins.

R. D. Britt. Biophysical chemistry: photosynthesis, biological metal and radical chemistry, advanced electron paramagnetic resonance methods.

T. Dieckmann. Biophysical chemistry: NMR spectroscopy, RNA and protein structure, interactions, catalysis, viral infections and cellular defense mechanisms.

W. R. Fawcett. Electrochemistry: double-layer structure and electrode kinetics at well-defined solid electrodes, FTIR studies of nonaqueous electrolytes and interfaces, lithium batteries.

W. H. Fink. Physical chemistry: theoretical and computational chemistry, especially electronic structure theory; quantum theory of structure and physical properties.

A. J. Fisher. Structural biology: protein structure-function, apoptosis, phytochrome.

W. M. Jackson. Chemical dynamics: laser photodissociation and laser detection, applications to comets, planetary atmospheres, combustion, and theoretical chemistry.

P. G. Jessop. Inorganic chemistry: homogeneous catalysis in supercritical fluids, green chemistry, fixation of greenhouse gases, coordination chemistry.

S. M. Kauzlarich. Solid-state inorganic and materials chemistry: synthesis and characterization of new materials, magnetic materials, Zintl compounds, semiconductor nanoclusters, magnetic nanoclusters.

P. B. Kelly. Analytical and physical chemistry: application of mass spectrometry to environmental chemistry, resonance Raman spectroscopy, combustion diagnostics.

M. J. Kurth. Organic chemistry: natural products synthesis, synthetic methodology, and immunochemistry.

G. N. LaMar. Biophysical and bioinorganic chemistry: NMR spectroscopy of metalloproteins, structure-function studies of heme and iron-sulfur cluster proteins, structural bases of hyperthermostability.

D. P. Land. Analytical and physical chemistry: surface analysis, laser desorption mass spectrometry, photoelectron spectroscopy, surface vibrational spectroscopy, surface microscopy, surface reaction mechanisms and kinetics.

C. B. Lebrilla. Analytical chemistry: bioanalytical mass spectrometry with specific applications to oligosaccharides, enantiomeric analysis of amino acids and peptides, application of Fourier transform mass spectrometry.

C. F. Meares. Biological chemistry: bioconjugate chemistry, molecular biology, mapping protein-protein interactions, bifunctional chelating agents, monoclonal antibodies.

T. F. Molinski. Organic chemistry: marine natural products isolation structure elucidation, NMR, synthesis.

K. P. Nambiar. Bioorganic chemistry: peptide design, synthesis, and folding; nucleic acid synthesis; synthesis of enzyme mimics.

M. H. Nantz. Organic chemistry: synthesis and methodology, lipids and liposome applications, organometallic chemistry.

A. Navrotsky. Solid-state and materials chemistry: microscopic features of structure and bonding to macroscopic thermodynamic behavior in minerals, ceramics, and other complex materials; high-temperature reaction calorimetry.

G. T. R. Palmore. Physical organic chemistry: biocatalysis, electrochemistry.

T. E. Patten. Polymer/materials chemistry: polymer synthesis and macromolecular architecture, development of living polymerization methods, synthesis of hybrid organic/inorganic nanoparticles and composites.

P. P. Power. Inorganic chemistry: synthesis, structure, and physical and chemical properties of inorganic and organometallic compounds.

P. A. Rock. Physical chemistry: chemical thermodynamics, environmental chemistry and aqueous geochemistry, energy utilization and conversion, biomineralization, chemical safety.

C. W. Schmid. Biophysical chemistry: structure and function of repetitive human DNA sequences.

N. E. Schore. Organic chemistry: applications of organometallic and polymer chemistry to organic synthesis.

B. Shen. Biological/bioorganic chemistry: chemistry, biochemistry, and genetics of secondary metabolite biosynthesis in microorganisms; combinatorial biosynthesis to create chemical diversity.

K. M. Smith. Organic and biological chemistry: synthesis, biosynthesis, biochemistry, and spectroscopy of porphyrins, hemes, chlorophylls, vitamin B_{12}, other tetrapyrrole pigments, and their metal complexes; heterocyclic chemistry; organic electrochemistry.

A. Stuchebrukhov. Theoretical chemistry and biophysics: electron transfer in biological molecules (proteins, DNA), molecular wires and molecular electronics, STM, molecular dynamics, relaxation processes.

D. S. Tinti. Physical chemistry: electronic spectroscopy of solids, magnetic resonance spectroscopy of excited triplet states, photophysics of excited states.

N. S. True. Physical chemistry: gas-phase NMR spectroscopy, applications to low-energy unimolecular processes and conformational kinetics, microwave spectra of flexible molecules.

S. C. Tucker. Theoretical physical chemistry: supercritical fluids, theoretical and computational methods for understanding dynamics in condensed phases, statistical mechanics, computer simulation.

University of California, Davis

SELECTED PUBLICATIONS

Cureton, S. M., S. Vyas, P. B. Kelly, and **M. P. Augustine.** Measurement of the Raman polarizability anisotropy for the v=1 pure rotational Raman transition in H2 by rotational Raman spectroscopy. *Mol. Phys.,* in press.

Augustine, M. P. and E. L. Hahn. Application of a nuclear magnetic resonance area theorem to multiple pulse sequences. *Mol. Phys.* 95:737–46, 1998.

Olmstead, M. M., K. Maitra, and **A. L. Balch.** Formation of a curved silver nitrate network that conforms to the shape of C_{60} and encapsulates the Fullerene-structural characterization of C_{60} {Ag(NO$_3$)}$_5$. *Angew. Chem. Int. Ed.* 38:231–3, 1999.

Balch, A. L., D. A. Costa, and K. Winkler. Formation of redox-active, two-component films by electrochemical reduction of C_{60} and transition metal complexes. *J. Am. Chem. Soc.* 120:9614–20, 1998.

Baldwin, E. P., et al. Generating ligand binding sites in T4 lysozyme by deficiency-creating substitutions. *J. Mol. Biol.* 277:467–85, 1998.

Baldwin, E. P., J. Xu, W. A. Baase, and B. W. Matthews. Thermodynamic and structural compensation in "size-switch" core repacking variants of T4 lysozyme. *J. Mol. Biol.* 259:542–59, 1996.

Peloquin, J. M., K. A. Campbell, and **R. D. Britt.** ^{55}Mn pulsed ENDOR demonstrates that the photosystem II "split" EPR signal arises from a magnetically-coupled mangano-tyrosyl complex. *J. Am. Chem. Soc.* 120:6840–1, 1998.

Campbell, K. A., et al. **(R.D. Britt).** Parallel polarization EPR detection of an S1-state "multiline" EPR signal in photosystem II particles from *Synechocystis* sp. PCC 6803. *J. Am. Chem. Soc.* 120:447–8, 1998.

Allain, F. H. T., et al. **(T. Dieckmann).** Solution structure of the HMG protein NHP6A and its interaction with DNA reveals the structural determinants for non-sequence specific binding. *EMBO J.* 18:2563–79, 1999.

Dieckmann, T., et al. The solution structure of the C-terminal UBA domain of the human DNA repair protein HHR23A and implications for its interaction with HIV-1 Vpr. *Nature Struct. Biol. 5:1042–6, 1998.*

Calvente, J. J., N. S. Marinkovic, Z. Kovacova, and **W. R. Fawcett.** SNIFTIRS studies of the double layer at the metal/solution interface. Part I. Single crystal gold electrodes in aqueous perchloric acid. *J. Electroanal. Chem.* 421:49–57, 1997.

Fawcett, W. R. The role of the metal and the solvent in simple heterogeneous electron transfer reactions. *Electrochim. Acta* 42:833–9, 1997.

Fink, W. H., P. P. Power, and T. L. Allen. Comparison of π-bond strengths in M-E (M=B, Al, Ga; E=O,N,S) compounds. *Ab initio* calculation of rotational barriers. *Inorgan. Chem.* 36:1431–6, 1997.

Jackson, W. M., et al. **(W. H. Fink).** Non-adiabatic interactions in excited C_2H molecules and the relationship to C_2 formation in comets. *Astrophys. Space Sci.* 236:29–47, 1996.

Fisher, A. J., et al. Crystal structure of baculovirus P35: Role of a novel reactive site loop in apoptotic caspase inhibition. *EMBO J.* 18:2031–9, 1999.

Rao-Naik, C., et al. **(A. J. Fisher).** The family of ubiquitin-like proteins: Crystal structure of Arabidopsis RUB1 and expression of multiple RUBs in Arabidopsis. *J. Biol. Chem.* 273:34976–982, 1998.

Jackson, W. M., et al. Ion imaging studies of the Lyman α photodissociation mechanism for H atom production from hydrocarbons. *J. Chem. Phys.,* in press.

Mebel, A. M., **W. M. Jackson,** A. H. H. Chang, and S. H. Lin. Photodissociation dynamics of propyne and allene: A view from ab initio calculations of the C_3H_n(n=1-4) species and the isomerization mechanism for C_3H_2. *J. Am. Chem. Soc.* 120:5751–63, 1998.

Wynne, D. and **P. G. Jessop.** Cyclopropanation enantioselectivity in pressure dependent in supercritical fluoroform. *Angew. Chem. Int. Ed. Engl.* 38:1143–4, 1999.

Jessop, P. G., T. Ikariya, and R. Noyori. Homogeneous catalysis in supercritical fluids. *Chem. Rev.* 99:475–93, 1999.

Ozawa, T., et al. **(S. M. Kauzlarich).** Synthesis and characterization of new compounds with alternating Mn022- and Zn2As22-layers: Ba2MnZn2As202. *Chem. Mater.* 10:392–6, 1998.

Taylor, B. R., **S. M. Kauzlarich,** H. W. H. Lee, and G. R. Delgado. Solution synthesis of germanium nanocrystals demonstrating quantum confinement. *Chem. Mater.* 10:22–4, 1998.

Bezabeh, D. Z., et al. **(P. B. Kelly).** Negative ion laser desorption ionization time-of-flight mass spectrometry of nitrated polycyclic aromatic hydrocarbons. *J. Am. Soc. Mass Spec.* 8:630–6, 1997.

Allen, T. M., et al. **(P. B. Kelly).** Speciation of arsenic oxides using laser desorption/ionization time-of-flight mass spectrometry. *Anal. Chem.* 68:4052–9, 1996.

Kizer, D. E., R. B. Miller, and **M. J. Kurth.** Fused pyrazolo heterocycles: Intramolecular [3+2]-nitrile oxide cycloadditions applied to syntheses of pyrazolo[3,4-g][2,1]dihydrobenzoisoxazol(in)es. *Tetrahedron Lett.* 40:3535–8, 1999.

Kantorowski, E. J., S. W. E. Eisenberg, W. H. Fink, and **M. J. Kurth.** Six- vs. seven-membered ring formation from the 1-bicyclo[4.1.0]heptanylmethyl radical: Synthetic and *ab initio* studies. *J. Org. Chem.* 64:570–80, 1999.

Nguyen, B. D., et al. **(G. N. LaMar).** Solution NMR determination of the anisotropy and orientation of the paramagnetic susceptibility tensor as a function of temperature for metmyoglobin cyanide: Implications for the population of excited electronic states. *J. Am. Chem. Soc.* 121:208–17, 1999.

Gorst, C. M., et al. **(G. N. LaMar).** Solution 1H NMR investigation of the molecular and electronic structure of the active site of substrate-bound human heme oxygenase: The nature of the distal hydrogen bond donor to bound ligands. *J. Am. Chem. Soc.* 120:8875–84, 1998.

Rocklein, M. N. and **D. P. Land.** Mass spectra of Fe(CO)(5) using Fourier transform mass spectrometry (FTMS) and laser induced thermal desorption FTMS with electron ionization, charge exchange, and proton transfer. *Int. J. Mass Spec.* 177:83–9, 1998.

Caldwell, T. E., I. M. Abdelrehim, and **D. P. Land.** Preadsorbed oxygen atoms affect the product distribution and kinetics of acetylene cyclization to benzene on Pd(111): A laser-induced thermal desorption Fourier transform mass spectrometry study. *J. Phys. Chem. B* 102:562–8, 1998.

Tseng, K., J. L. Hedrick, and **C. B. Lebrilla.** The catalog-library approach for the rapid and sensitive structural elucidation of oligosaccharides. *Anal. Chem.,* in press.

Wang, H., K. Tseng, and **C. B. Lebrilla.** A simple and general method for producing bio-affinity MALDI probes. *Anal. Chem.* 71:2014–20, 1999.

Traviglia, S. L., S. A. Datwyler, and **C. F. Meares.** Mapping protein-protein interactions with a library of tethered cutting reagents: The binding site of sigma (70) on *Escherichia coli* RNA polymerase. *Biochemistry* 38:4259–65, 1999.

DeNardo, G. L., et al. **(C. F. Meares).** Cu-67-versus I-131-labeled Lym-1 antibody: Comparative pharmacokinetics and dosimetry in patients with non-Hodgkin's lymphoma. *Clin. Cancer Res.* 5:533–41, 1999.

Bailey, K. L. and **T. F. Molinski.** Entropically favorable macrolactamization. Synthesis of isodityrosine peptide analogues by tandem Erlenmeyer condensation-macrolactamization. *J. Org. Chem.* 64:2500–4, 1999.

Searle, P. A., **T. F. Molinski,** L. J. Brzezinski, and J. W. Leahy. Absolute configuration of phorboxazoles A and B from the marine sponge Phorbas sp. 1. macrolide and hemiketal rings. *J. Am. Chem. Soc.* 118(39):9422–3, 1996.

Forood, B., H. R. Reddy, and **K. P. Nambiar.** Extraordinary helicity in short peptides via end capping design. *J. Am. Chem. Soc.* 116:6935–6, 1994.

Kuimelis, R. G. and **K. P. Nambiar.** Synthesis of oligodeoxynucleotides containing 2-thiopyrimidine residues: A new protection scheme. *Nucleic Acids Res.* 22:1429–36, 1994.

Aberle, A. M., et al. **(M. H. Nantz).** A novel tetraester construct that reduces cationic lipid-associated cytotoxicity. Implications for the onset of cytotoxicity. *Biochemistry* 37:6533–40, 1998.

Nantz, M. H., D. K. Moss, J. D. Spence, and M. M. Olmstead. Actuating cycloaromatization of a bicyclo[7.3.1] enediyne by annelation, an example of inverse dependence on bridge hybridization. *Angew. Chem. Int. Ed.* 37:470–3, 1998.

Navrotsky, A. Energetics and crystal chemical systematics among ilmenite, lithium niobate, and perovskite structures. *Chem. Mater.* 10:2787–93, 1998.

Kanke, Y. and **A. Navrotsky.** A calorimetric study of the lanthanide

University of California, Davis

Selected Publications (continued)

aluminum oxides and the lanthanide gallium oxides: Stability of the perovskites and the garnets. *J. Solid State Chem.* 141:424–36, 1998.

Palmore, G. T. R. and J. C. MacDonald. The role of amides in functional supramolecular aggregates and structures. In *Structure, Energetics and Reactivity in Chemistry.* eds. A. Greenberg, C. Breneman, and J. Liebman, in press.

Palmore, G. T. R., et al. Methanol/dioxygen biofuel cells: Application of an electro-enzymatic method to regenerate nicotinamide adenine dinucleotide. *J. Electroanal. Chem.* 155, 1998.

Patten, T. E. and K. Matyjaszewski. Atom transfer radical polymerization: The polymerization method and its use in the synthesis of polymeric materials. *Adv. Mater.* 10:901–5, 1998.

Matyjaszewski, K., **T. E. Patten,** and J. Xia. Controlled/"living" radical polymerization. Kinetics of the homogeneous atom transfer radical polymerization of styrene. *J. Am. Chem. Soc.* 119:674–80, 1997.

Twamley, B., C. D. Sofield, M. M. Olmstead, and **P. P. Power.** Homologous series of heavier element dipnictenes 2,6-Ar_2-$H_3C_6E+EC_6H_3$-2,6-Ar_2, (E=P, As, Sb, Bi; Ar=Mes=C_6H_2-2,4,6-Me_3; or Trip=C_6H_2-2,4,6-^{i}-Pr_3) stabilized by m-terphenyl ligands. *J. Am. Chem. Soc.* 121:3357–67, 1999.

Pu, L., M. O. Senge, M. M. Olmstead, and **P. P. Power.** Synthesis and characterization of $Na_2\{GeC_6H_3$-2,6-$Trip_2)\}_2$ and $K_2\{SnC_6H_3$-2,6-$Trip_2)\}_2(Trip=C_6H_3$-2,4,6-i-Pr_3): A new class of multiply bonded main group compounds. *J. Am. Chem. Soc.* 120:12682–3, 1998.

McBeath, M. K., **P. A. Rock,** W. H. Casey, and G. K. Mandell. Gibbs energies of formation of metal-carbonate solid solutions 3. The CaxMn1-xCO3 system at 298°K and 1 bar. *Geochim. Cosmochim. Acta* 62(16):2799–808, 1998.

Mandell, G. K., **P. A. Rock,** W. H. Fink, and W. H. Casey. Lattice energies of calcite-structure metal carbonates III. Theoretical excess energies for solid solutions (Ca,M)C03 [M = Cd, Mn, or Fe]. *J. Phys. Chem. Solids* 60:651–61, 1998.

Chu, W.-M., et al. **(C. W. Schmid).** Potential Alu function: Regulation of the activity of the double stranded RNA-activated kinase PKR. *Mol. Cell. Biol.* 18:58–68, 1998.

Schmid, C. W. Alu: Structure, origin, evolution, significance and function of one tenth of human DNA. *Prog. Nucl. Acids Mol. Biol.* 53:283–319, 1996.

Breczinski, P. M., et al. **(N. E. Schore).** Stereoselectivity in the intramolecular Pauson-Khand reaction: Towards a simple predictive model. *Tetrahedron,* in press.

Montierth, J. M., et al. **(N. E. Schore).** The polymer-supported Cadiot-Chodkiewicz coupling of acetylenes to produce unsymmetrical diynes. *Tetrahedron* 54:11741, 1998.

Thorson, J. S., et al. **(B. Shen).** Enediyne biosynthesis and self-resistance: A progress report. *Bioorg. Chem.* 27:172–88, 1999.

Shen, B., et al. Bleomycin biosynthesis in Streptomyces verticullus ATCC15003: A model of hybrid peptide and polyketide biosynthesis. *Bioorg. Chem.* 27:155–71, 1999.

Clement, T. E., D. J. Nurco, and **K. M. Smith.** Synthesis and characterization of a series of monometallo-, bimetallo-, and heterobimetallo-1,2-ethene linked cofacial bisporphyrins. *Inorg. Chem.* 37:1150–60, 1998.

Khoury, R. G., et al. **(K. M. Smith).** A calix[4]arenoporphyrin. *Angew. Chem. Int. Ed. Engl.* 36:2497–500, 1997.

Cheung, M. S., I. Daizadeh, **A. A. Stuchebrukhov,** and P. H. Heelis. Pathways of electron transfer in *E. coli* DNA photolyase: Trp306 to FADH. *Biophys. J.,* in press.

Stuchebrukhov, A. A. Tunneling currents in long-distance electron transfer reactions. III. Many-electron formulation. *J. Chem. Phys.* 108:8499–520, 1998.

Weissbart, B., D. V. Toronto, A. L. Balch, and **D. S. Tinti.** Optical and ODMR studies of luminescent halo(dimethylphenylphosphine) gold(I) crystals. *Inorg. Chem.* 35:2490–6, 1996.

Toronto, D. V., B. Weissbart, **D. S. Tinti,** and A. L. Balch. Solid state structures and gold-gold bonding in luminescent halo(dimethylphenylphosphine)gold(I) complexes. *Inorg. Chem.* 35: 2484–9, 1996.

Taha, A. N., S. M. Neugebauer-Crawford, and **N. S. True.** Determination of the internal rotation barrier of [^{15}N]formamide from gas-phase NMR spectra. *J. Am. Chem. Soc.* 120:1934–5, 1998.

Taha, A. N., S. M. Neugebauer-Crawford, and **N. S. True.** Gas-phase ^{1}H NMR studies of internal rotation activation energies and conformer stabilities of asymmetric *N,N*-disubstituted formamides and trifluoroacetamides. *J. Phys. Chem. A* 102:1425–30, 1998.

Goodyear, G. and **S. C. Tucker.** What causes the vibrational lifetime plateau in supercritical fluids? *J. Chem. Phys.* 110:3643–5, 1999.

Reese, S. K. and **S. C. Tucker.** Curvilinear-path based theory for the energy transfer limited rate of a two-dimensional solute in a dissipative bath. *Chem. Phys.* 235:171–87, 1998.

UNIVERSITY OF CALIFORNIA, SAN DIEGO

Department of Chemistry and Biochemistry

Program of Study

The goal of the program is to prepare students for careers in science as researchers and educators by expanding their knowledge of chemistry while developing their ability for critical analysis, creativity, and independent study. Admittance is to the Ph.D. program only, although the M.S. may be earned while in residence. Research opportunities are comprehensive and interdisciplinary, spanning biochemistry; biophysics; inorganic, organic, physical, and theoretical chemistry; surface and materials chemistry; and atmospheric and environmental chemistry. During the first year, students take courses, begin their teaching apprenticeships, choose a research adviser, and embark on their thesis research; students whose native language is not English must pass an English proficiency examination. In the second year, there is an oral examination, which includes critical discussion of a recent research article. In the third year, students advance to candidacy for the doctorate by defending the topic, preliminary findings, and future research plans for their dissertation. Subsequent years focus on thesis research and writing the dissertation. Most students graduate during their fifth year.

At the University of California, San Diego (UCSD), chemists and biochemists are part of a thriving community that stretches across campus and out into research institutions throughout the San Diego area, uniting researchers in substantive interactions and collaborations. Seminars are presented weekly in biochemistry and inorganic, organic, and physical chemistry. Interdisciplinary programs in nonlinear science, materials science, biophysics, and atmospheric and planetary chemistry also hold regular seminars. The Cal-biochem, SIBIA Neurosciences, and other endowed lectureships attract world-renowned speakers.

Research Facilities

State-of-the-art facilities include a national laboratory for protein crystal structure determination; high-field nuclear magnetic resonance (NMR) instruments; the Natural Sciences Graphics Laboratory, which provides high-end graphic workstation resources; and laser spectroscopic equipment. Buildings specially designed for chemical research, a computational center, a laboratory fabrication and construction facility, and machine, glass, and electronic shops are part of the high-quality research support system.

The UCSD library collection is one of the largest in the country, with superior computerized reference and research services. Access to the facilities at the Scripps Institute of Oceanography, the San Diego Supercomputer Center, the Salk Institute, the Scripps Research Institute, and a thriving technological park, all within blocks of campus, make the overall scope of available research facilities among the best in the world.

Financial Aid

All students who remain in good academic standing are provided year-round support packages of a stipend plus fees and tuition. Support comes from a variety of sources, including teaching assistantships, research assistantships, fellowships, and awards. Special fellowships, such as the GAANN, Urey, Cota Robles, and San Diego fellowships, are available to outstanding students. Students are strongly encouraged to apply for outside fellowships, and the department supplements such awards. The twelve-month stipend is adjusted periodically and for 1999–2000 is $16,200 for incoming students and $17,200 for advanced students. Emergency short-term as well as long-term loan programs are administered by the UCSD Student Financial Services office.

Cost of Study

Registration fees and tuition (paid by the department) are $4889 and $10,323, respectively, per year. Premiums for a primary health-care program, which covers most major medical expenses, are covered by registration fees. The Student Health Center treats minor illnesses and injuries. An inexpensive, optional dental insurance plan is available. Optional health and dental coverage for dependents is at the student's expense.

Living and Housing Costs

The University Housing Service operates more than 1,000 apartments for families, couples, and single graduate students. There are several apartment complexes near campus at comparable or higher rents; rental sharing is a common way to reduce the expense. Generally, rents become less expensive outside La Jolla and Del Mar. Rents range from $320 to $980 per month, excluding utilities. The Commuter Student Services Office, located on campus, maintains extensive current rental and rental-share opportunities.

Student Group

Students are drawn from the top ranks of U.S. and international colleges and universities. There are 2,400 graduate students on the general campus and at the Scripps Institute of Oceanography and 1,200 in the School of Medicine. Within the department, there are 175 graduate students and 600 undergraduate majors. The graduate student population reflects diversity in culture, gender, and ethnicity.

Student Outcomes

Graduates typically obtain jobs in academia (55 percent) or in the chemical industry (45 percent). Many take postdoctoral research positions in academic institutions or national laboratories that lead to future academic or industrial careers. The departmental Industrial Relations Office assists students with placement in industrial positions.

Location

The campus sits on 1,200 acres of eucalyptus groves near the Pacific Ocean. Surrounding the campus is La Jolla, a picturesque community of boutiques, bistros, and businesses. Seven miles south of campus is San Diego with its world-acclaimed zoo, museums, and theaters. The Laguna Mountains and the Anza-Borrego Desert are within a 2-hour drive east of campus.

The University

UCSD, a comparatively young university, has already achieved widespread recognition, ranking fifth in federal funding for research and development, and in the top ten of all doctoral degree–granting institutions in a study conducted by the National Research Council. Programs span the arts and humanities, engineering, international studies, and the social, natural, and physical sciences. The intellectual climate is enhanced by a variety of social, educational, professional, political, religious, and recreational opportunities and services.

Applying

Application packets include a completed UCSD application form, a statement of purpose, official transcripts from previous colleges, three letters of recommendation, GRE scores (general and advanced chemistry or biochemistry), and a TOEFL score (for noncitizens only; a minimum score of 550 is required). Research experience should be described. Copies of or references to any publications should be included with the application. Applications received by January 15 receive the highest priority.

Correspondence and Information

Graduate Admissions Coordinator
Department of Chemistry and Biochemistry 0301
University of California, San Diego
9500 Gilman Drive
La Jolla, California 92093-0301
Telephone: 619-534-6870
Fax: 619-534-7687
E-mail: gradinfo@chem.ucsd.edu
World Wide Web: http://www-chem.ucsd.edu/

University of California, San Diego

THE FACULTY AND THEIR RESEARCH

William S. Allison, Ph.D., Brandeis. Biochemistry: enzymology, structure-function relationships in proton translocating ATPases.

Robert E. Continetti, Ph.D., Berkeley. Experimental chemical physics: reaction dynamics and energetics of free radicals and reactive intermediates, negative-ion photodetachment spectroscopy and photodissociation processes, three-body dissociation dynamics.

John E. Crowell, Ph.D., Berkeley. Experimental physical chemistry: materials surface chemistry, kinetics at metal and semiconductor surfaces, semiconductor and oxide growth by CVD, photo-induced deposition, spectroscopy of thin films and interfaces.

Edward A. Dennis, Ph.D., Harvard. Biochemistry: biological, molecular biological, bioorganic, and biophysical approaches to enzyme catalysis; phospholipase A_2, C, and D; prostaglandin control; cloning and site-specific mutagenesis; signal transduction in macrophage cells.

Daniel J. Donoghue, Ph.D., MIT. Biochemistry: molecular and structural biochemistry of growth factors, cellular biochemistry of transformed cells and oncogenic protein kinases.

Nathaniel S. Finney, Ph.D., Caltech. Organic chemistry: solid-phase organic synthesis, asymmetric catalysis, and molecular recognition, with an emphasis on applying the methods of combinatorial chemistry where appropriate.

Gourisankar Ghosh, Ph.D., Yeshiva (Einstein). Regulation of gene expression: high-resolution X-ray crystallography, mutational and biochemical approaches to study biologically active protein/DNA and protein/RNA complexes.

Partho Ghosh, Ph.D., California, San Francisco. Biochemistry and biophysics: mechanisms of bacterial and protozoal pathogenesis, protein X-ray crystallography, structure and function of virulence factors and host-pathogen protein interactions.

Murray Goodman, Ph.D., Berkeley. Organic, biophysical, and biopolymer chemistry: peptide synthesis, peptidomimetics, conformation, computer-molecular dynamics, spectroscopy, structure–biological activity relationships.

Daniel F. Harvey, Ph.D., Yale. Organic chemistry: development of new methods and strategies for organic synthesis, application of organometallic chemistry to organic synthesis, bioorganic and bioinorganic chemistry.

David N. Hendrickson, Ph.D., Berkeley. Inorganic chemistry: bioinorganic chemistry, solid-state chemistry, magnetochemistry, dynamics of transition metal complexes.

Patricia A. Jennings, Ph.D., Penn State. Biophysical chemistry: protein structure, dynamics and folding, 2-, 3-, and 4-D NMR spectroscopy, PCR, equilibrium and kinetic-fluorescence, absorbance and circular dichroism spectroscopies.

Simpson Joseph, Ph.D., Vermont. Biochemistry: ribosome structure, function, and dynamics; interaction of antibiotics and ribosomes; RNA folding; RNA catalysis.

Timothy B. Karpishin, Ph.D., Berkeley. Inorganic chemistry: bioinorganic chemistry, supramolecular chemistry, design and synthesis of oxygenation catalysts, enzyme mimics, photocatalysts, molecular sensors.

Elizabeth A. Komives, Ph.D., California, San Francisco. Biochemistry: protein-protein interactions mediated by EGF-like domains, dynamics, structure, and function of the EGF domains from thrombomodulin calcium binding and structure of the EGF domains from Notch.

Clifford P. Kubiak, Ph.D., Rochester. Inorganic chemistry: organotransition metal chemistry, photochemistry, and electrochemistry; chemistry of carbon dioxide; electron transfer and electronic conduction in molecular nanostructures; chemically gated devices.

Andrew C. Kummel, Ph.D., Stanford. Chemical physics: chemistry of microelectronics processing using scanning tunneling microscopy and laser spectroscopy, chemical dynamics of gas-surface chemistry.

Jack E. Kyte, Ph.D., Harvard. Biochemistry: protein chemical studies of membrane-bound proteins catalyzing the transport of ions and of the active site of ribonucleotide reductase.

Katja Lindenberg, Ph.D., Cornell. Physical chemistry: nonequilibrium statistical mechanics, stochastic processes, nonlinear phenomena, condensed-matter theory.

Douglas Magde, Ph.D., Cornell. Experimental physical chemistry: photochemistry and photobiophysics, picosecond and femtosecond lasers.

Kurt Marti, Ph.D., Bern (Switzerland). Cosmochemistry: isotopic studies on the origins and evolution of the solar system, the asteroid-meteorite link, synthesis of the elements.

J. Andrew McCammon, Ph.D., Harvard. Statistical mechanics of macromolecules and liquids; theory of protein structure, dynamics, and function; development and application of computer models and simulation methods for molecular systems.

Trevor C. McMorris, Ph.D., London. Natural products chemistry: steroids, plant hormones, and antitumor compounds.

K. C. Nicolaou, Ph.D., University College, London. Synthetic and bioorganic chemistry: new synthetic technology and synthesis of natural and designed molecules, biologically active substances.

Joseph M. O'Connor, Ph.D., Wisconsin–Madison. Synthetic and mechanistic organotransition metal chemistry.

Hans Oesterreicher, Ph.D., Vienna. Solid-state science: magnetic information storage, superconductivity.

Charles L. Perrin, Ph.D., Harvard. Physical-organic chemistry: reaction mechanisms, proton exchange, anomeric effects and stereoelectronic control, hydrogen bonding, isotope effects, ionic solvation.

Michael J. Sailor, Ph.D., Northwestern. Inorganic chemistry, materials chemistry: synthesis and study of materials with novel electrical and photochemical properties, chemical and biochemical sensors, phosphors.

Barbara A. Sawrey, Ph.D., California, San Diego, and San Diego State. Chemical education: development of computer-based multimedia to assist student learning of complex scientific processes and concepts.

Jay S. Siegel, Ph.D., Princeton. Organic chemistry: stereochemistry of organic and organometallic compounds and reactions.

Amitabha Sinha, Ph.D., MIT. Experimental physical chemistry: gas phase laser spectroscopy, state-to-state reaction dynamics and photochemistry of vibrationally excited molecules.

Susan S. Taylor, Ph.D., Johns Hopkins. Biochemistry: structure and function of protein kinases, chemical modifications, genetic engineering, X-ray crystallography, NMR, microinjection.

Emmanuel A. Theodorakis, Ph.D., Paris XI (South). Synthesis and bioorganic studies of natural products and designed molecules with biological and medicinal interest, development of new strategies, reactions, and reagents for organic and bioorganic chemistry.

Mark H. Thiemens, Chair; Ph.D., Florida State. Atmospheric chemistry: measurements of stable isotopes in atmospheric species by ground and rocket sampling, physical chemistry of isotope effects, studies of solar system formation and nucleosynthesis.

Yitzhak Tor, Ph.D., Weizmann (Israel). Organic chemistry: biological, bioorganic, and biomimetic approaches to molecular recognition of carbohydrates and nucleic acids; synthesis and assembly of novel materials.

William C. Trogler, Ph.D., Caltech. Inorganic chemistry: homogeneous and heterogeneous catalysis; reaction mechanisms; electrochemistry; environmental chemistry related to nitrogen, oxides, chlorine dioxide, and carbonyl sulfide; photodeposition of carbon sulfide polymers.

Roger Y. Tsien, Ph.D., Cambridge. Organic chemistry and biochemistry: design and synthesis of molecular probes of cell function, photochemistry and spectroscopy applied to intracellular signal transduction.

Regitze R. Vold, Ph.D., Denmark Technical. Physical chemistry: nuclear magnetic resonance, liquid crystals and model membranes; solid paramagnetic material, peptides, and proteins.

John H. Weare, Ph.D., Johns Hopkins. Physical chemistry: calculations of the dynamics of complex systems, theoretical geochemistry.

John C. Wheeler, Ph.D., Cornell. Physical chemistry: thermodynamics and statistical mechanics, phase transitions and critical phenomena in molecularly complex systems, polymers and polymerization, microemulsions, surface motion in solids.

Kent R. Wilson, Ph.D., Berkeley. Chemical physics: molecular dynamics of chemical reactions; theoretical and experimental quantum control dynamics with tailored laser light, ultrafast X-ray diffraction, and spectroscopy; dynamic laser microscopy and cellular functioning.

Nguyen-Huu Xuong, Ph.D., Berkeley. Biophysical chemistry: structure of proteins, protein crystallography.

Research, Emeritus, and Adjunct Faculty

James R. Arnold, Ph.D., Princeton: Cosmochemistry. Kim Baldridge, Ph.D., North Dakota State: Electronic structure theory methodologies and computational chemistry. Marjorie Caserio, Ph.D., Bryn Mawr: Organic chemistry. Senyon Choe, Ph.D., Berkeley: Protein structures. Leigh B. Clark, Ph.D., Washington (Seattle): Experimental chemical physics. Russell F. Doolittle, Ph.D., Harvard: Biochemistry, structure and evolution of proteins. Robert C. Fahey, Ph.D., Chicago: Biochemistry. Elvin Harper, Ph.D., Yeshiva (Einstein): Biochemistry. John E. Johnson, Ph.D., Iowa State: Biochemistry. Martin D. Kamen, Ph.D., Chicago: Biochemistry. David R. Kearns, Ph.D., Berkeley: Experimental chemical physics. Joseph Kraut, Ph.D., Caltech: Biochemistry, protein structure and function. Stanley L. Miller, Ph.D., Chicago: Biochemistry, prebiotic synthesis, origin of living organisms. Joseph P. Noel, Ph.D., Ohio State: Protein X-ray crystallography. Leslie E. Orgel, D. Phil., Oxford: Prebiotic chemistry. Thomas D. Pollard, Ph.D., Harvard: Biochemistry. Gerhard Schrauzer, Ph.D., Munich: Inorganic chemistry and biochemistry. Kurt E. Shuler, Ph.D., Catholic University: Chemical physics. Peter R. Taylor, Ph.D., Sydney: Theoretical and computational chemistry. Ernest Wenkert, Ph.D., Harvard: Organic chemistry. Bruno H. Zimm, Ph.D., Columbia: Biophysical chemistry.

UNIVERSITY OF DETROIT MERCY

College of Engineering and Science
Department of Chemistry and Biochemistry

Programs of Study	The Department of Chemistry and Biochemistry offers the Doctor of Philosophy (Ph.D.) in macromolecular chemistry and the Master of Science (M.S.) in macromolecular chemistry and economic aspects of chemistry. The Ph.D. in macromolecular chemistry prepares well-trained chemists with demonstrated research ability and appropriate teaching experience. The Ph.D. and M.S. degrees in macromolecular chemistry draw upon the resources and research activities of the Polymer Institute and the Center for Excellence in Environmental Engineering Science, widely recognized research centers within the College of Engineering and Science. The M.S. in economic aspects of chemistry prepares chemists for an active and responsible role in activities involving the interaction of chemistry and technology. Chemistry programs are accredited by the American Chemical Society's Committee on Professional Training. The Ph.D. in macromolecular chemistry is based upon completion of doctoral degree course work, attainment of doctoral candidacy through satisfactory completion of written and oral comprehensive examinations, and completion of a doctoral dissertation. Required courses include Organic Mechanisms, Synthetic Methods of Organic Chemistry, Polymer Surface Coatings I, Polymer Synthesis and Characterization, Polymer Synthesis and Characterization Laboratory, Thermodynamics of Molecular Systems, Physical Chemistry of Macromolecules, and Introduction to Polymer Engineering and Science I. In Part 1 of the comprehensive examination requirement, the student must successfully complete a written exam in macromolecular chemistry. In Part 2, the student begins preparation for the oral examination and submits to the Research Advisory Committee an outline of a student-originated research proposal in his or her major area of study that is different from the student's dissertation research. Upon approval of the proposal outline by the research adviser and the chemistry department chairperson, the student must complete the written research proposal, submit it to the Research Advisory Committee, and orally defend the proposal before the committee within five months of satisfactorily completing the written examination. Successful completion of parts 1 and 2 constitute admission to Ph.D. candidacy. For the dissertation requirement, the student selects a research director by the end of two terms of graduate study. Within six weeks of this selection, a research advisory committee, composed of the research director and two other faculty members with expertise in the area of the student's dissertation research, is appointed. Degree requirements for the M.S. in macromolecular chemistry consist of 24 credit hours of formal course work and 6 hours of thesis research. All full-time graduate students must enroll in a graduate seminar for each term for which they register. Students also must select a research adviser by the end of two terms of study. Part-time students currently employed in industry may substitute 6 hours of course work for thesis research with the chairperson's approval. Required courses include Organic Mechanisms, Polymer Synthesis and Characterization, Polymer Synthesis and Characterization Laboratory, Thermodynamics of Molecular Systems, Physical Chemistry of Macromolecules, and Introduction to Polymer Engineering and Science I. Requirements for the M.S. in economic aspects of chemistry consist of 22 credit hours of chemistry courses, 9 credit hours of business courses, and 4 credit hours (two terms) of research. A written report may be accepted in place of the traditional thesis. This written report is presented orally to a committee for approval. The maximum time for completion of all degrees is seven years from the time of admission. Requirements for the chemistry and biochemistry programs may change due to current curriculum review by the faculty.
Research Facilities	Special research facilities are available for graduate students in chemistry. Equipment includes extensive modern instrumentation; one ESR and several UV-visible, infrared, and atomic absorption spectrometers; a differential thermal analyzer; a Guoy balance; a solution calorimeter; equipment for photochemical and kinetic work; a gas chromatograph/mass spectrometer; FTIR; an X-ray fluorescence spectrometer; a laser-based scanning densitometer; a spectrofluorometer; and an X-ray fluorescence spectrometer.
Financial Aid	Fellowships, assistantships, and tuition scholarships are available each year for selected full-time students. Fellowships and assistantships usually involve stipends and may include remission of tuition and academic fees for two academic terms or, in some circumstances, for the entire year. After admission, students should apply for fellowships and assistantships through the chemistry department. The Scholarship and Financial Aid Office provides applications for grants, loans, and work-study assistance. Aid includes the Michigan Tuition Grant for Michigan residents, various work-study programs and a variety of low-interest loans providing up to ten years for repayment. UDM accepts third-party payment from employers and offers deferred payment plans for equal installments throughout the academic year.
Cost of Study	Graduate tuition for 1999–2000 is $545 per credit hour for both regular semesters and summer sessions. Graduate students also pay a registration and student activities fee.
Living and Housing Costs	Housing is available in University residence halls. Double-occupancy rates begin at $1410 per semester. Single-occupancy rates begin at $2420 per semester. A variety of meal plans are available and cost about $1085 per semester.
Student Group	UDM enrolls about 6,700 students, including 1,766 graduate students. About 180 graduate students are enrolled in the College of Engineering and Science; of these students, 83 percent are men, 17 percent are women, 57 percent are Caucasian, 7 percent are African American, 3 percent are Asian American, and 26 percent are international. The average student age is 33. The majority of students enroll part-time and earn an average GPA of 3.66.
Location	UDM's Detroit location in southeastern Michigan places it amidst a corporate and educational community that rivals any in the world for its size and importance. Metropolitan Airport provides easy access to UDM from almost anywhere in the United States, and daily international flights offer links with major centers around the globe.
The University and The College	UDM, the largest private university in Michigan, operates under the sponsorship of the Society of Jesus and the Sisters of Mercy of the Americas. The College of Engineering and Science offers courses at UDM's McNichols campus in a residential area of northwest Detroit. The campus and the Detroit area offer a wide variety of cultural and recreational activities, including concerts and theatrical performances of national reputation plus museums, libraries, and four professional sports teams. Canada is just a few minutes away.
Applying	Ph.D. applicants must present an undergraduate major in chemistry or its equivalent, with a minimum GPA of 3.0 in the major field and an overall GPA of 2.75 (or at least in the last 60 hours). Such prior work must be essentially equivalent to that required by the chemistry department for a B.S. degree as set forth in the University of Detroit Mercy undergraduate catalog. Applicants whose undergraduate preparation does not satisfy these admission requirements may be admitted on probationary status with the approval of the College of Engineering and Science dean and the chemistry department chairperson. Courses taken to satisfy admission requirements may not be taken for graduate credits.
Correspondence and Information	Professor M. Caspers, Chair Department of Chemistry and Biochemistry University of Detroit Mercy P.O. Box 19900 Detroit, Michigan 48219-0900 Telephone: 313-993-1258 E-mail: schleyja@udmercy.edu (When using the Internet, students should include a mailing address where information can be sent.)

University of Detroit Mercy

THE FACULTY

Detailed faculty member profiles, including examples of chemistry research now in progress, are provided in the information package that students may request.

Mark A. Benvenuto, Assistant Professor of Chemistry; Ph.D., Virginia.

David Brook, Assistant Professor of Chemistry; Ph.D., Colorado.

Brian Buffin, Assistant Professor of Chemistry; Ph.D., Utah.

Mary Lou Caspers, Professor of Chemistry; Ph.D., Wayne State.

Kurt C. Frisch, Professor of Engineering and Chemistry and Director of Polymer Technologies Institute; Ph.D., Columbia.

Daniel Klempner, Associate Professor of Polymer Chemistry and Associate Director of Polymer Technologies Institute; Ph.D., SUNY at Albany.

Elizabeth Roberts-Kirchhoff, Assistant Professor of Chemistry; Ph.D., Michigan.

S. Shulamith Schlick, Professor of Chemistry; D.Sc., Israel Institute of Technology.

Jonathan Stevens, Assistant Professor of Chemistry; Ph.D, Chicago.

UNIVERSITY OF ILLINOIS AT CHICAGO

Department of Chemistry

Programs of Study

The department offers a Ph.D. program in chemistry with specializations in analytical chemistry, biochemistry, inorganic chemistry, organic chemistry, physical chemistry, and biophysical chemistry. There is considerable overlap between these areas, as well as opportunity for research involving other disciplines, such as biology and physics.

The doctoral programs require 96 semester hours beyond the B.S. degree. A thesis is the center of the program, and the course work is determined according to the student's background and interests. Candidates must successfully complete a program of cumulative examinations. The Ph.D. program is usually completed in four to five years.

The school year is divided into fall and spring semesters plus a shorter summer session in which no graduate courses are offered. Most students begin their graduate studies in the fall semester, which starts in late August. The department does not have evening graduate programs.

Research Facilities

The research activities are housed in modern, well-equipped laboratories and are supported by department-staffed electronics, machine, and glassblowing shops. Major special facilities are in the areas of surface chemistry, laser photochemical kinetics, synthetic organic and inorganic chemistry, vibrational circular dichroism, computational chemistry, light scattering, time-resolved fluorescence spectroscopy, optical spectroscopy, X-ray diffraction, fast kinetics, photoelectron spectroscopy, electron microscopy, and protein structure and function. The science library is in the same building as the chemistry department. A Research Resources Center (RRC) is housed in the chemistry department building. The RRC is equipped with modern NMR, mass spectrometry, electron microscopy, and X-ray diffraction instrumentation.

The Health Sciences Center, which has additional shared research facilities, is just 5 minutes away by shuttle bus, and Argonne National Laboratory and Fermilab are less than an hour's drive away, as are several major research institutions and industrial centers.

Financial Aid

Financial support is available to all qualified graduate students. Fellowships for outstanding students, as well as dedicated fellowships for minority students, are available through the department and the University. Support for newly admitted teaching assistants starts at $17,000 for the 1999–2000 calendar year. Most advanced graduate students are supported by research assistantships.

Cost of Study

The University waives tuition and service fees for all graduate assistants and fellows on a quarter-time to two-thirds-time appointment (graduate students have a half-time appointment); these students pay approximately $1200 per year for health insurance, health service, and general fees.

Living and Housing Costs

Housing is available in residence halls of the University; the cost for eleven months in 1999–2000 is $5020–$5934. Many graduate students secure housing in the immediate neighborhood, around town, or in the suburbs at a wide range of rents.

Student Group

The campus has more than 25,000 students, approximately 9,000 of whom are enrolled in graduate programs. The Department of Chemistry has approximately 130 graduate students.

Student Outcomes

Most University of Illinois at Chicago (UIC) graduates currently have research positions in industry (Abbott Laboratories, Motorola, B.P.-Amoco, Merck), in government laboratories, and in universities. While the geographical distribution of former students is high, UIC Department of Chemistry students have been particularly successful in obtaining positions in the Chicago area.

Location

Chicago, with a metropolitan population of about 7 million, is the cultural center of the Midwest, famous for its symphony, opera, theater companies, and museums. All forms of sports and indoor and outdoor recreation are readily accessible. The campus is located just a few blocks from the Loop, the business district of Chicago, and less than 2 miles from Lake Michigan. Transportation to the campus from the city and the suburbs is excellent.

The University

The University of Illinois at Chicago is one of three campuses of the University of Illinois and is the major public university in Chicago. UIC is classified as a Research I university and ranks fifty-seventh in the country in terms of total funds for research and development. It has fifteen colleges, including the nation's largest college of medicine, and a number of special institutes, centers, and laboratories.

Applying

Applications for admission may be submitted at any time, but should be received at least three months before the beginning of the desired term. Graduate students may start in fall or (in special cases) spring, and credit may be received for previous graduate work. Applicants from international institutions must provide scores on the TOEFL, and all students must submit scores on the chemistry Subject Test of the GRE.

Correspondence and Information

Further information and application forms may be obtained from:

Director of Graduate Studies
Department of Chemistry (M/C 111)
University of Illinois at Chicago
845 West Taylor Street, Room 4500
Chicago, Illinois 60607-7061

University of Illinois at Chicago

THE FACULTY AND THEIR RESEARCH

Albert S. Benight, Professor; Ph.D., Georgia Tech, 1983. Biophysical chemistry: dynamic light-scattering investigations of DNA, proteins, and DNA-protein complexes; experimental and theoretical investigations of DNA thermal denaturation.

Richard P. Burns, Associate Professor; Ph.D., Chicago, 1965. Physical chemistry: kinetics of evaporation, condensation, and chemical reaction between adsorbed species; high-temperature chemistry; mass spectrometry.

Lisheng Cai, Assistant Professor; Ph.D., Chicago, 1992. Inorganic chemistry: investigations of multiple electron redox catalysts involved in O_2 activation, multiple electron reductions, and photo-induced charge separation.

Wonhwa Cho, Associate Professor, Ph.D., Chicago, 1988. Biochemistry: protein engineering of phospholipase A_2 and its inhibitory proteins, development of anti-inflammatory agents, biophysical studies of surface-active proteins and peptides, design of novel protein catalysts.

David Crich, Professor; Ph.D., London, 1984. Organic chemistry: diastereoselective free-radical reactions, acyl radical cyclizations, asymmetric synthesis of amino acids.

Lucio Frydman, Associate Professor; Buenos Aires, 1990. Analytical chemistry: development of new analytical methods in nuclear magnetic resonance with emphasis on solid-state NMR and NMR imaging techniques.

Vladimir Gevorgyan, Associate Professor; Ph.D., Institute of Organic Synthesis (Latvia), 1984. Organic chemistry: development of novel transition metal catalyzed highly regioselective and chemoselective cycloaddition reactions, synthesis of polysubstituted aromatic and heteroaromatic compounds.

Arun K. Ghosh, Associate Professor; Ph.D., Pittsburgh, 1985. Organic chemistry: synthesis of peptide mimics that act as enzyme inhibitors, enantioselective reactions.

Eric A. Gislason, Professor and Head; Ph.D., Harvard, 1967, Physical chemistry: theoretical studies of ion-molecule reactions, neutral reactions, vibrational excitation, collisional dissociation, intermolecular potentials, and vibrational effects in electronic transitions; negative ion resonances.

Robert J. Gordon, Professor; Ph.D., Harvard, 1970. Physical chemistry: experimental studies of molecular reaction dynamics, gas phase kinetics, and photochemistry.

Luke Hanley, Associate Professor; Ph.D., SUNY at Stony Brook, 1988. Analytical chemistry: experimental studies of atomic and molecular ion-surface interactions at low collision energies employing mass, Auger electron, and infrared reflection-absorption spectroscopies.

Cynthia J. Jameson, Professor; Ph.D., Illinois, 1963. Physical and theoretical chemistry: nuclear magnetic resonance, theoretical calculations of NMR chemical shifts and coupling constants, polarizabilities, and other molecular electronic properties.

Caroline Jarrold, Assistant Professor; Ph.D., Berkeley, 1994. Physical chemistry: laser investigations of bare metal clusters.

Richard Kassner, Professor; Ph.D., Yale, 1966. Biochemistry: structure and properties of metalloproteins; model and protein studies of redox, ligand binding, spin-state, and catalytic properties of heme proteins; metalloporphyrin formation in heme and chlorophyll biosynthesis.

Timothy Keiderling, Professor; Ph.D., Princeton, 1974. Physical chemistry: vibrational optical activity applications to theory and molecular structural analyses (protein, peptide, and nucleic acid conformational studies), new spectroscopic instrumentation, electronic and vibrational magnetic circular dichroism, electronic spectroscopy of transition metal complexes, nonlinear spectroscopy.

Pierre R. LeBreton, Professor; Ph.D., Harvard, 1970. Physical and biophysical chemistry: photoemission and theoretical quantum mechanical probes of electronic properties of nucleic acids, mechanisms of DNA alkylation, and structures of genotoxic DNA lesions.

William L. Mock, Professor; Ph.D., Harvard, 1965. Organic chemistry:structure-reactivity relationships, synthetic methods, concerted reactions, organosulfur chemistry, bioorganic chemistry.

Robert M. Moriarty, Professor; Ph.D., Princeton, 1959. Organic chemistry: mechanism of oxygen fixation, singlet dioxygen oxidation, photolyses in lipid bilayer membranes, organic syntheses with lasers, polycyclic aromatic hydrocarbons, steroid synthesis, hypervalent iodine in synthesis, mechanism cholinesterase activity, alkyl azides.

John A. Morrison, Professor; Ph.D., Maryland, 1972. Inorganic chemistry: synthesis of inorganic and organometallic compounds and the study of their structure and reactivity, preparative reactions using discharge and high-temperature techniques, chemistry of the boron subhalides and fluorinated organometallic compounds.

Scott A. Shippy, Assistant Professor; Ph.D., Illinois at Urbana-Champaign, 1997. Analytical chemistry: development and characterization of assays to follow neurochemical signaling in freely behaving animals.

Boon K. Teo, Professor; Ph.D., Wisconsin, 1973. Inorganic chemistry:synthesis, structure, bonding, and properties of large metal clusters; magic numbers; X-ray crystallography and metal tetrathiolenes; EXAFS and synchrotron research.

Michael Trenary, Professor; Ph.D., MIT, 1982. Physical chemistry: structure, dynamics, and reactions of molecules adsorbed on well-defined crystal surfaces; adsorbate phase transitions; kinetics of surface diffusion; infrared spectroscopy of molecular adsorbates.

Duncan J. Wardrop, Assistant Professor; Ph.D., Glasgow, 1994. Organic chemistry: organosilicon chemistry and the use of small ring fragmentation in synthesis, development of new synthetic strategies with application to natural product synthesis.

Donald J. Wink, Associate Professor; Ph.D., Harvard, 1985. Inorganic chemistry: organometallic catalysts and X-ray crystallography.

Paul R. Young, Professor; Ph.D., South Florida, 1975. Physical organic chemistry and biochemistry: the mechanism and driving force for general acid-base catalysis, nucleophilic substitution at tricoordinate sulfur, evidence for sulfurane intermediates, biochemistry of methionine redox enzymes.

UIC's science complex with Chicago and Sears Tower, the world's tallest building, in the background.

SELECTED PUBLICATIONS

Lane, M. J., et al. **(A. S. Benight).** The thermodynamic advantage of oligonucleotide "stacking hybridization" reactions: Energetics of a DNA nick. *Nucleic Acids Res.* 25:611, 1997.

Budzynski, D. M., X. Gao, and **A. S. Benight.** Isolation, characterization and magnesium induced self-association kinetics of discrete aggregates of RecA protein from *Escherichia coli.* *Biopolymers* 38:471, 1996.

Paner, T. M., P. V. Riccelli, R. Owczarzy, and **A. S. Benight.** Studies of DNA dumbbells VI: Analysis of optical melting curves of dumbbells with a sixteen base-pair duplex stem and end-loops of variable size and sequence. *Biopolymers* 39:779, 1996.

Riccelli, P. V., et al. **(A. S. Benight).** DNA and RNA oligomer sequences from the 3' non-coding region of the chicken glutamine synthetase gene form intramolecular hairpins. *Biochemistry* 35: 15364, 1996.

Pierce, D. E., **R. P. Burns,** and K. A. Gabriel. Thermal desorption spectroscopy of palladium and copper on silica. *Thin Solid Films* 206:340, 1991.

Pierce, D. E., **R. P. Burns,** H. M. Dauplaise, and L. J. Mlzerka. Thermal desorption spectroscopy of sputtered molybdenum sulfide (MoSx) films. *Tribol. Trans.* 34:205, 1991.

Gannon, T., A. R. Anabro, and **R. P. Burns.** Incineration of hazardous wastes. *Environ. Monit. Assess.* 19:105, 1991.

Cai, L., et al. Preorganization of iron-centers for the activation of molecular dioxygen. *Inorg. Chem. Comm.* 1:70, 1998.

Cai, L., et al. Synthesis, characterization of chiral 1,1'-binaphthyl-2,2'-diamine sulfonamide and its ruthenium complex and evaluation of the catalytic properties in transfer hydrogenation reactions. *J. Organomet. Chem.* 568:77, 1998.

Mahmoud, H., **L. Cai,** Y. Han, and B. Segal. An improved resolution of 1,1'-binaphthyl-2-amino-2'-hydroxy. *Tetrahedron: Asymmetry* 9: 2035, 1998.

Cai, L., et al. **(D. J. Wink).** Synthesis and characterization of constricted and rigid ligand systems for five-coordinate binuclear complexes. *Inorg. Chim. Acta* 263:231, 1997.

Bittova, L., P. M. Sumandea, and **W. Cho.** A structure-function study of C2 domain of cytosolic phospholipase A₂: Identification of essential calcium ligands and hydrophobic membrane binding residues. *J. Biol. Chem.* 274:9665, 1999.

Han, S.-K., E. T. Yoon, and **W. Cho.** Functional expression and characterization of human secretory class V phospholipase A₂. *Biochem. J.* 331:353, 1998.

Medkova, M., and **W. Cho.** Mutagenesis of the C2 domain of protein kinase C-α: Differential roles of Ca²⁺ ligands and membrane binding residues. *J. Biol. Chem.* 273:17544, 1998.

Bitto, E., and **W. Cho.** Roles of individual domains of annexin I in its vesicle binding and vesicle aggregation: A comprehensive mutagenesis study. *Biochemistry* 37:10231, 1998.

Choi, S.-Y., **D. Crich** et al. **(D. J. Wink).** Absence of diffusively free radical cation intermediates in reactions of β-(phosphatoxy)alkyl radicals. *J. Am. Chem. Soc.* 120:211, 1998.

Crich, D., et al. **(D. J. Wink).** Stereoselective sulfoxidation of α-mannopyranosyl thioglycosides: The exo-anomeric effect in action. *Chem. Commun.* 2763, 1998.

Crich, D., and Q. Yao. Generation of acyl radicals from thiolesters by intramolecular homolytic substitution at sulfur. *J. Org. Chem.* 61:3566, 1996.

Crich, D., and S. Sun. Formation of b-mannopyransides of primary alcohols using the sulfoxide method. *J. Org. Chem.* 61:4506, 1996.

Crich, D. Free radical chemistry of lactones: Ring contractions and expansions. *J. Am. Chem. Soc.* 118:7422, 1996.

Crich, D., and X.-S. Mo. Nucleotide C3',4'-radical cations and the effect of a 2'-oxygen substituent. The DNA/RNA paradox. *J. Am. Chem. Soc.* 119:249, 1997.

Marinelli, L., S. Wi, and **L. Frydman.** A density matrix description of ¹⁴N overtone NMR in static and spinning solids. *J. Chem. Phys.* 110:3100, 1999.

Zhou, M., V. Frydman, and **L. Frydman.** Order determinations in liquid crystals by dynamic director NMR spectroscopy. *J. Am. Chem. Soc.* 120:2178, 1998.

Medek, A., V. Frydman, and **L. Frydman.** Solid and liquid phase ⁵⁹Co NMR studies of cobalamins and their derivatives. *Proc. Natl. Acad. Sci. U.S.A.* 94:14237, 1997.

Zhou, M., V. Frydman, and **L. Frydman.** NMR analyses of order and dynamics in poly(p-benzamide)/sulfuric acid solutions. *Macromolecules* 30:5416, 1997.

Quan, L. G., **V. Gevorgyan,** and Y. Yamamoto. Intramolecular nucleophilic addition of vinylpalladiums to aryl ketones. *J. Am. Chem. Soc.* 121:3545, 1999.

Weibel, D., **V. Gevorgyan,** and Y. Yamamoto. Synthesis of polyether exomethylene paracyclophanes via an intramolecular Pd-catalyzed bis-enyne benzannulation. *Protocol. J. Org. Chem.* 63:1217, 1998.

Imamura, K., E. Yoshikawa, **V. Gevorgyan,** and Y. Yamamoto. First exclusive *endo-dig* carbocyclization: HfCl₄-catalyzed intramolecular allylsilylation of alkynes. *J. Am. Chem. Soc.* 120:5339, 1998.

Gevorgyan, V., K. Tando, N. Uchiyama, and Y. Yamamoto. An efficient route to 2,6-disubstituted styrenes via the palladium-catalyzed homodimerization of conjugated enynes. *J. Org. Chem.* 63:7022, 1998.

Ghosh, A. K., and W.-M. Liu. Enantioselective total synthesis of (+)-sinefungin. *J. Org. Chem.* 61:6175, 1996.

Ghosh, A. K., P. Mathivanan, and J. Cappiello. Conformationally constrained bis(oxazoline) derived chiral catalyst: A highly effective enantioselective-catalytic Diels-Alder reaction. *Tetrahedron Lett.* 37:3815, 1996.

Ghosh, A. K., and M. Onishi. Synthesis of enantiomerically pure anti aldols: A highly stereoselective ester-derived titanium enolate aldol reaction. *J. Am. Chem. Soc.* 118:2527, 1996.

Ghosh, A. K., W.-M. Liu, Y. Xu, and Z. Chen. A convergent, enantioselective total synthesis of hapalosin with multidrug-resistance reversing activity. *Angew. Chem.* 35:74, 1996.

Sizun, M., J. B. Song, and **E. A. Gislason.** Theoretical study of the reactions of Ar⁺H₂ and Ar⁺+HD using the trajectory surface hopping method. *J. Chem. Phys.* 109:4815, 1998.

Song, J. B., and **E. A. Gislason.** Theoretical study of the effect of reagent rotation and vibration on the reactions of Cl+H₂ and Cl+HD. *Chem. Phys.* 237:159, 1998.

Lim, H., D. G. Schultz, **E. A. Gislason,** and **L. Hanley.** Activation energies for the fragmentation of thiophene ions by surface-induced dissociation. *J. Phys. Chem. B* 102:4573, 1998.

Song, J. B., and **E. A. Gislason.** Application of the pairwise energy model to various isotopic variations of the H+H₂ reaction. *Chem. Phys.* 214:23, 1997.

Song, J. B., and **E. A. Gislason.** A modified pairwise-energy model applied to exothermic ion-molecule reactions. *Chem. Phys. Lett.* 259:91, 1996.

Fiss, J. A., L. Zhu, **R. J. Gordon,** and T. Seideman. The origin of a phase lag in the coherent control of photoionization and photodissociation. *Phys. Rev. Lett.* 82:65, 1999.

Liyanage, R., **R. J. Gordon,** and R. W. Field. Diabatic analysis of the electronic states of hydrogen chloride. *J. Chem. Phys.* 109:8374, 1998.

Zhu, L., et al. **(R. J. Gordon).** The effect of resonances on the coherent control of the photoionization and photodissociation of HI and DI. *Phys. Rev. Lett.* 79:4108, 1997.

Zhu, L., et al. **(R. J. Gordon).** Coherent laser control of the product distribution obtained in the photoexcitation of HI. *Science* 270:77, 1995.

Ada, E. T., O. Kornienko, and **L. Hanley.** Chemical modification of polystyrene surfaces by low-energy polyatomic ion beams. *J. Phys. Chem. B* 102:3959, 1998.

Kornienko, O., et al. **(L. Hanley).** Organic surface analysis by two laser ion trap mass spectrometry. Part II: Improved desorption/photoionization configuration. *Anal. Chem.* 70:1208, 1998.

Schultz, D. G., et al. **(L. Hanley).** Classical dynamics simulations of SiMe₃⁺ ion-surface scattering. *J. Chem. Phys.* 106:10337, 1997.

ter Horst, M. A., and **C. J. Jameson.** A classical dynamics study of the anisotropic interactions in NNO-Ar and NNO-Kr systems: Comparison with transport and relaxation data. *J. Chem. Phys.* 109:10238, 1998.

de Dios, A. C., and **C. J. Jameson.** The ¹²⁹Xe nuclear shielding surfaces for Xe interacting with linear molecules CO, N₂ and CO₂. *J. Chem. Phys.* 107:4253, 1997.

Jameson, C. J., A. K. Jameson, R. E. Gerald II, and H. M. Lim. Anisotropic Xe chemical shifts in zeolites. The role of intra- and inter-crystallite diffusion. *J. Phys. Chem.* 101:8418, 1997.

Jameson, C. J., H. M. Lim, and A. K. Jameson. The role of

University of Illinois at Chicago

Selected Publications (continued)

polarization of Xe by di- and monovalent cations in ^{129}Xe NMR studies in zeolite A. *Solid State Nucl. Magn. Reson.* 9:277, 1997.

Klopcic, S. A., V. D. Moravec, and **C. C. Jarrold.** The photoelectron spectrum of PdO$^-$. *J. Chem. Phys.*, in press.

Klopcic, S. A., V. D. Moravec, and **C. C. Jarrold.** Anion photoelectron spectroscopy of PdCO$^-$ and PdCN$^-$: Reactivity of Pd$^-$. *J. Chem. Phys.*, in press.

Moravec, V. D., S. A. Klopcic, and **C. C. Jarrold.** Anion photoelectron spectroscopy of small tin clusters. *J. Chem. Phys.* 110:5079, 1999.

Moravec, V. D., and **C. C. Jarrold.** Study of the low-lying states of NiO$^-$ and NiO using anion photoelectron spectroscopy. *J. Chem. Phys.* 108:1804, 1998.

Marjan, M., **R. J. Kassner,** T. E. Meyer, and M. A. Cusanovich. Cyanide-linked dimer-monomer equilibrium of chromatium vinosum ferric cytochrome c'. *Biochim. Biophys. Acta* 1076:97, 1991.

Kassner, R. J. Ligand binding properties of cytochromes c'. *Biochim. Biophys. Acta* 1058:8, 1991.

Pancoska, P., V. Janota, and **T. A. Keiderling.** Novel matrix descriptor for secondary structure segments in proteins: Demonstration of predictability from circular dichroism spectra. *Anal. Biochem.* 267:72, 1999.

Yoder, G., P. Pancoska, and **T. A. Keiderling.** Characterization of alanine rich peptides of the general formula Ac-(AAKAA)$_n$-GY-NH2 using vibrational circular dichroism and Fourier transform IR. *Biochemistry* 36:15123, 1997.

Yoder, G., **T. A. Keiderling** et al. Conformational characterization of terminally blocked L-(α-Me)-Val homopeptides using vibrational and electronic circular dichroism: ^{3}10 helical stabilization by peptide-peptide interaction. *J. Am. Chem. Soc.* 119:10278, 1997.

Keiderling, T. A. Vibrational circular dichroism applications to conformational analysis of biomolecules. In *Circular Dichroism and the Conformational Analysis of Biomolecules,* pp. 555–98, ed. G. D. Fasman. New York: Plenum Press, 1996.

Fernando, H., G. A. Papadantonakis, N. S. Kim, and **P. R. LeBreton.** Conduction-band-edge ionization thresholds of DNA components in aqueous solution. *Proc. Natl. Acad. Sci. U.S.A.* 95:5550, 1998.

Fernando, H., et al. **(P. R. LeBreton).** The energetics of nucleotide ionization in water-counterion environments. In *Molecular Modeling of Nucleic Acids, ACS Symposium Series 682,* eds. N. B. Leontis and J. SantaLucia Jr. Washington, D.C.: American Chemical Society, 1998.

Kim, N. S., and **P. R. LeBreton.** UV photoelectron spectral corrections applied to the quantum mechanical evaluation of nucleotide ionization potentials in water, counterion environments: The valence electronic structure of anionic 2'-deoxyadenosine-5'-phosphate. *Biospectroscopy* 3:1, 1997.

Fetzer, M., et al. **(P. R. LeBreton).** Valence ionization potentials of anionic phosphate esters: An ab initio quantum mechanical study. *Int. J. Quantum Chem. Quantum Biol. Symp.* 65:1095, 1997.

Mock, W. L. Zinc proteinases. In *Comprehensive Biological Catalysis,* ed. M. Sinnott. United Kingdom: Academic Press, 1998.

Mock, W. L., and J. Yao. Kinetic characterization of the serralysins: A divergent catalytic mechanism pertaining to astacin-type metalloproteases. *Biochemistry* 36:4949, 1997.

Mock, W. L. Cucurbituril. In *Comprehensive Supramolecular Chemistry,* Vol. 2, Chap. 15, p. 477, ed F. Vögtle. Oxford: Pergamon Press, 1996.

Mock, W. L., and D. J. Stanford. Arazoformyl dipeptide substrates for thermolysin. Confirmation of a reverse protonation catalytic mechanism. *Biochemistry* 35:7369, 1996.

Moriarty, R. M., et al. **(G. L. Gould** and **D. J. Wink).** Michael addition to α,β-unsaturated arene ruthenium(II)cyclopentadiene complexes: endonucleophilic addition. *Chem. Commun.* 1155, 1998.

Moriarty, R. M., T. E. Hopkins, R. K. Vaid, and S. G. Levy. Hypervalent iodine oxidation of allenes: Synthesis of 3-acetoxy-3-alkoxypropynes, 2-alkoxy-3-tosyloxypropanals and phenyl-substituted propenals and propenones. *Synthesis* 847, 1992.

Prakash, O. P., and **R. M. Moriarty.** Use of hypervalent iodine oxidation in the synthesis of 2-(a-alkoxyacetyl)pyridine thiosemicarbazones as potential antimalarial agents. *Indian J. Chem. Sect. B* 31b:470, 1992.

Luk, T. S., **R. M. Moriarty** et al. Isotopic studies of atomic site selectivity in molecular multiphoton ionization of nitrogen oxide (N$_2$O). *Phys. Rev. A* 45:6744, 1992.

Moriarty, R. M., and W. R. Epa. Palladium catalyzed cross-coupling reactions of alkenyl(phenyl) iodonium salts with organotin compounds. *Tetrahedron Lett.* 33:4095, 1992.

Ahmed, L., J. Castillo, and **J. A. Morrison.** Reactivity of the diboron tetrahalides. Diboration of ethylene with diboron tetrabromide and thermal decomposition and ligand exchanges of diboron tetrabromide and carbon tetrachloride. *Inorg. Chem.* 31:706, 1992.

Ahmed, L., J. Castillo, and **J. A. Morrison.** Chemistry of tetraboron tetrachloride. Synthesis and characterization of tetraboron tetrabromide (B$_4$B$_4$) and observation of B$_4$BrCl$_3$, B$_4$Br$_2$Cl$_3$, and B$_4$Br$_3$Cl. *Inorg. Chem.* 31:1858, 1992.

Loizou, D. C., et al. **(J. A. Morrison).** Synthesis of cyclopentadienyl-dinitrosyl(trifluoromethyl)-chromium(0), CpCr(NO)$_2$CF$_3$, and cyclopentadienyldinitrosyl(trifluoromethyl)-molybdenum(0), CpMo(NO)$_2$CF$_3$, crystal structure of CpCr(NO)$_2$Cf$_3$. *Organometallics* 11:4189, 1992.

Morrison, J. A. Chemistry of the polyhedral boron halides and the diboron tetrahalides. *Chem. Rev.* 91:35, 1991.

Lockyear-Schultz, L. L., **S. A. Shippy,** T. A. Nieman, and J. V. Sweedler. Peroxyoxalate chemiluminescence detection for CE using membrane collection. *J. Microcol. Sep.* 10:329, 1998.

Garden, R. W., **S. A. Shippy** et al. Novel proteolytic processing of aplysia egg-laying hormone prohormone. *Proc. Natl. Acad. Sci. U.S.A.* 95:3972, 1998.

Cruz, L., **S. A. Shippy,** and J. V. Sweedler. CE detectors based on light. In *High Performance Capillary Electrophoresis,* ed. M. G. Khaledi. New York: John Wiley & Sons, 1998.

Teo, B. K., X. Shi, and H. Zhang. Pure gold cluster of 1:9:9:1:9:9:1 layered structure: A novel 39-metal-atom cluster [(Ph$_3$P)$_{14}$Au$_{39}$Cl$_6$]Cl$_2$ with an interstitial gold atom in a hexagonal antiprismatic cage. *J. Am. Chem. Soc.* 114:2743, 1992.

Teo, B. K., X. Shi, and H. Zhang Cluster rotamerism of a 25-metal-atom cluster [(Ph$_3$P)$_{10}$Au$_{13}$Ag$_{12}$Br$_8$]$^+$ monocation: A molecular rotary unit. *J. Chem. Soc. Chem. Commun.* 1195, 1992.

Teo, B. K., and H. Zhang. Molecular machines: molecular structure of [(p-Tol$_3$P)$_{10}$Au$_{13}$Ag$_{12}$Cl$_8$(PF$_6$)], a cluster with a biicosahedral core, rotor-like metal framework and an unusual arrangement of bridging ligand. *Angew. Chem.* 104:447, 1992.

Teo, B. K., and H. Zhang. Clusters of clusters: Self-organization and self-similarity in the intermediate stages of cluster growth of gold-silver supraclusters. *Proc. Natl. Acad. Sci. U.S.A.* 88:5067, 1991.

Perkins, C. L., **M. Trenary,** and T. Tanaka. Structure of the (100) surface of the icosahedral solid YB$_{66}$. *Phys. Rev. B.* 15:9980, 1998.

Celio, H., et al. **(M. Trenary).** Molecular adsorption of HCN on the Pt(111) and Cu(100) surfaces. *Langmuir* 14:379, 1998.

Celio, H., K. Mudalige, P. Mills, and **M. Trenary.** Formation of isocyanate on Cu(100) from the oxidation of cyanogen and from the decomposition of isocyanic acid. *Surf. Sci.* 394:L168, 1997.

Mills, P., D. Jentz, and **M. Trenary.** The chemistry of cyanogen (C$_2$N$_2$) and hydrogen on Pt(111). *J. Am. Chem. Soc.* 119:9002, 1997.

D. J. Wink. Is teaching instinctive? No, I'm afraid not. *J. Coll. Sci. Teach.* 28:315, 1999.

Young, P. R., and C. Karunatilake. Bovine brain cathepsin D: Inhibition by pepstatin and binding to concanavalin A. *Int. J. Biochem.* 24:229, 1992.

Young, P. R., and S. M. Spevacek. Substratum acidification by murine B$_{16}$F$_{10}$ melanoma cultures. *Biochim. Biophys. Acta* 1139:163, 1992.

Young, P. R., W. R. Snyder, and R. F. McMahon. Inhibition of *Clostridium perfringens* phospholipase C by ammonium and sulfonium dications. *Biochim. Biophys. Acta* 1121:297, 1992.

Young, P. R., C. Karunatilake, and A. P. Zygas. Binding of cathepsin D to the mannose receptor on rat peritoneal macrophages. *Biochim. Biophys. Acta* 1095:1, 1991.

UofL

UNIVERSITY OF LOUISVILLE

Department of Chemistry

Programs of Study

The Department of Chemistry offers both the M.S. and Ph.D. degrees in chemistry, with concentrations in analytical chemistry, biochemistry, chemical physics, inorganic chemistry, organic chemistry, and physical chemistry. The research projects are clustered into two main areas: chemical catalysis and biohealth-related chemical studies. Several of these projects involve strong and successful interactions with faculty members in other departments, such as chemical and electrical engineering and physics within the context of chemical catalysis, and the departments of biochemistry, ophthalmology and visual sciences, pharmacology, and toxicology in projects related to the synthesis of biologically relevant molecules and the understanding of complex biochemical phenomena. Chemistry graduates are well trained to enter their professional careers with expertise in cutting-edge technologies and scientific knowledge.

Research Facilities

The department is housed in a 1-million-square-foot building that is well equipped with modern instrumentation and computational facilities. Available in the department are solution nuclear magnetic resonance (NMR) spectrometers (500-MHz, 300-MHz, and smaller ones), solid-state NMR (500-MHz and 300-MHz), single-crystal X-ray diffractometer, UV-vis, mid- and near-infrared spectrometers, mass spectrometers, laser-based spectrofluorometers, and gas and high-pressure liquid chromatographs. In addition, students are not only trained to perform, for example, fairly sophisticated multidimensional experiments using a 500-MHz NMR spectrometer, but they also have easy access to the instrumentation. Hands-on experience and immediate access to state-of-the-art instrumentation enhance the quality of the graduate training.

Financial Aid

Most entering graduate students qualify for a graduate teaching assistantship (GTA). The GTA includes a yearly stipend of about $15,000 and full remission of tuition fees. For first-year graduate students, the responsibilities associated with a GTA include the teaching of undergraduate laboratories and/or recitations in introductory chemistry courses under the guidance of a senior instructor. Later into the graduate program, research assistantships (RAs) and GTAs for the instruction of upper-level undergraduate courses are also available. The experience gained in the teaching of undergraduate students is of great value in the professional careers of the students.

Cost of Study

Tuition costs are waived for graduate students in good standing who hold GTAs and RAs.

Living and Housing Costs

Although dormitory rooms are available, most graduate students rent privately owned apartments nearby and within commuting distance. The monthly rent for one-bedroom apartments varies between $300 and $450.

Student Group

There are about 4,000 graduate students in the University. The department has about 60 graduate students, half of whom are international students from Western and Eastern Europe and Asia.

Student Outcomes

Most Ph.D. students are employed by industries or pursue postdoctoral positions before taking permanent industrial or academic jobs. Research positions in government laboratories have also been accepted by Ph.D. graduates.

Location

A very positive aspect of the department is the city in which it is located. The Louisville metropolitan area has a population of about 500,000 people. It is affordable and clean, with a network of beautiful and well-cared-for parks that offer hiking and biking trails. Excellent and relatively inexpensive restaurants abound in the city, with a wide range of ethnic cuisines represented. Weekends in spring, summer, and early fall are filled with festivals and outdoor activities. The community of Louisville is noted for its commitment to and support for the arts. The Louisville Symphony Orchestra, the Louisville Ballet, and the Actors Theater of Louisville offer outstanding performances. Churchill Downs, home of the Kentucky Derby, is a popular attraction. The Run for the Roses is the exciting culmination of a week full of fun events in early May.

The University

Created in 1798, the University of Louisville is one of the oldest municipal universities in the nation. The University entered the state system of higher education in 1970, and excellence in research and teaching have continued to be the goal. With the remarkable commitment of Governor Patton and University President John Shumaker to improve the quality of higher education, the future of the research programs in the areas of chemical catalysis and biohealth seems most auspicious.

Applying

Applications for admission into the graduate program are accepted from students with bachelor's degrees or the equivalent. Applications must be received by January 15 for admission in the fall term. Students can request application packages from the address listed below.

Correspondence and Information

Graduate Student Admission Coordinator
Department of Chemistry
University of Louisville
Louisville, Kentucky 40292

Telephone: 502-852-6798
Fax: 502-852-8149
E-mail: sfbull01@homer.louisville.edu
World Wide Web: http://www.louisville.edu/a-s/chemistry

University of Louisville

THE FACULTY AND THEIR RESEARCH
Department of Chemistry

Richard P. Baldwin, Professor; Ph.D., Purdue, 1976. Electroanalytical chemistry, applications of chemically modified electrodes, bioseparations by HPLC and capillary electrophoresis.

Robert M. Buchanan, Professor; Ph.D., Colorado, 1980. Synthesis, structure, and magnetic properties of inorganic and bioinorganic compounds; active site models of μ-oxo iron proteins; polynuclear managanese complexes as models of PSII and pseudocatalase proteins; mixed valence complexes; C–H bond functionalization via metal-oxo catalyzed reactions.

Thomas H. Crawford, Professor Emeritus; Ph.D., Louisville, 1961. Chemical education, complexes of antimony trichloride with organic substrates.

Donald B. DuPré, Professor; Ph.D., Princeton, 1968. Polymers and liquid crystals, molecular modeling.

Peter W. Faguy, Associate Professor; Ph.D., Case Western Reserve, 1988. Infrared spectroscopic investigations of the electrode/electrolyte solution interface, development of in situ infrared reflection techniques, structural characterization and electrochemical application of conducting polymer/clay mineral composite materials.

Dorothy H. Gibson, Professor; Texas at Austin, 1965. Transition-metal organometallic chemistry, reactions of coordinated ligands, homogeneous catalysis, synthesis and characterization of transition-metal complexes of carbon dioxide and other C_1 ligands.

Pawel M. Kozlowski, Assistant Professor; Ph.D., Arizona, 1992. Computational quantum chemistry, theoretical modeling of biomolecules and prediction of spectral properties.

N. Thornton Lipscomb, Professor Emeritus; Ph.D., Louisville, 1961. Kinetics and mechanisms of radiation-induced polymerization, photosensitized polymerization, mechanisms of photosensitization, UV cure of thick (1 cm) samples.

Frederick A. Luzzio, Associate Professor; Ph.D., Tufts, 1982. Synthetic methods, total synthesis, natural products isolation.

Muriel C. Maurer, Assistant Professor; Ph.D., Virginia, 1993. Biochemistry, protein structure-function relationships, enzyme-ligand interactions, blood coagulation/anticoagulation, protein folding, site-directed mutagenesis, nuclear magnetic resonance, circular dichroism.

Mark E. Noble, Professor; Ph.D., Indiana, 1982. Synthesis, structural, and reactivity properties of metal-sulfur compounds of catalytic and enzymatic interest; bioinorganic chemistry.

George R. Pack, Professor; Ph.D., SUNY at Buffalo, 1973. Theoretical biophysical chemistry, electrostatic properties and their contribution to the regulation of nucleic acid structure and function.

John F. Richardson, Associate Professor; Ph.D., Western Ontario, 1981. The application of X-ray crystallography and molecular graphics to structure-function relationships and nonbonded contacts; homogeneous catalysts; bonding environments in heavier nonmetals, ceramics, oligosaccharides, and pseudopeptides.

Arno F. Spatola, Professor; Ph.D., Michigan, 1971. Structure-activity relationships of polypeptide hormones, solid-phase peptide synthesis, conformational studies using NMR, peptide backbone modifications, collagenase inhibitors, catalytic transfer hydrogenation, HPLC-based/peptide degradation assays, cyclic peptides, enzyme mimetics, cyclic peptide libraries, pseudopeptide macrocycles.

K. Grant Taylor, Professor; Ph.D., Wayne State, 1963. Radical and ionic chemistry of peroxides, carbohydrate and oligosaccharide chemistry, diallene oligomerizations.

Charles A. Trapp, Professor; Ph.D., Chicago, 1963. Magnetic properties of matter, electron spin resonance of transition-metal complexes and organic free radicals, cancer research.

Donald E. Williams, Professor Emeritus; Ph.D., Iowa State, 1964. Computational chemistry, molecular clusters and crystals, intermolecular potential energy, molecular packing analysis.

Richard J. Wittebort, Professor; Ph.D., Indiana, 1978. Experimental studies of structure and molecular dynamics in partially ordered solids and fibrous proteins by solid-state nuclear magnetic resonance spectroscopy.

John L. Wong, Professor; Ph.D., Berkeley, 1966. Molecular studies of environmental health problems, with focus on carcinogenesis, preparation of monoclonal antibodies for immunoassay of hemoblobin adducts as biomarkers, metal speciation, and cytoxicity by electrochemical bioassay and human dosimetry.

M. Cecilia Yappert, Associate Professor; Ph.D., Oregon State, 1985. Laser fluorescence spectroscopy; optical fibers for remote sensing; biological systems; infrared spectroscopy, deconvolution computational methods, lipid-lipid interactions, and lipid-protein interactions; lipid composition in ocular lenses.

UMBC

AN HONORS
UNIVERSITY
IN MARYLAND

UNIVERSITY OF MARYLAND, BALTIMORE COUNTY

Department of Chemistry and Biochemistry

Programs of Study

The Department of Chemistry and Biochemistry at the University of Maryland, Baltimore County (UMBC), offers programs of graduate study in chemistry and biochemistry leading to the M.S. and the Ph.D. degrees. The department also participates in a biotechnology M.S. program (applied molecular biology) in collaboration with the Department of Biological Sciences, an interdisciplinary Ph.D. program in molecular and cellular biology, an Interface Program that provides cross-disciplinary experience in chemistry and biology, and the Meyerhoff Program in Biomedical Sciences. The department's graduate programs in biochemistry and in molecular and cellular biology benefit from being part of larger intercampus joint programs in those fields, sponsored in conjunction with departments at the medical, dental, and pharmacy schools of the downtown Baltimore campus.

Upon entering the graduate program, both M.S. and Ph.D. students are required to take a set of placement examinations that are designed to test their proficiency at the senior undergraduate level and to indicate any areas of deficiency. Under the guidance of an advisory committee, they next complete a group of courses, constituting a core curriculum, which has been designed to bring them to a minimum level of proficiency in each of the major areas of chemistry. In addition, they are expected to take specialized courses in their field of interest. To fulfill the course requirements normally requires one to two years, depending upon the student's initial level of proficiency as demonstrated by the placement examinations.

To qualify for the degree, M.S. students must pass a comprehensive examination in their major field. Thesis research must be approved by a thesis committee, which also administers an oral examination based on the thesis research. Completing the course requirements, passing the comprehensive and oral examinations, and gaining approval of the thesis constitute fulfillment of the M.S. degree requirements. Candidates for the M.S. also have the option of substituting additional course work for the thesis. Graduate students in the Ph.D. program are expected to pass comprehensive examinations, prepare and defend an acceptable research proposal, present a dissertation based upon original research, and pass an oral defense.

The principal areas of thesis research for both the M.S. and Ph.D. degrees include analytical chemistry; biochemistry; bioinorganic chemistry; enzymology; mass spectrometry; models for enzymic reactions; organic mechanisms; organic synthesis; protein and nucleic acid chemistry; theoretical, physical, bioanalytical, biophysical, and carbohydrate chemistry; and chemistry at the biology interface.

Research Facilities

Extensive facilities are available for modern research. The specialized research instrumentation available includes calorimetry, chromatography, stopped-flow and temperature-jump kinetics, nanosecond laser flash photolysis, nuclear magnetic resonance spectroscopy (one 200-, one 300-, one 500-, two 600-, and one 800-MHz instruments), electron spin resonance spectroscopy, circular dichroism, X-ray diffraction, infrared spectroscopy, laser fluorescence spectroscopy, atomic absorption, gas chromatography–mass spectrometry, and scintillation and gamma counting apparatus as well as extensive molecular modeling computer facilities. Also located in the department is a Center for Structural Biochemistry, which specializes in the structural analysis of biological molecules (e.g., biopolymers, peptides, glycoproteins). In addition to TOF/FT, a laser desorption mass spectrometer, and two 500-MHz and 600-MHz NMRs, the center houses one of the few tandem mass spectrometers located in academic institutions worldwide. The Howard Hughes Medical Investigator Suite houses the second 600- and the 800-MHz NMRs, used for high-dimensional studies of HIV proteins, metallobiomolecules, and macromolecular interactions. The main University library contains more than 2,500 volumes of chemistry texts and subscribes to 150 chemistry and biochemistry periodicals. The department reference room also provides access to the principal journals.

Financial Aid

Financial aid packages with stipends of $13,300 to $16,500 per year, with health insurance and tuition remission, are offered to qualified students.

Cost of Study

Tuition in 1999–2000 is $268 per credit hour for Maryland residents and $470 per credit hour for nonresidents. Fees are $423 per semester.

Living and Housing Costs

There are a limited number of on-campus dormitory rooms available for graduate students. Most graduate students are housed in apartments or rooming houses in the nearby communities of Arbutus and Catonsville. A single graduate student can expect living and educational expenses of approximately $11,000 to $13,000 a year.

Student Group

In 1999–2000, the department's graduate students include 32 men and 21 women. Approximately 80 percent of the students are receiving some form of financial aid.

Student Outcomes

All of the students plan careers in chemistry and biochemistry in either teaching or research and in associated regulatory and financial areas.

Location

The University has a scenic location on the periphery of the Baltimore metropolitan area. Downtown Baltimore can be reached in 15 minutes by car, while Washington is an hour away. Both Baltimore and Washington have very extensive cultural facilities, including eight major universities, a number of museums and art galleries of international reputation, two major symphony orchestras, and numerous theaters. All the usual recreational facilities are available in both cities. Several excellent beaches are accessible by car.

The University

UMBC was established in 1966 on a 500-acre campus. The Department of Chemistry and Biochemistry of the University of Maryland Graduate School, Baltimore, is located at the UMBC campus. The University has about 10,400 students drawn primarily from Maryland, although an increasing number have enrolled from other states and countries. The undergraduates are predominantly interested in professional or business careers. Because a high percentage of the students are the first members of their families to attend college, UMBC has a very different atmosphere from that encountered in older institutions and has made a particular effort to attract minority students, who now account for about 36 percent of the undergraduate student body.

Applying

Applications should include an academic transcript, three references, and the results of the General Test of the Graduate Record Examinations.

Correspondence and Information

Graduate Program Director
Department of Chemistry and Biochemistry
University of Maryland, Baltimore County
1000 Hilltop Circle
Baltimore, Maryland 21250
Telephone: 410-455-2491
E-mail: chemgrad@umbc.edu

University of Maryland, Baltimore County

THE FACULTY AND THEIR RESEARCH

Bradley R. Arnold, Assistant Professor; Ph.D., Utah, 1991; postdoctoral studies at the National Research Council of Canada, Ottawa, and the Center for Photoinduced Charge Transfer, University of Rochester. Physical chemistry, application of time-resolved polarized spectroscopy.

Theodore A. Budzichowski, Assistant Professor; Ph.D., California, Irvine, 1991; postdoctoral studies at Indiana. Inorganic chemistry, synthetic and mechanistic organometallic chemistry, catalysis.

C. Allen Bush, Professor; Ph.D., Berkeley, 1965; postdoctoral studies at Cornell. Biophysical chemistry: conformation and dynamics of carbohydrates, glycoproteins, glycopeptides, and polysaccharides by NMR spectroscopy, computer modeling, and circular dichroism.

Donald Creighton, Professor; Ph.D., UCLA, 1972; postdoctoral studies at the Institute for Cancer Research. Enzyme mechanisms and protein structure, studies on sulfhydryl proteases and glyoxalase enzymes.

Dan Fabris, Assistant Professor; Ph.D., Padua (Italy), 1989; postdoctoral studies at the National Research Council, Area of Research of Padua (Italy), and the University of Maryland, Baltimore County. Bioanalytical and biomedical applications of mass spectrometry, nucleic acid adducts, and protein–nucleic acid interactions.

James C. Fishbein, Professor; Ph.D., Brandeis, 1985; postdoctoral studies at Toronto. Mechanisms of organic reactions in aqueous solutions; generation and study of reactive intermediates, particularly those involved in nitrosamine and nitrosamide carcinogenesis.

Ramachandra S. Hosmane, Professor; Ph.D., South Florida, 1978; postdoctoral studies at Illinois. Organic synthesis; biomedicinal chemistry, with applications in antiviral and anticancer therapy; and biomedical technology, with applications in artificial blood.

Richard L. Karpel, Professor; Ph.D., Brandeis, 1970; postdoctoral studies at Princeton. Interactions of helix destabilizing proteins with nucleic acids and the involvement of such proteins in various aspects of RNA function, metal ion–nucleic acid interactions.

Lisa A. Kelly, Assistant Professor; Ph.D., Bowling Green, 1993; postdoctoral studies at Brookhaven National Laboratory. Photoredox initiated chemical bond cleavage in biological and model systems.

William R. LaCourse, Associate Professor; Ph.D., Northeastern, 1987; postdoctoral studies at Ames Laboratory (USDOE) and Iowa State. Pulsed electrochemical detection techniques for bioanalytical separations.

Joel F. Liebman, Professor; Ph.D., Princeton, 1970; postdoctoral studies at Cambridge and the National Institute of Standards and Technology. Energetics of organic molecules, especially considerations of strain and aromaticity; gaseous ions; noble gas, fluorine, boron, and silicon chemistry; mathematical and quantum chemistry.

Ralph M. Pollack, Professor; Ph.D., Berkeley, 1968; postdoctoral studies at Northwestern. Enzyme reactions, model systems for enzyme mechanisms, organic reaction mechanisms.

Paul J. Smith, Assistant Professor; Ph.D., Pittsburgh, 1993; postdoctoral studies at Johns Hopkins. Bioorganic and physical organic chemistry, host-guest chemistry, DNA structure and DNA binding by small molecules.

Michael F. Summers, Professor and Howard Hughes Associate Medical Investigator; Ph.D., Emory, 1984; postdoctoral studies at the Center for Drugs and Biologics, FDA, Bethesda, Maryland. Elucidation of structural, dynamic, and thermodynamic features of metallobiomolecules utilizing advanced two-dimensional and multinuclear NMR methods.

James S. Vincent, Associate Professor; Ph.D., Harvard, 1963; postdoctoral studies at Caltech. Infrared and Raman spectroscopy of phospholipid membrane systems, magnetic spectroscopy of transition-metal complexes.

Dale L. Whalen, Professor; Ph.D., Berkeley, 1965; postdoctoral studies at UCLA. Reactions of carcinogenic polycyclic aromatic hydrocarbon epoxides, organic reaction mechanisms.

University of Maryland, Baltimore County

SELECTED PUBLICATIONS

Zaini, R. Y., A. C. Orcutt, and **B. R. Arnold.** Determination of equilibrium constants of weakly bound charge transfer complexes. *J. Photochem. Photobiol.* 69:443, 1999.

Wagner, B. D., **B. R. Arnold,** G. S. Brown, and J. Lusztyk. Spectroscopy and absolute reactivity of ketenes in acetonitrile studied by laser flash photolysis with time-resolved infrared detection. *J. Am. Chem. Soc.* 120:1827, 1998.

Arnold, B. R., et al. Combined application of picosecond transient absorption and emission measurements in studies of radical-ion pair dynamics. *Photochem. Photobiol.* 65(1):15–22, 1997.

Arnold, B. R., et al. Absolute energies of interconverting contact and solvent-separated radical-ion pairs. *J. Am. Chem. Soc.* 118(23):5482–3, 1996.

Arnold, B. R., et al. Dynamics of interconversion of contact and solvent-separated radical-ion pairs. *J. Am. Chem. Soc.* 117:4399–4400, 1995.

Feher, F. J., and **T. A. Budzichowski.** Heterosilsesquioxanes: Synthesis and characterization of gallium-containing polyhedral oligosilsesquioxanes. *Inorg. Chem.* 36:4082–6, 1997.

Budzichowski, T. A., M. H. Chisholm, and W. E. Streib. Preparation and structure of $Mo_2(OCH_2{}^rBu)_6(\eta^5\text{-}Cp)Na(DME)$. *Can. J. Chem.* 74:2386–91, 1996.

Budzichowski, T. A., M. H. Chisholm, K. S. Kramer, and K. Folting. $Mo_2(\mu\text{-}O)(OCH_2{}^rBu)_4(PMe_3)_4$. Preparation and structure of a partial hydrolysis product of $Mo_2(OCH_2{}^rBu)_6$. *Polyhedron* 15:3085–91, 1996.

Budzichowski, T. A., M. H. Chisholm, and K. Folting. Substrate uptake and activation by dimolybdenum and ditungsten hexaalkoxides. Factors influencing the cleavage of C-X multiple bonds as deduced from studies of the reactions between $[Mo_2(OR)_6]$ ($R={}^rBu$ and $CH_2{}^rBu$) and $Ar_2C=S$, Et_2NCN, and $P({}^nBu)_3$. *Chem. Eur. J.* 2:110–7, 1996.

Budzichowski, T. A., et al. Tetranuclear phosphinidine, phosphide, arsenide and oxide anionic clusters of molybdenum and tungsten supported by neopentoxide ligands: $Na(18\text{-crown-}6)[M_4(\mu\text{-}PSiMe_3)(OCH_2{}^rBu)_{11}]$, $K(18\text{-crown-}6)[M_4(\mu_3\text{-}E)(OCH_2{}^rBu)_{11}]$ where $E=P$ and As, and $K(18\text{-crown-}6)_2[Mo_4(\mu_3\text{-}O)(OCH_2{}^rBu)_{11}]$. *Inorg. Chem.* 35:3659–66, 1996.

Bush, C. A., M. Martin-Pastor, and A. Imberty. Structure and conformation of complex carbohydrates of glycoproteins, glycolipids and bacterial polysaccharides. *Annu. Rev. Biophys. Struct. Biol.,* in press.

Xu, Q., and **C. A. Bush.** Measurement of long-range carbon-carbon coupling constants in a uniformly enriched complex polysaccharide. *Carbohydr. Res.* 306:334–9, 1998.

Reddy, G. P., et al. **(C. A. Bush).** Structure determination of the capsular polysaccharide from *Vibrio vulnificus* strain 6353. *Eur. J. Biochem.* 255:279–88, 1998.

Gunawardena, S., et al. **(C. A. Bush).** Structure of a muramic acid containing capsular polysaccharide from the pathogenic strain of *Vibrio vulnificus* ATCC 27562. *Carbohydr. Res.* 309:65–76, 1998.

Bush, C. A., et al. Classification of *Vibrio vulnificus* strains by the carbohydrate composition of their capsular polysaccharides. *Anal. Biochem.* 250:186–95, 1997.

Xu, Q., and **C. A. Bush.** Molecular modeling of the flexible cell wall of *Streptococcus mitis* J22 on the basis of heteronuclear coupling constraints. *Biochemistry* 35:14521–9, 1996.

Cameron, A. D., et al. **(D. J. Creighton).** X-ray crystal structure of the complex between human glyoxalase I and an intermediate analog and implications for the reaction mechanism. *J. Mol. Biol.,* in press.

Hamilton, D. S., et al. **(D. J. Creighton).** A new method for rapidly generating inhibitors of glyoxalase I inside tumor cells using S-(N-aryl-n-hydroxycarbamoyl)ethylsulfoxide. *J. Med. Chem.,* in press.

Kavarana, M. J., E. G. Kovaleva, **D. J. Creighton,** and J. L. Eiseman. Mechanism based competitive inhibitors of glyoxalase I: Membrane transport properties, *in vitro* antitumor activities, and stabilities in human serum and mouse serum. *J. Med. Chem.* 42:221–8, 1999.

Saint-Jean, A. P., K. R. Phillips, **D. J. Creighton,** and M. J. Stone.

Active monomeric and dimeric forms of *Pseudomonas Putida* glyoxalase I: Evidence for 3D domain swapping. *Biochemistry* 37:10345, 1998.

Shih, M. J., J. W. Edinger, and **D. J. Creighton.** Diffusion-dependent kinetic properties of glyoxalase I and estimates of the steady-state concentrations of glyoxalase pathway intermediates in glycolyzing erythrocytes. *Eur. J. Biochem.* 244:852–7, 1997.

Lan, Y., T. Lu, P. Lovett, and **D. J. Creighton.** Evidence for a (triosephosphate isomerase-like) "catalytic loop" near the active site of glyoxalase I. *J. Biol. Chem.* 270:12957–60, 1995.

Fabris, D., Y. Hatout, and C. Fenselau. Investigation of zinc chelation in zinc-finger arrays by electrospray mass spectrometry. *Inorg. Chem.,* in press.

Fabris, D., and C. Fenselau. Characterization of allosteric insulin hexamers by electrospray ionization mass spectrometry. *Anal. Chem.* 71:384–7, 1999.

Zaia, J., **D. Fabris** et al. **(R. Karpel).** Monitoring metal ion flux in reactions of metallothionein and drug-modified metallothionein by electrospray mass spectrometry. *Protein Sci.* 7:2398–404, 1998.

Fabris, D., J. Zaia, Y. Hatout, and C. Fenselau. Retention of thiol protons in two classes of protein zinc coordination centers. *J. Am. Chem. Soc.* 118:12242–3, 1996.

Hatout, Y., and **D. Fabris** et al. Characterization of intermediates in the oxidation of zinc fingers in the HIV-1 nucleocapsid protein P7. *Drug Metab. Dispos.* 24:1395–400, 1996.

Chahoua, L., and **J. C. Fishbein.** Formation and nucleophilic capture of N-nitrosiminium ions. *Can. J. Chem.,* in press.

Chahoua, L., H. Cai, and **J. C. Fishbein.** Cyclic α-acetoxynitrosamines: Mechanisms of decomposition and stability of α-hydroxynitrosamine and nitrosiminium ion reactive intermediates. *J. Am. Chem. Soc.,* in press.

Cai, H., and **J. C. Fishbein.** α-acyloxydialkylnitrosamines: Effects of structure on the formation of N-nitrosiminium ions and a predicted change in mechanism. *J. Am. Chem. Soc.* 121:1826, 1999.

Cai, H., and **J. C. Fishbein.** Secondary α-deuterium kinetic isotope effects in the decomposition of simple α-acetoxydialkylnitrosamines: Nitrosiminium ion intermediates. *Tetrahedron* 53:10671–6, 1997.

Chahoua, L., M. Mesić, T. A. Vigroux, and **J. C. Fishbein.** Evidence for the formation of α-hydroxydialkylnitrosamines in the pH-independent solvolysis of α-acyloxydialkylnitrosamines. *J. Org. Chem.* 62:2500–4, 1997.

Mesić, M., C. Revis, and **J. C. Fishbein.** Effects of structure on the reactivity of α-hydroxydialkylnitrosamines in aqueous solutions. *J. Am. Chem. Soc.* 118:7412–3, 1996.

Peri, S. P., et al. **(R. S. Hosmane.)** Affinity reagents for cross-linking hemoglobin: Bis(phenoxycarbonylethyl)-phosphinic acid (BPCEP) and bis(3-nitrophenoxycarbonylethyl)phosphinic acid (BNCEP). *Hemoglobin* 23:1–20, 1999.

Skancke, A., **R. S. Hosmane,** and **J. F. Liebman.** Unification of some literature models of aromaticity: A calculational and conceptual study of a set of one-ring species. *Acta Chem. Scand.* 52:967–74, 1998.

Rajappan, V. P., and **R. S. Hosmane.** Synthesis and guanase inhibition studies of a novel ring-expanded purine analogue containing a 5:7-fused, planar, aromatic heterocyclic ring system. *Bioorg. Med. Chem.* 8:3649–52, 1998.

Agasimundin, Y. S., M. W. Mumper, and **R. S. Hosmane.** Inhibitors of glycogen phosphorylase B: Synthesis, biochemical screening, and molecular modeling studies of novel analogues of hydantocidin. *Bioorg. Med. Chem.* 6:911–23, 1998.

Rajappan, V. P., and **R. S. Hosmane.** Analogues of Azepinomcin as inhibitors of guanase. *Nucleosides Nucleotides* 17:1141–51, 1998.

Hosmane, R. S., S. P. Peri, V. S. Bhadti, and V. W. Macdonald. Bis[2-(4-carboxyphenoxy)-carbonylethyl]phosphinic acid (BCCEP): A novel affinity reagent for the β-cleft modification of human hemoglobin. *Bioorg. Med. Chem.* 6:767–83, 1998.

Wu, M., E. K. Flynn, and **R. L. Karpel.** Details of the nucleic acid binding site of T4 gene 32 protein revealed by proteolysis and DNA T_m depression methods. *J. Mol. Biol.* 286:1107–21, 1999.

University of Maryland, Baltimore County

Selected Publications (continued)

Karpel, R. L., H. I. Ziserman, and L. A. Waidner. Double-stranded DNA-interactive properties of intact and truncated gene 32 protein. *FASEB J.* 11:1951, 1997.

Herschaig, D., et al. **(R. L. Karpel).** An RNA chaperone activity of nonspecific RNA binding proteins in hammerhead ribozyme catalysis. *EMBO J.* 13:2913–24, 1994.

Delahunty, M. D., S. H. Wilson, and **R. L. Karpel.** Studies on primer binding of HIV-1 reverse transcriptase using a fluorescent probe. *J. Mol. Biol.* 236:469–79, 1994.

Rogers, J. E., and **L. A. Kelly.** Nucleic acid oxidation mediated by naphthalene and benzophenone imide and diimide derivatives. *J. Am. Chem. Soc.,* in press.

Kelly, L. A., J. G. Trunk, and J. C. Southerland. Time-resolved fluorescence polarization measurements for entire emission spectra with a resistive-anode, single-photon-counting detector: the Fluorescence Omnilyzer. *Rev. Sci. Instr.* 68:2279, 1997.

Chen, X. G., et al., **(L. A. Kelly).** Resonance Raman examination of the electronic excited states of glycylglycine and other dipeptides: Observation of a carboxylate -> amide charge transfer transition. *J. Am. Chem. Soc.* 118:9705, 1996.

Kelly, L. A., J. G. Trunk, K. Polewski, and J. C. Sutherland. Simultaneous resolution of spectral and temporal properties of UV and visible fluorescence using single-photon counting with a position-sensitive detector. *Rev. Sci. Instrum.* 66:1496, 1995.

Kelly, L. A., and M. A. J. Rodgers. Inter- and intramolecular oxidative quenching of mixed ligand tris(bipyridyl)ruthenium(II) complexes by methyl viologen. *J. Phys. Chem.* 99:13132, 1995.

LaCourse, W. R., and C. O. Dasenbrock. Pulsed electrochemical detection of sulfur-containing antibiotics following high performance liquid chromatography. *J. Pharm. Biomed. Anal.* 19:239–52, 1999.

Dasenbrock, C. O., and **W. R. LaCourse.** Assay for cephapirin and ampicillin in raw milk by high performance liquid chromatography-integrated pulsed electrochemical detection. *Anal. Chem.* 70:2415–20, 1998.

Zook, C. M., and **W. R. LaCourse.** Pulsed amperometric detection of microdialysates from the glucose oxidase reaction. *Anal. Chem.* 70:801–6, 1998.

LaCourse, W. R. *Pulsed Electrochemical Detection in High Performance Liquid Chroma-tography.* New York: John Wiley & Sons, 1997.

Owens, G. S., and **W. R. LaCourse.** Pulsed electrochemical detection of thiols and disulfides following capillary electrophoresis. *J. Chromatogr. B* 695:15–25, 1997.

Hunter, E. P., et al. **(J. F. Liebman).** The "thermochemical mimicry" of phenyl and vinyl groups: Can it be extended to charged species? *Int. J. Mass Spectrom. Ion Processes* 179/180:261–6, 1998.

Rogers, D. W., Y. Zhao, M. Hulce, and **J. F. Liebman.** Enthalpies of hydrogenation and formation of enones: Resonance energies of 2-cyclopentenone and 2-cyclohexenone. *J. Chem. Thermodyn.* 30:1393–400, 1998.

Liebman, J. F., H. L. Paige, and J. Passmore. Why aren't there any trioxygenyl or ozonium salts? Or, why does our reaction of O_3 and PtF_6 give O_2PtF_6? *Struct. Chem.* 9:315–7, 1998.

Liebman, J. F. Some thoughts on the solubility of carbon dioxide and silicon dioxide in water. *Struct. Chem.* 8:313–5, 1997.

Roux, M. V., et al. **(J. F. Liebman).** The elusive antiaromaticity of maleimides and maleic anhydride: Enthalpies of formation of N-methylmaleimide, N-methylsuccinimide, N-methylphthalimide and N-benzoyl-N-methylbenzamide. *J. Org. Chem.* 62:2732–7, 1997.

Yao, X., and **R. M. Pollack.** Electronic effects on enol acidity and keto-enol equilibrium constants for ring substituted 2-tetralones. *Can. J. Chem.,* in press.

Qi, L., and **R. M. Pollack.** The catalytic contribution of phenylalanine-101 of 3-oxo-delta-5-steroid isomerase. *Biochemistry* 37:6760–6, 1998.

Thornburg, L. D., et al. **(R. M. Pollack).** Electrophilic assistance by Asp-99 of 3-oxo-delta-5-steroid isomerase. *Biochemistry* 37:10499–506, 1998.

Petrounia, I., and **R. M. Pollack.** Substituent effects in the binding of phenols to the D38N mutant of 3-Oxo-Δ^5-steroid isomerase. *Biochemistry* 37:700, 1998.

Nevy, J. B., et al. **(R. M. Pollack).** Transition state imbalance in the deprotonation of substituted 2-tetralones by hydroxide ion. *J. Am. Chem. Soc.* 119:12722, 1997.

Wu, Z. R., et al. **(R. M. Pollack** and **M. F. Summers).** Solution structure of 3-oxo-Δ^5-steroid isomerase. *Science* 276:415–8, 1997.

Kumar, G., **P. J. Smith,** and G. F. Payne. Enzymatic grafting of a natural product onto chitosan to confer water solubility under basic conditions. *Biotechnol. Bioeng.* 63:154–65, 1999.

Hauser, S. L., E. S. Cotner, and **P. J. Smith.** Synthesis of a capped dicationic derivative of beta-cyclodextrin. *Tetrahedron Lett.* 40:2865–6, 1999.

Cotner, E. S., **P. J. Smith.** Phosphotyrosine-binding by ammonium- and guanidinium-modified cyclodextrins. *J. Org. Chem.* 63:1737–9, 1998.

Chatterjee, M., **P. J. Smith,** and C. A. Townsend. The role of the aminosugar and helix binding in the thiol-induced activation of calicheamicin for DNA cleavage. *J. Am. Chem. Soc.* 118:1938–48, 1996.

Turner, B. G., and **M. F. Summers.** Structural biology of HIV. *J. Mol. Biol.* 285:1–32, 1999.

DeGuzman, R. N., et al. **(M. F. Summers).** Structure of the HIV-1 nucleocapsid protein bound to the SL3 Ψ-RNA recognition element. *Science* 279:384–8, 1998.

McDonnell, N. B., W. G. Rice, and **M. F. Summers.** Zinc-ejection as a new rationale for the use of cystamine and thiamine disulfide in the treatment of AIDS. *J. Med. Chem.* 40:1969–76, 1997.

Rice, W. G., et al. **(M. F. Summers).** Azodicarbonamide inhibits HIV-1 replication by targeting the nucleocapsid protein. *Nature Med.* 3:341–5, 1997.

Gitti, R. K., et al. **(M. F. Summers).** Structure of the amino-terminal core domain of the HIV-I capsid protein. *Science* 273:231–5, 1996.

Shenoy, V., J. Rosenblatt, **J. Vincent,** and A. Gaigalas. Measurement of mesh sizes in concentrated rigid and flexible polyelectrolyte solutions by electron spin resonance technique. *Macromolecules* 28:525–30, 1995.

Vincent, J. S., S. D. Revak, C. D. Cochrane, and I. W. Levin. Interactions of model human pulmonary surfactants with a mixed phospholipid bilayer assembly: Raman spectroscopic studies. *Biochemistry* 32:8228–38, 1993.

Vincent, J. S., S. D. Revak, C. D. Cochrane, and I. W. Levin. Raman spectroscopic studies of model human pulmonary surfactant systems: Phospholipid interactions with peptide paradigms for the surfactant protein SP-B. *Biochemistry* 30:8395–401, 1991.

Vincent, J. S., and I. W. Levin. Raman spectroscopic studies of dimyristoyl-phosphatidic acid and its interactions with ferricytochrome c in cationic binary and ternary lipid-protein complexes. *Biophys. J.* 59:1007–21, 1991.

Lin, B., H. Yagi, D. M. Jerina, and **D. L. Whalen.** Halide effects in the hydrolysis reactions of (±)-7β,8α-dihydroxy-9α,10α-epoxy-7,8,9,10-tetrahydrobenzo[a]pyrene. *Chem. Res. Toxicol.* 11:630–8, 1998.

Lin, B., et al. **(D. Whalen).** Change in rate limiting step in general acid-catalyzed benzo[a]pyrene diol epoxide hydrolysis. *J. Am. Chem. Soc.* 120:4327–33, 1998.

Coxon, J. M., K. Morokuma, A. J. Thorpe, and **D. Whalen.** Molecular orbital studies of intramolecular reaction of protonated cis- and trans-3,4-epoxypentan-l-01. *J. Org. Chem.* 63:3875–83, 1998.

Coxon, J. M., et al. **(D. Whalen).** Rearrangement of protonated propene oxide to protonated propanal. *J. Am. Chem. Soc.* 119:4712–9, 1997.

Carrell, H. L., **D. L. Whalen,** and J. P. Glusker. Hydrogen bonding in cis-2,3-epoxycyclooctanol. *Struct. Chem.* 8:149–54, 1997.

UNIVERSITY OF MASSACHUSETTS AMHERST

Department of Chemistry

Programs of Study

The department offers courses of study leading to the degrees of M.S. and Ph.D. in chemistry. A multidisciplinary approach combines traditional fields to address research problems in frontier areas, including nanoengineered materials, molecular devices, and biomaterials; protein folding, protein–nucleic acid interactions, and membrane proteins; and molecular recognition and bioanalytical and environmental chemistry. The NIH-funded Chemistry/Biology Interface and the NSF-funded Materials Research Science and Engineering Center further expand opportunities for multidisciplinary research and learning. The graduate program is optimized to allow students the freedom to acquire the knowledge and skills necessary to become independent and effective researchers. The first year of study consists of course work that includes both a unified core course taken by all incoming students and several advanced-level and special topics courses, which are chosen by the student and build on the broad base provided by the core course. Research group choice is aided by a series of rotations in several research groups. For greater breadth of experience, joint appointments or pursuit of collaborative research with departments such as polymer science and engineering, biochemistry, and chemical engineering are common. Students also have opportunities for work in industrial or government laboratories through internships to acquire additional experience. Ph.D. candidacy is attained after passing an oral defense of an outline of the proposed research and an original research proposal. The Ph.D. is awarded for the production and successful defense of a dissertation that describes original, publishable research.

Research Facilities

Four interconnected buildings (the seventeen-story Lederle Graduate Research Tower, the two Goessmann Laboratories, and the Conte National Center for Polymer Research) provide spacious laboratory and facilities accommodations. The Department of Chemistry and the University of Massachusetts Materials Research Science and Engineering Center provide world-class instrumentation laboratories. Major equipment includes a single-crystal X-ray diffractometer with CCD detector; small- and wide-angle X-ray scattering, ORD-CD, and ESR spectrometers; and GC, HPLC, GPC, and electrophoresis with infrared, mass, and plasma-emission spectrometries detection as well as ICP optical and mass spectrometries and AA. The NMR laboratory operates six Bruker (200- to 500-MHz) instruments for liquid and solid samples, with probes for analysis of any magnetic nucleus using virtually any pulse sequence. Capabilities include advanced projects in liquids (including broadband detection); pulsed-field gradients; automated operation for 2-D experiments, including indirect detection; and solid-static, magic-angle, and wideline applications for virtually any magnetic nuclide. All spectrometers are Ethernet linked for transfer, storage, and offline processing of data. The Mass Spectrometry Facility performs analyses of molecules, biopolymers, and high–molecular weight synthetic polymers. Instruments include an electrospray ion trap; MALDI TOF; high-resolution, two-sector EI/CI, FAB, FDI, and electrospray ionization; and quadrupole GC/MS spectrometers. The vibrational spectroscopy laboratory houses three Raman instruments with dispersive or FT capabilities, high-throughput laser and high-resolution laser spectrometers, and four FTIR and vacuum FTIR spectrometers. Capabilities include temperature sweeps from 6°K to 900°K, time-resolved spectroscopy at 6-microsecond resolution, time-resolved dynamic-mechanical infrared spectroscopy, low-frequency Raman spectroscopy, and reflectance spectroscopy at air-solid, air-liquid, and liquid-liquid interfaces using Langmuir troughs. The surface spectroscopy laboratory contains two XPS spectrometers that are capable of analysis of surface elements and composition, depth profiling, and ion-scattering spectroscopy. The electron microscopy laboratory includes two SEMs, a 100-kV TEM, and 200- and 300-kV TEM/STEM instruments, with EELS capability and light- and heavy-element EDS for high-resolution imaging, electron diffraction, and spatially resolved composition analysis. An ultrahigh-resolution field emission gun SEM images surfaces to better than 50 Å with EDS spatial composition analysis.

Financial Aid

All students who are admitted to the program receive financial support. The current stipend for an academic-year teaching assistantship is at least $12,500, with a summer research fellowship of $3000. The financial offer may include a departmental fellowship carrying an additional stipend of $1000 to $2000.

Cost of Study

All financial offers include a waiver of tuition and a major part of the fees, for a total exemption of more than $11,000. Some fees, amounting to approximately $550, are not waived and must be paid by the student.

Living and Housing Costs

The cost of living in Amherst is comparable to other towns in the New England area. Cost-of-living estimates for an international student in residence are available through the University's Office for Foreign Students and Scholars. In 1998–99, the starting cost of residence hall room and board was approximately $4500 per year. Off-campus housing is available.

Student Group

The department has more than 120 graduate students and postdoctoral fellows. The student body is primarily domestic; however, students come from all over the world to study at the University of Massachusetts Amherst.

Student Outcomes

The vast majority of University of Massachusetts graduates go on to further employment in the U.S., divided almost equally between industrial and academic positions. Recent graduates have gone on to chemical companies, such as Dow, Monsanto, and Olin; pharmaceutical companies, including Eli Lilly, Merck, Pfizer, and Norwich Eaton; and instrument companies, such as Perkin Elmer and Hewlett-Packard. Others have taken postdoctoral positions or have become faculty members at such institutions as Caltech, MIT, and the Scripps Institute, among others.

Location

Amherst, founded in 1759 and situated in the scenically attractive section of the Connecticut River valley known as the Pioneer Valley, is the archetypical New England town, complete with town common and old homes on shady, tree-lined streets. Together with Northampton, Amherst is a thriving community offering amenities found only in larger urban centers, while retaining the relaxed atmosphere of a small town. Amherst is also centrally located and is 1½ hours away from Boston and 2½ hours away from New York City.

The University and The Department

The University of Massachusetts, founded under the Morrill Land Grant Act of 1863, has 23,000 students, occupies 1,400 acres, and operates on a semester system. The chemistry department has awarded higher degrees since 1890 and has a long history of excellence. The department is central to the chemical sciences at the University, with strong research and teaching links to the Departments of Polymer Science and Engineering, Biochemistry, Physics, and Chemical Engineering.

Applying

Applicants should have a bachelor's degree in chemistry or a closely-related subject and a GPA of 3.0 or better in chemistry courses. GRE test scores are not required but are strongly encouraged by the Graduate Admissions and Awards Committee, whose members evaluate applications as soon as they are complete. Decisions regarding admission and financial support are made as soon as possible.

Correspondence and Information

For program information and applications:

Chair, Graduate Admissions and Awards
  Committee
Department of Chemistry
Box 34510
University of Massachusetts
Amherst, Massachusetts 01003-4510

Telephone: 413-545-2291
Fax: 413-545-4490
E-mail: gpd@chem.umass.edu
World Wide Web: http://www.chem.umass.edu

For general information on graduate programs:

Graduate Admissions Office
Goodell Building
University of Massachusetts
Amherst, Massachusetts 01003

E-mail: gradinfo@umassp.edu
World Wide Web: http://www.umass.edu/gradschool

University of Massachusetts Amherst

THE FACULTY AND THEIR RESEARCH

Scott M. Auerbach, Assistant Professor; Ph.D., Berkeley, 1993. Physical chemistry: theoretical studies of molecular adsorption, diffusion, and reactivity in nanoporous materials; quantum, classical, and statistical mechanics of solid-fluid interfaces.

Ramon M. Barnes, Professor; Ph.D., Illinois, 1966. Analytical chemistry: spectrochemical analysis.

Patricia A. Bianconi, Associate Professor; Ph.D., MIT, 1986. Inorganic chemistry: inorganic network polymers, analogies to biomineralization, materials chemistry, interface between solid-state, organometallic, and polymer chemistry.

Paul E. Cade, Professor; Ph.D., Wisconsin, 1961. Theoretical chemistry.

Louis A. Carpino, Professor; Ph.D., Illinois, 1953. Organic chemistry: new amino protecting groups, new techniques for rapid synthesis of peptides.

Roberta O. Day, Professor; Ph.D., MIT, 1971. Inorganic chemistry: X-ray crystallography, computer-assisted instructional technology.

Lila M. Gierasch, Professor and Head; Ph.D., Harvard, 1975. Biophysical chemistry: conformational analysis of peptides and proteins, biophysical approaches to protein folding and localization in vivo.

Stephen S. Hixson, Professor; Ph.D., Wisconsin, 1970. Organic chemistry: organic photochemistry, photochemical probes of structure of biological macromolecules.

Bret E. Jackson, Professor; Ph.D., MIT, 1983. Physical chemistry: theoretical studies of molecule-surface interactions, time-dependent reactive and non-reactive scattering, charge and energy transfer in condensed matter.

Igor A. Kaltashov, Assistant Professor; Ph.D., Maryland, 1995. Mass spectrometry, analytical chemistry, study of supramolecular complexes, folding and conformation of biopolymers, architecture of synthetic polymers.

Paul M. Lahti, Professor; Ph.D., Yale, 1985. Organic chemistry: conducting organic doped polymers, organic ferromagnetism, electroluminescent polymers and materials, crystal engineering, computational chemistry.

Michael J. Maroney, Professor; Ph.D., Washington (Seattle), 1981. Inorganic chemistry: investigations of metal sites in metalloproteins, understanding structure-function relationship in biological or catalytic systems involving transition metals.

Craig T. Martin, Associate Professor; Ph.D., Caltech, 1984. Biological chemistry: enzymology of transcription, structure-function relationships in protein-DNA interactions.

Ricardo B. Metz, Assistant Professor; Ph.D., Berkeley, 1991. Physical chemistry: spectroscopy and dynamics of gas-phase adducts composed of a transition metal cation and a simple organic ligand.

Bernard Miller, Professor; Ph.D., Columbia, 1955. Organic chemistry: molecular rearrangements, reactions of cyclohexadienones and semibenzenes, chemistry of coal and coal analogs.

Marvin D. Rausch, Professor; Ph.D., Kansas, 1955. Organometallic and organic chemistry: synthesis and characterization of new metallocene derivatives of group 4 metals and their utility as catalysts for the stereoregular polymerization of $alpha$-olefins, functionally substituted cyclopentadienyl-metal compounds and their chemistry.

Marion B. Rhodes, Professor; Ph.D., Massachusetts, 1966. Analytical chemistry: correlation of the morphology with the physical properties of polymers, optical microscopy.

Vincent M. Rotello, Assistant Professor; Ph.D., Yale, 1990. Organic chemistry: bioorganic chemistry, structure and dynamics of peptides, mechanisms and modulation of redox cofactors.

Richard S. Stein, Professor; Ph.D., Princeton, 1949. Polymer chemistry: optical and mechanical properties of high polymers.

Howard D. Stidham, Professor; Ph.D., MIT, 1955. Physical chemistry: vibrational and spin resonance spectra, molecular spectra and structure.

Lynmarie K. Thompson, Assistant Professor; Ph.D., Yale, 1989. Biophysical chemistry: biophysical studies of mechanisms of transmembrane signaling by bacterial chemotaxis receptors, solid-state NMR studies of membrane proteins.

Julian F. Tyson, Professor; Ph.D., Imperial College (London), 1975. Analytical chemistry: flow-injection techniques for online sample pretreatment for analytical spectrometry, trace element characterization of environmental and biological materials by atomic spectrometry.

Peter C. Uden, Professor; Ph.D., Bristol (England), 1964. Analytical chemistry: gas, liquid, and supercritical fluid chromatography, capillary electromigration, elemental selective atomic and mass spectral detection, volatile metal compounds, organoselenium chemistry, humic materials, chemical analysis.

Richard W. Vachet, Assistant Professor; Ph.D., North Carolina at Chapel Hill, 1997. Analytical chemistry, mass spectrometry, metal ion studies in biological systems, metal-ligand complexes in marine organisms.

D. Venkataraman, Assistant Professor; Ph.D., Illinois, 1996. Organic chemistry, materials chemistry, design and control of solid-state structures, polymer-inorganic composites, self-regulating catalysis.

William J. Vining, Associate Professor; Ph.D., North Carolina at Chapel Hill, 1985. Chemical education: development of computer-based multimedia software systems.

Edward G. Voigtman Jr., Associate Professor; Ph.D., Florida, 1979. Analytical chemistry: laser spectrometry, computer simulations, S/N analysis.

Robert M. Weis, Associate Professor; Ph.D., Stanford, 1984. Biological and physical chemistry: physical chemistry of cell membranes, signal transduction in bacterial chemotaxis, phase behavior of phospholipid monolayers.

John S. Wood, Professor; Ph.D., Manchester (England), 1962. Inorganic chemistry: X-ray crystallography and inorganic stereochemistry, charge density distributions in simple coordination compounds.

O. Thomas Zajicek, Professor; Ph.D., Wayne State, 1961. Inorganic chemistry: chemistry of the aquatic environment, trace metals in water, the nature and impact of acid rain on the aquatic environment.

SELECTED PUBLICATIONS

Roy, A. H., R. R. Broudy, **S. M. Auerbach,** and **W. J. Vining.** Teaching materials that matter: An interactive, multi-media module on Zeolite and in general chemistry. *Chem. Edu.* 4(3), 1999.

Saravanan, C., F. Jousse, and **S. M. Auerbach.** Ising model of diffusion in molecular sieves. *Phys. Rev. Lett.* 80:5754–7, 1998.

Saravanan, C., and **S. M. Auerbach.** Simulations of high Tc vapor-liquid phase transitions in nanoporous materials. *J. Chem. Phys.* 109:8755–8, 1998.

Favre, D. E., D. J. Schaefer, **S. M. Auerbach,** and B. F. Chmelka. Direct measurement of intercage hopping in strongly adsorbing guest-zeolite systems. *Phys. Rev. Lett.* 81:5852–5, 1998.

Jousse, F., and **S. M. Auerbach.** Activated diffusion of benzene in Na-Y: Rate constants from transition state theory with dynamical corrections. *J. Chem. Phys.* 107:9629–39, 1997.

Gelinas, Y., A. Krushevska, and **R. M. Barnes.** Determination of total iodine in nutritional and biological samples by ICP-MS following their combustion within an oxygen stream. *Anal. Chem.* 70:1021–5, 1998.

Krushevska, A., et al. **(R. M. Barnes.)** Reducing polyatomic interferences in the ICP-MS determination of chromium and vanadium in biofluids and tissues. *Appl. Spectroscopy* 52:205–11, 1998.

Al-Ammar A. S., and **R. M. Barnes.** Correction for drift in ICP-AES measurements by internal standardization using spectral lines of the sample analyte as internal reference. *Atomic Spectroscopy* 19(1):18–22, 1998.

Bianconi, P. A., J. Lin, and E. Cates. A synthetic analog of the biomineralization process: Controlled crystallization of an inorganic phase by a polymer matrix. *J. Am. Chem. Soc.* 116:4738–41, 1994.

Bianconi, P. A., et al. Molecular precursors to lanthanide (II)-based semiconductors: Synthetic pathways toward the preparation of lanthanide monochalcogenide precursors. *Inorg. Chem.* 33:5188–94, 1994.

Bianconi, P. A., and G. Visscher. Synthesis and characterization of polycarbynes, a new class of carbon-based network polymers. *J. Am. Chem. Soc.* 116:1805–11, 1994.

Carpino, L. A., et al. New family of base- and nucleophile-sensitive amino-protecting groups. A Michael-acceptor-based deblocking process. Practical utilization of the 1,1-dioxobenzo[b]thiophene-2-ylmethyloxycarbonyl (Bsmoc) Group. *J. Am. Chem. Soc.* 119:9915–6, 1997.

Carpino, L. A., D. Ionescu, and A. El-Faham. Peptide coupling in the presence of highly hindered tertiary amines. *J. Org. Chem.* 61:2460–5, 1996.

Carpino, L. A., M. Beyermann, H. Wenschuh, and M. Biernert. Peptide synthesis via amino acid halides. *Acct. Chem. Res.* 29(6):268–74, 1996.

Allan, C. B., et al. **(R. O. Day** and **M. J. Maroney).** Protonation and alkylation of a dinuclear nickel thiolate complex. *Inorg. Chem.* 37:4166–7, 1998.

Sherlock, D., A. Chandrasekaran, **R. O. Day,** and **R. R. Holmes.** Hexacoordination via sulfur donor action in nitrogen and chorine bonded bicyclic tetraoxyphosphoranes. *J. Chem. Soc.* 119:1317, 1997.

Miriza, S. A., **R. O. Day,** and **M. J. Maroney.** The oxidation of a dimeric nickel thiolate with O_2. *Inorg. Chem.* 35:1992–5, 1996.

Montgomery, D. L., R. I. Morimoto, and **L. M. Gierasch.** Mutations in the substrate binding domain of the *Escherichia coli* 70kDa molecular chaperone, DnaK, which alter substrate affinity or interdomain coupling. *J. Mol. Biol.* 286:915–32, 1999.

Zheng, N., and **L. M. Gierasch.** Domain interactions in *E. coli* SRP; stabilization of M domain by RNA is required for effective signal sequence modulation of NG domain. *Mol. Cell* 1:79–87, 1997.

Clark, P. L, Z.-P. Liu, J. Rizo, and **L. M. Gierasch.** Cavity formation before stable hydrogen bonding in the folding of a β-clam protein. *Nature Struct. Biol.* 4:883–6, 1997.

Hixson, S., et al. Synthesis of 2,6-Diazido-9-(b-D-ribofuranosyl) purine 3',5'-bisphosphate: Incorporation into transfer RNA and photochemical labeling of *Escherichia coli* ribosomes. *Bioconjugate Chem.* 5:158–61, 1994.

Jackson, B. Reduced density matrix description of gas-solid interactions: Scattering, trapping and desorption. *J. Chem. Phys.* 108:1131–9, 1998.

Carre, M.-N., and **B. Jackson.** Dissociative chemisorption of CH_4 on Ni: The role of molecular orientation. *J. Chem. Phys.* 108:3722–30, 1998.

Caratzoulas, S., **B. Jackson,** and M. Persson. Eley-rideal and hot-atom reaction dynamics of H(g) with H Adsorbed on Cu(111). *J. Chem. Phys.* 107:6420–31, 1997.

Dotson, G. D., **I. A. Kaltashov,** R. J. Cotter, and C. R. Raetz.

Expression cloning of a *Pseudomonas* gene encoding a hydroxydecanoyl-acyl carrier protein-dependent UDP-GlcNAc acyltransferase. *J. Bacteriol.* 180:330–7, 1998.

Kaltashov, I. A., V. M. Doroshenko, and R. J. Cotter. Gas phase H/D exchange reactions of peptide ions studied in a quadrupole ion trap mass spectrometer. *Proteins Struct. Funct. Genet.* 28:53–8, 1997.

Kaltashov, I. A., et al. Confirmation of the structure of lipid A derived from the lipopolysaccharide of *Rhodobacter sphaeroides* by a combination of MALDI, LSIMS, and tandem mass spectrometry. *Anal. Chem.* 69:2317–22, 1997.

Liu, Y., **P. M. Lahti,** and F. La. Synthesis of a regiospecific, soluble poly(2-alkoxy-1,4-phenylenevinylene). *Polymer* 39:5241–4, 1998.

Lahti, P. M., B. Esat, and R. Walton. 2-(4-Nitrenophenyl)-4,4,5,5-tetramethyl-4,5-dihydro-*1H*-imidazole-3-oxide-1-oxyl: Photogeneration of a quartet state organic molecule with both localized and delocalized spins. *J. Am. Chem. Soc.* 120:5122–3, 1998.

Gurge, R. M., et al. **(P. M. Lahti).** Synthesis of a green-emitting alternating block copolymer. *Polym. Adv. Technol.* 9:504–10, 1998.

Choudhury, S. B., et al. **(M. J. Maroney).** Examination of the nickel site structure and reaction mechanism in *Streptomyces seoulensis* superoxide dismutase. *Biochemistry* 38:3744–52, 1999.

Allan, C. B., et al. **(M. J. Maroney).** An X-ray absorption spectroscopic structural investigation of the nickel site in *Escherichia coli* NikA protein. *Inorg. Chem.* 37:5952–5, 1998.

Maroney, M. J., G. Davidson, C. B. Allan, and J. Figlar. The structure and function of nickel sites in metalloproteins. In *Structure and Bonding*, pp. 1–65, ed. M. J. Clarke, 1998.

Weston, B. F., I. Kuzmine, and **C. T. Martin.** Positioning of the start site in the initiation of transcription by T7 RNA polymerase. *J. Mol. Biol.* 272:21–30, 1997.

Ujvári, A., and **C. T. Martin.** Identification of a minimal binding element within the T7 RNA polymerase promoter. *J. Mol. Biol.* 273:775–81, 1997.

Ujvári, A., and **C. T. Martin.** Thermodynamic and kinetic measurements of promoter binding by T7 RNA. *Polymerase Biochem.* 35:14574–82, 1996.

Husband, J., F. Aguirre, P. Ferguson, and **R. B. Metz.** Vibrationally resolved photofragment spectroscopy of FeO^+. *J. Chem. Phys.,* in press.

Brown, S. S., **R. B. Metz,** H. L. Berghout and F. F. Crim. Vibrationally mediated photodissociation of isocyanic acid (HNCO): Preferential N-H bond fission by excitation of the reaction coordinate. *J. Chem. Phys.* 105:6293, 1996.

Pfeiffer, J. M., et al. **(R. B. Metz).** Reactions of O, H, and Cl atoms with highly vibrationally excited HCN: Using product states to determine mechanisms. *J. Chem. Phys.* 104:4490, 1996.

Miller, B., and D. Ionescu. An addition-cyclization-elimination mechanism for dehydro Diels-Alder reactions. *Tetrahedron Lett.* 35,6615–8, 1994.

Miller, B., and X. Shi. Unusual regiochemistry in the hydroboration of 3,3-dibenzylcycloalkenes. *Tetrahedron Lett.* 35:223–6, 1994.

Miller, B., and X. Shi. Cyclization and rearrangement processes resulting from bromination of 3-benzylcycloalkenes. *J. Org. Chem.* 58:2907–9, 1993.

Rausch, M. D., and M. S. Blais. A new synthetic route to functionally substituted η5-cyclopentadienyl-dicarbonyliridium compounds *J. Organomet. Chem.* 502:1–8, 1995.

Rausch, M. D., Y. X. Chen, and J. C. W. Chien. C_{2v} and C_2 symmetric *ansa*-Bis-(fluoreny)zirconocene catalysts: synthesis and *alpha*-olefin catalysis. *Macromolecules* 28:5399–5404, 1995.

Rausch, M. D., J. C. Flores, and J. C. W. Chien. {[2-(Dimethylamino)ethyl]cyclopentadienyl}trichlorotitanium: A new type of polymerization catalyst. *Organometallics* 13:4140–2, 1994.

Rhodes, M. The quantitative characterization of the cellular structure in polymeric foams. *J. Therm. Insulation* 15:101–9, 1991.

Rhodes, M., and B. Khaykin. Multiple stereological parameter characterization of cellular structures. In *Proceedings of the Society of the Plastics Industry,* pp. 178–182, 1989.

Rhodes, M., and B. Khaykin. Foam characterization and quantitative stereology. *Langmuir* 2:643–9, 1986.

Deans, R., A. Niemz, E. Breinlinger, and **V. Rotello.** Electrochemical control of recognition processes: A three-component molecular switch. *J. Am. Chem. Soc.* 119:10863–4, 1997.

Greaves, M., and **V. Rotello.** Model systems for flovoenzyme activity. Hydrogen bond recognition of FMN in a sol-gel matrix. *J. Am. Chem. Soc.* 119:10569–72, 1997.

University of Massachusetts Amherst

Selected Publications (continued)

Nie, B., and **V. Rotello.** Thermally controlled formation of fullerene-diene oligomers and copolymers. *Macromolecules* 30:3949–51, 1997.

Deans, R., and **V. Rotello.** Model systems for flovoenzyme activity. Molecular recognition of flavin at the polymer-liquid interface. *J. Org. Chem.* 62:4528–59, 1997.

Stein, R., Y. Cheung, B. Chu, and G. Wu. Evolution of crystalline structures of poly(e-caprolactone)/polycarbonate blends. Isothermal crystallization kinetics as probed by synchrotron small-angle X-ray scattering. *Macromolecules* 27:3589–95, 1994.

Stein, R., and G. Beaucage. Mechanical behavior and morphology of tactic poly(vinyl methyl ether)/polystyrene blends. *Polymer* 35:2716–24, 1994.

Stein, R., V. Janarthanan, and P. Garrett. Role of entanglements on the fracture toughness of incompatible polymer interfaces. *Macromolecules* 27:4855–8, 1994.

Stidham, H., Y. Ren, C. Meuse and S. Hsu. Reflectance infrared spectroscopic analysis of monolayer films at the air-water interface. *J. Phys. Chem.* 98:8424–30, 1994.

Stidham, H., et al. Raman and infrared spectra, conformational stability, barrier to internal rotation, and ab initio calculations for 1,1-dichloromethyl methyl ether. *J. Raman Spectrosc.* 25:747–60, 1994.

Stidham, H., et al. Raman and infrared spectra, conformational stability, barriers to internal rotation and ab initio calculations of fluorocarbonyl isocyanate. *J. Raman Spectrosc.* 25:221–32, 1994.

Kumashiro, K. K., et al. **(L. K. Thompson).** A novel tool for probing membrane protein structure: Solid-state NMR with proton spin diffusion and X-nucleus detection. *J. Am. Chem. Soc.* 120:5043–51, 1998.

Wang, J., Y. S. Balazs, and **L. K. Thompson.** Solid-state REDOR NMR distance measurements at the ligand site of a bacterial chemotaxis membrane receptor. *Biochemistry* 36:1699–703, 1997.

Seeley, S. K., G. K. Wittrock, **L. K. Thompson,** and **R. M. Weis.** Oligomers of the cytoplasmic fragment from the *Escherichia coli* aspartate receptor dissociate through an unfolded transition state. *Biochemistry* 35:16336–45, 1996.

Wang, J., A. D. Parkhe, D. A. Tirrell, and **L. K. Thompson.** Crystalline aggregates of the repetitive polypeptide {(AlaGly)₃GluGly(GlyAla)₃GluGly}₁₀: Structure and dynamics by ^{13}C magic angle spinning nuclear magnetic resonance spectroscopy. *Macromolecules* 29:1548–53, 1996.

Fitzgerald, N., **J. F. Tyson,** and D. A. Leighty. Reduction of water loading effects in inductively coupled plasma mass spectrometry by a nafion membrane dryer device. *J. Anal. Atomic Spectrom.* 13:13–6, 1998.

Tyson, J. F., R. I. Ellis, S. A. McIntosh, and C. P. Hanna. Effect of sample volume on the limit of detection in flow injection hydride generation electrochemical atomic absorption spectrometry. *J. Anal. Atomic Spectrom.* 13:17–22, 1998.

Bird, S. M., et al. **(J. F. Tyson).** High performance liquid chromatography of selenoaminoacids and organo-selenium compounds. Speciation by inductively coupled plasma mass spectrometry. *J. Chromatogr. A* 789:349–59, 1997.

Rockwell, G, et al. **(P. C. Uden).** Oxalogenesis in parenteral nutrition solution components. *Nutrition* 14:836–9, 1999.

Uden, P. C., et al. Analytical selenoamino acid studies by chromatography with interfaced atomic mass spectrometry and atomic emission spectral detection. *Fresenius J. Anal. Chem.* 362:5447–56, 1998.

Khuhawar, M. Y., A. S. Yazdi, J. Seeley, and **P. C. Uden.** Capillary column GC determination of platinum using microwave induced plasma atomic emission detection. *J. Chromatogr.* 824:223–9, 1998.

Block, E., et al. **(P. C. Uden).** The Search for anticarcinogenic organoselenium compounds from natural sources. *Phosphorus Sulfur Silicon* 136:1–10, 1998.

Vachet, R. W., and G. L. Glish. Boundary-activated dissociation of peptide ions in a quadrupole ion trap. *Anal. Chem.* 70:340–6, 1998.

Vachet, R. W., B. M. Bishop, B. W. Erickson, and G. L. Glish. Novel peptide dissociation: Gas phase intramolecular rearrangement of internal amino acid residues. *J. Am. Chem. Soc.* 119:5481–8, 1997.

Vachet, R. W., M. R. Asam, and G. L. Glish. Secondary interactions affecting the dissociation patterns of arginine containing peptide ions. *J. Am. Chem. Soc.* 118:6252–6, 1996.

Venkataraman, D., et al. An improved high yield synthesis procedure and reactivity of W6S8(4-tert-butylpyridine)6. *J. Inorg. Chem.* 38:828–30, 1999.

Venkataraman, D., et al. A coordination geometry table of the d-block transition elements and their ions. *Chem. Educ.* 74:915–8, 1997.

Venkataraman, D., G. Gardner, S. Lee, and J. S. Moore. Zeolite-like behavior of a coordination network. *J. Am. Chem. Soc.* 117:11600–1, 1995.

Gardner, G. B., **D. Venkataraman,** J. S. Moore, and S. Lee. Spontaneous assembly of a hinged coordination network. *Nature* 374:792–5, 1995.

Venkataraman, D., S. Lee, J. Zhang, and J. S. Moore. An organic solid with wide channels based on hydrogen bonding between macrocycles. *Nature* 371:591–3, 1994.

Grosso, R., J. T. Fermann, and **W. J. Vining.** The madulung constant. *J. Chem. Educ.,* in press.

Vining, W. J., and R. S. Stein. *The World of Plastics* (CD-ROM). National Plastics Center and Museum, 1999.

Stamm, K., et al. **(W. J. Vining).** Designing interactive instructional software: Students as educators. *Chem. Educ.* 4(1), 1999.

Voigtman, E. Comparison of signal-to-noise ratios. *Anal. Chem.* 69:226–34, 1997.

Kale, U., and **E. Voigtman.** Signal processing of transient atomic absorption signals. *Spectrochim. Acta* 50B:E1531–41, 1995.

Kale, U., and **E. Voigtman.** Signal and noise analysis of non-modulated polarimeters using Mueller calculus simulations. *Analyst* 120:325–30, 1995.

Seeley, S. K., **R. M. Weis,** and **L. K. Thompson.** The cytoplasmic fragment of the aspartate receptor displays globally dynamic behavior. *Biochemistry* 35:5199–206, 1996.

Long, D. G., and **R. M. Weis.** Reversible dissociation and unfolding of the *Escherichia coli* aspartate receptor cytoplasmic fragment. *Biochemistry* 34:3056–65, 1995.

Lin, L.-N., J. Li, J. F. Brandts, and **R. M. Weis.** The serine receptor of bacterial chemotaxis exhibits half-site saturation for serine binding. *Biochemistry* 33:6564–70, 1994.

Wood, J. S., P. E. M. Wijnands, and W. J. Maaskant. Disordered CuN₆ Jahn-Teller active centers in hexa(1-methyltrazole) copper(II) tetrafluoroborate: A temperature dependent X-ray and EPR study. *Inorg. Chem.* 35:1214–22, 1996.

Wood, J. S., J. C. Flores, J. C. W. Chien, and **M. D. Rausch.** [(1-(2, Phenyl-ethyl))-2,3,4,5-tetramethylcyclopentadienyl] titanium compounds. Synthesis and their use for the syndiospecific polymerisation of styrene. *Organometallics* 15:4944–50, 1996.

Wood, J. S., R. D. Archer, M. J. Cook, and M. E. Lamet. The UEA/UMass student exchange program: 1978 to date. *J. Chem. Educ.* 74:486, 1997.

Zajicek, O. T. Why isn't my rain as acidic as yours? *J. Chem. Educ.* 62:158, 1985.

Zajicek, O. T., D. Atlas, and J. Coombs. The corrosion of copper by chlorinated drinking waters. *Water Res.* 16:693, 1982.

Zajicek, O. T. The effect of redox potential on iron valence in model systems and foods. *J. Food Sci.* 46:1265, 1981.

UNIVERSITY OF MINNESOTA

Department of Chemistry

Programs of Study

The graduate program in the Department of Chemistry centers on the research of students and leads to the Ph.D. degree. The research interests of the faculty cover all major areas, including analytical, biological, inorganic, materials, organic, and physical chemistry. There is also a program in chemical physics.

Upon entering the program, each student takes proficiency exams in analytical, inorganic, organic, and physical chemistry. Most students complete their course requirements (24 semester credits—usually eight courses) during the first year, and they pick a research adviser early during this period to begin research. The preliminary candidacy exam for the Ph.D. consists of a written and an oral section, each of which is completed during the second academic year in residence. After the first year, the majority of students' effort is directed toward their thesis research.

The excellent educational and research background prepares students for positions in academia or industry. During the fall of each year, the Department of Chemistry hosts a large number of interviewers from the major chemical companies in the United States. Many students accept job offers as a result of these preliminary on-campus interviews.

An M.S. degree is also offered, which requires 20 semester credits with a thesis or 30 semester credits without a thesis.

Research Facilities

The Department of Chemistry is housed in two large buildings, Smith and Kolthoff halls. Smith Hall was completely remodeled in 1987. The University library is adjacent and connected to Smith Hall. Many of the design and manufacturing needs of the chemistry program are carried out directly in the department in sophisticated machine, electronics, and glassblowing shops. The extensive instrumentation for research housed in the department includes multinuclear NMR spectrometers (one 100-, one 200-, two 300-, and one 500-MHz, one fitted with autosampler); a VG 7070 high-resolution mass spectrometer with fast-atom bombardment (FAB) capability, a Finnigan GC/MS with chemical ionization and electron impact ionization capability, and an AEI MS30 high-resolution spectrometer; an Enraf-Nonius CAD4 single-crystal X-ray diffractometer; and an ESCA/Auger/SIMS spectrometer for surface analysis. Computing capabilities include a VAX-11/780 computer and ready access to the extensive University mainframes and the Cray supercomputer. Many other instruments and facilities, such as FT-IR spectrophotometers, high-energy pulsed lasers, instrumentation for studying reactions in molecular beams, chromatographs, and cold rooms, are used and maintained by individual research groups.

Financial Aid

Research and teaching assistantships are both available, carrying nine-month stipends of about $14,000 and a waiver of tuition in 1990–2000. A number of fellowships are awarded each year to highly qualified students by the Department of Chemistry and the Graduate School. Summer support is independent of academic-year funding and may come in any of the forms mentioned above.

Cost of Study

Tuition is approximately $5000 per year but is waived for students holding assistantships and/or fellowships. Students also are assessed a yearly student services fee of approximately $450 and a computer fee of $300.

Living and Housing Costs

Dormitory room and board rates vary from about $1500 per semester for small double rooms to about $1800 per semester for large single rooms and suites. A variety of rooming houses and apartments are available close to campus. Excellent bus service in the metropolitan and suburban areas also makes the University readily accessible from other areas of the Twin Cities. Depending on the area, rents can range from approximately $300 per month for a room in a private home to $400 or more per month for a one-bedroom apartment.

Student Group

The Department of Chemistry has about 200 undergraduates and 230 graduate students; the graduate students come from many sections of the United States and several other countries. The vast majority of the graduate students in the Department of Chemistry receive financial assistance. Recent graduates of the department have been employed by universities, industrial firms, and government laboratories.

Location

The Twin Cities area, with a population of about 2 million people, has all the advantages of a major metropolitan area but few of the usual urban drawbacks. It offers two flourishing downtowns, sophisticated educational and cultural institutions, countless recreational opportunities, and citizens known for their friendliness. Within the city limits of both Minneapolis and St. Paul are numerous large lakes, parks, bicycle and walking trails, and parkways. The Twin Cities are home to professional baseball, basketball, and football teams, in addition to the numerous University teams. The Guthrie Theatre's reputation as a top regional theater is firmly established throughout the country. The Twin Cities are also the home of two internationally respected musical ensembles: the St. Paul Chamber Orchestra, which performs in the Ordway Center, and the Minnesota Orchestra, which performs in Orchestra Hall downtown.

The University

The University of Minnesota was chartered in 1851, seven years before the Minnesota Territory became a state. Today, the University has 4,500 full-time faculty members and 58,000 students enrolled in day classes, with tens of thousands more students in evening, continuing education, and noncredit courses. As one of the largest public institutions of higher learning in the United States, the University offers a rich variety of highly respected programs leading to baccalaureate, graduate, and professional degrees.

Applying

Interested students should complete both an application for admission to the Graduate School and an application for financial aid. These forms may be obtained from the department at the address listed below and should normally be returned, accompanied by the necessary supporting documents, by January 2 for fall semester admission. Transcripts from all colleges or universities attended and three letters of recommendation are required. Scores on the TOEFL and GRE General and Subject tests are required of all international applicants.

A strong background in the fundamental areas of chemistry, along with supporting course work in mathematics and physics, is highly recommended for admission to graduate work.

Correspondence and Information

Assistant to the Director of Graduate Studies
Department of Chemistry
University of Minnesota
207 Pleasant Street, SE
Minneapolis, Minnesota 55455
Telephone: 612-626-7444
           800-777-2431 (toll-free)
Fax: 612-626-7541
E-mail: inquiry@chem.umn.edu
World Wide Web: http://www.chem.umn.edu

University of Minnesota

THE FACULTY AND THEIR RESEARCH

Norma M. Allewell, Professor; Ph.D., Yale, 1969. Biophysical chemistry, protein interaction and regulation.

Edgar A. Arriaga, Assistant Professor; Ph.D., Dalhousie, 1990. Analytical chemistry, detection of biomolecules, mass spectrometry.

George Barany, Professor; Ph.D., Rockefeller, 1977. Bioorganic and peptide synthesis, organosulfur chemistry.

Paul F. Barbara, Professor; Ph.D., Brown, 1978. Photochemistry, spectroscopy.

Frank S. Bates, Associate Professor; Sc.D., MIT, 1982. Thermodynamics and dynamics of polymers and polymer mixtures.

Victor A. Bloomfield, Professor; Ph.D., Wisconsin–Madison, 1962. Biophysical chemistry.

Doyle Britton, Professor; Ph.D., Caltech, 1955. Crystal structure, intermolecular interactions.

Peter W. Carr, Professor; Ph.D., Penn State, 1969. Analytical chemistry, chromatography, biochemical analysis.

Christopher J. Cramer, Assistant Professor; Ph.D., Illinois, 1988. Theoretical organic chemistry.

John S. Dahler, Professor; Ph.D., Wisconsin–Madison, 1955. Theoretical chemistry.

H. Ted Davis, Professor; Ph.D., Chicago, 1962. Physical chemistry.

Mark D. Distefano, Assistant Professor; Ph.D., MIT, 1989. Biophysical chemistry.

John E. Ellis, Professor; Ph.D., MIT, 1971. Synthetic inorganic and organometallic chemistry.

John F. Evans, Professor; Ph.D., Delaware, 1977. Surface chemistry, plasma chemistry, electrochemistry.

Craig J. Forsyth, Assistant Professor; Ph.D., Cornell, 1989. Synthetic and biological organic chemistry.

W. Ronald Gentry, Professor; Ph.D., Berkeley, 1967. Chemical physics, molecular beams.

Wayne L. Gladfelter, Professor; Ph.D., Penn State, 1978. Organometallic and inorganic chemistry, metal clusters, catalysis.

Gary R. Gray, Professor; Ph.D., Iowa, 1969. Chemical immunology, polysaccharide structure determination.

Marc A. Hillmyer, Assistant Professor; Ph.D., Caltech, 1994. Polymer chemistry.

Thomas R. Hoye, Professor; Ph.D., Harvard, 1976. Organic synthesis, natural products, symmetry, organometallics.

Steven R. Kass, Associate Professor; Ph.D., Yale, 1984. Organic chemistry, gas phase reactions.

Doreen Geller Leopold, Associate Professor; Ph.D., Harvard, 1983. Physical chemistry, organometallic ion-molecule reactions.

Kenneth R. Leopold, Associate Professor; Ph.D., Harvard, 1983. Physical chemistry, Van der Waals molecules.

John D. Lipscomb, Professor; Ph.D., Illinois at Urbana-Champaign, 1944. Biological and bioinorganic chemistry.

Sanford Lipsky, Professor; Ph.D., Chicago, 1954. Physical chemistry, photophysics, photochemistry, electronic spectroscopy.

Hung-Wen Liu, Associate Professor; Ph.D., Columbia, 1981. Bioorganic chemistry, immunochemistry, biosynthesis, enzyme mechanisms.

Timothy P. Lodge, Professor; Ph.D., Wisconsin–Madison, 1980. Polymer and analytical chemistry, conformational dynamics, diffusion.

Kent R. Mann, Professor; Ph.D., Caltech, 1976. Inorganic and organometallic chemistry, photochemistry.

Larry L. Miller, Professor; Ph.D., Illinois, 1964. Organic chemistry, electrochemistry.

Wilmer G. Miller, Professor; Ph.D., Wisconsin–Madison, 1958. Polymer, surfactant, and physical chemistry.

Eric J. Munson, Assistant Professor; Ph.D., Texas A&M, 1992. Analytical, materials, and physical chemistry.

Karin Musier-Forsyth, Assistant Professor; Ph.D., Cornell, 1989. Biochemistry, biophysical chemistry, molecular biology.

Wayland E. Noland, Professor; Ph.D., Harvard, 1952. Organic chemistry, nitrogen heterocycles, nitro rearrangements.

George A. O'Doherty, Assistant Professor; Ph.D., Ohio State, 1993. Organic synthesis, organometallics, natural products.

Louis H. Pignolet, Professor; Ph.D., Princeton, 1969. Inorganic chemistry, organometallic chemistry, homogeneous catalysis.

Lawrence Que Jr., Professor; Ph.D., Minnesota, 1973. Bioinorganic chemistry, iron proteins, oxygen activation.

Michael A. Raftery, Professor; Ph.D., 1960, D.Sci., 1971, Ireland. Isolation and characterization of receptors and ion channels of the nervous system.

Jeffrey T. Roberts, Assistant Professor; Ph.D., Harvard, 1988. Surface chemistry of transition metals and semiconductors, physical chemistry.

J. Ilja Siepmann, Assistant Professor; Ph.D., Cambridge, 1991. Physical chemistry.

Marian T. Stankovich, Associate Professor; Ph.D., Texas at Austin, 1975. Bioanalytical chemistry, spectroelectrochemistry, electron transfer, flavoproteins.

Andreas Stein, Assistant Professor; Ph.D., Toronto, 1991. Physical chemistry.

Harold S. Swofford Jr., Professor; Ph.D., Illinois, 1962. Electrochemistry, electroanalytical chemistry, mechanisms and rates of electrooxidation and electroreduction.

William B. Tolman, Associate Professor; Ph.D., Berkeley, 1987. Synthetic inorganic and organometallic chemistry, biomimetic transition-metal complexes, chiral ligands.

Donald G. Truhlar, Professor; Ph.D., Caltech, 1970. Theoretical chemical dynamics, quantum chemistry, kinetics.

Michael D. Ward, Associate Professor; Ph.D., Princeton, 1981. Materials chemistry, electroanalytical chemistry.

Darrin M. York, Assistant Professor; Ph.D., North Carolina at Chapel Hill, 1993. Theoretical chemistry, quantum/classical simulations, macromolecule modeling.

UNIVERSITY OF MISSOURI–KANSAS CITY

Department of Chemistry

Programs of Study

The Department of Chemistry has a graduate program that offers both M.S. and Ph.D. degrees. The following areas of specialization are available: analytical, inorganic, organic, physical, and polymer chemistry. Doctoral degree programs at the University of MIssouri–Kansas City (UMKC) are interdisciplinary and provide academic training at the highest level, while allowing students' participation in other research areas. Currently, graduate students in the department have codisciplines in the following fields: education, physics, mathematics, pharmaceutical sciences, pharmacology, and geosciences. A maximum of 60 percent of the total credits (exclusive of dissertation credits) are allowed from chemistry.

A core course curriculum has been designed to prepare graduates for the changes in specialization within the field of chemistry that they often encounter after entering the job market. A minimum of four courses is taken within this curriculum, each from a different specialization. For the M.S. degree, two additional courses must be taken. Master's students may choose between nonthesis and thesis degrees. A Ph.D. candidate must take at least three codiscipline courses beyond the four required core courses. Ph.D. students must also pass a comprehensive examination with both written and oral portions in the area of specialization. The final requirement for a Ph.D. is to complete a research project culminating in a publishable dissertation.

Research Facilities

Research equipment includes four mass spectrometers (two GC/MS, one double-focusing MS, and one adapted to measure appearance potentials and photodissociation spectra of ions); one 250-MHz and one 400-MHz NMR spectrometer; an ESR spectrometer; UV-visible, Raman, and FT-IR spectrophotometers; several gas chromatographs; X-ray diffraction and fluorescence apparatus; a dynamic light scattering facility; positron annihilation lifetime, Doppler broadening, and angular correlation spectrometers; a slow positron beam; a peptide synthesizer; an HPLC; and apparatus for measuring the bulk and solution properties of synthetic polymers.

The University computer center provides access to a number of high-powered Alpha cluster computers from Digital Equipment Corporation. Additional workstations from several vendors are available in the department. Students can access computers in the chemistry student library. Well-equipped electronics and glassblower's shops are located in the chemistry building. Linda Hall Library of Science and Technology, 2½ blocks away, maintains active subscriptions to 16,000 serials and houses a collection of more than 150,000 technical books.

Financial Aid

Graduate teaching assistantships (GTAs) are awarded on a competitive level to a select number of entering graduate students; in 1999–2000, the stipend is more than $14,000 for twelve months. Graduate research assistantships are available to advanced graduate students through their research advisers. Out-of-state tuition and in-state fees for the first 6 credit hours each semester are waived for all graduate assistants. Assistantships are awarded preferentially to Ph.D. applicants. Exceptionally well-qualified entering students will be considered for an Arthur Mag Fellowship ($12,500 per year) or a Chancellor's Ph.D. Fellowship ($11,000 for ten months). Several other fellowship programs supplement the assistantship stipends by up to $1500 per year and/or provide either out-of-state fees or tuition remission.

Cost of Study

Fees for Missouri residents are $167.80 per credit hour (9–10 credit hours per semester is a typical course load for beginning graduate students) in 1999–2000. Out-of-state fees are $504.80 per credit hour for full-time graduate students. Books usually cost less than $500 per year.

Living and Housing Costs

A wide selection of rental housing is available near campus at monthly rents that range from $350 to $600 per month, depending on apartment size. The University Residence Hall also provides rooms and meals on an academic-year (nine-month) contract.

Student Group

There are approximately 35 graduate students in the Department of Chemistry, the majority of whom are full-time. Eight are women; 19 are international students. Nearly all the full-time students are supported by graduate teaching or research assistantships or graduate fellowships.

Location

UMKC is located in a residential area forty blocks south of Kansas City's central business district. The Brush Creek waterfront walkway runs along the north side of campus connecting the area to the Nelson Art Gallery and the Country Club Plaza. Kansas City is known for its professional sports franchises, but it also supports several theaters and museums and an extensive park system as well as a ballet company, a symphony, and an opera company. Offices of Hoechst Marion Roussel, the Midwest Research Institute, Bayer, and Pfizer are located in Kansas City. There is easy access to city bus routes from campus.

The University

UMKC has a student body of nearly 13,000 (45 percent graduate students, 8 to 10 percent international students) distributed among thirteen schools (College of Arts and Sciences, School of Biological Sciences, Computer Science Telecommunications Program, Henry W. Bloch School of Business and Public Administration, Conservatory of Music, School of Dentistry, School of Education, School of Graduate Studies, School of Law, School of Medicine, School of Nursing, School of Pharmacy, and Engineering Programs). UMKC originated in 1933 as the private, independent University of Kansas City and thirty years later merged into the University of Missouri System, which now has four campuses—Columbia, Kansas City, Rolla, and St. Louis.

Applying

Preferred applicants are expected to have the equivalent of an American Chemical Society-approved bachelor's degree in chemistry, which includes course work in general chemistry, analytical chemistry, inorganic chemistry, and one year of organic chemistry as well as one year of physical chemistry that requires prerequisites in both calculus and physics. Even though the University deadline is April 15, applications (including the assistantship application form) should be completed and submitted as soon as possible, because normal turnaround for applications is approximately three months. For the Master of Science program, the General Test and the Subject Test in chemistry of the Graduate Record Examinations are recommended but not required. Ph.D. applicants must score at least 1500 on the GRE. International applicants must submit TOEFL scores (minimum score of 550 for admission and 585 for GTAs). Application forms and other information may be obtained from the address given below.

Correspondence and Information

Graduate Recruiting Committee
Department of Chemistry
University of Missouri–Kansas City
5100 Rockhill Road
Kansas City, Missouri 64110

Telephone: 816-235-2273
Fax: 816-235-5502
E-mail: chemdept@umkc.edu
World Wide Web: http://www.umkc.edu/chem

University of Missouri–Kansas City

THE FACULTY AND THEIR RESEARCH

Jerry R. Dias, Professor; Ph.D., Arizona State, 1970. Organic chemistry: synthesis and properties of steroids and related natural products, structure elucidation by mass spectrometry, graph theoretical/molecular modeling studies, benzenoid hydrocarbon synthesis.

James R. Durig, Professor and Dean of Arts and Sciences; Ph.D., MIT. Physical chemistry: infrared and Raman spectroscopy and ab initio calculations emphasizing conformational stability, barriers to rotation, and molecular structure.

Andrew Holder, Associate Professor; Ph.D., Southern Mississippi, 1987. Physical chemistry: semiempirical and ab initio molecular orbital calculations, development of theoretical models for chemical systems.

Yan Ching Jean, Professor; Ph.D., Marquette, 1974. Physical chemistry: positron annihilation spectroscopy of polymers, membranes, and superconductors; chemistry of positronium and muonium; coating durability; electronic properties of materials.

Kathleen V. Kilway, Assistant Professor; Ph.D., California, San Diego, 1992. Physical organic chemistry: synthesis, conformational studies and modeling (molecular, semiempirical, and ab initio) of novel host-guest systems; interaction and communication of molecules in solution.

Zhonghua Peng, Assistant Professor; Ph.D., Chicago, 1997. Organic chemistry and material science: polymer chemistry, optical active and electroactive organic/polymer materials, novel polymer materials architectures and applications, polymer-template directed nanostructues.

Thomas C. Sandreczki, Associate Professor; Ph.D., Rochester, 1979. Physical chemistry: properties of advanced materials, electron spin resonance spectroscopy of polymeric materials, conduction in highly conjugated and ladder polymers, electrochemical applications to polymer properties, photodegradation of coatings.

Kenneth S. Schmitz, Professor; Ph.D., Washington (Seattle), 1972. Physical chemistry: dynamic light-scattering studies on polyelectrolytes and colloidal systems in presence and absence of an electric field, thermodynamics of small-molecule/polymer interactions.

Timothy F. Thomas, Professor; Ph.D., Oregon, 1964. Physical chemistry: laser spectroscopy of ions found in the stratosphere; photochemical methods of solar energy conversion; mass spectrometric appearance potentials; photophysical chemistry of small ring compounds and environmental pollutants; kinetics of surface-catalyzed reactions and of unimolecular reactions.

Zhe Wu, Assistant Professor; Ph.D., Caltech, 1994. Organic chemistry: transition metal mediated organic transformations, polymer syntheses, and mechanisms; synthesis of materials with optical properties and biomedical applications.

Charles J. Wurrey, Professor and Associate Dean of Arts and Sciences; Ph.D., MIT, 1973. Physical chemistry: infrared and Raman spectroscopy, conformational analysis, molecular structure, environmental applications of infrared spectroscopy, molecular modeling, theoretical calculations of molecular structure and spectra.

Associated Faculty

K. L. Cheng, Professor Emeritus; Ph.D., Illinois. Analytical chemistry.

John W. Connolly, Professor Emeritus; Ph.D., Purdue. Inorganic chemistry.

Wesley J. Dale, Professor Emeritus; Ph.D., Minnesota. Organic chemistry.

Henry A. Droll, Professor Emeritus; Ph.D., Penn State. Inorganic chemistry.

Eckhard W. Hellmuth, Professor Emeritus; Ph.D., Marburg (Germany). Polymer science.

Peter F. Lott, Professor Emeritus; Ph.D., Connecticut. Analytical chemistry.

Ronald A. MacQuarrie, Professor, Vice Provost, and Dean of the Graduate School; Ph.D., Oregon. Biochemistry.

Layton L. McCoy, Professor Emeritus; Ph.D., Washington (Seattle). Organic chemistry.

Frank Millich, Professor Emeritus; Ph.D., Polytechnic of Brooklyn. Polymer science.

Bob I.-Y. Yang, Associate Professor; Ph.D., Iowa State. Biochemistry.

SELECTED PUBLICATIONS

Dias, J. R. The most stable class of benzenoid hydrocarbons and their topological characteristics: Total resonant sextet benzenoids revisited. *J. Chem. Inf. Comput. Sci.* 39:144–50, 1999.

Dias, J. R. Correlations and applications of the circumscribing/excised internal structure concept. *Adv. Mol. Similarity* 2:257–62, 1998.

Dias, J. R. The complementarity principle and its uses in molecular similarity and related aspects. *Adv. Mol. Similarity* 2:243–56, 1998.

Gao, H., and J. R. Dias. Highly selective cyclotrimerization of lithocholic acid by DCC/DMAP reagent. *Croat. Chem. Acta* 71:827–31, 1998.

Dias, J. R. From small polyradical molecules to infinitely large π-electronic networks: Strongly subspectral molecular systems. *Z. Naturforsch.* 53a:909–18, 1998.

Gao, H., and J. R. Dias. Synthesis of cyclocholates and derivatives, part II. Selective synthesis of cyclocholates from linear dimers. *New J. Chem.* 579–83, 1998.

Gao, H., and J. R. Dias. Cyclocholates with 12-Oxo and 7,12-Oxo groups. *Eur. J. Chem.* 719–24, 1998.

Dias, J. R. *Molecular Orbital Calculation Using Chemical Graph Theory*. Berlin: Springer-Verlag, 1993.

Durig, J. R., et al. Infrared and Raman spectra, conformational stability, barriers to internal rotation, vibrational assignment, and ab initio calculations for methyl vinyl sulfide. *J. Mol. Struct.* 442:71, 1998.

Durig, J. R., et al. Infrared and Raman spectra, conformational stability, ab initio calculations, and vibrational assignments for cyclopropyldichlorosilane. *Chem. Phys.* 226:125, 1998.

Durig, J. R., and F. F. D. Daeyaert. Raman and infrared spectra, conformational stability, ab initio calculations, and vibrational assignment of fluoromethyl phosphonothioic dichloride. *J. Raman Spectrosc.* 29:191, 1998.

Guirgis, G. A., B. R. Drew, T. K. Gounev, and J. R. Durig. Conformational stability and vibrational assignment of propanal. *Spectrochim. Acta* 54:123, 1998.

Guirgis, G. A., Y. E. Nashed, T. K. Gounev, and J. R. Durig. Conformational stability, structural parameters, vibrational frequencies, and Raman and infrared intensities of allylsilane. *Struct. Chem.* 9:265, 1998.

Durig, J. R., J. Xiao, J. B. Robb II, and F. F. D. Daeyaert. Ab initio calculation of the conformational stability, vibrational wavenumbers, Raman and infrared intensities, and structural parameters of chloromethyldichlorophosphine. *J. Raman Spectrosc.* 29:463, 1998.

Durig, J. R., Y. Li, S. Shen, and D. T. Durig. Conformational stability and structural parameters of CH_3CH_2CCIO and other $(CH_3)_nCH_{3-n}$-CCIO molecules. *J. Mol. Struct.* 449:131, 1998.

Durig, J. R., et al. Raman and infrared spectra, conformational stability, normal coordinate analysis, vibrational assignment, and ab initio calculations of difluoromethylcyclopropane. *J. Phys. Chem.* 102:10460, 1998.

Durig, J. R., S. Shen, T. K. Gounev, and C. J. Wurrey. Conformational behavior of ethyloxirane from infrared and Raman spectra, temperature dependent FT-IR spectra of xenon solutions and ab initio calculations. *J. Mol. Struct.* 379:267–82, 1996.

Holder, A. J. AM1. In *Encyclopedia of Computational Chemistry*, vol. 1, pp. 8–11, eds. P. v. R. Schleyer et al. Chichester (United Kingdom): John Wiley and Sons, 1998.

Holder, A. J. CODESSA. In *Encyclopedia of Computational Chemistry*, vol. 5, pp. 3302–3, eds. P. v. R. Schleyer et al. Chichester (United Kingdom): John Wiley and Sons, 1998.

Holder, A. J. SAM1. In *Encyclopedia of Computational Chemistry*, vol. 4, pp. 2542–4, eds. P. v. R. Schleyer et al. Chichester (United Kingdom): John Wiley and Sons, 1998.

Holder, A. J., and R. D. Dennington II. An evaluation of SAM1 calculated vibrational frequencies. *Theochem* 401/3:207, 1997.

Holder, A. J. The future of semiempirical methods. *Theochem* 401/3:193, 1997.

Yuan, J.-P., H. Cao, E. W. Hellmuth, and Y. C. Jean. Subnanometer hole properties of CO_2-exposed polysulfone studied by positron annihilation spectroscopy. *J. Polym. Sci. B: Polym. Phys.* 36:3049–56, 1998.

Li, H.-L., Y. Ujihira, A. Nanasawa, and Y. C. Jean. Estimation of free volume in polystyrene-polyphenylene ether blend by positron annihilation lifetime technique. *Polymer* 40:349–55, 1998.

Cao, H., et al. (Y. C. Jean). Degradation of coating systems studied by positron annihilation spectroscopy: 1. Effect of UV irradiation. *Macromolecules* 31:6627–35, 1998.

Cao, H., et al. (Y. C. Jean). Free-volume hole model for positronium formation in polymers: Surface studies. *J. Phys.: Condens. Matter* 10:10429–42, 1998.

Huang, C.-M., E. W. Hellmuth, and Y. C. Jean. Positron annihilation studies of chromophore-doped polymers. *J. Phys. Chem. B* 102:2474–82, 1998.

Jean, Y. C., et al. Glass transition of polystyrene near the surface studied by slow positron annihilation spectroscopy. *Phys. Rev. B: Condens. Matter* 56:R8459–62, 1997.

Ching, W. Y., Y.-N. Xu, Y. C. Jean, and Y. Lou. Electronic states and Fermi surfaces in the organic superconductor k-(BEDT-TTF)$_2$CU[N(CN)$_2$]Br. *Phys. Rev. B: Condens. Matter* 55:2780–3, 1997.

Jean, Y. C., et al. Free-volume hole properties near the surface of polymers obtained from slow positron annihilation spectroscopy. *Appl. Surf. Sci.* 116:251–5, 1997.

Jean, Y. C. Comments on the paper: Can positron annihilation spectroscopy measure the free volume hole size distribution in amorphous polymers? *Macromolecules* 29:5767–8, 1996.

Jean, Y. C., et al. Anisotropy of hole structures in polymers probed by two-dimensional angular correlation of annihilation radiation. *Phys. Rev. B* 54:1785–90, 1996.

Jean, Y. C., et al. High sensitivity of positron annihilation lifetime to time and pressure effects in gas-exposed polymers. *J. Radioanal. Nucl. Chem.* 210:513–24, 1996.

Jean, Y. C., H. Yang, S. S. Jordan, and W. J. Koros. Free-volume hole properties of gas-exposed polycarbonate studied by positron annihilation lifetime spectroscopy. *Macromolecules* 29:7859–64, 1996.

Jean, Y. C., Y. Rhee, Y. Lou, D. Shelby, and G. L. Wilkes. Anisotropy of hole structures in oriented polycarbonate probed by two-dimensional angular correlation of annihilation radiation. *J. Polym. Sci. B: Polym. Phys.* 34:2979–85, 1996.

Lou, Y. M., et al. (Y. C. Jean). Hole structures of polymers and zeolites probed by two-dimensional angular correlation of annihilation radiation. *J. Radioanal. Nucl. Chem.* 211:85–91, 1996.

Abbotto, A., S. S.-W. Leung, A. Streitwieser, and K. V. Kilway. The role of monomer in the alkylation reaction of the lithium enolate of *p*-phenylisobutyrophenone in THF. *J. Am. Chem. Soc.* 120:10806–13, 1998.

Streitwieser, A., J. A. Krom, K. V. Kilway, and A. Abbotto. Aggregation and reactivity of the cesium enolate of *p*-phenylisobutyrophenone in tetrahydrofuran. *J. Am. Chem. Soc.* 120:10801–6, 1998.

Meltzheim, B., et al. (K. V. Kilway). Synthesis of various (pentamethylcyclopentadienyl) Ru(η^6-arene) complexes of phenalene derivatives. *Bull. Soc. Chim. Fr.* 133:979–85, 1996.

Kilway, K. V., and J. S. Siegel. The effect of transition-metal complexation on the stereodynamics of per-substituted arenes. Evidence for steric complementarity between arene and metal tripod. *J. Am. Chem. Soc.* 114:225, 1992.

Borchardt, A., A. Fuchicello, K. V. Kilway, K. K. Baldridge, and J. S. Siegel. Synthesis and dynamics of the corannulene nucleus. *J. Am. Chem. Soc.* 114:1921, 1992.

Kilway, K. V., and J. S. Siegel. Experimental observation of the barrier to rotation around the metal-arene bond in bis-1,4-(4,4-dimethyl-3-oxopentyl)-2,3,5,6-tetraethylbenzene molybdenum tricarbonyl. *Organometallics* 11:1426, 1992.

Peng, Z., and M. E. Galvin. Novel polymer structures for light-emitting-diode. *Acta Polym.* 49:244, 1998.

Peng, Z., and M. E. Galvin. Polymers with high electron affinities for light emitting diodes. *Chem. Mater.* 10(7):1785, 1998.

Peng, Z., Z. Bao, and M. E. Galvin. Oxadiazole-containing conjugated polymers for light-emitting diodes. *Adv. Mater.* 10(9):680, 1998.

Peng, Z., Z. Bao, and M. E. Galvin. Polymers with bipolar carrier transport abilities for light emitting diodes. *Chem. Mater.* 10(8):2086, 1998.

Peng, Z. H., A. Gharavi, and L. Yu. Conjugated photorefractive polymers containing ionic transition metal complex as sensitizer. *J. Am. Chem. Soc.* 119:4622, 1997.

University of Missouri–Kansas City

Selected Publications (continued)

Peng, Z. H., A. Gharavi, and L. Yu. A hybridized approach to new polymers exhibiting large photorefractivity. *Appl. Phys. Lett.* 69:4002, 1996.

Peng, Z. H., and L. Yu. Syntheses of conjugated polymers containing ionic transition metal complexes. *J. Am. Chem. Soc.* 118:3777, 1996.

Sandreczki, T. C., et al. Examination of photo-induced radicals in polyurethane clearcoats using ESR spectroscopy. *Polym. Preprints* 39(2):641, 1998.

Wilbur, J. M., et al. (T. C. Sandreczki). A representative of a new class of conducting oligomer: Acetylene-terminated polyaniline. *Synth. Met.* 82:175, 1996.

Leopold, D. J., I. M. Brown, and T. C. Sandreczki. Electronic states induced by ion irradiation in a conjugated ladder polymer. *Synth. Met.* 78:67, 1996.

Sandreczki, T. C., X. Hong, and Y. C. Jean. Sub-glass-transition temperature of annealing of polycarbonate studied by positron annihilation spectroscopy. *Macromolecules* 29:4015, 1996.

Morelli, J. J., and T. C. Sandreczki. The vacuum pyrolysis and thermal degradation in air of irradiated poly(ethylene-co-tetrafluoroethylene) films. *J. Anal. Appl. Pyrolysis* 35:121, 1995.

Brown, I. M., D. J. Leopold, S. Mohite, and T. C. Sandreczki. Conducting thermoset polymers: A comparative study of Schiff base precursors with different end groups. *Synth. Met.* 72:269, 1995.

Schmitz, K. S. A many-bodied interpretation of the attraction between macroions of like charge: Juxtaposition of potential fields. *Langmuir* 13:5849, 1997.

Schmitz, K. S. The pairwise "Gibbsian" free energy and screened coulombic interactions. *Langmuir* 12:3828–43, 1996.

Schmitz, K. S. Further developments on polyelectrolyte coupled dynamics. *Ber. Bunsen-Ges.* 100:748–56, 1996.

Schmitz, K. S. Effect of finite ion size on the "Overbeek correction" to the Sogami-Ise interaction potential between macroions of like charge. *Langmuir* 12:1407–10, 1996.

Schmitz, K. S. On the "attractive component" to the free energy of interaction between macroions of like charge. *Accounts Chem. Res.* 29:7–11, 1996.

Schmitz, K. S., and T. J. Pontalion. Quasielastic light scattering in the presence of a sinusoidal electric field: A comparison of theories to experimental data on poly(lysine). *J. Chem. Phys.* 103:794–7, 1995.

Schmitz, K. S. Re-analysis of Dapp(q) of polystyrene latex spheres in terms of the extended coupled mode model. *Macromolecules* 27:3442–3, 1994.

Schmitz, K. S. *Macroions in Solution and Colloidal Suspension.* New York: VCH Publishers, 1994.

Schmitz, K. S. Dynamic light scattering by polyelectrolyte solutions. *Macromolecular Symposia: Dynamics of Polymers* 79:57, 1994.

Schmitz, K. S., ed. An overview of polyelectrolytes: Six topics in search of an author. *ACS Symp. Ser. 548*, p. 1. Washington, D.C.: American Chemical Society, 1994.

Schmitz, K. S. *An Introduction to Dynamic Light Scattering by Macromolecules.* New York: Academic Press, 1990.

Fitzgibbons, S., and T. F. Thomas. A MIKES study of the energetics and mechanism of fragmentation of the ethylacetoacetate cation. *Proceedings of the 46th ASMS Conference on Mass Spectrometry* p. 1210, 1998.

Mohd Zabidi, N. A., D. Tapp, and T. F. Thomas. Kinetics of the rapid dark reaction between methanol and oxygen in the presence of a "photo-"catalyst. *J. Phys. Chem.* 99:14733, 1995.

Snow, K. B., and T. F. Thomas. Photodissociation spectroscopy of OCS^+ with momentum analysis of the photoproduction ion. *Proceedings of the 42nd Annual Conference on Mass Spectrometry*, p. 445, 1994.

Thomas, T. F., F. Dale, and J. F. Paulson. Rate constants for quenching the $\tilde{A}\ ^2A_2$ state of SO_2^+. *J. Chem. Phys.* 88:5553, 1988.

Thomas, T. F., F. Dale, and J. F. Paulson. The photo-dissociation spectrum of SO_2^+. *J. Chem. Phys.* 84:1215, 1986.

Thomas, T. F., F. Dale, and J. F. Paulson. Observation of a metastable state of SO_2^+ by ion photodissociation spectroscopy. *J. Chem. Phys.* 79:4078, 1983.

Thomas, T. F., T. L. Rose, and J. F. Paulson. On the photochemical stability of $H_3O^+\cdot(H_2O)_n$. *J. Chem. Phys.* 71:552, 1979.

Chang, J. C., and T. F. Thomas. Matrix photochemistry of cyclic ketones: ESR study. *J. Photochem.* 9:312, 1978.

Thomas, T. F., F. Dale, and J. F. Paulson. Photodissociation of positive ions. I. Photodissociation spectra of D_2^+, HD^+, and N_2O^+. *J. Chem. Phys.* 67:793, 1977.

Rodriguez, H. J., J. C. Chang, and T. F. Thomas. Thermal, photochemical and photophysical processes in cyclopropanone vapor. *J. Am. Chem. Soc.* 98:2027, 1976.

Wang, D. K., and Z. Wu. Facile synthesis of new unimolecular initiators for living radical polymerizations. *Macromolecules* 31:6727, 1998.

Ariffin, Z., D. K. Wang, and Z. Wu. Synthesis of polycarbonates using a cationic zirconocene complex. *Macromol. Rapid Commun.* 19:601, 1998.

Ayub, M., C.-T. Ko, and C. J. Wurrey. Conformational analysis of (aminomethyl)cyclopropane hydrochloride using vibrational spectroscopy and ab initio calculations. *J. Mol. Struct.* 449:159–76, 1998.

Wurrey, C. J., S. Shen, X. Zhu, H. Zhen, and J. R. Durig. Conformational studies of cyanomethylcyclopropane from temperature-dependent FT-IR spectra of xenon solutions and ab initio calculations. *J. Mol. Struct.* 449:203–17, 1998.

Wurrey, C. J., S. Shen, T. K. Gounev, and J. R. Durig. Conformational stability of ethylcyclopropane from Raman spectra, temperature dependent FT-IR spectra of xenon solutions and ab initio calculations. *J. Mol. Struct.* 406:207, 1997.

Gurka, D. F., et al. (C. J. Wurrey). Environmental analysis by ab initio quantum mechanical computation and gas chromatography/Fourier transform infrared spectrometry. *Anal. Chem.* 68:4221–7, 1996.

Guan, Y., C. J. Wurrey, and G. J. Thomas Jr. Vibrational analysis of nucleic acids. I. The phosphodiester group in dimethyl phosphate model compounds: $(CH_3O)_2PO_2^-$, $(CD_3O)_2PO_2^-$, and $(^{13}CH_3O)_2PO_2^-$. *Biophys. J.* 66:225–35, 1994.

Wurrey, C. J., et al. (A. J. Holder). Vibrational and rotational spectra and conformational behavior of (chloromethyl)thiirane. *Spectrochim. Acta* 50A:481, 1994.

Li, H., C. J. Wurrey, and G. J. Thomas Jr. Cysteine conformation and sulfhydryl interactions in proteins and viruses: 2. Normal coordinate analysis of the cysteine side chain and model compounds. *J. Am. Chem. Soc.* 114:7463, 1992.

UNIVERSITY OF NOTRE DAME

Department of Chemistry and Biochemistry

Program of Study

The Department of Chemistry and Biochemistry offers graduate programs of study that lead to the Ph.D. in chemistry (inorganic, organic, and physical) and biochemistry. Interdisciplinary programs in biochemistry, biophysics, and molecular biology; chemical physics; and materials and surface science that involve faculty members in the Departments of Biological Sciences, Physics, and Chemical Engineering, respectively, are also available. In addition, the Department of Chemistry and Biochemistry maintains research ties with the Radiation Research Laboratory.

The broad objective of the Ph.D. program is to prepare students for effective careers in research and teaching. Entering students in both chemistry and biochemistry programs normally take qualifying examinations in relevant subject areas, and their performance serves as a guideline for their future course of study. Ordinarily, formal courses and candidacy requirements are completed by the end of the second year. Students choose a thesis adviser and begin research during their first year. The dissertation defense includes the presentation of a departmental seminar followed by a committee examination.

The department has an active seminar program that includes the Lynch, Nieuwland, Reilly, and College of Science endowed lectureships. These memorial lectureships allow world-renowned chemists and biochemists to visit the campus for periods of up to one week. In addition, many other visiting scientists lecture throughout the year as part of a colloquium series.

Research Facilities

A modern research building provides ample laboratory space for chemical and biochemical research. The department maintains major instrumentation required for modern scientific research, including a 600-MHz, a 500-MHz, and two 300-MHz multinuclear NMR spectrometers; a variety of lasers; X-ray and UV photoelectron spectrometers; a microwave spectrometer; laser-Raman spectrometers; an EPR spectrometer; two high-resolution, double-focusing mass spectrometer systems with GC and LC sample delivery and varied modes of ionization, including FAB and electrospray; a DE MALDI-TOF mass spectrometer; two circular dichroism instruments; molecular beam facilities; two X-ray diffractometers, one equipped with an area detector; automated DNA and protein sequencing facilities; oligonucleotide and peptide synthesizers; GC, HPLC, and FPLC units; amino acid and peptide analyzers; stopped-flow spectrophotometers; spectrofluorometers; atomic absorption spectrometers; preparative and analytical ultracentrifuges; and other routine instrumentation. The Radiation Research Laboratory facilities include a picosecond flash photolysis apparatus, two Van de Graaff accelerators, high-pressure radiation equipment, and a linear electron accelerator. In addition, Silicon Graphics and Sun workstations for molecular structure analysis and visualization are found throughout the department.

Financial Aid

Graduate teaching assistantship stipends are $18,000 per year for the 1999–2000 session. Included are $13,500 for the nine-month academic year and guaranteed summer support prorated for the three-month summer period (based on satisfactory academic performance). Stipend levels are revised annually. Research fellowships for outstanding students and members of minority groups are also available. Advanced students are usually supported as research assistants from funds obtained from government, commercial, or private grants.

Cost of Study

Graduate tuition for the 1999–2000 academic year is $21,840. All students admitted to the program are granted full tuition scholarships by the Graduate School.

Living and Housing Costs

Housing for graduate students (Fischer and O'Hara-Grace Graduate Residences) is conveniently located within walking distance of the department. Married student housing is provided in University-owned apartments, and there are several apartment complexes near campus and in the greater South Bend area.

Student Group

Currently, there are approximately 110 graduate students in the Department of Chemistry and Biochemistry, drawn from colleges and universities throughout the U.S. and from top international institutions. The majority are full-time students working toward the doctoral degree. The University has an enrollment of 10,000 students, of whom 2,200 are enrolled in various graduate and professional programs.

Location

The University of Notre Dame is located north of the city of South Bend. Its geographical location makes the Chicago metropolitan area easily accessible. The Broadway Theatre League brings major New York theater productions to South Bend for multiple performances, and the South Bend Symphony Orchestra has an extensive concert schedule. Lake Michigan is nearby and provides facilities for water sports. Facilities for winter skiing can be found a short distance away.

The University and The Department

The University of Notre Dame, founded in 1842, is a private, independent, and fully coeducational institution. The intellectual, cultural, and athletic traditions at Notre Dame, coupled with the beauty of the campus, contribute to the University's international reputation. The University offers a variety of cultural and recreational activities, including plays, concerts, and lectures that bring world-famous figures to campus. There are ample facilities for indoor and outdoor sports; tennis and ice skating can be enjoyed throughout the year.

The department maintains strong ties with other departments in the College of Science, particularly Biological Sciences and Physics, and with the College of Engineering. As a result, interdisciplinary research and teaching occur in a cooperative and collaborative environment within the College of Science.

Applying

Applications from qualified students who possess the equivalent of an undergraduate degree in the fields of chemistry, biochemistry, biological sciences, or physics are encouraged without regard to nationality, religion, race, or gender. Scores on the General Test of the Graduate Record Examinations (GRE) are required, and submission of scores on the GRE Subject Test in chemistry or biochemistry is strongly recommended. For application forms and other information, students should contact the address below. Completed application forms should be submitted as early as possible in the academic year.

Correspondence and Information

Chairman, Graduate Admissions
Department of Chemistry and Biochemistry
251 Nieuwland Science Hall
University of Notre Dame
Notre Dame, Indiana 46556-5670

Telephone: 219-631-7058
Fax: 219-631-6652
World Wide Web: http://www.science.nd.edu/chemistry/

University of Notre Dame

THE FACULTY AND THEIR RESEARCH

K.-D. Asmus, Professor; Ph.D., Berlin Technical, 1965. Physical chemistry: structure and chemistry of free radicals.

S. C. Basu, Professor; Ph.D., Michigan, 1966; D.Sc., Calcutta, 1976. Biochemistry: structure, biosynthesis, and function of glycosphingolipids; studies on DNA polymerase-α.

R. K. Bretthauer, Professor; Ph.D., Michigan State, 1962. Biochemistry:glycoprotein biosynthesis, structure, and function.

S. Brown, Assistant Professor; Ph.D., Washington (Seattle), 1994. Inorganic chemistry: organic and inorganic reaction mechanisms, cooperative reactions.

F. J. Castellino, Kleiderer/Pezold Professor and Dean, College of Science; Ph.D., Iowa, 1968. Biochemistry: structure, function, and activation of proteins involved in blood coagulation and fibrinolysis.

M. J. Chetcuti, Associate Professor; Ph.D., Malta, 1976. Inorganic chemistry: transition-metal organometallic chemistry: synthesis and reactions of metal-metal bonded complexes.

X. Creary, Huisking Professor; Ph.D., Ohio State, 1973. Organic chemistry: synthetic methods for formation of strained polycyclic molecules; cationic, free-radical carbenic, and electron transfer processes.

T. P. Fehlner, Grace Rupley Professor; Ph.D., Johns Hopkins, 1963. Inorganic chemistry: synthesis, structure, and reactivity of metal boron clusters; clusters as substituents; cluster assemblies as precursors for novel catalysts.

R. W. Fessenden, Professor; Ph.D., MIT, 1958. Physical and radiation chemistry: structure and reactions of unstable species produced by radiolysis and photolysis as studied by ESR and related techniques.

S. Hammes-Schiffer, Clare Boothe Luce Assistant Professor; Ph.D., Stanford, 1993. Physical chemistry: theoretical and computational chemistry, incorporation of quantum effects in the simulation of biologically important reactions.

G. V. Hartland, Assistant Professor; Ph.D., UCLA, 1991. Physical chemistry: reaction and energy transfer dynamics of highly excited molecules, photophysics of nanometer-sized semiconductor particles, nonlinear Fourier-transform spectroscopy.

R. G. Hayes, Professor; Ph.D., Berkeley, 1962. Physical chemistry: electronic structure of molecules, Auger and X-ray photoelectron spectroscopy.

P. Helquist, Professor; Ph.D., Cornell, 1972. Organometallic and bioorganic chemistry: synthesis and activity of natural products, new synthetic methods.

P. W. Huber, Associate Professor; Ph.D., Purdue, 1978. Biochemistry:protein–nucleic acid interactions, nucleic acid structure.

D. C. Jacobs, Associate Professor; Ph.D., Stanford, 1988. Physical chemistry: dynamics of molecular ion collisions with metal and semiconductor surfaces, surface science, charge transfer and etching reactions, multiphoton laser ionization techniques.

J. S. Keller, Assistant Professor; Ph.D., Chicago, 1989. Physical chemistry: nonlinear optical probes of molecules undergoing multiresonant laser excitation, spectroscopy of high vibrationally excited species, investigation of reactive surfaces, control over excited-state geometries and product channels.

A. G. Lappin, Professor and Chairman; Ph.D., Glasgow, 1975. Inorganic and analytical chemistry: electron transfer reactions of transition-metal ion complexes and metalloproteins.

M. Lieberman, Assistant Professor; Ph.D., Washington (Seattle), 1994. Organic chemistry: surface and materials chemistry.

D. Meisel, Professor and Director, Radiation Laboratory; Ph.D., Hebrew (Jerusalem), 1974. Physical chemistry: radiation and photochemistry, kinetics and thermodynamics in microheterogeneous systems, nanoparticles and self-assembly, applications to energy conversion and environmental management.

M. J. Miller, George and Winifred Clark Professor; Ph.D., Cornell, 1976. Organic chemistry: synthetic methods; synthesis and study of biologically important nitrogen-containing compounds, such as amino acids, peptides, hydroxamic acids, carbocyclic nucleosides, β-lactam antibiotics, and siderophore (microbial iron chelators) antibiotics.

T. Nowak, Professor; Ph.D., Kansas, 1969. Biochemistry: enzyme mechanisms, catalysis, and regulation; monovalent and divalent cations in catalysis; stereochemistry; drug effects; biochemical applications of magnetic resonance spectroscopy.

W. R. Scheidt, Professor; Ph.D., Michigan, 1968. Inorganic chemistry: relation of chemistry, physical properties, and molecular structure of metalloporphyrins and closely related derivatives; models of the cytochromes.

R. H. Schuler, Zahm Professor; Ph.D., Notre Dame, 1949. Physical and radiation chemistry: studies of radiation-produced chemical intermediates using optical, ESR, and Raman techniques and chemical methods.

A. S. Serianni, Associate Professor; Ph.D., Michigan State, 1980. Biochemistry: carbohydrate and nucleotide chemistry and biochemistry, synthesis and applications of stable isotopically enriched biomolecules.

S. Sevov, Assistant Professor; Ph.D., Iowa State, 1993. Inorganic chemistry: inorganic and solid-state chemistry.

B. D. Smith, Associate Professor; Ph.D., Penn State, 1988. Organic chemistry: molecular recognition and switchable host/guest chemistry, enzyme inhibitors for photoregulation of enzyme activity and active-site mapping using NMR spectroscopy.

R. Taylor, Assistant Professor; Ph.D., Rensselaer, 1992. Organic chemistry: synthetic methodology and bioorganic recognition.

J. K. Thomas, Julius A. Nieuwland Professor; Ph.D., 1957, D.Sc., 1969, Manchester; Fellow, Royal Society of Chemistry. Physical and radiation chemistry: laser photocatalysis of reactions in assemblies, micelles, polymers, colloidal semiconductors, clay, and metal oxides.

O. Wiest, Assistant Professor; Ph.D., Bonn (Germany), 1993. Organic chemistry: physical and theoretical organic chemistry, electron transfer–induced processes.

SELECTED PUBLICATIONS

Asmus, K.-D. Glycine decarboxylation: The free radical mechanism. *J. Am. Chem. Soc.* 120:9930–40, 1998.

Basu, S. C. Purification and characterization of avian glycolipid: β-galactosyltransferases (GalT-4 and GalT-3): Cloning and expression of truncated βGalT-4. *Acta Biochim. Pol.* 45:451–67, 1998.

Bretthauer, R. K. O-Mannosylation of *Pichia pastoris* cellular and recombinant proteins. *Biotechnol. Appl. Biochem.* 28:39–45, 1998.

Brown, S. Phenyl-to-oxo migration in an electrophilic rhenium(VII) dioxo complex. *J. Am. Chem. Soc.* 118:12119–33, 1996.

Castellino, F. J. Inactivation of the gene for anticoagulant protein C causes lethal perinatal consumptive coagulopathy in mice. *J. Clin. Invest.* 102:1481–8, 1998.

Chetcuti, M. J. Group 6-Group 10 heterobimetallic complexes with sulfur ligands. *J. Cluster Sci.* 7:225–45, 1996.

Creary, X. Reaction of benzylic α-hydroxythioamides with thionyl chloride. *J. Org. Chem.* 63:4907–11, 1998.

Fehlner, T. P. Synthesis of mono- and ditungstaboranes from reaction of Cp*WCl$_4$ and [CP*WCl$_2$]$_2$ with BH$_3$THF or LiBH$_4$(CP*=η^5-C$_5$Me$_5$). Control of reaction pathway by choice of monoborane reagent and oxidation state of the metal center. *Organometallics* 18:53–64, 1999.

Fessenden, R. W. Dye capped semiconductor nanoclusters. Role of back electron transfer in the photosensitization of SnO$_2$ nanocrystallites with cresyl violet aggregates. *J. Phys. Chem. B* 101:2583–90, 1997.

Hammes-Schiffer, S. Mixed quantum/classical dynamics of hydrogen transfer reactions. *J. Phys. Chem. A* 102:10443–54, 1999.

Hartland, G. V. Spectroscopy and dynamics of nanometer sized noble metal particles. *J. Phys. Chem. B* 102:6958–67, 1998.

Hayes, R. G. Dynamical behavior of electronic states of NH$_3$$^{2+}$ prepared from NIs ionization of ammonia. *J. Electron Spectrosc. Rel. Phenomena* 75:83–96, 1995.

Helquist, P. Quantitative structure-reactivity relationships in palladium-catalyzed allylation derived from molecular mechanics (MM2) calculations. *Organometallics* 16:3015–21, 1997.

Huber, P. W. Binding of neomycin to the TAR element of HIV-1 RNA induces dissociation of Tat protein by an allosteric mechanism. *Biochemistry* 37:5549–57, 1998.

Jacobs, D. C. Dynamics of dissociative scattering: Hyperthermal energy collisions of state-selected OCS$^+$ on Ag(111). *J. Chem. Phys.* 107:6448–59, 1997.

Keller, J. S. Dissociation dynamics of CH$_3$SH at 222, 248, and 193 nm: An analog for probing non-adiabaticity in the transition state region of bimolecular reactions. *J. Chem. Phys.* 98:2882, 1993.

Lappin, A. G. Convenient synthesis and characterization of the chiral complexes *cis*- and *trans*-[Ru((*SS*)-(Pr^i)$_2$pybox)(py)Cl]PF$_6$ and [Ru((*SS*)-Pr^i)$_2$pybox)bpy)Cl]PF$_6$. *Inorg. Chem.* 36:3735–40, 1997.

Lieberman, M. Dynamic structure and potential energy surface of a 3-helix bundle protein. *J. Am. Chem. Soc.* 116:5035–44, 1994.

Meisel, D. Charge carrier transfer across the silica nanoparticle/water interface. *J. Phys. Chem.* 102:7225–30, 1998.

Miller, M. J. Polyoxins and nikkomycins progress in synthetic and biological studies. *Curr. Pharm. Design* 5:1–27, 1999.

Nowak, T. Chromium(III) modification of the first metal binding site of phosphoenolpyruvate carboxykinase. *Biochemistry* 37:8061–70, 1998.

Scheidt, W. R. Syntheses, characterization and structural studies of several (Nitro)(nitrosyl)iron(III) porphyrinates: [Fe(Porph)(NO$_2$)(NO)]. *Inorg. Chem.* 38:100–8, 1999.

Schuler, R. H. Track effects in water radiolysis: Yields of the Fricke dosimeter for carbo ions with energies up to 1700 MeV. *J. Am. Chem. Soc.* 116:7760–70, 1994.

Serianni, A. S. Three-bond C-O-C-C spin-coupling constants in carbohydrates: Development of a Karplus relationship. *J. Am. Chem. Soc.* 120:11158–73, 1998.

Sevov, S. Synthesis and structure of deltahedral nine-atom silicon clusters. *J. Am. Chem. Soc.* 120:3263–4, 1998.

Smith, B. D. Anionic saccharides activate liposomes containing phospholipids bearing a boronic acid for Ca^{2+}-dependent fusion. *J. Am. Chem. Soc.* 129:7141–2, 1998.

Taylor, R. A formal total synthesis of epothilone A: Enantioselective preparation of the C1-C6 and C7-C12 fragments. *J. Org. Chem.* 60:9580, 1998.

Thomas, J. K. Spectroscopic investigation of photoinduced charge separation and recombination in solid polymers. *J. Phys. Chem.* 102:5465–75, 1998.

Wiest, O. *Ab Initio* studies of the ring-opening reaction of the cyclobutene radical cation. *J. Am. Chem. Soc.* 117:5713–9, 1997.

UNIVERSITY OF PITTSBURGH

Department of Chemistry

Programs of Study

The department offers programs of study leading to the M.S. and Ph.D. degrees in analytical, inorganic, organic, and physical chemistry. A concentration in chemical physics is also available. Interdisciplinary research is currently conducted in the areas of surface science, natural product synthesis, combinatorial chemistry, laser spectroscopy, biosensors, materials science, organometallic chemistry, and theoretical chemistry. Both advanced degree programs involve original research and course work. Other requirements include a comprehensive examination, a thesis, a seminar, and, for the Ph.D. candidate, a proposal. For the typical Ph.D. candidate, this process takes four to five years.

Representative of current research activities in the department in analytical chemistry are techniques in electroanalytical chemistry, photoelectrochemistry, in vivo electrochemistry, chemical state imaging, capillary electrophoresis, UV resonance Raman spectroscopy, polymer analysis, and vibrational circular dichroism. In inorganic chemistry, studies are being conducted on organotransition metal complexes, redox reactions, complexes of biological interest, transition metal polymers, and optoelectronic materials; in organic chemistry, on reaction mechanisms, ion transport, total synthesis, drug design, molecular recognition, natural products synthesis, bioorganic chemistry, synthetic methodology, organometallics, enzyme mechanisms, and physical-organic chemistry. Research areas in physical chemistry include Raman, photoelectron, Auger, NMR, EPR, infrared, and mass spectroscopy; electron-stimulated desorption ion angular distribution (ESDIAD); condensed phase spectroscopy; high-resolution laser spectroscopy; molecular spectroscopy; electron and molecular beam scattering; electronic emission spectroscopy; atmospheric chemistry; and catalysis. Theoretical fields of research include electronic structure, reaction mechanisms, electron transfer theory, quantum mechanics, and new material design. Research on computer applications to chemistry is under way in a variety of areas.

Research Facilities

The Department of Chemistry is housed in a fifteen-story complex, which contains a vast array of modern research instruments and also offers in-house machine, electronics, and glassblowing shops. The Chemistry Library is a spacious 6,000-square-foot facility that contains more than 30,000 monographs and bound periodicals and more than 200 maintained journal subscriptions. Three other chemistry libraries are nearby. Shared instrumentation includes three 300-MHz NMRs and one 500-MHz NMR; two high-resolution, an LC/MS, and four low-resolution mass spectrometers; a light-scattering instrument; a circular dichroism spectrophotometer; a spectropolarimeter; X-ray systems—single crystal, powder, and fluorescence; a scanning electron microscope; a vibrating sample magnetometer; several FT-IR and UV-VIS spectrophotometers; and computer and workstation clusters.

Financial Aid

Seventy-five teaching assistantships and teaching fellowships are available. The former provide $15,900 in 1999 for the three trimesters of the year; the fellowships (awarded to superior students after their first year) carry an annual stipend of $16,545. Most advanced students are supported by research assistantships and fellowships, which pay up to $1390 per month. All teaching assistantships, fellowships, and research assistantships include a full scholarship that covers all tuition, fees, and medical insurance.

Special Kaufman Fellowships provide up to an additional $4000 award to truly outstanding incoming Ph.D. candidates. In addition, Bayer Fellowships, Ashe Fellowships, and Aristech Fellowships provide supplements to the three-term teaching assistantships that range from $2000 to $5000 annually. In some cases, these supplements may be used to begin research in the summer prior to the formal initiation of graduate study.

Cost of Study

All graduate assistants and fellows receive full tuition scholarships. Estimated tuition and fees for full-time study in 1999 are $8484 per term for out-of-state students and $4239 for state residents.

Living and Housing Costs

Most graduate students prefer private housing, which is available in a wide range of apartments and rooms in areas of Pittsburgh near the campus. The University maintains a housing office to assist students seeking off-campus housing. Living costs compare favorably with other urban areas.

Student Group

The University enrolls about 17,000 students, including about 9,500 graduate and professional school students. Most parts of the United States and many other countries are represented. About 170 full-time graduate chemistry students are supported by the various sources listed under Financial Aid. The University is coeducational in all schools and divisions; more than one third of the graduate chemistry students are women. An honorary chemistry society promotes a social program for all faculty members and graduate students in the department.

Location

Deservedly, Pittsburgh is currently ranked "among the most livable cities in the United States" by Rand McNally. It is recognized for its outstanding blend of cultural, educational, and technological resources. Pittsburgh's famous Golden Triangle is enclosed by the Allegheny and Monongahela rivers, which meet at the Point in downtown Pittsburgh to form the Ohio River. Pittsburgh has enjoyed a dynamic renaissance in the last few years. The city's cultural resources include the Pittsburgh Ballet, Opera Company, Symphony Orchestra, Civic Light Opera, and Public Theatre and the Three Rivers Shakespeare Festival. Many outdoor activities, such as rock climbing, rafting, sailing, skiing, and hunting, are also available within a 50-mile radius.

The University

The University of Pittsburgh, founded in 1787, is one of the oldest schools west of the Allegheny Mountains. Although privately endowed and controlled, the University is state-related to permit lower tuition rates for Pennsylvania residents and to provide a steady source of funds for all of its programs. Attracting more than $269 million in sponsored research annually, the University has continued to increase in stature.

Applying

Applications for September admission and assistantships should be made prior to February 1. However, special cases may be considered throughout the year. A background that includes a B.S. degree in chemistry, with courses in mathematics through integral calculus, is preferred. GRE scores, including the chemistry Subject Test, are required. International applicants must submit TOEFL results and GRE scores.

Correspondence and Information

Graduate Admissions
Department of Chemistry
University of Pittsburgh
Pittsburgh, Pennsylvania 15260

Telephone: 412-624-8501
E-mail: nsattler@vms.cis.pitt.edu
World Wide Web: http://www.chem.pitt.edu

University of Pittsburgh

THE FACULTY AND THEIR RESEARCH

P. A. Aker, Assistant Professor; Ph.D., Carleton, 1986. Physical chemistry: atmospheric chemistry; application of nonlinear laser Raman spectroscopic techniques to study gas-phase and gas-surface chemical reactions.

S. A. Asher, Professor; Ph.D., Berkeley, 1977. Analytical chemistry: resonance Raman spectroscopy; biophysical chemistry, material science, development of techniques for probing macromolecules and surface-adsorbed species, porphyrins, heme proteins, colloid optical devices.

D. N. Beratan, Professor; Ph.D., Caltech, 1985. Physical chemistry: theoretical bioinorganic chemistry and biochemistry; theoretical design of new materials for electronic and optical computing applications.

E. Borguet, Assistant Professor; Ph.D., Pennsylvania, 1993. Physical chemistry: surface science; ultrafast dynamics at interfaces; nonlinear vibrational (SFG) and electronic (SFG and SHF) spectroscopy of interfaces.

T. M. Chapman, Associate Professor; Ph.D., Polytechnic of Brooklyn, 1965. Organic chemistry: solid-phase synthesis, polyurethane chemistry, polymer surfactants, new polymers of uncommon architecture.

R. D. Coalson, Professor; Ph.D., Harvard, 1984. Physical chemistry: quantum theory of rate processes, optical spectroscopy, computational techniques for quantum dynamics; structure and energetics of macroions in solution; design of optical waveguides.

N. J. Cooper, Professor and Dean of the Faculty of Arts and Sciences; D.Phil., Oxford, 1976. Inorganic chemistry: synthetic and mechanistic inorganic and organometallic chemistry, heteroallene activation; anionic complexes containing metals in negative oxidation states, synthesis and reactivity of cationic alkylidene complexes of transition metals, organometallic photochemistry.

D. P. Curran, Distinguished Service Professor; Ph.D., Rochester, 1979. Organic chemistry: natural products total synthesis and new synthetic methodology, heterocycles in organic synthesis, synthesis via free-radical reactions.

M. F. Golde, Associate Professor; Ph.D., Cambridge, 1972. Physical chemistry: kinetic and spectroscopic studies of mechanisms of formation and removal of electronically excited atoms and small molecules, noble-gas halide excimers and similar species.

J. J. Grabowski, Associate Professor; Ph.D., Colorado, 1983. Physical-organic chemistry: mechanisms, reactive intermediates, dynamics and thermodynamics; gas and condensed phases; flowing afterglow, SIFT, Drift; photoacoustic calorimetry.

M. D. Hopkins, Professor; Ph.D., Caltech, 1986. Inorganic chemistry: electronically excited states of transition-metal complexes, linear-chain metal clusters, photochemistry and photophysics of multiple metal-metal and metal-ligand bonds.

K. D. Jordan, Professor; Ph.D., MIT, 1974. Physical chemistry: theoretical studies of the electronic structure of molecules, electron transmission and electron energy loss spectroscopy, computer simulations, chemical reactions at semiconductor surfaces, long-range intramolecular interactions.

J. P. Landers, Assistant Professor; Ph.D., Guelph, 1988. Bioanalytical chemistry: development of capillary electrophoresis-based clinical assays and diagnostic electrophoretic "chip" technology and methods.

T. Y. Meyer, Assistant Professor; Ph.D., Iowa, 1991. Inorganic chemistry: organometallic chemistry, polymer chemistry, application of transition metal catalysis to polymer synthesis; inorganic polymers; catalytic depolymerization; polymers with functionalized backbones.

A. C. Michael, Associate Professor; Ph.D., Emory, 1987. Analytical chemistry: in vivo voltammetry, voltammetry in supercritical fluids, voltammetry using microelectrodes, enzyme voltammetry.

S. G. Nelson, Assistant Professor; Ph.D., Rochester, 1991. Organic chemistry: natural products total synthesis, new synthetic methods, asymmetric catalysis.

D. W. Pratt, Professor; Ph.D., Berkeley, 1967. Physical chemistry: molecular structure and dynamics, as revealed by high-resolution laser and magnetic resonance spectroscopy, in the gas phase and in the condensed phase.

R. E. Shepherd, Professor; Ph.D., Stanford, 1971. Inorganic chemistry: reaction mechanisms and properties of biochemically related transition-metal complexes, electron transfer reactions, catalysis mechanisms.

J. A. Shin, Assistant Professor; Ph.D., Caltech, 1992. Organic and biological chemistry: protein-DNA and protein-protein interactions; molecular design and recognition; design, synthesis, and characterization of novel biomolecules.

P. E. Siska, Professor; Ph.D., Harvard, 1970. Physical chemistry: crossed molecular beam studies of intermolecular forces and chemical reaction dynamics.

D. H. Waldeck, Professor; Ph.D., Chicago, 1983. Physical chemistry: ultrafast spectroscopy as used to investigate the condensed phase, liquid-state dynamics, charge transfer events at the semiconductor-electrolyte interface.

G. C. Walker, Assistant Professor; Ph.D., Minnesota, 1991. Physical chemistry: structural dynamics of biological and model systems observed using time-resolved, including femtosecond, infrared spectroscopy; protein self-assembly and catalytic binding; charge transfer and vibrational relaxation.

S. G. Weber, Professor; Ph.D., McGill, 1979. Bioanalytical chemistry: separation and detection of peptides; sensors and smart materials; control over binding reactions using light and electrochemistry.

C. S. Wilcox, Professor; Ph.D., Caltech, 1979. Bioorganic chemistry: design, synthesis, and evaluation of stereoselective receptors and molecular aggregates; artificial enzymes based on binding and catalysis by functional group arrays; chemistry of ion pairs; new synthetic reactions.

P. Wipf, Professor and Director, Center for Combinatorial Chemistry; Ph.D., Zurich, 1987. Organic chemistry: synthesis and reactivity of bioactive molecules, peptidomimetics, synthesis of reactive functionalities.

J. T. Yates Jr., Mellon Chair Professor and Director, Surface Science Laboratory; Ph.D., MIT, 1960. Surface science: kinetics of surface processes; vibrational spectroscopy of surface species; electronic spectroscopy of surfaces; catalytic and surface chemistry on model clusters, oxides, and single crystals; semiconductor surfaces, scanning tunneling microscopy.

UNIVERSITY OF PUERTO RICO, RÍO PIEDRAS

Department of Chemistry

Programs of Study

The Department of Chemistry of the University of Puerto Rico, Río Piedras campus, offers programs of study that lead to the M.S. and Ph.D. degrees. Both degree programs require the presentation and oral defense of a thesis. Students should have a knowledge of Spanish and English. All students select research advisers and begin research by the end of the first year. Areas of concentration are biochemistry and analytical, inorganic, organic, and physical chemistry. An interdepartmental doctoral program in chemical physics is also offered.

M.S. students normally complete the thesis and the required 21 semester credits in courses during the second year. Students pursuing the Ph.D. degree must pass qualifying examinations in three major areas by the end of the first year, after which they must present two research proposals; one proposal is related to the student research project. Forty-two semester credits in courses and 24 in research are required for the Ph.D. One year as a teaching assistant is required for all students.

Research Facilities

The Facundo Bueso Building houses the Office of the Graduate Program and all the laboratories, classrooms, and services used by the program. Extensive renovation and modernization of the laboratories has been recently completed. Major equipment and instruments necessary for research are available, including lasers, a single photon-counting spectrofluorimeter, an X-ray diffractometer, and FT-NMR, FT-IR, and GC-MS spectrometers. There is a wide variety of equipment in individual research laboratories, including electrochemical analyzers, a quartz crystal microbalance, UV-Vis spectrophotometers, DSC, HPLC/GC, a fluorometer, and computers. The department has electronics, scientific illustration, machine, and glassblowing shops. Facilities to support research include the Materials Science and Surface Characterization, Biotesting, and Computational Chemistry Centers. Undergraduate chemistry classes and laboratories are held in another building. The Science Library is in a new building of the College of Natural Sciences.

Financial Aid

The research program of the department is supported by funds from the University and from government and industrial grants. Both teaching and research assistantships are available from these sources. Support for students from Latin America may also be obtained from foundations and from the OAS. Support of $700 to $1200 per month plus remission of tuition and fees is available, depending on the qualifications of the student.

Cost of Study

For 1999–2000, tuition and fees for students who are not teaching or research assistants are $75 per credit hour for residents. There is a nonresident fee, which is about $1750 per semester for international students or equal to the nonresident fee charged by the state university in the state where the student resides.

Living and Housing Costs

University housing is very limited, but private apartments and rooms are available in the University area. Housing costs vary from $150 to $300 per month per student.

Student Group

About 115 students (local and international) are enrolled in the graduate programs in chemistry, a number that permits careful supervision of each student's progress and needs. Postdoctorals and visiting scientists also participate in the program.

Location

The University is located in a residential suburb of San Juan, the capital and cultural center of Puerto Rico. The numerous historical sites and the carefully restored buildings of Old San Juan give the city a highly individual character. With its perennially pleasant climate, excellent beaches, and convenient transportation to North and South America and all the Caribbean, San Juan is the center of tourism in the Caribbean, and its residents enjoy a wide variety of entertainment and recreational facilities.

The University

The University of Puerto Rico, founded in 1903, is supported by the Commonwealth of Puerto Rico. Río Piedras, the oldest and largest campus, includes the Colleges of Natural Sciences, Social Sciences, Humanities, General Studies, Law, Education, and Business Administration, and a School of Architecture, a graduate School of Planning, and a School of Library Science. The Medical School is located near the Río Piedras campus and the Engineering Schools at the Mayagüez campus of the University. Facilities at the 288-acre Río Piedras campus are rapidly being expanded and remodeled. The student body of the Río Piedras campus consists of 22,000 full-time students in eight colleges.

Applying

The application for admission, including results of the General Test and chemistry Subject Test of the Graduate Record Examinations, should be addressed to the Department of Chemistry and returned no later than the first week of February. The application for financial assistance also should be sent to the Department of Chemistry.

Correspondence and Information

Graduate Program Coordinator
Department of Chemistry
University of Puerto Rico, Río Piedras
P.O. Box 23346
San Juan, Puerto Rico 00931-3346
Telephone: 787-764-0000 Ext. 2445, 4818, or 4817
Fax: 787-756-8242
E-mail: aguadal@upracd.upr.clu.edu
World Wide Web: http://web.uprr.pr/chemistry

University of Puerto Rico, Río Piedras

THE FACULTY AND THEIR RESEARCH

Rafael Arce Quintero, Professor; Ph.D., Wisconsin, 1971. Physical chemistry (photochemistry): photochemistry and photophysics of purine bases and their derivatives, heterogeneous photochemistry of organic pollutants, ESR, laser photolysis, fluorescence.

Carlos R. Cabrera, Professor; Ph.D., Cornell, 1987. Analytical chemistry (electrochemistry): photoelectrochemistry, batteries, electrocatalysis (fuel cells), surface analysis.

Néstor Carballeira, Professor; Ph.D., Würzburg (Germany), 1983. Organic chemistry: organic reaction mechanisms, lipid chemistry and biosynthesis of marine natural products.

Jorge L. Colón, Associate Professor; Ph.D., Texas A&M, 1989. Inorganic and bioinorganic chemistry: electron transfer and ligand binding in heme proteins, photophysics and photochemistry of luminescent molecules in inorganic layered materials and electropolymerized films, photo-induced charge separation.

Fernando A. González, Associate Professor; Ph.D., Cornell, 1989. Biochemistry and molecular biology: signal transduction by nucleotide P2 receptors.

Kai Griebenow, Assistant Professor; Ph.D., Max Planck Institute (Dusseldorf), 1992. Biochemistry: sustained delivery of proteins, nonaqueous enzymology, protein structure and stability.

Ana R. Guadalupe, Professor and Graduate Program Coordinator; Ph.D., Cornell, 1987. Analytical chemistry (electrochemistry): polymer-modified electrodes, chemical sensors and biosensors, electrocatalysis.

Yasuyuki Ishikawa, Professor; Ph.D., Iowa, 1976. Theoretical chemistry: relativistic effects in atoms and molecules, investigated by relativistic many-body theory; Monte Carlo simulations of quantum many-body systems.

Reginald Morales, Professor; Ph.D., Rutgers, 1976. Biochemistry: phospholipid organization on cell surfaces, phospholipases as probes of membrane structure, structure-function relationships of lipid analogues, phospholipid synthesis and analysis.

José A. Prieto, Professor; Ph.D., Puerto Rico, 1982. Organic chemistry: organic synthesis, synthesis of biologically active compounds, Lewis acid catalysis.

Edwin Quiñones, Associate Professor; Ph.D., Puerto Rico, 1986. Physical chemistry: dynamics of unimolecular and bimolecular elementary reactions, laser-induced reactions, energy-transfer collisions, photochemistry and chemiluminescence, spectroscopy of small molecules, photochemistry and photophysics of microheterogeneous solutions.

Raphael G. Raptis, Assistant Professor; Ph.D., Texas A&M, 1988. Inorganic chemistry: synthesis, X-ray crystallography, electrochemistry, spectroelectrochemistry, bioinorganic chemistry, metal clusters, metal-metal bonds, small molecule activation.

Abimael D. Rodriguez, Professor; Ph.D., Johns Hopkins, 1983. Organic chemistry: isolation, characterization, and synthesis of marine natural products.

Osvaldo Rosario, Professor; Ph.D., Puerto Rico, 1978. Analytical chemistry: development of methods for the analysis of environmental pollutants, analysis of air pollutants, gas chromatography–mass spectrometry, artifacts during sampling.

John A. Soderquist, Professor; Ph.D., Colorado, 1977. Organic chemistry: organometallic reagents in organic synthesis and natural product chemistry, stereochemically defined functional derivatives of main group organometallics, silicon-containing analogues of natural products, metal-metalloid combinations for organic synthesis.

Brad R. Weiner, Professor; Ph.D., California, Davis, 1986. Physical chemistry: laser studies of molecular reaction dynamics, photochemistry and photophysics with lasers, radical kinetics in gaseous phase, nonlinear processes, molecular energy transfer.

UNIVERSITY OF SAN FRANCISCO

Department of Chemistry

Program of Study

The University of San Francisco (USF) offers a program leading to the Master of Science degree in chemistry. Graduate research programs are available in selected areas of organic, physical, analytical, and inorganic chemistry as well as biochemistry.

The M.S. degree is research oriented and is awarded on the basis of completion of 24 semester units and the presentation of a thesis resulting from a research investigation. The individual research groups tend to be modest in size, and the student-professor interaction is highly valued.

Each student selects his or her research supervisor early in the first semester, and together they work out a specific program in consultation with the graduate adviser. Completion of the program generally requires eighteen months to two years.

Research Facilities

The Department of Chemistry is located in the Harney Science Center. The proximity of the various sciences has been particularly suitable for interdisciplinary research programs. Major research equipment includes FT-IR, GC, GC-MAS, HPLC, electrochemical and recently acquired UV-Vis-NIR and 400-Mhz FT NMR instruments.

Financial Aid

Teaching assistantships for the 1998–99 academic year carried stipends up to approximately $6200 for two laboratory sessions. Teaching assistants are generally responsible for recitation and lab sections in the lower-division chemistry courses. Research fellowships or assistantships may be provided through grants to faculty members by such agencies as NIH and NSF. Scholarships are also available each year; many students receive $3500, and some as much as $7100.

Cost of Study

Tuition in 1999–2000 is $701 per unit. The typical course load is 6 units per semester.

Living and Housing Costs

Housing is available in the immediate vicinity of the University at moderate rates. The central location of the University makes it readily accessible to students who live off campus.

Student Group

There are typically between 14 and 20 graduate students in the department. The majority of graduate students hold teaching assistantships. Students come to USF from virtually every other part of the world as well as from the United States, making the campus truly international.

Location

The University of San Francisco is situated in the heart of the city of San Francisco—the location itself is one of the great educational assets of the institution. San Francisco, with its world-famous natural setting, is the commercial center of the Pacific Coast. This industrial metropolis, with its tradition of promoting the arts and its cosmopolitan population, provides an environment for culture and for business contacts that is unobtainable in a small community. The climate is world renowned, and every conceivable type of recreation can be found in or near the Bay Area.

The University

The University of San Francisco, known for more than three quarters of a century as Saint Ignatius College, began its existence almost simultaneously with the city of San Francisco. The school was opened in 1855 during the glamorous Gold Rush days by a group of bold Jesuits. In 1906, fire and earthquake totally destroyed the majestic institution, its laboratories, its libraries, and its art treasures. Rebuilding began immediately with characteristic pioneer courage, and today the University consists of the College of Liberal Arts, the College of Science, the College of Business Administration, the School of Law, and the School of Nursing. Enrollment at present is about 8,000 students.

Applying

Applications should be received by March 15 for the fall semester and October 1 for the spring semester. Later applications will be given due consideration. Applicants should specify their areas of research interest to the department. The GRE General and Subject tests are required for domestic applicants and recommended for international applicants. TOEFL exam scores are required for international applicants.

Correspondence and Information

For more information on teaching assistantships, research fellowships, and the department's programs, students should write to the following addresses:

Dr. Tami Spector
Graduate Advisor
Department of Chemistry
University of San Francisco
San Francisco, California 94117-1080
Telephone: 415-422-2927
Fax: 415-422-2346

Office of Graduate Admissions
University of San Francisco
2130 Fulton Street
San Francisco, California 94117
Telephone: 415-422-2927
    800-CALL-USF (toll-free outside California)
Fax: 415-422-2578
E-mail: graduate@usfca.edu

University of San Francisco

THE FACULTY AND THEIR RESEARCH

Claire Castro, Assistant Professor; Ph.D., UCLA, 1993. Organic chemistry: synthesis of modified nucleosides.

John G. Cobley, Professor; Ph.D., Bristol (England), 1972; Fellow of the European Molecular Biology Organization, 1973. Molecular biology of chromatic adaptation in blue-green bacteria.

Jeff C. Curtis, Professor; Ph.D., North Carolina, 1980. Mechanistic/synthetic/physical inorganic chemistry: optically and thermally induced electron-transfer processes, solvent-solute interactions.

Arthur Furst, Distinguished University Professor Emeritus; Ph.D., Stanford, 1948. Toxicology of metals, carcinogenesis.

Thomas A. Gruhn, Professor; Ph.D., Berkeley, 1967. Use of polymers in radiation dosimetry.

Theodore H. D. Jones, Professor; Ph.D., MIT, 1966. Biochemistry: enzymology, hormone metabolism, peptide processing.

William Karney, Adjunct Professor; Ph.D., UCLA, 1994. Theoretical and computational studies of organic reaction mechanisms and reactive intermediates, especially those relevant to biological and atmospheric processes.

Lawrence D. Margerum, Assistant Professor; Ph.D., North Carolina, 1985. Bioanalytical and bioinorganic chemistry, physiochemical studies of metal ions with dendrimers, metal chelates in medicine.

William Melaugh, Adjunct Professor; Ph.D., California, San Francisco, 1994. Medicinal chemistry: application of mass spectrometry to the solution of biological problems, particularly structure-function relationships in the surface glycolipids of pathogenic bacteria, with a view to designing drugs for therapeutic intervention.

William J. Michaely, Ph.D., Indiana, 1971. Organometallic chemistry applied to synthetic reagents and organic synthesis.

Robert J. Seiwald, Emeritus Professor, member of the National Inventors Hall of Fame; Ph.D., Saint Louis, 1954. Organic chemistry: derivatives of uracil, protonation of weak bases in concentrated sulfuric acid.

Tami Spector, Associate Professor; Ph.D., Dartmouth, 1987. Organic chemistry: synthesis and spectroscopic investigations of small-ring organics, molecular dynamics and free energy calculations on biomolecules.

Kim D. Summerhays, Professor; Ph.D., California, Davis, 1971. Analytical and physical chemistry, computer applications in chemistry.

Robert F. Toia, Professor; Ph.D., Western Australia, 1977. Chemical toxicology of organophosphorus esters, with emphasis on the oxidative chemistry of phosphorioates; isolation and structure elucidation of natural products from both terrestrial and marine sources.

An aerial view of the USF campus.

University of San Francisco

SELECTED PUBLICATIONS

Jung, M. E., **C. Castro**, and S. I. Khan. Novel Lewis acid catalyzed rearrangement of sugar-base-hybrid to afford an anhydronucleoside. *Nucleosides Nucleotides* 17:2383, 1998.

Castro, C., and **W. Karney.** Incorporating organic name reactions and minimizing qualitative analysis in an unknown identification experiment. *J. Chem. Educ.* 75:472–5, 1998.

Jung, M. E., and **C. Castro.** New approach to the synthesis of β-2′-Deoxyribonucleosides: Intramolecular vorbrüggen coupling. *J. Org. Chem.* 58:807, 1993.

Krevor, J. V., et. al. **(C. Castro).** Determination of the magnitude and sign of the $^2J_{Pt-P}$ coupling constant in dinuclear platinum(I) phosphine complexes by two-dimensional ^{31}P NMR spectroscopy. *Inorg. Chem.* 31:312, 1992.

Jung, M. E., **C. Castro,** and J. M. Gardiner. Rapid synthesis of 2′-3′-Dideoxycytidine (ddC) from a simple archiral precursor. *Tetrahedron Lett.* 32:5717, 1991.

Cobley, J. G., et al. Transposition of Tn5 derivatives in the chromatically adapting cyanobacterium, *Fremyella diplosiphon.* In *The Phototrophic Prokaryotes,* eds. G. Peschek, W. Loffelhardt, and G. Schmetterer. New York: Plenum, 1998.

Cobley, J. G., et al. Construction of shuttle plasmids which can be efficiently mobilized from *Escherichia coli* into the chromatically adapting cyanobacterium, *Fremyella diplosiphon. Plasmid* 30:90–105, 1993.

Schaefer, M. R., G. G. Chiang, **J. G. Cobley,** and A. R. Grossman. Plasmids from two morphologically distinct cyanobacterial strains share a novel replication origin. *J. Bacteriol.* 175(17), 1993.

Yang, J., et al. **(J. C. Curtis).** Spectroscopic and electrochemical evidence for significant electronic coupling in mixed-valence hydrogen-bonded adducts of ruthenium cyano and ethylenediamine complexes. *J. Am. Chem. Soc.* 119:5329–36, 1997.

Mao, W., Z. Qian, H.-J. Yen, and **J. C. Curtis.** Deuterium NMR kinetic measurements of solvent effects on the biomolecular electron transfer self-exchange rates of ruthenium ammine complexes: A dominant role for solvent-solute hydrogen bonding. *J. Am. Chem. Soc.* 118(13):3247–52, 1996.

Salaymeh, F., et al **(J. C. Curtis).** Electronic coupling in mixed-valence binuclear ruthenium ammine complexes as probed by an electrochemical method and an extension of Mulliken's theory of donor-acceptor interactions. *Inorg. Chem.* 32:3895–4808, 1993.

Curtis, J. C., et al. Solvent-induced and polyether-ligand–induced redox isomerization within an asymmetrically coordinated mixed-valence ion: *trans*(pyridine) $(NH_3)_4$ Ru(4cyanopyridine) Ru(2,2′bpy)$_2$Cl^{4+}. *Inorg. Chem.* 30:3856–60, 1991.

Rendon, M. J., et al. **(T. A. Gruhn).** OMS-3000 optical dose and energy monitoring for ion implantation. *Future Fab Int.* 6:253–8, 1999.

Gruhn, T. A., and E. V. Benton. The chemical basis of the photo-oxidative enhancement of track etching in the polycarbonate of bisphenol A. In *Solid State Nuclear Track Detectors,* pp. 69–72, eds. P. H. Fowler and V. M. Clapham. Pergammon Press, 1982.

Choi, W. S., Q. Fu, and **T. H. D. Jones.** Purification and characterization of a novel dipeptidyl peptidase from *Dictyostelium discoideum. Biochem. Mol. Biol. Int.,* in press.

Krimper, R. P., and **T. H. D. Jones.** Purification and characterization of tripeptidyl peptidase I from *Dictyostelium discoideum. Biochem. Mol. Bio. Int.,* in press.

Jones, T. H. D. The purification, specificity, and role of dipeptidyl peptidase III in *Dictyostelium discoideum. Exp. Mycology* 16:102–9, 1992.

Jones, T. H. D. The biochemical basis of Parkinson's disease. In *Clinical Practice of Gerontological Nursing,* eds. C. Chenits, J. Takano-Stone, and S. Salisbury. Philadelphia: W. B. Saunders, 1990.

Kemnitz, C. R., **W. L. Karney,** and W. T. Borden. Why are nitrenes more stable than carbenes? *J. Am. Chem. Soc.* 120:3495–503, 1998.

Karney, W. L., and W. T. Borden. Ab initio study of the ring expansion of phenylnitrene and comparison with the ring expansion of phenylcarbene. *J. Am. Chem. Soc.* 119:1378–87, 1997.

Karney, W. L., and W. T. Borden. Why does o-fluorine substitution raise the barrier to ring expansion in phenylnitrene? *J. Am. Chem. Soc.* 119:3347–50, 1997.

Schreiner, P. R., et al. **(W. L. Karney).** Carbene rearrangements unsurpassed: Details of the C_7H_6 potential energy surface revealed. *J. Org. Chem.* 61:7030–9, 1996.

Margerum, L. D., et al. Gadolinium(III) DO3A macrocycles and polyethylene glycol coupled to dendrimers. Effect of molecular weight on physical and biological properties of macromolecular magnetic resonance imaging contrast agents. *J. Alloys Comp.* 249:185–90, 1997.

Melaugh, W., et al. Mass spectrometry as a tool to determine the structures and heterogeneity of bacterial lipooligosaccharides (LOS). In *Mass Spectrometry in Biological Sciences,* eds. A. L. Burlingame and S. Carr. Humana Press, 1996.

Melaugh, W., A. A. Campagnari, and B. W. Gibson. The lipooligosaccharides of *Haemophilus ducreyi* are highly sialylated. *J. Bacteriol.* 178(2):564–70, 1996.

Melaugh, W., et al. Structure of the major oligosaccharide from the lipooligosaccharide of *Haemophilus ducreyi* strain 35000 and evidence for additional glycoforms. *Biochemistry* 33:13070–8, 1994.

Michaely, W. J. Cyclizations of *omega*-alkynyl halides by chromium (II) reduction. *J. Org. Chem.* 49(22):4244–8, 1984.

Michaely, W. J., R. P. Hanzlik, M. Edelamn, and G. Scott. Enzymic hydration of [18O] expoxides. Role of nucleophilic mechanisms. *J. Am. Chem. Soc.* 98(7):1952–5, 1976.

Michaely, W. J., and R. P. Hanzlik. Metal-catalyzed hydration of 2-pyridyloxirane. *J. Chem. Soc., Chem. Commun.* 113–4, 1975.

University of San Francisco

Selected Publications (continued)

Michaely, W. J., and J. K. Crandall. Reactions of *omega*-iodoalkynes with nickel tetracarbonyl/potassium tert-butoxide. *J. Organometal. Chem.* 51:375–9, 1973.

Spector, T. I., and P. A. Kollman. Investigation of the anomalous solvatin free energies of amides and amines: FEP calculations in cyclohexane and PS-GVB calculations on amide-water complexes. *J. Phys. Chem.* 102:4004–10, 1998.

Spector, T. I. *No Universal Constants: Journeys of Women in Science and Engineering,* eds. S. A. Ambrose, et al. Philadelphia: Temple University Press, 1997.

Spector, T. I. Mary Fieser. In *Noted Women Scientists: A Biographical Dictionary, Vol. II, The Physical Sciences.* Greenwood Press, 1997.

Spector, T. I., T. E. Cheatham, and P. A. Kollman. Unrestrained molecular dynamics of photodamaged DNA in aqueous solution. *J. Am. Chem. Soc.* 119:7095–104, 1997.

Cheatham, T. E., et al. **(T. I. Spector).** Molecular dynamics simulations on nucleic acid systems using the Cornell et al. Force field and particle mesh ewald electrostatics. In *Molecular Modeling of Nucleic Acids,* eds. N. B. Leontis and J. SantaLucia Jr. Oxford University Press, 1997.

Spector, T. I. Review of *The structure, energetics and dynamics of organic ions. J. Amer. Chem. Soc.* 119:7905, 1997.

Spector, T. I. Naming names: A short biography of women in chemistry. *J. Chem. Ed.* 72:394–5, 1995.

Spector, T. I. Managing undergraduates for success in the research laboratory: Easing the transition from routine class work to independent research. *J. Chem. Ed.* 70:146–8, 1993.

Spector, T. I. The use of Fourier transform infrared spectroscopy for the curricular integration of general and organic chemistry. *J. Chem. Ed.,* 1993.

Rahmani, M., **R. F. Toia,** and K. D. Croft. Lignans from barks of *Hernandia nymphaefolia* and *H. peltata. Planta Med.* 61:487–8, 1995.

Kim, J. H., M. J. Gallagher, and **R. F. Toia.** Methanolysis of 1-methyl-4-phospha-3,5,8-trioxiabicyclo[2,2,2]octane 4-oxide and 4-sulfide: Mechanistic and stereochemical considerations. *Aust. J. Chem.* 47:715–20, 1994.

Kim, J. H., D. C. Craig, M. J. Gallagher, and **R. F. Toia.** Reaction of 2-ethoxy-5-methyl-1,3,2-dioxaphosphorinane-5-methanol 2-sulfide and 4-methyl-2,6,7-trioxa-1-phosphabicyclo[2,2,2] octane 1-sulfide with sulfuryl chloride: Mechanistic and stereochemical considerations. *Aust. J. Chem.* 47:2161–9, 1994.

Ando, T., N. Koseki, **R. F. Toia,** and J. E. Casida. Three-bond ^{13}C-^{1}H coupling constants for chrysanthemic acid and pehothrin metabolites: Detection by two-dimensional long-range ^{13}C-^{1}H J-resolution spectroscopy. *Magn. Reson. Chem.* 31:90–3, 1993.

Sun, C. M., and **R. F. Toia.** Biosynthetic studies on ant metabolites of meillein and 2,4-dihydroxyacetophenone from [1,2-$^{13}C_2$] acetate. *J. Nat. Prod.* 56:953–6, 1993.

Segall, Y., **R. F. Toia,** and J. E. Casida. Mechanism of the phosphorylation reaction of 2-haloalkylphosphonic acids. *Phosphorus, Sulfur Silicon Relat. Elem.* 75:191–4, 1993.

WAKE FOREST UNIVERSITY

Department of Chemistry

WAKE FOREST
U N I V E R S I T Y

Programs of Study

The Department of Chemistry offers graduate programs of study leading to the M.S. and Ph.D. degrees in the fields of analytical, inorganic, organic, and physical chemistry. For the M.S. degree, a student completes 24 hours of course work, submits a thesis based on his or her completed research, and passes an oral examination based on the thesis. Students normally complete the M.S. program in two years. The essence of the Ph.D. degree is the solution of an important chemical problem at the frontier of current knowledge. This is accomplished under the direction of a faculty adviser who is chosen by the student. The student's dissertation, based upon this research, is defended in an oral examination before a Ph.D. committee. The course requirement for the Ph.D. is determined by an advisory committee and is tailored to meet the needs of the individual student while providing a broad, well-balanced background. Competence in the student's selected area of study is tested by means of cumulative examinations. The requirements for the Ph.D. degree are normally completed in four to five years.

The emphasis of the program is on close interaction between faculty members and students. This ensures that the students develop to their full potential as quickly as possible. Choice of a research adviser is usually completed by the end of the first semester, and students may begin their research during the second semester.

Research Facilities

The Department of Chemistry occupies all of Salem Hall, which includes approximately 45,000 square feet of space for research, classrooms, and offices. Salem Hall was extensively renovated during 1990. Each graduate student has his or her own laboratory-office space. NMR facilities have been dramatically upgraded with the installation of 300- and 500-MHz Bruker systems in 1999. Other standard instrumentation that is available for graduate research includes an X-ray diffractometer, additional spectrometers (GC/MS and ESR; FT IR, laser Raman; visible-UV; luminescence; and atomic absorption), chromatographic systems (gas and high-performance liquid), inert-atmosphere glove boxes, and polarographic and electrochemical systems.

Additional instrumentation, including 300-MHz NMR and quadrupole mass spectrometers, are available at the School of Medicine. Computational facilities include a DEC Alpha 3000/600 cluster that is shared with the physics department, a Silicon Graphics workstation with SPARTAN, and several PCs. The department also has access to a Cray-T-90 supercomputer provided by the North Carolina Supercomputer Center. The campus central site has an IBM SP-2 that provides e-mail and other network/Internet services. The library contains more than 225 current journal subscriptions in chemistry and physics and holds complete runs in most chemistry titles. The chemistry collection is housed mainly in Salem Hall and is available to graduate students at all times. Online computer searching of more than 200 databases is available.

Financial Aid

In 1999–2000, graduate teaching assistantships and research assistantships provide $14,500 above tuition fees for the academic year. Support is included for the summer months for all students. Assuming a student's satisfactory progress, support is generally available for two years for an M.S. student and at least four years for a Ph.D. student.

Cost of Study

In 1999–2000, tuition for full-time study is $18,000, but this is remitted for all assistantship recipients. Other academic expenses are the cost of books, parking permit ($37.50), and thesis binding ($60).

Living and Housing Costs

Most graduate students live in apartments or rooms either on campus or near the University. The rent for one-bedroom apartments near the campus varies from $350 to $450 per month.

Student Group

During the academic year 1998–99, 550 graduate students were enrolled at Wake Forest University. Thirty graduate students were enrolled in the chemistry program, of whom 6 were from other countries. Due to the size of the student body, a close camaraderie exists between the students and extends to the faculty members. An active Graduate Student Association encourages interaction between disciplines through numerous social functions and discussion groups.

The department has offered the M.S. degree since 1961 and the Ph.D. since 1980. Recent graduates have obtained industrial offers from companies such as Eli Lilly, Burroughs-Wellcome, Pfizer, Wyeth-Ayerst, Hoechst, Rhône-Poulenc, Glaxo, Marion Merrill Dow, and Ortho, while others have gone on to postdoctoral positions.

Location

Winston-Salem is a city in northwestern North Carolina with a population of about 160,000. It is located about 200 miles from the ocean, 70 miles from the Blue Ridge Mountains, and 300 miles from Atlanta and Washington, D.C. Cultural opportunities include unusually good music, dance, and theater performances both on and off campus and a number of good historical and art museums. A wide selection of spectator sports is available.

The University

Wake Forest University has a rich tradition going back to its founding as a college in 1834. At the present time, its enrollment consists of about 3,700 undergraduates and 1,800 graduate and professional (law, medicine, and business) students. The main campus is a wooded 300-acre site on the northwest edge of Winston-Salem surrounded by numerous scenic walking and jogging paths, grassy picnic areas, and a beautiful public garden. An important part of the Wake Forest tradition is its continuing emphasis upon academic excellence.

Applying

Men and women who are completing a bachelor's degree or its equivalent are invited to obtain additional information and application materials by writing to the chemistry department at the address given below. Typically, GRE General Test scores, transcripts, and three letters of recommendation are required. Submission of scores on the GRE Subject Test in chemistry is recommended. Students may be admitted in either the fall or the spring semester. The deadline for fall application is March 15, but late applicants will be considered if positions are still available. The deadline for application for spring is flexible.

Correspondence and Information

Graduate Committee Chairman
Department of Chemistry
P.O. Box 7486
Winston-Salem, North Carolina 27109
Telephone: 336-758-5325

Wake Forest University

THE FACULTY AND THEIR RESEARCH

C. L. Colyer, Ph.D., Queen's at Kingston. Analytical chemistry; high efficiency separations of biologically-important molecules by capillary electrophoresis (CE); interaction of proteins with near infrared dyes for detection by semiconductor laser-induced fluorescence; on-column chemical reactions for derivatization and immunoanalysis; fundamental CE studies of flow rates, solution mixing, and electrokinetic phenomena.

J. C. Fishbein, Ph.D., Brandeis. Mechanisms of organic reactions in aqueous solutions; generation and study of reactive intermediates, particularly those involved in nitrosamine and nitrosamide carcinogenesis.

S. C. Haefner, Ph.D., Michigan State. Synthesis, spectroscopy, and structures of transition metal inorganic and organometallic complexes; small-molecule binding and activation, molecular recognition, development of supramolecular systems, one-dimensional clusters, and molecular wires.

R. A. Hegstrom, Ph.D., Harvard. Theoretical chemistry, quantum theory. Particular areas of interest are relativistic corrections to magnetic properties, parity violation in atoms and molecules, electron chirality, and macroscopic quantum coherence.

W. L. Hinze, Ph.D., Texas A&M. Analytical-clinical chemistry; separation science, including resolution of optical isomers; new extraction procedures for recovery of hazardous organic compounds from environmental matrices; luminescence spectroscopy, including coupled chemiluminescence assays; development of new enzyme immobilization techniques; utilization of cyclodextrin and surfactant organized assemblies in chemical analysis.

B. T. Jones, Ph.D., Florida. Spectrochemical analysis, instrument design, trace metal analysis; continuum source atomic absorption spectrometry; atomic absorption spectrometry with a flame emission source; development of a portable blood-lead analyzer; determination of lead in the blood of painters; investigation of urine-cadmium concentration as a biomarker for osteoporosis and prostate cancer; determination of silicone in breast tissue.

S. B. King, Ph.D., Cornell. Design and synthesis of new compounds capable of interaction with nitric oxide synthase; design, synthesis, and evaluation of new nitric oxide and nitroxyl delivery agents; total synthesis of biologically active natural products.

D. K. Kondepudi, Ph.D., Texas at Austin. Self-organization in nonequilibrium chemical systems with a particular focus on symmetry-breaking transitions; theoretical and experimental study of chiral symmetry breaking in crystallization and other chemical and physical processes; amplification of chiral asymmetry in physical and chemical processes.

A. Lachgar, Ph.D., Nantes. Synthesis and structural characterization of inorganic solid state materials: hydrothermal synthesis of new metal phosphates and metal oxohalides cluster chemistry.

R. A. Manderville, Ph.D., Queen's at Kingston. Bioorganic chemistry, synthesis and mechanism of action of DNA-targeting compounds, interaction of naturally occurring isocoumarins and conjugated pyrrole ring systems with nucleic acids, structural characterization using multidimensional NMR experiments and molecular modeling calculations.

G. A. Melson, Ph.D., Sheffield (England). Synthesis, characterization, and reactions of transition-metal compounds; supported metal catalysts for synthesis gas conversion and flue gas cleanup.

R. E. Noftle, Ph.D., Washington (Seattle). Main group chemistry; synthesis and characterization of novel compounds of the main group elements, especially carbon, nitrogen, sulfur, and the halogens; electrochemistry: cyclic voltammetry, chronoamperometry, rotating ring-disk voltammetry, electrochemical synthesis; spectroscopy of main group compounds; synthesis and electrochemistry of platinum compounds.

R. L. Swofford, Ph.D., Berkeley. Visible laser molecular spectroscopy of high vibrational overtones ($\Delta v = 5, 6, 7$, etc.) of X-H bonds (X = C, N, O, S, etc.) and the theoretical models that describe the spectral behavior; quantum chemical calculations of anharmonic vibrational potential energies; "isolated-molecule" spectroscopy: (1) emission line-narrowing in frozen alkane solutions: identification and determination of polyaromatic hydrocarbons (PAH) at part-per-million levels; (2) pulsed supersonic jet spectroscopy of vibrationally cooled molecules.

M. E. Welker, Ph.D., Florida State. Uses of transition-metal complexes in organic synthesis; synthesis and cycloaddition chemistry of transition-metal complexes containing propargyl, allyl, dienyl, and allenyl ligands; transition-metal mediated 3 + 2 and 4 + 2 cycloaddition chemistry as synthetic methods for the synthesis of functionalized cyclopentanoid and cyclohexanoid compounds; synthesis of potential anticarcinogenic enzyme inducers.

SELECTED PUBLICATIONS

Colyer, C. L., T. Tang, N. Chiem, and D. J. Harrison. Clinical potential of microchip capillary electrophoresis systems. *Electrophoresis* 18:1733–41, 1997.

Colyer, C. L., S. D. Mangru, and D. J. Harrison. Microchip-based capillary electrophoresis of human serum proteins. *J. Chromatogr. A* 781:271–6, 1997.

Colyer, C. L. Unusual peaks and baseline shifts in capillary electrophoresis. *J. Capillary Electrophoresis* 3:131–7, 1996.

Colyer, C. L., J. C. Myland, and K. B. Oldham. Diffusive analyte loss in capillary electrophoresis caused by delay in field application. *J. Chromatogr. A* 732:335–43, 1996.

Colyer, C. L., K. B. Oldham, and A. V. Sokirko. Electroosmotically-transported baseline perturbations in capillary electrophoresis. *Anal. Chem.* 67:3234–45, 1995.

Colyer, C. L., and K. B. Oldham. Emersion peaks in capillary electrophoresis. *J. Chromatogr. A* 716:3-15, 1995.

Cai, H., and **J. C. Fishbein.** a-acyloxydialkylnitrosamines: Effects of structure on the formation of n-nitrosiminium ions and a predicted change in mechanism. *J. Am. Chem. Soc.,* in press.

Chahoua, L., H. Cai, and **J. C. Fishbein.** Cyclic a-acetoxynitrosamines: Mechanisms of decomposition and stability of a-hydroxynitrosamine and nitrosiminium ion reactive intermediates. *J. Org. Chem.,* in press.

Chahoua, L., and **J. C. Fishbein.** Formation and nucleophilic capture of n-nitrosiminium ions. *Can. J. Chem.,* in press.

Chahoua, L., M. Mesić, A. Vigroux, and **J. C. Fishbein.** Evidence for the formation of α-Hydroxydialkynitrosamines in the pH-independent solvolysis of α-Acyloxydialkylnitrosamines. *J. Org. Chem.* 62:2500, 1997.

Mesić, M., C. Revis, and **J. C. Fishbein.** Effects of structure on the reactivity of α-Hydroxydialkylnitrosamines in aqueous solutions. *J. Am. Chem. Soc.* 7412, 1996.

Finneman, J. I., and **J. C. Fishbein.** Mechanisms of decomposition of (Z)-2,2,2-Trifluoromethyl-1-arylethanediazoates in aqueous media. *J. Am. Chem. Soc.* 7134, 1996.

Chahoua, L., M. Mesić, and **J. C. Fishbein.** Failure to isolate the first n-nitrosiminium cation. *J. Org. Chem.* 61:1512, 1996.

Finneman, J. I., and **J. C. Fishbein.** Mechanisms of benzyl group transfer in the decay of (E)-arylmethanediazoates and aryldiazomethanes in aqueous solutions. *J. Am. Chem. Soc.* 117:4288, 1995.

Cotton, F. A., **S. C. Haefner,** and A. P. Sattelberger. Metal-metal multiply-bonded complexes of technetium. 7. Oxidative decomposition of tetrachlorotetrakis(dimethylphenylphosphino)ditechnetium(II) by an aminium hexachloro-antimonate(V). *Inorg. Chim. Acta* 271:187, 1997.

Cotton, F. A., **S. C. Haefner,** and A. P. Sattelberger. Metal-metal multiply-bonded complexes of technetium 6. Reductive cleavage of the Tc≡Tc triple bond in [Tc$_2$(CH$_3$CN)$_{10}$][BF$_4$]$_4$. *Inorg. Chim. Acta* 266:55, 1997.

Cotton, F. A., L. M. Daniels, **S. C. Haefner,** and C. A. Murillo. Lewis- or Bronsted-acid assisted formation of open-chain vinamidinium salts from N,N'-diarylformamidines and acetone. *J. Chem. Soc., Chem. Commun.* 2507, 1996.

Cotton, F. A., **S. C. Haefner,** and A. P. Sattelberger. Metal-metal multiply-bonded complexes of technetium. 5. Tris- and tetra-formamidinate complexes of ditechnetium. *Inorg. Chem.* 35:7350, 1996.

Cotton, F. A., **S. C. Haefner,** and A. P. Sattelberger. Metal-metal multiply-bonded complexes of technetium. 4. Photodissociation of the Tc≡Tc triple bond in [Tc$_2$(CH$_3$CN)$_{10}$][BF$_4$]$_4$. *J. Am. Chem. Soc.* 118:5486, 1996.

Cotton, F. A., **S. C. Haefner,** and A. P. Sattelberger. Metal-metal multiply-bonded complexes of technetium, 3. Preparation and characterization of phosphine complexes of technetium possessing a metal-metal bond order of 3.5. *Inorg. Chem.* 35:1831, 1996.

Hegstrom, R. A. Spontaneous symmetry breaking in Bose-Einstein condensates. *Chem. Phys. Lett.* 288:248, 1998.

Hegstrom, R. A. B decay and the origins of biological chirality: Theoretical results. In *Physical Origin of Homochirality in Life,* p. 7, ed. D. B. Cline. Woodbury, New York: American Institute of Physics Press, 1996.

Hegstrom, R. A., and **D. K. Kondepudi.** Influence of static magnetic fields on chirally autocatalytic radical-pair reactions. *Chem. Phys. Lett.* 253:322–6, 1996.

Hegstrom, R. A., and F. Sols. A model of quantum measurement in Josephson junctions. *Found. Phys.* 25:681, 1995.

Hegstrom, R. A. Electron chirality. *J. Mol. Struct. Theochem.* 232:17, 1991.

Hegstrom, R. A., and **D. K. Kondepudi.** The handedness of the universe. *Sci. American* 262:108, 1990.

Nair, U. B., D. W. Armstrong, and **W. L. Hinze.** Characterization and evaluation of d(+)-tubocurarine chloride as a chiral selector for capillary electrophoretic enantioseparations. *Anal. Chem.* 70:1059, 1998.

Dai, F., V. P. Burkert, H. N. Singh, and **W. L. Hinze.** Evaluation of the effectiveness of different thiols and micellar media in Roth's fluorimetric method for the determination of primary amino compounds.*Microchem. J.* 57:166, 1997.

Hinze, W. L., F. Dai, R. P. Frankewich, and J. Szejtli. Cyclodextrins as reagents in analytical chemistry and diagnostics. In *Comprehensive Supramolecular Chemistry,* vol. 3 (Cyclodextrins), ch. 20, pp. 587–602, eds. J. Szejtli and T. Osa. Pergamon Press, 1996.

Hinze, W. L., I. Uemasu, F. Dai, and J. M. Braun. Analytical and related applications of organogels. *Curr. Opin. Colloid Interface Sci.* 1:502–13, 1996.

Rhoades, C. B., K. E. Levine, A. Salido, and **B. T. Jones.** Elemental analysis using microwave digestion and an environmental evaporation chamber. *Appl. Spectrosc.* 52:200–4, 1998.

Shepard, M. R., **B. T. Jones,** and D. J. Butcher. High resolution time-resolved spectra of indium and aluminum atoms, fluorides, chlorides, and oxides in a graphite furnace. *Appl. Spectrosc.* 52:430–7, 1998.

Besecker, K. D., C. B. Rhoades Jr., **B. T. Jones,** and K. W. Barnes. A simple closed-vessel nitric acid digestion method for cosmetic samples. *Atomic Spectrosc.* 19:48–54, 1998.

Besecker, K. D., C. B. Rhoades Jr., **B. T. Jones,** and K. W. Barnes. Closed vessel nitric acid microwave digestion of polymers. *Atomic Spectrosc.* 19:55–9, 1998.

Batchelor, J. D., S. E. Thomas, and **B. T. Jones.** Determination of cadmium with a portable, battery-powered tungsten coil atomic absorption spectrometer. *Appl. Spectrosc.* 52:1086–91, 1998.

Wagner, K. A., K. E. Levine, and **B. T. Jones.** A simple, low-cost, multielement atomic absorption spectrometer with a tungsten coil atomizer. *Spectrochim. Acta, Part B* 53:1507–16, 1998.

Levine, K. E., K. A. Wagner, and **B. T. Jones.** A low-cost, modular electrothermal vaporization system for inductively coupled plasma atomic emission spectrometry. *Appl. Spectrosc.* 52:1165–71, 1998.

Batchelor, J. D., and **B. T. Jones.** Development of a digital micromirror spectrometer for analytical atomic spectrometry. *Anal. Chem.* 70:4907–14, 1998.

King, S. B., and H. T. Nagasawa. Chemical approaches toward the generation of nitroxyl (HNO). In *Methods in Enzymology,* vol. 301, chapter 22, ed. L. Packer. San Diego: Academic Press, 1998.

Xu, Y., et al. **(S. B. King).** Nitrosylation of sickle cell hemoglobin by hydroxyurea. *J. Org. Chem.* 63:6452–3, 1998.

Kim-Shapiro, D. B., and **S. B. King** et al. Time resolved absorption study of the reaction of hydroxyurea with sickle cell hemoglobin. *Biochim. Biophys. Acta* 1380:64–74, 1998.

Atkinson, R. N., B. M. Storey, and **S. B. King.** Reactions of acyl nitroso compounds with amines: Production of nitroxyl with the preparation of amides. *Tetrahedron Lett.* 37:9287–90, 1996.

Becker, H. B., et al. **(S. B. King).** New ligands and improved enantioselectivities for the asymmetric dihydroxylation of olefins. *J. Org. Chem.* 60:3940–1, 1995.

King, S. B., and B. Ganem. Synthetic studies on Mannostatin A and its derivatives: A new family of glycoprotein processing inhibitors. *J. Am. Chem. Soc.* 116:562–70, 1994.

Wake Forest University

Selected Publications (continued)

Kondepudi, D. K., and M. Culha. Chiral interaction and stochastic interaction in stirred crystallization of amino acids. *Chirality,* in press.

Kondepudi, D. K., and I. Prigogine. Nonequilibrium thermodynamics.In *Encyclopedia of Applied Physics,* vol. 21. New York: VCH Publisher Inc., 1997.

Kondepudi, D. K., et al. Studies in chiral-symmetry-breaking crystallization I: The effects of stirring and evaporation rates. *Chirality* 7:61–8, 1995.

Kondepudi, D. K., et al. Stirring rate as a critical parameter in chiral symmetry breaking crystallization. *J. Am. Chem. Soc.* 117:401–4, 1995.

Anokhina, E. V., M. W. Essig, and **A. Lachgar.** $Ti_2Nb_6Cl_{14}O_4$: A unique 2D-1D network combination in niobium cluster chemistry. *Angew. Chem. Int. Ed. Engl.* 37:522–5, 1998.

Tang, X., and **A. Lachgar.** The missing link: Synthesis, crystal structure, and thermogravimetric studies in $InPO_4.H_2O$. *Inorg. Chem.* 37:6181–5, 1998.

Sitar, J., **A. Lachgar,** H. Womelsdorf, and H-J. Meyer. Niobium cluster compounds with transition metals: $K_2Mn[Nb_6Cl_{18}]$. *J. Solid State Chem.* 122:428 1996.

Buncel, E., J. M. Dust, and **R. A. Manderville.** Ambident reactivity of enolate ions toward 1,3,5-trinitrobenzene. The first observation of an oxygen-bonded enolate Meisenheimer complex. *J. Am. Chem. Soc.,* in press.

Manderville, R. A., J. F. Ellena, and S. M. Hecht. Interaction of Zn(II)•bleomycin with d(CGCTAGCG)$_2$, a binding model based on NMR experiments and restrained molecular dynamics calculations. *J. Am. Chem. Soc.* 117:7891–903, 1995.

Manderville, R. A., J. F. Ellena, and S. M. Hecht. Solution structure of a Zn(II)•bleomycin A$_5$-d(CGCTAGCG)$_2$ complex. *J. Am. Chem. Soc.* 116:10851–2, 1994.

Manderville, R. A., and E. Buncel. Regioselectivity and stereoelectronic factors in the reactions of aryloxide nucleophiles with 4-nitrobenzofuroxan. *J. Chem. Soc. Perkin Trans.* 2:1887–94, 1993.

Manderville, R. A., and E. Buncel. Inversion of kinetic and thermodynamic preferences in Meisenheimer complex formation: Regioselectivity in the reaction of 2,4,6-trimethylphenoxide ion with 2,4,6-trinitroanisole and the importance of stereoelectronic factors. *J. Am. Chem. Soc.* 115:8985–9, 1993.

Buncel, E., and **R. A. Manderville.** Ambient reactivity of aryloxide ions towards 1,3,5-trinitrobenzene, low-temperature characterization of the elusive oxygen-bonded σ-complexes by ^{1}H and ^{13}C NMR spectroscopy. *J. Phys. Org. Chem.* 6:71–82, 1993.

Melson, G. A. Bifunctional Ru/zeolite catalysts for CO hydrogenation.*Proceedings, 9th International Congress of Catalysis* 807, 1988.

Melson, G. A., and E. B. Zuckerman. ZSM-5 supported Fe and Ru catalysts from $Fe_3(CO)_{12}$ structure-activity correlations for synthesis gas conversion. *Preprints, Division of Fuel Chemistry,* American Chemical Society 31:59, 1986.

Narula, P. M., and **R. E. Noftle.** Investigation of the lifetimes of some pyrrole species by rapid scan cyclic voltammetry and double potential step techniques. *J. Electroanal. Chem.,* in press.

Ritter, S. K., et al. **(R. E. Noftle).** Synthesis and characterization of thiophenes with fluorinated substituents. *J. Fluorine Chem.* 93:73, 1999.

Odian, M. A., and **R. E. Noftle.** Preparation and oxidative polymerization of 3-thienylperfluoroacylimides. *J. Fluorine Chem.* 92:129, 1998.

Ye, F., and **R. E. Noftle.** Preparation of fluorinated imides. *J. Fluorine Chem.* 81:193, 1997.

Gregory, A. J., et al. **(R. E. Noftle).** Studies of platinum electroplating baths. Part III. The electrochemistry of $Pt(NH_3)_{4-x}(H_2O)_x{}^{2+}$ and $PtCl_{4-x}(H_2O)_x{}^{(2x)}$. *J. Electroanal. Chem.* 399:105, 1995.

Noftle, R. E., M. A. Odian, and S. K. Ritter. New fluorinated thiophenes and their electrochemical properties. *J. Fluorine Chem.* 71:177, 1995.

Long, J. W., Y. Wu, and **R. E. Noftle.** On the formation of tubules during the electropolymerization of pyrrole in the presence of perfluorobutyrate. *J. Fluorine Chem.* 68:261, 1994.

Spivey, S., and **R. L. Swofford.** Inclusion complexes of N-benzoyl-D-leucine and C-benzoyl-L-leucine with B-cyclodextrin by Raman spectroscopy. *Appl. Spectrosc.,* in press.

Dorshow, R. B., and **R. L. Swofford.** An adjustable-resolution surface laser-light scattering spectrometer and its application to the measurement of interfacial tension and viscosity in crude oil systems. *Colloids and Surfaces* 43:133–49, 1990.

Dorshow, R. B., and **R. L. Swofford.** Application of surface laser-light scattering spectroscopy to the photoabsorbing systems: The measurement of interfacial tension and viscosity in crude oil. *J. Appl. Phys.* 65:3756–9, 1989.

Dorshow, R. B., A. Hajiloo, and **R. L. Swofford.** A surface laser-light scattering spectrometer with adjustable resolution. *J. Appl. Phys.* 63:1265–78, 1988.

Dorshow, R. B., and **R. L. Swofford.** Surface laser-light scattering. *Phys. Today* 41(1):S49–50, 1988.

Findsen, L., H. L. Fang, **R. L. Swofford,** and R. R. Birge. Theoretical description of the overtone spectra of acetaldehyde using the local mode approach. *J. Chem. Phys.* 84:16–27, 1986.

Fang, H. L., **R. L. Swofford,** M. McDevitt, and A. B. Anderson. C–H stretching overtone spectrum of propylene: Molecular orbital analysis in the local mode model. *J. Phys. Chem.* 89:225–9, 1985.

Hayes, B. L., and **M. E. Welker.** Reactions of transition-metal cyclopropyl and n^1-allyl complexes with fulfur dioxide and disulfur monoxide. *Organometallics* 17:5334, 1998.

Adams, T. A., **M. E. Welker,** and C. S. Day. Transition-metal mediated dihydropyran syntheses. Exo selective hetero Diels-Alder reactions of cobaloxime dienyl complexes with aldehydes. *J. Org. Chem.* 63:3683, 1998.

Hurley, A. L., **M. E. Welker,** and C. S. Day. Reactions of transition-metal n^1-propargyl and n1-allenyl complexes with sulfur dioxide and transition-metal-carbon bond cleaving reactions of the cycloadducts which yield cyclic sulfenate esters. *Organometallics* 17:2832, 1998.

Adams, T. A., and **M. E. Welker.** Synthesis of cobaloxime substituted α,β-unsaturated acyl complexes via reactions of cobaloxime anions and/or hydrides with ynones, ynoates and α,β-unsaturated acyl electrophiles. *Organometallics* 16:1300, 1997.

Chapman, J. J., and **M. E. Welker.** Preparation of cobalt (III) salen-1,3-butadien-2-yl complexes and their utilization in facile and regioselective Diels-Alder reactions. *Organometallics* 16:747, 1997.

Richardson, B. M., and **M. E. Welker.** Transition-metal mediated exo selective Diels-Alder reactions used in the preparation of octalones with unusual stereochemistries. *J. Org. Chem.* 62:1299, 1997.

Wright, M. W., et al. **(M. E. Welker).** Preparation and *exo* selective 4+2 cycloaddition reactions of cobaloxime substituted 1,3-dienes. In *Advances in Cycloaddition,* vol. 4, pp. 149–206, ed. M. Lautens. Greenwich, Conn.: JAI Press, 1997.

WASHINGTON UNIVERSITY IN ST. LOUIS

Division of Biology and Biomedical Sciences
Bioorganic Chemistry Program

Program of Study

Bioorganic chemistry is an emerging field in which synthetic and physical organic chemistry are brought to bear on problems of critical biological relevance. During the last decade, truly remarkable advances in protein chemistry, molecular biology, and organic chemistry have been combined and exploited to gain insights into biological phenomena. The molecular mechanisms of cellular regulation and metabolism have been probed, experimental therapeutics are increasingly directed by an understanding of molecular recognition, and novel syntheses are often driven by modeling experiments. The fundamental principles of chemistry collectively form the foundation for understanding molecular structure/function relationships. Examples of research projects of the program's faculty members include studies of membrane function and novel synthetic membranes, protein conformation and function; synthetic receptors; mechanism-based drug development and modeling; novel magnetic resonance imaging agents development; novel peptide and peptidomimetic synthesis; protein structure-function relationships in genetically manipulable model organisms; RNA hydrolysis; and drugs designed to interact with DNA.

The program of study comprises four academic courses, three laboratory rotations, and a qualifying examination. The four courses cover bioorganic chemistry, synthetic organic chemistry for bioorganic chemists, a survey of molecular cell biology, and physical organic chemistry and spectroscopic methods applied to biological molecules. The qualifying examination is an oral exam given by 3 faculty members to each student to be certain that the background obtained in the first year of study is sufficient to begin full-time research. Students undertake laboratory rotations beginning in the first semester and normally choose a research mentor by the beginning of the second year, when full-time research usually begins.

Research Facilities

Specialized research facilities include an area detector facility for X-ray crystallography, Silicon Graphics computers for molecular modeling, femtosecond laser spectroscopy, and nuclear magnetic resonance (magnetic resonance imaging, high-resolution NMR, and solid-state magnetic resonance) apparatus. Additional facilities are available for microcalorimetry, analytical ultracentrifugation, stopped-flow instrumentation, and automated nucleic acid and peptide synthesis. The Washington University library system has 3.3 million volumes and significant journal holdings in the biological and chemical sciences.

Financial Aid

Each student in the Division of Biology and Biomedical Sciences is guaranteed a stipend ($15,500 for the 1999–2000 academic year), health coverage, life insurance, disability insurance, and tuition for the duration of training in the Division, provided that all academic standards are maintained.

Cost of Study

The 1999–2000 tuition charge of $23,400 per annum and the 1999–2000 health coverage cost of $1406 are paid for all students by the Graduate School and by the Division.

Living and Housing Costs

Students can choose from among numerous apartment buildings and rooms in private homes, often within walking distance of campus. Off-campus housing costs in St. Louis are modest compared to costs in most cities; accommodations for a student living with a roommate might range between $3000 and $4500 per year. Private rooms in the Medical Center's Olin Residence Hall cost between $288 and $382 per month during the 1999–2000 academic year.

Student Group

Approximately 6,000 undergraduate and nearly 6,000 graduate students are enrolled at Washington University. The Division of Biology and Biomedical Sciences admits about 68 Ph.D. and 22 M.D./Ph.D. students per year. Currently there are more than 450 graduate students in the Division.

Student Outcomes

As of 1997, 659 (428 Ph.D. and 231 M.D./Ph.D.) students have completed doctoral programs in the Division. Of those who have completed their postdoctoral training (55 percent of total graduates), 59 percent hold faculty positions at universities, 3 percent are NIH investigators, 20 percent hold industrial positions, 4 percent are museum curators, and 1 percent are faculty members at small colleges.

Location

Washington University's location at the boundary of St. Louis and St. Louis County allows students access to the cultural riches only a city can provide. Life in St. Louis also preserves the ease and convenience usually found only in suburban areas. Among St. Louis's many cultural and recreational facilities are the Missouri Botanical Garden, the St. Louis Science Center, the highly regarded St. Louis Zoo, and art and history museums. Several attractions are located in Forest Park, the city's largest, located between the University's East and West campuses. Music lovers enjoy the St. Louis Symphony, the Opera Theatre, and the Municipal Opera's outdoor presentations of musicals. Theater thrives in St. Louis; amateur groups abound, and resident and touring companies present professional productions at several locations. Area residents enthusiastically support professional football, baseball, hockey, and indoor soccer teams. The nearby Ozark Mountains are ideal for day or weekend trips and offer hiking, spelunking, fishing, and boating within an hour's drive of the city.

The University and The Division

Washington University in St. Louis is a private, nondenominational, coeducational institution located on the western edge of St. Louis in an area of parks and residences. The faculty has approximately 1,900 full-time members.

Organized in 1973, the Division of Biology and Biomedical Sciences is a graduate educational consortium that includes more than 320 faculty members affiliated with twenty basic science departments in the School of Medicine and in the College of Arts and Sciences, all at Washington University in St. Louis. Programs offered in the Division provide a broad interdisciplinary approach to graduate education. Each program is managed by a faculty steering committee, which provides advice to first- and second-year students, monitors progress of advanced students, and develops and maintains interdisciplinary courses.

Applying

Review of applications begins December 15, and early application is encouraged. Applications should be received by January 1 for fall admission. The GRE General Test is required, as are three letters of recommendation and transcripts from all universities attended. The GRE Subject Test is highly recommended. Applicants should have one year of the following courses: general chemistry, organic chemistry, physical chemistry (one semester acceptable), physics, calculus, and one or more courses of general biology, biochemistry, or molecular biology. Additional advanced courses in biology, biochemistry, chemistry, mathematics, and physics are recommended. Notification of admission is made February through April. Although classes start in late August or early September, students can start graduate work with a summer laboratory rotation (stipend available) beginning prior to June 15.

Correspondence and Information

Division of Biology and Biomedical Sciences
Campus Box 8226
Washington University in St. Louis
660 South Euclid Avenue
St. Louis, Missouri 63110
Telephone: 314-362-3365
            800-852-9074 (toll-free)
Fax: 314-362-3369
E-mail: admissions@dbbs.wustl.edu
World Wide Web: http://dbbs.wustl.edu

Washington University in St. Louis

THE FACULTY AND THEIR RESEARCH

Carolyn J. Anderson. Development of radiopharmaceuticals for cancer diagnosis and therapy.

Douglas Covey. Allosteric modulators of ion channels, enzyme inhibitors.

Laura L. Dugan. Free radicals and oxidative injury in nervous system diseases.

Scott Gilbertson. Stereoselective catalysis, metal-binding peptides, natural product synthesis.

George Gokel. Synthetic membranes, synthetic models for cation-conducting channels, mechanisms and molecular recognition in coenzyme A reactions and enzymes.

Gregory Grant. Neurotoxin-receptor interactions, allosteric mechanisms.

Michael Gross. Fourier Transform Mass Spectrometry, MS/MS, and FTMS combined with desorption ionization for determining biomolecules.

Richard Gross. Lipid second messengers, signal transduction, phospholipases.

Jay Heinecke. Molecular mechanisms for oxidative damage of lipids and proteins.

Garland Marshall. Peptidomimetics, molecular modeling and recognition, combinatorial libraries, antiviral agents and antibiotics.

Kevin Moeller. Development of novel synthetic methods for the construction of rigid peptide analogs, medicinally useful rigid peptide analogs.

Stephen M. Moerlein. Development of radiopharmaceuticals for PET and SPECT.

David R. Piwnica-Worms. Molecular pharmacology of multidrug resistance of P-glycoprotein and homologous transporters, functional imaging with metallopharmaceuticals.

Jay W. Ponder. Protein engineering, computer modeling of protein structure and folding.

John-Stephen Taylor. DNA-targeted design and synthesis of anticancer and antiviral drugs, SAR of DNA photoproducts.

John Turk. Phospholipid-derived mediators and insulin secretion.

Michael Welch. Radiopharmaceutical chemistry, development of new imaging agents.

Karen L. Wooley. Organic and polymer synthesis, novel macromolecular architectures as mimetics of biological delivery agents, degradable polymers.

WESLEYAN UNIVERSITY

Department of Chemistry

Program of Study

The Department of Chemistry offers a program of study leading to the Ph.D. degree. Students are awarded this degree upon demonstration of creativity and scholarly achievement. This demands intensive specialization in one field of chemistry as well as broad knowledge of related areas. The department provides coverage of physical, organic, inorganic, bioorganic, and biophysical chemistry.

The first year of graduate study contains much of the required course work, although most students also choose a research adviser and begin a research program at the beginning of the second semester. Students are expected to demonstrate knowledge of five core areas of chemistry, either by taking the appropriate course or by passing a placement examination. In addition, students take advanced courses in their area of specialization. Classes are small (5–10 students) and emphasize interaction and discussion. Student seminar presentations are also emphasized. Election of interdisciplinary programs in chemical physics and molecular biophysics in conjunction with the Departments of Physics and Molecular Biology and Biochemistry, respectively, is also possible. Students are admitted to Ph.D. candidacy, generally in the second year, by demonstrating proficiency in the core course curriculum, passing a specified number of regularly scheduled progress exams, demonstrating an aptitude for original research, and defending a research proposal. The progress and development of a student is monitored throughout by a 3-member faculty advisory committee. The Ph.D. program, culminating in the completion of a Ph.D. thesis, is normally completed within four to five years. Two semesters of teaching in undergraduate courses is required, where the load is, on average, about 5 hours per week during the academic year. This requirement is normally met in the first year.

An M.A. degree may be awarded on completion of two years of study, as described above, and with a written research thesis. Students who wish only a master's degree, however, are generally not admitted.

Research Facilities

The Hall-Atwater Laboratory is equipped with a wide variety of modern instrumentation appropriate to the research interests of the faculty. There are excellent machine and electronics shops and glassblowing facilities. A departmental computer network consisting of several IBM RS/6000, Silicon Graphics, Sun, and DEC Graphics workstations and connected to University and national computer networks is available to students. The Science Library, containing an excellent collection of journals, monographs, and reference materials, is located in a building directly adjacent to the Hall-Atwater Laboratory.

Financial Aid

All students receive a twelve-month stipend, which, for 1999–2000, is $16,321. In the first year, this stipend derives from a teaching assistantship. In later academic years, students may be supported by research assistantships where funds are available, or by further teaching assistantships.

Cost of Study

Tuition for 1999–2000 is $3000 per course credit, but remission of this is granted to all holders of teaching and research assistantships.

Living and Housing Costs

Most graduate students, both single and married, live in houses administered and maintained by the University, with rents ranging between $400 and $500 per month.

Student Group

The student body at Wesleyan is composed of some 2,600 undergraduates and 150 graduate students. Of the latter, most are in the sciences, with 32, equally divided between men and women, in the chemistry department. Most graduates obtain industrial positions, although some choose academic careers, normally after postdoctoral experience in each case.

Student Outcomes

All Ph.D. graduates in the last two years have gone on to postdoctoral fellowships at major universities such as Harvard, Yale, and California Institute of Technology. Most earlier graduates are now on college faculties or have research positions in the chemical industry.

Location

Middletown is a small city on the west bank of the Connecticut River, 15 miles south of Hartford, the state capital. New Haven is 24 miles to the southwest; New York City and Boston are 2 hours away by automobile. Middletown's population of 50,000 is spread over an area of 43 square miles, much of which is rural. Although Wesleyan is the primary source of cultural activity in Middletown, the city is not a "college town" but serves as a busy commercial center for the region between Hartford and the coast. Water sports, skiing, hiking, and other outdoor activities can be enjoyed in the hills, lakes, and river nearby.

The University

For more than 150 years, Wesleyan University has been identified with the highest aspirations and achievements of private liberal arts higher education. Wesleyan's commitment to the sciences dates from the founding of the University, when natural sciences and modern languages were placed on an equal footing with traditional classical studies. In order to maintain and strengthen this commitment, graduate programs leading to the Ph.D. degree in the sciences were established in the late 1960s. The program in chemistry was designed to be small, distinctive, and personal, emphasizing research, acquisition of a broad knowledge of advanced chemistry, and creative thinking.

Applying

By and large, a rolling admissions policy is in place, although applicants seeking admission in September are advised to submit applications (no application fee) as early as possible in the calendar year. Three letters of recommendation are required, and applicants are required to take the Graduate Record Examinations. Students whose native language is not English should take the TOEFL. Applicants are strongly encouraged to visit the University after arrangements are made with the department.

Correspondence and Information

Chairman
Graduate Admissions Committee
Department of Chemistry
Wesleyan University
Middletown, Connecticut 06459

Wesleyan University

THE FACULTY AND THEIR RESEARCH

Anne M. Baranger, Assistant Professor; Ph.D., Berkeley, 1993. Bioorganic chemistry: mechanism of RNA folding, molecular origins of RNA–protein complex affinity and specificity.

David L. Beveridge, Professor; Ph.D., Cincinnati, 1965. Theoretical physical chemistry and molecular biophysics: statistical thermodynamics and computer simulation studies of hydrated biological molecules, structure and motions of nucleic acid, environmental effects on conformational stability, organization of water in crystal hydrates.

Philip H. Bolton, Professor; Ph.D., California, San Diego, 1976. Biochemistry and physical chemistry: NMR and modeling studies of duplex DNA; the structure of DNA containing abasic sites and other damaged DNA; studies on aptamer, telomere, and triplet repeat DNA; development of NMR methodology.

Joseph W. Bruno, Associate Professor; Ph.D., Northwestern, 1983. Inorganic and organometallic chemistry: synthetic and mechanistic studies of transition-metal compounds; organometallic photochemistry, metal-mediated reactions of unsaturated organics.

Albert J. Fry, Professor; Ph.D., Wisconsin, 1963. Organic chemistry: mechanisms of organic electrode processes, development of synthetically useful organic electrochemical reactions.

Joseph L. Knee, Associate Professor; Ph.D., SUNY at Stony Brook, 1983. Chemical physics: investigation of ultrafast energy redistribution in molecules using picosecond laser techniques, emphasis on isolated molecule processes including unimolecular photodissociation reaction rates.

Stewart E. Novick, Professor; Ph.D., Harvard, 1973. Physical chemistry: pulsed-jet Fabry-Perot Fourier transform microwave spectroscopy, structure and dynamics of weakly bound complexes, high resolution spectroscopy of radicals important in the interstellar medium.

George A. Petersson, Professor; Ph.D., Caltech, 1970. Theoretical chemistry: development of improved methods for electronic structure calculations, with applications to small molecular systems and chemical reactions.

Rex F. Pratt, Professor; Ph.D., Melbourne (Australia), 1969. Bioorganic chemistry: enzyme mechanisms and inhibitor design, beta-lactam antibiotics and beta-lactamases, protein chemistry.

Wallace C. Pringle, Professor; Ph.D., MIT, 1966. Physical chemistry: spectroscopic studies of internal interactions in small molecules, collision-induced spectra, environmental chemistry.

Ganesan Ravishanker, Adjunct Associate Professor and Director of Technology Support Services; Ph.D., CUNY, Hunter, 1984. Molecular dynamics and Monte Carlo simulation studies of biomolecular systems, application of computer graphics techniques for the analysis of molecular dynamics simulations, complete correlation analysis of conformational parameters of DNA.

John W. Sease, Emeritus Professor; Ph.D., Caltech, 1946. Organic and analytical chemistry: mechanism of electrochemical reduction of the carbon-halogen bond, product analysis and voltammetry, chemical instrumentation.

T. David Westmoreland, Assistant Professor; Ph.D., North Carolina, 1985. Inorganic and bioinorganic chemistry: electronic structure and mechanism in molybdenum-containing enzymes, EPR spectroscopy of transition-metal complexes, fundamental aspects of atom transfer reactions in solution.

Peter S. Wharton, Professor; Ph.D., Yale, 1959. Organic chemistry.

The Hall-Atwater Laboratory, which houses the chemistry department.

SELECTED PUBLICATIONS

Baranger, A. M. Accessory factor-bZIP DNA interactions. *Curr. Opin. Chem. Biol.* 2:18, 1998.

Hanna, T. A., et al. **(A. M. Baranger).** Addition of organic 1,3-dipolar compounds across an early-late heterobinuclear (Zr-Ir) bond. Mechanism of nitrogen loss from an organoazido complex. *Angew. Chem.* 35:653, 1996.

Hanna, T. A., et al. **(A. M. Baranger).** Reactivity of zirconocene azametallacyclobutenes: Insertion of aldehydes, carbon monoxide, and formation of α,β-unsaturated imines. Formation and trapping of [$Cp_2Zr=O$] in a [4+2] retrocycloaddition. *J. Org. Chem.* 61:4532, 1996.

Hanna, T. A., et al. **(A. M. Baranger).** Reaction of carbon dioxide and heterocumulenes with an unsymmetrical metal-metal bond. Direct addition of CO_2 across a Zr-Ir bond and stoichiometric reduction of CO_2 to formate. *J. Am. Chem. Soc.* 117:11363, 1995.

Baranger, A. M., et al. Transfer of oxygen and sulfur from organic molecules to a Zr-Ir bond. Evidence for an unusually rapid atom abstraction reaction. *J. Am. Chem. Soc.* 117:10041, 1995.

Sprous, D., et al. **(D. L. Beveridge).** Molecular dynamics studies of axis bending in oligonucleotide duplexes d[$G_5(GA_4T_4C)_2$-C_5] and d[G_5-($GA_4T_4C_2$)-C_5]: Effects of sequence polarity on DNA curvature. *J. Mol. Biol.* 285:1623, 1999.

Young, M. A., et al. **(D. L. Beveridge).** The local dielectric environment of B-DNA in solution: Results from a 14 nanosecond molecular dynamics trajectory. *J. Phys. Chem.* 102:7666, 1998.

Jayaram, B., et al. **(D. L. Beveridge).** Solvation free energy of biomacromolecules: Parameters for a modified generalized born model consistent with the AMBER force field. *J. Phys. Chem.* 102:9571, 1998.

Jayaram, B., et al. **(D. L. Beveridge).** Free energy analysis of the conformational stability of A and B forms of DNA in solution. *J. Am. Chem. Soc.* 120:10629, 1998.

Beveridge, D. L. Molecular dynamics: DNA. In *Encyclopedia of Computational Chemistry,* Vol. 3., ed. P. von Ragué. John Wiley and Sons, 1998.

Young, M. A., and **D. L. Beveridge.** Molecular dynamics simulations of an oligonucleotide duplex with adenine tracts phased by a full helix turn. *J. Mol. Biol.* 281:675, 1998.

Jayaram, B., et al. **(D. L. Beveridge).** A modification of the generalized born theory for improved estimates of solvation energies and Pka shifts. *J. Chem. Phys.* 109:1465, 1998.

Sprous, D., et al. **(D. L. Beveridge).** Molecular dynamics studies of the conformational preferences of a DNA double helix in water and an ethanol/water mixture: Theoretical considerations of the A B transition. *J. Phys. Chem.* 102:4658, 1998.

Arthanari, H., et al. **(P. H. Bolton).** Fluorescent dyes specific for quadruplex DNA. *Nucl. Acids Res.* 26:2724, 1998.

McNulty, J. M., et al. **(P. H. Bolton).** Replication inhibition and miscoding properties of DNA templates containing a site specific cis-thymine glycol or urea residue. *Chem. Res. Toxicol.* 11:66, 1998.

Beger, R. D., and **P. H. Bolton.** Structures of apurinic and apyrimidinic sites in duplex DNA. *J. Biol. Chem.* 273:15565, 1998.

Beger, R. D., et al. **(P. H. Bolton).** Interresidue quiet NOEs for DNA structural studies. *J. Magn. Reson.* 132:34, 1998.

Jerkovic, B., et al. **(P. H. Bolton).** Purification of thymine glycol DNAs and nucleosides using boronate chromatography. *Anal. Biochem.* 255:90, 1998.

Wang, K. Y., et al. **(P. H. Bolton).** Solution structure of a duplex DNA with an abasic site in a dA tract. *Biochemistry* 39:11629, 1997.

Beger, R. D., and **P. H. Bolton.** Protein φ and ψ dihedral restraints determined from multidimensional hypersurface correlations of backbone chemical shifts and their use in the determination of protein tertiary structures. *J. Biomolecular NMR* 10:129, 1997.

Lundquist, A. J., et al. **(P. H. Bolton).** Site-directed mutagenesis and characterization of uracil-DNA glycosylase inhibitor protein: Role of specific carboxylic amino acids in complex formation with *Escherichia coli* uracil-DNA glycosylase. *J. Biol. Chem.* 272:21408, 1997.

Reardon, J. T., et al. **(P. H. Bolton).** In vitro repair of oxidative DNA damage by human nucleotide excision repair system: Possible explanation for neurodegeneration in *Xeroderma pigmentosum* patients. *Proc. Natl. Acad. Sci. U.S.A.* 94:9463, 1997.

Sarker, N. and **J. W. Bruno.** Thermodynamic and kinetic studies of hydride transfer for a series of molybdenum and tungsten hydrides. *J. Am. Chem. Soc.* 120:2174, 1999.

Zhang, X.-M., et al. **(J. W. Bruno).** Hydride affinities of arylcarbenium ions and iminium ions in dimethyl sulfoxide and acetonitrile. *J. Org. Chem.* 63:4671, 1998.

Thiyagarajan, B., et al. **(J. W. Bruno).** Niobium-mercury heterometallic compounds as sources of niobium(II): Radical paths to organoniobium species. *Organometallics* 16:5884, 1997.

Kerr, M. E., et al. **(J. W. Bruno).** Effects of the niobium(V) center on the energetics of ligand-centered proton and hydrogen atom transfer reactions in acyl and alkoxide complexes. *Organometallics* 16:3249 1997.

Kerr, M. E., and **J. W. Bruno.** Synthesis and reactivity of niobium-vinylketene complexes exhibiting ketene η^2-C,O complexation.*J. Am. Chem. Soc.* 119:3183, 1997.

Thiyagarajan, B., et al. **(J. W. Bruno).** Electrophilic attack on the carbon terminus of a niobium-bound formaldehyde ligand. *Organometallics* 16:1331, 1997.

Thiyagarajan, B., et al. **(J. W. Bruno).** Generation of organoniobium(II) radicals and synthesis of heterometallic niobium-mercury compounds.*Organometallics* 15:2588, 1996.

Kerr, M. E., et al. **(J. W. Bruno).** Luminescence studies on substituted niobocene ketene complexes: Evidence for thermally-activated excited state processes involving arene torsion. *J. Chem. Soc., Chem. Commun.* 1221, 1996.

Thiyagarajan, B., et al. **(J. W. Bruno).** Synthesis, structure and redox reactivity of a substituted niobocene formaldehyde complex. The importance of hydrogen-bonding in the redox chemistry. *Organometallics* 15:1989, 1996.

Fry, A. J., et al. Synthesis, chemistry, and anodic oxidation of 1,2-*bis*-(trialkylsilyl)ethanes. In *Novel Trends in Electroorganic Synthesis,* ed. S. Torii. Springer-Verlag, 1998.

Louie, J., et al. **(A. J. Fry).** Discrete high molecular weight triarylamine dendrimers prepared by palladium-catalyzed amination. *J. Am. Chem. Soc.* 119:11695, 1997.

Porter, J. M., et al. **(A. J. Fry).** 1,2-*Bis*-(trialkylsilyl)ethanes: Synthons for vicinal dications? *Tetrahedron Lett.* 38:7147, 1997.

Touster, J., and **A. J. Fry.** Stereoselective sonochemical reductive silylation of geminal dibromocyclopropanes by bulk magnesium. *Tetrahedron Lett.* 38:6553, 1997.

Fry, A. J., et al. New biopolymers for electroenzymatic synthesis of *alpha*-hydroxy acids. In *Fundamentals and Potential Applications of Electrochemical Synthesis,* eds. R. D. Weaver et al. Electrochemical Society, 1997.

Zhu, Q., et al. **(A. J. Fry).** Bond dissociation of antioxidants. *Polym. Degrad. Stab.* 57:2444, 1997.

Fry, A. J., and J. Touster. Stereoselective electrochemical and chemical reductive silylation of bicyclic geminal dihalocyclopropanes. Effects of ultrasound. *Electrochim. Acta* 42:2057, 1997.

Fry, A. J. The electrochemistry of the C=C, C=O, and C=N groups. In *The Chemistry of Double-bonded Functional Groups,* Supplement A3. John Wiley and Sons, 1997.

Fry, A. J. The electrochemistry of nitro, nitroso, and related compounds. In *The Chemistry of Amino, Nitroso, Nitro & Related Groups,* Supplement F2, ed. S. Patai. John Wiley and Sons, 1997.

Kaufman, S. A., et al. **(A. J. Fry).** Cobalt(salen)-electrocatalyzed conversion of benzotrichloride to tolane. A quintupled electrochemical transformation. *Tetrahedron Lett.* 37:8105, 1996.

Leonida, M. L., et al. **(A. J. Fry).** Co-electropolymerization of a viologen oligomer and lipoamide dehydrogenase on an electrode surface. Application to cofactor regeneration. *Bioorg. Med. Chem. Lett.* 6:1663, 1996.

Zhang, X.-M., et al. **(A. J. Fry).** Equilibrium acidities and homolytic bond dissociation enthalpies of the acidic C-H bonds in P-(*p*-substituted benzyl)triphenylphosphonium cations and related cations.*J. Org. Chem.* 61:4101, 1996.

Wesleyan University

Selected Publications (continued)

Pitts, J. D. and **J. L. Knee.** Structure and dynamics of 9-ethylfluorene-Ar_n van der Waals complexes. *J. Chem. Phys.* 110:3389, 1998.

Pitts, J. D., et al. **(J. L. Knee).** Conformational energy and dynamics of 9-ethylfluorene. *J. Chem. Phys.* 110:3378, 1998.

Pitts, J. D. and **J. L. Knee.** Electronic spectroscopy and dynamics of the monomer and Ar_n clusters of 9-phenylfluorene. *J. Chem. Phys.* 109:7113, 1998.

Pitts, J. D., and **J. L. Knee.** Dynamics of vibronically excited fluorene-Ar_n (n=4-5) cluster. *J. Chem. Phys.* 108:9632, 1998.

Zhang, X., et al. **(J. L. Knee).** Neutral and cation spectroscopy of fluorene-Ar_n clusters. *J. Chem. Phys.* 107:8239, 1997.

Knee, J. L., et al. Photoelectron spectroscopy of molecular clusters. In *Laser Techniques for State-Selected and State-to-State Chemistry III,* ed. J. W. Hepburn. *Proc. SPIE* 2548:48, 1995.

Knee, J. L. ZEKE studies with picosecond lasers. In *Highly Resolved Laser Photoionization and Photoelectron Studies, Current Topics in Ion Chemistry and Physics,* eds. T. Baer et al. John Wiley and Sons, 1995.

Knee, J. L. Time resolved threshold ionization spectroscopy. In *Femtosecond Chemistry,* eds. J. Manz and L. Woste. Verlag Chemie, 1995.

Chen, W., et al. **(S. E. Novick).** Microwave spectroscopy of the 2,4-Pentadiynyl Radical: $H_2CCCCCH$. *J. Chem. Phys.* 109:10190, 1998.

Chen, W., et al. **(S. E. Novick).** Microwave spectra of the methylcyanopolynes CH_3 $(C{\equiv}C)_n$ CN(n=2,3,4,5). *J. Mol. Spectrosc.* 192:1, 1998.

Chen, W., et al. **(S. E. Novick).** Laboratory detection of a new carbon radical: H_2CCCCN. *Astrophys. J.* 492:849, 1998.

Chen, W., et al. **(S. E. Novick).** Determination of the structure of HBr DBr. *J. Chem. Phys.* 106:10386, 1997.

McCarthy, M. J., et al. **(S. E. Novick).** Two new cumulene carbenes: H_2C_5 and H_2C_6. *Science* 275:518, 1997.

Travers, M. J., et al. **(S. E. Novick).** Structure of the cumulene carbene butatrieneylidene, H_2CCCC. *J. Mol. Spectrosc.* 180:75, 1996.

Novick, S. E., et al. Hyperfine structure in the microwave spectrum of NF_3. *J. Mol. Spectrosc.* 179:219, 1996.

Petersson, G. A. Complete basis set thermochemistry and kinetics. In *Computational Thermochemistry,* eds. K. K. Irikura et al. ACS Symposium Series No. 677, 1998.

Malick, D. K., et al. **(G. A. Petersson).** Transition states for chemical reactions. I. Geometry and barrier height. *J. Chem. Phys.* 108:5704, 1998.

Clifford, E. P., et al. **(G. A. Petersson).** Photoelectron spectroscopy of the NCN⁻ and HNCN⁻ ions. *J. Phys. Chem. A.* 101:4338, 1997.

Ochterski, J. W., et al. **(G. A. Petersson).** A complete basis set model chemistry. V. Extensions to six or more heavy atoms. *J. Chem. Phys.* 104:2598, 1996.

Harkins, P. C., et al. **(G. A. Petersson).** Distortion of O-P-O bond angles in phosphorus monoanions: *Ab initio* studies. *J. Inorg. Biochem.* 61:25, 1996.

Ochterski, J. W., et al. **(G. A. Petersson).** A comparison of model chemistries. *J. Am. Chem. Soc.* 117:11299, 1995.

Graves-Woodward, K., and **R. F. Pratt.** Reaction of soluble penicillin-binding protein 2a of methicillin-resistant *Staphylococcus aureus* with β-lactams and acyclic substrates: Kinetics in homogenous solution. *Biochem. J.* 332:755, 1998.

Pratt, R. F., and N. Li. Inhibition of serine β-lactamases by acyl phosph(on)ates: A new source of inert acyl [and phosphon(on)yl]-enzymes. *J. Am. Chem. Soc.* 120:4264, 1998.

Maveyraud, L., et al. **(R. F. Pratt).** Crystal structure of an acylation transition-state analog of the TEM-1 β-lactamase. Mechanistic implications for the class A β-lactamases. *Biochemistry* 37:2622, 1998.

Pratt, R. F., and N. J. Hammar. Salicyloyl cyclic phosphate, a "penicillin-like" inhibitor of β-lactamases. *J. Am. Chem. Soc.* 120:3004, 1998.

Li, N., et al. **(R. F. Pratt).** Structure-activity studies of the inhibition of serine β-lactamases by phosphonate monoesters. *Bioorg. Med. Chem.* 5:1783, 1997.

Curley K., and **R. F. Pratt.** Structure of an α-keto-β-amido acid, 3-(Phenylacetamido)pyruvic acid and its methyl ester in the solid state and in organic and aqueous solvents. *J. Org. Chem.* 62:4479, 1997.

Curley, K., and **R. F. Pratt.** Effectiveness of tetrahedral adducts as transition-state analogs and inhibitors of the class C β-lactamase of *Enterobacter cloacae* P99. *J. Am. Chem. Soc.* 119:1529, 1997.

Pratt, R. F., et al. 8-Hydroxypenillic acid from 6-aminopenicillanic acid: A new reaction catalyzed by a class C β-lactamase. *J. Am. Chem. Soc.* 118:8207, 1996.

Adediran, S. A., et al. **(R. F. Pratt).** β-secondary and solvent deuterium kinetic isotope effects on β-lactamase catalysis. *Biochemistry* 35:3604, 1996.

Xu, Y., et al. **(R. F. Pratt).** Kinetics and mechanism of the hydrolysis of depsipeptides by the β-lactamase of *Enterobacter cloacae* P99. *Biochemistry* 35:3595, 1996.

Pringle, W. C., et al. Collision induced far infrared spectrum of cyclopropane. *Mol. Phys.* 62:669, 1987.

Pringle, W. C., et al. Analysis of collision induced far infrared spectrum of ethylene. *Mol. Phys.* 62:661, 1987.

Cohen, R., and **W. C. Pringle.** Analysis of the collision induced far-infrared spectrum of ethane. *Spectrochim. Acta* 41A:291, 1986.

Sprous, D. et al. **(G. Ravishanker** and **D. L. Beveridge).** Molecular dynamics information extraction. In *IMA Volumes in Mathematics and its Applications,* "Mathematical and Computational Issues in Drug Design," ed. J. Blaney. Springer-Verlag, 1997.

Young, M.A., **G. Ravishanker,** and **D. L. Beveridge.** A five-nanosecond molecular dynamics trajectory for B-DNA: Analysis of structure motions and solvation. *Biophys. J.* 73:2313, 1997.

Vijayakumar, S., **G. Ravishanker, R. F. Pratt,** and **D. L. Beveridge.** Molecular dynamics simulation of a class A β-lactamase: Structural and mechanistic implications. *J. Am. Chem. Soc.* 117:1722, 1995.

Young, M. A., et al. **(G. Ravishanker** and **D. L. Beveridge).** Analysis of local helix bending in crystal structures of DNA oligonucleotides and DNA-proteins complexes. *Biophys. J.* 68:2454, 1995.

Holmer, S. A., et al. **(T. D. Westmoreland).** A new irreversibly inhibited form of xanthine oxidase from ethylisonitrile. *J. Inorg. Biochem.* 66:63, 1997.

Swann, J., and **T. D. Westmoreland.** Density functional calculations of *g* values and molybdenum hyperfine coupling constants for a series of molybdenum(V) oxyhalide anions. *Inorg. Chem.* 36:5348, 1997.

Nipales, N. S., and **T. D. Westmoreland.** Correlation of EPR parameters with electronic structure in the homologous series of low symmetry complexes Tp*MoOX₂ (Tp* = tris(3,5-dimethylpyrazol-1-yl)borate; X = F, Cl, Br). *Inorg. Chem.* 36:756, 1997.

Balagopalakrishna, C., et al. **(T. D. Westmoreland).** Electronic structural contributions to *g* values and molybdenum hyperfine coupling constants in oxyhalide anions of molybdenum (V). *Inorg. Chem.* 35:7758, 1996.

Deraniyagala, S. P., et al. **(T. D. Westmoreland).** Coupled two-electron/halide transfer reactions of ruthenoceniums and osmoceniums. *Inorg. Chem.* 35:7699, 1996.

Xu, A., et al. **(T. D. Westmoreland).** Hydride abstraction reactivity of haloruthenoceniums and haloosmoceniums. *Organometallics* 15:4888, 1996.

WEST VIRGINIA UNIVERSITY

Department of Chemistry

Programs of Study

The Department of Chemistry offers programs of study that lead to Master of Science (M.S.) and Doctor of Philosophy (Ph.D.) degrees. The principal component of both programs of study is the completion of a research project and defense of a thesis or dissertation describing the project. Although most research projects concentrate on problems in the general areas of analytical, inorganic, organic, and physical chemistry, some students pursue projects that bridge two or more of these subdisciplines or related disciplines in science.

Within their first year of graduate studies, all students must demonstrate proficiency in the discipline of chemistry at the bachelor's level through satisfactory performance on guidance examinations or successful completion of approved course work. Students also select a research group, a research problem, and a research advisory committee during their first year. The research advisory committee outlines a program of study, including course work, that develops the student's ability to formulate, evaluate, and undertake research strategies.

Ph.D. students begin candidacy examinations in their second year. Prospective Ph.D. students must first demonstrate their mastery of the discipline by passing six cumulative examinations before the end of their third year. Once the cumulative examinations are completed, the student then develops an original research proposal. The final component of the candidacy examinations for Ph.D. students is the defense of this proposal before the research advisory committee. Success entails a proven ability to consider a problem critically and to develop a creative strategy for solution of the problem.

Research Facilities

The Department of Chemistry occupies 100,000 square feet of space in two adjoining buildings: the Chemistry Research Laboratory and the Clark Hall of Chemistry. The Chemistry Research Laboratory houses modern research laboratories, the Physical Sciences Library, and research support facilities. The Clark Hall of Chemistry, renovated in 1983, serves as the location of secondary research facilities, teaching laboratories, and classrooms. Research grade FT-NMR, FT-IR, GC-MS, EPR, and UV-VIS systems and computational facilities are available in support of research efforts. Individual research group laboratories house instrumentation devoted to their research, such as electrokinetic separation, ion trap mass spectrometry, Raman spectroscopy, time-of-flight mass spectrometry, HPLC, electrochemical, and X-ray diffraction systems. Electronics, glass, and machine shops staffed with expert instrument specialists to support research projects are available in-house.

Financial Aid

The chemistry program offers financial support to all graduate students in the form of teaching or research assistantships. These assistantships include a stipend of up to $15,000 per year and a full waiver of tuition. The department seeks applicants with strong academic records and encourages them to pursue various fellowships offered by the University, the Eberly College of Arts and Sciences, and the department. A significant percentage of graduate students pursue their studies after the first year with support from externally funded research assistantships. This funding, along with the University's Doctoral Student Travel Grant Program, affords students the opportunity to attend major research conferences and present their work.

Cost of Study

All graduate students receive tuition waivers as part of their appointments as teaching or research assistants.

Living and Housing Costs

The University offers furnished efficiency and single-bedroom apartments for graduate students at $370 to $445 per month. For married graduate students and their families, unfurnished two-bedroom apartments are available from the University at $400 per month. In addition to University-owned housing, affordable housing is readily available from private sources in the Morgantown community.

Student Group

Currently 58 students are enrolled in the graduate program in the Department of Chemistry. The average research group consists of 3 graduate students. Many groups also include 1 or more postdoctoral research associates. The program has a mix of local, domestic, and international students.

Location

Morgantown is a pleasant community in the Appalachian highlands along the banks of the Monongahela River. The area is known for the abundance of outdoor recreational opportunities and natural scenic beauty. The University is the flagship institution of higher education in the state of West Virginia and enhances the small-town environment of Morgantown with a diversity of academic, cultural, and athletic programs. The presence of national and industrial laboratories such as the U.S. DoE Morgantown Energy Technology Center, the National Institute of Occupational Safety and Health, Mylan Pharmaceuticals, and GE Plastics, in conjunction with West Virginia University's (WVU) College of Engineering and Health Sciences Schools, provides an environment rich with opportunity for interdisciplinary research.

The University

Established in 1867, West Virginia University is the state's major research, doctoral degree–granting, land-grant institution. WVU provides high-quality programs of instruction, offering 164 degree programs at the undergraduate, graduate, and professional levels; fosters basic and applied research and scholarship; and engages in and encourages other creative and artistic work.

Applying

Application materials for admission and teaching assistantships must be obtained from and returned to the Director of Graduate Studies in the Department of Chemistry. A nonrefundable fee of $45 must accompany each application. Applications should be received at the department by February 1 to be considered for admission in the following fall or by June 1 to be considered for admission in the following spring. The qualifications of all candidates are considered without regard to race, color, national origin, religion, sex, or handicap.

Correspondence and Information

Director of Graduate Studies
Department of Chemistry
West Virginia University
Morgantown, West Virginia 26506-6045

West Virginia University

THE FACULTY AND THEIR RESEARCH

Kay M. Brummond, Assistant Professor; Ph.D., Penn State. Development of synthetic methods and their application to the preparation of small molecule libraries.

Harry O. Finklea, Associate Professor; Ph.D., Caltech. Development of methods for the preparation of organized monolayers and the investigation of long-range electron transfer processes, gas piezoelectric sensors.

Terry Gullion, Assistant Professor; Ph.D., William and Mary. Development and application of high-resolution solid-state NMR to biomolecules and polymers.

Charles Jaffe, Associate Professor; Ph.D., Colorado. Examination of the correspondence between classical and quantum mechanics and the role of chaos in molecular systems.

Paul W. Jagodzinski, Associate Professor; Ph.D., Texas A&M. Infrared, Raman, and surface-enhanced Raman spectroscopy; optical spectroscopy; molecular structure; amorphous materials; colloids; study of liquids and solutions; donor-acceptor molecules.

Fred L. King, Associate Professor; Ph.D., Virginia. Development of mass and optical spectroscopic methods for the characterization of trace species, bioanalytical chemistry, gas-phase chemistry.

Robert S. Nakon, Professor; Ph.D., Texas A&M. Transition metal chemistry, solution equilibria, kinetics and mechanisms of metal ion and metal chelate catalysis.

John H. Penn, Associate Professor; Ph.D., Wisconsin. Application of physical methods to study electron-transfer organic molecular complexes, photochemistry, and the dehalogenation of haloaromatics; chemical education.

Jeffrey L. Petersen, Professor; Ph.D., Wisconsin. Synthesis and reactivity of electrophilic organometallic complexes, X-ray crystallographic determination of molecular structure.

Kenneth Showalter, Bennet Professor; Ph.D., Colorado. Investigations of chemical kinetics, oscillatory reactions, reaction dynamics in open chemical systems, and chemical waves.

Reuben Simoyi, Professor; Ph.D., Brandeis. Fast reaction chemical kinetics, relaxation techniques, nonlinear dynamics in chemistry, clock reactions, chemical oscillations, chaos, spatial instabilities.

Ronald B. Smart, Associate Professor; Ph.D., Michigan. Environmental chemistry, voltammetric membrane electrode sensors, trace metal speciation, chemistry of water disinfection, coal chemistry.

Bjorn C. Soderberg, Assistant Professor; Ph.D., Royal Institute of Technology (Stockholm). Development of new synthetic methods, mediated or catalyzed by transitions metals and their use in the synthesis of physiologically active molecules.

Alan M. Stolzenberg, Associate Professor; Ph.D., Stanford. Bioinorganic and organometallic chemistry, inorganic synthesis, coordination chemistry, reactivity and chemical mechanisms.

Aaron Timperman, Assistant Professor; Ph.D., Illinois. Development of separation methods, mass spectrometry and its application to novel marine peptides.

Kung K. Wang, Professor; Ph.D., Purdue. Organoborane, organosilane, and organotin reagents in organic synthesis; biradical-forming reactions; synthesis of biologically active indole alkaloids.

SELECTED PUBLICATIONS

Brummond, K. M., and J. Lu. A solid-phase synthesis of BRL 49653. *J. Org. Chem.* 64:1723, 1999.

Brummond, K. M., and K. D. Gesenberg. Alpha-chlorination of ketones using p-toluenesulfonyl chloride. *Tetrahedron Lett.* 40:2231, 1999.

Brummond, K., and H. Wan. The allenic Pauson-Khand cycloaddition. Dependence in π-bond selectivity on substrate structure. *Tetrahedron Lett.* 39:931, 1998.

Brummond, K., H. Wan, and J. L. Kent. An intramolecular allenic [2+2+1] cycloaddition reaction. *J. Org. Chem.* 63:6535, 1998.

Brummond, K. M., K. D. Gesenberg, J. L. Kent, and A. D. Kerekes. A new method for the preparation of alkynes from vinyl triflates. *Tetrahedron Lett.* 39:8613, 1998.

Finklea, H. O., M. A. Phillippi, E. Lompert, and J. W. Grate. Highly sorbent films derived from Ni(SCN)2(4-picoline)4 for the detection of chlorinated and aromatic hydrocarbons with quartz crystal microbalance sensors. *Anal. Chem.* 70:1268–76, 1998.

Lowy, D. A., and **H. O. Finklea**. Gold electrodes with polyion multilayers and electrostatically bound redox centers. *Electrochim. Acta* 42:1325–35, 1997.

Finklea, H. O., and M. S. Ravenscroft. Temperature and overpotential dependence of long range electron transfer across a self-assembled monolayer with pendant ruthenium redox centers. *Isr. J. Chem.* 37:179–84, 1997.

Finklea, H. O. Electrochemistry of organized monolayers of thiols and related molecules on electrodes. *Electroanal. Chem.* 19:109–335, 1996.

Finklea, H. O., L. Liu, M. S. Ravenscroft, and S. Punturi. Multiple electron tunneling paths across self-assembled monolayers of alkane thiols with attached ruthenium(II/III) redox centers. *J. Phys. Chem.* 100:18852–8, 1996.

Gullion, T., and C. Pennington. REDOR: An MAS NMR method to simply multiple coupled heteronuclear spin systems. *Chem. Phys. Lett.* 90:88–93, 1998.

Chopin, L., S. Vega, and **T. Gullion**. A MAS NMR method for measuring 13C-17O distances. *J. Am. Chem. Soc.* 120:4406–9, 1998.

Cull, T. S., et al. **(T. Gullion)**. Counting spins with a new spin echo double resonance. *J. Magn. Reson.* 133:352–7, 1998.

Gullion, T. Introduction to rotational-echo, double resonance NMR. *Concepts Magn. Reson.* 10:277–89, 1998.

Ba, Y., et al. **(T. Gullion)**. Optimizing the 13C-14N REAPDOR NMR experiment: A theoretical and experimental study. *J. Magn. Reson.* 133:104–14, 1998.

Gullion, T. Measurement of heteronuclear dipolar interactions by rotational-echo, double-resonance, nuclear magnetic resonance. *Magn. Reson. Rev.* 12:83–131, 1997.

Chopin, L., R. Rosanske, and **T. Gullion**. Simple improvements in spinning-speed control for MAS NMR experiments. *J. Magn. Reson. A* 122:237–9, 1996.

Gullion, T. Detecting 13C-17O dipolar interactions by rotational-echo, adiabatic-passage, double-resonance NMR. *J. Magn. Reson. A* 117:326–9, 1995.

Gullion, T. Measurement of dipolar interactions between spin- and quadrupolar nuclei by rotational-echo, adiabatic-passage, double-resonance NMR. *Chem. Phys. Lett.* 246:325–30, 1995.

Anderson, R., and **T. Gullion** et al. Rotational-echo double-resonance nuclear magnetic resonance spectroscopy of [1-13C, 15N]acetyl-L-carnitine. *J. Am. Chem. Soc.* 117:10546–50, 1995.

Tovbis, A., M. Tsuchiya, and **C. Jaffé**. Exponential asymptotic expansions and approximations of the unstable and stable manifolds of singularly perturbed systems with the Hénon map as an example. *Chaos* 8:665, 1998.

Tovbis, A., M. Tsuchiya, and **C. Jaffé**. Exponential asymptotics and approximation of stable and unstable manifolds in singularly perturbed nonlinear systems. In *Hamiltonian Systems With Three or More Degrees of Freedom. NATO ASI Series.* Kluwer Academic Publishers, 1998.

Steckel, J., and **C. Jaffé**. The bifurcations of the Langmuir orbit in the two-electron atom. In *Hamiltonian Systems With Three or More Degrees of Freedom. NATO ASI Series.* Kluwer Academic Publishers, 1998.

Borondo, F., S. Miret-Artés, J. Bowers, and **C. Jaffé**. Chaotic scattering in atom-surface collisions. In *Hamiltonian Systems With Three or More Degrees of Freedom. NATO ASI Series.* Kluwer Academic Publishers, 1998.

Peters, A. D., **C. Jaffé**, and J. B. Delos. Closed-orbit theory and the photodetachment cross section of H in parallel electric and magnetic fields. *Phys. Rev. A* 56:31, 1997.

Peters, A. D., **C. Jaffé**, J. Gao, and J. B. Delos. Quantum manifestations of bifurcations of closed orbits in the photodetachment cross section of H- in parallel fields. *Phys. Rev. A* 56:45, 1997.

Guantes, R., F. Borondo, **C. Jaffé**, and S. Miret-Artés. Diffraction of atoms from stepped surfaces: A semiclassical chaotic S-matrix study. *Phys. Rev. B* 53:14117, 1996.

Miret-Artés, S., et al. **(C. Jaffé)**. Classical singularities in chaotic atom-surface scattering. *Phys. Rev. B* 54:10397, 1996.

Kushto, G. P., and **P. W. Jagodzinski**. Vibrational spectra and normal coordinate analysis of 4-(dimethylamino)benzaldehyde and selected isotopic derivatives. *Spectrochim. Acta* 54A:799–819, 1998.

Kao, E. C., et al. **(P. W. Jagodzinski)**. Setting reactions of amino-modified glass ionomer restoratives. *J. Dental Res.* 77:512, 1998.

Coyle, C. M., G. Chumanov, and **P. W. Jagodzinski**. Surface enhanced Raman spectra of the reduction product of 4-cyanopyridine on copper colloids. *J. Raman Spectrosc.* 29:757, 1998.

Lewis, C. L., et al. **(F. L. King)**. Determination of 40Ca+ in the presence of 40Ar+: An illustration of the utility of time-gated detection in pulsed glow discharge mass spectrometry. *Anal. Chem.* 71:230, 1999.

Barshick, C. M., et al. **(F. L. King)**. Investigation into the analytical utility of plasma etching in reactive glow discharge plasmas. *Appl. Spectrosc.* 53:65, 1999.

Steiner, R. E., C. L. Lewis, and **F. L. King**. Time-of-flight mass spectrometry with a pulsed glow discharge ionization source. *Anal. Chem.* 69:1715, 1997.

Barshick, C. M., et al. **(F. L. King)**. The periodic nature of noble gas adduct ions in glow discharge mass spectrometry. *Appl. Spectrosc.* 49:885, 1995.

King, F. L., J. Teng, and R. E. Steiner. Glow discharge mass spectrometry: Trace element determinations in solid samples. *J. Mass Spectrosc.* 30:1061, 1995.

Teng, J., et al. **(F. L. King)**. Factors influencing the quantitative determination of trace elements in soils by glow discharge mass spectrometry. *Appl. Spectrosc.* 49:1361, 1995.

Makarov, S. V., et al. **(J. H. Penn** and **J. L. Petersen)**. Structure and stability of aminoiminomethanesulfonic acid. *Inorg. Chim. Acta* 286: 149–54, 1999.

Makarov, S. V., et al. **(J. H. Penn)**. New and surprising experimental results from the oxidation of sulfinic and sulfonic acids. *J. Phys. Chem. A* 102:6786–92, 1998.

Penn, J. H., D.-L. Deng, and T. Q. Chang. Catalytic dechlorination of polycyclic chloroaromatics with dicyclopentadienyl yttrium chloride. *Chin. Chem. Lett.* 7:845–6, 1996.

Renton, J. J., Y.-T. Yu, and **J. H. Penn**. FTIR microspectroscopy of particular liptinite, lopinite rich late Permian coals from South China. *Int. J. Coal Geol.* 29:187–97, 1996.

Huang, J., E. D. Stevens, S. P. Nolan, and **J. L. Petersen**. Olefin metathesis-active ruthenium complexes bearing a nucleophilic carbene ligand. *J. Am. Chem. Soc.* 120:2674–8, 1999.

Close, M. R., **J. L. Petersen**, and E. L. Kugler. Synthesis and characterization of nanoscale molybdenum sulfide catalysts by controlled gas phase decompositions of Mo(CO)₆ and H₂S. *Inorg. Chem.* 38:1535–47, 1999.

Serron, S., et al. **(J. L. Petersen)**. Solution thermochemical and structural studies of ligand substitution of N-pyrrolyl phosphine ligands in the (p-cymene)RuCl2(PR3) system. *Organometallics* 17:104–10, 1998.

Huang, J., C. Li, S. P. Nolan, and **J. L. Petersen**. Solution calorimetric investigation of oxidative addition of HEAr (E=O, S, Se; Ar=C6H4X, X=CH3, H, Cl, NO2) to (PMe3) 4Ru(C2H4): Relationship between HEAr acidity and enthalpy of reaction. *Organometallics* 17:3516–21, 1998.

Cao, Y., **J. L. Petersen**, and **A. M. Stolzenberg**. Metalloradical chemistry of cobalt(II) porphyrins: The syntheses, structure, and reactivity of triphenyltin(II)- and trihalomethyl-cobalt(III) octaethylporphyrin. *Inorg. Chem.* 37:5173–9, 1998.

Haar, C. M., J. Huang, S. P. Nolan, and **J. L. Petersen**. Synthetic, thermochemical and catalytic studies involving novel R2P(ORf) [R=alkyl or aryl; Rf=CH2CH2(CF2)5CF3] ligands. *Organometallics* 17:5018–24, 1998.

Cao, Y., **J. L. Petersen**, and **A. M. Stolzenberg**. Do organocobalt

West Virginia University

Selected Publications (continued)

porphyrins have agostic alkyl groups? An investigation of the structure of ethyl cobalt(III) octaethylporphyrin and the nuclear magnetic resonance spectra of ^{13}C-labelled alkyl cobalt(III) porphyrin complexes. *Inorg. Chim. Acta* 263:139–48, 1997.

Reardon, D., et al. **(J. L. Petersen).** Reactivity of coordinatively unsaturated trivalent chromium complexes with sulfur. Preparation of novel sulfido-bridged dinuclear Cr(IV) derivatives. *Chem. Eur. J.* 3:1482–8, 1997.

Kloppenburg, L., and **J. L. Petersen.** Double isocyanide insertion and C,C-coupling reaction of [(C$_5$Me$_4$)SiMe$_2$(N-t-Bu)]ZrMe$_2$. Structural characterization of the two, 1,4-diaza-5-zircona-cyclopentene ring conformations for [(C$_5$Me$_4$)SiMe$_2$(N-t-Bu)]Zr[N(R)C(Me)=C(Me)N(R)] complexes. *Organometallics* 16:3548–56, 1997.

Chinake, C. R., O. Olojo, and **R. H. Simoyi.** Oxidation of formaldehyde by chlorite in basic and slightly acidic media. *J. Phys. Chem.* 102:606, 1998.

Bond, R. A., J. R. Mika, B. S. Martincigh, and **R. H. Simoyi.** The quasi-steady-state approximation: Numerical validation. *J. Chem. Educ.* 75:1158, 1998.

Darkwa, J., C. Mundoma, and **R. H. Simoyi.** Antioxidant chemistry: Reactivity and oxidation of DL-cysteine by some common oxidants. *J. Chem. Soc., Faraday Trans.* 94:1971, 1998.

Chinake, C. R., and **R. H. Simoyi.** Oxyhalogen-sulfur chemistry: Kinetics and mechanism of the formation of bromamines from the reaction between acidic bromate and aminomethanesulfonic acid. *J. Phys. Chem.* 102:10490–7, 1998.

Martincigh, B. S., C. Mundoma, and **R. H. Simoyi.** Antioxidant chemistry: Hypotaurine-taurine oxidation by chlorite. *J. Phys. Chem.* 102:9838–46, 1998.

Wang, J. C., S. Kadar, P. Jung, and **K. Showalter.** Noise driven avalanche behavior in subexcitable media. *Phys. Rev. Lett.* 82:855–8, 1999.

Kadar, S., J. Wang, and **K. Showalter.** Noise supported traveling waves in subexcitable media. *Nature* 391:770–2, 1998.

Merkin, J. H., et al. **(K. Showalter).** Competitive autocatalysis in reaction-diffusion systems: Exclusive product selectivity. *Faraday Trans. Roy. Chem. Soc.* 94:53–8, 1998.

Jung, P., et al. **(K. Showalter).** Noise sustained waves in subexcitable media: From chemical waves to brain waves. *Chaos* 8:567–75, 1998.

Amemiya, T., et al. **(K. Showalter).** Formation and evolution of scroll waves in photosensitive excitable media. *Chaos* 8:872–8, 1998.

Amemiya, T., et al. **(K. Showalter).** Perturbation-induced scroll waves in photosensitive excitable media. In *Proceedings of the 4th Experimental Chaos Conference*, pp. 19–24, eds. W. L. Ditto et al. Singapore: World Scientific, 1998.

Petrov, V., and **K. Showalter.** Nonlinear prediction, filtering, and control of chemical systems from time series. *Chaos* 7:614–20, 1997.

Scott, S. K., J. C. Wang, and **K. Showalter.** Modelling studies of spiral waves and target patterns in premixed flames. *J. Chem. Soc., Faraday Trans.* 93:733–9, 1997.

Kadar, S., T. Amemiya, and **K. Showalter.** Reaction mechanism for light sensitivity of the Ru(bpy)(3)(2+)-catalyzed Belousov-Zhabotinsky reaction. *J. Phys. Chem. A* 101:8200–6, 1997.

Ditto, W. L., and **K. Showalter.** Introduction: Control and synchronization of chaos. *Chaos* 7:509–11, 1997.

Li, H., and **R. B. Smart.** Square wave catalytic stripping voltammetry of molybdenum complexed with dihydroxynaphthalene. *J. Electroanal. Chem.* 429:169–74, 1997.

Li, H., and **R. B. Smart.** Determination of sub-nanomolar concentration of arsenic(III) in natural waters by square wave cathodic stripping voltammetry. *Anal. Chim. Acta* 325:25–32, 1996.

Li, H., and **R. B. Smart.** Catalytic stripping voltammetry of vanadium in the presence of dihydroxynaphthalene and bromate. *Anal. Chim. Acta* 333:131–8, 1996.

Söderberg, B. C., A. K. Berry, and P. C. Jones. Reactions of trimethylsilyl dienolethers with palladium(II) salts: Formation of α-oxa-η3-allylpalladium complexes and 4-acyloxy-substituted 2-alkenals. *Organometallics* 17:1069–78, 1998.

Söderberg, B. C., and J. A. Shriver. Palladium-catalyzed synthesis of indoles by reductive N-heteroannulation of 2-nitrostyrenes. *J. Org. Chem.* 62:5838–45, 1997.

Söderberg, B. C., J. Liu, T. W. Ball, and M. J. Turbeville. Thermal decomposition of pentacarbonyl [1-acyloxy-alkylidene]chromium(0) complexes: Formation of enol esters. *J. Org. Chem.* 62:5945–52, 1997.

Söderberg, B. C., and S. L. Fields. Expedient syntheses of espintanol, p-methoxycarvacrol, and thymoquinol dimethylether. *Org. Prep. Proc. Int.* 28:221–5, 1996.

Söderberg, B. C., and H. H. Odens. Photolytic reaction of a-hydroxy substituted Fischer carbene complexes: Synthesis of a-hydroxy esters. *Organometallics* 15:5080–4, 1996.

Söderberg, B. C., et al. Tetramethylammonium pentacarbonyl(1-oxyalkylidene)chromate(0) salts as acyl anion synthons. *Organometallics* 14:3712, 1995.

Stolzenberg, A. M., S. W. Simerly, B. D. Steffey, and G. S. Haymond. The synthesis, properties, and reactivities of free-base- and Zn(II)-N-methyl hydroporphyrin compounds. The unexpected selectivity of the direct methylation of free-base hydroporphyrin compounds. *J. Am. Chem. Soc.* 119:11843–54, 1997.

Stolzenberg, A. M., and Z. Zhang. F430 model chemistry. An investigation of nickel complexes as catalysts for the reduction of alkyl halides and methyl coenzyme-M by sodium borohydride. *Inorg. Chem.* 36:593–600, 1997.

Stolzenberg, A. M., J. L. Petersen, and Z. Zhang. F430 model chemistry. A reexamination of the [1,4,7,10,13-pentaazacyclohexa-decane-14,16-dionato(2-)]nickel(II)-induced formation of methane from methyl coenzyme-M. *Inorg. Chem.* 35:4649, 1996.

Renner, M. W., L. R. Furenlid, and **A. M. Stolzenberg.** Effects of metal-centered reduction on the structural, electronic, and coordination properties of nickel and copper octaethylisobacteriochlorin. *J. Am. Chem. Soc.* 117:293, 1995.

Shi, C. S., Q. Zhang, and **K. K. Wang.** Biradicals from thermolysis of N-[2-(1-alkynyl)phenyl]-N'-phenylcarbodiimides and their subsequent transformations to 6H-indolo[2,3-b] quinolines. *J. Org. Chem.* 64:925–32, 1999.

Wang, K. K., H.-R. Zhang, and **J. L. Petersen.** Thermolysis of benzoenyne-allenes to form biradicals and subsequent intramolecular trapping with a tetraarylallene to generate two triarylmethyl radical centers. *J. Org. Chem.* 64:1650–6, 1999.

Shi, C., and **K. K. Wang.** Generation of biradicals and subsequent formation of quinolines and 5H-benzo[b]carbazoles from N-[2-(1-alkynyl)phenyl]keteimines. *J. Org. Chem.* 63:3517–20, 1998.

Wang, K. K., C. Shi, and **J. L. Petersen.** A facile cascade synthesis of 5,6-diaryldibenzo[a,e]cyclooctenes from (Z,Z)-1-aryl-3,5-octadiene-1,7-diynes. *J. Org. Chem.* 63:4413–9, 1998.

Tarli, A., and **K. K. Wang.** Synthesis and thermolysis of enediynyl ethyl ethers as precursors of enyne-ketenes. *J. Org. Chem.* 62:8841–7, 1997.

Liu, B., **K. K. Wang,** and **J. L. Petersen.** Synthesis of (4z)-1,1-diphenyl-1,2,4,6-heptatrien-6-ynes and their facile cycloaromatizations to alpha,3-didehydrotoluene biradicals having a triarylmethyl radical center. *J. Org. Chem.* 61:8503–7, 1996.

Wang, K. K., Z. G. Wang, A. Tarli, and P. Gannett. Cascade radical cyclizations via biradicals generated from (Z)-1,2,4-heptatrien-6-ynes. *J. Am. Chem. Soc.* 118:10783–91, 1996.

Wang, K. K., B. Liu, and **J. L. Petersen.** Benzocyclobutadienes via electrocyclizations of (Z,Z)-3,5-octadiene-1,7-diynes leading to dimers with unusual polycyclic structures. *J. Am. Chem. Soc.* 118:6860–7, 1996.

Wang, K. K., Q. Zhang, and J. K. Liao. Synthesis of 5-methylene-1,3-cyclohexadienes (O-isotoluenes) via electrocyclization of (4z)-1,2,4,6-heptatetraenes. *Tetrahedron Lett.* 37:4087–90, 1996.

Wang, K. K., Z. G. Wang, and P. D. Sattsangi. Synthesis and cycloaromatization of (Z)-1,2,4-heptatrien-6-ynes and (Z)-2,4,5-hexatrienenitriles. *J. Org. Chem.* 61:1516–8, 1996.

YALE UNIVERSITY
Department of Chemistry

Programs of Study

The Department of Chemistry admits students for graduate study leading to the Ph.D. degree. Students may earn an M.S. while working toward the doctorate, but no students are admitted who wish to terminate their studies at the master's level.

The department is divided into four divisions:inorganic, organic, physical, and biophysical. Entering students select the division in which they wish to get their degrees at the beginning of their first semester of study. There are two stages to the Ph.D. program: qualification and the thesis. In order to qualify, the student must complete a certain number of courses with satisfactory grades and pass a qualifying examination. The courses to be taken vary from one division of the department to another and are arranged for each student, taking his or her previous experience into account. The format of the qualifying examination also depends on the division in which the student is enrolled. Qualification is normally completed by the end of the second year. All students are expected to participate in teaching by serving as a teaching assistant in departmental courses for two semesters. This requirement is met by most students in their first year.

Thesis research is unquestionably the most important part of a student's training in the Ph.D. program. By the beginning of the second term of study, students select the faculty member in whose laboratory they will do their research. Full-time research is carried out in the summer between the first and second years. Most students do research part-time while engaged in the final stages of qualifying for the degree in their second year of study and full-time thereafter.

Research Facilities

The Department of Chemistry is located in adjoining buildings, the Sterling Chemistry Laboratory and the Kline Chemistry Laboratory. A substantial amount of this laboratory space has been renovated recently. Most of the department's major research instrumentation is contained in the Yale Chemical Instrumentation Center, which is part of Sterling. Included in the center are two 500-MHz NMR spectrometers, one of them a Bruker WM500 and the second built by the personnel of the center. In addition, there are two Bruker 250-MHz NMR spectrometers, a Kratos mass spectrometer, and equipment for X-ray crystallography. The center also maintains UV, visible, IR, and CD spectrometers along with a laser spectroscopy laboratory. The laboratories of individual faculty members contain the more specialized instruments specific to their research.

The department operates a variety of computers, including a superminicomputer for the use of its faculty and students. These machines are connected to University and national computing networks. A small library devoted to chemical journals and monographs is housed in Sterling Chemistry, and the main science library covering all disciplines is a few steps away.

Financial Aid

Graduate students in the department, including the entering class, receive financial aid. Entering students who do not have outside support receive a nine-month University Fellowship that pays tuition plus a stipend. The details of this support are clearly spelled out in the letter of admission. After the spring of the first year, most students are supported by the research grants of their research director as assistants in research. Those students who are not supported in their later years by their directors' grants are awarded University Fellowships in an amount comparable to the aid they received as first-year students. The 1999–2000 stipend for those supported by teaching or as assistants in research is $17,000 for twelve months, plus tuition. Department fellowships for outstanding applicants increase stipends by modest amounts.

Cost of Study

Tuition is normally covered by a tuition fellowship or tuition remission from a research grant.

Living and Housing Costs

It is estimated that the standard budget for a single student for the academic year 1999–2000 (exclusive of tuition) is $12,000. This includes room and board, transportation, and academic and personal expenses. The estimated standard budget for a married couple is $19,730; this figure increases by approximately $4000 for each dependent.

Student Group

The total number of graduate students in the chemistry department is 135. Postdoctoral students number about 50. A wide variety of ethnic and national backgrounds are represented by these students.

Location

Yale enjoys many of the advantages of a cosmopolitan center without the disadvantages of a congested urban environment. The Greater New Haven area has a population of about 360,000. One of the most extensive urban redevelopment programs ever undertaken in a city of comparable size has made significant improvements to the center of New Haven and its very character. New Haven is 90 minutes from New York by train or car, and Boston is only 3 hours away. The University is an integral part of the worldwide community of scholars, and its central location makes it possible for many distinguished visitors to come to Yale, both from the United States and from abroad.

The University

Yale began to offer graduate education in 1847 and in 1861 conferred the first Ph.D. degrees awarded in North America. In 1876, Yale became the first American university to award the Ph.D. to a black American. With the appointment of a dean in 1892, the Graduate School was formally established. In the same year, women were first admitted as candidates for the doctorate. Today, the Graduate School community includes a growing number of postdoctoral students, fellows, and research associates in addition to its faculty and the many students enrolled in regular degree programs. Besides the Graduate School of Arts and Sciences, Yale's Schools of Architecture, Art, Music, Drama, Forestry and Environmental Studies, Organization and Management, Divinity, Nursing, Medicine, and Law offer graduate-level and professional programs.

Applying

Applications for admission may be obtained by writing to the address below. A nonrefundable fee of $65 must accompany each application. The application deadline is January 2; however, applications received after this date will be considered when possible. All applicants must take the GRE General Test and the Subject Test in chemistry. It is recommended that these tests be taken in September, if possible, and not later than December. Students whose native language is not English are also required to take the Test of English as a Foreign Language (TOEFL) and are strongly encouraged to take the Test of Spoken English (TSE).

Correspondence and Information

Department of Chemistry
Yale University
P.O. Box 208107
New Haven, Connecticut 06520-8107

Telephone: 203-432-3915
Fax: 203-432-6144
World Wide Web: http://www.chem.yale.edu

Yale University

THE FACULTY AND THEIR RESEARCH

Sidney Altman, Professor; Ph.D., Colorado, 1967. Biology: biochemical and biophysical analysis of catalytic RNA reaction mechanism and interaction of the enzyme (RNase P) with its substrates.

David J. Austin, Assistant Professor; Ph.D., Emory, 1993. Organic and bioorganic chemistry: synthesis of biologically interesting molecules, natural product directed target elucidation, protein engineering for biological catalysis.

Gary Brudvig, Professor; Ph.D., Caltech, 1981. Biophysical chemistry:structural and mechanistic studies of photosynthetic water oxidation, application of electron paramagnetic resonance spectroscopy to the study of metalloproteins, biological electron transfer reactions, manganese–enzyme active site model compounds.

Robert H. Crabtree, Professor; Ph.D., Sussex, 1973. Inorganic chemistry: exploratory synthetic and physical studies in transition-metal chemistry and catalysis; fluorocarbon chemistry and C-F activation; combinatorial catalysis.

R. James Cross Jr., Professor; Ph.D., Harvard, 1965. Physical chemistry: fullerene chemistry, detailed dynamics of organic reactions, using crossed molecular beams; theory of inelastic scattering.

Donald M. Crothers, Professor; Ph.D., California, San Diego, 1963. Biophysical chemistry: nucleic acid structure and protein interactions, mechanism of control of gene expression.

John W. Faller, Professor; Ph.D., MIT, 1967. Inorganic chemistry: synthesis and elucidation of structure and bonding of inorganic and organometallic compounds; mechanisms of catalysis; stereoselective and asymmetric synthesis utilizing transition-metal complexes.

Gary L. Haller, Professor; Ph.D., Northwestern, 1966. Chemical engineering and chemistry: heterogeneous catalysis and surface structure and mechanism of catalyzed reactions; catalyst characterization utilizes classical chemisorption and reaction kinetics of sample reactions with several physical methods: UV, IR, EXAFS, NMR, and ESR spectroscopies.

Andrew D. Hamilton, Irénée duPont Professor; Ph.D., Cambridge, 1980. Organic chemistry: organic synthesis applied to biological problems, artificial enzymes, molecular recognition, molecular intervention in cellular biochemistry, anti-cancer drug design.

John F. Hartwig, Professor; Ph.D., Berkeley, 1990. Inorganic and organic chemistry: development and mechanistic analysis of transition metal catalyzed chemistry, including polymerizations; exploratory synthesis of organometallic and transition metal-main group complexes.

Francesco Iachello, J. W. Gibbs Professor of Physics and Chemistry; Dott.Ing.Nucl., Politecnio di Torino (Italy), 1964; Ph.D., MIT, 1969. Physical chemistry: investigation of problems through application of advanced mathematical methods (Lie algebraic methods), algebraic evolution of multidimensional bound-bound/band-free Franck-Condon transition intensities (especially for transitions involving significant changes in equilibrium geometry), study of finite polymer chains (especially their vibrational response to infrared radiation).

Mark A. Johnson, Professor; Ph.D., Stanford, 1983. Physical chemistry: femtosecond kinetics of reactions in clusters, spectroscopic studies of hydrogen bonding in nanosolvated environments, energy transport through weakly bonded networks.

William L. Jorgensen, Professor; Ph.D., Harvard, 1975. Bioorganic chemistry: applications of molecular dynamics, quantum mechanics, and statistical mechanics in organic chemistry and biochemistry; computer simulations of reactions in solution; protein dynamics; protein-ligand binding; molecular recognition; drug design.

J. Michael McBride, Professor; Ph.D., Harvard, 1966. Organic chemistry: physical and chemical properties of organic solids, free-radical reactions, spectroscopic investigation of reactions in single crystals, growth and dissolution of crystals.

Peter B. Moore, Professor; Ph.D., Harvard, 1966. Biophysical chemistry: determination of the structure and function of ribonucleoproteins, especially ribosomes, using NMR and X-ray crystallography.

Martin Saunders, Professor; Ph.D., Harvard, 1956. Organic chemistry:structures and rearrangement processes in carbocations in stable solution, isotopic perturbation, search methods for finding conformers of flexible molecules, molecules containing atoms inside fullerenes.

Alanna Schepartz, Professor; Ph.D., Columbia, 1987. Organic and bioorganic chemistry: molecular recognition in cellular and viral gene expression, protein design, supramolecular chemistry, combinatorial chemistry.

Charles A. Schmuttenmaer, Associate Professor; Ph.D., Berkeley, 1991. Physical chemistry: liquid dynamics and solvation, hydrogen bonding, vibrational energy dissipation in liquids, and transient photoconductivity in solids, all studied with subpicosecond far-infrared pulses.

Robert G. Shulman, Professor; Ph.D., Columbia, 1949. Molecular biophysics and biochemistry and chemistry: study of metabolism in vivo by high-resolution NMR; living systems studied range from *Escherichia coli* to humans and the nuclei followed are ^{31}P, ^{13}C, ^{1}H, ^{23}Na, and ^{39}K; generally, metabolic fluxes are determined and the control of these pathways ascertained.

Dieter Söll, Professor; Ph.D., Stuttgart (Germany), 1962. Molecular biophysics and biochemistry and chemistry: RNA-protein interactions, evolution of translational apparatus in Archaea, functional bacterial genomics.

Thomas A. Steitz, Professor; Ph.D., Harvard, 1966. Molecular biophysics and biochemistry and chemistry: macromolecular structure and function; protein–nucleic acid interaction, including structures of proteins involved in transcription, protein synthesis, DNA replication, and recombination; enzyme mechanism, specificity, and conformational changes; protein crystallography; ribosome structure.

Scott A. Strobel, Ph.D., Caltech, 1992. Molecular biophysics and biochemistry and chemistry: function and structure of RNA utilizing tools of bioorganic chemistry, reaction mechanisms of catalytic RNAs and molecular recognition of RNA by proteins.

John C. Tully, Professor; Ph.D., Chicago, 1968. Theoretical chemistry: dynamics of chemical processes at surfaces and in condensed phases.

Patrick H. Vaccaro, Professor; Ph.D., MIT, 1986. Physical chemistry: state-selective preparation and characterization of energetic molecular species; state-to-state studies of reaction dynamics and relaxation phenomena; development and application of multiple-resonance laser techniques.

John L. Wood, Professor; Ph.D., Pennsylvania, 1991. Organic chemistry: synthetic methods and strategy development, natural product synthesis, and applications of synthesis at the organic chemistry/cellular biology interface.

Frederick E. Ziegler, Professor; Ph.D., Columbia, 1964. Organic chemistry: synthetic methods, free radicals, natural products synthesis.

Kurt W. Zilm, Professor; Ph.D., Utah, 1981. Physical chemistry: solid-state NMR, matrix-isolation NMR of reactive species, surface chemistry, transition-metal polyhydrides, tunneling in NMR, solid-state NMR of RNA and RNA complexes, development of new pulse sequences in solids NMR.

Sterling Chemistry Laboratory is part of the Science Hill quadrangle.

Section 3
Geosciences

This section contains a directory of institutions offering graduate work in geosciences, followed by in-depth entries submitted by institutions that chose to prepare detailed program descriptions. Additional information about programs listed in the directory but not augmented by an in-depth entry may be obtained by writing directly to the dean of a graduate school or chair of a department at the address given in the directory.

For programs offering related work, see all other areas in this book. In Book 2, see Geography; in Book 3, see Biological and Biomedical Sciences, Biophysics, and Botany and Plant Sciences; and in Book 5, see Aerospace/Aeronautical Engineering; Agricultural Engineering; Civil and Environmental Engineering; Engineering and Applied Sciences; Geological, Mineral/Mining, and Petroleum Engineering; Mechanical Engineering and Mechanics; and Energy and Power Engineering (Nuclear Engineering).

CONTENTS

Geochemistry

California Institute of Technology, Division of Geological and Planetary Sciences, Pasadena, CA 91125-0001. Offers cosmochemistry (PhD); geobiology (PhD); geochemistry (MS, PhD); geology (MS, PhD); geophysics (MS, PhD); planetary science (MS, PhD). *Faculty:* 32 full-time (1 woman). *Students:* 58 full-time (22 women); includes 1 minority (Hispanic American), 20 international. Terminal master's awarded for partial completion of doctoral program. *Degree requirements:* For master's, thesis not required; for doctorate, dissertation required. *Entrance requirements:* For doctorate, GRE General Test, GRE Subject Test, TOEFL. *Application deadline:* For fall admission, 1/15. Application fee: $0. *Unit head:* Dr. Edward M. Stolper, Chair, 626-395-6108, Fax: 626-795-6028, E-mail: divgps@gps.caltech.edu. *Application contact:* Dr. George R. Rossman, Division Academic Officer, 626-395-6125, Fax: 626-568-0935, E-mail: divgps@gps.caltech.edu.

California State University, Fullerton, Graduate Studies, School of Natural Science and Mathematics, Department of Chemistry and Biochemistry, Fullerton, CA 92834-9480. Offers analytical chemistry (MS); biochemistry (MS); geochemistry (MS); inorganic chemistry (MS); organic chemistry (MS); physical chemistry (MS). Part-time programs available. *Faculty:* 18 full-time, 14 part-time. *Students:* 8 full-time (3 women), 32 part-time (14 women); includes 19 minority (14 Asian Americans or Pacific Islanders, 5 Hispanic Americans), 6 international. *Degree requirements:* For master's, thesis, departmental qualifying exam required, foreign language not required. *Entrance requirements:* For master's, minimum GPA of 2.5 in last 60 units, major in chemistry or related field. Application fee: $55. Tuition, nonresident: part-time $264 per unit. *Unit head:* Dr. Bruce Weber, Chair, 714-278-3621. *Application contact:* Dr. Gregory Williams, Adviser, 714-278-2170.

Colorado School of Mines, Graduate School, Department of Chemistry and Geochemistry, Program in Geochemistry, Golden, CO 80401-1887. Offers MS, PhD. Part-time programs available. *Students:* 7 full-time (1 woman), 19 part-time (8 women); includes 2 minority (1 Asian American or Pacific Islander, 1 Hispanic American), 3 international. 19 applicants, 89% accepted. In 1998, 2 master's awarded (100% found work related to degree); 2 doctorates awarded (100% found work related to degree). *Degree requirements:* For master's, thesis required, foreign language not required; for doctorate, dissertation, comprehensive exam required, foreign language not required. *Entrance requirements:* For master's and doctorate, GRE General Test (combined average 1840 on three sections), minimum GPA of 3.0. *Application deadline:* Applications are processed on a rolling basis. Application fee: $40. Electronic applications accepted. *Financial aid:* In 1998–99, 18 students received aid, including 1 fellowship, 2 research assistantships, 5 teaching assistantships; unspecified assistantships also available. Aid available to part-time students. *Faculty research:* Geochemical analysis, organic geochemistry, hydrochemical systems, environmental microbiology, process control programming. *Unit head:* Dr. Wendy Harrison, Head, 303-273-3821, E-mail: wharriso@mines.edu.

Colorado School of Mines, Graduate School, Department of Geology and Geological Engineering, Golden, CO 80401-1887. Offers engineering geology (Diploma); exploration geosciences (Diploma); geochemistry (MS, PhD); geological engineering (ME, MS, PhD, Diploma); geology (MS, PhD); hydrogeology (Diploma). Part-time programs available. *Faculty:* 27 full-time (5 women), 23 part-time (0 women). *Students:* 53 full-time (16 women), 68 part-time (19 women); includes 6 minority (3 Asian Americans or Pacific Islanders, 2 Hispanic Americans, 1 Native American), 26 international. *Degree requirements:* For master's, thesis required, foreign language not required; for doctorate, dissertation, comprehensive exam required, foreign language not required; for Diploma, foreign language and thesis not required. *Entrance requirements:* For master's, doctorate, and Diploma, GRE General Test (combined average 1660 on three sections), GRE Subject Test, minimum GPA of 3.0. *Application deadline:* Applications are processed on a rolling basis. Application fee: $40. Electronic applications accepted. *Unit head:* Dr. Roger Slatt, Head, 303-273-3800, E-mail: rslatt@mines.edu. *Application contact:* Marilyn Schwinger, Administrative Assistant, 303-273-3800, Fax: 303-273-3859, E-mail: mschwing@mines.edu.

Columbia University, Graduate School of Arts and Sciences, Division of Natural Sciences, Department of Earth and Environmental Sciences, New York, NY 10027. Offers geochemistry (M Phil, MA, PhD); geodetic sciences (M Phil, MA, PhD); geophysics (M Phil, MA, PhD); oceanography (M Phil, MA, PhD). *Degree requirements:* For master's, thesis or alternative, fieldwork, written exam required, foreign language not required; for doctorate, one foreign language, dissertation required. *Entrance requirements:* For master's and doctorate, GRE General Test, GRE Subject Test, TOEFL, major in natural or physical science. *Faculty research:* Structural geology and stratigraphy, petrology, paleontology, rare gas, isotope and aqueous geochemistry.

Cornell University, Graduate School, Graduate Fields of Engineering, Field of Geological Sciences, Ithaca, NY 14853-0001. Offers economic geology (MS, PhD); engineering geology (MS, PhD); environmental geophysics (M Eng, MS, PhD); general geology (MS, PhD); geobiology (MS, PhD); geochemistry and isotope geology (MS, PhD); geohydrology (M Eng, MS, PhD); geomorphology (MS, PhD); geophysics (MS, PhD); geotectonics (MS, PhD); mineralogy (MS, PhD); paleontology (MS, PhD); petroleum geology (MS, PhD); petrology (MS, PhD); planetary geology (MS, PhD); Precambrian geology (MS, PhD); Quaternary geology (MS, PhD); rock mechanics (MS, PhD); sedimentology (MS, PhD); seismology (MS, PhD); stratigraphy (MS, PhD); structural geology (MS, PhD). *Faculty:* 28 full-time. *Students:* 36 full-time (12 women); includes 4 minority (1 African American, 1 Asian American or Pacific Islander, 2 Hispanic Americans), 16 international. *Degree requirements:* For master's, thesis (MS) required; for doctorate, dissertation required, foreign language not required. *Entrance requirements:* For master's and doctorate, GRE General Test, TOEFL (minimum score of 550 required). *Application deadline:* For fall admission, 1/15. Application fee: $65. Electronic applications accepted. *Unit head:* Director of Graduate Studies, 607-255-3474, Fax: 607-254-4780. *Application contact:* Graduate Field Assistant, 607-255-3474, Fax: 607-254-4780, E-mail: gradprog@geology.cornell.edu.

See in-depth description on page 273.

The George Washington University, Columbian School of Arts and Sciences, Department of Geology, Program in Geochemistry, Washington, DC 20052. Offers MS. *Degree requirements:* For master's, thesis or alternative, comprehensive exam required. *Entrance requirements:* For master's, GRE General Test, bachelor's degree in field, minimum GPA of 3.0. Application fee: $55. Tuition: Full-time $17,328; part-time $722 per credit hour. Required fees: $828; $35 per credit hour. Tuition and fees vary according to campus/location and program. *Financial aid:* Application deadline: 2/1. *Unit head:* Dr. John Lewis, Chair, Department of Geology, 202-994-6190.

Georgia Institute of Technology, Graduate Studies and Research, College of Sciences, School of Earth and Atmospheric Sciences, Atlanta, GA 30332-0001. Offers atmospheric chemistry (MS, PhD); atmospheric dynamics and physics (MS, PhD); geochemistry (MS, PhD); solid-earth geophysics (MS, PhD). Part-time programs available. Terminal master's awarded for partial completion of doctoral program. *Degree requirements:* For master's, thesis or alternative required, foreign language not required; for doctorate, dissertation, comprehensive exams required, foreign language not required. *Entrance requirements:* For master's and doctorate, GRE General Test, TOEFL (minimum score of 550 required), minimum GPA of 2.7. Electronic applications accepted. *Faculty research:* Geophysics, geochemistry, atmospheric chemistry, atmospheric dynamics, seismology.

See in-depth description on page 277.

Indiana University Bloomington, Graduate School, College of Arts and Sciences, Department of Geological Sciences, Program in Geochemistry, Bloomington, IN 47405. Offers MS, PhD. PhD offered through the University Graduate School. *Degree requirements:* For master's, one foreign language (computer language can substitute), thesis or alternative required; for doctorate, dissertation required, dissertation required. *Entrance requirements:* For master's and doctorate, GRE General Test, TOEFL. *Application deadline:* For fall admission, 1/15 (priority date); for spring admission, 9/1 (priority date). Applications are processed on a rolling basis. Application fee: $40. Tuition, state resident: part-time $161 per credit hour. Tuition, nonresident: part-time $468 per credit hour. Required fees: $360 per year. Tuition and fees vary according to course load and program. *Financial aid:* Fellowships with tuition reimbursements, research assistantships with tuition reimbursements, teaching assistantships with tuition reimbursements, career-related internships or fieldwork, Federal Work-Study, and institutionally-sponsored loans available. Financial aid application deadline: 2/15. *Faculty research:* Isotopic and molecular biogeochemistry, stable isotope geochemistry, aqueous and sedimentary geochemistry, trace element petrochemistry, theoretical and computational geochemistry. *Unit head:* Alpa Patel, Graduate Coordinator, 404-651-3120, Fax: 404-651-1416, E-mail: cheaup@panther.gsu.edu. *Application contact:* Mary Iverson, Secretary, Committee for Graduate Studies, 812-855-7214, Fax: 812-855-7899, E-mail: geograd@indiana.edu.

Johns Hopkins University, Zanvyl Krieger School of Arts and Sciences, Department of Earth and Planetary Sciences, Program in Geochemistry, Baltimore, MD 21218-2699. Offers MA, PhD. *Faculty:* 1 full-time (0 women). *Students:* 1 (woman) full-time. Average age 24. In 1998, 2 doctorates awarded (100% entered university research/teaching). Terminal master's awarded for partial completion of doctoral program. *Degree requirements:* For doctorate, dissertation required, foreign language not required. *Entrance requirements:* For master's and doctorate, GRE General Test. *Average time to degree:* Master's–2 years full-time; doctorate–5.5 years full-time. *Application deadline:* For fall admission, 1/15. Application fee: $55. Tuition: Full-time $23,660. Tuition and fees vary according to program. *Financial aid:* Federal Work-Study and institutionally-sponsored loans available. Financial aid application deadline: 3/14; financial aid applicants required to submit FAFSA. *Unit head:* Dr. John M. Ferry, Chair, Department of Earth and Planetary Sciences, 410-516-7135, Fax: 410-516-7933.

Massachusetts Institute of Technology, School of Science, Department of Earth, Atmospheric, and Planetary Sciences, Program in Geology and Geochemistry, Cambridge, MA 02139-4307. Offers SM, PhD, Sc D. *Faculty:* 9 full-time (1 woman). *Students:* 21 full-time (8 women); includes 2 minority (both Hispanic Americans), 4 international. Average age 28. 29 applicants, 24% accepted. In 1998, 2 master's, 2 doctorates awarded. Terminal master's awarded for partial completion of doctoral program. *Degree requirements:* For master's, thesis required, foreign language not required; for doctorate, dissertation, general exam required, foreign language not required. *Entrance requirements:* For master's and doctorate, GRE General Test. *Application deadline:* For fall admission, 1/15; for spring admission, 11/1. Application fee: $55. *Financial aid:* Fellowships, research assistantships, teaching assistantships available. Financial aid application deadline: 1/15. *Unit head:* Dr. Vernon R. Morris, Associate Professor, 202-806-5450, Fax: 202-806-4430, E-mail: vmorris@physics1.howard.edu. *Application contact:* Anastasia Frangos, Administrative Assistant, 617-253-3381, Fax: 617-253-8298, E-mail: eapsinfo@mit.edu.

McMaster University, School of Graduate Studies, Faculty of Science, School of Geography and Geology, Hamilton, ON L8S 4M2, Canada. Offers geochemistry (PhD); geology (M Sc, PhD); human geography (MA, PhD); physical geography (M Sc, PhD). Part-time programs available. *Faculty:* 23 full-time (3 women), 12 part-time (1 woman). *Students:* 49 full-time (24 women), 9 part-time (7 women), 8 international. Terminal master's awarded for partial completion of doctoral program. *Degree requirements:* For master's, thesis required, foreign language not required; for doctorate, dissertation, comprehensive exam required, foreign language not required. *Entrance requirements:* For master's, minimum B+ average. *Application deadline:* For fall admission, 3/15 (priority date). Applications are processed on a rolling basis. Application fee: $50. *Unit head:* Dr. Fred L. Hall, Director, 905-525-9140 Ext. 24196, Fax: 905-546-0463, E-mail: hallfl@mcmaster.ca. *Application contact:* Medy Espiritu, Graduate Secretary, 905-525-9140 Ext. 23535, Fax: 905-522-3141, E-mail: espiritu@mcmaster.ca.

Montana Tech of The University of Montana, Graduate School, Geoscience Program, Butte, MT 59701-8997. Offers geochemistry (MS); geological engineering (MS); geology (MS); geophysical engineering (MS); hydrogeological engineering (MS); hydrogeology (MS); mineral economics (MS). Part-time programs available. *Faculty:* 17 full-time (2 women). *Students:* 15 full-time (6 women), 7 part-time (1 woman); includes 1 minority (Native American) *Degree requirements:* For master's, thesis required (for some programs), foreign language not required. *Entrance requirements:* For master's, GRE General Test, TOEFL (minimum score of 525 required), minimum B average. *Application deadline:* For fall admission, 4/1 (priority date); for spring admission, 10/1 (priority date). Applications are processed on a rolling basis. Application fee: $30. Tuition, state resident: full-time $3,211; part-time $162 per credit hour. Tuition, nonresident: full-time $9,883; part-time $440 per credit hour. International tuition: $15,500 full-time. *Unit head:* Cindy Dunstan, Administrative Assistant, 406-496-4128, Fax: 406-496-4334, E-mail: cdunstan@mtech.edu. *Application contact:* Cindy Dunstan, Administrative Assistant, 406-496-4128, Fax: 406-496-4334, E-mail: cdunstan@mtech.edu.

New Mexico Institute of Mining and Technology, Graduate Studies, Department of Earth and Environmental Science, Program in Geochemistry, Socorro, NM 87801. Offers MS, PhD. *Faculty:* 2 full-time (0 women), 1 part-time (0 women). *Students:* 17 full-time (8 women); includes 1 minority (Hispanic American), 2 international. Average age 30. 14 applicants, 79% accepted. In 1998, 4 master's awarded. *Degree requirements:* For master's, thesis optional, foreign language not required; for doctorate, dissertation required, foreign language not required. *Entrance requirements:* For master's, GRE General Test, TOEFL (minimum score of 540 required); for doctorate, GRE General Test, GRE Subject Test, TOEFL (minimum score of 540 required). *Average time to degree:* Master's–3 years full-time; doctorate–7 years full-time. *Application deadline:* For fall admission, 3/1; for spring admission, 6/1. Applications are processed on a rolling basis. Application fee: $16. *Financial aid:* In 1998–99, 1 fellowship, 9 research assistantships (averaging $9,670 per year), 3 teaching assistantships (averaging $9,670 per year) were awarded.; Federal Work-Study and institutionally-sponsored loans also available. Financial aid application deadline: 3/1; financial aid applicants required to submit CSS PROFILE or FAFSA. *Unit head:* Dr. Phillip Kyle, Coordinator, 505-835-5995, Fax: 505-835-6436, E-mail: geos@nmt.edu. *Application contact:* Dr. David B. Johnson, Dean of Graduate Studies, 505-835-5513, Fax: 505-835-5476, E-mail: graduate@nmt.edu.

Pennsylvania State University University Park Campus, Graduate School, College of Earth and Mineral Sciences, Department of Geosciences, Program in Geochemistry, State College, University Park, PA 16802-1503. Offers MS, PhD. *Entrance requirements:* For master's and doctorate, GRE General Test, TOEFL.

Announcement: Penn State offers MS and PhD research opportunities in high- and low-temperature aqueous geochemistry and geochemical kinetics, igneous and metamorphic petrology, isotope studies, sedimentary geochemistry, organic geochemistry, mineralogy and mineral physics, ore deposits, environmental chemistry, paleoceanography, and the chemistry of global cycles.

Rensselaer Polytechnic Institute, Graduate School, School of Science, Department of Earth and Environmental Sciences, Troy, NY 12180-3590. Offers environmental chemistry (MS, PhD); geochemistry (MS, PhD); geology (MS, PhD); geophysics (MS, PhD); hydrogeology (MS); petrology (MS, PhD); planetary geology (MS, PhD); tectonics (MS, PhD). Part-time programs available. *Faculty:* 7 full-time (0 women), 2 part-time (0 women). *Students:* 19 full-time (8 women), 1 (woman) part-time; includes 2 minority (1 African American, 1 Native American) *Degree requirements:* For master's, thesis required (for some programs); for doctorate, dissertation required. *Entrance requirements:* For master's and doctorate, GRE General Test, TOEFL (minimum score of 550 required). *Application deadline:* For fall admission, 2/1 (priority date). Applications are processed on a rolling basis. Application fee: $35. *Unit head:* Dr. Robert McCaffrey, Chair, 518-276-6474, Fax: 518-276-6680, E-mail: ees@rpi.edu. *Application contact:* Dr. Steven Roecker, Associate Professor, 518-276-6474, Fax: 518-276-6680, E-mail: ees@rpi.edu.

See in-depth description on page 299.

University of California, Los Angeles, Graduate Division, College of Letters and Science, Department of Earth and Space Sciences, Program in Geochemistry, Los Angeles, CA 90095. Offers MS, PhD. *Students:* 4 full-time (2 women), 1 international. 6 applicants, 17% accepted. *Degree requirements:* For master's, comprehensive exams or thesis required; for doctorate, dissertation, oral and written qualifying exams required, foreign language not required. *Entrance requirements:* For master's, GRE General Test, minimum GPA of 3.0; for doctorate, GRE General Test, minimum undergraduate GPA of 3.0. *Application deadline:* For fall admission, 12/15. Application fee: $40. Electronic applications accepted. *Financial aid:* In 1998–99, 3 fellowships, 3 teaching assistantships were awarded.; research assistantships, Federal Work-Study, institutionally-sponsored loans, scholarships, and tuition waivers (full and partial) also available. Financial aid application deadline: 3/1. *Unit head:* Dr. S. Kwok, Chairman, Graduate Affairs, 403-220-5414, Fax: 403-289-3331, E-mail: kwok@acs.ucalgary.ca. *Application contact:* Departmental Office, 888-377-8252, E-mail: verity@ess.ucla.edu.

University of Georgia, Graduate School, College of Arts and Sciences, Department of Geology, Athens, GA 30602. Offers geochemistry (MS, PhD); geophysics (MS, PhD). *Faculty:* 19 full-time (3 women). *Students:* 37 full-time (12 women), 9 part-time (2 women). 35 applicants, 63% accepted. In 1998, 4 master's, 3 doctorates awarded. *Degree requirements:* For master's, thesis required, foreign language not required; for doctorate, one foreign language (computer language can substitute), dissertation required. *Entrance requirements:* For master's and doctorate, GRE General Test. *Application deadline:* For fall admission, 7/1 (priority date); for spring admission, 11/15. Application fee: $30. Electronic applications accepted. *Financial aid:* Fellowships, research assistantships, teaching assistantships, unspecified assistantships available. *Unit head:* Dr. David Wenner, Graduate Coordinator, 706-542-2427, E-mail: dwenner@arches.uga.edu.

University of Hawaii at Manoa, Graduate Division, School of Ocean and Earth Science and Technology, Department of Geology and Geophysics, Honolulu, HI 96822. Offers high-pressure geophysics and geochemistry (MS, PhD); hydrogeology and engineering geology (MS, PhD); marine geology and geophysics (MS, PhD); planetary geosciences and remote sensing (MS, PhD); seismology and solid-earth geophysics (MS, PhD); volcanology, petrology, and geochemistry (MS, PhD). *Faculty:* 84 full-time (10 women). *Students:* 48 full-time (15 women), 9 part-time (4 women); includes 3 minority (1 African American, 2 Asian Americans or Pacific Islanders), 15 international. Terminal master's awarded for partial completion of doctoral program. *Degree requirements:* For master's, thesis required, foreign language not required; for doctorate, dissertation, comprehensive exams required, foreign language not required. *Entrance requirements:* For master's and doctorate, GRE General Test, TOEFL, minimum GPA of 3.0. *Application deadline:* For fall admission, 1/15; for spring admission, 9/1. Application fee: $25 ($50 for international students). *Unit head:* Dr. John Sinton, Chair, 808-956-7640, Fax: 808-956-5512, E-mail: sinton@soest.hawaii.edu. *Application contact:* John Mahoney, Graduate Field Chairperson, 808-956-8763, Fax: 808-956-2538, E-mail: jmahoney@hawaii.edu.

University of Illinois at Chicago, Graduate College, College of Liberal Arts and Sciences, Department of Earth and Environmental Sciences, Chicago, IL 60607-7128. Offers crystallography (MS, PhD); environmental geology (MS, PhD); geochemistry (MS, PhD); geology (MS, PhD); geomorphology (MS, PhD); geophysics (MS, PhD); geotechnical engineering and geosciences (PhD); hydrogeology (MS, PhD); low-temperature and organic geochemistry (MS, PhD); mineralogy (MS, PhD); paleoclimatology (MS, PhD); paleontology (MS, PhD); petrology (MS, PhD); quaternary geology (MS, PhD); sedimentology (MS, PhD); water resources (MS, PhD). *Faculty:* 9 full-time (2 women). *Students:* 8 full-time (2 women), 1 part-time, 2 international. *Degree requirements:* For master's and doctorate, thesis/dissertation required. *Entrance requirements:* For master's and doctorate, GRE General Test, TOEFL (minimum score of 550 required), minimum GPA of 3.75 on a 5.0 scale. *Application deadline:* For fall admission, 7/3; for spring admission, 11/8. Application fee: $40 ($50 for international students). *Unit head:* A. F. Koster Van Groos, Acting Head, 312-996-3153. *Application contact:* Martin Flower, Graduate Director, 312-996-9662.

University of Illinois at Urbana–Champaign, Graduate College, College of Liberal Arts and Sciences, Department of Geology, Urbana, IL 61801. Offers earth sciences (MS, PhD); geochemistry (MS, PhD); geology (MS, PhD); geophysics (MS, PhD). *Faculty:* 14 full-time (1 woman), 4 part-time (0 women). *Students:* 20 full-time (4 women), 11 international. Terminal master's awarded for partial completion of doctoral program. *Degree requirements:* For master's and doctorate, thesis/dissertation required, foreign language not required. *Entrance requirements:* For master's and doctorate, GRE General Test, TOEFL. *Application deadline:* For fall admission, 9/15 (priority date); for spring admission, 1/15. Applications are processed on a rolling basis. Application fee: $40 ($50 for international students). Tuition, state resident: full-time $4,040. Tuition, nonresident: full-time $11,192. Full-time tuition and fees vary according to program. *Unit head:* Jay Bass, Head, 217-333-3540. *Application contact:* Barbara Elmore, Graduate Admissions Secretary, 217-333-3541, Fax: 217-244-4996.

University of Michigan, Horace H. Rackham School of Graduate Studies, College of Literature, Science, and the Arts, Department of Geological Sciences, Program in Oceanography: Marine Geology and Geochemistry, Ann Arbor, MI 48109. Offers MS, PhD. *Faculty:* 4 full-time (0 women), 1 part-time (0 women). *Students:* 4 full-time (3 women). 7 applicants, 57% accepted. Terminal master's awarded for partial completion of doctoral program. *Degree requirements:* For master's, thesis required, foreign language not required; for doctorate, variable foreign

language requirement, dissertation, oral defense of dissertation, preliminary exam required. *Entrance requirements:* For master's, GRE General Test, GRE Subject Test; for doctorate, GRE General Test, GRE Subject Test, master's degree. *Average time to degree:* Master's–2 years full-time; doctorate–5 years full-time. *Application deadline:* For fall admission, 1/15 (priority date). Applications are processed on a rolling basis. Application fee: $55. Electronic applications accepted. *Financial aid:* In 1998–99, 2 students received aid, including 2 research assistantships, 2 teaching assistantships; fellowships, career-related internships or fieldwork and Federal Work-Study also available. *Faculty research:* Paleoceanography, paleolimnology, marine geochemistry, seismic stratigraphy. *Unit head:* David K. Rea, Chair, Department of Geological Sciences, 734-764-1435, Fax: 734-763-4690.

University of Missouri–Rolla, Graduate School, School of Mines and Metallurgy, Department of Geology and Geophysics, Rolla, MO 65409-0910. Offers geochemistry (MS, PhD); geology (MS, PhD); geophysics (MS, PhD); groundwater and environmental geology (MS, PhD). Part-time programs available. *Faculty:* 8 full-time (1 woman). *Students:* 28 full-time (11 women), 7 international. *Degree requirements:* For master's, computer language, thesis required, foreign language not required; for doctorate, computer language, dissertation, departmental qualifying exam required, foreign language not required. *Entrance requirements:* For master's, GRE General Test (minimum combined score of 1100 required), GRE Subject Test, TOEFL (minimum score of 550 required), minimum GPA of 3.0 in last 4 semesters; for doctorate, GRE General Test (minimum combined score of 1100 required), GRE Subject Test, TOEFL (minimum score of 550 required). *Application deadline:* For fall admission, 7/1; for spring admission, 12/1. Applications are processed on a rolling basis. Application fee: $25. Electronic applications accepted. *Unit head:* Dr. Richard D. Hagni, Chairman, 573-341-4616, Fax: 573-341-6935, E-mail: rhagni@umr.edu.

University of Nevada, Reno, Graduate School, Mackay School of Mines, Department of Geological Sciences, Reno, NV 89557. Offers geochemistry (MS, PhD); geological engineering (MS, Geol E); geology (MS, PhD); geophysics (MS, PhD). *Degree requirements:* For master's, thesis optional, foreign language not required; for doctorate, one foreign language, dissertation required. *Entrance requirements:* For master's, GRE General Test, GRE Subject Test, TOEFL (minimum score of 500 required), minimum GPA of 2.75; for doctorate, GRE General Test, GRE Subject Test, TOEFL (minimum score of 500 required), minimum GPA of 3.0. *Faculty research:* Hydrothermal ore deposits, metamorphic and igneous petrogenesis, sedimentary rock record of earth history, field and petrographic investigation of magnetism, rock fracture mechanics.

University of New Hampshire, Graduate School, College of Engineering and Physical Sciences, Department of Earth Sciences, Durham, NH 03824. Offers earth sciences (MS, PhD), including geochemical (MS); geology, hydrology (PhD); oceanography; hydrology (MS). *Faculty:* 25 full-time. *Students:* 32 full-time (7 women), 36 part-time (15 women); includes 1 minority (Asian American or Pacific Islander), 10 international. *Degree requirements:* For master's, thesis required, foreign language not required; for doctorate, dissertation required. *Entrance requirements:* For master's and doctorate, GRE General Test. *Application deadline:* For fall admission, 4/1 (priority date). Applications are processed on a rolling basis. Application fee: $50. Tuition, area resident: Full-time $5,750; part-time $319 per credit. Tuition, state resident: full-time $8,625. Tuition, nonresident: full-time $14,640; part-time $598 per credit. Required fees: $224 per semester. Tuition and fees vary according to course load, degree level and program. *Unit head:* Wallace Bothner, Chairperson, 603-862-1718. *Application contact:* Dr. Francis Birch, Graduate Coordinator, 603-862-3142.

University of Victoria, Faculty of Graduate Studies, Faculty of Science, School of Earth and Ocean Sciences, Victoria, BC V8W 2Y2, Canada. Offers geochemistry (M Sc, PhD); geophysics (M Sc, PhD); marine geology and geophysics (M Sc, PhD); ocean acoustics (M Sc, PhD); oceanography (M Sc, PhD); paleobiology (M Sc, PhD); paleoceanography (M Sc, PhD); sedimentology (M Sc, PhD); stratigraphy (M Sc, PhD). Part-time programs available. *Faculty:* 15 full-time, 41 part-time. *Students:* 39 full-time (0 women), 1 part-time. *Degree requirements:* For master's and doctorate, thesis/dissertation required. *Application deadline:* For fall admission, 2/15. Applications are processed on a rolling basis. Application fee: $50. Electronic applications accepted. *Unit head:* Dr. C. R. Barnes, Director, 250-721-6120, Fax: 250-721-6200, E-mail: crbarnes@uvic.ca. *Application contact:* Dr. Dante Canil, Graduate Adviser, 250-721-6120, Fax: 250-721-6200, E-mail: dcanil@uvic.ca.

Washington University in St. Louis, Graduate School of Arts and Sciences, Department of Earth and Planetary Sciences, St. Louis, MO 63130-4899. Offers earth and planetary sciences (MA); geochemistry (PhD); geology (MA, PhD); geophysics (PhD); planetary sciences (PhD). *Students:* 26 full-time (11 women); includes 2 minority (1 Asian American or Pacific Islander, 1 Native American), 4 international. Terminal master's awarded for partial completion of doctoral program. *Degree requirements:* For master's and doctorate, thesis/dissertation required. *Entrance requirements:* For master's and doctorate, GRE General Test. *Application deadline:* For fall admission, 1/15 (priority date). Applications are processed on a rolling basis. Application fee: $35. *Unit head:* Dr. Raymond E. Arvidson, Chairman, 314-935-5610.

Yale University, Graduate School of Arts and Sciences, Department of Geology and Geophysics, New Haven, CT 06520. Offers geochemistry (PhD); geophysics (PhD); meteorology (PhD); mineralogy and crystallography (PhD); oceanography (PhD); paleoecology (PhD); paleontology and stratigraphy (PhD); petrology (PhD); structural geology (PhD). *Faculty:* 26. *Students:* 26 full-time (11 women), 9 international. *Degree requirements:* For doctorate, dissertation required, foreign language not required. *Entrance requirements:* For doctorate, GRE General Test, TOEFL. *Application deadline:* For fall admission, 1/4. Application fee: $65. *Unit head:* Chair, 203-432-3174. *Application contact:* Admissions Information, 203-432-2770.

See in-depth description on page 327.

Geodetic Sciences

Columbia University, Graduate School of Arts and Sciences, Division of Natural Sciences, Department of Earth and Environmental Sciences, New York, NY 10027. Offers geochemistry (M Phil, MA, PhD); geodetic sciences (M Phil, MA, PhD); geophysics (M Phil, MA, PhD); oceanography (M Phil, MA, PhD). *Degree requirements:* For master's, thesis or alternative, fieldwork, written exam required, foreign language not required; for doctorate, one foreign language, dissertation required. *Entrance requirements:* For master's and doctorate, GRE General Test, GRE Subject Test, TOEFL, major in natural or physical science. *Faculty research:* Structural geology and stratigraphy, petrology, paleontology, rare gas, isotope and aqueous geochemistry.

The Ohio State University, Graduate School, College of Engineering, Department of Civil and Environmental Engineering and Geodetic Science, Program in Geodetic Science and Surveying, Columbus, OH 43210. Offers MS, PhD. *Faculty:* 10 full-time, 3 part-time. *Students:* 55 full-time (6 women), 3 part-time; includes 6 minority (4 African Americans, 1 Asian American or Pacific Islander, 1 Hispanic American), 42 international. 50 applicants, 54% accepted. In 1998, 18 master's, 5 doctorates awarded. *Degree requirements:* For master's, computer language required, thesis optional, foreign language not required; for doctorate, computer language, dissertation required, foreign language not required. *Application deadline:* For fall admission, 8/15. Applications are processed on a rolling basis. Application fee: $30 ($40 for

international students). *Financial aid:* Fellowships, research assistantships, teaching assistantships, Federal Work-Study and institutionally-sponsored loans available. Aid available to part-time students. *Faculty research:* Photogrammetry, cartography, geodesy, land information systems. *Unit head:* Rongxing Li, Graduate Studies Committee Chair, 614-292-6753, Fax: 614-292-3780, E-mail: li.282@osu.edu.

Université Laval, Faculty of Graduate Studies, Faculty of Forestry and Geomatics, Department of Geomatics Sciences, Sainte-Foy, PQ G1K 7P4, Canada. Offers M Sc, PhD. *Students:* 37 full-time (9 women), 10 part-time (4 women). 29 applicants, 52% accepted. In 1998, 8 master's, 1 doctorate awarded. *Application deadline:* For fall admission, 3/1. Application fee: $30. *Unit head:* Jacques Jobin, Director, 418-656-2131 Ext. 7182, Fax: 418-656-7411, E-mail: scg@scg.ulaval.ca.

University of New Brunswick, School of Graduate Studies, Faculty of Engineering, Department of Geodesy and Geomatics, Fredericton, NB E3B 5A3, Canada. Offers land information management (Diploma); mapping, charting and geodesy (Diploma); surveying engineering (M Eng, M Sc E, PhD). Part-time programs available. *Degree requirements:* For master's, thesis required, foreign language not required; for doctorate, dissertation, qualifying exam required, foreign language not required; for degree. *Entrance requirements:* For master's and doctorate, TOEFL, TWE, minimum GPA of 3.0; for Diploma, TOEFL, TWE.

Geology

Acadia University, Faculty of Pure and Applied Science, Department of Geology, Wolfville, NS B0P 1X0, Canada. Offers M Sc. *Faculty:* 7 full-time (2 women), 1 part-time (0 women). *Students:* 2 full-time (1 woman), 1 part-time. Average age 37. 3 applicants, 33% accepted. *Degree requirements:* For master's, thesis required, foreign language not required. *Application deadline:* For fall admission, 2/1 (priority date). Applications are processed on a rolling basis. Application fee: $25. *Expenses:* Tuition and fees charges are reported in Canadian dollars. Tuition, state resident: full-time $4,361 Canadian dollars. International tuition: $8,722 Canadian dollars full-time. Required fees: $147 Canadian dollars. Full-time tuition and fees vary according to program and student level. *Financial aid:* Fellowships, teaching assistantships, career-related internships or fieldwork available. Financial aid application deadline: 2/1. *Faculty research:* Igneous, metamorphic, and Quaternary geology; stratigraphy; remote sensing; micropaleontology. Total annual research expenditures: $75,000. *Unit head:* Dr. Robert Raeside, Head, 902-585-1208, Fax: 902-585-1816, E-mail: geology@acadiau.ca. *Application contact:* Dr. Sandra Barr, Graduate Coordinator, 902-585-1340, Fax: 902-585-1816, E-mail: sandra.barr@acadiau.ca.

Auburn University, Graduate School, College of Sciences and Mathematics, Department of Geology, Auburn, Auburn University, AL 36849-0002. Offers MS. Part-time programs available. *Faculty:* 10 full-time (1 woman). *Students:* 7 full-time (3 women), 12 part-time (1 woman). 11 applicants, 55% accepted. In 1998, 7 degrees awarded. *Degree requirements:* For master's, computer language or G.I.S., field camp required. *Entrance requirements:* For master's, GRE General Test. *Application deadline:* For fall admission, 9/1; for spring admission, 3/1. Applications are processed on a rolling basis. Application fee: $25 ($50 for international students). Tuition, state resident: full-time $2,760; part-time $76 per credit hour. Tuition, nonresident: full-time $8,280; part-time $228 per credit hour. *Financial aid:* Research assistantships, teaching assistantships, Federal Work-Study available. Aid available to part-time students. Financial aid application deadline: 3/15. *Faculty research:* Empirical magma dynamics and melt migration, ore mineralogy, role of terrestrial plant biomass in deposition, metamorphic petrology and isotope geochemistry, reef development, crinoid taphology. *Unit head:* Dr. Robert B. Cook, Head, 334-844-4282. *Application contact:* Dr. John F. Pritchett, Dean of the Graduate School, 334-844-4700.

Announcement: The master's program offers a broad-based curriculum that takes advantage of Auburn's location on the boundary between the Appalachian front and the Gulf Coastal Plain. Low student-faculty ratio results in small class size, close relationships between students and faculty members, and relaxed and informal atmosphere. Research opportunities include aqueous and hydrothermal geochemistry; economic geology, petrochemistry, and tectonics of the southern Appalachians; environmental geophysics; coastal-plain stratigraphy/sedimentology; and taphonomy and paleoecology of Phanerozoic megafloral and invertebrate assemblages. Current investigations extend beyond the region to other areas in the US as well as the Bahamas, Borneo, Scandinavia, central Europe, and Bolivia. For additional information, visit the Web site: http://www.auburn.edu/academic/science_math/geology/docs.

Ball State University, Graduate School, College of Sciences and Humanities, Department of Geology, Muncie, IN 47306-1099. Offers MA, MS. *Faculty:* 5. *Students:* 4 full-time (2 women), 5 part-time (2 women). Average age 25. 15 applicants, 53% accepted. In 1998, 3 degrees awarded. *Degree requirements:* For master's, thesis (MS) required. Application fee: $15 ($25 for international students). *Financial aid:* Teaching assistantships, career-related internships or fieldwork available. *Faculty research:* Environmental geology, geophysics, stratigraphy. *Unit head:* Dr. Alan Samuelson, Chairman, 765-285-8270, E-mail: asamuels@bsu.edu. *Application contact:* Scott Rice-Snow, Director of Graduate Programs, E-mail: ricesnow@bsu.edu.

Baylor University, Graduate School, College of Arts and Sciences, Department of Geology, Waco, TX 76798. Offers earth science (MA); geology (MS, PhD). *Faculty:* 12 full-time (1 woman). *Students:* 24 full-time (8 women), 6 part-time (2 women); includes 2 minority (both Hispanic Americans), 4 international. In 1998, 10 master's, 1 doctorate awarded. *Degree requirements:* For master's, thesis required, foreign language not required; for doctorate, dissertation required, dissertation required. *Entrance requirements:* For master's, GRE General Test, GRE Subject Test; for doctorate, GRE General Test. *Application deadline:* For fall admission, 3/15 (priority date). Applications are processed on a rolling basis. Application fee: $25. *Financial aid:* In 1998–99, 18 teaching assistantships were awarded.; Federal Work-Study and institutionally-sponsored loans also available. *Faculty research:* Petroleum geology, geophysics, engineering geology, hydrogeology. *Unit head:* Dr. Thomas T. Goforth, Chairman, 254-710-2361, Fax: 254-710-2673, E-mail: thomas_goforth@baylor.edu. *Application contact:* Suzanne Keener, Administrative Assistant, 254-710-3588, Fax: 254-710-3870, E-mail: suzanne_keener@baylor.edu.

Boise State University, Graduate College, College of Arts and Sciences, Department of Geosciences, Program in Geology, Boise, ID 83725-0399. Offers MS. Part-time programs available. *Faculty:* 9 full-time (0 women), 21 part-time (3 women). *Students:* 12 full-time (1 woman), 10 part-time (2 women), 1 international. Average age 36. 9 applicants, 100% accepted. *Degree requirements:* For master's, computer language, thesis required. *Entrance requirements:* For master's, GRE General Test, minimum GPA of 3.0, BS in related field. *Application deadline:* For fall admission, 7/23 (priority date); for spring admission, 11/24. Applications are processed on a rolling basis. Application fee: $20 ($30 for international students). Electronic applications accepted. *Financial aid:* In 1998–99, 16 students received aid, including 4 research assistantships with full tuition reimbursements available (averaging $11,500 per year); career-related internships or fieldwork, Federal Work-Study, institutionally-sponsored loans, and unspecified assistantships also available. Aid available to part-time students. Financial aid application deadline: 3/1. *Unit head:* Dr. C. J. Northrup, Coordinator, 208-426-1009.

Boston College, Graduate School of Arts and Sciences, Department of Geology and Geophysics, Chestnut Hill, MA 02467-3800. Offers MS, MBA/MS. *Faculty:* 8 full-time (0 women). *Students:* 17 full-time (8 women), 12 part-time (6 women); includes 2 minority (1 Asian American or Pacific Islander, 1 Hispanic American), 4 international. 23 applicants, 78% accepted. In 1998, 6 degrees awarded. *Degree requirements:* For master's, thesis required, foreign language not required. *Entrance requirements:* For master's, GRE General Test, GRE Subject Test. *Application deadline:* For fall admission, 2/1 (priority date). Application fee: $40. *Financial aid:* Research assistantships, teaching assistantships, Federal Work-Study available. Aid available to part-time students. Financial aid application deadline: 3/15; financial aid applicants required to submit FAFSA. *Faculty research:* Coastal and marine geology, experimental sedimentology, geomagnetism, igneous petrology, paleontology. *Unit head:* Dr. Christopher Hepburn, Chairperson, 617-552-3640, E-mail: christopher.hepburn@bc.edu. *Application contact:* Dr. John Ebel, Graduate Program Director, 617-552-3640, E-mail: john.ebel@bc.edu.

Bowling Green State University, Graduate College, College of Arts and Sciences, Department of Geology, Bowling Green, OH 43403. Offers MAT, MS. Part-time programs available. *Faculty:* 7 full-time (1 woman). *Students:* 20 full-time (3 women), 1 (woman) part-time; includes 1 minority (African American), 2 international. 20 applicants, 75% accepted. In 1998, 9 degrees awarded. *Degree requirements:* For master's, thesis required, foreign language not required. *Entrance requirements:* For master's, GRE General Test, GRE Subject Test, TOEFL (minimum score of 570 required). *Application deadline:* For fall admission, 3/1; for spring admission, 11/1. Application fee: $30. Electronic applications accepted. *Financial aid:* Research assistantships with full tuition reimbursements, teaching assistantships with full tuition reimbursements, career-related internships or fieldwork, institutionally-sponsored loans, tuition waivers (full), and unspecified assistantships available. Financial aid applicants required to submit FAFSA. *Faculty research:* Remote sensing, environmental geology, geological information systems, structural geology, geochemistry, mineralogy, petrology. *Unit head:* Dr. Joseph Frizado, Chair, 419-372-2886. *Application contact:* Dr. Charles Onasch, Graduate Coordinator, 419-372-7197.

Brigham Young University, Graduate Studies, College of Physical and Mathematical Sciences, Department of Geology, Provo, UT 84602-1001. Offers MS. *Faculty:* 13 full-time (0 women), 1 part-time (0 women). *Students:* 19 full-time (6 women), 2 international. Average age 24. 8 applicants, 50% accepted. In 1998, 5 degrees awarded. *Degree requirements:* For master's, thesis required. *Entrance requirements:* For master's, GRE General Test (score in 50th percentile or higher required), minimum GPA of 3.0 in last 60 hours. *Average time to degree:* Master's–3 years full-time. *Application deadline:* For fall admission, 2/1 (priority date). Applications are processed on a rolling basis. Application fee: $30. Tuition: Full-time $3,330; part-time $185 per credit hour. Tuition and fees vary according to program and student's religious affiliation. *Financial aid:* In 1998–99, 17 students received aid, including 1 research assistantship (averaging $12,000 per year), 7 teaching assistantships (averaging $12,000 per year); fellowships, career-related internships or fieldwork, institutionally-sponsored loans, scholarships, and tuition waivers (partial) also available. Financial aid application deadline: 2/1. *Faculty research:* Regional tectonics, hydrogeochemistry, crystal chemistry and crystallography, stratigraphy, environmental geophysics. Total annual research expenditures: $48,500. *Unit head:* Dr. Bart J. Kowallis, Chairman, 801-378-3918, Fax: 801-378-8143. *Application contact:* Dr. Jeffrey D. Keith, Graduate Coordinator, 801-378-2189, Fax: 801-378-8143.

Brooklyn College of the City University of New York, Division of Graduate Studies, Department of Geology, Brooklyn, NY 11210-2889. Offers applied geology (MA); geology (MA, PhD). Evening/weekend programs available. *Faculty:* 5 full-time (0 women). Average age 24. 6 applicants, 67% accepted. In 1998, 1 degree awarded. *Degree requirements:* For master's, computer language, comprehensive and qualifying exams required, foreign language and thesis not required. *Entrance requirements:* For master's, TOEFL (minimum score of 550 required), bachelor's degree in geology or equivalent, fieldwork. *Average time to degree:* Master's–2 years full-time, 3 years part-time. *Application deadline:* For fall admission, 3/1; for spring admission, 11/1. Applications are processed on a rolling basis. Application fee: $40. *Financial aid:* In 1998–99, 9 students received aid, including 2 fellowships, 1 research assistantship, 6 teaching assistantships; career-related internships or fieldwork, Federal Work-Study, institutionally-sponsored loans, scholarships, and tuition waivers (full and partial) also available. Aid available to part-time students. Financial aid application deadline: 5/1; financial aid applicants required to submit FAFSA. *Faculty research:* Geochemistry, petrology, tectonophysics, hydrogeology, sedimentary geology, environmental geology. *Unit head:* Dr. Nehru Cherukupalli, Chairperson, 718-951-5416, Fax: 718-951-4753. *Application contact:* Dr. William H. Harris, Graduate Deputy, 718-951-4809, Fax: 718-951-4753, E-mail: wharris@brooklyn.cuny.edu.

Bryn Mawr College, Graduate School of Arts and Sciences, Department of Geology, Bryn Mawr, PA 19010-2899. Offers MA, PhD. *Faculty:* 5. *Students:* 1 (woman) full-time, 3 part-time. 2 applicants, 100% accepted. *Degree requirements:* For master's, thesis required; for doctorate, dissertation required. *Entrance requirements:* For master's and doctorate, GRE General Test. *Application deadline:* For fall admission, 6/30. Application fee: $40. *Financial aid:* Fellowships, research assistantships, teaching assistantships, Federal Work-Study, institutionally-sponsored loans, and tuition awards available. Aid available to part-time students. Financial aid application deadline: 1/2. *Unit head:* Dr. M. L. Crawford, Chairman, 610-526-5115. *Application contact:* Graduate School of Arts and Sciences, 610-526-5072.

California Institute of Technology, Division of Geological and Planetary Sciences, Pasadena, CA 91125-0001. Offers cosmochemistry (PhD); geobiology (PhD); geochemistry (MS, PhD); geology (MS, PhD); geophysics (MS, PhD); planetary science (MS, PhD). *Faculty:* 32 full-time (1 woman). *Students:* 58 full-time (22 women); includes 1 minority (Hispanic American), 20 international. Average age 26. 82 applicants, 32% accepted. In 1998, 4 master's awarded (0% continued full-time study); 14 doctorates awarded. Terminal master's awarded for partial completion of doctoral program. *Degree requirements:* For master's, thesis not required; for doctorate, dissertation required. *Entrance requirements:* For doctorate, GRE General Test, GRE Subject Test, TOEFL. *Average time to degree:* Master's–3 years full-time; doctorate–6 years full-time. *Application deadline:* For fall admission, 1/15. Application fee: $0. *Financial aid:* In 1998–99, 58 students received aid, including 3 fellowships with full tuition reimbursements available (averaging $17,660 per year), research assistantships with full tuition reimbursements available (averaging $17,660 per year); teaching assistantships, institutionally-sponsored loans also available. Financial aid applicants required to submit FAFSA. Total annual research expenditures: $11.2 million. *Unit head:* Dr. Edward M. Stolper, Chair, 626-395-6108, Fax: 626-795-6028, E-mail: divgps@gps.caltech.edu. *Application contact:* Dr. George R. Rossman, Division Academic Officer, 626-395-6125, Fax: 626-568-0935, E-mail: divgps@gps.caltech.edu.

California State University, Bakersfield, Graduate Studies and Research, School of Arts and Sciences, Program in Geology, Bakersfield, CA 93311-1099. Offers geology (MS); hydrology (MS). Part-time and evening/weekend programs available. *Degree requirements:* For master's, computer language, thesis required. *Entrance requirements:* For master's, GRE General Test, BS in geology.

California State University, Fresno, Division of Graduate Studies, School of Natural Sciences, Department of Geology, Fresno, CA 93740-0057. Offers MS. Part-time programs available. *Faculty:* 7 full-time (1 woman). *Students:* 4 full-time (0 women), 5 part-time, 1 international. Average age 31. 3 applicants, 67% accepted. *Degree requirements:* For master's, thesis required, foreign language not required. *Entrance requirements:* For master's, GRE General Test, GRE Subject Test, TOEFL (minimum score of 550 required), undergraduate geology degree, minimum GPA of 2.7. *Average time to degree:* Master's–3.5 years full-time. *Application deadline:* For fall admission, 8/1 (priority date); for spring admission, 12/1. Applications are processed on a rolling basis. Application fee: $55. Electronic applications accepted. Tuition, nonresident: part-time $246 per unit. Required fees: $1,906; $620 per semester. *Financial aid:* In 1998–99, 6 teaching assistantships were awarded.; fellowships, career-related internships or fieldwork, Federal Work-Study, and scholarships also available. Financial aid application deadline: 3/1; financial aid applicants required to submit FAFSA. *Faculty research:* Water drainage, pollution, cartography. *Unit head:* Dr. Fraka Harmsen, Chair, 559-278-3086, Fax: 559-278-5980, E-mail: fraka_harmsen@csufresno.edu.

California State University, Hayward, Graduate Programs, School of Science, Department of Geological Sciences, Hayward, CA 94542-3000. Offers geology (MS). Evening/weekend programs available. *Faculty:* 6 full-time (3 women). *Students:* 3 full-time (1 woman), 7 part-time (2 women). 2 applicants, 100% accepted. In 1998, 3 degrees awarded. *Degree requirements:* For master's, thesis required, foreign language not required. *Entrance requirements:* For master's, GRE, minimum GPA of 2.75 in field, 2.5 overall. Application fee: $55. Tuition, nonresident: part-time $164 per unit. Required fees: $587 per quarter. *Financial aid:* Career-related internships or fieldwork, Federal Work-Study, and institutionally-sponsored loans available. Aid available to part-time students. Financial aid application deadline: 3/1. *Unit head:* Dr. Nancy Fegan, Chair, 510-885-3486. *Application contact:* Jennifer Rice, Graduate Program Assistant, 510-885-3286, Fax: 510-885-4795, E-mail: gradprograms@csuhayward.edu.

California State University, Long Beach, Graduate Studies, College of Natural Sciences, Department of Geological Sciences, Long Beach, CA 90840. Offers MS. Part-time programs available. *Faculty:* 8 full-time (3 women), 2 part-time (0 women). Average age 35. 14 applicants, 79% accepted. *Degree requirements:* For master's, thesis required, foreign language not required. *Entrance requirements:* For master's, GRE General Test. *Application deadline:* For fall admission, 8/1; for spring admission, 12/1. Applications are processed on a rolling basis. Application fee: $55. Electronic applications accepted. Tuition, nonresident: part-time $246 per unit. Required fees: $569 per semester. Tuition and fees vary according to course load. *Financial aid:* In 1998–99, 9 students received aid; research assistantships, teaching assistantships, Federal Work-Study, grants, and institutionally-sponsored loans available. Financial aid application deadline: 3/2. *Faculty research:* Paleontology, geophysics, structural geology, organic geochemistry, sedimentary geology. *Unit head:* Dr. Stanley C. Finney, Chair, 562-985-4809, Fax: 562-985-8638, E-mail: scfinney@csulb.edu. *Application contact:* Dr. James Sample, Graduate Coordinator, 562-985-4589, Fax: 562-985-8638, E-mail: csample@csulb.edu.

California State University, Los Angeles, Graduate Studies, School of Natural and Social Sciences, Department of Geology, Los Angeles, CA 90032-8530. Offers MS. Offered jointly with California State University, Northridge. Part-time and evening/weekend programs available. *Faculty:* 6 full-time, 7 part-time. *Students:* 2 full-time (1 woman), 19 part-time (5 women); includes 3 minority (2 Asian Americans or Pacific Islanders, 1 Hispanic American), 2 international. In 1998, 3 degrees awarded. *Degree requirements:* For master's, comprehensive exam or thesis required. *Entrance requirements:* For master's, TOEFL (minimum score of 550 required). *Application deadline:* For fall admission, 6/30; for spring admission, 2/1. Applications are processed on a rolling basis. Application fee: $55. *Financial aid:* In 1998–99, 7 students received aid. Federal Work-Study available. Aid available to part-time students. Financial aid application deadline: 3/1. *Unit head:* Dr. Robert Stull, Chair, 323-343-2400.

California State University, Northridge, Graduate Studies, College of Science and Mathematics, Department of Geological Sciences, Northridge, CA 91330. Offers MS. Part-time and evening/weekend programs available. *Faculty:* 12 full-time, 1 part-time. *Students:* 3 full-time (1 woman), 12 part-time (5 women); includes 2 minority (both Hispanic Americans), 2 international. Average age 35. 11 applicants, 100% accepted. In 1998, 5 degrees awarded. *Degree requirements:* For master's, computer language, thesis required, foreign language not required. *Entrance requirements:* For master's, GRE General Test, TOEFL, minimum GPA of 2.75. *Application deadline:* For fall admission, 11/30. Application fee: $55. Tuition, nonresident: part-time $246 per unit. International tuition: $7,874 full-time. Required fees: $1,970. Tuition and fees vary according to course load. *Financial aid:* Research assistantships, teaching assistantships, Federal Work-Study available. Financial aid application deadline: 3/1. *Faculty research:* Petrology of California Miocene volcanics, sedimentology of California Miocene formations, Eocene gastropods, structure of White/Inyo Mountains, seismology of Californian and Mexican earthquakes. *Unit head:* Dr. Eugene Fritsche, Chair, 818-677-3541. *Application contact:* Dr. Eugene Fritsche, Chair, 818-677-3541.

Case Western Reserve University, School of Graduate Studies, Department of Geological Sciences, Cleveland, OH 44106. Offers MS, PhD. Part-time programs available. Terminal master's awarded for partial completion of doctoral program. *Degree requirements:* For master's, thesis or alternative required; for doctorate, dissertation required. *Entrance requirements:* For master's and doctorate, GRE General Test, GRE Subject Test, TOEFL (minimum score of 550 required). *Faculty research:* Geochemistry, hydrology, geochronology, paleoclimates, geomorphology.

Central Washington University, Graduate Studies and Research, College of the Sciences, Department of Geology, Ellensburg, WA 98926. Offers MS. *Faculty:* 7 full-time (3 women). *Students:* 9 full-time (6 women), 2 part-time; includes 1 minority (African American) 9 applicants, 56% accepted. In 1998, 1 degree awarded. *Degree requirements:* For master's, thesis required. *Entrance requirements:* For master's, GRE General Test, minimum GPA of 3.0. *Application deadline:* For fall admission, 4/1 (priority date); for winter admission, 10/1; for spring admission, 1/1. Applications are processed on a rolling basis. Application fee: $35. Tuition, state resident: full-time $4,389; part-time $146 per credit. Tuition, nonresident: full-time $13,365; part-time $446 per credit. Tuition and fees vary according to course load. *Financial aid:* In 1998–99, 2 research assistantships with partial tuition reimbursements (averaging $6,470 per year), 5 teaching assistantships with partial tuition reimbursements (averaging $6,470 per year) were awarded.; career-related internships or fieldwork and Federal Work-Study also available. Financial aid application deadline: 2/15; financial aid applicants required to submit FAFSA. *Unit head:* Dr. Lisa Ely, Chair, 509-963-2701. *Application contact:* Christie A. Fevergeon, Program Coordinator, Graduate Studies and Research, 509-963-3103, Fax: 509-963-1799, E-mail: masters@cwu.edu.

Cleveland State University, College of Graduate Studies, College of Arts and Sciences, Department of Biological, Geological and Environmental Sciences, Cleveland, OH 44115-2440. Offers MS, PhD. Part-time programs available. *Faculty:* 18 full-time (3 women). *Students:* 3 full-time (2 women), 45 part-time (25 women); includes 5 minority (3 African Americans, 2 Asian Americans or Pacific Islanders), 9 international. Average age 32. 30 applicants, 30% accepted. In 1998, 5 master's, 5 doctorates awarded. Terminal master's awarded for partial completion of doctoral program. *Degree requirements:* For doctorate, dissertation required, foreign language not required, foreign language not required. *Entrance requirements:* For master's and doctorate, GRE General Test, GRE Subject Test. *Application deadline:* For fall admission, 9/1 (priority date). Applications are processed on a rolling basis. Application fee: $25. *Financial aid:* In 1998–99, 12 research assistantships, 15 teaching assistantships were awarded.; institutionally-sponsored loans and unspecified assistantships also available. *Faculty research:* Physiology, biochemistry/neurochemistry, immunology, taxonomic botany, molecular parasitology. *Unit head:* Dr. Michael Gates, Interim Chairperson, 216-687-3917, Fax: 216-687-6972, E-mail: gates@biology.csuohio.edu. *Application contact:* Director, 216-687-2440.

Colgate University, Graduate Programs, Department of Geology, Hamilton, NY 13346-1386. Offers MA. Part-time programs available. *Degree requirements:* For master's, thesis required, foreign language not required. *Entrance requirements:* For master's, GRE General Test. *Application deadline:* For fall admission, 3/15. Application fee: $50. *Financial aid:* Research assistantships, institutionally-sponsored loans and tuition waivers (partial) available. Financial aid application deadline: 2/1. *Faculty research:* Geochemistry, clay mineralogy, sedimentology, sedimentary petrology. *Unit head:* Dr. Connie Soja, Chair, 315-228-7201.

Colorado School of Mines, Graduate School, Department of Geology and Geological Engineering, Golden, CO 80401-1887. Offers engineering geology (Diploma); exploration geosciences (Diploma); geochemistry (MS, PhD); geological engineering (ME, MS, PhD, Diploma); geology (MS, PhD); hydrogeology (Diploma). Part-time programs available. *Faculty:* 27 full-time (5 women), 23 part-time (0 women). *Students:* 53 full-time (16 women), 68 part-time (19 women); includes 6 minority (3 Asian Americans or Pacific Islanders, 2 Hispanic Americans, 1 Native American), 26 international. 90 applicants, 56% accepted. In 1998, 15 master's awarded (100% found work related to degree); 6 doctorates awarded (100% found work related to degree). *Degree requirements:* For master's, thesis required, foreign language not required; for doctorate, dissertation, comprehensive exam required, foreign language not required; for Diploma, foreign language and thesis not required. *Entrance requirements:* For master's, doctorate, and Diploma, GRE General Test (combined average 1660 on three sections), GRE Subject Test, minimum GPA of 3.0. *Application deadline:* Applications are processed on a rolling basis. Application fee: $40. Electronic applications accepted. *Financial aid:* In 1998–99, 54 students received aid, including 6 fellowships, 18 research assistantships, 15 teaching assistantships; unspecified assistantships also available. Aid available to part-time students. Financial aid applicants required to submit FAFSA. *Faculty research:* Predictive sediment modeling, petrophysics, aquifer-contaminant flow modeling, water-rock interactions, geotechnical engineering. Total annual research expenditures: $1.2 million. *Unit head:* Dr. Roger Slatt, Head, 303-273-3800, E-mail: rslatt@mines.edu. *Application contact:* Marilyn Schwinger, Administrative Assistant, 303-273-3800, Fax: 303-273-3859, E-mail: mschwing@mines.edu.

Colorado State University, Graduate School, College of Natural Resources, Department of Earth Resources, Program in Geology, Fort Collins, CO 80523-0015. Offers fluvial geomorphology (MS); hydrogeology (MS); petrology/geochemistry and economic geology (MS); stratigraphy/sedimentology (MS); structure/tectonics (MS). Part-time programs available. *Faculty:* 9 full-time (3 women), 1 (woman) part-time. *Students:* 9 full-time (7 women), 3 part-time (1 woman); includes 3 minority (1 Asian American or Pacific Islander, 1 Hispanic American, 1 Native American) Average age 28. 28 applicants, 43% accepted. In 1998, 3 degrees awarded. *Degree requirements:* For master's, thesis required, foreign language not required. *Entrance requirements:* For master's, GRE General Test (minimum score of 600 on each section required), GRE Subject Test, TOEFL (minimum score of 550 required), minimum GPA of 3.0. *Application deadline:* For fall admission, 2/1 (priority date). Applications are processed on a rolling basis. Application fee: $30. *Financial aid:* In 1998–99, 5 research assistantships, 1 teaching assistantship were awarded.; fellowships, career-related internships or fieldwork, Federal Work-Study, institutionally-sponsored loans, and traineeships also available. Financial aid application deadline: 2/15. *Faculty research:* Structural geology and tectonics, geochemistry and geochronology, economic geology, fluvial processes, groundwater hydrology. Total annual research expenditures: $500,000. *Unit head:* Frank G. Ethridge, Head, 970-491-5662, Fax: 970-491-6307, E-mail: fredpet@cnr.colostate.edu. *Application contact:* Barbara Holtz, Staff Assistant, 970-491-5662, Fax: 970-491-6307, E-mail: barbh@cnr.colostate.edu.

Cornell University, Graduate School, Graduate Fields of Engineering, Field of Geological Sciences, Ithaca, NY 14853-0001. Offers economic geology (MS, PhD); engineering geology (MS, PhD); environmental geophysics (M Eng, MS, PhD); general geology (MS, PhD); geobiology (MS, PhD); geochemistry and isotope geology (MS, PhD); geohydrology (M Eng, MS, PhD); geomorphology (MS, PhD); geophysics (MS, PhD); geotectonics (MS, PhD); mineralogy (MS, PhD); paleontology (MS, PhD); petroleum geology (MS, PhD); petrology (MS, PhD); planetary geology (MS, PhD); Precambrian geology (MS, PhD); Quaternary geology (MS, PhD); rock mechanics (MS, PhD); sedimentology (MS, PhD); seismology (MS, PhD); stratigraphy (MS, PhD); structural geology (MS, PhD). *Faculty:* 28 full-time. *Students:* 36 full-time (12 women); includes 4 minority (1 African American, 1 Asian American or Pacific Islander, 2 Hispanic Americans), 16 international. *Degree requirements:* For master's, thesis (MS) required; for doctorate, dissertation required, foreign language not required. *Entrance requirements:* For master's and doctorate, GRE General Test, TOEFL (minimum score of 550 required). *Application deadline:* For fall admission, 1/15. Application fee: $65. Electronic applications accepted. *Unit head:* Director of Graduate Studies, 607-255-3474, Fax: 607-254-4780. *Application contact:* Graduate Field Assistant, 607-255-3474, Fax: 607-254-4780, E-mail: gradprog@geology.cornell.edu.

See in-depth description on page 273.

Duke University, Graduate School, Department of Biological Anthropology and Anatomy, Durham, NC 27708-0586. Offers cellular and molecular biology (PhD); gross anatomy and physical anthropology (PhD), including comparative morphology of human and non-human primates, primate social behavior, vertebrate paleontology; neuroanatomy (PhD). *Faculty:* 13 full-time, 1 part-time. *Students:* 22 full-time (13 women); includes 3 minority (2 African Americans, 1 Hispanic American), 3 international. *Degree requirements:* For doctorate, dissertation required. *Entrance requirements:* For doctorate, GRE General Test. *Application deadline:* For fall admission, 12/31. Application fee: $75. *Unit head:* Kathleen Smith, Director of Graduate Studies, 919-684-4124, Fax: 919-684-8034, E-mail: rachel_hougom@baa.mc.duke.edu.

Duke University, Graduate School, Department of Earth and Ocean Sciences (Geology), Durham, NC 27708-0586. Offers MS, PhD. Part-time programs available. *Faculty:* 19 full-time. *Students:* 20 full-time (8 women), 4 international. 34 applicants, 53% accepted. In 1998, 4 master's, 2 doctorates awarded. Terminal master's awarded for partial completion of doctoral program. *Degree requirements:* For master's and doctorate, thesis/dissertation required. *Entrance requirements:* For master's and doctorate, GRE General Test, GRE Subject Test (recommended). *Application deadline:* For fall admission, 12/31; for spring admission, 11/1. Application fee: $75. *Financial aid:* Fellowships, research assistantships, teaching assistantships, Federal Work-Study available. Financial aid application deadline: 12/31. *Unit head:* Alan Boudreau, Director of Graduate Studies, 919-684-5847, Fax: 919-684-5833, E-mail: debbie@rogue.geo.duke.edu.

Announcement: Programs leading to degrees of MS and PhD in geology are offered, with specialized training in the active research areas of the staff. These include aquatic geochemistry, biogeochemistry, biological anthropology and anatomy, carbonate diagenesis, clastic and carbonate facies analysis, continental margin and deep-sea sedimentation, desert studies, economic geology, hydrogeology, igneous petrology and geochemistry focusing on layered intrusions, isotope geochemistry, limnology, marine micropaleontology, paleoecology, paleoceanography, paleoclimatology, sediment dynamics, seismology, structure and development of transform faults, rift basins, spreading centers and passive margins, and tectonics. Research projects have involved fieldwork throughout North and South America and across Africa, as well as in the world's oceans. Housed in a renovated building, the department includes the Duke University Program for the Study of Developed Shorelines and maintains a close connection with the Duke University Marine Laboratory on the North Carolina coast. Up-to-date information about the department and the faculty can be found on the World Wide Web at http://www.eos.duke.edu/

East Carolina University, Graduate School, College of Arts and Sciences, Department of Geology, Greenville, NC 27858-4353. Offers MS. Part-time programs available. *Faculty:* 7 full-time (2 women). *Students:* 8 full-time (7 women), 15 part-time (5 women); includes 1 minority (African American) Average age 28. 14 applicants, 86% accepted. In 1998, 8 degrees awarded. *Degree requirements:* For master's, one foreign language (computer language can substitute), thesis, comprehensive exams required. *Entrance requirements:* For master's, GRE General Test, TOEFL. *Application deadline:* For fall admission, 6/1 (priority date); for spring admission, 10/15. Applications are processed on a rolling basis. Application fee: $40. Tuition, state resident: full-time $1,012. Tuition, nonresident: full-time $8,578. Required fees: $1,006. Part-time tuition and fees vary according to course load. *Financial aid:* Research assistantships with partial tuition reimbursements, teaching assistantships with partial tuition reimbursements available. Aid available to part-time students. Financial aid application deadline: 6/1. *Unit head:* Dr. Terri Woods, Director of Graduate Studies, 252-328-6379, Fax: 252-328-4391, E-mail: woodst@mail.ecu.edu. *Application contact:* Dr. Paul D. Tschetter, Senior Associate Dean, 252-328-6012, Fax: 252-328-6071, E-mail: grad@mail.ecu.edu.

Eastern Kentucky University, The Graduate School, College of Natural and Mathematical Sciences, Department of Earth Sciences, Richmond, KY 40475-3101. Offers geology (MS, PhD). Part-time programs available. *Students:* 15. In 1998, 2 degrees awarded. *Degree requirements:* For master's, thesis required. *Entrance requirements:* For master's, GRE General Test, minimum GPA of 2.5. Application fee: $0. *Financial aid:* Research assistantships, teaching assistantships, Federal Work-Study available. Aid available to part-time students. *Unit head:* Dr. Gary Kuhnhenn, Chair, 606-622-1273.

Eastern Washington University, Graduate School, College of Science, Mathematics and Technology, Department of Geology, Cheney, WA 99004-2431. Offers MS. *Faculty:* 9 full-time (1 woman). *Students:* 1 (woman) full-time, 3 part-time (1 woman). In 1998, 1 degree awarded. *Degree requirements:* For master's, thesis, comprehensive oral exam required. *Entrance requirements:* For master's, minimum GPA of 3.0. *Application deadline:* For fall admission, 4/1 (priority date); for spring admission, 1/15. Applications are processed on a rolling basis. Application fee: $35. Tuition, state resident: full-time $4,368. Tuition, nonresident: full-time $13,284. *Financial aid:* Research assistantships, teaching assistantships, career-related internships or fieldwork, Federal Work-Study, and institutionally-sponsored loans available. Financial aid application deadline: 2/1. *Unit head:* Dr. Linda McCollum, Chair, 509-359-2286.

Florida Atlantic University, Charles E. Schmidt College of Science, Department of Geography and Geology, Program in Geology, Boca Raton, FL 33431-0991. Offers MS. *Faculty:* 6 full-time (0 women). *Students:* 8 full-time (1 woman), 12 part-time (2 women); includes 2 minority (both Hispanic Americans) Average age 32. In 1998, 11 degrees awarded. *Degree requirements:* For master's, thesis required, foreign language not required. *Entrance requirements:* For master's, GRE General Test (minimum combined score of 1000 required; average 1100), minimum GPA of 3.0. *Application deadline:* For fall admission, 6/1. Application fee: $20.

Geology

Florida Atlantic University (continued)

Tuition, state resident: part-time $148 per credit hour. Tuition, nonresident: part-time $509 per credit hour. *Financial aid:* In 1998–99, 2 research assistantships, 5 teaching assistantships were awarded.; Federal Work-Study also available. *Faculty research:* Paleontology, beach erosion, stratigraphy, hydrogeology, environmental geology. Total annual research expenditures: $30,000. *Application contact:* Jorge Restrepo, Graduate Coordinator, 561-297-2795, Fax: 561-297-2744.

Florida International University, College of Arts and Sciences, Department of Geology, Miami, FL 33199. Offers MS, PhD. Part-time and evening/weekend programs available. *Faculty:* 10 full-time (2 women), 2 part-time (1 woman). *Students:* 15 full-time (2 women), 10 part-time (5 women); includes 3 minority (2 African Americans, 1 Hispanic American), 12 international. Average age 32. 22 applicants, 23% accepted. In 1998, 2 master's awarded. *Degree requirements:* For master's, one foreign language, thesis required; for doctorate, dissertation required. *Entrance requirements:* For master's and doctorate, GRE General Test (minimum combined score of 1000 required), TOEFL (minimum score of 500 required). *Application deadline:* For fall admission, 4/1 (priority date); for spring admission, 10/1. Applications are processed on a rolling basis. Application fee: $20. Tuition, state resident: part-time $145 per credit hour. Tuition, nonresident: part-time $506 per credit hour. Required fees: $158; $158 per year. *Financial aid:* Research assistantships, teaching assistantships available. Financial aid application deadline: 4/1. *Faculty research:* Determination of dispersivity and hydraulic conductivity in the Biscayne Aquifer. *Unit head:* Dr. Gautam Sen, Chairperson, 305-348-2365, Fax: 305-348-3877, E-mail: seng@fiu.edu.

Florida State University, Graduate Studies, College of Arts and Sciences, Department of Geological Sciences, Tallahassee, FL 32306. Offers geological sciences (MS, PhD); geophysical fluid dynamics (PhD). *Faculty:* 15 full-time (1 woman). *Students:* 23 full-time (4 women), 11 part-time (5 women), 14 international. Average age 27. *Degree requirements:* For master's, thesis, departmental qualifying exam required, foreign language not required; for doctorate, dissertation, departmental qualifying exam required. *Entrance requirements:* For master's and doctorate, GRE General Test (minimum combined score of 1050 required), GRE Subject Test, TOEFL (minimum score of 550 required), minimum GPA of 3.0. *Application deadline:* Applications are processed on a rolling basis. Application fee: $20. Electronic applications accepted. Tuition, state resident: part-time $139 per credit hour. Tuition, nonresident: part-time $482 per credit hour. Tuition and fees vary according to program. *Financial aid:* In 1998–99, 12 students received aid; fellowships, research assistantships, teaching assistantships, career-related internships or fieldwork and Federal Work-Study available. Financial aid application deadline: 2/7; financial aid applicants required to submit FAFSA. *Faculty research:* Appalachian and collisional tectonics, surface and groundwater hydrogeology, micropaleontology, isotope and trace element geochemistry, coastal and estuarine studies. *Unit head:* Dr. David Jon Furbish, Chairman, 850-644-5892, E-mail: furbish@gly.fsu.edu. *Application contact:* Tami Karl, Program Assistant, 850-644-5861, Fax: 850-644-4214, E-mail: karl@gly.fsu.edu.

Fort Hays State University, Graduate School, College of Arts and Sciences, Department of Geosciences, Program in Geology, Hays, KS 67601-4099. Offers MS. *Faculty:* 6 full-time (0 women). *Students:* 3 full-time (0 women), 8 part-time (3 women); includes 1 minority (Hispanic American) Average age 27. 2 applicants, 100% accepted. In 1998, 4 degrees awarded. *Degree requirements:* For master's, thesis required, foreign language not required. *Entrance requirements:* For master's, GRE General Test. *Application deadline:* For fall admission, 7/1 (priority date). Applications are processed on a rolling basis. Application fee: $25 ($35 for international students). Tuition, state resident: part-time $94 per credit hour. Tuition, nonresident: part-time $248 per credit hour. Full-time tuition and fees vary according to course level and course load. *Financial aid:* Research assistantships, teaching assistantships, career-related internships or fieldwork and institutionally-sponsored loans available. Aid available to part-time students. *Faculty research:* Cretaceous and late Cenozoic stratigraphy, sedimentation, paleontology. *Unit head:* Dr. Paul Krutak, Chair, Department of Geosciences, 785-628-5389.

The George Washington University, Columbian School of Arts and Sciences, Department of Geology, Washington, DC 20052. Offers geochemistry (MS); geology (MS, PhD); hominid paleobiology (MS, PhD). Part-time and evening/weekend programs available. *Faculty:* 5 full-time (0 women). *Students:* 7 full-time (3 women), 12 part-time (5 women); includes 1 minority (Asian American or Pacific Islander), 7 international. Average age 30. 6 applicants, 100% accepted. In 1998, 4 master's, 2 doctorates awarded. Terminal master's awarded for partial completion of doctoral program. *Degree requirements:* For master's, thesis or alternative, comprehensive exam required; for doctorate, dissertation, general exam required. *Entrance requirements:* For master's, GRE General Test, bachelor's degree in field, interview, minimum GPA of 3.0; for doctorate, GRE General Test, interview, minimum GPA of 3.0. Application fee: $55. Tuition: Full-time $17,328; part-time $722 per credit hour. Required fees: $828; $35 per credit hour. Tuition and fees vary according to campus/location and program. *Financial aid:* Federal Work-Study available. Financial aid application deadline: 2/1. *Faculty research:* Engineering geology. *Unit head:* Dr. John Lewis, Chair, 202-994-6190.

Georgia State University, College of Arts and Sciences, Department of Geology, Atlanta, GA 30303-3083. Offers geology (MS). Part-time and evening/weekend programs available. *Faculty:* 7 full-time (1 woman). *Students:* 11 full-time (9 women), 5 part-time (1 woman); includes 1 African American, 1 international. Average age 27. 11 applicants, 64% accepted. In 1998, 6 degrees awarded (100% found work related to degree). *Degree requirements:* For master's, one foreign language (computer language can substitute), thesis, comprehensive exam required. *Entrance requirements:* For master's, GRE General Test, TOEFL (minimum score of 550 required), minimum GPA of 2.75. *Average time to degree:* Master's–2 years full-time, 3 years part-time. Application fee: $25. Tuition, state resident: full-time $2,896; part-time $121 per credit hour. Tuition, nonresident: full-time $11,584; part-time $483 per credit hour. Required fees: $468. Tuition and fees vary according to program. *Financial aid:* Research assistantships, teaching assistantships, career-related internships or fieldwork, Federal Work-Study, institutionally-sponsored loans, tuition waivers (partial), and unspecified assistantships available. Aid available to part-time students. Financial aid application deadline: 7/15. *Faculty research:* Clay mineralogy, metamorphism; hydrothermal rock-fluid interaction, fracture analysis, volcaniclastic sedimentation. *Unit head:* Dr. David A. Vanko, Chair, 404-651-2272, Fax: 404-651-1376, E-mail: geodav@asusai1.asu.edu. *Application contact:* Dr. Hassan Babaie, Director of Graduate Studies, 404-651-2272, Fax: 404-651-1376, E-mail: geohab@panther.gsu.edu.

See in-depth description on page 279.

ICR Graduate School, Graduate Programs, Santee, CA 92071. Offers astro/geophysics (MS); biology (MS); geology (MS); science education (MS). Part-time programs available. *Faculty:* 4 full-time (0 women), 6 part-time (0 women). *Students:* 13 full-time (5 women), 23 part-time (9 women). *Degree requirements:* For master's, thesis required (for some programs), foreign language not required. *Entrance requirements:* For master's, BS degree in field of graduate study. *Application deadline:* Applications are processed on a rolling basis. Application fee: $30. *Unit head:* Kenneth B. Cumming, Dean, 619-448-0900, Fax: 619-448-3469. *Application contact:* Dr. Jack Kriege, Registrar, 619-448-0900, Fax: 619-448-3469.

Idaho State University, Graduate School, College of Arts and Sciences, Department of Geology, Pocatello, ID 83209. Offers geology (MS); geophysics/hydrology (MS); natural science (MNS). MS (geophysics/hydrology) offered jointly with Boise State University. Part-time programs available. *Degree requirements:* For master's, thesis required, foreign language not required. *Entrance requirements:* For master's, GRE General Test (score in 35th percentile or higher on verbal or quantitative section required). *Faculty research:* Structural geography, stratigraphy, geochemistry, volcanography, geomorphology.

Indiana University Bloomington, Graduate School, College of Arts and Sciences, Department of Geological Sciences, Bloomington, IN 47405. Offers biogeochemistry (MS, PhD); environmental geosciences (MS, PhD); geobiology, stratigraphy, and sedimentology (MS, PhD); geochemistry (MS, PhD); geochemistry, mineralogy, and petrology (MS, PhD); geophysics (MS, PhD); geophysics, tectonics, and structural geology (MS, PhD). PhD offered through the University Graduate School. Part-time programs available. *Faculty:* 21 full-time (1 woman). *Students:* 27 full-time (8 women), 22 part-time (6 women); includes 3 minority (2 Asian Americans or Pacific Islanders, 1 Hispanic American), 9 international. In 1998, 12 master's, 5 doctorates awarded. *Degree requirements:* For master's, one foreign language (computer language can substitute), thesis or alternative required; for doctorate, dissertation required, dissertation required. *Entrance requirements:* For master's and doctorate, GRE General Test, TOEFL. *Application deadline:* For fall admission, 1/15 (priority date); for spring admission, 9/1 (priority date). Applications are processed on a rolling basis. Application fee: $40. Tuition, state resident: part-time $161 per credit hour. Tuition, nonresident: part-time $468 per credit hour. Required fees: $360 per year. Tuition and fees vary according to course load and program. *Financial aid:* In 1998–99, research assistantships with full and partial tuition reimbursements (averaging $11,000 per year); fellowships with tuition reimbursements, teaching assistantships with tuition reimbursements, career-related internships or fieldwork, Federal Work-Study, and institutionally-sponsored loans also available. Financial aid application deadline: 2/15. *Faculty research:* Geophysics, geochemistry, hydrogeology, igneous and metamorphic petrology and clay minerology. Total annual research expenditures: $289,139. *Unit head:* Dr. Christopher G. Maples, Chairman, 812-855-5582, Fax: 812-855-7899, E-mail: cmaples@indiana.edu. *Application contact:* Mary Iverson, Secretary, Committee for Graduate Studies, 812-855-7214, Fax: 812-855-7899, E-mail: geograd@indiana.edu.

See in-depth description on page 283.

Indiana University–Purdue University Indianapolis, School of Science, Department of Geology, Indianapolis, IN 46202-3272. Offers MS. Part-time and evening/weekend programs available. *Students:* 3 full-time (2 women), 8 part-time (5 women); includes 2 minority (1 African American, 1 Asian American or Pacific Islander) Average age 27. In 1998, 3 degrees awarded (100% found work related to degree). *Degree requirements:* For master's, computer language, thesis required (for some programs), foreign language not required. *Entrance requirements:* For master's, GRE General Test, minimum GPA of 3.0. *Average time to degree:* Master's–2 years full-time, 6 years part-time. Application fee: $35 ($55 for international students). Tuition, state resident: part-time $158 per credit hour. Tuition, nonresident: part-time $455 per credit hour. Required fees: $121 per year. Tuition and fees vary according to course load and degree level. *Financial aid:* In 1998–99, 1 fellowship with full tuition reimbursement (averaging $12,000 per year), 6 research assistantships with full tuition reimbursements (averaging $12,000 per year), 5 teaching assistantships with full tuition reimbursements (averaging $12,000 per year) were awarded.; scholarships also available. Financial aid application deadline: 3/1. *Faculty research:* Wetland hydrology, groundwater contamination, soils, sedimentology, sediment chemistry. *Unit head:* Andrew P. Barth, Chair, 317-274-7484, Fax: 317-274-7966, E-mail: ibsz100@iupui.edu. *Application contact:* Lenore P. Tedesco, Associate Professor, 317-274-7484, Fax: 317-274-7966, E-mail: ltedesco@iupui.edu.

Iowa State University of Science and Technology, Graduate College, College of Liberal Arts and Sciences, Department of Geological and Atmospheric Sciences, Ames, IA 50011. Offers earth science (MS, PhD); geology (MS, PhD); meteorology (MS, PhD); water resources (MS, PhD). *Faculty:* 17 full-time. *Students:* 28 full-time (8 women), 9 part-time (3 women); includes 1 minority (Asian American or Pacific Islander), 11 international. 43 applicants, 42% accepted. In 1998, 4 master's, 2 doctorates awarded. *Degree requirements:* For master's, thesis required (for some programs); for doctorate, dissertation required. *Entrance requirements:* For master's and doctorate, GRE General Test, TOEFL (minimum score of 530 required). *Application deadline:* For fall admission, 2/15 (priority date). Applications are processed on a rolling basis. Application fee: $20 ($50 for international students). Electronic applications accepted. Tuition, state resident: full-time $3,308. Tuition, nonresident: full-time $9,744. Part-time tuition and fees vary according to course load, campus/location and program. *Financial aid:* In 1998–99, 15 research assistantships with partial tuition reimbursements (averaging $9,915 per year), 11 teaching assistantships with partial tuition reimbursements (averaging $9,999 per year) were awarded.; fellowships, scholarships also available. *Unit head:* Dr. Paul G. Spry, Chair, 515-294-4477.

See in-depth description on page 285.

Johns Hopkins University, Zanvyl Krieger School of Arts and Sciences, Department of Earth and Planetary Sciences, Program in Geology, Baltimore, MD 21218-2699. Offers MA, PhD. *Faculty:* 8 full-time (1 woman). *Students:* 17 full-time (8 women). Average age 24. In 1998, 1 doctorate awarded. Terminal master's awarded for partial completion of doctoral program. *Degree requirements:* For doctorate, dissertation required, foreign language not required. *Entrance requirements:* For master's and doctorate, GRE General Test. *Average time to degree:* Master's–2 years full-time; doctorate–5.5 years full-time. *Application deadline:* For fall admission, 1/15. Application fee: $55. Tuition: Full-time $23,660. Tuition and fees vary according to program. *Financial aid:* Federal Work-Study and institutionally-sponsored loans available. Financial aid application deadline: 3/14; financial aid applicants required to submit FAFSA. *Unit head:* Dr. John M. Ferry, Chair, Department of Earth and Planetary Sciences, 410-516-7135, Fax: 410-516-7933.

Kansas State University, Graduate School, College of Arts and Sciences, Department of Geology, Manhattan, KS 66506. Offers MS. *Faculty:* 7 full-time (1 woman). *Students:* 10 full-time (4 women), 4 part-time (1 woman); includes 1 Hispanic American Average age 24. 10 applicants, 60% accepted. In 1998, 7 degrees awarded. *Degree requirements:* For master's, thesis required, foreign language not required. *Entrance requirements:* For master's, GRE General Test, GRE Subject Test, TOEFL. *Average time to degree:* Master's–1 year full-time. *Application deadline:* For fall admission, 3/15. Application fee: $0 ($25 for international students). Electronic applications accepted. *Financial aid:* In 1998–99, 3 research assistantships with full tuition reimbursements, 6 teaching assistantships with full tuition reimbursements were awarded.; career-related internships or fieldwork, Federal Work-Study, institutionally-sponsored loans, and scholarships also available. Aid available to part-time students. Financial aid application deadline: 3/1; financial aid applicants required to submit FAFSA. *Faculty research:* Sedimentary geology, paleobiology, geochemistry, tectonics, Quaternary geology. Total annual research expenditures: $100,000. *Unit head:* Charles G. Oviatt, Head, 785-532-6724, Fax: 785-532-5159, E-mail: joviatt@ksu.edu. *Application contact:* Mary Hubbard, Graduate Coordinator, 785-532-6724, Fax: 785-532-5159, E-mail: mhub@ksu.edu.

Kent State University, College of Arts and Sciences, Department of Geology, Kent, OH 44242-0001. Offers MS, PhD. *Faculty:* 16 full-time. *Students:* 30 full-time (13 women), 17 part-time (4 women); includes 2 minority (1 African American, 1 Hispanic American), 11 international. 30 applicants, 77% accepted. In 1998, 3 master's, 1 doctorate awarded. *Degree requirements:* For master's, thesis required, foreign language not required; for doctorate, dissertation required. *Entrance requirements:* For master's, minimum GPA of 2.75; for doctorate, GRE General Test, GRE Subject Test, minimum GPA of 3.0. *Application deadline:* For fall admission, 7/12; for spring admission, 11/29. Applications are processed on a rolling basis. Application fee: $30. *Financial aid:* Fellowships, research assistantships, teaching assistantships, career-related internships or fieldwork, Federal Work-Study, institutionally-sponsored loans, and tuition waivers (full) available. Financial aid application deadline: 2/1. *Faculty research:* Groundwater, surface water, engineering geology, petroleum geology, exploration geology. *Unit head:* Dr. Donald F. Palmer, Chairman, 330-672-2680, Fax: 330-672-7949.

Lakehead University, Graduate Studies and Research, Faculty of Arts and Science, Department of Geology, Thunder Bay, ON P7B 5E1, Canada. Offers M Sc. Part-time and evening/weekend programs available. *Degree requirements:* For master's, thesis required, foreign language not required. *Entrance requirements:* For master's, TOEFL (minimum score of 550 required), minimum B average. *Faculty research:* Rock physics, sedimentology, mineralogyand economic geology, geochemistry, petrology of alkaline rocks.

Laurentian University, School of Graduate Studies and Research, Programme in Geology, Sudbury, ON P3E 2C6, Canada. Offers M Sc. Part-time programs available. *Faculty:* 11

full-time (1 woman), 15 part-time (2 women). *Students:* 14 full-time (5 women), 8 part-time (2 women). 12 applicants, 50% accepted. In 1998, 2 degrees awarded. *Degree requirements:* For master's, thesis required, foreign language not required. *Entrance requirements:* For master's, honors degree with second class or better. *Application deadline:* For fall admission, 9/1. Applications are processed on a rolling basis. Application fee: $50. *Financial aid:* In 1998–99, 4 fellowships (averaging $2,000 per year), 9 teaching assistantships (averaging $6,500 per year) were awarded.; research assistantships, institutionally-sponsored loans and scholarships also available. *Faculty research:* Localization and metallogenesis of Ni-Cu-(PGE) sulphide mineralization in the Thompson Nickel Belt, mapping lithology and ore-grade by remote sensing, global reef expansion and collapse, monitoring dissolved organic carbon in lakes using remote sensing, volcanic environments and controls on VMS deposits. Total annual research expenditures: $780,530. *Unit head:* Dr. Darrel G. F. Long, Chairman, 705-675-1151 Ext. 2268, Fax: 705-673-6508. *Application contact:* 705-675-1151 Ext. 3909, Fax: 705-675-4843.

Lehigh University, College of Arts and Sciences, Department of Earth and Environmental Sciences, Bethlehem, PA 18015-3094. Offers environmental science (MS, PhD); geological sciences (MS, PhD). *Students:* 25 full-time (14 women); includes 1 minority (Hispanic American), 2 international. Average age 28. 33 applicants, 30% accepted. In 1998, 6 master's, 1 doctorate awarded (100% entered university research/teaching). *Degree requirements:* For master's, thesis required, foreign language not required; for doctorate, dissertation, language at the discretion of the PhD committee required. *Entrance requirements:* For master's and doctorate, GRE General Test (score in 75th percentile or higher required), TOEFL (minimum score of 550 required). *Average time to degree:* Master's–2 years full-time; doctorate–4.5 years full-time. *Application deadline:* For fall admission, 7/15; for spring admission, 12/1. Applications are processed on a rolling basis. Application fee: $40. *Financial aid:* In 1998–99, 3 fellowships, 4 research assistantships, 8 teaching assistantships were awarded.; Federal Work-Study, institutionally-sponsored loans, and tuition waivers (full and partial) also available. Financial aid application deadline: 1/15. *Faculty research:* Tectonics, surficial processes, aquatic ecology. Total annual research expenditures: $1.5 million. *Unit head:* Dr. Peter Zeitler, Chairman, 610-758-3667, Fax: 610-758-3677, E-mail: pkz0@lehigh.edu. *Application contact:* Dr. Donald Morris, Graduate Coordinator, 610-758-5831, Fax: 610-758-3677, E-mail: dpmz0@lehigh.edu.

See in-depth description on page 289.

Loma Linda University, Graduate School, Department of Geology, Loma Linda, CA 92350. Offers MS. Part-time programs available. *Degree requirements:* For master's, thesis required. *Entrance requirements:* For master's, GRE General Test (minimum combined score of 1500 on three sections required). Application fee: $40. *Financial aid:* Fellowships, Federal Work-Study and tuition waivers (partial) available. Aid available to part-time students. *Unit head:* Dr. Paul Buchheim, Coordinator, 909-824-4530.

Louisiana State University and Agricultural and Mechanical College, Graduate School, College of Basic Sciences, Department of Geology and Geophysics, Baton Rouge, LA 70803. Offers MS, PhD. *Faculty:* 19 full-time (4 women), 1 part-time (0 women). *Students:* 33 full-time (11 women), 14 part-time (5 women); includes 1 minority (Hispanic American), 11 international. Average age 29. 40 applicants, 40% accepted. In 1998, 8 master's, 6 doctorates awarded. Terminal master's awarded for partial completion of doctoral program. *Degree requirements:* For master's and doctorate, thesis/dissertation required, foreign language not required. *Entrance requirements:* For master's and doctorate, GRE General Test (minimum combined score of 1000 required), TOEFL (minimum score of 525 required, 550 for assistantships), minimum GPA of 3.0. *Application deadline:* For fall admission, 1/25 (priority date). Applications are processed on a rolling basis. Application fee: $25. *Financial aid:* In 1998–99, 4 fellowships, 3 research assistantships with partial tuition reimbursements, 21 teaching assistantships with partial tuition reimbursements were awarded.; career-related internships or fieldwork, Federal Work-Study, institutionally-sponsored loans, and unspecified assistantships also available. Financial aid application deadline: 3/15. *Faculty research:* Geophysics, geochemistry of sediments, isotope geochemistry, igneous and metamorphic petrology, micropaleontology. *Unit head:* Dr. G. Ray Byerly, Chair, 225-388-3353, Fax: 225-388-2302, E-mail: glbyer@lsuvm.sncc.lsu.edu. *Application contact:* Lui Chan, Graduate Coordinator, 225-388-6439, E-mail: glchan@lsuvm.sncc.lsu.edu.

Massachusetts Institute of Technology, School of Science, Department of Earth, Atmospheric, and Planetary Sciences, Program in Geology and Geochemistry, Cambridge, MA 02139-4307. Offers SM, PhD, Sc D. *Faculty:* 9 full-time (1 woman). *Students:* 21 full-time (8 women); includes 2 minority (both Hispanic Americans), 4 international. Average age 28. 29 applicants, 24% accepted. In 1998, 2 master's, 2 doctorates awarded. Terminal master's awarded for partial completion of doctoral program. *Degree requirements:* For master's, thesis required, foreign language not required; for doctorate, dissertation, general exam required, foreign language not required. *Entrance requirements:* For master's and doctorate, GRE General Test. *Application deadline:* For fall admission, 1/15; for spring admission, 11/1. Application fee: $55. *Financial aid:* Fellowships, research assistantships, teaching assistantships available. Financial aid application deadline: 1/15. *Unit head:* Dr. Vernon R. Morris, Associate Professor, 202-806-5450, Fax: 202-806-4430, E-mail: vmorris@physics1.howard.edu. *Application contact:* Anastasia Frangos, Administrative Assistant, 617-253-3381, Fax: 617-253-8298, E-mail: eapsinfo@mit.edu.

McMaster University, School of Graduate Studies, Faculty of Science, School of Geography and Geology, Hamilton, ON L8S 4M2, Canada. Offers geochemistry (PhD); geology (M Sc, PhD); human geography (MA, PhD); physical geography (M Sc, PhD). Part-time programs available. *Faculty:* 23 full-time (3 women), 12 part-time (1 woman). *Students:* 49 full-time (24 women), 9 part-time (7 women), 8 international. Average age 24. 51 applicants, 31% accepted. In 1998, 12 master's, 7 doctorates awarded. Terminal master's awarded for partial completion of doctoral program. *Degree requirements:* For master's, thesis required, foreign language not required; for doctorate, dissertation, comprehensive exam required, foreign language not required. *Entrance requirements:* For master's, minimum B+ average. *Application deadline:* For fall admission, 3/15 (priority date). Applications are processed on a rolling basis. Application fee: $50. *Financial aid:* In 1998–99, 33 students received aid; teaching assistantships, scholarships available. Financial aid application deadline: 3/15. *Unit head:* Dr. Fred L. Hall, Director, 905-525-9140 Ext. 24196, Fax: 905-546-0463, E-mail: hallfl@mcmaster.ca. *Application contact:* Medy Espiritu, Graduate Secretary, 905-525-9140 Ext. 23535, Fax: 905-522-3141, E-mail: espiritu@mcmaster.ca.

Memorial University of Newfoundland, School of Graduate Studies, Department of Earth Sciences, St. John's, NF A1C 5S7, Canada. Offers geology (M Sc, PhD); geophysics (M Sc, PhD). Part-time programs available. *Faculty:* 25 full-time (2 women), 4 part-time (0 women). *Students:* 32 full-time (11 women), 5 part-time (2 women), 15 international. *Degree requirements:* For master's, thesis required; for doctorate, dissertation, comprehensive exam required. *Entrance requirements:* For master's, honors B Sc; for doctorate, M Sc. *Application deadline:* For fall admission, 3/31; for spring admission, 12/31. Applications are processed on a rolling basis. Application fee: $40. *Unit head:* Dr. G. Quinlan, Head, 709-737-2334, Fax: 709-737-2589, E-mail: gquinlan@sparkyz.esd.ucs.mun.ca. *Application contact:* Dr. Ali Aksu, Graduate Officer, 709-737-8385, Fax: 709-737-2589, E-mail: aaksu@sparkyz.esd.ucs.mun.ca.

Miami University, Graduate School, College of Arts and Sciences, Department of Geology, Oxford, OH 45056. Offers MA, MS, PhD. Part-time programs available. *Faculty:* 12. *Students:* 21 full-time (7 women); includes 2 minority (1 African American, 1 Asian American or Pacific Islander), 2 international. 30 applicants, 67% accepted. In 1998, 6 master's, 1 doctorate awarded. *Degree requirements:* For master's, thesis (for some programs), final exam required; for doctorate, dissertation, comprehensive and final exams required. *Entrance requirements:* For master's, GRE General Test, GRE Subject Test, minimum undergraduate GPA of 3.0 during previous 2 years or 2.75 overall; for doctorate, GRE General Test, GRE Subject Test, minimum undergraduate GPA of 2.75 or 3.0 graduate. *Application deadline:* For fall admission, 3/1 (priority date); for spring admission, 12/1. Applications are processed on a rolling basis. Application fee: $35. *Financial aid:* Fellowships, research assistantships, teaching assistantships, Federal Work-Study and tuition waivers (full) available. Financial aid application deadline: 3/1. *Unit head:* Dr. Liz Widom, Director of Graduate Studies, 513-529-5048.

Michigan State University, Graduate School, College of Natural Science, Department of Geological Sciences, East Lansing, MI 48824-1020. Offers environmental geosciences (MS, PhD); geological sciences (MA, MS, PhD). Part-time programs available. *Faculty:* 15 full-time (2 women), 7 part-time (2 women). *Students:* 33 full-time (15 women), 4 part-time (2 women); includes 1 minority (Asian American or Pacific Islander), 2 international. Average age 27. 65 applicants, 65% accepted. In 1998, 8 master's awarded (13% entered university research/teaching, 74% found other work related to degree, 13% continued full-time study). *Degree requirements:* For master's, thesis required (for some programs), foreign language not required; for doctorate, dissertation required, foreign language not required. *Entrance requirements:* For master's and doctorate, GRE General Test, TOEFL. *Average time to degree:* Master's–3 years full-time. *Application deadline:* For fall admission, 6/1; for spring admission, 11/1. Applications are processed on a rolling basis. Application fee: $30 ($40 for international students). Electronic applications accepted. *Financial aid:* In 1998–99, 33 students received aid, including 27 fellowships (averaging $1,377 per year), 10 research assistantships with partial tuition reimbursements available (averaging $9,591 per year), 20 teaching assistantships with partial tuition reimbursements available (averaging $9,745 per year); institutionally-sponsored loans and scholarships also available. Financial aid application deadline: 1/15; financial aid applicants required to submit CSS PROFILE or FAFSA. *Faculty research:* Paleoenvironments and biological evolution, geochemical and biogeochemical cycles, fluids in and on the Earth, dynamics of the Earth's crust. Total annual research expenditures: $369,856. *Unit head:* Dr. Thomas Vogel, Chairperson, 517-355-4626, Fax: 517-353-8787, E-mail: geosci@pilot.msu.edu.

Michigan Technological University, Graduate School, College of Engineering, Department of Geology, Geophysics and Geological Engineering, Program in Geology, Houghton, MI 49931-1295. Offers geology (MS, PhD); geotechnical engineering (PhD). Part-time programs available. *Faculty:* 8 full-time (1 woman), 1 part-time (0 women). *Students:* 16 full-time (6 women); includes 1 minority (African American), 2 international. Average age 32. 16 applicants, 75% accepted. In 1998, 4 master's awarded. *Degree requirements:* For master's and doctorate, thesis/dissertation required, foreign language not required. *Entrance requirements:* For master's, GRE General Test (combined average 1714 on three sections), TOEFL (minimum score of 550 required; average 657); for doctorate, GRE General Test (combined average 1827 on three sections), TOEFL (minimum score of 550 required; average 596). *Average time to degree:* Master's–3.4 years full-time. *Application deadline:* For fall admission, 3/15 (priority date). Applications are processed on a rolling basis. Application fee: $30 ($35 for international students). Tuition, state resident: full-time $4,377. Tuition, nonresident: full-time $9,108. Required fees: $126. Tuition and fees vary according to course load. *Financial aid:* In 1998–99, 3 fellowships (averaging $3,318 per year), 4 research assistantships (averaging $6,825 per year), 1 teaching assistantship (averaging $9,189 per year) were awarded.; career-related internships or fieldwork, Federal Work-Study, institutionally-sponsored loans, and unspecified assistantships also available. Aid available to part-time students. Financial aid applicants required to submit FAFSA. *Faculty research:* Volcanic hazards, atmospheric remote sensing, groundwater engineering, subsurface visualization. *Unit head:* V. T. V. Nguyen, Chair, Graduate Admissions Committee, 514-398-6870, Fax: 514-398-7361, E-mail: sandy@civil.lan.mcgill.ca. *Application contact:* Dr. Jimmy Diehl, Graduate Coordinator, 906-487-2665, Fax: 906-487-3371, E-mail: jdiehl@mtu.edu.

Montana Tech of The University of Montana, Graduate School, Geoscience Program, Butte, MT 59701-8997. Offers geochemistry (MS); geological engineering (MS); geology (MS); geophysical engineering (MS); hydrogeological engineering (MS); hydrogeology (MS); mineral economics (MS). Part-time programs available. *Faculty:* 17 full-time (2 women). *Students:* 15 full-time (6 women), 7 part-time (1 woman); includes 1 minority (Native American) *Degree requirements:* For master's, thesis required (for some programs), foreign language not required. *Entrance requirements:* For master's, GRE General Test, TOEFL (minimum score of 525 required), minimum B average. *Application deadline:* For fall admission, 4/1 (priority date); for spring admission, 10/1 (priority date). Applications are processed on a rolling basis. Application fee: $30. Tuition, state resident: full-time $3,211; part-time $162 per credit hour. Tuition, nonresident: full-time $9,883; part-time $440 per credit hour. International tuition: $15,500 full-time. *Unit head:* Cindy Dunstan, Administrative Assistant, 406-496-4128, Fax: 406-496-4334, E-mail: cdunstan@mtech.edu. *Application contact:* Cindy Dunstan, Administrative Assistant, 406-496-4128, Fax: 406-496-4334, E-mail: cdunstan@mtech.edu.

New Mexico Institute of Mining and Technology, Graduate Studies, Department of Earth and Environmental Science, Program in Geology, Socorro, NM 87801. Offers MS, PhD. *Faculty:* 6 full-time (1 woman), 1 (woman) part-time. *Students:* 30 full-time (10 women), 5 international. Average age 30. 40 applicants, 63% accepted. In 1998, 11 master's, 3 doctorates awarded. *Degree requirements:* For master's, thesis optional, foreign language not required; for doctorate, dissertation required, foreign language not required. *Entrance requirements:* For master's, GRE General Test, TOEFL (minimum score of 540 required); for doctorate, GRE General Test, GRE Subject Test, TOEFL (minimum score of 540 required). *Average time to degree:* Master's–3 years full-time; doctorate–6 years full-time. *Application deadline:* For fall admission, 3/1 (priority date); for spring admission, 6/1. Applications are processed on a rolling basis. Application fee: $16. *Financial aid:* In 1998–99, 14 research assistantships (averaging $9,670 per year), 8 teaching assistantships (averaging $9,670 per year) were awarded.; fellowships, Federal Work-Study and institutionally-sponsored loans also available. Financial aid application deadline: 3/1; financial aid applicants required to submit CSS PROFILE or FAFSA. *Faculty research:* Mineralogy, petrology, sedimentology, stratigraphy, structure. *Unit head:* Dr. Andrew Campbell, Coordinator, 505-835-5327, Fax: 505-835-6436, E-mail: geos@nmt.edu. *Application contact:* Dr. David B. Johnson, Dean of Graduate Studies, 505-835-5513, Fax: 505-835-5476, E-mail: graduate@nmt.edu.

New Mexico State University, Graduate School, College of Arts and Sciences, Department of Geological Sciences, Las Cruces, NM 88003-8001. Offers MS. Part-time programs available. *Faculty:* 6 full-time (2 women). *Students:* 12 full-time (2 women), 10 part-time (1 woman); includes 2 minority (both Hispanic Americans), 2 international. Average age 27. 17 applicants, 94% accepted. In 1998, 3 degrees awarded. *Degree requirements:* For master's, thesis required, foreign language not required. *Entrance requirements:* For master's, GRE General Test. *Application deadline:* For fall admission, 7/1 (priority date); for spring admission, 11/1. Applications are processed on a rolling basis. Application fee: $15 ($35 for international students). Electronic applications accepted. Tuition, state resident: full-time $2,682; part-time $112 per credit. Tuition, nonresident: full-time $8,376; part-time $349 per credit. Tuition and fees vary according to course load. *Financial aid:* Teaching assistantships, career-related internships or fieldwork and Federal Work-Study available. Aid available to part-time students. Financial aid application deadline: 3/1. *Faculty research:* Geochemistry, tectonics, sedimentology, stratigraphy, igneous petrology. *Unit head:* Dr. Thomas Giordano, Head, 505-646-2708, Fax: 505-646-1056, E-mail: tgiordan@nmsu.edu.

North Carolina State University, Graduate School, College of Physical and Mathematical Sciences, Department of Marine, Earth, and Atmospheric Sciences, Raleigh, NC 27695. Offers geology (MS, PhD); geophysics (MS, PhD); marine, earth, and atmospheric sciences (MS, PhD); meteorology (MS, PhD); oceanography (MS, PhD). *Faculty:* 34 full-time (2 women), 39 part-time (1 woman). *Students:* 118 full-time (30 women), 12 part-time (3 women); includes 2 minority (both Asian Americans or Pacific Islanders), 37 international. Terminal master's awarded for partial completion of doctoral program. *Degree requirements:* For master's, thesis, final oral exam required, foreign language not required; for doctorate, dissertation, final oral exam, preliminary oral and written exams required, foreign language not required. *Entrance requirements:* For master's and doctorate, GRE General Test, minimum GPA of 3.0. *Application deadline:* For fall admission, 6/25 (priority date); for spring admission, 11/25. Applications are processed on a rolling basis. Application fee: $45. *Unit head:* Dr. Leonard J. Pietrafesa,

Geology

North Carolina State University (continued)

Head, 919-515-3717, Fax: 919-515-7802, E-mail: leonard_pietrafesa@ncsu.edu. *Application contact:* Dr. Gerald S. Janowitz, Director of Graduate Programs, 919-515-7837, Fax: 919-515-7802, E-mail: janowitz@ncsu.edu.

See in-depth description on page 293.

Northern Arizona University, Graduate College, College of Arts and Sciences, Department of Geology, Program in Geology, Flagstaff, AZ 86011. Offers MS. *Students:* 23 full-time (12 women), 11 part-time (2 women); includes 3 minority (all Hispanic Americans) 38 applicants, 37% accepted. In 1998, 13 degrees awarded. *Degree requirements:* For master's, thesis required, foreign language not required. *Application deadline:* For fall admission, 2/1. Application fee: $45. *Financial aid:* Research assistantships, teaching assistantships, career-related internships or fieldwork, Federal Work-Study, and tuition waivers (full and partial) available. Total annual research expenditures: $499,385. *Unit head:* Dr. Ronald Blakey, Coordinator, 520-523-2740, E-mail: ronald.blakey@nau.edu. *Application contact:* Dr. Ronald Blakey, Coordinator, 520-523-2740, E-mail: ronald.blakey@nau.edu.

Northern Arizona University, Graduate College, College of Arts and Sciences, Program in Quaternary Studies, Flagstaff, AZ 86011. Offers MS. *Faculty:* 10 full-time (1 woman). *Students:* 13 full-time (6 women), 9 part-time (3 women); includes 1 Hispanic American, 1 international. Average age 27. 11 applicants, 27% accepted. In 1998, 2 degrees awarded. *Degree requirements:* For master's, thesis required, foreign language not required. *Application deadline:* For fall admission, 2/15 (priority date); for spring admission, 10/15. Applications are processed on a rolling basis. Application fee: $45. *Financial aid:* In 1998–99, 5 research assistantships were awarded.; career-related internships or fieldwork, Federal Work-Study, tuition waivers (full and partial), and unspecified assistantships also available. *Faculty research:* Sandbar stability in the Grand Canyon; Stone Age site excavation in South Africa; neogene reptile and mammal evolution; mammoths of Hot Springs, South Dakota; Quaternary science of national parks on Colorado Plateau. *Unit head:* Dr. Jim Mead, Director, 520-523-7184.

Northern Illinois University, Graduate School, College of Liberal Arts and Sciences, Department of Geology and Environmental Geosciences, De Kalb, IL 60115-2854. Offers MS, PhD. Part-time programs available. *Faculty:* 12 full-time (1 woman), 1 (woman) part-time. *Students:* 21 full-time (6 women), 18 part-time (6 women); includes 3 minority (1 Asian American or Pacific Islander, 1 Hispanic American, 1 Native American), 10 international. Average age 32. 27 applicants, 63% accepted. In 1998, 8 master's, 1 doctorate awarded. Terminal master's awarded for partial completion of doctoral program. *Degree requirements:* For master's, comprehensive exam required, thesis optional, foreign language not required; for doctorate, variable foreign language requirement, candidacy exam, dissertation defense, internship required. *Entrance requirements:* For master's, GRE General Test, TOEFL (minimum score of 550 required; 213 for computer-based), bachelor's degree in engineering or science, minimum GPA of 2.75; for doctorate, GRE General Test, TOEFL (minimum score of 550 required; 213 for computer-based), bachelor's or master's degree in engineering or science, minimum graduate GPA of 3.2. *Application deadline:* For fall admission, 6/1; for spring admission, 11/1. Applications are processed on a rolling basis. Application fee: $30. *Financial aid:* In 1998–99, 2 research assistantships, 15 teaching assistantships were awarded.; fellowships, career-related internships or fieldwork, Federal Work-Study, tuition waivers (full), and unspecified assistantships also available. Aid available to part-time students. *Unit head:* Dr. Jonathan Berg, Chair, 815-753-1943. *Application contact:* Dr. James Walker, Director of Graduate Studies, 815-753-7936.

Northwestern University, The Graduate School, Judd A. and Marjorie Weinberg College of Arts and Sciences, Department of Geological Sciences, Evanston, IL 60208. Offers MS, PhD. Admissions and degrees offered through The Graduate School. Part-time programs available. *Faculty:* 9 full-time (1 woman), 1 part-time (0 women). *Students:* 14 full-time (5 women), 3 international. Average age 27. 23 applicants, 35% accepted. In 1998, 2 master's, 6 doctorates awarded. *Degree requirements:* For doctorate, dissertation required. *Entrance requirements:* For master's and doctorate, GRE General Test, TOEFL (minimum score of 560 required). *Application deadline:* For fall admission, 1/30 (priority date). Application fee: $50 ($55 for international students). *Financial aid:* In 1998–99, 3 fellowships with full tuition reimbursements (averaging $11,673 per year), 1 research assistantship with partial tuition reimbursement (averaging $16,128 per year), 7 teaching assistantships with full tuition reimbursements (averaging $12,042 per year) were awarded.; career-related internships or fieldwork, Federal Work-Study, institutionally-sponsored loans, scholarships, and tuition waivers (full and partial) also available. Financial aid application deadline: 1/15; financial aid applicants required to submit FAFSA. *Faculty research:* Tectonophysics, seismology, biogeochemistry, stratigraphy, paleocecology. Total annual research expenditures: $579,058. *Unit head:* Abraham Lerman, Chair, 847-491-3238, Fax: 847-491-8060, E-mail: abe@earth.nwu.edu. *Application contact:* Charlotte Hayes, Admission Contact, 847-491-3238, Fax: 847-491-8060, E-mail: geodept@earth.nwu.edu.

Nova Scotia Agricultural College, Research and Graduate Studies, Truro, NS B2N 5E3, Canada. Offers agriculture (M Sc), including animal behavior, animal genetics, animal management, animal nutrition, animal technology, botany, crop breeding, crop management, crop physiology, ecology, environmental microbiology, food science, geology, nutrient management, pest management, physiology, plant biotechnology, plant pathology, soil chemistry, soil fertility, soil physics, waste management. Part-time programs available. *Faculty:* 33 full-time (4 women), 14 part-time (1 woman). *Students:* 23 full-time (15 women), 17 part-time (8 women). *Degree requirements:* For master's, thesis, candidacy exam required. *Entrance requirements:* For master's, TOEFL (minimum score of 580 required), minimum GPA of 3.0. *Application deadline:* For fall admission, 6/1; for winter admission, 10/1; for spring admission, 2/1. Applications are processed on a rolling basis. Application fee: $55. *Unit head:* Jill L. Rogers-Langille, Coordinator, 902-893-6360, Fax: 902-897-9399, E-mail: jrogers-langille@cadmin.nsac.ns.ca. *Application contact:* Kari Duff, Assistant, 902-893-6502, Fax: 902-897-9399, E-mail: kduff@cadmin.nsac.ns.ca.

The Ohio State University, Graduate School, College of Mathematical and Physical Sciences, Department of Geological Sciences, Columbus, OH 43210. Offers MS, PhD. *Faculty:* 26 full-time, 8 part-time. *Students:* 48 full-time (17 women), 10 part-time (2 women), 15 international. 41 applicants, 51% accepted. In 1998, 15 master's, 4 doctorates awarded. *Degree requirements:* For master's, thesis required, foreign language not required; for doctorate, dissertation required. *Entrance requirements:* For master's and doctorate, GRE General Test, GRE Subject Test. *Application deadline:* For fall admission, 8/15. Applications are processed on a rolling basis. Application fee: $30 ($40 for international students). *Financial aid:* Fellowships, research assistantships, teaching assistantships, Federal Work-Study and institutionally-sponsored loans available. Aid available to part-time students. *Unit head:* William I. Ausich, Chairman, 614-292-2721, Fax: 614-292-7688, E-mail: ausich.1@osu.edu.

Ohio University, Graduate Studies, College of Arts and Sciences, Department of Geological Sciences, Athens, OH 45701-2979. Offers MS. *Faculty:* 10 full-time (2 women), 2 part-time (1 woman). *Students:* 19 full-time (5 women), 1 (woman) part-time, 2 international. 16 applicants, 38% accepted. In 1998, 6 degrees awarded. *Degree requirements:* For master's, thesis required. *Application deadline:* For fall admission, 3/1 (priority date). Application fee: $30. Tuition, state resident: full-time $5,754; part-time $238 per credit hour. Tuition, nonresident: full-time $11,055; part-time $457 per credit hour. Tuition and fees vary according to course load, campus/location and program. *Financial aid:* Research assistantships, teaching assistantships, Federal Work-Study, institutionally-sponsored loans, scholarships, and tuition waivers (full and partial) available. Financial aid application deadline: 3/15. *Faculty research:* Hydrology, geophysics, sedimentology, structure and tectonics. *Unit head:* Dr. Damian Nance, Chair, 740-593-1101. *Application contact:* Dr. Douglas Green, Graduate Chair, 740-593-1843, E-mail: green@ouvaxa.cats.ohiou.edu.

Oklahoma State University, Graduate College, College of Arts and Sciences, School of Geology, Stillwater, OK 74078. Offers MS. *Faculty:* 8 full-time (1 woman). *Students:* 14 full-time (4 women), 30 part-time (9 women); includes 4 minority (1 African American, 3 Native Americans), 2 international. Average age 30. In 1998, 8 degrees awarded. *Degree requirements:* For master's, thesis required, foreign language not required. *Entrance requirements:* For master's, TOEFL (minimum score of 550 required). *Application deadline:* For fall admission, 6/1 (priority date). Application fee: $25. *Financial aid:* In 1998–99, 16 students received aid, including 3 research assistantships (averaging $10,195 per year), 13 teaching assistantships (averaging $7,787 per year); career-related internships or fieldwork, Federal Work-Study, and tuition waivers (partial) also available. Aid available to part-time students. Financial aid application deadline: 3/1. *Faculty research:* Groundwater hydrology, petroleum geology. *Unit head:* Dr. Darwin Boardman, Interim Head, 405-744-6358.

Old Dominion University, College of Sciences, Department of Ocean, Earth and Atmospheric Sciences, Program in Geological Sciences, Norfolk, VA 23529. Offers MS. *Students:* 2 full-time (1 woman), 9 part-time (4 women), 2 international. Average age 29. In 1998, 4 degrees awarded. *Degree requirements:* For master's, comprehensive exam required, thesis optional, foreign language not required. *Entrance requirements:* For master's, GRE, TOEFL, minimum GPA of 3.0 in major, 2.5 overall. *Application deadline:* For fall admission, 7/1. Applications are processed on a rolling basis. Application fee: $30. Electronic applications accepted. *Financial aid:* In 1998–99, 10 students received aid, including 3 research assistantships (averaging $11,710 per year), 3 teaching assistantships (averaging $7,867 per year); career-related internships or fieldwork, grants, and tuition waivers (partial) also available. Aid available to part-time students. Financial aid application deadline: 2/15; financial aid applicants required to submit FAFSA. *Faculty research:* Environmental geology, low-temperature geochemistry, sedimentation, geomorphology, geophysics. *Unit head:* Dr. Randall S. Spencer, Graduate Director, 757-683-4301, Fax: 757-683-5303, E-mail: rspencer@odu.edu.

Oregon State University, Graduate School, College of Science, Department of Geosciences, Program in Geology, Corvallis, OR 97331. Offers MA, MAIS, MS, PhD. Part-time programs available. *Faculty:* 9 full-time (0 women), 11 part-time (1 woman). *Students:* 28 full-time (5 women), 5 part-time (3 women); includes 1 minority (Native American), 8 international. Average age 28. In 1998, 8 master's, 2 doctorates awarded. Terminal master's awarded for partial completion of doctoral program. *Degree requirements:* For master's, variable foreign language requirement, thesis required; for doctorate, one foreign language, dissertation required. *Entrance requirements:* For master's and doctorate, GRE General Test, GRE Subject Test, TOEFL (minimum score of 550 required), minimum GPA of 3.0 in last 90 hours. *Application deadline:* For fall admission, 2/1. Applications are processed on a rolling basis. Application fee: $50. *Financial aid:* Fellowships, research assistantships, teaching assistantships, Federal Work-Study and institutionally-sponsored loans available. Aid available to part-time students. Financial aid application deadline: 2/1. *Faculty research:* Hydrogeology, geomorphology, ocean geology, geochemistry, earthquake geology. *Unit head:* Dr. David Burdige, Graduate Program Director, Programs in Oceanography, 757-683-4930, Fax: 757-683-5303, E-mail: dburdige@odu.edu. *Application contact:* Joanne VanGeest, Graduate Admissions Coordinator, 541-737-1204, Fax: 541-737-1200, E-mail: vangeesj@terra.geo.orst.edu.

Pennsylvania State University University Park Campus, Graduate School, College of Earth and Mineral Sciences, Department of Geosciences, Program in Geology, State College, University Park, PA 16802-1503. Offers MS, PhD. *Entrance requirements:* For master's and doctorate, GRE General Test, TOEFL.

Announcement: Penn State offers MS and PhD research opportunities in paleoclimatology, paleontology, petroleum geology, sedimentology, sequence and biostratigraphy, basin analysis, structural geology and tectonophysics, rock mechanics, tectonic geomorphology, remote sensing, hydrogeology, and glaciology.

Portland State University, Graduate Studies, College of Liberal Arts and Sciences, Department of Geology, Portland, OR 97207-0751. Offers geology (MA, MS, PhD); science/geology (MAT, MST). Part-time programs available. *Faculty:* 5 full-time (1 woman), 3 part-time (1 woman). *Students:* 13 full-time (5 women), 11 part-time (6 women), 2 international. Average age 29. 15 applicants, 60% accepted. In 1998, 5 degrees awarded. *Degree requirements:* For master's, computer language, thesis, field comprehensive required, foreign language not required; for doctorate, computer language, dissertation, 2 years of residency required. *Entrance requirements:* For master's, GRE General Test, GRE Subject Test, TOEFL (minimum score of 550 required), minimum GPA of 3.0 in upper-division course work or 2.75 overall, BA/BS in geology. *Application deadline:* For fall admission, 4/1 (priority date). Applications are processed on a rolling basis. Application fee: $50. *Financial aid:* In 1998–99, 2 research assistantships, 7 teaching assistantships were awarded.; career-related internships or fieldwork, Federal Work-Study, and institutionally-sponsored loans also available. Aid available to part-time students. Financial aid application deadline: 3/1; financial aid applicants required to submit FAFSA. *Faculty research:* Sediment transport, volcanic environmental geology, coastal and fluvial processes. Total annual research expenditures: $208,547. *Unit head:* Dr. Ansel Johnson, Head, 503-725-3022, Fax: 503-725-3025, E-mail: ansel@ch1.ch.pdx.edu. *Application contact:* Nancy Eriksson, Office Coordinator, 503-725-3022, Fax: 503-725-3025, E-mail: erikssonn@pdx.edu.

Princeton University, Graduate School, Department of Geosciences, Princeton, NJ 08544-1019. Offers atmospheric and oceanic sciences (PhD); environmental engineering and water resources (PhD); geological and geophysical sciences (PhD). *Degree requirements:* For doctorate, dissertation required. *Entrance requirements:* For doctorate, GRE General Test, GRE Subject Test.

Queens College of the City University of New York, Division of Graduate Studies, Mathematics and Natural Sciences Division, Department of Geology, Flushing, NY 11367-1597. Offers MA. Part-time and evening/weekend programs available. *Faculty:* 14 full-time (4 women). 5 applicants, 100% accepted. *Degree requirements:* For master's, thesis, comprehensive exam required, foreign language not required. *Entrance requirements:* For master's, GRE, TOEFL (minimum score of 550 required), previous course work in calculus, physics, and chemistry; minimum GPA of 3.0. *Application deadline:* For fall admission, 4/1; for spring admission, 11/1. Applications are processed on a rolling basis. Application fee: $40. Tuition, state resident: full-time $4,350; part-time $185 per credit. Tuition, nonresident: full-time $7,600; part-time $320 per credit. Required fees: $114; $57 per semester. Tuition and fees vary according to course load and program. *Financial aid:* Career-related internships or fieldwork, Federal Work-Study, institutionally-sponsored loans, tuition waivers (partial), unspecified assistantships, and adjunct lectureships available. Aid available to part-time students. Financial aid application deadline: 4/1; financial aid applicants required to submit FAFSA. *Faculty research:* Sedimentology/stratigraphy, paleontology, field petrology. *Unit head:* Dr. Allan Ludman, Chairperson, 718-997-3300. *Application contact:* Dr. Daniel Habib, Graduate Adviser, 718-997-3300, E-mail: dxhageol@qcl.qc.edu.

Queen's University at Kingston, School of Graduate Studies and Research, Faculty of Arts and Sciences, Department of Geological Sciences, Kingston, ON K7L 3N6, Canada. Offers M Sc, M Sc Eng, PhD. Part-time programs available. *Students:* 36 full-time (12 women), 7 part-time (2 women). In 1998, 15 master's, 7 doctorates awarded. *Degree requirements:* For master's, thesis optional, foreign language not required; for doctorate, dissertation, comprehensive exam required. *Entrance requirements:* For master's and doctorate, TOEFL (minimum score of 550 required). *Application deadline:* For fall admission, 2/28 (priority date). Application fee: $60. Electronic applications accepted. *Financial aid:* Fellowships, research assistantships, teaching assistantships, institutionally-sponsored loans available. Financial aid application deadline: 3/1. *Faculty research:* Mineralogy, petrology, structural geology, stratigraphy, sedimentology. *Unit head:* Dr. H. Helmstaedt, Head, 613-533-2598. *Application contact:* Dr. D. L. Smith, Graduate Coordinator, 613-533-6183.

Rensselaer Polytechnic Institute, Graduate School, School of Science, Department of Earth and Environmental Sciences, Program in Geology, Troy, NY 12180-3590. Offers MS, PhD. Part-time programs available. *Faculty:* 7 full-time (0 women), 2 part-time (0 women). *Students:* 18 full-time (7 women); includes 2 minority (1 African American, 1 Native American) 18 applicants, 78% accepted. In 1998, 3 master's, 2 doctorates awarded. *Degree requirements:* For doctorate, dissertation required. *Entrance requirements:* For master's and doctorate, GRE General Test, TOEFL (minimum score of 550 required). *Application deadline:* For fall admission, 2/1 (priority date). Applications are processed on a rolling basis. Application fee: $35. *Financial aid:* In 1998–99, research assistantships with partial tuition reimbursements (averaging $10,500 per year), teaching assistantships with partial tuition reimbursements (averaging $10,500 per year) were awarded.; career-related internships or fieldwork and tuition waivers (partial) also available. Financial aid application deadline: 2/1. *Unit head:* Dr. Lisa White, Graduate Coordinator, 415-338-1209, E-mail: lwhite@sfsu.edu. *Application contact:* Dr. Steven Roecker, Associate Professor, 518-276-6474, Fax: 518-276-6680, E-mail: ees@rpi.edu.

Rice University, Graduate Programs, Wiess School of Natural Sciences, Department of Geology and Geophysics, Houston, TX 77005-1892. Offers geology and geophysics (MA, PhD). *Degree requirements:* For master's and doctorate, thesis/dissertation required, foreign language not required. *Entrance requirements:* For master's and doctorate, GRE General Test (score in 70th percentile or higher on either section required), GRE Subject Test, TOEFL (minimum score of 550 required), minimum GPA of 3.0. *Faculty research:* Stratigraphy/sedimentology, igneous petrology, carbonate petrology, meteoritics, geochemistry.

Rutgers, The State University of New Jersey, Newark, Graduate School, Department of Geology, Newark, NJ 07102-3192. Offers environmental geology (MS). Part-time and evening/weekend programs available. *Faculty:* 6 full-time (1 woman). *Students:* 1 (woman) full-time, 6 part-time (1 woman). 10 applicants, 100% accepted. *Degree requirements:* For master's, comprehensive exam required, thesis optional. *Entrance requirements:* For master's, GRE General Test, minimum B average. Application fee: $40. *Faculty research:* Environmental geology, plate tectonics, geoarchaeology, geophysics, mineralogy-petrology. Total annual research expenditures: $124,000. *Unit head:* Dr. Andreas Vassiliou, Director, 973-353-5109, Fax: 973-353-5100, E-mail: avhass@andromeda.rutgers.edu.

Rutgers, The State University of New Jersey, New Brunswick, Graduate School, Program in Geological Sciences, New Brunswick, NJ 08903. Offers MS, PhD. Part-time programs available. *Faculty:* 16 full-time (1 woman). *Students:* 15 full-time (9 women), 13 part-time (4 women). 16 applicants, 31% accepted. In 1998, 1 master's awarded (100% found work related to degree); 3 doctorates awarded (100% found work related to degree). *Degree requirements:* For master's, thesis required, foreign language not required; for doctorate, dissertation required. *Entrance requirements:* For master's and doctorate, GRE General Test. *Application deadline:* For fall admission, 7/1 (priority date); for spring admission, 12/1. Applications are processed on a rolling basis. Application fee: $50. *Financial aid:* In 1998–99, 13 students received aid, including 1 fellowship with full tuition reimbursement available (averaging $14,000 per year), 4 research assistantships with full tuition reimbursements available (averaging $12,136 per year), 8 teaching assistantships with full tuition reimbursements available (averaging $12,136 per year); Federal Work-Study and scholarships also available. Financial aid application deadline: 3/1; financial aid applicants required to submit FAFSA. *Faculty research:* Petrology, paleoecology, stratigraphy and sedimentology, geophysics, geochemistry, paleomagnetics. Total annual research expenditures: $605,000. *Unit head:* Michael J. Carr, Director, 732-445-3619.

St. Francis Xavier University, Graduate Studies, Program in Geology, Antigonish, NS B2G 2W5, Canada. Offers M Sc. *Faculty:* 3 full-time (0 women). *Students:* 1 (woman) full-time. 2 applicants, 50% accepted. In 1998, 2 degrees awarded. *Degree requirements:* Foreign language not required. *Entrance requirements:* For master's, minimum undergraduate B average. *Application deadline:* For fall admission, 9/1 (priority date). Applications are processed on a rolling basis. Application fee: $30. *Faculty research:* Petrogenesis, geochemistry, structural geology and tectonics, sedimentology, hydrogeology, paleontology. Total annual research expenditures: $105,000. *Unit head:* Dr. Alan Anderson, Chair, 902-867-2309, Fax: 902-867-2457, E-mail: aanderso@stfx.ca. *Application contact:* Admissions Office, 902-867-2219, Fax: 902-867-2329, E-mail: admit@stfx.ca.

San Diego State University, Graduate and Research Affairs, College of Sciences, Department of Geological Sciences, San Diego, CA 92182. Offers MS. *Students:* 15 full-time (7 women), 25 part-time (6 women); includes 7 minority (3 Asian Americans or Pacific Islanders, 2 Hispanic Americans, 2 Native Americans) Average age 27. 25 applicants, 72% accepted. In 1998, 8 degrees awarded. *Degree requirements:* For master's, thesis required, foreign language not required. *Entrance requirements:* For master's, GRE General Test (minimum combined score of 1000 required), TOEFL (minimum score of 550 required), bachelor's degree in related field. *Application deadline:* For fall admission, 7/1 (priority date); for spring admission, 12/1. Applications are processed on a rolling basis. Application fee: $55. *Financial aid:* Fellowships, research assistantships, teaching assistantships available. *Faculty research:* Earthquakes, hydrology, meteorological analysis and tomography studies. Total annual research expenditures: $575,000. *Unit head:* Gary Girty, Chair, 619-594-2552, Fax: 619-594-4372, E-mail: ggirty@geology.sdsu.edu. *Application contact:* David Kimbrough, Graduate Coordinator, 619-594-1385, Fax: 619-594-4372, E-mail: jkimbrough@geology.sdsu.edu.

San Jose State University, Graduate Studies, College of Science, Department of Geology, San Jose, CA 95192-0001. Offers MS. *Faculty:* 14 full-time (2 women), 12 part-time (2 women). *Students:* 9 full-time (3 women), 12 part-time (4 women); includes 1 minority (Hispanic American), 2 international. Average age 29. 14 applicants, 71% accepted. In 1998, 1 degree awarded. *Degree requirements:* For master's, thesis required, foreign language not required. *Entrance requirements:* For master's, GRE. *Application deadline:* For fall admission, 6/1. Applications are processed on a rolling basis. Application fee: $59. Tuition, nonresident: part-time $246 per unit. Required fees: $1,939; $1,309 per year. *Financial aid:* Teaching assistantships, Federal Work-Study available. *Unit head:* Dr. John Williams, Chair, 408-924-5050, Fax: 408-924-5053. *Application contact:* Dr. Cal Stevens, Graduate Adviser, 408-924-5029.

South Dakota School of Mines and Technology, Graduate Division, Department of Geology and Geological Engineering, Program in Paleontology, Rapid City, SD 57701-3995. Offers MS. Part-time programs available. *Faculty:* 3 part-time (0 women). *Students:* 10 full-time (5 women). Average age 24. In 1998, 2 degrees awarded. *Degree requirements:* For master's, thesis required, foreign language not required. *Entrance requirements:* For master's, GRE General Test, GRE Subject Test, TOEFL (minimum score of 520 required), TWE. *Application deadline:* For fall admission, 6/15 (priority date); for spring admission, 10/15. Applications are processed on a rolling basis. Application fee: $15. Electronic applications accepted. Tuition, state resident: part-time $89 per hour. Tuition, nonresident: part-time $261 per hour. Part-time tuition and fees vary according to program. *Financial aid:* In 1998–99, 1 research assistantship, 4 teaching assistantships were awarded.; fellowships, Federal Work-Study and institutionally-sponsored loans also available. Aid available to part-time students. Financial aid application deadline: 5/15. *Faculty research:* Cretaceous vertebrates, Miocene vertebrates, Oligocene vertebrates. *Unit head:* Dr. James Fox, Dean, 605-394-2461. *Application contact:* Brenda Brown, Secretary, 800-454-8162 Ext. 2493, Fax: 605-394-5360, E-mail: graduate_admissions@silver.sdmt.edu.

Southern Illinois University Carbondale, Graduate School, College of Science, Department of Geology, Carbondale, IL 62901-6806. Offers MS, PhD. *Faculty:* 11 full-time (0 women). *Students:* 17 full-time (9 women), 5 part-time (2 women). Average age 25. 12 applicants, 58% accepted. In 1998, 4 master's awarded. *Degree requirements:* For master's, thesis required, foreign language not required; for doctorate, one foreign language (computer language can substitute), dissertation required. *Entrance requirements:* For master's, GRE, TOEFL (minimum score of 550 required), minimum GPA of 2.7; for doctorate, GRE General Test, TOEFL (minimum score of 550 required), minimum GPA of 3.25. *Application deadline:* For fall admission, 2/15 (priority date). Applications are processed on a rolling basis. Application fee: $20. *Financial aid:* In 1998–99, 17 students received aid; fellowships with full tuition reimbursements available, research assistantships with full tuition reimbursements available, teaching assistantships with full tuition reimbursements available, Federal Work-Study, institutionally-sponsored loans, and tuition waivers (full) available. Aid available to part-time students. Total annual research expenditures: $720,000. *Unit head:* Dr. Jay Zimmerman, Chair, 618-453-3351, Fax: 618-453-7393, E-mail: zimmerman@qm.c_geo.siu.edu.

Announcement: Strong, broad-based MS and PhD programs are supported by excellent analytical laboratories for research in environmental geology, coal/organic petrology, organic geochemistry, SEM/EDS, GIS, sedimentology, and geophysics. Available are 2 drilling/coring rigs, a vibracorer, and a 40-foot-by-8-foot flume for hydrogeology/geomorphology research; field data acquisition equipment and data processing facilities for research in geophysics; and facilities for research in environmental geology, ore deposits, structural geology, sedimentary petrology, paleontology, environments of deposition, computer mapping, and coal geology. Graduate students currently are conducting research in environmental geology, organic geochemistry, sedimentology, paleoecology, hydrogeology, seismology, and geomorphology.

Southern Methodist University, Dedman College, Department of Geological Sciences, Program in Geology, Dallas, TX 75275. Offers MS, PhD. *Students:* 9 full-time (3 women), 10 part-time (5 women), 8 international. Average age 29. In 1998, 4 master's awarded. *Degree requirements:* For master's, thesis, qualifying exam required, foreign language not required; for doctorate, one foreign language, dissertation, qualifying exam required. *Entrance requirements:* For master's and doctorate, GRE General Test (minimum combined score of 1200 required), minimum GPA of 3.0. *Application deadline:* For fall admission, 6/30; for spring admission, 11/30. Application fee: $50. Tuition: Part-time $686 per credit hour. Required fees: $88 per credit hour. Part-time tuition and fees vary according to course load and program. *Financial aid:* Application deadline: 2/15; *Application contact:* Dr. Robert Gregory, Graduate Director, 214-768-3075, Fax: 214-768-2701, E-mail: bgregory@mail.smu.edu.

State University of New York at Albany, College of Arts and Sciences, Department of Earth and Atmospheric Sciences, Albany, NY 12222-0001. Offers atmospheric science (MS, PhD); geology (MS, PhD). Evening/weekend programs available. *Faculty:* 24 full-time (0 women). *Students:* 46 full-time (16 women), 4 part-time; includes 1 minority (African American), 25 international. *Degree requirements:* For master's, thesis, comprehensive exam required; for doctorate, dissertation, comprehensive and oral exams required. *Entrance requirements:* For master's and doctorate, GRE General Test. Application fee: $50. Tuition, state resident: full-time $5,100; part-time $213 per credit. Tuition, nonresident: full-time $8,416; part-time $351 per credit. Required fees: $31 per credit. *Unit head:* Dr. John Delano, Chair, 518-442-4466.

State University of New York at Binghamton, Graduate School, School of Arts and Sciences, Department of Geological Sciences, Binghamton, NY 13902-6000. Offers MA, PhD. *Faculty:* 14 full-time, 5 part-time. *Students:* 33 full-time (5 women), 4 part-time (all women); includes 2 minority (1 Asian American or Pacific Islander, 1 Hispanic American), 9 international. Average age 30. 28 applicants, 61% accepted. In 1998, 3 master's awarded. Terminal master's awarded for partial completion of doctoral program. *Degree requirements:* For master's, thesis or alternative required; for doctorate, dissertation, departmental qualifying exam required. *Entrance requirements:* For master's and doctorate, GRE General Test, GRE Subject Test, TOEFL. *Application deadline:* For fall admission, 4/15 (priority date); for spring admission, 11/1. Applications are processed on a rolling basis. Application fee: $50. Electronic applications accepted. Tuition, state resident: full-time $5,100; part-time $213 per credit. Tuition, nonresident: full-time $8,416; part-time $351 per credit. Required fees: $77 per credit. Part-time tuition and fees vary according to course load. *Financial aid:* In 1998–99, 23 students received aid, including 1 fellowship with full tuition reimbursement available (averaging $8,000 per year), 9 research assistantships with full tuition reimbursements available (averaging $8,325 per year), 12 teaching assistantships with full tuition reimbursements available (averaging $8,250 per year); career-related internships or fieldwork, Federal Work-Study, institutionally-sponsored loans, and unspecified assistantships also available. Aid available to part-time students. Financial aid application deadline: 2/15. *Unit head:* Dr. H. R. Naslund, Chairperson, 607-777-2264.

State University of New York at Buffalo, Graduate School, College of Arts and Sciences, Department of Geology, Buffalo, NY 14260. Offers MA, PhD. Part-time programs available. *Faculty:* 8 full-time (1 woman), 3 part-time (1 woman). *Students:* 21 full-time (9 women), 18 part-time (3 women); includes 3 minority (all African Americans), 7 international. Average age 30. 26 applicants, 69% accepted. In 1998, 14 master's awarded (100% found work related to degree); 4 doctorates awarded (100% entered university research/teaching). *Degree requirements:* For master's, variable foreign language requirement, comprehensive exam, project, or thesis required; for doctorate, variable foreign language requirement, dissertation, dissertation defense required. *Entrance requirements:* For master's and doctorate, GRE General Test, TOEFL (minimum score of 550 required). *Average time to degree:* Master's–4.8 years full-time; doctorate–4.1 years full-time. *Application deadline:* For fall admission, 3/1 (priority date); for spring admission, 10/1. Applications are processed on a rolling basis. Application fee: $35. Electronic applications accepted. Tuition, state resident: full-time $5,100; part-time $213 per credit hour. Tuition, nonresident: full-time $8,416; part-time $351 per credit hour. Required fees: $870; $75 per semester. Tuition and fees vary according to course load and program. *Financial aid:* In 1998–99, 30 students received aid, including 2 fellowships, 5 research assistantships, 15 teaching assistantships; Federal Work-Study and grants also available. Financial aid application deadline: 2/28; financial aid applicants required to submit FAFSA. *Faculty research:* Fracture and environmental geology, volcanology, basin analysis, evolutionary biology. Total annual research expenditures: $640,000. *Unit head:* Dr. Michael F. Sheridan, Chairman, 716-645-6800 Ext. 6100, Fax: 716-645-3999, E-mail: mfs@acsu.buffalo.edu. *Application contact:* Dr. Robert D. Jacobi, Director of Graduate Studies, 716-645-6800 Ext. 2468, Fax: 716-645-3999, E-mail: rdjacobi@acsu.buffalo.edu.

State University of New York at New Paltz, Graduate School, Faculty of Liberal Arts and Sciences, Department of Geological Sciences, New Paltz, NY 12561. Offers MA, MAT, MS Ed. *Degree requirements:* For master's, thesis, comprehensive exam required. *Entrance requirements:* For master's, GRE General Test, minimum GPA of 3.0. *Application deadline:* For fall admission, 3/15 (priority date). Applications are processed on a rolling basis. Application fee: $50. *Financial aid:* Research assistantships, teaching assistantships, Federal Work-Study and institutionally-sponsored loans available. *Unit head:* Dr. Frederick Vollmer, Chairman, 914-257-3760.

Stephen F. Austin State University, Graduate School, College of Sciences and Mathematics, Department of Geology, Nacogdoches, TX 75962. Offers MS, MSNS. *Faculty:* 6 full-time (0 women). *Students:* 8 full-time (2 women), 2 part-time. Average age 23. 4 applicants, 100% accepted. In 1998, 1 degree awarded. *Degree requirements:* For master's, comprehensive exam required. *Entrance requirements:* For master's, GRE General Test (minimum combined score of 1000 required), TOEFL, minimum GPA of 2.8 in last 60 hours, 2.5 overall. *Application deadline:* For fall admission, 8/1 (priority date); for spring admission, 12/15. Applications are processed on a rolling basis. Application fee: $0 ($50 for international students). Tuition, state resident: full-time $1,792. Tuition, nonresident: full-time $6,880. *Financial aid:* In 1998–99, teaching assistantships (averaging $6,750 per year); Federal Work-Study and unspecified assistantships also available. Financial aid application deadline: 3/1. *Faculty research:* Stratigraphy of Kaibab limestone, Utah; structure of Ouachita Mountains, Arkansas; groundwater chemistry of Carrizo Sand, Texas. *Unit head:* Dr. William Roberts, Chair, 409-468-3701. *Application contact:* Dr. R. LaRell Nielson, Director of Graduate Program, 409-468-2248.

Sul Ross State University, School of Arts and Sciences, Department of Geology and Chemistry, Alpine, TX 79832. Offers MS. Part-time programs available. *Degree requirements:* For master's, thesis optional, foreign language not required. *Entrance requirements:* For master's, GRE

Geology

Sul Ross State University (continued)
General Test (minimum combined score of 850 required), minimum GPA of 2.5 in last 60 hours of undergraduate work.

Announcement: Program stresses integrated field and laboratory research. The University is situated in an area of diverse and well-exposed geology. Research equipment includes GIS, XRF, SEM, XRD, AA, CL, and NAA. Current faculty research in environmental geology, volcanology, trace-element geochemistry, paleontology, carbonate depositional environments, paleoecology, planetary geology, and remote sensing.

Syracuse University, Graduate School, College of Arts and Sciences, Department of Earth Sciences, Syracuse, NY 13244-0003. Offers geology (MA, MS, PhD); hydrogeology (MS). *Faculty:* 9. *Students:* 24 full-time (9 women), 1 part-time, 4 international. Average age 29. 18 applicants, 28% accepted. In 1998, 1 master's, 1 doctorate awarded. *Degree requirements:* For master's, thesis (for some programs), research tool required; for doctorate, dissertation, 2 research tools required. *Entrance requirements:* For master's and doctorate, GRE General Test, GRE Subject Test. Application fee: $40. Tuition: Full-time $13,992; part-time $583 per credit hour. *Financial aid:* Fellowships, research assistantships, teaching assistantships, Federal Work-Study and tuition waivers (partial) available. Financial aid application deadline: 3/1. *Unit head:* Dr. Cathryn Newton, Chair, 315-443-2672.

Temple University, Graduate School, College of Science and Technology, Department of Geology, Philadelphia, PA 19122-6096. Offers MA. *Faculty:* 6 full-time (1 woman). *Students:* 15 (3 women); includes 1 minority (Asian American or Pacific Islander) 15 applicants, 80% accepted. In 1998, 6 degrees awarded. *Degree requirements:* For master's, thesis, qualifying exam required, foreign language not required. *Entrance requirements:* For master's, GRE General Test, minimum GPA of 3.0 during previous 2 years, 2.8 overall. *Application deadline:* For fall admission, 2/1 (priority date); for spring admission, 10/1. Application fee: $40. Electronic applications accepted. *Financial aid:* Fellowships, research assistantships, teaching assistantships, scholarships available. *Unit head:* Dr. George Myer, Chair, 215-204-7173, Fax: 215-204-3496, E-mail: gmyer@nimbus.ocis.temple.edu. *Application contact:* Dr. Edwin Anderson, Graduate Secretary, 215-204-8249, Fax: 215-204-3496, E-mail: sburgess@vm.temple.edu.

Announcement: Advanced study and research in stratigraphy, structural geology, mineralogy, petrology, geochemistry, environmental geology, geophysics, and hydrogeology. Financial support (teaching assistantship, research assistantship, fellowship) includes stipend, book allowance, and full tuition. Graduates of the program have an excellent record of employment and an outstanding rate of acceptance into doctoral programs.

Texas A&M University, College of Geosciences, Department of Geology and Geophysics, College Station, TX 77843. Offers MS, PhD. *Faculty:* 32 full-time (2 women). *Students:* 83 full-time (21 women), 17 part-time (6 women); includes 6 minority (4 Asian Americans or Pacific Islanders, 2 Hispanic Americans), 39 international. Average age 31. 53 applicants, 75% accepted. In 1998, 8 master's, 6 doctorates awarded. *Degree requirements:* For master's and doctorate, thesis/dissertation required, foreign language not required. *Entrance requirements:* For master's and doctorate, GRE General Test, TOEFL. *Application deadline:* For fall admission, 3/1 (priority date); for spring admission, 10/1. Applications are processed on a rolling basis. Application fee: $50 ($75 for international students). Electronic applications accepted. *Financial aid:* In 1998–99, 92 students received aid, including 24 fellowships with partial tuition reimbursements available, 16 research assistantships with partial tuition reimbursements available (averaging $11,475 per year), 66 teaching assistantships with partial tuition reimbursements available (averaging $11,475 per year); Federal Work-Study, institutionally-sponsored loans, and tuition waivers (partial) also available. Financial aid application deadline: 3/1; financial aid applicants required to submit FAFSA. *Faculty research:* Environmental and engineering geology and geophysics, petroleum geology, tectonophysics, geochemistry. Total annual research expenditures: $343,000. *Unit head:* Andrew Hajash, Head, 409-845-2451, Fax: 409-845-6162, E-mail: hajash@geo.tamu.edu. *Application contact:* Robert K. Popp, Graduate Adviser, 409-845-2451, Fax: 409-845-6162, E-mail: popp@geo.tamu.edu.

Texas A&M University–Kingsville, College of Graduate Studies, College of Arts and Sciences, Department of Geosciences, Kingsville, TX 78363. Offers applied geology (MS). Part-time and evening/weekend programs available. *Faculty:* 6 full-time (0 women). *Degree requirements:* For master's, thesis, comprehensive exam required, foreign language not required. *Entrance requirements:* For master's, GRE General Test (minimum combined score of 800 required), GRE Subject Test (geology), TOEFL (minimum score of 500 required), minimum GPA of 3.0. *Application deadline:* For fall admission, 6/1; for spring admission, 11/15. Applications are processed on a rolling basis. Application fee: $15 ($25 for international students). Tuition, state resident: full-time $2,062. Tuition, nonresident: full-time $7,246. *Financial aid:* Fellowships, teaching assistantships, career-related internships or fieldwork, Federal Work-Study, and institutionally-sponsored loans available. Aid available to part-time students. Financial aid application deadline: 5/15. *Faculty research:* Stratigraphy and sedimentology of modern coastal sediments, sandstone diagnosis, vertebrate paleontology, structural geology. Total annual research expenditures: $3,000. *Unit head:* Dr. Michael Jordan, Coordinator, 361-593-3310, Fax: 361-593-3107.

Texas Christian University, Add Ran College of Arts and Sciences, Department of Geology, Fort Worth, TX 76129-0002. Offers MS. Part-time and evening/weekend programs available. *Students:* 10 (3 women) 1 international. 10 applicants, 50% accepted. In 1998, 5 degrees awarded. *Degree requirements:* For master's, thesis, preliminary exam required, foreign language not required. *Entrance requirements:* For master's, GRE General Test (minimum combined score of 1000 required), TOEFL (minimum score of 550 required). *Application deadline:* For fall admission, 3/1; for spring admission, 12/1. Applications are processed on a rolling basis. Application fee: $0. *Financial aid:* Teaching assistantships, unspecified assistantships available. Financial aid application deadline: 3/1. *Unit head:* Dr. Ken Morgan, Chairperson, 817-921-7270.

Tulane University, Graduate School, Department of Geology, New Orleans, LA 70118-5669. Offers geology (MS, PhD); paleontology (PhD). *Students:* 8 full-time (3 women); includes 1 minority (Hispanic American), 1 international. *Degree requirements:* For master's, one foreign language, thesis or alternative required; for doctorate, one foreign language, dissertation required. *Entrance requirements:* For master's, GRE General Test (minimum combined score of 1000 required; average 1200), TOEFL (minimum score of 600 required), TSE (minimum score of 220 required), minimum B average in undergraduate course work; for doctorate, GRE General Test (minimum combined score of 1000 required; average 1200), TOEFL (minimum score of 600 required), TSE (minimum score of 220 required). *Application deadline:* For fall admission, 2/1. Application fee: $45. *Unit head:* Dr. Stephen Nelson, Chair, 504-865-5198.

See in-depth description on page 303.

Université de Montréal, Faculty of Graduate Studies, Faculty of Arts and Sciences, Department of Geology, Montréal, PQ H3C 3J7, Canada. Offers M Sc, PhD. *Faculty:* 14 full-time (1 woman). *Students:* 21 full-time (7 women). 15 applicants, 27% accepted. In 1998, 1 master's, 2 doctorates awarded. *Degree requirements:* For master's, thesis or alternative required, foreign language not required; for doctorate, one foreign language, dissertation, general exam required. *Entrance requirements:* For doctorate, M Sc in geology or related field. *Application deadline:* For fall admission, 3/1. Application fee: $30. *Financial aid:* Fellowships, teaching assistantships, tuition waivers (partial) available. Financial aid application deadline: 4/15. *Faculty research:* Geochemistry, petrology, stratigraphy, tectonics, geomorphology. *Unit head:* Bernard Mamet, Chairman, 514-343-7542. *Application contact:* Walter Trzcienski, Graduate Chairman, 514-343-5977.

Université Laval, Faculty of Graduate Studies, Faculty of Sciences and Engineering, Department of Geology and Geological Engineering, Sainte-Foy, PQ G1K 7P4, Canada. Offers earth sciences (PhD); geology (M Sc, PhD). *Students:* 30 full-time (12 women), 5 part-time. 17 applicants, 47% accepted. In 1998, 3 master's awarded. *Application deadline:* For fall admission, 3/1. Application fee: $30. *Faculty research:* Engineering, economics, regional geology. *Unit head:* Michel Rocheleau, Director, 418-656-2131 Ext. 7340, Fax: 418-656-7339, E-mail: michel.rocheleau@ggl.ulaval.ca.

The University of Akron, Graduate School, Buchtel College of Arts and Sciences, Department of Geology, Akron, OH 44325-0001. Offers earth science (MS); engineering geology (MS); environmental geology (MS); geophysics (MS). Part-time programs available. *Faculty:* 11 full-time, 5 part-time. *Students:* 10 full-time (4 women), 2 part-time (1 woman); includes 2 minority (1 African American, 1 Hispanic American), 1 international. Average age 28. In 1998, 6 degrees awarded. *Degree requirements:* For master's, thesis required, foreign language not required. *Entrance requirements:* For master's, minimum GPA of 2.75. *Average time to degree:* Master's–2 years full-time, 4 years part-time. *Application deadline:* For fall admission, 3/1. Applications are processed on a rolling basis. Application fee: $25 ($50 for international students). Tuition, state resident: part-time $189 per credit. Tuition, nonresident: part-time $353 per credit. Required fees: $7.3 per credit. *Financial aid:* Research assistantships with full tuition reimbursements, teaching assistantships with full tuition reimbursements, Federal Work-Study and tuition waivers (full) available. *Faculty research:* Broad-range geology, petrology (sedimentary, igneous, metamorphic, and clay), geochemistry, geophysics. *Unit head:* Dr. John Szabo, Chair, 330-972-7630, E-mail: jszabo@uakron.edu. *Application contact:* Dr. David McConnell, Director of Graduate Studies, 330-972-8047, E-mail: mcconnell@uakron.edu.

The University of Alabama, Graduate School, College of Arts and Sciences, Department of Geological Sciences, Tuscaloosa, AL 35487. Offers MS, PhD. *Faculty:* 13 full-time (1 woman), 2 part-time (0 women). *Students:* 33 full-time (9 women), 7 part-time (3 women); includes 1 Hispanic American, 7 international. Average age 27. 18 applicants, 67% accepted. In 1998, 9 master's awarded (78% found work related to degree, 22% continued full-time study); 1 doctorate awarded (100% entered university research/teaching). *Degree requirements:* For master's and doctorate, thesis/dissertation required, foreign language not required. *Entrance requirements:* For master's, GRE General Test (minimum combined score of 1500 on three sections required), minimum GPA of 3.0; for doctorate, GRE General Test. *Average time to degree:* Master's–2.9 years full-time; doctorate–2.5 years full-time. *Application deadline:* For fall admission, 3/15 (priority date); for spring admission, 11/15. Applications are processed on a rolling basis. Application fee: $25. Electronic applications accepted. *Financial aid:* In 1998–99, 4 fellowships with full tuition reimbursements (averaging $11,000 per year), 14 research assistantships with full tuition reimbursements, 13 teaching assistantships with full tuition reimbursements (averaging $9,200 per year) were awarded.; career-related internships or fieldwork, Federal Work-Study, and institutionally-sponsored loans also available. Financial aid application deadline: 3/15. *Faculty research:* Structure, petrology, stratigraphy, geochemistry, hydrogeology. Total annual research expenditures: $1.5 million. *Unit head:* W. Berry Lyons, Chairperson, 205-348-1876, Fax: 205-348-0818, E-mail: blyons@wgs.geo.ua.edu. *Application contact:* Richard H. Groshong, Director of Graduate Studies, 205-348-1882, Fax: 205-348-0818, E-mail: rgroshon@wgs.geo.ua.edu.

See in-depth description on page 305.

University of Alaska Fairbanks, Graduate School, College of Science, Engineering and Mathematics, Department of Geology and Geophysics, Fairbanks, AK 99775-7480. Offers geology (MS, PhD); geophysics (MS, PhD); geoscience (MAT). *Faculty:* 21 full-time (3 women). *Students:* 37 full-time (11 women), 17 part-time (6 women); includes 3 minority (2 Asian Americans or Pacific Islanders, 1 Native American), 12 international. Average age 30. 24 applicants, 71% accepted. In 1998, 2 master's, 4 doctorates awarded. *Degree requirements:* For master's, thesis, comprehensive exam required, foreign language not required; for doctorate, one foreign language (computer language can substitute), dissertation, comprehensive exam required. *Entrance requirements:* For master's and doctorate, GRE General Test, GRE Subject Test, TOEFL (minimum score of 550 required). *Application deadline:* For fall admission, 3/1. Application fee: $35. *Financial aid:* Research assistantships, teaching assistantships available. Financial aid application deadline: 3/1. *Faculty research:* Glacial surging, Alaska as geologic fragments, natural zeolites. *Unit head:* Dr. Paul Layer, Head, 907-474-7565. *Application contact:* Doug Christensen, Adviser, 907-474-7426.

University of Arkansas, Graduate School, J. William Fulbright College of Arts and Sciences, Department of Geosciences, Program in Geology, Fayetteville, AR 72701-1201. Offers MS. *Faculty:* 7 full-time (0 women). *Students:* 16 full-time (4 women), 3 part-time; includes 2 minority (1 African American, 1 Asian American or Pacific Islander), 1 international. 9 applicants, 89% accepted. In 1998, 7 degrees awarded. *Degree requirements:* For master's, thesis required, foreign language not required. Application fee: $40 ($50 for international students). Tuition, state resident: full-time $3,186. Tuition, nonresident: full-time $7,560. Required fees: $378. *Financial aid:* Research assistantships, teaching assistantships, career-related internships or fieldwork and Federal Work-Study available. Aid available to part-time students. Financial aid application deadline: 4/1; financial aid applicants required to submit FAFSA. *Unit head:* Ronald Konig, Chair, 501-575-3355, E-mail: rkonig@comp.uark.edu.

University of British Columbia, Faculty of Graduate Studies, Faculty of Science, Department of Earth and Ocean Sciences, Program in Geological Sciences, Vancouver, BC V6T 1Z2, Canada. Offers M Sc, PhD. Part-time programs available. *Degree requirements:* For master's, thesis required (for some programs); for doctorate, dissertation, comprehensive exam required. *Entrance requirements:* For master's and doctorate, TOEFL (minimum score of 600 required). Electronic applications accepted.

University of Calgary, Faculty of Graduate Studies, Faculty of Science, Department of Geology and Geophysics, Calgary, AB T2N 1N4, Canada. Offers geology (M Sc, PhD); geophysics (M Sc, PhD). Part-time programs available. *Faculty:* 29 full-time (3 women), 4 part-time (1 woman). *Students:* 81 full-time (40 women), 7 part-time (3 women). 45 applicants, 27% accepted. In 1998, 7 master's, 4 doctorates awarded. Terminal master's awarded for partial completion of doctoral program. *Degree requirements:* For master's, thesis required; for doctorate, dissertation, candidacy exam required. *Entrance requirements:* For master's, TOEFL (minimum score of 580 required), B Sc; for doctorate, TOEFL (minimum score of 580 required), B Sc or M Sc. *Average time to degree:* Master's–3 years full-time; doctorate–5 years full-time. *Application deadline:* For fall admission, 2/1 (priority date). Applications are processed on a rolling basis. Application fee: $60. *Financial aid:* In 1998–99, 50 students received aid, including 17 fellowships, 27 teaching assistantships; career-related internships or fieldwork, institutionally-sponsored loans, and research scholarships also available. Financial aid application deadline: 2/1. *Faculty research:* Geochemistry, petrology, paleontology, stratigraphy, exploration and solid-earth geophysics. *Unit head:* Donald C. Lawton, Head, 403-220-8863, Fax: 403-284-0074, E-mail: dclawton@geo.ucalgary.ca. *Application contact:* Gail Campbell, Graduate Student Administrator, 403-220-3254, Fax: 403-284-0074, E-mail: campbell@geo.ucalgary.ca.

University of California, Berkeley, Graduate Division, College of Letters and Science, Department of Geology and Geophysics, Division of Geology, Berkeley, CA 94720-1500. Offers MA, MS, PhD. *Students:* 42 full-time (16 women); includes 6 minority (3 Asian Americans or Pacific Islanders, 1 Hispanic American, 2 Native Americans), 10 international. 75 applicants, 29% accepted. In 1998, 2 master's, 2 doctorates awarded. Terminal master's awarded for partial completion of doctoral program. *Degree requirements:* For master's, oral exam (MA), thesis (MS) required; for doctorate, dissertation, candidacy and comprehensive exams required. *Entrance requirements:* For master's and doctorate, GRE General Test, TOEFL (minimum score of 570 required; 230 for computer-based), minimum GPA of 3.0. *Application deadline:* For fall admission, 1/12. Application fee: $40. *Financial aid:* Fellowships, research assistantships, teaching assistantships, Federal Work-Study available. Financial aid application deadline: 1/12. *Faculty research:* Tectonics, environmental geology, economic geology, mineralogy, geochemistry. *Unit head:* Dr. Joseph S. Thrasher, Professor and Director of Graduate Studies,

205-348-8434, Fax: 205-348-8448, E-mail: jthrashe@ua1vm.ua.edu. *Application contact:* Mei Griebenow, Graduate Assistant for Admission, 510-642-5574, Fax: 510-643-9980, E-mail: meig@seismo.berkeley.edu.

University of California, Davis, Graduate Studies, Program in Geology, Davis, CA 95616. Offers MS, PhD. *Faculty:* 16 full-time (3 women), 3 part-time (0 women). *Students:* 32 full-time (11 women); includes 1 minority (Asian American or Pacific Islander), 1 international. 40 applicants, 43% accepted. In 1998, 3 master's, 3 doctorates awarded. *Degree requirements:* For master's and doctorate, thesis/dissertation required. *Entrance requirements:* For master's and doctorate, GRE General Test, GRE Subject Test, minimum GPA of 3.0. *Application deadline:* For fall admission, 1/15. Application fee: $40. Electronic applications accepted. *Financial aid:* In 1998–99, 10 fellowships with full and partial tuition reimbursements, 10 research assistantships with full and partial tuition reimbursements, 14 teaching assistantships with full and partial tuition reimbursements were awarded.; grants, institutionally-sponsored loans, and scholarships also available. Financial aid application deadline: 1/15; financial aid applicants required to submit FAFSA. *Faculty research:* Petrology, paleontology, geophysics, sedimentology, structure/tectonics. *Unit head:* James McClain, Graduate Chair, 530-752-9100, Fax: 530-752-0951. *Application contact:* Judy Hendrickson, Graduate Coordinator, 530-752-9100, Fax: 530-752-0951.

University of California, Los Angeles, Graduate Division, College of Letters and Science, Department of Earth and Space Sciences, Program in Geology, Los Angeles, CA 90095. Offers MS, PhD. *Students:* 23 full-time (9 women); includes 5 minority (1 African American, 2 Asian Americans or Pacific Islanders, 2 Hispanic Americans) 35 applicants, 49% accepted. *Degree requirements:* For master's, comprehensive exams or thesis required; for doctorate, dissertation, oral and written qualifying exams required, foreign language not required. *Entrance requirements:* For master's, GRE General Test, minimum GPA of 3.0; for doctorate, GRE General Test, minimum undergraduate GPA of 3.0. *Application deadline:* For fall admission, 12/15. Application fee: $40. Electronic applications accepted. *Financial aid:* In 1998–99, 21 students received aid, including 18 fellowships, 19 teaching assistantships; research assistantships, Federal Work-Study, institutionally-sponsored loans, scholarships, and tuition waivers (full and partial) also available. Financial aid application deadline: 3/1. *Unit head:* Diane Swindall, Graduate Program Staff, 530-752-1669, Fax: 530-752-1552, E-mail: dgswindall@ucdavis.edu. *Application contact:* Departmental Office, 888-377-8252, E-mail: verity@ess.ucla.edu.

University of California, Riverside, Graduate Division, College of Natural and Agricultural Sciences, Department of Earth Sciences, Program in Geological Sciences, Riverside, CA 92521-0102. Offers MS, PhD. Part-time programs available. *Faculty:* 13 full-time (1 woman), 4 part-time (1 woman). *Students:* 15 full-time (5 women), 1 part-time, 1 international. Average age 30. 21 applicants, 52% accepted. In 1998, 8 master's, 3 doctorates awarded. Terminal master's awarded for partial completion of doctoral program. *Degree requirements:* For master's, thesis, thesis, final oral examination required, foreign language not required; for doctorate, one foreign language (computer language can substitute), dissertation, qualifying exams, final oral examination required. *Entrance requirements:* For master's and doctorate, GRE General Test (minimum combined score of 1100 required), TOEFL (minimum score of 550 required), minimum GPA of 3.2. *Average time to degree:* Master's–2.6 years full-time; doctorate–6 years full-time. *Application deadline:* For fall admission, 5/1; for winter admission, 9/1; for spring admission, 12/1. Applications are processed on a rolling basis. Application fee: $40. Electronic applications accepted. *Financial aid:* In 1998–99, 13 students received aid, including 4 fellowships with full and partial tuition reimbursements available (averaging $27,245 per year), research assistantships with full and partial tuition reimbursements available (averaging $12,111 per year), teaching assistantships with full and partial tuition reimbursements available (averaging $13,329 per year); career-related internships or fieldwork, Federal Work-Study, institutionally-sponsored loans, and tuition waivers (full and partial) also available. Financial aid application deadline: 1/15; financial aid applicants required to submit FAFSA. *Faculty research:* Applied and solid earth geophysics, tectonic geomorphology, fluid-rock interaction, paleobiology and ecology. *Unit head:* Prof. David F. Bocian, Graduate Adviser, 909-787-3520, Fax: 909-787-4713, E-mail: david.bocian@ucr.edu. *Application contact:* Carole Carpenter, Graduate Program Assistant, 909-787-3435, Fax: 909-787-4324, E-mail: carole.carpenter@ucr.edu.

Announcement: The geological sciences program includes geology, paleontology, geochemistry, geophysics, and geomorphology/Quaternary geology. Research strengths include orogenesis and neotectonics, arid-lands geomorphology, qualitative stratigraphy, evolution and paleoecology, vertebrate biostratigraphy, mineral deposits, hydrothermal geochemistry, geothermal resources, stable-isotope geochemistry, groundwater resources and hydrogeology, gravity, experimental tectonophysics, heat flow, geoelectricity, and geomagnetism.

University of California, San Diego, Graduate Studies and Research, Scripps Institution of Oceanography, La Jolla, CA 92093-5003. Offers biological oceanography (MS, PhD); geochemistry and marine chemistry (MS, PhD); marine biology (MS, PhD); physical oceanography and geological sciences (MS, PhD). *Faculty:* 73. *Students:* 170 (68 women). *Entrance requirements:* For master's and doctorate, GRE General Test, GRE Subject Test (marine biology). Application fee: $40. *Unit head:* W. Kendall Melville, Chair. *Application contact:* Yvonne Gaffney, Graduate Coordinator, 619-534-3206.

University of California, Santa Barbara, Graduate Division, College of Letters and Science, Division of Math, Life and Physical Science, Department of Geological Sciences, Santa Barbara, CA 93106. Offers geological sciences (MA, PhD); geophysics (MS). *Students:* 45 full-time (15 women). 64 applicants, 41% accepted. In 1998, 1 master's, 6 doctorates awarded. *Degree requirements:* For master's, one foreign language, thesis or exam required; for doctorate, variable foreign language requirement, dissertation required. *Entrance requirements:* For master's and doctorate, GRE General Test, TOEFL (minimum score of 550 required). *Application deadline:* For fall admission, 1/15. Application fee: $40. Electronic applications accepted. *Financial aid:* Fellowships, research assistantships, teaching assistantships, career-related internships or fieldwork, Federal Work-Study, institutionally-sponsored loans, and tuition waivers (full and partial) available. Financial aid application deadline: 1/15; financial aid applicants required to submit FAFSA. *Unit head:* Dr. Bruce Luyendyk, Chair, 805-893-2827. *Application contact:* Christina Foster, Graduate Program Assistant, 805-893-3329, E-mail: foster@magic.geol.ucsb.edu.

University of Cincinnati, Division of Research and Advanced Studies, McMicken College of Arts and Sciences, Department of Geology, Cincinnati, OH 45221-0091. Offers MS, PhD. *Faculty:* 10 full-time. *Students:* 19 full-time (8 women), 3 part-time (1 woman); includes 1 minority (Native American), 3 international. 27 applicants, 37% accepted. In 1998, 12 master's, 3 doctorates awarded. *Degree requirements:* For master's, thesis required, foreign language not required; for doctorate, dissertation required. *Entrance requirements:* For master's and doctorate, GRE General Test, GRE Subject Test, 1 year course in physics, chemistry, and calculus. *Average time to degree:* Master's–3.9 years full-time; doctorate–4.8 years full-time. *Application deadline:* For fall admission, 2/1. Application fee: $30. *Financial aid:* Fellowships, tuition waivers (full) and unspecified assistantships available. Aid available to part-time students. Financial aid application deadline: 5/1. Total annual research expenditures: $90,760. *Unit head:* Dr. I. Attila Kilinc, Head, 513-556-3732, Fax: 513-556-6931, E-mail: attila.kilinc@uc.edu. *Application contact:* Arnold Miller, Graduate Program Director, 513-556-4530, Fax: 513-556-6931, E-mail: arnold.miller@uc.edu.

University of Colorado at Boulder, Graduate School, College of Arts and Sciences, Department of Geological Sciences, Boulder, CO 80309. Offers MS, PhD. Terminal master's awarded for partial completion of doctoral program. *Degree requirements:* For master's, thesis or alternative, comprehensive exam required, foreign language not required; for doctorate, dissertation required. *Entrance requirements:* For master's and doctorate, GRE General Test.

University of Connecticut, Graduate School, College of Liberal Arts and Sciences, Department of Geological Sciences, Field of Geology, Storrs, CT 06269. Offers MS, PhD. *Degree requirements:* For doctorate, dissertation required. *Entrance requirements:* For master's and doctorate, GRE General Test, TOEFL.

University of Delaware, College of Arts and Science, Department of Geology, Newark, DE 19716. Offers MS, PhD. Part-time programs available. *Faculty:* 9 full-time (1 woman), 6 part-time (0 women). *Students:* 29 full-time (10 women), 1 part-time, 5 international. Average age 34. 22 applicants, 41% accepted. In 1998, 4 master's awarded (100% found work related to degree); 1 doctorate awarded (100% entered university research/teaching). *Degree requirements:* For master's and doctorate, thesis/dissertation required, foreign language not required. *Entrance requirements:* For master's and doctorate, GRE General Test (minimum combined score of 1050 required). *Average time to degree:* Master's–3 years full-time, 5 years part-time; doctorate–4 years full-time, 7 years part-time. *Application deadline:* For fall admission, 7/1. Application fee: $45. Electronic applications accepted. *Financial aid:* In 1998–99, fellowships with full tuition reimbursements (averaging $10,000 per year), 3 research assistantships with full tuition reimbursements (averaging $10,200 per year), 9 teaching assistantships with full tuition reimbursements (averaging $10,200 per year) were awarded.; Federal Work-Study, institutionally-sponsored loans, tuition waivers (full and partial), and full or partial tuition scholarships also available. Financial aid application deadline: 3/15; financial aid applicants required to submit FAFSA. *Faculty research:* Coastal plain mollusk geochemistry, taphonomy of marsh forams. Total annual research expenditures: $150,000. *Unit head:* Dr. John F. Wehmiller, Chairman, 302-831-2926, Fax: 302-831-4158, E-mail: jwehm@udel.edu.

Announcement: The department has 13 laboratories equipped for research in aminostratigraphy, biostratigraphy, environmental geophysics, micropaleontology, coastal and marine geology/geophysics, geoarchaeology, geomorphology, mineralogy, paleoceanography, petrology, sedimentology, stratigraphy, structure, taphonomy, tectonics. Major equipment includes X-ray diffractometer, liquid and gas chromatographs, SEM/EDS, drilling barge, high-resolution seismograph, ground-penetrating radar, laser theodolite system, and Sun Workstations.

University of Florida, Graduate School, College of Liberal Arts and Sciences, Department of Geology, Gainesville, FL 32611. Offers geology (MS, PhD); geology education (MST). *Faculty:* 19. *Students:* 29 full-time (11 women), 13 part-time (4 women); includes 2 minority (both Hispanic Americans), 5 international. 30 applicants, 70% accepted. In 1998, 6 master's, 1 doctorate awarded. Terminal master's awarded for partial completion of doctoral program. *Degree requirements:* For master's, thesis required (for some programs), foreign language not required; for doctorate, one foreign language, dissertation required. *Entrance requirements:* For master's and doctorate, GRE General Test (minimum combined score of 1000 required), GRE Subject Test, minimum GPA of 3.0. *Application deadline:* For fall admission, 6/1 (priority date). Applications are processed on a rolling basis. Application fee: $20. Electronic applications accepted. *Financial aid:* In 1998–99, 26 students received aid, including 2 fellowships, 8 research assistantships, 16 teaching assistantships; career-related internships or fieldwork, Federal Work-Study, and institutionally-sponsored loans also available. Aid available to part-time students. Financial aid application deadline: 3/1. *Faculty research:* Paleoclimatology, tectonophysics, petrochemistry, marine geology, geochemistry, hydrology. Total annual research expenditures: $1.5 million. *Unit head:* Dr. Paul Mueller, Chair, 352-392-2231, Fax: 352-392-9294, E-mail: mueller@geology.ufl.edu. *Application contact:* Dr. Michael R. Perfit, Graduate Coordinator, 352-392-2128, Fax: 352-392-9294, E-mail: perf@nervm.nerdc.ufl.edu.

University of Hawaii at Manoa, Graduate Division, School of Ocean and Earth Science and Technology, Department of Geology and Geophysics, Honolulu, HI 96822. Offers high-pressure geophysics and geochemistry (MS, PhD); hydrogeology and engineering geology (MS, PhD); marine geology and geophysics (MS, PhD); planetary geosciences and remote sensing (MS, PhD); seismology and solid-earth geophysics (MS, PhD); volcanology, petrology, and geochemistry (MS, PhD). *Faculty:* 84 full-time (10 women). *Students:* 48 full-time (15 women), 9 part-time (4 women); includes 3 minority (1 African American, 2 Asian Americans or Pacific Islanders), 15 international. 73 applicants, 23% accepted. In 1998, 5 master's, 10 doctorates awarded. Terminal master's awarded for partial completion of doctoral program. *Degree requirements:* For master's, thesis required, foreign language not required; for doctorate, dissertation, comprehensive exams required, foreign language not required. *Entrance requirements:* For master's and doctorate, GRE General Test, TOEFL, minimum GPA of 3.0. *Application deadline:* For fall admission, 1/15; for spring admission, 9/1. Application fee: $25 ($50 for international students). *Financial aid:* In 1998–99, 33 research assistantships (averaging $18,894 per year), 6 teaching assistantships (averaging $17,276 per year) were awarded. *Unit head:* Dr. John Sinton, Chair, 808-956-7640, Fax: 808-956-5512, E-mail: sinton@soest.hawaii.edu. *Application contact:* John Mahoney, Graduate Field Chairperson, 808-956-8763, Fax: 808-956-2538, E-mail: jmahoney@hawaii.edu.

University of Houston, College of Natural Sciences and Mathematics, Department of Geosciences, Program in Geosciences, Houston, TX 77004. Offers geology (MS, PhD). Part-time and evening/weekend programs available. *Faculty:* 11 full-time (2 women), 3 part-time (1 woman). *Students:* 17 full-time (2 women), 22 part-time (8 women); includes 4 minority (1 Asian American or Pacific Islander, 1 Hispanic American, 2 Native Americans), 9 international. Average age 36. 35 applicants, 86% accepted. In 1998, 3 degrees awarded. *Degree requirements:* For doctorate, dissertation required, foreign language not required. *Entrance requirements:* For master's and doctorate, GRE General Test (minimum combined score of 1700 on three sections required), TOEFL (minimum score of 550 required). *Application deadline:* For fall admission, 7/20 (priority date); for spring admission, 11/20. Applications are processed on a rolling basis. Application fee: $0 ($75 for international students). *Financial aid:* In 1998–99, 1 fellowship, 10 research assistantships, 14 teaching assistantships were awarded. *Faculty research:* Seismic and solid earth geophysics, tectonics, environmental hydrochemistry, carbonates, micropaleontology. *Application contact:* Henry Chafetz, Graduate Adviser, 713-743-3427, Fax: 713-748-7906, E-mail: hchafetz@uh.edu.

University of Idaho, College of Graduate Studies, College of Mines and Earth Resources, Department of Geology and Geological Engineering, Program in Geology, Moscow, ID 83844-4140. Offers MS, PhD. *Students:* 22 full-time (7 women), 18 part-time (4 women); includes 1 minority (African American), 4 international. In 1998, 6 master's awarded. *Degree requirements:* For master's, thesis required, foreign language not required; for doctorate, dissertation required. *Entrance requirements:* For master's, minimum GPA of 2.8; for doctorate, minimum undergraduate GPA of 2.8, 3.0 graduate. *Application deadline:* For fall admission, 8/1; for spring admission, 12/15. Application fee: $35 ($45 for international students). *Financial aid:* Application deadline: 2/15. *Faculty research:* Geological engineering, hydrology, earth sciences. *Unit head:* Dr. John Oldow, Head, Department of Geology and Geological Engineering, 208-885-7327.

University of Illinois at Chicago, Graduate College, College of Liberal Arts and Sciences, Department of Earth and Environmental Sciences, Chicago, IL 60607-7128. Offers crystallography (MS, PhD); environmental geology (MS, PhD); geochemistry (MS, PhD); geology (MS, PhD); geomorphology (MS, PhD); geophysics (MS, PhD); geotechnical engineering and geosciences (PhD); hydrogeology (MS, PhD); low-temperature and organic geochemistry (MS, PhD); mineralogy (MS, PhD); paleoclimatology (MS, PhD); paleontology (MS, PhD); petrology (MS, PhD); quaternary geology (MS, PhD); sedimentology (MS, PhD); water resources (MS, PhD). *Faculty:* 9 full-time (2 women). *Students:* 8 full-time (2 women), 1 part-time, 2 international. *Degree requirements:* For master's and doctorate, thesis/dissertation required. *Entrance requirements:* For master's and doctorate, GRE General Test, TOEFL (minimum score of 550 required), minimum GPA of 3.75 on a 5.0 scale. *Application deadline:* For fall admission, 7/3; for spring admission, 11/8. Application fee: $40 ($50 for international students). *Unit head:* A. F. Koster Van Groos, Acting Head, 312-996-3153. *Application contact:* Martin Flower, Graduate Director, 312-996-9662.

Announcement: The department offers MS and PhD programs in geomorphology, hydrogeology, environmental geology, low-temperature and organic geochemistry, sedimentology, paleoclimatology, quaternary geology, paleontology, geophysics, mineralogy, crystallography,

Geology

University of Illinois at Chicago (continued)

petrology, and geochemistry. The PhD program is offered jointly with the Department of Civil Engineering, Mechanics, and Metallurgy. Student research can include fieldwork, laboratory studies, theoretical investigations, or some combination of these. The department has modern and well-equipped laboratories and facilities and access to the UIC Research Resources Center and maintains close ties with the Field Museum of Natural History and Argonne National Laboratories. Geology or earth science majors and students with backgrounds in other fields of science are encouraged to apply.

University of Illinois at Urbana–Champaign, Graduate College, College of Liberal Arts and Sciences, Department of Geology, Urbana, IL 61801. Offers earth sciences (MS, PhD); geochemistry (MS, PhD); geology (MS, PhD); geophysics (MS, PhD). *Faculty:* 14 full-time (1 woman), 4 part-time (0 women). *Students:* 20 full-time (4 women), 11 international. Average age 26. 47 applicants, 9% accepted. In 1998, 3 master's, 4 doctorates awarded. Terminal master's awarded for partial completion of doctoral program. *Degree requirements:* For master's and doctorate, thesis/dissertation required, foreign language not required. *Entrance requirements:* For master's and doctorate, GRE General Test, TOEFL. *Application deadline:* For fall admission, 9/15 (priority date); for spring admission, 1/15. Applications are processed on a rolling basis. Application fee: $40 ($50 for international students). Tuition, state resident: full-time $4,040. Tuition, nonresident: full-time $11,192. Full-time tuition and fees vary according to program. *Financial aid:* In 1998–99, 35 students received aid; fellowships, research assistantships, teaching assistantships, Federal Work-Study and tuition waivers (full and partial) available. Financial aid application deadline: 2/15. *Faculty research:* Hydrogeology, structure/tectonics, mineral science. *Unit head:* Jay Bass, Head, 217-333-3540. *Application contact:* Barbara Elmore, Graduate Admissions Secretary, 217-333-3541, Fax: 217-244-4996.

The University of Iowa, Graduate College, College of Liberal Arts, Department of Geology, Iowa City, IA 52242-1316. Offers MS, PhD. *Faculty:* 15 full-time. *Students:* 18 full-time (6 women), 19 part-time (5 women); includes 4 minority (1 Asian American or Pacific Islander, 3 Hispanic Americans), 5 international. 24 applicants, 38% accepted. In 1998, 5 master's, 3 doctorates awarded. *Degree requirements:* For master's, thesis optional; for doctorate, dissertation, comprehensive exam required. *Entrance requirements:* For master's and doctorate, GRE General Test. Application fee: $30 ($50 for international students). *Financial aid:* In 1998–99, 4 fellowships, 16 research assistantships, 17 teaching assistantships were awarded. Financial aid application deadline: 3/1; financial aid applicants required to submit FAFSA. *Unit head:* Ann F. Budd, Chair, 319-335-1820, Fax: 319-335-1821.

University of Kansas, Graduate School, College of Liberal Arts and Sciences, Department of Geology, Lawrence, KS 66045. Offers MS, PhD. *Faculty:* 13 full-time. *Students:* 25 full-time (13 women), 29 part-time (9 women); includes 2 minority (both Native Americans), 6 international. In 1998, 7 master's, 4 doctorates awarded. *Degree requirements:* For master's, thesis or alternative required, foreign language not required; for doctorate, dissertation required, foreign language not required. *Entrance requirements:* For master's and doctorate, GRE General Test, GRE Subject Test, TOEFL (minimum score of 570 required). *Financial aid:* Fellowships, research assistantships, teaching assistantships available. *Unit head:* Anthony Walton, Chair, 785-864-4974. *Application contact:* W. R. Van Schmus, Graduate Director, 785-864-4974.

University of Kentucky, Graduate School, Graduate School Programs from the College of Arts and Sciences, Program in Geology, Lexington, KY 40506-0032. Offers MS, PhD. *Degree requirements:* For master's, thesis, comprehensive exam required, foreign language not required; for doctorate, dissertation, comprehensive exam required. *Entrance requirements:* For master's, GRE General Test, minimum undergraduate GPA of 2.5; for doctorate, GRE General Test, minimum graduate GPA of 3.0. *Faculty research:* Structure tectonics, geophysics, stratigraphy, hydrogeology, coal geology.

University of Maine, Graduate School, College of Natural Sciences, Forestry, and Agriculture, Department of Geological Sciences, Orono, ME 04469. Offers MS, PhD. Part-time programs available. *Faculty:* 12 full-time. *Students:* 17 (5 women). 24 applicants, 54% accepted. In 1998, 2 master's, 2 doctorates awarded. *Degree requirements:* For master's, thesis required, foreign language not required; for doctorate, one foreign language, computer language, dissertation required. *Entrance requirements:* For master's, GRE General Test, GRE Subject Test, TOEFL (minimum score of 550 required); for doctorate, GRE General Test, TOEFL (minimum score of 550 required). *Application deadline:* For fall admission, 2/1 (priority date); for spring admission, 10/15. Applications are processed on a rolling basis. Application fee: $50. *Financial aid:* In 1998–99, 4 research assistantships with tuition reimbursements (averaging $10,500 per year), 5 teaching assistantships with tuition reimbursements (averaging $7,900 per year) were awarded.; Federal Work-Study, institutionally-sponsored loans, and tuition waivers (full and partial) also available. Financial aid application deadline: 3/1. *Faculty research:* Appalachian bedrock geology, Quaternary studies, marine geology. *Unit head:* Dr. Stephen Norton, Chair, 207-581-2156, Fax: 207-581-2202. *Application contact:* Scott G. Delcourt, Director of the Graduate School, 207-581-3218, Fax: 207-581-3232, E-mail: graduate@maine.edu.

University of Maine, Graduate School, Institute for Quaternary Studies, Orono, ME 04469. Offers MS. Part-time programs available. *Faculty:* 13 full-time (2 women). *Students:* 12 (7 women). 9 applicants, 33% accepted. In 1998, 2 degrees awarded. *Degree requirements:* For master's, thesis required. *Entrance requirements:* For master's, GRE General Test, TOEFL (minimum score of 550 required). *Application deadline:* For fall admission, 2/1 (priority date); for spring admission, 10/15. Applications are processed on a rolling basis. Application fee: $50. *Financial aid:* In 1998–99, 6 research assistantships with tuition reimbursements (averaging $8,100 per year) were awarded.; tuition waivers (full and partial) also available. Financial aid application deadline: 3/1. *Faculty research:* Geology, glacial geology, anthropology, climate. *Unit head:* Dr. George Jacobson, Director, 207-581-2190, Fax: 207-581-1203. *Application contact:* Scott G. Delcourt, Director of the Graduate School, 207-581-3218, Fax: 207-581-3232, E-mail: graduate@maine.edu.

University of Manitoba, Faculty of Graduate Studies, Faculty of Science, Department of Geological Sciences, Winnipeg, MB R3T 2N2, Canada. Offers geology (M Sc, PhD); geophysics (M Sc, PhD). *Faculty:* 16 full-time. *Degree requirements:* For master's and doctorate, thesis/dissertation required. *Entrance requirements:* For master's and doctorate, GRE General Test, GRE Subject Test (geology), TOEFL, minimum GPA of 3.0. *Unit head:* G. S. Clark, Head.

University of Maryland, College Park, Graduate School, College of Computer, Mathematical and Physical Sciences, Department of Geology, College Park, MD 20742-5045. Offers MS, PhD. *Faculty:* 14 full-time (3 women), 1 (woman) part-time. *Students:* 12 full-time (4 women), 6 part-time (2 women); includes 1 minority (Hispanic American), 3 international. 33 applicants, 52% accepted. In 1998, 4 master's awarded. *Degree requirements:* For master's and doctorate, thesis/dissertation required. *Entrance requirements:* For master's, GRE General Test, minimum GPA of 3.0; for doctorate, GRE General Test. *Application deadline:* Applications are processed on a rolling basis. Application fee: $50 ($70 for international students). Tuition, state resident: part-time $272 per credit hour. Tuition, nonresident: part-time $475 per credit hour. Required fees: $632; $379 per year. *Financial aid:* In 1998–99, 7 research assistantships with tuition reimbursements (averaging $12,600 per year), 10 teaching assistantships with tuition reimbursements (averaging $9,920 per year) were awarded.; fellowships with full tuition reimbursements, Federal Work-Study and scholarships also available. Aid available to part-time students. Financial aid application deadline: 2/15; financial aid applicants required to submit FAFSA. *Faculty research:* Granite origin and evolution, metamorphic petrogenesis, phase equilibria, wetland hydrology, glacial geology, x-ray diffractometry. Total annual research expenditures: $1.2 million. *Unit head:* Dr. Michael Brown, Chairman, 301-405-4082, Fax: 301-314-9661. *Application contact:* Trudy Lindsey, Director, Graduate Admission and Records, 301-405-4198, Fax: 301-314-9305, E-mail: grschool@deans.umd.edu.

Announcement: MS/PhD degrees are offered in earth interior processes, including mineralogy, petrology, geochemistry, and tectonics, and in earth surface processes, including hydrology, sedimentation, geochemistry, paleoclimatology, global change, and geomorphology. Apply by February 15 for financial aid. For information, contact Graduate Office, Department of Geology, University of Maryland, College Park, MD 20742 (e-mail: jsmartin@geol.umd.edu; WWW: http://www.geol.umd.edu).

University of Massachusetts Amherst, Graduate School, College of Natural Sciences and Mathematics, Department of Geosciences, Program in Geology, Amherst, MA 01003. Offers MS, PhD. *Students:* 23 full-time (16 women), 13 part-time (9 women); includes 2 minority (1 Asian American or Pacific Islander, 1 Hispanic American), 1 international. Average age 29. 41 applicants, 71% accepted. In 1998, 6 degrees awarded. *Degree requirements:* For master's, thesis optional, foreign language not required. *Entrance requirements:* For master's, GRE General Test. *Application deadline:* For fall admission, 2/1 (priority date); for spring admission, 10/1. Applications are processed on a rolling basis. Application fee: $40. Tuition, state resident: full-time $2,640; part-time $165 per credit. Tuition, nonresident: full-time $9,756; part-time $407 per credit. Required fees: $1,221 per term. One-time fee: $110. Full-time tuition and fees vary according to course load, campus/location and reciprocity agreements. *Financial aid:* Fellowships with full tuition reimbursements, research assistantships with full tuition reimbursements, teaching assistantships with full tuition reimbursements, career-related internships or fieldwork, Federal Work-Study, grants, scholarships, traineeships, and unspecified assistantships available. Aid available to part-time students. Financial aid application deadline: 2/1. *Unit head:* Dr. Laurie Brown, Director, 413-545-5933, Fax: 413-545-1200, E-mail: lbrown@geo.umass.edu.

The University of Memphis, Graduate School, College of Arts and Sciences, Department of Geological Sciences, Memphis, TN 38152. Offers geology (MS); geophysics (MS, PhD). Part-time and evening/weekend programs available. *Faculty:* 13 full-time (1 woman). *Students:* 15 full-time (3 women), 5 part-time (2 women); includes 2 minority (1 African American, 1 Hispanic American), 9 international. Average age 29. 13 applicants, 46% accepted. In 1998, 4 degrees awarded. Terminal master's awarded for partial completion of doctoral program. *Degree requirements:* For master's, thesis, comprehensive exam, seminar presentation required; for doctorate, dissertation required. *Entrance requirements:* For master's, GRE General Test, GRE Subject Test. *Application deadline:* For fall admission, 8/1; for spring admission, 12/1. Applications are processed on a rolling basis. Application fee: $25 ($50 for international students). Tuition, state resident: full-time $3,410; part-time $178 per credit hour. Tuition, nonresident: full-time $8,670; part-time $408 per credit hour. Tuition and fees vary according to program. *Financial aid:* In 1998–99, 3 fellowships, 15 research assistantships, 4 teaching assistantships were awarded. *Faculty research:* Eocene and oligocene sediments, laboratory synthesis of dolomite, crystal structure of luenburgite, gregoryorite and lamprophyllite, heavy mineral distribution river investigation. *Unit head:* Dr. Phili Deboo, Chairman, 901-678-2177, Fax: 901-678-2178. *Application contact:* Dr. Daniel Larsen, Coordinator of Graduate Studies, 901-678-4358, Fax: 901-678-2178, E-mail: dlarsen@memphis.edu.

University of Miami, Graduate School, Rosenstiel School of Marine and Atmospheric Science, Division of Marine Geology and Geophysics, Coral Gables, FL 33124. Offers MA, MS, PhD. *Faculty:* 15 full-time (3 women), 1 (woman) part-time. *Students:* 19 full-time (10 women), 1 part-time, 6 international. Average age 27. 24 applicants, 42% accepted. In 1998, 1 master's, 7 doctorates awarded. Terminal master's awarded for partial completion of doctoral program. *Degree requirements:* For master's and doctorate, thesis/dissertation required, foreign language not required. *Entrance requirements:* For master's and doctorate, GRE General Test, TOEFL (minimum score of 550 required). *Average time to degree:* Master's–3 years full-time; doctorate–6 years full-time. *Application deadline:* For fall admission, 2/1 (priority date). Applications are processed on a rolling basis. Application fee: $35. Electronic applications accepted. Tuition: Full-time $15,336; part-time $852 per credit. Required fees: $174. Tuition and fees vary according to program. *Financial aid:* In 1998–99, 15 students received aid, including 1 fellowship with tuition reimbursement available, 11 research assistantships with tuition reimbursements available (averaging $17,000 per year), 3 teaching assistantships with tuition reimbursements available (averaging $17,000 per year); institutionally-sponsored loans also available. Financial aid application deadline: 2/1. *Faculty research:* Carbonate sedimentology, low-temperature geochemistry, paleoceanography, geodesy and tectonics. *Unit head:* Dr. Gregor Eberli, Chairperson, 305-361-4103, Fax: 305-361-4632. *Application contact:* Dr. Frank Millero, Associate Dean, 305-361-4155, Fax: 305-361-4771, E-mail: gso@rsmas.miami.edu.

University of Michigan, Horace H. Rackham School of Graduate Studies, College of Literature, Science, and the Arts, Department of Geological Sciences, Program in Oceanography: Marine Geology and Geochemistry, Ann Arbor, MI 48109. Offers MS, PhD. *Faculty:* 4 full-time (0 women), 1 part-time (0 women). *Students:* 4 full-time (3 women). 7 applicants, 57% accepted. Terminal master's awarded for partial completion of doctoral program. *Degree requirements:* For master's, thesis required, foreign language not required; for doctorate, variable foreign language requirement, dissertation, oral defense of dissertation, preliminary exam required. *Entrance requirements:* For master's, GRE General Test, GRE Subject Test; for doctorate, GRE General Test, GRE Subject Test, master's degree. *Average time to degree:* Master's–2 years full-time; doctorate–5 years full-time. *Application deadline:* For fall admission, 1/15 (priority date). Applications are processed on a rolling basis. Application fee: $55. Electronic applications accepted. *Financial aid:* In 1998–99, 2 students received aid, including 2 research assistantships, 2 teaching assistantships; fellowships, career-related internships or fieldwork and Federal Work-Study also available. *Faculty research:* Paleoceanography, paleolimnology, marine geochemistry, seismic stratigraphy. *Unit head:* David K. Rea, Chair, Department of Geological Sciences, 734-764-1435, Fax: 734-763-4690.

University of Minnesota, Duluth, Graduate School, College of Science and Engineering, Department of Geology, Duluth, MN 55812-2496. Offers MS. Part-time programs available. *Faculty:* 11 full-time (1 woman), 2 part-time (1 woman). *Students:* 14 full-time (5 women), 2 part-time, 1 international. Average age 23. 12 applicants, 42% accepted. In 1998, 6 degrees awarded (50% entered university research/teaching, 50% found other work related to degree). *Degree requirements:* For master's, thesis required (for some programs), foreign language not required. *Entrance requirements:* For master's, GRE General Test, TOEFL (minimum score of 600 required), minimum GPA of 3.0. *Average time to degree:* Master's–2 years full-time. *Application deadline:* For fall admission, 7/15; for spring admission, 11/15. Applications are processed on a rolling basis. Application fee: $50 ($55 for international students). *Financial aid:* In 1998–99, 13 students received aid, including 3 research assistantships with full and partial tuition reimbursements available (averaging $9,300 per year), 10 teaching assistantships with full and partial tuition reimbursements available (averaging $9,300 per year); career-related internships or fieldwork, Federal Work-Study, institutionally-sponsored loans, and tuition waivers (partial) also available. Aid available to part-time students. Financial aid application deadline: 3/15. *Faculty research:* Ore deposits, limnology, glacial geology. Total annual research expenditures: $500,000. *Unit head:* Dr. Penelope Morton, Director of Graduate Study, 218-726-7962, Fax: 218-726-8275, E-mail: pmorton@d.umn.edu.

Announcement: MS and PhD (UMTC) degrees are awarded in economic geology; igneous, sedimentary, and metamorphic petrology; hydrogeology; and Quaternary geology. The Large Lakes Observatory concentrates on physical processes in large lakes worldwide: sedimentology and paleoclimatology, circulation dynamics, remote sensing, and biogeochemistry. Duluth lies on Lake Superior, surrounded by classic Precambrian and Quaternary terrane.

University of Minnesota, Twin Cities Campus, Graduate School, Institute of Technology, Department of Geology and Geophysics, Minneapolis, MN 55455-0213. Offers geology (MS, PhD); geophysics (MS, PhD). Terminal master's awarded for partial completion of doctoral program. *Degree requirements:* For master's, thesis optional; for doctorate, dissertation required. *Entrance requirements:* For master's and doctorate, GRE General Test, TOEFL. *Faculty research:* Hydrogeology, geochemistry, structural geology, sedimentology.

University of Missouri–Columbia, Graduate School, College of Arts and Sciences, Department of Geological Sciences, Columbia, MO 65211. Offers MS, PhD. *Faculty:* 14 full-time (2 women). *Students:* 10 full-time (2 women), 10 part-time (6 women); includes 1 minority (Asian

American or Pacific Islander), 2 international. 5 applicants, 80% accepted. In 1998, 4 master's, 3 doctorates awarded. *Degree requirements:* For master's, thesis required, foreign language not required; for doctorate, dissertation required. *Entrance requirements:* For master's and doctorate, GRE General Test, minimum GPA of 3.0. *Application deadline:* Applications are processed on a rolling basis. Application fee: $30 ($50 for international students). *Financial aid:* Research assistantships, teaching assistantships, institutionally-sponsored loans available. *Unit head:* Dr. Kevin Shelton, Director of Graduate Studies, 573-882-6568.

University of Missouri–Kansas City, College of Arts and Sciences, Department of Geosciences, Kansas City, MO 64110-2499. Offers geosciences (PhD); urban environmental geology (MS). PhD offered through the School of Graduate Studies. Part-time programs available. *Faculty:* 7 full-time (1 woman). *Students:* 1 (woman) full-time, 8 part-time (3 women), 3 international. *Degree requirements:* For master's, thesis required, foreign language not required. *Entrance requirements:* For master's, GRE General Test (minimum combined score of 1400 on three sections required), TOEFL, minimum GPA of 3.0. *Application deadline:* For fall admission, 3/15. Application fee: $25. *Unit head:* Dr. Raymond M. Coveney, Chair, 816-235-1334, Fax: 816-235-5535, E-mail: rcoveney@cctr.umkc.edu. *Application contact:* Dr. Syed E. Hasan, Associate Professor, 816-235-1334, Fax: 816-235-5535, E-mail: shasan@cctr.umkc.edu.

University of Missouri–Rolla, Graduate School, School of Mines and Metallurgy, Department of Geology and Geophysics, Rolla, MO 65409-0910. Offers geochemistry (MS, PhD); geology (MS, PhD); geophysics (MS, PhD); groundwater and environmental geology (MS, PhD). Part-time programs available. *Faculty:* 8 full-time (1 woman). *Students:* 28 full-time (11 women), 7 international. Average age 33. 20 applicants, 100% accepted. In 1998, 4 master's awarded. *Degree requirements:* For master's, computer language, thesis required, foreign language not required; for doctorate, computer language, dissertation, departmental qualifying exam required, foreign language not required. *Entrance requirements:* For master's, GRE General Test (minimum combined score of 1100 required), GRE Subject Test, TOEFL (minimum score of 550 required), minimum GPA of 3.0 in last 4 semesters; for doctorate, GRE General Test (minimum combined score of 1100 required), GRE Subject Test, TOEFL (minimum score of 550 required). *Application deadline:* For fall admission, 7/1; for spring admission, 12/1. Applications are processed on a rolling basis. Application fee: $25. Electronic applications accepted. *Financial aid:* In 1998–99, 18 fellowships with full tuition reimbursements (averaging $6,600 per year), 2 research assistantships with partial tuition reimbursements (averaging $6,493 per year), 14 teaching assistantships with partial tuition reimbursements (averaging $6,493 per year) were awarded.; Federal Work-Study and institutionally-sponsored loans also available. Aid available to part-time students. Financial aid application deadline: 3/1; financial aid applicants required to submit FAFSA. *Faculty research:* Economic geology, geophysical modeling,seismic wave analysis. *Unit head:* Dr. Richard D. Hagni, Chairman, 573-341-4616, Fax: 573-341-6935, E-mail: rhagni@umr.edu.

The University of Montana–Missoula, Graduate School, College of Arts and Sciences, Department of Geology, Missoula, MT 59812-0002. Offers MS, PhD. Part-time programs available. *Faculty:* 12 full-time (1 woman). *Students:* 21 full-time (11 women), 5 part-time (2 women). Average age 25. 9 applicants, 100% accepted. In 1998, 8 degrees awarded. Terminal master's awarded for partial completion of doctoral program. *Degree requirements:* For master's, thesis required, foreign language not required; for doctorate, one foreign language (computer language can substitute), dissertation required. *Entrance requirements:* For master's and doctorate, GRE General Test. *Application deadline:* For fall admission, 2/15 (priority date). Applications are processed on a rolling basis. Application fee: $45. *Financial aid:* Teaching assistantships, Federal Work-Study available. Financial aid application deadline: 3/1. *Faculty research:* Environmental geoscience, regional structure and tectonics, groundwater geology, petrology, mineral deposits. *Unit head:* Dr. Steven D. Sheriff, Chair, 406-243-2341, Fax: 406-243-4028.

University of Nevada, Reno, Graduate School, Mackay School of Mines, Department of Geological Sciences, Reno, NV 89557. Offers geochemistry (MS, PhD); geological engineering (MS, Geol E); geology (MS, PhD); geophysics (MS, PhD). *Degree requirements:* For master's, thesis optional, foreign language not required; for doctorate, one foreign language, dissertation required. *Entrance requirements:* For master's, GRE General Test, GRE Subject Test, TOEFL (minimum score of 500 required), minimum GPA of 2.75; for doctorate, GRE General Test, GRE Subject Test, TOEFL (minimum score of 500 required), minimum GPA of 3.0. *Faculty research:* Hydrothermal ore deposits, metamorphic and igneous petrogenesis, sedimentary rock record of earth history, field and petrographic investigation of magnetism, rock fracture mechanics.

University of New Brunswick, School of Graduate Studies, Faculty of Science, Department of Geology, Fredericton, NB E3B 5A3, Canada. Offers M Sc, PhD. Part-time programs available. *Degree requirements:* For master's and doctorate, thesis/dissertation required. *Entrance requirements:* For master's and doctorate, TOEFL, TWE, minimum GPA of 3.0.

University of New Hampshire, Graduate School, College of Engineering and Physical Sciences, Department of Earth Sciences, Durham, NH 03824. Offers earth sciences (MS, PhD), including geochemical (MS), geology, hydrology (PhD), oceanography; hydrology (MS). *Faculty:* 25 full-time. *Students:* 32 full-time (7 women), 36 part-time (15 women); includes 1 minority (Asian American or Pacific Islander), 10 international. *Degree requirements:* For master's, thesis required, foreign language not required; for doctorate, dissertation required. *Entrance requirements:* For master's and doctorate, GRE General Test. *Application deadline:* For fall admission, 4/1 (priority date). Applications are processed on a rolling basis. Application fee: $50. Tuition, area resident: Full-time $5,750; part-time $319 per credit. Tuition, state resident: full-time $8,625. Tuition, nonresident: full-time $14,640; part-time $598 per credit. Required fees: $224 per semester. Tuition and fees vary according to course load, degree level and program. *Unit head:* Wallace Bothner, Chairperson, 603-862-1718. *Application contact:* Dr. Francis Birch, Graduate Coordinator, 603-862-3142.

University of New Orleans, Graduate School, College of Sciences, Department of Geology and Geophysics, New Orleans, LA 70148. Offers geology (MS); geophysics (MS). Evening/weekend programs available. *Faculty:* 16 full-time (1 woman), 2 part-time (1 woman). *Students:* 18 full-time (9 women), 17 part-time (7 women); includes 5 minority (4 African Americans, 1 Asian American or Pacific Islander), 1 international. Average age 29. 26 applicants, 50% accepted. In 1998, 11 degrees awarded. *Degree requirements:* For master's, thesis required, foreign language not required. *Entrance requirements:* For master's, GRE General Test. *Application deadline:* For fall admission, 7/1 (priority date). Applications are processed on a rolling basis. Application fee: $20. Tuition, state resident: full-time $2,362. Tuition, nonresident: full-time $7,888. Part-time tuition and fees vary according to course load. *Financial aid:* Fellowships, research assistantships, teaching assistantships, career-related internships or fieldwork, Federal Work-Study, and institutionally-sponsored loans available. *Faculty research:* Continental margin structure and seismology, burial diagenesis of siliclastic sediments, tectonics at convergent plate margins, continental shelf sediment stability, early diagenesis of carbonates. *Unit head:* Dr. William Busch, Chairman, 504-280-6793, Fax: 504-280-7396, E-mail: whbes@uno.edu. *Application contact:* Dr. Matthew Totten, Graduate Coordinator, 504-280-6800, Fax: 504-280-7396.

The University of North Carolina at Chapel Hill, Graduate School, College of Arts and Sciences, Department of Geology, Chapel Hill, NC 27599. Offers MS, PhD. *Faculty:* 15 full-time (0 women), 6 part-time (0 women). *Students:* 16 full-time (8 women), 4 part-time (2 women); includes 1 minority (Native American), 2 international. Average age 30. 30 applicants, 33% accepted. In 1998, 5 master's awarded (40% found work related to degree, 60% continued full-time study); 1 doctorate awarded (100% found work related to degree). *Degree requirements:* For master's, thesis, comprehensive exam required, foreign language not required; for doctorate, dissertation, comprehensive exam required. *Entrance requirements:* For master's and doctorate, GRE General Test (minimum combined score of 1000 required), minimum GPA of 3.0. *Application deadline:* For fall admission, 1/1 (priority date); for spring admission, 10/15 (priority date). Applications are processed on a rolling basis. Application fee: $55. Electronic applications accepted. *Financial aid:* In 1998–99, 3 research assistantships with full tuition reimbursements, 15 teaching assistantships with full tuition reimbursements were awarded.; fellowships Financial aid application deadline: 3/1. *Faculty research:* Paleoceanography, igneous petrology, paleontology, geophysics, structural geology. Total annual research expenditures: $429,464. *Unit head:* Dr. Timothy J. Bralower, Chair, 919-962-0704, Fax: 919-966-4519, E-mail: bralower@email.unc.edu. *Application contact:* Patsy H. Webb, Student Services Manager, 919-962-0679, Fax: 919-966-4519, E-mail: pwebb@email.unc.edu.

University of North Carolina at Wilmington, College of Arts and Sciences, Department of Earth Sciences, Wilmington, NC 28403-3201. Offers geology (MS). *Faculty:* 11 full-time (3 women). *Students:* 1 (woman) full-time, 22 part-time (12 women); includes 3 minority (2 Asian Americans or Pacific Islanders, 1 Native American) Average age 35. 10 applicants, 40% accepted. In 1998, 6 degrees awarded. *Degree requirements:* For master's, thesis, oral and written comprehensive exams required. *Entrance requirements:* For master's, GRE General Test, GRE Subject Test, minimum B average in undergraduate major and basic courses for prerequisite to geology. *Application deadline:* For fall admission, 2/15. Applications are processed on a rolling basis. Application fee: $35. *Financial aid:* In 1998–99, 9 teaching assistantships were awarded.; career-related internships or fieldwork and Federal Work-Study also available. Aid available to part-time students. Financial aid application deadline: 3/15. *Unit head:* Dr. Patricia Kelley, Chair, 910-962-3736. *Application contact:* Neil F. Hadley, Dean, Graduate School, 910-962-4117, Fax: 910-962-3787, E-mail: hadleyn@uncwil.edu.

University of North Dakota, Graduate School, School of Engineering and Mines, Department of Geology, Grand Forks, ND 58202. Offers MA, MS, PhD. *Faculty:* 11 full-time (0 women). *Students:* 11 full-time (3 women). 5 applicants, 100% accepted. In 1998, 4 master's awarded. *Degree requirements:* For master's, thesis required, thesis required; for doctorate, one foreign language (computer language can substitute), dissertation required. *Entrance requirements:* For master's, GRE General Test, TOEFL (minimum score of 550 required), minimum GPA of 3.0; for doctorate, GRE General Test, TOEFL (minimum score of 550 required), minimum GPA of 3.5. *Application deadline:* For fall admission, 3/1 (priority date). Applications are processed on a rolling basis. Application fee: $20. *Financial aid:* In 1998–99, 10 students received aid, including 4 research assistantships, 6 teaching assistantships; fellowships, career-related internships or fieldwork, Federal Work-Study, institutionally-sponsored loans, and tuition waivers (full and partial) also available. Financial aid application deadline: 3/15. *Unit head:* Dr. Phil Gerla, Director, 701-777-2811, Fax: 701-777-4449, E-mail: phil_gerla@mail.und.nodak.edu.

University of Oklahoma, Graduate College, College of Geosciences, School of Geology and Geophysics, Program in Geology, Norman, OK 73019-0390. Offers MS, PhD. *Students:* 14 full-time (5 women), 26 part-time (11 women); includes 1 minority (Asian American or Pacific Islander), 16 international. Average age 29. 25 applicants, 48% accepted. In 1998, 8 master's, 4 doctorates awarded. *Degree requirements:* For master's, computer language, thesis, comprehensive exam required, foreign language not required; for doctorate, one foreign language, computer language, dissertation, general exam required. *Entrance requirements:* For master's, GRE General Test, TOEFL (minimum score of 550 required), bachelor's degree in field; for doctorate, GRE General Test, TOEFL (minimum score of 550 required). *Application deadline:* For fall admission, 2/1 (priority date); for spring admission, 9/1. Applications are processed on a rolling basis. Application fee: $25. Tuition, state resident: part-time $86 per credit hour. Tuition, nonresident: part-time $275 per credit hour. Tuition and fees vary according to course level, course load and program. *Financial aid:* Research assistantships, teaching assistantships, Federal Work-Study, institutionally-sponsored loans, and tuition waivers (partial) available. Financial aid application deadline: 2/1. *Faculty research:* Petroleum geology, environmental geology and hydrogeology, geochemistry, mineralogy/petrology. *Application contact:* Dr. Barry Weaver, Graduate Liaison, 405-325-5325.

University of Oregon, Graduate School, College of Arts and Sciences, Department of Geological Sciences, Eugene, OR 97403. Offers MA, MS, PhD. *Faculty:* 14 full-time (2 women), 6 part-time (2 women). *Students:* 32 full-time (10 women), 5 part-time (2 women); includes 3 minority (2 Asian Americans or Pacific Islanders, 1 Hispanic American), 5 international. 61 applicants, 33% accepted. In 1998, 1 master's, 4 doctorates awarded (100% entered university research/teaching). *Degree requirements:* For master's, foreign language (MA) required, thesis not required; for doctorate, thesis not required. *Entrance requirements:* For master's and doctorate, GRE General Test, GRE Subject Test. *Application deadline:* For fall admission, 2/1. Application fee: $50. *Financial aid:* In 1998–99, 16 research assistantships, 24 teaching assistantships were awarded.; career-related internships or fieldwork and Federal Work-Study also available. Financial aid application deadline: 2/1. *Unit head:* A. Dana Johnston, Chair, 541-346-4573. *Application contact:* Pat Kallunki, Graduate Secretary, 541-346-4573.

University of Pennsylvania, School of Arts and Sciences, Graduate Group in Geology, Philadelphia, PA 19104. Offers MS, PhD. Part-time programs available. *Degree requirements:* For master's and doctorate, thesis/dissertation required. *Entrance requirements:* For master's, GRE General Test; for doctorate, GRE General Test, TOEFL. *Faculty research:* Isotope geochemistry, regional tectonics, environmental geology, metamorphic and igneous petrology, paleontology.

University of Pittsburgh, Faculty of Arts and Sciences, Department of Geology and Planetary Science, Pittsburgh, PA 15260. Offers MS, PhD. Part-time programs available. *Faculty:* 11 full-time (2 women), 1 part-time (0 women). *Students:* 18 full-time (9 women), 8 part-time (2 women). In 1998, 3 master's, 1 doctorate awarded. *Degree requirements:* For master's and doctorate, thesis/dissertation required, foreign language not required. *Entrance requirements:* For master's and doctorate, GRE General Test, TOEFL (minimum score of 550 required). *Average time to degree:* Master's–2.5 years full-time; doctorate–6.5 years full-time. *Application deadline:* For fall admission, 8/1 (priority date); for spring admission, 12/1. Applications are processed on a rolling basis. Application fee: $30 ($40 for international students). *Financial aid:* Career-related internships or fieldwork, Federal Work-Study, institutionally-sponsored loans, and tuition waivers (full and partial) available. Aid available to part-time students. Financial aid application deadline: 3/1; financial aid applicants required to submit FAFSA. *Faculty research:* Plate tectonics and basement studies, sedimentology and image analysis, marine paleoecology and geoarchaeology, geophysics and geomagnetism. *Unit head:* Dr. Thomas H. Anderson, Chairman, 412-624-8783, Fax: 412-624-3914, E-mail: taco@vms.cis.pitt.edu. *Application contact:* Dr. William A. Cassidy, Graduate Adviser, 412-624-8886, Fax: 412-624-3914, E-mail: ansmet@vms.cis.pitt.edu.

University of Puerto Rico, Mayagüez Campus, Graduate Studies, College of Arts and Sciences, Department of Geology, Mayagüez, PR 00681-5000. Offers MS. Part-time programs available. *Degree requirements:* For master's, thesis, comprehensive exam required, foreign language not required. *Entrance requirements:* For master's, GRE.

See in-depth description on page 311.

University of Regina, Faculty of Graduate Studies and Research, Faculty of Science, Department of Geology, Regina, SK S4S 0A2, Canada. Offers M Sc. *Faculty:* 6 full-time (2 women). *Students:* 6 full-time (2 women), 7 part-time (3 women). 6 applicants, 100% accepted. In 1998, 3 degrees awarded. *Degree requirements:* For master's, thesis required, foreign language not required. *Entrance requirements:* For master's, TOEFL (minimum score of 580 required). *Application deadline:* Applications are processed on a rolling basis. Application fee: $0. *Expenses:* Tuition and fees charges are reported in Canadian dollars. Tuition, state resident: full-time $1,688 Canadian dollars; part-time $94 Canadian dollars per credit hour. International tuition: $3,375 Canadian dollars full-time. Required fees: $65 Canadian dollars per course. Tuition and fees vary according to course load and program. *Financial aid:* In 1998–99, 3 research assistantships, 2 teaching assistantships were awarded.; fellowships, scholarships also available. Financial aid application deadline: 6/15. *Faculty research:* Geochemical, igneous, metamorphic, and structural studies of Canadian shield; Planerozoic carbonate; elastic and evaporite studies; energy. *Unit head:* Dr. B. Watters, Head, 306-585-4677, Fax: 306-585-5205.

Geology

University of Rhode Island, Graduate School, College of Arts and Sciences, Department of Geology, Kingston, RI 02881. Offers MS. *Degree requirements:* For master's, computer language required, thesis optional.

University of Rochester, The College, Arts and Sciences, Department of Earth and Environmental Science, Rochester, NY 14627-0250. Offers geology (MS, PhD). *Faculty:* 5. *Students:* 13 full-time (4 women), 2 part-time; includes 1 minority (Hispanic American), 4 international. 35 applicants, 23% accepted. In 1998, 4 master's, 2 doctorates awarded. Terminal master's awarded for partial completion of doctoral program. *Degree requirements:* For master's, thesis required, foreign language not required; for doctorate, dissertation, qualifying exam required, foreign language not required. *Entrance requirements:* For master's and doctorate, GRE General Test, TOEFL. *Application deadline:* For fall admission, 2/1 (priority date). Application fee: $25. *Financial aid:* Fellowships, research assistantships, teaching assistantships, career-related internships or fieldwork available. Financial aid application deadline: 2/1. *Unit head:* John Tarduno, Chair, 716-275-5713. *Application contact:* Kathy Lutz, Graduate Program Secretary, 716-275-5713.

University of Saskatchewan, College of Graduate Studies and Research, College of Arts and Sciences, Department of Geological Sciences, Saskatoon, SK S7N 5A2, Canada. Offers M Sc, PhD. *Degree requirements:* For master's and doctorate, thesis/dissertation required. *Entrance requirements:* For master's, CANTEST (minimum score of 4.5 required) or International English Language Testing System (minimum score of 6 required) or Michigan English Language Assessment Battery (minimum score of 80 required), orTOEFL (minimum score of 550 required; average 560); for doctorate, TOEFL.

University of South Carolina, Graduate School, College of Science and Mathematics, Department of Geological Sciences, Columbia, SC 29208. Offers IMA, MAT, MS, PhD. IMA and MAT offered in cooperation with the College of Education. *Faculty:* 24 full-time (0 women), 3 part-time (1 woman). *Students:* 42 full-time (15 women), 11 part-time (4 women); includes 3 minority (all Hispanic Americans), 16 international. Average age 31. 78 applicants, 27% accepted. In 1998, 13 master's, 8 doctorates awarded. Terminal master's awarded for partial completion of doctoral program. *Degree requirements:* For master's, thesis required, foreign language not required; for doctorate, dissertation, published paper required, foreign language not required. *Entrance requirements:* For master's and doctorate, GRE General Test, TOEFL. *Application deadline:* For fall admission, 7/1 (priority date); for spring admission, 11/15. Applications are processed on a rolling basis. Application fee: $35. Electronic applications accepted. Tuition, state resident: full-time $4,014; part-time $202 per credit hour. Tuition, nonresident: full-time $8,528; part-time $428 per credit hour. Required fees: $100; $4 per credit hour. Tuition and fees vary according to program. *Financial aid:* In 1998–99, 1 fellowship, 29 research assistantships with partial tuition reimbursements (averaging $15,000 per year), 25 teaching assistantships with partial tuition reimbursements (averaging $15,000 per year) were awarded.; career-related internships or fieldwork and Federal Work-Study also available. Financial aid application deadline: 3/1. *Faculty research:* Sedimentary geology, geochemistry, tectonics, marine geology, petrology. *Unit head:* Dr. Robert Thunell, Chair, 803-777-4535, Fax: 803-777-6610. *Application contact:* Dr. James Kellogg, Director of Graduate Studies, 803-777-3959, Fax: 803-777-6610, E-mail: kellogg@sc.edu.

See in-depth description on page 315.

University of Southern Mississippi, Graduate School, College of Science and Technology, Department of Geology, Hattiesburg, MS 39406-5167. Offers MS. Part-time programs available. *Faculty:* 6 full-time (1 woman). *Students:* 8 full-time (6 women), 5 part-time (4 women); includes 2 minority (both Asian Americans or Pacific Islanders) Average age 31. 6 applicants, 50% accepted. In 1998, 3 degrees awarded. *Degree requirements:* For master's, computer language, thesis required, foreign language not required. *Entrance requirements:* For master's, GRE General Test, TOEFL, BS in geology, minimum GPA of 2.75. *Application deadline:* For fall admission, 8/6 (priority date). Applications are processed on a rolling basis. Application fee: $0 ($25 for international students). Tuition, state resident: full-time $2,250; part-time $137 per semester hour. Tuition, nonresident: full-time $3,102; part-time $172 per semester hour. Required fees: $602. *Financial aid:* Fellowships, research assistantships, teaching assistantships, career-related internships or fieldwork, Federal Work-Study, and tuition waivers (full) available. Financial aid application deadline: 3/15. *Faculty research:* Volcanic rocks and associated minerals, marine stratigraphy and seismology, hydrology, micropaleontology, isotope geology. *Unit head:* Dr. Gail Russell, Chair, 601-266-4526.

University of South Florida, Graduate School, College of Arts and Sciences, Department of Geology, Tampa, FL 33620-9951. Offers geology (MS, PhD); hydrogeology (MS, Adv C). Part-time programs available. *Faculty:* 11 full-time (3 women), 3 part-time (0 women). *Students:* 37 full-time (13 women), 7 part-time; includes 1 minority (Hispanic American), 6 international. Average age 28. 37 applicants, 68% accepted. In 1998, 10 master's, 1 doctorate awarded. *Degree requirements:* For master's, thesis required (for some programs); for doctorate, dissertation required. *Entrance requirements:* For master's, GRE General Test (minimum combined score of 1000 required), minimum GPA of 3.0 in last 60 hours; for doctorate, GRE General Test. *Application deadline:* For fall admission, 6/1; for spring admission, 10/15. Application fee: $20. Electronic applications accepted. Tuition, state resident: part-time $148 per credit hour. Tuition, nonresident: part-time $509 per credit hour. *Financial aid:* In 1998–99, 2 fellowships with partial tuition reimbursements (averaging $6,000 per year), 5 research assistantships with partial tuition reimbursements (averaging $8,600 per year), 14 teaching assistantships with partial tuition reimbursements (averaging $8,600 per year) were awarded.; career-related internships or fieldwork, Federal Work-Study, and institutionally-sponsored loans also available. Aid available to part-time students. Financial aid application deadline: 2/15; financial aid applicants required to submit FAFSA. *Faculty research:* Coastal geology, environmental geology and hydrogeology, paleontology and geochemistry. *Unit head:* Mark T. Stewart, Chairperson, 813-974-0325, Fax: 813-974-2654, E-mail: mark@chuma.cas.usf.edu. *Application contact:* Nancy A. Mole, Graduate Coordinator, 813-974-2236, Fax: 813-974-2654, E-mail: nancym@chuma1.cas.usf.edu.

University of Southwestern Louisiana, Graduate School, College of Sciences, Department of Geology, Lafayette, LA 70504. Offers MS. Part-time programs available. *Faculty:* 7 full-time (0 women). *Students:* 14 full-time (4 women), 9 part-time (1 woman); includes 2 minority (1 Asian American or Pacific Islander, 1 Hispanic American), 6 international. 17 applicants, 65% accepted. In 1998, 4 degrees awarded. *Degree requirements:* For master's, thesis required, foreign language not required. *Entrance requirements:* For master's, GRE General Test, minimum GPA of 2.75. *Application deadline:* For fall admission, 5/15. Application fee: $5 ($15 for international students). *Financial aid:* In 1998–99, 6 research assistantships with full tuition reimbursements (averaging $5,417 per year) were awarded.; fellowships, teaching assistantships, Federal Work-Study and tuition waivers (full and partial) also available. Aid available to part-time students. Financial aid application deadline: 5/1. *Faculty research:* Aquifer contamination, coastal erosion, geochemistry of peat, petroleum geology and geophysics, remote sensing and geographic information systems applications. *Unit head:* Dr. Brian Lock, Head, 318-482-6468. *Application contact:* Dr. Daniel Tucker, Graduate Coordinator, 318-482-5353.

University of Tennessee, Knoxville, Graduate School, College of Arts and Sciences, Department of Geological Sciences, Knoxville, TN 37996. Offers geology (MS, PhD). Part-time programs available. *Faculty:* 17 full-time (1 woman). *Students:* 34 full-time (14 women), 9 part-time (2 women), 8 international. 30 applicants, 57% accepted. In 1998, 6 master's, 2 doctorates awarded. *Degree requirements:* For master's, thesis required, foreign language not required; for doctorate, dissertation required. *Entrance requirements:* For master's and doctorate, GRE General Test, TOEFL (minimum score of 550 required), minimum GPA of 2.7. *Application deadline:* For fall admission, 2/1 (priority date). Applications are processed on a rolling basis. Application fee: $35. Electronic applications accepted. *Financial aid:* In 1998–99, 28 research assistantships, 27 teaching assistantships were awarded.; fellowships, Federal Work-Study, institutionally-sponsored loans, and unspecified assistantships also available. Financial aid application deadline: 2/1; financial aid applicants required to submit FAFSA. *Unit head:* Dr. William Dunne, Head, 423-974-2366, Fax: 423-974-2368, E-mail: wdunne@utk.edu. *Application contact:* Dr. Steven Driese, Graduate Representative, 423-974-6002, E-mail: sdriese@utk.edu.

The University of Texas at Arlington, Graduate School, College of Science, Department of Geology, Arlington, TX 76019. Offers MS. *Faculty:* 8 full-time (0 women). *Students:* 6 full-time (4 women), 9 part-time (2 women), 1 international. 4 applicants, 75% accepted. In 1998, 2 degrees awarded. *Degree requirements:* For master's, computer language required, thesis optional, foreign language not required. *Entrance requirements:* For master's, GRE General Test. *Application deadline:* Applications are processed on a rolling basis. Application fee: $25 ($50 for international students). Tuition, state resident: full-time $1,368; part-time $76 per semester hour. Tuition, nonresident: full-time $5,454; part-time $303 per semester hour. Required fees: $66 per semester hour. $86 per term. Tuition and fees vary according to course load. *Financial aid:* Teaching assistantships, Federal Work-Study and institutionally-sponsored loans available. *Unit head:* Dr. John S. Wickham, Head, 817-272-2322, Fax: 817-272-2628, E-mail: wickham@uta.edu. *Application contact:* Dr. William L. Balsam, Graduate Adviser, 817-272-2987, Fax: 817-272-2628, E-mail: balsam@uta.edu.

The University of Texas at Austin, Graduate School, College of Natural Sciences, Department of Geological Sciences, Austin, TX 78712-1111. Offers MA, MS, PhD. Part-time programs available. *Faculty:* 38 full-time (3 women), 2 part-time (1 woman). *Students:* 141 full-time (42 women); includes 6 minority (1 African American, 2 Asian Americans or Pacific Islanders, 2 Hispanic Americans, 1 Native American), 44 international. 179 applicants, 33% accepted. In 1998, 23 master's, 16 doctorates awarded. *Degree requirements:* For master's, report (MA), thesis (MS) required; for doctorate, dissertation required, foreign language not required. *Entrance requirements:* For master's and doctorate, GRE General Test (minimum combined score of 1100 preferred). *Average time to degree:* Master's–3 years full-time; doctorate–7 years full-time. *Application deadline:* For fall admission, 2/1 (priority date); for spring admission, 10/1. Application fee: $50 ($75 for international students). Electronic applications accepted. *Financial aid:* In 1998–99, 125 students received aid, including 6 fellowships with partial tuition reimbursements available (averaging $18,000 per year), research assistantships with partial tuition reimbursements available (averaging $13,500 per year), 38 teaching assistantships with partial tuition reimbursements available (averaging $13,500 per year); career-related internships or fieldwork, Federal Work-Study, and institutionally-sponsored loans also available. Financial aid application deadline: 2/1. *Faculty research:* Sedimentary geology, geophysics, hydrogeology, structure/tectonics, vertebrate paleontology. Total annual research expenditures: $205,000. *Unit head:* Mark Cloos, Chairman, 512-471-5172, Fax: 512-471-9425, E-mail: cloos118@maestro.geo.utexas.edu. *Application contact:* Earle F. McBride, Graduate Adviser, 512-471-6098, Fax: 512-471-9425.

The University of Texas at El Paso, Graduate School, College of Science, Department of Geological Sciences, El Paso, TX 79968-0001. Offers geological sciences (MS, PhD); geophysics (MS). Part-time programs available. *Faculty:* 14 full-time (3 women), 4 part-time (3 women). *Students:* 36 full-time (15 women), 14 part-time (3 women); includes 13 minority (3 African Americans, 10 Hispanic Americans), 12 international. Average age 34. 17 applicants, 47% accepted. In 1998, 5 master's, 2 doctorates awarded. *Degree requirements:* For master's, thesis required, foreign language not required; for doctorate, one foreign language, dissertation required. *Entrance requirements:* For master's, TOEFL (minimum score of 550 required), minimum GPA of 3.0, BS in geology or equivalent; for doctorate, TOEFL (minimum score of 550 required), minimum GPA of 3.4, MS in geology or equivalent. *Average time to degree:* Master's–2.5 years full-time, 4 years part-time; doctorate–4.5 years full-time, 6 years part-time. *Application deadline:* Applications are processed on a rolling basis. Application fee: $15 ($65 for international students). Electronic applications accepted. Tuition, state resident: full-time $2,118. Tuition, nonresident: full-time $7,230. Tuition and fees vary according to program. *Financial aid:* In 1998–99, 36 students received aid, including 11 fellowships, 7 research assistantships, 17 teaching assistantships; career-related internships or fieldwork, institutionally-sponsored loans, scholarships, and tuition waivers (partial) also available. Aid available to part-time students. Financial aid applicants required to submit FAFSA. *Faculty research:* Igneous petrology, economic geology, paleontology, environmental geology, sedimentology. Total annual research expenditures: $581,939. *Unit head:* Dr. G. Randy Keller, Chairperson, 915-747-5501, Fax: 915-747-5073, E-mail: keller@geo.utep.edu. *Application contact:* Susan Jordan, Director, Graduate Student Services, 915-747-5491, Fax: 915-747-5788, E-mail: sjordan@utep.edu.

The University of Texas at San Antonio, College of Sciences and Engineering, Division of Earth and Physical Sciences, San Antonio, TX 78249-0617. Offers chemistry (MS); environmental sciences (MS); geology (MS). *Faculty:* 22 full-time (1 woman), 27 part-time (6 women). *Students:* 22 full-time (11 women), 83 part-time (29 women); includes 27 minority (2 African Americans, 6 Asian Americans or Pacific Islanders, 19 Hispanic Americans), 6 international. Average age 34. 30 applicants, 67% accepted. In 1998, 25 degrees awarded. *Entrance requirements:* For master's, GRE General Test. *Application deadline:* For fall admission, 7/1. Applications are processed on a rolling basis. Application fee: $25. *Financial aid:* Research assistantships, teaching assistantships available. *Unit head:* Dr. Weldon Hammond, Interim Director, 210-458-4455.

The University of Texas of the Permian Basin, Graduate School, College of Arts and Sciences, Department of Sciences and Mathematics, Program in Geology, Odessa, TX 79762-0001. Offers MS. *Degree requirements:* For master's, thesis or alternative required, foreign language not required. *Entrance requirements:* For master's, GRE General Test (minimum combined score of 1200 required).

University of Toledo, Graduate School, College of Arts and Sciences, Department of Geology, Toledo, OH 43606-3398. Offers MS. Part-time programs available. *Degree requirements:* For master's, thesis required, foreign language not required. *Entrance requirements:* For master's, GRE General Test (minimum combined score of 950 required), TOEFL. Electronic applications accepted. *Faculty research:* Environmental geochemistry, geophysics,petrology and mineralogy, paleontology, geohydrology.

University of Toronto, School of Graduate Studies, Physical Sciences Division, Department of Geology, Toronto, ON M5S 1A1, Canada. Offers M Sc, MA Sc, PhD. Part-time programs available. *Degree requirements:* For master's, thesis required (for some programs); for doctorate, dissertation required.

University of Tulsa, Graduate School, College of Business Administration, Department of Engineering and Technology Management, Tulsa, OK 74104-3189. Offers chemical engineering (METM); computer science (METM); electrical engineering (METM); geological science (METM); mathematics (METM); mechanical engineering (METM); petroleum engineering (METM). Part-time and evening/weekend programs available. *Students:* 3 full-time (1 woman), 1 part-time, 3 international. *Degree requirements:* For master's, foreign language and thesis not required. *Entrance requirements:* For master's, GRE General Test (minimum score of 430 on verbal section, 600 on quantitative required), TOEFL (minimum score of 575 required). *Application deadline:* Applications are processed on a rolling basis. Application fee: $30. Electronic applications accepted. Tuition: Full-time $8,640; part-time $480 per hour. Required fees: $3 per hour. One-time fee: $200 full-time. Tuition and fees vary according to program. *Unit head:* Dr. Richard C. Burgess, Assistant Dean/Director of Graduate Business Studies, 918-631-2242, Fax: 918-631-2142.

University of Utah, Graduate School, College of Mines and Earth Sciences, Department of Geology and Geophysics, Program in Geology, Salt Lake City, UT 84112-1107. Offers MS, PhD. *Students:* 19 full-time (6 women), 13 part-time (3 women), 2 international. In 1998, 5 master's awarded. *Degree requirements:* For master's, computer language, thesis, qualifying exam required; for doctorate, one foreign language, computer language, dissertation required. *Entrance requirements:* For master's and doctorate, GRE General Test, TOEFL (minimum score of 500 required), minimum GPA of 3.25. *Application deadline:* For fall admission, 7/1. Application fee: $30 ($50 for international students). *Financial aid:* Application deadline: 2/15. *Unit head:* Susan Jordan, Director, Graduate Student Services, 915-747-5491, Fax: 915-747-5788, E-mail: sjordan@utep.edu. *Application contact:* Marjorie Chan, Director of Graduate Studies, 801-581-7162, Fax: 801-581-7065.

University of Vermont, Graduate College, College of Arts and Sciences, Department of Geology, Burlington, VT 05405-0160. Offers geology (MS); geology education (MAT, MST). *Degree requirements:* For master's, thesis required, foreign language not required. *Entrance requirements:* For master's, GRE General Test, TOEFL (minimum score of 550 required). *Faculty research:* Mineralogy, lake sediments, structural geology.

University of Victoria, Faculty of Graduate Studies, Faculty of Science, School of Earth and Ocean Sciences, Victoria, BC V8W 2Y2, Canada. Offers geochemistry (M Sc, PhD); geophysics (M Sc, PhD); marine geology and geophysics (M Sc, PhD); ocean acoustics (M Sc, PhD); oceanography (M Sc, PhD); paleobiology (M Sc, PhD); paleoceanography (M Sc, PhD); sedimentology (M Sc, PhD); stratigraphy (M Sc, PhD). Part-time programs available. *Faculty:* 15 full-time, 41 part-time. *Students:* 39 full-time (0 women), 1 part-time. *Degree requirements:* For master's and doctorate, thesis/dissertation required. *Application deadline:* For fall admission, 2/15. Applications are processed on a rolling basis. Application fee: $50. Electronic applications accepted. *Unit head:* Dr. C. R. Barnes, Director, 250-721-6120, Fax: 250-721-6200, E-mail: crbarnes@uvic.ca. *Application contact:* Dr. Dante Canil, Graduate Adviser, 250-721-6120, Fax: 250-721-6200, E-mail: dcanil@uvic.ca.

University of Washington, Graduate School, College of Arts and Sciences, Department of Geological Sciences, Seattle, WA 98195. Offers MS, PhD. *Faculty:* 24 full-time (2 women), 18 part-time (2 women). *Students:* 29 full-time (7 women), 6 part-time (4 women). 105 applicants, 26% accepted. In 1998, 6 master's, 4 doctorates awarded. *Degree requirements:* For master's, thesis or alternative required, foreign language not required; for doctorate, dissertation required, foreign language not required. *Entrance requirements:* For master's and doctorate, GRE, TOEFL (minimum score of 500 required), minimum GPA of 3.0. *Average time to degree:* Master's–2.5 years full-time; doctorate–6 years full-time. *Application deadline:* For fall admission, 1/15. Applications are processed on a rolling basis. Application fee: $50. Tuition, state resident: full-time $5,196; part-time $475 per credit. Tuition, nonresident: full-time $13,485; part-time $1,285 per credit. Required fees: $387; $38 per credit. Tuition and fees vary according to course load. *Financial aid:* In 1998–99, 28 students received aid, including 2 fellowships with full tuition reimbursements available (averaging $10,701 per year), 8 research assistantships with full tuition reimbursements available (averaging $10,701 per year), 18 teaching assistantships with partial tuition reimbursements available (averaging $9,990 per year); Federal Work-Study also available. Financial aid application deadline: 3/1. *Faculty research:* Physics and chemistry of magmatic processes, Quaternary geology and environmental change, surface processes and geomorphology, remote sensing, cordilleran tectonics. Total annual research expenditures: $2.2 million. *Unit head:* Darrel Cowan, Acting Chairman, 206-543-1190, Fax: 206-543-3836, E-mail: darrel@u.washington.edu. *Application contact:* Bernadine Anderson, Coordinator, 206-543-5405, Fax: 206-543-3836, E-mail: bern@u.washington.edu.

University of Washington, Graduate School, College of Ocean and Fishery Sciences, School of Oceanography, Seattle, WA 98195. Offers biological oceanography (MS, PhD); chemical oceanography (MS, PhD); marine geology and geophysics (MS, PhD); physical oceanography (MS, PhD). *Faculty:* 52 full-time (6 women), 1 (woman) part-time. *Students:* 72 full-time (37 women), 3 part-time (2 women); includes 9 minority (1 African American, 4 Asian Americans or Pacific Islanders, 4 Hispanic Americans), 17 international. Terminal master's awarded for partial completion of doctoral program. *Degree requirements:* For master's, research project required, foreign language and thesis not required; for doctorate, dissertation required, foreign language not required. *Entrance requirements:* For master's and doctorate, GRE General Test, TOEFL (minimum score of 500 required), minimum GPA of 3.0. *Application deadline:* For fall and spring admission, 1/15. Application fee: $50. Electronic applications accepted. Tuition, state resident: full-time $5,196; part-time $475 per credit. Tuition, nonresident: full-time $13,485; part-time $1,285 per credit. Required fees: $387; $38 per credit. Tuition and fees vary according to course load. *Unit head:* Richard W. Sternberg, Director, 206-543-5039, Fax: 206-543-6073, E-mail: student@ocean.washington.edu. *Application contact:* Della Rogers, Student Services Coordinator, 206-543-5039, Fax: 206-543-6073, E-mail: drogers@ocean.washington.edu.

University of Windsor, College of Graduate Studies and Research, Faculty of Science, Earth Sciences, Windsor, ON N9B 3P4, Canada. Offers geological engineering (MA Sc); geology (M Sc). Part-time programs available. *Degree requirements:* For master's, thesis required. *Entrance requirements:* For master's, TOEFL (minimum score of 550 required), minimum B average. *Faculty research:* Paleontology, geochemistry, sedimentology.

University of Wisconsin–Madison, Graduate School, College of Letters and Science, Department of Geology and Geophysics, Program in Geology, Madison, WI 53706-1380. Offers MS, PhD. *Degree requirements:* For master's, thesis required; for doctorate, one foreign language, dissertation required. *Entrance requirements:* For master's and doctorate, GRE General Test. *Application deadline:* For fall admission, 12/15 (priority date). Application fee: $45. *Financial aid:* Application deadline: 12/15. *Unit head:* Sicrid Gerhardt, Graduate coordinator, 608-262-8544, Fax: 608-263-6386, E-mail: gerhardt@astro.wisc.edu. *Application contact:* Graduate Admissions Coordinator, 608-262-9266, Fax: 608-262-0693, E-mail: sharonm@geology.wisc.edu.

University of Wisconsin–Milwaukee, Graduate School, College of Letters and Sciences, Department of Geosciences, Milwaukee, WI 53201-0413. Offers geological sciences (MS, PhD). *Faculty:* 13 full-time (0 women). *Students:* 14 full-time (2 women), 12 part-time (1 woman); includes 1 minority (African American), 2 international. 13 applicants, 69% accepted. In 1998, 1 master's awarded. *Degree requirements:* For master's, thesis required, foreign language not required; for doctorate, one foreign language (computer language can substitute), dissertation required. *Entrance requirements:* For master's and doctorate, GRE General Test. *Application deadline:* For fall admission, 1/1 (priority date); for spring admission, 9/1. Applications are processed on a rolling basis. Application fee: $45 ($75 for international students). *Financial aid:* In 1998–99, 1 fellowship, 6 research assistantships, 10 teaching assistantships were awarded.; career-related internships or fieldwork and unspecified assistantships also available. Aid available to part-time students. Financial aid application deadline: 4/15. *Unit head:* Mark Harris, Chair, 414-229-6558.

University of Wyoming, Graduate School, College of Arts and Sciences, Department of Geology and Geophysics, Laramie, WY 82071. Offers geology and geophysics (MS, PhD); geology/water resources (MS); geophysics (MS, PhD). Part-time programs available. *Faculty:* 22 full-time (3 women), 2 part-time (1 woman). *Students:* 42 full-time (19 women), 23 part-time (7 women); includes 3 minority (1 Hispanic American, 2 Native Americans), 7 international. 30 applicants, 53% accepted. In 1998, 10 master's, 8 doctorates awarded. *Degree requirements:* For master's and doctorate, thesis/dissertation required. *Entrance requirements:* For master's and doctorate, GRE General Test (minimum combined score of 1200 required), minimum GPA of 3.0. *Application deadline:* For fall admission, 1/31. Applications are processed on a rolling basis. Application fee: $40. Tuition, state resident: full-time $2,520; part-time $140 per credit hour. Tuition, nonresident: full-time $7,790; part-time $433 per credit hour. Required fees: $400; $7 per credit hour. Full-time tuition and fees vary according to course load and program. *Financial aid:* Fellowships, research assistantships, teaching assistantships, career-related internships or fieldwork, Federal Work-Study, and institutionally-sponsored loans available. Financial aid application deadline: 3/1. *Faculty research:* Geochemistry and petroleum geology, tectonics and sedimentation, geomorphology and remote sensing, igneous and metamorphic petrology. *Unit head:* Dr. James R. Steidtman, Head, 307-766-3386. *Application contact:* Deayne M. Johnson, Admissions Coordinator, 307-766-3389, Fax: 307-766-6679, E-mail: acadcoord.geol@uwyo.edu.

Utah State University, School of Graduate Studies, College of Science, Department of Geology, Logan, UT 84322. Offers MS. *Faculty:* 7 full-time (0 women), 1 (woman) part-time. *Students:* 14 full-time (4 women), 8 part-time (4 women), 1 international. Average age 27. 21 applicants, 33% accepted. In 1998, 3 degrees awarded. *Degree requirements:* For master's, thesis required, foreign language not required. *Entrance requirements:* For master's, GRE General Test (score in 40th percentile or higher required), TOEFL (minimum score of 550 required), minimum GPA of 3.0. *Application deadline:* For fall admission, 2/15 (priority date); for spring admission, 10/15. Applications are processed on a rolling basis. Application fee: $40. Tuition, state resident: full-time $1,492. Tuition, nonresident: full-time $5,232. Required fees: $434. Tuition and fees vary according to course load. *Financial aid:* In 1998–99, 18 students received aid, including 1 fellowship with partial tuition reimbursement available (averaging $15,000 per year), 3 research assistantships with partial tuition reimbursements available (averaging $10,200 per year), 9 teaching assistantships with partial tuition reimbursements available (averaging $10,200 per year); career-related internships or fieldwork, Federal Work-Study, and institutionally-sponsored loans also available. Financial aid application deadline: 7/15. *Faculty research:* Sedimentary geology, structural geology, regional tectonics, hydrogeology. Total annual research expenditures: $250,000. *Unit head:* Dr. Don Fiesinger, Head, 435-797-1274, Fax: 435-797-1588, E-mail: geology@cc.usu.edu.

Vanderbilt University, Graduate School, Department of Geology, Nashville, TN 37240-1001. Offers MS. *Faculty:* 9 full-time (2 women), 1 part-time (0 women). *Students:* 10 full-time (6 women), 1 part-time. Average age 28. 21 applicants, 95% accepted. In 1998, 3 degrees awarded. *Degree requirements:* For master's, thesis or alternative required, foreign language not required. *Entrance requirements:* For master's, GRE General Test, GRE Subject Test (recommended). *Application deadline:* For fall admission, 1/15. Application fee: $40. *Financial aid:* In 1998–99, 11 students received aid, including 8 teaching assistantships with full tuition reimbursements available (averaging $10,750 per year); research assistantships, career-related internships or fieldwork, Federal Work-Study, and institutionally-sponsored loans also available. Financial aid application deadline: 1/15. *Faculty research:* Sedimentology, geochemistry, tectonics, environmental geology, biostratigraphy. *Unit head:* Leonard P. Alberstadt, Chair, 615-322-2976, Fax: 615-322-2138, E-mail: alberslp@ctrvax.vanderbilt.edu. *Application contact:* Calvin F. Miller, Director of Graduate Studies, 615-322-2976, Fax: 615-322-2138, E-mail: millercf@ctrvax.vanderbilt.edu.

Virginia Polytechnic Institute and State University, Graduate School, College of Arts and Sciences, Department of Geological Sciences, Program in Geological Sciences, Blacksburg, VA 24061. Offers MS, PhD. *Students:* 28 full-time (7 women), 6 part-time (3 women), 3 international. 32 applicants, 34% accepted. In 1998, 6 master's, 3 doctorates awarded. *Degree requirements:* For master's and doctorate, thesis/dissertation required. *Entrance requirements:* For master's and doctorate, GRE General Test, GRE Subject Test, TOEFL. *Application deadline:* For fall admission, 12/1 (priority date). Applications are processed on a rolling basis. Application fee: $25. *Financial aid:* Application deadline: 4/1. *Unit head:* Dr. Cahit Coruh, Head, Department of Geological Sciences, 540-231-6521, E-mail: coruh@vt.edu.

See in-depth description on page 323.

Washington State University, Graduate School, College of Sciences, Department of Geology, Pullman, WA 99164. Offers MS, PhD. *Faculty:* 13 full-time (1 woman), 11 part-time (2 women). *Students:* 24 full-time (8 women), 5 part-time (2 women), 1 international. Average age 25. In 1998, 12 master's, 1 doctorate awarded (100% found work related to degree). *Degree requirements:* For master's, thesis (for some programs), oral exam required, foreign language not required; for doctorate, one foreign language (computer language can substitute), dissertation, oral exam required. *Entrance requirements:* For master's and doctorate, GRE General Test, minimum GPA of 3.0. *Average time to degree:* Master's–3 years full-time; doctorate–4 years full-time. *Application deadline:* For fall admission, 3/1 (priority date). Applications are processed on a rolling basis. Application fee: $35. *Financial aid:* In 1998–99, 2 research assistantships, 19 teaching assistantships were awarded.; career-related internships or fieldwork, Federal Work-Study, institutionally-sponsored loans, and tuition waivers (partial) also available. Financial aid application deadline: 3/1; financial aid applicants required to submit FAFSA. *Faculty research:* Genesis of ore deposits, geohydrology of the Pacific Northwest, geochemistry and petrology of plateau basalts. Total annual research expenditures: $184,698. *Unit head:* Dr. P. Larson, Chairman, 509-335-3009, Fax: 509-335-7816, E-mail: plarson@wsu.edu.

Washington University in St. Louis, Graduate School of Arts and Sciences, Department of Earth and Planetary Sciences, St. Louis, MO 63130-4899. Offers earth and planetary sciences (MA); geochemistry (PhD); geology (MA, PhD); geophysics (PhD); planetary sciences (PhD). *Students:* 26 full-time (11 women); includes 2 minority (1 Asian American or Pacific Islander, 1 Native American), 4 international. Terminal master's awarded for partial completion of doctoral program. *Degree requirements:* For master's and doctorate, thesis/dissertation required. *Entrance requirements:* For master's and doctorate, GRE General Test. *Application deadline:* For fall admission, 1/15 (priority date). Applications are processed on a rolling basis. Application fee: $35. *Unit head:* Dr. Raymond E. Arvidson, Chairman, 314-935-5610.

Wayne State University, Graduate School, College of Science, Department of Geology, Detroit, MI 48202. Offers MS. *Degree requirements:* For master's, thesis required, foreign language not required. *Entrance requirements:* For master's, GRE General Test. *Faculty research:* Geologic history of southwestern U.S., heavy metal contamination of soils.

West Chester University of Pennsylvania, Graduate Studies, College of Arts and Sciences, Department of Geology and Astronomy, West Chester, PA 19383. Offers physical science (MA). Part-time and evening/weekend programs available. *Faculty:* 4 part-time. *Students:* 26. Average age 32. *Degree requirements:* For master's, comprehensive exam required, foreign language and thesis not required. *Application deadline:* For fall admission, 4/15 (priority date); for spring admission, 10/15. Applications are processed on a rolling basis. Application fee: $25. Tuition, state resident: full-time $3,780; part-time $210 per credit. Tuition, nonresident: full-time $6,610; part-time $367 per credit. Required fees: $684; $39 per credit. Tuition and fees vary according to course load. *Financial aid:* In 1998–99, 1 research assistantship with full tuition reimbursement (averaging $5,000 per year) was awarded. Aid available to part-time students. Financial aid application deadline: 2/15. *Unit head:* Dr. Gil Wiswall, Chair, 610-436-2570. *Application contact:* Dr. Steven Good, Graduate Coordinator, 610-436-2203, E-mail: sgood@wcupa.edu.

Western Michigan University, Graduate College, College of Arts and Sciences, Department of Geology, Program in Geology, Kalamazoo, MI 49008. Offers MS, PhD. *Students:* 8 full-time (1 woman), 25 part-time (10 women); includes 5 minority (4 African Americans, 1 Asian American or Pacific Islander), 5 international. 22 applicants, 77% accepted. In 1998, 12 master's, 3 doctorates awarded. *Degree requirements:* For master's, oral exam required; for doctorate, dissertation, oral exam required. *Entrance requirements:* For master's and doctorate, GRE General Test. *Application deadline:* For fall admission, 2/15 (priority date). Applications are processed on a rolling basis. Application fee: $25. *Financial aid:* Application deadline: 2/15. *Unit head:* Paula J. Boodt, Coordinator, Graduate Admissions and Recruitment, 616-387-2000, Fax: 616-387-2355, E-mail: paula.boodt@wmich.edu. *Application contact:* Paula J. Boodt, Coordinator, Graduate Admissions and Recruitment, 616-387-2000, Fax: 616-387-2355, E-mail: paula.boodt@wmich.edu.

Western Washington University, Graduate School, College of Arts and Sciences, Department of Geology, Bellingham, WA 98225-5996. Offers MS. Part-time programs available. *Faculty:* 11. *Students:* 24 full-time (12 women), 2 part-time (both women); includes 1 minority (Asian American or Pacific Islander), 1 international. 26 applicants, 88% accepted. In 1998, 7 degrees awarded. *Degree requirements:* For master's, thesis required (for some programs), foreign language not required. *Entrance requirements:* For master's, GRE General Test, TOEFL, minimum GPA of 3.0 in last 60 semester hours or last 90 quarter hours. *Application deadline:* For fall admission, 1/31 (priority date); for winter admission, 10/1; for spring admis-

Geology–Geophysics

Western Washington University (continued)

sion, 2/1. Applications are processed on a rolling basis. Application fee: $35. Tuition, state resident: full-time $3,247; part-time $146 per credit hour. Tuition, nonresident: full-time $13,364; part-time $445 per credit hour. Required fees: $254; $85 per quarter. *Financial aid:* In 1998–99, 7 teaching assistantships with partial tuition reimbursements (averaging $7,563 per year) were awarded.; career-related internships or fieldwork, Federal Work-Study, institutionally-sponsored loans, scholarships, and tuition waivers (partial) also available. Aid available to part-time students. Financial aid application deadline: 2/15; financial aid applicants required to submit FAFSA. *Unit head:* Dr. Thor Hansen, Chair, 360-650-3648. *Application contact:* Dr. Chris Suczek, Graduate Adviser, 360-650-3590.

West Virginia University, Eberly College of Arts and Sciences, Department of Geology and Geography, Program in Geology, Morgantown, WV 26506. Offers MS, PhD. Part-time programs available. Terminal master's awarded for partial completion of doctoral program. *Degree requirements:* For master's, thesis required, foreign language not required; for doctorate, dissertation, comprehensive exam required, foreign language not required. *Entrance requirements:* For master's, GRE General Test, GRE Subject Test, TOEFL (minimum score of 550 required), minimum GPA of 2.5; for doctorate, GRE General Test, GRE Subject Test, TOEFL (minimum score of 550 required), minimum GPA of 3.3.

Wichita State University, Graduate School, Fairmount College of Liberal Arts and Sciences, Department of Geology, Wichita, KS 67260. Offers MS. Part-time programs available. *Faculty:* 5 full-time (1 woman). *Students:* 4 full-time (1 woman), 6 part-time (2 women); includes 1 minority (Native American) Average age 32. 7 applicants, 57% accepted. In 1998, 2 degrees awarded. *Degree requirements:* For master's, thesis required, foreign language not required. *Entrance requirements:* For master's, GRE General Test (minimum combined score of 1000 required), TOEFL (minimum score of 550 required). *Application deadline:* For fall admission, 7/1 (priority date); for spring admission, 1/1. Applications are processed on a rolling basis. Application fee: $25 ($40 for international students). Electronic applications accepted. *Financial aid:* In 1998–99, 1 research assistantship (averaging $4,000 per year), 5 teaching assistantships with full tuition reimbursements (averaging $6,600 per year) were awarded.; Federal Work-Study and institutionally-sponsored loans also available. Aid available to part-time students. Financial aid application deadline: 4/1; financial aid applicants required to submit FAFSA. *Faculty research:* Midcontinent and Permian basin stratigraphy studies, recent sediments of Belize and Florida, image analysis of sediments and porosity. Total annual research expenditures: $10,544. *Unit head:* Dr. Collette Burke, Chairperson, 316-978-3140, E-mail: burke@twsuvm.uc.twsu.edu. *Application contact:* Dr. Michael Lydy, Coordinator, 316-978-3111, Fax: 316-978-3772, E-mail: lydy@wsuhub.uc.twsu.edu.

Wright State University, School of Graduate Studies, College of Science and Mathematics, Department of Geological Sciences, Program in Geological Sciences, Dayton, OH 45435. Offers environmental geology (MS); environmental sciences (MS); geological sciences (MS); geophysics (MS); hydrogeology (MS); petroleum geology (MS). Part-time programs available. *Students:* 32 full-time (14 women), 9 part-time (2 women), 1 international. Average age 26. 29 applicants, 72% accepted. In 1998, 20 degrees awarded. *Degree requirements:* For master's, computer language, thesis required, foreign language not required. *Entrance requirements:* For master's, TOEFL (minimum score of 550 required). Application fee: $25. *Financial aid:* Fellowships, research assistantships, teaching assistantships, Federal Work-Study and unspecified assistantships available. Aid available to part-time students. Financial aid application deadline: 3/1; financial aid applicants required to submit FAFSA. *Unit head:* Dr. Dennis Burns, Graduate Coordinator, 316-978-3120, Fax: 316-978-3431, E-mail: burns@twsuvm.uc.twsu.edu. *Application contact:* Deborah L. Cowles, Assistant to Chair, 937-775-3455, Fax: 937-775-3462.

Yale University, Graduate School of Arts and Sciences, Department of Geology and Geophysics, New Haven, CT 06520. Offers geochemistry (PhD); geophysics (PhD); meteorology (PhD); mineralogy and crystallography (PhD); oceanography (PhD); paleoecology (PhD); paleontology and stratigraphy (PhD); petrology (PhD); structural geology (PhD). *Faculty:* 26. *Students:* 26 full-time (11 women), 9 international. 21 applicants, 86% accepted. In 1998, 6 degrees awarded. *Degree requirements:* For doctorate, dissertation required, foreign language not required. *Entrance requirements:* For doctorate, GRE General Test, TOEFL. *Average time to degree:* Doctorate–7.9 years full-time. *Application deadline:* For fall admission, 1/4. Application fee: $65. *Financial aid:* Fellowships, research assistantships, teaching assistantships, Federal Work-Study and institutionally-sponsored loans available. Aid available to part-time students. *Unit head:* Chair, 203-432-3174. *Application contact:* Admissions Information, 203-432-2770.

Announcement: Department offers individualized programs of study leading to the doctorate (6 years). It welcomes applicants interested in earth sciences who have bachelor's or master's degree in biology, chemistry, engineering, mathematics, meteorology, or physics, as well as geology. Program has no required curriculum of credit courses but is designed to encourage development of individual interests under guidance of faculty advisory committee.

See in-depth description on page 327.

Geophysics

Boise State University, Graduate College, College of Arts and Sciences, Department of Geosciences, Program in Applied Geophysics, Boise, ID 83725-0399. Offers MS. Part-time programs available. *Faculty:* 9 full-time (0 women), 21 part-time (3 women). *Students:* 3 full-time (1 woman), 2 part-time. Average age 31. 1 applicants, 100% accepted. In 1998, 2 degrees awarded (100% found work related to degree). *Degree requirements:* For master's, computer language, thesis required. *Entrance requirements:* For master's, GRE General Test, TOEFL (minimum score of 550 required), minimum GPA of 3.0, BS in related field. *Application deadline:* For fall admission, 7/23 (priority date); for spring admission, 11/24. Applications are processed on a rolling basis. Application fee: $20 ($30 for international students). Electronic applications accepted. *Financial aid:* In 1998–99, 5 students received aid, including 4 research assistantships with full tuition reimbursements available (averaging $12,000 per year); career-related internships or fieldwork, Federal Work-Study, institutionally-sponsored loans, and graduate assistantships, grants also available. Aid available to part-time students. Financial aid application deadline: 3/1. *Faculty research:* Shallow seismic profile, seismic hazard, tectonics, hazardous waste disposal. *Unit head:* Dr. John R. Pelton, Coordinator, 208-426-1419, Fax: 208-426-4061.

Boston College, Graduate School of Arts and Sciences, Department of Geology and Geophysics, Chestnut Hill, MA 02467-3800. Offers MS, MBA/MS. *Faculty:* 8 full-time (0 women). *Students:* 17 full-time (8 women), 12 part-time (6 women); includes 2 minority (1 Asian American or Pacific Islander, 1 Hispanic American), 4 international. 23 applicants, 78% accepted. In 1998, 6 degrees awarded. *Degree requirements:* For master's, thesis required, foreign language not required. *Entrance requirements:* For master's, GRE General Test, GRE Subject Test. *Application deadline:* For fall admission, 2/1 (priority date). Application fee: $40. *Financial aid:* Research assistantships, teaching assistantships, Federal Work-Study available. Aid available to part-time students. Financial aid application deadline: 3/15; financial aid applicants required to submit FAFSA. *Faculty research:* Coastal and marine geology, experimental sedimentology, geomagnetism, igneous petrology, paleontology. *Unit head:* Dr. Christopher Hepburn, Chairperson, 617-552-3640, E-mail: christopher.hepburn@bc.edu. *Application contact:* Dr. John Ebel, Graduate Program Director, 617-552-3640, E-mail: john.ebel@bc.edu.

California Institute of Technology, Division of Geological and Planetary Sciences, Pasadena, CA 91125-0001. Offers cosmochemistry (PhD); geobiology (PhD); geochemistry (MS, PhD); geology (MS, PhD); geophysics (MS, PhD); planetary science (MS, PhD). *Faculty:* 32 full-time (1 woman). *Students:* 58 full-time (22 women); includes 1 minority (Hispanic American), 20 international. Terminal master's awarded for partial completion of doctoral program. *Degree requirements:* For master's, thesis not required; for doctorate, dissertation required. *Entrance requirements:* For doctorate, GRE General Test, GRE Subject Test, TOEFL. *Application deadline:* For fall admission, 1/15. Application fee: $0. *Unit head:* Dr. Edward M. Stolper, Chair, 626-395-6108, Fax: 626-795-6028, E-mail: divgps@gps.caltech.edu. *Application contact:* Dr. George R. Rossman, Division Academic Officer, 626-395-6125, Fax: 626-568-0935, E-mail: divgps@gps.caltech.edu.

Colorado School of Mines, Graduate School, Department of Geophysics, Golden, CO 80401-1887. Offers geophysical engineering (ME, MS, PhD); geophysics (MS, PhD, Diploma). Part-time programs available. *Faculty:* 11 full-time (0 women), 6 part-time (0 women). *Students:* 47 full-time (10 women), 8 part-time (3 women); includes 2 minority (1 Asian American or Pacific Islander, 1 Hispanic American), 27 international. 55 applicants, 69% accepted. In 1998, 6 master's awarded (100% found work related to degree); 7 doctorates awarded (100% found work related to degree). *Degree requirements:* For master's, thesis required, foreign language not required; for doctorate, one foreign language, dissertation, comprehensive and oral exams required; for Diploma, foreign language and thesis not required. *Entrance requirements:* For master's and doctorate, GRE General Test (combined average 1790 on three sections), minimum GPA of 3.0; for Diploma, GRE General Test, minimum GPA of 3.0. *Application deadline:* Applications are processed on a rolling basis. Application fee: $40. Electronic applications accepted. *Financial aid:* In 1998–99, 31 students received aid, including 5 fellowships, 14 research assistantships, 7 teaching assistantships; unspecified assistantships also available. Aid available to part-time students. Financial aid applicants required to submit FAFSA. *Faculty research:* Seismic exploration, gravity and geomagnetic fields, electrical mapping and sounding, bore hole measurements, environmental physics. Total annual research expenditures: $1.3 million. *Unit head:* Dr. Thomas Davis, Acting Head, 303-273-3938. *Application contact:* Sara Summers, Program Assistant, 303-273-3935, Fax: 303-273-3478, E-mail: ssummers@mines.edu.

Columbia University, Graduate School of Arts and Sciences, Division of Natural Sciences, Department of Earth and Environmental Sciences, New York, NY 10027. Offers geochemistry (M Phil, MA, PhD); geodetic sciences (M Phil, MA, PhD); geophysics (M Phil, MA, PhD); oceanography (M Phil, MA, PhD). *Degree requirements:* For master's, thesis or alternative, fieldwork, written exam required, foreign language not required; for doctorate, one foreign language, dissertation required. *Entrance requirements:* For master's and doctorate, GRE General Test, GRE Subject Test, TOEFL, major in natural or physical science. *Faculty research:* Structural geology and stratigraphy, petrology, paleontology, rare gas, isotope and aqueous geochemistry.

Cornell University, Graduate School, Graduate Fields of Engineering, Field of Geological Sciences, Ithaca, NY 14853-0001. Offers economic geology (MS, PhD); engineering geology (MS, PhD); environmental geophysics (M Eng, MS, PhD); general geology (MS, PhD); geobiology (MS, PhD); geochemistry and isotope geology (MS, PhD); geohydrology (M Eng, MS, PhD); geomorphology (MS, PhD); geophysics (MS, PhD); geotectonics (MS, PhD); mineralogy (MS, PhD); paleontology (MS, PhD); petroleum geology (MS, PhD); petrology (MS, PhD); planetary geology (MS, PhD); Precambrian geology (MS, PhD); Quaternary geology (MS, PhD); rock mechanics (MS, PhD); sedimentology (MS, PhD); seismology (MS, PhD); stratigraphy (MS, PhD); structural geology (MS, PhD). *Faculty:* 28 full-time. *Students:* 36 full-time (12 women); includes 4 minority (1 African American, 1 Asian American or Pacific Islander, 2 Hispanic Americans), 16 international. *Degree requirements:* For master's, thesis (MS) required; for doctorate, dissertation required, foreign language not required. *Entrance requirements:* For master's and doctorate, GRE General Test, TOEFL (minimum score of 550 required). *Application deadline:* For fall admission, 1/15. Application fee: $65. Electronic applications accepted. *Unit head:* Director of Graduate Studies, 607-255-3474, Fax: 607-254-4780. *Application contact:* Graduate Field Assistant, 607-255-3474, Fax: 607-254-4780, E-mail: gradprog@geology.cornell.edu.

See in-depth description on page 273.

Florida State University, Graduate Studies, College of Arts and Sciences, Department of Geological Sciences, Interdisciplinary Program in Geophysical Fluid Dynamics, Tallahassee, FL 32306. Offers PhD. *Faculty:* 21 full-time (1 woman). *Students:* 1 full-time (0 women), 1 international. Average age 30. 6 applicants, 17% accepted. *Degree requirements:* For doctorate, computer language, dissertation, departmental qualifying exam required, foreign language not required. *Entrance requirements:* For doctorate, GRE General Test, GRE Subject Test, TOEFL, minimum GPA of 3.0. *Application deadline:* For fall admission, 12/30. Application fee: $20. Tuition, state resident: part-time $139 per credit hour. Tuition, nonresident: part-time $482 per credit hour. Tuition and fees vary according to program. *Financial aid:* Fellowships, research assistantships available. Financial aid applicants required to submit FAFSA. *Faculty research:* Hurricane dynamics, topography, convection, air-sea interaction, wave-mean flow interaction, numerical models. *Unit head:* Dr. Albert I. Barcilon, Director, 850-644-2488, Fax: 850-644-8972, E-mail: blumsack@math.fsu.edu.

Georgia Institute of Technology, Graduate Studies and Research, College of Sciences, School of Earth and Atmospheric Sciences, Atlanta, GA 30332-0001. Offers atmospheric chemistry (MS, PhD); atmospheric dynamics and physics (MS, PhD); geochemistry (MS, PhD); solid-earth geophysics (MS, PhD). Part-time programs available. Terminal master's awarded for partial completion of doctoral program. *Degree requirements:* For master's, thesis or alternative required, foreign language not required; for doctorate, dissertation, comprehensive exams required, foreign language not required. *Entrance requirements:* For master's and doctorate, GRE General Test, TOEFL (minimum score of 550 required), minimum GPA of 2.7. Electronic applications accepted. *Faculty research:* Geophysics, geochemistry, atmospheric chemistry, atmospheric dynamics, seismology.

See in-depth description on page 277.

ICR Graduate School, Graduate Programs, Santee, CA 92071. Offers astro/geophysics (MS); biology (MS); geology (MS); science education (MS). Part-time programs available. *Faculty:* 4 full-time (0 women), 6 part-time (0 women). *Students:* 13 full-time (5 women), 23 part-time (9 women). *Degree requirements:* For master's, thesis required (for some programs), foreign language not required. *Entrance requirements:* For master's, BS degree in field of graduate study. *Application deadline:* Applications are processed on a rolling basis. Application fee: $30. *Unit head:* Kenneth B. Cumming, Dean, 619-448-0900, Fax: 619-448-3469. *Application contact:* Dr. Jack Kriege, Registrar, 619-448-0900, Fax: 619-448-3469.

Idaho State University, Graduate School, College of Arts and Sciences, Department of Geology, Pocatello, ID 83209. Offers geology (MS); geophysics/hydrology (MS); natural science (MNS). MS (geophysics/hydrology) offered jointly with Boise State University. Part-time programs available. *Degree requirements:* For master's, thesis required, foreign language not required. *Entrance requirements:* For master's, GRE General Test (score in 35th percentile or higher on verbal or quantitative section required). *Faculty research:* Structural geography, stratigraphy, geochemistry, volcanography, geomorphology.

Indiana University Bloomington, Graduate School, College of Arts and Sciences, Department of Geological Sciences, Program in Geophysics, Bloomington, IN 47405. Offers MS, PhD. PhD offered through the University Graduate School. *Degree requirements:* For master's, one foreign language (computer language can substitute), thesis or alternative required; for doctorate, dissertation required, dissertation required. *Entrance requirements:* For master's and doctorate, GRE General Test, TOEFL. *Application deadline:* For fall admission, 1/15 (priority date); for spring admission, 9/1 (priority date). Applications are processed on a rolling basis. Application fee: $40. Tuition, state resident: part-time $161 per credit hour. Tuition, nonresident: part-time $468 per credit hour. Required fees: $360 per year. Tuition and fees vary according to course load and program. *Financial aid:* Fellowships with tuition reimbursements, research assistantships with tuition reimbursements, teaching assistantships with tuition reimbursements, career-related internships or fieldwork, Federal Work-Study, and institutionally-sponsored loans available. Financial aid application deadline: 2/15. *Faculty research:* Seismology, tomography, potential fields, rock mechanics, volcanology and geodosy. Total annual research expenditures: $284,309. *Unit head:* Mary Iverson, Secretary, Committee for Graduate Studies, 812-855-7214, Fax: 812-855-7899, E-mail: geograd@indiana.edu. *Application contact:* Mary Iverson, Secretary, Committee for Graduate Studies, 812-855-7214, Fax: 812-855-7899, E-mail: geograd@indiana.edu.

Johns Hopkins University, Zanvyl Krieger School of Arts and Sciences, Department of Earth and Planetary Sciences, Program in Geophysics, Baltimore, MD 21218-2699. Offers MA, PhD. *Faculty:* 2 full-time (0 women). *Students:* 1 full-time (0 women). Average age 26. In 1998, 1 degree awarded. Terminal master's awarded for partial completion of doctoral program. *Degree requirements:* For doctorate, dissertation required, foreign language not required. *Entrance requirements:* For master's and doctorate, GRE General Test. *Average time to degree:* Doctorate–5.5 years full-time. *Application deadline:* For fall admission, 1/15. Application fee: $55. Tuition: Full-time $23,660. Tuition and fees vary according to program. *Financial aid:* Application deadline: 3/14; *Unit head:* Dr. John M. Ferry, Chair, Department of Earth and Planetary Sciences, 410-516-7135, Fax: 410-516-7933.

Louisiana State University and Agricultural and Mechanical College, Graduate School, College of Basic Sciences, Department of Geology and Geophysics, Baton Rouge, LA 70803. Offers MS, PhD. *Faculty:* 19 full-time (4 women), 1 part-time (0 women). *Students:* 33 full-time (11 women), 14 part-time (5 women); includes 1 minority (Hispanic American), 11 international. Average age 29. 40 applicants, 40% accepted. In 1998, 8 master's, 6 doctorates awarded. Terminal master's awarded for partial completion of doctoral program. *Degree requirements:* For master's and doctorate, thesis/dissertation required, foreign language not required. *Entrance requirements:* For master's and doctorate, GRE General Test (minimum combined score of 1000 required), TOEFL (minimum score of 525 required, 550 for assistantships), minimum GPA of 3.0. *Application deadline:* For fall admission, 1/25 (priority date). Applications are processed on a rolling basis. Application fee: $25. *Financial aid:* In 1998–99, 4 fellowships, 3 research assistantships with partial tuition reimbursements, 21 teaching assistantships with partial tuition reimbursements were awarded.; career-related internships or fieldwork, Federal Work-Study, institutionally-sponsored loans, and unspecified assistantships also available. Financial aid application deadline: 3/15. *Faculty research:* Geophysics, geochemistry of sediments, isotope geochemistry, igneous and metamorphic petrology, micropaleontology. *Unit head:* Dr. G. Ray Byerly, Chair, 225-388-3353, Fax: 225-388-2302, E-mail: glbyer@lsuvm.sncc.lsu.edu. *Application contact:* Lui Chan, Graduate Coordinator, 225-388-6439, E-mail: glchan@lsuvm.sncc.lsu.edu.

Massachusetts Institute of Technology, School of Science, Department of Earth, Atmospheric, and Planetary Sciences, Program in Geophysics, Cambridge, MA 02139-4307. Offers SM, PhD, Sc D. *Faculty:* 10 full-time (1 woman). *Students:* 28 full-time (8 women), 14 international. Average age 30. 33 applicants, 39% accepted. In 1998, 1 master's, 6 doctorates awarded. Terminal master's awarded for partial completion of doctoral program. *Degree requirements:* For master's, thesis required, foreign language not required; for doctorate, dissertation, general exam required, foreign language not required. *Entrance requirements:* For master's and doctorate, GRE General Test. *Application deadline:* For fall admission, 1/15; for spring admission, 11/1. Application fee: $55. *Financial aid:* Fellowships, research assistantships, teaching assistantships available. Financial aid application deadline: 1/15. *Unit head:* Bernard W. Sullivan, Associate Director of Admissions, 718-488-1011, Fax: 718-797-2399, E-mail: attend@liu.edu. *Application contact:* Anastasia Frangos, Administrative Assistant, 617-253-3381, Fax: 617-253-8298, E-mail: eapsinfo@mit.edu.

Memorial University of Newfoundland, School of Graduate Studies, Department of Earth Sciences, St. John's, NF A1C 5S7, Canada. Offers geology (M Sc, PhD); geophysics (M Sc, PhD). Part-time programs available. *Faculty:* 25 full-time (2 women), 4 part-time (0 women). *Students:* 32 full-time (11 women), 5 part-time (2 women), 15 international. *Degree requirements:* For master's, thesis required; for doctorate, dissertation, comprehensive exam required. *Entrance requirements:* For master's, honors B Sc; for doctorate, M Sc. *Application deadline:* For fall admission, 3/31; for spring admission, 12/31. Applications are processed on a rolling basis. Application fee: $40. *Unit head:* Dr. G. Quinlan, Head, 709-737-2334, Fax: 709-737-2589, E-mail: gquinlan@sparkyz.esd.ucs.mun.ca. *Application contact:* Dr. Ali Aksu, Graduate Officer, 709-737-8385, Fax: 709-737-2589, E-mail: aaksu@sparkyz.esd.ucs.mun.ca.

Michigan Technological University, Graduate School, College of Engineering, Department of Geology, Geophysics and Geological Engineering, Program in Geophysics, Houghton, MI 49931-1295. Offers MS. Part-time programs available. *Faculty:* 1 full-time (0 women), 2 part-time (1 woman). *Students:* 1 full-time (0 women). Average age 28. 1 applicants, 100% accepted. In 1998, 3 degrees awarded. *Degree requirements:* For master's, thesis required, foreign language not required. *Entrance requirements:* For master's, GRE General Test (combined average 1620 on three sections), TOEFL (minimum score of 550 required). *Average time to degree:* Master's–3.5 years full-time. *Application deadline:* For fall admission, 3/15 (priority date). Applications are processed on a rolling basis. Application fee: $30 ($35 for international students). Tuition, state resident: full-time $4,377. Tuition, nonresident: full-time $9,108. Required fees: $126. Tuition and fees vary according to course load. *Financial aid:* In 1998–99, 1 research assistantship (averaging $4,365 per year) was awarded.; fellowships, teaching assistantships, career-related internships or fieldwork, Federal Work-Study, and institutionally-sponsored loans also available. Aid available to part-time students. Financial aid applicants required to submit FAFSA. *Faculty research:* Paleomagnetism/rock magnetism, environmental geophysics, electromagnetic geophysics, magnetotellurics. *Application contact:* Dr. Jimmy Diehl, Graduate Coordinator, 906-487-2665, Fax: 906-487-3371, E-mail: jdiehl@mtu.edu.

New Mexico Institute of Mining and Technology, Graduate Studies, Department of Earth and Environmental Science, Program in Geophysics, Socorro, NM 87801. Offers MS, PhD. *Students:* 8 full-time (2 women), 2 international. Average age 30. 15 applicants, 93% accepted. *Degree requirements:* For master's, thesis optional, foreign language not required; for doctorate, dissertation required, foreign language not required. *Entrance requirements:* For master's, GRE General Test, TOEFL (minimum score of 540 required); for doctorate, GRE General Test, GRE Subject Test, TOEFL (minimum score of 540 required). *Average time to degree:* Master's–3 years full-time; doctorate–6 years full-time. *Application deadline:* For fall admission, 3/1 (priority date); for spring admission, 6/1. Applications are processed on a rolling basis. Application fee: $16. *Financial aid:* In 1998–99, 6 research assistantships (averaging $9,670 per year), 2 teaching assistantships (averaging $9,670 per year) were awarded.; fellowships, Federal Work-Study and institutionally-sponsored loans also available. Financial aid application deadline: 3/1; financial aid applicants required to submit CSS PROFILE or FAFSA. *Faculty research:* Crustal exploration, tectonophysics. *Unit head:* Dr. Rick Aster, Coordinator, 505-835-5924, Fax: 505-835-6436, E-mail: geos@nmt.edu. *Application contact:* Dr. David B. Johnson, Dean of Graduate Studies, 505-835-5513, Fax: 505-835-5476, E-mail: graduate@nmt.edu.

North Carolina State University, Graduate School, College of Physical and Mathematical Sciences, Department of Marine, Earth, and Atmospheric Sciences, Raleigh, NC 27695. Offers geology (MS, PhD); geophysics (MS, PhD); marine, earth, and atmospheric sciences (MS, PhD); meteorology (MS, PhD); oceanography (MS, PhD). *Faculty:* 34 full-time (2 women), 39 part-time (1 woman). *Students:* 118 full-time (30 women), 12 part-time (3 women); includes 2 minority (both Asian Americans or Pacific Islanders), 37 international. Terminal master's awarded for partial completion of doctoral program. *Degree requirements:* For master's, thesis, final oral exam required, foreign language not required; for doctorate, dissertation, final oral exam, preliminary oral and written exams required, foreign language not required. *Entrance requirements:* For master's and doctorate, GRE General Test, minimum GPA of 3.0. *Application deadline:* For fall admission, 6/25 (priority date); for spring admission, 11/25. Applications are processed on a rolling basis. Application fee: $45. *Unit head:* Dr. Leonard J. Pietrafesa, Head, 919-515-3717, Fax: 919-515-7802, E-mail: leonard_pietrafesa@ncsu.edu. *Application contact:* Dr. Gerald S. Janowitz, Director of Graduate Programs, 919-515-7837, Fax: 919-515-7802, E-mail: janowitz@ncsu.edu.

See in-depth description on page 293.

Oregon State University, Graduate School, College of Oceanic and Atmospheric Sciences, Program in Geophysics, Corvallis, OR 97331. Offers MA, MS, PhD. *Faculty:* 6 full-time (1 woman). *Students:* 2 full-time (0 women), (both international). Average age 30. In 1998, 1 master's awarded. Terminal master's awarded for partial completion of doctoral program. *Degree requirements:* For master's, thesis optional, foreign language not required; for doctorate, dissertation required, foreign language not required. *Entrance requirements:* For master's and doctorate, GRE General Test, TOEFL (minimum score of 550 required), minimum GPA of 3.0 in last 90 hours. *Application deadline:* For fall admission, 2/1. Applications are processed on a rolling basis. Application fee: $50. *Financial aid:* Fellowships, research assistantships, teaching assistantships, career-related internships or fieldwork, Federal Work-Study, and institutionally-sponsored loans available. Aid available to part-time students. Financial aid application deadline: 2/1. *Faculty research:* Seismic waves; gravitational, geothermal, and electromagnetic fields; rock magnetism; paleomagnetism. *Application contact:* Irma Delson, Assistant Director, Student Services, 541-737-5190, Fax: 541-737-2064, E-mail: student_adviser@oce.orst.edu.

Pennsylvania State University University Park Campus, Graduate School, College of Earth and Mineral Sciences, Department of Geosciences, Program in Geophysics, State College, University Park, PA 16802-1503. Offers MS, PhD. *Entrance requirements:* For master's and doctorate, GRE General Test, TOEFL.

Announcement: Penn State offers MS and PhD research opportunities in geodynamics, seismology, exploration geophysics, geophysical signal analysis, thermal-mechanical modeling of plate tectonics, and mineral physics and tectonophysics.

Princeton University, Graduate School, Department of Geosciences, Princeton, NJ 08544-1019. Offers atmospheric and oceanic sciences (PhD); environmental engineering and water resources (PhD); geological and geophysical sciences (PhD). *Degree requirements:* For doctorate, dissertation required. *Entrance requirements:* For doctorate, GRE General Test, GRE Subject Test.

Rensselaer Polytechnic Institute, Graduate School, School of Science, Department of Earth and Environmental Sciences, Troy, NY 12180-3590. Offers environmental chemistry (MS, PhD); geochemistry (MS, PhD); geology (MS, PhD); geophysics (MS, PhD); hydrogeology (MS); petrology (MS, PhD); planetary geology (MS, PhD); tectonics (MS, PhD). Part-time programs available. *Faculty:* 7 full-time (0 women), 2 part-time (0 women). *Students:* 19 full-time (8 women), 1 (woman) part-time; includes 2 minority (1 African American, 1 Native American) *Degree requirements:* For master's, thesis required (for some programs); for doctorate, dissertation required. *Entrance requirements:* For master's and doctorate, GRE General Test, TOEFL (minimum score of 550 required). *Application deadline:* For fall admission, 2/1 (priority date). Applications are processed on a rolling basis. Application fee: $35. *Unit head:* Dr. Robert McCaffrey, Chair, 518-276-6474, Fax: 518-276-6680, E-mail: ees@rpi.edu. *Application contact:* Dr. Steven Roecker, Associate Professor, 518-276-6474, Fax: 518-276-6680, E-mail: ees@rpi.edu.

See in-depth description on page 299.

Rice University, Graduate Programs, Wiess School of Natural Sciences, Department of Geology and Geophysics, Houston, TX 77005-1892. Offers geology and geophysics (MA, PhD). *Degree requirements:* For master's and doctorate, thesis/dissertation required, foreign language not required. *Entrance requirements:* For master's and doctorate, GRE General Test (score in 70th percentile or higher on either section required), GRE Subject Test, TOEFL (minimum score of 550 required), minimum GPA of 3.0. *Faculty research:* Stratigraphy/sedimentology, igneous petrology, carbonate petrology, meteoritics, geochemistry.

Southern Methodist University, Dedman College, Department of Geological Sciences, Program in Exploration Geophysics, Dallas, TX 75275. Offers MS. *Degree requirements:* For master's, qualifying exam required, thesis optional, foreign language not required. *Entrance requirements:* For master's, GRE General Test (minimum combined score of 1200 required), minimum GPA of 3.0. *Application deadline:* For fall admission, 6/30; for spring admission, 11/30. Application fee: $50. Tuition: Part-time $686 per credit hour. Required fees: $88 per credit hour. Part-time tuition and fees vary according to course load and program. *Financial aid:* Application deadline: 2/15; *Application contact:* Dr. Robert Gregory, Graduate Director, 214-768-3075, Fax: 214-768-2701, E-mail: bgregory@mail.smu.edu.

Southern Methodist University, Dedman College, Department of Geological Sciences, Program in Geophysics, Dallas, TX 75275. Offers applied geophysics (MS); geophysics (MS, PhD). Part-time programs available. Average age 36. In 1998, 1 master's, 2 doctorates awarded. *Degree requirements:* For master's, thesis (for some programs), qualifying exam required, foreign language not required; for doctorate, one foreign language, dissertation, qualifying exam required. *Entrance requirements:* For master's and doctorate, GRE General Test (minimum combined score of 1200 required), minimum GPA of 3.0. *Application deadline:* For fall admission, 6/30; for spring admission, 11/30. Application fee: $50. Tuition: Part-time $686 per credit hour. Required fees: $88 per credit hour. Part-time tuition and fees vary according to course load and program. *Financial aid:* Fellowships, research assistantships, teaching assistantships, tuition waivers (full and partial) available. Financial aid application deadline: 2/15; financial aid applicants required to submit FAFSA. *Faculty research:* Seismology, heat flow, tectonics. *Unit head:* Steve Scheiner, Chair, Graduate Admissions Committee, 618-453-6476, Fax: 618-453-6408, E-mail: scheiner@chem.siu.edu. *Application contact:* Dr. Robert Gregory, Graduate Director, 214-768-3075, Fax: 214-768-2701, E-mail: bgregory@mail.smu.edu.

Stanford University, School of Earth Sciences, Department of Geophysics, Stanford, CA 94305-9991. Offers MS, PhD. *Faculty:* 11 full-time (0 women). *Students:* 52 full-time (18 women), 7 part-time (1 woman); includes 2 minority (1 Asian American or Pacific Islander, 1 Hispanic American), 37 international. Average age 28. 38 applicants, 45% accepted. In 1998, 11 master's, 10 doctorates awarded. Terminal master's awarded for partial completion of doctoral program. *Degree requirements:* For master's, foreign language and thesis not required; for doctorate, dissertation required, foreign language not required. *Entrance requirements:* For master's and doctorate, GRE General Test, TOEFL. *Application deadline:* For fall admission, 1/

Geophysics

Stanford University (continued)
15. Application fee: $65 ($80 for international students). Electronic applications accepted. Tuition: Full-time $23,058. Required fees: $152. Part-time tuition and fees vary according to course load. *Financial aid:* Fellowships, research assistantships, teaching assistantships, institutionally-sponsored loans available. Aid available to part-time students. Financial aid application deadline: 1/1. *Unit head:* Amos Nur, Chair, 650-723-9526, Fax: 650-723-3118, E-mail: nur@pangea.stanford.edu. *Application contact:* Administrative Assistant, 650-723-4746.

Texas A&M University, College of Geosciences, Department of Geology and Geophysics, College Station, TX 77843. Offers MS, PhD. *Faculty:* 32 full-time (2 women). *Students:* 83 full-time (21 women), 17 part-time (6 women); includes 6 minority (4 Asian Americans or Pacific Islanders, 2 Hispanic Americans), 39 international. Average age 31. 53 applicants, 75% accepted. In 1998, 8 master's, 6 doctorates awarded. *Degree requirements:* For master's and doctorate, thesis/dissertation required, foreign language not required. *Entrance requirements:* For master's and doctorate, GRE General Test, TOEFL. *Application deadline:* For fall admission, 3/1 (priority date); for spring admission, 10/1. Applications are processed on a rolling basis. Application fee: $50 ($75 for international students). Electronic applications accepted. *Financial aid:* In 1998–99, 92 students received aid, including 24 fellowships with partial tuition reimbursements available, 16 research assistantships with partial tuition reimbursements available (averaging $11,475 per year), 66 teaching assistantships with partial tuition reimbursements available (averaging $11,475 per year); Federal Work-Study, institutionally-sponsored loans, and tuition waivers (partial) also available. Financial aid application deadline: 3/1; financial aid applicants required to submit FAFSA. *Faculty research:* Environmental and engineering geology and geophysics, petroleum geology, tectonophysics, geochemistry. Total annual research expenditures: $343,000. *Unit head:* Andrew Hajash, Head, 409-845-2451, Fax: 409-845-6162, E-mail: hajash@geo.tamu.edu. *Application contact:* Robert K. Popp, Graduate Adviser, 409-845-2451, Fax: 409-845-6162, E-mail: popp@geo.tamu.edu.

The University of Akron, Graduate School, Buchtel College of Arts and Sciences, Department of Geology, Program in Geophysics, Akron, OH 44325-0001. Offers MS. Average age 37. In 1998, 1 degree awarded. *Degree requirements:* For master's, thesis required, foreign language not required. *Entrance requirements:* For master's, minimum GPA of 2.75. *Average time to degree:* Master's–2 years full-time, 4 years part-time. *Application deadline:* For fall admission, 3/1. Applications are processed on a rolling basis. Application fee: $25 ($50 for international students). Tuition, state resident: part-time $189 per credit. Tuition, nonresident: part-time $353 per credit. Required fees: $7.3 per credit. *Unit head:* Dr. David McConnell, Director of Graduate Studies, 330-972-8047, E-mail: mcconnell@uakron.edu.

University of Alaska Fairbanks, Graduate School, College of Science, Engineering and Mathematics, Department of Geology and Geophysics, Fairbanks, AK 99775-7480. Offers geology (MS, PhD); geophysics (MS, PhD); geoscience (MAT). *Faculty:* 21 full-time (3 women). *Students:* 37 full-time (11 women), 17 part-time (6 women); includes 3 minority (2 Asian Americans or Pacific Islanders, 1 Native American), 12 international. Average age 30. 24 applicants, 71% accepted. In 1998, 2 master's, 4 doctorates awarded. *Degree requirements:* For master's, thesis, comprehensive exam required, foreign language not required; for doctorate, one foreign language (computer language can substitute), dissertation, comprehensive exam required. *Entrance requirements:* For master's and doctorate, GRE General Test, GRE Subject Test, TOEFL (minimum score of 550 required). *Application deadline:* For fall admission, 3/1. Application fee: $35. *Financial aid:* Research assistantships, teaching assistantships available. Financial aid application deadline: 3/1. *Faculty research:* Glacial surging, Alaska as geologic fragments, natural zeolites. *Unit head:* Dr. Paul Layer, Head, 907-474-7565. *Application contact:* Doug Christensen, Adviser, 907-474-7426.

University of Alberta, Faculty of Graduate Studies and Research, Department of Physics, Edmonton, AB T6G 2E1, Canada. Offers astrophysics (M Sc, PhD); condensed matter (M Sc, PhD); geophysics (M Sc, PhD); medical physics (M Sc, PhD); nuclear physics (M Sc, PhD); subatomic physics (M Sc, PhD). *Degree requirements:* For master's and doctorate, thesis/dissertation required. *Entrance requirements:* For master's and doctorate, TOEFL (minimum score of 550 required), minimum GPA of 7.0 on a 9.0 scale. *Faculty research:* Cosmology, astro-particle physics, high-intermediate energy, magnetism, superconductivity, electron microscopy, low-temperature physics, seismology, geodynamics, MRI.

University of British Columbia, Faculty of Graduate Studies, Faculty of Science, Department of Geophysics and Astronomy, Vancouver, BC V6T 1Z2, Canada. Offers astronomy (M Sc, MA Sc, PhD); geophysics (M Sc, MA Sc, PhD). *Degree requirements:* For master's, thesis required; for doctorate, dissertation, comprehensive exam required. *Entrance requirements:* For master's and doctorate, TOEFL. *Faculty research:* Stellar astronomy, cosmology, crustal and earthquake seismology, geophysical inverse theory, glacier and ice sheet physics.

University of Calgary, Faculty of Graduate Studies, Faculty of Science, Department of Geology and Geophysics, Calgary, AB T2N 1N4, Canada. Offers geology (M Sc, PhD); geophysics (M Sc, PhD). Part-time programs available. *Faculty:* 29 full-time (3 women), 4 part-time (1 woman). *Students:* 81 full-time (40 women), 7 part-time (3 women). 45 applicants, 27% accepted. In 1998, 7 master's, 4 doctorates awarded. Terminal master's awarded for partial completion of doctoral program. *Degree requirements:* For master's, thesis required; for doctorate, dissertation, candidacy exam required. *Entrance requirements:* For master's, TOEFL (minimum score of 580 required), B Sc; for doctorate, TOEFL (minimum score of 580 required), B Sc or M Sc. *Average time to degree:* Master's–3 years full-time; doctorate–5 years full-time. *Application deadline:* For fall admission, 2/1 (priority date). Applications are processed on a rolling basis. Application fee: $60. *Financial aid:* In 1998–99, 50 students received aid, including 17 fellowships, 27 teaching assistantships; career-related internships or fieldwork, institutionally-sponsored loans, and research scholarships also available. Financial aid application deadline: 2/1. *Faculty research:* Geochemistry, petrology, paleontology, stratigraphy, exploration and solid-earth geophysics. *Unit head:* Donald C. Lawton, Head, 403-220-8863, Fax: 403-284-0074, E-mail: dclawton@geo.ucalgary.ca. *Application contact:* Gail Campbell, Graduate Student Administrator, 403-220-3254, Fax: 403-284-0074, E-mail: campbell@geo.ucalgary.ca.

University of California, Berkeley, Graduate Division, College of Letters and Science, Department of Geology and Geophysics, Division of Geophysics, Berkeley, CA 94720-1500. Offers MA, MS, PhD. 28 applicants, 43% accepted. In 1998, 1 master's, 3 doctorates awarded. Terminal master's awarded for partial completion of doctoral program. *Degree requirements:* For master's, oral exam required; for doctorate, dissertation, candidacy and comprehensive exams required. *Entrance requirements:* For master's and doctorate, GRE General Test, minimum GPA of 3.0. *Application deadline:* For fall admission, 1/12; for spring admission, 9/1. Application fee: $40. *Financial aid:* Fellowships, research assistantships, teaching assistantships, Federal Work-Study available. Financial aid application deadline: 1/12. *Faculty research:* High-pressure geophysics and seismology. *Unit head:* Mei Griebenow, Graduate Assistant for Admission, 510-642-5574, Fax: 510-643-9980, E-mail: meig@seismo.berkeley.edu. *Application contact:* Mei Griebenow, Graduate Assistant for Admission, 510-642-5574, Fax: 510-643-9980, E-mail: meig@seismo.berkeley.edu.

University of California, Los Angeles, Graduate Division, College of Letters and Science, Department of Earth and Space Sciences, Program in Geophysics and Space Physics, Los Angeles, CA 90095. Offers MS, PhD. *Students:* 26 full-time (9 women); includes 2 minority (both Asian Americans or Pacific Islanders), 9 international. 35 applicants, 40% accepted. *Degree requirements:* For master's, comprehensive exams or thesis required; for doctorate, dissertation, oral and written qualifying exams required, foreign language not required. *Entrance requirements:* For master's, GRE General Test, minimum GPA of 3.0; for doctorate, GRE General Test, minimum undergraduate GPA of 3.0. *Application deadline:* For fall admission, 12/15. Application fee: $40. Electronic applications accepted. *Financial aid:* In 1998–99, 18 fellowships, 7 teaching assistantships were awarded.; research assistantships, Federal Work-Study, institutionally-sponsored loans, scholarships, and tuition waivers (full and partial) also available. Financial aid application deadline: 3/1. *Unit head:* Departmental Office, 310-825-2307, E-mail: apply@physics.ucla.edu. *Application contact:* Departmental Office, 888-377-8252, E-mail: verity@ess.ucla.edu.

University of California, Santa Barbara, Graduate Division, College of Letters and Science, Division of Math, Life and Physical Science, Department of Geological Sciences, Santa Barbara, CA 93106. Offers geological sciences (MA, PhD); geophysics (MS). *Students:* 45 full-time (15 women). *Degree requirements:* For master's, one foreign language, thesis or exam required; for doctorate, variable foreign language requirement, dissertation required. *Entrance requirements:* For master's and doctorate, GRE General Test, TOEFL (minimum score of 550 required). *Application deadline:* For fall admission, 1/15. Application fee: $40. Electronic applications accepted. *Unit head:* Dr. Bruce Luyendyk, Chair, 805-893-2827. *Application contact:* Christina Foster, Graduate Program Assistant, 805-893-3329, E-mail: foster@magic.geol.ucsb.edu.

University of Chicago, Division of the Physical Sciences, Department of the Geophysical Sciences, Chicago, IL 60637-1513. Offers atmospheric sciences (SM, PhD); earth sciences (SM, PhD); planetary and space sciences (SM, PhD). *Degree requirements:* For master's, thesis, seminar required; for doctorate, dissertation required. *Entrance requirements:* For master's and doctorate, GRE General Test, TOEFL (minimum score of 550 required). *Faculty research:* Climatology, evolutionary paleontology,petrology, geochemistry, oceanic sciences.

University of Colorado at Boulder, Graduate School, College of Arts and Sciences, Department of Physics, Boulder, CO 80309. Offers chemical physics (PhD); geophysics (PhD); mathematical physics (PhD); medical physics (PhD); physics (MS, PhD). Terminal master's awarded for partial completion of doctoral program. *Degree requirements:* For master's, thesis or alternative, comprehensive exam required, foreign language not required; for doctorate, dissertation, comprehensive exam required. *Entrance requirements:* For master's, GRE General Test, GRE Subject Test, TOEFL (minimum score of 575 required), minimum undergraduate GPA of 3.0; for doctorate, GRE General Test, GRE Subject Test, TOEFL (minimum score of 575 required).

University of Connecticut, Graduate School, College of Liberal Arts and Sciences, Department of Geological Sciences, Field of Geophysics, Storrs, CT 06269. Offers MS, PhD. *Degree requirements:* For doctorate, dissertation required. *Entrance requirements:* For master's and doctorate, GRE General Test, TOEFL.

University of Georgia, Graduate School, College of Arts and Sciences, Department of Geology, Athens, GA 30602. Offers geochemistry (MS, PhD); geophysics (MS, PhD). *Faculty:* 19 full-time (3 women). *Students:* 37 full-time (12 women), 9 part-time (2 women). 35 applicants, 63% accepted. In 1998, 4 master's, 3 doctorates awarded. *Degree requirements:* For master's, thesis required, foreign language not required; for doctorate, one foreign language (computer language can substitute), dissertation required. *Entrance requirements:* For master's and doctorate, GRE General Test. *Application deadline:* For fall admission, 7/1 (priority date); for spring admission, 11/15. Application fee: $30. Electronic applications accepted. *Financial aid:* Fellowships, research assistantships, teaching assistantships, unspecified assistantships available. *Unit head:* Dr. David Wenner, Graduate Coordinator, 706-542-2427, E-mail: dwenner@arches.uga.edu.

University of Hawaii at Manoa, Graduate Division, School of Ocean and Earth Science and Technology, Department of Geology and Geophysics, Honolulu, HI 96822. Offers high-pressure geophysics and geochemistry (MS, PhD); hydrogeology and engineering geology (MS, PhD); marine geology and geophysics (MS, PhD); planetary geosciences and remote sensing (MS, PhD); seismology and solid-earth geophysics (MS, PhD); volcanology, petrology, and geochemistry (MS, PhD). *Faculty:* 84 full-time (10 women). *Students:* 48 full-time (15 women), 9 part-time (4 women); includes 3 minority (1 African American, 2 Asian Americans or Pacific Islanders), 15 international. 73 applicants, 23% accepted. In 1998, 5 master's, 10 doctorates awarded. Terminal master's awarded for partial completion of doctoral program. *Degree requirements:* For master's, thesis required, foreign language not required; for doctorate, dissertation, comprehensive exams required, foreign language not required. *Entrance requirements:* For master's and doctorate, GRE General Test, TOEFL, minimum GPA of 3.0. *Application deadline:* For fall admission, 1/15; for spring admission, 9/1. Application fee: $25 ($50 for international students). *Financial aid:* In 1998–99, 33 research assistantships (averaging $18,894 per year), 6 teaching assistantships (averaging $17,276 per year) were awarded. *Unit head:* Dr. John Sinton, Chair, 808-956-7640, Fax: 808-956-5512, E-mail: sinton@soest.hawaii.edu. *Application contact:* John Mahoney, Graduate Field Chairperson, 808-956-8763, Fax: 808-956-2538, E-mail: jmahoney@hawaii.edu.

University of Houston, College of Natural Sciences and Mathematics, Department of Geosciences, Program in Geophysics, Houston, TX 77004. Offers MS, PhD. Part-time and evening/weekend programs available. *Faculty:* 4 full-time (0 women), 2 part-time (0 women). *Students:* 12 full-time (0 women), 12 part-time (3 women); includes 2 minority (both Asian Americans or Pacific Islanders), 10 international. Average age 35. 25 applicants, 40% accepted. In 1998, 8 master's, 1 doctorate awarded. *Degree requirements:* For master's, thesis required (for some programs); for doctorate, dissertation required. *Entrance requirements:* For master's and doctorate, GRE General Test (minimum combined score of 1700 on three sections required), TOEFL (minimum score of 550 required). *Application deadline:* For fall admission, 7/20 (priority date); for spring admission, 11/20. Applications are processed on a rolling basis. Application fee: $0 ($75 for international students). *Financial aid:* Fellowships, research assistantships, teaching assistantships, tuition waivers (full) available. *Faculty research:* Seismic modelling, exploration, paleomagnetics, seismology. *Unit head:* Dr. Gareth Wynn-Williams, Graduate Chair, 808-956-8807, E-mail: wynnwill@ifa.hawaii.edu. *Application contact:* Henry Chafetz, Graduate Adviser, 713-743-3427, Fax: 713-748-7906, E-mail: hchafetz@uh.edu.

University of Idaho, College of Graduate Studies, College of Mines and Earth Resources, Department of Geology and Geological Engineering, Program in Geophysics, Moscow, ID 83844-4140. Offers MS. *Students:* 1 full-time (0 women). *Entrance requirements:* For master's, minimum GPA of 2.8. *Application deadline:* For fall admission, 8/1; for spring admission, 12/15. Application fee: $35 ($45 for international students). *Financial aid:* Application deadline: 2/15. *Unit head:* Dr. John Oldow, Head, Department of Geology and Geological Engineering, 208-885-7327.

University of Illinois at Chicago, Graduate College, College of Liberal Arts and Sciences, Department of Earth and Environmental Sciences, Chicago, IL 60607-7128. Offers crystallography (MS, PhD); environmental geology (MS, PhD); geochemistry (MS, PhD); geology (MS, PhD); geomorphology (MS, PhD); geophysics (MS, PhD); geotechnical engineering and geosciences (PhD); hydrogeology (MS, PhD); low-temperature and organic geochemistry (MS, PhD); mineralogy (MS, PhD); paleoclimatology (MS, PhD); paleontology (MS, PhD); petrology (MS, PhD); quaternary geology (MS, PhD); sedimentology (MS, PhD); water resources (MS, PhD). *Faculty:* 9 full-time (2 women). *Students:* 8 full-time (2 women), 1 part-time, 2 international. *Degree requirements:* For master's and doctorate, thesis/dissertation required. *Entrance requirements:* For master's and doctorate, GRE General Test, TOEFL (minimum score of 550 required), minimum GPA of 3.75 on a 5.0 scale. *Application deadline:* For fall admission, 7/3; for spring admission, 11/8. Application fee: $40 ($50 for international students). *Unit head:* A. F. Koster Van Groos, Acting Head, 312-996-3153. *Application contact:* Martin Flower, Graduate Director, 312-996-9662.

University of Illinois at Urbana–Champaign, Graduate College, College of Liberal Arts and Sciences, Department of Geology, Urbana, IL 61801. Offers earth sciences (MS, PhD); geochemistry (MS, PhD); geology (MS, PhD); geophysics (MS, PhD). *Faculty:* 14 full-time (1 woman), 4 part-time (0 women). *Students:* 20 full-time (4 women), 11 international. Terminal master's awarded for partial completion of doctoral program. *Degree requirements:* For master's and doctorate, thesis/dissertation required, foreign language not required. *Entrance requirements:*

For master's and doctorate, GRE General Test, TOEFL. *Application deadline:* For fall admission, 9/15 (priority date); for spring admission, 1/15. Applications are processed on a rolling basis. Application fee: $40 ($50 for international students). Tuition, state resident: full-time $4,040. Tuition, nonresident: full-time $11,192. Full-time tuition and fees vary according to program. *Unit head:* Jay Bass, Head, 217-333-3540. *Application contact:* Barbara Elmore, Graduate Admissions Secretary, 217-333-3541, Fax: 217-244-4996.

University of Manitoba, Faculty of Graduate Studies, Faculty of Science, Department of Geological Sciences, Winnipeg, MB R3T 2N2, Canada. Offers geology (M Sc, PhD); geophysics (M Sc, PhD). *Faculty:* 16 full-time. *Degree requirements:* For master's and doctorate, thesis/dissertation required. *Entrance requirements:* For master's and doctorate, GRE General Test, GRE Subject Test (geology), TOEFL, minimum GPA of 3.0. *Unit head:* G. S. Clark, Head.

The University of Memphis, Graduate School, College of Arts and Sciences, Department of Geological Sciences, Memphis, TN 38152. Offers geology (MS); geophysics (MS, PhD). Part-time and evening/weekend programs available. *Faculty:* 13 full-time (1 woman). *Students:* 15 full-time (3 women), 5 part-time (2 women); includes 2 minority (1 African American, 1 Hispanic American), 9 international. Terminal master's awarded for partial completion of doctoral program. *Degree requirements:* For master's, thesis, comprehensive exam, seminar presentation required; for doctorate, dissertation required. *Entrance requirements:* For master's, GRE General Test, GRE Subject Test. *Application deadline:* For fall admission, 8/1; for spring admission, 12/1. Applications are processed on a rolling basis. Application fee: $25 ($50 for international students). Tuition, state resident: full-time $3,410; part-time $178 per credit hour. Tuition, nonresident: full-time $8,670; part-time $408 per credit hour. Tuition and fees vary according to program. *Unit head:* Dr. Phili Deboo, Chairman, 901-678-2177, Fax: 901-678-2178. *Application contact:* Dr. Daniel Larsen, Coordinator of Graduate Studies, 901-678-4358, Fax: 901-678-2178, E-mail: dlarsen@memphis.edu.

University of Miami, Graduate School, Rosenstiel School of Marine and Atmospheric Science, Division of Marine Geology and Geophysics, Coral Gables, FL 33124. Offers MA, MS, PhD. *Faculty:* 15 full-time (3 women), 1 (woman) part-time. *Students:* 19 full-time (10 women), 1 part-time, 6 international. Average age 27. 24 applicants, 42% accepted. In 1998, 1 master's, 7 doctorates awarded. Terminal master's awarded for partial completion of doctoral program. *Degree requirements:* For master's and doctorate, thesis/dissertation required, foreign language not required. *Entrance requirements:* For master's and doctorate, GRE General Test, TOEFL (minimum score of 550 required). *Average time to degree:* Master's–3 years full-time; doctorate–6 years full-time. *Application deadline:* For fall admission, 2/1 (priority date). Applications are processed on a rolling basis. Application fee: $35. Electronic applications accepted. Tuition: Full-time $15,336; part-time $852 per credit. Required fees: $174. Tuition and fees vary according to program. *Financial aid:* In 1998–99, 15 students received aid, including 1 fellowship with tuition reimbursement available, 11 research assistantships with tuition reimbursements available (averaging $17,000 per year), 3 teaching assistantships with tuition reimbursements available (averaging $17,000 per year); institutionally-sponsored loans also available. Financial aid application deadline: 2/1. *Faculty research:* Carbonate sedimentology, low-temperature geochemistry, paleoceanography, geodesy and tectonics. *Unit head:* Dr. Gregor Eberli, Chairperson, 305-361-4103, Fax: 305-361-4632. *Application contact:* Dr. Frank Millero, Associate Dean, 305-361-4155, Fax: 305-361-4771, E-mail: gso@rsmas.miami.edu.

University of Minnesota, Twin Cities Campus, Graduate School, Institute of Technology, Department of Geology and Geophysics, Minneapolis, MN 55455-0213. Offers geology (MS, PhD); geophysics (MS, PhD). Terminal master's awarded for partial completion of doctoral program. *Degree requirements:* For master's, thesis optional; for doctorate, dissertation required. *Entrance requirements:* For master's and doctorate, GRE General Test, TOEFL. *Faculty research:* Hydrogeology, geochemistry, structural geology, sedimentology.

University of Missouri–Rolla, Graduate School, School of Mines and Metallurgy, Department of Geology and Geophysics, Rolla, MO 65409-0910. Offers geochemistry (MS, PhD); geology (MS, PhD); geophysics (MS, PhD); groundwater and environmental geology (MS, PhD). Part-time programs available. *Faculty:* 8 full-time (1 woman). *Students:* 28 full-time (11 women), 7 international. Average age 33. 20 applicants, 100% accepted. In 1998, 4 master's awarded. *Degree requirements:* For master's, computer language, thesis required, foreign language not required; for doctorate, computer language, dissertation, departmental qualifying exam required, foreign language not required. *Entrance requirements:* For master's, GRE General Test (minimum combined score of 1100 required), GRE Subject Test, TOEFL (minimum score of 550 required), minimum GPA of 3.0 in last 4 semesters; for doctorate, GRE General Test (minimum combined score of 1100 required), GRE Subject Test, TOEFL (minimum score of 550 required). *Application deadline:* For fall admission, 7/1; for spring admission, 12/1. Applications are processed on a rolling basis. Application fee: $25. Electronic applications accepted. *Financial aid:* In 1998–99, 18 fellowships with full tuition reimbursements (averaging $6,600 per year), 2 research assistantships with partial tuition reimbursements (averaging $6,493 per year), 14 teaching assistantships with partial tuition reimbursements (averaging $6,493 per year) were awarded.; Federal Work-Study and institutionally-sponsored loans also available. Aid available to part-time students. Financial aid application deadline: 3/1; financial aid applicants required to submit FAFSA. *Faculty research:* Economic geology, geophysical modeling,seismic wave analysis. *Unit head:* Dr. Richard D. Hagni, Chairman, 573-341-4616, Fax: 573-341-6935, E-mail: rhagni@umr.edu.

University of Nevada, Reno, Graduate School, Mackay School of Mines, Department of Geological Sciences, Reno, NV 89557. Offers geochemistry (MS, PhD); geological engineering (MS, Geol E); geology (MS, PhD); geophysics (MS, PhD). *Degree requirements:* For master's, thesis optional, foreign language not required; for doctorate, one foreign language, dissertation required. *Entrance requirements:* For master's, GRE General Test, GRE Subject Test, TOEFL (minimum score of 500 required), minimum GPA of 2.75; for doctorate, GRE General Test, GRE Subject Test, TOEFL (minimum score of 500 required), minimum GPA of 3.0. *Faculty research:* Hydrothermal ore deposits, metamorphic and igneous petrogenesis, sedimentary rock record of earth history, field and petrographic investigation of magnetism, rock fracture mechanics.

University of New Orleans, Graduate School, College of Sciences, Department of Geology and Geophysics, New Orleans, LA 70148. Offers geology (MS); geophysics (MS). Evening/weekend programs available. *Faculty:* 16 full-time (1 woman), 2 part-time (1 woman). *Students:* 18 full-time (9 women), 17 part-time (7 women); includes 5 minority (4 African Americans, 1 Asian American or Pacific Islander), 1 international. Average age 29. 26 applicants, 50% accepted. In 1998, 11 degrees awarded. *Degree requirements:* For master's, thesis required, foreign language not required. *Entrance requirements:* For master's, GRE General Test. *Application deadline:* For fall admission, 7/1 (priority date). Applications are processed on a rolling basis. Application fee: $20. Tuition, state resident: full-time $2,362. Tuition, nonresident: full-time $7,888. Part-time tuition and fees vary according to course load. *Financial aid:* Fellowships, research assistantships, teaching assistantships, career-related internships or fieldwork, Federal Work-Study, and institutionally-sponsored loans available. *Faculty research:* Continental margin structure and seismology, burial diagenesis of siliclastic sediments, tectonics at convergent plate margins, continental shelf sediment stability, early diagenesis of carbonates. *Unit head:* Dr. William Busch, Chairman, 504-280-6793, Fax: 504-280-7396, E-mail: whbes@uno.edu. *Application contact:* Dr. Matthew Totten, Graduate Coordinator, 504-280-6800, Fax: 504-280-7396.

University of Oklahoma, Graduate College, College of Geosciences, School of Geology and Geophysics, Program in Geophysics, Norman, OK 73019-0390. Offers MS. *Students:* 4 full-time (1 woman), 2 part-time (1 woman); includes 1 minority (African American), 3 international. Average age 29. 4 applicants, 50% accepted. In 1998, 3 degrees awarded. *Degree requirements:* For master's, computer language, thesis, comprehensive exam required, foreign language not required. *Entrance requirements:* For master's, GRE General Test, TOEFL (minimum score of 550 required), bachelor's degree in field. *Application deadline:* For fall admission, 2/1 (priority date); for spring admission, 9/1. Applications are processed on a rolling basis. Application fee: $25. Tuition, state resident: part-time $86 per credit hour. Tuition, nonresident: part-time $275 per credit hour. Tuition and fees vary according to course level, course load and program. *Financial aid:* Fellowships, research assistantships, teaching assistantships, Federal Work-Study, institutionally-sponsored loans, and tuition waivers (partial) available. Financial aid application deadline: 2/1. *Faculty research:* Technophysics and solid-earth geophysics, exploration geophysics, paleomagnetics, geophysical imaging. *Application contact:* Dr. Barry Weaver, Graduate Liaison, 405-325-5325.

The University of Texas at El Paso, Graduate School, College of Science, Department of Geological Sciences, Program in Geophysics, El Paso, TX 79968-0001. Offers MS. Part-time programs available. 4 applicants, 75% accepted. *Degree requirements:* For master's, thesis required, foreign language not required. *Entrance requirements:* For master's, TOEFL (minimum score of 550 required), minimum GPA of 3.0, BS in geology or equivalent. *Average time to degree:* Master's–2.5 years full-time. *Application deadline:* Applications are processed on a rolling basis. Application fee: $15 ($65 for international students). Electronic applications accepted. Tuition, state resident: full-time $2,118. Tuition, nonresident: full-time $7,230. Tuition and fees vary according to program. *Financial aid:* In 1998–99, 1 fellowship, 2 research assistantships, 2 teaching assistantships were awarded.; career-related internships or fieldwork, institutionally-sponsored loans, scholarships, and tuition waivers (partial) also available. Aid available to part-time students. Financial aid applicants required to submit FAFSA. *Faculty research:* Crystal and earthquake seismology, environmental and engineering geophysics, tectonophysics. Total annual research expenditures: $500,000. *Unit head:* Dr. Kenneth Clark, Graduate Adviser, 915-747-5501. *Application contact:* Susan Jordan, Director, Graduate Student Services, 915-747-5491, Fax: 915-747-5788, E-mail: sjordan@utep.edu.

University of Utah, Graduate School, College of Mines and Earth Sciences, Department of Geology and Geophysics, Program in Geophysics, Salt Lake City, UT 84112-1107. Offers MS, PhD. *Students:* 13 full-time (0 women), 6 part-time (1 woman), 11 international. In 1998, 4 master's, 2 doctorates awarded. *Degree requirements:* For master's, computer language, thesis, qualifying exam required; for doctorate, one foreign language, computer language, dissertation required. *Entrance requirements:* For master's and doctorate, GRE General Test, TOEFL (minimum score of 500 required), minimum GPA of 3.25. *Application deadline:* For fall admission, 7/1. Application fee: $30 ($50 for international students). *Financial aid:* Application deadline: 2/15. *Unit head:* Martha D. Wheat, Director of Admissions and Student Records, 903-566-7201, Fax: 903-566-7068. *Application contact:* Marjorie Chan, Director of Graduate Studies, 801-581-7162, Fax: 801-581-7065.

University of Victoria, Faculty of Graduate Studies, Faculty of Science, Department of Physics and Astronomy, Victoria, BC V8W 2Y2, Canada. Offers astronomy and astrophysics (M Sc, PhD); condensed matter physics (M Sc, PhD); geophysics (M Sc, PhD); medical physics (PhD); nuclear and particle studies (M Sc, PhD); theoretical physics (M Sc, PhD). *Faculty:* 20 full-time (0 women), 22 part-time (1 woman). *Students:* 28 full-time (7 women). *Degree requirements:* For master's and doctorate, thesis/dissertation required, foreign language not required. *Application deadline:* For fall admission, 5/31 (priority date); for spring admission, 10/31. Applications are processed on a rolling basis. Application fee: $50. *Unit head:* Dr. C. E. Picciotto, Chair, 250-721-7698, E-mail: pic@uvic.ca. *Application contact:* Dr. A. Watton, Graduate Adviser, 250-721-7703, Fax: 250-721-7715, E-mail: awatt@uvvm.uvic.ca.

University of Victoria, Faculty of Graduate Studies, Faculty of Science, School of Earth and Ocean Sciences, Victoria, BC V8W 2Y2, Canada. Offers geochemistry (M Sc, PhD); geophysics (M Sc, PhD); marine geology and geophysics (M Sc, PhD); ocean acoustics (M Sc, PhD); oceanography (M Sc, PhD); paleobiology (M Sc, PhD); paleoceanography (M Sc, PhD); sedimentology (M Sc, PhD); stratigraphy (M Sc, PhD). Part-time programs available. *Faculty:* 15 full-time, 41 part-time. *Students:* 39 full-time (0 women), 1 part-time. *Degree requirements:* For master's and doctorate, thesis/dissertation required. *Application deadline:* For fall admission, 2/15. Applications are processed on a rolling basis. Application fee: $50. Electronic applications accepted. *Unit head:* Dr. C. R. Barnes, Director, 250-721-6120, Fax: 250-721-6200, E-mail: crbarnes@uvic.ca. *Application contact:* Dr. Dante Canil, Graduate Adviser, 250-721-6120, Fax: 250-721-6200, E-mail: dcanil@uvic.ca.

University of Washington, Graduate School, College of Arts and Sciences, Geophysics Program, Seattle, WA 98195. Offers MS, PhD. *Faculty:* 19 full-time (1 woman), 6 part-time (1 woman). *Students:* 34 full-time (7 women); includes 2 minority (both Asian Americans or Pacific Islanders), 14 international. Average age 29. 38 applicants, 32% accepted. In 1998, 2 master's awarded (50% found work related to degree); 7 doctorates awarded (71% entered university research/teaching, 29% found other work related to degree). *Degree requirements:* For master's, thesis or alternative, departmental qualifying exam, final exam required, foreign language not required; for doctorate, dissertation, departmental qualifying exam; general and final exams required, foreign language not required. *Entrance requirements:* For master's and doctorate, GRE General Test, TOEFL, minimum GPA of 3.0. *Average time to degree:* Master's–3.5 years full-time; doctorate–5.75 years full-time. *Application deadline:* For fall admission, 1/31 (priority date). Application fee: $50. Electronic applications accepted. Tuition, state resident: full-time $5,196; part-time $475 per credit. Tuition, nonresident: full-time $13,485; part-time $1,285 per credit. Required fees: $387; $38 per credit. Tuition and fees vary according to course load. *Financial aid:* In 1998–99, 32 students received aid, including 27 research assistantships with full tuition reimbursements available, 5 teaching assistantships with full tuition reimbursements available; fellowships with full tuition reimbursements available, Federal Work-Study also available. Financial aid application deadline: 1/31. *Faculty research:* Seismology and mineral physics, glaciology, geomagnetism and paleomagnetism, atmospheric sciences, space physics. Total annual research expenditures: $3.9 million. *Unit head:* Dr. J. Michael Brown, Chair, 206-543-8020, Fax: 206-543-0489, E-mail: brown@geophys.washington.edu. *Application contact:* Julie Van Buren, Graduate Program Assistant, 206-685-8992, Fax: 206-543-0489, E-mail: julie@geophys.washington.edu.

See in-depth description on page 319.

University of Wisconsin–Madison, Graduate School, College of Letters and Science, Department of Geology and Geophysics, Program in Geophysics, Madison, WI 53706-1380. Offers MS, PhD. *Degree requirements:* For master's, thesis required; for doctorate, one foreign language, dissertation required. *Entrance requirements:* For master's and doctorate, GRE General Test. *Application deadline:* For fall admission, 12/15 (priority date). Application fee: $45. *Financial aid:* Application deadline: 12/15. *Unit head:* Ann McLain, Student Services Coordinator, 608-263-3264, Fax: 608-265-2340, E-mail: asmclain@facstaff.wisc.edu. *Application contact:* Graduate Admissions Coordinator, 608-262-9266, Fax: 608-262-0693, E-mail: sharonm@geology.wisc.edu.

University of Wyoming, Graduate School, College of Arts and Sciences, Department of Geology and Geophysics, Laramie, WY 82071. Offers geology and geophysics (MS, PhD); geology/water resources (MS); geophysics (MS, PhD). Part-time programs available. *Faculty:* 22 full-time (3 women), 2 part-time (1 woman). *Students:* 42 full-time (19 women), 23 part-time (7 women); includes 3 minority (1 Hispanic American, 2 Native Americans), 7 international. 30 applicants, 53% accepted. In 1998, 10 master's, 8 doctorates awarded. *Degree requirements:* For master's and doctorate, thesis/dissertation required. *Entrance requirements:* For master's and doctorate, GRE General Test (minimum combined score of 1200 required), minimum GPA of 3.0. *Application deadline:* For fall admission, 1/31. Applications are processed on a rolling basis. Application fee: $40. Tuition, state resident: full-time $2,520; part-time $140 per credit hour. Tuition, nonresident: full-time $7,790; part-time $433 per credit hour. Required fees: $400; $7 per credit hour. Full-time tuition and fees vary according to course load and program. *Financial aid:* Fellowships, research assistantships, teaching assistantships, career-related internships or fieldwork, Federal Work-Study, and institutionally-sponsored loans available. Financial aid application deadline: 3/1. *Faculty research:* Geochemistry and petroleum geology, tectonics and sedimentation, geomorphology and remote sensing, igneous and metamorphic petrology. *Unit head:* Dr. James R. Steidtman, Head, 307-766-3386. *Application*

Geophysics–Geosciences

University of Wyoming (continued)
contact: Deayne M. Johnson, Admissions Coordinator, 307-766-3389, Fax: 307-766-6679, E-mail: acadcoord.geol@uwyo.edu.

Virginia Polytechnic Institute and State University, Graduate School, College of Arts and Sciences, Department of Geological Sciences, Program in Geophysics, Blacksburg, VA 24061. Offers MS, PhD. *Faculty:* 5 full-time (0 women). *Students:* 3 full-time (1 woman). 8 applicants, 50% accepted. *Degree requirements:* For master's and doctorate, thesis/dissertation required. *Entrance requirements:* For master's and doctorate, GRE General Test, GRE Subject Test, TOEFL. *Application deadline:* For fall admission, 12/1 (priority date). Applications are processed on a rolling basis. Application fee: $25. *Financial aid:* Fellowships, research assistantships, teaching assistantships, career-related internships or fieldwork, tuition waivers (full), and unspecified assistantships available. Financial aid application deadline: 4/1. *Faculty research:* Earthquake seismology, exploration seismology, reflection seismology, exploration geophysics, theoretical and observational seismology. *Unit head:* Dr. Cahit Coruh, Head, Department of Geological Sciences, 540-231-6521, E-mail: coruh@vt.edu.

Washington University in St. Louis, Graduate School of Arts and Sciences, Department of Earth and Planetary Sciences, St. Louis, MO 63130-4899. Offers earth and planetary sciences (MA); geochemistry (PhD); geology (MA, PhD); geophysics (PhD); planetary sciences (PhD). *Students:* 26 full-time (11 women); includes 2 minority (1 Asian American or Pacific Islander, 1 Native American), 4 international. Terminal master's awarded for partial completion of doctoral program. *Degree requirements:* For master's and doctorate, thesis/dissertation required. *Entrance requirements:* For master's and doctorate, GRE General Test. *Application deadline:* For fall admission, 1/15 (priority date). Applications are processed on a rolling basis. Application fee: $35. *Unit head:* Dr. Raymond E. Arvidson, Chairman, 314-935-5610.

Wright State University, School of Graduate Studies, College of Science and Mathematics, Department of Geological Sciences, Program in Geological Sciences, Dayton, OH 45435. Offers environmental geology (MS); environmental sciences (MS); geological sciences (MS); geophysics (MS); hydrogeology (MS); petroleum geology (MS). Part-time programs available. *Students:* 32 full-time (14 women), 9 part-time (2 women), 1 international. *Degree requirements:* For master's, computer language, thesis required, foreign language not required. *Entrance requirements:* For master's, TOEFL (minimum score of 550 required). Application fee: $25. *Unit head:* Dr. Dennis Burns, Graduate Coordinator, 316-978-3120, Fax: 316-978-3431, E-mail: burns@twsuvm.uc.twsu.edu. *Application contact:* Deborah L. Cowles, Assistant to Chair, 937-775-3455, Fax: 937-775-3462.

Yale University, Graduate School of Arts and Sciences, Department of Geology and Geophysics, New Haven, CT 06520. Offers geochemistry (PhD); geophysics (PhD); meteorology (PhD); mineralogy and crystallography (PhD); oceanography (PhD); paleoecology (PhD); paleontology and stratigraphy (PhD); petrology (PhD); structural geology (PhD). *Faculty:* 26. *Students:* 26 full-time (11 women), 9 international. 21 applicants, 86% accepted. In 1998, 6 degrees awarded. *Degree requirements:* For doctorate, dissertation required, foreign language not required. *Entrance requirements:* For doctorate, GRE General Test, TOEFL. *Average time to degree:* Doctorate–7.9 years full-time. *Application deadline:* For fall admission, 1/4. Application fee: $65. *Financial aid:* Fellowships, research assistantships, teaching assistantships, Federal Work-Study and institutionally-sponsored loans available. Aid available to part-time students. *Unit head:* Chair, 203-432-3174. *Application contact:* Admissions Information, 203-432-2770.

See in-depth description on page 327.

Geosciences

Adelphi University, Graduate School of Arts and Sciences, Department of Earth Sciences, Garden City, NY 11530. Offers earth sciences (MS); environmental management (Certificate). Part-time and evening/weekend programs available. In 1998, 2 degrees awarded. *Degree requirements:* For master's, computer language required, thesis optional, foreign language not required. *Application deadline:* Applications are processed on a rolling basis. Application fee: $50. *Financial aid:* Career-related internships or fieldwork available. Financial aid application deadline: 3/1. *Faculty research:* Environmental and marine sciences, hydrogeology, stratigraphy, palynology, paleontology. *Unit head:* Dr. Anthony Cok, Chairperson, 516-877-4170.

Ball State University, Graduate School, College of Sciences and Humanities, Department of Geography, Muncie, IN 47306-1099. Offers earth sciences (MA). *Faculty:* 5. *Students:* 1 (woman) full-time. 1 applicants, 0% accepted. In 1998, 1 degree awarded. *Degree requirements:* Foreign language not required. Application fee: $15 ($25 for international students). *Faculty research:* Remote sensing, tourism and recreation, Latin American urbanization. *Unit head:* Dr. Gopalan Venugopal, Chairman, 765-285-1776.

Baylor University, Graduate School, College of Arts and Sciences, Department of Geology, Waco, TX 76798. Offers earth science (MA); geology (MS, PhD). *Faculty:* 12 full-time (1 woman). *Students:* 24 full-time (8 women), 6 part-time (2 women); includes 2 minority (both Hispanic Americans), 4 international. *Degree requirements:* For master's, thesis required, foreign language not required; for doctorate, dissertation required, dissertation required. *Entrance requirements:* For master's, GRE General Test, GRE Subject Test; for doctorate, GRE General Test. *Application deadline:* For fall admission, 3/15 (priority date). Applications are processed on a rolling basis. Application fee: $25. *Unit head:* Dr. Thomas T. Goforth, Chairman, 254-710-2361, Fax: 254-710-2673, E-mail: thomas_goforth@baylor.edu. *Application contact:* Suzanne Keener, Administrative Assistant, 254-710-3588, Fax: 254-710-3870, E-mail: suzanne_keener@baylor.edu.

Boston University, Graduate School of Arts and Sciences, Department of Earth Sciences, Boston, MA 02215. Offers MA, PhD. *Faculty:* 9 full-time (1 woman), 6 part-time (0 women). *Students:* 7 full-time (5 women), 2 part-time (1 woman); includes 1 minority (African American), 1 international. Average age 29. 25 applicants, 32% accepted. In 1998, 3 master's awarded (100% entered university research/teaching); 1 doctorate awarded (100% entered university research/teaching). Terminal master's awarded for partial completion of doctoral program. *Degree requirements:* For master's, one foreign language, thesis, comprehensive exam required; for doctorate, one foreign language, dissertation, comprehensive/qualifying exam required. *Entrance requirements:* For master's and doctorate, GRE General Test, TOEFL (minimum score of 550 required). *Application deadline:* For fall admission, 7/1; for spring admission, 11/15. Application fee: $50. Tuition: Full-time $23,770; part-time $743 per credit. Required fees: $220. Tuition and fees vary according to class time, course level, campus/location and program. *Financial aid:* In 1998–99, 3 fellowships, 2 research assistantships with tuition reimbursements (averaging $11,500 per year), 5 teaching assistantships with tuition reimbursements (averaging $11,500 per year) were awarded.; Federal Work-Study and unspecified assistantships also available. Aid available to part-time students. Financial aid application deadline: 1/15; financial aid applicants required to submit FAFSA. *Faculty research:* Structural geology, geomorphology, coastal geology, geochemistry, marine geology, oceanography, tectonics, petrology. *Unit head:* Dr. Carol Simpson, Chairman, 617-353-2532, Fax: 617-353-3290, E-mail: csimpson@bu.edu. *Application contact:* Dr. Drew Coleman, Director of Graduate Studies, 617-353-2532, Fax: 617-353-3290, E-mail: dcoleman@bu.edu.

Brock University, Graduate Studies and Research, Faculty of Mathematics and Science, Department of Earth Sciences, St. Catharines, ON L2S 3A1, Canada. Offers M Sc. Part-time programs available. *Faculty:* 7 full-time (1 woman), 2 part-time (0 women). *Students:* 6 full-time (3 women), 3 part-time (1 woman). Average age 24. 14 applicants, 29% accepted. In 1998, 2 degrees awarded. *Degree requirements:* For master's, thesis required, foreign language not required. *Entrance requirements:* For master's, TOEFL (minimum score of 550 required), honors B Sc in geology. *Average time to degree:* Master's–2 years full-time, 4 years part-time. *Application deadline:* For fall admission, 3/30 (priority date). Applications are processed on a rolling basis. Application fee: $35. *Financial aid:* Fellowships, research assistantships, teaching assistantships, career-related internships or fieldwork, grants, scholarships, and unspecified assistantships available. Aid available to part-time students. Financial aid application deadline: 4/30. *Faculty research:* Quaternary geology, petrology, crustal studies, hydrology, carbonate geochemistry. *Unit head:* Dr. Greg Finn, Chair, 905-688-5550 Ext. 3528, Fax: 905-682-9020, E-mail: gfinn@craton.geol.brocku.ca. *Application contact:* Dr. Rick Cheel, Graduate Officer, 905-688-5550, Fax: 905-682-9020, E-mail: rcheel@craton.brocku.ca.

Brown University, Graduate School, Department of Geological Sciences, Providence, RI 02912. Offers MA, Sc M, PhD. *Degree requirements:* For master's, foreign language and thesis not required; for doctorate, dissertation, 1 semester of teaching experience, preliminary exam required, foreign language not required. *Faculty research:* Geochemistry, mineral kinetics, igneous and metamorphic petrology, tectonophysics including geophysics and structural geology, paleoclimatology, paleoceanography, sedimentation, planetary geology.

California State University, Chico, Graduate School, College of Natural Sciences, Department of Geosciences, Chico, CA 95929-0722. Offers geosciences (MS), including earth sciences, hydrology and hydrogeology. *Faculty:* 10 full-time (2 women), 4 part-time (1 woman). *Students:* 12 full-time (3 women), 4 part-time (2 women). *Degree requirements:* For master's, thesis, competency exam required, foreign language not required. *Entrance requirements:* For master's, GRE General Test (minimum combined score of 1500 recommended). *Application deadline:* For fall admission, 4/1. Applications are processed on a rolling basis. Application fee: $55. *Unit head:* Dr. Victor Fisher, Chair, 530-898-5262. *Application contact:* Dr. Gregory Taylor, Graduate Coordinator, 530-898-6369.

California State University, Chico, Graduate School, College of Natural Sciences, Department of Geosciences, Program in Geosciences, Option in Earth Sciences, Chico, CA 95929-0722. Offers MS. *Students:* 7 full-time (1 woman). Average age 27. *Degree requirements:* For master's, thesis, oral exam required, foreign language not required. *Entrance requirements:* For master's, GRE General Test (minimum combined score of 1500 recommended). *Application deadline:* For fall admission, 4/1. Applications are processed on a rolling basis. Application fee: $55.

California University of Pennsylvania, School of Graduate Studies, School of Liberal Arts, Program in Geography and Earth Sciences, California, PA 15419-1394. Offers earth science (MS); geography (M Ed, MA). Part-time and evening/weekend programs available. *Degree requirements:* For master's, comprehensive exam required, thesis optional, foreign language not required. *Entrance requirements:* For master's, MAT (minimum score of 33 required), TOEFL (minimum score of 550 required), minimum GPA of 2.5, teaching certificate (M Ed).

Carleton University, Faculty of Graduate Studies, Faculty of Science, Department of Earth Science, Ottawa, ON K1S 5B6, Canada. Offers M Sc, PhD. *Faculty:* 14 full-time (4 women). *Students:* 32 full-time (13 women), 8 part-time (3 women). Average age 32. In 1998, 3 master's, 6 doctorates awarded. *Degree requirements:* For master's, thesis, seminar required; for doctorate, dissertation, comprehensive exam, seminar required. *Entrance requirements:* For master's, TOEFL (minimum score of 550 required), honors degree in science; for doctorate, TOEFL (minimum score of 550 required), M Sc. *Average time to degree:* Master's–2 years full-time; doctorate–6.3 years full-time. *Application deadline:* For fall admission, 3/1. Applications are processed on a rolling basis. Application fee: $35. *Financial aid:* Fellowships, research assistantships, teaching assistantships available. Financial aid application deadline: 3/1. Total annual research expenditures: $939,000. *Unit head:* Sharon Carr, Associate Director, 613-520-2600 Ext. 4417, Fax: 613-520-5192, E-mail: sharon_carr@carleton.ca.

Case Western Reserve University, School of Graduate Studies, Department of Geological Sciences, Cleveland, OH 44106. Offers MS, PhD. Part-time programs available. Terminal master's awarded for partial completion of doctoral program. *Degree requirements:* For master's, thesis or alternative required; for doctorate, dissertation required. *Entrance requirements:* For master's and doctorate, GRE General Test, GRE Subject Test, TOEFL (minimum score of 550 required). *Faculty research:* Geochemistry, hydrology, geochronology, paleoclimates, geomorphology.

Central Connecticut State University, School of Graduate Studies, School of Arts and Sciences, Department of Physics and Earth Science, New Britain, CT 06050-4010. Offers earth science (MS); general science (MS); physics (MS). Part-time and evening/weekend programs available. *Faculty:* 12 full-time (4 women), 10 part-time (2 women). *Students:* 2 full-time (1 woman), 25 part-time (18 women). Average age 35. 30 applicants, 53% accepted. In 1998, 9 degrees awarded. *Degree requirements:* For master's, thesis or alternative, comprehensive exam required, foreign language not required. *Entrance requirements:* For master's, TOEFL (minimum score of 550 required), minimum GPA of 2.7. *Application deadline:* For fall admission, 6/1 (priority date); for spring admission, 12/1. Applications are processed on a rolling basis. Application fee: $40. *Financial aid:* Federal Work-Study available. Financial aid application deadline: 3/15; financial aid applicants required to submit FAFSA. *Faculty research:* Elementary/secondary science education, particle and solid states, weather patterns, planetary studies. *Unit head:* Dr. Ali Antar, Chair, 860-832-2930.

City College of the City University of New York, Graduate School, College of Liberal Arts and Science, Division of Science, Department of Earth and Atmospheric Sciences, New York, NY 10031-9198. Offers earth and environmental science (PhD); earth systems science (MA). PhD offered through the Graduate School and University Center of the City University of New York. *Degree requirements:* For master's, thesis, comprehensive exam required, foreign language not required. *Entrance requirements:* For master's, TOEFL (minimum score of 500 required), appropriate bachelor's degree. *Faculty research:* Water resources, high-temperature geochemistry, sedimentary basin analysis, tectonics.

Colorado School of Mines, Graduate School, Department of Geology and Geological Engineering, Golden, CO 80401-1887. Offers engineering geology (Diploma); exploration geosciences (Diploma); geochemistry (MS, PhD); geological engineering (ME, MS, PhD, Diploma); geology (MS, PhD); hydrogeology (Diploma). Part-time programs available. *Faculty:* 27 full-time (5 women), 23 part-time (0 women). *Students:* 53 full-time (16 women), 68 part-time (19 women); includes 6 minority (3 Asian Americans or Pacific Islanders, 2 Hispanic Americans, 1 Native American), 26 international. *Degree requirements:* For master's, thesis required, foreign language not required; for doctorate, dissertation, comprehensive exam required, foreign language not required; for Diploma, foreign language and thesis not required. *Entrance requirements:* For master's, doctorate, and Diploma, GRE General Test (combined average 1660 on three sections), GRE Subject Test, minimum GPA of 3.0. *Application deadline:* Applications are processed on a rolling basis. Application fee: $40. Electronic applications accepted. *Unit head:* Dr. Roger Slatt, Head, 303-273-3800, E-mail: rslatt@mines.edu. *Application contact:* Marilyn Schwinger, Administrative Assistant, 303-273-3800, Fax: 303-273-3859, E-mail: mschwing@mines.edu.

Colorado State University, Graduate School, College of Natural Resources, Department of Earth Resources, Fort Collins, CO 80523-0015. Offers earth resources (PhD); geology (MS), including fluvial geomorphology, hydrogeology, petrology/geochemistry and economic geology, stratigraphy/sedimentology, structure/tectonics; watershed science (MS, PhD), including earth resources (PhD), watershed science (MS). Part-time programs available. *Faculty:* 15 full-time (5 women), 2 part-time (1 woman). *Students:* 21 full-time (8 women), 22 part-time (4 women); includes 4 minority (2 Hispanic Americans, 2 Native Americans), 9 international. Average age 30. 63 applicants, 44% accepted. In 1998, 13 master's, 7 doctorates awarded. *Degree requirements:* For master's, thesis required, foreign language not required; for doctorate, one foreign language, dissertation required. *Entrance requirements:* For master's and doctorate, GRE General Test, TOEFL (minimum score of 550 required), minimum GPA of 3.0. *Application deadline:* For fall admission, 2/1 (priority date). Applications are processed on a rolling basis. Application fee: $30. *Financial aid:* In 1998–99, 3 fellowships, 12 research assistantships, 2 teaching assistantships were awarded.; career-related internships or fieldwork, Federal Work-Study, institutionally-sponsored loans, and traineeships also available. Financial aid application deadline: 2/15. *Faculty research:* Snow, surface, and groundwater hydrology; fluvial geomorphology; geographic information systems; geochemistry; bedrock geology. Total annual research expenditures: $1.3 million. *Unit head:* Dr. Judith L. Hannah, Head, 970-491-5662, Fax: 970-491-6307, E-mail: jhannah@cnr.colostate.edu. *Application contact:* Barbara Holtz, Staff Assistant, 970-491-5662, Fax: 970-491-6307, E-mail: barbh@cnr.colostate.edu.

Columbia University, Graduate School of Arts and Sciences, Division of Natural Sciences, Department of Earth and Environmental Sciences, New York, NY 10027. Offers geochemistry (M Phil, MA, PhD); geodetic sciences (M Phil, MA, PhD); geophysics (M Phil, MA, PhD); oceanography (M Phil, MA, PhD). *Degree requirements:* For master's, thesis or alternative, fieldwork, written exam required, foreign language not required; for doctorate, one foreign language, dissertation required. *Entrance requirements:* For master's and doctorate, GRE General Test, GRE Subject Test, TOEFL, major in natural or physical science. *Faculty research:* Structural geology and stratigraphy, petrology, paleontology, rare gas, isotope and aqueous geochemistry.

Cornell University, Graduate School, Graduate Fields of Engineering, Field of Geological Sciences, Ithaca, NY 14853-0001. Offers economic geology (MS, PhD); engineering geology (MS, PhD); environmental geophysics (M Eng, MS, PhD); general geology (MS, PhD); geobiology (MS, PhD); geochemistry and isotope geology (MS, PhD); geohydrology (M Eng, MS, PhD); geomorphology (MS, PhD); geophysics (MS, PhD); geotectonics (MS, PhD); mineralogy (MS, PhD); paleontology (MS, PhD); petroleum geology (MS, PhD); petrology (MS, PhD); planetary geology (MS, PhD); Precambrian geology (MS, PhD); Quaternary geology (MS, PhD); rock mechanics (MS, PhD); sedimentology (MS, PhD); seismology (MS, PhD); stratigraphy (MS, PhD); structural geology (MS, PhD). *Faculty:* 28 full-time. *Students:* 36 full-time (12 women); includes 4 minority (1 African American, 1 Asian American or Pacific Islander, 2 Hispanic Americans), 16 international. 105 applicants, 23% accepted. In 1998, 2 master's, 6 doctorates awarded. *Degree requirements:* For master's, thesis (MS) required; for doctorate, dissertation required, foreign language not required. *Entrance requirements:* For master's and doctorate, GRE General Test, TOEFL (minimum score of 550 required). *Application deadline:* For fall admission, 1/15. Application fee: $65. Electronic applications accepted. *Financial aid:* In 1998–99, 31 students received aid, including 11 fellowships with full tuition reimbursements available, 13 research assistantships with full tuition reimbursements available, 7 teaching assistantships with full tuition reimbursements available; institutionally-sponsored loans, scholarships, tuition waivers (full and partial), and unspecified assistantships also available. Financial aid applicants required to submit FAFSA. *Faculty research:* Geophysics, structural geology, and continental evolution; sedimentology and basin studies; biochemistry, geohydrology, and fluid-rock processes; remote sensing and terrestrial/climate interactions; igneous petrology; oceanography. *Unit head:* Director of Graduate Studies, 607-255-3474, Fax: 607-254-4780. *Application contact:* Graduate Field Assistant, 607-255-3474, Fax: 607-254-4780, E-mail: gradprog@geology.cornell.edu.

See in-depth description on page 273.

Dalhousie University, Faculty of Graduate Studies, College of Arts and Science, Faculty of Science, Department of Earth Sciences, Halifax, NS B3H 3J5, Canada. Offers M Sc, PhD. Part-time programs available. *Faculty:* 11 full-time (2 women), 15 part-time (4 women). *Students:* 24 full-time (9 women), 1 part-time, 9 international. 22 applicants, 36% accepted. In 1998, 4 master's, 4 doctorates awarded. *Degree requirements:* For master's and doctorate, thesis/dissertation required. *Entrance requirements:* For master's, TOEFL (minimum score of 580 required); for doctorate, TOEFL (minimum score of 580 required), M Sc. *Application deadline:* For fall admission, 6/1. Applications are processed on a rolling basis. Application fee: $55. *Financial aid:* Fellowships, career-related internships or fieldwork available. *Faculty research:* Marine geology and geophysics, Appalachian and Grenville geology, micropaleontology, geodynamics and structural geology, geochronology. *Unit head:* Dr. P. H. Reynolds, Chair, 902-494-2358. *Application contact:* Nicholas Culshaw, Graduate Coordinator, 902-494-3501, Fax: 902-494-6889, E-mail: nicholas.culshaw@dal.ca.

Dartmouth College, School of Arts and Sciences, Department of Earth Sciences, Hanover, NH 03755. Offers MS, PhD. *Faculty:* 8 full-time (2 women), 10 part-time (0 women). *Students:* 16 full-time (3 women), 2 international. 31 applicants, 23% accepted. In 1998, 1 doctorate awarded (100% entered university research/teaching). Terminal master's awarded for partial completion of doctoral program. *Degree requirements:* For master's, thesis required; for doctorate, dissertation required, foreign language not required. *Entrance requirements:* For master's and doctorate, GRE General Test, GRE Subject Test. *Application deadline:* For fall admission, 2/15. Application fee: $20. *Financial aid:* In 1998–99, 16 students received aid, including 5 research assistantships with full tuition reimbursements available; fellowships with full tuition reimbursements available, career-related internships or fieldwork, grants, institutionally-sponsored loans, scholarships, tuition waivers (full), and unspecified assistantships also available. *Unit head:* Richard Birnie, Chairman, 603-646-2373. *Application contact:* Grace Morse, Administrative Assistant, 603-646-2373.

Emporia State University, School of Graduate Studies, College of Liberal Arts and Sciences, Division of Physical Sciences, Emporia, KS 66801-5087. Offers chemistry (MS); earth science (MS); physics (MS). *Faculty:* 18 full-time (1 woman), 3 part-time (0 women). *Students:* 10 full-time (4 women), 11 part-time (3 women); includes 1 minority (Native American), 8 international. *Degree requirements:* For master's, comprehensive exam or thesis required. *Entrance requirements:* For master's, TOEFL (minimum score of 550 required), written exam. *Application deadline:* For fall admission, 8/15 (priority date). Applications are processed on a rolling basis. Application fee: $30 ($75 for international students). Electronic applications accepted. Tuition, state resident: full-time $2,356; part-time $106 per credit hour. Tuition, nonresident: full-time $6,158; part-time $264 per credit hour. *Unit head:* Dr. DeWayne Backhus, Chair, 316-341-5330, E-mail: backhusd@emporia.edu.

Georgia Institute of Technology, Graduate Studies and Research, College of Sciences, School of Earth and Atmospheric Sciences, Atlanta, GA 30332-0001. Offers atmospheric chemistry (MS, PhD); atmospheric dynamics and physics (MS, PhD); geochemistry (MS, PhD); solid-earth geophysics (MS, PhD). Part-time programs available. Terminal master's awarded for partial completion of doctoral program. *Degree requirements:* For master's, thesis or alternative required, foreign language not required; for doctorate, dissertation, comprehensive exams required, foreign language not required. *Entrance requirements:* For master's and doctorate, GRE General Test, TOEFL (minimum score of 550 required), minimum GPA of 2.7. Electronic applications accepted. *Faculty research:* Geophysics, geochemistry, atmospheric chemistry, atmospheric dynamics, seismology.

See in-depth description on page 277.

Graduate School and University Center of the City University of New York, Graduate Studies, Program in Earth and Environmental Sciences, New York, NY 10036-8099. Offers PhD. *Faculty:* 36 full-time (5 women). *Students:* 46 full-time (16 women), 9 part-time (2 women); includes 3 African Americans, 1 Asian American or Pacific Islander, 2 Hispanic Americans Average age 37. 44 applicants, 82% accepted. In 1998, 3 degrees awarded. *Degree requirements:* For doctorate, one foreign language (computer language can substitute), dissertation, comprehensive exam required. *Entrance requirements:* For doctorate, GRE General Test. *Application deadline:* For fall admission, 4/15. Application fee: $40. *Financial aid:* In 1998–99, 25 students received aid, including 13 fellowships, 1 teaching assistantship; research assistantships, career-related internships or fieldwork, Federal Work-Study, institutionally-sponsored loans, and tuition waivers (full and partial) also available. Financial aid application deadline: 2/1; financial aid applicants required to submit FAFSA. *Unit head:* Dr. Frederick Shaw, Executive Officer, 212-642-2202.

Harvard University, Graduate School of Arts and Sciences, Department of Earth and Planetary Sciences, Cambridge, MA 02138. Offers AM, PhD. *Students:* 33 full-time (12 women). 64 applicants, 22% accepted. In 1998, 1 master's, 6 doctorates awarded. Terminal master's awarded for partial completion of doctoral program. *Degree requirements:* For master's, thesis or alternative required; for doctorate, dissertation, general exams required. *Entrance requirements:* For master's and doctorate, GRE General Test, TOEFL (minimum score of 550 required). *Application deadline:* For fall admission, 12/15. Application fee: $60. *Financial aid:* Fellowships, research assistantships, teaching assistantships, career-related internships or fieldwork, Federal Work-Study, and institutionally-sponsored loans available. Financial aid application deadline: 12/30. *Faculty research:* Economic geography, geochemistry, geophysics, mineralogy, crystallography. *Unit head:* Dr. Michael B. McElroy, Chairman, 617-495-2351. *Application contact:* Office of Admissions and Financial Aid, 617-495-5315.

See in-depth description on page 281.

Indiana State University, School of Graduate Studies, College of Arts and Sciences, Department of Geography, Geology and Anthropology, Terre Haute, IN 47809-1401. Offers earth sciences (MS); economic geography (PhD); geography (MA); physical geography (PhD). *Faculty:* 22 full-time (4 women). *Students:* 27 full-time (11 women), 16 part-time (4 women); includes 2 minority (both African Americans), 11 international. *Degree requirements:* For doctorate, computer language, dissertation required. *Entrance requirements:* For doctorate, GRE General Test, departmental qualifying exam. *Application deadline:* For fall admission, 7/1 (priority date); for spring admission, 11/1 (priority date). Applications are processed on a rolling basis. Application fee: $20. Electronic applications accepted. *Unit head:* Dr. William Dando, Chairperson, 812-237-2261.

Indiana University Bloomington, Graduate School, College of Arts and Sciences, Department of Geological Sciences, Bloomington, IN 47405. Offers biogeochemistry (MS, PhD); environmental geosciences (MS, PhD); geobiology, stratigraphy, and sedimentology (MS, PhD); geochemistry (MS, PhD); geochemistry, mineralogy, and petrology (MS, PhD); geophysics (MS, PhD); geophysics, tectonics, and structural geology (MS, PhD). PhD offered through the University Graduate School. Part-time programs available. *Faculty:* 21 full-time (1 woman). *Students:* 27 full-time (8 women), 22 part-time (6 women); includes 3 minority (2 Asian Americans or Pacific Islanders, 1 Hispanic American), 9 international. In 1998, 12 master's, 5 doctorates awarded. *Degree requirements:* For master's, one foreign language (computer language can substitute), thesis or alternative required; for doctorate, dissertation required, dissertation required. *Entrance requirements:* For master's and doctorate, GRE General Test, TOEFL. *Application deadline:* For fall admission, 1/15 (priority date); for spring admission, 9/1 (priority date). Applications are processed on a rolling basis. Application fee: $40. Tuition, state resident: part-time $161 per credit hour. Tuition, nonresident: part-time $468 per credit hour. Required fees: $360 per year. Tuition and fees vary according to course load and program. *Financial aid:* In 1998–99, research assistantships with full and partial tuition reimbursements (averaging $11,000 per year); fellowships with tuition reimbursements, teaching assistantships with tuition reimbursements, career-related internships or fieldwork, Federal Work-Study, and institutionally-sponsored loans also available. Financial aid application deadline: 2/15. *Faculty research:* Geophysics, geochemistry, hydrogeology, igneous and metamorphic petrology and clay minerology. Total annual research expenditures: $289,139. *Unit head:* Dr. Christopher G. Maples, Chairman, 812-855-5582, Fax: 812-855-7899, E-mail: cmaples@indiana.edu. *Application contact:* Mary Iverson, Secretary, Committee for Graduate Studies, 812-855-7214, Fax: 812-855-7899, E-mail: geograd@indiana.edu.

See in-depth description on page 283.

Iowa State University of Science and Technology, Graduate College, College of Liberal Arts and Sciences, Department of Geological and Atmospheric Sciences, Ames, IA 50011. Offers earth science (MS, PhD); geology (MS, PhD); meteorology (MS, PhD); water resources (MS, PhD). *Faculty:* 17 full-time. *Students:* 28 full-time (8 women), 9 part-time (3 women); includes 1 minority (Asian American or Pacific Islander), 11 international. 43 applicants, 42% accepted. In 1998, 4 master's, 2 doctorates awarded. *Degree requirements:* For master's, thesis required (for some programs); for doctorate, dissertation required. *Entrance requirements:* For master's and doctorate, GRE General Test, TOEFL (minimum score of 530 required). *Application deadline:* For fall admission, 2/15 (priority date). Applications are processed on a rolling basis. Application fee: $20 ($50 for international students). Electronic applications accepted. Tuition, state resident: full-time $3,308. Tuition, nonresident: full-time $9,744. Part-time tuition and fees vary according to course load, campus/location and program. *Financial aid:* In 1998–99, 15 research assistantships with partial tuition reimbursements (averaging $9,915 per year), 11 teaching assistantships with partial tuition reimbursements (averaging $9,999 per year) were awarded.; fellowships, scholarships also available. *Unit head:* Dr. Paul G. Spry, Chair, 515-294-4477.

See in-depth description on page 285.

Lehigh University, College of Arts and Sciences, Department of Earth and Environmental Sciences, Bethlehem, PA 18015-3094. Offers environmental science (MS, PhD); geological sciences (MS, PhD). *Students:* 25 full-time (14 women); includes 1 minority (Hispanic American), 2 international. Average age 28. 33 applicants, 30% accepted. In 1998, 6 master's, 1 doctorate awarded (100% entered university research/teaching). *Degree requirements:* For master's, thesis required, foreign language not required; for doctorate, dissertation, language at the discretion of the PhD committee required. *Entrance requirements:* For master's and doctorate, GRE General Test (score in 75th percentile or higher required), TOEFL (minimum score of 550 required). *Average time to degree:* Master's–2 years full-time; doctorate–4.5 years full-time. *Application deadline:* For fall admission, 7/15; for spring admission, 12/1. Applications are processed on a rolling basis. Application fee: $40. *Financial aid:* In 1998–99, 3 fellowships, 4 research assistantships, 8 teaching assistantships were awarded.; Federal Work-Study, institutionally-sponsored loans, and tuition waivers (full and partial) also available. Financial aid application deadline: 1/15. *Faculty research:* Tectonics, surficial processes, aquatic ecology. Total annual research expenditures: $1.5 million. *Unit head:* Dr. Peter Zeitler, Chairman, 610-758-3667, Fax: 610-758-3677, E-mail: pkz0@lehigh.edu. *Application contact:* Dr. Donald Morris, Graduate Coordinator, 610-758-5831, Fax: 610-758-3677, E-mail: dpmz0@lehigh.edu.

See in-depth description on page 289.

Massachusetts Institute of Technology, School of Science, Department of Earth, Atmospheric, and Planetary Sciences, Cambridge, MA 02139-4307. Offers atmospheres, oceans, and climate (SM, PhD, Sc D); atmospheric chemistry (SM, PhD, Sc D); geology and geochemistry (SM, PhD, Sc D); geophysics (SM, PhD, Sc D); planetary science (SM, PhD, Sc D). *Faculty:* 39 full-time (4 women). *Students:* 164 full-time (68 women); includes 7 minority (3 Asian Americans

Geosciences

Massachusetts Institute of Technology (continued)
or Pacific Islanders, 4 Hispanic Americans), 59 international. Average age 29. 212 applicants, 34% accepted. In 1998, 12 master's, 27 doctorates awarded. Terminal master's awarded for partial completion of doctoral program. *Degree requirements:* For master's, thesis required, foreign language not required; for doctorate, dissertation, general exam required, foreign language not required. *Entrance requirements:* For master's and doctorate, GRE General Test. *Application deadline:* For fall admission, 1/15; for spring admission, 11/1. Application fee: $55. *Financial aid:* In 1998–99, 43 fellowships, 90 research assistantships, 15 teaching assistantships were awarded.; institutionally-sponsored loans also available. Financial aid application deadline: 1/15. *Faculty research:* Evolution of main features of the planetary system; origin, composition, structure, and state of the atmospheres, oceans, surfaces, and interiors of planets; dynamics of planets and satellite motions. *Unit head:* Dr. Ronald G. Prinn, Chairman, 617-253-3382. *Application contact:* Anastasia Frangos, Administrative Assistant, 617-253-3381, Fax: 617-253-8298, E-mail: eapsinfo@mit.edu.

See in-depth description on page 291.

McGill University, Faculty of Graduate Studies and Research, Faculty of Science, Department of Earth and Planetary Sciences, Montréal, PQ H3A 2T5, Canada. Offers earth and planetary sciences (M Sc, PhD, Diploma). *Faculty:* 11 full-time (2 women). *Students:* 37 full-time (12 women), 12 international. Average age 25. 65 applicants, 38% accepted. In 1998, 10 master's awarded (40% found work related to degree, 60% continued full-time study); 4 doctorates awarded. *Degree requirements:* For master's and doctorate, thesis/dissertation required, foreign language not required. *Entrance requirements:* For master's, TOEFL (minimum score of 550 required), minimum GPA of 3.0; for doctorate, TOEFL (minimum score of 550 required). *Average time to degree:* Master's–4 years full-time; doctorate–6 years full-time. *Application deadline:* For fall admission, 3/1 (priority date). Applications are processed on a rolling basis. Application fee: $60. *Financial aid:* Fellowships, research assistantships, teaching assistantships, institutionally-sponsored loans and tuition waivers (partial) available. *Faculty research:* Geochemistry, sedimentary petrology, igneous petrology, theoretical geophysics, economic geology, planetary sciences. *Unit head:* A. E. Williams-Jones, Chair, 514-398-6768, Fax: 514-398-4680, E-mail: willy_j@geosci.lan.mcgill.ca. *Application contact:* A. Hynes, Chair, Graduate Admissions, 514-398-5884, Fax: 514-398-4680, E-mail: andrew@geosci.lan.mcgill.ca.

McMaster University, School of Graduate Studies, Faculty of Science, School of Geography and Geology, Hamilton, ON L8S 4M2, Canada. Offers geochemistry (PhD); geology (M Sc, PhD); human geography (MA, PhD); physical geography (M Sc, PhD). Part-time programs available. *Faculty:* 23 full-time (3 women), 12 part-time (1 woman). *Students:* 49 full-time (24 women), 9 part-time (7 women), 8 international. Average age 24. 51 applicants, 31% accepted. In 1998, 12 master's, 7 doctorates awarded. Terminal master's awarded for partial completion of doctoral program. *Degree requirements:* For master's, thesis required, foreign language not required; for doctorate, dissertation, comprehensive exam required, foreign language not required. *Entrance requirements:* For master's, minimum B+ average. *Application deadline:* For fall admission, 3/15 (priority date). Applications are processed on a rolling basis. Application fee: $50. *Financial aid:* In 1998–99, 33 students received aid; teaching assistantships, scholarships available. Financial aid application deadline: 3/15. *Unit head:* Dr. Fred L. Hall, Director, 905-525-9140 Ext. 24196, Fax: 905-546-0463, E-mail: hallfl@mcmaster.ca. *Application contact:* Medy Espiritu, Graduate Secretary, 905-525-9140 Ext. 23535, Fax: 905-522-3141, E-mail: espiritu@mcmaster.ca.

Announcement: MA, M Sc, and PhD programs. Human and social geography areas: environment and health (strategic area), economic, population, transportation, and urban. Geology and physical geography areas: geochemistry, geophysics, near-surface environmental processes, climatology, and environmental science. Scholarships and teaching assistantships of $13,000–$15,000 (1999–2000). Write to Director, School of Geography and Geology.

Memorial University of Newfoundland, School of Graduate Studies, Department of Earth Sciences, St. John's, NF A1C 5S7, Canada. Offers geology (M Sc, PhD); geophysics (M Sc, PhD). Part-time programs available. *Faculty:* 25 full-time (2 women), 4 part-time (0 women). *Students:* 32 full-time (11 women), 5 part-time (2 women), 15 international. 30 applicants, 20% accepted. In 1998, 13 master's, 4 doctorates awarded. *Degree requirements:* For master's, thesis required; for doctorate, dissertation, comprehensive exam required. *Entrance requirements:* For master's, honors B Sc; for doctorate, M Sc. *Application deadline:* For fall admission, 3/31; for spring admission, 12/31. Applications are processed on a rolling basis. Application fee: $40. *Financial aid:* Fellowships, research assistantships, teaching assistantships available. *Faculty research:* Geochemistry, sedimentology, paleoceanography and global change, mineral deposits, petroleum geology, hydrology. Total annual research expenditures: $2.5 million. *Unit head:* Dr. G. Quinlan, Head, 709-737-2334, Fax: 709-737-2589, E-mail: gquinlan@sparkyz.esd.ucs.mun.ca. *Application contact:* Dr. Ali Aksu, Graduate Officer, 709-737-8385, Fax: 709-737-2589, E-mail: aaksu@sparkyz.esd.ucs.mun.ca.

Michigan State University, Graduate School, College of Natural Science, Department of Geological Sciences, East Lansing, MI 48824-1020. Offers environmental geosciences (MS, PhD); geological sciences (MA, MS, PhD). Part-time programs available. *Faculty:* 15 full-time (2 women), 7 part-time (2 women). *Students:* 33 full-time (15 women), 4 part-time (2 women); includes 1 minority (Asian American or Pacific Islander), 2 international. Average age 27. 65 applicants, 65% accepted. In 1998, 8 master's awarded (13% entered university research/teaching, 74% found other work related to degree, 13% continued full-time study). *Degree requirements:* For master's, thesis required (for some programs), foreign language not required; for doctorate, dissertation required, foreign language not required. *Entrance requirements:* For master's and doctorate, GRE General Test, TOEFL. *Average time to degree:* Master's–3 years full-time. *Application deadline:* For fall admission, 6/1; for spring admission, 11/1. Applications are processed on a rolling basis. Application fee: $30 ($40 for international students). Electronic applications accepted. *Financial aid:* In 1998–99, 33 students received aid, including 27 fellowships (averaging $1,377 per year), 10 research assistantships with partial tuition reimbursements available (averaging $9,591 per year), 20 teaching assistantships with partial tuition reimbursements available (averaging $9,745 per year); institutionally-sponsored loans and scholarships also available. Financial aid application deadline: 1/15; financial aid applicants required to submit CSS PROFILE or FAFSA. *Faculty research:* Paleoenvironments and biological evolution, geochemical and biogeochemical cycles, fluids in and on the Earth, dynamics of the Earth's crust. Total annual research expenditures: $369,856. *Unit head:* Dr. Thomas Vogel, Chairperson, 517-355-4626, Fax: 517-353-8787, E-mail: geosci@pilot.msu.edu.

Mississippi State University, College of Arts and Sciences, Department of Geosciences, Mississippi State, MS 39762. Offers MS. *Students:* 36 full-time (11 women), 59 part-time (31 women); includes 6 minority (3 African Americans, 2 Asian Americans or Pacific Islanders, 1 Hispanic American), 1 international. Average age 30. 75 applicants, 93% accepted. In 1998, 16 degrees awarded. *Degree requirements:* For master's, computer language, thesis (for some programs), comprehensive oral or written exam, statistics or a foreign language required, foreign language not required. *Entrance requirements:* For master's, TOEFL (minimum score of 550 required), minimum QPA of 2.75. *Application deadline:* For fall admission, 7/1; for spring admission, 11/1. Applications are processed on a rolling basis. Application fee: $25 for international students. *Financial aid:* Research assistantships with full tuition reimbursements, teaching assistantships with full tuition reimbursements, Federal Work-Study, institutionally-sponsored loans, tuition waivers (partial), and unspecified assistantships available. Financial aid applicants required to submit FAFSA. *Faculty research:* Climatology, hydrogeology, sedimentology, stratigraphy, speleology. Total annual research expenditures: $330,000. *Unit head:* Dr. Charles L. Wax, Head, 662-325-3915, Fax: 662-325-9423, E-mail: wax@geosci.msstate.edu. *Application contact:* Jerry B. Inmon, Director of Admissions, 662-325-2224, Fax: 662-325-7360, E-mail: admit@admissions.msstate.edu.

Montana State University–Bozeman, College of Graduate Studies, College of Letters and Science, Department of Earth Sciences, Bozeman, MT 59717. Offers MS. Part-time programs available. *Students:* 10 full-time (4 women), 15 part-time (9 women). Average age 30. 32 applicants, 13% accepted. In 1998, 7 degrees awarded. *Degree requirements:* For master's, thesis required, foreign language not required. *Entrance requirements:* For master's, GRE General Test, TOEFL (minimum score of 550 required). *Application deadline:* For fall admission, 6/1 (priority date); for spring admission, 11/1. Applications are processed on a rolling basis. Application fee: $50. *Financial aid:* In 1998–99, 2 research assistantships with tuition reimbursements (averaging $7,650 per year), 12 teaching assistantships with tuition reimbursements (averaging $7,210 per year) were awarded.; fellowships, Federal Work-Study, grants, and scholarships also available. Financial aid application deadline: 3/1; financial aid applicants required to submit FAFSA. *Faculty research:* Geology, geography, hydrology, geographic information systems, earth surface processes. Total annual research expenditures: $632,913. *Unit head:* Dr. James Schmidt, Head, 406-994-3331, Fax: 406-994-6923, E-mail: earth@montana.edu.

Montana Tech of The University of Montana, Graduate School, Geoscience Program, Butte, MT 59701-8997. Offers geochemistry (MS); geological engineering (MS); geology (MS); geophysical engineering (MS); hydrogeological engineering (MS); hydrogeology (MS); mineral economics (MS). Part-time programs available. *Faculty:* 17 full-time (2 women). *Students:* 15 full-time (6 women), 7 part-time (1 woman); includes 1 minority (Native American) 27 applicants, 56% accepted. In 1998, 7 degrees awarded. *Degree requirements:* For master's, thesis required (for some programs), foreign language not required. *Entrance requirements:* For master's, GRE General Test, TOEFL (minimum score of 525 required), minimum B average. *Application deadline:* For fall admission, 4/1 (priority date); for spring admission, 10/1 (priority date). Applications are processed on a rolling basis. Application fee: $30. Tuition, state resident: full-time $3,211; part-time $162 per credit hour. Tuition, nonresident: full-time $9,883; part-time $440 per credit hour. International tuition: $15,500 full-time. *Financial aid:* In 1998–99, 12 students received aid, including 5 research assistantships with partial tuition reimbursements available (averaging $7,216 per year), 4 teaching assistantships with partial tuition reimbursements available (averaging $5,950 per year); career-related internships or fieldwork, institutionally-sponsored loans, and tuition waivers (full and partial) also available. Financial aid application deadline: 4/1; financial aid applicants required to submit FAFSA. *Faculty research:* Water resource development, seismic processing, petroleum reservoir characterization, environmental geochemistry, molecular modeling, magmatic and hydrothermal ore deposits. Total annual research expenditures: $1.2 million. *Unit head:* Cindy Dunstan, Administrative Assistant, 406-496-4128, Fax: 406-496-4334, E-mail: cdunstan@mtech.edu. *Application contact:* Cindy Dunstan, Administrative Assistant, 406-496-4128, Fax: 406-496-4334, E-mail: cdunstan@mtech.edu.

Montclair State University, Office of Graduate Studies, College of Science and Mathematics, Department of Earth and Environmental Studies, Program in Geoscience, Upper Montclair, NJ 07043-1624. Offers MS. Part-time and evening/weekend programs available. *Degree requirements:* For master's, thesis, comprehensive exam required, foreign language not required. *Entrance requirements:* For master's, GRE General Test.

New Mexico Institute of Mining and Technology, Graduate Studies, Department of Earth and Environmental Science, Socorro, NM 87801. Offers geochemistry (MS, PhD); geology (MS, PhD); geophysics (MS, PhD); hydrology (MS, PhD). *Faculty:* 18 full-time (1 woman), 23 part-time (2 women). *Students:* 87 full-time (31 women); includes 1 minority (Hispanic American), 11 international. Average age 30. 109 applicants, 74% accepted. In 1998, 19 master's, 6 doctorates awarded. *Degree requirements:* For master's, thesis optional, foreign language not required; for doctorate, dissertation required, foreign language not required. *Entrance requirements:* For master's, GRE General Test, TOEFL (minimum score of 540 required); for doctorate, GRE General Test, GRE Subject Test, TOEFL (minimum score of 540 required). *Application deadline:* For fall admission, 3/1 (priority date); for spring admission, 6/1. Applications are processed on a rolling basis. Application fee: $16. *Financial aid:* In 1998–99, 1 fellowship, 42 research assistantships (averaging $9,670 per year), 17 teaching assistantships (averaging $9,670 per year) were awarded.; Federal Work-Study and institutionally-sponsored loans also available. Financial aid application deadline: 3/1; financial aid applicants required to submit CSS PROFILE or FAFSA. *Faculty research:* Crust-mantle geochemistry; volcanology (Southwest and Antarctic); ore genesis, stratigraphy, and sedimentation; coal petrology; fluid inclusions. *Unit head:* Dr. Fred Phillips, Chairman, 505-835-5634, Fax: 505-835-6436, E-mail: geos@nmt.edu. *Application contact:* Dr. David B. Johnson, Dean of Graduate Studies, 505-835-5513, Fax: 505-835-5476, E-mail: graduate@nmt.edu.

North Carolina Central University, Division of Academic Affairs, College of Arts and Sciences, Department of Earth Sciences, Durham, NC 27707-3129. Offers MS. *Faculty:* 5 full-time (0 women). *Students:* 2 full-time (both women), 4 part-time (1 woman); includes 4 minority (all African Americans) Average age 31. 1 applicants, 100% accepted. *Degree requirements:* For master's, comprehensive exam required. *Entrance requirements:* For master's, minimum GPA of 3.0 in major, 2.5 overall. *Application deadline:* For fall admission, 8/1. Application fee: $30. *Financial aid:* Application deadline: 5/1. *Unit head:* Dr. Albert P. Barnett, Chairperson, 919-560-5171. *Application contact:* Dr. Bernice D. Johnson, Dean, College of Arts and Sciences, 919-560-6368.

North Carolina State University, Graduate School, College of Physical and Mathematical Sciences, Department of Marine, Earth, and Atmospheric Sciences, Raleigh, NC 27695. Offers geology (MS, PhD); geophysics (MS, PhD); marine, earth, and atmospheric sciences (MS, PhD); meteorology (MS, PhD); oceanography (MS, PhD). *Faculty:* 34 full-time (2 women), 39 part-time (1 woman). *Students:* 118 full-time (30 women), 12 part-time (3 women); includes 2 minority (both Asian Americans or Pacific Islanders), 37 international. Average age 30. 95 applicants, 52% accepted. In 1998, 17 master's, 12 doctorates awarded. Terminal master's awarded for partial completion of doctoral program. *Degree requirements:* For master's, thesis, final oral exam required, foreign language not required; for doctorate, dissertation, final oral exam, preliminary oral and written exams required, foreign language not required. *Entrance requirements:* For master's and doctorate, GRE General Test, minimum GPA of 3.0. *Application deadline:* For fall admission, 6/25 (priority date); for spring admission, 11/25. Applications are processed on a rolling basis. Application fee: $45. *Financial aid:* In 1998–99, 1 fellowship (averaging $4,504 per year), 84 research assistantships (averaging $3,877 per year), 30 teaching assistantships (averaging $3,678 per year) were awarded.; institutionally-sponsored loans also available. Financial aid application deadline: 3/1. *Faculty research:* Boundary layer and air quality meteorology; climate and mesoscale dynamics; biological, chemical, geological, and physical oceanography; hard rock, soft rock, environmental, and paleogeology. Total annual research expenditures: $8.8 million. *Unit head:* Dr. Leonard J. Pietrafesa, Head, 919-515-3717, Fax: 919-515-7802, E-mail: leonard_pietrafesa@ncsu.edu. *Application contact:* Dr. Gerald S. Janowitz, Director of Graduate Programs, 919-515-7837, Fax: 919-515-7802, E-mail: janowitz@ncsu.edu.

See in-depth description on page 293.

Northeastern Illinois University, Graduate College, College of Arts and Sciences, Department of Earth Science, Program in Earth Science, Chicago, IL 60625-4699. Offers MS. Part-time and evening/weekend programs available. *Faculty:* 5 full-time (2 women), 1 (woman) part-time. *Students:* 1 full-time (0 women), 17 part-time (11 women); includes 3 minority (all Asian Americans or Pacific Islanders) Average age 38. In 1998, 3 degrees awarded. *Degree requirements:* For master's, oral presentation required, thesis optional, foreign language not required. *Entrance requirements:* For master's, 15 undergraduate hours in earth science, 8 undergraduate hours in chemistry and physics, minimum GPA of 2.75. *Application deadline:* For fall admission, 3/31 (priority date); for spring admission, 9/30. Applications are processed on a rolling basis. Application fee: $0. *Financial aid:* In 1998–99, 7 research assistantships were awarded.; career-related internships or fieldwork, Federal Work-Study, institutionally-sponsored loans, and tuition waivers (full and partial) also available. Aid available to part-time students. Financial aid applicants required to submit FAFSA. *Faculty research:* Coastal engineering, Paleozoic and Precambrian tectonics and volcanology, ravine erosion control, well head protection delineation, genesis and evolution of basaltic magma. *Unit head:* Dr. Karen Bartels, Graduate Adviser, 773-794-6564. *Application contact:* Dr. Mohan K. Sood, Dean of Graduate College, 773-583-4050 Ext. 6143, Fax: 773-794-6670, E-mail: m-sood@neiu.edu.

Northeast Louisiana University, Graduate Studies and Research, College of Pure and Applied Sciences, Department of Geosciences, Monroe, LA 71209-0001. Offers MS. *Faculty:* 11 full-time (0 women). *Students:* 9 full-time (3 women), 2 part-time (1 woman), 2 international. Average age 33. *Degree requirements:* For master's, thesis required, foreign language not required. *Entrance requirements:* For master's, GRE General Test (minimum combined score of 900 required), minimum GPA of 2.8 during previous two years or 3.0 in 21 hours of geosciences. *Application deadline:* For fall admission, 7/1 (priority date); for spring admission, 11/1. Applications are processed on a rolling basis. Application fee: $15 ($25 for international students). Tuition, state resident: full-time $1,650. Tuition, nonresident: full-time $7,608. Required fees: $378. *Financial aid:* Research assistantships, teaching assistantships, Federal Work-Study and unspecified assistantships available. Financial aid application deadline: 7/1. *Faculty research:* Sedimentology, environmental hydrology, planetary geosciences, micropaleontology. *Unit head:* Dr. Eric Pani, Head, 318-342-1878, Fax: 318-342-1755, E-mail: gepani@alpha.nlu.edu.

Northern Arizona University, Graduate College, College of Arts and Sciences, Department of Geology, Program in Earth Science, Flagstaff, AZ 86011. Offers MAT, MS. *Students:* 4 full-time (1 woman), 3 part-time (1 woman); includes 1 minority (Native American) 2 applicants, 0% accepted. In 1998, 4 degrees awarded. *Degree requirements:* Foreign language not required. *Application deadline:* For fall admission, 3/1 (priority date); for spring admission, 11/1. Applications are processed on a rolling basis. Application fee: $45. *Financial aid:* Career-related internships or fieldwork, Federal Work-Study, and tuition waivers (full and partial) available. *Unit head:* Dr. Dale Nations, Coordinator, 520-523-7180, E-mail: jack.nations@nau.edu. *Application contact:* Dr. Barbara Palermo, Secretary, 520-523-4561, Fax: 520-523-9220, E-mail: barbara.palermo@nau.edu.

Northwestern University, The Graduate School, Judd A. and Marjorie Weinberg College of Arts and Sciences, Department of Geological Sciences, Evanston, IL 60208. Offers MS, PhD. Admissions and degrees offered through The Graduate School. Part-time programs available. *Faculty:* 9 full-time (1 woman), 1 part-time (0 women). *Students:* 14 full-time (5 women), 3 international. Average age 27. 23 applicants, 35% accepted. In 1998, 2 master's, 6 doctorates awarded. *Degree requirements:* For doctorate, dissertation required. *Entrance requirements:* For master's and doctorate, GRE General Test, TOEFL (minimum score of 560 required). *Application deadline:* For fall admission, 1/30 (priority date). Application fee: $50 ($55 for international students). *Financial aid:* In 1998–99, 3 fellowships with full tuition reimbursements (averaging $11,673 per year), 1 research assistantship with partial tuition reimbursement (averaging $16,128 per year), 7 teaching assistantships with full tuition reimbursements (averaging $12,042 per year) were awarded.; career-related internships or fieldwork, Federal Work-Study, institutionally-sponsored loans, scholarships, and tuition waivers (full and partial) also available. Financial aid application deadline: 1/15; financial aid applicants required to submit FAFSA. *Faculty research:* Tectonophysics, seismology, biogeochemistry, stratigraphy, paleoecology. Total annual research expenditures: $579,058. *Unit head:* Abraham Lerman, Chair, 847-491-3238, Fax: 847-491-8060, E-mail: abe@earth.nwu.edu. *Application contact:* Charlotte Hayes, Admission Contact, 847-491-3238, Fax: 847-491-8060, E-mail: geodept@earth.nwu.edu.

Pennsylvania State University University Park Campus, Graduate School, College of Earth and Mineral Sciences, Department of Geosciences, State College, University Park, PA 16802-1503. Offers geochemistry (MS, PhD); geology (MS, PhD); geophysics (MS, PhD). *Students:* 65 full-time (28 women), 6 part-time (1 woman). *Entrance requirements:* For master's and doctorate, GRE General Test, TOEFL. Application fee: $50. *Unit head:* Dr. Rudy L. Slingerland, Head, 814-865-2622. *Application contact:* Dr. Lee Kump, Associate Head, 814-865-7394.

See in-depth description on page 295.

Princeton University, Graduate School, Department of Geosciences, Princeton, NJ 08544-1019. Offers atmospheric and oceanic sciences (PhD); environmental engineering and water resources (PhD); geological and geophysical sciences (PhD). *Degree requirements:* For doctorate, dissertation required. *Entrance requirements:* For doctorate, GRE General Test, GRE Subject Test.

Purdue University, Graduate School, School of Science, Department of Earth and Atmospheric Sciences, West Lafayette, IN 47907. Offers MS, PhD. *Faculty:* 23 full-time (1 woman), 4 part-time (0 women). *Students:* 44 full-time (16 women), 11 part-time (5 women); includes 1 minority (African American), 26 international. Average age 25. 97 applicants, 42% accepted. In 1998, 5 master's, 8 doctorates awarded. *Degree requirements:* For master's, thesis required, foreign language not required; for doctorate, dissertation required. *Entrance requirements:* For master's and doctorate, GRE General Test, TOEFL (minimum score of 550 required). *Application deadline:* For fall admission, 2/1 (priority date); for spring admission, 6/1 (priority date). Applications are processed on a rolling basis. Application fee: $30. Electronic applications accepted. *Financial aid:* In 1998–99, 4 fellowships with partial tuition reimbursements (averaging $14,400 per year), 18 research assistantships with partial tuition reimbursements (averaging $13,500 per year), 17 teaching assistantships with partial tuition reimbursements (averaging $13,500 per year) were awarded. Aid available to part-time students. Financial aid application deadline: 3/1; financial aid applicants required to submit FAFSA. *Faculty research:* Geology, geophysics, hydrogeology, paleoclimatology, environmental science. Total annual research expenditures: $2.7 million. *Application contact:* Kathy Kincade, Graduate Secretary, 765-494-5984, Fax: 765-496-1210, E-mail: kkincade@purdue.edu.

Radford University, Graduate College, College of Arts and Sciences, Department of Geology, Radford, VA 24142. Offers engineering geosciences (MS). Part-time programs available. Postbaccalaureate distance learning degree programs offered (minimal on-campus study). *Faculty:* 14 full-time (1 woman), 1 part-time (0 women). *Students:* 4 full-time (0 women), 7 part-time (4 women). Average age 31. 15 applicants, 53% accepted. In 1998, 1 degree awarded. *Degree requirements:* For master's, thesis (for some programs), comprehensive exam required, foreign language not required. *Entrance requirements:* For master's, GMAT, GRE General Test or MAT, TOEFL (minimum score of 550 required), minimum GPA of 2.7. *Average time to degree:* Master's–2 years full-time, 2.5 years part-time. *Application deadline:* For fall admission, 2/15 (priority date); for spring admission, 10/15. Applications are processed on a rolling basis. Application fee: $25. Electronic applications accepted. *Financial aid:* In 1998–99, 10 students received aid, including 2 fellowships (averaging $4,650 per year), 8 research assistantships (averaging $5,175 per year); teaching assistantships, career-related internships or fieldwork, Federal Work-Study, grants, institutionally-sponsored loans, and scholarships also available. Financial aid application deadline: 2/1; financial aid applicants required to submit FAFSA. *Unit head:* Dr. Stephen W. Lenhart, Chair, 540-831-5652, Fax: 540-831-5732, E-mail: slenhart@runet.edu. *Application contact:* Dr. Robert C. Whisonant, Coordinator, 540-831-5224.

Rensselaer Polytechnic Institute, Graduate School, School of Science, Department of Earth and Environmental Sciences, Troy, NY 12180-3590. Offers environmental chemistry (MS, PhD); geochemistry (MS, PhD); geology (MS, PhD); geophysics (MS, PhD); hydrogeology (MS); petrology (MS, PhD); planetary geology (MS, PhD); tectonics (MS, PhD). Part-time programs available. *Faculty:* 7 full-time (0 women), 2 part-time (0 women). *Students:* 19 full-time (8 women), 1 (woman) part-time; includes 2 minority (1 African American, 1 Native American) 20 applicants, 75% accepted. In 1998, 6 master's, 2 doctorates awarded. *Degree requirements:* For master's, thesis required (for some programs); for doctorate, dissertation required. *Entrance requirements:* For master's and doctorate, GRE General Test, TOEFL (minimum score of 550 required). *Application deadline:* For fall admission, 2/1 (priority date). Applications are processed on a rolling basis. Application fee: $35. *Financial aid:* In 1998–99, 9 research assistantships with partial tuition reimbursements (averaging $10,500 per year), 4 teaching assistantships with partial tuition reimbursements (averaging $10,500 per year) were awarded.; fellowships, career-related internships or fieldwork, institutionally-sponsored loans, and tuition waivers (partial) also available. Financial aid application deadline: 2/1. *Faculty research:* Groundwater modeling, asteroid chemistry, mantel geochemistry, contaminant geochemistry, seismology, GPS geodesy, remote sensing. Total annual research expenditures: $1.8 million. *Unit head:* Dr. Robert McCaffrey, Chair, 518-276-6474, Fax: 518-276-6680, E-mail: ees@rpi.edu. *Application contact:* Dr. Steven Roecker, Associate Professor, 518-276-6474, Fax: 518-276-6680, E-mail: ees@rpi.edu.

See in-depth description on page 299.

Saint Louis University, Graduate School, College of Arts and Sciences, Department of Earth and Atmospheric Sciences, Program in Geoscience, St. Louis, MO 63103-2097. Offers MS, MS(R), PhD. *Faculty:* 10 full-time (1 woman), 2 part-time (1 woman). *Students:* 7 full-time (1 woman), 3 part-time, 8 international. Average age 31. 10 applicants, 80% accepted. In 1998, 1 master's, 2 doctorates awarded. *Degree requirements:* For master's, computer language, comprehensive oral exam, thesis for MS(R) required; for doctorate, computer language, dissertation, preliminary exams required, foreign language not required. *Entrance requirements:* For master's and doctorate, GRE General Test. *Application deadline:* For fall admission, 7/1; for spring admission, 11/1. Applications are processed on a rolling basis. Application fee: $40. Tuition: Full-time $20,520; part-time $507 per credit hour. Required fees: $38 per term. Tuition and fees vary according to program. *Financial aid:* In 1998–99, 9 students received aid, including 4 research assistantships, 1 teaching assistantship Financial aid application deadline: 4/1. *Faculty research:* Seismic wave propagation, earthquake processes, crustal and fault-zone properties. *Unit head:* Dr. Brian Mitchell, Director, 314-977-3123. *Application contact:* Dr. Marcia Buresch, Assistant Dean of the Graduate School, 314-977-2240, Fax: 314-977-3943, E-mail: bureschm@slu.edu.

San Francisco State University, Graduate Division, College of Science and Engineering, Department of Geosciences, San Francisco, CA 94132-1722. Offers applied geosciences (MS). *Entrance requirements:* For master's, minimum GPA of 2.5 in last 60 units. *Application deadline:* For fall admission, 11/30 (priority date). Applications are processed on a rolling basis. Application fee: $55. *Financial aid:* Application deadline: 3/1. *Unit head:* Dr. Karen Grove, Chair, 415-338-2061, E-mail: kgrove@sfsu.edu. *Application contact:* Dr. Lisa White, Graduate Coordinator, 415-338-1209, E-mail: lwhite@sfsu.edu.

Simon Fraser University, Graduate Studies, Faculty of Science, Department of Earth Sciences, Burnaby, BC V5A 1S6, Canada. Offers M Sc. *Faculty:* 4 full-time (1 woman). *Students:* 5 full-time (2 women). Average age 26. *Degree requirements:* For master's, thesis required. *Entrance requirements:* For master's, TOEFL (minimum score of 570 required), TWE (minimum score of 5 required), or International English Language Test (minimum score of 7.5 required), minimum GPA of 3.0. Application fee: $55. *Financial aid:* In 1998–99, 3 fellowships were awarded. *Faculty research:* Earth surface processes, environmental geoscience, surficial and Quaternary geology, sedimentology. *Unit head:* M. Roberts, Director, 604-291-5387, Fax: 604-291-4198. *Application contact:* Graduate Secretary, 604-291-5387, Fax: 604-291-4198.

Southeast Missouri State University, Graduate School, Department of Geosciences, Cape Girardeau, MO 63701-4799. Offers MNS. *Degree requirements:* For master's, thesis or alternative required, foreign language not required. *Entrance requirements:* For master's, minimum GPA of 2.5. *Faculty research:* Earthquake studies, remote sensing.

Stanford University, School of Earth Sciences, Department of Geological and Environmental Sciences, Stanford, CA 94305-9991. Offers MS, PhD, Eng. *Faculty:* 20 full-time (3 women). *Students:* 72 full-time (23 women), 19 part-time (3 women); includes 7 minority (2 African Americans, 2 Asian Americans or Pacific Islanders, 2 Hispanic Americans, 1 Native American), 29 international. Average age 28. 94 applicants, 36% accepted. In 1998, 6 master's, 18 doctorates awarded. Terminal master's awarded for partial completion of doctoral program. *Degree requirements:* For master's and doctorate, thesis/dissertation required; for Eng, computer language, thesis required, foreign language not required. *Entrance requirements:* For master's, doctorate, and Eng, GRE General Test, TOEFL. *Application deadline:* For fall admission, 1/15. Application fee: $65 ($80 for international students). Tuition: Full-time $23,058. Required fees: $152. Part-time tuition and fees vary according to course load. *Financial aid:* Fellowships, research assistantships, teaching assistantships, Federal Work-Study and institutionally-sponsored loans available. Aid available to part-time students. Financial aid application deadline: 1/15. *Unit head:* Gail Mahood, Chair, 650-723-1429, Fax: 650-725-0979, E-mail: gail@pangea.stanford.edu. *Application contact:* Graduate Admissions Coordinator, 650-725-0574.

Stanford University, School of Earth Sciences, Earth Systems Program, Stanford, CA 94305-9991. Offers MS. Students admitted at the undergraduate level. *Students:* 15 full-time (10 women), 1 (woman) part-time; includes 3 minority (1 African American, 1 Asian American or Pacific Islander, 1 Hispanic American) Average age 23. In 1998, 12 degrees awarded. Application fee: $65 ($80 for international students). Electronic applications accepted. Tuition: Full-time $23,058. Required fees: $152. Part-time tuition and fees vary according to course load. *Unit head:* Joan Roughgarden, Director, 650-723-4961, Fax: 650-725-0958, E-mail: rough@pangea.stanford.edu.

State University of New York at Albany, College of Arts and Sciences, Department of Earth and Atmospheric Sciences, Albany, NY 12222-0001. Offers atmospheric science (MS, PhD); geology (MS, PhD). Evening/weekend programs available. *Faculty:* 24 full-time (0 women). *Students:* 46 full-time (16 women), 4 part-time; includes 1 minority (African American), 25 international. Average age 25. 50 applicants, 46% accepted. In 1998, 7 master's, 3 doctorates awarded. *Degree requirements:* For master's, thesis, comprehensive exam required; for doctorate, dissertation, comprehensive and oral exams required. *Entrance requirements:* For master's and doctorate, GRE General Test. Application fee: $50. Tuition, state resident: full-time $5,100; part-time $213 per credit. Tuition, nonresident: full-time $8,416; part-time $351 per credit. Required fees: $31 per credit. *Financial aid:* Fellowships, research assistantships, teaching assistantships, minority assistantships available. *Unit head:* Dr. John Delano, Chair, 518-442-4466.

State University of New York at Stony Brook, Graduate School, College of Arts and Sciences, Department of Geosciences, Stony Brook, NY 11794. Offers earth and space science (MS, PhD); earth science (MAT). MAT offered through the School of Professional Development and Continuing Studies. *Faculty:* 13 full-time (1 woman). *Students:* 27 full-time (11 women), 24 part-time (4 women); includes 4 minority (1 African American, 2 Asian Americans or Pacific Islanders, 1 Hispanic American), 14 international. 30 applicants, 77% accepted. In 1998, 11 master's, 1 doctorate awarded. Terminal master's awarded for partial completion of doctoral program. *Degree requirements:* For master's, thesis or alternative required, foreign language not required; for doctorate, dissertation required, foreign language not required. *Entrance requirements:* For master's and doctorate, GRE General Test, TOEFL, minimum GPA of 3.0. *Application deadline:* For fall admission, 1/15. Application fee: $50. *Financial aid:* In 1998–99, 4 fellowships, 15 research assistantships, 7 teaching assistantships were awarded. *Faculty research:* Astronomy, theoretical and observational astrophysics, paleontology, petrology, crystallography. Total annual research expenditures: $3.8 million. *Unit head:* Dr. Robert Libermann, Chairman, 516-632-8200, Fax: 516-632-8240. *Application contact:* Dr. John Parise, Director, 516-632-8200, Fax: 516-632-8240, E-mail: jparise@notes.cc.sunysb.edu.

State University of New York College at Oneonta, Graduate Studies, Department of Earth Sciences, Oneonta, NY 13820-4015. Offers MA. Part-time and evening/weekend programs available. *Faculty:* 9 full-time (0 women). *Students:* 2 full-time (0 women). *Degree requirements:* For master's, thesis required. *Entrance requirements:* For master's, GRE General Test. *Application deadline:* For fall admission, 4/15. Application fee: $50. *Financial aid:* Fellowships available. *Unit head:* Dr. P. Jay Fleisher, Chair, 607-436-3707.

Texas A&M University–Commerce, Graduate School, College of Arts and Sciences, Department of Biological and Earth Sciences, Commerce, TX 75429-3011. Offers M Ed, MS. *Faculty:*

Geosciences

Texas A&M University–Commerce (continued)
7 full-time (0 women), 3 part-time (0 women). *Students:* 5 full-time (all women), 9 part-time (6 women). Average age 36. In 1998, 9 degrees awarded. *Degree requirements:* For master's, thesis (for some programs), comprehensive exam required. *Entrance requirements:* For master's, GRE General Test (minimum combined score of 850 required). *Application deadline:* For fall admission, 6/1 (priority date); for spring admission, 11/1 (priority date). Applications are processed on a rolling basis. Application fee: $0 ($25 for international students). Electronic applications accepted. *Financial aid:* In 1998–99, research assistantships (averaging $7,750 per year), teaching assistantships (averaging $7,750 per year) were awarded.; Federal Work-Study, institutionally-sponsored loans, and scholarships also available. Financial aid application deadline: 5/1; financial aid applicants required to submit FAFSA. Total annual research expenditures: $8,356. *Unit head:* Dr. Don R. Lee, Interim Head, 903-886-5378. *Application contact:* Betty Hunt, Graduate Admissions Adviser, 903-886-5167, Fax: 903-886-5165, E-mail: betty_hunt@tamu_commerce.edu.

Texas Tech University, Graduate School, College of Arts and Sciences, Department of Geosciences, Lubbock, TX 79409. Offers atmospheric sciences (MS); geoscience (MS, PhD). Part-time programs available. *Faculty:* 13 full-time (1 woman). *Students:* 29 full-time (7 women), 11 part-time (2 women), 5 international. Average age 31. 16 applicants, 31% accepted. In 1998, 12 master's, 1 doctorate awarded. *Degree requirements:* For master's and doctorate, thesis/dissertation required. *Entrance requirements:* For master's, GRE General Test (combined average 1164); for doctorate, GRE General Test. *Application deadline:* For fall admission, 4/15 (priority date); for spring admission, 11/1 (priority date). Applications are processed on a rolling basis. Application fee: $25 ($50 for international students). Electronic applications accepted. *Financial aid:* In 1998–99, 2 research assistantships (averaging $10,800 per year), 24 teaching assistantships (averaging $11,674 per year) were awarded.; fellowships, Federal Work-Study and institutionally-sponsored loans also available. Aid available to part-time students. Financial aid application deadline: 5/15; financial aid applicants required to submit FAFSA. *Faculty research:* Thunderstorm complexes, properties of near-ground high-wind phenomena, Jurassic/Cretaceous magnetism in Kiamouth Mountains. Total annual research expenditures: $230,469. *Unit head:* Dr. Richard Peterson, Chairman, 806-742-3102, Fax: 806-742-0100.

Université du Québec à Chicoutimi, Graduate Programs, Program in Earth Sciences, Chicoutimi, PQ G7H 2B1, Canada. Offers M Sc A. Part-time programs available. *Degree requirements:* For master's, thesis required. *Entrance requirements:* For master's, appropriate bachelor's degree, proficiency in French.

Université du Québec à Montréal, Graduate Programs, Program in Earth Sciences, Montréal, PQ H3C 3P8, Canada. Offers M Sc. Part-time programs available. *Degree requirements:* For master's, thesis required. *Entrance requirements:* For master's, appropriate bachelor's degree or equivalent and proficiency in French.

Université du Québec, Institut national de la recherche scientifique, Graduate Programs, Research Center—Earth, Ste-Foy, PQ G1V 4C7, Canada. Offers earth sciences (M Sc, PhD). Part-time programs available. *Degree requirements:* For master's, thesis not required; for doctorate, dissertation required. *Entrance requirements:* For master's, appropriate bachelor's degree, proficiency in French; for doctorate, appropriate master's degree, proficiency in French.

Université Laval, Faculty of Graduate Studies, Faculty of Sciences and Engineering, Department of Geology and Geological Engineering, Sainte-Foy, PQ G1K 7P4, Canada. Offers earth sciences (PhD); geology (M Sc, PhD). *Students:* 30 full-time (12 women), 5 part-time. *Application deadline:* For fall admission, 3/1. Application fee: $30. *Unit head:* Michel Rocheleau, Director, 418-656-2131 Ext. 7340, Fax: 418-656-7339, E-mail: michel.rocheleau@ggl.ulaval.ca.

The University of Akron, Graduate School, Buchtel College of Arts and Sciences, Department of Geology, Program in Earth Science, Akron, OH 44325-0001. Offers MS. *Students:* 1 (woman) full-time, 1 part-time. *Degree requirements:* For master's, thesis required, foreign language not required. *Entrance requirements:* For master's, minimum GPA of 2.75. *Average time to degree:* Master's–2 years full-time, 4 years part-time. *Application deadline:* For fall admission, 3/1. Applications are processed on a rolling basis. Application fee: $25 ($50 for international students). Tuition, state resident: part-time $189 per credit. Tuition, nonresident: part-time $353 per credit. Required fees: $7.3 per credit. *Unit head:* Dr. David McConnell, Director of Graduate Studies, 330-972-8047, E-mail: mcconnell@uakron.edu.

University of Alberta, Faculty of Graduate Studies and Research, Department of Earth and Atmospheric Sciences, Edmonton, AB T6G 2E1, Canada. Offers M Sc, MA, PhD. *Degree requirements:* For master's and doctorate, thesis/dissertation, residency required. *Entrance requirements:* For master's and doctorate, TOEFL or Michigan English Language Assessment Battery. *Faculty research:* Geology, human geography, physical geography, meteorology.

The University of Arizona, Graduate College, College of Science, Department of Geosciences, Tucson, AZ 85721. Offers MS, PhD. Part-time programs available. *Students:* 70 full-time (29 women), 11 part-time (5 women); includes 5 minority (all Hispanic Americans), 14 international. 145 applicants, 26% accepted. In 1998, 6 master's, 13 doctorates awarded. *Degree requirements:* For master's, thesis or prepublication required; for doctorate, dissertation required. *Entrance requirements:* For master's and doctorate, GRE General Test, TOEFL (minimum score of 550 required). *Application deadline:* For fall admission, 2/1. Applications are processed on a rolling basis. Application fee: $45. *Financial aid:* Fellowships, research assistantships, teaching assistantships, institutionally-sponsored loans, scholarships, and tuition waivers (full) available. Financial aid application deadline: 2/15. *Faculty research:* Tectonics, geophysics, geochemistry/petrology, economic geology, Quaternary studies, stratigraphy/paleontology. *Application contact:* Graduate Program Office, 520-621-6004, E-mail: gradapps@geo.arizona.edu.

Announcement: The Department of Geosciences at the University of Arizona offers advanced study and research in the areas of tectonics (structural geology and regional tectonics), geophysics (earthquake and reflection seismology, paleomagnetism, and plate dynamics), geochemistry/petrology (isotope geochemistry, geochronology and thermodynamics, geohydrology, and chemical and isotopic studies of water), economic geology (genesis of ore deposits and regional metallogenesis), quaternary studies (geomorphology and paleoenvironmental studies), and stratigraphy/paleontology (paleoclimatology and paleobiology). Interdisciplinary approaches to research in the geosciences are encouraged. The department has a wide range of state-of-the-art laboratory and support facilities.

University of California, Irvine, Office of Research and Graduate Studies, School of Physical Sciences, Department of Earth System Science, Irvine, CA 92697. Offers MS, PhD. *Students:* 15 full-time (7 women); includes 2 minority (1 Asian American or Pacific Islander, 1 Hispanic American), 6 international. 11 applicants, 82% accepted. In 1998, 4 master's awarded. *Degree requirements:* For doctorate, dissertation required. *Entrance requirements:* For master's, GRE General Test, GRE Subject Test, minimum GPA of 3.0; for doctorate, GRE General Test, GRE Subject Test. *Application deadline:* For fall admission, 1/15 (priority date). Applications are processed on a rolling basis. Application fee: $40. Electronic applications accepted. *Financial aid:* Fellowships, research assistantships, teaching assistantships, career-related internships or fieldwork, institutionally-sponsored loans, and tuition waivers (full and partial) available. Financial aid application deadline: 3/2; financial aid applicants required to submit FAFSA. *Faculty research:* Atmospheric chemistry, climate change, isotope biogeochemistry, global environmental chemistry. *Unit head:* Ellen Druffel, Chair, 949-824-2116, Fax: 949-824-3256. *Application contact:* Kathy Vonk, Department Assistant, 949-824-3877, Fax: 949-824-3874, E-mail: kvonk@uci.edu.

University of California, Los Angeles, Graduate Division, College of Letters and Science, Department of Earth and Space Sciences, Los Angeles, CA 90095. Offers geochemistry (MS, PhD); geology (MS, PhD); geophysics and space physics (MS, PhD). *Students:* 53 full-time (20 women); includes 7 minority (1 African American, 4 Asian Americans or Pacific Islanders, 2 Hispanic Americans), 10 international. 76 applicants, 42% accepted. *Degree requirements:* For master's, comprehensive exams or thesis required; for doctorate, dissertation, oral and written qualifying exams required, foreign language not required. *Entrance requirements:* For master's, GRE General Test, minimum GPA of 3.0; for doctorate, GRE General Test, minimum undergraduate GPA of 3.0. *Application deadline:* For fall admission, 12/15. Application fee: $40. Electronic applications accepted. *Financial aid:* In 1998–99, 29 fellowships, 29 teaching assistantships were awarded.; research assistantships, Federal Work-Study, institutionally-sponsored loans, scholarships, and tuition waivers (full and partial) also available. Financial aid application deadline: 3/1. *Unit head:* Dr. T. Mark Harrison, Chair, 310-825-3917. *Application contact:* Departmental Office, 888-377-8252, E-mail: verity@ess.ucla.edu.

University of California, Riverside, Graduate Division, College of Natural and Agricultural Sciences, Department of Earth Sciences, Riverside, CA 92521-0102. Offers geography (MS, PhD); geological sciences (MS, PhD). Part-time programs available. *Faculty:* 13 full-time (1 woman), 4 part-time (1 woman). *Students:* 21 full-time (5 women), 1 part-time; includes 1 minority (Asian American or Pacific Islander), 1 international. 22 applicants, 64% accepted. In 1998, 9 master's, 4 doctorates awarded. Terminal master's awarded for partial completion of doctoral program. *Degree requirements:* For master's, thesis, thesis, final oral examination required, foreign language not required; for doctorate, one foreign language (computer language can substitute), dissertation, qualifying exams, final oral examination required. *Entrance requirements:* For master's and doctorate, GRE General Test (minimum combined score of 1100 required), TOEFL (minimum score of 550 required), minimum GPA of 3.2. *Application deadline:* For fall admission, 5/1; for winter admission, 9/1; for spring admission, 12/1. Applications are processed on a rolling basis. Application fee: $40. Electronic applications accepted. *Financial aid:* In 1998–99, 17 students received aid, including 5 fellowships with partial tuition reimbursements available (averaging $22,000 per year), research assistantships with full and partial tuition reimbursements available (averaging $12,111 per year), teaching assistantships with partial tuition reimbursements available (averaging $13,329 per year); career-related internships or fieldwork, Federal Work-Study, institutionally-sponsored loans, and tuition waivers (full and partial) also available. Financial aid application deadline: 1/15; financial aid applicants required to submit FAFSA. *Faculty research:* Physical geography, applied geophysics, geophysics, geochemistry, paleontology, sedimentology, geographic information systems. *Unit head:* Dr. Michael O. Woodburne, Chair, 909-787-5028, Fax: 909-787-4324, E-mail: michael.woodburne@ucr.edu. *Application contact:* Carole Carpenter, Graduate Program Assistant, 909-787-3435, Fax: 909-787-4324, E-mail: carole.carpenter@ucr.edu.

University of California, Santa Cruz, Graduate Division, Division of Natural Sciences, Program in Earth Sciences, Santa Cruz, CA 95064. Offers MS, PhD. *Faculty:* 17 full-time. *Students:* 54 full-time (26 women); includes 6 minority (2 Asian Americans or Pacific Islanders, 4 Hispanic Americans), 1 international. 76 applicants, 49% accepted. In 1998, 15 master's, 7 doctorates awarded. *Degree requirements:* For master's, thesis required; for doctorate, one foreign language (computer language can substitute), dissertation, qualifying exam required. *Entrance requirements:* For master's and doctorate, GRE General Test, GRE Subject Test. *Application deadline:* For fall admission, 1/15. Application fee: $40. *Financial aid:* Fellowships, research assistantships, teaching assistantships, career-related internships or fieldwork, Federal Work-Study, and institutionally-sponsored loans available. Financial aid application deadline: 1/15. *Faculty research:* Evolution of continental margins and orogenic belts, geologic processes occurring at plate boundaries, deep-sea sediment diagenesis, paleoecology, hydrogeology. *Unit head:* Thorne Lay, Chairperson, 831-459-3164. *Application contact:* Graduate Admissions, 831-459-2301.

University of Chicago, Division of the Physical Sciences, Department of the Geophysical Sciences, Chicago, IL 60637-1513. Offers atmospheric sciences (SM, PhD); earth sciences (SM, PhD); planetary and space sciences (SM, PhD). *Degree requirements:* For master's, thesis, seminar required; for doctorate, dissertation required. *Entrance requirements:* For master's and doctorate, GRE General Test, TOEFL (minimum score of 550 required). *Faculty research:* Climatology, evolutionary paleontology,petrology, geochemistry, oceanic sciences.

University of Illinois at Chicago, Graduate College, College of Liberal Arts and Sciences, Department of Earth and Environmental Sciences, Chicago, IL 60607-7128. Offers crystallography (MS, PhD); environmental geology (MS, PhD); geochemistry (MS, PhD); geology (MS, PhD); geomorphology (MS, PhD); geophysics (MS, PhD); geotechnical engineering and geosciences (PhD); hydrogeology (MS, PhD); low-temperature and organic geochemistry (MS, PhD); mineralogy (MS, PhD); paleoclimatology (MS, PhD); paleontology (MS, PhD); petrology (MS, PhD); quaternary geology (MS, PhD); sedimentology (MS, PhD); water resources (MS, PhD). *Faculty:* 9 full-time (2 women). *Students:* 8 full-time (2 women), 1 part-time, 2 international. Average age 29. 10 applicants, 40% accepted. In 1998, 2 master's awarded. *Degree requirements:* For master's and doctorate, thesis/dissertation required. *Entrance requirements:* For master's and doctorate, GRE General Test, TOEFL (minimum score of 550 required), minimum GPA of 3.75 on a 5.0 scale. *Application deadline:* For fall admission, 7/3; for spring admission, 11/8. Application fee: $40 ($50 for international students). *Financial aid:* In 1998–99, 7 students received aid; fellowships, research assistantships, teaching assistantships available. *Unit head:* A. F. Koster Van Groos, Acting Head, 312-996-3153. *Application contact:* Martin Flower, Graduate Director, 312-996-9662.

University of Illinois at Urbana–Champaign, Graduate College, College of Liberal Arts and Sciences, Department of Geology, Urbana, IL 61801. Offers earth sciences (MS, PhD); geochemistry (MS, PhD); geology (MS, PhD); geophysics (MS, PhD). *Faculty:* 14 full-time (1 woman), 4 part-time (0 women). *Students:* 20 full-time (4 women), 11 international. Terminal master's awarded for partial completion of doctoral program. *Degree requirements:* For master's and doctorate, thesis/dissertation required, foreign language not required. *Entrance requirements:* For master's and doctorate, GRE General Test, TOEFL. *Application deadline:* For fall admission, 9/15 (priority date); for spring admission, 1/15. Applications are processed on a rolling basis. Application fee: $40 ($50 for international students). Tuition, state resident: full-time $4,040. Tuition, nonresident: full-time $11,192. Full-time tuition and fees vary according to program. *Unit head:* Jay Bass, Head, 217-333-3540. *Application contact:* Barbara Elmore, Graduate Admissions Secretary, 217-333-3541, Fax: 217-244-4996.

University of Maine, Graduate School, College of Natural Sciences, Forestry, and Agriculture, Department of Geological Sciences, Orono, ME 04469. Offers MS, PhD. Part-time programs available. *Faculty:* 12 full-time. *Students:* 17 (5 women). 24 applicants, 54% accepted. In 1998, 2 master's, 2 doctorates awarded. *Degree requirements:* For master's, thesis required, foreign language not required; for doctorate, one foreign language, computer language, dissertation required. *Entrance requirements:* For master's, GRE General Test, GRE Subject Test, TOEFL (minimum score of 550 required); for doctorate, GRE General Test, TOEFL (minimum score of 550 required). *Application deadline:* For fall admission, 2/1 (priority date); for spring admission, 10/15. Applications are processed on a rolling basis. Application fee: $50. *Financial aid:* In 1998–99, 4 research assistantships with tuition reimbursements (averaging $10,500 per year), 5 teaching assistantships with tuition reimbursements (averaging $7,900 per year) were awarded.; Federal Work-Study, institutionally-sponsored loans, and tuition waivers (full and partial) also available. Financial aid application deadline: 3/1. *Faculty research:* Appalachian bedrock geology, Quaternary studies, marine geology. *Unit head:* Dr. Stephen Norton, Chair, 207-581-2156, Fax: 207-581-2202. *Application contact:* Scott G. Delcourt, Director of the Graduate School, 207-581-3218, Fax: 207-581-3232, E-mail: graduate@maine.edu.

University of Massachusetts Amherst, Graduate School, College of Natural Sciences and Mathematics, Department of Geosciences, Program in Geosciences, Amherst, MA 01003. Offers PhD. Postbaccalaureate distance learning degree programs offered. *Students:* 3 full-time (1 woman), 9 part-time (2 women), 6 international. Average age 33. 6 applicants, 17% accepted. *Degree requirements:* For doctorate, one foreign language, dissertation required. *Entrance requirements:* For doctorate, GRE General Test. *Application deadline:* For fall admission, 2/1; for spring admission, 10/1. Applications are processed on a rolling basis. Application fee: $40. Tuition, state resident: full-time $2,640; part-time $165 per credit. Tuition, nonresident: full-time $9,756; part-time $407 per credit. Required fees: $1,221 per term. One-time fee: $110. Full-time tuition and fees vary according to course load, campus/location and reciprocity agreements. *Financial aid:* Fellowships with full tuition reimbursements, research assistantships with full tuition reimbursements, teaching assistantships with full tuition reimbursements, career-related internships or fieldwork, Federal Work-Study, grants, scholarships, traineeships, and unspecified assistantships available. Aid available to part-time students. Financial aid application deadline: 2/1. *Unit head:* Dr. Raymond Bradley, Head, Department of Geosciences, 413-545-5932, Fax: 413-545-1200, E-mail: rbradley@geo.umass.edu.

University of Michigan, Horace H. Rackham School of Graduate Studies, College of Engineering, Department of Atmospheric, Oceanic, and Space Sciences, Ann Arbor, MI 48109. Offers atmospheric and space sciences (M Eng, MS, PhD); oceanography: physical (MS, PhD); remote sensing and geoinformation (M Eng); space and planetary physics (PhD); space systems (M Eng). Part-time programs available. *Faculty:* 21 full-time (2 women), 9 part-time (0 women). *Students:* 61 full-time (26 women), 1 part-time; includes 2 minority (both African Americans), 19 international. Terminal master's awarded for partial completion of doctoral program. *Degree requirements:* For master's, thesis required (for some programs); for doctorate, dissertation, oral defense of dissertation, preliminary exams required. *Entrance requirements:* For master's and doctorate, GRE General Test (combined average 2000 on three sections), TOEFL (minimum score of 600 required). *Application deadline:* For fall admission, 1/15 (priority date). Applications are processed on a rolling basis. Application fee: $60. *Unit head:* Lennard Fisk, Chair, 734-764-3335, Fax: 734-764-4585, E-mail: lafisk@umich.edu. *Application contact:* Susan Schreiber, Academic Services Assistant, 734-764-3336, Fax: 734-764-4585, E-mail: aoss.um@umich.edu.

University of Michigan, Horace H. Rackham School of Graduate Studies, College of Engineering, Program in Geoscience and Remote Sensing, Ann Arbor, MI 48109. Offers atmospheric, oceanic and space sciences (MS, PhD); electrical engineering (MS, PhD).

University of Missouri–Kansas City, College of Arts and Sciences, Department of Geosciences, Kansas City, MO 64110-2499. Offers geosciences (PhD); urban environmental geology (MS). PhD offered through the School of Graduate Studies. Part-time programs available. *Faculty:* 7 full-time (1 woman). *Students:* 1 (woman) full-time, 8 part-time (3 women), 3 international. Average age 36. In 1998, 2 master's awarded. *Degree requirements:* For master's, thesis required, foreign language not required. *Entrance requirements:* For master's, GRE General Test (minimum combined score of 1400 on three sections required), TOEFL, minimum GPA of 3.0. *Application deadline:* For fall admission, 3/15. Application fee: $25. *Financial aid:* In 1998–99, 2 research assistantships, 4 teaching assistantships were awarded.; Federal Work-Study, institutionally-sponsored loans, and tuition waivers (full and partial) also available. Aid available to part-time students. *Faculty research:* Quaternary environments, waste management, black shale geochemistry, geological mapping, history of cartography, neotectonics, fluvial geomorphology. Total annual research expenditures: $70,000. *Unit head:* Dr. Raymond M. Coveney, Chair, 816-235-1334, Fax: 816-235-5535, E-mail: rcoveney@cctr.umkc.edu. *Application contact:* Dr. Syed E. Hasan, Associate Professor, 816-235-1334, Fax: 816-235-5535, E-mail: shasan@cctr.umkc.edu.

Announcement: University of Missouri–Kansas City, Department of Geosciences, offers an urban environmental geology MS program and participates in an interdisciplinary PhD. Entrance requirements: GRE scores, minimum 3.0 GPA, and TOEFL scores. Application deadline: March 15. Application fee: $25. Fees: $181.70 per credit hour for state residents, $508.20 per credit hour for nonresidents. Contact R. M. Coveney, Chair, 816-235-1334.

University of Nebraska–Lincoln, Graduate College, College of Arts and Sciences, Department of Geosciences, Lincoln, NE 68588. Offers MS, PhD. *Faculty:* 12 full-time (1 woman), 1 part-time (0 women). *Students:* 27 full-time (9 women), 15 part-time (4 women); includes 2 minority (1 Asian American or Pacific Islander, 1 Hispanic American), 12 international. Average age 32. 24 applicants, 58% accepted. In 1998, 3 master's, 4 doctorates awarded. *Degree requirements:* For master's, departmental qualifying exam required, thesis optional; for doctorate, dissertation, comprehensive and departmental qualifying exams required. *Entrance requirements:* For master's and doctorate, GRE General Test, TOEFL (minimum score of 550 required). *Average time to degree:* Doctorate–6 years full-time. *Application deadline:* For fall admission, 3/1 (priority date). Applications are processed on a rolling basis. Application fee: $35. Electronic applications accepted. *Financial aid:* In 1998–99, 24 fellowships, 11 research assistantships, 20 teaching assistantships were awarded.; Federal Work-Study also available. Aid available to part-time students. Financial aid application deadline: 2/15. *Faculty research:* Hydrogeology, sedimentology, environmental geology, vertebrate paleontology. *Unit head:* Dr. Norman Smith, Chair, 402-472-2663, Fax: 402-472-4917.

University of Nevada, Las Vegas, Graduate College, College of Science, Department of Geoscience, Program in Geoscience, Las Vegas, NV 89154-9900. Offers MS, PhD. Part-time programs available. *Students:* 18 full-time (7 women), 19 part-time (8 women); includes 2 minority (both African Americans), 3 international. 17 applicants, 47% accepted. In 1998, 3 degrees awarded. *Degree requirements:* For master's, thesis, comprehensive exam required, foreign language not required. *Entrance requirements:* For master's, GRE Subject Test, minimum GPA of 2.75. *Application deadline:* Applications are processed on a rolling basis. Application fee: $40 ($95 for international students). *Financial aid:* In 1998–99, 4 research assistantships with partial tuition reimbursements (averaging $9,075 per year), 12 teaching assistantships with partial tuition reimbursements (averaging $8,608 per year) were awarded. Financial aid application deadline: 3/1. *Unit head:* Walter Trzcienski, Graduate Chairman, 514-343-5977. *Application contact:* Graduate College Admissions Evaluator, 702-895-3320.

University of New Hampshire, Graduate School, College of Engineering and Physical Sciences, Department of Earth Sciences, Durham, NH 03824. Offers earth sciences (MS, PhD), including geochemical (MS), geology, hydrology (PhD), oceanography; hydrology (MS). *Faculty:* 25 full-time. *Students:* 32 full-time (7 women), 36 part-time (15 women); includes 1 minority (Asian American or Pacific Islander), 10 international. Average age 31. 58 applicants, 69% accepted. In 1998, 10 master's, 4 doctorates awarded. *Degree requirements:* For master's, thesis required, foreign language not required; for doctorate, dissertation required. *Entrance requirements:* For master's and doctorate, GRE General Test. *Application deadline:* For fall admission, 4/1 (priority date). Applications are processed on a rolling basis. Application fee: $50. Tuition, area resident: Full-time $5,750; part-time $319 per credit. Tuition, state resident: full-time $8,625. Tuition, nonresident: full-time $14,640; part-time $598 per credit. Required fees: $224 per semester. Tuition and fees vary according to course load, degree level and program. *Financial aid:* In 1998–99, 4 fellowships, 15 research assistantships, 11 teaching assistantships were awarded.; career-related internships or fieldwork, Federal Work-Study, scholarships, and tuition waivers (full and partial) also available. Aid available to part-time students. Financial aid application deadline: 2/15. *Unit head:* Wallace Bothner, Chairperson, 603-862-1718. *Application contact:* Dr. Francis Birch, Graduate Coordinator, 603-862-3142.

University of New Mexico, Graduate School, College of Arts and Sciences, Department of Earth and Planetary Sciences, Albuquerque, NM 87131-2039. Offers MS, PhD. *Faculty:* 18 full-time (4 women), 5 part-time (2 women). *Students:* 26 full-time (9 women), 20 part-time (9 women); includes 1 minority (Native American), 1 international. Average age 31. 77 applicants, 23% accepted. In 1998, 4 master's, 2 doctorates awarded. Terminal master's awarded for partial completion of doctoral program. *Degree requirements:* For master's and doctorate, computer language, thesis/dissertation required, foreign language not required. *Entrance requirements:* For master's, GRE General Test (average 70th percentile); for doctorate, GRE General Test (average 70th percentile), GRE Subject Test (average 70th percentile). *Application deadline:* For fall admission, 1/31. Application fee: $25. *Financial aid:* In 1998–99, 8 fellowships (averaging $1,179 per year), 22 research assistantships with tuition reimbursements (averaging $3,301 per year), 14 teaching assistantships with tuition reimbursements (averaging $7,319 per year) were awarded.; career-related internships or fieldwork, Federal Work-Study, and institutionally-sponsored loans also available. Aid available to part-time students. Financial aid application deadline: 1/31. *Faculty research:* Geochemistry, meteoritics, tectonics, Quaternary studies, Precambrian geology. Total annual research expenditures: $1.3 million. *Unit head:* Dr. Les P. McFadden, Chair, 505-277-4204, Fax: 505-277-8843, E-mail: lmcfadnm@unm.edu.

University of North Carolina at Charlotte, Graduate School, College of Arts and Sciences, Department of Geography and Earth Sciences, Charlotte, NC 28223-0001. Offers MA. Part-time and evening/weekend programs available. *Faculty:* 21 full-time (2 women). *Students:* 25 full-time (8 women), 18 part-time (7 women); includes 2 minority (both African Americans), 2 international. Average age 29. 15 applicants, 93% accepted. In 1998, 15 degrees awarded. *Degree requirements:* For master's, written comprehensive exam, project required, thesis not required. *Entrance requirements:* For master's, GRE General Test or MAT, Doppelt Math Reasoning Test, minimum GPA of 3.0 in undergraduate major, 2.75 overall. *Application deadline:* For fall admission, 7/15; for spring admission, 11/15. Applications are processed on a rolling basis. Application fee: $35. Electronic applications accepted. *Financial aid:* In 1998–99, 11 research assistantships, 13 teaching assistantships were awarded.; career-related internships or fieldwork and Federal Work-Study also available. Financial aid application deadline: 4/1. *Faculty research:* Petrology, hydrology, transportation. *Unit head:* Dr. Wayne A. Walcott, Chair, 704-547-2293, Fax: 704-547-3182, E-mail: wawalcot@email.uncc.edu. *Application contact:* Kathy Barringer, Assistant Director of Graduate Admissions, 704-547-3366, Fax: 704-547-3279, E-mail: gradadm@email.uncc.edu.

University of Northern Colorado, Graduate School, College of Arts and Sciences, Department of Earth Sciences, Greeley, CO 80639. Offers MA. *Faculty:* 5 full-time (0 women). *Students:* 6 full-time (3 women), 1 (woman) part-time. Average age 32. 3 applicants, 100% accepted. In 1998, 3 degrees awarded. *Degree requirements:* For master's, comprehensive exams required, thesis not required. *Application deadline:* Applications are processed on a rolling basis. Application fee: $35. *Financial aid:* In 1998–99, 7 students received aid, including 2 fellowships, 1 research assistantship, 5 teaching assistantships; unspecified assistantships also available. Financial aid application deadline: 3/1. *Unit head:* Dr. William D. Nesse, Chairperson, 970-351-2647.

University of Notre Dame, Graduate School, College of Engineering, Department of Civil Engineering and Geological Sciences, Notre Dame, IN 46556. Offers bioengineering (MS); civil engineering (MS); civil engineering and geological sciences (PhD); environmental engineering (MS); geological sciences (MS). *Faculty:* 13 full-time (1 woman). *Students:* 35 full-time (10 women), 4 part-time; includes 4 minority (2 African Americans, 1 Asian American or Pacific Islander, 1 Hispanic American), 11 international. 86 applicants, 20% accepted. In 1998, 3 master's awarded (100% found work related to degree); 2 doctorates awarded (100% entered university research/teaching). Terminal master's awarded for partial completion of doctoral program. *Degree requirements:* For master's and doctorate, thesis/dissertation required, foreign language not required. *Entrance requirements:* For master's and doctorate, GRE General Test, TOEFL (minimum score of 600 required; 250 for computer-based). *Average time to degree:* Master's–2 years full-time; doctorate–5.5 years full-time. *Application deadline:* For fall admission, 2/1 (priority date); for spring admission, 10/15. Applications are processed on a rolling basis. Application fee: $40. *Financial aid:* In 1998–99, 35 students received aid, including 14 fellowships with full tuition reimbursements available (averaging $16,000 per year), 4 research assistantships with full tuition reimbursements available (averaging $11,500 per year), 17 teaching assistantships with full tuition reimbursements available (averaging $11,500 per year); tuition waivers (full) also available. Financial aid application deadline: 2/1. *Faculty research:* Structural analysis, finite-element methods, environmental modeling, biological-waste treatment, petrology, environmental geology. Total annual research expenditures: $2.1 million. *Unit head:* Dr. Billie F. Spencer, Director of Graduate Studies, 219-631-5381, Fax: 219-631-9236, E-mail: cegeos@nd.edu. *Application contact:* Dr. Terrence J. Akai, Director of Graduate Admissions, 219-631-7706, Fax: 219-631-4183, E-mail: gradad@nd.edu.

University of Ottawa, School of Graduate Studies and Research, Faculty of Science, Ottawa-Carleton Geoscience Centre, Ottawa, ON K1N 6N5, Canada. Offers earth sciences (M Sc, PhD). *Faculty:* 39 full-time, 8 part-time. *Students:* 60 full-time (16 women), 14 part-time (6 women), 17 international. Average age 33. In 1998, 19 master's, 10 doctorates awarded. *Degree requirements:* For master's and doctorate, thesis/dissertation required, foreign language not required. *Entrance requirements:* For master's, honors degree or equivalent, minimum B average; for doctorate, minimum B+ average. *Application deadline:* For fall admission, 3/1. Application fee: $35. *Financial aid:* Fellowships, research assistantships, teaching assistantships, career-related internships or fieldwork and Federal Work-Study available. Financial aid application deadline: 9/15. *Faculty research:* Precambrian geology, Arctic studies, geomathematics–computer application, environmental earth science. *Unit head:* Keith Benn, Director, 613-562-5800 Ext. 6858, Fax: 613-562-5192. *Application contact:* Hélène De Gouffe, Academic Adviser, 613-562-5800 Ext. 6870, Fax: 613-562-5192, E-mail: hdegout@science.uottawa.ca.

University of South Carolina, Graduate School, College of Science and Mathematics, Department of Geological Sciences, Columbia, SC 29208. Offers IMA, MAT, MS, PhD. IMA and MAT offered in cooperation with the College of Education. *Faculty:* 24 full-time (0 women), 3 part-time (1 woman). *Students:* 42 full-time (15 women), 11 part-time (4 women); includes 3 minority (all Hispanic Americans), 16 international. Average age 31. 78 applicants, 27% accepted. In 1998, 13 master's, 8 doctorates awarded. Terminal master's awarded for partial completion of doctoral program. *Degree requirements:* For master's, thesis required, foreign language not required; for doctorate, dissertation, published paper required, foreign language not required. *Entrance requirements:* For master's and doctorate, GRE General Test, TOEFL. *Application deadline:* For fall admission, 7/1 (priority date); for spring admission, 11/15. Applications are processed on a rolling basis. Application fee: $35. Electronic applications accepted. Tuition, state resident: full-time $4,014; part-time $202 per credit hour. Tuition, nonresident: full-time $8,528; part-time $428 per credit hour. Required fees: $100; $4 per credit hour. Tuition and fees vary according to program. *Financial aid:* In 1998–99, 1 fellowship, 29 research assistantships with partial tuition reimbursements (averaging $15,000 per year), 25 teaching assistantships with partial tuition reimbursements (averaging $15,000 per year) were awarded.; career-related internships or fieldwork and Federal Work-Study also available. Financial aid application deadline: 3/1. *Faculty research:* Sedimentary geology, geochemistry, tectonics, marine geology, petrology. *Unit head:* Dr. Robert Thunell, Chair, 803-777-4535, Fax: 803-777-6610. *Application contact:* Dr. James Kellogg, Director of Graduate Studies, 803-777-3959, Fax: 803-777-6610, E-mail: kellogg@sc.edu.

See in-depth description on page 315.

University of Southern California, Graduate School, College of Letters, Arts and Sciences, Department of Earth Sciences, Los Angeles, CA 90089. Offers MS, PhD. *Faculty:* 30 full-time (4 women). *Students:* 39 full-time (12 women), 1 part-time; includes 2 minority (1 Asian American or Pacific Islander, 1 Hispanic American), 13 international. Average age 30. 47 applicants, 47% accepted. In 1998, 5 master's, 4 doctorates awarded. *Degree requirements:* For master's and doctorate, thesis/dissertation required. *Entrance requirements:* For master's and doctorate, GRE General Test. *Application deadline:* For fall admission, 7/1 (priority date); for spring admission, 12/1. Application fee: $55. Tuition: Full-time $22,198; part-time $748 per unit. Required fees: $406. Tuition and fees vary according to program. *Financial aid:* In 1998–99, 19 fellowships, 12 research assistantships, 24 teaching assistantships were awarded.; Federal Work-Study, institutionally-sponsored loans, and scholarships also available. Aid available to part-time students. Financial aid application deadline: 2/15; financial aid applicants required to submit FAFSA. *Unit head:* Charlie Sammis, Chair, 213-740-6106.

The University of Texas at Austin, Graduate School, College of Natural Sciences, Department of Geological Sciences, Austin, TX 78712-1111. Offers MA, MS, PhD. Part-time programs available. *Faculty:* 38 full-time (3 women), 2 part-time (1 woman). *Students:* 141 full-time (42 women); includes 6 minority (1 African American, 2 Asian Americans or Pacific

Geosciences–Hydrology

The University of Texas at Austin (continued)
Islanders, 2 Hispanic Americans, 1 Native American), 44 international. 179 applicants, 33% accepted. In 1998, 23 master's, 16 doctorates awarded. *Degree requirements:* For master's, report (MA), thesis (MS) required; for doctorate, dissertation required, foreign language not required. *Entrance requirements:* For master's and doctorate, GRE General Test (minimum combined score of 1100 preferred). *Average time to degree:* Master's–3 years full-time; doctorate–7 years full-time. *Application deadline:* For fall admission, 2/1 (priority date); for spring admission, 10/1. Application fee: $50 ($75 for international students). Electronic applications accepted. *Financial aid:* In 1998–99, 125 students received aid, including 6 fellowships with partial tuition reimbursements available (averaging $18,000 per year), research assistantships with partial tuition reimbursements available (averaging $13,500 per year), 38 teaching assistantships with partial tuition reimbursements available (averaging $13,500 per year); career-related internships or fieldwork, Federal Work-Study, and institutionally-sponsored loans also available. Financial aid application deadline: 2/1. *Faculty research:* Sedimentary geology, geophysics, hydrogeology, structure/tectonics, vertebrate paleontology. Total annual research expenditures: $205,000. *Unit head:* Mark Cloos, Chairman, 512-471-5172, Fax: 512-471-9425, E-mail: cloos118@maestro.geo.utexas.edu. *Application contact:* Earle F. McBride, Graduate Adviser, 512-471-6098, Fax: 512-471-9425.

The University of Texas at Dallas, School of Natural Sciences and Mathematics, Program in Geosciences, Richardson, TX 75083-0688. Offers MS, PhD. Part-time and evening/weekend programs available. *Students:* 34 full-time (6 women), 20 part-time (10 women); includes 2 minority (1 Asian American or Pacific Islander, 1 Hispanic American), 24 international. Average age 35. In 1998, 6 master's, 5 doctorates awarded. *Degree requirements:* For master's, computer language, minimum GPA of 3.0 required, thesis optional, foreign language not required; for doctorate, computer language, dissertation, minimum GPA of 3.0 required, foreign language not required. *Entrance requirements:* For master's and doctorate, GRE General Test (minimum combined score of 1000 required), TOEFL (minimum score of 550 required), minimum GPA of 3.0 in upper-level course work in field. *Application deadline:* For fall admission, 7/15; for spring admission, 11/15. Applications are processed on a rolling basis. Application fee: $25 ($75 for international students). *Financial aid:* Fellowships, research assistantships, teaching assistantships, career-related internships or fieldwork, Federal Work-Study, grants, institutionally-sponsored loans, and scholarships available. Aid available to part-time students. Financial aid application deadline: 4/30; financial aid applicants required to submit FAFSA. *Unit head:* Dr. Robert Stern, Head, 972-883-2401, Fax: 972-883-2537. *Application contact:* Dr. Carlos Aiken, Graduate Adviser, 972-883-2450, E-mail: aiken@utdallas.edu.

University of Tulsa, Graduate School, College of Engineering and Applied Sciences, Department of Geosciences, Tulsa, OK 74104-3189. Offers MS, PhD. Part-time programs available. *Faculty:* 6 full-time (0 women). *Students:* 14 full-time (4 women), 5 part-time (2 women); includes 1 minority (Native American), 9 international. Average age 33. 13 applicants, 85% accepted. In 1998, 4 master's, 3 doctorates awarded. *Degree requirements:* For master's, computer language required, thesis optional, foreign language not required; for doctorate, computer language, dissertation required, foreign language not required. *Entrance requirements:* For master's and doctorate, GRE General Test, TOEFL (minimum score of 550 required). *Application deadline:* Applications are processed on a rolling basis. Application fee: $30. Electronic applications accepted. Tuition: Full-time $8,640; part-time $480 per hour. Required fees: $3 per hour. One-time fee: $200 full-time. Tuition and fees vary according to program. *Financial aid:* In 1998–99, 17 students received aid, including 1 fellowship (averaging $3,500 per year), 7 research assistantships (averaging $8,614 per year), 9 teaching assistantships (averaging $7,042 per year); career-related internships or fieldwork and tuition waivers (partial) also available. Aid available to part-time students. Financial aid application deadline: 2/1; financial aid applicants required to submit FAFSA. *Faculty research:* Petroleum geology, carbonate and marine geology, exploration geophysics, structural geology. *Unit head:* Dr. Colin G. Barker, Chairperson, 918-631-3014. *Application contact:* Dr. Peter J. Michael, Adviser, 918-631-3017, Fax: 918-631-2091.

University of Victoria, Faculty of Graduate Studies, Faculty of Science, School of Earth and Ocean Sciences, Victoria, BC V8W 2Y2, Canada. Offers geochemistry (M Sc, PhD); geophysics (M Sc, PhD); marine geology and geophysics (M Sc, PhD); ocean acoustics (M Sc, PhD); oceanography (M Sc, PhD); paleobiology (M Sc, PhD); paleoceanography (M Sc, PhD); sedimentology (M Sc, PhD); stratigraphy (M Sc, PhD). Part-time programs available. *Faculty:* 15 full-time, 41 part-time. *Students:* 39 full-time (0 women), 1 part-time. Average age 27. 137 applicants, 16% accepted. In 1998, 2 master's, 1 doctorate awarded. *Degree requirements:* For master's and doctorate, thesis/dissertation required. *Average time to degree:* Master's–3.11 years full-time; doctorate–4.5 years full-time. *Application deadline:* For fall admission, 2/15. Applications are processed on a rolling basis. Application fee: $50. Electronic applications accepted. *Financial aid:* In 1998–99, 16 fellowships, 22 research assistantships, 25 teaching assistantships were awarded.; career-related internships or fieldwork, institutionally-sponsored loans, and awards also available. Financial aid application deadline: 2/15. *Faculty research:* Climate modelling, geology. *Unit head:* Dr. C. R. Barnes, Director, 250-721-6120, Fax: 250-721-6200, E-mail: crbarnes@uvic.ca. *Application contact:* Dr. Dante Canil, Graduate Adviser, 250-721-6120, Fax: 250-721-6200, E-mail: dcanil@uvic.ca.

University of Waterloo, Graduate Studies, Faculty of Science, Department of Earth Sciences, Waterloo, ON N2L 3G1, Canada. Offers M Sc, PhD. Part-time programs available. *Faculty:* 24 full-time (4 women), 23 part-time (3 women). *Students:* 79 full-time (29 women), 15 part-time (3 women). 40 applicants, 30% accepted. In 1998, 22 master's, 4 doctorates awarded. *Degree requirements:* For master's; for doctorate, dissertation required. *Entrance requirements:* For master's, TOEFL (minimum score of 570 required), honors degree, minimum B average; for doctorate, TOEFL (minimum score of 570 required), master's degree. *Application deadline:* For fall admission, 8/1 (priority date). Applications are processed on a rolling basis. Application fee: $50. *Expenses:* Tuition and fees charges are reported in Canadian dollars. Tuition, state resident: full-time $3,168 Canadian dollars; part-time $792 Canadian dollars per term. Tuition, nonresident: full-time $8,000 Canadian dollars; part-time $2,000 Canadian dollars. Required fees: $45 Canadian dollars per term. Tuition and fees vary according to program. *Financial aid:* In 1998–99, research assistantships (averaging $5,500 per year), teaching assistantships (averaging $3,900 per year) were awarded.; career-related internships or fieldwork and institutionally-sponsored loans also available. *Faculty research:* Environmental geology, soil physics. *Unit head:* Dr. E. R. Sudicky, Chair, 519-888-4567 Ext. 3231. *Application contact:* S. Fisher, Graduate Secretary, 519-888-4567 Ext. 5836, Fax: 519-746-7484, E-mail: sfisher@sciborg.uwaterloo.ca.

Announcement: Department offers MSc and PhD in most areas of earth science. Special strength in hydrogeology, geological engineering, geophysics, hydrogeochemistry, isotope hydrology, isotope geochemistry, waste disposal, mine tailings, groundwater pollution, mathematical modeling, rock and soil mechanics, sedimentation, Quaternary and Paleozoic geology, paleontology and palynology, Precambrian geology, and mineral deposits. Excellent facilities; financial support available. Department houses the Institute for Groundwater Research and the Quaternary Sciences Institute.

The University of Western Ontario, Faculty of Graduate Studies, Physical Sciences Division, Department of Earth Sciences, London, ON N6A 5B8, Canada. Offers M Sc, PhD.

Washington University in St. Louis, Graduate School of Arts and Sciences, Department of Earth and Planetary Sciences, St. Louis, MO 63130-4899. Offers earth and planetary sciences (MA); geochemistry (PhD); geology (MA, PhD); geophysics (PhD); planetary sciences (PhD). *Students:* 26 full-time (11 women); includes 2 minority (1 Asian American or Pacific Islander, 1 Native American), 4 international. 41 applicants, 32% accepted. In 1998, 4 master's, 8 doctorates awarded. Terminal master's awarded for partial completion of doctoral program. *Degree requirements:* For master's and doctorate, thesis/dissertation required. *Entrance requirements:* For master's and doctorate, GRE General Test. *Application deadline:* For fall admission, 1/15 (priority date). Applications are processed on a rolling basis. Application fee: $35. *Financial aid:* Fellowships, research assistantships, teaching assistantships, Federal Work-Study, institutionally-sponsored loans, and tuition waivers (full and partial) available. Financial aid application deadline: 1/15. *Unit head:* Dr. Raymond E. Arvidson, Chairman, 314-935-5610.

Wesleyan University, Graduate Programs, Department of Earth Sciences, Middletown, CT 06459-0260. Offers MA. *Degree requirements:* For master's, thesis required. *Entrance requirements:* For master's, GRE General Test, GRE Subject Test. *Faculty research:* Tectonics, volcanology, stratigraphy, coastal processes, geochemistry.

Western Connecticut State University, Division of Graduate Studies, School of Arts and Sciences, Department of Physics, Astronomy and Meteorology, Danbury, CT 06810-6885. Offers earth and planetary sciences (MA). Part-time and evening/weekend programs available. *Degree requirements:* For master's, thesis required, foreign language not required. *Entrance requirements:* For master's, minimum GPA of 2.5. *Application deadline:* For fall admission, 8/1 (priority date). Applications are processed on a rolling basis. Application fee: $40. *Financial aid:* Fellowships, career-related internships or fieldwork and Federal Work-Study available. Aid available to part-time students. Financial aid application deadline: 5/1; financial aid applicants required to submit FAFSA. *Unit head:* Dr. Alice Chance, Chair, 203-837-8667. *Application contact:* Chris Shankle, Associate Director of Graduate Admissions, 203-837-8244, Fax: 203-837-8338, E-mail: shanklec@wcsu.edu.

Western Michigan University, Graduate College, College of Arts and Sciences, Department of Geology, Program in Earth Science, Kalamazoo, MI 49008. Offers MS. 3 applicants, 67% accepted. In 1998, 5 degrees awarded. *Degree requirements:* For master's, oral exam required. *Entrance requirements:* For master's, GRE General Test. *Application deadline:* For fall admission, 2/15 (priority date). Applications are processed on a rolling basis. Application fee: $25. *Financial aid:* Fellowships, research assistantships, teaching assistantships, Federal Work-Study available. Financial aid application deadline: 2/15; financial aid applicants required to submit FAFSA. *Unit head:* Allison M. Insall, Director of Graduate Office, 860-685-2390, Fax: 860-685-2439. *Application contact:* Paula J. Boodt, Coordinator, Graduate Admissions and Recruitment, 616-387-2000, Fax: 616-387-2355, E-mail: paula.boodt@wmich.edu.

Yale University, Graduate School of Arts and Sciences, Department of Geology and Geophysics, New Haven, CT 06520. Offers geochemistry (PhD); geophysics (PhD); meteorology (PhD); mineralogy and crystallography (PhD); oceanography (PhD); paleoecology (PhD); paleontology and stratigraphy (PhD); petrology (PhD); structural geology (PhD). *Faculty:* 26. *Students:* 26 full-time (11 women), 9 international. 21 applicants, 86% accepted. In 1998, 6 degrees awarded. *Degree requirements:* For doctorate, dissertation required, foreign language not required. *Entrance requirements:* For doctorate, GRE General Test, TOEFL. *Average time to degree:* Doctorate–7.9 years full-time. *Application deadline:* For fall admission, 1/4. Application fee: $65. *Financial aid:* Fellowships, research assistantships, teaching assistantships, Federal Work-Study and institutionally-sponsored loans available. Aid available to part-time students. *Unit head:* Chair, 203-432-3174. *Application contact:* Admissions Information, 203-432-2770.

See in-depth description on page 327.

York University, Faculty of Graduate Studies, Faculty of Science, Program in Earth and Space Science, Toronto, ON M3J 1P3, Canada. Offers M Sc, PhD. Part-time and evening/weekend programs available. *Degree requirements:* For master's, computer language required, thesis optional, foreign language not required; for doctorate, variable foreign language requirement, computer language, dissertation required.

Hydrology

Auburn University, Graduate School, College of Engineering, Department of Civil Engineering, Auburn, Auburn University, AL 36849-0002. Offers construction engineering and management (MCE, MS, PhD); environmental engineering (MCE, MS, PhD); geotechnical/materials engineering (MCE, MS, PhD); hydraulics/hydrology (MCE, MS, PhD); structural engineering (MCE, MS, PhD); transportation engineering (MCE, MS, PhD). Part-time programs available. *Faculty:* 22 full-time. *Students:* 24 full-time (6 women), 34 part-time (8 women); includes 2 minority (1 African American, 1 Hispanic American), 9 international. *Degree requirements:* For master's, project (MCE), thesis (MS) required; for doctorate, dissertation, comprehensive exam required, foreign language not required. *Entrance requirements:* For master's, GRE General Test; for doctorate, GRE General Test (minimum score of 400 on each section required). *Application deadline:* For fall admission, 9/1; for spring admission, 3/1. Applications are processed on a rolling basis. Application fee: $25 ($50 for international students). Tuition, state resident: full-time $2,760; part-time $76 per credit hour. Tuition, nonresident: full-time $8,280; part-time $228 per credit hour. *Unit head:* Dr. Joseph F. Judkins, Head, 334-844-4320. *Application contact:* Dr. John F. Pritchett, Dean of the Graduate School, 334-844-4700.

California State University, Bakersfield, Graduate Studies and Research, School of Arts and Sciences, Program in Geology, Bakersfield, CA 93311-1099. Offers geology (MS); hydrology (MS). Part-time and evening/weekend programs available. *Degree requirements:* For master's, computer language, thesis required. *Entrance requirements:* For master's, GRE General Test, BS in geology.

California State University, Chico, Graduate School, College of Natural Sciences, Department of Geosciences, Chico, CA 95929-0722. Offers geosciences (MS), including earth sciences, hydrology and hydrogeology. *Faculty:* 10 full-time (2 women), 4 part-time (1 woman). *Students:* 12 full-time (3 women), 4 part-time (2 women). *Degree requirements:* For master's, thesis, competency exam required, foreign language not required. *Entrance requirements:* For master's, GRE General Test (minimum combined score of 1500 recommended). *Application deadline:* For fall admission, 4/1. Applications are processed on a rolling basis. Application fee: $55. *Unit head:* Dr. Victor Fisher, Chair, 530-898-5262. *Application contact:* Dr. Gregory Taylor, Graduate Coordinator, 530-898-6369.

California State University, Chico, Graduate School, College of Natural Sciences, Department of Geosciences, Program in Geosciences, Option in Hydrology and Hydrogeology, Chico, CA 95929-0722. Offers MS. *Degree requirements:* For master's, thesis, oral exam required, foreign language not required. *Entrance requirements:* For master's, GRE General Test (minimum combined score of 1500 recommended). *Application deadline:* For fall admission, 4/1. Applications are processed on a rolling basis. Application fee: $55.

Clemson University, Graduate School, College of Engineering and Science, School of the Environment, Department of Geological Sciences, Clemson, SC 29634. Offers hydrogeology (MS). *Students:* 16 full-time (8 women), 1 (woman) part-time. Average age 25. 6 applicants, 100% accepted. In 1998, 4 degrees awarded. *Degree requirements:* For master's, thesis optional, foreign language not required. *Entrance requirements:* For master's, GRE General Test, TOEFL, minimum GPA of 3.0 during previous 2 years. *Application deadline:* For fall admission, 6/1. Application fee: $35. Electronic applications accepted. *Financial aid:* Fellowships, research assistantships, teaching assistantships, career-related internships or fieldwork and institutionally-sponsored loans available. Aid available to part-time students. Financial aid application deadline: 6/1; financial aid applicants required to submit FAFSA. *Faculty research:* Groundwater geology, environmental geology, geochemistry, remediation, stratigraphy. Total annual research expenditures: $670,000. *Unit head:* Richard D. Warner, Chair, 864-656-3438, Fax: 864-656-1041, E-mail: wrichar@clemson.edu.

Colorado School of Mines, Graduate School, Department of Geology and Geological Engineering, Golden, CO 80401-1887. Offers engineering geology (Diploma); exploration geosciences (Diploma); geochemistry (MS, PhD); geological engineering (ME, MS, PhD, Diploma); geology (MS, PhD); hydrogeology (Diploma). Part-time programs available. *Faculty:* 27 full-time (5 women), 23 part-time (0 women). *Students:* 53 full-time (16 women), 68 part-time (19 women); includes 6 minority (3 Asian Americans or Pacific Islanders, 2 Hispanic Americans, 1 Native American), 26 international. *Degree requirements:* For master's, thesis required, foreign language not required; for doctorate, dissertation, comprehensive exam required, foreign language not required; for Diploma, foreign language and thesis not required. *Entrance requirements:* For master's, doctorate, and Diploma, GRE General Test (combined average 1660 on three sections), GRE Subject Test, minimum GPA of 3.0. *Application deadline:* Applications are processed on a rolling basis. Application fee: $40. Electronic applications accepted. *Unit head:* Dr. Roger Slatt, Head, 303-273-3800, E-mail: rslatt@mines.edu. *Application contact:* Marilyn Schwinger, Administrative Assistant, 303-273-3800, Fax: 303-273-3859, E-mail: mschwing@mines.edu.

Colorado State University, Graduate School, College of Engineering, Department of Civil Engineering, Specialization in Water Resources, Hydrologic and Environmental Sciences, Fort Collins, CO 80523-0015. Offers MS, PhD. Part-time programs available. *Faculty:* 5 full-time (1 woman). In 1998, 7 master's, 6 doctorates awarded. Terminal master's awarded for partial completion of doctoral program. *Degree requirements:* For master's, thesis or alternative required, foreign language not required; for doctorate, dissertation required, foreign language not required. *Entrance requirements:* For master's and doctorate, GRE General Test, TOEFL (minimum score of 550 required; 213 for computer-based), minimum GPA of 3.0. *Average time to degree:* Master's–2 years full-time, 5 years part-time; doctorate–4 years full-time. *Application deadline:* For fall admission, 3/1 (priority date); for spring admission, 8/1 (priority date). Applications are processed on a rolling basis. Application fee: $30. Electronic applications accepted. *Financial aid:* Fellowships, research assistantships, teaching assistantships, Federal Work-Study and institutionally-sponsored loans available. *Faculty research:* Flood prediction, stochastic hydrology, drought analysis, watershed modeling, groundwater quality and contamination, drainage, flow through porous media, conjunctive use, numerical modeling. Total annual research expenditures: $600,000. *Unit head:* James W. Warner, Leader, 970-491-8381, Fax: 970-491-7727, E-mail: warner@engr.colostate.edu. *Application contact:* Laurie Howard, Student Adviser, 970-491-5844, Fax: 970-491-7727, E-mail: lhoward@engr.colostate.edu.

Colorado State University, Graduate School, College of Natural Resources, Department of Earth Resources, Program in Geology, Fort Collins, CO 80523-0015. Offers fluvial geomorphology (MS); hydrogeology (MS); petrology/geochemistry and economic geology (MS); stratigraphy/sedimentology (MS); structure/tectonics (MS). Part-time programs available. *Faculty:* 9 full-time (3 women), 1 (woman) part-time. *Students:* 9 full-time (7 women), 3 part-time (1 woman); includes 3 minority (1 Asian American or Pacific Islander, 1 Hispanic American, 1 Native American) *Degree requirements:* For master's, thesis required, foreign language not required. *Entrance requirements:* For master's, GRE General Test (minimum score of 600 on each section required), GRE Subject Test, TOEFL (minimum score of 550 required), minimum GPA of 3.0. *Application deadline:* For fall admission, 2/1 (priority date). Applications are processed on a rolling basis. Application fee: $30. *Unit head:* Frank G. Ethridge, Head, 970-491-5662, Fax: 970-491-6307, E-mail: fredpet@cnr.colostate.edu. *Application contact:* Barbara Holtz, Staff Assistant, 970-491-5662, Fax: 970-491-6307, E-mail: barbh@cnr.colostate.edu.

Colorado State University, Graduate School, College of Natural Resources, Department of Earth Resources, Program in Watershed Science, Fort Collins, CO 80523-0015. Offers earth resources (PhD); watershed science (MS). *Faculty:* 6 full-time (2 women), 1 part-time (0 women). *Degree requirements:* For master's, thesis required, foreign language not required; for doctorate, one foreign language, dissertation required. *Entrance requirements:* For master's, GRE General Test (minimum score of 640 on verbal section, 660 on quantitative required), GRE Subject Test, TOEFL (minimum score of 550 required), minimum GPA of 3.0. *Application deadline:* For fall admission, 2/1 (priority date). Applications are processed on a rolling basis. Application fee: $30. *Financial aid:* Fellowships, research assistantships, teaching assistantships, career-related internships or fieldwork, Federal Work-Study, and institutionally-sponsored loans available. Financial aid application deadline: 2/15. *Faculty research:* Land use hydrology, water quality, watershed planning and management, snow hydrology, hillslope-wetland hydrology, geographic information systems, risk management. Total annual research expenditures: $750,000. *Unit head:* Dr. John Stednick, Head, 970-491-5662, Fax: 970-491-6307, E-mail: jds@cnr.colostate.edu. *Application contact:* Barbara Holtz, Staff Assistant, 970-491-5662, Fax: 970-491-6307, E-mail: barbh@cnr.colostate.edu.

Cornell University, Graduate School, Graduate Fields of Engineering, Field of Civil and Environmental Engineering, Ithaca, NY 14853-0001. Offers environmental engineering (M Eng, MS, PhD); environmental fluid mechanics and hydrology (M Eng, MS, PhD); environmental systems engineering (M Eng, MS, PhD); geotechnical engineering (M Eng, MS, PhD); remote sensing (M Eng, MS, PhD); structural engineering (M Eng, MS, PhD); transportation engineering (M Eng, MS, PhD); water resource systems (M Eng, MS, PhD). *Faculty:* 29 full-time. *Students:* 143 full-time (32 women); includes 16 minority (11 Asian Americans or Pacific Islanders, 5 Hispanic Americans), 76 international. Terminal master's awarded for partial completion of doctoral program. *Degree requirements:* For master's, thesis (MS) required; for doctorate, dissertation required, foreign language not required. *Entrance requirements:* For master's, TOEFL (minimum score of 600required); for doctorate, GRE General Test, TOEFL (minimum score of 600 required). *Application deadline:* For fall admission, 1/15. Application fee: $65. Electronic applications accepted. *Unit head:* Director of Graduate Studies, 607-255-7560, Fax: 607-255-9004. *Application contact:* Graduate Field Assistant, 607-255-7560, E-mail: cee_grad@cornell.edu.

Cornell University, Graduate School, Graduate Fields of Engineering, Field of Geological Sciences, Ithaca, NY 14853-0001. Offers economic geology (MS, PhD); engineering geology (MS, PhD); environmental geophysics (M Eng, MS, PhD); general geology (MS, PhD); geobiology (MS, PhD); geochemistry and isotope geology (MS, PhD); geohydrology (M Eng, MS, PhD); geomorphology (MS, PhD); geophysics (MS, PhD); geotectonics (MS, PhD); mineralogy (MS, PhD); paleontology (MS, PhD); petroleum geology (MS, PhD); petrology (MS, PhD); planetary geology (MS, PhD); Precambrian geology (MS, PhD); Quaternary geology (MS, PhD); rock mechanics (MS, PhD); sedimentology (MS, PhD); seismology (MS, PhD); stratigraphy (MS, PhD); structural geology (MS, PhD). *Faculty:* 28 full-time. *Students:* 36 full-time (12 women); includes 4 minority (1 African American, 1 Asian American or Pacific Islander, 2 Hispanic Americans), 16 international. *Degree requirements:* For master's, thesis (MS) required; for doctorate, dissertation required, foreign language not required. *Entrance requirements:* For master's and doctorate, GRE General Test, TOEFL (minimum score of 550 required). *Application deadline:* For fall admission, 1/15. Application fee: $65. Electronic applications accepted. *Unit head:* Director of Graduate Studies, 607-255-3474, Fax: 607-254-4780. *Application contact:* Graduate Field Assistant, 607-255-3474, Fax: 607-254-4780, E-mail: gradprog@geology.cornell.edu.

See in-depth description on page 273.

Idaho State University, Graduate School, College of Arts and Sciences, Department of Geology, Pocatello, ID 83209. Offers geology (MS); geophysics/hydrology (MS); natural science (MNS). MS (geophysics/hydrology) offered jointly with Boise State University. Part-time programs available. *Degree requirements:* For master's, thesis required, foreign language not required. *Entrance requirements:* For master's, GRE General Test (score in 35th percentile or higher on verbal or quantitative section required). *Faculty research:* Structural geography, stratigraphy, geochemistry, volcanography, geomorphology.

Illinois State University, Graduate School, College of Arts and Sciences, Department of Geography-Geology, Normal, IL 61790-2200. Offers geohydrology (MS). *Faculty:* 11 full-time (0 women). *Students:* 10 full-time (1 woman), 4 part-time; includes 1 minority (Asian American or Pacific Islander), 1 international. 3 applicants, 100% accepted. In 1998, 1 degree awarded. *Entrance requirements:* For master's, GRE General Test. *Application deadline:* Applications are processed on a rolling basis. Application fee: $0. Tuition, state resident: full-time $2,526; part-time $105 per credit hour. Tuition, nonresident: full-time $7,578; part-time $316 per credit hour. Required fees: $1,082; $38 per credit hour. Tuition and fees vary according to course load and program. *Financial aid:* In 1998–99, 8 teaching assistantships were awarded.; research assistantships, unspecified assistantships also available. Financial aid application deadline: 4/1. *Faculty research:* Recharge area evaluations; Devonian biological crises and causes; geological mapping of LaSalle 7.5' Quadrangle, Illinois. Total annual research expenditures: $78,925. *Unit head:* Dr. Robert Corbett, Chairman, 309-438-7649.

Montana Tech of The University of Montana, Graduate School, Geoscience Program, Butte, MT 59701-8997. Offers geochemistry (MS); geological engineering (MS); geology (MS); geophysical engineering (MS); hydrogeological engineering (MS); hydrogeology (MS); mineral economics (MS). Part-time programs available. *Faculty:* 17 full-time (2 women). *Students:* 15 full-time (6 women), 7 part-time (1 woman); includes 1 minority (Native American) *Degree requirements:* For master's, thesis required (for some programs), foreign language not required. *Entrance requirements:* For master's, GRE General Test, TOEFL (minimum score of 525 required), minimum B average. *Application deadline:* For fall admission, 4/1 (priority date); for spring admission, 10/1 (priority date). Applications are processed on a rolling basis. Application fee: $30. Tuition, state resident: full-time $3,211; part-time $162 per credit hour. Tuition, nonresident: full-time $9,883; part-time $440 per credit hour. International tuition: $15,500 full-time. *Unit head:* Cindy Dunstan, Administrative Assistant, 406-496-4128, Fax: 406-496-4334, E-mail: cdunstan@mtech.edu. *Application contact:* Cindy Dunstan, Administrative Assistant, 406-496-4128, Fax: 406-496-4334, E-mail: cdunstan@mtech.edu.

New Mexico Institute of Mining and Technology, Graduate Studies, Department of Earth and Environmental Science, Program in Hydrology, Socorro, NM 87801. Offers MS, PhD. *Faculty:* 5 full-time (0 women). *Students:* 32 full-time (11 women), 2 international. Average age 30. 40 applicants, 78% accepted. In 1998, 4 master's, 3 doctorates awarded. *Degree requirements:* For master's, thesis optional, foreign language not required; for doctorate, dissertation required, foreign language not required. *Entrance requirements:* For master's, GRE General Test, TOEFL (minimum score of 540 required); for doctorate, GRE General Test, GRE Subject Test, TOEFL (minimum score of 540 required). *Average time to degree:* Master's–4 years full-time; doctorate–7 years full-time. *Application deadline:* For fall admission, 3/1 (priority date); for spring admission, 6/1. Applications are processed on a rolling basis. Application fee: $16. *Financial aid:* In 1998–99, 13 research assistantships (averaging $9,670 per year), 4 teaching assistantships (averaging $9,670 per year) were awarded.; fellowships, Federal Work-Study and institutionally-sponsored loans also available. Financial aid application deadline: 3/1; financial aid applicants required to submit CSS PROFILE or FAFSA. *Faculty research:* Surface and subsurface hydrology, numerical simulation, stochastic hydrology, water quality, modeling. *Unit head:* Dr. Robert Bowman, Coordinator, 505-835-5308, Fax: 505-835-6436, E-mail: geos@mnt.edu. *Application contact:* Dr. David B. Johnson, Dean of Graduate Studies, 505-835-5513, Fax: 505-835-5476, E-mail: graduate@nmt.edu.

Rensselaer Polytechnic Institute, Graduate School, School of Science, Department of Earth and Environmental Sciences, Program in Hydrogeology, Troy, NY 12180-3590. Offers MS. Part-time programs available. *Faculty:* 7 full-time (0 women), 1 part-time (0 women). *Students:* 1 (woman) full-time, 1 (woman) part-time. 2 applicants, 50% accepted. In 1998, 3 degrees awarded. *Degree requirements:* For master's, thesis or alternative required. *Entrance requirements:* For master's, GRE General Test, TOEFL (minimum score of 550 required). *Average time to degree:* Master's–1 year full-time. *Application deadline:* For fall admission, 2/1 (priority date). Applications are processed on a rolling basis. Application fee: $35. *Financial aid:* In 1998–99, 1 teaching assistantship with partial tuition reimbursement (averaging $10,500 per year) was awarded.; fellowships, research assistantships, career-related internships or fieldwork also available. Financial aid application deadline: 2/1. *Faculty research:* Groundwater modeling, contaminant geochemistry. *Unit head:* R. E. Wild, Chairman, Graduate Admissions, 765-494-5200, E-mail: wild@purdue.edu. *Application contact:* Dr. Steven Roecker, Associate Professor, 518-276-6474, Fax: 518-276-6680, E-mail: ees@rpi.edu.

Syracuse University, Graduate School, College of Arts and Sciences, Department of Earth Sciences, Program in Hydrogeology, Syracuse, NY 13244-0003. Offers MS. *Faculty:* 7. *Students:* 1 full-time (0 women). Average age 28. 1 applicants, 100% accepted. *Degree requirements:* For master's, research tool required. *Entrance requirements:* For master's, GRE General Test, GRE Subject Test. *Application deadline:* Applications are processed on a rolling basis. Application fee: $40. Tuition: Full-time $13,992; part-time $583 per credit hour. *Financial aid:* Fellowships, research assistantships, teaching assistantships, Federal Work-Study and tuition waivers (partial) available. Financial aid application deadline: 3/1. *Unit head:* Charles Driscoll, Graduate Director, 315-443-3434.

Syracuse University, Graduate School, L. C. Smith College of Engineering and Computer Science, Department of Civil and Environmental Engineering, Syracuse, NY 13244-0003. Offers civil engineering (MS, PhD); environmental engineering (MS); hydrogeology (MS). *Faculty:* 19. *Students:* 22 full-time (7 women), 15 part-time (4 women), 17 international. *Degree requirements:* For doctorate, computer language, dissertation required, foreign language not required, foreign language not required. *Entrance requirements:* For master's and doctorate, GRE General Test, GRE Subject Test. *Application deadline:* Applications are processed on a rolling basis. Application fee: $40. Tuition: Full-time $13,992; part-time $583 per credit hour. *Unit head:* Dr. Shobha Bhatia, Chair, 315-443-2311.

Texas A&M University, College of Engineering, Department of Civil Engineering, College Station, TX 77843. Offers construction engineering and project management (M Eng, MS, D Eng, PhD); engineering mechanics (M Eng, MS, PhD); environmental engineering (M Eng, MS, D Eng, PhD); geotechnical engineering (M Eng, MS, D Eng, PhD); hydraulic engineering (M Eng, MS, PhD); hydrology (M Eng, MS, PhD); materials engineering (M Eng, MS, D Eng, PhD); ocean engineering (M Eng, MS, D Eng, PhD); public works engineering and management (M Eng, MS, PhD); structural engineering and structural mechanics (M Eng, MS, D Eng, PhD); transportation engineering (M Eng, MS, D Eng, PhD); water resources engineering (M Eng, MS, D Eng, PhD). Part-time programs available. *Faculty:* 59 full-time (4 women), 7 part-time (2 women). *Students:* 249 full-time, 54 part-time; includes 13 minority (2 African Americans, 4 Asian Americans or Pacific Islanders, 7 Hispanic Americans), 162 international. *Degree requirements:* For master's, thesis (MS) required; for doctorate, dissertation (PhD), internship (D Eng) required. *Entrance requirements:* For master's and doctorate, GRE General Test, TOEFL. *Application deadline:* Applications are processed on a rolling basis. Application fee: $50 ($75 for international students). *Unit head:* Dr. John M. Niedzwecki, Head, 409-845-7435, Fax: 409-862-2800, E-mail: ce-grad@tamu.edu. *Application contact:* Dr. Peter B. Keating, Graduate Adviser, 409-845-2498, Fax: 409-862-2800, E-mail: ce-grad@tamu.edu.

Hydrology–Limnology

The University of Arizona, Graduate College, College of Engineering and Mines, Department of Hydrology and Water Resources, Tucson, AZ 85721. Offers hydrology (MS, PhD); water resource administration (MS, PhD). Part-time programs available. *Faculty:* 30. *Students:* 90 full-time (22 women), 38 part-time (18 women); includes 6 minority (1 African American, 3 Asian Americans or Pacific Islanders, 2 Hispanic Americans), 25 international. Average age 31. 80 applicants, 76% accepted. In 1998, 15 master's, 9 doctorates awarded (100% found work related to degree). *Degree requirements:* For master's and doctorate, computer language, thesis/dissertation required, foreign language not required. *Entrance requirements:* For master's, GRE General Test, TOEFL (minimum score of 550 required), minimum undergraduate GPA of 3.0; for doctorate, GRE General Test, TOEFL (minimum score of 550 required), minimum GPA of 3.2 (undergraduate), 3.4 (graduate). *Application deadline:* For fall admission, 4/15. Applications are processed on a rolling basis. Application fee: $35. *Financial aid:* Fellowships, research assistantships, teaching assistantships, institutionally-sponsored loans and scholarships available. Financial aid application deadline: 1/31. *Faculty research:* Subsurface and surface hydrology, water quality, hydrometeorology/climatology, applied remote sensing, water resource systems. *Unit head:* Dr. Soroosh Sorooshian, Head, 520-621-7121. *Application contact:* Teresa Handloser, Academic Adviser, 520-621-3131, Fax: 520-621-1422.

University of British Columbia, Faculty of Graduate Studies, Program in Hydrology, Vancouver, BC V6T 1Z2, Canada. Offers PhD. *Degree requirements:* For doctorate, dissertation required, foreign language not required. *Entrance requirements:* For doctorate, TOEFL (minimum score of 550 required). *Faculty research:* Mountain hydrology snowmelt, glaciermelt, sediment transport, river morphology.

University of California, Davis, Graduate Studies, Program in Hydrologic Sciences, Davis, CA 95616. Offers MS, PhD. *Faculty:* 38. *Students:* 39 full-time (13 women), 1 part-time; includes 4 minority (3 Asian Americans or Pacific Islanders, 1 Hispanic American), 11 international. Average age 24. 35 applicants, 63% accepted. In 1998, 8 master's, 1 doctorate awarded. *Degree requirements:* For master's and doctorate, thesis/dissertation required. *Entrance requirements:* For master's, GRE General Test, minimum GPA of 3.0; for doctorate, GRE. *Average time to degree:* Master's–2.5 years full-time. *Application deadline:* For fall admission, 6/1 (priority date). Application fee: $40. Electronic applications accepted. *Financial aid:* In 1998–99, 9 fellowships with full and partial tuition reimbursements, 17 research assistantships with full and partial tuition reimbursements, 3 teaching assistantships with full and partial tuition reimbursements were awarded.; career-related internships or fieldwork, Federal Work-Study, grants, institutionally-sponsored loans, and scholarships also available. Financial aid application deadline: 1/15; financial aid applicants required to submit FAFSA. *Faculty research:* Pollutant transport in surface and subsurface waters, subsurface heterogeneity, micrometerology evaporation, biodegradation. *Unit head:* Dr. Graham Fogg, Graduate Adviser, 530-752-6810, Fax: 530-752-5262, E-mail: gefogg@ucdavis.edu. *Application contact:* Diane Swindall, Graduate Program Staff, 530-752-1669, Fax: 530-752-1552, E-mail: dgswindall@ucdavis.edu.

University of Hawaii at Manoa, Graduate Division, School of Ocean and Earth Science and Technology, Department of Geology and Geophysics, Honolulu, HI 96822. Offers high-pressure geophysics and geochemistry (MS, PhD); hydrogeology and engineering geology (MS, PhD); marine geology and geophysics (MS, PhD); planetary geosciences and remote sensing (MS, PhD); seismology and solid-earth geophysics (MS, PhD); volcanology, petrology, and geochemistry (MS, PhD). *Faculty:* 84 full-time (10 women). *Students:* 48 full-time (15 women), 9 part-time (4 women); includes 3 minority (1 African American, 2 Asian Americans or Pacific Islanders), 15 international. Terminal master's awarded for partial completion of doctoral program. *Degree requirements:* For master's, thesis required, foreign language not required; for doctorate, dissertation, comprehensive exams required, foreign language not required. *Entrance requirements:* For master's and doctorate, GRE General Test, TOEFL, minimum GPA of 3.0. *Application deadline:* For fall admission, 1/15; for spring admission, 9/1. Application fee: $25 ($50 for international students). *Unit head:* Dr. John Sinton, Chair, 808-956-7640, Fax: 808-956-5512, E-mail: sinton@soest.hawaii.edu. *Application contact:* John Mahoney, Graduate Field Chairperson, 808-956-8763, Fax: 808-956-2538, E-mail: jmahoney@hawaii.edu.

University of Idaho, College of Graduate Studies, College of Mines and Earth Resources, Department of Geology and Geological Engineering, Program in Hydrology, Moscow, ID 83844-4140. Offers MS. *Students:* 6 full-time (2 women), 13 part-time (3 women). In 1998, 3 degrees awarded. *Entrance requirements:* For master's, minimum GPA of 2.8. *Application deadline:* For fall admission, 8/1; for spring admission, 12/15. Application fee: $35 ($45 for international students). *Financial aid:* Application deadline: 2/15. *Unit head:* Dr. John Oldow, Head, Department of Geology and Geological Engineering, 208-885-7327.

University of Illinois at Chicago, Graduate College, College of Liberal Arts and Sciences, Department of Earth and Environmental Sciences, Chicago, IL 60607-7128. Offers crystallography (MS, PhD); environmental geology (MS, PhD); geochemistry (MS, PhD); geology (MS, PhD); geomorphology (MS, PhD); geophysics (MS, PhD); geotechnical engineering and geosciences (PhD); hydrogeology (MS, PhD); low-temperature and organic geochemistry (MS, PhD); mineralogy (MS, PhD); paleoclimatology (MS, PhD); paleontology (MS, PhD); petrology (MS, PhD); quaternary geology (MS, PhD); sedimentology (MS, PhD); water resources (MS, PhD). *Faculty:* 9 full-time (2 women). *Students:* 8 full-time (2 women), 1 part-time, 2 international. *Degree requirements:* For master's and doctorate, thesis/dissertation required. *Entrance requirements:* For master's and doctorate, GRE General Test, TOEFL (minimum score of 550 required), minimum GPA of 3.75 on a 5.0 scale. *Application deadline:* For fall admission, 7/3; for spring admission, 11/8. Application fee: $40 ($50 for international students). *Unit head:* A. F. Koster Van Groos, Acting Head, 312-996-3153. *Application contact:* Martin Flower, Graduate Director, 312-996-9662.

University of Missouri–Rolla, Graduate School, School of Engineering, Department of Civil Engineering, Program in Hydrology and Hydraulic Engineering, Rolla, MO 65409-0910. Offers MS, DE, PhD. *Degree requirements:* For master's, thesis or alternative required, foreign language not required; for doctorate, dissertation required, foreign language not required. *Entrance requirements:* For master's and doctorate, GRE General Test (minimum combined score of 1100 required), TOEFL (minimum score of 550 required), minimum GPA of 3.0.

University of Nevada, Reno, Graduate School, Graduate Program in Hydrologic Sciences, Reno, NV 89557. Offers hydrogeology (MS, PhD); hydrology (MS, PhD). Offered through the M. C. Fleischmann College of Agriculture, the College of Engineering, the Mackay School of Mines, and the Desert Research Institute. Part-time programs available. Terminal master's awarded for partial completion of doctoral program. *Degree requirements:* For master's, thesis optional, foreign language not required; for doctorate, dissertation required, foreign language not required. *Entrance requirements:* For master's and doctorate, GRE General Test (minimum combined score of 1000 required), TOEFL (minimum score of 500 required), minimum GPA of 3.0. *Faculty research:* Groundwater, water resources, surface water, soil science.

University of New Brunswick, School of Graduate Studies, Faculty of Engineering, Department of Civil Engineering, Fredericton, NB E3B 5A3, Canada. Offers environmental engineering (M Eng, M Sc E, PhD); geotechnical engineering (M Eng, M Sc E); structures and structural foundations (M Eng, M Sc E, PhD); transportation engineering (M Eng, M Sc E, PhD); water resources and hydrology (M Eng, M Sc E, PhD). Part-time programs available. *Degree requirements:* For master's, thesis required, foreign language not required; for doctorate, dissertation, qualifying exam required, foreign language not required. *Entrance requirements:* For master's and doctorate, TOEFL, TWE, minimum GPA of 3.0.

University of New Hampshire, Graduate School, College of Engineering and Physical Sciences, Department of Earth Sciences, Program in Hydrology, Durham, NH 03824. Offers MS. *Students:* 3 full-time (1 woman), 9 part-time (5 women), 1 international. Average age 29. 14 applicants, 50% accepted. In 1998, 4 degrees awarded. *Degree requirements:* For master's, thesis required, foreign language not required. *Entrance requirements:* For master's, GRE General Test. *Application deadline:* For fall admission, 4/1 (priority date). Applications are processed on a rolling basis. Application fee: $50. Tuition, area resident: Full-time $5,750; part-time $319 per credit. Tuition, state resident: full-time $8,625. Tuition, nonresident: full-time $14,640; part-time $598 per credit. Required fees: $224 per semester. Tuition and fees vary according to course load, degree level and program. *Financial aid:* In 1998–99, 3 teaching assistantships were awarded.; fellowships, research assistantships, career-related internships or fieldwork, Federal Work-Study, scholarships, and tuition waivers (full and partial) also available. Financial aid application deadline: 2/15. *Faculty research:* Water quality, quantitative hydrology, surface water hydrology, water resource management. *Application contact:* Dr. Francis Birch, Graduate Coordinator, 603-862-3142.

University of South Florida, Graduate School, College of Arts and Sciences, Department of Geology, Tampa, FL 33620-9951. Offers geology (MS, PhD); hydrogeology (MS, Adv C). Part-time programs available. *Faculty:* 11 full-time (3 women), 3 part-time (0 women). *Students:* 37 full-time (13 women), 7 part-time; includes 1 minority (Hispanic American), 6 international. *Degree requirements:* For master's, thesis required (for some programs); for doctorate, dissertation required. *Entrance requirements:* For master's, GRE General Test (minimum combined score of 1000 required), minimum GPA of 3.0 in last 60 hours; for doctorate, GRE General Test. *Application deadline:* For fall admission, 6/1; for spring admission, 10/15. Application fee: $20. Electronic applications accepted. Tuition, state resident: part-time $148 per credit hour. Tuition, nonresident: part-time $509 per credit hour. *Unit head:* Mark T. Stewart, Chairperson, 813-974-0325, Fax: 813-974-2654, E-mail: mark@chuma.cas.usf.edu. *Application contact:* Nancy A. Mole, Graduate Coordinator, 813-974-2236, Fax: 813-974-2654, E-mail: nancym@chuma1.cas.usf.edu.

University of Washington, Graduate School, College of Forest Resources, Seattle, WA 98195. Offers forest economics (MS, PhD); forest ecosystem analysis (MS, PhD); forest engineering/forest hydrology (MS, PhD); forest products marketing (MS, PhD); forest soils (MS, PhD); pulp and paper science (MS, PhD); quantitative resource management (MS, PhD); silviculture (MFR); silviculture and forest protection (MS, PhD); social sciences (MS, PhD); urban horticulture (MFR, MS, PhD); wildlife science (MS, PhD). *Faculty:* 47 full-time (4 women), 16 part-time (2 women). *Students:* 161 full-time (65 women), 16 part-time (5 women); includes 15 minority (1 African American, 10 Asian Americans or Pacific Islanders, 1 Hispanic American, 3 Native Americans), 9 international. *Degree requirements:* For master's, thesis required (for some programs), foreign language not required; for doctorate, dissertation required, foreign language not required. *Entrance requirements:* For master's and doctorate, GRE, TOEFL (minimum score of 500 required), minimum GPA of 3.0. *Application deadline:* For fall admission, 2/1 (priority date); for winter admission, 11/1; for spring admission, 2/1. Applications are processed on a rolling basis. Application fee: $50. Electronic applications accepted. Tuition, state resident: full-time $5,196; part-time $475 per credit. Tuition, nonresident: full-time $13,485; part-time $1,285 per credit. Required fees: $387; $38 per credit. Tuition and fees vary according to course load. *Unit head:* Dr. David B. Thorud, Dean, 206-685-1928, Fax: 206-685-0790. *Application contact:* Michelle Trudeau, Student Services Manager, 206-616-1533, Fax: 206-685-0790, E-mail: michtru@u.washington.edu.

Wright State University, School of Graduate Studies, College of Science and Mathematics, Department of Geological Sciences, Program in Geological Sciences, Dayton, OH 45435. Offers environmental geology (MS); environmental sciences (MS); geological sciences (MS); geophysics (MS); hydrogeology (MS); petroleum geology (MS). Part-time programs available. *Students:* 32 full-time (14 women), 9 part-time (2 women), 1 international. *Degree requirements:* For master's, computer language, thesis required, foreign language not required. *Entrance requirements:* For master's, TOEFL (minimum score of 550 required). Application fee: $25. *Unit head:* Dr. Dennis Burns, Graduate Coordinator, 316-978-3120, Fax: 316-978-3431, E-mail: burns@twsuvm.uc.twsu.edu. *Application contact:* Deborah L. Cowles, Assistant to Chair, 937-775-3455, Fax: 937-775-3462.

Limnology

Baylor University, Graduate School, College of Arts and Sciences, Department of Biology, Waco, TX 76798. Offers biology (MA, MS, PhD); environmental biology (MS); limnology (MSL). Part-time programs available. *Faculty:* 13 full-time (3 women). *Students:* 18 full-time (10 women), 5 part-time (1 woman); includes 5 minority (1 African American, 3 Asian Americans or Pacific Islanders, 1 Hispanic American), 3 international. *Degree requirements:* For master's, thesis required (for some programs); for doctorate, dissertation required. *Entrance requirements:* For master's and doctorate, GRE General Test. *Application deadline:* For fall admission, 1/31 (priority date). Applications are processed on a rolling basis. Application fee: $25. *Unit head:* Dr. Richard E. Duhrkopf, Director of Graduate Studies, 254-710-2911, Fax: 254-710-2969, E-mail: rick_duhrkopf@baylor.edu. *Application contact:* Sandy Tighe, Administrative Assistant, 254-710-2911, Fax: 254-710-2969, E-mail: sandy_tighe@baylor.edu.

Cornell University, Graduate School, Graduate Fields of Agriculture and Life Sciences, Field of Ecology and Evolutionary Biology, Ithaca, NY 14853-0001. Offers ecology (PhD), including animal ecology, applied ecology, biogeochemistry, community and ecosystem ecology, limnology, oceanography, physiological ecology, plant ecology, population ecology, theoretical ecology, vertebrate zoology; evolutionary biology (PhD), including ecological genetics, paleobiology, population biology, systematics. *Faculty:* 41 full-time. *Students:* 55 full-time (29 women); includes 5 minority (1 African American, 2 Asian Americans or Pacific Islanders, 2 Hispanic Americans), 3 international. *Degree requirements:* For doctorate, dissertation, 2 semesters of teaching experience required, foreign language not required. *Entrance requirements:* For doctorate, GRE General Test, TOEFL (minimum score of 550 required). *Application deadline:* For fall admission, 12/15. Application fee: $65. Electronic applications accepted. *Unit head:* Director of Graduate Studies, 607-254-4230. *Application contact:* Graduate Field Assistant, 607-254-4230, E-mail: eeb_grad_req@cornell.edu.

University of Alaska Fairbanks, Graduate School, School of Fisheries and Ocean Sciences, Program in Marine Sciences and Limnology, Fairbanks, AK 99775-7480. Offers marine biology (MS); oceanography (MS, PhD), including biological oceanography (PhD), chemical oceanography (PhD), fisheries (PhD), physical oceanography (PhD). *Faculty:* 9 full-time (1 woman), 2 part-time (0 women). *Students:* 37 full-time (25 women), 6 part-time (4 women); includes 2 minority (1 African American, 1 Asian American or Pacific Islander), 10 international. Average age 30. 27 applicants, 44% accepted. In 1998, 2 master's, 1 doctorate awarded. *Degree requirements:* For master's, thesis, comprehensive exam required, foreign language not required; for doctorate, one foreign language (computer language can substitute), dissertation, comprehensive exam required. *Entrance requirements:* For master's and doctorate, GRE General Test, TOEFL (minimum score of 550 required). *Application deadline:* For fall admission, 3/1 (priority date). Applications are processed on a rolling basis. Application fee: $35. *Financial aid:* Research assistantships, teaching assistantships available. *Unit head:* Dr. Susan Henrichs, Head, 907-474-7289.

University of Florida, Graduate School, College of Agriculture, Department of Fisheries and Aquatic Science, Gainesville, FL 32611. Offers MFAS, MS, PhD. *Faculty:* 23. *Students:* 26 full-time (8 women), 12 part-time (5 women); includes 2 minority (both Hispanic Americans), 3 international. 34 applicants, 35% accepted. In 1998, 11 master's awarded. *Degree requirements:* For master's, thesis optional, foreign language not required; for doctorate, dissertation required, foreign language not required. *Entrance requirements:* For master's and doctorate, GRE General Test, TOEFL, minimum GPA of 3.0. *Application deadline:* For fall admission, 6/1. Applications are processed on a rolling basis. Application fee: $20. Electronic applications accepted. *Financial aid:* In 1998–99, 1 fellowship, 21 research assistantships were awarded.; unspecified assistantships also available. *Unit head:* Dr. Wallis H. Clark, Chair, 352-392-9617, Fax: 352-846-1088, E-mail: faa@gnv.ifas.ufl.edu. *Application contact:* Dr. Ed Philips, Graduate Coordinator, 352-392-9617 Ext. 248, Fax: 352-846-1088, E-mail: ejph@gnv.ifas.ufl.edu.

University of Wisconsin–Madison, Graduate School, College of Engineering, Program in Oceanography and Limnology, Madison, WI 53706-1380. Offers MS, PhD. *Faculty:* 15 full-time (2 women), 2 part-time (0 women). *Students:* 11 full-time (3 women); includes 5 minority (2

African Americans, 1 Hispanic American, 2 Native Americans) 21 applicants, 29% accepted. In 1998, 2 doctorates awarded (100% found work related to degree). Terminal master's awarded for partial completion of doctoral program. *Degree requirements:* For master's, thesis required, foreign language not required; for doctorate, one foreign language, dissertation required. *Entrance requirements:* For master's and doctorate, GRE General Test. *Application deadline:* For fall admission, 1/1 (priority date). Application fee: $45. Electronic applications accepted. *Financial aid:* In 1998–99, 9 students received aid; fellowships, research assistantships, teaching assistantships, Federal Work-Study and institutionally-sponsored loans available. Financial aid application deadline: 1/1. *Faculty research:* Lake ecosystems, ecosystem modeling, geochemistry, physiological ecology, chemical limnology. *Unit head:* Dr. William C. Sonzogni, Chair, 608-224-6200, Fax: 608-224-6201, E-mail: sonzogni@facstaff.wisc.edu. *Application contact:* Ann McLain, Student Services Coordinator, 608-263-3264, Fax: 608-265-2340, E-mail: asmclain@facstaff.wisc.edu.

William Paterson University of New Jersey, College of Science and Health, Department of Biology, General Biology Program, Wayne, NJ 07470-8420. Offers general biology (MA); limnology and terrestrial ecology (MA); molecular biology (MA); physiology (MA). Part-time and evening/weekend programs available. *Degree requirements:* For master's, comprehensive exam, independent study or thesis required. *Entrance requirements:* For master's, GRE General Test, minimum GPA of 2.75.

Planetary and Space Sciences

California Institute of Technology, Division of Geological and Planetary Sciences, Pasadena, CA 91125-0001. Offers cosmochemistry (PhD); geobiology (PhD); geochemistry (MS, PhD); geology (MS, PhD); geophysics (MS, PhD); planetary science (MS, PhD). *Faculty:* 32 full-time (1 woman). *Students:* 58 full-time (22 women); includes 1 minority (Hispanic American), 20 international. Average age 26. 82 applicants, 32% accepted. In 1998, 4 master's awarded (0% continued full-time study); 14 doctorates awarded. Terminal master's awarded for partial completion of doctoral program. *Degree requirements:* For master's, thesis not required; for doctorate, dissertation required. *Entrance requirements:* For doctorate, GRE General Test, GRE Subject Test, TOEFL. *Average time to degree:* Master's–3 years full-time; doctorate–6 years full-time. *Application deadline:* For fall admission, 1/15. Application fee: $0. *Financial aid:* In 1998–99, 58 students received aid, including 3 fellowships with full tuition reimbursements available (averaging $17,660 per year), research assistantships with full tuition reimbursements available (averaging $17,660 per year); teaching assistantships, institutionally-sponsored loans also available. Financial aid applicants required to submit FAFSA. Total annual research expenditures: $11.2 million. *Unit head:* Dr. Edward M. Stolper, Chair, 626-395-6108, Fax: 626-795-6028, E-mail: divgps@gps.caltech.edu. *Application contact:* Dr. George R. Rossman, Division Academic Officer, 626-395-6125, Fax: 626-568-0935, E-mail: divgps@gps.caltech.edu.

Columbia University, Graduate School of Arts and Sciences, Division of Natural Sciences, Program in Atmospheric and Planetary Science, New York, NY 10027. Offers M Phil, PhD. Offered jointly through the Departments of Geological Sciences, Astronomy, and Physics and in cooperation with NASA Goddard Space Flight Center's Institute for Space Studies. *Degree requirements:* For doctorate, variable foreign language requirement, dissertation required. *Entrance requirements:* For doctorate, GRE General Test, GRE Subject Test, TOEFL, previous course work in mathematics and physics. *Faculty research:* Climate, weather prediction.

Cornell University, Graduate School, Graduate Fields of Arts and Sciences, Field of Astronomy and Space Sciences, Ithaca, NY 14853-0001. Offers astronomy (PhD); astrophysics (PhD); general space sciences (PhD); infrared astronomy (PhD); planetary studies (PhD); radio astronomy (PhD); radiophysics (PhD); theoretical astrophysics (PhD). *Faculty:* 26 full-time. *Students:* 23 full-time (9 women); includes 3 minority (2 Asian Americans or Pacific Islanders, 1 Hispanic American), 8 international. 88 applicants, 27% accepted. In 1998, 6 doctorates awarded. *Degree requirements:* For doctorate, dissertation required, foreign language not required. *Entrance requirements:* For doctorate, GRE General Test, GRE Subject Test, TOEFL (minimum score of 600 required). *Application deadline:* For fall admission, 1/15. Application fee: $65. Electronic applications accepted. *Financial aid:* In 1998–99, 22 students received aid, including 6 fellowships with full tuition reimbursements available, 8 research assistantships with full tuition reimbursements available, 8 teaching assistantships with full tuition reimbursements available; institutionally-sponsored loans, scholarships, tuition waivers (full and partial), and unspecified assistantships also available. Financial aid applicants required to submit FAFSA. *Faculty research:* High energy astrophysics, cosmology, star formation. *Unit head:* Director of Graduate Studies, 607-255-4341, Fax: 607-255-5907. *Application contact:* Graduate Field Assistant, 607-255-4341, E-mail: oconnor@astrosun.tn.cornell.edu.

Florida Institute of Technology, Graduate School, College of Science and Liberal Arts, Department of Physics and Space Sciences, Program in Space Science, Melbourne, FL 32901-6975. Offers MS, PhD. Part-time programs available. *Faculty:* 5 full-time (0 women). *Students:* 4 full-time (1 woman). Average age 27. 6 applicants, 67% accepted. In 1998, 1 master's awarded. Terminal master's awarded for partial completion of doctoral program. *Degree requirements:* For master's, comprehensive exam required, thesis optional, foreign language not required; for doctorate, dissertation, comprehensive exam, oral defense of dissertation required, foreign language not required. *Entrance requirements:* For master's, GRE General Test, GRE Subject Test, minimum GPA of 3.0, proficiency in a computer language; for doctorate, GRE General Test, GRE Subject Test, minimum GPA of 3.2. *Application deadline:* Applications are processed on a rolling basis. Application fee: $50. Electronic applications accepted. Tuition: Part-time $575 per credit hour. Required fees: $100. Tuition and fees vary according to campus/location and program. *Financial aid:* In 1998–99, 3 students received aid, including 2 teaching assistantships with tuition reimbursements available (averaging $4,199 per year); research assistantships with tuition reimbursements available, tuition remissions also available. Financial aid application deadline: 3/1; financial aid applicants required to submit FAFSA. *Faculty research:* Observational astronomy, theoretical astrophysics, space plasma physics. *Unit head:* Anthony Jones, Director of Admissions, 615-329-8665, Fax: 615-329-8774, E-mail: ajones@dubois_fisk.edu. *Application contact:* Carolyn P. Farrior, Associate Dean of Graduate Admissions, 407-674-7118, Fax: 407-723-9468, E-mail: cfarrior@fit.edu.

Harvard University, Graduate School of Arts and Sciences, Department of Earth and Planetary Sciences, Cambridge, MA 02138. Offers AM, PhD. *Students:* 33 full-time (12 women). 64 applicants, 22% accepted. In 1998, 1 master's, 6 doctorates awarded. Terminal master's awarded for partial completion of doctoral program. *Degree requirements:* For master's, thesis or alternative required; for doctorate, dissertation, general exams required. *Entrance requirements:* For master's and doctorate, GRE General Test, TOEFL (minimum score of 550 required). *Application deadline:* For fall admission, 12/15. Application fee: $60. *Financial aid:* Fellowships, research assistantships, teaching assistantships, career-related internships or fieldwork, Federal Work-Study, and institutionally-sponsored loans available. Financial aid application deadline: 12/30. *Faculty research:* Economic geography, geochemistry, geophysics, mineralogy, crystallography. *Unit head:* Dr. Michael B. McElroy, Chairman, 617-495-2351. *Application contact:* Office of Admissions and Financial Aid, 617-495-5315.

See in-depth description on page 281.

Johns Hopkins University, Zanvyl Krieger School of Arts and Sciences, Department of Earth and Planetary Sciences, Baltimore, MD 21218-2699. Offers geochemistry (MA, PhD); geology

(MA, PhD); geophysics (MA, PhD); groundwater (MA, PhD); oceanography (MA, PhD); planetary atmosphere (MA, PhD). *Faculty:* 13 full-time (1 woman). *Students:* 21 full-time (9 women), 10 international. Terminal master's awarded for partial completion of doctoral program. *Degree requirements:* For doctorate, dissertation required, foreign language not required. *Entrance requirements:* For master's and doctorate, GRE General Test. *Application deadline:* For fall admission, 1/15 (priority date). Application fee: $55. Tuition: Full-time $23,660. Tuition and fees vary according to program. *Unit head:* Dr. John M. Ferry, Chair, 410-516-7135, Fax: 410-516-7933.

Massachusetts Institute of Technology, School of Science, Department of Earth, Atmospheric, and Planetary Sciences, Program in Planetary Science, Cambridge, MA 02139-4307. Offers SM, PhD, Sc D. *Faculty:* 4 full-time (1 woman). *Students:* 7 full-time (0 women). Average age 28. 21 applicants, 5% accepted. In 1998, 1 master's awarded. Terminal master's awarded for partial completion of doctoral program. *Degree requirements:* For master's, thesis required, foreign language not required; for doctorate, dissertation, general exam required, foreign language not required. *Entrance requirements:* For master's and doctorate, GRE General Test. *Application deadline:* For fall admission, 1/15; for spring admission, 11/1. Application fee: $55. *Financial aid:* Fellowships, research assistantships, teaching assistantships available. Financial aid application deadline: 1/15. *Unit head:* Dr. John Woolcock, Graduate Coordinator, 724-357-4828, E-mail: woolcock@grove.iup.edu. *Application contact:* Anastasia Frangos, Administrative Assistant, 617-253-3381, Fax: 617-253-8298, E-mail: eapsinfo@mit.edu.

McGill University, Faculty of Graduate Studies and Research, Faculty of Science, Department of Earth and Planetary Sciences, Montréal, PQ H3A 2T5, Canada. Offers earth and planetary sciences (M Sc, PhD, Diploma). *Faculty:* 11 full-time (2 women). *Students:* 37 full-time (12 women), 12 international. Average age 25. 65 applicants, 38% accepted. In 1998, 10 master's awarded (40% found work related to degree, 60% continued full-time study); 4 doctorates awarded. *Degree requirements:* For master's and doctorate, thesis/dissertation required, foreign language not required. *Entrance requirements:* For master's, TOEFL (minimum score of 550 required), minimum GPA of 3.0; for doctorate, TOEFL (minimum score of 550 required). *Average time to degree:* Master's–4 years full-time; doctorate–6 years full-time. *Application deadline:* For fall admission, 3/1 (priority date). Applications are processed on a rolling basis. Application fee: $60. *Financial aid:* Fellowships, research assistantships, teaching assistantships, institutionally-sponsored loans and tuition waivers (partial) available. *Faculty research:* Geochemistry, sedimentary petrology, igneous petrology, theoretical geophysics, economic geology, planetary sciences. *Unit head:* A. E. Williams-Jones, Chair, 514-398-6768, Fax: 514-398-4680, E-mail: willy_j@geosci.lan.mcgill.ca. *Application contact:* A. Hynes, Chair, Graduate Admissions, 514-398-5884, Fax: 514-398-4680, E-mail: andrew@geosci.lan.mcgill.ca.

Rensselaer Polytechnic Institute, Graduate School, School of Science, Department of Earth and Environmental Sciences, Troy, NY 12180-3590. Offers environmental chemistry (MS, PhD); geochemistry (MS, PhD); geology (MS, PhD); geophysics (MS, PhD); hydrogeology (MS); petrology (MS, PhD); planetary geology (MS, PhD); tectonics (MS, PhD). Part-time programs available. *Faculty:* 7 full-time (0 women), 2 part-time (0 women). *Students:* 19 full-time (8 women), 1 (woman) part-time; includes 2 minority (1 African American, 1 Native American) *Degree requirements:* For master's, thesis required (for some programs); for doctorate, dissertation required. *Entrance requirements:* For master's and doctorate, GRE General Test, TOEFL (minimum score of 550 required). *Application deadline:* For fall admission, 2/1 (priority date). Applications are processed on a rolling basis. Application fee: $35. *Unit head:* Dr. Robert McCaffrey, Chair, 518-276-6474, Fax: 518-276-6680, E-mail: ees@rpi.edu. *Application contact:* Dr. Steven Roecker, Associate Professor, 518-276-6474, Fax: 518-276-6680, E-mail: ees@rpi.edu.

See in-depth description on page 299.

State University of New York at Stony Brook, Graduate School, College of Arts and Sciences, Department of Physics and Astronomy, Program in Astronomy, Stony Brook, NY 11794. Offers earth and space sciences (MS, PhD). *Students:* 8 full-time (1 woman), 6 part-time (4 women); includes 1 minority (Hispanic American), 7 international. *Degree requirements:* For master's, thesis or alternative required, foreign language not required; for doctorate, dissertation required, foreign language not required. *Entrance requirements:* For master's and doctorate, GRE General Test, TOEFL, minimum GPA of 3.0. *Application deadline:* For fall admission, 1/15. Application fee: $50. *Application contact:* Dr. Peter Stephens, Director, 516-632-8279, Fax: 516-632-8176, E-mail: pstephens@ccmail.sunysb.edu.

The University of Arizona, Graduate College, College of Science, Department of Planetary Sciences, Tucson, AZ 85721. Offers MS, PhD. *Faculty:* 31. *Students:* 26 full-time (8 women), 2 part-time (1 woman); includes 1 minority (Hispanic American), 5 international. Average age 28. 46 applicants, 20% accepted. In 1998, 1 master's, 1 doctorate awarded (100% found work related to degree). *Degree requirements:* For master's, thesis required (for some programs), foreign language not required; for doctorate, dissertation required. *Entrance requirements:* For master's and doctorate, GRE General Test, GRE Subject Test, TOEFL (minimum score of 550 required). *Application deadline:* For fall admission, 1/15. Applications are processed on a rolling basis. Application fee: $35. *Financial aid:* Fellowships, research assistantships, teaching assistantships, scholarships and tuition waivers (partial) available. Financial aid application deadline: 2/15. *Faculty research:* Cosmochemistry, planetary geology, astronomy, space physics, planetary physics. *Unit head:* Dr. Michael Drake, Head, 520-621-6962. *Application contact:* Joan Weinberg, Assistant to the Director, 520-621-4128, Fax: 520-621-4933.

See in-depth description on page 309.

University of California, Los Angeles, Graduate Division, College of Letters and Science, Department of Earth and Space Sciences, Los Angeles, CA 90095. Offers geochemistry (MS,

Planetary and Space Sciences–Cross-Discipline Announcements

University of California, Los Angeles (continued)
PhD); geology (MS, PhD); geophysics and space physics (MS, PhD). *Students:* 53 full-time (20 women); includes 7 minority (1 African American, 4 Asian Americans or Pacific Islanders, 2 Hispanic Americans), 10 international. 76 applicants, 42% accepted. *Degree requirements:* For master's, comprehensive exams or thesis required; for doctorate, dissertation, oral and written qualifying exams required, foreign language not required. *Entrance requirements:* For master's, GRE General Test, minimum GPA of 3.0; for doctorate, GRE General Test, minimum undergraduate GPA of 3.0. *Application deadline:* For fall admission, 12/15. Application fee: $40. Electronic applications accepted. *Financial aid:* In 1998–99, 29 fellowships, 29 teaching assistantships were awarded.; research assistantships, Federal Work-Study, institutionally-sponsored loans, scholarships, and tuition waivers (full and partial) also available. Financial aid application deadline: 3/1. *Unit head:* Dr. T. Mark Harrison, Chair, 310-825-3917. *Application contact:* Departmental Office, 888-377-8252, E-mail: verity@ess.ucla.edu.

University of Chicago, Division of the Physical Sciences, Department of the Geophysical Sciences, Chicago, IL 60637-1513. Offers atmospheric sciences (SM, PhD); earth sciences (SM, PhD); planetary and space sciences (SM, PhD). *Degree requirements:* For master's, thesis, seminar required; for doctorate, dissertation required. *Entrance requirements:* For master's and doctorate, GRE General Test, TOEFL (minimum score of 550 required). *Faculty research:* Climatology, evolutionary paleontology,petrology, geochemistry, oceanic sciences.

University of Hawaii at Manoa, Graduate Division, School of Ocean and Earth Science and Technology, Department of Geology and Geophysics, Honolulu, HI 96822. Offers high-pressure geophysics and geochemistry (MS, PhD); hydrogeology and engineering geology (MS, PhD); marine geology and geophysics (MS, PhD); planetary geosciences and remote sensing (MS, PhD); seismology and solid-earth geophysics (MS, PhD); volcanology, petrology, and geochemistry (MS, PhD). *Faculty:* 84 full-time (10 women). *Students:* 48 full-time (15 women), 9 part-time (4 women); includes 3 minority (1 African American, 2 Asian Americans or Pacific Islanders), 15 international. Terminal master's awarded for partial completion of doctoral program. *Degree requirements:* For master's, thesis required, foreign language not required; for doctorate, dissertation, comprehensive exams required, foreign language not required. *Entrance requirements:* For master's and doctorate, GRE General Test, TOEFL, minimum GPA of 3.0. *Application deadline:* For fall admission, 1/15; for spring admission, 9/1. Application fee: $25 ($50 for international students). *Unit head:* Dr. John Sinton, Chair, 808-956-7640, Fax: 808-956-5512, E-mail: sinton@soest.hawaii.edu. *Application contact:* John Mahoney, Graduate Field Chairperson, 808-956-8763, Fax: 808-956-2538, E-mail: jmahoney@hawaii.edu.

University of Michigan, Horace H. Rackham School of Graduate Studies, College of Engineering, Department of Atmospheric, Oceanic, and Space Sciences, Program in Atmospheric and Space Sciences, Ann Arbor, MI 48109. Offers M Eng, MS, PhD. Part-time programs available. *Faculty:* 21 full-time (2 women), 9 part-time (0 women). *Students:* 42 full-time (15 women), 10 international. 72 applicants, 44% accepted. In 1998, 3 master's, 6 doctorates awarded. Terminal master's awarded for partial completion of doctoral program. *Degree requirements:* For master's, thesis required (for some programs); for doctorate, dissertation, oral defense of dissertation, preliminary exams required. *Entrance requirements:* For master's and doctorate, GRE General Test (combined average 2000 on three sections), TOEFL (minimum score of 600 required). *Application deadline:* For fall admission, 1/15 (priority date). Applications are processed on a rolling basis. Application fee: $60. *Financial aid:* In 1998–99, 8 fellowships, 4 teaching assistantships were awarded.; research assistantships, career-related internships or fieldwork, Federal Work-Study, and institutionally-sponsored loans also available. Aid available to part-time students. Financial aid application deadline: 3/15; financial aid applicants required to submit FAFSA. *Faculty research:* Air quality, remote sensing, meteorology aeronomy, planetary and comet atmospheres. Total annual research expenditures: $13.5 million. *Unit head:* William Kuhn, Adviser, 734-764-3335, Fax: 734-764-4585, E-mail: wkuhn@umich.edu. *Application contact:* Susan Schreiber, Academic Services Assistant, 734-764-3336, Fax: 734-764-4585, E-mail: aoss.um@umich.edu.

University of New Mexico, Graduate School, College of Arts and Sciences, Department of Earth and Planetary Sciences, Albuquerque, NM 87131-2039. Offers MS, PhD. *Faculty:* 18 full-time (4 women), 5 part-time (2 women). *Students:* 26 full-time (9 women), 20 part-time (9 women); includes 1 minority (Native American), 1 international. Average age 31. 77 applicants, 23% accepted. In 1998, 4 master's, 2 doctorates awarded. Terminal master's awarded for partial completion of doctoral program. *Degree requirements:* For master's and doctorate, computer language, thesis/dissertation required, foreign language not required. *Entrance requirements:* For master's, GRE General Test (average 70th percentile); for doctorate, GRE General Test (average 70th percentile), GRE Subject Test (average 70th percentile). *Application deadline:* For fall admission, 1/31. Application fee: $25. *Financial aid:* In 1998–99, 8 fellowships (averaging $1,179 per year), 22 research assistantships with tuition reimbursements (averaging $3,301 per year), 14 teaching assistantships with tuition reimbursements (averaging $7,319 per year) were awarded.; career-related internships or fieldwork, Federal Work-Study, and institutionally-sponsored loans also available. Aid available to part-time students. Financial aid application deadline: 1/31. *Faculty research:* Geochemistry, meteoritics, tectonics, Quaternary studies, Precambrian geology. Total annual research expenditures: $1.3 million. *Unit head:* Dr. Les P. McFadden, Chair, 505-277-4204, Fax: 505-277-8843, E-mail: lmcfadnm@unm.edu.

University of North Dakota, Graduate School, Center for Aerospace Studies, Space Studies Program, Grand Forks, ND 58202. Offers MS. Part-time programs available. Postbaccalaureate distance learning degree programs offered (minimal on-campus study). *Faculty:* 8 full-time (1 woman). *Students:* 21 full-time (5 women), 112 part-time (26 women). 52 applicants, 100% accepted. In 1998, 36 degrees awarded. *Degree requirements:* For master's, thesis or alternative, comprehensive exam required. *Entrance requirements:* For master's, TOEFL (minimum score of 550 required), minimum GPA of 3.0. *Application deadline:* For fall admission, 3/1 (priority date). Applications are processed on a rolling basis. Application fee: $20. *Financial aid:* In 1998–99, 7 students received aid, including 6 research assistantships, 1 teaching assistantship; fellowships, career-related internships or fieldwork, Federal Work-Study, institutionally-sponsored loans, tuition waivers (full and partial), and unspecified assistantships also available. Financial aid application deadline: 3/15. *Faculty research:* Earth-approaching asteroids, international remote sensing statutes, Mercury fly-by design, origin of meteorites, craters on Venus. *Unit head:* Joanne Gabrynowicz, Director, 701-777-2480, Fax: 701-777-3711, E-mail: gabrynow@aero.und.edu.

Announcement: The space studies MS program integrates the scientific, technical, medical, political, and legal impacts associated with the exploration and development of space. This program is available on campus and via the Internet for students of all backgrounds. Visit the program's Web site at http://www.space.edu or call 701-777-2480.

University of Pittsburgh, Faculty of Arts and Sciences, Department of Geology and Planetary Science, Pittsburgh, PA 15260. Offers MS, PhD. Part-time programs available. *Faculty:* 11 full-time (2 women), 1 part-time (0 women). *Students:* 18 full-time (9 women), 8 part-time (2 women). In 1998, 3 master's, 1 doctorate awarded. *Degree requirements:* For master's and doctorate, thesis/dissertation required, foreign language not required. *Entrance requirements:* For master's and doctorate, GRE General Test, TOEFL (minimum score of 550 required). *Average time to degree:* Master's–2.5 years full-time; doctorate–6.5 years full-time. *Application deadline:* For fall admission, 8/1 (priority date); for spring admission, 12/1. Applications are processed on a rolling basis. Application fee: $30 ($40 for international students). *Financial aid:* Career-related internships or fieldwork, Federal Work-Study, institutionally-sponsored loans, and tuition waivers (full and partial) available. Aid available to part-time students. Financial aid application deadline: 3/1; financial aid applicants required to submit FAFSA. *Faculty research:* Plate tectonics and basement studies, sedimentology and image analysis, marine paleo-ecology and geoarchaeology, geophysics and geomagnetism. *Unit head:* Dr. Thomas H. Anderson, Chairman, 412-624-8783, Fax: 412-624-3914, E-mail: taco@vms.cis.pitt.edu. *Application contact:* Dr. William A. Cassidy, Graduate Adviser, 412-624-8886, Fax: 412-624-3914, E-mail: ansmet@vms.cis.pitt.edu.

Washington University in St. Louis, Graduate School of Arts and Sciences, Department of Earth and Planetary Sciences, St. Louis, MO 63130-4899. Offers earth and planetary sciences (MA); geochemistry (PhD); geology (MA, PhD); geophysics (PhD); planetary sciences (PhD). *Students:* 26 full-time (11 women); includes 2 minority (1 Asian American or Pacific Islander, 1 Native American), 4 international. 41 applicants, 32% accepted. In 1998, 4 master's, 8 doctorates awarded. Terminal master's awarded for partial completion of doctoral program. *Degree requirements:* For master's and doctorate, thesis/dissertation required. *Entrance requirements:* For master's and doctorate, GRE General Test. *Application deadline:* For fall admission, 1/15 (priority date). Applications are processed on a rolling basis. Application fee: $35. *Financial aid:* Fellowships, research assistantships, teaching assistantships, Federal Work-Study, institutionally-sponsored loans, and tuition waivers (full and partial) available. Financial aid application deadline: 1/15. *Unit head:* Dr. Raymond E. Arvidson, Chairman, 314-935-5610.

Western Connecticut State University, Division of Graduate Studies, School of Arts and Sciences, Department of Physics, Astronomy and Meteorology, Danbury, CT 06810-6885. Offers earth and planetary sciences (MA). Part-time and evening/weekend programs available. *Degree requirements:* For master's, thesis required, foreign language not required. *Entrance requirements:* For master's, minimum GPA of 2.5. *Application deadline:* For fall admission, 8/1 (priority date). Applications are processed on a rolling basis. Application fee: $40. *Financial aid:* Fellowships, career-related internships or fieldwork and Federal Work-Study available. Aid available to part-time students. Financial aid application deadline: 5/1; financial aid applicants required to submit FAFSA. *Unit head:* Dr. Alice Chance, Chair, 203-837-8667. *Application contact:* Chris Shankle, Associate Director of Graduate Admissions, 203-837-8244, Fax: 203-837-8338, E-mail: shanklec@wcsu.edu.

York University, Faculty of Graduate Studies, Faculty of Science, Program in Earth and Space Science, Toronto, ON M3J 1P3, Canada. Offers M Sc, PhD. Part-time and evening/weekend programs available. *Degree requirements:* For master's, computer language required, thesis optional, foreign language not required; for doctorate, variable foreign language requirement, computer language, dissertation required.

Cross-Discipline Announcements

Boston College, The Graduate School of the Wallace E. Carroll School of Management, Chestnut Hill, MA 02467-3800.

Boston College's MBA Program and BC's master's programs in geology and geophysics offer a dual-degree program that allows students to obtain an MBA and a master's degree in these disciplines. See in-depth description in Book 6.

Indiana University Bloomington, School of Public and Environmental Affairs, Public Affairs Programs, Bloomington, IN 47405.

The MS in Environmental Science curriculum builds competence in various facets of environmental science while adding a management and policy dimension crucial to the environmental science professional. Concentration areas include applied ecology, environmental chemistry, hazardous materials management, and water resources. For more information, see in-depth description in the Natural Resources section in this volume or contact the school.

Oregon State University, Graduate School, College of Oceanic and Atmospheric Sciences, Corvallis, OR 97331.

The College invites students with earth sciences degrees to apply for graduate study in marine geology, interdisciplinary oceanography, and geophysics. Research areas include mid-ocean ridge and hotspot vulcanism, hydrothermal systems, biogeochemical cycles, sedimentation, coastal and shelf processes, marine geophysics, plate tectonics, and seismology. See description under Marine Sciences and Oceanography in this volume.

Princeton University, Graduate School, Princeton Materials Institute, Princeton, NJ 08540-5211.

The Princeton Materials Institute welcomes students interested in cross-disciplinary research involving any aspect of materials science and engineering. Faculty members from 8 academic departments collaborate in a remarkably broad range of programs, supported by outstanding facilities. Some fellowships are available. See the in-depth description in Book 5, Section 21.

CORNELL UNIVERSITY

Department of Geological Sciences

Programs of Study

The Department of Geological Sciences offers programs of study leading to a Master of Science or a Doctor of Philosophy degree in a wide range of geoscience disciplines. A one-year professional master's degree option (Master of Engineering) is also possible in selected areas. The program is highly flexible and allows students to tailor their graduate work to individual interests and career goals. Students take an active role in designing their graduate program, guided by a special committee of faculty members chosen by the student. This committee is usually chaired by the professor who directs the thesis research.

Research and study are often interdisciplinary; the committee may include faculty members in fields other than geological sciences. Cornell has special research strength in regional tectonics (Andes, Himalaya/Tibet, North Africa/Middle East, Urals, and Japan), lithospheric geophysics, geofluid flow, geochemistry, remote sensing, and climate change. Areas of concentration include environmental geophysics*; general geology; geobiology; geochemistry and isotope geology; geohydrology*; geomorphology; geophysics; geotectonics; mineralogy; paleontology; petroleum geoscience*; petrology; planetary geology; Quaternary geology; rock mechanics; sedimentology; seismology; stratigraphy; structural geology; and marine geology (* also available in the Master of Engineering program). A new option in geoarchaeology, emphasizing geochemical and geophysical methods, is under development.

Six residence units are required for the Ph.D. degree; two residence units are required for the master's. A residence unit equals one semester of satisfactory full-time study. Student progress in the Ph.D. program is evaluated by the committee with a qualifying exam in the first year and an admission to candidacy exam (A-exam) after course work is complete. The Committee judges both the M.S. and the Ph.D. thesis defenses.

Research Facilities

Facilities for geoscience research at Cornell are unusually comprehensive. They include specialized workstation clusters (UNIX and NT) for satellite image analysis, 3-D seismics (processing, modeling, and interpretation), and GIS. In addition, Cornell hosts unique digital libraries of global deep seismic reflection profiles, topographic and geologic data, and satellite imagery. Numerous personal computers and access to Cornell's IBM SP2 supercomputer round out the computational power. Geophysical equipment includes a multichannel seismograph, ground penetrating radar, a resistivity meter, a magnetometer, and a gravimeter.

Geochemical analysis is facilitated by an X-ray diffraction laboratory, an ICP-MS lab, a nearby nuclear reactor for neutron activation analysis, a high-pressure (diamond anvil) mineralogy lab, electron microprobes, and supporting laboratory facilities, including a clean room, a rock-prep lab, an electronics shop, and wood and metal workshops.

Cornell's nineteen libraries contain more than 6 million volumes, with special and rare collections, and access to hundreds of libraries throughout the country via interlibrary loan.

Financial Aid

Almost all doctoral candidates receive financial aid through fellowships and teaching or research assistantships. Fellowships, awarded by the Graduate School annually on a competitive basis, were $12,000 plus tuition for the nine-month period for 1998–99. Teaching and research assistants received a stipend of $12,000 and a full tuition fellowship. The application for merit-based aid is part of the application for admission. Summer fellowships are also available. Those applying for need-based aid, such as federal and private loans, must file the FAFSA.

Cost of Study

The 1999–2000 academic year tuition is $23,760.

Living and Housing Costs

Estimated living expenses for the twelve-month academic year, including books, housing and dining, personal expenses, and medical insurance for a single graduate student, are between $10,608 and $14,352. Married students should add about $7176 for a spouse. The stipend portion of assistantships is taxable and subject to withholding.

Student Group

The total number of graduate students in 1999–2000 is 31, including 16 women. Forty-three percent are international students. Ninety-eight percent receive financial aid. Current students are engaged in a wide range of research, including satellite monitoring of glaciers as a guide to climate change, the deep structure of the Tibet plateau, evolution of the Andes, evolution of the Atlas mountains of Morocco, lithospheric architecture of the Urals, fluid migration in complex oil structures, acoustic monitoring of oceanic biomass fluctuations, and geochemistry of Himalaya sediments, to mention but a few.

Student Outcomes

Most recent graduates have found subsequent employment in either academic institutions (postdoctoral or faculty positions) or private industry, particularly the oil exploration industry.

Location

Cornell is located in Ithaca in the Finger Lakes region of New York State. The countryside is one of rolling hills traversed by gorges, waterfalls, lakes, and streams. Outdoor recreation includes sailing, windsurfing, swimming, skiing, and hiking; three state parks lie within 10 miles of the city. Ithaca's cuisine, theaters, and exhibits typify the creative vitality of this pluralistic community.

The University

Founded by Ezra Cornell in 1865, Cornell is both the land-grant institution of New York State and a privately endowed university. The student population is almost 19,000. The graduate faculty has more than 1,600 members and includes Nobel laureates, Pulitzer Prize recipients, and members of the National Academy of Sciences. The Department of Geological Sciences is housed in Snee Hall, built in 1984. Beautiful as well as functional, the spacious four-story building includes a large atrium and a variety of modern research facilities.

Applying

Admission applications may be submitted at any time; however, the deadline to be considered for certain forms of financial aid is January 10. The admission application also serves as the application for fellowship, assistantship, or tuition awards. Basic GRE scores are required. All applicants whose native language is not English must meet English proficiency requirements (e.g., a TOEFL score of at least 550).

Correspondence and Information

Professor Larry D. Brown
Director of Graduate Studies
Department of Geological Sciences
Snee Hall
Cornell University
Ithaca, NY 14853
Telephone: 607-255-7357
Fax: 607-254-4780
Email: brown@geology.cornell.edu
World Wide Web: http://www.geo.cornell.edu

Cornell University

THE FACULTY AND THEIR RESEARCH

Richard W. Allmendinger, Professor; Ph.D., Stanford, 1979. Structural geology, tectonics, microscopic and mesoscopic rock fabrics, interpretation of seismic reflection profiles.

Warren Allmon, Adjunct Associate Professor; Ph.D., Harvard, 1988. Paleontology, ecology, paleoecology.

Muawia Barazangi, Professor; Ph.D., Columbia, 1971. Seismology, geophysics, tectonics.

William A. Bassett, Professor; Ph.D., Columbia, 1959. Optical microscopy, X-ray diffraction, light absorption, light scattering and electrical resistance at high pressures and temperatures in diamond cells, application to Earth's interior.

John M. Bird, Professor; Ph.D., Rensselaer, 1962. Geotectonics, plate tectonics, orogeny, economic geology, ophiolites, origin of terrestrial metals, geology of the Appalachians, paleostress indicators.

Larry D. Brown, Professor; Ph.D., Cornell, 1976. Exploration seismology, deep structure of continental crust, recent crustal movements, digital signal processing, computer graphics.

Lawrence M. Cathles, Professor; Ph.D., Princeton, 1971. Economic geology, extractive metallurgy, geophysics, geohydrology.

John L. Cisne, Professor; Ph.D., Chicago, 1973. Paleobiology, paleoceanography, biostratigraphy.

Kerry Cook, Associate Professor; Ph.D., North Carolina State, 1984. Climate dynamics, global and regional climate modeling.

Louis A. Derry, Assistant Professor; Ph.D., Harvard, 1989. Interaction of tectonic, geochemical, and biological processes; geochemistry; isotope geology.

Charles H. Greene, Associate Professor; Ph.D., Washington (Seattle), 1985. Physical oceanography, marine geology, acoustic monitoring of ocean biomass.

Bryan L. Isacks, Professor and Chair; Ph.D., Columbia, 1965. Tectonics, satellite remote sensing, earthquake seismology.

Teresa E. Jordan, Professor; Ph.D., Stanford, 1979. Stratigraphy, continental basin evolution, tectonics.

Robert W. Kay, Professor; Ph.D., Columbia, 1970. Petrology, geochemistry, trace-element and isotope geochemistry applied to the origin of igneous rocks and lower continental crust.

Suzanne Mahlburg Kay, Associate Professor; Ph.D., Brown, 1975. Petrology of convergent margin magmas, relation of tectonics processes to magmatic evolution, silicate mineralogy.

James Knapp, Adjunct Associate Professor; Ph.D., MIT, 1988. Structural geology, continental tectonics, geodynamics of Central Asia and the Urals.

K. Douglas Nelson, Adjunct Associate Professor; Ph.D., SUNY at Albany, 1979. Structural geology, stratigraphy and tectonics.

Donald L. Turcotte, Professor; Ph.D., Caltech, 1958. Geophysics, geomechanics, mantle convection, convection in porous media.

William M. White, Professor; Ph.D., Rhode Island, 1977. Isotope and trace-element geochemistry of oceanic igneous rocks and marine sediments, solid-source mass spectrometry, chemical evolution of the mantle and crust.

SELECTED PUBLICATIONS

Allmendinger, R. W., T. E. Jordan, **S. M. Kay,** and **B. L. Isacks.** The evolution of the Altiplano-Puna Plateau of the Central Andes. *Ann. Rev. Earth Planetary Sci.* 25:139–174, 1997.

Allmendinger, R. W., and T. Gubbels. Pure and simple shear plateau uplift, Altiplano-Puna, Argentina and Bolivia. *Tectonophysics* 259(1–3):1-13, 1996.

Brooks, B. A., **R. W. Allmendinger,** and I. G. Garrido. Fault spacing in the El Teniente Mine, central Chile; evidence for nonfractal fault geometry. *J. Geophys. Res.* 101(6):13553–633, 1996.

Cladouhos, T. T., and **R. W. Allmendinger.** Finite strain and rotation from fault slip data. *J. Struct. Geol.* 15:771–84, 1993.

Allmendinger, R. W. Thrust and fold tectonics of the western United States exclusive of the accreted terranes. In *The Cordilleran Orogen: Coterminous U.S.,* pp. 583–607, eds. B. C. Burchfiel, P. Lipman, and M. L. Zoback. Boulder, Colo.: Geological Society of America, 1992.

Allmon, W. D., S. D. Emslie, D. S. Jones, and G. S. Morgan. Late Neogene oceanographic change along Florida's West Coast: Evidence and mechanisms. *J. Geol.* 104:143–62, 1996.

Allmon, W. D. Taxic evolutionary paleoecology and the ecological context of macroevolutionary change. *Evolutionary Ecol.* 8:95–112, 1994.

Allmon, W. D., G. Rosenberg, R. W. Portell, and K. S. Schindler. Diversity of Atlantic coastal plain mollusks since the Pliocene. *Science* 260:1626–8, 1993.

Allmon, W. D. Role of nutrients and temperature in extinction of turritelline gastropods in the northwestern Atlantic and northeastern Pacific. *Palaeogeogr. Palaeoclimatol. Palaeoecol.* 92:41–54, 1992.

Allmon, W. D. Ecology of living turritelline gastropods (Prosobranchia, Turritellidae): Current knowledge and paleontological implications. *Palaios* 3:259–84, 1988.

Brew, G., et al. **(M. Barazangi).** Basement depth and sedimentary velocity structure in the northern Arabian platform, eastern Syria. *Geophys. J.* 128:617–31, 1997.

Seber, D., et al **(M. Barazangi).** Middle East tectonics: Applications of geographic information systems (GIS). *GSA Today* 7(2):1–6, 1997.

Beauchamp, W., **M. Barazangi,** A. Demnati, and M. El Alji. Intracontinental rifting and inversion: Missour Basin and Atlas Mountains, Morocco. *Am. Assoc. Petroleum Geologists Bull.* 80(9):1459–82, 1996.

Seber, D., **M. Barazangi,** A. Ibenbrahim, and A. Demnati. Geophysical evidence for lithospheric delamination beneath the Alboran Sea and Rif-Betic mountains. *Nature* 379:785–90, 1996.

Barazangi, M., and J. Ni. Velocities and propagation characteristics of Pn and Sn beneath the Himalayan arc and Tibetan plateau: Possible evidence for underthrusting of Indian continental lithosphere beneath Tibet. *Geology* 10:179, 1982.

Wu, T.-C., et al **(W. A. Bassett).** Montmorillonite under high H2O pressures; stability of hydrate phases, rehydration hysteresis, and the effect of interlayer cations. *Amer. Miner.* 82(1–2):69–78, 1997.

Bassett, W. A., et al. The hydrothermal diamond anvil cell (HDAC) and its applications. *Spec. Publ. Geochem. Soc.* 5:261–72, 1996.

Bassett, W. A., A. H. Shen, M. Bucknum, and I.-M. Chou. A new diamond anvil cell for hydrothermal studies to 2.5 GPa and from -190°C to 1200°C. *Rev. Sci. Instrum.* 64:2340–5, 1993.

Wu, T.-C., **W. A. Bassett,** P. C. Burnley, and M. S. Weathers. Shear-promoted phase transitions in Fe2SiO4 and Mg2SiO4 and mechanism of deep earthquakes. *J. Geophys. Res.* 98:19767–76, 1993.

Bassett, W. A., and G. E. Brown Jr. Synchrotron radiation: Applications in the earth sciences. In *Annual Reviews of Earth and Planetary Sciences,* vol. 18, pp. 387–447, ed. G. W. Wetherill. Palo Alto, Calif.: Annual Reviews, 1990.

Dickey, J. S., Jr., **W. A. Bassett, J. M. Bird,** and M. S. Weathers. Liquid carbon in the lower mantle? *Geology* 11:219–20, 1983.

Blythe, A. E., **J. M. Bird,** and G. I. Omar. Deformation history of the central Brooks Range, Alaska; results from fission-track and 40Ar/39Ar analyses. *Tectonics* 15(2):440–55, 1996.

Wirth, K. R., et al. **(J. M. Bird).** Age and evolution of western Brooks Range ophiolites, Alaska; results from 40Ar/39Ar thermochronometry. *Tectonics* 12(2):410–32, 1993.

Harding, D. J., K. R. Wirth, and **J. M. Bird.** Spectral mapping of Alaskan ophiolites using Landsat thematic mapper data. *Remote Sensing Environment* 28:219–32, 1989.

Goodrich, C. A., and **J. M. Bird.** Formation of iron-carbon alloys in basaltic magma at Uivfaq, Disko Island: The role of carbon in mafic magmas. *J. Geol.* 93:475–92, 1985.

Brown, L. D., et al. Bright spots, structure, and magmatism in southern Tibet from INDEPTH seismic reflection profiling. *Science* 274(5293):1688–90, 1996.

Steer, D. N., **L. D. Brown,** J. H. Knapp, and D. J. Baird. Comparison of explosive and vibroseis source energy penetration during COCORP deep seismic reflection profiling in the Williston Basin. *Geophysics* 61:211–21, 1995.

Pratt, T. L., et al **(L. D. Brown).** Determining properties of a deep reflector: Wide-angle shear and compressional-wave studies of the midcrustal Surrency Bright Spot beneath southeastern Georgia. *J. Geophys. Res.* 98:17723–35, 1993.

Matos, R., and **L. D. Brown.** Deep seismic profile of the Amazonian craton (northern Brazil). *Tectonics* 11:621–33, 1992.

Brown, L. D., and J. E. Oliver. Recent vertical crustal movements from leveling data and their relation to geologic structure in the eastern U.S. *Rev. Geophys. Space Phys.* 14:13–35, 1976.

Cathles, L. M., W. Fjeldskaar, and J. X. Mitrovica. The inference of mantle viscosity from an inversion of the Fennoscandian relaxation spectrum [discussion and reply]. *Geophys. Jour. Int.* 128(2):489–98, 1997.

Hunt, J. M., J. K. Whelan, L. B. Eglinton, and **L. M. Cathles.** Gas generation; a major cause of deep Gulf Coast overpressures. *Oil Gas J.* 92(29):59–63, 1994.

Cathles, L. M. Oxygen isotope alteration in the Noranda mining district, Abitibi greenstone belt, Quebec. *Econ. Geol.* 88:1483–511, 1993.

Cathles, L. M. A capless 350° flow zone model to explain megaplumes, salinity variations, and high temperature veins in ridge axis hydrothermal systems. *Econ. Geol.* 88:1977–99, 1993.

Cathles, L. M. *The Viscosity of the Earth's Mantle.* Princeton, N.J.: Princeton University Press, 1975.

Ackerly, S., **J. L. Cisne,** B. L. Railsback, and T. F. Anderson. Punctal density in the Ordovician orthide brachiopod Paucicrura rogata; anatomical and paleoenvironmental variation. *Lethaia* 26(1):17–24, 1993.

Muramoto, J. A., et al. **(J. L. Cisne).** Sulfur, iron and organic carbon fluxes in the Black Sea; sulfur isotopic evidence for origin of sulfur fluxes. *Deep-Sea Res. Part A Oceanogr. Res. Pap.* 38 Suppl. 2A:1151–87, 1991.

Gildner, R. F., and **J. L. Cisne.** Quantitative modeling of carbonate stratigraphy and water-depth history using depth-dependent sedimentation function. In *Quantitative Dynamic Stratigraphy,* pp. 417–32, ed. T. A. Cross. Englewood Cliffs, N.J.: Prentice-Hall, 1990.

Railsback, L. B., T. F. Anderson, S. C. Ackerly, and **J. L. Cisne.** Palaeontological and isotope evidence for warm saline deep waters in Ordovician oceans. *Nature* 343:156–9, 1990.

Cisne, J. L. Earthquakes recorded stratigraphically on carbonate platforms. *Nature* 323:320–2, 1986.

Cook, K. H. Large-scale atmospheric dynamics and Sahelian precipitation. *J. Climate* 10:1137–52, 1997.

Nayvelt, L., P. J. Gierasch, and **K. H. Cook.** Modeling and observations of Martian stationary waves. *J. Atmos. Sci.* 8: 986–1013, 1997.

Lenters, J. L., and **K. H. Cook.** On the origin of the Bolivian High and related circulation features of the South American climate. *J. Atmos. Sci.* 5:656–77, 1997.

Cook, K. H., and I. M. Held. The time-mean response of the atmosphere to large-scale orography. *J. Atmos. Sci.* 49:525–39, 1992.

Cook, K. H. The atmosphere's response to the ice sheets of the last glacial maximum. *Ann. Glaciol.* 14:32–8, 1990.

Derry, L. A., and C. France-Lanord. Neogene growth of the sedimentary organic carbon reservoir. *Paleoceanography* 11:267–75, 1996.

Derry, L. A., and C. France-Lanord. Neogene Himalayan weathering history and river 87Sr/86Sr: Impact on the marine Sr record. *Earth Planetary Sci. Lett.* 142:59–76, 1996.

Derry, L. A., et al. Sr and C isotopes in Lower Cambrian carbonates from the Siberian craton: A paleoenvironmental record during the "Cambrian Explosion." *Earth Planetary Sci. Lett.* 128:671–81, 1994.

France-Lanord, C., and **L. A. Derry.** d13C of organic carbon in the Bengal fan: Source evolution and transport of C3 and C4 plant carbon to marine sediments. *Geochim. Cosmochim. Acta* 58:4809–14, 1994.

Cornell University

Selected Publications (continued)

Derry, L. A., and S. B. Jacobsen. The chemical evolution of Precambrian seawater: Evidence from REEs in banded iron formations. *Geochim. Cosmochim. Acta* 54:2965–77, 1990.

Chandy, S. T., and **C. H. Greene.** Estimating the predatory impact of gelatinous zooplankton. *Limnol. Oceanogr.* 40:947–55, 1995.

Genin, A., et al. **(C. H. Greene).** Zooplankton patch dynamics: Daily gap formation over abrupt topography. *Deep-Sea Res.* 41:941–51, 1994.

Greene, C. H., T. K. Stanton, P. H. Wiebe, and S. McClatchie. Acoustic estimates of Antarctic krill. *Nature* 349:110, 1991.

Greene, C. H., and P. H. Wiebe. Bioacoustical oceanography: New tools for zooplankton and micromekton research in the 1990s. *Oceanography* 3:12–17, 1990.

Greene, C. H., P. H. Wiebe, J. Burczynski, and M. J. Youngbluth. Acoustical detection of high-density demersal krill layers in the submarine canyons off Georges Bank. *Science* 241:359–61, 1988.

Smith, L. C., R. R. Forster, **B. L. Isacks,** and D. K. Hall. Seasonal climatic forcings of alpine glaciers revealed with orbital synthetic aperture radar. *J. Glaciol.* 43(145):480–8, 1997.

Whitman, D., **B. L. Isacks,** and **S. M. Kay.** Lithospheric structure and along-strike segmentation of the Central Andean Plateau; seismic Q, magmatism, flexure, topography and tectonics. *Tectonophysics* 259(1–3):29–40, 1996.

Bevis, M., et al. **(B. L. Isacks).** Geodetic observations of very rapid convergence and back-arc extension at the Tonga Arc. *Nature* 374(6519):249–51, 1995.

Masek, J. G., **B. L. Isacks,** T. L. Gubbels, and E. J. Fielding. Erosion and tectonics of margins of continental plateaus. *J. Geophys. Res.* 99:13941–56, 1994.

Isacks, B. L. Uplift of the Central Andean plateau and the bending of the Bolivian Orocline. *J. Geophys. Res.* 93:13841–54, 1988.

Isacks, B. L., J. Oliver, and L. R. Sykes. Seismology and the new global tectonics. *J. Geophys. Res.* 73:5855–99, 1968.

Jordan, T. E., J. H. Reynolds III, and J. P. Erikson. Variability in age of initial shortening and uplift in the Central Andes, 16-33° 30'S. In *Tectonic Uplift and Climate Change,* ed. W. Ruddiman. New York: Plenum, 1997.

Jordan, T. E., R. W. Allmendinger, J. F. Damanti, and R. E. Drake. Chronology of motion in a complete thrust belt: The Precordillera, 30-31°S, Andes Mountains. *J. Geol.* 101:135–56, 1993.

Jordan, T. E., and P. B. Flemings. Large-scale stratigraphic architecture, eustatic variation, and unsteady tectonism: A theoretical evaluation. *J. Geophys. Res.* 96:6681–99, 1991.

Jordan, T. E., and R. N. Alonso. Cenozoic stratigraphy and basin tectonics of the Andes Mountains, 20-28° south latitude. *AAPG Bull.* 71:49–64, 1987.

Jordan, T. E., B. L. Isacks, R. W. Allmendinger, et al. Andean tectonics related to geometry of subducted Nazca plate. *Bull. Geol. Soc. Am.* 94:341–61, 1983.

Yogodzinski, G. M., et al. **(R. W. Kay** and **S. M. Kay).** Magnesian andesite in the western Aleutian Komandorsky region; implications for slab melting and processes in the mantle wedge. *Geol. Soc. Am. Bull.* 107(5):505–19, 1995.

Kay, R. W., and **S. M. Kay.** Delamination and delamination magmatism. *Tectonophysics* 219:177–89, 1993.

Fountain, D. M., R. Arculus, and **R. W. Kay.** *Continental Lower Crust.* New York: Elsevier, 1992.

Kay, R. W., and **S. M. Kay.** Crustal recycling and the Aleutian Arc. *Geochim. Cosmochim. Acta* 52:1351–9, 1988.

Gorring, M. L., et al. **(S. M. Kay).** Neogene Patagonian plateau lavas; continental magmas associated with ridge collision at the Chile triple junction. *Tectonics* 16(1):1–17, 1997.

Kay, S. M., and J. M. Abbruzzi. Magmatic evidence for Neogene lithospheric evolution of the central Andean "flat-slab" between 30° and 32°S. *Tectonophysics* 259(1–3):15–28, 1996.

Kay, S. M., S. Orrell, and J. M. Abbruzzi. Zircon and whole rock Nd-Pb isotopic evidence for a Grenville age and a Laurentian origin for the basement of the Precordilleran terrane in Argentina. *J. Geol.* 104(6):637–48, 1996.

Kay, S. M., B. Coira, and J. Viramonte. Young mafic back-ark volcanic rocks as guides to lithospheric delamination beneath the Argentine Puna Plateau, Central Andes. *J. Geophys. Res.* 99:24323–39, 1994.

Kay, S. M., and **R. W. Kay.** Aleutian magmatism in space and time. In *The Geology of Alaska,* vol. G-1, pp. 687–722, eds. G. Plafker and D. L. Jones. Boulder, Colo.: Geological Society of America. 1994.

Yogodzinski, G. M., J. L. Rubenstone, **S. M. Kay,** and **R. W. Kay.** Magmatic and tectonic development of the Western Aleutians: An oceanic arc in a strike-slip setting. *J. Geophys. Res.* 98:11807–34, 1993.

Steer, D. N., **J. H. Knapp,** and **L. D. Brown.** Super-deep reflection profiling; exploring the continental mantle lid. *Tectonophysics* 286(1–4):111–21, 1998.

Diaconescu, C. C., et al. **(J. H. Knapp).** Precambrian Moho offset and tectonic stability of the East European Platform from the URSEIS deep seismic profile. *Geology* 26(3):211–4, 1998.

Knapp, J. H., et al. Seismic reflection fabrics of continental collision and post-orogenic extension in the middle Urals, central Russia. *Tectonophysics* 288(1–4):115–26, 1998.

Knapp, J. H., et al. Lithosphere-scale seismic image of the Southern Urals from explosion-source reflection profiling. *Science* 274(5285):226–8, 1996.

Steer, D. N., et al. **(J. H. Knapp** and **L. D. Brown).** Crustal structure of the Middle Urals based upon reprocessing of Russian seismic reflection data. *Geophys. J. Int.* 123:673–82, 1995.

Wu, C., et al. **(K. D. Nelson).** Yadong cross structure and South Tibetan detachment in the east central Himalaya (89 degrees–90 degrees E). *Tectonics* 17(1):28–45, 1998.

Nelson, K. D., et al. Partially molten middle crust beneath southern Tibet; synthesis of Project INDEPTH results. *Science* 274(5293):1684–8, 1996.

Nelson, K. D. A unified view of craton evolution motivated by recent deep seismic reflection and refraction results. *Geophys. J.* 105(1):25–35, 1990.

Nelson, K. D., et al. **(L. D. Brown).** COCORP seismic reflection profiling in the Ouachita Mountains of western Arkansas: Geometry and geologic interpretation. *Tectonics* 1:413–30, 1982.

Nelson, K. D. Melange development in the Boones Point Complex: North central Newfoundland. *Can. J. Earth Sci.* 18:433–42, 1981.

Morein, G., **D. L. Turcotte,** and A. Gabrielov. On the statistical mechanics of distributed seismicity. *Geophys. J. Int.* 131(3):552–8, 1997.

Turcotte, D. L. *Chaos in Geology and Geophysics.* Cambridge, UK: Cambridge University Press, 1997.

Kellogg, L. H., and **D. L. Turcotte.** Mixing and the distribution of heterogeneities in a chaotically convecting mantle. *J. Geophys. Res.* 95:421–32, 1990.

Turcotte, D. L. A heat-pipe mechanism for volcanism and tectonics on Venus. *J. Geophys. Res.* 94:2779–85, 1989.

Turcotte, D. L. *Geodynamics.* John Wiley and Sons, 1982.

Godfrey, L. V., et al. **(W. M. White).** The Hf isotopic composition of ferromanganese nodules and crusts and hydrothermal manganese deposits; implications for seawater Hf. *Earth Planet Sci. Lett.* 151(1–2):91–105, 1997.

Keller, R. A., M. R. Fisk, R. A. Duncan, and **W. M. White.** 16 m.y. of hotspot and non-hotspot volcanism on the Patton-Murray seamont platform, Gulf of Alaska. *Geology* 25(6):511–4, 1997.

White, W. M. Crustal recycling; best friend hides a deep secret. *Nature* 379(6561):117–8, 1996.

White, W. M., A. McBirney, and R. A. Duncan. Petrology and geochemistry of the Galapagos Islands: Portrait of a pathological mantle plume. *J. Geophys. Res.* 98:19533–63, 1993.

White, W. M., and A. W. Hofmann. Sr and Nd isotope geochemistry of oceanic basalts and mantle evolution. *Nature* 296:821–5, 1982.

GEORGIA INSTITUTE OF TECHNOLOGY

School of Earth and Atmospheric Sciences

Programs of Study

The School of Earth and Atmospheric Sciences (EAS) offers graduate programs in the geosciences leading to the degrees of Master of Science (M.S.) and Doctor of Philosophy (Ph.D.) in four areas of specialization: geochemistry, solid-earth geophysics, atmospheric chemistry, and atmospheric dynamics and physics.

The core curricula in each area of specialization are designed to provide students from diverse academic backgrounds with a common introduction to fundamental chemical and physical principles. More advanced courses are also available to introduce students to current academic and research topics. Doctoral students pursue their thesis research upon successful completion of the comprehensive examination, which consists of a written original research paper or proposal and an oral examination that covers the paper and fundamental principles within the student's area of specialization.

In addition to the required courses in a student's area of specialization, doctoral candidates complete 10 credit hours of study in an academic minor. This can be satisfied in another discipline within the School or in other academic units at Georgia Tech, such as in Chemistry and Biochemistry, Physics, Mathematics, Public Policy, Computer Sciences, or Environmental Engineering. EAS students can also participate in a certificate program in geohydrology, which is based on educational criteria of the American Institute of Hydrology and is administered by the School of Civil and Environmental Engineering. To accomplish this, students supplement their graduate program of study with a specified set of engineering and EAS courses. Also, marine science research may be carried out in cooperation with the Skidaway Institute of Oceanography. Students conduct their thesis research at Skidaway after completing course work at Georgia Tech.

Research Facilities

The School is well equipped with a wide variety of computational, laboratory, and field measurement research tools. Computational facilities include an array of high-performance workstations and personal computers. Several chromatographs, spectrophotometers, inductively coupled plasma mass spectrometers, and various elemental analyzers are available for analytical measurements of volatile and nonvolatile chemical constituents in solid, liquid, and gaseous samples.

Field equipment includes a high-performance portable reverse osmosis system, a Ramac ground penetrating radar, an EM-31 conductivity meter, a proton precession magnetometer, a resistivity meter, a Lacoste-Romberg gravimeter, four broadband seismometers, geophones and a twelve-channel seismograph, and differential GPS units. The geophysics group maintains a seismic network in northern Georgia and a seismic observatory south of Atlanta. The atmospheric chemistry program maintains several mobile and fixed-site sampling facilities, including a 48-foot mobile laboratory, equipped with a variety of meteorological and analytical instruments for detailed studies of chemical processes. Several research vessels are also available for cooperative research with scientists at the Skidaway Institute of Oceanography.

Financial Aid

Graduate research and teaching assistantships are available to applicants with outstanding records and high research potential. Research and teaching assistants receive a tuition waiver plus a twelve-month stipend that ranges from $14,000 to $15,500. President's Fellowships and President's Minority Fellowships are awarded to qualified matriculants on a competitive basis. These fellowships provide modest stipend supplements and are renewable for up to four years. The Institute also participates in a number of fellowship and traineeship programs sponsored by federal agencies. Traineeships associated with specific programs, such as water resources planning and management, are also available through the Environmental Resources Center.

Cost of Study

Nonresident tuition is estimated to be $5620 per semester in 1999–2000 (see above for information regarding tuition waivers for graduate assistants). The 1999–2000 matriculation fees for graduate assistants are estimated to be $335 per semester.

Living and Housing Costs

Room and board costs for individual graduate students are estimated to be $2800 per semester for 1999–2000. Contemporary on-campus graduate student housing is available as well as private off-campus housing.

Student Group

There are currently about 50 graduate students in the School, representing a diverse body of academic, ethnic, and national backgrounds. Successful applicants typically have degrees in the physical sciences, biological sciences, or engineering and a keen desire to understand the chemistry and physics of the natural environment.

Location

Georgia Tech is located on a 360-acre campus in the heart of midtown Atlanta, a modern, cosmopolitan city with a variety of cultural, historical, and outdoor attractions. The city benefits from a moderate climate, which permits a broad range of year-round outdoor activities. Additional information on Atlanta can be found on the World Wide Web at http://www.accessatlanta.com.

The Institute

Georgia Tech was founded in 1888 and is a member of the University System of Georgia. The Institute has a tradition of excellence as a center of technological research and education, with a strong focus on interdisciplinary activities. The School of Earth and Atmospheric Sciences will soon become a cornerstone of a new campus building that will foster interdisciplinary research in environmental sciences and technology.

Applying

Application information is available from the Graduate Admissions Committee from the address listed below. Prospective applicants are also encouraged to directly contact faculty members with whom their interests best coincide. Applicants are required to submit scores from the General Test of the Graduate Record Examinations. Minimum TOEFL scores of 550 (paper-based) or 213 (computer-based) are required of all international applicants whose native language is not English. To ensure full consideration of available fellowships and assistantships, completed applications should be received by January 15.

Correspondence and Information

EAS Graduate Admissions Committee
School of Earth and Atmospheric Sciences
Georgia Institute of Technology
Atlanta, Georgia 30332-0340
Telephone: 404-894-3893
Fax: 404-894-5638
World Wide Web: http://www.eas.gatech.edu/admissions.html

Georgia Institute of Technology

THE FACULTY AND THEIR RESEARCH

ATMOSPHERIC SCIENCES

Michael H. Bergin, Assistant Professor; Ph.D., Carnegie Mellon, 1994. Aerosol formation, transport, and deposition; light scattering and absorption by aerosols; influence of aerosols on climate; estimation of past atmospheric chemistry based on ice cores.

Robert X. Black, Senior Research Scientist; Ph.D., MIT, 1990. Potential vorticity-based dynamical diagnoses of cyclogenesis, atmospheric blocking, storm tracks, and weather regime transitions; validation of general circulation models; stratosphere-troposphere interactions.

Glen R. Cass, Professor and Chair; Ph.D., Caltech, 1978. Design of regional air pollution control programs, air quality modeling, aerosol mechanics, visibility, air pollution source characteristics and control technology, fluid mechanics, indoor air quality, protection of museums and archaeological sites from damage due to environmental conditions, health effects of air pollutants, environmental economics.

William L. Chameides, Professor; Ph.D., Yale, 1974. Tropospheric gas-phase and aqueous-phase chemistry, air pollution, global chemical cycles, biospheric-atmospheric interaction, cloud chemistry, chemistry of atmospheric lightning.

George Chimonas, Professor; Ph.D., Sussex (England), 1965. Stability of atmospheric flows, internal gravity waves, severe storm theory, atmospheric turbulence.

Derek M. Cunnold, Professor; Ph.D., Cornell, 1965. Remote sensing of the atmosphere, atmospheric data analysis, numerical modeling of atmospheric chemistry and dynamics.

Douglas D. Davis, Professor; Ph.D., Florida, 1966. Airborne-based global atmospheric chemistry measurements, photochemistry, gas kinetics, environmental atmospheric chemistry, global biogeochemical cycles.

Robert E. Dickinson, Professor; Ph.D., MIT, 1966. Global change, climate modeling, remote sensing, tropical deforestation, interaction of terrestrial and atmospheric hydrological processes, drought.

Rong Fu, Associate Professor; Ph.D., Columbia, 1991. Atmospheric hydrological cycle involving water vapor distribution and transport within the troposphere and lower stratosphere, fluxes at the surface, and across tropopause, convection, cloud, and precipitation processes; global land-ocean-atmosphere interaction; satellite remote sensing.

L. Gregory Huey, Associate Professor; Ph.D., Wisconsin–Madison, 1992. Atmospheric chemistry, measurement of trace gases using chemical ionization mass spectrometry, chemical kinetics of both ions and neutrals, heterogeneous chemistry, aircraft sampling of condensible gases.

Chia S. Kiang, Professor; Ph.D., Georgia Tech, 1970. Atmospheric chemistry, nucleation theory, environmental science, public policy, international program development, interdisciplinary research and educational programs.

Shaw C. Liu, Professor; Ph.D., Pittsburgh, 1972. Global and regional budgets of tropospheric trace gases and aerosols, modeling anthropogenic aerosols and their effect on surface radiative processes, regional climate change due to aerosols.

Robert G. Roper, Professor; Ph.D., Adelaide, 1963. Application and interpretation of radar/sonar techniques as applied to the measurement of atmospheric motions, the application of imaging doppler interferometry to radar measurements of atmospheric dynamics.

Scott T. Sandholm, Senior Research Scientist; Ph.D., Michigan State, 1982. Tropospheric chemistry: nitrogen cycles, sources, and sinks; airborne measurements of nitrogen oxides; measurements elucidating the chemical cycles of atmospheric ammonia.

Rodney J. Weber, Assistant Professor; Ph.D., Minnesota, 1995. Atmospheric aerosols, gas-to-particle conversion, mechanisms and conditions for new particle formation by homogeneous nucleation, particle growth processes, aerosol sampling from aircraft.

Paul H. Wine, Professor; Ph.D., Florida State, 1974. Atmospheric free radical chemistry in both gas and condensed phases, chemical kinetics, photochemistry, reaction dynamics.

GEOCHEMISTRY

Patricia M. Dove, Associate Professor; Ph.D., Princeton, 1991. Kinetics and mechanisms of processes at the mineral surface–aqueous solution interfaces; experimental and theoretical methods to study mineral dissolution, crystal growth, and sorption reactions.

Philip N. Froelich, Professor, Ph.D., Rhode Island, 1979. Ocean biogeochemistry, paleoceanography, and paleoclimatology of the Antarctic; marine sedimentary geochemistry; environmental geochemistry of rivers and estuaries; continental chemical weathering; global biogeochemical dynamics; analytical geochemistry.

E. Michael Perdue, Professor; Ph.D., Georgia Tech, 1973. Chemical characterization of dissolved organic matter in natural waters, thermodynamics of acid-base and metal-ligand equilibria involving humic substances.

Philippe S. Van Cappellen, Associate Professor; Ph.D., Yale, 1990. Biogeochemistry of carbon, nitrogen, phosphorus, sulfur, and metals in aquatic environments; mineral-water interactions; geochemical kinetics; transport-reaction modeling; global biogeochemical cycles.

J. Marion Wampler, Associate Professor; Ph.D., Columbia, 1963. Nuclear geochemistry, radiometric age determinations, isotopic geochemistry of argon, geochemistry of radionuclides, trace element geochemistry, sorption on clays.

Charles E. Weaver, Professor Emeritus; Ph.D., Penn State, 1952. Petrology, mineralogy, and geochemistry of shales; global distribution of clay materials throughout geologic time; clay minerals as paleotemperature indicators; effects of filter feeders on clay minerals.

GEOPHYSICS

James B. Gaherty, Assistant Professor; Ph.D., MIT, 1995. Global seismology and mantle dynamics, seismic anisotropy and upper-mantle heterogeneity, subduction and fate of slabs, initiation of earthquake rupture, regional and tomographic modeling.

Daniel Lizarralde, Assistant Professor; Ph.D. MIT/Woods Hole Oceanic Institute, 1997. Evolution of Earth's crust and lithosphere studied via active source seismology, processes at continental margins, large igneous provinces, plume-ridge interaction, methane gas–hydrate reservoirs.

L. Timothy Long, Professor; Ph.D., Oregon State, 1968. Earthquake seismology and tectonophysics emphasizing mechanisms of intraplate earthquakes, seismic monitoring, near-surface geophysics, surface-wave tomography, seismic hazard analysis, gravity data acquisition and analysis.

Robert P. Lowell, Professor; Ph.D., Oregon State, 1972. Mathematical modeling of continental and seafloor hydrothermal systems, water-rock reactions and two-phase flow in porous media, evolution of permeability, physics of magmatic processes, methane gas hydrates, wetland hydrology.

Carolyn D. Ruppel, Assistant Professor; Ph.D., MIT, 1992. Methane gas hydrates, environmental geophysics for shallow hydrologic applications, three-dimensional structure of continental lithosphere, integrated geophysical and petrologic studies of mid-ocean ridges and orogenic belts.

GEORGIA STATE UNIVERSITY

College of Arts and Sciences
Department of Geology

Programs of Study

The department offers programs leading to the Master of Science (M.S.) degree in geology and the Doctor of Philosophy (Ph.D.) degree in geochemistry. Instruction and research opportunities are provided in the areas of low-temperature and aqueous geochemistry, soils and clay mineralogy, hydrogeology, mineralogy, paleontology, petrology, Quaternary geology, sedimentology, stratigraphy, structural geology/tectonics, experimental petrology and geoscience education. The department stresses but does not restrict students to field-related studies. Atlanta is situated on the Brevard Zone between the Piedmont and Blue Ridge provinces of the southern Appalachians, underlain by intrusive and high-grade metamorphic rocks. A wide variety of geologic settings are easily accessible for thesis research. The Valley and Ridge and Coastal Plain provinces are within a short drive of Atlanta. Faculty members have supervised M.S. thesis field research outside of Georgia and the United States. The department also offers an Advanced Certificate program in hydrogeology. A minimum of one academic year of residence is required for the M.S. degree. Thirty-six semester hours of graduate-level credit are required for the thesis-option master's degree, including 6 hours of thesis work and 3 to 6 hours of courses in related disciplines outside the department. A nonthesis M.S. degree option is also available to qualified applicants. Master's degree students must demonstrate knowledge of a foreign language or an approved alternative research skill, complete a thesis, take a written general examination, and orally defend the thesis. The Ph.D. program requires 80 semester hours, four semesters of residence, and a dissertation.

Research Facilities

The department has facilities and equipment for field and laboratory research, including vehicles; plane tables; fossil curation equipment; a sedimentological laboratory; a hydrogeochemistry laboratory; a clay mineral separation lab and soil collection equipment; microscopes with full accessories; a rock preparation laboratory; a heating/freezing fluid-inclusion stage; video, photographic, and drafting equipment; microcomputers and mainframes; computerized XRF and XRD facilities; an ICPMS and laser ablation laboratory; cathodoluminescence; a high-pressure, high-temperature rock deformation apparatus; an argon ion mill for TEM foil preparation; and access to scanning electron microscopes and microprobe. Hydrogeology students also have access to logging equipment and geophysical and water-quality instrumentation. The department has access to facilities of the Skidway Institute and the Marine Extension Center on Skidway Island. The Georgia State University (GSU) library receives all major and many minor journals devoted to geology; most extend back to the first volume. GSU is a repository for USGS publications, has a good map collection, and subscribes to GEOREF and many other databases. Students also have access to the libraries of the Georgia Institute of Technology, Emory University, and the Georgia Geological Survey, all located in Atlanta.

Financial Aid

Graduate research assistantships (GRAs) are available for qualified students. Stipends generally are $6000 to $12,000 for two semesters plus tuition waiver. Some summer assistantships are also available. Cooperative programs with Atlanta-based geotechnical companies or government agencies normally can be arranged.

Cost of Study

For current tuition figures, students may visit the University's Web site (http://www.gsu.edu).

Living and Housing Costs

Georgia State University has a nonresidential campus located in downtown Atlanta at the center of a network of highways and rapid-transit services extending throughout the greater metropolitan area. This transportation network makes it possible to live anywhere in the metropolitan area and get to downtown easily. The cost of living in Atlanta is moderate compared with that in other centers in the United States. Dormitory housing is available at the Georgia State Village, a short distance from Georgia State's downtown campus.

Student Group

Georgia State University is a public institution with more than 24,000 students. The graduate student population of more than 7,000 is one of the largest in the Southeast. The average age of graduate students is 33. Students from 113 countries and all fifty states attend the University.

Location

The University is located in the heart of Atlanta's central business district. The city is a rapidly growing metropolitan area characterized by a spectacular skyline and a culturally diverse population. Atlanta's Hartsfield International Airport is one of the world's largest and busiest, making the city easily accessible from anywhere in the world. The climate is moderate, with a mean July temperature of 23°C and a mean January temperature of 10°C. Atlanta is located in the foothills of the southern Appalachian mountain range and is close to both the Great Smokey Mountains and the Atlantic and Gulf coasts.

The University and The Department

Georgia State University is responsive to students' career goals and provides educational and research programs relevant to the practical needs of both the students and the community. The University offers nearly fifty undergraduate and graduate degree programs covering some 200 fields of study through its five colleges—Arts and Sciences, Business Administration, Education, Health and Human Sciences, Law–and its School of Policy Studies.

Applying

Application materials may be obtained from the department or from the Office of Graduate Studies of the College of Arts and Sciences. Applicants must submit the Application for Graduate Study and the University Information forms, a $25 application fee, official copies of transcripts from each institution attended, GRE General Test scores, three letters of recommendation, and a statement of educational and career goals. Applicants may obtain additional information about the Department of Geology by contacting the Director of Graduate Studies or by visiting the Web page, listed below.

Correspondence and Information

Director of Graduate Studies
Department of Geology
340 Kell Hall
Georgia State University
Atlanta, Georgia 30303-3083

Telephone: 404-651-2272
Fax: 404-651-1376
E-mail: geohab@panther.gsu.edu
World Wide Web: http://www.gsu.edu/~wwwgeo

Georgia State University

THE FACULTY AND THEIR RESEARCH

Hassan A. Babaie, Associate Professor; Ph.D., Northwestern, 1984. Structural geology and tectonics of fold-and-thrust belts, ophiolites, mylonitic shear zones, and accretionary prisms; neotectonics of southwest Montana.

Pamela C. Burnley, Assistant Professor; Ph.D., California, Davis, 1990. High-pressure experimental rock deformation, mantle phase transformation and computer modeling of these processes; effectiveness of teaching methods and outreach strategies for geosciences.

W. Crawford Elliott, Assistant Professor; Ph.D., Case Western Reserve, 1988. Clay mineralogy, K/Ar dating, soil geochemistry.

William J. Fritz, Professor; Ph.D., Montana, 1980. Sedimentology and stratigraphy, volcaniclastic sedimentation, influence of explosive volcanism on depositional environment, Tertiary stratigraphy and neotectonics of southwest Montana.

Vernon J. Henry, Professor Emeritus; Ph.D., Texas A&M, 1961. Geology of coasts, barrier islands, and coastal plains; monitoring of shoreline changes; sub-bottom profiling of continental shelves.

Timothy E. La Tour, Associate Professor; Ph.D., Western Ontario, 1979. Metamorphic and structural geology, mylonites and mylonite zones, metamorphic geochemistry.

Seth E. Rose, Associate Professor; Ph.D., Arizona, 1987. Aqueous geochemistry, controls on groundwater quality and hazardous-waste disposal, regional hydrogeology.

David A. Vanko, Professor and Chair; Ph.D., Northwestern, 1982. Igneous petrology, geochemistry, fluid-rock interactions, and metallogenesis, especially in the young ocean crust along the mid-ocean ridge system.

Research Scientist

A. Mohamad Ghazi, Ph.D., Nebraska, 1992. Analytical geochemistry, petrogenesis of Iranian ophiolites, development of new applications of ICPMS and laser ablation ICPMS.

Instructors

Kenneth J. Terrell, M.A., Cincinnati, 1980. Vertebrate paleontology and geomorphology.

Annette B. McCartney, M.S., Georgia State, 1995. Earth science education.

HARVARD UNIVERSITY

Department of Earth and Planetary Sciences

Programs of Study

The department offers instruction and opportunities for research in a wide variety of fields within the broad scope of earth and planetary sciences. Requirements for admission are highly flexible, but adequate undergraduate preparation in mathematics, physics, and chemistry is strongly recommended. Students whose undergraduate majors are in science, engineering, or mathematics and who desire a Ph.D. in one of the fields of earth and planetary sciences are encouraged to apply. The master's degree is not a prerequisite for entering the Ph.D. program. Students are not normally admitted to work toward a terminal A.M. degree. The student's Ph.D. research often includes interaction with several faculty members in addition to the primary thesis adviser.

Graduate study leading to the Ph.D. degree is supervised by a faculty advisory committee made up in accordance with each student's aims and interests. Fields of teaching and research include atmospheric chemistry, dynamic meteorology, economic geology, geochemistry, geophysics, mineralogy, oceanography, paleontology, petrology, sedimentology, seismology, stratigraphy, and structural geology. In addition, courses may be taken in chemistry, physics, engineering, or biology. Under reciprocal arrangements, graduate students at Harvard may take and receive credit for courses given at the Massachusetts Institute of Technology in Cambridge and the Woods Hole Oceanographic Institute.

Research Facilities

The department is housed in Hoffman Laboratory, the adjoining Geological Museum, and a building called "the Link" that joins Hoffman Laboratory with the Department of Chemistry. These buildings provide office, classroom, and laboratory space for the faculty, staff, and students. The facilities and equipment include a computing facility based on a network of Sun Workstations with a wide range of peripheral devices such as a massive online storage system for seismological data; a mass spectrometer facility that includes a coupled plasma mass spectrometer, a stable gas isotope ratio mass spectrometer, and two thermal ionization mass spectrometers; a high-pressure facility that includes two large hydraulic presses fitted with multianvil devices; an electron microprobe and X-ray laboratory; facilities for geophysical and paleontological fluid dynamics experiments; and associated laboratories for sample preparation and analysis.

Financial Aid

All students receive financial support for both tuition and living expenses while studying for advanced degrees. Support comes from Harvard University, independent fellowships, and research and teaching assistantships. The base living expenses stipend is $1500 per month.

Cost of Study

The cost of tuition is paid in full by the department for the first four years. Tuition costs include health insurance and cover the use of facilities and services of the University.

Living and Housing Costs

Unmarried students may live at the Graduate Center dormitories at costs ranging from $4000 to $5500 during the 1999–2000 academic year. Married students may rent University-owned apartments near campus.

Student Group

The department has from 30 to 35 graduate students and about 50 undergraduates. The GeoClub, a student organization more than sixty years old, organizes lectures and activities.

Student Outcomes

Students who earn graduate degrees from the Department of Earth and Planetary Sciences pursue a range of careers in academia, government, and industry. In addition to teaching, recent graduates have found research positions in planetary magnetism, climatology, atmospheric chemistry, geodynamics, and other areas of earth science. Other graduates are employed in mining, petroleum exploration, and environmental fields.

Location

The Cambridge-Boston area is one of the most concentrated centers of educational, intellectual, and cultural activity in the world. At the same time, there is ready access to the scenic and historic New England countryside, which is of diverse and abundant geologic interest. Recreational activities range from the full scope of indoor athletic activities provided by Harvard to sailing and skiing. The great concentration of educational organizations in the area makes the total student population quite large, and the services offered for the benefit of students are correspondingly numerous.

The University

Harvard, the oldest institution of higher learning in the United States, offers an educational life covering the entire span of the fields of learning, old and new. Tradition is strong, but innovation and change are characteristic. Graduate students in the Department of Earth and Planetary Sciences mingle with students from other graduate departments, with undergraduates, and with students at the various professional schools.

Applying

Completed applications for admission and scholarship aid should be submitted before the end of December. Scores on the GRE General Test are required, but it is not required that a student take a Subject Test. The examination should be taken early in the fall to ensure completion before the admission application deadline.

Correspondence and Information

Professor Michael B. McElroy, Department Chair
Department of Earth and Planetary Sciences
Hoffman Laboratory
Harvard University
20 Oxford Street
Cambridge, Massachusetts 02138-2902
Telephone: 617-495-2351

Harvard University

THE FACULTY AND THEIR RESEARCH

James G. Anderson, Philip S. Weld Professor of Atmospheric Chemistry; Ph.D., Colorado, 1970. Gas-phase kinetics of free radicals, catalytic processes in the atmosphere controlling global change of ozone, high-altitude experiments from balloons and aircraft, development of laser systems for stratospheric and tropospheric studies, development of high-altitude long-duration unmanned aircraft for studies of global change.

Jeremy Bloxham, Professor of Geophysics; Ph.D., Cambridge, 1986. Planetary magnetic fields, dynamo theory, structure and dynamics of the earth's core and lower mantle, inverse theory, mathematical geophysics.

James N. Butler, Gordon McKay Professor of Applied Chemistry; Ph.D., Harvard, 1959. Chemistry of natural and polluted waters, physical chemistry of interfaces, electrochemistry, oil pollution of the oceans.

Adam M. Dziewonski, Frank B. Baird Jr. Professor of Science; Ph.D., Polish Academy of Sciences, 1965. Theoretical seismology, internal structure of the earth, seismic tomography, earthquake source mechanisms, geodynamics.

Göran A. Ekström, Professor of Geophysics; Ph.D., Harvard, 1987. Seismology, forward and inverse problems of seismic source.

Brian F. Farrell, Robert P. Burden Professor of Meteorology; Ph.D., Harvard, 1981. Explosive development of tropical and mid-latitude cyclones, predictability of weather regimes, dynamics of glacial and equable paleoclimates.

Stephen J. Gould, Professor of Geology and Alexander Agassiz Professor of Zoology in the Museum of Comparative Zoology; Ph.D., Columbia, 1967. Stochastic simulation of evolutionary patterns, the evolution of growth, Pleistocene and recent evolution of the Bahamian land snail *Cerion,* the evolution of brain size, relationship of ontogeny and phylogeny.

Paul F. Hoffman, Sturgis Hooper Professor of Geology; Ph.D., Johns Hopkins, 1970. Global tectonics, evolution of the earth's crust in the Precambrian, sedimentology and stratigraphy.

Heinrich D. Holland, Harry C. Dudley Professor of Economic Geology; Ph.D., Columbia, 1952. Chemistry and chemical evolution of the ocean-atmosphere-crust system, chemistry of ore-forming solutions.

Daniel J. Jacob, Gordon McKay Professor of Atmospheric Chemistry and Environmental Engineering; Ph.D., Caltech, 1985. Air pollution, atmospheric transport, regional and global atmospheric chemistry, biosphere-atmosphere interactions, climate change.

Stein B. Jacobsen, Professor of Geochemistry; Ph.D., Caltech, 1980. Isotope and trace-element geochemistry, chemical evolution of earth's crust-mantle system, isotopic and chemical evolution of seawater.

Andrew H. Knoll, Professor of Biology; Ph.D., Harvard, 1977. Paleontology and sedimentary geology of Precambrian terrains, evolution of vascular plants in geologic time.

James J. McCarthy, Alexander Agassiz Professor of Biological Oceanography; Ph.D., California, San Diego (Scripps), 1971. Biological oceanography, phytoplankton ecology, nitrogen nutrition of phytoplankton.

Michael B. McElroy, Gilbert Butler Professor of Environmental Studies and Department Chair; Ph.D., Queen's at Kingston, 1962. Chemistry of atmosphere and oceans, including interactions with the biosphere; evolution of planetary atmospheres.

Richard J. O'Connell, Professor of Geophysics; Ph.D., Caltech, 1969. Geodynamics: mantle flow, convection, and plate tectonics; models of tectonic processes; elasticity and rheology of rocks and minerals.

James R. Rice, Gordon McKay Professor of Engineering Sciences and Geophysics; Ph.D., Lehigh, 1963. Crustal stressing and earthquake source processes, fracture theory, solid mechanics, materials science.

Allan R. Robinson, Gordon McKay Professor of Geophysical Fluid Dynamics; Ph.D., Harvard, 1959. Physical and dynamical oceanography, geophysical fluid dynamics, numerical models of ocean currents and interdisciplinary modeling, design and interpretation of field experiments.

Roberta L. Rudnick, Associate Professor of Geology; Ph.D., Australian National, 1988. Geochemistry of continental crust and mantle materials: crustal growth processes, nature of the lower crust; origin of peridotites, eclogites, diamonds, and their inclusions.

Daniel P. Schrag, John L. Loeb Associate Professor of the Natural Sciences; Ph.D., Berkeley, 1993. Geochemical oceanography, paleoclimatology, stable isotope geochemistry.

John H. Shaw, Assistant Professor of Structural and Economic Geology; Ph.D., Princeton, 1993. Structure of the Earth's crust, active faulting and folding, earthquake hazards assessment, petroleum exploration methods, remote sensing.

Jeroen Tromp, Professor of Geophysics; Ph.D., Princeton, 1992. Theoretical global seismology: free oscillations, surface waves, and body waves; structure of the earth; seismic tomography.

Nikolaas J. van der Merwe, Landon T. Clay Professor of Scientific Archaeology; Ph.D., Yale, 1966. Chemical applications in archaeology, light-stable isotopes in dietary and environmental reconstruction, history of metallurgy.

Steven C. Wofsy, Gordon McKay Professor of Atmospheric and Environmental Sciences; Ph.D., Harvard, 1971. Chemistry of the atmosphere on global and regional scales, including stratospheric and tropospheric chemistry.

INDIANA UNIVERSITY BLOOMINGTON

Department of Geological Sciences

Programs of Study

The Department of Geological Sciences at Indiana University offers training at the master's and doctoral levels in many fields of the geological sciences, including biogeochemistry, economic geology, aqueous and isotope geochemistry, geomorphology, geophysics, hydrogeology, mineralogy and petrology, paleoecology, paleontology, petroleum geology, sedimentology, stratigraphy, structural geology, and tectonics. The programs are open to students with undergraduate degrees in geology, chemistry, engineering, mathematics, physics, and the biological sciences.

Graduate courses are structured within a three-tier system: introductory seminars on integrated research topics and quantitative skills; core courses in environmental geology and hydrology, geobiology, geochemistry, geophysics, and sedimentology/stratigraphy; and a combination of advanced courses and seminars in specialized research areas.

A minimum of three years of graduate work (90 hours), completion of a dissertation in the major area, proficiency in one language or a tool skill, and an minor area are required for the Ph.D. degree. Three major examinations are part of the Ph.D. program: a preliminary examination usually taken during the second semester of post-master's study; a qualifying examination taken after completion of course work, including the language or tool skill requirement; and a defense-of-thesis examination. The program of course work is flexible, depending on individual goals and background, but consists of a minimum of 35 hours at the graduate level.

The M.S. program consists of 30 hours of graduate study combined with a thesis or by either demonstrated proficiency in a foreign language or through designated course work in a research tool skill. The thesis may include a maximum of 8 hours toward the 30-hour requirement.

Research Facilities

The diverse needs of various research programs for sample preparation and for geochemical and mineralogical measurements are fulfilled by various facilities. Analytical instruments include molecular and stable isotopic mass spectrometers; gas chromatographs; preparation lines for stable isotopes; an automated electron microprobe and X-ray diffraction units; atomic absorption and emission spectrometric equipment (including inductively coupled plasma); and ion and elemental analyzers and high-temperature experimental facilities. There is a seismic station. The instruments, ancillary facilities for other analytical determinations, and field equipment are maintained by dedicated support staff members who assist students in gaining hands-on experience in their use. Several analytical and computer laboratories that serve the needs of various research groups (including biochemistry, geophysics, inorganic geochemistry, and hydrology) have benefitted from major renovations in recent years. The department maintains a geological field station in southwest Montana. This permanent facility is used as a teaching center for field geology and also serves as a base for geological research in the Rockies.

Computers equipped with relevant software are available for specific activities within individual research groups. Many are dedicated to the particular needs of projects in geological and geophysical modeling and imaging; others fulfill the needs for data processing capabilities. There is a departmental computing laboratory, and the Geology Building also houses a computer UNIX cluster, which is one of many campuswide computing facilities (Macintosh, PC, and UNIX) maintained by University Information Technology Services. The University is involved in the development of Internet 2.

The Geology Library houses an extensive collection of geological publications and maps and carries subscriptions to all periodicals that are pertinent to the research activities of the faculty members and graduate students. It provides electronic access to library catalogs, geologic information, and facilities for literature searches, including GeoRef.

Financial Aid

A substantial number of teaching assistantships, research assistantships, and fellowships are available to qualified students. The stipends and fee support that are offered are competitive. Prestigious University-wide fellowships are awarded to outstanding applicants. The department and University offer funds to support field and/or laboratory expenses connected with dissertation research. A number of summer assistantships at the field station and on campus are also available.

Cost of Study

Tuition for 1999–2000 is $152.90 per credit hour for Indiana residents and $445.40 for nonresidents. Currently, teaching and research assistants and students with fellowships ordinarily pay a fee of $260 each semester for a maximum of 12 hours per semester.

Living and Housing Costs

Housing for unmarried students in the Eigenmann Graduate Center ranges from about $5000 to $6250 for the academic year, including meals and other fees. Rent for University married student housing ranges from about $450 to $900 per month.

Student Group

Forty-two graduate students are currently enrolled in the department, and about 90 percent of them receiving financial support. Approximately half are studying toward the Ph.D. degree. The student body is drawn from all regions of the United States and from a number of other countries. The department also has 81 undergraduate majors.

Location

Bloomington is located in the south-central part of the state in a scenic region of low but rugged relief. There are many recreational opportunities (fishing, boating, hiking, canoeing, cycling, camping, spelunking, skiing, and swimming) and several state parks and state and national forests in the immediate vicinity. Lake Monroe, the largest lake wholly within the state, is a major recreational site about 10 miles south of the city. The city of Bloomington has a permanent population of about 65,000, with an economy based largely on the University and several mechanical and electronic firms. Indianapolis (population about 750,000) is 50 miles northeast and offers all the facilities of a large city, including an international airport. Cincinnati, Louisville, Chicago, and St. Louis are all just a few hours' drive away.

The University

Indiana University was founded as a small seminary in Bloomington in 1820. This makes it the second-oldest state-supported university in the Midwest. It is also one of the largest, with approximately 36,000 students on the Bloomington campus studying within the College of Arts and Sciences in all major fields of science, social science, humanities, and the arts. The campus is comprised of various professional schools, including education, law, business, journalism, library and information science, and music. Despite its size, the campus has retained much of the charm of smaller settings, preserving much open space and wooded areas. Many cultural events are supported by the University community, including a full and varied program of theater, dance, opera, symphony, jazz, and pop concerts, performed by both professional touring companies and student groups. The University also has a well-balanced athletic program of both intramural and major collegiate sports.

Applying

Applications for admission to graduate study can be made at any time, but applications requesting financial assistance should be made before January 15 for consideration for support in the following fall semester. An official transcript and three letters of reference must be supplied. The Graduate Record Examinations General Test results are required. The Subject Test in geology is optional.

Correspondence and Information

Chair
Committee for Graduate Studies
Department of Geological Sciences
Indiana University
Bloomington, Indiana 47405
Telephone: 812-855-7214
　　　　　800-553-2592 (toll-free)
E-mail: geograd@indiana.edu
World Wide Web: http://www.indiana.edu/~geosci

Indiana University Bloomington

THE FACULTY AND THEIR RESEARCH

Christopher G. Maples, Professor and Chair; Ph.D., Indiana. Paleoecology and invertebrate paleantology, lagerstötten, paleobiogeography, statigraphy.

Abhijit Basu, Professor; Ph.D., Indiana. Mineralogy and petrology, lunar geology.

Simon C. Brassell, Professor; Ph.D., Bristol (England). Molecular organic geochemistry, biogeochemistry, paleoclimatology, petroleum geochemistry.

Jeremy Dunning, Professor; Ph.D., North Carolina. Structural geology, rock mechanics, and fracturing; stress corrosion.

Erle G. Kauffman, Professor; Ph.D., Michigan. Mesozoic-Cenozoic molluscan evolutional and paleontologic theory, Jurassic through Paleogene stratigraphy, depositional environments.

Noel C. Krothe, Professor; Ph.D., Penn State. Hydrogeology, hydrochemistry and stable isotopes, water–rock interactions.

Enrique Merino, Professor; Ph.D., Berkeley. Chemical sedimentology, solution chemistry, dynamic fluid-mineral systems.

Peter J. Ortoleva, Distinguished Professor; Ph.D., Cornell. Geochemistry, thermodynamics, kinetics, and transport mechanisms, modeling geochemical systems, basin diagenesis.

Gary L. Pavlis, Professor; Ph.D., Washington (Seattle). Seismology, geophysical inversion, seismic wave propogation, 3-D tomography.

Lisa M. Pratt, Professor; Ph.D., Princeton. Organic geochemistry, stable-isotope geochemistry, sulfer cycles, sedimentology, cyclic stratigraphy.

Edward M. Ripley, Professor; Ph.D., Penn State. Metallic ore deposits, geochemical exploration, stable isotopes and fluid inclusions.

Lee J. Suttner, Professor; Ph.D., Wisconsin. Physical stratigraphy, sedimentology, sedimentary petrology, ancient fluviol systems, foreland basins.

Robert P. Wintsch, Professor; Ph.D., Brown. Metamorphic, structural, and theoretical petrology, geochronology, phase equilibria.

James G. Brophy, Associate Professor and Director, Indiana Geologic Field Station; Ph.D., Johns Hopkins. Igneous petrology, tectonophysics of magma ascension, magmatic differentiation.

Michael Hamburger, Associate Professor; Ph.D., Cornell. Observational seismology, tectonics, earthquake prediction, geodynamics, geodetic measurements.

Gregory Olyphant, Associate Professor; Ph.D., Iowa. Surface and subsurface hydrology, acide mine drainage and erosion, computer modeling.

Lawrence Onesti, Associate Professor; Ph.D., Wisconsin. Geomorphology, environmental geology.

David G. Towell, Associate Professor; Ph.D., MIT. Trace-element and isotope geochemistry, geochemistry and petrology of plutons and volcanics.

Claudia Johnson, Assistant Professor; Ph.D., Colorado. Caribbean geology, evolution of rudistid bivalves, ancient reefs and tropical geobiology, paleoclimatology.

Arndt Schimmelmann, Associate Scientist; Ph.D., UCLA. Chemical oceanography, stable isotopes in organic matter, paleoclimatology.

Michael D. Dorais, Assistant Scientist; Ph.D., Georgia. Igneous petrology, alkaline magma genesis, emplacement processes, mafic enclaves.

Bruce Douglas, Assistant Scientist; Ph.D., Princeton. Regional tectonics, field and experimental study of deformation mechanisms.

Erika Elswick, Assistant Scientist; Ph.D., Cincinnati. Geochemistry, sedimentary ore deposits, depositional environments and diagenetic processes.

Emeritus Faculty

Robert F. Blakely, Professor Emeritus; Ph.D., Indiana. Geophysics.

J. Robert Dodd, Professor Emeritus; Ph.D., Caltech. Paleoecology, carbonate petrology, biogeochemistry, marine geology.

John B. Droste, Professor Emeritus; Ph.D., Illinois. Sedimentary petrology, clay mineralogy, evaporites, environmental geology.

Donald E. Hattin, Professor Emeritus; Ph.D., Kansas. Stratigraphy, paleoecology, Cretaceous sedimentology and biostratigraphy.

Norman C. Hester, Professor Emeritus; Ph.D., Cincinnati. Depositional environments, Carboniferous stratigraphy, coal and petroleum geology.

N. Gary Lane, Professor Emeritus; Ph.D., Kansas. Paleontology, crinoids, Mississippian and Pennsylvanian fauna, Paleozoic geology, paleoecology.

Judson Mead, Professor Emeritus; Ph.D., MIT. Geophysics, rock magnetism, experimental seismology.

Haydn H. Murray, Professor Emeritus; Ph.D., Illinois. Clay mineralogy, nonmetallic mineral deposits, economic geology, coal geology.

Albert J. Rudman, Professor Emeritus; Ph.D., Indiana. Geophysics, gravity, magnetics.

Charles J. Vitaliano, Professor Emeritus; Ph.D., Columbia. Petrology, igneous and metamorphic geology, ignimbrites.

Adjunct Faculty

Gordon S. Fraser, Associate Professor (Indiana Geological Survey); Ph.D., Illinois. Pleistocene and Holocene sedimentology.

Brian D. Keith, Associate Professor (Indiana Geological Survey); Ph.D., RPI. Carbonate depositional models and facies, carbonate petrology, petroleum geology.

Hendrik M. Haitjema, Professor (School of Public and Environmental Affairs); Ph.D., Minnesota. Hydrology, groundwater flow modeling.

Erik Kvale, Associate Professor (Indiana Geological Survey); Ph.D., Iowa State. Clastic sedimentology, coal-bearing sequences, tidal rhythmites.

Carl B. Rexroad, Professor (Indiana Geological Survey); Ph.D., Iowa. Conodonts, paleontology, Paleozoic stratigraphy.

Jeffrey R. White, Professor (School of Public and Environmental Affairs); Ph.D., Syracuse. Aquatic chemistry, limnology, biogeochemistry.

Indiana Geologic Field Station, Montana.

Indiana University Geology Building.

IOWA STATE UNIVERSITY

Department of Geological and Atmospheric Sciences

Programs of Study

The department offers M.S. and Ph.D. degrees in geology and earth science with specializations in hydrogeology, environmental geology, geochemistry, petrology, mineralogy, structural geology/tectonics, stratigraphy/sedimentation, economic geology, and earth science education.

Graduate degree programs in geology include specific requirements but remain flexible so that individual programs can be formulated to suit individual students. The earth science programs have different specified requirements and even greater flexibility to provide opportunities in more broadly defined areas of earth science. The department participates in interdisciplinary water resources and mineral resources programs and in the Center for Coal and the Environment program. A double major in geology and water resources is available to students who are studying some aspect of hydrogeology and/or aqueous geochemistry.

The M.S. program typically requires 2–2½ years of study, particularly for those who hold assistantships. The degree requires preparation of a thesis. The Ph.D. program typically requires three to four years beyond the master's degree and focuses strongly on completing a significant dissertation research project.

Research Facilities

The department has research laboratories with a variety of instrumentation, including an X-ray diffractometer; an X-ray fluorescence unit; an automated electron microprobe; high-temperature and high-pressure experimental laboratories that contain high-temperature furnaces; cold-seal Stellite and TZM pressure vessels; a piston cylinder apparatus; large-volume hydrothermal reaction vessels; fluid inclusion stages; low-temperature crystal growth chambers; ultraviolet, visible, and infrared spectrophotometers; a liquid scintillation counter; a high-pressure liquid chromatograph; a refrigerated incubator-shaker; a 500 MHz Alpha workstation; a 36-inch HP Design Jet color printer; and equipment for the field hydrogeology program. The department maintains a teaching/research lab with 486 and Pentium microcomputers connected to the Iowa State high-speed, fiber-optic Ethernet network. Iowa State maintains numerous high-speed DEC and SGI workstations and access to a Cray supercomputer.

Equipment available on campus includes ICP, GC/MS, and FT-IR spectroscopy; NMR spectroscopy; laser-Raman spectroscopy, TEM, SEM, and computerized single-crystal X-ray diffraction; and drafting and photographic facilities. The on-campus DOE National Laboratory and USDA National Soil Tilth Laboratory also have specialized equipment.

Financial Aid

The department offers teaching assistantships and research assistantships to qualified students with stipends starting at $1111 per month for a half-time appointment. Teaching assistantships involve 20 hours per week of preparation, teaching, and grading for laboratory or discussion classes. High-quality applicants are nominated for Graduate College Premium for Academic Excellence (PACE) Awards for one to three years; these awards can cover half of resident tuition.

A Graduate College Scholarship Credit covers a portion of the resident fee for each teaching and research assistant on full admission. The scholarships award $792 per semester to students on quarter- or half-time appointments.

Cost of Study

Full-time tuition and fees for the academic year are currently $1583 per semester for Iowa residents and $4662 per semester for nonresidents (nonresidents with assistantships pay resident tuition).

Living and Housing Costs

It is estimated that for the typical single student, the cost of room, board, books, supplies, and personal expenses totals approximately $7000 (not counting tuition) for a nine-month academic year.

Student Group

There are approximately 25,000 students at Iowa State University; about 4,500 are graduate students. The department currently has 25 graduate students, of whom 8 are pursuing Ph.D. degrees. These students come from all parts of the United States and from several other countries.

Location

Ames has a population of approximately 50,000 and is surrounded by some of the most fertile farmland on Earth. The city maintains twenty-seven parks and 650 acres of streams and woods and offers outstanding indoor and outdoor recreational facilities. The campus is 30 miles north of Des Moines, the capital and largest city in Iowa (with a population of approximately 250,000). Chicago, Minneapolis, St. Louis, and Kansas City are within a few hours' drive.

The University

Iowa State University, which encompasses 1,700 acres, was founded in 1858 as the land-grant institution for the state of Iowa. The University is an outstanding cultural center and offers an excellent program of popular and symphonic concerts and theater performed by international, national, and local companies. The University offers a wide variety of major intercollegiate and intramural sports.

Applying

Completed applications for admission and financial assistance, a statement of purpose, TOEFL scores for applicants whose native language is not English, three letters of recommendation, and official transcripts should be received before February 15 for funding consideration for the following fall semester. The department requires submission of GRE General Test scores and recommends submission of scores on the GRE Subject Test in geology.

Correspondence and Information

Graduate Applications Coordinator
Department of Geological and Atmospheric Sciences
253 Science Hall 1
Iowa State University
Ames, Iowa 50011
Telephone: 515-294-4477
Fax: 515-294-6049
E-mail: dfrisk@iastate.edu

Iowa State University

THE FACULTY AND THEIR RESEARCH

Igor A. Beresnev, Assistant Professor; Ph.D., Moscow, 1986. Applied geophysics, earthquake source physics, earthquake ground motions, numerical modeling of geophysical processes, signal processing, stimulated fluid flow in porous media, nonlinear waves.

Michael R. Burkart, Collaborating Associate Professor; Ph.D., Iowa, 1976. Regional-scale water resource responses to agrichemicals, hydrogeology, application of GIS technology.

Anita M. Cody, Adjunct Instructor; M.S., Colorado, 1967. Crystallography, biological mineralization, geochemical reactions in concrete degradation.

Robert D. Cody, Associate Professor; Ph.D., Colorado, 1968. Geochemical sedimentology, experimental growth of authigenic minerals, diagenesis, evaporites, environmental geochemistry, geochemical reactions in concrete.

Frederick P. DeLuca, Associate Professor and Coordinator of Earth Science Education Program; Ph.D., Oklahoma, 1970.

George R. Hallberg, Adjunct Professor; Ph.D., Iowa, 1975. Nonpoint source pollution and water quality; Quaternary geology and geomorphology; stratigraphic, hydrologic, pedologic, and engineering properties of the unconsolidated materials of Iowa.

Blythe L. Hoyle, Assistant Professor; Ph.D., California, Davis, 1994. Contaminant hydrogeology, biodegradation of organic contaminants, microbial interactions with porous media, biodegradation kinetics modeling, environmental geochemistry.

Neal R. Iverson, Assistant Professor; Ph.D., Minnesota, 1989. Geomorphology, field and experimental studies of glacial and hillslope processes, soil mechanics.

Carl E. Jacobson, Professor; Ph.D., UCLA, 1980. Structural geology, metamorphic petrology, tectonics of the western United States, computer mapping.

Alfred Kracher, Adjunct Assistant Professor; Ph.D., Vienna, 1974. Microanalysis of earth materials, geochemistry of meteorites, theory of natural science.

Matthew J. Kramer, Adjunct Assistant Professor; Ph.D., Iowa State, 1988. Experimental determination of the rheology of minerals, analytical electron microscopy, computer applications to geosciences.

Karl E. Seifert, Professor; Ph.D., Wisconsin, 1963. Igneous petrology, trace element geochemistry of mafic and ultramafic igneous rocks, modeling of geochemical processes of magma modification and source characteristics.

William W. Simpkins, Associate Professor; Ph.D., Wisconsin, 1989. Hydrogeology, hydrogeochemistry of till, agricultural water quality, isotope hydrology, field methods in hydrogeology.

Paul G. Spry, Professor and Chairman; Ph.D., Toronto, 1984. Economic geology, metallic mineral deposits, mineralogy, fluid inclusion and stable isotope studies, geochemistry of concrete.

Tracy L. Vallier, Collaborating Associate Professor; Ph.D., Oregon State, 1967. Marine geology, tectonics and petrology of island arcs, oceanography.

Carl F. Vondra, Distinguished Professor; Ph.D., Nebraska, 1963. Cenozoic fluvial stratigraphy and sedimentation of North America, Asia, and Africa; geology of early Hominids.

Kenneth E. Windom, Associate Professor; Ph.D., Penn State, 1976. Experimental and theoretical mineralogy and petrology, nature of the Earth's crust and upper mantle.

Geologist analyzing mineral composition with a University-owned electron microprobe.

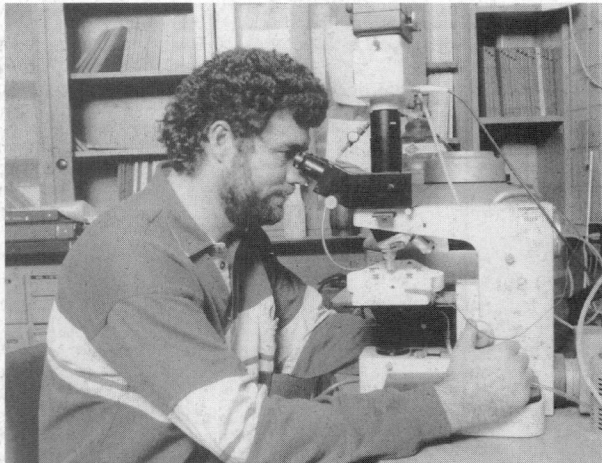

Geologist working on a polished ore section with a fluid inclusion stage.

Geology students working on class problems in the departmental computer laboratory.

SELECTED PUBLICATIONS

Beresnev, I. A., and G. M. Atkinson. FINSIM–a FORTRAN program for stimulating stochastic acceleration time histories from finite faults. *Seismol. Res. Lett.* 69:27–32, 1998.

Beresnev, I. A., and G. M. Atkinson. Shear-wave velocity survey of seismographic sites in eastern Canada: Calibration of empirical regression method of estimating site response. *Seismol. Res. Lett.* 68:981–7, 1997.

Beresnev, I. A., and G. M. Atkinson. Modeling finite-fault radiation from the omega**n spectrum. *Bull. Seismol. Soc. Am.* 87:67–84, 1997.

Beresnev, I. A., and K.-L. Wen. The possibility of observing nonlinear path effect in earthquake-induced seismic wave propagation.*Bull. Seismol. Soc. Am.* 86:1028–41, 1996.

Beresnev, I. A., and P. A. Johnson. Elastic-wave stimulation of oil production: A review of methods and results. *Geophysics* 59:1000–17, 1994.

Squillace, P. J., **M. R. Burkart,** and **W. W. Simpkins.** Infiltration of agrichemicals from a tributary stream into an alluvial aquifer. *Water Res. Bull.,* 33:89–95, 1997.

Burkart, M. R. and J. Feher. Estimation of regional ground water vulnerability to diffuse sources of agricultural chemicals. *Water Sci. and Technol.* 33:3–4; 241–7, 1996.

James, D., **M. R. Burkart,** and M. J. Hewitt III. Regional spatial analysis using the national resources inventory. *Proceedings of the 15th Annual ESRI Users' Conference, 1995.* Available only on World Wide Web (URL:http://www.esri.com/resources/userconf/proc95/to200/p168.html).

Burkart, M. R., D. E. James, S. L. Oberle, and M. J. Hewitt III. Exporing diversity within regional agroecosystems. In *Exploring the Role of Diversity in Sustainable Agriculture,* pp. 195–223, eds. R. Olson and C. Francis. Madison, Wisconsin: American Society of Agronomy (special publication), 1995.

Burkart, M. R., S. L. Oberle, M. J. Hewitt, and J. Pickus. A framework for regional agroecosystems characterization using the national resources inventory. *J. Environ. Quality* 23(5):866–74, 1994.

Oberle, S., and **M. R. Burkart.** Agroecosystems and water resource protection. *J. Environ. Quality* 23(1):4–9, 1994.

Burkart, M. R., and D. W. Kolpin. Hydrologic and land-use factors associated with herbicides and nitrate in near-surface aquifers. *J. Environ. Quality* 22(4): 646–56, 1993.

Cody, A. M., and **R. D. Cody.** Dendrite formation by apparent repeated twinning of calcium oxalate dihydrate. *J. Cryst. Growth* 151:369–74, 1995.

Cody, A. M., and **R. D. Cody.** Calcium oxalate trihydrate phase control by structurally-specific carboxylic acids. *J. Cryst. Growth* 135:235–45, 1994.

Cody, A. M., and **R. D. Cody.** Chiral habit modifications of gypsum from epitaxial-like adsorption of stereospecific growth inhibitors. *J. Cryst. Growth* 113:508–19, 1991.

Mazzella, F. and **R. D. Cody.** Analysis of anomalous quaternary river channel alignments in north central Iowa using GIS techniques. *Zeitschrift fur Geomorphologie,* 41:445–60, 1997.

Cody, R. D., A. M. Cody, P. G. Spry, and G.-L. Gan. Experimental deterioration of concrete by chloride deicing salts. *Environ. Eng. Geosci.* 2:575–88, 1996.

Cody, R. D. Organo-crystalline interactions in evaporite systems: The effects of crystallization inhibition. *J. Sed. Petrol.* 61:704–18, 1991.

Schilling, K. E. and **B. L. Hoyle.** Tracer test to evaluate dilution of ground water due to lost circulation during drilling. *Ground Water Monitoring Remediation* 16:124–30, 1996.

Hoyle, B. L., K. M. Scow, G. E. Fogg, and J. L. Darby. Effect of carbon-nitrogen ratio on kinetics of phenol biodegradation by *Acinetobacter johnsonii* in saturated sand. *Biodegradation* 6:283–93, 1995.

Rößner, U., **B. L. Hoyle,** and K. M. Scow. Effect of carbon-nitrogen ratios on growth kinetics of *Acinetobacter johnsonii* metabolizing phenol in liquid and saturated sand. In *Proceedings of the Second International Conference on Ground Water Ecology,* pp. 239–47, eds. J. A. Stanford and H. M. Valett. Herndon, Virginia: American Water Resources Association, 1994.

Hooke, R. LeB., et al. **(N. R. Iverson).** Rheology of subglacial till, Storglaciaren, Sweden. *J. Glaciology* 43:172–9, 1997.

Iverson, N. R., T. Hooyer, and R. LeB. Hooke. A laboratory study of sediment deformation: Stress heterogeneity and grain-size evolution. *Ann. Glaciology* 22:167–75, 1996.

Iverson, N. R., and R. Souchez. Isotopic signature of debris-rich ice formed by regelation into a subglacial sediment bed. *Geophysics Res. Lett.* 23:1151–3, 1996.

Hooke, R. LeB., and **N. R. Iverson.** Grain-size distribution in deforming subglacial tills: Role of grain fracture. *Geology* 23:57–60, 1995.

Iverson, N. R. Processes of erosion. In *Glacial Environments— Processes, Sediments, and Landforms,* vol. 1, pp. 241–59, ed. J. Menzies. Oxford: Butterworth Heinemann, 1995.

Iverson, N. R., B. Hanson, R. LeB. Hooke, and P. Jansson. Flow mechanism of glaciers on soft beds. *Science* 267:80–1, 1995.

Iverson, N. R., and D. Semmens. Intrusion of ice into porous media by regelation: A mechanism of sediment entrainment by glaciers. *J. Geophysical Res.* 100:10219–30, 1995.

Iverson, N. R., P. Jansson, and R. LeB. Hooke. In situ measurement of the strength of deforming subglacial sediment. *J. Glaciology* 40:497–503, 1994.

Iverson, N. R. Regelation of ice through debris at glacier beds: Implications for sediment transport. *Geology* 21:559–62, 1993.

Iverson, N. R. Potential effects of subglacial water-pressure fluctuations on quarrying. *J. Glaciology* 37:27–36, 1991.

Iverson, N. R. Morphology of glacial striae: Implications for abrasion of glacier beds and fault surfaces. *Geological Soc. Am. Bull.* 103:1308–16, 1991.

Iverson, N. R. Laboratory simulations of glacial abrasion: Comparison with theory. *J. Glaciology* 32:304–14, 1990.

Oyarzabal, F. R., **C. E. Jacobson,** and G. B. Haxel. Extensional reactivation of the Chocolate Mountains subduction thrust in the Gavilan Hills of southeastern California. *Tectonics* 16:650–61, 1997.

Jacobson, C. E. Metamorphic convergence of the upper and lower plates of the Vincent thrust, San Gabriel mountains, southern California. *J. Metamorphic Geol.* 15:155–65, 1997.

Jacobson, C. E. SpheriCAD: An AutoCAD program for analysis of structural orientation data. In *Structural Geology and Personal Computers,* pp. 181–93, ed. D. DePaor. Amsterdam, Elsevier, 1996.

Jacobson, C. E., F. R. Oyarzabal, and G. B. Haxel. Subduction and exhumation of the Pelona-Orocopia-Rand Schists, southern California.*Geology* 24:547–50, 1996.

Jacobson, C. E. Qualitative thermobarometry of inverted metamorphism in the Pelona and Rand Schists of southern California using calciferous amphibole in mafic schist. *J. Metamorphic Geol.* 13:79–92, 1995.

Jacobson, C. E., and M. R. Dawson. Structural and metamorphic evolution of the Orocopia Schist and related rocks, southern California: Evidence for late movement on the Orocopia fault. *Tectonics* 14:933–44, 1995.

Barth, A. P., **C. E. Jacobson,** and D. J. May. Mesozoic evolution of basement terranes of the San Gabriel Mountains, southern California: Summary and field guide. In *Geological Excursions in Southern California and Mexico, Guidebook 1991 Annual Meeting,* pp. 186–98, eds. M. J. Walawender and B. B. Hanan. Geological Society of America, 1991.

Dokka, R. K., et al. **(C. E. Jacobson).** Aspects of the Mesozoic and Cenozoic geologic evolution of the Mojave Desert. In *Geological Excursions in Southern California and Mexico, Guidebook 1991 Annual Meeting,* pp. 1–43, eds. M. J. Walawender and B. B. Hanan. Boulder, Colorado. Geological Society of America, 1991.

Jacobson, C. E. The $^{40}Ar/^{39}Ar$ geochronology of the Pelona Schist and related rocks, southern California. *J. Geophys. Res.* 95:509–28, 1990.

Kracher, A. Iron meteorites. In *Encyclopedia of Planetary Sciences,* pp. 361–3, eds. J. H. Shirley and R. W. Fairbridge. London: Chapman Hall, 1997.

Koeberl, C., et al. **(A. Kracher).** Mineralogical, petrological, and geochemical studies of drill core samples from the Manson impact structure, Iowa. In *The Manson Impact Structure, Iowa: Anatomy of an Impact Crater,* eds. C. Koeberl and R. R. Anderson, *Geol. Soc. Amer. Special Pap.* 302:145–219, 1996.

Fahey, A. J., E. Zinner, G. Kurat, and **A. Kracher.** Hibonite-hercynite inclusion HH-1 from the Lance (CO3) meteorite: The history of an ultrarefractory CAI. *Geochim. Cosmchim. Acta* 58:4779–93, 1994.

Kracher, A., et al. **(K. E. Windom).** Analysis of highly moisture-

Iowa State University

Selected Publications (continued)

sensitive samples in an electron microprobe. In *Microbeam Analysis*, eds. D. R. Howitt, San Francisco Press, 319–21, 1991.

Kurat, G., A. Embey-Isztin, **A. Kracher**, and H. G. Scharbert. The upper mantle beneath Kapfenstein and the Transdanubian volcanic region, E. Austria and W. Hungary: a comparison. *Min. Petrol* 44:21–38, 1991.

Dobosi, G., R. Schultz-Guttler, G. Kurat, and **A. Kracher**. Pyroxene chemistry and evolution of alkali basaltic rocks from Burgenland and Styria, Austria. *Min. Petrol.* 43:275–92, 1991.

Seifert, K. E., C.-W. Chang, and D. Brunotte. Evidence from Ocean Drilling Program Leg 149 mafic igneous rocks for oceanic crust in the Iberia Abyssal Plain ocean-continent transition zone. *J. Geophys. Res.* 102:7915–28, 1997.

Seifert, K. E. and R. R. Anderson. Geochemistry of midcontinent rift volcanic rocks in Iowa: data from well samples. *J. Iowa Acad. Sci. U.S.A.* 103:63–73, 1996.

Gibson, I. L., et al. **(K. E. Seifert)**. Major and trace-element seawater alteration profiles in serpentinite formed during the development of the Galicia Margin, ODP Site 897. In *Proceedings of the Ocean Drilling Program, Scientific Results,* 149. pp. 519–27, College Station, Texas: Ocean Drilling Program, 1996.

Milliken, K. L., F. L. Lynch, and **K. E. Seifert**. Marine weathering of serpentinites and serpentinite breccias, Sites 897 and 899, Iberia Abyssal Plain. In *Proceedings of the Ocean Drilling Program, Scientific Results*, 149. College Station, Texas: Ocean Drilling Program, pp. 529–40, 1996.

Seifert, K. E., and D. Brunotte. Geochemical nature of ODP Leg 149 Site 897 serpentinized peridotites from the Iberia Abyssal Plain. In *Proceedings of the Ocean Drilling Program, Scientific Results,* 149 pp. 413–34. College Station, Texas: Ocean Drilling Program, 1996.

Seifert, K. E., and D. Brunotte. Geochemistry of ODP Leg 149 Hole 899B MORB basalt and diabase clasts from the Iberia Abyssal Plain. In *Proceedings of the Ocean Drilling Program, Scientific Results,* 149 pp. 497–515. College Station, Texas: Ocean Drilling Program, 1996.

Seifert, K. E., I. Gibson, D. Weis, and D. Brunotte. Geochemistry and petrology of ODP Leg 149 Hole 900A metamorphosed cumulate oceanic gabbros from the Iberia Abyssal Plain. In *Proceedings of the Ocean Drilling Program, Scientific Results,* 149pp. 471–88. College Station, Texas: Ocean Drilling Program, 1996.

Seifert, K. E., Z. E. Peterman, and S. E. Thieben. Possible crustal contamination of Midcontinent Rift igneous rocks: Examples from the Mineral Lake intrusions, Wisconsin. *Can. J. Earth Sci.* 29:1140–53, 1992.

Kramer, M. J., and **K. E. Seifert**. Strain-enhanced diffusion in feldspar. In *Diffusion and Flow in Minerals and Fluids*, vol. 9, Advances in Physical Geochemistry, pp. 286–303, ed. J. Ganguly. New York: Springer-Verlag, 1991.

Simpkins, W. W. and M. R. Burkart. Hydrogeology and water quality of the Walnut Creek watershed. *Iowa Geol. Sur. Bur. Guidebook Series* 20:105, 1996.

Parkin, T. B., and **W. W. Simpkins**. Contemporary groundwater methane production from Pleistocene carbon. *J. Environ. Quality* 24:367–72, 1995.

Schultz, R. C., et al. **(W. W. Simpkins)**. Design and placement of a multi-species riparian buffer strip system. *J. Agroforest. Res.* 29:201–26, 1995.

Simpkins, W. W. Isotopic composition of precipitation in central Iowa. *J. Hydrology* 172:185–207, 1995.

Simpkins, W. W., and T. B. Parkin. Hydrogeology and redox geochemistry of methane in a late Wisconsin till and loess sequence in central Iowa. *Water Resour. Res.* 29:3643–57, 1993.

Simpkins, W. W. *Water, water everywhere..., Guidebook for the 57th Annual Tri-State Geol. Field Conf. and Geol. Soc. Iowa Field Trip Guidebook* 58. Iowa Geological Survey, 1993.

Simpkins, W. W., and K. R. Bradbury. Groundwater flow, velocity, and age in a thick, fine-grained till unit in southeastern Wisconsin. *J. Hydrology* 132:283–319, 1992.

Spry, P. G., F. Foster, J. Truckle, and T. H. Chadwick. The mineralogy of the Golden Sunlight gold-silver telluride deposit, Montana, U.S.A. *Mineralogy and Petrology* 59:143–164, 1997.

Gan, G. L., **P. G. Spry, R. D. Cody,** and **A. M. Cody**. Rim formation on Iowa highway concrete dolomite aggregate: the effects of dedolomitization reactions. *Environ. Eng. Geosci.* 2:59–72, 1996.

Spry, P. G., et al. A genetic link between gold-silver telluride and porphyry molybdenum mineralization at the Golden Sunlight deposit, Whitehall, Montana: Fluid inclusion and stable isotope studies. *Econ. Geol.* 91:507–26, 1996.

Spry, P. G. and S. E. Thieben. Two occurrences of benleonardite, a rare silver-tellurium sulfosalt, and a possible new occurrence of cervelleite. *Min. Mag.* 60:871–6, 1996.

Spry, P. G., J. L. Rosenberg, **C. E. Jacobson**, and F. M. Vokes. A metamorphic sulphidation-oxidation halo associated with the Bleikvassli Zn-Pb-(Cu) deposit. Nordland, Norway, *Mineral Deposits: From their Origin to their Environmental Impacts.* eds. Pasava, Kribek, and Zak. Balkema, Rotterdam, pp. 909–12, 1995.

Spry, P. G., and G. D. Fuhrmann. Additional fluid inclusion data for the Illinois-Kentucky fluorspar district: Implications for the lack of a regional thermal gradient. *Econ. Geol.* 89:288–306, 1994.

Spry, P. G., et al. New occurrences and refined crystal chemistry of colusite with comparisons to arsenosulvanite. *Amer. Min.* 79:750–62, 1994.

Zhang, X., and **P. G. Spry**. Petrological, mineralogical, fluid inclusion and stable isotope studies of the Gies gold-silver telluride deposit, Judith Mountains, Montana. *Econ. Geol.* 89:602–28, 1994.

Zhang, X., and **P. G. Spry**. Calculated stability of aqueous tellurium species, calaverite and hessite at elevated temperatures. *Econ. Geol.* 89:1152–66, 1994.

Zhang, X. and **P. G. Spry**. FO_2pH: A Quickbasic program to calculate mineral stabilities and sulfur isotope contours in $logf0_2$-pH space. *Min. Petrol.* 50:287–91, 1994.

Chesley, J. T., A. N. Halliday, T. K. Kyser, and **P. G. Spry**. Direct dating of Mississippi Valley-type mineralization: use of Sm/Nd in fluorite. *Econ. Geol.* 89:1192–9, 1994.

Spry, P. G. The genetic relationship between coticules and metamorphosed massive sulfide deposits. In *Regional Metamorphism of Ore Deposits and Genetic Implications*, pp. 49–75, eds. P. G. Spry and L. T. Bryndzia. Utrecht, the Netherlands: VSP, 1990.

Spry, P. G., and L. T. Bryndzia, eds. *Regional Metamorphism of Ore Deposits and Genetic Implications*. Utrecht, the Netherlands: VSP, 1990.

Spry, P. G., C. K. Richardson, M. S. Koellner, and H. Jones. Thermochemical changes in the ore fluid during deposition at the Denton mine, Cave-in-Rock fluorspar district, Illinois. *Econ. Geol.* 85:172–81, 1990.

Bryndzia, L. T., S. D. Scott, and **P. G. Spry**. The sphalerite and hexagonal pyrrhotite geobarometer: Correction in calibration and application. *Econ. Geol.* 85:408–11, 1990.

Enzl, C., J. Trappe, and **C. F. Vondra**. Silicified stromatolites, paleokarst and diagenetic overprinting along sequence boundary beds, Madison/Darwin contact, Bighorn Basin, Wyoming—a tool for low-stand carbonate deposystem investigation. *Wyoming Geol. Assoc. Guidebook*, 47th Ann. Field Conf., 137–44, 1996.

Forster, A., A. Irmen, and **C. F. Vondra**. Structural Interpretation of Sheep Mountain Anticline, Bighorn Basin, Wyoming. *Wyoming Geol. Assoc. Guidebook,* 47th Ann. Field Conf., 239–51, 1996.

Kimbel, W. H., et al. **(C. F. Vondra)**. Late Pliocene *Homo* and Oldowan tools from the Hadar Formation (Kada Hadar Member) Ethiopia. *J. Human Evol.* 31:549–61, 1996.

Trappe, J. and **C. F. Vondra**. Microstructure and origin of fibrous phosphate concretions from the Cretaceous Thermopolis Shale—An example of apatite replacement of a Fe-precursor? *Neus Jahrb. Geol. Palantl. Monstshefte* 198: 363–74, 1995.

Kvale, E. P. and **C. F. Vondra**. Effects of relative sea-level changes and local tectonics on a Lower Cretaceous fluvial to transitional marine sequence, Bighorn, Basin, Wyoming, USA. ed. by M. Marzo and C. Puigdefabregas, Alluvial Sedimentation, Spec. Publ. 17, *Intern. Assoc. Sedimentologist* 383–99, 1994.

Windom, K. E., et al. **(K. E. Seifert)**. Archean and Proterozoic tectono-magmatic activity along the southern margin of the Superior Province in northwestern Iowa, United States. *Can. J. Earth Sci.* 30:1275–85, 1993.

Windom, K. E., K. E. Seifert, and R. R. Anderson. Studies of the Precambrian geology of Iowa: Part 1. The Otter Creek layered igneous complex. *J. Iowa Acad. Sci.* 98:170–7, 1991.

Windom, K. E., K. E. Seifert, and R. R. Anderson. Studies of the Precambrian geology of Iowa: Part 2. The Matlock keratophyre. *J. Iowa Acad. Sci.* 98:178–81, 1991.

LEHIGH UNIVERSITY

Department of Earth and Environmental Sciences

Programs of Study

Lehigh's Department of Earth and Environmental Sciences (EES) offers graduate programs leading to the M.S. and Ph.D. degrees in earth and environmental sciences. M.S. programs typically require two years of full-time effort, a Ph.D. about four years. Faculty research programs include aquatic ecosystems, aquatic ecology, aqueous geochemistry, fluvial and tectonic geomorphology, geochronology, glacial geology, high-resolution geophysics, hydrogeology, metamorphic petrology, microbial ecology, sedimentation, paleolimnology, paleomagnetism, seismology, structural geology, and tectonics (those interested can see details on the World Wide Web site listed below). The intermediate size of the department (13 faculty members) and its range of active research programs provide an intimate atmosphere in which graduate students receive extensive experience with diverse analytical and theoretical approaches to the study of geological, ecological, and environmental processes.

Research Facilities

Equipment for environmental biological research includes microscopes, environmental chambers, centrifuges, sampling nets, current meters, incubators, and autoclaves. The department is home to the Aquatic Ecosystems Program, which supports diverse, multidisciplinary research on aquatic systems, and the Pocono Comparative Lakes Program, which focuses on three "core" lakes (in the Pocono Mountains) that serve as model systems for experimental and comparative studies of aquatic communities and ecosystems. Faculty members operate facilities for sediment coring and analysis, aqueous geochemistry, and plankton ecology. They also maintain automated meteorological and hydrological facilities as well as terrestrial and water-column instrumentation for measuring solar UV radiation.

The department houses a Philips APD-3600 X-ray powder diffractometer and complete petrographic facilities, including cathodoluminescence and camera lucida digitizing apparatus. Other facilities include a noble-gas and fission-track geochronology laboratory with a low-blank, double-vacuum resistance furnace and a VG Isotopes model 3600 mass spectrometer; a stable-isotope chemistry laboratory with a Finnigan MAT model 252 mass spectrometer and extraction lines for stable-isotope analyses; an aqueous geochemistry laboratory with an ARL 34000 inductively coupled plasma atomic emission spectrometer and a high-pressure core-holder/column reactor for flow-through experiments; a Carlo Erba 1106 elemental analyzer, a Shimadzu TOC-5000 carbon analyzer, a Latchet Quick Chem 4000 automated ion analyzer, and assorted HPLCs, HPICs, GCs, fluorometers, and spectrophotometers; and a sedimentation laboratory equipped with a Particle Data computer-based particle-size analyzer and a rapid sediment analyzer. Geophysical equipment includes a paleomagnetism laboratory with a Molspin spinner magnetometer, a 2-axis CTF cryogenic rock magnetometer, a Schonstedt tumbling AF demagnetizer, and a Schonstedt thermal demagnetizer; a reflection seismology laboratory with computer workstations for seismic processing and a Bison DIFP multichannel seismograph; field geophysical equipment, including a Bison shallow refraction seismic unit and a Bison shallow resistivity apparatus, a master Wordon gravimeter, a Geometrics portable proton precession magnetometer; and Keck borehole logging equipment, including caliper, natural gamma, electrical resistivity, and self-potential probes.

The department's computing facilities include Sun SPARCstations, Silicon Graphics workstations, networked computer laboratories, and numerous stand-alone PCs and Macintoshes. The workstations support a geographic information system for multiattribute locational database management and inquiry and graphic information analysis and presentation. The University supports high-speed networking to offices, labs, and classrooms and provides access to high-performance workstations for computationally intensive tasks.

Financial Aid

Financial assistance in the form of teaching assistantships, research assistantships, scholarships, and University and departmental fellowships is awarded to applicants on a competitive basis. Teaching assistant stipends begin at $11,450 for the nine-month academic year. In addition, teaching assistants receive tuition remission for up to 9 credits per semester and 3 credits during the summer. Fellowship and research assistantship stipends are comparable to the stipends for teaching assistants. Students making satisfactory progress are normally supported until the completion of their degree program.

Cost of Study

Tuition for the 1998–99 academic year was $800 per credit; tuition expenses are paid for teaching assistants and research assistants.

Living and Housing Costs

Students live in a wide variety of accommodations, and expenses can be reasonable, especially if shared. Lehigh operates a 148-unit garden apartment complex for single and married students located in nearby Saucon Valley; rent for a one-bedroom unfurnished apartment is $430 per month. Day care is available nearby, and hourly bus service is provided. Private rental units are also available. Costs average $5000 per year.

Student Group

In 1998–99, there were 25 students in the EES graduate program. Students come from many states and several other countries. It is the policy of the University to provide equal opportunity based on merit and without discrimination due to race, color, religion, gender, age, national origin, citizenship, status, handicap, or veteran status.

Student Outcomes

Graduates from the department typically find employment in environmental consulting firms and oil companies, as postdoctoral researchers, in governmental agencies, and as faculty members at colleges and universities.

Location

Bethlehem, Pennsylvania (population 72,000), is located 50 miles north of Philadelphia and 90 miles west of New York City; best access is via Interstate 78, U.S. Route 22, or the Lehigh Valley International Airport. Founded in 1741, Bethlehem has a rich cultural heritage in the Moravian tradition. Historic buildings have been well preserved, giving the community a charming Colonial atmosphere. The Lehigh Valley (Allentown, Bethlehem, and Easton) is the chief commercial and industrial center of east-central Pennsylvania.

The University

Lehigh is an independent, nondenominational, coeducational university. Founded in 1865, it has approximately 4,500 undergraduates within its three major colleges: Arts and Sciences, Engineering and Applied Science, and Business and Economics. There are approximately 2,000 students enrolled in various graduate programs and in the graduate-only College of Education. The 700-acre campus includes superb athletic facilities, a health club, and cultural venues, including a new $33-million arts center.

Applying

Applications for admission as a regular graduate student are accepted until July 15 for the fall term, December 1 for the spring term, April 30 for the first summer term, and May 30 for the second summer term. To be considered for financial aid, completed applications must be received by the College of Arts and Sciences Graduate Programs Office by January 15 for the following academic year. Students should send all admission forms to CAS Graduate Programs, Maginnes Hall, Lehigh University, 9 West Packer Avenue, Bethlehem, Pennsylvania 18015.

Correspondence and Information

Donald P. Morris, Graduate Coordinator
Department of Earth and Environmental Sciences
Lehigh University
31 Williams Drive
Bethlehem, Pennsylvania 18015-3188
Telephone: 610-758-3660
Fax: 610-758-3677
World Wide Web: http://www.ees.lehigh.edu

Lehigh University

THE FACULTY AND THEIR AREAS OF SCHOLARSHIP

Peter K. Zeitler, Professor and Chair; Ph.D., Dartmouth, 1983. Geochronology, tectonics. (e-mail: pkz0@lehigh.edu)

Gray E. Bebout, Associate Professor and Graduate Coordinator; Ph.D., UCLA, 1989. Petrology, high-temperature geochemistry, tectonics, stable-isotope geochemistry. (e-mail: geb0@lehigh.edu)

David J. Anastasio, Associate Professor; Ph.D., Johns Hopkins, 1988. Structural geology, tectonics. (e-mail: dja2@lehigh.edu)

Bobb Carson, Professor; Ph.D., Washington (Seattle), 1971. Sedimentary processes, sedimentation, tectonics, marine geology, submarine hydrology. (e-mail: bc00@lehigh.edu)

Edward B. Evenson, Professor; Ph.D., Michigan, 1972. Glacial and Quaternary geology, environmental geology and soils. (e-mail: ebe0@lehigh.edu)

Bruce Hargreaves, Associate Professor; Ph.D., Berkeley, 1977. Physiological and ecosystem ecology, biooptics, limnology. (e-mail: brh0@lehigh.edu)

Kenneth P. Kodama, Professor; Ph.D., Stanford, 1977. Paleomagnetism, rock magnetism, environmental magnetism. (e-mail: kpk0@lehigh.edu)

Anne S. Meltzer, Associate Professor; Ph.D., Rice, 1989. Reflection seismology, tectonics. (e-mail: asm3@lehigh.edu)

Donald P. Morris, Associate Professor; Ph.D., Colorado, 1990. Microbial ecology, limnology. (e-mail: dpm2@lehigh.edu)

Carl Moses, Associate Professor; Ph.D., Virginia, 1988. Aqueous geochemistry, mineral-solution interface. (e-mail: com0@lehigh.edu)

Paul B. Myers Jr., Professor; Ph.D., Lehigh, 1960. Hydrogeology, geographic information systems. (e-mail: pbm1@lehigh.edu)

Frank J. Pazzaglia, Associate Professor; Ph.D. Penn State, 1993. Fluvial and tectonic geomorphology. (e-mail: fjp3@lehigh.edu)

Craig Williamson, Professor; Ph.D., Dartmouth, 1981. Ecology of UV-B radiation, predation risk, freshwater zooplankton communities. (e-mail: cew0@lehigh.edu)

RECENT GRADUATE RESEARCH

Brian K. Altheim. Low-Grade Metamorphism in the Catalina Schist: Tectonic and Kinetic Implications; 1997. (adviser: Bebout)

Lore Ayoub. UV Absorption in Lakes: Relative Contributions of Dissolved and Particulate Material; 1997. (coadvisers: Hargreaves and Morris)

Gregory S. Baker. An Examination of Triassic Cyclostratigraphy in the Newark Basin from Shallow Seismic Profiles and Geophysical Logs; 1994. (adviser: Meltzer)

Patrick A. Burkhart. Hydrogeologic Characterization and Modeling of Soil Water-Groundwater-Surface Water Interactions in a Forested Catchment with a Chain of Lakes, Pocono Mountains, Pa.; 1994. (adviser: Moses)

Scot G. Davidson. Passive Concentration and Metasomatism during Cleavage Formation in Carbonate Rocks; 1997. (coadvisers: Anastasio and Bebout)

Kris Egers. Solution-Composition Influence on the Stimulation of 1HNMR Relaxation Rates by Mineral-Water Interactions in Porous Sandstones; 1993. (adviser: Moses)

Staci Ensminger. Pressurized Subglacial Water: Relation to Velocity and Uplift Measurements and Debris Band Origins at the Matanuska Glacier, Alaska; 1997. (adviser: Evenson)

John C. Gosse. Alpine Glacial History Reconstruction: 1. Application of the Cosmogenic 10Be Exposure Age Method to Reconstruct the Glacial Chronology of the Wind River Mountains, Wyoming, USA. 2. Relative Dating of Quaternary Deposits in the Rio Atuel Valley, Mondoza, Argentina; 1994. (adviser: Evenson)

Carla Gutierrez-Rodriquez. Influences of Solar Ultraviolet Light on Early Life Stages of the Bluegill, *Leponis macrochirus*. Effects of UV Light on Fish Larva in Lakes with Contrasting DOC Concentrations; 1997. (adviser: Williamson)

Christopher A. Hedlund. Kinematics of Fault-Related Folding in a Duplex, Lost River Range, Idaho; 1993. (adviser: Anastasio)

James E. Holl. Foreland Deformation Processes, Southern Pyrenees, Spain; 1994. (adviser: Anastasio)

Michael Krol. Thermal and Tectonic Evolutions of the Cenozoic Himalayan Orogen and the Mesozoic Newark Rift Basin: Evidence from 40Ar/39Ar Thermochronology; 1996. (adviser: Zeitler)

Kathyleen Kresge. The Impact of UV Radiation on Bacterial Growth in Lakes in the Pocono Plateau; 1996 (adviser: Morris)

Amy Ondrus. Deformation of the Point Arena Basin and the Location of the San Andreas Fault Zone, Offshore Northern California; 1997. (adviser: Meltzer)

Elizabeth J. Screaton. Investigation of Fluid Sources and Movement at the Cascadia Margin; 1995. (adviser: Carson)

Elizabeth R. Sherwood. Remagnetization of the Scott Peak Formation Associated with Tertiary Igneous Activity; 1994. (adviser: Kodama)

John Stamatakos. Paleomagnetism Applied to Tectonic Problems in South-Central Alaska and in the Central Appalachian Valley and Ridge Province; 1990. (adviser: Kodama)

Joanne Tenore-Nortrup. Metasomatism of Gabbroic and Dioritic Cobbles in Blueschist Facies Metaconglomerate: Sources and Sinks for High-P/T Metamorphic Fluids; 1996. (adviser: Bebout)

Mary Colleen Costello Walker. Surface Water Alkalinity in the Neversink Basin, Catskill Mountains, New York; 1995 (adviser: Moses)

Yin Zhong. Estimation of Underwater Scalar PAR: Models and Measurements in Lakes; 1995 (adviser: Hargreaves)

MASSACHUSETTS INSTITUTE OF TECHNOLOGY

Department of Earth, Atmospheric, and Planetary Sciences

Programs of Study

The department offers graduate degrees in all fields of the earth and planetary sciences, including geology and geochemistry, geophysics, planetary science, oceanography, atmospheric science, and climate physics and chemistry.

A professional master's degree program, which can be completed in one academic year, is available for students seeking careers in industry as professional geoscientists or for working professionals who wish to expand their knowledge and career opportunities. This program is open to highly motivated students with undergraduate degrees in geoscience, physics, chemistry, mathematics, or engineering and prepares students for careers in the environmental, natural resources, and technical consulting industries. Students are introduced to all areas of geoscience through a two-semester course sequence in geosystems that focuses on physical and chemical processes, systems concepts, and numerical simulation of a wide range of natural systems. The program is computer-intensive and highly quantitative and requires a concentration in a specific disciplinary field along with subjects in economics and geoscience inference, as well as a thesis project. In addition to the professional master's degree program, a research-oriented Master of Science degree, which generally takes two years to complete, is also offered.

Programs of study leading to the Ph.D. or Sc.D. degree are tailored to each student's background and goals in consultation with a personal faculty adviser and a department committee. Thesis research normally begins immediately after the General Examination, taken by the end of the second year. The thesis is expected to meet high professional standards and be a significant original contribution to the scientific field. Doctoral degrees in oceanography are also offered jointly with the Woods Hole Oceanographic Institution through the joint program in oceanography.

Research Facilities

Special facilities range from MIT-based laboratories to remote field and marine stations. On campus the department operates wave flumes, high-pressure/high-temperature apparatus, electron and ion probes, mass spectrometers, an array of analytical chemical facilities, a Doppler radar facility, a synoptic meteorology laboratory, and an extensive network of computers. Off-campus studies take place on four continents and in four oceans and include the measurement of worldwide ocean and atmospheric dynamics and chemistry, observations of extratropical cyclones and winter storms, and usage of a variety of optical and radio telescopes. The department operates a geology field camp in the eastern Mojave desert and an astronomy field camp in Flagstaff, Arizona. MIT is also one of the important centers in seismologic and tectonic applications on the global digital network. The facilities of the Woods Hole Oceanographic Institution (WHOI) are also available to students through the joint program in oceanography. The Center for Global Change Science combines the resources of the department with six other MIT departments to study the complexities of global climate change. The Earth Resource Lab (ERL) operates a geophysical field test site in Michigan for petroleum reservoir studies.

Financial Aid

Research and teaching assistantships are offered on a competitive basis to students accepted for admission to the Ph.D. program. All prospective students should explore outside fellowship opportunities. Research and teaching assistants receive full tuition plus a stipend for living expenses. Several departmental fellowships are awarded annually to highly qualified applicants.

Scholarships are available to exceptional students admitted to the professional master's degree program. Students admitted to the department's research-oriented Master of Science program receive financial support only if additional funds are available after support has been provided for all qualified doctoral candidates.

Cost of Study

The 1999–2000 tuition is $25,000 for nine months. The mandatory student health insurance fee is $636.

Living and Housing Costs

Estimated room and board expenses for one year total $13,800. Approximately 25 percent of MIT's graduate students live in MIT's residential system, with the remainder finding housing in the Boston area. Graduate students' costs for housing, food, books, and incidentals vary.

Student Group

There are currently 164 graduate students in the department (96 men, 68 women). More than 90 percent of the department's graduate students are working toward a Ph.D. Slightly fewer than half of the student population is international students. All students are full-time.

Student Outcomes

Students completing graduate studies in the department enter jobs in academic research or industry in about equal numbers. Many graduates go on to jobs as faculty members or research scientists at a university, national lab, or industrial research facility. Graduates are working in the oil, environmental, computer, and financial industries.

Location

MIT is one of more than fifty schools in the Boston area, and the concentration of academic, cultural, and intellectual activities is one of the highest in the country. MIT is also a short drive from mountain skiing, ocean beaches, and the many outdoor recreational parks of New England.

The Institute

MIT is an independent, coeducational university with twenty-two academic departments. The Institute seeks to create an atmosphere of intellectual excitement and a climate of inquiry and innovation in which each student develops a consuming interest in understanding for its own sake. MIT's total enrollment is approximately 9,800 students, of which more than half are graduate students. The MIT faculty numbers approximately 1,100, with a total teaching staff of more than 2,000.

Applying

Deadline for fall admission is January 15, and for spring admission, November 1. GRE General Test scores are required; GRE Subject Test scores are required only for applicants to the MIT/WHOI joint program in oceanography. The application fee of $55 is waived only for U.S. underrepresented minority applicants. TOEFL scores are required for all international students, with a minimum score of 233 out of 300 total points (or 577 under the former scoring system).

Correspondence and Information

EAPS Education Office, 54-913
Department of Earth, Atmospheric, and Planetary Sciences
77 Massachusetts Avenue
Cambridge, Massachusetts 02139
Telephone: 617-253-3381
Fax: 617-253-8298
E-mail: eapsinfo@mit.edu
World Wide Web: http://www-eaps.mit.edu/

Massachusetts Institute of Technology

THE FACULTY AND THEIR RESEARCH

Richard P. Binzel, Professor; Ph.D., Texas, 1986. Planetary astronomy, collisional evolution of asteroids. (Telephone: 617-253-6486)

Samuel A. Bowring, Professor; Ph.D., Kansas, 1985. Origin and evolution of continental lithosphere, U-Pb geochronology, early history of the Earth. (Telephone: 617-253-3775)

Edward A. Boyle, Professor; Ph.D., MIT, 1976. Paleoceanography and paleoclimatology, trace element chemistry of seawater. (Telephone: 617-253-3388)

Rafael L. Bras, Professor; Ph.D., MIT, 1975. Surface and groundwater hydrology. (Telephone: 617-253-2117)

B. Clark Burchfiel, Professor; Ph.D., Yale, 1961. Origin, development, and structural evolution of the continental crust. (Telephone: 617-253-7919)

Edmund Chang, Assistant Professor; Ph.D., MIT, 1993. Baroclinic instability, life cycle of extratropical cyclones. (Telephone: 617-253-9397)

John M. Edmond, Professor; Ph.D., California, San Diego (Scripps), 1970. Geochemical cycle of the elements, trace element geochemistry of the oceans. (Telephone: 617-253-5739)

James L. Elliot, Professor; Ph.D., Harvard, 1972. Structure and orbits of planetary rings, stellar occultation observations. (Telephone: 617-253-6308)

Kerry A. Emanuel, Professor; Ph.D., MIT, 1981. Relationship between cumulus convection and large-scale circulations, mesoscale dynamics of fronts and cyclones. (Telephone: 617-253-2462)

Dara Entekhabi, Associate Professor; Ph.D., MIT, 1990. Hydrometeorological predictability, hydrological processes, inversion of remote-sensing data for surface conditions. (Telephone: 617-253-9698)

J. Brian Evans, Professor; Ph.D., MIT, 1978. Strength of rocks; the effect of fluids and impurities on strength; interrelationships of porosity, permeability, and plastic flow. (Telephone: 617-253-2856)

Glenn R. Flierl, Professor; Ph.D., Harvard, 1975. Modeling of the physics, chemistry, and biology of strongly nonlinear eddies and meandering jets. (Telephone: 617-253-4692)

Fred A. Frey, Professor; Ph.D., Wisconsin, 1967. Origin and evolution of igneous rocks, upper mantle composition and processes. (Telephone: 617-253-2818)

John P. Grotzinger, Professor; Ph.D., Virginia Tech, 1985. Sedimentary geology, tectonics and sedimentation, biogeology; earth history. (Telephone: 617-253-3498)

Timothy L. Grove, Professor; Ph.D., Harvard, 1976. Igneous petrology, magma generation processes in island arc-continental settings and mid-ocean ridges. (Telephone: 617-253-2878)

Bradford H. Hager, Professor; Ph.D., Harvard, 1978. Mantle dynamics, numerical modeling of solid-state convection, space-geodetic observations of surface deformation. (Telephone: 617-253-0126)

Thomas A. Herring, Professor; Ph.D., MIT, 1983. Techniques of space geodesy, including Very Long Baseline Interferometry and the use of the Global Positioning System. (Telephone: 617-253-5941)

Kip V. Hodges, Professor; Ph.D., MIT, 1982. Structural and thermal evolution of compressional and extensional orogens; structural geology, metamorphic petrology, and geochronology. (Telephone: 617-253-2927)

Thomas H. Jordan, Professor; Ph.D., Caltech, 1972. Seismological study of earth structure, geodetic observations of plate motions and interplate deformation. (Telephone: 617-253-0149)

Richard S. Lindzen, Professor; Ph.D., Harvard, 1964. Baroclinic instability, transient planetary waves. (Telephone: 617-253-2432)

Chris Marone, Associate Professor; Ph.D., Columbia, 1989. Experimental studies of the physics of rock deformation, micromechanics of rock friction, fault and earthquake mechanics. (Telephone: 617-253-4352)

John C. Marshall, Professor; Ph.D., Imperial College (London), 1980. Dynamics and causes of the general circulation of the atmosphere and ocean, global-scale ocean modeling. (Telephone: 617-253-9615)

Mario J. Molina, Professor; Ph.D., Berkeley, 1972. Experimental atmospheric chemistry, kinetics of free radicals, heterogeneous chemistry of the polar stratosphere. (Telephone: 617-253-5081)

Dale Morgan, Professor; Ph.D., MIT, 1981. Geoelectromagnetism, inverse methods, applied seismology, environmental geophysics. (Telephone: 617-253-7857)

Reginald E. Newell, Professor; Ph.D., MIT, 1960, MIT. Climate diagnostic studies, influence of volcanic activity on global temperature, sea-air interaction. (Telephone: 617-253-2940)

R. Alan Plumb, Professor; Ph.D., Manchester (England), 1972. Eddy transport processes, dynamics of the middle atmosphere. (Telephone: 617-253-6281)

Ronald G. Prinn, Professor and Department Head; Sc.D., MIT, 1971. Chemical-dynamical models of the atmosphere, measurement and modeling of the long-lived gases involved in the greenhouse effect and ozone depletion, atmospheric chemistry. (Telephone: 617-253-2452)

Maureen Raymo, Associate Professor; Ph.D., Columbia, 1989. Studies of past climate changes, in particular the glacial-interglacial cycles of recent ice ages. (Telephone: 617-253-0474)

Paola M. Rizzoli, Professor; Ph.D., California, San Diego (Scripps), 1978. Numerical modeling of the ocean general circulation, assimilation of oceanographic data sets. (Telephone: 617-253-2451)

Daniel H. Rothman, Professor; Ph.D., Stanford, 1986. Numerical models of nonlinear dynamical systems. (Telephone: 617-253-7861)

Leigh H. Royden, Professor; Ph.D., MIT, 1982. Regional geology and geophysics, mechanics of large-scale continental deformation. (Telephone: 617-253-1292)

John B. Southard, Professor; Ph.D., Harvard, 1966. Dynamics of sediment transport by currents and waves. (Telephone: 617-253-3397)

Peter H. Stone, Professor; Ph.D., Harvard, 1964. Baroclinic stability theory, climate modeling, coupled atmosphere–ocean models. (Telephone: 617-253-2443)

M. Nafi Toksöz, Professor; Ph.D., Caltech, 1963. Seismology and tectonics of the eastern Mediterranean, seismic tomography for characterization of the earth's crust and petroleum reservoirs. (Telephone: 617-253-7852)

Robert D. van der Hilst, Associate Professor; Ph.D., Utrecht (Netherlands), 1990. Seismic tomography, tectonic evolution of subduction systems, mantle dynamics. (Telephone: 617-253-6977)

Kelin X. Whipple, Assistant Professor; Ph.D., Washington (Seattle), 1994. Process geomorphology; interaction of climate, tectonics, and surface processes; debris-flow rheology. (Telephone: 617-253-2578)

Jack Wisdom, Professor; Ph.D., Caltech, 1981. Solar system dynamics, long-term evolution of the orbits and spins of the planets and natural satellites, dynamical systems, chaotic behavior. (Telephone: 617-253-7730)

Carl I. Wunsch, Professor; Ph.D., MIT, 1967. General circulation of the ocean, development of satellite altimeters and scatterometers and acoustic tomography, global-scale ocean modeling. (Telephone: 617-253-5937)

Maria T. Zuber, Professor; Ph.D., Brown, 1986. Theoretical modeling of geophysical processes, mechanical structures and states of stress in planetary lithospheres, space-based laser ranging systems. (Telephone: 617-253-6397)

NORTH CAROLINA STATE UNIVERSITY

Department of Marine, Earth and Atmospheric Sciences

Programs of Study

The department offers M.S. and Ph.D. degrees in oceanography, meteorology, and geology.

In oceanography, students specialize in biological, chemical, geological, or physical oceanography. In the biological area, research topics are in benthic, plankton, or invertebrate physiological ecology. Research in the chemical area exists in the study of organic and inorganic processes in estuarine, coastal, and deep-sea environments. Emphasis in geological oceanography is in sedimentology and micropaleontology. In physical oceanography, research topics include the study of the dynamics of estuarine, shelf-slope, and deep-sea waters.

In meteorology, research topics exist in modeling and parameterizing the planetary atmospheric boundary layer, in physically and theoretically modeling dispersion over complex terrain, in air-sea interaction, in atmospheric chemistry, and in climate dynamics. Other research areas are those of cloud-aerosol interaction, cloud chemistry and acid rain deposition, plant-atmosphere interaction, severe localized storm systems, and mesoscale phenomena and processes related to East Coast fronts and cyclones.

In earth science, research topics are in the areas of hard-rock and soft-rock geology, tectonics, and sedimentary geochemistry. In hard-rock geology the emphasis is on igneous and metamorphic petrology. Soft-rock studies span both recent and ancient detrital deposits, including economic deposits, with field-based studies of facies relationships and associated depositional environments.

The M.S. degree program requires 30 semester credit hours of course work, a research thesis, and a final oral examination. A nonthesis option is available to students on leave from government or industry. The Ph.D. program requires at least 36 credit hours beyond the M.S. degree, as well as a thesis, preliminary written and oral examinations, and a dissertation defense.

Research Facilities

Jordan Hall, the department's home, is a modern structure dedicated to research in natural resources, which has been specially designed to accommodate department research laboratories. Modern facilities currently exist in all program areas. Students have access to the million-volume D. H. Hill Library and the University Computing Center IBM 3090 and the Supercomputer Center CRAY Y-MP computers, which link the department to local, national, and international networks. The department operates an IBM-sponsored facility for ocean/atmosphere modeling and visualization, composed of eight network parallelized IBM RS/6000 390 Risc Workstations, as well as Nextlab, with seventeen networked Sun SPARCstations, a general computer facility with twelve networked Sun SPARCstations, and a MicroVAX 3500. Other specialized departmental equipment includes a Quorum Communications HRTP satellite receiver, a Finnigan MAT 251 Ratio Mass Spectrometer, a McIDAS workstation, an electron microprobe, an X-ray diffractometer, and an atomic absorption spectrometer. Elsewhere on campus, students have access to electron microscopes, ion microprobes, and a nuclear reactor for neutron activation analyses. Students also have access to the EPA Fluid Modeling Facility tow tank and wind tunnel in nearby Research Triangle Park. The department is a member of the Duke/UNC consortium, which operates the 131-foot R/V *Cape Hatteras*, a vessel used for both educational and research cruises. Students have also used facilities at the Duke University Marine Laboratory and the National Marine Fisheries Laboratory, both at Pivers Island, North Carolina. The department is a member of the University Corporation for Atmospheric Research, which provides access to the computing and observational systems of the National Center for Atmospheric Research.

Financial Aid

A number of teaching and research assistantships are available on a competitive basis. The stipends for 1999–2000, for 20 hours of service per week, are $1000 per month on a nine-month basis for teaching assistants and a twelve-month basis for research assistants. Students on assistantships receive paid health insurance and have tuition waived; they are responsible only for in-state fees of $457 per semester.

Cost of Study

Tuition and fees for 1999–2000 for a full course load of 9 or more credits are $1185 per semester for in-state students and $5768 per semester for out-of-state students. U.S. citizens may be able to establish North Carolina residence after one year and then be eligible for in-state tuition rates.

Living and Housing Costs

The University has graduate dormitory rooms that cost about $1210 per semester. Married student housing is available at King Village for about $415 per month for a one-bedroom apartment. Off-campus housing is available starting at about $450 per month.

Student Group

University enrollment is approximately 27,200, with an undergraduate enrollment of 18,700, a graduate enrollment of 4,400, and a continuing-education enrollment of 4,100. The department has approximately 227 undergraduate majors and 130 graduate students, with 30 in marine science, 30 in earth science, and 70 in atmospheric science. Approximately 26 of the graduate students are women.

Location

Raleigh, a modern growing city with a population of more than 200,000 in a metropolitan area of more than 1 million, is situated in rolling terrain in the eastern Piedmont near the upper Coastal Plain. Raleigh, the state capital, is one vertex of the Research Triangle area, with Durham and Chapel Hill the other vertices. Numerous colleges and industrial and government laboratories are located in the Triangle area, which each year also attracts some of the world's foremost symphony orchestras and ballet companies. Located within a 3-hour drive of the campus are both the seashore and the mountains, which offer many opportunities for skiing, hiking, swimming, boating, and fishing.

The University

North Carolina State University, the state's land-grant and chief technological institution, recently celebrated its centennial year. A graduate faculty of 1,400 and more than 100 major buildings are located on the 623-acre main campus. The 780-acre Centennial Campus, which has just been acquired adjacent to the main campus, ensures room for future expansion. The University is organized into nine colleges plus the Graduate School. The department is one of six in the College of Physical and Mathematical Sciences.

Applying

For fall admission, the completed application form, transcripts, recommendation forms, GRE scores, and TOEFL scores (for international students) should be received no later than March 1 to ensure full consideration for assistantship support. Applications for summer and spring admission are also considered, but assistantship support is less likely.

Correspondence and Information

Graduate Administrator
Department of Marine, Earth and Atmospheric Sciences
North Carolina State University
Box 8208
Raleigh, North Carolina 27695-8208
Telephone: 919-515-7837
E-mail: janowitz@ncsu.edu

North Carolina State University

THE FACULTY AND THEIR RESEARCH

Viney Aneja, Research Professor; Ph.D., North Carolina State, 1977. Atmospheric chemistry.

S. Pal Arya, Professor; Ph.D., Colorado State, 1968. Micrometeorology, atmospheric turbulence and diffusion, air-sea interaction.

Reese Barrick, Visiting Assistant Professor; Ph.D., USC, 1993. Dinosaur paleobiology and paleoecology.

Neal E. Blair, Professor; Ph.D., Stanford, 1980. Chemical oceanography, biogeochemistry, organic geochemistry.

Roscoe R. Braham, Scholar in Residence; Ph.D., Chicago, 1951. Cloud physics, thunderstorms, weather modification.

Victor V. Cavaroc, Professor; Ph.D., LSU, 1969. Sedimentary petrology/petrography, lithostratigraphy, coal stratigraphy.

Tony F. Clark, Visiting Professor; Ph.D., North Carolina at Chapel Hill, 1974. Geophysical oceanography.

Jerry M. Davis, Professor; Ph.D., Ohio State, 1971. Agricultural meteorology, climatology, statistical meteorology, planetary boundary layer.

David J. DeMaster, Professor; Ph.D., Yale, 1979. Marine geochemistry and radio chemistry in the nearshore and deep-sea environments.

Thomas Drake, Assistant Professor; Ph.D., UCLA, 1988. Geology, physics of surficial processes.

David B. Eggleston, Associate Professor; Ph.D., William and Mary, 1991. Marine benthic ecology, epifauna.

Ronald V. Fodor, Professor; Ph.D., New Mexico, 1972. Igneous petrology, volcanoes, meteorites.

James Hibbard, Associate Professor; Ph.D., Cornell, 1988. Structural geology.

Thomas S. Hopkins, Visiting Professor; Ph.D., Washington (Seattle), 1971. Physical oceanography.

Gerald S. Janowitz, Professor and Graduate Administrator; Ph.D., Johns Hopkins, 1967. Geophysical fluid mechanics, continental shelf and ocean circulation.

Daniel L. Kamykowski, Professor; Ph.D., California, San Diego, 1973. Effects of physical factors on phytoplankton behavior and physiology, global plant nutrient distributions.

Michael M. Kimberley, Associate Professor; Ph.D., Princeton, 1974. Sedimentary geochemistry, sedimentary ore deposits, chemistry of natural and polluted water.

Charles E. Knowles, Associate Professor; Ph.D., Texas A&M, 1970. Estuarine and coastal processes, surface gravity wave measurements.

Steven E. Koch, Associate Professor; Ph.D., Oklahoma, 1979. Severe storms, mesoscale and cloud scale processes.

Gary M. Lackmann, Assistant Professor; Ph.D., SUNY at Albany, 1995. Synoptic and mesoscale meteorology.

Elana L. Leithold, Associate Professor; Ph.D., Washington (Seattle), 1987. Nearshore and shelf sedimentation and stratigraphy, sediment transport.

Yuh Lang Lin, Professor; Ph.D., Yale, 1984. Modeling of mesoscale atmospheric dynamics.

Thomas F. Malone, University Distinguished Scholar; Sc.D., MIT, 1946. Meteorology.

John M. Morrison, Associate Professor; Ph.D., Texas A&M, 1977. Descriptive physical oceanography, general ocean circulation, air-sea interaction and climatic problems.

Leonard J. Pietrafesa, Professor and Head; Ph.D., Washington (Seattle), 1973. Estuarine and continental margin physical processes, seismology.

Sethu S. Raman, Professor; Ph.D., Colorado State, 1972. Air-sea interactions, boundary layer meteorology and air pollution.

Henry G. Reichle Jr., Visiting Professor; Ph.D., Michigan, 1969. Air pollution detection by satellite.

Allen J. Riordan, Associate Professor; Ph.D., Wisconsin, 1977. Satellite meteorology, Antarctic meteorology.

Dale A. Russell, Visiting Professor; Ph.D., Columbia, 1964. Dinosaurian ecology.

Vin K. Saxena, Professor; Ph.D., Rajasthan, 1969. Cloud physics, acid precipitation, weather modification.

Frederick Semazzi, Associate Professor; Ph.D., Nairobi, 1983. Climate dynamics.

Ping Tung Shaw, Associate Professor; Ph.D., Woods Hole/MIT, 1982. Shelf-slope physical oceanography and Lagrangian analysis.

William J. Showers, Associate Professor; Ph.D., Hawaii, 1982. Stable-isotope geochemistry, paleoceanography, micropaleontology, environmental monitoring, geoarchaeology.

Stephen Snyder, Assistant Professor; Ph.D., South Florida, 1994. Geological oceanography.

Edward F. Stoddard, Associate Professor; Ph.D., UCLA, 1976. Metamorphic petrology, silicate mineralogy, Piedmont geology.

Donna L. Wolcott, Associate Professor; Ph.D., Berkeley, 1972. Physiological ecology of terrestrial crabs.

Thomas G. Wolcott, Professor; Ph.D., Berkeley, 1971. Physiological ecology of marine invertebrates, biotelemetry.

Lian Xie, Visiting Assistant Professor; Ph.D., Miami (Florida), 1992. Air-sea interaction processes.

Jordan Hall, home of the department.

PENNSYLVANIA STATE UNIVERSITY

PENNSTATE

Department of Geosciences

Programs of Study

The Department of Geosciences offers M.S. and Ph.D. degree programs. A wide range of faculty interests (see reverse side of page) and exceptional laboratory and other support facilities provide an extensive variety of areas of specialization in which students may choose their course work and research topics. These areas include the Earth System Science Center (ESSC), which is an interdepartmental program directed toward a global, multidisciplinary view of the earth and its variability.

Research Facilities

The department maintains a variety of unsurpassed modern facilities and equipment for research, including an extensive computer network with direct access to ESSC's Cray supercomputer. Students have access to laboratories for research on the petrography and petrology of igneous, metamorphic, and sedimentary rocks, including coal and organic sediments; rock preparation and rock mechanics laboratories; high-temperature and high-pressure/high-temperature equipment for dry or hydrothermal experiments; mass spectrometers and ancillary equipment for isotope analysis; a seismic observatory, ultrasonic model laboratories, and field equipment for seismic, electrical, magnetic, and gravity surveys; facilities and data for remote sensing of earth resources; laboratories and field facilities for the study of the hydrogeology and geochemistry of natural waters; and coastal marine laboratories in Virginia. The department and the Materials Characterization Laboratories are equipped for both classical methods of chemical analysis and modern instrumental methods, such as atomic absorption, emission, and absorption spectroscopy; electron microscopy and scanning transmission electron microscopy; automated X-ray diffractometry; ICP-MS; and ion microprobe and automated electron microprobe analysis. The department has excellent collections of rocks, minerals, and ore and coal samples; paleontological, paleobotanical, and palynological collections; lunar photographs and data; and maps. More than 50,000 volumes related to earth sciences are housed in the library of the College of Earth and Mineral Sciences. A nuclear reactor is available on campus.

Financial Aid

All of the department's on-campus graduate students receive support from assistantships, fellowships, or traineeships. Half-time teaching or research assistantships of $5603 per semester, plus full tuition and limited medical coverage, were available to qualified applicants in 1998–99. One-quarter-time and three-quarter-time assistantships are awarded in special cases. Most research assistantships involve the study of problems appropriate for thesis research. Financial support for thesis research unsupported by grants is available through a special fund.

Cost of Study

For 1998–99, the self-supporting Pennsylvania resident paid $3267 per semester; nonresidents paid $6730 per semester.

Living and Housing Costs

Living costs are moderate. In 1998–99, for single students, a room in the coeducational University residence halls and board were available for $2420 per semester. Privately owned housing can be found within walking distance of the campus. For married students, ample accommodations are available locally at a wide range of prices, and graduate student apartments on campus rented for $345 and $420 per month for one- and two-bedroom units, respectively.

Student Group

In the department there are approximately 90 graduate students. The total student enrollment at the main University Park campus is about 34,000.

Location

The University Park campus of Pennsylvania State University is in the town of State College—a metropolitan area of more than 100,000 people in the center of the commonwealth. Located in a rural and scenic part of the Appalachian Mountains, the area is only 3 to 4 hours away from Washington, D.C., Pittsburgh, and Philadelphia. Varied cultural, educational, and athletic activities are available throughout the year.

The University and The Department

Founded in 1855, Penn State is the land-grant university of Pennsylvania. The University Park campus has 258 major buildings on 4,786 acres, of which 540 acres constitute the beautifully landscaped central campus. The College of Earth and Mineral Sciences, of which the department is a part, has approximately 130 faculty members and 450 graduate students in the earth sciences and closely related fields in the Departments of Geography, Materials Science and Engineering, Meteorology, Mineral Economics, and Mineral Engineering. The College occupies a complex of four buildings on the west side of the campus, with the Department of Geosciences housed primarily in the modern, air-conditioned Deike Building. Facilities for graduate student research are available within the department and in the Materials Characterization Labs, the Energy and Fuels Research Center, the Materials Research Lab, and the Earth System Science Center. The size of the faculty promotes close personal relationships between faculty and students. Each faculty member works with a research group averaging 2–4 students. In cooperation with a faculty adviser and committee, each student designs and pursues a course and research program tailored to his or her individual interests and needs.

Applying

The University offers two 15-week semesters and an 8-week summer session beginning approximately August 26, January 10, and June 10, respectively. Candidates may apply for admission in either fall or spring. Applications must be received by July for admission to the fall semester; if financial support is required, applications must be received by January 15. All correspondence regarding admission and financial aid should be sent to the address given below.

Correspondence and Information

Associate Head for the Geosciences Graduate Program
303 Deike Building
Pennsylvania State University
University Park, Pennsylvania 16802

Telephone: 814-865-7394
Fax: 814-863-7823
E-mail: admissions@geosc.psu.edu
World Wide Web: http://www.geosc.psu.edu

Pennsylvania State University

THE FACULTY AND THEIR RESEARCH

M. A. Arthur, Professor; Ph.D., Princeton, 1979. Marine geology, stable isotope geochemistry, sedimentary geochemistry, paleoceanography.
S. S. Alexander, Professor of Geophysics; Ph.D., Caltech, 1963. Seismology, time-series analysis, remote sensing.
R. B. Alley, Professor; Ph.D., Wisconsin–Madison, 1987. Glaciology, ice sheet stability, paleoclimates from ice cores.
E. J. Barron, Professor and Director, Earth System Science Center; Ph.D., Miami (Florida), 1980. Earth system science, paleoclimatology.
S. L. Brantley, Professor; Ph.D., Princeton, 1987. Aqueous geochemistry, geochemical kinetics.
D. W. Burbank, Professor; Ph.D., Dartmouth, 1982. Geomorphology, surficial processes, sedimentation, and tectonics.
R. J. Cuffey, Professor of Paleontology; Ph.D., Indiana, 1966. Paleontology, evolution, systematics, paleoecology, bryozoans, reefs.
P. Deines, Professor of Geochemistry; Ph.D., Penn State, 1967. Isotope geochemistry.
D. H. Eggler, Professor of Petrology; Ph.D., Colorado, 1967. Experimental mineralogy and petrology of the upper mantle.
T. Engelder, Professor; Ph.D., Texas A&M, 1973. Rock mechanics, structural geology.
D. M. Fisher, Associate Professor; Ph.D., Brown, 1988. Regional tectonics, structural geology.
P. B. Flemings, Associate Professor; Ph.D., Cornell, 1990. Stratigraphy, basin analysis, basin-scale fluid flow.
K. H. Freeman, Associate Professor; Ph.D., Indiana, 1991. Organic geochemistry, isotopic biogeochemistry.
K. P. Furlong, Professor; Ph.D., Utah, 1981. Plate tectonics, thermal and mechanical evolution of the lithosphere.
T. Furman, Associate Professor; Ph.D., MIT, 1989. Geochemistry, igneous petrogenesis, watershed biogeochemistry.
E. K. Graham, Professor and Associate Head of Undergraduate Programs; Ph.D., Penn State, 1969. Experimental solid-state geophysics, planetary models.
R. J. Greenfield, Professor of Geophysics; Ph.D., MIT, 1965. Magnetic and electrical fields, seismology.
P. J. Heaney, Associate Professor; Ph.D., Johns Hopkins, 1989. Mineral and materials sciences, crystallography.
J. F. Kasting, Professor; Ph.D., Michigan, 1979. Atmospheric evolution, planetary atmospheres, paleoclimates.
D. M. Kerrick, Professor; Ph.D., Berkeley, 1968. Metamorphic and igneous petrogenesis, fluids in the earth, role of Earth degassing in global geochemical cycles.
J. D. Kubicki, Assistant Professor; Ph.D., Yale, 1990. Theoretical geochemistry, environmental geochemistry.
L. R. Kump, Professor and Associate Head of Graduate Programs; Ph.D., South Florida, 1986. Biogeochemical cycles, low-temperature sedimentary geochemistry, evolution of oceans, atmosphere, and climate.
C. A. Langston, Professor of Geophysics; Ph.D., Caltech, 1976. Seismology, inversion theory, tectonics.
R. G. Najjar, Assistant Professor; Ph.D., Princeton, 1990. Marine biogeochemistry, air-sea gas exchange, oceans and climate.
A. A. Nyblade, Assistant Professor; Ph.D., Michigan, 1992. Geophysics, tectonics, applied seismology.
H. Ohmoto, Professor of Geochemistry; Ph.D., Princeton, 1969. Astrobiology, stable isotopes, ore deposits.
R. R. Parizek, Professor of Geology; Ph.D., Illinois, 1961. Groundwater, glacial, and environmental geology.
M. E. Patzkowsky, Assistant Professor; Ph.D., Chicago, 1992. Invertebrate paleontology, stratigraphy, paleoecology.
R. L. Slingerland, Professor and Head of the Department; Ph.D., Penn State, 1977. Sedimentology, deterministic models.
T. A. Sowers, Assistant Professor; Ph.D., Rhode Island, 1991. Paleoclimatology, ice core and marine climate.
B. Voight, Professor of Geology; Ph.D., Columbia, 1964. Volcanology, engineering, and geology.
W. B. White, Professor of Geochemistry; Ph.D., Penn State, 1962. Carbonate groundwaters, mineralogy, spectroscopy.

Emeriti

H. L. Barnes, Distinguished Professor Emeritus of Geochemistry; Ph.D., Columbia, 1958. Hydrothermal processes, ore deposits, geothermal systems.
T. F. Bates, Professor Emeritus of Mineralogy; Ph.D., Columbia, 1944. Clay mineralogy, public education in geosciences.
C. W. Burnham, Professor Emeritus of Geochemistry; Ph.D., Caltech, 1955. Experimental petrology, geochemistry of ore deposits.
A. Davis, Professor of Geology; Ph.D., Durham (England), 1965. Organic geology, coal petrology, paleogeology of coal deposits.
D. P. Gold, Professor of Geology; Ph.D., McGill, 1963. Petrology, structural geology, remote sensing, economic geology.
A. L. Guber, Professor Emeritus of Geology; Ph.D., Illinois, 1962. Paleozoology, evolution, paleoecology.
B. F. Howell Jr., Professor Emeritus of Geophysics and Associate Dean Emeritus of the Graduate School; Ph.D., Caltech, 1949. Seismology, tectonics.
M. L. Keith, Professor Emeritus of Geochemistry; Ph.D., MIT, 1939. General geochemistry, geotectonics.
P. M. Lavin, Professor Emeritus of Geophysics; Ph.D., Penn State, 1962. Gravity and magnetic surveying, crustal tectonics.
A. W. Rose, Professor Emeritus of Geochemistry; Ph.D., Caltech, 1958. Geochemical exploration, ore deposits, environmental geochemistry.
R. F. Schmalz, Professor Emeritus of Geology; Ph.D., Harvard, 1959. Oceanography, chemistry of sedimentation.
R. Scholten, Professor Emeritus of Petroleum Geology; Ph.D., Michigan, 1950. Tectonics, Rocky Mountain geology, habitat of oil.
D. K. Smith, Professor Emeritus of Mineralogy; Ph.D., Minnesota, 1956. X-ray crystallography.
W. Spackman, Professor Emeritus of Paleobotany; Ph.D., Harvard, 1949. Paleobotany, coal petrology, modern organic sediments.
C. P. Thornton, Professor Emeritus of Petrology; Ph.D., Yale, 1953. Volcanology, igneous petrology.
A. Traverse, Professor Emeritus of Palynology; Ph.D., Harvard, 1951. Palynology of Paleozoic-Recent sediments.
E. G. Williams, Professor Emeritus of Geology; Ph.D., Penn State, 1957. Carboniferous stratigraphy, sedimentation.
L. A. Wright, Professor Emeritus of Geology; Ph.D., Caltech, 1951. Industrial minerals, Great Basin geology, tectonics.

The Deike Building, which houses the Department of Geosciences.

SELECTED PUBLICATIONS

Alley, R. B., et al. Holocene climatic instability: A prominent, widespread event 8200 years ago. *Geology* 25(6):483–6, 1997.

Fischer, M., **R. B. Alley,** and **T. Engelder.** Fracture toughness of ice and firm determined from the modified ring test. *J. Glaciol.* 41:383–94, 1995.

Alley, R. B., and D. R. MacAyeal. Ice-rafted debris associated with binge/purge oscillations of the Laurentide ice sheet. *Paleoceanography* 9(4):503–11, 1994.

Alley, R. B., et al. Abrupt increase in snow accumulation at the end of the Younger Dryas event. *Nature* 362:527–9, 1993.

Yan, B., and **S. S. Alexander.** Source mechanism of the 1982 New Brunswick, Canada, earthquake sequence using combined surface wave methods. *Bull. Seism. Soc. Am.* 80:296–312, 1990.

Alexander, S. S. The association of lineaments in satellite and geophysical data with present and past tectonic stress conditions. *Memoirs, Geolog. Soc. India* 12:75–83, 1989.

Arthur, M. A., and W. E. Dean. Preservation of organic matter on the Holocene Peru Margin. *Chem. Geol.* 153:272–86, 1998.

Arthur, M. A., and W. E. Dean. Organic-matter production and preservation and evolution of anoxia in the Holocene Black Sea. *Paleoceanography* 13:395–411, 1998.

D'Hondt, S., and **M. A. Arthur.** Late Cretaceous oceans and the cool tropics paradox. *Science* 271:1838–41, 1996.

Gibbs, M. T., **E. J. Barron,** and **L. R. Kump.** An atmospheric pCO_2 threshold for glaciation in the late Ordovician. *Geology* 25:447–50, 1997.

Dutton, J. F., and **E. J. Barron.** Miocene to present vegetation changes: A possible piece of the Cenozoic cooling puzzle. *Geology* 25(1):39–41, 1997.

Gibbs, M. T., **E. J. Barron,** and **L. R. Kump.** An atmospheric pCO_2 threshold for glaciation in the Late Ordovician. *Geology* 25(5):447–50, 1997.

Jenkins, G. S., and **E. J. Barron.** Global climate model and coupled regional climate model simulations over the eastern United States: GENESIS and RegCM2 simulations. *Global Planet. Change* 3–32, 1997.

Brantley, S. L., J. T. Chesley, and L. L. Stillings. Isotopic ratios and release rates of Sr measured from weathering feldspars. *Geochim. Cosmochim. Acta* 62:1492–500, 1998.

Nugent, M. A., **S. L. Brantley,** C. G. Pantano, and P. A. Maurice. The influence of natural mineral coatings on feldspar weathering. *Nature* 396:527–622, 1998.

Brantley, S. L., and K. Koepenick. Carbon dioxide emissions from Ol Doinyo Lengai and the skewed distribution of passive degassing from volcanoes. *Geology* 23:933–6, 1995.

Brantley, S. L., and Y. Chen. Chemical weathering rates of pyroxenes and amphiboles. In *Chemical Weathering Rates of Silicate Minerals, Mineralogical Society of America Short Course,* vol. 31, A. F. White and S. L. Brantley, eds. Chelsea, Mass: MSA Publications, 1995.

Brozovic, N., **D. W. Burbank,** and A. J. Meigs. Climatic limits on landscape development in the northwestern Himalaya. *Science* 276:571–4, 1997.

Burbank, D. W., A. Meigs, and N. Brozovic. Interactions of growing folds and coeval depositional systems. *Basin Res.* 8:199–223, 1996.

Burbank, D. W., et al. Bedrock incision, rock uplift, and threshold hillslopes in the northwestern Himalaya. *Nature* 379:505–10, 1996.

Tang, S., and **R. J. Cuffey.** *Inconobotopora lichenoporoides,* a new genus and species of cystoporate bryozoan from the Silurian of Gotland, and its evolutionary implications. *J. Paleontol.* 72:256–64, 1998.

Cuffey, R. J. Prasopora-bearing event beds in the Coburn Limestone (Bryozoa; Ordovician; Pennsylvania). In *Paleontological Events: Stratigraphic, Ecological, and Evolutionary Implications,* pp. 110–30, eds. C. E. Brett and G. C. Baird. New York: Columbia University Press, 1997.

Butler, K. L., and **R. J. Cuffey.** Reduced bryozoan diversity and paleoenvironmental stress in the Saluda Dolomite (uppermost Ordovician, southeastern Indiana). In *Bryozoans in Space and Time,* pp. 55–61, eds. D. P. Gordon, A. M. Smith, and J. A. Grant-Mackie. Wellington, New Zealand: National Institute of Water and Atmospheric Research, 1996.

Taylor, G. H., et al. **(A. Davis).** *Organic Petrology.* Berlin, Stuttgart: Gebrüder Borntraeger, 1998.

Deines, P., J. W. Harris, and J. J. Gurney. Carbon isotope ratios, nitrogen content and aggregation state, and inclusion chemistry of diamonds from Jwaneng, Botswana. *Geochim. Cosmochim. Acta* 61(18):3993–4005, 1997.

Deines, P., and J. W. Harris. Sulfide inclusion chemistry and carbon isotopes of African diamonds. *Geochim. Cosmochim. Acta* 59(15): 3173–88, 1995.

Ayers, J. C., and **D. H. Eggler.** Partitioning of elements between silicate melt and H_2O-NaCl fluids at 1.5 and 2.0 Gpa pressure: Implications for mantle metasomatism. *Geochim. Cosmochim. Acta* 59:4237–46, 1995.

Eggler, D. H., and J. P. Lorand. Mantle sulfide geobarometry. *Geochim. Cosmochim. Acta* 57:2213–22, 1993.

Younes, A., **T. Engelder,** and W. Bosworth. Factors contributing to fracture density and distribution in faulted basement blocks; Structural geology in reservoir characterization. Gulf of Suez, Egypt. Eds. M. P. Coward, T. S. Daltaban, and H. Johnson. *Geological Soc. London,* special publication 127:167–90, 1998.

Engelder, T., M. R. Gross, and P. Pinkerton. Joint development in clastic rocks of the Elk Basin anticline, Montana-Wyoming: An analysis of fracture spacing versus bed thickness in a basement-involved Laramide structure. In *Rocky Mountain Association of Geologists 1997 Guidebook,* pp. 1–18, eds. T. Hoak, A. Klawitter, and P. Blomquist. Denver, Colorado, 1997.

Engelder, T., and J. T. Leftwich. A pore-pressure limit in overpressured South Texas oil and gas fields: Seals, traps, and the petroleum system (ed. R. C. Surdam). *Am. Assoc. Petroleum Geologists Mem.* 67:255–67, 1997.

Fisher, D. M., and D. J. Anastasio. Kinematic analysis of a large-scale leading edge fold, Lost River Range, Idaho. *J. Struct. Geol.* 16(3):337–54, 1994.

Fisher, D. M., T. W. Gardner, and J. J. Marshall. Kinematics associated with late Tertiary and Quaternary deformation in central Costa Rica: Western boundary of the Panama microplate. *Geology* 22:263–6, 1994.

Fisher, D. M., and **S. L. Brantley.** Models of quartz overgrowth and vein formation: Deformation and episodic fluid flow in an ancient subduction zone. *J. Geophys. Res.* 97:20043–61, 1992.

Poulsen, C. J., **P. B. Flemings,** R. A. J. Robinson, and J. M. Metzger. Three-dimensional stratigraphic evolution of the Miocene Baltimore Canyon region: Implications for eustatic interpretations and the systems tract model. *GSA Bull.* 110:1105–22, 1998.

Gordon, D. S., and **P. B. Flemings.** Generation of overpressure and compaction-driven fluid flow in a Plio-Pleistocene growth-faulted basin, Eugene Island 330, offshore Louisiana. *Basin Res.* 10:177–96, 1998.

Alexander, L. L., and **P. B. Flemings.** Geologic evolution of a Plio-Pleistocene salt withdrawal mini-basin: Block 330, Eugene Island, south addition, offshore Louisiana. *AAPG Bull.* 79:1737–56, 1995.

Pancost, R. D., **K. H. Freeman,** S. G. Wakeham, and C. Y. Robertson. Controls on carbon isotope fractionation by diatoms in the Peru Upwelling Region. *Geochim. Acta* 61:4983–92, 1997.

Dias, R. F., and **K. H. Freeman.** Carbon-isotope analyses of semivolatile organic compounds in aqueous media using solid-phase microextraction and isotope-ratio-monitoring GCMS. *Anal. Chem.* 69:944–50, 1997.

Freeman, K. H., S. G. Wakeham, and J. M. Hayes. Predictive isotopic biogeochemistry: Hydrocarbons from anoxic marine basins. *Org. Geochem.* 21:629–44, 1994.

Furlong, K. P., and R. Govers. Ephemeral crustal thickening at a triple junction: The Mendocino crustal conveyor. *Geology* 27:127–30, 1999.

Kreemer, C., R. Govers, **K. P. Furlong,** and W. E. Holt. Plate boundary deformation between the Pacific and North America in the Explorer Region. *Tectonophysics* 293:225–38, 1998.

Prims, J., **K. P. Furlong,** K. M. M. Rohr, and R. Govers. Lithospheric structure along the Queen Charlotte margin in western Canada: Constraints from flexural modeling. *Geo-Marine Lett.* 17:94–9, 1996.

Furman, T., P. Thompson, and B. Hatchl. Primary mineral weathering in the central Appalachians: A mass balance approach. *Geochim. Cosmochim. Acta,* in press.

Fitzhugh, R. D., **T. Furman,** and B. J. Cosby. Controls on longitudinal and seasonal variation of stream acidity in a headwater catchment on the Appalachia Plateau, West Virginia. *Biogeochemistry,* in press.

Furman, T., and D. Graham. Erosion of lithospheric mantle beneath the East African Rift system: Evidence from the Kivu volcanic province. *Lithos,* in press.

Furman, T. Melting of metasomatized subcontinental lithosphere:

Pennsylvania State University

Selected Publications (continued)

Undersaturated mafic lavas from Rungwe, Tanzania. *Contrib. Mineral. Petrol.* 122:97–115, 1995.

Pacalo, R. E., and **E. K. Graham.** Pressure and temperature dependence of the elastic properties of synthetic MnO. *Phys. Chem. Miner.* 18:69–80, 1991.

Greenfield, R. J., and **E. K. Graham.** Application of a simple relation for describing wave velocity as a function of pressure in rocks containing microcracks. *J. Geophys. Res.* 101(B3):5643–52, 1996.

De, S., and **P. J. Heaney** et al. Microstructural observations of polycrystalline diamond: A contribution to the carbonado conundrum. *Earth Planet. Sci. Lett.,* in press.

Yates, D. M., K. J. Joyce, and **P. J. Heaney.** Complexation of copper with polymeric silica in aqueous solution. *Appl. Geochem.* 13:235–41, 1998.

Heaney, P. J., et al. Structural effects of Sr-substitution in La_2.xSr$_x$NiO$_{4+\delta}$. *Phys. Rev. B* 57:10370–8, 1998.

Heaney, P. J., and **A. M. Davis.** Observation and origin of self-organized textures in agates. *Science* 269:1562–5, 1995.

Kasting, J. F. Why a water world? *Sci. Am. Presents* 9(3):16–22, 1998.

Williams, D. M., **J. F. Kasting,** and R. A. Wade. Habitable moons around extrasolar giant planets. *Nature* 385:234–6, 1997.

Kasting, J. F. Habitable zones around low mass stars and the search for extraterrestrial life. *Origins Life* 27:291–307, 1997.

Schultz, P. A., and **J. F. Kasting.** Optimal reductions in CO_2 emissions. *Energy Policy* 25:491–500, 1997.

Taubman, S. J., and **J. F. Kasting.** Carbonyl sulfide: No remedy for global warming. *Geophys. Res. Lett.* 22:803–5, 1995.

Kerrick, D. M., and K. Caldeira. Metamorphic CO_2 degassing from orogenic belts. *Chem. Geol.* 145:213–32, 1998.

Kerrick, D. M., and J. A. D. Connolly. Subduction of ophicarbonates and recycling of CO_2 and H_2O. *Geology* 26:375–8, 1998.

Seward, T. M., and **D. M. Kerrick.** Hydrothermal CO_2 emission from the Taupo Volcanic Zone, New Zealand. *Earth Planet. Sci. Lett.* 139:105–13, 1996.

Nesbitt, B. E., C. A. Mendoza, and **D. M. Kerrick.** Surface fluid convection during Cordilleran extension and generation of metamorphic CO_2 contributions to Cenozoic atmospheres. *Geology* 23:99–101, 1995.

Kubicki, J. D., M. J. Itoh, L. M. Schroeter, and S. E. Apitz. The bonding mechanisms of salicylic acid adsorbed onto illite clay: An ATR-FTIR and MO study. *Environ. Sci. Technol.* 31:1151–6, 1997.

Kubicki, J. D., G. A. Blake, and S. E. Apitz. Ab initio calculations on Q^3Si^{4+} and Al^{3+} species: Implications for atomic structure of mineral surfaces. *Am. Mineral.* 81:789–99, 1996.

Kubicki, J. D., and E. M. Stolper. Structural roles of CO_2 and $[CO_3]^{2-}$ in fully-polymerized sodium aluminosilicate melts and glasses. *Geochim. Cosmochim. Acta* 59:683–98, 1995.

Machusak, D., and **L. R. Kump.** Environmental controls on groundwater chemistry in an offshore island aquifer: Fiesta Key, Florida. *Aquatic Geochem.* 3:129–67, 1997.

Kump, L. R., and **M. A. Arthur.** Global chemical erosion during the Cenozoic: Weatherability balances the budgets. In *Tectonics Uplift and Climate Change,* pp. 399–426, ed. W. Ruddiman. New York: Plenum Press, 1997.

Lovelock, J. E., and **L. R. Kump.** Failure of climate regulation in a geophysiological model. *Nature* 369:732–4, 1994.

Langston, C. A., R. Brazier, **A. A. Nyblade,** and T. J. Owens. Local magnitude scale and seismicity rate for Tanzania, East Africa. *Bull. Seism. Soc. Am.* 88:712–21, 1998.

Zhao, M., **C. A. Langston,** and **A. A. Nyblade.** Lower crustal rifting in the Rukwa graben, East Africa. *Geophys. J. Int.* 129:412–20, 1997.

Hammer, J. K., and **C. A. Langston.** Modeling the effect of San Andreas fault structure on receiver functions using elastic 3D finite difference. *Bull. Seism. Soc. Am.* 86:1608–22, 1996.

Najjar, R. G., and R. K. Keeling. Analysis of the mean annual cycle of the dissolved oxygen anomaly in the World Ocean. *J. Marine Res.* 55:117–51, 1997.

Najjar, R. G., D. J. Erickson III, and S. Madronich. Modeling the air-sea fluxes of gases formed from the decomposition of dissolved organic matter: Carbonyl sulfide and carbon monoxide. In *The Role of Non-living Organic Matter in the Earth's Carbon Cycle,* pp. 106–32, eds. R. Zepp and C. Sonntag. New York: John Wiley, 1995.

Najjar, R. G. Marine biogeochemistry. In *Climate System Modeling,* pp. 241–80, ed. K. Trenberth. Cambridge, England: Cambridge University Press, 1992.

Ritsema, J., and **A. A. Nyblade** et al. **(C. A. Langston).** Upper mantle seismic velocities beneath Tanzania, East Africa: Implications for the stability of cratamic lithosphere. *J. Geophys. Res.* 103:21201–13, 1998.

Nyblade, A. A., K. S. Vogfjard, and **C. A. Langston.** P wave velocity structure of Proterozoic upper mantle beneath central and Southern Africa. *J. Geophys. Res.* 101:11159–71, 1996.

Nyblade, A. A., and S. W. Robinson. The African superswell. *Geophys. Res. Lett.* 21:765–8, 1994.

Watanabe, Y., et al. **(H. Ohmoto).** Carbon, nitrogen, and sulfur geochemistry of Archean and Proterozoic shales from the Kaapvaal Craton, South Africa. *Geochim. Cosmochim. Acta* 61(16):3441–59, 1997.

Ohmoto, H., and M. B. Goldhaber. Sulfur and carbon isotopes. In *Geochemistry of Hydrothermal Ore Deposits,* third edition, pp. 517–612, ed. H. L. Barnes. New York: John Wiley & Sons, 1997.

Ohmoto, H. Evidence in pre-2.2 Ga paleosols for the early evolution of atmospheric oxygen and terrestrial biota. *Geology* 24:1135–8, 1996.

Cohen, J., et al. **(R. R. Parizek).** *Report to the U.S. Congress and Secretary of Energy.* Arlington, Va.: U.S. Nuclear Waste Technical Review Board, 1998.

Kim, J. M., and **R. R. Parizek.** Numerical simulation of the Noordbergum effect resulting from groundwater pumping in a layered aquifer system. *J. Hydrol.* 202:231–43, 1997.

Kim J. M., **R. R. Parizek,** and D. Elsworth. Evaluation of fully-coupled strata deformation and groundwater flow in response to longwall mining. *Int. J. Rock Mech. Miner. Sci.* 34(8):1187–99, 1997.

Patzkowsky, M. E., and S. M. Holland. Patterns of turnover in Middle and Upper Ordovician brachiopods of the eastern United States: A test of coordinated stasis. *Paleobiology* 23(4):420–43, 1997.

Patzkowsky, M. E., M. A. Arthur, and **K. H. Freeman.** Late Middle Ordovician environmental change and extinction: Harbinger of the Late Ordovician or continuation of Cambrian patterns? *Geology* 25(10):911–4, 1997.

Patzkowsky, M. E. A hierarchical branching model of evolutionary radiations. *Paleobiology* 21:440–60, 1995.

Slingerland, R., and N. D. Smith. Necessary conditions for a meandering-river avulsion. *Geology* 26:435–8, 1998.

Tucker, G. E., and **R. Slingerland.** Drainage basin responses to climate change. *Water Resources Res.* 33(8):2031–47, 1997.

Slingerland, R. L., and **L. R. Kump** et al. **(M. A. Arthur** and E. J. **Barron).** Estuarine Circulation in the Turonian Western Interiod Seaway of North America. *Geol. Soc. Am. Bull.* 108:941–52, 1996.

Slingerland, R. L., K. Furlong, and J. Harbaugh. *Simulating Clastic Sedimentary Basins/Physical Fundamentals and Computing Procedures.* Englewood Cliffs, N.J.: Prentice Hall, 1993.

Sowers, T. A., et al. An inter-laboratory comparison of techniques for extracting and analyzing trapped gases in ice cores. *J. Geophys. Res.* 102(26):527–39, 1997.

Sowers, T. A., and M. Bender. Climate records during the last deglaciation. *Science* 269:210–4, 1995.

Sowers, T., et al. 135,000 year Vostok-SPECMAP common temporal framework. *Paleoceanography* 8:737–66, 1993.

Voight, B., et al. Magma flow instability and cyclic activity at Soufriere Hills Volcano, Montserrat, B.W.I. *Science* 283:1138–42, 1999.

Voight, B., et al. Remarkable cyclic ground deformation monitored in real time on Montserrat and its use in eruption forecasting. *Geophys. Res. Lett.* 25(18):3405–8, 1998.

Young, S., and **B. Voight** et al. Eruption of Soufriere Hills Volcano, Montserrat, B.W.I. Special Section, *Geophys. Res. Lett.* 25(18):3387–440; 25(19):3651–700, 1998.

Voight, B., and D. Elsworth. Failure of volcano slopes. *Geotechnique* 46(4):1–40, 1997.

Voight, B. The management of volcanic emergencies: Nevado del Ruiz. In *Volcano Emergency Management,* pp. 719–69, eds. R. Scarpa and R. Tilling. UNESCO/Int. Assoc. Volcanology and Chemistry of Earth's Interior. Geneva, 1996.

White, W. B. Groundwater flow in karstic aquifers. In *The Handbook of Groundwater Engineering,* 18.1–18.36, ed. J. W. Delleur. Boca Raton, Fla.: CRD Press, 1998.

Boldish, S. R., and **W. B. White.** Optical band gaps of selected sulfide minerals. *Am. Miner.* 83:865–71, 1998.

White, W. B. Thermodynamic equilibrium, kinetics, activation barriers, and reaction mechanisms for chemical reactions in karst terrains. *Environ. Geol.* 30:46–58, 1997.

RENSSELAER POLYTECHNIC INSTITUTE

Department of Earth and Environmental Sciences

Programs of Study

As its name suggests, the department is committed to education and research not only in solid-earth geoscience but also those branches of earth science that bear on present day and future environmental concerns. Because of its small size (7 faculty members and 25–35 graduate students), the department is also able to maintain a commitment to personalized education and informal traditions, which promote emphasis on individual abilities and intellectual development. Programs leading to the degrees of Master of Science and Doctor of Philosophy are offered in the fields of environmental chemistry, geochemistry, geophysics, hydrogeology, petrology, planetary science, and tectonics. These programs recognize the interdependence of geology and other sciences. Students with undergraduate majors in geology have the opportunity and are generally expected to broaden their education, while those with undergraduate majors in biology, chemistry, engineering, mathematics, and physics are given the opportunity to complement their backgrounds with formal and reading courses in geology. The program for the master's degree usually includes a thesis of 6 to 9 credit hours, with exceptions made under special circumstances.

Research Facilities

The department is equipped for research in a number of fields. In addition to routine equipment for specimen preparation and sampling, the following are available: solid media high-pressure equipment, hydrothermal apparatus, a 5-spectrometer electron microprobe, a gamma-ray spectrometer, an X-ray diffractometer, two isotope ratio mass spectrometers with dual microinlet, an elemental analyzer, and gas chromatographic sample introduction systems for continuous flow and compound-specific analyses. Seismology and neotectonic studies are supported by a seismograph station, a twelve-channel seismic system, GPS receivers, gravity meters, magnetometers, a resistivity meter, and a computing lab with Sun, HP, and IBM workstations as well as PC and Macintosh computers. Petrology, fission-track studies, and asteroid spectrography are also supported by exceptional software. Essential geology is well represented, since classical areas of Proterozoic, Paleozoic, and Pleistocene geology are located close to campus.

Research is supported by such state-of-the-art facilities as the Rensselaer Libraries, whose electronic information systems provide access to collections, databases, and Internet resources from campus and remote terminals; the Rensselaer Computing System, which permeates the campus with a coherent array of advanced workstations, a shared toolkit of applications for interactive learning and research, and high-speed Internet connectivity; a visualization laboratory for scientific computation; and a high-performance computing facility that includes a 36-node SP2 parallel computer.

Financial Aid

Financial aid is available in the form of fellowships, research or teaching assistantships, and scholarships. The stipend for assistantships ranges up to $11,000 for the nine-month 1999–2000 academic year. In addition, full tuition scholarships are granted. Additional compensation for research during the summer months is also available. Outstanding students may qualify for University-supported Rensselaer Scholar Fellowships, which carry a stipend of $15,000 and a full tuition scholarship. Low-interest, deferred-repayment graduate loans are also available to U.S. citizens with demonstrated need. Most enrolled students receive some kind of financial assistance.

Cost of Study

Tuition for 1999–2000 is $665 per credit hour. Other fees amount to approximately $535 per semester. Books and supplies cost about $1700 per year.

Living and Housing Costs

The cost of rooms for single students in residence halls or apartments ranges from $3356 to $5298 for the 1999–2000 academic year. Family student housing with monthly rents of $592 to $720 is available. Local telephone service is included in all residences and apartments.

Student Group

There are about 4,300 undergraduates and 1,750 graduate students representing all fifty states and more than eighty countries at Rensselaer.

Student Outcomes

Eighty-eight percent of Rensselaer's 1998 graduate students were hired after graduation, earning starting salaries that averaged $56,259 for master's degree recipients and $57,000 to $75,000 for doctoral degree recipients.

Location

Rensselaer is situated on a scenic 260-acre hillside campus in Troy, New York, across the Hudson River from the state capital of Albany. Troy's central Northeast location provides students with a supportive, active, medium-sized community in which to live and an easy commute to Boston, New York, and Montreal and some of the country's finest outdoor recreation sites, including Lake George, Lake Placid, and the Adirondack, Catskill, Berkshire, and Green Mountains. The Capital Region has one of the largest concentrations of academic institutions in the United States. Sixty thousand students attend fourteen area colleges and benefit from shared activities and courses.

The University

Founded in 1824 and the first American college to award degrees in engineering and science, Rensselaer Polytechnic Institute today is accredited by the Middle States Association of Colleges and Schools and is a private, nonsectarian, coeducational university. Rensselaer has five schools—Architecture, Engineering, Management, Science, and Humanities and Social Sciences—that offer a total of ninety-eight graduate degrees in forty-seven fields.

Applying

Admissions applications and all supporting credentials should be submitted well in advance of the preferred semester of entry to allow sufficient time for departmental review and processing. The application fee is $35. GRE scores on the General Test are required. Since the first departmental awards are made in February and March for the next full academic year, applicants requesting financial aid are encouraged to submit all required credentials by February 1 to ensure that they will receive consideration.

Correspondence and Information

For written information about graduate work:
Department of Earth and Environmental
    Sciences
Rensselaer Polytechnic Institute
Troy, New York 12180-3590
Telephone: 518-276-6474
E-mail: ees@rpi.edu
World Wide Web: http://www.rpi.edu/dept/geo

For admissions information and applications:
Director of Graduate Academic and Enrollment
    Services, Graduate Center
Rensselaer Polytechnic Institute
110 8th Street
Troy, New York 12180-3590
Telephone: 518-276-6789
E-mail: grad-services@rpi.edu
World Wide Web: http://www.rpi.edu

Rensselaer Polytechnic Institute

THE FACULTY AND THEIR RESEARCH

Institute Professor
E. B. Watson, Ph.D., MIT. Experimental geochemistry and petrology.

Professors
T. A. Abrajano Jr., Ph.D., Washington (St. Louis). Biogeochemistry.
M. J. Gaffey, Ph.D., MIT. Planetary science.
S. Roecker, Ph.D., MIT. Geophysics, seismology and geodesy.
F. S. Spear, Ph.D., UCLA. Petrology, geochemistry.

Associate Professors
R. F. Bopp, Ph.D., Columbia. Environmental geochemistry.
R. McCaffrey, Ph.D., California, Santa Cruz. Tectonics, seismology, geodesy.

Professors Emeriti
M. B. Bayly, Ph.D., Chicago. Structural geology, rheological properties of earth materials.
G. M. Friedman, Ph.D., Columbia; D.Sc., London. Sedimentology.
S. Katz, Ph.D., Columbia. Geophysics.
R. G. LaFleur, Ph.D., Rensselaer. Geomorphology, glacial geology, water resources.
D. S. Miller, Ph.D., Columbia. Geochemistry, isotope geology, fission-track research.

Adjunct Faculty
K. E. Brewer, Ph.D., Nevada. Hydrogeology, contaminant transport.
Y. W. Isachsen, Ph.D., Cornell. Metamorphic petrology, Precambrian geology.
T. Morgan, Ph.D., Houston. Geophysics.

Research Associate Professor
D. A. Wark, Ph.D., Texas at Austin. Igneous petrology, volcanology.

Research Scientists
D. Cherniak, Ph.D., SUNY at Albany. Geochemical kinetics.
G. Gaetani, Ph.D., MIT. Experimental geochemistry.
J. Price, Ph.D., Oklahoma. Experimental petrology.
E. Shuster, Ph.D., Rensselaer. Environmental geology/hydrology.

Visiting Scientist
T. Winther, Ph.D., Chicago. Experimental petrology/materials science.

Selected Current Research Projects
Zircon dissolution kinetics.
Diffusion of cations in zircon.
Diffusion of sulfur in magma.
Evolution of fluids in subduction zones.
Structure and evolution of the Toba caldera.
GPS study of tectonics in Indonesia and New Guinea.
Mechanics of oblique convergence at subduction zones.
Why great earthquakes occur where they do.
Inversion of earthquake waveforms.
P-T-t paths of the Valhalla Complex, B.C., the Adirondack Mountains, and the Limpopo Belt, R.S.A.
Inverted metamorphism in central New England.
A petrogenetic grid for pelitic schists.
Sediment coring in Hudson River tributaries and reservoirs.
PCB-TSS-DOC sampling and analysis in the Hudson River.
Telescopic characterization of asteroid compositions.
Early solar system processes.
Seismic tomography.
Persistent contaminant sources and chronologies.
Remote sensing.
High-resolution geophysics.

SELECTED PUBLICATIONS

Abrajano, T., T. Bieger, and J. Hellou. Reply to Grossi and de Leeuw. *Org. Geochem.* 28:137, 1998.

Aksu, A., **T. Abrajano,** P. Mudie, and D. Yasar. Organic geochemical and palynological evidence for terrigenous origin of the Aegean Sea sapropel S1. *Mar. Geol.,* in press.

Aravena, R., et al. **(T. Abrajano).** Application of isotopic fingerprinting for biodegradation studies of chlorinated solvents in groundwater. In *Risk, Resource, and Regulatory Issues: Remediation of Chlorinated and Recalcitrant Compounds,* pp. 67–71, eds. G. B. Wickramanayake and R. E. Hinchee. Columbus, Ohio: Battelle Press, 1998.

Dayan, H., **T. Abrajano,** N. Sturchio, and L. Winsor. Carbon isotopic fractionation during reductive dehalogenation of chlorinated ethenes by metallic iron. *Org. Geochem.,* in press.

Heraty, L., et al. **(T. Abrajano).** Isotopic fractionation of carbon and chlorine by microbial degradation of dichloromethane. *Org. Geochem.,* in press.

Holt, B. D., N. C. Sturchio, and **T. Abrajano.** High-temperature method for conversion of chlorinated organic compounds to methyl chloride and CO_2 for isotopic analysis of chlorine and carbon. *Anal. Chem.* 69:2727–33, 1997.

Li, M., et al. **(T. Abrajano).** Unusual polycyclic alkanes in Lower Cretaceous Ostracode sediments and related oils of the western Canadian sedimentary basin. *Org. Geochem.* 25:199–209, 1997.

Pulchan, K., **T. Abrajano,** and R. Helleur. Characterization of tetramethylammonium hydroxide thermocatalysis products of near-shore marine sediments using gas chromatography/mass spectrometry and gas chromatography/combustion/isotope ratio mass spectrometry. *J. Anal. Appl. Pyrolysis* 42:135, 1997.

Todd, S., P. Ostrom, J. Lien, and **T. Abrajano.** Use of biopsy samples of humpback whale (*Megaptera novaeangliae*) skin for stable isotope determination. *J. Northwest Atlantic Fisheries Sci.* 22:71–6, 1998.

Pelayo, R., and **T. Abrajano.** Understanding generic soil cleanup levels: Implication on agricultural chemicals. *J. Soil Contam.* 7(3):357, 1998.

Huang, L., et al. **(T. Abrajano).** C and C1 isotope fractionation of chlorinated aliphatic hydrocarbons during evaporation: Comparison with that in biodegradation. *Org. Geochem.,* in press.

Smirnova, A., **T. Abrajano,** A. Smirnov, and A. Stark. Distribution and sources of polycyclic aromatic hydrocarbons in the sediments of Lake Erie. *Org. Geochem.,* in press.

Sturchio, N., et al. **(T. Abrajano).** Chlorine isotope investigation of natural attenuation of trichloroethene in an aerobic aquifer. *Env. Sci. Tech.* 32:3037–42, 1998.

Bieger, T., **T. A. Abrajano,** and J. Hellou. Generation of biogenic hydrocarbons during a spring bloom in NW Atlantic waters. *Org. Geochem.* 26:207–18, 1997.

Bopp, R. F., et al. **(E. L. Shuster).** Trends in chlorinated hydrocarbon levels in Hudson River Basin sediments. *Environ. Health Perspect,* supplement 4, 106:1075–81, 1998.

Chaky, D. A., et al. **(R. F. Bopp** and **E. L. Shuster).** Chlorinated hydrocarbon contamination of the New York/New Jersey metropolitan area: The urban atmospheric influence. In *Eos. Transactions of the American Geophysical Union, Spring Meeting Supplement S86.* 79(17), 1998.

Kroenke, A. E., et al. **(R. F. Bopp** and **E. L. Shuster).** Atmospheric deposition and fluxes of mercury in remote and urban areas of the Hudson River Basin. In *Eos. Transactions of the American Geophysical Union, Spring Meeting Supplement, S86.* 79(17), 1998.

D. P. Keane, **R. F. Bopp,** and **E. L. Shuster.** Saturated petroleum hydrocarbons in sediments of the Hudson basin. *Northeastern Geol. Soc. Am. Abstracts with Programs, Spring Meeting,* 1997.

McNulty, A. K., and **R. F. Bopp.** In situ anaerobic dechlorination of PCBs in Hudson River sediments. *Abstract, SETAC, 17th Annual Meeting,* 1996.

Cherniak, D. J., J. M. Hanchar, and **E. B. Watson.** Rare-earth diffusion in zircon. *Chem. Geol.* 134:289–301.

Cherniak, D. J. Strontium diffusion in sanidine and albite, and general comments on strontium diffusion in alkali feldspars. *Geochim. Cosmochim. Acta* 60(24):5037–43.

Gaffey, M. J. Surface lithologic heterogeneity of asteroid 4 Vesta. *Icarus,* in press.

Gaffey, M. J. Spectral identification of asteroid 6 Hebe as the mainbelt parent body of the H-type ordinary chondrites. *Meteoritics* 31:A47.

Gaffey, M. J. The search for the asteroidal parent bodies of the meteorites. *Asteroids, Comets, Meteors 96, COSPAR Coll. 10,* pp. 83–4.

Gaffey, M. J. Asteroid 6 Hebe: Spectral evaluation of the prime large mainbelt ordinary chondrite parent body candidate with implications from space weathering of Gaspra and the da-Dactyl system. *LPSC XXVII* 391–2.

Gaffey, M. J. Surface lithologic heterogeneity of asteroid 4 Vesta. *Icarus* 127:130–57.

Gaffey, M. J. The early solar system. *Origins of Life and Evolution of the Biosphere-Special Astronomy,* 27:185–203.

Jarvis K. S., F. Vilas, S. M. Larson, and **M. J. Gaffey.** S4 Hyperion and S9 Phoebe: Testing a link with Iapetus. *LPSC XXVIII,* 661–2.

Jarvis K. S., F. Vilas, S. M. Larson, and **M. J. Gaffey.** A search for variation in the surface mineralogical composition of J VI Himalia. *Bull. Am. Astron. Soc.* 28:1072.

Reed, K. L., **M. J. Gaffey,** and L. A. Lebofsky. Relative projected area and relative albedo variations of asteroid 15 Eunomia. *Icarus* 125:446–54.

Kelley, M. S., and **M. J. Gaffey.** Investigation of the validity of highly evolved asteroid families. *LPSC XXVIII,* 711–2.

Kelley, M. S., and **M. J. Gaffey.** A genetic study of the Ceres (Williams #67) asteroid family. *Bull. Am. Astron. Soc.* 28:1097.

Vilas, F., et al. **(M. J. Gaffey).** Unraveling the zebra: Clues to the Iapetus dark material composition. *Icarus* 124:262–7.

Thomas, P. C., et al. **(M. J. Gaffey).** Impact excavation on asteroid 4 Vesta: Hubble Space Telescope results. *Science* 277:1492–5.

Thomas, P. C., et al. **(M. J. Gaffey).** Vesta: Spin pole, size, and shape from HST images. *Icarus* 128:88–94.

Zellner, B., et al. **(M. J. Gaffey).** HST images of Vesta at perihelion. *Bull. Am. Astron. Soc.* 28:1100.

Stockstill K. R., S. M. Larson, F. Vilas, and **M. J. Gaffey.** The composition of the Iapetus dark material, Hyperion and Phoebe. *Bull. Am. Astron. Soc.* 28:1071.

Allen R. A., F. Vilas, A. Fitzsimmons, and **M. J. Gaffey.** Confirmation of the 0.43-mm Fe^{3+} feature in low-albedo asteroids. *Bull. Am. Astron. Soc. 28,* 1100.

Binzel R. P., et al. **(M. J. Gaffey).** Geologic mapping of Vesta from 1994 Hubble Space Telescope images. *Icarus* 128:95–103.

Masturyono, et al. **(R. McCaffrey).** Rupture zone of the Biak earthquake of February 17, 1996 inferred from aftershocks, coseismic deformation, and waveform analysis. *EOS* 79:F573, 1998.

Masturyono, et al. **(R. McCaffrey, D. Wark,** and **S. Roecker).** Imaging magma system of Toba Caldera using P velocity tomography. *EOS* 78, 1997.

McCaffrey, R., and L. Seeber. Shortening parallel to convergent plate boundaries at cusps between broad bends toward the lower Plate. *EOS* 79:F913, 1998.

McCaffrey, R., and J. Nabelek. Role of oblique convergence in the active deformation of southern Tibet. *Geology* 26:691–4, 1998.

McCaffrey, R., and P. Zwick. Strain partitioning at convergent margins: GPS constraints and numerical modeling. *EOS* 79, 1998.

McCaffrey, R., et al. GPS constraints on forearc sliver motion, plate coupling, and strain partitioning in northwestern Oregon. *EOS* 79:F874, 1998.

McCaffrey, R. Estimates of modern arc-parallel strain rates in fore arcs. *Geology* 24:27–30.

McCaffrey, R. Influences of recurrence times and fault zone temperatures on the age-rate dependence of subduction zone seismicity. *J. Geophys. Res.* 102:22839–54, 1997.

McCaffrey, R., J. Nabelek, and P. Zwick. Role of oblique convergence in the active deformation of southern Tibet. *EOS* 77, 1996.

McCaffrey, R., et al. Geodetic evidence for full strain partitioning in north Sumatra. *EOS* 78, 1997.

McCaffrey, R. Slip partitioning at convergent plate boundaries of SE Asia. *Tectonic Evolution of Southeast Asia Symposium, Geol. Soc. London Special Publication* 106:3–18.

McCaffrey, R. Strain partitioning as applied to Southern Tibet. *EOS* 78, 1997.

McCaffrey, R. Thermal view of the age-rate dependence of subduction zone seismicity: How Cascadia fits in. *GSA Abstracts with Program* 28(5):89, 1996.

McCaffrey, R. Statistical significance of the seismic coupling coefficient. *Bull. Seismol. Soc. Am.* 87:1069–73, 1997.

Rensselaer Polytechnic Institute

Selected Publications (continued)

Prawirodirdjo, L., Y. Bock, **R. McCaffrey,** and J. Genrich. Strain rates along the Sumatra subduction fault from traingulation and GPS. *EOS* 79:F185, 1998.

Prawirodirdjo, L., et al. **(R. McCaffrey).** Geodetic observations of interseismic strain segmentation at the Sumatra subduction zone. *Geophys. Res. Lett.* 24:2601–4, 1997.

Schurr, B., et al. **(R. McCaffrey).** RAMP aftershock survey of the Feb. 17, 1996 Mw=8.2 Irian Jaya earthquake. *IRIS Workshop,* 1996.

Stevens, C., et al. **(R. McCaffrey).** GPS measurements across the eastern Ramu-Markham fault, Papua New Guinea. *EOS* 79: F863, 1998.

Stevens, C., et al. **(R. McCaffrey).** GPS measurements of interseismic, co-seismic, and post-seismic slip at the central Ramu-Markham fault in Papua New Guinea. *EOS* 79:F601, 1998.

Stevens, C., et al. **(R. McCaffrey).** The Feb. 17 1996 Mw=8.2 Biak earthquake: Dislocation models constrained by GPS measurements, co-seismic sea-level changes and aftershocks. *EOS* 77, 1996.

Stevens, C., et al. **(R. McCaffrey).** Mid-crystal detachment and ramp faulting in the Markham Valley, Papua New Guinea. *Geology* 26:847–50, 1998.

Zwick, P., et al. **(R. McCaffrey** and **D. Wark).** The Toba Seismic Experiment: Imaging a large silicic magma chamber. *EOS* 77:S182, 1996.

Fauzi, et al. **(R. McCaffrey** and **D. Wark).** Lateral variation in slap orientation beneath Toba caldera, northern Sumatra. *Geophys. Res. Lett.* 23:443–6.

Genrich, J., et al. **(R. McCaffrey).** Accretion of the southern Banda arc to the Australian plate margin determined by Global Positioning System measurements. *Tectonics* 15:288–95.

Dricker, I. G., **S. W. Roecker,** G. L. Kosarev, and L. P. Vinnik. Shear-wave velocity structure of the crust and upper mantle beneath the Kola peninsula. *Geophys. Res. Lett.* 23(23):3389–92.

Dricker, I. G., and **S. W. Roecker.** Lateral heterogeneity in the upper mantle beneath the Tibetan Plateau and its surroundings from SS-S travel time residuals. *Eos Trans. AGU,* supplemental, 77(46):691, 1996.

Chen, Y. H., **S. W. Roecker,** C. Thurber, and W. Lutter. High resolution three-dimensional tomographic imaging of the San Andreas fault in the Bear Valley region of Central California. *Eos Trans. AGU,* 1997.

Chen, Y. H., **S. W. Roecker,** and G. L. Kosarev. Elevation of the 410-km discontinuity beneath the central Tien Shan; evidence for a detached lithospheric root. *Geophys. Res. Lett.* 24:1531–4, 1997.

Lin, C. H., and **S. W. Roecker.** Evidence for active crustal subduction and exhumation in Taiwan. In *When Continents Collide: Geodynamics and Geochemistry of Ultra-high Pressure Rocks.* eds. Hacker and Liou. 1997.

Lin, C. H., et al. **(S. W. Roecker).** Three-dimensional elastic wave velocity structure of the Hualien region of Taiwan: Evidence of active crustal exhumation. *Tectonics* 17:89–103, 1998.

Lin, C. H., and **S. W. Roecker.** Three-dimensional P-wave velocity structure of the Bear Valley region of central California. *Pure Appl. Geophys.* 149:667–88, 1997.

Lin, C. H., and **S. W. Roecker.** P-wave backazimuth anomalies observed by a small-aperture seismic array at Pinyon Flat, Southern California, implications for structure and source location. *Bull. Seismol. Soc. Am.* 86(2):470–6, 1996.

Thurber, C., et al. **(S. W. Roecker).** Two-dimensional seismic image of the San Andreas fault in the Northern Gabilan Range, central California: Evidence for fluids in the fault zone. *Geophys. Res. Lett.* 24:1591–4, 1997.

Roecker, S. W. Effects of global scale laterally varying structure on the travel times and bounce point locations of reflected shear waves. *Eos Trans. AGU* 77(17):179, 1996.

Pyle, J. M., and **F. S. Spear.** Trace element distributions in garnet: A road map for following pelite reaction histories. *Geological Society of America Abstracts with Programs* 30:A-231, 1998.

Pyle, J. M., and **F. S. Spear.** Yttrium zonation in pelitic garnet, central New England: A record of Y saturation? *EOS* 79:S-380, 1998.

Spear, F. S., and M. J. Kohn. Trace element zoning in garnet as a monitor of dehydration melting in pelites. *Geological Society of America Abstracts with Programs* 1–7, 1996.

Daniel, C. G., and **F. S. Spear.** The 3-D reconstruction of metamorphic rocks: Insights into garnet and plagioclase growth. *EOS* 78:S336, 1997.

Daniel, C. G., and **F. S. Spear.** The interface controlled growth of garnet in regional metamorphic rocks from NW Connecticut. *Geological Society of America Abstracts with Programs* 29:A338, 1997.

Spear, F. S., and R. R. Parrish. Petrology and cooling rates of the Valhalla Complex, British Columbia, Canada. *J. Petrol.* 37(4):733–65.

Spear, F. S., and C. G. Daniel. Garnet growth in the garnet zone. *Geological Society of America Abstracts with Programs* 29:A338, 1997.

Watson, E. B. Surface enrichment and trace-element uptake during crystal growth. *Geochim. Cosmochim. Acta* 60(24):5013–20.

Watson, E. B., and **D. J. Cherniak.** Oxygen diffusion in zircon. *Earth Planet. Sci. Lett.* 148:527–44.

Watson, E. B. Dissolution, growth and survival of zircons during crustal fusion: Kinetic principles, geological models and implications for isotopic inheritance. *Trans. Roy. Soc. Edinburgh: Earth Sci.* 87:43–56.

Minarik, W. G., F. J. Ryerson, and **E. B. Watson.** Textural entrapment of core-forming melts. *Science* 272.

Minarik, W. G., and **E. B. Watson.** Interconnectivity of carbonate melt at low melt fraction. *Earth Planet. Sci. Lett.* 133:423–37.

Rapp, R. P., and **E. B. Watson.** Dehydration melting of metabasalt at 8-32 kbar: Implications for continental growth and crust-mantle recycling. *J. Petrol.* 36(4):P891–931.

TULANE UNIVERSITY

Department of Geology

Programs of Study

The Department of Geology offers graduate programs leading to the degrees of Master of Science in broad areas of geology and paleontology and Doctor of Philosophy in geology and, in cooperation with the Department of Biology, a program leading to the degree of Doctor of Philosophy in paleontology. Two master's degree programs are available: the principal one requires 24 semester hours of graduate course work and successful completion, presentation, and defense of a thesis that reflects individual research accomplishments. A second, nonthesis, program requires 36 semester hours of course work and a significant research paper. The Ph.D. programs in both geology and paleontology each require course work, oral and written examinations, and an original contribution in the form of a written dissertation suitable for publication in a learned journal. Areas of research in geology and paleontology include sedimentary geochemistry, theoretical geochemistry, sedimentary geology, environmental geology, igneous petrology, volcanology, and paleontology of primitive echinoderms. Special emphasis is given to geology of the Gulf Coast region and Latin America, especially Mexico.

Research Facilities

The department's research facilities, partially supported by a departmental endowment, include a scanning electron microscope with an energy-dispersive X-ray system, an X-ray fluorescence spectrometer, an electron microprobe, an X-ray diffractometer, a cathodoluminescence microscope, an ICP spectrometer, a wet chemistry laboratory, and a computer laboratory with microcomputers, a graphics laboratory, and terminals to the University Computer Center. In addition, single-crystal X-ray diffraction equipment, a transmission electron microscope with an energy-dispersive X-ray system, a high-resolution optical microscope, and other equipment are available in a coordinated instrumentation facility.

Financial Aid

Graduate teaching and research assistantships are available to all qualified students and provide nine-month stipends, including departmental supplements, ranging from $9000 to $13,000. All assistantships and fellowships are accompanied by a tax-free full tuition scholarship. Funding to support research activities during the summer months is available each year.

Cost of Study

Full-time tuition for 1999–2000 is $11,080 per semester plus a $280 University fee. Tuition on a part-time basis is $1231 per credit hour plus fees.

Living and Housing Costs

A limited amount of University housing is available for graduate students. Most graduate students choose to live off campus, where costs vary greatly depending on the type of accommodation selected. A cost-of-living figure of $750 per month is quoted to international graduate students for purposes of entry.

Student Group

Tulane currently enrolls 8,750 full-time and 2,320 part-time students. Of these, approximately 800 are registered in the Graduate School. In recent years, graduate students have come to Tulane from more than 380 colleges and universities, from all fifty states, and from thirty-six other countries.

The department seeks to admit 2 to 4 students per year. There are currently 10 students in residence. Graduate students, in coordination with a member of the faculty and with departmental support, organize a program of speakers.

Location

Tulane's eleven colleges and schools, with the exception of the medical divisions, are located on 100 acres in a residential area of New Orleans. New Orleans' mild climate, many parks, and proximity to the Gulf Coast provide opportunities for a wide variety of outdoor activities. The city's many art galleries and museums offer regularly scheduled exhibits throughout the year. New Orleans is famous for its French Quarter, Mardi Gras, Creole cuisine, and jazz.

The University and The Department

Tulane is a private nonsectarian university offering a wide range of undergraduate, graduate, and professional courses of study for men and women. The University's history dates from 1834, when it was founded as the Medical College of Louisiana. Graduate work was first offered in 1883. In 1884, the University was organized under its present form of administration and renamed for Paul Tulane, a wealthy New Orleans merchant who endowed it generously. Tulane is a member of the American Association of Universities, a group of fifty-six major North American research universities. It is among the top twenty-five private universities in the amount of outside support received for research each year.

The Department of Geology is in the Liberal Arts and Sciences division of the University, which has strong programs in biology, chemistry, mathematics, and physics as well as in geology. Graduate students in geology are encouraged to enroll in appropriate courses in one or more of these disciplines. Cross-enrollment with the School of Engineering is also available, as are environmental courses offered by the School of Law.

Applying

The general deadline for applying is July 1; for those requesting financial aid, however, the application deadline is February 1. Students should write to the Dean of the Graduate School for application forms, or they can download the application forms from the Web site listed below. The Graduate School will not forward the application to the department for consideration for admission until all of the following documents, plus the $35 application fee, have been received: a completed application form, three completed recommendation forms, official transcripts of all undergraduate and graduate work, and official results of the Graduate Record Examinations General Test, taken within the past five years. International applicants for admission must present satisfactory evidence of competence in English by submitting a score of at least 220 on the TSE (Test of Spoken English) or, if this test is not available, a minimum score of 600 on the TOEFL. Admission is based on academic accomplishments and promise. Admission preference is given to students applying to the Ph.D. program. Tulane is an affirmative action/equal employment opportunity institution.

Correspondence and Information

For application forms and admission:
Dean of the Graduate School
Tulane University
New Orleans, Louisiana 70118
Telephone: 504-865-5100
World Wide Web: http://www.tulane.edu/~gradprog/

For specific information regarding programs:
Director of Graduate Studies
Department of Geology
Tulane University
New Orleans, Louisiana 70118
Telephone: 504-865-5198
E-mail: jhughes@mailhost.tcs.tulane.edu

Tulane University

THE FACULTY AND THEIR RESEARCH

Mead A. Allison, Ph.D., SUNY at Stony Brook, 1993. Continental margin sedimentology, high-concentration suspended-sentiment/cohesive seabed interactions, contaminated sediment depocenters, use of GIS/image analysis.

Bernard J. Coakley, Ph.D., Columbia, 1991. Tectonics and geophysics of oceanic basins.

George C. Flowers, Ph.D., Berkeley, 1979. Theoretical geochemistry, sedimentary geochemistry, and environmental geochemistry of estuarine sediments.

Franco Marcantonio, Ph.D., Columbia, 1994. Isotope geochemistry, using isotopic tracers to investigate issues in environmental science, paleoclimatology, environmental hydrogeology.

Brent A. McKee, Ph.D., North Carolina State, 1986. Sedimentary geology, sedimentary geochemistry, coastal marine geology.

Stephen A. Nelson, Ph.D., Berkeley, 1979. Igneous petrology: petrologic studies of volcanoes; relationships between volcanism and tectonism, particularly in Mexico; volcanic hazards studies; mechanisms of explosive volcanism; thermodynamic modeling of silicate systems; fluid mechanical processes in magmatic systems.

Ronald L. Parsley, Ph.D., Cincinnati, 1969. Paleontology: paleobiology, paleoecology, and evolution of lower Paleozoic primitive Echinodermata; Paleozoic faunas in general.

Recent Publications

Allison, M. A., et al. Sources and sinks of sediment to the Amazon margin: The Amapa coast. *Geo-Marine Lett.* 16:36–40, 1996.

Allison, M. A., C. A. Nittrouer, and L.E.C. Faria. Rates and mechanisms of muddy shoreline progradation and retreat downdrift of the Amazon River mouth. *Marine Geol.* 125:373–92,1995.

Allison, M. A., C. A. Nittrouer, and G. C. Kineke. Seasonal sediment storage on mudflats adjacent to the Amazon River. *Marine Geol.* 125:303–28, 1995.

Coakley, B. J., and M. Gurnis. Far-field tilting of Laurentia during the Ordovician and constraints on the evolution of a slab under an ancient continent. *J. Geophys. Res.* 100:6313–27, 1995.

Coakley, B. J., G. Nadon, and H. F. Wang. Spatial variations in Ordovician tectonic subsidence across the Michigan basin. *Basin Res.* 6:131–40, 1994.

Pratson, L., and **B. J. Coakley.** A model for the headward erosion of submarine canyons induced by downslope-eroding sediment flows. *Geol. Soc. Ame. Bull.* 107:225–34, 1996.

Flowers, G. C. Environmental sedimentology of the Pontchartrain Estuary. *Trans. Gulf Coast Assoc. Geological Soc.* 40:237–50, 1990.

Marcantonio, F., et al. Terrigenous helium in deep-sea sediments. *Geochim. Cosmochim. Acta.*, in press.

Marcantonio, F., G. Flowers, L. Thien, and E. Ellgaard. Pb isotopes in tree rings: Chronology of pollution in Bayou Trepagnier, LA. *Environ. Sci. Tecnhol.*, in press.

Williams, G., **F. Marcantonio,** and K. K. Turekian. The behavior of natural and anthropogenic osmium in Long Island Sound, an urban estuary in the eastern U.S. *Earth Planet. Sci. Lett.* 148:341–7, 1997.

Marcantonio, F., A. Zindler, T. Elliot, and H. Staudigel. A comparative study of accumulation rates determined by He and Th isotope analysis of marine sediments. *Earth Planet. Sci. Lett.* 133:549-55, 1995.

McKee, B. A., D. J. DeMaster, and C. A. Nittrouer. Removal of Th, Po, and Pb by marine particulates. *Geochim. Cosmochim. Acta.*, in press.

McKee, B. A. and M. Baskaran. Sedimentary processes in Gulf of Mexico estuaries: Inputs and dynamics. In *Biogeochemistry of Gulf of Mexico Estuaries,* eds. T. Bianchi, J. Pennock, and R. Twilley. New York: John Wiley and Sons, 1998.

McKee, B. A., P. W. Swarzenski, and J. G. Booth. The flux of uranium isotopes from river-dominated shelf sediments. In *Geochemistry of the Earth's Surface,* pp. 85–91, ed. S. H. Bottrell. Leeds: University of Leeds Press, 1996.

Nelson, S. A., and J. Hegre. Volcán Las Navajas, a Plio-Pleistocene trachyte/peralkaline rhyolite volcano in the northwestern Mexican Volcanic Belt. *Bull. Volcanology* 52:186–204, 1990.

Nelson, S. A., and E. Gonzalez-Caver. Geology and K-Ar dating of the Tuxtla volcanic field, Veracruz, Mexico. *Bull. Volcanology.* 55:85–96, 1992.

Nelson, S. A., E. Gonzalez-Caver, and T. K. Kyser. Constraints on the origin of alkaline and calc-alkaline magmas from the Tuxtla Volcanic Field, Veracruz, Mexico. *Contr. Mineral. Petrol.* 122:191-211, 1995.

Verma, S. P., and **S. A. Nelson.** Isotopic and trace-element constraints on the origin and evolution of calc-alkaline and alkaline magmas in the northwestern portion of the Mexican Volcanic Belt. *J. Geophys. Res.* 94:4531–44, 1989.

Parsley, R. L. *Aristocystites:* A recumbent diploporid (Echinodermata) from the Middle and Upper Ordovician of Bohemia, CSSR. *J. Paleontol.* 64:278–93, 1990.

Parsley, R. L. Review of selected North American mitrate stylophorans (Homalozoa: Echinodermata). *Bull. Am. Paleontol.* 100:1–57, 1991.

Recent Thesis and Dissertation Topics

"Depositional Environment and Diagenesis of Vicksburg Sandstones, Tabasco Field, Hidalgo County, Texas," Sydney A. Rasbury (1986).

"The Biostratigraphy and Paleoecology of Miocene Benthic Foraminiferida from the Salina Basin, State of Veracruz, Mexico," Betsy M. Strachan (1986).

"The Genus *Strombus* in Western Atlantic," Samuel C. Kindervater (1987).

"A Survey of Modern Peritidal Stromatolitic Mats of the Yucatan Peninsula and a Depositional Model of a Carbonate Tidal Flat in Rio Lagartos, Yucatan, Mexico," Jerry B. Pennington (1987).

"The Effect of Lithology, Diagenesis, and Low-Grade Metamorphism on the Ultrastructure and Surface Sculpture of Acritarchs from the Late Proterozoic Chuar Group, Grand Canyon, Arizona," Yvonne Halprin (1988).

"Provenance of Sandstones from the Belt Supergroup (Middle Proterozoic), Montana," Kathleen Kordesh (1988).

"A Neotectonic Study Along the Rio Ameca—Implications of the Northern Boundary of the Jalisco Block of Western Mexico," Troy Rasbury (1990).

"Petrologic Study of the Volcanic Rocks in the Chiconquiaco–Palma Sola Area, Central Veracruz, Mexico," Manuel Lopez Infanzon (1991).

"The Stratigraphy and Volcanic History of Post Tertiary Volcanics, Tuxtla Volcanic Field, Veracruz, Mexico," Bentley K. Reinhardt (1991).

"The Systematics and Paleoecology of the Prosobranch Gastropods of the Pleistocene Moín Formation, Costa Rica," David C. Robinson (1991).

"Petrology of the "Older Volcanic Sequence' of the Tuxtla Volcanic Field, Veracruz, Mexico," Erika L. Gonzalez-Caver (1992).

"Geology and Petrology of Socorro Island, Revillagigedo Archipelago, Mexico," Enrique Carballido-Sanchez (1994).

"Environmental Assessment of the Eustis and Capelton Mining Areas Ascot County, Southeastern Quebec," Geoffrey Gallant (1996).

THE UNIVERSITY OF ALABAMA

Department of Geological Sciences

Programs of Study

The Department of Geological Sciences at the University of Alabama (UA) offers programs of study leading to Master of Science and Doctor of Philosophy degrees in a wide range of geoscience disciplines.

Research Facilities

The Department is well equipped for modern quantitative geoscience research. For sample preparation there are rock sawing, crushing, pulverizing, sieving, and mineral separation labs; a rock fusion lab; thin-sectioning, grinding, and polishing labs; electron optical and microanalytical preparation labs with ion mill, disk punch/cutter/grinder, electrolytic thinner, vacuum evaporator, and ion sputter coater; and a low-temperature asher. For wet chemistry and spectroscopy there are complete wet chemical labs with clean room; an automated inductively coupled plasma mass spectrometer; an automated twenty-channel simultaneous and sequential, inductively coupled plasma emission spectrograph; an ion chromatograph; a graphite furnace atomic absorption spectrophotometer; a semiautomated atomic absorption spectrophotometer; a total organic carbon analyzer; a microprocessor-controlled selective ion analyzer, gold film mercury detector, and fluorimeter; a low-temperature hydrothermal experimental flow-through system; and access to multinuclear magnetic resonance spectrometers, mass spectrometers, gas chromatographs, and an S-C analyzer elsewhere on campus. For X-ray diffraction/fluorescence there is a sequential X-ray spectrometer system, an automated X-ray powder diffraction system, and access to computer-controlled, single-crystal X-ray diffractometers elsewhere on campus. For electron optical/microanalytical purposes there is a high-sensitivity, multitechnique electron spectroscope with scanning auger and mono and micro XPS; an automated electron probe microanalyzer with five wavelength dispersive spectrometers, energy dispersive X-ray analysis system, and image analysis system; an automated 200 keV transmission electron microscope with energy dispersive X-ray analysis system; and an automated scanning electron microscope with backscattered electron detector, automated energy dispersive X-ray analysis system, and an image analysis system (shared with the Department of Biology). Geophysical equipment includes a U/Th field spectrometer; a torsion magnetometer; a twelve-channel signal enhancement seismograph; an ORE 3.5 KHz high-resolution reflection seismic system; an ELICS-DELPHI-1 digital seismic acquisition and processing system; a PROMAX interactive seismic data processing system; a GPS navigation system; global digital gravity, magnetic, topography, and heat flow datasets with manipulation and visualization software; access to global seismological datasets and survey equipment through University membership in the Incorporated Research Institutions for Seismology (IRIS); access to earth resistivity and ground-penetrating radar systems elsewhere on campus; and access to the Dauphin Island Sea Lab research vessel. For optical/photographic research there are microscopes for transmitted and reflected light microscopy, photomicrography, cathodoluminescence, epifluorescence, coal reflectometry, and universal stage microscopy; and heating/freezing stage for fluid inclusion microthermometry and a photographic darkroom with variable dodging and standard color enlargers. Computing facilities include numerous Macintosh and IBM-compatible microcomputers; several IBM, Sun, and Silicon Graphics UNIX workstations; laser printers; slide maker; scanners; digitizers; workstation-based Arc/Info geographic information system; and Ethernet local area network with routing to UA fiber-optic/broadband network providing high-speed access to a CRAY C94A/264 supercomputer, an IBM 3090/400E mainframe computer, and the Internet. There is access to additional experimental and analytical equipment on campus and through University of Alabama membership in the Oak Ridge Associated Universities.

Financial Aid

A variety of teaching and research assistantships and fellowships are available. Teaching assistantships are awarded by the department on the basis of the student's background, academic credentials, and curriculum requirements. Research assistantships are awarded at the discretion of the professor holding the research grant. Fellowships are awarded by the University, the graduate school, or the College and are highly competitive (minimum GPA of 3.8, minimum GRE score of 2000). Stipends are adjusted continuously to reflect increases in living expenses and are currently $9200 for nine-month teaching assistantships and $11,000 for nine-month Graduate Council Research Fellowships. Research assistantship stipends vary from $9200 to $16,000 for nine months. The College of Arts and Sciences Dean's Merit Assistantships carry an additional award of $4000. All assistantships and fellowships include full tuition waivers worth about an additional $5700, representing total award packages between about $15,000 and $21,000. Additional summer support is often available. In addition, the department has endowed funds to support graduate student fieldwork, research, and travel. Travel and research funds are also available from the graduate school and the Student Government Association.

Cost of Study

The 1999–2000 academic year tuition is $2820 for residents of Alabama and $7580 for nonresidents. All tuition and fees are waived for students who have been awarded assistantships and fellowships.

Living and Housing Costs

The cost of living and housing in Tuscaloosa is average to below average for a typical U.S. city.

Student Group

The total number of graduate students in the geological sciences is about 40. A wide variety of academic and geographic backgrounds are represented among these students.

Student Outcomes

Most recent graduates have found subsequent employment in either academic institutions (postdoctoral or faculty positions) or private industry, particularly the environmental and petroleum industries.

Location

The University of Alabama is located in Tuscaloosa, a city of approximately 90,000 in the west-central part of the state. The Gulf Coastal Plain and Appalachian Plateau and Valley and Ridge intersect at Tuscaloosa. The Appalachian Piedmont is less than an hour's drive away.

The University

The University of Alabama was founded in 1831, twelve years after Alabama gained statehood. Most of the campus was burned to the ground by Union troops during the Civil War but was quickly rebuilt and has grown into a major teaching, research, and service institution made up of seventeen colleges, divisions, and schools with more than 120 academic departments and 270 accredited undergraduate and graduate degree programs. Total student enrollment on the Tuscaloosa campus is about 19,000, of which about 3,000 are graduate students, representing all fifty states and more than sixty-five countries.

Applying

Applications may be submitted at any time. However, to receive full consideration for financial assistance they should be received before March 15 for August admission and before August 31 for January admission. All applicants must submit the following: the official Graduate School application form, a statement of purpose, and an application fee; three original letters of recommendation; official transcripts of all college or university course work; official scores for the Graduate Record Examinations (GRE); and official scores on the Test of English as a Foreign Language (TOEFL) and the Test of Spoken English (TSE), for applicants whose first language is not English.

Correspondence and Information

Director of Graduate Studies
Department of Geological Sciences
Box 870338
The University of Alabama
Tuscaloosa, Alabama 35487-0338

Telephone: 205-348-5095
Fax: 205-348-0818
E-mail: gradstud@wgs.geo.ua.edu
World Wide Web: http://www.geo.ua.edu

The University of Alabama

THE FACULTY AND THEIR RESEARCH

Sridhar Anandakrishnan, Assistant Professor; Ph.D., Wisconsin, 1990. Seismology, glaciology, seismic imaging.

Louis R. Bartek III, Associate Professor; Ph.D., Rice, 1989. Seismic and sequence stratigraphy, sedimentology, depositional environments.

D. Joe Benson, Associate Professor and Assistant Dean; Ph.D., Cincinnati, 1976. Carbonate petrology, diagenesis, depositional environments.

Daniel A. Cenderelli, Assistant Professor; Ph.D., Colorado State, 1998. Fluvial geomorphology, slope process, Quaternary geology.

Rona J. Donahoe, Associate Professor; Ph.D., Stanford, 1984. Aqueous geochemistry, environmental geochemistry.

Jen-Ho Fang, Professor Emeritus; Ph.D., Penn State, 1961. Geostatistics, well log analysis, expert systems, neural networks.

Nathan L. Green, Associate Professor; Ph.D., British Columbia, 1978. Volcanology, igneous petrology, geochemistry, mineralogy.

Richard H. Groshong Jr., Professor; Ph.D., Brown, 1971. Quantitative structural geology.

Dennis L. Harry, Assistant Professor; Ph.D., Texas at Dallas, 1989. Geophysics, geodynamics, tectonophysics.

W. Gary Hooks, Professor Emeritus; Ph.D., North Carolina, 1961. Geomorphology, environmental geology, sedimentology.

W. Berry Lyons, Loper Professor of Environmental Geology; Ph.D., Connecticut, 1979. Aqueous geochemistry, global climate change.

Ernest A. Mancini, Professor, Ph.D., Texas A&M, 1974. Petroleum geology, lithostratigraphy, paleoecology.

Carl W. Stock, Professor; Ph.D., North Carolina, 1977. Invertebrate paleontology, paleobiogeography, paleoecology, biostratigraphy.

Harold H. Stowell, Professor and Chair; Ph.D., Princeton, 1987. Metamorphic petrology, tectonics, structural geology, ore deposits.

Chunmiao Zheng, Associate Professor, Ph.D., Wisconsin, 1988. Hydrogeology, flow and transport modeling, groundwater remediation.

SELECTED PUBLICATIONS

Anandakrishnan, S., D. D. Blankenship, R. B. Alley, and P. A. Stoffa. Influence of subglacial geology on the position of a West Antarctic ice stream from seismic observations. *Nature* 394:62–5, 1998.

Gow, A. J., et al. **(S. Anandakrishnan).** Physical and structural properties of the GISP2 ice cores. *J. Geophys. Res.* 102(C12):26559–76, 1997.

Anandakrishnan, S., and R. B. Alley. Stagnation of ice stream C, West Antarctica by water piracy. *Geophys. Res. Lett.* 24:265–6, 1997.

Anandakrishnan, S., S. R. Taylor, and B. W. Stump. Quantification and characterization of regional seismic signals from cast blasting in mines: A linear elastic model. *Geophys. Res. Int.* 131:45–60, 1997.

Anandakrishnan, S., and R. B. Alley. Tidal forcing of basal seismicity of ice stream C, West Antarctica, observed far inland. *J. Geophys. Res.* 102(B7):15183–96, 1997.

Shuman, C. A., et al. **(S. Anandakrishnan).** Temperature and accumulation at the Greenland Summit: Comparison of high-resolution isotope profiles and satellite passive microwave brightness temperature trends. *J. Geophys. Res.* 100(D5):9165–77, 1995.

Alley, R. B., et al. **(S. Anandakrishnan).** Changes in continental and sea-salt atmospheric loadings in central Greenland during the most recent deglaciation: Model-based estimates. *J. Glac.* 41:503–14, 1995.

Alley, R. B., and **S. Anandakrishnan.** Variations in melt-layer frequency in the GISP2 ice core: Implications for Holocene summer temperatures in central Greenland. *Ann. Glac.* 40:341–9, 1995.

Bartek, L. R., J. L. R. Andersen, and T. A. Oneacre. Substrate control on distribution and subglacial and glaciomarine seismic facies based on stochastic models of glacial seismic facies deposition on the Ross Sea Continental Margin, Antarctica. *Mar. Geol.* 143:223–62, 1997.

Bartek, L. R., S. A. Henrys, J. B. Anderson, and P. J. Barrett. Seismic stratigraphy of McMurdo Sound, Antarctica: Implications for glacially influenced Early Cenozoic Eustatic Change? *Mar. Geol.* 130:79–98, 1996.

Barrett, P. J., et al. **(L. R. Bartek).** Geology of the margin of the Victoria Land basin off Cape Roberts, southwest Ross Sea. In *Geology and Seismic Stratigraphy of the Antarctic Margin,* eds. A. K. Cooper, P. F. Barker, and G. Brancholini. *Am. Geophys. Union Antarctic Res. Ser.* 68:183–207, 1995.

Benson, D. J., and **E. A. Mancini.** Diagenetic influence on reservoir development and quality in the Smackover updip basement ridge play, southwest Alabama. *Trans. Gulf Coast Assoc. Geol. Socs.,* in press.

Carlson, E. C., **D. J. Benson, R. H. Groshong Jr.,** and **E. A. Mancini.** Improved oil recovery from heterogeneous carbonate reservoirs associated with paleotopographic basement structures: Appleton Field, Alabama. *Proc. Eleventh SPE/DOE Symp. Improved Oil Recovery,* 2:99–105, 1998.

Benson, D. J., et al. **(E. A. Mancini, R. H. Groshong Jr.,** and **J. H. Fang).** Petroleum geology of Appleton Field, Escambia County, Alabama. *Trans. Gulf Coast Assoc. Geol. Socs.* 47:35–42, 1997.

Benson, D. J., L. M. Pultz, and D. D. Bruner. The influence of paleotopography, sea-level fluctuation, and carbonate productivity on deposition of the Smackover and Buckner Formations, Appleton Field, Escambia County, Alabama. *Trans. Gulf Coast Assoc. Geol. Socs.* 46:15–23, 1996.

Benson, D. J. Classification of heterogeneities in Smackover reservoirs, southwest Alabama. *Geol. Soc. Am. Abs. Prog.* 28(2):3, 1996.

Benson, D. J., L. M. Pultz, D. D. Bruner, and G. Lu. Depositional history of the Smackover Formation, Appleton Field, Escambia County, Alabama. *Am. Assoc. Petrol. Geol. Ann. Conv. Prog.* 5:A14, 1996.

Cenderelli, D. A., and B. Cluer. Depositional patterns, sedimentology, and sediment supply in boundary-resistant channels. In *Bedrock Channels,* eds. E. E. Wohl and K. J. Tinker. Washington: American Geophysical Union, in press.

Wohl, E. E., and **D. A. Cenderelli.** Flooding in the Himalaya Mountains. In *Flood Studies in India,* ed. V. S. Kale. Geological Society of India, in press.

Wohl, E. E., **D. A. Cenderelli,** and M. Mejia-Navarro. Geomorphic hazards from extreme floods in canyon rivers. In *Proceedings from the Schumm Symposium,* eds. M. D. Harvey, P. Mosley, and D. A. Anthony, in press.

Cenderelli, D. A. Floods from the failure of natural and artificial dams. In *Inland Flood Hazards: Human, Riparian, and Aquatic Communities,* ed. E. E. Wohl. Cambridge University Press, in press.

Cenderelli, D. A., and E. E. Wohl. Sedimentology and clast orientation of deposits produced by glacial-lake outburst floods in the Mount Everest Region, Nepal. In *Geomorphological Hazards in*

High Mountain Areas, pp. 1–26, eds. J. Kalvoda and C. L. Rosenfield. Kluwar Academic Publishers, 1998.

Cenderelli, D. A., and J. S. Kite. Geomorphic effects of large debris flows on channel morphology at North Fork Mountain, eastern West Virginia, U.S.A. *Earth Surf. Proc. Landforms* 23:1–19, 1998.

Howell, J. R., **R. J. Donahoe,** E. E. Roden, and F. G. Ferris. Effects of microbial iron oxide reduction on pH and alkalinity in anaerobic bicarbonate-buffered media: Implications for metal mobility. *Miner. Mag.* 62A:657–8, 1998.

Donahoe, R. J., and C. Liu. Porewater geochemistry near the sediment-water interface of a zoned, freshwater wetland in the southeastern United States. *Environ. Geol.* 33:143–53, 1998.

Gong, C., and **R. J. Donahoe.** An experimental study of heavy metal attenuation and mobility in sandy loam soils. *Appl. Geochem.* 12:243–54, 1997.

Jones, S. C., **R. J. Donahoe,** and E. Roden. Iron and iron-reducing bacteria: Their distribution within a freshwater riparian wetland system. *Program and Abstracts: 4th Symposium on Biogeochemistry of Wetlands,* Wetland Biogeochemistry Institute, Louisiana State University, and University of Florida. 86, 1996.

Donahoe, R. J., C. Liu, K. Dobson, and E. Graham. Cycling of iron and manganese in a riparian wetland. *Miner. Mag.* 58A:237–8, 1994.

Green, N. L. Mechanism for middle to upper crustal contamination: Evidence from continental margin magmas. *Geology* 22:231–4, 1994.

Green, N. L. Mount St. Helens: Potential example of the partial melting of the subducted lithosphere in a volcanic arc. Comment. *Geology* 22:188–9, 1994.

Groshong Jr., R. H. *3-D Structural Geology.* Heidelberg: Springer-Verlag, 1999.

Pashin, J. C., and **R. H. Groshong Jr.** Structural control of coalbed methane in Alabama. *Int. J. Coal Geol.* 38:89–113, 1998.

Pashin, J. C., and **R. H. Groshong Jr.** Structural modeling of a fractured chalk reservoir: Toward revitalizing Gilbertown field, Choctaw County, Alabama. *Trans. Gulf Coast Assoc. Geol. Socs.* 48:335–47, 1998.

Qi, J., J. C. Pashin, and **R. H. Groshong Jr.** Structure and evolution of North Choctaw Ridge Field, Alabama, a salt-related footwall uplift along the peripheral fault system, Gulf Coast Basin. *Trans. Gulf Coast Assoc. Geol. Socs.* 48:349–59, 1998.

Groshong Jr., R. H. Construction and validation of extensional cross sections using lost area and strain, with application to the Rhine Graben. In *Modern Developments in Structural Interpretation, Validation and Modelling,* eds. P. G. Buchanan and D. A. Nieuwland. *Geol. Soc. (London) Spec. Pub.* 99:79–87, 1996.

Groshong Jr., R. H., and J.-L. Epard. Computerized cross section balance and restoration. In *Structural Geology and Personal Computers,* pp. 477–98, ed. D. G. DePoar. Amsterdam: Elsevier, 1996.

Epard, J.-L., and **R. H. Groshong Jr.** Kinematic model of detachment folding including limb rotation, fixed hinges and layer-parallel strain. *Tectonophysics* 247:85–103, 1995.

Harry, D. L., and **N. L. Green.** Slab dehydration and basalt petrogenesis in subduction systems involving very young oceanic lithosphere. *Chem. Geol.,* in press.

Harry, D. L. 4-D gravity surveying and active tectonics in the subsurface: A first year campaign in western Nevada and eastern California. *Proc. Am. Geophys. Union Chapman Conf. Migrogal Gravimetry Instruments, Observations Appl., IfAG,* in press.

Harry, D. L., and K. Mickus. Gravity constraints on lithosphere flexure and the structure of the late Paleozoic Quachita orogen in Arkansas and Oklahoma, south-central North America. *Tectonics* 17:187–202, 1998.

Harry, D. L., and M. Batzle. Acoustic properties of ultramafic rocks from the Iberia abyssal plain, eds. R. B. Whitmarsh, D. S. Sawyer, and A. Klaus. *Proc. ODP, Sci. Results* 149:425–9, 1996.

Harry, D. L., J. S. Oldow, and D. S. Sawyer. The growth of orogenic belts and the role of crustal heterogeneities in decollement tectonics. *Geol. Soc. Am. Bull.* 107:1411–26, 1995.

Harry, D. L., and W. P. Leeman. Partial melting of melt metasomatized subcontinental mantle and the magma source potential of the lower lithosphere. *J. Geophys. Res.* 100:10255–69, 1995.

Lyons, W. B., et al. Geochemical linkages among glaciers, streams and lakes within the Taylor Valley, Antarctica. In *Ecosystem Dynamics in a Polar Desert: The McMurdo Dry Valleys,* pp. 77–92, ed. J. Priscu. Antarctica Res. Ser., AGU. 1998.

Mayewski, P. A., et al. **(W. B. Lyons).** Major features and forcing of

The University of Alabama

Selected Publications (continued)

high-latitude northern hemisphere atmospheric circulation using a 110,000-year-long glaciochemical series. *J. Geophys. Res.* 102:26345–66, 1998.

Lyons, W. B., K. A. Welch, and P. Sharma. Chlorine-36 in the waters of the McMurdo Dry Valley lakes, Southern Victoria Land, Antarctica: Revisited. *Geochim. Cosmochim. Acta* 62:185–92, 1998.

Lyons, W. B., D. M. Wayne, J. J. Warwick, and G. A. Doyle. The Hg geochemistry of a geothermal stream, Steamboat Creek, Nevada: Natural vs. anthropogenic influences. *Environ. Geol.* 34:143–50, 1998.

Tyler, S. W., et al. **(W. B. Lyons).** Evidence of deep circulation in two perennially ice-covered Antarctic lakes. *Limnol. Oceanogr.* 43:625–35, 1998.

Lyons, W. B., et al. A late Holocene desiccation of Lake Hoare and Lake Fryxell, McMurdo Dry Valleys, Antarctica. *Antarctica Sci.* 10:245–54, 1998.

Johannesson, K. H., et al. **(W. B. Lyons).** Oxyanion concentrations in eastern Sierra Nevada rivers: 2. Arsenic and phosphate. *Aqueous Geochem.* 3:61–97, 1997.

Toxey, J. K., D. A. Meese, K. A. Welch, and **W. B. Lyons.** The measurement of reactive silicate in saline-hypersaline lakes: Examples of the problem. *Int. J. Salt Lake Res.* 6:17–23, 1997.

Lyons, W. B., et al. Chemical weathering rates and reactions in the Lake Fryxell Basin, Taylor Valley: Comparison to temperature river basins. In *Ecosystem Processes in Antarctic Ice-Free Landscapes.* pp. 147–54, Rotterdam: Balkema Press, 1997.

Lyons, W. B., P. A. Mayewski, **L. R. Bartek,** and P. M. Doran. Climate history of the McMurdo Dry Valleys since the Last Glacial Maximum. In *Ecosystem Processes in Antarctic Ice-Free Landscapes.* pp. 15–22, Rotterdam: Balkema Press, 1997.

Lyons, W. B., S. W. Tyler, H. E. Gaudette, and D. T. Long. The use of strontium isotopes in determining groundwater mixing and brine fingering in a playa spring zone, Lake Tyrrell, Australia. *J. Hydrol.* 167:225–39, 1995.

Yang, W. T., H. Chen, and **E. A. Mancini.** A data mining approach. *Trans. Gulf Coast Assoc. Geol. Socs.,* in press.

Puckett, T. M., and **E. A. Mancini.** Stratigraphic framework of the Mesozoic sediments of the Mississippi Interior Salt Basin. *Trans. Gulf Coast Assoc. Geol. Socs.,* in press.

Li, H., H. Chen, and **E. A. Mancini.** Classification of porosity and permeability category with regression trees. *Trans. Gulf Coast Assoc. Geol. Socs.,* in press.

Mancini, E. A., W. C. Parcell, and T. M. Puckett. Modeling of the burial and thermal histories of strata in the Mississippi Interior Salt Basin. *Trans. Gulf Assoc. Geol. Socs.,* in press.

Mancini, E. A., and **D. J. Benson.** Upper Jurassic carbonate reservoir, Appleton Field, Escambia County, Alabama: 3-D seismic case history. In *3-D Seismic Case Histories from the Gulf Coast Basin.* pp. 1–14, 1998.

Puckett, T. M., and **E. A. Mancini.** Planktonic foraminiferal *Globotruncanitacalcarata* Total Range Zone: Its global significance and importance to chronostratigraphic correlation in the Gulf Coastal Plain, U.S.A. *J. Foram. Res.* 28:124–34, 1998.

Mancini, E. A., et al. Sequence stratigraphy and biostratigraphy of Upper cretaceous strata of the Alabama Coastal Plain. In *Guidebook for the Annual Alabama Geological Society Field Trip,* pp. 1–41, 1998.

Mancini, E. A., et al. **(D. J. Benson).** Geologic and computer modeling of Upper Jurassic Smackover reef and carbonate shoal lithofacies, Eastern Gulf Coastal Plain. *Trans. Gulf Coast Assoc. Geol. Socs.* 48:225–34, 1998.

Mancini, E. A., and D. J. Benson. Fracture porosity and stylolites in Upper Jurassic Norphlet sandstone and Smackover carbonate deep gas reservoirs, northeastern Gulf of Mexico. In *Symposium on Fractured Reservoirs: Practical Exploration and Development Strategies.* pp. 365–8, Denver: Rocky Mountain Association of Geologists, 1998.

Mancini, E. A., and B. H. Tew. Recognition of maximum flooding events in mixed siliciclastic-carbonate systems: Key to global chronostratigraphic correlation. *Geology* 25:351–4, 1997.

Mancini, E. A., M. L. Epsman, and D. D. Steif. Characterization and evaluation of the Upper Jurassic Frisco City sandstone reservoir in southwestern Alabama utilizing fullbore formation micro imager technology. *Trans. Gulf Coast Assoc. Geol. Socs.* 47:329–35, 1997.

Mancini, E. A., T. M. Puckett, and B. H. Tew. Integrated biostratigraphic and sequence stratigraphic framework for Upper Cretaceous strata of the eastern Gulf Coastal Plain, U.S.A. *Cret. Res.* 17:645–69, 1996.

Mancini, E. A., B. H. Tew, and T. M. Puckett. Comparison of Upper Cretaceous and Paleogene depositional sequences. *Trans. Gulf Coast Assoc. Geol. Socs.* 46:281–86, 1996.

Mancini, E. A., and B. H. Tew. Geochronology, biostratigraphy and sequence stratigraphy of a marginal marine to marine shelf stratigraphic succession: Upper Paleocene and lower Eocene Wilcox Group, eastern Gulf Coastal Plain, U.S.A. *SEPM Spec. Pub.* 54:281–93, 1995.

Tew, B. H., and **E. A. Mancini.** An integrated stratigraphic method for paleogeographic reconstruction: Examples from the Jackson and Vicksburg Groups of the eastern Gulf Coastal Plain. *Palaios* 10:133–53, 1995.

Stearn, C. W., B. D. Webby, H. Nestor, and **C. W. Stock.** Revision and terminology of Paleozoic stromatoporoids. *Acta Palaeo. Polonica* 44:1–70, 1999.

Stock, C. W., and J. A. Burry-Stock. Two new genera of Upper Silurian actinostromatid stromatoporoids. *J. Paleo.* 72:190–201, 1998.

Stock, C. W. Lower Devonian (Lochkovian) Stromatoporoidea form the Coeymans Formation of central New York. *J. Paleo.* 71:539–53, 1997.

Stock, C. W. Paleobiogeographical range of North American Devonian stromatoporoids: The roles of global and regional controls. *Bol. Real Soc. Esp. Hist. Nat. (Sec. Geol.)* 92:279–86, 1997.

Stowell, H. H., and S. A. Goldberg. Sm-Nd garnet dating of polyphase metamorphism: Northern Coast Mountains, southeastern Alaska. *J. Met. Geol.* 15:439–50, 1997.

Stowell, H. H., T. Menard, and C. K. Ridgway. Chemical zonation of garnet and Cametasomatism in contact metamorphic aureoles, Juneau gold belt, southeastern Alaska. *Can. Miner.* 34:1195-1209, 1996.

Stowell, H. H., et al. **(N. L. Green).** Metamorphism and gold mineralization in the Blue Ridge, southernmost Appalachians. *Econ. Geol.* 91:1115–44, 1996.

Menard, T., et al. **(H. H. Stowell).** Geology, genesis and metamorphic history of the Namew Lake Ni-Cu deposit, Manitoba. *Econ. Geol.* 91:1394–413, 1996.

Zheng, C., and P. P. Wang. An integrated global and local optimization approach for remediation system design. *Water Resource Res.,* in press.

Poeter, E. P., **C. Zheng,** and M. C. Hill, eds. *Proceedings of the MODFLOW98 International Conference.* Golden, Colo.: Colorado Schools of Mines, 1998.

Zheng, C., and P. P. Wang. *MT3DMS: A Modular Multi-Species Three-Dimensional Transport Model, Documentation and User's Guide.* Technical Publication of the U.S. Army Corps of Engineers Waterway Experiment Station, 1998.

Zheng, C., and J. J. Jiao. Numerical simulation of tracer tests in heterogeneous aquifer. *J. Environ. Eng.* 124:510–6, 1998.

Wang, M., and **C. Zheng.** Application of genetic algorithms and simulated annealing in groundwater management: formulation and comparison. *J. Am. Water Resource Assoc.* 34:519–30, 1998.

Jiao, J. J., and **C. Zheng.** Abnormal fluid pressures caused by erosion and subsidence of sedimentary basins. *J. Hydr.* 204:124–37, 1998.

Wang, P. P., and **C. Zheng.** An efficient approach for successively perturbed groundwater models. *Adv. Water Resource* 21:499–508, 1998.

Wang, M., and **C. Zheng.** Optimal remediation policy selection under general conditions. *Ground Water* 35:757–64, 1997.

Jiao, J. J., **C. Zheng,** and R. J.-C. Hennet. Analysis of underpressured geological formations for disposal of hazardous wastes. *Hydrogeol. J.* 5(3):19–31, 1997.

Zheng, C., and P. P. Wang. Parameter structure identification using tabu search and simulated annealing. *Adv. Water Resource* 19:215–24, 1996.

Zheng, C., and G. D. Bennett. *Applied Contaminant Transport Modeling: Theory and Practice.* New York: John Wiley and Sons, 1995.

Zheng, C., and G. D. Bennett. More on the role of simulation in hydrogeology. *Ground Water* 33:1040–1, 1995.

THE UNIVERSITY OF ARIZONA

Department of Planetary Sciences / Lunar and Planetary Laboratory

Program of Study

The graduate program prepares students for careers in solar system research. For this interdisciplinary enterprise, the department maintains faculty expertise in the important areas of planetary science. Through a combination of core courses, minor requirements, and interaction with faculty and research personnel, students are provided with a comprehensive education in modern planetary science. The program is oriented toward granting the Ph.D., although M.S. degrees are now awarded as well.

Upon admission, a student is assigned an adviser in his or her general scientific area. Students advance to Ph.D. candidacy by passing an oral preliminary examination after completing the required major and minor course work. The examination is normally taken two years after matriculation. Students typically complete their dissertations and receive the Ph.D. three to four years later.

Because of the low student-faculty ratio, students receive close supervision and guidance. Dissertation areas include, but are not limited to, observational planetary astronomy; physics of the sun and interplanetary medium; observational, experimental, and theoretical studies of planetary atmospheres, surfaces, and interiors; studies of the interstellar medium and the origin of the solar system; and the geology and chemistry of the surfaces and interiors of solar system bodies.

Research Facilities

The Lunar and Planetary Laboratory (LPL) and the Department of Planetary Sciences function as a single unit to carry out solar system research and education. The department and laboratory are housed in the Gerard P. Kuiper Space Sciences and the Gould-Simpson Buildings on the campus. Neighboring facilities include the Tucson headquarters of the National Optical Astronomy Observatory, the National Radio Astronomy Observatory, Steward Observatory, the Optical Sciences Center, the Flandrau Planetarium, the Department of Geosciences, and the Planetary Sciences Institute.

The facilities of the University observatories are available to all researchers in LPL. These include the multiple-mirror telescope as well as numerous midsize and smaller telescopes. For cosmochemical research, LPL operates a scanning electron microprobe, high-temperature and pressure apparatus for rock-melting experiments, a noble gas mass spectrometry laboratory, and a radiochemistry separation facility for neutron activation analysis; these are used for studying meteorites, lunar samples, and terrestrial analogues. Also available in LPL are well-equipped electronics, machine, and photo shops as well as a graphic arts facility.

The Space Imagery Center at the LPL is one of several regional facilities supported by NASA as a repository for spacecraft images and maps of planets and satellites. The Planetary Image Research Laboratory is a modern remote sensing and image processing center for analysis of astronomical and spacecraft data. The Laboratory maintains an extensive computer network; various research groups maintain specialized computer systems for particular applications. University central computing facilities include a variety of systems and network facilities as well as several superminicomputers.

Financial Aid

Most planetary sciences graduate students receive graduate research assistantships for the academic year. These assistantships normally require 20 hours of work per week on a sponsored research project. For the nine-month academic year, such assistantships pay $12,391. For students who pass their preliminary examination and are advanced to Ph.D. candidacy, the pay increases to $13,862. In addition, most students work full-time (40 hours per week) on research projects during the summer term, earning $5728 more.

Cost of Study

For 1998–99, fees for Arizona residents taking 1–6 units are $110 per unit. For 7 or more units, the cost is $1081 per semester. Out-of-state students who do not have a research or teaching assistantship are also charged tuition, but tuition scholarships are frequently available.

Living and Housing Costs

Typical costs for off-campus housing, food, and entertainment for a single graduate student total about $600 to $850 per month. Housing is generally inexpensive and plentiful.

Student Group

In 1998–99, there are 28 graduate students enrolled in the planetary science program. Most come from undergraduate or M.S. programs in chemistry, physics, geology, and astronomy, and some have been employed for several years prior to entering graduate school.

Location

Tucson is located in the Sonoran Desert, about 100 kilometers north of the Mexican border. The climate is dry and warm; hiking, mountain climbing, horseback riding, swimming, golf, and tennis are popular year-round activities.

The University

The University is a state-supported institution with an enrollment of approximately 35,000 and ranks in the top twenty research universities. In addition to the planetary sciences program, major research efforts and graduate programs exist in chemistry, engineering, physics, astronomy, optical sciences, and geosciences. LPL interacts closely with these groups.

Applying

Completed application forms, three letters of reference, and GRE scores must be received by January 15 in order to receive full consideration. All applicants are required to submit GRE General Test scores as well as the Subject Test score in a physical science or other relevant area.

Correspondence and Information

Graduate Admissions Secretary
Lunar and Planetary Laboratory
Kuiper Space Sciences Building
The University of Arizona
1629 East University Boulevard
Tucson, Arizona 85721-0092
Telephone: 520-621-6954
E-mail: acad_info@lpl.arizona.edu
World Wide Web: http://www.lpl.arizona.edu/

The University of Arizona

THE FACULTY AND THEIR RESEARCH

Victor R. Baker, Professor; Ph.D., Colorado, 1971. Planetary geomorphology.

Stephen W. Bougher, Assistant Research Scientist; Ph.D., Michigan, 1985. Planetary atmospheres, with emphasis on comparative study of terrestrial planet processes and global change implications.

William V. Boynton, Professor; Ph.D., Carnegie Mellon, 1971. Trace-element cosmochemistry and geochemistry, chemistry of planetary bodies by spacecraft remote sensing and in situ instrumentation, neutron activation analysis.

Lyle A. Broadfoot, Senior Research Scientist and *Voyager* Experiment Principal Investigator; Ph.D., Saskatchewan, 1963. Ultraviolet spectroscopy, planetary atmospheres, instrument development.

Robert H. Brown, Professor; Ph.D., Hawaii, 1982. Ground-based, space-based, and theoretical studies of surfaces and satellites in the outer solar system.

Alexander J. Dessler, Senior Research Scientist Emeritus; Ph.D., Duke, 1956. Magnetospheric physics.

Michael J. Drake, Professor, Head of the Department, and Director of the Laboratory; Ph.D., Oregon, 1972. Experimental and theoretical geochemistry, petrology and geochemistry of lunar samples and meteorites.

Uwe Fink, Professor; Ph.D., Penn State, 1965. Infrared Fourier spectroscopy, planetary atmospheres.

Tom Gehrels, Professor; Ph.D., Chicago, 1956. Asteroid astronomy, survey and origin of the solar system.

Richard J. Greenberg, Professor; Ph.D., MIT, 1972. Celestial mechanics, studies of planetary accumulation, satellite and ring dynamics.

Jay B. Holberg, Senior Research Scientist; Ph.D., Berkeley, 1974. Far-UV spectra, interstellar medium, planetary rings and atmospheres.

Lon L. Hood, Senior Research Scientist; Ph.D., UCLA, 1979. Geophysics, space physics, solar-terrestrial physics.

William B. Hubbard, Professor; Ph.D., Berkeley, 1967. High-pressure physics, planetary interiors and atmospheres.

Donald M. Hunten, Professor; Ph.D., McGill, 1950. Earth and planetary atmospheres, composition, structure, aeronomy.

J. R. Jokipii, Professor; Ph.D., Caltech, 1965. Theoretical astrophysics, cosmic rays, solar wind, astrophysical plasmas.

Harold P. Larson, Professor; Ph.D., Purdue, 1967. High-resolution interferometry, infrared Fourier spectroscopy, planetary atmospheres.

Larry A. Lebofsky, Senior Research Scientist; Ph.D., MIT, 1974. Planetary astronomy.

Eugene H. Levy, Professor; Ph.D., Chicago, 1971. Theoretical astrophysics, generation and behavior of magnetic fields, solar physics, cosmic rays.

John S. Lewis, Professor; Ph.D., California, San Diego, 1968. Cosmochemistry, planetary atmospheres.

Jonathan I. Lunine, Professor; Ph.D., Caltech, 1985. Theoretical planetary physics, condensed-matter studies, structure of planets.

Alfred McEwen, Associate Research Scientist; Ph.D., Arizona State, 1988. Multispectral studies of many bodies, volcanism on Io, calderas in Guatemala, mass movements of Earth and Mars, Copernican craters on the moon, remote sensing.

Robert S. McMillan, Associate Research Scientist; Ph.D., Texas, 1977. Doppler spectroscopy and asteroid detection survey.

H. Jay Melosh, Professor; Ph.D., Caltech, 1972. Planetary geophysics, planetary surfaces.

Carolyn C. Porco, Associate Professor; Ph.D., Caltech, 1983. Planetary rings, image processing.

George H. Rieke, Professor; Ph.D., Harvard, 1969. Gamma-ray, infrared astronomy, cosmic radiation.

Elizabeth Roemer, Professor; Ph.D., Berkeley, 1955. Comets, minor planets, astrometry.

Bill R. Sandel, Senior Research Scientist; Ph.D., Rice, 1972. Astrophysical plasmas, planetary atmospheres, airglow emissions, instrument development.

Peter H. Smith, Associate Research Scientist; M.S., Arizona, 1977. Optical sciences and radiative transfer in planetary atmospheres.

Charles P. Sonett, Professor Emeritus; Ph.D., UCLA, 1954. Planetary physics, solar wind.

Robert G. Strom, Professor; M.S., Stanford, 1957. Lunar and planetary surfaces, spacecraft imaging of planetary surfaces.

Timothy D. Swindle, Associate Professor; Ph.D., Washington (St. Louis), 1986. Cosmochemistry, noble gas studies of meteorites.

Martin G. Tomasko, Research Professor; Ph.D., Princeton, 1969. Planetary atmospheres, radiative transfer theory.

Space Sciences Building, which houses the Department of Planetary Sciences and the Lunar and Planetary Laboratory.

UNIVERSITY OF PUERTO RICO

Department of Geology

Program of Study

The Department of Geology in the College of Arts and Sciences at the Mayaguez Campus of the University of Puerto Rico is the only degree program in geology on the island of Puerto Rico. The department currently offers B.S. and M.S. degrees. Research emphasizes geological, geophysical, geochemical, and geobiological problems of the circum-Caribbean region with particular focus on surficial, tectonic, and volcanic processes and their associated hazards; the development of Cretaceous to Holocene reefs; carbonate petrology and stratigraphy; fluid history and hydrothermal mineralization; island arc formation and evolution; and accretionary and transcurrent plate boundary tectonics.

Research Facilities

The Department of Geology occupies the western third of the Physics Building, shared by geology, physics, and marine sciences. Facilities consist of a rock preparation room, a wet geochemistry laboratory, an X-ray analysis laboratory, a high-pressure and temperature experimental petrology laboratory, and a remote sensing/geophysical laboratory. Analytical instrumentation includes an electron microprobe, an X-ray diffractometer, an X-ray fluorescence spectrometer, a luminoscope, and various ancillary equipment. Development is underway for a fully automated stable isotope laboratory capable of measuring a range of geological and environmental materials. High-pressure and temperature experimental equipment includes bench-top piston cylinders, one-atmosphere gas-mixing furnaces, and a one-atmosphere heating/freezing stage. Geophysical equipment includes a gravimeter, a magnetometer, a portable seismometer, a ground-penetrating radar system, geodetic and hand-held GPS receivers, and a Total Station. Computing facilities consist of Macintosh, PC, SUN, and Silicon Graphics workstations linked by TCP/IP LAN with direct T1 connection to the Internet. The Puerto Rican Seismic Network is administered by the Department of Geology. The staff oversees a network of short period and broadband seismometers installed in Puerto Rico and nearby islands.

Financial Aid

Teaching assistantships pay $7000 for ten months. Assistantships from externally funded research projects are also available with a monthly stipend of up to $1000. University-funded assistantships also carry a tuition waiver. Students should indicate financial need when applying for admission.

Cost of Study

Residents of Puerto Rico pay $75 per credit hour. Nonresident U.S. citizens pay the nonresident rates of their state universities (except for students from U.S. institutions having reciprocal tuition-reduction agreements with Puerto Rico). Residency for U.S. citizens can be obtained after one year of study. Non-U.S. citizens who are not permanent residents pay $1750 per semester.

Living and Housing Costs

A typical annual budget for a single student (exclusive of tuition) ranges from $7000 to $9000. This includes room and board, local transportation, and academic and personal expenses. There are limited University living facilities for married graduate students off campus.

Student Group

The total enrollment at the Mayaguez campus is around 12,000, about 600 of whom are graduate students. The Department of Geology has approximately 15 graduate students and more than 100 undergraduate majors. The Student Geological Society, which includes both graduate and undergraduate students, organizes lectures and field trips and aids in the running of the Annual Symposium on Caribbean Geology.

Location

Mayaguez, the largest city in western Puerto Rico, has a population of 150,000. While offering all major services, the atmosphere remains casual. Cosmopolitan San Juan is only 120 miles away, and uncrowded sand beaches and pristine turquoise waters are reached in minutes. The climate is tropical with sunny blue skies in the morning and, particularly from April to October, frequent downpours in the late afternoon.

The University

Founded in 1911, the University of Puerto Rico, Mayaguez (UPRM) is an autonomous campus of the University of Puerto Rico. UPRM offers a wide variety of degree programs in its four colleges: arts and sciences, agricultural sciences, business administration, and engineering. Instruction is in both English and Spanish.

Applying

Application materials for graduate study can be obtained from the Graduate Admissions Committee. Applications are due on or before February 15 for admission for the first semester and on or before September 15 for the second semester. The GRE General Test is required, and the GRE Subject Test in geology is recommended. The minimum GPA for acceptance into the department is 2.8.

Correspondence and Information

Graduate Admissions Committee
Department of Geology
Box 9017
University of Puerto Rico
Mayaguez, Puerto Rico 00681-9017

Telephone: 787-265-3845
Fax: 787-265-3845
E-mail: webmaster@geology.upsm.edu
World Wide Web: http://geology.uprm.edu/GeologyHome.html

University of Puerto Rico

FACULTY AND THEIR RESEARCH

Ivan P. Gill, Assistant Professor; Ph.D., LSU, 1989. Carbonate petrology, low temperature geochemistry, geology of reef systems, paleoclimates.

Pamela E. Jansma, Associate Professor; Ph.D., Northwestern, 1988. Structural geology and tectonics, remote sensing.

James Joyce, Professor; Ph.D., Northwestern, 1985. Caribbean surficial and tectonic processes, structural and engineering geology, metamorphic petrology.

Glen S. Mattioli, Associate Professor; Ph.D., Northwestern, 1987. Experimental petrology and geochemistry, remote sensing, geodesy.

Robert L. Ripperdan, Assistant Professor; Ph.D., Caltech, 1990. Stable isotope geochemistry, geobiology, paleoclimatology.

Hernan Santos, Instructor; M.S., Colorado, 1990. Paleontology and stratigraphy of Caribbean Cretaceous carbonate platforms, development of rudist-coral framework.

Johannes H. Schellekens, Professor; Ph.D., Syracuse, 1993. Igneous geochemistry, mineral deposits in island arcs, Caribbean metallogenesis.

Alan L. Smith, Professor; Ph.D., Berkeley, 1969. Volcanology, stratigraphy and petrology of island arc volcanoes, volcanic hazard assessment.

SELECTED PUBLICATIONS

Hubbard, D. K., R. P. Burke, and **I. P. Gill**. Where's the reef: The role of framework in the Holocene. *Carbonates Evaporates,* in press.

Gill, I. P., P. P. McLaughlin, and D. K. Hubbard. The Neogene sedimentologic evolution of St. Croix. In *Sedimentary Basins of the World, vol 4: Caribbean Basins,* pp. 341–64, ed. P. A. Mann, 1999.

Gill, I. P., D. K. Hubbard, P. P. McLaughlin, and C. H. Moore Jr. The geology and hydrology of St. Croix. In *The Geology and Hydrogeology of Carbonate Islands, Developments in Sedimentology,* vol. 54, pp. 359–80, eds. L. Vacher and T. Quinn, 1997.

Gill, I. P., C. H. Moore, and P. Aharon. Evaporitic mixed-water dolomitization on St. Croix. *J. Sed. Res.* A65:591–604, 1995.

Gill, I. P., J. J. Olson, and D. K. Hubbard. Corals, paleotemperature and the aragonite-calcite transformation. *Geology* 23:333–6, 1995.

McLaughlin, P. P., **I. P. Gill,** and W. van den Bold. Biostratigraphy, paleoenvironments and stratigraphic evolution of the Neogene of St. Croix, U.S. Virgin Islands. *Micropalentology* 41:293–320, 1995.

Gill, I. P. Groundwater geochemistry of the Kingshill aquifer system, St. Croix. *Environ. Geosciences* 1:40–9, 1994.

Dixon, E., et al. **(P. Jansma).** Relative motion between the Caribbean and North American plates and related boundary zone deformation from a decade of GPS observations. *J. Geophys. Res.* 103:15157–83, 1998.

Jansma, P. E., and H. R. Lang. The Arcelia Graben: Basin and range extension south of the Trans-Mexican volcanic belt in northern Guerrero State, Mexico. *Geology* 25:455–8, 1998.

Jansma, P. E., and H. R. Lang. Spectral stratigraphy of the Balsas Group, northern Guerrero, Mexico. *Trans. 14th Caribbean Geol. Conference,* in press.

Jansma, P. E., and H. R. Lang. Applications of spectral stratigraphy to upper Cretaceous and Tertiary rocks in southern Mexico: Tertiary Graben control on volcanism. *Photogrammetric Eng. Remote Sensing* 62:1371–8, 1996.

Lang, H. R., et al. **(P. E. Jansma).** Terrane deletion in northern Guerrero. *Geofisica Internacional* 35:349–59, 1996.

Jansma, P. E., and R. C. Speed. Kinematics of underthrusting in the Paleozoic Antler foreland basin. *J. Geology* 103:559–75, 1995.

Jansma, P. E., and **G. S. Mattioli.** Fluid flow in brittle shear zones and the formation of nodular chert layer in Upper Paleozoic carbonates in the hinterland of the Sevier Orogenic belt at Carlin Canyon, Nevada. *Mountain Geologist* 31:85–94, 1994.

Jansma, P. E., and R. C. Speed. Deformation, dewatering, and decollement development in the Antler foreland basin during the Antler orogeny. *Geology* 21:1035–8, 1993.

Jansma, P. E., H. R. Lang, and C. A. Johnson. Preliminary stratigraphy of the Tertiary Balsas Group, Mesa Los Caballos area, central Mexico, from Landsat Thematic Mapper data. *Mountain Geologist* 28:137–50, 1991.

Jansma, P. E., and R. C. Speed. Omissional faulting during regional contraction, Carlin Canyon, Nevada. *Geol. Soc. Amer. Bull.* 102:417–27, 1990.

Joyce, J. Blueschist metamorphism and deformation on the Samana Peninsula—A record of subduction and collision in the Greater Antilles. In *Geologic and Tectonic Development of the North America-Caribbean Plate Boundary in Hispaniola, GSA Special Paper,* vol 262, pp. 47–76, eds. P. Mann, G. Draper, and J. F. Lewis, 1991.

Larue, D. K., **J. Joyce,** and H. F. Ryan. Neotectonics of the Puerto Rico Trench: Extensional tectonism and forearc subsidence. *Trans. 12th Caribbean Geol. Conference,* pp. 231–48, 1990.

Taggart, B. E., and **J. Joyce.** Radiometrically dated marine terraces on northwestern Puerto Rico. *Trans. 12th Caribbean Geol. Conference,* pp. 248–57, 1990.

Mattioli, G. S., et al. **(P. E. Jansma** and **A. L. Smith**). GPS measurements of surface deformation around Soufriere Hills Volcano, Montserrat from October 1995 to July 1996. *Geophys Res. Lett.* 25:3417–20, 1998.

Hooper, D. M., **G. S. Mattioli,** and T. P. Kover. Computer-simulation models of pyroclastic flows and lahars at Soufriere Hills volcano, Montserrat: Applications to hazard assessment. *Proc. Second Caribbean Conference Natural Hazards and Disasters,* in press.

Hooper, D. M., and **G. S. Mattioli.** Numerical simulation and experimental constraints of bubble growth in rhyolite glasses. In *NASA University Research Centers Technical Advances on Education, Aeronautics, Space, Earth, and Environment,* vol. 1, pp. 337–42, ed. M. Jamshidi et al., 1997.

Hooper, D. M., **G. S. Mattioli,** and T. P. Kover. Kinematic flow modeling and computer simulation for volcanic hazard assessment at Soufriere Hills volcano, Montserrat, B. W. I. In *NASA University Research Centers Technical Advances on Education, Aeronautics, Space, Earth, and Environment,* vol. 1, pp. 343–8, ed. M. Jamshidi et al., 1997.

Mattioli, G. S., **P. Jansma,** L. Jaramillo, and **A. L. Smith.** A desktop image processing and photometric method for rapid volcanic hazard mapping: Application to air photo interpretation of Mt. Pelée, Martinique. *Bull. Volcanol.* 58:401–10, 1996.

Mattioli, G. S., **P. Jansma,** L. Jaramillo, and **A. L. Smith.** Sector collapse in island arc volcanoes: A digital topographic and bathymetric investigation of the Qualibou depression, St. Lucia, Lesser Antilles. *Caribbean J. Sci.* 31:163–73, 1995.

Dixon, T. H., ed. **(G. S. Mattioli and A. L. Smith).** SAR interferometry and surface change detection: Results from the NASA Boulder Workshop, February 3–4, 1994. *RSMAS Tech. Rep. University Miami.* 54 pages, 1995.

Mattioli, G. S., N. Bashir, and E. Stolper. In situ, real-time determination of H_2O bubble formation and growth in rhyolitic glasses at 500° to 700°C: Preliminary results and interpretations. *Prog. et Abs. WOVO meeting, St. Francois, Guadeloupe, FWI,* pp. 111–13, 1993.

Mattioli, G. S., M. B. Baker, M. J. Rutter, and E. M. Stolper. Upper mantle oxygen fugacity and its relation to metamorphism. *J. Geology* 97:521–36, 1989.

Ripperdan, R. L., et al. Oxygen isotope ratios in authigenic magnetites from the Belden Formation, Colorado. *J. Geophys. Res.,* in press.

Kirschvink, J. L., **R. L. Ripperdan,** and D. Evans. Evidence for a large-scale reorganization of Early Cambrian continental masses by inertial interchange true polar wander. *Science* 227:541–5, 1997.

Holser, W. T., M. Magaritz, and **R. L. Ripperdan.** Global isotopic events. In *Global Events and Event Stratigraphy,* pp. 63–88, ed. O. Walliser. Berlin: Springer, 1995.

Ripperdan, R. L. A review of carbon isotope variations during the Late Neoproterozoic and Early Cambrian. *Ann. Rev. Earth Planet. Sci.* 26:385–417, 1994.

Ripperdan, R. L., M. Magaritz, and J. L. Kirschvink. Carbon isotope and magnetic polarity evidence for non-depositional events within the Cambrian-Ordovician boundary section at Dayangcha, Jilin Province, China. *Geology Mag.* 130:443–52, 1993.

Apollonov, M. K., et al. **(R. L. Ripperdan).** Paleomagnetic scale of Upper Cambrian and Lower Ordovician in Batyrbai section (Lesser Karatau, South Kazakhstan) in Russia. *Izvestiya Akad. Nauk Kazakhskoy SSR, Ser. Geolog.* 4:51–7, 1992.

Ripperdan, R. L., M. Magaritz, R. S. Nicoll, and J. H. Shergold. Simultaneous changes in carbon isotopes, sea level, and conodont

University of Puerto Rico

Selected Publications (continued)

biozones within the Cambrian-Ordovician boundary interval at Black Mountain, Australia. *Geology* 20:1039–42, 1992.

Schellekens, J. H. Composition, metamorphic grade, and origin of metabasites in the Bermeja Complex, Southwest Puerto Rico. *Int. Geol. Rev.* 40:722, 1998.

Schellekens, J. H. Geochemical evolution and tectonic history of Puerto Rico. In *Tectonics and Geochemistry of the Northeastern Caribbean, GSA Special Paper 322,* pp. 35–66, eds. E. G. Lidiak and D. K. Larue, 1998.

Frost, C. D., **J. H. Schellekens,** and **A. L. Smith.** Nd, Sr, and Pb isotopic characterization of Cretaceous and Paleogene volcanic and plutonic island arc rocks from Puerto Rico. In *Tectonics and Geochemistry of the Northeastern Caribbean, GSA Special Paper 322,* pp. 123–32, eds. E. G. Lidiak and D. K. Larue, 1998.

Jolly, W. T., E. Lidiak, **J. H. Schellekens,** and **H. Santos.** Volcanism, tectonics, and stratigraphic correlations in Puerto Rico. In *Tectonics and Geochemistry of the Northeastern Caribbean, GSA Special Paper 322,* pp. 1–34, eds. E. G. Lidiak and D. K. Larue, 1998.

Montgomery, H., E. A. Pessagno, J. F. Lewis, and **J. H. Schellekens.** Paleogeographic history of Jurassic terranes in Puerto Rico and Hispaniola. *Tectonics* 13:725–32, 1994.

Lipin, B., **J. H. Schellekens,** and A. L. Meir. Geology and PGE potential. In *Mineral Resource Assessment of Puerto Rico, U.S. Geological Survey Open-File report,* vol. 92-567, pp. 12–17, ed. J. N. Weaver, 1992.

Frost, C. D., and **J. H. Schellekens.** Rb-Sr and Sm-Nd isotopic characterization of Eocene volcanic rocks from the Toa Baja borehole and Eocene volcanic sequence, Puerto Rico. *Geophys. Res. Lett.* 18:545–8, 1991.

Reid, J., P. W. Plumley, and **J. H. Schellekens.** Paleomagnetic evidence for Late Miocene counterclockwise rotation of north coast carbonate sequence, Puerto Rico. *Geophys. Res. Lett.* 18:565–8, 1991.

Schellekens, J. H. Late Jurassic to Eocene geochemical evolution of volcanic rocks of Puerto Rico. *Geophys. Res. Lett.* 18:553–6, 1991.

Donnelly, T. W., et al. **(J. H. Schellekens** and **A. L. Smith).** History and tectonic setting of Caribbean magmatism. In Geological Society of America, *Geology of the Caribbean, DNAG,* eds. G. Dengo and J. Case. H:339–74, 1990.

Schellekens, J. H., H. Montgomery, **J. Joyce,** and **A. L. Smith.** Late Jurassic to late Cretaceous development of island arc crust in southwestern Puerto Rico. *Trans. 12th Caribbean Geol. Conference,* pp. 268–81, 1990.

Roobol, M. J., and **A. L. Smith.** Pyroclastic stratigraphy of the Soufriere Hills Volcano, Montserrat—Implications for the present eruption. *Geophys. Res. Lett.* 25:3393–6, 1998.

Smith, A. L., J. H. Schellekens, M. J. Roobol, and **J. Joyce.** The stratigraphy and age of the White Wall-Sugar Loaf sequence, St. Eustatius. *Trans. 14th Caribbean Geol. Conference,* in press.

Larue, D. K., R. Torrini, **A. L. Smith,** and **J. Joyce.** North Coast Tertiary basin of Puerto Rico: From arc basin to carbonate platform to arc-massif slope. In *Tectonics and Geochemistry of the Northeastern Caribbean, GSA Special Paper 322,* pp. 155–76, eds. E. G. Lidiak and D. K. Larue, 1998.

Smith, A. L., J. H. Schellekens, and A.-L. Muriel Diaz. Batholith emplacement in the northeastern Caribbean: Markers of tectonic change. In *Tectonics and Geochemistry of the Northeastern Caribbean, GSA Special Paper 322,* pp. 99–122, eds. E. G. Lidiak and D. K. Larue, 1998.

Roobol, M. J., **A. L. Smith,** and J. F. Tomlin. An assessment of the volcanic hazard on the islands of Saba and St. Eustatius in the northern Lesser Antilles. In *Report of the Geological Survey of the Netherlands,* 134, 1997.

Smith, A. L., and M. J. Roobol. Eastern Caribbean volcanic hazards. *Trans. Caribbean Conference on Volcanoes, Earthquakes, Windstorms and Floods,* pp. 220–9, 1994.

Harkness, D. D., et al. **(A. L. Smith).** A Reappraisal of the radiocarbon dating of the Mansion "Series." *Bull. Volcanol.* 56:326–34, 1994.

Smith, A. L., K. Severin, and D. K. Larue. Stratigraphy, geochemistry, and mineralogy of Eocene rocks from the Toa Baja Drillhole. *Geophys. Res. Lett.* 18:521–4, 1991.

Larue, D. K., **A. L. Smith,** and **J. H. Schellekens.** Oceanic island arc stratigraphy in the Caribbean region: Don't take it for granite: *Sed. Geology* 74:289–308, 1991.

Smith, A. L., and M. J. Roobol. Mt. Pelée, Martinique—A study of an active island arc volcano. *Geol. Soc. Amer. Memoir* 175:105, 1990.

Roobol, M. J., and **A. L. Smith.** Volcanic and associated hazards in the Lesser Antilles. *IAVCEI Proc. Volcanol.* 1:57–85, 1989.

UNIVERSITY OF SOUTH CAROLINA

Department of Geological Sciences

Programs of Study	The Department of Geological Sciences offers programs leading to the M.S. and Ph.D. degrees. The department also offers a geology-oriented specialization within the Master of Earth and Environmental Resource Management (M.E.E.R.M.) program. The Master of Arts in Teaching and the Interdisciplinary Master of Arts are offered in cooperation with the College of Education. There are several emphasis areas. Environmental geosciences examines the geological aspects of environmental sciences, including hydrology, hydrogeology, aqueous geochemistry, and contaminant transport, and how these play a crucial role in environmental hazard assessment and mitigation. The evolution of orogenic systems provides students with an understanding of the physical and chemical processes controlling the formation and evolution of the planet Earth, which is critical to many issues of fundamental and societal importance, including identification and mitigation of geologic hazards and the maintenance of a sufficient supply of natural resources. Finally, global climate change allows students to gain an understanding of minimization of and adjustment to geological, geochemical, and geophysical influences on global climate change and how these are of critical concern for the coming decades. Available fields of specialization include environmental geosciences, geochemistry, geophysics, global climate change, hydrocarbon exploration, marine sciences, oceanography, petrology, satellite geodesy, sedimentology, seismology, structural geology, and tectonics.
	Degree requirements generally follow those of the Graduate School. The M.S. degree requires the satisfactory completion of 30 semester hours of graduate credit, a thesis proposal presentation, a written thesis, and a comprehensive exam, in which the thesis must be successfully defended. Requirements for the Ph.D. degree include 12 semester hours of GEOL 899 and additional course work as determined by the advisory committee and depending on the student's background and specific needs. Qualifying and comprehensive exams must be successfully completed. The oral portion of the comprehensive exam consists, in part, of the defense of a paper written by the student that has been submitted for publication in an approved peer-reviewed journal. All Ph.D. candidates are required to publish a paper in a refereed scientific journal. A written dissertation is required that must be successfully defended. Additional details are available from the Director of Graduate Studies in geological sciences.
Research Facilities	The Department of Geological Sciences at the University of South Carolina (USC) is well supplied with field and laboratory equipment for extensive geologic research and maintains a network of workstations and servers. One server, a Sun 4/280, is dedicated to departmental use, and the second, a Sun 4/670MP, is dedicated for use by the geophysics program. A variety of state-of-the-art laboratories exist in the department, including Andean geophysical research; coastal plain research; estuarine, coastal, and satellite oceanography; deep sea sediments; geological image analysis; ocean circulation modeling; radioisotope geochemistry; sediment dynamics; seismology-geophysics; stable isotope; structural geology and tectonics research; and X-ray fluorescence and diffraction. In addition, the department houses the Southeastern Regional Electron Microprobe Facility and has access to the College Electron Microscopy Center.
Financial Aid	All students accepted into the graduate program receive a teaching or research assistantship. Approximately twenty-six teaching assistantships, carrying a nine-month stipend of $11,000 in 1999–2000 for 20 hours of employment per week, are awarded each academic year. Research assistantships sponsored by individual professors are also available. Regardless of the source of funding, all M.S. candidates are guaranteed support for two academic years and Ph.D. candidates for three years. Additional duration of support from grant funds is at the discretion of the research adviser. Special fellowships and awards are also available through the department.
Cost of Study	Students holding teaching or research assistantships pay reduced tuition of about $700 per semester.
Living and Housing Costs	Graduate students generally prefer to live off campus, but the University maintains on-campus housing, including the Bates House Graduate Wing and Cliff Apartments. There is a waiting list for these apartments, so application should be made early. Shuttle-bus service is available, and assistance in locating off-campus housing is available from Campus Housing and Residential Services.
Student Group	The department has 70 graduate students. There are full- and part-time students in both the M.S. and Ph.D. programs.
Location	Columbia, the state capital, serves a two-county metropolitan area of 400,000 by offering a variety of cultural activities, including excellent community theaters, two ballet companies, several music organizations, and museums. For recreation, Columbia offers attractive city and state parks, the acclaimed Riverbanks Zoo, and the University's varsity sports program. Just 15 miles from downtown Columbia, 50,000-acre man-made Lake Murray has some of the nation's best largemouth bass fishing and is ideal for camping and water sport. Columbia is only a few hours' drive from the Appalachian Mountains, with their excellent ski areas, and from South Carolina's beautiful beaches and primeval coastal islands. Like the entire Palmetto State, Columbia is rich in history and a delight to explore.
The University and The Department	Chartered in 1801 as South Carolina College, USC is one of the oldest state universities and the first to be supported continuously by annual state appropriations. Of more than 2,000 faculty members in the USC system, more than 1,500 are on the Columbia campus. The Columbia campus enrollment of almost 26,000 students includes more than 10,000 graduate students.
	In 1981, the Department of Geological Sciences moved into the Earth and Water Sciences Building. With this move the Departments of Geological Sciences, Chemistry, Physics and Astronomy, and Biology and the Marine Science Program were brought together in one centrally located science complex. The Department of Geological Sciences has expanded rapidly, both in size and direction, during the last fifteen years—from 12 faculty members and 25 graduate students in 1970 to 26 faculty members and 70 graduate students in 1998–99.
Applying	Application forms for admission to the graduate program can be obtained from the department. The admissions application should be completed and returned no later than April 1 for fall registration and October 1 for spring. Late applications will be considered if enrollment limits have not been reached. Most financial aid is offered by April 15. The General Test of the Graduate Record Examinations is required, and, in addition, international students must take the TOEFL.
Correspondence and Information	Director of Graduate Studies Department of Geological Sciences University of South Carolina Columbia, South Carolina 29208 Telephone: 803-777-4535 or 4501 E-mail: kellogg@sc.edu World Wide Web: http://inlet.geol.sc.edu/tappa/opening.htm

University of South Carolina

THE FACULTY AND THEIR RESEARCH

John R. Carpenter, Professor, Geological Education and Director, Center for Science Education; Ph.D., Florida State, 1964. Implementation and evaluation of innovative approaches to introductory-level earth science courses and teacher education courses.

Frank T. Caruccio, Professor Emeritus, Groundwater and Environmental Geology and Associate Chairman; Ph.D., Penn State, 1967. Environmental hydrology, groundwater geology and applied geochemistry, the evaluation of hydrogeochemical responses to land perturbations, urban development, waste disposal.

Arthur D. Cohen, Professor, Organic Sedimentology and Coal Research; Ph.D., Penn State, 1968. Coal and peat petrology, palynology and paleoecology, climate and sea-level changes, peat resources and utilization, hazardous waste and groundwater remediation utilizing organics.

Donald J. Colquhoun, Professor Emeritus, Coastal Plain Stratigraphy; Ph.D., Illinois, 1960. Surface and subsurface stratigraphy and hydrostratigraphy, quaternary geology, coastal plain geomorphology, Holocene sea-level history.

Robert Ehrlich, Professor Emeritus, Sedimentology and Petrophysics; Ph.D., LSU, 1965. Relating petrography to physics, especially porous rocks and fluids; image analysis and pattern recognition; quantifying diagenesis.

James C. Evans, Associate Professor, Physical Oceanography, Modeling, and Oceanic Policy; Ph.D., Florida State, 1984. Physical oceanography on the mesoscale, basin, and global scales; numerical ocean modeling; oceanic and coastal policy.

Leonard Gardner, Professor, Low Temperature Geochemistry; Ph.D., Penn State, 1968. Aqueous geochemistry and geomorphology; the geochemistry and mineralogy of soils and saprolites; origin of caliche; hydrologic, geologic, and geochemical processes in salt marshes; watershed biogeochemistry; modeling of geochemical processes in aqueous systems.

Miguel A. Goñi, Assistant Professor, Organic Geochemistry; Ph.D., Washington (Seattle), 1992. Organic geochemistry and the role of organic matter in global biogeochemical cycles of major elements (carbon, nitrogen, oxygen); sources, transport, transformations, and fate of organic matter in marine and other aquatic environments; paleoceanography.

Michael W. Howell, Assistant Professor, Marine Geology and Micropaleontology; Ph.D., South Carolina, 1988. Application of geochemical and micropaleontological methods in paleoceanographic and paleoclimatic reconstruction and modeling, paleontology.

William H. Kanes, Professor Emeritus, International Geology and Director, Earth Sciences and Resources Institute; Ph.D., West Virginia, 1965. Petroleum geology, regional geology, sedimentology.

James N. Kellogg, Professor, Applied Geophysics and Director of Graduate Studies; Ph.D., Princeton, 1981. Applied geophysics, GPS geodesy, gravity-tectonic studies, tectonics of convergent margins, Andean orogenic belt, seamounts.

Christopher G. St. C. Kendall, Professor, Sequence Stratigraphy, Computer Simulation of Basin Sedimentation, and Oil Exploration and Carbonates; Ph.D., Imperial College (London), 1966. Graphical simulation of basin stratigraphy in terms of sediment geometry responding to eustasy, tectonic history, and rates of sedimentation; Middle East stratigraphy and hydrocarbons; carbonate facies, geometry, and cementation.

Björn Kjerfve, Professor, Oceanography; Ph.D., LSU, 1973. Oceanography of estuaries, lagoons, and coastal waters; application of satellite remote sensing to coastal oceanography; ecology and modeling of transport processes in salt marshes and mangrove wetlands.

James H. Knapp, Associate Professor, Tectonics, Geophysics, and Petroleum Geology; Ph.D., MIT, 1989. Structural and geodynamic evolution of the continental lithosphere, controlled-source seismology, petroleum geology, structural geology, and tectonics, with emphasis on the former Soviet Union.

Matthew J. Kohn, Assistant Professor, Metamorphic Petrology and Stable Isotope Geochemistry; Ph.D., Rensselaer, 1991. Development and application of geochemical and stable isotope techniques to investigate orogenesis.

Venkataraman Lakshmi, Assistant Professor, Hydrology; Ph.D., Princeton, 1996. Land surface and subsurface hydrological modeling; scaling in hydrology; remote sensing of land surface variables, such as surface temperature and soil moisture; calculation of global warming using satellite data; assimilation of satellite data in land surface and general circulation models.

David R. Lawrence, Associate Professor Emeritus, Paleontology; Ph.D., Princeton, 1966. Paleoenvironmental reconstructions and the use of case studies to elucidate taxonomic and paleoecologic theory.

Ian Lerche, Professor, Geophysics; Ph.D., Manchester, 1965. Diagenetic and thermal history of sediments, basin modeling, salt and shale tectonics; paleosealevel determination, seismic wave propagation, inversion theory, stratigraphic signal filtering, surface waves, mineral coagulation and solubility, relation of diagenesis; cosmic rays and astrophysics; risk theory.

Willard S. Moore, Professor, Geochemistry and Chemical Oceanography; Ph.D., SUNY at Stony Brook, 1969. Natural radionuclides as tracers of geological and oceanographic processes, groundwater discharge and seawater cycling in coastal aquifers, coastal mixing rates.

Alan E. M. Nairn, Professor Emeritus, Regional Geology and Environmental Geology; Ph.D., Glasgow, 1954. Applicability to geological problems.

Thomas J. Owens, Professor, Seismology; Ph.D., Utah, 1984. Seismology and earth structure, crust and upper mantle geophysical processes, application of quantitative seismological methods to constrain the structure and physical properties of the continental lithosphere.

Evangelos K. Paleologos, Assistant Professor, Hydrology; Ph.D., Arizona, 1994. Saturated and unsaturated zone physics, stochastic subsurface hydrology, surface hydrology, numerical methods and modeling in groundwater and surface hydrology, contaminant transport, groundwater remediation.

Donald T. Secor Jr., Professor Emeritus, Structural Geology; Ph.D., Stanford, 1963. Structural geology and tectonics of the Appalachians.

W. Edwin Sharp, Professor Emeritus, Exploration Mineralogy; Ph.D., UCLA, 1964. Sampling design, statistical petrology, exploration geochemistry, computer simulations.

John W. Shervais, Professor, Petrology and Geochemistry and Director of Undergraduate Studies; Ph.D., California, Santa Barbara, 1979. Igneous petrology, major- and trace-element geochemistry, phase equilibria.

Pradeep Talwani, Professor, Geophysics and Seismology; Ph.D., Stanford, 1973. Seismotectonics of intraplate regions, paleoseismicity, neotectonics, crustal structure in the Southeast U.S., reservoir-induced seismicity.

Robert C. Thunell, Carolina Distinguished Professor and Chairman, Paleoceanography, Paleoclimatology, and Deep Sea Sediments; Ph.D., Rhode Island, 1978. Reconstructing paleoceanographic and paleoclimatic conditions using deep sea sediments, sedimentation and dissolution of calcium carbonate in the deep sea, production and flux of biogenic particles in the open ocean, plankton ecology/paleoecology.

Raymond Torres, Assistant Professor, Near-Surface Hydrology, Geomorphology; Ph.D., Berkeley, 1997. The interactions between water and sediment transport processes and how they control landscape evolution.

George Voulgaris, Assistant Professor, Coastal Processes, Sediment Dynamics, Coastal Oceanography; Ph.D., Southampton (United Kingdom), 1993. Hydrodynamics, marine turbulence, sediment transport mechanisms and pathways, coastline evolution.

Douglas F. Williams, Professor, Paleoceanography and Stable Isotope Geochemistry; Ph.D., Rhode Island, 1976. Application of stable isotope geochemistry to a wide variety of paleoenvironments and geological phenomena, including paleoclimatology and paleoceanography.

SELECTED PUBLICATIONS

Carpenter, J. R. The role of geosciences faculty in the undergraduate education of science and mathematics teachers. In *Proceedings of the National Science Foundation Workshop on the Role of Faculty from the Scientific Disciplines in the Undergraduate Education of Future Science and Mathematics Teachers*, pp. 208–17. Washington, D.C.: National Science Foundation, 1993.

Carpenter, J. R. An overview of geoscience education reform in the United States. *J. Geol. Educ.* 41:304–11, 1993.

Carpenter, J. R. The importance of earth science in the pre-college curriculum. *J. Geol. Educ.* 38:445–51, 1990.

Cohen, A. D., C. P. Gage, and **W. S. Moore.** Combining organic petrography and palynology to assess anthropogenic impacts on peatlands Part I: An example from the northern Everglades of Florida. *Int. J. Coal Geol.* 39(1–3):3–45, 1999.

Rizzuti, A. M., **A. D. Cohen,** P. P. G. Hunt, and M. B. Vanotti. Testing of peats for removal of odors from liquid swine manure. *J. Environ. Sci. Health Part A* A33(8):1719–39, 1998.

Cohen, A. D., et al. Applications of atomic force microscopy to study of artificially coalified peats. *Soc. Org. Petrol.* 15:23–7, 1998.

Evans, J. C., Y. Zhang, **R. Ehrlich,** and W. Li. Implications of transport synchrony for loop current intrusion and ring formation. *J. Phys. Oceanogr.,* in press.

Castro, J. E., and **L. R. Gardner.** A geochemical model for the aquifer storage and recovery project at Myrtle Beach, South Carolina. In *Proceedings of AWRA Symposium, Conjunctive Use of Water Resources: Aquifer Storage and Recovery, TPS-97-2,* pp. 201–10, ed. D. R. Kendall. Herndon, Va.: American Water Resources Association, 1997.

Michener, W. K., et al. **(L. R. Gardner).** Climate change, hurricanes and tropical storms, and rising sea level in coastal wetlands. *Ecol. Appl.* 7(3):770–801, 1997.

Gardner, L. R. Simulation of the diagenesis of carbon, sulfur and dissolved oxygen in salt marsh sediments. *Ecol. Monographs* 60:91–111, 1990.

Goñi, M. A. Record of terrestrial organic matter composition in Amazon fan sediments. In *Proceedings of the Ocean Drilling Program, Scientific Results,* vol. 155, pp. 519–30, eds. R. D. Flood, D. J. W. Piper, A. Klaus, and L. C. Peterson. College Station, Tex.: Ocean Drilling Program, 1997.

Goñi, M.A., K. C. Ruttenberg, and T. I. Eglinton. Sources and contribution of terrigenous organic carbon to surface sediments in the Gulf of Mexico. *Nature* 389:275–8, 1997.

Ruttenberg, K. C., and **M. A. Goñi.** Phosphorous distribution, C:N:P ratios, and δ13COC in arctic, temperate, and tropical coastal sediments: Tools for characterizing bulk sedimentary organic matter. *Marine Geol.* 139:123–45, 1997.

Emeis, K.-C., et al. **(M. W. Howell).** Stable isotope and alkenone temperature records of sapropels from ODP Sites 964 and 967: Constraining the physical environment of sapropel formation in the eastern Mediterranean Sea. In *Proceedings of the Ocean Drilling Program, Scientific Results 160,* eds. A. H. F. Robertson, K.-C. Emeis, C. Richter, and A. Camerlenghi. College Station, Tex.: Ocean Drilling Program, 1998.

Howell, M. W., R. C. Thunell, R. Sprovieri, and E. DiStefano. Stable isotope chronology and paleoceanographic history of ODP Sites 963 and 964, Eastern Mediterranean Sea. In *Proceedings of the Ocean Drilling Program, Scientific Results 160,* eds. A. H. F. Robertson, K.-C. Emeis, C. Richter, and A. Camerlenghi. College Station, Tex.: Ocean Drilling Program, 1998.

Sprovieri, R., et al. **(M. W. Howell).** Integrated calcareous plankton biostratigraphy and planktonic foraminifera abundance fluctuations at ODP Leg 160, Site 964. In *Proceedings of the Ocean Drilling Program, Scientific Results 160,* eds. A. H. F. Robertson, K.-C. Emeis, C. Richter, and A. Camerlenghi. College Station, Tex.: Ocean Drilling Program, 1998.

Kellogg, J. N., R. Trenkamp, and J. T. Freymueller. Subduction of the Southwestern Caribbean plate boundary–CASA GPS results 1991–1996. *Trans. Am. Geophys. Union,* 78:S114, 1997.

Kellogg, J. N., and V. Vega. Tectonic development of Panama, Costa Rica, and the Colombian Andes: Constraints from global positioning system geodetic studies and gravity. In *Geologic and Tectonic Development of the Caribbean Plate Boundary in Southern Central America, Special Paper 295,* ed. P. Mann, pp. 75–90. Boulder, Colo.: Geological Society of America, 1995.

Liu, K., T. C. K. Liang, L. Paterson, and **C. G. St. C. Kendall.** Computer simulation of the influence of basin physiography on condensed section deposition and maximum flooding. *Sedimentary Geol.* 122:181–91, 1998.

Perlmutter, M. A., B. J. Radovich, M. D. Matthews, and **C. G. St. C. Kendall.** The impact of high-frequency sedimentation cycles on stratigraphic interpretation. In *Sequence Stratigraphy—Concepts and Applications,* Norwegian Petroleum Society Special Publication No. 8, pp. 141–70, eds. F. M. Gradstein, K. O. Sandvick, and N. J. Milton. Amsterdam: Elsevier Science, 1998.

Quaternary Deserts and Climatic Change, Proc. Int. Conf. Quaternary Deserts Climatic Change, Al Ain, United Arab Emirates, 9–11 December 1995, eds. A. S. Alsharhan, K. W. Glennie, G. L. Whittle, and **C. G. St. C. Kendall.** A. A. Balkema Publishers, 1998.

Kendall, C. G. St. C., and A. Sen. Use of sedimentary simulations for dating sequence boundaries and measuring the size of eustatic sea level changes: An example from the Neogene of the Bahamas. In *Computerized Modeling of Sedimentary Systems,* pp. 291–306, eds. J. Harff, W. Lemke, and K. Stattegger. Berlin: Springer Verlag, 1998.

Kjerfve, B., et al. Oceanographic characteristics of an impacted coastal bay: Baía de Guanabara, Rio de Janeiro, Brazil. *Continent. Shelf Res.* 17(13):1609–43, 1997.

Kjerfve, B., et al. Hydrology and salt balance in large hypersaline coastal lagoon: Lagoa de Araruama, Brazil. *Estuarine Coast. Shelf Sci.* 42(6):701–25, 1996.

Kjerfve, B., H. E. Seim, A. F. Blumberg, and L. D. Wright. Modeling of the residual circulation in Broken Bay and the lower Hawkesbury River, NSW. *Aust. J. Marine Freshwater Res.* 43:1339–57, 1992.

Diaconescu, C. C., and **J. H. Knapp** et al. Precambrian Moho offset and tectonic stability of the East European platform from the URSEIS deep seismic profile. *Geology* 26:211–4, 1998.

Knapp, J. H., et al. Seismic reflection fabrics of continental collision and post-orogenic extension in the Middle Urals, central Russia. *Tectonophysics* 288:115–26, 1998.

Steer, D. N., and **J. H. Knapp** et al. Deep structure of the continental lithosphere in an unextended orogen: An explosive-source seismic reflection profile in the Urals (Urals Seismic Experiment and Integrated Studies (URSEIS 95)). *Tectonics* 17:143–57, 1998.

Kohn, M. J. Why most "dry" rocks should cool "wet." *Am. Mineral.* 84:570–80, 1999.

Kohn, M. J. You are what you eat. *Science* 283:335–6, 1999.

Kohn, M. J., F. S. Spear, and J. W. Valley. Dehydration-melting and fluid recycling during metamorphism: Rangeley Formation, New Hampshire, U.S.A. *J. Petrol.* 38:1255–77, 1997.

Lakshmi, V., and E. F. Wood. Diurnal cycle of evaporation over FIFE using observations and modeling. *J. Hydrol.* 204:37–51, 1998.

Lakshmi, V., E. F. Wood, and B. J. Choudhury. A soil-canopy-atmosphere model for use in satellite microwave remote sensing. *J. Geophys. Res.* 102(D6):6911–27, 1997.

Lakshmi, V., E. F. Wood, and B. J. Choudhury. Evaluation of SSM/I satellite data for regional soil moisture estimation over the Red River Basin. *J. Appl. Meteorol.* 36(10):1309–28, 1997.

Wood, E. F., and **V. Lakshmi.** Scaling water and energy fluxes in climate systems: Three land-atmospheric modeling experiments. *J. Climate* 6(5):839–57, 1993.

Lerche, I., and X. Pang. Establishment of a quantitative index for evaluation of cap rock sealing, and application to the Shongliao Basin, China. *Energy Explor. Exploitation* 15:369–86, 1997.

Lerche, I., E. Bagirov, and R. Nadirov. Hydrocarbon evolution for a north-south section of the South Caspian Basin. *Marine Petrol. Geol.* 14:773–854, 1997.

Lerche, I., and E. Bagirov. Deformation and stress caused by a rising mud diapir. In *Neotectonics and Its Influence on the Formation and Distribution of Oil and Gas Fields,* pp. 120–2. Baku Nafta Press, 1997.

University of South Carolina

Selected Publications (continued)

Moore, W. S., and K. K. Falkner. Cycling of radium and barium in the Black Sea. *J. Environ. Radioactivity* 43:247–54, 1999.

Moore, W. S., and T. J. Shaw. Chemical signals from submarine fluid advection onto the continental shelf. *J. Geophys. Res.* 103:21543–52, 1998.

Moore, W. S. Large groundwater inputs to coastal waters revealed by 226Ra enrichments. *Nature* 380:612–4, 1996.

Rama, and **W. S. Moore.** Using the radium quartet for evaluating groundwater input and water exchange in salt marshes. *Geochim. Cosmochim. Acta* 60:4645–52, 1996.

Zhao, M., C. A. Langston, A. A. Nyblade, and **T. J. Owens.** Upper mantle velocity structure beneath southern Africa from modeling regional seismic data. *J. Geophys. Res.* 104:4783–94, 1999.

Ritsema, J., et al. **(T. J. Owens).** Upper mantle seismic velocity structure beneath Tanzania, east Africa: Implications for the stability of cratonic lithosphere. *J. Geophys. Res.* 103:21201–13, 1999.

Owens, T. J., and G. Zandt. The implications of crustal property variations on models of Tibetan Plateau evolution. *Nature* 387:37–43, 1997.

Bene, K. J., and **E. K. Paleologos.** Geostatistical analyses of laboratory and in-situ measurements of saturated hydraulic conductivity. *Southeastern Sec. Geol. Soc. Am.* 29(3):A4, 1997.

Paleologos, E. K., S. P. Neuman, and D. Tartakovsky. Effective hydraulic conductivity of bounded, strongly heterogeneous porous media. *Water Resources Res.* 32(5):1333–41, 1996.

Paleologos, E. K., and S. P. Neuman. Effective hydraulic conductivity of bounded, strongly nonuniform porous media. *EOS Trans. Am. Geophys. Union* 74(16):157, 1993.

Broman, C., A. P. Watkins, and **W. E. Sharp.** A study of the fluid inclusions from quartzitic tectonites of the Bomfa/Beposo area, NW Ashanti belt, Ghana, West Africa. *Ghana Mining J.* 3(1–2):18–27, 1997.

Sharp, W. E. Distribution of heavy metals in the brown alga, *Ascophyllum nodosum*, along the fjords of the Trondheim region, Norway. *Norwegian Geol. Survey 95.028,* 56 pp., 1997.

Turner, B. F., and **W. E. Sharp.** Unilateral ARMA processes on a square net by the herringbone method. *Math. Geol.* 26(5):557–64, 1994.

Shervais, J. W., and J. J. McGee. KREEP cumulates in the western lunar highlands: Ion and electron microprobe study of alkali anorthosites and norites from Apollo 14. *Am. Mineral.,* in press.

Shervais, J. W. Highlands crust at the Apollo 14 site: Surfing the Fra Mauro shoreline. *Int. Geol. Rev.* 41:141–53, 1999.

Shervais, J. W., and J. J. McGee. Ion and electron microprobe study of Mg suite troctolites, norite, and anorthosites from Apollo 14:

Evidence for urKREEP assimilation during petrogenesis of Apollo 14 Mg-suite rocks. *Geochim. Cosmochim. Acta* 62(17):3009–23, 1998.

Talwani, P. Fault geometry and earthquakes in continental interiors. *Tectonophysics,* in press.

Talwani, P., et al. In situ measurements of hydraulic properties of a shear zone in northwestern South Carolina. *J. Geophys. Res.,* in press.

Talwani, P. On the nature of reservoir-induced seismicity. *Pure Appl. Geophys.* 150:473–92, 1997.

Talwani, P. Seismotectonics of the Koyna-Warna area. *Pure Appl. Geophys.* 150:511–50, 1997.

Thunell, R. Seasonal and annual variability in particle fluxes in the Gulf of California: A response to climate forcing. *Deep-Sea Res.* 45:2131–55, 1998.

Thunell, R. Continental margin particle flux: Seasonal cycles and archives of global change. *Oceanus* 40:15–9, 1998.

Patrick, A., and **R. Thunell.** Tropical Pacific sea surface temperatures and upper water column thermal structure during the last glacial maximum. *Paleoceanography* 12:649–57, 1997.

Torres, R., et al. Unsaturated zone processes and the hydrologic response of a steep, unchanneled catchment. *Water Resources Res.* 34(8):1865–77, 1998.

Anderson, S. P., et al. **(R. Torres).** Concentration-discharge relationships in runoff from a steep, unchanneled catchment. *Water Resources Res.* 33(1):211–25, 1997.

Montgomery, D. R., et al. **(R. Torres).** Piezometric response of a small catchment. *Water Resources Res.* 33(1):93–109, 1997.

Wallbridge, S., **G. Voulgaris,** B. N. Tomlinson, and M. B. Collins. Initial motion and pivoting characteristics of sand particles in uniform and heterogeneous beds: Experiments and modelling. *Sedimentology* 46:17–32, 1999.

Voulgaris, G., and J. H. Trowbridge. Evaluation of the Acoustic Doppler Velocimeter (ADV) for turbulence measurements. *J. Atmos. Oceanog. Technol.* 15(1):272–89, 1998.

Voulgaris, G., et al. Measuring and modelling sediment transport on a macrotidal ridge and runnel beach: An intercomparison. *J. Coastal Res.* 14(1):315–30, 1998.

Karabanov, E. B., A. A. Prokopenko, **D. F. Williams,** and G. K. Khursevich. Evidence for mid-Eemian cooling in continental climatic record from Lake Baikal. *J. Paleolimnol.,* in press.

Karabanov, E. B., A. A. Prokopenko, **D. F. Williams,** and S. M. Colman. Evidence from Lake Baikal for Siberian glaciation during oxygen-isotope substage 5d. *Quaternary Res.* 50:46–55, 1998.

Williams, D. F., et al. Lake Baikal record of continental climate response to orbital insolation during the past 5 million years. *Science* 278:1114–7, 1997.

UNIVERSITY OF WASHINGTON

Geophysics Program

Programs of Study

Geophysics is the study of the earth's physical makeup, behavior, and planetary environment. Based directly on physical laws and encompassing many different mathematical and observational methods, geophysics examines the complex nature of the solid, liquid, and gaseous components of the earth and its environment. Current research also focuses increasingly on the interactions of these components, for example, the climate system. Modern geophysics is thus an interdisciplinary science, not a separate and isolated area of knowledge.

All students are required to take a core curriculum of courses on the earth's interior, the oceans, the atmosphere, and the solar-terrestrial environment. Beyond this sequence, students select a course of study from offerings in the Geophysics Program and the participating Departments of Astronomy, Atmospheric Sciences, Civil Engineering, Electrical Engineering, Geological Sciences, Oceanography, and Physics. Because of the diversity of disciplines represented in geophysics, there are few formal course requirements, and it is the responsibility of the student and his or her advisory committee to plan a course of study that is appropriate as a background for thesis research. The principal areas of activity in the program today are seismology, geomagnetism, high-pressure experimental geophysics, glaciology, geophysical fluid dynamics, space physics, and aeronomy.

Qualification for the Ph.D. program is a process that considers course and research performance with the results of a research proposition-based oral exam normally given to students at the beginning of their second year. Students who do not qualify for the Ph.D. program by means of this process may be reconsidered following completion of an M.S. program. During the second year, M.S. students either prepare a thesis or satisfy the nonthesis option by preparing a manuscript suitable for publication. Ph.D. students pursue a course of study selected in conjunction with the advisory committee and prepare a dissertation proposal for presentation at a general examination. Work then proceeds on the dissertation until it is ready to be presented at the final examination. The Ph.D. program typically requires five to six years.

Research Facilities

Laboratory facilities are available for a wide range of experimental work. They include a high-pressure/temperature laboratory, including diamond anvil cells for studying rock and mineral properties; cold room facilities for glaciological research; geophysical fluid laboratories; a space physics laboratory for preparing balloon and satellite experiments; a laboratory for the development of optical instrumentation; and assorted electronics and machine shop facilities. Computer systems are used for various types of online experiments and for modeling calculations. Extensive support facilities are available, as are major facilities, including ocean-bottom seismographs, seismic profiling equipment, a magnetotelluric array, gravimeters, magnetometers, and GPS survey equipment. The Pacific Northwest Seismograph Network (PNSN), which locates earthquakes in Washington and Oregon, is centered in the Geophysics Program. The research facilities of all participating departments are available to students through their thesis supervisor.

Financial Aid

Most graduate students receive support in the form of research assistantships. A limited number of teaching assistantships are available in the Departments of Geological Sciences and Physics. All assistantship appointments require 20 hours of service per week and provide a beginning monthly income of $1110, with a 3 percent increase projected for the 1999–2000 academic year. The student's interests are matched as closely as possible with fields of available support. Changes can be made after the first year, if appropriate.

Cost of Study

Tuition for the 1999–2000 academic year is estimated at $1865 per quarter for in-state students and $4625 per quarter for out-of-state students. However, students holding assistantships are required to pay only a minor portion (estimated to be $140 per quarter) of these tuition costs.

Living and Housing Costs

Housing for single students is available on campus through the Office of Housing and Food Services. In 1999–2000, on-campus costs are about $377 per month for shared student apartments to $426 per month for one-bedroom married student apartments. Off-campus housing arrangements are typically $300 to $400 per person per month for group-living rentals.

Student Group

Geophysics usually has about 40 students, most of whom are working toward a Ph.D. Backgrounds are diverse, but an entering student normally has the equivalent of a B.S. in physics. Graduates at both the M.S. and Ph.D. levels have found excellent employment opportunities during the past decade, and this is expected to continue.

Location

Seattle's University District is both environmentally attractive and culturally interesting. It lies between Lake Washington and Puget Sound at the northern end of downtown Seattle. All the cultural advantages of a large city are available, while some of the country's most spectacular natural environments, from mountains to ocean beaches, can be found nearby.

The University

The University, founded in 1861, is the oldest state-assisted institution of higher education on the Pacific Coast. The campus is large, with a total enrollment of nearly 33,000 and a national reputation for quality in graduate research and education. The Geophysics Program is administered by the College of Arts and Sciences.

Applying

Applications for admission and for financial support should be sent to the Graduate Program Assistant (address below). The deadline for applications is January 31 for optimum admission and funding consideration. Admission for the fall quarter can be requested as late as July 1, but earlier application is strongly recommended. Scores on the General Test of the Graduate Record Examinations are required for consideration for both admission and financial aid. Assistantship applications, statements of purpose, three letters of recommendation, transcripts, and test scores should be sent directly to the Geophysics Program. The Graduate School application and fee should be sent to Graduate Admissions, Box 351245.

Correspondence and Information

Graduate Program Assistant
Geophysics Program
Box 351650
University of Washington
Seattle, Washington 98195-1650
Telephone: 206-543-8020

University of Washington

THE FACULTY AND THEIR RESEARCH

Marcia B. Baker, Professor of Geophysics and Atmospheric Sciences; Ph.D., Washington (Seattle), 1971. Atmospheric geophysics.

John R. Booker, Professor of Geophysics; Ph.D., California, San Diego, 1968. Geomagnetic induction, magnetotellurics, inverse theory, geophysical fluid dynamics.

J. Michael Brown, Professor of Geophysics and Geological Sciences and Chair, Geophysics Program; Ph.D., Minnesota, 1980. Experimental and theoretical mineral and rock physics.

Robert A. Charlson, Professor of Atmospheric Sciences, Chemistry, Civil Engineering, and Geophysics; Ph.D., Washington (Seattle), 1964. Atmospheric chemistry, tropospheric aerosols.

Kenneth C. Clark, Professor Emeritus of Physics and Geophysics; Ph.D., Harvard, 1947. Optical spectroscopy, upper atmosphere.

Howard Conway, Research Associate Professor; Ph.D., Canterbury (New Zealand), 1986. Physical processes in snow and ice.

Kenneth C. Creager, Professor of Geophysics; Ph.D., California, San Diego, 1984. Seismology and geophysical inverse theory.

Robert S. Crosson, Professor of Geophysics and Geological Sciences; Ph.D., Stanford, 1966. Seismology, structure and tectonics, earthquake hazards.

Janice DeCosmo, Research Assistant Professor; Ph.D., Washington (Seattle), 1991. Experimental air-sea interaction, science education.

John T. Ely, Research Associate Professor Emeritus of Geophysics; Ph.D., Washington (Seattle), 1969. Background radiation as part of the geophysical environment.

Gonzalo Hernandez, Research Professor; Ph.D., Rochester, 1962. Optical interference phenomena, remote sensing of atmospheres.

Robert H. Holzworth, Professor of Geophysics and Physics; Ph.D., Berkeley, 1977. Experimental space plasma physics, atmospheric and magnetospheric electric fields, thunderstorm electrodynamics.

Conway B. Leovy, Professor of Atmospheric Sciences, Geophysics, and Astronomy; Ph.D., MIT, 1963. Dynamics and radiative transfer of the stratosphere and mesosphere, the atmospheres of other planets.

Brian T. R. Lewis, Professor of Oceanography and Geophysics; Ph.D., Wisconsin, 1970. Processes of lithosphere generation and consumption using seismology, gravity, and magnetics.

Stephen D. Malone, Research Professor; Ph.D., Nevada, 1972. Seismicity of Mt. St. Helens, the Cascade volcanoes, and eastern Washington; computer applications in seismic network analysis.

Gary Maykut, Research Professor of Atmospheric Sciences and Geophysics; Ph.D., Washington (Seattle), 1969. Sea-air-ice interaction in the polar oceans.

Michael McCarthy, Research Associate Professor; Ph.D., Washington (Seattle), 1988. Solar wind and magnetospheric physics.

James A. Mercer, Research Associate Professor; Ph.D., Washington (Seattle), 1983. Seismic acoustic studies, oceanacoustic tomography.

Ronald T. Merrill, Professor of Geophysics, Geological Sciences, and Oceanography; Ph.D., Berkeley, 1967. Geomagnetism, geophysics of solids, rock magnetism.

Robert I. Odom Jr., Research Associate Professor; Ph.D., Washington (Seattle), 1980. Seismic acoustic studies, oceanacoustic tomography, theoretical seismology, elastic wave scattering.

George K. Parks, Professor of Geophysics and Physics; Ph.D., Berkeley, 1966. Particles and waves in auroral, magnetospheric, and interplanetary space plasma phenomena.

Anthony Qamar, Research Associate Professor of Geophysics; Ph.D., Berkeley, 1971. GPS-based geodesy, earthquake tectonics in the Pacific Northwest, earthquakes associated with volcanoes and glaciers, earth-structure and earthquake hazards.

Charles F. Raymond, Professor of Geophysics, Quaternary Research, and Geological Sciences; Ph.D., Caltech, 1969. Glaciology, glacier and ice sheet dynamics.

John D. Sahr, Associate Professor of Electrical Engineering and Geophysics; Ph.D., Cornell, 1990. Ionospheric physics, ion acoustic plasma turbulence, ground-based radar remote sensing.

Stewart W. Smith, Professor Emeritus; Ph.D., Caltech, 1961. Seismology, earthquake risk, seismotectonics.

Brian D. Swanson, Research Assistant Professor; Ph.D., Washington (Seattle), 1992. Atmospheric geophysics.

Martyn J. Unsworth, Research Associate Professor; Ph.D., Cambridge, 1991. Geomagnetic induction, magnetotellurics, electromagnetic geophysics.

Norbert Untersteiner, Professor Emeritus of Atmospheric Sciences and Geophysics; Ph.D., Innsbruck, 1950. Glaciology, arctic sea ice.

Edwin D. Waddington, Professor of Geophysics; Ph.D., British Columbia, 1981. Glacier and ice sheet modeling, interpretation of ice sheet stratigraphy and paleoclimate from ice cores.

Stephen G. Warren, Professor of Atmospheric Sciences, Geophysics, and Quaternary Research; Ph.D., Harvard, 1973. Atmospheric radiation; radiative properties of clouds, snow, and sea ice; Antarctic climate.

William S. D. Wilcock, Associate Professor of Oceanography and Geophysics; Ph.D., MIT (WHOI), 1992. Marine seismology, mid-ocean ridges, hydrothermal circulation.

Robert Winglee, Associate Professor of Geophysics; Ph.D., Sydney, 1984. Energetic phenomena in the plasmas about the sun and earth, excitation of waves, acceleration of high-energy particles, magnetic reconnection.

A seismology graduate student waits to board a helicopter to Karymsky Volcano in Petropavlovsk, Kamchatka, to study the volcano with seismic and acoustic instrumentation. The volcano has been active since 1996.

A glaciology graduate student takes GPS data for measurements of surface velocity of the ice on Siple Dome, West Antarctica. The measurements will be used in ice dynamics studies.

SELECTED PUBLICATIONS

Schroeder, V., **M. B. Baker,** and J. Latham. A model study of corona emission from hydrometeors. *Q. J. Roy. Meteorol. Soc.,* in press.

Solomon, R., and **M. B. Baker.** Lightning frequency and type in convective thunderstorms. *J. Geophys. Res.* 103(D12):14041–57, 1998.

Baker, M. B. Cloud microphysics and climate. *Science* 276:1072–8, 1997.

Booker, J. R., C. Aprea, **M. J. Unsworth,** and N. Wu. Electrical conductivity structure in major continental tectonic zones. *Geowissenschaften* 15:111–5, 1997.

Chen, L., and **J. R. Booker** et al. **(M. J. Unsworth).** Electrically conductive rust in southern Tibet from INDEPTH magnetotelluric surveying. *Science* 274:1694–6, 1996.

Chai, M., **J. M. Brown,** and Y. Wang. Yield strength, slip systems and deformation induced phase transition of San Carlos olivine up to transition zone pressure at room temperature. In *Properties of Earth and Planetary Materials at High Pressure and Temperature,* pp. 483–94, eds. M. H. Manghnani and T. Yagi. Washington, D.C.: American Geophysical Union, 1998.

Hearn, E., G. Humphreys, M. Chai, and **J. M. Brown.** Effect of anisotropy on oceanic upper mantle temperatures, structure, and dynamics. *J. Geophys. Res.* 102:11943–56, 1997.

Chai, M., **J. M. Brown,** and L. J. Slutsky. Thermal diffusivity of mantle minerals. *Phys. Chem. Miner.* 23:470–5, 1996.

Zaug, J., E. Abramson, **J. M. Brown,** and L. J. Slutsky. Sound velocities for olivine under mantle conditions of pressure. *Science* 260:1487–9, 1993.

Conway, H., and C. Wilbour. Evolution of snow slope stability during storms. *Cold Regions Sci. Technol.,* in press.

Conway, H., L. A. Rasmussen, and H.-P. Marshall. Annual mass balance of Blue Glacier, U.S.A.: 1957–97. *Geografiska Ann.,* in press.

Conway, H. The impact of surface perturbations on snow slope stability. *Ann. Glaciol.* 26:307–12, 1998.

Conway, H., et al. Observations of basal sliding at sub-freezing temperatures: A report on studies at Meserve Glacier, Antarctica. *Antarctic J. U.S.* 31(2):67–8, 1996.

Castle, J. C., and **K. C. Creager.** A steeply dipping discontinuity in the lower mantle beneath Izu-Bonin. *J. Geophys. Res.,* in press.

Castle, J. C., and **K. C. Creager.** Northwest Pacific slabs steepen at seismicity cutoff. *Earth Planets Space* 50:977–85, 1998.

Castle, J. C., and **K. C. Creager.** Topography of the 660-km seismic discontinuity beneath Izu-Bonin: Implications for tectonic history and slab deformation. *J. Geophys. Res.* 103:12511–28, 1998.

Creager, K. C. Inner core rotation rate from small-scale heterogeneity and time-varying travel times. *Science* 278:1284–8, 1997.

Symons, N. P., and **R. S. Crosson.** Seismic velocity structure of the Puget Sound region from 3-D non-linear tomography. *Geophys. Res. Lett.* 24:2593–6, 1997.

Schultz, A. P., and **R. S. Crosson.** Seismic velocity structure across the central Washington Cascade Range from refraction interpretation with earthquake sources. *J. Geophys. Res.* 101:27899–915, 1996.

Dewberry, S. R., and **R. S. Crosson.** The M 5.0 earthquake of January 29, 1995 in the Puget Lowland of western Washington. *Bull. Seism. Soc. Am.* 86:1167–72, 1996.

Thomas, G. C., **R. S. Crosson,** D. L. Carver, and T. S. Yelin. The 25 March 1993 Scotts Mills, Oregon, earthquake and aftershock sequence: Spatial distribution, focal mechanisms, and the Mount Angel fault. *Bull. Seism. Soc. Am.* 86:925–35, 1996.

Andreas, E. L., and **J. DeCosmo.** Sea spray production and influence on air-sea heat and moisture fluxes over the open ocean. In *Air-Sea Fluxes of Momentum, Heat, and Chemicals,* ed. G. Geernaerdt, in press.

Winn, W., **J. DeCosmo,** T. Emerson, and R. Yu. Global change, virtual reality and learning. In *Proceedings of the National Science Foundation Workshop.* Seattle, Wash., 1997.

DeCosmo, J., et al. Air-sea exchange of water vapor and sensible heat: The humidity exchange over the sea (HEXOS) results. *J. Geophys. Res. Oceans* 101:12001–16, 1996.

Hernandez, G. Time series, periodograms and significance. *J. Geophys. Res.* 104:10355–68, 1999.

Hernandez, G., et al. Optical determination of the vertical wavelength of propagating 12-hour period upper atmosphere oscillations. *Geophys. Res. Lett.* 22:2389–92, 1995.

Hernandez, G., and R. G. Roble. Nighttime thermospheric neutral gas temperature and winds over Fritz Peak Observatory: Observed and calculated solar cycle variation. *J. Geophys. Res.* 99:14647–59, 1995.

Hernandez, G. *Fabry-Perot Interferometers.* Cambridge University Press, 1988.

Holzworth, R. H., and **R. M. Winglee** et al. Lightning whistler waves in the high latitude magnetosphere. *J. Geophys. Res.,* in press.

Holzworth, R. H., and E. A. Bering III. Ionospheric electric fields from stratospheric balloon-borne probes. In *Measurement Techniques in Space Plasmas,* vol. 103, pp. 79–85, *Geophysical Monographs* series, eds. J. Borovsky, R. Pfaff, and D. Young. American Geophysical Union, 1998.

Kelley, M. C., et al. **(R. H. Holzworth).** LF and MF observations of the lightning electromagnetic pulse at ionospheric altitudes. *Geophys. Res. Lett.* 24:1111, 1997.

Hu, H., and **R. H. Holzworth.** An inertial wave driven stratospheric horizontal electric field: New evidence. *J. Geophys. Res.* 102:19717–30, 1997.

Bajuk, L. J., and **C. B. Leovy.** Seasonal and interannual variations in stratiform and convective clouds over the Pacific and Indian Oceans from ship observations. *J. Climate,* in press.

Orsolini, Y. J., V. Limpasuvan, and **C. B. Leovy.** The tropical stratopause in the UKMO stratospheric analyses: Evidence for a 2-day wave and inertial circulations. *Q. J. R. Met. Soc.* 123:1707–24, 1997.

Murphy, J. R., et al. **(C. B. Leovy).** Three-dimensional numerical simulations of Martian global dust storms. *J. Geophys. Res.* 100(E12):26357–76, 1996.

Norris, J. R., and **C. B. Leovy.** Interannual variability in stratiform cloudiness and sea surface temperature. *J. Climate* 7:1915–25, 1993.

Malone, S. D. The Council of the National Seismic System—The first five years. *Seism. Res. Lett.* 69(2):164, 1998.

Malone, S. D., and **A. I. Qamar.** Stress conditions in the United States Pacific Northwest: Focal mechanisms, tectonics, and geodesy. In *Earthquake Fault Plane Solutions: Databases, Derived Parameters, Geodynamic Inferences, Proc.,* eds. G. Neri and C. Eva. Taormina-Messina, Italy, 1998.

Malone, S. D., and S. C. Moran. Deep long-period earthquakes in the Washington Cascades. *EOS* 78(46):F438, 1997.

Malone, S. D. "Near" realtime seismology. *Seism. Res. Lett.* 67(6):52–4, 1997.

Maykut, G. A., and M.G. McPhee. Solar heating of the arctic mixed layer. *J. Geophys. Res.* 100(C12):24691–703, 1995.

Maykut, G. A., and B. Light. Refractive index measurements in freezing sea ice and sodium chloride brines. *Appl. Opt.* 34:950–61, 1995.

Perovich, D. K., and **G. A. Maykut.** Solar heating of a stratified ocean in the presence of a static ice cover. *J. Geophys. Res.* 95:18233–45, 1990.

McCarthy, M. P., and J. P. McFadden. Measurement of 0-25~eV ions with a retarding potential analyzer on the cluster ion spectroscopy experiment. In *Measurement Techniques in Space Plasmas: Particles,* vol. 102, *Geophysical Monographs* series, eds. J. Borovsky, R. Pfaff, and D. Young. American Geophysical Union, 1998.

Datta, S., R. M. Skoug, **M. P. McCarthy,** and **G. K. Parks.** Modeling of microburst electron precipitation using pitch angle diffusion theory. *J. Geophys. Res.* 102:17325–33, 1997.

Marshall, T. C., **M. P. McCarthy,** and W. D. Rust. Electric field magnitudes and lightning initiation in thunderstorms. *J. Geophys. Res.* 100:7097–103, 1995.

University of Washington

Selected Publications (continued)

McElhinny, M. W., P. L. McFadden, and **R. T. Merrill.** The time-averaged paleomagnetic field. *J. Geophys. Res.* 101:25007–28, 1996.

Merrill, R. T., M. W. McElhinny, and P. L. McFadden. In *The Magnetic Field of the Earth: Paleomagnetism, the Core, and the Deep Mantle,* p. 531. San Diego, Calif.: Academic Press, 1996.

Merrill, R. T., and S. Halgedahl. Theoretical and experimental studies of magnetic domains. *Rev. Geophys.* 33(Iss. S):137–144, 1995.

McFadden, P. L., and **R. T. Merrill.** History of the earth's magnetic field and the core-mantle boundary. *J. Geophys. Res.* 100:307–16, 1995.

Park, M., and **R. I. Odom.** The effect of stochastic rough interfaces on coupled-mode elastic waves. *Geophys. J. Int.* 136:123–43, 1999.

Park, M., and **R. I. Odom.** Effects of elastic heterogeneities and anisotropy on mode coupling and signals in shallow water. *J. Acoust. Soc. Am.* 104:747–57, 1998.

Odom, R. I., and **J. A. Mercer.** Spectral diffusion of elastic wave energy. *Geophys. J. Int.* 127:111–24, 1996.

Odom, R. I., et al. (**J. A. Mercer** and **R. S. Crosson**). Effects of transverse isotropy on modes and mode coupling in shallow water. *J. Acoust. Soc. Am.* 100:2079–92, 1996.

Parks, G. K., et al. (**M. P. McCarthy**). Does the UVI on Polar detect cosmic snowballs. *Geophys. Res. Lett.* 24:3109–12, 1997.

Parks, G. K., et al. (**M. P. McCarthy**). Ion beams observed in the near-earth plasma sheet region on May 10, 1996. *Geophys. Res. Lett.* 24(8):975–8, 1997.

Lee, N. C., and **G. K. Parks.** Ponderomotive acceleration of ions by circularly polarized electromagnetic waves. *Geophys. Res. Lett.* 23:327–30, 1996.

Qamar, A. I., S. D. Malone, and R. S. Ludwin. Rapid earthquake notification in the Pacific Northwest. *Washington Geol.,* 25(4):33–6, 1997.

Dragovich, J. D., J. E. Zollweg, **A. I. Qamar,** and D. K. Norman. The Macaulay Creek thrust, the 1990 5.2-magnitude Deming earthquake, and Quaternary geologic anomalies in the Deming area, western Whatcom County, Washington—cause and effects. *Wash. Geol.* 25(2):15–27, 1997.

Stanley, W. D., et al. (**A. I. Qamar**). Tectonics and seismicity of the southern Washington Cascade Range. *Bull. Seism. Soc. Am.* 86:1–18, 1996.

Nereson, N. A., **C. F. Raymond, E. D. Waddington,** and R. W. Jacobel. Migration of the Siple Dome Ice Divide, West Antarctica. *J. Glaciol.,* in press.

Jacobson, H. P., and **C. F. Raymond.** Thermal effects on the location of ice stream margins. *J. Geophys. Res.* 103:12111–22, 1998.

Boudreaux, A., and **C. F. Raymond.** Geometry response of glaciers to changes in spatial pattern of mass balance. *Ann. Glaciol.* 25:407–11, 1997.

Raymond, C. F., et al. Geometry, motion and mass balance of Dyer Plateau, Antarctica. *J. Glaciol.* 42(142):510–8, 1996.

Sahr, J. D., and F. D. Lind. The Manastash Ridge radar: A passive bistatic radar for upper atmospheric radio science. *Radio Sci.* 32(6):2345–58, 1997.

Sahr, J. D., and B. G. Fejer. Auroral electrojet plasma irregularity theory and experiment: A critical review of present understanding and future directions. *J. Geophys. Res.* 101(A12):26893–909, 1996.

Sahr, J. D. Application of closure phase and self-calibration to radar interferometric imaging of atmospheric and ionospheric irregularities. *J. Atmospheric Terrestrial Phys.* 58(8–9):959–64, 1996.

Bacon, N. J., **B. D. Swanson, M. B. Baker,** and E. J. Davis. Laboratory measurements of light scattering by single ice particles. *J. Aerosol Sci.* 29:S1317–8, 1998.

Bacon, N. J., **B. D. Swanson, M. B. Baker,** and E. J. Davis. The breakup of levitated frost particles. *J. Geophys. Res.* 103:13763–75, 1998.

Aardahl, C. L., et al. (**B. D. Swanson**). Trapping two-particle arrays in a double-ring electrodynamic balance. *J. Aerosol Sci.* 28:1491–505, 1997.

Unsworth, M. J., G. D. Egbert, and **J. R. Booker.** High resolution electromagnetic imaging of the San Andreas fault in Central California. *J. Geophys. Res.* 104:1131–50, 1999.

Aprea, C. M., **M. J. Unsworth,** and **J. R. Booker.** Resistivity structure of the Olympic Mountains and Puget Lowland: Implications for subduction zone seismicity. *Geophys. Res. Lett.* 25:109, 1998.

Unsworth, M. J., P. E. Malin, G. D. Egbert, and **J. R. Booker.** Internal structure of the San Andreas fault zone at Parkfield, California. *Geology* 25:359–62, 1997.

Unsworth, M. J. Exploration of mid-ocean ridges with a frequency domain electromagnetic system. *Geophys. J. Int.* 116:447–67, 1994.

Vaughan, D. G., H. F. J. Corr, C. S. M. Doake, and **E. D. Waddington.** Distortion of isochronous layers in ice revealed by ground-penetrating radar. *Nature* 398(6725):323–6, 1999.

Steig, E. J., et al. (**E. D. Waddington**). Synchronous climate changes in Antarctica and the North Atlantic. *Science* 282(5386):92–5, 1998.

Morse, D. L., **E. D. Waddington,** and E. J. Steig. Ice age storm trajectories inferred from radar stratigraphy at Taylor Dome, Antarctica. *Geophys. Res. Lett.* 25(17):3383–6, 1998.

Alley, R. B., et al. (**E. D. Waddington**). Grain-scale processes, folding and stratigraphic disturbance in the GISP2 ice core. *J. Geophys. Res.* 102(C12):26819–30, 1997.

Walden, V. P., **S. G. Warren,** and F. J. Murcray. Measurement of the downward longwave radiation spectrum over the Antarctic Plateau, and comparison to a line-by-line radiative transfer model for clear skies. *J. Geophys. Res.* 103:3825–46, 1998.

Warren, S. G., C. S. Roesler, and R. E. Brandt. Solar radiation processes in the East Antarctic sea ice zone. *Antarctic J. U.S.* 32:85–187, 1997.

Brandt, R. E., and **S. G. Warren.** Temperature measurements and heat transfer in the near-surface snow at the South Pole. *J. Glaciol.* 43:339–51, 1997.

Warren, S. G., G. E. Thomas, **G. Hernandez,** and R. W. Smith. Noctilucent cloud observed in autumn at South Pole Station: Temperature anomaly or meteoritic debris. *J. Geophys. Res.* 102:1991–2000, 1997.

Cherkaoui, A. S. M., and **W. S. D. Wilcock.** Characteristics of high Rayleigh number two-dimensional convection in an open-top porous layer heated from below. *J. Fluid Mech.,* in press.

Toomey, D. R., et al. (**W. S. D. Wilcock**). Mantle seismic structure beneath the MELT region of the East Pacific Rise from P and S wave tomography. *Science* 280:1224–7, 1998.

Wilcock, W. S. D. Cellular convection models of mid-ocean ridge hydrothermal circulation and the temperatures of black smoker fluids. *J. Geophys. Res.* 103:2585–96, 1998.

Winglee, R. M., S. Kokubun, R. P. Lin, and R. P. Lepping. Flux rope structures in the magnetotail: Comparison between WIND/Geotail observations and global simulations. *J. Geophys. Res.* 103:135, 1998.

Goodson, A. P., **R. M. Winglee,** and K. H. Bohm. Time dependent accretion of magnetic young stellar objects as a launching mechanism for stellar jets. *Astrophys. J.* 489:199–209, 1997.

Winglee, R. M., V. O. Papitashvili, and D. R. Weimer. Comparison of the high latitude ionospheric electrodynamics inferred from global simulations and semi-empirical models for the January 1992 GEM campaign. *J. Geophys. Res.* 102:26961, 1997.

Winglee, R. M., et al. IMF induced changes in the nightside magnetosphere using WIND/Geotail/IMP 8 observations and modeling. *Geophys. Res. Lett.* 24:829, 1997.

VIRGINIA POLYTECHNIC INSTITUTE AND STATE UNIVERSITY

Department of Geological Sciences

Programs of Study

The Department of Geological Sciences offers graduate programs leading to the Master of Science (M.S.) and Doctor of Philosophy (Ph.D.) degrees in geological and geophysical sciences that cover the fields of aqueous/environmental geochemistry, earthquake seismology, exploration geophysics, hydrogeosciences, petrogenesis and isotope geology, mineralogy, petrology, ore deposits, paleontology, sedimentology, stratigraphy, structural geology, and tectonics. Graduate programs are flexible, and students with degrees in majors other than the geological sciences are encouraged to apply.

Individual student programs are established through close cooperation between the student and his or her advisory committee. The specific course requirements for the M.S. and Ph.D. degrees are as follows: 30 credits are required for the M.S., including a maximum of 12 credits from allowable 4000-level courses and a minimum of 12 credits from 5000-level courses. Also, a minimum of 6 credits and a maximum of 12 credits of 5994-level courses can be counted. A maximum of 6 credits obtained at an accredited institution can be considered for transfer credit. Ninety credits are required for the Ph.D. degree, including a maximum of 6 credits from allowable 4000-level courses and a minimum of 27 credits from 5000-level courses. The minimum and maximum number of credits of 5994-level courses or 7994-level courses are 30 and 60, respectively. A maximum of 42 credits can be transferred; however, no more than 10 credits can be applied to a master's thesis. Transfer students must take at least 15 credits at the 5000 level or higher (not including thesis or dissertation hours) at Virginia Tech. The preliminary examination must be taken before the end of the third semester of enrollment in the Ph.D. program.

Research Facilities

Located in Derring Hall, a five-story teaching and research center, the department is equipped with excellent facilities that are supported by faculty members and qualified technical staff members. Major items of equipment include a Scintag fully automated powder X-ray diffractometer; a Cameca SX-50 four-spectrometer microprobe with image analysis capability; a scanning electron microscope with electron channeling capability; micro-Raman and FTIR spectrometers; two solid-source mass spectrometers with multicollection capability; Digital Instruments ambient scanning tunneling and atomic force microscopes; an ultrahigh-vacuum Omicron system, including a scanning tunneling microscope, X-ray and ultraviolet photoelectron spectroscopies, low-energy electron diffraction, and a borehole heat-pulse flowmeter with data acquisitions and processing software and hardware; and a portable winch with 500 meters of single-conductor cable. In addition, facilities are available for high-temperature/high-pressure investigations of mineral equilibria and for fluid inclusion studies of ores and rocks. Currently, operational and well-equipped laboratories include radiogenic isotope and petrogenesis, geochemistry, sedimentology and stratigraphy, paleontology, mineral surface geochemistry, tectonics, structure, earthquake seismology, exploration geophysics 3-D subsurface imaging, and hydrogeosciences. Equipment for geophysics also includes portable sixty-channel seismic equipment, multichannel resistivity, ground-penetrating radar, and 3-D seismic reflection data processing, modeling, and interpretation systems. The department operates a regional telemetered network for earthquake monitoring and houses a United States National Network Seismic Network station. The laboratories are equipped with state-of-the-art computing hardware and software (3D Focus, Landmark, and 2D and 3D AIMS).

The Geological Sciences Museum houses extensive mineralogical and paleontological collections. The Geological Sciences Library, with more than 28,000 volumes, is also located in Derring Hall. Detailed information about the department's research facilities can be obtained from the World Wide Web at the address listed below.

Financial Aid

Twenty-hour-per-week graduate assistantships include a stipend of about $10,000 as well as $4125 for tuition each year.

Cost of Study

In-state tuition is approximately $4125 per year for 1999–2000; the cost of study is often met by graduate assistantships, as described above. Health and student fees are approximately $820 per year for 1999–2000.

Living and Housing Costs

The Blacksburg area has many rooms, apartments, and mobile homes for rent at costs ranging from $250 to $450 per month. Students should apply early to ensure that they have housing when the school year commences.

Student Group

There are approximately 140 undergraduate and 50 graduate students currently enrolled in geology, geochemistry, and geophysics. Most resident graduate students receive financial aid.

Location

Blacksburg, first settled in 1757, lies high in the folded and thrust-faulted southern Appalachians on the watershed between the Roanoke and the New Rivers—a natural geological laboratory. Nearby lakes, rivers, forests, caves, and mountains provide a variety of recreational opportunities. The community of 50,000 provides shopping, athletic, recreational, educational, and cultural activities for a broad range of interests. Several research-oriented industries, the University, Radford Army Ammunition Plant, and many businesses and services offer a wide range of employment opportunities. Blacksburg is connected to major airline routes through nearby Roanoke Airport.

The University

Founded as a land-grant college in 1872, the University now enrolls about 25,000 students, including more than 4,500 graduate students, from all fifty states and forty-six countries. Instruction is offered by more than fifty departments in eight colleges—Arts and Sciences, Agriculture and Life Sciences, Architecture and Urban Studies, Business, Engineering, Forestry and Wildlife Resources, Human Resources and Education, and Veterinary Medicine. University research services for agriculture, industry, and government agencies are coordinated by the Research Division and the Extension Division.

Applying

Applications for admission and financial aid are accepted at any time during the year; however, most financial aid is offered by April 15. The General Test of the Graduate Record Examinations is required. In addition, international students must take the TOEFL, TSE, and TWE for admission and financial assistance.

Correspondence and Information

Dr. C. Çoruh, Chairman
Department of Geological Sciences
Virginia Polytechnic Institute and State University
Blacksburg, Virginia 24061-0420
Telephone: 540-231-6521
Fax: 540-231-3386
E-mail: records@vt.edu
          coruh@vt.edu
World Wide Web: http://www.geol.vt.edu

Virginia Polytechnic Institute and State University

THE FACULTY AND THEIR RESEARCH

Economic Geology
B. M. Bekken, Ph.D., Stanford, 1990. Geology and geochemistry of metallic mineral deposits.
J. R. Craig, Ph.D., Lehigh, 1965. Ore mineralogy and phase equilibria, gold, ore deposits, mineral resources.

Earthquake Seismology
J. A. Snoke, Ph.D., Yale, 1969. Theoretical and observational seismology, structure of the mantle, seismic source studies, regional seismicity, earthquake hazard mitigation.

Exploration Geophysics
C. Çoruh, Ph.D., Istanbul, 1970. Exploration seismology, seismic data processing, crustal structures.
J. A. Hole, Ph.D., British Columbia, 1993. Reflection and refraction seismology, crustal structure and tectonics, inverse modeling.
M. G. Imhof, Ph.D., MIT, 1996. Exploration seismology, seismic data processing, theoretical wave propagation, reservoir delineation and characterization.

Geochemistry
R. J. Bodnar, Ph.D., Penn State, 1985. Experimental determination of properties of hydrothermal fluids at high temperatures and pressures, fluid inclusion studies of various geologic environments.
M. F. Hochella Jr., Ph.D., Stanford, 1981. Mineral-water interface geochemistry, general geochemistry.
J. D. Rimstidt, Ph.D., Penn State, 1979. Geochemical kinetics, geothermal and hydrothermal chemistry, applied geochemistry.
N. L. Ross, Ph.D., Arizona State, 1985. Thermochemical and lattice vibrational study of high-pressure phase transitions in silicates and germanates.

Hydrogeosciences
T. J. Burbey, Ph.D., Nevada, Reno, 1994. Aquifer mechanics, applied and theoretical groundwater modeling, groundwater and well hydraulics, contaminant transport, wellhead protection and water resources evaluation.
M. E. Schreiber, Ph.D., Wisconsin–Madison, 1999. Contaminant hydrogeology, bioremediation, wetlands geochemistry, groundwater quality, contaminant transport modeling.

Mineralogy and Petrology
S. C. Eriksson, Ph.D., Witwatersrand (South Africa), 1983; Director of Museum. Geochemistry of alkaline rocks.
A. K. Sinha, Ph.D., California, Santa Barbara, 1969. Geochemical and isotopic studies of igneous and metamorphic rocks, application to tectonics and petrogenesis, geologic assessment of nuclear waste.
R. J. Tracy, Ph.D., Massachusetts, 1975. Metamorphic and igneous petrology.

Paleontology
R. K. Bambach, Ph.D., Yale, 1969. Community paleoecology; functional morphology; evolution, systematics of Bivalvia; paleogeography and paleobiogeography.
M. Kowalewski, Ph.D., Arizona, 1995. Taphonomy, time-averaging, paleoecology, predation, trace fossils, morphometrics, statistical methods, lingulide brachiopods, benthic mollusks.

Stratigraphy and Sedimentology
K. A. Eriksson, Ph.D., Witwatersrand (South Africa), 1977. Clastic sedimentology, Precambrian geology.
J. F. Read, Ph.D., Western Australia, 1971. Carbonate sedimentology and diagenesis.

Structure Tectonics and Geomorphology
R. D. Law, Ph.D., London, 1981. Relationships between tectonics and structural processes, microstructural and crystallographic analysis of ductile fabrics, evolution of thrust belts and extensional terranes, exhumation of high-pressure rocks in Himalayas and Alaska.
J. A. Spotila, Ph.D., Caltech, 1998. Neotectonics, geomorphology, and paleoseismology, with emphasis on the long-term evolution and interaction between crustal deformations and surficial processes in mountain systems.

Emeritus Faculty
F. D. Bloss, Ph.D., Chicago, 1951. New methods in optical crystallography.
G. A. Bollinger, Ph.D., Saint Louis, 1967. Earthquake seismology, seismicity of the southeastern United States, aftershock sequences.
J. K. Costain, Ph.D., Utah, 1960. Terrestrial heat flow and geothermal studies, reflection seismology, hydroseismicity.
G. V. Gibbs, Ph.D., Penn State, 1962. Crystal chemistry of minerals.
L. Glover III, Ph.D., Princeton, 1967. Tectonics of the Appalachian and Caledonide orogens; plate tectonics; evolution of passive, collisional, and oblique-slip margins.
G. C. Grender, Ph.D., Penn State, 1960. Quantitative exploration modeling, computer analysis of terrain.
D. A. Hewitt, Ph.D., Yale, 1970. Experimental and metamorphic petrology.
W. D. Lowry, Ph.D., Rochester, 1943. Tectonic history: juncture of the southern and central Appalachians.
D. M. McLean, Ph.D., Stanford, 1969. Dynamics and thermodynamics of bioevolution; taxonomy, biostratigraphy, paleoecology, and evolution of dinoflagellates.
P. H. Ribbe, Ph.D., Cambridge, 1963. Crystal chemistry of silicate minerals, electron probe microanalysis.
E. S. Robinson, Ph.D., Wisconsin, 1964. Earth and ocean tides, exploration geophysics.

Virginia Polytechnic Institute and State University

SELECTED PUBLICATIONS

Knoll, A. H., **R. K. Bambach,** J. P. Grotzinger, and D. Canfield. Comparative Earth history and late Permian mass extinction. *Science* 273:452–7, 1996.

Dorsch, J., **R. K. Bambach,** and S. G. Driese. Basin-rebound origin for the "Tuscarora unconformity" in southwestern Virginia and its bearing on the nature of the Taconic orogeny. *Am. J. Sci.* 294:237–55, 1994.

Bambach, R. K. Seafood through time: Changes in biomass, energetics and productivity in the marine ecosystem. *Paleobiology* 19:372–97, 1993.

Bekken, B. M. A revised physical geology laboratory curriculum based on group learning. *J. Geol. Educ.* 43(4):361–5, 1995.

Fleming, R. H., and **B. M. Bekken.** Isotope ratio and trace elements imaging of pyrite grains in gold ores. *Int. J. Ion Phys. Mass Spectrom.* 143:213–24, 1995.

Bekken, B. M. Wall-rock alteration, gold mineralization and the geochemical evolution of the hydrothermal system in the main ore body, Carlin Mine, Nevada. *Great Basin Symposium Proceedings April 1990.* In Reno, Nevada, 1992.

Bekken, B. M., R. H. Fleming, and **M. F. Hochella Jr.** High-resolution microscopy of auriferous pyrite from the Post deposit, Carlin district, Nevada. In *Process Mineralogy XI—Characterization of Metallurgical and Recyclable Products,* pp. 13–23, eds. D. M. Hausen, W. Petruck, R. D. Hagni, and A. Vassiliou. The Minerals, Metals, and Materials Society, 1991.

Schmidt, C., I.-M. Chou, **R. J. Bodnar,** and W. A. Bassett. Microthermometric analysis of synthetic fluid inclusions in the hydrothermal diamond-anvil cell. *Am. Mineral.* 83:995–1007, 1998.

Szabó, C., **R. J. Bodnar,** and A. V. Sobolev. Fluid inclusion evidence for an upper mantle origin for green clinopyroxenes in late Cenozoic basanites from the Nógrad-Gömör Volcanic Field, North Hungary/South Slovakia. *Int. Geol. Rev.* 40(9):765–73, 1998.

Roedder, E., and **R. J. Bodnar.** *Fluid Inclusion Studies of Hydrothermal Ore Deposits in Geochemistry of Hydrothermal Ore Deposits,* 3rd ed., pp. 657–98, ed. H. L. Barnes. New York: John Wiley & Sons, 1997.

Bodnar, R. J. Fluid inclusion evidence for a magmatic source for metals in porphyry copper deposits. In *Mineralogical Association of Canada Short Course Volume 23, Magmas, Fluids and Ore Deposits,* pp. 139–52, ed. J. F. H. Thompson. 1995.

Bodnar, R. J. Experimental determination of the PVTx properties of aqueous solutions at elevated temperatures and pressures using synthetic fluid inclusions: H_2O-NaCl as an example. *J. Pure Appl. Chem.* 67(6):873–80, 1995.

Burbey, T. J. Modeling three-dimensional deformation in response to pumping of unconsolidated aquifers. *Environ. Eng. Geosci.,* in press.

Burbey, T. J. Quantifying subsidence in the vicinity of basin-fill faults. *Proceedings of the Association of Engineering Geologists 39th Annual Meeting,* in press.

Burbey, T. J. Hydrogeology and potential for ground-water development, carbonate rock aquifers, southern Nevada and southeastern California. *U.S. Geological Survey Water-Resources Investigations Report 95-4168,* 1997.

Burbey, T. J. Validity of Jacob's assumptions for calculating subsidence due to pumping of confined aquifers. In *Proceedings of the 17th Annual American Geophysical Union Hydrology Days,* pp. 29–44, ed. H. J. Morel-Seytoux. Fort Collins, Colo.: Colorado State University, 1997.

Burbey, T. J. State of subsidence modeling within the U.S. Geological Survey. In *U.S. Geological Survey Subsidence Interest Group Conference–Proceedings of the Technical Meeting, Las Vegas, Nevada, February 14–16, 1995,* eds. K. R. Prince and S. A. Leake. U.S. Geological Survey Open-File Report 97–47:15–19, 1997.

Prudic, D. E., J. R. Harrill, and **T. J. Burbey.** Conceptual evaluation of regional ground-water flow in the carbonate-rock province of the Great Basin, Nevada, Utah, and adjacent states. *U.S. Geological Survey Professional Paper 1409-D:102,* 1995.

Burbey, T. J. Shallow ground water in the Whitney area southeastern Las Vegas Valley, Clark County, Nevada—Part II Assessment of a proposed strategy to reduce the contribution of salts to Las Vegas Wash. *U.S. Geological Survey Water-Resources Investigations Report 92-4051,* 1993.

Domoracki, W. J., D. E. Stephenson, **C. Çoruh,** and **J. K. Costain.** Seismotectonic structures along the Savannah River corridor, South Carolina, U.S.A. *J. Geodynamics* 27:97–118, 1999.

Balog, A., J. Haas, and **C. Çoruh.** Shallow marine record of orbitally forced cyclicity in a Late Triassic carbonate platform, Hungary. *J. Sedimentary Res.* 67(4):661–75, 1997.

Doll, W. E., et al **(C. Çoruh).** Seismic reflection evidence for the evolution of a transcurrent fault system: The Norumbega fault zone, Maine. *Geology* 24(3):251–4, 1996.

Çoruh, C., et al. Composite refraction-reflection stack sections: Imaging shallow subsurface structures. In *Proceedings of the Symposium on the Application of Geophysics to Engineering and Environmental Problems, SAGEEP* 95:937–46, 1995.

Lampshire, L. D., **C. Çoruh,** and **J. K. Costain.** Crustal structures and the eastern extent of the lower Paleozoic shelf strata within the central Appalachians: A seismic reflection interpretation. *Geol. Soc. Am. Bull.* 106:1018, 1994.

Demirbag, E., **C. Çoruh,** and **J. K. Costain.** Inversion of P-wave AVO in offset-dependent reflectivity—theory and practice of AVO analysis. In *Investigations in Geophysics,* vol. 8, pp. 287–302, eds. J. P. Castagna and M. M. Backus. Tulsa, Oklahoma: Society of Exploration Geophysicists, 1993.

Craig, J. R., F. M. Vokes, and T. N. Solberg. Pyrite: Physical and chemical textures. *Mineralium Deposita,* in press.

Craig, J. R., and J. D. Rimstidt. United States gold production history. *Ore Geol. Rev.* 13:407–64, 1998.

Vaughan, D. J., and **J. R. Craig.** Sulfide ore mineral stabilities, morphologies, and intergrowth textures. In *Geochemistry of Hydrothermal Ore Deposits,* 3rd ed., pp. 367–434, ed. H. L. Barnes. New York: John Wiley & Sons, 1996.

Craig, J. R., D. J. Vaughan, and B. J. Skinner. *Resources of the Earth: Origin, Use, and Environmental Impact,* 2nd ed. Upper Saddle River, New Jersey: Prentice Hall, Inc., 1996.

Groen, J. C., and **J. R. Craig.** The inorganic geochemistry of coal, petroleum, and their gasification combustion products. *Fuel Processing Technol.* 40:15–48, 1994.

Callahan, J. E., J. W. Miller, and **J. R. Craig.** Mercury pollution as a result of gold extraction in North Carolina, U.S.A. *Appl. Geochem.* 9:235–41, 1994.

Craig, J. R., and D. J. Vaughan. *Ore Microscopy and Ore Petrography,* 2nd ed. New York: Wiley Interscience, 1994.

Adkins, R. M., and **K. A. Eriksson.** Rhythmic sedimentation in a mid-Pennsylvanian delta front succession, Four Corners Formation (Breathitt Group), eastern Kentucky: A near complete record of daily, semi-monthly and monthly tidal periodicities. *SEPM Spec. Publ.,* in press.

Miller, D. J., and **K. A. Eriksson.** Linked sequence development and global climate change: The upper Mississippian record in the Appalachian basin. *Geology,* in press.

Eriksson, K. A., and E. L. Simpson. Precambrian eolianites: Preservational bias? *Sedimentary Geol.* 120:275–94, 1998.

Eriksson, K. A., B. Krapez, and P. W. Fralick. Sedimentology aspects of greenstone belts. In *Tectonic Evolution of Greenstone Belts,* pp. 33–54, eds. M. J. de Wit and L. Ashwal. Oxford: Oxford University Press, 1997.

Miller, D. J., and **K. A. Eriksson.** Late Mississippian prodeltaic rhythmites in the Appalachian basin: A hierarchical record of tidal and climatic periodicities. *J. Sediment. Res.* B67:653–60, 1997.

Junta-Rosso, J., **M. F. Hochella Jr.,** and J. D. Rimstidt. Linking microscopic and macroscopic data for heterogeneous reactions illustrated by the oxidation of manganese (II) at mineral surfaces. *Geochim. Cosmochim. Acta* 61:149–59, 1997.

Becker, U., **M. F. Hochella Jr.,** and D. Vaughan. The adsorption of gold to galena surfaces: Calculations of adsorption/reduction energies, reaction mechanisms XPS spectra, and STM images. *Geochim. Cosmochim. Acta* 61:3565–85, 1997.

Barron, V., N. Galvez, **M. F. Hochella Jr.,** and J. Torrent. Epitaxial

Virginia Polytechnic Institute and State University

Selected Publications (continued)

overgrowth of goethite on hematite synthesized in phosphate media: A scanning force and transmission electron microscopy study. *Am. Mineral.* 82:1091–100, 1997.

Hochella, M. F., Jr., and J. Banfield. Chemical weathering of silicates in nature: A microscopic perspective with theoretical considerations. In *Chemical Weathering Rates of Silicate Minerals,* eds. A. White and S. Brantley. *Rev. Mineral.* 31:353–406, 1995.

Hochella, M. F., Jr. Mineralogy scratches new surfaces. *Geotimes* 40:16–8, 1995.

Hochella, M. F., Jr. Mineral surfaces: Characterization methods, and their chemical, physical, and reactive nature. In *Mineral Surfaces,* pp. 17–60, eds. D. Vaughan and R. Pattrick. London: Chapman and Hall, 1994.

Hole, J. A., B. C. Beaudoin, and T. J. Henstock. Wide-angle seismic constraints on the evolution of the deep San Andreas plate boundary by Mendocino triple junction migration. *Tectonics* 17:802–18, 1998.

Henstock, T. J., A. Levander, and **J. A. Hole.** Deformation in the lower crust of the San Andreas Fault system in northern California. *Science* 278:650–3, 1997.

Hole, J. A., H. Thybo, and S. L. Klemperer. Seismic reflections from the near-vertical San Andreas Fault. *Geophys. Res. Lett.* 23:237–40, 1996.

Hole, J. A., and B. C. Zelt. 3-D finite-difference reflection travel times. *Geophys. J. Int.* 121:427–34, 1995.

Hole, J. A. Nonlinear high-resolution three-dimensional seismic travel time tomography. *J. Geophys. Res.* 97:6553–62, 1992.

Imhof, M. G., and M. N. Toksöz. Acousto-elastic multiple scattering: A comparison of ultrasonic experiments with multiple multipole expansion. *J. Acoust. Soc. Am.* 101(4):1836–46, 1997.

Imhof, M. G. Scattering of acoustic and elastic waves using a hybrid multiple multipole expansions—Finite element technique. *J. Acoust. Soc. Am.* 100(3):1325–38, 1996.

Imhof, M. G. Multiple multipole expansions for acoustic scattering. *J. Acoust. Soc. Am.* 97(2):754–63, 1995.

Kowalewski, M., A. Dulai, and F. T. Fuersich. A fossil record full of holes: The Phaneorozoic history of drilling predation. *Geology* 26:1091–4.

Kowalewski, M., G. A. Goodfriend, and K. W. Flessa. The high-resolution estimates of temporal mixing in shell beds: The evils and virtues of time-averaging. *Paleobiology* 24:287–304, 1998.

Kowalewski, M., et al. The phentic discrimination of biometric simpletons: Paleobiological implications of morphospecies in the lingulide brachiopod Glottidia. *Paleobiology* 23:444–69, 1997.

Kowalewski, M., and K. W. Flessa. The fossil record of lingulide brachiopods and the nature of taphonomic megabiases. *Geology* 24:977–80, 1996.

Kowalewski, M. Time-averaging, overcompletness and the geological record. *J. Geol.* 104:317–26, 1996.

Morgan, S. S., **R. D. Law,** and M. W. Nyman. Lacolith-like emplacement model for the Papoose Flat pluton based on porphyroblast-matrix analysis. *Geol. Soc. Am. Bull.* 110:96–110, 1998.

Nyman, M. W., **R. D. Law,** and S. S. Morgan. Conditions of contact metamorphism, Papoose Flat pluton, eastern California, U.S.A.: Implications for cooling and strain histories. *J. Metamorph. Geol.* 13:627–43, 1995.

Law, R. D., E. L. Miller, T. A. Little, and J. Lee. Extensional origin of ductile fabrics in the Schist Belt, Central Brooks Range, Alaska. Part 2: Microstructural and petrofabric evidence. *J. Struct. Geol.* 16:919–40, 1994.

Read, J. F. Overview of carbonate platform sequences, cycle stratigraphy and reservoirs in greenhouse and icehouse worlds. In *Milankovitch Sea Level Changes, Cycles and Reservoirs on Carbonate Platforms in Greenhouse and Icehouse Worlds, SEPM Short Course Notes,* no. 35, pp. 1–102, eds. J. F. Read et al., 1995.

Read, J. F., and A. D. Horbury. Eustatic and tectonic controls on porosity evolution beneath sequence bounding unconformities and parasequence disconformities on carbonate platforms. In *Diagenesis and Basin Development, AAPG Studies in Geology,* vol. 36, pp. 155–97, eds. A. D. Horbury and A. G. Robinson, 1993.

Montanez, I. P., and **J. F. Read.** Fluid rock interaction history during stabilization of early dolomites, Upper Knox Group (Lower Ordovician), US Appalachians. *J. Sedimentary Petrol.* 62:753–78, 1992.

Read, J. F. Carbonate platform models. *AAPG Bull.* 69:1–21, 1985.

Rimstidt, J. D., and W. D. Newcomb. Measurement and analysis of rate data: The rate of reaction of ferric iron with pyrite. *Geochim. Cosmochim. Acta* 57:1919–34, 1993.

Rimstidt, J. D., and H. L. Barnes. The kinetics of silica-water reactions. *Geochim. Cosmochim. Acta* 44:1683–99, 1989.

Chermak, J. A., and **J. D. Rimstidt.** Estimating the thermodynamic properties (G and H) of silicate minerals at 298 K from the sum of polyhedral contributions. *Am. Mineral.* 74:1023–31, 1989.

Sinha, A. K., D. A. Hewitt, and **J. D. Rimstidt.** Metamorphic petrology and isotope geochemistry associated with the development of mylonites. In *Frontiers in Petrology,* vol. 288-A, pp. 115–47, eds. A. K. Sinha and D. A. Hewitt. *Am J. Sci. Spec.,* 1988.

Schreiber, M. E, G. R. Moline, and J. M. Bahr. Hydrochemical facies analysis to delineate groundwater flowpaths in fractured media. *Ground Water Monitoring Remediation* 19(1):95–109, 1999.

Moline, G. R., **M. E. Schreiber,** and J. M. Bahr. Representative groundwater monitoring in fractured porous systems. *J. Environ. Eng.* 124(6):530–8, 1998.

Schreiber, M. E., et al. Field and laboratory studies of BTEX bioremediation under denitrifying conditions. In *Proceedings of the Fourth International Symposium on In Situ and On-Site Bioremediation.* 5:13–8, 1997.

Sinha, A. K., D. M. Wayne, and B. Hanan. U-Pb zercon age and petrogeneses of the Baltimore Mafic Complex, Maryland Piedmont. In *The Nature of Magmatism in the Appalachian Orogen,* eds. A. K. Sinha, J. B. Whalen, and J. Hogan. *Geol. Soc. Am. Mem.* 191:275–86, 1997.

Sinha, A. K., J. P. Hogan, and J. Parks. Lead isotope mapping of crustal reservoirs within the Grenville superterrane: I Central and southern Appalachians. *Am. Geophys. Union Monograph* 95:293–305, 1996.

Condie, K. C., and **A. K. Sinha.** Rare earth and other trace element mobility during mylonitization: A comparison of the Brevard and Hope Valley shear zones in the Appalachian Mountains, U.S.A. *J. Metamorph. Geol.* 14:213–26, 1996.

Sinha, A. K., D. M. Wayne, and D. A. Hewitt. The hydrothermal stability of zircon: Preliminary experimental and isotopic studies. *Geochim. Cosmochim. Acta* 56:3551–60, 1992.

Huang, S., I. S. Sacks, and **J. A. Snoke.** Topographic and seismic effects of long-term coupling between the subducting and overriding plates beneath northeast Japan. *Tectonophysics* 269:279–97, 1997.

Snoke, J. A., and D. E. James. Lithospheric structure of the Chaco and Paran and acute basins of South America from surface-wave inversion. *J. Geophys. Res.* 102:2939–51, 1997.

Norabuena, E. O., **J. A. Snoke,** and D. E. James. Structure of the subducting Nazca plate beneath Peru. *J. Geophys. Res.* 99:9215–26, 1994.

Taylor, D. W. A., **J. A. Snoke,** I. S. Sacks, and T. Takarami. Seismic quiescence before the Urakawa-Oki earthquake. *Bull. Seism. Soc. Am.* 81(4):1255–71, 1991.

Snoke, J. A. Stable determinations of (Brune) stress drops. *Bull. Seism. Soc. Am.* 77:530–8, 1987.

Spotila, J. A., K. A. Farley, and K. Sieh. Uplift and erosion of the San Bernardino Mountains associated with transpression along the San Andreas fault, California, as constrained by radiogenic helium thermochronometry. *Tectonics* 17:360–78, 1998.

Blatt, H., and **R. J. Tracy.** *Petrology: Igneous, Sedimentary and Metamorphic.* New York: W. H. Freeman, 1996.

Winslow, D. M., R. J. Bodnar, and **R. J. Tracy.** Fluid inclusion evidence for an anti-clockwise P-T path in the CMT, central Massachusetts. *J. Metamorph. Geol.* 12:361–71, 1994.

Nyman, M. W., and **R. J. Tracy.** Petrologic evolution of amphibolite shear zones, Cheyenne Belt, southeastern Wyoming. *J. Metamorph.Geol.* 11:757–73, 1993.

YALE UNIVERSITY

Department of Geology and Geophysics

Programs of Study

The Department of Geology and Geophysics offers instruction and opportunities for research leading to the Ph.D. degree in a broad range of earth sciences. Fields represented in the department include geochemistry, geophysics, structural geology, tectonics, paleontology, petrology, and oceans and atmosphere. Requirements for admission are flexible, but adequate preparation in the related sciences of physics, chemistry, mathematics, and biology is important for graduate study in geology and geophysics. Those with majors in another science are encouraged to apply. The program includes course work during the first two years, a comprehensive qualifying examination in the area of specialty in the middle of the second year, research on a dissertation topic, and the completion and oral defense of the dissertation. The average time for completion is about six years; at least three full years in residence are required. All entering graduate students are advised by a faculty committee selected by the student and the Director of Graduate Studies. Generally, 3 to 8 new students are admitted each year; approximately 25 students are currently enrolled.

Research Facilities

The department is located in the modern Kline Geology Laboratory adjacent to Yale's Peabody Museum of Natural History. This building occupies approximately 100,000 square feet and contains laboratories for research in geophysical fluid dynamics, geophysics, geochemistry, structural geology, and experimental petrology. Laboratories are fully equipped with microscopes, instrumentation, and extensive computer facilities, including a state-of-the-art electron microprobe, mass spectrometers, an X-ray diffractometer, an AA/AE spectrophotometer, and equipment for measurement of mineral surface reaction kinetics. Computational facilities include thirty-four UNIX workstations (DEC, Sun, and Silicon Graphics machines), numerous personal computers, and network connections to parallel-processing computers elsewhere on campus and supercomputers off campus. Also available in the Peabody Museum is one of the world's most important collections of fossil vertebrates, invertebrates, and minerals. The Geology Library is located in the department and contains more than 112,000 volumes and 181,000 maps. The Kline Science Library is nearby.

Financial Aid

All entering students are guaranteed a four-year scholarship that includes a stipend for living expenses (currently $16,680 per year) and tuition. In addition, each student is given a budget of $2000 for travel and scientific conferences in the first two years. After the fourth year, if not sooner, students are typically supported by a research grant or fellowship.

Cost of Study

All students are guaranteed a four-year scholarship, as stated above. Enrollment includes coverage in the University health plan. Spouses and dependents may be enrolled in the health plan for an additional fee.

Living and Housing Costs

Most students live in the attractive residential neighborhood adjacent to the Kline Geology Laboratory. Rooms are available to single students in the Hall of Graduate Studies and Helen Hadley Hall for $3810 to $4530 for the academic year. Additional rooms for single students are available in small residence halls in other nearby locations. The University maintains a number of housing units for married students, ranging from efficiency apartments ($500–$570 per month) to one-, two-, and three-bedroom apartments ($560–$800 per month).

Student Group

Graduate education at Yale is directed toward training the next generation of scholars. The Department of Geology and Geophysics has a diverse Ph.D. program that draws top students from North America and abroad. There are currently 21 full-time graduate students and 35 undergraduate majors. The Dana Club (the graduate student club named after James Dwight Dana) sponsors student activities and social events and consults with the faculty.

Location

The Kline Geology Laboratory is located on Science Hill, which is next to Yale's central campus and close to downtown New Haven. Located on the north shore of Long Island Sound, New Haven is approximately 90 miles from New York City and 150 miles from Boston. Recreational activities include boating, sailing, swimming, fishing, hiking, cycling, and (nearby) skiing. New Haven and Hartford (40 miles away) feature frequent sports events, concerts, theater, ballet, and films.

The University

Yale was founded in 1701 and began offering graduate education in 1847. The Graduate School is one of twelve schools constituting the University. Yale was the first university in North America to award the Ph.D. degree, conferring three in 1861. The University community consists of approximately 5,000 undergraduates, 6,000 students in the various graduate and professional schools, 1,500 faculty members, and hundreds of supporting research staff members. Among the facilities for research and study, beyond those of the department, are the University Library (with more than 6 million volumes), the Beinecke Rare Book and Manuscript Library, the Becton Engineering and Applied Science Center, the Arthur W. Wright Nuclear Structure Laboratory, the Peabody Museum of Natural History, and many other laboratories in various science departments, the School of Medicine, and the School of Forestry and Environmental Studies. Interdepartmental and interdisciplinary study is encouraged throughout the University.

Applying

Inquiries should be made directly to the Department of Geology and Geophysics, Director of Graduate Studies. Applications for admission should be submitted by January 3 to the Office of Admissions, Graduate School, Yale University, Box 1504A Yale Station, New Haven, Connecticut 06520. Scores on the General Test of the Graduate Record Examinations are required, and the examination should be taken before December; applicants are encouraged but not required to submit GRE Subject Test scores. The TOEFL is required for all applicants for whom English is a second language.

Correspondence and Information

Director of Graduate Studies
Department of Geology and Geophysics
Box 208109
Yale University
New Haven, Connecticut 06520-8109
E-mail: dgs@geology.yale.edu
World Wide Web: http://www.yale.edu/geology

Yale University

THE FACULTY AND THEIR RESEARCH

Jay Ague, Associate Professor. Igneous and metamorphic petrology, crustal metamorphism, genesis of granitic batholiths.

Robert Berner, Alan M. Bateman Professor. Earth surface geochemistry cycles.

Mark Brandon, Associate Professor and Director of Graduate Studies. Tectonic evolution of convergent margins, low-temperature deformation, circum-Pacific tectonics.

Leo Buss, Adjunct Professor and Professor of Biology. Evolutionary biology and paleobiology.

Jacques Gauthier, Professor. Vertebrate paleontology, evolution of reptiles, phylogenetic systematics.

Robert Gordon, Professor of Geophysics and Applied Mechanics. Mechanics of earth materials and surficial processes, utilization of earth resources.

Thomas Graedel, Adjunct Professor and Professor of Forestry and Environmental Studies. Atmospheric chemistry, industrial ecology.

Leo Hickey, Professor. Paleobotany, evolution of flowering plants, Cretaceous and Tertiary climates.

Phillip Ihinger, Lecturer. Igneous petrology, hotspot magmatism, volatiles in silicate melts.

Antonio Lasaga, Professor. Theoretical and experimental geochemistry; kinetics, coupled reactions, and transport in geochemical systems.

Jonathan Lees, Associate Professor. Earthquake and crustal seismology; tomographic imaging of fault zones and volcanoes.

Jeffrey Park, Associate Professor and Director of Undergraduate Studies. Global seismology, mantle anisotrophy, geologic time-series analysis.

Neil Ribe, Professor. Mantle convection, global geodynamics.

Danny Rye, Professor and Chairman. Isotope geochemistry related to ore deposits, metamorphic rocks, and paleoenvironments.

Barry Saltzman, Professor. Dynamical meteorology, theory of climate.

Adolf Seilacher, Adjunct Professor. Latest Precambrian and Paleozoic trace fossils, taphonomy, and morphology.

Brian Skinner, Eugene Higgins Professor. Geochemistry of mineral deposits, sulfide mineralogy.

Ronald B. Smith, Professor and Adjunct Professor of Mechanical Engineering and Director, Center for Earth Observation. Geophysical fluid dynamics, dynamical meteorology, remote sensing.

Karl Turekian, Silliman Professor and Director, Center for the Study of Global Change. Geochemistry of the earth's surface, oceans, and atmosphere; planetary evolution.

George Veronis, Henry Barnard Davis Professor of Geophysics and Applied Science. Physical oceanography, geophysical fluid dynamics.

Elisabeth S. Vrba, Professor and Adjunct Professor of Biology. Evolutionary paleobiology, vertebrate paleotology, evolution of mammals, phylogenetic systematics, evolutionary theory.

Wendell Welch, Lecturer. Large-scale and meoscale atmospheric dynamics.

Professors Emeriti

Sydney P. Clark Jr., Sidney J. Weinberg Professor of Geophysics Emeritus. Constitution of the earth's interior, heat flow and the thermal state of the earth.

John H. Ostrom, Professor of Geology and Geophysics Emeritus. Functional morphology; evolution and paleoecology of ancient reptiles, particularly archosaurs.

John Rodgers, Silliman Professor of Geology Emeritus. Structural and regional geology of mountain ranges.

Karl M. Waage, Alan M. Bateman Professor of Geology Emeritus. Invertebrate paleontology and stratigraphy, Mesozoic paleoenvironments.

Associates

Edward Bolton, Associate Research Scientist. Geophysical fluid dynamics, coupled modeling of geochemical systems.

Mark Davis, Associate Research Scientist. Experimental petrology.

James Eckert, Associate Research Scientist. Petrology.

John Kingston, Anthropologist.

Vadim Levin, Associate Research Scientist. Seismology.

Postdoctoral Associates

Joydeep Bhattacharyya. Seismology.

Edouard Kaminsky. Geophysical fluid dynamics.

Zavareh Kothavala. Climatology.

Prasad Thenkabail. Remote sensing.

Postdoctoral Fellows

Geoffrey Batt. Tectonics and dynamic modeling.

Ruth Blake. Geomicrobiology and isotope geochemistry.

Christopher Carson. Metamorphic petrology.

Denis Cohen. Glaciology.

Research Affiliates

Dorothy Koch. Atmospheric chemistry, climate modeling.

Mikhail Verbitsky. Climate modeling.

Section 4
Marine Sciences and Oceanography

This section contains a directory of institutions offering graduate work in marine sciences and oceanography, followed by in-depth entries submitted by institutions that chose to prepare detailed program descriptions. Additional information about programs listed in the directory but not augmented by an in-depth entry may be obtained by writing directly to the dean of a graduate school or chair of a department at the address given in the directory.

For programs offering related work, see also in this book Chemistry, Geosciences, Meteorology and Atmospheric Sciences, and Physics. In Book 3, see Biological and Biomedical Sciences; Ecology, Environmental Biology, and Evolutionary Biology; and Marine Biology; and in Book 5, see Civil and Environmental Engineering, Engineering and Applied Sciences, and Ocean Engineering.

CONTENTS

Marine Sciences

California State University, Fresno, Division of Graduate Studies, School of Natural Sciences, Program in Marine Sciences, Fresno, CA 93740-0057. Offers MS. Part-time programs available. Postbaccalaureate distance learning degree programs offered. *Faculty:* 10 full-time (1 woman), 6 part-time (1 woman). *Students:* 1 full-time (0 women), 2 part-time (1 woman); includes 1 minority (African American) Average age 31. 5 applicants, 60% accepted. In 1998, 3 degrees awarded. *Degree requirements:* For master's, thesis required, foreign language not required. *Entrance requirements:* For master's, GRE General Test, GRE Subject Test, TOEFL (minimum score of 550 required), minimum GPA of 3.0. *Application deadline:* For fall admission, 3/15 (priority date); for spring admission, 10/15. Applications are processed on a rolling basis. Application fee: $55. Electronic applications accepted. Tuition, nonresident: part-time $246 per unit. Required fees: $1,906; $620 per semester. *Financial aid:* Career-related internships or fieldwork, Federal Work-Study, scholarships, and unspecified assistantships available. Financial aid application deadline: 3/1; financial aid applicants required to submit FAFSA. *Faculty research:* Wetlands ecology, land/water conservation, water irrigation. *Unit head:* Dr. Thomas Mallory, Chair, 559-278-2001, Fax: 559-278-3936, E-mail: thomas_mallory@csufresno.edu. *Application contact:* Dr. Greg Calliet, Coordinator, 831-755-8656, E-mail: cailliet@mlml.calstate.edu.

California State University, Hayward, Graduate Programs, School of Science, Department of Biological Sciences, Moss Landing Marine Laboratory, Hayward, CA 94542-3000. Offers marine sciences (MS). *Faculty:* 9 full-time. 1 applicants, 0% accepted. In 1998, 1 degree awarded. *Degree requirements:* For master's, thesis required, foreign language not required. *Entrance requirements:* For master's, GRE Subject Test, minimum GPA of 3.0 in field, 2.75 overall. Application fee: $55. Tuition, nonresident: part-time $164 per unit. Required fees: $587 per quarter. *Financial aid:* Application deadline: 3/1. *Unit head:* Director, 408-633-3304. *Application contact:* Jennifer Rice, Graduate Program Assistant, 510-885-3286, Fax: 510-885-4795, E-mail: gradprograms@csuhayward.edu.

California State University, Sacramento, Graduate Studies, School of Natural Sciences and Mathematics, Department of Biological Sciences, Sacramento, CA 95819-6048. Offers biological sciences (MA, MS); immunohematology (MS); marine science (MS). Part-time programs available. *Degree requirements:* For master's, thesis, writing proficiency exam required, foreign language not required. *Entrance requirements:* For master's, TOEFL (minimum score of 550 required), bachelor's degree in biology or equivalent; minimum GPA of 3.0 in biology, 2.75 overall during previous 2 years. *Application deadline:* For fall admission, 4/15; for spring admission, 11/1. Application fee: $55. *Unit head:* Dr. Laurel Heffernan, Chair, 916-278-6535. *Application contact:* Dr. Michael Baad, Coordinator, 916-278-6494.

College of William and Mary, School of Marine Science/Virginia Institute of Marine Science, Gloucester Point, VA 23062. Offers MS, PhD. *Faculty:* 46 full-time (5 women). *Students:* 115 full-time (50 women), 10 part-time (4 women); includes 11 minority (3 African Americans, 4 Asian Americans or Pacific Islanders, 3 Hispanic Americans, 1 Native American), 8 international. Average age 27. 220 applicants, 22% accepted. In 1998, 9 master's, 4 doctorates awarded (75% entered university research/teaching, 25% found other work related to degree). *Degree requirements:* For master's and doctorate, one foreign language, thesis/dissertation, defense, qualifying exam required. *Entrance requirements:* For master's, GRE, TOEFL (minimum score of 550 required), appropriate bachelor's degree; for doctorate, GRE, TOEFL (minimum score of 550 required), appropriate master's degree. *Average time to degree:* Master's–3.42 years full-time; doctorate–7.17 years full-time. *Application deadline:* For fall admission, 2/1. Application fee: $30. *Financial aid:* In 1998–99, 25 fellowships, 92 research assistantships were awarded.; teaching assistantships, career-related internships or fieldwork and Federal Work-Study also available. Financial aid application deadline: 2/1. *Faculty research:* Physical, biological, geological, and chemical oceanography; marine fisheries science; resource management. Total annual research expenditures: $15.6 million. *Unit head:* Dr. L. Donelson Wright, Dean and Director, 804-684-7102, Fax: 804-684-7009, E-mail: wright@vims.edu. *Application contact:* Dr. John D. Milliman, Dean of Graduate Studies, 804-684-7105, Fax: 804-684-7097, E-mail: milliman@vims.edu.

See in-depth description on page 337.

Duke University, Nicholas School of the Environment, Durham, NC 27708-0328. Offers coastal environmental management (MEM); environmental science and policy (PhD); environmental toxicology, chemistry, and risk assessment (MEM); forest resource management (MF); resource ecology (MEM); resource economics and policy (MEM); water and air resources (MEM). PhD offered through the Graduate School. *Accreditation:* SAF (one or more programs are accredited). Part-time programs available. *Faculty:* 61 full-time (10 women), 23 part-time (3 women). *Students:* 228 full-time (136 women); includes 7 minority (2 African Americans, 4 Asian Americans or Pacific Islanders, 1 Hispanic American), 24 international. Average age 25. 400 applicants, 63% accepted. In 1998, 116 master's, 10 doctorates awarded. Terminal master's awarded for partial completion of doctoral program. *Degree requirements:* For master's, thesis required (for some programs), foreign language not required; for doctorate, dissertation required, foreign language not required. *Entrance requirements:* For master's, GRE General Test, TOEFL, previous course work in biology or ecology, calculus, statistics, and microeconomics; computer familiarity with word processing and data analysis; for doctorate, GRE General Test, TOEFL. *Average time to degree:* Master's–2 years full-time, 3 years part-time; doctorate–5 years full-time, 8 years part-time. *Application deadline:* For fall admission, 2/1; for spring admission, 10/15. Applications are processed on a rolling basis. Application fee: $75. *Financial aid:* In 1998–99, 29 fellowships (averaging $11,500 per year), 53 research assistantships (averaging $2,600 per year), 15 teaching assistantships (averaging $6,000 per year) were awarded.; career-related internships or fieldwork, Federal Work-Study, institutionally-sponsored loans, scholarships, and unspecified assistantships also available. Financial aid application deadline: 2/1; financial aid applicants required to submit FAFSA. *Faculty research:* Ecosystem management, conservation ecology, earth systems, risk assessment. *Unit head:* Dr. Norman L. Christensen, Dean, 919-613-8004, Fax: 919-684-8741. *Application contact:* Bertie S. Belvin, Associate Dean for Academic Services, 919-613-8070, Fax: 919-684-8741, E-mail: envadm@duke.edu.

Announcement: Two-year professional program provides excellent preparation for careers in coastal environmental management. Core courses emphasize coastal sedimentary and biological processes, ecology, economics, policy, and quantitative analytical methods. Program includes courses on the main Durham campus and at the Duke University Marine Laboratory located at Beaufort, North Carolina. See in-depth description in the Natural Resources section of this volume.

Florida Institute of Technology, Graduate School, College of Engineering, Division of Marine and Environmental Systems, Program in Oceanography, Melbourne, FL 32901-6975. Offers biological oceanography (MS); chemical oceanography (MS); coastal zone management (MS); geological oceanography (MS); oceanography (PhD); physical oceanography (MS). Part-time programs available. *Faculty:* 6 full-time (0 women), 5 part-time (1 woman). *Students:* 6 full-time (2 women), 28 part-time (10 women), 13 international. Terminal master's awarded for partial completion of doctoral program. *Degree requirements:* For master's, thesis required (for some programs), foreign language not required; for doctorate, one foreign language (computer language can substitute), dissertation, comprehensive and departmental qualifying exams required. *Entrance requirements:* For master's, GRE General Test, minimum GPA of 3.0; for doctorate, GRE General Test, minimum GPA of 3.2. *Application deadline:* Applications are processed on a rolling basis. Application fee: $50. Electronic applications accepted. Tuition: Part-time $575 per credit hour. Required fees: $100. Tuition and fees vary according to campus/location and program. *Unit head:* Dr. Dean R. Norris, Chair, 407-674-7377, Fax: 407-674-7212, E-mail: norris@marine.fit.edu. *Application contact:* Carolyn P. Farrior, Associate Dean of Graduate Admissions, 407-674-7118, Fax: 407-723-9468, E-mail: cfarrior@fit.edu.

See in-depth description on page 343.

Memorial University of Newfoundland, School of Graduate Studies, Interdisciplinary Program in Marine Studies, St. John's, NF A1C 5S7, Canada. Offers fisheries resource management (MMS). *Students:* 2 full-time (1 woman), 10 part-time (2 women). 12 applicants, 67% accepted. Application fee: $40. *Financial aid:* Fellowships, research assistantships, teaching assistantships available. *Unit head:* Dr. Peter Fisher, Chair, 709-778-0461, E-mail: pfisher@gill.ifmt.nf.ca.

Murray State University, College of Science, Department of Water Science, Murray, KY 42071-0009. Offers MS. Part-time programs available. *Students:* 3 full-time (1 woman), 3 part-time (1 woman). 2 applicants, 100% accepted. *Application deadline:* Applications are processed on a rolling basis. Application fee: $20. *Financial aid:* Application deadline: 4/1. *Unit head:* Dr. David White, Graduate Coordinator, 502-762-3194, E-mail: david.white@murraystate.edu.

North Carolina State University, Graduate School, College of Physical and Mathematical Sciences, Department of Marine, Earth, and Atmospheric Sciences, Raleigh, NC 27695. Offers geology (MS, PhD); geophysics (MS, PhD); marine, earth, and atmospheric sciences (MS, PhD); meteorology (MS, PhD); oceanography (MS, PhD). *Faculty:* 34 full-time (2 women), 39 part-time (1 woman). *Students:* 118 full-time (30 women), 12 part-time (3 women); includes 2 minority (both Asian Americans or Pacific Islanders), 37 international. Average age 30. 95 applicants, 52% accepted. In 1998, 17 master's, 12 doctorates awarded. Terminal master's awarded for partial completion of doctoral program. *Degree requirements:* For master's, thesis, final oral exam required, foreign language not required; for doctorate, dissertation, final oral exam, preliminary oral and written exams required, foreign language not required. *Entrance requirements:* For master's and doctorate, GRE General Test, minimum GPA of 3.0. *Application deadline:* For fall admission, 6/25 (priority date); for spring admission, 11/25. Applications are processed on a rolling basis. Application fee: $45. *Financial aid:* In 1998–99, 1 fellowship (averaging $4,504 per year), 84 research assistantships (averaging $3,877 per year), 30 teaching assistantships (averaging $3,678 per year) were awarded.; institutionally-sponsored loans also available. Financial aid application deadline: 3/1. *Faculty research:* Boundary layer and air quality meteorology; climate and mesoscale dynamics; biological, chemical, geological, and physical oceanography; hard rock, soft rock, environmental, and paleogeology. Total annual research expenditures: $8.8 million. *Unit head:* Dr. Leonard J. Pietrafesa, Head, 919-515-3717, Fax: 919-515-7802, E-mail: leonard_pietrafesa@ncsu.edu. *Application contact:* Dr. Gerald S. Janowitz, Director of Graduate Programs, 919-515-7837, Fax: 919-515-7802, E-mail: janowitz@ncsu.edu.

Nova Southeastern University, Oceanographic Center, Fort Lauderdale, FL 33314-7721. Offers coastal-zone management (MS); marine biology (MS); marine environmental science (MS); oceanography (PhD). Part-time and evening/weekend programs available. *Students:* 13 full-time (9 women), 59 part-time (30 women); includes 5 minority (1 Asian American or Pacific Islander, 3 Hispanic Americans, 1 Native American), 2 international. *Degree requirements:* For master's, thesis optional, foreign language not required; for doctorate, dissertation, departmental qualifying exam required. *Entrance requirements:* For master's, GRE General Test (minimum combined score of 1000 required); for doctorate, GRE General Test (minimum combined score of 1100 required), master's degree. *Application deadline:* Applications are processed on a rolling basis. Application fee: $50. Tuition: Part-time $417 per credit hour. Required fees: $50 per semester. Tuition and fees vary according to degree level and program. *Unit head:* Dr. Julian P. McCreary, Dean, 954-920-1909, Fax: 954-947-8559, E-mail: jay@ocean.nova.edu. *Application contact:* Dr. Richard Dodge, Associate Dean, 954-920-1909, Fax: 954-947-8559, E-mail: dodge@ocean.nova.edu.

See in-depth description on page 351.

Oregon State University, Graduate School, College of Oceanic and Atmospheric Sciences, Program in Marine Resource Management, Corvallis, OR 97331. Offers MA, MS. *Students:* 23 full-time (14 women), 1 (woman) part-time; includes 1 minority (Asian American or Pacific Islander), 3 international. Average age 28. In 1998, 7 degrees awarded. *Degree requirements:* For master's, thesis optional, foreign language not required. *Entrance requirements:* For master's, GRE General Test, TOEFL (minimum score of 550 required), minimum GPA of 3.0 in last 90 hours. *Application deadline:* For fall admission, 2/1 (priority date). Applications are processed on a rolling basis. Application fee: $50. *Financial aid:* Fellowships, research assistantships, teaching assistantships, career-related internships or fieldwork, Federal Work-Study, and institutionally-sponsored loans available. Aid available to part-time students. Financial aid application deadline: 2/1. *Faculty research:* Ocean and coastal resources, fisheries resources, marine pollution, marine recreation and tourism. *Unit head:* Jim W. Good, Coordinator, 541-737-1340, Fax: 541-737-2064, E-mail: good@oce.orst.edu. *Application contact:* Irma Delson, Assistant Director, Student Services, 541-737-5190, Fax: 541-737-2064, E-mail: student_adviser@oce.orst.edu.

San Jose State University, Graduate Studies, College of Science, Program in Marine Science, San Jose, CA 95192-0001. Offers MS. *Faculty:* 8 full-time (0 women), 14 part-time (0 women). *Students:* 4 full-time (all women), 28 part-time (14 women); includes 1 minority (Hispanic American), 1 international. Average age 32. 32 applicants, 34% accepted. In 1998, 7 degrees awarded. *Degree requirements:* For master's, thesis, qualifying exam required, foreign language not required. *Entrance requirements:* For master's, GRE. *Application deadline:* For fall admission, 6/1. Applications are processed on a rolling basis. Application fee: $59. Tuition, nonresident: part-time $246 per unit. Required fees: $1,939; $1,309 per year. *Financial aid:* Teaching assistantships, career-related internships or fieldwork available. Aid available to part-time students. *Faculty research:* Physical oceanography, marine geology, ecology, ichthyology, invertebrate zoology. *Unit head:* Dr. Kenneth Coale, Acting Director, 408-755-8671, Fax: 408-753-2826. *Application contact:* Gail Johnson, Administrative Assistant, 408-755-8650.

State University of New York at Stony Brook, Graduate School, Marine Sciences Research Center, Program in Marine Environmental Sciences, Stony Brook, NY 11794. Offers MS. Evening/weekend programs available. *Faculty:* 19 full-time (6 women), 1 (woman) part-time. *Students:* 58 full-time (35 women), 8 part-time (7 women); includes 3 minority (1 African American, 1 Asian American or Pacific Islander, 1 Hispanic American), 9 international. Average age 24. 54 applicants, 54% accepted. In 1998, 24 degrees awarded. *Degree requirements:* For master's, thesis, written comprehensive exam required, foreign language not required. *Entrance requirements:* For master's, GRE General Test, TOEFL (minimum score of 550 required), minimum GPA of 3.0. *Application deadline:* For fall admission, 1/15. Application fee: $50. *Financial aid:* Fellowships, research assistantships, teaching assistantships available. *Application contact:* Dr. Henry Bokuniewicz, Director, 516-632-8681, Fax: 516-632-8200, E-mail: hbokuniewicz@ccmail.sunysb.edu.

University of Alaska Fairbanks, Graduate School, School of Fisheries and Ocean Sciences, Program in Marine Sciences and Limnology, Fairbanks, AK 99775-7480. Offers marine biology (MS); oceanography (MS, PhD), including biological oceanography (PhD), chemical oceanography (PhD), fisheries (PhD), physical oceanography (PhD). *Faculty:* 9 full-time (1 woman), 2 part-time (0 women). *Students:* 37 full-time (25 women), 6 part-time (4 women); includes 2 minority (1 African American, 1 Asian American or Pacific Islander), 10 international. Average age 30. 27 applicants, 44% accepted. In 1998, 2 master's, 1 doctorate awarded. *Degree requirements:* For master's, thesis, comprehensive exam required, foreign language not required; for doctorate, one foreign language (computer language can substitute), dissertation, comprehensive exam required. *Entrance requirements:* For master's and doctorate, GRE General Test, TOEFL (minimum score of 550 required). *Application deadline:* For fall admission, 3/1 (priority date). Applications are processed on a rolling basis. Application fee: $35. *Financial aid:* Research assistantships, teaching assistantships available. *Unit head:* Dr. Susan Henrichs, Head, 907-474-7289.

University of California, San Diego, Graduate Studies and Research, Scripps Institution of Oceanography, La Jolla, CA 92093-5003. Offers biological oceanography (MS, PhD); geochemistry and marine chemistry (MS, PhD); marine biology (MS, PhD); physical oceanography and geological sciences (MS, PhD). *Faculty:* 73. *Students:* 170 (68 women). *Entrance requirements:* For master's and doctorate, GRE General Test, GRE Subject Test (marine biology). Application fee: $40. *Unit head:* W. Kendall Melville, Chair. *Application contact:* Yvonne Gaffney, Graduate Coordinator, 619-534-3206.

University of California, Santa Barbara, Graduate Division, College of Letters and Science, Division of Math, Life and Physical Science, Interdepartmental Program in Marine Science, Santa Barbara, CA 93106. Offers MS, PhD. *Students:* 9 full-time (5 women); includes 2 minority (both Asian Americans or Pacific Islanders) 9 applicants, 100% accepted. *Degree requirements:* For master's and doctorate, thesis/dissertation required, foreign language not required. *Entrance requirements:* For master's and doctorate, GRE, TOEFL (minimum score of 550 required). *Application deadline:* For fall admission, 12/15 (priority date). Application fee: $40. Electronic applications accepted. *Financial aid:* In 1998–99, 7 students received aid, including 1 fellowship, 5 research assistantships, 1 teaching assistantship; career-related internships or fieldwork, Federal Work-Study, institutionally-sponsored loans, and tuition waivers (full and partial) also available. Aid available to part-time students. Financial aid application deadline: 12/15; financial aid applicants required to submit FAFSA. *Faculty research:* Biological oceanography, paleoceanography, ocean physical processes, ecology of marine organisms, marine geophysics. *Unit head:* Alice Alldredge, Chair, 805-893-3997, E-mail: alldredg@lifesci.ucsb.edu. *Application contact:* Melanie Fujii-Abe, Graduate Program Assistant, 805-893-8162, E-mail: marinegp-gradasst@lifesci.ucsb.edu/.

See in-depth description on page 361.

University of California, Santa Cruz, Graduate Division, Division of Natural Sciences, Program in Marine Sciences, Santa Cruz, CA 95064. Offers MS. *Faculty:* 6 full-time. *Students:* 18 full-time (11 women), 1 international. 86 applicants, 35% accepted. In 1998, 7 degrees awarded. *Degree requirements:* For master's, thesis required. *Entrance requirements:* For master's, GRE General Test, GRE Subject Test. *Application deadline:* For fall admission, 1/15. Application fee: $40. *Financial aid:* Fellowships, research assistantships, teaching assistantships, career-related internships or fieldwork, Federal Work-Study, and institutionally-sponsored loans available. Financial aid application deadline: 1/15. *Faculty research:* Oceanography, biology of higher marine vertebrates, ecology of coastal zone, marine geology. *Unit head:* Dr. Margaret Delaney, Chairperson, 831-459-4736, E-mail: delaney@cats.ucsc.edu. *Application contact:* Graduate Admissions, 831-459-2301.

University of California, Santa Cruz, Graduate Division, Division of Natural Sciences, Program in Ocean Sciences, Santa Cruz, CA 95064. Offers PhD. *Faculty:* 6 full-time. *Students:* 6 full-time (3 women), 1 international. 21 applicants, 43% accepted. *Degree requirements:* For doctorate, dissertation required. *Entrance requirements:* For doctorate, GRE General Test, GRE Subject Test. *Application deadline:* For fall admission, 1/1. *Unit head:* Dr. Margaret Delaney, Chairperson, 831-423-9117, E-mail: delaney@cats.ucsc.edu. *Application contact:* Graduate Admissions, 831-459-2301.

University of Connecticut, Graduate School, College of Liberal Arts and Sciences, Field of Oceanography, Storrs, CT 06269. Offers MS, PhD. *Degree requirements:* For doctorate, dissertation required. *Entrance requirements:* For master's and doctorate, GRE General Test, GRE Subject Test, TOEFL.

University of Delaware, College of Marine Studies, Newark, DE 19716. Offers MMP, MS, PhD. *Faculty:* 30 full-time (2 women), 24 part-time (2 women). *Students:* 108 full-time (53 women), 7 part-time (2 women); includes 7 minority (3 Asian Americans or Pacific Islanders, 4 Hispanic Americans), 27 international. Average age 25. 126 applicants, 23% accepted. In 1998, 12 master's, 5 doctorates awarded. *Degree requirements:* For master's and doctorate, thesis/dissertation required, foreign language not required. *Entrance requirements:* For master's and doctorate, GRE General Test, GRE Subject Test. *Average time to degree:* Master's–2.75 years full-time; doctorate–4.6 years full-time. *Application deadline:* For fall admission, 3/1; for spring admission, 10/1. Applications are processed on a rolling basis. Application fee: $45. Electronic applications accepted. *Financial aid:* In 1998–99, 14 fellowships with full tuition reimbursements, 54 research assistantships with full tuition reimbursements were awarded.; teaching assistantships, career-related internships or fieldwork, Federal Work-Study, and tuition waivers (full and partial) also available. Financial aid application deadline: 4/1. *Faculty research:* Marine biology and biochemistry, oceanography, marine policy, physical ocean science and engineering. *Unit head:* Dr. Carolyn A. Thoroughgood, Dean, 302-831-2841. *Application contact:* Doris Manship, Academic Affairs Coordinator, 302-645-4226, Fax: 302-645-4007, E-mail: dmanship@udel.edu.

University of Florida, Graduate School, College of Agriculture, Department of Fisheries and Aquatic Science, Gainesville, FL 32611. Offers MFAS, MS, PhD. *Faculty:* 23. *Students:* 26 full-time (8 women), 12 part-time (5 women); includes 2 minority (both Hispanic Americans), 3 international. 34 applicants, 35% accepted. In 1998, 11 master's awarded. *Degree requirements:* For master's, thesis optional, foreign language not required; for doctorate, dissertation required, foreign language not required. *Entrance requirements:* For master's and doctorate, GRE General Test, TOEFL, minimum GPA of 3.0. *Application deadline:* For fall admission, 6/1. Applications are processed on a rolling basis. Application fee: $20. Electronic applications accepted. *Financial aid:* In 1998–99, 1 fellowship, 21 research assistantships were awarded.; unspecified assistantships also available. *Unit head:* Dr. Wallis H. Clark, Chair, 352-392-9617, Fax: 352-846-1088, E-mail: faa@gnv.ifas.ufl.edu. *Application contact:* Dr. Ed Philips, Graduate Coordinator, 352-392-9617 Ext. 248, Fax: 352-846-1088, E-mail: ejph@gnv.ifas.ufl.edu.

University of Georgia, Graduate School, College of Arts and Sciences, Department of Marine Sciences, Athens, GA 30602. Offers biological oceanography (MS, PhD); chemical oceanography (MS, PhD); physical oceanography (MS, PhD). *Faculty:* 16 full-time (4 women). *Students:* 24 full-time (10 women), 1 part-time. 59 applicants, 25% accepted. In 1998, 2 master's awarded. *Degree requirements:* For doctorate, dissertation required. *Entrance requirements:* For master's and doctorate, GRE General Test. *Application deadline:* For fall admission, 7/1 (priority date); for spring admission, 11/15. Application fee: $30. Electronic applications accepted. *Unit head:* Dr. Mary Ann Moran, Graduate Coordinator, 706-542-5863, Fax: 706-542-5888, E-mail: mmoran@arches.uga.edu.

See in-depth description on page 363.

University of Maine, Graduate School, College of Natural Sciences, Forestry, and Agriculture, School of Marine Sciences, Program in Marine Policy, Orono, ME 04469. Offers MS. *Students:* 3 (all women) 6 applicants, 83% accepted. *Degree requirements:* For master's, thesis required, foreign language not required. *Entrance requirements:* For master's, GRE General Test, GRE Subject Test, TOEFL (minimum score of 550 required). *Application deadline:* For fall admission, 2/1 (priority date); for spring admission, 10/15. Applications are processed on a rolling basis. Application fee: $50. *Financial aid:* Tuition waivers (full and partial) available. Financial aid application deadline: 3/1. *Unit head:* Dr. Melissa McDonald, Coordinator, 978-934-3683, E-mail: melissa_mcdonald@woods.uml.edu. *Application contact:* Scott G. Delcourt, Director of the Graduate School, 207-581-3218, Fax: 207-581-3232, E-mail: graduate@maine.edu.

University of Maryland, Graduate School, Program in Marine-Estuarine-Environmental Sciences (an intercampus, interdisciplinary program), Baltimore, MD 21201-1627. Offers MS, PhD. *Faculty:* 5 full-time (1 woman). *Students:* 4 (1 woman) 1 international. 4 applicants, 75% accepted. In 1998, 2 degrees awarded. *Degree requirements:* For master's, thesis required; for doctorate, dissertation, comprehensive exam, proposal defense required. *Entrance requirements:* For master's and doctorate, minimum GPA of 3.0. *Application deadline:* For fall admission, 3/1; for spring admission, 11/1. Application fee: $50. *Financial aid:* Research assistantships, teaching assistantships available. *Unit head:* Dr. Kennedy T. Paynter, Director, 301-405-6938.

University of Maryland, Baltimore County, Graduate School, Program in Marine-Estuarine-Environmental Sciences (an intercampus, interdisciplinary program), Baltimore, MD 21250-5398. Offers MS, PhD. *Faculty:* 15. *Students:* 8 full-time (6 women), 2 part-time (both women); includes 1 minority (Hispanic American), 1 international. 12 applicants, 33% accepted. In 1998, 1 doctorate awarded. *Degree requirements:* For master's, thesis required, foreign language not required; for doctorate, dissertation, comprehensive exam, proposal defense required, foreign language not required. *Entrance requirements:* For master's and doctorate, GRE General Test, TOEFL, minimum GPA of 3.0. *Application deadline:* For fall admission, 3/1; for spring admission, 11/1. Applications are processed on a rolling basis. Application fee: $45. Electronic applications accepted. *Financial aid:* Fellowships, research assistantships with tuition reimbursements, teaching assistantships with tuition reimbursements, career-related internships or fieldwork available. *Unit head:* Dr. Kennedy T. Paynter, Director, 301-405-6938, Fax: 301-314-4139, E-mail: mees@mees.umd.edu. *Application contact:* Dr. Kennedy T. Paynter, Director, 301-405-6938, Fax: 301-314-4139, E-mail: mees@mees.umd.edu.

University of Maryland, College Park, Graduate School, College of Life Sciences, Program in Marine-Estuarine-Environmental Sciences (an intercampus, interdisciplinary program), College Park, MD 20742-5045. Offers MS, PhD. Part-time programs available. *Faculty:* 138. *Students:* 219 (104 women); includes 14 minority (3 African Americans, 5 Asian Americans or Pacific Islanders, 5 Hispanic Americans, 1 Native American) 45 international. 243 applicants, 37% accepted. In 1998, 16 master's, 17 doctorates awarded. Terminal master's awarded for partial completion of doctoral program. *Degree requirements:* For master's, thesis required; for doctorate, dissertation, comprehensive exam, proposal defense required. *Entrance requirements:* For master's and doctorate, GRE General Test, minimum GPA of 3.0. *Application deadline:* For fall admission, 3/1; for spring admission, 11/1. Applications are processed on a rolling basis. Application fee: $70. Electronic applications accepted. Tuition, state resident: part-time $272 per credit hour. Tuition, nonresident: part-time $475 per credit hour. Required fees: $632; $379 per year. *Financial aid:* In 1998–99, 1 fellowship with full tuition reimbursement (averaging $5,000 per year), 3 teaching assistantships with tuition reimbursements (averaging $12,903 per year) were awarded.; research assistantships, Federal Work-Study, grants, and scholarships also available. Aid available to part-time students. Financial aid applicants required to submit FAFSA. *Faculty research:* Marine and estuarine organisms, terrestrial and freshwater ecology, remote environmental sensing. *Unit head:* Dr. Kennedy T. Paynter, Director, 301-405-6938, Fax: 301-314-4139, E-mail: mees@mees.umd.edu. *Application contact:* 301-405-6938, Fax: 301-314-4139, E-mail: meesgrad@mees.umd.edu.

See in-depth description on page 367.

University of Massachusetts Boston, Graduate Studies, College of Arts and Sciences, Faculty of Sciences, Program in Environmental, Coastal and Ocean Sciences, Track in Environmental, Coastal and Ocean Sciences, Boston, MA 02125-3393. Offers PhD. *Degree requirements:* For doctorate, dissertation, comprehensive exams required, foreign language not required. *Entrance requirements:* For doctorate, GRE General Test, minimum GPA of 2.75.

University of Miami, Graduate School, Rosenstiel School of Marine and Atmospheric Science, Division of Applied Marine Physics, Coral Gables, FL 33124. Offers applied marine physics (MA, MS, PhD), including coastal ocean circulation dynamics (MS, PhD), dynamics and air-sea interaction physics (MA), ocean acoustics and geoacoustics (PhD), ocean acoustics and geoacoutics (MA), small-scale ocean surface (MA), small-scale ocean surface dynamics and air-sea interaction physics (PhD); ocean engineering (MS). Part-time programs available. *Faculty:* 11. *Students:* 10 full-time (0 women), 5 international. Average age 30. 9 applicants, 44% accepted. In 1998, 1 master's, 2 doctorates awarded. Terminal master's awarded for partial completion of doctoral program. *Degree requirements:* For master's and doctorate, thesis/dissertation required, foreign language not required. *Entrance requirements:* For master's and doctorate, GRE General Test, TOEFL (minimum score of 550 required). *Average time to degree:* Master's–3 years full-time; doctorate–6 years full-time. *Application deadline:* For fall admission, 2/1 (priority date). Applications are processed on a rolling basis. Application fee: $35. Electronic applications accepted. Tuition: Full-time $15,336; part-time $852 per credit. Required fees: $174. Tuition and fees vary according to program. *Financial aid:* In 1998–99, 10 students received aid, including 2 fellowships with tuition reimbursements available, 4 research assistantships with tuition reimbursements available (averaging $17,000 per year), teaching assistantships with tuition reimbursements available (averaging $17,000 per year); institutionally-sponsored loans also available. Financial aid application deadline: 2/1. Total annual research expenditures: $2.5 million. *Unit head:* Dr. Harry A. De Ferrari, Chair, 305-361-4644, Fax: 305-261-4701. *Application contact:* Dr. Frank Millero, Associate Dean, 305-361-4155, Fax: 305-361-4771, E-mail: gso@rsmas.miami.edu.

University of Miami, Graduate School, Rosenstiel School of Marine and Atmospheric Science, Division of Marine Affairs, Coral Gables, FL 33124. Offers MA, MS, JD/MA. Part-time programs available. *Faculty:* 6 full-time (1 woman). *Students:* 29 full-time (13 women), 8 part-time (7 women). Average age 25. 41 applicants, 73% accepted. In 1998, 11 degrees awarded. *Degree requirements:* For master's, thesis (for some programs), internship, paper required, foreign language not required. *Entrance requirements:* For master's, GRE General Test, TOEFL (minimum score of 550 required). *Average time to degree:* Master's–1.5 years full-time, 3 years part-time. *Application deadline:* For fall admission, 2/1 (priority date). Applications are processed on a rolling basis. Application fee: $35. Electronic applications accepted. Tuition: Full-time $15,336; part-time $852 per credit. Required fees: $174. Tuition and fees vary according to program. *Financial aid:* In 1998–99, 4 students received aid, including 2 fellowships with partial tuition reimbursements available (averaging $5,000 per year), 2 teaching assistantships (averaging $5,000 per year); research assistantships, career-related internships or fieldwork, Federal Work-Study, and institutionally-sponsored loans also available. Financial aid application deadline: 3/1; financial aid applicants required to submit FAFSA. *Unit head:* Sarah Meltzoff, Chair, 305-361-4085. *Application contact:* Dr. Frank Millero, Associate Dean, 305-361-4155, Fax: 305-361-4771, E-mail: gso@rsmas.miami.edu.

University of Miami, Graduate School, Rosenstiel School of Marine and Atmospheric Science, Division of Marine and Atmospheric Chemistry, Coral Gables, FL 33124. Offers MA, MS, PhD. *Faculty:* 14 full-time (2 women). *Students:* 10 full-time (4 women), 5 international. Average age 25. 21 applicants, 29% accepted. In 1998, 3 master's, 2 doctorates awarded. Terminal master's awarded for partial completion of doctoral program. *Degree requirements:* For master's and doctorate, thesis/dissertation required. *Entrance requirements:* For master's and doctorate, GRE General Test, TOEFL (minimum score of 550 required). *Average time to degree:* Master's–3 years full-time; doctorate–6 years full-time. *Application deadline:* For fall admission, 2/1 (priority date). Applications are processed on a rolling basis. Application fee: $35. Electronic applications accepted. Tuition: Full-time $15,336; part-time $852 per credit. Required fees: $174. Tuition and fees vary according to program. *Financial aid:* In 1998–99, 8 students received aid, including 1 fellowship with tuition reimbursement available, 7 research assistantships with tuition reimbursements available (averaging $17,000 per year), teaching assistantships with tuition reimbursements available (averaging $17,000 per year); institutionally-sponsored loans also available. Financial aid application deadline: 2/1. *Faculty research:* Global change issues, chemistry of marine waters and marine atmosphere. Total annual research expenditures: $4 million. *Unit head:* Dr. Rod Zika, Chairperson, 305-361-4722, Fax: 305-361-4689. *Application contact:* Dr. Frank Millero, Associate Dean, 305-361-4155, Fax: 305-361-4771, E-mail: gso@rsmas.miami.edu.

The University of North Carolina at Chapel Hill, Graduate School, College of Arts and Sciences, Curriculum in Marine Sciences, Chapel Hill, NC 27599. Offers MS, PhD. *Degree requirements:* For master's, thesis, comprehensive exam required, foreign language not required; for doctorate, dissertation, comprehensive exam required. *Entrance requirements:* For master's

Marine Sciences–Oceanography

The University of North Carolina at Chapel Hill (continued)
and doctorate, GRE General Test (minimum combined score of 1000 required), GRE Subject Test, minimum GPA of 3.0.

University of Puerto Rico, Mayagüez Campus, Graduate Studies, College of Arts and Sciences, Department of Marine Sciences, Mayagüez, PR 00681-5000. Offers biological oceanography (MMS, PhD); chemical oceanography (MMS, PhD); geological oceanography (MMS, PhD); physical oceanography (MMS, PhD). *Degree requirements:* For master's, one foreign language, thesis, departmental and comprehensive final exams required; for doctorate, one foreign language, dissertation, qualifying, comprehensive, and final exams required. *Faculty research:* Marine botany, ecology, chemistry, and parasitology; fisheries; ichthyology; aquaculture.

See in-depth description on page 369.

University of San Diego, College of Arts and Sciences, Program in Marine and Environmental Studies, San Diego, CA 92110-2492. Offers marine science (MS). Part-time programs available. *Faculty:* 5 full-time (3 women), 9 part-time (3 women). *Students:* 30 (15 women); includes 4 minority (1 Asian American or Pacific Islander, 2 Hispanic Americans, 1 Native American) 2 international. Average age 25. 23 applicants, 70% accepted. In 1998, 7 degrees awarded. *Degree requirements:* For master's, thesis required, foreign language not required. *Entrance requirements:* For master's, GRE, TOEFL (minimum score of 580 required), TWE (minimum score of 4.5 required), minimum GPA of 3.0, undergraduate major in science. *Application deadline:* For fall admission, 5/1 (priority date). Applications are processed on a rolling basis. Application fee: $45. Tuition: Part-time $630 per unit. Tuition and fees vary according to degree level. *Financial aid:* Fellowships with partial tuition reimbursements, teaching assistantships with partial tuition reimbursements, career-related internships or fieldwork, Federal Work-Study, institutionally-sponsored loans, tuition waivers (partial), and unspecified assistantships available. Aid available to part-time students. Financial aid application deadline: 5/1; financial aid applicants required to submit FAFSA. *Faculty research:* Marine ecology; paleoclimatology; geochemistry; functional morphology; marine zoology of mammals, birds and turtles. *Unit head:* Dr. Hugh I. Ellis, Director, 619-260-4075, Fax: 619-260-6804, E-mail: ellis@acusd.edu. *Application contact:* Mary Jane Tiernan, Director of Graduate Admissions, 619-260-4524, Fax: 619-260-4158, E-mail: grads@acusd.edu.

University of South Alabama, Graduate School, College of Arts and Sciences, Department of Marine Sciences, Mobile, AL 36688-0002. Offers MS, PhD. *Faculty:* 3 full-time (0 women). *Students:* 27 full-time (13 women), 17 part-time (5 women), 1 international. 36 applicants, 56% accepted. In 1998, 3 master's, 1 doctorate awarded. *Degree requirements:* For master's, comprehensive exam required; for doctorate, one foreign language (computer language can substitute), dissertation, comprehensive exam, research project required. *Entrance requirements:* For master's, GRE, minimum GPA of 3.0. *Application deadline:* For fall admission, 9/1 (priority date). Applications are processed on a rolling basis. Application fee: $25. Tuition, state resident: part-time $116 per semester hour. Tuition, nonresident: part-time $230 per semester hour. Required fees: $121 per semester. Part-time tuition and fees vary according to course load and program. *Financial aid:* In 1998–99, 7 fellowships, 4 research assistantships were awarded. Financial aid application deadline: 4/1. *Unit head:* Dr. Robert Shipp, Chair, 334-460-7136.

University of South Carolina, Graduate School, College of Science and Mathematics, Marine Science Program, Columbia, SC 29208. Offers MS, PhD. *Faculty:* 32 full-time (3 women), 2 part-time (0 women). *Students:* 24 full-time (16 women), 6 part-time (4 women); includes 2 minority (both African Americans), 5 international. Average age 29. 60 applicants, 18% accepted. In 1998, 2 master's, 3 doctorates awarded. *Degree requirements:* For master's and doctorate, thesis/dissertation required, foreign language not required. *Entrance requirements:* For master's and doctorate, GRE General Test. *Average time to degree:* Master's–2.25 years full-time; doctorate–5.67 years full-time. *Application deadline:* For fall admission, 2/1 (priority date). Applications are processed on a rolling basis. Application fee: $35. Electronic applications accepted. Tuition, state resident: full-time $4,014; part-time $202 per credit hour. Tuition, nonresident: full-time $8,528; part-time $428 per credit hour. Required fees: $100; $4 per credit hour. Tuition and fees vary according to program. *Financial aid:* In 1998–99, 10 students received aid, including 5 fellowships, 10 research assistantships, 10 teaching assistantships; career-related internships or fieldwork, Federal Work-Study, and institutionally-sponsored loans also available. Financial aid application deadline: 2/1. *Faculty research:* Biological, chemical, geological, and physical oceanography; policy. *Unit head:* Dr. Madilyn M. Fletcher, Director, 803-777-5288, Fax: 803-777-3935, E-mail: fletcher@biol.sc.edu. *Application contact:* Dr. John Mark Dean, Graduate Studies Director, 803-777-0075, Fax: 803-777-3935, E-mail: jmdean@sc.edu.

University of Southern California, Graduate School, College of Letters, Arts and Sciences, Department of Biological Sciences, Program in Marine Biology and Biological Oceanography, Los Angeles, CA 90089. Offers MS, PhD. *Faculty:* 8 full-time (1 woman). *Students:* 18 full-time (6 women), 2 part-time; includes 1 minority (Asian American or Pacific Islander), 8 international. Average age 30. 14 applicants, 43% accepted. In 1998, 3 master's, 6 doctorates awarded. *Degree requirements:* For master's and doctorate, thesis/dissertation required. *Entrance requirements:* For master's and doctorate, GRE General Test. *Application deadline:* For fall admission, 2/1 (priority date); for spring admission, 10/15. Application fee: $55. Tuition: Full-time $22,198; part-time $748 per unit. Required fees: $406. Tuition and fees vary according to program. *Financial aid:* In 1998–99, 3 fellowships, 6 research assistantships, 10 teaching assistantships were awarded.; Federal Work-Study, institutionally-sponsored loans, and scholarships also available. Aid available to part-time students. Financial aid application deadline: 2/15; financial aid applicants required to submit FAFSA. *Unit head:* Dr. Donald Manahan, Chair.

University of Southern Mississippi, Graduate School, Institute of Marine Sciences, Department of Marine Science, Hattiesburg, MS 39406-5167. Offers MS, PhD. Part-time programs available. *Faculty:* 7 full-time (1 woman). *Students:* 15 full-time (8 women), 15 part-time (6 women); includes 5 minority (1 African American, 4 Asian Americans or Pacific Islanders) Average age 25. 40 applicants, 23% accepted. In 1998, 6 master's awarded. *Degree requirements:* For master's, thesis required, foreign language not required; for doctorate, 2 foreign languages (computer language can substitute for one), dissertation required. *Entrance requirements:* For master's, GRE General Test, minimum GPA of 3.0; for doctorate, GRE General Test, minimum GPA of 3.0 (undergraduate), 3.5 (graduate). *Application deadline:* For fall admission, 8/9 (priority date); for spring admission, 12/7. Applications are processed on a rolling basis. Application fee: $0 ($25 for international students). Electronic applications accepted. Tuition, state resident: full-time $2,250; part-time $137 per semester hour. Tuition, nonresident: full-time $3,102; part-time $172 per semester hour. Required fees: $602. *Financial aid:* Research assistantships with full tuition reimbursements, teaching assistantships with full tuition reimbursements, institutionally-sponsored loans and co-op program with U.S. Navy available. Financial aid application deadline: 3/15. *Faculty research:* Chemical, biological, physical, and geological marine science; remote sensing. Total annual research expenditures: $1.2 million. *Unit head:* Dr. Denis A. Wiesenburg, Director, 228-688-3177, Fax: 228-688-1121, E-mail: marine.science@usm.edu.

University of South Florida, Graduate School, College of Arts and Sciences, Department of Marine Science, Tampa, FL 33620-9951. Offers marine biology (MS, PhD); marine science (MS, PhD); oceanography (MS, PhD). Part-time and evening/weekend programs available. *Faculty:* 25 full-time (4 women). *Students:* 92 full-time (52 women), 16 part-time (4 women); includes 2 minority (1 African American, 1 Asian American or Pacific Islander), 10 international. Average age 30. 210 applicants, 11% accepted. In 1998, 13 master's, 5 doctorates awarded. *Degree requirements:* For master's, thesis required; for doctorate, 2 foreign languages (computer language can substitute for one), dissertation required. *Entrance requirements:* For master's and doctorate, GRE General Test (minimum combined score of 1100 required), minimum GPA of 3.0 in last 60 hours. *Average time to degree:* Master's–3.5 years full-time; doctorate–6 years full-time. *Application deadline:* For fall admission, 6/1; for spring admission, 10/15. Applications are processed on a rolling basis. Application fee: $20. Tuition, state resident: part-time $148 per credit hour. Tuition, nonresident: part-time $509 per credit hour. *Financial aid:* In 1998–99, 12 fellowships with partial tuition reimbursements (averaging $12,000 per year), 74 research assistantships with partial tuition reimbursements (averaging $12,000 per year), 12 teaching assistantships with partial tuition reimbursements (averaging $12,000 per year) were awarded. *Faculty research:* Trace metal analysis, water quality, organic and isotope geochemistry, physical chemistry, optical oceanography, satellite imagery, sedimentology, geophysics, physical oceanography. *Unit head:* Dr. Peter R. Betzer, Chairperson, 727-553-1130, Fax: 727-553-1189, E-mail: pbetzer@marine.usf.edu. *Application contact:* Edward VanVleet, Coordinator, 727-553-1165, Fax: 727-553-1189, E-mail: vanvleet@marine.usf.edu.

See in-depth description on page 371.

The University of Texas at Austin, Graduate School, College of Natural Sciences, Department of Marine Science, Austin, TX 78712-1111. Offers MA, PhD. *Students:* 28 (12 women) 3 international. 39 applicants, 10% accepted. In 1998, 5 master's, 4 doctorates awarded. *Entrance requirements:* For master's and doctorate, GRE General Test (minimum combined score of 1000 required). Application fee: $50 ($100 for international students). *Financial aid:* Application deadline: 2/1. *Unit head:* Wayne S. Gardner, Chairman, 512-749-6730, E-mail: gardner@utmsi.utexas.edu. *Application contact:* Lee A. Fuiman, Graduate Adviser, 512-749-6721.

See in-depth description on page 375.

University of Washington, Graduate School, College of Ocean and Fishery Sciences, School of Marine Affairs, Seattle, WA 98195. Offers MMA, MMA/MAIS. *Degree requirements:* For master's, thesis required, foreign language not required. *Entrance requirements:* For master's, GRE General Test, TOEFL (minimum score of 500 required), minimum GPA of 3.0. Tuition, state resident: full-time $5,196; part-time $475 per credit. Tuition, nonresident: full-time $13,485; part-time $1,285 per credit. Required fees: $387; $38 per credit. Tuition and fees vary according to course load. *Faculty research:* Marine pollution, port authorities, fisheries management, global climate change, marine environmental protection.

University of Wisconsin–Madison, Graduate School, College of Letters and Science, Department of Atmospheric and Oceanic Sciences, Madison, WI 53706-1380. Offers MS, PhD. Part-time programs available. *Faculty:* 19 full-time (0 women), 2 part-time (0 women). *Students:* 48 full-time (14 women), 6 part-time (1 woman), 11 international. Average age 25. 84 applicants, 44% accepted. In 1998, 8 master's awarded (12% entered university research/teaching, 63% found other work related to degree, 25% continued full-time study); 5 doctorates awarded (20% entered university research/teaching, 80% found other work related to degree). *Degree requirements:* For master's, thesis required (for some programs), foreign language not required; for doctorate, dissertation required, foreign language not required. *Entrance requirements:* For master's and doctorate, GRE General Test (minimum score of 650 on quantitative section, 500 on analytical required), minimum GPA of 3.0; previous course work in chemistry, mathematics, and physics. *Average time to degree:* Master's–2 years full-time, 3.5 years part-time; doctorate–4 years full-time, 5 years part-time. *Application deadline:* For fall admission, 8/1 (priority date); for spring admission, 12/1 (priority date). Applications are processed on a rolling basis. Application fee: $45. Electronic applications accepted. *Financial aid:* In 1998–99, 47 students received aid, including 1 fellowship with full tuition reimbursement available (averaging $17,500 per year), 29 research assistantships with full tuition reimbursements available (averaging $14,600 per year), 8 teaching assistantships with full tuition reimbursements available; career-related internships or fieldwork, Federal Work-Study, institutionally-sponsored loans, and scholarships also available. Aid available to part-time students. *Faculty research:* Satellite meteorology, weather systems, global climate change, numerical modeling, atmosphere-ocean interaction. Total annual research expenditures: $1.4 million. *Unit head:* Matthew Hitchman, Chair, 608-262-2828, Fax: 608-262-0166, E-mail: matt@adams.meteor.wisc.edu. *Application contact:* Connie Linehan, Graduate Coordinator, 608-262-2827, Fax: 608-262-0166, E-mail: linehan@facstaff.wisc.edu.

Oceanography

Columbia University, Graduate School of Arts and Sciences, Division of Natural Sciences, Department of Earth and Environmental Sciences, New York, NY 10027. Offers geochemistry (M Phil, MA, PhD); geodetic sciences (M Phil, MA, PhD); geophysics (M Phil, MA, PhD); oceanography (M Phil, MA, PhD). *Degree requirements:* For master's, thesis or alternative, fieldwork, written exam required, foreign language not required; for doctorate, one foreign language, dissertation required. *Entrance requirements:* For master's and doctorate, GRE General Test, GRE Subject Test, TOEFL, major in natural or physical science. *Faculty research:* Structural geology and stratigraphy, petrology, paleontology, rare gas, isotope and aqueous geochemistry.

Cornell University, Graduate School, Graduate Fields of Agriculture and Life Sciences, Field of Ecology and Evolutionary Biology, Ithaca, NY 14853-0001. Offers ecology (PhD), including animal ecology, applied ecology, biogeochemistry, community and ecosystem ecology, limnology, oceanography, physiological ecology, plant ecology, population ecology, theoretical ecology, vertebrate zoology; evolutionary biology (PhD), including ecological genetics, paleobiology, population biology, systematics. *Faculty:* 41 full-time. *Students:* 55 full-time (29 women); includes 5 minority (1 African American, 2 Asian Americans or Pacific Islanders, 2 Hispanic Americans), 3 international. *Degree requirements:* For doctorate, dissertation, 2 semesters of teaching experience required, foreign language not required. *Entrance requirements:* For doctorate, GRE General Test, TOEFL (minimum score of 550 required). *Application deadline:* For fall admission, 12/15. Application fee: $65. Electronic applications accepted. *Unit head:* Director of Graduate Studies, 607-254-4230. *Application contact:* Graduate Field Assistant, 607-254-4230, E-mail: eeb_grad_req@cornell.edu.

Dalhousie University, Faculty of Graduate Studies, College of Arts and Science, Faculty of Science, Department of Oceanography, Halifax, NS B3H 3J5, Canada. Offers M Sc, PhD. Part-time programs available. *Faculty:* 22 full-time (1 woman), 16 part-time (2 women). *Students:* 35 full-time (19 women), 1 part-time, 10 international. Average age 27. 45 applicants, 36% accepted. In 1998, 5 master's, 5 doctorates awarded. *Degree requirements:* For master's and doctorate, thesis/dissertation required, foreign language not required. *Entrance requirements:* For master's and doctorate, TOEFL (minimum score of 600 required). *Average time to degree:* Master's–2.5 years full-time, 3 years part-time; doctorate–5.5 years full-time. *Application deadline:* For fall admission, 5/1. Applications are processed on a rolling basis. Application fee: $55. *Financial aid:* In 1998–99, 32 fellowships, 13 teaching assistantships were awarded. *Faculty research:* Biological and physical oceanography, chemical and geological oceanography, atmospheric sciences. *Unit head:* Dr. R. M. Moore, Chair, 902-494-3557, Fax: 902-494-3877,

E-mail: oceanography@dal.ca. *Application contact:* Dr. B. Boudreau, Graduate Coordinator, 902-494-8895, Fax: 902-494-3877.

See in-depth description on page 341.

Florida Institute of Technology, Graduate School, College of Engineering, Division of Marine and Environmental Systems, Program in Oceanography, Melbourne, FL 32901-6975. Offers biological oceanography (MS); chemical oceanography (MS); coastal zone management (MS); geological oceanography (MS); oceanography (PhD); physical oceanography (MS). Part-time programs available. *Faculty:* 6 full-time (0 women), 5 part-time (1 woman). *Students:* 6 full-time (2 women), 28 part-time (10 women), 13 international. Average age 28. 30 applicants, 67% accepted. In 1998, 9 master's, 1 doctorate awarded. Terminal master's awarded for partial completion of doctoral program. *Degree requirements:* For master's, thesis required (for some programs), foreign language not required; for doctorate, one foreign language (computer language can substitute), dissertation, comprehensive and departmental qualifying exams required. *Entrance requirements:* For master's, GRE General Test, minimum GPA of 3.0; for doctorate, GRE General Test, minimum GPA of 3.2. *Application deadline:* Applications are processed on a rolling basis. Application fee: $50. Electronic applications accepted. Tuition: Part-time $575 per credit hour. Required fees: $100. Tuition and fees vary according to campus/location and program. *Financial aid:* In 1998–99, 14 students received aid, including 8 research assistantships (averaging $3,426 per year), 4 teaching assistantships with tuition reimbursements available (averaging $3,420 per year); career-related internships or fieldwork and tuition remissions also available. Financial aid application deadline: 3/1; financial aid applicants required to submit FAFSA. *Faculty research:* Marine geochemistry, ecosystem dynamics, coastal processes, marine pollution, environmental modeling. Total annual research expenditures: $960,780. *Unit head:* Dr. Dean R. Norris, Chair, 407-674-7377, Fax: 407-674-7212, E-mail: norris@marine.fit.edu. *Application contact:* Carolyn P. Farrior, Associate Dean of Graduate Admissions, 407-674-7118, Fax: 407-723-9468, E-mail: cfarrior@fit.edu.

See in-depth description on page 343.

Florida State University, Graduate Studies, College of Arts and Sciences, Department of Oceanography, Tallahassee, FL 32306. Offers MS, PhD. *Faculty:* 18 full-time (4 women), 4 part-time (0 women). *Students:* 46 full-time (15 women), 2 part-time (1 woman), 20 international. Average age 26. 50 applicants, 16% accepted. In 1998, 6 master's, 3 doctorates awarded. *Degree requirements:* For master's, thesis required, foreign language not required; for doctorate, dissertation, comprehensive exam required, foreign language not required. *Entrance requirements:* For master's and doctorate, GRE General Test (minimum combined score of 1100 required), TOEFL (minimum score of 550 required; 213 for computer-based). *Average time to degree:* Master's–2 years full-time; doctorate–4 years full-time. *Application deadline:* For fall admission, 2/1 (priority date); for spring admission, 7/1. Applications are processed on a rolling basis. Application fee: $20. Electronic applications accepted. Tuition, state resident: part-time $139 per credit hour. Tuition, nonresident: part-time $482 per credit hour. Tuition and fees vary according to program. *Financial aid:* In 1998–99, 41 students received aid, including 2 fellowships with full tuition reimbursements available, 36 research assistantships with full tuition reimbursements available, 3 teaching assistantships with full tuition reimbursements available Financial aid application deadline: 2/1; financial aid applicants required to submit FAFSA. *Faculty research:* Trace metals in seawater, currents and waves, modeling, benthic ecology, marine biogeochemistry. Total annual research expenditures: $3.8 million. *Unit head:* Dr. David Thistle, Chair, 850-644-6700, Fax: 850-644-2581, E-mail: thistle@ocean.fsu.edu. *Application contact:* Academic Coordinator, 850-644-6700, Fax: 850-644-2581, E-mail: admissions@ocean.fsu.edu.

See in-depth description on page 347.

Johns Hopkins University, Zanvyl Krieger School of Arts and Sciences, Department of Earth and Planetary Sciences, Program in Oceanography, Baltimore, MD 21218-2699. Offers MA, PhD. *Faculty:* 1 full-time (0 women). *Students:* 2 full-time (0 women). In 1998, 1 degree awarded. Terminal master's awarded for partial completion of doctoral program. *Degree requirements:* For doctorate, dissertation required, foreign language not required. *Entrance requirements:* For master's and doctorate, GRE General Test. *Average time to degree:* Doctorate–5.5 years full-time. *Application deadline:* For fall admission, 1/15. Application fee: $55. Tuition: Full-time $23,660. Tuition and fees vary according to program. *Financial aid:* Federal Work-Study and institutionally-sponsored loans available. Financial aid application deadline: 3/14; financial aid applicants required to submit FAFSA. *Unit head:* Dr. John M. Ferry, Chair, Department of Earth and Planetary Sciences, 410-516-7135, Fax: 410-516-7933.

Louisiana State University and Agricultural and Mechanical College, Graduate School, Center for Coastal, Energy and Environmental Resources, Department of Oceanography and Coastal Sciences, Baton Rouge, LA 70803. Offers MS, PhD. *Faculty:* 21 full-time (2 women). *Students:* 37 full-time (14 women), 30 part-time (7 women); includes 6 minority (4 Asian Americans or Pacific Islanders, 1 Hispanic American, 1 Native American), 12 international. Average age 32. 20 applicants, 40% accepted. In 1998, 17 master's, 6 doctorates awarded. *Degree requirements:* For master's, thesis required (for some programs), foreign language not required; for doctorate, dissertation required. *Entrance requirements:* For master's, GRE General Test (minimum combined score of 1100 required), TOEFL (minimum score of 550 required), minimum GPA of 3.0; for doctorate, GRE General Test (minimum combined score of 1100 required), TOEFL (minimum score of 550 required), MA or MS, minimum GPA of 3.0. *Application deadline:* For fall admission, 1/25 (priority date). Applications are processed on a rolling basis. Application fee: $25. *Financial aid:* In 1998–99, 12 fellowships, 19 research assistantships with partial tuition reimbursements, 1 teaching assistantship with partial tuition reimbursement were awarded.; Federal Work-Study, institutionally-sponsored loans, and unspecified assistantships also available. *Faculty research:* Management and development of estuarine and coastal areas and resources; physical, chemical, geological, and biological research. *Unit head:* Dr. Charles Wilson, Chair, 225-388-6308, Fax: 225-388-6307. *Application contact:* Dr. Lawrence Rouse, Graduate Adviser, 225-388-6308, Fax: 225-388-6307, E-mail: ocean@lsuvm.sncc.lsu.edu.

Massachusetts Institute of Technology, Program in Oceanography/Applied Ocean Science and Engineering, Cambridge, MA 02139-4307. Offers biological oceanography (PhD, Sc D); chemical oceanography (PhD, Sc D); marine geochemistry (PhD, Sc D); marine geology (PhD, Sc D); oceanographic engineering (MS, PhD, Sc D, Eng); physical oceanography (PhD, Sc D). MS, PhD, and Sc D offered jointly with Woods Hole Oceanographic Institution. *Faculty:* 170 full-time. *Students:* 133 full-time, 43 international. Average age 27. 187 applicants, 26% accepted. In 1998, 6 master's, 23 doctorates, 2 other advanced degrees awarded. Terminal master's awarded for partial completion of doctoral program. *Degree requirements:* For master's and Eng, thesis required (for some programs), foreign language not required; for doctorate, dissertation required, foreign language not required. *Entrance requirements:* For master's, GRE General Test; for doctorate, GRE General Test, GRE Subject Test. *Average time to degree:* Master's–2.5 years full-time; doctorate–6 years full-time; Eng–2 years full-time. *Application deadline:* For fall admission, 1/15 (priority date). Application fee: $55. *Financial aid:* Fellowships, research assistantships, teaching assistantships available. *Unit head:* Paola Rizzoli, Director, 617-253-2451. *Application contact:* Ronni Schwartz, Administrator, 617-253-7544, Fax: 617-253-9784.

See in-depth description on page 349.

Massachusetts Institute of Technology, School of Science, Department of Biology, Program in Biological Oceanography, Cambridge, MA 02139-4307. Offers PhD, Sc D. *Degree requirements:* For doctorate, dissertation, general exam required, foreign language not required. *Entrance requirements:* For doctorate, GRE General Test, GRE Subject Test (biology). *Application deadline:* For fall admission, 1/1. Application fee: $55. *Financial aid:* Application deadline: 1/1. *Application contact:* Jo-Ann Murray, Educational Administrator, 617-253-3717, Fax: 617-258-9329, E-mail: gradbio@mit.edu.

Massachusetts Institute of Technology, School of Science, Department of Earth, Atmospheric, and Planetary Sciences, Program in Atmospheres, Oceans, and Climate, Cambridge, MA 02139-4307. Offers SM, PhD, Sc D. *Faculty:* 16 full-time (2 women). *Students:* 61 full-time (24 women), 32 international. Average age 27. 79 applicants, 35% accepted. In 1998, 4 master's, 11 doctorates awarded. Terminal master's awarded for partial completion of doctoral program. *Degree requirements:* For master's, thesis required, foreign language not required; for doctorate, dissertation, general exam required, foreign language not required. *Entrance requirements:* For master's and doctorate, GRE General Test, GRE Subject Test. *Application deadline:* For fall admission, 1/15; for spring admission, 11/1. Application fee: $55. *Financial aid:* Fellowships, research assistantships, teaching assistantships, institutionally-sponsored loans available. Financial aid application deadline: 1/15. *Faculty research:* Origin, composition, structure, and state of atmospheres and oceans. *Unit head:* Dr. Carl I. Wunsch, Director, 617-253-5937, E-mail: paoc@mit.edu. *Application contact:* Anastasia Frangos, Administrative Assistant, 617-253-3381, Fax: 617-253-8298, E-mail: eapsinfo@mit.edu.

McGill University, Faculty of Graduate Studies and Research, Faculty of Science, Department of Atmospheric and Oceanic Sciences, Montréal, PQ H3A 2T5, Canada. Offers atmospheric science (M Sc, PhD); physical oceanography (M Sc, PhD). *Faculty:* 13 full-time (1 woman), 5 part-time (0 women). *Students:* 41 full-time (4 women), 2 part-time. Average age 24. 53 applicants, 23% accepted. In 1998, 6 master's awarded (50% found work related to degree, 50% continued full-time study); 4 doctorates awarded (75% entered university research/teaching, 25% found other work related to degree). Terminal master's awarded for partial completion of doctoral program. *Degree requirements:* For master's and doctorate, thesis/dissertation required, foreign language not required. *Entrance requirements:* For master's, GRE General Test, TOEFL (minimum score of 550 required), minimum GPA of 3.0, or 3.2 during last 2 years of full-time study; for doctorate, GRE, TOEFL (minimum score of 550 required), master's degree in meteorology or related field. *Average time to degree:* Master's–2 years full-time; doctorate–4 years full-time. *Application deadline:* For fall admission, 7/1 (priority date); for winter admission, 12/1 (priority date). Applications are processed on a rolling basis. Application fee: $60. *Financial aid:* In 1998–99, 43 research assistantships (averaging $16,000 per year), 15 teaching assistantships (averaging $1,000 per year) were awarded.; fellowships, tuition waivers (partial) also available. Financial aid application deadline: 7/1. *Faculty research:* Dynamic meteorology and climate dynamics, synoptic meteorology, mesometeorology, radar meteorology, physical oceanography. Total annual research expenditures: $2.7 million. *Unit head:* Prof. C. A. Lin, Chair, 514-398-3760, Fax: 514-398-6115, E-mail: lin@zephyr.meteo.mcgill.ca. *Application contact:* Prof. H. G. Leighton, Chair, Graduate Admissions, 514-398-3766, Fax: 514-398-6115, E-mail: gradinfo@zephyr.meteo.mcgill.ca.

Memorial University of Newfoundland, School of Graduate Studies, Department of Physics and Physical Oceanography, St. John's, NF A1C 5S7, Canada. Offers condensed matter physics (PhD); molecular physics (PhD); physical oceanography (M Sc, PhD); physics (M Sc). Part-time programs available. *Students:* 12 full-time (2 women), 3 part-time, 10 international. 27 applicants, 22% accepted. In 1998, 1 master's, 2 doctorates awarded (100% entered university research/teaching). *Degree requirements:* For master's, thesis required; for doctorate, dissertation, comprehensive exam required. *Entrance requirements:* For master's, honors B Sc or equivalent; for doctorate, M Sc or equivalent. *Average time to degree:* Doctorate–4 years full-time. *Application deadline:* Applications are processed on a rolling basis. Application fee: $40. *Financial aid:* Fellowships, research assistantships, teaching assistantships available. *Faculty research:* Experiment and theory in atomic and molecular physics. Total annual research expenditures: $2.1 million. *Unit head:* Dr. Mike Morrow, Acting Head, 709-737-8737, Fax: 709-737-8739. *Application contact:* Dr. J. de Bruyn, Deputy Head, Graduate Studies, 709-737-2113, Fax: 709-737-8739, E-mail: jdebruyn@kelvin.physics.mun.ca.

Naval Postgraduate School, Graduate Programs, Department of Oceanography, Monterey, CA 93943. Offers MS, PhD. Program only open to commissioned officers of the United States and friendly nations and selected United States federal civilian employees. Part-time programs available. *Students:* 11 full-time, 5 international. In 1998, 8 degrees awarded. *Degree requirements:* For master's, computer language, thesis required, foreign language not required; for doctorate, one foreign language, computer language, dissertation required. *Unit head:* Dr. Roland W. Garwood, Chairman, 831-656-2673. *Application contact:* Theodore H. Calhoon, Director of Admissions, 831-656-3093, Fax: 831-656-2891, E-mail: tcalhoon@nps.navy.mil.

North Carolina State University, Graduate School, College of Physical and Mathematical Sciences, Department of Marine, Earth, and Atmospheric Sciences, Raleigh, NC 27695. Offers geology (MS, PhD); geophysics (MS, PhD); marine, earth, and atmospheric sciences (MS, PhD); meteorology (MS, PhD); oceanography (MS, PhD). *Faculty:* 34 full-time (2 women), 39 part-time (1 woman). *Students:* 118 full-time (30 women), 12 part-time (3 women); includes 2 minority (both Asian Americans or Pacific Islanders), 37 international. Terminal master's awarded for partial completion of doctoral program. *Degree requirements:* For master's, thesis, final oral exam required, foreign language not required; for doctorate, dissertation, final oral exam, preliminary oral and written exams required, foreign language not required. *Entrance requirements:* For master's and doctorate, GRE General Test, minimum GPA of 3.0. *Application deadline:* For fall admission, 6/25 (priority date); for spring admission, 11/25. Applications are processed on a rolling basis. Application fee: $45. *Unit head:* Dr. Leonard J. Pietrafesa, Head, 919-515-3717, Fax: 919-515-7802, E-mail: leonard_pietrafesa@ncsu.edu. *Application contact:* Dr. Gerald S. Janowitz, Director of Graduate Programs, 919-515-7837, Fax: 919-515-7802, E-mail: janowitz@ncsu.edu.

Nova Southeastern University, Oceanographic Center, Fort Lauderdale, FL 33314-7721. Offers coastal-zone management (MS); marine biology (MS); marine environmental science (MS); oceanography (PhD). Part-time and evening/weekend programs available. *Students:* 13 full-time (9 women), 59 part-time (30 women); includes 5 minority (1 Asian American or Pacific Islander, 3 Hispanic Americans, 1 Native American), 2 international. Average age 30. In 1998, 14 master's awarded. *Degree requirements:* For master's, thesis optional, foreign language not required; for doctorate, dissertation, departmental qualifying exam required. *Entrance requirements:* For master's, GRE General Test (minimum combined score of 1000 required); for doctorate, GRE General Test (minimum combined score of 1100 required), master's degree. *Average time to degree:* Master's–2 years full-time, 3 years part-time; doctorate–4 years full-time, 6 years part-time. *Application deadline:* Applications are processed on a rolling basis. Application fee: $50. Tuition: Part-time $417 per credit hour. Required fees: $50 per semester. Tuition and fees vary according to degree level and program. *Financial aid:* Research assistantships, teaching assistantships, career-related internships or fieldwork, Federal Work-Study, and tuition waivers (partial) available. Aid available to part-time students. *Faculty research:* Physical, geological, chemical, and biological oceanography. *Unit head:* Dr. Julian P. McCreary, Dean, 954-920-1909, Fax: 954-947-8559, E-mail: jay@ocean.nova.edu. *Application contact:* Dr. Richard Dodge, Associate Dean, 954-920-1909, Fax: 954-947-8559, E-mail: dodge@ocean.nova.edu.

See in-depth description on page 351.

Old Dominion University, College of Sciences, Department of Ocean, Earth and Atmospheric Sciences, Programs in Oceanography, Norfolk, VA 23529. Offers MS, PhD. Part-time programs available. *Faculty:* 20 full-time (2 women). *Students:* 32 full-time (12 women), 7 part-time (2 women); includes 1 minority (Asian American or Pacific Islander), 17 international. Average age 30. 28 applicants, 57% accepted. In 1998, 9 master's, 2 doctorates awarded. Terminal master's awarded for partial completion of doctoral program. *Degree requirements:* For master's, 10 days of ship time, comprehensive exam required, thesis optional, foreign language not required; for doctorate, computer language, dissertation, 10 days of ship time, comprehensive exam required, foreign language not required. *Entrance requirements:* For master's, GRE General Test, GRE Subject Test, TOEFL (minimum score of 550 required), minimum GPA of 3.0 in major, 2.7 overall; for doctorate, GRE General Test (minimum combined score of 1000 required), GRE Subject Test (minimum score of 600 required), TOEFL (minimum score of 550 required). *Application deadline:* For fall admission, 2/15 (priority date). Applica-

Oceanography

Old Dominion University (continued)

tions are processed on a rolling basis. Application fee: $30. Electronic applications accepted. *Financial aid:* In 1998–99, 39 students received aid, including 26 research assistantships (averaging $11,088 per year), 3 teaching assistantships (averaging $9,000 per year); career-related internships or fieldwork, grants, and tuition waivers (partial) also available. Aid available to part-time students. Financial aid application deadline: 2/15; financial aid applicants required to submit FAFSA. Total annual research expenditures: $1.8 million. *Unit head:* Dr. David Burdige, Graduate Program Director, 757-683-4930, Fax: 757-683-5303, E-mail: dburdige@odu.edu. *Application contact:* Dr. David Burdige, Graduate Program Director, 757-683-4930, Fax: 757-683-5303, E-mail: dburdige@odu.edu.

Oregon State University, Graduate School, College of Oceanic and Atmospheric Sciences, Program in Oceanography, Corvallis, OR 97331. Offers MA, MS, PhD. *Faculty:* 63 full-time (4 women), 12 part-time (0 women). *Students:* 42 full-time (17 women), 2 part-time, 12 international. Average age 31. Terminal master's awarded for partial completion of doctoral program. *Degree requirements:* For master's, thesis optional, foreign language not required; for doctorate, dissertation required, foreign language not required. *Entrance requirements:* For master's and doctorate, GRE General Test, TOEFL (minimum score of 550 required), minimum GPA of 3.0 in last 90 hours. *Application deadline:* For fall admission, 2/1 (priority date). Applications are processed on a rolling basis. Application fee: $50. *Financial aid:* Fellowships, research assistantships, teaching assistantships, career-related internships or fieldwork, Federal Work-Study, and institutionally-sponsored loans available. Aid available to part-time students. Financial aid application deadline: 2/1. *Faculty research:* Biological, chemical, geological, and physical oceanography. *Unit head:* Dr. Tim Cowles, Associate Dean, 541-737-3268, Fax: 541-737-2064, E-mail: tjc@oce.orst.edu. *Application contact:* Irma Delson, Assistant Director, Student Services, 541-737-5190, Fax: 541-737-2064, E-mail: student_adviser@oce.orst.edu.

See in-depth description on page 353.

Princeton University, Graduate School, Department of Geosciences, Program in Atmospheric and Oceanic Sciences, Princeton, NJ 08544-1019. Offers PhD. *Degree requirements:* For doctorate, dissertation required. *Entrance requirements:* For doctorate, GRE General Test, GRE Subject Test. *Faculty research:* Climate dynamics, middle atmosphere dynamics and chemistry, oceanic circulation, marine geochemistry, numerical modelling.

Rutgers, The State University of New Jersey, New Brunswick, Graduate School, Program in Oceanography, New Brunswick, NJ 08903. Offers MS, PhD. *Faculty:* 40 full-time (5 women). *Students:* 25 full-time (10 women), 1 (woman) part-time, 6 international. Average age 29. 31 applicants, 29% accepted. In 1998, 1 master's awarded (0% continued full-time study); 2 doctorates awarded. Terminal master's awarded for partial completion of doctoral program. *Degree requirements:* For master's and doctorate, thesis/dissertation required. *Entrance requirements:* For master's, GRE General Test (minimum combined score of 1680 on three sections required; average 1902), 1 year of calculus, physics, chemistry; for doctorate, GRE General Test (minimum combined score of 1510 on three sections required; average 1911), 1 year of calculus, physics, chemistry. *Average time to degree:* Master's–2.5 years full-time; doctorate–4 years full-time. *Application deadline:* For fall admission, 2/1 (priority date); for spring admission, 11/1. Applications are processed on a rolling basis. Application fee: $50. *Financial aid:* In 1998–99, 20 students received aid, including 2 fellowships with full tuition reimbursements available (averaging $14,500 per year), 15 research assistantships with full tuition reimbursements available (averaging $14,000 per year), 3 teaching assistantships with full tuition reimbursements available (averaging $12,336 per year); career-related internships or fieldwork and institutionally-sponsored loans also available. Financial aid application deadline: 3/1; financial aid applicants required to submit FAFSA. *Faculty research:* Coastal observations and modeling, estuarine ecology/fish/benthos, geochemistry, deep sea ecology/hydrothermal vents, molecular biology applications. Total annual research expenditures: $7.2 million. *Unit head:* Dr. Dale Haidvogel, Director, 732-932-6555 Ext. 256.

See in-depth description on page 357.

State University of New York at Stony Brook, Graduate School, Marine Sciences Research Center, Program in Coastal Oceanography, Stony Brook, NY 11794. Offers PhD. Evening/weekend programs available. *Students:* 38 full-time (11 women), 24 part-time (9 women); includes 1 minority (Asian American or Pacific Islander), 33 international. Average age 29. 53 applicants, 38% accepted. In 1998, 7 degrees awarded (100% entered university research/teaching). *Degree requirements:* For doctorate, dissertation, written comprehensive exam required. *Entrance requirements:* For doctorate, GRE General Test, TOEFL (minimum score of 550 required), minimum graduate GPA of 3.0. *Application deadline:* For fall admission, 1/15. Application fee: $50. *Financial aid:* Fellowships, research assistantships, teaching assistantships, career-related internships or fieldwork available. *Application contact:* Dr. Henry Bokuniewicz, Director, 516-632-8681, Fax: 516-632-8200, E-mail: hbokuniewicz@ccmail.sunysb.edu.

Texas A&M University, College of Geosciences, Department of Oceanography, College Station, TX 77843. Offers MS, PhD. *Faculty:* 26 full-time (2 women), 2 part-time (0 women). *Students:* 70 full-time (23 women), 9 part-time (4 women); includes 6 minority (1 African American, 4 Hispanic Americans, 1 Native American), 26 international. Average age 30. 56 applicants, 73% accepted. In 1998, 3 master's, 7 doctorates awarded (57% entered university research/teaching, 29% found other work related to degree, 14% continued full-time study). *Degree requirements:* For master's and doctorate, thesis/dissertation required, foreign language not required. *Entrance requirements:* For master's and doctorate, GRE General Test, TOEFL. *Average time to degree:* Master's–3.5 years full-time; doctorate–5 years full-time. *Application deadline:* For fall admission, 3/1 (priority date); for spring admission, 10/1. Applications are processed on a rolling basis. Application fee: $50 ($75 for international students). Electronic applications accepted. *Financial aid:* In 1998–99, 65 students received aid, including 8 fellowships with partial tuition reimbursements available (averaging $18,000 per year), 45 research assistantships with partial tuition reimbursements available (averaging $17,000 per year), 17 teaching assistantships with partial tuition reimbursements available (averaging $17,000 per year); Federal Work-Study, scholarships, and foreign government supports also available. Financial aid application deadline: 3/1. *Faculty research:* Ocean circulation, climate studies, coastal and shelf dynamics, marine phytoplankton, stable isotope geochemistry, paleoceanography. Total annual research expenditures: $5.3 million. *Unit head:* Dr. William R. Bryant, Head, 409-845-7211, Fax: 409-845-6331. *Application contact:* Pat Swigert, Academic Adviser, 409-845-7412, Fax: 409-845-6331, E-mail: pat@ocean.tamu.edu.

Université du Québec à Rimouski, Graduate Programs, Program in Oceanography, Rimouski, PQ G5L 3A1, Canada. Offers M Sc, PhD. Part-time programs available. *Degree requirements:* For master's and doctorate, thesis/dissertation required. *Entrance requirements:* For master's, appropriate bachelor's degree, proficiency in French; for doctorate, appropriate master's degree, proficiency in French.

University of Alaska Fairbanks, Graduate School, School of Fisheries and Ocean Sciences, Program in Marine Sciences and Limnology, Fairbanks, AK 99775-7480. Offers marine biology (MS); oceanography (MS, PhD), including biological oceanography (PhD), chemical oceanography (PhD), fisheries (PhD), physical oceanography (PhD). *Faculty:* 9 full-time (1 woman), 2 part-time (0 women). *Students:* 37 full-time (25 women), 6 part-time (4 women); includes 2 minority (1 African American, 1 Asian American or Pacific Islander), 10 international. *Degree requirements:* For master's, thesis, comprehensive exam required, foreign language not required; for doctorate, one foreign language (computer language can substitute), dissertation, comprehensive exam required. *Entrance requirements:* For master's and doctorate, GRE General Test, TOEFL (minimum score of 550 required). *Application deadline:* For fall admission, 3/1 (priority date). Applications are processed on a rolling basis. Application fee: $35. *Unit head:* Dr. Susan Henrichs, Head, 907-474-7289.

University of British Columbia, Faculty of Graduate Studies, Faculty of Science, Department of Earth and Ocean Sciences, Program in Oceanography, Vancouver, BC V6T 1Z2, Canada. Offers M Sc, PhD. Part-time programs available. *Degree requirements:* For master's, thesis required; for doctorate, dissertation, oral comprehensive exam required. *Entrance requirements:* For master's and doctorate, TOEFL (minimum score of 550 required), minimum GPA of 3.0.

University of California, San Diego, Graduate Studies and Research, Scripps Institution of Oceanography, La Jolla, CA 92093-5003. Offers biological oceanography (MS, PhD); geochemistry and marine chemistry (MS, PhD); marine biology (MS, PhD); physical oceanography and geological sciences (MS, PhD). *Faculty:* 73. *Students:* 170 (68 women). 282 applicants, 22% accepted. In 1998, 3 master's, 27 doctorates awarded. *Entrance requirements:* For master's and doctorate, GRE General Test, GRE Subject Test (marine biology). Application fee: $40. *Financial aid:* Fellowships, research assistantships available. *Unit head:* W. Kendall Melville, Chair. *Application contact:* Yvonne Gaffney, Graduate Coordinator, 619-534-3206.

University of Connecticut, Graduate School, College of Liberal Arts and Sciences, Field of Oceanography, Storrs, CT 06269. Offers MS, PhD. *Degree requirements:* For doctorate, dissertation required. *Entrance requirements:* For master's and doctorate, GRE General Test, GRE Subject Test, TOEFL.

University of Georgia, Graduate School, College of Arts and Sciences, Department of Marine Sciences, Athens, GA 30602. Offers biological oceanography (MS, PhD); chemical oceanography (MS, PhD); physical oceanography (MS, PhD). *Faculty:* 16 full-time (4 women). *Students:* 24 full-time (10 women), 1 part-time. 59 applicants, 25% accepted. In 1998, 2 master's awarded. *Degree requirements:* For doctorate, dissertation required. *Entrance requirements:* For master's and doctorate, GRE General Test. *Application deadline:* For fall admission, 7/1 (priority date); for spring admission, 11/15. Application fee: $30. Electronic applications accepted. *Unit head:* Dr. Mary Ann Moran, Graduate Coordinator, 706-542-5863, Fax: 706-542-5888, E-mail: mmoran@arches.uga.edu.

See in-depth description on page 363.

University of Hawaii at Manoa, Graduate Division, School of Ocean and Earth Science and Technology, Department of Oceanography, Honolulu, HI 96822. Offers MS, PhD. Part-time programs available. *Faculty:* 54 full-time (3 women). *Students:* 43 full-time (23 women), 14 part-time (3 women); includes 2 minority (both Asian Americans or Pacific Islanders), 12 international. Average age 31. 81 applicants, 22% accepted. In 1998, 7 master's awarded (22% found work related to degree, 78% continued full-time study); 5 doctorates awarded (75% entered university research/teaching, 25% found other work related to degree). Terminal master's awarded for partial completion of doctoral program. *Degree requirements:* For master's, computer language, thesis, field experience required, foreign language not required; for doctorate, one foreign language, computer language, dissertation, field experience required. *Entrance requirements:* For master's and doctorate, GRE. *Average time to degree:* Master's–3.3 years full-time; doctorate–4 years full-time. *Application deadline:* For fall admission, 2/1; for spring admission, 9/1. Application fee: $25 ($50 for international students). *Financial aid:* In 1998–99, 40 students received aid, including 26 research assistantships (averaging $17,644 per year), 6 teaching assistantships (averaging $15,381 per year); fellowships, career-related internships or fieldwork, institutionally-sponsored loans, and tuition waivers (full and partial) also available. Financial aid applicants required to submit FAFSA. *Faculty research:* Physical oceanography, marine chemistry, biological oceanography, atmospheric chemistry, marine geology. Total annual research expenditures: $6.6 million. *Unit head:* Dr. Michael Mottl, Chairperson, 808-956-7633, Fax: 808-956-9225, E-mail: mmottl@soest.hawaii.edu.

University of Maine, Graduate School, College of Natural Sciences, Forestry, and Agriculture, School of Marine Sciences, Program in Oceanography, Orono, ME 04469. Offers MS, PhD. Part-time programs available. *Students:* 23 (11 women). 26 applicants, 42% accepted. In 1998, 2 master's, 2 doctorates awarded. *Degree requirements:* For master's and doctorate, thesis/dissertation required, foreign language not required. *Entrance requirements:* For master's and doctorate, GRE General Test, GRE Subject Test, TOEFL (minimum score of 550 required). *Application deadline:* For fall admission, 2/1 (priority date); for spring admission, 10/15. Applications are processed on a rolling basis. Application fee: $50. *Financial aid:* Fellowships, research assistantships, teaching assistantships, career-related internships or fieldwork, Federal Work-Study, and tuition waivers (full and partial) available. Aid available to part-time students. Financial aid application deadline: 3/1. *Faculty research:* Coastal processes, microbial ecology, crustacean systematics. *Application contact:* Scott G. Delcourt, Director of the Graduate School, 207-581-3218, Fax: 207-581-3232, E-mail: graduate@maine.edu.

University of Miami, Graduate School, Rosenstiel School of Marine and Atmospheric Science, Division of Meteorology and Physical Oceanography, Coral Gables, FL 33124. Offers atmospheric science (MA, MS, PhD); physical oceanography (MA, MS, PhD). *Faculty:* 18 full-time (1 woman). *Students:* 38 full-time (15 women), 1 (woman) part-time; includes 1 minority (African American), 26 international. Average age 27. 59 applicants, 22% accepted. In 1998, 3 master's, 2 doctorates awarded. Terminal master's awarded for partial completion of doctoral program. *Degree requirements:* For master's and doctorate, thesis/dissertation required, foreign language not required. *Entrance requirements:* For master's and doctorate, GRE General Test, TOEFL (minimum score of 550 required). *Average time to degree:* Master's–3 years full-time; doctorate–6 years full-time. *Application deadline:* For fall admission, 2/1 (priority date). Applications are processed on a rolling basis. Application fee: $35. Electronic applications accepted. Tuition: Full-time $15,336; part-time $852 per credit. Required fees: $174. Tuition and fees vary according to program. *Financial aid:* In 1998–99, 35 students received aid, including 1 fellowship with tuition reimbursement available, 31 research assistantships with tuition reimbursements available (averaging $17,000 per year), teaching assistantships with tuition reimbursements available (averaging $17,000 per year); institutionally-sponsored loans also available. Financial aid application deadline: 2/1. *Faculty research:* Large-scale ocean circulation, mesocale process, climate studies. *Unit head:* Dr. Kevin R. Leaman, Chair, 305-361-4045. *Application contact:* Dr. Frank Millero, Associate Dean, 305-361-4155, Fax: 305-361-4771, E-mail: gso@rsmas.miami.edu.

Announcement: The Division emphasizes research apprenticeships in its exclusively graduate-level education program. A student-faculty ratio of about 3:2 provides ample opportunity for personal guidance. Research programs encompass satellite-based remote sensing, computer-based modeling of atmospheric and oceanic systems, and worldwide ocean observations, with ties to biology as well as to climate, providing a wide range of choices for student research specialization. MPO graduate students may focus either on diagnostic observations of environmental processes or on any part of a spectrum of theoretical or modeling problems that range from mathematical aspects of fluid mechanics to problems of physical constraints on living systems. Financial aid is provided for all students in good academic standing, mainly as research assistantships.

University of Michigan, Horace H. Rackham School of Graduate Studies, College of Engineering, Department of Atmospheric, Oceanic, and Space Sciences, Program in Oceanography: Physical, Ann Arbor, MI 48109. Offers MS, PhD. Part-time programs available. *Faculty:* 2 full-time (0 women). *Students:* 3 full-time (1 woman), 1 international. In 1998, 1 doctorate awarded. Terminal master's awarded for partial completion of doctoral program. *Degree requirements:* For master's, thesis required (for some programs); for doctorate, dissertation, oral defense of dissertation, preliminary exams required. *Entrance requirements:* For master's and doctorate, GRE General Test (combined average 2000 on three sections), TOEFL (minimum score of 600 required). *Application deadline:* For fall admission, 1/15 (priority date). Applications are processed on a rolling basis. *Financial aid:* In 1998–99, 1 student received aid, including 1 fellowship, 1 research assistantship, 1 teaching assistantship; career-related internships or fieldwork, Federal Work-Study, and institutionally-sponsored loans also available. Aid available to part-time students. Financial aid application deadline: 3/15; financial aid applicants required to submit FAFSA. *Faculty research:* Fluid dynamics, physical oceanography air-sea boundary layer, remote sensing global change. Total annual research expenditures: $13.5 million. *Unit head:* Stanley Jacobs, Adviser, 734-764-3335, Fax: 734-764-4585, E-mail: sjj@umich.edu. *Application contact:* Susan Schreiber, Academic Services Assistant, 734-764-3336, Fax: 734-764-4585, E-mail: aoss.um@umich.edu.

University of Michigan, Horace H. Rackham School of Graduate Studies, College of Literature, Science, and the Arts, Department of Geological Sciences, Program in Oceanography: Marine Geology and Geochemistry, Ann Arbor, MI 48109. Offers MS, PhD. *Faculty:* 4 full-time (0 women), 1 part-time (0 women). *Students:* 4 full-time (3 women). 7 applicants, 57% accepted. Terminal master's awarded for partial completion of doctoral program. *Degree requirements:* For master's, thesis required, foreign language not required; for doctorate, variable foreign language requirement, dissertation, oral defense of dissertation, preliminary exam required. *Entrance requirements:* For master's, GRE General Test, GRE Subject Test; for doctorate, GRE General Test, GRE Subject Test, master's degree. *Average time to degree:* Master's–2 years full-time; doctorate–5 years full-time. *Application deadline:* For fall admission, 1/15 (priority date). Applications are processed on a rolling basis. Application fee: $55. Electronic applications accepted. *Financial aid:* In 1998–99, 2 students received aid, including 2 research assistantships, 2 teaching assistantships; fellowships, career-related internships or fieldwork and Federal Work-Study also available. *Faculty research:* Paleoceanography, paleolimnology, marine geochemistry, seismic stratigraphy. *Unit head:* David K. Rea, Chair, Department of Geological Sciences, 734-764-1435, Fax: 734-763-4690.

University of New Hampshire, Graduate School, College of Engineering and Physical Sciences, Department of Earth Sciences, Durham, NH 03824. Offers earth sciences (MS, PhD), including geochemical (MS), geology, hydrology (PhD), oceanography; hydrology (MS). *Faculty:* 25 full-time. *Students:* 32 full-time (7 women), 36 part-time (15 women); includes 1 minority (Asian American or Pacific Islander), 10 international. *Degree requirements:* For master's, thesis required, foreign language not required; for doctorate, dissertation required. *Entrance requirements:* For master's and doctorate, GRE General Test. *Application deadline:* For fall admission, 4/1 (priority date). Applications are processed on a rolling basis. Application fee: $50. Tuition, area resident: Full-time $5,750; part-time $319 per credit. Tuition, state resident: full-time $8,625. Tuition, nonresident: full-time $14,640; part-time $598 per credit. Required fees: $224 per semester. Tuition and fees vary according to course load, degree level and program. *Unit head:* Wallace Bothner, Chairperson, 603-862-1718. *Application contact:* Dr. Francis Birch, Graduate Coordinator, 603-862-3142.

University of Puerto Rico, Mayagüez Campus, Graduate Studies, College of Arts and Sciences, Department of Marine Sciences, Mayagüez, PR 00681-5000. Offers biological oceanography (MMS, PhD); chemical oceanography (MMS, PhD); geological oceanography (MMS, PhD); physical oceanography (MMS, PhD). *Degree requirements:* For master's, one foreign language, thesis, departmental and comprehensive final exams required; for doctorate, one foreign language, dissertation, qualifying, comprehensive, and final exams required. *Faculty research:* Marine botany, ecology, chemistry, and parasitology; fisheries; ichthyology; aquaculture.

See in-depth description on page 369.

University of Rhode Island, Graduate School, Graduate School of Oceanography, Kingston, RI 02881. Offers MS, PhD.

University of Southern California, Graduate School, College of Letters, Arts and Sciences, Department of Biological Sciences, Program in Marine Biology and Biological Oceanography, Los Angeles, CA 90089. Offers MS, PhD. *Faculty:* 8 full-time (1 woman). *Students:* 18 full-time (6 women), 2 part-time; includes 1 minority (Asian American or Pacific Islander), 8 international. Average age 30. 14 applicants, 43% accepted. In 1998, 3 master's, 6 doctorates awarded. *Degree requirements:* For master's and doctorate, thesis/dissertation required. *Entrance requirements:* For master's and doctorate, GRE General Test. *Application deadline:* For fall admission, 2/1 (priority date); for spring admission, 10/15. Application fee: $55. Tuition: Full-time $22,198; part-time $748 per unit. Required fees: $406. Tuition and fees vary according to program. *Financial aid:* In 1998–99, 3 fellowships, 6 research assistantships, 10 teaching assistantships were awarded.; Federal Work-Study, institutionally-sponsored loans, and scholarships also available. Aid available to part-time students. Financial aid application deadline: 2/15; financial aid applicants required to submit FAFSA. *Unit head:* Dr. Donald Manahan, Chair.

University of South Florida, Graduate School, College of Arts and Sciences, Department of Marine Science, Tampa, FL 33620-9951. Offers marine biology (MS, PhD); marine science (MS, PhD); oceanography (MS, PhD). Part-time and evening/weekend programs available. *Faculty:* 25 full-time (4 women). *Students:* 92 full-time (52 women), 16 part-time (4 women); includes 2 minority (1 African American, 1 Asian American or Pacific Islander), 10 international. *Degree requirements:* For master's, thesis required; for doctorate, 2 foreign languages (computer language can substitute for one), dissertation required. *Entrance requirements:* For master's and doctorate, GRE General Test (minimum combined score of 1100 required), minimum GPA of 3.0 in last 60 hours. *Application deadline:* For fall admission, 6/1; for spring admission, 10/15. Applications are processed on a rolling basis. Application fee: $20. Tuition, state resident: part-time $148 per credit hour. Tuition, nonresident: part-time $509 per credit hour. *Unit head:* Dr. Peter R. Betzer, Chairperson, 727-553-1130, Fax: 727-553-1189, E-mail: pbetzer@marine.usf.edu. *Application contact:* Edward VanVleet, Coordinator, 727-553-1165, Fax: 727-553-1189, E-mail: vanvleet@marine.usf.edu.

See in-depth description on page 371.

University of Victoria, Faculty of Graduate Studies, Faculty of Science, School of Earth and Ocean Sciences, Victoria, BC V8W 2Y2, Canada. Offers geochemistry (M Sc, PhD); geophysics (M Sc, PhD); marine geology and geophysics (M Sc, PhD); ocean acoustics (M Sc, PhD); oceanography (M Sc, PhD); paleobiology (M Sc, PhD); paleoceanography (M Sc, PhD); sedimentology (M Sc, PhD); stratigraphy (M Sc, PhD). Part-time programs available. *Faculty:* 15 full-time, 41 part-time. *Students:* 39 full-time (0 women), 1 part-time. Average age 27. 137 applicants, 16% accepted. In 1998, 2 master's, 1 doctorate awarded. *Degree requirements:*

For master's and doctorate, thesis/dissertation required. *Average time to degree:* Master's–3.11 years full-time; doctorate–4.5 years full-time. *Application deadline:* For fall admission, 2/15. Applications are processed on a rolling basis. Application fee: $50. Electronic applications accepted. *Financial aid:* In 1998–99, 16 fellowships, 22 research assistantships, 25 teaching assistantships were awarded.; career-related internships or fieldwork, institutionally-sponsored loans, and awards also available. Financial aid application deadline: 2/15. *Faculty research:* Climate modelling, geology. *Unit head:* Dr. C. R. Barnes, Director, 250-721-6120, Fax: 250-721-6200, E-mail: crbarnes@uvic.ca. *Application contact:* Dr. Dante Canil, Graduate Adviser, 250-721-6120, Fax: 250-721-6200, E-mail: dcanil@uvic.ca.

University of Washington, Graduate School, College of Ocean and Fishery Sciences, School of Oceanography, Programs in Biological Oceanography, Seattle, WA 98195. Offers MS, PhD. *Faculty:* 11 full-time (4 women). *Students:* 20 full-time (15 women); includes 3 minority (1 African American, 1 Asian American or Pacific Islander, 1 Hispanic American), 3 international. Average age 25. 68 applicants, 12% accepted. In 1998, 5 master's awarded (% continued full-time study); 2 doctorates awarded (100% entered university research/teaching). Terminal master's awarded for partial completion of doctoral program. *Degree requirements:* For master's, research project required, foreign language and thesis not required; for doctorate, dissertation required, foreign language not required. *Entrance requirements:* For master's and doctorate, GRE General Test, TOEFL (minimum score of 500 required), minimum GPA of 3.0. *Average time to degree:* Master's–2.5 years full-time; doctorate–5.5 years full-time. *Application deadline:* For fall and spring admission, 1/15. Application fee: $49. Electronic applications accepted. Tuition, state resident: full-time $5,196; part-time $475 per credit. Tuition, nonresident: full-time $13,485; part-time $1,285 per credit. Required fees: $387; $38 per credit. Tuition and fees vary according to course load. *Financial aid:* In 1998–99, 20 students received aid, including 7 fellowships with full tuition reimbursements available (averaging $18,333 per year), 10 research assistantships with full tuition reimbursements available (averaging $18,333 per year), 3 teaching assistantships with full tuition reimbursements available (averaging $18,333 per year) Aid available to part-time students. Financial aid application deadline: 1/15. *Faculty research:* Immunological techniques, thermophilic and archae-bacteria in hydrothermal systems, remote sensing, astrobiology. Total annual research expenditures: $2.4 million. *Application contact:* Della Rogers, Student Services Coordinator, 206-543-5039, Fax: 206-543-6073, E-mail: drogers@ocean.washington.edu.

University of Wisconsin–Madison, Graduate School, College of Engineering, Program in Oceanography and Limnology, Madison, WI 53706-1380. Offers MS, PhD. *Faculty:* 15 full-time (2 women), 2 part-time (0 women). *Students:* 11 full-time (3 women); includes 5 minority (2 African Americans, 1 Hispanic American, 2 Native Americans) 21 applicants, 29% accepted. In 1998, 2 doctorates awarded (100% found work related to degree). Terminal master's awarded for partial completion of doctoral program. *Degree requirements:* For master's, thesis required, foreign language not required; for doctorate, one foreign language, dissertation required. *Entrance requirements:* For master's and doctorate, GRE General Test. *Application deadline:* For fall admission, 1/1 (priority date). Application fee: $45. Electronic applications accepted. *Financial aid:* In 1998–99, 9 students received aid; fellowships, research assistantships, teaching assistantships, Federal Work-Study and institutionally-sponsored loans available. Financial aid application deadline: 1/1. *Faculty research:* Lake ecosystems, ecosystem modeling, geochemistry, physiological ecology, chemical limnology. *Unit head:* Dr. William C. Sonzogni, Chair, 608-224-6200, Fax: 608-224-6201, E-mail: sonzogni@facstaff.wisc.edu. *Application contact:* Ann McLain, Student Services Coordinator, 608-263-3264, Fax: 608-265-2340, E-mail: asmclain@facstaff.wisc.edu.

University of Wisconsin–Madison, Graduate School, College of Letters and Science, Department of Atmospheric and Oceanic Sciences, Madison, WI 53706-1380. Offers MS, PhD. Part-time programs available. *Faculty:* 19 full-time (0 women), 2 part-time (0 women). *Students:* 48 full-time (14 women), 6 part-time (1 woman), 11 international. Average age 25. 84 applicants, 44% accepted. In 1998, 8 master's awarded (12% entered university research/teaching, 63% found other work related to degree, 25% continued full-time study); 5 doctorates awarded (20% entered university research/teaching, 80% found other work related to degree). *Degree requirements:* For master's, thesis required (for some programs), foreign language not required; for doctorate, dissertation required, foreign language not required. *Entrance requirements:* For master's and doctorate, GRE General Test (minimum score of 650 on quantitative section, 500 on analytical required), minimum GPA of 3.0; previous course work in chemistry, mathematics, and physics. *Average time to degree:* Master's–2 years full-time, 3.5 years part-time; doctorate–4 years full-time, 5 years part-time. *Application deadline:* For fall admission, 8/1 (priority date); for spring admission, 12/1 (priority date). Applications are processed on a rolling basis. Application fee: $45. Electronic applications accepted. *Financial aid:* In 1998–99, 47 students received aid, including 1 fellowship with full tuition reimbursement available (averaging $17,500 per year), 29 research assistantships with full tuition reimbursements available (averaging $14,600 per year), 8 teaching assistantships with full tuition reimbursements available; career-related internships or fieldwork, Federal Work-Study, institutionally-sponsored loans, and scholarships also available. Aid available to part-time students. *Faculty research:* Satellite meteorology, weather systems, global climate change, numerical modeling, atmosphere-ocean interaction. Total annual research expenditures: $1.4 million. *Unit head:* Matthew Hitchman, Chair, 608-262-2828, Fax: 608-262-0166, E-mail: matt@adams.meteor.wisc.edu. *Application contact:* Connie Linehan, Graduate Coordinator, 608-262-2827, Fax: 608-262-0166, E-mail: linehan@facstaff.wisc.edu.

Yale University, Graduate School of Arts and Sciences, Department of Geology and Geophysics, New Haven, CT 06520. Offers geochemistry (PhD); geophysics (PhD); meteorology (PhD); mineralogy and crystallography (PhD); oceanography (PhD); paleoecology (PhD); paleontology and stratigraphy (PhD); petrology (PhD); structural geology (PhD). *Faculty:* 26. *Students:* 26 full-time (11 women), 9 international. *Degree requirements:* For doctorate, dissertation required, foreign language not required. *Entrance requirements:* For doctorate, GRE General Test, TOEFL. *Application deadline:* For fall admission, 1/4. Application fee: $65. *Unit head:* Chair, 203-432-3174. *Application contact:* Admissions Information, 203-432-2770.

Cross-Discipline Announcement

Florida Institute of Technology, Graduate School, College of Science and Liberal Arts, Department of Biological Sciences, Melbourne, FL 32901-6975.

MS and PhD in marine biology with research emphases in mollusks, echinoderms, coral reef fishes, and manatees and community studies of lagoonal, mangrove, and reef systems. Applications range from physiological and ecological systematics to biochemical and molecular biological studies in these areas.

COLLEGE OF WILLIAM AND MARY

School of Marine Science
Virginia Institute of Marine Science

Programs of Study

The School of Marine Science offers the Master of Science and the Doctor of Philosophy degrees in marine science. Programs of study in biological oceanography, physical oceanography, environmental chemistry and toxicology, geological oceanography, marine fisheries oceanography, and marine resource management and policy are available at both levels.

The M.S. degree requires 36 semester hours of graduate work completed with a grade of B or better, of which at least 9 hours must be in advanced courses; no more than 6 hours of thesis credit; successful completion of a qualifying examination and defense of the thesis; and a reading knowledge of one foreign language. The Ph.D. requires a minimum of three years of study beyond the baccalaureate and at least 42 semester hours of advanced work (with at least 9 credit hours in advanced courses); students must also be registered for at least 9 credit hours of dissertation, have a reading knowledge of one foreign language, successfully complete a course of study determined by the student's committee, pass a qualifying examination, and give a dissertation defense. To fulfill the full-time academic residency requirement of the School of Marine Science, students working on either degree must successfully complete the core course requirements and be registered full-time and in good standing for two consecutive semesters. All active degree-seeking students must register for a minimum of nine credit hours each semester and 1 hour during each summer session. The program is interdisciplinary; all students are required to take core courses in biological, chemical, physical, and geological oceanography and statistics. Students interested in careers in government and industry are encouraged to take courses in environmental law and marine affairs.

The primary orientation of the faculty is toward estuarine, coastal zone, and tidal freshwater environments. Many of the faculty members are actively engaged in applied research of direct concern to industry and management agencies. Students often find that their assistantship duties and/or research topics bring them into close contact with industry and management agencies at state, federal, and regional levels.

There is ample opportunity for students to engage in field-oriented thesis and dissertation research, and all students are encouraged to participate in field studies to gain experience in research at sea.

Research Facilities

The main research campus of the School of Marine Science/Virginia Institute of Marine Science is located at Gloucester Point on the York River. There is a branch laboratory at Wachapreague on Virginia's Eastern Shore that is ideally suited for research on the barrier island and lagoon systems. The Institute is well equipped with modern laboratory and seagoing instrumentation. Computer support is provided by a campuswide network connecting several high-performance workstations and more than 400 desktop computers. The Institute is equipped with running salt water. Major equipment includes transmission and scanning electron microscopes, a gas chromatograph/mass spectrometer, computer-interfaced gas chromatographs, an atomic absorption spectrometer, computer-assisted image analysis, sidescan sonar, a multifrequency echo sounder, and a hydraulic flume. The Institute has several vessels for estuarine and coastal operations research.

Financial Aid

Financial aid in the form of research assistantships, teaching assistantships, workships, and fellowships is available to a large percentage of the student body. Twelve-month assistantships for 1999–2000 are $14,900 for M.S. candidates and $15,300 for Ph.D. candidates. The majority of research assistantships are funded through grants and contracts. A limited number of outstanding applicants are awarded three-year fellowships that include full tuition and fee waiver in addition to the research assistantship. Several two- to three-year minority fellowships are awarded each year. All students on assistantships are eligible for consideration for resident tuition rates. Hourly workships are also available.

Cost of Study

The 1999–2000 cost of full-time study (9 or more hours) is $2650 for Virginia residents and $8088 for nonresidents per semester. Hourly fees are $165 per hour for residents and $510 per hour for nonresidents.

Living and Housing Costs

No student housing is available in Gloucester Point. Apartments and housing in the area rent for $325 or more per month. An automobile is strongly recommended. A list of apartments and houses in the area is available from the graduate dean's office.

Student Group

The School enrolls about 125 students; 8 to 10 percent of the students are from other countries. The majority of students have a biological orientation. About 43 percent are women. Recruiting initiatives in the coming years will be focused on increasing enrollment in the physical, geological, and chemical sciences and increasing the number of students who are members of minority groups in all disciplines. Graduates assume a wide range of marine and environmental science–related positions in federal, state, or other agencies and programs, as well as academic institutions, both public and private.

Location

Gloucester Point offers easy access by automobile to the urban regions surrounding Hampton Roads. Williamsburg, the site of the main campus of William and Mary, is 20 minutes away. The urban areas and the College support a vigorous cultural program, including theater, opera, ballet, and art. Two large coliseums with full programs are within an hour's drive.

The College and The School

The College of William and Mary, the second-oldest university in the United States, celebrated its 300th anniversary in 1993. It is a state-supported institution that prides itself on a dedication to excellence in its undergraduate program and a few select graduate programs.

The School of Marine Science of the College of William and Mary draws its faculty and academic support facilities from the Virginia Institute of Marine Science (VIMS), a research laboratory of the College whose origins go back to 1940. The dean of the School is also the director of VIMS.

Applying

Applications close on February 1 for the following academic year. The majority of students are admitted for the fall semester; students are admitted to the spring semester only under exceptional circumstances. Applications must be submitted on an appropriate form obtainable from the College of William and Mary and must include appropriate transcripts, scores on the General Test of the Graduate Record Examinations, and three letters of recommendation. Personal interviews are encouraged and may be arranged by advance appointment.

Correspondence and Information

Dean of Graduate Studies
School of Marine Science
Virginia Institute of Marine Science
College of William and Mary
P.O. Box 1346
Gloucester Point, Virginia 23062-1346
Telephone: 804-642-7106 or 7105

College of William and Mary

THE FACULTY AND THEIR RESEARCH

L. Donelson Wright, Dean and Director; Ph.D., LSU, 1970. Sediment transport, benthic boundary layer and morphodynamics of coastal zone.
John D. Milliman, Dean of Graduate Studies; Ph.D., Miami (Florida), 1966. Marine geology, transport, deposition, and diagenesis of sediments; applied marine geology; coastal zone processes.

Professors

Standish K. Allen Jr., Ph.D., Washington (Seattle), 1987. Genetics and breeding technologies in aquaculture, fisheries genetics.
Herbert M. Austin, Ph.D, Florida State, 1971. Fisheries oceanography, physical environmental parameters and interannual variability abundance of living marine resources.
John D. Boon III, Ph.D., William and Mary, 1974. Geological oceanography, mathematical geology, tidal hydraulics.
Eugene M. Burreson, Director of Research and Advisory Services; Ph.D., Oregon State, 1975. Parasitology; ecology, pathology, and immunology of marine parasitic protozoa; systematics and zoogeography of marine leeches.
Mark E. Chittenden Jr., Ph.D., Rutgers, 1969. Marine fisheries ecology and population dynamics.
Fu-Lin Chu, Ph.D., William and Mary, 1982. Nutrition-biochemistry studies of mollusks, diseases and immunopathology of shellfish, oyster, and algal culture.
Robert J. Diaz, Ph.D., Virginia, 1977. Benthic ecology; population dynamics, energetics, and quantitative analyses of benthic communities; sediment resuspension and accumulation rates; invertebrate taxonomy.
Hugh W. Ducklow, Ph.D., Harvard, 1977. Marine microbial ecology and biogeochemistry, global ocean carbon cycle.
William D. DuPaul, Ph.D., William and Mary, 1972. Fisheries science, marine advisory services, commercial fisheries development.
John E. Graves, Ph.D., California, San Diego (Scripps), 1981. Fishery genetics.
John M. Hoenig, Ph.D., Rhode Island, 1983. Stock assessment methods, commercial and sport fishery management, statistical parameter estimation.
Stephen L. Kaattari, Ph.D., California, Davis, 1979. Cellular immunology, immunochemistry, immunotoxicology, immunodiagnosis, and vaccine design.
Steven A. Kuehl, Ph.D., North Carolina State, 1985. Sediment geology and radioisotope geochemistry.
Albert Y. Kuo, Ph.D., Johns Hopkins, 1970. Physical oceanography, estuarine hydrodynamics, estuarine circulation and water quality, turbulence, mathematical modeling.
Maurice P. Lynch, Ph.D., William and Mary, 1972. Management resource and policy, physiological ecology.
William G. MacIntyre, Ph.D., Dalhousie, 1965. Chemical oceanography, groundwater contaminant transport theory, organic solute transport solubility.
Roger L. Mann, Ph.D., University College of North Wales, 1976. Physiology, biochemistry, and ecology of marine bivalve mollusks; larval behavior; ecology.
John A. Musick, Acuff Professor; Ph.D., Harvard, 1969. Ecology of marine fishes, sea turtles, and marine mammals; systematics and ecology of marine fishes.
Michael C. Newman, Ph.D., Rutgers, 1981. Ecological toxicology, quantitative prediction of pollutant bioaccumulation and effects.
Robert J. Orth, Ph.D., Maryland, 1975. Biology and ecology of submerged aquatic vegetation, benthic communities.
Morris H. Roberts Jr., Ph.D., William and Mary, 1969. Aquatic toxicology, culture of marine invertebrates.
Gene M. Silberhorn, Ph.D., Kent State, 1970. Coastal and wetlands plant ecology and systematics, coastal-zone management, submerged aquatic vegetation reproductive life cycles.
Dennis L. Taylor, Ph.D., Wales, 1967. Algal physiology.
N. Bartlett Theberge, LL.M., Miami (Florida), 1974. Ocean and coastal law, marine affairs, marine resource management.
Richard L. Wetzel, Ph.D., Georgia, 1975. Estuarine and coastal ecology, energetics, systems ecology.

Associate Professors

James E. Bauer, Ph.D., Maryland, 1989. Isotope geochemistry of marine organic matter, marine biogeochemistry and microbial ecology.
John M. Brubaker, Ph.D., Oregon State, 1979. Physical oceanography, estuarine hydrodynamics, shallow-water fronts.
Rebecca M. Dickhut, Ph.D., Wisconsin–Madison, 1989. Chemical fate and transport in aquatic environments.
J. Emmett Duffy, Ph.D., North Carolina at Chapel Hill, 1989. Ecology, evolution, and systematics; origin, maintenance, and function of biological diversity.
David A. Evans, D.Phil., Oxford, 1964. Applied mathematics and physics, numerical analysis.
Mohamed Faisal, Ph.D./D.V.M., Ludwig-Maximillian, 1982. Pathogenesis, immunotoxicology, disease of aquatic animals.
Robert C. Hale, Ph.D., William and Mary, 1983. Fate and effects of pollutants in the marine environment.
Carl H. Hershner, Ph.D., Virginia, 1977. Estuarine and coastal ecology, marine resource management.
Howard I. Kator, Ph.D., Florida State, 1971. Microbiology, ecology of estuarine and marine bacteria, biodegradation processes, sanitary microbiology of estuarine waters.
James E. Kirkley, Ph.D., Maryland, 1986. Resource economics, production, trade, resource management, quantitative methods and bioeconomics.
Romuald N. Lipcius, Ph.D., Florida State, 1984. Ecology, behavior and population dynamics of crustaceans, benthic predator-prey and recruitment dynamics, biostatistics, quantitative ecology.
Jerome P.-Y. Maa, Ph.D., Florida, 1986. Geological oceanography, sediment transport.
Mark R. Patterson, Ph.D., Harvard, 1985. Biomechanics and physical biology of lower invertebrates and algae, bioenergetics of corals and sponges, underwater instrumentation.
Linda C. Schaffner, Ph.D., William and Mary, 1987. Biological oceanography, invertebrate ecology and behavior (general and blue crabs), animal-sediment interactions, effects of disturbance on marine ecosystems.
Peter A. Van Veld, Ph.D., Georgia, 1987. Biochemical responses of marine organisms to pollutants, detoxification enzymes.
Wolfgang K. Vogelbein, Ph.D., LSU, 1991. Pathobiology of pollution/disease association in aquatic animals, particularly the relationship between chemical exposure and cancer in fishes.

Assistant Professors

Elizabeth A. Canuel, Ph.D., North Carolina at Chapel Hill, 1992. Organic geochemistry of particulate matter, lipid biomarkers.
Catherine J. Chisholm-Brause, Ph.D., Stanford, 1991. Aqueous and surface geochemistry, chemical reactions at solid-water interfaces.
Carl T. Friedrichs, Ph.D., MIT/Woods Hole Oceanographic Institution, 1993. Coastal and estuarine hydrodynamics and sediment transport.
Harry V. Wang, Ph.D., Johns Hopkins, 1983. Physical oceanography, estuarine and coastal hydrodynamics, coastal engineering, numerical modeling.

College of William and Mary

SELECTED PUBLICATIONS

Bushek, D., and **S. K. Allen Jr.** et al. Response of *Crassostrea virginica* to *in vitro* cultured *Perkinsus marinus:* Preliminary comparisons of three innoculation methods. *J. Shellfish Res.* 16:479–85, 1997.

Guo, X., and **S. K. Allen Jr.** Fluorescence in situ hybridization of the vertebrate telomere sequence to chromosome ends of the Pacific oyster, *Crassostrea gigas* (Thunberg). *J. Shellfish Res.* 16:87–9, 1997.

Que, H., X. Guo, F. Zhang, and **S. K. Allen Jr.** Chromosome segregation in fertilized eggs from triploid Pacific oysters, *Crassostrea gigas* (Thunberg), following inhibition of polar body 1. *Biol. Bull.* 193:14–9, 1997.

Austin, H. M., D. Scoles, and A. Abell. Morphometric separation of annual cohorts in mid-Atlantic bluefish, *Pomatomus saltatrix,* using discriminant function analysis. *Fish. Bull.,* in press.

Wagner, C. M., and **H. M. Austin.** Correspondence between environmental gradients and summer littoral fish assemblages across the freshwater/marine ecotone of the lower Chesapeake Bay, U.S.A. *Mar. Ecol. Prog. Ser.,* in press.

Spraker, H., and **H. M. Austin.** Diel feeding periodicity of Atlantic silverside, *Menidia menidia,* in the York River, Chesapeake Bay, Virginia. *J. Eliaha Mitchell Sci. Soc.* 113(4):171–82, 1997.

Cherrier, J., and **J. E. Bauer** et al. Radiocar in oceanic bacteria: Evidence of the age of assimilated carbon. *Limnol. Oceanogr.,* in press.

Bauer, J. E., et al. Temporal variability in dissolved organic carbon and radiocarbon in the eastern North Pacific Ocean. *J. Geophys. Res.* 103(C2):2867–82, 1998.

Bauer, J. E., et al. Distributions of dissolved organic and inorganic carbon and radiocarbon in the eastern North Pacific continental margin. *Deep-Sea Res. II* 45:689–714, 1998.

Brubaker, J. M., and J. H. Simpson. Flow convergence and stability at a tidal estuarine front: Acoustic Doppler current observations. *J. Geophys. Res.,* in press.

Siddall, M. E., and **E. M. Burreson.** Leeches (Oligochaeta?: Euhirudinea), their phylogeny and the evolution of life-history strategies. *Hydrobiologia* 334:277–85, 1996.

Flores, B. S., M. E. Siddall, and **E. M. Burreson.** Phylogeny of the *Haplosporidia* (Eukaryota: Alveolata) based on small subunit ribosomal RNA gene sequence. *J. Parasitol.* 82(4):616–23, 1996.

Burreson, E. M., and L. M. Ragone Calvo. Epizootiology of *Perkinsus marinus* disease of oysters in Chesapeake Bay, with emphasis on data since 1985. *J. Shellfish Res.* 15(1):17–34, 1996.

Canuel, E. A., K. H. Freeman, and S. G. Wakeham. Isotopic compositions of lipid biomarker compounds in estuarine plants and surface sediments. *Limnol. Oceanogr.* 42(7):1570–84, 1997.

Canuel, E. A., and C. S. Martens. Reactivity of recently-deposited organic matter: Degradation of lipid compounds near the sediment-water interface. *Geochim. Cosmochim. Acta* 60:1793–806, 1996.

Canuel, E. A., et al. Using molecular and isotopic tracers to examine sources of organic matter and its incorporation into the food webs of San Francisco Bay. *Limnol. Oceanogr.* 40:67–81, 1995.

Barbieri, L. R., **M. E. Chittenden Jr.,** and C. M. Jones. Yield-per-recruit analysis and management strategies for Atlantic croaker, *Micropogonias undulatus,* in the Middle Atlantic Bight. *Fish. Bull. U.S.* 95:637–45, 1997.

Lowerre-Barbieri, S. K., **M. E. Chittenden Jr.,** and L. R. Barbieri. Variable spawning activity and annual fecundity of weakfish in Chesapeake Bay. *Trans. Am. Fish. Soc.* 125:532–45, 1996.

Lowerre-Barbieri, S. K., **M. E. Chittenden Jr.,** and L. R. Barbieri. The multiple spawning pattern of weakfish *(Cynoscion regalis)* in the Chesapeake Bay and Middle Atlantic Bight. *J. Fish. Biol.* 48:1139–63, 1996.

Chu, F.-L. E., and S. Ozkizilcik. Lipid and fatty acid composition of striped bass *(Morone saxatilis)* larvae during development. *Comp. Biochem. Physiol.* 111B:665–74, 1995.

Volety, A. K., and **F.-L. E. Chu.** Suppression of chemiluminescence of eastern oyster *(Crassostrea virginica)* hemocytes by the protozoan parasite *Perkinsus marinus. Dev. Comp. Immunol.* 19:135–42, 1995.

Nestlerode, J. A., and **R. J. Diaz.** Effects of periodic environmental hypoxia on predation of a tethered polychaete, *Glycera americana:* Implication for trophic dynamics. *Mar. Ecol. Prog. Ser.* 172:185–95, 1998.

Bonsdorff, E., **R. J. Diaz** et al. Characterization of soft-bottom benthic habitats of the Aland Islands, northern Baltic Sea. *Mar. Ecol. Prog. Ser.* 142:235–45, 1996.

Diaz, R. J., and R. Rosenberg. Marine benthic hypoxia—review of ecological effects and behavioral responses on macrofauna. *Oceanogr. Mar. Biol. Ann. Rev.* 33:245–303, 1995.

Liu, K., and **R. M. Dickhut.** Effects of wind speed and particulate matter source on surface microlayer characteristics and enrichment of organic matter in southern Chesapeake Bay. *J. Geophys. Res., Atmos.* 103:10571–7, 1998.

Gustafson, K. E., and **R. M. Dickhut.** Gaseous exchange of polycyclic aromatic hydrocarbons across the air-water interface of southern Chesapeake Bay. *Environ. Sci. Technol.* 31:1623–9, 1997.

Carlson, C., **H. W. Ducklow,** and T. D. Sleeter. Stocks and dynamics of bacterioplankton in the northwestern Sargasso Sea. *Deep-Sea Res. II* 43:491–516, 1996.

Carlson, C., and **H. W. Ducklow.** Growth of bacterioplankton and consumption of dissolved organic carbon in the Sargasso Sea. *Aq. Microb. Ecol.* 10:69–85, 1996.

Oguz, T., **H. W. Ducklow** et al. Simulation of annual plankton productivity cycles in the Black Sea by one-dimensional, physical-biological model. *J. Geophys. Res.* 101:16585–99, 1996.

Duffy, J. E. On the frequency of eusociality in snapping shrimps with description of a new eusocial species. *Bull. Marine Sci.,* in press.

Duffy, J. E. Eusociality in a coral-reef shrimp. *Nature* 381:512–4, 1996.

Duffy, J. E. Resource-associated population subdivision in a symbiotic coral-reef shrimp. *Evolution* 50:360–73, 1996.

DuPaul, W. D., J. C. Brust, and **J. E. Kirkley.** Bycatch in the United States and Canadian Sea Scallop Fishery. In *Solving Bycatch: Considerations for Today and Tomorrow,* pp. 175–81. University of Alaska, Sea Grant College Program Report No. 96–103, 1996.

Loesch, J. G., and **D. A. Evans.** Seasonal variation in surf clam yields. *J. Shellfish Res.* 13(2):425–31, 1994.

La Peyre, J. F., D. Y. Schafhauser, E. M. Rizkalla, and **M. Faisal.** Production of serine proteases by the oyster pathogen *Perkinsus marinus* (Apicomplexa) in vitro. *J. Euk. Microbiol.* 42(5):451–8, in press.

Faisal, M., B. J. Rutan, and S. Sami-Demmerle. Development of continuous liver cell cultures from the marine teleost, spot *(Leiostomus xanthurus,* Pisces: sciaenidae). *Aquaculture* 132:59–72, 1995.

La Peyre, J. F., and **M. Faisal.** *Perkinsus marinus* produces extracellular proteolytic factor(s) in vitro. *Bull. Eur. Assoc. Fish Pathol.* 15:28–31, 1995.

Friedrichs, C. T., and **L. D. Wright.** Sensitivity of bottom stress and bottom roughness estimates to density stratification, Eckernförde Bay, Southern Baltic Sea. *J. Geophys. Res.* 102:5721–32, 1997.

Aubrey, D. G., and **C. T. Friedrichs,** editors. *Buoyancy Effects on Coastal Dynamics.* Washington, D.C.: American Geophysical Union, 1996.

Scoles, D. R., B. B. Collette, and **J. E. Graves.** Global phylogeography of mackerels of the genus *Scomber. Fish. Bull.* 96:823–42, 1998.

Graves, J. E. Molecular insights into the population structures of cosmopolitan marine fishes. *J. Heredity* 89:427–37, 1998.

Carlini, D. B., and **J. E. Graves.** Phylogenetic analysis of cytochrome *c* oxidase I sequences to determine higher-level relationships with the coleoid cephalopods. *Bull. Mar. Sci.,* in press.

Hale, R. C., C. Enos, and K. Gallagher. Sources and distribution of polychlorinated terphenyls (PTCs) at a major U.S. aeronautics research facility. *Environ. Manage.* 22:937–46, 1998.

Hale, R. C., and K. M. Aneiro. Detection of coal tar and creosote constituents in the aquatic environment. *J. Chromatogr. A* 774:79–95, 1997.

Hale, R. C., et al. Robustness of supercritical fluid extraction (SFE) in environmental studies: Analysis of chlorinated pollutants in tissues from the osprey *(Pandion haliaetus)* and several fish species. *Intern. J. Environ. Anal. Chem.* 64:11–19, 1996.

Varnell, L. M., K. J. Havens, and **C. Hershner.** Daily variability in the population levels and characteristics of aquatic wildlife using tidal salt marshes. *Estuaries* 18(2):326–34, 1995.

Hoenig, J. M., et al. Models for tagging data that allow for incomplete mixing of newly tagged animals. *Can. J. Fish. Aquat. Sci.,* in press.

Chen, C. L., K. H. Pollock, and **J. M. Hoenig.** Combining change-in-ratio, index-removal and removal models for estimating population size. *Biometrics,* in press.

Kaattari, S. L., D. Evans, and J. Klemer. Varied redox forms of teleost IgM: An alternative to isotypic diversity? *Immunol. Rev.* 166:133–42, 1998.

Ottinger, C. A., and **S. L. Kaattari.** Sensitivity of rainbow trout leukocytes to aflatoxin B1. *Fish Shellfish Immunol.* 8:515–30, 1998.

Kaattari, S. L., and J. D. Piganelli. Vaccination against bacterial kidney disease. In *Developments in Biological Standardization.* International Association of Biological Standardization 90:145–52, 1997.

Kator, H., and R. A. Fisher. Bacterial spoilage of processed sea scallop *(Placopecten magellanicus)* meats. *J. Food Protect.* 58:1351–6, 1995.

Rhodes, M. W., and **H. Kator.** Seasonal occurrence of *Mesophilic aeromonas* spp. as a function of biotype and water quality in temperate freshwater lakes. *Water Res.* 28:2241–51, 1994.

Dellapenna, T. M., **S. A. Kuehl,** and **L. C. Schaffner.** Seabed mixing

College of William and Mary

Selected Publications (continued)

and particle residence times in biologically and physically dominated estuarine systems: A comparison of lower Chesapeake Bay and the York River subestuary. *Estuar. Coastal Shelf Sci.* 46:777–95, 1998.

Kuehl, S. A., T. D. Pacioni, and J. M. Rine. Seabed dynamics of the inner Amazon continental shelf: Temporal and spatial variability of surficial strata. *Mar. Geol.* 125:283–302, 1995.

Dukat, D. A., and **S. A. Kuehl.** Non-steady-state 210pb flux and the use of 228Ra/226Ra as a geochronometer on the Amazon continental shelf. *Mar. Geol.* 125:329–50, 1995.

Nittrouer, C. A., **S. A. Kuehl** et al. An introduction to the geological significance of sediment transport and accumulation on the Amazon continental shelf. *Mar. Geol.* 125:177–92, 1995.

Shen, J., and **A. Y. Kuo.** Inverse estimation of parameters for an estuarine eutrophication model. *ASCE J. Environ. Eng.* 122(11):1031–40, 1996.

Park, K., and **A. Y. Kuo.** A multi-step computation scheme decoupling kinetic processes from physical transport in water quality models. *Water Res.* 30(10):2255–64, 1996.

Park, K., and **A. Y. Kuo.** A numerical model study of hypoxia in the tidal Rappahannock River of Chesapeake Bay. *Estuarine Coastal Shelf Sci.* 42(5):563–81, 1996.

Lipcius, R. N., et al. Hydrodynamic decoupling of recruitment, habitat quality and adult abundance in the Caribbean spiny lobster: Source-sink dynamics? *Mar. Freshwater Res.* 48:1–9, 1997.

Moksnes, P., **R. N. Lipcius,** L. Pihl, and J. van Montfrans. Cannibal-prey dynamics in young juveniles and postlarvae of the blue crab. *J. Exp. Mar. Biol. Ecol.* 215:157–87, 1997.

Pile, A. J., **R. N. Lipcius,** J. van Montfrans, and **R. J. Orth.** Density-dependent settler-recruit-juvenile relationships in blue crabs. *Ecol. Monogr.* 66(3):277–300, 1996.

Lynch, M. P., and S. A. Walton. Talking trash on the Internet: Working real data into your classroom. *Learning Leading Technol.* 25(5), February 1998.

Walton, S. A., and **M. P. Lynch.** The Menhaden mystery. *Sci. Scope* 20(8):10–13, 1997.

Walton, S. A., and **M. P. Lynch.** The virtual "surf" zone: Environmental studies on the Internet. *Science Scope* 19(6):19–21, 1996.

Maa, J. P.-Y., and C. H. Hobbs III. Physical impact of waves on adjacent coasts resulting from dredging at Sandbridge Shoal, VA. *J. Coastal Res.* 14(2):525–36, 1998.

Maa, J. P.-Y., L. Sandord, and J. P. Halka. Sediment resuspension characteristics in the Baltimore Harbor. *Mar. Geol.* 146:137–45, 1998.

Maa, J. P.-Y., K.-J. Sun, and Q. He. Ultrasonic characterization of marine sediments. *Mar. Geol.* 141:183–92, 1997.

MacIntyre, W. G., C. P. Antworth, T. B. Stauffer, and R. G. Young. Heterogeneity of sorption and transport related properties in a sand-gravel aquifer at Columbus, MS. *J. Contaminant Hydrology,* in press.

Stauffer, T. B., J. M. Boggs, and **W. G. MacIntyre.** Ten years of research in groundwater transport at Columbus A.F.B., MS. In *Biotechnology in the Sustainable Environments,* pp. 85–96, chapter 9, ed. G. Sayler. New York: Plenum Press, 1997.

Gundersen, J. L., **W. G. MacIntyre,** and **R. C. Hale.** pH dependent sorption of chloroguiacols on estuarine sediments: The effects of humic acids and TOC. *Environ. Sci. Tech.* 31(1):188–93, 1997.

Bartol, I., and **R. Mann.** Small-scale settlement patterns of the oyster *Crassostrea virginica* on a constructed intertidal reef. *Bull. Marine Sci.,* in press.

Baker, P., and **R. Mann.** The postlarval phase of bivalve mollusks: A review of functional ecology and new records of postlarval drifting of Chesapeake Bay bivalves. *Bull. Marine Sci.,* in press.

Roegner, G. C., and **R. Mann.** Early recruitment and growth patterns of *Crassostrea virginica* Gmelin with respect to tidal zonation. *Mar. Ecol. Prog. Ser.* 117:91–101, 1995.

Milliman, J. D. Fluvial sediment discharge to the sea and the importance of regional tectonics. In *Tectonic Uplift and Climate Change,* pp. 239–57, ed. W. F. Ruddiman. New York: Plenum Press, 1997.

Milliman, J. D., and A. W. Droxler. Neritic and pelagic carbonate sedimentation in the marine environment: Ignorance is not bliss. *Geol. Rundschau* 85:496–504, 1996.

Milliman, J. D., and B. U. Haq. *Sea-Level Rise and Coastal Subsidence: Causes, Consequences and Strategies.* Amsterdam: Kluwer Press, 1996.

Musick, J. A. Endangered marine fishes: Criteria and identification of North American stocks at risk. *Fisheries* 23(2):28–30, 1998.

Murdy, E., R. Birdsong, and **J. A. Musick.** *The Fishes of Chesapeake Bay,* 324 pp. Washington, D.C.: Smithsonian Press, 1997.

Musick, J. A., et al. Historical comparison of the structure of demersal fish communities near a deep-sea disposal site in the western North Atlantic. *J. Mar. Environ. Eng.* 3:149–71, 1996.

Newman, M. C. *Fundamentals of Ecotoxicology,* 415 pp. Chelsea, Mich.: Ann Arbor Press, 1998.

Newman, M. C., and R. M. Jagoe. Bioaccumulation models with time lags: Dynamics and stability criteria. *Ecol. Model.* 84:281–6, 1996.

Newman, M. C. *Quantitative Methods in Aquatic Ecotoxicology,* 426 pp. Chelsea, Mich.: Lewis Publishers, 1995.

Orth, R. J., M. Luckenbach, and K. A. Moore. Seed dispersal in a marine macrophyte: Implications for colonization and restoration. *Ecology* 75:1927–39, 1994.

Savarese, M., **M. R. Patterson,** V. I. Chernykh, and V. A. Fialkov. Trophic effects of sponge feeding within Lake Baikal's littoral zone: 1. In situ pumping rates. *Limnol. Oceanogr.* 42(1):171–8, 1997.

Pile, A. J., **M. R. Patterson** et al. Trophic effects of sponge feeding within Lake Baikal's littoral zone: 2. Sponge abundance, diet, feeding efficiency, and carbon flux. *Limnol. Oceanogr.* 42(1):178–84, 1997.

Reece, K. S., D. Bushek, and **J. E. Graves.** Molecular markers for population genetic analysis of *Perkinsus marinus. Mol. Mar. Biol. Biotechnol.* 6(3):197–206, 1997.

Reece, K. S., M. E. Siddall, **E. M. Burreson,** and **J. E. Graves.** Phylogenetic analysis of *Perkinsus* based upon actin gene sequences. *J. Parasitol.* 83(3):417–23, 1997.

Siddall, M. E., **K. S. Reece, J. E. Graves,** and **E. M. Burreson.** "Total evidence" refutes the inclusion of *Perkinsus* species in the phylum Apicomplexa. *Parasitology* 115:165–76, 1997.

Sved, D. W., **M. H. Roberts Jr.,** and **P. A. Van Veld.** Toxicity of sediments contaminated with fractions of creosote. *Water Res.* 31:294–300, 1997.

Roberts, M. H., Jr., R. J. Huggett et al. Tributyltin bioconcentration from solution and suspended sediments by oysters with a comparison to uptake in a field experiment. In *Tributyltin: Fate and Effects,* pp. 357–68, eds., M. Champ and P. Seligman, 1996.

Sved, D. W., and **M. H. Roberts Jr.** A novel use for the continuous-flow serial diluter: Aquatic toxicity testing of contaminated sediments in suspension. *Water Res.* 29:1169–77, 1995.

Kane-Driscoll, S. B., **L. C. Schaffner,** and **R. M. Dickhut.** Toxicokinetics of fluoranthene to the amphipod, *Leptocheirum plumulosus,* in water-only and sediment exposures. *Mar. Environ. Res.* 45:269–84, 1998.

Schaffner, L. C., and **R. M. Dickhut** et al. Role of physical-chemistry and bioturbation by estuarine macrogauna on the transport and fate of hydrophobic organic contaminants in the benthos. *Environ. Sci. Technol.* 31:3120–5, 1997.

Schaffner, L. C., R. M. Dickhut, S. Mitra, and P. W. Lay. Effects of physical chemistry and bioturbation by estuarine macrofauna on the transport of hydrophobic organic contaminants in the benthos. *Environ. Sci. Technol.* 31:3120–5, 1997.

Silberhorn, G. M., S. Dewing, and P. A. Mason. Production of reproductive shoots, vegetative shoots, and seeds in populations of *Ruppia maritima* L. from Chesapeake Bay, Virginia. *Wetlands* 16:232–9, 1996.

Armknecht, S. L., **P. A. Van Veld,** and **S. L. Kaattari.** An elevated glutathione S–transferase in creosote-resistant mummichog *(Fundulus heteroclitus). Aquat. Toxicol.,* in press.

Van Veld, P. A., W. K. Vogelbein et al. Route-specific cellular expression of cytochrome P4501A (CYPIA) in fish *(Fundulus heteroclitus)* following exposure to aqueous and dietary benzo[a]pyrene. *Toxicol. Appl. Pharmacol.* 143:348–59, 1997.

Cooper, P. S., **W. K. Vogelbein,** and **P. A. Van Veld.** Immunohistochemical and immunoblot detection of P-glycoprotein in normal and neoplastic fish liver. In *Techniques in Aquatic Toxicology,* pp. 307–25, ed. G. K. Ostrander. Boca Raton: CRC/Lewis Publishers, 1996.

Wright, L. D., C. R. Sherwood, and R. W. Sternberg. Field measurements of fairweather bottom boundary layer processes and sediment suspension on the Louisiana inner continental shelf. *Marine Geol.* 140:329–45, 1997.

Wright, L. D., L. C. Schaffner, and **J. P.-Y. Maa.** Biological mediation of bottom boundary layer processes and sediment suspension in the lower Chesapeake Bay. *Marine Geol.* 141:27–50, 1997.

Wright, L. D., C. T. Friedrichs, and D. A. Hepworth. Effects of benthic biology on bottom boundary layer processes, Dry Tortugas Bank, Florida Keys. *Geo-Marine Lett.* (Special Issue on NRL-CBBL Dry Tortugas Results) 17:291–8, 1997.

DALHOUSIE UNIVERSITY

Department of Oceanography

Program of Study

The Department of Oceanography offers a program leading to M.Sc. and Ph.D. degrees in oceanography. The program is designed to provide students with a general knowledge of the field as a whole and with advanced training in one of the specialties. Introductory and advanced courses are available in atmospheric sciences, physical and chemical oceanography, marine geology and geophysics, and biological oceanography. Students also commonly take courses at the graduate level in appropriate basic sciences. However, the main emphasis is on thesis research rather than formal course work, particularly after the first year. Ph.D. candidates make an oral defence of the research proposal, normally during the second year. All students must make an oral thesis defence. Mastery of shipboard oceanographic techniques is an integral part of the program.

The University term is from mid-September to mid-April, but scholarships are granted on a year-round basis and students are expected to be in residence during the summer to carry on their thesis research.

Research Facilities

The department's facilities within the Life Sciences Centre include a large running-seawater system with environmentally controlled rooms, high-pressure facilities for simulation of deep-sea conditions, and large tanks for fish studies. Seagoing facilities are supplied by federal oceanographic ships. The department is equipped with the collecting gear and laboratory instrumentation required for oceanographic research. Library facilities are centralized in a science library nearby. In addition to numerous terminals to the University's RISC 6000 computer, the department has a variety of microcomputers and workstations with plotters and laser printers.

Financial Aid

Virtually all students not receiving external scholarships are supported by Dalhousie Fellowships. For the 1998–99 academic year, the base graduate stipend for oceanography students is Can$15,000 per annum. During the years that a student pays full fees, a supplement will be added to the base stipend to help offset some of the tuition fees. Some larger scholarships are available for outstanding students. Applicants are urged to seek external scholarships that may be available to them.

Cost of Study

In 1999–2000, the cost of tuition is Can$4889 per year for M.Sc. students, Can$5089 for Ph.D. students, and Can$1509 for students who are completing their thesis. International students pay an additional Can$2950 per year. International students are also required to pay medical insurance fees, which are Can$416 for single students and Can$798 for married students.

Living and Housing Costs

The cost of living in Halifax is higher than in the eastern United States. In general, scholarship support is adequate for an unmarried student. Married students find that their spouses need to get a job to supplement their income. University housing is limited, and most students live off campus, although finding good housing at a reasonable cost is one of the most troublesome problems that graduate students have.

Student Group

There are currently about 45 graduate students in the Department of Oceanography; the student-faculty ratio is 2:1.

Location

Halifax, a city of about 114,000 with a metropolitan population of 320,000, is built on a peninsula that is surrounded by arms of the sea. Dalhousie is situated in a residential area in the southwestern part of the peninsula, 0.6 kilometres from the water. Halifax is a mixture of the old and the new—high-rise apartments, modern office buildings, fine residential areas, and some historic neighborhoods. There is an unusual amount of park area. Museums, several repertory theatres, and a symphony orchestra supplement the variety of cultural activities sponsored by the University. By large-city standards the pace of life is leisurely. Halifax is surrounded by rugged granite country, largely forested and with numerous lakes. Wild country a half-hour drive from the centre of the city provides ample opportunity for outdoor activities.

The University

Dalhousie, founded in 1818, has a current enrolment of 13,700 students. In addition to the undergraduate and graduate faculties of arts and sciences, there are schools of law, medicine, dentistry, and other professions. The Life Sciences Centre houses the Departments of Oceanography, Biology, Earth Sciences, and Psychology. There is student representation on the Senate and Board of Governors and in most academic departments. The Dalhousie Association of Graduate Students has a year-round social facility.

Applying

Requests for application forms for admission and scholarship support should be directed to the registrar at Dalhousie University. In order to be considered for scholarships, students must submit applications for fall admission before January 15. Admission is granted primarily on the basis of the undergraduate record and letters of recommendation; scores on the General Test of the Graduate Record Examinations or the equivalent are required if available. If English is not their first language, students must demonstrate a knowledge of English by taking the TOEFL. A bachelor's degree in mathematics, atmospheric sciences, or in one of the basic sciences is ordinarily required for admission, although consideration is also given to applicants with a background in engineering. Non-Canadian students normally enter Canada on a student visa with a Dalhousie Fellowship. For more specific details, applicants should refer to the international student information letter provided by the Dalhousie Association of Graduate Students.

Correspondence and Information

The Graduate Co-ordinator
Department of Oceanography
Dalhousie University
Halifax, Nova Scotia B3H 4J1
Canada
Telephone: 902-494-3557
Fax: 902-494-3877
E-mail: oceanography@dal.ca
World Wide Web: http://www.phys.ocean.dal.ca

Dalhousie University

THE FACULTY AND THEIR RESEARCH

H. Barker, Adjunct Professor; Ph.D., McMaster. Atmospheric radiation, cloud physics.

C. Beaumont, Professor (Inco Fellow of the CIAR); Ph.D., Dalhousie. Geodynamics.

B. P. Boudreau, Associate Professor; Ph.D., Yale. Diagenesis, sediment-water interactions, geochemical modelling.

A. J. Bowen, Professor; Ph.D., California, San Diego (Scripps). Physical oceanography, nearshore dynamics, sediment transport.

C. M. Boyd, Adjunct Professor; Ph.D., California, San Diego (Scripps). Zooplankton distribution, behaviour, and sensory physiology.

M. Bricelj, Adjunct Professor; Ph.D., SUNY at Stony Brook. Physiological ecology, bioenergetics, aquaculture of bivalve molluscs.

A. D. Cembella, Adjunct Professor; Ph.D., British Columbia. Population dynamics, genetics and ecophysiology of toxic marine algae and transfer of biotoxins in marine food webs.

P. Chylek, Professor; Ph.D., California, Riverside. Radiation physics; radiative transfer in theory, in the laboratory, and in the atmosphere.

J. S. Craigie, Adjunct Professor; Ph.D., Queen's at Kingston. Algal physiology, algal membrane structure, storage products.

J. Cullen, Professor; Ph.D., California, San Diego (Scripps); NSERC/SATLANTIC Industrial Research Chair. Phytoplankton processes, optical measurements, effects of ultraviolet radiation.

I. Folkins, Associate Professor; Ph.D., Toronto. Stratospheric ozone modelling, atmospheric chemistry.

R. O. Fournier, Professor; Ph.D., Rhode Island. Biological oceanography.

K. T. Frank, Adjunct Professor; Ph.D., Toledo; Bedford Institute of Oceanography. Population dynamics, stock assessment, fisheries oceanography, recruitment.

Q. Fu, Associate Professor; Ph.D., Utah. Atmospheric radiative transfer modelling emphasizing interaction among radiation, clouds, and climate; atmospheric remote sensing.

J. Grant, Professor; Ph.D., South Carolina. Benthic ecology, shellfisheries.

R. J. Greatbatch, Professor; Ph.D., Cambridge; NSERCH/AES/MARTECH Industrial Research Chair. Oceanic atmosphere dynamics.

B. T. Hargrave, Adjunct Professor; Ph.D., British Columbia; Bedford Institute of Oceanography. Benthic ecology.

A. Hay, Professor; Ph.D., British Columbia; NSERC/SATLANTIC Industrial Research Chair. Physical oceanography, ocean acoustics.

P. S. Hill, Associate Professor; Ph.D., Washington (Seattle). Fine sediment transport, particle aggregation.

G. Isaac, Adjunct Professor; Ph.D., McGill; Atmospheric Environment Service. Cloud physics and chemistry, tropospheric aerosols.

D. Kelley, Associate Professor; Ph.D., Dalhousie. Ocean mixing, deep convection, double diffusion, arctic mixing.

M. D. King, Adjunct Professor; Ph.D., Arizona; NASA, Goddard Space Flight Center. Atmospheric radiation, remote sensing, cloud physics.

M. R. Lewis, Professor; Ph.D., Dalhousie. Biological oceanography, marine ecosystem modelling.

Z. Li, Adjunct Professor; Ph.D., McGill. Atmospheric radiation and aerosols.

U. Lohmann, Assistant Professor; Ph.D., Hamburg. Cloud physics, climate modelling, aerosol-cloud-radiation interactions.

K. E. Louden, Professor; Ph.D., MIT/Woods Hole. Marine geophysics.

A. Metaxas, Assistant Professor; Ph.D., Dalhousie; NSERCH UFA. Benthic ecology, larval settlement, deep-sea biology.

W. Miller, Associate Professor; Ph.D., Rhode Island. Trace element cycles, aquatic photochemistry, chemical-biological interactions.

E. L. Mills, Professor; Ph.D., Yale. Benthic ecology, history of oceanography.

R. M. Moore, Professor; Ph.D., Southampton. Chemical oceanography, low molecular weight halocarbons in the marine environment.

N. S. Oakey, Adjunct Professor; Ph.D., McMaster; Bedford Institute of Oceanography. Physical oceanography, mixing processes in the ocean, instrumentation related to mixing processes.

D. J. W. Piper, Adjunct Professor; Ph.D., Cambridge; Atlantic Geoscience Center, Bedford Institute of Oceanography. Marine sedimentology.

H. Ritchie, Adjunct Professor; Ph.D., McGill. Numerical methods for atmosphere and oceans, atmosphere-ocean coupling, environmental prediction.

B. R. Ruddick, Professor; Ph.D., MIT/Woods Hole. Physical oceanography.

S. Sathyendranath, Adjunct Professor; Ph.D., Paris VI (Curie); Bedford Institute of Oceanography. Optical oceanography, remote sensing of ocean colour, marine primary production.

J. Sheng, Assistant Professor; Ph.D., Memorial University of Newfoundland; NSERC/AES/MARTEC Industrial Research Chair. Shelf circulation, ocean modeling, data assimilation.

P. C. Smith, Adjunct Professor; Ph.D., MIT/Woods Hole; Coastal Oceanography, Bedford Institute of Oceanography. Continental shelf dynamics, air-sea interaction, data assimilation.

C. T. Taggart, Associate Professor; Ph.D., McGill. Fisheries oceanography and early life history phenomena, biological-physical interactions, population genetics.

K. R. Thompson, Professor; Ph.D., Liverpool. Physical oceanography/climatology.

D. Wright, Adjunct Professor; Ph.D., British Columbia; Bedford Institute of Oceanography. Climate dynamics, coastal oceanography, geophysical fluid dynamics.

FLORIDA INSTITUTE OF TECHNOLOGY
Division of Marine and Environmental Systems
Programs in Oceanography,
Applied Marine Science,
and Coastal Zone Management

Programs of Study

Florida Institute of Technology offers programs of research and study options in the fields of biological, chemical, geological, and physical oceanography and in environmental and marine chemistry that lead to M.S. and Ph.D. degrees in oceanography. An M.S. in oceanography with an option in coastal zone management is also offered. Those students interested in the graduate program in ocean engineering should consult the program description in Book 5 of these guides.

Research Facilities

Florida Institute of Technology is conveniently located on the Indian River Lagoon, a major east-central Florida estuarine system recently designated an Estuary of National Significance. Marine and environmental laboratories and field research stations are located on the lagoon and at an oceanfront marine research facility. Marine operations, located just 5 minutes from campus, house a fleet of small outboard-powered craft and medium-sized work boats. These boats are available to students and faculty members for teaching and research in the freshwater tributaries and the Indian River Lagoon. In addition, the College of Engineering operates the 60-foot Research Vessel *Delphinus,* which is berthed at Port Canaveral. With its own captain and crew; requisite marine and oceanographic cranes, winches, and state-of-the-art sampling equipment; and instrumentation and laboratories, the vessel is the focal point of both marine and estuarine research in the region. The ship can accommodate a scientific team and crew for periods of seven to ten days. The *Delphinus* conducts short research and teaching cruises throughout the year and teaching trips to the Atlantic Ocean each summer.

The Institute's oceanfront marine research facility, the Vero Beach Marine Laboratory, located at Vero Beach just 40 minutes from campus, provides facilities, including flowing seawater from the Atlantic Ocean, to support research in such areas as aquaculture, biofouling, and corrosion. There is also a permanent research platform, centrally located in the Indian River Lagoon, to support marine research projects. On the campus, the departmental teaching and research facilities include separate laboratories for biological, chemical, physical, geological, and instrumentation investigations. In addition, high-pressure, hydroacoustics, fluid dynamics, and GIS/remote sensing facilities are available in the Division. An electron microscope is also available for research work.

About an hour from campus is the Harbor Branch Oceanographic Institution; scientists and engineers there pursue their own research and development activities and interact with the Institute's students and faculty on projects of mutual interest.

The Biological Oceanography Laboratory is fully equipped for research on plankton, benthos, and fishes of coastal and estuarine ecosystems. Collection gear; analytical equipment, including a flow-through fluorometer; and a controlled environment room are available for student and research use. Areas of research have included toxic algal blooms, seagrass ecology, and artificial and natural reef communities.

The Chemical Oceanography Laboratory is equipped to do both routine and research-level operations on open ocean and coastal lagoonal waters. Major and minor nutrients, heavy-metal contaminants, and biological pollutants can be quantitatively determined. Analytical methods available include gas and liquid chromatography, infrared and visible light spectrophotometry, and atomic absorption spectrometry. The Physical Oceanography and the Hydrodynamics laboratories support graduate research in ocean waves, coastal processes, circulation, and pollutant transport. In addition, CTD and XBT systems, current meters, tide and wind recorders, salinometers, wave-height gauges, side-scan sonar, and other oceanographic instruments are available for field work. A remote sensing and optics lab provides capabilities for analyzing ocean color data and collecting in situ hydrologic optics data.

The Coastal Processes Laboratory is used to study near-shore sedimentation and stratigraphy. The lab equipment includes a state-of-the-art computerized rapid sediment analyzer, a magnetic heavy mineral separator, and computer-assisted sieve systems.

Financial Aid

Graduate teaching and research assistantships are available to qualified students. For 1999–2000, financial support ranges from approximately $9000 to $16,000, including stipend and tuition, per academic year for approximately half-time duties. Stipend-only assistantships are sometimes awarded for less time commitment. Most coastal zone management students receive support through internship appointments.

Cost of Study

In 1999–2000, tuition is $575 per graduate semester credit hour.

Living and Housing Costs

Room and board on campus cost approximately $2400 per semester in 1999–2000. On-campus housing (dormitories and apartments) is available for full-time single and married graduate students, but priority for dormitory rooms is given to undergraduate students. Many apartment complexes and rental houses are available near the campus.

Student Group

The College of Engineering has 450 graduate students. Oceanography currently has approximately 30 graduate and 40 undergraduate students.

Student Outcomes

Graduates have gone on to careers with such institutions as NOAA, EPA, Florida Water Management Districts, Western Geophysical, Naval Oceanographic Office, Digicon, and with county and state agencies.

Location

The campus is located in Melbourne, on Florida's east coast. It is an area, located 4 miles from the Atlantic Ocean beaches, with a year-round subtropical climate. The area's economy is supported by a well-balanced mix of industries in electronics, aviation, light manufacturing, optics, communications, agriculture, and tourism. Many industries support activities at the Kennedy Space Center.

The Institute

Florida Institute of Technology is a distinctive, independent university, founded in 1958 by a group of scientists and engineers to fulfill a need for specialized advanced educational opportunities on the Space Coast of Florida. Florida Tech is the only independent technological university in the Southeast. Supported by both industry and the community, Florida Tech is the recipient of many research grants and contracts, a number of which provide financial support for graduate students.

Applying

Forms and instructions for applying for admission and assistantships are sent on request. Admission is possible at the beginning of any semester, but admission in the fall semester is recommended. It is advantageous to apply early.

Correspondence and Information

Chairman
Oceanography Program
Florida Institute of Technology
Melbourne, Florida 32901-6975

Telephone: 407-674-8096
Fax: 407-674-7212
E-mail: norris@marine.fit.edu

Graduate Admissions Office
Florida Institute of Technology
Melbourne, Florida 32901-6975

Telephone: 407-674-8027
        800-944-4348 (toll-free)
Fax: 407-723-9468
World Wide Web: http://www.fit.edu

Florida Institute of Technology

THE FACULTY AND THEIR RESEARCH

Charles R. Bostater Jr., Assistant Professor; Ph.D., Delaware. Remote sensing, hydrologic optics, particle dynamics in estuaries, modeling of toxic substances, physical oceanography of coastal waters, environmental modeling.

Iver W. Duedall, Professor; Ph.D., Dalhousie. Chemical oceanography, physical chemistry of seawater, geochemistry, marine pollution, ocean management.

Lee Harris, Associate Professor; Ph.D., Florida Atlantic; PE. Coastal engineering, coastal structures, beach erosion and control, physical oceanography.

Elizabeth A. Irlandi, Assistant Professor; Ph.D., North Carolina. Landscape ecology in aquatic environments, seagrass ecosystems, coastal zone management.

George A. Maul, Professor; Ph.D., Miami (Florida). Physical oceanography, marine meteorology, climate and sea level change, satellite oceanography, earth system science.

Dean R. Norris, Professor; Ph.D., Texas A&M. Taxonomy and ecology of marine phytoplankton, particularly dinoflagellates; ecology and life cycles of toxic dinoflagellates.

Randall W. Parkinson, Associate Professor; Ph.D., Miami (Florida); PG. Geological oceanography, sea level and climatic change, coastal and shelf processes, sedimentation and stratigraphy.

Geoffrey W. J. Swain, Associate Professor; Ph.D., Southampton. Materials corrosion, biofouling, offshore technology, ship operations.

John H. Trefry, Professor; Ph.D., Texas A&M. Trace metal geochemistry and pollution, geochemistry of rivers, global chemical cycles, deep-sea hydrothermal systems.

John G. Windsor, Professor; Ph.D., William and Mary. Trace organic analysis, organic chemistry, sediment-sea interaction, air-sea interaction, mass spectrometry, hazardous/toxic substance research.

Gary Zarillo, Professor; Ph.D., Georgia; PG. Sediment transport and morphodynamics, tidal inlet–barrier dynamics, numerical modeling of inlet hydrodynamics.

SELECTED PUBLICATIONS

Belanger, T. V., H. H. Heck, and M. Sohn. Sediment analyses to answer lake management questions: A case study for Lake Panasoffkee, Florida. *Chem. Ecol.* 11:229–54, 1995.

Belanger, T. V., and R. A. Kirkner. Groundwater–surface water interaction in a Florida augmentation lake. *Lake Reservoir Manage.* 8(2):165–74, 1994.

Belanger, T. V., and M. E. Montgomery. Seepage meter errors. *Limnol. Oceanogr.* 37(8):1787–95, 1992.

Belanger, T. V., and E. A. Korzun. Critique of the floating dame technique for estimating recreation rates. *ASCE J. Environ. Eng.* 117(1):144–55, 1991.

Belanger, T. V., and E. A. Korzun. Rainfall reaeration effects. In *Air Water Mass Transfer,* eds. S. Wilhelms and J. Gulliver. ASCE Publishers, 1991.

Belanger, T. V., D. Scheidt, and J. Platkoll. Effects of nutrient enrichment on the Florida Everglades. *Lake Reservoir Manage.* 5(1):101–11, 1989.

Bostater, C. Remote sensing methods using aircraft and ships for estimating optimal bands and coefficients related to ecosystem responses. *Int. Soc. Opt. Eng. (SPIE)* 1930:1051–62, 1992.

Bostater, C. Mathematical techniques for spectral discrimination between corals, seagrasses, bottom and water types using high spectral resolution reflectance signatures. In *ISSSR, Spectral Sensing Research,* pp. 526–36, 1992.

Williams, J., F. Doehring, and **I. W. Duedall.** History of Florida hurricanes. *Oceanus,* submitted.

Shieh, C. S., and **I. W. Duedall.** Disposal of wastes at sea in tropical areas. In *Pollution in Tropical Aquatic Systems,* pp. 218–29, eds. D. W. Connell and D. W. Hawker. Boca Raton: CRC Press, 1992.

Shieh, C. S., and **I. W. Duedall.** Cd and Pb in waste-to-energy residues. *Chemistry and Ecology* 6:247–58, 1992.

Duedall, I. W., and M. A. Champ. Artificial reefs: Emerging science and technology. *Oceanus* 34:94–101, 1991.

Duedall, I. W. A brief history of ocean disposal. *Oceanus* 33(2):29–38, 1990.

Harris, L. E., Childress, Winder, and Perry. Real-time wave data collection system at Sebastian Inlet, Florida. In *Fifth International Workshop on Wave Hindcasting and Forecasting,* pp. 146–53. Ontario: Environment Canada, 1998.

Smith, J. T., **L. E. Harris,** and J. Tabar. *Preliminary Evaluation of the Vero Beach, FL Prefabricated Submerged Breakwater.* Tallahassee, Fla.: FSBPA, 1998.

Zadikovv, Covello, **L. E. Harris,** and Skornick. Concrete tetrahedrons and sand-filled geotextile containers: New technologies for shoreline stabilization. In *Proceedings of the International Coastal Symposium (ICS98), Journal of Coastal Research,* special issue no. 26, pp. 261–8, 1998.

Harris, L. E. Dredged material used in sand-filled containers for scour and erosion control. In *Dredging 94,* American Society of Civil Engineers (ASCE), 1994.

Chambers, P. A., R. E. DeWreede, **E. A. Irlandi,** and H. Vandermeulen. Management issues in aquatic macrophyte ecology: A Canadian perspective. *Can. J. Botany,* in press.

Irlandi, E. A., B. A. Orlando, and W. G. Ambrose Jr. The effect of habitat patch size on growth and survival of juvenile bay scallops (*Argopecten irradians*). *J. Exp. Marine Biol. Ecol.* 235:21–43, 1999.

Irlandi, E. A. Seagrass patch size and survivorship of an infaunal bivalve. *Oikos* 78:511–8, 1997.

Irlandi, E. A., S. Macia, and J. Serafy. Salinity reduction from freshwater canal discharge: Effects on mortality and feeding of an urchin (*Lytechinus variegatus*) and a gastropod (*Lithopoma tectum*). *Bull. Marine Sci.* 61:869–79, 1997.

Irlandi, E. A. The effects of seagrass patch size and energy regime on growth of a suspension-feeding bivalve. *J. Marine Res.* 54:161–85, 1996.

Irlandi, E. A., and M. E. Mehlich. The effect of tissue cropping and disturbance by browsing fishes on growth of two species of suspension-feeding bivalves. *J. Exp. Marine Biol. Ecol.* 197:279–93, 1996.

Pugh, D. T., and **G. A. Maul.** Coastal sea level prediction for climate change. In *Coastal Ocean Prediction,* num. 56, pp. 377–404, ed. C. N. K. Mooers. Washington: American Geophysical Union, Coastal and Estuarine Studies, 1999.

Mooers, C. N. K., and **G. A. Maul.** Intra-Americas sea circulation. In *The Sea,* chap. 7, pp. 183–208, eds. A. R. Robinson and K. H. Brink, 1998.

Maul, G. A. *Small Islands: Marine Science and Sustainable Development.* Washington: American Geophysical Union, Coastal and Estuarine Studies, number 51, 1996.

Maul, G. A. *Climatic Changes in the Intra-Americas Sea.* United Nations Environment Programme. London: Edward Arnold Publishers, 1993.

Maul, G. A., and D. M. Martin. Sea level rise at Key West, Florida, 1846–1992: America's longest instrument record? *Geophys. Res. Lett.* 20(18):1955–59, 1993.

Hanson, D. V., and **G. A. Maul.** Anticyclonic current rings in the eastern tropical Pacific Ocean. *J. Geophys. Res.* 96(C4):6965–79, 1991.

Hanson, K., **G. A. Maul,** and T. R. Karl. Are atmospheric greenhouse effects apparent in the climatic record of the contiguous U.S. (1895–1987)? *Geophys. Res. Lett.* 16(1):49–52, 1989.

Maul, G. A. *Introduction to Satellite Oceanography.* Martinus Nijhoff Publishers, Dordrecht/Boston/Lancaster, 1985.

Nelsen, T. A., et al. **(S. Metz).** Time-based correlation of biogenic, lithogenic and authigenic sediment components with anthropogenic inputs in the Gulf of Mexico. *Estuaries* 1:873–85, 1994.

Eadie, B. J., et al. **(S. Metz** and **J. H. Trefry).** Records of nutrient-enhanced coastal ocean productivity in sediments from the Louisiana continental shelf. *Estuaries* 17:754–65, 1994.

Metz, S., and **J. H. Trefry.** Field and laboratory studies of metal uptake and release by hydrothermal precipitates. *J. Geophys. Res.* 98:9661–66, 1993.

Metz, S., J. H. Trefry, and T. A. Nelsen. History and geochemistry of a metalliferous sediment core from the Mid-Atlantic Ridge at 26 N. *Geochim. Cosmochim. Acta* 52:2369–78, 1988.

Metz, S., and **J. H. Trefry.** Trace metal considerations in experimental oil ash reefs. *Mar. Poll. Bull.* 19:633–36, 1988.

Morton, S. L., **D. R. Norris,** and J. W. Bomber. Effect of temperature, salinity and light intensity on the growth and seasonality of toxic dinoflagellates associated with Ciguatera. *J. Exp. Mar. Biol. Ecol.* 157:79–90, 1992.

Morton, S. L., and **D. R. Norris.** Role of temperature, salinity and light on the seasonality of Prorocentrum lima (Ehrenberg) Dodge. In *Toxic Marine Phytoplankton,* pp. 201–5, eds. E. Graneli, B. Sundstrom, L. Edler, and E. M. Anderson. New York: Elsevier, 1990.

Bomber, J. W., M. G. Rubio, and **D. R. Norris.** Epiphytism of dinoflagellates associated with Ciguatera: Substrate specificity and nutrition. *Phycologia* 82:360–68, 1989.

Bomber, J. W., et al. **(D. R. Norris).** Epiphytic dinoflagellates of drift algae—another toxigenic community in the ciguatera food chain. *Bull. Mar. Sci.* 43(2):204–14, 1988.

Parkinson, R. W. Managing biodiversity from a geological perspective. *Bull. Mar. Sci.,* in press.

Parkinson, R. W., and J. R. White. Late Holocene erosional shoreface retreat within a siliciclastic to carbonate transition zone, East Central Florida, USA. *J. Sedim. Res.* B64(3), 1994.

Florida Institute of Technology

Selected Publications (continued)

Parkinson, R. W., R. D. DeLaune, and J. R. White. Holocene sea-level rise and the fate of mangrove forests within the wider Caribbean region. *J. Coastal Res.* 10(4), 1994.

Parkinson, R. W., et al. Distribution and migration of pesticide residue in mosquito control impoundments, St. Lucie County, Florida. *Env. Geol. Water Sci.* 22:26–32, 1993.

Parkinson, R. W. Building a conceptual model of mangrove ecosystem response to global climate change: Sea-level rise and the geological record. *Jaina* 3:6, 1992.

Parkinson, R. W., and J. F. Meeder. Mudbank destruction and the formation of a transgressive sand sheet, Southwest Florida. *Geol. Soc. Am. Bull.* 103:1543–51, 1991.

Parkinson, R. W. Stratigraphic evidence of onshore sand transport throughout the Holocene marine transgression, Southwest Florida. *Mar. Geol.* 96:269–77, 1991.

Rae, G. J. S., and S. E. Dunn. On-line damage detection for autonomous underwater vehicles. In *Proc. IEEE AUV-94,* Boston, 1994.

Smith, S. M., and **G. J. S. Rae.** Fuzzy logic control of autonomous underwater vehicles. *Control Eng. Pract.* 2:321–31, 1994.

Rae, G. J. S., and S. M. Smith. A fuzzy rule based docking procedure for two moving autonomous underwater vehicles. In *Proceedings of the American Control Conference '93,* San Francisco, 1993.

Swain, G. W. J., J. Griffith, D. Bultman, and H. Vincent. Barnacle adhesion measurements for the field evaluation of candidate anti-fouling surfaces. *Biofouling* 6:105–14, 1992.

Swain, G. W. J., and E. Muller. Oxygen concentration cells and corrosion in a seawater aquarium. *Corrosion* 92(394), 1992.

Swain, G. W. J., and J. Patrick-Maxwell. The effect of biofouling on the performance of Al-Zn-Hg anodes. *Corrosion* 46(3):256–60, 1990.

Swain, G. W. J., and W. Thomason. Cathodic protection and the use of copper anti-fouling systems on fixed offshore steel structures. Presented at Offshore Mechanics and Arctic Engineering 9th International Conference, Houston, February 1990.

Hanes, D. M., and **E. D. Thosteson** et al. Field observations of small scale sediment suspension. In *Proceedings of the 26th International Conference on Coastal Engineering.* Copenhagen, Denmark: ASCE, 1998.

Thosteson, E. D., D. M. Hanes, and S. L. Schonfield. Design of a littoral sedimentation processes monitoring system. *J. Oceanic Eng.,* in press.

Thosteson, E. D., and D. M. Hanes. The time lag between fluid forcing and wave generated sediment suspension. *AGU Fall Meeting,* 1998.

Thosteson, E. D., and D. M. Hanes. A simplified method for determining sediment size and concentration from multiple frequency acoustic backscatter measurements. *J. Acoust. Soc. Am.* 104(2): 820, 1998.

Trefry, J. H., R. P. Trocine, K. L. Naito, and **S. Metz.** Assessing the potential for enhanced bioaccumulation of heavy metals from produced water discharges to the Gulf of Mexico. In *Produced Water: Environmental Issues and Mitigation Technologies,* pp. 339–54. New York: Plenum Press, 1996.

Trefry, J. H., S. Metz, et al. Transport of particulate organic carbon by the Mississippi River and its fate in the Gulf of Mexico. *Estuaries* 17:839–49, 1994.

Grguric, G., **J. H. Trefry,** and J. J. Keaffaber. Reactions of bromine and chlorine in ozonated artificial seawater systems. *Water Res.* 28:1087–94, 1994.

Trefry, J. H., et al. **(S. Metz).** Trace metals in hydrothermal solutions from Cleft segment on the southern Juan de Fuca Ridge. *J. Geophys. Res.* 99:4925–35, 1994.

Feely, R. A., et al. **(J. H. Trefry).** Composition and sedimentation of hydrothermal plume particles from North Cleft segment, Juan de Fuca Ridge. *J. Geophys. Res.* 99:4985–5006, 1994.

Trocine, R. P., and **J. H. Trefry.** Metal concentrations in sediment water, and clams from the Indian River Lagoon, Florida. *Marine Pollut. Bull.* 32:754–9, 1996.

Trocine, R. P., and **J. H. Trefry.** Distribution and chemistry of suspended particles from an active hydrothermal vent site on the Mid-Atlantic Ridge at 26 N. *Earth Planet. Sci. Lett.* 88:1–15, 1988.

Frease, R. A., and **J. G. Windsor Jr.** Behavior of selected polycyclic aromatic hydrocarbons associated with a stabilized oil and coal ash reef. *Marine Poll. Bull.* 22:15–19, 1991.

Windsor Jr., J. G. Fate and transport of oil, dispersants, and dispersed oil in the Florida coastal environment. Oil Spill Dispersant Research Program: Technical Advisory Group Workshop, University of Florida, Gainesville, Florida, April 25–26, 1991.

Windsor Jr., J. G., and **L. E. Harris.** SEEAS—Science and Engineering Education At Sea. *MTS '90, Marine Technology Society,* Washington, D.C., September 1990.

Holm, S. E., and **J. G. Windsor Jr.** Exposure assessment of sewage treatment plant effluent by a selected chemical marker method. *Arch. Environ. Contaminat. Toxicol.* 19:674–79, 1990.

Windsor Jr., J. G. Marine Field Projects: An established, unique undergraduate curriculum in ocean science. Presented at the 200th National Meeting of the American Chemical Society, August 26–31, 1990.

Wood, S. L. Function driven design selection of plastic injection molding features. In *1996 ASME Design for Manufacturing Conference,* DFM A W2, Los Angeles, California, 1996.

Wood, S. L. Design reasoning using plastic injection molding primary features. In *1996 ASME Design for Manufacturing Conference,* DFM M4, Los Angeles, California, 1996.

Ullman, D. G., **S. L. Wood,** and D. Craig. The importance of drawing in the mechanical design process. *Comput. Graphics* 14(2), 1990.

Zarillo, G. A., and T. S. Bacchus. Application of seismic profile measurements to sand source studies. In *Handbook of Geophysical Exploration at Sea,* 2nd ed., *Hard Minerals,* pp. 241–58, ed. R. A. Geyer. Boca Raton: CRC Press, 1992.

Zarillo, G. A., and J. Liu. Resolving components of the upper shoreface of a wave-dominated coast using empirical orthogonal functions. *Mar. Geol.* 82:169–86, 1988.

Zarillo, G. A., and M. J. Park. Prediction of sediment transport in a tide-dominated environment using a numerical model. *J. Coastal Res.* 3:429–44, 1987.

Zborowski, A., and H. S. Chu. *Hard Chine Versus Round Bottom Hull Form: A Comparison of Stability in Waves and Sea-Keeping Performance of Small Displacement Ships.* SNAME Annual Meeting, 1992.

Zborowski, A., and M. Taylan. Influence of main form parameters on stability margin of ships rolling in beam synchronous waves. In *International Conference on Stability of Ships and Ocean Vehicles,* Naples, Italy, 1990.

FLORIDA STATE UNIVERSITY

Department of Oceanography

Programs of Study

A graduate program in oceanography has existed at Florida State University since 1949, first in an interdisciplinary institute and since 1966 in a department within the College of Arts and Sciences. The Department of Oceanography, which offers both the M.S. and Ph.D. degrees in oceanography with specializations in physical, biological, or chemical oceanography, is the center for marine studies at the University. Additional marine and environmental research is conducted by the Departments of Biological Sciences, Chemistry, Geology, Mathematics, Meteorology, Physics, and Statistics, as well as the Geophysical Fluid Dynamics Institute and the Institute of Molecular Biophysics. Both formal and informal cooperative efforts between these science departments and the Department of Oceanography have flourished for years.

The M.S. degree program requires the completion of 33 semester hours of course work and a thesis covering an original research topic. Students pursuing the Ph.D. degree must complete 18 semester hours of formal course work beyond the master's degree course requirements and perform original research leading to a dissertation that makes a contribution to the science of oceanography.

The first year of graduate study is generally concerned with required course work and examinations. A supervisory committee, chosen by the individual student, directs the examinations and supervises the student's progress. Under its direction, the student begins thesis research as soon as possible. There is no foreign language requirement for either the M.S. or the Ph.D.

Research Facilities

Oceanography department headquarters, offices, and laboratories are located in the Oceanography-Statistics Building in the science area of the campus. Some of the laboratories currently in operation are for water quality analysis, organic geochemistry, trace-element analysis, radiochemistry, microbial ecology, phytoplankton ecology, numerical modeling, and fluid dynamics. The department also has the benefit of a fully equipped machine shop and a current-meter facility using state-of-the-art instruments. The Florida State University Marine Laboratory on the Gulf of Mexico is located at Turkey Point near Carrabelle, about 45 miles southwest of Tallahassee. The R/V *Bellows,* a 65-foot research vessel, is shared by FSU and other campuses of the State University System of Florida.

Departmental facilities are augmented by those in other FSU departments and institutes, such as the Van de Graaff accelerator in the physics department, the Antarctic Marine Geology Research Facility and Core Library in the geology department, the Geophysical Fluid Dynamics Institute laboratories, the Electron Microscopy Laboratory in the biological sciences department, the Statistical Consulting Center in the statistics department, and the CRAY Y-MP in the Supercomputer Computations Research Institute.

The research activities of the faculty members are heavily supported by federal funding, and these programs involve fieldwork, often at sea, all over the world. Faculty members and students have worked aboard a great many of the major research vessels of the U.S. fleet; because this kind of active collaboration works so well, it has not seemed necessary for the University to have its own major research vessel.

Financial Aid

Fellowships and teaching and research assistantships are available on a competitive basis. University fellowships pay $10,000 per academic year. Research and teaching assistantships range from $9438 to $14,950 for the year, including summer. In addition, out-of-state tuition waivers are available for assistantship and fellowship recipients. Currently, most of the full-time students in the department receive financial assistance.

Cost of Study

Tuition for 1999–2000 is $146.01 per credit hour for Florida residents; out-of-state students pay $506.74 per credit hour. The normal course load is 9 credit hours per semester for research and teaching assistants receiving tuition waivers.

Living and Housing Costs

A double room for single students in the graduate dormitories on campus costs about $300 per month (including utilities and local telephone). Married student housing at Alumni Village costs $254 to $442 per month. There are many off-campus apartment complexes in Tallahassee, with rents beginning at about $275 per month.

Student Group

The department currently has 49 full-time graduate students enrolled in the program (17 M.S., 32 Ph.D.). The students come from all areas of the country, with the greatest number representing the Northeast, South, and Midwest. Fifteen of the students are women. During the last five years, twenty-five M.S. and eighteen Ph.D. degrees were awarded in oceanography. Graduates have taken positions in federal and state agencies, universities, and private companies.

Location

Florida State University is located in Tallahassee, the state capital. Although it is among the nation's fastest-growing cities, Tallahassee has managed to preserve its natural beauty. The northern Florida location has a landscape and climate that are substantially different from those of southern Florida. Heavy forest covers much of the area, with the giant live oak being the chief tree of the clay hills. Five large lakes and the nearby Gulf of Mexico offer numerous recreational opportunities. Life in Tallahassee has been described as a combination of the ambience of traditional southern living with the bustle of a modern capital city.

The University

Florida State University is a public coeducational institution founded in 1857. Current enrollment is more than 28,000. The University has great diversity in its cultural offerings and is rich in traditions. It has outstanding science departments and excellent schools and departments in law, music, theater, and religion.

Applying

Applications should be submitted as early as possible in the academic year prior to anticipated enrollment. The deadline for applications for fall semester enrollment is in February for international students and in July for domestic students. Each prospective candidate must have a bachelor's degree, with a major pertinent to the student's chosen specialty area in oceanography. Minimum undergraduate preparation must include one year of calculus, chemistry, and physics. A minimum undergraduate GPA of 3.0 and a minimum GRE General Test score of 1100 (combined verbal and quantitative scores) are required. The average undergraduate GPA and the average GRE score of currently enrolled students are 3.45 and 1230 (verbal and quantitative), respectively.

Correspondence and Information

Academic Coordinator
Department of Oceanography
Florida State University
Tallahassee, Florida 32306-4320

Telephone: 850-644-6700
Fax: 850-644-2581
E-mail: admissions@ocean.fsu.edu
World Wide Web: http://ocean.fsu.edu/

Florida State University

THE FACULTY AND THEIR RESEARCH

William C. Burnett, Professor of Oceanography; Ph.D., Hawaii. Uranium-series isotopes and geochemistry of authigenic minerals of the seafloor, elemental composition of suspended material from estuaries and the deep ocean, environmental studies.

Jeffrey P. Chanton, Professor of Oceanography; Ph.D., North Carolina at Chapel Hill. Major element cycling, light stable isotopes, methane production and transport, coastal biogeochemical processes.

Allan J. Clarke, Professor of Oceanography; Ph.D., Cambridge. Climate dynamics, coastal oceanography, equatorial dynamics, tides.

William K. Dewar, Professor of Oceanography; Ph.D., MIT/Woods Hole. Gulf Stream ring dynamics, general circulation theory, intermediate- and large-scale interaction, mixed layer processes.

Ya Hsueh, Professor of Oceanography; Ph.D., Johns Hopkins. Variabilities in sea level, coastal currents, water density in continental shelf waters.

Richard L. Iverson, Professor of Oceanography; Ph.D., Oregon State. Physiology and ecology of marine phytoplankton.

Joel E. Kostka, Assistant Professor of Oceanography; Ph.D., Delaware. Microbial ecology and biogeochemistry, carbon and nutrient cycling in coastal marine environments, bacteria-mineral interactions.

Ruby E. Krishnamurti, Professor of Oceanography; Ph.D., UCLA. Ocean circulation, atmospheric convection, bioconvection, stability and transition to turbulence. Fellow, American Meteorological Society.

William M. Landing, Professor of Oceanography; Ph.D., California, Santa Cruz. Biogeochemistry of trace elements in the oceans, with emphasis on the effects of biological and inorganic processes on dissolved/particulate fractionation.

Nancy H. Marcus, Professor of Oceanography; Ph.D., Yale. Population biology and genetics of marine zooplankton dormancy, photoperiodism, biological rhythms. Fellow, AAAS.

Doron Nof, Professor of Oceanography; Ph.D., Wisconsin–Madison. Fluid motions in the ocean, dynamics of equatorial outflows and formation of eddies, geostrophic adjustment in sea straits and estuaries, generation of oceanfronts. Fellow, American Meteorological Society.

James J. O'Brien, Professor of Oceanography; Ph.D., Texas A&M. Modeling of coastal upwelling and equatorial circulation, upper oceanfronts, climate scale fluctuations. Fellow, American Meteorological Society; Recipient, Sverdrup Gold Medal in Air-Sea Interactions.

Lita M. Proctor, Assistant Professor of Oceanography; Ph.D., SUNY at Stony Brook. Microbiology, microscopy, biochemistry, molecular biology.

Kevin G. Speer, Assistant Professor of Oceanography; Ph.D., MIT. Deep-ocean circulation, observations and dynamics; water-mass formation; thermohaline flow; hydrothermal sources and circulation.

Melvin E. Stern, Professor of Oceanography; Ph.D., MIT. Theory of ocean circulation, salt fingers. Fellow, American Geophysical Union; Member, National Academy of Sciences.

Wilton Sturges III, Professor of Oceanography; Ph.D., Johns Hopkins. Ocean currents.

David Thistle, Professor and Chair, Department of Oceanography; Ph.D., California, San Diego (Scripps). Ecology of sediment communities, meiofauna ecology, deep-sea biology, crustacean systematics.

Georges L. Weatherly, Professor of Oceanography; Ph.D., Nova. Deep-ocean circulation and near-bottom currents.

John W. Winchester, Professor of Oceanography; Ph.D., MIT. Atmospheric chemistry, trace-element and aerosol-particle analysis.

AFFILIATED FACULTY

These faculty members are important in the academic program of students in the Department of Oceanography. This list includes faculty members from other departments who interact regularly with the department's faculty members and students.

Lawrence G. Abele, Professor of Biological Sciences and Provost; Ph.D., Miami (Florida). Ecology, community biology, systematics of decapod crustaceans.

Steven L. Blumsack, Associate Professor of Mathematics; Ph.D., MIT. Theory of rotating fluids.

William F. Herrnkind, Professor of Biological Sciences; Ph.D., Miami (Florida). Behavior and migration of marine animals.

Louis N. Howard, Professor of Mathematics; Ph.D., Princeton. Theory of rotating and stratified flows, hydrodynamic stability, bifurcation theory, geophysical fluid dynamics, chemical waves, biological oscillations. Member, National Academy of Sciences.

Christopher Hunter, Professor of Mathematics; Ph.D., Cambridge. Dynamics of fluids and stellar systems.

Charles L. Jordan, Professor of Meteorology; Ph.D., Chicago. Synoptic meteorology.

Michael Kasha, Professor of Chemistry, Institute of Molecular Biophysics; Ph.D., Berkeley. Molecular electronic spectroscopy, molecular quantum mechanics. Member, National Academy of Sciences.

Fred A. Leysieffer, Professor of Statistics; Ph.D., Michigan. Environmental statistics, sample surveys, stochastic processes.

Robley J. Light, Professor of Chemistry; Ph.D., Duke. Biosynthesis, metabolism, and structure of lipids and related compounds.

Robert J. Livingston, Professor of Biological Sciences; Ph.D., Miami (Florida). Estuarine ecology, aquatic pollution biology.

Richard N. Mariscal, Professor of Biological Sciences; Ph.D., Berkeley. Marine biology; behavior, physiology, and ultrastructure of invertebrates.

Duane A. Meeter, Professor of Statistics; Ph.D., Wisconsin–Madison. Ecological statistics, computer applications.

John K. Osmond, Professor of Geology; Ph.D., Wisconsin–Madison. Uranium-series isotopes.

Paul C. Ragland, Professor of Geology; Ph.D., Rice. Petrology, geochemistry.

David W. Stuart, Professor of Meteorology; Ph.D., UCLA. Mesoscale observational studies of the meteorology of upwelling regions, global weather, air-sea interactions. Principal Scientist, Field Experiments on El Niño.

William F. Tanner, Professor of Geology; Ph.D., Oklahoma. Fluid dynamics, paleoceanography, sedimentology, structural geology.

Thomas J. Vickers, Professor of Chemistry; Ph.D., Florida. Spectroscopic techniques for chemical analysis of trace elements relating to human health.

Sherwood W. Wise, Professor of Geology; Ph.D., Illinois. Micropaleontology, marine geology, diagenesis of pelagic sediments, biomineralization.

MASSACHUSETTS INSTITUTE OF TECHNOLOGY / WOODS HOLE OCEANOGRAPHIC INSTITUTION

Joint Program in Oceanography / Applied Ocean Science and Engineering

Program of Study

The Massachusetts Institute of Technology (MIT) and the Woods Hole Oceanographic Institution (WHOI) offer joint doctoral and professional degrees in oceanography and in applied ocean science and engineering. The Joint Program leads to a single degree awarded by both institutions. Graduate study in oceanography encompasses virtually all of the basic sciences as they apply to the marine environment: physics, chemistry, geochemistry, geology, geophysics, and biology. Oceanographic engineering allows for concentration in the major engineering fields of civil, mechanical, electrical, and ocean engineering. The graduate programs are administered by joint MIT/WHOI committees drawn from the faculty and staff of both institutions. The Joint Program involves several departments at MIT: Earth, Atmospheric, and Planetary Sciences and Biology in the School of Science; and Civil and Environmental Engineering, Electrical Engineering and Computer Science, Mechanical Engineering, and Ocean Engineering in the School of Engineering. WHOI departments are Physical Oceanography, Biology, Marine Chemistry and Geochemistry, Geology and Geophysics, and Applied Ocean Physics and Engineering. Upon admission, students register in the appropriate MIT department and at WHOI simultaneously and are assigned academic advisers at each institution. The usual steps to a doctoral degree are entering the program the summer preceding the first academic year and working in a laboratory at WHOI, following an individually designed program in preparation for a general (qualifying) examination to be taken before the third year, submitting a dissertation of significant original theoretical or experimental research, and conducting a public oral defense of the thesis. The normal time it takes to achieve the doctoral degree is about five years from the bachelor's degree. Students entering with a master's degree in the field may need less time. Each student is expected to become familiar with the principal areas of oceanography in addition to demonstrating a thorough knowledge of at least one major field. Subjects, seminars, and opportunities for research participation are offered at both MIT and WHOI. Courses and seminars are supplemented by cross-registration privileges with Harvard, Brown, and the Boston University Marine Program. Students also have the opportunity to participate in oceanographic cruises during graduate study.

Research Facilities

A broad spectrum of equipment and facilities are available. The wide-ranging deep-sea research vessels at WHOI include *Oceanus, Atlantis,* and *Knorr.* In addition, the deep-diving submersible *ALVIN,* which is carried on *Atlantis,* is operated by WHOI, as are several smaller coastal vessels. Both MIT and WHOI utilize the latest developments in computer technology, from personal computers to large multiuser access systems. Videoconferencing between MIT and WHOI provides interactive transmission for classes, and a high-speed data link for research is provided. Broad-based engineering design and support shop facilities (machining, electronics) are available at both MIT and WHOI. There are more than twelve libraries at MIT containing more than 2 million volumes. Cooperative arrangements with other libraries in the Boston area provide students with access to substantial research collections. WHOI library facilities are shared with the Marine Biological Laboratory and are supplemented by collections of the Northeast Fisheries Center and the U.S. Geological Survey, all located in Woods Hole.

Financial Aid

Research assistantships are available to most entering graduate students in the Joint Program and are usually awarded on a full-year basis. Such awards, as well as a few special fellowships, cover full tuition and provide a stipend adjusted periodically to current living expenses. For the 1999–2000 academic year, the stipend is $1540 per month.

Cost of Study

Because tuition and stipend are usually paid for students in good standing, the main costs to the student are for medical insurance, books, and supplies.

Living and Housing Costs

Place of residence is determined by the student's selected program of study and research interests. Graduate students traditionally live off campus at both MIT and WHOI, although there is some graduate housing at both campuses. Housing and living costs tend to be expensive in both the Cambridge and Woods Hole areas, although reasonable housing is available. Estimated twelve-month living costs for 1998–99 were $19,200 for a single graduate student and $25,800 for a married student.

Student Group

There are 134 graduate students registered in the Joint Program. They are divided among the five disciplines as follows: physical oceanography (28), marine geology and geophysics (24), biological oceanography (36), chemical oceanography (17), and applied ocean science and engineering (29).

Student Outcomes

Graduates of the program are employed in a various number of areas. Fifty-four percent are employed in academic/universities, 11 percent are in civilian government, 15 percent are employed in the private sector, 9 percent are in the military service, and 11 percent are employed in a variety of other areas. Places that have employed graduates recently include Scripps Institution of Oceanography, Lamont Doherty Earth Observatory, Princeton University, University of Texas at Austin, Harvard University, University of North Carolina at Chapel Hill, NASA-Goddard, Carnegie Institution, World Wildlife Fund of Canada, CSIRO in Australia, the Japan Defense Agency, and Anderson Consulting, Seattle.

Location

MIT's 146-acre campus extends more than a mile along the Cambridge side of the Charles River, overlooking downtown Boston. Metropolitan Boston offers diverse recreational and cultural opportunities. New England beaches and mountains are within easy reach. WHOI is in the small fishing village of Woods Hole, about 80 miles southeast of Boston and 20 miles west of Hyannis.

The University and The Institution

MIT is an independent, coeducational, privately endowed university. It is broadly organized into five academic schools: Architecture and Planning, Engineering, Humanities and Social Sciences, Management, and Science. Within these schools there are twenty-two academic departments. Total enrollment is approximately 9,800 divided almost evenly between undergraduate and graduate students. The MIT faculty numbers approximately 1,000 with a total teaching staff of 1,940. WHOI is one of the largest independent, unaffiliated oceanographic institutions and research fleet operators in the world. There is a staff of approximately 900 scientists, engineers, technicians, research vessel crews, and support personnel.

Applying

Application for admission to the Joint Program is made on the MIT graduate school application forms. Complete application files, including college transcripts, three letters of recommendation, test scores, and the application fee should be filed no later than January 15 for admission beginning in June or September. The General Test and one Subject Test of the GRE are required. The TOEFL is required of all international students whose schooling has not been predominantly in English.

Admission is offered on a competitive basis to those who appear most likely to benefit from the Joint Program. Notification of admission decisions are sent out prior to March 31.

Correspondence and Information

Education Office
MS #31
Woods Hole Oceanographic Institution
360 Wood Hole Road, Clark 223
Woods Hole, Massachusetts 02543-1546
Telephone: 508-289-2219
World Wide Web: http://www.whoi.edu/

MIT/WHOI Joint Program Office
54-911
Massachusetts Institute of Technology
77 Massachusetts Avenue
Cambridge, Massachusetts 02139
Telephone: 617-253-7544
World Wide Web: http://web.mit.edu/mit-whoi/www

Massachusetts Institute of Technology/Woods Hole Oceanographic Institution

THE DEPARTMENTS AND THEIR RESEARCH

Oceanography and applied ocean science and engineering are fields that naturally lead to interdisciplinary research. In the following departmental program sections, brief descriptions of the research areas covered by the faculty are given. It is quite common for students to pursue research problems that cross the disciplinary lines of the given departments.

BIOLOGICAL OCEANOGRAPHY

Rafael L. Bras, Ph.D., Chairman, Civil and Environmental Engineering Department, MIT.
Phillip A. Sharp, Ph.D., Chairman, Biology Department, MIT.
Laurence P. Madin, Ph.D., Chairman, Biology Department, WHOI.

Phytoplankton and zooplankton ecology; regulation of primary and secondary production; population biology; natural history and biology of oceanic fishes; comparative physiology; biochemical toxicology in marine species; biochemical and physiological adaptations; toxic algae and red tides; theoretical and experimental population ecology; estuarine and salt marsh ecology; ecology of deep and coastal benthos; microbial ecology and biochemistry; development and reproductive biology of marine invertebrates; larval dispersal mechanisms; behavior of marine mammals; symbiotic relationships; biogeochemistry of aquatic systems; biodegradation of aquatic contaminants; cell biology; molecular biology and evolution; synthesis, shape, and structure of macromolecules; cellular and molecular immunology; gene expression.

CHEMICAL OCEANOGRAPHY

Rafael L. Bras, Ph.D., Chairman, Civil and Environmental Engineering Department, MIT.
Ronald G. Prinn, Ph.D., Chairman, Department of Earth, Atmospheric, and Planetary Sciences, MIT.
Mark D. Kurz, Ph.D., Chairman, Marine Chemistry and Geochemistry Department, WHOI.

Water columns (open and coastal oceans, estuaries, rivers): organic and inorganic cycles of particulate and dissolved carbon, oxygen, nitrogen, phosphorous, sulfur, and trace metals (redox transformations, rare earths); stable and radioisotopic tracers; noble gases; air-sea exchange; remote sensing and modeling; environmental quality; oil and gas geochemistry; colloids and particle-reactive tracers; weathering. Sedimentary geochemistry: major and minor elements, radionuclides and their paleoceanographic applications, diagenesis and preservation of organic matter, modeling.
Seawater-basalt interactions: major and trace elements, stable isotopes, solid phases and hydrothermal solutions, laboratory experiments, modeling.

MARINE GEOLOGY AND GEOPHYSICS

Ronald G. Prinn, Ph.D., Chairman, Department of Earth, Atmospheric, and Planetary Sciences, MIT.
William B. Curry, Ph.D., Chairman, Geology and Geophysics Department, WHOI.

Micropaleontological biostratigraphy, planktonic and benthonic foraminifera, paleoceanography, paleobiogeography, benthic boundary-layer processes, paleocirculation and paleoecology, igneous petrology and volcanic processes, crustal structure and tectonics, marine magnetic anomalies, heat flow of the ocean floor, upper mantle petrology, seismic stratigraphy, fractionation processes of stable isotopes and stable isotope stratigraphy, metamorphosis of high-strain zones, gravity, observational and theoretical reflection and refraction seismology, earthquake seismology, relative and absolute plate motions, coastal processes, marine sedimentation.

OCEANOGRAPHIC ENGINEERING

Rafael L. Bras, Ph.D., Chairman, Civil and Environmental Engineering Department, MIT.
Paul L. Penfield Jr., Ph.D., Chairman, Electrical Engineering and Computer Sciences Department, MIT.
Nam Pyo Suh, Ph.D., Chairman, Mechanical Engineering Department, MIT.
Chryssostomos Chryssostomidis, Ph.D., Chairman, Ocean Engineering Department, MIT.
Timothy K. Stanton, Ph.D., Chairman, Applied Ocean Physics and Engineering Department, WHOI.

Optical instrumentation, laser velocimetry; volcanic, tectonic, and hydrothermal processes; deep submergence systems (imaging, control, robotics); underwater acoustics (acoustic tomography, scattering, remote sensing, Arctic acoustics, bottom acoustics propagation through the ocean interior and sediments, array design); buoy and mooring engineering; ocean instrumentation; signal processing theory; fluid dynamics, sediment transport, nearshore processes, bottom boundary layer and mixed layer dynamics; turbulence, wave prediction, numerical modeling; seismic profiling; data acquisition and communication systems, microprocessor-based instrumentation; fiber optics; sonar systems; marsh ecology; ship design; offshore structures; material science; groundwater flow.

PHYSICAL OCEANOGRAPHY

Ronald G. Prinn, Ph.D., Chairman, Department of Earth, Atmospheric, and Planetary Sciences, MIT.
Terrence M. Joyce, Ph.D., Chairman, Physical Oceanography Department, WHOI.

General circulation: distribution of tracer fields, models of idealized gyres, abyssal circulation, heat transport.
Air-sea interaction: water mass transportation, upper ocean response to atmospheric forcing, equatorial ocean circulation.
Shelf dynamics: coastal upwelling and fronts, coastal-trapped waves, deep ocean-shelf exchange.
Mesoscale processes: Gulf Stream Rings, oceanic fronts, barotropic and baroclinic instability, eddy-mean interactions.
Small-scale processes: double diffusion, intrusion, internal waves, convection.

NOVA SOUTHEASTERN UNIVERSITY

Oceanographic Center
Programs in Marine Biology, Coastal Zone Management,
Marine Environmental Sciences, and Oceanography

Programs of Study

The Oceanographic Center through the Institute of Marine and Coastal Studies offers the M.S. degree in marine biology, coastal zone management, and marine environmental science; the joint M.S. degree in marine biology/coastal zone management/marine environmental science; and the Ph.D. degree in oceanography. The M.S. and Ph.D. programs contain a common core of five marine courses: concepts in physical oceanography, ecosystems, geology, chemistry, and biostatistics. Specialty and tutorial courses in each program provide depth. The Oceanographic Center operates on a quarter-term system with twelve-week courses.

Classes for the M.S. programs meet one evening per week in a 3-hour session. Capstone Review and Thesis tracks are offered. The Capstone Review Track requires a minimum of 42 credits, which includes thirteen 3-credit courses and a 3-credit paper. The paper is usually an extended literature review of an approved subject, which the student defends before the Advisory Committee. The Thesis Track requires a minimum of 39 credits, including ten 3-credit courses and at least 9 credits of master's thesis research. The number of research credits depends upon the time needed to complete the thesis research, typically a minimum of three terms. The thesis is formally defended before the committee. All students admitted to the program are placed in the Capstone Review Track. To enter the Thesis Track, students must have approval of the major professor and complete an approved thesis proposal.

The joint M.S. degree in marine biology/coastal zone management/marine environmental science requires a minimum of 48 to 54 credits, depending upon the student's track—Capstone Review or Thesis, and thesis research or the Capstone Review Paper. The total minimum requirement for the M.S. degree ranges from 48 to 54 credits, taking an equal number of courses within each specialty.

The Ph.D. program consists of upper-level course work and original research on a selected topic of importance in the ocean sciences. Requirements include general core courses as well as tutorial studies with the major professor. The Ph.D. degree requires a minimum of 90 credits beyond the baccalaureate; at least 48 credits must consist of dissertation research and at least 42 credits must consist of upper-level course work, usually tutorial studies with the major professor. The student must successfully complete the Ph.D. comprehensive examination and defend the dissertation before Oceanographic Center faculty members. Students are expected to complete the Ph.D. program in nine years or less, a minimum of three years of which must be in residence.

Research Facilities

The center is composed of three main buildings, several modulars, and a two-story houseboat that contains a student center and ten student offices. The main buildings contain a conference room, a classroom, a warehouse bay staging area, an electron microscopy laboratory, a darkroom, a machine shop, a carpentry shop, an electronics laboratory, a computer center with ready room, a wetlab/classroom, a coral workshop, a filtered seawater facility, eight working biology laboratories, and twenty-four additional offices.

The William Springer Richardson Library contains 2,700 books as well as 80 active and 33 inactive periodicals. Audiovisual equipment is available as well as computer-assisted CD-ROM and Internet database searches. A general library facility is maintained on the main campus in Davie.

The computer center operates a multinode OpenVMS cluster consisting of DEC AXP workstations, with high-resolution color monitors, DAT tape drives, and CD-ROM readers. Also available are two networked HP 4SiMX PostScript printers, a networked Tektronix Phaser 550 color laser printer, a color flatbed scanner, and imaging hardware and software. The center also operates a LAN consisting of approximately forty PCs for faculty and staff member and student use that is connected to the Internet via a T-1 link.

Financial Aid

There is limited financial aid available in the form of undergraduate laboratory teaching assistantships and graduate research assistantships. The Office of Student Financial Aid helps students finance tuition, fees, books, and other costs, drawing on a variety of public and private aid programs. For more information, students should call 800-541-6682 Ext. 7411.

Cost of Study

In 1999–2000, tuition costs are $397 per credit hour for students enrolled in the M.S. programs and $2600 per term for students enrolled in the Ph.D. program.

Living and Housing Costs

All full-time students are eligible for main-campus housing, which is located 12 miles due west of the Oceanographic Center. Furnished one- and two-bedroom apartments are available. For more information, students should call 800-541-6682 Ext. 7052. Numerous apartments, condominiums, and other rental housing are available in Hollywood, Dania, and Ft. Lauderdale.

Student Group

There are approximately 100 students enrolled in the M.S. programs and 5 students enrolled in the Ph.D. program.

Student Outcomes

M.S. graduates find positions in city, county, and state governments or private industry, including consulting companies. Graduates also go on for further education and enter Ph.D. programs.

Location

The Center is located in Dania Beach, Florida, just south of Ft. Lauderdale, on a 10-acre site on the ocean side of Port Everglades and is easily accessible from I-95 and the Ft. Lauderdale airport. The Center has a 1-acre boat basin, and its location affords immediate access to the Gulf Stream and the open sea, the Florida Straits, and the Bahama Banks.

The University

Nova Southeastern University was chartered by the State of Florida in 1964 and currently, with nearly 15,000 students, is the largest independent university in Florida. The main campus is situated on 227 acres in Davie, Florida, near Ft. Lauderdale.

Applying

When applying, students must submit an application form, application fee, transcripts from other schools attended, GRE scores, and letters of recommendation. Applicants interested in the M.S. program in marine biology should hold a bachelor's degree in biology, oceanography, or a closely related field, including science education. Due to the discipline's diversity, applicants with any undergraduate major will be considered for admission into the M.S. program in coastal zone management or marine environmental science. However, a science major is most useful, and a science background is essential.

Correspondence and Information

Nova Southeastern University
Oceanographic Center
Institute of Marine and Coastal Studies
8000 North Ocean Drive
Dania Beach, Florida 33004
Telephone: 954-920-1909
Fax: 954-921-7764
E-mail: imcs@ocean.nova.edu
World Wide Web: http://www.nova.edu/ocean/

Nova Southeastern University

THE FACULTY AND THEIR RESEARCH

The Oceanographic Center pursues studies and investigations in biological oceanography and observational and theoretical oceanography. Research interests include: modeling of large-scale ocean circulation, coastal dynamics, ocean-atmosphere coupling, surface gravity waves, biological oceanography, chemical oceanography, coral reef assessment, Pleistocene and Holocene sea level changes, benthic ecology, marine biodiversity, calcification of invertebrates, marine fisheries, molecular ecology and evolution, wetlands ecology, aquaculture, and nutrient dynamics. Regions of interest include not only Florida's coastal waters and the continental shelf/slope waters of the southeastern United States, but also the waters of the Caribbean Sea, the Gulf of Mexico, and the Antarctic, Atlantic, Indian, and Pacific oceans.

Professors

Richard E. Dodge: Coral reefs and reef-building corals, effects of pollution and past climatic changes.
Russell Snyder: Development of instrumentation for remote monitoring of the wave field.
Richard Spieler: Fish chronobiology, artificial reefs, and habitat assessment.

Associate Professors

Patricia Blackwelder: Calcification and distribution of marine microfauna, a historical record of the past.
Curtis Burney: Dissolved nutrients and marine microbes, especially bacteria.
Edward Keith: Structure, function, and evolution of milk and tear proteins, physiological ecology of terrestrial and marine mammals, molecular phylogenetics and evolution of marine mammals.
Charles Messing: Systematics of crinoids and macroinvertebrate communities.
Andrew Rogerson: Ecology of the eukaryotic microbes (the protists) in the cycling of carbon and nutrients in coastal waters, particularly the amoeboid protozoa.
Alexander Soloviev: Measurement and modeling of near-surface turbulence and air/sea exchange.
James Thomas: Marine biodiversity, invertebrate systematics.

Assistant Professors

Veljko Dragojlovic: Isolation, characterization, and synthesis of natural products.
Joshua Feingold: Coral reef ecology.
Barry Klinger: Numerical, analytical, and laboratory modeling of geophysical fluid dynamics of ocean and climate processes.
Robert Pomeroy: Marine chemistry.
Venkatesh Shanbhag: Spectroscopic, potentiometric, and modeling studies of humic and fulvic acids, stability constants and contaminant transport in nature.
Mahmood Shivji: Conservation biology, biodiversity, evolution, molecular ecology, and population biology.
Alexander Yankovsky: Wind- and buoyancy-driven currents on the continental shelf and slope and their mesoscale variability and adjustment to realistic shelf topography.

Adjunct Professors

Bart Baca, Director of Aquaculture Programs: Wetlands ecology, marine botany, aquaculture.
Robert Baer: Public policy and marine archeology.
Mark Farber: Biostatistics.
Nancy Gassman: Marine biology, coastal zone management, and marine environmental sciences internships.
Gary Hitchcock: Marine plankton.
Stephen King: Coastal law.
Donald McCorquodale: Microbiology, marine chemistry.
Stacy Myers: GIS and remote sensing, coastal zone management.
Brian Polkinghorn: Environmental dispute resolution.
Gary Rand: Aquatic toxicology, biostatistics.
Keith Ronald: Marine mammals.
Alan Sosnow: Ports and harbors.
Thomas Thompson: Environmental health.
William Venezia: Coastal dynamics.

The Oceanographic Center.

OREGON STATE UNIVERSITY

College of Oceanic and Atmospheric Sciences

Programs of Study

The College offers M.A., M.S., and Ph.D. degrees in oceanography, atmospheric sciences, and geophysics. Specializations in biological, chemical, geological, and physical oceanography are available. An interdisciplinary program is also available. A master's degree in marine resource management is offered. These degree programs prepare students for research, teaching, management, and policy positions in the academic, governmental, and private sectors. Master's degrees in oceanography, atmospheric sciences, and geophysics require 45 quarter credits of graduate courses and thesis and a final oral examination. The Ph.D. degree in these fields requires about 100 credits of courses and thesis research, including any M.S. degree credits, a qualifying examination, and a final thesis presentation and oral defense. The marine resources management degree requires 60 credits of multidisciplinary courses; 6 credits of thesis, research, or internship; and a final oral examination. Each of the graduate programs requires a group of multidisciplinary core courses. The residence requirement for the master's degree is 30 credits taken at OSU and for the Ph.D., one academic year and 36 credits at OSU. Students accepted initially at the master's level may transfer into the Ph.D. program by passing a qualifying examination. The usual time taken to earn the M.S. degree is two to three years and for the Ph.D. degree, four or five years. Research opportunities for students are available in a diverse range of faculty research programs. In all fields, student thesis research involves extensive laboratory and field or at-sea activities. Persons interested in interdisciplinary research areas such as air-sea interactions, global climate change, geochemistry, and satellite oceanography are invited to apply.

Research Facilities

The College occupies two large research buildings, several smaller buildings, and portions of other research buildings. Major facilities and equipment include an electron microprobe, an inductively coupled plasma mass spectrometer, other mass spectrometers, gamma spectrometers, atomic absorption and UV spectrometers, multichannel autoanalyzers, N and C analyzers, an image analysis system with multispectral processing, and controlled environment rooms. The 54-meter research vessel *Wecoma*, capable of working in all oceans, has a wide array of laboratory and overside research equipment. The College is the repository for deep sea cores from the NORCOR program. The Environmental Computing Center of the College has two Thinking Machine supercomputers and a group of IBM RS/6000 workstations for high-performance computing. Three Sun 690 file servers provide file and application service. An advanced GIS system runs on dedicated equipment. Graduate students and faculty members access these computing facilities through an extensive network of 120 UNIX workstations and 150 microcomputers.

Financial Aid

Almost all graduate students are supported on graduate research assistantships, funded by research grants and contracts. A small number of teaching assistantships are also available. Both types of assistantships provided a yearly stipend of $16,000 for 1998–99 and full tuition remission. Assistantship duties average 20 hours per week. Space Grant Graduate Fellowships, funded by NASA, are available to qualified applicants with aerospace-related interests; they provide a stipend of $12,000 and full tuition remission. Graduate research and teaching assistantship stipends are taxable.

Cost of Study

For graduate students not on assistantships, tuition and fees are $6825 for Oregon residents and $11,097 for nonresidents for the 1999–2000 academic year. All students paid fees of about $300 per term. Tuition and fees are subject to change without notice.

Living and Housing Costs

The Cost of Living Index for the Corvallis area is at the national average, with the costs for utilities and housing slightly lower. Basic living costs (e.g., housing, food, utilities, and medical insurance) for a single graduate student are about $9000 per year and for a couple about $14,000. University housing for single students and some University student family housing are available. Most graduate students find private housing in the community.

Student Group

Students come from all parts of the United States and many other countries. In February 1997, there were 94 students enrolled in the College graduate programs: 12 in atmospheric sciences, 48 in oceanography, 7 in geophysics, and 27 in marine resource management. Of these, 70 percent were men, 30 percent were women, 30 percent were international students, and 4 percent were members of underrepresented U.S. minorities. Recent graduates are employed in colleges and universities, research organizations, consulting firms, and governmental agencies in the United States and other countries.

Location

The University is in the small city of Corvallis, situated in the Willamette valley, a mild-climate region of agriculture, timber, and vineyards between the Cascade Mountains and the Coast range. The metropolitan area of Portland is about an hour and a half away by freeway. Oregon offers superb living conditions and year-round outdoor activities. Spectacular coastal headlands, beaches and bays, mountains and skiing, and white-water rivers are within an hour of Corvallis.

The University and The College

Oregon State, with 3,000 graduate students among its enrollment of 15,000, is a strong research university in the basic and applied sciences, agriculture, and engineering. It is among the top 100 U.S. universities in research funding and operates many research facilities, such as a research reactor, large wave tanks, and the Marine Science Center, a coastal laboratory. The College, with 98 research scientists on its faculty, is among the leading U.S. oceanographic programs. It is a member of UCAR and the Joint Oceanographic Institutions and shares in major national oceanographic research efforts. In 1991, NASA designated the College a data analysis site for the Earth Observation System project.

Applying

For all applicants, the following are required: a strong background in a basic or applied science or mathematics; one year each of chemistry, physics, and calculus; the General Test of the GRE; and the relevant Subject Test. Applicants for fall term must submit application forms, test scores, transcripts, three reference letters, and a statement of research interests and objectives by February 1. Applicants whose education was not in English must submit TOEFL scores. There is a nonrefundable University application fee of $50. Students can request forms from the address below.

Correspondence and Information

Student Services Office
College of Oceanic and Atmospheric Sciences
104 Oceanography Administration Building
Oregon State University
Corvallis, Oregon 97331-5503
Telephone: 541-737-5190
E-mail: student_adviser@oce.orst.edu

Oregon State University

THE FACULTY AND THEIR RESEARCH

Biological Oceanography
M. R. Abbott. Mesoscale biological and physical process coupling, satellite study of phytoplankton spatiotemporal patterns.
T. J. Cowles. Zooplankton ecology; phytoplankton physiology and zooplankton food selection interactions; remote detection.
B. R. Mate. Marine mammals: behavior and population studies; migration, feeding, trophic relationships, and diving physiology.
C. B. Miller. Zooplankton ecology, oceanic ecodynamics.
D. M. Nelson. Biogeochemistry of the upper ocean, nutrient cycling, nutrient limitation of phytoplankton growth, marine silica cycle.
B. F. Sherr. Microbial roles in carbon-energy flow and nutrient regeneration in pelagic systems, dynamics of phagotrophic protista.
E. B. Sherr. Pelagic microbial food webs, microbes in carbon and nitrogen cycles in aquatic ecosystems.
R. A. Wheatcroft. Interdependence between sedimentological and biological processes in the marine environment, continental shelf processes.
P. A. Wheeler. Phytoplankton physiological ecology, nutrient and nitrogen cycles and metabolism in phytoplankton and bacteria.

Chemical Oceanography
R. W. Collier. Trace metal cycles, chemistry of environmental systems, geochemistry of suspended particulate matter.
K. K. Falkner. Inorganic element cycles in aquatic environments, application of isotopic systems to geochemical problems.
B. Hales. Benthic biogeochemistry; analysis and modeling of the physics, biology, and chemistry of the ocean surface.
F. G. Prahl. Biogeochemical cycling of natural and anthropogenic organic matter in aquatic environments, molecular geochemistry.
B. R. T. Simoneit. Organic, environmental, and petroleum geochemistry; paleobiogeochemistry; organic matter in the geobiosphere.

Geological Oceanography
D. M. Christie. Geochemistry and petrology of submarine lavas from mid-ocean ridges and oceanic hotspots.
G. B. Dalrymple. Geological isotopic dating, geomagnetic field reversals, Pacific plate tectonics, vulcanism, age of earth.
R. A. Duncan. Geochronology of ocean floor and island basalts, linear volcanism as a reference for crustal plate motion.
M. R. Fisk. Chemistry and mineralogy of mid-ocean ridge and island basalts, experimental petrology, volcanic process modeling.
D. W. Graham. Isotope geochemistry (especially helium and rare gases) of ocean floor, island, and continental volcanic systems.
R. A. Holman. Coastal processes, nearshore wave and current effects, dynamics of nearshore waves, beach morphology.
G. Klinkhammer. Sediment geochemistry and biogeochemical cycles, geochemistry of deep sea hydrothermal systems.
A. C. Mix. Deep-sea sediments, paleoceanography, paleoclimatology, micropaleontology of foraminifera, isotope geochemistry.
R. L. Nielsen. Modeling of the geochemical evolution of magmas, partitioning behavior of trace elements in igneous rocks.
N. G. Pisias. Marine stratigraphy and micropaleontology, paleoceanography and paleoclimatology, numerical and statistical analysis.

Physical Oceanography
J. S. Allen. Theoretical physical oceanography, geophysical fluid dynamics, studies of flow over the continental shelf and slope.
J. A. Barth. Coastal ocean dynamics, frontal instability, computational fluid dynamics, eastern boundary current modeling.
A. F. Bennett. Inverse methods, theory of turbulent diffusion.
D. B. Chelton. Satellite remote sensing, large-scale wind forced ocean circulation, air-sea interaction, statistical modeling.
R. A. deSzoeke. Upper ocean turbulent process modeling, Pacific circulation, Antarctic Circumpolar Current.
T. M. Dillon. Turbulent transport of energy and momentum, boundary layers, thermal microstructure and fine structure.
M. Freilich. Surface wave modeling, nearshore processes, satellite microwave ocean remote sensing.
A. Huyer. Coastal upwelling, continental shelf circulation, eastern boundary currents, hydrography of the Pacific Ocean.
P. M. Kosro. Physical oceanography, coastal circulation and exchange processes, eastern boundary currents.
M. D. Levine. Internal waves of the upper ocean, Arctic Ocean, response to storms, satellite altimetry.
R. P. Matano. Large-scale ocean circulation, dynamics of western boundary currents, ocean modeling.
R. N. Miller. Tropical Pacific sea level height, analysis and prediction of ENSO, use of remotely sensed data in dynamical models.
J. N. Moum. Small-scale ocean physics, turbulent processes, upper ocean dynamics, instrumentation, tropical oceanography.
J. G. Richman. Large-scale ocean circulation, upper ocean dynamics, satellite remote sensing, Antarctic Circumpolar Current.
W. D. Smyth. Turbulence in geophysical fluid systems, equatorial oceanography, vortex dynamics, numerical modeling.
P. T. Strub. Coastal oceanography, eastern boundary currents, air-sea interaction, vertical and horizontal transport modeling.
J. R. V. Zaneveld. Optical oceanography.

Atmospheric Sciences
J. R. Barnes. Large-scale atmospheric dynamics and planetary atmospheres.
J. A. Coakley Jr. Role of clouds in the earth's energy budget and climate.
S. K. Esbensen. Air-sea interaction, dynamical analysis of tropical climate and weather.
G. Levy. Mesoscale and synoptic scale dynamics, marine meteorology, boundary layer and mesoscale analytical modeling.
L. Mahrt. Turbulence, convection, and the atmospheric boundary layer.
M. H. Unsworth. Vegetation-atmosphere interactions, plant responses to ozone, ultraviolet radiation, global modeling of methane.
R. J. Vong. Aerosol, cloud, and rainwater chemistry; wet and dry deposition; air pollution source emissions and transport; modeling.

Geophysics
J. Y. Chen. Marine geophysics, geodynamics, continental tectonic processes, tectonics of Venus.
G. D. Egbert. Electromagnetic induction, geomagnetism, data processing, inversion and interpretation, stochastic modeling.
R. J. Lillie. Reflection seismology, continental geophysics, structure and evolution of collisional mountain ranges.
J. L. Nabelek. Applied and theoretical seismology, earthquake source mechanisms, tectonics.
A. M. Tréhu. Crustal structure from seismic reflection and refraction, continental margin tectonics, ocean bottom seismometers.

Marine Resource Management
B. R. De Young. Coastal service enterprise management and marketing, strategic planning of coastal recreation and tourism.
J. W. Good. Ocean and coastal policy, management, and planning; natural hazards and wetland management; mitigation.
R. G. Hildreth. Ocean and coastal law, water law, sustainable development, International Law of the Sea.
J. Jacobson. Ocean and coastal law, water law, sustainable development, International Law of the Sea.
G. E. Matzke. Biotic resources, Third World resource issues, resource conflicts.
M. T. Morrissey. Seafood product development, waste minimization, and utilization; seafood biochemistry, processing, and safety.
D. Sampson. Population dynamics of marine fish and mammals, groundfish stock assessment.
C. L. Smith. Cultural ecology, resource management, economic development, distributive justice, complex organizations.
G. R. Sylvia. Marine economics, seafood marketing.

SELECTED PUBLICATIONS

Abbott, M. R., et al. Scales of variability of bio-optical properties as observed from near-surface drifters. *J. Geophys. Res.* 100:13345–67, 1995.

Allen, J. S., P. A. Newberger, and **R. A. Holman.** Nonlinear shear instabilities of alongshore currents on plane beaches. *J. Fluid Mech.* 310:181–213, 1996.

Barnes, J. R., et al. Mars atmospheric dynamics as simulated by the NASA-Ames general circulation-model. *J. Geophys. Res.* 101:12753–76, 1996.

Barnes, J. R., et al. Winter quasi-stationary eddies. *J. Geophys. Res.* 101:12753–76, 1996.

Barth, J. A. Coastal ocean circulation off Oregon: Recent observations of spatial and temporal variability. In *Estuarine and Ocean Survival of Northeastern Pacific Salmon,* NOAA Technical Memorandum, NMFS, MWFSC, in press.

Bennett, A. F. Generalized inversion of a global numerical weather prediction model. *Meteor. Atmos. Phys.,* June 1996.

Morrow, R., R. Coleman, J. Church, and **D. B. Chelton.** Surface eddy momentum flux and velocity variances in the Southern Ocean from Geosat altimetry. *J. Phys. Oceanogr.* 24:2050–71, 1994.

Mestas-Nunez, A. M., **D. B. Chelton, M. H. Freilich,** and **J. G. Richman.** An evaluation of ECMWF-based climatological wind stress fields. *J. Phys. Oceanogr.* 24:1532–49, 1994.

Chelton, D. B., and M. G. Schlax. Global observations of oceanic Rossby waves. *Science* 272:234–8.

Morgan, J. P., and **Y. J. Chen.** Dependence of ridge-axis morphology on magma supply and spreading rate. *Nature* 364:706–8, 1993.

Chen, Y. J. Oceanic crustal thickness versus spreading rate. *Geophys. Res. Lett.* 19:753–6, 1992.

Christie, D. M., et al. **(R. L. Nielsen).** Near-primary melt inclusions in anorthite phenocrysts from the Galapagos platform. *Earth Planet. Sci. Lett.* 105:368–77, 1993.

Bretherton, C. S., E. Klinker, A. K. Betts, and **J. A. Coakley Jr.** Comparison of ceilometer, satellite and synoptic measurements of boundary layer cloudiness and the ECMWF diagnostic cloud parameterization scheme during ASTEX. *J. Atmos. Sci.* 52:2736–3751, 1995.

Ramaswamy, V., et al. **(J. A. Coakley Jr.).** Group Report: What are the observed and anticipated meteorological and climatic responses to aerosol forcing? In *Aerosol Forcing of Climate,* pp. 385–99, eds. R. J. Charlson and J. Heintenberg. New York: John Wiley & Sons, 1995.

Collier, R. W., et al. **(F. G. Prahl).** A biomarker perspective on Prymnesiophyte productivity in the Northeast Pacific Ocean. *Deep-Sea Res.* 40:2061–76, 1993.

Cowles, T. J., and R. A. Desiderio. Resolution of biological microstructure through in situ fluorescence emission spectra: An oceanographic application using optical fibers. *Oceanography* 6:105–11, 1993.

Ryder, G., et al. **(G. B. Dalrymple).** A glass spherule of questionably impact origin from the Apollo 15 landing site: Unique target more basalt. *Geochim. Cosmochim. Acta* 60:693–710, 1996.

de Szoeke, R. A. A model of wind and buoyancy-driven ocean circulation. *J. Phys. Oceanogr.* 25:918–41, 1995.

de Szoeke, R. A., and **A. F. Bennett.** Microstructure fluxes across density surfaces. *J. Phys. Oceanogr.* 23:2254–64, 1993.

Dillon, T. M. On the zonal momentum balance at the equator. *J. Phys. Oceanogr.* 19:561–70, 1989.

Dillon, T. M. Thermal microstructure and internal waves in an oceanic diffusive staircase. *Deep-Sea Res.* 36:531–42, 1989.

Gallahan, W. E., and **R. A. Duncan.** Spatial and temporal variability in crystallization of celadonites within the Troodos ophiolite, Cyprus: Implications for low-temperature alteration of the oceanic crust. *J. Geophys. Res.* 99:3147–61, 1994.

Egbert, G. D., and J. R. Booker. Imaging crustal structure in southwestern Washington with small magnetometer arrays. *J. Geophys. Res.* 98:15967–85, 1993.

Sun, J., **S. K. Esbensen,** and **L. Mahrt.** Estimation of surface heat flux. *J. Atmos. Sci.* 52:3162–71, 1995.

Esbensen, S. K., D. B. Chelton, D. Vickers, and J. Sun. An analysis of errors in special sensor microwave imager evaporation estimates over the global oceans. *J. Geophys. Res.* 98:7081–101, 1993.

Falkner, K. K., G. P. Klinkhammer, A. Ungerer, and **D. Christie.** Inductively coupled plasma mass spectrometry in geochemistry. *Earth Planet. Sci. Annu. Rev.* 23:409–49, 1995.

Keller, R. A., **M. R. Fisk,** W. M. White, and K. Birkenmajer. Istopic and trace element constraints on mixing and melting models of marginal basin volcanism, Bransfield Strait, Antarctica. *Earth Planet. Sci. Lett.* 111:287–303, 1992.

Fox, C. G., W. W. Chadwick, and R. W. Embley. Detection of changes in ridge-crest morphology using repeated multibeam sonar surveys. *J. Geophys. Res.* (97)B7:11149–62, 1992.

Freilich, M. H., and P. G. Challenor. A new approach for determining fully empirical altimeter wind speed model functions. *J. Geophys. Res.* 99:25051–62, 1994.

Goldfinger, C., et al. Active strike-slip faulting and folding of the Cascadia plate boundary and forearc in central and northern Oregon. In *U.S.G.S. Professional Paper 1560,* Earthquake Hazards in the Pacific Northwest, eds. Rogers, et al., in press.

McCaffrey, R., and **C. Goldfinger.** Forearc deformation and great subduction earthquakes: Implications for Cascadia offshore earthquake potential. *Science* 267:856–9, 1995.

Hanan, B. B., and **D. W. Graham.** Lead and helium isotope evidence from oceanic basalts for a common deep source of mantle plumes. *Science* 272:991–5, 1996.

Holman, R. A. Nearshore processes. *U.S. National Report to the IUGG* (1991-1994), in press.

Holland, K. T., C. Valentine, and **R. A. Holman.** Wavenumber-frequency structure of infragravity swash motions. *J. Geophys. Res.,* in review.

Holman, R. A., A. H. Sallenger Jr., T. C. Lippmann, and J. Haines. The application of video image processing to the study of nearshore processes. *Oceanography* 6(3):78–85, 1994.

Huyer, A., et al. **(P. M. Kosro** and **T. J. Cowles).** Currents and water masses of the coastal transition zone off northern California, June to August 1988. *J. Geophys. Res.* 96:14809–31, 1991.

Klinkhammer, G. P. Fiber optic spectrometers for in situ measurements in the oceans: The ZAPS probe. *Mar. Chem.* 47:13–20, 1994.

Kosro, P. M. Cross-shelf sediment transport by anticybric eddy off northern California. *Science* 261:1560–4, 1994.

Kosro, P. M., and E. D. Barton. Supersquirt: Dynamics of the Gulf of Tehuantepec, Mexico. *Oceanography* 6(1):23–30, 1993.

Levine, M. D., et al. **(T. Dillon).** A comparison of internal wave dissipation models with CEAREX observations. *J. Phys. Ocean.* 23:269–96, 1993.

Levy, G. Southern hemisphere low level wind circulation statistics from the Seasat scatterometer. *Ann. Geophys.* 12:65–79, 1994.

Levy, G. Surface dynamics of observed maritime fronts. *J. Atmos. Sci.* 46:1219–32, 1989.

Lillie, R. J., M. Bielik, V. Babuska, and J. Plomerová. Gravity modeling of the lithosphere in the Eastern Alpine-Western Carpathian-Pannonlan Basin Region. *Tectonophysics* 23:215–35, 1994.

Sun, J., **S. K. Esbensen,** and **L. Mahrt.** Estimation of surface heat flux. *J. Atmos. Sci.,* in press.

Mahrt, L., and J. Sun. The subgrid velocity scale in the bulk aerodynamic relationship for spatiality averaged acolor flues. *Mon. Wea. Rev.,* in press.

Mahrt, L. Dependence of surface exchange coefficients on averaging scale and grid size. *Quart. J. Roy. Met. Soc.,* in press.

Palacios, D., and **B. R. Mate.** Attack by false killer whales *(Pseudorca crassidens)* on sperm whales *(Phseter macrocephalus)* in the Galapagos Islands. *Mar. Mammal Sci.,* in press.

Miller, C. B. Development of large copepods during spring in the Gulf of Alaska. *Prog. Oceanogr.* 32:295–317, 1993.

Miller, C. B., and K. S. Tande. Stage duration estimation for *Colonus* populations, a modeling study. *Mar. Ecol. Prog. Ser.* 102:15–34, 1993.

Oregon State University

Selected Publications (continued)

Miller, R. N., M. Ghil, and F. Gauthiez. Advanced data assimilation in strongly nonlinear dynamical systems. *J. Atmos. Sci.* 51:1037–56, 1994.

Mix, A. C., W. Rugh, **N. G. Pisias,** S. Veirs, and the Leg 138 Scientific Party. Color reflectance spectroscopy: A tool for rapid characterization of deep sea sediments. In *Proc ODP. Init. Repts. 138,* eds. L. Mayer, N. G. Pisias, T. Janacek, et al. College Station, TX: Ocean Drilling Program, 677–8, 1992.

Moum, J. N. Energy-containing scales of turbulence in the ocean thermocline. *J. Geophys. Res.,* in press.

Moum, J. N. Efficiency of mixing in the main thermocline. *J. Geophys. Res.* 101:12057–69, 1996.

McCaffrey, R., and **J. L. Nabelek.** Earthquakes, gravity, and the origin of the Bali basin: An example of nascent continental fold-and-thrust belt. *J. Geophys. Res.* 92:441–60, 1987.

Nelson, D. M., et al. Production and dissolution of biogenic silica in the ocean: Revised global estimates, comparison with regional data and relationship to biogenic sedimentation. In *Global Biogeochemical Cycles: An International Journal for Global Change.* 9:3, Paper 95GB01070, 1995.

Nielsen, R. L., D. M. Christie, and F. M. Sprtel. Anomalous low Na magmas: Evidence for depleted MORB or analytical artifact? *Geochim. Cosmochim. Acta* 59:5023–6, 1995.

Nielsen, R. L., et al. **(D. M. Christie).** Melt inclusions in high-An plagioclase from the Gorda Ridge: An example of the local diversity of MORB parent magmas. *Contrib. Mineral. Petrol.* 122:34–5, 1995.

Pisias, N., and T. Moore Jr. Radiolarian response to oceanographic changing in the eastern equatorial Pacific at 2.2 and 4.7 Ma: Relationship between changing carbonate deposition and surface oceanography. In *Proc. ODP. Sci. Results 138,* eds. N. Pisias, L. Mayer, T. Janacek, et al. College Station, TX: Ocean Drilling Program, in press.

Prahl, F. G., L. A. Pinto, and M. A. Sparrow. Phytone from chemolytic analysis of modern marine sediments: A product of desulfurization or not? *Geochim. Cosmochim. Acta* 60:1065–73, 1995.

Stanton, B. R., and **J. G. Richman.** Density driven currents and sea level adjustment off the West Coast, South Island, New Zealand. *Cont. Shelf Res.,* in press.

Choi, J. W., **E. B. Sherr,** and **B. F. Sherr.** Relations between presence/absence of a visible nucleoid and metabolic actuity in bacterioplankton cells. *Limnol. Oceanogr.* 41:1161–8, 1996.

Sherr, E. B., and **B. F. Sherr.** Temporal offset in oceanic production and respiration processes implied by seasonal changes in atmospheric oxygen: The role of heterotrophic microbes. *Aquat. Microb. Ecol.* 11:91–100, 1996.

Sherr, E. B., and **B. F. Sherr.** Bacterivory and herbivory: Key roles of phagotrophic prosits in pelagic food webs. *Microb. Ecol.* 28:223–35, 1994.

Shifrin, K., and I. G. Zolotov. The information content of the spectral transmittance of the marine atmospheric boundary layer. *Appl. Opt.* 25, N24, 1996.

Shifrin, K., and I. G. Zolotov. Non-stationary scattering of electromagnetic pulse by spherical particles. *Appl. Opt.* 33(N3):552–8, 1995.

Simoneit, B. R. T., et al. Composition of higher molecular weight organic matter in smoke aerosol from biomass combustion in Amazonia. *Chemosphere* 30:995–1015, 1995.

Smyth, W. D., and W. R. Peltier. Three-dimensionalization of barotropic vortices on the f-plane. *J. Fluid Mech.* 265:25–64, 1994.

Smyth, W. D., and W. R. Peltier. Two-dimensional turbulence in homogeneous and stratified shear layers. *Geophys. Astrophys. Fluid Dynam.* 69:1–32, 1993.

Strub, P. T., J. M. Mesias, and C. James. Satellite observations of the Peru-Chile countercurrent. *Geophys. Res. Lett.* 22:211–4, 1995.

Strub, P. T., and C. James. The large-scale summer circulation of the California Current. *Geophys. Res. Lett.* 22:207–10, 1994.

Tréhu, A. M., and Mendocino Working Group. Pulling the rug out from under California: Seismic images of the Mendocino Triple Junction region, EOS. *Trans. Am. Geophys. Un.* 76:369, 380–1, 1995.

Tréhu, A. M., et al. A seismic reflection profile across the Cascadian subduction zone offshore central Oregon: New constraints on methane distribution and crustal structure. *J. Geophys. Res.* 100:15101–15, 15116, 1995.

Unsworth, M. H., J. J. Colls, and G. E. Sanders. Air pollutants as constraints for crop yields. In *Physiology and Determination of Crop Yield,* pp. 467–86, eds. K. J. Boote, T. R. Sinclaire, J. M. Bennent, and G. M. Paulson. Madison, WI: American Society of Agronomy, 1994.

Vong, R. J., and A. S. Kowalski. Eddy correlation measurements of size-dependent cloud droplet turbulent fluxes to complex terrain. *Tellus* 47B:331–52, 1995.

Mohnen, V. A., and **R. J. Vong.** A climatology of cloud chemistry for the eastern U.S. derived from the mountain cloud chemistry project. *Environ. Rev.* 1:38–54, 1993.

Libby, P. S., and **P. A. Wheeler.** Particulate and dissolved organic nitrogen on the central equatorial pacific. *Deep-Sea Res.,* in press.

Wheeler, P. A., et al. **(E. B. Sherr).** Active cycling of organic carbon in the central Arctic Ocean. *Nature* 380:697–9, 1996.

Zaneveld, J. R. V. Optical closure: From theory to measurement. In *Ocean Optics,* pp. 59–72, eds. R. S. Spinrad, K. L. Carder, and M. J. Perry. New York: Oxford University Press, 1994.

THE STATE UNIVERSITY OF NEW JERSEY

RUTGERS
Campus at New Brunswick

RUTGERS, THE STATE UNIVERSITY OF NEW JERSEY, NEW BRUNSWICK

Institute of Marine and Coastal Sciences
Graduate Program in Oceanography

Programs of Study

Oceanography is the discipline that encompasses all aspects of the scientific study of the oceans, including their physical, biological, chemical, and geological properties. The basic goals of oceanography are to obtain a systematic description of the oceans and a quantitative understanding sufficient for prediction of their behavior. The Graduate Program in Oceanography is centered in the Institute of Marine and Coastal Sciences, which serves as a focus of interdisciplinary studies and research in estuarine, coastal, and open-ocean environments. A broad range of research opportunities are available, including real-time studies in the coastal ocean using advanced underwater instrumentation, biological and geological processes at deep-sea hydrothermal vents, remote sensing and ocean modeling, advanced underwater optics and fish behavior, biodiversity and marine molecular biology, coastal geomorphology, organism-sediment interactions, cycling of organic and inorganic materials in the ocean, and watershed ecosystems.

Candidates with a baccalaureate degree may apply for either the Doctor of Philosophy (Ph.D.) or Master of Science (M.S.) degree program. The Ph.D. degree requires the completion of 72 credit hours of course work and research beyond the baccalaureate degree and the writing and defense of a dissertation resulting from the candidate's independent, original research in oceanography. The M.S. degree requires the completion of 30 credit hours of course work and research beyond the baccalaureate degree and the writing and defense of a thesis. All students are required to complete a program of core courses in oceanography; additional courses are chosen by students in consultation with their major professors and program committees. Ph.D. students must pass a written and oral qualifying examination upon completion of their course work.

Research Facilities

The Institute of Marine and Coastal Sciences is housed in a state-of-the-art research building that includes seawater, morphometrics, molecular biology, remote sensing, ocean modeling, and cartography laboratories. Major equipment includes seawater flumes; a satellite receiving station; a network of small (PCs), medium (UNIX-based workstations) and large (SGI Power Challenge, Thinking Machines CM-200 and CM-5) computer platforms; and electron microscopes. The Rutgers University Marine Field Station, located at the northern entrance to Great Bay, is the site of a large tract of pristine marsh and a major estuary that retains most of its natural characteristics. Great Bay connects with adjoining bays and has direct access to the Atlantic Ocean. An extensive program of long-term oceanographic and ecosystems research is underway at the station. The Haskin Shellfish Research Laboratory, located on Delaware Bay, includes microbiology, histopathology, shell structure, shellfish physiology and pathophysiology, and cytogenetics laboratories.

Financial Aid

Graduate assistantships are available from sponsored research grants and contracts awarded to the faculty. In addition, a limited number of state-supported teaching assistantships and fellowships are available each year. All assistantships and fellowships include a stipend (up to $12,800 per year) and full tuition remission. Typically, 90 percent of students who are accepted receive financial aid.

Cost of Study

For 1999–2000, tuition for full-time New Jersey residents is $3295.68 per semester. Tuition for out-of-state residents is $6061.38 per semester.

Living and Housing Costs

Graduate students traditionally live off campus. University housing is also available in dormitories ($3532.50 per year) and apartments ($2263 per year). A variety of meal plans that average $2430 per year are also available through the University.

Student Group

Currently, there are 24 full-time students in the program, 9 women and 15 men. Seventeen are pursuing the Ph.D. degree. Due to the highly interdisciplinary nature of much of the research conducted at the Institute, students share an unusual rapport with each other and faculty members.

Student Outcomes

The graduate program was established in 1994 and has graduated 3 Ph.D. students and 4 M.S. students, 2 of whom are continuing for the Ph.D. degree.

Location

The Institute of Marine and Coastal Sciences is located on Rutgers University's Cook Campus in New Brunswick, New Jersey. A wealth of cultural and recreational opportunities are nearby. Several accomplished repertory companies are housed in New Brunswick and nearby Princeton. The major metropolitan areas of New York City and Philadelphia are only short (less than 1 hour) train rides away. The world-famous New Jersey shore, with its beaches, swimming, and fishing, is readily accessible.

The University and The Institute

Rutgers, The State University of New Jersey, traces its origins back to 1766 when it was chartered as Queen's College, the eighth institution of higher learning founded in the colonies. Today, more than 47,000 students are enrolled on campuses in New Brunswick, Camden, and Newark. The Institute of Marine and Coastal Sciences was established in 1989 to develop research programs in marine and coastal sciences and to provide a center for the education of marine scientists.

Applying

Applicants to the program are expected to have an undergraduate degree in either mathematics, science, or engineering. Scores on the GRE General Test are required. International students must show proficiency in English. Application deadlines are February 1 for admission the following fall semester and November 1 for admission the following spring semester. Early submission is encouraged, especially for students seeking financial aid. Applicants are strongly encouraged to contact faculty members with complementary interests before and during the application process.

Correspondence and Information

Graduate Program in Oceanography
Institute of Marine and Coastal Sciences
Rutgers, The State University of New Jersey
71 Dudley Road
New Brunswick, New Jersey 08901-8521
Telephone: 732-932-6555 Ext. 501
Fax: 732-932-8578
E-mail: doremus@ahab.rutgers.edu
World Wide Web: http://marine.rutgers.edu/gpo/GradProg.html

Rutgers, The State University of New Jersey, New Brunswick

THE FACULTY AND THEIR RESEARCH

Kenneth W. Able, Professor; Ph.D., William and Mary. Life history, ecology, and behavior of fishes.

Hernan G. Arango, Assistant Research Professor; Ph.D., Texas A&M. Development and application of ocean models and data assimilation.

Gail Ashley, Professor; Ph.D., British Columbia. Sedimentology, geomorphology, environmental ecology, modern processes.

Roni Avissar, Associate Professor; Ph.D., Hebrew (Jerusalem). Micrometeorology, boundary-layer meteorology, atmospheric modeling.

Paul Falkowski, Professor; Ph.D., British Columbia. Biological oceanography: photosynthesis and biogeochemical cycles, application of molecular and biophysical techniques to the marine environment.

Jennifer A. Francis, Assistant Research Professor; Ph.D., Washington (Seattle). Satellite remote sensing of polar regions, air/ice/ocean transfer.

Scott Glenn, Associate Professor; Sc.D., MIT/Woods Hole Oceanographic Institution. Physical oceanography, satellite remote sensing.

J. Frederick Grassle, Professor; Ph.D., Duke. Marine ecology, oceanography.

Judith P. Grassle, Professor; Ph.D., Duke. Population genetics, marine benthic ecology.

Ximing Guo, Assistant Professor; Ph.D., Washington (Seattle). Aquaculture genetics and biotechnology, cytogenetic manipulation and analysis, genetic mapping, shellfish and fish breeding, biology and culture of mollusks.

Dale B. Haidvogel, Professor; Ph.D., MIT/Woods Hole Oceanographic Institution. Physical oceanography, numerical ocean circulation modeling.

Mohamed Iskandarani, Assistant Research Professor; Ph.D., Cornell. Numerical modeling in fluids, pollutant/sediment transport, wave hydrodynamics.

Michael J. Kennish, Research Marine Scientist; Ph.D., Rutgers. Marine geology, estuarine and marine ecology, marine pollution.

Lee J. Kerkhof, Assistant Professor; Ph.D., California, San Diego (Scripps). Marine microbiology–molecular biology, microbial population dynamics.

Uwe Kils, Associate Professor; Ph.D., Christian-Albrechts Universität zu Kiel (Germany). Behavior and microdistribution of juvenile fish, in situ optics.

David S. Kosson, Professor; Ph.D., Rutgers. Hazardous waste control.

Richard Lutz, Professor; Ph.D., Maine. Marine ecology and paleoecology, shellfish ecology, biology of deep-sea hydrothermal vents.

George R. McGhee, Professor; Ph.D., Rochester. Marine paleoecology, evolutionary theory, mass extinction.

James R. Miller, Professor; Ph.D., Maryland. Air-sea interactions, remote sensing, climate modeling, earth system science.

Kenneth G. Miller Sr., Professor; Ph.D., MIT/Woods Hole Oceanographic Institution. Cenozoic stratigraphy and paleoceanograpy; integrated biostratigraphy, isotope stratigraphy, magnetostratigraphy, and seismic stratigraphy.

Michael R. Muller, Associate Professor; Ph.D., Brown. Fluid mechanics, internal gravity waves and thermals.

Andreas Münchow, Assistant Professor; Ph.D., Delaware. Observational oceanography, dynamics of coastal oceans and estuaries.

Karl F. Nordstrom, Professor; Ph.D., Rutgers. Geomorphology, sedimentology.

Richard K. Olsson, Professor; Ph.D., Princeton. Micropaleontology, stratigraphy, paleoecology, paleobathymetry of Cretaceous and Cenozoic formations.

Eric N. Powell, Professor; Ph.D., North Carolina. Shellfish biology/modeling, carbonate preservation, reproductive biology.

Norbert P. Psuty, Professor; Ph.D., LSU. Coastal geomorphology, shoreline erosion, coastal zone management.

Clare Reimers, Associate Professor; Ph.D., Oregon State. Marine geochemistry, carbon cycling and fluxes.

John R. Reinfelder, Assistant Professor; Ph.D., SUNY at Stony Brook. Trace element biogeochemistry, phytoplankton physiology and marine primary production, marine carbon cycle.

Anna-Louise Reysenbach, Assistant Professor; Ph.D., Cape Town (South Africa). Hydrothermal vent microbial ecology, thermophilic microorganisms.

Alan Robock, Professor; Ph.D., MIT. Climatological data analysis, climate modeling, impacts of climate change, soil moisture, remote sensing.

Peter A. Rona, Professor; Ph.D., Yale. Seafloor hydrothermal system, ocean ridge processes, geology of Atlantic continental margins, genesis of seafloor mineral and energy resources.

Oscar M. E. Schofield, Assistant Professor; Ph.D., California, Santa Barbara. Marine phytoplankton ecology, biooptics, effects of UV radiation on phytoplankton.

Sybil P. Seitzinger, Visiting Professor; Ph.D., Rhode Island. Nutrient dynamics in marine, freshwater, and terrestrial ecosystems.

Robert E. Sheridan, Professor, Ph.D.; Columbia. Geology and geophysics of the Atlantic continental margin.

Robert Sherrell, Assistant Professor; Ph.D., MIT/Woods Hole Oceanographic Institution. Trace metals in the oceanic water column, environmental chemistry.

Peter Smouse, Professor; Ph.D., North Carolina State. Genetics and ecology.

Gary L. Taghon, Associate Professor; Ph.D., Washington (Seattle). Marine benthic ecology.

Christopher G. Uchrin, Professor; Ph.D., Michigan. Mathematical modeling of contaminant transport in surface and ground waters.

Robert J. Vrijenhoek, Professor; Ph.D., Connecticut. Evolutionary genetics, ecology.

Sam C. Wainright, Assistant Professor; Ph.D., Georgia. Ecosystems ecology.

W. Waldo Wakefield, Assistant Research Professor; Ph.D., California, San Diego (Scripps). Biological oceanography, marine fisheries, deep-sea biology.

Michael P. Weinstin, Visiting Professor; Ph.D., Florida State. Coastal ecology, habitat utilization (nekton) secondary production, restoration ecology, ecological engineering.

Rutgers, The State University of New Jersey, New Brunswick

SELECTED PUBLICATIONS

Able, K. W., M. P. Fahay, and G. R. Shephard. Early life history of black sea bass *Centroprislis striata* in the Mid-Atlantic Bight and a New Jersey estuary. *Fish. Bull.* 93:429–45, 1995.

Heck, K. L., K. W. Able, C. T. Roman, and M. P. Fahay. Composition, abundance, biomass, and production of macrofauna in a New England estuary: Companions among eelgrass meadows and other nursery habitats. *Estuaries* 18:379–89, 1995.

Miller, A. J., et al. (H. G. Arango). Quantitative skill of quasigeostrophic forecasts of a baroclinically unstable Iceland-Faroe front. *J. Geophys. Res.* 100:10633–49, 1995.

Miller, A. J., H. G. Arango et al. Quasigeostrophic forecasting and physical processes of Iceland-Faroe frontal variability. *J. Phys. Oceanogr.* 26:1273–95, 1995.

Malyk-Selivanova, N., et al. (G. M. Ashley). Geological-geochemical approach to "sourcing" of prehistoric chart artifacts, Brooks Range, northwestern Alaska. *Geoarchaeology Int. J.* 13:673–708, 1998.

Smith, N. D., and G. M. Ashley. A study of brash ice in the proximal marine zone of a sub-polar tidewater glacier. *Marine Geol.* 133:75–87, 1996.

Liu, Y., and R. Avissar. A study of persistence in the land-atmosphere system using a general circulation model and observations. *J. Climate*, in press.

Avissar, R. Which type of soil-vegetation-atmosphere transfer scheme is needed for general circulation models: A proposal for a higher-order scheme. *J. Hydrol.* 212:136–54, 1998.

Falkowski, P. G., R. T. Barber, and V. Smetcek. Biogeochemical controls and feedbacks on ocean primary production. *Science* 281:200–6, 1998.

Falkowski, P. G., and R. Raven. Aquatic Photosynthesis, in *Blackwell Scientific*, p. 375. Oxford: Oxford University Press, 1997.

Francis, J. A. Improvements to TOVS retrievals over sea ice and applications to estimating Arctic energy fluxes. *J. Geophys. Res.* 99:10395–408, 1994.

Glenn, S. M., and M. F. Crowley. Gulf stream and ring feature analyses for forecast model validation. *J. Am. Oceanic Tech.* 14:1366–78, 1997.

Glenn, S. M., and A. R. Robinson. Verification of an operational gulf stream forecasting model. In *Qualitative Skill Assessment for Coastal Ocean Models, Coastal and Estuarine Studies*, vol. 47, pp. 469–99, eds. D. Lynch and A. Davies. American Geophysical Union, 1995.

Grassle, J. F., S. Glenn, and C. von Alt. Ocean observing systems for marine habitats. *Ocean Community Conference '98*, 1998.

Snelgrove, V. R., J. F. Grassle, and C. A. Butman. Experimental evidence for aging food patches as a factor contributing to high deep-sea macrofaunal diversity. *Limnol. Oceanogr.* 41(4):605–14, 1996.

Snelgrove, V. R., J. P. Grassle, and C. A. Butman. Sediment choice by settling larvae of the bivalve, *Spisula solidissima* (Dillwyn), in flow and still water. *J. Exp. Mar. Biol. Ecol.* 231:171–90, 1998.

Bell, J. L., and J. P. Grassle. A DNA probe for identification of larvae of the commercial surfclam (*Spisula solidissima*). *Mol. Mar. Biol. Biotech.* 7:127–37, 1998.

Guo, X., et al. Genetic determinants of protandric sex in Crassostrea oyster. *Evolution* 52(2):394–402, 1998.

Guo, X., and S. K. Allen Jr. Sex determination and polyploid gigantism in the dwarf-surf clam, *Mulinia lateralis* Say. *Genetics* 138:1199–206, 1994.

Haidvogel, D. B., and A. Beckmann. *Numerical Ocean Circulation Modelling*. London: Imperial College Press, in press.

E. N. Curchitser, D. B. Haidvogel, and M. Iskandarani. On the transient adjustment of a midlatitude abyssal ocean basin with realistic geometry: The constant depth limit. *Dynamics Atmosphere Oceans*, in press.

Wunsch, C., D. B. Haidvogel, M. Iskandarani, and R. Hughes. Dynamics of the long-period tides. *Prog. Oceanogr.* 10:81–108, 1998.

Iskandarani, M., D. B. Haidvogel, and J. F. Boyd. A staggered spectral element model for the shallow water equations. *Int. J. Num. Methods Fluids* 20(5):393–414, 1995.

Kennish, M. J., and R. A. Lutz. Morphology and distribution of lava flows on mid-ocean ridges: A review. *Earth-Sci. Rev.* 43:63–90, 1998.

Kennish, M. J., R. A. Lutz, and A. S. Tan. Deep-sea vesicomyid clams from hydrothermal vent and cold seep environments: Analysis of shell microstructure. *Veliger* 41:195–200, 1998.

Scala, D., and L. Kerkhof. Nitrous oxide reductase (nosZ) gene-specific PCR primers for detection of denitrifiers and three nosZ genes from marine sediments. *FEMS Micro. Lett.* 162:61–8, 1998.

Kerkhof, L., and M. Speck. Ribsomal RNA gene dosage in marine bacteria. *Mol. Mar. Biol. Biotech.* 6:264–71, 1997.

Rademacher, K., and U. Kils. Predator-prey dynamics of fifteen-spined stickleback (*Spinachia spinachia*) and the mysid (*Neomysis integer*). *Arch. Fish. Mar. Res.* 43:171–201, 1995.

Thectmeyer, H., and U. Kils. To see and not be seen—the visibility of predator and prey with respect to feeding behavior. *Mar. Ecol. Prog. Ser.* 126:1–8, 1995.

Lutz, R. A., et al. Rapid rates of colonization and growth of vestimentiferan tube worms at newly formed hydrothermal vents. *Nature* 371:663–4, 1994.

Lutz, R. A., and R. M. Haymon. Rebirth of a deep-sea vent. *Natl. Geographic* 186:114–26, 1994.

McGhee, G. R. Jr. *Theoretical Morphology*. New York: Columbia University Press, 1999.

McGhee, G. R. Jr. *The Late Devonian Mass Extinction*. New York: Columbia University Press, 1996.

Miller, J. R., and G. L. Russell. Climate change and the Arctic hydrologic cycle as calculated by a global coupled atmosphere-ocean model. *Ann. Glactol.* 21:91–5, 1995.

Miller, J. R., G. L. Russell, and G. Caliri. Continental scale river flow in climate models. *J. Climate* 7:914–28, 1994.

Olsson, R. K., et al. (K. G. Miller). Ejecta layer at the Cretaceous-Tertiary boundary, Bass River, New Jersey (Ocean Drilling Program Leg 174AX). *Geology* 25:759–62, 1997.

Miller, K. G., G. S. Mountain, the Leg 150 Shipboard Party, and members of the New Jersey Coastal Plain Drilling Project. Drilling and dating New Jersey Oligocene-Miocene sequences: Ice volume, global sea level, and Exxon records. *Science* 271:1092–4, 1996.

Münchow, A., and R. J. Chant. Kinematics of inner shelf motions during the summer stratified season of New Jersey. *J. Phys. Oceanogr.*, in press.

Münchow, A., T. Weingartner, and L. Cooper. The summer hydrography and surface circulation of the East Siberian Sea. *J. Phys. Oceanogr.*, in press.

Münchow, A., and E. C. Carmack. Synoptic flow and density observations near an Arctic shelf break. *J. Phys. Oceanogr.* 27:1402–19, 1997.

Nordstrom, K. F., N. L. Jackson, J. R. Allen, and D. J. Sherman. Wave and current processes and beach changes on a microtidal lagoon beach at Fire Island, New York. In *Estuarine Shores*, eds. K. F. Nordstrom and C. T. Roman. London: John Wiley & Sons, 1996.

Nordstrom, K. F., and N. L. Jackson. Temporal and spatial scales of landscape change following storms on human-altered coasts. *J. Coastal Conserv.* 1:51–62, 1995.

Powell, E. N., W. R. Callender, and R. J. Stanton Jr. Can shallow- and deep-water chemoautotrophic and heterotrophic communities be discriminated in the fossil record? *Palaeogeogr. Palaeoclimatol. Palasoecal.* 144:85–114, 1998.

Kim, Y., et al. (E. N. Powell). Parasites of sentinel bivalves in the NOAA Status and Trends Program: Distribution and relationship to contaminant body burden. *Mar. Pollut. Bull.* 37:45–55, 1998.

Psuty, N. P., and M. E. Moreira. Holocene sedimentation and sea-level rise in the Sado Estuary, Portugal. *J. Coastal Res.*, in press.

Rutgers, The State University of New Jersey, New Brunswick

Selected Publications (continued)

Kalletat, D. H., and **N. P. Psuty**, eds. *Field Methods and Models to Quantity Rapid Coastal Changes.* Suppl. Bpl. 102. Berlin: Zeitschrift für Geomorphologie, 1996.

Bauer, J. E., **C. E. Reimers**, E. R. Druffel, and P. M. Williams. Isotopic constraints on carbon exchange between deep ocean sediments and sea water. *Nature* 373:666–9, 1995.

Cai, W.-J., and **C. E. Reimers**. Benthic oxygen flux, bottom water oxygen concentration and core top organic carbon content in the deep northeast Pacific Ocean. *Deep-Sea Res.* 42:1661–99, 1995.

Reinfelder, J. R., et al. Trace element trophic transfer in aquatic organisms: A critique of the kinetic model approach. *Sci. Total Environ.* 219:117–35, 1998.

Tortell, P. D., **J. R. Reinfelder**, and F. M. M. Morel. Active uptake of bicarbonate by diatoms. *Nature* 390:243–4, 1997.

Vinnikov, K. Y., et al. **(A. Robock)**. Satellite remote sensing of soil moisture in Illinois, U.S.A. *J. Geophys. Res.* 104:4145–68, 1999.

Stenchikov, G. L., et al. **(A. Robock)**. Radiative forcing from the 1991 Mount Pinatubo volcanic eruption. *J. Geophys. Res.* 103(13):837–57, 1998.

Lowell, R. P., **P. A. Rona**, and R. P. Von Herzen. Seafloor hydrothermal systems, *J. Geophys. Res.* 100:327–52, 1995.

Rona, P. A., and S. D. Scott. Preface: A special issue on seafloor hydrothermal mineralization: New perspectives. *Econ. Geol.* 88(8):1935–75, 1993.

Schofield, O., et al. Impact of temperature on photosynthesis in the red-tide dinoflagellate *Alexandrium fundyense* (Ca28). *J. Plankton Res.* 20(7):1241–58, 1998.

Schofield, O., T. J. Evens, D. F. Millie. Photosystem II quantum yields and xanthophyll-cycle pigments of the macroalga, *Sargassum natans* (Phacophyta): Dynamic responses under natural sunlight. *J. Phycology* 34(1):104–12, 1998.

Seitzinger, S. P., and C. Kroeze. Global distribution of nitrous oxide production and N inputs in freshwater and coastal marine ecosystems. *Global Biogeochem. Cycles* 12(1):93–113, 1998.

Seitzinger, S. P., and R. W. Sanders. Biologically reactive dissolved organic nitrogen inputs from rivers to estuaries. *Mar. Ecol. Progr. Ser.* 159:1–12, 1997.

Seitzinger, S. P., and A. E. Gibiln. Estimating denitrification in North Atlantic continental shelf sediments. *Biogeochemistry* 35:235–59, 1996.

Sherrell, R. M., M. P. Field, and Y. Gao. Temporal variability of suspended mass and composition in the Northeast Pacific water column: Relationships to sinking flux and lateral advection. *Deep-Sea Res. II* 45:733–61, 1998.

Field, M. P., and **R. M. Sherrell**. Magnetic sector ICP-MS with desolvating micro-nebulization: Interference-free sub-picogram determination of rare earth elements in natural samples. *Anal. Chem.* 70:4480–6, 1998.

Tso, S.-F., and **G. L. Taghon**. Factors affecting predation by *Cyclidium sp.* and *Euplotes sp.* on PAH-degrading and non-degrading bacteria. *Microbial Ecology* 37:3–12, 1999.

Krasnow, L. D., and **G. L. Taghon**. Rates of tube building and sediment particle size selection during tube construction by the crustacean *Leptochelia dubla. Estuaries* 20:534–46, 1997.

Taghon, G. L., F. G. Prahl, M. Sparrow, and C. M. Fuller. Lipid class and glycogen contents of the lugworm *Abarenicola pacifica* in relation to age, growth rate and reproductive condition. *Mar. Biol.* 120:287–95, 1994.

Taghon, G. L., and R. R. Greene. Utilization of deposited and suspended particulate matter by benthic "interface" feeders. *Limn. Oceanogr.* 37:1370–91, 1992.

Bartone, D. M., and **C. G. Uchrin**. Comparison of pollutant removal efficiency for two residential storm water basins. *J. Environ. Eng. ASCE*, in press.

Shaffer, K. L., and **C. G. Uchrin**. Uptake of methyl tertiary butyl ether (MTBE) by groundwater solids. *Bull. Environ. Contam. Toxicol.* 59:744, 1997.

Park, S. S., and **C. G. Uchrin**. A stoichiometric model for water quality interactions in macrophyte dominated water bodies. *Ecol. Modelling* 96:165, 1997.

Fischer, D., and **C. G. Uchrin**. Laboratory simulations of VOC entry into residence basements from soil gas. *Environ. Sci. Technol.* 30:2598, 1996.

Wainwright, S. C., et al. Utilization of nitrogen derived from seabird guano by terrestrial and marine plants at St. Paul, Pribilof Islands, Bering Sea, Alaska. *Mar. Biol.* 131:63–71, 1998.

Wainwright, S. C. Stimulation of heterotrophic microplankton production by resuspended marine sediments. *Science* 238:1710–2, 1987.

Adams, P. B., et al. **(W. W. Wakefield)**. Population estimates of Pacific Coast groundfishes from video transects and swept-area trawls. *Fish. Bull.* 93:446–55, 1995.

Smith, K. L., R. A. Kaufmann, and **W. W. Wakefield**. Mobile megafaunal activity monitored with a time-lapse camera in the abyssal North Pacific. *Deep-Sea Res.* 40:2307–24, 1993.

UNIVERSITY OF CALIFORNIA, SANTA BARBARA

The Interdepartmental Graduate Program in Marine Science

Programs of Study	The Interdepartmental Graduate Program in Marine Science offers graduate studies that lead to the Master of Science and the Doctor of Philosophy degrees in marine science. At the University of California, Santa Barbara (UCSB), the intrinsic interdisciplinary nature of modern marine science and the necessity for cross-disciplinary training is accomplished through a graduate program that brings together 33 marine faculty members from five departments on the UCSB campus. The program strives to provide students with an interdisciplinary perspective of the ocean as an integrated system through course work in physical, chemical, geological, and biological oceanography during the first year, which is followed by specialization in a marine subdiscipline in subsequent years. Research specialization in areas such as biological, chemical, and physical oceanography; marine optics and remote sensing; marine geology; marine geophysics; marine biology; paleoceanography; and ocean engineering are typically pursued by students in this program. The majority of students work toward a doctorate. The master's degree is by thesis only.
	Located directly on the California coast, UCSB is within close range of many unique marine features, including the oceanic Pacific and California Current; deep coastal basins; areas of extensive coastal upwelling; a variety of oceanic, coastal, deep-sea, estuarine, subtidal, and intertidal habitats near major faunal boundaries, submarine faults, and seeps; and an unsurpassed marine sedimentary global climate record. The marine faculty members on campus are an active and cooperative group of dynamic scientists who interact extensively with each other and students on multidisciplinary projects, grants, and research cruises. Study sites include such regions as the tropical and northern Pacific, the north Atlantic, the Sargasso Sea, and Antarctica, as well as the California region. Numerous professional marine researchers associated with the Marine Science Institute and the participating departments provide additional research opportunities and expertise for graduate study.
Research Facilities	The departments that participate in the interdepartmental program provide a full spectrum of modern facilities in marine science. These include a flow-through seawater system serving three main buildings on campus, electron and laser confocal microscopes, a fleet of coastal boats, scuba facilities, collection services for marine organisms, and extensive modern computing, GIS, and mapping facilities. A TeraScan ground station on campus automatically receives and processes global satellite imagery, including sea surface temperature and ocean color. Extensive chemical analysis is available through the Marine Science Institute Analytical Laboratory. The University maintains field stations on Santa Cruz Island and two local estuaries, which are part of the University of California Natural Reserve System.
Financial Aid	Faculty members in the program aim to fully support their students in good standing for the duration of the students' studies through a combination of University fellowships and research and teaching assistantships. Teaching assistantships are available through the participating departments, and applicants should discuss this option with their potential advisers. Prospective students are encouraged to apply for national fellowships such as NSF or ONR Graduate Fellowships. The salary for students with a research assistantship is approximately $1126 per month (at 49-percent time) plus fees and health insurance. The nine-month salary for teaching assistants is $13,329. Teaching assistants receive a fee offset. Additional summer support is available for most students.
Cost of Study	In 1999–2000, fees per quarter for students who do not receive tuition remission are approximately $1400, plus $270 for mandatory health insurance. In addition, out-of-state and international students who do not receive tuition remission pay nonresident tuition of approximately $3400 per quarter. Out-of-state students can establish California residency after one year. All fees are subject to revision without notification by the Regents of the University of California or by action of the California Legislature.
Living and Housing Costs	Unfurnished, University-operated apartments located near the campus are available for married and single students with children at a cost of approximately $470 to $660 per month in 1999–2000. In addition, a large selection of privately owned rental units are available in the vicinity of the campus. Costs range from $625 per month for a studio to $1350 per month for a two-bedroom accommodation.
Student Group	The Santa Barbara campus of the University of California had a total of 19,363 students enrolled during the 1998–99 year, including 2,304 graduate students. The Marine Graduate Program had 15 students in residence during 1998–99, the second year since its inception.
Location	UCSB is located on the Pacific seashore, 10 miles from the city of Santa Barbara, which has a population of 85,000. With the Santa Ynez Mountains on one side, the ocean on the other, and an ideal climate for year-round outdoor activities, the area around the campus provides field research and recreational resources, including the adjacent 2-million-acre Los Padres National Forest and the Channel Islands. The campus is situated on a promontory of 850 acres, with varied landscaping and two natural lagoons. A pier and county beach park are within walking distance. A wide range of cultural, entertainment, and intercollegiate athletic events that are characteristic of a major university campus are scheduled throughout the year. Santa Barbara is located about 100 miles from Los Angeles, in an area noted for its natural beauty, cultural sophistication, and mild climate.
The University	The University of California was established in 1868. The Santa Barbara campus was transformed into one of the nine major branches of the University in 1958. The UCSB campus serves the needs of more than 19,000 students and carries on research and professional training programs in forty academic fields.
Applying	Applicants are expected to have a bachelor's degree or its equivalent in a biological or physical science or in mathematics and a GPA of at least 3.0. An M.S. degree is not required to enter the Ph.D. program. Applications are considered for fall admission only and should be received with all supporting materials by December 15. All applicants are required to submit official transcripts, three letters of recommendation, and Graduate Record Examinations (GRE) General Test scores. International students whose native language is not English are required to provide satisfactory scores (minimum of 550) on the Test of English as a Foreign Language (TOEFL) or its equivalent. Applicants must be accepted by a major professor with whom they wish to work; therefore, applicants are strongly encouraged to directly contact individual faculty members whose research interests coincide with their own.
Correspondence and Information	Interdepartmental Graduate Program in Marine Science Room 1206, Building 478 University of California, Santa Barbara Santa Barbara, California 93106 Telephone: 805-893-8162 Fax: 805-893-4724 E-mail: marinegp-gradasst@lifesci.ucsb.edu World Wide Web: http://marinegp.ucsb.edu

University of California, Santa Barbara

THE FACULTY AND THEIR RESEARCH

Biological Oceanography/Marine Biology

Alice L. Alldredge, Professor, Department of Ecology, Evolution, and Marine Biology; Ph.D., California, Davis. Biological oceanography, ecology of marine gelatinous plankton, marine particulate matter and marine snow. (e-mail: alldredg@lifesci.ucsb.edu)

Mark A. Brzezinski, Associate Professor, Department of Ecology, Evolution, and Marine Biology; Ph.D., Oregon State. Phytoplankton ecology and physiology, phytoplankton cell cycles, elemental cycling in surface ocean. (e-mail: brzezins@lifesci.ucsb.edu)

David J. Chapman, Professor, Department of Ecology, Evolution, and Marine Biology; Ph.D., California, San Diego. Biochemistry and physiology of macroalgae and phytoplankton, biosynthesis and function of algal natural products, evolution of biochemical systems. (e-mail: chapman@lifesci.ucsb.edu)

James J. Childress, Professor, Department of Ecology, Evolution, and Marine Biology; Ph.D., Stanford. Ecological physiology of invertebrates and fishes, biological oceanography, physiology of deep-sea animals, metabolic adaptations of hydrothermal vent animals, chemoautotrophic endosymbioses. (e-mail: childres@lifesci.ucsb.edu)

Peter M. Collins, Professor, Department of Ecology, Evolution, and Marine Biology; Ph.D., London. Endocrinology, hormone regulation of reproduction in vertebrates. (e-mail: collins@lifesci.ucsb.edu)

Kathleen R. Foltz, Assistant Professor, Department of Molecular, Cellular, and Developmental Biology; Ph.D., Purdue. Biochemistry, cellular and molecular biology of fertilization, signal transduction during egg activation, evolution of gamete recognition molecules in free-spawning marine invertebrates. (e-mail: foltz@lifesci.ucsb.edu)

Steven D. Gaines, Associate Professor, Department of Ecology, Evolution, and Marine Biology; Ph.D., Oregon State. Population and community ecology; dispersal; marine biogeography; biostatistics. (e-mail: gaines@lifesci.ucsb.edu)

Sally J. Holbrook, Professor, Department of Ecology, Evolution, and Marine Biology; Ph.D., Berkeley. Community ecology, marine vertebrate predation and competition. (e-mail: holbrook@lifesci.ucsb.edu)

Robert S. Jacobs, Professor, Department of Ecology, Evolution, and Marine Biology; Ph.D., Loyola. Cellular and molecular mechanisms of action of marine natural products and toxins. (e-mail: r_jacobs@lifesci.ucsb.edu)

Armand M. Kuris, Professor, Department of Ecology, Evolution, and Marine Biology; Ph.D., Berkeley. Parasite population and community ecology, marine ecology, crustacean biology. (e-mail: kuris@lifesci.ucsb.edu)

John M. Melack, Professor, Department of Ecology, Evolution, and Marine Biology; Ph.D., Duke. Limnology of tropical, saline, and alpine lakes; phytoplankton and zooplankton ecology; biogeochemistry; wetland ecology; remote sensing. (e-mail: melack@lifesci.ucsb.edu)

Daniel E. Morse, Professor, Department of Molecular, Cellular, and Developmental Biology; Ph.D., Yeshiva (Einstein). Molecular marine biology and molecular genetics, mechanisms of regulation governing gene expression and development, molecular signals controlling metamorphosis. (e-mail: d_morse@lifesci.ucsb.edu)

Roger Nisbet, Professor, Department of Ecology, Evolution, and Marine Biology; Ph.D., St. Andrews (Scotland). Theoretical population ecology, marine toxicology. (e-mail: nisbet@lifesci.ucsb.edu)

Barbara B. Prezelin, Professor, Department of Ecology, Evolution, and Marine Biology; Ph.D., California, San Diego (Scripps). Primary productivity of phytoplankton in marine environments; bio-optical modeling; molecular, cellular, and environmental regulation of marine photosynthesis. (e-mail: prezelin@lifesci.ucsb.edu)

Russell J. Schmitt, Professor, Department of Ecology, Evolution, and Marine Biology; Ph.D., UCLA. Population and community ecology, applied ecology, consumer-resource interactions, marine invertebrates and reef fishes. (e-mail: schmitt@lifesci.ucsb.edu)

William C. Smith, Assistant Professor, Department of Molecular, Cellular, and Developmental Biology; Ph.D., California, Santa Cruz. Chordate embryogenesis and morphogenesis, developmental genetics of marine urochordates (Ciona savignyi), inductive interactions in amphibian development. (e-mail: w_smith@lifesci.ucsb.edu)

Robert K. Trench, Professor, Department of Ecology, Evolution, and Marine Biology; Ph.D., UCLA. Coral reef biology; biochemistry, physiology, and phylogenetics of symbiosis. (e-mail: trench@lifesci.ucsb.edu)

J. Herbert Waite, Professor, Department of Molecular, Cellular, and Developmental Biology; Ph.D., Duke. Protein chemistry, biomolecular materials in marine invertebrates (such as mussels, polychaetes, and ascidians), adhesive proteins and protein cross-linking. (e-mail: waite@lifesci.ucsb.edu)

Robert R. Warner, Professor, Department of Ecology, Evolution, and Marine Biology; Ph.D., California, San Diego (Scripps). Evolutionary ecology and population biology, ecology and behavior of coral reef fishes. (e-mail: warner@lifesci.ucsb.edu)

Ocean Physics, Optics, and Remote Sensing

Tommy Dickey, Professor, Department of Geography; Ph.D., Princeton. Atmosphere-ocean interactions and upper-ocean mixing, turbulence and internal waves. (e-mail: tommy@icess.ucsb.edu)

Catherine Gautier, Professor, Department of Geography; Ph.D., Paris. Earth radiation budget and cloud processes, large-scale hydrology and surface/atmosphere interaction, radiative transfer and remote sensing, global climate processes and earth system science. (e-mail: gautier@icess.ucsb.edu)

Leal Mertes, Assistant Professor, Department of Geography; Ph.D., Washington (Seattle). Fluvial geomorphology, remote sensing of wetlands, long-term evolution of large river systems, Amazon River. (e-mail: leal@icess.ucsb.edu)

Joel Michaelsen, Professor, Department of Geography; Ph.D., Berkeley. Climatology/meteorology, climate change, marine resources, temporal and spatial statistics. (e-mail: joel@elvis.geog.ucsb.edu)

David Siegel, Associate Professor, Department of Geography; Ph.D., USC. Physical oceanography, numerical modeling and supercomputing, bio-optical oceanography, turbulence, air-sea interaction and theoretical ecology. (e-mail: davey@icess.ucsb.edu)

Libe Washburn, Associate Professor, Department of Geography; Ph.D., California, San Diego. Physical oceanography, ocean turbulence and mixing processes, ocean bio-optics, air-sea interaction and marine pollution. (e-mail: washburn@icess.ucsb.edu)

Marine Geology/Geophysics/Paleoceanography

Jordan F. Clark, Assistant Professor, Department of Geological Sciences; Ph.D., Columbia. Hydrogeology. (e-mail: clark@magic.ucsb.edu)

Rachel M. Haymon, Associate Professor, Department of Geological Sciences; Ph.D., California, San Diego (Scripps). Marine geology and geochemistry, seafloor hydrothermal systems, seafloor volcanism. (e-mail: haymon@magic.ucsb.edu)

James P. Kennett, Professor, Department of Geological Sciences; Ph.D., Victoria (New Zealand). Paleoceanography, marine geology, micropaleontology. (e-mail: kennett@magic.ucsb.edu)

David W. Lea, Associate Professor, Department of Geological Sciences; Ph.D., MIT. Chemical oceanography and paleoceanography. (e-mail: lea@magic.ucsb.edu)

Bruce P. Luyendyk, Professor, Department of Geological Sciences; Ph.D., California, San Diego (Scripps). Tectonics, geophysics, paleomagnetism. (e-mail: luyendyk@quake.crustal.ucsb.edu)

Ken C. Macdonald, Professor, Department of Geological Sciences; Ph.D., MIT. Marine tectonics and magnetism. (e-mail: ken@magic.geol.ucsb.edu)

Ocean Engineering

Wilbert J. Lick, Professor, Department of Mechanical and Environmental Engineering; Ph.D., Rensselaer. Environmental engineering, fluid mechanics, numerical methods, oceanography, applied mathematics. (e-mail: willy@ferkel.ucsb.edu)

Stephen R. McLean, Associate Professor, Department of Mechanical and Environmental Engineering; Ph.D., Washington (Seattle). Sediment transport, bedform stability, boundary-layer fluid mechanics, coastal processes, physical oceanography. (e-mail: mclean@ocean.ucsb.edu)

UNIVERSITY OF GEORGIA

Department of Marine Sciences

Program of Study

The Department of Marine Sciences offers advanced training leading to the Ph.D. and M.S. degrees. Students develop an individualized program of study in one of three areas of marine sciences: biological oceanography, chemical oceanography, or physical oceanography. Coastal marine systems and processes is a specialization of the department, although the pursuit of study in other areas is encouraged.

The Ph.D. requires a minimum of 30 hours of graduate-level credit; of these, 9 hours consist of core courses covering biological, chemical, and physical oceanography. Additional graduate courses from marine sciences and other departments, chosen by the student in conjunction with their major professor and faculty advisory committee, complete each student's program of study. Typically, students begin research and course work during their first year of study, take written and oral qualifying exams during their third year, and defend their dissertation during their fifth year. Field experience in the form of participation in at least one major oceanographic cruise and one extended shore-based study is also required.

The M.S. program has two tracks, a traditional research track designed to prepare the student for further graduate training at the doctoral level, and an applied marine studies track designed as a terminal and/or in-service degree for students whose career goals are management and policy positions with government or industry. The M.S. requires a minimum of 30 hours of graduate-level credit; of these, 9 hours consists of core courses covering biological, chemical, and physical oceanography. Students on either track conduct an independent research project and submit and defend a thesis.

Research Facilities

The Department of Marine Sciences is housed within the School of Marine Programs on the University of Georgia campus. Faculty research laboratories are located on campus and at the Riverbend Research Facility and have state-of-the-art instrumentation for research in carbon and nitrogen cycling, molecular microbial ecology, ecosystem processes at the land-sea interface, organic biogeochemistry, biology of phytoplankton and bacteria, coastal physical processes, benthic carbon and oxygen cycling, and bioacoustics. Campus libraries and excellent research shops (such as an Instrument Shop, an Electronics Design and Maintenance Shop, and a Molecular Genetics Instrumentation Facility) and research centers (such as the Center for Advanced Ultrastructural Research, a Flow Cytometry Laboratory, the Center for Applied Isotope Study, and the Center for Remote Sensing and Mapping) provide additional support for research.

Graduate research can be conducted at any of several field facilities. The University of Georgia Marine Institute is located on a barrier island off the coast of Georgia. This pristine setting provides estuarine, salt marsh, and beach habitats for research, with laboratory and accommodations available on-site. The Marine Extension Education Service facility on Skidaway Island has additional research sites and boat facilities. The department also has a research/teaching facility at Clark Hill Reservoir, with a 60-foot boat equipped for research.

Financial Aid

Teaching assistantships and research assistantships are awarded to new and continuing students based on merit and availability of funds. Standard teaching assistantships (18 hours per week) are for nine months; summer funding is usually available. Awards cover tuition and provide a monthly stipend; nine- and twelve-month stipends for the 1999–2000 academic year range from $1237 to $1318 per month, depending on the period of award and the experience of the student. A number of University-level assistantships are also available annually and are awarded based on GRE scores and other measures of scholarship. Students may receive up to three years of support on university-level awards, after which they are eligible for standard research and teaching assistantships.

Cost of Study

Tuition is waived for graduate students supported on assistantships, regardless of residency. All students must pay a matriculation fee ($38 per semester) and an activity fee ($300 per semester); fees to cover health services and the use of athletic facilities are extra but optional.

Living and Housing Costs

Graduate students traditionally live off campus in apartments and houses. Living costs in the Athens area are very reasonable, with rents typically about $300 per month. Graduate housing is also available on campus for $1200 per semester in residence halls or $280 per month in family apartments.

Student Group

The department began accepting students in 1996 and anticipates approximately 50 full-time graduate students enrolled in the M.S. and Ph.D. programs. Current students of the marine sciences faculty come from all areas of the U.S. and from several other countries.

Student Outcomes

The department is just graduating its first students. It is expected that the students will enter professions in academia, government research and management, and industry.

Location

Athens is a small college town with a warm and eclectic personality. Located about 70 miles northeast of Atlanta amid forests and farms, Athens is the heart of a three-county region of 126,000 people. Downtown Athens is known for its music. Abundant opportunities for hiking, kayaking, bicycling, and many other outdoor activities are available all year round in the surrounding rural areas and in the nearby mountains of north Georgia.

The University and The Department

The University of Georgia was chartered in 1785 as the first land-grant college in the nation and became a Sea Grant College in 1980. Current enrollment is more than 30,000 students, with 8,000 (25 percent) pursuing graduate or professional degrees. The Department of Marine Sciences was established in 1992 and continues the long tradition of marine research and extension at the University of Georgia.

Applying

Applications should be submitted as early as possible in the academic year prior to anticipated enrollment and must be sent to the Graduate School of the University of Georgia. Decisions on financial support for the fall semester are made by the department the previous February. Complete applications include undergraduate college transcripts, three letters of recommendation, and GRE scores (plus TOEFL scores for international students). Potential students are encouraged to contact faculty members in their area of research interest.

Correspondence and Information

Graduate Coordinator
Department of Marine Sciences
University of Georgia
Athens, Georgia 30602-2206
Telephone: 706-542-5863
Fax: 706-542-5888
E-mail: gradmar@arches.uga.edu
World Wide Web:http://www.marsci.uga.edu

Office of Graduate Admissions
534 Boyd Graduate Studies Research Center
University of Georgia
Athens, Georgia 30602-7402

University of Georgia

THE FACULTY AND THEIR RESEARCH

Regular Faculty

Merryl Alber, Assistant Professor; Ph.D. Boston University, 1992. Elemental and material cycling through nearshore ecosystems; role of organic aggregates in detrital food webs and the linkage between microbial and metazoan consumers; particle dynamics in estuarine ecosystems, with an emphasis on particulate organic matter and the role of particle-attached bacteria in organic matter cycling.

Brian J. Binder, Assistant Professor; Ph.D., MIT, 1986. Physiology and ecology of marine phytoplankton, with emphasis on the picoplankton; regulation of cell growth and division among the picoplankton; applying flow cytometry and molecular biology approaches to the taxonomy and physiology of phytoplankton; field studies to assess the abundance and activity of specific phytoplankton groups in coastal and oceanic waters.

Deborah A. Bronk, Assistant Professor; Ph.D., Maryland, 1992. Fluxes of nitrogen in marine and estuarine environments, with emphasis on the role of dissolved organic nitrogen (DON) in microbial food webs; release of DON from phytoplankton and zooplankton and subsequent reincorporation of DON as a nitrogen source by phytoplankton and bacteria; phytoplankton and bacterial nitrogen metabolism, nitrogen fixation, and organic nitrogen biogeochemistry.

Wei-Jun Cai, Assistant Professor; Ph.D., California, San Diego (Scripps), 1992. Development of microsensors (pH and pCO_2) for biogeochemical studies in marine sediments, early diagenesis of organic C and $CaCO_3$; estuarine and coastal wetland biogeochemistry.

Changsheng Chen, Assistant Professor; Ph.D., MIT, 1992. Observational and numerical studies of coastal circulation, biological/physical interactions, coastal frontal dynamics, ecosystem modeling.

Daniela Di Iorio, Assistant Professor; Ph.D., Victoria (British Columbia), 1994. High-frequency acoustic propagation through random media (scintillation), ocean mixing and turbulent boundary layer processes, coastal ocean dynamics.

Robert E. Hodson, Professor and Department Head; Ph.D., California, San Diego (Scripps), 1977. Physiological ecology of marine microorganisms, microbial biogeochemistry, molecular microbial ecology, microbial decomposition of organic compounds of natural and pollutional origin in the sea, biochemical adaptations of microorganisms to low nutrient marine environments, decomposition of detrital lignocellulose in marine environments.

James T. Hollibaugh, Professor and Associate Director; Ph.D., Dalhousie, 1977. Structure and function of microbial communities, role of bacteria in biogeochemical processes, net ecosystem metabolism, polar oceanography, estuaries, human impacts in the coastal zone.

Samantha B. (Mandy) Joye, Assistant Professor; Ph.D., North Carolina at Chapel Hill, 1993. Biogeochemical cycling of nutrients, trace metals, and organic materials in coastal environments; biological production and consumption of trace gases; ecosystem and geochemical modeling; land-ocean exchange processes; microbial ecology, metabolism and physiology; molecular biology; marine nitrogen cycle.

Mary Ann Moran, Assistant Professor; Ph.D., Georgia, 1987. Microbial ecology and biogeochemistry in coastal marine environments, molecular approaches to bacterial community structure, bacterial degradation of lignin and humic substances in aquatic environments, fate of terrestrially derived organic matter in marine environments, identification and characterization of lignin-degrading bacteria.

J. Owens Smith, Assistant Professor; J.D., South Carolina, 1971. Marine and coastal margin law, environmental protection and natural resources law, administrative procedure law, constitutional constraints on regulatory limitations of private property.

Ming-Yi Sun, Assistant Professor; Ph.D., SUNY at Stony Brook, 1992. Fates of organic compounds in estuarine and coastal sediments, role of benthic fauna in preservation and degradation of organic carbon, oxygen effects on cycling of organic matter, application of molecular stable isotopes in organic geochemistry.

Randal L. Walker, Assistant Professor and Director, Marine Extension Service; Ph.D., Georgia, 1994. Marine bivalve life histories, population dynamics, fisheries management, gametogenesis, spawning, hatchery rearing, and aquaculture.

William J. Wiebe, Professor; Ph.D., Washington (Seattle), 1965. Bacterial responses to low temperature and the interaction of organic nutrients on these responses; field studies of nutrient fluxes in mangrove forests and temperate estuaries; rate of and controls on nitrogen fixation, denitrification, and sulfate reduction in marine environments.

Richard G. Wiegert, Professor; Ph.D., Michigan, 1962. Ecology of southeastern intertidal wetlands, ecology of thermal spring communities, theoretical ecology and modeling.

Patricia L. Yager, Assistant Professor; Ph.D., Washington (Seattle), 1996. Microbial biogeochemistry; role of marine microorganisms in global climate; biological feedbacks to physical or chemical changes in marine environments; Arctic ecosystems, changing role of Arctic Ocean in the global carbon cycle.

Joint-Staffed Faculty

William Fitt, Professor, Department of Ecology.
Susan T. Goldstein, Associate Professor, Department of Geology.
Steven M. Holland, Assistant Professor, Department of Geology.
Yao-wen Huang, Associate Professor, Department of Food Science and Technology.
John E. Noakes, Professor, Department of Geology.
Lawrence R. Pomeroy, Emeritus Professor, Institute of Ecology.
James W. Porter, Professor, Institute of Ecology.
Sally Walker, Associate Professor, Department of Geology.
Roy A. Welch, Research Professor, Department of Geography.
William B. Whitman, Professor, Department of Microbiology.

Adjunct Faculty

James J. Alberts, Senior Research Scientist, University of Georgia Marine Institute.
Clark R. Alexander, Assistant Professor, Skidaway Institute of Oceanography.
Jackson O. Blanton, Professor, Skidaway Institute of Oceanography.
John C. Briggs, Adjunct Professor, University of South Florida.
Alice Chalmers, Research Coordinator II, University of Georgia.
James E. Eckman, Associate Professor, Skidaway Institute of Oceanography.
Marc Frischer, Assistant Professor, Skidaway Institute of Oceanography.
Matthew R. Gilligan, Professor, Savannah State University.
Thomas F. Gross, Associate Professor, Skidaway Institute of Oceanography.
Richard A. Jahnke, Professor, Skidaway Institute of Oceanography.
Ronald T. Knieb, Associate Research Scientist, University of Georgia Marine Institute.
Joel Kostka, Assistant Professor, Skidaway Institute of Oceanography.
Richard F. Lee, Professor, Skidaway Institute of Oceanography.
Roberta L. Marinelli, Assistant Professor, Skidaway Institute of Oceanography.
Keith Maruya, Assistant Professor, Skidaway Institute of Oceanography.
James R. Nelson, Assistant Professor, Skidaway Institute of Oceanography.
Steven Y. Newell, Senior Research Scientist, University of Georgia Marine Institute.
Gustav-A. Paffenhofer, Professor, Skidaway Institute of Oceanography.
Steven C. Pennings, Assistant Research Scientist, University of Georgia Marine Institute.
Michael Perdue, Professor, Georgia Institute of Technology.
Mac C. Rawson, Director, Georgia Sea Grant.
Joseph P. Richardson, Professor, Skidaway Institute of Oceanography.
Harvey Seim, Assistant Professor, Skidaway Institute of Oceanography.
Stuart A. Stevens, Assistant Professor, Department of Natural Resources.
Maryellen Timmons, Public Service Assistant, University of Georgia Marine Extension Service.
Peter G. Verity, Professor, Skidaway Institute of Oceanography.
Stuart G. Wakeham, Professor, Skidaway Institute of Oceanography.
Herbert L. Windom, Professor, Skidaway Institute of Oceanography.

University of Georgia

SELECTED PUBLICATIONS

Alber, M., and I. Valiela. Utilization of microbial organic aggregates by bay scallops, *Argopecten irradians*. *J. Exp. Mar. Biol. Ecol.* 195:71–89, 1996.

Alber, M., and I. Valiela. Organic aggregates in detrital food webs: Incorporation by bay scallops, *Argopecten irradians*. *Mar. Ecol. Prog. Ser.* 121:117–24, 1995.

Alber, M., and I. Valiela. Production of microbial organic aggregates from macrophytederived dissolved organic material. *Limnol. Oceanogr.* 39:37–50, 1994.

Alber, M., and I. Valiela. Biochemical composition of organic aggregates produced from macrophyte-derived dissolved organic matter. *Limnol. Oceanogr.* 39:717–23, 1994.

Alber, M., and I. Valiela. Incorporation of organic aggregates by marine mussels. *Mar. Biol.* 121:259–65, 1994.

D'Avanzo, C., M. Alber, and I. Valiela. Nitrogen assimilation of amorphous detritus by two coastal consumers. *Est. Coast. Shelf Sci.* 33:203–9, 1991.

Valiela, I., M. Alber, and M. LaMontagne. Fecal coliform loadings and stocks in Buttermilk Bay, Mass., and management implications. *Environ. Manage.* 15:659–74, 1991.

Binder, B. J., and Y. C. Liu. Growth rate-regulation of ribosomal RNA content in a marine *Synechococcus* (Cyanobacterium) strain. *Appl. Environ. Microbiol.* 64:3346–51, 1998.

Mori, T., B. J. Binder, and C. H. Johnson. Circadian gating of cell division in cyanobacteria with average doubling times of less than 24 hours. *Proc. Natl. Acad. Sci.* 93:10183–8, 1996.

Binder, B. J., et al. Dynamics of pico-phytoplankton, ultra-phytoplankton, and bacteria in the central equatorial Pacific. *Deep-Sea Res. II* 43:907–31, 1996.

Zettler, E. R., et al. (B. J. Binder). Iron-enrichment bottle experiments in the Equatorial Pacific: Responses of individual phytoplankton cells. *Deep-Sea Res. II* 43:1017–29, 1996.

Frankel, D. S., S. L. Frankel, B. J. Binder, and R. F. Vogt. Application of neural networks to flow cytometry data: Analysis and real-time cell classification. *Cytometry* 23:290–302, 1996.

Binder, B. J., and S. W. Chisholm. Cell cycle regulation in marine *Synechococcus sp.* strains. *Appl. Environ. Microbiol.* 61:708–17, 1995.

Binder, B. J., and S. W. Chisholm. Relationship between DNA cycle and growth rate in *Synechococcus* sp. strain PCC 6301. *J. Bact.* 172:2313–9, 1990.

Amann, R., and B. J. Binder et al. Combining 16S rRNA-targeted oligonucleotide probes with flow cytometry for analyzing mixed microbial populations. *Appl. Environ. Microbiol.* 56:1919–25, 1990.

Bronk, D. A., and B. B. Ward. Gross and net nitrogen uptake and DON release in the euphotic zone of Monterey Bay, California. *Limnol. Oceanogr.*, in press.

Bronk, D. A., et al. Inorganic and organic nitrogen cycling in Chesapeake Bay: Autotrophic versus heterotrophic processes and relationships to carbon flux. *Aquat. Microbiol. Ecol.* 15:177–89. 1998.

Bronk, D. A., and P. M. Glibert. The fate of the missing ^{15}N differs among marine systems. *Limnol. Oceanogr.* 39:189–94, 1994.

Bronk, D. A., P. M. Glibert, B. B. Ward. Nitrogen uptake, dissolved organic nitrogen release, and new production. *Science* 265:1843–6, 1994.

Glibert, P. M., and D. A. Bronk. Release of dissolved organic nitrogen by marine diazotrophic cyanobacteria, *Trichodesmium spp*. *Appl. Environ. Microbiol.* 60:3996–4000, 1994.

Bronk, D. A., and P. M. Glibert. Application of a ^{15}N tracer method to the study of dissolved organic nitrogen uptake during spring and summer in Chesapeake Bay. *Mar. Biol.* 115:501–8, 1993.

Bronk, D. A., and P. M. Glibert. Contrasting patterns of dissolved organic nitrogen release by two size fractions of estuarine plankton during a period of rapid NH_4^+ consumption and NO_2 production. *Mar. Ecol. Prog. Ser.* 96:291–9, 1993.

Bronk, D. A., and P. M. Glibert. A ^{15}N tracer method for the measurement of dissolved organic nitrogen release by phytoplankton. *Mar. Ecol. Prog. Ser.* 77:171–82, 1991.

Cai, W.-J., L. R. Pomeroy, M. A. Moran, and Y. Wang. Oxygen and carbon dioxide mass balance for the estuarine/intertidal marsh complex of five rivers in the southeastern U.S. *Limnol. Oceanogr.*, in press.

Cai, W.-J., Y. Wang. The chemistry, fluxes and sources of carbon dioxide in the estuarine waters of the Satilla and Altamaha Rivers, Georgia. *Limnol. Oceanogr.*, in press.

Cai, W.-J., Y. Wang, and R. E. Hodson. Acid-base properties of dissolved organic matter in the estuarine waters of Georgia. *Geochim. Cosmochim. Acta,* in press.

Zhao, P., and W.-J. Cai. An improved pCO$_2$ microelectrode. *Anal. Chem.* 69:5052–8, 1997.

Cai, W.-J., and F. L. Sayles. Oxygen penetration depths and fluxes in marine sediments. *Mar. Chem.* 52:123–31, 1996.

Cai, W.-J., and C. E. Reimers. Benthic oxygen flux, bottom water oxygen concentration and core top organic carbon content in the deep northeast Pacific Ocean. *Deep-Sea Res.* 42:1681–99, 1995.

Cai, W.-J., C. E. Reimers, and T. Shaw. Microelectrode studies of organic carbon degradation and calcite dissolution at a California continental rise site. *Geochim. Cosmochim. Acta.* 59(3):497–511, 1995.

Franks, P. J. S., and C. Chen. Plankton production in tidal fronts: A model of Georges Bank in summer. *J. Mar. Res.* 54:631–51, 1998.

Chen, C., D. A. Wiesenburg, and L. Xie. Influences of river discharge on biological production in the inner shelf. A coupled biological and physical model of the Louisiana-Texas shelf. *J. Mar. Res.* 55:193–320, 1997.

Chen, C., R. O. Reid, and W. D. Nowlin. Near-inertial oscillations over the Texas-Louisiana shelf. *J. Geophys. Res.* 101:3509–24, 1996.

Chen, C., and R. Beardsley. A numerical study of stratified tidal rectification over finite-amplitude banks, part I: Symmetric banks. *J. Phys. Oceanogr.* 25:2090–110, 1995.

Chen, C., R. Beardsley, and R. Limeburner. A numerical study of stratified tidal rectification over finite-amplitude banks, part II: Georges Bank. *J. Phys. Oceanogr.* 25:2111–28, 1995.

Chen, C., R. Beardsley, and R. Limeburner. Variability of currents in late spring in the northern Great South Channel. *Cont. Shelf Res.* 15:451–73, 1995.

Chen, C., R. Beardsley, and R. Limeburner. Variability of water properties in late spring in the northern Great South Channel. *Cont. Shelf Res.* 15:415–31, 1995.

Chen, C., R. Beardsley, and R. Limeburner. Comparison of winter and summer hydrographic observations in the Yellow and East China Seas and adjacent Kuroshio during 1986. *Cont. Shelf Res.* 14:909–29, 1994.

Chen, C., R. Beardsley, and R. Limeburner. The structure of the Kuroshio southwest of Kyushu: Velocity, transport and potential vorticity fields. *Deep-Sea Res.* 39(2):245–68, 1992.

Farmer, D. M., and D. Di Iorio. Measurement of small-scale flow characteristics with acoustic scintillation. *J. Atmos. Ocean. Technol.*, in press.

Di Iorio, D., and H. Yuce. Observations of Mediterranean flow into the Black Sea. *J. Geophys. Res.* 104:3091–108, 1999.

Di Iorio, D., and D. M. Farmer. Separation of current and sound speed in the effective refractive index for a turbulent environment using reciprocal acoustic transmission. *J. Acoust. Soc. Am.* 103:321–9, 1998.

Di Iorio, D., and D. M. Farmer. Two-dimensional angle of arrival fluctuations. *J. Acoust. Soc. Am.* 100:814–24, 1996.

Di Iorio, D., and D. M. Farmer. Path averaged turbulent dissipation measurements using high frequency acoustical scintillation analysis. *J. Acoust. Soc. Am.* 96:1056–69, 1994.

Porter, K. G., et al. (R. E. Hodson). Linkages between chemical and physical responses and biological populations. *Limnol. Oceanogr.* 41(5):1041–51, 1996.

Bushaw, K. L., et al. (R. E. Hodson, D. A. Bronk, and M. A. Moran). Photochemical release of biologically available nitrogen from aquatic dissolved organic matter. *Nature* 381:404–7.

Hodson, R. E., W. A. Dustman, R. P. Garg, and M. A. Moran. Prokaryotic in situ PCR: Visualization of microscale distribution of specific genes and gene products in prokaryotic communities. *Appl. Environ. Microbiol.* 61:4074–82, 1995.

Spratt, H., E. Siekman, and R. E. Hodson. Microbial manganese oxidation in saltmarsh surface sediments using a highly sensitive leuco-crystal violet assay. *Est. Coast. Shelf Sci.* 38:91–112, 1994.

Chen, F., et al. (M. A. Moran and R. E. Hodson). In situ reverse transcription: An approach to characterize genetic diversity and activity of prokaryotes. *Appl. Environ. Microbiol.* 63:4907–13, 1997.

Hollibaugh, J. T., and P. S. Wong. Microbial processes in the San Francisco Bay estuarine turbidity maximum. *Estuaries,* in press.

Ferrari, V. C., and J. T. Hollibaugh. Distribution of microbial assemblages in the central Arctic Ocean basin studied by PCR/DGGE: Analysis of a large data set. *Hydrobiologia,* in press.

Murrell, M. C., J. T. Hollibaugh, M. W. Silver, and P. S. Wong. Bacterioplankton dynamics in northern San Francisco Bay: Role of particle association and seasonal freshwater flow. *Limnol. Oceanogr.*, in press.

Murrell, M. C., and J. T. Hollibaugh. Microzooplankton grazing in northern San Francisco Bay measured by the dilution method. *Aquat. Microb. Ecol.* 15:53–63, 1998.

Werner, I., K. F. Kline, and J. T. Hollibaugh. Stress proteins expression in *Ampelisca abdita* (Amphipoda) exposed to sediments from San Francisco Bay. *Mar. Environ. Res.* 45:417–30, 1998.

Fourqurean, J. W., T. O. Moore, B. Fry, and J. T. Hollibaugh. Spatial and temporal variation in C:N:P ratios, 15N, and morphology of eelgrass (*Zostera marina L.*) as indicators of ecosystem processes, Tomales Bay, California, U.S.A. *Mar. Ecol. Prog. Ser.* 157:147–57, 1997.

Smith, S. V., and J. T. Hollibaugh. Annual cycle and interannual variability of ecosystem metabolism in a temperate climate embayment. *Ecol. Monogr.* 67:509–33, 1997.

Murray, A. E., J. T. Hollibaugh, and C. Orrego. Comparison of the

University of Georgia

Selected Publications (continued)

phylogenetic compositions of bacterioplankton in two California estuaries by denaturing gradient gel electrophoresis of 16S rRNA gene fragments. *Appl. Environ. Microbiol.* 62:2676–80, 1996.

An, S., and **S. B. Joye.** An improved gas chromatographic method for measuring nitrogen, oxygen, argon and methane in gas or liquid samples. *Mar. Chem.,* in press.

Lee, R., **S. B. Joye,** B. Roberts, and I. Valiela. Release of N_2 and N_2O from salt marsh sediments subject to different land-derived N loads. *Biol. Bull.,* in press.

Connell, T., **S. B. Joye,** L. G. Miller, and R. S. Oremland. Bacterial oxidation of methyl bromide in Mono Lake, California. *Environ. Sci. Tech.* 31:1489–95, 1997.

Joye, S. B., S. V. Smith, **J. T. Hollibaugh,** and H. W. Paerl. Estimating denitrification in estuarine sediments: Comparisons of stoichiometric and acetylene based methods. *Biogeochem.* 33:197-215, 1996.

Joye, S. B., M. L. Mazzotta, and **J. T. Hollibaugh.** Community metabolism in intertidal microbial mats: The importance of iron and manganese reduction. *Est. Coast. Shelf Sci.* 43:746–66, 1996.

Currin, C. A., **S. B. Joye,** and H. W. Paerl. Nitrogen fixation and denitrification in a transplanted *Spartina* marsh: Implications for nitrogen budgets. *Est. Coast. Shelf Sci.* 42:597–616, 1996.

Joye, S. B., and **J. T. Hollibaugh.** Sulfide inhibition of nitrification influences nitrogen regeneration in sediments. *Science* 270:623–5, 1995.

Joye, S. B., and H. W. Paerl. Nitrogen cycling in marine microbial mats: Rates and patterns of nitrogen fixation and denitrification. *Mar. Biol.* 119:285–95, 1994.

Moran, M. A., and R. G. Zepp. Role of photoreactions in the formation of biologically labile compounds from dissolved organic matter. *Limnol. Oceanogr.* 42:1307–16, 1997.

Chen, F., et al. (**M. A. Moran** and **R. E. Hodson**). In situ reverse transcription: An approach to characterize genetic diversity and activity of prokaryotes. *Appl. Environ. Microbiol.* 63:4907–13, 1997.

Miller, W. L., and **M. A. Moran.** Interaction of photochemical and microbial processes in the degradation of refractory dissolved organic matter from a coastal marine environment. *Limnol. Oceanogr.* 42:1317–24, 1997.

González, J. M., and **M. A. Moran.** Numerical dominance of a group of marine bacteria in the α-subclass of Proteobacteria in coastal seawater. *Appl. Environ. Microbiol.* 63:4237–42, 1997.

Sobecky, P. A., **M. A. Moran,** M. Schell, and **R. E. Hodson.** Impact of a genetically engineered bacterium with enhanced alkaline phosphatase activity on marine phytoplankton communities. *Appl. Environ. Microbiol.* 62:6–12, 1996.

Moran, M. A., and **R. E. Hodson.** Dissolved humic substances of vascular plant origin in a coastal marine environment. *Limnol. Oceanogr.* 39:762–71, 1994.

Moran, M. A., and **R. E. Hodson.** Support of bacterioplankton production by dissolved humic substances from three marine environments. *Mar. Ecol. Prog. Ser.* 110:241–7, 1994.

Moran, M. A., et al. (**R. E. Hodson**). Distribution of terrestrially-derived dissolved organic matter on the southeastern U.S. continental shelf. *Limnol. Oceanogr.* 36:1134–49, 1991.

Sun, M.-Y., and S. G. Wakeham. Diagenesis of planktonic fatty acids and sterols in Long Island Sound sediments: Influences of a phytoplankton bloom inputs and bottom water oxygen content. *J. Mar. Res.* 57:357–85, 1999.

Sun, M.-Y., S. G. Wakeham, R. C. Aller, and C. Lee. Impact of seasonal hypoxia on diagenesis of phytol and its derivatives in Long Island Sound. *Mar. Chem.* 62:157–73, 1998.

Sun, M.-Y., and S. G. Wakeham. A study of oxic/anoxic effects on degradation of sterols at the simulated sediment-water interface of coastal sediments. *Org. Geochem.* 28:773–84, 1998.

Sun, M.-Y., S. G. Wakeham, and C. Lee. Rates and mechanisms of fatty acid degradation in oxic and anoxic coastal marine sediments of Long Island Sound. *Geochim. Cosmochim. Acta* 61:341–56, 1997.

Sun, M.-Y., R. C. Aller, and C. Lee. Spatial and temporal distributions of sedimentary chloropigments as indicators of benthic processes in Long Island Sound sediments. *J. Mar. Res.* 52:147–76, 1994.

Sun, M.-Y., and S. G. Wakeham. Molecular evidences for degradation and preservation of organic matter in the anoxic Black Sea basin. *Geochim. Cosmochim. Acta* 58:3395–406, 1994.

Sun, M.-Y., C. Lee, and R. C. Aller. Laboratory studies of oxic and anoxic degradation of chlorophyll-*a* in Long Island Sound sediment. *Geochim. Cosmochim. Acta* 57:147–57, 1993.

Sun, M.-Y., C. Lee, and R. C. Aller. Anoxic and oxic degradation of ^{14}C-labeled chloropigments and a ^{14}C-labeled diatom in Long Island Sound sediments. *Limnol. Oceanogr.* 38:1438–51, 1993.

O'Beirn, F. X., **R. L. Walker,** M. L. Jansen, and P. B. Heffernan. Microgeographic variation of gametogenesis and sex ratios in *Crassostrea virginica. Trans. Am. Fisheries Soc.* 128:298–308, 1998.

Sweeney, M. L., and **R. L. Walker.** The gametogenic cycle of the scorched mussel, *Brachidontes exustus* (Linnaeus, 1758), at Wassaw Island, Georgia. *Am. Malacol. Bull.* 14:149–56, 1998.

Walker, R. L. Comparative gametogenesis of *Spisula solidissima solidissima* and *Spisula solidissima similis* cultured in coastal Georgia. *J. World Aquacult. Soc.* 29:304–12, 1998.

Walker, R. L., D. H. Hurley, and R. Kupfer. Growth and survival of Atlantic surfclams, *Spisula solidissima,* larvae and juveniles fed various microalga diets. *J. Shellfish Res.* 17:211–4, 1998.

Walker, R. L., D. H. Hurley, and D. A. Moroney. Culture of juvenile Atlantic surfclams, *Spisula solidissima solidissima* and *Spisula solidissima similis,* in force-flow upwellers in a bivalve hatchery in coastal Georgia. *J. World Aquacult. Soc.* 28:28–33, 1997.

Dove, T. J., J. C. Ogden, and **W. J. Wiebe.** Coral reefs. In *Global Biodiversity Assessment,* pp. 381–6, eds. V. H. Heywood and R. T. Watson. New York: Cambridge University Press, 1995.

Nedwell, D. B., T. H. Blackburn, and **W. J. Wiebe.** Dynamic nature of the turnover of organic carbon and nitrogen in the sediments of a Jamaican mangrove forest. *Mar. Ecol. Prog. Ser.* 110:223–31, 1994.

Pomeroy, L. R., and **W. J. Wiebe.** Energy sources for microbial food webs. *Mar. Microb. Food Webs* 7:101–18, 1993.

Wiebe, W. J., W. M. Sheldon Jr., and L. R. Pomeroy. Evidence for an enhanced substrate requirement by marine mesophilic bacterial isolates at minimal growth temperatures. *Microb. Ecol.* 25:151–9, 1993.

Wiebe, W. J., W. M. Sheldon Jr. and L. R. Pomeroy. Bacterial growth and metabolism in the cold: Evidence for an enhanced substrate requirement. *Appl. Environ. Microbiol.* 58:359–64, 1992.

Wiebe, W. J., and L. R. Pomeroy. Possible effects of global warming on marine foodwebs at low temperature. In *The Unity of Evolutionary Biology: Proceedings of the 4th International Congress of Systematics and Evolutionary Biology,* pp 179– 83, ed. E.C. Dudley. Portland: Dioscorides Press, 1991.

Pomeroy, L. R., and **W. J. Wiebe,** et al. Bacterial responses to temperature and substrate concentration during the Newfoundland spring bloom. *Mar. Ecol. Prog. Ser.* 75:143–59, 1991.

Fitz, H. C., and **R. G. Wiegert.** Local population dynamics of estuarine blue crabs: Abundance, recruitment and loss. *Mar. Ecol. Prog. Ser.* 87:23–40, 1992.

Wiegert, R. G. Multicompartmental Models. In *Biological Data Analysis: A Practical Approach,* chapter 9, ed. J.C. Fry. Oxford: Oxford University Press, 1992.

Montague, C. L., and **R. G. Wiegert.** Salt Marshes. In *Ecosystems of Florida,* pp. 481–516, eds. R. L. Myers and J. J. Ewel. Orlando: University of Central Florida Press, 1990.

Wiegert, R. G. Modeling spatial and temporal variability in a salt marsh: Sensitivity to rates of primary production, tidal migration and microbial degradation. In *Estuarine Variability,* pp. 405–26, ed. D. A. Wolfe. New York: Academic Press, 1986.

Chalmers, A. G., **R. G. Wiegert,** and P. L. Wolfe. Carbon balance in a salt marsh: Interactions of diffusive export, tidal deposition and rainfall-caused erosion. *Est. Coast. Shelf Sci.* 21:757–71, 1985.

Wiegert, R. G., A. G. Chalmers, and P. F. Randerson. Productivity gradients in salt marshes: The response of *Spartina alterniflora* to experimentally manipulated soil water movement. *Oikos* 41:1–6, 1983.

King, G. M., M. J. Klug, A. G. Chalmers, and **R. G. Wiegert.** Relation of soil water movement and sulfide concentration to *Spartina alterniflora* production in a Georgia salt marsh. *Science* 218(4567): 61–3, 1982.

Daly, K. L., et al. (**P. L. Yager**). Anomalous carbon and nitrogen cycling in the Arctic: Effects of ecosystem structure and dynamics. *J. Geophys. Res.* 104:3185–99, 1999.

Smith, C. R., et al. (**P. L. Yager**). Sediment community structure around a whale skeleton in the deep North East Pacific: Macrofaunal, microbial, and bioturbation effects. *Deep-Sea Res. II* 45:335–64, 1998.

Yager, P. L., et al. The Northeast Water Polynya as an atmospheric CO_2 sink: A seasonal rectification hypothesis. *J. Geophys. Res.* 100:4389–98, 1995.

Jumars, P. A., et al. (**P. L. Yager**). Physical constraints on marine osmotrophy in an optimal foraging context. *Mar. Microb. Food Webs* 7:121–59, 1993.

Yager, P. L., A. R. M. Nowell, and P. A. Jumars. Enhanced deposition to pits: A local food source for benthos. *J. Mar. Res.* 51:1–28, 1993.

Deming, J. W., and **P. L. Yager.** Natural bacterial assemblages in deep-sea sediments: Toward a global view. In *Deep-Sea Food Chains and the Global Carbon Cycle,* pp. 11–27, eds. G. T. Rowe and V. Pariente. The Netherlands: Kluwer Academic Publishers, 1992.

UNIVERSITY OF MARYLAND

Graduate Program in Marine-Estuarine-Environmental Sciences

Program of Study

The specific objective of the all-University Graduate Program in Marine-Estuarine-Environmental Sciences (MEES) is the training of qualified graduate students, working toward the M.S. or Ph.D. degree, who have research interests in fields of study that involve interactions between biological systems and physical or chemical systems in the marine, estuarine, or terrestrial environments. The program comprises six Areas of Specialization (AOS): Oceanography, Environmental Chemistry (and toxicology), Ecology, Environmental Molecular Biology/Biotechnology, Fisheries Science, and Environmental Science (including management, policy, and economics). Students work with their Research Advisory Committee to develop a customized course of study based on research interests and previous experience.

All students must demonstrate competence in statistics. Each student is required to complete a thesis or dissertation reporting the results of an original investigation. The research problem is selected and pursued under the guidance of the student's adviser and advisory committee.

Research Facilities

Students may conduct their research either in the laboratories and facilities of the College Park (UMCP), Baltimore (UMB), Baltimore County (UMBC), or Eastern Shore (UMES) campuses or in one of the laboratories of the University of Maryland Center for Environmental Studies: Chesapeake Biological Laboratory (CBL) at Solomons, Maryland; the Horn Point Laboratory (HPL) in Cambridge, Maryland; and the Appalachian Laboratory (AL) in Frostburg, Maryland; or at the Center of Marine Biotechnology (COMB). CBL and HPL are located on the Chesapeake Bay. They include excellent facilities for the culture of estuarine organisms. The laboratories are provided with running salt water, which may be heated or cooled and may be filtered. Berthed at CBL are the University's research vessels, which range from the 65-foot *Aquarius* and the 52-foot *Orion* to a variety of smaller vessels for various specialized uses. At HPL there are extensive marshes, intertidal areas, oyster shoals, tidal creeks, and rock jetties. AL, located in the mountains of western Maryland, specializes in terrestrial and freshwater ecology.

Specialized laboratory facilities for environmental research are located on the campuses. These facilities provide space for microbiology, biotechnology, water chemistry, and cellular, molecular, and organismal biology, as well as specialized facilities for the rearing and maintenance of both terrestrial and aquatic organisms of all kinds. There are extensive facilities for remote sensing of the environment. Extensive field sites for environmental research are available through the University's agricultural programs and through cooperation with many other organizations in the state.

Financial Aid

University fellowships, research assistantships and traineeships, and teaching assistantships are available. In general, aid provides for full living and educational expenses. Some partial assistance may also be available. Research support from federal, state, and private sources often provides opportunities for additional student support through either research assistantships or part-time employment on research projects.

Cost of Study

In 1998–99, course fees for graduate students were $272 for Maryland residents and $400 for nonresidents for each credit hour. In addition, stipulated fees were $171 for up to 8 credits and $282 for 9 or more credits per semester for each student.

Living and Housing Costs

Commercial housing is plentiful in the area around the campuses. For students who are working at HPL or CBL, limited dormitory-type housing is available on site. Minimum living expenses for a year's study at College Park or in the Baltimore area are about $10,000, exclusive of tuition and fees. Costs are lower at the UMES campus.

Student Group

About 290 students are enrolled in the program. They come from a variety of academic backgrounds. There are a number of international students. About 50 percent of the students are in the doctoral program, and 50 percent are working toward the M.S. Some of the master's students expect to continue toward the doctorate. While most of the students are biologists, some come with undergraduate majors in chemistry, biochemistry, geology, economics, political science, or engineering. The program encourages and accommodates such diversity in its students.

Location

The MEES program is offered on campuses of the University at College Park, Baltimore, Baltimore County, and Eastern Shore (Princess Anne). Students normally enroll on the campus where their adviser is located. Of particular relevance for the MEES program is the University's location near Chesapeake Bay, one of the world's most important estuarine systems, which in many aspects serves as the program's principal laboratory resource.

The University

The University of Maryland is the state's land-grant and sea-grant university. It has comprehensive programs at both the undergraduate and graduate levels on the campuses at College Park, Baltimore County, and Eastern Shore. Programs in the health sciences and the professions are located in Baltimore. There are approximately 8,400 graduate students at College Park, 800 at Baltimore, 300 at Baltimore County, and 75 at Eastern Shore.

Applying

Applications for admission in the fall semester should be filed by February 1; if financial assistance is needed, it is better to apply by December 1. Some students will be admitted for the semester starting in January, for which the deadline is November 1. Applicants must submit an official application to the University of Maryland Graduate School, along with official transcripts of all previous collegiate work, three letters of recommendation, and scores on the General Test (aptitude) of the Graduate Record Examinations. It is particularly important that a student articulate clearly in the application a statement of goals and objectives pertaining to their future work in the field. Because of the interdisciplinary and interdepartmental nature of the program, only students for whom a specific adviser is identified in advance can be admitted. Prior communication with individual members of the faculty is encouraged.

Correspondence and Information

Graduate Program in Marine-Estuarine-Environmental Sciences
2113 Agriculture/Life Sciences Surge Building
University of Maryland
College Park, Maryland 20742
Telephone: 301-405-6938
Fax: 301-314-4139
E-mail: mees@mees.umd.edu
World Wide Web: http://www.mees.umd.edu

University of Maryland

THE FACULTY AND THEIR RESEARCH

Baltimore Campus. Raymond T. Jones: pathophysiology of elasmobranch and teleost fishes. Andrew S. Kane: aquatic toxicology, pathology. Robert K. Nauman: spirochetes and their relationship with marine mollusks. Renate Reimschuessel: aquatic pathology and toxicology. Henry N. Williams: ecology of the bacterial predator, *Bdellovibrio*, in the Chesapeake Bay.

Baltimore County Campus. Brian P. Bradley: zooplankton physiology and genetics. C. Allen Bush: environmental molecular biology, molecular structure determination. Thomas W. Cronin: vision in marine animals. Robert R. Provine: fish and waterfowl behavioral ecology. Philip G. Sokolove: endogenous rhythms and neuroendocrinology. Richard Tankersley: invertebrate physiology and behavior. Carl Weber: benthic ecology, systems ecology.

College Park Campus. Lowell W. Adams: wildlife biology, ecology, and management. J. Scott Angle: application of organic wastes to soil, aflatoxin ecology. Andrew H. Baldwin: wetland ecology, plant community ecology of coastal marshes and mangroves. Dale G. Bottrell: effects of pesticides on aquatic ecosystems. Amy Brown: toxicology, epidemiology, effects of pesticides on human health. Peter Brown: environmental management, policy, and ethics. James Carton: physical oceanography, ocean modeling, atmosphere/ocean interactions. Allen P. Davis: environmental chemistry as related to water/wastewater treatment. James Dietz: mammalian ecology and conservation. E. Kudjo Dzantor: use of plants for cleaning up environmental pollution, use of biological processes in combination with chemical/physical processes to address disposal of pesticides. Irwin Forseth: plant ecology and physiology. Oliver J. Hao: waste management and environmental engineering. George Helz: estuarine and marine geochemistry. Robert L. Hill: soil runoff, nonpoint source pollution in soil systems. Elmina J. Hilsenrath: suburban land use planning and site design, conservation of sensitive natural areas, reforestation and environmental restoration. David W. Inouye: terrestrial ecology, especially plant-animal interactions. Patrick Kangas: modeling and measuring of whole ecosystems with emphasis on management and ecology. Michael S. Kearney: pollen analytical investigations of tidal marsh sediments. Wayne J. Kuenzel: ecological studies of waterfowl. William O. Lamp: crop protection from arthropods through integration of crop management practices with arthropod/plant interactions, development of non-pesticide management tactics. Marla McIntosh: sludge utilization in woodlands, genetic diversity of food crops. Charles L. Mulchi: agricultural and environmental sciences, stress physiology. Judd O. Nelson: environmental toxicology of pesticides. Mary Ann Ottinger: effect of toxic substances on avian reproduction. Margaret Palmer: stream and estuarine ecology and hydrodynamics. Kennedy T. Paynter Jr.: physiology and biochemistry of estuarine organisms. Karen Prestegaard: watershed and wetland hydrology. Marjorie Reaka-Kudla: zoogeography, symbiosis, and behavior of marine crustaceans. Robert Ridky: Drainage basin analysis, siting factors for hazardous-waste management. Estelle Russek-Cohen: statistical problems in wildlife management, biomonitoring and sampling. Paul D. Schreuders: cryobiology/cryopreservation, biofilm function in nitrification processes. Kenneth P. Sebens: community ecology of subtidal benthos, coral reef ecology. Adel Shirmohammadi: impact of agricultural pest management practices on water quality. Eugene B. Small: estuarine and marine protozoology. Joseph H. Soares Jr.: waterfowl nutrition, calcification, vitamin and mineral metabolism. Ivar E. Strand Jr.: management models for commercial and recreational marine fisheries. Alba Torrents: organic pollutants, soil/water interface. Ray R. Weil: disturbed-land revegetation, land application of organic wastes. Ronald M. Weiner: environmental bacteriology. Richard Weismiller: agriculture and natural resources, remote sensing. L. Curry Woods: aquaculture, larviculture.

Eastern Shore Campus. Marianita Albano: microbial ecology, bioremediation. Eugene L. Bass: algal toxins, acclimatization of animals to environmental variables. Dixie Bounds: wildlife ecology and management, natural resources. Carolyn B. Brooks: microbial insecticides: symbiotic nitrogen fixation. Robert B. Dadson: soybean breeding, insect resistance, biological nitrogen fixation. Joseph Dodoo: coal technology, kinetic studies of coal pyrolysis. Gian C. Gupta: environmental chemistry, soil science, water and wastewater recycling. Youssef Hafez: nutrition, effects of processing on bioavailability of peptides. Thomas Handwerker: small-scale alternative crops. Jeannine M. Harter-Dennis: roasters chicken nutrition, reduction of fat. George E. Heath: food safety and drug residues, pharmokinetics. Steven G. Hughes: fish physiology, nutrition, feeding behavior, and ecology. Roman Jesien: coastal and inland fish habitat assessment, stock assessment. Jagmohan Joshi: plant breeding and genetics. Charles Loshon: spore formation and germination in bacteria. F. Joseph Margraf: population and community ecology of fishes. Joseph Okoh: carbon reaction chemistry. DeLois Powell: isolation and characterization of novel biomolecules of agricultural and biomedical significance. Steve Rebach: biological rhythms of marine invertebrates, ecology of decapod Crustacea. Douglas E. Ruby: population ecology and behavior of reptiles. Yan Waguespeck: spectroscopic studies of temperature- and gas pressure–induced chemical changes.

Appalachian Laboratory. Mark S. Castro: atmosphere-biosphere interactions. William S. Currie: biogeochemistry, nutrient cycling in plants and soils, decomposition in terrestrial systems. Keith N. Eshleman: watershed and wetlands hydrology and hydrobiogeochemistry. Robert H. Gardner: landscape ecology, ecosystem modeling. J. Edward Gates: behavioral ecology of vertebrates, habitat analysis and evaluation. Dan M. Harman: forestry and forest entomology. John L. Hoogland: vertebrate behavioral ecology, evolutionary biology of mammals. Kenneth R. McKaye: evolution, behavior, and community ecology of fishes. Raymond P. Morgan: pollution ecology, fisheries genetics. Louis Pitelka: plant ecology, including population biology and ecosystem dynamics. Steven Seagle: ecosystem and landscape simulation modeling.

Chesapeake Biological Laboratory. Robert Anderson: biochemical toxicology, effects of stress on marine invertebrate immunology. Joel Baker: behavior of organic contaminants in marine/estuarine systems. Walter R. Boynton: nutrient cycling in estuarine systems, food-web studies. Robert Costanza: ecological economics, environmental policy and management. Michael J. Fogarty: stock assessment, population dynamics, and fisheries management. Mary L. Haasch: aquatic toxicology, biochemical-molecular toxicology. H. Rodger Harvey: sources and fates of organic compounds in aquatic environments. Edward D. Houde: fishery science, population dynamics, ecology of the larval stage. Robert P. Mason: environmental chemistry, trace metals. Joseph A. Mihursky: population and community dynamics, temperature effects on estuarine organisms. Thomas J. Miller: fish ecology, population dynamics. Donald L. Rice: chemical sedimentology and early diagenesis of trace elements, marine benthic biogeochemistry. G. Roesijadi: physiology and toxicology of marine animals, metabolism of trace metals. David H. Secor: fisheries ecology, demographics, migration. Ronald L. Siefert: aqueous chemistry and photochemistry of metals in natural environments, aerosol dynamics. Kenneth Tenore: bioenergetics of detritus-based food chains, nutrition of marine invertebrates. Robert E. Ulanowicz: estuarine food-chain dynamics, hydrological-biological modeling. David A. Wright: comparative physiology of marine and estuarine animals, inorganic pollutants.

Horn Point Laboratory. Donald F. Boesch: benthic communities and sediment dynamics. William Boicourt: physical oceanography, continental shelf and estuarine circulation. Shenn-yu Chao: physical oceanography, continental shelf and slope circulation, western boundary currents. Jeffrey C. Cornwell: nutrient, metal, and sulfur cycling in estuaries and wetlands. Paul A. del Giorgio: comparative studies in aquatic microbial ecology, bacterial activity, carbon cycling and bioavailability. Thomas R. Fisher Jr.: nitrogen cycles in Atlantic coastal plain estuaries, nutrient cycling in tropical lakes. Patricia M. Glibert: phytoplankton and microplankton ecology, nitrogen cycling, photosynthesis. Lawrence W. Harding: biological oceanography, phytoplankton physiology and ecology. Reginald M. Harrell: warm-water aquaculture, particularly striped bass; larval fish nutrition and predator-prey interactions. Raleigh R. Hood: phytoplankton production and light response, modeling of primary production. Todd M. Kana: phytoplankton physiology. W. Michael Kemp: systems ecology, watershed nutrient budgets, submerged aquatic vegetation. Victor S. Kennedy: ecology and dynamics of benthic communities, particularly bivalves. Evamaria W. Koch: ecology of submerged aquatic vegetation and coastal seagrass ecosystems. Thomas Malone: phytoplankton ecology and nutrient cycling. Laura Murray: wetlands, seagrass ecology. Roger I. E. Newell: physiological and behavioral adaptations of invertebrates, especially bivalve mollusks. Jennifer Purcell: zooplankton ecology and trophic interactions. Michael R. Roman: zooplankton ecology, plankton food-chain energetics, detrital food chains. Lawrence P. Sanford: physical oceanography, geophysical boundary layers, turbulence and mixing processes. J. Court Stevenson: marsh ecology, nutrient loading in coastal watersheds. Diane Stoecker: role of heterotrophic and mixotrophic protists in food webs. William Van Heukelem: behavior of crab and oyster larvae as related to dispersal. Leonard J. Walstad: physical oceanography, ocean circulation.

Center of Marine Biotechnology. Robert M. Belas Jr.: sensory transduction and genetic regulation of gram-negative bacteria. Paul V. Dunlap: microbial diversity, physiology of microorganisms, bacterial phylogeny. Rosemary Jagus: developmental regulation of gene expression in sea urchin embryos. William Jones: marine microbes and microbial products, environmental biotechnology and marine ecosystems. Morris A. Levin: forecasting and trend analysis, environmental microbiology, virology, epidemiology. Allen Place: biochemical adaptations in marine organisms. Frank T. Robb: genetics of thermophilic marine bacteria. Kevin R. Sowers: molecular genetics and adaptation of anaerobic archaebacteria. John M. Trant: reproductive physiology, molecular endocrinology. Gerardo Vasta: cellular nonself recognition and cell-cell interactions. Yonathan Zohar: physiology and endocrinology of fish reproduction.

UNIVERSITY OF PUERTO RICO, MAYAGÜEZ

Department of Marine Sciences

Programs of Study

The Department of Marine Sciences is a graduate department offering instruction leading to Master of Science and Doctor of Philosophy degrees in marine sciences. The primary aim of the department is to train marine scientists for careers in teaching, research, and management of marine resources. Students specialize in biological, chemical, geological, or physical oceanography; fisheries biology; aquaculture; or through core courses and electives. Much of the teaching and research is carried out at the marine station, 22 miles south of Mayagüez, but students are able to elect courses in other departments and to use facilities at the computer center and the Research Development Center.

A minimum of 36 semester hours of credit in approved graduate courses is required for the M.S. degree; 72 for the Ph.D. Courses in the Department of Marine Sciences are taught in English and Spanish. Because Puerto Rico has a Spanish culture and the University is bilingual, candidates are expected to gain a functional knowledge of Spanish as well as English before finishing their degree. Further requirements for the M.S. are residence of at least one academic year, passing a departmental examination, completing a satisfactory thesis, and passing a comprehensive final examination; for the Ph.D., residence of at least two years, passing a qualifying examination, subsequently passing a comprehensive examination, completing a satisfactory thesis, and passing a final examination in defense of the thesis are required.

Research Facilities

Modern teaching and sophisticated research facilities are available both on campus and at the field station. A department library specializing in marine science publications is located at the main campus. The field station is on 18-acre Magueyes Island within a protected embayment off La Parguera, 22 miles from Mayagüez. In addition to classroom and laboratory facilities, the marine station has indoor and outdoor aquaria and tanks with running seawater and three museums containing reference collections of fish, invertebrates, and algae. Boats include the 127-foot R/V Chapman, a 51-foot Thompson trawler; the 72-foot R/V *Isla Magueyes* trawler; a 35-foot diesel Downeast; and a number of small open boats. Research facilities for warmwater aquaculture include some 8 acres of earthen ponds, two hatcheries and numerous concrete tanks, plastic pools, and aquaria facilities with running water available for controlled environmental studies.

Financial Aid

Some graduate students receive tuition waivers and stipends for their work as teaching or research assistants. Student support is also available through research grants that are awarded to faculty members and through UPRM's Financial Aid Office.

Cost of Study

Residents carrying a full program (9 to 12 credits) paid $75 per credit hour in 1998–99. General fees of approximately $75 per semester are added to these costs. Resident status may be established in one year. Nonresidents, including aliens, pay $3500 per year except for students from U.S. institutions having reciprocal tuition-reduction agreements with Puerto Rico (a list of states is available on request).

Living and Housing Costs

Apartments and houses can be found in Mayagüez, San Germán, Lajas, and La Parguera for roughly $200 to $350 per month and single rooms for less. Single students in the department frequently share apartments.

Student Group

Total enrollment at the Mayagüez campus of the University of Puerto Rico is about 12,000. The department's enrollment is about 90 graduate students.

Location

Mayagüez, the third-largest city in Puerto Rico, has a population of 150,000. It is a seaport on the west coast of the island. The economy of the city centers largely on shipping, commercial fishing, light industry, and the University. San Germán and Lajas, where many University people live, are 10 and 15 miles south of Mayagüez, respectively. The main campus of Inter-American University is located in San Germán. An increasing number of concerts, art exhibits, and other cultural activities are arranged in Mayagüez, Lajas, and San Germán, although San Juan, a 3-hour drive from Mayagüez, remains the center for music (with, for instance, the yearly Casals Festival), drama, art, and other activities sponsored by various civic entities and the Institute of Puerto Rican Culture. Many of these events are held at the Center for Fine Arts. In addition, repertory theaters are becoming very popular in the metropolitan area.

The University and The Department

The University of Puerto Rico, Mayagüez, had its beginning in 1911 as the College of Agriculture, an extension of the University in Río Piedras. In 1912 the name was changed to the College of Agriculture and Mechanic Arts. Following a general reform of the University in 1942, the college became a regular campus of the University under a vice-chancellor and, in 1966, an autonomous campus with its own chancellor.

The marine sciences program of the University of Puerto Rico is in Mayagüez. It began in 1954 with the establishment of the Institute of Marine Biology. A master's degree program in marine biology was initiated in 1963. In 1968 the institute became the Department of Marine Sciences, a graduate department, with its own academic staff. The doctoral program began in 1972. Research remains an important function of the department.

Applying

Application forms are available from the Graduate School and at http://mayaweb.upr.clu.edu/acad_aff/graduate/estgrad.htm. An undergraduate science degree is required. The applicant should have had at least basic courses in biology, chemistry, physics, geology, and mathematics through calculus. An engineering degree may be acceptable in some circumstances. Applications should be submitted before February 28 for the fall semester and before September 15 for the spring semester.

Correspondence and Information

Director, Graduate School
Box 9020
University of Puerto Rico
Mayagüez, Puerto Rico 00681-9020

Director, Department of Marine Sciences
Box 9013
University of Puerto Rico
Mayagüez, Puerto Rico 00681-9013
E-mail: director@rmocfis.uprm.edu
World Wide Web: http://rmocfis.uprm.edu

University of Puerto Rico, Mayagüez

THE FACULTY AND THEIR RESEARCH

Dallas E. Alston, Professor; Ph.D. (invertebrate aquaculture), Auburn. Culture of invertebrate organisms.

Nilda E. Aponte, Associate Professor and Acting Director of the Department; Ph.D. (marine botany), Puerto Rico, Mayagüez. Taxonomy, morphology and life history of marine algae.

Richard S. Appeldoorn, Professor; Ph.D. (fisheries biology), Rhode Island. Fisheries biology.

Roy Armstrong, Assistant Professor; Ph.D., (bio-optical oceanography), Puerto Rico, Mayagüez. Remote sensing and water optics.

David L. Ballantine, Professor; Ph.D. (marine botany), Puerto Rico, Mayagüez. Taxonomy and ecology of marine algae.

Jorge E. Capella, Associate Professor; Ph.D. (physical oceanography), Texas A&M. Multidisciplinary modeling.

Milton Carlo, Director of Underwater Activity; B.S. (geology), Puerto Rico. Geological surveys.

Jorge E. Corredor, Professor; Ph.D. (chemical oceanography), Miami (Florida). Chemical oceanography, pollution.

Ricardo Cortés Maldonado, Professor; M.S. (aquaculture), Puerto Rico, Mayagüez. Aquaculture.

Jorge R. García Sais, Associate Investigator; Ph.D. (biological oceanography), Rhode Island. Zooplankton ecology.

Juan G. González Lagoa, Professor and Associate Director of the Resource Center for Science and Engineering Office; Ph.D. (planktology), Rhode Island. Biological oceanography, planktology.

Dannie A. Hensley, Professor; Ph.D. (ichthyology), South Florida. Systematics and ecology of fishes.

Manuel L. Hernández Avila, Professor; Ph.D. (physical oceanography), LSU. Coastal physical oceanography.

Jeffrey G. Holmquist, Associate Professor; Ph.D. (marine ecology), Florida State. Marine ecology, invertebrate biology, seagrass and algae systems.

Aurelio Mercado Irizarry, Professor; M.S. (physical oceanography), Miami (Florida). Geophysical fluid dynamics.

John Kubaryk, Professor; Ph.D. (seafood technology), Auburn. Seafood technology, aquatic nutrition and water quality.

José M. López-Diaz, Associate Professor; Ph.D. (environmental chemistry), Texas. Water pollution control.

Jack Morelock, Professor; Ph.D. (geological oceanography), Texas A&M. Sediments, beach and littoral studies, reef sediments and marine terraces, geophysical surveys.

Julio Morell, Associate Investigator; M.S. (chemical oceanography), Puerto Rico. Biogeochemistry and environmental chemistry.

Govind S. Nadathur, Professor and Associate Director of the Department; Ph.D. (molecular microbiology), Baroda (India). Genetics and biotechnology of marine organisms.

Thomas R. Tosteson, Professor; Ph.D. (physiology), Pennsylvania. Marine physiology and pharmacology.

Ernesto Weil, Assistant Professor; Ph.D. (zoology), Texas at Austin. Coral systematics, ecology and evolution, coral reef ecology.

Ernest H. Williams, Professor; Ph.D. (parasitology), Auburn. Systematics and culture of parasites of fishes.

Amos Winter, Professor; Ph.D. (paleoceanography), Hebrew University (Jerusalem). Paleoceanography.

Paul Yoshioka, Professor; Ph.D. (marine ecology), California, San Diego. Marine ecology.

Baqar R. Zaidi, Investigator; Ph.D. (marine microbiology and physiology), Puerto Rico, Mayagüez. Marine physiology and bioremediation.

Field station at Magueyes Island, La Parguera, Puerto Rico.

Graduate student documenting underwater observations for thesis research.

UNIVERSITY OF SOUTH FLORIDA

Department of Marine Science

Programs of Study	The St. Petersburg Campus of the University of South Florida offers M.S. and Ph.D. degrees with specializations in biological, chemical, geological, and physical oceanography. Students are strongly encouraged to take interdisciplinary programs encompassing two or more of the four basic disciplines.
	Both M.S. and Ph.D. candidates are required to complete a core course program covering the four basic oceanographic disciplines. Requirements for the M.S. degree include 32 credit hours of course and research work and defense of a thesis that makes an original contribution to oceanography. Ph.D. candidates are required to demonstrate proficiency in two computer techniques or foreign languages and successfully complete a written and oral comprehensive examination. After completing 90 credit hours of course and research work, they must defend a dissertation that represents a publishable contribution to marine science. Students are encouraged to participate in oceanographic research cruises during the course of their enrollment.
	As part of a variety of national and international programs supported by the National Science Foundation and other federal agencies, over the past five years the department's students and faculty have conducted research in the Pacific, Atlantic, Indian, and Antarctic oceans; the Gulf of Mexico; and the Norwegian, Arabian, and Bering seas.
Research Facilities	The Department of Marine Science is located at Bayboro Harbor, Port of St. Petersburg. The harbor has immediate access to Tampa Bay and can accommodate any ship in the fleet of U.S. oceanographic vessels. Bayboro Harbor is home port to the R/V *Suncoaster* (110 feet) and the R/V *Bellows* (71 feet), the principal vessels operated by the Florida Institute of Oceanography (FIO) for the entire state university system. FIO is located within the original building (82,000 square feet) of the Department of Marine Science. The department's research facilities are adjacent to the Florida Marine Research Institute, the research arm of the Florida Department of Environmental Protection. In 1988, the St. Petersburg Campus became the site of the Center for Coastal Geology of the United States Geological Survey.
	The department's specialized laboratories include those for trace-metal analysis, physical chemistry, water quality, organic and isotope geochemistry, optical oceanography, satellite imagery and numerical modeling, sedimentology, micropaleontology, physiology, benthic ecology, microbiology, ichthyology, planktology, and geophysics. Major items of equipment include an ISI (DS-130) scanning electron microscope, a Fisons Plasma Quad II inductively coupled plasma mass spectrometer, a Hitachi H-7100 transmission electron microscope, a Finnigan MAT 252 stable isotope ratio mass spectrometer, high-resolution gas chromatographs, a combined gas chromatograph–mass spectrometer, flame and graphite furnace atomic absorption spectrometers, multichannel autoanalyzer systems, UV-visible scanning spectrophotometers, an EG&G uniboom high-resolution continuous seismic reflection profiling system, an EG&G side-scan sonar system, a Simrad EM 3000 multibeam bathymetric mapper, X-ray diffraction systems, and a Mössbauer spectroscopy system. The department has its own marine science library collection on the St. Petersburg Campus as well as access to the University's Tampa Campus facilities.
Financial Aid	Approximately fifteen state-supported assistantships are available each year for beginning students. In addition, approximately ten fellowships are available from endowments. After their first year, students are expected to pursue research on grant-supported projects. Assistantships pay in the range of $12,000 to $15,000 for twelve months. A number of out-of-state tuition waivers are available for first-year students.
Cost of Study	For 1999–2000, tuition is $140.55 per semester hour for state residents and $501.29 per semester hour for nonresident students. Out-of-state students who are American citizens may establish Florida residency after one year if certain criteria are met.
Living and Housing Costs	There are no on-campus accommodations in St. Petersburg, but students easily find apartments or houses near the campus. The rents range between $250 and $500 per month, and single students often share rental expenses. The average total living expenses for students are currently about $500 per month.
Student Group	For the 1998–99 academic year, there were more than 100 graduate students enrolled in the marine science program. More than half are working toward a Ph.D. degree. Approximately 45 students are in biological oceanography, 20 in chemical oceanography, 25 in geological oceanography, and 10 in physical oceanography. Most program graduates have obtained positions in their field or have gone on to other universities for their Ph.D.'s.
Location	The department is situated just a few blocks from downtown St. Petersburg and the Bayfront Center Arena-Theater (where major performing groups entertain), museums (including the Salvador Dali Museum), Al Lang Baseball Stadium (where major-league spring training games are held), Albert Whitted Airport (a general aviation airport servicing the USF Flying Club), numerous restaurants, department stores, shops, the St. Petersburg Yacht Club, and marinas. The Gulf Coast beaches are within a 20-minute drive of the campus. Because the marine environment is extremely important in this area—both from a commercial and a leisure-activity point of view—the department receives considerable attention and support from the community.
The University and The Department	The University of South Florida was founded in 1956. The first major state university in America to be planned and built entirely in this century, it is the second-largest public university in Florida. The Department of Marine Science, established in 1967, is a department in the College of Arts and Sciences and is the only department located entirely on the St. Petersburg Campus. The main campus in Tampa, with its wealth of supportive and cultural activities, is just 35 miles away via Interstate Highway 275. The department's newest building, opened in 1994, is the 50,000-square-foot Knight Oceanographic Research Center. Renovation of the department's original building is ongoing and has added 10,000 square feet of laboratory and office space to accommodate the department's new Center for Ocean Technology.
Applying	Applications should be submitted by June 1 for the fall semester and November 1 for the spring semester. (The deadlines for international applicants are May 1 for the fall and September 1 for the spring semesters.) The financial aid deadlines are February 15 and October 1, respectively. Minimum requirements for admission are an undergraduate major in biology, chemistry, engineering, geology, math, or physics; an upper-level GPA of 3.0; and a GRE General Test (verbal and quantitative sections) score of 1100. Applicants are also expected to have successfully completed 1 year of calculus.
Correspondence and Information	Graduate Program Coordinator Department of Marine Science University of South Florida 140 7th Avenue, South St. Petersburg, Florida 33701 Telephone: 813-553-1130

University of South Florida

THE FACULTY AND THEIR RESEARCH

Peter R. Betzer, Professor and Chairman; Ph.D., Rhode Island, 1971. Chemical oceanography, chemical tracers, pollutant transfer, particle fluxes, role of organisms in modifying chemistry of seawater.

Norman J. Blake, Professor; Ph.D., Rhode Island, 1972. Ecology and physiology of marine invertebrates, inshore environmental ecology and pollution, reproductive physiology of mollusks and crustaceans.

Robert H. Byrne, Professor; Ph.D., Rhode Island, 1974. Chemical oceanography, physical chemistry of seawater, ionic interactions, marine surface chemistry, oceanic CO_2 system chemistry.

Kendall L. Carder, Professor; Ph.D., Oregon State, 1970. Physical oceanography, ocean optics, suspended-particle dynamics, instrument development, ocean remote sensing.

Paula G. Coble, Associate Professor; Ph.D., MIT (Woods Hole Joint Program), 1990. Chemical oceanography, marine organic geochemistry, fluorescence and remote sensing of dissolved organic matter in seawater.

Larry J. Doyle, Professor; Ph.D., USC, 1973. Marine geology, sedimentology, sedimentary processes of the continental margins.

Kent A. Fanning, Professor; Ph.D., Rhode Island, 1973. Chemical oceanography, pore-water geochemistry, nutrients in the ocean, marine radiochemistry.

Benjamin P. Flower, Assistant Professor; Ph.D., California, Santa Barbara, 1993. Paleoceanography, paleoclimatology, isotope geochemistry.

Boris Galperin, Associate Professor; Ph.D., Technion (Israel), 1982. Physical oceanography, boundary layers, turbulence, renormalization group theory, numerical modeling of oceanic circulation.

Pamela Hallock-Muller, Professor; Ph.D., Hawaii, 1977. Micropaleontology, paleoceanography, carbonate sedimentology, coral reef ecology.

Albert C. Hine, Professor; Ph.D., South Carolina, 1975. Carbonate sedimentology, coastal sedimentary processes, geological oceanography, sequence stratigraphy.

Thomas L. Hopkins, Professor; Ph.D., Florida State, 1964. Biological oceanography, marine plankton and micronekton ecology, oceanic food webs.

Peter A. Howd, Assistant Professor; Ph.D., Oregon State, 1991. Beach and inner-shelf processes, beach morphodynamics, wave-driven processes on coral reefs.

Mark E. Luther, Associate Professor; Ph.D., North Carolina at Chapel Hill, 1982. Physical oceanography, numerical modeling of ocean circulation, equatorial dynamics, air-sea interaction, climate variability, estuarine circulation.

Gary T. Mitchum, Associate Professor; Ph.D., Florida State, 1984. Physical oceanography, ocean's role in climate variability, physical factors influencing biological variability.

Frank E. Müller-Karger, Associate Professor; Ph.D., Maryland, 1988. Marine, estuarine, and environmental science; biological oceanography; remote sensing; nutrient cycles.

David F. Naar, Assistant Professor; Ph.D., California, San Diego (Scripps), 1990. Marine geophysics, plate tectonics, marine tectonics, midocean ridge processes, physical modeling using molten wax.

John H. Paul, Professor; Ph.D., Miami (Florida), 1980. Marine microbiology and genetics, gene transfer mechanisms.

Terrence M. Quinn, Associate Professor; Ph.D., Brown, 1989. Paleoclimatology and carbonate geochemistry.

Joan B. Rose, Associate Professor; Ph.D., Arizona, 1985. Water pollution microbiology, risk assessment, coastal water quality, parasites and viruses.

Sarah F. Tebbens, Assistant Professor; Ph.D., Columbia, 1994. Marine geophysics, aeromagnetics, plate boundary processes, triple junction evolution, natural hazard assessment.

Joseph J. Torres, Professor; Ph.D., California, Santa Barbara, 1980. Biological oceanography, deep-sea biology, bioenergetics of pelagic animals, comparative physiology.

Edward S. Van Vleet, Professor; Ph.D., Rhode Island, 1978. Chemical oceanography, organic geochemistry, molecular biomarkers, hydrocarbon pollution.

Gabriel A. Vargo, Associate Professor; Ph.D., Rhode Island, 1976. Biological oceanography; phytoplankton ecology, physiology, and nutrient dynamics.

John J. Walsh, Distinguished Professor; Ph.D., Miami (Florida), 1969. Continental shelf ecosystems, systems analysis of marine food webs, global carbon and nitrogen cycles.

Robert W. Weisberg, Professor; Ph.D., Rhode Island, 1975. Physical oceanography, equatorial ocean dynamics, estuarine and nearshore circulation studies.

Adjunct Faculty

Thomas G. Bailey, Assistant Professor; Ph.D., California, Santa Barbara, 1984. Physiology and ecology of deep-sea fishes and invertebrates.

Theresa M. Bert, Assistant Professor; Ph.D., Yale, 1985. Evolution, systematics, population biology, physiology, genetics of fish and shellfish.

Greg R. Brooks, Assistant Professor; Ph.D., South Florida, 1986. Sediments and sedimentary processes in coastal and offshore environments.

Roy E. Crabtree, Assistant Professor; Ph.D., William and Mary, 1984. Ecology, physiology, and early life history of gamefish; ichthyology.

Richard A. Davis Jr., Distinguished Professor; Ph.D., Illinois, 1964. Dynamics and sediments of beach and barrier island systems.

John V. Gartner Jr., Assistant Professor; Ph.D., South Florida, 1990. Ecology, life history and energetics of marine fishes, deep-sea biology, ichthyology.

Robert B. Halley (U.S. Geological Survey), Professor; Ph.D., SUNY at Stony Brook, 1974. Carbonate sedimentation, chemistry and diagenesis, stratigraphy, coastal sedimentation, coral reefs, paleoclimate records and climate variability.

Gary W. Litman, Professor; Ph.D., Minnesota, 1972. Molecular genetics, evolution, immunology, developmental regulation.

R. Edmond Matheson, Assistant Professor; Ph.D., Texas A&M, 1983. Ecology and population biology of estuarine fish, ichthyology.

Anne Meylan, Assistant Professor; Ph.D., Florida, 1984. Ecology, migrations, and evolution of marine turtles; biology of demosponges.

Robert G. Muller, Assistant Professor; Ph.D., Hawaii, 1976. Fisheries biology, population dynamics, modeling of exploited populations, fisheries statistics.

Esther C. Peters, Assistant Professor; Ph.D., Rhode Island, 1985. Comparative histopathology, coral biology, invertebrate oncology.

John E. Reynolds III, Associate Professor; Ph.D., Miami (Florida), 1980. Marine mammals: population dynamics, management, and functional anatomy.

Gary E. Rodrick, Associate Professor; Ph.D., Oklahoma, 1971. Medical malacology, comparative physiology and immunology of invertebrates, biochemistry of mitochondrial enzymes and nucleic acids, parasite metabolism.

Asbury H. Sallenger Jr. (U.S. Geological Survey), Professor; Ph.D., Virginia, 1975. Nearshore sedimentary and wave processes, coastal erosion, sediment transport.

Eugene A. Shinn (U.S. Geological Survey), Professor; H.C., Kensington, 1987. Carbonate diagenesis, tidal flat deposition, reef development, coral reef ecology and geology.

Karen A. Steidinger, Ph.D., South Florida, 1979. Dinoflagellates, red tides, ultrastructure of unicells, cytology.

Rick Stumpf, Assistant Professor; Ph.D., Delaware, 1984. Estuarine sediments and remote sensing.

Yves Tardy, Distinguished Professor; Ph.D., Louis Pasteur (Strasbourg), 1969. Geochemical thermodynamics, mineral-solution equilibria, global chemical cycles, weathering and erosion.

University of South Florida

SELECTED PUBLICATIONS

Young, R. W., et al. **(K. L. Carder** and **P. R. Betzer).** Atmospheric iron inputs and primary productivity: Phytoplankton responses in the north Pacific. *Global Biogeochem. Cycles* 5:119–34, 1991.

Betzer, P. R., et al. **(K. L. Carder).** Long range transport of giant mineral aerosol particles. *Nature* 336:568–71, 1988.

Coble, P. G. Characterization of marine and terrestrial DOM in seawater rising excitation–emission matrix spectroscopy. *Mar. Chem.* 52:325–46, 1996.

Coble, P. G., S. Green, R. B. Gagosian, and N. Blough. Characterization of dissolved organic matter in the Black Sea by fluorescence spectroscopy. *Nature* 348:432–5, 1990.

Fanning, K. A. Nutrient provinces in the sea: Concentration ratios, reaction rate ratios, and ideal co–variation. *J. Geophys. Res.* 97:5693–712, 1992.

Fanning, K. A., and L. M. Torres. Rn-222 and Ra-226: Indicators of sea-ice effects on air–sea gas exchange. *Polar Res.* 10:51–8, 1991.

Flower, B. P. Overconsolidated section on the Yermak Plateau, Arctic Ocean: Ice sheet grounding prior to ca. 660 ka? *Geology* 25:147–50, 1997.

Zachos, J. C., **B. P. Flower,** and H. Paul. Orbitally paced climate oscillations across the Oligocene/Miocene boundary. *Nature* 388: 567–70, 1997.

Hallock, P. Reefs and reef limestones in Earth history. In *Life and Death of Coral Reefs,* pp. 13–42, ed. C. Birkeland. Chapman and Hall, 1997.

Hallock, P., H. K. Talge, E. M. Cockey, and R. G. Muller. A new disease in reef-dwelling foraminifera: Implications for coastal sedimentation. *J. Foraminiferal Res.* 25:280–6, 1995.

Hine, A. C. Structural, stratigraphic, paleoceanographic development of the margins of the Florida Platform. In *Geology of Florida,* pp. 169–94, eds. A. F. Randazzo and D. S. Jones. Gainesville, Fla.: University of Florida Press, 1997.

Hine, A. C., et al. Megabreccia shedding from modern, low-relief carbonate platforms; Nicaraguan Rise. *Geolog. Soc. Am. Bull.* 104:928–43, 1992.

Bryan, K., **P. A. Howd,** and A. J. Bowen. Field observations of bar-trapped edge waves. *J. Geophys. Res.* 103:1285–305, 1998.

Nelsen, C., and **P. A. Howd.** Surf as coastal resource: The wave of the future. *Geotimes* 41:19–22, 1996.

Leonard, L. A., and **M. E. Luther.** Flow hydrodynamics in tidal marsh canopies. *Limnol. Oceanography* 40:1474–84, 1995.

Luther, M. E., J. J. O'Brien, and W. L. Prell. Variability in upwelling fields in the northwestern Indian ocean: Part 1: Model experiments over the past 18,000 years. *Paleoceanography* 5:433–45, 1990.

Mitchum, G. T. A context for the Hawaiian Ocean Timeseries Measurements as estimated from TOPEX/Poseidon Latimetric heights. *Deep–Sea Res.* 43:257–80, 1996.

Mitchum, G. T. The source of 90-day oscillations at Wake Islands. *J. Geophys. Res.* 100:2459–75, 1995.

Müller-Karger, F. E., P. L. Richardson, and D. McGillicuddy. On the offshore dispersal of the Amazon's Plume in the North Atlantic. *Deep-Sea Res. I* 42(11/12):2127–37, 1995.

Müller-Karger, F. E., et al. Pigment distribution in the Caribbean Sea: Observations from space. *Prog. Oceanography* 23:23–69, 1989.

Tebbens, S. F., P. G. Coble, and T. Greely. Innovative programs for 6th–8th graders gain momentum. *Eos Trans. AGU* 79(11):137–41, 1998.

Tebbens, S. F., and S. C. Cande. Southeast Pacific tectonic evolution from early Oligocene to present. *J. Geophys. Res.* 102:12061–84, 1997.

Greely, T. M., J. V. Gartner, and **J. J. Torres.** Age and growth of Electrona antarctica, dominant mesopelagic fish of the Southern Ocean. *Mar. Biol.,* in press.

Torres, J. J., et al. **(T. L. Hopkins).** Proximate composition and overwintering strategies of Antarctic micronektonic Crustacea. *Mar. Ecol. Prog. Ser.* 113:221–32, 1994.

Pease, T. K., **E. S. Van Vleet,** J. S. Barre, and H. D. Dickens. Degradation of gyceryl ethers by hydrous and flash pyrolysis. *Org. Geochem.,* in press.

Wetzel, D. L., et al. **(E. S. Van Vleet).** Environmental distribution of oil-related hydrocarbons following a spill of No. 6 fuel oil in Tampa Bay. *Gulf Mex. Caribbean Oil Spills Coastal Ecosyst. Assess. Effects Natl. Recovery Prog. Remediation Res.,* pp. 32–54, 1997.

Weisberg, R. H., and C. Wang. Slow variability in the equatorial west-central Pacific in relation to ENSO. *J. Climate* 10:1998–2017, 1997.

Weisberg, R. H., and C. Wang. A western Pacific oscillator paradigm for the El Niño–Southern oscillation. *Geophys. Res. Lett.* 24:779–82, 1997.

THE UNIVERSITY OF TEXAS AT AUSTIN

Department of Marine Science

Programs of Study

The Department of Marine Science offers research opportunities and course work leading to the M.A. and Ph.D. degrees in marine science. Graduate students usually begin their academic program with course work on the Austin campus and move to the University of Texas Marine Science Institute at Port Aransas for specialized advanced courses and thesis or dissertation research. Core courses are required in several subdisciplines, including marine ecosystem dynamics, marine biogeochemistry, and adaptations to the marine environment. Areas of research available in Port Aransas include physiology and ecology of marine organisms, biological oceanography, geochemistry, marine environmental quality, coastal processes, and mariculture.

Research Facilities

The Marine Science Institute at Port Aransas is located near Corpus Christi and provides opportunities to study living organisms in the laboratory and under field conditions. A wide variety of environments are readily accessible, such as the pass connecting Corpus Christi Bay with the Gulf of Mexico, the continental shelf, and many bays and estuaries, including brackish estuaries and the hypersaline Laguna Madre. There are outside open and covered seawater tanks, a pier lab with running seawater, a reference collection of most of the plants and animals of the area, and controlled-environment chambers. Vessels include the R/V *Longhorn*, a 105-foot research vessel with navigation and laboratory capabilities for most research projects; the R/V *Katy*, a 54-foot boat with dredge and trawl equipment for collection of specimens; and several smaller boats. A remote terminal is linked with the computation center in Austin. Laboratories are equipped to study animal physiology, toxicology, bacterial and algal physiology, bacterial and algal ecology, fish ecology, marine phycology, mariculture, sea grass ecology and physiology, and geochemistry. Research is under way in benthic ecology, biological oceanography, fish behavior, invertebrate biology, phytoplankton ecology, and taxonomy of marine organisms. The Institute also provides teaching facilities in Port Aransas, including upper-division and graduate course offerings during the summer. Facilities are available on the Austin campus for research in marine sedimentology and in marine mineral deposits, including genesis, exploration, and recovery.

Financial Aid

Research and teaching assistantships are available through graduate advisers or the department chairman. E. J. Lund Fellowships and Scholarships for research at the Marine Science Institute are awarded annually.

Cost of Study

In 1999–2000, tuition and required fees for Texas residents and any students holding an assistantship are approximately $1400 per semester for 9 credit hours. Nonresident tuition and required fees for 9 credit hours total $3200 per semester.

Living and Housing Costs

In Port Aransas, furnished University apartments are available for students at approximately $150–$200 per month plus utilities. Non-University housing off campus costs approximately $400–$500 per month. For the Department of Marine Science's Summer Program, dormitory and dining facilities are also available to registered students.

In Austin, University dormitories and apartments, furnished and unfurnished, are available. Rooms and apartments are conveniently situated near the campus. There is also a shuttle bus service.

Student Group

The enrollment of the University of Texas at Austin is more than 47,500, including approximately 10,975 graduate students. The College of Natural Sciences has about 1,585 students. An average of 25 graduate students reside at the Marine Science Institute in Port Aransas.

Location

Austin is the state capital, with a population of approximately 500,000. Cultural events sponsored by the University are abundant, and there are many recreational facilities available. Port Aransas is a small coastal town approximately 200 miles south of Austin, where the Gulf of Mexico and surrounding bays and estuaries provide excellent boating, fishing, and swimming.

The University

The University of Texas at Austin was founded in 1883 and is part of the University of Texas System. The Department of Marine Science is in the College of Natural Sciences.

Applying

Prospective students must apply to both the Director of Admissions of the Graduate School and the Graduate Studies Committee of the Department of Marine Science in order to be considered for admission to the department. Application forms may be obtained from the Graduate School and from the department office. Only admission applications completed by January 1 can be considered for fellowship or teaching assistantship awards.

Correspondence and Information

Graduate Adviser
Marine Science Institute
The University of Texas at Austin
750 Channel View Drive
Port Aransas, Texas 78373-5015
Telephone: 512-749-6721
E-mail: gradinfo@utmsi.utexas.edu

Chairman
Department of Marine Science
The University of Texas at Austin
750 Channel View Drive
Port Aransas, Texas 78373-5015
Telephone: 512-749-6721

The University of Texas at Austin

THE FACULTY AND THEIR RESEARCH

Connie R. Arnold, Professor, Port Aransas; Ph.D., Texas A&M, 1968. Maturation and spawning, egg and larval development, growth requirements of marine organisms, designing and testing seawater systems, fish and invertebrate utilization of seagrass meadows as a nursery area.

Jay Brandes, Assistant Professor, Port Aransas; Ph.D., Washington (Seattle), 1996. Biogeochemical cycles of C, H, N, O, and S in present-day and prebiotic oceans.

Edward J. Buskey, Professor, Port Aransas; Ph.D., Rhode Island, 1983. Marine plankton ecology, sensory perception and behavior of marine organisms, bioluminescence of marine organisms, role of planktonic grazers in harmful algal bloom dynamics.

Kenneth H. Dunton, Associate Professor, Port Aransas (also Professor in the School of Biological Sciences, Austin); Ph.D., Alaska Fairbanks, 1985. Physiological ecology of marine algae and seagrasses, in situ production, nutrient and carbon cycling in marine macrophytes, trophic relations in seagrass marsh and algal communities, temperature and UV effects on photosynthesis in polar microalgae and subtropical seagrasses.

Lee A. Fuiman, Associate Professor, Port Aransas; Ph.D., Michigan, 1983. Fish ecology, especially developmental ecology of fish larvae; predation, sensory systems, development, behavior.

Wayne S. Gardner, Professor, Port Aransas; Ph.D., Wisconsin, 1971. Nitrogen dynamics in water column and sediments, nutrient-organism interactions in coastal ecosystems.

G. Joan Holt, Associate Professor, Port Aransas; Ph.D., Texas A&M, 1976. Larval fish feeding dynamics and nutrition, transport and recruitment, reef fishes, RNA-DNA ratio, condition indices, osmoregulation.

Ellery D. Ingall, Assistant Professor, Port Aransas; Ph.D., Yale, 1991. Marine chemistry, sediment diagenesis, nutrient cycles, phosphorus geochemistry.

Paul A. Montagna, Associate Professor, Port Aransas; Ph.D., South Carolina, 1983. Benthic ecology, especially invertebrate community structure, population genetics, and trophic dynamics; environmental science, modeling, and biostatistics.

Peter Thomas, Professor, Port Aransas (also Professor in the School of Biological Sciences, Austin); Ph.D., Leicester (England), 1977. Fish reproductive physiology, purification and molecular actions of hormones, endocrine disrupting chemicals, environmental endocrinology, applications of endocrinology to fish culture, environmental toxicology of marine fishes, especially reproduction.

Tracy A. Villareal, Assistant Professor, Port Aransas; Ph.D., Rhode Island, 1989. Marine phytoplankton, autecology of harmful algal species, biological oceanography.

SELECTED PUBLICATIONS

Lazo, J. P., D. A. Davis, and **C. R. Arnold.** The effects of dietary protein levels on growth, feed efficiency and survival of juvenile Florida pompano *(Trachinotus carolinus). Aquaculture* 169(3–4): 225–32, 1998.

Davis, D. A., and **C. R. Arnold.** The design, management and production of a recirculating raceway system for the production of marine shrimp. *Aquaculture Eng.* 17:193–211, 1998.

Davis, D. A., and **C. R. Arnold.** Tolerance of the rotifer *Brachionus plicatilis* to ozone and total oxidative residuals. *Ozone* 12(5):457–69, 1997.

Davis, D. A., and **C. R. Arnold.** Response of Atlantic croaker fingerlings to practical diet formulations with varying protein and energy contents. *J. World Aquaculture Soc.* 28(3):241–8, 1997.

Jirsa, D. O., D. A. Davis, and **C. R. Arnold.** Effects of dietary nutrient density on water quality and growth of red drum, *Sciaenops ocellatus,* in closed systems. *J. World Aquaculture Soc.* 28(1):68–78, 1997.

Brandes, J. A., et al. Isotopic composition of nitrate in the central Arabian Sea and eastern tropical North Pacific: a tracer for mixing and nitrogen cycles. *Limnol. Oceanogr.* 43(7):1680–9, 1999.

Brandes, J. A., et al. Abiotic nitrogen reduction in the early Earth. *Nature* 395:365–7, 1998.

Naqvi, S. W. A., et al. **(J. A. Brandes).** Budgetary and biogeochemical implications of N20 isotope signatures in the Arabian Sea. *Nature* 394:462–4, 1998.

Brandes, J. A., and A. H. Devol. Isotopic fractionation of nitrogen and oxygen in coastal marine sediments. *Geochim. Cosmochim. Acta* 61(9):1793–801, 1997.

Brandes, J. A., and A. H. Devol. Simultaneous NO3 and O2 respiration in coastal sediments: Evidence for discrete diagenesis. *J. Marine Res.* 53:771–97, 1995.

Buskey, E. J., B. Wysor, and C. Hyatt. The role of hypersalinity in the persistence of the Texas "brown tide" bloom in the Laguna Madre. *J. Plankton Res.* 20:1553–65, 1998.

Buskey, E. J. Components of mating behavior in planktonic copepods. *J. Marine Syst.* 15:13–21, 1998.

Buskey, E. J. Energetic costs of swarming behavior for the copepod *Dioithona oculata. Marine Biol.* 130:417–23, 1998.

Buskey, E. J., P. A. Montagna, A. F. Amos, and T. E. Whitledge. The initiation of the Texas brown tide algal bloom: Disruption of grazer populations as a contributing factor. *Limnol. Oceanogr.* 42:1215–22, 1997.

Buskey, E. J. Behavioral components of feeding selectivity of the heterotrophic dinoflagellate *Protoperidinium pellucidum. Marine Ecol. Prog. Ser.* 153:77–89, 1997.

Dunton, K. H., and S. V. Schonberg. The benthic faunal assemblage of the Boulder Patch kelp community. In *Wildlife and Fish in Arctic Alaska: Populations, Processes, and Habitats,* ed. J. Truett. Academic Press, in press.

Lee, K.-S., and **K. H. Dunton.** Inorganic nitrogen acquisition in the seagrass *Thalassia testudinum:* Development of a whole-plant nitrogen budget. *Limnol. Oceanogr.,* in press.

Herzka, S. Z., and **K. H. Dunton.** Light and carbon balance in the seagrass *Thalassia testudinum:* Evaluation of current production models. *Marine Biol.* 132:711–21, 1998.

Henley, W. J., and **K. H. Dunton.** Effects of nitrogen supply and seven months of continuous darkness on growth and photosynthesis of the arctic kelp, *Laminaria solidungula. Limnol. Oceanogr.* 42(2):209–16, 1997.

Dunton, K. H. Photosynthetic production and biomass of the subtropical seagrass *Halodule wrightii* along an estuarine gradient. *Estuaries* 19:436–47, 1996.

Faulk, C. K., **L. A. Fuiman,** and **P. Thomas.** Parental exposure to ortho, para-dichlorodiphenyltrichloroethane impairs survival skills of Atlantic croaker *(Micropogonias undulatus)* larvae. *Environ. Toxicol.Chem.* 18:254–62, 1999.

Fuiman, L. A., K. R. Poling, and D. M. Higgs. Quantifying developmental progress for comparative studies of larval fishes. *Copeia* 1998:602–11, 1998.

Fuiman, L. A., and B. C. Delbos. Developmental changes in visual sensitivity of red drum, *Sciaenops ocellatus. Copeia* 1998:936–43, 1998.

Fuiman, L. A. What can flatfish ontogenies tell us about pelagic and benthic lifestyles? *J. Sea Res.* 37:257, 1997.

Fuiman, L. A., and D. M. Higgs. Ontogeny, growth, and the recruitment process. In *Early Life History and Recruitment in Fish Populations,* pp. 225–49, eds. R. C. Chambers and E. A. Trippel. Chapman and Hall, 1997.

Gardner, W. S., et al. Nitrogen cycling rates and light effects in tropical Lake Maracaibo, Venezuela. *Limnol. Oceanogr.* 43(8):1814–25, 1998.

Lavrentyev, P. J., et al. **(W. S. Gardner).** Microbial plankton response to resource limitation: Insights from the community structure and seston stoichiometry in Florida Bay, USA. *Marine Ecol. Prog. Ser.* 165:45–57, 1998.

Tomaszek, J. A., **W. S. Gardner,** and T. H. Johengen. Denitrification in sediments of a Lake Erie coastal wetland (Old Woman Creek, Huron, Ohio, USA). *J. Great Lakes Res.* 23(4):403–15, 1997.

Bauer, R. T., and **G. J. Holt.** Simultaneous hermaphroditism in the marine shrimp *(Lysmata wurdemanni)*(Caridea: Hippolytidae): An undescribed sexual system in the decapod Crustacea. *Marine Biol.* 132:223–35, 1998.

Brinkmeyer, R. L., and **G. J. Holt.** Highly unsaturated fatty acids in diets of red drum *(Sciaenops ocellatus)* larvae. *Aquaculture* 161:253–68, 1998.

Rooker, J. R., **G. J. Holt,** and S. A. Holt. Vulnerability of newly settled red drum *(Sciaenops ocellatus)* to predatory fish: Is early-life survival enhanced by seagrass meadows? *Marine Biol.* 131:145–51, 1998.

Rooker, J. R., S. A. Holt, M. A. Soto, and **G. J. Holt.** Postsettlement patterns of habitat use by sciaenid fishes in subtropical seagrass meadows. *Estuaries* 21(2):318–27, 1998.

Rooker, J. R., Q. R. Dokken, C. V. Pattengill, and **G. J. Holt.** Fish assemblages on artificial and natural reefs in the Flower Garden Banks National Marine Sanctuary, U.S.A. *Coral Reefs* 16:83–92, 1997.

Clark, L. L., **E. D. Ingall,** and R. Benner. Marine phosphorus is selectively remineralized. *Nature* 393:426, 1998.

Ingall, E. D., and R. Jahnke. Influence of water column anoxia on the elemental fractionation of carbon and phosphorus during sediment diagenesis. *Marine Geol.* 139:219–29, 1997.

Van Cappellen, P., and **E. D. Ingall.** Redox stabilization of the atmosphere and oceans by phosphorus-limited marine productivity. *Science* 271:493–6, 1996.

Ingall, E. D., and R. A. Jahnke. Evidence for enhanced phosphorus regeneration from marine sediments overlain by oxygen depleted waters. *Geochim. Cosmochim. Acta* 58:2571–5, 1994.

Montagna, P. A., and J. Li. Modelling contaminant effects on deposit feeding nematodes near Gulf of Mexico production platforms. *Ecol. Modelling* 98:151–62, 1997.

Montagna, P. A., and D. E. Harper Jr. Benthic infaunal long-term response to offshore production platforms. *Can. J. Fisheries Aquatic Sci.* 53:2567–88, 1996.

Street, G. T., and **P. A. Montagna.** Loss of genetic variability in harpacticoid copepods associated with offshore platforms. *Marine Biol.* 126:271–82, 1996.

Montagna, P. A., and R. D. Kalke. Ecology of infaunal Mollusca in south Texas estuaries. *Am. Malacolog. Bull.* 11:163–75, 1995.

Montagna, P. A. Rates of Meiofaunal microbivory: A review. *Vie Milieu* 45:1–10, 1995.

Thomas, P. Nontraditional sites of endocrine disruption by chemicals on the hypothalamus-pituitary-gonadal axis: Interactions with steroid membrane receptors, monoaminergic pathways and signal transduction systems. In *Endocrine Disruptors: Effects on Male and Female Reproductive Systems,* pp. 3–38, ed. R. K. Naz. Boca Raton, Fla.: CRC Press, 1999.

Thomas, P., D. Breckenridge-Miller, and C. Detweiler. The teleost sperm membrane progestogen receptor: Interactions with xenoestrogens. *Marine Environ. Res.* 46:163–7, 1998.

The University of Texas at Austin

Selected Publications (continued)

Khan, I. A., and **P. Thomas.** Estradiol-17β and o,p'-DDT stimulate gonadotropin release in Atlantic croaker. *Marine Environ. Res.* 46:149–52, 1998.

Zhu, Y., and **P. Thomas.** Effects of light on plasma somatolactin levels in red drum *(Sciaenops ocellatus). Gen. Comp. Endocrinol.* 111:76–82, 1998.

Thomas, P., and S. Das. Correlation between binding affinities of C21 steroids for the maturation-inducing steroid membrane receptor in spotted seatrout ovaries and their agonist and antagonist activities in an oocyte maturation bioassay. *Biol. Reprod.* 57:999–1007, 1997.

Thomas, P., D. Breckenridge-Miller, and C. Detweiler. Binding characteristics and regulation of the 17,20β, 21-trihydroxy-4-pregnen-3-one (20β-S) receptor on testicular and sperm plasma membranes of spotted seatrout *(Cynoscion nebulosus). Fish Physiol. Biochem.* 17:109–16, 1997.

Villareal, T. A., et al. New estimates of vertical nitrate transport by migrating diatom mats. *Nature* (London) 397:423–5, 1999.

Morton, S. L., and **T. A. Villareal.** Bloom of *Gonyalulax polygramma* Stein (dinophyceae) in a mangrove lagoon, Douglas Cay, Belize. *Bull. Marine Sci.* 63(3):639–42, 1998.

Brzezinksi, M. A., **T. A. Villareal,** and F. Lipschultz. Silica production and the contribution of diatoms to new and primary production in the central North Pacific. *Marine Ecol. Prog. Ser.* 167:89–101, 1998.

Joseph, L., and **T. A. Villareal.** Nitrate reductase activity as a measure of nitrogen incorporation in *Rhizosolenia formosa* (H. Peragallo): Internal nitrate and diel effects. *J. Exp. Marine Biol. Ecol.* 229:159–76, 1998.

Hegarty, S. G., and **T. A. Villareal.** Effects of light levels and N:P supply ratio on the competition between *Phaeocystis* cf. *pouchetii* (Hariot) Lagerheim (Prymnesiophyceae) and five diatom species. *J. Exp. Marine Biol. Ecol.* 226:241–58, 1998.

Section 5
Meteorology and Atmospheric Sciences

This section contains a directory of institutions offering graduate work in meteorology and atmospheric sciences, followed by in-depth entries submitted by institutions that chose to prepare detailed program descriptions. Additional information about programs listed in the directory but not augmented by an in-depth entry may be obtained by writing directly to the dean of a graduate school or chair of a department at the address given in the directory.

For programs offering related work, see also in this book Astronomy and Astrophysics, Geosciences, Marine Sciences and Oceanography, and Physics. In Book 3, see Biological and Biomedical Sciences and Biophysics; and in Book 5, see Aerospace/Aeronautical Engineering, Civil and Environmental Engineering, Engineering and Applied Sciences, and Mechanical Engineering and Mechanics.

CONTENTS

Atmospheric Sciences

City College of the City University of New York, Graduate School, College of Liberal Arts and Science, Division of Science, Department of Earth and Atmospheric Sciences, New York, NY 10031-9198. Offers earth and environmental science (PhD); earth systems science (MA). PhD offered through the Graduate School and University Center of the City University of New York. *Degree requirements:* For master's, thesis, comprehensive exam required, foreign language not required. *Entrance requirements:* For master's, TOEFL (minimum score of 500 required), appropriate bachelor's degree. *Faculty research:* Water resources, high-temperature geochemistry, sedimentary basin analysis, tectonics.

Clemson University, Graduate School, College of Engineering and Science, Department of Physics and Astronomy, Clemson, SC 29634. Offers physics (MS, PhD), including astronomy and astrophysics, atmospheric physics, biophysics. Part-time programs available. *Students:* 33 full-time (8 women), 4 part-time; includes 1 minority (African American), 11 international. Terminal master's awarded for partial completion of doctoral program. *Degree requirements:* For master's, thesis or alternative required, foreign language not required; for doctorate, dissertation required, foreign language not required. *Entrance requirements:* For master's and doctorate, GRE General Test, TOEFL. *Application deadline:* For fall admission, 2/15 (priority date). Applications are processed on a rolling basis. Application fee: $35. *Unit head:* Dr. Peter J. McNulty, Chair, 864-656-3419, Fax: 864-656-0805, E-mail: mpeter@clemson.edu. *Application contact:* Dr. Miguel F. Larsen, Graduate Coordinator, 864-656-5309, Fax: 864-656-0805, E-mail: mlarson@clemson.edu.

Colorado State University, Graduate School, College of Engineering, Department of Atmospheric Science, Fort Collins, CO 80523-0015. Offers MS, PhD. *Faculty:* 15 full-time (1 woman). *Students:* 67; includes 2 minority (1 African American, 1 Hispanic American), 10 international. Average age 28. 124 applicants, 27% accepted. In 1998, 14 master's, 9 doctorates awarded. *Degree requirements:* For master's, thesis or alternative required, foreign language not required; for doctorate, dissertation required, foreign language not required. *Entrance requirements:* For master's, GRE General Test, TOEFL (minimum score of 550 required), minimum GPA of 3.0; for doctorate, GRE General Test, TOEFL, minimum GPA of 3.0. *Application deadline:* For fall admission, 2/1 (priority date). Applications are processed on a rolling basis. Application fee: $30. Electronic applications accepted. *Financial aid:* In 1998–99, 1 fellowship, 52 research assistantships were awarded.; teaching assistantships, traineeships also available. Financial aid application deadline: 4/15. *Faculty research:* Global circulation and climate, atmospheric chemistry, radiation and remote sensing, marine meteorology, mesoscale meteorology. Total annual research expenditures: $7.1 million. *Unit head:* Dr. Steven A. Rutledge, Head, 970-491-8360, Fax: 970-491-8449, E-mail: rutledge@olympic.atmos.colostate.edu. *Application contact:* Dr. Jeffrey L. Collett, Student Counselor, 970-491-8680, Fax: 970-491-8449, E-mail: collett@lamar.colostate.edu.

Columbia University, Graduate School of Arts and Sciences, Division of Natural Sciences, Program in Atmospheric and Planetary Science, New York, NY 10027. Offers M Phil, PhD. Offered jointly through the Departments of Geological Sciences, Astronomy, and Physics and in cooperation with NASA Goddard Space Flight Center's Institute for Space Studies. *Degree requirements:* For doctorate, variable foreign language requirement, dissertation required. *Entrance requirements:* For doctorate, GRE General Test, GRE Subject Test, TOEFL, previous course work in mathematics and physics. *Faculty research:* Climate, weather prediction.

See in-depth description on page 385.

Cornell University, Graduate School, Graduate Fields of Agriculture and Life Sciences, Field of Soil, Crop, and Atmospheric Sciences, Ithaca, NY 14853. Offers agronomy (MPS, MS, PhD); atmospheric sciences (MPS, MS, PhD); environmental management (MPS); field crop science (MPS, MS, PhD); soil science (MPS, MS, PhD). *Faculty:* 44 full-time. *Students:* 42 full-time (14 women); includes 1 minority (Hispanic American), 21 international. 54 applicants, 24% accepted. In 1998, 8 master's, 11 doctorates awarded. Terminal master's awarded for partial completion of doctoral program. *Degree requirements:* For master's, thesis (MS), project paper (MPS) required; for doctorate, dissertation required, foreign language not required. *Entrance requirements:* For master's and doctorate, GRE General Test, TOEFL (minimum score of 550 required). *Application deadline:* For fall admission, 2/1. Application fee: $65. Electronic applications accepted. *Financial aid:* In 1998–99, 34 students received aid, including 5 fellowships with full tuition reimbursements available, 24 research assistantships with full tuition reimbursements available, 5 teaching assistantships with full tuition reimbursements available; institutionally-sponsored loans, scholarships, tuition waivers (full and partial), and unspecified assistantships also available. Financial aid applicants required to submit FAFSA. *Faculty research:* Environmental modeling, soil chemistry, international agriculture, weather and climate, crop physiology. *Unit head:* Director of Graduate Studies, 607-255-5457, Fax: 607-255-8615. *Application contact:* Graduate Field Assistant, 607-255-5457, E-mail: scas_grad_field@cornell.edu.

Creighton University, Graduate School, College of Arts and Sciences, Program in Atmospheric Sciences, Omaha, NE 68178-0001. Offers MS. *Faculty:* 3 full-time, 10 part-time. *Students:* 2 full-time (1 woman), 1 part-time. In 1998, 2 degrees awarded. *Degree requirements:* For master's, computer language, thesis required. *Entrance requirements:* For master's, GRE General Test, TOEFL (minimum score of 550 required). *Application deadline:* For fall admission, 3/1. Applications are processed on a rolling basis. Application fee: $30. *Unit head:* Dr. Dean Morss, Chair, 402-280-2420. *Application contact:* Dr. Barbara J. Braden, Dean, Graduate School, 402-280-2870, Fax: 402-280-5762.

Drexel University, Graduate School, College of Arts and Sciences, Department of Physics and Atmospheric Science, Philadelphia, PA 19104-2875. Offers MS, PhD. *Faculty:* 21 full-time (1 woman), 1 part-time (0 women). *Students:* 26 full-time (7 women), 9 part-time (2 women); includes 2 minority (1 Asian American or Pacific Islander, 1 Hispanic American), 23 international. Average age 31. 94 applicants, 19% accepted. In 1998, 9 master's, 3 doctorates awarded. Terminal master's awarded for partial completion of doctoral program. *Degree requirements:* For master's, foreign language and thesis not required; for doctorate, dissertation required, foreign language not required. *Entrance requirements:* For master's and doctorate, GRE, TOEFL (minimum score of 570 required). *Application deadline:* For fall admission, 8/21. Applications are processed on a rolling basis. Application fee: $35. *Financial aid:* In 1998–99, 8 research assistantships, 23 teaching assistantships were awarded.; unspecified assistantships also available. Financial aid application deadline:2/1. *Faculty research:* Nuclear structure, mesoscale meteorology, numerical astrophysics, numerical weather prediction, earth energy radiation budget. *Unit head:* Dr. Michael Vallieres, Head, 215-895-2709. *Application contact:* Director of Graduate Admissions, 215-895-6700, Fax: 215-895-5939.

Georgia Institute of Technology, Graduate Studies and Research, College of Sciences, School of Earth and Atmospheric Sciences, Atlanta, GA 30332-0001. Offers atmospheric chemistry (MS, PhD); atmospheric dynamics and physics (MS, PhD); geochemistry (MS, PhD); solid-earth geophysics (MS, PhD). Part-time programs available. Terminal master's awarded for partial completion of doctoral program. *Degree requirements:* For master's, thesis or alternative required, foreign language not required; for doctorate, dissertation, comprehensive exams required, foreign language not required. *Entrance requirements:* For master's and doctorate, GRE General Test, TOEFL (minimum score of 550 required), minimum GPA of 2.7. Electronic applications accepted. *Faculty research:* Geophysics, geochemistry, atmospheric chemistry, atmospheric dynamics, seismology.

Howard University, Graduate School of Arts and Sciences, Program in Atmospheric Sciences, Washington, DC 20059-0002. Offers MS, PhD. Part-time programs available. *Faculty:* 3 full-time (1 woman), 4 part-time (0 women). *Students:* 4 full-time (2 women), 1 part-time; all minorities (all African Americans) Average age 25. 6 applicants, 100% accepted. Terminal master's awarded for partial completion of doctoral program. *Degree requirements:* For master's, thesis required, foreign language not required; for doctorate, dissertation, comprehensive exams required. *Entrance requirements:* For master's and doctorate, GRE General Test, TOEFL, minimum GPA of 3.0. *Application deadline:* For fall admission, 4/1; for spring admission, 11/1. Applications are processed on a rolling basis. Application fee: $45. *Financial aid:* In 1998–99, 5 fellowships with full tuition reimbursements (averaging $15,000 per year), research assistantships with full tuition reimbursements (averaging $16,000 per year) were awarded.; career-related internships or fieldwork, grants, scholarships, tuition waivers (partial), and unspecified assistantships also available. Financial aid application deadline: 4/1. *Faculty research:* Atmospheric chemistry, climate, ionospheric physics, gravity waves, aerosols, extraterrestrial atmospheres, turbulence. Total annual research expenditures: $550,000. *Unit head:* Dr. Arthur N. Thorpe, Director, 202-806-5172, Fax: 202-806-4430, E-mail: thorpe@cstea.cstea.howard.edu. *Application contact:* Dr. Vernon R. Morris, Associate Professor, 202-806-5450, Fax: 202-806-4430, E-mail: vmorris@physics1.howard.edu.

Massachusetts Institute of Technology, School of Science, Department of Earth, Atmospheric, and Planetary Sciences, Cambridge, MA 02139-4307. Offers atmospheres, oceans, and climate (SM, PhD, Sc D); atmospheric chemistry (SM, PhD, Sc D); geology and geochemistry (SM, PhD, Sc D); geophysics (SM, PhD, Sc D); planetary science (SM, PhD, Sc D). *Faculty:* 39 full-time (4 women). *Students:* 164 full-time (68 women); includes 7 minority (3 Asian Americans or Pacific Islanders, 4 Hispanic Americans), 59 international. Average age 29. 212 applicants, 34% accepted. In 1998, 12 master's, 27 doctorates awarded. Terminal master's awarded for partial completion of doctoral program. *Degree requirements:* For master's, thesis required, foreign language not required; for doctorate, dissertation, general exam required, foreign language not required. *Entrance requirements:* For master's and doctorate, GRE General Test. *Application deadline:* For fall admission, 1/15; for spring admission, 11/1. Application fee: $55. *Financial aid:* In 1998–99, 43 fellowships, 90 research assistantships, 15 teaching assistantships were awarded.; institutionally-sponsored loans also available. Financial aid application deadline: 1/15. *Faculty research:* Evolution of main features of the planetary system; origin, composition, structure, and state of the atmospheres, oceans, surfaces, and interiors of planets; dynamics of planets and satellite motions. *Unit head:* Dr. Ronald G. Prinn, Chairman, 617-253-3382. *Application contact:* Anastasia Frangos, Administrative Assistant, 617-253-3381, Fax: 617-253-8298, E-mail: eapsinfo@mit.edu.

McGill University, Faculty of Graduate Studies and Research, Faculty of Science, Department of Atmospheric and Oceanic Sciences, Montréal, PQ H3A 2T5, Canada. Offers atmospheric science (M Sc, PhD); physical oceanography (M Sc, PhD). *Faculty:* 13 full-time (1 woman), 5 part-time (0 women). *Students:* 41 full-time (4 women), 2 part-time. Average age 24. 53 applicants, 23% accepted. In 1998, 6 master's awarded (50% found work related to degree, 50% continued full-time study); 4 doctorates awarded (75% entered university research/teaching, 25% found other work related to degree). Terminal master's awarded for partial completion of doctoral program. *Degree requirements:* For master's and doctorate, thesis/dissertation required, foreign language not required. *Entrance requirements:* For master's, GRE General Test, TOEFL (minimum score of 550 required), minimum GPA of 3.0, or 3.2 during last 2 years of full-time study; for doctorate, GRE, TOEFL (minimum score of 550 required), master's degree in meteorology or related field. *Average time to degree:* Master's–2 years full-time; doctorate–4 years full-time. *Application deadline:* For fall admission, 7/1 (priority date); for winter admission, 12/1 (priority date). Applications are processed on a rolling basis. Application fee: $60. *Financial aid:* In 1998–99, 43 research assistantships (averaging $16,000 per year), 15 teaching assistantships (averaging $1,000 per year) were awarded.; fellowships, tuition waivers (partial) also available. Financial aid application deadline: 7/1. *Faculty research:* Dynamic meteorology and climate dynamics, synoptic meteorology, mesometeorology, radar meteorology, physical oceanography. Total annual research expenditures: $2.7 million. *Unit head:* Prof. C. A. Lin, Chair, 514-398-3760, Fax: 514-398-6115, E-mail: lin@zephyr.meteo.mcgill.ca. *Application contact:* Prof. H. G. Leighton, Chair, Graduate Admissions, 514-398-3766, Fax: 514-398-6115, E-mail: gradinfo@zephyr.meteo.mcgill.ca.

New Mexico Institute of Mining and Technology, Graduate Studies, Department of Physics, Socorro, NM 87801. Offers astrophysics (MS, PhD); atmospheric physics (MS, PhD); instrumentation (MS); mathematical physics (PhD). *Faculty:* 11 full-time (1 woman), 5 part-time (0 women). *Students:* 26 full-time (6 women), 8 international. *Degree requirements:* For master's and doctorate, thesis/dissertation required, foreign language not required. *Entrance requirements:* For master's, GRE General Test, TOEFL (minimum score of 540 required); for doctorate, GRE General Test, GRE Subject Test, TOEFL (minimum score of 540 required). *Application deadline:* For fall admission, 3/1 (priority date); for spring admission, 6/1. Applications are processed on a rolling basis. Application fee: $16. *Unit head:* Dr. Alan Blyth, Chairman, 505-835-5744, Fax: 505-835-5707, E-mail: blyth@kestrel.nmt.edu. *Application contact:* Dr. David B. Johnson, Dean of Graduate Studies, 505-835-5513, Fax: 505-835-5476, E-mail: graduate@nmt.edu.

North Carolina State University, Graduate School, College of Physical and Mathematical Sciences, Department of Marine, Earth, and Atmospheric Sciences, Raleigh, NC 27695. Offers geology (MS, PhD); geophysics (MS, PhD); marine, earth, and atmospheric sciences (MS, PhD); meteorology (MS, PhD); oceanography (MS, PhD). *Faculty:* 34 full-time (2 women), 39 part-time (1 woman). *Students:* 118 full-time (30 women), 12 part-time (3 women); includes 2 minority (both Asian Americans or Pacific Islanders), 37 international. Average age 30. 95 applicants, 52% accepted. In 1998, 17 master's, 12 doctorates awarded. Terminal master's awarded for partial completion of doctoral program. *Degree requirements:* For master's, thesis, final oral exam required, foreign language not required; for doctorate, dissertation, final oral exam, preliminary oral and written exams required, foreign language not required. *Entrance requirements:* For master's and doctorate, GRE General Test, minimum GPA of 3.0. *Application deadline:* For fall admission, 6/25 (priority date); for spring admission, 11/25. Applications are processed on a rolling basis. Application fee: $45. *Financial aid:* In 1998–99, 1 fellowship (averaging $4,504 per year), 84 research assistantships (averaging $3,877 per year), 30 teaching assistantships (averaging $3,678 per year) were awarded.; institutionally-sponsored loans also available. Financial aid application deadline: 3/1. *Faculty research:* Boundary layer and air quality meteorology; climate and mesoscale dynamics; biological, chemical, geological, and physical oceanography; hard rock, soft rock, environmental, and paleogeology. Total annual research expenditures: $8.8 million. *Unit head:* Dr. Leonard J. Pietrafesa, Head, 919-515-3717, Fax: 919-515-7802, E-mail: leonard_pietrafesa@ncsu.edu. *Application contact:* Dr. Gerald S. Janowitz, Director of Graduate Programs, 919-515-7837, Fax: 919-515-7802, E-mail: janowitz@ncsu.edu.

The Ohio State University, Graduate School, College of Social and Behavioral Sciences, Program in Atmospheric Sciences, Columbus, OH 43210. Offers MS, PhD. *Faculty:* 10 full-time, 2 part-time. *Students:* 15 full-time (6 women); includes 1 minority (Hispanic American), 5 international. 31 applicants, 39% accepted. In 1998, 1 master's, 1 doctorate awarded. *Degree requirements:* For master's and doctorate, computer language, thesis/dissertation required, foreign language not required. *Entrance requirements:* For master's and doctorate, GRE General Test, minimum GPA of 3.0. *Application deadline:* For fall admission, 8/15. Applications are processed on a rolling basis. Application fee: $30 ($40 for international students). *Financial aid:* Fellowships, research assistantships, teaching assistantships, Federal Work-Study and institutionally-sponsored loans available. Aid available to part-time students. *Faculty research:* Climatology, aeronomy, solar-terrestrial physics, air environment. *Unit head:* Jay S. Hobgood, Director, 614-292-2514, Fax: 614-292-6213, E-mail: hobgood.1@osu.edu.

Oregon State University, Graduate School, College of Oceanic and Atmospheric Sciences, Program in Atmospheric Sciences, Corvallis, OR 97331. Offers MA, MS, PhD. *Faculty:* 5 full-time (0 women), 2 part-time (0 women). *Students:* 7 full-time (2 women), 2 international. Average age 36. In 1998, 1 master's, 1 doctorate awarded. Terminal master's awarded for partial completion of doctoral program. *Degree requirements:* For master's, variable foreign language requirement, thesis, qualifying exams required; for doctorate, dissertation, qualifying exams required, foreign language not required. *Entrance requirements:* For master's and doctorate, GRE General Test, TOEFL (minimum score of 600 required), minimum GPA of 3.0 in last 90 hours. *Application deadline:* For fall admission, 2/1 (priority date). Applications are processed on a rolling basis. Application fee: $50. *Financial aid:* Fellowships, research assistantships, teaching assistantships, career-related internships or fieldwork, Federal Work-Study, and institutionally-sponsored loans available. Aid available to part-time students. Financial aid application deadline: 2/1. *Faculty research:* Planetary atmospheres, boundary layer dynamics, climate, statistical meteorology, satellite meteorology, atmospheric chemistry. *Unit head:* Dr. Mike Unsworth, Director, 541-737-4557, Fax: 541-737-2540, E-mail: unsworts@oce.orst.edu. *Application contact:* Irma Delson, Assistant Director, Student Services, 541-737-5190, Fax: 541-737-2064, E-mail: student_adviser@oce.orst.edu.

Princeton University, Graduate School, Department of Geosciences, Program in Atmospheric and Oceanic Sciences, Princeton, NJ 08544-1019. Offers PhD. *Degree requirements:* For doctorate, dissertation required. *Entrance requirements:* For doctorate, GRE General Test, GRE Subject Test. *Faculty research:* Climate dynamics, middle atmosphere dynamics and chemistry, oceanic circulation, marine geochemistry, numerical modelling.

Purdue University, Graduate School, School of Science, Department of Earth and Atmospheric Sciences, West Lafayette, IN 47907. Offers MS, PhD. *Faculty:* 23 full-time (1 woman), 4 part-time (0 women). *Students:* 44 full-time (16 women), 11 part-time (5 women); includes 1 minority (African American), 26 international. Average age 25. 97 applicants, 42% accepted. In 1998, 5 master's, 8 doctorates awarded. *Degree requirements:* For master's, thesis required, foreign language not required; for doctorate, dissertation required. *Entrance requirements:* For master's and doctorate, GRE General Test, TOEFL (minimum score of 550 required). *Application deadline:* For fall admission, 2/1 (priority date); for spring admission, 6/1 (priority date). Applications are processed on a rolling basis. Application fee: $30. Electronic applications accepted. *Financial aid:* In 1998–99, 4 fellowships with partial tuition reimbursements (averaging $14,400 per year), 18 research assistantships with partial tuition reimbursements (averaging $13,500 per year), 17 teaching assistantships with partial tuition reimbursements (averaging $13,500 per year) were awarded. Aid available to part-time students. Financial aid application deadline: 3/1; financial aid applicants required to submit FAFSA. *Faculty research:* Geology, geophysics, hydrogeology, paleoclimatology, environmental science. Total annual research expenditures: $2.7 million. *Application contact:* Kathy Kincade, Graduate Secretary, 765-494-5984, Fax: 765-496-1210, E-mail: kkincade@purdue.edu.

Saint Louis University, Graduate School, College of Arts and Sciences, Department of Earth and Atmospheric Sciences, Program in Atmospheric Science, St. Louis, MO 63103-2097. Offers M Pr Met, MS(R), PhD. *Faculty:* 6 full-time (0 women), 2 part-time (0 women). *Students:* 5 full-time (1 woman), 13 part-time, 4 international. Average age 29. 19 applicants, 68% accepted. In 1998, 5 master's, 1 doctorate awarded. *Degree requirements:* For master's, computer language, comprehensive oral exam, thesis for MS(R) required; for doctorate, computer language, dissertation, preliminary exams required, foreign language not required. *Entrance requirements:* For master's and doctorate, GRE General Test. *Application deadline:* For fall admission, 7/1; for spring admission, 11/1. Applications are processed on a rolling basis. Application fee: $40. Tuition: Full-time $20,520; part-time $507 per credit hour. Required fees: $38 per term. Tuition and fees vary according to program. *Financial aid:* In 1998–99, 8 students received aid, including 1 research assistantship, 4 teaching assistantships Financial aid application deadline: 4/1; financial aid applicants required to submit FAFSA. *Faculty research:* Dynamic meteorology, radar meteorology,climate, satellite meteorology, tropical meteorology. *Unit head:* Dr. Yeong Jer Lin, Director, 314-977-3116, Fax: 314-977-3117. *Application contact:* Dr. Marcia Buresch, Assistant Dean of the Graduate School, 314-977-2240, Fax: 314-977-3943, E-mail: bureschm@slu.edu.

South Dakota School of Mines and Technology, Graduate Division, Department of Atmospheric Sciences, Rapid City, SD 57701-3995. Offers MS, PhD. Part-time programs available. *Faculty:* 9 part-time (0 women). *Students:* 17 full-time (5 women), 8 international. Average age 27. In 1998, 2 master's awarded. *Degree requirements:* For master's, thesis required, foreign language not required; for doctorate, dissertation required. *Entrance requirements:* For master's and doctorate, TOEFL (minimum score of 520 required), TWE. *Application deadline:* For fall admission, 6/15 (priority date); for spring admission, 10/15. Applications are processed on a rolling basis. Application fee: $15. Electronic applications accepted. Tuition, state resident: part-time $89 per hour. Tuition, nonresident: part-time $261 per hour. Part-time tuition and fees vary according to program. *Financial aid:* In 1998–99, 17 students received aid; fellowships, research assistantships, teaching assistantships, Federal Work-Study and institutionally-sponsored loans available. Aid available to part-time students. Financial aid application deadline: 5/15. *Faculty research:* Hailstorm observations and numerical modeling, microbursts and lightning, radiative transfer, remote sensing. Total annual research expenditures: $1.3 million. *Unit head:* Dr. Mark Hjelmselt, Chair, 605-394-1987. *Application contact:* Brenda Brown, Secretary, 800-454-8162 Ext. 2493, Fax: 605-394-5360, E-mail: graduate_admissions@silver.sdmt.edu.

South Dakota School of Mines and Technology, Graduate Division, Joint PhD Program in Atmospheric, Environmental, and Water Resources, Rapid City, SD 57701-3995. Offers PhD. *Students:* 15 full-time (5 women), 9 international. Average age 47. *Degree requirements:* For doctorate, dissertation required. *Entrance requirements:* For doctorate, GRE General Test, GRE Subject Test, TOEFL (minimum score of 520 required), TWE. *Application deadline:* For fall admission, 6/15 (priority date); for spring admission, 10/15. Applications are processed on a rolling basis. Application fee: $15. Electronic applications accepted. Tuition, state resident: part-time $89 per hour. Tuition, nonresident: part-time $261 per hour. Part-time tuition and fees vary according to program. *Financial aid:* In 1998–99, 2 students received aid, including 1 research assistantship, 1 teaching assistantship *Unit head:* Admissions Office, 902-867-2219, Fax: 902-867-2329, E-mail: admit@stfx.ca. *Application contact:* Brenda Brown, Secretary, 800-454-8162 Ext. 2493, Fax: 605-394-5360, E-mail: graduate_admissions@silver.sdmt.edu.

See in-depth description on page 387.

South Dakota State University, Graduate School, College of Engineering, Joint PhD Program in Atmospheric, Environmental, and Water Resources, Brookings, SD 57007. Offers PhD. Offered jointly with the South Dakota School of Mines and Technology. *Degree requirements:* For doctorate, dissertation, preliminary oral and written exams required. *Entrance requirements:* For doctorate, GRE General Test, GRE Subject Test, TOEFL. *Faculty research:* Use of fabric-reinforced soil wall for internal abutment bridge, end treatment performance evaluation of water and wastewater treatment.

See in-depth description on page 387.

State University of New York at Albany, College of Arts and Sciences, Department of Earth and Atmospheric Sciences, Albany, NY 12222-0001. Offers atmospheric science (MS, PhD); geology (MS, PhD). Evening/weekend programs available. *Faculty:* 24 full-time (0 women). *Students:* 46 full-time (16 women), 4 part-time; includes 1 minority (African American), 25 international. Average age 25. 50 applicants, 46% accepted. In 1998, 7 master's, 3 doctorates awarded. *Degree requirements:* For master's, thesis, comprehensive exam required; for doctorate, dissertation, comprehensive and oral exams required. *Entrance requirements:* For master's and doctorate, GRE General Test. Application fee: $50. Tuition, state resident: full-time $5,100; part-time $213 per credit. Tuition, nonresident: full-time $8,416; part-time $351 per credit. Required fees: $31 per credit. *Financial aid:* Fellowships, research assistantships, teaching assistantships, minority assistantships available. *Unit head:* Dr. John Delano, Chair, 518-442-4466.

See in-depth description on page 391.

State University of New York at Stony Brook, Graduate School, Institute for Terrestrial and Planetary Atmospheres, Stony Brook, NY 11794. Offers PhD. *Application deadline:* For fall admission, 3/1. Application fee: $50. *Financial aid:* Fellowships available. *Unit head:* Marvin A. Geller, Director, 516-632-6170.

See in-depth description on page 393.

State University of New York at Stony Brook, Graduate School, Marine Sciences Research Center, Stony Brook, NY 11794. Offers coastal oceanography (PhD); marine environmental sciences (MS); terrestrial and planetary atmospheres (PhD). Evening/weekend programs available. *Faculty:* 34 full-time (7 women), 2 part-time (both women). *Students:* 96 full-time (46 women), 32 part-time (16 women); includes 4 minority (1 African American, 2 Asian Americans or Pacific Islanders, 1 Hispanic American), 42 international. Application fee: $50. *Unit head:* Dr. Marvin A. Geller, Dean, 516-632-8700, Fax: 516-632-8200. *Application contact:* Dr. Henry Bokuniewicz, Director, 516-632-8681, Fax: 516-632-8200, E-mail: hbokuniewicz@ccmail.sunysb.edu.

Texas Tech University, Graduate School, College of Arts and Sciences, Department of Geosciences, Lubbock, TX 79409. Offers atmospheric sciences (MS); geoscience (MS, PhD). Part-time programs available. *Faculty:* 13 full-time (1 woman). *Students:* 29 full-time (7 women), 11 part-time (2 women), 5 international. *Degree requirements:* For master's and doctorate, thesis/dissertation required. *Entrance requirements:* For master's, GRE General Test (combined average 1164); for doctorate, GRE General Test. *Application deadline:* For fall admission, 4/15 (priority date); for spring admission, 11/1 (priority date). Applications are processed on a rolling basis. Application fee: $25 ($50 for international students). Electronic applications accepted. *Unit head:* Dr. Richard Peterson, Chairman, 806-742-3102, Fax: 806-742-0100.

Université du Québec à Montréal, Graduate Programs, Programs in Atmospheric Sciences and Meteorology, Montréal, PQ H3C 3P8, Canada. Offers atmospheric sciences (M Sc); meteorology (PhD, Diploma). PhD offered jointly with McGill University. Part-time programs available. *Degree requirements:* For master's, thesis required, foreign language not required; for Diploma, thesis not required. *Entrance requirements:* For master's and Diploma, appropriate bachelor's degree or equivalent and proficiency in French; for doctorate, appropriate master's degree or equivalent and proficiency in French.

The University of Alabama in Huntsville, School of Graduate Studies, College of Science, Department of Atmospheric and Environmental Science, Huntsville, AL 35899. Offers MS, PhD. Part-time and evening/weekend programs available. *Faculty:* 6 full-time (0 women), 2 part-time (0 women). *Students:* 24 full-time (5 women), 5 part-time; includes 2 minority (1 Asian American or Pacific Islander, 1 Hispanic American), 10 international. Average age 31. 9 applicants, 100% accepted. In 1998, 2 master's, 4 doctorates awarded. *Degree requirements:* For master's, oral and written exams required, thesis optional, foreign language not required; for doctorate, dissertation, oral and written exams required, foreign language not required. *Entrance requirements:* For master's and doctorate, GRE General Test (minimum combined score of 1650 on three sections required), minimum GPA of 3.0. *Application deadline:* For fall admission, 7/24 (priority date); for spring admission, 11/15 (priority date). Applications are processed on a rolling basis. Application fee: $20. Tuition and fees vary according to course load. *Financial aid:* In 1998–99, 22 students received aid, including 21 research assistantships with full and partial tuition reimbursements available (averaging $11,248 per year), 1 teaching assistantship with full and partial tuition reimbursement available (averaging $9,450 per year); fellowships with full and partial tuition reimbursements available, career-related internships or fieldwork, Federal Work-Study, grants, institutionally-sponsored loans, scholarships, and tuition waivers (full and partial) also available. Aid available to part-time students. Financial aid application deadline: 4/1; financial aid applicants required to submit FAFSA. *Faculty research:* Air pollution, climate dynamics, severe storms, remote sensing, satellite meteorology, statistical climatology. *Unit head:* Dr. Ronald Welch, Chair, 256-922-5754, Fax: 256-922-5755, E-mail: ron.welch@atmos.uah.edu.

University of Alaska Fairbanks, Graduate School, College of Science, Engineering and Mathematics, Department of Physics, Fairbanks, AK 99775-7480. Offers atmospheric science (MS, PhD); physics (MS, PhD); space physics (MS, PhD). Part-time programs available. *Faculty:* 19 full-time (1 woman). *Students:* 24 full-time (8 women), 2 part-time; includes 2 minority (1 African American, 1 Hispanic American) Terminal master's awarded for partial completion of doctoral program. *Degree requirements:* For master's, thesis, comprehensive exam required, foreign language not required; for doctorate, one foreign language (computer language can substitute), dissertation, comprehensive exam required. *Entrance requirements:* For master's and doctorate, GRE General Test, GRE Subject Test, TOEFL (minimum score of 550 required). *Application deadline:* For fall admission, 2/15. Application fee: $35. *Unit head:* Dr. Brenton Watkins, Head, 907-474-7339. *Application contact:* Dr. Brenton Watkins, Head, 907-474-7339.

The University of Arizona, Graduate College, College of Science, Department of Atmospheric Sciences, Tucson, AZ 85721. Offers MS, PhD. *Faculty:* 11. *Students:* 21 full-time (6 women), 5 part-time (1 woman); includes 2 minority (1 Asian American or Pacific Islander, 1 Hispanic American), 9 international. Average age 30. 19 applicants, 32% accepted. In 1998, 6 master's, 3 doctorates awarded. *Degree requirements:* For master's, computer language, thesis or alternative required, foreign language not required; for doctorate, computer language, dissertation required, foreign language not required. *Entrance requirements:* For master's, GRE, TOEFL (minimum score of 550 required); for doctorate, TOEFL (minimum score of 550 required). *Application deadline:* For fall admission, 4/15. Applications are processed on a rolling basis. Application fee: $35. *Financial aid:* Fellowships, research assistantships, teaching assistantships, scholarships and tuition waivers (full) available. *Faculty research:* Climate dynamics, radiative transfer and remote sensing, atmospheric chemistry, atmosphere dynamics, atmospheric electricity. *Unit head:* Dr. Benjamin M. Herman, Head, 520-621-6831. *Application contact:* Dawn Winsor-Hibble, Graduate Secretary, 520-621-6831, Fax: 520-621-6833.

University of British Columbia, Faculty of Arts, Department of Geography, Vancouver, BC V6T 1Z2, Canada. Offers atmospheric science (M Sc, PhD); geography (M Sc, MA, PhD). Part-time programs available. *Faculty:* 26 full-time (4 women), 6 part-time (2 women). *Students:* 96 full-time (46 women), 4 part-time (2 women); includes 5 minority (4 Asian Americans or Pacific Islanders, 1 Native American), 33 international. Terminal master's awarded for partial completion of doctoral program. *Degree requirements:* For master's, thesis required; for doctorate, dissertation, comprehensive exam required. *Application deadline:* For fall admission, 2/15. Application fee: $65 Canadian dollars. *Unit head:* Prof. Graeme Wynn, Head, 604-822-2148, Fax: 604-822-6150, E-mail: wynn@geog.ubc.ca. *Application contact:* Elaine Cho, Graduate Secretary, 604-822-2663, Fax: 604-822-6150, E-mail: echo@geog.ubc.ca.

University of California, Davis, Graduate Studies, Program in Atmospheric Science, Davis, CA 95616. Offers MS, PhD. *Faculty:* 8. *Students:* 19 full-time (9 women); includes 2 minority (both Asian Americans or Pacific Islanders), 6 international. 22 applicants, 23% accepted. In 1998, 2 master's, 6 doctorates awarded. *Degree requirements:* For master's, comprehensive exam or thesis required; for doctorate, dissertation, 3-part qualifying exam required. *Entrance requirements:* For master's and doctorate, GRE General Test, TOEFL (minimum score of 550 required), minimum GPA of 3.0. *Application deadline:* For fall admission, 1/15. Application fee: $40. Electronic applications accepted. *Financial aid:* In 1998–99, 4 fellowships with full and partial tuition reimbursements, 14 research assistantships with full and partial tuition reimbursements, 3 teaching assistantships with full and partial tuition reimbursements were awarded.; career-related internships or fieldwork, Federal Work-Study, and institutionally-sponsored loans also available. Financial aid application deadline: 1/15; financial aid applicants required to submit FAFSA. *Faculty research:* Air quality, biometeorology, climate dynamics, boundary layer large-scale dynamics. Total annual research expenditures: $1.2 million. *Unit head:* Terrance Nathan, Graduate Adviser, 530-752-1669. *Application contact:* Diane Swindall, Graduate Staff Adviser, 530-752-1669, Fax: 530-752-5262, E-mail: dgswindall@ucdavis.edu.

Atmospheric Sciences

University of California, Los Angeles, Graduate Division, College of Letters and Science, Department of Atmospheric Sciences, Los Angeles, CA 90095. Offers MS, PhD. *Students:* 34 full-time (15 women); includes 7 minority (1 African American, 6 Asian Americans or Pacific Islanders), 17 international. 68 applicants, 75% accepted. *Degree requirements:* For master's, comprehensive exam or thesis required; for doctorate, dissertation, oral and written qualifying exams required, foreign language not required. *Entrance requirements:* For master's, GRE General Test, minimum GPA of 3.0; for doctorate, GRE General Test, minimum undergraduate GPA of 3.0. *Application deadline:* For fall admission, 12/15. Application fee: $40. Electronic applications accepted. *Financial aid:* In 1998–99, 33 fellowships, 18 teaching assistantships were awarded.; research assistantships, Federal Work-Study, institutionally-sponsored loans, scholarships, and tuition waivers (full and partial) also available. Financial aid application deadline: 3/1. *Unit head:* Dr. Roger Walcimoto, Chair, 310-825-1217. *Application contact:* Departmental Office, 310-825-1217, E-mail: lori@atmos.ucla.edu.

University of Chicago, Division of the Physical Sciences, Department of the Geophysical Sciences, Chicago, IL 60637-1513. Offers atmospheric sciences (SM, PhD); earth sciences (SM, PhD); planetary and space sciences (SM, PhD). *Degree requirements:* For master's, thesis, seminar required; for doctorate, dissertation required. *Entrance requirements:* For master's and doctorate, GRE General Test, TOEFL (minimum score of 550 required). *Faculty research:* Climatology, evolutionary paleontology,petrology, geochemistry, oceanic sciences.

University of Colorado at Boulder, Graduate School, College of Arts and Sciences, Department of Astrophysical, Planetary, and Atmospheric Sciences, Boulder, CO 80309. Offers astrophysical and geophysical fluid dynamics (MS, PhD); astrophysics (MS, PhD); plasma physics (MS, PhD). Terminal master's awarded for partial completion of doctoral program. *Degree requirements:* For master's, thesis or alternative, comprehensive exam required, foreign language not required; for doctorate, dissertation required. *Entrance requirements:* For master's and doctorate, GRE General Test, GRE Subject Test.

University of Delaware, College of Arts and Science, Department of Geography, Program in Climatology, Newark, DE 19716. Offers PhD. *Faculty:* 12 full-time (3 women), 4 part-time (0 women). *Students:* 9 full-time (3 women), 3 part-time (1 woman); includes 1 African American Average age 28. 5 applicants, 20% accepted. In 1998, 2 degrees awarded (100% entered university research/teaching). *Degree requirements:* For doctorate, computer language, dissertation required, foreign language not required. *Entrance requirements:* For doctorate, GRE General Test. *Application deadline:* For fall admission, 2/1. Application fee: $45. *Financial aid:* In 1998–99, 2 fellowships with full tuition reimbursements (averaging $11,200 per year), 5 research assistantships with full tuition reimbursements (averaging $11,200 per year), 1 teaching assistantship with full tuition reimbursement (averaging $11,200 per year) were awarded. *Faculty research:* Physical and applied climatology, waterbudgets, synoptic climatology, glaciology, computer methods. *Unit head:* Dr. Cort J. Willmott, Chairman, 302-831-8998, Fax: 302-831-6654, E-mail: willmott@udel.edu. *Application contact:* Janice Spry, Assistant to the Chair, 302-831-8998, Fax: 302-831-6654, E-mail: janice.spry@mvs.udel.edu.

University of Guelph, Faculty of Graduate Studies, Ontario Agricultural College, Department of Land Resource Science, Guelph, ON N1G 2W1, Canada. Offers atmospheric science (M Sc, PhD); land science (M Sc, PhD). Part-time programs available. *Faculty:* 17 full-time (1 woman), 3 part-time (0 women). *Students:* 42 full-time (19 women), 11 part-time (2 women), 9 international. *Degree requirements:* For master's and doctorate, thesis/dissertation required. *Entrance requirements:* For master's, minimum B- average during previous 2 years. *Application deadline:* Applications are processed on a rolling basis. Application fee: $60. *Expenses:* Tuition and fees charges are reported in Canadian dollars. Tuition, area resident: Full-time $4,725 Canadian dollars; part-time $1,055 Canadian dollars per term. International tuition: $6,999 Canadian dollars full-time. Required fees: $295 Canadian dollars per term. *Unit head:* Dr. T. J. Gillespie, Chairman, 519-824-4120 Ext. 2447, Fax: 519-824-5730, E-mail: tgillesp@lrs.uoguelph.ca. *Application contact:* Dr. W. Chesworth, Graduate Coordinator, 519-824-4120 Ext. 2457, Fax: 519-824-5730, E-mail: wcheswor@lrs.uoguelph.ca.

University of Illinois at Urbana–Champaign, Graduate College, Department of Atmospheric Science, Urbana, IL 61801. Offers MS, PhD. *Faculty:* 11 full-time (1 woman). *Students:* 32 full-time (14 women); includes 1 minority (Hispanic American), 15 international. 61 applicants, 5% accepted. In 1998, 5 master's, 4 doctorates awarded. *Degree requirements:* For master's and doctorate, thesis/dissertation required. *Entrance requirements:* For master's and doctorate, GRE General Test. *Application deadline:* Applications are processed on a rolling basis. Application fee: $40 ($50 for international students). Tuition, state resident: full-time $4,040. Tuition, nonresident: full-time $11,192. Full-time tuition and fees vary according to program. *Financial aid:* In 1998–99, 32 students received aid, including 30 research assistantships, 2 teaching assistantships; fellowships, tuition waivers (full and partial) also available. Financial aid application deadline: 2/15. *Unit head:* Robert B. Wilhelmson, Acting Head, 217-333-2046, Fax: 217-244-4393. *Application contact:* Robert Rauber, Director of Graduate Studies, 217-333-2835, Fax: 217-244-4393, E-mail: rauber@uiatma.atmos.uiuc.edu.

University of Maryland, Baltimore County, Graduate School, Department of Physics, Baltimore, MD 21250-5398. Offers applied physics (MS, PhD), including optics, solid state physics; atmospheric physics (MS, PhD). Part-time programs available. *Faculty:* 15 full-time (0 women), 4 part-time (0 women). *Students:* 18 full-time (1 woman), 3 part-time, 7 international. Terminal master's awarded for partial completion of doctoral program. *Degree requirements:* For master's, thesis optional, foreign language not required; for doctorate, dissertation required, foreign language not required. *Entrance requirements:* For master's and doctorate, GRE General Test, GRE Subject Test, TOEFL (minimum score of 600 required), minimum GPA of 3.0. *Application deadline:* For fall admission, 7/1 (priority date); for spring admission, 12/1 (priority date). Applications are processed on a rolling basis. Application fee: $45. *Unit head:* Dr. Geoffrey P. Summers, Chairman, 410-455-2513, Fax: 410-455-1072. *Application contact:* 410-455-2513, Fax: 410-455-1072, E-mail: physics@umbc.edu.

University of Miami, Graduate School, Rosenstiel School of Marine and Atmospheric Science, Division of Meteorology and Physical Oceanography, Coral Gables, FL 33124. Offers atmospheric science (MA, MS, PhD); physical oceanography (MA, MS, PhD). *Faculty:* 18 full-time (1 woman). *Students:* 38 full-time (15 women), 1 (woman) part-time; includes 1 minority (African American), 26 international. Terminal master's awarded for partial completion of doctoral program. *Degree requirements:* For master's and doctorate, thesis/dissertation required, foreign language not required. *Entrance requirements:* For master's and doctorate, GRE General Test, TOEFL (minimum score of 550 required). *Application deadline:* For fall admission, 2/1 (priority date). Applications are processed on a rolling basis. Application fee: $35. Electronic applications accepted. Tuition: Full-time $15,336; part-time $852 per credit. Required fees: $174. Tuition and fees vary according to program. *Unit head:* Dr. Kevin R. Leaman, Chair, 305-361-4045. *Application contact:* Dr. Frank Millero, Associate Dean, 305-361-4155, Fax: 305-361-4771, E-mail: gso@rsmas.miami.edu.

University of Michigan, Horace H. Rackham School of Graduate Studies, College of Engineering, Department of Atmospheric, Oceanic, and Space Sciences, Program in Atmospheric and Space Sciences, Ann Arbor, MI 48109. Offers M Eng, MS, PhD. Part-time programs available. *Faculty:* 21 full-time (2 women), 9 part-time (0 women). *Students:* 42 full-time (15 women), 10 international. 72 applicants, 44% accepted. In 1998, 3 master's, 6 doctorates awarded. Terminal master's awarded for partial completion of doctoral program. *Degree requirements:* For master's, thesis required (for some programs); for doctorate, dissertation, oral defense of dissertation, preliminary exams required. *Entrance requirements:* For master's and doctorate, GRE General Test (combined average 2000 on three sections), TOEFL (minimum score of 600 required). *Application deadline:* For fall admission, 1/15 (priority date). Applications are processed on a rolling basis. Application fee: $60. *Financial aid:* In 1998–99, 8 fellowships, 4 teaching assistantships were awarded.; research assistantships, career-related internships or fieldwork, Federal Work-Study, and institutionally-sponsored loans also available. Aid available to part-time students. Financial aid application deadline: 3/15; financial aid applicants required to submit FAFSA. *Faculty research:* Air quality, remote sensing, meteorology aeronomy, planetary and comet atmospheres. Total annual research expenditures: $13.5 million. *Unit head:* William Kuhn, Adviser, 734-764-3335, Fax: 734-764-4585, E-mail: wkuhn@umich.edu. *Application contact:* Susan Schreiber, Academic Services Assistant, 734-764-3336, Fax: 734-764-4585, E-mail: aoss.um@umich.edu.

University of Missouri–Columbia, Graduate School, School of Natural Resources, Department of Soil and Atmospheric Sciences, Columbia, MO 65211. Offers MS, PhD. *Faculty:* 9 full-time (1 woman). *Students:* 7 full-time (3 women), 9 part-time (2 women); includes 2 minority (1 Asian American or Pacific Islander, 1 Hispanic American), 5 international. 3 applicants, 67% accepted. In 1998, 7 master's, 3 doctorates awarded. Terminal master's awarded for partial completion of doctoral program. *Degree requirements:* For master's and doctorate, thesis/dissertation required, foreign language not required. *Entrance requirements:* For master's and doctorate, GRE General Test, minimum GPA of 3.0. *Application deadline:* Applications are processed on a rolling basis. Application fee: $30 ($50 for international students). *Financial aid:* Research assistantships, teaching assistantships, grants and institutionally-sponsored loans available. *Unit head:* Dr. Steve Anderson, Director of Graduate Studies, 573-882-6303.

University of Nevada, Reno, Graduate School, Center for Environmental Sciences and Engineering, Reno, NV 89557. Offers atmospheric sciences (MS, PhD); ecology, evolution and conservation biology (PhD); environmental sciences and health (MS, PhD). *Entrance requirements:* For master's and doctorate, GRE, TOEFL. *Faculty research:* Air, water, and soil pollution; endangered species habitats; restoration ecology; environmental analytical chemistry; control of pollution from mining.

University of North Dakota, Graduate School, Center for Aerospace Studies, Department of Atmospheric Sciences, Grand Forks, ND 58202. Offers MS. *Faculty:* 5 full-time (0 women). *Students:* 4 full-time (1 woman), 4 part-time. 8 applicants, 100% accepted. *Degree requirements:* For master's. *Entrance requirements:* For master's, GRE General Test, TOEFL (minimum score of 550 required), minimum GPA of 3.0. *Application deadline:* For fall admission, 3/1 (priority date). Applications are processed on a rolling basis. Application fee: $20. *Financial aid:* In 1998–99, 3 students received aid, including 2 research assistantships, 1 teaching assistantship *Unit head:* Dr. Ronald Rinehart, Director, 701-777-2184, Fax: 701-777-5032, E-mail: rinehart@aero.und.edu.

University of Washington, Graduate School, College of Arts and Sciences, Department of Atmospheric Sciences, Seattle, WA 98195. Offers MS, PhD. Terminal master's awarded for partial completion of doctoral program. *Degree requirements:* For master's, thesis required, foreign language not required; for doctorate, dissertation, qualifying exam required, foreign language not required. *Entrance requirements:* For master's and doctorate, GRE General Test, TOEFL (minimum score of 500 required), minimum GPA of 3.0. Tuition, state resident: full-time $5,196; part-time $475 per credit. Tuition, nonresident: full-time $13,485; part-time $1,285 per credit. Required fees: $387; $38 per credit. Tuition and fees vary according to course load. *Faculty research:* Climate change, synoptic and mesoscale meteorology, atmospheric chemistry, cloud physics, dynamics of the atmosphere.

See in-depth description on page 401.

University of Wisconsin–Madison, Graduate School, College of Letters and Science, Department of Atmospheric and Oceanic Sciences, Madison, WI 53706-1380. Offers MS, PhD. Part-time programs available. *Faculty:* 19 full-time (0 women), 2 part-time (0 women). *Students:* 48 full-time (14 women), 6 part-time (1 woman), 11 international. Average age 25. 84 applicants, 44% accepted. In 1998, 8 master's awarded (12% entered university research/teaching, 63% found other work related to degree, 25% continued full-time study); 5 doctorates awarded (20% entered university research/teaching, 80% found other work related to degree). *Degree requirements:* For master's, thesis required (for some programs), foreign language not required; for doctorate, dissertation required, foreign language not required. *Entrance requirements:* For master's and doctorate, GRE General Test (minimum score of 650 on quantitative section, 500 on analytical required), minimum GPA of 3.0; previous course work in chemistry, mathematics, and physics. *Average time to degree:* Master's–2 years full-time, 3.5 years part-time; doctorate–4 years full-time, 5 years part-time. *Application deadline:* For fall admission, 8/1 (priority date); for spring admission, 12/1 (priority date). Applications are processed on a rolling basis. Application fee: $45. Electronic applications accepted. *Financial aid:* In 1998–99, 47 students received aid, including 1 fellowship with full tuition reimbursement available (averaging $17,500 per year), 29 research assistantships with full tuition reimbursements available (averaging $14,600 per year), 8 teaching assistantships with full tuition reimbursements available; career-related internships or fieldwork, Federal Work-Study, institutionally-sponsored loans, and scholarships also available. Aid available to part-time students. *Faculty research:* Satellite meteorology, weather systems, global climate change, numerical modeling, atmosphere-ocean interaction. Total annual research expenditures: $1.4 million. *Unit head:* Matthew Hitchman, Chair, 608-262-2828, Fax: 608-262-0166, E-mail: matt@adams.meteor.wisc.edu. *Application contact:* Connie Linehan, Graduate Coordinator, 608-262-2827, Fax: 608-262-0166, E-mail: linehan@facstaff.wisc.edu.

University of Wyoming, Graduate School, College of Engineering, Department of Atmospheric Science, Laramie, WY 82071. Offers MS, PhD. *Faculty:* 8 full-time (0 women). *Students:* 10 full-time (1 woman), 9 part-time (2 women), 7 international. 13 applicants, 54% accepted. In 1998, 2 master's, 2 doctorates awarded. Terminal master's awarded for partial completion of doctoral program. *Degree requirements:* For master's and doctorate, thesis/dissertation required, foreign language not required. *Entrance requirements:* For master's and doctorate, GRE General Test, TOEFL, minimum GPA of 3.0. *Application deadline:* For fall admission, 4/15 (priority date). Applications are processed on a rolling basis. Application fee: $40. Tuition, state resident: full-time $2,520; part-time $140 per credit hour. Tuition, nonresident: full-time $7,790; part-time $433 per credit hour. Required fees: $400; $7 per credit hour. Full-time tuition and fees vary according to course load and program. *Financial aid:* Research assistantships, career-related internships or fieldwork, Federal Work-Study, and institutionally-sponsored loans available. Aid available to part-time students. Financial aid application deadline: 3/1. *Faculty research:* Cloud and precipitation processes, mesoscale dynamics, weather modification, winter storms, aircraft instrumentation. Total annual research expenditures: $1.1 million. *Unit head:* Dr. Thomas R. Parish, Head, 307-766-3246, Fax: 307-766-2635. *Application contact:* Dr. Derek Montague, Graduate Coordinator, 307-766-4949, Fax: 307-766-2635, E-mail: montague@grizzly.uwyo.edu.

Meteorology

Air Force Institute of Technology, School of Engineering, Department of Engineering Physics, Program in Meteorology, Wright-Patterson AFB, OH 45433-7765. Offers MS, PhD. Part-time programs available. *Faculty:* 4 full-time (1 woman). *Students:* 26 full-time. In 1998, 12 master's awarded (100% found work related to degree). *Degree requirements:* For master's and doctorate, thesis/dissertation required, foreign language not required. *Entrance requirements:* For master's, GRE General Test (minimum score of 500 on verbal section, 600 on quantitative required), minimum GPA of 3.0, must be military officer or U.S. citizen; for doctorate, GRE General Test (minimum score of 550 on verbal section, 650 on quantitative required), minimum GPA of 3.0, must be military officer or U.S. citizen. Application fee: $0. *Faculty research:* Space environment, military weather. *Unit head:* Lt. Col. Mike Walters, Curriculum Chair, 937-255-3636 Ext. 4681, Fax: 937-255-2921, E-mail: mwalters@afit.af.mil.

Florida State University, Graduate Studies, College of Arts and Sciences, Department of Meteorology, Tallahassee, FL 32306. Offers MS, PhD. *Faculty:* 12 full-time (2 women), 3 part-time (0 women). *Students:* 60 full-time (10 women), 4 part-time; includes 15 minority (3 African Americans, 10 Asian Americans or Pacific Islanders, 2 Hispanic Americans) Average age 28. 90 applicants, 39% accepted. In 1998, 18 master's awarded (67% found work related to degree, 33% continued full-time study); 6 doctorates awarded (67% entered university research/teaching, 33% found other work related to degree). Terminal master's awarded for partial completion of doctoral program. *Degree requirements:* For master's, foreign language and thesis not required; for doctorate, dissertation required, foreign language not required. *Entrance requirements:* For master's and doctorate, GRE General Test (minimum combined score of 1000 required) or minimum GPA of 3.0. *Average time to degree:* Master's–2.6 years full-time, 5.5 years part-time; doctorate–3.5 years full-time. *Application deadline:* For fall admission, 6/15; for spring admission, 11/1. Applications are processed on a rolling basis. Application fee: $20. Tuition, state resident: part-time $139 per credit hour. Tuition, nonresident: part-time $482 per credit hour. Tuition and fees vary according to program. *Financial aid:* In 1998–99, 38 students received aid, including 2 fellowships, 25 research assistantships, 7 teaching assistantships; career-related internships or fieldwork also available. *Faculty research:* Physical, dynamic, and synoptic meteorology; climatology. *Unit head:* Dr. Peter Ray, Chairman, 850-644-6205, Fax: 850-644-9642. *Application contact:* Anna R. Nelson Smith, Coordinator of Academic Support Services, 850-644-8582, Fax: 850-644-9642, E-mail: ansmith@met.fsu.edu.

Iowa State University of Science and Technology, Graduate College, College of Liberal Arts and Sciences, Department of Geological and Atmospheric Sciences, Ames, IA 50011. Offers earth science (MS, PhD); geology (MS, PhD); meteorology (MS, PhD); water resources (MS, PhD). *Faculty:* 17 full-time. *Students:* 28 full-time (8 women), 9 part-time (3 women); includes 1 minority (Asian American or Pacific Islander), 11 international. *Degree requirements:* For master's, thesis required (for some programs); for doctorate, dissertation required. *Entrance requirements:* For master's and doctorate, GRE General Test, TOEFL (minimum score of 530 required). *Application deadline:* For fall admission, 2/15 (priority date). Applications are processed on a rolling basis. Application fee: $20 ($50 for international students). Electronic applications accepted. Tuition, state resident: full-time $3,308. Tuition, nonresident: full-time $9,744. Part-time tuition and fees vary according to course load, campus/location and program. *Unit head:* Dr. Paul G. Spry, Chair, 515-294-4477.

Massachusetts Institute of Technology, School of Science, Department of Earth, Atmospheric, and Planetary Sciences, Program in Atmospheres, Oceans, and Climate, Cambridge, MA 02139-4307. Offers SM, PhD, Sc D. *Faculty:* 16 full-time (2 women). *Students:* 61 full-time (24 women), 32 international. Average age 27. 79 applicants, 35% accepted. In 1998, 4 master's, 11 doctorates awarded. Terminal master's awarded for partial completion of doctoral program. *Degree requirements:* For master's, thesis required, foreign language not required; for doctorate, dissertation, general exam required, foreign language not required. *Entrance requirements:* For master's and doctorate, GRE General Test, GRE Subject Test. *Application deadline:* For fall admission, 1/15; for spring admission, 11/1. Application fee: $55. *Financial aid:* Fellowships, research assistantships, teaching assistantships, institutionally-sponsored loans available. Financial aid application deadline: 1/15. *Faculty research:* Origin, composition, structure, and state of atmospheres and oceans. *Unit head:* Dr. Carl I. Wunsch, Director, 617-253-5937, E-mail: paoc@mit.edu. *Application contact:* Anastasia Frangos, Administrative Assistant, 617-253-3381, Fax: 617-253-8298, E-mail: eapsinfo@mit.edu.

McGill University, Faculty of Graduate Studies and Research, Faculty of Agricultural and Environmental Sciences, Department of Natural Resource Sciences, Montréal, PQ H3A 2T5, Canada. Offers agrometeorology (M Sc, PhD); entomology (M Sc, PhD); forest science (M Sc, PhD); microbiology (M Sc, PhD); soil science (M Sc, PhD); wildlife biology (M Sc, PhD). *Faculty:* 18 full-time (1 woman), 26 part-time (3 women). *Students:* 83 full-time (35 women), 10 international. *Degree requirements:* For master's and doctorate, thesis/dissertation required. *Entrance requirements:* For master's, TOEFL (minimum score of 550 required), minimum GPA of 3.0; for doctorate, TOEFL (minimum score of 550 required), M Sc. *Application deadline:* For fall admission, 1/1 (priority date); for winter admission, 5/1 (priority date); for spring admission, 9/1 (priority date). Applications are processed on a rolling basis. Application fee: $60. *Unit head:* Dr. W. H. Hendershot, Chair, 514-398-7942, Fax: 514-398-7990, E-mail: chair@nrs.mcgill.ca. *Application contact:* 514-398-7708, Fax: 514-398-7968, E-mail: grad@macdonald.mcgill.ca.

Naval Postgraduate School, Graduate Programs, Department of Meteorology, Monterey, CA 93943. Offers MS, PhD. Program only open to commissioned officers of the United States and friendly nations and selected United States federal civilian employees. Part-time programs available. *Students:* 45 full-time. In 1998, 21 master's, 1 doctorate awarded. *Degree requirements:* For master's, computer language, thesis required, foreign language not required; for doctorate, one foreign language, computer language, dissertation required. *Unit head:* Dr. Carlyle H. Wash, Chairman, 831-656-2517. *Application contact:* Theodore H. Calhoon, Director of Admissions, 831-656-3093, Fax: 831-656-2891, E-mail: tcalhoon@nps.navy.mil.

North Carolina State University, Graduate School, College of Physical and Mathematical Sciences, Department of Marine, Earth, and Atmospheric Sciences, Raleigh, NC 27695. Offers geology (MS, PhD); geophysics (MS, PhD); marine, earth, and atmospheric sciences (MS, PhD); meteorology (MS, PhD); oceanography (MS, PhD). *Faculty:* 34 full-time (2 women), 39 part-time (1 woman). *Students:* 118 full-time (30 women), 12 part-time (3 women); includes 2 minority (both Asian Americans or Pacific Islanders), 37 international. Terminal master's awarded for partial completion of doctoral program. *Degree requirements:* For master's, thesis, final oral exam required, foreign language not required; for doctorate, dissertation, final oral exam, preliminary oral and written exams required, foreign language not required. *Entrance requirements:* For master's and doctorate, GRE General Test, minimum GPA of 3.0. *Application deadline:* For fall admission, 6/25 (priority date); for spring admission, 11/25. Applications are processed on a rolling basis. Application fee: $45. *Unit head:* Dr. Leonard J. Pietrafesa, Head, 919-515-3717, Fax: 919-515-7802, E-mail: leonard_pietrafesa@ncsu.edu. *Application contact:* Dr. Gerald S. Janowitz, Director of Graduate Programs, 919-515-7837, Fax: 919-515-7802, E-mail: janowitz@ncsu.edu.

Pennsylvania State University University Park Campus, Graduate School, College of Earth and Mineral Sciences, Department of Meteorology, State College, University Park, PA 16802-1503. Offers MS, PhD. *Students:* 60 full-time (13 women), 5 part-time. In 1998, 27 master's, 2 doctorates awarded. *Entrance requirements:* For master's and doctorate, GRE General Test. Application fee: $50. *Unit head:* Dr. William H. Brune, Head, 814-865-0478. *Application contact:* Dr. Johannes Verlinde, Chair, 814-865-0478.

San Jose State University, Graduate Studies, College of Science, Department of Meteorology, San Jose, CA 95192-0001. Offers MS. *Faculty:* 5 full-time (2 women), 4 part-time (0 women). *Students:* 1 full-time (0 women), 8 part-time (1 woman); includes 1 minority (Asian American or Pacific Islander), 2 international. Average age 33. 11 applicants, 45% accepted. In 1998, 1 degree awarded. *Degree requirements:* For master's, thesis or alternative required, foreign language not required. *Entrance requirements:* For master's, GRE. *Application deadline:* For fall admission, 6/1. Applications are processed on a rolling basis. Application fee: $59. Tuition, nonresident: part-time $246 per unit. Required fees: $1,939; $1,309 per year. *Unit head:* Dr. Jindra Goodman, Chair, 408-924-5200, Fax: 408-924-5191. *Application contact:* Dr. Alison Bridger, Graduate Adviser, 408-924-5206.

Texas A&M University, College of Geosciences, Department of Atmospheric Sciences, College Station, TX 77843. Offers MS, PhD. *Faculty:* 15 full-time (0 women). *Students:* 52 full-time (13 women), 12 part-time (1 woman); includes 14 minority (12 Asian Americans or Pacific Islanders, 2 Hispanic Americans), 12 international. Average age 30. 74 applicants, 55% accepted. In 1998, 12 master's, 4 doctorates awarded. *Degree requirements:* For master's and doctorate, thesis/dissertation required, foreign language not required. *Entrance requirements:* For master's and doctorate, GRE General Test, TOEFL. *Average time to degree:* Master's–2.5 years full-time; doctorate–4 years full-time. *Application deadline:* For fall admission, 3/1; for spring admission, 10/1. Applications are processed on a rolling basis. Application fee: $50 ($75 for international students). Electronic applications accepted. *Financial aid:* In 1998–99, 50 students received aid, including 3 fellowships (averaging $16,500 per year), 39 research assistantships with tuition reimbursements available (averaging $15,500 per year), 8 teaching assistantships (averaging $15,500 per year); career-related internships or fieldwork, grants, institutionally-sponsored loans, scholarships, and tuition waivers (partial) also available. Financial aid application deadline: 3/1; financial aid applicants required to submit FAFSA. *Faculty research:* Radar- and satellite-rainfall relationships, mesoscale dynamics and numerical modeling, climatology. Total annual research expenditures: $2.1 million. *Unit head:* Dr. Gerald North, Head, 409-845-7688, Fax: 409-862-4466. *Application contact:* Patricia Price, Staff Assistant, 409-845-7671, Fax: 409-862-4466, E-mail: pprice@ariel.net.tamu.edu.

Université du Québec à Montréal, Graduate Programs, Programs in Atmospheric Sciences and Meteorology, Montréal, PQ H3C 3P8, Canada. Offers atmospheric sciences (M Sc); meteorology (PhD, Diploma). PhD offered jointly with McGill University. Part-time programs available. *Degree requirements:* For master's, thesis required, foreign language not required; for Diploma, thesis not required. *Entrance requirements:* For master's and Diploma, appropriate bachelor's degree or equivalent and proficiency in French; for doctorate, appropriate master's degree or equivalent and proficiency in French.

University of Hawaii at Manoa, Graduate Division, School of Ocean and Earth Science and Technology, Department of Meteorology, Honolulu, HI 96822. Offers MS, PhD. Part-time programs available. *Faculty:* 12 full-time (1 woman). *Students:* 18 full-time (3 women), 19 part-time (5 women); includes 6 minority (2 African Americans, 3 Asian Americans or Pacific Islanders, 1 Hispanic American), 16 international. Average age 27. 25 applicants, 44% accepted. In 1998, 3 master's awarded (100% found work related to degree); 2 doctorates awarded (100% found work related to degree). *Degree requirements:* For master's and doctorate, computer language, thesis/dissertation required, foreign language not required. *Entrance requirements:* For master's, GRE General Test (minimum combined score of 1600 on three sections required; average 1850); for doctorate, GRE General Test (minimum combined score of 1800 on three sections required; average 2000). *Average time to degree:* Master's–3 years full-time; doctorate–5 years full-time. *Application deadline:* For fall admission, 3/1; for spring admission, 9/1. Application fee: $25 ($50 for international students). *Financial aid:* In 1998–99, 28 research assistantships (averaging $17,131 per year), 1 teaching assistantship (averaging $14,958 per year) were awarded.; fellowships, Federal Work-Study and tuition waivers (full) also available. *Faculty research:* Tropical cyclones, air-sea interactions, mesoscale meteorology, intraseasonal oscillations, tropical climate. Total annual research expenditures: $1.2 million. *Unit head:* Dr. Gary M. Barnes, Chairperson, 808-956-2565, Fax: 808-956-2877, E-mail: garyb@soest.hawaii.edu.

University of Maryland, College Park, Graduate School, College of Computer, Mathematical and Physical Sciences, Department of Meteorology, College Park, MD 20742-5045. Offers MS, PhD. Postbaccalaureate distance learning degree programs offered. *Faculty:* 42 full-time (3 women), 8 part-time (3 women). *Students:* 26 full-time (4 women), 20 part-time (8 women); includes 1 minority (Asian American or Pacific Islander), 31 international. 58 applicants, 38% accepted. In 1998, 16 master's, 1 doctorate awarded. *Degree requirements:* For master's, computer language, comprehensive exams, scholarly paper required, thesis not required; for doctorate, dissertation, exam required. *Entrance requirements:* For master's, GRE General Test, minimum GPA of 3.0, previous undergraduate course work in calculus, differential equations, linear algebra, physics, chemistry, scientific computer language; for doctorate, GRE General Test. *Application deadline:* Applications are processed on a rolling basis. Application fee: $50 ($70 for international students). Tuition, state resident: part-time $272 per credit hour. Tuition, nonresident: part-time $475 per credit hour. Required fees: $632; $379 per year. *Financial aid:* In 1998–99, 36 research assistantships with tuition reimbursements (averaging $15,785 per year), 4 teaching assistantships with tuition reimbursements (averaging $14,884 per year) were awarded.; fellowships with full tuition reimbursements, Federal Work-Study, grants, and scholarships also available. Aid available to part-time students. Financial aid applicants required to submit FAFSA. *Faculty research:* Weather, atmospheric chemistry, air pollution, global change, radiation. Total annual research expenditures: $5.9 million. *Unit head:* Dr. Russell Dickerson, Acting Chairman, 301-405-5391, Fax: 301-314-9482. *Application contact:* Trudy Lindsey, Director, Graduate Admission and Records, 301-405-4198, Fax: 301-314-9305, E-mail: grschool@deans.umd.edu.

See in-depth description on page 397.

University of Miami, Graduate School, Rosenstiel School of Marine and Atmospheric Science, Division of Meteorology and Physical Oceanography, Coral Gables, FL 33124. Offers atmospheric science (MA, MS, PhD); physical oceanography (MA, MS, PhD). *Faculty:* 18 full-time (1 woman). *Students:* 38 full-time (15 women), 1 (woman) part-time; includes 1 minority (African American), 26 international. Average age 27. 59 applicants, 22% accepted. In 1998, 3 master's, 2 doctorates awarded. Terminal master's awarded for partial completion of doctoral program. *Degree requirements:* For master's and doctorate, thesis/dissertation required, foreign language not required. *Entrance requirements:* For master's and doctorate, GRE General Test, TOEFL (minimum score of 550 required). *Average time to degree:* Master's–3 years full-time; doctorate–6 years full-time. *Application deadline:* For fall admission, 2/1 (priority date). Applications are processed on a rolling basis. Application fee: $35. Electronic applications accepted. Tuition: Full-time $15,336; part-time $852 per credit. Required fees: $174. Tuition and fees vary according to program. *Financial aid:* In 1998–99, 35 students received aid, including 1 fellowship with tuition reimbursement available, 31 research assistantships with tuition reimbursements available (averaging $17,000 per year), teaching assistantships with tuition reimbursements available (averaging $17,000 per year); institutionally-sponsored loans also available. Financial aid application deadline: 2/1. *Faculty research:* Large-scale ocean circulation, mesoscale process, climate studies. *Unit head:* Dr. Kevin R. Leaman, Chair, 305-361-4045. *Application contact:* Dr. Frank Millero, Associate Dean, 305-361-4155, Fax: 305-361-4771, E-mail: gso@rsmas.miami.edu.

Announcement: The Division emphasizes research apprenticeships in its exclusively graduate-level education program. A student-faculty ratio of about 3:2 provides ample opportunity for personal guidance. Research programs encompass satellite-based remote sensing, computer-based modeling of atmospheric and oceanic systems, and worldwide ocean observations, with ties to biology as well as to climate, providing a wide range of choices for student research specialization. MPO graduate students may focus either on diagnostic observations of environmental processes or on any part of a spectrum of theoretical or modeling problems that range from mathematical aspects of fluid mechanics to problems of physical constraints on living

Meteorology

University of Miami (continued)

systems. Financial aid is provided for all students in good academic standing, mainly as research assistantships.

University of Oklahoma, Graduate College, College of Geosciences, School of Meteorology, Norman, OK 73019-0390. Offers MS Metr, PhD. Part-time programs available. *Faculty:* 17 full-time (2 women). *Students:* 24 full-time (2 women), 55 part-time (13 women), 11 international. Average age 27. 42 applicants, 29% accepted. In 1998, 15 master's, 7 doctorates awarded. *Degree requirements:* For master's, thesis or alternative, comprehensive exam required, foreign language not required; for doctorate, one foreign language (computer language can substitute), dissertation, departmental qualifying exam required. *Entrance requirements:* For master's, GRE, TOEFL (minimum score of 550 required), bachelor's degree in related area; for doctorate, GRE, TOEFL (minimum score of 550 required). *Application deadline:* For fall admission, 2/1 (priority date). Applications are processed on a rolling basis. Application fee: $25. Tuition, state resident: part-time $86 per credit hour. Tuition, nonresident: part-time $275 per credit hour. Tuition and fees vary according to course level, course load and program. *Financial aid:* In 1998–99, 58 research assistantships, 6 teaching assistantships were awarded.; fellowships, career-related internships or fieldwork, Federal Work-Study, and institutionally-sponsored loans also available. Aid available to part-time students. Financial aid application deadline: 2/1. *Faculty research:* Atmospheric dynamics, cloud physics, climatology, synoptic and mesometeorology. *Unit head:* Dr. Frederick H. Carr, Director, 405-325-6561. *Application contact:* Dr. Brian H. Zielder, Graduate Liaison, 405-325-2860.

University of Utah, Graduate School, College of Mines and Earth Sciences, Department of Meteorology, Salt Lake City, UT 84112-1107. Offers MS, PhD. *Faculty:* 7 full-time (1 woman), 8 part-time (1 woman). *Students:* 11 full-time (2 women), 6 part-time (2 women); includes 1 minority (Asian American or Pacific Islander), 4 international. Average age 31. In 1998, 7 master's, 2 doctorates awarded. *Degree requirements:* For master's, thesis optional, foreign language not required; for doctorate, dissertation required, foreign language not required. *Entrance requirements:* For master's and doctorate, GRE General Test, TOEFL (minimum score of 500 required), minimum GPA of 3.0. *Application deadline:* For fall admission, 7/1. Application fee: $30 ($50 for international students). *Financial aid:* In 1998–99, 10 research assistantships were awarded.; teaching assistantships Financial aid application deadline: 2/15. *Faculty research:* Micrometeorology, cloud physics, air pollution, dynamical processes, satellite meteorology. *Unit head:* Dr. Jan Paegle, Acting Chair, 801-581-6136, Fax: 801-585-3681.

Yale University, Graduate School of Arts and Sciences, Department of Geology and Geophysics, New Haven, CT 06520. Offers geochemistry (PhD); geophysics (PhD); meteorology (PhD); mineralogy and crystallography (PhD); oceanography (PhD); paleoecology (PhD); paleontology and stratigraphy (PhD); petrology (PhD); structural geology (PhD). *Faculty:* 26. *Students:* 26 full-time (11 women), 9 international. *Degree requirements:* For doctorate, dissertation required, foreign language not required. *Entrance requirements:* For doctorate, GRE General Test, TOEFL. *Application deadline:* For fall admission, 1/4. Application fee: $65. *Unit head:* Chair, 203-432-3174. *Application contact:* Admissions Information, 203-432-2770.

COLUMBIA UNIVERSITY / NASA GODDARD SPACE FLIGHT CENTER'S INSTITUTE FOR SPACE STUDIES

Atmospheric and Planetary Science Program

Program of Study

The Departments of Earth and Environmental Sciences and Applied Physics jointly offer a graduate program in atmospheric and planetary science leading to the Ph.D. degree. Four to six years are generally required to complete the Ph.D., including the earning of M.A. and M.Phil. degrees. Applicants should have a strong background in physics and mathematics, including advanced undergraduate courses in mechanics, electromagnetism, advanced calculus, and differential equations.

The program is conducted in cooperation with the NASA Goddard Space Flight Center's Institute for Space Studies, which is adjacent to Columbia University. Members of the Institute hold adjunct faculty appointments, offer courses, and supervise the research of graduate students in the program. The Institute holds colloquia and scientific conferences in which the University community participates. Opportunities for visiting scientists to conduct research at the Institute are provided by postdoctoral research programs administered by the National Academy of Sciences–National Research Council and Columbia and supported by NASA.

Research at the Institute focuses on broad studies of natural and anthropogenic global changes. Areas of study include global climate, biogeochemical cycles, earth observations, planetary atmospheres, and related interdisciplinary studies. The global climate program involves basic research on climatic variations and climate processes, including the development of one-, two-, and three-dimensional numerical models to study the climatic effects of increasing carbon dioxide and other trace gases, aerosols, solar variability, and changing surface conditions. Biogeochemical cycles research utilizes three-dimensional models to study the distribution of trace gases in the troposphere and stratosphere and to examine the role of the biosphere in the global carbon cycle. The earth observations program entails research in the retrieval of cloud, aerosol, and surface radiative properties from global satellite radiance data to further understanding of their effects on climate. The planetary atmospheres program includes comparative modeling of radiative transfer and dynamics applied to Venus, Titan, Mars, and the Jovian planets; participation in spacecraft experiments; and analysis of ground-based observations. Interdisciplinary research includes studies of turbulence and solar system formation, and evolution of solar-type stars.

Research Facilities

The Institute operates a modern general-purpose scientific computing facility consisting of two IBM 4381 mainframe computers; eighty workstations, including sixty-five IBM RISC 6000, and one each of 4-, 8-, and 64-processor SGI Origin 2000 servers; one 8-processor SGI Power Challenge development server; one 12-processor SGI Power Challenge user server; and peripheral equipment. Spyglass, AVS, IDL, NCAR graphics, and in-house software permit interactive processing, display, and analysis of satellite imagery and other digital data. Daily weather maps, analyses, and satellite images are received from the National Weather Service. The Institute conducts the Photopolarimeter Radiometer experiment on the *Galileo Jupiter Orbiter* spacecraft and maintains data from the earlier Cloud Photopolarimeter experiment on the *Pioneer Venus Orbiter*. The Institute is the Global Processing Center for the International Satellite Cloud Climatology Project and the Global Aerosol Climatology Project, which use satellite observations to create a multidecadal record of cloud, aerosol, and surface variants. Institute personnel frequently collaborate with scientists at the Goddard Space Flight Center in Greenbelt, Maryland. Close research ties also exist with the Lamont-Doherty Earth Observatory of Columbia University, especially in the areas of geochemistry, oceanography, and paleoclimate studies. All facilities, including the Institute's library containing approximately 17,000 volumes, are made available to students in the program.

Financial Aid

Research assistantships are available to most students in the program. Graduate assistantships in 1999–2000 carry a twelve-month stipend of between $1450 and $1500 per month and include a tuition waiver and payment of fees.

Cost of Study

Tuition and fees for 1999–2000 are estimated at $26,180. As noted above, tuition and fees are paid for graduate students holding research assistantships.

Living and Housing Costs

Limited on-campus housing is available for single and married graduate students on 350-day contracts. Rates range from $5100 for a double room to $7500 for a single room. Studios, suites, and one-bedroom apartments range from $7200 to $11,580. Most students live off campus, many of them in apartments owned and operated by the University within a few blocks of the campus.

Student Group

Of the 18,500 students at Columbia, 3,500 are students in the Graduate School of Arts and Sciences. In 1999–2000, there are 16 Columbia students at the Institute for Space Studies, all of whom are Ph.D. candidates in the Atmospheric and Planetary Science Program. There are also 56 University and 1 National Academy of Sciences research associates in residence at the Institute.

Location

Columbia University is located in the Morningside Heights section of Manhattan in New York City. New York's climate is moderate, with average maximum and minimum temperatures of 85 and 69 degrees in July and 40 and 28 in January. New York is one of the top cultural centers in the United States and, as such, provides unrivaled opportunities for attending concerts, operas, and plays and for visiting world-renowned art, scientific, and historical museums. Student discount tickets for many musical and dramatic performances are available in the Graduate Student Lounge. A comprehensive network of public transportation alleviates the need for keeping an automobile in the city. The superb beaches of Long Island, including the Fire Island National Seashore, are within easy driving distance, as are the numerous ski slopes, state parks, and other mountain recreational areas of upstate New York and southern New England.

The University

Columbia University, founded in 1754 by royal charter of King George II of England, is a member of the Ivy League. It is the oldest institution of higher learning in New York State and the fifth-oldest in the United States. It consists of sixteen separate schools and colleges with more than 1,700 full-time faculty members.

Applying

To enter the program, an application must be submitted to one of the participating departments. Completed forms should be received by January 15 from students applying for September admission.

Correspondence and Information

Dr. Anthony D. Del Genio
Atmospheric and Planetary Science Program
Armstrong Hall—GISS
Columbia University
2880 Broadway
New York, New York 10025
Telephone: 212-678-5588
E-mail: adelgenio@giss.nasa.gov

Columbia University/NASA Goddard Space Flight Center's Institute for Space Studies

THE INSTITUTE STAFF AND THEIR RESEARCH

Michael Allison, Ph.D., Rice, 1982. Planetary atmospheric dynamics, remote sensing meteorology of Mars, Jupiter, and the outer planets.

Vittorio M. Canuto, Ph.D., Turin (Italy), 1960. Theory of fully developed turbulence, analytical models for large-scale turbulence and their applications to geophysics and astrophysics.

Barbara E. Carlson, Ph.D., SUNY at Stony Brook, 1984. Radiative transfer in planetary atmospheres, remote sensing and cloud modeling of Earth and Jovian planets.

Mark A. Chandler, Ph.D., Columbia, 1992. Paleoclimate reconstruction and modeling, role of oceans in climate change.

Anthony D. Del Genio, Ph.D., UCLA, 1978. Dynamics of planetary atmospheres, parameterization of clouds and cumulus convection, climate change, general circulation.

Leonard M. Druyan, Ph.D., NYU, 1971. Tropical climate, African climate, Sahel drought, regional climate remodeling.

James E. Hansen, Head of the Institute for Space Studies; Ph.D., Iowa, 1967. Remote sensing of Earth and planetary atmospheres, global modeling of climate processes and climate sensitivity.

Andrew A. Lacis, Ph.D., Iowa, 1970. Radiative transfer, climate modeling, remote sensing of Earth and planetary atmospheres.

Ron L. Miller, Ph.D., MIT, 1990. Tropical climate, coupled ocean-atmosphere dynamics, interannual and decadal variability.

Michael I. Mishchenko, Ph.D., Ukrainian Academy of Sciences, 1987. Radiative transfer, electromagnetic scattering, remote sensing of Earth and planetary atmospheres.

Dorothy M. Peteet, Ph.D., NYU, 1983. Paleoclimatology, palynology, ecology, botany.

Jennifer G. Phillips, Ph.D., Cornell, 1994. Soil-plant-atmosphere modeling, interannual climate variability impacts on agriculture, applications of seasonal climate forecasts to agricultural management.

David H. Rind, Ph.D., Columbia, 1976. Atmospheric and climate dynamics, stratospheric modeling and remote sensing.

Cynthia Rosenzweig, Ph.D., Massachusetts at Amherst, 1991. Parameterization of ground hydrology and biosphere, impacts of climate change on agriculture.

William B. Rossow, Ph.D., Cornell, 1976. Planetary atmospheres and climate, cloud physics and climatology, general circulation.

Gary L. Russell, Ph.D., Columbia, 1976. Numerical methods, general circulation modeling.

Gavin A. Schmidt, Ph.D., London, 1994. Physical oceanography, paleoclimate, coupled atmosphere-ocean general circulation models.

Drew T. Shindell, Ph.D., SUNY at Stony Brook, 1995. Atmospheric chemistry and climate change.

Richard B. Stothers, Ph.D., Harvard, 1964. Astronomy, climatology, geophysics, solar physics, history of science.

Larry D. Travis, Associate Chief of the Institute for Space Studies; Ph.D., Penn State, 1971. Remote sensing of Earth and planetary atmospheres, radiative transfer, numerical modeling.

Francesco N. Tubiello, Ph.D., NYU, 1995. Terrestrial carbon cycle, plant response to CO_2, impacts of climate change on agriculture.

The Institute hosts conferences and workshops that bring scientists together to discuss relevant dynamics, radiation, and chemistry issues. Conferences and workshops on satellite cloud data analysis, long-term climate monitoring, and tropospheric aerosols have been held recently.

Fossil pollen and spores obtained by coring swamp sediments are used by Institute scientists to document ancient climate changes.

Graduate students can use a variety of workstations to process and analyze visible and infrared data from earth-orbiting satellites and to conduct and view the results of global climate model simulations.

SOUTH DAKOTA SCHOOL OF MINES AND TECHNOLOGY/ SOUTH DAKOTA STATE UNIVERSITY

Joint Program in Atmospheric, Environmental, and Water Resources

Program of Study
This joint program provides Ph.D. education and degrees in the three fields of atmospheric, environmental, and water resources (AEWR). The primary departments and disciplines involved in the programs are atmospheric sciences, civil and environmental engineering (CEE), geology and geological engineering, mining engineering, and chemical engineering and chemistry at South Dakota School of Mines and Technology (SDSM&T); and CEE, agricultural engineering, chemistry, agriculture, biology, water resources, and hydrology at South Dakota State University (SDSU). Degree candidates are expected to complete an approved program of study that integrates course work from among these disciplines to provide both breadth and a focus for their research areas. A common program core is required of all students, which includes seminars taken by all students in the joint program. A modern audio/video telecommunications network is used to provide instruction from one university to the other. A minimum of 50 semester course credit hours beyond the bachelor's degree and 40 dissertation credit hours are required in the program. Entering students with an appropriate Master of Science degree are allowed to apply a maximum of 24 semester credit hours of prior course work to the Ph.D. requirement. The program includes qualifying and comprehensive examinations and a dissertation that represents the culmination of between one and two academic years of full-time research. The residence requirement is two consecutive semesters.

Research Facilities
At SDSM&T, the library has 104,000 volumes and more than 800 periodicals and is also a selective depository of U.S. government documents. The Institute of Atmospheric Sciences provides a specially instrumented, armored T-28 aircraft to collect storm data. At SDSU, the Briggs Library collections contain more than 450,000 bound volumes, 375,000 government publications, and 500,000 items in microfilm, microfiche, or microcards in addition to newspapers, maps, and pamphlet materials. More than 3,400 periodical titles are received currently. Open 98 hours per week, the library contains seating for more than 1,000 readers. A computerized system links Briggs with other major academic and research libraries nationwide.

Financial Aid
Information about aid for U.S. students is available upon request from the Financial Aid Office at each institution. Teaching and research assistantships and a few teaching associateships are available. These awards range from about $8000 to $9000 for nine months to about $16,000 for twelve months.

Cost of Study
Graduate tuition in 1999–2000 is $85.25 per semester hour for state residents and $251.45 for nonresidents. Students on an assistantship pay one third the resident tuition rate. In addition, students are assessed fees that range from $50 to $95 per credit hour, depending on the type of course. Other fees are added for a guarantee deposit, parking, late registration, and health insurance, as applicable.

Living and Housing Costs
At SDSM&T, assistance in finding off-campus rooms and apartments is available from the Director of Housing. Off-campus rooms range in cost from $75 to $100 per week. Apartments rent for a minimum of $275 per month. On-campus board is payable by the meal or is available through various plans that range from $476 to $838 per semester. When available to graduate students, dormitory rooms cost $658 per semester for double occupancy or $875 for a single room. At SDSU, assistance in finding on-campus housing (i.e., family housing, residence halls, or residence apartments) is available from the Office of Residential Life. For 1998–99, family apartments ranged in cost from $275 to $290 per month. Assistance in finding off-campus housing is available in the Off-Campus Housing Office. Students may purchase a discounted food program either at registration or at the University Food Service Office, or meals may be purchased on a walk-in basis.

Student Group
Total enrollment (primarily science and engineering) at SDSM&T is more than 2,000 students, with approximately 200 to 250 students registered in graduate programs. Of all students, 32 percent are either nonresident or international, and 32 percent are women. Total enrollment at SDSU is more than 8,000 students, making SDSU the state's largest university, with eight colleges and a fully accredited graduate school. There are about 850 students registered in graduate degree programs. Of all graduate students, 19 percent are either nonresident or international, and 49.6 percent are women.

Location
Rapid City, the home of SDSM&T, has a population of about 60,000 residents. Described as the gateway to the Black Hills, it is located a short distance from the Mount Rushmore Memorial and the White River Badlands. SDSU is located on the eastern edge of South Dakota in Brookings, a city of 16,270 residents. McCrory Gardens, the State Agricultural Heritage Museum, and the South Dakota Art Museum are located on the SDSU campus. The Brookings Art Festival, held every summer, draws thousands of people from across the United States. Climatic conditions in both locations are favorable in winter and summer for a variety of recreational activities—skiing, hunting, fishing, hiking, biking, and camping—with easy access to many area lakes, streams, and rivers.

The School and The University
In 1885, the territorial legislature established the Dakota School of Mines in Rapid City, where it served the frontier communities of the Black Hills as a mining college and prospectors' analytical laboratory. Since 1900, however, the educational emphasis at SDSM&T has shifted to include a broad spectrum of engineering and scientific disciplines. About sixty graduate degrees are awarded annually. SDSM&T is accredited by the North Central Association of Colleges and Schools. An act of the Territorial Legislature, approved in 1881, provided that an "Agricultural College for the Territory of Dakota be established at Brookings." As a land-grant university, South Dakota State University subscribes to the land-grant philosophy of education, research, and extension as its threefold mission. The main campus includes more than 109 major buildings on 282 acres. More than 200 majors, minors, and options are available, with more than 1,600 different course offerings. Students may join any of the more than 170 organizations and clubs at SDSU. Career and academic planning, counseling, health services, and legal aid are available to all students.

Applying
Applications from U.S. residents should normally be received at SDSM&T sixty days before the beginning of the semester; at SDSU, thirty days prior. International students should apply 120 days prior to their expected date of matriculation at SDSM&T. For SDSU, international students residing outside of the U.S. should apply five months prior to matriculation; students in the United States, three months prior. All applicants are required to submit GRE General Test and Subject Test scores. A minimum TOEFL score of 520 is required (560 for admission without additional English tutoring) of applicants from non-English-speaking countries.

Correspondence and Information
Program Director, AEWR Program
Graduate Education and Research Office
South Dakota School of Mines and Technology
501 East Saint Joseph Street
Rapid City, South Dakota 57701-3995

Program Director, AEWR Program
College of Engineering
South Dakota State University
P.O. Box 2219
Brookings, South Dakota 57007

South Dakota School of Mines and Technology / South Dakota State University

DEPARTMENTS AND RESEARCH AREAS

SOUTH DAKOTA SCHOOL OF MINES AND TECHNOLOGY

Institute of Atmospheric Sciences
Director: P. R. Zimmerman, Ph.D., Colorado State. Telephone: 605-394-2291.
Trace gas biogeochemistry, tropospheric chemistry, airborne measurements, atmospheric electricity, cloud physics, hailstorms, nucleation processes, mesoscale meteorology, numerical cloud modeling, radar meteorology, radiative transfer, land use and change, weather modification, climate change, hydrology.

Department of Atmospheric Sciences
Department Chair: M. R. Hjelmfelt, Ph.D., Chicago. Telephone: 605-394-2291.
Research areas are listed under the Institute of Atmospheric Sciences above.

Department of Chemical Engineering
Department Chair: M. S. McDowell, Ph.D., Iowa State. Telephone: 605-394-2421.
HPLC, NMR, FTIR, molecular modeling, biomass conversions, mining wastes characterization, hazardous waste incineration pollutants, environmental and forensic chemistries, combustion syntheses, natural products, synthetic plant growth regulators, organophosphorous chemistry, polymers and polymer/composites, kinetics and mechanisms of inorganic reactions, supermolecular assemblies, nanotechnology, supercritical fluids, process control.

Department of Civil and Environmental Engineering
Department Chair: W. H. Hovey, Ph.D., California, Davis. Telephone: 605-394-2439.
Advanced materials, environmental engineering, geotechnical engineering, hazardous waste treatment and remediation, soil mechanics and hydraulics, structural engineering, water and wastewater treatment, water resources, water quality engineering.

Department of Geology and Geological Engineering
Department Chair: J. E. Fox, Ph.D., Wyoming. Telephone: 605-394-2461.
Bioremediation, Black Hills geology, economic geology, engineering geophysics, geochemistry, geographic information systems, geohydrology, gold deposits, groundwater, igneous and metamorphic petrology, mineralogy, ore-forming systems, pegmatite petrogenesis, remote sensing, sedimentology, stratigraphy, surficial processes, tectonics, vertebrate paleontology.

Graduate Education and Research Office
Dean: S. O. Farwell, Ph.D., Montana State. Telephone: 605-394-2493.
Analytical atmospheric chemistry; tropospheric chemistry; air pollution; instrumentation for airborne sampling and measurements; calibration techniques and intercomparison experiments; biogeochemistry of S, N, and C compounds; climate change; remote sensing; land use and change; atmospheric water; statistics and sampling strategy; experimental design.

SOUTH DAKOTA STATE UNIVERSITY

Department of Agricultural Engineering
Department Head: R. Alcock, Ph.D., Reading (England). Telephone: 605-688-5141.
Machine vision, biomaterials processing, soil and water engineering, irrigation and drainage, climatology, groundwater in agriculture, structures and machine design.

Department of Civil and Environmental Engineering
Department Head: D. A. Rollag, Ph.D., Purdue. Telephone: 605-688-5427.
Structural engineering; transportation; engineering; geotechnical and geoenvironmental engineering; water resources; hydrology; hydraulics; environmental engineering; engineering mechanics; water quality; solid, hazardous, and industrial waste; water and wastewater treatment plant design; land application of wastes.

Department of Plant Science
Department Head: F. A. Cholick, Ph.D., Colorado State. Telephone: 605-688-5125.
Soil chemistry, water management, crop-water relationships, water quality, soil physics, weed science, entomology, nutrient movement in the subsurface, best management practices.

Department of Biology/Microbiology
Department Head: C. R. McMullen, Ph.D., South Dakota State. Telephone: 605-688-6141.
Ecology, environmental stress, aquatics, environmental management, industrial microbiology, wetlands.

Department of Chemistry
Department Head: L. I. Peterson, Ph.D., Yale. Telephone: 605-688-4526.
Biochemistry, physical chemistry, organic chemistry, analytical chemistry, environmental chemistry, plant biochemistry, geochemistry.

Department of Wildlife and Fisheries
Department Head: C. G. Scalet, Ph.D., Oklahoma. Telephone: 605-688-4777.
Limnology, ecology and management, aquatic ecology, wetland ecology and management, aquaculture.

Northern Great Plains Water Resources Research Center
Director: V. R. Schaefer, Ph.D., Virginia Tech. Telephone: 605-688-6252.
Artificial recharge of groundwater, numerical modeling, solid and hazardous landfill design, till hydrology, drinking water, wastewater, wetland groundwater modeling, watershed management, expert systems, statistical hydrology, animal waste lagoons.

South Dakota School of Mines and Technology / South Dakota State University

SELECTED PUBLICATIONS

Capehart, W. J., and T. N. Carlson. Decoupling of surface and near-surface soil water content: A remote sensing perspective. *Water Resources Res.* 33:1383–95, 1997.

Davis, A. D., C. J. Webb, and T. V. Durkin. A watershed approach to evaluating impacts of abandoned mines in the Bear Butte Creek basin of the Black Hills. *SME Pre-Print 97-2.* Littleton, Colo.: Society for Mining, Metallurgy, and Exploration, Inc., 1997.

Davis, A. D., and **C. J. Webb.** Ground-water flow simulations and geochemical modeling of arsenic transport in the Madison aquifer of the Black Hills. *SME Pre-Print 97-81.* Littleton, Colo.: Society for Mining, Metallurgy, and Exploration, Inc., 1997.

Davis, A. D., C. J. Paterson, and **C. J. Webb.** Comprehensive inventory of abandoned mines in the Black Hills of South Dakota. *SME Pre-Print 97-147.* Littleton, Colo.: Society for Mining, Metallurgy, and Exploration, Inc., 1997.

Davis, A. D., and P. H. Rahn. Karstie gypsum problems at wastewater stabilization sites in the Black Hills of South Dakota. *Carbonates Evaporites* 12(1):73–80, 1997.

Rahn, P. H., and **A. D. Davis.** An educational and research well field. *J. Geosci. Educ.* 44:506–17, 1996.

Davis, A. D., A. Heriba, and **C. J. Webb.** Prediction of nitrate concentrations in effluent from spent ore. *Mining Eng.* 48(2):79–83, 1996.

Davis, A. D., and G. A. Zabolotney. Ground-water flow simulations for the determination of post-mining recharge rates at the Belle Ayr Mine. *Mining Eng.* 48(11):80–3, 1996.

Rahn, P. H., and **A. D. Davis.** Gypsum foundation problems in the Black Hills area, South Dakota. *Environ. Eng. Geosci.* 2(2):213–23, 1996.

Rahn, P. H., **A. D. Davis, C. J. Webb,** and A. D. Nichols. Water quality impacts from mining in the Black Hills, South Dakota, USA. *Environ. Geology* 27(1):38–53, 1996.

Rahn, P. H., and **A. D. Davis.** Engineering geology of the central and northern Black Hills. Road Log. Field Trip 7. In *Guidebook to the Geology of the Black Hills, South Dakota, Bulletin No. 19,* pp. 38–50, eds. C. J. Paterson and J. G. Kirchner. Rapid City, S. Dak.: South Dakota School of Mines and Technology, 1996.

Bloomer, M. C., and **A. G. Detwiler.** Implications that the North Dakota Tracer Experiment of 1993 may have for the glaciogenic seeding of supercooled convective clouds to suppress hail. *J. Weather Modif.* 28:86–91, 1996.

Farwell, S. O., J. R. Burdge, and D. L. MacTaggart. Realistic detection limits from confidence bands. *J. Chem. Educ.,* in press.

Farwell, S. O., et al. A continuous monitor-sulfur chemiluminescence detector (CM-SCD) system for the measurement of total gaseous sulfur species in air. *Atmos. Environ.,* in press.

Farwell, S. O., et al. Generation and evaluation of test gas mixtures for the Gaseous Sulfur Intercomparison Experiment (GASIE). *J. Geophys. Res.* 102(D13):16237, 1997.

Farwell, S. O. *Modern Gas Chromatographic Instrumentation in Analytical Instrumentation Handbook,* 2nd edition, pp. 1205–85. New York: Marcel Dekker, Inc., 1997.

Farwell, S. O., et al. Results of the Gas-Phase Sulfur Intercomparison Experiment (GASIE): Overview of experimental setup, results, and general conclusions. *J. Geophys. Res.* 102(D13):16219, 1997.

Farwell, S. O., et al. Airborne measurements of total sulfur gases during NASA GTE/CITE 3. *J. Geophys. Res.* 100:7223, 1995.

Farwell, S. O., et al. A modified microcomputer-controlled proportioning valve instrument for programmable dilution of gases. *Instrum. Sci. Technol.* 23:277, 1995.

Farwell, S. O., J. R. Burdge, Z. Cei, and J. Papillon. A novel focusing injection technique for chemiluminescent detection of volatile sulfur compounds separated by GC. *J. High Resolution Chromatogr.* 17:1, 1994.

French, J. R., **J. H. Helsdon, A. G. Detwiler,** and **P. L. Smith.** Microphysical and electrical evolution of a Florida thunderstorm. Part 1: Observations. *J. Geophys. Res.* 101:18961–77, 1996.

Kilmowski, B. A., et al. **(M. R. Hjelmfelt** and **L. R. Johnson).** Hailstorm damage observed from the GOES-B satellite: The 05-06 July Butte-Meade Storm. *Monthly Weather Rev.* 126:352–5, 1997.

Nair, U. S., **M. R. Hjelmfelt,** and R. A. Pielke. Numerical simulation of the June 9-10, 1972 Black Hills storm using CSU RAMS. *Monthly Weather Rev.* 125:1753–66, 1997.

Orville, H. D. Comments on "Weather modification—A theoritician's viewpoint." *Bull. Am. Meteorol. Soc.* 78:2010–1, 1997.

Orville, H. D., and D. Rosenfeld. MEDREP meeting report. *Bull. Am. Meteorol. Soc.* 78:2007–9, 1997.

Dennis, A. S., and **H. D. Orville.** Comments on "A new look at the Israeli cloud seeding experiments." *J. Appl. Meteorol.* 36:277–8, 1997.

Farley, R. D., D. L. Hjermstad, and **H. D. Orville.** Numerical simulation of cloud seeding effects during a four-day storm period. *J. Weather Modif.* 29:49–55, 1997.

Orville, H. D. History of research in cloud dynamics and microphysics. *Historical Essays on Meteorology 1919–1995,* pp. 225–59, ed. J. R. Fleming. Boston: American Meteorological Society, 1996.

Orville, H. D. A review of cloud modeling in weather modification. *Bull. Am. Meteorol. Soc.* 77:1535–55, 1996.

Tanaka K. L., D. A. Senske, **M. Price,** and R. L. Kirk. Physiography, geomorphic/geologic mapping, and stratigraphy of Venus. In *Venus II-Geology, Geophysics, Atmosphere, and Solar Wind Environment,* eds. R. J. Phillips et al. Tucson, Ariz.: University of Arizona Press, 1997.

Herrick, R., and **M. Price.** It's a dry heat: The geology of Venus from Magellan. Set of 40 slides. *Lunar and Planetary Institute.* Houston, Texas, 1997.

Price, M., G. Watson, J. Suppe, and C. Brankman. Dating volcanism and rifting on Venus using impact crater densities. *J. Geophys. Res.* 101(E2):4657–71, 1996.

Price, M., and J. Suppe. Constraints on the resurfacing history of Venus from the hypsometry and distribution of tectonism, volcanism, and impact craters. *Earth Moon Planets* 71:99–145, 1995.

Price, M., and J. Suppe. Mean age of rifting and volcanism on Venus deduced from impact crater densities. *Nature* 372:756–9, 1994.

Harley, P., A. Guenther, and **P. Zimmerman.** Environmental controls over isoprene emission in deciduous oak canopies. *Tree Phys.* 17:705–14, 1997.

Singh, G. P., and **P. Zimmerman.** A new method for estimation of methane from ruminant using sulphur hexafluoride tracer technique. *Pashudhan* 12(7):50488/87. Bengalore, India: Brindavan Printers and Publishers (P) Ltd., 1997.

Darlington, J. P. E. C., and **P. Zimmerman,** et al. Production of metabolic gases by nests of the termite *Macrotermes jeanneli* in Kenya. *J. Trop. Ecol.* 13:491–510, 1996.

Greenberg, J. P., D. Helmig, and **P. Zimmerman.** Seasonal measurements of nonmethane hydrocarbon and carbon monoxide at the Mauna Loa observatory during MLOPEX II. *J. Geophys. Res.* MLOPEX2 special issue 101:14581–98, 1996.

South Dakota School of Mines and Technology / South Dakota State University

Selected Publications (continued)

Guenther, A., et al. **(P. Zimmerman).** Leaf, branch, stand and landscape scale measurements of volatile organic compound flexes from U.S. woodlands. *Tree Phys.* 16:17–24, 1996.

Guenther, A., and **P. Zimmerman,** et al. Estimates of regional natural volatile organic compound fluxes from enclosure and ambient concentrations measurements. *J. Geophys. Res.* 101:1345–59, 1996.

Guenther, A., et al. **(P. Zimmerman).** Isoprene fluxes measured by enclosure, relaxed eddy accumulation, surface gradient, mixed-layer gradient, and mixed layer mass balance techniques. *J. Geophys. Res.* 101:18555–67, 1996.

Harley, P., A. Guenther, and **P. Zimmerman.** Effects of light, temperature and canopy position on net photosynthesis and isoprene emission from leaves of sweetgum *(Liquidambar styraciflua L.)*. *Tree Phys.* 16:25–32, 1996.

Helmig, D., W. Pollack, J. Greenberg, and **P. Zimmerman.** Gas chromatography/mass spectrometry analysis of volatile organic trace gases at Mauna Loa Observatory/Hawaii. *J. Geophys. Res.* MLOPEX2 special issue 101:14697–710, 1996.

Lamb, B., et al. **(P. Zimmerman).** Evaluation of forest canopy models for estimating isoprene emissions. *J. Geophys. Res.* 101:22787–97, 1996.

STATE UNIVERSITY OF NEW YORK AT ALBANY

Department of Earth and Atmospheric Sciences

Programs of Study

The Department of Earth and Atmospheric Sciences offers programs of study leading to master's and doctoral degrees in geological sciences and atmospheric science. The areas of active research include cloud and precipitation physics, solar energy meteorology, aerosol physics, dynamical and theoretical meteorology, synoptic-scale and mesoscale meteorology, numerical weather prediction, tropical meteorology, micrometeorology, atmospheric electricity, atmospheric chemistry, environmental and climate change research, paleoceanography, geochemistry of lunar and terrestrial igneous systems, structural geology, tectonics, physical limnology, and permafrost/periglacial geomorphology.

Research Facilities

The department's research facilities include the National Lightning Detection Network; an interactive computer weather data-handling system; Fisons Instruments VG Optima stable isotope mass spectrometer; 2 Deltech furnace 1-atm, high-temperature, gas-mixing experiments; JEOL-733 electron microprobe located only 14 km from campus; and a field station at Whiteface Mountain in the Adirondacks.

Financial Aid

Fellowships and assistantships in the amounts of $12,000 to $17,000 for fall 1999 through summer 2000, inclusive, are available to students admitted to graduate study. Tuition scholarships are available for students who are receiving financial support.

Cost of Study

Resident tuition in 1999–2000 is expected to be $2550 per semester, and nonresident tuition is expected to be $4208 per semester.

Living and Housing Costs

Residence hall facilities plus meals per day are available. There is no University campus housing for married students. Off-campus accommodations include apartments renting for about $400 per month, if shared with other students.

Student Group

For the 1999–2000 academic year there are 50 full-time students in the graduate programs.

Location

The Albany area has abundant cultural and recreational opportunities. Located nearby are the Saratoga Performing Arts Center, summer home of the New York City Ballet and the Philadelphia Orchestra; Tanglewood, summer home of the Boston Symphony Orchestra; a full range of theatrical activities and concerts at the Palace Theater in Albany, Proctor's Theater in Schenectady, Troy Music Hall, and Cohoes Music Hall; and the New York State Cultural Education Center, which includes the State Museum, Convention Center, and Performing Arts Center at the Nelson A. Rockefeller Empire State Plaza in downtown Albany. The area also lends itself to winter and summer recreational activities. It is surrounded by the Berkshire, Adirondack, Helderberg, and Catskill Mountains. Historical and vacation spots within leisurely driving distance include New York City, Boston, Cape Cod, Vermont, Montreal, Lake George, and Lake Placid.

The University

The State University of New York at Albany, the oldest unit and one of four University Centers of the statewide system, is home to 585 full-time faculty members, 11,175 undergraduates, and 4,926 graduate students. It acknowledges the three traditional obligations of the University—teaching, research, and service to its community.

Applying

Applications for general admission are handled through the Office of Graduate Admissions. Applicants are required to submit scores on the General Test of the Graduate Record Examinations.

Correspondence and Information

For admission and applications:
Office of Graduate Admissions
State University of New York at Albany
1400 Washington Avenue
Albany, New York 12222
Telephone: 800-440-4723 (toll-free)
E-mail: graduate@poppa.fab.albany.edu

State University of New York at Albany

THE FACULTY AND THEIR RESEARCH

John G. Arnason, Visiting Assistant Professor; Ph.D., Stanford, 1995. Geochemistry and petrology.
Lance F. Bosart, Professor; Ph.D., MIT, 1969. Synoptic and mesoscale meteorology.
*Julius S. Chang, Senior Research Professor; Ph.D., SUNY at Stony Brook, 1971. Atmospheric chemistry, numerical modeling.
Petr Chylek, Visiting Professor; Ph.D., California, Riverside, 1970. Radiation and remote sensing.
John W. Delano, Associate Professor, Ph.D., SUNY at Stony Brook, 1977. Igneous and sedimentary geochemistry.
Kenneth L. Demerjian, Professor and Director, Atmospheric Sciences Research Center; Ph.D., Ohio State, 1973. Atmospheric chemistry.
*David R. Fitzjarrald, Senior Research Professor; Ph.D., Virginia, 1980. Boundary-layer meteorology.
Gregory D. Harper, Associate Professor, Ph.D., Berkeley, 1980. Structural geology and tectonics.
*Lee C. Harrison, Research Professor; Ph.D., Washington (Seattle), 1982. Aerosol physics.
Vincent P. Idone, Associate Professor; Ph.D., SUNY at Albany, 1982. Atmospheric electricity and physical meteorology.
Robert G. Keesee, Associate Professor; Ph.D., Colorado, 1979. Atmospheric chemistry and aerosols.
Daniel Keyser, Professor; Ph.D., Penn State, 1981. Synoptic-dynamic and mesoscale meteorology.
William S. F. Kidd, Professor, Ph.D., Cambridge, 1974. Tectonics and structural geology.
David Knight, Research Associate; Ph.D., Washington (Seattle), 1987. Mesoscale meteorology, numerical modeling.
*G. Garland Lala, Senior Research Professor; Ph.D., SUNY at Albany, 1972. Cloud and precipitation physics.
Michael G. Landin, Lecturer; M.S., SUNY at Albany, 1982. Synoptic meteorology.
Andrei G. Lapenis, Assistant Professor (joint appointment with the Department of Geography and Planning); Ph.D., State Hydrological Institute (St. Petersburg), 1986. Climate change, quaternary paleogeography, soils.
Braddock K. Linsley, Assistant Professor, Ph.D., New Mexico, 1990. Environmental geochemistry and climate change.
Arthur Z. Loesch, Professor; Ph.D., Chicago, 1973. Geophysical fluid dynamics.
Winthrop D. Means, Professor Emeritus, Ph.D., Berkeley, 1960. Structural geology.
*Joseph J. Michalsky, Research Professor; Ph.D., Kentucky, 1974. Solar radiation measurement.
Volker A. Mohnen, Professor; Ph.D., Munich, 1966. Air pollution, aerosol physics.
John E. Molinari, Professor; Ph.D., Florida State, 1979. Numerical weather prediction, tropical meteorology.
*Richard R. Perez, Research Professor; Ph.D., SUNY at Albany, 1983. Solar energy.
S. T. Rao, Research Professor; Ph.D., SUNY at Albany, 1973. Atmospheric turbulence and dispersion.
*James J. Schwab, Research Professor; Ph.D., Harvard, 1983. Atmospheric chemistry.
Jon T. Scott, Associate Professor Emeritus; Ph.D., Wisconsin–Madison, 1963. Bioclimatology, physical oceanography.
*Christopher J. Walcek, Research Professor; Ph.D., UCLA, 1983. Cloud physics, cloud chemistry.
*Wei-Chyung Wang, Senior Research Professor; D.Eng.Sc., Columbia, 1973. Global climatic change.

Special Academic and Research Facilities

An active synoptic-dynamic and mesometeorology research and teaching program is supported by a fully equipped map room, a synoptic laboratory, and interactive computer systems. Domestic and international surface and upper-air weather observations, radar data, satellite observations can be accessed, displayed, and analyzed by using the departmental computing facilities. National Weather Service conventional data and facsimile maps are also available through a DIFAX map plotter and weather data printer. Diagnostic and prognostic research investigations can also be conducted through the University VAX and IBM mainframes or by remote link to the NCAR supercomputers. Year-round forecasting is open to students to help them apply their theoretical knowledge to real-world situations. An on-campus meteorological/geophysical observatory is available for student and faculty research projects.

The department is the birthplace of the National Lightning Detection Network (NLDN). Data coverage is national, with real-time and archived NLDN data available to students for thesis research. Other lightning research opportunities exist via a substantial inventory of high-speed photographic observations of lightning.

The Atmospheric Sciences Research Center (ASRC) is a University-wide research center affiliated with the SUNY Albany campus and has close ties with the Department of Earth and Atmospheric Sciences; most of the researchers in ASRC hold joint appointments with the department. ASRC maintains a specialized field station at Whiteface Mountain, which is located in the midst of the Adirondack Mountains' high peak area. The Whiteface Mountain research observatory provides routine monitoring instrumentation for numerous atmospheric chemical and geophysical parameters.

The petrology and geochemistry of Cambro-Ordovician clastic sedimentary rocks are being studied to follow the transition from passive to active continental margin sedimentation. Volcanic ash layers of Late Orodivican age are being geochemically analyzed by X-ray fluorescence and electron microprobe. Apollo lunar samples are being analyzed for major- and trace-elements to place additional constraints on the nature of basaltic volcanism on the Moon.

Research emphasizes tectonic, structural, and petrologic studies of processes at divergent plate boundaries, focusing on ancient ocean crust (ophiolites) in California and northern Italy. Additional research involving regional geology and tectonic evolution of Jurassic rocks of the western U.S., such as ophiolite generation and emplacement as deduced from field, structural, stratigraphic, and geochronological data, is being conducted.

Research is being focused on the tectonics of continental collision, specifically the Tibetan Plateau and Himalaya using surface geological observations and thermochronological studies. Structural and tectonic research into some aspects of older collisional orogens, especially the Taconic belt of the northern Appalachians, is also an active interest.

Research involving the generation of stable isotopic and geochemical time-series data from corals and sediment cores for paleoclimatic reconstruction on time scales that range from sub-seasonal to millennia is being conducted using the mass spectrometer. This is important in understanding "base state" climatic variability. Specific research projects include developing the use of eastern and central Pacific coral skeletal oxygen isotopic ($\delta^{18}O$) composition and growth density bands as tracers of past oceanographic and climatic conditions over the last 300 years; reconstruction of late Pleistocene millennial-scale paleoclimatic variability from high accumulation rate sediments in the Sulu Sea of the tropical western Pacific.

Additional research centers on the relationship between microstructure and micromotion in deforming rocks, permitting direct observation of progressive microstructure changes and observation of the associated particle motions. Future research planned includes behavior of crystal/fluid systems and systems deforming by particulate flow and cataclasis.

Primary affiliation with the Atmospheric Sciences Research Center.

STATE UNIVERSITY OF NEW YORK AT STONY BROOK

Institute for Terrestrial and Planetary Atmospheres

Program of Study	The Institute for Terrestrial and Planetary Atmospheres conducts a teaching and research program for students interested in the physics, chemistry, and dynamics of the atmospheres of Earth and other planets. The Institute is organizationally within the Marine Sciences Research Center. Opportunities are offered by the center for research in a broad range of activities in atmospheric science and atmosphere-ocean interactions. Approximately five years are generally required to complete the Ph.D. after receiving the bachelor's degree.
	Each graduate student's program of study begins with learning the fundamental principles of atmospheric sciences through course work. At the same time, students are encouraged to join an ongoing research activity, increasing their degree of responsibility. Completion of the degree program thus entails a thorough understanding of the principles of atmospheric science and their application to significant problems.
	Research is done on a wide range of problems relating to terrestrial and planetary atmospheres. Research is carried out in state-of-the-art laboratories, by ground-based remote sensing at various locations around the earth, by analysis of conventional and satellite data, and by the development and analysis of theoretical and numerical models. Research is being performed to better understand past climate changes as well as to predict the future climate. Comprehensive data sets are analyzed as are the results of global three-dimensional climate models together with results of simplified models. Cloud-radiative effects on climate are of particular interest and are investigated in models and by analyzing satellite data from the Earth Radiation Budget Experiment. Satellite data, models, and conventional data are also analyzed to better understand the influences of latent heat release in the tropics on global climate. There is extensive activity aimed at better understanding the physical basis for predictions of the size and timing of future greenhouse warming. There are also research efforts within the Institute to understand the environmental effects on the atmosphere of current and future aircraft operations.
	Atmospheric chemistry is another area of emphasis. Experimental research has been carried out for nearly a decade using state-of-the-art remote-sensing equipment to measure stratospheric ozone and those chemicals that catalyze its destruction. Mass spectrometric measurement of the abundance of stable isotopes of atmospheric gases, including methane and carbon monoxide, are carried out to help obtain better estimates of their sources and sinks. The Institute is analyzing daily global measurements of stratospheric energetics, composition, and dynamics from NASA's Upper Atmospheric Research Satellite. The Institute is involved in continuing activity in the modeling of global tropospheric chemistry. Several faculty members are investigators on NASA's Earth Observation System, which is the most comprehensive planned international investigation of the global climate system. There is also research activity on the physics, chemistry, and evolution of terrestrial and planetary thermospheres-ionospheres, including those of Mars, Venus, and the outer planets and their satellites. Research is also carried out in a state-of-the-art infrared spectroscopy laboratory to determine those molecular parameters, such as line shape and strength, that are needed for atmospheric heating calculations as well as for remote sensing.
Research Facilities	The Institute computer facilities include DEC-based central processing capabilities, as well as workstations, printers, graphics terminals, and hard-copy plotters. The spectroscopy laboratories are equipped with infrared (grating) spectrometers, low-temperature absorption cells, a tunable diode laser spectrometer, and a high-resolution Fourier-transform spectrometer. A stable isotope mass spectrometer is the centerpiece of the atmospheric isotope laboratory. Students have access to millimeter-wave remote-sensing equipment, specially developed at Stony Brook, and to data from numerous NASA missions.
Financial Aid	Assistantships and fellowships provide a base stipend of $10,000 for the 1999–2000 academic year, depending on student status after tuition payments. In addition, summer research assistantships generally are available.
Cost of Study	The tuition fee for the 1999–2000 academic year is $5100 for residents of New York State and $8400 for out-of-state students. Miscellaneous fees, such as insurance and activity fees, total approximately $300. Tuition waivers are generally available for graduate assistants.
Living and Housing Costs	In 1999–2000, estimated living costs are approximately $500 to $900 per month for single students living on campus. Off-campus rentals in communities surrounding the Stony Brook campus are also popular with graduate students.
Student Group	At any given time, about 25 graduate students are engaged in research in atmospheric sciences in collaboration with the faculty members shown on the reverse side of this page.
Location	Stony Brook is located about 60 miles east of Manhattan on the wooded North Shore of Long Island, convenient to New York City's cultural life and Suffolk County's tranquil, recreational countryside and seashores. Long Island's hundreds of miles of magnificent coastline attract many swimming, boating, and fishing enthusiasts from around the world.
The University	Established forty years ago as New York's comprehensive State University Center for Long Island and metropolitan New York, Stony Brook offers excellent programs in a broad spectrum of academic subjects. The University conducts major research and public service projects. Over the past decade, externally funded support for Stony Brook's research programs has grown faster than that of any other university in the United States and now exceeds $110 million per year. The University's internationally renowned faculty members teach courses from the undergraduate to the doctoral level to more than 18,000 students. More than 100 undergraduate and graduate departmental and interdisciplinary majors are offered. Extensive resources and expert support services help foster intellectual and personal growth.
Applying	Students applying for graduate study should hold a B.S. degree in such fields as physics, chemistry, mathematics, engineering, or atmospheric science. Applicants may write for additional information about admission and financial aid to a graduate program faculty member whose research is of primary interest to them or write to the Institute director. Applications should be received by March 1 for September admission.
Correspondence and Information	Institute for Terrestrial and Planetary Atmospheres State University of New York at Stony Brook Stony Brook, New York 11794-5000 Telephone: 516-632-8009 Fax: 516-632-6251 E-mail: bwornow@notes.cc.sunysb.edu

State University of New York at Stony Brook

THE FACULTY AND THEIR RESEARCH

Robert D. Cess, Distinguished Professor; Ph.D., Pittsburgh, 1959. Radiative transfer and climate modeling, greenhouse effect, intercomparison of global climate models.

Brian A. Colle, Assistant Professor; Ph.D., Washington (Seattle), 1997. Synaptic meteorology, weather forecasting, mesoscale modeling.

Robert L. de Zafra, Professor (Department of Physics with joint appointment in Marine Sciences Research Center); Ph.D., Maryland, 1958. Monitoring and detection of trace gases in the terrestrial stratosphere, changes in the ozone layer, remote-sensing instrumentation.

Jane L. Fox, Professor; Ph.D., Harvard, 1978. Aeronomy of Earth and other planets, chemical and thermal structures of thermospheres and ionospheres, airglow and aurora, atmospheric evolution.

Marvin A. Geller, Professor and Dean of Marine Sciences Research Center; Ph.D., MIT, 1969. Atmospheric dynamics, stratosphere dynamics and transport, climate dynamics.

Sultan Hameed, Professor; Ph.D., Manchester (England), 1968. Analysis of climate change using observational data and climate models, interannual variations in climate, climate predictability.

John E. Mak, Assistant Professor; Ph.D., California, San Diego, 1992. Isotopic analysis of atmospheric gases.

Prasad Varanasi, Professor; Ph.D., California, San Diego, 1967. Infrared spectroscopic measurements in support of NASA's space missions, atmospheric remote sensing, greenhouse effect and climate research, molecular physics at low temperatures.

Duane E. Waliser, Assistant Professor; Ph.D., California, San Diego, 1992. Observational, numerical, and theoretical studies of ocean-atmosphere coupling.

Valery Yudin, Research Assistant Professor; Ph.D., Leningrad State (Russia), 1985. Middle- and upper-atmosphere dynamics, transport-chemistry modeling.

Minghua Zhang, Associate Professor; Ph.D., Academia Sinica (China), 1987. Atmospheric dynamics and climate modeling.

State University of New York at Stony Brook

SELECTED PUBLICATIONS

Cess, R. D., and X. Jing. Comparison of atmospheric clear-sky shortwave radiation models to collocated satellite and surface measurements. *JGR Atmos. J. Geophys. Res.* 103: 28817–24, 1998.

Cess, R. D., M. H. Zhang, et al. Comparison of the seasonal change in cloud-radiative forcing from atmospheric general circulation models and satellite observations. *J. Geophys. Res.* 102:16593–603, 1997.

Cess, R. D., M. H. Zhang, et al. Absorption of solar radiation by clouds: Interpretation of satellite, surface, and aircraft measurements. *J. Geophys. Res.* 101:23299–309, 1996.

Cess, R. D., M. H. Zhang, et al. Cloud feedback in atmospheric general circulation models: An update. *J. Geophys. Res.* 101:12791–4, 1996.

Chen, M. H., **R. D. Cess,** and **M. H. Zhang.** Effects of longwave cloud radiative forcing anomalies on the atmospheric response to equatorial Pacific sea surface temperature anomalies. *J. Geophys. Res.* 100:13791–810, 1995.

Cess, R. D., et al. Absorption of solar radiation by clouds: Observations versus models. *Science* 267:496–9, 1995.

Colle, B. A., and C. F. Mass. Windstorms along the western side of the Washington Cascade Mountains, part I: An observational and modeling study of the 12 February 1995 event. *Monthly Weather Rev.* 126:28–52, 1998.

Colle, B. A., and C. F. Mass. Windstorms along the western side of the Washington Cascade Mountains, part II: Characteristics of past events and three-dimensional idealized simulations. *Monthly Weather Rev.* 126:53–71, 1998.

Bond, N. A., et al. **(B. A. Colle).** The coastal observation and simulation with topography (COAST) experiment. *Bull. Am. Meteorol. Soc.* 78:1941–55, 1997.

Colle, B. A., and C. F. Mass. An observational and modeling study of the interaction of low-level southwesterly flow with the Olympic Mountains during COAST IOP 4. *Monthly Weather Rev.* 124:2153–75, 1996.

Colle, B. A., and C. F. Mass. Structural evolution of northerly cold surges along the eastern side of the Rocky Mountains. *Monthly Weather Rev.* 123:2577–610, 1995.

Shindell, D. T., and **R. L. de Zafra.** Limits on heterogeneous processing in the Antarctic spring vortex from a comparison of measured and modeled chlorine. *J. Geophys. Res.* 102:1441–9, 1997.

Cheng, D., et al. **(R. L. de Zafra).** Millimeter-wave spectroscopic measurements over the South Pole, 4: O_3 and N_2 during 1995 and their correlations for two quasi-annual cycles. *J. Geophys. Res.* 102:6109–16, 1997.

Cheng, D., **R. L. de Zafra,** and C. Trimble. Millimeter-wave spectroscopic measurements over the South Pole, 3: The behavior of stratospheric nitric acid through polar fall, winter, and spring. *J. Geophys. Res.* 102:1399–1410, 1997.

Shindell, D. T., and **R. L. de Zafra.** Chlorine monoxide in the Antarctic spring vortex, 2: A comparison of measured and modeled diurnal cycling over McMurdo Station, 1993. *J. Geophys. Res.* 101:1475–87, 1996.

Klein, U., S. Crewell, and **R. L. de Zafra.** Correlated millimeter-wave measurements of ClO, N_2O, and HNO_3 from McMurdo, Antarctica, during polar spring, 1995. *J. Geophys. Res.* 101:20925–32, 1996.

Cheng, D., **R. L. de Zafra,** and C. Trimble. Millimeter-wave spectroscopic measurements over the South Pole, 2: An 11-month cycle of stratospheric ozone observations during 1993–94. *J. Geophys. Res.* 101:6781–9, 1996.

Crewell, S., D. Cheng, **R. L. de Zafra,** and C. Trimble. Millimeter-wave spectroscopic measurements over the South Pole, 1: A study of stratospheric dynamics using N_2O observations. *J. Geophys. Res.* 100:20839–44, 1995.

Emmons, L. K., J. M. Reeves, D. T. Shindell, and **R. L. de Zafra.** Stratospheric ClO profiles from McMurdo Station, Antarctica, spring 1992. *J. Geophys. Res.* 100:3049–55, 1995.

Fox, J. L., and A. Hac'. $^{15}N/^{14}N$ isotope fractionation in N_2^+ dissociative recombination. *J. Geophys. Res.* 102:9191–204, 1997.

Kim, Y. H., **J. L. Fox,** and J. J. Caldwell. Temperatures and altitudes of Jupiter's ultraviolet aurora inferred from GHRS observations with the Hubble Space Telescope. *Icarus* 128:189–201, 1997.

Fox, J. L., and A. Hac'. The spectrum of hot O at the exobases of the terrestrial planets. *J. Geophys. Res.* 102:24005–11, 1997.

Fox, J. L., and R. V. Yelle. Hydrocarbon ions in the ionosphere of Titan. *Geophys. Res. Lett.* 24:2179–82, 1997.

Fox, J. L. Upper limits to the outflow of ions at Mars: Implications for atmospheric evolution. *Geophys. Res. Lett.* 24:2901–4, 1997.

Fox, J. L., and A. J. Kliore. Ionosphere: Solar activity variations. In *Venus II,* pp. 161–88, eds. S. Bougher, D. Hunten, and R. Phillips. Tucson, Ariz.: University of Arizona Press, 1997.

Fox, J. L. Aeronomy. In *Atomic, Molecular and Optical Physics Handbook,* pp. 940–68, ed. G. W. F. Drake. Woodbury, New York: American Institute of Physics Press, 1996.

Fox, J. L. Hydrocarbon ions in the ionospheres of Titan and Jupiter. In *Dissociative Recombination: Theory, Experiment and Applications,* pp. 40–6, eds. D. Zajfman, J. B. A. Mitchell, and B. Rowe. River Edge, N.J.: World Scientific Publishing Co, 1996.

Dobe, Z., A. F. Nagy, and **J. L. Fox.** A theoretical study concerning the solar cycle dependence of the nightside ionosphere of Venus. *J. Geophys. Res.* 100:14507, 1995.

Kim, Y. H., J. J. Caldwell, and **J. L. Fox.** High resolution ultraviolet spectroscopy of the Jovian aurora. *Astrophys. J.* 447:906–14, 1995.

Dvortsov, V. L., **M. A. Geller, V. A. Yudin,** and S. P. Smyshlyaev. Parameterazation of the convective transport in a two-dimensional chemistry-transport model and its validation with radon 222 and other tracer simulations. *J. Geophys. Res.* 103:22047–62, 1998.

Smyshlyaev, S. P., V. L. Dvortsov, **M. A. Geller,** and **V. A. Yudin.** A two-dimensional model with input parameters from a general circulation model: Ozone sensitivity to different formulations for the longitudinal temperature variation. *J. Geophys. Res.* 103:28373–87, 1998.

Khattatov, B. V., et al. **(M. A. Geller).** Diurnal migrating tide as seen by the high-resolution Doppler imager/UARS. 1. Monthly mean global meridional winds. *J. Geophys. Res.* 102:4405–22, 1997.

Khattatov, B. V., et al. **(M. A. Geller).** Diurnal migrating tide as seen by the high-resolution Doppler imager/UARS. 2. Monthly mean global zonal and vertical velocities, pressure, temperature, and inferred dissipation. *J. Geophys. Res.* 102:4423–35, 1997.

Geller, M. A., V. A. Yudin, B. V. Khattatov, and M. E. Hagen. Modelling the diurnal tide with dissipation derived from UARS/HRDI measurements. *Ann. Geophys.* 15:1198–1204, 1997.

Geller, M. A., W. Shen, **M. H. Zhang,** and W.-Y. Tan. Calculations of the stratospheric quasi-biennial oscillation for time-varying wave forcing. *J. Atmos. Sci.* 54:883–94, 1997.

Yudin, V. A., **M. A. Geller,** et al. A UARS study of lower stratospheric polar processing in the early stages of northern and southern winters. *J. Geophys. Res.* 102:19137–48, 1997.

Geller, M. A. Dynamics. In *Encyclopedia of Climate and Weather,* pp. 263–7, ed. S. Schneider. New York: Oxford University Press, 1996.

Shen, W., **M. A. Geller,** and **M. H. Zhang.** Generalization of the effect of vertical shear of the mean zonal flow on tropical CISK-wave excitation. *J. Atmos. Sci.* 53:2166–85, 1996.

Khattatov, B., et al. **(M. A. Geller).** Dynamics of the mesosphere and lower thermosphere as seen by MF radars and by HRDI/UARS. *J. Geophys. Res.* 101:10393–404, 1996.

Geller, M. A., et al. UARS PSC, CX1ONO₂, HCl, and ClO measurements in early winter: Additional verification of the paradigm for chlorine activation. *Geophys. Res. Lett.* 22:2937–40, 1995.

Conversi, A., and **S. Hameed.** Evidence for quasi-biennial oscillations in zooplankton biomass in the subarctic Pacific. *J. Geophys. Res.* 102:15659–65, 1997.

Hameed, S., and **M. H. Zhang.** Chaos and predictability of climate. *Int. J. Bifurcation Chaos* 7:1–10, 1997.

Christoforou, P., and **S. Hameed.** Solar cycle and the Pacific centers of action. *Geophys. Res. Lett.* 24:293–6, 1997.

Hameed, S., I. I. Pittalwala, and W. Shi. Predictability of the Icelandic low and the Azores high. In *Proceedings of the 21st Annual Climate*

State University of New York at Stony Brook

Selected Publications (continued)

Diagnostics and Prediction Workshop, pp. 304–7. Huntsville, Ala.: National Oceanic and Atmospheric Administration, 1996.

Shi, W., and **S. Hameed**. Effects of local diabatic heating on the subtropical high pressure systems. In *Proceedings of the 21st Annual Climate Diagnostics and Predictions Workshop*, pp. 308–11. Huntsville, Ala.: National Oceanic and Atmospheric Administration, 1996.

Christoforou, P., and **S. Hameed**. An attempt to predict California precipitation. In *Proceedings of the Conference on Coastal Oceanic and Atmospheric Prediction*, pp. 243–9. Atlanta: American Meteorological Society, 1996.

Hameed, S., and R. G. Currie. The discrete spectrum of observed sea level pressure variations with time scale of months to decades. In *Proceedings of the 13th Conference on Probability and Statistics in Atmospheric Sciences*, pp. 355–60. San Francisco: American Meteorological Society, 1996.

Pittalwala, I. I., and **S. Hameed**. Atmosphere-ocean interactions in the North Atlantic Ocean. In *Proceedings of the Conference on the Global Ocean-Atmosphere-Land System (GOALS)*, pp. 269–73. Atlanta: American Meteorological Society, 1996.

Hameed, S., R. G. Currie, and H. LaGrone. Signals in atmospheric pressure variations from 2 to ca. 70 months; Part I, simulations by two coupled ocean-atmospheric GCMs. *Int. J. Climatol.* 15:853–71, 1995.

Hameed, S., W. Shi, J. Boyle, and B. Santer. Investigation of the centers of action in the North Atlantic and North Pacific in the ECHAM AMIP simulation. In *Proceedings of the First International AMIP Scientific Conference*, pp. WCRP-92221–6. Monterey, Calif., 1995.

Hameed, S., and A. Conversi. Signals in the interannual variations of zooplankton mass in the Gulf of Alaska. *J. Coastal Res.* 17:21–7, 1995.

Mak, J. E., C. A. M. Brenninkmeijer, and J. Tamaresis. Atmospheric ^{14}CO observations and their use for estimating carbon monoxide removal rates. *J. Geophys. Res.* 99:22915, 1994.

Mak, J. E., and C. A. M. Brenninkmeijer. Compressed air sample technology for the isotopic analysis of atmospheric carbon monoxide. *J. Atmos. Ocean. Tech.* 11(2):425–31, 1994.

Mak, J. E., C. A. M. Brenninkmeijer, and M. R. Manning. Evidence for a missing carbon monoxide sink based on tropospheric measurement of ^{14}CO. *Geophys. Res. Lett.* 19(14):1467–70, 1992.

Mak, J. E. The isotopes of carbon monoxide in the free troposphere and their implications to atmospheric chemistry. Ph.D. Thesis, University of California, San Diego, April 1992.

Varanasi, P., and V. Nemtchinov. Thermal infrared absorption coefficients of CFC-12 at atmospheric conditions. *J. Quantum Spectrosc. Radiat. Transfer* 51:679, 1994.

Li, Z., and **P. Varanasi**. Measurement of the absorption cross-sections of CFC-11 at conditions representing various model atmospheres. *J. Quantum Spectrosc. Radiat. Transfer* 52:137, 1994.

Varanasi, P., Z. Li, V. Nemtchinov, and A. Cherukuri. Spectral absorption-coefficient data on HCFC-22 and SF_6 for remote-sensing applications. *J. Quantum Spectrosc. Radiat. Transfer* 52:323, 1994.

Varanasi, P., and A. Gopalan. Line widths of $^{14}NH_3$ and $^{15}NH_3$ applicable to planetary atmospheric observations. *J. Quantum Spectrosc. Radiat. Transfer* 49:383, 1993.

Varanasi, P., U. Shin, and A. Gopalan. Infrared spectroscopic measurements needed for atmospheric remote sensing. Optical Society of America. *Tech. Digest Ser.* 5:330–3, 1993.

Varanasi, P. Thermal infrared absorption of atmospheric radiation by water vapour and its effect on climate. In *Modern Developments in Energy, Combustion, and Spectroscopy in honor of S. S. Penner*, Chapter 11. Tarrytown, N.Y.: Pergamon Press, 1993.

Varanasi, P., V. Nemtchinov, Z. Li, and A. Cherukuri. Infrared spectroscopy of high latitude atmospheric layers. In *SPIE Proceedings of the Symposium of High Latitude Optics held in Tromso, Norway*, 1993.

Waliser, D. E., C. Jones, J. K. Schemm, and N. E. Graham. A statistical extended-range tropical forecast model based on the slow evolution of the Madden-Julian Oscillation. *J. Climate*, in press.

Waliser, D. E., K. M. Lau, and J. H. Kim. The influence of coupled sea surface temperatures on the Madden-Julian Oscillation: A model perturbation experiment. *J. Atmos. Sci.* 56:333–58, 1998.

Waliser, D. E., and W. Zhou. Removing satellite equatorial crossing time biases from the OLR and HRC data sets. *J. Climate* 10:2125–46, 1997.

Waliser, D. E. Formation and limiting mechanism for very high SST: Linking the dynamics and thermodynamics. *J. Climate* 9:161–88, 1996.

Waliser, D. E. Some considerations on the thermostat hypothesis. *Bull. Am. Met. Soc.* 77:357–60, 1996.

Waliser, D. E., W. D. Collins, and S. P. Anderson. An estimate of the surface shortwave cloud forcing over the Western Pacific during TOGA COARE. *Geophys. Res. Lett.* 23:519–22, 1996.

Waliser, D. E. Climate controls on high sea surface temperatures. *World Resource Rev.* 8:289–310, 1996.

Waliser, D. E., and R. C. J. Somerville. The preferred latitudes of the intertropical convergence zone. *J. Atmos. Sci.* 51:1619–39, 1994.

Waliser, D. E., B. Blanke, J. D. Neelin, and C. Gautier. Shortwave feedbacks and ENSO: Forced ocean and coupled ocean-atmosphere modeling experiments. *J. Geophys. Res.* 99:25109–25, 1994.

Yudin, V. A., and **M. A. Geller** et al. TMTM simulations of tides: Comparisons with UARS observations. *Geophys. Res. Lett.* 25:221–4, 1998.

Yudin, V. A., and **M. A. Geller** et al. A UARS study of lower stratospheric polar processing in the early stages of northern and southern winters. *J. Geophys. Res.* 102:19137–48, 1997.

Yudin, V. A., **M. A. Geller**, and B. V. Khattatov. Estimate of atmospheric dissipation derived from UARS/HRDI measurements. *NATO ASI Ser. I* 50:187–97, 1997.

Lin, W. Y., **M. H. Zhang**, and **M. A. Geller**. Diabatic subsidence in the subtropical upper troposphere derived from SAGE II measurements. *Geophys. Res. Lett.* 25:4181–4, 1998.

Zhang, M. H., and J. L. Lin. Constrained variational analysis of sounding data based on column-integrated budgets of mass, heat, moisture and momentum: Approach and application to ARM measurements. *J. Atmos. Sci.* 54:1503–24, 1997.

Zhang, M. H., R. D. Cess, and X. D. Jing. Concerning the interpretation of enhanced cloud shortwave absorption using monthly-mean earth radiation budget experiment/global energy balance archive measurement. *J. Geophys. Res.* 102:25899–905, 1997.

Zhang, M. H., and Q. C. Zeng. Discrete and continuous spectra of the barotropic quasi-geostrophic vorticity model, Part 1. *J. Atmos. Sci.* 54:1910–22, 1997.

Zhang, M. H., **R. D. Cess**, and S. C. Xie. Relationship between cloud radiative forcing and sea surface temperatures over the entire tropical oceans. *J. Climate* 9:1374–84, 1996.

Zhang, M. H. Implication of the convection-evaporation-wind feedback to surface climate simulation in climate models. *Climate Dynam.* 12:299–312, 1996.

Zhang, M. H., **R. D. Cess**, and S. C. Xie. Relationships between sea surface temperatures and cloud-radiative-forcings over the entire tropical oceans. *J. Climate* 9:1374–84, 1996.

Zhang, M. H., and **R. D. Cess**. How much solar radiation do clouds absorb? *Science* 271:1133–4, 1996.

Zhang, M. H. Assessment of the SAGE sampling strategy in the derivation of tropospheric water vapor in a general circulation model. *Geophys. Res. Lett.* 22:1353–6, 1995.

Zhang, M. H., **R. D. Cess**, T. Y. Kwon, and M. H. Chen. Approaches to compare clear-sky radiative fluxes from GCMs with ERBE data. *J. Geophys. Res.* 99:5515–23, 1994.

Zhang, M. H., **R. D. Cess**, J. J. Hack, and J. T. Kiehl. Diagnostic study of climate feedback processes in atmospheric general circulation models. *J. Geophys. Res.* 99:5525–37, 1994.

UNIVERSITY OF MARYLAND, COLLEGE PARK

Department of Meteorology

Programs of Study

The Department of Meteorology offers rigorous graduate study programs leading to the M.S. and Ph.D. degrees. As an integral part of their graduate education, students are expected to take an active role in one of a variety of research areas, such as biosphere-atmosphere interactions, chemistry, climate theory and modeling, cloud studies, fluid dynamics, general circulation, mesoscale modeling, numerical weather prediction, oceanography, pollution, radiation, remote sensing, and turbulence and diffusion. Interdisciplinary programs in areas such as chemical physics and applied mathematics are encouraged, as are collaborative endeavors with neighboring institutions such as the NASA Goddard Space Flight Center, National Oceanic and Atmospheric Administration (NOAA), and National Institute of Standards and Technology (NIST).

Students wishing to earn a Ph.D. are required to demonstrate an understanding of the basics of meteorology by passing (usually in the second year) a written comprehensive examination in the areas of general meteorology, dynamics, radiation, and a specialty area. To show the ability to plan and conduct original research, Ph.D. students must pass an oral defense of a research proposal and later, a final defense of the dissertation. Master's students must pass the comprehensive exam at a lower level and prepare a scholarly paper.

Research Facilities

Students and faculty members in the department enjoy access to extensive research facilities. The department operates a network of DEC and SGI workstations, with ample nodes available to students, allowing state-of-the-art computer and interactive graphics. Access to Cray supercomputers is provided by high-speed links to the San Diego Supercomputer Center, the National Center for Atmospheric Research, the NASA Goddard Space Flight Center, the National Meteorological Center, and other national facilities. The department has an instrumented weather station and is an NOAA cooperative observing station. For air chemistry, a mobile laboratory for surface measurements and an airborne setup for aircraft such as the NOAA Hurricane Hunters have been developed. The local office of the state climatologist provides an extensive data collection and research opportunities.

Financial Aid

The Department of Meteorology offers graduate research assistantships to qualified students. Additionally, the department nominates exceptionally qualified incoming students for prestigious University fellowships. The stipends given to research assistants and fellows include an additional increment to cover the full cost of tuition.

Cost of Study

Tuition for the fall 1999 semester is $272 per credit hour for Maryland residents and $400 per credit hour for nonresidents. These figures are subject to change.

Living and Housing Costs

A limited amount of space in University dormitories and apartments is available to students attending University of Maryland, College Park. Apartments off campus are plentiful; rent decreases dramatically with distance from downtown Washington.

Student Group

The department's typical graduate student enrollment is about 75, with members drawn from across the United States and many other countries. Some students are employed by one of the many nearby government agencies.

Location

Situated in the Maryland suburbs of Washington, D.C., the University is in an ideal location for interaction with the large scientific community in the area. Cooperative research agreements have been made with NOAA, NASA, and NIST, and government scientists often collaborate with students on research projects. Nearby Washington (the White House is less than 10 miles away) offers a truly international atmosphere and a rich variety of cultural and recreational opportunities, such as the Kennedy Center and the Smithsonian Institution. The University lies between the Blue Ridge Mountains (about 50 miles, or 80 kilometers, to the west) and Chesapeake Bay (about 35 miles, or 55 kilometers, to the east). Summers are warm and sometimes humid, and the winters are mild; especially pleasant weather prevails in the spring and fall. The coldest weather occurs in late January and early February, with an average daily maximum temperature of 7°C (45°F) and an average daily minimum of −2°C (28°F). The warmest time is late July, when daily high temperatures commonly exceed 30°C (86°F). Sunny weather is common the year round, with most precipitation falling in showers; thunderstorms occur on about one out of every ten days in the summer.

The University

The University of Maryland is a land-grant university, originating in 1807. The entire University system includes about 2,600 faculty members and 9,000 graduate students. The College Park campus, where the Department of Meteorology is located, is the system's flagship institution and is undergoing a period of sustained growth.

Applying

The department requires at least a bachelor's degree in meteorology, oceanography, physics, chemistry, mathematics, engineering, or another program that suitably emphasizes the physical and mathematical sciences. Previous education in meteorology is favorably considered but is not required. The application deadlines for the fall semester are May 15 for American students and February 1 for international students. The application deadlines for the spring semester are October 15 for American students and June 1 for international students. American students applying for financial aid should submit applications by the deadlines for international students.

Correspondence and Information

Chair, Admissions Committee
Department of Meteorology
University of Maryland, College Park
College Park, Maryland 20742-2425

Telephone: 301-405-5390
E-mail: metograd@deans.umd.edu
World Wide Web: http://www.meto.umd.edu

University of Maryland, College Park

THE FACULTY AND THEIR RESEARCH

Ferdinand Baer, Professor; Ph.D., Chicago. Numerical weather prediction and atmospheric modeling. (baer@atmos.umd.edu)

Ernesto H. Berbery, Assistant Research Scientist; Ph.D., Buenos Aires. Climate diagnostics. (berbery@atmos.umd.edu)

Lahouari Bounoua, Assistant Research Scientist; Ph.D., Florida State. Atmospheric radiation.

James Carton, Professor; Ph.D., Princeton. Physical oceanography, ocean atmosphere interactions. (carton@atmos.umd.edu)

David B. Considine, Assistant Research Scientist; Ph.D., Boston University. Stratospheric photochemistry and polar heterogeneous chemistry. (dbc@atmos.umd.edu)

Andrew E. Dessler, Assistant Research Scientist; Ph.D., Harvard. Stratospheric chemistry, tropospheric and stratospheric water vapor, atmospheric effects of clouds. (dessler@atmos.umd.edu)

Russell Dickerson, Professor; Ph.D., Michigan. Atmospheric chemistry and air pollution. (russ@atmos.umd.edu)

Bruce Doddridge, Associate Research Scientist; Ph.D., Adelaide. Atmospheric chemistry. (bruce@atmos.umd.edu)

Robert Ellingson, Professor and Director of the Cooperative Institute for Climate Studies; Ph.D., Florida State. Atmospheric radiation and remote sensing. (bobe@atmos.umd.edu)

Mark Fahnestock, Assistant Research Scientist; Ph.D., Caltech. Cryospheric processes. (mark@atmos.umd.edu)

Michael Fox-Rabinovitz, Senior Research Scientist; Ph.D., World Meteorological Center. Atmospheric dynamics. (foxrab@stratan.gsfc.nasa.gov)

Robert D. Hudson, Professor and Chairman; Ph.D., Reading (England). Atmospheric chemistry, satellite measurements. (hudson@atmos.umd.edu)

Istvan Laszlo, Associate Research Scientist; Ph.D., Eötvös Loránd (Budapest). Atmospheric radiation and remote sensing. (laszlo@atmos.umd.edu)

Peter Lyster, Associate Research Scientist; Ph.D., Cornell. Data assimilation modeling. (lys@dao.gsfc.nasa.gov)

Vikram Mehta, Assistant Research Scientist; Ph.D., Florida State. Atmospheric dynamics. (mehta@climate.gsfc.nasa.gov)

Ferenc Miskolczi, Assistant Research Scientist; Ph.D., Budapest. Remote sensing of atmospheric and surface parameters from space, modeling of transfer of radiation in the atmosphere. (miskolczi@atmos.umd.edu)

Raghuram Murtugudde, Assistant Research Scientist; Ph.D., Columbia. Simulation of different climate scenarios resulting from anthropogenic effects using state-of-the-art coupled biospheric atmospheric general circulation models. (ragu@atmos.umd.edu)

Sumant Nigam, Senior Research Scientist; Ph.D., Princeton. Climate dynamics, ocean-atmosphere interactions, monsoon variability. (nigam@atmos.umd.edu)

Kenneth Pickering, Associate Research Scientist; Ph.D., Maryland. Atmospheric chemistry and chemical transport meteorology. (pickering@atmos.umd.edu)

Rachel Pinker, Professor; Ph.D., Maryland. Surface-atmosphere interactions, remote sensing. (pinker@atmos.umd.edu)

Eugene Rasmusson, Senior Research Scientist; Ph.D., MIT. Diagnostic studies of short-term climate variability. (erasmu@atmos.umd.edu)

Alan Robock, Professor; Ph.D., MIT. Climate change. (alan@atmos.umd.edu)

Piers Sellers, Adjunct Professor; Ph.D., Leeds. Atmosphere-biosphere interaction. (piers@imogen.gsfc.nasa.gov)

Georgiy L. Stenchikov, Associate Research Scientist; Ph.D., Moscow Physical Technical Institute. Climate modeling, cloud modeling, air pollution and numerical methods. (gera@atmos.umd.edu)

Anne M. Thompson, Senior Research Scientist; Ph.D., Bryn Mawr. Atmospheric chemistry, remote sensing of tropical ozone, air-sea gas exchange, ozone in convective systems, prediction of tropospheric ozone changes, simulation of pre-industrial troposphere. (thompson@gator1.gsfc.nasa.gov)

Owen Thompson, Professor; Ph.D., Missouri. Satellite meteorology, remote sensing. (owen@atmos.umd.edu)

Huug van den Dool, Associate Research Scientist; Ph.D., Utrecht (Netherlands). Climate variability, climate modeling, long-range weather prediction.

Anandu Vernekar, Professor; Ph.D., Michigan. Climate modeling, general circulation, monsoon dynamics. (adv@atmos.umd.edu)

Konstantin Vinnikov, Senior Research Scientist; Ph.D., Voeikov Main Geophysical Observatory (Leningrad). Climate change. (kostya@atmos.umd.edu)

Roxana Wajsowicz, Associate Research Scientist; Ph.D., Cambridge. Physical oceanography. (roxana@atmos.umd.edu)

Liping Wang, Assistant Research Scientist; Ph.D., MIT. Ocean circulations, data analysis, theoretical modeling and numerical simulation. (lwang@atmos.umd.edu)

Lisan Yu, Assistant Research Scientist; Ph.D., Florida State. Physical oceanography, numerical modeling, data analysis and assimilation of the large-scale ocean circulations, dynamics of the tropical and midlatitude oceans. (lyu@atmos.umd.edu)

Da-Lin Zhang, Associate Professor; Ph.D., Penn State. Mesoscale meteorology, numerical weather predictions. (dalin@atmos.umd.edu)

The Inner Harbor in nearby Baltimore.

University of Maryland, College Park campus.

Historic landmark in nearby Annapolis.

University of Maryland, College Park

SELECTED PUBLICATIONS

Goyer, G. C., J. E. McDonald, **F. Baer,** and R. R. Braham. Effects of electric fields on water-droplet coalescence. *J. Meteorology* 17:442–5, 1990.

Baer, F., and J. J. Tribbia. On complete filtering of gravity of modes through nonlinear initialization. *Monthly Weather Rev.* 105:1536–9, 1977.

Baer, F. An alternate scale representation of atmospheric energy spectra. *J. Atmospheric Sci.* 29:649–64, 1972.

Berbery, E. H., E. M. Rasmusson, and K. E. Mitchell. Studies of North American continental-scale hydrology using Eta model forecast products. *J. Geophys. Res.* 101(D3):7305–19, 1996.

Berbery, E. H. Intraseasonal interactions between the tropics and extratropics in the Southern-Hemisphere. *J. Atmospheric Sci.* 50:1950–65, 1993.

Berbery, E. H., J. Nogues-Paegle, and J. Horel. Wave-like southern hemisphere extratropical teleconnections. *J. Atmospheric Sci.* 49:155–77, 1992.

Bounoua, L., and T. N. Krishnamurti. Influence of soil moisture on the Sahelian climate prediction I. *Meteorology Atmospheric Phys.* 52:183, 203, 1993.

Bounoua, L., and T. N. Krishnamurti. Influence of soil moisture on the Sahelian climate prediction II. *Meteorology Atmospheric Phys.* 52:205, 224, 1993.

Bounoua L., and T. N. Krishnamurti. Thermodynamic budget of the five wave over the Saharan Desert during summer. *Meteorology Atmospheric Phys.* 47:1, 25, 1991.

Carton, J. A., and E. J. Katz. Estimates of the zonal slope and seasonal transport of the Atlantic north equatorial countercurrent. *J. Geophys. Res.* 95:3091–100, 1990.

Robinson, A. R., **J. A. Carton,** N. Pinardi, and C. N. K. Mooers. Dynamical forecasting and dynamical interpolation: An experiment in the California current. *J. Phys. Oceanography* 16:1561–79, 1986.

Carton, J. A. The variation with frequency of the long period tides. *J. Geophys. Res.* 8:7563–72, 1983.

Chandra, S., et al. **(D. B. Considine).** Chlorine catalyzed destruction of ozone: Implications for ozone variability in the upper stratosphere. *Geophys. Res. Lett.* 20:351–4, 1993.

ben-Avraham, D., S. Redner, **D. B. Considine,** and P. Meakin. Finite-size "poisoning" in heterogeneous catalysis. *J. Phys. A: Math. Gen.* 23:L615–9, 1990.

ben-Avraham, D., **D. B. Considine,** et al. Saturation transition in a monomer-monomer model of heterogeneous catalysis. *J. Phys. A: Math. Gen.* 23:4297–312, 1990.

Salawitch, R. J., et al. **(A. E. Dessler).** The diurnal variation of hydrogen, nitrogen, and chlorine radicals: Implications for the heterogeneous production of HNO_2. *Geophys. Res. Lett.* 21:2551–4, 1994.

Salawitch, R. J., et al. **(A. E. Dessler).** The distribution of hydrogen, nitrogen, and chlorine radicals in the lower stratosphere: Implications for changes in O_3 due to emission of NO_y from supersonic aircraft. *Geophys. Res. Lett.* 21:2547–50, 1994.

Wennberg, P. O., et al. **(A. E. Dessler).** A test of modeled stratospheric Ho_x chemistry: Simultaneous measurements of OH, HO_2, O_3, and H_2O. *Geophys. Res. Lett.* 17:1909–12, 1990.

Poulida, O., et al. **(R. R. Dickerson** and **B. G. Doddridge).** Trace gas concentrations and meteorology in rural Virginia 1: Ozone and carbon monoxide. *J. Geophys. Res.* 96:22461–75, 1991.

Fehsenfeld, F. C., et al. **(R. R. Dickerson** and **K. Pickering).** A ground-based intercomparison of NO, No_x, No_y measurement techniques. *J. Geophys. Res.* 92(12):14710–22, 1987.

Dickerson, R. R., et al. **(K. Pickering).** Thunderstorm: An important mechanism in the transport of air pollutants. *Science* 235:460–5, 1987.

Chameides, W. L., et al. **(R. R. Dickerson).** No_x production in lightning. *J. Atmospheric Sci.* 34(1):143–9, 1977.

Chin, M., et al. **(B. G. Doddridge).** Relationship of ozone and carbon monoxide over North America and its implication of ozone production and transport. *J. Geophys. Res.* 99:14565–73, 1994.

Doddridge, B. G., and **R. R. Dickerson,** et al. Trace gas concentrations and meteorology in rural Virginia 2: Reactive nitrogen compound. *J. Geophys. Res.* 97:20631–46, 1992.

Luther, F. M., et al. **(R. G. Ellingson).** Intercomparison of radiation codes in climate models (ICRCCM): Longwave clear-sky results—A workshop summary. *Bull. Am. Meteorological Soc.* 69:40–8, 1988.

Ohring, G., A. Gruber, and **R. G. Ellingson.** Satellite determinations of the relationship between total longwave radiation flux and infrared window radiance. *J. Climate Appl. Meteorology* 23:416–25, 1984.

Ellingson, R. G. On the effects of cumulus dimensions on longwave irradiance and heating rate calculations. *J. Atmospheric Sci.* 39:886–96, 1982.

Fahnestock, M., R. Bindschadler, R. Kwok, and K. Jezek. Greenland ice-sheet surface-properties and ice dynamics from ERS-1 synthetic aperture radar imager. *Science* 262:1530–4, 1993.

Humprey, N., B. Kamb, **M. Fahnestock,** and H. Engelhardt. Characteristics of the bed of the Lower Columbia Glacier, Alaska. *J. Geophys. Res.–Solid Earth* 98:837–46, 1993.

Engelhardt, H., N. Humphrey, B. Kamb, and **M. Fahnestock.** Physical conditions at the base of a fast moving Antarctic ice stream. *Science* 248:57–9, 1990.

Fox-Rabinovitz, M. S., and B. D. Gross. Diabatic dynamic initialization. *Monthly Weather Rev.* 121(2):549–64, 1993.

Fox-Rabinovitz, M. S. Computational dispersion properties of horizontal staggered grids for atmospheric and ocean models. *Monthly Weather Rev.* 119(7):1624–39, 1991.

Lindzen, R. S., and **M. S. Fox-Rabinovitz.** Consistent vertical and horizontal resolution. *Monthly Weather Rev.* 117(11):2575–83, 1989.

Herman, J. R., **R. D. Hudson,** et al. A new self-calibration method applied to TOMS/SBUV backscattered ultraviolet data to determine long term global ozone change. *J. Geophys. Res.* 96:7531–45, 1991.

Frederick, J. E., and **R. D. Hudson.** Predissociation line widths and oscillator strengths for the 2-0 to 13-0 Schumann-Runge bands of O_2. *J. Mol. Spectrosc.* 74:247–58, 1979.

Hudson, R. D. Absorption cross section of stratospheric molecules. *Can. J. Chem.* 52:1465, 1974.

Kalnay, E., et al. The NCEP/NCAR 40-year reanalysis project. *Bull. Am. Meteorological Soc.* 77(3):437–71, 1996.

Toth, Z., and **E. Kalnay.** Ensemble forecasting at NMC—The generation of perturbations. *Bull. Am. Meteorological Soc.* 74(12): 2317–30, 1993.

Kalnay, E., and R. Jenne. Summary of the NMC/NCAR reanalysis workshop of April 1991. *Bull. Am. Meteorological Soc.* 72(12):1897–904, 1991.

Lyster, P. M., P. C. Liewer, R. D. Ferraro, and V. K. Decyk. Implementation and characterization of three-dimensional particle-in-cell codes on multiple-instruction-multiple-data parallel supercomputers. *Computational Phys.* 9(4):420–32, 1995.

Lyster, P. M., and R. N. Sudan. The dynamics of ion rings in highly conductive plasmas. *Phys. Fluids B* 2:2661–78, 1990.

Sudan, R. N., and **P. M. Lyster.** Injection and trapping of energetic ions in compact torus configurations. *Comments Plasma Phys. Controlled Fusion* 9:23–34, 1984.

Power, S., et al. **(V. M. Mehta).** Decadal climate variability in Australia during the 20th century. *J. Climate* 1919:169–84, 1998.

Mehta, V. M., and T. Delworth. Decadal variability of the tropical Atlantic Ocean surface temperature in shipboard measurements and in a global ocean-atmosphere model. *J. Climate* 8:172–90, 1995.

Koehler, J., G. Sofko, and **V. M. Mehta.** A statistical study of magnetic aspect effects associated with VHF auroral backscatter. *Radio Sci.* 20:689–95, 1985.

Miskolczi, F., M. Bonzagni, and R. Rizzi. High resolution atmospheric radiance-transmittance code (HARTCODE). In *Meteorology and Environmental Sciences,* pp. 743–90. World Scientific Publishing, Co., 1990.

Miskolczi, F. *Technical Report: High Resolution Atmospheric Radiance-Transmittance Code (HARTCODE),* Version 1. IMGA-CNR1-222, 1989.

Miskolczi, F., R. Rizzi, R. Guzzi, and M. Bonzagni. A new high

University of Maryland, College Park

Selected Publications (continued)

resolution transmittance code and its application in the field of remote sensing. In IRS 88: *Current Problems in Atmospheric Radiation*, pp. 388–91. A. Deepak Publishing, 1989.

Cane, M., et al. **(R. Murtugudde)**. 20th century sea surface temperature trends. *Science* 275:957–60, 1997.

Seager, R., and **R. Murtugudde**. Ocean dynamics, thermocline adjustment and regulation of tropical SST. *J. Climate* 10:521–34, 1997.

Murtugudde, R. G., R. Seager, and A. J. Busalacchi. Simulations of tropical oceans with an ocean GCM coupled to an atmospheric mixed layer model. *J. Climate* 9:1795–815, 1996.

Fennessy, M. J., et al. **(S. Nigam** and **A. D. Vernekar)**. The simulated Indian monsoon: A GCM sensitivity study. *J. Climate* 7:33–43, 1991.

Held, I. M., S. W. Lyons, and **S. Nigam**. Transients and the extratropical response to El Nino. *J. Atmospheric Sci.* 46:163–74, 1989.

Nigam, S., and R. S. Lindzen. The sensitivity of stationary waves to variations in the basic state zonal flow. *J. Atmospheric Sci.* 46:1746–68, 1989.

Lindzen, R. S., and **S. Nigam**. On the role of sea surface temperature gradients in forcing low-level winds and convergence in the tropics. *J. Atmospheric Sci.* 44:2418–36, 1987.

Pickering, K., et al. Heating, moisture and water budgets of tropical and midlatitude squall lines: Comparisons and sensitivity to longwave radiation. *J. Atmospheric Sci.* 50:673–90, 1993.

Whitlock, C. H., et al. **(R. T. Pinker** and **I. Laszlo)**. First global WCRP shortwave radiation budget dataset. *Bull. Am. Meteorological Soc.* 76(6):1–18, 1995.

Pinker, R. T., and **I. Laszlo**. Modeling surface solar irradiance for satellite applications on a global scale. *J. Appl. Meteorology* 31:192–211, 1992.

Pinker, R. T., and **I. Laszlo**. Global distribution of photosynthetically active radiation as observed from satellites. *J. Climate* 5:56–65, 1992.

Pinker, R. T., and J. A. Ewing. On the modeling of surface solar radiation: Model formulation and validation. *J. Climate Appl. Meteorology* 24:389–401, 1985.

Pinker, R. T., T. Eck, and **O. E. Thompson**. Albedo of a tropical evergreen forest. *Q. J. Roy. Meteorological Soc.* 107:551–8, 1981.

Pinker, R. T., T. Eck, and **O. E. Thompson**. The energy balance of a tropical evergreen forest. *J. Appl. Meteorology* 19:1341–50, 1980.

Pinker, R. T., **O. E. Thompson**, and T. F. Eck. The albedo of a tropical forest. *Q. J. Roy. Meteorological Soc.* 106:551–8, 1980.

Rasmusson, E. M., and J. M. Wallace. Meteorological aspects of the El Nino/Southern Oscillation. *Science* 222:1195–202, 1983.

Rasmusson, E. M., and T. H. Carpenter. Variations in tropical sea surface temperature and surface wind fields associated with the Southern Oscillation/El Nino. *Monthly Weather Rev.* 110:354–84, 1982.

Rasmusson, E. M. Atmospheric water vapor transport and the water balance of North America: Part I. Characteristics of the water vapor flux field. *Monthly Weather Rev.* 95:403–27, 1967.

Sellers, P., C. A. Kelly, J. W. M. Rudd, and A. R. MacHutchon. Photodegradation of methylmercury in lakes. *Nature* 308(6576):694–7, 1996.

Sellers, P., et al. The boreal ecosystem-atmosphere study (BOREAS): An overview and early results from the 1994 field year. *Bull. Am. Meteorological Soc.* 76(9):1549–77, 1995.

Goutorbe, J. P., et al. **(P. Sellers)**. Hapex-Sahel—A large-scale study of land-atmosphere interactions in the semiarid tropics. *Ann. Geophys.-Atmospheres Hydrospheres Space Sci.* 12(1):53–64, 1994.

Alley, R. B., et al. **(C. A. Shuman)**. Changes in continental and sea salt atmospheric loadings in central Greenland during the most recent deglaciation. *J. Glaciology* 41:139, 503–14, 1995.

Kapsner, W. R., et al. **(C. A. Shuman)**. Dominant influence of atmospheric circulation on snow accumulation in Greenland over the past 18,000 years. *Nature* 373, 6509, 52–4, 1995.

Alley, R. B., et al. **(C. A. Shuman)**. Abrupt accumulation increase at the Younger Dryas termination in the GISP2 ice core. *Nature* 362, 6420, 527–9, 1993.

Thompson, A. M. The oxidizing capacity of the Earth's atmosphere: Probable past and future changes. *Science* 256:1157–65, 1992.

Thompson, A. M., et al. **(K. Pickering** and **R. R. Dickerson)**. Convective events. *J. Geophys. Res.* 95:14049–62, 1990.

Thompson, A. M., and R. J. Cicerone. Possible perturbations to atmospheric CO, CH_4, and OH. *J. Geophys. Res.* 91:10853–64, 1986.

Thompson, A. M., and R. J. Cicerone. Clouds and wet removal as causes of variability in the trace gas composition of the marine troposphere. *J. Geophys. Res.* 87:8811–26, 1982.

Thompson, O. E., and **R. T. Pinker**. Wind and temperature profile characteristics in a tropical evergreen forest in Thailand. *Tellus* 27(6):562–73, 1975.

Vernekar, A. D., and B. Saltzman. A solution for the Northern Hemisphere climate zonation during a glacial maximum. *Quaternary Res.* 5:307–20, 1975.

Vernekar, A. D., and B. Saltzman. An equilibrium solution for the axially-symmetric component of the Earth macroclimate. *J. Geophys. Res.* 76:1498–524, 1971.

Stouffer, R. J., S. Manabe, and **K. Y. Vinnikov**. Model assessment of the role of natural variability. *Nature* 367:634–6, 1994.

Vinnikov, K. Y., P. Y. Groisman, and K. M. Lugina. Empirical data on contemporary climate change (temperature and precipitation). *J. Climate* 3:662–77, 1990.

Vinnikov, K. Y., et al. Current climate changes of the climate in the Northern Hemisphere. *Soviet Meteorology Hydrology* 6:1–10, 1980.

Wajsowicz, R. C. Free planetary waves in finite-difference numerical models. *J. Phys. Oceanography* 16:773–89, 1986.

Wajsowicz, R. C. The circulation of the depth-integrated flow around an island with application to the Indonesian throughflow. *J. Phys. Oceanography* 23:1470–84, 1993.

Wajsowicz, R. C., and A. E. Gill. Adjustment of the ocean under buoyancy forces, I: The role of Kelvin waves. *J. Phys. Oceanography* 16:2097–114, 1986.

Wang, L., and R. X. Huang. A linear homogeneous model of wind-driven circulation in a beta-plane channel. *J. Phys. Oceanography* 25:587–603, 1995.

Wang, L., and R. X. Huang. A simple model of the abyssal circulation in the circumpolar ocean. *J. Phys. Oceanography* 24:1040–58, 1994.

Wang, L., and C. Koblinsky. Influence of mid-ocean ridge on Rossby wave. *J. Geophys. Res.* 99(12):25, 143–25, 153, 1994.

Yu, L., and P. Malanotte-Rizzoli. Analysis of the North Atlantic climatologies using the combined OGCM/adjoint approach. *J. Marine Res.* 54:867–913, 1996.

Yu, L., and J. J. O'Brien. On the initial condition in parameter estimation. *J. Phys. Oceanography* 22:1361–4, 1992.

Yu, L., and J. J. O'Brien. Variational estimation of the wind stress drag coefficient and the oceanic eddy viscosity profile. *J. Phys. Oceanography* 21:709–19, 1991.

Zhang, D.-L., K. Gao, and D. B. Parsons. Numerical simulation of an intense squall line during 10–11 June 1985 PRE-STORM, Part I: Model verification. *Monthly Weather Rev.* 117:960–94, 1989.

Zhang, D.-L., and J. M. Fritsch. Numerical simulation of the meso-B scale structure and evolution of the 1977 Johnstown flood. Part I: Model description and verification. *J. Atmospheric Sci.* 43:1913–43, 1986.

Zhang, D.-L., and R. A. Anthes. A high-resolution model of the planetary boundary layer: Sensitivity tests and comparisons with SESAME-79 data. *J. Appl. Meteorology* 21:1594–609, 1982.

UNIVERSITY OF WASHINGTON

Department of Atmospheric Sciences

Programs of Study	The Department of Atmospheric Sciences offers programs of graduate study leading to the degrees of Master of Science and Doctor of Philosophy. The department also cooperates in offering studies leading to degrees of M.S. and Ph.D. under the interdepartmental Geophysics and Atmospheric Chemistry programs and under less formal arrangements with other degree-granting units on campus. The department maintains active programs in atmospheric chemistry, atmospheric dynamics, atmospheric radiation, boundary-layer processes, cloud and aerosol research, glaciology, and planetary atmospheres. Research areas of current emphasis include global climate change, stratospheric ozone depletion, acid rain, mesoscale meteorology and forecasting, ocean-atmosphere interaction, and extended-range forecasting. These research efforts employ a wide range of research methods, including laboratory experimentation, field observations using surface or airborne platforms, remote sensing from satellites, numerical modeling, and mathematical analysis. In some of these activities, there is close cooperation with the nearby Pacific Marine Environmental Laboratories at the National Oceanic and Atmospheric Administration (NOAA) Regional Center and through the Joint Institute for the Study of the Atmosphere and Ocean (JISAO).

For most students, the first year of study is devoted largely to basic courses in atmospheric sciences and mathematical methods. Virtually all students devote at least half-time to research. Research projects and graduate courses in the Department of Atmospheric Sciences are closely related, and the well-prepared graduate student may expect to begin research work rather quickly.

Research Facilities
Weather data is received from a satellite link, through the Internet national network, and from local networks. Current weather satellite pictures and DIFAX facsimile weather maps are displayed in the map room, and copies are archived for use in research. A wide array of data is available on line on workstations linked to a file server, and satellite film loops are on display. The department is a leader in the use of optical disks as high-volume weather data storage devices, and archives of past data are available on disks and on microfilm. Instruments for taking local observations and a radiosonde system for upper-air observations are maintained.

A wide range of computing resources are available. Networks of Sun and VAX workstations provide the most-used research computing environment. The networks and file servers provide access to an array of software and data storage devices within the department and are linked to supercomputer facilities at NCAR, SDSC, NCSA, and NOAA. The University also maintains an array of minicomputers and an IBM 3090 mainframe for research computing.

An instrumented Convair C 131 research aircraft; a mobile Doppler radar; and a series of cold rooms, clean rooms, and chemistry laboratories are maintained by the cloud and aerosol research group. A state-of-the-art clean room and laboratory for research on trace gases in the atmosphere has recently been completed for the air chemistry group, a joint atmospheric sciences–chemistry project.

Students in the department have access to a machine shop, two electronic laboratories, field stations, and a slow-speed wind tunnel for instrument calibration.

Financial Aid
For qualified students, the department offers research assistantships. For the 1999–2000 academic year, an assistantship pays from $17,400 to $20,085 per year, in addition to tuition.

Cost of Study
Tuition and fees are $1861 per quarter for the academic year. The department pays $1720 of this amount for research assistants, leaving $141 per quarter in fees for building and activities expenses to be paid by the student. Out-of-state tuition is waived.

Living and Housing Costs
Housing for students is available on campus through the Housing Assignment Office. In 1998–99, on-campus costs were about $700 per month, including meals. Off-campus housing arrangements were typically $350–$450 per month for group-living rentals.

Student Group
There are typically about 60 to 70 graduate students in the atmospheric sciences from a variety of disciplines: physics, chemistry, engineering, atmospheric or geophysical sciences, and applied mathematics. Opportunities are broad enough that each of these backgrounds is valuable for specific fields within the atmospheric sciences. However, students of atmospheric sciences should have in common a background in the fundamentals of physics and applied mathematics and an interest in complex natural phenomena.

Location
Seattle lies between Lake Washington and Puget Sound, with the Cascade Range to the east and the Olympic Mountains to the west. Easily accessible are skiing, boating, and hiking, in addition to fine restaurants, theaters, opera, ballet, symphony, and sports events such as can be found in a cosmopolitan area. The public transportation system is good, and there are many biking trails and parks within the city.

The University
The University of Washington was founded in 1861 and is the oldest state-assisted institution of higher education on the Pacific Coast. There are approximately 41,700 students studying in a variety of fields, including arts and sciences, business administration, engineering, and medicine; approximately 8,500 graduate students; and 1,900 faculty members. All of the major earth science disciplines are represented on campus, including the Departments of Oceanography, Geophysics, Geology, and Forestry and institutes with programs in environmental studies, quaternary sciences, and marine studies. Comprehensive intercollegiate and intramural athletics programs are offered, plus a range of musical and cultural programs. The beautiful green campus encompasses 680 acres and is bordered on the east by Lake Washington and on the south by Lake Union. The University of Washington is ranked among the top twenty universities in the United States and is an outstanding center of academic excellence in the Northwest.

Applying
Applications for admission and financial support should be sent to the address listed below. Applications for research assistantships must be submitted by February 1 for admission the following autumn quarter. The General Test of the GRE is a requirement. Students whose native language is not English must take the TOEFL.

Correspondence and Information
Academic Counselor
Department of Atmospheric Sciences, Box 351640
University of Washington
Seattle, Washington 98195
Telephone: 206-543-6471
Fax: 206-543-0308
E-mail: kathryn@atmos.washington.edu
World Wide Web: http://www.atmos.washington.edu

University of Washington

THE FACULTY AND THEIR RESEARCH

Academic Faculty

Marcia B. Baker, Professor; Ph.D., Washington (Seattle). Cloud microphysics, electrification, entrainment.

David S. Battisti, Associate Professor; Ph.D., Washington (Seattle). Large-scale atmosphere-ocean dynamics, tropical circulation, climate dynamics.

Christopher S. Bretherton, Professor; Ph.D., MIT. Role of clouds in atmospheric convection, mesoscale meteorology, climate theory.

Dale R. Durran, Professor; Ph.D., MIT. Atmospheric dynamics, mesoscale meteorology, numerical modeling.

Gregory J. Hakim, Assistant Professor; Ph.D., SUNY at Albany. Synoptic and mesoscale meteorology, atmospheric dynamics, balanced turbulence.

Dennis L. Hartmann, Professor; Ph.D., Princeton. Climate theory, dynamic meteorology, earth radiation budget.

Peter V. Hobbs, Professor; Ph.D., Imperial College (London). Aerosol/cloud/precipitation physics, atmospheric chemistry, air pollution, mesoscale meteorology.

James R. Holton, Professor and Chair; Ph.D., MIT. Dynamic meteorology, middle atmosphere meteorology.

Robert A. Houze, Professor; Ph.D., MIT. Mesoscale meteorology, cloud physics and dynamics, radar meteorology, tropical meteorology.

Conway B. Leovy, Professor; Ph.D., MIT. Planetary atmospheres, middle atmosphere meteorology, remote sensing.

Clifford F. Mass, Professor; Ph.D., Washington (Seattle). Synoptic meteorology, mesoscale meteorology.

Peter B. Rhines, Professor; Ph.D., Cambridge. Theoretical physical oceanography, geophysical fluid dynamics, general circulation of the atmosphere and ocean.

Edward S. Sarachik, Professor; Ph.D., Brandeis. Atmospheric dynamics, large-scale atmosphere-ocean interactions, greenhouse warming, equatorial dynamics, El Niño/southern oscillation, climate change.

John Michael Wallace, Professor; Ph.D., MIT. Atmospheric dynamics, large-scale motions.

Stephen G. Warren, Professor; Ph.D., Harvard. Atmospheric radiation, climatology, glaciology.

Research Faculty

Robert A. Brown, Research Professor; Ph.D., Washington (Seattle). Planetary boundary layers, air-sea interaction, turbulence, satellite remote sensing.

David S. Covert, Research Professor; Ph.D., Washington (Seattle). Aerosol instrumentation, aerosol physics and chemistry, atmospheric chemistry.

Ronald J. Ferek, Research Associate Professor; Ph.D., Florida State. Atmospheric chemistry, global tropospheric chemistry, acid precipitation.

Thomas C. Grenfell, Research Professor; Ph.D., Washington (Seattle). Atmospheric radiation, radiative transfer, microwave remote sensing, sea-ice optics, microwave theory.

Dean A. Hegg, Research Professor; Ph.D., Washington (Seattle). Atmospheric chemistry, cloud physics.

John D. Locatelli, Research Associate Professor; B.S., Washington (Seattle). Cloud and precipitation physics, synoptic and mesoscale meteorology.

Gary A. Maykut, Research Professor; Ph.D., Washington (Seattle). Polar air-sea-ice interaction, radiative transfer in ice and snow.

Bradley F. Smull, Research Associate Professor; Ph.D., Washington (Seattle). Mesoscale and radar meteorology; tropical meteorology; large-scale atmosphere-ocean interactions.

James E. Tillman, Research Professor; M.S., MIT. Mars meteorology, humidity and temperature instrumentation, planetary boundary layer.

Sandra E. Yuter, Research Assistant Professor; Ph.D., Washington (Seattle). Physical meteorology, mesoscale meteorology, radar and remote sensing.

The University of Washington campus with Mount Rainier in the background.

Aerial view of the University of Washington campus, with Lake Washington Ship Canal, Lake Union, Elliot Bay, and Puget Sound.

Section 6
Physics

This section contains a directory of institutions offering graduate work in physics, followed by in-depth entries submitted by institutions that chose to prepare detailed program descriptions. Additional information about programs listed in the directory but not augmented by an in-depth entry may be obtained by writing directly to the dean of a graduate school or chair of a department at the address given in the directory.

For programs offering related work, see all other areas in this book. In Book 3, see Biological and Biomedical Sciences and Biophysics; in Book 5, see Aerospace/Aeronautical Engineering, Electrical and Computer Engineering, Energy and Power Engineering (Nuclear Engineering), Engineering and Applied Sciences, Engineering Physics, Materials Sciences and Engineering, and Mechanical Engineering and Mechanics; and in Book 6, see Allied Health and Optometry and Vision Sciences.

CONTENTS

CONTENTS

Acoustics

The Catholic University of America, School of Engineering, Department of Mechanical Engineering, Program in Ocean and Structural Acoustics, Washington, DC 20064. Offers MME, MS Engr, PhD. Part-time and evening/weekend programs available. 1 applicants, 0% accepted. In 1998, 1 master's, 3 doctorates awarded. *Degree requirements:* For master's, comprehensive exam required, thesis optional, foreign language not required; for doctorate, dissertation, comprehensive and oral exams required, foreign language not required. *Entrance requirements:* For master's, minimum GPA of 3.0; for doctorate, minimum GPA of 3.5. *Application deadline:* For fall admission, 8/1 (priority date); for spring admission, 12/1. Applications are processed on a rolling basis. Application fee: $50. *Financial aid:* Research assistantships, teaching assistantships, career-related internships or fieldwork, Federal Work-Study, institutionally-sponsored loans, and tuition waivers (full and partial) available. Aid available to part-time students. Financial aid application deadline: 2/1. *Unit head:* Dr. John J. Gilheany, Director, 202-319-5170.

Naval Postgraduate School, Graduate Programs, Program in Engineering Acoustics, Monterey, CA 93943. Offers MS, D Eng, PhD. Program only open to commissioned officers of the United States and friendly nations and selected United States federal civilian employees. Part-time programs available. In 1998, 8 degrees awarded. *Degree requirements:* For master's, computer language, thesis required, foreign language not required; for doctorate, one foreign language, computer language, dissertation required. *Unit head:* Dr. Kevin B. Smith, Academic Committee Chairman, 831-656-2084. *Application contact:* Theodore H. Calhoon, Director of Admissions, 831-656-3093, Fax: 831-656-2891, E-mail: tcalhoon@nps.navy.mil.

Pennsylvania State University University Park Campus, Graduate School, Intercollege Graduate Programs, Intercollege Graduate Program in Acoustics, State College, University Park, PA 16802-1503. Offers M Eng, MS, PhD. *Students:* 34 full-time (7 women), 32 part-time (6 women). *Degree requirements:* For doctorate, dissertation required, foreign language not required. *Entrance requirements:* For master's and doctorate, GRE General Test. Application fee: $50. *Unit head:* Dr. Anthony Atchley, Chair, 814-865-6364.

Applied Physics

Alabama Agricultural and Mechanical University, School of Graduate Studies, School of Arts and Sciences, Department of Natural and Physical Sciences, Area in Physics, Normal, AL 35762-1357. Offers applied physics (PhD); materials science (PhD); optics (PhD); physics (MS). Part-time programs available. *Faculty:* 11 full-time (1 woman). *Students:* 15 full-time (3 women), 17 part-time (8 women); includes 22 minority (all African Americans), 7 international. *Degree requirements:* For master's, thesis optional, foreign language not required; for doctorate, computer language, dissertation required, foreign language not required. *Entrance requirements:* For master's, GRE General Test, BS in electrical engineering or physics; for doctorate, GRE General Test (minimum combined score of 1000 required). *Application deadline:* For fall admission, 5/1 (priority date). Applications are processed on a rolling basis. Application fee: $15 ($20 for international students). Tuition, state resident: full-time $1,932. Tuition, nonresident: full-time $3,864. Tuition and fees vary according to course load. *Unit head:* J. C. Wang, Chairperson, 256-851-6662.

Appalachian State University, Cratis D. Williams Graduate School, College of Arts and Sciences, Department of Physics and Astronomy, Boone, NC 28608. Offers applied physics (MS). *Faculty:* 10 full-time (3 women). *Students:* 5 full-time (2 women), 5 part-time (2 women); includes 1 minority (Asian American or Pacific Islander) 2 applicants, 50% accepted. In 1998, 4 degrees awarded (100% found work related to degree). *Degree requirements:* For master's, comprehensive exam required, thesis optional. *Entrance requirements:* For master's, GRE General Test. *Application deadline:* For fall admission, 7/15 (priority date). Application fee: $35. *Financial aid:* In 1998–99, 1 fellowship (averaging $1,000 per year), 6 research assistantships (averaging $7,000 per year) were awarded.; teaching assistantships, career-related internships or fieldwork, scholarships, and unspecified assistantships also available. Aid available to part-time students. Financial aid application deadline: 7/15; financial aid applicants required to submit FAFSA. *Faculty research:* Raman spectroscopy, applied electrostatics, scanning tunneling microscope/atomic force microscope (STM/AFM), stellar spectroscopy and photometry, surface physics, remote sensing. *Unit head:* Chairperson, 828-262-3090. *Application contact:* Dr. Sid Clements, Director, 828-262-2447, E-mail: clementsjs@appstate.edu.

Brooklyn College of the City University of New York, Division of Graduate Studies, Department of Physics, Brooklyn, NY 11210-2889. Offers applied physics (MA); physics (MA, PhD). Part-time programs available. Terminal master's awarded for partial completion of doctoral program. *Degree requirements:* For master's, comprehensive exam required; for doctorate, dissertation, comprehensive exam required, foreign language not required. *Entrance requirements:* For master's and doctorate, GRE, TOEFL (minimum score of 500 required). *Application deadline:* For fall admission, 3/1; for spring admission, 11/1. Application fee: $40. *Unit head:* Dr. Peter M. S. Lesser, Chairperson, 718-951-5418, Fax: 718-951-4407. *Application contact:* Dr. Ming Kung Liou, Graduate Deputy, 718-951-5811, Fax: 718-951-4407.

California Institute of Technology, Division of Engineering and Applied Science, Option in Applied Physics, Pasadena, CA 91125-0001. Offers applied physics (MS, PhD); plasma physics (MS, PhD). *Faculty:* 7 full-time (0 women). *Students:* 35 full-time (5 women), 16 international. 80 applicants, 6% accepted. In 1998, 9 master's, 10 doctorates awarded. *Degree requirements:* For master's, foreign language and thesis not required; for doctorate, dissertation required, foreign language not required. *Application deadline:* For fall admission, 1/15. Application fee: $0. *Financial aid:* Research assistantships, teaching assistantships available. *Faculty research:* Solid-state electronics, quantum electronics, plasmas, linear and nonlinear laser optics, electromagnetic theory. *Unit head:* Dr. Kerry F. Vahala, Representative, 626-395-2144.

Carnegie Mellon University, Mellon College of Science, Department of Physics, Pittsburgh, PA 15213-3891. Offers applied physics (PhD); physics (MS, PhD). Part-time programs available. *Faculty:* 56 full-time (3 women), 2 part-time (0 women). *Students:* 44 full-time (7 women), 3 part-time (1 woman), 28 international. Terminal master's awarded for partial completion of doctoral program. *Degree requirements:* For master's, qualifying exam required, foreign language and thesis not required; for doctorate, dissertation, qualifying exam required, foreign language not required. *Entrance requirements:* For master's, GRE General Test; for doctorate, GRE General Test (minimum combined score of 1900 on three sections required; average 2110). *Application deadline:* For fall admission, 2/1 (priority date). Applications are processed on a rolling basis. Application fee: $0. *Unit head:* Dr. Robert H. Swendsen, Head, 412-268-6681, Fax: 412-681-0648, E-mail: swendsen@andrew.cmu.edu. *Application contact:* Ned S. Vanderven, Chair of Graduate Admissions, 412-268-2766, Fax: 412-268-0648, E-mail: nsvr@andrew.cmu.edu.

See in-depth description on page 439.

Christopher Newport University, Graduate Studies, Department of Physics, Computer Science, and Engineering, Newport News, VA 23606-2998. Offers applied physics and computer science (MS). Part-time and evening/weekend programs available. *Faculty:* 14 full-time (2 women), 1 part-time (0 women). *Students:* 2 full-time (1 woman), 25 part-time (3 women); includes 5 minority (3 African Americans, 1 Asian American or Pacific Islander, 1 Hispanic American) Average age 36. In 1998, 3 degrees awarded (100% found work related to degree). *Degree requirements:* For master's, computer language, comprehensive exam required, thesis optional, foreign language not required. *Entrance requirements:* For master's, GRE, minimum GPA of 3.0. *Average time to degree:* Master's–2 years full-time, 3 years part-time. *Application deadline:* For fall admission, 7/1 (priority date); for spring admission, 12/15. Applications are processed on a rolling basis. Application fee: $40. Electronic applications accepted. Tuition, state resident: part-time $145 per credit hour. Tuition, nonresident: part-time $351 per credit hour. Required fees: $20 per year. *Financial aid:* In 1998–99, 1 research assistantship with full tuition reimbursement (averaging $5,000 per year) was awarded.; career-related internships or fieldwork and Federal Work-Study also available. Aid available to part-time students. Financial aid application deadline: 3/1; financial aid applicants required to submit FAFSA. *Faculty research:* Advanced programming methodologies, experimental nuclear physics, computer architecture, semiconductor nanophysics, laser and optical fiber sensors. *Unit head:* Dr. David Hibler, Coordinator, 757-594-7360, Fax: 757-594-7919, E-mail: dhibler@pcs.cnu.edu. *Application contact:* Gary Clark, Graduate Admissions, 757-594-7993, Fax: 757-594-7333, E-mail: admit@cnu.edu.

Colorado School of Mines, Graduate School, Department of Physics, Golden, CO 80401-1887. Offers applied physics (PhD); physics (MS). Part-time programs available. *Faculty:* 15 full-time (0 women), 7 part-time (0 women). *Students:* 19 full-time (3 women), 5 part-time (1 woman); includes 1 minority (Asian American or Pacific Islander), 10 international. *Degree requirements:* For master's, thesis required, foreign language not required; for doctorate, dissertation, oral and written comprehensive exams required, foreign language not required. *Entrance requirements:* For master's and doctorate, GRE General Test, GRE Subject Test, TOEFL, minimum GPA of 3.0, BS in physics. *Application deadline:* Applications are processed on a rolling basis. Application fee: $40. Electronic applications accepted. *Unit head:* Dr. Don Williamson, Head, 303-273-3830, E-mail: dwilliam@mines.edu. *Application contact:* Reuben Collins, Professor, 303-273-3851, Fax: 303-273-3919, E-mail: rtcollin@mines.edu.

Columbia University, Fu Foundation School of Engineering and Applied Science, Department of Applied Physics and Applied Mathematics, New York, NY 10027. Offers applied physics (MS, PhD), including applied mathematics (PhD), plasma physics (PhD), quantum electronics (PhD), solid state physics (PhD); applied physics and applied mathematics (Eng Sc D); medical physics (MS). Part-time programs available. *Faculty:* 11 full-time (0 women), 4 part-time (0 women). *Students:* 43 full-time (9 women), 16 part-time (7 women); includes 14 minority (2 African Americans, 9 Asian Americans or Pacific Islanders, 3 Hispanic Americans), 27 international. 159 applicants, 18% accepted. In 1998, 28 master's, 7 doctorates awarded (43% entered university research/teaching, 57% found other work related to degree). Terminal master's awarded for partial completion of doctoral program. *Degree requirements:* For master's, foreign language and thesis not required; for doctorate, dissertation, qualifying exam required, foreign language not required. *Entrance requirements:* For master's and doctorate, GRE General Test, GRE Subject Test (strongly recommended), TOEFL. *Application deadline:* For fall admission, 1/5; for spring admission, 10/1. Application fee: $55. *Financial aid:* In 1998–99, 40 students received aid, including 1 fellowship, 31 research assistantships, 4 teaching assistantships; Federal Work-Study and unspecified assistantships also available. Financial aid application deadline: 1/5; financial aid applicants required to submit FAFSA. Total annual research expenditures: $4.7 million. *Unit head:* Dr. Gerald A. Navratil, Chairman, 212-854-4457, E-mail: seasinfo.ap@columbia.edu.

See in-depth description on page 449.

Cornell University, Graduate School, Graduate Fields of Engineering, Field of Applied Physics, Ithaca, NY 14853-0001. Offers applied physics (PhD); engineering physics (M Eng, PhD). *Faculty:* 42 full-time. *Students:* 62 full-time (13 women); includes 6 minority (2 African Americans, 2 Asian Americans or Pacific Islanders, 2 Hispanic Americans), 20 international. 101 applicants, 55% accepted. In 1998, 8 master's, 7 doctorates awarded. *Degree requirements:* For doctorate, dissertation, oral and written exams required, foreign language not required, foreign language not required. *Entrance requirements:* For master's, TOEFL (minimum score of 550 required); for doctorate, GRE General Test, GRE Subject Test, TOEFL (minimum score of 550 required). *Application deadline:* For fall admission, 1/15. Application fee: $65. *Financial aid:* In 1998–99, 55 students received aid, including 12 fellowships with full tuition reimbursements available, 35 research assistantships with full tuition reimbursements available, 8 teaching assistantships with full tuition reimbursements available; institutionally-sponsored loans, scholarships, tuition waivers (full and partial), and unspecified assistantships also available. *Faculty research:* Quantum and nonlinear optics; plasma physics; solid state physics, condensed matter physics, and nanotechnology; condensed matter physics; biophysics; electron and x-ray spectroscopy. *Unit head:* Graduate Faculty Representative, 607-255-0638. *Application contact:* Graduate Field Assistant, 607-255-0638, E-mail: aep_info@cornell.edu.

DePaul University, College of Liberal Arts and Sciences, Department of Physics, Program in Applied Physics, Chicago, IL 60604-2287. Offers MS. *Faculty:* 7 full-time (1 woman), 3 part-time (0 women). *Students:* 4 full-time (0 women); includes 1 minority (Asian American or Pacific Islander) Average age 25. 12 applicants, 42% accepted. In 1998, 2 degrees awarded (0% continued full-time study). *Degree requirements:* For master's, thesis, oral exams required, foreign language not required. *Entrance requirements:* For master's, minimum GPA of 2.7. *Average time to degree:* Master's–2 years full-time. *Application deadline:* For fall admission, 6/15 (priority date); for spring admission, 9/1. Applications are processed on a rolling basis. Application fee: $25. *Financial aid:* Teaching assistantships available. *Faculty research:* Optics, solid-state physics, computational physics, atomic physics, laser physics. *Unit head:* Shelley Parker, Admissions Coordinator, Graduate Studies and Research, 902-494-1288, Fax: 902-494-3149, E-mail: shelley.parker@dal.ca. *Application contact:* Department Office, 773-325-7330, Fax: 773-325-7334, E-mail: cogoedde@condor.depaul.edu.

George Mason University, College of Arts and Sciences, Department of Physics, Fairfax, VA 22030-4444. Offers applied and engineering physics (MS). *Faculty:* 14 full-time (5 women), 4 part-time (1 woman). *Students:* 2 full-time (0 women), 11 part-time (4 women); includes 1 minority (Hispanic American) Average age 31. 8 applicants, 75% accepted. In 1998, 4 degrees awarded. *Degree requirements:* For master's, thesis optional. *Entrance requirements:* For master's, minimum GPA of 2.75 in last 60 hours. *Application deadline:* For fall admission, 5/1; for spring admission, 11/1. Application fee: $30. Electronic applications accepted. Tuition, state resident: full-time $4,416; part-time $184 per credit hour. Tuition, nonresident: full-time $12,516; part-time $522 per credit hour. Tuition and fees vary according to program. *Financial aid:* Research assistantships, teaching assistantships available. Aid available to part-time

Applied Physics

George Mason University *(continued)*
students. Financial aid application deadline: 3/1; financial aid applicants required to submit FAFSA. *Unit head:* Dr. Joseph Lieb, Chairman, 703-993-1280, Fax: 703-993-1269, E-mail: jlieb@osf1.gmu.edu.

Georgia Institute of Technology, Graduate Studies and Research, College of Sciences, School of Physics, Atlanta, GA 30332-0001. Offers applied physics (MSA Phy); physics (MS, MS Phys, PhD). Part-time programs available. Terminal master's awarded for partial completion of doctoral program. *Degree requirements:* For doctorate, dissertation, comprehensive exam required, foreign language not required, foreign language not required. *Entrance requirements:* For master's, TOEFL (minimum score of 600 required), minimum GPA of 3.0; for doctorate, TOEFL (minimum score of 600 required), minimum GPA of 3.4. Electronic applications accepted. *Faculty research:* Atomic and molecular physics, chemical physics, condensed matter, optics, nonlinear physics and chaos.

Harvard University, Graduate School of Arts and Sciences, Department of Physics, Cambridge, MA 02138. Offers experimental physics (AM, PhD); medical engineering/medical physics (PhD, Sc D), including applied physics (PhD), engineering sciences (PhD), medical engineering/medical physics (Sc D), physics (PhD); theoretical physics (AM, PhD). *Students:* 80 full-time (26 women). *Degree requirements:* For doctorate, dissertation, final exams, laboratory experience required, foreign language not required. *Entrance requirements:* For master's, GRE General Test, TOEFL (minimum score of 550 required); for doctorate, GRE General Test, GRE Subject Test, TOEFL (minimum score of 550 required). *Application deadline:* For fall admission, 12/14. Application fee: $60. *Unit head:* Dr. David Nelson, Chairperson, 617-495-2866. *Application contact:* Office of Admissions and Financial Aid, 617-495-5315.

See in-depth description on page 469.

Harvard University, Graduate School of Arts and Sciences, Division of Engineering and Applied Sciences, Cambridge, MA 02138. Offers applied mathematics (ME, SM, PhD); applied physics (ME, SM, PhD); computer science (ME, SM, PhD); computing technology (PhD); engineering science (ME); engineering sciences (SM, PhD); medical engineering/medical physics (PhD, Sc D), including applied physics (PhD), engineering sciences (PhD), medical engineering/medical physics (Sc D), physics (PhD). *Students:* 143 full-time (31 women); includes 10 minority (1 African American, 9 Asian Americans or Pacific Islanders), 57 international. Terminal master's awarded for partial completion of doctoral program. *Degree requirements:* For master's, foreign language and thesis not required; for doctorate, dissertation required, foreign language not required. *Entrance requirements:* For master's and doctorate, GRE General Test, GRE Subject Test, TOEFL (minimum score of 550 required). Application fee: $60. *Unit head:* Dr. Paul C. Martin, Dean, 617-495-2833. *Application contact:* Office of Admissions and Financial Aid, 617-495-5315.

Harvard University, Medical School, Division of Health Sciences and Technology, Program in Medical Engineering/Medical Physics, Cambridge, MA 02138. Offers applied physics (PhD); engineering sciences (PhD); medical engineering/medical physics (Sc D); physics (PhD). Offered jointly with Massachusetts Institute of Technology. *Degree requirements:* For doctorate, dissertation, oral and written qualifying exams required, foreign language not required.

Laurentian University, School of Graduate Studies and Research, Programme in Applied Physics, Sudbury, ON P3E 2C6, Canada. Offers M Sc. Part-time programs available. *Faculty:* 9 full-time (0 women), 9 part-time (0 women). *Students:* 9 full-time (1 woman), 1 part-time, 1 international. 6 applicants, 50% accepted. *Degree requirements:* For master's, thesis or alternative required, foreign language not required. *Entrance requirements:* For master's, honors degree with second class or better. *Application deadline:* For fall admission, 9/1. Application fee: $50. *Financial aid:* In 1998–99, 3 fellowships (averaging $2,000 per year), 6 teaching assistantships (averaging $6,500 per year) were awarded.; institutionally-sponsored loans and scholarships also available. *Faculty research:* Fibre optic sensors for underground mining applications, powder science and technology, including aerosols. Total annual research expenditures: $196,625. *Unit head:* Dr. Ian Robb, Chairman, 705-675-1151 Ext. 2230, Fax: 705-675-4868. *Application contact:* 705-675-1151 Ext. 3909, Fax: 705-675-4843.

Michigan Technological University, Graduate School, College of Sciences and Arts, Department of Physics, Houghton, MI 49931-1295. Offers applied physics (PhD); physics (MS, PhD). Part-time programs available. *Faculty:* 19 full-time (1 woman), 1 part-time (0 women). *Students:* 3 full-time (all women), 18 part-time; includes 1 minority (African American), 11 international. *Degree requirements:* For master's, thesis optional, foreign language not required; for doctorate, dissertation required, foreign language not required. *Entrance requirements:* For master's, GRE General Test, TOEFL (minimum score of 570 required), BS in physics or related area, minimum GPA of 3.0; for doctorate, GRE General Test (combined average 1816 on three sections), TOEFL (minimum score of 570 required; average 600), BS in physics or related area, minimum GPA of 3.0. *Application deadline:* For fall admission, 3/15 (priority date). Applications are processed on a rolling basis. Application fee: $30 ($35 for international students). Tuition, state resident: full-time $4,377. Tuition, nonresident: full-time $9,108. Required fees: $126. Tuition and fees vary according to course load. *Unit head:* Dr. James B. Rafert, Head, 906-487-2086, Fax: 906-487-2933, E-mail: jbrafert@mtu.edu.

See in-depth description on page 485.

New Jersey Institute of Technology, Office of Graduate Studies, Department of Physics, Program in Applied Physics, Newark, NJ 07102-1982. Offers MS, PhD. Program offered jointly with Rutgers, The State University of New Jersey, Newark. Part-time and evening/weekend programs available. Terminal master's awarded for partial completion of doctoral program. *Degree requirements:* For master's, thesis required, foreign language not required; for doctorate, dissertation, residency required, foreign language not required. *Entrance requirements:* For master's, GRE General Test (minimum score of 450 on verbal section, 600 on quantitative, 550 on analytical required); for doctorate, GRE General Test (minimum score of 450 on verbal section, 600 on quantitative, 550 on analytical required), minimum graduate GPA of 3.5. Electronic applications accepted.

Pittsburg State University, Graduate School, College of Arts and Sciences, Department of Physics, Pittsburg, KS 66762-5880. Offers applied physics (MS); physics (MS); professional physics (MS). *Students:* 2 full-time (1 woman), 1 international. *Degree requirements:* For master's, thesis or alternative required, foreign language not required. Application fee: $0 ($40 for international students). Tuition, state resident: full-time $2,466; part-time $105 per credit hour. Tuition, nonresident: full-time $6,268; part-time $264 per credit hour. *Unit head:* Dr. Charles Blatchley, Chairperson, 316-235-4398. *Application contact:* Marvene Darraugh, Administrative Officer, 316-235-4220, Fax: 316-235-4219, E-mail: mdarraug@pittstate.edu.

Princeton University, Graduate School, School of Engineering and Applied Science, Department of Mechanical and Aerospace Engineering, Princeton, NJ 08544-1019. Offers applied physics (M Eng, MSE, PhD); computational methods (M Eng, MSE); dynamics and control systems (M Eng, MSE, PhD); energy and environmental policy (M Eng, MSE, PhD); energy conversion, propulsion, and combustion (M Eng, MSE, PhD); flight science and technology (M Eng, MSE, PhD); fluid mechanics (M Eng, MSE, PhD). *Faculty:* 26 full-time (2 women). *Students:* 46 full-time (6 women); includes 5 minority (4 Asian Americans or Pacific Islanders, 1 Hispanic American), 17 international. *Degree requirements:* For master's and doctorate, thesis/dissertation required, foreign language not required. *Entrance requirements:* For master's and doctorate, GRE General Test. *Application deadline:* For fall admission, 1/3. Electronic applications accepted. *Unit head:* Prof. Richard B. Miles, Director of Graduate Studies, 609-258-4683, Fax: 609-258-6109, E-mail: maegrad@princeton.edu. *Application contact:* Etta Recke, Graduate Administrator, 609-258-4683, Fax: 609-258-6109, E-mail: etta@princeton.edu.

Rensselaer Polytechnic Institute, Graduate School, School of Science, Department of Physics, Applied Physics and Astronomy, Troy, NY 12180-3590. Offers physics (MS, PhD). Part-time programs available. *Faculty:* 19 full-time (1 woman), 2 part-time (0 women). *Students:* 53

full-time (13 women), 6 part-time; includes 2 minority (1 Asian American or Pacific Islander, 1 Hispanic American), 26 international. 87 applicants, 55% accepted. In 1998, 6 master's, 6 doctorates awarded. Terminal master's awarded for partial completion of doctoral program. *Degree requirements:* For doctorate, dissertation required, foreign language not required, foreign language not required. *Entrance requirements:* For master's and doctorate, GRE General Test, GRE Subject Test, TOEFL (minimum score of 575 required). *Application deadline:* For fall admission, 2/1 (priority date). Applications are processed on a rolling basis. Application fee: $35. *Financial aid:* In 1998–99, 56 students received aid, including 9 fellowships (averaging $11,800 per year), 22 research assistantships (averaging $11,800 per year), 25 teaching assistantships (averaging $11,800 per year); career-related internships or fieldwork and institutionally-sponsored loans also available. Financial aid application deadline: 2/1. *Faculty research:* Astrophysics, condensed matter, nuclear physics, optics, physics education. Total annual research expenditures: $2 million. *Unit head:* Dr. Leo Schowalter, Chair, 518-276-6435, Fax: 518-276-6680. *Application contact:* Dr. Gary Adams, Chair, Graduate Recruitment Committee, 518-276-8391, Fax: 518-276-6680, E-mail: fanchj@rpi.edu.

See in-depth description on page 501.

Rice University, Graduate Programs, Wiess School of Natural Sciences, Department of Physics, Applied Physics Program, Houston, TX 77251-1892. Offers MS, PhD. Offered jointly with the George R. Brown School of Engineering. *Degree requirements:* For master's and doctorate, thesis/dissertation required, foreign language not required. *Entrance requirements:* For master's, GRE General Test, GRE Subject Test (physics), TOEFL (minimum score of 550 required), minimum GPA of 3.0; for doctorate, GRE General Test (score in 70th percentile or higher required), GRE Subject Test (physics), TOEFL, minimum GPA of 3.0.

See in-depth description on page 503.

Stanford University, School of Humanities and Sciences, Department of Applied Physics, Stanford, CA 94305-9991. Offers MS, PhD. *Faculty:* 9 full-time (1 woman). *Students:* 82 full-time (10 women), 23 part-time (2 women); includes 10 minority (3 African Americans, 5 Asian Americans or Pacific Islanders, 2 Hispanic Americans), 50 international. Average age 26. 108 applicants, 31% accepted. In 1998, 10 master's, 12 doctorates awarded. Terminal master's awarded for partial completion of doctoral program. *Degree requirements:* For master's, thesis optional, foreign language not required; for doctorate, dissertation required, foreign language not required. *Entrance requirements:* For master's and doctorate, GRE General Test, GRE Subject Test, TOEFL. *Application deadline:* For fall admission, 1/1. Application fee: $65 ($80 for international students). Electronic applications accepted. Tuition: Full-time $23,058. Required fees: $152. Part-time tuition and fees vary according to course load. *Financial aid:* Fellowships, research assistantships, Federal Work-Study and institutionally-sponsored loans available. *Unit head:* Aharon Kapitulnik, Chair, 650-723-3847, Fax: 650-725-2189, E-mail: ak@loki.stanford.edu. *Application contact:* Graduate Admissions Coordinator, 650-723-4028.

State University of New York at Binghamton, Graduate School, School of Arts and Sciences, Department of Physics, Applied Physics, and Astronomy, Binghamton, NY 13902-6000. Offers applied physics (MS); physics (MA, MS). *Faculty:* 9 full-time, 2 part-time. *Students:* 9 full-time (1 woman), 1 part-time; includes 1 minority (African American), 2 international. Average age 26. 12 applicants, 58% accepted. In 1998, 1 degree awarded. *Degree requirements:* For master's, thesis or alternative required. *Entrance requirements:* For master's, GRE General Test, GRE Subject Test, TOEFL. *Application deadline:* For fall admission, 4/15 (priority date); for spring admission, 11/1. Applications are processed on a rolling basis. Application fee: $50. Electronic applications accepted. Tuition, state resident: full-time $5,100; part-time $213 per credit. Tuition, nonresident: full-time $8,416; part-time $351 per credit. Required fees: $77 per credit. Part-time tuition and fees vary according to course load. *Financial aid:* In 1998–99, 6 students received aid, including 3 research assistantships with full tuition reimbursements available (averaging $9,000 per year), 3 teaching assistantships with full tuition reimbursements available (averaging $7,600 per year); fellowships, career-related internships or fieldwork, Federal Work-Study, institutionally-sponsored loans, and unspecified assistantships also available. Aid available to part-time students. Financial aid application deadline: 2/15. *Unit head:* Dr. Robert L. Pompi, Chairperson, 607-777-2217.

Texas Tech University, Graduate School, College of Arts and Sciences, Department of Physics, Lubbock, TX 79409. Offers applied physics (MS, PhD); physics (MS, PhD). Part-time programs available. *Faculty:* 16 full-time (2 women), 1 part-time (0 women). *Students:* 30 full-time (5 women), 7 part-time (1 woman); includes 7 minority (4 Asian Americans or Pacific Islanders, 3 Hispanic Americans), 8 international. *Degree requirements:* For master's and doctorate, thesis/dissertation required. *Entrance requirements:* For master's, GRE General Test (combined average 1184); for doctorate, GRE General Test. *Application deadline:* For fall admission, 4/15 (priority date); for spring admission, 11/1 (priority date). Applications are processed on a rolling basis. Application fee: $25 ($50 for international students). Electronic applications accepted. *Unit head:* Dr. Lynn L. Hatfield, Chairman, 806-742-3767, Fax: 806-742-1182.

University of California, San Diego, Graduate Studies and Research, Department of Electrical and Computer Engineering, La Jolla, CA 92093-5003. Offers applied ocean science (MS, PhD); applied physics (MS, PhD); communication theory and systems (MS, PhD); computer engineering (MS, PhD); electrical engineering (M Eng, MS, PhD); electronic circuits and systems (MS, PhD); intelligent systems, robotics and control (MS, PhD); photonics (MS, PhD); signal and image processing (MS, PhD). *Faculty:* 35. *Students:* 251 (24 women). *Entrance requirements:* For master's and doctorate, GRE General Test. Application fee: $40. *Unit head:* William Coles, Chair. *Application contact:* Graduate Coordinator, 619-534-6606.

University of Central Oklahoma, Graduate College, College of Mathematics and Science, Department of Industrial and Applied Physics, Edmond, OK 73034-5209. Offers MS. Part-time programs available. *Faculty:* 8 full-time (0 women), 3 part-time (0 women). *Students:* 1 full-time (0 women), 4 part-time (1 woman); includes 1 minority (Asian American or Pacific Islander), 3 international. Average age 34. 1 applicants, 100% accepted. In 1998, 2 degrees awarded. *Degree requirements:* For master's, thesis optional, foreign language not required. *Entrance requirements:* For master's, 24 hours of physics course work. *Application deadline:* For fall admission, 8/23 (priority date). Applications are processed on a rolling basis. Application fee: $15. *Financial aid:* Unspecified assistantships available. Financial aid application deadline: 3/31; financial aid applicants required to submit FAFSA. *Faculty research:* Acoustics, solid-state physics/optical properties, molecular dynamics, nuclear physics, crystallography. *Unit head:* Dr. Baha Jassemnejad, Chairperson, 405-974-5461, Fax: 405-974-3824.

University of Maryland, Baltimore County, Graduate School, Department of Physics, Baltimore, MD 21250-5398. Offers applied physics (MS, PhD), including optics, solid state physics; atmospheric physics (MS, PhD). Part-time programs available. *Faculty:* 15 full-time (0 women), 4 part-time (0 women). *Students:* 18 full-time (1 woman), 3 part-time, 7 international. Terminal master's awarded for partial completion of doctoral program. *Degree requirements:* For master's, thesis optional, foreign language not required; for doctorate, dissertation required, foreign language not required. *Entrance requirements:* For master's and doctorate, GRE General Test, GRE Subject Test, TOEFL (minimum score of 600 required), minimum GPA of 3.0. *Application deadline:* For fall admission, 7/1 (priority date); for spring admission, 12/1 (priority date). Applications are processed on a rolling basis. Application fee: $45. *Unit head:* Dr. Geoffrey P. Summers, Chairman, 410-455-2513, Fax: 410-455-1072. *Application contact:* 410-455-2513, Fax: 410-455-1072, E-mail: physics@umbc.edu.

See in-depth description on page 535.

University of Massachusetts Boston, Graduate Studies, College of Arts and Sciences, Faculty of Sciences, Program in Applied Physics, Boston, MA 02125-3393. Offers MS. *Degree requirements:* For master's, thesis optional, foreign language not required. *Entrance requirements:* For master's, minimum GPA of 2.75.

University of Massachusetts Lowell, Graduate School, College of Arts and Sciences, Department of Physics and Applied Physics, Program in Applied Physics, Lowell, MA 01854-2881. Offers applied mechanics (PhD); applied physics (MS, PhD), including optical sciences (MS). Terminal master's awarded for partial completion of doctoral program. *Degree requirements:* For master's, thesis required; for doctorate, 2 foreign languages (computer language can substitute for one), dissertation required. *Entrance requirements:* For master's and doctorate, GRE General Test. *Application deadline:* For fall admission, 4/1 (priority date); for spring admission, 10/1. Applications are processed on a rolling basis. Application fee: $20 ($35 for international students). *Financial aid:* Fellowships, research assistantships, teaching assistantships, career-related internships or fieldwork, Federal Work-Study, and institutionally-sponsored loans available. Aid available to part-time students. Financial aid application deadline: 4/1. *Application contact:* Dr. Gus Couchell, Coordinator, 978-934-3772, E-mail: gus_couchell@uml.edu.

University of Michigan, Horace H. Rackham School of Graduate Studies, College of Engineering, Interdepartmental Program in Applied Physics, Ann Arbor, MI 48109. Offers PhD. *Faculty:* 30 full-time (5 women), 1 part-time (0 women). *Students:* 41 full-time (8 women); includes 19 minority (6 African Americans, 10 Asian Americans or Pacific Islanders, 3 Hispanic Americans), 9 international. Average age 23. 78 applicants, 18% accepted. In 1998, 5 degrees awarded. *Degree requirements:* For doctorate, dissertation, oral defense of dissertation, preliminary and qualifying exams required, foreign language not required. *Entrance requirements:* For doctorate, GRE General Test, GRE Subject Test (recommended). *Average time to degree:* Doctorate–5.2 years full-time. *Application deadline:* For fall admission, 2/1. Applications are processed on a rolling basis. Application fee: $55. Electronic applications accepted. *Financial aid:* In 1998–99, 12 fellowships with full tuition reimbursements, 2 research assistantships with full tuition reimbursements were awarded.; teaching assistantships with full tuition reimbursements, traineeships also available. Financial aid application deadline: 2/1; financial aid applicants required to submit FAFSA. *Faculty research:* Optical sciences, materials research, quantum structures, medical imaging, environment and science policy. Total annual research expenditures: $16 million. *Unit head:* Roy Clarke, Director, 734-936-0653. *Application contact:* Administrative Assistant, 734-936-0653, Fax: 734-764-2193, E-mail: ap.phys@umich.edu.

University of Missouri–St. Louis, Graduate School, College of Arts and Sciences, Department of Physics and Astronomy, St. Louis, MO 63121-4499. Offers applied physics (MS); astro physics (MS); physics (PhD). Part-time and evening/weekend programs available. *Faculty:* 11. *Students:* 7 full-time (0 women), 6 part-time (1 woman); includes 1 minority (Asian American or Pacific Islander), 6 international. Terminal master's awarded for partial completion of doctoral program. *Degree requirements:* For master's, thesis optional, foreign language not required; for doctorate, dissertation required, foreign language not required. *Entrance requirements:* For master's and doctorate, GRE General Test. *Application deadline:* For fall admission, 4/1 (priority date); for spring admission, 12/1 (priority date). Applications are processed on a rolling basis. Application fee: $24 ($40 for international students). Electronic applications accepted. *Unit head:* Dr. Bruce Wilking, Director of Graduate Studies, 314-516-5023, Fax: 314-516-6152, E-mail: graduate@newton.umsl.edu. *Application contact:* Graduate Admissions, 314-516-5458, Fax: 314-516-6759, E-mail: gradadm@umsl.edu.

University of New Orleans, Graduate School, College of Sciences, Department of Physics, New Orleans, LA 70148. Offers applied physics (MS); physics (MS). Part-time and evening/weekend programs available. *Faculty:* 9 full-time (1 woman). *Students:* 9 full-time (2 women), 7 part-time (2 women); includes 8 minority (6 African Americans, 1 Asian American or Pacific Islander, 1 Hispanic American), 1 international. *Degree requirements:* For master's, thesis required (for some programs), foreign language not required. *Entrance requirements:* For master's, GRE General Test (minimum combined score of 1000 required), TOEFL (minimum score of 500 required). *Application deadline:* For fall admission, 7/1 (priority date). Applications are processed on a rolling basis. Application fee: $20. Tuition, state resident: full-time $2,362. Tuition, nonresident: full-time $7,888. Part-time tuition and fees vary according to course load. *Unit head:* Dr. Milton Slaughter, Chair, 504-280-6341, Fax: 504-280-6048, E-mail: mdsph@uno.edu. *Application contact:* Dr. Ashok Puri, Graduate Coordinator, 504-280-6682, Fax: 504-280-6048, E-mail: apph@uno.edu.

University of North Carolina at Charlotte, Graduate School, College of Arts and Sciences, Department of Physics, Charlotte, NC 28223-0001. Offers applied physics (MS). *Faculty:* 17 full-time (1 woman), 1 part-time (0 women). *Students:* 6 full-time (1 woman), 6 part-time; includes 1 minority (African American), 5 international. Average age 29. 9 applicants, 89% accepted. In 1998, 3 degrees awarded. *Degree requirements:* For master's, thesis optional. *Entrance requirements:* For master's, GRE General Test, minimum GPA of 3.0 during previous 2 years, 2.75 overall. *Application deadline:* For fall admission, 7/15; for spring admission, 11/15. Applications are processed on a rolling basis. Application fee: $35. Electronic applications accepted. *Financial aid:* In 1998–99, 4 research assistantships, 11 teaching assistantships were awarded. Financial aid application deadline: 4/1. *Unit head:* Dr. Thomas Michael Corwin, Chair, Interim, 704-547-2537 Ext. 704, Fax: 704-547-3160, E-mail: mcorwin@email.uncc.edu. *Application contact:* Kathy Barringer, Assistant Director of Graduate Admissions, 704-547-3366, Fax: 704-547-3279, E-mail: gradadm@email.uncc.edu.

University of Puerto Rico, Río Piedras, Faculty of Natural Sciences, Department of Physics, San Juan, PR 00931. Offers applied physics (MS); physics (MS); physics-chemical (PhD). Part-time and evening/weekend programs available. *Faculty:* 19. *Students:* 19 full-time (4 women), 13 part-time (2 women); includes 19 minority (all Hispanic Americans), 13 international. *Degree requirements:* For master's and doctorate, one foreign language, thesis/dissertation, comprehensive exam required. *Entrance requirements:* For master's, GRE, TOEFL, interview, minimum GPA of 3.0; for doctorate, GRE, master's degree, minimum GPA of 3.0. *Application deadline:* For fall admission, 2/1. Application fee: $17. *Unit head:* Dr. Luftul Bari Bhuiyan, Coordinator of Master Program, 787-764-0000 Ext. 2307, Fax: 787-764-4063. *Application contact:* Luis F. Fonseca, Coordinator of Doctoral Program, 787-764-0000 Ext. 4773, Fax: 787-764-4063.

See in-depth description on page 563.

University of South Florida, Graduate School, College of Arts and Sciences, Department of Physics, Tampa, FL 33620-9951. Offers applied physics (MS); engineering science/physics (MS, PhD); physics (MA, MS). Part-time programs available. *Faculty:* 11 full-time (0 women), 4 part-time (0 women). *Students:* 16 full-time (3 women), 2 part-time (1 woman); includes 9 minority (2 African Americans, 6 Asian Americans or Pacific Islanders, 1 Hispanic American) *Degree requirements:* For master's, thesis optional, foreign language not required; for doctorate, 2 foreign languages (computer language can substitute for one), dissertation required. *Entrance requirements:* For master's, GRE General Test (minimum combined score of 1000 required), minimum GPA of 3.0 in last 60 hours; for doctorate, GRE General Test (minimum combined score of 1000 required), minimum graduate GPA of 3.2. *Application deadline:* For fall admission, 6/1 (priority date); for spring admission, 10/15. Applications are processed on a rolling basis. Application fee: $20. Electronic applications accepted. Tuition, state resident: part-time $148 per credit hour. Tuition, nonresident: part-time $509 per credit hour. *Unit head:* R. S. Chang, Chairperson, 813-974-2871, Fax: 813-974-5813, E-mail: chang@chuma.cas.usf.edu. *Application contact:* Pritish Mukherjee, Director, 813-974-5230, Fax: 813-974-5813, E-mail: pritish@chuma.cas.usf.edu.

University of Southwestern Louisiana, Graduate School, College of Sciences, Department of Physics, Lafayette, LA 70504. Offers applied physics (MS); physics (MS). Part-time programs available. *Faculty:* 6 full-time (0 women). *Students:* 5 full-time (2 women), 2 part-time, 1 international. *Degree requirements:* For master's, thesis required, foreign language not required. *Entrance requirements:* For master's, GRE General Test, minimum GPA of 2.75. *Application deadline:* For fall admission, 5/15. Application fee: $5 ($15 for international students). *Unit head:* Dr. John Meriwether, Head, 318-482-6691. *Application contact:* Dr. Daniel Whitmire, Graduate Coordinator, 318-482-6185.

University of Washington, Graduate School, College of Arts and Sciences, Department of Physics, Seattle, WA 98195. Offers MS, PhD. Part-time and evening/weekend programs available. *Faculty:* 64 full-time (4 women), 9 part-time (2 women). *Students:* 119 full-time (16 women), 35 part-time (3 women); includes 16 minority (1 African American, 10 Asian Americans or Pacific Islanders, 4 Hispanic Americans, 1 Native American), 38 international. Average age 30. 305 applicants, 51% accepted. In 1998, 21 master's, 2 doctorates awarded. Terminal master's awarded for partial completion of doctoral program. *Degree requirements:* For master's, foreign language and thesis not required; for doctorate, dissertation required, foreign language not required. *Entrance requirements:* For master's, GRE, TOEFL; for doctorate, GRE General Test, GRE Subject Test, TOEFL (minimum score of 580 required), minimum GPA of 3.0. *Average time to degree:* Master's–2.3 years full-time, 4.3 years part-time; doctorate–7 years full-time. *Application deadline:* For fall admission, 1/15 (priority date). Applications are processed on a rolling basis. Application fee: $50. Electronic applications accepted. Tuition, state resident: full-time $5,196; part-time $475 per credit. Tuition, nonresident: full-time $13,485; part-time $1,285 per credit. Required fees: $387; $38 per credit. Tuition and fees vary according to course load. *Financial aid:* In 1998–99, 121 students received aid, including 7 fellowships with full tuition reimbursements available (averaging $14,676 per year), 68 research assistantships with full tuition reimbursements available (averaging $15,708 per year), 41 teaching assistantships with full tuition reimbursements available (averaging $15,372 per year); Federal Work-Study also available. Financial aid application deadline: 2/15; financial aid applicants required to submit FAFSA. *Faculty research:* Astro-, atomic, condensed-matter, nuclear, and particle physics; physics education. Total annual research expenditures: $10.8 million. *Unit head:* David G. Boulware, Chairman, 206-543-2770, Fax: 206-685-0635, E-mail: dgb@phys.washington.edu. *Application contact:* Kimberly Hawley, Graduate Program Assistant, 206-543-2488, Fax: 206-685-0635, E-mail: grad@phys.washington.edu.

Virginia Commonwealth University, School of Graduate Studies, College of Humanities and Sciences, Department of Physics, Richmond, VA 23284-9005. Offers applied physics (MS); physics (MS). Part-time programs available. *Students:* 5 full-time (1 woman), 3 part-time; includes 3 minority (all Asian Americans or Pacific Islanders) *Degree requirements:* For master's, thesis required (for some programs), foreign language not required. *Entrance requirements:* For master's, GRE. *Application deadline:* For fall admission, 8/1; for spring admission, 12/1. Applications are processed on a rolling basis. Application fee: $30. Tuition, state resident: full-time $4,031; part-time $224 per credit hour. Tuition, nonresident: full-time $11,946; part-time $664 per credit hour. Required fees: $1,081; $40 per credit hour. Tuition and fees vary according to campus/location and program. *Unit head:* Dr. Robert H. Gowdy, Chair, 804-828-1821, Fax: 804-828-7073, E-mail: rgowdy@atlas.vcu.edu. *Application contact:* Marilyn F. Bishop, Graduate Program Director, 804-828-1819, Fax: 804-828-7073.

Yale University, Graduate School of Arts and Sciences, Programs in Engineering and Applied Science, Department of Applied Physics, New Haven, CT 06520. Offers MS, PhD. *Faculty:* 14 full-time (2 women). *Students:* 16 full-time (2 women); includes 1 minority (Asian American or Pacific Islander), 8 international. 36 applicants, 14% accepted. In 1998, 1 degree awarded. Terminal master's awarded for partial completion of doctoral program. *Degree requirements:* For master's, foreign language and thesis not required; for doctorate, dissertation, area exam required, foreign language not required. *Entrance requirements:* For master's and doctorate, GRE General Test, TOEFL. *Average time to degree:* Doctorate–6 years full-time. *Application deadline:* For fall admission, 1/4. Application fee: $65. *Financial aid:* Fellowships, Federal Work-Study and institutionally-sponsored loans available. Aid available to part-time students. *Unit head:* Chair, 203-432-4282. *Application contact:* Admissions Information, 203-432-2770.

Announcement: Applied physics at Yale University, a department within the Faculty of Engineering, encompasses numerous areas of theoretical and experimental condensed-matter and laser physics. Specific programs include localization, surface science, microlithography and quantum transport, optical properties of micro-objects, structural and electronic properties of complex crystals theory, MRI, and medical instrumentation. For more information, visit the Web site at http://www.eng.yale.edu/aphy.

Mathematical Physics

New Mexico Institute of Mining and Technology, Graduate Studies, Department of Physics, Socorro, NM 87801. Offers astrophysics (MS, PhD); atmospheric physics (MS, PhD); instrumentation (MS); mathematical physics (PhD). *Faculty:* 11 full-time (1 woman), 5 part-time (0 women). *Students:* 26 full-time (6 women), 8 international. *Degree requirements:* For master's and doctorate, thesis/dissertation required, foreign language not required. *Entrance requirements:* For master's, GRE General Test, TOEFL (minimum score of 540 required); for doctorate, GRE General Test, GRE Subject Test, TOEFL (minimum score of 540 required). *Application deadline:* For fall admission, 3/1 (priority date); for spring admission, 6/1. Applications are processed on a rolling basis. Application fee: $16. *Unit head:* Dr. Alan Blyth, Chairman, 505-835-5744, Fax: 505-835-5707, E-mail: blyth@kestrel.nmt.edu. *Application contact:* Dr. David B. Johnson, Dean of Graduate Studies, 505-835-5513, Fax: 505-835-5476, E-mail: graduate@nmt.edu.

Princeton University, Graduate School, Department of Mathematics, Princeton, NJ 08544-1019. Offers applied and computational mathematics (PhD); mathematical physics (PhD); mathematics (PhD). *Degree requirements:* For doctorate, dissertation required. *Entrance requirements:* For doctorate, GRE General Test, GRE Subject Test.

Princeton University, Graduate School, Department of Physics, Program in Mathematical Physics, Princeton, NJ 08544-1019. Offers PhD. *Degree requirements:* For doctorate, dissertation required. *Entrance requirements:* For doctorate, GRE General Test, GRE Subject Test.

University of Alberta, Faculty of Graduate Studies and Research, Department of Mathematical Sciences, Edmonton, AB T6G 2E1, Canada. Offers applied mathematics (M Sc, PhD); mathematical finance (M Sc); mathematical physics (M Sc, PhD); mathematics (M Sc, PhD); statistics (M Sc, PhD, Postgraduate Diploma). Part-time programs available. Terminal master's awarded for partial completion of doctoral program. *Degree requirements:* For master's, thesis required (for some programs), foreign language not required; for doctorate, dissertation required, foreign language not required. *Faculty research:* Classical and functional analysis, algebra, differential equations, geometry.

Mathematical Physics–Optical Sciences

University of Colorado at Boulder, Graduate School, College of Arts and Sciences, Department of Physics, Boulder, CO 80309. Offers chemical physics (PhD); geophysics (PhD); mathematical physics (PhD); medical physics (PhD); physics (MS, PhD). Terminal master's awarded for partial completion of doctoral program. *Degree requirements:* For master's, thesis or alternative, comprehensive exam required, foreign language not required; for doctorate, dissertation, comprehensive exam required. *Entrance requirements:* For master's, GRE General Test, GRE Subject Test, TOEFL (minimum score of 575 required), minimum undergraduate GPA of 3.0; for doctorate, GRE General Test, GRE Subject Test, TOEFL (minimum score of 575 required).

Virginia Polytechnic Institute and State University, Graduate School, College of Arts and Sciences, Department of Mathematics, Blacksburg, VA 24061. Offers applied mathematics (MS, PhD); mathematical physics (MS, PhD); pure mathematics (MS, PhD). Part-time programs available. *Faculty:* 55 full-time (5 women). *Students:* 66 full-time (26 women), 81 part-time (45 women); includes 12 minority (10 African Americans, 2 Asian Americans or Pacific Islanders), 14 international. Terminal master's awarded for partial completion of doctoral program. *Degree requirements:* For master's, thesis required (for some programs), foreign language not required; for doctorate, dissertation required. *Entrance requirements:* For master's and doctorate, TOEFL. *Application deadline:* For fall admission, 12/1 (priority date). Applications are processed on a rolling basis. Application fee: $25. *Unit head:* Dr. Robert F. Olin, Head, 540-231-6536, E-mail: olin@math.vt.edu. *Application contact:* Dr. E. L. Green, Graduate Administrator, 540-231-6536.

Optical Sciences

Alabama Agricultural and Mechanical University, School of Graduate Studies, School of Arts and Sciences, Department of Natural and Physical Sciences, Area in Physics, Normal, AL 35762-1357. Offers applied physics (PhD); materials science (PhD); optics (PhD); physics (MS). Part-time programs available. *Faculty:* 11 full-time (1 woman). *Students:* 15 full-time (3 women), 17 part-time (8 women); includes 22 minority (all African Americans), 7 international. *Degree requirements:* For master's, thesis optional, foreign language not required; for doctorate, computer language, dissertation required, foreign language not required. *Entrance requirements:* For master's, GRE General Test, BS in electrical engineering or physics; for doctorate, GRE General Test (minimum combined score of 1000 required). *Application deadline:* For fall admission, 5/1 (priority date). Applications are processed on a rolling basis. Application fee: $15 ($20 for international students). Tuition, state resident: full-time $1,932. Tuition, nonresident: full-time $3,864. Tuition and fees vary according to course load. *Unit head:* J. C. Wang, Chairperson, 256-851-6662.

Cleveland State University, College of Graduate Studies, College of Arts and Sciences, Department of Physics, Cleveland, OH 44115-2440. Offers applied optics (MS); condensed matter physics (MS). Part-time programs available. *Faculty:* 9 full-time (0 women). *Degree requirements:* For master's, computer language required, foreign language and thesis not required. *Application deadline:* For fall admission, 7/15 (priority date). Applications are processed on a rolling basis. Application fee: $25. *Unit head:* Dr. Clyde B. Bratton, Chairperson, 216-687-2427. *Application contact:* Dr. James A. Locke, Director, 216-687-2425.

École Polytechnique de Montréal, Graduate Programs, Department of Engineering Physics, Montréal, PQ H3C 3A7, Canada. Offers optical engineering (M Eng, M Sc A, PhD); solid-state physics and engineering (M Eng, M Sc A, PhD). Part-time programs available. *Degree requirements:* For master's and doctorate, one foreign language, computer language, thesis/dissertation required. *Entrance requirements:* For master's, minimum GPA of 2.75; for doctorate, minimum GPA of 3.0. *Faculty research:* Optics, thin-film physics, laser spectroscopy, plasmas, photonic devices.

Indiana University Bloomington, School of Optometry, Graduate Program in Visual Sciences and Physiological Optics, Bloomington, IN 47405. Offers MS, PhD. PhD offered through the University Graduate School. *Students:* 4 full-time (2 women), 3 part-time (1 woman); includes 1 minority (Asian American or Pacific Islander), 4 international. 11 applicants, 18% accepted. In 1998, 1 master's, 1 doctorate awarded. Terminal master's awarded for partial completion of doctoral program. *Degree requirements:* For master's and doctorate, thesis/dissertation required, foreign language not required. *Entrance requirements:* For master's and doctorate, GRE, TOEFL. *Application deadline:* For fall admission, 2/15 (priority date). Application fee: $40. Tuition, state resident: part-time $196 per credit hour. Tuition, nonresident: part-time $544 per credit hour. Required fees: $360 per year. *Financial aid:* In 1998–99, 5 fellowships with full tuition reimbursements (averaging $10,000 per year), 2 research assistantships with full tuition reimbursements (averaging $7,600 per year), 1 teaching assistantship with full tuition reimbursement (averaging $4,000 per year) were awarded.; scholarships also available. Financial aid application deadline: 3/1; financial aid applicants required to submit FAFSA. *Faculty research:* Visual psychophysics, neurophysiology of visual systems, anatomy of visual system, biochemistry of visual system, corneal pathophysiology. Total annual research expenditures: $362,783. *Unit head:* P. Sarita Soni, Associate Dean, 812-855-4475, Fax: 812-855-7045, E-mail: sonip@indiana.edu. *Application contact:* Jacqueline S. Olson, Director of Student Affairs, 812-855-1917, Fax: 812-855-8664, E-mail: iubopt@indiana.edu.

The Ohio State University, College of Optometry, Program in Physiological Optics, Columbus, OH 43210. Offers MS, PhD, OD/MS. *Faculty:* 17 full-time (7 women). *Students:* 25 full-time (13 women); includes 3 minority (1 African American, 2 Asian Americans or Pacific Islanders), 1 international. In 1998, 5 master's awarded. *Degree requirements:* For master's and doctorate, thesis/dissertation required, foreign language not required. *Entrance requirements:* For master's and doctorate, GRE General Test. *Average time to degree:* Master's–2 years full-time; doctorate–4 years full-time. *Application deadline:* For fall admission, 4/15 (priority date). Applications are processed on a rolling basis. Application fee: $30 ($40 for international students). *Financial aid:* In 1998–99, 9 students received aid, including teaching assistantships with full tuition reimbursements available (averaging $21,000 per year); Federal Work-Study and institutionally-sponsored loans also available. Financial aid application deadline: 2/1; financial aid applicants required to submit FAFSA. *Application contact:* Dr. Ronald Jones, Graduate Studies Chair and Associate Dean, 614-292-1665, Fax: 614-292-7493, E-mail: rjones@optometry.ohio-state.edu.

Rochester Institute of Technology, Part-time and Graduate Admissions, College of Science, Center for Imaging Science, Rochester, NY 14623-5604. Offers MS, PhD. *Students:* 41 full-time (8 women), 39 part-time (13 women); includes 8 minority (2 African Americans, 4 Asian Americans or Pacific Islanders, 2 Hispanic Americans), 31 international. 67 applicants, 61% accepted. In 1998, 18 master's, 3 doctorates awarded. *Degree requirements:* For master's, thesis required. *Entrance requirements:* For master's, TOEFL, minimum GPA of 3.0. *Application deadline:* For fall admission, 3/1 (priority date). Applications are processed on a rolling basis. Application fee: $40. *Financial aid:* Research assistantships, teaching assistantships available. *Unit head:* Dr. Ian Gatley, Director, 716-475-6220, E-mail: ixgpci@rit.edu.

See in-depth description on page 507.

Rose-Hulman Institute of Technology, Faculty of Engineering and Applied Sciences, Program in Applied Optics, Terre Haute, IN 47803-3920. Offers MS. Part-time programs available. *Faculty:* 13 full-time (1 woman). *Students:* 7 full-time (1 woman), 5 international. Average age 24. 7 applicants, 43% accepted. In 1998, 7 degrees awarded. *Degree requirements:* For master's, thesis required, foreign language not required. *Entrance requirements:* For master's, GRE, TOEFL (minimum score of 580 required), minimum GPA of 3.0. *Average time to degree:* Master's–2 years full-time. *Application deadline:* For fall admission, 2/1 (priority date). Applications are processed on a rolling basis. Application fee: $0. Tuition: Full-time $19,305; part-time $540 per credit hour. Required fees: $800. *Financial aid:* In 1998–99, 5 students received aid, including 3 fellowships (averaging $6,000 per year); research assistantships, teaching assistantships, grants, institutionally-sponsored loans, and tuition waivers (full and partial) also available. Financial aid application deadline: 2/1. *Unit head:* Dr. Arthur B. Western, Chairman, Department of Physics, 812-877-8337, Fax: 812-877-8895. *Application contact:* Dr. Buck F. Brown, Dean for Research and Graduate Studies, 812-877-8403, Fax: 812-877-8102, E-mail: buck.brown@rose-hulman.edu.

Tufts University, Division of Graduate and Continuing Studies and Research, Professional and Continuing Studies, Electro-Optics Technology Program, Medford, MA 02155. Offers Certificate. Part-time and evening/weekend programs available. In 1998, 2 degrees awarded. *Average time to degree:* 1 year part-time. *Application deadline:* For fall admission, 8/15 (priority date); for spring admission, 12/12. Applications are processed on a rolling basis. Application fee: $40. *Financial aid:* Available to part-time students. Application deadline: 5/1;

The University of Alabama in Huntsville, School of Graduate Studies, Interdisciplinary Program in Optical Science and Engineering, Huntsville, AL 35899. Offers PhD. Part-time and evening/weekend programs available. *Faculty:* 2 full-time (0 women). *Students:* 19 full-time (7 women), 4 part-time; includes 1 minority (Asian American or Pacific Islander), 8 international. Average age 32. 12 applicants, 83% accepted. In 1998, 3 degrees awarded. *Degree requirements:* For doctorate, dissertation, written and oral exams required, foreign language not required. *Entrance requirements:* For doctorate, GRE General Test (minimum combined score of 1600 on three sections required), minimum GPA of 3.0, BS in physical science or engineering. *Application deadline:* For fall admission, 7/24 (priority date); for spring admission, 11/15 (priority date). Applications are processed on a rolling basis. Application fee: $20. Tuition and fees vary according to course load. *Financial aid:* In 1998–99, 12 students received aid, including 6 research assistantships with full and partial tuition reimbursements available (averaging $10,646 per year); fellowships with full and partial tuition reimbursements available, teaching assistantships with full tuition reimbursements available, career-related internships or fieldwork, Federal Work-Study, grants, institutionally-sponsored loans, scholarships, and tuition waivers (full and partial) also available. Aid available to part-time students. Financial aid application deadline: 4/1; financial aid applicants required to submit FAFSA. *Faculty research:* Laser technology, holography, optical communications, medical image processing, computer design. *Unit head:* Dr. Reza Adhami, Director, 256-890-6316, Fax: 256-890-6803, E-mail: adhami@eb.uah.edu.

University of Alberta, Faculty of Graduate Studies and Research, Department of Electrical and Computer Engineering, Edmonton, AB T6G 2E1, Canada. Offers computational optics (PhD); computer engineering (M Eng, M Sc, PhD); control systems (M Eng, M Sc, PhD); engineering management (M Eng); laser physics (M Sc, PhD); oil sands (M Eng, M Sc, PhD); plasma physics (M Sc, PhD); power engineering (M Eng, M Sc, PhD); telecommunications (M Eng, M Sc, PhD). Terminal master's awarded for partial completion of doctoral program. *Degree requirements:* For master's and doctorate, thesis/dissertation required, foreign language not required. *Entrance requirements:* For master's and doctorate, TOEFL (minimum score of 580 required; average 610). Electronic applications accepted. *Faculty research:* Controls, communications, microelectronics, electromagnetics.

The University of Arizona, Graduate College, Department of Optical Sciences, Tucson, AZ 85721. Offers MS, PhD. Part-time programs available. *Faculty:* 52. *Students:* 97 full-time (17 women), 35 part-time (6 women); includes 16 minority (1 African American, 8 Asian Americans or Pacific Islanders, 7 Hispanic Americans), 42 international. Average age 29. 119 applicants, 29% accepted. In 1998, 23 master's, 19 doctorates awarded. *Degree requirements:* For master's, thesis (for some programs), exam required, foreign language not required; for doctorate, dissertation, oral and written exams required, foreign language not required. *Entrance requirements:* For master's and doctorate, GRE General Test, GRE Subject Test, TOEFL (minimum score of 550 required). *Application deadline:* For fall admission, 3/1. Applications are processed on a rolling basis. Application fee: $35. *Financial aid:* Fellowships, research assistantships, teaching assistantships, scholarships available. *Faculty research:* Medical optics, medical imaging, optical data storage, optical bistability, nonlinear optical effects. *Unit head:* Dr. Richard C. Powell, Director, 520-621-6997, Fax: 520-621-9613. *Application contact:* Dr. Richard L. Shoemaker, Associate Director, Academic Affairs, 520-621-4111, Fax: 520-621-6778.

University of Central Florida, College of Engineering, Department of Electrical and Computer Engineering, Program in Optical Science and Engineering, Orlando, FL 32816. Offers MS, PhD. Part-time and evening/weekend programs available. *Faculty:* 28 full-time, 14 part-time. *Students:* 33 full-time (4 women), 6 part-time (2 women); includes 2 minority (1 African American, 1 Asian American or Pacific Islander), 21 international. Average age 28. 56 applicants, 27% accepted. In 1998, 5 master's, 6 doctorates awarded. *Degree requirements:* For master's, thesis or alternative required, foreign language not required; for doctorate, dissertation, departmental qualifying exam, candidacy exam required, foreign language not required. *Entrance requirements:* For master's, GRE General Test (minimum combined score of 1000 required), TOEFL (minimum score of 550 required; 213 computer-based), minimum GPA of 3.0 in last 60 hours; for doctorate, GRE General Test (minimum combined score of 1100 required), TOEFL (minimum score of 550 required; 213 computer-based), minimum GPA of 3.5 in last 60 hours. *Application deadline:* For fall admission, 2/1 (priority date); for spring admission, 12/15. Application fee: $20. Tuition, state resident: full-time $2,054; part-time $137 per credit. Tuition, nonresident: full-time $7,207; part-time $480 per credit. Required fees: $47 per term. *Financial aid:* In 1998–99, 37 students received aid, including 36 fellowships with partial tuition reimbursements available (averaging $2,848 per year); research assistantships with partial tuition reimbursements available, teaching assistantships with partial tuition reimbursements available, career-related internships or fieldwork, Federal Work-Study, institutionally-sponsored loans, tuition waivers (partial), and unspecified assistantships also available. Financial aid application deadline: 3/1; financial aid applicants required to submit FAFSA. *Unit head:* Dr. M. G. Moharam, Head, 407-823-6833. *Application contact:* Dr. Jim Moharam, Coordinator, 407-823-6833.

See in-depth description on page 521.

University of Dayton, Graduate School, School of Engineering, Program in Electro-Optics, Dayton, OH 45469-1300. Offers MSEO, PhD. Part-time and evening/weekend programs available. *Faculty:* 4 full-time (0 women), 19 part-time (0 women). *Students:* 22 full-time (0 women), 7 part-time; includes 3 minority (1 African American, 2 Asian Americans or Pacific Islanders), 9 international. Average age 25. In 1998, 4 master's, 1 doctorate awarded. *Degree requirements:* For master's, thesis optional, foreign language not required; for doctorate, dissertation, departmental qualifying exam required. *Entrance requirements:* For master's, TOEFL. *Applica-*

tion deadline: For fall admission, 8/1. Application fee: $30. *Financial aid:* In 1998–99, 24 students received aid, including 24 research assistantships with full tuition reimbursements available (averaging $14,000 per year); fellowships, teaching assistantships, institutionally-sponsored loans also available. Financial aid application deadline: 2/1. *Faculty research:* Fiber optics, optical materials, computational optics, holography, laser diagnostics. *Unit head:* Dr. Perry Yaney, Interim Director, 937-229-2797, Fax: 937-229-2471, E-mail: yaney@neelix.udayton. edu. *Application contact:* Dr. Donald L. Moon, Associate Dean, 937-229-2241, Fax: 937-229-2471, E-mail: dmoon@engr.udayton.edu.

University of Maryland, Baltimore County, Graduate School, Department of Physics, Baltimore, MD 21250-5398. Offers applied physics (MS, PhD), including optics, solid state physics; atmospheric physics (MS, PhD). Part-time programs available. *Faculty:* 15 full-time (0 women), 4 part-time (0 women). *Students:* 18 full-time (1 woman), 3 part-time, 7 international. Terminal master's awarded for partial completion of doctoral program. *Degree requirements:* For master's, thesis optional, foreign language not required; for doctorate, dissertation required, foreign language not required. *Entrance requirements:* For master's and doctorate, GRE General Test, GRE Subject Test, TOEFL (minimum score of 600 required), minimum GPA of 3.0. *Application deadline:* For fall admission, 7/1 (priority date); for spring admission, 12/1 (priority date). Applications are processed on a rolling basis. Application fee: $45. *Unit head:* Dr. Geoffrey P. Summers, Chairman, 410-455-2513, Fax: 410-455-1072. *Application contact:* 410-455-2513, Fax: 410-455-1072, E-mail: physics@umbc.edu.

See in-depth description on page 535.

University of Massachusetts Lowell, Graduate School, College of Arts and Sciences, Department of Physics and Applied Physics, Program in Applied Physics, Lowell, MA 01854-2881. Offers applied mechanics (PhD); applied physics (MS, PhD), including optical sciences (MS). Terminal master's awarded for partial completion of doctoral program. *Degree requirements:* For master's, thesis required; for doctorate, 2 foreign languages (computer language can substitute for one), dissertation required. *Entrance requirements:* For master's and doctorate, GRE General Test. *Application deadline:* For fall admission, 4/1 (priority date); for spring admission, 10/1. Applications are processed on a rolling basis. Application fee: $20 ($35 for international students). *Application contact:* Dr. Gus Couchell, Coordinator, 978-934-3772, E-mail: gus_couchell@uml.edu.

University of New Mexico, Graduate School, College of Arts and Sciences, Department of Physics and Astronomy, Albuquerque, NM 87131-2039. Offers optical sciences (PhD); physics (MS, PhD). *Faculty:* 43 full-time (5 women), 7 part-time (1 woman). *Students:* 52 full-time (10 women), 45 part-time (5 women); includes 4 minority (1 African American, 3 Asian Americans or Pacific Islanders), 32 international. Terminal master's awarded for partial completion of doctoral program. *Degree requirements:* For master's, proficiency in 1 computer language recommended required, thesis optional, foreign language not required; for doctorate, dissertation required, foreign language not required. *Entrance requirements:* For master's, GRE General Test (combined average 1850 on three sections); for doctorate, GRE General Test (combined average 1930 on three sections). *Application deadline:* For fall admission, 2/1 (priority date). Application fee: $25. *Unit head:* John K. McIver, Chairman, 505-277-2616, Fax: 505-277-1520, E-mail: jmciver@unm.edu. *Application contact:* Academic Adviser, 505-277-1514, Fax: 505-277-1520, E-mail: panda8@unm.edu.

See in-depth description on page 547.

University of Rochester, The College, School of Engineering and Applied Sciences, Institute of Optics, Rochester, NY 14627-0250. Offers MS, PhD. Part-time programs available. *Faculty:* 14. *Students:* 86 full-time (20 women), 6 part-time; includes 8 minority (7 Asian Americans or Pacific Islanders, 1 Hispanic American), 19 international. 157 applicants, 34% accepted. In 1998, 10 master's, 12 doctorates awarded. Terminal master's awarded for partial completion of doctoral program. *Degree requirements:* For master's, comprehensive exam required, foreign language and thesis not required; for doctorate, dissertation, preliminary and qualifying exams required, foreign language not required. *Entrance requirements:* For master's and doctorate, GRE, TOEFL. *Application deadline:* For fall admission, 2/1 (priority date). Application fee: $25. *Financial aid:* Fellowships, research assistantships, teaching assistantships, tuition waivers (full and partial) available. Financial aid application deadline: 2/1. *Unit head:* Dennis Hall, Chair, 716-275-2322. *Application contact:* Joan Christian, Graduate Program Secretary, 716-275-7764.

See in-depth description on page 567.

Physics

Adelphi University, Graduate School of Arts and Sciences, Department of Physics, Garden City, NY 11530. Offers MS. Part-time and evening/weekend programs available. *Students:* 1 full-time (0 women), 1 part-time; includes 1 minority (African American) Average age 35. In 1998, 2 degrees awarded. *Degree requirements:* For master's, thesis or alternative required, foreign language not required. *Application deadline:* Applications are processed on a rolling basis. Application fee: $50. *Financial aid:* Fellowships, research assistantships, teaching assistantships, tuition waivers (partial) available. Financial aid application deadline: 3/1. *Faculty research:* General relativity, solid-state physics, atomic physics, optics. *Unit head:* Dr. Gottipaty Rao, Chairman, 516-877-4880.

Alabama Agricultural and Mechanical University, School of Graduate Studies, School of Arts and Sciences, Department of Natural and Physical Sciences, Area in Physics, Normal, AL 35762-1357. Offers applied physics (PhD); materials science (PhD); optics (PhD); physics (MS). Part-time programs available. *Faculty:* 11 full-time (1 woman). *Students:* 15 full-time (3 women), 17 part-time (8 women); includes 22 minority (all African Americans), 7 international. In 1998, 6 master's awarded (100% found work related to degree); 5 doctorates awarded (20% entered university research/teaching, 80% found other work related to degree). *Degree requirements:* For master's, thesis optional, foreign language not required; for doctorate, computer language, dissertation required, foreign language not required. *Entrance requirements:* For master's, GRE General Test, BS in electrical engineering or physics; for doctorate, GRE General Test (minimum combined score of 1000 required). *Application deadline:* For fall admission, 5/1 (priority date). Applications are processed on a rolling basis. Application fee: $15 ($20 for international students). Tuition, state resident: full-time $1,932. Tuition, nonresident: full-time $3,864. Tuition and fees vary according to course load. *Financial aid:* In 1998–99, 1 fellowship with tuition reimbursement (averaging $18,000 per year), 4 research assistantships with tuition reimbursements (averaging $9,000 per year) were awarded.; career-related internships or fieldwork, Federal Work-Study, grants, and unspecified assistantships also available. Aid available to part-time students. Financial aid application deadline: 4/1. *Faculty research:* Optics/lasers, nonlinear optics, crystal growth modeling. *Unit head:* J. C. Wang, Chairperson, 256-851-6662.

American University, College of Arts and Sciences, Department of Physics, Washington, DC 20016-8001. Offers MS. Part-time and evening/weekend programs available. *Faculty:* 8 full-time (1 woman), 4 part-time (0 women). *Students:* 5 full-time (4 women), 9 part-time (2 women), 7 international. 21 applicants, 19% accepted. In 1998, 3 degrees awarded. *Degree requirements:* For master's, thesis or alternative, comprehensive exams required, thesis or alternative, comprehensive exams required. *Application deadline:* For fall admission, 2/1 (priority date); for spring admission, 10/1. Applications are processed on a rolling basis. Application fee: $50. *Financial aid:* Fellowships, research assistantships, teaching assistantships, career-related internships or fieldwork, Federal Work-Study, institutionally-sponsored loans, and tuition waivers (partial) available. Aid available to part-time students. Financial aid application deadline: 2/1. *Faculty research:* Nuclear particle experimental physics, solid-state physics, quantum electronics, critical phenomena, intense fields. Total annual research expenditures: $852,000. *Unit head:* Dr. Robert DeWitt, Chair, 202-885-2743. *Application contact:* Graduate Studies Adviser, 202-885-2766.

See in-depth description on page 431.

Andrews University, School of Graduate Studies, College of Arts and Sciences, Department of Physics, Berrien Springs, MI 49104. Offers MS. *Application deadline:* Applications are processed on a rolling basis. Application fee: $40. *Unit head:* Dr. Robert E. Kingman, Chairman, 616-471-3431.

Arizona State University, Graduate College, College of Liberal Arts and Sciences, Department of Physics and Astronomy, Tempe, AZ 85287. Offers MNS, MS, PhD. *Faculty:* 44 full-time (5 women). *Students:* 59 full-time (14 women), 11 part-time (2 women); includes 3 minority (all Hispanic Americans), 26 international. Average age 29. 83 applicants, 51% accepted. In 1998, 10 master's, 10 doctorates awarded. *Degree requirements:* For master's, thesis, oral and written exams required; for doctorate, dissertation required. *Entrance requirements:* For master's and doctorate, GRE. Application fee: $45. *Faculty research:* Electromagnetic interaction of hadrons, investigation of tripartition fission, and beta activity of various elements formed in fission processes; phase transitions in solids. *Unit head:* Dr. Howard G. Voss, Chair, 480-965-3561. *Application contact:* Dr. Kevin Schmidt, 480-965-4702.

Auburn University, Graduate School, College of Sciences and Mathematics, Department of Physics, Auburn, Auburn University, AL 36849-0002. Offers MS, PhD. Part-time programs available. *Faculty:* 22 full-time (1 woman). *Students:* 13 full-time (2 women), 16 part-time (1 woman); includes 2 minority (1 African American, 1 Hispanic American), 9 international. 9 applicants, 67% accepted. In 1998, 8 master's, 5 doctorates awarded. *Degree requirements:*

For doctorate, dissertation, oral and written exams required, foreign language not required, foreign language not required. *Entrance requirements:* For master's, GRE General Test; for doctorate, GRE General Test (minimum score of 400 on each section required). *Application deadline:* For fall admission, 9/1; for spring admission, 3/1. Applications are processed on a rolling basis. Application fee: $25 ($50 for international students). Tuition, state resident: full-time $2,760; part-time $76 per credit hour. Tuition, nonresident: full-time $8,280; part-time $228 per credit hour. *Financial aid:* Research assistantships, teaching assistantships, career-related internships or fieldwork and Federal Work-Study available. Aid available to part-time students. Financial aid application deadline: 3/15. *Faculty research:* Atomic/radiative physics, plasma physics, condensed matter physics, space physics, nonlinear dynamics. *Unit head:* Dr. Joe D. Perez, Head, 334-844-4264. *Application contact:* Dr. John F. Pritchett, Dean of the Graduate School, 334-844-4700.

Ball State University, Graduate School, College of Sciences and Humanities, Department of Physics and Astronomy, Program in Physics, Muncie, IN 47306-1099. Offers MA, MS. *Faculty:* 14. *Students:* 8 full-time (3 women), 5 part-time (2 women). Average age 27. 3 applicants, 67% accepted. In 1998, 7 degrees awarded. *Degree requirements:* Foreign language not required. Application fee: $15 ($25 for international students). *Financial aid:* Research assistantships available. *Faculty research:* Solar energy, particle physics, atomic spectroscopy. *Unit head:* Dr. John F. Pritchett, Dean of the Graduate School, 334-844-4700.

Baylor University, Graduate School, College of Arts and Sciences, Department of Physics, Waco, TX 76798. Offers MA, MS, PhD. *Students:* 11 full-time (1 woman), 3 part-time, 5 international. In 1998, 2 master's, 2 doctorates awarded. *Degree requirements:* For master's, thesis or alternative required, foreign language not required; for doctorate, one foreign language (computer language can substitute), dissertation required. *Entrance requirements:* For master's and doctorate, GRE General Test. *Application deadline:* Applications are processed on a rolling basis. Application fee: $25. *Financial aid:* Fellowships, teaching assistantships, Federal Work-Study and institutionally-sponsored loans available. *Unit head:* Dr. Truell W. Hyde, Director of Graduate Studies, 254-710-2511, Fax: 254-710-3878, E-mail: truell_hyde@baylor. edu. *Application contact:* Suzanne Keener, Administrative Assistant, 254-710-3588, Fax: 254-710-3870, E-mail: suzanne_keener@baylor.edu.

Boston College, Graduate School of Arts and Sciences, Department of Physics, Chestnut Hill, MA 02467-3800. Offers MS, PhD. *Faculty:* 13 full-time (0 women). *Students:* 7 full-time (2 women), 12 part-time (2 women). 35 applicants, 57% accepted. In 1998, 2 master's, 5 doctorates awarded. Terminal master's awarded for partial completion of doctoral program. *Degree requirements:* For master's, thesis required (for some programs), foreign language not required; for doctorate, dissertation required, foreign language not required. *Entrance requirements:* For master's and doctorate, GRE General Test, GRE Subject Test. *Application deadline:* For fall admission, 2/1. Application fee: $40. *Financial aid:* Fellowships, research assistantships, teaching assistantships, Federal Work-Study and scholarships available. Aid available to part-time students. Financial aid application deadline: 3/15; financial aid applicants required to submit FAFSA. *Faculty research:* Atmospheric/space physics, astrophysics, atomic and molecular physics, fusion and plasmas, solid-state physics. *Unit head:* Dr. Kevin Bedell, Chairperson, 617-552-3576, E-mail: kevin.bedell@bc.edu. *Application contact:* Dr. Michael Graf, Graduate Program Director, 617-552-4128, E-mail: michael.graf@bc.edu.

Boston University, Graduate School of Arts and Sciences, Department of Physics, Boston, MA 02215. Offers MA, PhD. *Faculty:* 35 full-time (4 women), 24 part-time (1 woman). *Students:* 75 full-time (7 women); includes 4 minority (all Hispanic Americans), 51 international. Average age 26. 190 applicants, 44% accepted. In 1998, 3 master's awarded (67% found work related to degree, 33% continued full-time study); 15 doctorates awarded (40% entered university research/teaching, 60% found other work related to degree). Terminal master's awarded for partial completion of doctoral program. *Degree requirements:* For master's, one foreign language, thesis or alternative, comprehensive exam required; for doctorate, one foreign language, dissertation, qualifying and oral exams required. *Entrance requirements:* For master's and doctorate, GRE General Test, GRE Subject Test, TOEFL (minimum score of 600 required). *Average time to degree:* Master's–2 years full-time; doctorate–6 years full-time. *Application deadline:* For fall admission, 1/15; for spring admission, 11/1. Applications are processed on a rolling basis. Application fee: $50. Tuition: Full-time $23,770; part-time $743 per credit. Required fees: $220. Tuition and fees vary according to class time, course level, campus/location and program. *Financial aid:* In 1998–99, 38 research assistantships, 41 teaching assistantships were awarded.; fellowships, Federal Work-Study and scholarships also available. Aid available to part-time students. Financial aid application deadline: 1/15; financial aid applicants required to submit FAFSA. *Faculty research:* Condensed matter, surfaces, elementary particles, biophysics, statistical physics. Total annual research expenditures: $5.6 million. *Unit head:* Dr. Lawrence R. Sulak, Chairman, 617-353-9454, Fax: 617-353-9393,

Physics

Boston University (continued)

E-mail: sulak@bu.edu. *Application contact:* Mirtha Cabello, Administrative Coordinator, 617-353-2623, Fax: 617-353-9393, E-mail: cabello@buphyk.bu.edu.

See in-depth description on page 433.

Bowling Green State University, Graduate College, College of Arts and Sciences, Department of Physics and Astronomy, Bowling Green, OH 43403. Offers physics (MAT, MS); physics and astronomy (MAT). *Faculty:* 5 full-time (0 women). *Students:* 8 full-time (1 woman), 1 part-time, (all international). 28 applicants, 61% accepted. In 1998, 3 degrees awarded. *Degree requirements:* For master's, thesis or alternative required, foreign language not required. *Entrance requirements:* For master's, GRE General Test, TOEFL (minimum score of 550 required). Application fee: $30. Electronic applications accepted. *Financial aid:* Research assistantships with full tuition reimbursements, teaching assistantships with full tuition reimbursements, career-related internships or fieldwork, institutionally-sponsored loans, and unspecified assistantships available. Financial aid applicants required to submit FAFSA. *Faculty research:* Computational physics, solid-state physics, materials science, theoretical physics. *Unit head:* Dr. Robert I. Boughton, Chair, 419-372-2421. *Application contact:* Dr. Lewis Fulcher, Graduate Coordinator, 419-372-2635.

Brandeis University, Graduate School of Arts and Sciences, Program in Physics, Waltham, MA 02454-9110. Offers MS, PhD. Part-time programs available. *Faculty:* 20 full-time (1 woman). *Students:* 24 full-time (5 women), 5 part-time; includes 11 minority (9 Asian Americans or Pacific Islanders, 2 Hispanic Americans) Average age 25. 66 applicants, 64% accepted. In 1998, 5 master's awarded (60% found work related to degree, 20% continued full-time study); 2 doctorates awarded. Terminal master's awarded for partial completion of doctoral program. *Degree requirements:* For master's, qualifying exam required, foreign language and thesis not required; for doctorate, dissertation required, foreign language not required. *Entrance requirements:* For doctorate, GRE General Test, GRE Subject Test. *Average time to degree:* Doctorate–7 years full-time. *Application deadline:* For fall admission, 2/15 (priority date). Application fee: $60. *Financial aid:* In 1998–99, 22 students received aid; fellowships, research assistantships, teaching assistantships, scholarships and tuition waivers (full) available. Financial aid application deadline: 4/15; financial aid applicants required to submit CSS PROFILE or FAFSA. *Faculty research:* Theoretical physics, experimental physics, astrophysics, computational neuroscience, condensed matter, high energy physics. Total annual research expenditures: $1.9 million. *Unit head:* Dr. James R. Bensinger, Chair, 781-736-2875, Fax: 781-736-2915, E-mail: bensinger@brandeis.edu. *Application contact:* Chairman, Graduate Admissions Committee, 781-736-2835, Fax: 781-736-2915, E-mail: physics1@brandeis.edu.

Brigham Young University, Graduate Studies, College of Physical and Mathematical Sciences, Department of Physics and Astronomy, Provo, UT 84602-1001. Offers physics (MS, PhD); physics and astronomy (PhD). Part-time programs available. *Faculty:* 30 full-time (0 women), 2 part-time (1 woman). *Students:* 21 full-time (2 women), 4 part-time; includes 1 minority (Hispanic American), 11 international. Average age 28. 28 applicants, 29% accepted. In 1998, 5 master's awarded (40% found work related to degree, 40% continued full-time study); 3 doctorates awarded (100% entered university research/teaching). Terminal master's awarded for partial completion of doctoral program. *Degree requirements:* For master's, thesis required; for doctorate, dissertation required, dissertation required. *Entrance requirements:* For master's and doctorate, GRE Subject Test, minimum GPA of 3.0 in last 60 hours. *Average time to degree:* Master's–2.5 years full-time, 4.7 years part-time; doctorate–6.8 years full-time. *Application deadline:* For fall admission, 2/1. Application fee: $30. Electronic applications accepted. Tuition: Full-time $3,330; part-time $185 per credit hour. Tuition and fees vary according to program and student's religious affiliation. *Financial aid:* In 1998–99, 19 students received aid, including 2 research assistantships with tuition reimbursements available (averaging $4,160 per year), 17 teaching assistantships with tuition reimbursements available (averaging $4,289 per year); fellowships with tuition reimbursements available, career-related internships or fieldwork, institutionally-sponsored loans, and tuition waivers (partial) also available. Aid available to part-time students. Financial aid application deadline: 2/1. *Faculty research:* Acoustics; astrophysics; atomic, molecular, and optical physics; plasma; theoretical and mathematical physics; condensed matter. *Unit head:* Dr. Dorian M. Hatch, Chair, 801-378-4361, Fax: 801-378-2265, E-mail: hatchd@wigner.byu.edu. *Application contact:* Dr. Jean-Francois S. Van Huele, Graduate Coordinator, 801-378-4481, Fax: 801-378-2265, E-mail: graduatep_physics@byu.edu.

Brock University, Graduate Studies and Research, Faculty of Mathematics and Science, Department of Physics, St. Catharines, ON L2S 3A1, Canada. Offers M Sc. Part-time programs available. *Faculty:* 8 full-time (1 woman). *Students:* 7 full-time (3 women), 1 part-time, 3 international. Average age 24. 18 applicants, 44% accepted. In 1998, 2 degrees awarded. *Degree requirements:* For master's, thesis required, foreign language not required. *Entrance requirements:* For master's, TOEFL (minimum score of 550 required), honors B Sc in physics. *Average time to degree:* Master's–2 years full-time, 4 years part-time. *Application deadline:* For fall admission, 3/1 (priority date). Applications are processed on a rolling basis. Application fee: $35. *Financial aid:* Fellowships, research assistantships, teaching assistantships, career-related internships or fieldwork, grants, scholarships, and unspecified assistantships available. Aid available to part-time students. *Faculty research:* Tunneling spectroscopy of superconductors; structure, stability, and transport structure of quasi crystals; NMR spectroscopy. *Unit head:* Dr. Bodizar Mitrovic, Chair, 905-688-5550 Ext. 3343, Fax: 905-682-9020, E-mail: mitrovic@newton.physics.brocku.ca. *Application contact:* Dr. S. Bose, Graduate Studies Officer, 905-688-5550 Ext. 3876, Fax: 905-682-9020, E-mail: saar@newton.physics.brocku.ca.

Brooklyn College of the City University of New York, Division of Graduate Studies, Department of Physics, Brooklyn, NY 11210-2889. Offers applied physics (MA); physics (MA, PhD). Part-time programs available. In 1998, 1 degree awarded (100% found work related to degree). Terminal master's awarded for partial completion of doctoral program. *Degree requirements:* For master's, comprehensive exam required; for doctorate, dissertation, comprehensive exam required, foreign language not required. *Entrance requirements:* For master's and doctorate, GRE, TOEFL (minimum score of 500 required). *Average time to degree:* Master's–2 years full-time. *Application deadline:* For fall admission, 3/1; for spring admission, 11/1. Application fee: $40. *Financial aid:* Fellowships, research assistantships, teaching assistantships, Federal Work-Study, institutionally-sponsored loans, scholarships, and tuition waivers (full and partial) available. Aid available to part-time students. Financial aid application deadline: 5/1; financial aid applicants required to submit FAFSA. Total annual research expenditures: $1.2 million. *Unit head:* Dr. Peter M. S. Lesser, Chairperson, 718-951-5418, Fax: 718-951-4407. *Application contact:* Dr. Ming Kung Liou, Graduate Deputy, 718-951-5811, Fax: 718-951-4407.

Announcement: All research leading to the PhD may be pursued on Brooklyn College campus. Research facilities include extremely well-equipped solid-state and applied physics laboratories for UHV surface science, low-energy electron diffraction photoreflectance, Raman scattering, near-field scanning optical microscopy and STM, and electrochemistry. Major areas of research include experimental: applied, surface, and condensed-matter physics; theoretical: applied, atomic, nuclear, and solid-state physics. Teaching and/or research assistantships available at approximately $22,000 per year.

Brown University, Graduate School, Department of Physics, Providence, RI 02912. Offers Sc M, PhD. *Degree requirements:* For master's, foreign language and thesis not required; for doctorate, dissertation, qualifying and oral exams required, foreign language not required.

See in-depth description on page 435.

Bryn Mawr College, Graduate School of Arts and Sciences, Department of Physics, Bryn Mawr, PA 19010-2899. Offers MA, PhD. *Faculty:* 6. *Students:* 2 full-time (1 woman), 3 part-time (1 woman); includes 1 Native American, 3 international. In 1998, 1 master's, 1 doctorate awarded. *Degree requirements:* For master's and doctorate, thesis/dissertation required. *Entrance requirements:* For master's and doctorate, GRE General Test, GRE Subject Test. *Application deadline:* For fall admission, 6/30. Application fee: $40. *Financial aid:* Fellowships, research assistantships, teaching assistantships, Federal Work-Study, institutionally-sponsored loans, and tuition awards available. Aid available to part-time students. Financial aid application deadline: 1/2. *Unit head:* Dr. Alfonso Albano, Chairman, 610-526-5358. *Application contact:* Graduate School of Arts and Sciences, 610-526-5072.

California Institute of Technology, Division of Physics, Mathematics and Astronomy, Department of Physics, Pasadena, CA 91125-0001. Offers PhD. *Faculty:* 55. *Students:* 137 full-time (16 women); includes 4 minority (all Asian Americans or Pacific Islanders), 56 international. Average age 25. 405 applicants, 20% accepted. In 1998, 11 degrees awarded. *Degree requirements:* For doctorate, dissertation, candidacy and final exams required, foreign language not required. *Entrance requirements:* For doctorate, GRE General Test, GRE Subject Test, TOEFL. *Application deadline:* For fall admission, 1/15. Application fee: $0. *Financial aid:* In 1998–99, 127 students received aid, including 20 fellowships with full tuition reimbursements available (averaging $18,300 per year), 70 research assistantships with full tuition reimbursements available (averaging $18,030 per year), 47 teaching assistantships with full tuition reimbursements available (averaging $11,754 per year); Federal Work-Study, institutionally-sponsored loans, and outside awards also available. Financial aid application deadline: 1/15. *Faculty research:* High-energy physics, nuclear physics, condensed-matter physics, theoretical physics and astrophysics, gravity physics. *Unit head:* Dr. Ken Libbrecht, Executive Officer, 626-395-3722. *Application contact:* Donna Driscoll, Graduate Secretary, 626-395-4244, E-mail: donnad@cco.caltech.edu.

See in-depth description on page 437.

California State University, Fresno, Division of Graduate Studies, School of Natural Sciences, Department of Physics, Fresno, CA 93740-0057. Offers MS. Part-time programs available. *Faculty:* 9 full-time (1 woman). *Students:* 4 full-time (2 women), 3 part-time, 3 international. Average age 31. 14 applicants, 57% accepted. In 1998, 1 degree awarded. *Degree requirements:* For master's, thesis or alternative required, foreign language not required. *Entrance requirements:* For master's, GRE General Test, TOEFL (minimum score of 550 required), minimum GPA of 2.5. *Average time to degree:* Master's–3.5 years full-time. *Application deadline:* For fall admission, 8/1 (priority date); for spring admission, 12/1. Applications are processed on a rolling basis. Application fee: $55. Electronic applications accepted. Tuition, nonresident: part-time $246 per unit. Required fees: $1,906; $620 per semester. *Financial aid:* In 1998–99, 3 teaching assistantships were awarded.; career-related internships or fieldwork, Federal Work-Study, scholarships, and unspecified assistantships also available. Financial aid application deadline: 3/1; financial aid applicants required to submit FAFSA. *Faculty research:* Energy, astronomy. *Unit head:* Dr. Michael Zender, Chair, 559-278-2371, Fax: 559-278-7741, E-mail: michael_zender@csufresno.edu. *Application contact:* Dr. Manfred Bucher, Graduate Coordinator, 559-278-2357, Fax: 559-278-7741, E-mail: manfred_bucher@csufresno.edu.

Announcement: MS program in preparation for PhD studies, industry, or teaching. Faculty involved in scanning probe microscopy, Raman spectroscopy, biophysics, field theory, solid-state theory, CCD variable star photometry, dielectric properties of fullerenes, laser cooling, pedagogy, and particle theory. Teaching assistantships approximately $10,000. Near Yosemite National Park. World Wide Web: http://maxwell.phys.csufresno.edu:8001/Dept/grad.html.

California State University, Fullerton, Graduate Studies, School of Natural Science and Mathematics, Department of Physics, Fullerton, CA 92834-9480. Offers MA. *Faculty:* 8 full-time (3 women), 13 part-time. *Students:* 1 full-time (0 women), 13 part-time (3 women); includes 2 minority (1 Asian American or Pacific Islander, 1 Hispanic American) 21 applicants, 62% accepted. In 1998, 2 degrees awarded. Application fee: $55. Tuition, nonresident: part-time $264 per unit. Required fees: $1,947; $1,281 per year. *Financial aid:* Grants available. Financial aid application deadline: 3/1. *Unit head:* Dr. Mark Shapiro, Chair, 714-278-3366.

California State University, Long Beach, Graduate Studies, College of Natural Sciences, Department of Physics and Astronomy, Long Beach, CA 90840. Offers metals physics (MS); physics (MS). Part-time programs available. *Faculty:* 13 full-time (1 woman). *Students:* 2 full-time (1 woman), 20 part-time (2 women); includes 5 minority (4 Asian Americans or Pacific Islanders, 1 Hispanic American), 3 international. Average age 35. 24 applicants, 42% accepted. In 1998, 3 degrees awarded. *Degree requirements:* For master's, comprehensive exam or thesis required. *Application deadline:* For fall admission, 8/1; for spring admission, 12/1. Applications are processed on a rolling basis. Application fee: $55. Electronic applications accepted. Tuition, nonresident: part-time $246 per unit. Required fees: $569 per semester. Tuition and fees vary according to course load. *Financial aid:* Federal Work-Study, grants, and institutionally-sponsored loans available. Financial aid application deadline: 3/2. *Faculty research:* Musical acoustics, modern optics, neutrino physics, quantum gravity, atomic physics. *Unit head:* Dr. Alfred Leung, Chair, 562-985-4924, Fax: 562-985-7924, E-mail: aleung@csulb.edu. *Application contact:* Dr. Edwin Woollett, Graduate Coordinator, 562-985-4910, Fax: 562-985-7924, E-mail: woollett@csulb.edu.

California State University, Los Angeles, Graduate Studies, School of Natural and Social Sciences, Department of Physics and Astronomy, Los Angeles, CA 90032-8530. Offers physics (MS). Part-time and evening/weekend programs available. *Faculty:* 11 full-time, 10 part-time. *Students:* 1 full-time (0 women), 9 part-time (2 women); includes 5 minority (2 Asian Americans or Pacific Islanders, 3 Hispanic Americans), 2 international. In 1998, 2 degrees awarded. *Degree requirements:* For master's, comprehensive exam or thesis required. *Entrance requirements:* For master's, TOEFL (minimum score of 550 required). *Application deadline:* For fall admission, 6/30; for spring admission, 2/1. Applications are processed on a rolling basis. Application fee: $55. *Financial aid:* In 1998–99, 2 students received aid. Federal Work-Study available. Aid available to part-time students. Financial aid application deadline: 3/1. *Faculty research:* Intermediate energy, nuclear physics, condensed-matter physics, biophysics. *Unit head:* Dr. Konrad Aniol, Chair, 323-343-2100.

California State University, Northridge, Graduate Studies, College of Science and Mathematics, Department of Physics and Astronomy, Northridge, CA 91330. Offers physics (MS). Part-time and evening/weekend programs available. *Faculty:* 21 full-time, 8 part-time. *Students:* 1 full-time (0 women), 8 part-time (2 women); includes 2 minority (1 African American, 1 Asian American or Pacific Islander), 1 international. Average age 36. 15 applicants, 60% accepted. In 1998, 7 degrees awarded. *Degree requirements:* For master's, thesis optional, foreign language not required. *Entrance requirements:* For master's, TOEFL, GRE General Test or minimum GPA of 3.0. *Application deadline:* For fall admission, 11/30. Application fee: $55. Tuition, nonresident: part-time $246 per unit. International tuition: $7,874 full-time. Required fees: $1,970. Tuition and fees vary according to course load. *Financial aid:* Teaching assistantships available. Financial aid application deadline: 3/1. *Unit head:* Dr. Adrian D. Herzog, Chair, 818-677-2775.

Carleton University, Faculty of Graduate Studies, Faculty of Science, Department of Physics, Ottawa, ON K1S 5B6, Canada. Offers M Sc, PhD. *Faculty:* 14 full-time (1 woman). *Students:* 17 full-time (6 women), 2 part-time (1 woman). Average age 27. In 1998, 4 master's, 3 doctorates awarded. *Degree requirements:* For master's, seminar required, thesis optional; for doctorate, dissertation, comprehensive exam, seminar required. *Entrance requirements:* For master's, TOEFL (minimum score of 550 required), honors degree in science; for doctorate, TOEFL (minimum score of 550 required), M Sc. *Average time to degree:* Master's–2.3 years full-time; doctorate–5.1 years full-time. *Application deadline:* For fall admission, 3/1 (priority date). Applications are processed on a rolling basis. Application fee: $35. *Financial aid:* Application deadline: 3/1. *Faculty research:* Experimental and theoretical elementary particle physics, medical physics. Total annual research expenditures: $3.6 million. *Unit head:* Dean Karlen, Director, 613-520-4377, Fax: 613-520-4061. *Application contact:* Dean Karlen, Director, 613-520-4377, Fax: 613-520-4061.

Carnegie Mellon University, Mellon College of Science, Department of Physics, Pittsburgh, PA 15213-3891. Offers applied physics (PhD); physics (MS, PhD). Part-time programs available. *Faculty:* 56 full-time (3 women), 2 part-time (0 women). *Students:* 44 full-time (7 women), 3 part-time (1 woman), 28 international. Average age 28. In 1998, 9 master's, 6 doctorates awarded. Terminal master's awarded for partial completion of doctoral program. *Degree requirements:* For master's, qualifying exam required, foreign language and thesis not required; for doctorate, dissertation, qualifying exam required, foreign language not required. *Entrance requirements:* For master's, GRE General Test; for doctorate, GRE General Test (minimum combined score of 1900 on three sections required; average 2110). *Average time to degree:* Master's–2 years full-time; doctorate–5 years full-time. *Application deadline:* For fall admission, 2/1 (priority date). Applications are processed on a rolling basis. Application fee: $0. *Financial aid:* In 1998–99, 32 research assistantships, 22 teaching assistantships were awarded.; fellowships *Faculty research:* Astrophysics, condensed matter physics, biological physics, medium energy and nuclear physics, high-energy physics. Total annual research expenditures: $4.7 million. *Unit head:* Dr. Robert H. Swendsen, Head, 412-268-6681, Fax: 412-681-0648, E-mail: swendsen@andrew.cmu.edu. *Application contact:* Ned S. Vanderven, Chair of Graduate Admissions, 412-268-2766, Fax: 412-268-0648, E-mail: nsvr@andrew.cmu.edu.

See in-depth description on page 439.

Case Western Reserve University, School of Graduate Studies, Department of Physics, Cleveland, OH 44106. Offers MS, PhD. Part-time programs available. Terminal master's awarded for partial completion of doctoral program. *Degree requirements:* For master's, exam required, foreign language and thesis not required; for doctorate, dissertation, qualifying exam, topical exam required, foreign language not required. *Entrance requirements:* For master's and doctorate, TOEFL (minimum score of 550 required). *Faculty research:* Condensed-matter physics, imaging physics, nonlinear optics, high-energy physics, cosmology and astrophysics.

The Catholic University of America, School of Arts and Sciences, Department of Physics, Washington, DC 20064. Offers MS, PhD. Part-time programs available. *Faculty:* 9 full-time (1 woman). *Students:* 15 full-time (0 women), 18 part-time (2 women); includes 5 minority (1 African American, 2 Asian Americans or Pacific Islanders, 2 Hispanic Americans), 18 international. Average age 29. 97 applicants, 36% accepted. In 1998, 7 master's, 4 doctorates awarded (100% found work related to degree). Terminal master's awarded for partial completion of doctoral program. *Degree requirements:* For master's, comprehensive exam required, thesis optional, foreign language not required; for doctorate, dissertation, comprehensive exam required, foreign language not required. *Entrance requirements:* For master's, GRE General Test (minimum combined score of 1150 required), minimum GPA of 2.5; for doctorate, GRE General Test (minimum combined score of 1150 required), TOEFL (minimum score of 600 required), minimum GPA of 2.5. *Average time to degree:* Master's–2.5 years full-time, 4 years part-time; doctorate–6 years full-time, 9 years part-time. *Application deadline:* For fall admission, 8/1 (priority date); for spring admission, 12/1. Applications are processed on a rolling basis. Application fee: $50. *Financial aid:* In 1998–99, 28 students received aid, including 7 fellowships, 15 research assistantships, 4 teaching assistantships; career-related internships or fieldwork, Federal Work-Study, institutionally-sponsored loans, scholarships, and tuition waivers (full and partial) also available. Aid available to part-time students. Financial aid application deadline: 2/1. *Faculty research:* Condensed-matter physics, intermediate-energy physics, astrophysics, biophysics. Total annual research expenditures: $4 million. *Unit head:* Dr. Charles Montrose, Chair, 202-319-5315. *Application contact:* Gail Hershey, Assistant to the Chair, 202-319-5315, Fax: 202-319-4448, E-mail: hershey@cua.edu.

The Catholic University of America, School of Arts and Sciences, Department of Politics, Washington, DC 20064. Offers American government (MA, PhD); congressional studies (MA); international affairs (MA); international political economics (MA); political theory (MA, PhD); world politics (MA, PhD). Part-time programs available. *Faculty:* 16 full-time (2 women), 10 part-time (1 woman). *Students:* 28 full-time (10 women), 94 part-time (22 women); includes 12 minority (2 African Americans, 6 Asian Americans or Pacific Islanders, 3 Hispanic Americans, 1 Native American), 11 international. *Degree requirements:* For master's, one foreign language (computer language can substitute), thesis or alternative, comprehensive exam required; for doctorate, 2 foreign languages (computer language can substitute for one), dissertation, comprehensive exam required. *Entrance requirements:* For master's, GRE General Test, TOEFL; for doctorate, GRE General Test. *Application deadline:* For fall admission, 8/1 (priority date); for spring admission, 12/1. Applications are processed on a rolling basis. Application fee: $50. *Unit head:* Dr. Stephen Schneck, Chairman, 202-319-6228, Fax: 202-319-6289, E-mail: schneck@cua.edu. *Application contact:* Helen Foggo, Office Manager, 202-319-5130.

Central Connecticut State University, School of Graduate Studies, School of Arts and Sciences, Department of Physics and Earth Science, New Britain, CT 06050-4010. Offers earth science (MS); general science (MS); physics (MS). Part-time and evening/weekend programs available. *Faculty:* 12 full-time (4 women), 10 part-time (2 women). *Students:* 2 full-time (1 woman), 25 part-time (18 women). Average age 35. 30 applicants, 53% accepted. In 1998, 9 degrees awarded. *Degree requirements:* For master's, thesis or alternative, comprehensive exam required, foreign language not required. *Entrance requirements:* For master's, TOEFL (minimum score of 550 required), minimum GPA of 2.7. *Application deadline:* For fall admission, 6/1 (priority date); for spring admission, 12/1. Applications are processed on a rolling basis. Application fee: $40. *Financial aid:* Federal Work-Study available. Financial aid application deadline: 3/15; financial aid applicants required to submit FAFSA. *Faculty research:* Elementary/secondary science education, particle and solid states, weather patterns, planetary studies. *Unit head:* Dr. Ali Antar, Chair, 860-832-2930.

Central Michigan University, College of Graduate Studies, College of Science and Technology, Department of Physics, Mount Pleasant, MI 48859. Offers MS. *Faculty:* 14 full-time (0 women). *Students:* 5 full-time (1 woman), 7 part-time, 8 international. Average age 28. In 1998, 1 degree awarded. *Degree requirements:* For master's, thesis or alternative required, foreign language not required. *Entrance requirements:* For master's, GRE, TOEFL, bachelor's degree in physics, minimum GPA of 2.6. *Application deadline:* For fall admission, 3/1 (priority date). Applications are processed on a rolling basis. Application fee: $30. Tuition, state resident: part-time $144 per credit hour. Tuition, nonresident: part-time $285 per credit hour. Required fees: $240 per semester. Tuition and fees vary according to degree level and program. *Financial aid:* In 1998–99, 5 research assistantships with tuition reimbursements, 7 teaching assistantships with tuition reimbursements were awarded.; fellowships with tuition reimbursements, career-related internships or fieldwork and Federal Work-Study also available. Financial aid application deadline: 3/7. *Faculty research:* Polymer physics, laser spectroscopy, observational astronomy, nuclear physics, thin films. *Unit head:* Dr. Stanley Hirschi, Chairperson, 517-774-3321, Fax: 517-774-7106, E-mail: hirschi@dune.phy.cmich.edu.

City College of the City University of New York, Graduate School, College of Liberal Arts and Science, Division of Science, Department of Physics, New York, NY 10031-9198. Offers MA, PhD. PhD offered through the Graduate School and University Center of the City University of New York. Terminal master's awarded for partial completion of doctoral program. *Degree requirements:* For master's, comprehensive exam required; for doctorate, dissertation required, foreign language not required. *Entrance requirements:* For master's, TOEFL (minimum score of 500 required); for doctorate, GRE.

See in-depth description on page 443.

Clark Atlanta University, School of Arts and Sciences, Department of Physics, Atlanta, GA 30314. Offers MS. Part-time programs available. *Students:* 6 full-time (2 women), 5 part-time (3 women); all minorities (all African Americans) In 1998, 5 degrees awarded. *Degree requirements:* For master's, one foreign language (computer language can substitute), thesis required. *Entrance requirements:* For master's, GRE General Test, minimum GPA of 2.5. *Application deadline:* For fall admission, 4/1; for spring admission, 11/1. Applications are processed on a rolling basis. Application fee: $40. *Financial aid:* Fellowships, research assistantships available. Financial aid application deadline: 4/30. *Faculty research:* Fusion energy, investigations of nonlinear differential equations, difference schemes, collisions in dense plasma. *Unit head:* Dr. Denise Stephenson-Hawk, Chairperson, 404-880-8798. *Application contact:* Michelle Clark-Davis, Graduate Program Assistant, 404-880-8709.

Clarkson University, Graduate School, School of Science, Department of Physics, Potsdam, NY 13699. Offers MS, PhD. *Faculty:* 8 full-time (0 women). *Students:* 11 full-time (1 woman), 6 international. Average age 26. 30 applicants, 83% accepted. In 1998, 4 master's, 1 doctorate awarded. *Degree requirements:* For master's, foreign language and thesis not required; for doctorate, dissertation, departmental qualifying exam required, foreign language not required. *Entrance requirements:* For master's, GRE, TOEFL. *Application deadline:* For fall admission, 5/15 (priority date); for spring admission, 10/15 (priority date). Applications are processed on a rolling basis. Application fee: $25 ($35 for international students). Tuition: Part-time $661 per credit hour. Required fees: $215 per semester. *Financial aid:* In 1998–99, 2 research assistantships, 8 teaching assistantships were awarded.; fellowships *Faculty research:* Computer simulation, stochastic processes, adhesion mechanisms, metals and alloys, thin film. Total annual research expenditures: $73,569. *Unit head:* Vladimir Privman, Chair, 315-268-2396, Fax: 315-268-6670, E-mail: privman@clarkson.edu. *Application contact:* Dr. Philip K. Hopke, Dean of the Graduate School, 315-268-6447, Fax: 315-268-7994, E-mail: hopkepk@clarkson.edu.

Clark University, Graduate School, Department of Physics, Worcester, MA 01610-1477. Offers MA, PhD. Part-time programs available. *Students:* 11 (3 women). 68 applicants, 7% accepted. In 1998, 3 doctorates awarded. Terminal master's awarded for partial completion of doctoral program. *Degree requirements:* For master's, computer language, thesis or alternative required, foreign language not required; for doctorate, one foreign language, computer language, dissertation required. *Entrance requirements:* For master's and doctorate, TOEFL (minimum score of 575 required). *Application deadline:* For fall admission, 3/1 (priority date). Applications are processed on a rolling basis. Application fee: $40. *Financial aid:* Research assistantships, teaching assistantships, Federal Work-Study and tuition waivers (full and partial) available. Financial aid application deadline: 4/1. *Faculty research:* Statistical and thermal physics, magnetic properties of materials, computer simulation. *Unit head:* Dr. S. Leslie Blatt, Chair, 508-793-7169. *Application contact:* Sujata Davis, Department Secretary, 508-793-7169.

Clemson University, Graduate School, College of Engineering and Science, Department of Physics and Astronomy, Clemson, SC 29634. Offers physics (MS, PhD), including astronomy and astrophysics, atmospheric physics, biophysics. Part-time programs available. *Students:* 33 full-time (8 women), 4 part-time; includes 1 minority (African American), 11 international. Average age 25. 48 applicants, 73% accepted. In 1998, 9 master's, 2 doctorates awarded. Terminal master's awarded for partial completion of doctoral program. *Degree requirements:* For master's, thesis or alternative required, foreign language not required; for doctorate, dissertation required, foreign language not required. *Entrance requirements:* For master's and doctorate, GRE General Test, TOEFL. *Application deadline:* For fall admission, 2/15 (priority date). Applications are processed on a rolling basis. Application fee: $35. *Financial aid:* Fellowships, research assistantships, teaching assistantships available. Financial aid application deadline: 6/1; financial aid applicants required to submit FAFSA. *Faculty research:* Radiation physics, solid-state physics, nuclear physics, radar and lidar studies of atmosphere. *Unit head:* Dr. Peter J. McNulty, Chair, 864-656-3419, Fax: 864-656-0805, E-mail: mpeter@clemson.edu. *Application contact:* Dr. Miguel F. Larsen, Graduate Coordinator, 864-656-5309, Fax: 864-656-0805, E-mail: mlarson@clemson.edu.

See in-depth description on page 445.

Cleveland State University, College of Graduate Studies, College of Arts and Sciences, Department of Physics, Cleveland, OH 44115-2440. Offers applied optics (MS); condensed matter physics (MS). Part-time programs available. *Faculty:* 9 full-time (0 women). Average age 39. 2 applicants, 100% accepted. In 1998, 3 degrees awarded. *Degree requirements:* For master's, computer language required, foreign language and thesis not required. *Application deadline:* For fall admission, 7/15 (priority date). Applications are processed on a rolling basis. Application fee: $25. *Faculty research:* Statistical mechanics of phase transitions, low-temperature and solid-state physics, superconductivity, theoretical light scattering. Total annual research expenditures: $350,000. *Unit head:* Dr. Clyde B. Bratton, Chairperson, 216-687-2427. *Application contact:* Dr. James A. Locke, Director, 216-687-2425.

College of William and Mary, Faculty of Arts and Sciences, Department of Physics, Williamsburg, VA 23187-8795. Offers MA, MS, PhD. *Faculty:* 29 full-time (2 women). *Students:* 43 full-time (7 women); includes 4 minority (1 African American, 2 Asian Americans or Pacific Islanders, 1 Hispanic American), 19 international. Average age 28. 88 applicants, 56% accepted. In 1998, 12 master's, 8 doctorates awarded. Terminal master's awarded for partial completion of doctoral program. *Degree requirements:* For master's, comprehensive exam, minimum GPA of 3.0 required, foreign language and thesis not required; for doctorate, dissertation, comprehensive and final exams required, foreign language not required. *Entrance requirements:* For master's and doctorate, GRE General Test, GRE Subject Test, minimum GPA of 2.5. *Average time to degree:* Master's–1.5 years full-time; doctorate–4.5 years full-time, 7.5 years part-time. *Application deadline:* For fall admission, 3/1 (priority date). Applications are processed on a rolling basis. Application fee: $30. *Financial aid:* In 1998–99, 36 research assistantships with full tuition reimbursements (averaging $11,250 per year), 19 teaching assistantships with full tuition reimbursements (averaging $11,250 per year) were awarded.; career-related internships or fieldwork also available. Financial aid applicants required to submit FAFSA. *Faculty research:* Nuclear/particle, condensed-matter, atomic, and plasma physics; accelerator physics; molecular/optical physics; plasma/nonlinear physics. Total annual research expenditures: $2.7 million. *Unit head:* Dr. J. Dirk Walecka, Chair, 757-221-3540. *Application contact:* Dr. Marc Sher, Chair of Admissions, 757-221-3538, Fax: 757-221-3540, E-mail: grad@physics.wm.edu.

Colorado School of Mines, Graduate School, Department of Physics, Golden, CO 80401-1887. Offers applied physics (PhD); physics (MS). Part-time programs available. *Faculty:* 15 full-time (0 women), 7 part-time (0 women). *Students:* 19 full-time (3 women), 5 part-time (1 woman); includes 1 minority (Asian American or Pacific Islander), 10 international. 25 applicants, 48% accepted. In 1998, 3 master's awarded (100% found work related to degree); 2 doctorates awarded (50% found work related to degree). *Degree requirements:* For master's, thesis required, foreign language not required; for doctorate, dissertation, oral and written comprehensive exams required, foreign language not required. *Entrance requirements:* For master's and doctorate, GRE General Test, GRE Subject Test, TOEFL, minimum GPA of 3.0, BS in physics. *Application deadline:* Applications are processed on a rolling basis. Application fee: $40. Electronic applications accepted. *Financial aid:* In 1998–99, 18 students received aid, including 1 fellowship, 12 research assistantships, 5 teaching assistantships; unspecified assistantships also available. Aid available to part-time students. Financial aid applicants required to submit FAFSA. *Faculty research:* Light scattering, low-energy nuclear physics, high fusion plasma diagnostics, laser operations, mathematical physics. Total annual research expenditures: $536,758. *Unit head:* Dr. Don Williamson, Head, 303-273-3830, E-mail: dwilliam@mines.edu. *Application contact:* Reuben Collins, Professor, 303-273-3851, Fax: 303-273-3919, E-mail: rtcollin@mines.edu.

Colorado State University, Graduate School, College of Natural Sciences, Department of Physics, Fort Collins, CO 80523-0015. Offers MS, PhD. *Faculty:* 20 full-time (1 woman), 4 part-time (1 woman). *Students:* 23 full-time (7 women), 17 part-time (2 women), 15 international. Average age 31. 150 applicants, 19% accepted. In 1998, 4 master's, 4 doctorates awarded. Terminal master's awarded for partial completion of doctoral program. *Degree requirements:* For doctorate, dissertation required, foreign language not required, foreign language not required. *Entrance requirements:* For master's and doctorate, GRE General Test, TOEFL (minimum score of 600 required), minimum GPA of 3.0. *Application deadline:* For fall admission, 2/15 (priority date). Applications are processed on a rolling basis. Application fee: $30. Electronic applications accepted. *Financial aid:* In 1998–99, 2 fellowships, 14 research assistantships, 18

Physics

Colorado State University (continued)

teaching assistantships were awarded.; career-related internships or fieldwork, Federal Work-Study, and traineeships also available. *Faculty research:* Experimental condensed-matter physics, laser spectroscopy, optics, theoretical condensed-matter physics, particle physics. Total annual research expenditures: $1.8 million. *Unit head:* James R. Sites, Chair, 970-491-6206. *Application contact:* Martin Gelfand, Chairman, Graduate Admissions Committee, 970-491-5263, E-mail: gelfand@lamar.colostate.edu.

Columbia University, Graduate School of Arts and Sciences, Division of Natural Sciences, Department of Physics, New York, NY 10027. Offers M Phil, MA, PhD. *Degree requirements:* For master's, foreign language and thesis not required; for doctorate, dissertation required, foreign language not required. *Entrance requirements:* For master's and doctorate, GRE General Test, GRE Subject Test, TOEFL, 3 years of course work in physics. *Faculty research:* Theoretical physics; astrophysics; low-, medium-, and high-energy physics.

Concordia University, School of Graduate Studies, Faculty of Arts and Science, Department of Physics, Montréal, PQ H3G 1M8, Canada. Offers M Sc, PhD. *Students:* 21 full-time (3 women), 2 part-time. *Degree requirements:* For master's, thesis or alternative required; for doctorate, dissertation, comprehensive exam required. *Entrance requirements:* For master's, honors degree in physics or equivalent; for doctorate, M Sc. Application fee: $50. *Financial aid:* Research assistantships, teaching assistantships available. *Faculty research:* Fundamental physics, applied physics, nuclear physics, statistical physics, stochastic quantum mechanics. *Unit head:* Dr. J. D. Cheeke, Chair, 514-848-3270, Fax: 514-848-2828. *Application contact:* Dr. M. Frank, Director, 514-848-3271, Fax: 514-848-2828.

Cornell University, Graduate School, Graduate Fields of Arts and Sciences, Field of Physics, Ithaca, NY 14853-0001. Offers experimental physics (MS, PhD); physics (MS, PhD); theoretical physics (MS, PhD). *Faculty:* 55 full-time. *Students:* 151 full-time (31 women); includes 12 minority (1 African American, 9 Asian Americans or Pacific Islanders, 2 Hispanic Americans), 57 international. 399 applicants, 26% accepted. In 1998, 16 master's, 27 doctorates awarded. Terminal master's awarded for partial completion of doctoral program. *Degree requirements:* For master's and doctorate, thesis/dissertation required, foreign language not required. *Entrance requirements:* For master's and doctorate, TOEFL (minimum score of 550 required). *Application deadline:* For fall admission, 1/1. Application fee: $65. Electronic applications accepted. *Financial aid:* In 1998–99, 150 students received aid, including 35 fellowships with full tuition reimbursements available, 66 research assistantships with full tuition reimbursements available, 49 teaching assistantships with full tuition reimbursements available; institutionally-sponsored loans, scholarships, tuition waivers (full and partial), and unspecified assistantships also available. Financial aid applicants required to submit FAFSA. *Faculty research:* Experimental condensed matter physics, theoretical condensed matter physics, experimental high energy particle physics, particle and field theory physics, theoretical astrophysics. *Unit head:* Director of Graduate Studies, 607-255-6016, Fax: 607-255-2643. *Application contact:* Graduate Field Assistant, 607-255-6016, E-mail: phys_dpt@cornell.edu.

Creighton University, Graduate School, College of Arts and Sciences, Program in Physics, Omaha, NE 68178-0001. Offers MS. *Faculty:* 3 full-time. *Students:* 8 full-time (0 women); includes 2 minority (1 Asian American or Pacific Islander, 1 Hispanic American), 1 international. In 1998, 4 degrees awarded. *Degree requirements:* For master's, thesis or alternative required. *Entrance requirements:* For master's, GRE General Test, GRE Subject Test, TOEFL (minimum score of 550 required). *Application deadline:* For fall admission, 3/1. Applications are processed on a rolling basis. Application fee: $30. *Unit head:* Dr. Robert Kennedy, Chair, 402-280-2835. *Application contact:* Dr. Barbara J. Braden, Dean, Graduate School, 402-280-2870, Fax: 402-280-5762.

Dalhousie University, Faculty of Graduate Studies, College of Arts and Science, Faculty of Science, Department of Physics, Halifax, NS B3H 3J5, Canada. Offers M Sc, PhD. *Faculty:* 13 full-time (1 woman), 14 part-time (1 woman). *Students:* 14 full-time (1 woman), 1 part-time; includes 1 African American Average age 26. In 1998, 2 master's, 3 doctorates awarded. *Degree requirements:* For master's and doctorate, thesis/dissertation required, foreign language not required. *Entrance requirements:* For master's and doctorate, TOEFL (minimum score of 600 required). *Application deadline:* For fall admission, 4/1. Applications are processed on a rolling basis. Application fee: $55. *Financial aid:* Fellowships, teaching assistantships available. Financial aid application deadline: 3/1. *Faculty research:* Applied, experimental, and solid-state physics. Total annual research expenditures: $1.4 million. *Unit head:* Dr. D. Kiang, Chair, 902-494-2337, Fax: 902-494-5191, E-mail: physics@dal.ca. *Application contact:* Dr. R. A. Dunlap, Graduate Coordinator, 902-494-2394, Fax: 902-494-5191, E-mail: gradc@fizz.phys.dal.ca.

Dartmouth College, School of Arts and Sciences, Department of Physics and Astronomy, Hanover, NH 03755. Offers MS, PhD. *Faculty:* 18 full-time (1 woman), 4 part-time (0 women). *Students:* 30 full-time (12 women); includes 1 minority (African American), 7 international. 184 applicants, 16% accepted. In 1998, 2 master's awarded (100% found work related to degree); 5 doctorates awarded (20% entered university research/teaching, 80% found other work related to degree). Terminal master's awarded for partial completion of doctoral program. *Degree requirements:* For master's and doctorate, thesis/dissertation required. *Entrance requirements:* For master's and doctorate, GRE General Test, GRE Subject Test. *Application deadline:* For fall admission, 2/28 (priority date). Application fee: $15. *Financial aid:* In 1998–99, 30 students received aid, including 10 research assistantships with full tuition reimbursements available; fellowships with full tuition reimbursements available, grants, institutionally-sponsored loans, scholarships, and tuition waivers (full) also available. *Unit head:* Dr. Mary Hudson, Chair, 603-646-2359. *Application contact:* Judy Lowell, Administrative Assistant, 603-646-2359.

See in-depth description on page 453.

Delaware State University, Graduate Programs, Department of Physics, Dover, DE 19901-2277. Offers physics (MS); physics teaching (MS). Part-time and evening/weekend programs available. *Degree requirements:* For master's, foreign language and thesis not required. *Entrance requirements:* For master's, minimum GPA of 2.75 overall, 3.0 in major. *Faculty research:* Thermal properties of solids, nuclear physics, radiation damage in solids.

DePaul University, College of Liberal Arts and Sciences, Department of Physics, Chicago, IL 60604-2287. Offers applied physics (MS); teaching of physics (MS). Part-time and evening/weekend programs available. *Faculty:* 7 full-time (1 woman), 3 part-time (0 women). *Students:* 4 full-time (0 women); includes 1 minority (Asian American or Pacific Islander) Average age 25. 12 applicants, 42% accepted. In 1998, 4 degrees awarded (0% continued full-time study). *Degree requirements:* For master's, thesis, oral exams required, foreign language not required. *Entrance requirements:* For master's, minimum GPA of 2.7. *Average time to degree:* Master's–2 years full-time. *Application deadline:* For fall admission, 6/15 (priority date); for spring admission, 9/1. Applications are processed on a rolling basis. Application fee: $25. *Financial aid:* In 1998–99, teaching assistantships (averaging $5,000 per year); tuition waivers (partial) also available. *Faculty research:* Optics, solid-state physics, computational physics, atomic physics, laser physics. Total annual research expenditures: $54,000. *Unit head:* Dr. Anthony F. Behof, Chairman, 773-325-7330, Fax: 773-325-7334, E-mail: abehof@wppost.depaul.edu. *Application contact:* Department Office, 773-325-7330, Fax: 773-325-7334, E-mail: cgoedde@condor.depaul.edu.

Drexel University, Graduate School, College of Arts and Sciences, Department of Physics and Atmospheric Science, Philadelphia, PA 19104-2875. Offers MS, PhD. *Faculty:* 21 full-time (1 woman), 1 part-time (0 women). *Students:* 26 full-time (7 women), 9 part-time (2 women); includes 2 minority (1 Asian American or Pacific Islander, 1 Hispanic American), 23 international. Average age 31. 94 applicants, 19% accepted. In 1998, 9 master's, 3 doctorates awarded. Terminal master's awarded for partial completion of doctoral program. *Degree requirements:* For master's, foreign language and thesis not required; for doctorate, dissertation required,

foreign language not required. *Entrance requirements:* For master's and doctorate, GRE, TOEFL (minimum score of 570 required). *Application deadline:* For fall admission, 8/21. Applications are processed on a rolling basis. Application fee: $35. Tuition: Full-time $15,795; part-time $585 per credit. Required fees: $375; $67 per term. Tuition and fees vary according to program. *Financial aid:* In 1998–99, 8 research assistantships, 23 teaching assistantships were awarded.; unspecified assistantships also available. Financial aid application deadline: 2/1. *Faculty research:* Nuclear structure, mesoscale meteorology, numerical astrophysics, numerical weather prediction, earth energy radiation budget. *Unit head:* Dr. Michael Vallieres, Head, 215-895-2709. *Application contact:* Director of Graduate Admissions, 215-895-6700, Fax: 215-895-5939.

See in-depth description on page 455.

Duke University, Graduate School, Department of Physics, Durham, NC 27708-0586. Offers PhD. Part-time programs available. *Faculty:* 27 full-time, 19 part-time. *Students:* 61 full-time (11 women), 24 international. 64 applicants, 58% accepted. In 1998, 11 doctorates awarded. *Degree requirements:* For doctorate, dissertation required. *Entrance requirements:* For doctorate, GRE General Test, GRE Subject Test. *Application deadline:* For fall admission, 12/31. Application fee: $75. *Financial aid:* Fellowships, research assistantships, teaching assistantships, Federal Work-Study available. Financial aid application deadline: 12/31. *Unit head:* Dr. Henry Weller, Director of Graduate Studies, 919-660-2502, Fax: 919-660-2525, E-mail: donna@phy.duke.edu.

See in-depth description on page 457.

East Carolina University, Graduate School, College of Arts and Sciences, Department of Physics, Greenville, NC 27858-4353. Offers applied and biomedical physics (MS, PhD), including applied and biomedical physics (MS), biomedical physics (PhD); medical physics (MS). Part-time programs available. *Faculty:* 12 full-time (0 women). *Students:* 16 full-time (5 women), 1 part-time; includes 3 minority (1 African American, 2 Asian Americans or Pacific Islanders), 6 international. Average age 27. 23 applicants, 57% accepted. In 1998, 4 master's awarded. *Degree requirements:* For master's, one foreign language (computer language can substitute), comprehensive exam required. *Entrance requirements:* For master's, GRE General Test, TOEFL. *Application deadline:* Applications are processed on a rolling basis. Application fee: $40. Tuition, state resident: full-time $1,012. Tuition, nonresident: full-time $8,578. Required fees: $1,006. Part-time tuition and fees vary according to course load. *Financial aid:* Research assistantships with partial tuition reimbursements, teaching assistantships with partial tuition reimbursements, Federal Work-Study available. Aid available to part-time students. Financial aid application deadline: 6/1. *Unit head:* Dr. Mumtaz A. Dinno, Chairman, 252-328-6739, E-mail: dinnom@mail.ecu.edu. *Application contact:* Dr. Xin-Hua Hu, Director of Graduate Studies, 252-328-1860, Fax: 252-328-6314, E-mail: hux@mail.ecu.edu.

Announcement: The department offers MS and PhD degrees in applied and biomedical physics. Research areas include atomic collisions, biomedical lasers, biophysics, bioacoustics, musical acoustics, and solar physics. Teaching and research assistantships, scholarships, and summer research are available. Visit the Web site at http://www.physics.ecu.edu.

Eastern Michigan University, Graduate School, College of Arts and Sciences, Department of Physics and Astronomy, Program in Physics, Ypsilanti, MI 48197. Offers MS. In 1998, 4 degrees awarded. *Degree requirements:* For master's, thesis required (for some programs), foreign language not required. *Entrance requirements:* For master's, TOEFL (minimum score of 500 required). *Application deadline:* For fall admission, 5/15; for spring admission, 3/15. Applications are processed on a rolling basis. Application fee: $30. *Financial aid:* Fellowships, teaching assistantships available. Aid available to part-time students. Financial aid application deadline: 3/15; financial aid applicants required to submit FAFSA. *Unit head:* Dr. Daniel Trochet, Coordinator, 734-487-4144.

Emory University, Graduate School of Arts and Sciences, Department of Physics, Atlanta, GA 30322-1100. Offers physics (PhD), including biophysics, radiological physics, solid-state physics. *Faculty:* 17 full-time (1 woman), 3 part-time (0 women). *Students:* 10 full-time (1 woman); includes 1 minority (Asian American or Pacific Islander), 8 international. Average age 24. 22 applicants, 41% accepted. In 1998, 3 doctorates awarded. *Degree requirements:* For doctorate, dissertation, comprehensive exams required, foreign language not required. *Entrance requirements:* For doctorate, GRE General Test, TOEFL, minimum GPA of 3.0. *Application deadline:* For fall admission, 1/20 (priority date). Application fee: $45. *Financial aid:* Fellowships, teaching assistantships, institutionally-sponsored loans, scholarships, and tuition waivers (partial) available. Financial aid application deadline: 1/20; financial aid applicants required to submit FAFSA. *Faculty research:* Theory of semiconductors and superlattices, experimental laser optics and submillimeter spectroscopy theory, neural networks and stereoscopic vision, experimental studies of the structure and function of metalloproteins. *Unit head:* Dr. Vincent Huynh, Director of Graduate Studies, 404-727-4295, Fax: 404-727-8073, E-mail: phsbhh@physics.emory.edu. *Application contact:* Brenda J. Wingo, Coordinator of Academic Services, 404-727-8037, Fax: 404-727-8073, E-mail: phsbw@physics.emory.edu.

See in-depth description on page 459.

Emporia State University, School of Graduate Studies, College of Liberal Arts and Sciences, Division of Physical Sciences, Emporia, KS 66801-5087. Offers chemistry (MS); earth science (MS); physics (MS). *Faculty:* 18 full-time (1 woman), 3 part-time (0 women). *Students:* 10 full-time (4 women), 11 part-time (3 women); includes 1 minority (Native American), 8 international. *Degree requirements:* For master's, comprehensive exam or thesis required. *Entrance requirements:* For master's, TOEFL (minimum score of 550 required), written exam. *Application deadline:* For fall admission, 8/15 (priority date). Applications are processed on a rolling basis. Application fee: $30 ($75 for international students). Electronic applications accepted. Tuition, state resident: full-time $2,356; part-time $106 per credit hour. Tuition, nonresident: full-time $6,158; part-time $264 per credit hour. *Unit head:* Dr. DeWayne Backhus, Chair, 316-341-5330, E-mail: backhusd@emporia.edu.

Fairleigh Dickinson University, Teaneck–Hackensack Campus, University College: Arts, Sciences, and Professional Studies, School of Natural Sciences, Program in Physics, Teaneck, NJ 07666-1914. Offers MS. *Degree requirements:* For master's, foreign language and thesis not required. *Entrance requirements:* For master's, GRE General Test. *Faculty research:* Aquatic ecology, toxicology, desalination, lightwave technology, neuroendocrinology.

Fisk University, Graduate Programs, Department of Physics, Nashville, TN 37208-3051. Offers MA. *Faculty:* 4 full-time (0 women). *Students:* 8 full-time (1 woman). Average age 25. In 1998, 3 degrees awarded (33% entered university research/teaching, 67% continued full-time study). *Degree requirements:* For master's, thesis, comprehensive exam required, foreign language not required. *Entrance requirements:* For master's, GRE General Test, GRE Subject Test, minimum GPA of 3.0. *Average time to degree:* Master's–2.4 years full-time. *Application deadline:* For fall admission, 6/15 (priority date). Applications are processed on a rolling basis. Application fee: $25. Tuition: Full-time $8,480; part-time $471 per semester hour. Required fees: $540; $270 per semester. *Financial aid:* In 1998–99, 12 research assistantships with full tuition reimbursements (averaging $15,000 per year) were awarded. *Faculty research:* Molecular physics, astrophysics. *Unit head:* Dr. Eugene Collins, Director, 615-329-8605. *Application contact:* Anthony Jones, Director of Admissions, 615-329-8665, Fax: 615-329-8774, E-mail: ajones@dubois_fisk.edu.

Florida Agricultural and Mechanical University, Division of Graduate Studies, Research, and Continuing Education, College of Arts and Sciences, Department of Physics, Tallahassee, FL 32307-3200. Offers MS. *Students:* 2 (1 woman); both minorities (1 African American, 1 Asian American or Pacific Islander). *Degree requirements:* For master's, thesis required. *Entrance requirements:* For master's, GRE General Test (minimum combined score of 1000 required), minimum GPA of 3.0. *Application deadline:* For fall admission, 5/13. Application fee: $20. *Unit head:* Dr. C. A. Weatherford, Chairperson, 850-599-3470, Fax: 850-599-3577.

Physics

Florida Atlantic University, Charles E. Schmidt College of Science, Department of Physics, Boca Raton, FL 33431-0991. Offers MS, MST, PhD. Part-time programs available. *Faculty:* 11 full-time (1 woman), 4 part-time (0 women). *Students:* 16 full-time (6 women), 4 part-time (1 woman); includes 2 minority (1 Asian American or Pacific Islander, 1 Hispanic American), 4 international. Average age 35. 42 applicants, 48% accepted. In 1998, 4 master's, 2 doctorates awarded. *Degree requirements:* For master's, thesis required (for some programs), foreign language not required; for doctorate, dissertation required, foreign language not required. *Entrance requirements:* For master's, GRE General Test (minimum combined score of 1100 required; average 1142), minimum GPA of 3.0; for doctorate, GRE General Test (minimum combined score of 1100 required; average 1230). Application fee: $20. Tuition, state resident: part-time $148 per credit hour. Tuition, nonresident: part-time $509 per credit hour. *Financial aid:* In 1998–99, 3 research assistantships with full tuition reimbursements (averaging $14,000 per year), 17 teaching assistantships with full tuition reimbursements (averaging $14,000 per year) were awarded.; fellowships, Federal Work-Study and tuition waivers (partial) also available. *Faculty research:* Astrophysics, spectroscopy, mathematical physics, theory of metals, superconductivity. Total annual research expenditures: $150,000. *Unit head:* Dr. Fernando Medina, Chair, 561-297-3380, Fax: 561-297-2662, E-mail: medina@acc.fau.edu. *Application contact:* Bjorn Lamborn, Graduate Coordinator, 561-297-3304, Fax: 561-297-2662, E-mail: lamborn@acc.fau.edu.

Florida Institute of Technology, Graduate School, College of Science and Liberal Arts, Department of Physics and Space Sciences, Program in Physics, Melbourne, FL 32901-6975. Offers MS, PhD. Part-time programs available. *Faculty:* 7 full-time (0 women). *Students:* 1 (woman) full-time, 5 part-time (1 woman); includes 1 minority (Asian American or Pacific Islander), 1 international. Average age 33. 21 applicants, 43% accepted. In 1998, 1 master's awarded. Terminal master's awarded for partial completion of doctoral program. *Degree requirements:* For master's, comprehensive exam required, thesis optional, foreign language not required; for doctorate, dissertation, comprehensive exam, oral defense of dissertation required, foreign language not required. *Entrance requirements:* For master's, GRE General Test, GRE Subject Test, minimum GPA of 3.0, proficiency in a computer language; for doctorate, GRE General Test, GRE Subject Test, minimum GPA of 3.2. *Application deadline:* Applications are processed on a rolling basis. Application fee: $50. Electronic applications accepted. Tuition: Part-time $575 per credit hour. Required fees: $100. Tuition and fees vary according to campus/location and program. *Financial aid:* In 1998–99, 3 students received aid, including 3 teaching assistantships (averaging $4,394 per year); research assistantships, tuition remissions also available. Financial aid application deadline: 3/1; financial aid applicants required to submit FAFSA. *Faculty research:* Lasers, semiconductors, magnetism, quantum devices, solid state physics, optics. Total annual research expenditures: $272,260. *Unit head:* Bonita Evans, Coordinator, 360-866-6000 Ext. 6707, Fax: 360-866-6794, E-mail: evansb@evergreen.edu. *Application contact:* Carolyn P. Farrior, Associate Dean of Graduate Admissions, 407-674-7118, Fax: 407-723-9468, E-mail: cfarrior@fit.edu.

See in-depth description on page 461.

Florida International University, College of Arts and Sciences, Department of Physics, Miami, FL 33199. Offers MS, PhD. Part-time and evening/weekend programs available. *Faculty:* 15 full-time (2 women), 4 part-time (0 women). *Students:* 19 full-time (6 women), 3 part-time (1 woman); includes 9 minority (all Hispanic Americans), 10 international. Average age 30. 18 applicants, 61% accepted. In 1998, 5 degrees awarded. *Degree requirements:* For master's and doctorate, one foreign language, thesis/dissertation required. *Entrance requirements:* For master's and doctorate, GRE General Test (minimum combined score of 1000 required), TOEFL (minimum score of 500 required). *Application deadline:* For fall admission, 4/1 (priority date); for spring admission, 10/1. Applications are processed on a rolling basis. Application fee: $20. Tuition, state resident: part-time $145 per credit hour. Tuition, nonresident: part-time $506 per credit hour. Required fees: $158; $158 per year. *Financial aid:* Application deadline: 4/1. *Faculty research:* Molecular collision processes (molecular beams), biophysical optics. *Unit head:* Dr. Stephan L. Mintz, Chairperson, 305-348-2605, Fax: 305-348-3053, E-mail: mintz@fiu.edu.

Florida State University, Graduate Studies, College of Arts and Sciences, Department of Physics, Tallahassee, FL 32306. Offers chemical physics (MS, PhD); physics (MS, PhD). *Faculty:* 42 full-time (3 women). *Students:* 65 full-time (9 women), 4 part-time (1 woman); includes 4 minority (1 African American, 1 Asian American or Pacific Islander, 2 Hispanic Americans) Average age 24. 200 applicants, 7% accepted. In 1998, 2 master's, 5 doctorates awarded. Terminal master's awarded for partial completion of doctoral program. *Degree requirements:* For master's, thesis required (for some programs), foreign language not required; for doctorate, dissertation required, foreign language not required. *Entrance requirements:* For master's and doctorate, GRE General Test (minimum combined score of 1100 required), minimum GPA of 3.0. *Average time to degree:* Master's–2 years full-time; doctorate–6 years full-time. *Application deadline:* Applications are processed on a rolling basis. Application fee: $20. Electronic applications accepted. Tuition, state resident: part-time $139 per credit hour. Tuition, nonresident: part-time $482 per credit hour. Tuition and fees vary according to program. *Financial aid:* In 1998–99, 7 fellowships with full tuition reimbursements, 54 research assistantships with full tuition reimbursements (averaging $15,200 per year), 15 teaching assistantships with full tuition reimbursements (averaging $15,200 per year) were awarded.; career-related internships or fieldwork and Federal Work-Study also available. Financial aid application deadline: 3/1; financial aid applicants required to submit FAFSA. *Faculty research:* Surface physics, elementary particles and fields, nanostructure condensed matter. Total annual research expenditures: $4 million. *Unit head:* Dr. Kirby W. Kemper, Chairman, 850-644-2867, Fax: 850-644-2338, E-mail: kirby@phy.fsu.edu.

Announcement: Extensive research opportunities exist in theoretical and experimental physics in the areas of atomic, condensed-matter, high-energy, and nuclear physics. This research makes use of extensive computers and instrumentation at FSU, as well as the Supercomputer Computations Research Institute and the National High-Magnetic Field Laboratory. Each full-time graduate student has an assistantship.

See in-depth description on page 465.

The George Washington University, Columbian School of Arts and Sciences, Department of Physics, Washington, DC 20052. Offers physics (PhD). Part-time and evening/weekend programs available. *Faculty:* 5 full-time (0 women), 1 (woman) part-time. *Students:* 7 full-time (0 women), 11 part-time (1 woman), 12 international. Average age 32. 19 applicants, 63% accepted. In 1998, 2 doctorates awarded. *Degree requirements:* For doctorate, dissertation, general exam required. *Entrance requirements:* For doctorate, GRE General Test, GRE Subject Test, minimum GPA of 3.0. Application fee: $55. Tuition: Full-time $17,328; part-time $722 per credit hour. Required fees: $828; $35 per credit hour. Tuition and fees vary according to campus/location and program. *Financial aid:* In 1998–99, 9 fellowships, 8 teaching assistantships were awarded.; research assistantships, Federal Work-Study also available. Financial aid application deadline: 2/1. *Unit head:* Dr. Barry L. Berman, Chair, 202-994-6275.

Georgia Institute of Technology, Graduate Studies and Research, College of Sciences, School of Physics, Atlanta, GA 30332-0001. Offers applied physics (MSA Phy); physics (MS, MS Phys, PhD). Part-time programs available. Terminal master's awarded for partial completion of doctoral program. *Degree requirements:* For doctorate, dissertation, comprehensive exam required, foreign language not required. *Entrance requirements:* For master's, TOEFL (minimum score of 600 required), minimum GPA of 3.0; for doctorate, TOEFL (minimum score of 600 required), minimum GPA of 3.4. Electronic applications accepted. *Faculty research:* Atomic and molecular physics, chemical physics, condensed matter, optics, nonlinear physics and chaos.

Announcement: Presidential Fellowships may be awarded to particularly well-qualified students; these fellowships add $5000 per annum to the standard assistantship stipend, for a total of $20,000. Tuition and other fees for students with assistantships are reduced to $245 per quarter. Applications received by January 15 receive full consideration.

Georgia State University, College of Arts and Sciences, Department of Physics and Astronomy, Program in Physics, Atlanta, GA 30303-3083. Offers MS, PhD. Part-time and evening/weekend programs available. *Students:* 21 full-time (2 women), 9 part-time (3 women); includes 4 minority (1 African American, 2 Asian Americans or Pacific Islanders, 1 Native American), 12 international. Average age 26. 50 applicants, 22% accepted. In 1998, 8 master's, 3 doctorates awarded. Terminal master's awarded for partial completion of doctoral program. *Degree requirements:* For master's, one foreign language (computer language can substitute), thesis or alternative required; for doctorate, 2 foreign languages (computer language can substitute for one), dissertation required. *Entrance requirements:* For master's and doctorate, GRE General Test, GRE Subject Test, TOEFL (minimum score of 550 required), minimum GPA of 3.0. *Average time to degree:* Master's–2 years full-time, 4 years part-time; doctorate–5 years full-time. Application fee: $25. Tuition, state resident: full-time $2,896; part-time $121 per credit hour. Tuition, nonresident: full-time $11,584; part-time $483 per credit hour. Required fees: $468. Tuition and fees vary according to program. *Financial aid:* Research assistantships, teaching assistantships, Federal Work-Study, institutionally-sponsored loans, and tuition waivers (full and partial) available. Financial aid application deadline: 5/1. *Faculty research:* Biophysics; nuclear, condensed-matter, and atomic physics; astrophysics. Total annual research expenditures: $630,700. *Unit head:* Renee Loew, Director of Graduate Admissions and Records, 732-367-1717, Fax: 732-364-4516. *Application contact:* Dr. Unil Perera, Director of Graduate Studies, 404-651-2279, Fax: 404-651-1427, E-mail: phyuup@panther.gsu.edu.

See in-depth description on page 467.

Graduate School and University Center of the City University of New York, Graduate Studies, Program in Physics, New York, NY 10036-8099. Offers PhD. *Faculty:* 105 full-time (3 women). *Students:* 90 full-time (12 women), 1 part-time; includes 1 African American, 2 Asian Americans or Pacific Islanders, 2 Hispanic Americans Average age 31. 103 applicants, 62% accepted. In 1998, 8 degrees awarded. *Degree requirements:* For doctorate, dissertation required, foreign language not required. *Entrance requirements:* For doctorate, GRE General Test. *Application deadline:* For fall admission, 4/15. Application fee: $40. *Financial aid:* In 1998–99, 49 students received aid, including 45 fellowships, 2 teaching assistantships; research assistantships, career-related internships or fieldwork, Federal Work-Study, institutionally-sponsored loans, and tuition waivers (full and partial) also available. Financial aid application deadline: 2/1; financial aid applicants required to submit FAFSA. *Faculty research:* Condensed-matter, particle, nuclear, and atomic physics. *Unit head:* Dr. Louis S. Celenza, Executive Officer, 212-642-2454.

Hampton University, Graduate College, Department of Physics, Hampton, VA 23668. Offers MS, PhD. Part-time and evening/weekend programs available. *Faculty:* 17 full-time (1 woman). *Students:* 30 full-time (8 women), 6 part-time (3 women); includes 29 minority (22 African Americans, 7 Asian Americans or Pacific Islanders), 4 international. In 1998, 3 master's, 4 doctorates awarded. Terminal master's awarded for partial completion of doctoral program. *Degree requirements:* For master's, thesis optional, foreign language not required; for doctorate, dissertation, oral defense, qualifying exam required, foreign language not required. *Entrance requirements:* For master's, GRE General Test (minimum score of 450 on verbal section required); for doctorate, GRE General Test (minimum score of 550 on quantitative section required), minimum GPA of 3.0 or master's degree in physics or related field. *Application deadline:* For fall admission, 6/1 (priority date); for spring admission, 11/1. Applications are processed on a rolling basis. Application fee: $25. Tuition: Full-time $9,490; part-time $230 per semester hour. Required fees: $60; $35 per semester. Tuition and fees vary according to course load. *Financial aid:* Fellowships, research assistantships, teaching assistantships, career-related internships or fieldwork, Federal Work-Study, institutionally-sponsored loans, and scholarships available. Aid available to part-time students. Financial aid application deadline: 5/1; financial aid applicants required to submit FAFSA. *Faculty research:* Laser optics, remote sensing. *Unit head:* Dr. Donald Whitney, Interim Chair, 757-727-5277. *Application contact:* Erika Henderson, Director, Graduate Programs, 757-727-5454, Fax: 757-727-5084.

Harvard University, Graduate School of Arts and Sciences, Committee on Chemical Physics, Cambridge, MA 02138. Offers chemical physics (PhD); chemistry (AM); physics (AM). *Students:* 2 full-time (0 women); includes 1 minority (Hispanic American) *Degree requirements:* For doctorate, dissertation, cumulative exams required. *Entrance requirements:* For master's, GRE General Test, TOEFL (minimum score of 550 required); for doctorate, GRE General Test, GRE Subject Test, TOEFL (minimum score of 550 required). *Application deadline:* For fall admission, 1/1. Application fee: $60. *Unit head:* Dr. William Klemperer, Director of Graduate Studies, 617-495-4094. *Application contact:* Department of Chemistry and Chemical Biology, 617-496-3208.

Harvard University, Graduate School of Arts and Sciences, Department of Physics, Cambridge, MA 02138. Offers experimental physics (AM, PhD); medical engineering/medical physics (PhD, Sc D), including applied physics (PhD), engineering sciences (PhD), medical engineering/medical physics (Sc D), physics (PhD); theoretical physics (AM, PhD). *Students:* 80 full-time (26 women). 311 applicants, 16% accepted. In 1998, 18 master's, 22 doctorates awarded. *Degree requirements:* For doctorate, dissertation, final exams, laboratory experience required, foreign language not required. *Entrance requirements:* For master's, GRE General Test, TOEFL (minimum score of 550 required); for doctorate, GRE General Test, GRE Subject Test, TOEFL (minimum score of 550 required). *Application deadline:* For fall admission, 12/14. Application fee: $60. *Financial aid:* Fellowships, research assistantships, teaching assistantships, career-related internships or fieldwork, Federal Work-Study, and institutionally-sponsored loans available. Financial aid application deadline: 12/30. *Faculty research:* Particle physics, condensed matter physics, atomic physics. *Unit head:* Dr. David Nelson, Chairperson, 617-495-2866. *Application contact:* Office of Admissions and Financial Aid, 617-495-5315.

See in-depth description on page 469.

Harvard University, Graduate School of Arts and Sciences, Division of Engineering and Applied Sciences, Cambridge, MA 02138. Offers applied mathematics (ME, SM, PhD); applied physics (ME, SM, PhD); computer science (ME, SM, PhD); computing technology (PhD); engineering science (ME); engineering sciences (SM, PhD); medical engineering/medical physics (PhD, Sc D), including applied physics (PhD), engineering sciences (PhD), medical engineering/medical physics (Sc D), physics (PhD). *Students:* 143 full-time (31 women); includes 10 minority (1 African American, 9 Asian Americans or Pacific Islanders), 57 international. Terminal master's awarded for partial completion of doctoral program. *Degree requirements:* For master's, foreign language and thesis not required; for doctorate, dissertation required, foreign language not required. *Entrance requirements:* For master's and doctorate, GRE General Test, GRE Subject Test, TOEFL (minimum score of 550 required). Application fee: $60. *Unit head:* Dr. Paul C. Martin, Dean, 617-495-2833. *Application contact:* Office of Admissions and Financial Aid, 617-495-5315.

Harvard University, Medical School, Division of Health Sciences and Technology, Program in Medical Engineering/Medical Physics, Cambridge, MA 02138. Offers applied physics (PhD); engineering sciences (PhD); medical engineering/medical physics (Sc D); physics (PhD). Offered jointly with Massachusetts Institute of Technology. *Degree requirements:* For doctorate, dissertation, oral and written qualifying exams required, foreign language not required.

Howard University, Graduate School of Arts and Sciences, Department of Physics and Astronomy, Washington, DC 20059-0002. Offers physics (MS, PhD). Part-time programs available. *Faculty:* 17 full-time (1 woman), 2 part-time (0 women). *Students:* 32 full-time (3 women), 1 part-time; includes 21 minority (all African Americans), 11 international. Average age 35. 9 applicants, 78% accepted. In 1998, 5 master's awarded (60% found work related to degree, 40% continued full-time study); 1 doctorate awarded (100% found work related to degree). Terminal master's awarded for partial completion of doctoral program. *Degree requirements:* For master's, comprehensive exam required, thesis optional, foreign language not required; for doctorate, dissertation, departmental qualifying exam, final comprehensive exam required, foreign language not required. *Entrance requirements:* For master's, GRE General Test,

Physics

Howard University (continued)

bachelor's degree in physics or related field, minimum GPA of 3.0; for doctorate, GRE General Test, bachelor's or master's degree in physics or related field. *Average time to degree:* Master's–4 years full-time; doctorate–7 years full-time. *Application deadline:* For fall admission, 4/1; for spring admission, 11/1. Applications are processed on a rolling basis. Application fee: $45. *Financial aid:* In 1998–99, 4 fellowships with tuition reimbursements (averaging $15,000 per year), 18 research assistantships with tuition reimbursements (averaging $15,000 per year), 11 teaching assistantships with tuition reimbursements (averaging $10,000 per year) were awarded.; career-related internships or fieldwork, grants, institutionally-sponsored loans, and tuition waivers (partial) also available. Financial aid application deadline: 4/1. *Faculty research:* Atmospheric physics, spectroscopy and optical physics, high energy physics, condensed matter. Total annual research expenditures: $2.5 million. *Unit head:* Dr. Demetrius D. Venable, Chairman, 202-806-6245, Fax: 202-806-5830, E-mail: dvenable@howard.edu.

Hunter College of the City University of New York, Graduate School, Division of Sciences and Mathematics, Department of Physics, New York, NY 10021-5085. Offers MA, PhD. PhD offered jointly with the Graduate School and University Center of the City University of New York. Part-time programs available. Terminal master's awarded for partial completion of doctoral program. *Degree requirements:* For master's, comprehensive exam or thesis required. *Entrance requirements:* For master's, GRE General Test, TOEFL (minimum score of 550 required), minimum 36 credits in mathematics and physics. Tuition, state resident: full-time $4,350; part-time $185 per credit. Tuition, nonresident: full-time $7,600; part-time $320 per credit. Required fees: $8 per term. *Faculty research:* Experimental and theoretical quantum optics, experimental and theoretical condensed matter, mathematical physics.

Idaho State University, Graduate School, College of Arts and Sciences, Department of Physics, Pocatello, ID 83209. Offers natural science (MNS); physics (MS). Part-time programs available. *Degree requirements:* For master's, thesis required (for some programs), foreign language not required. *Entrance requirements:* For master's, GRE General Test. *Faculty research:* Ion beam applications, low-energy nuclear physics, relativity and cosmology, observational astronomy.

Illinois Institute of Technology, Graduate College, Armour College of Engineering and Sciences, Department of Biological, Chemical and Physical Sciences, Physics Division, Chicago, IL 60616-3793. Offers health physics (MHP); physics (MS, PhD). Part-time programs available. *Faculty:* 13 full-time (0 women), 2 part-time (0 women). *Students:* 14 full-time (2 women), 62 part-time (28 women); includes 24 minority (21 African Americans, 3 Asian Americans or Pacific Islanders), 21 international. 56 applicants, 27% accepted. In 1998, 4 master's, 3 doctorates awarded. Terminal master's awarded for partial completion of doctoral program. *Degree requirements:* For master's, thesis (for some programs), comprehensive exam required, foreign language not required; for doctorate, dissertation, qualifying comprehensive exam required, foreign language not required. *Entrance requirements:* For master's and doctorate, GRE (minimum score of 1200 required), TOEFL (minimum score of 550 required), undergraduate GPA of 3.0 required. *Application deadline:* For fall admission, 7/1; for spring admission, 11/1. Applications are processed on a rolling basis. Application fee: $30. Electronic applications accepted. *Financial aid:* In 1998–99, 5 research assistantships, 6 teaching assistantships were awarded.; fellowships, Federal Work-Study, institutionally-sponsored loans, scholarships, and graduate assistantships also available. Financial aid application deadline: 3/1. *Faculty research:* Atomic structure, quantum physics. *Unit head:* Mary Beth Carey, Vice President of Enrollment Services, 516-463-6700, Fax: 516-560-7660, E-mail: hofstra@hofstra.edu. *Application contact:* Dr. S. Mohammad Shahidehpour, Dean of Graduate College, 312-567-3024, Fax: 312-567-7517, E-mail: grad@minna.cns.iit.edu.

Indiana State University, School of Graduate Studies, College of Arts and Sciences, Department of Physics, Terre Haute, IN 47809-1401. Offers MA, MS. Part-time programs available. *Faculty:* 7 full-time (1 woman). *Students:* 1 full-time (0 women), 3 part-time (1 woman), 2 international. Average age 28. 13 applicants, 77% accepted. *Degree requirements:* For master's, thesis required (for some programs), foreign language not required. *Entrance requirements:* For master's, GRE General Test, TOEFL. *Average time to degree:* Master's–2 years full-time, 5 years part-time. *Application deadline:* For fall admission, 7/1 (priority date); for spring admission, 11/1 (priority date). Applications are processed on a rolling basis. Application fee: $20. Electronic applications accepted. *Financial aid:* Research assistantships with partial tuition reimbursements, teaching assistantships, Federal Work-Study and tuition waivers (partial) available. Aid available to part-time students. Financial aid application deadline: 3/1; financial aid applicants required to submit FAFSA. *Faculty research:* Holography, solid-state physics, fluorescent spectroscopy. *Unit head:* Dr. Torsten Alvager, Chairperson, 812-237-2064.

Indiana University Bloomington, Graduate School, College of Arts and Sciences, Department of Physics, Bloomington, IN 47405. Offers MAT, MS, PhD. PhD offered through the University Graduate School. Part-time programs available. *Faculty:* 48 full-time (3 women). *Students:* 47 full-time (11 women), 19 part-time (1 woman); includes 2 minority (1 Asian American or Pacific Islander, 1 Hispanic American), 37 international. In 1998, 11 master's, 9 doctorates awarded. Terminal master's awarded for partial completion of doctoral program. *Degree requirements:* For master's, qualifying exam required, foreign language and thesis not required; for doctorate, dissertation, qualifying exam required, foreign language not required. *Entrance requirements:* For master's and doctorate, GRE General Test, GRE Subject Test (physics), TOEFL (minimum score of 550 required). *Average time to degree:* Master's–1.5 years full-time; doctorate–6.2 years full-time. *Application deadline:* For fall admission, 1/15 (priority date); for spring admission, 9/1. Application fee: $40. Tuition, state resident: part-time $161 per credit hour. Tuition, nonresident: part-time $468 per credit hour. Required fees: $360 per year. Tuition and fees vary according to course load and program. *Financial aid:* In 1998–99, research assistantships with partial tuition reimbursements (averaging $16,464 per year), teaching assistantships with partial tuition reimbursements (averaging $11,280 per year) were awarded.; career-related internships or fieldwork also available. Financial aid application deadline: 2/1. *Unit head:* Dr. V. Alan Kostelecký, Chair, 812-855-1247, Fax: 812-855-5533. *Application contact:* June Dizer, Student Affairs Administrator, 812-855-3973, E-mail: gradphys@indiana.edu.

Announcement: Theoretical and experimental nuclear, particle, condensed matter, accelerator, astrophysics, plasma, and chemical physics. IUCF electron-cooled storage ring; nuclear theory center, supercomputers. Low-temperature clean room, photolithographic, STM, UHV analysis, 14T magnet, X-ray diffraction, and microwave facilities. Experiments at several national and international laboratories. Financial support available.

See in-depth description on page 471.

Indiana University of Pennsylvania, Graduate School, College of Natural Sciences and Mathematics, Department of Physics, Indiana, PA 15705-1087. Offers MA, MS. Part-time programs available. *Students:* 8 full-time (3 women), 1 part-time; includes 1 minority (African American), 4 international. Average age 31. 17 applicants, 53% accepted. In 1998, 4 degrees awarded. *Degree requirements:* For master's, thesis required (for some programs), foreign language not required. *Entrance requirements:* For master's, TOEFL (minimum score of 500 required). *Application deadline:* For fall admission, 7/1 (priority date); for spring admission, 11/1. Applications are processed on a rolling basis. Application fee: $30. *Financial aid:* Research assistantships, Federal Work-Study available. Aid available to part-time students. Financial aid application deadline: 3/15. *Unit head:* Richard D. Roberts, Chairperson, 724-357-2370, E-mail: rroberts@grove.iup.edu. *Application contact:* Dr. Muhammad Numan, Graduate Coordinator, 724-357-2318, E-mail: mznuman@grove.iup.edu.

Indiana University–Purdue University Indianapolis, School of Science, Department of Physics, Indianapolis, IN 46202-2896. Offers MS, PhD. Part-time programs available. *Students:* 6 full-time (0 women), 4 part-time (1 woman); includes 1 minority (African American), 3 international. Average age 26. In 1998, 2 master's awarded (0% continued full-time study); 1 doctorate awarded (100% entered university research/teaching). Terminal master's awarded for partial completion of doctoral program. *Degree requirements:* For master's, thesis optional, foreign language not required; for doctorate, dissertation required, foreign language not required. *Entrance requirements:* For master's and doctorate, TOEFL (minimum score of 550 required). *Average time to degree:* Master's–2 years full-time; doctorate–6 years full-time. *Application deadline:* For fall admission, 3/1 (priority date). Applications are processed on a rolling basis. Application fee: $25 ($50 for international students). Tuition, state resident: part-time $158 per credit hour. Tuition, nonresident: part-time $455 per credit hour. Required fees: $121 per year. Tuition and fees vary according to course load and degree level. *Financial aid:* Fellowships, research assistantships, teaching assistantships, Federal Work-Study, institutionally-sponsored loans, and tuition waivers (full and partial) available. Aid available to part-time students. Financial aid application deadline: 3/1. *Faculty research:* Magnetic resonance, photosynthesis, optical physics, biophysics, physics of materials. *Unit head:* B. D. Nageswara Rao, Chair, 317-274-6901. *Application contact:* G. Vemuri, Chair, Graduate Committee, 317-274-0002, Fax: 317-274-2393.

Institute of Paper Science and Technology, Graduate Programs, Program in Physics/Mathematics, Atlanta, GA 30318-5794. Offers MS, PhD. Part-time programs available. Terminal master's awarded for partial completion of doctoral program. *Degree requirements:* For master's, industrial experience, research project required, foreign language and thesis not required; for doctorate, dissertation required, foreign language not required. *Entrance requirements:* For master's and doctorate, GRE (score in 50th percentile or higher required), minimum GPA of 3.0. *Application deadline:* For fall admission, 3/1 (priority date). Application fee: $0. *Financial aid:* Career-related internships or fieldwork and institutionally-sponsored loans available. Financial aid applicants required to submit FAFSA. *Unit head:* John Waterhouse, Acting Director,Fiber and Paper Physics Division, 404-894-1621, Fax: 404-894-4778, E-mail: john.waterhouse@ipst.edu. *Application contact:* Dana Carter, Student Development Counselor, 404-894-5745, Fax: 404-894-4778, E-mail: dana.carter@ipst.edu.

Iowa State University of Science and Technology, Graduate College, College of Liberal Arts and Sciences, Department of Physics and Astronomy, Ames, IA 50011. Offers MS, PhD. Part-time programs available. *Faculty:* 51 full-time, 3 part-time. *Students:* 83 full-time (12 women), 5 part-time; includes 2 minority (1 Asian American or Pacific Islander, 1 Hispanic American), 44 international. 102 applicants, 58% accepted. In 1998, 7 master's, 15 doctorates awarded. Terminal master's awarded for partial completion of doctoral program. *Degree requirements:* For master's, thesis or alternative required; for doctorate, dissertation required. *Entrance requirements:* For master's and doctorate, GRE General Test, GRE Subject Test (physics), TOEFL (minimum score of 550 required). *Application deadline:* For fall admission, 2/15 (priority date). Applications are processed on a rolling basis. Application fee: $20 ($50 for international students). Electronic applications accepted. Tuition, state resident: full-time $3,308. Tuition, nonresident: full-time $9,744. Part-time tuition and fees vary according to course load, campus/location and program. *Financial aid:* In 1998–99, 37 research assistantships with partial tuition reimbursements (averaging $12,241 per year), 43 teaching assistantships with partial tuition reimbursements (averaging $11,646 per year) were awarded.; fellowships, Federal Work-Study, institutionally-sponsored loans, and scholarships also available. Aid available to part-time students. Financial aid application deadline: 2/15. *Faculty research:* Condensed-matter physics, including superconductivity and new materials; high-energy and nuclear physics; astronomy and astrophysics; atmospheric and environmental physics. Total annual research expenditures: $8.8 million. *Unit head:* Dr. Douglas K. Finnemore, Chair, 515-294-5441, Fax: 515-294-6027, E-mail: phys_astro@iastate.edu.

John Carroll University, Graduate School, Department of Physics, University Heights, OH 44118-4581. Offers MS. Part-time programs available. *Faculty:* 6 full-time (1 woman). *Students:* 4 full-time (0 women), 3 part-time (1 woman). 3 applicants, 100% accepted. In 1998, 1 degree awarded (100% found work related to degree). *Degree requirements:* For master's, comprehensive exam, essay or thesis required. *Entrance requirements:* For master's, bachelor's degree in electrical engineering or physics. *Average time to degree:* Master's–2 years full-time, 4 years part-time. *Application deadline:* For fall admission, 8/15 (priority date); for spring admission, 1/3. Applications are processed on a rolling basis. Application fee: $25 ($35 for international students). *Financial aid:* Teaching assistantships available. Financial aid application deadline: 3/1; financial aid applicants required to submit FAFSA. *Faculty research:* Fiber optics, ultrasonics, complex fluids, light scattering, atomic force microscopy. Total annual research expenditures: $200,000. *Unit head:* Dr. Joseph Trivisonno, Chairperson, 216-397-4301, E-mail: trivisonno@jcvaxa.jcu.edu.

Johns Hopkins University, Zanvyl Krieger School of Arts and Sciences, Department of Physics and Astronomy, Baltimore, MD 21218-2699. Offers astronomy (PhD); physics (PhD). *Faculty:* 32 full-time (2 women), 8 part-time (1 woman). *Students:* 79 full-time (16 women); includes 5 minority (2 African Americans, 3 Asian Americans or Pacific Islanders), 39 international. Average age 25. 259 applicants, 21% accepted. In 1998, 17 doctorates awarded. *Degree requirements:* For doctorate, dissertation, comprehensive exam required, foreign language not required. *Entrance requirements:* For doctorate, GRE General Test, GRE Subject Test, TOEFL. *Average time to degree:* Doctorate–6.5 years full-time. *Application deadline:* For fall admission, 1/15 (priority date). Application fee: $55. Tuition: Full-time $23,660. Tuition and fees vary according to program. *Financial aid:* In 1998–99, 1 fellowship, 34 research assistantships, 33 teaching assistantships were awarded.; career-related internships or fieldwork, Federal Work-Study, institutionally-sponsored loans, and tuition waivers (full and partial) also available. Financial aid application deadline: 3/14; financial aid applicants required to submit FAFSA. *Faculty research:* High-energy physics, condensed-matter astrophysics, particle and experimental physics, physics theory. Total annual research expenditures: $34.7 million. *Unit head:* Dr. Paul D. Feldman, Chair, 410-516-7346, Fax: 410-516-7239. *Application contact:* Janet Krupsaw, Academic Program Coordinator, 410-516-7344, Fax: 410-516-7239, E-mail: krupsaw@pha.jhu.edu.

See in-depth description on page 475.

Kansas State University, Graduate School, College of Arts and Sciences, Natural Resources and Environmental Sciences, Manhattan, KS 66506. Offers MS, PhD. *Faculty:* 29 full-time (3 women). *Students:* 45 full-time (8 women); includes 13 minority (all Asian Americans or Pacific Islanders) 30 applicants, 60% accepted. In 1998, 4 master's, 5 doctorates awarded. Terminal master's awarded for partial completion of doctoral program. *Degree requirements:* For master's, thesis required, foreign language not required; for doctorate, dissertation required. *Entrance requirements:* For master's, GRE Subject Test; for doctorate, GRE Subject Test, TOEFL (minimum score of 550 required). *Average time to degree:* Master's–2 years full-time; doctorate–6 years full-time. Application fee: $0 ($25 for international students). Electronic applications accepted. *Financial aid:* Fellowships, research assistantships, teaching assistantships, career-related internships or fieldwork and Federal Work-Study available. *Faculty research:* Ion-atom collisions, neutrinos, physics education, surfaces, materials. Total annual research expenditures: $4.1 million. *Unit head:* James C. Legg, Head, 785-532-6786, Fax: 785-532-6806, E-mail: graduate@phys.ksu.edu. *Application contact:* Jane Peterson, Secretary, 785-532-1603, Fax: 785-532-6806, E-mail: graduate@phys.ksu.edu.

Kent State University, College of Arts and Sciences, Department of Physics, Kent, OH 44242-0001. Offers MA, MS, PhD. *Faculty:* 32 full-time. *Students:* 47 full-time (10 women), 4 part-time (3 women); includes 1 minority (African American), 35 international. 39 applicants, 46% accepted. In 1998, 5 master's, 7 doctorates awarded. Terminal master's awarded for partial completion of doctoral program. *Degree requirements:* For master's, thesis optional, foreign language not required; for doctorate, computer language, dissertation required. *Entrance requirements:* For master's, minimum GPA of 2.75; for doctorate, minimum GPA of 3.0. *Application deadline:* For fall admission, 6/1. Application fee: $30. *Financial aid:* Fellowships, research assistantships, teaching assistantships, Federal Work-Study, institutionally-sponsored loans, and tuition waivers (full) available. Financial aid application deadline: 2/1. *Unit head:* Dr. David W. Allender, Chairman, 330-672-2880.

See in-depth description on page 477.

Lakehead University, Graduate Studies and Research, Faculty of Arts and Science, Department of Physics, Thunder Bay, ON P7B 5E1, Canada. Offers M Sc. *Degree requirements:* For master's, thesis or alternative required, foreign language not required. *Entrance requirements:* For master's, TOEFL (minimum score of 550 required), minimum B average. *Faculty research:* Absorbed water, radiation reaction, superlattices and quantum well structures, polaron interactions.

Lehigh University, College of Arts and Sciences, Department of Physics, Bethlehem, PA 18015-3094. Offers MS, PhD. *Students:* 30 full-time (5 women), 1 part-time, 12 international. 104 applicants, 16% accepted. In 1998, 6 master's awarded (0% continued full-time study); 11 doctorates awarded. Terminal master's awarded for partial completion of doctoral program. *Degree requirements:* For master's, research project required, foreign language and thesis not required; for doctorate, dissertation, exam required, foreign language not required. *Entrance requirements:* For master's, TOEFL (minimum score of 550 required; average 600), TSE (strongly recommended); for doctorate, GRE General Test, TOEFL (minimum score of 550 required; average 600), TSE (strongly recommended). *Average time to degree:* Master's–2 years full-time; doctorate–5.5 years full-time. *Application deadline:* For fall admission, 7/15; for spring admission, 12/1. Applications are processed on a rolling basis. Application fee: $40. *Financial aid:* In 1998–99, 6 fellowships, 8 research assistantships, 14 teaching assistantships were awarded.; Federal Work-Study and institutionally-sponsored loans also available. Financial aid application deadline: 1/15. *Faculty research:* Solid-state physics, fluids and plasmas, atomic physics, high-energy physics, polymers. Total annual research expenditures: $1.9 million. *Unit head:* Dr. Arnold Kritz, Chairman, 610-758-3930, Fax: 610-758-5730, E-mail: ahk3@lehigh.edu. *Application contact:* Dr. Shelden Radin, Graduate Admissions Officer, 610-758-3919, Fax: 610-758-5730, E-mail: shr0@lehigh.edu.

Louisiana State University and Agricultural and Mechanical College, Graduate School, College of Basic Sciences, Department of Physics and Astronomy, Baton Rouge, LA 70803. Offers astronomy (PhD); astrophysics (PhD); physics (MS, PhD). *Faculty:* 32 full-time (0 women). *Students:* 58 full-time (10 women), 4 part-time; includes 3 minority (all African Americans), 30 international. Average age 29. 39 applicants, 51% accepted. In 1998, 5 master's, 9 doctorates awarded. Terminal master's awarded for partial completion of doctoral program. *Degree requirements:* For master's, thesis or alternative required, foreign language not required; for doctorate, dissertation required, foreign language not required. *Entrance requirements:* For master's, GRE General Test, TOEFL (minimum score of 550 required for admission, 560 required for assistantships), minimum GPA of 3.0; for doctorate, GRE General Test, TOEFL (minimum score of 550 required), minimum GPA of 3.0. *Average time to degree:* Master's–2.9 years full-time; doctorate–6.6 years full-time. *Application deadline:* For fall admission, 1/25 (priority date). Applications are processed on a rolling basis. Application fee: $25. *Financial aid:* In 1998–99, 9 fellowships, 16 research assistantships with partial tuition reimbursements, 31 teaching assistantships with partial tuition reimbursements were awarded.; institutionally-sponsored loans and unspecified assistantships also available. Financial aid application deadline: 3/15. *Faculty research:* Experimental and theoretical atomic, nuclear, particle, cosmic-ray, low-temperature, and condensed-matter physics. *Unit head:* Dr. William Metcalf, Chair, 225-388-2261, Fax: 225-388-5855, E-mail: metcalf@phzeus.phys.lsu.edu. *Application contact:* Dr. Philip Adams, Chair, Assistantship Committee, 225-388-1194, Fax: 225-388-5855, E-mail: phadan@lsuvm.sncc.lsu.edu.

See in-depth description on page 479.

Louisiana Tech University, Graduate School, College of Engineering and Science, Department of Physics, Ruston, LA 71272. Offers applied computational analysis and modeling (PhD); physics (MS). Part-time programs available. *Degree requirements:* For master's, computer language, thesis or alternative required, foreign language not required; for doctorate, computer language, dissertation required, foreign language not required. *Entrance requirements:* For master's, GRE General Test (minimum combined score of 1070 required; average 1245), TOEFL (minimum score of 550 required), minimum GPA of 3.0 in last 60 hours; for doctorate, TOEFL (minimum score of 550 required). *Faculty research:* Experimental high energy physics, laser/optics, computational physics, quantum gravity.

Maharishi University of Management, Graduate Studies, Program in Physics, Fairfield, IA 52557. Offers MS, PhD. Admissions temporarily suspended. Terminal master's awarded for partial completion of doctoral program. *Degree requirements:* For master's, seminar presentation required, foreign language and thesis not required; for doctorate, dissertation, comprehensive exam, qualifying exam required, foreign language not required. *Faculty research:* Particle physics and cosmology, critical phenomena and phase transitions, quantum optics, nonlinear dynamical systems theory.

Marshall University, Graduate College, College of Science, Department of Physical Science and Physics, Huntington, WV 25755-2020. Offers physical science (MS). *Faculty:* 7 full-time (0 women). *Students:* 11 full-time (4 women), 3 part-time (2 women), 4 international. In 1998, 12 degrees awarded. *Degree requirements:* For master's, thesis optional, foreign language not required. *Entrance requirements:* For master's, GRE General Test. *Unit head:* Dr. Nicola Orsini, Chairperson, 304-696-6738, E-mail: orsini@marshall.edu. *Application contact:* Ken O'Neal, Assistant Vice President, Adult Student Services, 304-746-2500 Ext. 1907, Fax: 304-746-1902, E-mail: oneal@marshall.edu.

Massachusetts Institute of Technology, School of Science, Department of Physics, Cambridge, MA 02139-4307. Offers SM, PhD, Sc D. *Faculty:* 76 full-time (5 women). *Students:* 252 full-time (28 women); includes 32 minority (11 African Americans, 15 Asian Americans or Pacific Islanders, 5 Hispanic Americans, 1 Native American), 121 international. 546 applicants, 23% accepted. In 1998, 7 master's, 38 doctorates awarded. *Degree requirements:* For master's and doctorate, thesis/dissertation required, foreign language not required. *Entrance requirements:* For master's and doctorate, GRE General Test, GRE Subject Test. *Application deadline:* For fall admission, 1/15; for spring admission, 11/1. Application fee: $55. Electronic applications accepted. *Financial aid:* In 1998–99, 47 fellowships, 169 research assistantships, 36 teaching assistantships were awarded.; career-related internships or fieldwork also available. Financial aid application deadline: 1/15. *Unit head:* Prof. Marc A. Kastner, Head, 617-253-4801. *Application contact:* Peggy Berkovitz, Education Coordinator, 617-253-4851.

McGill University, Faculty of Graduate Studies and Research, Faculty of Science, Department of Physics, Montréal, PQ H3A 2T5, Canada. Offers M Sc, PhD. *Faculty:* 32 full-time (0 women). *Students:* 80 full-time (10 women), 28 international. Average age 25. 117 applicants, 34% accepted. In 1998, 7 master's, 6 doctorates awarded. Terminal master's awarded for partial completion of doctoral program. *Degree requirements:* For master's and doctorate, thesis/dissertation required. *Entrance requirements:* For master's, TOEFL (minimum score of 550 required), minimum GPA of 3.0; for doctorate, TOEFL (minimum score of 550 required). *Average time to degree:* Master's–2 years full-time; doctorate–5 years full-time. *Application deadline:* For fall admission, 2/1; for winter admission, 8/1. Applications are processed on a rolling basis. Application fee: $60. *Financial aid:* In 1998–99, teaching assistantships (averaging $3,250 per year); fellowships, research assistantships, bursaries also available. Financial aid application deadline: 2/1. *Faculty research:* High-energy, condensed-matter, and nuclear physics; biophysics; mathphyiscs; geophysics/atmospheric physics. *Unit head:* R. Myers, Chair, Graduate Studies Commitee, 514-398-4345, Fax: 514-398-3733, E-mail: myers@physics.mcgill.ca. *Application contact:* P. Domingues, Student Affairs Assistant, 514-398-6485, Fax: 514-398-8434, E-mail: domingues@physics.mcgill.ca./paulad@physics.lan.mcgill.ca.

McMaster University, School of Graduate Studies, Faculty of Science, Department of Physics and Astronomy, Hamilton, ON L8S 4M2, Canada. Offers astrophysics (PhD); chemical physics (M Sc, PhD); health and radiation physics (M Sc); physics (PhD). Part-time programs available. *Degree requirements:* For master's, thesis or alternative required, foreign language not required; for doctorate, dissertation, comprehensive exam required, foreign language not required. *Entrance requirements:* For master's and doctorate, minimum B+ average. *Faculty research:* Condensed matter, astrophysics, nuclear, medical, nonlinear dynamics.

Memorial University of Newfoundland, School of Graduate Studies, Department of Physics and Physical Oceanography, St. John's, NF A1C 5S7, Canada. Offers condensed matter physics (PhD); molecular physics (PhD); physical oceanography (M Sc, PhD); physics (M Sc). Part-time programs available. *Students:* 12 full-time (2 women), 3 part-time, 10 international. 27 applicants, 22% accepted. In 1998, 1 master's, 2 doctorates awarded (100% entered university research/teaching). *Degree requirements:* For master's, thesis required; for doctorate, dissertation, comprehensive exam required. *Entrance requirements:* For master's, honors B Sc or equivalent; for doctorate, M Sc or equivalent. *Average time to degree:* Doctorate–4 years full-time. *Application deadline:* Applications are processed on a rolling basis. Application fee: $40. *Financial aid:* Fellowships, research assistantships, teaching assistantships available. *Faculty research:* Experiment and theory in atomic and molecular physics. Total annual research expenditures: $2.1 million. *Unit head:* Dr. Mike Morrow, Acting Head, 709-737-8737, Fax: 709-737-8739. *Application contact:* Dr. J. de Bruyn, Deputy Head, Graduate Studies, 709-737-2113, Fax: 709-737-8739, E-mail: jdebruyn@kelvin.physics.mun.ca.

Miami University, Graduate School, College of Arts and Sciences, Department of Physics, Oxford, OH 45056. Offers MA, MAT, MS. Part-time programs available. *Faculty:* 17. *Students:* 17 full-time (3 women), 2 part-time (1 woman), 3 international. 36 applicants, 86% accepted. In 1998, 8 degrees awarded. *Degree requirements:* For master's. *Entrance requirements:* For master's, minimum undergraduate GPA of 3.0 during previous 2 years or 2.75 overall. *Application deadline:* For fall admission, 3/1 (priority date); for spring admission, 12/1. Applications are processed on a rolling basis. Application fee: $35. *Financial aid:* Fellowships, research assistantships, teaching assistantships, Federal Work-Study and tuition waivers (full) available. Financial aid application deadline: 3/1. *Unit head:* Perry Rice, Director of Graduate Studies, 513-529-5636.

Michigan State University, Graduate School, College of Natural Science, Department of Physics and Astronomy, East Lansing, MI 48824-1020. Offers astrophysics (MS, PhD); chemical physics (MS); physics (MAT, MS, PhD). *Faculty:* 57. *Students:* 111 full-time (22 women), 12 part-time (2 women); includes 8 minority (3 African Americans, 5 Asian Americans or Pacific Islanders), 53 international. Average age 27. 244 applicants, 20% accepted. In 1998, 17 master's, 19 doctorates awarded. Terminal master's awarded for partial completion of doctoral program. *Degree requirements:* For master's, thesis or alternative required, foreign language not required; for doctorate, dissertation required, foreign language not required. *Entrance requirements:* For master's, GRE. *Application deadline:* For fall admission, 3/15. Applications are processed on a rolling basis. Application fee: $30 ($40 for international students). *Financial aid:* In 1998–99, 68 research assistantships with tuition reimbursements (averaging $11,968 per year), 45 teaching assistantships with tuition reimbursements (averaging $11,185 per year) were awarded.; fellowships Financial aid applicants required to submit FAFSA. *Faculty research:* Nuclear and accelerator physics, high-energy physics, condensed-matter physics. Total annual research expenditures: $3.7 million. *Unit head:* Dr. Raymond Brock, Chairperson, 517-353-5286, Fax: 517-353-4500.

See in-depth description on page 483.

Michigan Technological University, Graduate School, College of Sciences and Arts, Department of Physics, Houghton, MI 49931-1295. Offers applied physics (PhD); physics (MS, PhD). Part-time programs available. *Faculty:* 19 full-time (1 woman), 1 part-time (0 women). *Students:* 3 full-time (all women), 18 part-time; includes 1 minority (African American), 11 international. Average age 32. 58 applicants, 28% accepted. In 1998, 1 master's, 5 doctorates awarded. *Degree requirements:* For master's, thesis optional, foreign language not required; for doctorate, dissertation required, foreign language not required. *Entrance requirements:* For master's, GRE General Test, TOEFL (minimum score of 570 required), BS in physics or related area, minimum GPA of 3.0; for doctorate, GRE General Test (combined average 1816 on three sections), TOEFL (minimum score of 570 required; average 600), BS in physics or related area, minimum GPA of 3.0. *Average time to degree:* Master's–1.3 years full-time; doctorate–4.9 years full-time. *Application deadline:* For fall admission, 3/15 (priority date). Applications are processed on a rolling basis. Application fee: $30 ($35 for international students). Tuition, state resident: full-time $4,377. Tuition, nonresident: full-time $9,108. Required fees: $126. Tuition and fees vary according to course load. *Financial aid:* In 1998–99, 6 fellowships (averaging $3,115 per year), 4 research assistantships (averaging $11,500 per year), 10 teaching assistantships (averaging $8,889 per year) were awarded.; Federal Work-Study, institutionally-sponsored loans, and unspecified assistantships also available. Aid available to part-time students. Financial aid application deadline: 3/1; financial aid applicants required to submit FAFSA. *Faculty research:* Atomic and molecular physics, remote sensing physics, materials physics, astrophysics, high-energy astrophysics. Total annual research expenditures: $803,095. *Unit head:* Dr. James B. Rafert, Head, 906-487-2086, Fax: 906-487-2933, E-mail: jbrafert@mtu.edu.

See in-depth description on page 485.

Minnesota State University, Mankato, College of Graduate Studies, College of Science, Engineering and Technology, Department of Physics and Astronomy, Mankato, MN 56002-8400. Offers MS, MT. *Faculty:* 10 full-time (2 women). *Students:* 1 full-time (0 women), 1 part-time. Average age 34. *Degree requirements:* For master's, thesis or alternative, comprehensive exam required. *Entrance requirements:* For master's, minimum GPA of 3.0 during previous 2 years. *Application deadline:* For fall admission, 7/9 (priority date); for spring admission, 11/27. Applications are processed on a rolling basis. Application fee: $20. *Financial aid:* Teaching assistantships with partial tuition reimbursements, Federal Work-Study available. Aid available to part-time students. Financial aid application deadline: 3/15; financial aid applicants required to submit FAFSA. *Unit head:* Dr. Sandford Schuster, Chairperson, 507-389-5743. *Application contact:* Joni Roberts, Admissions Coordinator, 507-389-2321, Fax: 507-389-5974, E-mail: grad@mankato.msus.edu.

Mississippi State University, College of Arts and Sciences, Department of Physics and Astronomy, Mississippi State, MS 39762. Offers physics (MS). Part-time programs available. *Students:* 5 full-time (1 woman), 1 part-time; includes 4 minority (3 African Americans, 1 Asian American or Pacific Islander) Average age 30. 8 applicants, 25% accepted. *Degree requirements:* Foreign language not required. *Entrance requirements:* For master's, TOEFL. *Application deadline:* For fall admission, 7/1; for spring admission, 11/1. Applications are processed on a rolling basis. Application fee: $25 for international students. *Financial aid:* Federal Work-Study, institutionally-sponsored loans, and unspecified assistantships available. Financial aid applicants required to submit FAFSA. *Faculty research:* Atomic/molecular spectroscopy, theoretical optics, gamma-ray astronomy, experimental nuclear physics, physics education. Total annual research expenditures: $351,310. *Unit head:* Dr. Rodney B. Piercey, Head, 662-325-2806, Fax: 662-325-8898, E-mail: rbp1@ra.msstate.edu. *Application contact:* Jerry B. Inmon, Director of Admissions, 662-325-2224, Fax: 662-325-7360, E-mail: admit@admissions.msstate.edu.

Announcement: The Department of Physics and Astronomy at MSU offers an engineering physics (EP) PhD, an MS in physics, and 3 different BS options (physics, premed, applied physics). The EP PhD program, offered in collaboration with the College of Engineering, combines a foundation in physics with an engineering perspective. Research opportunities include astrophysics (exploring the mysteries of gamma-ray and hard X-ray cosmic sources), atomic/molecular physics (applications of lasers/optical techniques to environmental problems and molecular structure), optics (coherence theory, quantum optics, visualization), nuclear physics (nuclei far from stability, nuclei in high spin states), particle physics (elementary particle interactions at fundamental level), and physics education (Web-based instruction, curriculum development, physics in the workplace). Contact: Rodney Piercey, Professor and Head, Department of Physics and Astronomy, Mississippi State University, Mississippi State, MS 39762-516 7. 601-325-2806, fax: 601-325-8898, e-mail: physics@ra.msstate.edu, Web: http://

Physics

Mississippi State University (continued)
www.msstate.edu/dept/physics. MSU does not discriminate on the basis of race, color, religion, national origin, sex, age, disability, or veteran status.

Montana State University–Bozeman, College of Graduate Studies, College of Letters and Science, Department of Physics, Bozeman, MT 59717. Offers MS, PhD. Part-time programs available. *Students:* 38 full-time (5 women), 5 part-time (2 women); includes 1 minority (Asian American or Pacific Islander) Average age 29. 39 applicants, 38% accepted. In 1998, 2 master's, 6 doctorates awarded. Terminal master's awarded for partial completion of doctoral program. *Degree requirements:* For master's, thesis or alternative required, foreign language not required; for doctorate, dissertation required, foreign language not required. *Entrance requirements:* For master's and doctorate, GRE General Test, TOEFL (minimum score of 580 required). *Application deadline:* For fall admission, 6/1 (priority date); for spring admission, 11/1. Applications are processed on a rolling basis. Application fee: $50. *Financial aid:* In 1998–99, 42 students received aid, including 1 fellowship with full tuition reimbursement available (averaging $11,250 per year), 23 research assistantships with full tuition reimbursements available (averaging $10,594 per year), 17 teaching assistantships with full tuition reimbursements available (averaging $10,288 per year); Federal Work-Study, scholarships, and traineeships also available. Aid available to part-time students. Financial aid application deadline: 3/1; financial aid applicants required to submit FAFSA. *Faculty research:* Surface science, laser/nonlinear optics, relativity, astrophysics, solar physics, physics teaching. Total annual research expenditures: $3 million. *Unit head:* Dr. John C. Hermanson, Head, 406-994-3614, Fax: 406-994-4452, E-mail: gradinfo@physics.montana.edu.

Murray State University, College of Science, Department of Physics, Murray, KY 42071-0009. Offers MAT, MS. Part-time programs available. *Students:* 1 full-time (0 women), 1 international. *Degree requirements:* For master's, thesis required (for some programs), foreign language not required. *Entrance requirements:* For master's, GRE General Test, TOEFL (minimum score of 500 required). *Application deadline:* Applications are processed on a rolling basis. Application fee: $20. *Financial aid:* Research assistantships, teaching assistantships, Federal Work-Study available. Financial aid application deadline: 4/1. *Unit head:* Dr. Steve Cobb, Chairman, 502-762-6186, Fax: 502-762-6107, E-mail: steve.cobb@murraystate.edu.

Naval Postgraduate School, Graduate Programs, Department of Physics, Monterey, CA 93943. Offers MS, PhD. Program only open to commissioned officers of the United States and friendly nations and selected United States federal civilian employees. Part-time programs available. *Students:* 81 full-time, 26 international. In 1998, 29 degrees awarded. *Degree requirements:* For master's, computer language, thesis required, foreign language not required; for doctorate, one foreign language, computer language, dissertation required. *Unit head:* Dr. William B. Maier, Chairman, 831-656-2896. *Application contact:* Theodore H. Calhoon, Director of Admissions, 831-656-3093, Fax: 831-656-2891, E-mail: tcalhoon@nps.navy.mil.

New Mexico Institute of Mining and Technology, Graduate Studies, Department of Physics, Socorro, NM 87801. Offers astrophysics (MS, PhD); atmospheric physics (MS, PhD); instrumentation (MS); mathematical physics (PhD). *Faculty:* 11 full-time (1 woman), 5 part-time (0 women). *Students:* 26 full-time (6 women), 8 international. Average age 30. 38 applicants, 18% accepted. In 1998, 4 master's, 1 doctorate awarded. *Degree requirements:* For master's and doctorate, thesis/dissertation required, foreign language not required. *Entrance requirements:* For master's, GRE General Test, TOEFL (minimum score of 540 required); for doctorate, GRE General Test, GRE Subject Test, TOEFL (minimum score of 540 required). *Average time to degree:* Master's–4 years full-time; doctorate–8 years full-time. *Application deadline:* For fall admission, 3/1 (priority date); for spring admission, 6/1. Applications are processed on a rolling basis. Application fee: $16. *Financial aid:* In 1998–99, 16 research assistantships (averaging $10,000 per year), 5 teaching assistantships (averaging $10,000 per year) were awarded.; fellowships, Federal Work-Study and institutionally-sponsored loans also available. Financial aid application deadline: 3/1; financial aid applicants required to submit CSS PROFILE or FAFSA. *Faculty research:* Cloud physics, stellar and extragalactic processes. *Unit head:* Dr. Alan Blyth, Chairman, 505-835-5744, Fax: 505-835-5707, E-mail: blyth@kestrel.nmt.edu. *Application contact:* Dr. David B. Johnson, Dean of Graduate Studies, 505-835-5513, Fax: 505-835-5476, E-mail: graduate@nmt.edu.

New Mexico State University, Graduate School, College of Arts and Sciences, Department of Physics, Las Cruces, NM 88003-8001. Offers MS, PhD. Part-time programs available. *Faculty:* 9 full-time (0 women), 1 part-time (0 women). *Students:* 35 full-time (6 women), 5 part-time (1 woman); includes 2 minority (1 Asian American or Pacific Islander, 1 Hispanic American), 20 international. Average age 31. 47 applicants, 83% accepted. In 1998, 3 master's, 6 doctorates awarded. Terminal master's awarded for partial completion of doctoral program. *Degree requirements:* For master's, computer language required, thesis optional, foreign language not required; for doctorate, computer language, dissertation required, foreign language not required. *Entrance requirements:* For master's and doctorate, GRE General Test. *Application deadline:* For fall admission, 7/1 (priority date); for spring admission, 11/1 (priority date). Applications are processed on a rolling basis. Application fee: $15 ($35 for international students). Electronic applications accepted. Tuition, state resident: full-time $2,682; part-time $112 per credit. Tuition, nonresident: full-time $8,376; part-time $349 per credit. Tuition and fees vary according to course load. *Financial aid:* Research assistantships, teaching assistantships available. Financial aid application deadline: 3/15. *Faculty research:* Nuclear and particle physics, optics, materials science, neutron scattering, geophysics. *Unit head:* Dr. George Burleson, Head, 505-646-3831, Fax: 505-646-1934, E-mail: burleson@nmsu.edu.

New York University, Graduate School of Arts and Science, Department of Physics, New York, NY 10012-1019. Offers MS, PhD. Part-time programs available. *Faculty:* 26 full-time (1 woman), 5 part-time. *Students:* 47 full-time (5 women), 2 part-time (1 woman); includes 1 minority (Hispanic American), 41 international. Average age 26. 94 applicants, 30% accepted. In 1998, 8 master's, 7 doctorates awarded. Terminal master's awarded for partial completion of doctoral program. *Degree requirements:* For master's, thesis required (for some programs), foreign language not required; for doctorate, one foreign language, dissertation, research seminar, teaching experience required. *Entrance requirements:* For master's, GRE General Test, GRE Subject Test, TOEFL, bachelor's degree in physics; for doctorate, GRE General Test, GRE Subject Test, TOEFL. *Application deadline:* For fall admission, 1/4 (priority date); for spring admission, 11/1. Application fee: $60. Tuition: Full-time $17,880; part-time $745 per credit. Required fees: $1,140; $35 per credit. Tuition and fees vary according to course load and program. *Financial aid:* Fellowships, research assistantships, teaching assistantships, Federal Work-Study, institutionally-sponsored loans, and tuition waivers (full and partial) available. Financial aid application deadline: 1/4; financial aid applicants required to submit FAFSA. *Faculty research:* Atomic physics, elementary particles and fields, astrophysics, condensed-matter physics, neuromagnetism. *Unit head:* Glennys Farrar, Chairman, 212-998-7700. *Application contact:* Daniel Zwanziger, Director of Graduate Studies, 212-998-7700, Fax: 212-995-4016, E-mail: dgsphys@nyu.edu.

North Carolina State University, Graduate School, College of Physical and Mathematical Sciences, Department of Physics, Raleigh, NC 27695. Offers MS, PhD. Part-time programs available. *Faculty:* 41 full-time (3 women), 12 part-time (1 woman). *Students:* 77 full-time (12 women), 7 part-time; includes 4 minority (3 African Americans, 1 Asian American or Pacific Islander), 16 international. Average age 29. 71 applicants, 28% accepted. In 1998, 3 master's, 16 doctorates awarded. Terminal master's awarded for partial completion of doctoral program. *Degree requirements:* For master's and doctorate, thesis/dissertation required. *Entrance requirements:* For master's and doctorate, GRE General Test, GRE Subject Test. *Application deadline:* For fall admission, 6/25 (priority date); for spring admission, 11/25. Applications are processed on a rolling basis. Application fee: $45. *Financial aid:* In 1998–99, 2 fellowships (averaging $6,906 per year), 62 research assistantships (averaging $3,911 per year), 36 teaching assistantships (averaging $5,552 per year) were awarded.; institutionally-sponsored loans also available. Financial aid application deadline: 3/1. *Faculty research:* Atomic, biological, nuclear, particle computational, educational, and solid-state physics; astrophysics; optics. Total annual research expenditures: $9.2 million. *Unit head:* Dr. Christopher Gould, Head, 919-515-2522, Fax: 919-515-6538, E-mail: chris_gould@ncsu.edu. *Application contact:* Dr. Michael A. Paesler, Director of Graduate Programs, 919-515-3155, Fax: 919-515-7331, E-mail: paesler@ncsu.edu.

North Dakota State University, Graduate Studies and Research, College of Science and Mathematics, Department of Physics, Fargo, ND 58105. Offers MS, PhD. Part-time programs available. *Faculty:* 4 full-time (0 women), 1 part-time (0 women). *Students:* 6 full-time (0 women), 1 part-time, 2 international. Average age 32. 16 applicants, 50% accepted. In 1998, 2 master's awarded (0% continued full-time study). Terminal master's awarded for partial completion of doctoral program. *Degree requirements:* For master's and doctorate, thesis/dissertation required, foreign language not required. *Entrance requirements:* For master's and doctorate, TOEFL (minimum score of 600 required). *Average time to degree:* Master's–3 years full-time. *Application deadline:* For fall admission, 3/1 (priority date). Applications are processed on a rolling basis. Application fee: $25. *Financial aid:* In 1998–99, 7 students received aid, including 2 research assistantships with tuition reimbursements available (averaging $8,561 per year), teaching assistantships with tuition reimbursements available (averaging $8,561 per year); career-related internships or fieldwork and unspecified assistantships also available. Aid available to part-time students. Financial aid application deadline: 4/15; financial aid applicants required to submit FAFSA. *Faculty research:* Biophysics; condensed matter; thermodynamics; surface physics; general relativity, gravitation, and space physics; nonlinear physics. Total annual research expenditures: $201,000. *Unit head:* Dr. Douglas T. Kurtze, Interim Chair, 701-231-7048, Fax: 701-231-7088, E-mail: kurtze@plains.nodak.edu. *Application contact:* Dr. Craig Rottman, Graduate Advisory Committee Chair, 701-231-7045, Fax: 701-231-7088, E-mail: rottman@plains.nodak.edu.

Northeastern University, College of Arts and Sciences, Department of Physics, Boston, MA 02115-5096. Offers MAT, MS, PhD. Part-time programs available. *Faculty:* 29 full-time (1 woman). *Students:* 50 full-time (5 women), 6 part-time. Average age 27. 90 applicants, 58% accepted. In 1998, 5 master's, 11 doctorates awarded. Terminal master's awarded for partial completion of doctoral program. *Degree requirements:* For master's, thesis optional, foreign language not required; for doctorate, dissertation required, foreign language not required. *Entrance requirements:* For master's and doctorate, TOEFL (minimum score of 550 required; average 615). *Average time to degree:* Master's–2 years full-time; doctorate–7 years full-time. *Application deadline:* For fall admission, 4/15 (priority date). Application fee: $50. *Financial aid:* In 1998–99, 20 research assistantships with tuition reimbursements, 31 teaching assistantships with tuition reimbursements were awarded.; Federal Work-Study, tuition waivers (full and partial), and unspecified assistantships also available. Financial aid application deadline: 2/15; financial aid applicants required to submit FAFSA. *Faculty research:* High-energy theory and experimentation, astrophysics, biophysics, condensed-matter theory and experimentation. *Unit head:* Dr. Paul Champion, Chairman, 617-373-2902, Fax: 617-373-2943, E-mail: grad-admin@physics.neu.edu. *Application contact:* Timothy Emrick, Administrative Secretary, 617-373-4240, Fax: 617-373-2943, E-mail: grad-admin@physics.neu.edu.

See in-depth description on page 489.

Northern Illinois University, Graduate School, College of Liberal Arts and Sciences, Department of Physics, De Kalb, IL 60115-2854. Offers MS. Part-time programs available. *Faculty:* 12 full-time (2 women). *Students:* 12 full-time (2 women), 15 part-time (3 women); includes 1 minority (Asian American or Pacific Islander), 5 international. Average age 32. 12 applicants, 83% accepted. In 1998, 10 degrees awarded. *Degree requirements:* For master's, thesis or alternative, comprehensive exam, research seminar required, foreign language not required. *Entrance requirements:* For master's, GRE General Test, TOEFL (minimum score of 550 required; 213 for computer-based), minimum GPA of 2.75. *Application deadline:* For fall admission, 6/1; for spring admission, 11/1. Applications are processed on a rolling basis. Application fee: $30. *Financial aid:* In 1998–99, 5 research assistantships, 10 teaching assistantships were awarded.; fellowships, career-related internships or fieldwork, Federal Work-Study, and unspecified assistantships also available. Aid available to part-time students. Financial aid application deadline: 3/1. *Unit head:* Dr. John Shaffer, Chair, 815-753-6470.

Northwestern University, The Graduate School, Judd A. and Marjorie Weinberg College of Arts and Sciences, Department of Physics and Astronomy, Evanston, IL 60208. Offers astronomy (PhD); astrophysics (PhD); physics (PhD). Admissions and degrees offered through The Graduate School. *Faculty:* 27 full-time (3 women). *Students:* 74 full-time (13 women); includes 6 minority (5 Asian Americans or Pacific Islanders, 1 Hispanic American), 51 international. 87 applicants, 59% accepted. In 1998, 5 doctorates awarded. *Degree requirements:* For doctorate, dissertation, qualifying exam required, foreign language not required. *Entrance requirements:* For doctorate, GRE General Test, GRE Subject Test, TOEFL (minimum score of 600 required; average 630). Application fee: $50 ($55 for international students). *Financial aid:* In 1998–99, 12 fellowships with full tuition reimbursements (averaging $11,673 per year), 27 research assistantships with partial tuition reimbursements (averaging $17,016 per year), 19 teaching assistantships with full tuition reimbursements (averaging $12,042 per year) were awarded.; career-related internships or fieldwork, Federal Work-Study, and institutionally-sponsored loans also available. Financial aid application deadline: 1/15; financial aid applicants required to submit FAFSA. *Faculty research:* Nuclear and particle physics, condensed-matter physics, nonlinear physics, astrophysics. Total annual research expenditures: $5.2 million. *Unit head:* David E. Buchholz, Chair, 847-491-3644, Fax: 847-491-9982, E-mail: physics-astronomy@nwu.edu. *Application contact:* Mary Rosenthal, Admission Contact, 847-491-3644, Fax: 847-491-9982, E-mail: physics-astronomy@nwu.edu.

Oakland University, Graduate Studies, College of Arts and Sciences, Department of Physics, Rochester, MI 48309-4401. Offers medical physics (PhD); physics (MS). *Faculty:* 11 full-time. *Students:* 13 full-time (1 woman), 3 part-time (1 woman); includes 2 minority (1 African American, 1 Asian American or Pacific Islander), 3 international. Average age 35. 8 applicants, 50% accepted. In 1998, 2 doctorates awarded. *Degree requirements:* For master's, foreign language and thesis not required; for doctorate, dissertation required, foreign language not required. *Entrance requirements:* For master's, minimum GPA of 3.0 for unconditional admission; for doctorate, GRE Subject Test, minimum GPA of 3.0 for unconditional admission. *Application deadline:* For fall admission, 7/15; for spring admission, 3/15. Application fee: $30. Tuition, state resident: part-time $221 per credit hour. Tuition, nonresident: part-time $488 per credit hour. Required fees: $214 per semester. Part-time tuition and fees vary according to program. *Financial aid:* Fellowships, career-related internships or fieldwork, Federal Work-Study, institutionally-sponsored loans, and tuition waivers (full) available. Financial aid application deadline: 3/1; financial aid applicants required to submit FAFSA. *Unit head:* Dr. Beverly Berger, Chair, 248-370-3410. *Application contact:* Dr. Gopalan Srinivasan, Coordinator, 248-370-3416.

The Ohio State University, Graduate School, College of Mathematical and Physical Sciences, Department of Physics, Columbus, OH 43210. Offers MS, PhD. *Faculty:* 52 full-time, 6 part-time. *Students:* 124 full-time (19 women), 2 part-time; includes 3 minority (1 African American, 2 Asian Americans or Pacific Islanders), 59 international. 267 applicants, 4% accepted. In 1998, 13 master's, 26 doctorates awarded. *Degree requirements:* For master's, thesis optional, foreign language not required; for doctorate, dissertation required, foreign language not required. *Entrance requirements:* For master's and doctorate, GRE General Test, GRE Subject Test. *Application deadline:* For fall admission, 8/15. Applications are processed on a rolling basis. Application fee: $30 ($40 for international students). *Financial aid:* Fellowships, research assistantships, teaching assistantships, Federal Work-Study and institutionally-sponsored loans available. Aid available to part-time students. *Unit head:* Frank DeLucia, Chairman, 614-292-5713, Fax: 614-292-7557, E-mail: de-lucia.2@osu.edu.

Ohio University, Graduate Studies, College of Arts and Sciences, Department of Physics and Astronomy, Athens, OH 45701-2979. Offers physics (MS, PhD). *Faculty:* 21 full-time (2 women),

2 part-time (0 women). *Students:* 51 full-time (12 women), 3 part-time; includes 1 minority (Hispanic American), 39 international. Average age 27. 63 applicants, 43% accepted. In 1998, 6 master's, 5 doctorates awarded. Terminal master's awarded for partial completion of doctoral program. *Degree requirements:* For master's, thesis or alternative required, foreign language not required; for doctorate, dissertation, oral and written comprehensive exams required. *Application deadline:* For fall admission, 4/1 (priority date). Applications are processed on a rolling basis. Application fee: $30. Tuition, state resident: full-time $5,754; part-time $238 per credit hour. Tuition, nonresident: full-time $11,055; part-time $457 per credit hour. Tuition and fees vary according to course load, campus/location and program. *Financial aid:* In 1998–99, 50 students received aid, including 1 fellowship, 20 research assistantships, 30 teaching assistantships; Federal Work-Study, institutionally-sponsored loans, and tuition waivers (full) also available. Financial aid application deadline: 4/1. *Faculty research:* Nuclear physics, condensed-matter physics, nonlinear systems, acoustics, astrophysics. Total annual research expenditures: $1.9 million. *Unit head:* Dr. David Onley, Chair, 740-593-1718, E-mail: onley@ohiou.edu. *Application contact:* Dr. Charlotte Elster, Graduate Admissions Chair, 740-593-1697, E-mail: elster@stingray.phy.ohiou.edu.

See in-depth description on page 493.

Oklahoma State University, Graduate College, College of Arts and Sciences, Department of Physics, Stillwater, OK 74078. Offers MS, PhD. *Faculty:* 19 full-time (2 women). *Students:* 27 full-time (5 women), 19 part-time (2 women); includes 6 minority (5 Asian Americans or Pacific Islanders, 1 Hispanic American), 17 international. Average age 28. In 1998, 4 master's, 3 doctorates awarded. *Degree requirements:* For doctorate, dissertation required, foreign language not required, foreign language not required. *Entrance requirements:* For master's and doctorate, TOEFL (minimum score of 550 required). *Application deadline:* For fall admission, 7/1 (priority date). Application fee: $25. *Financial aid:* In 1998–99, 41 students received aid, including 17 research assistantships (averaging $14,693 per year), 24 teaching assistantships (averaging $13,507 per year); Federal Work-Study and tuition waivers (partial) also available. Aid available to part-time students. Financial aid application deadline: 3/1. *Faculty research:* Lasers and photonics, non-linear optical materials, turbulence, structure and function of biological membranes, particle theory. *Unit head:* Dr. Stephen McKeever, Head, 405-744-5796.

Old Dominion University, College of Sciences, Department of Physics, Norfolk, VA 23529. Offers MS, PhD. *Faculty:* 19 full-time (2 women). *Students:* 26 full-time (8 women), 14 part-time (4 women), 25 international. Average age 31. In 1998, 5 master's, 2 doctorates awarded. Terminal master's awarded for partial completion of doctoral program. *Degree requirements:* For master's, comprehensive exam required, thesis optional, foreign language not required; for doctorate, dissertation, comprehensive exam required, foreign language not required. *Entrance requirements:* For master's, TOEFL, BS in physics or related field, minimum GPA of 3.0 in major; for doctorate, GRE General Test (minimum combined score of 1000 required), GRE Subject Test (minimum score of 600 required), TOEFL, minimum GPA of 3.0. *Application deadline:* For fall admission, 7/1. Applications are processed on a rolling basis. Application fee: $30. Electronic applications accepted. *Financial aid:* In 1998–99, 40 students received aid, including 30 research assistantships (averaging $13,962 per year), 1 teaching assistantship (averaging $9,900 per year); fellowships, career-related internships or fieldwork, grants, and tuition waivers (partial) also available. Aid available to part-time students. Financial aid application deadline: 2/15; financial aid applicants required to submit FAFSA. *Faculty research:* Atomic physics, nuclear physics, gamma ray optics, condensed-matter physics, plasma physics, ultra-cold physics. Total annual research expenditures: $852,708. *Unit head:* Dr. J. Wallace Van Orden, Chair, 757-683-3468, Fax: 757-683-3038, E-mail: vanorden@physics.odu.edu. *Application contact:* Dr. J. Wallace Van Orden, Chair, 757-683-3468, Fax: 757-683-3038, E-mail: vanorden@physics.odu.edu.

Oregon State University, Graduate School, College of Science, Department of Physics, Corvallis, OR 97331. Offers MA, MS, PhD. Part-time programs available. *Faculty:* 18 full-time (2 women). *Students:* 46 full-time (9 women), 2 part-time; includes 3 minority (all Asian Americans or Pacific Islanders), 14 international. Average age 28. In 1998, 7 master's, 3 doctorates awarded (33% entered university research/teaching, 67% found other work related to degree). Terminal master's awarded for partial completion of doctoral program. *Degree requirements:* For master's, qualifying exam required, thesis optional, foreign language not required; for doctorate, dissertation, qualifying exam required, foreign language not required. *Entrance requirements:* For master's and doctorate, TOEFL (minimum score of 550 required), minimum GPA of 3.0 in last 90 hours. *Average time to degree:* Master's–3 years part-time. *Application deadline:* For fall admission, 3/1. Application fee: $50. *Financial aid:* Fellowships, research assistantships, teaching assistantships, Federal Work-Study and institutionally-sponsored loans available. Aid available to part-time students. Financial aid application deadline: 2/1. *Unit head:* Dr. Henri Jansen, Chair, 541-737-4631, Fax: 541-737-1683, E-mail: henri@physics.orst.edu. *Application contact:* Dr. Henri Jansen, Chair, 541-737-4631, Fax: 541-737-1683, E-mail: henri@physics.orst.edu.

Announcement: Solid-state research: high-temperature superconductors, defects in semiconductors, magnetic anisotropy theory, thin-film superconductors, superlattices, microstructures. Nuclear/particle research: nuclear astrophysics, symmetry violations, nucleon structure, exotic nuclear matter, superstring theory. Optics research: nonlinear optics, surface physics, laser cooling and trapping, atomic interferometry. Teaching apprentice program for future college teachers.

Pennsylvania State University University Park Campus, Graduate School, Eberly College of Science, Department of Physics, State College, University Park, PA 16802-1503. Offers M Ed, MS, D Ed, PhD. *Students:* 63 full-time (9 women), 18 part-time (5 women). In 1998, 4 master's, 13 doctorates awarded. *Entrance requirements:* For master's and doctorate, GRE General Test. Application fee: $50. *Unit head:* Dr. Jayanth Banavar, Head, 814-865-7533. *Application contact:* Dr. Jorge Pullin, Director, Admissions, 814-865-7534.

See in-depth description on page 497.

Pittsburg State University, Graduate School, College of Arts and Sciences, Department of Physics, Pittsburg, KS 66762-5880. Offers applied physics (MS); physics (MS); professional physics (MS). *Students:* 2 full-time (1 woman), 1 international. In 1998, 2 degrees awarded. *Degree requirements:* For master's, thesis or alternative required, foreign language not required. Application fee: $0 ($40 for international students). Tuition, state resident: full-time $2,466; part-time $105 per credit hour. Tuition, nonresident: full-time $6,268; part-time $264 per credit hour. *Financial aid:* Teaching assistantships, career-related internships or fieldwork and Federal Work-Study available. *Unit head:* Dr. Charles Blatchley, Chairperson, 316-235-4398. *Application contact:* Marvene Darraugh, Administrative Officer, 316-235-4220, Fax: 316-235-4219, E-mail: mdarraug@pittstate.edu.

Polytechnic University, Brooklyn Campus, Department of Chemical Engineering, Chemistry and Materials Science, Major in Physics, Brooklyn, NY 11201-2990. Offers MS, PhD. Part-time and evening/weekend programs available. *Students:* 1 (woman) full-time, 10 part-time; includes 2 minority (1 African American, 1 Asian American or Pacific Islander), 5 international. Average age 33. 13 applicants, 0% accepted. In 1998, 3 master's, 3 doctorates awarded. *Degree requirements:* For master's, thesis not required; for doctorate, dissertation required, foreign language not required. *Entrance requirements:* For master's, BA in physics; for doctorate, departmental qualifying exam, BS in physics. *Application deadline:* Applications are processed on a rolling basis. Application fee: $45. Electronic applications accepted. *Financial aid:* Fellowships, research assistantships, teaching assistantships, institutionally-sponsored loans available. Aid available to part-time students. Financial aid applicants required to submit FAFSA. *Faculty research:* Combining microdroplets, UHV cryogenic scanning, tunneling, surface spectroscopy of a single aerosol particle. Total annual research expenditures: $523,071.

Polytechnic University, Farmingdale Campus, Graduate Programs, Department of Chemical Engineering, Chemistry and Material Science, Major in Physics, Farmingdale, NY 11735-3995. Offers MS, PhD. *Degree requirements:* For doctorate, dissertation required. *Application deadline:* Applications are processed on a rolling basis. Application fee: $45. Electronic applications accepted. *Application contact:* John S. Kerge, Dean of Admissions, 718-260-3200, Fax: 718-260-3446, E-mail: admitme@poly.edu.

Portland State University, Graduate Studies, College of Liberal Arts and Sciences, Department of Physics, Portland, OR 97207-0751. Offers MA, MS, PhD. Part-time programs available. *Faculty:* 7 full-time (0 women), 3 part-time (0 women). *Students:* 3 full-time (1 woman), 4 part-time (1 woman); includes 1 minority (Asian American or Pacific Islander), 4 international. Average age 32. 4 applicants, 50% accepted. In 1998, 7 degrees awarded. *Degree requirements:* For master's, thesis, oral exam required; for doctorate, dissertation required. *Entrance requirements:* For master's, TOEFL (minimum score of 550 required), minimum GPA of 3.0 in upper-division course work or 2.75 overall. *Application deadline:* For fall admission, 4/1 (priority date). Applications are processed on a rolling basis. Application fee: $50. *Financial aid:* In 1998–99, 2 research assistantships were awarded.; teaching assistantships, career-related internships or fieldwork, Federal Work-Study, and institutionally-sponsored loans also available. Aid available to part-time students. Financial aid application deadline: 3/1; financial aid applicants required to submit FAFSA. *Faculty research:* Statistical physics, membrane biophysics, low-temperature physics, electron microscopy, atmospheric physics. Total annual research expenditures: $567,616. *Unit head:* Dr. Eric Bodegom, Head, 503-725-3812, Fax: 503-725-3888, E-mail: bodegome@pdx.edu. *Application contact:* Peter Leung, Coordinator, 503-725-3812, Fax: 503-725-3888, E-mail: leungp@pdx.edu.

Princeton University, Graduate School, Department of Physics, Princeton, NJ 08544-1019. Offers applied and computational mathematics (PhD); mathematical physics (PhD); physics (PhD); physics and chemical physics (PhD). *Degree requirements:* For doctorate, dissertation required. *Entrance requirements:* For doctorate, GRE General Test, GRE Subject Test.

Purdue University, Graduate School, School of Science, Department of Physics, West Lafayette, IN 47907. Offers MS, PhD. Part-time programs available. *Faculty:* 49 full-time (2 women). *Students:* 74 full-time (7 women), 20 part-time (4 women); includes 8 minority (2 African Americans, 6 Asian Americans or Pacific Islanders), 56 international. Average age 25. 161 applicants, 36% accepted. In 1998, 9 master's, 12 doctorates awarded. Terminal master's awarded for partial completion of doctoral program. *Degree requirements:* For master's, qualifying exam required, foreign language and thesis not required; for doctorate, dissertation, qualifying exam required, foreign language not required. *Entrance requirements:* For master's and doctorate, GRE General Test, GRE Subject Test, TOEFL (minimum score of 550 required). *Average time to degree:* Master's–2 years full-time; doctorate–5.5 years full-time. *Application deadline:* For fall admission, 2/1 (priority date). Applications are processed on a rolling basis. Application fee: $30. Electronic applications accepted. *Financial aid:* In 1998–99, 93 students received aid, including 4 fellowships with partial tuition reimbursements available (averaging $15,000 per year), 30 research assistantships with partial tuition reimbursements available (averaging $16,500 per year), 59 teaching assistantships with partial tuition reimbursements available (averaging $13,700 per year) Aid available to part-time students. Financial aid application deadline: 2/1; financial aid applicants required to submit FAFSA. *Faculty research:* Solid-state, elementary particle, and nuclear physics; biological physics; acoustics; astrophysics. Total annual research expenditures: $6.1 million. *Unit head:* Dr. A. S. Hirsch, Head, 765-494-3000, Fax: 765-494-0706. *Application contact:* Russell Coverdale, Graduate Coordinator, 765-494-5383, Fax: 765-494-0706, E-mail: russ@physics.purdue.edu.

Queens College of the City University of New York, Division of Graduate Studies, Mathematics and Natural Sciences Division, Department of Physics, Flushing, NY 11367-1597. Offers MA. Part-time and evening/weekend programs available. *Faculty:* 12 full-time (1 woman). 5 applicants, 100% accepted. In 1998, 3 degrees awarded. *Degree requirements:* For master's, comprehensive exam required, foreign language and thesis not required. *Entrance requirements:* For master's, TOEFL (minimum score of 500 required), previous course work in calculus, minimum GPA of 3.0. *Application deadline:* For fall admission, 4/1; for spring admission, 11/1. Applications are processed on a rolling basis. Application fee: $40. Tuition, state resident: full-time $4,350; part-time $185 per credit. Tuition, nonresident: full-time $7,600; part-time $320 per credit. Required fees: $114; $57 per semester. Tuition and fees vary according to course load and program. *Financial aid:* Career-related internships or fieldwork, Federal Work-Study, institutionally-sponsored loans, and tuition waivers (partial) available. Aid available to part-time students. Financial aid application deadline: 4/1; financial aid applicants required to submit FAFSA. *Faculty research:* Solid-state physics, low temperature physics, elementary particles and fields. *Unit head:* Dr. Kenneth Rafanelli, Chairperson, 718-997-3350. *Application contact:* Dr. J. Marion Dickey, Graduate Adviser, 718-997-3350.

Queen's University at Kingston, School of Graduate Studies and Research, Faculty of Arts and Sciences, Department of Physics, Kingston, ON K7L 3N6, Canada. Offers M Sc, M Sc Eng, PhD. Part-time programs available. *Students:* 47 full-time (6 women). In 1998, 8 master's, 7 doctorates awarded. *Degree requirements:* For master's, thesis required, foreign language not required; for doctorate, dissertation, comprehensive exam required, foreign language not required. *Entrance requirements:* For master's and doctorate, TOEFL (minimum score of 600 required). *Application deadline:* For fall admission, 2/28 (priority date). Application fee: $60. Electronic applications accepted. *Financial aid:* Fellowships, research assistantships, teaching assistantships, institutionally-sponsored loans available. Financial aid application deadline: 3/1. *Faculty research:* Experimental nuclear physics, experimental solid-state physics, applied solid-state and nuclear physics, theoretical physics, astronomy and astrophysics. *Unit head:* Dr. M. Duncan, Head, 613-533-2706. *Application contact:* Dr. I. P. Johnstone, Graduate Coordinator, 613-533-2695.

Rensselaer Polytechnic Institute, Graduate School, School of Science, Department of Physics, Applied Physics and Astronomy, Troy, NY 12180-3590. Offers physics (MS, PhD). Part-time programs available. *Faculty:* 19 full-time (1 woman), 2 part-time (0 women). *Students:* 53 full-time (13 women), 6 part-time; includes 2 minority (1 Asian American or Pacific Islander, 1 Hispanic American), 26 international. 87 applicants, 55% accepted. In 1998, 6 master's, 6 doctorates awarded. Terminal master's awarded for partial completion of doctoral program. *Degree requirements:* For doctorate, dissertation required, foreign language not required, foreign language not required. *Entrance requirements:* For master's and doctorate, GRE General Test, GRE Subject Test, TOEFL (minimum score of 575 required). *Application deadline:* For fall admission, 2/1 (priority date). Applications are processed on a rolling basis. Application fee: $35. *Financial aid:* In 1998–99, 56 students received aid, including 9 fellowships (averaging $11,800 per year), 22 research assistantships (averaging $11,800 per year), 25 teaching assistantships (averaging $11,800 per year); career-related internships or fieldwork and institutionally-sponsored loans also available. Financial aid application deadline: 2/1. *Faculty research:* Astrophysics, condensed matter, nuclear physics, optics, physics education. Total annual research expenditures: $2 million. *Unit head:* Dr. Leo Schowalter, Chair, 518-276-6435, Fax: 518-276-6680. *Application contact:* Dr. Gary Adams, Chair, Graduate Recruitment Committee, 518-276-8391, Fax: 518-276-6680, E-mail: fanchj@rpi.edu.

See in-depth description on page 501.

Rice University, Graduate Programs, Wiess School of Natural Sciences, Department of Physics, Houston, TX 77251-1892. Offers applied physics (MS, PhD); physics (MA, PhD). *Degree requirements:* For master's and doctorate, thesis/dissertation required, foreign language not required. *Entrance requirements:* For master's, GRE General Test, GRE Subject Test (physics), TOEFL (minimum score of 550 required), minimum GPA of 3.0; for doctorate, GRE General Test (score in 70th percentile or higher required), GRE Subject Test (physics), TOEFL, minimum GPA of 3.0. *Faculty research:* Atomic, solid-state, and molecular physics; biophysics; medium- and high-energy physics.

Rutgers, The State University of New Jersey, New Brunswick, Graduate School, Program in Physics and Astronomy, New Brunswick, NJ 08903. Offers astrophysics (MS, PhD); condensed matter physics (MS, PhD); elementary particle physics (MS, PhD); intermediate energy nuclear

Physics

Rutgers, The State University of New Jersey, New Brunswick (continued)
physics (MS, PhD); nuclear physics (MS, PhD); physics (MST); theoretical physics (MS, PhD). Part-time programs available. *Faculty:* 67 full-time (5 women). *Students:* 87 full-time (14 women), 3 part-time; includes 5 minority (2 African Americans, 3 Hispanic Americans), 63 international. Average age 24. 178 applicants, 30% accepted. In 1998, 8 master's, 10 doctorates awarded. Terminal master's awarded for partial completion of doctoral program. *Degree requirements:* For master's, thesis optional, foreign language not required; for doctorate, dissertation required, foreign language not required. *Entrance requirements:* For master's and doctorate, GRE General Test, GRE Subject Test. *Average time to degree:* Doctorate–6 years full-time. *Application deadline:* For fall admission, 1/2 (priority date); for spring admission, 11/1. Applications are processed on a rolling basis. Application fee: $50. *Financial aid:* In 1998–99, 19 fellowships with full tuition reimbursements (averaging $14,400 per year), 29 research assistantships with full tuition reimbursements (averaging $12,000 per year), 38 teaching assistantships with full tuition reimbursements (averaging $12,000 per year) were awarded. Financial aid application deadline: 1/2; financial aid applicants required to submit FAFSA. *Faculty research:* Astronomy, high energy, condensed matter, surface physics, physics. Total annual research expenditures: $5.3 million. *Unit head:* Dr. Jolie A. Cizewski, Director, 732-445-3884, Fax: 732-445-4343, E-mail: cizewski@physics.rutgers.edu.

See in-depth description on page 509.

St. Francis Xavier University, Graduate Studies, Department of Physics, Antigonish, NS B2G 2W5, Canada. Offers M Sc. *Faculty:* 6 full-time (0 women), 1 (woman) part-time. *Degree requirements:* For master's, computer language, thesis required, foreign language not required. *Entrance requirements:* For master's, minimum B average in undergraduate course work, honors degree in physics or related area. *Application deadline:* For fall admission, 9/1 (priority date). Applications are processed on a rolling basis. Application fee: $30. *Faculty research:* Atomic and molecular spectroscopy, quantum theory, many body theory, mathematical physics. Total annual research expenditures: $160,000. *Unit head:* Dr. D. Hunter, Chair, 902-867-2104, Fax: 902-867-2414, E-mail: dhunter@stfx.ca. *Application contact:* Admissions Office, 902-867-2219, Fax: 902-867-2329, E-mail: admit@stfx.ca.

Sam Houston State University, College of Arts and Sciences, Department of Physics, Huntsville, TX 77341. Offers MS. *Students:* 6 full-time (0 women), 1 (woman) part-time; includes 4 minority (all Asian Americans or Pacific Islanders), 2 international. Average age 29. In 1998, 10 degrees awarded. *Degree requirements:* For master's, thesis required, foreign language not required. *Entrance requirements:* For master's, GRE General Test (minimum combined score of 1000 required), TOEFL (minimum score of 550 required). *Application deadline:* For fall admission, 3/15 (priority date); for spring admission, 11/1. Applications are processed on a rolling basis. Application fee: $15. *Financial aid:* Research assistantships, teaching assistantships, institutionally-sponsored loans available. *Faculty research:* Solid-state physics, optical propertiesof semiconductors, EPR of semiconductors, meteorites, ion sources. Total annual research expenditures: $650,000. *Unit head:* Dr. Charles Meitzler, Chair, 409-294-1600, Fax: 409-294-1585.

San Diego State University, Graduate and Research Affairs, College of Sciences, Department of Physics, Program in Physics, San Diego, CA 92182. Offers MA, MS. *Students:* 3 full-time (0 women), 8 part-time (3 women); includes 1 minority (Hispanic American), 2 international. 12 applicants, 58% accepted. In 1998, 1 degree awarded. *Degree requirements:* For master's, thesis, oral exam required. *Entrance requirements:* For master's, GRE General Test (minimum combined score of 950 required), TOEFL (minimum score of 550 required). *Application deadline:* For fall admission, 6/1 (priority date); for spring admission, 11/1. Applications are processed on a rolling basis. Application fee: $55. *Financial aid:* Career-related internships or fieldwork available. *Application contact:* Patrick Papin, Graduate Adviser, 619-594-6154, Fax: 619-594-5485, E-mail: ppapin@sciences.sdsu.edu.

San Francisco State University, Graduate Division, College of Science and Engineering, Department of Physics and Astronomy, San Francisco, CA 94132-1722. Offers physics and astrophysics (MS). *Students:* 56 full-time (12 women). In 1998, 11 degrees awarded. *Degree requirements:* For master's, computer language, thesis required. *Entrance requirements:* For master's, minimum GPA of 2.5 in last 60 units. *Average time to degree:* Master's–2.5 years full-time. *Application deadline:* For fall admission, 11/30 (priority date). Applications are processed on a rolling basis. Application fee: $55. *Financial aid:* In 1998–99, 35 students received aid; research assistantships, teaching assistantships, career-related internships or fieldwork, Federal Work-Study, institutionally-sponsored loans, and tuition waivers (partial) available. Financial aid application deadline: 3/1. *Faculty research:* Quark search, thin-films, dark matter detection, search for planetary systems, low temperature. Total annual research expenditures: $705,000. *Unit head:* Dr. Robert Rogers, Chair, 415-338-1659, E-mail: rrogers@stars.sfsu.edu. *Application contact:* Dr. Susan Lea, Graduate Coordinator, 415-338-1691, E-mail: lea@stars.sfsu.edu.

San Jose State University, Graduate Studies, College of Science, Department of Physics, San Jose, CA 95192-0001. Offers MS. Part-time and evening/weekend programs available. *Faculty:* 18 full-time (1 woman). *Students:* 3 full-time (1 woman), 10 part-time (2 women); includes 2 minority (1 Asian American or Pacific Islander, 1 Hispanic American), 2 international. Average age 36. 13 applicants, 69% accepted. In 1998, 8 degrees awarded. *Degree requirements:* For master's, thesis optional, foreign language not required. *Entrance requirements:* For master's, GRE. *Application deadline:* For fall admission, 6/1. Applications are processed on a rolling basis. Application fee: $59. Tuition, nonresident: part-time $246 per unit. Required fees: $1,939; $1,309 per year. *Financial aid:* In 1998–99, 7 teaching assistantships were awarded.; career-related internships or fieldwork, Federal Work-Study, and institutionally-sponsored loans also available. Aid available to part-time students. Financial aid application deadline: 3/1. *Faculty research:* Astrophysics, atmospheric physics, elementary particles, dislocation theory, general relativity. *Unit head:* Dr. Joseph Becker, Chair, 408-924-5210, Fax: 408-924-2917. *Application contact:* Dr. Franklin Muirhead, Graduate Adviser, 408-924-5258.

Simon Fraser University, Graduate Studies, Faculty of Science, Department of Physics, Burnaby, BC V5A 1S6, Canada. Offers biophysics (M Sc, PhD); chemical physics (M Sc, PhD); physics (M Sc, PhD). *Faculty:* 23 full-time (2 women). *Students:* 51 full-time (5 women). Average age 29. In 1998, 5 master's, 7 doctorates awarded. *Degree requirements:* For master's and doctorate, thesis/dissertation required, foreign language not required. *Entrance requirements:* For master's, TOEFL (minimum score of 570 required), TWE (minimum score of 5 required), or International English Language Test (minimum score of 7.5 required), minimum GPA of 3.0; for doctorate, TOEFL (minimum score of 570 required), TWE (minimum score of 5 required), or International English Language Test (minimum score of 7.5 required), minimum GPA of 3.5. Application fee: $55. *Financial aid:* In 1998–99, 14 fellowships were awarded.; research assistantships, teaching assistantships *Faculty research:* Solid-state physics, magnetism, energy research, superconductivity, nuclear physics. *Unit head:* R. F. Frindt, Chair, 604-291-4465, Fax: 604-291-3592. *Application contact:* Graduate Secretary, 604-291-4465, Fax: 604-291-3592, E-mail: physics_grad_office@sfu.ca.

South Dakota School of Mines and Technology, Graduate Division, Division of Material Engineering and Science, Doctoral Program in Materials Engineering and Science, Rapid City, SD 57701-3995. Offers chemical engineering (PhD); chemistry (PhD); civil engineering (PhD); electrical engineering (PhD); mechanical engineering (PhD); metallurgical engineering (PhD); physics (PhD). Part-time programs available. *Students:* 14 full-time (2 women), 9 international. *Degree requirements:* For doctorate, dissertation required, foreign language not required. *Entrance requirements:* For doctorate, TOEFL (minimum score of 520 required), TWE, minimum graduate GPA of 3.0. *Application deadline:* For fall admission, 6/15 (priority date); for spring admission, 10/15. Applications are processed on a rolling basis. Application fee: $15. Electronic applications accepted. Tuition, state resident: part-time $89 per hour. Tuition, nonresident: part-time $261 per hour. Part-time tuition and fees vary according to program. *Unit head:* Dr. Chris Jenkins, Coordinator, 605-394-2406. *Application contact:* Brenda Brown, Secretary, 800-454-8162 Ext. 2493, Fax: 605-394-5360, E-mail: graduate_admissions@silver.sdmt.edu.

South Dakota School of Mines and Technology, Graduate Division, Division of Material Engineering and Science, Master's Program in Materials Engineering and Science, Rapid City, SD 57701-3995. Offers chemistry (MS); metallurgical engineering (MS); physics (MS). *Students:* 17. *Degree requirements:* Foreign language not required. *Entrance requirements:* For master's, TOEFL (minimum score of 520 required), TWE. *Application deadline:* For fall admission, 6/15 (priority date); for spring admission, 10/15. Applications are processed on a rolling basis. Application fee: $15. Electronic applications accepted. Tuition, state resident: part-time $89 per hour. Tuition, nonresident: part-time $261 per hour. Part-time tuition and fees vary according to program. *Unit head:* James W. Smolka, Coordinator, 805-258-5936. *Application contact:* Brenda Brown, Secretary, 800-454-8162 Ext. 2493, Fax: 605-394-5360, E-mail: graduate_admissions@silver.sdmt.edu.

South Dakota State University, Graduate School, College of Engineering, Department of Physics, Brookings, SD 57007. Offers MS. *Degree requirements:* For master's, thesis, oral exam required, foreign language not required. *Entrance requirements:* For master's, TOEFL (minimum score of 580 required). *Faculty research:* Materials science, astrophysics, remote sensing and atmospheric corrections, theoretical and computational physics, applied physics.

Southern Illinois University Carbondale, Graduate School, College of Science, Department of Physics, Carbondale, IL 62901-6806. Offers MS. *Faculty:* 11 full-time (0 women). *Students:* 15 full-time (2 women), 3 part-time (1 woman), 15 international. 11 applicants, 55% accepted. In 1998, 3 degrees awarded. *Degree requirements:* For master's, one foreign language (computer language can substitute), thesis required. *Entrance requirements:* For master's, TOEFL (minimum score of 550 required), minimum GPA of 2.7. *Application deadline:* Applications are processed on a rolling basis. Application fee: $20. *Financial aid:* In 1998–99, 14 students received aid, including 1 fellowship with full tuition reimbursement available, 3 research assistantships with full tuition reimbursements available, 14 teaching assistantships with full tuition reimbursements available; career-related internships or fieldwork, Federal Work-Study, institutionally-sponsored loans, and tuition waivers (full) also available. Aid available to part-time students. Financial aid application deadline: 2/15. *Faculty research:* Atomic, molecular, nuclear, and mathematical physics; statistical mechanics; solid-state and low-temperature physics; rheology; material science. Total annual research expenditures: $773,352. *Unit head:* Dr. Rongila Tao, Chairperson, 618-453-2643. *Application contact:* Graduate Admissions Committee, 618-453-2643.

Southern Illinois University Edwardsville, Graduate Studies and Research, College of Arts and Sciences, Department of Physics, Edwardsville, IL 62026-0001. Offers MS. *Students:* 1 full-time (0 women), 5 part-time (2 women), 3 international. 15 applicants, 7% accepted. In 1998, 3 degrees awarded. *Degree requirements:* For master's, final exam required. *Entrance requirements:* For master's, TOEFL (minimum score of 550 required). *Application deadline:* For fall admission, 7/24. Application fee: $25. *Financial aid:* In 1998–99, 1 research assistantship with full tuition reimbursement was awarded.; fellowships with full tuition reimbursements, teaching assistantships with full tuition reimbursements, Federal Work-Study, institutionally-sponsored loans, and unspecified assistantships also available. Aid available to part-time students. *Unit head:* Dr. Arthur Braundmeier, Chair, 618-650-2359, E-mail: abraund@siue.edu.

Southern Methodist University, Dedman College, Department of Physics, Dallas, TX 75275. Offers MS, PhD. *Faculty:* 8 full-time (0 women). *Students:* 6 full-time (2 women), 3 part-time, 7 international. Average age 28. 15 applicants, 27% accepted. In 1998, 2 master's, 2 doctorates awarded. *Degree requirements:* For master's, oral exam required, thesis optional, foreign language not required; for doctorate, dissertation, written exam required, foreign language not required. *Entrance requirements:* For master's, GRE General Test, minimum GPA of 3.0; for doctorate, GRE General Test, GRE Subject Test (physics), minimum GPA of 3.0. *Average time to degree:* Master's–2 years full-time; doctorate–5 years full-time. *Application deadline:* For fall admission, 6/30 (priority date); for spring admission, 11/30 (priority date). Applications are processed on a rolling basis. Application fee: $50. Tuition: Part-time $686 per credit hour. Required fees: $88 per credit hour. Part-time tuition and fees vary according to course load and program. *Financial aid:* In 1998–99, 8 students received aid, including 4 research assistantships with full tuition reimbursements available (averaging $14,400 per year), 4 teaching assistantships with full tuition reimbursements available (averaging $13,200 per year) Financial aid applicants required to submit FAFSA. *Faculty research:* Particle physics, cosmology. Total annual research expenditures: $500,000. *Unit head:* Dr. Gary McCartor, Chair, 214-768-2495. *Application contact:* Dr. Ryszard Stroynowski, Graduate Adviser, 214-768-4076, Fax: 214-768-4095.

Southern University and Agricultural and Mechanical College, Graduate School, College of Sciences, Department of Physics, Baton Rouge, LA 70813. Offers MS. *Faculty:* 14 full-time (0 women), 1 part-time (0 women). *Students:* 10 full-time (2 women), 3 part-time; includes 7 minority (all African Americans), 6 international. In 1998, 9 degrees awarded. *Degree requirements:* For master's, thesis required, foreign language not required. *Entrance requirements:* For master's, GMAT or GRE General Test, TOEFL. *Average time to degree:* Master's–2 years full-time, 4 years part-time. *Application deadline:* For fall admission, 6/1 (priority date); for spring admission, 11/1. Applications are processed on a rolling basis. Application fee: $5. *Financial aid:* In 1998–99, fellowships with tuition reimbursements (averaging $15,000 per year), research assistantships with partial tuition reimbursements (averaging $12,000 per year), teaching assistantships with partial tuition reimbursements (averaging $12,000 per year) were awarded. Financial aid application deadline: 4/15. *Faculty research:* Piezoelectric materials and devices, predictive ab-instio calculations, high energy physics, surface growth studies. *Unit head:* Dr. Stephen G. McGuire, Chair, 225-771-4130 Ext. 12, Fax: 225-771-2310, E-mail: mcguire@grant.phys.subr.edu.

Southwest Texas State University, Graduate School, School of Science, Department of Physics, San Marcos, TX 78666. Offers MA, MS. Part-time programs available. *Faculty:* 5 full-time (1 woman). *Students:* 4 full-time (1 woman), 11 part-time (2 women); includes 3 minority (all Hispanic Americans) Average age 31. In 1998, 5 degrees awarded. *Degree requirements:* For master's, thesis (for some programs), comprehensive exam required, foreign language not required. *Entrance requirements:* For master's, GRE General Test (minimum combined score of 900 required), TOEFL (minimum score of 550 required), minimum GPA of 2.75 in last 60 hours. *Application deadline:* For fall admission, 6/15 (priority date); for spring admission, 10/15 (priority date). Applications are processed on a rolling basis. Application fee: $25 ($50 for international students). Tuition, state resident: full-time $684; part-time $38 per semester hour. Tuition, nonresident: full-time $4,572; part-time $254 per semester hour. *Financial aid:* Teaching assistantships, career-related internships or fieldwork, Federal Work-Study, and institutionally-sponsored loans available. Aid available to part-time students. Financial aid application deadline: 4/1; financial aid applicants required to submit FAFSA. *Faculty research:* High-temperature superconductors, historical astronomy, general relativity. *Unit head:* Dr. James R. Crawford, Chair, 512-245-2131, Fax: 512-245-8233, E-mail: jc03@swt.edu.

Stanford University, School of Humanities and Sciences, Department of Physics, Stanford, CA 94305-9991. Offers MAT, PhD. *Faculty:* 27 full-time (2 women). *Students:* 94 full-time (18 women), 25 part-time (4 women); includes 19 minority (3 African Americans, 11 Asian Americans or Pacific Islanders, 4 Hispanic Americans, 1 Native American), 37 international. Average age 26. 332 applicants, 19% accepted. In 1998, 8 master's, 14 doctorates awarded. *Degree requirements:* For doctorate, dissertation, oral exam required, foreign language not required. *Entrance requirements:* For doctorate, GRE General Test, GRE Subject Test, TOEFL. *Application deadline:* For fall admission, 1/1. Application fee: $65 ($80 for international students). Electronic applications accepted. Tuition: Full-time $23,058. Required fees: $152. Part-time tuition and fees vary according to course load. *Financial aid:* Fellowships, research assistantships, teaching assistantships, institutionally-sponsored loans available. *Unit head:* Blas Cabrera,

Chair, 650-723-4228, E-mail: cabrera@leland.stanford.edu. *Application contact:* Graduate Administrator, 650-723-0830.

State University of New York at Albany, College of Arts and Sciences, Department of Physics, Albany, NY 12222-0001. Offers MS, PhD. Evening/weekend programs available. *Faculty:* 17 full-time (2 women), 3 part-time (0 women). *Students:* 65 full-time (13 women), 7 part-time (3 women); includes 4 minority (1 African American, 1 Asian American or Pacific Islander, 2 Hispanic Americans), 42 international. Average age 27. 50 applicants, 60% accepted. In 1998, 19 master's, 6 doctorates awarded. *Degree requirements:* For master's, one foreign language required, (computer language can substitute); for doctorate, one foreign language (computer language can substitute), dissertation required. *Application deadline:* For fall admission, 6/1. Application fee: $50. Tuition, state resident: full-time $5,100; part-time $213 per credit. Tuition, nonresident: full-time $8,416; part-time $351 per credit. Required fees: $31 per credit. *Financial aid:* Fellowships, research assistantships, teaching assistantships, minority assistantships available. Financial aid application deadline: 3/15. *Faculty research:* Condensed-matter physics, high-energy physics, applied physics, electronic materials. *Unit head:* Hassa Bakhru, Chairman, 518-442-4500.

State University of New York at Binghamton, Graduate School, School of Arts and Sciences, Department of Physics, Applied Physics, and Astronomy, Binghamton, NY 13902-6000. Offers applied physics (MS); physics (MA, MS). *Faculty:* 9 full-time, 2 part-time. *Students:* 9 full-time (1 woman), 1 part-time; includes 1 minority (African American), 2 international. Average age 26. 12 applicants, 58% accepted. In 1998, 1 degree awarded. *Degree requirements:* For master's, thesis or alternative required. *Entrance requirements:* For master's, GRE General Test, GRE Subject Test, TOEFL. *Application deadline:* For fall admission, 4/15 (priority date); for spring admission, 11/1. Applications are processed on a rolling basis. Application fee: $50. Electronic applications accepted. Tuition, state resident: full-time $5,100; part-time $213 per credit. Tuition, nonresident: full-time $8,416; part-time $351 per credit. Required fees: $77 per credit. Part-time tuition and fees vary according to course load. *Financial aid:* In 1998–99, 6 students received aid, including 3 research assistantships with full tuition reimbursements available (averaging $9,000 per year), 3 teaching assistantships with full tuition reimbursements available (averaging $7,600 per year); fellowships, career-related internships or fieldwork, Federal Work-Study, institutionally-sponsored loans, and unspecified assistantships also available. Aid available to part-time students. Financial aid application deadline: 2/15. *Unit head:* Dr. Robert L. Pompi, Chairperson, 607-777-2217.

State University of New York at Buffalo, Graduate School, College of Arts and Sciences, Department of Physics, Buffalo, NY 14260. Offers MS, PhD. Part-time programs available. *Faculty:* 18 full-time (0 women), 2 part-time (1 woman). *Students:* 41 full-time (9 women), 29 part-time (5 women); includes 1 minority (Asian American or Pacific Islander), 58 international. Average age 29. 95 applicants, 51% accepted. In 1998, 6 master's, 10 doctorates awarded. Terminal master's awarded for partial completion of doctoral program. *Degree requirements:* For master's, thesis, qualifying exam required, foreign language not required; for doctorate, dissertation, qualifying exams required, foreign language not required. *Entrance requirements:* For master's and doctorate, GRE Subject Test, TOEFL (minimum score of 550 required). *Average time to degree:* Master's–2 years full-time, 5.5 years part-time; doctorate–7 years full-time. *Application deadline:* For fall admission, 2/15 (priority date). Applications are processed on a rolling basis. Application fee: $35. Tuition, state resident: full-time $5,100; part-time $213 per credit hour. Tuition, nonresident: full-time $8,416; part-time $351 per credit hour. Required fees: $870; $75 per semester. Tuition and fees vary according to course load and program. *Financial aid:* In 1998–99, 54 students received aid, including 2 fellowships (averaging $4,000 per year), 14 research assistantships with full tuition reimbursements available (averaging $12,742 per year), 35 teaching assistantships with full tuition reimbursements available (averaging $9,600 per year); Federal Work-Study, institutionally-sponsored loans, and tuition waivers (full and partial) also available. Aid available to part-time students. Financial aid application deadline: 3/1; financial aid applicants required to submit FAFSA. *Faculty research:* Condensed-matter physics (experimental and theoretical), high energy and particle physics (experimental and theoretical), computational physics, medical physics, materials physics. Total annual research expenditures: $1 million. *Unit head:* Dr. Richard J. Gonsalves, Chairman, 716-645-2017, Fax: 716-645-2507, E-mail: phygons@acsu.buffalo.edu. *Application contact:* Dr. Athos C. Petrou, Director of Graduate Studies, 716-645-2987, Fax: 716-645-2507, E-mail: petrou@acsu.buffalo.edu.

State University of New York at Stony Brook, Graduate School, College of Arts and Sciences, Department of Physics and Astronomy, Program in Physics, Stony Brook, NY 11794. Offers MA, MAT, MS, PhD. *Students:* 108 full-time (16 women), 55 part-time (7 women); includes 11 minority (1 African American, 7 Asian Americans or Pacific Islanders, 3 Hispanic Americans), 101 international. *Degree requirements:* For master's, foreign language and thesis not required; for doctorate, dissertation required. *Entrance requirements:* For master's and doctorate, GRE General Test, TOEFL. *Application deadline:* For fall admission, 1/15. Application fee: $50. *Financial aid:* Fellowships, research assistantships, teaching assistantships available. Financial aid application deadline: 2/1. *Application contact:* Dr. Peter Stephens, Director, 516-632-8279, Fax: 516-632-8176, E-mail: pstephens@ccmail.sunysb.edu.

Stephen F. Austin State University, Graduate School, College of Sciences and Mathematics, Department of Physics and Astronomy, Nacogdoches, TX 75962. Offers physics (MS). Part-time programs available. *Faculty:* 6 full-time, 1 part-time (0 women). *Students:* 5 full-time (1 woman), 2 part-time (1 woman); includes 1 minority (Hispanic American), 1 international. Average age 30. 2 applicants, 100% accepted. In 1998, 1 degree awarded. *Degree requirements:* For master's, comprehensive exam required, foreign language and thesis not required. *Entrance requirements:* For master's, GRE General Test (minimum combined score of 1000 required), TOEFL, minimum GPA of 2.8 in last 60 hours, 2.5 overall. *Application deadline:* For fall admission, 8/1 (priority date); for spring admission, 12/15. Applications are processed on a rolling basis. Application fee: $0 ($50 for international students). Tuition, state resident: full-time $1,792. Tuition, nonresident: full-time $6,880. *Financial aid:* Teaching assistantships, institutionally-sponsored loans available. Financial aid application deadline: 3/1. *Faculty research:* Low-temperature physics, x-ray spectroscopy and metallic glasses, infrared spectroscopy. *Unit head:* Dr. Harry D. Downing, Chair, 409-468-3001.

Stevens Institute of Technology, Graduate School, School of Applied Sciences and Liberal Arts, Department of Physics and Engineering Physics, Hoboken, NJ 07030. Offers applied optics (Certificate); engineering physics (M Eng), including engineering optics, engineering physics; physics (MS, PhD); surface physics (Certificate). Part-time and evening/weekend programs available. Terminal master's awarded for partial completion of doctoral program. *Degree requirements:* For master's, thesis optional, foreign language not required; for doctorate, dissertation required, foreign language not required; for Certificate, computer language required, foreign language not required. *Entrance requirements:* For master's and doctorate, GRE, TOEFL. Electronic applications accepted. *Faculty research:* Laser spectroscopy, physical kinetics, semiconductor-device physics, condensed-matter theory.

Syracuse University, Graduate School, College of Arts and Sciences, Department of Physics, Syracuse, NY 13244-0003. Offers biophysics (PhD); physics (MS, PhD). *Faculty:* 23. *Students:* 44 full-time (2 women), 2 part-time (both women); includes 1 minority (African American), 28 international. Average age 29. 172 applicants, 15% accepted. In 1998, 1 master's, 4 doctorates awarded. Terminal master's awarded for partial completion of doctoral program. *Degree requirements:* For master's, thesis or alternative required, foreign language not required; for doctorate, dissertation required, foreign language not required. *Entrance requirements:* For master's and doctorate, GRE General Test, GRE Subject Test, TOEFL. *Application deadline:* Applications are processed on a rolling basis. Application fee: $40. Tuition: Full-time $13,992; part-time $583 per credit hour. *Financial aid:* Fellowships, research assistantships, teaching assistantships, Federal Work-Study and tuition waivers (partial) available. Financial aid application deadline: 3/1. *Unit head:* Eric Schiff, Chair, 315-443-3901. *Application contact:* Edward Lipson, Graduate Program Director, 315-443-5958.

Temple University, Graduate School, College of Science and Technology, Department of Physics, Philadelphia, PA 19122-6096. Offers MA, PhD. *Faculty:* 15 full-time (2 women). *Students:* 17 (3 women); includes 6 minority (all Asian Americans or Pacific Islanders) 2 international. 17 applicants, 71% accepted. In 1998, 6 master's, 2 doctorates awarded. Terminal master's awarded for partial completion of doctoral program. *Degree requirements:* For master's, computer language, thesis or alternative, comprehensive exam required, foreign language not required; for doctorate, computer language, dissertation, 2 comprehensive exams required, foreign language not required. *Entrance requirements:* For master's and doctorate, minimum GPA of 3.0 during previous 2 years, 2.8 overall. *Application deadline:* For fall admission, 7/15; for spring admission, 11/15. Applications are processed on a rolling basis. Application fee: $40. Electronic applications accepted. *Financial aid:* Fellowships, research assistantships, teaching assistantships, tuition waivers (full and partial) available. *Faculty research:* Laser-based molecular spectroscopy, elementary particle physics, statistical mechanics, solid-state physics. *Unit head:* Dr. Edward Gawlinski, Chair, 215-204-7624, Fax: 215-204-5652, E-mail: ed@egs.phys.temple.edu. *Application contact:* Dr. Robert Intemann, Chair, Graduate Program Committee, 215-204-1791, Fax: 215-204-5652, E-mail: intemann@vm.temple.edu.

See in-depth description on page 511.

Texas A&M University, College of Science, Department of Physics, College Station, TX 77843. Offers MS, PhD. *Faculty:* 40 full-time (0 women), 2 part-time (0 women). *Students:* 110 full-time (10 women), 5 part-time (1 woman); includes 3 minority (1 African American, 2 Hispanic Americans), 76 international. Average age 28. 99 applicants, 75% accepted. In 1998, 10 master's awarded (40% found work related to degree, 60% continued full-time study); 10 doctorates awarded (20% entered university research/teaching, 60% found other work related to degree, 20% continued full-time study). Terminal master's awarded for partial completion of doctoral program. *Degree requirements:* For doctorate, dissertation required, foreign language not required, foreign language not required. *Entrance requirements:* For master's, GRE General Test (minimum score of 400 on verbal section, 650 on quantitative, 600 on analytical required), GRE Subject Test (minimum score of 600 rquired), TOEFL (minimum score of 550 required); for doctorate, GRE General Test (minimum score of 400 on verbal section, 650 on quantitative, 600 on analytical required), GRE Subject Test (minimum score of 600 required), TOEFL (minimum score of 550 required). *Average time to degree:* Master's–3.1 years full-time; doctorate–5.4 years full-time. *Application deadline:* For fall admission, 3/1 (priority date); for spring admission, 8/1. Application fee: $50 ($75 for international students). Electronic applications accepted. *Financial aid:* In 1998–99, 30 research assistantships (averaging $15,392 per year), 79 teaching assistantships (averaging $15,604 per year) were awarded.; fellowships Financial aid application deadline: 3/1; financial aid applicants required to submit FAFSA. *Faculty research:* Condensed-matter, atomic/molecular, high-energy, medical, and nuclear physics. Total annual research expenditures: $6.1 million. *Unit head:* Dr. Thomas W. Adair, Head, 409-845-7717, Fax: 409-845-2590, E-mail: adair@phys.tamu.edu. *Application contact:* Dr. George W. Kattawar, Professor, 409-845-1180, Fax: 409-845-2590, E-mail: kattawar@silly.tamu.edu.

See in-depth description on page 513.

Texas A&M University–Commerce, Graduate School, College of Arts and Sciences, Department of Physics, Commerce, TX 75429-3011. Offers M Ed, MS. Part-time programs available. *Faculty:* 2 full-time (0 women), 1 part-time (0 women). *Students:* 2 full-time (1 woman), 6 part-time (1 woman); includes 1 minority (African American) Average age 36. In 1998, 3 degrees awarded. *Degree requirements:* For master's, thesis (for some programs), comprehensive exam required. *Entrance requirements:* For master's, GRE General Test (minimum combined score of 850 required). *Average time to degree:* Master's–2 years full-time, 2.75 years part-time. *Application deadline:* For fall admission, 6/1 (priority date); for spring admission, 11/1 (priority date). Applications are processed on a rolling basis. Application fee: $0 ($25 for international students). Electronic applications accepted. *Financial aid:* In 1998–99, research assistantships (averaging $7,750 per year), teaching assistantships (averaging $7,750 per year) were awarded.; Federal Work-Study, institutionally-sponsored loans, and scholarships also available. Financial aid application deadline: 5/1; financial aid applicants required to submit FAFSA. Total annual research expenditures: $7,345. *Unit head:* Dr. Ben Doughty, Head, 903-886-5488. *Application contact:* Betty Hunt, Graduate Admissions Adviser, 903-886-5167, Fax: 903-886-5165, E-mail: betty_hunt@tamu_commerce.edu.

Texas Christian University, Add Ran College of Arts and Sciences, Department of Physics, Fort Worth, TX 76129-0002. Offers MA, MS, PhD. Part-time and evening/weekend programs available. *Students:* 15 (2 women); includes 2 minority (1 African American, 1 Hispanic American) 7 international. 40 applicants, 8% accepted. In 1998, 1 master's, 3 doctorates awarded. *Degree requirements:* For master's, foreign language (MA) required, thesis optional; for doctorate, dissertation, qualifying exams required, foreign language not required. *Entrance requirements:* For master's, GRE General Test (minimum combined score of 1000 required), TOEFL (minimum score of 550 required); for doctorate, GRE General Test, TOEFL (minimum score of 550 required). *Application deadline:* For fall admission, 3/1; for spring admission, 12/1. Applications are processed on a rolling basis. Application fee: $0. *Financial aid:* Fellowships, teaching assistantships available. Financial aid application deadline: 3/1. *Unit head:* Dr. C. A. Quarles, Chairperson, 817-257-7375.

Texas Tech University, Graduate School, College of Arts and Sciences, Department of Physics, Lubbock, TX 79409. Offers applied physics (MS, PhD); physics (MS, PhD). Part-time programs available. *Faculty:* 16 full-time (2 women), 1 part-time (0 women). *Students:* 30 full-time (5 women), 7 part-time (1 woman); includes 7 minority (4 Asian Americans or Pacific Islanders, 3 Hispanic Americans), 8 international. Average age 28. 14 applicants, 64% accepted. In 1998, 8 master's, 6 doctorates awarded. *Degree requirements:* For master's and doctorate, thesis/dissertation required. *Entrance requirements:* For master's, GRE General Test (combined average 1184); for doctorate, GRE General Test. *Application deadline:* For fall admission, 4/15 (priority date); for spring admission, 11/1 (priority date). Applications are processed on a rolling basis. Application fee: $25 ($50 for international students). Electronic applications accepted. *Financial aid:* In 1998–99, 28 students received aid, including 12 research assistantships, 11 teaching assistantships (averaging $11,986 per year); fellowships, career-related internships or fieldwork, Federal Work-Study, and institutionally-sponsored loans also available. Aid available to part-time students. Financial aid application deadline: 5/15; financial aid applicants required to submit FAFSA. *Faculty research:* Laser detection of latent fingerprints/criminology, physics of semiconductor materials, particle physics. Total annual research expenditures: $1.5 million. *Unit head:* Dr. Lynn L. Hatfield, Chairman, 806-742-3767, Fax: 806-742-1182.

Trent University, Graduate Studies, Program in Applications of Modelling in the Natural and Social Sciences, Department of Physics, Peterborough, ON K9J 7B8, Canada. Offers M Sc. Part-time programs available. 1 applicants, 100% accepted. *Degree requirements:* For master's, thesis required, foreign language not required. *Entrance requirements:* For master's, honours degree. *Application deadline:* For fall admission, 2/1 (priority date). Applications are processed on a rolling basis. Application fee: $45. *Financial aid:* Research assistantships, teaching assistantships available. *Faculty research:* Radiation physics, chemical physics. *Unit head:* Dr. J. Jury, Chair, 705-748-1549, E-mail: jjury@trentu.ca. *Application contact:* Graduate Studies Officer, 705-748-1245, Fax: 705-748-1587.

Tufts University, Division of Graduate and Continuing Studies and Research, Graduate School of Arts and Sciences, Department of Physics and Astronomy, Medford, MA 02155. Offers physics (MS, PhD). *Faculty:* 14 full-time, 3 part-time. *Students:* 32 (5 women) 20 international. 39 applicants, 44% accepted. In 1998, 4 master's, 2 doctorates awarded. Terminal master's awarded for partial completion of doctoral program. *Degree requirements:* For master's, thesis optional, foreign language not required; for doctorate, dissertation required, foreign language not required. *Entrance requirements:* For master's and doctorate, GRE General Test, GRE Subject Test, TOEFL (minimum score of 550 required). *Application deadline:* For fall admission, 2/15; for spring admission, 10/15. Applications are processed on a rolling basis.

Physics

Tufts University (continued)

Application fee: $50. *Financial aid:* Research assistantships with full and partial tuition reimbursements, teaching assistantships with full and partial tuition reimbursements, Federal Work-Study, scholarships, and tuition waivers (partial) available. Financial aid application deadline: 2/15; financial aid applicants required to submit FAFSA. *Unit head:* Dr. David L. Weaver, Chair, 617-627-3029. *Application contact:* Dr. Yaacov Shapira, 617-627-3029.

See in-depth description on page 515.

Tulane University, Graduate School, Department of Physics, New Orleans, LA 70118-5669. Offers MS, PhD. *Students:* 20 full-time (8 women), 12 international. 28 applicants, 25% accepted. In 1998, 2 doctorates awarded. *Degree requirements:* For master's, computer language, thesis or alternative required; for doctorate, computer language, dissertation required. *Entrance requirements:* For master's, GRE General Test (minimum combined score of 1000 required; average 1200), TOEFL (minimum score of 600 required), TSE (minimum score of 220 required), minimum B average in undergraduate course work; for doctorate, GRE General Test (minimum combined score of 1000 required; average 1200), TOEFL (minimum score of 600 required), TSE (minimum score of 220 required). *Average time to degree:* Master's–2 years full-time; doctorate–6 years full-time. *Application deadline:* For fall admission, 2/1. Application fee: $45. *Financial aid:* In 1998–99, 15 students received aid; fellowships, research assistantships, teaching assistantships, career-related internships or fieldwork, Federal Work-Study, and institutionally-sponsored loans available. Financial aid application deadline: 2/1. *Faculty research:* Surface physics, condensed-matter experiment, condensed-matter theory, nuclear theory, polymers. Total annual research expenditures: $700,000. *Unit head:* Dr. Wayne F. Reed, Chair, 504-865-5520, Fax: 504-862-8702. *Application contact:* Dr. Jim McGuire, Murchison Mallory Professor, E-mail: mcguire@mcguire.phy.tcs.tulane.edu.

Université de Moncton, Faculty of Science, Department of Physics, Moncton, NB E1A 3E9, Canada. Offers M Sc. *Faculty:* 8 full-time (0 women). *Students:* 4 full-time (0 women), 2 international. Average age 24. In 1998, 3 degrees awarded (100% found work related to degree). *Degree requirements:* For master's, thesis required, foreign language not required. *Application deadline:* For fall admission, 6/1 (priority date); for winter admission, 11/15 (priority date). Applications are processed on a rolling basis. Application fee: $50 Canadian dollars. Electronic applications accepted. *Financial aid:* Fellowships, research assistantships, teaching assistantships, institutionally-sponsored loans available. Financial aid application deadline: 6/30. *Faculty research:* Thin films, optical properties, solar selective surfaces, microgravity and photonic materials. *Unit head:* Dr. Francis Weil, Director, 506-858-4339, Fax: 506-858-4541, E-mail: weilf@umoncton.ca.

Université de Montréal, Faculty of Graduate Studies, Faculty of Arts and Sciences, Department of Physics, Montréal, PQ H3C 3J7, Canada. Offers M Sc, PhD. *Faculty:* 60 full-time (7 women), 1 part-time (0 women). *Students:* 102 full-time (16 women). 54 applicants, 24% accepted. In 1998, 12 degrees awarded. *Degree requirements:* For doctorate, dissertation, general exam required. Application fee: $30. *Financial aid:* Fellowships, research assistantships, teaching assistantships available. *Faculty research:* Astronomy; biophysics; solid-state, plasma, and nuclear physics. *Unit head:* Raynald Laprade, Chairman, 514-343-6669. *Application contact:* François Wesemael, Graduate Chairman, 514-343-7355.

Université de Sherbrooke, Faculty of Sciences, Department of Physics, Sherbrooke, PQ J1K 2R1, Canada. Offers M Sc, PhD. *Degree requirements:* For master's and doctorate, thesis/dissertation required, foreign language not required. *Entrance requirements:* For doctorate, master's degree. *Faculty research:* Solid-state physics.

Université Laval, Faculty of Graduate Studies, Faculty of Sciences and Engineering, Department of Physics, Sainte-Foy, PQ G1K 7P4, Canada. Offers M Sc, PhD. *Students:* 79 full-time (16 women), 7 part-time (1 woman). 38 applicants, 58% accepted. In 1998, 17 master's, 18 doctorates awarded. *Application deadline:* For fall admission, 3/1. Application fee: $30. *Unit head:* Pierre Amiot, Director, 415-656-2131 Ext. 3938, Fax: 418-656-2040, E-mail: pierre.amiot@phy.ulaval.ca.

The University of Akron, Graduate School, Buchtel College of Arts and Sciences, Department of Physics, Akron, OH 44325-0001. Offers MS. Part-time and evening/weekend programs available. *Faculty:* 6 full-time, 2 part-time. *Students:* 11 full-time (1 woman), 1 (woman) part-time; includes 1 minority (Hispanic American), 5 international. Average age 36. In 1998, 2 degrees awarded. *Degree requirements:* For master's, thesis or alternative required, foreign language not required. *Entrance requirements:* For master's, minimum GPA of 2.75. *Average time to degree:* Master's–2 years full-time, 4 years part-time. *Application deadline:* For fall admission, 8/15. Applications are processed on a rolling basis. Application fee: $25 ($50 for international students). Tuition, state resident: part-time $189 per credit. Tuition, nonresident: part-time $353 per credit. Required fees: $7.3 per credit. *Financial aid:* In 1998–99, 5 research assistantships with full tuition reimbursements, 9 teaching assistantships with full tuition reimbursements were awarded.; tuition waivers (full) also available. *Faculty research:* Polymer physics, statistical physics, NMR, electron tunneling, solid-state physics. *Unit head:* Dr. Ernst von Meerwall, Chair, 330-972-7078, E-mail: evonmeerwall@uakron.edu. *Application contact:* Dr. Purushottam Gujrati, 330-972-7136, E-mail: pgujrati@uakron.edu.

The University of Alabama, Graduate School, College of Arts and Sciences, Department of Physics and Astronomy, Tuscaloosa, AL 35487. Offers physics (MS, PhD). *Faculty:* 21 full-time (0 women), 3 part-time (1 woman). *Students:* 30 full-time (8 women), 15 international. Average age 28. 25 applicants, 48% accepted. In 1998, 5 master's awarded (60% found work related to degree, 40% continued full-time study); 6 doctorates awarded (17% entered university research/teaching, 83% found other work related to degree). Terminal master's awarded for partial completion of doctoral program. *Degree requirements:* For master's, oral exam required, thesis optional, foreign language not required; for doctorate, dissertation, oral and written exams required, foreign language not required. *Entrance requirements:* For master's and doctorate, GRE General Test (minimum combined score of 1500 on three sections required), TOEFL (minimum score of 550 required), minimum GPA of 3.0. *Average time to degree:* Master's–4 years full-time; doctorate–5.7 years full-time. *Application deadline:* For fall admission, 7/6 (priority date); for spring admission, 11/22. Applications are processed on a rolling basis. Application fee: $25. Electronic applications accepted. *Financial aid:* In 1998–99, 28 students received aid, including 3 fellowships with full tuition reimbursements available (averaging $10,000 per year), 9 research assistantships with full tuition reimbursements available (averaging $10,000 per year), 16 teaching assistantships with full tuition reimbursements available (averaging $10,000 per year); career-related internships or fieldwork and institutionally-sponsored loans also available. Financial aid application deadline: 4/1. *Faculty research:* Condensed-matter, high-energy physics; optics; molecular spectroscopy; astrophysics. Total annual research expenditures: $1.1 million. *Unit head:* Dr. Stanley T. Jones, Chairperson, 205-348-5050, Fax: 205-348-5051, E-mail: sjones@physics.as.ua.edu.

The University of Alabama at Birmingham, Graduate School, School of Natural Sciences and Mathematics, Department of Physics, Birmingham, AL 35294. Offers MS, PhD. *Students:* 20 full-time (4 women), 2 part-time; includes 4 minority (2 African Americans, 1 Asian American or Pacific Islander, 1 Hispanic American), 5 international. 18 applicants, 83% accepted. In 1998, 4 master's, 4 doctorates awarded. Terminal master's awarded for partial completion of doctoral program. *Degree requirements:* For master's, thesis optional; for doctorate, dissertation required. *Entrance requirements:* For master's, GRE General Test (minimum score of 500 on each of the three sections), TOEFL (minimum score of 600 required), minimum GPA of 3.0; for doctorate, GRE General Test (minimum score of 550 required on each of the three sections), TOEFL (minimum score of 600 required), minimum GPA of 3.0. *Application deadline:* Applications are processed on a rolling basis. Application fee: $30 ($60 for international students). Electronic applications accepted. *Financial aid:* In 1998–99, 12 students received aid, including 9 fellowships with full tuition reimbursements available (averaging $16,898 per year), 4 research assistantships (averaging $15,170 per year), 8 teaching assistantships with full tuition reimbursements available (averaging $12,825 per year); career-related internships or fieldwork, Federal Work-Study, grants, institutionally-sponsored loans, scholarships, traineeships, and unspecified assistantships also available. Aid available to part-time students. Financial aid application deadline: 4/15; financial aid applicants required to submit FAFSA. *Faculty research:* Laser physics, space physics, optics, biophysics, material physics. *Unit head:* Dr. David L. Shealy, Chairman, 205-934-4736, Fax: 205-934-8042, E-mail: dls@uab.edu.

The University of Alabama in Huntsville, School of Graduate Studies, College of Science, Department of Physics, Huntsville, AL 35899. Offers MS, PhD. Part-time and evening/weekend programs available. *Faculty:* 18 full-time (1 woman). *Students:* 35 full-time (6 women), 9 part-time (1 woman); includes 2 minority (both Asian Americans or Pacific Islanders), 8 international. Average age 30. 20 applicants, 100% accepted. In 1998, 9 master's, 4 doctorates awarded. *Degree requirements:* For master's, oral and written exams required, thesis optional, foreign language not required; for doctorate, dissertation, oral and written exams required, foreign language not required. *Entrance requirements:* For master's and doctorate, GRE General Test (minimum combined score of 1500 on three sections required), minimum GPA of 3.0. *Application deadline:* For fall admission, 7/24 (priority date); for spring admission, 11/15 (priority date). Applications are processed on a rolling basis. Application fee: $20. Tuition and fees vary according to course load. *Financial aid:* In 1998–99, 35 research assistantships with full and partial tuition reimbursements (averaging $10,768 per year), 15 teaching assistantships with full and partial tuition reimbursements (averaging $9,930 per year) were awarded.; fellowships with full and partial tuition reimbursements, career-related internships or fieldwork, Federal Work-Study, grants, institutionally-sponsored loans, scholarships, and tuition waivers (full and partial) also available. Aid available to part-time students. Financial aid application deadline: 4/1; financial aid applicants required to submit FAFSA. *Faculty research:* Space sciences, solid state/materials, optics/quantum electronics, astrophysics, crystal growth. Total annual research expenditures: $1.5 million. *Unit head:* Dr. Gordon Emslie, Chair, 256-890-6276, Fax: 256-890-6873, E-mail: emslieg@email.uah.edu.

University of Alaska Fairbanks, Graduate School, College of Science, Engineering and Mathematics, Department of Physics, Fairbanks, AK 99775-7480. Offers atmospheric science (MS, PhD); physics (MS, PhD); space physics (MS, PhD). Part-time programs available. *Faculty:* 19 full-time (1 woman). *Students:* 24 full-time (8 women), 2 part-time; includes 2 minority (1 African American, 1 Hispanic American) Average age 30. 14 applicants, 93% accepted. In 1998, 3 doctorates awarded (100% found work related to degree). Terminal master's awarded for partial completion of doctoral program. *Degree requirements:* For master's, thesis, comprehensive exam required, foreign language not required; for doctorate, one foreign language (computer language can substitute), dissertation, comprehensive exam required. *Entrance requirements:* For master's and doctorate, GRE General Test, GRE Subject Test, TOEFL (minimum score of 550 required). *Application deadline:* For fall admission, 2/15. Application fee: $35. *Financial aid:* Research assistantships, teaching assistantships available. Financial aid application deadline: 2/15. *Unit head:* Dr. Brenton Watkins, Head, 907-474-7339. *Application contact:* Dr. Brenton Watkins, Head, 907-474-7339.

University of Alberta, Faculty of Graduate Studies and Research, Department of Electrical and Computer Engineering, Edmonton, AB T6G 2E1, Canada. Offers computational optics (PhD); computer engineering (M Eng, M Sc, PhD); control systems (M Eng, M Sc, PhD); engineering management (M Eng); laser physics (M Sc, PhD); oil sands (M Eng, M Sc, PhD); plasma physics (M Sc, PhD); power engineering (M Eng, M Sc, PhD); telecommunications (M Eng, M Sc, PhD). Terminal master's awarded for partial completion of doctoral program. *Degree requirements:* For master's and doctorate, thesis/dissertation required, foreign language not required. *Entrance requirements:* For master's and doctorate, TOEFL (minimum score of 580 required; average 610). Electronic applications accepted. *Faculty research:* Controls, communications, microelectronics, electromagnetics.

University of Alberta, Faculty of Graduate Studies and Research, Department of Physics, Edmonton, AB T6G 2E1, Canada. Offers astrophysics (M Sc, PhD); condensed matter (M Sc, PhD); geophysics (M Sc, PhD); medical physics (M Sc, PhD); nuclear physics (M Sc, PhD); subatomic physics (M Sc, PhD). *Degree requirements:* For master's and doctorate, thesis/dissertation required. *Entrance requirements:* For master's and doctorate, TOEFL (minimum score of 550 required), minimum GPA of 7.0 on a 9.0 scale. *Faculty research:* Cosmology, astro-particle physics, high-intermediate energy, magnetism, superconductivity, electron microscopy, low-temperature physics, seismology, geodynamics, MRI.

The University of Arizona, Graduate College, College of Science, Department of Physics, Tucson, AZ 85721. Offers M Ed, MS, PhD. Part-time programs available. *Faculty:* 54. *Students:* 46 full-time (8 women), 15 part-time (1 woman); includes 4 minority (2 Asian Americans or Pacific Islanders, 2 Hispanic Americans), 19 international. Average age 29. 79 applicants, 15% accepted. In 1998, 5 master's, 6 doctorates awarded. Terminal master's awarded for partial completion of doctoral program. *Degree requirements:* For master's, thesis optional, foreign language not required; for doctorate, one foreign language, dissertation required. *Entrance requirements:* For master's and doctorate, GRE General Test, GRE Subject Test, TOEFL (minimum score of 550 required), minimum GPA of 3.0. *Application deadline:* For fall admission, 2/1. Applications are processed on a rolling basis. Application fee: $35. *Financial aid:* Fellowships, research assistantships, teaching assistantships, Federal Work-Study, scholarships, and tuition waivers (full) available. Aid available to part-time students. Financial aid application deadline: 5/1. *Faculty research:* Astrophysics; high-energy, condensed-matter, atomic, and molecular physics; optics. *Unit head:* Dr. Daniel L. Stern, Acting Head, 520-621-6801. *Application contact:* Iris Wright, Graduate Secretary, 520-621-2453, Fax: 520-621-4721.

University of Arkansas, Graduate School, J. William Fulbright College of Arts and Sciences, Department of Physics, Fayetteville, AR 72701-1201. Offers MA, MS, PhD. *Faculty:* 15 full-time (1 woman). *Students:* 36 full-time (5 women), 2 part-time; includes 1 minority (Hispanic American), 14 international. 27 applicants, 70% accepted. In 1998, 6 master's, 4 doctorates awarded. *Degree requirements:* For master's and doctorate, thesis/dissertation required, foreign language not required. Application fee: $40 ($50 for international students). Tuition, state resident: full-time $3,186. Tuition, nonresident: full-time $7,560. Required fees: $378. *Financial aid:* In 1998–99, 23 research assistantships, 19 teaching assistantships were awarded.; career-related internships or fieldwork and Federal Work-Study also available. Aid available to part-time students. Financial aid application deadline: 4/1; financial aid applicants required to submit FAFSA. *Unit head:* Dr. Surendra Singh, Chair, 501-575-2506. *Application contact:* Raj Gupta, Graduate Coordinator, 501-575-5933, E-mail: rgupta@comp.uark.edu.

University of British Columbia, Faculty of Graduate Studies, Faculty of Science, Department of Physics and Astronomy, Vancouver, BC V6T 1Z2, Canada. Offers engineering physics (MA Sc); physics (M Sc, PhD). *Degree requirements:* For master's, thesis required; for doctorate, dissertation, comprehensive exam required. *Entrance requirements:* For master's, GRE General Test, TOEFL, honors degree; for doctorate, GRE General Test, TOEFL, master's degree. *Faculty research:* Applied physics, astrophysics, condensed matter, plasma physics, subatomic physics, astronomy.

University of Calgary, Faculty of Graduate Studies, Faculty of Science, Department of Physics and Astronomy, Calgary, AB T2N 1N4, Canada. Offers M Sc, PhD. Part-time programs available. *Faculty:* 18 full-time (1 woman), 1 part-time (0 women). *Students:* 17 full-time (7 women). Average age 28. 25 applicants, 16% accepted. In 1998, 3 master's awarded (67% found work related to degree, 33% continued full-time study); 1 doctorate awarded (100% found work related to degree). *Degree requirements:* For master's, thesis required; for doctorate, dissertation, oral candidacy exam, written qualifying exam required. *Entrance requirements:* For master's and doctorate, GRE General Test, GRE Subject Test, TOEFL (minimum score of 550 required). *Application deadline:* For fall admission, 3/1. Applications are processed on a rolling basis. Application fee: $60. *Financial aid:* Fellowships, research assistantships, teaching assistantships, institutionally-sponsored loans available. Financial aid application deadline: 5/31. *Faculty research:* Astronomy and astrophysics, mass spectrometry, atmospheric physics, space physics, condensed–matter physics, medical physics. Total annual research expenditures: $3.3 million. *Unit head:* Dr. J. S. Murphree, Head, 403-220-5385, Fax: 403-289-3331, E-mail: murphree@phys.ucalgary.ca. *Application contact:* Dr. S. Kwok, Chairman, Graduate Affairs, 403-220-5414, Fax: 403-289-3331, E-mail: kwok@acs.ucalgary.ca.

University of California, Berkeley, Graduate Division, College of Letters and Science, Department of Physics, Berkeley, CA 94720-1500. Offers PhD. *Students:* 221 full-time (27 women); includes 34 minority (1 African American, 26 Asian Americans or Pacific Islanders, 7 Hispanic Americans), 34 international. 532 applicants, 21% accepted. In 1998, 28 degrees awarded. *Degree requirements:* For doctorate, dissertation, qualifying exam required. *Entrance requirements:* For doctorate, GRE General Test, GRE Subject Test, minimum GPA of 3.0. *Application deadline:* For fall admission, 1/5. Application fee: $40. *Financial aid:* Fellowships, research assistantships, teaching assistantships available. Financial aid application deadline: 1/5. *Unit head:* Dr. Roger W. Falcone, Chair, 510-642-3316. *Application contact:* Donna Sakima, Graduate Assistant for Admission, 510-642-0596, Fax: 510-643-8497, E-mail: sakima@physics.berkeley.edu.

University of California, Davis, Graduate Studies, Program in Physics, Davis, CA 95616. Offers MS, PhD. *Faculty:* 28 full-time (2 women), 3 part-time (0 women). *Students:* 75 full-time (11 women); includes 11 minority (1 African American, 7 Asian Americans or Pacific Islanders, 3 Hispanic Americans), 6 international. 79 applicants, 73% accepted. In 1998, 14 master's, 7 doctorates awarded. Terminal master's awarded for partial completion of doctoral program. *Degree requirements:* For master's, thesis optional, foreign language not required; for doctorate, dissertation required, foreign language not required. *Entrance requirements:* For master's and doctorate, GRE General Test, GRE Subject Test, minimum GPA of 3.0. *Average time to degree:* Master's–2 years full-time; doctorate–6 years full-time. *Application deadline:* For fall admission, 1/15 (priority date). Application fee: $40. Electronic applications accepted. *Financial aid:* In 1998–99, 17 fellowships with full and partial tuition reimbursements, 20 research assistantships with full and partial tuition reimbursements, 46 teaching assistantships with full and partial tuition reimbursements were awarded.; Federal Work-Study, grants, institutionally-sponsored loans, scholarships, and tuition waivers (full and partial) also available. Financial aid application deadline: 1/15; financial aid applicants required to submit FAFSA. *Faculty research:* Astrophysics, condensed-matter physics, nuclear physics, particle physics, quantum optics. Total annual research expenditures: $3.7 million. *Unit head:* Barry M. Klein, Chair, 530-752-1501, E-mail: klein@bethe.ucdavis.edu. *Application contact:* Lynn Rabena, Administrative Assistant, 530-752-1501, Fax: 530-752-4717, E-mail: rabena@physics.ucdavis.edu.

University of California, Irvine, Office of Research and Graduate Studies, School of Physical Sciences, Department of Physics and Astronomy, Irvine, CA 92697. Offers physics (MS, PhD). *Faculty:* 32 full-time (3 women), 2 part-time (0 women). *Students:* 45 full-time (7 women), 1 part-time; includes 10 minority (9 Asian Americans or Pacific Islanders, 1 Hispanic American), 13 international. 73 applicants, 47% accepted. In 1998, 9 master's, 10 doctorates awarded. Terminal master's awarded for partial completion of doctoral program. *Degree requirements:* For doctorate, dissertation required, foreign language not required, foreign language not required. *Entrance requirements:* For master's, GRE General Test, GRE Subject Test, minimum GPA of 3.0; for doctorate, GRE General Test, GRE Subject Test. *Application deadline:* For fall admission, 1/15 (priority date). Applications are processed on a rolling basis. Application fee: $40. Electronic applications accepted. *Financial aid:* Fellowships, research assistantships, teaching assistantships, institutionally-sponsored loans and tuition waivers (full and partial) available. Financial aid application deadline: 3/2; financial aid applicants required to submit FAFSA. *Faculty research:* High-energy physics, condensed-matter physics, low-temperature physics, plasma physics, astrophysics, particle physics, chemical and materials physics. *Unit head:* Dr. Gary Chanan, Chair, 949-824-6619, Fax: 949-824-2174, E-mail: gachanan@uci.edu. *Application contact:* Graduate Adviser, 949-824-5438, Fax: 949-824-2174.

University of California, Los Angeles, Graduate Division, College of Letters and Science, Department of Physics and Astronomy, Program in Physics, Los Angeles, CA 90095. Offers physics (PhD); physics education (MAT). MAT admits only applicants whose objective is PhD. *Students:* 107 full-time (15 women); includes 17 minority (14 Asian Americans or Pacific Islanders, 3 Hispanic Americans), 28 international. 246 applicants, 30% accepted. *Degree requirements:* For master's, comprehensive exam or thesis required; for doctorate, dissertation, oral and written qualifying exams required, foreign language not required. *Entrance requirements:* For master's, GRE General Test, GRE Subject Test (physics), minimum GPA of 3.0; for doctorate, GRE General Test, GRE Subject Test (physics), minimum undergraduate GPA of 3.0. *Application deadline:* For fall admission, 12/15. Application fee: $40. Electronic applications accepted. *Financial aid:* In 1998–99, 76 fellowships, 92 teaching assistantships were awarded.; research assistantships, Federal Work-Study, institutionally-sponsored loans, scholarships, and tuition waivers (full and partial) also available. Financial aid application deadline: 3/1. *Unit head:* Judy Erwin, Graduate Assistant, 530-752-1926, Fax: 530-752-5660, E-mail: gjerwin@ucdavis.edu. *Application contact:* Departmental Office, 310-825-2307, E-mail: apply@physics.ucla.edu.

Announcement: Strong, broad research and graduate student programs in both experimental and theoretical physics: condensed matter, low temperature, plasma, astrophysics, high energy, intermediate energy, nuclear physics. Approximately 55 faculty members, 125 graduate students; 20 PhDs per year. Strong research funding. Financial support for essentially all graduate students. Near ocean in attractive West Los Angeles. WWW: http://www.physics.ucla.edu.

University of California, Riverside, Graduate Division, College of Natural and Agricultural Sciences, Department of Physics, Riverside, CA 92521-0102. Offers MS, PhD. Part-time programs available. *Faculty:* 18 full-time (0 women), 2 part-time (0 women). *Students:* 39 full-time (2 women); includes 4 minority (1 African American, 3 Asian Americans or Pacific Islanders), 20 international. Average age 29. In 1998, 2 master's, 6 doctorates awarded. Terminal master's awarded for partial completion of doctoral program. *Degree requirements:* For master's, comprehensive exams or thesis required; for doctorate, dissertation, qualifying exams required, foreign language not required. *Entrance requirements:* For master's and doctorate, GRE General Test (minimum combined score of 1100 required), TOEFL (minimum score of 550 required), minimum GPA of 3.2. *Average time to degree:* Master's–1.6 years full-time; doctorate–6 years full-time. *Application deadline:* For fall admission, 5/1; for winter admission, 9/1; for spring admission, 12/1. Applications are processed on a rolling basis. Application fee: $40. Electronic applications accepted. *Financial aid:* Fellowships, research assistantships, teaching assistantships, career-related internships or fieldwork, Federal Work-Study, grants, institutionally-sponsored loans, and tuition waivers (full and partial) available. Financial aid application deadline: 2/1; financial aid applicants required to submit FAFSA. *Faculty research:* Laser physics and surface science, elementary particle and heavy ion physics, plasma physics, optical physics, astrophysics, space physics. *Unit head:* Dr. Allen Zych, Chair, 909-787-5332, Fax: 909-787-5136, E-mail: gophysics@ucrac1.ucr.edu. *Application contact:* Pat Brooks, Graduate Program Assistant, 909-787-5332, Fax: 909-787-4529, E-mail: gophysics@ucrac1.ucr.edu.

University of California, San Diego, Graduate Studies and Research, Department of Physics, La Jolla, CA 92093-5003. Offers biophysics (MS, PhD); physics (MS, PhD). *Faculty:* 47. *Students:* 119 (12 women). 221 applicants, 38% accepted. In 1998, 10 master's, 15 doctorates awarded. *Degree requirements:* For doctorate, dissertation required. *Entrance requirements:* For master's and doctorate, GRE General Test, GRE Subject Test. Application fee: $40. *Unit head:* Thomas M. O'Neil, Professor, 619-534-4176, E-mail: toneil@ucsd.edu. *Application contact:* Debra Bomar, Graduate Coordinator, 619-534-3293.

See in-depth description on page 519.

University of California, Santa Barbara, Graduate Division, College of Letters and Science, Division of Math, Life and Physical Science, Department of Physics, Santa Barbara, CA 93106. Offers PhD. *Students:* 104 full-time (14 women). 251 applicants, 37% accepted. In 1998, 22 doctorates awarded. *Degree requirements:* For doctorate, dissertation required, foreign language not required. *Entrance requirements:* For doctorate, GRE General Test, GRE Subject Test, TOEFL (minimum score of 550 required). *Application deadline:* For fall admission, 3/15. Application fee: $40. *Financial aid:* Fellowships, research assistantships, teaching assistantships, career-related internships or fieldwork, Federal Work-Study, institutionally-sponsored loans, and tuition waivers (full and partial) available. Financial aid application deadline: 1/15; financial aid applicants required to submit FAFSA. *Unit head:* Rollin Morrison, Chair, 805-893-4888. *Application contact:* Kathy Upton, Graduate Secretary, 805-893-4646, E-mail: kmu@orca.physics.ucsb.edu.

University of California, Santa Cruz, Graduate Division, Division of Natural Sciences, Program in Physics, Santa Cruz, CA 95064. Offers MS, PhD. *Faculty:* 18 full-time. *Students:* 42 full-time (8 women); includes 3 minority (2 Asian Americans or Pacific Islanders, 1 Hispanic American), 9 international. 63 applicants, 41% accepted. In 1998, 16 master's, 5 doctorates awarded. *Degree requirements:* For master's, thesis required; for doctorate, one foreign language (computer language can substitute), dissertation, qualifying exam required. *Entrance requirements:* For master's and doctorate, GRE General Test, GRE Subject Test. *Application deadline:* For fall admission, 1/15. Application fee: $40. *Financial aid:* Fellowships, research assistantships, teaching assistantships, career-related internships or fieldwork, Federal Work-Study, and institutionally-sponsored loans available. Financial aid application deadline: 1/15. *Faculty research:* Theoretical and experimental high-energy physics, theoretical and experimental solid-state physics, critical phenomena, theoretical fluid dynamics, experimental biophysics. *Unit head:* Dr. George Brown, Chair, 831-459-2327. *Application contact:* Graduate Admissions, 831-459-2301.

University of Central Florida, College of Arts and Sciences, Program in Physics, Orlando, FL 32816. Offers MS, PhD. Part-time and evening/weekend programs available. *Faculty:* 16 full-time, 16 part-time. *Students:* 29 full-time (8 women), 11 part-time; includes 3 minority (1 African American, 2 Hispanic Americans), 16 international. Average age 32. 19 applicants, 37% accepted. In 1998, 14 master's, 5 doctorates awarded. *Degree requirements:* For master's, thesis or alternative required, foreign language not required; for doctorate, dissertation, candidacy and qualifying exams required, foreign language not required. *Entrance requirements:* For master's, GRE General Test (minimum combined score of 1000 required), TOEFL (minimum score of 550 required; 213 computer-based), minimum GPA of 3.0 in last 60 hours; for doctorate, GRE General Test (minimum combined score of 1000 required), GRE Subject Test, TOEFL (minimum score of 550 required; 213 computer-based), minimum GPA of 3.0 in last 60 hours or master's qualifying exam. *Application deadline:* For fall admission, 2/15. Application fee: $20. Tuition, state resident: full-time $2,054; part-time $137 per credit. Tuition, nonresident: full-time $7,207; part-time $480 per credit. Required fees: $47 per term. *Financial aid:* In 1998–99, 37 students received aid, including 13 fellowships with partial tuition reimbursements available (averaging $2,354 per year), research assistantships with partial tuition reimbursements available (averaging $3,082 per year), 28 teaching assistantships with partial tuition reimbursements available (averaging $4,868 per year); career-related internships or fieldwork, Federal Work-Study, institutionally-sponsored loans, tuition waivers (partial), and unspecified assistantships also available. Financial aid application deadline: 3/1; financial aid applicants required to submit FAFSA. *Faculty research:* Atomic-molecular physics, condensed-matter physics, biophysics of proteins, laser physics. *Unit head:* Dr. B. P. Tonner, Acting Chair, 407-823-2325. *Application contact:* Dr. Michael Johnson, Coordinator, 407-823-5199, Fax: 407-823-5112.

University of Chicago, Division of the Physical Sciences, Department of Physics, Chicago, IL 60637-1513. Offers SM, PhD. Terminal master's awarded for partial completion of doctoral program. *Degree requirements:* For master's, foreign language and thesis not required; for doctorate, dissertation required, foreign language not required. *Entrance requirements:* For master's and doctorate, GRE General Test, GRE Subject Test, TOEFL. *Faculty research:* Astrophysics, particle physics, condensed-matter physics, statistical physics, electron and ion microscopy.

University of Chicago, Division of the Physical Sciences, Program in the Physical Sciences, Chicago, IL 60637-1513. Offers MS.

University of Cincinnati, Division of Research and Advanced Studies, McMicken College of Arts and Sciences, Department of Physics, Cincinnati, OH 45221-0091. Offers MS, PhD. *Faculty:* 20 full-time. *Students:* 55 full-time (15 women), 7 part-time (3 women); includes 5 minority (2 Asian Americans or Pacific Islanders, 3 Hispanic Americans), 43 international. 185 applicants, 8% accepted. In 1998, 5 master's, 7 doctorates awarded. *Degree requirements:* For master's, thesis optional; for doctorate, dissertation required. *Entrance requirements:* For master's and doctorate, GRE General Test, GRE Subject Test, TOEFL. *Average time to degree:* Master's–1.9 years full-time; doctorate–5.4 years full-time. *Application deadline:* For fall admission, 2/1. Application fee: $30. *Financial aid:* Fellowships, tuition waivers (full) and unspecified assistantships available. Aid available to part-time students. Financial aid application deadline: 5/1. Total annual research expenditures: $1.5 million. *Unit head:* Dr. Frank Pinski, Head, 513-556-0511, Fax: 513-556-3425, E-mail: frank.pinski@uc.edu. *Application contact:* Dr. Frank Pinski, Head, 513-556-0511, Fax: 513-556-3425, E-mail: frank.pinski@uc.edu.

University of Colorado at Boulder, Graduate School, College of Arts and Sciences, Department of Physics, Boulder, CO 80309. Offers chemical physics (PhD); geophysics (PhD); mathematical physics (PhD); medical physics (PhD); physics (MS, PhD). Terminal master's awarded for partial completion of doctoral program. *Degree requirements:* For master's, thesis or alternative, comprehensive exam required, foreign language not required; for doctorate, dissertation, comprehensive exam required. *Entrance requirements:* For master's, GRE General Test, GRE Subject Test, TOEFL (minimum score of 575 required), minimum undergraduate GPA of 3.0; for doctorate, GRE General Test, GRE Subject Test, TOEFL (minimum score of 575 required).

University of Colorado at Colorado Springs, Graduate School, College of Letters, Arts and Sciences, Department of Physics, Colorado Springs, CO 80933-7150. Offers MBS, MS. Part-time and evening/weekend programs available. *Faculty:* 7 full-time (0 women). *Students:* 7 full-time (1 woman), 3 part-time; includes 1 minority (Hispanic American) Average age 29. 15 applicants, 33% accepted. In 1998, 3 degrees awarded (100% found work related to degree). *Degree requirements:* Foreign language not required. *Entrance requirements:* For master's, GRE or minimum GPA of 2.75. *Application deadline:* For fall admission, 6/15; for spring admission, 12/1. Applications are processed on a rolling basis. Application fee: $40 ($50 for international students). Tuition, state resident: full-time $2,124. Tuition, nonresident: full-time $10,881. Required fees: $432. *Financial aid:* In 1998–99, 2 students received aid; research assistantships, teaching assistantships, career-related internships or fieldwork and Federal Work-Study available. Financial aid application deadline: 5/1. *Faculty research:* Solid-state/condensed-matter physics, surface science, electron spectroscopies, nonlinear physics. Total annual research expenditures: $57,000. *Unit head:* Dr. Thomas M. Christensen, Chairman, 719-262-3130, Fax: 719-262-3013, E-mail: tchriste@mail.uccs.edu. *Application contact:* Dr. Robert Camley, Graduate Adviser, 719-262-3512, Fax: 719-262-3013, E-mail: rcamley@mail.uccs.edu.

University of Connecticut, Graduate School, College of Liberal Arts and Sciences, Field of Physics, Storrs, CT 06269. Offers MS, PhD. *Degree requirements:* For doctorate, dissertation required. *Entrance requirements:* For master's and doctorate, GRE General Test, GRE Subject Test.

See in-depth description on page 525.

University of Delaware, College of Arts and Science, Joint Graduate Program of Department of Physics and Astronomy and Bartol Research Institute, Newark, DE 19716. Offers MS, PhD. Part-time programs available. *Faculty:* 22 full-time (1 woman), 5 part-time (1 woman). *Students:* 43 full-time (4 women), 2 part-time; includes 8 minority (1 African American, 7 Asian Americans

Physics

University of Delaware (continued)
or Pacific Islanders), 16 international. 180 applicants, 29% accepted. In 1998, 2 master's awarded (100% entered university research/teaching); 9 doctorates awarded (67% entered university research/teaching, 33% found other work related to degree). Terminal master's awarded for partial completion of doctoral program. *Degree requirements:* For master's and doctorate, thesis/dissertation required, foreign language not required. *Entrance requirements:* For master's and doctorate, GRE General Test, GRE Subject Test. *Application deadline:* For fall admission, 7/1. Application fee: $45. *Financial aid:* In 1998–99, 41 students received aid, including 5 fellowships, 9 research assistantships, 26 teaching assistantships; career-related internships or fieldwork, Federal Work-Study, institutionally-sponsored loans, and corporate sponsorship also available. *Faculty research:* Magnetoresistance and magnetic materials, ultrafast optical phenomena, superfluidity, elementary particle physics, stellar atmospheres. Total annual research expenditures: $1.4 million. *Unit head:* Dr. Henry R. Glyde, Chair, 302-831-3361. *Application contact:* Dr. S. B. Woo, 302-831-1995, Fax: 302-831-1637, E-mail: grad.physics@udel.edu.

University of Denver, Graduate Studies, Faculty of Natural Sciences, Mathematics and Engineering, Department of Physics and Astronomy, Denver, CO 80208. Offers MS, PhD. Part-time programs available. *Faculty:* 8. *Students:* 7 (6 women); includes 1 minority (Asian American or Pacific Islander) 3 international. 9 applicants, 89% accepted. In 1998, 1 doctorate awarded. Terminal master's awarded for partial completion of doctoral program. *Degree requirements:* For master's, thesis optional, foreign language not required; for doctorate, dissertation required, foreign language not required. *Entrance requirements:* For master's and doctorate, GRE General Test, TOEFL (minimum score of 550 required), TSE (minimum score of 230 required), minimum GPA of 3.0. *Application deadline:* Applications are processed on a rolling basis. Application fee: $40 ($45 for international students). *Financial aid:* In 1998–99, 4 research assistantships with full and partial tuition reimbursements (averaging $16,896 per year), 3 teaching assistantships with full and partial tuition reimbursements (averaging $14,376 per year) were awarded.; career-related internships or fieldwork, Federal Work-Study, institutionally-sponsored loans, and scholarships also available. Aid available to part-time students. Financial aid application deadline: 3/1; financial aid applicants required to submit FAFSA. *Faculty research:* Atomic and molecular beams and collisions, infrared astronomy, acoustic emission from stressed solids. Total annual research expenditures: $2.3 million. *Unit head:* Dr. Kevin Guy Murcray, Chair, 303-871-2238.

Announcement: The Department of Physics and Astronomy at the University of Denver has teaching and research assistantship positions available for qualified graduate students pursuing doctoral or master's degrees. The University of Denver is a small, private university with significant sponsored research in several areas of physics and astronomy, including atomic and molecular physics, atmospheric physics, astrophysics, observational astronomy, solid-state physics, and materials physics. Some of the research projects have both experimental and theoretical components, with laboratory and field components. Because of the University's size, it is able to offer individualized programs. Visit the department's Web site at http://www.du.edu/physastron.

University of Florida, Graduate School, College of Liberal Arts and Sciences, Department of Physics, Gainesville, FL 32611. Offers physics (MS, PhD); physics education (MST). *Accreditation:* NCATE (one or more programs are accredited). *Faculty:* 68 full-time. *Students:* 70 full-time (9 women), 4 part-time; includes 2 minority (both Hispanic Americans), 33 international. 100 applicants, 36% accepted. In 1998, 6 master's, 7 doctorates awarded. *Degree requirements:* For master's, thesis required (for some programs); for doctorate, dissertation required. *Entrance requirements:* For master's and doctorate, GRE General Test, minimum GPA of 3.0. *Application deadline:* For fall admission, 6/1 (priority date). Applications are processed on a rolling basis. Application fee: $20. Electronic applications accepted. *Financial aid:* In 1998–99, 69 students received aid, including 1 fellowship, 30 research assistantships, 38 teaching assistantships; unspecified assistantships also available. *Faculty research:* Astrophysics, condensed-matter physics, elementary particle physics, statistical mechanics, quantum theory. *Unit head:* Dr. Neil Sullivan, Chair, 352-392-0521, Fax: 352-392-0524, E-mail: sullivan@phys.ufl.edu. *Application contact:* Dr. John Yelton, Graduate Coordinator, 352-392-8475, Fax: 352-392-6694, E-mail: yelton@phys.ufl.edu.

See in-depth description on page 527.

University of Georgia, Graduate School, College of Arts and Sciences, Department of Physics and Astronomy, Athens, GA 30602. Offers physics (MS, PhD). *Faculty:* 27 full-time (0 women). *Students:* 36 full-time (7 women), 3 part-time; includes 3 minority (1 African American, 1 Asian American or Pacific Islander, 1 Native American), 18 international. 40 applicants, 38% accepted. In 1998, 4 master's, 3 doctorates awarded. *Degree requirements:* For master's, thesis required, foreign language not required; for doctorate, one foreign language (computer language can substitute), dissertation required. *Entrance requirements:* For master's and doctorate, GRE General Test. *Application deadline:* For fall admission, 7/1 (priority date); for spring admission, 11/15. Application fee: $30. Electronic applications accepted. *Financial aid:* Fellowships, research assistantships, teaching assistantships, unspecified assistantships available. *Unit head:* Dr. Jean-Pierre Caillault, Graduate Coordinator, 706-542-2818, Fax: 706-542-2492, E-mail: jpc@akbar.physast.uga.edu.

University of Guelph, Faculty of Graduate Studies, College of Physical and Engineering Science, Guelph-Waterloo Program for Graduate Work in Physics, Guelph, ON N1G 2W1, Canada. Offers M Sc, PhD. Part-time programs available. *Faculty:* 61 full-time (6 women), 4 part-time (0 women). *Students:* 59 full-time. 43 applicants, 81% accepted. In 1998, 20 master's, 9 doctorates awarded. *Degree requirements:* For master's; for doctorate, dissertation required. *Entrance requirements:* For master's, GRE Subject Test, TOEFL (minimum score of 600 required), minimum B average during previous 2 years; for doctorate, minimum B average. *Average time to degree:* Master's–2.3 years full-time; doctorate–4.3 years full-time. *Application deadline:* Applications are processed on a rolling basis. Application fee: $60. *Expenses:* Tuition and fees charges are reported in Canadian dollars. Tuition, area resident: Full-time $4,725 Canadian dollars; part-time $1,055 Canadian dollars per term. International tuition: $6,999 Canadian dollars full-time. Required fees: $295 Canadian dollars per term. *Financial aid:* Fellowships, research assistantships, teaching assistantships, career-related internships or fieldwork available. *Faculty research:* Subatomic and nuclear physics, astronomy and astrophysics, atomic and molecular physics, chemical physics, biophysics, photonics, applied physics, condensed-matter physics, conductivity and superconductivity. Total annual research expenditures: $2.8 million. *Unit head:* Dr. K. Jeffrey, Director, 519-885-1211 Ext. 3909, Fax: 519-836-9967. *Application contact:* M. Mayne, Administrative Assistant, 519-824-4120 Ext. 2263, E-mail: gwp@physics.uoguelph.ca.

University of Hawaii at Manoa, Graduate Division, College of Arts and Sciences, College of Natural Sciences, Department of Physics and Astronomy, Honolulu, HI 96822. Offers MS, PhD. *Faculty:* 58 full-time (5 women). *Students:* 32 full-time (8 women), 1 (woman) part-time. 54 applicants, 20% accepted. In 1998, 6 master's, 7 doctorates awarded. *Degree requirements:* For master's, qualifying exam or thesis required; for doctorate, dissertation, oral comprehensive and qualifying exams required. *Entrance requirements:* For master's and doctorate, GRE General Test, GRE Subject Test. *Application deadline:* For fall admission, 2/1 (priority date). Application fee: $25 ($50 for international students). *Financial aid:* In 1998–99, 27 research assistantships (averaging $17,641 per year), 18 teaching assistantships (averaging $14,829 per year) were awarded. *Unit head:* Dr. James R. Gaines, Chairperson, 808-956-7087, E-mail: gaines@uhhepg.phys.hawaii.edu. *Application contact:* Dr. Gareth Wynn-Williams, Graduate Chair, 808-956-8807, E-mail: wynnwill@ifa.hawaii.edu.

University of Houston, College of Natural Sciences and Mathematics, Department of Physics, Houston, TX 77004. Offers MS, PhD. Part-time programs available. *Faculty:* 28 full-time (1 woman), 1 part-time (0 women). *Students:* 37 full-time (7 women), 8 part-time (1 woman); includes 5 minority (1 African American, 2 Asian Americans or Pacific Islanders, 2 Hispanic Americans), 26 international. Average age 30. In 1998, 5 master's, 5 doctorates awarded. Terminal master's awarded for partial completion of doctoral program. *Degree requirements:* For master's, foreign language and thesis not required; for doctorate, dissertation required, foreign language not required. *Entrance requirements:* For master's and doctorate, GRE General Test, TOEFL (minimum score of 550 required). *Application deadline:* For fall admission, 7/20 (priority date); for spring admission, 11/20. Applications are processed on a rolling basis. Application fee: $25. *Financial aid:* Research assistantships, teaching assistantships available. *Faculty research:* Condensed-matter, superconductivity, space chaos, particle physics, high-temperature physics. *Unit head:* Dr. Lawrence Pinsky, Chairman, 713-743-3550. *Application contact:* Richard Frazier, Advising Assistant, 713-743-3550, Fax: 713-743-3589, E-mail: frazier@uh.edu.

See in-depth description on page 529.

University of Idaho, College of Graduate Studies, College of Letters and Science, Department of Physics, Moscow, ID 83844-4140. Offers physics (MS, PhD); physics education (MAT). *Accreditation:* NCATE (one or more programs are accredited). *Faculty:* 10 full-time (2 women). *Students:* 4 full-time (0 women), 2 part-time, (all international). In 1998, 2 master's, 4 doctorates awarded. *Degree requirements:* For master's and doctorate, thesis/dissertation required, foreign language not required. *Entrance requirements:* For master's, GRE, minimum GPA of 2.8; for doctorate, GRE, minimum undergraduate GPA of 2.8, 3.0 graduate. *Application deadline:* For fall admission, 8/1; for spring admission, 12/15. Application fee: $35 ($45 for international students). *Financial aid:* In 1998–99, 5 teaching assistantships (averaging $11,795 per year) were awarded.; research assistantships Financial aid application deadline: 2/15. *Unit head:* Dr. Henry Willmes, Chair, 208-885-6380.

University of Illinois at Chicago, Graduate College, College of Liberal Arts and Sciences, Department of Physics, Chicago, IL 60607-7128. Offers MS, PhD. *Faculty:* 26 full-time (2 women), 3 part-time (0 women). *Students:* 35 full-time (7 women), 14 part-time (3 women); includes 1 minority (African American), 32 international. Average age 26. 116 applicants, 17% accepted. In 1998, 8 master's, 8 doctorates awarded. Terminal master's awarded for partial completion of doctoral program. *Degree requirements:* For master's, foreign language and thesis not required; for doctorate, dissertation required, foreign language not required. *Entrance requirements:* For master's and doctorate, GRE General Test, TOEFL (minimum score of 550 required), minimum GPA of 4.0 on a 5.0 scale. *Application deadline:* For fall admission, 7/3; for spring admission, 11/8. Application fee: $40 ($50 for international students). *Financial aid:* In 1998–99, 31 students received aid; fellowships, research assistantships, teaching assistantships available. *Faculty research:* High-energy, laser, and solid-state physics. *Unit head:* Uday Sukhatme, Head, 312-996-3400. *Application contact:* James S. Kouvel, Director of Graduate Studies, 312-996-5348.

See in-depth description on page 531.

University of Illinois at Urbana–Champaign, Graduate College, College of Engineering, Department of Physics, Urbana, IL 61801. Offers MS, PhD. *Faculty:* 73 full-time (2 women). *Students:* 224 full-time (14 women); includes 17 minority (15 Asian Americans or Pacific Islanders, 2 Hispanic Americans), 79 international. 189 applicants, 18% accepted. In 1998, 48 master's, 40 doctorates awarded. *Degree requirements:* For master's, foreign language and thesis not required; for doctorate, dissertation, departmental qualifying exam required, foreign language not required. *Entrance requirements:* For master's, minimum GPA of 4.0 on a 5.0 scale. *Application deadline:* Applications are processed on a rolling basis. Application fee: $40 ($50 for international students). Tuition, state resident: full-time $4,616. Tuition, nonresident: full-time $11,768. Full-time tuition and fees vary according to course load. *Financial aid:* In 1998–99, 7 fellowships, 163 research assistantships, 66 teaching assistantships were awarded. Financial aid application deadline: 2/15. *Unit head:* Miles V. Klein, Interim Head, 217-333-3760. *Application contact:* Jack M. Mochel, Director of Graduate Studies, 217-333-8702, Fax: 217-333-9819, E-mail: j-mochel@physics.uiuc.edu.

The University of Iowa, Graduate College, College of Liberal Arts, Department of Physics and Astronomy, Program in Physics, Iowa City, IA 52242-1316. Offers MS, PhD, JD/PhD. *Students:* 18 full-time (0 women), 33 part-time (2 women); includes 2 minority (both Asian Americans or Pacific Islanders), 27 international. 101 applicants, 31% accepted. In 1998, 3 master's, 8 doctorates awarded. *Degree requirements:* For master's, thesis optional; for doctorate, dissertation, comprehensive exam required. *Entrance requirements:* For master's and doctorate, GRE General Test, GRE Subject Test. *Application deadline:* For fall admission, 1/1. Applications are processed on a rolling basis. Application fee: $30 ($50 for international students). *Financial aid:* In 1998–99, 1 fellowship, 20 research assistantships, 25 teaching assistantships were awarded. Financial aid applicants required to submit FAFSA. *Unit head:* Wayne N. Polyzou, Chair, Department of Physics and Astronomy, 319-335-1688, Fax: 319-335-1753.

University of Kansas, Graduate School, College of Liberal Arts and Sciences, Department of Physics and Astronomy, Lawrence, KS 66045. Offers computational physics and astronomy (MS); physics (MS, PhD). *Faculty:* 24 full-time. *Students:* 16 full-time (5 women), 24 part-time (4 women); includes 1 minority (Hispanic American), 23 international. In 1998, 7 master's, 8 doctorates awarded. *Degree requirements:* For master's, foreign language and thesis not required; for doctorate, computer language, dissertation required. *Entrance requirements:* For master's and doctorate, TOEFL (minimum score of 570 required). *Financial aid:* Fellowships, research assistantships, teaching assistantships available. *Faculty research:* Condensed-matter and chaos cosmology, elementary particles, nuclear physics, space physics. *Unit head:* Dr. Raymond G. Ammar, Chair, 785-864-4626. *Application contact:* Douglas McKay, Graduate Director.

See in-depth description on page 533.

University of Kentucky, Graduate School, Graduate School Programs from the College of Arts and Sciences, Program in Physics and Astronomy, Lexington, KY 40506-0032. Offers MS, PhD. *Degree requirements:* For master's, comprehensive exam required, thesis optional, foreign language not required; for doctorate, dissertation, comprehensive exam required, foreign language not required. *Entrance requirements:* For master's, GRE General Test, minimum undergraduate GPA of 2.5; for doctorate, GRE General Test, minimum graduate GPA of 3.0. *Faculty research:* Astrophysics, active galactic nuclei, interstellar masses, and radio astronomy; atomic physics, Rydbert atoms, and electron scattering; TOF neutron and (n, n'o) spectroscopy, hyperon interactions and muons; solid-state, STM, charge-density waves, fulleneus, and 1-dimensional systems; particle theory, lattice gauge theory, quark, and skyrmion models.

University of Louisville, Graduate School, College of Arts and Sciences, Department of Physics, Louisville, KY 40292-0001. Offers MS. *Faculty:* 12 full-time (1 woman), 5 part-time (1 woman). *Students:* 10 full-time (3 women), 1 part-time; includes 1 minority (Hispanic American), 7 international. Average age 28. In 1998, 8 degrees awarded. *Degree requirements:* For master's, thesis required. *Entrance requirements:* For master's, GRE General Test. *Application deadline:* Applications are processed on a rolling basis. Application fee: $25. *Unit head:* Dr. Joseph S. Chalmers, Chair, 502-852-6787, Fax: 502-852-0742, E-mail: chalmers@louisville.edu.

University of Maine, Graduate School, College of Liberal Arts and Sciences, Department of Physics and Astronomy, Orono, ME 04469. Offers engineering physics (M Eng); physics (MS, PhD). *Faculty:* 17 full-time (1 woman), 1 part-time (0 women). *Students:* 19 full-time (5 women), 7 part-time (1 woman), 11 international. Average age 29. 54 applicants, 19% accepted. In 1998, 3 doctorates awarded (100% entered university research/teaching). Terminal master's awarded for partial completion of doctoral program. *Degree requirements:* For doctorate, dissertation required, foreign language not required, foreign language not required. *Entrance requirements:* For master's, GRE General Test, GRE Subject Test, TOEFL (minimum score of 550 required); for doctorate, GRE General Test, TOEFL (minimum score of 550 required).

Application deadline: For fall admission, 2/1 (priority date); for spring admission, 10/15. Applications are processed on a rolling basis. Application fee: $50. *Financial aid:* In 1998–99, 2 fellowships with tuition reimbursements (averaging $11,250 per year), 11 research assistantships with tuition reimbursements (averaging $11,200 per year), 14 teaching assistantships with tuition reimbursements (averaging $9,735 per year) were awarded.; tuition waivers (full and partial) also available. Financial aid application deadline: 3/1. *Faculty research:* Solid-state physics, fluids, biophysics, plasma physics, surface physics. *Unit head:* Dr. Susan McKay, Chair, 207-581-1015, Fax: 207-581-3410. *Application contact:* Scott G. Delcourt, Director of the Graduate School, 207-581-3218, Fax: 207-581-3232, E-mail: graduate@maine.edu.

University of Manitoba, Faculty of Graduate Studies, Faculty of Science, Department of Physics, Winnipeg, MB R3T 2N2, Canada. Offers M Sc, PhD. *Degree requirements:* For master's, thesis required, foreign language not required; for doctorate, dissertation required. *Unit head:* R. C. Barber, Head.

University of Maryland, Baltimore County, Graduate School, Department of Physics, Baltimore, MD 21250-5398. Offers applied physics (MS, PhD), including optics, solid state physics; atmospheric physics (MS, PhD). Part-time programs available. *Faculty:* 15 full-time (0 women), 4 part-time (0 women). *Students:* 18 full-time (1 woman), 3 part-time, 7 international. Average age 25. 31 applicants, 32% accepted. In 1998, 10 master's, 2 doctorates awarded (75% entered university research/teaching, 25% found other work related to degree). Terminal master's awarded for partial completion of doctoral program. *Degree requirements:* For master's, thesis optional, foreign language not required; for doctorate, dissertation required, foreign language not required. *Entrance requirements:* For master's and doctorate, GRE General Test, GRE Subject Test, TOEFL (minimum score of 600 required), minimum GPA of 3.0. *Average time to degree:* Doctorate–4 years full-time. *Application deadline:* For fall admission, 7/1 (priority date); for spring admission, 12/1 (priority date). Applications are processed on a rolling basis. Application fee: $45. *Financial aid:* In 1998–99, 20 students received aid, including 1 fellowship with tuition reimbursement available, 3 research assistantships with tuition reimbursements available, 10 teaching assistantships with tuition reimbursements available; grants and unspecified assistantships also available. Financial aid application deadline: 3/1. *Faculty research:* Physics of solids, atmospheric research, materials science, quantum optics, nonlinear optics. Total annual research expenditures: $1.2 million. *Unit head:* Dr. Geoffrey P. Summers, Chairman, 410-455-2513, Fax: 410-455-1072. *Application contact:* 410-455-2513, Fax: 410-455-1072, E-mail: physics@umbc.edu.

See in-depth description on page 535.

University of Maryland, College Park, Graduate School, College of Computer, Mathematical and Physical Sciences, Department of Physics, College Park, MD 20742-5045. Offers MS, PhD. *Faculty:* 119 full-time (12 women), 31 part-time (3 women). *Students:* 133 full-time (13 women), 44 part-time (9 women); includes 8 minority (1 African American, 4 Asian Americans or Pacific Islanders, 2 Hispanic Americans, 1 Native American), 85 international. 308 applicants, 42% accepted. In 1998, 10 master's, 29 doctorates awarded. *Degree requirements:* For master's, thesis optional, foreign language not required; for doctorate, dissertation required. *Entrance requirements:* For master's, GRE General Test, Advanced Physics Test (minimum score of 700 required), minimum GPA of 3.0; for doctorate, GRE General Test, Advanced Physics Test (minimum score of 700 required). *Application deadline:* Applications are processed on a rolling basis. Application fee: $50 ($70 for international students). Tuition, state resident: part-time $272 per credit hour. Tuition, nonresident: part-time $475 per credit hour. Required fees: $632; $379 per year. *Financial aid:* In 1998–99, 8 fellowships with full tuition reimbursements (averaging $14,438 per year), 82 research assistantships with tuition reimbursements (averaging $15,370 per year), 66 teaching assistantships with tuition reimbursements (averaging $11,877 per year) were awarded.; Federal Work-Study, grants, and scholarships also available. Aid available to part-time students. Financial aid applicants required to submit FAFSA. *Faculty research:* Astrometrology, superconductivity, gravitation, particle astrophysics, plasma physics. Total annual research expenditures: $16.1 million. *Unit head:* Dr. Stephen Wallace, Chair, 301-405-5946, Fax: 301-314-9525. *Application contact:* Linda O'Hara, Administrative Assistant, 301-405-5982.

Announcement: Department of Physics, one of the nation's major recipients of research grants, has programs in chemical, condensed-matter, elementary particles, high-energy, nuclear, plasma, and space physics, as well as in astrometrology, chaos and nonlinear dynamics, general relativity, material science, particle astrophysics, quantum electronics, and superconductivity. Contact Jean Clement, 301-405-5982; WWW: http://www.physics.umd.edu

University of Massachusetts Amherst, Graduate School, College of Natural Sciences and Mathematics, Department of Physics and Astronomy, Program in Physics, Amherst, MA 01003. Offers MS, PhD. Part-time programs available. *Faculty:* 38 full-time (3 women). *Students:* 16 full-time (3 women), 41 part-time (7 women); includes 4 minority (2 Asian Americans or Pacific Islanders, 2 Hispanic Americans), 36 international. Average age 29. 85 applicants, 28% accepted. In 1998, 7 master's, 12 doctorates awarded. Terminal master's awarded for partial completion of doctoral program. *Degree requirements:* For master's, foreign language and thesis not required; for doctorate, dissertation required, foreign language not required. *Entrance requirements:* For master's and doctorate, GRE General Test, GRE Subject Test. *Application deadline:* For fall admission, 2/1 (priority date); for spring admission, 10/1. Applications are processed on a rolling basis. Application fee: $40. Tuition, state resident: full-time $2,640; part-time $165 per credit. Tuition, nonresident: full-time $9,756; part-time $407 per credit. Required fees: $1,221 per term. One-time fee: $110. Full-time tuition and fees vary according to course load, campus/location and reciprocity agreements. *Financial aid:* Fellowships with full tuition reimbursements, research assistantships with full tuition reimbursements, teaching assistantships with full tuition reimbursements, career-related internships or fieldwork, Federal Work-Study, grants, scholarships, traineeships, and unspecified assistantships available. Aid available to part-time students. Financial aid application deadline: 2/1. *Unit head:* Dr. William Gerace, Director, 413-545-2548, Fax: 413-545-0648, E-mail: gerace@phast.umass.edu. *Application contact:* Dr. Donald Candela, Chair, Admissions Committee, 413-545-2407, E-mail: candela@phast.umass.edu.

University of Massachusetts Dartmouth, Graduate School, College of Engineering, Department of Physics, North Dartmouth, MA 02747-2300. Offers MS. Part-time programs available. *Faculty:* 13 full-time (2 women), 1 part-time (0 women). *Students:* 13 full-time (6 women), 6 part-time (1 woman), 12 international. 28 applicants, 100% accepted. In 1998, 5 degrees awarded. *Degree requirements:* For master's, thesis or alternative required, foreign language not required. *Entrance requirements:* For master's, GRE General Test, TOEFL. *Application deadline:* For fall admission, 4/20 (priority date); for spring admission, 11/15 (priority date). Applications are processed on a rolling basis. Application fee: $40 for international students. Tuition, area resident: Full-time $3,107; part-time $129 per credit. Tuition, state resident: full-time $2,071; part-time $86 per credit. Tuition, nonresident: full-time $7,845; part-time $327 per credit. Required fees: $2,888. Full-time tuition and fees vary according to program and reciprocity agreements. Part-time tuition and fees vary according to course load and reciprocity agreements. *Financial aid:* In 1998–99, 1 research assistantship with full tuition reimbursement (averaging $3,500 per year), 11 teaching assistantships with full tuition reimbursements (averaging $4,984 per year) were awarded.; Federal Work-Study and unspecified assistantships also available. Aid available to part-time students. Financial aid application deadline: 3/15; financial aid applicants required to submit FAFSA. *Faculty research:* Astrophysics, computational physics, elementary particle/nuclear physics, liquid crystals, physical and satellite oceanography, theoretical physics (foundations, atomic/solid-state). Total annual research expenditures:$95,000. *Unit head:* Dr. Jong-Ping Hsu, Director, 508-999-8363, Fax: 508-999-9115, E-mail: jhsu@umassd.edu. *Application contact:* Carol A. Novo, Graduate Admissions Office, 508-999-8026, Fax: 508-999-8183, E-mail: graduate@umassd.edu.

Announcement: MS programs lead to careers and graduate study in physics, physical oceanography, engineering, computer science, and teaching. A collaborative PhD program with the University of Massachusetts Amherst is offered. Full assistantships typically pay a 9-month stipend of $7000 (15 hours per week) plus tuition. Specialties include computational physics, applied astrophysics, theoretical atomic and solid-state physics, oceanography, and traffic flow; physical and satellite oceanography in conjunction with the Center for Marine and Science Technology (CMAST); theoretical physics (foundations); liquid crystals; and, with faculty members in other departments, optics, acoustics, and mathematical physics. World Wide Web: http://www.umassd.edu/physics.

University of Massachusetts Lowell, Graduate School, College of Arts and Sciences, Department of Physics and Applied Physics, Program in Physics, Lowell, MA 01854-2881. Offers MS, PhD. *Degree requirements:* For master's, thesis required; for doctorate, 2 foreign languages (computer language can substitute for one), dissertation required. *Entrance requirements:* For master's and doctorate, GRE General Test. *Application deadline:* For fall admission, 4/1 (priority date); for spring admission, 10/1. Applications are processed on a rolling basis. Application fee: $20 ($35 for international students). *Financial aid:* Fellowships, research assistantships, teaching assistantships, career-related internships or fieldwork, Federal Work-Study, and institutionally-sponsored loans available. Aid available to part-time students. Financial aid application deadline: 4/1. *Unit head:* Dr. Lee M. Larson, Graduate Studies Director, 502-852-6826, Fax: 502-852-7132, E-mail: llarson@louisville.edu. *Application contact:* Dr. Gus Couchell, Coordinator, 978-934-3772, E-mail: gus_couchell@uml.edu.

See in-depth description on page 537.

The University of Memphis, Graduate School, College of Arts and Sciences, Department of Physics, Memphis, TN 38152. Offers MS. Part-time programs available. *Faculty:* 10 full-time (1 woman), 4 part-time (0 women). *Students:* 7 full-time (2 women), 4 international. Average age 28. 8 applicants, 50% accepted. In 1998, 4 degrees awarded. *Degree requirements:* For master's, thesis or alternative, comprehensive exam required. *Entrance requirements:* For master's, GRE General Test or MAT, 20 undergraduate hours in physics. *Application deadline:* For fall admission, 8/1; for spring admission, 12/1. Applications are processed on a rolling basis. Application fee: $25 ($50 for international students). Tuition, state resident: full-time $3,410; part-time $178 per credit hour. Tuition, nonresident: full-time $8,670; part-time $408 per credit hour. Tuition and fees vary according to program. *Financial aid:* In 1998–99, 6 students received aid, including 1 research assistantship, 5 teaching assistantships; Federal Work-Study and institutionally-sponsored loans also available. Financial aid application deadline: 5/1; financial aid applicants required to submit CSS PROFILE. *Faculty research:* Solid-state physics, materials science. Total annual research expenditures: $500,000. *Unit head:* Dr. Michael Garland, Chairman, 901-678-2620, Fax: 901-678-4733, E-mail: mgarland@memphis.edu. *Application contact:* Dr. M. Shah Jahan, Coordinator of Graduate Studies, 901-678-3115, Fax: 901-678-4733, E-mail: sjahan@memphis.edu.

University of Miami, Graduate School, College of Arts and Sciences, Department of Physics, Coral Gables, FL 33124. Offers MS, DA, PhD. *Faculty:* 18 full-time (2 women). *Students:* 23 full-time (3 women); includes 1 minority (Hispanic American), 20 international. Average age 25. 124 applicants, 3% accepted. In 1998, 4 master's awarded. Terminal master's awarded for partial completion of doctoral program. *Degree requirements:* For master's, foreign language and thesis not required; for doctorate, dissertation required, foreign language not required. *Entrance requirements:* For master's and doctorate, GRE General Test, GRE Subject Test, TOEFL (minimum score of 550 required). *Application deadline:* For fall admission, 3/1 (priority date). Applications are processed on a rolling basis. Application fee: $35. Tuition: Full-time $15,336; part-time $852 per credit. Required fees: $174. Tuition and fees vary according to program. *Financial aid:* In 1998–99, 22 students received aid, including 1 fellowship, 5 research assistantships, 18 teaching assistantships *Faculty research:* High-energy theory, marine and atmospheric optics, plasma physics, solid-state physics. Total annual research expenditures: $1.5 million. *Unit head:* Dr. George Alexandrakis, Chairman, 305-284-2323, Fax: 305-284-4222. *Application contact:* Dr. Josef Ashkenazi, Chairman, Graduate Recruitment Committee, 305-284-2323 Ext. 3, Fax: 305-284-4222.

See in-depth description on page 541.

University of Michigan, Horace H. Rackham School of Graduate Studies, College of Literature, Science, and the Arts, Department of Physics, Ann Arbor, MI 48109. Offers MS, PhD. *Faculty:* 58 full-time (4 women), 5 part-time (1 woman). *Students:* 96 full-time (20 women); includes 12 minority (6 African Americans, 3 Asian Americans or Pacific Islanders, 3 Hispanic Americans), 40 international. Average age 29. 300 applicants, 24% accepted. In 1998, 2 master's awarded (0% continued full-time study); 18 doctorates awarded (77% entered university research/teaching, 22% found other work related to degree). Terminal master's awarded for partial completion of doctoral program. *Degree requirements:* For master's, foreign language and thesis not required; for doctorate, dissertation, oral defense of dissertation, preliminary exam required, foreign language not required. *Entrance requirements:* For master's and doctorate, GRE General Test. *Average time to degree:* Master's–3 years full-time; doctorate–7 years full-time. *Application deadline:* For fall admission, 1/15. Applications are processed on a rolling basis. Application fee: $55. *Financial aid:* Fellowships with full tuition reimbursements, research assistantships with full tuition reimbursements, teaching assistantships with full tuition reimbursements available. *Faculty research:* Elementary particle, solid-state, atomic, and molecular physics (theoretical and experimental). Total annual research expenditures: $9.5 million. *Unit head:* Dr. Ctirad Uher, Chair, 734-764-4437. *Application contact:* Dr. Fred C. Adams, Associate Chair for Graduate Studies, 734-764-5539, E-mail: physics.550@umich.edu.

See in-depth description on page 545.

University of Minnesota, Duluth, Graduate School, College of Science and Engineering, Department of Physics, Duluth, MN 55812-2496. Offers MS. Part-time programs available. *Faculty:* 8 full-time (1 woman). *Students:* 8 full-time (2 women), 5 international. Average age 26. 20 applicants, 40% accepted. In 1998, 2 degrees awarded (0% continued full-time study). *Degree requirements:* For master's, thesis required (for some programs), foreign language not required. *Entrance requirements:* For master's, minimum GPA of 3.0. *Average time to degree:* Master's–2 years full-time. *Application deadline:* For fall admission, 7/15; for spring admission, 11/15. Applications are processed on a rolling basis. Application fee: $50 ($55 for international students). *Financial aid:* In 1998–99, 8 students received aid, including 8 teaching assistantships; research assistantships, Federal Work-Study and institutionally-sponsored loans also available. Aid available to part-time students. Financial aid application deadline: 2/15. *Faculty research:* Computer modeling, solid-state physics, surface phenomena, physical limnology. Total annual research expenditures: $70,000. *Unit head:* Dr. John Hiller, Head, 218-726-7594, Fax: 218-726-6942, E-mail: jhiller@ub.d.umn.edu. *Application contact:* Dr. Bo Casserberg, Director of Graduate Studies, 218-726-8247, Fax: 218-726-6942, E-mail: bcasserb@d.umn.edu.

Announcement: MS in physics: concentrations in condensed matter, theoretical particle physics, and physical limnology. Thesis projects provide experience in computational physics, instrumentation, optics, and cryogenics. Current research areas include fundamental quantum mechanics, quark models, scanning-tunneling microscopy, semiconductor photoreflectance, environmental optics, dynamics of large and mesoscale circulation, upper ocean dynamics, and small particle concentrations.

University of Minnesota, Twin Cities Campus, Graduate School, Institute of Technology, School of Physics and Astronomy, Department of Physics, Minneapolis, MN 55455-0213. Offers MS, PhD. Part-time programs available. *Degree requirements:* For master's and doctorate, thesis/dissertation required. *Entrance requirements:* For master's and doctorate, GRE General Test, GRE Subject Test. *Faculty research:* Condensed matter, elementary particle, space, nuclear and atomic physics.

University of Mississippi, Graduate School, College of Liberal Arts, Department of Physics and Astronomy, Oxford, University, MS 38677-9702. Offers physics (MA, MS, PhD). *Faculty:*

Physics

University of Mississippi (continued)

13 full-time (1 woman). *Students:* 19 full-time (2 women), 2 part-time (1 woman); includes 1 minority (African American), 1 international. In 1998, 3 master's, 2 doctorates awarded. *Degree requirements:* For master's, thesis required (for some programs), foreign language not required; for doctorate, dissertation required, foreign language not required. *Entrance requirements:* For master's, GRE General Test, TOEFL, minimum GPA of 3.0; for doctorate, GRE General Test, TOEFL. *Application deadline:* For fall admission, 8/1. Applications are processed on a rolling basis. Application fee: $0 ($25 for international students). Tuition, state resident: full-time $3,053; part-time $170 per credit hour. Tuition, nonresident: full-time $6,155; part-time $342 per credit hour. Tuition and fees vary according to program. *Financial aid:* Application deadline: 3/1. *Unit head:* Thomas C. Marshall, Chairman, 601-232-5325, Fax: 601-232-5045, E-mail: marshall@beauty1.phy.olemiss.edu.

University of Missouri–Columbia, Graduate School, College of Arts and Sciences, Department of Physics, Columbia, MO 65211. Offers MS, PhD. *Faculty:* 18 full-time (1 woman). *Students:* 27 full-time (8 women), 11 part-time (1 woman), 17 international. 7 applicants, 71% accepted. In 1998, 4 master's, 9 doctorates awarded. Terminal master's awarded for partial completion of doctoral program. *Degree requirements:* For master's, foreign language and thesis not required; for doctorate, dissertation required. *Entrance requirements:* For master's and doctorate, GRE General Test, minimum GPA of 3.0. *Application deadline:* Applications are processed on a rolling basis. Application fee: $30 ($50 for international students). *Financial aid:* Research assistantships, teaching assistantships, institutionally-sponsored loans available. *Unit head:* Dr. H. R. Chandrasekhav, Director of Graduate Studies, 573-882-6086.

University of Missouri–Kansas City, College of Arts and Sciences, Department of Physics, Kansas City, MO 64110-2499. Offers MS, PhD. PhD offered through the School of Graduate Studies. Part-time and evening/weekend programs available. *Faculty:* 10 full-time (1 woman), 1 part-time (0 women). *Students:* 2 full-time (0 women), 2 part-time (1 woman). Average age 30. In 1998, 5 master's awarded. Terminal master's awarded for partial completion of doctoral program. *Degree requirements:* For master's, comprehensive exam required, thesis optional, foreign language not required; for doctorate, dissertation, comprehensive exam required, foreign language not required. *Entrance requirements:* For master's, TOEFL (minimum score of 675 required); for doctorate, GRE General Test (minimum combined score of 1500 required). *Average time to degree:* Master's–2 years full-time, 3 years part-time. *Application deadline:* For fall admission, 6/1 (priority date); for spring admission, 11/1. Applications are processed on a rolling basis. Application fee: $25. *Financial aid:* In 1998–99, research assistantships with full and partial tuition reimbursements (averaging $10,000 per year), teaching assistantships with full and partial tuition reimbursements (averaging $9,800 per year) were awarded.; Federal Work-Study, institutionally-sponsored loans, and tuition waivers (full and partial) also available. Aid available to part-time students. Financial aid application deadline: 4/1. *Faculty research:* Surface physics, material science, statistical mechanics, computational physics, relativity and quantum theory, condensed-matter theory and experiment. Total annual research expenditures: $639,400. *Unit head:* Dr. David Wieliczka, Chairperson, 816-235-2505, E-mail: wieliczka@umkc.edu. *Application contact:* Da Ming Zhu, Principal Graduate Adviser, 816-235-2509, Fax: 816-235-5221, E-mail: zhud@cctr.umkc.edu.

University of Missouri–Rolla, Graduate School, College of Arts and Sciences, Department of Physics, Rolla, MO 65409-0910. Offers MS, PhD. *Faculty:* 19 full-time (1 woman). *Students:* 26 full-time (4 women), 5 part-time; includes 2 minority (1 Asian American or Pacific Islander, 1 Native American), 19 international. Average age 30. 23 applicants, 87% accepted. In 1998, 1 master's awarded (0% continued full-time study); 3 doctorates awarded (100% found work related to degree). Terminal master's awarded for partial completion of doctoral program. *Degree requirements:* For master's, thesis optional, foreign language not required; for doctorate, dissertation required. *Entrance requirements:* For master's and doctorate, GRE General Test (minimum combined score of 1100 required), TOEFL (minimum score of 570 required). *Average time to degree:* Master's–1.8 years full-time; doctorate–6.2 years full-time. *Application deadline:* For fall admission, 7/1. Applications are processed on a rolling basis. Application fee: $25. Electronic applications accepted. *Financial aid:* In 1998–99, 26 students received aid, including 1 fellowship (averaging $2,000 per year), 11 research assistantships with partial tuition reimbursements available (averaging $12,985 per year), 14 teaching assistantships with partial tuition reimbursements available (averaging $12,985 per year); Federal Work-Study and institutionally-sponsored loans also available. Financial aid application deadline:7/1. *Faculty research:* Atomic and molecular physics, condensed-matter physics, atmosphere/cloud physics. Total annual research expenditures: $935,830. *Unit head:* Dr. Edward B. Hale, Chairman, 573-341-4701.

University of Missouri–St. Louis, Graduate School, College of Arts and Sciences, Department of Physics and Astronomy, St. Louis, MO 63121-4499. Offers applied physics (MS); astro physics (MS); physics (PhD). Part-time and evening/weekend programs available. *Faculty:* 11. *Students:* 7 full-time (0 women), 6 part-time (1 woman); includes 1 minority (Asian American or Pacific Islander), 6 international. Average age 25. In 1998, 3 master's, 1 doctorate awarded. Terminal master's awarded for partial completion of doctoral program. *Degree requirements:* For master's, thesis optional, foreign language not required; for doctorate, dissertation required, foreign language not required. *Entrance requirements:* For master's and doctorate, GRE General Test. *Application deadline:* For fall admission, 4/1 (priority date); for spring admission, 12/1 (priority date). Applications are processed on a rolling basis. Application fee: $24 ($40 for international students). Electronic applications accepted. *Financial aid:* In 1998–99, 1 research assistantship with partial tuition reimbursement (averaging $11,000 per year), 8 teaching assistantships with partial tuition reimbursements (averaging $11,784 per year) were awarded.; fellowships, career-related internships or fieldwork also available. *Faculty research:* Biophysics, atomic physics, nonlinear dynamics, materials science. Total annual research expenditures: $769,358. *Unit head:* Dr. Bruce Wilking, Director of Graduate Studies, 314-516-5023, Fax: 314-516-6152, E-mail: graduate@newton.umsl.edu. *Application contact:* Graduate Admissions, 314-516-5458, Fax: 314-516-6759, E-mail: gradadm@umsl.edu.

University of Nebraska–Lincoln, Graduate College, College of Arts and Sciences, Department of Physics and Astronomy, Lincoln, NE 68588. Offers astronomy (MS, PhD); physics (MS, PhD). *Faculty:* 24 full-time (1 woman), 2 part-time (0 women). *Students:* 40 full-time (6 women), 6 part-time (1 woman); includes 3 minority (1 African American, 2 Asian Americans or Pacific Islanders), 25 international. Average age 30. 72 applicants, 33% accepted. In 1998, 10 master's, 10 doctorates awarded. *Degree requirements:* For master's, thesis optional, foreign language not required; for doctorate, dissertation, comprehensive exams required. *Entrance requirements:* For master's and doctorate, GRE General Test, TOEFL (minimum score of 550 required). *Average time to degree:* Doctorate–4 years full-time. *Application deadline:* For fall admission, 2/1 (priority date). Applications are processed on a rolling basis. Application fee: $35. Electronic applications accepted. *Financial aid:* In 1998–99, 4 fellowships, 28 research assistantships, 23 teaching assistantships were awarded.; Federal Work-Study also available. Aid available to part-time students. Financial aid application deadline: 2/15. *Faculty research:* Electromagnetics of solids and thin films, photoionization, ion collisions with atoms, molecules and surfaces, search for top quark. *Unit head:* Dr. Roger Kirby, Chair, 402-472-2784.

University of Nevada, Las Vegas, Graduate College, College of Science, Department of Physics, Las Vegas, NV 89154-9900. Offers MS, PhD. *Faculty:* 15 full-time (2 women). *Students:* 7 full-time (0 women), 4 part-time (1 woman); includes 4 minority (1 African American, 2 Asian Americans or Pacific Islanders, 1 Hispanic American), 2 international. 7 applicants, 29% accepted. In 1998, 3 master's, 1 doctorate awarded. *Degree requirements:* For master's, thesis, oral exam required, foreign language not required; for doctorate, dissertation, qualifying exam required. *Entrance requirements:* For master's and doctorate, GRE General Test, GRE Subject Test, minimum GPA of 3.0 during previous 2 years, 2.75 overall. *Application deadline:* For fall admission, 6/15 (priority date); for spring admission, 11/15. Applications are processed on a rolling basis. Application fee: $40 ($95 for international students). *Financial aid:* In 1998–99, teaching assistantships with partial tuition reimbursements (averaging $8,388 per year); research assistantships, unspecified assistantships also available. Financial aid application deadline: 3/1. *Faculty research:* Laser (atomic, molecular, and optical) physics, astronomy/astrophysics, condensed-matter physics. *Unit head:* Dr. Victor Kwong, Chair, 702-895-3084. *Application contact:* Graduate College Admissions Evaluator, 702-895-3346.

University of Nevada, Reno, Graduate School, College of Arts and Science, Department of Physics, Reno, NV 89557. Offers MS, PhD. Terminal master's awarded for partial completion of doctoral program. *Degree requirements:* For master's, thesis optional, foreign language not required; for doctorate, dissertation required, foreign language not required. *Entrance requirements:* For master's, TOEFL (minimum score of 500 required), minimum GPA of 2.75; for doctorate, TOEFL (minimum score of 500 required), minimum GPA of 3.0. *Faculty research:* Atomic and molecular physics.

University of New Brunswick, School of Graduate Studies, Faculty of Science, Department of Physics, Fredericton, NB E3B 5A3, Canada. Offers M Sc, PhD. Part-time programs available. *Degree requirements:* For master's and doctorate, thesis/dissertation required. *Entrance requirements:* For master's and doctorate, TOEFL, TWE, minimum GPA of 3.0.

University of New Hampshire, Graduate School, College of Engineering and Physical Sciences, Department of Physics, Durham, NH 03824. Offers MS, PhD. *Faculty:* 29 full-time. *Students:* 25 full-time (6 women), 17 part-time (2 women); includes 3 minority (all Asian Americans or Pacific Islanders), 16 international. Average age 27. 44 applicants, 57% accepted. In 1998, 7 master's, 2 doctorates awarded. Terminal master's awarded for partial completion of doctoral program. *Degree requirements:* For master's, thesis or alternative required, foreign language not required; for doctorate, dissertation required, foreign language not required. *Entrance requirements:* For master's and doctorate, GRE General Test. *Application deadline:* For fall admission, 4/1 (priority date). Applications are processed on a rolling basis. Application fee: $50. Tuition, area resident: Full-time $5,750; part-time $319 per credit. Tuition, state resident: full-time $8,625. Tuition, nonresident: full-time $14,640; part-time $598 per credit. Required fees: $224 per semester. Tuition and fees vary according to course load, degree level and program. *Financial aid:* In 1998–99, 3 fellowships, 23 research assistantships, 11 teaching assistantships were awarded.; Federal Work-Study, scholarships, and tuition waivers (full and partial) also available. Aid available to part-time students. Financial aid application deadline: 2/15. *Faculty research:* Astrophysics and space physics, nuclearphysics, atomic and molecular physics, nonlinear dynamical systems. *Unit head:* L. Christian Balling, Chairperson, 603-862-2829. *Application contact:* James Ryan, Graduate Coordinator, 603-862-3516.

University of New Mexico, Graduate School, College of Arts and Sciences, Department of Physics and Astronomy, Albuquerque, NM 87131-2039. Offers optical sciences (PhD); physics (MS, PhD). *Faculty:* 43 full-time (5 women), 7 part-time (1 woman). *Students:* 52 full-time (10 women), 45 part-time (5 women); includes 4 minority (1 African American, 3 Asian Americans or Pacific Islanders), 32 international. Average age 31. 23 applicants, 26% accepted. In 1998, 7 master's, 9 doctorates awarded. Terminal master's awarded for partial completion of doctoral program. *Degree requirements:* For master's, proficiency in 1 computer language recommended required, thesis optional, foreign language not required; for doctorate, dissertation required, foreign language not required. *Entrance requirements:* For master's, GRE General Test (combined average 1850 on three sections); for doctorate, GRE General Test (combined average 1930 on three sections). *Application deadline:* For fall admission, 2/1 (priority date). Application fee: $25. *Financial aid:* In 1998–99, 76 students received aid, including 2 fellowships (averaging $376 per year), 56 research assistantships with tuition reimbursements available (averaging $3,841 per year), 12 teaching assistantships with tuition reimbursements available (averaging $7,071 per year); career-related internships or fieldwork, institutionally-sponsored loans, and unspecified assistantships also available. Aid available to part-time students. Financial aid application deadline: 3/15. *Faculty research:* Astrophysics, high-energy and particle physics, optical and laser sciences, condensed matter. Total annual research expenditures: $3.8 million. *Unit head:* John K. McIver, Chairman, 505-277-2616, Fax: 505-277-1520, E-mail: jmciver@unm.edu. *Application contact:* Academic Adviser, 505-277-1514, Fax: 505-277-1520, E-mail: panda8@unm.edu.

See in-depth description on page 547.

University of New Orleans, Graduate School, College of Sciences, Department of Physics, New Orleans, LA 70148. Offers applied physics (MS); physics (MS). Part-time and evening/weekend programs available. *Faculty:* 9 full-time (1 woman). *Students:* 9 full-time (2 women), 7 part-time (2 women); includes 8 minority (6 African Americans, 1 Asian American or Pacific Islander, 1 Hispanic American), 1 international. Average age 31. 23 applicants, 43% accepted. In 1998, 1 degree awarded (100% found work related to degree). *Degree requirements:* For master's, thesis required (for some programs), foreign language not required. *Entrance requirements:* For master's, GRE General Test (minimum combined score of 1000 required), TOEFL (minimum score of 500 required). *Application deadline:* For fall admission, 7/1 (priority date). Applications are processed on a rolling basis. Application fee: $20. Tuition, state resident: full-time $2,362. Tuition, nonresident: full-time $7,888. Part-time tuition and fees vary according to course load. *Financial aid:* Research assistantships, teaching assistantships, career-related internships or fieldwork available. *Faculty research:* Underwater acoustics, applied electromagnetics, experimental atomic beams, digital signal processing, astrophysics. *Unit head:* Dr. Milton Slaughter, Chair, 504-280-6341, Fax: 504-280-6048, E-mail: mdsph@uno.edu. *Application contact:* Dr. Ashok Puri, Graduate Coordinator, 504-280-6682, Fax: 504-280-6048, E-mail: apph@uno.edu.

University of North Dakota, Graduate School, College of Arts and Sciences, Department of Physics, Grand Forks, ND 58202. Offers MS, PhD. *Faculty:* 9 full-time (0 women). *Students:* 9 full-time (2 women), 2 part-time. 9 applicants, 78% accepted. In 1998, 1 master's awarded. *Degree requirements:* For master's, thesis required; for doctorate, dissertation required. *Entrance requirements:* For master's, TOEFL (minimum score of 550 required), minimum GPA of 3.0; for doctorate, TOEFL (minimum score of 550 required), minimum GPA of 3.5. *Application deadline:* For fall admission, 3/1 (priority date). Applications are processed on a rolling basis. Application fee: $20. *Financial aid:* In 1998–99, 8 students received aid, including 1 research assistantship, 7 teaching assistantships; fellowships, Federal Work-Study, institutionally-sponsored loans, and tuition waivers (full and partial) also available. Financial aid application deadline:3/15. *Unit head:* Dr. Sesh Rao, Chairperson, 701-777-2911, Fax: 701-777-3523, E-mail: serao@badlands.nodak.edu.

University of North Texas, Robert B. Toulouse School of Graduate Studies, College of Arts and Sciences, Department of Physics, Denton, TX 76203. Offers MA, MS, PhD. *Faculty:* 20 full-time (1 woman), 2 part-time (0 women). *Students:* 30 full-time (4 women), 9 part-time (1 woman); includes 1 minority (Hispanic American), 18 international. Average age 26. In 1998, 8 doctorates awarded. Terminal master's awarded for partial completion of doctoral program. *Degree requirements:* For master's, thesis or problems, comprehensive exam required; for doctorate, one foreign language (computer language can substitute), dissertation, comprehensive exam required. *Entrance requirements:* For master's and doctorate, GRE General Test (minimum combined score of 1100 required). *Application deadline:* For fall admission, 7/17. Application fee: $25 ($50 for international students). *Financial aid:* Fellowships, research assistantships, teaching assistantships available. *Faculty research:* Accelerator physics, chaos. *Unit head:* Dr. Samuel E. Matteson, Chair, 940-565-2626, Fax: 940-565-2515, E-mail: matteson@unt.edu. *Application contact:* Dr. William Deering, Graduate Adviser, Fax: 940-565-2515, E-mail: deering@cas.unt.edu.

Announcement: BA, BS, MS, and PhD degrees offered with full program of graduate courses in experimental and theoretical physics. Undergraduate scholarships of $2500 and $1000, with out-of-state tuition waiver available for physics majors, and opportunities for additional merit aid. Graduate teaching assistantships and fellowships with tuition waiver are also available.

University of Notre Dame, Graduate School, College of Science, Department of Physics, Notre Dame, IN 46556. Offers PhD. *Faculty:* 34 full-time (4 women), 1 part-time (0 women). *Students:* 74 full-time (18 women), 1 part-time; includes 3 minority (1 Asian American or Pacific Islander, 1 Hispanic American, 1 Native American), 42 international. 184 applicants, 24% accepted. In 1998, 9 doctorates awarded (55% entered university research/teaching, 45% found other work related to degree). *Degree requirements:* For doctorate, dissertation required, foreign language not required. *Entrance requirements:* For doctorate, GRE General Test, GRE Subject Test, TOEFL (minimum score of 600 required; 250 for computer-based). *Average time to degree:* Doctorate–7 years full-time. *Application deadline:* For fall admission, 2/1 (priority date); for spring admission, 10/15. Applications are processed on a rolling basis. Application fee: $40. *Financial aid:* In 1998–99, 71 students received aid, including 4 fellowships with full tuition reimbursements available (averaging $16,000 per year), 26 research assistantships with full tuition reimbursements available (averaging $12,500 per year), 40 teaching assistantships with full tuition reimbursements available (averaging $12,500 per year); tuition waivers (full) also available. Financial aid application deadline: 2/1. *Faculty research:* Elementary particle, nuclear, atomic, and condensed-state physics; astrophysics. Total annual research expenditures: $4.5 million. *Unit head:* Dr. James J. Kolata, Director of Graduate Studies, 219-631-6387, Fax: 219-631-5952, E-mail: clark.15@nd.edu. *Application contact:* Dr. Terrence J. Akai, Director of Graduate Admissions, 219-631-7706, Fax: 219-631-4183, E-mail: gradad@nd.edu.

See in-depth description on page 551.

University of Oklahoma, Graduate College, College of Arts and Sciences, Department of Physics and Astronomy, Program in Physics, Norman, OK 73019-0390. Offers M Nat Sci, MS, PhD. Part-time programs available. *Students:* 21 full-time (6 women), 18 part-time (3 women); includes 1 minority (Native American), 11 international. Average age 28. 3 applicants, 67% accepted. In 1998, 1 master's, 3 doctorates awarded. Terminal master's awarded for partial completion of doctoral program. *Degree requirements:* For master's, thesis or alternative, departmental qualifying exam required, foreign language not required; for doctorate, dissertation, comprehensive, departmental qualifying, oral, and written exams required, foreign language not required. *Entrance requirements:* For master's and doctorate, GRE General Test, GRE Subject Test, TOEFL (minimum score of 600 required), previous course work in physics. *Application deadline:* For fall admission, 3/1 (priority date); for spring admission, 10/1. Applications are processed on a rolling basis. Application fee: $25. Tuition, state resident: part-time $86 per credit hour. Tuition, nonresident: part-time $275 per credit hour. Tuition and fees vary according to course level, course load and program. *Financial aid:* In 1998–99, 28 students received aid; fellowships, research assistantships, teaching assistantships, Federal Work-Study, institutionally-sponsored loans, and tuition waivers (full and partial) available. Aid available to part-time students. Financial aid application deadline: 3/1. *Faculty research:* Atomic and molecular physics, high-energy physics, solid-state physics, atmospheric science. *Application contact:* Dr. John Furneaux, Chair, Graduate Selection Committee, 405-325-3961, Fax: 405-325-7557.

University of Oregon, Graduate School, College of Arts and Sciences, Department of Physics, Eugene, OR 97403. Offers MA, MS, PhD. *Faculty:* 30 full-time (1 woman), 19 part-time (4 women). *Students:* 70 full-time (12 women), 3 part-time, 35 international. 16 applicants, 94% accepted. In 1998, 7 master's, 11 doctorates awarded. Terminal master's awarded for partial completion of doctoral program. *Degree requirements:* For master's, foreign language and thesis not required; for doctorate, dissertation required, foreign language not required. *Entrance requirements:* For master's and doctorate, GRE General Test, TOEFL (minimum score of 500 required), GRE Subject Test. *Average time to degree:* Master's–1 year full-time; doctorate–5 years full-time. *Application deadline:* For fall admission, 2/15. Applications are processed on a rolling basis. Application fee: $50. *Financial aid:* In 1998–99, 59 teaching assistantships were awarded.; Federal Work-Study, institutionally-sponsored loans, and traineeships also available. Financial aid application deadline: 2/15. *Faculty research:* Solid-state and chemical physics, optical physics, elementary particle physics, astrophysics, atomic and molecular physics. *Unit head:* Dr. Nilendra Deshpande, Head, 541-346-4751. *Application contact:* Sandy Ryan, Graduate Secretary, 541-346-4787, Fax: 541-346-4787.

See in-depth description on page 555.

University of Ottawa, School of Graduate Studies and Research, Faculty of Science, Ottawa-Carleton Institute for Physics, Ottawa, ON K1N 6N5, Canada. Offers M Sc, PhD. *Faculty:* 50 full-time, 6 part-time. *Students:* 46 full-time (12 women), 2 part-time, 5 international. Average age 28. In 1998, 9 master's, 10 doctorates awarded. *Degree requirements:* For master's, thesis or alternative required, foreign language not required; for doctorate, dissertation required, foreign language not required. *Entrance requirements:* For master's, honors degree or equivalent, minimum B average; for doctorate, minimum B+ average. *Application deadline:* For fall admission, 3/1. Application fee: $35. *Financial aid:* Fellowships, research assistantships, teaching assistantships, Federal Work-Study available. *Faculty research:* Low-temperature, condensed-matter, ion,and high-energy physics. *Unit head:* Ivan L'Heureux, Director, 613-562-5800 Ext. 6750, Fax: 613-562-5190. *Application contact:* Madeleine Thomas, Academic Secretary, 613-562-5800 Ext. 6750, Fax: 613-562-5190, E-mail: mthomas@science.uottawa.ca.

University of Pennsylvania, School of Arts and Sciences, Graduate Group in Physics and Astronomy, Philadelphia, PA 19104. Offers physics (PhD). Part-time programs available. *Degree requirements:* For doctorate, dissertation, oral, preliminary and final exams required, foreign language not required. *Entrance requirements:* For doctorate, GRE General Test, GRE Subject Test, TOEFL, TSE (recommended). Electronic applications accepted. *Faculty research:* Astrophysics, condensed matter experiment, condensed matter theory, particle experiment, particle theory.

See in-depth description on page 559.

University of Pittsburgh, Faculty of Arts and Sciences, Department of Physics and Astronomy, Pittsburgh, PA 15260. Offers astronomy (MS, PhD); physics (MS, PhD). Part-time programs available. *Faculty:* 39 full-time (4 women). *Students:* 69 full-time (5 women), 2 part-time (1 woman); includes 5 minority (2 African Americans, 2 Asian Americans or Pacific Islanders, 1 Hispanic American), 41 international. 173 applicants, 26% accepted. In 1998, 13 master's, 3 doctorates awarded. Terminal master's awarded for partial completion of doctoral program. *Degree requirements:* For master's, thesis optional, foreign language not required; for doctorate, dissertation required, foreign language not required. *Entrance requirements:* For master's and doctorate, GRE General Test, GRE Subject Test, TOEFL (minimum score of 575 required), minimum QPA of 3.0. *Average time to degree:* Master's–2 years full-time, 3.5 years part-time; doctorate–5.5 years full-time. *Application deadline:* For fall admission, 1/31 (priority date). Applications are processed on a rolling basis. Application fee: $30 ($40 for international students). Electronic applications accepted. *Financial aid:* In 1998–99, 7 fellowships with full tuition reimbursements (averaging $15,150 per year), 31 research assistantships with full tuition reimbursements (averaging $10,600 per year), 32 teaching assistantships with full tuition reimbursements (averaging $10,815 per year) were awarded.; scholarships also available. Financial aid application deadline: 1/31; financial aid applicants required to submit FAFSA. *Faculty research:* Astrophysics, general relativity and condensed-matter physics, atomic physics, particle physics, nuclear physics. Total annual research expenditures: $4 million. *Unit head:* Dr. Frank Tabakin, Chairman, 412-624-6381, Fax: 412-624-9163, E-mail: frankt@tabakin.phyast.pitt.edu. *Application contact:* Peter M. Koehler, Admissions, 412-624-9000, Fax: 412-624-9163.

See in-depth description on page 561.

University of Puerto Rico, Mayagüez Campus, Graduate Studies, College of Arts and Sciences, Department of Physics, Mayagüez, PR 00681-5000. Offers MS. Part-time programs available. *Degree requirements:* For master's, thesis, comprehensive exam required, foreign language not required. *Faculty research:* Atomic and molecular physics, nuclear physics, nonlinear thermostatics, fluid dynamics, molecular spectroscopy.

University of Puerto Rico, Río Piedras, Faculty of Natural Sciences, Department of Physics, San Juan, PR 00931. Offers applied physics (MS); physics (MS); physics-chemical (PhD). Part-time and evening/weekend programs available. *Faculty:* 19. *Students:* 19 full-time (4 women), 13 part-time (2 women); includes 19 minority (all Hispanic Americans), 13 international. Average age 29. 12 applicants, 50% accepted. In 1998, 4 master's, 1 doctorate awarded. *Degree requirements:* For master's and doctorate, one foreign language, thesis/dissertation, comprehensive exam required. *Entrance requirements:* For master's, GRE, TOEFL, interview, minimum GPA of 3.0; for doctorate, GRE, master's degree, minimum GPA of 3.0. *Average time to degree:* Master's–6 years full-time; doctorate–8 years full-time. *Application deadline:* For fall admission, 2/1. Application fee: $17. *Financial aid:* Fellowships, research assistantships, teaching assistantships, Federal Work-Study, institutionally-sponsored loans, and tuition waivers (partial) available. Financial aid application deadline: 5/31. *Faculty research:* Low frequency radio studies of active extragalactic sources, structural studies of cylindrical polyelectrolyte solutions, spectroscopy of small clusters of hydrogen, light scattering and infrared spectroscopy of solids, spontaneously broken global symmetrics in supersymmetric theories. *Unit head:* Dr. Luftul Bari Bhuiyan, Coordinator of Master Program, 787-764-0000 Ext. 2307, Fax: 787-764-4063. *Application contact:* Luis F. Fonseca, Coordinator of Doctoral Program, 787-764-0000 Ext. 4773, Fax: 787-764-4063.

See in-depth description on page 563.

University of Regina, Faculty of Graduate Studies and Research, Faculty of Science, Department of Physics, Regina, SK S4S 0A2, Canada. Offers M Sc, PhD. *Faculty:* 11 full-time (0 women), 1 part-time (0 women). *Students:* 4 full-time (1 woman), 4 part-time. 20 applicants, 50% accepted. In 1998, 2 master's, 1 doctorate awarded. *Degree requirements:* For master's, thesis required, foreign language not required; for doctorate, variable foreign language requirement, dissertation required. *Entrance requirements:* For master's, TOEFL (minimum score of 550 required), honors degree or equivalent; for doctorate, TOEFL (minimum score of 550 required), M Sc or equivalent. *Application deadline:* Applications are processed on a rolling basis. Application fee: $0. *Expenses:* Tuition and fees charges are reported in Canadian dollars. Tuition, state resident: full-time $1,688 Canadian dollars; part-time $94 Canadian dollars per credit hour. International tuition: $3,375 Canadian dollars full-time. Required fees: $65 Canadian dollars per course. Tuition and fees vary according to course load and program. *Financial aid:* In 1998–99, 4 research assistantships, 2 teaching assistantships were awarded.; fellowships, career-related internships or fieldwork and scholarships also available. Financial aid application deadline: 6/15. *Faculty research:* Intermediate energy, nuclear and particle physics, condensed-matter/x-ray crystallography, theoretical physics. *Unit head:* Dr. G. Lolos, Head, 306-585-4149, Fax: 306-585-4894. *Application contact:* Dr. N. Mobed, Graduate Coordinator, 306-585-4359, Fax: 306-585-4894, E-mail: mobed@meena.cc.uregina.ca.

University of Rhode Island, Graduate School, College of Arts and Sciences, Department of Physics, Kingston, RI 02881. Offers MS, PhD.

University of Rochester, The College, Arts and Sciences, Department of Physics and Astronomy, Rochester, NY 14627-0250. Offers physics (MA, MS, PhD); physics and astronomy (PhD). Part-time programs available. *Faculty:* 28. *Students:* 89 full-time (12 women); includes 1 minority (Hispanic American), 36 international. 273 applicants, 30% accepted. In 1998, 13 master's, 16 doctorates awarded. Terminal master's awarded for partial completion of doctoral program. *Degree requirements:* For master's, thesis (for some programs), comprehensive exam required, foreign language not required; for doctorate, dissertation, comprehensive exam, qualifying exam required, foreign language not required. *Entrance requirements:* For master's, GRE General Test; for doctorate, GRE General Test, TOEFL. *Application deadline:* For fall admission, 2/1 (priority date). Application fee: $25. *Financial aid:* Fellowships, research assistantships, teaching assistantships, tuition waivers (full and partial) available. Financial aid application deadline: 2/1. *Unit head:* Arie Bodek, Chair, 716-275-4351. *Application contact:* Barbara Warren, Graduate Program Secretary, 716-275-4351.

See in-depth description on page 565.

University of Saskatchewan, College of Graduate Studies and Research, College of Arts and Sciences, Department of Physics, Saskatoon, SK S7N 5A2, Canada. Offers M Sc, PhD. *Degree requirements:* For master's and doctorate, thesis/dissertation required. *Entrance requirements:* For master's, CANTEST (minimum score of 4.5 required) or International English Language Testing System (minimum score of 6 required) or Michigan English Language Assessment Battery (minimum score of 80 required), orTOEFL (minimum score of 550 required; average 560); for doctorate, TOEFL.

University of South Carolina, Graduate School, College of Science and Mathematics, Department of Physics and Astronomy, Columbia, SC 29208. Offers IMA, MAT, MS, PhD. IMA and MAT offered in cooperation with the College of Education. Part-time programs available. *Faculty:* 23 full-time (0 women), 2 part-time (0 women). *Students:* 26 full-time (2 women), 4 part-time (1 woman); includes 1 minority (Asian American or Pacific Islander), 18 international. Average age 30. 28 applicants, 18% accepted. In 1998, 1 master's awarded (0% continued full-time study); 2 doctorates awarded (100% entered university research/teaching). Terminal master's awarded for partial completion of doctoral program. *Degree requirements:* For master's, thesis required, foreign language not required; for doctorate, one foreign language, dissertation required. *Entrance requirements:* For master's and doctorate, GRE General Test, GRE Subject Test. *Application deadline:* For fall admission, 8/1 (priority date). Applications are processed on a rolling basis. Application fee: $35. Electronic applications accepted. Tuition, state resident: full-time $4,014; part-time $202 per credit hour. Tuition, nonresident: full-time $8,528; part-time $428 per credit hour. Required fees: $100; $4 per credit hour. Tuition and fees vary according to program. *Financial aid:* Fellowships, research assistantships, teaching assistantships, Federal Work-Study available. Aid available to part-time students. *Faculty research:* Mechanics, electron-spin resonance, foundations of quantum magnetism, intermediate-energy nuclear physics, high-energy physics. Total annual research expenditures: $2.2 million. *Unit head:* Dr. James M. Knight, Chair, 803-777-4121, Fax: 803-777-3065, E-mail: knight@sc.edu. *Application contact:* Dr. Milind V. Purohit, Director of Graduate Studies, 803-777-6996, Fax: 803-777-3065, E-mail: purohit@charm.psc.sc.edu.

See in-depth description on page 571.

University of Southern California, Graduate School, College of Letters, Arts and Sciences, Department of Physics and Astronomy, Los Angeles, CA 90089. Offers physics (MA, MS, PhD). *Faculty:* 29 full-time (0 women). *Students:* 40 full-time (4 women), 7 part-time; includes 1 minority (Asian American or Pacific Islander), 38 international. Average age 27. 168 applicants, 4% accepted. In 1998, 5 master's, 1 doctorate awarded. *Degree requirements:* For master's, thesis required (for some programs); for doctorate, dissertation required. *Entrance requirements:* For master's and doctorate, GRE General Test, GRE Subject Test. *Application deadline:* For fall admission, 7/1 (priority date); for spring admission, 12/1. Application fee: $55. Tuition: Full-time $22,198; part-time $748 per unit. Required fees: $406. Tuition and fees vary according to program. *Financial aid:* In 1998–99, 1 fellowship, 17 research assistantships, 33 teaching assistantships were awarded.; Federal Work-Study, institutionally-sponsored loans, and scholarships also available. Aid available to part-time students. Financial aid application deadline: 2/15; financial aid applicants required to submit FAFSA. *Faculty research:* Low-temperature physics, ultralow-temperature physics, superconductivity, electron quantum interference in disordered metals, space physics, solar astronomy, laser physics, nonlinear optics, quantum electronics, atomic physics, high-energy particle theory. *Unit head:* Dr. Tu-nan Chang, Chairman, 213-740-0848.

University of Southern Mississippi, Graduate School, College of Science and Technology, School of Mathematical Sciences, Department of Physics and Astronomy, Hattiesburg, MS 39406-5167. Offers MS. *Faculty:* 7 full-time (0 women), 1 part-time (0 women). *Students:* 4 full-time (0 women). Average age 27. 18 applicants, 17% accepted. In 1998, 1 degree awarded. *Degree requirements:* For master's, thesis, oral/written comprehensive exam required, foreign language not required. *Entrance requirements:* For master's, GRE General Test (minimum

Physics

University of Southern Mississippi (continued)
combined score of 1000 required), TOEFL (minimum score of 580 required), minimum GPA of 2.75. *Application deadline:* For fall admission, 8/6 (priority date). Applications are processed on a rolling basis. Application fee: $0 ($25 for international students). Tuition, state resident: full-time $2,250; part-time $137 per semester hour. Tuition, nonresident: full-time $3,102; part-time $172 per semester hour. Required fees: $602. *Financial aid:* Teaching assistantships, Federal Work-Study available. Financial aid application deadline: 3/15. *Faculty research:* Polymers, atomic physics, fluid mechanics, liquid crystals, refractory materials. Total annual research expenditures: $80,000. *Unit head:* Dr. William E. Hughes, Chairman, 601-266-4934, Fax: 601-266-5149.

University of South Florida, Graduate School, College of Arts and Sciences, Department of Physics, Tampa, FL 33620-9951. Offers applied physics (MS); engineering science/physics (MS, PhD); physics (MA, MS). Part-time programs available. *Faculty:* 11 full-time (0 women), 4 part-time (0 women). *Students:* 16 full-time (3 women), 2 part-time (1 woman); includes 9 minority (2 African Americans, 6 Asian Americans or Pacific Islanders, 1 Hispanic American). Average age 26. 8 applicants, 88% accepted. In 1998, 7 master's, 2 doctorates awarded (50% entered university research/teaching, 50% found other work related to degree). *Degree requirements:* For master's, thesis optional, foreign language not required; for doctorate, 2 foreign languages (computer language can substitute for one), dissertation required. *Entrance requirements:* For master's, GRE General Test (minimum combined score of 1000 required), minimum GPA of 3.0 in last 60 hours; for doctorate, GRE General Test (minimum combined score of 1000 required), minimum graduate GPA of 3.2. *Average time to degree:* Master's–2 years full-time; doctorate–5 years full-time. *Application deadline:* For fall admission, 6/1 (priority date); for spring admission, 10/15. Applications are processed on a rolling basis. Application fee: $20. Electronic applications accepted. Tuition, state resident: part-time $148 per credit hour. Tuition, nonresident: part-time $509 per credit hour. *Financial aid:* In 1998–99, 8 research assistantships with full tuition reimbursements (averaging $12,000 per year), 8 teaching assistantships with full tuition reimbursements (averaging $11,000 per year) were awarded.; fellowships, Federal Work-Study, institutionally-sponsored loans, and scholarships also available. Aid available to part-time students. Financial aid applicants required to submit FAFSA. *Faculty research:* Laser, medical, and solid-state physics. *Unit head:* R. S. Chang, Chairperson, 813-974-2871, Fax: 813-974-5813, E-mail: chang@chuma.cas.usf.edu. *Application contact:* Pritish Mukherjee, Director, 813-974-5230, Fax: 813-974-5813, E-mail: pritish@chuma.cas.usf.edu.

University of Southwestern Louisiana, Graduate School, College of Sciences, Department of Physics, Lafayette, LA 70504. Offers applied physics (MS); physics (MS). Part-time programs available. *Faculty:* 6 full-time (0 women). *Students:* 5 full-time (2 women), 2 part-time, 1 international. 17 applicants, 65% accepted. In 1998, 5 degrees awarded. *Degree requirements:* For master's, thesis required, foreign language not required. *Entrance requirements:* For master's, GRE General Test, minimum GPA of 2.75. *Application deadline:* For fall admission, 5/15. Application fee: $5 ($15 for international students). *Financial aid:* In 1998–99, 1 fellowship with full tuition reimbursement (averaging $13,000 per year), 7 research assistantships (averaging $6,107 per year) were awarded.; teaching assistantships, Federal Work-Study also available. Financial aid application deadline: 5/1. *Faculty research:* Environmental physics, geophysics, astrophysics, acoustics, atomic physics. *Unit head:* Dr. John Meriwether, Head, 318-482-6691. *Application contact:* Dr. Daniel Whitmire, Graduate Coordinator, 318-482-6185.

University of Tennessee, Knoxville, Graduate School, College of Arts and Sciences, Department of Physics and Astronomy, Knoxville, TN 37996. Offers physics (MS, PhD). Part-time programs available. *Faculty:* 41 full-time (2 women), 15 part-time (0 women). *Students:* 74 full-time (9 women), 16 part-time (2 women); includes 1 minority (Asian American or Pacific Islander), 44 international. 89 applicants, 51% accepted. In 1998, 9 master's, 4 doctorates awarded. *Degree requirements:* For master's, thesis or alternative required, foreign language not required; for doctorate, dissertation required, foreign language not required. *Entrance requirements:* For master's and doctorate, TOEFL (minimum score of 550 required), minimum GPA of 2.7. *Application deadline:* For fall admission, 2/1 (priority date). Applications are processed on a rolling basis. Application fee: $35. Electronic applications accepted. *Financial aid:* In 1998–99, 17 fellowships, 38 research assistantships, 37 teaching assistantships were awarded.; Federal Work-Study and institutionally-sponsored loans also available. Financial aid application deadline: 2/1; financial aid applicants required to submit FAFSA. *Unit head:* Dr. Lee Riedinger, Head, 423-974-3342, Fax: 423-974-7843, E-mail: lrieding@utk.edu. *Application contact:* Dr. C. C. Shih, Graduate Representative, 423-974-7806, E-mail: chia-shih@utk.edu.

See in-depth description on page 573.

University of Tennessee Space Institute, Graduate Programs, Program in Physics, Tullahoma, TN 37388-9700. Offers MS, PhD. *Faculty:* 4 full-time (0 women). *Students:* 11 full-time (3 women), 4 part-time; includes 1 minority (Asian American or Pacific Islander), 5 international. 15 applicants, 87% accepted. In 1998, 2 master's, 1 doctorate awarded. *Degree requirements:* For master's, thesis required (for some programs), foreign language not required; for doctorate, dissertation required. *Entrance requirements:* For master's and doctorate, GRE General Test, GRE Subject Test. *Application deadline:* Applications are processed on a rolling basis. Application fee: $35. *Financial aid:* Fellowships, research assistantships, career-related internships or fieldwork, Federal Work-Study, and tuition waivers (full and partial) available. Financial aid applicants required to submit FAFSA. *Unit head:* Dr. Horace Crater, Degree Program Chairman, 931-393-7469, E-mail: hcrater@utsi.edu. *Application contact:* Dr. Edwin M. Gleason, Assistant Dean for Admissions and Student Affairs, 931-393-7432, Fax: 931-393-7346, E-mail: egleason@utsi.edu.

The University of Texas at Arlington, Graduate School, College of Science, Department of Physics, Arlington, TX 76019. Offers physics (MS, PhD); radiological physics (MS). *Faculty:* 12 full-time (1 woman), 2 part-time (0 women). *Students:* 21 full-time (6 women), 7 part-time (1 woman); includes 1 minority (Asian American or Pacific Islander), 14 international. 17 applicants, 53% accepted. In 1998, 1 master's, 4 doctorates awarded. *Degree requirements:* For doctorate, dissertation, comprehensive exam required, foreign language not required. *Entrance requirements:* For master's and doctorate, GRE General Test, TOEFL. *Application deadline:* Applications are processed on a rolling basis. Application fee: $25 ($50 for international students). Tuition, state resident: full-time $1,368; part-time $76 per semester hour. Tuition, nonresident: full-time $5,454; part-time $303 per semester hour. Required fees: $66 per semester hour. $86 per term. Tuition and fees vary according to course load. *Financial aid:* Research assistantships, teaching assistantships available. *Unit head:* Dr. John L. Fry, Acting Chairman, 817-272-2266, Fax: 817-272-3637, E-mail: fry@uta.edu. *Application contact:* Dr. John L. Fry, Acting Chairman, 817-272-2266, Fax: 817-272-3637, E-mail: fry@uta.edu.

The University of Texas at Austin, Graduate School, College of Natural Sciences, Department of Physics, Austin, TX 78712-1111. Offers MA, MS, PhD. *Students:* 237 full-time (29 women), 19 part-time. 321 applicants, 36% accepted. In 1998, 16 master's, 28 doctorates awarded. *Entrance requirements:* For master's and doctorate, GRE General Test (minimum combined score of 1000 required; average 1228), GRE Subject Test (physics). Application fee: $50 ($75 for international students). *Financial aid:* Fellowships, research assistantships, teaching assistantships available. Financial aid application deadline: 1/15. *Unit head:* Kenneth W. Gentle, Chairman, 512-471-7581, Fax: 512-471-9637, E-mail: gentle@fusion.ph.utexas.edu. *Application contact:* Dr. Takeshi Udagawa, Graduate Adviser, 512-471-1984, Fax: 512-471-9637, E-mail: udagawa@physics.utexas.edu.

See in-depth description on page 575.

The University of Texas at Dallas, School of Natural Sciences and Mathematics, Program in Physics, Richardson, TX 75083-0688. Offers MS, PhD. Part-time and evening/weekend programs available. *Students:* 35 full-time (10 women), 24 part-time (5 women); includes 4

minority (3 Asian Americans or Pacific Islanders, 1 Hispanic American), 14 international. Average age 34. In 1998, 9 master's, 9 doctorates awarded. *Degree requirements:* For master's, minimum GPA of 3.0, industrial internship required, thesis optional, foreign language not required; for doctorate, dissertation, minimum GPA of 3.5, publishable paper required, foreign language not required. *Entrance requirements:* For master's and doctorate, GRE General Test (minimum combined score of 1100 or minimum score of 700 on quantitative section required), TOEFL (minimum score 550 required), minimum GPA of 3.0 in upper-level course work in field. *Application deadline:* For fall admission, 7/15; for spring admission, 11/15. Applications are processed on a rolling basis. Application fee: $25 ($75 for international students). *Financial aid:* Research assistantships, teaching assistantships, career-related internships or fieldwork, Federal Work-Study, grants, institutionally-sponsored loans, scholarships, and unspecified assistantships available. Aid available to part-time students. Financial aid application deadline: 4/30; financial aid applicants required to submit FAFSA. *Faculty research:* Atomic, molecular, atmospheric, chemical, solid-state, and space physics; optics and quantum electronics; relativity and astrophysics; high-energy particles. *Unit head:* Dr. John H. Hoffman, Associate Dean and College Master, 972-883-2846, Fax: 972-883-2848, E-mail: jhoffman@utdallas.edu.

The University of Texas at El Paso, Graduate School, College of Science, Department of Physics, El Paso, TX 79968-0001. Offers MS. Part-time programs available. *Faculty:* 13 full-time (2 women), 5 part-time (0 women). *Students:* 13 full-time (2 women), 1 part-time; includes 5 minority (1 African American, 4 Hispanic Americans), 9 international. Average age 30. 12 applicants, 58% accepted. In 1998, 4 degrees awarded. *Degree requirements:* For master's, thesis optional, foreign language not required. *Entrance requirements:* For master's, GRE General Test, TOEFL (minimum score of 550 required). *Application deadline:* Applications are processed on a rolling basis. Application fee: $15 ($65 for international students). Tuition, state resident: full-time $2,118. Tuition, nonresident: full-time $7,230. Tuition and fees vary according to program. *Financial aid:* In 1998–99, 13 students received aid, including 10 teaching assistantships; Federal Work-Study, institutionally-sponsored loans, and tuition waivers (partial) also available. Financial aid applicants required to submit FAFSA. *Faculty research:* Surface physics, condensed matter theory, nuclear theory, geophysics. Total annual research expenditures: $16,485. *Unit head:* Dr. James Craig, Chairperson, 915-747-5715. *Application contact:* Susan Jordan, Director, Graduate Student Services, 915-747-5491, Fax: 915-747-5788, E-mail: sjordan@utep.edu.

The University of Texas at Tyler, Graduate Studies, College of Liberal Arts, Department of Social Sciences, Tyler, TX 75799-0001. Offers interdisciplinary studies (MA, MS); political science (MA, MAT); public administration (MPA). Part-time and evening/weekend programs available. *Faculty:* 13 full-time (1 woman), 1 (woman) part-time. *Students:* 7. *Degree requirements:* For master's, research methods course required, foreign language and thesis not required. *Entrance requirements:* For master's, GRE General Test (minimum score of 1000 required), minimum GPA of 3.0. Application fee: $0. *Unit head:* Dr. Barbara L. Hart, Chair, 903-566-7371 Ext. 7426, Fax: 903-566-7377, E-mail: bhart@mail.uttyl.edu. *Application contact:* Martha D. Wheat, Director of Admissions and Student Records, 903-566-7201, Fax: 903-566-7068.

University of Toledo, Graduate School, College of Arts and Sciences, Department of Physics and Astronomy, Toledo, OH 43606-3398. Offers physics (MS, MS Ed, PhD). *Degree requirements:* For master's, thesis required, foreign language not required; for doctorate, dissertation, departmental qualifying exam required, foreign language not required. *Entrance requirements:* For master's and doctorate, GRE General Test, GRE Subject Test, TOEFL (minimum score of 550 required). Electronic applications accepted. *Faculty research:* Atomic physics, solid-state physics, materials science, astrophysics.

University of Toronto, School of Graduate Studies, Physical Sciences Division, Department of Physics, Toronto, ON M5S 1A1, Canada. Offers M Sc, PhD. *Degree requirements:* For master's, thesis optional; for doctorate, dissertation required.

University of Utah, Graduate School, College of Science, Department of Physics, Salt Lake City, UT 84112-1107. Offers chemical physics (PhD); physics (M Phil, MA, MS, PhD). Part-time programs available. *Faculty:* 25 full-time (1 woman), 23 part-time (0 women). *Students:* 65 full-time (9 women), 11 part-time (2 women), 30 international. Average age 31. In 1998, 6 master's, 6 doctorates awarded. Terminal master's awarded for partial completion of doctoral program. *Degree requirements:* For master's, thesis or alternative, teaching experience required; for doctorate, dissertation, departmental qualifying exam required, foreign language not required. *Entrance requirements:* For master's, GRE General Test, GRE Subject Test, TOEFL (minimum score of 500 required), minimum GPA of 3.0; for doctorate, GRE Subject Test, TOEFL (minimum score of 500 required), minimum GPA of 3.0. *Application deadline:* For fall admission, 7/1. Application fee: $30 ($50 for international students). *Financial aid:* In 1998–99, 40 teaching assistantships were awarded.; fellowships, research assistantships, Federal Work-Study and institutionally-sponsored loans also available. Financial aid application deadline: 3/31. *Faculty research:* High-energy physics, crystal growth, low-temperature physics, cosmic-ray physics, solid-state physics. *Unit head:* Craig Taylor, Chair, 801-581-6901, Fax: 801-581-4801, E-mail: craig@mail.physics.utah.edu. *Application contact:* Lynn Higgs, Director of Graduate Studies, 801-581-7140.

University of Vermont, Graduate College, College of Arts and Sciences, Department of Physics, Burlington, VT 05405-0160. Offers engineering physics (MS); physical sciences (MST); physics (MAT, MS). *Degree requirements:* For master's, computer language required, foreign language not required. *Entrance requirements:* For master's, GRE General Test, TOEFL (minimum score of 550 required).

University of Victoria, Faculty of Graduate Studies, Faculty of Science, Department of Physics and Astronomy, Victoria, BC V8W 2Y2, Canada. Offers astronomy and astrophysics (M Sc, PhD); condensed matter physics (M Sc, PhD); geophysics (M Sc, PhD); medical physics (PhD); nuclear and particle studies (M Sc, PhD); theoretical physics (M Sc, PhD). *Faculty:* 20 full-time (0 women), 22 part-time (1 woman). *Students:* 28 full-time (7 women). Average age 25. 56 applicants, 16% accepted. In 1998, 5 master's, 2 doctorates awarded. *Degree requirements:* For master's and doctorate, thesis/dissertation required, foreign language not required. *Average time to degree:* Master's–3.06 years full-time; doctorate–4.33 years full-time. *Application deadline:* For fall admission, 5/31 (priority date); for spring admission, 10/31. Applications are processed on a rolling basis. Application fee: $50. *Financial aid:* Fellowships, research assistantships, teaching assistantships, career-related internships or fieldwork and institutionally-sponsored loans available. Financial aid application deadline: 2/15. *Faculty research:* Old stellar populations in globular clusters; observational cosmology and large scale structure; muonium-antimuonium conversion; kaon rare decay modes; geomagnetism, seismology, and space physics. *Unit head:* Dr. C. E. Picciotto, Chair, 250-721-7698, E-mail: pic@uvic.ca. *Application contact:* Dr. A. Watton, Graduate Adviser, 250-721-7703, Fax: 250-721-7715, E-mail: awatt@uvvm.uvic.ca.

University of Virginia, College and Graduate School of Arts and Sciences, Department of Physics, Charlottesville, VA 22903. Offers MA, MAT, MS, PhD. *Faculty:* 34 full-time (4 women), 7 part-time (1 woman). *Students:* 65 full-time (11 women); includes 1 minority (African American), 32 international. Average age 26. 106 applicants, 36% accepted. In 1998, 4 master's, 12 doctorates awarded. *Degree requirements:* For master's and doctorate, thesis/dissertation required, foreign language not required. *Entrance requirements:* For master's and doctorate, GRE General Test, GRE Subject Test. *Application deadline:* For fall admission, 7/15; for spring admission, 12/1. Applications are processed on a rolling basis. Application fee: $60. *Financial aid:* Application deadline: 3/15. *Unit head:* Michael Fowler, Chairman, 804-924-3781. *Application contact:* Duane J. Osheim, Associate Dean, 804-924-7184, E-mail: grad-a-s@virginia.edu.

See in-depth description on page 577.

University of Washington, Graduate School, College of Arts and Sciences, Department of Physics, Seattle, WA 98195. Offers MS, PhD. Part-time and evening/weekend programs available. *Faculty:* 64 full-time (4 women), 9 part-time (2 women). *Students:* 119 full-time (16 women), 35 part-time (3 women); includes 16 minority (1 African American, 10 Asian Americans or Pacific Islanders, 4 Hispanic Americans, 1 Native American), 38 international. Average age 30. 305 applicants, 51% accepted. In 1998, 21 master's, 2 doctorates awarded. Terminal master's awarded for partial completion of doctoral program. *Degree requirements:* For master's, foreign language and thesis not required; for doctorate, dissertation required, foreign language not required. *Entrance requirements:* For master's, GRE, TOEFL; for doctorate, GRE General Test, GRE Subject Test, TOEFL (minimum score of 580 required), minimum GPA of 3.0. *Average time to degree:* Master's–2.3 years full-time, 4.3 years part-time; doctorate–7 years full-time. *Application deadline:* For fall admission, 1/15 (priority date). Applications are processed on a rolling basis. Application fee: $50. Electronic applications accepted. Tuition, state resident: full-time $5,196; part-time $475 per credit. Tuition, nonresident: full-time $13,485; part-time $1,285 per credit. Required fees: $387; $38 per credit. Tuition and fees vary according to course load. *Financial aid:* In 1998–99, 121 students received aid, including 7 fellowships with full tuition reimbursements available (averaging $14,676 per year), 68 research assistantships with full tuition reimbursements available (averaging $15,708 per year), 41 teaching assistantships with full tuition reimbursements available (averaging $15,372 per year); Federal Work-Study also available. Financial aid application deadline: 2/15; financial aid applicants required to submit FAFSA. *Faculty research:* Astro-, atomic, condensed-matter, nuclear, and particle physics; physics education. Total annual research expenditures: $10.8 million. *Unit head:* David G. Boulware, Chairman, 206-543-2770, Fax: 206-685-0635, E-mail: dgb@phys.washington.edu. *Application contact:* Kimberly Hawley, Graduate Program Assistant, 206-543-2488, Fax: 206-685-0635, E-mail: grad@phys.washington.edu.

University of Waterloo, Graduate Studies, Faculty of Science, Guelph-Waterloo Program in Physics, Waterloo, ON N2L 3G1, Canada. Offers M Sc, PhD. Part-time programs available. *Faculty:* 24 full-time (2 women), 9 part-time (0 women). *Students:* 60 full-time (5 women), 4 part-time. 35 applicants, 37% accepted. In 1998, 10 master's, 3 doctorates awarded. *Degree requirements:* For master's; for doctorate, dissertation required. *Entrance requirements:* For master's, GRE Subject Test, TOEFL (minimum score of 600 required), honors degree, minimum B average; for doctorate, GRE Subject Test, TOEFL (minimum score of 600 required), master's degree. *Application deadline:* For fall admission, 7/1 (priority date); for winter admission, 11/1 (priority date); for spring admission, 3/1 (priority date). Applications are processed on a rolling basis. Application fee: $60. *Expenses:* Tuition and fees charges are reported in Canadian dollars. Tuition, state resident: full-time $3,168 Canadian dollars; part-time $792 Canadian dollars per term. Tuition, nonresident: full-time $8,000 Canadian dollars; part-time $2,000 Canadian dollars. Required fees: $45 Canadian dollars per term. Tuition and fees vary according to program. *Financial aid:* In 1998–99, 49 research assistantships, 51 teaching assistantships were awarded.; career-related internships or fieldwork also available. *Faculty research:* Condensed-matter physics; applied physics; subatomic physics; astrophysics and gravitation; atomic, molecular, and optical physics. Total annual research expenditures: $3.2 million. *Unit head:* Dr. R. L. Brooks, Director, 519-824-4120 Ext. 3991, Fax: 519-836-9967, E-mail: rbrooks@uoguelph.ca. *Application contact:* M. M. Mayne, Administrative Assistant, 519-824-4120 Ext. 2263, Fax: 519-836-9967, E-mail: gwp@physics.uoguelph.ca.

The University of Western Ontario, Faculty of Graduate Studies, Physical Sciences Division, Department of Physics and Astronomy, Program in Physics, London, ON N6A 5B8, Canada. Offers M Sc, PhD. *Degree requirements:* For master's and doctorate, comprehensive exam required, thesis optional, foreign language not required. *Faculty research:* Condensed-matter and surface science, space and atmospheric physics, atomic and molecular physics, medical physics.

University of Windsor, College of Graduate Studies and Research, Faculty of Science, Physics, Windsor, ON N9B 3P4, Canada. Offers M Sc, PhD. Part-time programs available. *Degree requirements:* For master's, thesis required (for some programs); for doctorate, dissertation required. *Entrance requirements:* For master's, GRE, TOEFL, minimum B average; for doctorate, TOEFL (minimum score of 550 required), GRE General Test (score in 80th percentile or higher required), master's degree. *Faculty research:* Electrodynamics, plasma physics, atomic structure/particles, spectroscopy, quantum mechanics.

University of Wisconsin–Madison, Graduate School, College of Letters and Science, Department of Physics, Madison, WI 53706-1380. Offers MA, MS, PhD. *Faculty:* 45 full-time (2 women). *Students:* 129 full-time (14 women); includes 5 minority (2 Asian Americans or Pacific Islanders, 2 Hispanic Americans, 1 Native American), 37 international. 234 applicants, 42% accepted. In 1998, 8 master's awarded (75% found work related to degree, 25% continued full-time study); 27 doctorates awarded. Terminal master's awarded for partial completion of doctoral program. *Degree requirements:* For master's, qualifying exam, thesis (MS) required; for doctorate, dissertation, preliminary and qualifying exams required. *Entrance requirements:* For master's and doctorate, GRE, TOEFL (minimum score of 600 required). *Average time to degree:* Master's–2.4 years full-time; doctorate–7 years full-time. *Application deadline:* For fall admission, 1/1; for spring admission, 11/1. Application fee: $45. Electronic applications accepted. *Financial aid:* In 1998–99, 124 students received aid, including 6 fellowships with full tuition reimbursements available, 78 research assistantships with full tuition reimbursements available, 39 teaching assistantships with full tuition reimbursements available; traineeships and unspecified assistantships also available. Financial aid application deadline: 1/1. *Faculty research:* Atomic, physics, condensed matter, astrophysics, particles and fields, nuclear physics, plasma, phenomenology. Total annual research expenditures: $13.7 million. *Unit head:* Lee G. Pondrom, Chair, 608-263-3279, Fax: 608-262-3077, E-mail: pondrom@wishep.physics.wisc.edu. *Application contact:* Barb Schutz, Graduate Program Assistant, 608-262-9678, Fax: 608-262-3077, E-mail: physgrad@macc.wisc.edu.

University of Wisconsin–Milwaukee, Graduate School, College of Letters and Sciences, Department of Physics, Milwaukee, WI 53201-0413. Offers MS, PhD. *Faculty:* 13 full-time (2 women). *Students:* 19 full-time (1 woman), 9 part-time (1 woman), 13 international. 26 applicants, 46% accepted. In 1998, 6 master's, 2 doctorates awarded. *Degree requirements:* For master's, thesis or alternative required, foreign language not required; for doctorate, dissertation required. *Entrance requirements:* For master's and doctorate, GRE General Test. *Application deadline:* For fall admission, 1/1 (priority date); for spring admission, 9/1. Applications are processed on a rolling basis. Application fee: $45 ($75 for international students). *Financial aid:* In 1998–99, 3 fellowships, 6 research assistantships, 15 teaching assistantships were awarded.; career-related internships or fieldwork and unspecified assistantships also available. Aid available to part-time students. Financial aid application deadline: 4/15. *Unit head:* John Norbury, Chair, 414-229-4474.

University of Wisconsin–Oshkosh, Graduate School, College of Letters and Science, Department of Physics and Astronomy, Oshkosh, WI 54901. Offers physics (MS), including instrumentation, physics education. Part-time programs available. *Faculty:* 7 full-time (1 woman). *Students:* 2 full-time (1 woman), 5 part-time (1 woman), 1 international. Average age 27. In 1998, 3 degrees awarded. *Degree requirements:* For master's, thesis required, foreign language not required. *Entrance requirements:* For master's, minimum GPA of 2.75, BS in physics or related field. *Application deadline:* Applications are processed on a rolling basis. Application fee: $45. *Financial aid:* In 1998–99, 1 research assistantship with partial tuition reimbursement was awarded.; fellowships, institutionally-sponsored loans also available. Financial aid application deadline: 3/15; financial aid applicants required to submit FAFSA. *Faculty research:* Digital signal processing, stellar atmospheres and abundances, phase transitions, thin-film magnetism. *Unit head:* Dr. Roy Knispel, Chair, 920-424-4431, E-mail: knispel@uwosh.edu. *Application contact:* Dr. Sandra Gade, Coordinator, 920-424-7103, E-mail: gade@uwosh.edu.

University of Wyoming, Graduate School, College of Arts and Sciences, Department of Physics and Astronomy, Laramie, WY 82071. Offers MS, MST, PhD. *Faculty:* 17. *Students:* 14 full-time (7 women), 5 part-time, 5 international. 9 applicants, 67% accepted. In 1998, 4 doctorates awarded. *Degree requirements:* For doctorate, dissertation required, foreign language not required, foreign language not required. *Entrance requirements:* For master's and doctorate, GRE General Test, GRE Subject Test, minimum GPA of 3.0. *Application deadline:* For fall admission, 6/1 (priority date). Applications are processed on a rolling basis. Application fee: $40. Tuition, state resident: full-time $2,520; part-time $140 per credit hour. Tuition, nonresident: full-time $7,790; part-time $433 per credit hour. Required fees: $400; $7 per credit hour. Full-time tuition and fees vary according to course load and program. *Financial aid:* In 1998–99, 6 research assistantships, 15 teaching assistantships were awarded.; institutionally-sponsored loans also available. Financial aid application deadline: 3/1. *Faculty research:* Astrophysics; atomic, molecular, and optic physics; atmospheric physics; medium-energy, nuclear, and particle physics. *Unit head:* Dr. Paul Johnson, Head, 307-766-6150.

Utah State University, School of Graduate Studies, College of Science, Department of Physics, Logan, UT 84322. Offers MS, PhD. Part-time programs available. *Faculty:* 26 full-time (1 woman), 16 part-time (1 woman). *Students:* 23 full-time (1 woman), 6 part-time (1 woman); includes 1 minority (Hispanic American), 8 international. Average age 28. 22 applicants, 91% accepted. In 1998, 1 master's awarded (100% found work related to degree); 4 doctorates awarded. Terminal master's awarded for partial completion of doctoral program. *Degree requirements:* For master's and doctorate, thesis/dissertation required, foreign language not required. *Entrance requirements:* For master's and doctorate, GRE General Test (score in 40th percentile or higher required), GRE Subject Test (score in 40th percentile or higher required), TOEFL (minimum score of 550 required), minimum GPA of 3.0. *Application deadline:* For fall admission, 6/15 (priority date); for spring admission, 10/15. Applications are processed on a rolling basis. Application fee: $40. Tuition, state resident: full-time $1,492. Tuition, nonresident: full-time $5,232. Required fees: $434. Tuition and fees vary according to course load. *Financial aid:* In 1998–99, 17 students received aid, including 1 fellowship with partial tuition reimbursement available (averaging $10,000 per year), 9 research assistantships with partial tuition reimbursements available (averaging $14,000 per year), 12 teaching assistantships with partial tuition reimbursements available (averaging $10,500 per year); Federal Work-Study and institutionally-sponsored loans also available. Aid available to part-time students. Financial aid application deadline: 3/1. *Faculty research:* Upper-atmosphere physics, relativity, gravitational magnetism, particle physics, medium-energy nuclear physics. Total annual research expenditures: $1.5 million. *Unit head:* Dr. W. John Raitt, Head, 435-797-2848, Fax: 435-797-2492, E-mail: physics@cc.usu.edu. *Application contact:* Dr. David Peak, Assistant Head, 435-797-2884, Fax: 435-797-2492, E-mail: physics@cc.usu.edu.

Vanderbilt University, Graduate School, Department of Physics and Astronomy, Nashville, TN 37240-1001. Offers astronomy (MS); physics (MA, MAT, MS, PhD). *Faculty:* 29 full-time (1 woman), 6 part-time (0 women). *Students:* 54 full-time (8 women), 2 part-time (1 woman), 29 international. Average age 28. 54 applicants, 37% accepted. In 1998, 4 master's, 6 doctorates awarded. *Degree requirements:* For master's, thesis required; for doctorate, dissertation, final and qualifying exams required. *Entrance requirements:* For master's, GRE General Test; for doctorate, GRE General Test, GRE Subject Test. *Application deadline:* For fall admission, 1/15. Application fee: $40. *Financial aid:* In 1998–99, 52 students received aid, including 26 research assistantships with full tuition reimbursements available (averaging $13,000 per year), 26 teaching assistantships with full tuition reimbursements available (averaging $13,000 per year); career-related internships or fieldwork, Federal Work-Study, and institutionally-sponsored loans also available. Financial aid application deadline: 1/15. *Faculty research:* Experimental and theoretical physics, free electron laser, living-state physics, heavy-ion physics, nuclear structure. *Unit head:* David J. Ernst, Chair, 615-322-2828, Fax: 615-343-7263, E-mail: e.waters@ctrvax.vanderbilt.edu. *Application contact:* Royal G. Albridge, Director of Graduate Studies, 615-322-2774, Fax: 615-343-7263, E-mail: albridrg@ctrvax.vanderbilt.edu.

Virginia Commonwealth University, School of Graduate Studies, College of Humanities and Sciences, Department of Physics, Richmond, VA 23284-9005. Offers applied physics (MS); physics (MS). Part-time programs available. *Students:* 5 full-time (1 woman), 3 part-time; includes 3 minority (all Asian Americans or Pacific Islanders) In 1998, 3 degrees awarded. *Degree requirements:* For master's, thesis required (for some programs), foreign language not required. *Entrance requirements:* For master's, GRE. *Application deadline:* For fall admission, 8/1; for spring admission, 12/1. Applications are processed on a rolling basis. Application fee: $30. Tuition, state resident: full-time $4,031; part-time $224 per credit hour. Tuition, nonresident: full-time $11,946; part-time $664 per credit hour. Required fees: $1,081; $40 per credit hour. Tuition and fees vary according to campus/location and program. *Financial aid:* Fellowships, teaching assistantships, Federal Work-Study, institutionally-sponsored loans, and tuition waivers (full and partial) available. Aid available to part-time students. *Faculty research:* Condensed-matter theory and experimentation, electronic instrumentation, relativity. *Unit head:* Dr. Robert H. Gowdy, Chair, 804-828-1821, Fax: 804-828-7073, E-mail: rgowdy@atlas.vcu.edu. *Application contact:* Marilyn F. Bishop, Graduate Program Director, 804-828-1819, Fax: 804-828-7073.

Virginia Polytechnic Institute and State University, Graduate School, College of Arts and Sciences, Department of Physics, Blacksburg, VA 24061. Offers MS, PhD. *Students:* 39 full-time (6 women), 19 part-time (3 women); includes 3 minority (1 African American, 1 Asian American or Pacific Islander, 1 Hispanic American), 28 international. 29 applicants, 72% accepted. In 1998, 12 master's, 3 doctorates awarded. *Entrance requirements:* For master's and doctorate, TOEFL. *Application deadline:* For fall admission, 12/1 (priority date). Applications are processed on a rolling basis. Application fee: $25. *Financial aid:* In 1998–99, 17 research assistantships, 13 teaching assistantships were awarded.; fellowships, unspecified assistantships also available. Financial aid application deadline: 4/1. *Unit head:* Dr. Laynam N. Chang, Head, 540-231-6544, E-mail: laynam@vt.edu.

Virginia State University, School of Graduate Studies and Continuing Education, School of Agriculture, Science and Technology, Department of Physics, Petersburg, VA 23806-0001. Offers MS. *Faculty:* 2 full-time (0 women). *Degree requirements:* For master's, thesis required. *Entrance requirements:* For master's, GRE General Test. *Application deadline:* For fall admission, 8/15. Applications are processed on a rolling basis. Application fee: $25. Tuition, state resident: full-time $2,306; part-time $106 per credit hour. Tuition, nonresident: full-time $7,824; part-time $346 per credit hour. Required fees: $29 per credit hour. *Financial aid:* Application deadline: 5/1. *Unit head:* Dr. James C. Davenport, Chair, 804-524-5913. *Application contact:* Dr. Wayne F. Virag, Dean, Graduate Studies and Continuing Education, 804-524-5985, Fax: 804-524-5104, E-mail: wvirag@vsu.edu.

Wake Forest University, Graduate School, Department of Physics, Winston-Salem, NC 27109. Offers MS, PhD. Part-time programs available. *Faculty:* 9 full-time (1 woman), 2 part-time (0 women). *Students:* 12 full-time (1 woman), 5 part-time. Average age 27. 20 applicants, 25% accepted. In 1998, 4 master's awarded (0% continued full-time study); 1 doctorate awarded. *Degree requirements:* For master's, one foreign language (computer language can substitute), thesis required; for doctorate, 2 foreign languages (computer language can substitute for one), dissertation required. *Entrance requirements:* For master's, GRE General Test, GRE Subject Test, TOEFL; for doctorate, GRE General Test. *Application deadline:* For fall admission, 2/15. Application fee: $25. *Financial aid:* In 1998–99, 16 students received aid, including 3 research assistantships, 10 teaching assistantships; scholarships also available. Aid available to part-time students. Financial aid application deadline: 2/15; financial aid applicants required to submit FAFSA. *Unit head:* Dr. George M. Holzwarth, Director, 336-758-5337, E-mail: gholz@wfu.edu.

Washington State University, Graduate School, College of Sciences, Department of Physics, Pullman, WA 99164. Offers chemical physics (PhD); material science (MS, PhD); physics (MS, PhD). *Faculty:* 20 full-time (1 woman). *Students:* 31 full-time (2 women), 5 part-time (1 woman); includes 3 minority (1 African American, 1 Asian American or Pacific Islander, 1 Hispanic American), 12 international. In 1998, 6 master's awarded (0% continued full-time study); 6 doctorates awarded (100% found work related to degree). *Degree requirements:* For master's, thesis (for some programs), oral exam required; for doctorate, dissertation, oral exam required. *Entrance requirements:* For master's and doctorate, GRE General Test, GRE

Peterson's Graduate Programs in the Physical Sciences, Mathematics, Agricultural Sciences, the Environment & Natural Resources 2000 427

Physics–Plasma Physics

Washington State University (continued)

Subject Test, minimum GPA of 3.0. *Average time to degree:* Master's–2 years full-time; doctorate–4 years full-time. *Application deadline:* For fall admission, 3/1 (priority date). Applications are processed on a rolling basis. Application fee: $35. *Financial aid:* In 1998–99, 1 fellowship, 17 research assistantships, 16 teaching assistantships were awarded.; Federal Work-Study, institutionally-sponsored loans, tuition waivers (partial), and teaching associateship also available. Financial aid application deadline: 4/1; financial aid applicants required to submit FAFSA. *Faculty research:* Linear and nonlinear acoustics and optics, shock wave dynamics, solid-state physics, surface physics, high-pressure physics. Total annual research expenditures: $2.4 million. *Unit head:* Dr. Miles Dresser, Chair, 509-335-1698, Fax: 509-335-7816, E-mail: physics@wsu.edu. *Application contact:* Dr. Y. Gupta, 509-335-3140.

Washington University in St. Louis, Graduate School of Arts and Sciences, Department of Physics, St. Louis, MO 63130-4899. Offers MA, PhD. Part-time programs available. *Students:* 56 full-time (13 women), 1 part-time; includes 4 minority (2 African Americans, 1 Asian American or Pacific Islander, 1 Hispanic American), 19 international. 90 applicants, 33% accepted. In 1998, 6 master's, 10 doctorates awarded. Terminal master's awarded for partial completion of doctoral program. *Degree requirements:* For master's, thesis or alternative required; for doctorate, dissertation required. *Entrance requirements:* For master's and doctorate, GRE General Test. *Application deadline:* For fall admission, 1/15 (priority date). Applications are processed on a rolling basis. Application fee: $35. *Financial aid:* Fellowships, research assistantships, teaching assistantships, Federal Work-Study, institutionally-sponsored loans, and tuition waivers (full and partial) available. Aid available to part-time students. Financial aid application deadline: 1/15. *Unit head:* Dr. Clifford M. Will, Chairperson, 314-935-6250.

See in-depth description on page 579.

Wayne State University, Graduate School, College of Science, Department of Physics and Astronomy, Detroit, MI 48202. Offers physics (MA, MS, PhD). *Degree requirements:* For doctorate, dissertation required, foreign language not required. *Faculty research:* High-energy physics, nuclear thermal wave imaging, quantum theory of fields, HgCdTe, positron and atomic scattering, relativistic heavy-ion physics.

Wesleyan University, Graduate Programs, Department of Physics, Middletown, CT 06459-0260. Offers MA, PhD. Terminal master's awarded for partial completion of doctoral program. *Degree requirements:* For master's and doctorate, thesis/dissertation required. *Entrance requirements:* For master's, GRE General Test, GRE Subject Test; for doctorate, GRE Subject Test. *Faculty research:* Low-temperature physics, magnetic resonance, atomic collisions, laser spectroscopy, surface physics.

Western Carolina University, Graduate School, College of Arts and Sciences, Department of Chemistry and Physics, Cullowhee, NC 28723. Offers MAT, MS. Part-time and evening/weekend programs available. *Faculty:* 13. *Students:* 6 full-time (3 women), 2 part-time (1 woman); includes 1 minority (African American) 12 applicants, 58% accepted. In 1998, 7 degrees awarded. *Degree requirements:* For master's, variable foreign language requirement, thesis, comprehensive exam required. *Entrance requirements:* For master's, GRE General Test. *Application deadline:* For fall admission, 5/1 (priority date); for spring admission, 10/1 (priority date). Applications are processed on a rolling basis. Application fee: $35. Tuition, state resident: full-time $918. Tuition, nonresident: full-time $8,188. Required fees: $881. *Financial aid:* In 1998–99, 7 students received aid, including 1 research assistantship with full and partial tuition reimbursement available (averaging $7,000 per year), 6 teaching assistantships with full and partial tuition reimbursements available (averaging $7,583 per year); fellowships, Federal Work-Study, grants, and institutionally-sponsored loans also available. Financial aid application deadline: 3/15; financial aid applicants required to submit FAFSA. *Unit head:* Paul Brandt, Head, 828-227-7260. *Application contact:* Kathleen Owen, Assistant to the Dean, 828-227-7398, Fax: 828-227-7480, E-mail: kowen@wcu.edu.

Western Illinois University, School of Graduate Studies, College of Arts and Sciences, Department of Physics, Macomb, IL 61455-1390. Offers MS. Part-time programs available. *Faculty:* 8 full-time (1 woman). *Students:* 8 full-time (2 women), 1 (woman) part-time; includes 1 minority (Asian American or Pacific Islander), 7 international. Average age 29. 8 applicants, 50% accepted. In 1998, 6 degrees awarded. *Degree requirements:* For master's, thesis or alternative required, foreign language not required. *Application deadline:* Applications are processed on a rolling basis. Application fee: $0 ($25 for international students). *Financial aid:* In 1998–99, 8 students received aid, including 8 research assistantships with full tuition reimbursements available (averaging $4,880 per year) Financial aid applicants required to submit FAFSA. *Faculty research:* Optimized hybrid collector, secondary physics instrumentation laboratory, high-energy physics, metaphysics. *Unit head:* Dr. Harold Hart, Chairperson, 309-298-1596. *Application contact:* Barbara Baily, Director of Graduate Studies, 309-298-1806, Fax: 309-298-2245, E-mail: barb_baily@ccmail.wiu.edu.

Western Michigan University, Graduate College, College of Arts and Sciences, Department of Physics, Kalamazoo, MI 49008. Offers MA, PhD. *Students:* 6 full-time (1 woman), 11 part-time (4 women), 11 international. 25 applicants, 56% accepted. In 1998, 4 master's, 2 doctorates awarded. *Degree requirements:* For master's, thesis required, foreign language not required; for doctorate, dissertation, oral exam required. *Entrance requirements:* For doctorate, GRE General Test. *Application deadline:* For fall admission, 2/15 (priority date). Applications are processed on a rolling basis. Application fee: $25. *Financial aid:* Fellowships, research assistantships, teaching assistantships, Federal Work-Study available. Financial aid application deadline: 2/15; financial aid applicants required to submit FAFSA. *Unit head:* Dr. Robert Shamu, Chairperson, 616-387-4940. *Application contact:* Paula J. Boodt, Coordinator, Graduate Admissions and Recruitment, 616-387-2000, Fax: 616-387-2355, E-mail: paula.boodt@wmich.edu.

West Virginia University, Eberly College of Arts and Sciences, Department of Physics, Morgantown, WV 26506. Offers MS, PhD. Terminal master's awarded for partial completion of doctoral program. *Degree requirements:* For master's, thesis or alternative, qualifying exam required, foreign language not required; for doctorate, dissertation, qualifying exam required, foreign language not required. *Entrance requirements:* For master's and doctorate, GRE General Test, GRE Subject Test, TOEFL (minimum score of 550 required), minimum GPA of 3.0. *Faculty research:* Experimental and theoretical condensed-matter, plasma, high-energy theory, nonlinear dynamics, laser physics.

Wichita State University, Graduate School, Fairmount College of Liberal Arts and Sciences, Department of Physics, Wichita, KS 67260. Offers MS. Part-time programs available. *Faculty:* 7 full-time (1 woman), 4 part-time (0 women). Average age 35. 14 applicants, 57% accepted. In 1998, 3 degrees awarded. *Degree requirements:* For master's, qualifying exam required, thesis optional. *Entrance requirements:* For master's, GRE, TOEFL (minimum score of 550 required). *Application deadline:* For fall admission, 7/1 (priority date); for spring admission, 1/1. Applications are processed on a rolling basis. Application fee: $25 ($40 for international students). Electronic applications accepted. *Financial aid:* In 1998–99, research assistantships (averaging $7,000 per year), teaching assistantships with full tuition reimbursements (averaging $2,000 per year) were awarded.; Federal Work-Study, institutionally-sponsored loans, and unspecified assistantships also available. Aid available to part-time students. Financial aid application deadline: 4/1; financial aid applicants required to submit FAFSA. *Faculty research:* Condensed matter experiment and theory, low-mass stellar atmospheres. *Unit head:* Dr. Hussein Hamdeh, Chair, 316-978-5224, E-mail: hamdeh@twsuvm.uc.twsu.edu. *Application contact:* Dr. Elizabeth Behrman, Graduate Coordinator, 316-978-3990, E-mail: behrman@wsuhub.uc.twsu.edu.

Wilkes University, Graduate Studies, Department of Physics, Wilkes-Barre, PA 18766-0002. Offers MS, MS Ed. *Degree requirements:* For master's, thesis or alternative required, foreign language not required. *Entrance requirements:* For master's, GRE.

Worcester Polytechnic Institute, Graduate Studies, Department of Physics, Worcester, MA 01609-2280. Offers MS, PhD. *Faculty:* 14 full-time (0 women), 2 part-time (0 women). *Students:* 5 full-time (0 women), 1 part-time, 5 international. 46 applicants, 7% accepted. In 1998, 1 master's, 2 doctorates awarded. *Degree requirements:* For master's and doctorate, thesis/dissertation required, foreign language not required. *Entrance requirements:* For master's, TOEFL (minimum score of 550 required; average 599); for doctorate, TOEFL (minimum score of 550 required; average 599. *Average time to degree:* Master's–2 years full-time; doctorate–5 years full-time. *Application deadline:* For fall admission, 2/15 (priority date); for spring admission, 10/15 (priority date). Applications are processed on a rolling basis. Application fee: $50. Electronic applications accepted. *Financial aid:* In 1998–99, 1 fellowship with full tuition reimbursement (averaging $15,000 per year), 4 research assistantships with full tuition reimbursements (averaging $15,000 per year), teaching assistantships with full tuition reimbursements (averaging $11,970 per year) were awarded.; career-related internships or fieldwork, grants, institutionally-sponsored loans, and scholarships also available. Financial aid application deadline: 2/15; financial aid applicants required to submit FAFSA. *Faculty research:* Chemical and biochemical physics, materials research, classical and quantum optics, relativity, solid state physics, statistical mechanics. Total annual research expenditures: $164,591. *Unit head:* Dr. Thomas Keil, Head, 508-831-5419, Fax: 508-831-5886, E-mail: thkeil@wpi.edu. *Application contact:* P. K. Aravind, Graduate Coordinator, 508-831-5559, Fax: 508-831-5886, E-mail: paravind@wpi.edu.

Wright State University, School of Graduate Studies, College of Science and Mathematics, Department of Physics, Program in Physics, Dayton, OH 45435. Offers medical physics (MS); physics (MS). Part-time and evening/weekend programs available. *Students:* 3 full-time (0 women), 1 part-time; includes 2 minority (1 African American, 1 Hispanic American), 1 international. Average age 34. 4 applicants, 50% accepted. In 1998, 3 degrees awarded. *Degree requirements:* For master's, computer language, thesis required, foreign language not required. *Entrance requirements:* For master's, TOEFL (minimum score of 550 required). *Application deadline:* For fall admission, 3/1 (priority date). Applications are processed on a rolling basis. Application fee: $25. *Financial aid:* Fellowships, research assistantships, teaching assistantships, Federal Work-Study, institutionally-sponsored loans, and tuition waivers (full and partial) available. Aid available to part-time students. Financial aid application deadline: 3/1; financial aid applicants required to submit FAFSA. *Faculty research:* Solid-state physics, optics, geophysics. *Unit head:* Dr. Gust Bambakidis, Chair, Department of Physics, 937-775-2954, Fax: 937-775-2571.

Announcement: Kettering Medical Center/Cox Institute houses PET and MRI systems. Miami Valley Hospital houses X-ray imaging systems. Physics department houses 2-MeV electron Van de Graaff accelerator, 400-keV ion Van de Graaff with RBS/channeling, 120-keV ion implanter, Polaron DLTS, an X-ray diffraction unit, and high-resolution spectrometers.

Yale University, Graduate School of Arts and Sciences, Department of Physics, New Haven, CT 06520. Offers PhD. *Faculty:* 62. *Students:* 80 full-time (9 women); includes 3 minority (2 Asian Americans or Pacific Islanders, 1 Hispanic American), 50 international. 145 applicants, 41% accepted. In 1998, 15 degrees awarded. *Degree requirements:* For doctorate, dissertation required. *Entrance requirements:* For doctorate, GRE General Test, GRE Subject Test. *Average time to degree:* Doctorate–6 years full-time. *Application deadline:* For fall admission, 1/4. Application fee: $65. *Financial aid:* Fellowships, research assistantships, teaching assistantships, Federal Work-Study and institutionally-sponsored loans available. Aid available to part-time students. *Unit head:* Chair, 203-432-3650. *Application contact:* Admissions Information, 203-432-2770.

See in-depth description on page 581.

York University, Faculty of Graduate Studies, Faculty of Science, Program in Physics and Astronomy, Toronto, ON M3J 1P3, Canada. Offers M Sc, PhD. Part-time and evening/weekend programs available. *Degree requirements:* For master's, thesis optional, foreign language not required; for doctorate, dissertation required, foreign language not required.

Plasma Physics

California Institute of Technology, Division of Engineering and Applied Science, Option in Applied Physics, Pasadena, CA 91125-0001. Offers applied physics (MS, PhD); plasma physics (MS, PhD). *Faculty:* 7 full-time (0 women). *Students:* 35 full-time (5 women), 16 international. *Degree requirements:* For master's, foreign language and thesis not required; for doctorate, dissertation required, foreign language not required. *Application deadline:* For fall admission, 1/15. Application fee: $0. *Unit head:* Dr. Kerry F. Vahala, Representative, 626-395-2144.

Columbia University, Fu Foundation School of Engineering and Applied Science, Department of Applied Physics and Applied Mathematics, New York, NY 10027. Offers applied physics (MS, PhD), including applied mathematics (PhD), plasma physics (PhD), quantum electronics (PhD), solid state physics (PhD); applied physics and applied mathematics (Eng Sc D); medical physics (MS). Part-time programs available. *Faculty:* 11 full-time (0 women), 4 part-time (0 women). *Students:* 43 full-time (9 women), 16 part-time (7 women); includes 14 minority (2 African Americans, 9 Asian Americans or Pacific Islanders, 3 Hispanic Americans), 27 international. Terminal master's awarded for partial completion of doctoral program. *Degree requirements:* For master's, foreign language and thesis not required; for doctorate, dissertation, qualifying exam required, foreign language not required. *Entrance requirements:* For master's and doctorate, GRE General Test, GRE Subject Test (strongly recommended), TOEFL. *Application deadline:* For fall admission, 1/5; for spring admission, 10/1. Application fee: $55. *Unit head:* Dr. Gerald A. Navratil, Chairman, 212-854-4457, E-mail: seasinfo.ap@columbia.edu.

See in-depth description on page 449.

Princeton University, Graduate School, Department of Astrophysical Sciences, Program in Plasma Physics, Princeton, NJ 08544-1019. Offers PhD. *Degree requirements:* For doctorate, dissertation required, foreign language not required. *Entrance requirements:* For doctorate, GRE General Test, GRE Subject Test. *Faculty research:* Magnetic fusion energy research, plasma physics, x-ray laser studies.

Rensselaer Polytechnic Institute, Graduate School, School of Engineering, Department of Electrical, Computer, and Systems Engineering, Troy, NY 12180-3590. Offers computer and systems engineering (M Eng, MS, D Eng, PhD); electrical engineering (M Eng, MS, D Eng, PhD); plasma physics (M Eng, MS, D Eng, PhD). Part-time programs available. Post-baccalaureate distance learning degree programs offered (no on-campus study). *Faculty:* 36 full-time (1 woman), 4 part-time (0 women). *Students:* 151 full-time (16 women), 49 part-time (3 women); includes 19 minority (3 African Americans, 13 Asian Americans or Pacific Islanders, 3 Hispanic Americans), 86 international. Terminal master's awarded for partial completion of doctoral program. *Degree requirements:* For master's, thesis required (for some programs), foreign language not required; for doctorate, dissertation required, foreign language not required. *Entrance requirements:* For master's and doctorate, GRE, TOEFL (minimum score of 600 required). *Application deadline:* For fall admission, 2/1; for spring admission, 10/1. Applications are processed on a rolling basis. Application fee: $35. *Unit head:* Dr. Joe H. Chow, Acting Chair, 518-276-2879, Fax: 518-276-2433. *Application contact:* Ann Bruno, Manager of Graduate Admissions and Financial Aid, 518-276-2554, Fax: 518-276-2433, E-mail: bruno@ecse.rpi.edu.

University of Alberta, Faculty of Graduate Studies and Research, Department of Electrical and Computer Engineering, Edmonton, AB T6G 2E1, Canada. Offers computational optics

(PhD); computer engineering (M Eng, M Sc, PhD); control systems (M Eng, M Sc, PhD); engineering management (M Eng); laser physics (M Sc, PhD); oil sands (M Eng, M Sc, PhD); plasma physics (M Sc, PhD); power engineering (M Eng, M Sc, PhD); telecommunications (M Eng, M Sc, PhD). Terminal master's awarded for partial completion of doctoral program. *Degree requirements:* For master's and doctorate, thesis/dissertation required, foreign language not required. *Entrance requirements:* For master's and doctorate, TOEFL (minimum score of 580 required; average 610). Electronic applications accepted. *Faculty research:* Controls, communications, microelectronics, electromagnetics.

University of Colorado at Boulder, Graduate School, College of Arts and Sciences, Department of Astrophysical, Planetary, and Atmospheric Sciences, Boulder, CO 80309. Offers astrophysical and geophysical fluid dynamics (MS, PhD); astrophysics (MS, PhD); plasma physics (MS, PhD). Terminal master's awarded for partial completion of doctoral program. *Degree requirements:* For master's, thesis or alternative, comprehensive exam required, foreign language not required; for doctorate, dissertation required. *Entrance requirements:* For master's and doctorate, GRE General Test, GRE Subject Test.

Theoretical Physics

Cornell University, Graduate School, Graduate Fields of Arts and Sciences, Field of Physics, Ithaca, NY 14853-0001. Offers experimental physics (MS, PhD); physics (MS, PhD); theoretical physics (MS, PhD). *Faculty:* 55 full-time. *Students:* 151 full-time (31 women); includes 12 minority (1 African American, 9 Asian Americans or Pacific Islanders, 2 Hispanic Americans), 57 international. Terminal master's awarded for partial completion of doctoral program. *Degree requirements:* For master's and doctorate, thesis/dissertation required, foreign language not required. *Entrance requirements:* For master's and doctorate, TOEFL (minimum score of 550 required). *Application deadline:* For fall admission, 1/1. Application fee: $65. Electronic applications accepted. *Unit head:* Director of Graduate Studies, 607-255-6016, Fax: 607-255-2643. *Application contact:* Graduate Field Assistant, 607-255-6016, E-mail: phys_dpt@cornell.edu.

Harvard University, Graduate School of Arts and Sciences, Department of Physics, Cambridge, MA 02138. Offers experimental physics (AM, PhD); medical engineering/medical physics (PhD, Sc D), including applied physics (PhD), engineering sciences (PhD), medical engineering/medical physics (Sc D), physics (PhD); theoretical physics (AM, PhD). *Students:* 80 full-time (26 women). *Degree requirements:* For doctorate, dissertation, final exams, laboratory experience required, foreign language not required. *Entrance requirements:* For master's, GRE General Test, TOEFL (minimum score of 550 required); for doctorate, GRE General Test, GRE Subject Test, TOEFL (minimum score of 550 required). *Application deadline:* For fall admission, 12/14. Application fee: $60. *Unit head:* Dr. David Nelson, Chairperson, 617-495-2866. *Application contact:* Office of Admissions and Financial Aid, 617-495-5315.

See in-depth description on page 469.

Rutgers, The State University of New Jersey, New Brunswick, Graduate School, Program in Physics and Astronomy, New Brunswick, NJ 08903. Offers astrophysics (MS, PhD); condensed

matter physics (MS, PhD); elementary particle physics (MS, PhD); intermediate energy nuclear physics (MS, PhD); nuclear physics (MS, PhD); physics (MST); theoretical physics (MS, PhD). Part-time programs available. *Faculty:* 67 full-time (5 women). *Students:* 87 full-time (14 women), 3 part-time; includes 5 minority (2 African Americans, 3 Hispanic Americans), 63 international. Terminal master's awarded for partial completion of doctoral program. *Degree requirements:* For master's, thesis optional, foreign language not required; for doctorate, dissertation required, foreign language not required. *Entrance requirements:* For master's and doctorate, GRE General Test, GRE Subject Test. *Application deadline:* For fall admission, 1/2 (priority date); for spring admission, 11/1. Applications are processed on a rolling basis. Application fee: $50. *Unit head:* Dr. Jolie A. Cizewski, Director, 732-445-3884, Fax: 732-445-4343, E-mail: cizewski@physics.rutgers.edu.

See in-depth description on page 509.

University of Victoria, Faculty of Graduate Studies, Faculty of Science, Department of Physics and Astronomy, Victoria, BC V8W 2Y2, Canada. Offers astronomy and astrophysics (M Sc, PhD); condensed matter physics (M Sc, PhD); geophysics (M Sc, PhD); medical physics (PhD); nuclear and particle studies (M Sc, PhD); theoretical physics (M Sc, PhD). *Faculty:* 20 full-time (0 women), 22 part-time (1 woman). *Students:* 28 full-time (7 women). *Degree requirements:* For master's and doctorate, thesis/dissertation required, foreign language not required. *Application deadline:* For fall admission, 5/31 (priority date); for spring admission, 10/31. Applications are processed on a rolling basis. Application fee: $50. *Unit head:* Dr. C. E. Picciotto, Chair, 250-721-7698, E-mail: pic@uvic.ca. *Application contact:* Dr. A. Watton, Graduate Adviser, 250-721-7703, Fax: 250-721-7715, E-mail: awatt@uvvm.uvic.ca.

Cross-Discipline Announcements

Boston University, College of Engineering, Department of Aerospace and Mechanical Engineering, Boston, MA 02215.

The department offers graduate programs leading to the PhD and MS degrees. Research is focused in waves and acoustics; dynamics, control, and robotics; fluid mechanics; and precision engineering. Areas of specialization include aerodynamics, biomechanics, biomedical acoustics, multiphase flow, noise and vibrational control, structural dynamics, thermal processes, theoretical fluid dynamics, and turbulence.

Cornell University, Graduate School, Graduate Fields of Engineering, Field of Nuclear Science and Engineering, Ithaca, NY 14853-0001.

Research areas include delayed and prompt neutron activation analysis, neutron transmission radiography, neutron autoradiography, neutron depth profiling, atomic physics of highly charged ions, reactor accident analysis, reactor physics, nuclear fuel-cycle economics, seismology and reactor siting, plasma physics, and controlled thermonuclear fusion. See in-depth description in Book 5, Energy and Power Engineering section.

Dartmouth College, Thayer School of Engineering, Hanover, NH 03755.

Thayer School offers MS and PhD programs in applied sciences. The interdisciplinary character of the institution, modern laboratories, computing facilities, and active collaborations with other departments provide unique opportunities for study and research in space plasma physics, nonlinear optics, electromagnetism, fluid mechanics, and oceanography. See in-depth description in Section 1, Book 5 of this series.

Johns Hopkins University, Zanvyl Krieger School of Arts and Sciences, Thomas C. Jenkins Department of Biophysics, Baltimore, MD 21218-2699.

The Department of Biophysics offers a comprehensive and rigorous training program in the major areas of biophysical inquiry. The program emphasizes the understanding of key biological processes through insights and techniques of the physical sciences. Areas of active research include structural thermodynamics, signal transduction, intermolecular forces, mechanical basis of allostery, electrostatic and regulatory interactions in proteins and macromolecular assemblies, physical chemistry of proteins and nucleic acids, computer-aided drug design, computer methods for structure-based energy calculations, computational and experimental studies of folding and stability of proteins and nucleic acids, membrane biophysics and regulation membrane proteins, X-ray analysis of proteins and protein–nucleic acid complexes, NMR and EPR, fluorescence spectroscopy, and microcalorimetry. Most successful applicants are physics majors with research interests in biological problems. See in-depth description in Book 3, Biophysics section.

Johns Hopkins University, Zanvyl Krieger School of Arts and Sciences, Department of Chemistry, Baltimore, MD 21218-2699.

Applications from undergraduate physics majors to the graduate program in the Department of Chemistry at Johns Hopkins University are encouraged. A number of faculty members have active research programs at the interface between chemistry and physics. These include research in gas-phase atomic and molecular systems, clusters, and surfaces.

Johns Hopkins University, Intercampus Program in Molecular Biophysics, Baltimore, MD 21218-2699.

The Intercampus Program in Molecular Biophysics (IPMB) is staffed by about 40 faculty members with interests in molecular biophysics. It offers special opportunities to applicants trained in the physical sciences or mathematics for graduate study in areas such as protein crystallography, NMR and ESR, thermodynamics, statistical mechanics, computer modeling, biophysical chemistry, and biochemistry. It emphasizes studies on macromolecules, or on interacting assemblies of macromolecules, for which a combination of approaches—molecular genetics and structural studies, for example—may be necessary for real progress. Collaborative projects between faculty members are encouraged. For information, contact IPMB Office, 410-516-5197, fax: 410-516-5199, e-mail: ipmb@jhu.edu, World Wide Web: http://www.jhu.edu/~ipmb/

Louisiana State University and Agricultural and Mechanical College, Graduate School, College of Engineering, Department of Electrical and Computer Engineering, Baton Rouge, LA 70803.

A flexible curriculum featuring theory, design, fabrication, and characterization of semiconductor devices and circuits is emphasized. The laboratory has a clean room for device processing. The Center for Advanced Microstructures and Devices (CAMD) supports X-ray lithography and microelectromechanical (MEM) devices research. Students may enter the program with a BS in engineering or another science discipline such as physics or chemistry.

Oregon State University, Graduate School, College of Oceanic and Atmospheric Sciences, Corvallis, OR 97331.

The College invites students with physics and mathematics degrees to apply for graduate study in physical oceanography, interdisciplinary oceanography, atmospheric physics, and geophysics. Research areas include ocean circulation, turbulence, air-sea interactions, atmospheric dynamics, ocean and atmosphere modeling, satellite applications, geodynamics, geomagnetism, electromagnetic induction, and seismology. See description under Marine Sciences and Oceanography in this volume.

Cross-Discipline Announcements

Princeton University, Graduate School, Princeton Materials Institute, Princeton, NJ 08540-5211.

The Princeton Materials Institute welcomes students interested in cross-disciplinary research involving any aspect of materials science and engineering. Faculty members from 8 academic departments collaborate in a remarkably broad range of programs, supported by outstanding facilities. Some fellowships are available. See the in-depth description in Book 5, Section 21.

University of California, Berkeley, Graduate Division, Group in Applied Science and Technology, Berkeley, CA 94720-1500.

The program areas of emphasis are applied physics, engineering science, and mathematical sciences. Faculty members are drawn from College of Engineering departments as well as from the departments of physics, chemistry, chemical engineering, and mathematics. Topics of interest include the novel properties and applications of nanostructures, thin films and interface science, microelectromechanical systems (MEMS), X-ray microimaging, and laser-induced chemical processes.

University of Kentucky, Graduate School, Graduate School Programs from the College of Allied Health, Program in Radiation Sciences, Lexington, KY 40506-0032.

Accredited two-year MS in radiological medical physics emphasizing academic and laboratory training in therapy and imaging physics using modern linacs and treatment planning systems, Gammaknife, and CT, SPECT, simulator, and traditional imaging systems. Campus visits welcomed. For information contact 606-323-1100 Ext. 248 or e-mail rcchri1@pop.uky.edu. Visit the Web site at http://radweb.hosp.uky.edu.

University of Michigan, Horace H. Rackham School of Graduate Studies, College of Engineering, Department of Nuclear Engineering and Radiological Sciences, Ann Arbor, MI 48109.

The department offers master's and doctoral programs in nuclear engineering and nuclear science and a joint-degree program in scientific computing. Students may elect to study plasma physics, fusion, fission reactor physics, materials, measurements, imaging, medical applications, and radiation protection (health physics). Students with degrees in engineering, computer science, or the physical sciences are encouraged to apply.

University of Michigan, Horace H. Rackham School of Graduate Studies, College of Engineering, Department of Materials Science and Engineering, Ann Arbor, MI 48109.

Interdisciplinary curriculum leads to master's and PhD degrees in materials science and engineering for physics students interested in condensed-matter physics; metals; ceramics; polymers; composites; electronic, magnetic, and optical materials; and other engineering materials. Research assistantships and fellowships available on a competitive basis. See in-depth description of the department in the Engineering and Applied Sciences volume of this series.

University of Virginia, College and Graduate School of Arts and Sciences, Interdisciplinary Program in Biophysics, Charlottesville, VA 22903.

The Interdisciplinary Program in Biophysics at the University of Virginia offers training and research opportunities with more than 35 faculty members in the Schools of Graduate Arts and Sciences, Engineering, and Medicine. Macromolecular structure and physical biochemistry, membrane biophysics, and radiological physics are areas of specific research strength. All students are financially supported.

University of Virginia, College and Graduate School of Arts and Sciences, Department of Molecular Physiology and Biological Physics, Charlottesville, VA 22903.

The Department of Molecular Physiology and Biological Physics at the University of Virginia provides opportunities for multidisciplinary doctoral training in structural biology, physiology, and biophysics. Internationally recognized faculty members employ state-of-the-art research approaches, including X-ray diffraction, electron microscopy, probe microscopy, NMR and EPR spectroscopy, and molecular biology, offering the opportunity for a broadly based educational experience. Interdisciplinary research is especially encouraged and promoted. For an in-depth description, see Physiology section in the Biological Sciences volume of this series. To apply, contact Avril V. Somlyo, Graduate Program Director, 804-982-0825.

AMERICAN UNIVERSITY

Department of Physics

Programs of Study

The Department of Physics offers a program leading to the M.S. degree. The department recognizes that the development of a mature, professional physicist is accomplished through a variety of experiences. Therefore, in addition to taking formal courses, graduate students are provided with an early opportunity to become acquainted with the various areas of ongoing research and to develop graduate projects. On-campus research projects include experiments in magnetism using the Mössbauer technique, acoustics, laser experiments, and electron impact in excitation of atoms. There is ongoing theoretical research in intense-field electrodynamics and critical phenomena. The University also offers a strong experimental high-energy nuclear physics program. Research is conducted in nuclear physics, condensed-matter physics, acoustics, astronomy, and intense-field/laser physics. Students in the program participate in research at the Stanford Linear Accelerator Center (SLAC). In some areas of research, joint programs are operated with government research laboratories that provide students with an opportunity to enrich their experience by contact with other professional scientists. Graduate students in physics complete a series of core courses and select additional course work to round out their individual programs. Classes are small, enabling students to work closely with faculty members and fellow students.

Research Facilities

Research facilities of the Department of Physics, housed in the McKinley Building, include general and advanced laboratories (for example, Mössbauer, critical phenomena, kinetic molecular, and laser laboratories), a minicomputer room, and electronics and audio technology equipment. Nuclear research is carried out under a cooperative arrangement with SLAC. The current research program receives financial support from such federal agencies as the National Science Foundation, the Office of Naval Research, the U.S. Department of Energy, and the National Aeronautics and Space Administration, in addition to internal funds from the University.

The Bender Library and Learning Resources Center houses more than 700,000 volumes and 3,000 periodical titles as well as extensive microform collections and a nonprint media center. In addition, more than fourteen indexes in compact disc format are searchable using library microcomputers. Graduate students have unlimited borrowing privileges at six other college and university libraries in the Washington Research Library Consortium, all accessible through the online catalog. Microcomputer resources are extensive and can be used 24 hours a day at various campus locations.

Financial Aid

Fellowships, scholarships, and graduate assistantships are available to full-time students. Special opportunity grants for members of minority groups parallel the regular honor awards and take the form of assistantships and scholarships. Research and teaching fellowships provide stipends plus tuition. Graduate assistantships provide up to 18 credit hours of tuition remission per year.

Cost of Study

For the 1999–2000 academic year, tuition is $721 per credit hour.

Living and Housing Costs

Although many graduate students live off campus, the University provides graduate dormitory rooms and apartments. The Off-Campus Housing Office maintains a referral file of rooms and apartments. Housing costs in Washington, D.C., are comparable to those in other major metropolitan areas.

Student Group

The graduate students in the department represent many cultures and nationalities. Formal classes are generally small, ensuring that students receive individual attention. There are close working relationships between faculty members and students in research activities.

Student Outcomes

Previous graduates have found employment at government laboratories, universities, and national research laboratories such as the NASA/Goddard Space Flight Center, the National Bureau of Standards, the National Research Laboratory, the Naval Surface Warfare Center, the University of Rochester, and Deutsches Elektronen-Synchrotron (DESY).

Location

The national capital area offers students access to a variety of educational, governmental, and cultural resources that enrich the student's degree program with opportunities for practical applications of theoretical studies. Opportunities exist for research, internships, cooperative educational placements, and part-time jobs. Local bus and rail transportation from the campus provides easy access to sites such as the National Institutes of Health, the National Institutes of Standards and Technology, and numerous other government and private research laboratories.

The University

American University was founded as a Methodist institution, chartered by Congress in 1893, and originally intended for graduate study only. The University is located on an 84-acre site in a residential area of northwest Washington. As a member of the Consortium of Universities of the Washington Metropolitan Area, American University offers its degree candidates the option of taking courses at other consortium universities for residence credit.

Applying

Applications for admission should be submitted prior to February 1 if the student is also applying for financial aid. Deadlines vary for different fields of study, but early application is always encouraged. The application fee is $50.

Correspondence and Information

To contact faculty members and for specific program information:

Department of Physics
College of Arts and Sciences
American University
4400 Massachusetts Avenue, NW
Washington, D.C. 20016-8058
Telephone: 202-885-2743
Fax: 202-885-2723
E-mail: physics@american.edu
World Wide Web: http://kotzebue.physics.american.edu

For an application and University catalog:

Graduate Admissions Office
American University
4400 Massachusetts Avenue, NW
Washington, D.C. 20016-8001
Telephone: 202-885-6000
E-mail: afa@american.edu

American University

THE FACULTY AND THEIR RESEARCH

Robert N. DeWitt, Professor and Chairperson; Ph.D., American (e-mail: rdewitt@american.edu). Intense-field electrodynamics, plasma physics and applications of electromagnetism.
The Behavior of Systems in the Space Environment. The Netherlands: Kluwer Academic Publishers.

Raymond Arnold, Research Professor and Project Director, American University Group at the Stanford Linear Accelerator Center; Ph.D., Boston University. Nuclear high-energy physics, nucleon–few nucleon structure.

Richard Berendzen, Professor; Ph.D., Harvard. History of science, cosmology, solar astrophysics, astronomy education, sociology of science. A founding editor of the *Journal of College Science Teaching,* former consultant to the U.S. National Academy of Sciences, and Fellow of the American Association for the Advancement of Science.

Peter Bosted, Research Associate Professor; Ph.D., MIT. Nuclear high-energy physics, nucleon–few nucleon structure.

Teresa L. Hein, Assistant Professor; Ph.D., Kansas State (e-mail: thein@american.edu). Physics/science education.

Richard B. Kay, Professor Emeritus; Ph.D., Arkansas (e-mail: rkay@american.edu). Laser research and development, quantum electronics.

Howard R. Reiss, Professor; Ph.D., Maryland (e-mail: reiss@american.edu). Quantum theory; interaction of very intense fields with matter, including applications to external-field interactions with nuclei and atoms.
Radioactive Processes in Atomic Physics. New York: John Wiley & Sons, Inc.

Stephen Rock, Research Professor, American University Group at the Stanford Linear Accelerator Center; Ph.D., Berkeley. High-energy physics.

Romeo A. Segnan, Professor; Ph.D., Carnegie Mellon (e-mail: rsegnan@american.edu). Mössbauer spectroscopy, amorphous magnetism, magnetic alloys, audio techniques.
Twinning in epilayer of CdTe on [211] Si: Influence of ZnTe buffer layer. *Mat. Res. Soc. J.*

Zenon Szalata, Research Associate Professor; Ph.D., Massachusetts. Nuclear high-energy physics, nucleon–few nucleon structure.

John A. White, Professor Emeritus; Ph.D., Yale. Light scattering, critical point phenomena in fluids, magnetism, speed of light, experimental foundation of relativity theory, renormalization theory of fluids.

RESEARCH ACTIVITIES

Innovative Teaching Strategies (Hein): Classroom research that focuses on the use of interactive and innovative teaching strategies in the introductory physics curriculum, particularly in the introductory course for nonscience majors. Current studies involve the assessment of multimedia learning tools such as interactive digital video and of student learning styles for physics teaching. A broad goal is to develop and assess instructional tools and techniques to better reach an increasingly diverse group of learners.

Intense-Field/Laser Physics (DeWitt, Kay, Reiss): Experimental and theoretical studies are being performed on the interaction of very intense electromagnetic fields with matter. The focus of interest is on multiphoton processes of high order in a domain of intensity beyond the scope of perturbation theory. Applications are made to atomic photoionization and to the new field of alteration of radioactivity by external means.

Nuclear Physics (Arnold, Bosted, Rock, Szalata): The American University Group at the Stanford Linear Accelerator Center is carrying out experimental studies to measure nuclear electromagnetic structure functions. The major work is to measure electron scattering from deuterium at a scattering angle of 180 degrees, using the electron beam from the new Nuclear Physics Injector at SLAC. The purpose of this experiment is to measure the magnetic structure functions of the deuteron over a large range of momentum transfer $Q2$, up to the largest possible $Q2$ allowed by the data rates.

Solid-State Physics (Segnan): Work is being done on magnetic materials by using the Mössbauer technique. The nitrogenation process of Tb-Fe intermetallic compounds is being studied. Mössbauer investigations are also being performed on early Greek, Etruscan, and Phoenician ceramics to establish a reliable basis for assessing ancient trade routes in the western Mediterranean.

Statistical Mechanics (White): Theoretical studies are in progress on the nature of phase transitions and critical point phenomena in condensable gases. A new renormalization group theory of fluids is being developed to test nonuniversal as well as universal properties and predict thermal behavior over the entire range of densities from zero to more than twice the critical point density.

BOSTON UNIVERSITY

Department of Physics

Programs of Study	The Department of Physics offers programs leading to the Ph.D. and M.A. degrees in physics. The time it takes to obtain a Ph.D. degree is approximately 5½ years, although students have obtained their degree in as short a time as 2 years and as long as 8.
	The master's degree requires the completion of eight semester courses, passed with a grade of B– or better; evidence of having successfully completed advanced courses in French, German, or Russian or passed the departmental language exam; and the achievement of a passing grade on the departmental comprehensive exam or the completion of a master's thesis. Each student must satisfy a residency requirement of a minimum of two consecutive semesters of full-time graduate study at Boston University.
	The doctorate requires the completion of eight semester courses beyond the master's degree passed with a grade of B– or better; passing of the departmental language exam in French, Russian, or German; an honors grade on the departmental comprehensive exam; passing of an oral exam; and the completion of a dissertation and a dissertation defense. The dissertation must exhibit an original contribution to the field. Each student must satisfy a residency requirement of a minimum of two consecutive semesters of full-time graduate study at Boston University.
	In addition to the programs mentioned above, a Ph.D. program in cellular biophysics and an interdisciplinary Ph.D. program are also available.
Research Facilities	The Department of Physics is part of Boston University's $250-million Science and Engineering Complex, centrally located on the main Charles River Campus. Condensed-matter physics facilities include STM spectroscopy and manipulation of individual atoms, metastable-helium-atom probes of magnetic order, photoemission and soft X-ray fluorescence probes of electronic structure in novel materials, X-ray diffractometers, nanolithography, optics and transport at high fields and low temperatures, and fabrication of bulk and thin-film high-Tc superconductors. Biophysics/polymer labs include dynamical light scattering, Raman and Brillouin scattering, and infrared and far-infrared absorption spectroscopy as well as modern facilities for genetically manipulating biomolecules. Physicists at the Center for Photonics Research develop and use near-field-scanning optical and infrared microscopy, atomic-force microscopy, and a full complement of molecular beam epitaxy and device processing facilities, the latter primarily with InGaAl-nitride wide-band-gap semiconductor materials and devices. The high-energy physics labs include facilities for the design, production, and testing of key components of various particle detectors. Examples are the muon detectors for the D0 detector at Fermilab, the forward muon system of the ATLAS detector at CERN, the muon g-2 experiment at Brookhaven, the MACRO cosmic-ray-shower detector in Italy, and the SuperKamiokande neutrino detector in Japan. All experimental groups benefit from uniquely strong scientific instrument and electronics design facilities. For computation, terminals and high-powered workstations are networked to two major departmental servers (SGI Challenge L and Sun UltraSPARC Enterprise 3000) as well as computer clusters provided by the University for general student use. In addition, students can have access to the University's high-end computational resources, which include an SGI/Cray Origin 2000 supercomputer with 192 processors (75 Gflops), a 38-processor SGI PowerChallengeArray, advanced visualization facilities, and an external connection to the new vBNS (a prototype of Internet II).
Financial Aid	Financial aid is available for qualified students in the form of teaching fellowships, research assistantships, and University fellowships, as well as many national fellowships such as that sponsored by the NSF. Typically, these awards provide between $12,500 and $18,750 in stipend support and a full-tuition scholarship.
Cost of Study	For 1998–99, tuition costs for a normal two-semester load for graduate students (three semester courses) were $22,108, including fees. Books and other expenses cost an additional $400.
Living and Housing Costs	There is limited graduate housing available on the Boston University campus at approximately $9500 per year for room and board. However, students generally rent apartments in the Boston area. The cost of apartments varies widely, depending on the area.
Student Group	Currently, the department has approximately 75 graduate students engaged in work toward the Ph.D. and M.A. degrees, and it prides itself on the close contact maintained between students and faculty members.
Student Outcomes	Recent Ph.D. recipients from the Department of Physics have been awarded the Wigner Fellowship at Oak Ridge, National Research Council Postdoctoral Fellowships, and the IBM Supercomputer Research Award, among others. Other graduates have gone on to permanent positions at Bell Laboratories, NEC Corporation, NASA, and NIST.
Location	Boston University is located in Boston, Massachusetts, which is a major metropolitan center of cultural, scholarly, scientific, and technological activity. Besides Boston University, there are many major academic institutions in the area. Facilities of the local universities, if needed, are easily accessible. Colloquium programs in the area give graduate students a special opportunity to learn the current status of physics research.
The University and The Department	Boston University is a private urban university with a faculty of 3,133 members and a student population of 29,171. The University consists of fifteen schools and colleges.
	The Department of Physics is part of the College of Arts and Sciences and the Graduate School. In the recent past, the department has experienced significant growth. The department was the first to move into the Science and Engineering Complex. The Graduate Student Association is represented on the faculty Graduate Committee and has a major input in policies concerning graduate affairs in the department.
Applying	The application deadlines are January 15 for fall admission and November 1 for spring admission. For admission to the graduate programs, a bachelor's degree in physics or astronomy is required, with no minimum undergraduate GPA specified. Scores on the General Test and the Subject Test in physics of the GRE are required. The acceptable score for admission is dependent on the applicant's overall record; there is no specified minimum. Students from non-English-speaking countries are required to demonstrate proficiency in English by earning a minimum acceptable score of 280 on the computer-based Test of English as a Foreign Language (TOEFL).
Correspondence and Information	Chair, Graduate Admissions Committee Department of Physics Boston University 590 Commonwealth Avenue Boston, Massachusetts 02215 Telephone: 617-353-2623

Boston University

THE FACULTY AND THEIR RESEARCH

Professors
Steven Paul Ahlen, Ph.D., Berkeley, 1976. Experimental astrophysics, heavy-ion physics, monopole and quark searches.
Rama Bansil, Ph.D., Rochester, 1974. Biophysics, polymers.
Edward C. Booth, Emeritus; Ph.D., Johns Hopkins, 1955. Intermediate-energy particle physics.
Kenneth Brecher, joint appointment with the Department of Astronomy; Ph.D., MIT, 1969. Theoretical astrophysics, relativity, cosmology.
Bernard Chasan, Ph.D., Cornell, 1961. Biophysics.
Robert S. Cohen, Emeritus; Ph.D., Yale, 1948. Philosophical and historical foundations of physics.
Ernesto Corinaldesi, Emeritus; Ph.D., Manchester (England), 1951. Quantum mechanics.
Alvaro DeRújula, joint appointment with CERN; Ph.D., Madrid, 1968. Theoretical particle physics, phenomenology.
Dean S. Edmonds Jr., Emeritus; Ph.D., MIT, 1958. Electronics and instrumentation.
Maged El-Batanouny, Ph.D., California, Davis, 1978. Surface physics, solitons.
Wolfgang Franzen, Emeritus; Ph.D., Pennsylvania, 1949. Atomic physics, surface physics.
Sheldon Glashow, Distinguished Physicist and Research Scholar (Harvard); Ph.D., Harvard, 1958. Theoretical particle physics.
William S. Hellman, Ph.D., Syracuse, 1961. Elementary particle theory.
William Klein, Ph.D., Temple, 1972. Condensed-matter theory.
Frank Krienen, Emeritus Professor of Engineering and Applied Physics; I.R., Amsterdam, 1947. Experimental particle and accelerator physics, muon g-2.
Kenneth D. Lane, Ph.D., Johns Hopkins, 1970. Theoretical high-energy physics.
James Miller, Ph.D., Carnegie Mellon, 1974. Intermediate- and high-energy experimental physics, muon g-2, CP violation.
Theodore Moustakas, joint appointment in the College of Engineering; Ph.D., Columbia, 1974. Synthetic novel materials.
So-Young Pi, Ph.D., SUNY at Stony Brook, 1974. Field theory, theoretical elementary particle physics.
Claudio Rebbi, Ph.D., Turin (Italy), 1967. Theoretical physics, lattice quantum chromodynamics, computational physics.
Sidney Redner, Ph.D., MIT, 1977. Statistical and polymer physics.
B. Lee Roberts, Ph.D., William and Mary, 1974. Intermediate- and high-energy experimental physics, muon g-2, CP violation.
James Rohlf, Ph.D., Caltech, 1980. Experimental particle physics, hadron collider physics.
Kenneth Rothschild, Ph.D., MIT, 1973. Biophysics, molecular electronics, physics of vision.
Abner Shimony, Emeritus; Ph.D. (philosophy), Yale, 1953; Ph.D. (physics), Princeton, 1962. Philosophical and historical foundations of physics, theoretical quantum mechanics.
William J. Skocpol, Ph.D., Harvard, 1974. Experimental condensed-matter physics.
John Stachel, Curator of Einstein papers in the United States; Ph.D., Stevens, 1952. General relativity, foundations of relativistic space-time theories.
H. Eugene Stanley, Ph.D., Harvard, 1967. Phase transitions, scaling, polymer physics, fractals and chaos.
James L. Stone, Ph.D., Michigan, 1976. Experimental particle physics and astrophysics, neutrinos, proton decay, monopole studies.
Lawrence R. Sulak, Ph.D., Princeton, 1970. Experimental particle physics, proton decay, monopoles, muon g-2, neutrinos.
Charles R. Willis, Emeritus; Ph.D., Syracuse, 1957. Theory of interaction of radiation with matter, statistical physics.
J. Scott Whitaker, Ph.D., Berkeley, 1976. Experimental colliding-beam physics, supersymmetric particle searches.
George O. Zimmerman, Ph.D., Yale, 1963. Low-temperature physics, magnetism.

Associate Professors
John Butler, Ph.D., Stanford, 1986. Experimental high-energy physics.
R. Sekhar Chivukula, Ph.D., Harvard, 1987. Elementary particle theory.
Andrew G. Cohen, Ph.D., Harvard, 1986. Elementary particle physics.
Shyamsunder Erramilli, Ph.D., Illinois, 1986. Biophysics.
Bennett B. Goldberg, Ph.D., Brown, 1987. Condensed-matter physics.
Karl Ludwig, Ph.D., Stanford, 1986. Experimental condensed-matter physics.
Ganpathy Murthy, Ph.D., Yale, 1987. Condensed-matter theory.
Elizabeth H. Simmons, Ph.D., Harvard, 1990. Theoretical elementary particle physics.
Kevin E. Smith, Ph.D., Yale, 1988. Experimental condensed-matter physics.

Assistant Professors
Robert Carey, Ph.D., Harvard, 1989. Experimental high-energy physics.
Claudio Chamon, Ph.D., MIT, 1996. Condensed matter theory.
Michael F. Crommie, Ph.D., Berkeley, 1991. Surface physics.
Ulrich Heintz, Ph.D., SUNY at Stony Brook, 1991. High-energy physics.
William Worstell, Ph.D., Harvard, 1986. Experimental particle physics, monopole searches, muon g-2.

Lecturers
Andrew G. Duffy, Ph.D., Queen's at Kingston, 1995.
Thomas C. Hayes, J.D., Harvard, 1969. Electronics.

Research Faculty and Staff
Yakir Aharonov, Ph.D., Bristol (England), 1960.
Luis Amaral, Ph.D., Boston University, 1996.
Sergey Buldyrev, Ph.D., Leningrad State, 1988.
Yu-Cheng Chao, Ph.D., Linköping (Sweden), 1996.
Antonio Coniglio, Ph.D., Naples, 1962.
Luis Cruz, Ph.D., MIT, 1994.
Laurent Duda, Ph.D., Uppsala (Sweden), 1996.
Efstratios Efstathiadis, Ph.D., CUNY, City College, 1996.
Nicholas Evans, Ph.D., Southampton (England), 1993.
David Francis, Ph.D., Liverpool, 1988.
Peter Garik, Ph.D., Cornell, 1981.
Paul Gerald, Ph.D., MIT, 1992.
Alec Habig, Ph.D., Indiana, 1996.
Shlomo Havlin, Ph.D., Bar-Ilan.
Mi Kyuny Hong, Ph.D., Illinois, 1988.
Michael Kaplan, Ph.D., Moscow, 1985.
Edward Kearns, Ph.D., Harvard, 1990.
Paul Krapivsky, Ph.D., Moscow Physical Technical Institute, 1991.
Edyta Kryzmanska-Olejnik, M.S., Mickiewicz (Poland), 1986.
Brigitia Kutnjak-Urbanc, Ph.D., Ljubljana (Slovenia), 1993.
Kent Lauritsen, Ph.D., Aarhus (Denmark), 1994.

Jacques Mainville, Ph.D., McGill, 1991.
Sergey Mamaev, Ph.D., Novosibirsk (Russia), 1987.
Margaret Marynowski, Ph.D., Boston University, 1997.
Martin Meyer, Ph.D., Giessen (Germany), 1996.
Sava Milosevic, Ph.D., MIT, 1972.
Theodore Moustakas, Ph.D., Columbia, 1974.
Meenakshi Narain, Ph.D., SUNY at Stony Brook, 1991.
Jerzy Olejnik, Ph.D., Mickiewica (Poland), 1991.
C. K. Peng, Ph.D., Boston University, 1993.
Martin Schmaltz, Ph.D., California, San Diego, 1995.
Kate Scholberg, Ph.D., Caltech, 1996.
Francesco Sciortino, Ph.D., Palermo (Italy), 1988.
Hannah M. Sevian, Ph.D., Columbia, 1992.
James Shank, Ph.D., Berkeley, 1988.
James Sullivan, Ph.D., Chicago, 1970.
Raman Sundrum, Ph.D., Yale, 1990.
Cristopher Walter, Ph.D., Caltech, 1996.
Stacey Williams, Ph.D., California, Santa Cruz, 1993.
Jinyu Xue, Ph.D., La Trobe (Australia), 1998.
Hui Zhong, Ph.D., CUNY, 1998.

BROWN UNIVERSITY

Department of Physics

Program of Study	The department offers a program of study designed primarily for students seeking the degree of Doctor of Philosophy in physics. The Master of Science in physics is also offered.
	Requirements for the Ph.D. are a core of nine semester courses at the graduate level in physics and mathematics; some specialization, normally three semester courses, in advanced graduate study; a qualifying examination and a preliminary examination in general physics; a thesis describing the results of independent research; and an oral examination based on the thesis and research. Students normally complete their formal course work and begin research after two years. All graduate students are encouraged to remain on campus during the summer for study and research.
Research Facilities	The physics department is housed in the seven-story Barus and Holley Building, built in 1965. Nearby are the University computing laboratory, with two IBM computers, linked to the Barus and Holley Building, and a fourteen-story science library that houses the University's excellent collection. High-energy facilities at the Stanford Linear Accelerator Center, at Brookhaven National Laboratory, and at Fermi National Accelerator Laboratory are used by Brown research groups.
Financial Aid	Financial aid includes University fellowships, which cover full tuition and include a stipend sufficient for living costs, and NSF graduate fellowships, which are awarded directly by the granting organization. The most common form of aid is an assistantship—teaching, research, or a combination—which allows three-quarter-time study. Stipends for assistantships cover tuition and defray some living costs. Assistantships carry a total equivalent value of $32,116 for the nine-month academic year 1999–2000. Almost all graduate students in the department receive some type of financial aid.
Cost of Study	Tuition is $24,624 for the academic year 1999–2000, and $18,468 for assistants studying three-quarter time. After the equivalent of three full-time years, the student pays only a registration fee of $1477 per semester while completing his or her work.
Living and Housing Costs	The University's Graduate Center provides housing for both men and women at moderate cost. Students also live in apartments and rented rooms in the residential area surrounding the University. Meals are available at campus dining halls.
Student Group	There are 5,722 undergraduate students and 1,579 graduate students at Brown University. There are 82 graduate students in physics.
Location	The Brown University campus is a few minutes' walk from the center of the city of Providence, the capital of Rhode Island. The metropolitan area has a population of half a million. It is an active commercial center and port and has theaters, concert and symphony halls, and museums. It is on main highway, rail, bus, and air routes. Boston is an hour away by car and 45 minutes by train. New York City is about 3½ hours away by car, train, or bus and 40 minutes by plane. Rhode Island has an extensive coastline, and there are many excellent beaches. Newport is a half-hour drive away. The rest of New England is also within easy driving distance: Cape Cod, 1½ hours; the Berkshires, 2 hours; the White Mountains of New Hampshire, 4½ hours; and the Maine coast, a little over 2 hours.
The University	Founded in 1764, Brown University first awarded advanced degrees in 1888. Instruction and research in the sciences are carried on within the framework of a strong and comprehensive program in the liberal arts. The University has consciously maintained a small, select student body and a faculty that is active in research and enthusiastic in teaching. A low student-faculty ratio permits small classes and individual attention to each student.
Applying	Completed applications for the following fall are due in the Office of the Dean of the Graduate School by January 2. Applications received after this date will be considered, although much of the available financial aid is committed by mid-March. It is strongly recommended that applicants take the Graduate Record Examinations. Applicants whose native language is not English must submit scores on the Test of English as a Foreign Language (TOEFL).
Correspondence and Information	Professor D. Cutts, Chairman Department of Physics Brown University Providence, Rhode Island 02912 Telephone: 401-863-2644

Brown University

THE FACULTY AND AREAS OF RESEARCH

T. Ala-Nissila, J. C. Baird, R. H. Brandenberger, L. N. Cooper, E. Crisman, D. Cutts, C. Elbaum, P. J. Estrup, G. S. Guralnik, J. S. Hoftan, A. Houghton, A. Jevicki, K. Kang, J. M. Kosterlitz, G. Landsberg, R. E. Lanou, N. M. Lawandy, X. S. Ling, D. A. Lowe, H. J. Maris, J. B. Marston, A. V. Nurmikko, R. Partridge, R. A. Pelcovits, G. L. Petersen, S. Ramgoolam, G. M. Seidel, C -I. Tan, D. M. Targan, G. S. Tucker, J. M. Valles Jr., G. Watts, G. Xiao, S. C. Ying.

RESEARCH ACTIVITIES

Physics of Elementary Particles:
Theory: Current activities include studies in quantum field theory, quantum chromodynamics, functional formulations and path-integral techniques, nonperturbative methods in field theory, solitons, monopoles, spontaneous symmetry breaking, lattice field theories, renormalization group, field theoretic approaches to condensed matter, gauge theories of weak and electromagnetic interactions, grand unification theory and phenomenology, flavor dynamics and mixings, phenomenology of scattering and production processes, the quantum theory of gravitation, supersymmetry, supergravity, superstrings, and cosmology.
Experiment: The properties of elementary particles and their interactions are being investigated, with current effort focused on the study of proton-antiproton collisions at the highest available energy in the D0 experiment at Fermilab and the study of low-energy neutrinos originating in the sun. The D0 program is involved in a wide range of investigations, including studies of top quark properties, searches for supersymmetry, and measurement of the properties of the electroweak and strong interactions. High-performance computer networks and videoconferencing provide a close link between Brown and Fermilab. The Heron project is seeking to understand the solar neutrino problem and search for dark matter using a novel liquid helium detector.

Physics of Condensed Matter:
Theory: Research problems currently under investigation include the quantum mechanical many-body problem; the properties of models relevant to high Tc superconductors and heavy fermion systems, e.g., the Anderson and Hubbard models, and quantum antiferromagnets; the study of the elementary excitations and the optical and transport properties of artificially structured materials; the effect of disorder in solids; Josephson junction arrays in a magnetic field—classical and quantum aspects; liquid crystals (including large-scale numerical simulations); surface reconstruction; microscopic theory of surface diffusion and vibrational relaxation; stability and growth of strained epitaxial layers; and charge transfer at surfaces.
Experiment: Studies of magnetoconductive, optical, and mechanical properties of amorphous metals and semiconductors, magnetic solids, and high Tc superconductors; mesoscopic superconducting arrays and colloidal model systems; flux lattices in type-II superconductors; low-temperature scanning probe techniques and devices; giant and colossal magnetoresistance effects in magnetic superlattices, granular solids, and oxides; electron-electron interactions in two-dimensional electron systems at low temperatures, electronic and magnetic properties of artificial superlattices, quantum wires, and dots; the quantum Hall effect; nonlinear optical phenomena and plasma dynamics studies in semiconductors using picosecond and femtosecond laser pulses; studies of ultrasonic and thermal properties of solids using picosecond laser pulses; holographic studies; properties of liquid and solid He4 and He3, including elementary excitations and their interactions cavitation and levitation of superfluid He4; NMR studies of the structure and bonding of crystalline and glassy solids; nuclear quadrupole resonance (NQR) studies of electronic distributions in molecules of biological importance and in inorganic solids; studies of chemisorption phenomena, surface band structure, reconstruction, and two-dimensional phase transitions by low-energy electron diffraction, Auger and photoelectron spectroscopy, electron energy-loss spectroscopy (EELS), and related techniques.

Astrophysics and Cosmology:
Work to develop detectors for solar neutrinos and dark matter is in progress. Theories of the origin of structure based on quantum field theory and elementary particle physics (e.g., inflationary Universe model, cosmic string theory) are being developed, and new quantitative predictions of these theories for new experiments are being derived. An active program to measure the anisotropy and polarization of the cosmic microwave background is underway. X-ray detectors for astrophysics and laboratory applications are being developed.

Neural Science:
The major goal of the research is to elucidate the biological mechanisms that underlie learning and memory and to find principles of organization that can account for experimental data on the cellular level. Detailed objectives include clarifying the dependence of learning on synaptic modification, elucidating the principles that govern synapse formation or modification, and using principles of organization that can account for observations on a cellular level to construct network models that can learn, associate, and reproduce such higher-level cognitive acts as abstraction, computation, and language acquisition.

A view of the Sciences Library and CIT Building.

A graduate student studying in the Barus and Holley Building, Physics Library.

The Barus and Holley Building.

CALIFORNIA INSTITUTE OF TECHNOLOGY

Department of Physics
Department of Astronomy

Programs of Study

The departments offer programs of study leading to the degree of Doctor of Philosophy (Ph.D.) in physics or astronomy. A Master of Science (M.S.) degree may be awarded upon completion of a one-year program of courses. Students are not admitted to work toward a terminal M.S. degree. Requirements for the Ph.D. include passing a written and oral candidacy exam, writing a thesis that describes the results of independent research, and passing a final oral exam based on this thesis and research.

Some students admitted into the physics department find their research interests are best matched to Caltech faculty members outside the department. Students whose interests are primarily in applied physics may condider applying directly to that department. Students whose interests are primarily in pure astronomy may consider applying to the astronomy department.

Research Facilities

A 6-MeV tandem accelerator features high-intensity, high-transmission efficiency and superb energy and position resolution. Equipment is also available for precision investigations of nuclear gamma and beta rays. Equipment for experiments in high-energy physics is designed and constructed, and the resulting data analyzed, in Caltech laboratories. Other experimental facilities include one 130-foot and two 90-foot movable and steerable radio antennas with a 10-meter millimeter dish, a low-temperature laboratory, and facilities for cosmic-ray research on the ground, in balloons, and in spacecraft. The facilities of the nearby Jet Propulsion Laboratory (JPL) are often used. The Mount Palomar observatory is an outstanding facility, as is the 10-meter Keck telescope on Mauna Kea in Hawaii. The Infrared Processing and Analysis Center (IPAC) is a major participant in several infrared astrophysics missions, including the Space Infrared Telescope Facility (SIRTF).

Financial Aid

Institute fellowships are available with a current stipend of $16,224 plus tuition for the academic year and summer. In addition, the physics department awards the Robert A. Millikan and the Richard P. Feynman fellowships with current stipends of $17,730. The astronomy department awards the Van Maanen Fellowship, which carries a stipend of $18,500.

Graduate teaching assistants are assigned duties requiring a total of 15 hours per week during the academic year. The current stipend ranges from $11,187 to $12,780. Additional financial support is also available for graduate teaching assistants to continue their research during the summer.

Graduate research assistants work on various research projects for 15 hours per week during the academic year and 30 hours per week during the summer. Physics stipends currently range from $17,730 to $19,170 per calendar year, and astronomy stipends range from $18,500 to $19,100.

Cost of Study

Tuition in 1999–2000 is $19,260 for the academic year. There is a general deposit of $25. Books and supplies vary in cost; a typical figure might be $500 per year. All students receive a special award to cover tuition.

Living and Housing Costs

The cost of accommodations for single students in the Catalina graduate apartment complex ranges from $4224 to $5028; the range is $8700 to $10,056 for married students. This covers rent for twelve months; utilities are extra. Housing is also available in the residential areas that surround the campus.

Student Group

Caltech has approximately 1,000 undergraduate students and about 1,000 graduate students, 25 percent of whom are women. There are about 135 graduate students in physics and about 30 in astronomy, all of whom are receiving financial support. Admission to graduate study is highly competitive; about 30 new students are admitted each year in physics, and about 5 are admitted in astronomy.

There are more than 19,000 Institute alumni around the world, many of whom are eminent in their fields of science and engineering. Twenty-six alumni are recipients of the Nobel Prize.

Location

Pasadena, a city of approximately 140,000 inhabitants, is located 10 miles northeast of Los Angeles and 30 miles inland from the Pacific Ocean, at the foot of the San Gabriel Mountains. The city contains both residential and light industrial areas. Caltech's 124-acre campus is located in the center of a residential area close to shopping, entertainment, and recreational facilities. Hiking, camping, skiing, and many cultural activities of the large metropolitan area may be reached in an hour or less by car. Any part of southern California can be explored on a weekend.

There are numerous recreational facilities in the vicinity. Hiking, camping, and occasionally skiing are immediately at hand in the mountains. The Pacific Ocean is less than an hour away by car, and any part of southern California can be explored on a weekend.

The Institute

Throughout its history, Caltech has maintained a small, select student body and a faculty that is unusually active in research. The faculty currently numbers about 1,100 members, including postdoctoral scholars; of this number, more than 275 are full professors.

There is a strong emphasis on fundamental studies in science and engineering with a minimum of specialization. There is also considerable emphasis on humanistic studies. Humanities have always played an essential role in the undergraduate curriculum, and undergraduates can major in these areas.

Musical and dramatic events are presented on campus throughout the year.

Applying

Students are admitted only in September, and applications should be received by January 15. It is strongly advised that applicants take the GRE General Test and physics Subject Test by the October test date. Application materials may be obtained from the Institute Graduate Office, mail code 02-31.

Correspondence and Information

For the physics program:
Donna Driscoll
Physics Graduate Coordinator
Mail Code 103-33
California Institute of Technology
Pasadena, California 91125
World Wide Web: http://www.pma.caltech.edu/GSR/

For the astronomy program:
S. Phinney
Astronomy Option Representative
Mail Code 130-33
California Institute of Technology
Pasadena, California 91125
World Wide Web: http://www.astro.caltech.edu

California Institute of Technology

THE FACULTY AND THEIR RESEARCH

B. C. Barish, Ph.D., Berkeley, 1962. Experimental high-energy physics, monopole searches, e^+e^- collisions.

R. D. Blandford, Ph.D., Cambridge, 1974. Astrophysical plasmas, pulsars, active galactic nuclei.

J. G. Cohen, Ph.D., Caltech, 1971. Interstellar medium, stellar spectroscopy, globular clusters, astronomical instrumentation.

M. C. Cross, Ph.D., Cambridge, 1975. Condensed-matter theory, nonequilibrium physics.

S. G. Djorgovski, Ph.D., Berkeley, 1985. Galaxies at high redshift, structures and dynamics of globular clusters.

R. P. W. Drever, Ph.D., Glasgow, 1958. Experimental gravitation, gravitational wave detection.

J. P. Eisenstein, Ph.D., Berkeley, 1980. Experimental condensed matter, low-dimensional electronic systems.

B. W. Filippone, Ph.D., Chicago, 1982. Experimental nuclear physics, nuclear astrophysics.

S. C. Frautschi, Ph.D., Stanford, 1958. Theoretical physics.

P. M. Goldreich, Ph.D., Cornell, 1960. Theoretical astrophysics.

D. L. Goodstein, Ph.D., Washington (Seattle), 1965. Two-dimensional matter, surfaces, phase transitions and interfaces, ballistic phonons, high-temperature superconductivity.

F. A. Harrison, Ph.D., Berkeley, 1993. X-ray and gamma-ray astrophysics and instrumentation.

D. Hitlin, Ph.D., Columbia, 1968. Experimental high-energy physics.

E. W. Hughes, Ph.D., Columbia, 1987. Experimental high-energy and nuclear physics.

C. E. Jones, Ph.D., Caltech, 1991. Experimental nuclear physics, parity violations and electron scattering.

R. W. Kavanagh, Ph.D., Caltech, 1956. Experimental nuclear physics, nuclear astrophysics.

H. J. Kimble, Ph.D., Rochester, 1978. Experimental quantum optics.

S. E. Koonin, Ph.D., MIT, 1975. Theoretical nuclear and many-body physics.

S. R. Kulkarni, Ph.D., Berkeley, 1983. Interstellar medium, pulsars, compact objects, radio and optical interferometry.

A. E. Lange, Ph.D., Berkeley, 1987. Submillimeter-wave astronomy.

K. G. Libbrecht, Ph.D., Princeton, 1984. Experimental quantum optics, solar and stellar acoustic oscillations, solar phenomena, solar oblateness.

H. Mabuchi, Ph.D., Caltech, 1998. Experimental quantum optics.

C. Martin, Ph.D., Berkeley, 1986. Ultraviolet astronomy.

J. K. McCarthy, Ph.D., Caltech, 1988. Observational astronomy.

R. D. McKeown, Ph.D., Princeton, 1979. Experimental nuclear physics, electromagnetic structure of nuclear matter and nucleons at high-momentum transfer, development of optically pumped polarized ^{3}He targets.

M. R. Metzger, Ph.D., MIT, 1994. Astronomical observations and instrumentation.

R. A. Mewaldt, Ph.D., Washington (St. Louis), 1971. Experimental galactic, solar, and interplanetary cosmic rays.

R. P. Mount, Ph.D., Cambridge, 1975. Experimental high-energy physics.

G. Neugebauer, Ph.D., Caltech, 1960. Observational infrared astronomy.

H. Newman, Sc.D., MIT, 1973. Experimental high-energy physics.

T. J. Pearson, Ph.D., Cambridge, 1977. Active galactic nuclei, cosmic background radiation, radio interferometry.

C. W. Peck, Ph.D., Caltech, 1964. Experimental high-energy physics, electron-positron colliding beams, monopole searches.

T. Phillips, D.Phil., Oxford, 1964. Submillimeter-wave astronomy.

E. S. Phinney, Ph.D., Cambridge, 1983. Active galactic nuclei, high-energy and relativistic astrophysics.

J. Pine, Ph.D., Cornell, 1956. Biophysics, experimental physics.

H. D. Politzer, Ph.D., Harvard, 1974. Theoretical physics.

F. C. Porter, Ph.D., Berkeley, 1977. Experimental high-energy physics, e^+e^- collisions.

J. Preskill, Ph.D., Harvard, 1980. Elementary particle theory.

T. Prince, Ph.D., Chicago, 1978. Gamma-ray astronomy, ground-based optical interferometry, concurrent computing.

A. C. S. Readhead, Ph.D., Cambridge, 1972. Astrophysics.

I. N. Reid, Ph.D., Edinburgh, 1983. Galactic structure, low-mass stars, chromospheric and coronal activity, stellar mass function.

M. L. Roukes, Ph.D., Cornell, 1985. Experimental condensed-matter physics, mesoscopic systems at ultralow temperatures, biophysics with nanostructures.

A. I. Sargent, Ph.D., Caltech, 1977. Millimeter and infrared studies of star and planetary system formation.

W. L. W. Sargent, Ph.D., Manchester, 1959. Astrophysics, radio galaxies, evolution of galaxies, absorption-line spectra of quasars.

A. Scherer, Ph.D., New Mexico Tech, 1985. Nanofabrication, microoptics and integrated optoelectronics, surface micromachining.

J. H. Schwarz, Ph.D., Berkeley, 1966. Theoretical high-energy physics, especially superstring theory.

N. Z. Scoville, Ph.D., Princeton, 1972. Millimeter and infrared studies of star formation and galactic structure.

B. Simon, Ph.D., Princeton, 1970. Mathematical physics.

T. Soifer, Ph.D., Cornell, 1972. Infrared astronomy.

C. Steidel, Ph.D., Caltech, 1990. Optical astronomy, quasars.

E. C. Stone, Ph.D., Chicago, 1963. Experimental galactic and solar cosmic rays, magnetosphere physics.

K. S. Thorne, Ph.D., Princeton, 1965. Relativistic astrophysics, gravitational physics.

T. A. Tombrello, Ph.D., Rice, 1961. Application of ion beam techniques to material science and surface science, modeling of geophysical processes, radiation damage.

P. Vogel, Ph.D., Joint Institute for Nuclear Research (Russia), 1966. Nuclear theory, mesic X rays, neutrinos, fission.

R. E. Vogt, Ph.D., Chicago, 1961. Experimental astrophysics, experimental gravitation, gravitational wave detection.

A. J. Weinstein, Ph.D., Harvard, 1983. Experimental high-energy physics.

M. B. Wise, Ph.D., Stanford, 1980. Theoretical particle physics, cosmology.

N. C. Yeh, Ph.D., MIT, 1988. Experimental condensed-matter physics, superconductivity, magnetism, phase transitions.

F. Zachariasen, Ph.D., Chicago, 1957. Theory of high-energy physics.

A. H. Zewail, Ph.D., Pennsylvania, 1974. Chemical physics.

H. Zirin, Ph.D., Harvard, 1953. Solar phenomena; flares, stellar spectroscopy, solar radio astronomy.

J. Zmuidzinas, Ph.D., Berkeley, 1987. Submillimeter astronomy and instrumentation.

RESEARCH AREAS

Theoretical

Astrophysics, condensed matter, elementary particles and fields, mathematical physics, nuclear physics, and relativity.

Experimental

Applied physics, astronomy, biophysics, condensed-matter physics, elementary particles and fields, gravitational physics, high-energy astrophysics, low-temperature physics, nuclear astrophysics, nuclear physics, observational astrophysics, solar physics, and quantum optics.

CARNEGIE MELLON UNIVERSITY

Mellon College of Science
Department of Physics

Programs of Study	The department is committed to providing an outstanding graduate education in a broad range of areas at the leading edge of scientific research. Students have the opportunity to study the areas of astrophysics, high-energy physics, nuclear physics, or condensed-matter physics or to do interdisciplinary work with chemistry, biology, materials, science, computer science, robotics, and engineering. The department has a student-faculty ratio in the area of 2:1.

Candidates for the degree of Doctor of Philosophy in the field of physics or applied physics should expect to spend at least four years or the academic equivalent in full-time graduate study that includes a minimum of one year at CMU. The first three semesters emphasize concentrated study of fundamental courses. The normal course sequence can be altered as appropriate to accommodate advanced students or the need to provide additional background course work at the advanced undergraduate level. After two and three semesters, respectively, students take the first and second parts of the Qualifying Examination. Following successful completion of these examinations, or sooner, the student seeks affiliation with one of the department's research groups and selects a subject area for thesis. Formal admission to candidacy for the Ph.D. depends on acceptable performance in course work, teaching, and research, as well as the qualifying examinations.

The Master of Science degree in physics is awarded to those who demonstrate a mastery of advanced topics beyond the B.S. degree level. Wide latitude exists for students to tailor their programs toward professional goals. While it is possible to complete the requirements for a master's in physics in one semester, most students complete the program in three. Candidates must complete 96 units of course work with a B average or better, including at least 48 units in the Department of Physics, at least 24 additional units in physics or closely allied fields, and 10–12 units in advanced physics laboratory or equivalent.

Research Facilities

The department maintains facilities for condensed-matter and biological physics research, including apparatus for X-ray diffraction and reflection, laser spectroscopies, calorimetry, magnetic and electrical transport measurements, optical characterization of interfaces, scanning tunneling and atomic force microscopies, and sample preparation. Scattering experiments are carried out at a new X-ray facility that includes fix tube and rotating anode sources as well as at national synchrotron and neutron facilities. Collaborations with other departments provide access to additional facilities, including electron microscopies, optical microscopies, magnetic measurements, and fluids and interface characterization. High-energy research is carried out by colliding beams and counter groups, utilizing facilities at the Fermi National Accelerator Laboratory in Chicago, at CERN in Geneva, and at CESR in New York. A data analysis laboratory is maintained on campus, as are laboratories for the development of detection systems. The medium-energy nuclear physics group uses the facilities of CERN in Geneva, Brookhaven in New York, and the Thomas Jefferson National Accelerator Facility (formerly CEBAF) in Virginia. Astrophysical research is carried out using a variety of space-based and ground-based telescopes, including a facility at the South Pole. Departmental facilities include electronic and machine stops, numerous computer clusters, and a stock room. The University Computing Center operates an extensive system of networked scientific workstations and microcomputers with central file servers for research and educational applications.

Financial Aid

The Department of Physics generally provides full tuition and fees for all graduate students who are not supported in full by outside scholarships. Living stipends are provided via scholarships, teaching fellowships, and research assistantships. Additional financial support is usually available for research or teaching during the summer months.

Cost of Study

Tuition and fees are provided for all graduate students as described above.

Living and Housing Costs

In 1999, rental rates in the Pittsburgh area ranged from $475 to $725 per month for a one-bedroom apartment and $725 to $1225 per month for a three-bedroom apartment, depending upon location and amenities. Single rooms in shared houses ranged from $275 to $525 per month. Campus dining facilities are available.

Student Group

Currently, the physics department has approximately 60 graduate students, all fully supported on assistantships or fellowships. Carnegie Mellon University has 4,876 undergraduates and 2,894 graduate students and a faculty of 535.

Location

CMU is located in the Oakland section of Pittsburgh, an area known for its academic, cultural, and recreational attributes. The campus is minutes from downtown by public transportation in a city rated one of the most safe in America.

The University

The Mellon College of Science is part of a university that includes four undergraduate and three graduate schools renowned in the sciences, engineering, business, public policy, and the fine arts. Because CMU is small, its faculty members and students engage in an unusual degree of interdisciplinary research.

Applying

Application materials from qualified applicants should be received by February 1 to be assured priority consideration. Applications received before February 1 will be eligible for early decision consideration. Applications should include appropriate CMU forms, transcripts from colleges attended, three letters of professional reference, GRE scores, and, if the student's native language is not English, a TOEFL score.

Correspondence and Information

Chairman, Graduate Admissions Committee
Department of Physics
Carnegie Mellon University
Pittsburgh, Pennsylvania 15213-3890
Telephone: 412-268-2740
Fax: 412-681-0648
E-mail: physgrad@andrew.cmu.edu
World Wide Web: http://info.phys.cmu.edu/info_phys.html

Carnegie Mellon University

THE FACULTY AND THEIR RESEARCH

Luc Berger, Professor Emeritus, Ph.D., Lausanne (Switzerland), 1960. Experimental and theoretical solid-state physics, studies of metallic ferromagnets.

Roy A. Briere, Assistant Professor; Ph.D., Chicago, 1995. Experimental elementary particle physics, CP violation.

Richard M. Edelstein, Professor; Ph.D., Columbia, 1960. Experimental high-energy physics, dynamics of strong interactions.

Arnold Engler, Professor; Ph.D., Bern (Switzerland), 1953. Experimental high-energy physics, colliding beam techniques.

Randall M. Feenstra, Professor; Ph.D., Caltech, 1982. Experimental solid-state physics, scanning tunnelling microscopy of semiconductor surfaces.

Thomas A. Ferguson, Professor; Ph.D., UCLA, 1978. Experimental high-energy physics, colliding beam techniques.

John G. Fetkovich; Professor; Ph.D., Carnegie Mellon, 1959.

Gregg B. Franklin, Professor; Ph.D., MIT, 1980. Experimental nuclear physics, strangeness in nucleon and nuclei.

Simeon A. Friedberg, Professor Emeritus; Sc.D., Carnegie Mellon, 1951. Experimental solid-state and low-temperature physics, magnetic and thermal properties of solids.

Stephen Garoff, Professor and Associate Department Head; Ph.D., Harvard, 1977. Experimental condensed-matter physics, surfaces and interfaces.

Frederick Gilman, Buhl Professor of Physics; Ph.D., Princeton, 1965. Theoretical elementary particle physics, CP violation, physics of heavy quarks and heavy lepton.

Richard E. Griffiths, Professor; Ph.D., Leicester (England), 1972. Experimental astrophysics, observational cosmology using Hubble Space Telescope.

Robert B. Griffiths, Otto Stern Professor of Physics; Ph.D., Stanford, 1962. Theoretical physics, statistical mechanics and thermodynamics of phase transitions, foundations of quantum mechanics.

James B. Hannon, Assistant Professor; Ph.D., Pennsylvania, 1994. Experimental condensed-matter physics, metal and semiconductor surface science, surface growth mechanisms.

Richard F. Holman, Professor; Ph.D., John Hopkins, 1982. Theoretical particle physics/cosmology.

Leonard S. Kisslinger, Professor; Ph.D., Indiana, 1956. Theoretical nuclear and particle physics, nonperturbative QCD.

Robert W. Kraemer, Professor; Ph.D., Johns Hopkins, 1962. Experimental particle physics, colliding beam techniques.

Michael J. Levine, Professor; Ph.D., Caltech, 1963. Theoretical elementary particle physics, symbolic computer methods in quantum electrodynamics.

Ling-Fong Li, Professor; Ph.D., Pennsylvania, 1970. Theoretical elementary particle physics, unified theories of particle interactions.

Sara A. Majetich, Professor; Ph.D., Georgia, 1987. Experimental condensed-matter physics, semiconductor and magnetic nanocrystalites.

Curtis A. Meyer, Associate Professor; Ph.D., Berkeley, 1987. Experimental medium energy, nuclear physics; meson and glueball spectroscopy; strangeness in physics.

John F. Nagle, Professor; Ph.D., Yale, 1965. Experimental and theoretical biological physics, statistical mechanics of phase transitions, biomembranes.

Robert C. Nichol, Assistant Professor; Ph.D., Edinburgh, 1992. Experimental astrophysics, observational cosmology using X-ray and optical observations.

Jeffrey B. Peterson, Associate Professor; Ph.D., Berkeley, 1985. Astrophysics, observational cosmology.

Michael Procario, Associate Professor; Ph.D., Wisconsin, 1986. Experimental high-energy physics, hadrons containing charm or bottom quarks.

Brian P. Quinn, Associate Professor; Ph.D., MIT, 1984. Experimental medium energy/nuclear physics, production and interactions of strange hadrons, strange sea quarks in the nucleon.

Kavan U. Ratnatunga, Senior Research Scientist; Ph.D., Australian National, 1983. Experimental astrophysics, observational cosmology using the Hubble Space Telescope.

John A. Rayne, Professor Emeritus; Ph.D., Chicago, 1954. Experimental solid-state physics, electronic and magnetic properties of metals and alloys, ultrasonic absorption in solids.

Frederick Reif, Professor; Ph.D., Harvard, 1953. Physics education.

A. Katherine Romer, Research Scientist; Ph.D., Edinburgh, 1995. Experimental astrophysics, observational cosmology.

Ira Z. Rothstein, Assistant Professor; Ph.D., Maryland College Park, 1992. Theoretical elementary particle physics, heavy quark physics, interface of cosmological and particle physics.

James S. Russ, Professor; Ph.D., Princeton, 1966. Experimental high-energy physics, heavy quark physics.

Reinhard A. Schumacher, Professor; Ph.D., MIT, 1983. Experimental medium energy/nuclear physics, production and interactions of strange hadrons, strange sea quarks in the nucleon.

Robert T. Schumacher, Professor Emeritus; Ph.D., Illinois, 1955. Musical acoustics, magnetic resonance in solids.

Robert F. Sekerka, University Professor of Physics; Ph.D., Harvard, 1965. Theoretical problems in materials science.

Bruce A. Sherwood, Professor; Ph.D., Chicago, 1967. Development of computer-based education systems and physics education.

Raymond A. Sorensen, Professor Emeritus; Ph.D., Carnegie Mellon, 1958. Theoretical nuclear physics, static and dynamic properties of nuclei.

Roger B. Sutton, Professor Emeritus; Ph.D., Princeton, 1943. Elementary particle physics, experimental physics.

Robert H. Swendsen, Professor and Department Head; Ph.D., Pennsylvania, 1971. Theoretical physics, computer simulations in condensed matter, statistical mechanics of phase transitions and biological molecules.

Robert M. Suter, Professor; Ph.D., Clark, 1978. Experimental condensed-matter physics, X-ray and neutron scattering studies.

Ned S. VanderVen, Professor; Ph.D., Princeton, 1962. Experimental solid-state physics, electron and nuclear spin resonance in solids.

Helmut Vogel, Professor; Ph.D., Erlangen (Germany), 1979. Experimental high-energy physics, colliding beam techniques.

Michael Widom, Professor; Ph.D., Chicago, 1983. Theoretical condensed-matter physics, quasicrystals, ferrofluids.

Lincoln Wolfenstein, University Professor of Physics; Ph.D., Chicago, 1949. Theoretical elementary particle physics, weak interactions and symmetry principles.

Hugh D. Young, Professor; Ph.D., Carnegie Mellon, 1959. Physics education.

Research Activities

Experimental Astrophysics: Observational cosmology, measurements of anisotropy in the 2.7K cosmic background radiation at millimeter wavelengths using telescopes at the South Pole, development of high-sensitivity receivers at millimeter wavelengths, studies of galactic clustering and gravitational lensing. Early evolution of galaxies and the universe, using data from the Hubble Space Telescope. Study of clusters of galaxies, using X-ray and optical observation to provide information on the evolution of large-scale structure in the universe.

Experimental High-Energy Physics: Study of heavy quark production and decay properties at Fermilab. Studies of the properties of the Z° boson using the L3 detector at LEP (CERN). Preparation for physics at the LHC collider.

Theoretical High-Energy Physics: Quantum gauge field theories and their applications to experiments, weak interaction phenomenology, CP violation, heavy quark physics, problems at the interface between particle physics and cosmology, quantum electrodynamics and large-scale computations.

Experimental Medium-Energy Physics: Formation of hyper-nuclear and exotic strange systems, strangeness-changing weak decays, meson spectroscopy, electromagnetic reactions, antiproton reactions.

Theoretical Medium-Energy Physics: Nuclear models, nuclear reactions at medium and high energies, nuclear quark/glucon structure and interactions, QCD and weak interactions in nuclei.

Experimental Biological Physics: Structure and function of biomembranes employing x-ray scattering and density measurements. NMR studies of the structure of proteins and optical microscopic studies of cell structure (in collaboration with faculty members from other departments).

Theoretical Biological Physics: Theoretical analysis of biomembranes, Monte Carlo simulations of proteins.

Experimental Condensed-Matter Physics and Applied Physics: Properties and applications of nanoparticles and nanostructures; structure of thin organic and metal solid films; structure and properties of liquid/solid interfaces; wetting of fluids on solids; structure of semiconductor surfaces; influence of surface properties on semiconductor devices; magnetic films for data storage; development of NMR imaging and spectroscopy techniques; development of new optical microscopic techniques; computer vision; robotics, electron paramagnetic resonance; x-ray scattering from thin films and surfaces; physics of musical oscillators. Some activities are carried out in active collaboration with other departments, institutes, and centers in the science and engineering colleges.

Theoretical Condensed-Matter Physics: Nonlinear analysis and simulation of crystal growth; Monte Carlo studies of complex fluids, biological molecules, disordered solids, and phase transitions; modeling of quasicrystals, ferroelectrics, and incommensurate phases.

Foundations of Quantum Mechanics: Reformulation of quantum theory using consistent histories and decoherence.

SELECTED PUBLICATIONS

Berger, L. Multilayers as spin-wave emitting diodes. *J. Appl. Phys.* 81:4880, 1997.

Cleo Collaboration: Asner, D., et al. **(R. A. Briere).** Radiative decay modes of the D^0 meson. *Phys. Rev. D* 58:09001, 1998.

Cleo Collaboration: Asner, D., et al. **(R. A. Briere).** New limits for neutrinoless tau decays. *Phys. Rev. D* 57:5903, 1998.

Cleo Collaboration: Asner, D., et al. **(R. A. Briere).** Study of semileptonic decays of b mesons to charmed baryons. *Phys. Rev. D* 57:6604, 1998.

FNAL E731/E773/E779 Collaboration: Arisaka, K., et al. **(R. A. Briere).** Search for the lepton-family number violating decay $K_L \to \pi^0 \mu^\pm e^\mp$. *Phys. Lett. B* 432:230, 1998.

L3 Collaboration: Acciarri, M., et al. **(A. Engler, T. A. Ferguson, R. W. Kraemer, and H. Vogel).** Test of CP invariance in $Z \to \mu^+ \mu^- \gamma$ decay. *Phys. Lett. B* 436:428–36, 1998.

L3 Collaboration: Acciarri, M., et al. **(A. Engler, T. A. Ferguson, R. W. Kraemer, and H. Vogel).** Measurement of the inclusive charmless semileptonic branching fraction of beauty hadrons and a determination of $|V_{ub}|$ at LEP. *Phys. Lett. B* 436:174–86, 1998.

L3 Collaboration: Acciarri, M., et al. **(A. Engler, T. A. Ferguson, R. W. Kraemer, and H. Vogel).** Study of anomalous ZZγ and Z$\gamma\gamma$ couplings at LEP. *Phys. Lett. B* 436:187–98, 1998.

L3 Collaboration: Acciarri, M., et al. **(A. Engler, T. A. Ferguson, R. W. Kraemer, and H. Vogel).** Measurement of radiative bhabha and quasi-real compton scattering. *Phys. Lett. B* 439:183–96, 1998.

L3 Collaboration: Acciarri, M., et al. **(A. Engler, T. A. Ferguson, R. W. Kraemer, and H. Vogel).** Measurement of w-pair cross sections in e^+e^- interactions at $\sqrt{s}$=183 GeV and w-decay branching fractions. *Phys. Lett. B* 436:437–52, 1998.

L3 Collaboration: Acciarri, M., et al. **(A. Engler, T. A. Ferguson, R. W. Kraemer, and H. Vogel).** Measurement of the michel parameters and the average tau-neutrino helicity from tau decays at lep. *Phys. Lett. B* 438:405–16, 1998.

L3 Collaboration: Acciarri, M., et al. **(A. Engler, T. A. Ferguson, R. W. Kraemer, and H. Vogel).** Measurement of the effective weak mixing angle by jet-charge asymmetry in hadronic decays of the z boson. *Phys. Lett. B* 439:225–36, 1998.

L3 Collaboration: Acciarri, M., et al. **(A. Engler, T. A. Ferguson, R. W. Kraemer, and H. Vogel).** Upper limit on the lifetime difference of short- and long-lived B^0_s mesons. *Phys. Lett. B* 438:417–29, 1998.

Smith, A. R., and **R. M. Feenstra** et al. Determination of wurtzite GaN lattice polarity based on surface reconstruction. *Appl. Phys. Lett.* 72:2114, 1998.

Piva, P. G., et al. **(R. M. Feenstra).** A comparison of spectroscopic and microscopic observations of ion-induced intermixing in InGaAs/InP quantum wells. *Appl. Phys. Lett.* 72:1599, 1998.

Chen, H., and **R. M. Feenstra** et al. Strain variations in InGaAsP/InGaP superlattices studied by scanning probe microscopy. *Appl. Phys. Lett.* 72:1727, 1998.

Feenstra, R. M., and B. G. Briner. The search for residual resistivity dipoles by scanning tunneling potentiometry. *Superlattices Microstruct.* 23:699, 1998.

BNL E836 Collaboration: Stotzer, R. W., et al. **(G. B. Franklin, C. A. Meyer, B. P. Quinn, and R. A. Schumacher).** Search for the H-dibaryon in ^{3}He(K$^-$, K$^+$)Hn. *Phys. Rev. Lett.* 78:3646, 1997.

Barnes, P. D., et al. **(G. B. Franklin and R. A. Schumacher).** Measurement of the reactions $\bar{p}\,p \to \bar{\Sigma}^+ \Sigma^+$ and $\bar{p}\,p \to \bar{\Sigma}^- \Sigma^-$ close to threshold. *Phys. Lett. B* 402:227, 1997.

Barnes, P. D., et al. **(G. B. Franklin, B. P. Quinn, and R. A. Schumacher).** A measurement of the $\bar{p}\,p \to \bar{\Lambda}\,\Lambda$ and $\bar{p}\,p \to \bar{\Sigma}^0\,\Lambda$+ c.c. reactions at 1.726 and 1.771 GeV/c. *Phys. Rev. C* 54:2831, 1996.

Barnes, P. D., et al. **(G. Franklin, B. Quinn, and R. A. Schumacher).** Observables in high-statistics measurements of the reaction $\bar{p}p \to \Lambda\bar{\Lambda}$. *Phys. Rev. C* 54:1877, 1996.

Stoev, K., E. Ramé, T. Leonhardt, and **S. Garoff.** The effects of thin films on the hydrodynamics near moving contact lines. *Phys. Fluids* 10:1793, 1998.

Decker, E., and **S. Garoff.** Contact angle hysteresis on ambient surfaces: The need for new experimental and theoretical models. *J. Adhesion* 63:159, 1997.

Chen, Q., R. Rame, and **S. Garoff.** The velocity field near moving contact lines. *J. Fluid Mech.* 337:49, 1997.

Gilman, F. J. CP violation. *Z. Naturforsch.* 52a:149, 1997.

Gilman, F. J. Tau/charm workshop summary. In *Workshop on the Tau/Charm Factory,* Argonne National Laboratory, June 21–23, 1995, ed. J. Repond. *American Institute of Physics Conference Proceedings* 349:491. New York, 1996.

Gilman, F. J., K. Kleinknecht, and B. Renk. The Cabibbo-Kobayashi-Maskawa matrix. In *Review of Particle Physics, Phys. Rev. D* 54:94, 1996.

Im, M., et al. **(R. E. Griffiths** and **K. U. Ratnatunga).** The morphologically divided redshift distribution of faint galaxies. *Astrophys. J.* 510:82, 1999.

Griffiths, R. B. Choice of consistent family, and quantum incompatibility. *Phys. Rev. A* 57:1604, 1998.

Griffiths, R. B., and J. B. Hartle. Comment on "Consistent sets yield contrary inferences in quantum theory." *Phys. Rev. Lett.* 81:1981, 1998.

Griffiths, R. B. Reply to "Comment on consistent histories and quantum reasoning." *Phys. Rev. A* 58:3356, 1998.

Griffiths, R. B. Consistent histories and quantum delayed choice. *Fortschr. Phys.* 46:741, 1998.

Niu, C. S., and **R. B. Griffiths.** Optimal copying of one quantum bit. *Phys. Rev. A* 58:4377, 1998.

Stapelfeldt, K. R., et al. **(R. E. Griffiths).** Hubble space telescope imaging of the circumstellar nebulosity of t tauri. *Astrophys. J.* 508:736, 1998.

Trauger, J. T., et al. **(R. E. Griffiths).** Saturn's hydrogen aurora: Wide field and planetary camera 2 imaging from the hubble space telescope. *J. Geophys. Res.* 1032:0237, 1998.

Hannon, J. B., M. C. Bartelt, N. C. Bartelt, and G. L. Kellogg. Etching of the Si(001) surface with molecular oxygen. *Phys. Rev. Lett.* 81:4676, 1998.

Klünker, C., and **J. B. Hannon** et al. Activation energy for the decay of two-dimensional islands on Cu(100). *Phys. Rev. B* 58:R7556, 1998.

Hannon, J. B., G. L. Kellogg, M. C. Bartelt, and N. C. Bartelt. Quantitative analysis of the evolution of surface growth morphology in LEEM. *Surf. Rev. Lett.* 5:1151, 1998.

Hannon, J. B., B. S. Swartzentruber, G. L. Kellogg, and N. C. Bartelt. LEEM measurements of step energies at the (001) surface of heavily boron-doped silicon. *Surf. Rev. Lett.* 5:1159, 1998.

Boyanovsky, D., et al. **(R. Holman).** Non-perturbative quantum dynamics of a new inflation model. *Phys. Rev. D* 57:2166, 1998.

Boyanovsky, D., D. Cormier, H. J. De Vega, and **R. Holman.** Non-equilibrium evolution of a tsunami: Dynamical symmetry breaking. *Phys. Rev. D* 57:3653, 1998.

Boyanovsky, D., et al. **(R. Holman).** Asymptotic dynamics in scalar field theory: Anomalous relaxation. *Phys. Rev. D* 57:7388, 1998.

Johnson, M. B., and **L. S. Kisslinger.** Hadronic couplings via QCD sum rules using three-point functions I: Vacuum susceptibilities. *Phys. Rev. D* 57:2841, 1998.

Kisslinger, L. S., T. Goldman, and Z. Li. QCD penguin contributions to ispspin splittings of heavy-light quark systems. *Phys. Lett. B* 141:263, 1998.

Kisslinger, L. S., and T. Meissner. Structure of vacuum condensates. *Phys. Rev. C* 57:1528, 1998.

Henley, E. M., W.-Y. P. Hwang, and **L. S. Kisslinger.** The weak parity-violating pion-nucleon coupling (addendum). *Phys. Rev. B* 440:449, 1998.

Cheng, T. P., and **L.-F. Li.** Why naive quark model can yield a good account of the baryon magnetic moments. *Phys. Rev. Lett.* 80:2789, 1998.

Cheng, T. P., and **L.-F. Li.** Chiral quark model of nucleon spin flavor structure with SU(3) and axial U(1) breaking. *Phys. Rev. D* 57:344, 1998.

Majetich, S. A., K. M. Chowdary, and E. M. Kirkpatrick. Size and interaction effects in the magnetization reversal in SmCo5 nanoparticles. *IEEE Trans. Magn.* 34:985, 1998.

Scalzetti, E. M., G. M. Gagne, J. H. Scott, and **S. A. Majetich.** Electron microscopic observations on technegas and pertechnegas. *Aerosol Sci. Technol.* 28:523, 1998.

Turgut, Z., et al. **(S. A. Majetich).** Magnetic properties and ordering in c-coated FexCo1-x alloy nanocrystals. *J. Appl. Phys.* 83:6468, 1998.

Carnegie Mellon University

Selected Publications (continued)

Crystal Barrel Collaboration: Abele, A., et al. **(C. A. Meyer).** Decay dynamics of the process $\eta \rightarrow 3\pi^0$. *Phys. Lett. B* 417:193, 1998.

Crystal Barrel Collaboration: Abele, A., et al. **(C. A. Meyer).** Momentum dependence of the decay $\eta \rightarrow \pi^+\pi^-\pi^0$. *Phys. Lett. B* 417:197, 1998.

Crystal Barrel Collaboration: Abele, A., et al. **(C. A. Meyer).** Exotic $\eta\pi$ state in $\bar{p}d$ annihilation at rest into $\pi^-\pi^0\eta p_{spectator}$. *Phys. Lett. B* 423:175, 1998.

Crystal Barrel Collaboration: Abele, A., et al. **(C. A. Meyer).** Study of $\bar{p}p$ annihilation into $\eta\pi^0\pi^0\pi^0$ at rest. *Nucl. Phys. B* 514:45, 1998.

Tristram-Nagle, S., H. I. Petrache, and **J. F. Nagle.** Structure and interactions of fully hydrated dioleoylphosphatidylcholine bilayers. *Biophys. J.* 75:917–25, 1998.

Gouliaev, N., and **J. F. Nagle.** Simulations of interacting membranes. *Phys. Rev. Lett.* 81:2610–3, 1998.

Petrache, H. I., S. Tristram-Nagle, and **J. F. Nagle.** Fluid phase structure of EPC and DMPC bilayers. *Chem. Phys. Lipids* 95:83–94, 1998.

Nagle, J. F., et al. **(R. M. Suter).** Multiple mechanisms for critical behavior in the biologically relevant phase of lecithin bilayers. *Phys. Rev. E* 58:7769–76, 1998.

Adami et al. **(R. C. Nichol).** Deep probing of the coma cluster. *A&A* 334:765, 1998.

Ostrander, E. J., **R. C. Nichol, K. U. Ratnatunga,** and **R. E. Griffiths.** The hubble space telescope medium deep survey cluster sample: Methodology and data. *Astron. J.* 116:2644, 1998.

Nichol, R. C., et al. Evolution in the x-ray cluster luminosity function revisited. *Astrophys. J.* 481:644, 1997.

Burke, D. J., et al. **(R. C. Nichol).** The SHARC survey: X-ray cluster luminosity function out to z=0.7. *Astrophys. J.* 488:L83, 1997.

Nichol, R. C., et al. **(A. K. Romer).** Evolution in the x-ray cluster luminosity function revisited. *Astrophys. J.* 481:644, 1997.

Peterson, J. B. Anisotropy in the microwave suy at 90 GHZ: Results from Python III. *Astrophys. J. Lett.* 475:1, 1997.

Peterson, J. B. Single mode bolometers. *Appl. Phys. Lett.* December 1997.

Procario, M. B Physics beyond the year 2000. In *Proceedings of the 10th Topical Workshop on Proton-Antiproton Collider Physics,* eds. R. Raja and J. Yoh, 1996.

CLEO Collaboration: Barish, B., et al. **(M. Procario).** Measurement of the $\bar{B} \rightarrow D^*\ell\nu$ branching fractions and $|V_{ob}|$. *Phys. Rev. D* 51:256, 1995.

Lubin, L. M., et al. **(K. U. Ratnatunga).** A study of nine high-redshift clusters of galaxies. III. Hubble space telescope morphology of clusters 0023+0423 and 1604+4304. *Astrophys. J.* 116:584–622, 1998.

Tyson, J. A., et al. **(K. U. Ratnatunga** and **R. E. Griffiths).** Deep optical imaging of the bright seyfert galaxy NGC 5548: A long, very low surface brightness tail. *Astrophys. J.* 116:102–10, 1988.

Collins, C. A., et al. **(A. K. Romer** and **R. C. Nichol).** On the evolution of x-ray clusters at high redshift. *Astrophys. J.* 479:L117, 1997.

Burke, D. J., et al. **(A. K. Romer** and **R. C. Nichol).** The southern SHARC survey: The z=0.3–0.7 cluster XLF. *Astrophys. J.* 488:L83, 1997.

Holden, B. P., **A. K. Romer, R. C. Nichol,** and M. P. Ulmer. X-ray observations of distant optically selected clusters. *Astron. J.* 114:1701, 1997.

Boyd, C. G., and **I. Z. Rothstein.** Phenomenology at inclusive sum rules. *Phys. Lett. B* 420:350, 1998.

Grinstein, B., and **I. Z. Rothstein.** Effective field theory and mutchins in non-relativistic gauge theories. *Phys. Lett. D* 57:78, 1998.

Boyd, C. G., Z. Ligeti, **I. Z. Rothstein,** and M. B. Wise. Corrections to the Bjorken and Voloshin sum rules. *Phys. Lett. D* 55:3027–37, 1997.

Rothstein, I. Z., and M. B. Wise. The octet structure function and radiative quarkonia decays. *Phys. Lett. B* 402:346–50, 1997.

Neuostroev, P., et al. **(J. Russ).** A fastbus-based silicon strip readout system. *Nucl. Phys. B (Proc. Suppl.)* 44:583–6, 1995.

Schumacher, R. A. Photoproduction evidence for and against hidden-strangeness states near 2 GeV. *Phys. Rev. C* 56:2774, 1997.

Schumacher, R. T., and J. Woodhouse. Computer modelling of violin playing. *Contemp. Phys.* 36:79, 1995.

Schumacher, R. T., and J. Woodhouse. The transient behaviour of models of bowed-string motion. *Chaos* 5:509, 1995.

Tsulomoto, K., et al. **(R. F. Sekerka).** Transient crystal growth rate in microgravity: Report from TR-IA-4 rocket experiment. *J. Japan Microgravity Appl.* 15:2–9, 1998.

Coriell, S. R., G. B. McFadden, **R. F. Sekerka,** and W. J. Boettinger. Multiple similarity solutions for solidification and melting. *J. Crys. Growth* 191:573–85, 1998.

Bi, Z., and **R. F. Sekerka.** Phase-field model of solidification of a binary alloy. *Phys. A* 261:95–106, 1998.

Sherwood, B. A., and R. W. Chabay. Integrating theory and experiment in lecture using desktop experiments. In *The Changing Role of Physics Departments in Modern Universities,* pp. 1053–60, eds. E. F. Redish and J. S. Rigden. College Park: AIP Press, 1997.

Sherwood, B. A. Getting computer science students to take more physics courses. In *The Changing Role of Physics Departments in Modern Universities,* pp. 95–8, eds. E. F. Redish and J. S. Rigden. College Park: AIP Press, 1997.

Chabay, R. W., and **B. A. Sherwood.** 3D visualization of fields. In *The Changing Role of Physics Departments in Modern Universities,* pp. 763–5, eds. E. F. Redish and J. S. Rigden. College Park: AIP Press, 1997.

Tristram-Nagle, S., H. I. Petrache, **R. M. Suter,** and **J. F. Nagle.** Effect of substrate roughness on D spacing supports theoretical resolution of vapor pressure paradox. *Biophys. J.* 74:1421–7, 1998.

Petrache, H. I., et al. **(R. M. Suter** and **J. F. Nagle).** Interbilayer interactions: High resolution x-ray study. *Phys. Rev. E* 57:7014–24, 1998.

Tristam-Nagle, S., **R. M. Suter,** and **J. F. Nagle.** Effect of substrate roughness on D-spacing supports theoretical resolution of vapor pressure paradox. *Biophys. J.* 74:1421–7, 1998.

Rahman, S., E. Rush, and **R. H. Swendsen.** Intermediate-temperature ordering in a three-state antiferromagnetic Potts model. *Phys. Rev. B* 58:9125, 1998.

Heilmann, R. K., J.-S. Wang, and **R. H. Swendsen.** Rotationally symmetric ordered phase in the three-state antiferromagnetic Potts model. *Phys. Rev. B* 53:2210, 1996.

Swendsen, R. H. Histogram analysis of Monte Carlo simulation. *Int. J. Modern Phys.* 7:281–5, 1996.

Thong, C. J., S. Simizu, and **N. S. VanderVen.** Microwave absorption studies of high-T_c superconductors. *Bull. Am. Phys. Soc.* 39(1):786, 1994.

Miranda, J. A., and **M. Widom.** Weakly nonlinear investigation of the Saffman-Taylor problem in a rectangular Hele-Shaw cell. *Int. J. Mod. Phys. B* 12:931–49, 1998.

Cockayne, E., and **M. Widom.** Ternary model of an Al-Cu-Co decagonal quasicrystal. *Phys. Rev. Lett.* 81:598–601, 1998.

Miranda, J. A., and **M. Widom.** Radial fingering in a Hele-Shaw cell: A weakly nonlinear analysis. *Phys. D* 120:315, 1998.

Widom, M., and J. A. Moriarty. First principles interatomic potentials for transition metal aluminides. II. Application to Al-Co and Al-Ni phase diagrams. *Phys. Rev. B* 58:8967–79, 1998.

Widom, M., and J. A. Miranda. Viscous fingering patterns in ferrofluids. *J. Stat. Phys.* 95:411–26, 1998.

Wolfenstein, L. Lepton asymmetry in B decays. *Phys. Rev. D* 57:5453, 1998.

Wolfenstein, L. New physics effects in CP-violating B decay. *Phys. Rev. D* 57:6857, 1998.

Wolfenstein, L., and T. G. Trippe. Tests of conservation laws. In *Review of Particle Physics. Eur. J. Phys.* 3:62–7, 1998.

Wolfenstein, L. CP violation. In *Review of Particle Physics. Eur. J. Phys.* 3:107–8, 487, 1998.

Young, H. D., and R. Freedman. *University Physics,* ninth edition. Reading, Mass.: Addison-Wesley, 1996.

CITY COLLEGE
OF THE CITY UNIVERSITY OF NEW YORK

Department of Physics

Programs of Study

The Department of Physics offers students the opportunity for study and research leading to the degrees of Doctor of Philosophy and Master of Arts.

Students in the Ph.D. program usually take a year of graduate courses before the first qualifying examination, although some advanced students take the examination after half a year of course work or even upon entering the program. The examination tests classical mechanics and electromagnetism, quantum theory, and general undergraduate physics. Students entering the biophysics subspecialty are allowed to substitute a biophysics examination for classical mechanics. Sixty credits of course work are normally required for the Ph.D. degree program; advanced students with an M.A. degree can usually transfer 30 credits of previous graduate work. In addition, arrangements are always made so that advanced students meet course requirements by working at their appropriate level in connection with their anticipated thesis research. After passing the qualifying examination, students choose faculty mentors for their thesis research. When student and mentor feel confident of the area of thesis research, the student takes an oral second examination before an appropriately chosen thesis committee. During this examination, the student describes the proposed research and demonstrates familiarity with the physics in the area of research. When students complete their original research, they defend a written thesis before their thesis committee at a final thesis defense.

Students in the M.A. program normally take the qualifying examination after 1 or 1½ years, when they have completed the necessary course work. Students who pass the qualifying examination are often admitted to the Ph.D. program. Students who do not pass the qualifying examination but show satisfactory performance at the master's level are awarded a master's degree when they have completed 30 credits of course work. The M.A. program normally requires 1½ years to complete.

Research Facilities

The physics department is housed on three floors (about 70,000 square feet) of the thirteen-story Marshak Science Building, which also houses the other CCNY science departments. FT-IR, X-ray diffraction, UV-visible spectrometers, ultrafast laser instrumentation in picosecond and femtosecond regimes, and departmental computers are available to students. In addition, high-resolution FT-NMR spectrometers and mass spectrometers are run by operators for any research group. A wide variety of equipment is used by individual research groups, including lasers of many kinds, molecular beam instrumentation, a microwave spectrometer, computers, ultrahigh-vacuum systems for surface studies, two He3-He4 dilution refrigerators, a SQUID-based magnetometer, e-beam evaporators, crystal growing equipment, Raman spectrometers, ultrafast time-resolving instrumentation, and atomic beam systems. The department has an electronics shop, a machine shop, a student machine shop, and a glassblower available for designing and building equipment. The Institute for Ultrafast Spectroscopy and Lasers has eight laboratories in the Science Building and the Engineering Building. The New York State Center for Advanced Technology in Ultrafast Photonic Materials and Applications focuses on photonics research with commercial applications.

Financial Aid

Students accepted into the Ph.D. program are normally offered financial support by the Department of Physics. The support is in the form of fellowships and/or research assistantships, for a total stipend of $12,500–$13,500 (taxable) per year, plus tuition. The exact amount depends on the student's progress in the program, tuition costs, and need. Some New York State residents are also eligible for other stipends or awards. More advanced students are generally awarded research assistantships.

Cost of Study

Tuition for spring 1999 was $3800 for an entering student ($2175 for New York residents), $3025 for an intermediate-level student ($1360 for New York residents), and $1080 for an advanced student ($540 for New York residents).

Living and Housing Costs

There is no on-campus housing available at City College. Graduate student housing run by the City University of New York is available in midtown Manhattan; rooms are $455–$555 per month. Many students live in rooms and apartments throughout New York City, paying $350–$650 per person per month.

Student Group

The total number of graduate students in the physics department is currently about 55. There are about 25 postdoctoral assistants. A wide variety of academic, ethnic, and national backgrounds are represented among these students.

Location

The City College is located in an urban setting in the upper part of Manhattan. The College is part of the City University of New York, which includes eighteen campuses—among them Brooklyn, Hunter, and Queens colleges. Physics research at these other branches of the City University complements that at City College. The College is near many other institutions in the New York metropolitan area, including Columbia University, Rockefeller University, and Polytechnic University of New York, and has cooperative arrangements with Brookhaven National Laboratory on Long Island. A number of world-famous industrial research laboratories are near New York City, including AT&T Bell Laboratories, IBM's Thomas J. Watson Laboratory, RCA's David Sarnoff Laboratory, and the Exxon Research Center.

New York City is a major cultural, artistic, communications, medical, and scientific center with numerous resources and opportunities. The city is also a focus of international travel, and visiting scientists often come to City College as part of their itinerary in the United States.

The College

The City College of the City University of New York is the lineal descendant of the Free Academy of New York City, founded in 1847. City College is the oldest and best-known component of the City University of New York.

Applying

Information and application forms can be obtained from the Department of Physics at the address below. An application fee of $40 must accompany the application, with the exception of international students with financial difficulties, for whom the fee can be deferred until registration.

Correspondence and Information

Chairman
Graduate Admissions Committee
Department of Physics
City College of the City University of New York
New York, New York 10031
Fax: 212-650-6940

City College of the City University of New York

THE FACULTY AND THEIR RESEARCH

Adolf A. Abrahamson, Professor; Ph.D., NYU. Atomic and nuclear structure, properties of superheavy elements.

Robert R. Alfano, Distinguished Professor; Ph.D., NYU. Ultrafast picosecond and femtosecond laser spectroscopy applied to physical and biological systems: nonlinear optics, optical imaging, medical applications of photonics, laser development.

Philip Baumel, Professor; Ph.D., Columbia. Physics instruction.

Kurt Becker, Professor; Ph.D., Saarlandes (Germany). Experimental atomic and chemical physics, especially electron collision processes.

Joseph L. Birman, Distinguished Professor; Ph.D., Columbia. Theoretical physics—condensed matter theory; symmetry and symmetry breaking and restoration; optical response of matter, including nonlinear response and response of strongly correlated electronic systems (quantum Hall systems); microscopic theory of high-Tc superconductors; many-body theory, including use of quantum deformed algebras.

Timothy Boyer, Professor; Ph.D., Harvard. Connections between classical and quantum theories: zero-point radiation, stochastic electrodynamics, van der Waals forces, classical electromagnetism.

Ngee-Pong Chang, Professor; Ph.D., Columbia. Unification and dynamical symmetry breaking: origin of mass and chirality, quark-gluon plasma and handedness of the early universe.

Victor Chung, Professor; Ph.D., Berkeley. Administration, physics instruction.

Herman Z. Cummins, Distinguished Professor; Ph.D., Columbia. Light-scattering studies of liquids and solids: phase transitions and critical phenomena, crystal-growth kinetics, pattern formation in nonequilibrium crystal growth, biological problems, liquid-glass transition.

Harold Falk, Professor; Ph.D., Washington (Seattle). Statistical mechanics, especially exact results for spin-systems: discrete-time, nonlinear, and stochastic models.

Joel Gersten; Professor and Chair; Ph.D., Columbia. Solid-state theory: interactions involving small solid-state particles or solid-state surfaces, sonoluminescence.

Daniel M. Greenberger, Professor; Ph.D., Illinois. Fundamental problems in quantum mechanics: the neutron interferometer, coherence in and interpretation of quantum theory, relativistic considerations.

Marilyn Gunner, Assistant Professor; Ph.D., Pennsylvania. Experimental and theoretical biophysics: proteins in electron and proton transfer reactions, time-resolved spectroscopic measurements in photosynthesis.

Michio Kaku, Professor; Ph.D., Berkeley. Superstring theory, supersymmetry, supergravity, string field theory, quantum gravity, quantum chromodynamics.

Joel Koplik, Professor; Ph.D., Berkeley. Molecular dynamics of microscopic fluid flow: transport in disordered systems, superfluid vortex dynamics, pattern selection in nonequilibrium growth processes.

Melvin Lax, Distinguished Professor; Ph.D., MIT. Theoretical studies of radiative and nonradiative interactions in ordered systems, coherent systems, and disordered systems: semiconductors, heterostructures, quantum wells, lasers, random process techniques.

Michael S. Lubell, Professor; Ph.D., Yale. Photon-atom interactions, synchrotron radiation studies, polarized electron physics, two-electron systems, science and technology policy.

V. Parameswaran Nair, Assistant Professor; Ph.D., Syracuse. Mathematical and topological aspects of quantum field theory: skyrmions, quantum breaking of classical symmetries, conformal field theory, black holes, quantum chromodynamics, interaction of anyons.

Vladimir Petricevic, Assistant Professor; Ph.D., CUNY. Growth of solid-state laser materials, laser development, photonics, spectroscopy of ions in solids, ultrafast phenomena.

Stuart Samuel, Professor; Ph.D., Berkeley. Theoretical elementary particle physics: quark confinement, quantum chromodynamics, standard model, string theory, neutrino oscillations; solid-state theory: ferromagnetic and ferroelectric systems, C60 molecule.

Myriam P. Sarachik, Distinguished Professor; Ph.D., Columbia. Low-temperature studies of metal-insulator transitions, Anderson localization, disordered systems, strongly correlated systems; mesoscopic tunneling of magnetization.

David Schmeltzer, Associate Professor; D.Sc., Technion (Israel). Many-body physics of strongly correlated fermions: Fermi and non-Fermi liquids, Luttinger liquids, fractional quantum Hall effect, renormalization group, bosonization; metal-insulator transition, persistent currents; high-Tc superconductivity.

David I. Shelupsky, Associate Professor; Ph.D., Princeton. General relativity and quantum gravity, abstract harmonic analysis.

Frederick W. Smith, Professor; Ph.D., Brown. Deposition and characterization of semiconducting and dielectric thin films; modeling of local atomic bonding in amorphous films; chemical vapor deposition of diamond.

Peter L. Tea, Professor; Ph.D., Columbia. Physics instruction.

Martin Tiersten, Professor; Ph.D., Columbia. Classical mechanics and electromagnetic theory.

Narkis Tzoar, Professor; Ph.D., Pennsylvania. Theoretical investigations of optically produced plasmas in solids: nonlinear propagation in solids and plasmas, optical and transport properties of electron-gas systems.

Professors Emeriti

Michael E. Arons, Joseph Aschner, Alvin Bachman, Arthur Bierman, M. Vertner Brown, Erich Erlbach, Truly C. Hardy, Paul Harris, Hiram Hart, Morton Kaplon, Martin Kramer, Robert M. Lea, S. J. Lindenbaum, Harry Lustig, William Miller, Marvin Mittleman, Leonard Roellig, Fred C. Rose, Kenneth Rubin, Bunji Sakita, Harry Soodak, Harold L. Stolov, Lawrence A. Wills, Robert Wolff, Chi Yuan.

CLEMSON UNIVERSITY

Programs in Physics and Astronomy

Programs of Study

Clemson University offers programs leading to the M.S. and Ph.D. degrees in physics through the Department of Physics and Astronomy. Master's and doctoral programs in astronomy and astrophysics, atmospheric physics, and biophysics are also available; the degree awarded is in physics.

Requirements for the Ph.D. degree include the passing of qualifying exams on undergraduate- and graduate-level physics and an oral exam on the subject of the dissertation. There are no formal course requirements. A program of study is worked out with the student's advisory committee and the graduate advisers.

Requirements for the M.S. degree include the completion of 30 semester hours of credit for research and courses and the passing of an oral exam on the subject of the thesis. A nonthesis option, requiring 36 semester hours of credit, is also available.

Research Facilities

The Department of Physics and Astronomy is housed in a completely air-conditioned building containing 64,000 square feet of teaching and research space. Major equipment and facilities include a computer-controlled microdensitometer; a superconducting magnet (split coil 8T and axial 12T); low-temperature apparatus for studies at temperatures down to 1K; a UHV, low temperature, STM optics facility for luminescence, absorption, and Raman studies; electrostatically shielded rooms; complete electronics and machine shops; and microcomputers that are used in both teaching and research laboratories. An atmospheric observatory with radar and lidar instrumentation is under construction. Students and faculty members have direct access to a departmental UNIX workstation laboratory along with more than twenty-five UNIX workstations throughout the building. Students have access to major astronomical observatories and lidar and radar facilities for atmospheric studies both in the United States and around the world, as well as SEM and atomic force microscopy on campus.

Financial Aid

For students entering with a B.S. or M.S. degree, University assistantships are $13,000 in 1999–2000. Graduate teaching assistants' duties usually involve teaching two or three elementary laboratories each week as well as tutoring or grading in elementary courses. These stipends may be supplemented by fellowships for highly qualified students. More advanced students often receive research assistantships. The University employs students' spouses, as do many local businesses and schools.

Cost of Study

The total cost of study for assistants was about $480 per semester and $320 for summer school in 1998, for in-state and out-of-state students alike. This cost is subject to change without notice.

Living and Housing Costs

Dormitories ranged in cost from $810 to $1185 per semester for double occupancy in 1998–99. All are air conditioned, and most include the cost of a room telephone. University apartments range in cost from $1050 to $1280 per semester for modern units for 4 people; the cost of utilities varies. Many privately owned apartments are available. Costs vary considerably.

Food at University dining facilities in 1998–99 cost $797 per semester for three meals a day five days a week. University health care costs $95 per semester.

Student Group

There are approximately 40 graduate students and 40 undergraduate students in the department.

Student Outcomes

Departmental alumni hold positions at a number of educational institutions, including Max Planck Institut für Aeronomie, Iowa State, Indiana, Southern Illinois, Appalachian State, and Georgia Tech. Graduates also hold various industrial positions at places such as Los Alamos National Laboratory, the Naval Electronics Lab, the Naval Research Lab, NASA Goddard, and Intel Supercomputer Division.

Location

Clemson University is located in Clemson, South Carolina, a small university town (population 11,000) in northwestern South Carolina in the foothills of the Blue Ridge Mountains. It is midway between Charlotte, North Carolina, and Atlanta, Georgia, and is about 10 miles north of Interstate Highway 85. In addition to the normal University activities, there are extensive opportunities for outdoor recreation. For example, Lake Hartwell, with its 1,000-mile shoreline and beautifully clear water, is just west of the campus.

The University

Clemson University is a fully accredited, state-supported land-grant university. The main campus is situated on a 1,400-acre site, part of which was once the John C. Calhoun plantation. The campus is surrounded by 21,000 acres of agricultural research land and bordered by Lake Hartwell. Enrollment is about 17,000, including approximately 3,600 graduate students. Clemson offers seventy-eight undergraduate and fifty-five graduate curriculums.

Applying

Prospective students should write to the address below for the necessary application forms. International students should apply directly to the Graduate School for a special self-managed application package. Applications are normally due by February 15 but are considered at any time. The General Test of the Graduate Record Examinations is required for admission. The physics Subject Test is recommended but not required.

Correspondence and Information

Miguel Larsen
Graduate Student Recruiter
Department of Physics and Astronomy
Clemson University
Clemson, South Carolina 29634-1911

Telephone: 864-656-3416
E-mail: mlarsen@maxwell.phys.clemson.edu
World Wide Web: http://physicsnt.clemson.edu

Clemson University

THE FACULTY AND THEIR RESEARCH

Professors: P. B. Burt; D. D. Clayton; M. S. Daw; L. L. Larcom; M. F. Larsen; J. R. Manson; P. J. McNulty, Chair; J. W. Meriwether; G. X. Tessema. **Associate Professors:** P. J. Flower; D. H. Hartmann; M. D. Leising; B. S. Meyer. **Assistant Professors:** D. L. Carroll; J. A. Clayhold; M. P. Hickey; D. L. Hysell; H. Jiang; D. C. Marinescu; J. P. McCarten; T. M. Tritt. **Research Professors:** Y. K. Kuo; M. V. Nevitt; M. J. Skove; L. S. The; C. W. Ulbrich.

RESEARCH AREAS

Astronomy and Astrophysics
Gamma-ray and X-ray astronomy. (Clayton, Hartmann, Leising, The)
Origin of the solar system and of meteorites, presolar dust. (Clayton, Meyer)
Stellar structure and evolution. (Clayton, Flower, Hartmann, Meyer, The)
Galactic structure and evolution. (Clayton, Hartmann, Leising, Meyer)
Compact stellar objects. (Hartmann, Leising, Meyer, The)
Galactic and cosmological chemodynamics. (Clayton, Hartmann, Meyer)

Atmospheric Physics
Numerical simulation studies of atmospheric wave propagation, dissipation, and interaction with atmosperic chemical processes. (Hickey)
Radar observations of space plasma waves and instabilities, plasma turbulence, ionospheric modifications. (Hysell)
Vertical profiling of atmospheric winds with MST radars; applications in turbulence theory and dynamic meteorology. (Larsen)
Optical studies of atmospheric dynamics using lidar and Fabry-Perot interferometer instrumentation. (Meriwether)
Millimeter-wave-length radar techniques for remote sensing of geophysical atmospheric and oceanographic parameters. (Miller)
Physics of precipitation-forming processes in clouds and methods of remotely sensing precipitation parameters; multiparameter observations of lightning flashes and their effects on precipitation. (Ulbrich)

Biophysics
DNA damage and its repair; effects of nonionizing radiation on biological systems; mechanisms of carcinogenesis. (Larcom)
Biomedical optics; optical imaging for breast cancer detection; fluorescence imaging and spectroscopy for biodiagnostics; image processing; finite element computations of light propagation in tissues. (Jiang)
Photon migration analysis of particles in biological, mechanical, and ceramic systems; particle sizing for online process monitoring in chemical/pharmaceutical industries. (Jiang)

Computational Physics
Solid-state theory: defects in solids and relationship to mechanical properties; surface structure and growth modes; dynamical phase transitions. (Daw)
Modeling radiation environments in space and the effects on microstructures. (McNulty)

Solid-State Physics
Solid-state theory: defects in solids and relationship to mechanical properties; surface structure and growth modes; dynamical phase transitions. (Daw)
Interaction of radiation with matter; microdosimetry; elementary particle theory; interaction of electromagnetic radiation with atoms and molecules; soft errors and microelectronic circuits. (McNulty)
Low-dimensional conductors: charge density waves, superconductivity, nonlinear electron transport, learned behavior. (McCarten)
Transport and magnetotransport in quasi-one-dimensional conductors (charge density waves), superconductivity under very high magnetic fields. (Skove, Tessema)
Conducting polymers: thermopower and electrical conductivity. (Tessema)
High-temperature superconductivity: stress effects, specific heat, thermal conductivity. (Nevitt, Skove, Tessema)
Investigation of solid-state materials for thermoelectric applications; colossal magnetoresistance systems, thermal conductivity and electronic properties of low-dimensional conductors. (Tritt)
Applications of scanning tunneling microscopy (STM)/spectroscopy (STS) and scanning near-field optical microscopy (SNOM) to nanostructures and systems of reduced dimension; macromolecular devices; nanoscale, optical, and electronic phenomena. (D. L. Carroll)
Correlated-electron systems; transport and thermal properties; superconductivity; magnetism; re-entrant superconductivity; precision measurements; thermoelectric effects. (J. A. Clayhold)

Solid-state Theory
Magnetic, optic, and transport properties of semiconductors mesoscopic structures (quantum wells, superlattices); broken symmetry states, charge, and spin density waves; nonequilibrium superconductivity. (Marinescu)

Theoretical Physics
Quantum theory and quantum field theory: persistent interactions and nonperturbative interactions. (P. B. Burt)
Mathematical physics: construction of intrinsically nonlinear solutions of nonlinear field equations. (P. B. Burt)
Solid-state theory: defects in solids and relationship to mechanical properties; surface structure and growth modes; dynamical phase transitions. (M. S. Daw)
Surface physics and solid-state theory: information about the nature of surface structure and surface interactions, obtained by studying the interactions of atomic and molecular beams impinging upon solid surfaces. (J. R. Manson)

SELECTED PUBLICATIONS

Burt, P. B. Solutions of the Riccati equation by the method of base equations. In *Modeling and Simulation,* Chap. 10, eds. J. Brawley, G. Proctor, and T. Wallenius. Chemical Rubber Corporation, 1999.

Burt, P. B. Solution of the Riccati equation by the method of base equations. In *Modeling in the Mathematical Sciences,* chapt. 10. Chemical Rubber Corporation, 1997.

Burt, P. B. Huygens' Principle and the unification of dynamics. In *Proceedings of the Conference in Theoretical Physics,* Chap. 2, ed. G. Strobel. University of Georgia, 1997.

Burt, P. B. Boundary conditions in quantum field theories II; the role of the vacuum. In *Foundations of Physics,* 1997.

Carroll, D. L., T. Wagner, and M. Rühle. Nano-phase formation in LiNbO3 substrates studied by STM. *Appl. Phys. Lett.* 75(1):46–8, 1999.

Carroll, D. L., et al. Nano-domain formation in B-doped carbon nanotubes. *Phys. Rev. Lett.* 81(11):2332–5, 1998.

Carroll, D. L., et al. Picking a needle from the nano-haystack. *Adv. Mater.* 10(7):871, 1998.

Curran, S., et al. **(D. L. Carroll).** A composite from poly (m-phenylenevinylene-co-2,5-dioctoxy-p-phenylenevinylene) and carbon nanotubes: A novel material for molecular optoelectronics. *Adv. Mater.* 10(14):1091 and cover feature, 1998.

Carroll, D. L., et al. Electronic structure and localized states at carbon nanotube tips. *Phys. Rev. Lett.* 78(14):2811–4, 1997.

Clayhold, J. A., et al. Thermomagnetic effects above and below T$_c$ in the cuprate superconductors. *Proc. 2nd Conf. Oxide Superconductor Phys. Nano-Eng., SPIE* 28:2967, 1996.

Frenkel, D. M., and **J. A. Clayhold.** Current instabilities in reentrant superconductors. *Proc. 10th Anniversary Workshop High-T$_c$ Superconductors,* p. 589. World Scientific, 1996.

Clayhold, J. A. The Nernst effect in anisotropic metals. *Phys. Rev. B* 54:6103, 1996.

Clayhold, J. A., et al. Unusual magnetic-field dependence of the electrothermal conductivity in the mixed state of cuprate superconductors. *Phys. Rev. B* 53:8681, 1996.

Timmes, F. X., and **D. D. Clayton.** Galactic evolution of silicon isotopes. *Astrophys. J.* 472:723–41, 1996.

Clayton, D. D., and L. Jin. Gamma rays, cosmic rays and extinct radioactivity in molecular clouds. *Astrophys. J.* 451:681, 1995.

Band, D., and **D. H. Hartmann.** A statistical treatment of the gamma-ray burst no-host galaxy problem. *Astrophys. J.* 493:555, 1998.

Hartmann, D. H., et al. On Flamsteed's Supernova Cas A. *Nucl. Phys. A* 621:83c–91c, 1997.

Hartmann, D. H., and S. E. Woosley. The cosmic supernova neutrino background. *Astron. Particle Phys.* 7:137, 1997.

Hakkila, J., J. M. Myers, B. J. Stidham, and **D. H. Hartmann.** A computerized model of large scale visual interstellar extinction. *Astron. J.* 114:2043, 1997.

Fishman, G. J., and **D. H. Hartmann.** Gamma-ray bursts. *Sci. Am.* 277:46–51, 1997.

Hickey, M. P., and R. L. Walterscheid. A note on gravity wave-driven volume emission rate weighted temperature perturbations inferred from O$_2$ atmospheric and O I 5577 airglow observations. *J. Geophys. Res.* 104:4279, 1999.

Hickey, M. P., M. J. Taylor, C. S. Gardner, and C. R. Gibbons. Full-wave modeling of small-scale gravity waves using airborne lidar and observations of the Hawaiian airglow (ALOHA-93)O(^{1}S) images and coincident Na wind/temperature lidar measurements. *J. Geophys. Res.* 103:6439, 1998.

Hickey, M. P., et al. Numerical simulations of gravity waves imaged over Arecibo during the 10-day January 1993 campaign. *J. Geophys. Res.* 102:11475, 1997.

Hysell, D. L., and J. D. Burcham. JULIA radar studies of equatorial spread F. *J. Geophys.* 103:29155, 1998.

Hysell, D. L., and C. E. Seyler. A renormalization group approach to estimation of anomalous diffusion in the unstable equatorial F region. *J. Geophys. Res.* 103:26731, 1998.

Hysell, D. L. Imaging coherent scatter radar studies of bottomside equatorial spread F. *J. Atmos. Sol. Terr. Phys.* 60:1109, 1998.

Jiang, H. Frequency-domain fluorescent diffusion tomography, A finite element algorithm and simulations. *Appl. Opt.* 37:5337–43, 1999.

Jiang, H., G. Marquez, and L. Wang. Particle sizing in concentrated suspensions using steady-state, continuous-wave photon migration techniques. *Opt. Lett.* 23:394–6, 1998.

Jiang, H., K. D. Paulsen, and U. L. Osterberg. Optical image reconstruction using DC data: Simulations and experiments. *Phys. Med. Biol.* 41:1483–98, 1996.

Paulsen, K. D., and **H. Jiang.** Enhanced frequency-domain optical image reconstruction in tissues through total variation minimization. *Appl. Opt.* 35:3447–58, 1996.

Jiang, H., et al. Optical image reconstruction using frequency-domain data: Simulations and experiments. *J. Opt. Soc. Am. A* 13:253–66, 1996.

Watanabe, K., **M. D. Leising, D. H. Hartmann,** and **L.-S. The.** The extragalactic X-ray background due to cosmological supernovae. *Astrophys. J.,* in press.

Leising, M. D., et al. Compton Observatory OSSE observations of supernova 1991T. *Astrophys. J.* 444:244, 1995.

Manson, J. R. Atom-surface scattering in the classical limit: Temperature and energy dependence. *Phys. Rev. B* 58:2253, 1998.

Bertino, M. F., **J. R. Manson,** W. Silverstri, and J. P. Toennies. A comparative experimental study of the scattering of highly energetic atomic and molecular beams from metallic surfaces. *J. Chem. Phys.* 108:10239, 1998.

Glebov, A. **J. R. Manson** et al. Inelastic focusing effects in atom-surface scattering. *Phys. Rev. B* 57:R9455, 1998.

Glebov, A., **J. R. Manson,** J. G. Skofronick, and J. P. Toennies. Defect-mediated diffraction resonances in surface scattering. *Phys. Rev. Lett.* 78:1508, 1997.

Balzer, F., R. Gerlach, **J. R. Manson,** and H.-G. Rubahn. Photodesorption of Na atoms from rough Na surfaces. *J. Chem. Phys.* 106:7995, 1997.

Marinescu, D. C., and J. J. Quinn. Long wavelength collective excitations in a 2D spin polarized electron gas—A Fermi liquid approach. *Phys. Rev. B* 58:15688, 1998.

Marinescu, D. C., and J. J. Quinn. Collective excitations in an asymmetrically spin-polarized quantum well. *Phys. Rev. B* 58:13762, 1998.

Marinescu, D. C., and J. J. Quinn. Exchange and correlation corrections to the response functions of a spin polarized electron gas. *Phys. Rev. B* 56:114, 1997.

Marinescu, D. C., J. J. Quinn, P. Sitko, and K. S. Yi. Composite fermions and the half-filled state. *Phys. Rev. B* 56:14941, 1997.

Marinescu, D. C., and A. W. Overhauser. Thermoelectric flux in superconducting rings. *Phys. Rev. B* 55:11637, 1997.

Coppersmith, S. N., et al. **(J. P. McCarten).** Self organized short term memories. *Phys. Rev. Lett.* 78:3983, 1997.

Scheick, L. Z., **P. J. McNulty** and D. R. Roth. Dosimetry based on the erasure of floating gates in the natural radiation environments of space. *IEEE Trans. Nucl. Sci.* 45:2681–8, 1998.

Savage, M. W., **P. J. McNulty,** D. R. Roth, and C. C. Foster. Possible role for secondary particles in proton-induced single event upsets of modern devices. *IEEE Trans. Nucl. Sci.* 45:2745.

Reed, R. A., et al. **(P. J. McNulty).** *IEEE Trans. Nucl. Sci.* 44:2224–9, 1997.

McNulty, P. J., M. W. Savage, D. R. Roth, and C. C. Foster. In *Radiations and Their Effects on Systems,* pp. 570–5. 1997.

Meriwether, J. W., S. Collins, and M. E. Hagan. Observed coupling of the mesosphere inversion layer to the thermal tidal structure. *Geophys. Res. Lett.* 25:1479–82, 1998.

Gao, X., **J. W. Meriwether,** V. B. Wickwar, and T. Wilkerson. Rayleigh lidar measurements of the temporal frequency and vertical wavenumber spectra in the mesosphere over the Rocky Mountain region. *J. Geophys. Res.* 103:6405–16, 1998.

Clemson University

Selected Publications (continued)

Gao, X., and **J. W. Meriwether.** Mesoscale spectral analysis of in situ horizontal and vertical wind measurements at 6 km. *J. Geophys. Res.* 103:6405–16, 1998.

Gao, X., and **J. W. Meriwether.** Mesoscale airborne in situ and lidar observations of variance and spatial structure in the troposphere and stratosphere regions. *J. Geophys. Res.* 103:6391–6, 1998.

Meriwether, J. W., et al. Optical interferometric studies of the nighttime equatorial thermosphere: Enhanced temperatures and zonal wind gradients. *J. Geophys. Res.* 102:20041–58, 1997.

Meyer, B. S., T. D. Krishnan, and **D. D. Clayton.** Theory of quasi-equilibrium nucleosynthesis and applications to matter expanding from high temperature and density. *Astrophys. J.* 498:808, 1998.

Meyer, B. S., G. C. McLaughlin, and G. M. Fuller. Neutrino capture and r-process nucleosynthesis. *Phys. Rev. C* 58:3696, 1998.

Meyer, B. S., T. D. Krishnan, and **D. D. Clayton.** Ca production in matter expanding from high temperature and density. *Astrophys. J.* 462:825–38, 1996.

Tessema, G. X., et al. Effect of magnetic and nonmagnetic impurities (Ni, Zn) substitution for CU in BiSCCO whiskers. *Phys. Rev. B,* in press.

Kuh, J., et al. **(G. X. Tessema** and **M. J. Skove).** NbSe$_3$: Effect of aniaxial stress on the threshold field and fermiology. *Phys. Rev. B* 57(23), 1998.

Eaiprasertasak, K., R. V. Gregory, and **G. X. Tessema.** Conductivity and thermopower of doped polyaniline as-spum fibers from leucoemeraldine base. *ANTEC,* 1998.

Verebeleyi, D., and **G. X. Tessema.** Thermoelectric properties of $M_2Mo_6X_6$(M-Tl, In, Rb, Cs and X-Se, Te). *MRS Proc.,* Vol. 478, 1998.

The, L.-S., D. D. Clayton, L. Jin, and **B. S. Meyer.** Nuclear reactions governing the nucleosynthesis of ^{44}Ti. *Astrophys. J.* 504:500, 1998.

The, L.-S., et al. **(M. D. Leising).** OSSE observations of the Cassiopeia A. supernova remnant. *Astrophys. J.* 444:244, 1995.

Tritt, T. M. Thermoelectric materials run hot and cold. *Science* 272:1276, 1996.

Tritt, T. M., et al. Low temperature transport properties of the filled and unfilled IrSb$_3$ skutterudite system. *J. Appl. Phys.* 79:8412, 1996.

Nolas, G. S., et al. **(T. M. Tritt).** The effect of rare earth filling on the lattice thermal conductivity of skutterudites. *J. Appl. Phys.* 79:4002, 1996.

Nolas, G. S., V. G. Harris, **T. M. Tritt,** and G. A. Slack. Low temperature transport properties of the mixed-valence $Ru_{0.5}Pd_{0.5}Sb_3$. *J. Appl. Phys.* 80:6304, 1996.

Tritt, T. M., et al. Low temperature transport properties of IrSb$_3$. *Proc. XIV Int. Conf. Thermoelectrics.* St. Petersburg, Russia. 240, 1995.

COLUMBIA UNIVERSITY

Department of Applied Physics and Applied Mathematics

Programs of Study

The Department of Applied Physics and Applied Mathematics offers graduate study leading to the degrees of Master of Science (M.S), Doctor of Engineering Science (Eng.Sc.D.), and Doctor of Philosophy (Ph.D.).

The following fields of research (topics of emphasis in parentheses) are available for doctoral study: theoretical and experimental plasma physics (fusion and space plasmas), applied mathematics (scientific computation and geophysical fluid dynamics), solid-state physics (semiconductor, surface, and low-dimensional physics), quantum electronics (free electron lasers and laser interactions with matter), nuclear science (medical applications), and atmospheric science (global climate modeling and remote sensing). Successful completion of thirty points (semester hours) or more of approved graduate course work beyond the master's degree is required for the doctoral degree. Candidates must pass written and oral qualifying exams and successfully defend an approved dissertation based on original research. For the M.S. degree, candidates must successfully complete a minimum of 30 points of credit of approved graduate course work at Columbia. A 34-point M.S. degree with a concentration in medical physics is offered in collaboration with faculty from the College of Physicians and Surgeons. It prepares students for careers in medical physics and provides preparation for the ABMP certification exam.

Research Facilities

Research equipment in the Plasma Physics Laboratory includes a toroidal high-beta Tokamak, HBT-EP (R=0.92m, a=0.15m, B=0.5T), a relativistic electron beam machine (1 MeV, 20kA, 200nsec) that powers a millimeter-wave free-electron laser, a steady-state plasma experiment using a linear magnetic mirror, a large laboratory collisionless terrella used to investigate space plasma physics, a microwave plasma source for material processing, high-voltage capacitor banks, and switching circuits. A visible free-electron laser is available for research at Brookhaven National Laboratory, and an rf linac accelerator test facility is available at Yale. The plasma physics group is jointly constructing a new plasma confinement experiment with MIT, incorporating a levitated superconducting ring. The plasma physics group is also actively involved in experiments at the Princeton Plasma Physics Laboratory and on the DIII-D Tokamak at General Atomics in San Diego.

Research equipment in the solid-state physics and quantum electronics laboratories and the associated Microelectronics Sciences Laboratories include extensive laser and spectroscopy facilities, a microfabrication laboratory, ultra high-vacuum surface preparation and analysis chambers, direct laser writing stations, a molecular beam epitaxy machine, picosecond and femtosecond lasers, and diamond anvil cells. Facilities and research opportunities also exist within the interdisciplinary Materials Research Science and Engineering Center, which focuses on complex films composed of nanoparticles.

There are research opportunities in medical physics at the Columbia–Presbyterian Medical Center, as well as at other medical institutes, employing state-of-the-art medical diagnostic imaging and treatment equipment.

There is ongoing cooperative research between the Applied Mathematics Division and the NASA Goddard Institute for Space Studies, located nearby. Joint research, instruction, and supervision of graduate students exist in the fields of atmospheric science, geophysical fluid dynamics, and large-scale scientific computation.

In addition to the University Computer Center, the department maintains an extensive network of workstations, minicomputers, and desktop computers. The research of the Plasma Lab is supported by a dedicated data acquisition/data analysis system, and the applied math group maintains an SGI Power Challenge. Through the Internet, researchers in the department are currently using supercomputing facilities at the National Center for Atmospheric Research; the San Diego Supercomputing Center; the National Energy Research Supercomputer Center in Livermore, California; and others.

Financial Aid

Financial support is awarded on a competitive basis in the form of assistantships that provide a stipend and a tuition allowance that covers a full 15-point program each semester. For 1999–2000, the stipend for teaching assistants is $13,125 for nine months; for research assistants, stipends are $17,500 for twelve months. Hours of service per week range up to 15 for first-year students. The FAFSA is required for U.S. citizens and permanent residents.

Cost of Study

For 1999–2000, full-time tuition for the academic year is approximately $24,450; for part-time study, the cost is approximately $815 per credit. Annual fees are approximately $1400, and the cost of books is approximately $700.

Living and Housing Costs

The cost of on-campus, single student housing (dormitories, suites, apartments) ranges from $2000 to $3600 per term; married student accommodations range from $750 to $1050 per month. For the single student, a minimum of $12,200 should be allowed for board, room, and personal expenses for the academic year.

Student Group

Approximately 20,000 students attend the fifteen schools and colleges of Columbia University; more than half are graduate students. On average, the department has 65 graduate and 35 undergraduate students. The student population has a diverse and international character. Admission is highly competitive; in 1998–99, approximately 16 percent of the application pool of 154 was admitted.

Student Outcomes

Recent Ph.D. recipients have found employment as postdoctoral research scientists at universities in the U.S. and abroad and as staff members in advanced technology industries and at national laboratories such as NRL. Some have secured college-level faculty positions. Most M.S. graduates continued for the doctorate; a few went to medical school. M.S. graduates from the program in medical physics have secured positions in hospital departments of radiology and nuclear medicine or have entered doctoral programs.

Location

The 32-acre campus is situated in Morningside Heights on the upper west side of Manhattan, between Riverside Park and the Hudson River to the west, and Morningside Park to the east. This location, 15 minutes from the heart of New York City, allows Columbia to be an integral part of the city while maintaining the character of a unique neighborhood. Cultural, recreational, and athletic opportunities abound at city museums, libraries, concert halls, theaters, restaurants, stadiums, parks, and beaches.

The University and The Department

The Department of Applied Physics and Applied Mathematics was established at Columbia University in 1978 as part of the Graduate School of Arts and Sciences and the Fu Foundation School of Engineering and Applied Science, incorporating the Plasma Physics Program, which was started in 1961; Division of Nuclear Science and Engineering, which was started in 1962; and Division of Applied Mathematics, which was formed within the department in 1989 to recognize the growing role played by applied mathematics.

Applying

For fall admission, applications should be submitted as follows: January 5 for doctoral, doctoral-track, and all financial aid applicants; applications for master of science, part-time, and nondegree candidates are reviewed on a rolling basis. Scores from the GRE General Test are required; GRE Subject Test scores are strongly urged. TOEFL scores are required for students from non-English-speaking countries.

Correspondence and Information

Chairman, Graduate Admissions Committee
202 S. W. Mudd Building, MC 4701
Columbia University
New York, New York 10027

Telephone: 212-854-4457
E-mail: seasinfo.ap@columbia.edu
World Wide Web: http://www.ap.columbia.edu

Columbia University

THE FACULTY AND THEIR RESEARCH

In the Department of Applied Physics, theoretical and experimental research is conducted by 20 full-time faculty members, 5 adjunct professors, and 29 postdoctoral research scientists. Areas of research include applied mathematics, atmospheric/space physics, surface physics, computational and geophysical fluid dynamics, condensed-matter physics, electromagnetism, free-electron lasers, materials science, medical physics, nuclear science, oceanography, optical physics, plasma physics, and fusion.

Allen H. Boozer, Professor; Ph.D., Cornell, 1970. Plasma theory, theory of magnetic confinement for fusion energy, nonlinear dynamics.

Siu-Wai Chan, Associate Professor (joint with H. K. School of Mines); Sc.D., MIT, 1985. Electronic ceramics, grain boundaries and interfaces in thin films.

C. K. Chu, Professor; Ph.D., NYU (Courant), 1959. Applied mathematics, large-scale scientific computing, fluid dynamics.

Bjorn Engquist, Professor; Ph.D., Uppsala (Sweden), 1975. Applied and computational mathematics, numerical analysis, scientific computing.

Morton B. Friedman, Professor (joint with Civil Engineering); D.Sc., NYU, 1948. Applied mathematics and mechanics, numerical analysis, parallel computing.

Irving P. Herman, Professor; Ph.D., MIT, 1977. Lasers, laser diagnostics of thin-film processing, optical spectroscopy of semiconductors and heterostructures, physics of solids at high pressure, laser and plasma processing of materials.

James Im, Associate Professor (joint with H. K. School of Mines); Ph.D., MIT, 1985. Excimer laser-induced crystallization of amorphous Si films, nucleation in condensed systems.

Thomas C. Marshall, Professor; Ph.D., Illinois, 1960. Free-electron lasers, relativistic beam dynamics and radiation, accelerators.

Michael E. Mauel, Professor; Sc.D., MIT, 1983. Plasma physics, waves and instabilities, fusion and equilibrium control; space physics; plasma processing.

Gerald A. Navratil, Professor; Ph.D., Wisconsin–Madison, 1976. Plasma physics, plasma diagnostics, fusion reactor design.

Gertrude Neumark, Professor (joint with H. K. School of Mines); Ph.D., Columbia, 1979. Material science and physics of semiconductors, with emphasis on optical and electrical properties of wide semiconductors and their light-emitting devices.

Richard M. Osgood, Professor (joint with Electrical Engineering); Ph.D., MIT, 1973. Lasers, quantum electronics, surface physics, integrated optics, nanofabrication.

Aron Pinczuk, Professor (joint with Physics); Ph.D., Pennsylvania, 1969. Spectroscopy of semiconductors and insulators; quantum structures and interfaces; electrons in systems of reduced dimensions.

Lorenzo M. Polvani, Associate Professor; Ph.D., MIT, 1988. Atmospheric, oceanic, and planetary science; geophysical fluid dymanics; computational fluid mechanics; vortex dynamics; turbulence.

Yue-Hong Qian, Assistant Professor; Ph.D., Ecole Normale Supérieure de Paris, 1990. Computational fluid dynamics, numerical analysis, lattice Bolzmann methods, lattice gas cellular automata, nonlinear systems, parallel computation.

Malvin A. Ruderman, Professor (joint with Physics); Ph.D., Caltech, 1947. Theoretical astrophysics, neutron stars, pulsars, early universe, cosmic gamma rays.

Amiya K. Sen, Professor (joint with Electrical Engineering); Ph.D., Columbia, 1963. Plasma physics, fluctuations and anomalous transport in plasmas, control of plasma instabilities.

Horst Stormer, Professor (joint with Physics); Ph.D., Stuttgart, 1977. Semiconductors, electronic transport, lower-dimensional physics.

Wen I. Wang, Professor (joint with Electrical Engineering); Ph.D., Cornell, 1981. Heterostructure devices and physics, materials properties, molecular beam epitaxy.

Marco Zaider, Professor (joint with Radiation Oncology and Public Health); Ph.D., Tel Aviv, 1976. Medical physics, biophysical modeling, microdosimetry, quantum chemistry, radiation transport.

The Schapiro Center for Engineering and Physical Science Research; to the right, the Seeley W. Mudd Building, home of the Fu Foundation School of Engineering and Applied Science.

Faculty, research staff, and students of the Plasma Physics Laboratory in front of the Tokamak, HBT-EP.

Low Memorial Library and grounds.

SELECTED PUBLICATIONS

Boozer, A. H. What is a stellarator? *Phys. Plasmas* 5:1647–55, 1998.

Boozer, A. H. Equations for studies of feedback stabilization. *Phys. Plasmas* 5:3350–7, 1998.

Boozer, A. H. Stellarator optimization. *Fiz. Plazmy* 23:483–90, 1997. *Plasma Phys. Rep.* 23:449–55, 1997.

Sasinowski, M., and **A. H. Boozer.** A delta-f Monte Carlo method to calculate plasma parameters. *Phys. Plasmas* 4(10):3509–17, 1997.

Tang, X. Z., and **A. H. Boozer.** Hamiltonian structure of Hamiltonian chaos. *Phys. Lett. A* 236:476–82, 1997.

Christensen-Dalsgaard, J., and **V. M. Canuto.** Turbulence in astrophysics. *Ann. Rev. Fluid Mech.*, in press.

Dubovidov, M. S., and **V. M. Canuto.** Towards a statistical theory of turbulence. *Int. J. Theoret. Phys.* 12:3121, 1997.

Canuto, V. M. Compressible turbulence. *Ap. J.* 482:827, 1997.

Canuto, V. M. A dynamical model for turbulence: IV buoyancy driven flows. *Phys. Fluids* 9:2118, 1997.

Canuto, V. M. A dynamical model for turbulence: V, the effect of rotation. *Phys. Fluids* 9:2132, 1997.

Chan, S. -W. Nature of grain boundaries as related to critical currents in superconducting YBa2Cu307-x. *J. Phys. Chem. Solids* 55:1415–32, 1995.

Chan, S. -W. Degenerate epitaxy, coincidence epitaxy and the origin of 'special' boundaries in thin films. *J. Phys. Chem. Solids* 55:1137–45, 1995.

Chopra, M., et al. **(S. -W. Chan).** Growth of superconducting Y-Ba-Cu-O films on spinel and garnet. *Appl. Phys. Lett.* 63:2964, 1993.

Chefter, J. G., **C. K. Chu,** and E. E. Keyes. Domain decomposition for shallow water equations. In *Contemporary Mathematics, Proceedings of the 7th International Conference on Domain Decomposition Methods in Science and Engineering,* October 1993.

Yin, F. L., I. Y. Fung, and **C. K. Chu.** Equilibrium response of ocean deep-water circulation to variations in Ekman pumping and deep-water sources. *J. Phys. Oceanogr.* 22:1129, 1992.

Chaiken, J., **C. K. Chu,** M. Tabor, and Q. M. Tan. Lagrangian turbulence in Stokes flow. *Phys. Fluids* 30:687, 1987.

Chu, C. K., L. W. Xiang, and Y. Baransky. Solitary waves generated by boundary motion. *Comm. Pure Appl. Math.* 36:495, 1983.

Chu, C. K. Numerical methods in fluid dynamics. In *Advances in Applied Mechanics,* vol. 17, ed. C. S. Yih. New York: Academic Press, 1977.

Yao, M. -S., W. Kovari, K. K. -W. Lo, and **A. D. Del Genio.** A prognostic cloud water parameterization for global climate models. *J. Climate* 9:270, 1996.

Kovari, W., M. -S. Yao, and **A. D. Del Genio.** Climatic implications of the seasonal variation of upper troposphere water vapor. *Geophys. Res. Lett.* 21:2701, 1994.

Miller, R. L., and **A. D. Del Genio.** Tropical cloud feedbacks and decadal variability of climate. *J. Climate* 7:1388, 1994.

Zhou, W., T. P. Eichler, and **A. D. Del Genio.** Equatorial superrotation in a slowly rotating GCM: Implications for Titan and Venus. *Icarus* 101:1, 1993.

Aggarwal, R., D. R. Dellwo, and **M. B. Friedman.** Parallel solution of Fredholm integral equations of the second kind by accelerated projection methods. *Parallel Computing* 19:1105–15, 1993.

Dellwo, D. R., and **M. B. Friedman.** Accelerated projection and iterated projection methods with applications to nonlinear integral equations. *SIAM J. Numer. Anal.* 28:236–50, 1991.

Luo, J.-C., and **M. B. Friedman.** A study of decomposition methods. *Computers and Mathematics with Applications* 21(8):79–84, 1991.

Dellwo, D. R., **M. B. Friedman,** and R. Aggarwal. Computational aspects of accelerated projection methods for nonlinear integral equations. In *Proceedings of the Second International Conference on Integral Methods in Science and Engineering,* Arlington, Texas, 1990.

Luo, J.-C., and **M. B. Friedman.** Implicit decomposition as a tool for solving large-scale structural systems in a parallel environment. *Computers and Structures* 35(3):215–20, 1990.

Eryigit, R., and **I. P. Herman.** Optical anisotropy of the GaAs001 surface. *Phys. Rev. B* 56:9263, 1997.

Herman, I. P. *Optical Diagnostics for Thin Film Processing.* San Diego, California: Academic Press, 1996.

Herman, I. P., V. M. Donnelly, K. V. Guinn, and C. C. Cheng. Laser induced thermal desorption as an *in situ* surface probe during plasma etching. *Phys. Rev. Lett.* 72:2801, 1994.

Sui, Z., and **I. P. Herman.** Effect of strain on phonons in Si, Ge, and Si/Ge heterostructures. *Phys. Rev. B* 48:17938, 1993.

Tuchman, J. A., S. Kim, Z. Sui, and **I. P. Herman.** Exciton photoluminescence of bulk ZnSe and ZnSe epilayers under hydrostatic pressure. *Phys. Rev. B* 46:3371, 1992.

Im, J. S., et al. Controlled super-lateral growth of Si films for microstructural manipulation and optimization. *Phys. Status Solidi* 166:603, 1998.

Crowder, M. A., et al. **(J. S. Im).** Low-temperature single-crystal Si TFTs fabricated on Si films processed via sequential lateral solidification. *IEEE Electron Device Lett.* 19:306, 1998.

Im, J. S., V. V. Gupta, and M. A. Crowder. On determining the relevance of athermal nucleation in rapidly quenched liquids. *Appl. Phys. Lett.* 72:662, 1998.

Gupta, V. V., H. J. Song, and **J. S. Im.** Numerical analysis of excimer-laser induced melting and solidification of thin Si films. *Appl. Phys. Lett.* 71:99, 1997.

Sposili, R. S., and **J. S. Im.** Sequential lateral solidification of thin silicon films on SiO_2. *Appl. Phys. Lett.* 69:2864, 1996.

Zhang, T. -Z., **T. C. Marshall,** and J. L. Hirshfield. A cerenkov source of high power picosecond microwaves. *IEEE J. Plasma Sci.* (special microwave issue) 26:787, 1998.

Zhang, T. -Z., J. L. Hirshfield, and **T. C. Marshall.** Stimulated dielectric wakefield accelerator. *Phys. Rev. E* 56:4647, 1997.

Liu, Y. -H., and **T C. Marshall.** Harmonic millimeter radiation from a microwave free electron laser. *Phys. Rev. E* 56:2161, 1997.

Zhang, T. B., and **T. C. Marshall.** Possibility of generating a high-power self-similar radiation pulse from a free electron laser. *Phys. Rev. Lett.* 74:916, 1995.

Zhang, T. B., and **T. C. Marshall.** Microwave inverse FEL accelerator using a small "phase window." *Phys. Rev. E* 50:1491, 1994.

Garofalo, A. M., et al. **(M. E. Mauel** and **G. A. Navratil).** Stabilization of kink instabilities by eddy currents in a segmented wall and comparison with ideal MHD theory. *Nucl. Fusion* 38:1029, 1998.

Warren, H. P., **M. E. Mauel,** D. Brennan, and S. Taromina. Observation of wave-induced chaotic radial transport in a laboratory terrella experiment. *Phys. Plasmas* 3:1996, 1996.

Ivers, T. H., et al. **(M. E. Mauel** and **G. A. Navratil).** Observation of wall stabilization and active control of low-*n* MHD instabilities in a tokamak. *Phys. Plasmas* 3:1926, 1996.

Strait, E. J., et al. **(M. E. Mauel).** Enhanced confinement and stability in DIII-D discharges with reversed magnetic shear. *Phys. Rev. Lett.* 75:4421, 1995.

Warren, H. P., and **M. E. Mauel.** Wave-induced chaotic radial transport of energetic electrons in a laboratory terrella experiment. *Phys. Plasmas* 2:4185, 1995.

Warren, H. P., and **M. E. Mauel.** Observation of chaotic particle transport induced by drift-resonant fluctuations in a magnetic dipole field. *Phys. Rev. Lett.* 74:1351, 1995.

Taylor, T. S., et al. **(M. E. Mauel).** Wall stabilization of high beta plasmas in DIII-D. *Phys. Plasmas* 2:2390, 1995.

Sabbagh, S. A., et al. **(M. E. Mauel** and **G. A. Navratil).** Deuterium-tritium TFTR plasmas in the high poloidal beta regime. In *Plasma Physics and Controlled Fusion Research 1994,* vol. 1, p. 663, Vienna: IAEA, 1995.

Mauel, M. E., and **G. A. Navratil,** et al. Operation at the tokamak equilibrium poloidal beta limit in TFTR. *Nucl. Fusion* 32:1468, 1992.

Navratil, G. A., et al. **(A. H. Boozer** and **M. E. Mauel).** Active control of MHD modes in a tokamak. In *Proceedings of the 25th European Physical Society Conference on Controlled Fusion and Plasma Science,* Part II, p. 730, Prague, 1998.

Navratil, G. A., et al. **(M. E. Mauel).** Active control of 2/1 magnetic islands in a tokamak. *Phys. Plasmas* 5:1855, 1998.

Lazarus, E. A., and **G. A. Navratil** et al. Higher fusion power gain with profile control in DIII-D tokamak plasmas. *Nucl. Fusion* 37:7, 1997.

Lazarus, E. A., and **G. A. Navratil** et al. Higher fusion power gain with pressure profile control in strongly-shaped DIII-D plasmas. *Phys. Rev. Lett.* 77:2714, 1996.

Columbia University

Selected Publications (continued)

Xiao, Q., and **G. Navratil.** A photodiode for the measurement of soft X-ray radiation from plasma. *Rev. Sci. Instrum.* 67:3334, 1996.

Neumark, G. F. Deep impurity levels in widegap II-VI's. Section of Propetrties of Wide Bandgar, II-VI Semiconductors. *EMIS Data Reviews Series, IEEE* 17:166, 1997.

Neumark, G. F. Defects In wide bandgap II-VI crystals. *Mat. Sci. Eng. Rep.* R,21:1. Amsterdam: Elsevier, 1997.

Neumark, G. F. Wide bandgap light-emitting device materials and doping problems. *Mat. Lett.* 30:131, 1997 (published as materials update).

Neumark, G. F. Blue-green semiconductor diode lasers. *1995 McGraw-Hill Yearbook of Science and Technology.* New York: McGraw-Hill, 1995.

Neumark, G. F., and G. -J. Yi. II-VI semiconductors: Crystal defects. *Enc. Adv. Mat.* 4:2383-9, 1994.

Luo, Y., et al. **(R. M. Osgood Jr.).** Low-temperature, chemically driven atomic layer epitaxy: In situ monitored growth of CdS/ZnSe100.*Appl. Phys. Lett.,* in press.

Levy, D. S., R. Scarmozzino, Y. M. Li, and **R. M. Osgood Jr.** A new design for ultracompact multimode interference-based 2x2 couplers. *IEEE Photon. Tech. Lett.,* in press.

Osgood Jr., R. M., and X. Wang. Image states on single-crystal metal surfaces. Chapter in *Solid State Physics,* eds. H. Ehrenreich and F. Spaepen. Academic Press, 1997.

Yang, Q. Y., et al. **(R. M. Osgood Jr.).** Highly anisotropic angular dependence of CH_3 fragmentation from electron-transfer reaction on CH_3Br/GaAs(110). *Phys. Rev. Lett.* 72:3068, 1994.

Levy, M., I. Ilic, R. Scarmozzino, and **R. M. Osgood Jr.** Thin-film-magnet magneto-optic waveguide isolator. *IEEE Photon Technol. Lett.* 5:198–200, 1993.

Pellegrini, P., and **A. Pinczuk,** et al. Collapse of spin excitations in quantum hall states of electron double layers. *Phys. Rev. Lett.* 78:310, 1997.

Pinczuk, A., B. S. Dennis, L. N. Pfeiffer, and K. W. West. Observation of collective excitations in the fractional quantum Hall effect. *Phys. Rev. Lett.* 70:3983, 1993.

Pinczuk, A., et al. Observation of roton density of states in two-dimensional landau-level excitations. *Phys. Rev. Lett.* 61:2701, 1988.

Olego, D., **A. Pinczuk,** A. C. Gossard, and W. Wiegmann. Plasma dispersion in a layered electron gas: A determination in GaAs-A1GaAs heterostructures. *Phys. Rev. B* 26:7867, 1982.

Pinczuk, A., J. Shah, A. C. Gossard, and W. Wiegman. Light scattering by photoexcited two dimensional electron plasma in GaAs-A1GaAs heterostructures. *Phys. Rev. Lett.* 46:1341, 1981.

Polvani, L. M., J. G. Esler, and R. A. Plumb. Time variability and Simmons-Wallace-Branstator instability in a simple nonlinear model. *J. Atmos. Sci.,* in press.

Kuo, A., and **L. M. Polvani.** Time-dependent fully nonlinear geostrophic adjustment. *J. Phys. Oceanogr.* 27(8):1614, 1997.

Cho, J. Y.-K., and **L. M. Polvani.** The morphogenesis of bands and zonal winds with the atmospheres of the giant outer plants. *Science* 273:335–7, 1996.

Polvani, L. M., D. Waugh, and R. A. Plumb. On the subtropical edge of the stratospheric surf zone. *J. Atmos. Sci.* 59:1288–309, 1995.

Polvani, L. M., J. C. McWilliams, M. Spall, and R. Ford. The coherent structures of shallow water turbulence. *Chaos* 4:177–86, 1994.

Ruderman, M., F. Wang, J. Halpern, and T. Zhu. X-rays from isolated pulsars. *Astrophys. J.,* in press.

Ruderman, M., T. Zhu, and K. Chen. Pulsar magnetic field evolution, spindown indices, and glitches. *Astrophys. J.,* in press.

Ruderman, M., K. Chen, and T. Zhu. Alignment of spun-up millisecond pulsars. *Astrophys. J.,* in press.

Ruderman, M., and T. Zhu. Pulsed e annihilation -ray line from a crab-like pulsar. *Astrophys. J.* 478:201, 1997.

Sen, A. K., J. S. Chiu, J. Chen, and P. Tham. Basic studies of fluctuations, transport, and their control. *Plasma Phys., Control Fusion* May, 1997.

Chiu, J. S., and **A. K. Sen.** Studies of transport scaling and reduction under feedback. *Phys. Plasmas* 4:2933, 1997.

Sen, A. K. Feedback control of major disruptions in tokamaks. *Phys. Rev. Lett.* 76:1252, 1996.

Sen, A. K. Quasi-coherent structure in ITG turbulence. *Phys. Plasmas* 3:4287–9, 1996.

Chiu, J. S., M. Tinkle, and **A. K. Sen.** Feedback reduction of anomalous transport. *Phys. Rev. E* 54:2158–61, 1996.

Stormer, H. L., and D. C. Tsui. Composite fermions in the fractional quantum hall effect. Chapter in *Perspectives in Quantum Hall Effects,* eds. S. DasSarma and A. Pinczuk. New York: John Wiley & Sons, 1997.

Yacoby, A., and **H. L. Stormer,** et al. Non-universal conductance quantitatisation in quantum wire. *Phys. Rev. Lett.* 77:4612, 1996.

Ashoori, R. C., and **H. L. Stormer,** et al. N-electron ground state energies of a quantum dot in magnetic field. *Phys. Rev. Lett.* 71:613, 1993.

Kang, W., and **H. L. Stormer,** et al. How real are composite fermions? *Phys. Rev. Lett.* 71:3850, 1993.

Eisenstein, J. P., and **H. L. Stormer.** The fractional quantum hall effect. *Science* 248:1510, 1990.

Katz, J., Y. Zhang, and **W. I. Wang.** Normal incidence intervalence subband absorption in GaSb quantum well enhanced by coupling to InAs conduction band. *Appl. Phys. Lett.* 62:609–11, 1993.

Katz, J., Y. Zhang, and **W. I. Wang.** Normal incidence infrared absorption in AlAs/AlGaAs x-valley multiquantum wells. *Appl. Phys. Lett.* 61:1697–99, 1992.

Li, X., K. F. Longenbach, Y. Wang, and **W. I. Wang.** High breakdown voltage AlSbAs/InAs n-channel field effect transistors. *IEEE Electron Dev. Lett.* 13:192–94, 1992.

Li, X., K. F. Longenbach, and **W. I. Wang.** Observation of piezoelectric field induced carriers in AlGaAs/InGaAs strained-layer heterostructures. *Appl. Phys. Lett.* 60:1513–16, 1992.

Amols, H. I., **M. Zaider,** M. K. Hayes, and P. B. Schiff. Physician/patent-driven risk assignment in radiation oncology: Reality or fancy. *Int. J. Rad. Oncol. Biol. Phys.* 38:455–61, 1997.

Rossi, H. H., and **M. Zaider.** Raiogenic lung cancer: The effects of low doses of low -LET radiation. *Radiat. Environ. Biophys.* 36:85–8, 1997.

Etheridge, E. C., J. L. Fry, and **M. Zaider.** Quasiparticle spectra of trans-polyacetylene. *Phys. Rev. B* 53:3662–8, 1996.

Zaider, M., and M. N. Varma. Carcinogenic risk coefficients at environmental levels of random exposures. *Health Phys.* 70:837–44, 1996.

Zaider, M. Microdosimetric-based risk factors for radiation recieved in space activities during a trip to Mars. *Health Phys.* 70:845–51, 1996.

DARTMOUTH COLLEGE

Department of Physics and Astronomy

Program of Study

The department offers a program of graduate study leading to the Doctor of Philosophy (Ph.D.) degree in physics and participates in Dartmouth's M.D./Ph.D. program. The primary areas of experimental and theoretical research in the department are condensed-matter physics (nanostructures, quantum transport, low-temperature physics, ultrafast scanning tunneling microscopy, superconductivity theory, laser spectroscopy, biomedical optics), plasma and beam physics (magnetohydrodynamics and turbulence, plasma theory and experiment, physics of fusion devices, compact free-electron lasers), space physics (space plasma physics, studies of the ionosphere and magnetosphere, ring-currents, and ground-, satellite-, and rocket-based observations of the ionosphere), astronomy (large-scale structure of the universe, supernovae, X-ray binaries, cataclysmic variables), and cosmology (field theory, phase transitions in the early universe). The Master of Science (M.S.) in physics is also offered.

Requirements for the Ph.D. include satisfactory performance in a core curriculum of graduate-level physics and mathematics, advanced graduate study in a chosen field of specialization, a qualifying examination in general physics, an oral exam in the field of specialization, and successful defense of a written thesis describing the results of independent scholarly research. Two terms of Supervised Undergraduate Teaching are also required. Students with normal preparation usually complete the requirements for the Ph.D. in four to six years.

Research Facilities

The Department of Physics and Astronomy is located in Wilder Laboratory, part of the Sherman Fairchild Physical Sciences Center. The research facilities include fast-pulsed lasers and ultrafast imaging systems, scanning tunneling and atomic force microscopes, ultrahigh-vacuum systems, high field magnets, facilities for low-temperature measurements down to .01 Kelvin, plasma chambers, electron beams, and free electron lasers. Complete machine shop and electronic design and fabrication facilities are available. Computer facilities include a network of Silicon Graphics workstations and network access to supercomputing centers. Facilities for nanostructure fabrication include a clean room, thin-film deposition systems, electron-beam lithography, reactive ion etching, and analytical electron microscopes. Astronomical research facilities include the 2.4m Hiltner and 1.3m McGraw-Hill telescopes at Kitt Peak, Arizona. Field work in experimental space physics includes rocket- and satellite-based observation as well as travel to the Arctic and Antarctic for ground-based remote sensing. The physical sciences library subscribes to more than 1,500 journals.

Financial Aid

Financial aid is available in the form of teaching fellowships and research assistantships as well as national fellowships from NSF, DOD, and NASA. Most students are admitted with Dartmouth Fellowships, which provide a stipend for living expenses and cover the full cost of tuition for five years of study.

Cost of Study

Tuition and fees are provided for almost all graduate students.

Living and Housing Costs

Married students may apply for off-campus College housing. The cost is $450 to $600 per month. There is a limited amount of additional housing for single graduate students (both on and off campus) and a wide variety of housing in the private rental market. The Rental Housing Office can assist students with finding appropriate accommodations.

Student Group

There are 4,000 undergraduates and 1,500 graduate and professional students at Dartmouth College. About 35 students are pursuing graduate study in physics and astronomy.

Location

Dartmouth is located in Hanover, New Hampshire. Concerts, dance and theatrical productions, and film series are provided by the College's Hopkins Center. Both the Green Mountains of Vermont and the White Mountains of New Hampshire are nearby and offer skiing, hiking, and climbing. Boston, Montreal, and New York City may be reached by car in 2, 3, and 5 hours, respectively.

The College

Dartmouth was founded in 1769 and awarded its first Ph.D. in 1885. In addition to doctoral programs in the sciences, the College has graduate programs in business, engineering, and medicine. As the smallest of the Ivy League institutions, Dartmouth maintains a tradition of close student-faculty interaction and excellence in both research and teaching.

Applying

Students may obtain application materials by writing to the department or accessing the World Wide Web. Review of applications begins February 1 for admission the following fall. Later applications are considered, but opportunities for financial aid may be limited.

Correspondence and Information

All inquiries should be directed to:
Graduate Admissions Committee
6127 Wilder Laboratory
Department of Physics and Astronomy
Dartmouth College
Hanover, New Hampshire 03755-3528
Telephone: 603-646-2854
Fax: 603-646-1446
E-mail: physics@dartmouth.edu
World Wide Web: http://www.dartmouth.edu/~physics

Dartmouth College

THE FACULTY AND THEIR RESEARCH

Miles P. Blencowe, Assistant Professor; Ph.D., London, 1989. Condensed-matter theory; electronic and mechanical properties of mesoscopic systems, field theory applied to problems in condensed matter and statistical physics.

Brian C. Chaboyer, Assistant Professor; Ph.D., Yale, 1993. Theoretical astrophysics: structure and evolution of stars, astroseismology, globular cluster ages, formation of the Milky Way.

Richard E. Denton, Research Associate Professor; Ph.D., Maryland, 1986. Computational plasma physics involving linear theory and nonlinear particle and fluid simulations.

Robert A. Fesen, Professor; Ph.D., Michigan, 1981. Optical, UV, and X-ray studies of supernovae and supernova remnants, the interstellar medium, shock waves, and Wolf-Rayet stars.

Marcelo Gleiser, Professor; Ph.D., London, 1986. Field theory, cosmology, and nonequilibrium physics.

Joseph D. Harris, Professor; Ph.D., Purdue, 1955. General relativity and cosmology.

Mary K. Hudson, Robert E. Maxwell Professor in the Arts and Sciences and Department Chair; Ph.D., UCLA, 1974. Space plasma theory, plasma simulation; auroral particle acceleration and heating, solar wind–magnetosphere coupling, magnetosphere-ionosphere interaction, radiation belts and effects of geomagnetic storms.

James W. LaBelle, Associate Professor; Ph.D., Cornell, 1985. Ionospheric and magnetospheric physics, plasma measurements in space, remote sensing of ionospheric plasma processes.

Walter E. Lawrence, Professor; Ph.D., Cornell, 1970. Condensed-matter theory; mechanisms of normal transport and superconductivity.

John G. Lyon, Research Professor; Ph.D., Maryland, 1972. Space plasma physics and magnetospheric physics, numerical simulation and computational physics.

David C. Montgomery, Eleanor and A. Kelvin Smith Professor of Physics; Ph.D., Princeton, 1959. Nonlinear magnetohydrodynamics, MHD turbulence theory, disruptions in fusion devices, magnetic reconnection in laboratory and space plasmas, relaxation processes, statistical fluid mechanics.

Delo E. Mook, Professor; Ph.D., Michigan, 1970. Physics education.

Mary-Ann Mycek, Assistant Professor; Ph.D., Berkeley, 1995. Medical physics, biomedical optics: laser spectroscopy for noninvasive disease diagnosis, fluorescence lifetime imaging microscopy, computational models of optical response in inhomogenous media.

Geoffrey Nunes Jr., Assistant Professor; Ph.D., Cornell, 1991. Experimental condensed-matter physics; mesoscopic systems, low-temperature scanning probe microscopy, ultrafast scanning tunneling microscopy.

John R. Thorstensen, Professor; Ph.D., Berkeley, 1980. Optical studies of close binary stars; large-scale structure of the universe.

John E. Walsh, Frances and Mildred Sears Professor of Physics; Ph.D., Columbia, 1968. Free-electron lasers, millimeter-wave and far-infrared physics, plasma physics, geophysical instruments.

Gary A. Wegner, Margaret Anne and Edward Leede '49 Distinguished Professor; Ph.D., Washington, 1971. Cosmology, large-scale structure of the universe, end states of stellar evolution.

Martin Wybourne, Professor; Ph.D., Nottingham, 1980. Experimental condensed-matter physics; electrical and thermal properties of nanostructures.

DREXEL UNIVERSITY

College of Arts and Sciences
Physics Program

Programs of Study

The 20 faculty members and 30 graduate students who comprise the Department of Physics and Atmospheric Science are a highly diverse group united in the common pursuit of understanding nature at its deepest levels. Despite the relatively small size of the faculty, their interests span a wide range of physics and provide a stimulating collegial atmosphere. This professional diversity has been incorporated into the curriculum in which first- and second-year students see some of the contemporary fields of physics firsthand as well as learn the fundamental subjects. This is especially helpful to the student who is undecided about the field he or she wishes to pursue; specialization does not occur until after the second year. Both Ph.D. and master's-level programs are offered. Students interested solely in the M.S. degree are also welcomed and find the opportunities to broaden their professional understanding through traditional courses as well as the possibility of viewing forefront topics in a classroom setting.

Research Facilities

Available facilities include a laboratory for high-performance parallel computation; a detector development laboratory, which includes state-of-the-art fast electronics; a magnetic material and thin-film laboratory; a surface science laboratory, which includes high vacuum systems, various surface spectroscopies, and AFM and STMs; a pulsed-laser laboratory with dye, holmium oxide, and YLF lasers; a modulated excitation kinetics laboratory with Argon Ion and CW dye lasers that use frequency domain techniques; two spatially resolved kinetics laboratories (with argon ion and pulsed nitrogen laser) with microscopic resolution; and computational facilities for study and display of biomolecules.

Financial Aid

Virtually all full-time students in chemistry, mathematics, and physics hold teaching or research assistantships. Job requirements vary according to department. Stipends range from $12,000 to $15,000 per calendar year, and most assistantships include tuition remission. Information on general loan programs may be obtained from the Financial Aid Office.

Cost of Study

In 1999–2000, tuition in the physics department at Drexel University is $585 per credit hour. The general University fee is $125 per term for full-time students and $67 per term for part-time students.

Living and Housing Costs

Accommodations for single students are available in University residence halls. Ample housing is also available in the neighborhood bordering the campus. For the nine-month academic year, transportation and living expenses for a single student are estimated at $11,450.

Student Group

The University has a total enrollment of about 9,590 students, including 2,785 at the graduate level. The Department of Physics and Atmospheric Sciences enrolls about 30 graduate students. Virtually all Ph.D. graduates from the physics program assume faculty or postdoctoral fellow positions at first-rate research institutions, including, in recent years, Harvard, MIT, California Institute of Technology, the National Institutes of Health, and Brookhaven National Laboratory.

Location

A city of more than 2 million, Philadelphia is a center of science, industry, and culture. With some forty colleges and universities in the metropolitan area, it is the second-largest community of institutions of higher education in the country. The University, easily reached from all parts of the area by bus, subway, railroad, and auto, is only a few minutes' walk from the heart of a city steeped in history. The city's flourishing cultural life is based in its museums and centers for theater, opera, symphony concerts, and ballet. Philadelphia also supports a number of major sports, including professional football, ice hockey, baseball, and basketball. Facilities for a variety of intramural sports are available at colleges and universities throughout the city.

The University

Drexel, founded in 1891 by Anthony J. Drexel, Philadelphia financier and philanthropist, was originally the Drexel Institute of Art, Science and Industry. For many years designated the Drexel Institute of Technology, Drexel formally became a university in the 1969–70 academic year. It now comprises five coeducational units: the Colleges of Arts and Sciences, Design Arts, Engineering, Business and Administration, and Information Studies.

Applying

Students are normally admitted for the fall quarter, which begins in late September, but they may enter the program at the beginning of any quarter. A bachelor's degree or its equivalent from an accredited university is a prerequisite. Applicants who wish to be considered for assistantships must submit their application by February 1. Application forms and additional information may be obtained from the address below.

Correspondence and Information

Office of Graduate Admissions, Box P
Drexel University
Philadelphia, Pennsylvania 19104
Telephone: 215-895-6700
E-mail: admissions-grad@post.drexel.edu

Drexel University

THE FACULTY AND THEIR RESEARCH

Shyamalendu M. Bose, Ph.D., Maryland, 1967. Theory of surfaces and interfaces, disordered systems, electronic and X-ray spectroscopy of solids, superconductivity.

Joan Centrella, Ph.D., Cambridge, 1980. Large-scale computations of galactic structures, numerical modeling of the universe, gravitational radiation.

N. John DiNardo, Ph.D., Pennsylvania, 1982. Surfaces and interfaces of semiconductors, metals, and biomaterials; scanning tunneling, photoemission, and electron-scattering spectroscopies.

Da Hsuan Feng, Ph.D., Minnesota, 1972. Development of symmetry-dictated truncations of the spherical shell model for collective states in nuclei, electromagnetic properties of nuclei, high-spin spectroscopy, properties of nuclei far from B-stability, nuclear astrophysics, quantum chaos.

Frank A. Ferrone, Ph.D., Princeton, 1974. Experimental and theoretical protein dynamics, kinetics of biological self-assembly.

Leonard X. Finegold, Ph.D., London, 1959. Biological physics, phase transitions in biomembranes.

Robert Gilmore, Ph.D., MIT, 1967. Applications of compact and noncompact Lie algebras to problems in nuclear, atomic, and molecular physics; nonlinear dynamics and chaos; laser instabilities.

Richard D. Haracz, Ph.D., Wayne State, 1964. Electromagnetic scattering of irregular objects, atmospheric physics.

Frederick B. House, Ph.D., Wisconsin, 1965. Satellite meteorology, earth energy budget.

Charles E. Lane, Ph.D., Caltech, 1987. Experimental nuclear physics, experimental tests of invariance principles and conservation laws, magnetic monopoles and high-energy cosmic neutrinos, solar neutrinos and neutrino oscillations.

Donald C. Larson, Ph.D., Harvard, 1962. Optical waveguides in semiconductors, fiber-optical sensors, heat transfer.

Teck-Kah Lim, Ph.D., Adelaide (Australia), 1968. Structures and dynamics of small nuclear and molecular systems, spin-polarized quantum systems, physics in two dimensions, computer-aided physics education.

James A. McCray, Ph.D., Caltech, 1962. Pulsed-laser and synchroton radiation (Brookhaven and DESY), kinetic studies of the molecular mechanism of muscle contraction and neural transmitter function, laser photolysis of caged compounds, development of laser temperature-jump instrumentation systems.

Stephen L. McMillan, Ph.D., Harvard, 1983. Stellar dynamics, large-scale computations of stellar systems.

Lorenzo M. Narducci, Ph.D., Milan, 1964. Laser physics, quantum optics, nonlinear dynamical systems, spatial patterns.

Richard I. Steinberg, Ph.D., Yale, 1969. Experimental tests of invariance principles and conservation laws, experimental search for magnetic monopoles and high-energy cosmic neutrinos, solar neutrinos and neutrino oscillations.

Somdev Tyagi, Ph.D., Brigham Young, 1976. High-temperature superconductivity, magnetic properties of thin sputtered films of amorphous metallic allies, fiber-optical sensors.

Michel Vallieres, Ph.D., Pennsylvania, 1972. Large-scale (supercomputer) calculations of nuclear and quark structures, computer architecture for nuclear physics problems.

Jian-Min Yuan, Ph.D., Chicago, 1973. Nonlinear dynamics and chaos for atomic and molecular systems, group theoretical studies of scattering processes, protein folding.

Huan-Xiang Zhou, Ph.D., Drexel, 1993. Computational biophysics, electrostatics and protein dynamics.

DUKE UNIVERSITY

School of Arts and Sciences
Department of Physics

Programs of Study
The Department of Physics offers graduate work for students who wish to earn the A.M., M.S., or Ph.D. degree. In addition to a balanced program of basic graduate courses, the department offers specialized courses and seminars in several fields in which research is being performed by faculty and staff members. A typical first-year program provides one year each of quantum mechanics and mathematics and one semester each of classical mechanics, electromagnetism, and statistical mechanics. Quantum mechanics and electromagnetism are studied further in the second year, along with distribution courses in several areas of physics. The emphasis shifts heavily to research in the third year, with perhaps some courses and seminars to complete the specialized work.

Full-time students making good progress are advised to work directly toward the Ph.D. The option of taking the A.M. (oral exam without a thesis) or taking the M.S. (oral exam with a thesis) is subject to approval by a departmental committee. The average time needed to complete the Ph.D. is approximately six years, including summers; the minimum residency requirement is two years of full-time study and research.

A written qualifying exam is given at the end of the first year. A supervisory committee is appointed for each student and is responsible for making decisions about progress. The committee also administers two oral examinations: the Preliminary Examination, normally completed by the end of the third year, and the Final Examination, primarily concerned with the quality of the research reported in the dissertation.

Research Facilities
The research groups are not large but are very active; this provides the opportunity for students to play a major role in research and fosters a strong interaction between students and faculty members. The department is the site of the Triangle Universities Nuclear Laboratory and the Duke Free Electron Laser Laboratory.

The high-energy physics group works with researchers at major accelerator labs (e.g., Fermilab and CERN). The Center for Nonlinear Studies is a cooperative program involving faculty members of the Departments of Physics, Mathematics, Computer Science, and Chemistry and the School of Engineering.

Financial Aid
A number of teaching and research assistantships and fellowships are available each year to incoming students. In addition to a stipend, all awards provide funds that cover tuition and fees. The James B. Duke Fellowship is a four-year University award that requires no service during the first year. Charles H. Townes Teaching Fellowships are also available from the department. Research assistantships are available to advanced students and to first-year students with special experience. Excellent opportunities exist for summer employment as research assistants after the first academic year. Applicants who ask to be considered for an award are automatically considered for both assistantships and fellowships. The department does not ordinarily offer financial aid to students who intend to work toward only the A.M. or M.S. degree.

Cost of Study
In 1999–2000, the tuition rate for full-time graduate students is $17,520. Additional charges include a registration fee of $2500, a health fee of $480, and a one-time transcript charge of $30.

Living and Housing Costs
On-campus single graduate student housing (for twelve months) is $5012 for a 1-student efficiency, $3825 per student for a two-bedroom apartment, and $3251 per student for a three-bedroom apartment.

On-campus married graduate student housing (for twelve months) is $5012 for an efficiency (with spouse only), $7632 for two bedrooms (with spouse and 1 or 2 children), and $9715 for three bedrooms (with spouse and 2 or 3 children). Off-campus housing information is available at http://housing.bootp.duke.edu/grad/centrate.html or http://housing.bootp.duke.edu/grad/marrate.html.

Student Group
Currently, the Department of Physics has 60 full-time graduate students, all of whom receive financial aid. When reviewing applications for admission, the recruiting committee looks at the student's GPA, GRE and TOEFL scores, classes taken in undergraduate school, recommendation letters, and statement of purpose. At this time the physics department has 50 men and 10 women, 20 of whom are international students.

Student Outcomes
Duke graduates continue their careers in physics in a variety of positions all over the world in government laboratories, universities and colleges, and industry. Former students include an astronaut, the Science Advisors to Presidents Clinton and Reagan, a 1997 Nobel Laureate, and well over 100 university professors.

Location
Duke University and the surrounding area provide an exceptional environment for study and living. Neo-Gothic West Campus, where the Department of Physics is located, was built in the early 1930s. Duke's beautiful wooded campus, together with the adjacent Duke Forest, comprise about 8,000 acres. The pleasant climate invites outdoor activities; swimming pools, tennis courts, golf courses, jogging trails, and baseball fields abound. Cultural opportunities at Duke include numerous film series, the Broadway at Duke program, the Duke Artists series, an excellent series of chamber music concerts, and frequent visits by popular music groups.

The Department
The Department of Physics is a part of the School of Arts and Sciences. Interdisciplinary collaborations between the various departments within the School are a special feature of Duke, as are collaborations among the Schools of Arts and Sciences, Medicine, Business, and Law.

Nuclear physics and low-temperature physics have a long-standing history in the department. Currently, the department is active in optical and free-electron laser physics, experimental photon physics, medical physics, experimental condensed-matter physics, nuclear and particle theory, experimental high-energy physics, condensed-matter theory, experimental nuclear physics, nonlinear dynamics and complex systems, and string theory.

Applying
Application deadlines are December 31 for fall admission and financial aid. An offer of admission is made beginning April 15. The application fee is $75.

For admission to the graduate programs, a bachelor's degree in physics or a related subject is required, with a minimum undergraduate GPA of 3.2. GRE General and Subject Test scores are required.

Correspondence and Information
Pat Yonaitis
The Graduate School
127 Allen Building
Box 90065
Duke University
Durham, North Carolina 27708-0065
Telephone: 919-684-3913
E-mail: grad-admissions@acpub.duke.edu
World Wide Web: http://www.gradschool.duke.edu/reqapp.htm

Duke University

THE FACULTY AND THEIR RESEARCH

Professors

Robert P. Behringer, Ph.D., Duke, 1975. Low-temperature physics, nonlinear phenomena.
Edward G. Bilpuch (Emeritus), Ph.D., North Carolina, 1956. Experimental nuclear physics.
Mikael Ciftan (Adjunct), Ph.D., Duke, 1968. Theoretical physics, solid-state theory, statistical thermodynamics.
Lawrence Evans, Ph.D., Johns Hopkins, 1960. Theoretical physics, elementary particle physics.
Alfred T. Goshaw, Ph.D., Wisconsin, 1966. Experimental elementary particle physics, instrumentation.
Bob D. Guenther (Adjunct), Ph.D., Missouri, 1968. Optical and laser physics.
Moo-Young Han, Ph.D., Rochester, 1963. Theoretical physics, elementary particle physics.
G. Allan Johnson, Ph.D., Duke, 1974. Imaging physics, magnetic resonance imaging (primary appointment with Radiology).
Horst Meyer, Ph.D., Zurich, 1953. Experimental low-temperature and solid-state physics.
Berndt Müller, Chairman of the Department; Ph.D., Frankfurt, 1973. Theoretical nuclear and particle physics.
Richard G. Palmer, Ph.D., Cambridge, 1973. Theoretical condensed-matter physics, complex systems.
N. Russell Roberson, Ph.D., Johns Hopkins, 1960. Experimental nuclear physics, tests of fundamental symmetries.
John E. Thomas, Ph.D., MIT, 1979. Experimental quantum optics, atomic and molecular collision physics.
Werner Tornow (Research), Director of TUNL; Ph.D., Tuebingen (Germany), 1972. Experimental nuclear physics, few-nucleon systems.
Richard L. Walter, Ph.D., Notre Dame, 1960. Experimental nuclear physics.
Henry R. Weller, Director of Graduate Studies; Ph.D., Duke, 1967. Experimental nuclear physics, nuclear structure, gamma-ray studies.

Associate Professors

Daniel J. Gauthier, Director of Undergraduate Studies; Ph.D., Rochester, 1989. Quantum optics and laser physics.
Henry S. Greenside, Ph.D., Princeton, 1981. Nonlinear dynamics and computational physics.
Calvin R. Howell, Ph.D., Duke, 1984. Nuclear physics, few-nucleon systems.
Vladimir Litvinenko, Ph.D., Novosibirsk (Russia), 1990. Free-electron laser physics.
Seog H. Oh, Ph.D., MIT, 1981. Experimental elementary particle physics.
David D. Skatrud (Adjunct), Ph.D., Duke, 1984. Millimeter and submillimeter spectroscopy.
Stephen W. Teitsworth, Ph.D., Harvard, 1986. Experimental condensed-matter physics.

Assistant Professors

Robert G. Brown (Visiting), Ph.D., Duke, 1982. Theoretical physics.
Shailesh Chandrasekharan, Ph.D., Columbia, 1995. Lattice gauge theory.
Ludwig C. DeBraeckeleer, Ph.D., Louvain (Belgium), 1989. Experimental nuclear physics, weak interactions.
Henry Everitt (Adjunct), Ph.D., Duke, 1990. Molecular physics, quantum optics.
John Kolena (Adjunct), Ph.D., Indiana, 1978. Experimental atomic and molecular physics, astrophysics.
Ashutosh Kotwal, Ph.D., Harvard, 1995. Experimental elementary particle physics.
Alfred M. Lee, Ph.D., Yale, 1989. Experimental particle physics.
Konstantin Matveev, Ph.D., Chernogolovka, 1991. Theoretical condensed-matter physics.
Thomas J. Phillips (Research), Ph.D., Harvard, 1986. Experimental elementary particle physics, instrumentation.
Ronen M. Plesser, Ph.D., Harvard, 1991. String theory, supersymmetry.
Joshua E. S. Socolar, Ph.D., Pennsylvania, 1987. Theoretical condensed-matter physics.
Roxanne Springer, Ph.D., Caltech, 1990. Theoretical nuclear and particle physics.

EMORY UNIVERSITY
Department of Physics

Programs of Study

The Department of Physics offers programs leading to the Master of Arts, Master of Science, and Doctor of Philosophy degrees in physics. Current research activities in the department focus on two main areas: theoretical condensed-matter physics and experimental biological physics. The department's low student-faculty ratio guarantees high levels of personal interaction. Regular colloquia and seminars provide additional stimulation. To better prepare students to meet the rapidly changing environments in academia, industry, commerce, and government, the Department of Physics, together with other science departments at Emory University, including the Departments of Biology, Biochemistry, Chemistry, and Mathematics and Computer Science, has developed a new, multidisciplinary graduate program in physical, material, and computational sciences. It is comprised of three interrelated multidisciplinary research areas: molecular biophysics, material science, and theory and modeling. Students admitted into this program may choose to conduct research in one or more of these three areas and take graduate training courses from several of the above-mentioned departments. This new program provides students with in-depth, cross-disciplinary training that will enhance their pursuit of an independent career and increase their competitiveness in employment opportunities.

The Graduate School requirements for the master's degrees include 24 semester hours of course, seminar, or research credit and a general examination and/or a thesis. These requirements take an average of two to three semesters to complete. The requirements for the Ph.D. include the master's degree or the equivalent, full residence (12 semester hours) for at least four semesters beyond the master's level, a general doctoral examination, and a doctoral dissertation. During the full-residence period, 48 semester hours of credit must be accumulated. Of these, 24 hours must be in courses, directed study, or seminars, and 8 hours must be in areas outside physics.

Research Facilities

The Department of Physics is located in the Rollins Research Center, a state-of-the-art building designed for interdisciplinary scientific research. The departmental research facilities include Raman, EPR, and Mössbauer spectrometers; SQUID susceptometer and equipment for sample synthesis and preparation. Other facilities include an electronics shop and a machine shop. The department operates an internal computer network, connected both to the University Computer Center and to external networks, including the Internet. Graduate students have unlimited access to these facilities. The library facilities include a 75,000-volume science library, a chemistry library, and a health sciences library that subscribe to all of the major U.S. and foreign physics, chemistry, mathematics, and biophysics journals. Emory University is a sponsoring member of the UNISOR facility at Oak Ridge and has access to the infrared beam at the Brookhaven National Laboratory Synchrotron light source.

Financial Aid

Graduate students in the department receive full funding, including a full tuition waiver and a fellowship. First-year students do not teach. Second-year teaching assistants are assigned teaching duties that require a light load of 10–12 hours of teaching per week. Research assistantships and fellowships are available, allowing graduate students beyond the second year to carry out full-time research.

Cost of Study

Tuition for the 1999–2000 academic year is $22,770. Admitted graduate students are granted full tuition waivers and receive a yearly fellowship of $15,235 that covers expenses while they are earning their degree.

Living and Housing Costs

Atlanta's cost of living ranks among the lowest of the nation's metropolitan areas. Housing in University apartments ranges from $361 to $1071 per month. In addition, students have a wide range of options in rooms and apartments in the residential neighborhoods surrounding the campus.

Student Group

Emory has a total enrollment of 11,353 students. Enrollment in the various schools of the University is restricted to maintain the most favorable use possible of facilities and resources. There are 4,044 students in the undergraduate college and 5,011 students in the eight graduate and professional schools.

Location

Atlanta is a metropolitan area with a population of more than 2 million. It offers many cultural and recreational opportunities, including the Atlanta Symphony Orchestra, a resident opera company, a resident repertory theater, a ballet company, and major-league sports. Emory is located in the northeastern part of the city in a residential area, within a short drive or bus ride of the downtown area. Within an hour's drive are the Blue Ridge Mountains and several large lakes that offer opportunities for camping, hiking, swimming, and boating.

The University and The Department

Emory University is a private university with a national reputation for scholarly and educational excellence. Expansion at Emory accelerated after 1980, when the Robert W. Woodruff gift boosted Emory's endowment, now fifth in the nation. The Emory University Graduate School has awarded advanced degrees since 1919, and many of its graduates occupy positions of leadership in education and research. Nearly 140 Ph.D. degrees were awarded last year. The physics department has a tradition of emphasizing personal contact among faculty and students, as well as offering high-quality training in scholarship and research.

Applying

Applications should be submitted as early as possible. Applications for financial aid and scores on the GRE General Test and Subject Test in physics are to be submitted by January 20. International students whose native language is not English must provide scores on the Test of English as a Foreign Language (TOEFL) in addition to the GRE scores. Awards are generally made by April 1. Emory University does not discriminate on the basis of race, color, religion, sex, national origin, handicap, age, or veteran status.

Correspondence and Information

Director of Graduate Studies
Department of Physics
Emory University
Atlanta, Georgia 30322
Telephone: 404-727-8037
        800-727-6028 (toll-free)

Emory University

THE FACULTY AND THEIR RESEARCH

Scott R. Anderson, Teaching Affiliate; Ph.D., Chicago, 1987. Computational condensed-matter physics.

Krishan K. Bajaj, Charles T. Winship Professor of Physics; Ph.D., Purdue, 1966. Theoretical solid-state physics: electronic properties of semiconductors and superlattices, solid-state devices.

Katherine Benson, Assistant Professor; Ph.D., Harvard, 1991. Particle theory.

Keith M. Berland, Assistant Professor; Ph.D., Illinois, 1995. Experimental biophysics.

Stefan Boettcher, Lecturer; Ph.D., Washington (St. Louis), 1993. Statistical physics, critical phenomena.

Robert L. W. Chen, Professor; Ph.D., Syracuse, 1960. Theoretical physics, quantum mechanics.

Robert N. Coleman, Lecturer; M.S., Emory, 1974. Radioecology.

Christopher Dawson, Teaching Affiliate; B.S., Emory, 1996. Applied physics.

Edmund P. Day, Associate Professor; Ph.D., Stanford, 1973. Experimental biophysics: magnetic susceptibility measurement of metalloenzymes and synthetic models of these proteins.

Raymond C. DuVarney, Associate Professor and Chair of the Department; Ph.D., Clark, 1968. Adaptive optics.

Robert L. Eisner, Adjunct Assistant Professor; Ph.D., Purdue, 1968. Nuclear medicine.

Fereydoon Family, Samuel Candler Dobbs Professor of Condensed Matter Physics; Ph.D., Clark, 1974. Theoretical condensed-matter physics: nonequilibrium growth phenomena, pattern formation, fractals, surface and interface physics.

Peter Fong, Professor; Ph.D., Chicago, 1953. Theoretical nuclear physics, molecular biophysics, geophysics.

Ernest V. Garcia, Adjunct Associate Professor; Ph.D., Miami (Florida), 1974. Medical imaging.

H. George E. Hentschel, Associate Professor; Ph.D., Cambridge, 1978. Theoretical condensed-matter and statistical physics: neural networks, spin glasses, nonlinear dynamics, chaos and turbulence.

Boi Hanh Huynh, Samuel Candler Dobbs Professor of Physics and Director of Graduate Studies; Ph.D., Columbia, 1974. Experimental biophysics: Mössbauer and EPR studies of metalloenzymes.

James P. Kinney III, Teaching Affiliate; M.S., Georgia State, 1997. Physics.

Susannah Lomant, Teaching Affiliate; M.S., Ball State, 1999. Physics.

John A. Malko, Adjunct Assistant Professor; Ph.D., Ohio, 1970. Nuclear medicine.

Paul Meakin, Adjunct Professor; Ph.D., California, Santa Barbara, 1973. Simulational condensed-matter physics: growth and aggregation phenomena, fractals.

John Palms, Adjunct Professor; Ph.D., New Mexico, 1966. Environmental physics.

Sidney Perkowitz, Charles Howard Candler Professor of Condensed Matter Physics; Ph.D., Pennsylvania, 1967. Experimental condensed-matter physics: Raman, far-infrared, and photoluminescence spectroscopy of semiconductor superlattices and superconductors.

P. Venugopala Rao, Associate Professor; Ph.D., Oregon, 1964. Experimental nuclear and atomic physics.

Robert H. Rohrer, Professor Emeritus; Ph.D., Duke, 1954. Experimental radiological physics.

Christopher Summers, Adjunct Assistant Professor; Ph.D., Reading (England), 1966. Experimental solid-state physics: semiconductor physics.

Kurt Warncke, Assistant Professor; Ph.D., Pennsylvania, 1989. Experimental biophysics; pulsed EPR investigations of radical mediated enzyme catalysis.

Richard M. Williamon, Adjunct Assistant Professor; Ph.D., Florida, 1972. Astronomy.

RESEARCH INTERESTS

Theoretical

Condensed-matter physics: Nonequilibrium growth phenomena, pattern formation, fractals, spin glasses, dynamical systems. Family, Hentschel.

Neural networks and dynamical systems: Statistical theory of stereoscopic vision. Hentschel.

Solid-state physics: Theory of semiconductors, heterostructures, and optoelectronic devices. Bajaj.

Experimental

Biological Physics: Investigation of structure and function relations of proteins and enzymes using optical, Mössbauer, EPR, and time-resolved pulsed-EPR spectroscopies and saturation magnetization techniques. Investigation of cellular and biomolecular structure and dynamics using fluorescence imaging and spectroscopy. Development of ultrasensitive single-molecule techniques. Near-field optics. Berland, Day, Huynh, Warncke.

FLORIDA INSTITUTE OF TECHNOLOGY

College of Science and Liberal Arts
Department of Physics and Space Sciences

Programs of Study

The master's degree in physics requires a minimum of 33 graduate semester credit hours of study, including two graduate-level mathematics courses and seven core courses in physics. A master's thesis is optional. A special program involving 35 credits also earns the Certificate in Materials Science and Engineering.

The master's degree in space sciences requires 33 semester credit hours of graduate study, including three graduate-level mathematics and computer science courses and six core courses in space science, physics, and engineering. A master's thesis is optional. There are no foreign language requirements.

The minimum course requirements for the doctoral program of study in physics or in space sciences are 81 credits beyond the bachelor's degree or 48 credits beyond the master's degree. After some semesters of individual study and research under a faculty member's guidance, the candidate must demonstrate competence by passing a comprehensive written examination. Original research that has been accepted for publication must be performed. A dissertation based on original research must be submitted. This is followed by an oral dissertation defense examination. There are no foreign language requirements.

Research Facilities

Experimental research in physics and space sciences is carried out within a variety of laboratories operated by the department. Facilities that are currently available include the Applied Optics Laboratory, Geospace Physics Laboratories, Image Processing Laboratory, Nanoscale Materials Fabrication and Characterization Laboratory, a SARA 0.9-m telescope at Kitt Peak National Observatory, and the Scanning Probe Microscope Laboratory. Computational facilities in the Department of Physics and Space Sciences include four Sun SPARCstations running UNIX/X-windows and a number of Macintoshes and PCs. In addition, the department has access to a wide range of campus computers and can also access supercomputers via the Internet.

Financial Aid

Financial support that includes a stipend and the cost of tuition is available for teaching assistants. Stipends are awarded by the department. The stipend for two semesters at the master's level is $8400. The stipend for two semesters at the Ph.D. level is $9000.

Cost of Study

Tuition for 1998–99 was $550 per credit hour, and yearly increases are to be expected.

Living and Housing Costs

Room and board on campus cost approximately $2200 per semester in 1998–99. On-campus housing (dormitories and apartments) is available for full-time single and married graduate students, but priority for dormitory rooms is given to undergraduate students. Many apartment complexes and rental houses are available near the campus.

Student Group

There are approximately 25 graduate students in the Physics and Space Sciences graduate program. Two to 4 students enroll in the Ph.D. program each year.

Student Outcomes

Graduates have gone on to careers with such corporations as NASA, Harris Corporation, Texas Instruments, Rockwell International, Lockheed Martin, Barrios Technology, McDonnell Douglas, I-NET, Westinghouse, Computer Sciences Raytheon, Boeing, and PRC System Devices.

Location

Florida Tech is located in Melbourne, on the east central coast of Florida, approximately 60 miles southeast of Orlando. The Space Coast offers a delightful year-round subtropical climate and is 10 minutes from the ocean beaches. The Kennedy Space Center and Disney World in Orlando are within an hour's drive of Melbourne. Melbourne International Airport connects the area with other major Florida cities and other domestic destinations.

The University

Florida Institute of Technology was founded in 1958 in Melbourne, Florida, as Brevard Engineering College. Florida Tech has grown rapidly as a major scientific and technological university with both full- and part-time undergraduate and graduate programs. It is the only independent technological university in the Southeast.

Applying

Prospective students for the physics and space sciences programs may apply for admission at any time. The minimum requirement is an undergraduate degree in any of the physical sciences, engineering, or mathematics. Copies of undergraduate and graduate transcripts, GRE scores, and three letters of recommendation should be sent to the Office of Graduate Admissions. International students should include copies of their TOEFL scores; those applying for assistantships should have a TOEFL score of at least 600 and a TSE of at least 45.

Correspondence and Information

Department of Physics and Space Sciences
Florida Institute of Technology
150 West University Boulevard
Melbourne, Florida 32901-6975

Telephone: 407-674-8098
Fax: 407-674-7482
E-mail: blatt@pss.fit.edu

For Application and Catalog:
Graduate Admissions Office
150 West University Boulevard
Melbourne, Florida 32901-6975

Telephone: 407-674-8027
           800-944-4348 (toll-free)
Fax: 407-723-9468
World Wide Web: http://www.fit.edu

Florida Institute of Technology

THE FACULTY AND THEIR RESEARCH

Joel H. Blatt, Professor; Ph.D., Alabama, 1970. Applied optics, machine vision and human vision, optical processors, computer-interfaced video systems and instrumentation, biomedical engineering problems, electromigration.

Jay Burns, Professor Emeritus; Ph.D., Chicago, 1959. Dispersive transport in amorphous materials, elastic and dielectric properties of elastomeric polymers.

Rong-Sheng Jin, Associate Professor; Ph.D., Ohio State, 1965. Geomagnetic field variations, length-of-day fluctuations, planetary magnetic fields, time-series analysis, geodynamo.

James G. Mantovani, Assistant Professor; Ph.D., Clemson, 1985. Surface physics, scanning probe microscopy.

Mark B. Moldwin, Assistant Professor; Ph.D., Boston University, 1993. In-situ plasma observations from space platforms that sample a variety of plasma regions in the Earth's magnetosphere and in the solar wind.

Terry D. Oswalt, Professor; Ph.D., Ohio State, 1981. Ground- and space-based studies of late stages of stellar evolution, binary and multiple systems of stars, and collapsed stars called white dwarfs.

Ryne P. Raffaelle, Assistant Professor; Ph.D., Missouri–Rolla, 1990. Scanning probe microscopy, electrochemical deposition of superlattices, nanophysics, photovoltaic solar cells.

Hamid K. Rassoul, Assistant Professor; Ph.D., Texas at Dallas, 1987. Aeronomy, middle atmospheric chemistry, ionospheric modeling, solar wind–magnetosphere interaction.

Matthew A. Wood, Assistant Professor; Ph.D., Texas at Austin, 1990. Astrophysics, stellar evolution, white dwarf evolution, stellar pulsation, cataclysmic variables, astrophysical fluid dynamics.

James A. Gering, Instructor and Laboratory Supervisor; M.S., Indiana, 1984. Physics education.

Florida Institute of Technology

SELECTED PUBLICATIONS

Gilbert III, B., and **J. H. Blatt.** Multicolor fringe projection system with enhanced 3-D reconstruction of surfaces. In *SPIE Proceedings,* vol. 3520, *Three-Dimensional Imaging, Optical Metrology and Inspection IV,* pp. 13–20, 1998.

Andrade, R., et al. **(J. H. Blatt).** Real-time, optically processed face recognition system based on arbitrary moiré contours. *Opt. Eng.* 35(9):2534–40, 1996.

Caimi, F. M., and **J. H. Blatt** et al. Advanced underwater laser systems for ranging, size estimation, and profiling. *Marine Tech. Soc. J.* 21(1):31–41, 1993.

Blatt, J. H., J. A. Hooker, H.-C. C. Ho, and E. H. Young. The application of acousto-optic cells and video processing to achieve signal-to-noise improvements in variable resolution moiré profilometry. *Opt. Eng.* 31(10):2129–38, 1992.

Jin, R.-S. Cross correlation of the variations of the geomagnetic dipole moment and the fluctuations of the Earth's rotation. *J. Geophys. Res.* 97(B12):1725–60, 1992.

Jin, R.-S., and S. Jin. The 60-year power spectral peak of the magnetic variations around London and the Earth's rotation rate fluctuations. *J. Geophys. Res.* 94(B10):13673–9, 1989.

Fillingim, M. O., and **M. B. Moldwin** et al. Pitch-angle distributions of suprathermal electrons observed at geosynchronous orbit. *J. Geophys. Res.* 104:4457, 1999.

Moldwin, M. B., et al. A reexamination of the local time asymmetry of lobe encounters at geosynchronous orbit: CRRES, ATS5 and LANL observations. *J. Geophys. Res.* 103:9207, 1998.

Moldwin, M. B. Outer plasmaspheric plasma properties: What we know from satellite data. *Space Sci. Rev.* 80, 1997.

Dietrich, M., et al. **(T. D. Oswalt).** Steps toward determination of the size and structure of the broad-line region in active galactic nuclei XII: Ground-based monitoring of 3C 390.3. *Astrophys. J. Suppl.* 115:185, 1998.

Oswalt, T. D. Preserving the future of small observatories: Another good reason for amateur-professional cooperation! In *Proceedings of the Third Mini-Workshop for Asian Astronomers* (Okayama, Japan), p. 35, 1998.

Raffaelle, R. P., et al. **(J. G. Mantovani).** Electrodeposited CdS on CIS pn junctions. *Solar Energy Mater. Solar Cells* 57:167, 1999.

Raffaelle, R. P., J. G. Mantovani, and R. Friedfeld. Scanning microscopy of electrodeposited $CuInSe_2$ nanoscale multilayers. *Solar Energy Mater. Solar Cells* 46:201, 1997.

Switzer, J. A., and **R. P. Raffaelle** et al. Scanning tunneling microscopy of electrodeposited ceramic superlattices. *Science* 258:1918, 1992.

Ringwald, F. A., W. R. J. Rolleston, R. A. Saffer, and J. R. Thorstensen. PG 1002+506: A Be star apparently at $Z > +10$ kpc. *Astrophys J.* 497:717, 1998.

Ringwald, F. A., J. R. Thorstensen, R. K. Honeycutt, and R. C. Smith. The orbital period and variability of the dwarf nova WW Ceti. *Astron. J.* 111:2077, 1996.

Montgomery, M. H., E. W. Klumpe, D. E. Winget, and **M. A. Wood.** Evolutionary calculations of phase separation in crystallizing white dwarf stars. *Astrophys. J.,* in press.

Simpson, J. C., and **M. A. Wood.** Time-series energy production in SPH accretion disks: Superhumps in the AM CVn stars. *Astrophys. J.* 506:360, 1998.

Wood, M. A., and T. Oswalt. White dwarf cosmochronology 1: Monte Carlo simulations proper-motion and magnitude-limited samples using Schmidt's $1/V_{max}$ estimator. *Astrophys. J.* 497:870, 1997.

Provencal, J., et al. **(M. A. Wood).** Whole Earth telescope observations of the helium interacting binary PG1346+082 (CR Boo). *Astrophys. J.* 480:383, 1997.

FLORIDA STATE UNIVERSITY
Department of Physics

Programs of Study	Programs of study are offered that lead to the M.S. and Ph.D. degrees. The Department of Physics has approximately 40 teaching faculty members, including Nobel Laureate Professor Robert Schrieffer, and another 40 Ph.D. physicists engaged in a variety of research programs. The graduate program has approximately 90 students and almost all hold research or teaching assistantships. The programs of study include experimental and theoretical, atomic, and nuclear physics; computational physics; material science; and high-energy physics. Three University institutes have major physics research components—Supercomputer Computations Research Institutes (SCRI) for computational intensive research, Material Science and Technology Center (MARTECH) for condensed-matter physics, and the National High Magnetic Field Laboratory (NHMFL) for research on materials using very high magnetic fields.

The department offers both course-work only and thesis-type M.S. degrees. All students are required to pass a proficiency examination before the middle of their second year. Students studying for the Ph.D. degree are also required to pass a comprehensive examination on electrodynamics, quantum, classical, and statistical mechanics. Within six months of passing the comprehensive examination, students should pass an oral examination on the subject of the student's prospective research. The only formal course requirement is to take four advanced topics courses.

Research Facilities
The department occupies three adjacent buildings: an eight-story Physics Research Building, a Nuclear Research Building, and an undergraduate physics classroom and laboratory building. The experimental facilities include a 9.5-MV Super FN Tandem Van de Graaff accelerator with superconducting post accelerator; a large gamma detection array; 3- and 4-MeV Van de Graaffs; a detector development laboratory for high-energy particle detectors; high-resolution Fourier-transform IR spectrometers; facilities for ion implantation; liquid helium temperature research facilities; UHV facilities (including surface characterization, molecular beam epitaxy, and surface analysis by He atom scattering); facilities for high- and low-temperature superconductivity, small-angle and standard X-ray diffractometry, scanning electron and tunneling microscopy, image analysis, quasi-elastic light scattering, polarized electron energy loss spectroscopy, thick- and thin-film preparation, and high magnetic field studies; and the National High Magnetic Field Laboratory. In addition to using in-house facilities, those engaged in ongoing experiments use accelerator and other research equipment at Fermilab, Brookhaven, Los Alamos, MIT-Bates, TJNAF, Oak Ridge, and CERN. The Department of Physics and the University have extensive computational facilities that are networked throughout the world through T1 and T3 lines. Within the department there are several clusters of state-of-the-art computer workstations comprising more than 100 individual units. Computer facilities at SCRI are also available to students on a need basis. More information on individual faculty research can be found on the department's Web site (listed below).

Financial Aid
The department offers teaching and research assistantships and fellowships. The fellowships include several that are designed to help develop promising young minority physicists. The assistantship stipend is $16,000 for twelve months, with a workload equivalent to 6 contact hours in an elementary laboratory. In general, summer assistantships are provided for all students. Students are teaching assistants during the first academic year but most are supported by research assistantships after that year.

Cost of Study
All tuition and fees for Florida residents are covered by the department in 1999–2000. The additional charge for out-of-state tuition is normally waived for assistants and fellows.

Living and Housing Costs
Apartments and houses are readily available in Tallahassee. A typical one-bedroom unfurnished apartment within walking distance of the physics building rents for $425 per month. The University has married student housing with rents that range from $270 to $291 per month for a one-bedroom apartment to $364 to $428 per month for a two or three-bedroom apartment in 1999–2000. National surveys show that the cost of living in Tallahassee is 10 to 15 percent lower than that in most areas of the United States.

Student Group
Florida State University is a comprehensive university with a total of 29,371 students, of whom 5,685 are graduate or professional students. The physics department has about 90 graduate students. The average time for achieving a Ph.D. for students entering with a B.S. degree in physics is about 5½ years.

Location
Tallahassee is the capital city of the state of Florida. Its population is about 180,000. Many employment opportunities exist for students' spouses in Tallahassee. Students can live in relatively rural surroundings and still be only 20 minutes from the University. Extensive sports facilities and active city leagues exist in the city. Because of the mild winter climate, people in this region tend to be outdoor oriented. Numerous sinkholes provide enjoyable nontraditional swimming areas. The Gulf of Mexico is about 30 miles from campus.

The University and The Department
The presentations of the Schools of Fine Arts and Music provide cultural opportunities that are usually available only in much larger cities. The University Symphony, the Flying High Circus, and other theater and music groups give students the opportunity to participate in many activities in addition to their physics studies. FSU has active programs in intercollegiate and intramural sports.

Recent major additions in the FSU Science Center have been the development of the Supercomputer Computations Research Institute (SCRI), an interdisciplinary Materials Sciences and Technology (MARTECH) center, the completion of the P. A. M. Dirac Science Library, and the National High Magnetic Field Laboratory (NHMFL). The NHMFL houses the world's highest field magnets, making FSU one of the principal centers for magnetic research. Besides the teaching faculty at the Department of Physics (listed on the back of this page), there are 15 full-time research faculty members at SCRI and 13 in MARTECH.

Applying
Assistantship decisions are based on a student's transcript, GRE General Test scores, and three letters of reference. The deadline for completed applications to be on file with the physics department is January 15, 1999 for international students and March 1, 1999 for U.S. citizens. Application forms can be printed from the department's Web site (listed below).

Correspondence and Information
Professor Kirby Kemper
Graduate Physics Program
Department of Physics
Florida State University
Tallahassee, Florida 32306-4350
Telephone: 850-644-4473 or 2340
Fax: 850-644-8630
E-mail: graduate@hep.fsu.edu
World Wide Web: http://www.physics.fsu.edu

Florida State University

THE FACULTY AND THEIR RESEARCH

Howard Baer, Professor; Ph.D., Wisconsin–Madison, 1984. Theoretical physics: elementary particle physics.

Bernd Berg, Professor; Ph.D., Berlin, 1977. Theoretical physics: statistical mechanics, lattice gauge theory, quantum measurement process, computational physics.

Susan K. Blessing, Assistant Professor; Ph.D., Indiana, 1989. Experimental physics: elementary particle physics.

Nicholas Bonesteel, Assistant Professor; Ph.D., Cornell, 1991. Theoretical physics: condensed-matter physics, many-body theory, magnetism, quantum Hall effect.

James S. Brooks, Professor; Ph.D., Oregon, 1973. Experimental physics: low temperature, high magnetic field condensed matter, organic conductor, quantum fluid physics.

Simon C. Capstick, Assistant Professor; Ph.D., Toronto, 1986. Theoretical physics: theoretical nuclear and particle physics, computational physics.

Paul Cottle, Professor; Ph.D., Yale, 1986. Experimental physics: heavy-ion nuclear physics.

Jack Crow, Professor and Director, National High Magnetic Field Laboratory; Ph.D., Rochester, 1967. Experimental physics: correlated electron systems, high-T_c superconductors and heavy fermions.

Elbio Dagotto, Professor; R.A., Ph.D., Bariloche (Argentina), 1985. Theoretical physics: condensed matter, computational physics, superconductors.

Lawrence C. Dennis, Professor; Ph.D., Virginia, 1979. Experimental physics: intermediate-energy, electron scattering, computational physics.

Vladimir Dobrosavljivic, Assistant Professor; Ph.D, Brown, 1988. Theoretical condensed matter physics; disordered systems and glasses; metal-insulator transitions.

Dennis Duke, Professor; Ph.D., Iowa State, 1974. Theoretical physics: elementary particle physics, computational physics.

Steve Edwards, Professor; Ph.D., Johns Hopkins, 1960. Theoretical physics: low-energy nuclear physics.

Zachary Fisk, Professor; Ph.D., California, San Diego, 1969. Experimental physics: condensed matter physics, superconductivity, magnetism, heavy Fermions.

Neil R. Fletcher, Professor; Ph.D., Duke, 1961. Experimental physics: low-energy nuclear physics.

Vasken Hagopian, Professor; Ph.D., Pennsylvania, 1963. Experimental physics: elementary particle physics.

Kirby Kemper, Professor and Chairman of the Department; Ph.D., Indiana, 1968. Experimental physics: polarization studies of nuclear reactions, radioactive-beam physics.

J. Daniel Kimel, Professor; Ph.D., Wisconsin–Madison, 1966. Theoretical physics: elementary particle physics, computational physics.

David M. Lind, Associate Professor; Ph.D., Rice, 1986. Experimental physics: surfaces, thin films, magnetic properties of solids, magnetic and oxide superlattices.

Efstratios Manousakis, Professor; Ph.D., Illinois at Urbana-Champaign, 1985. Theoretical physics: condensed-matter physics, many-body theory, superfluidity, superconductivity.

Adriana Moreo, Associate Professor; Ph.D., Bariloche (Argentina), 1985. Theoretical physics: condensed matter, strongly correlated electronic systems, superconductivity, computational physics.

William G. Moulton, Professor; Ph.D., Illinois, 1952. Experimental physics: low-temperature solid-state physics.

H. K. Ng, Associate Professor; Ph.D., McMaster, 1984. Experimental condensed-matter physics: far-infrared spectroscopy, superconductivity, highly correlated electron systems, spectroscopy in high-magnetic fields.

Joseph F. Owens, Professor; Ph.D., Tufts, 1973. Theoretical physics: elementary particle theory.

Fred L. Petrovich, Professor; Ph.D., Michigan State, 1970. Theoretical physics: nuclear structure; reaction theory.

Hans S. Plendl, Professor Emeritus; Ph.D., Yale, 1958. Experimental physics: medium-energy nuclear and particle physics.

Harrison B. Prosper, Professor; Ph.D., Manchester (England), 1980. Experimental physics: particle physics, computational physics.

Laura Reina, Assistant Professor; Ph.D., Trieste, 1992. Theoretical physics; elementary particle physics.

Per Arne Rikvold, Professor; Ph.D., Temple, 1983. Theoretical physics: condensed-matter physics, surface and interface science, computational physics.

Mark A. Riley, Professor; Ph.D., Liverpool, 1985. Experimental physics: nuclear structure physics.

Don Robson, Professor; Ph.D., Melbourne, 1963. Theoretical physics: interface between high-energy and nuclear theory.

Adam Sarty, Assistant Professor; Ph.D., Saskatchewan, 1993. Experimental nuclear physics; intermediate-energy electron-scattering.

Pedro Schlottmann, Professor; Ph.D., Technical University Munich, 1973. Theoretical physics: condensed-matter physics, heavy fermions, magnetism, correlated electrons in one dimension.

Robert Schrieffer, Professor; Ph.D., Illinois, 1957. Theoretical physics: condensed matter, many-body theory, superconductivity, magnetism.

Shahid A. Shaheen, Associate Professor; Ph.D., Ruhr-Bochum, 1985. Experimental physics: permanent magnets, superconductivity, magnetism, materials science.

Neil Shelton, Professor; Ph.D., Florida State, 1962. Experimental physics: electron scattering on atoms, atomic collision calculations.

James G. Skofronick, Professor; Ph.D., Wisconsin–Madison, 1964. Experimental physics: He atom scattering studies of surface physics and epitaxial growth.

Samuel L. Tabor, Professor; Ph.D., Stanford, 1972. Experimental physics: high-spin states in nuclei.

David Van Winkle, Associate Professor; Ph.D., Colorado, 1984. Experimental physics: liquid crystals, colloids, macromolecules.

Stephan von Molnár, Professor; Ph.D., California, Riverside, 1965. Experimental physics: correlation effects in electronic systems, magnetic semiconductors, magnetic nanostructures.

Horst Wahl, Professor; Ph.D., Vienna, 1969. Experimental physics: particle physics.

Peng Xiong, Assistant Professor; Ph.D., Brown, 1994. Experimental physics, mesoscopic physics, quantum-phase transitions in low-dimensional systems, electron tunneling into complex solids.

Kun Yang, Assistant Professor; Ph.D., Indiana, 1994. Theoretical physics: condensed matter, computational physics.

RESEARCH ACTIVITIES

Theoretical

Condensed Matter. Many-body theory of magnetism, magnetic properties of solids, high-temperature superconductivity, adsorption, phase transitions, numerical simulations, heavy fermions.

Elementary Particles and Fields. Strong and electroweak interaction phenomenology in high-energy particle physics, lattice gauge theory, numerical simulations, computational quantum gravity.

Nuclear Theory. Nuclear shell-model calculations, nuclear structure studies via direct reactions at intermediate energies, quark models of hadrons and quark dynamics in nuclei, electro- and photo-production studies of hadronic systems.

Other Theoretical/Mathematics. The many-body problem, mathematical, and computational physics.

Experimental

Atomic and Molecular Physics. Electron scattering by atoms and molecules, infrared studies of gases of planetary atmospheres, radiation effects, studies of He-like ions.

Condensed-Matter Physics/Materials Science. Liquid crystals, magnetic nanostructures, modulated structures, surface physics, electron and optical spectroscopy, magnetic properties of solids, highly correlated electron systems.

Elementary Particles and Fields. Collider physics, strong and electroweak interactions in high-energy particle physics, detector development and simulation.

Nuclear Physics. Reactions using polarized alkali beams, studies of fragmentation, fusion, fission, properties of nuclear systems at high angular momentum and extreme shapes, electro- and photo-production of hypernuclei and hyperons, nuclear octupole excitations, relativistic heavy-ion reactions, fast radioactive beams.

Surface physics. He-surface scattering, clusters, electron spectroscopies.

GEORGIA STATE UNIVERSITY

College of Arts and Sciences
Department of Physics and Astronomy

Programs of Study

The Department of Physics and Astronomy offers programs of study leading to the Master of Science (M.S.) degree in physics and the Doctor of Philosophy (Ph.D.) degree in physics and in astronomy. It is possible to earn the M.S. degree through evening study; the Ph.D. program must include a minimum of two years of full-time residence.

Requirements for the M.S. degree include the completion of 24 semester hours of course work, a general examination, a foreign language reading or approved alternative research skill examination, and a thesis.

Requirements for the Ph.D. in physics include passing a written qualifying examination at the end of the first year, two foreign language reading or alternative research skill exams, and an oral defense of the dissertation. Course work requirements depend on the student's previous preparation.

Research Facilities

Research in the department is currently supported by the National Science Foundation, the Department of Energy, the National Institutes of Health, and the Office of Naval Research. Research apparatus within the department includes X-band and K-band EPR/ENDOR spectrometers; X-ray diffraction apparatus; UV-, X-, and gamma-irradiation facilities; a wide assortment of CAMAC and NIM modules; positron annihilation lifetime, high-resolution Ge detector and closed-cycle He refrigerators; a CO_2 laser; monochromators; a 32-channel logic analyzer with a dual-channel digital scope; 0.5–3.0-mil hybrid wedge wire bonder; an ultrahigh vacuum surface science apparatus; and a Fourier-transform IR spectrometer. Nuclear researchers utilize the particle accelerators at Fermi Lab and Brookhaven National laboratories. The numerous workstations, microprocessors, and minicomputers in the department are networked through the University Computer Center in order to provide access to the center's four mainframe and two Silicon Graphics minisupercomputers. The Georgia State University (GSU) library subscribes to more than 250 physics and astronomy journals. The department has occupied a new building since 1993.

Financial Aid

All full-time students accepted into the program receive financial assistance. The minimum level of support covers tuition, fees, and books and provides a small stipend. The majority of the students are fully supported. Full support in 1999–2000 includes a tuition waiver and a stipend of $12,000 per year for first-year students and $14,400 per year after successful completion of the qualifying exam.

Cost of Study

For current tuition figures, students should visit the University's Web site at http://www.gsu.edu.

Living and Housing Costs

Georgia State University has a nonresidential campus located in downtown Atlanta at the center of a network of highways and rapid-transit services that extend throughout the greater metropolitan area. This transportation network makes it possible to live anywhere in the metropolitan area and get to downtown easily. The cost of living in Atlanta is moderate compared with that in other urban centers in the United States. Dormitory housing is available at the Georgia State Village, which is a short distance from the downtown campus.

Student Group

Georgia State University is a public institution with more than 24,000 students. Its graduate student population of more than 7,000 is one of the largest in the Southeast. The average age of graduate students is 33. Students from 113 countries and all fifty states attend the University.

Location

The University is located in the heart of Atlanta's central business district. The city is a rapidly growing metropolitan area characterized by a spectacular skyline and a culturally diverse population. Atlanta's Hartsfield International Airport is the world's largest and busiest and makes the city easily accessible from anywhere in the world. The climate is moderate, with a mean July temperature of 23°C and a mean January temperature of 10°C. Atlanta is located in the foothills of the southern Appalachian range and is close to the Great Smoky Mountains and the Atlantic and Gulf coasts.

The University

Georgia State University is responsive to students' career goals and provides educational and research programs that are relevant to the practical needs of both the students and the community. The University offers nearly fifty undergraduate and graduate degree programs covering some 200 fields of study through its School of Policy Studies and five colleges: Arts and Sciences, Business Administration, Education, Health Sciences, and Law.

Applying

Application materials may be obtained from the department or from the Office of Graduate Studies of the College of Arts and Sciences. Applicants must submit the Application for Graduate Study and the University Information forms, a $25 application fee, official copies of transcripts from each institution attended, GRE General Test scores, and three letters of recommendation. Applicants have the option of submitting scores from the Subject Test in physics. Applicants to the astronomy program must submit a statement of education and career goals. Applicants may obtain additional information about the Department of Physics and Astronomy by contacting the Director of Graduate Studies or by viewing the Web page, listed below.

Correspondence and Information

For more information:
Dr. A. G. U. Perera
Director of Graduate Studies, Physics
Department of Physics and Astronomy
Georgia State University
Atlanta, Georgia 30303-3083
Telephone: 404-651-2709
Fax: 404-651-1427
E-mail: uperera@panther.gsu.edu
World Wide Web: http://www.phy-astr.gsu.edu

For application information:
Mrs. Donna Bravard
Graduate Secretary
Department of Physics and Astronomy
Georgia State University
Atlanta, Georgia 30303-3083
E-mail: admdlb@panther.gsu.edu

Georgia State University

THE FACULTY AND THEIR RESEARCH

Professors
Joseph H. Hadley Jr., Ph.D., Duke. (Emeritus)
Ronald J. Henry, Ph.D., Belfast.
Frank H. Hsu, Ph.D., Columbia.
William C. Mallard, Ph.D., North Carolina. (Emeritus)
Steven T. Manson, Ph.D., Columbia.
Martin R. Meder, Ph.D., Tulane. (Emeritus)
William H. Nelson, Ph.D., Duke.
Gus A. Petitt, Ph.D., Duke. (Emeritus)
Paul J. Wiita, Ph.D., Princeton.

Associate Professors
Carl R. Nave, Ph.D., Georgia Tech.
A. G. Unil Perera, Ph.D., Pittsburgh.

James E. Purcell, Ph.D., Case Tech. (Emeritus)
Mark I. Stockman, D.Sc., Russian Academy of Sciences.

Assistant Professors
Maxim Ershov, Ph.D., Russian Academy of Sciences.
Gary Hastings, Ph.D., Imperial College (London).
Xiao-chun He, Ph.D., Tennessee.
Brian D. Thoms, Ph.D., Cornell.

Adjunct Professors
Maurice H. Francombe, Ph.D., London.
Hui C. Liu, Ph.D., Pittsburgh.

Research Areas
Theoretical astrophysics: models of extragalactic radio sources and active galactic nuclei, defects in crystals, electron spin resonance in solids, electron-nuclear double resonance, radiation biophysics, positron annihilation studies, heavy-ion collisions, atomic collision, nuclear scattering, condensed-matter and optical theory, semiconductor optoelectronics, nonlinear dynamical applications in IR detectors, surface physics of wide bandgap semiconductors.

Physics Faculty Selected Publications (1997–98)
Ershov, M. Lateral photocurrent spreading in single quantum well infrared photodetectors. *Appl. Phys. Lett.* 72:2865–7, 1998.

Ershov, M., et al. Negative capacitance effect in semiconductor devices. *IEEE Trans. Elect. Dev.* 45:2196–206, 1998.

Ershov, M. Photoconductivity mechanism of quantum well infrared photodetectors under localized photoexcitation. *Appl. Phys. Lett.* 73:3432–4, 1998.

Hadley, J. H., F. H. Hsu et al. Rare earth incorporation in $CaTiO_3$. In *Ceramic Interfaces*, 229–37, eds. Smart and Nowotny. United Kingdom: IOM Communications, 1998.

Hadley, J. H., F. H. Hsu, et al. Positron trapping in Ce-doped zirconotiles. *J. Am. Ceramic Soc.*, 1999.

He, X. C., et al. Soft photon production in central 200-gev/nucleon S-32 + Au collisions. *Phys. Rev.* C56:1160–3, 1997.

Hsu, F. H., J. H. Hadley Jr. et al. Temperature dependence of positron annihilation studies in β-cyclodextrin complexes. *Mater. Sci. Forum* 255–7:466–8, 1997.

Kim, D.-S., et al. **(S. T. Manson)**. Photodetachment of (1s2s2p) ^{4}P He$^-$ in the vicinity of the 1s threshold. *J. Phys. B* 30:L1–7, 1997.

Kim, D.-S., et al. **(S. T. Manson)**. Photodetachment of the 1s2s2p ^{4}P state of He$^-$ from threshold to 100eV. *Phys. Rev. A* 55:414–25, 1997.

Manson, S. T., et al. Photoelectron angular distribution of the 2p subshell of the 1s2s2p ^{4}P state of He$^-$, Li, and Be$^+$. *J. Phys B* 30:3379–86, 1997.

Manson, S. T. Non-dipole angular distributions of the neon valence lines. *J. Phys. B* 30:L727–33, 1997.

Manson, S. T., et al. Breakdown of the independent particle approximation in high-energy photoionization. *Phys. Rev. Lett.* 78:4553–6, 1997.

Manson, S. T., et al. Photoabsorption by inner shells in the X-ray range: Recent results. *Indian J. Phys. B* 71B:335–47, 1997.

Dolmatov, V. K., and **S. T. Manson**. Masking effect in the photoelectron beta-parameter spectrum. *J. Phys. B* 30:L517–21, 1997.

Manson, S. T. Relativistic effects in the photoexcitation of neon. *Phys. Rev. A* 58:3661–72, 1998.

Manson, S. T., et al. Inner-shell photoionization cross section on outer-shell structure: Application to MN$^+$. *J. Phys. B* 31:999–1001, 1998.

Manson, S. T. Photoionization cross sections for excited laser-cooled cesium atoms. *Phys. Rev. A* 57:R4110–3, 1998.

Manson, S. T., and D. W. Lindle. Photoionization of some closed-shell atoms and ions. *Pranama: J. Phys.* 50:607–16, 1998.

Dolmatov, V. K., and **S. T. Manson**. Photoionization experiments yielding "complete" information. *Phys. Rev. A* 58:R2635–7, 1998.

Nave, C. R. Exploring hyperphysics, a search for cross-platform deployment. *Am. Assoc. Phys. Teachers, Denver, Colorado*, August 13, 1997.

Nelson, W. H. Alanine radicals. Structure determination by EPR and ENDOR of irradiated single crystals at 295 K. *J. Phys. Chem.* 101:9763–72, 1997.

Nelson, W. H. ESR and ENDOR study of X-irradiated deoxyadenosine: Protein transfer behavior of primary ionic radicals. *Radiat. Res.* 149:75–86, 1998.

Nelson, W. H., et al. Part I: Free radical formation at 10 K following high radiation dose. *Radiat. Res.* 149:109–19, 1998.

Nelson, W. H., et al. II. EPR and ENDOR study of single crystals of the base pair complex X-irradiated at 10 K. *Radiat. Res.* 149:120–7, 1998.

Nelson, W. H. EPR and ENDOR studies of X-irradiated single crystal deoxycytidine 5'-monophosphate at 10 and 77 K. *J. Phys. Chem.* 34:6737–44, 1998.

Perera, A. G. U., et al. FIR free hole absorption in epitaxial silicon films for homojunction far-infrared detectors. *Appl. Phys. Lett.* 71:515–7, 1997.

Perera, A. G. U. Performance analysis of Si n^+-i-n^+ homojunction FIR detectors by including space charge effect. *IEEE Trans. Elect. Dev.* 44:2180–6, 1997.

Perera, A. G. U., et al. A spectroscopic study of GaAs homojunction internal photoemission FIR detectors. *Infrared Phys. Tech.* 38:133–8, 1997.

Perera, A. G. U., H. C. Liu et al. GaAs multilayer p-i homojunction far-infrared detectors. *J. Appl. Phys.* 81:3316–9, 1997.

Perera, A. G. U., H. C. Liu et al. Demonstration of Si homojunction photoconductors for far-infrared detection. *Appl. Phys. Lett.* 72:2307–9, 1998.

Perera, A. G. U., H. C. Liu et al. GaAs/AlGaAs quantum well photodetectors with a cutoff wavelength at 28 mm. *Appl. Phys. Lett.* 72:1596–8, 1998.

Perera, A. G. U. Photoconductive generation mechanism and gain in internal photoemission infrared detectors. *J. Appl. Phys.* 83:3923–5, 1998.

Perera, A. G. U., et al **(H. C. Liu** and **M. Ershov)**. Nonuniform vertical charge in quantum well infrared detectors. *J. Appl. Phys.* 83:991–7, 1998.

Perera, A. G. U., et al. FIR free hole absorption in epitaxial silicon films for homojunction FIR detectors. *Appl. Phys. Lett.* 71:515–7, 1997.

Stockman, M. I. On mechanism of nonlinear laser cleavage of DNA. *Biofizika (Moscow)* 42(3):607–10, 1997.

Stockman, M. I. Chaos and spatial correlations for dipolar eigenproblem. *Phys. Rev. Lett.* 79(22):4562–5, 1997.

Stockman, M. I. Inhomogeneous eigenmode localization, chaos, and correlations in large disordered clusters. *Phys. Rev. E* 56(6):6494–507, 1997.

Stockman, M. I., et al. Absorption saturation study of Landau levels in quasi–two-dimensional systems. *Superlattices Microstructures* 21(4):501–8, 1997.

Thoms, B. D., et al. GaAs surface chemistry and surface damage in a chlorine high density etch process. *J. Electronic Mat.* 26:1320, 1997.

Pehrsson, P. E., and **B. D. Thoms**. Surface oxidation chemistry of β-SiC. *J. Vacuum Sci. Tech. A* 15:1, 1997.

Wiita, P. J., et al. General relativistic effects on the spectrum reflected by accretion disks around black holes. *Astrophys. J.* 504:58–63, 1998.

Wiita, P. J. Instabilities in three-dimensional simulations of astrophysical jets crossing angled interfaces. *Astrophys. J.* 493:81–90 and Plates 5–7, 1998.

Wiita, P. J. Accretion disks around black holes. In *Black Holes, Gravitational Radiation, and the Universe*, pp. 249–63, eds. Iyer and Bhawal. Dordrecht: Kluwer Academic Publishers, 1998.

Bao, G., and **P. J. Wiita**. The flux ratio of a jet to its counterjet revisited. *Astrophys. J.* 485:136–42, 1997.

Bao, G., P. Hadrava, **P. J. Wiita**, and Y. Xiong. Polarization variability of active galactic nuclei and X-ray binaries. *Astrophys. J.* 487:142–52, 1997.

Wiita, P. J. On the variability coherence observed in black hole candidates at different X-ray energies. *Astrophys. J.* 489:819–21, 1997.

HARVARD UNIVERSITY

Department of Physics

Program of Study

The Department of Physics offers a program of graduate study leading to the Ph.D. degree in physics. The primary areas of experimental and theoretical research in the physics department are high-energy particle physics, atomic and molecular physics, physics of solids and fluids, astrophysics, quantum field theory, statistical mechanics, mathematical physics, quantum optics, and relativity. The department is closely linked with the Division of Applied Sciences, which has an extensive program in theoretical and experimental studies of the properties of crystalline and disordered solids; the division also studies nonlinear optics and light scattering, earth and planetary physics, computer science, and applied mathematics.

The first year and a half of graduate study is normally spent on lecture courses. In the second year, students are expected to pass an oral examination on a subject of their choice and choose a field and adviser for their Ph.D. work. The requirements for the Ph.D. degree are demonstration of competence (usually through a year course in each field) in four fields of physics, satisfactory performance on a preliminary oral examination, and a Ph.D. dissertation based on independent scholarly research, which, upon conclusion, is defended in an oral examination before a Ph.D. committee. With normal preparation, students can usually complete the requirements for the Ph.D. degree in four to six years. The research interests of the faculty members in the physics department are listed on the reverse of this page.

A limited number of openings for postdoctoral research, with or without a stipend, are available each year to qualified applicants without regard to race, color, sex, or creed. Inquiries should be addressed to individual professors, under whose sponsorship these appointments are made.

Research Facilities

The facilities of the Department of Physics are concentrated in several buildings. Lyman Laboratory and Jefferson Laboratory form the center of departmental activity. These two buildings contain facilities for atomic physics experiments with fast atomic beams, apparatus for trapping and studying individual electrons and ions, equipment for producing nuclear and atomic polarization, superconducting magnets, lasers, dilution refrigerators for attaining very low temperatures, equipment for high-pressure studies, and equipment for optical and ultrasonic measurements. Additional facilities for the study of solid-state physics, laser physics, and materials science are located in Gordon McKay Laboratory. These include high-resolution electron microscopes, low-temperature facilities, a clean room for fabricating submicrometer structures, an MeV heavy-ion accelerator, high-resolution X-ray facilities, and materials preparation and characterization equipment. Studies of condensed-matter systems using synchrotron radiation are carried out at Brookhaven National Laboratory. Current projects in particle physics are being carried out at the Fermi National Accelerator Laboratory; at the European Center for Nuclear Research (CERN) in Geneva, Switzerland; and at the Cornell Wilson Synchrotron Laboratory. Apparatus for these projects is built and data from these experiments is analyzed in part at the High Energy Physics Laboratory at Harvard. A VAXcluster computer facility, located at the High Energy Physics Laboratory, is accessible from terminals in Lyman Laboratory.

Financial Aid

The Department of Physics has generally provided full tuition and fees for all graduate students who are not supported in full by outside scholarships. Living stipends are provided via scholarships, teaching fellowships, and research assistantships. Summer support is also included and is available in the form of either a teaching fellowship or a research assistantship.

Cost of Study

Tuition and fees are provided for all graduate students as described above.

Living and Housing Costs

There are a wide variety of dormitory rooms for single students, with costs that range from $3280 (for a small single room) up to $5260 (for a two-room suite) per academic year. These figures do not include meals.

Married students and single graduate students may apply for apartments in graduate student housing or other University-owned apartments. The monthly cost is $718–$976 for a one-room studio apartment, $876–$1265 for a one-bedroom apartment, $1113–$1708 for a two-bedroom apartment, and $1583 and up for a three-bedroom apartment. There are also many privately owned accommodations nearby and within commuting distance.

Student Group

The Graduate School of Arts and Sciences has an enrollment of 3,065. About 140 men and women are pursuing Ph.D. research in the physics laboratories with physics department faculty. Students come from all parts of the United States, and about one third are from other countries.

Student Outcomes

In recent years, three quarters of Harvard's doctoral students in physics received scientific positions in universities or government laboratories after graduation. Another one eighth acquired scientific jobs in industrial laboratories. Of the remaining one eighth, most secured jobs involving consulting or financial management. Only 3 percent of the recent graduates did not have definite employment plans upon graduation.

Location

Cambridge, Massachusetts, is a city of 96,000, adjacent to Boston and its cultural benefits, yet suburban in nature. All of New England is within driving distance—the mountains of New Hampshire and Vermont with camping and skiing, the beaches and woodlands of Maine, and the seashore and seaports of Massachusetts, as well as the great array of colleges and universities spread across all six states. Cambridge itself is a scientific and intellectual center teeming with activity in all areas of creativity and study.

The University

Harvard College was established in 1636, and its charter, which still guides the University, was granted in 1650. Today, Harvard University, with its network of graduate schools, occupies a noteworthy position in the academic world, and the Department of Physics offers an educational program in keeping with the University's long-standing record of achievement.

Applying

Men and women who are completing a bachelor's degree or the equivalent should write to the Admissions Office of the Graduate School of Arts and Sciences for application material and to the Department of Physics for additional information on the program. Completed application forms and all supporting material should be returned to the Admissions Office by December 14.

Correspondence and Information

Information on the program:

Chairman
Department of Physics
Jefferson 364
Harvard University
Cambridge, Massachusetts 02138

Application forms for admission:

Admissions Office
Graduate School of Arts and Sciences
Harvard University
8 Garden Street, 2nd Floor
Cambridge, Massachusetts 02138

Harvard University

THE FACULTY AND THEIR RESEARCH

Howard C. Berg, Ph.D., Professor of Molecular and Cellular Biology and Professor of Physics. Motile behavior of bacteria.

George Brandenburg, Ph.D., Senior Research Fellow and Director of the High Energy Physics Laboratory.

Sidney R. Coleman, Ph.D., Donner Professor of Science. Quantum field theory, relativity.

John Doyle, Ph.D., John L. Loeb Associate Professor of Natural Sciences. Experimental atomic, molecular, and elementary particle physics.

Henry Ehrenreich, Ph.D., Clowes Professor of Science (joint appointment with the Division of Engineering and Applied Sciences). Theoretical condensed-matter physics.

Gary Feldman, Ph.D., Frank B. Baird Jr. Professor of Science. Experimental high-energy physics.

Daniel S. Fisher, Ph.D., Professor of Physics and Professor of Applied Physics. Statistical physics, condensed-matter theory.

Melissa Franklin, Ph.D., Professor of Physics. Experimental high-energy physics.

Gerald Gabrielse, Ph.D., Professor of Physics. Experimental atomic, optical, plasma, and elementary particle physics.

Peter L. Galison, Ph.D., Mallinckrodt Professor of the History of Science and of Physics (joint appointment with the Department of History of Science). History and philosophy of physics.

Howard Georgi, Ph.D., Mallinckrodt Professor of Physics. Field theory, elementary particle physics.

Sheldon L. Glashow, Ph.D., Higgins Professor of Physics. Theoretical elementary particle physics.

Roy J. Glauber, Ph.D., Mallinckrodt Professor of Physics. Elementary particle theory, high-energy nuclear physics, quantum optics, statistical mechanics.

Jene A. Golovchenko, Ph.D., Gordon McKay Professor of Applied Physics and Professor of Physics (joint appointment with the Division of Engineering and Applied Sciences). Solid-state and atomic physics.

Bertrand I. Halperin, Ph.D., Hollis Professor of Mathematicks and Natural Philosophy. Condensed-matter theory, statistical theory.

Eric J. Heller, Ph.D., Professor of Chemistry and Physics. Theoretical atomic, molecular, and optical physics.

Paul Horowitz, Ph.D., Professor of Physics. Experimental astrophysics, search for extraterrestrial intelligence.

John Huth, Ph.D., Professor of Physics. Experimental high-energy physics.

Arthur M. Jaffe, Ph.D., Landon T. Clay Professor of Mathematics and Theoretical Science (joint appointment with the Department of Mathematics). Mathematical physics.

Efthimios Kaxiras, Ph.D., Gordon McKay Professor of Applied Physics and Professor of Physics. Theoretical and computational condensed-matter physics.

Margaret E. Law, Ph.D., Director of the Physics Laboratories and Senior Lecturer on Physics.

Juan Maldacena, Ph.D., Associate Professor of Physics. String theory, quantum gravity and field theory.

Paul C. Martin, Ph.D., John H. Van Vleck Professor of Pure and Applied Physics and Dean of the Division of Engineering and Applied Sciences (joint appointment with the Division of Engineering and Applied Sciences). Statistical physics, condensed-matter theory.

Eric Mazur, Ph.D., Gordon McKay Professor of Applied Physics and Professor of Physics (joint appointment with the Division of Engineering and Applied Sciences). Quantum optics, experimental molecular and condensed-matter physics.

David R. Nelson, Ph.D., Mallinckrodt Professor of Physics, Professor of Applied Physics, and Chairman. Statistical physics, condensed-matter theory.

Costas D. Papaliolios, Ph.D., Professor of Physics. Experimental astrophysics.

William Paul, Ph.D., Mallinckrodt Professor of Applied Physics and Professor of Physics (joint appointment with the Division of Engineering and Applied Sciences). Experimental condensed-matter physics, amorphous semiconductors.

Peter S. Pershan, Ph.D., Gordon McKay Professor of Applied Physics and Professor of Physics (joint appointment with the Division of Engineering and Applied Sciences). Experimental condensed-matter physics, synchrotron radiation studies of properties of matter at interfaces and surfaces.

Mara Prentiss, Ph.D., Professor of Physics. Experimental atomic physics, optical devices, optical tweezers, biophysics.

William H. Press, Ph.D., Professor of Astronomy and of Physics (joint appointment with the Department of Astronomy). Cosmology, theoretical astrophysics, computational physics.

Michael Schmitt, Ph.D., Assistant Professor of Physics. Experimental high-energy physics.

Irwin I. Shapiro, Ph.D., Timken University Professor (joint appointment with the Department of Astronomy). Radar and radio astronomy, experimental relativity.

Isaac F. Silvera, Ph.D., Thomas D. Cabot Professor of the Natural Sciences. Low-temperature physics of quantum fluids and solids, ultrahigh-pressure physics.

Andrew Strominger, Ph.D., Professor of Physics. String theory, field theory and general relativity.

Michael Tinkham, Ph.D., Rumford Professor of Physics and Gordon McKay Professor of Applied Physics (joint appointment with the Division of Engineering and Applied Sciences). Superconductivity, mesoscopic physics.

Cumrun Vafa, Ph.D., Professor of Physics. Elementary particle theory and string theory.

Robert M. Westervelt, Ph.D., Gordon McKay Professor of Applied Physics and Professor of Physics (joint appointment with the Division of Engineering and Applied Sciences). Experimental condensed-matter physics.

Richard Wilson, D.Phil., Mallinckrodt Professor of Physics. Experimental nuclear physics, elementary particle physics, energy-related environmental and medical physics.

Tai T. Wu, Ph.D., Gordon McKay Professor of Applied Physics and Professor of Physics (joint appointment with the Division of Engineering and Applied Sciences). Theoretical elementary particle physics, electromagnetic theory, statistical mechanics.

Professors Emeriti

Nicolaas Bloembergen, Ph.D., Gerhard Gade University Professor. Nonlinear optics.

Gerald Holton, Ph.D., Mallinckrodt Professor of Physics and Professor of the History of Science. Experimental physics, history of nineteenth- and twentieth-century physics.

Robert V. Pound, D.Sc., Mallinckrodt Professor of Physics. Experimental physics.

Norman F. Ramsey, Ph.D., Higgins Professor of Physics. Experimental physics, tests of time reversal symmetry.

Karl Strauch, Ph.D., George Vasmer Leverett Professor of Physics. Experimental high-energy particle physics.

INDIANA UNIVERSITY BLOOMINGTON

Department of Physics

Programs of Study

Physics research at Indiana University (IU) is conducted in the subfields of nuclear physics, accelerator physics, plasma physics, particle physics, condensed-matter physics, physics education, astrophysics, chemical physics, and theoretical physics. M.S., M.A.T., and Ph.D. degrees are offered. An interdisciplinary scientific computing minor and an M.S. in beam physics and technology sponsored by the U.S. Particle Accelerator School have recently been established.

M.S. candidates must complete 30 credit hours of graduate work (including a minimum of 20 hours in physics) and either pass a written comprehensive exam or, for some programs, complete a thesis. The M.A.T. requires 20 hours in physics and an additional 16 hours in mathematics, astronomy, chemistry, and education.

Course work is not the main criterion for obtaining the Ph.D. The candidate must demonstrate an ability to do research by carrying out an investigation and presenting a publishable thesis and must show a broad grasp of physics. The requirements for the Ph.D. include a minimum of 90 hours of graduate credit that consists of course work, supervised reading, and research. A qualifying exam is required no later than one year after arrival; two attempts at the exam are allowed. The great majority of students at IU pass the qualifying exam and are soon involved in thesis research. The final oral exam is conducted by the candidate's doctoral committee and consists of questions on the major and minor fields of work as well as on the thesis.

Research Facilities

The Indiana University Cyclotron Facility/Nuclear Theory Center is a national facility for nuclear physics research. It consists of an electron-cooled light ion storage ring with polarized beam and polarized internal target capability and extensive experimental support facilities. Other experiments in nuclear, particle and accelerator physics, and astrophysics are conducted at Fermilab, Thomas Jefferson Lab, Brookhaven, NIST, Los Alamos, Argonne, CERN, Grand Sasso, and CIDA. Local facilities include high-bay assembly areas, machine shops, electronic design facilities, a large open-bore superconducting magnet for balloon studies, a high-vacuum sputtering system, X-ray diffractometers, ultrahigh-vacuum surface analysis systems, a scanning tunneling microscope, a class 1000 clean room with photolithographic equipment, a 14-Tesla superconducting magnet with pumped ^{3}He and dilution refrigerator inserts, and several standard cryostats for transport measurements from DC to 20 GHz. Computing facilities include numerous workstations, a 32-node Linux cluster, and two supercomputers (64-node SGI Origin 2000 and 47-node IBM SP).

Financial Aid

Teaching assistantships carried stipends of at least $11,280 for the ten-month 1998–99 academic year. Research assistantship stipends average $16,464 for twelve months. Students are eligible for a number of University fellowships which pay $18,000 per year for five years. Teaching and research positions are also available that pay at least $2150 for the two summer months. Over the last ten years, 98 percent of the students who finished the Ph.D. received full financial support throughout their graduate careers.

Cost of Study

In 1998–99, fees per credit hour for in-state graduate students were $152.90; for out-of-state graduate students, $445.40. Teaching and research assistants ordinarily pay only a fee of $429.55 per semester.

Living and Housing Costs

University housing and meals for single graduate students (men and women) were available for $4714 for the 1998–99 academic year. Married students chose from efficiency apartments and one-, two-, and three-bedroom apartments ranging in cost from $453 to $924 per month. Both furnished and unfurnished units are available in University housing.

Student Group

Indiana University is a large institution, with 35,600 students enrolled at the Bloomington campus, including 7,345 graduate and professional school students. In fall 1998, there were 71 graduate students in physics, almost all of whom receive full financial support.

Student Outcomes

IU physics Ph.D. graduates are currently employed by national laboratories such as FNAL, BNL, SLAC, LANL, ORNL, NASA, LBL, NRL, and LLNL; by universities such as Rutgers, Rice, Brown, Vanderbilt, Michigan, Penn, Purdue, Virginia, North Carolina, Michigan State, Rensselaer, Missouri–Rolla, Arizona, Washington, Ohio State, and Ohio University; and by companies such as Lucent, Intel, IBM, Microsoft, McDonnell-Douglas, Silicon Graphics, LeCroy, Hewlett-Packard, General Motors, TRW, RAND, Exxon, Rockwell, and Spectra-Physics. Recent postdoctoral students are currently at Argonne, Lawrence Berkeley Lab, Northwestern University, MIT, Princeton University, the University of Maryland, and the National High Magnetic Field Lab.

Location

Bloomington is located in the picturesque hills of southern Indiana, 50 miles south of Indianapolis, the state capital. It is close to five state parks, two state forests, and the state's largest lake. It has consistently been chosen in national rankings as having a high quality of life.

The University

Indiana University is the oldest state university west of the Allegheny Mountains. It was founded in 1820 and has been a pioneer in higher education in the Midwest. It is widely recognized for the beauty of its campus and for the diversity and high quality of its graduate programs in the arts, humanities, and sciences. The campus provides numerous facilities for all types of indoor and outdoor sports. The School of Music presents concerts and opera. Lectures, dramatic and musical Broadway productions, ballet, drama, and concerts are presented by the Auditorium and the University Theatre.

Applying

The deadline for assistantship and fellowship applications for the fall semester is January 15. For further information, students should write to one of the addresses or call one of the numbers given below. Applications can be submitted over the World Wide Web at http://www.gradapp.indiana.edu.

Correspondence and Information

Chairperson
Department of Physics
Indiana University
Bloomington, Indiana 47405-4201
Telephone: 812-855-1247

Graduate Admissions Committee
Department of Physics
Indiana University
Bloomington, Indiana 47405-4201
Telephone: 812-855-3973
E-mail: gradphys@indiana.edu
World Wide Web: http://physics.indiana.edu

Indiana University Bloomington

THE FACULTY AND THEIR RESEARCH

Professors Emeriti
Ethan D. Alyea, Ph.D., Caltech, 1962. Astrophysics (experimental).
Robert D. Bent, Ph.D., Rice, 1954. Experimental nuclear physics: nuclear structure, reactions, astrophysics.
Ray R. Crittenden, Ph.D., Wisconsin, 1960. Elementary particle physics (experimental).
Charles Goodman, Ph.D., Rochester, 1959. Nuclear physics (experimental).
Richard R. Hake, Ph.D., Illinois, 1955. Condensed-matter and low-temperature physics.
Lawrence M. Langer, Ph.D., NYU, 1938. Nuclear physics: radioactivity, nuclear spectroscopy.
Andrew A. Lenard, Ph.D., Iowa, 1953. Theoretical physics, mathematical physics.
Don B. Lichtenberg, Ph.D., Illinois, 1955. Elementary particle physics (theory).
Hugh J. Martin, Ph.D., Caltech, 1956. Elementary particle physics (experimental).
Daniel W. Miller, Ph.D., Wisconsin, 1951. Nuclear physics (experimental): nuclear reactions.
Roger G. Newton, Distinguished Professor Emeritus; Ph.D., Harvard, 1953. Theoretical and mathematical physics: scattering theory.
P. Paul Singh, Ph.D., British Columbia, 1960. Nuclear physics, nuclear reactions, nuclear spectroscopy.
John G. Wills, Ph.D., Washington (Seattle), 1963. Theoretical nuclear physics: intermediate energy.

Professors
Andrew D. Bacher, Ph.D., Caltech, 1967. Intermediate-energy nuclear physics (experimental).
Bennet B. Brabson, Ph.D., MIT, 1966. Elementary particle physics (experimental).
John M. Cameron, Ph.D., UCLA, 1967. Nuclear physics (experimental).
John L. Challifour, Ph.D., Cambridge, 1963. Theoretical physics, mathematical physics.
Alex R. Dzierba, Ph.D., Notre Dame, 1969. Elementary particle physics (experimental).
Steven M. Girvin, Distinguished Professor; Ph.D., Princeton, 1977. Condensed-matter theory.
Steven A. Gottlieb, Ph.D., Princeton, 1978. Theoretical physics.
Gail G. Hanson, Distinguished Professor; Ph.D., MIT, 1973. Elementary particle physics (experimental).
Richard M. Heinz, Ph.D., Michigan, 1964. Astrophysics (experimental).
Archibald W. Hendry, Ph.D., Glasgow, 1962. Theoretical physics: elementary particles.
Charles J. Horowitz, Ph.D., Stanford, 1981. Nuclear theory.
Larry L. Kesmodel, Ph.D., Texas, 1974. Condensed-matter physics (experimental).
V. Alan Kostelecky, Ph.D., Yale, 1982. Theoretical physics.
S. Y. Lee, Ph.D., SUNY at Stony Brook, 1972. Accelerator physics.
J. Timothy Londergan, D.Phil., Oxford, 1969. Theoretical physics, nuclear theory.
Allan H. MacDonald, Distinguished Professor; Ph.D., Toronto, 1978. Condensed-matter theory.
Malcolm Macfarlane, Ph.D., Rochester, 1959. Nuclear theory.
Hans Otto Meyer, Ph.D., Basel, 1970. Nuclear physics (experimental).
James A. Musser, Ph.D., Berkeley, 1984. Astrophysics (experimental).
Hermann Nann, Ph.D., Frankfurt, 1967. Intermediate-energy nuclear physics (experimental).
Harold Ogren, Ph.D., Cornell, 1970. Elementary particle physics (experimental).
Catherine Olmer, Ph.D., Yale, 1976. Intermediate-energy nuclear physics (experimental).
Robert E. Pollock, Distinguished Professor; Ph.D., Princeton, 1963. Nuclear physics: nuclear reactions, cyclotron design.
William L. Schaich, Ph.D., Cornell, 1970. Condensed-matter theory.
Peter Schwandt, Ph.D., Wisconsin, 1967. Nuclear physics (experimental).
Brian D. Serot, Ph.D., Stanford, 1979. Nuclear theory.
James C. Swihart, Ph.D., Purdue, 1955. Condensed-matter theory.
Steven E. Vigdor, Ph.D., Wisconsin, 1973. Nuclear physics (experimental).
George E. Walker, Ph.D., Case Tech, 1966. Nuclear theory.
Andrej Zieminski, Ph.D., Warsaw, 1971. Elementary particle physics (experimental).

Associate Professors
David V. Baxter, Ph.D., Caltech, 1984. Condensed-matter physics (experimental).
Leslie C. Bland, Ph.D., Pennsylvania, 1983. Nuclear physics (experimental).
John P. Carini, Ph.D., Chicago, 1988. Condensed-matter physics (experimental).
Scott W. Wissink, Ph.D., Stanford, 1986. Nuclear physics (experimental).

Assistant Professors
J. Scott Berg, Ph.D., Stanford, 1996. Accelerator physics.
Michael S. Berger, Ph.D., Berkeley, 1991. Elementary particle physics (theory).
Robert W. Gardner, Ph.D., Notre Dame, 1991. Elementary particle physics (experimental).
William M. Snow, Ph.D., Harvard, 1990. Nuclear physics (experimental).
Adam P. Szczepaniak, Ph.D., Washington (Seattle), 1990. Theoretical physics.
Richard J. Vankooten, Ph.D., Stanford, 1990. Elementary particle physics (experimental).
H. P. Wei, Ph.D., Princeton, 1986. Condensed-matter physics (experimental).

Indiana University Bloomington

SELECTED PUBLICATIONS

Lisantti, J., et al. **(A. D. Bacher, C. Olmer, E. J. Stephenson,** and **S. W. Wissink).** Neutron transition densities for low lying states in ^{58}Ni obtained by using 200~MeV inelastic proton scattering. *Phys. Rev. C: Nucl. Phys.* 58:2217, 1998.

Baxter, **D. V.,** S. D. Steenwyk, J. Bass, and W. P. Pratt Jr. Resistance and spin-direction memory loss at Nb/Cu interfaces. *J. Appl. Phys.,* in press.

Baxter, **D. V.,** K. G. Caulton, M. H. Chisholm, S.-H. Chuang, and C. D. Minear. A two-step low pressure chemical vapor deposition process for the production of tungsten metal thin films. *Chem. Commun.* 1447–8, 1998.

Wen, C., W. P. Pratt Jr., M. Herrold, and **D. V. Baxter.** The effect of sputtering pressure on the CPP magnetotransport and structure of Co/Ag multilayered films. *Phys. Rev. B: Condens. Matter* 58:5602–10, 1998.

Fadnis, A. N., and **D. V. Baxter.** Measuring transport anisotrophy in Cu/Si multilayers using weak localization. *J. Phys. Condens. Matter* 8:1389–401, 1996.

Palarczyk, M., et al. **(L. C. Bland).** Cross sections and analyzing powers for (p,n) on ^{3}He and ^{4}He. *Phys. Rev. C: Nucl. Phys.* 58:645, 1998.

Brenschede, A., et al. **(L. C. Bland).** Production of ϕ and ω mesons in near-threshold pp reactions. *Phys. Rev. Lett.* 81:4572, 1998.

Cameron, **J. M.** Studying nuclear quark-gluon manifestations using multi-GeV polarized protons. *Nucl. Phys. A* 629:567C, 1998.

Lee, H.-L., **J. P. Carini, D. V. Baxter,** and G. Gruner. Temperature-frequency scaling in niobium-silicon near the metal-insulator transition.*Phys. Rev. Lett.* 78:4261–4, 1998.

Brunner, A., et al. **(R. R. Crittenden, A. R. Dzierba,** and **R. W. Gardner).** A cockcroft-wallton base for the EU84-3 photomultiplier tube. *Nucl. Instrum. Methods Phys. Res., Sect. A* 414:466, 1998.

Teige, S., et al. **(A. R. Dzierba).** Properties of the a$_0$ (980) meson. *Phys. Rev. D: Part. Fields* 59:1, 1999.

Adams, G. S., et al. **(A. R. Dzierba).** Observation of a new J^{PC} = 1^{-+} exotic state in the reaction πρ$^-$→π$^-$π$^-$π$^+$ρ at 18 GeV/c. *Phys. Rev. Lett.* 81:5760, 1988.

Frabetti, P. L., et al. **(R. W. Gardner).** Observation of a narrow state decaying into Ξ^0_cπ$^+$. *Phys. Lett. B* 426:403, 1998.

Frabetti, P. L., et al. **(R. W. Gardner).** A new measurement of the lifetime of the Ξ^+_c. *Phys. Lett. B* 57:11457, 1998.

Timm, **C., S. M. Girvin,** P. Henelius, and A. W. Sandvik. 1/N expansion for two-dimensional quantum ferromagnets. *Phys. Rev. B: Condens. Matter* 58:1464, 1998.

Girvin, **S. M.** Exotic quantum order in low-dimensional systems. In *Proceedings of the Conference on Advancing Frontiers of Condensed Matter Science. Solid State Comm.* 107:623, 1998.

Girvin, **S. M.** Duality in perspective. *Science* 274:524, 1996.

Sondhi, S. L., **S. M. Girvin, J. C. Carini,** and D. Shahar. Continuous quantum phase transitions. Invited Colloquium. *Rev. Mod. Phys.* 69:315, 1997.

Gottlieb, **S. A.,** et al. Quenched hadron spectroscopy with improved staggered quark action. *Phys. Rev. Lett.* D58:1453, 1998.

Gottlieb, **S. A.,** et al. Continuum limit of lattice QCD with staggered quarks in the quenched approximation. *Phys. Rev. Lett.* 81:3087, 1998.

Gottlieb, **S. A.** Lattice determination of heavy-light decay constants. *Phys. Rev. Lett.* 81:4812, 1998.

Ankenbrandt, **C. M.,** et al. **(G. G. Hanson).** Ionization cooling research and development program for a high luminosity muon collider. *Fermilab-P-0904* April 15, 1998.

Ackerstaff, K., et al. **(G. G. Hanson, H. O. Ogren,** and **R. J. Van Kooten).** A search for neutral higgs bosons in the MSSM and models with two scalar field doublets. CERN-EP/98-029. *Eur. Phys. J.* C5:19, 1998.

Hanson, **G. G.** Workshop summary. In *Proceedings of the Sixth International Workshop on Vertex Detectors. Nucl. Instrum. Methods Phys. Res., Sect. A* 418:210, 1998.

Anderson, S., et al. **(G. G. Hanson** and **R. J. Van Kooten).** The extended OPAL silicon strip microvertex detector. CERN-PPE/97-092.*Nucl. Instrum. Methods Phys. Res., Sect. A* 403:326, 1998.

Abbiendi, G., et al. **(G. G. Hanson, H. O. Ogren,** and **R. J. Van Kooten).** First measurement of Z/γ* production in compton scattering of quasi-real photons. *Phys. Lett. B* 438:391, 1998.

Ackerstaff, K., et al. **(G. G. Hanson, H. O. Ogren,** and **R. J. Van Kooten).** Production of X$_{c2}$ mesons in photon-photon collisions at LEP. *Phys. Lett. B* 439:197, 1998.

Ackerstaff, K., et al. **(G. G. Hanson, H. O. Ogren,** and **R. J. Van Kooten).** Test of the standard model and constraints on new physics from measurements of fermion-pair production at 183 GeV at LEP. *Eur. Phys. J.* 6:1, 1998.

Ackerstaff, K., et al. **(G. G. Hanson, H. O. Ogren,** and **R. J. Van Kooten).** Bose-Einstein correlations of three charged pions in hadronic Z^0 decays. *Eur. Phys. J.* 5:239, 1998.

Ackerstaff, K., et al. **(G. G. Hanson, H. O. Ogren,** and **R. J. Van Kooten).** An upper limit for the τ-neutrino mass from τ→5π±υ$_τ$ decays. *Eur. Phys. J.* C5:239, 1998.

Heinz, **R. M.,** et al. **(J. A. Musser).** Real time supernova neutrino burst detection with MACRO. *Astropart. Phys.* 8:123, 1998.

Heinz, **R. M.,** et al. **(J. A. Musser).** The observation of upgoing charged particles produced by high energy muons in underground detectors. *Astropart. Phys.* 9:105, 1998.

Heinz, **R. M.,** et al. **(J. A. Musser).** Measurement of the atmospheric neutrino-induced upgoing muon flux using MACRO. *Phys. Lett. B* 434:451, 1998.

Horowitz, **C. J.,** and J. Piekarewicz. Macroscopic parity violation and supernovae symmetries. *Nucl. Phys. A* 640:281, 1998.

Horowitz, **C. J.,** and G. Li. Cumulative parity violation in supernovae. *Phys. Rev. Lett.* 80:3694, 1998; 81:1985, 1998.

Horowitz, **C. J.** Parity violating elastic electron scattering and coulomb distortions. *Phys. Rev. C: Nucl. Phys.* 57:3430, 1998.

Kesmodel, **L. L.** Applications of high-resolution electron energy loss spectroscopy to technical surfaces. *Langmuir* 14:1355, 1998.

Kostelecký, **V. A.,** and D. Colladay. Lorentz-violating extension of the standard model. *Phys. Rev. D: Part. Fields* 58:116002, 1998.

Kostelecký, **V. A.** Sensitivity of CPT tests with neutral mesons. *Phys. Rev. Lett.* 80:1818, 1998.

Kostelecký, **V. A.,** R. Bluhm, and N. Russell. Testing CPT with anomalous magnetic moments. *Phys. Rev. Lett.* 79:1432, 1997.

Kostelecký, **V. A.,** and R. Potting. CPT and strings. *Nucl. Phys. B* 359:545, 1991.

Kostelecký, **V. A.,** and S. Samuel. Phenomenological constraints on strings and higher-dimensional theories. *Phys. Rev. Lett.* 63:224, 1989.

Kostelecký, **V. A.,** L. Hall, and S. Raby. New flavor violations in supergravity models. *Nucl. Phys. B* 267:415, 1986.

Kostelecký, **V. A.,** and M. M. Nieto. Evidence for a phenomenological supersymmetry in atomic physics. *Phys. Rev. Lett.* 53:2285, 1984.

Jeon, D., et al. **(S. Y. Lee).** A mechanism of anomalous diffusion in beams. *Phys. Rev. Lett.* 80:2314, 1998.

Bai, M., et al. **(S. Y. Lee).** Overcoming intrinsic spin resonances with an rf dipole. *Phys. Rev. Lett.* 80:4673, 1998.

Lee, **S. Y.,** and H. Okamoto. Space charge dominated beams in synchrotrons. *Phys. Rev. Lett.* 80:5133, 1998.

Chu, C. M., et al. **(S. Y. Lee** and **P. Schwandt).** Unexpectedly wide rf-induced synchrotron sideband depolarizing resonances. *Phys. Rev. E* 58:4973, 1998.

Lichtenberg, **D. B.** Are there quasistable strange baryons with anticharm or antibeauty? *J. Phys. G: Nucl. Part. Phys.* 24:2065, 1998.

Bhalerao, R. S., and **J. T. Londergan.** Using drell-yan processes to measure flavor symmetry violation in the nucleon sea. *Phys. Rev. D: Part. Fields* 57:3065, 1998.

Londergan, **J. T.** Validity of flavor symmetry and charge symmetry for parton distributions. *Nucl. Phys. A* 629:457c, 1998.

Londergan, **J. T.,** S. Braendler, and A. W. Thomas. Testing parton charge symmetry at HERA. *Phys. Lett. B* 424:185, 1998.

Benesh, C., and **J. T. Londergan.** Charge symmetry in parton valence and sea distributions. *Phys. Rev. C.: Nucl. Phys.* 58:1218, 1998.

Indiana University Bloomington

Selected Publications (continued)

Krippa, B. V., and **J. T. Londergan.** Estimates of hypernuclear production via the exclusive (p,K^+) reaction. *Phys. Rev. C: Nucl. Phys.* 58:1634, 1998.

Boros, C., **J. T. Londergan,** and A. W. Thomas. Shadowing in neutrino deep inelastic scattering and the determination of the strange quark distribution. *Phys. Rev. D: Part. Fields* 58:114030, 1998.

Boros, C., **J. T. Londergan,** and A. W. Thomas. Evidence for substantial charge symmetry violation in parton distributions. *Phys. Rev. Lett.* 81:4075, 1998.

Radtke, R. J., S. Das Sarma, and **A. H. MacDonald.** Mode mixing in antiferromagnetically coupled double quantum wells. *Phys. Rev. B: Condens. Matter* 57:2342, 1998.

Bønsager, M. C., K. Flensberg, B. Y.-K. Hu, and **A. H. MacDonald.** Frictional drag between quantum wells mediated by phonon exchange. *Phys. Rev. B: Condens. Matter* 57:7085, 1998.

Conti, S., G. Vignale, and **A. H. MacDonald.** Engineering superfluidity in electron-hole double layers. *Phys. Rev. B: Condens. Matter* 57:R6846, 1998.

Palacios, J. J., and **A. H. MacDonald.** Bulk charge distributions on integer and fractional quantum Hall plateaus. *Phys. Rev. B: Condens. Matter* 57:7119, 1998.

MacDonald, A. H., T. Jungwirth, and M. Kasner. Temperature dependence of itinerant electron junction magnetoresistance. *Phys. Rev. Lett.* 81:705, 1998.

Jungwirth, T., et al. **(A. H. MacDonald).** Magnetic anisotropy in quantum Hall ferromagnets. *Phys. Rev. Lett.* 81:2328, 1998.

Jungwirth, T., and **A. H. MacDonald.** Spin-bottleneck resistance in magnetic-tunnel-junction devices. *Solid State Commun.* 108:127, 1998.

Zülicke, U., **A. H. MacDonald,** and M. D. Johnson. Observability of counterpropagating modes at fractional Hall edges. *Phys. Rev. B: Condens. Matter* 58:13778, 1998.

Côté, R., et al. **(A. H. MacDonald** and **S. M. Girvin).** Collective excitations, NMR, and phase transitions in skyrme crystals. *Phys. Rev. Lett.* 78:4825, 1997.

Macfarlane, M. H. A high-precision study of anharmonic-oscillator spectra. *Ann. Phys.* 271:159, 1999.

Roncaglia, R., and **M. H. Macfarlane.** Monte Carlo methods for nuclear reactions. *Nucl. Phys. A* 633:651, 1998.

Rohdjess, H., et al. **(H. O. Meyer** and **R. E. Pollock).** Elastic pd scattering with 200-300 MeV protons. *Phys. Rev. C: Nucl. Phys.* 57:2111, 1998.

Przewoski, B. v., et al. **(H. O. Meyer** and **R. E. Pollock).** Proton-proton analyzing power and spin correlation coefficients between 250 and 450 MeV at 7<cm<90 with an internal target in a storage ring. *Phys. Rev. C: Nucl. Phys.* 58:1897, 1998.

Przewoski, B. v., et al. **(H. O. Meyer** and **R. E. Pollock).** Polarization lifetime near an induced depolarizing resonance. *Rev. Sci. Instrum.* 69:3146, 1998.

Meyer, H. O., et al. **(R. E. Pollock).** Dependence of pp→pp^0 near threshold on the spin of the colliding nucleons. *Phys. Rev. Lett.* 81:3096, 1998.

Musser, J. A., et al. Cosmic ray reentrant electron albedo: High energy antimatter telescope measurements from Fort Sumner, New Mexico. *J. Geophys. Res.* 103:4817, 1998.

Musser, J. A., et al. The energy spectra and relative abundances of electrons and positrons in the galactic cosmic radiation. *Astrophys. J.* 498:779, 1998.

Betigeri, M., et al. **(H. Nann).** The germanium wall of the GEM detector system. *Nucl. Instrum. Methods Phys. Res., Sect. A* 421:447, 1999.

Betigeri, M., et al. **(H. Nann).** Precision momentum calibration of the external COSY proton beam near 1930 MeV/c. *Nucl. Instrum. Methods Phys. Res.,* in press.

Wilburn, W. S., et al. **(H. Nann).** Measurement of the parity violating asymmetry A$_\gamma$ in n+p→. In *Applications of Accelerators in Research and Industry,* eds. J. L. Duggan and I. L. Morgan. AIP Conference Proceedings, 1999.

Bilger, R., et al. **(H. Nann).** Strangeness production in the reaction pp→K$^+$ Λp close to threshold. *Phys. Lett. B* 420: 217, 1998.

Bilger, R., et al. **(H. Nann).** Proton-proton bremsstrahlung at 797 MeV/c. *Phys. Lett. B* 429:195, 1998.

Newton, R. G. *The Truth of Science: Physical Theories and Reality.* Cambridge: Harvard University Press, 1997.

Newton, R. G. *What Makes Nature Tick?* Cambridge: Harvard University Press, 1993.

Schaich, W. L., and J. E. Goff. Hydrodynamic theory of photon drag. *Phys. Rev. B: Condens. Matter* 56:15421, 1997.

Schaich, W. L. On the dispersion of electrostatic surface plasmons. *Phys. Rev. B: Condens. Matter* 55:9379, 1997.

Schaich, W. L., M. R. Geller, and G. Vignale. Classical continuum theory of the dipole-forbidden collective excitation in quantum strips. *Phys. Rev. B: Condens. Matter* 53:13016, 1996.

Schaich, W. L., et al. Effects of nonlocal response and level quantization on electronic excitations of a bimetallic jellium film in an AlGaAs heterostructure. *Phys. Rev. B: Condens. Matter* 54:11467, 1996.

Schaich, W. L., and A. Liebsch. Influence of a polarizable medium on the nonlocal optical response of a metal surface. *Phys. Rev. B: Condens. Matter* 14:219, 1995.

Schwandt, P., et al. Reaction cross sections in Si of light proton-halo candidates ^{12}N and ^{17}Ne. *Nucl. Phys. A* 635:292, 1998.

Schwandt, P., et al. Spin flipping in the presence of a full Siberian snake. *Phys. Rev. Lett.* 81:2906, 1998.

Furnstahl, R. J., J. J. Rusnak, and **B. D. Serot.** The nuclear spin-orbit force in chiral effective field theories. *Nucl. Phys. A* 632:607, 1998.

Richardson, J. M., **W. M. Snow,** Z. Chowdhuri, and G. L. Greene. Accurate determination of thermal neutron flux via cryogenic calorimetry. *IEEE Trans. Nucl. Sci.* 45:550, 1998.

Keith, C. D., et al. **(W. M. Snow).** Neutron polarizers based on polarized ^{3}He. *Nucl. Instrum. Methods Phys. Res., Sect. A* 402:236, 1998.

Stephenson, E. J., et al. **(A. D. Bacher, C. Olmer,** and **S. W. Wissink).** Effective isovector NN interaction strengths determined from the ^{28}Si(p,p')^{28}Si(6$^-$,T=1) reaction. *Phys. Rev. Lett.* 78:1636, 1997.

Szczepaniak, A. P., A. V. Radyushkin, and C.-R. Ji. Consistent analysis of O(α_8) corrections to pion elastic form Factor. *Phys. Rev. D: Part. Fields* 57:2813, 1998.

Ji, C.-R., et al. **(A. P. Szczepaniak).** Coupled channel analysis of S wave ππ and KK photoproduction. *Phys. Rev. C: Nucl. Phys.* 58:1205, 1998.

Cotanch, S. R., **A. P. Szczepaniak,** E. S. Swanson, and C.-R. Ji. QCD Hamiltonian approach for the glueball. *Nucl. Phys. A* 631:640c, 1998.

Wells, S. P., and **S. W. Wissink.** Model-independent determination of the ^{12}C$(p,p')^{12}$C* (15.11 MeV, 1+T=1) transition amplitude at 200~MeV. *Phys. Rev. C: Nucl. Phys.,* in press.

Wissink, S. W. Spin transfer coefficients for pp elastic scattering at 200~MeV: Implications for the πNN coupling constant. *Nucl. Phys. A* 631:441c, 1998.

May, M., et al. **(S. W. Wissink).** First observation of the $p\Lambda\to s\Lambda$ γ-ray transition in $^{13}\Lambda$C. *Phys. Rev. Lett.* 78:4343, 1997.

Abbott, B., et al. **(A. T. Zieminski).** Measurement of dijet angular distributions and search for quark compositeness. *Phys. Rev. Lett.* 80:666, 1998.

Abbott, B., et al. **(A. T. Zieminski).** Search for the trilepton signature from the associated production of SUSY $_{\chi1\chi2}$ gauginos. *Phys. Rev. Lett.* 80:1591, 1998.

Abbott, B., et al. **(A. T. Zieminski).** Measurement of the top quark mass using dilepton events. *Phys. Rev. Lett.* 80:2063, 1998.

Abbott, B., et al. **(A. T. Zieminski).** A measurement of the W boson mass. *Phys. Rev. Lett.* 80:3000, 1998.

Abbott, B., et al. **(A. T. Zieminski).** Determination of the mass of the W boson using the D0 detector at the Tevatron. *Phys. Rev. D: Part. Fields* 58:12002, 1998.

JOHNS HOPKINS UNIVERSITY

Henry A. Rowland Department of Physics and Astronomy

Program of Study

The department offers a broad program for graduate and postdoctoral study in physics and astronomy in which intermediate, advanced, and specialized courses are offered. These courses and student research, begun as soon as possible, form the basis of the Ph.D. program. Considerable flexibility is available in each student's program, which is geared to individual needs by recommendation from faculty and staff advisers. Students may choose to specialize in either physics or astrophysics, with a full curriculum of graduate courses available in both areas. In addition to required courses, candidates take written and oral preliminary examinations. The written examinations, covering intermediate-level material, are offered in two parts during September, January, and May and are ordinarily passed by the end of three semesters. These exams are followed by an intermediate-level oral examination in the second year. A comprehensive oral examination is taken at the beginning of full-time research (usually in the third year). After completion of the student's research, an oral defense of the thesis is required. During residence, some teaching is usually required. Only those students who expect to complete the Ph.D. are admitted.

Research Facilities

The high-energy-physics group has facilities for constructing the electronics and detectors needed in experiments and also has independent computing capabilities that allow full analyses of data. Nuclear physics equipment includes facilities for relativistic heavy-ion collision studies. Facilities for condensed matter physics include systems for molecular beam epitaxy, He^3-He^4 dilution refrigeration, high-rate sputtering, ultrahigh-vacuum thin-film deposition, automatic X-ray diffraction, scanning electron microscopy, X-ray fluorescence, LEED/Auger spectroscopy, SQUID and vibrating-sample magnetometry, ferromagnetic resonance, magnetooptics, neutron diffraction Mössbauer spectroscopy, four-circle X-ray diffractometry, and optical and electron-beam lithography. For atomic, molecular, and plasma physics, facilities include high-resolution and very sensitive spectrometers for measurements of infrared to ultraviolet wavelengths, a high-precision X-ray spectrometer, extensive spectroscopic facilities, and lasers. The astrophysics group maintains a calibration and test facility for testing instrumentation for rocket and space flights. Computer facilities in the department include a large number of Sun, DEC, SGI, HP, and Intel-based workstations. These machines support a wide range of functions, including data reduction, image processing, and simulation of physical processes. All are networked to universities, national laboratories, and supercomputer facilities throughout the world, and Hopkins is part of Internet II and VBNS. Johns Hopkins University is the home of the Space Telescope Science Institute, is a partner in the Sloan Digital Sky Survey, and owns a share of the ARC 3.5 meter optical/infrared telescope. The University and its partners are constructing a space astronomy mission (FUSE) to be launched in late 1999. The Materials Research Science and Engineering Center (MRSEC) at Hopkins is one of twenty-four centers funded by the National Science Foundation to confront major challenges in the field of materials research. Facilities at the following laboratories and observatories are also frequently used: Brookhaven National Laboratory, Stanford Linear Accelerator Center, Fermi National Accelerator Laboratory, CERN, the University's own Applied Physics Laboratory, National Institute of Standards and Technology, Lawrence Berkeley Laboratory, Francis Bitter National Magnet Laboratory, Lawrence Livermore National Laboratory, the White Sands Missile Range, Kitt Peak National Observatory, Cerro Tololo Interamerican Observatory, the Very Large Array of the National Radio Astronomy Observatory, the Las Campanas Observatory, and NASA's Goddard Space Flight Center and Space Telescope Science Institute.

Financial Aid

Various tuition fellowships are usually awarded to all full-time Ph.D. candidates. Nonservice University fellowships and teaching assistantships offer a minimum of $12,500 (plus full tuition remission) for the nine-month academic year in 1999–2000. Summer research assistantships may be available at approximately $4200. Holders of teaching assistantships must assist in teaching general physics and introductory courses. This experience is useful for students interested in a college teaching career. In addition to teaching assistantships, research assistantships that pay approximately $1400 per month (plus full tuition remission) are also available for graduate students. These assistantships are awarded on the basis of experience, merit, and academic performance. (These awards are not usually given to first-year students unless they have special experience.) Loans and work-study arrangements are available from the Office of Student Financial Services.

Cost of Study

Tuition is $23,660 for the 1999–2000 academic year. A one-time matriculation fee of $500 is required at registration. The average thesis cost is about $100 (microfilming, binding, and copyrighting).

Living and Housing Costs

The University owns apartment buildings adjacent to the campus. In 1999–2000, rates for unfurnished and furnished rooms and apartments vary from $300 to $800 per month. A campus housing office assists students in finding rooms and apartments in the surrounding residential area.

Student Group

The University's Homewood Campus (the Schools of Arts and Sciences and of Engineering) had 3,583 undergraduates and 1,240 graduate students in 1998–99. There were 79 graduate students in physics and astronomy; all received financial support of some kind. Admission to graduate study in the department is highly competitive. An average of 15 new students are admitted each year; the majority enroll directly from college.

Location

Located in the northern section of Baltimore, the University is adjacent to one of the finest residential areas of the city, while most of the cultural activities of the large metropolitan area are but minutes away.

The University

The concept of graduate study came into being in America with the founding of the Johns Hopkins University in 1876. From the beginning, the hallmark of the University has been one of creative scholarship.

Applying

Requirements for admission after completion of the bachelor's or master's degree are transcripts of previous academic work, letters of recommendation, and GRE scores, including the General Test and the Subject Test in physics. International students whose native language is not English must submit their scores on the Test of English as a Foreign Language. Students are admitted only in September. Applications and all supporting materials must be received by January 15. The application fee is $55, but it is temporarily waived for students with either financial need or foreign exchange problems. Application materials may be obtained from the Henry A. Rowland Department of Physics and Astronomy, Graduate Admissions, Bloomberg Center.

Correspondence and Information

Graduate Admissions
The Henry A. Rowland Department of Physics and Astronomy
Bloomberg Center
Johns Hopkins University
Homewood Campus
Baltimore, Maryland 21218-2686
Telephone: 410-516-7344
Fax: 410-516-7239
E-mail: krupsaw@pha.jhu.edu
World Wide Web: http://www.pha.jhu.edu

Johns Hopkins University

THE FACULTY AND THEIR RESEARCH

Ronald J. Allen, Adjunct Professor (Space Telescope Science Institute); Ph.D., MIT, 1967. Spiral structure of galaxies, interstellar medium, radio and optical imaging.

Jonathan A. Bagger, Professor and Director, Theoretical Interdisciplinary Physics and Astrophysics Center; Ph.D., Princeton, 1983. Theoretical high-energy physics.

Bruce A. Barnett, Professor; Ph.D., Maryland, 1970. High-energy physics.

Steven Beckwith, Professor and Director, Space Telescope Science Institute; Ph.D., Caltech, 1978. Infrared astronomy.

William P. Blair, Associate Research Professor; Ph.D., Michigan, 1981. Astrophysics, shockwaves, spectroscopy of plasmas.

Barry J. Blumenfeld, Professor; Ph.D., Columbia, 1974. High-energy physics, neutrino physics.

Collin Broholm, Professor; Ph.D., Copenhagen, 1988. Experimental condensed-matter physics.

Chia-Ling Chien, Professor; Ph.D., Carnegie Mellon, 1972. Condensed-matter physics, artificially structured solids.

Chih-Yung Chien, Professor; Ph.D., Yale, 1966. High-energy physics.

Arthur F. Davidsen, Professor; Ph.D., Berkeley, 1975. Astronomy, astrophysics.

Gabor Domokos, Professor; Ph.D., Dubna (Russia), 1963. Theoretical high-energy physics, astro particle physics.

Sasha Dukan, Adjunct Assistant Professor; Ph.D., Johns Hopkins, 1996. Theoretical condensed-matter physics, theory of superconductivity in magnetic fields.

Adam Falk, Associate Professor; Ph.D., Harvard, 1991. Theoretical high-energy physics.

William G. Fastie, Research Professor Emeritus. Planetary atmospheres.

Gordon Feldman, Professor; Ph.D., Birmingham (England), 1953. Quantum field theory, theory of elementary particles.

Paul D. Feldman, Professor and Chair; Ph.D., Columbia, 1964. Astrophysics, spectroscopy, space physics, planetary and cometary atmospheres.

Michael Finkenthal, Visiting Professor (Hebrew University, Jerusalem) and Principal Research Scientist; Ph.D., Hebrew (Jerusalem), 1977. Plasma physics.

Holland Ford, Professor; Ph.D., Wisconsin, 1970. Stellar dynamics, evolution of galaxies, active galactic nuclei, astronomical instrumentation.

Thomas Fulton, Professor; Ph.D., Harvard, 1954. Quantum electrodynamics, atomic theory, high-energy particle physics.

Riccardo Giacconi, Research Professor; Ph.D., Milan, 1954. Astrophysics.

Michael G. Hauser, Adjunct Professor (Space Telescope Science Institute); Ph.D., Caltech, 1967. Astrophysics, cosmology, especially infrared background radiation.

Timothy Heckman, Professor; Ph.D., Washington (Seattle), 1978. Astrophysics, active galaxies and quasars.

Richard C. Henry, Professor and Director, Maryland Space Grant Consortium; Ph.D., Princeton, 1967. Astronomy, astrophysics.

Brian R. Judd, Gerhard H. Dieke Professor Emeritus; D.Phil., Oxford, 1955. Theoretical atomic and molecular physics, group theory, solid-state theory.

Chung W. Kim, Professor and President of the Korean Institute of Advanced Studies; Ph.D., Indiana, 1963. Nuclear theory, elementary particle theory, cosmology. (On leave)

Anne Kinney, Adjunct Associate Professor (Space Telescope Science Institute); Ph.D., NYU, 1984. Astrophysics.

Susan Kövesi-Domokos, Professor; Ph.D., Budapest, 1963. Theoretical high-energy physics, astroparticle physics.

Gerard A. Kriss, Adjunct Associate Professor; Ph.D., MIT, 1982. Astrophysics, observation of galactic nuclei.

Julian H. Krolik, Professor; Ph.D., Berkeley, 1977. Theoretical astrophysics.

Yung Keun Lee, Professor; Ph.D., Columbia, 1961. Nuclear physics.

Mario Livio, Adjunct Professor (Space Telescope Science Institute); Ph.D., Tel-Aviv, 1978. Theoretical astrophysics, accretion onto white dwarfs, neutron stars and black holes, novae and supernovae.

Knox S. Long, Adjunct Professor (Space Telescope Science Institute); Ph.D., Caltech, 1976. Supernova remnants, normal galaxies, cataclysmic variables.

Leon Madansky, Decker Professor Emeritus; Ph.D., Michigan, 1948. Nuclear physics, fundamental particles.

John March-Russell, Assistant Professor; Ph.D., Harvard, 1990. Theoretical high energy physics.

H. Warren Moos, Professor; Ph.D., Michigan, 1962. Astrophysics, plasma physics.

Jack Morava, Professor (Mathematics); Ph.D., Rice, 1967. Conformal field theory, topological gravity.

Ganpathy Murthy, Adjunct Associate Professor (Boston University); Ph.D., Yale, 1987. Theoretical condensed-matter physics.

Richard Mutshotzky, Adjunct Professor (Goddard Space Flight Center); Ph.D., California, San Diego, 1976. Astrophysics, active galactic nuclei, clusters of galaxies, elliptical galaxies, evolution of the element, cosmology.

David A. Neufeld, Professor; Ph.D., Harvard, 1987. Theoretical astrophysics, interstellar medium, astrophysical masers.

Colin A. Norman; D.Phil., Oxford, 1973. Theoretical astrophysics.

Aihud Pevsner, Jacob L. Hain Professor; Ph.D., Columbia, 1954. High-energy physics.

Marc Postman, Adjunct Associate Professor (Space Telescope Science Institute); Ph.D., Harvard, 1986. Observational cosmology and large-scale structures.

Daniel H. Reich, Professor; Ph.D., Chicago, 1988. Experimental condensed-matter physics.

Mark O. Robbins, Professor; Ph.D., Berkeley, 1983. Theoretical condensed-matter physics.

Darrell F. Strobel, Professor (Earth and Planetary Sciences); Ph.D., Harvard, 1969. Planetary atmospheres and astrophysics.

Alexander S. Szalay, Professor; Ph.D., Eötvös Loránd (Budapest), 1975. Theoretical astrophysics, galaxy formation.

Zlatko Tesanovic, Professor; Ph.D., Minnesota, 1985. Theoretical condensed-matter physics.

J. C. Walker, Professor; Ph.D., Princeton, 1961. Condensed-matter physics, thin films and surfaces, nuclear physics.

Kimberly Weaver, Adjunct Assistant Professor (Goddard Space Flight Center); Ph.D., Maryland, 1993. High-energy astrophysics.

Robert Williams, Adjunct Professor; Ph.D., Wisconsin–Madison, 1965. Astronomy and astrophysics, novae, space science.

Rosemary F. G. Wyse, Professor; Ph.D., Cambridge, 1982. Astrophysics: galaxy formation and evolution.

RESEARCH ACTIVITIES

Astrophysics. Observational programs include the use of ground-based optical and radio telescopes, analysis of archival data from previous space experiments, new research with existing satellites and sounding rockets, and space experiments. There is extensive laboratory work on detectors and instrument development for ultraviolet and optical astronomy. Research is concentrated in the following areas of astrophysics: cosmology, active galactic nuclei and quasars, galaxies and galaxy dynamics, stellar populations, the interstellar medium, comets and planetary atmospheres, and diffuse ultraviolet background studies.

Atomic Physics. Research in this area includes theoretical work on the electronic structure of atoms and molecules.

Condensed-Matter Physics. Research programs involve studies of very thin magnetic films, interfaces and surfaces, amorphous materials, conducting, superconducting, and magnetic properties of artificially structured materials, nanocrystals of metals and alloys, low-dimensional quantum magnets, highly correlated electron systems, high-T_c superconductors, and nonequilibrium phenomena. Techniques involve SQUID magnetometry, X-ray diffraction, Mössbauer spectroscopy, neutron diffraction, He^3-He^4 dilution refrigerator, DC and AC conductivity, LEED and Auger spectroscopies, ferromagnetic resonance, and vibrating-sample magnetometry.

High-Energy Physics. Current programs involve the study of strong, electromagnetic, and weak interactions. Experiments currently in progress are being performed at the Tevatron pp⁻ collider at Fermilab, at LEP and SPS, in CERN in Switzerland, and an experiment CMS at LHC in CERN. Data analysis is in progress at these facilities and at the Homewood Campus. Facilities for the construction and testing of particle detectors and associated electronics are available.

Plasma Spectroscopy. Extreme ultraviolet and soft X-ray diagnostic instrumentation is used to study high-temperature plasma devices used in controlled thermonuclear research.

Relativistic Heavy-Ion and Medium-Energy Nuclear Physics. The heavy-ion physics program includes the study of quark gluon plasma at the RHIC collider with the STAR and the BRAMS detectors at the Brookhaven National Laboratory.

Theoretical Physics. Areas of current research include condensed-matter physics, molecular and atomic structure, quantum optics, and astrophysics. The particle theory group currently conducts research in supersymmetric theories, heavy quark theory, and astroparticle physics. The condensed-matter theory group studies superconductivity, quantum Hall effect, "colossal" magnetoresistance, quantum critical phenomena, and various forms of nonequilibrium and growth phenomena. Members of the theory group specializing in different areas maintain close contact with each other and with the experimental groups.

KENT STATE UNIVERSITY

Department of Physics

Programs of Study

The Department of Physics offers a diverse program of graduate study and research leading to the Master of Arts, Master of Science, and Doctor of Philosophy degrees. Areas of concentration currently include experimental and theoretical research into the physics of condensed matter phases, with emphasis on liquid crystal systems and on novel electron systems, (e.g., high-T_c superconductors) and experimental and theoretical research in high-energy nuclear physics, with emphasis on electron and hadron scattering and on nuclear collisions. Theoretical research opportunities also provide training in quantum many-body techniques and in computational physics.

The physics graduate program provides solidly-based fundamental course work and the opportunity to specialize in the above areas with guidance and individual attention from internationally known scientists. The quality of the program is reflected in the University's success in competing nationally for research support and in the strong publication record of the faculty and students.

A student typically takes core courses during the first two years of study. The M.A. and M.S. degrees require 32 semester hours of courses. The M.S. degree requires a thesis. The Ph.D. degree requires 90 semester hours of courses, seminars, and research work beyond the bachelor's degree or 60 semester hours beyond the master's degree. Doctoral students normally will be expected to pass the candidacy examination by the start of their third year. Over the past ten years, the average time to completion of the Ph.D. degree from the first enrollment in the graduate program has been 5.7 years—about nine months shorter than the national average for physics over the same period.

Research Facilities

The Department of Physics has extensive facilities for condensed-matter research, including nonlinear optics, electro-optics, tunneling and atomic force microscopy, nuclear magnetic resonance, electron paramagnetic resonance, X-ray scattering, light scattering, microcalorimetry, millikelvin refrigeration, SQUID magnetometry, and magnetoresistance and Hall effect measurement. The experimental nuclear physics group has an extensive pool of state-of-the-art fast electronics and a transportable data-acquisition computer. Of special note are the large-volume, ultrafast neutron detectors and neutron polarimeters developed by the Kent faculty and their students. The Center for Nuclear Research (CNR) has the mission to support, enhance, and promote academic activities in the nuclear physics program of the physics department. The Liquid Crystal Institute (LCI) at Kent State University is a strong academic center of liquid-crystal research. Members of the department are also part of the Science and Technology Center for Research in Advanced Liquid Crystalline Optical Materials (ALCOM), a major NSF-funded center.

Financial Aid

In 1999–2000, graduate appointments for the nine-month academic year carry a stipend of $12,690, plus a full tuition scholarship. Half-time appointments are available that carry the same tuition scholarship as full-time appointments but have only half the stipend and half the service load. It is possible to enter the program at midyear. Students generally receive support during the summer. Approximately half of the continuing students hold research assistantships. The usual loans and work-study programs are available.

Cost of Study

The 1999–2000 annual tuition is $6789 for in-state residents pursuing full-time study and $13,031 for out-of-state residents pursuing full-time study. All appointees receive a full tuition scholarship.

Living and Housing Costs

Rooms are available for single graduate students in dormitories. Current costs per month are $361 for a single, $336 for a double, and $435 for a deluxe single. Furnished apartments (1-, 1½-, and 2-bedroom) for married students are available in the University-owned Allerton Apartments. Current costs per month are $455 for 1 bedroom, $470 for 1½ bedrooms, and $480 for 2 bedrooms. Reasonably priced rental housing can also be found. Campus Bus Service provides transportation on campus and to the surrounding area; this service is free to all Kent students.

Student Group

The approximately 20,000 students on the Kent campus include about 4,600 graduate students. The physics department has 51 graduate students with more than twelve countries represented. Kent State University emphasizes diversity; the school has been successful in attracting students from traditionally underrepresented groups, including minorities and women. Essentially all graduate students are full-time.

Student Outcomes

Students find rewarding positions in academic, government, and industrial institutions. Graduates enter initial employment in permanent positions at a higher rate than national norms. In the United States, the doctoral program at Kent is a major source of Ph.D. physicists employed in the liquid-crystal and flat-panel display industry. The 130 graduates (1968–1994) currently include four chairs of physics departments, presidents and vice-presidents of companies, managers, and directors.

Location

Kent is a city of about 30,000 located in northeastern Ohio. The Appalachian foothills to the east and Lake Erie to the north are within an hour's drive. The nearby Cuyahoga Valley National Recreation Area provides excellent recreational opportunities throughout the seasons and houses Blossom Music Center, summer home of the Cleveland Orchestra and the Porthouse Theatre.

The University and The Department

Kent State University offers degree programs ranging from undergraduate degrees in creative and performing arts to graduate degrees in the sciences. Kent is a strong research institution in the Carengie Research II category, ranking in the top dozen or so universities in income from patents and has a research library of more than 2 million volumes.

The physics department has offices, classrooms, and laboratories in Smith Hall and the adjacent Science Research Laboratory. There are 19 regular faculty members (all with Ph.D. degrees), who receive about $1.6 million per year in research support.

Applying

Application forms for admission and financial assistance may be obtained by writing to the Department of Physics. Graduate study may be initiated during any term, including the summer. Early application is recommended for consideration for financial aid.

Correspondence and Information

Dr. David W. Allender, Chairman
Department of Physics
Kent State University
Kent, Ohio 44242-0001

Telephone: 330-672-2880
Fax: 330-672-2959
E-mail: grad_prog@ksuvxd.kent.edu
World Wide Web: http://cnr2.kent.edu

Kent State University

THE FACULTY AND THEIR RESEARCH

David W. Allender, Professor and Chair; Ph.D., Illinois, 1975. Theoretical physics of condensed matter, liquid crystals.
Carmen C. Almasan, Assistant Professor; Ph.D., South Carolina, 1989. Experimental condensed-matter physics, superconductivity, magnetism, low-temperature and high-temperature physics.
Bryon D. Anderson, Professor; Ph.D., Case Western Reserve, 1972. Experimental nuclear physics, nuclear force, nucleon structure.
Brett D. Ellman, Assistant Professor; Ph.D., Chicago, 1992. Superconductivity, conduction mechanisms in insulators and semiconductors, phonon physics, disordered magnets.
George Fai, Professor; Ph.D., Roland Eötvös (Budapest), 1974. Theoretical nuclear physics, relativistic nuclear collisions.
Daniele Finotello, Professor; Ph.D., SUNY at Buffalo, 1985. Low-temperature and liquid-crystal physics, superconductivity.
James T. Gleeson, Assistant Professor; Ph.D., Kent State, 1991. Nonequilibrium dynamics and pattern formation.
Wilbert N. Hubin, Professor; Ph.D., Illinois, 1969. Computer hardware and physics education.
Declan Keane, Professor; Ph.D., University College (Dublin), 1981. Relativistic nuclear collisions.
Satyendra Kumar, Professor; Ph.D., Illinois at Urbana-Champaign, 1981. Liquid-crystal physics, superconductivity, liquid-crystal electrooptical effects.
Michael A. Lee, Professor; Ph.D., Northwestern, 1977. Condensed-matter theory.
D. Mark Manley, Professor; Ph.D., Wyoming, 1981. Experimental nuclear physics, baryon resonances.
Elizabeth K. Mann, Assistant Professor; Ph.D., Paris VI (Curie), 1992. Experimental soft-matter physics.
Spyridon Margetis, Assistant Professor; Ph.D., Frankfurt, 1990. Experimental high-energy nuclear physics.
Gerassimos Petratos, Associate Professor; Ph.D., American, 1988. Nuclear/particle physics.
Khandker F. Quader, Associate Professor; Ph.D., SUNY at Stony Brook, 1983. Theoretical condensed-matter physics, superconductivity, strongly correlated systems, low-temperature physics.
Samuel N. Sprunt Jr., Assistant Professor; Ph.D., MIT, 1989. Experimental liquid-crystal physics, phase transitions.
Peter C. Tandy, Professor and Director of the Center for Nuclear Research; Ph.D., Flinders (Australia), 1973. Nuclear reaction theory, multiparticle-scattering theory.
John W. Watson, Professor; Ph.D., Maryland, 1970. Medium-energy nuclear physics.

Faculty in Related Disciplines
Philip J. Bos, Associate Professor, Chemical Physics Interdisciplinary Program; Ph.D., Kent State, 1978. Liquid-crystal applications.
Jack R. Kelly, Associate Professor, Chemical Physics Interdisciplinary Program; Ph.D., Clarkson, 1979. Electrooptic and dielectric properties of liquid crystals.
Oleg Lavrentovich, Associate Professor, Chemical Physics Interdisciplinary Program; Ph.D., 1984, D.Sc., 1990, Ukrainian Academy of Sciences. Defects in liquid crystals, electrooptics of smectic liquid crystals, physics of liquid crystalline dispersions.
Peter Palffy-Muhoray, Professor, Chemical Physics Interdisciplinary Program; Ph.D., British Columbia, 1977. Nonlinear optics, pattern formation in liquid crystals.
John L. West, Professor, Chemistry; Ph.D., Carnegie-Mellon, 1980. Polymer-dispersed liquid crystals, surface-anchoring studies.
Deng-ke Yang, Assistant Professor, Chemical Physics Interdisciplinary Program; Ph.D., Hawaii, 1989. Liquid-crystal applications.

Active Research Topics
Theoretical investigation of fluctuation phenomena and mechanisms of superconductivity.
High-performance parallel computing: Research on scientific algorithms for study of the physics of many-body systems, using teraflop massively parallel computers.
Finite-size effects in superfluid helium.
Quantum fluids in porous media: Thermodynamic properties.
Nonlinear optics of ordered fluids.
Pattern formation in liquid crystals.
Phase transitions in liquid crystals under confinement.
High-precision heat capacity measurements of phase transitions in lytotropic liquid crystals and nonionic surfactant solutions.
Surface effects on liquid crystals.
High-resolution synchrotron X-ray diffraction and small-angle neutron scattering studies of structure and critical phenomena in complex fluids and thermotropic, polymer, and lyotropic liquid crystals.
X-ray studies of discotic liquid crystals.
Liquid-crystal display physics.
Ferroelectric liquid-crystal displays.
High-definition systems: Theoretical and experimental research in the use of liquid crystals in high-resolution display devices, including high-definition television.
Dynamics, thermodynamics, and microrheology in Langmuir films.
Experimental and theoretical investigations of the nuclear matter equation of state.
Signals of the quark-gluon phase in relativistic nuclear collisions.
Extended field-theory model studies of nucleons, mesons, and nuclear systems in terms of elementary (quark) degrees of freedom.
Measurements to probe the charge and magnetic structure of the neutron.
Nuclear structure studies with electron scattering and charge-exchange reactions.
Spin structure of the nucleons from polarized deep inelastic electron scattering.
Electromagnetic form-factors of deuterium and helium.
Studies of nucleon resonances with electromagnetic and hadronic probes.
Few-nucleon reaction studies.
Spin-transfer studies in nuclear reactions.

LOUISIANA STATE UNIVERSITY

Department of Physics and Astronomy

Programs of Study

The department offers studies leading to the Master of Natural Science (M.N.S.), Master of Science (M.S.), and Doctor of Philosophy (Ph.D.) degrees. For the M.N.S., 36 hours of graduate courses are required. This degree program provides depth in science subjects, as well as the breadth in physics that is required of teachers in junior and senior high schools. The M.S. degree requires 24 hours of graduate work with a thesis or 36 hours without a thesis. Formal requirements for the Ph.D. degree include 18 hours of advanced graduate courses beyond the core level; the Ph.D. general examination; publication of research results; and the final examination. The Ph.D. general examination is offered twice each year. It is comprehensive and is based primarily on graduate physics; students should approach it as the central formal examination of their graduate career. Those with normal preparation must take the general examination within two years of their entrance into the department. The final examination is an oral defense of the thesis. Through ongoing interdisciplinary interactions with faculty members in the LSU Department of Computer Science, students pursuing a graduate degree in physics have the opportunity to simultaneously earn an M.S. degree in system science from the Department of Computer Science.

Research Facilities

LSU has fully staffed machine shops and electronics shops. A full-time staff member operates a liquid-helium facility for the entire University. The department has two parallel computing laboratories that feature excellent computational facilities to support various research and educational programs. With $2.5 million in infrastructure enhancement grants, these labs have been equipped with a forty-six-processor Digital Alpha system on two Gigaswitches, an 8,192-node MasPar, a sixty-four-cell Intel iWarp systolic architecture, and an Intel iPSC/860 system. The visualization facilities in these labs include an eight-processor Silicon Graphics Power Center, an SGI workstation, and stereographic equipment. Two professional computer programmers are staff members of the department. Research resources include a dilution refrigerator–high magnetic field (18 tesla) apparatus; a 1.3-GeV electron synchrotron (CAMD) for materials science, surface physics, and X-ray lithography applications; and laser optics and crystal growing laboratories. Other experimental groups are involved in high-energy experiments at LAMPF, Fermilab, and CERN; nuclear physics measurements at Oak Ridge and RHIC; condensed-matter experiments at NIST and Brookhaven; cosmic-ray and neutrino studies with the SuperKamiokande, AUGER experiments, and balloon-launching sites from Canada to the Antarctic; and gravity-wave observations. Astronomers are involved in observations at Kitt Peak and Mauna-Kea, and in Chile and with the Hubble Space Telescope, ROSAT, ASCA, GRO, and AXAF satellites.

Financial Aid

The department provides about sixty-nine teaching and research assistantships. Stipends for fall 1999 are approximately $12,900 to $17,400 for the calendar year (twelve months), depending on qualifications. The University offers Graduate School, Board of Regents, NSF Traineeships, and NASA Space Grant Fellowships with yearly stipends of $17,000 to $20,000. To apply for financial aid, applicants should attach a statement to their application for admission indicating that they wish to be considered for an assistantship or a fellowship. Fellowship applicants must also report their scores on the GRE Subject Test in physics and prepare a statement of their intellectual and professional goals. Research assistantships are usually available to students after their first year. There are currently twenty-six grant-funded research assistantship positions for thesis research.

Cost of Study

For 1999, fees are $1362 per semester for Louisiana residents and $3312 per semester for nonresidents. For the summer (full-time), the fees are $1109 and $1576. Students on research or teaching assistantships pay resident fees.

Living and Housing Costs

The cost of a room in a dorm ranges from $798 to $1244 per semester. There are also 600 married student apartments that rented for $305 to $405 per month. In addition, many moderately priced apartments are available near the campus. The cost of living in Baton Rouge is moderate.

Student Group

The physics graduate student body is geographically diverse; students come from all parts of the United States and the world. The 1998–99 entering class of 12 was selected from more than 300 applicants, and the enrollment for the fall is expected to be about 70.

Location

Baton Rouge, located on the Mississippi River, is the capital of Louisiana. It has many of the recreational opportunities of a big city, while remaining a residential community of about 400,000 people.

The University

Louisiana State University, established more than a hundred years ago, is a statewide system of higher education, with headquarters on the main campus in Baton Rouge. Other campuses are located in Alexandria, Eunice, New Orleans, and Shreveport. On the Baton Rouge campus, the student enrollment is about 24,000, of whom about 4,500 are graduate students. The bachelor's degree is awarded in 125 major fields. Master's degrees are awarded in 56 departmental fields and the Ph.D. in 45.

Applying

Students may request an application packet from the department. All application materials should be sent directly to the department at the address below. Students must submit an Application for Admission for Advanced Studies; a score for the GRE General Test (a score on the GRE Subject Test in physics is recommended for U.S. students and required for international students); two official transcripts of all college and university course work, with a minimum GPA of 3.0 required for all undergraduate and graduate work (A = 4.0); and three letters of reference from people acquainted with the student's academic ability. Students whose native language is not English must submit a score of at least 600 on the TOEFL. U.S. applicants must submit all credentials at least sixty days before the beginning of the fall semester and thirty days before the beginning of the spring semester or summer session; International students must submit all credentials at least ninety days before the beginning of any term. The application deadline for fellowships and assistantships is January 25. Students are advised to apply well before these deadlines but are not discouraged from applying for assistantships after the deadline or for openings for the spring semester.

Correspondence and Information

Department of Physics and Astronomy
Graduate Student Secretary
Louisiana State University
Baton Rouge, Louisiana 70803-4001
Telephone: 225-388-1193

Louisiana State University

THE FACULTY AND THEIR RESEARCH

Astronomy and Astrophysics

Geoffrey C. Clayton, Assistant Professor; Ph.D., Toronto, 1983. Interstellar and extragalactic dust, circumstellar dust, R Coronae Borealis stars.

John S. Drilling, Professor; Ph.D., Case Western Reserve, 1967. Stellar astrophysics, galactic structure.

Juhan Frank, Professor; Ph.D., Cambridge, 1978. Accretion in close binaries and active galactic nuclei.

Arlo U. Landolt, Professor; Ph.D., Indiana, 1962. Stellar photometry.

Joel Tohline, Professor; Ph.D., California, Santa Cruz, 1978. Star formation, galaxy dynamics.

Atomic/Condensed-Matter Theory

Dana Browne, Professor; Ph.D., Stanford, 1981. Transport properties of very small devices, macroscopic quantum coherence effects, exotic forms of superconductivity.

Rajiv Kalia, Professor; Ph.D., Northwestern, 1976. Computational solid-state physics.

Robert F. O'Connell, Boyd Professor; Ph.D., Notre Dame, 1962. Inversion layers at insulator-semiconductor interface, Wigner distribution, two-dimensional degenerate electron gas.

A. R. P. Rau, Professor; Ph.D., Chicago, 1970. Atoms in electric and magnetic fields, threshold laws, mathematical physics.

Ken Schafer, Assistant Professor; Ph.D., Arizona, 1989. Theory of high-intensity ultrafast laser-matter interactions.

Priya Vashishta, FPS Chaired Professor of Computational Methods; Ph.D., Indian Institute of Technology, 1967. Materials science, molecular dynamics, computational physics.

Condensed-Matter/Solid-State/Atomic Experiment

Philip W. Adams, Associate Professor; Ph.D., Rutgers, 1986. Transport properties in two-dimensional systems, transport properties in quench condensed superconducting films.

John F. DiTusa, Assistant Professor; Ph.D., Cornell, 1992. Low-temperature physics, thin films, neutron scattering.

Roy G. Goodrich, Professor; Ph.D., California, Riverside, 1965. Electrical conduction in metals, magnitude and anisotropies in electron scattering.

Richard L. Kurtz, Professor; Ph.D., Yale, 1983. Surface science, synchrotron radiation studies.

Erwin Poliakoff, Adjunct Professor; Ph.D., Berkeley, 1979. Surface science, electronic properties of materials.

Roger Stockbauer, Professor; Ph.D., Chicago, 1973. Surface science, electronic properties of materials.

Elementary Particle Theory

Lai-Him Chan, Professor; Ph.D., Harvard, 1966. Quark phenomenology, low-energy hadron dynamics, chiral symmetry and α model, derivative expansion, effective action expansion.

Richard W. Haymaker, Professor; Ph.D., Berkeley, 1967. Dynamical symmetry breaking, lattice gauge theories.

Experimental General Relativity

William O. Hamilton, Professor; Ph.D., Stanford, 1963. Gravitational radiation instrumentation, cryogenic antenna to detect supernova collapses, cavity accelerometer detector, superconducting oscillator.

Warren W. Johnson, Associate Professor; Ph.D., Rutgers, 1974. Gravitational radiation detectors, Josephson devices, parametric transducers and quantum non-demolition.

Fluid Mechanics

R. G. Hussey, Professor; Ph.D., LSU, 1962. Low Reynolds number, boundary effects on axial motion.

High-Energy Astrophysics and Space Physics

Michael L. Cherry, Professor; Ph.D., Chicago, 1978. Neutrinos, cosmic rays, high-energy-particle astrophysics.

T. Gregory Guzik, Professor of Research; Ph.D., Chicago, 1980. Solar flares, particle interactions, accelerator experiments, cosmic rays.

W. Vernon Jones, Professor Emeritus; Ph.D., LSU, 1967. Cosmic rays.

James M. Matthews, Associate Professor; Ph.D., Wisconsin–Madison, 1984. Experimental cosmic-ray research at extreme energy.

J. Gregory Stacy, Assistant Professor; Ph.D., Maryland, 1980. Gamma-ray detector development, millimeter- and centimeter-wave radio astronomy, galactic structure and star formation regions.

Robert Svoboda, Associate Professor; Ph.D., Hawaii, 1985. Neutrino physics, proton decay, high-energy-particle astrophysics.

John P. Wefel, Professor; Ph.D., Washington (St. Louis), 1971. Astrophysics—experimental and theoretical; galactic cosmic radiation, solar energetic particles.

High-Energy Experiment

Richard L. Imlay, Professor; Ph.D., Princeton, 1967. Neutrino oscillations at Los Alamos National Laboratory (LANL), ep collisions at HERA.

Roger McNeil, Associate Professor; Ph.D., California, Davis, 1986. ep collisions at HERA, e^+e^- interactions, hadron collier physics.

William J. Metcalf, Professor and Chairman; Ph.D., Caltech, 1974. Neutrino oscillations at LANL, ep collisions at HERA, SSC detector development.

Nuclear Experiment

Paul N. Kirk, Professor; Ph.D., MIT, 1969. Nuclear and quark matter, quark condensation.

Edward F. Zganjar, Professor; Ph.D., Vanderbilt, 1966. Nuclei far from stability, heavy-ion accelerator, nuclear spectroscopy.

Nuclear Theory

Jerry P. Draayer, Professor; Ph.D., Iowa State, 1968. Shell model, statistical spectroscopy, group theory.

Calvin W. Johnson, Assistant Professor; Ph.D., Washington (Seattle), 1989. Theoretical nuclear physics and astrophysics.

Pedagogical Applications of Current Research on Physics Teaching and Learning

Donald F. Kirwan, Professor; Ph.D., Missouri–Columbia, 1969.

SELECTED PUBLICATIONS

Wu, W., J. Williams, and **P. W. Adams.** Zeeman splitting of the Coulomb anomaly: A tunneling study in two dimensions. *Phys. Rev. Lett.* 77:1139, 1996.

Wu, W., and **P. W. Adams.** Avalanches and slow relaxation: Dynamics of thin-film superconductors in a parallel magnetic field. *Phys. Rev. Lett.* 74:610, 1995.

Wu, W., and **P. W. Adams.** Superconductor-insulator transition in parallel magnetic field. *Phys. Rev. Lett.* 73:1412, 1994.

Bassler, K. E., and **D. A. Browne.** Nonequilibrium critical phenomena in a three species monomer-monomer model. *Phys. Rev. Lett.* 77:4094, 1996.

Helmkamp, B. S., and **D. A. Browne.** The role of the environment in chaotic quantum dynamics. *Phys. Rev. Lett.* 76:3691, 1996.

Helmkamp, B. S., and **D. A. Browne.** Inhibition of mixing in chaotic quantum dynamics. *Phys. Rev. E* 51:1849, 1995.

Chan, L.-H. Generalized derivative expansion and one-loop corrections to the vacuum energy of static background fields. *Phys. Rev. D* 55:6223–44, 1997.

Chan, L.-H. Unified effective theory for light mesons and heavy mesons. *Phys. Rev. D* 55:5362–75, 1997.

Chan, L.-H. Extended isoscalar-flavor-spin symmetries for baryons with a single spectator isoscalar quark. *Phys. Rev.* 54:6890–6, 1996.

Asakomori, K., et al. **(M. L. Cherry).** Cosmic ray proton and helium spectra—results from the JACEE experiment. *Astrophys. J.* 502:278, 1998.

Deincs-Jones, P., et al. **(M. L. Cherry).** High multiplicity lead-lead interactions at 158 GeV/nucleon. *Phys. Rev.* C53:3044, 1996.

Cherry, M. L., et al. Charge-coupled devices with fast timing for astrophysics and space physics research. *Proc. SPIE Conference 2806, Denver,* 551, 1996.

Cherry, M. L., et al. Large area sub-millimeter resolution CdZnTe strip detector for astronomy. *Nucl. Instrum. Methods Phys. Res. A* 380:490, 1996.

Clayton, G. C., et al. Evidence for a bipolar geometry in R Coronae Borealis? *Astrophys. J.,* in press.

Clayton, G. C., et al. Astro-2 observations of interstellar dust and gas in the Large Magellanic Cloud. *Astrophys. J.* 460:313, 1996.

Clayton, G. C. The R. Coronae Borealis stars. *Publ. Astron. Soc. Pacific* 108:225, 1996.

DiTusa, J. F., et al. Heavy fermion metal-Kondo insulator transition in $FeSi_{1-x}Al_x$. *Phys. Rev. B.* 58:10288–301, 1998.

DiTusa, J. F., et al. Metal-insulator transitions in the Kondo insulator FeSi and classic semiconductors are similar. *Phys. Rev. Lett.* 78:2831, 1997.

DiTusa, J. F., et al. Magnetic and charge dynamics in a doped one-dimensional transition metal oxide. *Phys. Rev. Lett.* 73:1857, 1994.

Draayer, J. P., and A. Ludu. Liquid drop non-linear modes as solitary waves. *Phys. Rev. Lett.* 80:2125, 1998.

Beuschel, T., A. L. Blokhin, and **J. P. Draayer.** On the validity of the pseudo-spin concept for triaxially deformed nuclei. *Nucl. Phys.* A619:119, 1997.

Blokhin, A. L., **J. P. Draayer,** and C. Bahri. On the origin of pseudospin symmetry. *Phys. Rev. Lett.* 74:4149–53, 1995.

Drilling, J. S., et al. The ultraviolet extinction curve for circumstellar dust formed in the hydrogen-poor environment of V348 Sagittarii. *Astrophys. J.,* in press.

Drilling, J. S. Basic data on hydrogen-deficient stars. *Astron. Soc. Pacific Conf. Ser.* 96:46, 1996.

Drilling, J. S., and T. C. Beers. UV spectrophotometry of the hottest stars in the southern HK survey. *Astrophys. J. Lett.* 446:L27, 1995.

McCormick, P., and **J. Frank.** Evolutionary effects of irradiation in cataclysmic variables. *Astrophys. J.* 500:923, 1998.

King, A. R., **J. Frank,** U. Kolb, and H. Ritter. Mass transfer cycles in close binaries with evolved companions. *Astrophys. J.* 482:919, 1997.

King, A. R., **J. Frank,** U. Kolb, and H. Ritter. Global analysis of mass transfer cycles in cataclysmic variables. *Astrophys. J.* 467:761, 1996.

Goodrich, R. G., P. W. Adams, D. H. Lowndes, and D. Norton. Origin of the variation of Tc with superconducting layer thickness and separation in YBCO/PrBCO superlattices. *Phys. Rev. B* 56:R14299, 1997.

Wu, W., **R. G. Goodrich,** and **P. W. Adams.** Spin-paramagnetic transition of ultrathin superconducting Al films in a tilted magnetic field. *Phys. Rev. B.,* 1995.

Goodrich, R. G. Thick-film chips in cryo temperature sensors. *Superconductor Industry* 24, Spring 1994.

Knott, C. N., et al. **(T. G. Guzik).** Interactions of relativistic neon to nickel projectiles in hydrogen. Elemental production cross sections. *Phys. Rev.* C 53:347, 1996.

Ryan, J. M., et al. **(M. L. Cherry** and **T. G. Guzik).** Large area sub-millimeter resolution CdZnTe strip detector for astronomy. In *EUV, X-Ray, and Gamma-Ray Instrumentation for Astronomy VI, SPIE* 2518:292, 1995.

Chen, J., **T. G. Guzik,** and **J. P. Wefel.** The ^{3}He/^{4}He ratios for solar energetic particle events during the combined release and radiation effects satellite mission. *Astrophys. J.* 442:875, 1995.

Morales, G. A., J. Faulkner, and **R. W. Hall.** Reply to comment on 'tight-binding simulations of argon cation clusters.' *J. Chem. Phys.,* in press.

Kestner, N. R., P. A. Limbach, **R. W. Hall,** and L. G. Butler. If you build it, will they come? *Campus-Wide Information Syst.,* in press.

Hall, R. W., L. G. Butler, N. R. Kestner, and P. A. Limbach. Combining feedback and assessment via Web-based homework. *Campus-Wide Information Syst.,* in press.

Mauceli, E., et al. **(W. O. Hamilton).** The Allegro gravitational radiation detector: Data acquisition and analysis. *Phys. Rev. D* 54:1264–75, 1996.

Astone, P., et al. **(W. O. Hamilton).** Result of a preliminary data analysis in coincidence between the LSU and Rome gravitational wave antennas. In *Proceedings of the X Italian Conference on General Relativity and Gravitational Physics Bardonecchia, TO,* Italy: World Scientific, 1994.

Solomonson, N., **W. O. Hamilton,** W. Johnson, and B. Xu. Construction and performance of a low noise inductive transducer for the Louisiana State University gravitational wave detector. *Rev. Sci. Instrum.* 65:174–81, 1994.

Haymaker, R. W., V. Singh, Y. Peng, and J. Wosiek. Distribution of the color fields around static quarks: Flux tube profiles. *Phys. Rev. D* 53:389–403, 1996.

Singh, V., D. A. Browne, and **R. W. Haymaker.** Structure of Abrikosov vortices in SU (2) lattice gauge theory. *Phys. Lett. B* 306:115–9, 1993.

Singh, V., D. A. Browne, and **R. W. Haymaker.** London relation and fluxoid quantization for monopole currents in U(1) lattice gauge theory. *Phys. Rev. D* 47:1715–8, 1993.

Pulley, J. W., **R. G. Hussey,** and A. M. J. Davis. Low nonzero Reynolds number drag of a thin disk settling axisymmetrically within a cylindrical outer boundary. *Phys. Fluids* 8:2275, 1996.

Wehbeh, E. G., T. J. Ui, and **R. G. Hussey.** End effects for the falling cylinder viscometer. *Phys. Fluids A* 5:25–33, 1993.

Trahan, J. F., R. F. Folse, and **R. G. Hussey.** Combined sidewall and bottom wall effects on the Stokes velocity of a disk moving broadside. *Phys. Fluids A* 1:1625, 1989.

Athanassopoulos, C., et al. **(R. Imlay).** Candidate events in a search for $^\mu\overline{v} \rightarrow ^e\overline{v}$ coscillations. *Phys. Rev. Lett.* 75:2650, 1995.

Chen, L., et al. **(R. Imlay).** Initial study of deep inelastic scattering with ZEUS at HERA. *Phys. Lett. B* 303:183–97, 1993.

Freedman, S. J., et. al. **(R. Imlay).** Limits on neutrino oscillations from $^e\overline{v}$ appearance. *Phys. Rev. D* 47:811, 1993.

Ginocchio, J. N., and **C. W. Johnson.** Unified theory of fermion pair to bosom mapping in full and truncated spaces. *Phys. Rev. C* 51:1861, 1995.

Johnson, C. W., S. E. Koonin, G. H. Lang, and W. E. Ormand. Monte Carlo methods for the nuclear shell model. *Phys. Rev. Lett.* 69:3157, 1992.

Koonin, S. E., **C. W. Johnson,** and P. Vogel. Optical model description of parity-nonconserving neutron resonances. *Phys. Rev. Lett.* 69:1163, 1992.

Magalhaes, N. S., **W. W. Johnson,** C. Frajuca, and O. D. Aguiar. A geometric method for location of gravitational wave sources. *Astrophys. J.,* accepted.

Merkowitz, S. M., and **W. W. Johnson.** First tests of a truncated icosahedral gravitational wave antenna. *Phys. Rev.* D53:5377, 1996.

Mauceli, E., et al. **(W. W. Johnson).** The Allegro gravitational wave detector: Data acquisition and analysis. *Phys. Rev.* D4:1264, 1996.

New, K. C. B., G. Chanmugam, **W. W. Johnson,** and **J. E. Tohline.** Millisecond pulsars: Detectable sources of continuous gravitational waves? *Astrophys. J.* 450:757–62, 1995.

Kalia, R. K., et al. Role of ultrafine microstructures in dynamic fracture in nanophase silicon nitride. *Phys. Rev. Lett.* 78:2144, 1997.

Kalia, R. K., A. Nakano, K. Tsuruta, and **P. Vashishta.** Morphology of pores and interfaces and mechanical behavior of nanocluster-assembled silicon nitride ceramic. *Phys. Rev. Lett.* 78:689, 1997.

Omeltchenko, A., J. Yu, **R. K. Kalia,** and **P. Vashishta.** Crack-front propagation and fracture in graphine: A molecular-dynamics. *Phys. Rev. Lett.* 78:2148, 1997.

Sahu, S. K., et al. **(P. N. Kirk).** A high-Q^2 measurement of the photon structure function F^2_γ. *Phys. Lett. B* 346:208, 1995.

Li, Y. K., et al. **(P. N. Kirk).** A determination of $^\alpha$s, in e^+e^- annihilation at $\sqrt{s}$ = 57.3 GeV. *Phys. Lett. B* 355:394, 1995.

Choi, S. K., et al. **(P. N. Kirk).** A measurement of Bose-Einstein correlations in e^+e^- annihilation at TRISTAN. *Phys. Lett. B* 355:406, 1995.

Kirwan, D. F., ed. *Properties and Behavior.* Baton Rouge, Louisiana: Louisiana State University, 1996.

Kirwan, D. F., ed. *Constancy and Change.* Baton Rouge, Louisiana: Louisiana State University, 1996.

Louisiana State University

Selected Publications (continued)

Kirwan, D. F., ed. *Powerful Ideas in Physical Science*. College Park, Maryland: American Association of Physics Teachers, 1995.

Hudson, L. T., et al. **(R. L. Kurtz and R. L. Stockbauer)**. A photoelectron spectroscopic study of the valence and core-level electronic structure of $BaTiO_3$. *Phys. Rev. B* 47:1174, 1993.

Kurtz, R. L., et al. **(R. L. Stockbauer)**. Photoelectron imaging of fermi surfaces. *Nucl. Instrum. Methods* A319:257, 1992.

Schaefer, B. E., et al. **(A. U. Landolt)**. The photometric period of the recurrent nova T Pyxidis. *Astrophys. J. Suppl.* 81:321, 1992.

Landolt, A. U. UBVRI photometric standard stars in the magnitude range 11.5 ⟨ V ⟨ 16.0 around the Celestial Equator. *Astron. J.* 104:340, 1992.

Landolt, A. U. Broadband UBVRI photometry of the Baldwin-Stone southern hemisphere spectrophotometric standards. *Astron. J.* 104:372, 1992.

Borione, A., et al. **(J. Matthews)**. Constraints on gamma-ray emission from the galactic plane at 300 TeV. *Astrophys. J.* 493:175, 1998.

Borione, A., et al. **(J. Matthews)**. A high statistics search for ultra-high energy gamma-ray emission from Cygnus X-3 and Hercules X-l. *Phys. Rev. D* 55:1714, 1997.

Borione, A., et al. **(J. Matthews)**. A search for ultrahigh energy gamma-ray emission from the Crab nebula and pulsar. *Astrophys. J.* 481:313, 1997.

Felps, W. S., J. D. Scott, and **S. P. McGlynn**. Magnetic circular dichroism of CD_3I in the vacuum ultraviolet. *J. Chem. Phys.* 104:419, 1996.

Klasine, L., I. Novak, and **S. P. McGlynn**. Photoelectron spectra of compounds with carbon-halogen bonds. In *Organic Chemistry of the Carbon-Halogen Bond*, Chapter 4, eds. S. Patai and P. Rappaport. New York: J. Wiley & Sons, 1995.

Kumar, D., R. R. Zinn, T. D. Armstrong, and **S. P. McGlynn**. The optogalvanic effect as a probe of plasma processes. *J. Phys. Chem.* (M.F.A. El-Sayed Festschrift). 99:7530, 1995.

McNeil, R. (L3 Collaboration). Search for heavy neutral and charged leptons in e+e- annihilation at 161GeV < √s < 172GeV. *Phys. Lett. B* 412:189, 1997.

McNeil, R. (L3 Collaboration). Measurement of the mass, width and gauge couplings of the W Boson at LEP. *Phys. Lett. B* 413:176, 1997.

McNeil, R. (L3 Collaboration). Measurement of hadron and lepton-pair production at 161GeV < √s < 172GeV. *Phys. Lett. B* 407:361, 1997.

Derrick, M., et al. **(W. J. Metcalf)**. Measurement of the reaction $\gamma p \to {}^{\gamma} \wp$ deep inelastic scattering at HERA. *Phys. Lett.* B380:220, 1996.

Athanassopoulos, C., et al. **(W. J. Metcalf)**. Candidate events in a search for $\bar{\nu}\mu \to \bar{\nu}e$ oscillations. *Phys. Rev. Lett.* 75:2650, 1995.

Derrick, M., et al. **(W. J. Metcalf)**. A search for excited fermions in electron-proton collisions at HERA. *Zeit. f. Physik* C65:627, 1995.

Ford, G. W., and **R. F. O'Connell**. The radiating electron: Fluctuations without dissipation in the equation of motion. *Phys. Rev. A* 57:3112, 1998.

Hu, G. Y., **R. F. O'Connell**, and J. Y. Ryu. Slanting coupling of one-dimensional arrays of small tunnel junctions. *J. Appl. Phys.* 84:6713, 1998.

Ford, G. W., and **R. F. O'Connell**. There is no quantum regression theorem. *Phys. Rev. Lett.* 77:798, 1996.

Ormand, W. E. Properties of proton drip-line nuclei at the sd-fp-shell interface. *Phys. Rev. C* 53:214, 1996.

Ormand, W. E., P. M. Pizzochero, P. F. Bortignon, and R. A. Broglia. Neutrino capture cross section for Ar-40 and the beta-decay of Ti-40. *Phys. Lett. B* 345:343, 1995.

Ormand, W. E., P. M. Pizzochero, P. F. Bortignon, and R. A. Broglia. The solar neutrino capture cross section for Na-23. *Phys. Lett. B* 308:207, 1993.

Piller, H. Lead-tin-telluride. In *Handbook of Optical Constants of Solids*, vol. 2, p. 725, ed. E. D. Palik. New York: Academic Press, 1991.

Piller, H. Cadmium-selenide, *Handbook of Optical Constants of Solids*, vol. 2, p. 59, ed. E. D. Palik. New York: Academic Press, 1991.

Piller, H., and J. Wagner. Faraday rotation and ellipticity in electron inversion layers of Si MOS structures. In *Application of High Magnetic Fields in Semiconductor Physics*, vol. 177, p. 199, ed. G. Landwehr. Berlin: Springer Verlag, 1983.

Rao, R. M., **E. D. Poliakoff**, K. Wang, and V. McKoy. Global Franck-Condon breakdown resulting from cooper minima. *Phys. Rev. Lett.* 76:2666–9, 1996.

Poliakoff, E. D., and R. M. Rao. Rotational and vibrational effects in photoionization: Bridging the gap from microvolts to kolovolts. *J. Electron Spectrosc. Rel. Phenom.* 79:361–6, 1996.

Poliakoff, E. D., et al. Photon rotational distributions from near-threshold to deep in the continuum. *J. Chem. Phys.* 103:1773–87, 1995.

Rau, A. R. P. Unitary integration of quantum Liouville-Bloch equations. *Phys. Rev. Lett.* 81:4785–9, 1998.

Fano, U., and **A. R. P. Rau**. Symmetries in quantum physics. *Academic Pr.*, 1996.

Heim, T. A., and **A. R. P. Rau**. Excitation of high-lying Pair-Rydberg states. *J. Phys. B* 28:5309–15, 1995.

Rose-Petruck, C., **K. J. Schafer**, K. R. Wilson, and C. P. J. Barty. Ultrafast electron dynamics and inner-shell ionization in laser driven clusters. *Phys. Rev. A*, 1996.

Schafer, K. J., and K. C. Kulander. High harmonic generation from ultrafast pump lasers. *Phys. Rev. Lett.*, 1996.

Schafer, K. J., B. Yang, L. F. DiMauro, and K. C. Kulander. Above threshold ionization beyond the high harmonic cutoff. *Phys. Rev. Lett.* 70:1599, 1993.

Stacy, J. G., et al. The gamma-ray blazar PKS 0208-512 from MeV to GeV energies. *Proc. 25th ICRC (Durban)* 3:105, 1997.

Stacy, J. G., et al. First results of an all-sky search for MeV-emission from active galaxies with COMPTEL. In *Fourth Compton Symposium, AIP Conference Proceedings 410*, p. 1356, eds. C. D. Dermer and J. D. Kurfess. New York: AIP, 1997.

Stacy, J. G., W. T. Vestrand, and R. B. Phillips. Coordinated millimeter-wave observations of bright, variable gamma-ray blazars with the Haystack Radio Telescope. In *Fourth Compton Symposium, AIP Conference Proceedings 410*, p. 1442, eds. C. D. Dermer and J. D. Kurfess. New York: AIP, 1997.

Mankey, G. J., K. Subramanian, **R. L. Stockbauer**, and **R. L. Kurtz**. Hybridization and charge transfer at magnetic interfaces measured by the observation of band filing. *Phys. Rev. B*, submitted.

Mankey, G. J., K. Subramanian, **R. L. Stockbauer**, and **R. L. Kurtz**. Observation of a bulklike fermi surface for a monolayer of Ni on Cu(001). *Phys. Rev. Lett.* 78:1146, 1997.

Becker-Szendy, R., et al. **(R. Svoboda)**. Neutrino measurements with the IMB detector. *Nucl. Phys. B* 38:331, 1995.

Becker-Szendy, R., et al. **(R. Svoboda)**. A search for moderate- and high-energy neutrino emission correlated with gamma-rays bursts. *Astrophys. J.* 444:415, 1995.

Miller, R. S., et al. **(R. Svoboda)**. A search for astrophysical sources of low-energy neutrinos using the IMB detector. *Astrophys. J.* 428:629, 1994.

New, K. C. B, and **J. E. Tohline**. The relative stability against merger of close, compact binaries. *Astrophys. J.* 490:311–27, 1997.

Cohl, H. S., X.-H. Sun, **J. E. Tohline**, and D. M. Christodoulou. Parallel implementation of a data-transpose technique for the solution of Poisson's equation in cylindrical coordinates. In *Proceedings of the 8th SIAM Conference on Parallel Processing for Scientific Computing, Minneapolis, Minnesota*, March, 1997.

Seo, E.-S., et al. **(J. P. Wefel)**. Advanced thin ionization calorimeter to measure ultrahigh energy cosmic rays. *Advances Space Res.* 19:711–8, 1997.

Chen, J., et al. **(J. P. Wefel)**. Energetic helium isotopes trapped in the magnetosphere. *J. Geophys. Res.* 101:24787, 1996.

Deines-Jones, P., et al. **(J. P. Wefel)**. High multiplicity lead-lead interactions at 158 GeV/c per nucleon. *Phys. Rev. C* 53:3044, 1996.

Wood, J. L., **E. F. Zganjar**, and K. Heyde. The strength of electric monopole transitions and the decay out of superdeformed bands. *Z. Phys. A* 353:355, 1996.

Batchelder, J. C., et al. **(E. F. Zganjar)**. Observation of the exotic nucleus ^{145}Tm via its direct proton decay. *Phys. Rev. C* 57, 1998.

von Schwarzenberg, J., J. L. Wood, and **E. F. Zganjar**. The identification of spherical states at low energy in the deformed nucleus ^{185}Pt. *Phys. Rev. C* 57:R15, 1998.

MICHIGAN STATE UNIVERSITY

Department of Physics and Astronomy

Programs of Study

M.S. and Ph.D. degrees are offered with specializations in accelerator physics, biomolecular physics, chemical physics, elementary particle theory, experimental particle physics, low-temperature physics, many-body theory, nuclear physics, solid-state physics, and observational and theoretical astrophysics. The semester system is followed. The ratio of faculty members to graduate students is about 1:2, and formal class sizes range from 5 to 40.

Research Facilities

Research facilities include two superconducting cyclotrons, K500 and K1200, each injected by ECR ion sources and associated apparatus, including the modern A1200 fragment separator that allows efficient production and in-flight separation of rare isotopes; the recently completed high-resolution S800 superconducting magnetic spectrograph; a large 92-inch scattering chamber; a recoil mass separator; 4-pi neutron and charged-particle detectors; a high-energy gamma ray detector array; neutron and charged-particle detector hodoscopes; a number of data acquisition and analysis computers; X-ray apparatus for study of structure on atomic and mesoscopic length scales; extensive photo and electron-beam lithographic facilities, housed in a clean room and including an atomic force natos, field-emission SEM, and a micro-Raman spectrometer, for device fabrication with 50-nm resolution; cryogenic facilities, including one helium-3 refrigerator and four helium-3/helium-4 dilution refrigerators; five (5T, 6T, 9T, 9T, and 14T) superconducting magnets; two automated SQUID magnetometers; an electron spin resonance laboratory; an ultrahigh-vacuum four-gun sputtering system; electron photo emission spectrometer; a high-energy physics laboratory, which is a state-of-the-art electronics design facility where detectors for experiments are developed, tested, and constructed; and numerous minicomputers and microcomputers in all research areas. Important off-campus facilities in the high-energy area include the accelerator at Fermilab in Batavia, Illinois, and CERN in Geneva, Switzerland, where experiments are currently being carried out by MSU faculty members and students. MSU faculty members and students are participating in studies and workshops in which the aim is to design experiments to operate at high-energy frontier facilities. The experimental high-energy group makes use of well-equipped high-energy physics laboratories in which state-of-the-art detectors are being constructed for use at the CDF and DZero experiments at Fermilab and the ATLAS experiment at the Large Hadron Collider at CERN. The departmental electronics shop's up-to-date electronic design facilities where the fast-trigger system for the DZero experiment was designed are now occupied with upgrade efforts in DZero as well as with designs of portions of the fast trigger for ATLAS. A large number of workstations, including some late-model DEC Alpha-based processors, are available for use for design and analysis. Facilities and software packages to analyze the large data sets resulting from running at the DZero and CDF collider detectors are available for use. Also available are full complements of programs for simulation and modeling of complex triggering systems such as those used in DZero and planned for ATLAS. The astronomy faculty makes use of the facilities on campus, which include a 0.6m telescope, and of the observatories at Kitt Peak (Arizona), WIRO (Wyoming), Mounts Wilson and Palomar (California), Siding Springs (Australia), and Cerro Tololo and Las Campanas (Chile). MSU has joined the SOAR consortium to build the 4-meter telescope in Chile. A department library has up-to-date collections of books and journals. Current research programs are described in materials available from the department.

Financial Aid

Half-time graduate assistantship stipends began at $15,300 for the 1998–99 academic year. Summer assistantships are available. Assistants spend up to 20 hours a week on their duties. In-class contact hours for teaching assistants range from 6 to 8 hours for recitation and laboratory classes. The normal course load for assistants is 6 to 9 credit hours. The duties of research assistants are commonly in the general area in which the Ph.D. thesis will be written. Fellowships and scholarships are also available.

Cost of Study

Tuition for 1999–2000 is $222.50 per credit hour for Michigan residents. Teaching and research assistants pay in-state rates and receive a full tuition waiver. Out-of-state tuition is $450 per credit hour. Half of the matriculation fees are paid by MSU for all graduate assistants beginning 1999–2000. Registration fees for students in 1999–2000 are $566 per year.

Living and Housing Costs

Single rooms in Owen Hall, the graduate residence center, rented for $1928 per semester and double rooms for $1649 per student per semester for 1998–99. This cost includes credit toward one meal per day (approximately $280 per month). Food may be obtained from several campus cafeterias and local restaurants. The University owns and operates more than 2,000 one- and two-bedroom apartments to help meet the housing needs of married students. These rent for $390 to $465 per month, respectively, and include all utilities, essential furniture, and a private telephone. Privately owned off-campus rooms and apartments are also available.

Student Group

The on-campus enrollment at Michigan State University for the 1998 fall semester was 43,189, including 7,838 graduate and professional students. There were 125 physics graduate students, including 96 Ph.D. candidates, and there were 20 postdoctoral research associates.

Location

East Lansing is a residential city adjacent to the Michigan State University campus and close to Lansing, the state capital. Many opportunities for cultural and social development are offered by the University and neighboring civic groups. Examples include the Wharton Center for the Performing Arts, the Kresge Art Center, the University Museum, and the lecture-concert, World Travel, and foreign film series.

The University and The Department

Michigan State University, one of the oldest land-grant colleges, was founded in 1855 for the purpose of furthering the interests of agriculture and the mechanic arts. From this modest beginning it has grown to become one of America's largest universities, with many educational innovations to its credit. Through its 14 colleges and more than 100 departments, it offers 200 different programs leading to undergraduate and graduate degrees.

Applying

Application forms may be obtained by writing to the address listed below. Applications for admission and supporting documents should be received at least one month prior to the first enrollment together with a $30 application fee. Applicants should request that registrars of colleges previously attended send transcripts directly to the department office listed below. Applications for a graduate assistantship, fellowship, or scholarship should reach the office no later than six months prior to the first anticipated enrollment. Acceptance of graduate students is decided by a departmental committee maintained for this purpose.

Correspondence and Information

Professor Phillip M. Duxbury, Associate Chairperson–Graduate Program
Department of Physics and Astronomy
Michigan State University
East Lansing, Michigan 48824-1116
Telephone: 517-355-9666
Fax: 517-353-4500
E-mail: duxbury@pa.msu.edu
World Wide Web: http://www.pa.msu.edu/

Michigan State University

THE FACULTY

Physics

Maris A. Abolins, Professor; Ph.D., California, San Diego, 1965.
Sam M. Austin, University Distinguished Professor; Ph.D., Wisconsin–Madison, 1960.
Jack Bass, Professor; Ph.D., Illinois, 1964.
Wolfgang Bauer, Professor and Associate Chairperson, Undergraduate Program; Ph.D., Giessen (Germany), 1987.
Walter Benenson, University Distinguished Professor; Ph.D., Wisconsin–Madison, 1962.
Martin Berz, Professor; Ph.D., Giessen (Germany), 1986.
Simon Billinge, Associate Professor; Ph.D., Pennsylvania, 1992.
Norman Birge, Associate Professor; Ph.D., Chicago, 1986.
Henry G. Blosser, University Distinguished Professor Emeritus; Ph.D., Virginia, 1954.
Jerzy Borysowicz, Professor; Ph.D., Institute for Nuclear Research (Warsaw), 1965.
Raymond L. Brock, Professor and Chairperson; Ph.D., Carnegie Mellon, 1980.
Carl M. Bromberg, Professor; Ph.D., Rochester, 1974.
B. Alex Brown, Professor; Ph.D., SUNY at Stony Brook, 1974.
Edward H. Carlson, Professor Emeritus; Ph.D., Johns Hopkins, 1959.
Pawel Danielewicz, Professor; Ph.D., Warsaw, 1981.
Phillip M. Duxbury, Professor and Associate Chairperson, Graduate Program; Ph.D., New South Wales (Australia), 1983.
Mark Dykman, Professor; Ph.D., Kiev, 1973.
Aaron Galonsky, Professor; Ph.D., Wisconsin–Madison. 1954.
C. Konrad Gelbke, University Distinguished Professor and Director, National Superconducting Cyclotron Laboratory; Ph.D., Heidelberg (Germany), 1972.
Thomas Glasmacher, Associate Professor; Ph.D., Florida State, 1992.
Brage Golding, Professor and Director, Center for Sensor Materials; Ph.D., MIT, 1966.
Morton M. Gordon, Emeritus Professor; Ph.D., Washington (St. Louis), 1950.
Gregers Hansen, Hannah Professor; Ph.D., Copenhagen, 1965.
Michael J. Harrison, Professor; Ph.D., Chicago, 1960.
William M. Hartmann, Professor; D.Phil., Oxford, 1965.
Jack Hetherington, Professor; Ph.D., Illinois, 1962.
Joey W. Huston, Professor; Ph.D., Rochester, 1982.
Thomas Kaplan, Emeritus Professor; Ph.D., Pennsylvania, 1954.
Edwin Kashy, University Distinguished Professor; Ph.D., Rice, 1959.
Gabor Kemeny, Emeritus Professor; Ph.D., NYU, 1962.
Julius S. Kovacs, Professor; Ph.D., Indiana, 1955.
James T. Linnemann, Professor; Ph.D., Cornell, 1978.
Rong Liu, Assistant Professor; Ph.D., Iowa State, 1990.
William G. Lynch, Professor; Ph.D., Washington (Seattle), 1980.
S. D. Mahanti, Professor; Ph.D., California, Riverside, 1968.
Hugh McManus, Emeritus Professor; Ph.D., Birmingham (England), 1947.
Paul M. Parker, Emeritus Professor; Ph.D., Ohio State, 1958.
Gerald L. Pollack, Professor; Ph.D., Caltech, 1962.
Bernard G. Pope, Professor and Associate Chairperson; Ph.D., Columbia, 1971.
Scott Pratt, Assistant Professor; Ph.D., Minnesota, 1985.
William Pratt, Professor; Ph.D., Minnesota, 1969.
Jon Pumplin, Professor; Ph.D., Michigan, 1968.
Wayne Repko, Professor; Ph.D., Wayne State, 1967.
Carl Schmidt, Assistant Professor; Ph.D., Harvard, 1990.
Peter A. Schroeder, Emeritus Professor; Ph.D., Bristol (England), 1955.
Bradley Sherrill, Professor; Ph.D., Michigan State, 1985.
Peter S. Signell, Professor; Ph.D., Rochester, 1958.
Daniel R. Stump, Associate Professor; Ph.D., MIT, 1976.
Stuart Tessmer, Assistant Professor; Ph.D., Illinois, 1995.
Michael Thoennessen, Professor; Ph.D., SUNY at Stony Brook, 1988.
Michael F. Thorpe, University Distinguished Professor; D.Phil., Oxford, 1968.
David Tomanek, Professor; Ph.D., Berlin, 1983.
Wu-ki Tung, Professor; Ph.D., Yale, 1966.
Hendrik J. Weerts, Professor; Ph.D., Aachen (Germany), 1981.
Gary D. Westfall, Professor; Ph.D., Texas at Austin, 1975.
Richard York, Professor; Ph.D., Iowa, 1976.
Chien-Peng Yuan, Associate Professor; Ph.D., Michigan, 1988.
Vladimir Zelevinsky, Professor; Ph.D., Budker Institute of Nuclear Physics, 1974.

Astronomy

Timothy C. Beers, Associate Professor; Ph.D., Harvard, 1983.
Suzanne Hawley, Associate Professor; Ph.D., Texas at Austin, 1989.
Jeffrey R. Kuhn, Professor; Ph.D., Princeton, 1981.
Albert P. Linnell, Emeritus Professor; Ph.D., Harvard, 1958.
Edwin D. Loh, Associate Professor; Ph.D., Princeton, 1977.
Susan M. Simkin, Professor; Ph.D., Wisconsin–Madison, 1967.
Horace Smith, Professor; Ph.D., Yale, 1980.
Robert F. Stein, Professor; Ph.D., Columbia, 1966.

MICHIGAN TECHNOLOGICAL UNIVERSITY

Department of Physics

Programs of Study

The Department of Physics offers programs that lead to the Master of Science and Doctor of Philosophy degrees in physics. The Master of Science in physics may be obtained via either a thesis or a course work option. Students who plan to complete their graduate studies with the Master of Science in physics are encouraged to pursue the thesis option. The course work option is intended for students who wish to pursue the Ph.D., and the requirements are more stringent than the minimum requirements of the Graduate School for a master's-level degree.

The focus of the graduate program in physics is on the Ph.D. in physics. Students are generally admitted into the department's graduate program based on an assessment of their ability to succeed as doctoral degree students. A minimum of 36 course and/or research credit hours beyond the M.S. degree (or its equivalent) or a minimum of 81 course and/or research credit hours beyond the bachelor's degree are required. The course work requirement for the Ph.D. in physics is determined by the student's Advisory Committee.

Students accepted into the graduate program must take the qualifying examination in the first fall quarter following their matriculation in the University. After the qualifying examination is taken and passed, the preliminary examination is administered by the student's Advisory Committee to review the student's proposed plan of research. The final oral examination may be scheduled anytime after a period of two quarters following the successful completion of the qualifying examination and completion of the dissertation in satisfactory form.

Multidisciplinary research is encouraged, and significant opportunities exist to collaborate with researchers in geophysics, materials and metallurgy, electrical engineering, chemistry, mathematics, and computer science.

Research Facilities

Research is conducted in the Fisher Hall physics laboratories as well as other University facilities in adjoining buildings. University facilities routinely used by physics faculty members and graduate students include SEMs, X-ray diffraction facilities, and materials processing and characterization facilities in the Institute for Materials Processing. The physics department has numerous faculty laboratories, including the hyperspectral imaging, high-field NMR, dislocation physics, computational atomic physics, and laser spectroscopy laboratories. Each faculty member and graduate student has immediate access to a variety of high-performance workstations and has access to local and distributed computation through the Center for Experimental Computation, which is jointly operated by the physics and computer science departments. The department has an electronics shop, student machine shop, and machine shop, and each has a professional support staff.

Financial Aid

Teaching assistantships (TAs), research assistantships (RAs), and fellowships are normally available for highly qualified applicants. The 1998–99 stipend (three quarters) for TAs and RAs was $8040 for master's candidates and $9330 for doctoral degree candidates. Fellowships carry a stipend of $13,080 for twelve months. Tuition is included with these awards. Summer stipends and tuition are generally supplied for first-year students on TA appointments and all students on RA appointments. The Miles Fellowship is awarded to exceptional applicants and carries a stipend of $19,000.

Cost of Study

Tuition is included as part of the TA, RA, or fellowship appointment, in addition to the stipend. Full-time in-state tuition is $1292 per quarter, while out-of-state tuition is $2769 per quarter. Other fees include $18 per copy for thesis binding (minimum three copies required), $104 per quarter for student health insurance (if not covered by a policy), $17 matriculation fee, Memorial Student Union expansion fee of $15 per quarter, student activity fee of $10 per quarter, and any lab fees in the curriculum. The department supplies some support for student conference travel and internship expenses on a competitive basis.

Living and Housing Costs

On-campus single student housing costs are $1530 per term (double occupancy, non-suite, with board). On-campus married student housing costs are $338 per month (one bedroom), $375 per month (two bedrooms), or $483 per month (three bedrooms). Off-campus housing in proximity to the University is also available.

Student Group

The usual number of graduate students in physics is about 30. A wide variety of academic, ethnic, and national backgrounds are represented. Approximately four to eight graduate degrees are awarded per year. An active undergraduate program in physics of about the same size (19 faculty members) and postdoctoral researchers bring the total membership in the Department of Physics to more than 100 scientists.

Student Outcomes

The graduate program prepares students for careers in academia, the national laboratories, or industry. Recent graduates have found employment primarily in industry, including IBM (San Jose), Ford (Dearborn), Argonne National Laboratory, Integraph, and Chrysler.

Location

Michigan Technological University (MTU) is located on the shore of Portage Lake, about 1 mile from downtown Houghton, in the heart of the scenic Keweenaw Peninsula. Nearby Lake Superior is the world's largest freshwater lake. The "Copper Country," as this region in known, includes many forests, lakes, and Precambrian geological formations—excellent resources for particular areas of study and an ideal environment in which to live. MTU was rated the safest public university campus in the state and among the top ten in the nation.

The University

Michigan Tech is a comprehensive university located in Michigan's scenic Upper Peninsula, with more than 6,500 students (700 graduate students) and 355 faculty members. Recently rated as one of the nation's "Top Ten" best buys for science and technology by *U.S. News & World Report,* Michigan Tech combines a mixture of graduate course work and uncompromising one-on-one student/faculty research partnerships to create an outstanding academic environment. Founded as the Michigan Mining School in 1885, the University has recently been cited as one of the nation's top educational values.

Applying

A student who wishes to apply for admission to the Graduate School for study in physics should obtain an application packet from the Department of Physics at the address below. The enclosed forms should be completed and returned to the Graduate School Office, along with the nonrefundable application fee. The registrar of each college or university the student attended should directly send official transcripts to the Graduate School Office. International students must submit TOEFL sores. All students are required to take the GRE General Test. Applicants with undergraduate majors in physics, materials science, mathematics, or engineering are particularly encouraged to apply.

Correspondence and Information

Graduate Studies Chairman
Department of Physics
Michigan Technological University
1400 Townsend Drive
Houghton, Michigan 49931
E-mail: physics@phy.mtu.edu
World Wide Web: http://www.phy.mtu.edu/

Michigan Technological University

THE FACULTY AND THEIR RESEARCH

Gary P. Agin, Associate Professor; Ph.D., Kansas State, 1968. Low-energy nuclear physics. (e-mail: gagin@mtu.edu)

Donald R. Beck, Professor; Ph.D., Lehigh, 1968. Theoretical atomic physics, properties of transition metal and rare earth atoms and ions, discovery of new negative ions, including correlation and relativistic effects. (e-mail: donald@mtu.edu)

Aleksandra Borysow, Associate Professor; Ph.D., Texas at Austin, 1985. Molecular physics; development of classical and quantum mechanical computational techniques to quantitatively describe collision-induced absorption and light scattering by dense nonpolar gases such as hydrogen, nitrogen, carbon dioxide, and methane, particularly for planetary and stellar atmosphere studies. (e-mail: aborysow@mtu.edu)

Jacek Borysow, Associate Professor; Ph.D., Texas at Austin, 1986. Atomic, molecular, and laser physics; ionization, dissociation, and collisional energy transfer; plasma diagnostics and laser development. (e-mail: jborysow@mtu.edu)

Larry Coke, Research Assistant Professor; Ph.D., Michigan Tech, 1994. Atmospheric physics research. (e-mail: lrcoke@mtu.edu)

Donald A. Daavettila, Associate Professor; M.S., Michigan Tech, 1958. Radiation safety. (e-mail: daavetti@mtu.edu)

Christ Ftaclas, Associate Professor; Ph.D., CUNY, 1978. Cosmology and extra-solar planets. (e-mail: ftaclas@mtu.edu)

Ulrich Hansmann, Assistant Professor; Ph.D., Berlin, 1990. Biomolecular modeling. (e-mail: hansmann@mtu.edu)

John A. Jaszczak, Assistant Professor and Adjunct Curator, Seaman Mineral Museum; Ph.D., Ohio State, 1989. Simulations of materials, Monte Carlo simulations of dynamics and etching of silicon surfaces with intersecting dislocations, molecular dynamics studies of structure-property correlations in metallic superlattices and amorphous alloys. (e-mail: jaszczak@mtu.edu)

Alexander B. Kostinski, Associate Professor; Ph.D., Illinois, 1984. Fluid dynamics; random waves, including applications to radar meteorology and geophysics, polarization optics, statistical signal analysis in atmospheric science, remote sensing, and waves in fluids. (e-mail: kostinsk@mtu.edu)

Kenneth Morgan, Visiting Instructor; Ph.D. candidate, Michigan Tech. Physics. (e-mail: kjmorgan@mtu.edu)

Robert H. Mount, Assistant Professor; B.Sc., Ohio State, 1952. General physics pedagogy.

Edward Nadgorny, Presidential Professor; Ph.D., 1963, D.Sc., 1971, Ioffe Physical-Technical Institute (Russia). Dislocation physics, dislocation dynamics in semiconductors and intermetallics, selective etching of dislocations by plasma and chemicals, fundamental processes for nanoscale engineering involving dislocations ("dislocation engineering"). (e-mail: nadgorny@mtu.edu)

Robert Nemiroff, Assistant Professor; Ph.D., Pennsylvania, 1987. Gravitational lensing, gamma ray burst data analysis. (e-mail: nemiroff@mtu.edu)

David Nitz, Research Professor; Ph.D., Rochester, 1978. Remote sensing/astrophysics. (e-mail: dfnitz@mtu.edu)

Ravindra Pandey, Associate Professor; Ph.D., Manitoba, 1988. Atomistic and quantum mechanical modeling of materials, oxide clusters, surface reconstruction in III-V nitrides, defects in chalcopyrites. (e-mail: pandey@mtu.edu)

Robert Pastel, Visiting Assistant Professor; Ph.D., New Mexico, 1994. Laser physics. (e-mail: rpastel@mtu.edu)

Warren F. Perger, Associate Professor; Ph.D., Colorado State, 1986. Quantum electronics, use of atomic physics theory to calculate electro-weak parameters of the Standard Model, the calculation of relativistic continuum orbitals with application to atomic many-body theory, scattering. (e-mail: wfp@mtu.edu)

Andrew N. Pilant, Research Assistant Professor; Ph.D., Michigan Tech, 1997. Remote sensing, geology, digital image processing, cryospheric phenomena, geographic information systems, Lake Superior ecosystem. (e-mail: anpilant@mtu.edu)

J. Bruce Rafert, Professor and Chair; Ph.D., Florida, 1978. Hyperspectral sensing, astrophysics, application of SPH models to eclipsing binary star systems with accretion disks, observational astrophysics of close binary stars, development of autonomous telescope systems, construction of advanced tomographic visible hyperspectral imagers for remote sensing from aircraft and small satellites. (e-mail: jbrafert@mtu.edu)

Michael J. Renn, Assistant Professor; Ph.D., Virginia, 1993. Atom interferometry, development of atomic wave guides (applications include atom-fiber interferometry and nanofabrication of electronic circuits). (e-mail: renn@mtu.edu)

Raymond Shaw, Assistant Professor; Ph.D., Penn State, 1998. Atmospheric sciences. (e-mail: shaw@mtu.edu)

Bryan H. Suits, Associate Professor; Ph.D., Illinois, 1981. NMR of materials, inorganic nanometer-sized particles and nanophase materials made from those particles, NMR and NQR imaging for materials exhibiting quadrupolar broadened resonances, development of NMR theory for slowly rotating solids containing quadrupole nuclei. (e-mail: suits@mtu.edu)

Robert S. Weidman, Associate Professor; Ph.D., Illinois, 1980. Physics education. (e-mail: weidman@mtu.edu)

Michael Wertheim, Professor; Ph.D., Yale, 1957. Theory of liquids. (e-mail: wertheim@mtu.edu)

Associated Faculty

P. E. Doak, Professor Emeritus, University of Southhampton (U.K.); senior editor, *Journal of Sound and Vibration*. Fluid dynamics and acoustics.

U. G. Jorgensen, Copenhagen University Observatory, Niels Bohr Institute. Astrophysics.

J. M. Vail, Department of Physics, University of Manitoba (Canada). Solid-state theory.

Michigan Technological University

SELECTED PUBLICATIONS

Avgoustoglou, E. N., and **D. R. Beck.** All-order relativistic many body calculations for the electron affinities of Ca⁻, Sr⁻, Ba⁻ and Yb⁻ negative ions. *Phys. Rev. A* 55:4143, 1997.

Beck, D. R. Hyperfine structure constants of $(d+s)^3$ states in La I and the Zr II and Hf II isoelectronic sequences. *Int. J. Quantum Chem.* 65:555, 1997.

Beck, D. R. Relativistic configuration interaction results for Xe^{32+}, Ba^{34+}, Nd^{38+} and Gd^{42+} "⁵D" J=2 to J=3 energy differences. *Phys. Rev. A* 56:2428, 1997.

Scheer, M., H. K. Haugen, and **D. R. Beck.** Single- and multiphoton infrared laser spectroscopy of Sb⁻: A case study. *Phys. Rev. Lett.* 79:4104, 1997.

Dinov, K. D., and **D. R. Beck.** Electron affinity and hyperfine structure of Pa⁻:7p attachment. *Phys. Rev. A* 53:4031, 1996.

O'Malley, S. M., and **D. R. Beck.** Relativistic configuration interaction results for hyperfine structure constants of ^{133}Cs II and ^{137}Ba III 5p5 (5d+6s+6p) levels. *Phys. Rev. A* 54:3894, 1996.

Young, L., et al. **(D. R. Beck).** Hyperfine structure studies of Nb II: Experimental and relativistic configuration interaction results. *Phys. Rev. A* 51:3534, 1995.

Beck, D. R., and D. Datta. Theoretical lifetimes of Nb II z $4d^3$ $5p^5G_3$ and $^3D_3$ levels. *Phys. Rev. A* 52:2436, 1995.

Dinov, K., and **D. R. Beck.** Electron affinities and hyperfine structure for U⁻ and UI obtained from relativistic configuration interaction calculations. *Phys. Rev. A* 52:2632, 1995.

Datta, D., and **D. R. Beck.** Relativistic many-body effects in the fine and hyperfine structure of LaII $(5d+6s)^2$ states: The need for second order electrostatic corrections. *Phys. Rev. A* 52:3622, 1995.

Dinov, K., and **D. R. Beck.** Electron affinities of 6p electrons in Pr⁻. *Phys. Rev. A* 51:1680, 1995.

Samuelson, R. E., N. Nath, and **A. Borysow.** Gaseous abundances and methane supersaturation in Titan's troposphere. *Planet. Space Sci.* 45(8):959–80, 1997.

Borysow, A., U. G. Joergensen, and C. Zheng. Model atmospheres of cool, low metallicity stars: The importance of collision-induced absorption. *Astron. Astrophys.* 324:185–95, 1997.

Gruszka, M., and **A. Borysow.** Roto-translational collision-induced absorption of CO_2 for the atmosphere of Venus at frequencies from 0 to 250 cm⁻¹ and at temperature from 200 to 800 K. *Icarus* 129:172–7, 1997.

Birnbaum, G., **A. Borysow,** and G. S. Orton. Collision-induced absorption of H_2-H_2 and H_2-He in the rotational and fundamental bands (0–6,000cm⁻¹) for planetary applications. *Icarus* 123:4–22, 1996.

Fu, Y., **A. Borysow,** and M. Moraldi. Light scattering in gaseous nitrogen. *Phys. Rev. A* 53:201–5, 1996.

Gruszka, M., and **A. Borysow.** New analysis of the spectral moments of collision induced absorption in gaseous N_2 and CO_2. *Mol. Phys.* 88:1173–85, 1996.

Fu, Y., **A. Borysow,** and M. Moraldi. Light scattering in gaseous nitrogen. *Phys. Rev. A* 53:201–5, 1996.

Borysow, A. Collision-induced molecular absorption in stellar atmospheres. In *Collision- and Interaction-Induced Spectroscopy,* pp. 529–39, eds. G. Tabisz and M. N. Neuman. Dordrecht: Kluver, 1995.

Borysow, A., and M. Moraldi. Collision-induced and allowed Raman spectra in hydrogen gas. In *Collision- and Interaction-Induced Spectroscopy,* pp. 395–406, eds. G. Tabisz and M. N. Neuman. Dordrecht: Kluver, 1995.

Zheng, C., and **A. Borysow.** Rototranslational CIA spectra of H_2-H_2 at temperatures between 600 and 7,000K. *Astrophys. J.* 441:960–5, 1995.

Zheng, C., and **A. Borysow.** Modeling of collision-induced infrared absorption spectra of H_2-H_2 pairs in the first overtone band at temperatures from 20 to 500K. *Icarus* 113:84–90, 1995.

Borysow, A., and O. Ruehr. On the desymmetrization of the rototranslational spectra of freely rotating linear molecules. *Mol. Phys.* 85:349–61, 1995.

Pati, B., and **J. Borysow.** Single mode tunable Ti:Sapphire laser over a wide range of frequency. *J. Opt. Soc. Am. A: Appl. Opt.* 36:9337–41, 1997.

Pakhomov, A., W. Nichols, and **J. Borysow.** Laser induced breakdown spectroscopy for detection of lead in concrete. *Appl. Spectrosc.* 50:880, 1996.

Ershov, A., and **J. Borysow.** Actinometry measurements of atomic densities in an ownstream microwave plasma source. *Bull. Am. Phys. Soc.* 40:1555, 1995.

Borysow, J., E. Augustyniak, and A. Ershov. Kinetics of Cs formation from CsCl in the positive column of hydrogen discharge. *Bull. Am. Phys. Soc.* 40:570, 1995.

Pakhomov, A., and **J. Borysow.** Laser induced breakdown spectroscopy for detection of lead and cadmium in concrete. *Bull. Am. Phys. Soc.* 40:588, 1995.

Filimonov, S., and **J. Borysow.** Long range tunable diode laser. *J. Opt. Soc. Am. A: Appl. Opt.* 34:438, 1995.

Ershov, A., and **J. Borysow.** Dynamic of OH(X2-Π, v=0) in high energy electric pulsed corona discharge. *J. Phys. D: Appl. Phys.* 28:68, 1995.

Augustyniak, E., and **J. Borysow.** Time evolution of the population inversion between (A3-ς-u+v″) and (B3-Π-g,v′) states in the positive column of nitrogen pulsed discharge. *J. Phys. D: Appl. Phys.* 28:55, 1995.

Terrile, R. J., and **C. Ftaclas.** Astronomical and biochemical origins and the search for life in the universe. *Proc. Astron. Union Colloq.* 162:359–66, 1997.

Harvey, J. E., and **C. Ftaclas.** Field-of-view limitations of phased telescope arrays. *J. Opt. Soc. Am. A.: Appl. Opt.* 34(25):5787–98, 1995.

Jaszczak, J. A. Unusual graphite crystals from Lime Crest Quarry, Sparta, New Jersey. *Rocks Miner.* 72:330–4, 1997.

Woodraska, D. L., and **J. A. Jaszczak.** Roughening and preroughening of diamond-cubic {111} surfaces. In *MRS Symposium Proceedings,* vol. 440, *Structure and Evolution of Surfaces,* eds. R. C. Cammarata, E. H. Chason, T. L. Einstein, and E. D. Williams. Warrendale, Pa.: Materials Research Society, 1997.

Woodraska, D. L., and **J. A. Jaszczak.** Preroughening of diamond-cubic {111} surfaces. In *Maui High Performance Computer Center Application Briefs,* p. 38, 1997.

Woodraska, D. L., and **J. A. Jaszczak.** Roughening and preroughening of diamond-cubic {111} surfaces. *Phys. Rev. Lett.* 78:258–61, 1997.

Woodraska, D. L., and **J. A. Jaszczak.** A Monte Carlo simulation method for {111} surfaces of silicon and other diamond-cubic materials. *Surf. Sci.* 374:319–32, 1997.

Woodraska, D. L., J. LaCosse, and **J. A. Jaszczak.** Monte Carlo simulation of dislocation-nucleated etching of silicon {111} surfaces. In *MRS Symposium Proceedings,* vol. 389, *Modeling and Simulation of Thin-Film Processing,* pp. 209–14, eds. C. A. Volkert, R. J. Kee, D. J. Srolovitz, and M. J. Fluss. Warrendale, Pa.: Materials Research Society, 1995.

Woodraska, D. L., and **J. A. Jaszczak.** The physics of diamond-cubic {111} surfaces. In *Maui High Performance Computer Center Application Briefs,* 1995.

Jaszczak, J. A. Graphite: Flat, fibrous and spherical. In *Mesomolecules: From Molecules to Materials,* pp. 161–80, eds. G. D. Mendenhall, J. F. Liebman, and F. Greenberg. New York: Chapman and Hall, 1995.

Jameson, A. R., and **A. B. Kostinski.** Fluctuation properties of precipitation. Part II: Reconsideration of the meaning and measurement of raindrop size distributions. *J. Atmos. Sci.* 55:283–94, 1998.

Kostinski, A. B., and A. R. Jameson. Fluctuation properties of precipitation. Part I: On deviations of single size drop counts from the Poisson distribution. *J. Atmos. Sci.* 54:2174–86, 1997.

Schulz, T., and **A. B. Kostinski.** Variance bounds on the estimation of reflectivity and polarization parameters in radar meteorology. *IEEE Trans. Geosci. Remote Sensing* 35(2):248–55, 1997.

Jameson, A. R., and **A. B. Kostinski.** Non-Rayleigh signal statistics caused by relative motion during measurements. *J. Appl. Meteorol.* 35(10):1846–9, 1996.

Adams, R., W. F. Perger, W. I. Rose, and **A. B. Kostinski.** Measurement of dielectric constant of volcanic ash. *J. Geophys. Res.* 101:8175–85, 1996.

Michigan Technological University

Selected Publications (continued)

Kulkarni, M. D., and **A. B. Kostinski.** A simple formula for monitoring quadrature phase error with arbitrary signals. *IEEE Trans. Geosci. Remote Sensing* 33(3):799–802, 1995.

Rose, W. I., **A. B. Kostinski,** L. Kelley. Real time C-band radar observations of 1992 eruption clouds from Crater Peak/Spurr Volcano, Alaska. *U.S. Geol. Survey Bull.* 2139:19–26, 1995.

Baranova, G. K., Y. L. Iunin, and **E. M. Nadgorny.** Chemical etching of dislocations and grain boundaries in ordered Ni₃Al single crystals. *Scripta Mater.* 34(7):1027–33, 1996.

Nadgorny, E. M., and Y. L. Iunin. Temperature dependence of dislocation mobility in Ni₃Al. In *MRS Symposium Proceedings,* vol. 364, *High-Temperature Ordered Intermetallic Alloys VI,* pp. 707–12, eds. J. Horton et al. Warrendale, Pa.: Materials Research Society, 1995.

Nemiroff, R. J., J. P. Norris, J. T. Bonnell, and G. F. Marani. Gamma-ray burst spikes could resolve stars. *Astrophys. J.* 494:L173, 1998.

Nemiroff, R. J. Bright lenses and optical depth. *Astrophys. J.* 486:693–6, 1997.

Bonnell, J. T., J. P. Norris, **R. J. Nemiroff,** and J. D. Scargle. Brightness-independent measurements of gamma-ray burst durations.*Astrophys. J.* 490:79–91, 1997.

Marani, G. F., **R. J. Nemiroff,** J. P. Norris, and J. T. Bonnell. On suggestive correlations between gamma-ray bursts and clusters of galaxies. *Astrophys. J.* 474:576–9, 1997.

Nemiroff, R. J., J. T. Bonnell, and J. P. Norris. Temporal and spectral characteristics of terrestrial gamma flashes. *J. Geophys. Res.* 102:9659, 1997.

Norris, J. P., and **R. J. Nemiroff** et al. Attributes of pulses in long bright gamma-ray bursts. *Astrophys. J.* 495:393–412, 1996.

Bonnell, J. T., **R. J. Nemiroff,** and J. J. Goldstein. The scale of the universe debate in 1996. *Publications Astron. Soc. Pacific* 108:1065–7, 1996.

Pandey, R., P. Zapol, and M. Causa. Theoretical study of nonpolar surfaces of AlN. *Phys. Rev. B* 55:16009, 1997.

Zapol, P., **R. Pandey,** and J. Gale. An interatomic potential study of the properties of GaN. *J. Phys. Condens. Matter* 9:9517, 1997.

Pandey, R., M. Causa, N. Harrison, and M. Seel. The high pressure phase transitions of silicon and gallium nitride. *J. Phys. Condens. Matter* 8:1, 1996.

Jaffe, J., **R. Pandey,** and P. Zapol. Surface relaxations in GaN (110) surface. *Phys. Rev. B* 53:R4209, 1996.

Groh, D., **R. Pandey,** and J. M. Recio. Local relaxations and optical properties of Cr³⁺ in MgO. *Radiat. Eff. Defects Solids* 134:201, 1996.

Zapol, P., **R. Pandey,** M. Ohmer, and J. Gale. Atomistic calculations of defects in ZnGeP₂. *J. Appl. Phys.* 79:671–5, 1996.

Groh, D., **R. Pandey,** and J. Recio. Electronic structure and optical properties of Cr³⁻ in MgO. *Phys. Rev. B* 50:14860, 1995.

Veliah, S., **R. Pandey,** Y. Li, and J. Newsam. Density functional study of structural and electronic properties of cube-like MgO clusters. *Chem. Phys. Lett.* 235:53–7, 1995.

Sutjianto, A., S. W. Tam, **R. Pandey,** and L. Curtiss. Ab initio calculations for dissociative hydrogen adsorption on Li₂O surfaces. *J. Nucl. Mater.* 219:250–8, 1995.

Adams, R., **W. F. Perger,** W. Rose, and A. Kostinski. Measurements of the complex dielectric constant of volcanic ash from 4 to 19 GHz. *J. Geol. Res.* 101:8175–85, 1996.

Perger, W. F., and M. Idrees. Relativistic calculation of specific mass shifts for Ar+, Ni, Kr+, and Ce+ using a multi-configuration Dirac-Fock approach. *Comput. Phys. Commun.* 85:389–97, 1995.

Halabuka, Z., **W. F. Perger,** and D. Trautmann. SCA calculations of the proton induced alignment. *J. Phys. B: At. Mol. Opt. Phys.* 28:83–9, 1995.

Griffiths, J. D., **A. N. Pilant,** and C. Smith. Quantitative estimates of the geology of large regions and their application to mineral resource assessment. *Nonrenewable Resources* 6(3):157–236, 1997.

Meigs, A. D., et al. **(J. B. Rafert).** LWIR and MWIR Ultraspectral Fourier Transform Imager. *SPIE Proc.* 3221:421–8, 1997.

Leckenby, H. J., and **J. B. Rafert.** A light curve analysis of the cataclysmic variable AR Cancri. *Bull. Am. Astron. Soc.* 190(27):2, 1997.

Otten, L. J., and **J. B. Rafert** et al. The engineering model for the MightySat II.1 Hyperspectral Imager. *SPIE Proc.* 3221:412–20, 1997.

Oswalt, T. D., and **J. B. Rafert** et al. Progress report on the SARA 0.9-m telescope project at Kitt Peak. *IAPPP Commun.* 61, 1996.

Neal, A. J., and **J. B. Rafert.** Computer modeling of W Serpentis binaries through the use of smoothed particle hydrodynamics. *IAPPP Commun.* 64:9, 1996.

Zable, S., and **J. B. Rafert.** Determining the effects of accretion disks on W Serpentis type stars through the comparison of theoretical and observed lights curves. *IAPPP Commun.* 64:47, 1996.

Rafert, J. B., R. G. Sellar, and J. H. Blatt. Monolithic Fourier-transform imaging spectrometer. *Appl. Opt.* 34:7228, 1995.

Sellar, R. G., and **J. B. Rafert.** A Fourier-transform imaging spectrometer with a single torroidal optic. *Appl. Opt.* 34:2931, 1995.

Otten, L. J., A. D. Meigs, R. G. Sellar, and **J. B. Rafert.** MightySat II.1 Fourier-transform hyperspectral imager payload performance. *SPIE Proc.* 2583:566–75, 1995.

Rafert, J. B., R. G. Sellar, and L. J. Otten. An interactive performance model for spatially modulated imaging Fourier transform spectrometers. *SPIE Proc.* 2480:410–7, 1995.

Otten, L. J., et al. **(J. B. Rafert).** The design of an airborne Fourier transform visible hyperspectral imaging system for light aircraft environmental sensing. *SPIE Proc.* 2480:418–24, 1995.

Otten, L. J., et al. **(J. B. Rafert).** Hyperspectral measurements of common camouflages. *SPIE Proc.* 2469:517–25, 1995.

Gauck, H., et al. **(M. J. Renn).** External radiative quantum efficiency of 96% from a GaAs/GaInP hererostructure. *Appl. Phys. A* 64:143, 1997.

Renn, M. J., et al. Optical dipole force fiber guiding and heating of atoms. *Phys. Rev. A* 55(5):R3684–96, 1997.

Renn, M. J., et al. Evanescent-wave guiding of atoms in hollow optical fibers. *Phys. Rev. A* 53:R648, 1996.

Renn, M. J., et al. Laser-guided atoms in hollow-core optical fibers. *Phys. Rev. Lett.* 75:3253, 1995.

Gauck, H. G., **M. J. Renn,** E. A. Cornell, and K. A. Bertness. Laser refrigeration in the solid state. *QELS Tech. Digest Ser.* 16, 1995.

Renn, M. J., et al. Laser atom guiding in hollow core optical fibers. *QELS Tech. Digest Ser.* 16, 1995.

Suits, B. H. DTMF/LT decoding made easy. *QST* 81(4):34–6, 1997.

Apte, P., **B. H. Suits,** and R. W. Siegel. Hardness measurements of nanophase Al/Al-oxide composites. *Nanostructured Mater.* 9:501, 1997.

Sepa, J., R. J. Gorte, **B. H. Suits,** and D. White. ¹³C Chemical shielding anisotropy in solid phases of CH₃¹³CN. *Chem. Phys. Lett.* 252:281–6, 1996.

Suits, B. H., J. Sepa, and D. White. Simulations of slow variable angle NMR spectra: Application to ¹³C bonded to N. *J. Magn. Reson. A* 120:88–96, 1996.

Suits, B. H., and G. Y. Plude. Gradient coils and NQR imaging of powders. *J. Magn. Reson. A* 117:84–7, 1995.

Suits, B. H., P. Apte, D. E. Wilken, and R. W. Siegel. NMR study of nanophase Al/Al-oxide powder and consolidated composites. *Nanostructured Mater.* 6:609, 1995.

Busch, N. A., **M. S. Wertheim,** and M. L. Yarmush. Monte Carlo simulation of n-member associating fluids. *J. Chem. Phys.* 104:3962–75, 1996.

Wertheim, M. S. Fluids of hard convex molecules: II. Two-point measures. *Mol. Phys.* 89:989–1004, 1996.

Wertheim, M. S. Fluids of hard convex molecules: III. The third virial coefficient. *Mol. Phys.* 89:1005–17, 1996.

Busch, N. A., Y. C. Chiew, M. L. Yarmush, and **M. S. Wertheim.** Development and validation of a simple antigen-antibody model. *Am. Inst. Chem. Eng. J.* 41:974–84, 1995.

NORTHEASTERN UNIVERSITY

Department of Physics

Programs of Study	The department offers a full-time program leading to the Ph.D. and full-time and part-time evening programs leading to the M.S. Requirements for the Ph.D. include 62 quarter hours of course work, a written qualifying examination, a thesis describing the results of independent research, and a final oral examination. Students may pursue basic research in elementary particle physics, condensed-matter physics, and molecular biophysics or in interdisciplinary areas such as materials science, surface sciences, chemical physics, biophysics, and applied engineering physics. They also may carry out cooperative research at technologically advanced industrial, governmental, and national and international laboratories and at medical research institutions in the Boston area. Requirements for the M.S. are 42 quarter hours of credit, up to 12 of which may be transfer credit, if approved. Subject to approval, graduate courses in other science and engineering fields may be taken for up to 12 quarter hours. The department offers alternative M.S. options with concentrations in optics and instrumentation. There is no language requirement for either degree.
Research Facilities	The department is housed in the Dana Research Center, with optics and condensed matter labs in the new Egan Research Center. There are ample modern research laboratories, department and student machine shops, an electronics shop, conference and seminar rooms, and faculty and graduate student offices. The Egan Center provides a direct interface with materials researchers in chemistry and engineering and includes extensive meeting space in the Technology Transfer Center. The High Energy Group has an Alpha cluster, an NT cluster, several Linux machines, and links to computer facilities at Fermilab and CERN. The Condensed Matter Theory Group carries out large-scale simulations with Cray and Connection Machine supercomputers as well as locally on Alphas. In addition to the research they do at campus facilities, faculty members and graduate students also work at research centers located in the United States and Europe. High-energy physics experiments are underway at Fermilab in Batavia, Illinois, and at the Organisation Europeene pour la Recherche Nucleaire (CERN), Geneva, Switzerland. High-magnetic-field experiments are in progress at the National High-Field Magnet Laboratory in Tallahassee, Florida, and Los Alamos National Laboratory, New Mexico.
Financial Aid	Northeastern awards financial aid through the Federal Perkins Loan, Federal Work-Study, and Federal Stafford Student Loan programs and through minority fellowships, including G. E. Fellowships and Martin Luther King, Jr. Scholarships. The Graduate School offers teaching and research assistantships that include tuition remission and a stipend (currently $16,667 for four quarters) and require 20 hours of work per week. Tuition assistantships provide tuition remission and require 10 hours of work per week. The department's newly established Lawrence Award Program honors students with Excellence in Teaching awards, Academic Excellence awards, and a Speaker's Prize.
Cost of Study	Tuition for the 1998–99 academic year was $440 per quarter hour. Books and supplies cost about $850 per year. (Figures are subject to increase for the 1999–2000 academic year.) Tuition charges are made for Ph.D. thesis and continuation. Other charges include the Student Center fee and health and accident insurance fee, which are required of all full-time students.
Living and Housing Costs	For 1998–99, on-campus room rates were $1575 to $1780 per quarter for a single, oversized room and $2105 to $2325 for a single efficiency. Shared living accommodations ranged from $1340 to $1650 per quarter. While there are several board options available, graduate students typically pay $1085 per quarter for a plan offering ten meals per week. Off-campus living accommodations also exist in the vicinity of the University.
Student Group	In the fall of 1998, 24,325 students were enrolled at the University, representing a wide variety of academic, professional, geographic, and cultural backgrounds. The department enrolled 53 full-time students, of whom 92 percent received some form of financial support. A small number of students were enrolled in the part-time, evening M.S. program. The department awards roughly ten Ph.D. degrees and eight M.S. degrees per year. Most graduates have continued to pursue research careers, either in academic institutions as postdoctoral fellows or in industrial, medical, or government laboratories.
Location	The University is located in the Back Bay section of Boston, close to the Museum of Fine Arts, the New England Conservatory of Music, Symphony Hall, and historic Copley Square. Greater Boston is home to more universities and research facilities than any other area in the world. It is a place where the past is appreciated, the present enjoyed, and the future anticipated.
The University and The Department	Founded in 1898, Northeastern University is a privately endowed, nonsectarian institution of higher learning. It offers a variety of curricula through seven undergraduate colleges, nine graduate and professional schools, two part-time undergraduate divisions, a number of continuing education programs, an extensive research division, and several institutes. The department offers opportunities for students to work on a wide range of groundbreaking research programs with an internationally recognized faculty whose goal is to provide an effective education to students with varied backgrounds.
Applying	Although there is no absolute deadline for applying, completed applications should be received by February 15 to secure priority consideration for September acceptance, especially if financial assistance is sought. Scores on the GRE Subject Test in physics are highly desirable. The latter is given considerable weight in the admissions and assistantship awarding process when the number of applicants is high. For international students, a TOEFL score is required for admission.
Correspondence and Information	Graduate Coordinator (Admissions) Department of Physics Northeastern University Boston, Massachusetts 02115 Telephone: 617-373-2902 Fax: 617-373-2943 E-mail: grad-admin@physics.neu.edu World Wide Web: http://www.physics.neu.edu

Northeastern University

THE FACULTY AND THEIR RESEARCH

Professors
Paul M. Champion, Chairperson; Ph.D., Illinois at Urbana-Champaign, 1975. Molecular biophysics.
Ronald Aaron, Ph.D., Pennsylvania, 1961. Medical physics.
Petros Argyres (Emeritus), Ph.D., Berkeley, 1954. Condensed-matter theory.
Arun Bansil, Ph.D., Harvard, 1974. Condensed-matter theory.
Alan H. Cromer, Ph.D., Cornell, 1960. Education.
William L. Faissler (Emeritus), Ph.D., Harvard, 1967. High-energy experimental physics.
David A. Garelick, Ph.D., MIT, 1963. High-energy experimental physics.
Michael J. Glaubman (Emeritus), Ph.D., Illinois, 1953. High-energy experimental physics.
Hyman Goldberg, Ph.D., MIT, 1963. Particle theory.
Walter Hauser (Emeritus), Ph.D., MIT, 1950. Education.
Donald Heiman, Ph.D., California, Irvine, 1975. Condensed-matter experimental physics.
Jorge V. José, D.Sc., National of Mexico, 1976. Condensed-matter theory.
Robert P. Lowndes, Ph.D., London, 1966. Condensed-matter experimental physics.
Bertram J. Malenka (Emeritus), Ph.D., Harvard, 1951. Particle theory.
Robert S. Markiewicz, Graduate Coordinator; Ph.D., Berkeley, 1975. Condensed-matter experimental physics.
Pran Nath, Ph.D., Stanford, 1964. Particle theory.
Clive H. Perry, Ph.D., London, 1960. Condensed-matter experimental physics.
Stephen Reucroft, Ph.D., Liverpool, 1969. High-energy experimental physics.
Eugene J. Saletan (Emeritus), Ph.D., Princeton, 1962. High-energy experimental physics.
Carl A. Shiffman, D.Phil., Oxford, 1956. Condensed-matter experimental physics.
Jeffrey B. Sokoloff, Ph.D., MIT, 1967. Condensed-matter theory.
Srinivas Sridhar, Ph.D., Caltech, 1983. Condensed-matter experimental physics.
Yogendra N. Srivastava, Ph.D., Indiana, 1964. Particle theory.
Michael T. Vaughn, Ph.D., Purdue, 1960. Particle theory.
Eberhard von Goeler, Ph.D., Illinois, 1961. High-energy experimental physics.
Allan Widom, Ph.D., Cornell, 1967. Condensed-matter theory.
Fa-Yueh Wu, Ph.D., Washington (St. Louis), 1963. Condensed-matter theory.

Associate Professors
George Alverson, Ph.D., Illinois at Urbana-Champaign, 1979. High-energy experimental physics.
Alain Karma, Ph.D., California, Santa Barbara, 1986. Condensed-matter theory.
Marie E. Machacek, Ph.D., Iowa, 1973. Particle theory.
Tomasz Taylor, Ph.D., Warsaw, 1981. Particle theory.

Assistant Professors
Nathan Israeloff, Ph.D., Illinois at Urbana-Champaign, 1990. Condensed-matter experimental physics.
Sergey Kravchenko, Ph.D., Institute of Solid State Physics (Chernogolovka), 1988. Condensed-matter experimental physics.
J. Timothy Sage, Ph.D., Illinois at Urbana-Champaign, 1986. Molecular biophysics.
John D. Swain, Ph.D., Toronto, 1990. High-energy experimental physics.
Darien Wood, Ph.D., Berkeley, 1987. High-energy experimental physics.

Research Associates
Andrey Demidov, Ph.D., Moscow, 1981. Molecular biophysics.
Pierrick Hanlet, Ph.D., Virginia, 1995. High-energy experimental physics.
Stanislaw Kaprzyk, Ph.D., Stanislaw Staszic (Poland), 1981. Condensed-matter theory.
Youngyih Lee, Ph.D., Northeastern, 1998. Condensed-matter theoretical physics.
Matti Lindroos, Ph.D., Tampere Tech (Finland), 1979. Condensed-matter theory.
Lakshmi Muthuswamy, Ph.D., McMaster, 1997. Molecular biophysics.
Muthusamy Mylrajan, Ph.D., Indian Institute of Technology, 1988. Condensed-matter experimental physics.
Neeti Parashar, M.Sc., Delhi (India), 1991. High-energy experimental physics.
Mathis Plapp, Ph.D., Paris XI (South), 1997. Condensed-matter theory.
Theodore Sjodin, Ph.D., Pennsylvania, 1998. Molecular biophysics.

Adjunct Professors
Nathaniel Alpert, Ph.D., Northeastern, 1970. Biomedical physics.
Thomas Deutsch, Ph.D., Harvard, 1961. Biomedical physics.
Graham Farmelo, Ph.D., Liverpool, 1977. High-energy experimental physics.
Howard Fenker, Ph.D., Vanderbilt, 1978. High-energy experimental physics.
Peter Mijnarends, Ph.D., Delft (the Netherlands), 1969. Condensed-matter theory.
Jorge H. Moromisato, Ph.D., Northeastern, 1971. High-energy experimental physics.
Fabio Sauli, Ph.D., Trieste (Italy), 1963. High-energy experimental physics.
Alfred Smith, Ph.D., Texas Tech, 1970. Biomedical physics.
Goran Svensson, Ph.D., Lund (Sweden), 1967. Biomedical physics.
Lucas Taylor, Ph.D., London, 1988. High-energy experimental physics.

RESEARCH ACTIVITIES

Experimental Condensed-Matter Physics. Research activities focus on high-temperature superconductors (HTSC), semiconductors, and magnetic materials. HTSC research includes fundamental studies of order parameter symmetry and vortex dynamics; flux-lattice melting; Josephson-junction arrays; low-field HTSC magnets; linear and nonlinear electrodynamics of HTSCs; electromagnetic response of HTSCs at far infrared, microwave, and radio frequencies; growth and characterization of new HTSC ceramics and single crystals; and factors limiting critical currents. Research on semiconductors includes correlated electron and quantum Hall effects, 2-D metal-insulator transition and electron solid; magnetooptical spectroscopy of nanostructures and quantum layers and molecular-beam epitaxy (MBE) crystal growth. Other areas under investigation are electromagnetic and quantum chaos; Raman, FT-IR, mesoscopic systems, noise, and superconducting networks.

Experimental High-Energy Physics. The group is participating in the DZero experiment at Fermilab, which studies proton-antiproton collisions at 2 TeV, and the L3 experiment at CERN, which studies the collisions of electrons and positrons at the Z^{0} and up to and beyond the $W^{+}W^{-}$ threshold near 200 GeV. The group is also involved in a program of detector development at Northeastern University. The far-into-the-future activity involves participation in the CMS experiment at the LHC collider at CERN to continue the high-mass and high-transverse momentum studies up to 14 TeV.

Molecular Biophysics. The group probes the structure and function of macromolecules, metalloproteins, and protein complexes. Specific research areas include electron transport, macromolecular structure, enzyme catalysis, and ligand binding and protein dynamics, using quasi-elastic scattering; transient absorption spectroscopy; Raman, FTIR and fluorescence spectroscopy; and femtosecond coherence spectroscopy.

Theoretical Condensed-Matter Physics. Research topics include transport theory, quantum chaos, Fermi liquid theory, charge density waves, and dense dipolar suspensions; and theory of Josephson junctions, catalytic properties of alloys, transport in nanostructures, structural phase transitions in DNA, nanotribology (atomic-level friction), electronic structure of disordered materials, magnetism, ferrites, Fermiology of HTSCs, Van Hove scenario and stripes in HTSCs, exact and rigorous results in statistical mechanics, localization and percolation in order-disorder phase transitions, positron annihilation and photoemission spectroscopy, and nonlinear dynamics and pattern formation.

Theoretical Elementary Particle Physics. Fundamental research includes the study of unified models based on supersymmetry and superstrings; unified gauge theories in the TeV range, and precision calculations within and beyond the Standard Model; particle physics in the early universe; proton stability and neutrino masses; electroweak anomaly in the observed asymmetry of the baryon number, gravitational theory and quantum gravity, Kaluza-Klein theories and large-radius compactification, and computer simulations of topological structures in field theory; and finite temperature effects in quantum chromodynamics.

SELECTED PUBLICATIONS

Aaron, R., M. Huang, and **C. A. Shiffman.** Anisotropy of human muscle via non-invasive impedance measurements. *Phys. Med. Biol.* 42:1245, 1997.

Huang, M., **R. Aaron,** and **C. A. Shiffman.** Maximum entropy method for magnetoencephalography. *IEEE Trans. Biomed. Eng.* 44:98, 1997.

Schlitt, H. A., et al. **(R. Aaron).** Evaluation of boundary element methods for the EEG forward problem: Effect of linear interpolation. *IEEE Trans. Biomed. Eng.* 42:52, 1995.

Acciarri, M., et al. **(G. Alverson)** (the L3 Collaboration). Pair-production of W bosons in e$^+$e$^-$ interactions at $\sqrt{s} = 161$ GeV. CERN-PPE/97–12, 1997.

Alverson, G. (the LEP Collaborations: ALEPH, DELPHI, L3, OPAL, and the LEP Electroweak Working Group). A combination of preliminary LEP electroweak measurements and constraints on the standard model. CERN-PPE/95–172, 1995.

Bansil, A., and M. Lindroos. A novel direct method of Fermi surface determination using constant initial energy angle-scanned photoemission. *Phys. Rev. Lett.* 77:2985, 1996.

Bansil, A., and M. Lindroos. Surface states and angle-resolved photoemission spectra from Nd-Ce-Cu-O superconductor. *Phys. Rev. Lett.* 75:1182, 1995.

Bansil, A., et al. A high-resolution Compton scattering study of Li: Asphericity of the Fermi surface and electron correlation effects. *Phys. Rev. Lett.* 74:2252, 1995.

Bansil, A., et al. Observation of an "extended" van Hove singularity in Y124 by ultra-high energy resolution angle resolved photoemission. *Phys. Rev. Lett.* 73:3302, 1994.

Champion, P. A multidimensional Landau-Zener description of chemical reaction dynamics and vibrational coherence. *J. Chem. Phys.* 107:2859, 1997.

Champion, P. Femtosecond coherence spectroscopy of heme proteins. *Biospectroscopy* 2:301, 1996.

Champion, P. Femtosecond time resolved vibrational spectroscopy of heme proteins. *J. Raman Spectrosc.* 26:527, 1995.

Champion, P. Observation of coherent reaction dynamics in heme proteins. *Science* 266:629, 1994.

Cromer, A. *Connected Knowledge: Science, Philosophy, and Education.* New York: Oxford University Press, 1997.

Cromer, A. New educational standards: Danger ahead. *Boston Globe,* Letters to the Editor, p. A22, Oct. 10, 1996.

Cromer, A. Skeptical wonderment. *Nature* 380:307–8, 1996.

Cromer, A. *Experiments in Introductory Physics.* Denton, Tex.: RonJon Publishing Co., 1994.

Garelick, D. A. (Co-Leader), et al. Balance evaluation with an ultrasonic measuring system. In *Proceedings of the January 1994 Meeting jointly sponsored by the Association of Academic Physiatrists and the American Academy of Physical Medicine and Rehabilitation,* 1994.

Garelick, D. A., and **G. Alverson** et al. Production of direct photons and neutral mesons at large transverse momenta by π^- and p beams at 500 GeV/c. *Phys. Rev. D* 48:5, 1993.

Garelick, D. A., and **G. Alverson** et al. Direct photon production at high-PT in π^--Be and p-Be collisions at 500 GeV/c. *Phys. Rev. Lett.* 68:2584–7, 1992.

Goldberg, H. Thermodynamics of hidden sector gaugino condensation in the expanding universe. *Phys. Lett. B* 394:43, 1997.

Goldberg, H., and M. Gómez. Lepton flavor violation in SUSY SO(10) with predictive Yukawa texture. *Phys. Rev. D* 53:5244, 1996.

Goldberg, H. Can hidden gauginos form condensates? *Phys. Lett. B* 357:588, 1995.

Plentz, F., **D. Heiman,** L. N. Pfeiffer, and K. W. West. Spin effects in polarized luminescence at v=1. *Phys. Rev. B* 57:1370, 1998.

Heiman, D. Spectroscopy of magnetic ions in high magnetic fields. In *High Magnetic Fields in the Physics of Semiconductors II,* p. 847, eds. G. Landwehr and W. Ossau. Singapore: World Scientific, 1997.

Lee, Z. K., and **D. Heiman** et al. Faraday-Stark optoelectronic effect. *Appl. Phys. Lett.* 69:3731, 1996; Lee, Z. K., and D. Heiman, U.S. Patent #5,640,021 (June 17, 1997).

Vidal Russell, E., and **N. E. Israeloff** et al. Nanometer scale dielectric fluctuations at the glass transition. *Phys. Rev. Lett.* 81:1461, 1998.

Bonetto, C., **N. E. Israeloff,** N. Pokrovskiy, and R. Bojko. Field enhanced superconductivity in disordered wire networks. *Phys. Rev. B* 58:128, 1998.

Israeloff, N. E., M. Kagalenko, and K. Chan. Can Zipf distinguish language from noise in non-coding DNA? *Phys. Rev. Lett.* 76:1976, 1996.

Tiesinga, P., **J. V. José,** and T. Hagenaars. 1/omega flux noise and dynamical critical properties of two-dimensional XY models. *Phys. Rev. Lett.* 78:3, 519, 1997.

Badrinarayanan, R., and **J. V. José.** Classical and quantum chaos in a quantum dot in time-periodic magnetic fields. *Phys. Rev. E* 54:3, 2419, 1996.

José, J. V., and C. Rojas. Critical properties of two-dimensional Josephson-junction arrays with zero-point quantum fluctuations. *Phys. Rev. B* 54:17, 12361, 1996.

Kopczynski, P., W.-J. Rappel, and **A. Karma.** Critical role of crystalline anisotropy in the stability of cellular array structures in directional solidification. *Phys. Rev. Lett.* 77:3387, 1996.

Karma, A., and W.-J. Rappel. Numerical simulation of three-dimensional dendritic growth. *Phys. Rev. Lett.* 77:4050, 1996.

Karma, A. Spiraling to destruction at the edge of chaos. *Nature* 379:118, 1996.

Simonian, D., **S. V. Kravchenko,** and M. P. Sarachik. Reflection symmetry at a B=0 metal-insulator transition in two dimensions. *Phys. Rev. B* 55:R13421, 1997.

Simonian, D., **S. V. Kravchenko,** M. P. Sarachik, and V. M. Pudalov. Suppression of the conducting phase in a 2D electron system by a magnetic field. *Phys. Rev. Lett.* 78:2304, 1997.

Kravchenko, S. V., et al. Electric field scaling at a B=0 metal-insulator transition in two dimensions. *Phys. Rev. Lett.* 77:4938, 1996.

Machacek, M. E. Growth of adiabatic perturbations in self-interacting dark matter. *Astrophys. J.* 431:41–51, 1994.

Machacek, M. E., E. Carlson, and L. Hall. Self-interacting dark matter. *Astrophys. J.* 398:43–52, 1992.

Markiewicz, R. S. A survey of the Van Hove scenario for high-T_c superconductivity. *J. Phys. Chem. Solids* 58:1179, 1997.

Markiewicz, R. S., et al. Biaxial alignment of high-T_c superconductor polycrystals (VIII): Phi-circle scan of EuBa$_2$Cu$_3$O$_7$ (Eu-123). *J. Mater. Res.* 11:1108, 1996.

Nath, P. Hierarchies and textures in supergravity unification. *Phys. Rev. Lett.* 76:2218, 1996.

Nath, P. Textured minimal and extended supergravity unification and implications for proton stability. *Phys. Lett. B* 381:147, 1996.

Nath, P., and U. Chattopadhyay. Probing supergravity grand unification in the Brookhaven g-2 experiment. *Phys. Rev. D* 53:1648, 1996.

Perry, C. H. Spectroscopic studies of quantum well heterostructures in pulsed magnetic fields. *Phys. Rev.,* in press; *Bull. Am. Phys. Soc.* 43:104–5, 1998.

Perry, C. H. Photoluminescence studies of semiconductor heterostructures in pulsed magnetic fields. *Phys. B* 246–7:182, 1998; in *Proceedings of the 5th International Symposium on Research in High Magnetic Fields,* Sydney, Australia, August 1997.

Kim, Y., and **C. H. Perry** et al. Photoluminescence studies of modulation-doped couple double quantum wells in pulsed magnetic fields. In *Physics of Semiconductors,* pp. 1859–62, eds. M. Scheffler and R. Zimmermann. Singapore: World Scientific, 1996.

Acciarri, M., et al. **(S. Reucroft)** (the L3 Collaboration). Measurement of the lifetime of the τ-lepton. *Phys. Lett. B* 389:187, 1996.

Abachi, S., et al. **(S. Reucroft)** (the DZero Collaboration). Measurement of the W-boson mass. *Phys. Rev. Lett.* 77:3309, 1996.

Northeastern University

Selected Publications (continued)

Abachi, S., et al. **(S. Reucroft** and **D. Wood)** (the DZero Collaboration). Observation of the top quark. *Phys. Rev. Lett.* 74:2632, 1995.

Sage, J. T. Infrared crystallography: Structural refinement through spectroscopy. *Appl. Spectrosc.* 51:329, 1997.

Sage, J. T. Structural characterization of the myoglobin active site using infrared crystallography. *J. Mol. Biol.* 274:2, 1997.

Sage, J. T. Myoglobin and CO: Structure, energetics, and disorder. *J. Biol. Inorg. Chem.* 2:537, 1997.

Shiffman, C. A., and R. Aaron. Angular dependence of resistance in non-invasive electrical measurements of human muscle: The tensor model. *Phys. Med. Biol.* 43:1317, 1998.

Sokoloff, J. B., and M. S. Tomassone. Effects of defects on friction for a thin film sliding over a solid surface. *Phys. Rev. B* 57:4888, 1998.

Tomassone, M. S., J. B. Sokoloff, A. Widom, and J. Krim. Dominance of phonon friction for a xenon film on a silver (111) surface. *Phys. Rev. Lett.* 79:4798, 1997.

Srikanth, H., et al. **(S. Sridhar).** Microwave response of $YBa_2Cu_3O_{6.95}$ crystals: Evidence for a multi-component order parameter. *Phys. Rev. B (Rapid Commun.)* 55:R14733, 1997.

Eskildesn, M. R., et al. **(S. Sridhar).** Observation of a field-driven structural phase transition in the flux line lattice in $ErNi_2B_2C$. *Phys. Rev. Lett.* 78:1968, 1997.

Kudrolli, A., V. Kidambi, and **S. Sridhar.** Experimental studies of chaos and localization in quantum wavefunctions. *Phys. Rev. Lett.* 75:822, 1995.

Swain, J., and S. Reucroft et al. Neutron irradiation studies of avalanche photodiodes using californium-252. *Nucl. Instrum. Methods A,* in press.

Swain, J., and L. Taylor. Constraints on the τ neutrino mass and mixing from precise measurements of τ decay rates. *Phys. Rev. D* 55:R1, 1997.

Acciarri, M., et al. **(J. Swain).** Measurement of the Michel parameters and the average tau-neutrino helicity from tau decays in $e^+e^-\rightarrow\tau^+\tau^-$. *Phys. Lett. B* 377:313, 1996.

Swain, J. Multiplicity distributions in $b\rightarrow s$ gluon decays. *Z. Phys. C* 71(3):455, 1996.

Dova, M. T., et al. **(J. Swain).** A method to determine the tau-neutrino helicity using polarized taus. *Phys. Lett. B* 366:360–4, 1996.

Taylor, T. R., et al. Aspects of type I-type II-heterotic triality in four dimensions. *Nucl. Phys. B* 489:160, 1997.

Taylor, T. R., and I. Antoniadis. Dual N=2 SUSY breaking. *Fortschr. Phys.* 44:487, 1996.

Taylor, T. R., et al. Topological amplitudes in heterotic superstring theory. *Nucl. Phys. B* 476:133, 1996.

Vaughn, M. T., and R. S. Markiewicz. The spectrum-generating algebra of the van Hove scenario is SO(8). *Phys. Rev. B* 57:14052, 1998.

Vaughn, M. T., and S. P. Martin. Two-loop renormalization group equations for soft supersymmetry-breaking couplings. *Phys. Rev. D* 50:3537, 1994.

Vaughn, M. T., H. Goldberg, and D. Nash. Classical ϕ^4 theory in 3 + 1 dimensions. *Phys. Rev. D* 46:2585, 1992.

Adams, D., et al. **(E. von Goeler)** (SMC Collaboration). Spin structure of the proton from polarized inclusive deep-inelastic muon-proton scattering. *Phys. Rev. D* 56:5330, 1997.

Adams, D., et al. **(E. von Goeler).** The spin dependent structure function g1(x) of the deuteron from polarized deep inelastic muon scattering. *Phys. Lett. B* 396:338, 1997.

Wood, D. (DZero Collaboration). A measurement of the W boson mass. *Phys. Rev. Lett.* 80:3000, 1998.

Lu, W. T., and F. Y. Wu. On the duality relation for correlation functions of the Potts model. *J. Phys. A* 31:2823, 1998.

Wu, F. Y., and H. Y. Huang. New sum rule identities and duality relation for the Potts correlation function. *Phys. Rev. Lett.* 79:4954, 1997.

Huang, H. Y., F. Y. Wu, and V. Popkov. Exact solution of a three-dimensional Dimer system. *Phys. Rev. Lett.* 78:405, 1997.

Pant, P., F. Y. Wu, and J. H. Barry. A lattice-statistical model for ternary polymer mixtures: Exact phase diagrams. *Physica* 238:149, 1997.

OHIO UNIVERSITY

Department of Physics and Astronomy

Programs of Study

The Department of Physics and Astronomy offers graduate study and research programs leading to the Master of Arts, Master of Science, and Doctor of Philosophy degrees. The program of study emphasizes individual needs and interests in addition to essential general requirements of the discipline. Major areas of current research are experimental and theoretical nuclear and intermediate-energy physics, experimental condensed-matter and surface physics, theoretical condensed-matter and statistical physics, nonlinear dynamics and chaos, biophysics, thermoacoustics, astronomy, and astrophysics.

A student typically takes core courses (mechanics, math, quantum, E & M) during the first year in preparation for the comprehensive exam that is given at the end of the summer following the first year. Students can usually retake the exam during the winter break of the second year if necessary. The courses in the second year cover more advanced topics. Master's degrees require completion of 45 graduate credits in physics and have both thesis and nonthesis options. Applied master's degrees (e.g., computational physics) are under development. The Ph.D. requirements include passing the comprehensive exam and writing and orally defending the dissertation.

Research Facilities

The physics department occupies two wings of Clippinger Laboratories, a modern, well-equipped research building; the recently expanded Edwards Accelerator Building, which contains Ohio University's 4.5-MV high-intensity tandem accelerator; and the Surface Science Research Laboratory, which is isolated from mechanical and electrical disturbances. Specialized facilities for measuring structural, thermal, transport, optical, and magnetic properties of condensed matter are available. In addition to research computers in laboratories, students have access to minicomputers and workstation clusters and the Ohio Supercomputer Center, where massively parallel systems (e.g. a CRAY T3E, an IBM SP2, and a CRAY T90) are located.

Financial Aid

Financial aid is available in the form of graduate assistantships (GAs), teaching assistantships (TAs), and research assistantships (RAs). All cover the full cost of tuition plus a stipend from which a quarterly fee of about $370 must be paid by the student. Current stipend levels for GAs are $14,000 per year; for TAs, $14,900 per year. The stipend levels for RAs are set by the research grant holders but are at or above the level of the TA stipends. Both GAs and TAs require approximately 15 hours per week of laboratory and/or teaching duties. Special assistantships through the Condensed Matter and Surface Science (CMSS) program are also available.

Cost of Study

Tuition and fees are approximately $1810 per quarter for Ohio residents and approximately $3477 per quarter for out-of-state students. Tuition and fees for part-time students are prorated.

Living and Housing Costs

On-campus rooms for single students are $1184 per quarter, while married student apartments cost from $556 to $680 per month. A number of off-campus apartments and rooms are available at various costs.

Student Group

About 19,000 students study on the main campus of the University, and about 2,500 of these are graduate students. The graduate student enrollment in the physics department ranges from 50 to 60.

Location

Athens is a city of about 25,000, situated in the rolling Appalachian foothills of southeastern Ohio. The surrounding landscape consists of wooded hills rising about the Hocking River valley, and the area offers many outdoor recreational opportunities. Eight state parks lie within easy driving distance of the campus and are popular spots for relaxation. The outstanding intellectual and cultural activities sponsored by this diverse university community are pleasantly blended in Athens with a lively tradition of music and crafts.

The University and The Department

Ohio University, founded in 1804 and the oldest institution of higher education in the Northwest Territory, is a comprehensive university with a wide range of graduate and undergraduate programs. The Ph.D. program in physics began in 1959, and more than 200 doctoral degrees have been awarded. Currently, the department has 21 regular faculty members, and additional part-time faculty and postdoctoral fellows. Sponsored research in the department amounts to approximately $2.8 million per year and comes from NSF, DOE, DOD, ARPA, ONR, BMDO, NASA, EPRI, and the state of Ohio.

Applying

Application forms for admission and for financial assistance may be obtained by writing to the Office of Graduate Students Services or to the Department of Physics and Astronomy. The deadline for assistantship and scholarship applications is April 1. Further information can be obtained from the department's home page on the World Wide Web (http://www.phy.ohiou.edu) or by writing to one of the addresses given below.

Correspondence and Information

Graduate Appointments Committee
Department of Physics and Astronomy
Ohio University
Athens, Ohio 45701
Telephone: 740-593-1718
E-mail: gradapp@helios.phy.ohiou.edu

Professor Louis E. Wright
Chair, Department of Physics and Astronomy
Ohio University
Athens, Ohio 45701
Telephone: 740-593-1713
Fax: 740-593-0433

Ohio University

THE FACULTY AND THEIR RESEARCH

Distinguished Professors
Roger W. Finlay, Emeritus, Ph.D., Johns Hopkins, 1962. Nuclear and intermediate-energy physics.
Jacobo Rapaport, Emeritus, Ph.D., MIT, 1963. Nuclear and intermediate-energy physics.

Professors
James P. Dilley, Emeritus, Ph.D., Syracuse, 1963. Planetary physics.
Steven M. Grimes, Ph.D., Wisconsin–Madison, 1968. Nuclear physics.
Kenneth H. Hicks, Ph.D., Colorado, 1984. Nuclear and intermediate-energy physics.
Earle R. Hunt, Emeritus, Ph.D., Rutgers, 1962. Nonlinear systems and chaos.
Martin E. Kordesch, Ph.D., Case Western Reserve, 1984. Surface physics.
David S. Onley, Emeritus, D.Phil., Oxford, 1960. Nuclear theory, electrodynamics.
Roger W. Rollins, Ph.D., Cornell, 1967. Solid-state physics, superconductivity, chaotic systems.
Sergio E. Ulloa, Ph.D., SUNY at Buffalo, 1984. Theoretical condensed-matter physics.
Louis E. Wright, Ph.D., Duke, 1966; Chair of the Department. Nuclear theory, electrodynamics, intermediate-energy theory.
Seung S. Yun, Emeritus, Ph.D., Brown, 1964. Physical acoustics, ultrasonics.

Associate Professors
Charles E. Brient, Ph.D., Texas at Austin, 1963. Nuclear physics, surface physics.
David A. Drabold, Ph.D., Washington (St. Louis), 1989. Theoretical condensed-matter, computational methodology for electronic structure, theory of topologically disordered materials.
Charlotte Elster, Dr.rer.nat, Bonn, 1986. Nuclear and intermediate-energy theory.
David C. Ingram, Ph.D., Salford (England), 1980. Atomic collisions in solids, thin films, deposition and analysis.
Peter Jung, Ph.D., Ulm (Germany), 1985. Nonequilibrium statistical physics, nonlinear stochastic processes, pattern formation.
Thomas S. Statler, Ph.D., Princeton, 1986. Astrophysics, galactic structure and dynamics.

Assistant Professors
Daniel S. Carman, Ph.D., Indiana, 1995. Experimental nuclear and particle physics.
Jean Heremans, Ph.D., Princeton, 1994. Experimental condensed-matter and surface physics.
Normand Mousseau, Ph.D., Michigan State, 1993. Theoretical condensed matter, nonequilbrium dynamical systems.
Allena K. Opper, Ph.D., Indiana Bloomington, 1991. Nuclear and intermediate-energy physics.
Daniel Phillips, Ph.D., Flinders (Australia), 1995. Theoretical nuclear and particle physics.
Joseph C. Shields, Ph.D., Berkeley, 1991. Astrophysics, interstellar medium, active galactic nuclei.
Arthur Smith, Ph.D., Texas at Austin, 1995. Experimental condensed-matter and surface physics.
Victoria Soghomonian, Ph.D., Syracuse, 1995. Experimental chemical physics.
Larry A. Wilen, Ph.D., Princeton, 1986. Experimental acoustics, condensed-matter physics, surface melting.

RESEARCH ACTIVITIES

Acoustics. Experimental studies of solids and liquids using ultrasonics. Experiments in thermoacoustics. Novel acoustic techniques to investigate surface melting and other surface phase transitions. Ultrasonic studies using surface acoustic wave (SAW) devices and development of new piezo-electric devices employing GaN and A1N films.

Astrophysics. Research is directed at understanding the origin and structure of galaxies and the nature of quasars and emission nebulae. These investigations utilize large ground-based telescopes, as well as the Hubble Space Telescope, Infrared Space Observatory, and orbiting X-ray telescopes. Major theoretical efforts are directed at understanding the stellar dynamics of elliptical galaxies and galactic nuclei and the interpretation of nebular emission spectra.

Condensed Matter and Surface Science. Current projects include neutron scattering (at NIST and Grenoble) and heat capacity measurements of fullerenes and glassy systems, the fabrication of diamond and diamondlike films and their characterization via novel electron microscopes and MeV ion-beam techniques, growth of metallic multilayer systems using sputtering techniques, and optical studies of interfacial melting in ice. There are also several project on hyperthermal beam growth, chemical vapor deposition of thin films, their characterization and fabrication of devices based on wide bandgap semiconductors such as GaN and A1N. Current theoretical research includes electronic states in novel semiconductor nanostructures and heterojunctions, theory of topologically disordered materials, ab initio density functional and empirical studies of structural and dynamical properties of alloys and amorphous and glassy systems, semiclassical and ab initio modeling of growth, and development of efficient algorithms for long-time microscopic activated dynamics and electronic structure calculations. Some of these projects in the Department of Physics and Astronomy are being pursued as an interdisciplinary effort with the Department of Chemistry and several engineering departments through the CMSS Program.

Nonlinear Systems and Chaos. Recent work has focused on analyzing and controlling chaotic systems as well as on the application of the methods of nonlinear dynamics and statistical physics to model biological processes. Electronic systems, lasers, and a chemical system have been successfully stabilized under conditions where they would normally show erratic behavior. Currently, the feasibility of controlling the much more complicated spatiotemporal systems is being studied both experimentally and with numerical modeling. In biological systems, there is work being done on the dynamics of single neurons and networks of neurons and neuron-like cells in the context of brain functions and pathologies. These projects are interdisciplinary in nature and pursued in collaboration with the Neurobiology Program at Ohio University; several other universities and an industrial partner are also involved.

Nuclear and Intermediate Energy (Institute of Nuclear and Particle Physics). Goals of this program are theoretical and experimental investigations of phenomena on the femtometer (10^{-15} meter) length scale. This spans the range from conventional nuclear physics at the larger end to quark degrees of freedom in nuclei at the smaller end of the scale. Various probes used for these investigations include photons, electrons, mesons, protons, neutrons, and heavier ions. Experimental work with nucleon beams is performed at Ohio University's 9-MeV tandem Van de Graaf accelerator and at intermediate-energy facilities: the Indiana University Cyclotron, Los Alamos National Laboratory, and Tri-University Meson Facility (TRIUMF) in Vancouver. Work with photon and electron beams is underway at the Laser-Electron Gamma Source (LEGS) at Brookhaven National Laboratory and the Continuous Electron Beam Accelerator (CEBAF) at Thomas Jefferson National Accelerator Facility. Experimental work on neutron sources for application to cancer therapy is also continuing. Future plans involve experiments at the BLAST detector at MIT, the SPRING8 laboratory in Japan, and at several European laboratories. Theoretical work includes description of few-nucleon systems, hadronic reactions of light and heavy nuclei at intermediate energies, electron scattering from nuclei, electroproduction and photoproduction of mesons, constituent-quark models of baryon structure and photo-hadron reactions, and studies of nuclear structure and models of the nucleon-nucleon interaction derived from meson degrees of freedom. Some of the investigations involve high-performance computation carried out at the Ohio Supercomputer Center and the National Energy Research Supercomputer Center.

SELECTED PUBLICATIONS

Brient, C. E., S. M. Grimes, and **D. C. Ingram.** Mass-energy telescope for materials analysis and charged-particle spectroscopy. *AIP Conf. Proc.* 392:1043–6, 1997.

Dilley, J. P. Energy loss in collisions of icy spheres: Loss mechanism and size-mass dependence. *Icarus* 105:225, 1993.

Stephan, U., and **D. A. Drabold.** Order-N projection method for first principles calculation of electronic quantities and Wannier functions. *Phys. Rev. B* 57:6391, 1998.

Dong, J., and **D. A. Drabold.** Atomistic structure of bandtail states in amorphous Si. *Phys. Rev. Lett.* 80:1928, 1998.

Stumm, P., and **D. A. Drabold.** Can amorphous GaN serve as a useful electronic material? *Phys. Rev. Lett.* 79:677, 1997.

M. Cobb, R. L. Cappelletti, and **D. A. Drabold.** Structure, dynamics and electronic properties of liquid and glassy $GeSe_2$. *J. Noncrystal. Solids* 222:348, 1997.

Dong, J., and **D. A. Drabold.** Bandtail states and the localized to extended transition in amorphons diamond. *Phys. Rev. B* 54:10284, 1996.

Cobb, M., **D. A. Drabold,** and R. L. Cappelletti. Ab initio study of glassy $GeSe_2$. *Phys. Rev. B* 54:12162, 1996.

Cappelletti, R. L., et al. **(D. A. Drabold).** Neutron scattering and ab initio molecular-dynamics study of vibrations in glassy $GeSe_2$. *Phys. Rev.* 52:9133, 1995.

Ordejon, P., and **D. A. Drabold** et al. Linear system size scaling methods for electronic structure calculations. *Phys. Rev. B* 51:1456, 1995.

Elster, C., W. Schadow, H. Kamada, and W. Glöckle. Two-body T-matrices without angular momentum decomposition: Energy and momentum dependencies. *Few-Body Syst.* 24:55, 1998.

Weppner, S. P., **C. Elster,** and D. Hüber. Off-shell structures of nucleon-nucleon t-matrices and their influence on nucleon nucleus elastic scattering observables. *Phys. Rev. C* 57:1378, 1998.

Elster, C., W. Schadow, H. Kamada, and W. Glöckle. Shadowing and antishadowing effects in a model for the n+d total cross section. *Phys. Rev. C* 58:3109, 1998.

Abfalterer, W. P., et al. **(C. Elster** and **R. W. Finlay).** Inadequacies on the nonrelativistic 3N Hamiltonian in describing the n+d total cross section above 100 MeV. *Phys. Rev. Lett.* 81:57, 1998.

Elster, C., and W. Glöckle. Nucleon scattering from very light nuclei: Intermediate energy expansions for transition potentials and breakup processes. *Phys. Rev. C* 55:1058, 1997.

Elster, C., E. E. Evans, H. Kamada, and W. Glöckle. Nonlocality in the nucleon-nucleon force due to minimal relativity factors: Effects on two-nucleon observables and the three nucleon binding energy. *Few-Body Syst.* 21:25, 1996.

Chinn, C. R., **C. Elster,** R. M. Thaler, and S. P. Weppner. Propagator modifications in elastic nucleon-nucleus scattering within the spectator expansion. *Phys. Rev. C* 52:1992, 1995.

Elster, C., K. Holinde, D. Schütte, and R. Machleidt. Extension of the Bonn meson exchange NN potential above pion production threshold. II. Role of the Delta Isobar. *Phys. Rev. C* 38:1828, 1988.

Machleidt, R., K. Holinde, and **C. Elster.** The Bonn meson exchange model for the nucleon-nucleon interaction. *Phys. Rep. B149:1, 1987.

Jin, Y., and **R. W. Finlay.** Analysis of total neutron-nucleus cross sections using relativistic impulse approximation. *Phys. Rev. C* 47:1697, 1993.

Clark, B. C., et al. **(R. W. Finlay).** Empirical determination of the mean free path of a nucleon in the nuclear medium. *Phys. Lett. B* 299:189, 1993.

Abfalterer, W., **R. W. Finlay, S. M. Grimes,** and V. Mishra. Level densities of ^{28}Al, ^{29}Si, and ^{41}Ca inferred from fluctuation measurements. *Phys. Rev. C* 47:1033, 1993.

Finlay, R. W., et al. Neutron total cross sections at intermediate energies. *Phys. Rev. C* 47:237, 1993.

Grimes, S. M., et al. A measurement of the $^{27}Al(d,w)$ spectrum for use in neutron detector calibration. *Nucl. Sci. Eng.* 129:175, 1998.

Grimes, S. M., et al. Justification of a simple Ramsauer model for neutron total cross sections. *Nucl. Sci. Eng.* 130:340, 1998.

Haight, R. C., et al. **(S. M. Grimes** and **C. E. Brient).** Measurement of the angular distribution of neutron-proton scattering at 10 MeV. *Fusion Eng. Des.* 37:49–56, 1997.

Grimes, S. M., and **C. E. Brient** et al. The $^{59}Co(n,x\alpha)$ reaction from 5 to 50 MeV. *Nucl. Sci. Eng.* 124:271, 1996.

Grimes, S. M., et al. Low-lying Gamow-Teller states in ^{92}Nb. *Phys. Rev. C* 53:6, 1996.

Stolla, T., et al. **(S. M. Grimes).** Spectroscopy of excited states of ^8He. *Z. Phys. A* 356:233, 1996.

Howard, W. B., et al. **(S. M. Grimes).** Measurements of the ^9Be (p,n) thick target spectrum for use in accelerator-based Boron Neutron Capture Therapy. *Med. Phys.* 23:7, 1996.

Bateman, F. B., et al. **(S. M. Grimes** and **C.E. Brient).** Determination of the ^{29}Si level density from 3 to 22 MeV. *Phys. Rev. G55:133, 1996.

Grimes, S. M., and T. N. Massey. New expansion technique for spectral distribution calculations. *Phys. Rev. C* 51:606, 1995.

Bohlen, H. G., et al. **(S. M. Grimes).** Spectroscopy of excited states of ^{11}Li. *Z. Phys. A351:7, 1995.

Bateman, F. B., et al. **(S. M. Grimes** and **C. E. Brient).** Determination of the ^{29}Si level density from 3 to 22 MeV. Institute of nuclear and particle physics and R. C. Haight, Los Alamos National Laboratory. *Phys. Rev. C* 55:133–43, 1997.

Michael, R., et al. **(K. H. Hicks).** K^+ elastic scattering from C and ^6Li at 715 MeV/c. *Phys. Lett. B* 382:29–34, 1996.

Blanpied, G., et al. **(K. Hicks).** Polarized compton scattering from the proton. *Phys. Rev. Lett.* 76:1023, 1996.

Larson, B., and **K. Hicks** et al. Polarization transfer in inelastic proton scattering from ^{4}states in oxygen at 350 MeV. *Phys. Rev. C* 53:1774,1996.

Löcher, M., G. A. Johnson, and **E. R. Hunt.** Spatiotemporal stochastic resonance in a system of coupled diode resonators. *Phys. Rev. Lett.* 77:4698–701, 1997.

Löcher, M., and **E. R. Hunt.** Control of high-dimensional chaos in systems with symmetry. *Phys. Rev. Lett.* 79:63–6, 1997.

Johnson, G. A., M. Löcher, and **E. R. Hunt.** Stabilized spatiotemporal waves in a convectively unstable open flow system: Coupled diodide resonators. *Phys. Rev. E, Rapid Comm.* 51:R1, 1995.

Maldei, M., and **D. C. Ingram.** Amorphous carbon solar cells. U.S. Patent 5562781.

Seo, S.-C., and **D. C. Ingram.** Fine structures of valance-band, X-ray excited auger electron, and plasmon loss spectra of diamond-like carbon films obtained using X-ray photoelectron spectroscopy. *J. Vac. Sci. Technol. A* 15:2579, 1997.

Ingram, D. C., C. E. Brient, and **S. M. Grimes**. Mass-energy telescope for materials analysis and charged-particle spectroscopy. *Proceedings of the 14th International Conference on Applications of Accelerators in Research & Industry, AIP Conference Proceedings* 392:1043, 1997.

Voevodin, A. A., et al. **(D. C. Ingram).** Structure and properties of diamond-like carbon films produced by pulsed laser deposition. *J. Vacuum Sci. Tech. A* 14:1927, 1996.

Wang, J., S. Kádár, **P. Jung,** and K. Showalter. Noise-driven avalanche behavior in subexcitable media. *Phys. Rev. Lett.* 82:855–8, 1998.

Jung, P., et al. Noise-sustained waves in subexcitable media: From chemical waves to brain waves. *Chaos* 8:567, 1998.

Jung, P., A. Cornell-Beck, K. Madden, and F. Moss. Noise-induced spiral waves in astrocyte syncytia show evidence of self-organized criticality. *J. Neurophysiol.* 79:1098, 1998.

Thorwart, M., P. Reimann, **P. Jung,** and R. F. Fox. Quantum steps in hysteresis. *Chem. Phys.* 235:62, 1998.

Marchesoni, F., **P. Jung,** P. Hänggi, and L. Gammaitoni. Stochastic resonance. *Rev. Modern Phys.* 70:223–87, 1998.

Jung, P., and K. Wiesenfeld. Too quiet for a whisper. *Nature* January 23, 1997.

Jung, P., and G. Mayer-Kress. Spatio-temporal stochastic resonance in excitable media. *Phys. Rev. Lett.* 74:2130, 1995.

Hänggi, P., and **P. Jung.** Colored noise in dynamical systems. *Adv. Chem. Phys.* 89:239, 1994.

Grossmann, F., T. Dittrich, **P. Jung,** and P. Hänggi. Coherent destruction of tunneling. *Phys. Rev. Lett.* 67:516, 1991.

Montei, E. L., V. W. Ballarotto, M. E. Little, and **M. E. Kordesch.** Applications for small photoelectron emission microscopes. *J. Elec. Spec. Rel. Phenom.* 84:129–36, 1997.

Montei, E.L., and **M. E. Kordesch.** High resolution electron loss spectroscopy and photoelectron emission microscopy study of fomblin Y on molybdenum surfaces. *J. Vac. Sci. Technol. A* 15:1173–8, 1997.

Montei, E. L., and **M. E. Kordesch.** High resolution electron energy loss spectroscopy of low vapor pressure liquid lubricants: Fomblin Y and Z. *Tribology Lett.* 3:205–8, 1997.

Montei, E. L., and **M. E. Kordesch.** The detection of tribochemical reactions using photoelectron emission microscopy. *J. Vac. Sci. Technol. A* 14:1352–6, 1996.

Unertl, W. N., and **M. E. Kordesch.** Direct imaging and geometrical

Ohio University

Selected Publications (continued)

methods. *Handbook of Surface Science, Vol. 1, Physical Structure,* pp. Chapter 8:361–421, ed. N. Richardson. Amsterdam: Elsevier North Holland, 1996.

Kordesch, M. E. Photoelectron emission microscopy. In *Handbook of Surfaces Imaging and Visualization,* ed. A. T. Hubbard. CRC Press, 1995.

Mousseau, N., and G. T. Barkema. Exploring high-dimensional energy landscapes. Invited review. *Comp. Sci. Eng.* 1:74–82, 1999.

Barkema, G. T., and **N. Mousseau.** Identification of relaxation and diffusion mechanisms in amorphous silicon. *Phys. Rev. Lett.* 81:1865, 1998.

Boisvert, G., **N. Mousseau,** and L. J. Lewis. Surface diffusion coefficients by thermodynamic integration: Cu on Cu(100). *Phys. Rev. B* 58:12667, 1998.

Mousseau, N., and G. T. Barkema. Traveling through potential energy landscapes of disordered materials: The activation-relaxation technique. *Phys. Rev. E* 57:2419, 1998.

Mousseau, N., and L. J. Lewis. Topology of amorphous tetrahedral semiconductors on intermediate length scales. *Phys. Rev. Lett.* 78:1484, 1997.

Mousseau, N. Synchronization by disorder in coupled systems. *Phys. Rev. Lett.* 77:968, 1996.

Mousseau, N. Randomly connected cellular automata: A search for critical connectivities. *Europhys. Lett.* 33:509, 1996.

Mousseau, N., and M. F. Thorpe. Size-mismatch disorder at the surface of semiconductors. *Phys. Rev. B* 52:2660, 1995.

Jin, Y., **D. S. Onley,** and **L. E. Wright.** Effects of Coulomb distortion and final state interaction on the fourth and fifth structure functions. *Phys. Rev. C* 50:168, 1994.

Zhang, J.-K., and **D. S. Onley.** Systematic relativistic Hartree-Fock calculation of deformed nuclei in s-d shell. *Phys. Rev. C* 49:762, 1994.

Jin, Y., J.-K. Zhang, **D. S. Onley,** and **L. E. Wright.** Quasielastic ^{40}Ca(e,e'p) cross sections in a many particle self-consistent Hartree model. *Phys. Rev. C* 47:2024, 1993.

Zhang, J.-K., Y. Jin, and **D. S. Onley.** QHD parametrization: A least-squares fit to nuclear ground state properties. *Phys. Rev. C* 48:2697, 1993.

Zhao, J., et al. **(A. K. Opper).** Precision measurement of charge symmetry breaking in np elastic scattering at 347 MeV. *Phys. Rev. C-Nucl. Phys.* 57:(5) 2126–41, 1998.

Davis, C. A., et al. **(A. K. Opper).** The zero-crossing angle of the *n - p* analyzing power. *Phys. Rev. C* 53:2052, 1996.

Hackett, E. D., et al. **(A. K. Opper).** Reaction mechanisms in $^{12}C(\gamma,pp)$ near 200 MeV. *Phys. Rev. C* 53:R1047–51, 1996.

Kolb, N. R., et al. **(A. K. Opper).** ^{3}He(γ,pd) cross sections with tagged photons below the Δ resonance. *Phys. Rev. C* 49:2586, 1994.

Abegg, R., et al. **(A. K. Opper).** Search for charge symmetry violation in np elastic scattering. *Nucl. Inst. Meth.* B79:318, 1993.

Rapaport, J. Medium effects on masses on couplings. *Proceedings of 20 years of Meson Factory Physics,* pp. 219, Ed. Gibson, Hoffman, Barnes and Hughes. World Scientific Publishing Co. 1997.

Rapaport, J., and E. Sugarbaker. Isovector excitations in nuclei. *Annual Review of Nuclear Particle Science* 44:109, 1994.

Chen, X. Y., et al. **(J. Rapaport).** Polarization transfer in quasifree (p,n) reactions at 495 MeV. *Phys. Rev. C* 47:2159, 1993.

Yang, X., et al. **(J. Rapaport).** Dipole and spin dipole resonances in charge-exchange reactions on 12C. *Phys. Rev. C* 48:1158, 1993.

Rapaport, J. Recent results of (n,p) studies at intermediate energies. In *Spin and Isospin in Nuclear Reactions,* vol. 433, eds. S. W. Wissink, C. D. Goodman, and G. E. Walker. Plenum Press, 1991.

Rhode, M. A., **R. W. Rollins,** and H. D. Dewald. On a simple recursive control algorithm automated and applied to an electrochemical experiment. *Chaos* 7:653–63, 1997.

Rhode, M. A., et al. **(R. W. Rollins).** Automated adaptive recursive control of unstable orbits in high-dimensional chaotic systems. *Phys. Rev. E* 54:4880–7, 1996.

Johnson, I., et al. **(R. W. Rollins).** *Solid State Physics Simulations.* New York: Wiley, 1996.

Rhode, M. A., and **R. W. Rollins** et al. Controlling chaos in a model of thermal pulse combustion. *J. Appl. Phys.* 78:2224–32, 1995.

Parmananda, P., et al. **(R. W. Rollins).** Stabilization of unstable steady state in an electrochemical system using derivative control. *Phys. Rev. E* 49:5007, 1994.

Shields, J. C., and F. Hamann. On the nature of ultraviolet and X-ray absorption in NGC 3783. *Astrophys. J.,* 481:752, 1997.

Shields, J. C., and F. Hamann. On the reality of extended Seyfert 1 emission in NGC 4388. *Astrophys. J.* 311:393, 1996.

Shields, J. C., and R. C. Kennicutt. Consequences of dust in metal-rich H II regions. *Astrophys. J.* 454:807, 1995.

Shields, J. C., G. J. Ferland, and B. M. Peterson. Optically thin broad-line clouds in active galactic nuclei. *Astrophys. J.* 441:507, 1995.

Smith, A. R., et al. Surface reconstruction during molecular beam epitaxial growth of GaN(0001). *MRS Internet J. Nitride Semicond. Res.* 3:12, 1998.

Smith, A. R., et al. Determination of Wurtzite GaN lattice polarity based on surface reconstruction. *Appl. Phys. Lett.* 72:2114, 1998.

Smith, A. R., et al. Reconstructions of the GaN(0001) surface. *Phys. Rev. Lett.* 79:3934, 1997.

Smith, A. R., K.-J. Chao, Q. Niu, and C.-K. Shih. Formation of atomically flat silver films on GaAs with a "silver mean" quasi periodicity. *Science* 273:226, 1996.

Smith, A. R., F. K. Men, K.-J. Chao, and C. K. Shih. Variable low-temperature scanning tunneling microscopy study of Si(001): Nature of the 2 x 1→ c(2x4) phase transition. *J. Vac. Sci. Technol. B* 14:914, 1996.

Smith, A. R., et al. Identification of first and second layer aluminum atoms in dilute AlGaAs using cross-sectional scanning tunneling microscopy. *Appl. Phys. Lett.* 69:1214, 1996.

Smith, A. R., et al. Cross-sectional scanning tunneling microscopy study of GaAs/AlAs short period superlattices: The influence of growth interrupt on the interfacial structure. *Appl. Phys. Lett.* 66:478, 1995.

Statler, T. S., H. Dejonghe, and T. Smecker-Hane. The three-dimensional mass distribution in NGC 1700. *Astron. J.* 117:126, 1999.

Statler, T. S., I. R. King, P. Crane, R. I. Jedrzejewski. Stellar kinematics of the double nucleus of M31. *Astron. J.* 117:894, 1999.

Statler, T. S., and T. Smecker-Hane. The stellar kinematic fields of NGC 3379. *Astron. J.* 117:839, 1999.

Meza-Montes, L., and **S. E. Ulloa.** Dynamics of two interacting particles in classical billiards. *Rapid Comm. Phys. Rev. E* 55:6315–8, 1997.

Shahbazyan, T. V., and **S. E. Ulloa.** Resonant scattering in a strong magnetic field: exact density of states. *Phys. Rev. Lett.* 79:3478–81, 1997.

Kato, H., F. M. Peeters, and **S. E. Ulloa.** The remote Wigner polaron in a two-dimensional electron systems. *Europhys. Lett.* 40:551–6, 1997.

Noguez, C., and **S. E. Ulloa.** Anisotropic optical response of the diamond(111) 2 x 1 surface. *Phys Rev. B* 53:13138–45, 1996.

Pfannkuche, D., and **S. E. Ulloa.** Selection rules for transport excitation spectroscopy of few-electron quantum dots. *Phys. Rev. Lett.* 74:1194, 1995.

Wilen, L. A. Measurements of thermoacoustic functions for single pores. *J. Acoustic. Soc. Am.,* in press.

Wilen, L. A. Measurements of scaling properties for acoustic propagation in a single pore. *Acoust. Soc. Am.* 101:1388, 1997.

Wilen, L. A., and J. G. Dash. Frost heave dynamics at a single crystal interface. *Phys. Rev. Lett.* 74:5076, 1995.

Wilen, L. A., et al. Dispersion force effects in interfacial premelting of ice. *Phys. Rev. B* 52:12426, 1995.

Wilen, L. A., and J. G. Dash. Giant facets at ice grain boundary grooves. *Science* 270:1184–6, 1995.

Kim, K. S., and **L. E. Wright.** Approximate Coulomb distortion effects in (e, e'p) reactions. *Phys. Rev. C* 56:302, 1997.

Lee, F. X., **L. E. Wright,** and C. Bennhold. Quasifree pion electroproduction from nuclei in the Δ region. *Phys. Rev. C* 55:318, 1997.

Lee, F. X., **L. E. Wright,** and C. Bennhold. Quasifree pion electroproduction from nuclei in the Δ region. *Phys. Rev. C* 55:318, 1997.

Lee, F. X., **L. E. Wright,** C. Bennhold, and L. Tiator. Quasifree eta photoproduction from nuclei. *Nucl. Phys. A* 603:345, 1996.

So, J., R. Esquivel-Sirvent, **S. S. Yun,** and **F. B. Stumpf.** Ultrasonic velocity of absorption measurements for poly(acrylic acid) and water solutions. *J. Acoust. Soc. Am.* 98:659, 1995.

PENNSTATE

PENNSYLVANIA STATE UNIVERSITY

Department of Physics

Programs of Study

The department is committed to offering an outstanding graduate education in a broad range of fields in experimental and theoretical physics, including condensed-matter physics, elementary particle physics, materials physics, atomic and molecular physics, optics, particle astrophysics, and gravitational physics. The department has 38 faculty members and 90 graduate students. Ninety percent of the faculty members have externally funded research, and one third was hired in the last five years. The department is thus very dynamic in research. There is a weekly colloquium series and several series of special lectures from distinguished physicists, in addition to approximately three to five specialized weekly physics seminars.

The graduate program is aimed primarily at the attainment of a Ph.D. degree in physics. An M.S. program is also offered. Upon arrival, each graduate student is appointed a mentoring committee to provide personalized guidance during graduate school. The first year of study covers basic courses in graduate physics. Arriving students with advanced backgrounds obtain course exemptions, thus effectively becoming second-year students. During the second year, after advancement to candidacy, students take advanced courses in their area of specialization, form a thesis committee, and choose a research adviser. Completion of all the Ph.D. requirements is typically accomplished in a total of five years. The M.S. degree is typically conferred after one year of research beyond the first-year graduate course work through the submission of a thesis.

Research Facilities

The department occupies two buildings on campus. Extensive state-of-the-art equipment is available for research, including thin-film preparation by sputtering and molecular beam epitaxy; photoelectron spectrometers; numerous pulsed and continuous lasers; a variety of cryostats operating between 77K and 5mK; atomic-scale microscopes, including scanning tunneling microscopes (STM), field ion microscopes (FIM), and a field emission microscope (FEM); a low-energy electron diffraction apparatus (LEED); and an in situ ultra-high vacuum ellipsometry. Condensed-matter experiments are also conducted at national facilities such as Argonne National Laboratory (outside Chicago), the National Institute for Science and Technology (NIST) in Maryland, and at Brookhaven National Laboratory in Long Island. Experimental high-energy physics research is carried out at various laboratories, including Brookhaven, Fermilab (near Chicago), and DESY (Hamburg, Germany). A convenient, excellent Physical Sciences Library is available in the same building as the physics department. A complete mathematics library is across the street from the physics department. The department has several clusters of networked UNIX workstations and various other computer facilities, including specially designed rooms for computer-based physics instruction. A SP2 parallel supercomputer is available at the University.

Financial Aid

The department offers incoming students teaching assistantships with full coverage of tuition. The nine-month stipend for the assistantships is approximately $12,200, with additional summer support typically available. Students from their second year on are commonly supported by the research grants of their advisers through research assistantships. The graduate school and the Eberly College of Science provide a few research fellowships and several supplemental fellowships for qualified students. Including summer support and supplemental fellowships, total first-year support for recent entering classes averages approximately $16,500.

Cost of Study

Tuition in 1998–99 was $266 per credit for Pennsylvania residents and $541 per credit for nonresidents, with a mandatory $75 computer fee and a $25 activity fee. For 1998, tuition for a normal two-semester load was $12,980. However, a tuition waiver is typically granted along with the teaching assistantship for incoming students.

Living and Housing Costs

There is limited graduate student housing on campus. Rentals in State College for a one-bedroom apartment range from $350 to $600 per month. Health-care coverage is offered at a rate of approximately $120 a year to teaching assistants.

Student Group

The department typically hosts about 90 graduate students with a variety of ethnic backgrounds and nationalities. The vast majority of students are on teaching or research assistantships. About 50 percent of the students are from the United States.

Location

The University Park campus of Penn State is home to 39,000 undergraduate and 6,000 graduate students and more than 3,000 faculty members. It is located in the municipality of State College, nestled amid the picturesque valleys and wooded mountains of central Pennsylvania. State College has an airport with twenty-four flights a day. The town is within 3½ hours' driving distance to Pittsburgh, Philadelphia, and Washington, D.C. New York City is 4½ hours away. In 1988, *Psychology Today* chose State College as the least stressful place to live in the U.S.

The University

Penn State, founded in 1855, is Pennsylvania's land-grant university and has twenty-four campuses throughout the state. Penn State has more than 340,000 living alumni. One in every 720 Americans and one in every 70 Pennsylvanians are graduates of Penn State. One in every 50 professional engineers and one in 4 meteorologists are also Penn State graduates. The University hosts a legendary football team and its home turf, Beaver Stadium (capacity 93,967), is the fourth largest in the U.S.

Applying

The formal deadline for applications for the fall is April 15, but applications are reviewed beginning in late January until all assistantships are offered. GRE (especially Subject Test in Physics) scores are strongly preferred. TOEFL and TSE scores are mandatory for students from non-English-speaking countries. Applications sent directly to the physics department do not initially require an application fee.

Correspondence and Information

Chair, Graduate Admissions
104 Davey Laboratory
Pennsylvania State University
University Park, Pennsylvania 16802-6300
Telephone: 814-863-9597
        800-876-5348 (toll-free within the United States)
Fax: 814-865-3604
E-mail: graduate-admissions@phys.psu.edu
World Wide Web: http://www.phys.psu.edu

Pennsylvania State University

THE FACULTY AND THEIR RESEARCH

A. Ashtekar, Eberly Professor and Director of Center for Gravitational Physics and Geometry; Ph.D., Chicago, 1974. General relativity, quantum gravity and quantum field theory.

J. R. Banavar, Professor and Department Head; Ph.D., Pittsburgh, 1978. Condensed-matter theory.

J. J. Beatty, Associate Professor; Ph.D., Chicago, 1986. Particle astrophysics.

M. H. W. Chan, Evan Pugh Professor; Ph.D., Cornell, 1974. Low-temperature physics.

S. Chaudhuri, Assistant Professor; Ph.D., Cornell, 1989. String theory, duality, supersymmetry, brane dynamics.

M. W. Cole, Professor; Ph.D., Chicago, 1970. Chemical physics and condensed-matter theory.

J. Collins, Professor; Ph.D., Cambridge, 1975. Perturbative quantum chromodynamics.

R. W. Collins, Professor; Ph.D., Harvard, 1982. Thin-film optical phenomena.

S. Coutu, Assistant Professor; Ph.D., Caltech, 1993. High-energy cosmic-ray positrons and antiprotons as a possible signal for annihilating dark matter particles; the highest-energy cosmic rays.

V. H. Crespi, Assistant Professor; Ph.D., Berkeley, 1994. Theory of superconducting, transport, electronic, and structural/mechanical properties of novel materials.

R. D. Diehl, Associate Professor; Ph.D., Washington (Seattle), 1982. Surface structure and phase transitions.

P. Eklund, Professor; Ph.D., Purdue, 1974. Fundamental properties and applications of new materials, spectroscopy and thermal/electrical transport.

W. E. Ernst, Professor; Dr.rer.nat., Hannover (Germany), 1977. Laser spectroscopy of molecules and clusters.

K. A. Fichthorn, Associate Professor; Ph.D., Michigan, 1989. Condensed-matter simulation and theory.

L. S. Finn, Professor; Ph.D., Caltech, 1987. Detection of gravitational waves, gravitational wave astronomy, relativistic astrophysics, numerical relativity.

G. Gonzalez, Assistant Professor; Ph.D., Syracuse, 1995. Gravitational wave astronomy, interferometric detectors of gravitational waves.

M. Gunaydin, Professor; Ph.D., Yale, 1973. Superstrings and supergravity.

S. F. Heppelmann, Associate Professor; Ph.D., Minnesota, 1981. Experimental high-energy physics.

R. M. Herman, Professor; Ph.D., Yale, 1963. Optical and atomic coherence.

J. Jain, Erwin W. Mueller Professor of Physics; Ph.D., SUNY at Stony Brook, 1985. Condensed-matter theory and the composite Fermion description of the fractional quantum Hall effect.

D. Larson, Professor and Dean of Eberly College of Science; Ph.D., Harvard, 1971. Atomic, molecular, and optical physics.

Q. Li, Assistant Professor; Ph.D., Peking, 1989. Superconducting and magnetic thin films and artificial structures.

Y. Liu, Assistant Professor; Ph.D., Minnesota, 1991. Superconductivity and related phenomena in disordered mesoscopic systems and perovskite compounds.

J. D. Maynard, Professor; Ph.D., Princeton, 1974. Quantum and acoustic wave phenomena.

B. Y. Oh, Professor; Ph.D., Wisconsin, 1969. Experimental high-energy physics.

J. Patel, Professor; Ph.D., SUNY at Stony Brook, 1982. Liquid crystals materials and device research.

R. Penrose, Pentz Professor; Ph.D., Cambridge, 1957. General relativity.

J. Pullin, Associate Professor; Ph.D., Instituto Balseiro, Bariloche (Argentina), 1988. Classical general relativity, colliding black holes, and quantum gravity.

R. W. Robinett, Associate Professor; Ph.D., Minnesota, 1981. Collider physics.

N. Samarth, Associate Professor and Director of Center for Materials Physics; Ph.D., Purdue, 1986. Spin transport and coherence in mesoscopic and nanostructured magnetic systems.

G. A. Smith, Professor and Director of Laboratory for Elementary Particle Science; Ph.D., Yale, 1961. Experimental high-energy physics.

L. Smolin, Professor; Ph.D., Harvard, 1979. Quantum gravity.

P. E. Sokol, Associate Professor; Ph.D., Ohio State, 1981. Neutron scattering and phase transitions.

M. Strikman, Professor; Ph.D., St. Petersburg Nuclear Physics Institute, 1978. High-energy probes of hadron and nuclear structure.

J. J. Whitmore, Professor; Ph.D., Illinois, 1970. Experimental high-energy physics.

R. F. Willis, Professor; Ph.D., Cambridge, 1967. Electronic states of atomic layers.

X. Xi, Assistant Professor; Ph.D., Peking, 1987. Materials physics of electronic and photonic thin films.

J. Yeazell, Assistant Professor; Ph.D., Rochester, 1989. Quantum chaos and the classical atom.

SELECTED PUBLICATIONS

Ashtekar, A., and M. Pierri. Probing quantum gravity through exactly soluble midisuperspaces I. *J. Math. Phys.* 37:6250–70, 1996.

Ashtekar, A. Generalized Wick transform for gravity. *Phys. Rev. D* 53:R2865–9, 1996.

Ashtekar, A. Large quantum gravity effects: Unforeseen limitations of the classical theory. *Phys. Rev. Lett.* 77:4864–7, 1996.

Maritan, A., et al. **(J. R. Banavar).** Universality classes of optimal channel networks. *Science* 272(5264):984–6, 1996.

Marsili, M., A. Martian, F. Toigo, and **J. R. Banavar.** Stochastic growth equations and reparameterization invariance. *Rev. Mod. Phys.* 68:963–83, 1996.

Seno, F., M. Vendruscolo, A. Maritan, and **J. R. Banavar.** Optimal protein design procedure. *Phys. Rev. Lett.* 77(9):1901–4, 1996.

Csathy, G. A., et al. **(M. H. W. Chan).** Heat capacity and superfluid density of thin ^{4}He films on porous gold and on H_2. *Phys. Rev. Lett.* 80:4482, 1998.

Evans, B., and **M. H. W. Chan.** To wet or not to wet. *Phys. World* 9:48–52, 1996.

Mulders, N., and **M. H. W. Chan.** Fourth sound in ^{4}He in reinforced aerogels. *Czech. J. Phys.* 46(Supp. S1):151–2. *Proceedings of the 21st International Conference on Low Temperature Physics,* Prague, August 8–14, 1996.

Mulders, N., et al. **(M. H. W. Chan).** Ordering of ^{3}He-^{4}He mixtures in aerogel. *J. Phys.: Condens. Matter* 8:9609–12, 1996.

Tulimeri, D., N. Mulders, and **M. H. W. Chan.** Heat capacity measurements in ^{3}He-^{4}He mixture in aerogel. *Czech. J. Phys.* 46(Supp. S1):199–200, 1996.

Yoon, J., N. Mulders, L. Hruberk, and **M. H. W. Chan.** Phase diagram of ^{3}He-^{4}He mixture in aerogel of 87% porosity. *Czech. J. Phys.* 46(Supp. S1):157–8, 1996.

Chan, M. H. W. Phase transitions of helium in aerogel. *Czech. J. Phys.,* 46(Supp. S6):2915–22, 1996. *Proceedings of the 21st International Conference on Low Temperature Physics,* Prague, August 8–14, 1996.

Chan, M. H. W., N. Mulders, and J. Reppy. Helium in aerogel. *Phys. Today* 49:30–7, 1996.

Artru, X., and **J. C. Collins.** Measuring transverse spin correlations by 4-particle correlations in e^+e^- to 2 jets. *Z. Phys. C* 69:277–86, 1996.

Berera, A., and **J. C. Collins.** Double pomeron jet cross sections. *Nucl. Phys.* B474:183–216, 1996.

Collins, J. C. The problem of scales: Renormalization and all that. In *Theoretical Advanced Study Institute in Elementary Particle Physics,* pp. 269–323 1995: QCD and Beyond (TASI '95)," ed. D. E. Soper. Singapore: World Scientific, 1996.

Lee, J., et al. **(R. W. Collins** and **N. Samarth).** Spectroellipsometry studies of Zn(1-x)Cd(x)Se: From optical functions to heterostructure characterization. In *Diagnostic Techniques for Semiconductor Materials Processing,* vol. 406, eds. S. W. Pang et al. Pittsburgh: Materials Research Society Symposium Proceedings, 1996.

Lee, J., et al. **(R. W. Collins** and **N. Samarth).** Spectroellipsometric characterization of Zn(1-x)Cd(x)Se multilayered structures on GaAs. *Appl. Phys. Lett.* 69:2273–775, 1996.

Crespi, V. H. Local temperature during growth of multiwalled carbon nanotubes. *Phys. Rev. Lett.* 82:2908, 1999.

Chopra, N. G., et al. **(V. H. Crespi).** Fully collapsed carbon nanotubes. *Nature* 377:135, 1995.

Chopra, N. G., et al. **(V. H. Crespi).** Boron nitride nanotubes. *Science* 269:966, 1995.

Leatherman, G. S., and **R. D. Diehl.** Phase diagrams and rotated incommensurate phases for K, Rb and Cs on Ag(111). *Phys. Rev. B* 53:4939–46, 1996.

Leatherman, G. S., and **R. D. Diehl.** Unexpected adsorption sites for potassium and rubidium adsorption on Ag(111). *Phys. Rev. B* 53:10254–60, 1996.

Diehl, R. D., and R. McGrath. Structural studies of alkali metal adsorption and coadsorption on metal surfaces. *Surf. Sci. Rep.* 23:143–71, 1996.

Higgins, J., et al. **(W. E. Ernst).** Photoinduced chemical dynamics of high-spin alkali trimers. *Science* 273:629–31, 1996.

Higgins, J., and **W. E. Ernst** et al. Spin polarized alkali clusters: Observation of quartet states of the sodium trimer. *Phys. Rev. Lett.* 77:4532–5, 1996.

Stienkemeier, F., et al. **(W. E. Ernst).** Spectroscopy of alkali atoms (Li, Na, K) attached to large helium clusters. *Z. Phys. D* 38:253–63, 1996.

Vituccio, D. T., et al. **(W. E. Ernst).** Photoionization spectroscopy of small alkali and superalkali clusters. In *Resonance Ionization Spectroscopy 1996 Conference Proceedings.* New York: AIP Press, 1996.

Ernst, W. E., D. Farson, and J. Sames. Determination of copper in A533b steel for the assessment of radiation embrittlement using laser-induced breakdown spectroscopy. *Appl. Spectrosc.* 50:306–9, 1996.

Fritschel, P., and **G. Gonzalez** et al. High power interferometric phase measurement limited by quantum noise and application to detection of gravitational waves. *Phys. Rev. Lett.* 80:3181, 1998.

Gunaydin, M., and S. Ketov. Seven-sphere and the exceptional N=7 and N=8 superconformal algebras. (PSU preprint PSU-95-166, December 1995) *Nucl. Phys. B* 467:215–46, 1996.

Armstrong, T., et al. **(M. A. Hasan** and **G. A. Smith).** (Fermilab E760 Collaboration) Light-quark meson spectroscopy. *Phys. Atomic Nuclei* 59:1307, 1996.

Armstrong, T., et al. **(M. A. Hasan** and **G. A. Smith).** (Fermilab E760 Collaboration) Precisions measurements of proton-antiproton forward elastic scattering parameters in the 3.7 to 6.2 GeV/c region. *Phys. Lett. B* 385:479, 1996.

Armstrong, T., et al. **(M. A. Hasan** and **G. A. Smith).** (Fermilab E760 Collaboration) Observation of the radiative decay $J/\Psi \rightarrow e^+e^-\gamma$. *Phys. Rev. D* 54:7067, 1996.

Gasparov, V. A., I. E. Batov, C. Kwon, and **Q. Li.** Observation of Berezinski-Kosterlitz-Thouless transition in (PrY)BaCuO/YBaCuO/(PrY)BaCuO trilayers. *Phys. Low-Dimens. Struct.* 12:361, 1996.

Ham, K. M., et al. **(Q. Li).** Reply to charge transfer in high Tc(Y/Pr)Ba$_2$Cu$_3$O$_7$ superlattices. *Phys. Rev. B* 53:6838, 1996.

Kwon, C., and **Q. Li** et al. Superconducting properties of ultrathin YBa$_2$Cu$_3$O$_7$ trilayers. *Physica C* 266:75–80, 1996.

Kwon, C., and **Q. Li** et al. Pulsed laser deposited superlattices based on perovskite oxides. *Superlattices Microstruct.* 19:169–81, 1996.

Repaci, J., et al. **(Q. Li).** Absence of a Kosterlitz-Thouless transition in ultrathin YBa$_2$Cu$_3$O$_7$ films. *Phys. Rev. B* 54:9674, 1996.

Xiong, G. C., et al. **(Q. Li).** Anomalous magnetoconductivity of epitaxial Nd$_{0.7}$Sr$_{0.3}$MnO$_x$ and Pr$_{0.7}$Sr$_{0.3}$MnO$_x$ films. *Solid State Commun.* 97:599, 1996.

Suh, S. W., et al. **(J. S. Patel).** Precise determination of the cholesteric pitch of a chiral liquid crystal in a circularly aligned configuration. *Appl. Phys. Lett.* 70:2547, 1997.

Hawking, S. W., and **R. Penrose.** The nature of space and time. *Sci. Am.* 275:60, 1996.

Penrose, R. On gravity's role in quantum state reduction. *Gen. Relativ. Gravit.* 28(5):581–600, 1996.

Armand-Ugon, D., R. Gambini, O. Obregon, and **J. Pullin.** Towards a loop representation of quantum canonical supergravity. *Nucl. Phys. B* 460:615–31, 1996.

Gambini, R., and **J. Pullin.** Knot theory and the dynamics of quantum gravity. *Class. Quantum Gravit.* 13:L129–34, 1996.

Gleiser, R., O. Nicasio, R. Price, and **J. Pullin.** Colliding black holes: How far can the close approximation go? *Phys. Rev. Lett.* 77:4483–6, 1996.

Gleiser, R., O. Nicasio, R. Price, and **J. Pullin.** Second order perturbations of a Schwarzschild black hole. *Class. Quantum Gravit.* 13:L117–24, 1996.

Price, R., and **J. Pullin.** Analytic approximations to the spacetime of a critical gravitational collapse. *Phys. Rev. D* 54:3792–9, 1996.

Pullin, J., and R. Gambini. *Loops, Knots, Gauge Theories and Quantum Gravity.* New York: Cambridge University Press, 1996.

Pennsylvania State University

Selected Publications (continued)

Kikkawa, J. M., I. P. Smorchkova, **N. Samarth**, and D. D. Awschalom. Room-temperature spin memory in two-dimensional electron gases. *Science* 277:1284, 1997.

Lopinski, G., et al. **(N. Samarth)**. Reconstruction-induced changes in the electronic states of ZnSe (100). *Surf. Sci. Lett.* 355:L355–60, 1996.

Crooker, S. A., et al. **(N. Samarth)**. Terahertz spin precession and coherent transfer of spin angular momenta in magnetic quantum wells. *Phys. Rev. Lett.* 77:2814–7, 1996.

Crowell, P. A., et al. **(N. Samarth)**. Spatiotemporal near-field spin spectroscopy of digital magnetic heterostructures. In *Proceedings of the International Conference on the Physics of Semiconductors*. Singapore: World Scientific Press, 1996.

Flack, F., et al. **(N. Samarth)**. Growth dynamics and exciton localization in CdSe quantum structures. In *Optoelectronic Materials: Ordering, Composition, Modulation, and Self-assembled Structures*, vol. 417, eds. E. D. Jones, A. Mascarenhas, and P. Petroff. Pittsburgh: Materials Research Society Symposium Proceedings, 1996.

Flack, F., and **N. Samarth** et al. Near-field optical spectroscopy of localized excitons in strained CdSe quantum dots. *Phys. Rev. B* 54:R17312–5, 1996.

Levy, J., et al. **(N. Samarth)**. Spatiotemporal near-field spin microscopy in patterned magnetic heterostructures. *Phys. Rev. Lett.* 76:1948–51, 1996.

Smorchkova, I., and **N. Samarth**. Fabrication of n-doped magnetic semiconductor heterostructures. *Appl. Phys. Lett.* 69:1640–2, 1996.

Samarth, N., and D. D. Awschalom. Spin coherence and imaging in magnetic quantum systems. In *Quantum Circuits and Devices*, eds. K. Ismail, S. Bandopadhyay, and J. P. LeBurton. London: Imperial College Press, 1996.

Goebel, W. A., et al. **(G. A. Smith)**. Trapping antimatter for space propulsion applications. Space Technology and Applications International Forum, Albuquerque, N.M., ed. M. El-Genk. *AIP Conf. Proc.* 361:1415. New York: AIP, 1996.

Holzscheiter, M. H., et al. **(G. A. Smith)**. Are antiprotons forever? *Phys. Lett. A* 214:279, 1996.

Lewis R. A., and **G. A. Smith** et al. Antiproton-catalyzed microfission/fusion propulsion systems for exploration of the outer solar system and beyond. In *Missions to the Outer Solar Systems and Beyond, Proceedings of the First IAA Symposium on Realistic Near-Term Advanced Scientific Space Missions*, p. 251. Torino, Italy: Levrotto & Bella, 1996.

Lewis R. A., **G. A. Smith,** F. M. Huber, and E. W. Messerschmid. Measuring the gravitational force on antiprotons in space. In *ESA Symposium Proceedings on "Space Station Utilisation,"* p. 439. Darmstadt, Germany: ESOC, 1996.

Lewis R. A., and **G. A. Smith** et al. Antiproton-catalyzed microfission/fusion propulsion. Space Technology and Applications International Forum, Albuquerque, N.M., ed. M. El-Genk. *AIP Conf. Proc.* 361:1423, New York: AIP, 1996.

Borrisov, R., S. Major, and **L. Smolin**. The geometry of quantum spin networks. *Class. Quantum Gravit.* 13:3181, 1996.

Major, S., and **L. Smolin**. Quantum deformation of quantum gravity. *Nucl. Phys. B* 473:267, 1996.

Sokol, P. E., et al. Microscopic origins of superfluidity in confined geometries. *Nature* 379:616, 1996.

Schirato, B. S., et al. **(P. E. Sokol)**. The structure of confined oxygen in silica xerogels. *Science* 267:369, 1995.

Gerland, L., et al. **(M. I. Strikman)**. J/Psi production, chi polarization, and color fluctuations. *Phys. Rev. Lett.* 81:762, 1998.

Frankfurt, L. L., and **M. I. Strikman**. Diffraction of nuclei in color singlet models of shadowing. *Phys. Lett. B* 382:6, 1996.

Frankfurt, L., W. Koepf, and **M. I. Strikman**. Hard diffractive electro-production of vector mesons in QCD. *TAUP*, pp. 2290–5, 1995. *Phys. Rev. D* 54:3194–215, 1996.

Koepf, W., L. L. Frankfurt, and **M. Strikman**. The nucleon's virtual meson cloud and deep inelastic lepton scattering. *Phys. Rev. D* 53:2586–98, 1996.

Derrick, M., et al. **(J. Whitmore)**. (ZEUS Collaboration) Rapidity gaps between jets in photoproduction at HERA. *Phys. Lett. B* 369:55, 1996.

Whitmore, J. (ZEUS Collaboration) Measurement of the proton structure function F_2 at low x and low Q^2 at HERA. *Z. Phys. C* 69:607, 1996.

Whitmore, J. (E672-706 Ph Collaboration) Production of J/Ψ and Ψ(2S)in π^-. *Phys. Rev. D* 53:4723, 1996.

Whitmore, J. (ZEUS Collaboration) Dijet angular distributions in direct and resolved photoproduction at HERA. *Phys. Lett. B* 384:401, 1996.

Whitmore, J. (ZEUS Collaboration) Inclusive charged particle distributions in deep inelastic scattering events at HERA. *Z. Phys. C* 70:1, 1996.

Whitmore, J. (ZEUS Collaboration) Measurement of elastic ϕ photoproduction at HERA. *Phys. Lett. B* 377:259, 1996.

Whitmore, J. (ZEUS Collaboration) Measurement of elastic ω photoproduction at HERA. *Z. Phys. C* 73:73, 1996.

Whitmore, J. (ZEUS Collaboration) Measurement of reaction $\gamma^*p\rightarrow\phi p$ in deep inelastic e$^+$p scattering at HERA. *Phys. Lett. B* 380:200, 1996.

Whitmore, J. (ZEUS Collaboration) Measurement of the diffractive cross section in deep inelastic scattering. *Z. Phys. C* 70:391, 1996.

Whitmore, J. (ZEUS Collaboration) Measurement of the F_2 structure function in deep inelastic e$^+$p scattering using 1994 data from the ZEUS detector at HERA. *Z. Phys. C* 72:399, 1996.

Whitmore, J. (ZEUS Collaboration) Observation of events with an energetic forward neutron in deep inelastic scattering at HERA. *Phys. Lett. B* 384:388, 1996.

Whitmore, J. (ZEUS Collaboration) Rapidity gaps between jets in photoproduction at HERA. *Phys. Lett. B* 369:55, 1996.

Whitmore, J. (ZEUS Collaboration) Study of charged-current ep interactions at $Q^2 > 200$ GeV^2 with the ZEUS detector at HERA. *Z. Phys. C* 72:47, 1996.

Lin, X. F., I. Chizhov, H. A. Mai, and **R. F. Willis**. Interaction of Sn atoms with the intrinsic dangling bond states of Si(111)-7x7. *Surf. Sci.* 366:51, 1996.

Lin, X. F., I. Chizhov, H. A. Mai, and **R. F. Willis**. Scanning tunneling spectroscopy examination of surface electronic structures of Si(111)(2$\sqrt{}$3x2$\sqrt{}$3)30°-Sn surface. *Proc. ICFSI-5*, Princeton, New Jersey, July 1995. *Appl. Surf. Sci.* 104/105:223, 1996.

Schumann, F. O., S. Z. Wu, G. J. Mankey, and **R. F. Willis**. Growth and magnetic properties of Fe$_x$Ni$_{1-x}$ ultrathin films on Cu(100). *Proc. MMM '95, J. Appl. Phys.* 79:5635, 1996.

Tobin, J. G., et al. **(R. F. Willis)**. MXLD photoemission and MXCD absorption of magnetic alloy ultrathin films. *Proc. AVAS '95, JVST B* 14:3171, 1996.

Tobin, J. G., et al. **(R. F. Willis)**. Magnetic x-ray linear dichroism in the photoelectron spectroscopy of ultrathin magnetic alloy films. *Proc. MMM '95, J. Appl. Phys.* 79:5626, 1996.

Tobin, J. G., et al. **(R. F. Willis)**. Magnetic x-ray dicroism in spectroscopy of ultrathin alloy films. *J. Vac. Sci. Technol. B* 14:3171, 1996.

Wu, S. Z., F. O. Schumann, G. J. Mankey, and **R. F. Willis**. Magnetic behavior of Fe$_x$Ni$_{1-x}$ and Co$_x$Ni$_{1-x}$ pseudomorphic films on Cu(100). *Proc. AVS '95, JVST B* 14:3189, 1996.

RENSSELAER POLYTECHNIC INSTITUTE

Department of Physics, Applied Physics and Astronomy

Programs of Study

The department offers opportunities for research leading to Master of Science and Doctor of Philosophy degrees in physics. Major areas of research are in astrophysics, condensed-matter physics, optics, and subatomic physics. There is also a smaller program in biophysics and an emerging program in educational physics. Faculty members work closely with each student to develop his or her interest in the chosen area. Graduate courses are offered in quantum mechanics, electromagnetic theory, advanced mechanics, statistical mechanics, nuclear and particle physics, theory of solids, quantum optics, methods in mathematical physics, interstellar matter, star formation, and infrared astronomy.

For the degree of Doctor of Philosophy, a candidate must complete a minimum of 90 credit hours beyond the bachelor's degree, satisfy preliminary examination requirements, pass the candidacy examination, and complete the research thesis and final thesis defense. The degree of Master of Science is based upon 30 credits of courses and research; the residence requirement is at least two terms (24 credits).

Research Facilities

The department has extensive on-campus facilities, including X-ray scattering and absorption spectroscopy systems, molecular beam epitaxy systems, surface magneto-optical Kerr effect experiments, Auger electron spectroscopy, and femtosecond pulsed laser systems. The Astrophysics group has an on-campus observatory equipped with modern detector systems, used for training of graduate students in observational techniques. The Astrophysics and Subatomic Physics groups make extensive use of major off-campus facilities in the United States and abroad, including the Brookhaven Alternating Gradient Synchrotron and the Jefferson Laboratory electron accelerator facility, and ground and satellite-based observatories such as the Hubble Space Telescope and the Infrared Space Observatory.

Research is supported by such state-of-the-art facilities as the George M. Low Center for Industrial Innovation; the Rensselaer Libraries, whose library systems allow access to collections, databases, and Internet resources from campus terminals; the Rensselaer Computing System, which permeates the campus with a coherent array of advanced workstations, a shared toolkit of applications for interactive learning and research, and high-speed Internet connectivity; a visualization laboratory for scientific computation; and a high-performance computing facility that includes a 36-node SP2 parallel computer. In addition, the academic departments have extensive research capabilities and equipment. There are also numerous centers and institutes, including Integrated Electronics and Electronics Manufacturing, Multiphase Research, Composite Materials and Structures, Lighting Research, Science and Technology Policy, Infrastructure and Transportation Studies, and the Geotechnical Centrifuge Research Center. Other research support units include the Fresh Water Institute and the Scientific Computation Center.

Financial Aid

Most support is in the form of research or teaching assistantships. Stipends are $12,150 for the 1999–2000 academic year. In addition, full tuition is granted. Additional compensation of $4000 for the summer months is often available from funded research grants and contracts. Outstanding students may qualify for Rensselaer Scholar Fellowships or other fellowships. Low-interest, deferred-repayment graduate loans are also available to U.S. citizens with demonstrated need.

Cost of Study

Tuition for 1999–2000 is $665 per credit hour. Other fees amount to approximately $535 per semester. Books and supplies cost about $1700 per year.

Living and Housing Costs

The cost of rooms for single students in residence halls or apartments ranges from $3356 to $5298 for the 1999–2000 academic year. Family student housing, with monthly rents of $592 to $720, is available.

Student Group

There are about 4,300 undergraduates and 1,750 graduate students representing all fifty states and more than eighty countries at Rensselaer. In fall 1998, there were approximately 60 graduate students enrolled in the department.

Location

Rensselaer is situated on a scenic 260-acre hillside campus in Troy, New York, across the Hudson River from the state capital of Albany. Troy's central Northeast location provides students with a supportive, active, medium-sized community in which to live; an easy commute to Boston, New York, and Montreal; and some of the country's finest outdoor recreation sites, including Lake George, Lake Placid, and the Adirondack, Catskill, Berkshire, and Green Mountains. The Capital Region has one of the largest concentrations of academic institutions in the United States. Sixty thousand students attend fourteen area colleges and benefit from shared activities and courses.

The University

Founded in 1824 and the first American college to award degrees in engineering and science, Rensselaer Polytechnic Institute today is accredited by the Middle States Association of Colleges and Schools and is a private, nonsectarian, coeducational university. Rensselaer has five schools—Architecture, Engineering, Management, Science, and Humanities and Social Sciences—that offer a total of ninety-eight graduate degrees in forty-seven fields.

Applying

Admissions applications and all supporting credentials, including GRE General and Subject Test results, should be submitted well in advance of the preferred semester of entry to allow sufficient time for departmental review and processing. The application fee is $35. Applicants requesting financial aid are encouraged to submit all required credentials by February 1 to ensure consideration for the fall term.

Correspondence and Information

For written information:
Department of Physics, Applied
    Physics and Astronomy
Graduate Admissions Committee
Rensselaer Polytechnic Institute
110 8th Street
Troy, New York 12180-3590
Telephone: 518-276-8391
E-mail: gradphysics@rpi.edu
World Wide Web: http://www.rpi.edu/dept/phys/

For applications and admissions information:
Director of Graduate Academic Enrollment
    Services, Graduate Center
Rensselaer Polytechnic Institute
110 8th Street
Troy, New York 12180-3590
Telephone: 518-276-6789
E-mail: grad-services@rpi.edu
World Wide Web: http://www.rpi.edu

Rensselaer Polytechnic Institute

THE FACULTY AND THEIR RESEARCH

G. S. Adams, Professor; Ph.D., Indiana, 1977. Experimental nuclear and particle physics.
P. A. Casabella, Professor and Curriculum Chair; Ph.D., Brown, 1959. Nuclear magnetic resonance in solids.
K. Cummings, Clinical Assistant Professor; Ph.D., SUNY at Albany, 1996. Educational physics.
R. M. Davidson, Research Assistant Professor; Ph.D., Rensselaer, 1987. Theoretical nuclear physics.
I. Giaever, Institute Professor of Science; Ph.D., Rensselaer, 1964. Biological physics.
J. W. Haus Jr., Professor; Ph.D., Catholic University, 1975. Quantum optics, statistical mechanics.
T. M. Hayes, Professor; Ph.D., Harvard, 1968. Condensed-matter physics.
R. Kersting, Assistant Professor; Ph.D., Rhenish-Westphalian Technical (Aachen), 1994. Ultrafast optics.
C. M. Leung, Professor; Ph.D., Berkeley, 1975. Computational astrophysics, radiation transport, astrochemistry.
T.-M. Lu, Professor; Ph.D., Wisconsin, 1976. Thin films and interfaces.
K. Min, Professor; Ph.D., Illinois, 1963. Experimental nuclear physics.
N. C. Mukhopadhyay, Professor; Ph.D., Chicago, 1972. Theoretical nuclear and particle physics.
J. Napolitano, Associate Professor and Associate Chair; Ph.D., Stanford, 1982. Experimental nuclear and particle physics.
H. Newberg, Associate Professor; Ph.D., Berkeley, 1992. Observational astronomy.
P. D. Persans, Professor; Ph.D., Chicago, 1982. Spectroscopy of semiconductors, thin films.
W. G. Roberge, Professor; Ph.D., Harvard, 1981. Theoretical astrophysics.
L. Schowalter, Professor and Chairman; Ph.D., Illinois, 1981. Material physics.
J. Schroeder, Professor; Ph.D., Catholic University, 1974. Optical properties of solids, high pressure.
G. A. Slack, Research Professor; Ph.D., Cornell, 1956. Thermoelectric materials.
D. Sperber, Professor; Ph.D., Princeton, 1960. Theoretical nuclear and particle physics.
P. Stoler, Professor; Ph.D., Rutgers, 1966. Experimental nuclear and particle physics.
D. J. Wagner, Clinical Assistant Professor; Ph.D., Vanderbilt, 1997. Educational physics.
G.-C. Wang, Professor; Ph.D., Wisconsin–Madison, 1978. Surface physics.
D. C. B. Whittet, Professor; Ph.D., St. Andrews (United Kingdom), 1975. Astrophysics, optical and infrared observations, interstellar dust.
J. Wilson, Professor; Ph.D., Kent State, 1972. Computers in physics, physics education.
X.-C. Zhang, Professor; Ph.D., Brown, 1986. Ultrafast photonic and optoelectronic science and technology.

RESEARCH SPECIALTIES AND STAFF

Theoretical

Astrophysics. Physics and chemistry of interstellar molecular clouds and circumstellar envelopes, interstellar shocks, and magnetohydrodynamics; application of radiative transport theory to astrophysical problems: theory of interstellar polarization. Leung, Roberge. One postdoctoral associate.

Theoretical Intermediate Energy and Elementary Particle Physics. Physics of hadrons in the context of the standard model and beyond, with emphasis on the study of meson and baryon spectroscopy accessible at accelerators such as the AGS at the Brookhaven National Laboratory and the Jefferson Laboratory; theory of hybrids and glueballs; interface between particles and nuclei; dynamics and transport phenomena in heavy-ion collisions; nuclear equation of state. Mukhopadhyay, Sperber. One postdoctoral associate.

Theory of Solids and Optical Physics. Simulations of electromagnetic band structure in periodic lattices and applications to cavity quantum electrodynamics and nonlinear optical effects; dynamic evolution of quantum coherence in atomic and solid media; models describing the structure of surfaces and interfaces and the binding and mobility of adsorbed atoms on metal surfaces; theory for the quantum confinement of carriers in semiconductor nanoparticles, especially the relationship of these properties to linear and nonlinear optical phenomena; optical soliton propagation and interactions in optical fibers and optical fiber laser models, including dynamic instabilities and mode-locking. Haus, Lu.

Experimental

Astrophysics. Data collected at wavelengths from ultraviolet to radio are used to study dust and molecules in interstellar clouds, particularly those giving birth to new stars and planetary systems. Millimeter wave observations are used to study molecular clouds in the Milky Way and other galaxies. Infrared observations are used to probe the physical conditions and chemical composition of protostars and protoplanetary disks. There is an emerging interest in the study of organic matter in interstellar clouds and its relevance to exobiology. Newburg, Roberge, Whittet.

Biophysics and Crystallography. Research includes X-ray crystallographic studies of DNA, the motion of nucleic acids through gels under the influence of an electric field, new means to detect the antibody-antigen interaction, and the motion of single cells in culture by a novel electrical method. The aim of this research is to characterize cells and their interactions with surfaces and to measure the effects of various chemical agents on cell motility. Giaever. One postdoctoral associate.

Educational Development in Physics. Research centers on development of new introductory course models; development of video tapes and disks, films, and laboratory and demonstration experiments; use of computers in physics instruction; production of written materials; computational physics activities; and computer-based multimedia programs. Casabella, Cummings, Min, Wilson.

Experimental Condensed Matter Physics. Measurements are made to establish the fundamental concepts important to the understanding of solids and liquids and their surfaces and interfaces. Novel and technologically interesting materials are prepared by a variety of techniques, including molecular beam and ionized cluster beam deposition, plasma-assisted chemical vapor deposition, and quenching from the melt. Optical interactions (Raman, Rayleigh, and Brillouin scattering; absorption; photoluminescence; electro- and photomodulation spectroscopy) are used to study structure and defects in semiconductors, quantum dots, quantum wires, glasses, and solids under high pressure. X-ray diffraction, high-resolution electron diffraction, scanning tunneling microscopy, and ballistic-electron emission microscopy are applied to study surfaces and overlayers. X-ray absorption spectroscopy and X-ray scattering are used to study the atomic-scale structure of a variety of materials of current interest, including semiconductor nanocrystals and dopants and defects in nanocrystalline semiconductors. Hayes, Lu, Persans, Schowalter, Schroeder, Slack, Wang, Zhang. Two visiting scholars. Three postdoctoral associates.

Experimental Particle and Nuclear Physics. Research centers mainly on properties of hadronic systems using lepton and hadron beams. A primary center of activities is Jefferson Laboratory, where research is on the electromagnetic structure of hadrons and, especially, the properties of exotic mesons and excited baryons. Collaboration on Experiment E852 at Brookhaven focuses on a search for exotic mesons. Adams, Napolitano, Stoler. Three postdoctoral associates.

Optical Physics. Research uses a broad range of optical and optoelectronic techniques to characterize and investigate linear and nonlinear properties of materials. Raman and Brillouin scattering and photoluminescence from samples at low temperature and high pressure have recently been applied to study of electron-phonon coupling in semiconductor nanocrystals. Optical techniques also include electromodulation and photoluminescence used to probe the nature of confined electronic and vibrational states in quantum dots and of the nucleation and growth of clusters in glass. Linear, nonlinear, electrooptic, and acoustooptic materials are being developed and studied for waveguide and integrated optic devices. Ultrafast linear and nonlinear time-resolved spectroscopy is developed from the visible to the far infrared (terahertz) regime using picosecond and femtosecond laser pulses. Kersting, Persans, Schroeder, Zhang. Two visiting scholars.

RICE UNIVERSITY

Applied Physics Program

Programs of Study

Rice University offers the Ph.D. degree in applied physics. A joint effort of both the natural sciences and the engineering divisions at Rice, the Applied Physics Program is overseen by a committee comprising representative members of the Physics, Electrical and Computer Engineering, Chemistry, Materials Science, and Space Physics and Astronomy departments. The objective is to provide an interdisciplinary graduate education in the basic science that underlies new technology. The faculty believes that the experience obtained performing research at the intellectually stimulating interface of physical science and engineering is particularly effective in producing graduates who succeed in careers based on new and emerging technologies.

The Applied Physics Program is closely allied with the Rice Quantum Institute (RQI) and a new Center for Nanoscale Science and Technology, which together involve about 45 faculty members, 120 graduate students, and about 30 postdoctoral fellows and research professionals. This interactive group of diverse individuals provides graduate students with a remarkably interdisciplinary environment. Rice is a national leader in nanoscale science. New laboratories for this research direction have been completed, and about a dozen new faculty members in this area are being hired. The Applied Physics Committee works with each student individually to set a curriculum that usually takes from both engineering and natural science. Students typically interact with faculty members in several departments and may choose a research adviser from any department. The only requirement placed on a student's choice of research topic is that it must arguably be "applied physics," which has ranged from theoretical chemistry through experimental chemistry and physics to bioengineering.

Successful completion of nine one-semester graduate-level courses is required for the master's degree in applied physics. For students who demonstrate a thorough knowledge of material, the Applied Physics Committee may waive some course requirements. Students are normally expected to complete the course requirements in three semesters and maintain a grade average of 3.0. There are four required one-semester graduate-level courses: Quantum Mechanics I, Quantum Mechanics II, Classical Electrodynamics, and Solid State Physics. An adequate undergraduate background in classical mechanics, electrostatics, and statistical and thermal physics is assumed. Students are also required to complete five other one-semester graduate-level courses in subjects that relate to applied physics. Each student's curriculum, research, and thesis topics receive individual consideration by the Applied Physics Committee and must be approved by that committee. Normally students defend a research-based master's thesis in order to become candidates for the Ph.D.

Research Facilities

Because of the interdisciplinary nature of the program, the student can access virtually any of the research facilities in either the natural sciences or engineering schools of Rice University. With a broad range of research opportunities available, the Applied Physics Committee urges prospective students to contact individual departments or the Rice Quantum Institute for detailed descriptions of research facilities and ongoing research projects.

Financial Aid

Most students receive financial aid in the form of a stipend. For the academic year 1998–99, this was nominally $1200 per month.

Cost of Study

Tuition for 1999–2000 is $16,300. Currently, all students in the Applied Physics Program receive tuition waivers or are exempt from tuition payment. Health insurance, if covered, ranges from $600 to $785 per year. Other fees, including Graduate Student Association fees, shuttle service, and Honor Council fees, amount to approximately $250 per year.

Living and Housing Costs

Graduate student housing is available adjacent to the campus at the Graduate House. Monthly rents range from $305 to $420 for singles and $195 to $330 for doubles. Inexpensive off-campus housing is available in the area. The cost of living in Houston is below the national average for U.S. cities.

Student Group

At present, there are approximately 30 graduate students in the Applied Physics Program. These students, however, work in the same research groups as students from the RQI-affiliated departments. The group size for social and intellectual interaction actually numbers about 175 graduate students, 20 postdoctoral students, and 20 undergraduate students who are working on special projects.

Location

Set in a 300-acre academic park near downtown Houston, the campus is adjacent to the Texas Medical Center, where world-famous labs, hospitals, and medical schools offer added opportunities for collaborative research. There is a wide range of social, cultural, and recreational activities available within the metropolitan area.

The University

Opened in 1912, Rice University is a private, coeducational, nondenominational university founded in 1891 from the estate of William Marsh Rice. The University has faculties of liberal arts, science, engineering, administration, and music. Current enrollment is about 3,000 undergraduates and 1,400 graduate students. The academic year consists of two semesters of fifteen weeks each.

Applying

Application materials for admission may be obtained at the World Wide Web site below. Completed applications, together with transcripts and four letters of recommendation, should be sent to the address below by February 1. The program requires official scores from the Graduate Record Examinations. International students whose native language is not English must have an official score sent from TOEFL.

Correspondence and Information

Applied Physics Program
Rice Quantum Institute—MS 104
Rice University
P. O. Box 1892
Houston, Texas 77251-1892
Telephone: 713-527-6028
Fax: 713-285-5935
E-mail: quantum@rice.edu
World Wide Web: http://cnst.rice.edu
http://www.rice.edu/rqi

Rice University

THE FACULTY AND THEIR RESEARCH

David Auston, Professor of Electrical and Computer Engineering; Ph.D., Berkeley, 1969. Electronic circuits and devices.

Enrique V. Barrera, Assistant Professor of Materials Science; Ph.D., Texas at Austin, 1984. Structural-mechanical property relations of materials; interface science; composites, coatings, and thin films.

Andrew Barron, Professor of Chemistry, Mechanical Engineering, and Materials Science; Ph.D., Imperial College (London), 1986. Inorganic and materials chemistry.

Philip R. Brooks, Professor of Chemistry; Ph.D., Berkeley, 1964. Experimental chemical physics studies on the nature of the chemical reaction process using molecular beams and lasers.

Franz R. Brotzen, Professor Emeritus of Materials Science; Ph.D., Case Tech, 1954. Physical properties of solid materials and electronic materials.

Daniel L. Callahan, Assistant Professor of Materials Science; Ph.D., Berkeley, 1989. Microstructural design and defect characterization with emphasis on advanced ceramic and composite systems.

Vicki Colvin, Assistant Professor of Chemistry; Ph.D., Berkeley, 1994. Fabrication of novel nanostructured materials.

Robert F. Curl, Harry C. and Olga K. Weiss Professor of Natural Sciences and Professor of Chemistry; Ph.D., Berkeley, 1957. Chemical kinetics and dynamics, semiconductor and carbon clusters.

F. Barry Dunning, Professor of Physics and of Space Physics and Astronomy; Ph.D., University College (London), 1969. Experimental atomic, molecular, and surface physics; laser physics; magnetism.

Paul S. Engel, Professor of Chemistry; Ph.D., Harvard, 1968. Physical-organic chemistry.

Graham P. Glass, Professor of Chemistry; Ph.D., Cambridge, 1953. Kinetics of fast reactions.

Naomi J. Halas, Assistant Professor of Electrical and Computer Engineering; Ph.D., Bryn Mawr, 1986. Carrier dynamics in electronic materials and structures.

Robert H. Hauge, Distinguished Faculty Fellow in Chemistry; Ph.D., Berkeley, 1965. Spectroscopy and diamond films.

Randall G. Hulet, Associate Professor of Physics; Ph.D., MIT, 1984. Quantum optics, laser cooling and atom trapping.

John S. Hutchinson, Associate Professor of Chemistry; Ph.D., Texas, 1981. Quantum and classical dynamics of chemical processes.

Bruce R. Johnson, Faculty Fellow in Chemistry; Ph.D., Wisconsin, 1981. Theoretical chemical dynamics.

James L. Kinsey, D.R. Bullard-Welch Foundation Professor of Science (Chemistry) and Dean of the Wiess School of Natural Sciences; Ph.D., Rice, 1959. Chemical dynamics, spectroscopy, lasers, and theoretical chemistry.

Carter Kittrell, Senior Research Scientist in Chemistry; B.S., Allegheny, 1971. Chemical dynamics, spectroscopy, and lasers.

Bruce M. Lairson, Assistant Professor of Materials Science; Ph.D., Stanford, 1991. Magnetic data storage, nanometer-scale magnetics, metal multilayers, ultrathin films, information storage materials.

John L. Margrave, E.D. Butcher Professor of Chemistry; Ph.D., Kansas, 1950. High-temperature/high-pressure chemistry.

Daniel Mittleman, Faculty Fellow, Electrical and Computer Engineering; Ph.D., Berkeley, 1994. Ultrafast laser pulses and spectroscopy.

Peter Nordlander, Associate Professor of Physics; Ph.D., Chalmers (Sweden), 1985. Condensed-matter theory, surfaces.

Thomas A. Rabson, Professor of Electrical and Computer Engineering; Ph.D., Rice, 1959. Semiconductor device physics and thin-film ferroelectrics.

Carl Rau, Professor of Physics; Ph.D., Munich Technical, 1970. Surface physics.

Alex Rimberg, Assistant Professor of Physics; Ph.D., Harvard, 1992. Condensed matter experiment, transport properties of nanostructures.

Marc A. Robert, Professor of Chemical Engineering; Ph.D., Swiss Federal Institute of Technology, 1980. Thermodynamics and statistical mechanics.

Gustavo E. Scuseria, Associate Professor of Chemistry; Ph.D., Buenos Aires, 1983. Electronic structure and calculations on novel chemical systems.

Qimiao Si, Assistant Professor of Physics; Ph.D., Chicago, 1991. Condensed matter theory.

Richard E. Smalley, Gene and Norman Hackerman Professor of Chemistry and Professor of Physics; Ph.D., Princeton, 1973. Molecular physics, chemical physics, and clusters.

Ken Smith, Distinguished Faculty Fellow in Physics and in Space Physics and Astronomy; Ph.D., Rice, 1976. Atomic and molecular collisions.

Ronald F. Stebbings, Professor of Physics and of Space Physics and Astronomy; Ph.D., University College (London), 1956. Experimental atomic and molecular physics.

Frank K. Tittel, J.S. Abercrombie Professor of Electrical and Computer Engineering; D.Phil., Oxford, 1959. Quantum electronic devices, laser spectroscopy, nonlinear optics and laser-materials interactions.

G. King Walters, Professor of Physics and of Space Physics and Astronomy; Ph.D., Duke, 1956. Experimental atomic, molecular, and surface physics.

Jon C. Weisheit, Professor of Space Physics and Astronomy; Ph.D., Rice, 1970. Theoretical astrophysics, plasma spectroscopy, and intense magnetic field phenomena.

R. Bruce Weisman, Professor of Chemistry; Ph.D., Chicago, 1977. Molecular photochemistry and photophysics.

William L. Wilson Jr., Professor of Electrical and Computer Engineering; Ph.D., Cornell, 1973. Semiconductor materials growth and electrooptic devices.

James F. Young, Associate Professor of Electrical and Computer Engineering; Ph.D., Stanford, 1970. Experimental quantum electronics, ultraviolet lasers, imaging, and communications.

SELECTED PUBLICATIONS

Sheng, X., and **E. V. Barrera.** A model for optical property degradation of anodic coatings by vacuum-ultraviolet radiation. In *The 9th International Conference on Surface Modification Technology,* TMS Proc., 233–45, 1996.

Barrera, E. V. Investigations of metal-fullerene interactions: A study of aluminum-fullerene interactions and materials synthesis. *NASA-Johnson Space Center Final Report,* March 1996.

Sheng, X., B. Klampfl, and **E. V. Barrera.** Effects of vacuum and vacuum-ultraviolet radiation on sulfuric acid anodized aluminum oxide coatings. 35(2):205–10, 1996.

Barron, A. R. CVD of SiO_2 and related materials: An overview. *Adv. Mater. Optics Electron.,* 6:101, 1996.

Barron, A. R. A FETISH for gallium arsenide. *Mater. Res. Soc.* 410: 23, Symp. Proc., 1996.

Aitken, C. L., and **A. R. Barron.** Crystal structure of $Al(tBu)3(NH_2CH_2CH_2Ph)$: A molecular slinky. *J. Chem. Cryst.* 26:297, 1996.

Koide, Y., S. G. Bott, and **A. R. Barron.** Alumoxanes as co-catalysts in palladium catalysed co-polymerization of carbon monoxide and ethylene: Genesis of a structure activity relationship. *Organometallics* 15:2213, 1996.

Landry, C. C., et al. **(A. R. Barron).** Gallium and indium compounds of sulfur donor ligands: pyridine-2-thiolates and diphenylthiophosphates. *Polyhedron* 15: 391, 1996

Brooks, P. R., and P. W. Harland. Effect of molecular orientation on electron transfer and electron impact ionization. In *Advances in Gas Phase Ion Chemistry,* vol. 2, pp. 1–39, eds. N. G. Adams and L. M. Babcock. Greenwich, Connecticut: JAI Press, 1996.

Bayazitoglu, Y., **F. R. Brotzen,** and Y. Zhang. Metal vapor condensation in a converging nozzle. *NanoStruct. Mat.* 7:789, 1996.

Wasz, M. L., **F. R. Brotzen,** R. B. McLellan, and A. J. Griffin Jr. Effect of oxygen and hydrogen on mechanical properties of commercial-purity titanium. *Int. Mat. Rev.* 41:1, 1996.

Callahan, D. Construction of contact deformation maps on ceramics. *Microscopy and Microanalysis 1996,* 636–7.

Callahan, D., et al. Hardness, elastic modulus, and structure of very hard carbon films produced by cathodic-arc deposition with substrate pulse-biasing. *Appl. Phys. Lett.* 68(6)779–81, 1996.

Callahan, D. Comment on diffraction method detection of local lattice distortion in AIN ceramics by convergent beam electron. *J. Am. Ceramic Soc.* 79(7):1982, 1996.

Eckhoff, W. C., et al. **(R. F. Curl** and **F. K. Tittel).** Continuously tunable long wavelength CW IR source for high-resolution spectroscopy and trace gas detection. *Appl. Phys. B,* 1996.

Petrov, K. P., et al. **(R. F. Curl** and **F. K. Tittel).** Detection of CO in air using diode-pumped 4.6 m difference frequency generation in quasi-phase matched $LiNbO_3$. *Opt. Lett.* 2186–8, 1996.

Frey, M. T., C. O. Reinhold, **F. B. Dunning,** and J. Burgdörfer. Ionisation of very-high-n Rydberg atoms by half-cycle pulses in the short-pulse regime. *Phys. Rev. A* 53:R2929, 1996.

Hill, S. B., M. T. Frey, **F. B. Dunning,** and I. I. Fabrikant. Electron-hydrogen fluoride scattering at ultra-low electron energies: Possible role of dipole supported states. *Phys. Rev. A* 53:3348, 1996.

Popple, R. A., C. D. Finch, **F. B. Dunning,** and **K. A. Smith.** Use of Rydberg atoms as a nanoscale laboratory to investigate dissociative electron attachment to CCl_4. *J. Chem. Phys.* 104:8485, 1996.

Compton, R. N., **F. B. Dunning,** and **P. Nordlander.** On the binding of electrons to CS_2: Possible role of quadrupole-bound states. *Chem. Phys. Lett.* 253:8, 1996.

Reinhold, C. O., J. Burgdörfer, M. T. Frey, and **F. B. Dunning.** Dynamics of Rydberg wave packets generated by half-cycle pulses. *Phys. Rev. A* 54:R33, 1996.

Dunning, F. B. Rydberg atoms: A microscale laboratory to study electron-molecule scattering at ultralow electron energies. *Comm. At. Mol. Phys.* 32:179, 1996.

Dunning, F. B., and **P. Nordlander.** Interaction of Rydberg atoms with a metal surface in the presence of an external electric field. *Phys. Rev. B* 53:8083, 1996.

Compton, R. N., **F. B. Dunning,** and **P. Nordlander.** Electric-field induced detachment from CS2: Possible role of quadrupole-bound states. *Chem. Phys. Lett.* 253:8–12, 1996.

Wallace, et al. **(F. B. Dunning** and **G. K. Walters).** Use of a diode laser to measure the polarization of an optically-pumped ensemble of He(23S) atoms. *Rev. Sci. Instrum.* 67:1684, 1996.

Jursic, B. S., J. W. Timberlake, and **P. S. Engel.** Computation of bond dissociation energies of substituted methanes with density functional theory. *Tetrahedron Lett.* 37:6473, 1996.

Adamson, J. D., et al. **(G. P. Glass** and **R. F. Curl).** Propargyl from the reaction of singlet methylene with acetylene. *J. Phys. Chem.* 100:2125, 1996.

Smith, C., J. C. Chu, L. Margrave, and **R. H. Hauge.** Metal catalyzed hydrogenation of diamonds. *Diamond and Related Materials,* 1997.

Abraham, E. R. I., W. I. McAlexander, **R. G. Hulet,** and H. T. C. Stoof. Hyperfine structure in photoassociative spectra of 6Li2 and 7Li2. *Phys. Rev. A* 53:3092–7, 1996.

Abraham, E. R. I., et al. **(R. G. Hulet).** Singlet s-wave scattering lengths of ^{6}Li and ^{7}Li. *Phys. Rev. A* 53:R3713, 1996.

Bradley, C. C., and **R. G. Hulet.** Laser cooling and atom trapping. *Atomic, Molecular and Optical Physics,* v. 29B, eds. F. B. Dunning and R. G. Hulet. San Diego: Academic, 1996.

McAlexander, W. I., E. R. I. Abraham, and **R. G. Hulet.** Radiative lifetime of the 2P state of lithium. *Phys. Rev. A* 54:5, 1996.

Stoof, H. T. C., M. Houbiers, C. A. Sackett, and **R. G. Hulet.** Superfluidity of spin-polarized ^{6}Li. *Phys. Rev. Lett.* 76: 10, 1996.

Abraham, E. R. I., N. W. M. Ritchie, W. I. McAlexander, and **R. G. Hulet.** Photoassociative spectroscopy of long-range states of ultracold 6Li2 and 7Li2. *J. Chem. Phys.* 103:7773–8, 1995.

Bradley, C. C., C. A. Sackett, J. J. Tollett, and **R. G. Hulet.** Evidence of Bose-Einstein condensation in an atomic gas with attractive interactions. *Phys. Rev. Lett.* 75:1687–90, 1995.

Côté, R., A. Dalgarno, Y. Sun, and **R. G. Hulet.** Photoabsorption and the scattering length. *Phys. Rev. Lett.* 74:3581–4, 1995.

Hutchinson, J. S. Nonlinear classical dynamics and unimolecular reactions. In *Dynamics of Moleculars and Chemical Reactions,* pp. 561–88, eds. R. E. Wyatt and J. Zhang, 1996.

Nunes, N. L., K. Chen, and **J. S. Hutchinson.** Flexible lattice model to study protein folding. *J. Phys. Chem.* 100(24):10443–9, 1996.

Lewis, L., **B. Johnson, P. R. Brooks,** and **R. F. Curl.** Role of fine structure states in a chemical reaction: Na*+KBr->NaBr+K*. *J. Phys. Chem.* 100:8008, 1996.

Johnson, B. R., and **J. L. Kinsey.** Joint analysis of absorption, magnetic circular dichronism and resonance Raman spectra of CH3I excited in the A Band. *J. Phys. Chem.* 100:18937, 1996.

Kinsey, J. L. Resonance Raman spectroscopy of dissociative polyatomic molecules. *J. Phys. Chem.* 100:7743, 1996.

Kittrell, C. Pulsed laser Raman spectroscopy of dynamic systems. In *Atomic, Molecular, and Optical Physics: Atoms and Molecules,* vol. 29B, Experimental Methods in the Physical Sciences, p. 393, eds. F. B. Dunning and R. G. Hulet, 1996.

Liu, W., S. Fleming, and **B. Lairson.** Reduction of intergranular exchange coupling in Pd/Co multilayers. *J. Appl. Phys.* 179:3651, 1996.

Lairson, B., W. Liu, and A. P. Payne. Magnetic relaxation at high linear densities in thin films with perpendicular magnetic anistropy. *J. Appl. Phys.* 179:7920, 1996.

Lairson, B., T. Coughlin, and B. Gooch. High density data storage with keepered media. *Data Storage,* September 1996.

Liu, W. H., et al. **(B. M. Lairson).** High linear density written transitions in exchange isolated Pt/CoCrTa multilayers. *Appl. Phys. Lett.* 69:124, 1996.

Wang, J., **J. L. Margrave,** and **R. H. Hauge.** Metal oxide catalyzed dry CO_2 oxidation of diamond. *Diamond and Related Materials,* 1997.

Wang, J., **J. L. Margrave,** and **R. H. Hauge.** Metal oxide catalyzed wet CO_2 oxidation of diamond. *Diamond and Related Materials,* 1997.

Rice University

Selected Publications (continued)

Park, M. A., **J. L. Margrave,** and **R. H. Hauge.** Reactions of Fe, Co, and Ni atoms/clusters with H_2 and H_2O in low temperature matrices. *Proceedings of Conference on Low Temperature Chemistry,* Kansas City, Missouri, Aug. 4–9, 1996.

Shukla, A., S. S. Shukla, and **J. L. Margrave.** The applications of microemulsions for analytical determinations. In *Industrial Applications of Microemulsions,* pp. 47–67. New York: Marrel Dekker, Inc., 1996.

Nordlander, P., and L. Lou. Carbon atomic chains in strong electric fields. *Phys. Rev. B* 54:16659–62, 1996.

Shao, H., D. C. Langreth, and **P. Nordlander.** Probing the highly correlated mixed-valent state via charge transfer with atoms moving out from a surface. *Phys. Rev. Lett.* 77:948–51, 1996.

Nordlander, P. Energies and lifetimes of atomic Rydberg states near metal surfaces. *Phys. Rev. B* 53:4125–32, 1996.

Akpati, H., J. Mackey, L. Lou, and **P. Nordlander.** Density functional study of cluster reactivity III:NH_3 reacting with $Ga_5As_5^+$. *J. Chem. Phys.* 104:1477–82, 1996.

Avouris, Ph., et al. **(P. Nordlander).** Breaking individual chemical bonds via STM-induced excitations. *Surf. Sci.* 363:368–77, 1996.

Modisette, J. P., **P. Nordlander, J. L. Kinsey,** and **B. R. Johnson.** Wavelet bases in eigenvalue problems in quantum mechanics. *Chem. Phys. Lett.* 250:485–94, 1996.

Pippinger, P. M., et al. **(P. Nordlander** and **N. J. Halas).** An excimer model for excitations in single crystal C60. *J. Phys. Chem.* 100:2854–61, 1996.

Rau, C., and **M. Robert.** Anisotropic XY model for two-dimensional Fe. *Mod. Phys. Lett. B* 10:223, 1996.

Rau, C., and **M. Robert.** Magnetic phase transitions of ultra-thin Fe films. *IEEE Trans. Magn.* 32:4553, 1996.

Robert, M., I. Reaney, and P. Stadelmann. Critical interface in two dimensions. *Physica A* 229:47, 1996.

Burant, J. C., M. C. Strain, M. J. Frisch, and **G. E. Scuseria.** Kohn-Sham analytic energy second derivatives with the Gaussian Very Fast Multipole Method (GvFMM). *Chem. Phys. Lett.* 258:45, 1996.

Scuseria, G. E., and A. R. Maclagan. An ab initio study of VC: A comparison of different levels of theory including density functional methods. *Chem. Phys. Lett.* 262:87, 1996.

Burant, J. C., **G. E. Scuseria,** and M. J. Frisch. A linear scaling method for Hartree-Fock exchange calculations of large molecules. *J. Chem. Phys.* 105:8969, 1996.

Scuseria, G. E. Ab initio calculations of fullerenes. *Science* 271:942–5, 1996.

Strain, M. C., **G. E. Scuseria,** and M. J. Frisch. Achieving linear scaling for the electronic quantum Coulomb problem. *Science* 271:51, 1996.

Strout, D. L., and **G. E. Scuseria.** A cycloaddition model for fullerene formation. *J. Phys. Chem.* 100:6492–8, 1996.

Thess, A., et al. **(G. Scuseria** and **R. E. Smalley).** Crystalline ropes of metallic carbon nanotubes. *Science* 273:483–7, 1996.

Si, Q. Non-Fermi liquids in the extended Hubbard model. *J. Phys. Condens. Matter* 8:9953–84, 1996.

Si, Q., and G. Kotliar. Fermi-liquid and non-Fermi liquid phases of an extended Hubbard model in infinite dimensions. *Phys. Rev. Lett.* 70:3143, 1996.

Si, Q., and J. L. Smith. Kosterlitz-Thouless transition and short range spatial correlations in an extended Hubbard model. *Phys. Rev. Lett.* 77:3391, 1996.

Moeller, G., et al. **(Q. Si).** Critical behavior near the Mott transition in the Hubbard model. *Phys. Rev. Lett.* 74:2082, 1995.

Dai, H., et al. **(R. E. Smalley).** Nanotubes as nanoprobes in scanning probe microscopy. *Nature* 384:147–51, 1996.

Dai, H., et al. **(R. E. Smalley).** Single-wall nanotubes produced by metal-catalyzed disproportionation of carbon monoxide. *Chem. Phys. Lett.* 260:471, 1996.

Rinzler, A., et al. **(R. E. Smalley).** Metal tipped carbon nanotubes. In *Fullerenes: Recent Advances in the Chemistry and Physics of Fullerenes and Related Materials.* ECS Conference Proceedings, vol. 3, May 1996.

Colbert, D. T., and **R. E. Smalley.** Fullerene tinkertoys. In *Proceedings from NATO Advanced Research Workshop on Modular Chemistry,* Estes Park, Colorado, September 1995.

Lindsay, B. G., et al. **(K. A. Smith** and **R. F. Stebbings).** Charge transfer of 0.5, 1.5, and 5keV protons with atomic oxygen: Absolute differential and integral cross sections. *Phys. Rev. A* 53:212, 1996.

Straub, H. C., B. G. Lindsay, **K. A. Smith,** and **R. F. Stebbings.** Absolute partial cross sections for electron-impact ionization of CO_2 from threshold to 1000 eV. *J. Chem. Phys.* 105:4015–22, 1996.

Tittel, F. K., et al. High resolution microlithography applications of Deep-UV excimer lasers. *XI International Conference on Gas Flow, Chemical Lasers and High Power Lasers,* Edinburgh, Scotland, August 1996.

Oraevsky, A. A., S. L. Jacques, R. O. Esenaliev, and **F. K. Tittel.** Pulsed laser ablation of soft tissues, gels, and aqueous solutions at temperatures below 100. *Lasers Surg. Med.* 18:231–40, 1996.

Weisheit, J. Spallation in active galactic nuclei. *Astrophys. J.* 465:659–65, 1996.

Murillo, M. S., and **J. Weisheit.** The electronic structure of dense plasmas. *J. Quant. Spectrosc. Radiat. Transfer* 54:271, 1996.

Ausman, K. D., and **R. B. Weisman.** Temperature-dependent kinetic studies of fullerene triplet states in solution. In *Recent Advances in the Chemistry and Physics of Fullerenes and Related Materials,* pp. 276–86, eds. K. M. Kadish and R. S. Ruoff. Pennington, New Jersey: The Electrochemical Society, 1996.

R·I·T

ROCHESTER INSTITUTE OF TECHNOLOGY

College of Science
Chester F. Carlson Center for Imaging Science

Programs of Study

The College of Science, through the Center for Imaging Science, offers both Master of Science and Doctor of Philosophy degrees within the field of imaging science. The Master of Science program consists of 45 quarter credit hours of core and elective courses in the areas of digital imaging processing, medical imaging, electrooptical imaging systems, remote sensing, color imaging, and hard-copy materials and processes. Students must enroll in either the research-thesis option or the graduate paper/project option at the beginning of their studies. The Doctor of Philosophy program signifies high achievement in scholarship and independent investigation in the diverse aspects of imaging science. Doctoral students must complete a core curriculum, successfully pass a series of examinations, and complete an acceptable dissertation.

Research Facilities

The Chester F. Carlson Center for Imaging Science is housed in a 70,000-square-foot building with thirty-six research and teaching laboratories that are dedicated to specialized areas of imaging science, including electronic imaging, digital-image processing, remote sensing, medical imaging, color science, optics, and chemical imaging.

Financial Aid

Federal, state, and institutional aid is available to those who qualify.

Cost of Study

In 1999–2000, tuition fees are $546 per credit hour for 1 to 11 credits and $6487 per quarter (12–18 credits). Fees for internships in the Master of Engineering degree programs are $290 per credit hour. An estimated cost for books and supplies for full-time students ranges from $500 to $2500. Depending on the number of courses, part-time students' books and supplies cost approximately $300 to $450. All full-time graduate students are required to pay a student activities fee of $48 per quarter. All fees are subject to change.

Living and Housing Costs

In 1999–2000, room and board for full-time students are $2284 per quarter (double-room occupancy and a standard meal plan). A variety of residence hall and apartment housing options and meal plans are available, and costs vary according to the options selected. Housing within the surrounding community is plentiful and moderately priced.

Student Group

Current enrollment for the Institute is approximately 13,000, including 8,000 full-time and 2,700 part-time undergraduates and 2,200 graduate students. The College of Science has approximately 950 undergraduates and 120 graduate students, of whom 590 are women.

Location

The campus occupies 1,300 acres in suburban Rochester, the third-largest city in New York State. Rochester has a thriving arts community that includes the International Museum of Photography, the Memorial Art Gallery, the Rochester Philharmonic Orchestra, the Eastman School of Music, and the Rochester Museum and Science Center and Planetarium. Also close by are the vineyards and wine-tasting region of the Finger Lakes and Lake Ontario. The population of the metropolitan area is approximately 1 million, with industries such as Eastman Kodak, Xerox, and Bausch & Lomb providing the area's economic base.

The Institute

Founded in 1829 and emphasizing career education, Rochester Institute of Technology (RIT) is a privately endowed coeducational university that consists of seven colleges. RIT is the fourth-oldest and one of the largest cooperative education institutions in the world, annually placing 2,600 students in co-op positions with approximately 1,300 employers. Enrolled students represent all fifty states and more than eighty other countries. The National Technical Institute for the Deaf has a current enrollment of approximately 1,200 students.

Applying

Admission to the degree programs is granted to qualified holders of a bachelor's degree from a regionally accredited university or college who have a grade point average of 3.0 on a 4.0 scale. A personal interview, the ability to write in simple computer language, and experience with a high-level language such as Pascal, FORTRAN, or C are also required. Applicants for the Doctor of Philosophy program must demonstrate proficiency on the Graduate Record Examinations (GRE). To be considered for admission, it is necessary to submit an Application for Admission to Graduate Study, accompanied by the appropriate undergraduate and graduate transcripts and two letters of recommendation. Applications are accepted on a rolling basis and must be submitted along with a $40 application fee. In addition, TOEFL scores may be required of students whose native language is not English. Applicants who seek financial aid must have all documents submitted to the Office of Financial Aid by February 15 to be considered for entry with support for the following September.

Correspondence and Information

Office of Part-Time and Graduate Enrollment Services
Rochester Institute of Technology
58 Lomb Memorial Drive
Rochester, New York 14623-5604

Telephone: 716-475-2229
E-mail: opes@rit.edu
World Wide Web: http://www.rit.edu

Rochester Institute of Technology

THE FACULTY

Jonathan S. Arney, Associate Professor; Ph.D., North Carolina.
Roy S. Berns, Richard S. Hunter Professor; Ph.D., Rensselaer.
Roger L. Easton, Associate Professor; Ph.D., Arizona.
Mark D. Fairchild, Associate Professor and Director of Munsell Color Science Laboratory; Ph.D., Rochester.
Richard Hailstone, Associate Professor; M.S., Indiana.
Joseph P. Hornak, Professor; Ph.D., Notre Dame.
Pantazis Mouroulis, Associate Professor; Ph.D., Reading (England).
Zoran Ninkov, Associate Professor; Ph.D., British Columbia.
Navalgund Rao, Associate Professor; Ph.D., Minnesota.
Harvey E. Rhody, Professor; Ph.D., Syracuse.
John Scott, Professor; Ph.D., Syracuse.

Extended Graduate Faculty

Peter G. Anderson, Professor; Ph.D., MIT.
Lynn F. Fuller, Professor; Ph.D., SUNY at Buffalo.
Guifang Li, Assistant Professor; Ph.D., Wisconsin.
Mysore Raghuveer, Associate Professor; Ph.D., Connecticut.
Bruce Smith, Assistant Professor; Ph.D., RIT.

RUTGERS, THE STATE UNIVERSITY OF NEW JERSEY, NEW BRUNSWICK

Department of Physics and Astronomy

Programs of Study

The Department of Physics and Astronomy offers programs leading to the Ph.D., M.S., M.S.T. (Master of Science for Teachers), and M.Phil. (Master of Philosophy) degrees in physics. The program for the Ph.D. degree involves an appropriate combination of research and course work, including several required courses. Most students should expect to obtain the Ph.D. degree in about five years. The qualifying examinations, including both written and oral sections, are normally taken at the beginning of the second year. No foreign languages are required. The M.S. requires a minimum of 30 credit hours, of which 6 can be devoted to research. In addition to passing an oral examination, the candidate must present either a critical essay or a thesis on some research problem. Two years are normally required to complete the M.S. program. While almost all of the currently enrolled graduate students are in the Ph.D. program, the master's programs provide attractive and useful alternatives to students who wish to complete their advanced education more quickly.

Research Facilities

The department has more than 60 faculty members. This includes new faculty members in experimental high-energy and condensed-matter physics and astronomy and expansion of programs in theoretical condensed-matter and high-energy physics and experimental surface and nuclear physics. The department is housed in a modern, fully equipped research laboratory with networks of Sun Workstations that provide easy computer access for all students and faculty members. The astrophysics group is focused on galactic dynamics and cosmology and has developed a Fabry-Perot interferometer, permanently located at the Cerro-Tololo observatory in Chile. Condensed-matter theory faculty members study strongly correlated electron systems and electronic properties of materials. The multidisciplinary Laboratory for Surface Modification includes 6 physics faculty members and members of the chemistry, materials science, and engineering departments. The research in low-temperature physics is supported by three dilution refrigerators to study the properties of liquid ^{3}He and two-dimensional electron systems. New research initiatives in experimental condensed matter probe the properties of new materials using a variety of spectroscopic probes and transport studies. High-energy theory research includes phenomenological studies and abstract approaches such as string theory and supersymmetric gauge theories. High-energy experimentalists do research with the CDF and KTeV detectors at Fermilab and SLD at SLAC. They have been involved in the discovery of the top quark, rare decay modes of neutral K mesons, and the properties of the Z0 vector boson. Nuclear physics research in both theory and experiment span a broad range of questions, from few-body systems to the limits of angular momentum and stability. Experiments are carried out at Berkeley and Argonne national labs, Yale, TJNAF in Virginia, and MAMI at Mainz, Germany.

Financial Aid

Virtually all students receive financial support from the department. First-year students are generally awarded teaching assistantships with stipends of at least $12,136 for the academic year, a waiver of tuition, and comprehensive health insurance. More advanced students frequently have research assistantships, with a current stipend of $13,956 to $14,186 for the calendar year and a waiver of tuition. Outstanding applicants may be eligible for fellowships of up to $14,000 for the calendar year. Summer jobs for teaching and research assistants are available, and research assistants and fellows may supplement their income with limited teaching assignments.

Cost of Study

The tuition for 1998–99 was $6492 per year for New Jersey residents and $9520 per year for nonresidents and is waived for students with assistantships or internships. In 1998–99, fees were $800 per year.

Living and Housing Costs

Assistantships provide modest but adequate support for students. For 1998–99, the cost of rooms in University housing for single students ranged from $4242 per academic year in a dormitory to $4844 in a University apartment shared with 3 other students. The cost of University apartments for married students for 1998–99 ranged from $563 to $716 per month.

Student Group

About 100 full-time graduate students are currently enrolled in the department; almost all of these are supported by assistantships or fellowships. Students come from a number of countries as well as from all parts of the United States.

Location

The department is located in Rutgers' Science Center in Piscataway, a pleasant suburban community about 10 minutes from urban New Brunswick in central New Jersey. Rutgers is about 35 miles from New York City, 40 miles from the New Jersey ocean beaches, and 16 miles from Princeton. Academic life in New Brunswick is enriched by lecture series, films, and, in particular, an extensive program of high-quality musical events. Athletic fields, a student center, and a recreation center are within easy walking distance.

The University and The Department

Rutgers was founded in 1766 and is now the State University of New Jersey. There are more than 48,000 students on six campuses. About 33,300 of these students, including about 4,500 graduate students, are in New Brunswick and Piscataway. The Department of Physics and Astronomy has grown significantly in recent years, with new faculty members in condensed-matter theory, high-energy theory, surface science, and astronomy. The department currently receives research support from outside sources in excess of $5.3 million per year.

Applying

All necessary forms for admission to the Graduate School and for appointment as an assistant or fellow may be obtained by writing to the address below. Applications are accepted until about July 15; applicants for financial aid are expected to apply before January 2. The GRE General Test and the Subject Test in physics are required. The Test of English as a Foreign Language (TOEFL) is required of students whose native language is not English.

Correspondence and Information

Dr. Jolie Cizewski, Graduate Program Director
Department of Physics and Astronomy
Rutgers University
136 Freylinghuysen Road
Piscataway, New Jersey 08854-8019
Telephone: 732-445-2502
Fax: 732-445-4343
E-mail: graduate@physics.rutgers.edu
World Wide Web: http://www.physics.rutgers.edu/

Rutgers, The State University of New Jersey, New Brunswick

THE FACULTY AND THEIR RESEARCH

Professors
Elihu Abrahams, Bernard Serin Professor of Physics and Astronomy; Ph.D., Berkeley, 1952. Theoretical condensed-matter physics.
Eva Y. Andrei, Ph.D., Rutgers, 1980. Experimental condensed-matter physics.
Natan Andrei, Ph.D., Princeton, 1979. Theoretical elementary particle/condensed-matter physics.
Thomas Banks, Ph.D., MIT, 1973. Theoretical elementary particle physics.
Robert Bartynski, Ph.D., Pennsylvania, 1986. Experimental condensed-matter physics.
John B. Bronzan, Ph.D., Princeton, 1963. Theoretical elementary particle physics.
Herman Y. Carr, Ph.D., Harvard, 1953. Experimental condensed-matter physics.
Sang-Wook Cheong, Ph.D. UCLA, 1989. Experimental condensed-matter physics and material science.
Jolie A. Cizewski, Associate Chair and Director of Graduate Program; Ph.D., SUNY at Stony Brook, 1978. Experimental nuclear physics.
Piers Coleman, Ph.D., Princeton, 1984. Theoretical condensed-matter physics.
Mark Croft, Ph.D., Rochester, 1977. Experimental condensed-matter physics.
Thomas Devlin, Ph.D., Berkeley, 1961. Experimental elementary particle physics.
Michael Douglas, Ph.D., Caltech, 1988. Theoretical particle physics.
Daniel Friedan, Ph.D., Berkeley, 1980. Theoretical elementary particle physics.
Eric Garfunkel, Ph.D., Berkeley, 1983. Experimental surface science.
Charles Glashausser, Ph.D., Princeton, 1966. Experimental nuclear physics.
Torgny Gustafsson, D.Sc., Chalmers (Sweden), 1973. Experimental condensed-matter physics, experimental surface physics.
David Harrington, Ph.D., Carnegie Tech, 1961. Theoretical nuclear physics.
George K. Horton, Ph.D., Birmingham (England), 1949. Theoretical condensed-matter physics.
Mohan S. Kalelkar, Undergraduate Coordinator and Associate Chair; Ph.D., Columbia, 1975. Experimental elementary particle physics.
Willem M. Kloet, Ph.D., Utrecht (Netherlands), 1973. Theoretical nuclear physics.
Haruo Kojima, Ph.D., UCLA, 1972. Experimental condensed-matter physics.
Noémie B. Koller, Associate Dean, Faculty of Arts and Science; Ph.D., Columbia, 1958. Experimental nuclear physics.
B. Gabriel Kotliar, Ph.D., Princeton, 1983. Theoretical condensed-matter physics.
Antti Kupiainen, Ph.D., Princeton, 1979. Statistical mechanics theory, math physics.
David C. Langreth, Ph.D., Illinois, 1964. Theoretical condensed-matter physics.
Paul L. Leath, Chair of the Department; Ph.D., Missouri–Columbia, 1966. Theoretical condensed-matter physics.
Joel Lebowitz, George William Hill Professor of Mathematics and Physics; Ph.D., Syracuse, 1956. Theoretical statistical mechanics, math physics.
Peter Lindenfeld, Ph.D., Columbia, 1954. Experimental condensed-matter physics.
Claud Lovelace, B.S., Cape Town (South Africa), 1954. Theoretical elementary particle physics.
Theodore Madey, Director, Surface Modification and Interface Dynamics Lab; Ph.D., Notre Dame, 1963. Experimental surface science physics, experimental condensed-matter physics.
Aram Mekjian, Ph.D., Maryland, 1968. Theoretical nuclear physics.
Andrew Millis, Ph.D., MIT, 1986. Theoretical condensed-matter physics.
Daniel E. Murnick, Ph.D., MIT, 1966. Experimental nuclear and atomic physics.
Herbert Neuberger, Ph.D., Tel Aviv, 1979. Theoretical elementary particle physics.
Joe H. Pifer, Ph.D., Illinois, 1966. Experimental condensed-matter physics.
Richard J. Plano, Ph.D., Chicago, 1956. Experimental elementary particle physics.
Ronald Rockmore, Ph.D., Columbia, 1957. Theoretical nuclear physics.
Andrei E. Ruckenstein, Ph.D., Cornell, 1984. Theoretical condensed-matter physics.
Joseph Sak, Ph.D., Institute of Solid-State Physics (Czechoslovakia), 1968. Theoretical condensed-matter physics.
Stephen R. Schnetzer, Ph.D., Berkeley, 1981. Experimental elementary particle physics.
Nathan Seiberg, Ph.D., Weizmann (Israel), 1980. Theoretical elementary particle physics.
Jeremy Sellwood, Ph.D., Manchester (England), 1977. Theoretical astrophysics.
Joel Shapiro, Ph.D., Cornell, 1967. Theoretical elementary particle physics.
Earl D. Shaw, Ph.D., Berkeley, 1969. Experimental laser physics.
Michael Stephen, D.Phil., Oxford, 1955. Theoretical condensed-matter physics.
Gordon Thomson, Ph.D., Harvard, 1972. Experimental elementary particle physics.
David Vanderbilt, Ph.D., MIT, 1981. Theoretical condensed-matter physics, theoretical surface physics.
Russell E. Walstedt, Ph.D., Berkeley, 1961. Experimental condensed-matter physics.
Terence Watts, Ph.D., Yale, 1963. Experimental elementary particle physics.
Theodore B. Williams, Ph.D., Caltech, 1974. Experimental astrophysics.
Larry Zamick, Ph.D., MIT, 1961. Theoretical nuclear physics.
Alexander Zamolodchikov, Ph.D., Institute of Theoretical and Experimental Physics (Moscow), 1978. Theoretical particle physics.
Harold S. Zapolsky, Ph.D., Cornell, 1962. Theoretical astrophysics.

Associate Professors
Ronald Gilman, Ph.D., Pennsylvania, 1985. Experimental nuclear physics.
B. Jane Hinch, Ph.D., Cambridge, 1987. Surface studies using atomic and molecular scattering.
Lev Ioffe, Ph.D., Landau Institute for Theoretical Physics (Russia), 1985. Theoretical condensed-matter physics.
Terry A. Matilsky, Ph.D., Princeton, 1971. Experimental astrophysics.
David R. Merritt, Ph.D., Princeton, 1982. Theoretical astrophysics.
Carlton Pryor, Ph.D., Harvard, 1982. Experimental astrophysics.
Ronald Ransome, Ph.D., Texas at Austin, 1981. Experimental nuclear physics.
Sunil Somalwar, Ph.D., Chicago, 1988. Experimental elementary particle physics.

Assistant Professors
John Conway, Ph.D., Chicago, 1987. Experimental elementary particle physics.
Michael E. Gershenson, Ph.D., Institute of Radio Engineering and Electronics (Moscow), 1982. Experimental condensed-matter physics.
John Hughes, Ph.D., UCLA, 1984. Observational astronomy.
Charles L. Joseph, Ph.D., Colorado, 1985. Observational astronomy and detector development.
Arthur Kosowsky, Ph.D., Chicago, 1994. Theoretical astrophysics.
Frank M. Zimmermann, Ph.D., Cornell, 1995. Experimental surface science physics.

TEMPLE UNIVERSITY
of the Commonwealth System of Higher Education

Department of Physics

Programs of Study

The department offers the M.A. and Ph.D. degrees. The M.A. program requires 24 semester hours of credit. Normally, required courses for the M.A. degree encompass 18 hours; the other 6 semester hours are used for thesis research or for additional courses. The student must also pass the M.A. comprehensive examination in physics. No specific number of graduate credits is required for the Ph.D. degree, but an approved program of graduate courses must be satisfactorily completed. A dissertation and dissertation examination are required. An M.A. degree is not necessary for the Ph.D. degree. The Ph.D. qualifying examination in physics is taken after completion of one year of graduate study. There is a one-year residence requirement for the Ph.D. degree. Students whose native language is not English must pass an examination in spoken and written English. There is no other language requirement for either the M.A. or the Ph.D. degree. Each full-time graduate student is given a desk in one of several student offices. Lecturers from other institutions describe their research activities at a weekly colloquium, and informal discussions with members of the faculty are frequent.

Research Facilities

The department is housed in completely air-conditioned Barton Hall, which has lecture halls, offices, classrooms, and laboratories. The Physics Department Library contains frequently used journals and books; several thousand additional volumes are located in the Paley Library across the street from Barton Hall. A student shop and a materials preparation facility are available. The University computer facilities include a UNIX cluster, composed of two DEC Alpha 4100s and an Alpha 8200, and an IBM 3090K (VM/XA) with two FPS-264 array processors attached. The departmental computer facilities include a local area network (LAN) of six Silicon Graphics IRIS Indigo R4000 workstations, two DEC workstations, and a Silicon Graphics R4400 workstation, all of which run the UNIX operating system. In addition, the department has numerous Pentium-class personal computers, an X terminal, and WYSE-50 terminals. The departmental local area network is connected to a fiber-optic (FDI, TCP/IP) campus backbone through which the University mainframe computers can be reached. High-speed access to the worldwide Internet is readily available to all departmental computers. Electronic information retrieval is provided by Temple University's library in the form of a GEAC online card catalog and a CD-ROM–based Scholars Information System, both of which can be searched across the network. The research laboratories are conducting a variety of studies on optical holeburning and multiple quantum well structures; laser-based molecular spectroscopy; low-temperature properties of alloys and intermetallics, including valence fluctuations and heavy fermion behavior; high temperature superconductivity; Mössbauer spectroscopy; neutrino oscillation; nucleon structure; and dark matter detectors. The department also uses outside facilities, including the Los Alamos Meson Physics Facility, the Brookhaven National Laboratory, the Stanford Linear Accelerator Center, the Thomas Jefferson National Accelerator Facility, and the National High Magnetic Laboratory. Theoretical work is being conducted in such areas as elementary particles and their interactions, statistical mechanics, biophysics, general relativity, and condensed-matter theory.

Financial Aid

Aid is available to qualified full-time students in the form of assistantships and fellowships funded by the University and various extramural agencies. All forms of financial aid include a stipend plus tuition. The specific type of aid offered to a particular student depends on the student's qualifications and program of study. Summer support for qualified students is also normally available. Current stipends are $12,400 for the academic year. For students with grant-supported research assistantships, the stipend is much higher.

Cost of Study

The annual tuition for full-time graduate study in 1998–99 was $323 per credit hour for residents of Pennsylvania and $444 per credit hour for nonresidents. Minimal fees are charged for various services, such as microfilming theses.

Living and Housing Costs

Room and board costs for students living on campus were approximately $3900 per year in 1998–99. University-sponsored apartments, both furnished and unfurnished, are also available on the edge of the campus.

Student Group

The department has approximately 25 full-time graduate students; nearly all are supported by assistantships or fellowships.

Location

Philadelphia is the fifth-largest city in the country, with a metropolitan population of more than 2 million. The city has a world-renowned symphony orchestra, a ballet company, two professional opera companies, and a chamber music society. Besides attracting touring plays, Philadelphia has a professional repertory theater and many amateur troupes. All sports and forms of recreation are easily accessible. The city is world famous for its historic shrines and parks and for the eighteenth-century charm that is carefully maintained in the oldest section. The climate is temperate, with an average winter temperature of 33 degrees and an average summer temperature of 75 degrees.

The University

The development of Temple University has been in line with the ideal of "educational opportunity for the able and deserving student of limited means." With a rich heritage of social purpose, Temple seeks to provide the opportunity for high-quality education without regard to a student's race, creed, or station in life. Affiliation with the Commonwealth System of Higher Education undergirds Temple's character as a public institution.

Applying

All application material, both for admission and for financial awards, should be received by early March for admission in the fall semester. Notification regarding admission and the awarding of an assistantship is made as soon as the application has been screened.

Correspondence and Information

For program information and all applications:
Graduate Chairman
Department of Physics 009-00
Barton Hall
Temple University
Philadelphia, Pennsylvania 19122-6052
Telephone: 215-204-7736
Fax: 215-204-5652
E-mail: physics@blue.temple.edu
World Wide Web: http://www.temple.edu/physics

For general information on graduate programs:
Dean
Graduate School
Temple University
Philadelphia, Pennsylvania 19122

Temple University

THE FACULTY AND THEIR RESEARCH

Condensed-Matter Physics
Z. Hasan, Associate Professor; Ph.D., Australian National, 1979. Optical and magneto-optical properties of solids.
C. L. Lin, Associate Professor; Ph.D., Temple, 1985. Heavy fermions, crystal fields, valence fluctuations, the Kondo effect, high-temperature superconductivity.
T. Mihalisin, Professor; Ph.D., Rochester, 1967. Crystal fields, valence fluctuations and the Kondo effect in magnetic systems.
R. Tahir-Kheli, Professor; D.Phil., Oxford, 1962. Theory of magnetism, randomly disordered systems.
T. Yuen, Associate Professor; Ph.D., Temple, 1990. Experimental condensed-matter physics, Mössbauer spectroscopy.

Educational Development Physics
The teaching of physics, creation of innovative teaching methods; use of mass media.
L. Dubeck, Professor; Ph.D., Rutgers, 1965. Development, publication, and testing of precollege science materials.
J. Karra, Associate Professor; Ph.D., Rutgers, 1964. Teaching physicist.
R. B. Weinberg, Professor Emeritus; Ph.D., Columbia, 1963. Teaching physicist.

Elementary Particle Physics and Cosmology
L. B. Auerbach, Professor; Ph.D., Berkeley, 1962. Experimental particle physics; investigations of the properties of fundamental particles at Los Alamos Meson Physics Facility, Brookhaven National Laboratory, and CERN.
Z. Dziembowski, Associate Professor; Ph.D., Warsaw, 1975. Theoretical particle physics.
J. Franklin, Professor Emeritus; Ph.D., Illinois, 1956. Theoretical particle physics; quark and parton theory, S-matrix theory.
C. J. Martoff, Professor; Ph.D., Berkeley, 1980. Experimental particle physics: investigation of weak interactions and dynamics of nuclei and particles, development of particle detectors for the study of "dark matter" using superconductivity.
Z.-E. Meziani, Professor; Ph.D., Paris, 1984. Experimental high-energy nuclear physics: investigation of the flavor and spin structure of the nucleon at the Stanford Linear Accelerator Center, search for transition region between nucleon-meson to quark-gluon description of few-body nuclear systems at the Continuous Electron Beam Accelerator Facility.
D. E. Neville, Professor; Ph.D., Chicago, 1962. Theoretical particle physics; symmetries and quark models, quantum gravity.

Optics
Z. Hasan, Associate Professor; Ph.D., Australian National, 1979. Laser materials, laser spectroscopy of solids.
M. Lyyra, Professor; Ph.D., Stockholm, 1984. Laser spectroscopy.

Relativity
P. Havas, Professor Emeritus; Ph.D., Columbia, 1944. Special and general relativity, elementary particle physics, mathematical physics.

Statistical Physics
T. Burkhardt, Professor; Ph.D., Stanford, 1967. Statistical mechanics and many-body theory.
D. Forster, Professor; Ph.D., Harvard, 1969. Statistical mechanics and many-body theory.
E. Gawlinski, Associate Professor and Chairman; Ph.D., Boston University, 1983. Statistical mechanics and computational physics.
S. Y. Larsen, Professor Emeritus; Ph.D., Columbia, 1962. Quantum statistical physics, few-body problem, hyperspherical harmonics, molecular physics, chemical reactions.

Theoretical Atomic Physics
R. L. Intemann, Professor; Ph.D., Stevens, 1964. Atomic physics, inner-shell processes.

Barton Hall, the physics building.

The Elementary Particle Physics Laboratory.

TEXAS A&M UNIVERSITY

Department of Physics

Programs of Study	The Department of Physics offers graduate studies leading to the degrees of Master of Science and Doctor of Philosophy. Major areas of research include atomic physics, quantum optics and light scattering, laser spectroscopy, low-temperature and condensed-matter physics, nuclear physics, high-energy physics, and accelerator physics, with both theoretical and experimental programs. An experimental program in medical physics is also available.
	Both thesis and nonthesis options are available for the M.S. The nonthesis option may be satisfied by successfully completing 36 hours of approved course work, including a 6-hour research project and comprehensive written and oral exams. The thesis option requires 32 hours of approved course work, including research, a research thesis, and an oral exam. The M.S. can be completed within two years. Qualified students may proceed directly to the Ph.D. program without first obtaining the M.S.
	Students in the doctoral program must pass a Ph.D. qualifying exam, usually taken at the end of the second semester of graduate study. The exam covers the material in introductory graduate courses. The Ph.D. program is tailored to the individual student's needs and normally includes several specialty or research-oriented courses in the student's field of research as well as introductory graduate courses and research. There is no language requirement. Most students take about five years to complete the requirements for the Ph.D.
Research Facilities	The physics building provides many well-equipped laboratories for experimental research. Optics and atomic research equipment includes CW narrow-bandwidth ring dye laser systems and diode laser systems; excimer, Nd:YAG, and flashlamp-pumped pulsed dye laser systems; and a 100-kV ion accelerator. Equipment for low-temperature studies includes several superconducting solenoids ranging up to 140 kG, four dilution refrigerator cryostats for studies to 0.003K, and a CTI 1400 helium liquefier. For nanostructure device fabrication, there are two molecular beam epitaxy machines operating in an 800-square-foot clean room, along with an electron-beam writer for nanolithography. For materials research, there are a clean high-vacuum thin-film evaporation facility, extensive facilities for rapid quenching of alloys, and a UHV scanning tunneling microscopy system for semiconductor surface science studies. The department has large, well-equipped machine and electronics shops and a variety of workstations. Students also have access to the University's VMS cluster, UNIX systems, a 24-processor SGI Power Challenge 1000XL, and a 16-processor Cray J90. Physics faculty and students have major programs at the Cyclotron Institute, which contains a K500 superconducting cyclotron and a powerful electron cyclotron resonance external ion source. Experimental equipment includes a K-400 magnetic spectrometer, a momentum achromat recoil mass spectrometer, a diproton spectrometer, a 4π neutron calorimeter, and a 57-element BaF_2 array.
Financial Aid	The research programs of the department are supported by University funds and grants from the federal government and private sponsors. Teaching or research fellowships and assistantships support about 105 graduate students. Research fellowships and assistantships are provided by the Office of Graduate Studies; government agencies, such as the NSF; research grants given to faculty members by private foundations, such as the Robert A. Welch Foundation; and industrial sponsors. In 1999–2000, stipends begin at $1200 per month for the academic year. Job opportunities for spouses are quite plentiful.
Cost of Study	In 1999–2000, graduate tuition and fees for Texas residents are approximately $1600 per semester for full-time students taking a total of 13 hours or $68 per semester hour for part-time students. Tuition and fees for nonresidents are approximately $4300 per semester for full-time students taking a total of 13 hours and $282 per semester hour for part-time students. Nonresident students on assistantships or fellowships pay resident tuition.
Living and Housing Costs	A limited number of University-owned apartments, both furnished and unfurnished, are available for students at $211 to $330 per month plus electricity. Further information is available from University Owned Apartments, University Mail Service, M.S. 3365. A large number of private apartments are also available in the community. For an information booklet, students can call 409-845-1741 or write to Off-Campus Center, MS1257.
Student Group	Texas A&M University has an enrollment of 43,389, including 6,746 graduate students.
Location	The Bryan–College Station area is located in south-central Texas, approximately 95 miles from Houston and 175 miles from Dallas. With a population of nearly 155,200, including the Texas A&M student body, the two cities constitute the largest urban area in this part of the state. Community facilities include excellent public and private schools, churches representing approximately twenty denominations, hospitals, cinemas, and various shopping centers.
The University	Founded in 1876 as a land-grant college under the Morrill Act, Texas A&M University began graduate training leading to the Master of Science in 1888. The first doctoral degree was conferred by the University in 1940. In recent years, the Office of Graduate Studies has grown quite rapidly, from 500 students in 1957 to its current enrollment of 6,746. More than 75 percent of all master's and professional degrees conferred by Texas A&M University and more than 85 percent of its doctorates have been granted in the past twenty years.
Applying	Inquiries regarding admission to graduate studies should be addressed to the Department of Physics. Inquiries about facilities for advanced studies, research, and requirements for graduate work in physics should also be addressed to the department. Applications for admission should be filed no later than six weeks prior to the opening of the semester. Students seeking admission with financial aid should send copies of all application materials by February 1 preceding the academic year for which the awards are sought. An application for financial aid will be considered independently of the admission decision.
Correspondence and Information	For admission: Chairman, Graduate Admissions Committee Department of Physics Texas A&M University College Station, Texas 77843-4242

For departmental information or aid:
Department of Physics
Texas A&M University
College Station, Texas 77843-4242
Telephone: 409-845-7717
E-mail: s-jones@physics.tamu.edu

Texas A&M University

THE FACULTY AND THEIR RESEARCH

Professors

Thomas W. Adair III, Head; Ph.D., Texas A&M, 1965. Magnetic effects at low temperatures.

Roland E. Allen, Ph.D., Texas at Austin, 1968. Condensed-matter theory and theory of materials.

R. L. Arnowitt, Distinguished Professor; Ph.D., Harvard, 1953. High-energy theory.

William H. Bassichis, Ph.D., Case Tech, 1963. Physics education and integrated engineering curriculum.

Ronald A. Bryan, Ph.D., Rochester, 1961. Theory of nucleon-nucleon interaction, elementary particles.

Siu Ah Chin, Ph.D., Stanford, 1975. Theoretical nuclear physics, relativistic and quantum man-body theory, Monte Carlo simulations of diverse physical systems.

David A. Church, Ph.D., Washington (Seattle), 1969. Stored-ion collisions and spectroscopy, polarization spectroscopy, multicharged ions.

Robert B. Clark, Ph.D., Yale, 1968. Theoretical particle physics, physics education.

Michael Duff, Distinguished Professor; Ph.D., Imperial College (London), 1972. High-energy theory.

Nelson M. Duller, Ph.D., Rice, 1953. Nuclear magnetic resonance, development of instrumentation for advanced undergraduate laboratories.

A. Lewis Ford, Ph.D., Texas at Austin, 1972. Theoretical atomic physics, ion-atom collisions.

Edward S. Fry, Ph.D., Michigan, 1969. Atomic and molecular spectroscopy, quantum optics, foundations of quantum mechanics, electromagnetic scattering by particles, ocean optics.

Carl A. Gagliardi, Ph.D., Princeton, 1982. Weak interactions, nuclear reactions and structure.

John C. Hiebert, Ph.D., Yale, 1964. Physics education, computers in physics education.

Chia-Ren Hu, Ph.D., Maryland, 1968. Theory of superconductivity, superfluid ^{3}He, quantum Hall effect, electromagnetic scattering, semiconductor lasers based on "lasing without inversion."

George W. Kattawar, Ph.D., Texas A&M, 1963. Atmospheric/oceanic optics, radiative transfer with both elastic and inelastic scattering in the atmosphere-ocean system.

Robert A. Kenefick, Ph.D., Florida State, 1962. High-energy atomic collision processes, ion sources, ion trap.

Wiley P. Kirk, Ph.D., SUNY at Stony Brook, 1970. Nanostructure materials and quantum device fabrication, low-temperature and condensed-matter physics, quantum solids and fluids, quantum Hall studies, low-dimensional systems, transport properties.

Che-Ming Ko, Ph.D., SUNY at Stony Brook, 1973. Theoretical nuclear physics.

Peter M. McIntyre, Ph.D., Chicago, 1972. High-energy accelerator physics, colliding beams at very high energy.

Dimitri Nanopoulos, Distinguished Professor; Ph.D., Sussex (England), 1973. High-energy theory, supersymmetry, supergravity, superstrings, astroparticle physics, neurophysics.

Donald G. Naugle, Ph.D., Texas A&M, 1965. Superconductivity, metallic glasses, calorimetry of small particles, thin metal films.

Valery Pokrovsky, Distinguished Professor; Ph.D., Kharkov (Russia), 1953. Theoretical condensed matter.

Christopher N. Pope, Ph.D., Cambridge, 1980. High-energy theory.

John F. Reading, Ph.D., Birmingham (England), 1964. Scattering theory, inner-shell ionization of atoms.

Wayne M. Saslow, Ph.D., California, Irvine, 1968. Theoretical condensed matter, electromagnetism, superfluidity.

Hans A. Schuessler, Ph.D., Heidelberg (Germany), 1964. Spectroscopy of free ions, ion storage, laser spectroscopy, online experiments at high-energy accelerators, collinear fast-beam laser spectroscopy of short-lived isotopes.

Marlan O. Scully, Distinguished Professor; Ph.D., Yale, 1966. Laser physics, quantum optics, nonequilibrium statistical mechanics, bioengineering.

Ergin Sezgin, Ph.D., SUNY at Stony Brook, 1980. High-energy theory.

Robert E. Tribble, Ph.D., Princeton, 1973. Mass measurement of exotic nuclei, nuclear reactions, weak interactions.

Robert C. Webb, Ph.D., Princeton, 1972. Electronic counter experiments in high-energy particle physics, pp and colliding-beam experiments, experimental astroparticle physics, searches for new particles.

Dave H. Youngblood, Ph.D., Rice, 1965. Nuclear structure and reactions, giant multipole resonances.

Associate Professors

Glenn Agnolet, Ph.D., Cornell, 1983. Two-dimensional phase transitions, quantum liquids, roughening transition in quantum crystals.

Teruki Kamon, Ph.D., Tsukuba (Japan), 1986. Experimental high-energy physics, CDF experiment at Fermilab.

Olga A. Kocharovskaya, Ph.D., Nizhi (Russia), 1986. Theoretical atomic physics, quantum optics, laser physics.

Joseph H. Ross Jr., Ph.D., Illinois, 1986. Magnetic resonance in solids, semiconductor structures, metal alloy ordering, low-dimensional materials, magnetic and optical coherences.

Michael B. Weimer, Ph.D., Caltech, 1986. Experimental condensed matter, surfaces and interfaces, scanning and tunneling microscopy and spectroscopy.

George R. Welch, Ph.D., MIT, 1989. Experimental atomic physics.

James T. White, Ph.D., California, San Diego, 1985. Experimental high-energy physics.

Asssistant Professor

Thomas Walther, Ph.D., Zurich (Switzerland), 1995. Experimental atomic physics, laser physics.

TUFTS UNIVERSITY

Department of Physics and Astronomy

Programs of Study

The Department of Physics and Astronomy offers programs of study leading to both M.S. and Ph.D. degrees for students interested in pursuing a wide variety of careers, including both teaching and research. Because there is a combined faculty of 21, many areas of physics and astronomy are available for study, and close faculty-student contact permits a deeper and more complete involvement in studies and research.

Candidates for the master's degree must complete eight graduate-level courses with grades of B– or better in their approved program; submission of a thesis is optional. While two semesters of residence are required, there are no language or examination requirements. The option of including research courses is also available. Each candidate is aided and advised by his or her own special committee of faculty members. Entering students should be familiar with intermediate-level physics and with mathematics through the level of calculus.

Ph.D. candidates need not fulfill a specific number of graduate courses but must demonstrate their proficiency in fundamental physics, quantum mechanics, their doctoral field, and a suitable fourth field. This may be done through course work or examinations. A preliminary oral examination is required on a subject determined by the candidate's committee, and, upon its successful completion, the committee will advise the student on further research work. Three academic years of study are required, at least one of which must be in residence; a dissertation and dissertation examination will conclude the Ph.D. program.

The areas of research in the department include experimental and theoretical particle physics, experimental and theoretical condensed-matter physics, cosmology and general relativity, theoretical molecular biophysics, and radio astronomy.

Research Facilities

Research is carried out at Tufts as well as at national institutions such as the Arecibo Laboratory, the Brookhaven National Laboratory, the Fermi National Accelerator Laboratory, the National High Magnetic Field Laboratory, the Soudan II Underground Laboratory, and the Very Large Array at the National Radio Astronomy Observatory.

Financial Aid

Both teaching and research assistantships are available, as are tuition scholarships. Stipends are intended to provide financial support adequate for basic living costs in the area. Summer research and teaching appointments are available to qualified students.

Cost of Study

Tuition for the 1999–2000 academic year is $24,804. Teaching and research assistants are charged only half this amount, which is usually covered by a tuition scholarship. For part-time students, the tuition is $2480 per course.

Living and Housing Costs

Some on-campus housing is provided for single students. In addition, the local area contains many private apartment facilities that customarily accommodate several persons, thus rendering living costs quite economical. Local public transportation is modestly priced and readily accessible.

Student Group

There are about 35 graduate students enrolled in the physics program, about half of whom conduct research during any given year. In 1997–98, one M.S. and four Ph.D. degrees were awarded.

Student Outcomes

The first jobs of the department's graduates during the past four years have been as follows: 6 have obtained postdoctoral positions in universities, 7 have obtained positions in information technology, 1 has taken a teaching position in a university, 2 have taken positions in private companies engaged in research and development, and 1 has become the president of a construction company.

Location

The Boston area offers an unusual combination of historical, cultural, and educational experiences and opportunities. Tufts University, on a small wooded campus in the suburb of Medford, is in a convenient location to take advantage of these opportunities.

The University

The University dates back to 1852 and has a proud heritage of both undergraduate and graduate achievement. There are about 5,500 students and 325 faculty members in the Faculty of Arts and Sciences. The moderate size of the student body and good student-faculty ratio foster an informal family environment not found in many larger institutions. There are many active organizations on campus, as well as a variety of local activities available for student participation.

Applying

Applications for fall admission should be received by February 15. Relevant materials may be obtained from the World Wide Web (http://www.tufts.edu/as/gsas), and applications should be sent to the Graduate School of Tufts University. There is a $50 application fee. The GRE General Test is required and appropriate Subject Tests are strongly recommended. Applicants will be considered on their individual merits for any and all available positions.

Correspondence and Information

Director of Graduate Studies
Department of Physics and Astronomy
Tufts University
Medford, Massachusetts 02155
E-mail: grasp@tuhepa.phy.tufts.edu
World Wide Web: http://www.tufts.edu/as/physics

Tufts University

THE FACULTY AND THEIR RESEARCH

David L. Weaver, Chairman; Ph.D., Iowa State, 1963. Molecular biophysics.

Peggy Cebe, Ph.D., Cornell, 1984. Experimental solid-state physics.
Allen E. Everett, Ph.D., Harvard, 1960. Theoretical particle physics, cosmology.
Lawrence H. Ford, Ph.D., Princeton, 1974. General relativity and cosmology, quantum field theory.
Gary R. Goldstein, Ph.D., Chicago, 1968. Theoretical particle physics.
Robert P. Guertin, Ph.D., Rochester, 1968. Experimental solid-state physics.
Leon Gunther, Ph.D., MIT, 1964. Theoretical solid-state physics.
Tomas Kafka, Ph.D., SUNY at Stony Brook, 1974. Experimental particle physics.
Kenneth R. Lang, Ph.D., Stanford, 1969. Astrophysics, radio astronomy.
W. Anthony Mann, Ph.D., Massachusetts, 1970. Experimental particle physics.
Kathryn A. McCarthy, Emerita; Ph.D., Harvard, 1957. Experimental solid-state physics.
Richard H. Milburn, Ph.D., Harvard, 1954. Experimental particle physics.
George S. Mumford, Emeritus; Ph.D., Virginia, 1954. Astronomy, astrophysics.
Austin Napier, Ph.D., MIT, 1978. Experimental particle physics.
William P. Oliver, Ph.D., Berkeley, 1969. Experimental particle physics.
J. Schneps, Ph.D., Wisconsin–Madison, 1956. Experimental particle physics.
Yaacov Shapira, Ph.D., MIT, 1964. Experimental solid-state physics.
Krzysztof Sliwa, Ph.D., Jagiellonian (Krakow), 1980. Experimental particle physics.
Roger G. Tobin, Ph.D., Berkeley, 1985. Experimental solid-state physics.
Alexander Vilenkin, Ph.D., SUNY at Buffalo, 1977. General relativity and cosmology, quantum field theory.
Robert F. Willson, Ph.D., Tufts, 1980. Radio astronomy, astrophysics.

RESEARCH ACTIVITIES

Theoretical
Molecular Biophysics. Dynamics of large biological molecules, models of protein folding and unfolding. (Weaver)
Condensed Matter. Macroscopic quantum tunneling, phase transitions, magnetism, superconductivity, Mössbauer effect. (Gunther)
High Energy. Quarks and quantum chromodynamics, electroweak theory, high-energy phenomenology. (Goldstein)
Cosmology and General Relativity. Physical processes in the very early universe, cosmic strings, cosmological phase transitions, quantum gravity, quantum field theory in curved space-time. (Everett, Ford, Vilenkin, 1 research associate, 2 visiting scholars)

Experimental
Astronomy. Radio interferometry of the sun, X-ray and gamma ray studies of the sun, radio observations of active stars. (Lang, Willson)
Condensed Matter. Magnetic properties of solids, high-temperature superconductors, polymer physics, surface physics. (Cebe, Guertin, Shapira, Tobin)
High Energy. Search for neutrino oscillations using atmospheric neutrinos and neutrinos at accelerators, nucleon decay, study of the top quark, search for Higgs particles, supersymmetry, physics beyond the standard model, charm and bottom spectroscopy, development of software tools for collider experiments, design of fully distributed computing systems.

SELECTED PUBLICATIONS

Cebe, P. Introduction to scattering from polymers. In *Scattering from Polymers: X-ray, Neutron, and Light*, pp. 1–20, eds. P. Cebe, B. Hsiao, and D. Lohse. ACS Symposium Series, 1999.

Rich, D. C., et al. **(P. Cebe).** Alignment layer relaxation: A method for assessing thermal transitions in polymer films. *Polymer Commun.* 39:7135, 1998.

Lu, S. X., et al. **(P. Cebe).** Effects of molecular weight on amorphous phase structure in poly(phenylene sulfide). *Macromolecules* 30: 6243, 1997.

Cheng, Y.-Y. et al. **(P. Cebe).** Modulated differential scanning calorimetry study of blends of poly(butylene terephthalate) with polycarbonate. *Thermochim. Acta*, special issue: "Temperature Modulated Calorimetry" 304(305):369, 1997.

Everett, A. E., and T. A. Roman. Superluminal subway: The Krasniko v Tube. *Phys. Rev. D* 56:2100, 1997.

Everett, A. E. Warp drive and causality. *Phys. Rev. D.* 53:7365, 1996.

Everett, A. E. Colored monopoles, Cheshire color, and fractional electric charge. *Phys. Rev. D* 50:2920, 1994.

Pfenning, M. J., and **L. H. Ford.** Quantum inequalities on the energy density in static Robertson-Walker spacetimes. *Phys. Rev. D* 55:4813, 1997.

Pfenning, M. J., and **L. H. Ford.** The unphysical nature of warp drive. *Class. Quant. Grav.* 14:1743, 1997.

Ford, L. H., and N. F. Svaiter. Cosmological and black hole horizon fluctuations. *Phys. Rev. D* 56:2226, 1997.

Ford, L. H. Electromagnetic vacuum fluctuations and electron coherence II: Effects of wave packet size. *Phys. Rev. A* 56:1812, 1997.

Ford, L. H., and T. A. Roman. Quantum field theory constrains traversable wormhole geometries. *Phys. Rev. D* 53:5496, 1996.

Goldstein, G. R. Spin correlations in top quark production and the top quark mass. *Proc. 12th Intl. Symp. on High Energy Spin Physics, "Spin 96,"* ed. C. W. deJager. Singapore: World Scientific, 1997.

Adamov, A., and **G. R. Goldstein.** Fragmentation functions for baryons in a diquark-quark model. *Phys. Rev. D* 56:7381, 1997.

Dharmaratna, W. G., and **G. R. Goldstein.** Single particle polarizations in QCD subprocesses. *Phys. Rev. D* 53:1073, 1996.

Chen, K., **G. R. Goldstein,** R. L. Jaffe, and X. Ji. Probing quark fragmentation functions for spin-1/2 Baryon production in unpolarized e+e-annihilation. *Nucl. Phys.* B445:380, 1995.

Goldstein, G. R., R. L. Jaffe, and X. Ji. Soffer's inequality. *Phys. Rev. D* 52:5006, 1995.

Liebl, H., and **G. R. Goldstein.** Electromagnetic polarizabilities and charge radii of the nucleons in the diquark-model. *Phys. Letters B* 343:363, 1995.

Dalitz, R. H., and **G. R. Goldstein.** Where is top? *Int. J. Modern Phys.* A9:635, 1994.

Gunther, L. Spin tunneling in a swept field. *Europhys. Lett.* 39:1, 1997.

Gunther, L. Hysteresis research is a priority issue. *Phys. Today* 50:98, 1997.

Gunther, L., and H. Simanjuntak. Nucleation of the phase of a finite Josephson junction. *J. Phys. Cond. Matt.* 9:2075, 1997.

Gunther, L., et al. Determination of the energy barrier distribution and prefactor for switching in a heterogeneous magnetic system. *J. Magn. Magn. Mat.* 140:661, 1995.

Gunther, L., and B. Barbara. Quantum tunneling across a domain wall junction—The DWJ. *Phys. Rev. B* 49:3926, 1994.

Benjamin, D., et al. **(T. Kafka, W. A. Mann, R. Milburn, A. Napier, W. Oliver,** and **J. Schneps).** Tracking calorimeter modules for the Soudan-2 detector. *Nucl. Inst. Methods*, in press.

Benjamin, D., et al. **(T. Kafka, W. A. Mann, R. Milburn, A. Napier, W. Oliver,** and **J. Schneps).** Ultra high energy cosmic ray composition from simultaneous surface air shower and underground measurements at Soudan 2. *Phys. Rev. D* 52:2760, 1995.

Lang, K. R. Magnificent cosmos. *Sci. Am.*, in press.

Lang, K. R. *Astrophysical Formulae*, third completely revised edition. New York: Springer-Verlag, 1998.

Lang, K. R. SOHO reveals secrets of the sun. *Sci. Am.* 276:32, 1997.

Lang, K. R. Radio evidence for nonthermal magnetic activity on main-sequence stars of late spectral type. *Int. Astronom. Union Colloq. No. 143, Magnetodynamic phenomena in the solar atmosphere.* Makuhari, Japan, 1996.

Lang, K. R. *Sun, Earth and Sky.* New York: Springer-Verlag, 1995.

Lang, K. R. Radio evidence for nonthermal particle acceleration on stars of late spectral type. *Astrophys. J. Supp.* 90:753, 1994.

Lang, K. R. Very large array observations of large-scale coronal structures. *Int. Astronom. Union Colloq. No. 144. Solar Coronal Structures.* Veda Pub., 1994.

Lang, K. R., et al. Particle acceleration and flare triggering in large-scale magnetic loops joining widely-spaced active regions. *Astrophys. J.* 418:490, 1993.

Lang, K. R., et al. Magnetospheres of solar active regions inferred from spectral-polarization observations with high spatial resolution. *Astrophys. J.* 419:398, 1993.

Lang, K. R. *Astrophysical Data—Planets and Stars.* New York: Springer-Verlag, 1992.

Lang, K. R. *Wanderers in Space—Exploration and Discovery in the Solar System.* New York: Cambridge University Press, 1991.

Mann, W. A., et al. Search for the proton decay mode p into nu K+ in Soudan 2. *Phys. Lett. B* 427:217, 1998.

Mann, W. A., et al. Measurements of the atmospheric neutrino flavor composition in Soudan 2. *Phys. Lett. B* 391:491, 1997.

Alves, G. A., et al. **(A. Napier).** Feynman-x and transverse momentum dependence of D meson production in 250 GeV π, K, and p interactions with nuclei. *Phys. Rev. Lett.* 77:2392, 1996.

Aitala, E. M., et al. **(A. Napier).** Search for D^0-$\bar{D}^0$ mixing in semileptonic decay modes. *Phys. Rev. Lett.* 77:2384, 1996.

Napier, A., et al. Asymmetries between the production of D+ and D-mesons from 500-GEV/C PI-nucleon interactions as a function of X_F and P_T**2. Fermilab-pub-96-001-E, Jan. 1996. *Phys. Lett. B* 371:157, 1996.

Napier, A., et al. Search for the flavor changing neutral current decays D+ - pi+mu+mu- and D+ - pi+e+e-, Fermilab-pub-95-142-E, June 1995. *Phys. Rev. Lett.* 76:364–7, 1996.

Napier, A. Results on D0/Anti-D0 mixing and doubly cabibbo suppressed decays. Fermilab E791, 5th Conference on the Intersections Between Particle and Nuclear Physics, St. Petersburg, FL, June 1994. In *AIP Conference Proceedings 338*, p. 243, ed. S. Seestrom. AIP Press, 1995.

Napier, A., et al. Ultrahigh-energy cosmic ray composition from surface air shower and underground muon measurements at Soudan-2. *Phys. Rev. D* 52:2760–5, 1995.

Oliver, W., et al. The atmospheric neutrino anomaly in Soudan-2. *Nucl. Phys. B (Proc. Suppl.)* 38:337, 1995.

Oliver, W., et al. Ultra high energy cosmic ray composition from simultaneous surface air shower and underground measurements at Soudan 2. *Phys. Rev. D* 52:2769, 1995.

Schneps, J. Neutrino oscillation projects in the U.S.A. Proceedings of the 16th international conference on neutrino physics and astrophysics, Eilat, Israel. *Nucl. Phys. (Proc. Suppl.)* 38:220–8, 1995.

Schneps, J., et al. Ultra high energy cosmic ray composition from surface air shower and underground muon measurements at Soudan 2. *Phys. Rev. D* 52:2760, 1995.

Schneps, J., et al. Neutral strange particle production in neutrino and antineutrino charged-current interactions on neon. *Phys. Rev. D* 50:6691, 1994.

Schneps, J. High-energy physics (Death of a supercollider). *Issues: Arts, Sciences and Technology at Tufts* Vol. 1, No. 2, Spring 1994.

Shapira, Y., et al. Magnetization steps in [Fe(salen)Cl]2. *Phys. Rev. B* 59:1046, 1999.

Tufts University

Selected Publications (continued)

Bindilatti, V., et al. **(Y. Shapira)**. Distant-neighbor exchange constants in dilute magnetic semiconductors. *Phys. Rev. Lett.* 80:5425, 1998.

Fries, T., et al. **(Y. Shapira)**. Magnetic ordering of the antiferromagnet Cu_2MnSnS_4 from magnetization and neutron-diffraction measurements. *Phys. Rev. B* 56:5424, 1997.

McCabe, G. H., et al. **(Y. Shapira)**. Bound magnetic polarons in p-type $Cu_2Mn_{0.9}Zn_{0.1}SnS_4$. *Phys. Rev. B* 56:6673, 1997.

Abe, F., et al. **(K. Sliwa)**. Search for chargino-neutrlino production in pp collisions at $\sqrt{s}$=1.8 TeV. *Phys. Rev. Lett.* 7:4307, 1996.

Abe, F., et al. **(K. Sliwa)**. Search of charged Higgs decays of the top quark using hadronic tau decays. *Phys. Rev. D* 54:735, 1996.

Wang, H., et al. **(R. G. Tobin)**. Reactions of N and NO on Pt(335). *J. Chem. Phys.* 107:9569, 1997.

Krastev, E. T., et al. **(R. G. Tobin)**. Multiple mechanisms for adsorbate-induced resistivity: Oxygen and formate on Cu(100). *Surface Sci. Lett.* 387:L1051, 1997.

Skelton, D. C., et al. **(R. G. Tobin)**. Oxidation of CO on gold-covered Pt(335). *J. Phys. Chem.* 103:964, 1999.

Wang, H., et al. **(R. G. Tobin)**. Absorption and dissociation of oxygen on Pt(335). *Surf. Sci.* 372:267, 1997.

Cho, I., and **A. Vilenkin**. Vacuum defects without vacuum. *Phys. Rev. D* 59:1701, 1999.

Vilenkin, A. Unambiguous probabilities in an externally inflating universe. *Phys. Rev. Lett.* 81:5501, 1998.

Garriga, J., and **A. Vilenkin**. Recycling universe. *Phys. Rev. D* 57:2230, 1998.

Berezinsky, M., et al. **(A. Vilenkin)**. Ultrahigh-energy cosmic rays without GZK cutoff. *Phys. Rev. Lett.* 79:4302, 1997.

Damour, T., and **A. Vilenkin**. Cosmic strings and string dilation. *Phys. Rev. Lett.* 78:2288, 1997.

Vilenkin, A. String theory and inflation. *Phys. Rev. D* 53:2981, 1996.

Vilenkin A. Predictions from quantum cosmology. *Phys. Rev. Lett.* 74:846, 1995.

Vilenkin, A., E. Chudnovsky, and A. Ferrera. Quantum depinning of flux lines from columnar defects. *Phys. Rev. B* 51:1181, 1995.

Vilenkin, A., and T. Kibble. Phase equilibration in bubble collisions. *Phys. Rev. D* 52:679, 1995.

Vilenkin, A. Defect production in slow first-order phase transitions. *Phys. Rev. D* 52:1934, 1995.

Vilenkin, A. Making predictions in an eternally inflating universe. *Phys. Rev. D.* 52:3365, 1995.

Vilenkin, A., and E. Chudnovsky. Vortex pairs in 2-d superconductors. *J. Phys. C*7:6501, 1995.

Weaver, D. L. Connection between back-reaction boundary conditions and approach to equilibrium for double square wells. *J. Chem. Phys.,* in press.

Pappu, R. V., and **D. L. Weaver**. The early folding of kinetics of apomyoglobin. *Protein Sci.* 7:480, 1998.

Pappu, R. V., W. J. Schneller, and **D. L. Weaver**. Electrostatic multipole representation of polypeptide chain: An algorithm for the simulation of polypeptide properties. *J. Comput. Chem.* 17:1033, 1996.

Yapa, K. K., and **D. L. Weaver**. Protein folding dynamics: Application of the diffusion-collision model to the folding of a four-helix bundle. *J. Phys. Chem.* 100:2498–509, 1996.

Fezoui, Y., **D. L. Weaver,** and J. J. Osterhout. Strategies and rationales for the de novo design of a helical hairpin peptide. *Prot. Sci.* 4:286–95, 1995.

Karplus, M., and **D. L. Weaver**. Protein folding dynamics: The diffusion-collision model and experimental data. *Prot. Sci.* 3:650–68, 1994.

Fezoui, Y., **D. L. Weaver,** and J. J. Osterhout. DeNova design and structural characterization of an α-helical hairpin peptide ($\alpha t\alpha$): A novel model for the study of protein folding intermediates. *Proc. Natl. Acad. Sci. U.S.A.* 91:3675–9, 1994.

Weaver, T. D., S. A. Islam, and **Weaver, D. L.** MacMolecular: A program for visualization of molecular structures on the Macintosh. *J. Mol. Graph.* 12:231–4, 1994.

Willson, R. F. VLA Observations of interconnected noise storm emission on the sun. In *Proceedings of the 9th Workshop on Cool Stars, Stellar Systems and the Sun,* in press.

Willson, R. F., J. N. Kile, and B. Rothberg. Very large array observations in evolving noise storm sources on the sun. *Solar Phys.,* 1996.

Willson, R. F., et al. **(R. F. Lang)**. Noise storms, soft X-rays and inversion of radio polarization. *Adv. Space Res.* 17:265, 1995.

Bogod, V. M., et al. **(R. F. Willson** and **K. R. Lang)**. Noise storms and the structure of microwave emission of solar active regions. *Solar Phys.* 160:133, 1995.

UNIVERSITY OF CALIFORNIA, SAN DIEGO

Department of Physics

Programs of Study

Graduate students from the Department of Physics are drawn from the upper ranks of the finest colleges and universities throughout the world. The department offers curricula leading to the M.S. and Ph.D. degrees in physics and the Ph.D. in physics/biophysics. A flexible program consisting of course work, research apprenticeships, teaching experience, and thesis research permits students to emphasize their special interests while simultaneously providing a broad, advanced education. Since its inception, the Department of Physics at the University of California, San Diego (UCSD), has been counted among the leading departments in the country. The faculty includes 9 members of the National Academy of Science, 13 members of the American Academy of Arts and Sciences, and 2 fellows of the Royal Society of London. Faculty members have received many prestigious prizes, including the National Medal of Science, Fermi Prize, Maxwell Prize, Matteucci Medal of the Accademia Nationale Delle Scienze of Italy, Heinemann Prize, Buckley Prize, Warner Prize, APS Biophysics Prize, and London Prize. Research activity occurs in an unusually broad range of areas. Substantial groups exist in astrophysics and astronomy, biophysics, condensed-matter physics, controlled fusion and plasma physics, elementary particle physics, and nonlinear dynamics. The requirements for the Ph.D. are written and oral qualifier exams, five advanced courses, teaching experience, advancement to candidacy, and defense of the thesis. Graduates go on to faculty, research, and industrial positions.

Research Facilities

The wide range of research interests represented in the department is reflected in its association with a number of campus research institutes and centers, including the Center for Astrophysics & Space Science (CASS), the Center for Magnetic Recording Research (CMRR), the Institute for Nonlinear Science (INLS), the Institute for Pure and Applied Physics Sciences (IPAPS), and the California Space Institute. Interdisciplinary collaborations with colleagues in other natural science and engineering departments, the Scripps Institution of Oceanography, and the School of Medicine are common. Weekly colloquia and seminars promote social interaction while introducing participants to a wide range of forefront research. Departmental facilities include excellent electronics and machine shops, a liquid He facility, and extensive computing facilities. Additional computing support is available from the campus-based San Diego Supercomputing Center (SDSC). The campus libraries maintain a superb collection of books and journals in physics and related fields.

Financial Aid

The department generally provides full tuition and fees for all graduate students not supported by outside scholarships, typically by a combination of research fellowships, research assistantships, and teaching assistantships. Support is also usually available during the summer.

Cost of Study

Tuition and fees are provided in almost all cases for graduate students as described above.

Living and Housing Costs

UCSD provides 802 apartments for graduate students. Monthly rates start at $495 for a coast studio, $318 for a single room in single graduate apartments, and $657 for married graduate student housing. There is also a variety of off-campus housing available in the surrounding communities. Prevailing rates range from $270 per month for a room in a private home to $1000 or more for a two bedroom apartment. Information about housing may be obtained from the UCSD Housing Office Web site (http://hdsu.ucsd.edu/hsgaffil/affhome.htm).

Student Group

Current campus enrollment is 19,282, which includes 15,840 undergraduate students and 3,442 graduate students. The Department of Physics has a current graduate enrollment of 109 (32 international students and 77 domestic students).

Location

UCSD overlooks the Pacific Ocean from a 1,000-acre site in La Jolla. The Mexican border at Tijuana is 30 miles south of the campus; beyond it stretches the isolated and beautiful seacoast of Baja California. Fifty miles to the east, the Cuyamaca Mountains rise 6,000 feet, and beyond them is the Anza-Borrego Desert. The climate is one of the finest in the world; winters are frost-free, with little rain, and ocean breezes guarantee pleasant summers. San Diego's scenic beauty and superb climate provide an unparalleled setting in which to live and study. Local cultural activities include off-Broadway premiers at the Old Globe Theatre and La Jolla Playhouse, musical events ranging from rock-and-roll to opera, and many film and fine arts exhibitions. Recreational opportunities abound; cycling, jogging, and sailing are year-round activities and winter sports venues are within easy driving distance. San Diego is also home to a vibrant research community that includes many companies and research institutes in the high-technology and biomedical industries. Nearby universities include California Institute of Technology; University of California, Los Angeles; University of California, Riverside; and University of California, Irvine.

The University

The University of California, San Diego, is recognized throughout the academic world for the eminence of its faculty members and for the quality of its instructional programs. One of the youngest of the nine campuses of the University of California, UCSD has already achieved a stature comparable to that of institutions founded a century or more ago. The high caliber of faculty members and research staff members attracts federal research grant funding equaled by few other academic centers in the nation. UCSD ranks third in the nation and first in the UC system, according to the amount of federal research dollars the campus spends on research development.

Applying

The graduate application deadline is February 15, 2000. Applicants must complete the UCSD application and a statement of purpose and submit official school transcripts, three letters of recommendation, and official GRE exam score reports (General and Subject Tests). Students from non-English-speaking countries are required to demonstrate proficiency in English via the TOEFL. The minimum TOEFL score required is 550 (paper-based) and 220 (computer-based).

Correspondence and Information:

Graduate Program Coordinator
Graduate Admissions Office
Department of Physics
University of California, San Diego
9500 Gilman Drive
La Jolla, California 92093-0354
Telephone: 858-534-3293
Fax: 858-534-0262
E-mail: dbomar@physics.ucsd.edu
World Wide Web: http://physics.ucsd.edu

University of California, San Diego

THE FACULTY AND THEIR RESEARCH

D. I. Abarbanel, Professor; Ph.D. Princeton, 1966. Nonlinear dynamics of fluids, optical systems and neural assemblies, geophysical fluid dynamics and physical oceanography.

Daniel P. Arovas, Professor; California, Santa Barbara, 1986. Condensed-matter theory, statistical mechanics.

Dmitri N. Bassov, Assistant Professor; Ph.D., Lebedev Institute (Russia), 1991. Experimental condensed matter.

Ami E. Berkowitz, Research Professor; Ph.D., Pennsylvania, 1953. Magnetic materials investigations, correlation of microstructures with magnetic behavior, surface effects, relaxation phenomena.

James G. Branson, Professor; Ph.D., Princeton, 1977. Experimental elementary particle physics.

Keith A. Brueckner, Professor Emeritus and Research Professor; Ph.D., Berkeley, 1950. Theoretical nuclear physics, statistical mechanics, plasma physics, interaction of lasers with matter, magnetohydrodynamics, theory of metals.

E. Margaret Burbidge, University Professor Emeritus; Ph.D., London Observatory, 1943. Extragalactic studies, spectrophotometric, and imaging; observational work on normal galaxies; galaxies; galaxies with active nuclei, especially radio galaxies; quasars.

Geoffrey R. Burbidge, Professor; Ph.D., London, 1951. Theoretical astrophysics, extragalactic astronomy, nuclear astrophysics, observational cosmology.

Joseph C. Y. Chen, Professor; Ph.D., Notre Dame, 1961. Theory of atomic and molecular structure and processes, history and philosophy of science.

Patrick H. Diamond, Professor; Ph.D., MIT, 1979. Theoretical plasma physics and astrophysics, nonlinear dynamics.

C. Fred Driscoll, Professor; Ph.D., California, San Diego, 1976. Experimental plasma physics, waves and transport in pure electron and pure ion plasmas, 2-D fluid dynamics and turbulence.

Daniel H. E. Dubin, Associate Professor; Ph.D. Princeton, 1984. Theoretical plasma physics.

Robert C. Dynes, Professor and Chancellor; Ph.D., McMaster, 1968. Experimental condensed-matter physics, low-temperature physics, superconductivity, transport.

George Feher, Research Professor Emeritus; Ph.D., Berkeley, 1954. Biophysics, photosynthesis, magnetic resonance, mechanisms of crystallization of macromolecules.

Donald R. Fredkin, Professor; Ph.D., Princeton, 1961. Solid-state theory, applied magnetics, biophysics.

George M. Fuller, Professor; Ph.D., Caltech, 1981. Theoretical astrophysics, nuclear and elementary particle physics.

Marvin L. Goldberger, Professor; Ph.D., Chicago, 1948. Elementary particle physics, quantum field theory, collision theory.

John M. Goodkind, Professor; Ph.D., Duke, 1960. Low-temperature experimental research, 2-D electrons, solid He, gravity, geophysical and fundamental quantum physics.

Robert J. Gould, Research Professor Emeritus; Ph.D., Cornell, 1963. Theoretical physics; statistical mechanics, atomic, and electromagnetic processes, with applications in astrophysics.

Kim Griest, Professor; Ph.D., California, Santa Cruz, 1987. Theoretical and observational astrophysics, theoretical elementary particle physics, dark matter.

Benjamin Grinstein, Professor; Ph.D., Harvard, 1984. Elementary particle theory.

Frances Hellman, Associate Professor; Ph.D., Stanford, 1985. Experimental condensed-matter physics and materials science; biophysics, magnetism, and amorphous metals; superconductivity; high-sensitivity calorimetry.

Jorge E. Hirsch, Professor; Ph.D., Chicago, 1980. Condensed-matter theory.

Terence T.-L. Hwa, Professor; Ph.D., MIT, 1990. Phase transition and critical phenomena, statistical mechanics, biopolymers, condensed-matter physics, dynamics of complex systems.

Kenneth A. Intriligator, Associate Professor; Ph.D., Harvard, 1992. Theoretical high-energy physics.

Elizabeth E. Jenkins, Associate Professor; Ph.D., Harvard, 1989. Elementary particle theory.

Barbara Jones, Professor; Ph.D., London, 1976. Infrared astrophysics, galactic and extragalactic astronomy, astronomical instrumentation.

David Kleinfeld, Professor; California, San Diego, 1984. Computational neuroscience and membrane biophysics.

Norman M. Kroll, Research Professor Emeritus; Ph.D., Columbia, 1948. Elementary particle theory and the quantum theory of fields, nonlinear optics and quantum electronics, free-electron lasers, accelerator.

Julius Kuti, Professor; Ph.D., Hungary, 1967. Elementary particles and fields.

Herbert Levine, Professor; Ph.D., Princeton, 1979. Theoretical nonlinear dynamics, biophysics, condensed-matter physics.

David B. MacFarlane, Professor; Ph.D., Caltech, 1984. Experimental high-energy physics.

Aneesh V. Manohar, Professor; Ph.D., Harvard, 1983. Elementary particle physics.

M. Brian Maple, Professor; Ph.D., California, San Diego, 1969. Superconductivity, magnetism, properties of alloys, high-pressure physics, surface physics, catalysis.

George E. Masek, Research Professor Emeritus; Ph.D., Stanford, 1956. Experimental high-energy physics.

Carl E. McIlwain, Research Professor Emeritus; Iowa, 1960. Space physics, experimental and theoretical studies of planetary magnetospheres, observational and instrumental astrophysics.

Xuong Nguyen-Huu, Professor; Ph.D., Berkeley, 1962. Biophysics, protein crystallography, advanced pixel array detectors for X-rays.

Melvin Y. Okamura, Professor; Ph.D., Northwestern, 1970. Biophysical (optical and magnetic resonance) studies of photosynthetic reaction centers.

Thomas M. O'Neil, Professor and Chairman; California, San Diego, 1965. Theoretical plasma physics.

Jose N. Onuchic, Professor; Ph.D., Caltech, 1987. Theoretical biophysics and chemical physics, theoretical studies in electron transfer reactions in chemical and biological systems.

Hans P. Paar, Professor; Ph.D., Columbia, 1974. Experimental high-energy physics.

Laurence E. Peterson, Research Professor Emeritus; Ph.D., Minnesota, 1960. X-ray and gamma-ray astronomy, cosmic rays, space physics, balloon and satellite instrumentation.

Oreste Piccioni, Professor Emeritus; Ph.D., Rome, 1938. Properties of elementary particles, theory and experiments on the Einstein-Podolsky-Rosen paradox.

Andreas Quirrenbach, Professor; Ph.D., Bonn, 1990. Observational astronomy.

Scot R. Renn, Assistant Professor; Ph.D., Pennsylvania, 1987. Condensed-matter theory and mesoscopic physics.

Sally K. Ride, Professor; Ph.D., Stanford, 1978. Beam wave interactions, free-electron lasers, space plasma physics.

Marshall N. Rosenbluth, Research Professor Emeritus; Ph.D., Chicago, 1949. Theoretical plasma physics.

Ivan K. Schuller, Professor; Ph.D., Northwestern, 1976. Experimental condensed-matter physics and materials science.

Sheldon Schultz, Research Professor Emeritus; Ph.D., Columbia, 1960. Magnetic recording particles; photonic band gap structures; plasmon resonant particles; advanced instrumentation in biotechnology, magnetic recording, and scanning near-field optical microscopy.

Lu J. Sham, Professor; Ph.D., Cambridge, 1963. Condensed-matter theory.

Vitali D. Shapiro, Professor; Sc., Novosibirsk (Russia), 1967. Space plasma physics: nonlinear plasma theory, fluid turbulence.

Vivek A. Sharma, Associate Professor; Ph.D., Syracuse, 1990. Experimental high-energy physics.

H. Gene Smith, Professor; Ph.D., Berkeley, 1974. Observational extragalactic astrophysics; infrared galaxies, active galaxies, and quasi-stellar objects; galaxy evolution and observational cosmology.

Harry Suhl, Research Professor Emeritus; Ph.D., Oxford, 1948. Theoretical solid state physics, particularly superconductivity, magnetism, and surface kinetics; nonlinear dynamics.

Clifford M. Surko, Professor; Ph.D., Berkeley, 1968. Experimental studies of nonlinear and nonequilibrium phenomena; plasma physics, using positrons and positron-matter interactions.

Robert A. Swanson, Research Professor Emeritus; Ph.D., Chicago, 1958. Experiments involving properties and interactions of elementary particles, interference and decay of neutral K-mesons, deep inelastic muon scattering, nucleon structure and fragmentation.

Harold Ticho, Professor Emeritus; Ph.D., Chicago, 1949. Experimental elementary particle physics.

David R. Tytler, Professor; Ph.D., London, 1982. Cosmology and galaxy formation; quasars; ultraviolet, optical, and infrared observations; telescopes and astronomical instrumentation; other planetary systems.

Wayne Vernon, Research Professor Emeritus; Ph.D., Princeton, 1965. Properties of elementary particles and their interactions, neutrino physics and astrophysics, particle detectors and acceleration techniques.

Arthur M. Wolfe, Professor; Texas, 1967. Observational cosmology, galaxy formation, velocity fields in protogalaxies.

David Y. Wong, Research Professor Emeritus; Ph.D., Maryland, 1958. Theoretical high-energy physics.

Herbert F. York, Professor Emeritus; Ph.D., Berkeley, 1949. Science and public policy.

UNIVERSITY OF CENTRAL FLORIDA

School of Optics

Programs of Study

The School of Optics is a graduate institute for optical science and engineering education and research that offers master's (M.S.) and doctoral (Ph.D.) degree programs in optics for qualified students who hold undergraduate degrees in engineering, physics, or a closely related field. It is one of only three independent academic departments in the nation offering degrees in optics. The Center for Research and Education in Optics and Lasers (CREOL) is the research arm of the School of Optics. The M.S. program has two options. The thesis option requires 36 credit hours (including 6 thesis hours), and the nonthesis option requires 36 credit hours. The Ph.D. program requires a total of 57 credit hours of course work (including up to 36 hours from the M.S. program) and 15 dissertation hours. The University of Central Florida (UCF) also offers M.S. and Ph.D. degree programs in electrical engineering (electrooptics) and in optical physics.

Research Facilities

Research activities are performed at the state-of-the-art, 82,000-square-foot building dedicated to optics, photonics, and laser education and research. The facility houses ninety research laboratories equipped with more than $40 million of state-of-the-art equipment. Current active research areas include guided-wave optics and devices, ultrafast photonics, nonlinear optics, optoelectronics, fiber communication devices, photonic information processing, infrared systems, image analysis, medical imaging, diffractive optics, solid-state lasers, development and growth of laser-host and nonlinear crystals, X-ray optics and applications, optical glasses, laser materials processing, high-intensity lasers, and wave propagation in random media. These research programs are supported by more than $7 million in research grants and contracts from numerous federal and state agencies and from industry.

Financial Aid

National Science Foundation Graduate Traineeships, CREOL Fellowships, and graduate research assistantships are available to qualified students. The stipend ranges from $14,000 to $18,000 per calendar year. Exceptional students are considered for additional Litton Fellowships of up to $4000. Full tuition, estimated at $9000 per year, is provided for students receiving graduate fellowships and research assistantships.

Cost of Study

Current tuition is $136.89 per credit hour for in-state students and $480.45 per credit hour for out-of-state students. Health fees and books and supplies are estimated at $350 per semester.

Living and Housing Costs

The cost of living is at or below the national average, and Florida does not impose a state income tax. University housing is not available for graduate students. Many apartments are available near campus, with rent ranging from $400 per month for one-bedroom units to $600 per month for two-bedroom units.

Student Group

Local student chapters of IEEE-LEOS, the Optical Society of America (OSA), and the International Society for Optical Engineering (SPIE) are very active at the School of Optics and CREOL. Currently, there are more than 100 graduate students performing M.S. thesis and Ph.D. dissertation research in optics, photonics, electrooptics, and optical physics at CREOL.

Student Outcomes

M.S. and Ph.D. graduates with specializations in optical science and engineering, electrooptics, and lasers are currently in high demand and are employed in high-technology corporations, small start-up companies, government and corporate research laboratories, and academia (Ph.D. graduates).

Location

UCF is located in Orlando, Florida, which has a metropolitan population of more than 1 million residents. The region has been experiencing dramatic growth, particularly in high-technology industries, including aerospace, electrooptics, lasers, and microelectronics. The region enjoys moderate temperatures year-round. Extensive outdoor activities are available at nearby lakes, waterways, wetlands, and the Atlantic Ocean.

The University

UCF is a growing metropolitan university, with enrollment exceeding 29,900 students. The University offers advanced graduate programs that match institutional strengths with evolving regional and national needs. The School of Optics/CREOL is the Florida State University System Center of Excellence for research and education in optical science and engineering. It has grown to be an internationally recognized institute with 21 tenured and tenure-track faculty members and 7 associate members from other academic units at UCF as well as 25 Ph.D.-level research scientists.

Applying

The optics program is intended for students with B.S. and/or M.S. degrees in electrical engineering, physics, or optics. Students with degrees in related fields may be required to take articulation courses. The minimum admission requirements for the M.S. program are a GPA of 3.0 (on a 4.0 scale) in the last 60 attempted semester hours of the B.S. degree and a GRE combined score of 1000 in the quantitative and verbal portions. For the Ph.D. program, the minimum requirements are a GPA of 3.5 in the M.S. program and a combined GRE score of 1100. A minimum TOEFL score of 213 (computer-based) is required if the applicant's previous degree(s) were obtained in a country in which English is not the official language. The priority application deadline for traineeship/fellowship/assistantship support is February 1.

Correspondence and Information

To obtain more information or to receive an admission packet, students should complete the preapplication form found on line at the Web address below or contact:

Dr. M. G. Moharam
Professor of Optics and Electrical and Computer Engineering and Associate Director
School of Optics/CREOL
University of Central Florida
P.O. Box 162700
Orlando, Florida 32816-2700
Telephone: 407-823-6833
Fax: 407-823-6810
E-mail: moharam@creol.ucf.edu
World Wide Web: http://www.creol.ucf.edu

University of Central Florida

THE FACULTY AND THEIR RESEARCH
SCHOOL OF OPTICS
Mike Bass, Professor of Optics, Physics, and Electrical and Computer Engineering; Ph.D., Michigan. Solid-state lasers, laser machining, laser medicine, light-matter interactions.

Glenn Boreman, Professor of Optics and Electrical and Computer Engineering; Ph.D., Arizona. Infrared detection, technology, and systems.

Bruce H. T. Chai, Professor of Optics; Physics; Mechanical, Materials, and Aerospace Engineering; and Electrical and Computer Engineering; Ph.D., Yale. Crystal growth, laser-host and nonlinear optical crystals.

Peter Delfyett, Professor of Optics, Electrical and Computer Engineering, and Physics; Ph.D., CUNY. High-speed optoelectronics, semiconductor lasers and amplifiers.

Luis Elias, Professor of Optics and Physics; Ph.D., Wisconsin. Free-electron lasers.

David J. Hagan, Associate Professor of Optics, Physics, and Electrical and Computer Engineering; Ph.D., Heriot-Watt (Edinburgh). Nonlinear optical material characterization, optical power limiting.

James Harvey, Associate Professor of Optics and Electrical and Computer Engineering; Ph.D., Arizona. Image analysis, optical design, optical scattering.

Aravinda Kar, Associate Professor of Optics and Mechanical, Materials, and Aerospace Engineering; Ph.D., Indian Institute of Technology. Laser-aided manufacturing and materials processing.

Guifang Li, Associate Professor of Optics, Physics, and Electrical and Computer Engineering; Ph.D., Wisconsin. Fiber optics and photonic communications.

Patrick LiKamWa, Associate Professor of Optics and Electrical and Computer Engineering; Ph.D., Sheffield (England). Optoelectronics, multiple quantum well devices.

Jim Moharam, Professor of Optics and Electrical and Computer Engineering; Ph.D., British Columbia. Diffractive and holographic optics, photorefraction, electromagnetic diffraction.

Kathleen Richardson, Associate Professor of Optics, Chemistry, and Mechanical, Materials, and Aerospace Engineering; Ph.D., Alfred. Glass fabrication, processing, and characterization.

Martin Richardson, Professor of Optics, Physics, and Electrical and Computer Engineering; Ph.D., London. Laser-induced plasmas, high-intensity lasers, X-ray sources and applications.

Nabeel Riza, Associate Professor of Optics and Electrical and Computer Engineering; Ph.D., Caltech. Photonic information processing systems.

Jannick Rolland, Assistant Professor of Optics, Electrical and Computer Engineering, and Computer Science; Ph.D., Arizona. Image analysis, medical imaging, 3-D visualization and virtual reality.

William Silfvast, Professor of Optics, Physics, and Electrical and Computer Engineering; Ph.D., Utah. Laser physics, X-ray sources, X-ray lithography.

M. J. Soileau, Professor of Optics, Electrical and Computer Engineering, and Physics; Ph.D., USC. Laser-induced damage, nonlinear optics.

George Stegeman, Professor of Optics, Physics, and Electrical Engineering and Cobb Family Chair; Ph.D., Toronto. Nonlinear guided-wave optics, nonlinear optics devices.

Eric Van Stryland, Professor of Optics, Physics, and Electrical and Computer Engineering; Ph.D., Arizona. Nonlinear optics materials characterization, ultrafast optics, optical damage.

Boris Ya. Zel'dovich, Professor of Optics and Physics; Ph.D., Lebedev Physics Institute (Russia). Theory of electromagnetic propagation, nonlinear holography, liquid-crystal technology.

FACULTY WITH JOINT APPOINTMENTS AT THE SCHOOL OF OPTICS
Larry Andrews, Professor of Mathematics, Electrical and Computer Engineering, and Optics; Ph.D., Michigan State. Laser beam propagation through random media.

Robert Peale, Associate Professor of Physics, Optics, and Electrical and Computer Engineering; Ph.D., Cornell. Fourier spectroscopy.

Ronald Phillips, Professor of Electrical and Computer Engineering, Mathematics, and Optics; Ph.D., Arizona State. Optical propagation through random media.

Mubarak Shah, Professor of Computer Science and Optics; Ph.D., Wayne State. Computer vision, biomedical imaging, gesture recognition, visual surveillance.

Arthur Weeks, Associate Professor of Electrical and Computer Engineering and Optics; Ph.D., Central Florida. Multiple-aperture optical communication systems, color image processing, optical image reconstruction.

University of Central Florida

SELECTED PUBLICATIONS

Zhang, X. X., P. Hong, **M. Bass,** and **B. H. T. Chai.** Blue upconversion with excitation into Tm ions at 780 nm in Yb and Tm Co-doped fluoride crystals. *Phys. Rev. B* 51:9298–303, 1995.

Zhang, X. X., P. Hong, **M. Bass,** and **B. H. T. Chai.** Multi-site fature and efficient lasing at 1041 and 1302 nm in Nd^{3+} doped potassium yttrium fluoride. *Appl. Phys. Lett.* 66:926–39, 1995.

Hong, P., et al. **(M. Bass** and **B. H. T. Chai).** Spectroscopic characteristics of Nd^{3+} doped strontium fluorovanadate and their effects on laser performance. *J. Appl. Phys.* 77:294–5, 1995.

Dogariu, A., and **G. Boreman.** Enhanced backscattering in a converging-beam configuration. *Opt. Lett.* 21:1718–20, 1996.

Boreman, G., A. Dogariu, C. Christodoulou, and D. Kotter. Modulation transfer function of antenna-coupled infrared detector arrays. *Appl. Opt.* 35:6110–4, 1996.

Effenberger, F., and **G. Boreman.** Dual-carrier transport model of SPRITE detectors. *Solid-State Electron.* 39:217–23, 1996.

Effenberger, F., and **G. Boreman.** Modal analysis of noise in SPRITE detectors. *Appl. Opt.* 35:566–71, 1996.

Boreman, G., and C. Dainty. Zernike expansions for non-Kolmogorov turbulence. *J. Opt. Soc. Am. A* 13:517–22, 1996.

Effenberger, F., and **G. Boreman.** MTF-enhanced readout for SPRITE detectors. *Appl. Opt.* 35:1022–4, 1996.

Boreman, G., A. Dogariu, C. Christodoulou, and D. Kotter. Dipole-on-dielectric model for infrared lithographic spiral antennas. *Opt. Lett.* 21:309–11, 1996.

Dogariu, A., and **G. Boreman.** Facet model for photon-flux transmission through rough dielectric interfaces. *Opt. Lett.* 21:701–3, 1996.

Fredin, P., and **G. Boreman.** Resolution-equivalent D* for SPRITE detectors. *Appl. Opt.* 34:7179–82, 1995.

Delfyett, P. J., et al. **(M. Richardson).** Ultrafast semiconductor laser diode seeded Cr:LiSAF regenerative amplifier system. *Appl. Opt.* 36:3375–80, 1997.

Delfyett, P. J. High power ultrafast semiconductor diode lasers. In *Compact Sources of Ultrashort Pulses: Studies in Modern Optics.* New York: Cambridge University Press, 1995.

Delfyett, P. J. Real world compact ultrafast semiconductor laser diode sources. In *Ultrafast Phenomena IX, Springer Series in Chemical Physics,* vol. 60, p. 22. New York: Springer-Verlag, 1995.

Rizvi, N., et al. **(P. J. Delfyett).** Modelocked Cr:LiSAF lasers. In *Ultrafast Phenomena IX, Springer Series in Chemical Physics,* vol. 60, p. 161. New York: Springer-Verlag, 1995.

Wang, Z., et al. **(D. J. Hagan** and **E. W. Van Stryland).** Cascaded second order effects in npp, a molecular single crystal. *J. Opt. Soc. Am. B* 14:76–86, 1997.

Dogariu, A., et al. **(D. J. Hagan** and **E. W. Van Stryland).** Purely refractive transient energy transfer via stimulated rayleigh wing scattering. *J. Opt. Soc. Am. B* 14, 1996.

DeSalvo, J. R., A. A. Said, **D. J. Hagan,** and **E. Van Stryland.** Infrared to ultraviolet measurements of 2-photon absorption and n_2 in wide bandgap solids. *IEEE J. Quantum Electron.* 32:1324–30, 1996.

Wang, Z., **D. J. Hagan, E. W. Van Stryland,** and G. Assanto. Phase-insensitive, single wavelength, all-optical transistor based on second-order nonlinearities. *Electron. Lett.* 32:1135–40, 1996.

Torruellas, W. E., et al. **(D. J. Hagan, E. W. Van Stryland, G. I. Stegeman,** and **L. Torner).** Observation of 2D solitary waves in a quadratic nonlinear medium. *Phys. Rev. Lett.* 74:5036–9, 1995.

Harvey, J. E., K. L. Lewotsky, and A. Kotha. Performance predictions of a Schwarzschild imaging microscope for soft x-ray applications. *Opt. Eng.* 35:2423–36, 1996.

Harvey, J. E., S. P. Reddy, and **R. L. Phillips.** Precision pointing and tracking through random media by exploiting the enhanced backscatter phenomenon. *Appl. Opt.* 35:4220–8, 1996.

Harvey, J. E., and W. J. Gressler. Image degradation due to assembly and alignment errors in conical foil x-ray telescopes. *Opt. Eng.* 35:3037–47, 1996.

Harvey, J. E., and C. Ftaclas. Field-of-view limitations of phased telescope arrays. *Appl. Opt.* 34:5787–98, 1995.

Kar, A., J. E. Scott, and W. P. Latham. Theoretical and experimental studies of thick-section cutting with a chemical oxygen-iodine laser. *J. Laser Appl.* 8:125–30, 1996.

Kar, A., J. E. Scott, and W. P. Latham. Effects of mode structure on three-dimensional laser heating due to single or multiple rectangular laser beams. *J. Appl. Phys.* 80:667–74, 1996.

Kar, A., and M. D. Langlais. Opto-thermal effects of laser modes in laser materials processing. *Opt. Quantum Electron.* 27:234–40, 1995.

Kar, A., and J. Mazumder. Mathematical modeling of keyhole laser welding. *J. Appl. Phys.* 79:114–21, 1995.

LiKamWa, P., and A. M. Kanan. Ultrafast all-optical switching in multiple quantum well Y-junction waveguides at the band gap resonance. *IEEE J. Selected Top. Quantum Electron.* 3(3), 1997.

Wang, H. S., F. Effenberger, **P. LiKamWa,** and A. Miller. Ultrafast cross-well carrier transport in a strained InGaAs/GaAs pin modulator. *IEEE J. Quantum Electron.* 33(2):192–7, 1997.

Kanan, A. M., **P. LiKamWa,** M. Dutta, and J. Pamulapati. Area-selective disordering of multiple quantum well structures and its applications to all-optical devices. *J. Appl. Phys.* 80(6):3179–83, 1996.

Kanan, A. M., **P. LiKamWa,** M. Dutta, and J. Pamulapati. Integrated all-optical routing Y-junction device with ultrafast on-off switching. *Electron. Lett.* 32(16):1476–7, 1996.

Kanan, A. M., **P. LiKamWa,** M. Dutta, and J. Pamulapati. 1.7ps consecutive switching in an integrated multiple-quantum-well y-junction optical switch. *IEEE Photonics Technol. Lett.* 8(12):1641–3, 1996.

Grann, E. B., and **M. G. Moharam.** Hybrid two-dimensional subwavelength surface-relief grating/mesh structures. *Appl. Opt.* 35:795–9, 1996.

Grann, E. B., and **M. G. Moharam.** Comparison between continuous and discrete subwavelength grating structure for antireflection surfaces. *J. Opt. Soc. Am. A* 13:988–93, 1996.

Grann, E. B., **M. G. Moharam,** and D. A. Pommet. Optimal graded index surfaces for tapered two-dimensional subwavelength gratings structures. *J. Opt. Soc. Am. A* 12:333–9, 1995.

Moharam, M. G., E. B. Grann, D. A. Pommet, and T. K. Gaylord. Formulation for stable implementation of the rigorous coupled-wave analysis of binary gratings. *J. Opt. Soc. Am. A* 12:1068–76, 1995.

Moharam, M. G., D. A. Pommet, E. B. Grann, and T. K. Gaylord. Enhanced transmission matrix approach for the stable implementation of the rigorous coupled wave analysis of surface-relief gratings. *J. Opt. Soc. Am. A* 12:1077–82, 1995.

Pommet, D. A., E. B. Grann, and **M. G. Moharam.** Effect of fabrication process errors of the performance of multi-level binary phase gratings. *Appl. Opt.* 34:2430, 1995.

Torres, D., F. Jin, **M. Richardson,** and C. DePriest. Characterization of mass-limited ice droplet laser plasmas. *OSA Trends Opt. Photonics Extreme Ultraviolet Lithography* 4:75–9, 1996.

Riza, N. A. Scanning heterodyne optical interferometers. *Rev. Sci. Instruments Am. Inst. Phys. J.* 67:2466–76, 1996.

Riza, N. A., M. M. K. Howlader, and N. Madamopoulos. Photonic security system using spatial codes and remote coded coherent optical communications. *Opt. Eng.* 35(9):2487–98, 1996.

Riza, N. A., and M. M. K. Howlader. Acousto-optic system for the generation and control of tunable low frequency signals. *Opt. Eng.* 35:920–5, 1996.

Riza, N. A., and M. M. K. Howlader. Narrowband ultrasonic phased array control using a photonic controller. *Ultrasonics* 34:9–18, 1996.

Riza, N. A., and N. Madamopoulos. High signal-to-noise ratio birefringence compensated optical delay line using a noise reduction scheme. *Opt. Lett.* 20(22):2351–3, 1995.

Klosner, M. A., H. A. Bender, **W. T. Silfvast,** and J. J. Rocca. Intense plasma discharge source at 13.5 nm for extreme-ultraviolet lithography. *Opt. Lett.* 22(1):34–6, 1997.

University of Central Florida

Selected Publications (continued)

Baek, Y., et al. **(G. I. Stegeman).** All-optical integrated Mach-Zehnder switching in lithium niobate waveguides due to cascaded nonlinearities. *Appl. Phys. Lett.* 68:2055–7, 1996.

Jägger, M., et al. **(G. I. Stegeman).** Comparison of quasi-phase-matching geometries for second harmonic generation in poled polymer channel waveguides at 1.55 μm. *Appl. Phys. Lett.* 68:1183–5, 1996.

Kang, J. U., **G. I. Stegeman,** and J. S. Aitchison. One-dimensional spatial soliton dragging, trapping and all-optical switching in AlGaAs waveguides. *Opt. Lett.* 21:189–92, 1996.

Kang, J. U., **G. I. Stegeman,** J. S. Aitchison, and N. Akhmediev. Observation of Manakov spatial solitons in AlGaAs planar waveguides. *Phys. Rev. Lett.* 76:3699–706, 1996.

Kang, J. U., **G. I. Stegeman,** A. Villeneuve, and J. S. Aitchison. AlGaAs below half bandgap: A laboratory for spatial soliton physics. *J. Eur. Opt. Soc. A, Pure Appl. Opt.* 5:583–94, 1996.

Krijnen, G. J. M., et al. **(G. I. Stegeman).** Optimisation of second harmonic generation and nonlinear phase-shifts in the Cerenkov regime. *IEEE J. Quantum Electron.* 32:729–38, 1996.

Otomo, A., **G. I. Stegeman,** W. H. G. Horsthuis, and G. R. Mohlmann. Quasi-phase-matched surface emitting second harmonic generation in poled polymer waveguides. *Appl. Phys. Lett.* 68:3683–5, 1996.

Schiek, R., Y. Baek, and **G. I. Stegeman.** One-dimensional spatial solitons due to cascaded second-order nonlinearities in planar waveguides. *Phys. Rev. A* 53:1138–41, 1996.

Schiek, R., et al. **(G. I. Stegeman).** All-optical switching in lithium niobate directional couplers with the cascaded nonlinearity. *Opt. Lett.* 21:940–2, 1996.

Stegeman, **G. I.,** and W. E. Torruellas. Nonlinear optical materials for information processing and communications. *Philos. Trans. R. Soc. London* 354:745–56, 1996.

Torruellas, W. E., **G. I. Stegeman,** and G. Assanto. All-optical switching by spatial walk-off compensation and solitary wave locking. *Appl. Phys. Lett.* 68:1449–51, 1996.

Treviño-Palacios, C. G., **G. I. Stegeman,** and P. Baldi. Spatial nonreciprocity in waveguide second order processes. *Opt. Lett.* 21:1442–4, 1996.

Schiek, R., et al. **(E. Van Stryland, D. J. Hagan,** and **G. Stegeman).** Cascading: A promising approach to nonlinear optical phenomena revisited. Invited contribution in *Novel Optical Materials and Applications,* eds. I. C. Khoo, F. Simoni, and C. Umeton. New York: John Wiley & Sons, 1997.

Gatt, P., et al. **(A. R. Weeks** and **C. M. Stickley).** Coherent optical array receivers for the mitigation of atmospheric turbulence and speckle effects. *Appl. Opt.* 35:5999–6009, 1996.

Bolshtyansky, M. A., **B. Ya. Zel'dovich,** and N. V. Tabiryan. BRIEFING: Beam reconstruction by iteration of an electromagnetic field with an induced nonlinearity gauge. *Opt. Lett.* 22(31):22–4, 1997.

Savchenko, A. Yu., and **B. Ya. Zel'dovich.** Wave propagation in a guiding structure: One step beyond the paraxial approximation. *J. Opt. Soc. Am. B* 13(2):273–81, 1996.

Anderson, D. Z., M. A. Bolshtyansky, and **B. Ya. Zel'dovich.** Stabilization of the speckle pattern of a multimode fiber undergoing bending. *Opt. Lett.* 21(11):785–7, 1996.

Bolshtyansky, M. A., and **B. Ya. Zel'dovich.** Random transverse tomography and phase conjugate scanning for image acquisition through a multimode fiber. *Opt. Eng.* 35(3):769–74, 1996.

UNIVERSITY OF CONNECTICUT

Department of Physics

Programs of Study

The department offers programs of study and research leading to both the M.S. and Ph.D. degrees in atomic and molecular physics (experimental and theoretical), condensed-matter physics (experimental and theoretical), elementary particle and field theory, theory of general relativity and cosmology, nuclear physics (experimental and theoretical), and quantum optics and lasers (experimental and theoretical). The master's degree may be earned under either of two plans. One requires at least 15 credits and a thesis. The second plan, appropriate for those intending to pursue a Ph.D., requires 24 credits of course work but no thesis. Ordinarily, 24 credits of course work beyond the master's degree are included in the doctoral plan of study. Students continuing toward the Ph.D. must pass a general examination. The doctoral dissertation, written under the immediate and continuous supervision of an advisory committee, is expected to represent a significant contribution to the field of physics.

Admission to the graduate programs is limited and selective. Ordinarily, students who do not qualify for assistantships are not admitted. The master's degree generally requires one to two years to complete. The Ph.D. degree represents the equivalent of at least an additional two years of full-time study and research.

Research Facilities

The physics department is located in the Edward Gant Science Complex, which also houses the Institute of Materials Science, the Departments of Mathematics and Statistics, and the University's Computer Center. A wide variety of research facilities are located in the physics department. A 2-MeV positive ion and a 2-MeV electron Van de Graaff accelerator and several smaller accelerators and ion sources are available for research in atomic collisions and in applications of ion beams to materials modification and surface analysis. Instruments available include argon-ion and krypton-ion lasers, YAG-pumped pulsed dye laser systems, an excimer laser, an ultrashort pulsed laser, CW ring dye lasers, standing-wave dye lasers, a grazing-incidence XUV spectrometer, spectrometers for electron spin resonance and both CW and pulsed nuclear magnetic resonance studies, a superconducting SQUID magnetometer, a SPEX double monochromator, a diamond-anvil high-pressure cell, and a fast transient digitizer. The Institute of Materials Science, where some students do their research, contains extensive facilities for materials research studies, including X-ray physics, surface physics, and investigations of biomaterials. In addition, a University of Connecticut Laser Facility has been established. The University Computer Center has a supercomputer, an IBM ES/9000-580 with triadic processor, available for research. In addition, the physics department has its own research computers and Macintosh and Pentium 400 MHz computers linked to an Ethernet network for a Sun SPARC20 workstation and other Sun Workstations. A substantial main library and the department's own research library are conveniently available. Joint research programs have been established with the Thomas Jefferson National Accelerator Facility, the Lawrence Livermore National Laboratory, and the National Institute for Science and Technology.

Financial Aid

For the 1999–2000 academic year, the nine-month graduate assistantship stipend ranges from $14,155 for entering students to $16,555 for those who have passed the general examinations. In addition, health insurance and tuition waivers (but not a waiver of fees) are provided to those holding assistantships. Assistantships are awarded competitively, and fellowship support is available for exceptionally well qualified candidates. Summer support is also available.

Cost of Study

In 1999–2000, the cost per semester for carrying 6 credits is $1706 (tuition) plus $339 (fees) for Connecticut residents and $4433 (tuition) plus $339 (fees) for out-of-state students. The tuition portion is waived for those holding assistantships.

Living and Housing Costs

A limited amount of space is available in a graduate dormitory. The cost is $1605 per semester for 1999–2000 (not including meals). In addition, rental units are available off campus. A description of University-owned apartments is available on the World Wide Web at http://www.drl.uconn.edu.

Student Group

There are 50 full-time graduate students, almost all of whom are enrolled in the doctoral program. Nearly all the students have financial support, teaching or research assistantships, or fellowships. The atmosphere in the department is friendly and informal; students conducting thesis research can expect to work individually and closely with their faculty advisers.

Location

The University of Connecticut is located in the scenic New England community of Storrs, 25 miles northeast of Hartford, near Interstate 84. Boston (90 miles), New York (130 miles), and the Rhode Island beaches are all within easy driving distance. Hiking, cross-country skiing, canoeing, and fishing may be enjoyed within a 10-minute drive from campus. Many students ski in Vermont and New Hampshire during the winter. The University hosts a number of cultural and social events during the academic year.

The University and The Department

The University is a state-supported institution with an enrollment of approximately 13,000 undergraduate and 4,000 graduate students on its Storrs campus. It is the flagship institution in the state's system of higher education and has strong research programs in many areas. The physics faculty currently numbers 37, of whom 32 are at the Storrs campus. There are several adjunct professors from other institutions. In addition to the core curriculum, the department provides a variety of courses and seminar series in several specialized areas. There is also a weekly colloquium series.

Applying

Prospective students are encouraged to apply in January for the following fall semester. While applications are considered at any time, early application optimizes the probability of receiving financial aid. International applications must include a TOEFL score for those whose native language is not English. All applicants must submit GRE General Test scores, and the Subject Test in physics is recommended, though optional. There is a $40 application fee for domestic students ($45 for international students). Prospective students should consult the *Graduate Education and Research in Physics at the University of Connecticut* brochure, which can be obtained from the department. The brochure is also available at the department's Web site (http://www.phys.uconn.edu).

Correspondence and Information

Professor William C. Stwalley, Head
Department of Physics, U-3046
University of Connecticut
2152 Hillside Road
Storrs, Connecticut 06269-3046
Telephone: 860-486-4924

University of Connecticut

THE FACULTY AND THEIR RESEARCH

William C. Stwalley, Professor and Head; Ph.D., Harvard. Experimental atomic and molecular interactions, laser spectroscopy and dynamics of atoms and molecules.

Gary D. Bent, Assistant Department Head; Ph.D., Connecticut. Theoretical atomic and molecular physics.

Philip E. Best, Professor; Ph.D., Western Australia. Experimental condensed-matter physics: X-ray and electron spectrometry, surface physics.

Joseph I. Budnick, Professor; Ph.D., Rutgers. Experimental condensed-matter physics: nuclear magnetic resonance, superconductivity, X-ray studies using synchrotron radiation.

Robin Côté, Assistant Professor; Ph.D., MIT. Theoretical atomic and molecular physics, ultracold collisions, Bose-Einstein condensation.

Gerald V. Dunne, Associate Professor; Ph.D., Imperial College (London). Theoretical high-energy physics: particle theory, quantum field theory.

Niloy K. Dutta, Professor; Ph.D., Cornell. Experimental condensed matter and optical physics, semiconductor laser technology, quantum wires, fiber optic transmission systems.

Edward E. Eyler, Professor; Ph.D., Harvard. Experimental atomic, molecular, and optical physics; precision laser spectroscopy.

Gayanath W. Fernando, Associate Professor; Ph.D., Cornell. Condensed-matter theory: electronic structure calculations.

Moshe Gai, Professor; Ph.D., SUNY at Stony Brook. Experimental nuclear physics and astrophysics.

George N. Gibson, Associate Professor; Ph.D., Illinois at Chicago. High-intensity short-pulse laser physics.

Phillip L. Gould, Professor; Ph.D., MIT. Experimental quantum optics: laser cooling and trapping of atoms.

Yukap Hahn, Professor; Ph.D., Yale. Theoretical atomic physics: scattering theory, hyperfine structure theory, electron-ion collisions in plasmas.

Kurt Haller, Professor; Ph.D., Columbia. Theoretical high-energy physics: particle theory, quantum field theory.

Douglas S. Hamilton, Professor; Ph.D., Wisconsin–Madison. Experimental condensed-matter physics: laser spectroscopy.

William A. Hines, Professor; Ph.D., Berkeley. Experimental condensed-matter physics: nuclear magnetic resonance, magnetic susceptibility of metals and alloys.

Muhammad M. Islam, Professor; Ph.D., Imperial College (London). Theoretical high-energy physics: scattering, nucleon substructure.

Juha Javanainen, Professor; Ph.D., Helsinki Tech. Theoretical quantum optics, interaction of light with atoms.

Richard T. Jones, Assistant Professor; Ph.D., Virginia Tech. Experimental nuclear physics: meson spectroscopy, low-energy QCD.

Lawrence A. Kappers, Professor; Ph.D., Missouri. Experimental condensed-matter physics: optical properties, color centers, radiation damage.

Quentin C. Kessel, Professor; Ph.D., Connecticut. Experimental atomic and molecular physics: ionization, X rays, and Auger electrons.

David P. Madacsi, Professor; Ph.D., Connecticut. Condensed-matter physics: paramagnetic resonance, computer modeling of lattice defects.

Ronald L. Mallett, Professor; Ph.D., Penn State. Theory of general relativity and cosmology.

Philip D. Mannheim, Professor; Ph.D., Weizmann (Israel). Elementary particle theory, field theory, general relativity, cosmology and astrophysics.

Douglas M. Pease, Professor; Ph.D., Connecticut. Experimental condensed-matter physics: X-ray studies of alloys.

Cynthia W. Peterson, Professor; Ph.D., Cornell. Experimental condensed-matter physics.

Edward Pollack, Professor; Ph.D., NYU. Experimental atomic physics: atomic and molecular beams, atom-molecule collisions.

Michael J. Ramsey-Musolf, Associate Professor; Ph.D., Princeton. Theoretical nuclear physics, electroweak interactions in nuclei, low energy QCD.

George H. Rawitscher, Professor; Ph.D., Stanford. Theoretical nuclear physics: nuclear reactions, electron-nucleus scattering.

Jeffrey S. Schweitzer, Research Professor in Residence; Ph.D., Purdue. Experimental nuclear physics, nuclear astrophysics, solar physics.

Boris Sinkovic, Associate Professor; Ph.D., Hawaii. Experimental condensed-matter physics: spin-polarized photoemission, magnetic properties of films, surfaces, and nanostructures.

Winthrop W. Smith, Professor; Ph.D., MIT. Atomic and molecular physics: ion-atom collisions, XUV and laser spectroscopy.

Mark S. Swanson, Professor; Ph.D., Missouri. Theoretical high-energy physics: quantum field theory.

Barrett O. Wells, Assistant Professor; Ph.D., Stanford. Experimental condensed-matter physics: neutron scattering, photoemission, superconductivity.

Associate and Adjunct Faculty

Steven A. Boggs, Research Professor of Materials Science; Ph.D., Toronto. High voltage dielectrics.

Philip C. Clapp, Professor of Metallurgy; Ph.D., MIT. Theoretical condensed matter physics.

David B. Fenner, Manager, Superconductivity Group, Advanced Fuel Research, Inc.

A. Marjatta Lyyra, Associate Professor; Ph.D., Stockholm. Experimental atomic, molecular, and optical physics.

H. Harvey Michels, Senior Consulting Scientist, Chemical Sciences, United Technologies Research Center.

Peter B. Mumola, Business Director, Precision Materials Operations, Hughes Danbury Optical Systems, Inc.

Fred A. Otter. Research in condensed-matter physics and nanoscale physics.

Bernard R. Weinberger, Senior Research Scientist, United Technologies Research Center.

A teaching assistant lends a helping hand in an introductory laboratory.

The physics building.

UNIVERSITY OF FLORIDA

Department of Physics

Programs of Study	The Department of Physics offers programs of study leading to the M.S. and Ph.D. degrees. The master's degree is not a prerequisite for the Ph.D., and a nonthesis M.S. program is available. Usually, a Ph.D. student devotes the first year to core courses, after which the qualifying exams are taken. Specialized courses and dissertation research are begun the following year. Some teaching is required of degree candidates. Students generally need five or six years to complete the Ph.D. program.
	Experimental research areas in the department include ultralow-temperature physics, condensed-matter physics, high-energy particle physics, development of advanced radiation detectors, synchrotron radiation, surface physics, X-ray and neutron scattering, NMR spectroscopy and imaging, atomic physics, and optical physics. Theoretical research is pursued in statistical mechanics, scattering, quantum fields, astrophysics and general relativity, and atomic, molecular, chemical, condensed-matter, and high-energy particle physics.
	The student-faculty ratio in the department is low. Arrangements with other departments provide opportunities for study in the interdisciplinary areas of astrophysics, chemical physics, material science, and medical physics. Through cooperative programs, research may be conducted at Oak Ridge National Laboratory, Los Alamos National Laboratory, Cornell University, Fermi National Accelerator Laboratory, CERN, Laser Interferometer Gravitational Observatory (LIGO), and other facilities. Many faculty members are involved in work at the National High Magnetic Field Laboratory, a joint University of Florida/Florida State University/Los Alamos National Laboratory project located in Tallahassee, Florida.
Research Facilities	The department is housed in a 225,000-square-foot building. Facilities include machine and electronics shops. Specialized equipment includes a 4-MV Van de Graaff accelerator, a helium liquefier and recovery system, ultra-low temperature and high–magnetic field labs, magnetic resonance spectrometers, high-pressure equipment, an electron energy loss spectrometer, a rotating anode X-ray source, a small-sample calorimeter for low temperatures, and ultrahigh-vacuum surface analytical systems. Superb computing facilities are available in the department. A terminal room for graduate students provides access to all systems and many software packages. The central science library holds more than 800,000 books and periodicals and offers extensive computer-search facilities.
Financial Aid	Each year, based on undergraduate and graduate records, GRE scores, and letters of recommendation, the department provides approximately fifty graduate teaching assistantships. In 1998–99, one-third-time stipends provided about $16,000 for twelve months. Duties, which require approximately 16 hours per week, include teaching undergraduate laboratory or discussion sections or grading in advanced courses. Advanced students are supported by research grants.
Cost of Study	For Florida residents, fees were $129 per credit in 1998–99. The out-of-state surcharge is $310 per credit. Tuition fees are normally waived for assistants or fellows. A health fee of $60 is required for each semester.
Living and Housing Costs	On- and off-campus housing accommodations are readily available for both single and married students. University-operated apartment complexes provide varying environments and living quarters at costs ranging from $941 per term for a one-bedroom apartment to $1236 per term for a four-bedroom town house. Privately owned housing, in either suburban or rural settings, is available at reasonable rates. The cost of living is generally lower than in the urban areas of the northern and western United States.
Student Group	The University enrollment is 42,000, including 7,000 graduate and professional students. The Department of Physics has 70 graduate students, who come from all parts of the United States and several countries.
Student Outcomes	Recent graduates are successfully pursuing careers both in the academic world and in industrial and government laboratories.
Location	Gainesville, a city of 95,000 people, is situated in north-central Florida, 65 miles from the Atlantic Ocean and 55 miles from the Gulf of Mexico; both offer excellent beaches and recreational opportunities. In addition, Gainesville is surrounded by numerous freshwater lakes, springs, and rivers. A moderate climate, with mean temperatures of 81°F in July and 58°F in January, permits year-round outdoor activities. There is a center for performing arts, and cultural offerings include two local theater groups, a civic ballet, a chorus, an orchestra, and a number of festivals. Tampa, the Kennedy Space Center, and Disney World are all less than 3 hours away by car.
The University	The University is the focus of a lively cultural, intellectual, and political life. Eminent scholars, artists, and public officials bring enlightening and stimulating ideas to the campus on a regular basis. Prominent musicians give concerts, many of them free, of classical and contemporary music. Frontiers of Science, a campuswide lecture series sponsored by the Department of Physics, brings several distinguished researchers to the University each year. The Sanibel Symposia program, conducted jointly by physicists and chemists of the Quantum Theory Project, is an annual event that brings internationally known scientists to the area.
Applying	Assistantships are usually awarded for the fall semester, with the financial aid decision made the previous spring. Up-to-date transcripts and current GRE General Test scores should be on file with the University admissions office as early as possible, preferably by January 1. The GRE Subject Test in physics is also required. Application forms can be obtained by writing to the address below.
Correspondence and Information	Graduate Affairs Office Department of Physics University of Florida P.O. Box 118440 Gainesville, Florida 32611-8440 Telephone: 352-392-9472 E-mail: grad_ad@phys.ufl.edu

University of Florida

THE FACULTY AND THEIR RESEARCH

Darin E. Acosta, Assistant Professor; Ph.D., California, San Diego, 1993. Experimental high-energy physics.
E. Dwight Adams, Professor; Ph.D., Duke, 1960. Ultralow-temperature physics: liquid and solid ^{3}He.
Bohdan Andraka, Associate Scientist; Ph.D., Temple, 1986. Condensed-matter experiment.
E. Raymond Andrew, Graduate Research Professor Emeritus; Ph.D., Cambridge, 1948. Nuclear magnetic resonance.
Paul R. Avery, Professor; Ph.D., Illinois, 1980. Experimental high-energy physics.
Rodney J. Bartlett, Graduate Research Professor; Ph.D., Florida, 1971. Many electron theory of atoms, molecules, and solids.
Arthur A. Broyles, Professor Emeritus; Ph.D., Yale, 1949. Quantum electrodynamics and foundations of physics.
J.-Robert Buchler, Professor; Ph.D., California, San Diego, 1969. Astrophysics.
Hai-Ping Cheng, Assistant Professor; Ph.D., Northwestern, 1988. Computational condensed-matter cluster physics.
Steven L. Detweiler, Professor; Ph.D., Chicago, 1975. Relativistic astrophysics.
Alan Dorsey, Professor; Ph.D., Illinois, 1987. Condensed-matter theory.
James W. Dufty, Professor; Ph.D., Lehigh, 1967. Nonequilibrium statistical mechanics.
F. Eugene Dunnam, Professor; Ph.D., LSU, 1958. Nuclear physics.
Richard D. Field Jr., Professor; Ph.D., Berkeley, 1971. Elementary particle theory.
James N. Fry, Professor; Ph.D., Princeton, 1979. Theoretical astrophysics, cosmology.
John M. Graybeal, Associate Professor; Ph.D., Stanford, 1985. Condensed-matter experiment.
Arthur F. Hebard, Professor; Ph.D., Stanford, 1970. Condensed-matter experiment.
Selman P. Hershfield, Associate Professor; Ph.D., Cornell, 1989. Condensed-matter theory.
Peter J. Hirschfeld, Associate Professor; Ph.D., Princeton, 1985. Condensed-matter theory.
Charles F. Hooper Jr., Professor; Ph.D., Johns Hopkins, 1963. Statistical mechanics, dense plasma physics.
Gary G. Ihas, Professor; Ph.D., Michigan, 1971. Ultralow-temperature physics: superfluid helium.
J. Kevin Ingersent, Associate Professor; Ph.D., Pennsylvania, 1990. Condensed-matter theory.
James R. Ipser, Professor; Ph.D., Caltech, 1969. Relativistic astrophysics.
Dallas C. Kennedy, Assistant Professor; Ph.D., Stanford, 1989. Elementary particle and particle astrophysics theory.
John R. Klauder, Professor; Ph.D., Princeton, 1959. Mathematical physics.
J. Konigsberg, Assistant Scientist, Ph.D., UCLA, 1989. High-energy experiment.
Andrey Korytov, Assistant Professor; Ph.D., Dubna (Russia), 1991. Experimental high-energy physics.
Pradeep Kumar, Professor; Ph.D., California, San Diego, 1973. Condensed-matter theory.
Per-Olov Löwdin, Graduate Research Professor Emeritus; Ph.D., Uppsala (Sweden), 1948. Quantum theory of matter.
Dmitrii Maslov, Assistant Professor; Ph.D., Landau Institute of Theoretical Physics (Moscow), 1989. Condensed-matter theory.
Mark W. Meisel, Professor; Ph.D., Northwestern, 1983. Condensed-matter experiment, ultralow-temperature physics.
David A. Micha, Professor; Ph.D., Uppsala (Sweden), 1966. Theoretical chemical physics, quantum theory of matter.
Guenakh Mitselmakher, Professor; Ph.D., Moscow, 1974. Experimental particle physics, gravitational wave searches.
Hendrik J. Monkhorst, Professor; Ph.D., Groningen (Netherlands), 1968. Theoretical chemical physics, colliding beam fusion reactor.
Khandker A. Muttalib, Associate Professor; Ph.D., Princeton, 1982. Condensed-matter theory.
Sergei P. Obukhov, Associate Professor; Ph.D., Landau Institute of Theoretical Physics (Moscow), 1978. Condensed-matter theory.
N. Yngve Öhrn, Professor; Ph.D., Uppsala (Sweden), 1963. Molecular physics and dynamics.
Lennart R. Peterson, Professor; Ph.D., MIT, 1966. Atmospheric and atomic physics.
Zongan Qiu, Associate Professor; Ph.D., Chicago, 1986. High-energy theory.
Pierre Ramond, Professor; Ph.D., Syracuse, 1969. Elementary particle theory.
David Reitze, Associate Professor; Ph.D., Texas, 1990. Femtosecond spectroscopy.
Andrew Rinzler, Assistant Professor; Ph.D., Connecticut, 1991. Condensed matter experiment.
John R. Sabin, Professor; Ph.D., New Hampshire, 1966. Quantum theory of matter, theory of interaction of radiation with matter.
J. Robert Schrieffer, University Chancellor Professor; Ph.D., Illinois, 1957. Condensed-matter theory.
L. Elizabeth Seiberling, Professor; Ph.D., Caltech, 1980. Condensed-matter experiment.
Fred Sharifi, Associate Professor; Ph.D., Illinois, 1989. Condensed-matter experiment.
Pierre Sikivie, Professor; Ph.D., Yale, 1975. Elementary particle theory.
Chris J. Stanton, Professor; Ph.D., Cornell, 1986. Condensed-matter theory.
Gregory R. Stewart, Professor; Ph.D., Stanford, 1975. Solid-state physics, novel materials.
Neil S. Sullivan, Professor and Chairman; Ph.D., Harvard, 1972. Condensed-matter physics, quantum crystals, nuclear magnetic resonance.
Yasumasa Takano, Professor; Ph.D., Helsinki, 1978. Ultralow-temperature physics.
David B. Tanner, Professor; Ph.D., Cornell, 1972. Condensed-matter experiment, axion search.
Charles B. Thorn, Professor; Ph.D., Berkeley, 1971. Elementary particle theory.
Samuel B. Trickey, Professor; Ph.D., Texas A&M, 1968. Theory and computation of solid and ultrathin film properties.
Henri A. Van Rinsvelt, Professor; Ph.D., Utrecht (Netherlands), 1965. Nuclear physics, X-ray analysis, ion-solid interactions.
James W. Walker, Professor; Ph.D., Glasgow, 1960. Medical physics.
Bernard F. Whiting, Associate Professor; Ph.D., Melbourne, 1979. Theoretical astrophysics.
Richard P. Woodard, Associate Professor; Ph.D., Harvard, 1984. Quantum gravity and quantum field theory.
John M. Yelton, Professor; D.Phil., Oxford, 1981. Experimental high-energy particle physics.

RESEARCH ACTIVITIES

Applied Physics. Investigations are carried out with particle-induced X-ray emission and on proton microprobe development.
Astrophysics. Research includes stellar structure and evolution, stellar variability, nonlinear fluid dynamics and chaos, high energy astrophysics, effects of general relativity in problems of astrophysics, cosmology and large-scale structure, and gravitational wave detection, (LIGO).
Atomic and Molecular Physics. Studies are being made of collisions of low-energy electrons with isolated molecules and high-intensity laser-solid interactions, experimental investigations of solid density plasmas. The introduction of relativistic and radiative effects into the formulas for the structure of atoms is underway.
Chemical Physics. This program is concerned with theoretical, experimental, and computational aspects of problems at the interface between chemistry and physics. Electronic structure, spectroscopy, atomic and molecular scattering, and surface phenomena are studied in atoms, molecules, and materials.
Condensed-Matter Experiment. Studies include NMR in solids, liquids, and polymers; optical spectroscopy and electronic properties of high-T_c superconductors, polymers, fullerenes, and low-dimensional conductors; ion scattering; calorimetry; UHV surface spectroscopy; ultrafast optical spectroscopy.
Condensed-Matter Theory. Research areas include properties of highly correlated quantum fluids and solids, semiconductors and superconductors, disordered metals and insulators, quasicrystals, and mesoscopic systems.
Experimental Particle Physics. Colliding beam studies are conducted at the Cornell University Laboratory for Nuclear Studies, Fermi National Accelerator Laboratory, and CERN in Geneva, Switzerland. Nonaccelerator studies also include axion searches.
Low-Temperature Physics. Work focuses on quantum fluids and solids and nuclear magnets at temperatures from the millikelvin range down to 10 microkelvin.
Medical Physics. Research includes nuclear magnetic resonance imaging, in vivo NMR spectroscopy, digital X-ray and neutron imaging, endoscopy, and single photon emission computed tomography.
Particle Physics. Elementary particles and high-energy interactions are studied. Superstring theories are explored for unification of all fundamental interactions. Implications of particle physics for cosmology and astrophysics are explored.
Statistical Mechanics. Research on fluctuations and transport includes plasma line broadening, nonlinear dynamics of systems far from equilibrium, nonequilibrium phase transitions, the physics of amorphous- and lattice-spin systems, and heavy fermions.

UNIVERSITY OF HOUSTON

Department of Physics

Program of Study	The Department of Physics offers a program of study leading to the Master of Science and Doctor of Philosophy degrees.
	A candidate for the M.S. degree must complete a minimum of 30 graduate credit hours, including courses in classical mechanics, quantum mechanics, statistical physics, electromagnetic theory, and mathematical physics; present an acceptable thesis; and defend the thesis before a thesis committee. A nonthesis M.S. degree can be awarded after the successful completion of 36 graduate credit hours and an examination.
	A candidate for the Ph.D. degree must successfully complete a minimum of 48 semester hours and pass a comprehensive examination covering classical mechanics, quantum mechanics, statistical physics, and electromagnetic theory at the graduate level. As part of the comprehensive examination, a student is required to make a research proposal. The final oral examination is primarily, but not exclusively, a defense of the dissertation.
	The comprehensive examination may be attempted a maximum of two times. There is no language requirement for the M.S. or Ph.D. degree.
	Current research programs involve investigations in condensed matter including high-T_c superconductivity, growth and properties of semiconductors, structures of materials and theoretical physics, high-energy and particle physics, intermediate-energy physics, space physics, optics, and theoretical chemical physics. These programs are supported by University and federal research grants and involve students as research assistants, usually after they have had a year or more of graduate study.
Research Facilities	The research facilities of the department are located on the fourth through seventh floors of the Science and Research One Building. The department has twenty-one large, well-equipped laboratories for carrying out experimental research in atmospheric physics; complexity, cosmology, and general relativity; condensed-matter physics; high-pressure low-temperature physics; high-energy physics; intermediate-energy physics; nonlinear dynamics; particle physics; space physics; statistical physics; and surface physics. To support these activities, the department maintains a large, comprehensive machine shop. The department has diverse and current computer facilities available for use by students. Many faculty members and graduate students collaborate closely with scientists at other universities and national laboratories. The department is also closely aligned in its research endeavors with two major research centers at the University: the Space Vacuum Epitaxy Center and the Texas Center for Superconductivity. The two centers, focused on material research, have total research and support staff of more than 200 personnel and laboratory space of more than 100,000 square feet.
Financial Aid	The department typically supports 20 to 25 students on teaching assistantships; awards average $1116 per month for the nine-month academic year. Approximately half of these are awarded to new graduate students. In addition, at any given time, there are 35 to 45 students supported by research assistantships, which also carry awards of $1116 per month for the nine-month academic year. The department usually supports all of its full-time graduate students with either teaching assistantships or with research assistantships. Supported students pay Texas-resident tuition and fees.
	The new Graduate Assistant Tuition Fellowship program pays $855 of the student's Texas resident tuition per semester, excluding the summer. To qualify, new or current students must be receiving a research or teaching assistantship and must be enrolled for 9 or more semester hours, and current students must have a GPA of 3.0 (B) or higher.
Cost of Study	In 1999–2000, the tuition and fees for graduate students who are Texas residents are approximately $1359 per semester for the normal course load of 12 semester hours. Nonresident students who are not supported pay approximately $3639 per semester for tuition and fees. Costs are subject to change. Students should contact the department for current costs. Students engaged solely in thesis research are permitted to register for a reduced load.
Living and Housing Costs	The University has limited space in residence halls, which cost $2798 for a single room and $2503 for a double room for the 1999–2000 academic year. In addition, upper-level housing is available in Cougar Place for $2763 per semester or $2988 per semester with kitchenette; all utilities included. The University offers optional meal plans in debit card form. They are available in amounts of $960, $1350, $1640, $1960, and $2260.
Student Group	In fall 1998, the University had 32,296 students, including 5,824 graduate students. The department had 75 full- and part-time graduate students. All of the full-time students in the department received financial support in the form of teaching or research assistantships.
Location	The University is located in the center of a growing science complex that includes the Johnson Space Center, chemical companies, petrochemical laboratories, the Texas Accelerator Center, and a large medical center. Houston has approximately 2,400 manufacturing companies, thus providing excellent employment opportunities. Many recreational opportunities are available; Galveston beach is only 45 miles away, and the central Texas hill country is only a 3-hour drive from Houston. There are also numerous sports and cultural events.
The University	The University of Houston was founded in 1927 and became a four-year institution in 1934. It has made rapid progress toward national recognition of its academic programs since becoming state supported in 1963.
Applying	Application forms for admission and financial aid may be obtained by writing to the Department of Physics. To be considered for a teaching assistantship for the fall semester, applicants should submit by March 15 an application, three letters of recommendation, official transcripts of previous college work, and GRE General Test scores (plus TOEFL scores, for international students). Texas residents must pay a $25 application fee; nonresidents pay $75. The application deadline for teaching assistantships for the spring semester is October 15.
Correspondence and Information	Chairman, Graduate Studies Committee Department of Physics, 617 S&R 1 University of Houston Houston, Texas 77204-5506 Telephone: 713-743-3550 Fax: 713-743-3589 E-mail: nixon@shasta.phys.uh.edu

University of Houston

THE FACULTY AND THEIR RESEARCH

James R. Benbrook, Professor; Ph.D., Washington (Seattle), 1969. Space physics, cosmic-ray physics. (E-mail: jrbenbrook@uh.edu)

Edgar A. Bering III, Professor; Ph.D., Berkeley, 1974. Space physics. (E-mail: eabering@uh.edu)

C. W. Paul Chu, Professor and T. L. L. Temple Chair of Science; Ph.D., California, San Diego, 1968. Solid-state physics, superconductivity, magnetism. (E-mail: cwchu@uh.edu)

W. K. Chu, Distinguished University Professor; Ph.D., Baylor, 1969. Superconductivity, ion beam processing. (E-mail: wkchu@uh.edu)

Terry Golding, Associate Professor; Ph.D., Cambridge, 1989. Semiconductor physics. (E-mail: golding@uh.edu)

Michael Gorman, Associate Chairman; Ph.D., Chicago, 1977. Nonlinear phenomena, fluid dynamics, optics. (E-mail: gorman@uh.edu)

Gemunu Gunaratne, Assistant Professor; Ph.D., Cornell, 1986. Nonlinear phenomena, hydrodynamics, pattern formation. (E-mail: gemunu@uh.edu)

Robert Helleman, Professor; Ph.D., Yeshiva, 1971. Theoretical physics, nonlinear dynamics.

Pei Herng Hor, Associate Professor; Ph.D., Houston, 1990. Condensed-matter physics, magnetism. (E-mail: phor@uh.edu)

Bambi Hu, Professor; Ph.D., Cornell, 1974. Nonlinear dynamics, critical phenomena, quantum field theory. (E-mail: hu@uh.edu)

Ed V. Hungerford III, Professor; Ph.D., Georgia Tech, 1967. Intermediate-energy physics. (E-mail: hunger@uh.edu)

Alex Ignatiev, Distinguished University Professor; Ph.D., Cornell, 1972. Surface physics, solid-state physics, chemical physics. (E-mail: ignatiev@uh.edu)

Donald J. Kouri, Professor; Ph.D., Wisconsin–Madison, 1965. Chemical physics. (E-mail: kouri@uh.edu)

Kwong Lau, Associate Professor; Ph.D., Maryland, 1981. High-energy particle physics. (E-mail: lau@uh.edu)

Billy W. Mayes II, Professor; Ph.D., MIT, 1969. Intermediate-energy physics. (E-mail: mayes@uh.edu)

Joseph L. McCauley, Professor; Ph.D., Yale, 1972. Theoretical physics. (E-mail: jmccauley@uh.edu)

John Miller, Assistant Professor; Ph.D., Illinois at Urbana-Champaign, 1985. Condensed-matter physics, superconductivity. (E-mail: jhmiller@uh.edu)

Simon C. Moss, Professor and M. D. Anderson Chair in Physics; Ph.D., MIT, 1962. Solid-state physics, materials science. (E-mail: smoss@uh.edu)

Carlos R. Ordóñez, Assistant Professor; Ph.D., Texas at Austin, 1986. Quantum field theory applications to high, medium-energy, and condensed-matter physics. (E-mail: ordonez@uh.edu)

Maya Paczuski, Assistant Professor; Ph.D., MIT, 1991. Theoretical physics. (E-mail: maya@uh.edu)

Lawrence S. Pinsky, Professor and Department Chairman; Ph.D., Rochester, 1973. Elementary particle and intermediate-energy physics. (E-mail: pinsky@uh.edu)

George F. Reiter, Professor; Ph.D., Stanford, 1967. Nonlinear phenomena, condensed-matter theory. (E-mail: greiter@uh.edu)

William R. Sheldon, Professor; Ph.D., Missouri–Columbia, 1960. Cosmic-ray physics, space physics. (E-mail: sheldon@uh.edu)

Wu-Pei Su, Associate Professor; Ph.D., Pennsylvania, 1981. Theoretical solid-state physics. (E-mail: wpsu@uh.edu)

Chin-Sen Ting, Professor; Ph.D., California, San Diego, 1970. Theoretical solid-state physics. (E-mail: csting@jetson.uh.edu)

Lorin L. Vant-Hull, Professor; Ph.D., Caltech, 1966. Solar energy.

Roy Weinstein, Professor; Ph.D., MIT, 1954. Magnetic properties of superconductors. (E-mail: weinstein@uh.edu)

Lowell T. Wood, Associate Professor; Ph.D., Texas at Austin, 1968. Physics of optical fibers, electrodynamics of composite media, optical properties of high critical temperature superconductors. (E-mail: ltwood@uh.edu)

UIC
UNIVERSITY OF ILLINOIS AT CHICAGO
Department of Physics

Programs of Study

Programs lead to the Doctor of Philosophy and Master of Science degrees. The general requirement for the Master of Science degree is satisfactory completion of 32 semester hours of work in courses approved by the department. At least 20 of these hours must be at the 500 level. Minimum requirements for a Doctor of Philosophy degree are the satisfactory completion of 96 semester hours of course work approved by the department, including at least 36 hours of 500-level courses; satisfactory performance in a comprehensive preliminary examination consisting of 400-level problems on classical mechanics, electricity and magnetism, quantum mechanics, thermal and statistical physics, and modern physics; satisfactory performance on an oral exam in the general area of the student's doctoral thesis research, which is to be taken within two years after passing the preliminary examination; satisfactory completion and defense of a doctoral dissertation; and two semesters of service as a teaching assistant.

Research Facilities

The research laboratories located in the department contain many notable resources, including the world's highest spectral brightness tunable ultraviolet laser. There are facilities for scanning tunneling microscopy; high-resolution electron microscopy; ultrahigh-power laser beams (used for the development of an X-ray microscope); ultrafast (picosecond) pulsed laser sources; optical and electron microscopes; laboratory X-ray sources; semiconductor optical, electrical, and structural characterization facilities; device fabrication capabilities; and a unique facility for the development of scintillating fiber detectors. The laboratories also contain dye laser systems, CW and pulsed CO_2 lasers, various excimer lasers, high-resolution spectrometers, and other computer-assisted optical equipment for Raman and Brillouin scattering and electroreflectance and photoluminescence studies. The Microphysics Laboratory has three Molecular Beam Epitaxial ultrahigh-vacuum growth chambers and surface analytical facilities (with in situ real-time characterization capabilities). The department has a recently constructed area dedicated to condensed matter and biophysics experiments. The facilities of Fermilab and the Argonne National Laboratory have been extensively used by University of Illinois at Chicago (UIC) students and faculty members for research projects and doctoral degree thesis work. Computing needs of the experimental groups are supported by computers within the department. These are accessible and interconnected through an Ethernet network. This network, via the University computer center, is connected to the rest of the world. The University computer center has an IBM 3090 mainframe and ample peripherals, several computers running UNIX, campuswide networks (ADN and ADN-II), and high-bandwidth connections to the Internet and to the National Supercomputer Center at Urbana. The experimental program is supported by a 4-person machine shop with ample equipment and a 3-person electronics shop with complete facilities for printed circuit layout and construction.

Financial Aid

Graduate students, in general, receive a full waiver of tuition and fees and are eligible for financial support in the form of teaching or research assistantships. Students are given a percentage of full-time employment, with the usual offer for an entering student ranging from 33 to 50 percent. The 50 percent appointment for academic year 1999–2000 carries a stipend of approximately $12,500 (including tuition) for the nine-month academic year, with summer assistantships also available. Various other types of financial assistance, such as fellowships, are available each year to promising students. They are described in the graduate catalog.

Cost of Study

For academic year 1999–2000, in-state residents pay $5300 ($2650 per semester) and out-of-state students pay $12,200 ($6100 per semester), although most graduate students receive a full tuition and fee waiver. A deferred tuition payment plan is also available.

Living and Housing Costs

The cost of living in Chicago is comparable to that of most cities in the United States. Housing inquires should be directed to the University of Illinois at Chicago (M/C 048), 750 South Halsted #704, Chicago, Illinois 60607-7016.

Student Group

There are approximately 60 graduate students in the Department of Physics. Students come from virtually every part of the world as well as from the United States, making the department truly international.

Student Outcomes

Graduates of the department have gone on to positions such as founder and president of Excel Technology Inc., a biomedical laser applications company; senior scientist at Sandia National Laboratories; high school physics and mathematics teacher; a fellowship position at the National Institute of Standards and Technology; and senior analyst with C&D Commodities Inc. Graduates have also gone on to postdoctoral study at such institutions as the Max Planck Institute for Physics in Munich, Germany.

Location

UIC is located in the heart of the Chicago metropolitan area. The immediate environment is totally urban, with a fine view of downtown Chicago's skyscrapers. A short distance away is beautiful Lake Michigan, which has beaches and parks that are full of activities and one of the most spectacular city skylines in the world.

The University

UIC is the largest center of higher education in the Chicago metropolitan area and has Research I status. The total enrollment is about 25,000 students, including approximately 8,000 graduate and professional students in various academic fields in its fifteen colleges and professional schools.

Applying

Application forms may be obtained directly from the Department of Physics. The department has established a policy of admitting new students only in the fall semester. Applications for the fall semester requesting financial aid must be mailed by January 15. If no financial aid is requested, applications must be submitted before March 15. Applicants are considered on an individual basis. Students must have a baccalaureate from an accredited college or university, a grade point average of at least 3.75 (A=5.0) for the final 60 semester hours (90 quarter hours) of undergraduate study, and at least 20 semester hours of courses in physics, including electricity and magnetism 1, quantum mechanics 1, and theoretical mechanics 1, or their equivalents.

Correspondence and Information

Department of Physics (M/C 273)
University of Illinois at Chicago
845 West Taylor Street, Room 2236
Chicago, Illinois 60607-7059
Telephone: 312-996-3400
Fax: 312-996-9016
E-mail: physics@uic.edu
World Wide Web: http://www.uic.edu/depts/phys

University of Illinois at Chicago

THE FACULTY AND THEIR RESEARCH

Experimental Condensed-Matter Physics

Nigel Browning, Associate Professor; Ph.D., Cambridge, 1992. Use of high-resolution electron microscopy techniques to characterize atomic scale defects in materials used in both electrical and mechanical device applications and correlate them with bulk device properties.

Juan-Carlos Campuzano, Professor; Ph.D., Wisconsin–Milwaukee, 1978. Critical phenomena and two-dimensional phase transitions, electronic structure of high-temperature superconductors, development of techniques for studying empty electron energy levels in solids.

Jean-Pierre Faurie, Professor; Ph.D., Clermont-Ferrand (France), 1970. Semiconductors (II-VI, III-V, and group IV), heteroepitaxial growth of semiconductors, semiconductor heterointerface formation and in situ characterization, semiconductor material characterization, optoelectronic devices.

James S. Kouvel, Professor; Ph.D., Yale, 1951. Vortex pinning studied very directly by means of unconventional magnetic measurements on superconducting samples as they are rotated slowly in fixed magnetic fields.

Pedro A. Montano, Professor; D.Sc., Technion (Israel), 1971. Structural studies of surfaces and artificial structures (i.e., superlattices); the main purpose has been in understanding the epitaxial growth process in metal films.

Mark Schlossman, Assistant Professor; Ph.D., Cornell, 1987. Structural studies of surfaces and interfaces in soft condensed matter, effect of fluctuations on interfaces, phase transitions in monolayer films, X-ray coherence.

W. Andreas Schroeder, Associate Professor; Ph.D., Imperial College (London), 1987. Investigation of ultrafast optical and electronic properties of wide-gap semiconductors using femtosecond laser pulses.

Sivalingam Sivananthan, Professor; Ph.D., Illinois at Chicago, 1988. Aspects of molecular beam epitaxy and the properties of II-VI semiconducting alloys, heterostructures, superlattices, and quantum structures.

Theoretical Condensed-Matter Physics

Inder P. Batra, Professor and Department Head; Ph.D., Simon Fraser, 1968. Electronic properties of materials, surface science, nanostructures, scanning tunneling microscopy.

Christoph Grein, Associate Professor; Ph.D., Princeton, 1989. Study of transport, structural, and optical properties of semiconductors, emphasizing nonradiative recombination in superlattices and epitaxial growth.

Walter Poetz, Professor; Ph.D., Graz (Austria), 1982. Mesoscopic semiconductor systems—both their transport properties and electronic structure.

Ram R. Sharma, Professor; Ph.D., California, Riverside, 1965. Dipolon excitations and dipolon theory of high-temperature superconductivity; nuclear quadruple interactions in solids and macromolecules; biophysics: theory of extraction in blood-brain barrier, single photon emission–computed tomography imaging.

Theoretical High-Energy Physics

Henrik Aratyn, Associate Professor; Ph.D., Copenhagen (Denmark), 1984. Quantum field theory, especially models characterized by a huge number of symmetries such as strings and conformal and integrable models, which all play a key role in modern theoretical physics.

Gloria T. Hoff, Associate Professor; Ph.D., Chicago, 1964. A proponent of a "strongly correlated resonances" model originally motivated by striking regularities observed in plots of pi-plus proton elastic differential-cross-section data and a background-resonance amplitude analysis based on it.

Tom Imbo, Associate Professor; Ph.D., Texas at Austin, 1988. Applications of group theory and algebraic topology in quantum field theory; exotic statistics for identical particles; novel topological aspects of gauge theories, nonlinear sigma models, and gravitational theories.

Wai-Yee Keung, Professor; Ph.D., Wisconsin–Madison, 1980. Symmetries in gauge theories, particularly on the phenomenology of the nonconservation of lepton numbers; CP parity.

A. Lewis Licht, Associate Professor; Ph.D., Maryland, 1963. Simple models of bound states in the continuum, Dirac particles in multiple connected spaces, knots and physics, ancient comets.

Antonio Pagnamenta, Professor; Ph.D., Maryland, 1965. Development of phenomenological models for the strong interactions and for the internal structure of the elementary particles.

Uday Sukhatme, Professor; Sc.D., MIT, 1971. Phenomenology of high-energy elementary particle collisions, consequences of supersymmetric quantum mechanics.

Experimental High-Energy Physics

Mark Adams, Professor; Ph.D., SUNY at Stony Brook, 1981. Fermi National Accelerator Laboratory Experiment E672 (fixed-target experiment that detects muon pairs produced in the interaction of pions and protons with nuclear targets) and the D-0 experiment (studies proton-antiproton collisions at an energy of 2 TeV).

Julius Solomon, Professor; Ph.D., Berkeley, 1963. Fermi National Accelerator Laboratory Experiment E672 (see M. Adams).

Nikos Varelas, Assistant Professor; Ph.D., Rochester, 1994. Fermi National Accelerator Laboratory Experiment (D0) to study the properties of hard interactions in proton-antiproton collisions at short distances (at an energy of 2 TeV).

Intermediate- and High-Energy Nuclear Physics

R. Russell Betts, Professor; Ph.D., Pennsylvania, 1972. Argonne National Laboratory experiment on strong field effects in heavy ion collisions, experiment (PHOBOS) to be run at the Relativistic Heavy Ion Collider.

Clive Halliwell, Professor; Ph.D., Manchester (England), 1971. Relativistic heavy ion collider experiment. (see R. Betts).

Donald W. McLeod, Professor; Ph.D., Cornell, 1962. Relativistic heavy ion collider experiment. (see R. Betts).

Atomic, Molecular, and Laser Physics

Charles K. Rhodes, Albert A. Michelson Professor of Physics; Ph.D., MIT, 1969. Interaction of matter with high-intensity radiation leading to the observation of new physical phenomena and the production of new classes of highly excited matter.

Discrete Dynamical Systems

Nino Boccara, Professor; Ph.D., Collège de France, 1961. Building up various models in epidemiology and ecology, including a report on street gang growth control.

Biophysics

Anjum Ansari, Assistant Professor; Ph.D., Illinois at Urbana-Champaign, 1988. Exploring the dynamics of macromolecules, in particular, the folding and unfolding of proteins and of DNA following a nanosecond laser-induced temperature jump.

John F. Marko, Assistant Professor; Ph.D., MIT, 1989. Structure and dynamics of large DNA molecules; single molecule micromanipulation; chromosome structure and dynamics.

Environmental Physics and Fluid Dynamics

Richard A. Carhart, Associate Professor; Ph.D., Wisconsin, 1964. Basic and applied theoretical studies of turbulent fluid flows, fundamental studies of turbulence characteristics of round nonbuoyant and buoyant fluid jets.

History of Physics

Edward Jurkowitz, Assistant Professor, Ph.D., Toronto, 1995. History of science, especially modern physics; quantum physics, superconductivity and superfluidity.

Adjunct Professors

Alexei Abrikosov, Darwin Chang, James Longworth, David Price, Robert Sporken, and Jerry Zajac.

Emeritus Professors

William Anderson, Arnold Bodmer, Keith Boyer, Helmut Claus, James Garland, Howard Goldberg, and Jared Haslett.

UNIVERSITY OF KANSAS

Department of Physics and Astronomy

Programs of Study

The Department of Physics and Astronomy offers programs of study leading to the Ph.D. in physics and the M.S. in physics, geophysics, and computational physics and astronomy.

The master's degree in physics requires 30 hours of advanced courses (up to 6 of which may be transferred from another accredited university) and at least 2 hours of master's research with satisfactory progress. A minimum average of B is required, as is a general examination in physics. The various master's programs differ in their detailed requirements.

The Ph.D. program begins with formal course work (which typically extends over two years for a well-prepared student) and, after admission to candidacy, is followed by Ph.D. research. The required courses include those needed for the M.S. in physics, so it is possible to obtain the M.S. on the way to the Ph.D. degree. Course work should average better than a B. There is no language requirement, but a demonstrated skill in computer programming related to the student's field of study is required. A written preliminary exam and a comprehensive oral exam are required for admission to candidacy. Following the oral exam, the student may choose a research project from the broad spectrum of experimental and theoretical research areas represented within the department. These include high-energy particle physics, astrophysics and cosmology, space physics, plasma physics, solid-state and condensed-matter physics, chaos and dynamical systems, and nuclear physics. After carrying out the research project under the guidance of a faculty member, the student must submit a dissertation showing the results of original research and must defend it in a final oral examination. A minimum of three full academic years of residency is required; the actual time taken to complete the Ph.D. varies considerably.

Research Facilities

Extensive computing facilities exist both in the department and at the University. The campus computer center has a small supercomputer system (a 16-processor SGI Origin 2000) and several high-end DEC Alphaservers (UNIX and VMS). The department has eight DEC Alpha computers, ten Sun SPARCstations, eight SGI O2 and Indigo workstations, two HP C240 workstations, numerous PCs and Macs, and two full-time system managers. A large collection of books and journals is contained in the adjacent Anschutz Science Library. Other facilities include the Tombaugh Astronomical Observatory, and a professionally staffed machine shop plus "student" shop. Condensed matter physics facilities include a well-equipped high-temperature superconductivity lab, multitarget magnetron sputtering and laser ablation systems, scanning and transmission electron microscopes, an X-ray diffractometer, a dc SQUID magnetometer, and photo and electron beam lithography. The high-energy physics and nuclear physics groups utilize experimental facilities at various universities and national laboratories as part of collaborative experiments. There is an extensive library of magnetic tapes of spacecraft data (from *Voyager, Ulysses, Galileo, Geotail,* and *Explorer)* for space physics research. The Kansas Institute of Theoretical and Computational Science sponsors interdisciplinary research among the Departments of Physics and Astronomy, Mathematics, and Chemistry.

Financial Aid

The principal form of financial aid is the graduate teaching assistantship; most first-year graduate students in the department have this type of support. A half-time teaching assistantship, which is the usual appointment, carries a nine-month stipend of $10,800 plus a 100 percent tuition fee waiver. Summer support is also available. Beginning graduate students may also be considered for graduate school fellowships in a University-wide competition. A few research assistantships are available for qualified first-year students, although the tendency is to award such assistantships to more advanced students.

Cost of Study

Full-time students with private support or with fellowships from sources outside the University paid tuition of $101 per credit hour for graduate-level courses in 1998–99 if they were Kansas residents and $330 per credit hour if they were nonresidents. Typical enrollments range from about 9 to 12 credit hours per semester during the first year. (University fees are set by the Board of Regents and are subject to change at any time; the fees listed here are not expected to change greatly for 1999–2000.)

Living and Housing Costs

Room and board are available in University dormitories; the cost for the 1998–99 academic year was $3832–$4660. There are a limited number of furnished one- and two-bedroom University apartments for married students and their families; the rent for 1998–99 was $226–$342 per month plus utilities. Many rooms and apartments, both furnished and unfurnished, are available off campus.

Student Group

The University of Kansas has an enrollment of approximately 25,150 students, including about 5,930 graduate students. The department enrolls approximately 40 graduate students drawn from throughout the United States and abroad. Most of these students are supported as either teaching assistants or research assistants.

Location

The University's main campus occupies 1,000 acres on and around Mount Oread in the city of Lawrence, a growing community of 65,000 located among the forested, rolling hills of eastern Kansas. Near Lawrence are four lake resort areas for boating, fishing, and swimming. Metropolitan Kansas City lies about 40 miles east of Lawrence via interstate highway and offers a variety of cultural and recreational activities.

The University

The University of Kansas is a state-supported school founded in 1866. Long known for its commitment to academic excellence, the University considers research an important part of the educational process. In addition to the College of Liberal Arts and Sciences and the Graduate School, the University houses a number of professional schools and programs, which include Engineering, Medicine, Law, Business, Journalism, and many others.

Applying

Completed applications should be received by March 1, for those requesting graduate teaching assistantships for the fall semester; applications are accepted until all the positions are filled, but preference is given to those received by the priority date. Applications for admissions that do not require assistantships should be completed by July 1. Application forms and additional information may be obtained by writing to the address given below or by calling the number indicated.

Correspondence and Information

Chairman, Admissions and Assistantships Committee
Department of Physics and Astronomy
University of Kansas
Lawrence, Kansas 66045
Telephone: 785-864-4626
World Wide Web: http://www.phsx.ukans.edu

University of Kansas

THE FACULTY AND THEIR RESEARCH

Raymond G. Ammar, Professor and Department Chairman; Ph.D., Chicago, 1959. Experimental high-energy physics.

Barbara J. Anthony-Twarog, Professor; Ph.D., Yale, 1981. Observational astronomy, stellar evolution in open star clusters, CCD and photoelectric photometry, globular clusters.

Thomas P. Armstrong, Professor; Ph.D., Iowa, 1966. Space physics, plasma physics.

Scott R. Baird, Adjunct Professor; Ph.D., Washington (Seattle), 1979. Stellar spectroscopy, variable stars.

Philip S. Baringer, Professor; Ph.D., Indiana, 1985. Experimental high-energy physics.

Alice L. Bean, Associate Professor; Ph.D., Carnegie Mellon, 1987. Experimental high-energy physics.

Robert C. Bearse, Professor Emeritus; Ph.D., Rice, 1964. Experimental nuclear physics, nuclear safeguards, materials control and accounting, computer database applications.

David Z. Besson, Associate Professor; Ph.D., Rutgers, 1986. Experimental high-energy physics.

David A. Braaten, Associate Professor; Ph.D., California, Davis, 1988. Atmospheric science.

Wai-Yim Ching, Adjunct Professor; Ph.D., LSU, 1974. Solid-state physics, electronic structures.

Thomas E. Cravens, Professor; Ph.D., Harvard, 1975. Space physics, plasma physics.

Jack W. Culvahouse, Professor Emeritus; Ph.D., Harvard, 1957. Experimental condensed-matter physics, magnetic properties of solids, computer simulations of transport in solids.

John P. Davidson, Professor Emeritus; Ph.D., Washington (St. Louis), 1952. Theoretical nuclear structure physics, atomic physics, astrophysics.

Robin E. P. Davis, Professor and Associate Chairman; D.Phil., Oxford, 1962. Experimental high-energy physics.

Gisela Dreschhoff, Courtesy Associate Professor; Dr.Sc., Braunschweig Technical (Germany), 1972. Geophysics, energy storage in solids.

Joe R. Eagleman, Professor; Ph.D., Missouri, 1963. Atmospheric science.

Jacob Enoch, Associate Professor Emeritus; Ph.D., Wisconsin, 1956. Theoretical physics.

Hume A. Feldman, Assistant Professor; Ph.D., SUNY at Stony Brook, 1989. Astrophysics and cosmology.

Robert J. Friauf, Professor Emeritus; Ph.D., Chicago, 1953. Experimental condensed-matter physics, diffusion and color centers, molecular dynamics and Monte Carlo simulations.

Paul Goldhammer, Professor Emeritus; Ph.D., Washington (St. Louis), 1956. Theoretical physics, nuclear structure physics, atomic physics.

Gregory S. Hackman, Assistant Professor; Ph.D., McMaster University, 1995. Experimental nuclear physics.

Curtis Hall, Instructor; M.S., Wisconsin, 1977. Atmospheric science.

Siyuan Han, Associate Professor; Ph.D., Iowa State, 1986. Experimental condensed-matter physics.

Ralph W. Krone, Professor Emeritus; Ph.D., Johns Hopkins, 1949. Experimental nuclear physics.

Nowhan Kwak, Professor; Ph.D., Tufts, 1962. Experimental high-energy physics.

Ying-Cheng Lai, Associate Professor; Ph.D., Maryland, 1992. Theoretical physics, chaos and dynamical systems, computational biology, mathematics.

Carl D. McElwee, Courtesy Professor; Ph.D., Kansas, 1970. Geophysics, magnetic properties of solids.

Douglas W. McKay, Professor; Ph.D., Northwestern, 1968. Theoretical elementary particle physics and particle astrophysics.

Adrian L. Melott, Professor; Ph.D., Texas, 1981. Astrophysics and cosmology, computational physics.

Herman A. Munczek, Professor Emeritus; Ph.D., Buenos Aires, 1958. Theoretical elementary particle physics.

Jeffrey S. Olafsen, Assistant Professor; Ph.D., Duke, 1994. Experimental physics, nonlinear dynamics and granular media.

Linda J. Olafsen, Assistant Professor; Ph.D., Duke, 1997. Experimental condense matter physics, semiconductor physics.

Francis W. Prosser, Professor Emeritus; Ph.D., Kansas, 1955. Experimental nuclear physics.

John P. Ralston, Professor; Ph.D., Oregon, 1980. Theoretical elementary particle physics and particle astrophysics.

Stephen J. Sanders, Professor; Ph.D., Yale, 1977. Experimental nuclear physics.

Richard C. Sapp, Professor Emeritus; Ph.D., Ohio State, 1955. Experimental solid-state physics.

Sergei F. Shandarin, Professor; Ph.D., Moscow Physical Technical Institute, 1971. Astrophysics and cosmology, large-scale structure, nonlinear dynamics, computational physics.

Stephen J. Shawl, Professor; Ph.D., Texas, 1972. Observational astronomy, stellar astronomy, polarization, globular clusters.

Jicong Shi, Assistant Professor; Ph.D., Houston, 1991. Theoretical physics, nonlinear dynamics, beam dynamics, accelerator physics.

Don W. Steeples, Courtesy Professor; Ph.D., Stanford, 1975. Geophysics.

Robert Stump, Professor Emeritus; Ph.D., Illinois, 1950. Experimental high-energy physics, atmospheric science.

Donna F. Tucker, Assistant Professor; Ph.D., Colorado State, 1987. Atmospheric science.

Bruce A. Twarog, Professor; Ph.D., Yale, 1980. Observational astronomy, stellar nucleosynthesis, chemical evolution of galaxies, stellar photometry.

Gordon G. Wiseman; Professor Emeritus; Ph.D., Kansas, 1950. Experimental solid-state physics.

Kai-Wai Wong, Professor; Ph.D., Northwestern, 1962. Many-body theory, superconductivity, liquid helium.

Judy Z. Wu, Associate Professor; Ph.D., Houston, 1993. Experimental condensed-matter physics, low-temperature physics.

UNIVERSITY OF MARYLAND, BALTIMORE COUNTY

College of Arts and Sciences
Department of Physics

Programs of Study

The Department of Physics at the University of Maryland, Baltimore County (UMBC), offers graduate programs that lead to M.S. and Ph.D. degrees in applied physics. The programs are structured to provide concentrations in two fields: materials and optics. The materials concentration covers the classical and quantum properties of condensed matter with emphases on material characterization, phase transitions, interfaces, defects, modeling, and band structure. The optics concentration emphasizes the interaction of electromagnetic radiation with matter and is concerned with such topics as visible and infrared spectroscopy, nonlinear optics, light scattering, quantum optics, and optical information processing.

The two areas of concentration in the program have sufficient overlap that students in either one can benefit from courses required in the other. Also, both areas have relevance to electrical engineering and photonics, so students may interact with students and faculty members in the engineering graduate programs.

Faculty members in the department have expertise in a wide range of fields, including nonlinear optical studies of inorganic crystals and polymers, laser physics, infrared spectroscopy, metal and semiconductor physics, radiation effects, ceramics, fluid dynamics, phase transformations, thermodynamics and statistical mechanics, and surface physics.

After completion of the Ph.D. core curriculum, prospective Ph.D. students are required to pass a written qualifying examination covering both undergraduate physics and graduate-level electromagnetism and classical, quantum, and statistical mechanics in order to qualify for candidacy for the Ph.D. degree. During the semester following the successful completion of the qualifying exam, each Ph.D. student selects an adviser to supervise the dissertation research. Upon completion of the research, the student is required to write and to defend a dissertation before a committee constituted in accordance with the graduate school regulations.

M.S. students who have satisfied the lecture course requirements may choose a thesis or a nonthesis option to complete their degree requirements. Nonthesis students are required to take a written comprehensive examination.

Research Facilities

The Department of Physics has a wide range of research equipment including two delayed-coincidence gamma-ray spectrometers with ultrafast CsF and BaF_2 detectors; a Ge-detector-based positron annihilation spectrometer; a Mössbauer spectrometer; an infrared tunable diode laser with closed-cycle helium refrigerator; a specialized "White Cell" capable of optical path lengths greater than 100 meters; several argon, Ti-sapphire, and YAG lasers; a deep-level transient spectrometer; an energy-dispersive X-ray diffractometer; and a radioisotope preparation room. Departmental research computing facilities include several Silicon Graphics Indigo color graphics workstations and a large number of PCs and Macintoshes. In the computational physics laboratory, graduate students have access to a network of several PCs and Macintoshes.

University-wide facilities include an electron microscope facility (scanning and transmission), fully staffed machine and glassblowing shops, and an electronics design and repair shop. The University computer center houses a Silicon Graphics Challenge XL 16-processor system running at 1000 MIPS. Several laboratories containing a large number of Silicon Graphics workstations are also available in the Computer Science building. The Albin Kuhn Library houses a large collection of physics, engineering, mathematics, and chemistry journals and monographs. It also provides access to a complete collection of science journals and books through interlibrary loan as well as access to several database systems.

Financial Aid

A number of graduate assistantships are available through the department. Students holding assistantships receive a twelve-month stipend of $16,000 and a tuition waiver for up to 10 credits per semester. University fellowships and merit awards may also be obtained by specially qualified students. In 1998–99, 18 students received full support on assistantships or fellowships.

Cost of Study

Tuition in 1998–99 was $260 per credit for Maryland residents and $468 per credit for nonresidents.

Living and Housing Costs

There are a limited number of on-campus dormitory rooms available for graduate students. Most graduate students are housed in apartments in the nearby communities of Catonsville and Arbutus. A single graduate student can expect living and educational expenses to be between $11,000 and $13,000 per year.

Student Group

In 1998–99, the graduate student enrollment was 18 full-time and 3 part-time students.

Location

The University has a scenic location on a 400-acre campus on the periphery of the Baltimore metropolitan area. Downtown Baltimore can be reached in 15 minutes by car; Washington, D.C., is an hour away. Both Baltimore and Washington have extensive cultural facilities, including eight major universities, a number of museums and art galleries of international reputation, two major symphony orchestras, and numerous theaters. Baltimore-Washington International Airport can be reached in only 6 minutes.

The University

The University of Maryland, Baltimore County, was established in 1966. The Department of Physics of the University of Maryland Graduate School, Baltimore, is located on the UMBC campus. The University has approximately 10,400 students drawn primarily from Maryland, although an increasing number have enrolled from other states and countries. UMBC has made a particular effort to attract students who are members of minority groups, who now account for about 30 percent of the undergraduate student body.

Applying

Students applying for admission to the Ph.D. or the M.S. programs in applied physics should have an undergraduate degree in physics or in a related field such as chemistry, engineering, or mathematics. All students must also meet the minimum standards for admission to the University of Maryland Graduate School. Applications should include an academic transcript, three letters of reference, and Graduate Record Examinations scores (General Test and Subject Test in physics). In some instances, the Subject Test requirement may be waived and a personal interview may be required.

Correspondence and Information

Graduate Admissions
Department of Physics
University of Maryland, Baltimore County
5401 Wilkens Avenue
Baltimore, Maryland 21228

Telephone: 410-455-2513
E-mail: physics@umbc.edu
World Wide Web: http://physics.umbc.edu

University of Maryland, Baltimore County

THE FACULTY AND THEIR RESEARCH

L. Michael Hayden, Associate Professor; Ph.D., California, Davis, 1987. Nonlinear optical properties of polymers, electrooptic techniques, photonic devices. *J. Appl. Phys.* 68:456, 1990.

Ivan Kramer, Associate Professor; Ph.D., Berkeley, 1967. Theoretical particle physics, mathematical modeling of infectious diseases. *Math. Comput. Modelling* 16:25, 1992.

Wallace McMillan, Assistant Professor; Ph.D., Johns Hopkins.

Harvey Melfi, Professor; Ph.D., William and Mary, 1970. Atmospheric physics, laser physics, LIDAR. *Appl. Opt.* 31:3068–82, 1992.

Robert L. Rasera, Professor; Ph.D., Purdue, 1965. Perturbed gamma-ray angular correlation spectroscopy, metal physics, ceramics, physical instrumentation. *Phys. Rev.* B45:5015, 1992.

Robert C. Reno, Associate Professor; Ph.D., Brandeis, 1970. Hyperfine interactions in solids, positron annihilation, electron microscopy, neutron diffraction. *Res. Nondestr. Eval.* 2:239, 1990.

Philip J. Rous, Associate Professor; Ph.D., Imperial College (London), 1986. Theoretical condensed matter and surface physics, low-energy electron diffraction theory, resonance states, surface dynamics. *Phys. Rev. Lett.* 67:1298, 1991.

Morton H. Rubin, Associate Professor; Ph.D., Princeton, 1964. Theoretical physics, quantum theory of measurement, theoretical quantum optics. *Phys. Rev.* A45:8138, 1992.

Yanhua Shih, Associate Professor; Ph.D., Maryland, 1987. Quantum optics, laser physics, nonlinear optics. *Phys. Rev.* A47:1288, 1993.

L. Larrabee Strow, Associate Professor; Ph.D., Maryland, 1981. High-resolution infrared molecular spectroscopy, remote sensing, atmospheric radiative transport. *J. Geophys. Res.* 96:20859, 1991.

Geoffrey P. Summers, Professor and Chair; D.Phil., Oxford, 1969. Radiation effects in semiconductors, fluorescence, photoconductivity. *J. Appl. Phys.* 71:4201, 1992.

Laszlo Takacs, Associate Professor; Ph.D., Eötvös Loránd (Budapest), 1978. Amorphous and metastable crystalline alloys, X-ray diffraction, mechanical alloying. *Materials Lett.* 13:119, 1992.

Gavin Watson, Assistant Professor; Ph.D., Pennsylvania, 1992. Experimental surface physics, X-ray diffraction.

En-Shinn Wu, Associate Professor; Ph.D., Cornell, 1972. Laser light scattering, fluorescence spectroscopy, microlithography. *Biochim. Biophys. Acta* 1058:400, 1991.

UNIVERSITY OF MASSACHUSETTS LOWELL

Department of Physics and Applied Physics

Programs of Study

The Department of Physics and Applied Physics offers programs leading to the degrees of Master of Science and Doctor of Philosophy.

The M.S. degree may be taken in physics or radiological science and protection (health physics) or in the applied physics option in optical sciences. Course requirements for the M.S. program consist of a total of 30 credits, including work on a thesis or project. The M.S. may serve as a basis for further study toward a Ph.D. degree. Students are expected to complete the M.S. program in two years.

The Ph.D. program requires 60 credits, including thesis research. Candidates for the degree must pass a written and oral comprehensive examination and a doctoral research admission examination (taken after successfully completing two semesters of an advanced research project) and demonstrate a proficiency in computer programming. Areas of research include experimental and theoretical nuclear physics, experimental and theoretical solid-state physics and materials science, optics, laser physics and far-infrared spectroscopy, scattering theory, quantum optics, relativity, particle physics, atmospheric and environmental physics, energy applications, applied mechanics, and radiological sciences.

Research Facilities

The University of Massachusetts Lowell (UML) Radiation Laboratory contains a 5.5-MV Van de Graaff accelerator with a Mobley bunching system for high-resolution neutron time-of-flight studies, a 1-MW research reactor, a 300-kCi Co-60 gamma-ray source, a fast neutron irradiation source, and radiological health physics equipment. The Submillimeter Technology Laboratory houses microwave through IR spectrometers for design and characterization of material dielectric properties, a CO_2 and far-IR laser magnetospectroscopy facility, and submillimeter-wave compact ranges for electromagnetic scattering studies. The Center for Advanced Materials has electron and atomic force microscopes and a full range of optical, X-ray, and ion spectrometers. Using MBE systems, the Photonics and Optoelectronics Device Center makes and characterizes photonics and optoelectronics devices for optical systems, communication, and computing applications. The HI-SPIN program combines experiments at national HI accelerator facilities with a cluster of workstations on campus to study gamma rays from rapidly spinning nuclei.

Financial Aid

In 1998–99, financial aid was available in the form of teaching assistantships at $14,380 to $15,850 and research assistantships at $15,850 for the academic year. Summer research stipends are available for qualified students at $1100 per month. In addition, INPO and Department of Energy fellowships are available for students in radiological sciences.

Cost of Study

In 1998–99, tuition and fees for full-time students were $3656 for Massachusetts residents and $7712 for nonresidents. Health insurance was $480 per year. The international student fee was $76.

Living and Housing Costs

The Lowell area offers a great variety of living accommodations. There is a limited amount of on-campus housing available for graduate students, including single-student accommodations with cooking facilities and unfurnished apartments for married students. Early application for these is essential. Cost per month for single students is approximately $300. Married student apartments cost approximately $400–$500 per month.

Student Group

In September 1998, the total University enrollment was approximately 12,325, including about 2,790 graduate students. There are about 60 full-time graduate students in physics. Thirty of these students receive financial support. Approximately 15 percent of the physics graduate students are women, and about 33 percent are international students.

Student Outcomes

Advanced degree recipients currently hold positions in academia, government laboratories, major medical facilities, and industry. Recent graduates have been successful in gaining employment in areas dealing with properties of materials, fiber optics, electrooptics, computer modeling, data analysis software development, radiation safety and protection, and medical physics. Others have obtained postdoctoral appointments at major research universities such as Chicago, Kentucky, Rutgers, and California, Santa Barbara, as well as at national laboratories, such as Los Alamos.

Location

The University is located in the city of Lowell, a community of about 100,000 residents, 30 miles northwest of Boston. The campus is located on both sides of the Merrimack River. Within an hour's drive of Lowell are the cultural, educational, and recreational activities of the Boston area as well as many nationally known sites. The locale is also ideally situated for the pursuit of outdoor activities. The lake and mountain regions of New Hampshire and the Atlantic beaches are easily accessible.

The University and The Department

The University of Massachusetts Lowell was formerly the University of Lowell and in 1991 became one of the five campuses of the University of Massachusetts. The Department of Physics and Applied Physics has offered the Ph.D. since 1967; the total number of students who have received graduate degrees from the department is about 350.

Applying

Applications must be submitted no later than April 1 preceding the fall term in which the applicant wishes to enroll. The General Test of the GRE, the TOEFL for international students whose native language is not English, transcripts in duplicate, and three letters of reference are required. There is an application fee of $20 for Massachusetts residents and $35 for nonresidents.

Correspondence and Information

Dr. Gus P. Couchell
Physics Graduate Coordinator
Department of Physics and Applied Physics
University of Massachusetts Lowell
Lowell, Massachusetts 01854
Telephone: 978-934-3772
E-mail: gus_couchell@uml.edu

University of Massachusetts Lowell

THE FACULTY AND THEIR RESEARCH

Professors
A. Altman, Ph.D., Maryland. Theoretical atomic physics.
A. Baker (Emeritus), Ph.D., Brandeis. Atomic theory.
L. E. Beghian (Emeritus), D.Phil., Oxford. Experimental nuclear physics, food irradiation.
G. Carr (Emeritus), Ph.D., Cornell. Physics education.
G. E. Chabot, Ph.D., Massachusetts Lowell. Radiation science and protection, dosimetry, radiation shielding.
G. P. Couchell, Ph.D., Columbia. Experimental nuclear physics.
J. J. Egan, Chairman; Ph.D., Kentucky. Experimental nuclear physics.
C. S. French, Ph.D., Massachusetts Lowell. Radiation science and protection, medical physics.
Z. Fried, Ph.D., Brandeis. Radiation theory, optics.
W. Goodhue, Ph.D., Massachusetts Lowell. Submicron devices.
P. Harihar, Ph.D., Columbia. Experimental nuclear physics.
J. Y. Harris (Emeritus), Ph.D., Rutgers. Radiological science and protection, radiation biology.
L. C. Kannenberg, Ph.D., Northeastern. Relativity, radiation theory.
A. S. Karakashian, Ph.D., Maryland. Theoretical solid-state physics, optics.
G. H. R. Kegel, Ph.D., MIT. Experimental nuclear physics, radiation effects in materials.
J. Kumar, Ph.D., Rutgers. Optics.
D. M. Larsen, Ph.D., MIT. Theoretical solid-state physics.
A. Liuzzi (Emeritus), Ph.D., NYU. Physics education.
A. Mittler, Ph.D., Kentucky. Experimental nuclear physics.
D. J. Pullen, D.Phil., Oxford. Experimental nuclear physics.
W. A. Schier, Ph.D., Notre Dame. Experimental nuclear physics.
K. J. Sebastian, Ph.D., Maryland. Particle physics theory.
E. Sheldon (Emeritus), Ph.D., D.Sc., London. Theoretical nuclear physics, astrophysics.
K. W. Skrable (Emeritus), Ph.D., Rutgers. Radiological science and protection, internal dosimetry.
R. W. Stimets, Ph.D., MIT. Experimental laser physics, astronomy, image processing.
J. Waldman, Ph.D., MIT. Experimental laser physics, infrared spectroscopy.
M. Wilner, Ph.D., MIT. Theoretical solid-state physics, optics.

Associate Professors
P. Chowdhury, Ph.D., SUNY at Stony Brook. Experimental nuclear physics, materials.
T. V. Marcella (Emeritus), Ph.D., Boston College. Physics education.
R. D. McLeod, M.S., Lowell Technological Institute. Theory of vision.
P. J. Ring (Emeritus), Ph.D., Brown. Physics education.
A. Sachs, Ph.D., New Hampshire. Theoretical mechanics.
C. Wong, Ph.D., Case Tech. Experimental solid-state physics, optics.

Adjunct Faculty
L. Bobek, M.S., Massachusetts Lowell. UML reactor supervisor, radiological sciences.
M. W. Carter, Ph.D., Florida. Radiological science.
T. G. Castner, Ph.D., Illinois. Solid-state theory.
J. F. Copeland, Ph.D., Massachusetts Lowell. Medical physics.
D. J. DeSimone, Ph.D., Massachusetts Lowell. Accelerator physics.
J. P. Donnelly, Ph.D., Carnegie Tech. Electrooptic devices.
R. Giles, Ph.D., Massachusetts Lowell. Solid-state physics, optics.
J. L. Lazewatsky, Ph.D., MIT. Biomedical engineering.
L. Li, Ph.D., Massachusetts Lowell. Nonlinear optics.
M. Montesalvo, M.S., M.B.A., Massachusetts Lowell. Radiological science.
C. Reinhardt, Ph.D., Massachusetts Lowell. Medical physics.
J. P. Ring, Ph.D., Lowell. Radiological science.
J. Segedy, Ph.D., Adelphi. Computational and solid-state physics.
N. L. B. Sullivan, Ph.D., Massachusetts Lowell. Radiological science.
Y. X. Wu, Ph.D., Shandong (China). Optoelectronics.
X.-Z. Yao, B.S., Nanjing (China). Photonics and optoelectronics.

RESEARCH ACTIVITIES AND PARTICIPATING FACULTY

Theoretical Physics
Atomic and molecular physics: electron emission and radiative transitions, inelastic electron-atom scattering, mesic atoms. (Altman, Fried)
Elementary particles and fields: current algebra, quark models, renormalization groups, quantum field theory, quantum electrodynamics, gauge theory, supersymmetry, general relativity. (Kannenberg, Sebastian)
Optics and solid-state physics: quantum optics, dielectric waveguides, surface plasmons, ultraviolet and far-infrared spectra, electronic and vibrational cluster calculations, optical and electronic properties of semiconductors and multiple-quantum-well structures, theory of vision. (Fried, Kannenberg, Karakashian, Larsen, McLeod, Sachs, Stimets, Wilner)

Experimental Physics
Applied physics: radiation effects, Rutherford back-scattering, food irradiation, PIXE, nuclear instrumentation. (Beghian, Egan, Kegel, Mittler)
Nuclear physics: neutron cross-sections, fission reaction studies, inelastic neutron scattering, fission-product studies, in-beam gamma-ray spectroscopy, high-spin nuclear structure, heavy-ion fusion reactions. (Beghian, Egan, Chowdhury, Couchell, Kegel, Mittler, Pullen, Schier)
Optics and solid-state physics: holography, tunable visible-infrared and far-infrared lasers, optoelectronic materials and devices, photonics and optoelectronics, molecular beam epitaxy, image processing, surface plasmons, radiation damage in optical and electronic materials and devices. (Goodhue, Karakashian, Kumar, Stimets, Waldman, Wong)

Radiological Sciences
Internal and external radiation dosimetry, biological effects of radiation, radon and radioactive aerosol collection and measurement systems and techniques, environmental sampling and analysis. (Chabot, French)

University of Massachusetts Lowell

SELECTED PUBLICATIONS

Beghian, L. E. Stochastic dynamics and the classical equations of motion. *Il Nuovo Cimento* 112B:727, 1996.

Beghian, L. E. Fluctuations and the second law of thermodynamics. *Il Nuovo Cimento* 110B:1369, 1995.

Beghian, L. E. The interrelationship between mechanics and thermodynamics. *Il Nuovo Cimento* 110B:377, 1995.

Castner, T. G. Low-frequency antiferromagnetic resonance of RbMnF$_3$ near the néel temperature. *Solid State Commun.* 105:627, 1998.

Zarifis, V. and **T. G. Castner.** Observation of the conduction-electron spin resonance from metallic antimony-doped silicon. *Phys. Rev.* B57, 1998.

Castner, T. G. Einstein relations near the metal-insulator transition. *Phys. Rev.* B55:4003, 1997.

Castner, T. G. Temperature dependence of the electrical conductivity and diffusivity of barely metallic n-type silicon. *23rd International Conference on the Physics of Semiconductors* 1:181, 1996.

Diehl, R., D. M. Wheatley, and **T. G. Castner.** The electromagnetic modes of a helical resonator. *Rev. Sci. Instrum.* 67:3904, 1996.

Copeland, J. F., et al. **(G. E. Chabot).** Energy effects in ESR bone dosimetry: Photons and electrons. *Appl. Radiat. Isotopes* 44:1/2–H, 1993.

Chabot, G. E., et al. **(C. S. French** and **K. W. Skrable).** A technique to correct for self absorption in beta radiation sources and for attenuation in other media. *Radiat. Prot. Manage.* 9(4):50–62, 1992.

Chabot, G. E., et al. Calibration of survey instruments used in radiation protection for the assessment of ionizing radiation fields and radioactive surface contamination. National Council on Radiation Protection and Measurements. *NCRP Report* 112, 1991.

Chabot, G. E., and **K. W. Skrable.** Beta-gamma point source on the skin problem—activity estimation and dose analysis. *Health Phys.* 55(5):729–39, 1988.

Chabot, G. E., K. W. Skrable, and **C. S. French.** When hot particles are not on the skin. *Radiat. Prot. Manage.* 5(6):31–42, 1988.

D'Alarcao, R., et al. **(P. Chowdhury).** High-K isomers in neutron-rich hafnium nuclei at and beyond the stability line. *Phys. Rev. C* 59:R1227, 1999.

Wheldon, C., et al. **(P. Chowdhury).** Opening up the A=180 K-isomer landscape: Inelastic excitation of new multi-quasiparticle yrast traps. *Phys. Lett. B* 425:239, 1998.

Nisius, D., et al. **(P. Chowdhury).** Differential lifetime measurements and configuration-dependent quadrupole moments for superdeformed bands in nuclei near 152Dy. *Phys. Lett.* B329:18, 1997.

Chowdhury, P., et al. K-isomers at gammasphere. *Proc. Workshop Gammasphere Phys.* 212, 1996.

Crowell, B., et al. **(P. Chowdhury).** High-K isomers in ^{176}W and mechanisms of K-violation. *Phys. Rev.* C53:1173, 1996.

Crowell, B., et al. **(P. Chowdhury).** Novel decay modes of high-K isomers: Tunneling in a triaxial landscape. *Phys. Rev. Lett.* 72:1164, 1994.

Nguyen, H. V., et al. **(G. P. Couchell, D. J. Pullen,** and **W. A. Schier).** Programs in C for parameterizing measured 5"x5" NaI gamma response functions and unfolding of continuous gamma spectra. *Comput. Phys. Comm.* 93:303, 1996.

Couchell, G. P., et al. **(D. J. Pullen** and **W. A. Schier).** A study of gamma-ray and beta-particle decay heat following thermal neutron induced fission of ^{235}U. *Proc. Int. Conf. on Nuclear Data Sci. Technol.* 966, 1994.

Staples, P., **J. J. Egan, G. H. R. Kegel,** and **A. Mittler.** The ^{14}N (n,n'g) cross section of the 2,313-MeV first excited state. *Nucl. Sci. Eng.* 126:168–75, 1997.

Egan, J. J., et al. **(G. H. R. Kegel** and **A. Mittler).** Use of barium fluoride detectors to signal fission events in fission neutron spectroscopy. *Proc. Int. Conf. Nucl. Data Sci. Technol., Trieste, Italy, SIF Bologna,* p. 544, 1997.

DeSimone, D. J., et al. **(J. J. Egan** and **G. H. R. Kegel).** Studies of a poenitz-type black neutron detector as a neutron flux monitor. *Nucl. Instrum. Methods Phys. Res.* A443, 1997.

Yue, G., M. O'Connor, **J. J. Egan,** and **G. H. R. Kegel.** Neutron scattering angular distributions in ^{239}Pu at 570 keV and 700 keV. *Nucl. Sci. Eng.* 122:366, 1996.

Staples, P., et al. **(J. J. Egan, G. H. R. Kegel,** and **A. Mittler).** Prompt fission neutron energy spectra induced by fast neutrons. *Nucl. Phys. A* 591:41, 1995.

Goodhue, W. D., et al. Bromine ion-beam assisted etching of III-V semiconductors. *J. Electron. Mater.* 28:364, 1999.

Goodhue, W. D., et al. Bromine ion-beam assisted etching of III-V semiconductors. *MIT Lincoln Lab. Solid State Res. Q. Tech. Rep.* V23:15, 1998.

Krishnaswami, K., R. J. Tremblay, **W. D. Goodhue,** and **A. S. Karakashian.** A comparative study of surface plasma enhanced grating coupled detectors. *Proc. SPIE* 2999, 1997.

Chai, Y. H., **W. D. Goodhue,** E. R. Mueller, and **J. Waldman.** Far-infrared photoconductive magnetospectroscopy as a tool for studying shallow donor concentration profiles in wide GaAs/A1GaAs quantum wells. *J. Vac. Sci. Technol.* B13:674, 1995.

Golubovic, B., et al. **(W. D. Goodhue).** Basic mode for an integrated optical phase difference measurement and correction system. *IEEE Photon. Technol. Lett.* 7:649, 1995.

Goodhue, W. D., et al. Bright field analysis of field-emission cones using high-resolution transmission electron microscopy and the effect of structural properties on current stability. *J. Vac. Sci. Technol.* B12:693, 1994.

Donnelly, J. P., and **W. D. Goodhue** et al. CW operation of monolithic arrays of surface-emitting A1GaAs diode lasers with dry-etched vertical facets and parabolic deflecting mirrors. *IEEE Photon. Technol. Lett.* 5:1146, 1993.

Le, H. Q., **W. D. Goodhue,** P. A. Maki, and S. Di Cecca. Diode-laser-pumped in GaAs/GaAs/A1GaAs heterostructure lasers with low internal loss and 4-W average power. *Appl. Phys. Lett.* 63:1465, 1993.

Harihar, P., H. Chen, and W. J. Stapor. Ultraviolet fluorescence lifetime in a trans-stilbene crystal. *Nucl. Instrum. Methods* A345:500, 1994.

Harihar, P., H. Chen, W. J. Stapor, and A. R. Knudson. Scintillation decays in a trans-stilbene crystal. *Nucl. Instrum. Methods* A336:176, 1993.

Harihar, P., et al. Rise time spectroscopy of nuclear radiations in cerussite scintillator. *Nucl. Instrum. Methods* A332:40, 1992.

Kannenberg, L. (Translator). *A New Branch of Mathematics: The "Ausdehnungslehre" of 1844 and Other Works by Hermann Grassman.* Chicago: Open Court, 1995.

Kannenberg, L. Response to 'Comment on "Quantum formalism via signal analysis."' *Found. Phys. Lett.* 4:475, 1992.

Kannenberg, L. Quantum formalism via signal analysis. *Found. Phys.* 19:367, 1989.

Kannenberg, L. Uniqueness of solutions to Helmholtz's equation with linear boundary conditions. *Am. J. Phys.* 57:60, 1989.

Chen, S. D., C. Narayan, **A. S. Karakashian.** The stark effect for surface states in a finite superlattice structure. *Physica* B228:239, 1996.

Frederickson, A. R., and **A. S. Karakashian.** Capacitance-voltage measurement of charged defect concentration profile near semiconductor depletion zones. *J. Appl. Phys.* 77:1627, 1995.

Kegel, G. H. R., et al. **(J. J. Egan** and **A. Mittler).** High resolution neutron total cross sections of ^{235}U from 200 to 400 keV. *Proc. Int. Conf. Nucl. Data Sci. Technol., Trieste, Italy, SIF Bologna,* p. 589, 1997.

Kegel, G. H. R., et al. **(J. J. Egan).** Studies of neutron dosimetry. *Nucl. Instrum. Methods Phys. Res.* A440, 1997.

Narayan, C., et al. **(G. H. Kegel).** PIXE studies on artifacts from Saugus Ironworks. *Nucl. Instr. Meth.* B118:396, 1996.

DeSimone, D. J., et al. **(G. H. R. Kegel, J. J. Egan,** and **A. Mittler).** Application of a Poenitz-type black neutron detector in the development of a neutron standard. *Proc. Int. Conf. on Nuclear Data Sci. Technol.* 145, 1994.

O'Connor, M., et al. **(G. H. R. Kegel** and **J. J. Egan).** Elastic and

University of Massachusetts Lowell

Selected Publications (continued)

inelastic neutron scattering in ^{197}Au at 1.5 MeV. *Proc. Int. Conf. Nuclear Data Sci. Technol.* 260, 1994.

Jiang, X. L., et al. **(J. Kumar).** Unusual polarization dependent optical erasure of surface relief gratings on azobenzene polymer films. *Appl. Phys. Lett.* 72:2502, 1998.

Kumar, J., et al. Gradient force: The mechanism for surface relief grating formation in azobenzene functionalized polymers. *Appl. Phys. Lett.* 72:2096, 1998.

Viswanathan, N. K., et al. **(J. Kumar).** Surface-initiated mechanism for the formation of relief gratings on azopolymer films. *J. Phys. Chem.* B102(31):6064, 1998.

He, J. A., et al. **(J. Kumar).** Photoelectric properties of oriented bacteriorhodopsin/polycation multiplayers by electrostatic layer-by-layer assembly. *J. Phys. Chem.* B102(36):7076, 1998.

Bian, S., et al. **(J. Kumar).** Single laser beam-induced deformation on azobenzene polymer films. *Appl. Phys. Lett.* 73(13):1817, 1998.

Yang, K., et al. **(J. Kumar).** Electroabsorption spectroscopy study of an azopolymer film fabricated by electrostatic absorption. *Appl. Phys. Lett.* 73(23):3345, 1998.

Chen, Z., et al. **(J. Kumar).** Two photon induced fluorescence from the phycoerythren protein. *Appl. Opt.* 36(7):1655, 1997.

Gonsalves, K. E., et al. **(J. Kumar).** Optical and microstructural characterization of chemically synthesized gallium nitride nanopowders. *Appl. Phys. Lett.* 71:2175, 1997.

Larsen, D. M. Effect of intersite electron-electron interaction on the concentration of D⁻ ions in quantum wells. *Phys. Rev.* B53:15719, 1996.

Fox, H. L., and **D. M. Larsen.** Exact solutions for barrier D⁻ states at high magnetic fields. *Phys. Rev. B* 51:10709, 1995.

Mueller, E. R., **D. M. Larsen, W. D. Goodhue,** and **J. Waldman.** Band nonparabolicity and central-cell corrections for D⁻ centers in GaAs quantum wells. *Phys. Rev. B* 51:2326, 1995.

Kaufman, R., **T. V. Marcella,** and **E. Sheldon.** Reflections on the pedagogic motive power of unconventional thermodynamic cycles. *Am. J. Phys.* 64:1507, 1996.

Mellen, W. R. Aligner for elastic collisions of dropped balls. *Phys. Teacher* 33:56, 1995.

Sachs, A., and J. H. Lee. Numerical solution of the fifth-order kdV equator for shallow-water solitary waves. *Il Nuovo Cimento* IIIB:1429, 1996.

Tipnis, S. V., et al. **(W. A. Schier, G. P. Couchell,** and **D. J. Pullen).** Yields of short-lived fission products produced following ^{235}U (n$_{th}$,f). *Phys. Rev. C* 58:905, 1998.

Schier, W. A., et al. **(G. P. Couchell** and **D. J. Pullen).** Beta particle spectrometer for measuring aggregate beta spectra following fission. *Nucl. Instrum. Methods Phys. Res.* A404:173, 1998.

Bennett, P. R., et al. **(W. A. Schier, G. P. Couchell** and **D. J. Pullen).**

Relative efficiency measurements of fission fragment transfer with a helium jet. *Nucl. Instrum. Methods Phys. Res.* A369:263, 1996.

Schier, W. A., et al. **(G. P. Couchell** and **D. J. Pullen).** Energy distributions of gamma and of beta decay heat as function of decay time for ^{238}U(n,f). *Proc. Int. Conf. on Nuclear Data Sci. Technol.* 111, 1994.

Sebastian, K. J., H. Grotch, and F. L. Ridener Jr. Leptonic decay rates of charmonium S and D states. *Phys. Rev.* D56:5885, 1997.

Mok, W. A., and **K. J. Sebastian.** Angular distribution in the decays of the ψ' charmonium state directly produced in polarized proton-antiproton collisions. *Il Nuovo Cimento* 110A:429, 1997.

Sebastian, K. J., and X. G. Zhang. Radiative transitions of the D states of charmonium in potential models. *Phys. Rev.* D55:225, 1997.

Sebastian, K. J., and F. L. Ridener Jr. Signals for the formation of the singlet D and P states of charmonium in proton-antiproton collisions. *Phys. Rev. D* 51:1172, 1995.

Sebastian, K. J., and F. L. Ridener Jr. Angular distribution functions in the decays of Psi' and Psi" directly produced in unpolarized proton-antiproton collisions. *Phys. Rev. D* 51:1177, 1995.

Sebastian, K. J., H. Grotch, and X. Zhang. The mass and the E1 decay-rate of the singlet P state of charmonium. *Phys. Rev. D* 49:1639, 1994.

Sebastian, K. J., and J. Anthony. Relativistic corrections to the Zeeman effect in hydrogen-like atoms and positronium. *Phys. Rev.* A49:192, 1994.

Kaufman, R. D., and **E. Sheldon.** Studies of unconventional heat engine design, operation and efficiency. *J. Phys.* D30(20):2853–64, 1997.

Sheldon, E. Cosmochronology and nucleochronometry. *Frontier Topics in Nuclear and Astrophysics (Graduate Lectures XXII, Int. Summer School on Nuclear Physics,* Piaski, Masuria, Poland) 227, 1992.

Sheldon, E., et al. Measured and calculated neutron scattering cross sections for the actinide nuclei ^{232}Th, ^{238}U and ^{239}Ps. *Sel. Topics in Nuclear Physics: Seminar at the XXII Int. Summer School on Nuclear Physics,* Piaski, Masuria, Poland, SINS-2124/A, 88, 1991.

Traut, S., D. A. Pommet, M. A. Fiddy, and **Y.-Y. Teng.** Low-power fault-tolerant laser-to-fiber coupling with photorefractive BaTiO$_3$. *Appl. Opt.* 36(23):5805, 1997.

Jacobs, E. S., **J. Waldman,** and **W. D. Goodhue.** 77 K far-infrared hot electron multiple-quantum-well detectors. *J. Vac. Sci. Technol.* B16:1430, 1998.

Wilner, M., D. Adler, M. E. Eberhart, and K. H. Johnson. Effects of bond bending on the electronic structure of silane. *J. Chem. Phys.* 84:6312, 1986.

Wilner, M. Effective local environment model for vibrational states in pure amorphous germanium and silicon. *J. Noncryst. Solids* 51:1, 1982.

UNIVERSITY OF MIAMI

Department of Physics

Programs of Study

The Department of Physics offers programs leading to the M.S. and Ph.D. degrees, and both thesis and nonthesis M.S. tracks are available. Usually a Ph.D. student devotes most of the first year to basic courses and takes the qualifying exam in the first January following arrival. Students should become involved with a research project by the second year and, after passing the qualifying exam, must present the beginnings of a research project to a committee within six months. This presentation normally turns into a dissertation, but the student is not bound to it and can switch to another project or even another area of research later.

Experimental research in the Department of Physics is in the areas of nonlinear phenomena and chaos, optics, optical oceanography, plasmas, and solid-state physics. Theoretical research is in elementary particles, environmental optics, plasmas, nonlinear phenomena and chaos, and solid-state physics. In addition to the research projects, the activities of research groups include seminars where both visitors and the department faculty members and graduate students present results of their research.

Research Facilities

The physics building includes 20,000 square feet of research laboratories and workshops. Major experimental instrumentation includes lasers, a radiometric calibration facility, CCD camera systems for measurements of radiance distribution and the point spread function under water, a very high resolution spectroradiometer, instruments for measuring spectral attenuation and scattering under water, an optical and a microwave spectrum analyzer, a UHV pumping station, vibration isolated optical tables, high-speed data acquisition systems, RF power sources, high-resolution video data systems, a transmission resonance spectrometer, cryogenic probes (0.3–330 K), a SQUID magnetometer, a 12-tesla superconducting magnet, thin films deposition systems (evaporator and pulsed excimer laser), high-temperature furnaces, polishing and cutting instruments, and a Philips MRD thin-film X-ray diffractometer.

Computing services are provided by the University Computing Center and by the physics department and include a number of VAX, DEC, and IBM computers in addition to numerous IBM PCs and Macintosh computers scattered in the various PC labs in the dorms and the computer center. Research groups utilize many VAX and DEC workstations, including Alpha AXP Digital DECstations, and have access to supercomputers.

Financial Aid

Financial support is available in several forms. Research assistantships (RAs) and teaching assistantships (TAs) include a stipend of $12,880 per year (additional stipend for summer teaching may be available) plus tuition for 9 credits per semester. Fellowships, with no teaching duties, include a stipend of $11,250 per year plus tuition for 9 credits per semester. For some teaching and/or research duties, the support is upgraded to the level of TA support. Summer research fellowships are available on a competitive basis.

Cost of Study

In 1999–2000, the tuition for one semester of full-time graduate study (9 credits) is $7668. An additional $195 per semester covers student activity and athletics fees.

Living and Housing Costs

The cost of a single room in the dormitories is $5836 per year (an additional $1679 for meals) per person per semester. Typical rents for off-campus apartments are $600–$700 per month for one bedroom and $700–$800 per month for two bedrooms. A typical rent for a room in a house off campus is $400–$500 per month, and the cost of living is generally lower than in the urban areas of the northern and western United States.

Student Group

In fall 1998, 22 graduate students were enrolled in the department. All of them received financial aid in the form of a TA, an RA, a fellowship, or external support (exchange students). The majority of the students are international.

Student Outcomes

Recent Ph.D. graduates have chosen a variety of work environments. One teaches at Washtenan Community College in Ann Arbor, Michigan; one works at Coulter Corporation; one works at NASA; one works at the NOAA government laboratory; and another has a postdoctoral appointment in Miami. Others have postdoctoral appointments at the University of Chicago, Brown University, and Durham University in the United Kingdom.

Location

The department is housed in the James L. Knight Physics Building on the Coral Gables campus. This campus occupies 260 beautifully landscaped acres in a predominantly residential area. Coral Gables is an affluent suburb of metropolitan Miami, which is the largest urban area in Florida. Downtown Miami is readily accessible by Metrorail train, which has a stop next to the campus. Miami is a center of Latin culture and is the commercial gateway to Latin America. It offers all the amenities of a large and prosperous city, as well as an excellent oceanside climate of warm winters and moderate summers.

The University

The University of Miami was founded in 1925 and is accredited by the Southern Association of Colleges and Schools. Individual programs are accredited by a total of twelve professional agencies. The University of Miami is the largest private university in the Southeast and has a full-time enrollment of more than 14,000, including more than 3,000 graduate students and 2,000 law and medical students. Two colleges and ten schools are located on the main campus in Coral Gables. The University's medical school, the fourth largest in the United States, is situated in Miami's civic center, and the Rosentiel School of Marine and Atmospheric Science is located on Virginia Key. Funded research activities total more than $100 million per year.

Applying

Consideration is given to applicants who have a B.S. degree in physics with a minimum undergraduate GPA of 3.0 (B). The GRE is required. Applicants from non-English-speaking countries must demonstrate proficiency in English via the TOEFL, and the minimum acceptable score for admission is 550.

The application deadline for the fall semester is February 1, and application for financial aid is made at the time of application for admission. Forms should be requested from the address below.

Correspondence and Information

Professor Josef Ashkenazi
Chairman of the Graduate Recruitment Committee
Department of Physics
University of Miami
P.O. Box 248046
Coral Gables, Florida 33124
Telephone: 305-284-2323/3
Fax: 305-284-4222
E-mail: ashkenazi@phyvax.ir.miami.edu

University of Miami

THE FACULTY AND THEIR RESEARCH

George C. Alexandrakis, Professor and Chairman of the Department; Ph.D., Princeton, 1968. Solid-state experiment, transmission resonance, magneto-acoustic propagation in ferromagnetic metals.

Orlando Alvarez, Professor; Ph.D., Harvard, 1979. Theory of elementary particles.

Josef Ashkenazi, Associate Professor; Ph.D., Hebrew (Jerusalem), 1975. Solid-state theory, first-principles band structure methods, many-body physics, high-temperature superconductors.

Stewart E. Barnes, Professor; Ph.D., UCLA, 1972. Solid-state theory, many-body theory, superconductivity and magnetism.

Joshua L. Cohn, Associate Professor; Ph.D., Michigan, 1989. Condensed matter, experiment, materials physics, electronic and lattice transport.

Thomas L. Curtright, Professor; Ph.D., Caltech, 1977. Theory of elementary particles.

Howard R. Gordon, Professor; Ph.D., Penn State, 1965. Optical oceanography, light scattering, radiative transfer, remote sensing.

Manuel A. Huerta, Professor; Ph.D., Miami (Florida), 1970. Statistical mechanics, plasma physics, numerical simulations in MHD.

Luca Mezincescu, Professor; Ph.D., Bucharest, 1978. Theory of elementary particles.

James C. Nearing, Associate Professor and Associate Chairman of the Department; Ph.D., Columbia, 1965. Theoretical physics, bifurcation theory in fully nonlinear plasma systems.

Rafael I. Nepomechie, Professor; Ph.D., Chicago, 1982. Theory of elementary particles.

William B. Pardo, Associate Professor; Ph.D., Northwestern, 1957. Experimental physics, plasma physics, nonlinear dynamics.

Arnold Perlmutter, Professor; Ph.D., NYU, 1955. Nuclear and particle physics.

Yaakov Shevy, Assistant Professor; Ph.D., Bar Ilan (Israel), 1987. Laser spectroscopy, quantum optics.

Kumble R. Subbaswamy, Professor; Ph.D., Indiana, 1976. Solid-state theory, lattice dynamics, optical properties.

Kenneth J. Voss, Professor; Ph.D., Texas A&M, 1984. Hydrologic optics, light scattering, atmospheric optics.

Fulin Zuo, Associate Professor; Ph.D., Ohio State, 1988. Condensed matter, experiment.

RESEARCH ACTIVITIES

Experimental and Theoretical Nonlinear Dynamics. Study of instabilities and chaotic oscillations in systems exhibiting complex dynamical behavior; dripping faucets, electronic circuits, lasers, athletes, inert-gas plasmas at low fractional ionization, phase synchronization and communication with chaos. More information is available through http://ndl.physics.miami.edu (Pardo)

Experimental Ocean Optics. Light scattering and absorption by marine particulates; instrumentation for measurement of optical properties of ocean water and of the atmosphere. (Voss)

Experimental Solid State Physics. Ferromagnetic transmission resonance in metals, spin relaxation, exchange energy, phonon excitation and propagation, nonlinear phenomena. (Alexandrakis)

Transport and magnetic properties of materials at low temperatures; high-temperature and organic superconductors and reduced dimensional systems (e.g., layered systems and thin films); electrical and thermal conduction, thermoelectric effects; vortex dynamics, critical currents, quantum tunneling. (Cohn, Zuo)

Quantum Optics. Mechanical effects of light, laser cooling of atoms, semiconductor lasers, quantum noise, nonclassical states of light. (Shevy)

Theoretical Elementary Particles Physics. Quantum field theory, supergravity, superstrings. (Alvarez, Curtright, Mezincescu, Nepomechie).

Theoretical Environmental Optics. Radiative transfer, remote determination of ocean chlorophyll concentrations. (Gordon)

Theoretical Plasma Physics. Numerical simulations in plasmas and other systems. (Huerta, Nearing)

Theoretical Solid State Physics. Electronic structure of solids, many-body physics, high-temperature superconductivity, magnetism, lattice dynamics. (Ashkenazi, Barnes, Subbaswamy)

More information is available through http://www.miami.edu/physics/

The James L. Knight Physics Building.

University of Miami

SELECTED PUBLICATIONS

Zuo, F., et al. **(G. C. Alexandrakis).** Anomalous magnetization in single-crystal κ-[bis(ethylenedithiotetrathiafulvalene)]$_2$Cu[N(CN)$_2$]Br superconductors. *Phys. Rev. B* 52:R13126, 1995.

Rittenmyer, K. M., **G. C. Alexandrakis,** and P. S. Dubbelday. Detection of fluid velocity and hydroacoustic particle velocity using a temperature autostabilized nonlinear dielectric element (Tandel). *J. Acoust. Soc. Am.* 84:2002, 1988.

Alexandrakis, G. C., and G. Dewar. Electromagnetic generation of 9.4 GHz phonons in Fe and Ni. *J. Appl. Phys.* 55:2467, 1984.

Abeles, J. H., T. R. Carver, and **G. C. Alexandrakis.** Microwave transmission measurement of the critical exponent beta in iron and iron-silicon. *J. Appl. Phys.* 53:8116, 1982.

Alexandrakis, G. C., R. A. B. Devine, and J. H. Abeles. High frequency sound as a probe of exchange energy in nickel. *J. Appl. Phys.* 53:2095, 1982.

Alexandrakis, G. C. Determination of the molecular size and the Avogadro number: A student experiment. *Am. J. Phys.* 46:810, 1978.

Alvarez, O., I. M. Singer, and P. Windey. The supersymmetric σ-model and the geometry of the Weyl-Kac character formula. *Nucl. Phys. B* 373:647, 1992.

Alvarez, O., T. P. Killingback, M. Mangano, and P. Windey. The Dirac-Ramond operator in string theory and loop space index theorems. *Nucl. Phys. Proc. Suppl.* B1A:189, 1987.

Alvarez, O., T. P. Killingback, M. Mangano, and P. Windey. String theory and loop space index theorems. *Comm. Math. Phys.* 111:1, 1987.

Alvarez, O., I. M. Singer, and B. Zumino. Gravitational anomalies and the family's index theorem. *Comm. Math. Phys.* 96:409, 1984.

Alvarez, O. Theory of strings with boundaries: Fluctuations, topology and quantum geometry. *Nucl. Phys. B* 216:125, 1983.

Ashkenazi, J. Stripes, non-Fermi-liquid behavior, and two-component transport in the high-T_c cuprates. *J. Phys. Chem. Solids* 59:1788–90, 1998.

Ashkenazi, J. Stripes, non-Fermi-liquid behavior, and high-T_c superconductivity. *J. Supercond.* 10:379–82, 1997.

Ashkenazi, J. A realistic theory for the "normal state" and pairing mechanism in the high-T_c cuprates. *J. Supercond.* 8:559–62, 1995.

Ashkenazi, J. A realistic microscopic theory for the high-T_c cuprates. *J. Supercond.* 7:719–36, 1994.

Ashkenazi, J., D. Vacaru, and C. G. Kuper. Search for the correct theory for the high temperature cuprate superconductors. In *High Temperature Superconductivity: Physical Properties, Microscopic Theory, and Mechanisms; Proceedings of the University of Miami Workshop on Electronic Structure and Mechanisms of High-Temperature Superconductivity, held January 3–9, 1991, in Coral Gables, Florida,* pp. 569–82, eds. J. Ashkenazi, S. E. Barnes, F. Zuo, G. C. Vezzoli, and B. M. Klein. New York: Plenum Press, 1992.

Ashkenazi, J., and C. G. Kuper. Charge-fluctuation excitations as mechanisms for high-T_c. In *Studies of High-Temperature Superconductors,* vol. III, pp. 1–49, ed. A. V. Narlikar. New York: Nova Science Publishers, Inc., 1989.

Vacaru, D., and **S. E. Barnes.** A new auxiliary particle method for the Hubbard, t-J and Heisenberg models. *J. Phys.: Condens. Matter* 6:719, 1994.

Nagashpur, M., and **S. E. Barnes.** Nonuniversality in the Kondo effect. *Phys. Rev. Lett.* 69:3824, 1992.

Barnes, S. E. Spinon-holon statistics, and broken statistical symmetry for the t-J and Hubbard models in 2D. In *High Temperature Superconductivity: Physical Properties, Microscopic Theory, and Mechanisms; Proceedings of the University of Miami Workshop on Electronic Structure and Mechanisms of High-Temperature Superconductivity, held January 3–9, 1991, in Coral Gables, Florida,* pp. 95–105, eds. J. Ashkenazi, S. E. Barnes, F. Zuo, G. C. Vezzoli, and B. M. Klein. New York: Plenum Press, 1992.

Barnes, S. E. Theory of the Jahn-Teller-Kondo effect. *Phys. Rev.* 37:3671, 1988.

Barnes, S. E. Theory of electron paramagnetic resonance of ions in metals. *Adv. Physics* 30:801–938, 1981.

Cohn, J. L. Superconducting-state enhancement of thermal conductivity in the cuprates: Correlation with the pair density. *Phys. Rev. B* 53:R2963, 1996.

Cohn, J. L. Anomalous phonon damping in insulating cuprates. *Phys. Rev. B* 52:R13134, 1995.

Cohn, J. L., E. F. Skelton, S. A. Wolf, and J. Z. Liu. In-plane thermoelectric power of untwinned YBa$_2$Cu$_3$O$_{7-\delta}$. *Phys. Rev. B* 45:13140, 1992.

Cohn, J. L., S. A. Wolf, V. Selvamanickam, and K. Salama. Thermoelectric power of YBa$_2$Cu$_3$O$_{7-\delta}$: Phonon-drag and multiband conduction. *Phys. Rev. Lett.* 66:1098, 1991.

Cohn, J. L., E. Ben-Jacob, and C. Uher. Low temperature electronic transport and the Coulomb blockade in oxidized films of bismuth. *Phys. Lett.* A148:110, 1990.

Cohn, J. L., S. D. Peacor, and C. Uher. Thermal conductivity of YBa$_2$Cu$_3$O$_{7-\delta}$ below 1K: Evidence for normal-carrier transport well below T_c. *Phys. Rev. B* 38:2892, 1988.

Cohn, J. L., et al. Upper critical fields of periodic and quasiperiodic Nb/Ta superlattices. *Phys. Rev. B* 38:2326, 1988.

Curtright, T. L., and C. Zachos. Canonical non-Abelian dual transformations in supersymmetric field theories. *Phys. Rev D* 52:R572–6, 1995.

Curtright, T. L., and G. Ghandour. Quantum effects in Liouville theory using functional methods. In *Quantum Field Theory, Statistical Mechanics, Quantum Groups, and Topology,* proceedings of the January 1991 NATO Advanced Research Workshop at the University of Miami, pp. 333–45, eds. T. Curtright, L. Mezincescu, and R. Nepomechie. World Scientific, 1992.

Curtright, T. L. Extrinsic geometry of superimmersions. In *Perspectives in String Theory,* pp. 437–80, eds. P. Di Vechia and J. L. Petersen. World Scientific, 1988.

Curtright, T. L., and C. K. Zachos. Geometry, topology, and supersymmetry in nonlinear models. *Phys. Rev. Lett.* 53:1799–801, 1984.

Curtright, T. L., and C. B. Thorn. Conformally invariant quantization of the Liouville theory. *Phys. Rev. Lett.* 48:1309–13, 1982.

Gordon, H. R., and G. C. Boynton. A radiance-irradiance inversion algorithm for estimating the absorption and backscattering coefficients of natural water: Homogenous waters. *Appl. Optics* 36:2636–41, 1997.

Gordon, H. R., T. Zhang, F. He, and K. Ding. Effects of stratospheric aerosols and thin cirrus clouds on atmospheric correction of ocean color imagery: Simulations. *Appl. Optics* 36:682–97, 1997.

Gordon, H. R., and T. Zhang. How well can radiance reflected from the ocean-atmosphere system be predicted from measurements at the sea surface? *Appl. Optics* 35:6527–43, 1996.

Gordon, H. R., et al. Phytoplankton pigment concentrations in the Middle Atlantic bight: Comparison of ship determinations and coastal zone color scanner measurements. *Appl. Optics* 22:20–36, 1983.

Gordon, H. R., D. K. Clark, J. L. Mueller, and W. A. Hovis. Phytoplankton pigments derived from the Nimbus-7 CZCS: Initial comparisons with surface measurements. *Science* 210:63–66, 1980.

Thio, Y. C., **M. A. Huerta,** and G. C. Boynton. The projectile-wall interface in rail launchers. *IEEE Trans. Magnetics* 29:1213–8, 1993.

Thio, Y. C., **M. A. Huerta,** and **J. C. Nearing.** On some techniques to achieve ablation free operation of electromagnetic rail launchers. *IEEE Trans. Magnetics* 29, 1993.

Castillo, J. L., and **M. A. Huerta.** Effect of resistivity on the Rayleigh-Taylor instability in an accelerated plasma. *Phys. Rev. E* 48:3849–66, 1993.

Boynton, G. C., **M. A. Huerta,** and Y. C. Thio. 2-D MHD numerical simulations of EML plasma armatures with ablation. *IEEE Trans. Magnetics* 29:751–56, 1993.

Huerta, M. A., and J. C. Nearing. Conformal mapping calculation of the railgun skin inductance. *IEEE Trans. Magnetics* 27:112–15, 1991.

Huerta, M. A. Steady detonation waves with losses. *Phys. Fluids* 28:2735–43, 1985.

University of Miami

Selected Publications (continued)

Huerta, M. A., and J. Magnan. Spatial structures in plasmas with metastable states as bifurcation phenomena. *Phys. Rev. A* 26:539–55, 1982.

Grisaru, M. T., **L. Mezincescu,** and **R. I. Nepomechie.** Direct calculation of boundary S matrix for open Heisenberg chain. *J. Phys. A* 28:1027–45, 1995.

de Vega, H. J., **L. Mezincescu,** and **R. I. Nepomechie.** Scalar kinks. *Intl. J. Mod. Phys. B* 8:3473–85, 1994.

Mezincescu, L., and **R. I. Nepomechie.** Analytical Bethe ansatz for quantum-algebra-invariant spin chains. *Nucl. Phys. B* 372:597–621, 1992.

Mezincescu, L., and **R. I. Nepomechie.** Integrability of open spin chains with quantum algebra symmetry. *Intl. J. Mod. Phys.* A6:5231–48, 1991 (Addendum—A7:5657–59, 1992).

Mezincescu, L., and M. Henneaux. A σ model interpretation of Green-Schwarz covariant superstrings. *Phys. Lett.* 152B:340–42, 1985.

Jones, D. R. T., and **L. Mezincescu.** The chiral anomaly and a class of two-loop finite supersymmetric theories. *Phys. Lett.* 138B:293–95, 1984.

Mezincescu, L. On the superfield approach for 0(2) supersymmetry. Preprint JINR Dubna P2-12572 (in Russian), pp. 1–19, 1979.

Nearing, J. C., and **M. A. Huerta.** Skin and heating effects of railgun currents. *IEEE Trans. Magnetics* 25:381–86, 1989.

Nepomechie, R. I. Non-Abelian symmetries from higher dimensions in string theories. *Phys. Rev. D* 33:3670–77, 1986; erratum, D36: 3290, 1987.

Nepomechie, R. I. String models with twisted currents. *Phys. Rev. D* 34:1129–35, 1986.

Nepomechie, R. I. Magnetic monopoles from antisymmetric tensor gauge fields. *Phys. Rev. D* 31:1921–24, 1985.

Buch, T. N., and **W. B. Pardo** et al. **(E. Rosa Jr.).** Experimental issues in the observation of water drop dynamics. *Phys. Lett. A* 248:353, 1998.

Johns, T. S., and **W. B. Pardo** et al. Bifurcation analysis of symmetrical structures in argon plasma as specified by experimental boundary conditions. *Proc. 4th Exp. Chaos Conf., August 6–8, 1997, Boca Raton, Florida,* pp. 161–6, eds. M. Ding et al. Singapore: World Scientific, 1998.

Walkenstein, J. A., **W. B. Pardo,** H. S. Robertson, and M. Monti. An inexpensive hybrid video imaging system. *Sci. Instr.* 66 (11), November 1995.

Magnan, J. F., **W. B. Pardo,** et al. Video based analysis of bifurcation phenomena in radio-frequency-excited inert gas plasmas. In *Proceedings of the 2nd Experimental Chaos Conference.* World Scientific Publishing Co., 1995.

Perlmutter, A., et al. Spin analyzing power in p-p elastic scattering at 28 GeV/c. *Phys. Rev. Lett.* 50:802–6, 1983.

Perlmutter, A., et al. Spin-spin forces in 6 GeV/c neutron-proton elastic scattering. *Phys. Rev. Lett.* 43:983–86, 1979.

Friedmann, M., D. Kessler, A. Levy, and **A. Perlmutter.** The coulomb field in $\Sigma\pi$ production by slow K-mesons in complex nuclei. *Nuovo Cimento* 35:355–76, 1965.

Cox, J., and **A. Perlmutter.** A method for the determination of the S matrix for scattering by a tensor potential. *Nuovo Cimento* 37:76–87, 1965.

Rosa Jr., E., and E. Ott. Mixed basin boundary structures of chaotic systems. *Phys. Rev. E* 59:343, 1999.

Shevy, Y., J. Kitching, and A. Yariv. Linewidth reduction and frequency stabilization of semiconductor laser with a combination of FM sideband locking and optical feedback. *Optics Lett.* 18:1071, 1993.

Shevy, Y., J. Iannelli, J. Kitching, and A. Yariv. Self quenching of semiconductor laser linewidth below the Schawlow-Townes limit. *Optics Lett.* 17:661, 1992.

Shevy, Y., B. Crosignani, and A. Yariv. Quantum fluctuations of the optical forces on atoms in squeezed vacuum. *Phys. Rev. A* 46:1421, 1992.

Shevy, Y. Laser cooling of atoms in squeezed vacuum. *Phys. Rev. Lett.* 64:2905, 1990.

Shevy, Y., D. S. Weiss, P. J. Ungar, and S. Chu. Bimodal velocity distribution in laser cooled atoms. *Phys. Rev. Lett.* 62:1118, 1989.

Rao, A. M., et al. **(K. R. Subbaswamy).** Diameter-selective Raman scattering from vibrational modes in carbon nanotubes. *Science* 275:187, 1997.

Madhu, M., E. Richter, and **K. R. Subbaswamy.** Structural and vibrational properties of Fullerenes and nanotubes in a nonorthogonal tight-binding scheme. *J. Chem. Phys.* 104:5875, 1996.

Mahan, G. D., and **K. R. Subbaswamy.** *Local Density Theory of Polarizability.* New York: Plenum Press, 1991.

Hawrylak, P., and **K. R. Subbaswamy.** Kinetics of stage transformation in intercalated graphite. *Phys. Rev. Lett.* 53:2098, 1984.

Subbaswamy, K. R., and M. Grabowski. Bond alteration, on-site Coulomb correlations, and solitons in Polyacetylene. *Phys. Rev. B* 24:2168, 1981.

Li, X., et al. **(K. Voss).** Dominance of mineral dust in aerosol light-scattering in the North Atlantic trade winds. *Nature* 380:416–9, 1996.

Ge, Y., **K. J. Voss,** and **H. Gordon.** In situ measurements of inelastic light scattering in Monterey Bay using solar Fraunhofer lines. *J. Geophys. Res.* 100:13227–36, 1995.

Morel, A., **K. J. Voss,** and B. Gentili. Bidirectional reflectance of oceanic water: A comparison of modeled and measured upward radiance fields. *J. Geophys. Res.* 100:13143–50, 1995.

Voss, K. J., and R. W. Austin. Beam attenuation measurement error due to small-angle scattering acceptance. *J. Atmos. Ocean. Techn.* 10:113–21, 1993.

Maffione, R. A., **K. J. Voss,** and R. C. Honey. Measurement of the spectral absorption coefficient in the ocean with an isotropic source. *Appl. Optics* 32:3273–79, 1993.

Voss, K. J. A spectral model of the beam attenuation coefficient in the ocean and coastal areas. *Limnol. Oceanogr.* 37:501–9, 1992.

Voss, K. J., and J. S. Schoonmaker. Temperature dependence of beam scattering in young sea ice. *Appl. Optics* 31:3388–89, 1992.

Voss, K. J., and A. L. Chapin. Measurement of the point spread function in the ocean. *Appl. Optics* 29:3638–42, 1990.

Su, X., and **F. Zuo** et al. Anisotropic magnetoresistance in the organic superconductor β''-$(ET)_2SF_5CH_2CF_2SO_3$. *Phys. Rev. B* 59:4376, 1999.

Zuo, F., X. Su, and W. K. Wu. Magnetic properties of the pre-martensitic transition in Ni_2MnGa alloys. *Phys. Rev. B* 58:11127, 1998.

Su, X., and **F. Zuo** et al. Structural disorder and its effect on the superconducting transition temperature in organic superconductor k-$(BEDT-TTF)_2Cu[N(CN)_2]Br$. *Phys. Rev. B* 57:R14056, 1998.

Zuo, F., J. Schlueter, and J. W. Williams. Mixed state magnetoresistance in organic superconductors k-$(ET)_2Cu[N(CN)_2]Br$. *Phys. Rev. B* 54:11973, 1996.

Zuo, F., S. Khizroev, **G. C. Alexandrakis,** and V. N. Kopylov. Anomalous magnetization in single-crystal $Tl_2Ba_2CuO_6$: Evidence for dimensional crossover. *Phys. Rev. B* 52:R755–8, 1995.

Zuo, F., et al. Josephson decoupling in single crystal $Nd_{1.85}Ce_{0.15}CuO_{4-y}$ superconductors. *Phys. Rev. Lett.* 72:1746–9, 1994.

Zuo, F., et al. Quantum tunneling of vortices in single crystal $Tl_2Ca_2Ba_2Cu_3O_{10}$ superconductors. *J. Low Temp. Phys.* 97:393–401, 1994.

UNIVERSITY OF MICHIGAN

Department of Physics

Programs of Study

The department offers programs leading to the Master of Science and Doctor of Philosophy in physics. The department offers research opportunities in theoretical and experimental fields, including atomic physics, astrophysics, biophysics, optical physics, condensed-matter physics, elementary particle physics, and nuclear physics. The requirements for the Ph.D. are as follows. Students must pass, with a grade of B or better, nine prescribed graduate physics courses (500 level) or show equivalent competence, 4 credits of cognate courses, one advanced graduate physics course (600 level) on a special topic, and a 4-credit course of supervised nonthesis research. Students must also pass a two-part written qualifying examination on advanced undergraduate material no later than the beginning of their third year. Ph.D. students are expected to attain candidacy by the end of their fifth term. Completion of the degree involves writing a thesis based on independent research done under the supervision of a faculty adviser and passing a final oral exam. Students in the M.S. degree program must have passing grades (B– or above) in 24 credit hours of courses at the 400 level and above, including 4 credits of cognate courses with a grade of C– or better, and they must maintain an overall grade average of B or better. At least 12 hours of courses must be in physics, and the students must pass two courses from a selected group of 500-level courses with a grade of B– or better.

Research Facilities

Physics research is focused at the Randall Laboratory/West Hall complex, which includes a 65,000-square-foot laboratory addition. The physics laboratories house state-of-the-art space and facilities that support the department's research activities. Individual investigators use tools such as atomic scale and positron microscopes, lasers of all sorts (CW, pulsed, Q-switched, mode-locked, ultrafast, frequency-stabilized, ion, dye, solid-state, and diode), dilution refrigerators and cryogenic equipment, laser tweezers, and a Mössbauer spectrometer for the study of active sites in protein. Nuclear and high-energy physics groups use campus laboratories to build and test apparatus used at accelerator facilities around the world. Apparatus for beams of radioactive nuclei, for polarized beams and targets, and for detector facilities used in fixed target and colliding beam experiments are among those developed on the University of Michigan campus. Collaborations in the medical sciences take place at the University Hospital and Medical School. The School of Engineering on the University's North Campus is the site of the Center for Ultrafast Optical Sciences, an NSF science and technology center exploring ultrafast and high-intensity laser science. Also on North Campus is the Phoenix Memorial Reactor used by physics department researchers for neutron and radiation studies. Department computer facilities are state-of-the-art, based on a professionally managed, distributed network with powerful workstations and high-speed network connections among department and University computers and to the Internet. Department shop facilities include a well-equipped student shop, a large instrument shop with computerized numerically controlled milling machines, and an electronics shop with custom VLSI circuit design facilities. Other University shop facilities complete the technical support necessary for state-of-the-art research. The University of Michigan libraries house one of the country's largest science libraries and employ modern computerized catalogs, databases, and information retrieval.

Financial Aid

The University's Regents' Fellowships paid a stipend of $18,000, plus full tuition and fees, in 1998–99. Several other merit-based scholarships are available through the department, to both incoming and advanced students. Graduate teaching assistantships cover a period of eight months and paid a stipend of $11,330 plus tuition in 1998–99; teaching loads usually consist of two to four 2-hour elementary lab sections per week. Graduate TAs are represented by a union. Graduate research assistantship stipends were $16,248 for twelve months in 1998–99. Summer RA appointments are available for most students. A very small number of summer TA appointments are also available. Students who have at least a one-quarter-time appointment (half a normal appointment) as a research or teaching assistant are eligible to participate in the University's group health insurance plan.

Cost of Study

For 1998–99, tuition was $5004 per term for full-time in-state residents and $10,150 per term for full-time out-of-state students; candidates paid $3235 per term. Tuition is waived for students with one-quarter-time or more teaching or research assistantships. Most fees are included in the tuition; fees not included total about $95 each semester. Books and supplies cost approximately $400 per term.

Living and Housing Costs

Living costs, including room and board, transportation, and personal needs, are estimated at $6400 per academic year for a single student with no dependents.

Student Group

The University of Michigan has approximately 35,000 students, of whom 13,500 are graduate students. The Department of Physics has approximately 130 graduate students.

Location

The University is in Ann Arbor, 40 miles west of Detroit in the Huron River Valley, in a beautiful, tree-lined town that combines the charm of a small city with the sophistication of cities many times its size. Regarded as a cultural center of the Midwest, it offers numerous opportunities for recreation and enjoyment.

The University and The Department

The University of Michigan, founded in 1817, is one of the nation's oldest public institutions of higher education. Consistently ranked among the great universities in the world, Michigan has a strong tradition of leadership in the development of the modern American research university—a tradition sustained by the wide-ranging interests and activities of its faculty members and students. Exceptional facilities and programs, both academic and nonacademic, are available. The Department of Physics has played a leading role in the development of modern physics, with accomplishments ranging from the discovery of spin, the invention of the racetrack synchrotron, and the bubble chamber to the birth of nonlinear optics, the detection of neutrinos from supernova 1987A, and evidence of the top quark.

Applying

Applications for admission in the fall term are due by January 15 of the preceding spring. The GRE General Test is required, and the GRE Subject Test in physics is recommended. For further information on admission requirements, students should write to the address given below.

Correspondence and Information

Associate Professor Fred C. Adams, Associate Chair for Graduate Studies
2464 Randall Laboratory of Physics
University of Michigan
Ann Arbor, Michigan 48109-1120
Telephone: 734-764-5539
World Wide Web: http://www.physics.lsa.umich.edu/

University of Michigan

THE FACULTY AND THEIR RESEARCH

Fred C. Adams, Associate Professor; Ph.D., Berkeley, 1988. Theoretical astrophysics.

Carl W. Akerlof, Professor; Ph.D., Cornell, 1967. Experimental high-energy physics, astrophysics, cosmic rays.

Ratindranath Akhoury, Professor; Ph.D., SUNY at Stony Brook, 1980. Theoretical high-energy physics.

James W. Allen, Professor; Ph.D., Stanford, 1968. Experimental condensed-matter physics.

Dante E. Amidei; Associate Professor; Ph.D., Berkeley, 1984. Experimental high-energy physics.

Meigan C. Aronson, Associate Professor; Ph.D., Illinois at Urbana-Champaign, 1988. Experimental condensed-matter physics.

Daniel Axelrod, Professor; Ph.D., Berkeley, 1974. Experimental biophysics.

Frederick D. Becchetti Jr., Professor; Ph.D., Minnesota, 1969. Experimental nuclear physics.

Paul Berman, Professor; Ph.D., Yale, 1969. Theoretical atomic, molecular, and optical physics.

Michael Bretz, Professor; Ph.D., Washington (Seattle), 1971. Experimental low-temperature physics, condensed-matter physics.

Philip H. Bucksbaum, Otto Laporte Professor of Physics and Associate Director, NSF Center for Ultrafast Optical Science; Ph.D., Berkeley, 1980. Experimental atomic and optical physics.

Myron Campbell, Professor; Ph.D., Yale, 1982. Experimental high-energy physics, elementary particles.

J. Wehrley Chapman, Professor; Ph.D., Duke, 1966. Experimental high-energy physics.

Timothy E. Chupp, Professor; Ph.D., Washington (Seattle), 1983. Experimental atomic physics.

Roy Clarke, Professor and Director, Applied Physics Program; Ph.D., Queen Mary College (London), 1973. Experimental condensed-matter physics.

C. Tristram Coffin, Emeritus Professor; Ph.D., Washington (Seattle), 1956. Biophysics.

H. Richard Crane, Emeritus Professor; Ph.D., Caltech, 1934. Nuclear physics, precision measurements, biophysics.

Steven Dierker, Professor; Ph.D., Illinois at Urbana-Champaign, 1983. Experimental condensed-matter physics.

Martin B. Einhorn, Professor; Ph.D., Princeton, 1968. Theoretical high-energy physics, elementary particles.

August Evrard, Associate Professor; Ph.D., SUNY at Stony Brook, 1980. Theoretical astrophysics.

George W. Ford, Emeritus Professor; Ph.D., Michigan, 1954. Theoretical physics.

Katherine Freese, Associate Professor; Ph.D., Chicago, 1984. Theoretical astrophysics.

David Gerdes, Assistant Professor; Ph.D., Chicago, 1992. High-energy physics.

David W. Gidley, Professor; Ph.D., Michigan, 1979. Experimental physics, atomic physics.

Walter S. Gray, Associate Professor; Ph.D., Colorado, 1964. Experimental nuclear physics.

Wayne E. Hazen, Emeritus Professor; Ph.D., California, 1941. Cosmic rays, nuclear physics, elementary particles.

Karl T. Hecht, Emeritus Professor; Ph.D., Michigan, 1955. Theoretical nuclear physics.

Dennis J. Hegyi, Professor; Ph.D., Princeton, 1968. Experimental physics, astrophysics.

Alfred Z. Hendel, Emeritus Professor; Ph.D., Paris, 1955. Cosmic rays, elementary particles.

Joachim W. Jänecke, Emeritus Professor; Dr.rer.nat., Heidelberg, 1955. Experimental nuclear physics.

Lawrence W. Jones, Professor; Ph.D., Berkeley, 1952. Experimental high-energy physics, elementary particles.

Gordon L. Kane, Professor; Ph.D., Illinois, 1963. Theoretical physics, elementary particles.

Ernst Katz, Emeritus Professor; Ph.D., Utrecht (Netherlands), 1941. Solid-state physics.

Samuel Krimm, Professor and Director of the Protein Structure and Design Program; Ph.D., Princeton, 1950. Experimental biophysics.

Alan D. Krisch, Professor; Ph.D., Cornell, 1964. Experimental high-energy physics, elementary particles.

Jean P. Krisch, Professor; Ph.D., Cornell, 1965. Theoretical physics, elementary particles, physics teaching.

Cagliyan Kurdak, Assistant Professor; Ph.D., Princeton, 1995. Condensed-matter physics.

Robert R. Lewis, Emeritus Professor; Ph.D., Michigan, 1954. Theoretical low-energy physics.

Michael J. Longo, Professor; Ph.D., Berkeley, 1961. Experimental high-energy physics, instrumentation.

Wolfgang B. Lorenzon, Assistant Professor; Ph.D., Basel (Switzerland), 1988. Experimental high-energy physics.

Frederick MacKintosh, Associate Professor; Ph.D., Princeton, 1989. Condensed-matter theory.

Timothy McKay, Assistant Professor; Ph.D., Chicago, 1992. Astrophysics.

Roberto D. Merlin, Professor; Dr.rer.nat., Stuttgart, 1978. Experimental condensed-matter physics, applied physics.

Donald I. Meyer, Emeritus Professor; Ph.D., Washington (Seattle), 1953. Astrophysics, experimental high-energy physics.

Margaret M. Murnane, Associate Professor; Ph.D., Berkeley, 1989. Experimental atomic physics.

Homer A. Neal, Professor, Vice President Emeritus for Research, and Director, Project ATLAS; Ph.D., Michigan, 1966. Experimental high-energy physics.

Franco Nori, Associate Professor; Ph.D., Illinois at Urbana-Champaign, 1987. Condensed-matter theory.

Bradford G. Orr, Associate Professor; Ph.D., Minnesota, 1985. Experimental condensed-matter physics, applied physics.

Oliver E. Overseth, Emeritus Professor; Ph.D., Brown, 1958. Experimental high-energy physics, elementary particles.

William C. Parkinson, Emeritus Professor; Ph.D., Michigan, 1948. Nuclear physics, biophysics.

Jian-Ming Qian, Associate Professor; Ph.D., MIT, 1991. Experimental high-energy physics.

Steven Rand, Associate Professor; Ph.D., Toronto, 1978. Optical physics, applied physics.

John Keith Riles, Associate Professor; Ph.D., Stanford, 1989. Experimental high-energy physics.

Byron P. Roe, Professor; Ph.D., Cornell, 1959. Experimental high-energy physics, elementary particles.

Alberto Rojo, Assistant Professor; Ph.D., Universidad Nacional de Cuyo (Argentina), 1990. Condensed-matter theory.

Marc H. Ross, Professor; Ph.D., Wisconsin, 1952. Energy resources, theoretical physics.

Leonard M. Sander, Professor; Ph.D., Berkeley, 1968. Theoretical physics, condensed matter.

T. Michael Sanders, Professor; Ph.D., Columbia, 1954. Experimental physics, low temperatures, condensed matter.

Richard H. Sands, Emeritus Professor; Ph.D., Washington (St. Louis), 1954. Biophysics.

Robert S. Savit, Professor; Ph.D., Stanford, 1973. Theoretical condensed-matter physics, elementary particles.

Daniel Sinclair, Emeritus Professor; Ph.D., Glasgow, 1957. Experimental high-energy physics, particle astrophysics.

Duncan G. Steel, Professor; Ph.D., Michigan, 1976. Experimental atomic and optical physics.

Gregory Tarlé, Professor; Ph.D., Berkeley, 1978. Experimental astrophysics, nuclear physics.

Rudolf P. Thun, Professor; Ph.D., SUNY at Stony Brook, 1980. Experimental high-energy physics, elementary particles.

Robert S. Tickle, Emeritus Professor; Ph.D., Virginia, 1960. Experimental nuclear physics.

Yukio Tomozawa, Professor; Ph.D., Tokyo, 1961. Theoretical high-energy physics, astrophysics.

Ctirad Uher, Professor and Chair; Ph.D., New South Wales, 1975. Experimental condensed-matter physics, applied physics.

John C. van der Velde, Emeritus Professor; Ph.D., Michigan, 1958. Experimental high-energy physics, astrophysics.

Martinus J. G. Veltman, MacArthur Professor Emeritus of Theoretical Physics; Ph.D., Utrecht (Netherlands), 1963. Elementary particles.

John F. Ward, Professor; D.Phil., Oxford, 1961. Experimental atomic and optical physics.

Marc Weidenbeck, Emeritus Professor; Ph.D., Alberta, 1944. Nuclear physics.

Gabriel Weinreich, Emeritus Professor; Ph.D., Columbia, 1954. Experimental physics, atomic physics, musical acoustics.

David N. Williams, Emeritus Professor; Ph.D., Berkeley, 1964. Theoretical physics, elementary particles.

Alfred C. T. Wu, Emeritus Professor; Ph.D., Maryland, 1960. Theoretical physics.

Y. P. Edward Yao, Professor; Ph.D., Harvard, 1964. Theoretical high-energy physics, elementary particles.

Bing Zhou, Associate Professor; Ph.D., MIT, 1987. High-energy physics.

Jens C. Zorn, Professor; Ph.D., Yale, 1961. Experimental physics, atomic physics.

UNIVERSITY OF NEW MEXICO

Department of Physics and Astronomy

Programs of Study

The Department of Physics and Astronomy offers M.S. and Ph.D. degrees in physics and a Ph.D. degree in optical sciences. An undergraduate major in physics or its equivalent is required. The master's degree includes courses in the areas of classical mechanics, statistical mechanics and thermodynamics, electrodynamics, and quantum mechanics. The degree is offered either with or without a thesis, with additional course work required for the latter option. The Ph.D. in physics includes course work in the above four areas, a laboratory or problems course, and additional seminars and electives. The Ph.D. in optical sciences includes classes in advanced optics, nonlinear optics, laser physics, methods in theoretical physics, electrodynamics, quantum mechanics, and one elective. Some additional courses may be required if not taken in the student's prior education. The student must pass written and oral comprehensive examinations to proceed to Ph.D. candidacy.

In theoretical physics, areas of specialization include general relativity, plasma physics, statistical mechanics, and nuclear physics; in experimental physics, areas include atomic physics, biophysics and medical physics, condensed matter and surface physics, cosmic radiation and space physics, and medium- and high-energy particle physics; in optical sciences, areas include lasers, relativity, Raman scattering, nonlinear optics, optical signal processing, interferometry, and gratings; and in astrophysics, areas include large-scale structure of the universe, clusters of galaxies, ISM and star formation in galaxies, galaxy halos, cosmic rays, galactic nuclei, star surveys, and close binary stars.

Research Facilities

Associated with the department are the Center for Advanced Studies, the New Mexico Center for Particle Physics, and the Institute for Astrophysics, all located in the department building; the Center for High Technology Materials, located in the University of New Mexico's Research Park; and the Capilla Peak Observatory. Considerable interaction occurs between these centers and the optical research interests at the Air Force Research Laboratory and Sandia National Laboratories. Opportunities for research are also available at the Los Alamos National Laboratory and the Very Large Array in Socorro. Other facilities with cooperative agreements include the Fermi National Accelerator Laboratory and the Brookhaven National Laboratory. Astrophysical research also employs the Kitt Peak National Observatory and the OVRO and BIMA millimeter-wave interferometers.

Financial Aid

Teaching or graduate assistantships (TAs or GAs) are normally available to all entering students. For a work load of 15–20 hours per week, the 1999–2000 stipend is $10,462 ($11,130 for post-master's degree students), with a tuition scholarship of $9456. Appointments are guaranteed for two years, with the possibility of extension dependent on special circumstances. While the department cannot guarantee summer research assistantships (RAs), they are usually available. Compensation for teaching, graduate, and research assistantships is taxable.

Cost of Study

New Mexico state resident full-time tuition is $2600 for the two-semester academic year. Nonresident full-time tuition is $9456 for the two-semester academic year. All graduate students currently pay an annual $32 Graduate and Professional Student Association (GPSA) fee.

Living and Housing Costs

Combination dormitory/meal plans are available at a cost of $4388 to $4800 for the two-semester academic year. University apartments for married students currently rent for $410 to $553 a month, including utilities. A variety of accommodations are also available in the Albuquerque area.

Student Group

The number of graduate students in the Department of Physics and Astronomy is currently about 100. These students represent a wide variety of academic, ethnic, and national backgrounds.

Location

The University of New Mexico is located in Albuquerque, a metropolitan area of more than 600,000. The campus lies a mile above sea level on a plateau overlooking the Rio Grande to the west. About twelve miles to the east are the Sandia Mountains, rising to 10,700 feet. Albuquerque is noted for its dry and sunny climate, which, combined with its physical setting, provides nearly year-round outdoor recreational opportunities. Historic Santa Fe, renowned as a center for the arts and music, lies 60 miles to the north. The University offers an opportunity to work and study in a distinctive setting rich in the traditions of Native American, Hispanic, Anglo, and African-American cultures. The excellent learning and research environment at the University of New Mexico is further enhanced by its proximity to the Los Alamos and Sandia National Laboratories and to the U.S. Air Force's Research Laboratory.

The University

The University of New Mexico was created by an act of the territorial legislature in 1889, twenty-three years before New Mexico became a state. Opening as a summer normal school on June 15, 1892, it began full-time instruction on September 21 of the same year. It has grown to be fifty-fifth in public and private research expenditures and is one of the premier research universities in the United States.

Applying

Applications, specifying the Department of Physics and Astronomy, must be made on a form available from the Graduate Admissions Coordinator, Humanities 107, University of New Mexico, Albuquerque, New Mexico 87131 (telephone: 505-277-2711 or 800-CALL-UNM, toll-free; fax: 505-277-7406). A nonrefundable fee of $25 must accompany the application. Applications requesting financial assistance and those from international students must be received by March 1. For best consideration, applications should be received by February 1. Other applications may be considered until June 30 (fall semester), October 31 (spring semester), or April 30 (summer session). Admission consideration is open to all qualified candidates without regard to race, color, national origin, religion, sex, or handicap.

Students need not submit a GAPSFAS form unless they are requesting a loan.

Correspondence and Information

Academic Advisor
Department of Physics and Astronomy
University of New Mexico
Albuquerque, New Mexico 87131
E-mail: panda8@unm.edu

University of New Mexico

THE FACULTY AND THEIR RESEARCH

The following list highlights areas of research interest for each faculty member. Although the department emphasizes optics, astrophysics, particle physics, condensed matter physics, materials science, and high-energy physics, active work is being conducted in nearly every area of physics.

H. S. Ahluwalia. Cosmic radiation, plasma physics, space physics, solar physics, nuclear electronics.

B. Bassalleck. Strangeness physics, including multistrange objects, rare K-decays, CP violation, spin physics at RHIC/PHENIX.

H. C. Bryant. Experimental atomic physics, the structure of the negative ion of hydrogen.

K. Cahill. Particle theory, lattice gauge theory, protein folding, medical physics.

B. G. Campbell. Infrared, optical, and radio astronomy; multiwavelength observations of the radiative and morphological properties of young stellar objects; star formation.

C. M. Caves. Information physics, quantum information theory, quantum chaos, quantum optics, quantum measurement theory.

C. Chandler. Multichannel quantum scattering theory for ionization of atoms and for nuclear few-body reactions, including low-energy pions.

I. H. Deutsch. Theoretical quantum optics, atom optics, photonic devices, quantum information processing.

J.-C. Diels. Ultrashort and ultra-intense pulse generation, amplification and measurement, ring lasers as gyros and sensors for small («0.01 Angstrom) displacements, interaction of intense laser fields with matter, laser-induced discharges.

B. D. Dieterle. Experimental neutrino physics.

R. V. Duncan. Low-temperature physics, superfluid transition in 4He under a heat flux, nonequilibrium critical phenomena, high-resolution experiments on low Earth orbit.

D. H. Dunlap. Theory of charge transport in disordered molecular solids.

N. Duric. Origin of cosmic rays, nature of galaxy halos, evolution of supernova remnants, search for extrasolar planets.

D. Finley. General relativity, exact solutions of Einstein's field equations, gravitational radiation, complex manifolds and HH spaces, symmetries of nonlinear partial differential equations, (infinite-dimensional) Lie algebras of symmetries.

M. S. Gold. Experimental high-energy physics.

S. A. Gregory. Extragalactic astronomy, galaxy clusters and superclusters, voids, image processing and red shifts.

P. A. Henning. Neutral hydrogen in galaxies, large-scale structure of the universe, material content of cosmic voids.

V. M. Kenkre. Theoretical solid-state physics, nonequilibrium statistical mechanics, nonlinear physics, granular materials, chemical physics.

J. A. J. Matthews. High-energy collider physics, extremely high-energy cosmic ray physics, particle physics instrumentation.

J. T. McGraw. Astronomy from the moon; photometric surveys of stars, galaxies, and galactic structure.

J. K. McIver. Symmetries of nonlinear partial differential equations, multiphoton effects in intense laser fields, nonlinear frequency conversion, kinetics in gas lasers, systems of coupled nonlinear elements.

J. A. Panitz. High-field, ion microscopy; solid-liquid interfaces.

R. M. Price. Galactic and extragalactic radio astronomy, radio properties of nuclei of galaxies.

S. Prasad. Optical interferometric imaging, information dynamics in image processing, quantum optics, optical fibers.

R. J. Rand. Interstellar matter and star formation in galaxies, disk-halo connection, starbursts, interstellar magnetic fields.

W. G. Rudolph. Nonlinear optics, laser physics, optical spectroscopy and imaging, ultrashort light pulses and applications.

S. C. Seidel. Experimental elementary particle physics and instrumentation.

M. Sheik-Bahae. Nonlinear optics, ultrafast phenomena, solid-state physics.

D. M. Wolfe. Experimental intermediate-energy physics.

M. Zeilik II. Infrared astronomy, cultural astronomy, astronomy education research.

University Professor

M. Gell-Mann. Complex systems, measures of complexity, decoherent histories in quantum mechanics.

Jointly Appointed Faculty

S. R. J. Brueck (Electrical and Computer Engineering). Nonlinear optics, optical lithography, silicon manufacturing methodology, nanoscale fabrication, laser-material interactions.

R. K. Jain (Electrical and Computer Engineering). Quantum electronics, optoelectronics, experimental solid-state physics.

C. A. Kelsey (Radiology). Biomedical physics.

M. Osiński (Electrical and Computer Engineering). Semiconductor lasers, optoelectronic devices and materials, group-III nitrides, degradation mechanisms and reliability, computer simulation.

Research and Affiliated Faculty

D. Emin. Transport in condensed matter, polaron theory, phonon-assisted processes.

D. Fields. High-energy spin physics, astrophysics, space-based research.

G. Herling. Atomic physics and quantum optics, computational physics.

J. Lowe. Experimental intermediate-energy physics.

G. Moore. Optical parametric oscillators, nonlinear optics, free-electron lasers.

G. Stephenson Jr. Neutrino physics, low-energy QCD.

SELECTED PUBLICATIONS

Ahluwalia, H. S., and M. D. Wilson. Present status of the recovery phase of cosmic ray eleven year modulation. *J. Geophys. Res.* 101:4879, 1996.

Ahluwalia, H. S., and M. M. Fikani. Cosmic ray solar semidiurnal anisotropy. 1. Treatment of experimental data. *J. Geophys. Res.* 101:11075, 1996.

Ahluwalia, H. S., and M. M. Fikani. Cosmic ray solar semidiurnal anisotropy. 2. Heliospheric relationships of anisotropy parameters. *J. Geophys. Res.* 101:11087, 1996.

Ahluwalia, H. S., G. R. Gisler, and L. I. Dorman. Milagro: An ideal detector for monitoring space weather? In *Solar Drivers of Interplanetary and Terrestrial Disturbances,* vol. 95, p. 518, eds. K. S. Balasubramanian, S. L. Keil, and R. N. Smart. Astronomical Society of the Pacific Conference Series, 1996.

Stotzer, R. W., et al. **(B. Bassalleck).** Search for the H-dibaryon in $^3He(K^-, K^+)Hn$. *Phys. Rev. Lett.* 78:3646–9, 1997.

Appel, R., et al. **(B. Bassalleck).** Experimental studies of rare K^+ decays. In *Proceedings of the 28th International Conference on High Energy Physics,* pp. 1188–94, eds. Ajduk and Wroblewski. World Scientific, 1997.

Eilerts, S., et al. **(B. Bassalleck).** Experimental studies of rare K^+ and π^0 decays. In *Intersections between Particle and Nuclear Physics, AIP Conf. Proc.* vol. 412, pp. 774–8, ed. T. W. Donnelly, 1997.

Gulley, M. S., et al. **(H. C. Bryant).** Measurement of H^-, H^0, and H^+ cross sections produced by foil-stripping of 800 MeV H^- ions. *Phys. Rev. A* 53:3201–10, 1996.

Bryant, H. C., and M. Halka. H^- spectroscopy. In *Coulomb Interactions in Nuclear and Atomic Few-Body Collisions,* pp. 221–80, eds. F. S. Levin and D. A. Micha. New York and London: Plenum Press, 1996.

Rislove, D. C., et al. **(H. C. Bryant).** Detachment of H^- using a broadly-tunable VUV source. *Bull. Amer. Phys. Soc.* 44:1095, 1996.

Cahill, K., and G. Herling. Noncompact, gauge-invariant simulations of U(1), SU(2), and SU(3). *Phys. Lett. B* 365:239, 1996.

Cahill, K. Lattice fermions without doublers. Published electronically *(hep-lat/9508013),* 1996.

Cahill, K. Random gauge transformations in noncompact SU(2) lattice simulations. Published electronically *(hep-lat/940600)* and *Phys. G: Nucl. Part. Phys.* 22:1373, 1996.

Nielsen, M., **C. M. Caves,** B. Schumacher, and H. Barnum. Information-theoretic approach to quantum error correction and reversible measurement. *Proc. Roy. Soc. London A* 454:277, 1998.

Barnum, H., **C. M. Caves** et al. Noncommuting mixed states cannot be broadcast. *Phys. Rev. Lett.* 76:2818–21, 1996.

Schack, R., and **C. M. Caves.** Chaos for Liouville probability densities. *Phys. Rev. E* 53:3387–401, 1996.

Chandler, C. On electron induced ionization of hydrogen. In *Proceedings of the 15th International Conference on Few-Body Problems in Physics,* in press.

Chandler, C., and A. G. Gibson. N-body quantum scattering theory in two Hilbert spaces. VIII. N-body integral equations. In *Few-Body Systems,* in press.

Chandler, C., and G. Bencze. Nonexistence of the Oppenheimer-Phillips process in low-energy deuteron-nucleus collisions. *Phys. Rev. C: Nucl. Phys.* 53:880–6, 1996.

Deutsch, I. H., J. Grondalski, and P. M. Alsing. Local dynamics of laser cooling in optical lattices. *Phys. Rev. A,* in press.

Jessen, P. S., and **I. H. Deutsch.** Optical lattices. In *Advances in Atomic, Molecular, and Optical Physics 37,* pp. 95–138, eds. B. Bederson and H. Walther. San Diego: Academic Press, 1996.

Deutsch, I. H., R. J. C. Spreeuw, S. L. Rolston, and W. D. Phillips. Photonic bandgaps in optical lattices. *Phys. Rev. A* 52:1394, 1995.

Diddams, S., B. Atherton, and **J.-C. Diels.** Frequency locking and unlocking in a femtosecond ring laser with the application to intracavity phase measurements. *Appl. Phys. B* 63:473–80, 1996.

Umbrasas, A., **J.-C. Diels** et al. Generation of femtosecond pulses through second harmonic compression of the output of a Nd:YAG laser. *Opt. Lett.* 20:2228–30, 1995.

Moeur, W. A., et al. **(R. V. Duncan).** Observation of self-organized criticality near the superfluid transition in 4He. *Phys. Rev. Lett.* 78:2421, 1997.

Moeur, W. A., et al. **(R. V. Duncan).** Cryogenic design of the liquid helium experiment: Critical dynamics in microgravity. *Cryogenics* 36:787–94, 1996.

Duncan, R. V. SQUID instrumentation. In *Encyclopedia of Physics.* Riverside, N.J.: Macmillan, 1996.

Dunlap, D. H. Hopping transport in molecularly doped polymers: On the relation between disorder and a field-dependent mobility. *J. Imaging Sci. Technol.* 40:291–7, 1996.

Dunlap, D. H., P. E. Parris, and **V. M. Kenkre.** Charge-dipole model for the universal field dependence of mobilities in molecularly doped polymers. *Phys. Rev. Lett.* 77:542–5, 1996.

Dunlap, D. H. Photoconduction in molecularly doped polymers: Establishing a relationship between experimental observations and the predictions of transport theory. In *SPIE Proceedings,* vol. 2850, *Organic Photorefractive Materials and Xerographic Photoreceptors,* pp. 110–20, eds. S. Ducharme and J. W. Stasiak. Bellingham, Wash., 1996.

Lacey, C., **N. Duric,** and W. M. Goss. A survey of compact radio sources in NGC 6946. *Astron. J. Suppl.* 109:417, 1997.

Devereux, N., **N. Duric,** and P. Scowen. Halpha, far infrared and thermal radio continuum emission within the late-type spiral galaxy M33. *Astron. J.* 113:236, 1997.

Duric, N., et al. Radial light distributions in five spiral galaxies: The relationship between young stars and the relativistic gas. *Astrophys. J.* 470:814, 1996.

McGraw, J. T., **N. Duric** et al. Friendly command, control, and information system for astronomy. In *Astronomical Data Analysis Software and Systems V,* vol. 101, eds. G. H. Jacoby and J. Barnes, A.S.P. Conference Series, 1996.

Jaime, M., et al. **(D. Emin).** Hall effect sign anomaly and small-polaronic conduction in $(La_{1-x}Gd_x)_{0.67}Ca_{0.33}MnO_3$. *Phys. Rev. Lett.* 78:951, 1997.

Aselage, T. L., D. R. Tallant, and **D. Emin.** Raman spectra of isotopically enriched $B_{12}As_2$, $B_{12}P_2$, $B_{12}O_2$ and $B_{12+x}C_{3-x}$: Compositions and relative stiffness of icosahedra and chain. *Phys. Rev. B* 56:3122, 1997.

Finley, D., J. F. Plebanski, and M. Przanowski. An iterative approach to twisting and diverging, type-N, vacuum Einstein equations: A (third-order) resolution of Stephani's "paradox." *Class. Quantum Grav.* 14:489–97, 1997.

Finley, D. The Robinson-Trautman type III prolongation structure contains K_2. *Commun. Math. Phys.* 178:375–90, 1996.

Finley, D., and **J. McIver.** Infinite-dimensional Estabrook-Wahlquist prolongations for the sine-Gordon equation. *J. Math. Phys.* 36:5707–34, 1995.

The CDF Collaboration, F. Abe et al. **(M. S. Gold).** Limits on quark-lepton compositeness scales from dileptons produced in 1.8 TeV *p-p* collisions. *Phys. Rev. Lett.* 79:2198–203, 1997.

The CDF Collaboration, F. Abe et al. **(M. S. Gold).** Search for new gauge bosons decaying into dileptons in *p-p* collisions at $\sqrt{s} = 1.8$ TeV. *Phys. Rev. Lett.* 79:2192–7, 1997.

The CDF Collaboration, F. Abe et al. **(M. S. Gold).** Observation of top quark production in *p-p* collisions. *Phys. Rev. Lett.* 74:2626–31, 1995.

Gregory, S. A. Digging the clues to galaxy formation in large-scale structure. *Mercury Magazine* 27(2):25, 1998.

Henning, P., et al. **(R. M. Price).** The first results from the HI Parkes Southern Zone of Avoidance survey. *BAAS* 192:5208, 1998.

Henning, P. A., et al. Galaxies discovered behind the Milky Way by the Dwingeloo Obscured Galaxies Survey. *Astron. J.* 115:584–91, 1998.

Henning, P. A. HI searches in the zone of avoidance: Past and present (and future). *Pub. Astron. Soc. Australia* 14:21–4, 1997.

Herling, G. H., and K. Wodkiewicz. Classical and nonclassical interference. *Phys. Rev. A* 57:815, 1998.

Silverman, J. D., D. E. Harris, and **W. Junor.** Multiwavelength

University of New Mexico

Selected Publications (continued)

observations of 26W20, a radio galaxy which displays BL lacertae characteristics. *Astron. Astrophys.* 335:443, 1998.

Mantovani, F., and **W. Junor** et al. Large bent jets in the inner region of CSSs. *Astron. Astrophys.* 332:10, 1998.

Kenkre, V. M. What do polarons owe to their harmonic origins? In *Fluctuations and Nonlinearity*, ed. G. P. Tsironis and E. Economou. *Physica D* 113:233–41, 1998.

Kenkre, V. M. Four stages in the study of electron-phonon interactions. *J. Luminescence* 76/77:511–7, 1998.

Parris, P. E., M. Kus, D. H. Dunlap, and **V. M. Kenkre.** Nonlinear response theory: Transport coefficients for driving fields of arbitrary magnitude. *Phys. Rev. E* 56:5295–305, 1997.

Lowe, J., et al. **(B. Bassalleck).** No Λ oscillations. *Phys. Lett. B* 384:288–92, 1996.

Matthews, J. A. J. Bulk radiation damage in silicon detectors and implications for LHC experiments. *Nucl. Instrum. Methods Phys. Res. Sect. A* 381:338–48, 1996.

The CDF Collaboration, F. Abe et al. **(J. A. J. Matthews).** Observation of top quark production in *p-p* collisions. *Phys. Rev. Lett.* 74:2626–31, 1995.

Antos, J., et al. **(J. A. J. Matthews).** The SVX II silicon vertex detector upgrade at CDF. *Nucl. Instrum. Methods Phys. Res. Sect. A* 360:118–24, 1995.

Sanchez, D. J., and **J. K. McIver.** Use of the analyticity of the generalized Fourier spectrum in object reconstruction. *JOSA A* 14:792–8, 1997.

Becker, W., S. Long, and **J. K. McIver.** Nonperturbative behavior of higher-harmonic production in a model atom. *Z. Naturforsch.* 52a:105–7, 1997.

Becker, W., et al. **(J. K. McIver).** Intensity dependence of the phase of the field-induced atomic dipole in high-harmonic generation. *Laser Phys.* 7:88–98, 1997.

Moore, G. T., K. Koch, and M. E. Dearborn. Gain enhancement of multi-stage parametric intracavity frequency conversion. *IEEE J. Quantum Electron.* 33:1734–42, 1997.

Moore, G. T., and K. Koch. The tandem optical parametric oscillator. *IEEE J. Quantum Electron.* 32:2085–94, 1996.

Moore, G. T., and K. Koch. Phasing of tandem crystals for nonlinear optical frequency conversion. *Opt. Commun.* 124:292–4, 1996.

Condon, G. R., and **J. A. Panitz.** Nanoscale imaging of the electronic tunneling barrier at a metal surface. *J. Vac. Sci. Technol. B* 16(1):23–9, 1998.

Panitz, J. A. Anecdotes from an atom-probe original. *Microscopy Microanal.* 4(supplement 2):74–5, 1998.

Olson, R. T., and **J. A. Panitz.** An instrument for investigating high electric field phenomena at small electrode separations. *Rev. Sci. Instrum.* 69(5):2067–71, 1998.

Prasad, S., and W. Guo. Multiple-scattering approach to Mie scattering from a sphere of arbitrary size. *Opt. Commun.* 136:447–60, 1997.

Prasad, S. Focusing light into a multiple-core fiber. I. Theory. *Opt. Commun.* 115:354–67, 1995.

Prasad, S. Focusing light into a multiple-core fiber. II. Application to ground-based interferometry. *Opt. Commun.* 115:368–78, 1995.

Putman, M., et al. **(R. M. Price).** Tidal disruption of the Magellanic Clouds by the Milky Way. *Nature* 394:752, 1998.

Stavely-Smith, L., et al. **(R. M. Price).** New HI-detected galaxies in the Zone of Avoidance. *Astron. J.* 116:2717, 1998.

Rand, R. J. A very deep spectrum of the diffuse ionized gas in NGC 891. *Astrophys. J.* 474:129, 1997.

Rand, R. J., and J. M. Stone. Modeling the HI supershell in the edge-on galaxy NGC 4631 as an energetic HVC impact. *Astron. J.* 111:190, 1996.

Rand, R. J. Diffuse ionized gas in nine edge-on galaxies. *Astrophys. J.* 462:712, 1996.

Dorn, P., J. Zeller, **W. Rudolph,** and **M. Sheik-Bahae.** Femtosecond nonlinear microscopy of photodetectors. In *Ultrafast Phenomena XI,* eds. T. Elsasser, J. G. Fujimoto, D. Wiersma, and W. Zinth. Springer Series in Chemical Physics, 1998.

Zeller, J., **W. Rudolph,** and **M. Sheik-Bahae.** Theoretical and experimental investigation of a quenched cavity laser with saturable absorber. *Appl. Phys. B* 66:295–303, 1998.

Rudolph, W., and M. Kempe. Trends in optical biomedical imaging. *J. Mod. Optics.* 44:1617–42, 1997.

Nicholson, J., J. Bienfang, **W. Rudolph,** and G. Hager. Intrinsic gigahertz modulation of photolytic iodine lasers. *IEEE J. Quant. Electron.* QE-33:324–8, 1997.

Ming, L., J. Nicholson, and **W. Rudolph.** Multiple pulse operation of a fs Ti:sapphire laser. *Opt. Commun.* 142:45–9, 1997.

Rudolph, W., M. Sheik-Bahae, A. Bernstein, and L. Lester. Femtosecond autocorrelation measurements based on two-photon photoconductivity in ZnSe. *Opt. Lett.* 22:313–5, 1997.

Seidel, S. C., et al. Studies of double-sided silicon microstrip detectors. *Nucl. Instrum. Methods Phys. Res. Sect. A* 383:128–36, 1996.

Frautschi, M. A., M. R. Hoeferkamp, and **S. C. Seidel.** Capacitance measurements of double-sided silicon microstrip detectors. *Nucl. Instrum. Methods Phys. Res. Sect. A* 378:284–96, 1996.

Hasselbeck, M. P., A. A. Said, E. W. Van Stryland, and **M. Sheik-Bahae.** Three-photon absorption in InAs. *Opt. Quantum Electronics* 30:193, 1998.

Stephenson, G., T. Goldman, and B. H. J. McKellar. MSW-like enhancements without matter. *Modern Phys. Lett. A* 12(31):2391–8, 1997.

Akiba, Y., et al. **(D. Wolfe).** The PHENIX experiment at RHIC. *Nucl. Phys. A* 638:565–70, 1998.

Akiba, Y., et al. **(D. Wolfe).** Spin physics with the PHENIX detector system. *Nucl. Phys. A* 638:575–578, 1998.

Ahn, J. K., et al. **(D. Wolfe).** Hyperon-proton scattering experiments with a scintillating fiber detector at KEK. *Nucl. Phys. A* 639L:21c–8c, 1998.

Yamamota, K., et al. **(D. Wolfe).** H-dibaryon search via the (K^-,K^+) reaction using a diamond target (BNL-E885). *Nucl. Phys. A* 639:371c–4c, 1998.

Zeilik, M., II. Conceptual astronomy: A novel model for teaching postsecondary science classes. *Am. J. Phys.* 65(10):987–96, 1997.

UNIVERSITY OF NOTRE DAME

Department of Physics

Programs of Study

The Department of Physics offers programs of study leading to the Ph.D. degree and the M.S. degree. Major areas of research include astronomy, astrophysics, atomic physics, elementary particle physics, general relativity, nuclear physics, condensed-matter physics, statistical physics, and the history and philosophy of science. Interdisciplinary programs are available in biophysics, radiation physics, and chemical physics.

Requirements for the Ph.D. include 72 course credit hours, seminars, and research. Students are expected to become actively involved in research during the first year and take a first-year qualifying exam. Both oral and written candidacy examinations are normally completed early in the third year. The candidate must demonstrate the ability to perform research and must show a broad understanding of physics. A thesis is required and must be approved by the student's doctoral committee and defended orally by the student before this committee.

Research Facilities

The Department of Physics, housed in Nieuwland Science Hall, has a well-equipped research library. Research facilities include 1-MV, 4-MV, and 9-MV Van de Graaff nuclear accelerators; a 1-meter magnetic spectrograph; a multidetector array for gamma-ray spectroscopy; and a dual superconducting solenoid system for radioactive beam studies. Nuclear physics programs are also under way at the Argonne National Laboratory (ANL), the National Superconducting Cyclotron Laboratory, and Thomas Jefferson National Laboratory, among others. Facilities for accelerator-based atomic physics research include vacuum ultraviolet monochromators, high-resolution position-sensitive photon detectors, and a 200-KV electrostatic accelerator system for heavy ions at Notre Dame and at ANL. Precision measurements in atomic Cs, which are necessary for interpretation of parity nonconservation experiments, are carried out using Ti-sapphire, dye, and diode lasers. Elementary particle physics research is carried out at the Tevatron Collider at Fermi National Accelerator Laboratory, Brookhaven National Laboratory (BNL), Stanford Linear Accelerator (SLAC), and the Large Hadron Collider at the CERN Laboratory in Geneva, Switzerland. On-campus facilities are used for the development of new particle detection systems, including scintillating fiber tracking and tile-fiber calorimeter detectors, and for detector development and instruction for the Quark Net National education and outreach project. An air-shower array studies high- (30–300 GeV) and ultrahigh-energy (greater than 100 TeV) cosmic rays, utilizing position-sensitive proportional wire detectors for precision angle measurements and particle identification; the array is located adjacent to the campus. Solid-state physics facilities are available for molecular-beam epitaxy (MBE) of semiconductor films, superlattices, and microstructures and for bulk crystal growth; low-temperature electron tunneling; microwave, optical, and infrared photoresponse studies of superconductors; resonance studies in ferromagnetic and paramagnetic materials; surface physics; X-ray and fluorescence characterization of solids; low-temperature thermodynamic studies; and optical and far-infrared studies of semiconductors, including photoluminescence and magnetooptical measurements. XAFS and X-ray-scattering experiments are also carried out at the ANL, and neutron diffraction studies are performed at the National Institute of Standards and Technology. In biophysics, cell culture and neurobiology facilities are available. Computing facilities include the University's IBM SP-1 and SP-2 highly parallel supercomputers and numerous workstation clusters. Departmental UNIX workstations include Suns, IBMs, SGIs, and HPs.

Financial Aid

Graduate teaching assistantships are normally available to all Ph.D. students and for 1999–2000 include a minimum nine-month stipend of $12,750, plus payment of tuition and fees. In 1999–2000, most incoming graduate assistants are supported at a level of $13,250 for nine months. Higher stipends are available for exceptionally well qualified applicants. Summer support is normally provided from federal and external research funding. Research fellowships are available on a competitive basis. Advanced students often receive support as research assistants.

Cost of Study

Graduate tuition for 1999–2000 is $21,840; summer tuition and fees are $260. Payment of tuition and fees is provided in addition to the student stipends.

Living and Housing Costs

Accommodations for single students are available on campus at a cost of $2750 to $3300 for nine months. Accommodations for married students are available near the campus for $290 to $398 (utilities extra) per month. Privately owned rooms and apartments are also for rent near the campus.

Student Group

There are 70 graduate students in the Department of Physics. In 1998–99, the University had an enrollment of 10,301 students, of whom 2,426 were graduate students.

Student Outcomes

The department has current employment data on most former graduate students. Of students who have completed their degrees over the past five years, roughly one third have accepted academic or research faculty positions, one third are employed by the government or industry, and one third hold postdoctoral positions.

Location

The University of Notre Dame is located adjacent to the city of South Bend in northern Indiana. South Bend enjoys an active social and cultural life and has numerous parks and recreation areas. Chicago is readily accessible and is less than 2 hours away by car. Nearby Lake Michigan provides excellent facilities for water sports. Skiing and other winter sports are also available in the area.

The University

The University of Notre Dame, founded in 1842, is a private, independent, coeducational school. The campus of 1,250 acres offers an uncrowded setting with two attractive lakes and numerous wooded areas. The intellectual, cultural, and athletic traditions at Notre Dame, coupled with the beauty of the campus, contribute to the University's fine reputation. The University offers a variety of cultural and recreational activities, including plays, concerts, and lecture series. On the campus are facilities for indoor and outdoor sports; tennis and ice-skating can be enjoyed the year round. The students and faculty represent a rich diversity of religious, racial, and ethnic backgrounds.

Applying

Applications are invited from qualified students without regard to sex, race, religion, or national or ethnic origin. Both the General Test and the Subject Test in physics of the GRE and three letters of recommendation are required. Complete applications should be submitted by February 1. A detailed departmental brochure and application information are available by writing to the address below or visiting the University's Web page.

Correspondence and Information

Chair, Admissions Committee
Department of Physics
University of Notre Dame
Notre Dame, Indiana 46556

Telephone: 219-631-6386
E-mail: physics@nd.edu
World Wide Web: http://www.science.nd.edu/physics/

University of Notre Dame

THE FACULTY AND THEIR RESEARCH

Ani Aprahamian, Ph.D., Clark, 1986. Experimental nuclear physics: gamma-ray spectroscopy.

Gerald B. Arnold, Ph.D., UCLA, 1977. Theoretical solid-state physics: magnetism, high-temperature superconductivity.

Albert-L. Barabasi, Ph.D., Boston University, 1994. Theoretical physics, statistical mechanics, nonlinear systems, surface science.

David P. Bennett, Ph.D., Stanford, 1986. Theoretical and observational cosmology/astrophysics, gravitational microlensing.

H. Gordon Berry, Ph.D., Wisconsin, 1967. Experimental atomic physics.

Ikaros I. Bigi, Ph.D., Munich, 1976. Theoretical high-energy physics.

Nripendra N. Biswas, Ph.D., Calcutta, 1954. Experimental physics: high-energy elementary particle physics, boson resonances and inclusive reactions.

Howard A. Blackstead, Ph.D., Rice, 1967. Experimental physics: solid-state physics, magnetism and acoustics.

Samir K. Bose, Ph.D., Rochester, 1962. Theoretical physics: black holes and other astrophysical objects in general relativity, applications of group theory to elementary particles.

Bruce A. Bunker, Ph.D., Washington (Seattle), 1980. Experimental physics: X-ray, UV, and electron spectroscopy.

Neal M. Cason, Ph.D., Wisconsin, 1964. Experimental physics: high-energy elementary particle physics, particle spectroscopy.

James T. Cushing, Ph.D., Iowa, 1963. Theoretical physics: foundational problems in quantum theory, history and philosophy of twentieth-century physics.

Malgorzata Dobrowolska-Furdyna, Ph.D., Polish Academy of Sciences, 1979. Experimental solid-state physics.

Stefan G. Frauendorf, Ph.D., Dresden Technical (Germany), 1971. Theoretical nuclear physics, atomic physics, mesoscopic systems.

Jacek K. Furdyna, Marquez University Professor; Ph.D., Northwestern, 1960. Experimental solid-state physics: man-made materials.

Alejandro Garcia, Ph.D., Washington (Seattle), 1991. Experimental nuclear physics.

Umesh Garg, Ph.D., SUNY at Stony Brook, 1978. Experimental nuclear physics: nuclear structure, giant resonances, gamma-ray spectroscopy, high-spin states.

James A. Glazier, Ph.D., Chicago, 1987. Experimental solid state, nonlinear systems, pattern formation, and biophysics.

Walter R. Johnson, Freimann Professor of Physics; Ph.D., Michigan, 1957. Theoretical physics: quantum electrodynamics, atomic physics.

Gerald L. Jones, Ph.D., Kansas, 1961. Theoretical physics: statistical mechanics.

James J. Kolata, Ph.D., Michigan State, 1969. Experimental physics: nuclear structure, heavy-ion reactions, radioactive beam physics.

A. Eugene Livingston, Ph.D., Alberta, 1974. Experimental physics: atomic physics, spectroscopy of highly ionized atoms.

John M. LoSecco, Ph.D., Harvard, 1976. Experimental and theoretical physics: high-energy elementary particle physics.

Eugene R. Marshalek, Ph.D., Berkeley, 1962. Theoretical nuclear physics.

Grant J. Mathews, Ph.D., Maryland, 1977. Theoretical astrophysics/cosmology, general relativity.

William D. McGlinn, Ph.D., Kansas, 1959. Theoretical physics: elementary particle physics.

Kathie E. Newman, Associate Dean of Science; Ph.D., Washington (Seattle), 1981. Theoretical physics: statistical mechanics, semiconductors.

John A. Poirier, Ph.D., Stanford, 1959. Experimental physics: high-energy elementary particle physics.

Terrence W. Rettig, Ph.D., Indiana, 1976. Observational astronomy: comets, solar system formation, and T Tauri stars.

Randal C. Ruchti, Ph.D., Michigan State, 1973. Experimental physics: high-energy elementary particle physics.

Steven T. Ruggiero, Ph.D., Stanford, 1981. Experimental physics: condensed-matter and low-temperature physics, superconductivity.

Jonathan R. Sapirstein, Ph.D., Stanford, 1979. Theoretical physics: quantum electrodynamics.

Uri Sarid, Ph.D., Harvard, 1990. Theoretical physics: elementary particle physics, particle astrophysics.

Peter E. Schiffer, Ph.D., Stanford, 1992. Condensed-matter experiment.

Paul E. Shanley, Ph.D., Northeastern, 1966. Theoretical physics: nuclear reactions, few-body problems, quantum chaos.

William D. Shephard, Ph.D., Wisconsin, 1962. Experimental physics: high-energy elementary particle physics, hadron and photon interactions and multiparticle systems.

Carol E. Tanner, Ph.D., Berkeley, 1985. Experimental physics: atomic physics.

Mitchell R. Wayne, Ph.D., UCLA, 1985. Experimental high-energy elementary particle physics.

Michael Wiescher, Ph.D., Münster (Germany), 1980. Experimental nuclear physics: nuclear astrophysics.

RESEARCH ACTIVITIES

Theoretical

Astrophysics/Cosmology: inflationary cosmology, primordial nucleosynthesis, cosmic microwave background, galaxy formation and evolution, large-scale structure, neutrino physics, dark matter, stellar evolution and nucleosynthesis, neutron star binaries, gravity waves, gamma-ray bursts, supernovae. (Bennett, Mathews, Sarid, Wiescher, 1 research professor, 1 postdoctoral fellow)

Atomic Physics: quantum electrodynamics, weak interactions, atomic many-body theory, photoionization and photoexcitation. (Johnson, Sapirstein, 1 visiting professor, 1 postdoctoral fellow)

Elementary Particle Physics: formal properties of quantum field theories, supersymmetry, grand unification, spontaneous breaking symmetry, phenomenology of strong and weak processes, rare decays, CP violation, supergravity and new particles. (Bigi, Bose, McGlinn, Sarid)

General Relativity: black holes in a magnetic field, charged black holes, neutron stars, numerical relativity, gravity waves. (Bose, Mathews)

History and Philosophy of Science: interpretative problems in quantum mechanics. (Cushing)

Nuclear Physics: many-body problem, nuclear reactions, few-body problem, boson expansions. (Frauendorf, Marshalek, Mathews, Shanley)

Solid State: many-body problem, superconductivity, tunneling phenomena, metal-metal interfaces, inhomogeneous and layered superconductors, hopping transport, studies of ordering in semiconductors. (Arnold, Barabasi, Newman)

Statistical Mechanics: phase transitions, critical phenomena in fluids. (Barabasi, Jones, Newman)

Experimental

Astrophysics/Astronomy: air shower array measurements of ultrahigh-energy cosmic rays, spectra and images of comets, stellar nuclear reaction rates. (Bennett, LoSecco, Poirier, Rettig, Wiescher, 2 research professors, 1 postdoctoral fellow)

Atomic Physics: atomic structure, parity violation, tests of fundamental symmetries, excitation mechanisms, and radiative decays in neutral and ionized atoms; precision lifetimes. (Berry, Livingston, Tanner, 1 visiting scholar, 1 postdoctoral fellow)

Biophysics: cell migration, neural architecture and neural computation. (Glazier)

High-Energy Elementary Particle Physics: fixed target production of heavy and light particle states, including charm, beauty particles, and gluonic matter; p$\bar{\text{p}}$ colliding beam multiparticle production, including jets and quark-gluon plasma, W, Z, and top quark production. (Biswas, Cason, LoSecco, Poirier, Ruchti, Shephard, Wayne, 3 research professors and specialists, 1 postdoctoral fellow)

Nuclear Physics: nuclear structure, reaction energies, electromagnetic transitions, gamma-ray spectroscopy, high-spin states, polarized particles, giant resonances, heavy-ion reactions, radioactive beam studies, nuclear astrophysics. (Aprahamian, Garcia, Garg, Kolata, Wiescher, 4 research professors and specialists, 2 postdoctoral fellows)

Solid-State Physics: low-temperature physics, superconducting microwave absorption, metal and semiconductor superlattices, magnetism, granular materials, magnetic resonance, magnetoelastic effects, high-temperature superconductivity, optical and far-infrared spectroscopy of semiconductors, crystal growth and MBE of semiconductors, magnetostatic effects, layered superconductors, single-electron tunneling, optical and infrared photoresponse of superconductors, X-ray absorption spectroscopy (EXAFS and XANES), condensed-matter systems. (Blackstead, Bunker, Dobrowolska-Furdyna, Furdyna, Glazier, Ruggiero, Schiffer, 2 research professors and specialists, 3 postdoctoral fellows)

University of Notre Dame

SELECTED PUBLICATIONS

Döring, J., and **A. Aprahamian** et al. Radioactive decay of ^{80}Y and low-lying states in ^{80}Sr. *Phys. Rev. C* 59:59–70, 1999.

Schatz, H., and **A. Aprahamian** et al. Reaction parameters for rp-process calculations above Z=32. *Phys. Rep.* 294:167, 1998.

Döring, J., and **A. Aprahamian** et al. New isomer in ^{80}Y. *Phys. Rev. C* 57:1159, 1998.

Wu, X., **A. Aprahamian**, et al. Multiphonon vibrational states in deformed nuclei. *Phys. Rev. C* 49:1837, 1994.

Hornbaker, D. J., et al. **(A.-L. Barabasi** and **P. Schiffer).** What keeps sandcastles standing. *Nature* 387:765, 1997.

Barabasi, A.-L., G. Grinstein, and M. A. Munoz. Directed surfaces in disordered media. *Phys. Rev. Lett.* 76:1481, 1996.

Barabasi, A.-L., and H.E. Stanley. Fractal concepts in surface growth. Cambridge University Press, Cambridge, 1995.

Vasilyev, A., et al. **(H. G. Berry** and **A. E. Livingston).** Lifetimes of the 3p ^{2}P$_{3/2}$ in sodium-like bromine (Br XXV). *Phys. Rev. A* 58:732, 1998.

Dunford, R. W., et al. **(H. G. Berry** and **A. E. Livingston).** E1-M1 damping interference in the electric field quenching of metastable Ar^{17+} ions. *Phys. Rev. Lett.* 79:3359–62, 1997.

Berry, H. G. Experiments on the fragmentation of C_{60} molecules. In *Application of Accelerators in Research & Industry,* p. 511, eds. J. L. Duggan and I. L. Morgan. AIP Press, 1997.

Ali, R., et al. **(H. G. Berry** and **A. E. Livingston).** Shape of the two-photon-continuum emission from the 1s2s ^{1}S$_0$ state in He-like krypton. *Phys. Rev. A* 55:994, 1997.

Bigi, I. I., et al. Sum rules for heavy flavor transitions in the small velocity limit. *Phys. Rev. D* 52:196, 1995.

Bigi, I. I., et al. QCD predictions for lepton spectra in inclusive heavy flavor decays. *Phys. Rev. Lett.* 71:496, 1993.

Bigi, I. I., et al. The question of CP noninvariance—as seen through the eyes of neutral beauty. In *CP Violation,* ed. C. Jarlskog. Singapore: World Scientific, 1989.

Blackstead, H. A., and J. D. Dow. Evidence of the direct role of dopant oxygen in high temperature superconductivity. *Philos. Mag. B* 73:223–230, 1996.

Blackstead, H. A., and J. D. Dow. Anomalous charge-transfer in La$_{2-x}$Sr.CuO$_4$ and in Nd$_{2-x}$Ce$_x$CuO$_4$. *J. Appl. Phys* 78:7175–7180, 1995.

Blackstead, H. A., et al. Superconductivity in PrBa$_2$Cu$_3$O$_7$. *Phys. Lett. A* 207:109, 1995.

Blackstead, H. A., and J. D. Dow. Implications of Abrikosov-Gor'kov exchange scattering for theories of high temperature superconductivity. *Phys. Lett. A* 206:107–10, 1995.

Bose, S. K. The structure of QCD vacuum and related topics. *Z. Naturforschung* 52a:133, 1997.

Bose, S. K. Projective representations of the 1 + 1 dimensional Poincaré group. *J. Math. Phys.* 37:2376, 1996.

Bose, S. K. The Galilean group in 2 + 1 space-times and its central extension. *Commun. Math. Phys.* 169:385, 1995.

Kropf, A. J., and **B. A. Bunker** et al. XAFS studies of Fe sites in synthetic and natural neuromelanins. *Biophys. J.* 75:3135–42, 1998.

Bunker, B. A., et al. XAFS and X-ray reflectivity studies of buried interfaces. *Nucl. Instrum. Methods Phys. Res. B* 133:102, 1997.

Mayanovic, R. M., and **B. A. Bunker.** Observation of anisotropic vibrational amplitudes due to thermal motion at the Cu/Al$_2$O$_3$ interface. *Phys. Lett. A* 202:225–9, 1995.

Kemner, K. M., et al. **(B. A. Bunker** and **K. E. Newman).** Atomic rearrangement at interfaces in ZnTe/CdSe superlattices. *Phys. Rev. B* 50:4327, 1994.

Bunker, B. A., Z. Wang, and Q. Islam. X-ray studies of off-center ions and ferroelectricity in PbS$_x$Te$_{1-x}$ and Zn$_x$Cd$_{1-x}$ Te alloys. *Ferroelectrics* 150:171, 1993.

Adams, G. S., et al. **(N. M. Cason, J. M. LoSecco,** and **W. D. Shephard).** Evidence for a new J^{PC}=1$^+$ exotic state in the reaction π^-p→$\pi^+\pi^-\pi^-$p state at 18 GeV/c. Brookhaven, I.H.E.P. Protvino, Indiana, Massachusetts-Dartmouth, Moscow State, Northwestern, Rensselaer Collaboration. *Phys. Rev. Lett.* 81:5760–3, 1998.

Frabetti, P. L., et al. **(N. M. Cason, R. C. Ruchti,** and **W. D. Shephard).** Analysis of the D$^+$,D$_s$$^+$→$\pi^-\pi^+\pi^+$ Dalitz plots. I.N.F.N. Bologna; Colorado; Fermilab; I.N.F.N. Frascati; Illinois; I.N.F.N. Milan; Northwestern; I.N.F.N. Pavia; Puerto Rico; California, Davis; South Carolina; Vanderbilt; North Carolina at Asheville; Tennessee; Korea Collaboration. *Phys. Lett. B* 407:79–91, 1997.

Thompson, D. R., et al. **(N. M. Cason, J. M. LoSecco,** and **W. D. Shephard).** Evidence for exotic meson production in the reaction π^-p→$\eta\pi^-$p. Brookhaven, I.H.E.P. Protvino, Indiana, Massachusetts-Dartmouth, Moscow State, Northwestern, Rensselaer Collaboration. *Phys. Rev. Lett.* 79:1630–3, 1997.

Adams, T., **N. Cason, J. M. LoSecco, W. D. Shephard,** et al. Design and performance of a cesium iodide detector. *Nucl. Instrum. Methods A* 368:617–27, 1996.

Cushing, J. T. *Philosophical Concepts in Physics.* Cambridge University Press, 1998.

Cushing, J. T. *Quantum Mechanics: Historical Contingency and the Copenhagen Hegemony.* University of Chicago Press, 1994.

Cushing, J. T., and E. McMullin. *Philosophical Consequences of Quantum Theory,* University of Notre Dame Press, 1989.

Dobrowolska, M., H. Luo, and **J. K. Furdyna.** Optical properties of diluted magnetic semiconductor quantum structures. *Acta Phys. Polonica A* 87:95, 1995 (invited).

Dobrowolska, M., and H. Luo. Diluted magnetic semiconductors as a tool for wave function mapping in semiconductor heterostructures. *J. Luminescence* 60/61:308, 1994 (invited).

Dai, N., **M. Dobrowolska,** et al. Observation of above-barrier transitions in superlattices with small magnetically induced band offsets. *Phys. Rev. B* 50:18153, 1994.

Luoi, H. M., **M. Dobrowolska,** et al. Observation of quasi-bound states in semiconductor single quantum barriers. *Phys. Rev. Lett.* 70:1307, 1993.

Shen, Q., H. Luo, and **J. K. Furdyna.** Spatial dependence of exchange interaction in Heisenberg antiferromagnet ZnMnTe. *Phys. Rev. Lett.* 75:2590, 1995.

Luo H., and **J. K. Furdyna.** The II-VI semiconductor blue-green laser: Challenges and solutions. *Semicond. Sci. Technol.* 10:1041, 1995 (invited).

Short, S. W., **J. K. Furdyna,** et al. Quantum-confined Stark effect in ZnSe/ZnCdSe quantum wells. *Appl. Phys. Lett.* 67:503, 1995.

Ahrenkiel, S. P., **J. K. Furdyna,** et al. Self-organized formation of compositionally modulated ZnSeTe superlattices. *Phys. Rev. Lett.* 75:1586, 1995.

Bhattacharya, M., and **A. Garcia** et al. Neutrino absorption efficiency of an ^{40}Ar detector from the β decay of ^{40}Ti. M. *Phys. Rev. C* 58:3677, 1998.

Bhattacharya, M., and **A. Garcia** et al. Electron capture decay of ^{116}In and nuclear structure of double beta decays. *Phys. Rev. C* 58:1247, 1998.

Kaloskamis, N. I., and **A. Garcia** et al. Isospin mixing in ^{37}K and spin decomposition of GT strength in ^{37}Ca decay. *Phys. Rev. C* 54:2047, 1997.

Hahn, K. I., and **A. Garcia** et al. Structure of ^{18}Ne and the breakout from the CNO cycle. *Phys. Rev. C* 54:1999, 1996.

Kharraja, B., and **U. Garg** et al. Quadrupole moments and identical superdeformed bands in ^{149}Tb. *Phys. Rev. C* 58:1422, 1998.

Kharraja, B., et al. **(U. Garg).** Level structures of ^{96,97,98}Ru at high angular momentum. *Phys. Rev. C* 57:85, 1998.

Kharraja, B., and **U. Garg** et al. Description of superdeformed bands in terms of incremental alignments and predictions of new superdeformed bands in $^{145-148}$Eu, ^{148,149}Tb, and ^{149,150}Dy. *Phys. Rev. Lett.* 80:1845, 1998.

Davis, B. F., and **U. Garg** et al. Evidence for the isoscalar giant dipole resonance in ^{208}Pb using inelastic α scattering at and near 0°. *Phys. Rev. Lett.* 79:609, 1997.

Glazier, J. A., S. Raghavachari, C. L. Berthelsen, and M. H. Skolnick. Reconstructing phylogeny from the multifractal spectrum of mitochondrial DNA. *Phys. Rev. E* 51:2665–8, 1995.

Gonatas, C. P., et al. **(J. A. Glazier).** Magnetic resonance images of coarsening inside a foam. *Phys. Rev. Lett.* 75:573–6, 1995.

Raghavachari, S., and **J. A. Glazier.** Partially coherent states in fractally coupled map lattices. *Phys. Rev. Lett.* 74:3297–3300, 1995.

Mombach, J. C. M., **J. A. Glazier,** R. C. Raphael, and M. Zajac. Quantitative comparison between differential adhesion models and cell sorting in the presence and absence of fluctuations. *Phys. Rev. Lett.* 75:2244–7, 1995.

Derevianko, A., **W. R. Johnson,** and S. Fritzsche. Many-body calculations of the static atom-wall interaction potential for alkali-metal atoms. *Phys. Rev. A* 57:2629–34, 1998.

Johnson, W. R., M. S. Safronova, and A. Dereviako. All-order methods in relativistic atomic structure theory. In *Atomic Processes in Plasmas AIP Conference Proceedings,* ed. M. Pindzola. New York: AIP Press, 1998.

Johnson, W. R. QED effects on inner shells of heavy atoms. In

University of Notre Dame

Selected Publications (continued)

Frontier Tests of QED and Physics of the Vacuum State, pp. 320–33, eds. E. Zavattini, D. Bakalov, and C. Rizzo. Sofia, Bulgaria: Heron Press, 1998.

Avgoustoglou, E., **W. R. Johnson**, Z. W. Liu, and **J. Sapirstein.** Relativistic many-body calculations of [2p5 3s] excited-state energy levels of neonlike ions. *Phys. Rev. A* 51:1196, 1995.

Jones, G. L. Symmetries and conservation laws of differential equations. *Il Nuovo Cimento* 112B:1053–9, 1997.

Kolata, J. J., et al. Subbarrier fusion of ^{6}He with ^{209}Bi. *Phys. Rev. Lett.* 81:4580–3, 1998.

Zecher, P. D., et al. **(J. J. Kolata).** Measurement of the ^{8}Li (n, γ) ^{9}Li cross section at astrophysical energies by reverse kinematics. *Phys. Rev. C* 57:959–66, 1998.

Tostevin, J. A., et al. **(J. J. Kolata).** Elastic and quasielastic scattering of ^{8}He from ^{12}C. *Phys. Rev. C* 56 (Rapid Communications):R2929–33, 1997.

Belbot, M. D., **J. J. Kolata,** et al. β-delayed neutron decay of ^{14}Be. *Phys. Rev. C* 51:2372–80, 1995.

Schaeffer, H. W., et al. **(A. E. Livingston).** Measurement of the two-photon spectral distribution from decay of the 1s2s $^1S_0$ level in He-like nickel. *Phys. Rev. A* 59:245–50, 1999.

Bosselmann, Ph., et al. **(A. E. Livingston).** Measurements of 2s-2p transition energies in lithiumlike Ni^{25+} and Zn^{27+}. *Phys. Rev. A* 58:3516–23, 1998.

Livingston, A. E., et al. The extreme ultraviolet spectrum of Ne III. *J. Opt. Soc. Am. B* 14:522–5, 1997.

Kukla, K. W., et al. **(A. E. Livingston** and **H. G. Berry).** Fine structure energies for the 1s2s ^{3}S - 1s2p ^{3}P transition in heliumlike Ar16+. *Phys. Rev. A* 51:1905–17, 1995.

LoSecco, J. M., G. E. A. Matsas, A. A. Natale, and J. A. F. Pacheco. Pulsar test of a violation of discrete symmetries in gravitation. *Phys. Lett. A* 138:5, 1989.

LoSecco, J. M., F. Reines, and D. Sinclair. The search for proton decay. In *Particle Physics in the Cosmos: A Scientific American Reader,* ed. R. A. Carrigan Jr. and W. P. Trower, New York: W. H. Freeman and Company, 1989.

Mathews, G. J., T. Kajino, and M. Orito. Inhomogeneous primordial nucleosynthesis and new abundance constraints on Ω_b. *Astrophys. J.* 456:98, 1996.

Wilson, J. R., and **G. J. Mathews.** Instabilities in close neutron star binaries. *Phys. Rev. Lett.* 75:4161, 1995.

Lee, S., D. N. Schramm, and **G. J. Mathews.** A merger model and globular cluster formation. *Astrophys. J.* 449:616, 1995.

Woosley, S. E., et al. **(G. J. Mathews).** The r-process and neutrino-heated supernova ejecta. *Astrophys. J.* 433:229, 1994.

McGlinn, W. D., L. O'Raifeartaigh, S. Sen, and R. D. Sorkin. Morse theory and the topology of configuration space. *Int. J. Mod. Phys. A,* 2(5):823–43, 1996.

McGettrick, M., N. Gorman, L. O'Raifeartaigh, and **W. D. McGlinn.** Virasoro operators for arbitrarily twisted Kac-Moody algebras. *Int. J. Mod. Phys. A* 7:2547, 1992.

Balachandran, A. P., et al. **(W. D. McGlinn).** The spin-statistics connection from homology groups of configuration space and an Anyon Wess-Zumino Term. *Int. J. Mod. Phys. A* 7:27, 6887, 1992.

Vandeworp, E. M., and **K. E. Newman.** Coherent alloy separation: Differences in canonical and grand canonical ensembles. *Phys. Rev. B* 55:14222–9, 1997.

Vandeworp, E. M., and **K. E. Newman.** Order-disorder in a model lattice-mismatched binary alloy. *Phys. Rev. B* 52:4086–92, 1995.

Poirier, J., et al. A new visible, Hh, to use in measuring the chemical composition of cosmic ray primaries. *Proc. 24th Int. Cosmic Ray Conf.,* I.U.P.A.P., Vol. 3, pp. 532–35, Rome, Italy, 1995.

Trzupek, A., Y. Lu, and **J. Poirier.** Survey for stellar sources using identified single muons at sea level. *Proc. 23rd Int. Cosmic Ray Conf.,* Vol. 4, pp. 454–7, Calgary, Alberta, Canada, 1993.

Trzupek, A., J. Kochocki, Y. Lu, and **J. Poirier.** The secondary gamma composition from hadronic and electromagnetic extensive air showers at 10, 100, 1000, and 10,000 TeV. *J. Phys. G: Nucl. Part. Phys.* 18:1849–61, 1992.

Hahn, J. M., W. R. Ward, and **T. W. Rettig.** Resonant trapping in a self gravitating planetesimal disk. *Icarus* 117:25–44, 1995.

Tegler, S. C., et al. **(T. W. Rettig).** Evidence for chemical processing of pre-cometary icy grains in circumstellar environments of pre-main-sequence stars. *Astrophys. J.* 439:279, 1995.

Weintraub, D. A., S. C. Tegler, J. H. Kastner, and **T. W. Rettig.** Infrared spectroscopy and imaging polarimetry of the disk around the T Tauri star RNO 91. *Astrophys. J.* 423:674, 1994.

Ruchti, R. Physics prospects with the upgraded D0 detector. *Proc. 10th Topical Workshop on Proton-Antiproton Collider Physics,* eds. R. Raja and J. Yoh. Fermi National Accelerator Laboratory, Batavia, IL, pp. 421–435, 1996.

Ruchti, R., and **M. R. Wayne.** The D0 collaboration, observation of the top quark. *Phys. Rev. Lett.* 74, 2632–7, 1995.

Ruchti, R., and **M. R. Wayne.** The D0 collaboration, W and Z Boson production in p collisions at = 1.8 TeV. *Phys. Rev. Lett.* 75:1466, 1995.

Ruchti, R. Tracking with scintillating fibers. *Nucl. Physics B.* (Proc. Suppl.) 44:308, 1995.

Ruggiero, S. T., et al. **(C. E. Tanner).** Wavelength dependent photo response in YBCO thin-film systems. *IEEE Trans. Appl. Superconductivity,* in press.

Ruggiero, S. T. Tunneling and Josephson junctions. In *Encyclopedia of Electrical and Electronics Engineering.* New York: Wiley, in press.

Nolen, S., and **S. T. Ruggiero.** Tunneling spectroscopy of fullerene/Ge multilayer systems. *Chem. Phys. Lett.,* in press.

Nolen, S., and **S. T. Ruggiero.** Tunneling in multilayer fullerene/ $A\ell_2O_3$ and fullerene/Ge systems. *Phys. Rev. B* 79:10942, 1998.

Sapirstein, J. Theory of many-electron atoms. *Physica Scripta* T46:52, 1993.

Rattazzi R., and **U. Sarid.** Unified minimal supersymmetric model with large Yukawa couplings. *Phys. Rev. D* 53:1553, 1996.

Hall, L. J., R. Rattazzi, and **U. Sarid.** The top quark mass in supersymmetric SO(10) unification. *Phys. Rev. D* 50:7048, 1994.

Hall, L. J., and **U. Sarid.** Gravitational smearing of minimal supersymmetric unification. *Phys Rev. Lett.* 70:2673, 1993.

Albert, R., M. A. Pfeiffer, **P. Schiffer,** and **A.-L. Barabasi.** Slow drag in a granular medium. *Phys. Rev. Lett.* 82:205, 1999.

Schiffer, P., et al. Frustration induced spin freezing in a site-ordered magnet: Gadolinium gallium garnet. *Phys. Rev. Lett.* 74:2379, 1995.

Schiffer, P., and D. D. Osheroff. The AB transition in superfluid helium-3: Baked Alaska and surface effects. *Rev. of Mod. Phys.* 67:491, 1995.

Schiffer, P., A. P. Ramirez, W. Bao, and S-W. Cheong. Low temperature magnetoresistance and the magnetic phase diagram of La (1-x)Ca(x)MnO(3). *Phys. Rev. Lett.* 75:3336, 1995.

Frabetti, P. L., **W. D. Shephard** et al. Study of higher mass charm baryons decaying to Λ_c^+. *Phys. Lett. B* 365:461–469, 1996.

Frabetti, P.L., **W. D. Shephard** et al. Study of charged hadronic four body decays of the D$_0$. *Phys. Lett. B* 354:486, 1995.

Rafac, R. J., et al. **(C. E. Tanner, A. E. Livingston,** and **H. G. Berry).** Precision lifetime measurements of the 6p 2P1/2,3/2 states in atomic cesium. *Phys. Rev. A* 50:R1976–9, 1994.

Wayne, M. R. The D0 upgrade tracker and projections for B physics. *Nucl. Instrum. Methods Phys. Res. A* 351:77, 1994.

Baumbaugh, B., **M. R. Wayne** et al. Performance of multiclad scintillating and clear waveguide fibers read out with visible light photon counters. *Nucl. Instrum. Methods Phys. Res. A* 345:271, 1994.

Meissner, J., et al. **(M. Wiescher).** Neutron capture cross section of 18O and its astrophysical implications. *Phys. Rev. C* 53:459, 1996.

Ross, J. G., et al. **(M. Wiescher).** Indirect study of resonances in ^{31}P$(p,\alpha)^{28}$Si and ^{35}Cl$(p,\alpha)^{32}$S. *Phys. Rev. C* 52:1681, 1995.

Gorres, J., H. Herndl, I. J. Thompson, and **M. Wiescher.** Two-neutron capture reactions in supernovae neutrino bubbles. *Phys. Rev. C* 52:2231, 1995.

Champagne, A. E., and **M. Wiescher.** Explosive hydrogen burning. *Ann. Rev. Nucl. Part. Sci.* 42:39, 1992.

UNIVERSITY OF OREGON

Department of Physics

Programs of Study

The Department of Physics offers graduate programs that lead to the Doctor of Philosophy, Master of Arts, and Master of Science degrees. Most of the broadly defined research areas of interest in physics are represented in the Department of Physics at Oregon. These include theoretical and experimental programs in astrophysics, cosmology, and relativity; atomic, molecular, and optical physics; biophysics; condensed-matter physics; elementary particle physics; fluid and superfluid mechanics; nuclear physics; and physics education research. Interdisciplinary doctoral research is fostered by several research institutes, which provide facilities, support, and research guidance for graduate students and postdoctoral fellows. The institutes most closely associated with physics are the Institute of Molecular Biology, the Institute of Theoretical Science, the Oregon Center for Optics, and the Materials Science Institute. Research opportunities in geophysics are available in cooperation with the Department of Geological Sciences. Research in physics education can be pursued at the master's level. A master's program in applied physics will be offered starting in fall 2000.

The doctoral program emphasizes research work in addition to course work and generally requires five to six years of graduate study. The physics department has minimal course requirements for the Doctor of Philosophy (Ph.D.) degree and relies primarily on demonstrated competence in the qualifying examination, comprehensive examination, and doctoral-dissertation research. The master's degree programs consist primarily of course work and require one to two years to complete. Opportunities for industrial internships in partial fulfillment of the requirements for the master's degree are available.

Research Facilities

The science facilities are closely clustered on the University's 280-acre campus. The complex includes the science library and four buildings that were recently constructed at a cost of $44 million. The physics building, completed in 1989, contains 136,000 square feet of laboratory, classroom, and office space. The science departments support professionally staffed, well-equipped machine, electronics, and glass shops. For experimental elementary particle physics research, access to beamlines and detectors at the forefront particle accelerators at Fermi Lab, SLAC, and CERN is available in addition to clean room facilities for the assembly of state-of-the-art solid-state detectors and associated electronics. For astrophysics research, the department operates the Pine Mountain Observatory 32-inch network-accessible telescope with wide-field CCD camera. A wide array of instrumentation exists within the Department of Physics for advanced materials research, including molecular beam epitaxy and plasma-enhanced chemical vapor deposition facilities. Facilities for transport measurement, capacitance spectroscopy, magnetic susceptibility, electron spin resonance, and low-angle X-ray reflectometry are available, as is access to synchrotron radiation facilities and end stations at the Advanced Light Source. A variety of state-of-the-art laser systems for spectroscopy, materials processing, and characterization are available through the University of Oregon Shared Laser Facility. A 5-MeV ion accelerator with ns bunched beam MeV-ion microprobe is available. Facilities are under construction that will generate the highest Reynolds number flows and the highest Reynolds number convective flows available in any academic institution. The Computational Science Institute provides supercomputer facilities on campus that include two Silicon Graphics Power Challenges with eight and twelve R8000 CPUs and a Power Onyx with eight R10000 CPUs. The University is part of the new high-speed Internet and is extending its internal asynchronous network.

Financial Aid

Financial aid is competitively awarded to Ph.D. students in the form of teaching or research fellowships. Both require 17½ hours of work per week and provide an annual stipend of $14,400 and a tuition waiver.

Cost of Study

For 1999–2000, the proposed tuition and required fees per term for 9–16 quarter hours (the typical course load for graduate students) are $2230 for Oregon residents and $3780 for nonresidents and international students. The tuition portion is waived for those students who hold assistantships. It then costs the new graduate student only $222 per term, as set by the State Board of Higher Education.

Living and Housing Costs

The University offers housing to both single students and students with families. On-campus housing consists of residence halls, which are reserved for single students. Three off-campus family-housing facilities are also available. The Westmoreland development consists of 404 furnished one- and two-bedroom apartments. Rent is $250 and $285 per month, respectively (subject to change). Spencer View, the newest complex, has 272 apartments and is located about a half mile southwest of campus. Two-bedroom apartments are $445 per month, and three-bedroom apartments are $545 (subject to change). Located a short distance from campus, Agate is a twenty-unit complex of one- and two-bedroom apartments. Rent starts at $445 a month and is subject to change.

Student Group

There are 77 full-time graduate students, almost all of whom are enrolled in the doctoral program. Nearly all the students have financial support, teaching or research assistantships, or fellowships. The atmosphere in the department is friendly and informal; students conducting thesis research can expect to work individually and closely with their faculty advisers.

Location

The University is located in Eugene, a city that offers many cultural, entertainment, and recreational opportunities, including an award-winning performing arts center, yet retains a friendly, small-town atmosphere. Skiing, hiking, mountaineering, white-water boating, hunting, and fishing are available in the Cascade Mountains just to the east, and the coast of the Pacific Ocean, 70 miles to the west, offers more opportunities for outdoor activities.

The University and The Department

The University of Oregon enrolls close to 16,780 students. Of this total, 26 percent come from states other than Oregon, 9 percent come from other countries, and 21 percent are graduate students. In the Department of Physics there are currently more than 85 graduate students. Graduate students in physics find excellent faculty members and facilities for the pursuit of advanced studies in many exciting areas. Classroom teaching loads are held to a level that encourages excellence in teaching and research and allows research students to receive maximum attention. Frequent seminars and weekly colloquia attract many distinguished visiting physicists to the campus, which further stimulates an active research environment.

Applying

Correspondence concerning admission should be directed to the Graduate Selection Committee. Graduate study requires a bachelor's degree in physics or a related area, with an undergraduate grade point average of 3.0 (B average) in advanced physics and mathematics courses. Also required for admission are the Graduate Record Examinations (GRE) General Test and the Subject Test in Physics. The Test of English as a Foreign Language (TOEFL), with a score above 600, is required for all international students. Applications from students who are requesting a teaching assistantship should be submitted by February 15 for fall admission.

Correspondence and Information

Graduate Selection Committee
Department of Physics
1274 University of Oregon
Eugene, Oregon 97403-1274

Telephone: 541-346-4751
Fax: 541-346-5861
World Wide Web: http://zebu.uoregon.edu/

University of Oregon

THE FACULTY AND THEIR RESEARCH

Dietrich Belitz. Theoretical research at the boundary between statistical mechanics and condensed matter.

Gregory Bothun. Extragalactic observational astronomy, electronic curriculum development.

James Brau. Experiments to test and extend the standard model of elementary particle interactions and to search for gravitational radiation.

Howard J. Carmichael. Theoretical research in the area of quantum optics and nonlinear optics.

J. David Cohen. Experimental solid-state physics, defects in semiconductors, electronic properties of amorphous semiconductors.

Paul Csonka. Particle beams, accelerators, coherence properties, X-ray lasers.

N. G. Deshpande. Electroweak interactions and grand-unification.

Russell J. Donnelly. Application of liquid and gaseous cryogenic helium to the study of high Reynold's number turbulence.

Raymond Frey. Experimental studies of electroweak interactions of elementary particles and search for gravitational radiation.

Stephen Gregory. Optical and electronic properties of microscopic cavity resonators, molecular electronics.

Roger Haydock. Electronic structure and dynamics of solids.

Stephen D. H. Hsu. Applications of quantum field theory to particle physics and cosmology.

James N. Imamura. High-energy astrophysics and astrophysical fluid flows.

Stephen Kevan. Experimental surface, interface, and 2-D physics.

Dean Livelybrooks. Physics education in hands-on laboratory settings, the use of magnetotellurics and ground-penetrating radar to characterize earthquake faults.

Brian Matthews. Protein structure and function, X-ray crystallography.

Thomas Mossberg. Experimental optical physics: quantum optics, cavity QED, lasing without inversion, time-domain frequency-selective optical memory, all-optical routing and switching technologies.

Kwangjai Park. High-precision far-infrared spectroscopy, using a Tunable Far Infrared Spectrometer; spectroscopic investigation of the atmosphere.

George Rayfield. Biophysics, particularly genetically engineered proteins for optical information storage devices.

Michael G. Raymer. Quantum optics, quantum dynamics in nonlinear optics and semiconductors, ultrafast lasers, light transport in random media.

S. J. Remington. X-ray crystallography, protein structure/function relationships.

James Schombert. Galaxy evolution and formation, observational cosmology.

Peter C. Sercel. Electronic and optical properties of quantized electronic structures; quantum optics in mesoscopic semiconductor systems.

Dave Soper. Theoretical elementary particle physics.

David Strom. Experimental study of high-energy electron-positron collisions.

Richard Taylor. Electronic properties of mesoscopic semiconductor devices, wave chaos, fractal analysis of biological systems.

John Toner. Strongly fluctuating extended systems: liquid crystals, membranes, bird flocks.

Hailin Wang. Quantum optics and optical spectroscopy of semiconductors.

Robert L. Zimmerman. Astrophysics, general relativity, and cosmology.

SELECTED PUBLICATIONS

Belitz, D., T. R. Kirkpatrick, and T. Vojta. First order transitions and multicritical points in weak itinerant ferromagnets. *Phys. Rev. Lett.* 82:4707–10, 1999.

Belitz, D., and T. R. Kirkpatrick. Theory of many-fermion systems. *Phys. Rev. B* 56:6513–41, 1997.

Kirkpatrick, T. R., and **D. Belitz.** Metal-superconductor transition at zero temperature: A case of unusual scaling. *Phys. Rev. Lett.* 79:3042–5, 1997.

Belitz, D., T. R. Kirkpatrick, and T. Vojta. Nonanalytic behavior of the spin susceptibility in clean Fermi systems. *Phys. Rev. B* 55:9452–62, 1997.

Belitz, D., and T. R. Kirkpatrick. The Anderson-Mott transition. *Rev. Mod. Phys.* 66:261, 1994.

Bothun, G. H-alpha velocity mapping of ultraluminous IRAS galaxies. *Astrophys. J.,* in press.

Bothun, G. *Modern Cosmological Observations and Problems.* London: Taylor and Francis, Ltd., 1998.

Bothun, G. The ghostliest galaxies. *Sci. Am.* 276:40, 1997.

Bothun, G. Low surface brightness galaxies: Hidden galaxies revealed. *Publ. Astron. Soc. Pacific* 108:743, 1997.

Abe, K., et al. **(J. Brau).** A measurement of R(b) using a vertex mass tag. *Phys. Rev. Lett.* 80:660, 1998.

Abe, K., et al. **(J. Brau).** An improved measurement of the left-right Z0 cross-section asymmetry. *Phys. Rev. Lett.* 78:2075, 1997.

Abe, K., et al. **(J. Brau).** Design and performance of the SLD vertex detector, a 307 Mpixel tracking system. *Nucl. Instrum. Methods A* 400:287, 1997.

Abe, K., et al. **(J. Brau).** A study of the orientation and energy partition of three jet events in hadronic Z0 decays. *Phys. Rev.* 55:2533, 1997.

Carmichael, H. J. Coherence and decoherence in the interaction of light with atoms. *Phys. Rev. A* 56:5065, 1997.

Carmichael, H. J., P. Kochan, and B. C. Sanders. Photon correlation spectroscopy. *Phys. Rev. Lett.* 77:631, 1996.

Carmichael, H. J. Stochastic Schroedinger equations: What they mean and what they can do. In *Coherence and Quantum Optics VII,* pp. 177–92, eds. J. H. Eberly, L. Mandel, and E. Wolf. Plenum Press: New York, 1996.

Carmichael, H. J. Quantum trajectory theory for cascaded open systems. *Phys. Rev. Lett.* 70:2273, 1993.

Palinginis, K. C., et al. **(J. D. Cohen).** Defect densities in tetrahedrally bonded amorphous carbon deduced by junction capacitance techniques. *Appl. Phys. Lett.* 74:371, 1999.

Chen, C.-C., et al. **(J. D. Cohen).** Evidence for charged defects in intrinsic glow discharge hydrogenated amorphous silicon-germanium alloys. *Phys. Rev. B* 57:R4210, 1998.

Cohen, J. D., and D. Kwon. Identification of the dominant electron deep trap in amorphous silicon from ESR and modulated photocurrent measurements: Implications for defect models. *J. Non-Cryst. Solids* 227:348, 1998.

Kwon, D., et al. **(J. D. Cohen).** Optical spectra of crystalline silicon particles embedded in an amorphous silicon matrix. *J. Non-Cryst. Solids* 227:1040, 1998.

Csonka, P. Secondary X-ray imaging: An alternative approach to angiography and other applications. *Nucl. Instrum. Methods Phys. Res.* 431:306, 1999.

Csonka, P. Optical beam energy modulators. *J. Quantum Electronics* 33:2, 1997.

Csonka, P. Method to generate femto and attosecond electron and X-ray pulses. *Nucl. Instrum. Methods Phys. A* 376:283, 1986.

Csonka, P. Production of Multy 100 MeV gamma ray beams for nuclear and other physics research. *Nucl. Instrum. Methods Phys. Res. A* 352:579, 1995.

Deshpande, N. G., B. Dutta, and S. Oh. Susy guts contributions and model independent extractions of CP phases. *Phys. Rev. Lett.* 77:4499–502, 1996.

Deshpande, N. G., and X.-G. He. CP asymmetry in neutral B system at symmetric colliders. *Phys. Rev. Lett.* 76:360–3, 1996.

Deshpande, N. G., B. Dutta, and E. Keith. Intermediate scale as a source of lepton flavor violation in susy SO(10). *Phys. Rev. D* 54:730–4, 1996.

Deshpande, N. G., X.-G. He, and J. Trampetic. Importance of dipole penguin operator in B decays. *Phys. Lett.* B377:161–7, 1996.

Barenghi, C. F., C. J. Swanson, and **R. J. Donnelly.** Emerging issues in helium turbulence. *Low Temp. Phys.* 100:1–29, 1995.

Abe, K., et al. **(R. Frey).** An improved measurement of the left-right Z⁰ cross-section asymmetry. *Phys. Rev. Lett.* 78:2075, 1997.

Abe, K., et al. **(R. Frey).** Measurements of Rb with impact parameters and displaced vertices. *Phys. Rev. D* 53:1023, 1996.

Frey, R. Top quark physics at a future electron-position collider. *Proceedings of Third Workshop on Physics and Experiments with Electron-Positron Linear Colliders.* World Scientific, 1996.

Kuhlman, S., et al. **(R. Frey).** Physics and technology of the next linear collider. *SLAC Report 485,* June 1996.

Im, C. I., K. M. Engenhardt, and **S. Gregory.** Light-induced transient currents from molecular films in a tunneling microscope. *Phys. Rev. B* 59:3153, 1999.

Gregory, S. Experimental observation of the scattering of tunneling electrons by a single magnetic moment. *Phys. Rev. Lett.* 68:2070, 1992.

Haydock, R., C. M. M. Nex, and B. D. Simons. Calculation of relaxation rates from microscopic equations of motion. *Phys. Rev. E* 59:5292–302, 1999.

Haydock, R., and R. L. Te. Numerical evidence of an electronic localization transition in a disordered layer of metal atoms. *Phys. Rev. B* 57:296–301, 1998.

Haydock, R. Efficient electronic energy functionals for tight-binding. In *Tight Binding Approach to Computational Materials Science. MRS Symposium Proceedings 491,* pp. 35–44, eds. P. E. A. Turchi, A. Gonis, and L. Colombo. Warrendale, PA: Materials Research Society, 1998.

Arnold, W. T., and **R. Haydock.** A parallel, object-oriented implementation of the dynamic recursion method. In *Computing in Object-Oriented Parallel Environments, Second International Symposium, ISCOPE98,* pp. 199–206, eds. D. Caromel, R. R. Oldehoeft, and M. Tholburn. Berlin: Springer, 1998.

Evans, N., **S. D. H. Hsu,** and M. Schwetz. An effective field theory approach to color superconductivity at high quark density. *Nucl. Phys. B* 551:275–89, 1999.

Hormuzdiar, J. N., and **S. D. H. Hsu.** Pion breather states in QCD. *Phys. Rev. C* 59:889–93, 1999

Hsu, S. D. H., and M. Schwetz. On the QCD phase transition at finite baryon density. *Phys. Lett. B* 432:203–8, 1998.

Hsu, S. D. H., N. Evans, and M. Schwetz. Phase transitions in softly broken N=2 SQCD at non-zero theta-angle. *Nucl. Phys. B* 484:124, 1997

Steiman-Cameron, T. Y., and **J. N. Imamura.** V2301 Ophiucus: A bright eclipsing AM Herculis object. *Astrophys. J.,* in press.

Toman, J., **J. N. Imamura,** R. H. Durisen, and B. Pickett. Nonaxisymmetric instabilities of rotating polytropes. I Kelvin Modes. *Astrophys. J.* 498:370, 1998.

Fornacis, U. Z., **J. N. Imamura,** and T. Y. Steiman-Cameron. High state observations of the eclipsing AM Herculis object. *Astrophys. J.* 501:830, 1998.

Yeom, H. W., et al. **(S. D. Kevan).** Instability and charge density wave of metallic quantum chains on a silicon surface. *Phys. Rev. Lett.* 82, 1999.

Price, A. C., et al. **(S. D. Kevan).** t X-ray dynamic light scattering from smectic A films. *Phys. Rev. Lett.* 82:755, 1999.

Rotenberg, E., J. W. Chung, and **S. D. Kevan.** Spin-orbit coupling induced surface band splitting in Li/W(110) and Li/Mo(110). *Phys. Rev. Lett.* 82:4066, 1999.

Rotenberg, E., and **S. D. Kevan.** Evolution of the electronic and structural properties of W(011) with H coverage. *Phys. Rev. Lett.* 80:2905, 1998.

Mackie, R. L., **D. W. Livelybrooks,** T. R. Madden, and J. C. Larsen. A magnetotelluric investigation of the San Andreas fault at Carrizo Plain, California. *Geophys. Res. Lett.* 24:1847, 1997.

Livelybrooks, D., M. Mareschal, E. Blais, and J. T. Smith. Magnetotelluric delineation of the Trillabelle Sulfide Body in Sudbury, Ontario. *Geophysics* 61(4):971–86, 1996.

Albright, R. A., and **B. W. Matthews.** How Cro and lambda-repressor distinguish between operators: The structural basis underlying a genetic switch. *Proc. Natl. Acad. Sci. U.S.A.* 95:3431–6, 1998.

Rupert, P. B., G. W. Daughdrill, B. Bowerman, and **B. W. Matthews.** A new DNA-binding motif in the Skn-1 binding domain-DNA complex. *Nat. Struct. Biol.* 5:484–91, 1998.

Juers, D. H., R. E. Huber, and **B. W. Matthews.** Structural comparisons of TIM barrel proteins suggest functional and evolutionary relationships between beta-galactosidase and other glycohydrolases. *Protein Sci.* 8:122–36, 1999.

Sagermann, M., W. A. Baase, and **B. W. Matthews.** Structural

University of Oregon

Selected Publications (continued)

characterization of an engineered tandem repeat contrasts the importance of context and sequence in protein folding. *Proc. Natl. Acad. Sci. U.S.A.* 96:6078–83, 1999.

Sellin, P. B., C. C. Yu, J. R. Bochinski, and **T. W. Mossberg.** Intrinsically irreversible multi-photon laser gain mechanisms. *Phys. Rev. Lett.* 78:1432, 1997.

Lin, H., T. Wang, and **T. W. Mossberg.** Demonstration of 8 Gbit/in2 areal storage density using swept-carrier frequency-selective optical memory. *Opt. Lett.* 20:1658, 1995.

Mossberg, T. W., and M. Lewenstein. Quantum optics of driven atoms in colored vacua. In *Adv. At. Molec. Opt. Phys.*, supplement 2, ed. P. Berman. Academic Press, 1994.

Morin, S. E., C. C. Yu, and **T. W. Mossberg.** Optical design from a quantum optical perspective: Realizing a strong atom-cavity coupling. *Phys. Rev. Lett.* 73:1489, 1994.

Gauthier, D., Q. Wu, S. Morin, and **T. W. Mossberg.** Realization of a continuous-wave, two-photon optical laser. *Phys. Rev. Lett.* 68:464, 1992.

Park, K., et al. Pressure broadening of the 118.455 cm^{-1} rotational Lines of OH by N_2, O_2, H_2, and He. *J. Quantum Spectrosc. Rad. Transfer* 61:715, 1999.

Chance, K. V., **K. Park,** and K. M. Evenson. Pressure broadening of far infrared rotational transitions: 88.65 cm^{-1} H_2O and 114.47 cm^{-1} O_3. *J. Quantum Spectrosc. Rad. Transfer* 59:687, 1998.

Nolt, I. G., et al. **(K. Park).** Stratospheric HBr concentration profile obtained from far-infrared emission spectroscopy. *Geophys. Res. Lett.* 24:281, 1997.

Hsu, K. C., **G. W. Rayfield,** and R. Needleman. Reversal of the surface charge asymmetry in purple membrane due to single amino acid substitutions. *Biophys. J.* 70:2358–65, 1996.

Schmidt, P. K., and **G. W. Rayfield.** Hyper-Rayleigh light scattering from an aqueous suspension of purple membrane. *Appl. Optics.* 33:4286–92, 1994.

Cheng, C.-C., and **M. G. Raymer.** Long-range saturation of spatial decoherence in wave-field transport in multiple-scattering media. *Phys. Rev. Lett.* 82:4807, 1999.

Anderson, M. A., D. F. McAlister, **M. G. Raymer,** and M. C. Gupta. Pulsed squeezed light generation in chi-two nonlinear waveguides. *J. Opt. Soc. Am. B* 14:3180, 1997.

Raymer, M. G. Measuring the quantum mechanical wave function. *Contemp. Phys.* 38:343, 1997.

Leonhardt, U., and **M. G. Raymer.** Observation of moving wave packets reveals their quantum state. *Phys. Rev. Lett.* 76:1985, 1996.

Munroe, M., D. Boggavarapu, M. E. Anderson, and **M. G. Raymer.** Photon number statistics from phase-averaged quadrature field distribution: Theory and ultrafast measurement. *Phys. Rev. A* 52:R924, 1995.

Ormo, M., et al. **(S. J. Remington).** Crystal structure of the aequorea victoria green fluorescent protein. *Science* 273:1392–5, 1996.

Brejc, K., et al. **(S. J. Remington).** Structural basis for dual excitation and photoisomerization of the Aequorea victoria green fluorescent protein. *Proc. Natl. Acad. Sci. U.S.A.* 94:2306–11, 1996.

Feese, M., et al. **(S. J. Remington).** Cation promoted association (CPA) of a regulatory and target protein is controlled by protein phosphorylation. *Proc. Natl. Acad. Sci. U.S.A.* 91:3544–8, 1994.

Usher, K. C., **S. J. Remington,** D. P. Martin, and D. G. Drueckhammer. A very short hydrogen bond provides only moderate stabilization of an enzyme-inhibitor complex of citrate synthase. *Biochemistry* 33:7753–9, 1994.

O'Neil, K., et al. **(J. Schombert).** A wide field survey for low surface brightness galaxies: II. Color distributions, stellar populations, and missing baryons. *Appl. J.* 114:2448, 1997.

Rakos, K., A. Odell, and **J. Schombert.** The Butcher-Oemler effect in Abell 2317. *Appl. J.* 490:194, 1997.

Pildis, R., **J. Schombert,** and J. Eder. Gas-rich dwarfs from the PSS-II II. Optical properties. *Appl. J.* 481:157, 1997.

Schombert, J., R. Pildis, and J. Eder. Gas-rich dwarfs from the PSS-II I. Catalog and characteristics. *Appl. J. Suppl.* 111:233, 1997.

Lee, H., W. Yang, and **P. C. Sercel.** The shape of self-assembled InAs islands grown by molecular beam epitaxy. *J. Electron. Mater.* 28:481–5, 1999.

Lee, H., R. Lowe-Webb, W. Yang, and **P. C. Sercel.** Determination of the shape of InAs/GaAs quantum dots by reflection high-energy electron diffraction. *Appl. Phys. Lett.* 72:812, 1998.

Yang, W., R. Lowe-Webb, H. Lee, and **P. C. Sercel.** Effect of carrier emission and trapping on luminescence time decays in InAs/GaAs quantum dots. *Phys. Rev. B* 56:13314, 1997.

Lee, H., R. Lowe-Webb, W. Yang, and **P. C. Sercel.** Formation of InAs/GaAs quantum dots by molecular beam epitaxy: Reversibility of the islanding transition. *Appl. Phys Lett.* 71:2325, 1997.

Soper, D. E. QCD calculations by numerical integration. *Phys. Rev. Lett.* 81:2638, 1998.

Soper, D. E., J. C. Collins, and G. Sterman. Factorization is not violated. *Phys. Lett. B* 438:184, 1998.

Soper, D. E., F. Hautmann, and Z. Kunszt. Diffractive deeply inelastic scattering of hadronic states with small transverse size. *Phys. Rev. Lett.* 81:3333, 1998.

Ackerstaff, K., et al. **(D. Strom).** Tests of the standard model and constraints on new physics from measurements of fermion-pair production at 183 GeV at LEP. The OPAL Collaboration. *Eur. Phys. J.* C6:1–18, 1999.

Strom, D. Measurement of the ratio of the invisible to leptonic widths of the Z0 using the OPAL Detector at LEP. In *Proceedings of the 8th Meeting, Divisions of Particles and Fields of the American Physical Society, Albuquerque, New Mexico, August 2–5, 1994.*

Micolich, A. P., et al. **(R. P. Taylor).** Geometry-induced fractal behaviour in a semiconductor billiard. *J. Phys. Condens. Matter* 10: 1339, 1998.

Taylor, R. P., et al. Self-similar magnetoresistance in a semiconductor Sinai billiard. *Phys. Rev. Lett.* 78:1952, 1997.

Taylor, R. P., et al. Can Ohmic spikes define quantum systems? *Jpn. J. Appl. Phys.* 36:3964, 1997.

Toner, J., P. E. Lammert, and D. S. Rokhsar. Topology and nematic ordering. II. Observable critical behavior. *Phys. Rev. Lett. E* 1801, 1995.

Toner, J., and Y.-h. Tu. Long-range order in a two-dimensional dynamical XY model: How birds fly together. *Phys. Rev. Lett.* 4326, 1995.

Radzihovsky, L., and **J. Toner.** A new phase of tethered membranes: Tubules. *Phys. Rev. Lett.* 4725, 1995.

Wang, H., and B. E. Hammons. Biexciton effects in the nonperturbative regime of semiconductor microcavities. *Phys. Rev. B* 57:R9451, 1998.

Fan, X., **H. Wang,** and B. E. Hammons. Laser emission from semiconductor microcavities: The role of cavity polaritons. *Phys. Rev. A* 56:3233, 1997.

Fan, X., **H. Wang,** and B. E. Hammons. Laser emission from semiconductor microcavities: Transition from nonperturbative to perturbative regimes. *Phys. Rev. B* 56:15256, 1997.

Ivanov, A. L., **H. Wang,** and L. N. Pfeiffer. Coherent transients in photoluminescence of excitonic molecules in GaAs quantum wells. *Phys. Rev. B* 56:3941, 1997.

Cresswell, A., and **R. L. Zimmerman.** Gravitational synchrotron radiation from cosmic strings. *Phys. Rev. D* 42:2527, 1990.

UNIVERSITY OF PENNSYLVANIA

Department of Physics and Astronomy

Program of Study

The Department of Physics and Astronomy offers an outstanding program of graduate study leading to the Ph.D. degree in physics. The primary areas of research in the department are particle physics, condensed-matter physics, and astrophysics. Experimental and theoretical research is performed in all concentrations.

The program attempts to provide students with a comprehensive overview of the discipline while challenging them to explore in detail an area of particular interest. The department requires all students to take an introductory seminar, one-semester graduate-level courses in laboratory techniques and statistical mechanics, and two courses from a selection outside the student's major field of specialization. In addition, credit for thesis research partially fulfills the University requirement of twenty courses for the Ph.D. degree. Most students in the program serve as teaching assistants during their first year.

In order to gain admission to Ph.D. candidacy, students must pass a written examination on first-year courses and an oral examination in a subfield of their choice. Doctoral candidates must complete a dissertation based on independent scientific research and defend it orally before a committee of faculty members. There is no foreign language requirement. For students with normal undergraduate preparation, the Ph.D. degree requires four to six years to complete. In cooperation with the Department of Radiology, a two-year professional Master of Medical Physics degree is also offered.

Research Facilities

Available to students on campus is the interdisciplinary Laboratory for Research on the Structure of Matter (LRSM). The department participates in high-energy physics experiments at CERN (ATLAS), Fermilab (CDF-II), and the Stanford Linear Accelerator Center (BABAR). The department operates two observatories: the Homestake Neutrino and Cosmic Ray Observatory, a leading extraterrestrial cosmic ray observatory, and the Flower and Cook Observatory, which focuses on interacting and astrometric binaries. In addition, the department participates in the Sudbury Neutrino Observatory in Canada and the Baksan Neutrino Observatory in Russia. The department is mounting astrophysical experiments in Chile and participates in the Hubble Space Telescope, the Very Large Array of the National Radio Astronomy Observatory, the Keck Observatory in Hawaii, and the Owens Valley Radio Observatory. Closer to home, members of the department collaborate with researchers at the hospital of the University of Pennsylvania.

Financial Aid

Generally, all students in physics are fully supported by teaching assistantships, research assistantships, or fellowships. The academic-year stipend for 1998–99 was $11,333. Summer support is included, usually in the form of research assistantships. The summer stipend for 1998 was $5500.

Cost of Study

Tuition and fees ($24,200 in 1998–99) are provided for all supported graduate students.

Living and Housing Costs

Students have a number of housing options, including on-campus and off-campus apartments. On-campus housing—generally single apartments—averages about $660 per month. Off-campus rentals are slightly less expensive, ranging from $400 per month for an efficiency apartment to $750 per month for a three-bedroom apartment. The University offers a variety of meal plans for graduate students, and these are priced from $1050 to $3198 per academic year. In addition, many on-campus apartments feature small kitchens.

Student Group

The University has about 10,300 graduate and professional students, of whom about 2,250 are in Arts and Sciences. Currently, 85 graduate students are enrolled in physics. In the past twelve months, fourteen Ph.D. degrees in physics were awarded. Approximately 19 new students arrive each year.

Student Outcomes

Many of the department's graduates have contributed significantly to the field in the areas of research, industry, and academia. About 50 percent of current graduates obtain postdoctoral positions in academia, the remaining 50 percent choosing positions in major national lab facilities such as Oak Ridge National Laboratory or Los Alamos National Laboratory or in private industry.

Location

The University is located in historic Philadelphia, a city composed of many distinctive neighborhoods. This colorful array includes such sections as Colonial Society Hill, Chinatown, and University City, the area surrounding Penn. Center City, with its museums, theaters, concert halls, and markets, lies just east of Penn across the Schuylkill River, which challenges rowers from all over the world. Those who wish to explore still further can easily drive to the beaches of New Jersey, to the mountains of Pennsylvania, or even to New York or Washington, D.C.

The University

A member of the Ivy League, the University was founded in 1740 by Benjamin Franklin, the noted statesman, author, and inventor. Since its inception and throughout its 250-year history, Penn has been at the forefront of educational and research developments. With its wide range of rigorous graduate programs, Penn has set new standards of excellence in the arts and sciences, engineering, medicine (including dental and veterinary), and business.

Applying

The GRE General Test is required for admission, and the Subject Test in physics is required for financial aid consideration. Applicants whose native language is not English must take the Test of English as a Foreign Language (TOEFL) and the Test of Spoken English (TSE). Applications should be sent to the address indicated below; those sent directly to the department will be delayed in processing. Completed applications and all supporting materials must be submitted by January 1 for financial aid consideration. Applicants who are admitted to the program will be notified during the months of February and March. Students can access the graduate catalog on the World Wide Web (http://www.physics.upenn.edu/guide/).

Correspondence and Information

For additional information:
Admissions Coordinator
Department of Physics and Astronomy
University of Pennsylvania
209 South 33rd Street
Philadelphia, Pennsylvania 19104-6396

Telephone: 215-898-3125
E-mail: walter@dept.physics.upenn.edu
World Wide Web: http://www.physics.upenn.edu/

To submit completed applications:
Graduate Admissions Office
University of Pennsylvania
16 College Hall
Philadelphia, Pennsylvania 19104-6378

University of Pennsylvania

THE FACULTY AND THEIR RESEARCH

Fay Ajzenberg-Selove, Ph.D., Professor of Physics. Nuclear experiments.
Ralph D. Amado, D.Phil., Professor of Physics. Nuclear theory.
David P. Balamuth, Ph.D., Professor of Physics. Nuclear experiments.
Eugene W. Beier, Ph.D., Professor of Physics. Elementary particle experiments.
Sidney Bludman, Ph.D., Professor of Physics. Astrophysics theory.
Howard Brody, Ph.D., Professor of Physics, Emeritus. Physics of sports.
Elias A. M. Burstein, Ph.D., Professor of Physics, Emeritus. Condensed-matter experiments.
Max E. Caspari, Ph.D., Professor of Physics, Emeritus. Condensed-matter experiments.
Bruce T. Cleveland, Ph.D., Research Associate Professor of Astronomy.
Jeffrey M. Cohen, Ph.D., Associate Professor of Physics. Astrophysics theory.
Michael Cohen, Ph.D., Professor of Physics, Emeritus. Condensed-matter theory.
Douglas Cowen, Ph.D., Assistant Professor of Physics. Elementary particle experiment.
Mirjam Cvetic, Ph.D., Associate Professor of Physics. Elementary particle theory.
Raymond Davis Jr., Ph.D., Research Professor of Astronomy.
Mark J. Devlin, Ph.D., Assistant Professor of Physics. Observational astrophysics.
Gerald Dolan, Ph.D., Professor of Physics, Emeritus. Condensed-matter experiments.
H. Terry Fortune, Ph.D., Professor of Physics. Nuclear experiments.
Sherman Frankel, Ph.D., Professor of Physics, Emeritus. High-energy and nuclear experiments.
William Frati, Ph.D., Research Professor of Physics. Experimental particles.
Anthony F. Garito, Ph.D., Professor of Physics. Condensed-matter experiments.
Larry Gladney, Ph.D., Associate Professor of Physics. Elementary particle experiments.
A. Brooks Harris, Ph.D., Professor of Physics. Condensed-matter theory.
Paul A. Heiney, Ph.D., Professor of Physics. Condensed-matter experiments.
Robert Hollebeek, Ph.D., Professor of Physics and Graduate Group Chair. Elementary particle experiments.
Alan T. Johnson, Ph.D., Assistant Professor of Physics. Condensed-matter experiments.
Randall Kamien, Ph.D., Assistant Professor of Physics. Condensed-matter theory.
Charles Kane, Ph.D., Associate Professor of Physics. Condensed-matter theory.
Abraham Klein, Ph.D., Professor of Physics, Emeritus. Nuclear theory.
Robert H. Koch, Ph.D., Professor of Astronomy, Emeritus.
David Koerner, Ph.D., Assistant Professor of Physics. Observational astrophysics.
Joseph Kroll, Ph.D., Assistant Professor of Physics. Elementary particle experiments.
Kenneth Lande, Ph.D., Professor of Physics and Astronomy. Astrophysics experiments.
Paul Langacker, Ph.D., William Smith Term Professor of Physics and Chair. Elementary particle theory.
Nigel Lockyer, Ph.D., Professor of Physics. Elementary particle experiments.
Tom C. Lubensky, Ph.D., Professor of Physics. Condensed-matter theory.
Chung-Pei Ma, Ph.D., Assistant Professor of Physics. Theoretical astrophysics.
Alfred K. Mann, Ph.D., Professor of Physics, Emeritus. Elementary particle experiments.
Eugene J. Mele, Ph.D., Professor of Physics. Condensed-matter theory.
Roy Middleton, Ph.D., Professor of Physics, Emeritus. Nuclear experiments.
Philip Nelson, Ph.D., Professor of Physics. Condensed-matter theory.
Burt Ovrut, Ph.D., Professor of Physics. Elementary particle theory.
Gino Segrè, Ph.D., Professor of Physics. Elementary particle theory.
Walter Selove, Ph.D., Professor of Physics, Emeritus. Elementary particle experiments.
Benjamin P. Shen, Ph.D., Professor of Astronomy, Emeritus.
Paul Soven, Ph.D., Professor of Physics. Condensed-matter theory.
Paul J. Steinhardt, Ph.D., Mary Amanda Wood Professor of Physics. Elementary particle and condensed-matter theory.
Walter D. Wales, Ph.D., Professor of Physics. Elementary particle experiments.
Roger Walmsley, Ph.D., Associate Professor of Physics, Emeritus. Statistical physics.
Hugh H. Williams, Ph.D., Professor of Physics. Elementary particle experiments.
Thomas H. Wood, Ph.D., Professor of Physics, Emeritus. Biophysics.
Arjun Yodh, Ph.D., Professor of Physics. Condensed-matter experiments.
Robert W. Zurmühle, Ph.D., Professor of Physics, Emeritus. Nuclear experiments.

Benjamin Franklin, founder of the University of Pennsylvania.

Philadelphia is an exciting array of skyscrapers, museums, markets, and theaters surrounded by a number of distinctive neighborhoods.

Begun in 1895, the Quadrangle, the University's oldest dormitory, houses almost 1,700 students.

UNIVERSITY OF PITTSBURGH

Department of Physics and Astronomy

Programs of Study	The graduate programs in the Department of Physics and Astronomy are designed primarily for students who wish to obtain the Ph.D. degree, although the M.S. degree is also offered. The Ph.D. program provides high-quality training for students without needlessly emphasizing formal requirements. Upon arrival, each graduate student is appointed an adviser to provide personalized guidance through the core curriculum. A set of basic courses is to be taken by all graduate students unless the equivalent material has been demonstrably mastered in other ways. These basic courses are one term of classical mechanics and modern physical laboratory methods and two terms each of quantum mechanics, electromagnetic theory, and statistical mechanics. More specialized courses in advanced nuclear physics, quantum mechanics, condensed-matter and statistical physics, astrophysics, astronomical physics, particle physics, relativity, and other subjects are offered.

Graduate students normally take a written examination, based on undergraduate physics, during the spring term of the first year and a written comprehensive examination, based on graduate physics, at the end of the second year. Students can then select a thesis adviser, choose a thesis topic, and apply for admission to candidacy for the Ph.D. Preparation and defense of a satisfactory dissertation complete the requirements. Most students with a baccalaureate degree should find it possible to attain the Ph.D. within five years.

Students have a wide variety of programs from which to choose a thesis topic. The University faculty members have active research programs in atomic physics (experiment and theory), astrophysics and astronomy using both ground- and space-based optical and radio telescopes, particle astrophysics (theory), condensed-matter and solid-state physics (experiment and theory), elementary particle physics (experiment and theory), general relativity (theory), intermediate-energy physics (experiment and theory), and chemical physics.

Under the department program in applied physics, students can arrange to do their thesis research in other departments of the University in, for example, biophysics, geophysics, radiation physics, material science, surface science, laser physics, or magnetic resonance imaging.

Research Facilities   The department's facilities include the physics library, an electronics shop, a glassblowing shop, a professionally staffed machine shop, and extensive departmental and University computer resources. Large CPU-intensive computer programs may be run by connecting to powerful campus time-sharing services accessible via public computing labs, dial-up access, the Internet, or to the nation's most powerful vector and massively parallel machines at the Pittsburgh Supercomputing Center, which is a joint effort of the University of Pittsburgh and Carnegie Mellon University, together with Westinghouse Electric Corporation. Other facilities include the Allegheny Observatory (for positional astronomy). Many of the experiments in particle and nuclear physics are carried out at such national and international facilities as Brookhaven National Laboratory; Fermi National Laboratory in Chicago; CERN in Geneva, Switzerland; Thomas Jefferson Accelerator Facility in Virginia; and Oak Ridge National Laboratory in Tennessee. Similarly, programs are conducted at national and international observatories, such as at Arecibo, Puerto Rico; at the Very Large Array in New Mexico; at Kitt Peak and Mount Hopkins, Arizona; at Cerro Tololo and Las Campanis, Chile; at the IRTF telescope in Hawaii; and on the Hubble Space Telescope and other space observatories.

Financial Aid   Financial aid is normally provided through teaching assistantships during the first year and through research assistantships thereafter. The department has recently established several fellowships for entering graduate students. They are awarded on a competitive basis, with all qualified applicants automatically entered into a pool. Some University fellowships are also available and are awarded in a University-wide competition. The department endeavors to support each student throughout his or her entire graduate career, provided good academic standing is maintained. Teaching assistantship appointments carry a stipend of $11,025 for two terms in 1999–2000, and all tuition charges are exempted. Research assistantship appointments may be held in connection with most of the department's research programs. In 1999–2000, the stipend is $11,025 for two terms, and all tuition charges are exempted.

Cost of Study   For full-time students who are not Pennsylvania residents, tuition and fees per term in 1999–2000 are $8824. Part-time students pay $707 per credit plus fees. Full-time Pennsylvania residents pay $4409 per term, including fees, and part-time Pennsylvania residents pay $342 per credit plus fees.

Living and Housing Costs   Most University of Pittsburgh students live in rooms or apartments in the Oakland area. The typical cost of rooms or apartments ranges from $340 to $550 per month for housing. Meals range from $300 to $400 per month.

Student Group   The department's graduate student body in 1998–99 consisted of 72 students, of whom 67 were men; 71 students received financial aid. These figures are typical of the department's graduate enrollment.

Student Outcomes   Ph.D. graduates accept postdoctoral positions at major research universities and industrial laboratories, often leading to teaching and research positions at outstanding universities. Recent graduates are employed at AT&T, Radiological Imaging Company, the Advanced Nuclear Magnetic Resonance Corporation, General Electric, Fisher Scientific, Columbia University, and the University of California and as faculty members in Korea, New South Wales, Sir Lanka, and Argentina. One graduate received the American Physical Society's 1999 Nicholas Metropolis Award for Outstanding Doctoral Thesis Work in Computational Physics.

Location   Pittsburgh is situated in a hilly and wooded region of western Pennsylvania where the Allegheny and Monongahela rivers join to form the Ohio. The region has a natural beauty. The terrain of western Pennsylvania is excellent for outdoor activities, including cycling, hiking, downhill and cross country skiing, white-water rafting and kayaking, rock climbing, hunting, and fishing. The University is located about 3 miles east of downtown Pittsburgh in the city's cultural center. Adjacent to the campus are Carnegie Mellon University, the Carnegie Institute, the Museum of Art and the Museum of Natural History, the public library, and the Music Hall. Schenley Park adjoins the campus; it has picnic areas, playing fields, trails, and an excellent botanical conservatory.

The Department   The department has long been active in research and in the training of more than 500 Ph.D. alumni. Close cooperation exists between this department and the physics department of Carnegie Mellon University; all seminars, colloquia, and joint courses are shared. The graduate students of both institutions benefit from belonging to one of the largest communities of active physicists in the country.

Applying   Students who wish to apply for admission or financial aid should take the GRE, including the Subject Test in physics. Applicants should request that the registrars of their undergraduate and graduate schools send transcripts of their records to the department. Three letters of recommendation are required for admission with aid. Unless English is the applicant's native language, the TOEFL is required. All applications must be received by January 31.

Correspondence and Information
Professor Peter F. M. Koehler
Admissions Committee
Department of Physics and Astronomy
University of Pittsburgh
Pittsburgh, Pennsylvania 15260
Telephone: 412-624-9066
E-mail: gradsec@physast1.phyast.pitt.edu
World Wide Web: http://www.phyast.pitt.edu/

University of Pittsburgh

THE FACULTY AND THEIR RESEARCH

Elizabeth U. Baranger, Professor and Vice Provost for Graduate Studies; Ph.D., Cornell. Theoretical nuclear physics.
James E. Bayfield, Professor; Ph.D., Yale. Experimental atomic physics and quantum optics.
Joseph Boudreau, Assistant Professor; Ph.D., Wisconsin. Experimental particle physics.
Daniel Boyanovsky, Professor; Ph.D., California, Santa Barbara. Condensed-matter physics, particle astrophysics.
Robert D. Carlitz, Professor; Ph.D., Caltech. Theoretical high-energy physics, computer networking.
Wolfgang J. Choyke, Research Professor; Ph.D., Ohio State. Solid-state physics, defect states in semiconductors, large bandgap spectroscopy physics.
Rob Coalson, Professor; Ph.D., Harvard. Chemical physics.
Andrew Connolly, Assistant Professor; Ph.D., Imperial College (London). Astrophysics.
Robert P. Devaty, Associate Professor; Ph.D., Cornell. Experimental solid-state physics.
H. E. Anthony Duncan, Professor; Ph.D., MIT. Theoretical high-energy physics.
Steven A. Dytman, Professor; Ph.D., Carnegie Mellon. Experimental intermediate-energy physics.
Peter W. Erdman, Adjunct Associate Professor; Ph.D., Pittsburgh. Experimental atomic and atmospheric physics.
George D. Gatewood, Professor; Ph.D., Pittsburgh. Astronomy, astrometry, search for planetary systems orbiting neighboring stars.
Yadin Y. Goldschmidt, Professor; Ph.D., Hebrew (Jerusalem). Condensed-matter theory, statistical mechanics.
Cyril Hazard, R. K. Mellon Professor; Ph.D., Manchester. Astrophysics.
D. John Hillier, Assistant Professor; Ph.D., Australian National. Astrophysics.
David M. Jasnow, Professor; Ph.D., Illinois. Theory of phase transitions, statistical mechanics.
Rainer Johnsen, Professor; Ph.D., Kiel (Germany). Experimental atomic and plasma physics.
Peter F. M. Koehler, Professor; Ph.D., Rochester. Experimental high-energy physics.
Jeremy Levy, Assistant Professor; Ph.D., California, Santa Barbara. Experimental condensed matter.
Irving J. Lowe, Professor; Ph.D., Washington (St. Louis). Experimental solid-state physics, nuclear magnetic resonance, nuclear magnetic resonance imaging.
James V. Maher, Professor and Provost; Ph.D., Yale. Experimental solid-state physics, critical phenomena, physics of fluids.
James Mueller, Assistant Professor; Ph.D., Cornell. Experimental intermediate-energy particle physics.
Donna Naples, Assistant Professor; Ph.D., Maryland. Experimental high-energy physics.
Vittorio Paolone, Assistant Professor; Ph.D., California, Davis. Experimental high-energy physics.
Ralph Z. Roskies, Professor; Ph.D., Princeton. Experimental high-energy physics, use of computer in theoretical physics.
Carlo Rovelli, Professor; Dottorato di Ricerca, Padua. General relativity.
Regina E. Schulte-Ladbeck, Associate Professor; Ph.D., Heidelberg. Astrophysics.
Paul F. Shepard, Professor; Ph.D., Princeton. Experimental high-energy physics.
David Snoke, Assistant Professor; Ph.D., Illinois at Urbana-Champaign. Solid-state experimental.
G. Alec Stewart, Associate Professor and Dean, University Honors College; Ph.D., Washington (Seattle). Experimental solid-state physics.
Frank Tabakin, Professor and Department Chairman; Ph.D., MIT. Theoretical nuclear physics.
Julia A. Thompson, Professor; Ph.D., Yale. Experimental high-energy physics, optical instrumentation.
David A. Turnshek, Professor; Ph.D., Arizona. Observational extragalactic astronomy.
C. Martin Vincent, Professor; Ph.D., Witwatersrand (South Africa). Theoretical intermediate-energy physics.
Xiao-Lun Wu, Associate Professor; Ph.D., Cornell. Experimental condensed matter.
John T. Yates, Professor; Ph.D., MIT. Physical chemistry.
Edward C. Zipf, Professor; Ph.D., Johns Hopkins. Experimental atomic and atmospheric physics.

EMERITUS FACULTY

Manfred A. Biondi, Professor Emeritus; Ph.D., MIT. Experimental atomic physics and aeronomy.
Wilfred W. Cleland, Professor Emeritus; Ph.D., Yale. Experimental high-energy physics.
Bernard L. Cohen, Professor Emeritus; Ph.D., Carnegie Mellon. Energy and environment.
Wilfried A. W. Daehnick, Professor Emeritus; Ph.D., Washington (St. Louis). Experimental nuclear physics.
Richard M. Drisko, Professor Emeritus; Ph.D., Carnegie Mellon. Theoretical nuclear physics.
Eugene Engels Jr., Professor Emeritus; Ph.D., Princeton. Experimental high-energy physics.
Myron P. Garfunkel, Professor Emeritus; Ph.D., Rutgers. Experimental low-temperature physics, superconductivity.
Edward Gerjuoy, Professor Emeritus; Ph.D., Berkeley. Theoretical atomic physics.
Walter I. Goldburg, Professor Emeritus; Ph.D., Duke. Experimental solid-state physics, phase transitions, light scattering, turbulence.
Allen I. Janis, Professor Emeritus; Ph.D., Syracuse. General relativity, philosophy of science.
Ezra T. Newman, Professor Emeritus; Ph.D., Syracuse. General relativity, twistor theory.
Richard H. Pratt, Professor; Ph.D., Chicago. Theoretical atomic and low-energy particle physics, bremsstrahlung, hot plasma processes, photon scattering.
Jurg X. Saladin, Professor Emeritus; Ph.D., Swiss Federal Institute of Technology. Experimental nuclear physics.
Raymond S. Willey, Professor Emeritus; Ph.D., Stanford. Theoretical high-energy physics.
Jeffrey Winicour, Research Professor; Ph.D., Syracuse. General relativity.

The department is centered in Allen Hall.

The 30-inch Thaw refractor at Allegheny Observatory.

UNIVERSITY OF PUERTO RICO, RÍO PIEDRAS

Department of Physics

Programs of Study
The Department of Physics at the Río Piedras Campus of the University of Puerto Rico offers a program leading to the M.S. degree in physics. It also offers, jointly with the Department of Chemistry, a program leading to the Ph.D. degree in chemical physics.

Candidates for the M.S. degree in physics must complete at least 24 credit hours, with an overall grade index of no less than 3, and then pass a comprehensive exam. Completion of thesis research in physics or astronomy (6 credits) and an oral defense are required.

Candidates for the Ph.D. degree in chemical physics are required to complete a minimum of 45 credit hours in graduate courses in physics or chemistry, with an overall grade index of no less than 3, and pass three written qualifying examinations. One of the qualifying examinations must be in physical chemistry and the other two in areas of physics to be selected by the student with the approval of his or her adviser. Completion of original thesis research (24 credit hours) and an oral defense of the thesis are also required.

Research Facilities
The department has laboratories for experimental work in various research areas of solid-state physics, including thin films, crystallography, and spectroscopy. Several members of the faculty use the facilities of the National Astronomy and Ionosphere Center at Arecibo for their research. Theoretical research is carried out in the areas of particle physics, general relativity, and condensed-matter physics.

Financial Aid
All regular students receive some type of financial aid. In 1998–99, teaching and laboratory assistantships paid, in addition to the exemption from tuition, $7000 for ten months for students in the M.S. program and $8500 for Ph.D. candidates.

Cost of Study
Tuition was $75 per credit for residents of Puerto Rico and $3500 per year for nonresidential students in 1998–99.

Living and Housing Costs
Cost of housing and living expenses vary considerably but are usually similar to those in the main metropolitan areas of the United States.

Student Group
The department has more than 30 graduate students who come from Puerto Rico, Central and South America, China, and several other countries.

Student Outcomes
After completion of the physics master's program, about 30 percent of the students enroll in a Ph.D. program in the United States. About half of the remaining students continue Ph.D. studies in the chemical physics program on campus, and the rest are either hired by industries located on the island or in the U.S. or teach in small colleges islandwide.

Location
San Juan is the capital and cultural center of Puerto Rico. Old San Juan is a fascinating city, with numerous historic sites, excellent beaches, and other tourist attractions. The cultural life in the city, and especially around the University, is fairly active and includes frequent concerts, plays, lectures, and other events. The internationally known Casals Festival of Music is held each year in June.

The University
The University was founded in 1903. The Río Piedras Campus is the oldest and largest and includes, among other divisions, the College of Natural Sciences and the Schools of Medicine and Architecture. Graduate programs in many disciplines are well established, including Ph.D. programs in chemistry and biology and an M.S. program in mathematics.

Applying
Applications should be filed no later than February 28 for the fall semester. Students should apply to the Department of Physics by May 1 for fellowships and teaching and laboratory assistantships.

Correspondence and Information
Dr. José F. Nieves, Chairman
Department of Physics
P.O. Box 23343, UPR Station
University of Puerto Rico
Río Piedras, Puerto Rico 00931-3343
Telephone: 787-764-0620
Fax: 787-764-4063
E-mail: chairman@physd.upr.clu.edu
World Wide Web: http://physd.upr.clu.edu

University of Puerto Rico, Río Piedras

THE FACULTY AND THEIR RESEARCH

F. Aliev, Professor; Ph.D., Leningrad, 1989. Experimental solid-state physics.
D. R. Altschuler, Professor; Ph.D., Brandeis, 1974. Astronomy.
L. B. Bhuiyan, Professor; Ph.D., London, 1977. Statistical mechanics.
L. Blum, Professor; Ph.D., Buenos Aires, 1956. Statistical mechanics and thermodynamics.
P. Coleman, Associate Professor; Ph.D., Pittsburgh, 1985. Astrophysics.
L. Fonseca, Professor; Ph.D., Puerto Rico, 1985. Theoretical solid-state physics.
M. Gómez, Professor; Ph.D., Cornell, 1968. Theoretical solid-state physics.
P. Hofner, Assistant Professor; Ph.D., Wisconsin, 1995. Astronomy.
R. S. Katiyar, Professor; Ph.D., Indian Institute of Science, 1967. Experimental solid-state physics.
A. Martínez, Associate Professor; Ph.D., American, 1990. Experimental solid-state physics.
J. F. Nieves, Professor; Ph.D., Pennsylvania, 1980. Theoretical high-energy physics.
C. A. Pantoja, Assistant Professor; Ph.D., Oklahoma, 1995. Astronomy.
J. Ponce de León, Professor; Ph.D., Venezuela (Caracas), 1985. General relativity.
R. G. Selsby, Professor; Ph.D., Ohio State, 1969. Quantum chemistry.
J. M. Tharrats, Professor; Ph.D., Madrid, 1952. Theoretical physics.
A. J. Torruella, Professor; Ph.D., Yale, 1965. Theoretical nuclear physics.
M. R. Ubriaco, Professor; Ph.D., North Carolina, 1989. Theoretical high-energy physics.
Z. S. Weisz, Professor; Ph.D., Hebrew (Jerusalem), 1962. Experimental solid-state physics.

SELECTED FACULTY PUBLICATIONS

Panarin, Y. P., C. Rosenblatt, and **F. Aliev.** The appearance of ferroelectric phases in a confined liquid crystal investigated by photon correlation spectroscopy. *Phys. Rev. Lett.* 81:2699, 1998.

Sinha, G. P., and **F. M. Aliev.** Dielectric spectroscopy of liquid crystals in smectic, nematic and isotropic phases confined in random porous media. *Phys. Rev. E* 58:2001, 1998.

Altschuler, D. R. The centiarcsecond structure of 16 low-frequency variable sources at 92 cm. *Astron. Astrophys. Suppl. Ser.* 114:197, 1995.

Rescic, J., V. Vlachy, **L. B. Bhuiyan,** and C. W. Outhwaite. Monte Carlo simulations of a mixture of an asymmetric electrolyte and a Neutral Species. *Mol. Phys.* 95:233, 1998.

Das, T., D. Bratko, **L. B. Bhuiyan,** and C. W. Outhwaite. Polyelectrolyte solutions containing mixed valency ions in the cell model. A simulation and modified Poisson-Boltzmann study. *J. Chem. Phys.* 107:9197, 1997.

Blum, L., F. Vericat, and L. Degreve. The Multiyukawa model of water. *Physica A* 265(A):396, 1999.

Legault, M., **L. Blum,** and D. A. Huckaby. An extended hard hexagon model for copper upd on Au(111). *J. Electroanal. Chem.* 409:79, 1996.

Taylor, A. R., et al. **(P. H. Coleman).** A WSRT 327 MHz survey of the Galactic Plane. *Astrophys. J. Suppl. Ser.* 107:239, 1996.

Rapaport, R., Y. Lubianiker, I. Balberg, and **L. Fonseca.** Sensitization of the minority carrier lifetime in $a - Si:H$. *Appl. Phys. Lett.* 72:103, 1998.

Lubianiker, Y., I. Balberg, and **L. F. Fonseca.** Thermal quenching of the minority-carrier lifetime in $a - Si:H$. *Phys. Rev. B* 55:15997, 1997.

Fonseca, L. F., and R. I. Rodriguez. Study of the enhancement effects of composite films on the magneto-optic Kerr effect. *J. Magn. Magn. Mater.* 161:379, 1996.

Vargas, W., **L. Fonseca,** and **M. Gómez.** A model to consider clustering effects for composites. In *Springer Proceeding in Physics,* vol. 62, Surface Science: 231, eds. F. A. Ponce and M. Cardona. Berlin: Springer-Verlag, 1992.

Hofner, P., and E. Churchwell. A hard X-ray source in the W3 core. *Astrophys. J.* L39:486, 1997.

Hofner, P., et al. Massive star formation in the hot, dense Cluod core of G9. 62+0.19. *Astrophys. J.* 460:359, 1996.

Cheng, Z.-Y., **R. S. Katiyar,** and A. S. Bhalla. Temperature dependence of the dielectric constant of relaxor ferroelectrics. *Phys Rev. B* 57:8166, 1998.

Meng, J. F., **R. S. Katiyar,** and G. T. Zou. Grain size effects on ferroelectric phase transitions in $Pb1-xBaxTiO3$ system. *J. Phys. Chem. Solids* 59:1161, 1998.

Martínez, A., A. R. Berrios, R. Collazo, and G. O. Ducoudray. Growth and characterization of Bismuth and Antimony thin films. *J. Cryst. Growth* 174:845, 1997.

Mohanty, S., **J. F. Nieves,** and P. B. Pal. Optical activity of a neutrino gas. *Phys. Rev. D* 58:093007, 1998.

Nieves, J. F., and P. B. Pal. Gravitational couplings of neutrinos in a medium. *Phys. Rev. D* 58:096005, 1998.

Pantoja, C. A., C. Giovanardi, **D. R. Altschuler,** and R. Giovanelli. HI observations of Weinberger Galaxies in the galactic anticenter region. *Astron. J.* 108:3, 1994.

Pantoja, C. A., D. R. Altschuler, C. Giovanardi, and R. Giovanelli. 21 cm line observations of galaxies in the Zone of Avoidance. *Astron. J.* 103:905, 1994.

Ponce de León, J., and P. S. Wesson. The equation of motion in higher-dimensional gravity. *Fields Inst. Commun.* 15:325, 1997.

Ubriaco, M. R. Lambda-transition in low dimensional systems with $SU_q(2)$ symmetry. *Phys. Lett. A* 241:1, 1998.

Ubriaco, M. R. Effect of quantum group invariance on trapped Fermi gases. *Phys. Rev. E* 58:4194, 1998.

Weisz, S. Z., et al. **(M. Gómez).** Relation between luminescence electronic surface characteristics in p-type porous silicon. *J. Lumin.* 729:72, 1997.

Li, F., et al. **(S. Z. Weisz).** Effects of aquaregia treatment on indium tin oxide substrates on the behavior of double layered organic light emitting diodes. *Appl. Phys. Lett.* 70:2441, 1997.

UNIVERSITY OF ROCHESTER

Department of Physics and Astronomy

Programs of Study

The department offers programs of study leading to the Ph.D. degree in physics or physics and astronomy. Students normally earn the M.A. or M.S. degree in physics en route to the Ph.D. The M.A. can be awarded after the completion of 30 semester hours of course work and a comprehensive examination; the M.S. degree in physics requires a thesis in addition to the course work. Students are not usually admitted to work toward a master's degree unless they are also working toward a Ph.D.

Most candidates for the Ph.D. degree take two years of course work and a written preliminary examination during their second year. Requirements for the Ph.D. include demonstrating competence in quantum mechanics, mathematical methods, electromagnetic theory, and statistical physics, as well as in an advanced area of specialization. A doctoral thesis, based on a significant piece of original research, and a final oral thesis defense are required of all Ph.D. candidates. A typical program of study takes five or six years to complete. A minor is not required, although students are encouraged to broaden their understanding of other subfields of physics or astronomy beyond the area of their thesis research. There is no foreign language requirement.

The department provides opportunities for research in observational astronomy, theoretical astrophysics, biological physics, experimental and theoretical condensed-matter physics, experimental and theoretical elementary particle physics, experimental and theoretical nuclear physics, theoretical plasma physics, and experimental and theoretical quantum optics.

Research Facilities

Infrared-astronomical instrumentation has been constructed and is in use on a variety of telescopes, including national facilities in Arizona and Hawaii. The C. E. Kenneth Mees Observatory houses a 61-cm reflector equipped for imaging spectroscopy and photometry. The quantum optics group offers extensive research facilities. These include a broad range of laser systems: ultraviolet, visible, and infrared gas lasers; several ultra-high-stability CW dye, solid-state, and diode laser systems; ultrafast lasers (femtosecond); and an ultra-high-power (psec, chirped-pulse, regeneratively amplified) pulsed solid-state laser system. The group's laboratories include sophisticated photon-counting facilities, laser cooling and trapping facilities, atomic beam systems, and a laser physics lab. For research on condensed systems, the department offers a unique magnetooptical spectroscopy lab and an advanced surface science research lab that is equipped with X-ray, ultraviolet, and inverse photoemission spectroscopy; scanning-tunneling, atomic-force, and near-field microscopy; low-energy electron and photoelectron diffraction facilities; and advanced thin-film deposition systems. In its low-temperature lab, there is a helium dilution refrigerator and superconducting magnet for measurements in correlated and mesoscopic systems. Nuclear physics research is focused primarily at major accelerator facilities, such as the Relativistic Heavy-Ion Collider at Brookhaven, the ATLAS Heavy-Ion Accelerator at Argonne, and the Gammasphere facility at Berkeley. In addition, the department has advanced facilities for the design and construction of large, sensitive, high-energy physics detectors. These are developed on campus and assembled and operated at the national laboratories, including Fermilab, Brookhaven, the Stanford Linear Accelerator Center, and Cornell's Wilson Lab. Departmental general computing facilities include more than two dozen Sun Workstations and VAXstations as well as Power Macs and PCs connected to the campus Ethernet backbone; each of the research groups has additional major computing facilities. The Physics-Optics-Astronomy Library, within the physics building, provides ready access to more than 350 journals. The facilities of the University's Laboratory for Laser Energetics (including a CRAY Y-MP supercomputer), the Center for Optoelectronics and Imaging, and the Center for Photoinduced Charge Transfer are also available.

Financial Aid

In 1999–2000, graduate teaching and research assistantships, which require 16 hours of work per week during the academic year, carry stipends of $13,000 for nine months. Additional support is available for participation in summer research. A graduate assistant who also takes part in full-time summer research receives a total of $16,720 for the calendar year. A few special University and departmental fellowships provide stipends of up to $18,860 for the calendar year. In addition, the Robert E. Marshak Fellowships for academic excellence are available to supplement teaching or research assistantships for outstanding international students.

Cost of Study

For students with fewer than 90 credit hours of accumulated graduate course work, tuition for the 1999–2000 academic year is $22,304. Tuition for more advanced students is $1070 per academic year. (Currently, all graduate students in the department receive special awards to cover tuition.) All full-time graduate students are charged a health service fee of $984 per year. The cost of books and supplies is about $600 per year.

Living and Housing Costs

The cost of living in Rochester is among the lowest for metropolitan areas. Supermarkets with moderate prices are located near the University, or meals can be obtained on campus. University-operated housing for either single or married graduate students is available within easy walking distance of the campus, with costs starting at $366 per person per month in 1999–2000. Free shuttle-bus service is available within the University complex. Additional privately owned rooms and apartments are available in the residential areas near the University.

Student Group

There are approximately 90 graduate students in physics and astronomy; about 10 percent are women, and about 20 percent of the students are married. All full-time students receive some form of financial aid. Admission to graduate study is highly competitive, with only about 15 new students admitted each year; about 50 percent have undergraduate degrees from institutions outside the United States. The department has trained more than 1,000 doctorate recipients, many of whom have achieved international eminence.

Location

With approximately 800,000 inhabitants, the Rochester metropolitan area is the third largest in the state. A city with its economy based on high-technology industries, it is located on the southern shore of Lake Ontario. Niagara Falls, the scenic Finger Lakes district, and the rugged Adirondack Mountains are all within a few hours' drive. The Rochester Philharmonic Orchestra and the Rochester Americans ice-hockey team provide two examples of the range of experiences available. Rochester is readily accessible both by air and by car.

The University and The Department

The University of Rochester is a private institution with approximately 4,400 undergraduates, 2,400 graduate students, and 1,025 faculty members. The Department of Physics and Astronomy, one of the largest and strongest departments within the University, has a reputation for excellence in graduate education and research spanning more than fifty years. Many faculty members of the department have been awarded major fellowships and prizes in recognition of their research accomplishments.

Applying

Catalogs and application forms can be obtained upon request from the address below. Students are admitted only in September, and completed applications should be received by February 1 in order for applicants to be considered for financial aid. Applicants should take the GRE General Test and physics Subject Test in time for scores to arrive by February 1. TOEFL scores are required of international students whose native language is not English.

Correspondence and Information

Graduate Student Counselor
Department of Physics and Astronomy
University of Rochester
Rochester, New York 14627

Telephone: 716-275-4356
World Wide Web: http://www.pas.rochester.edu

University of Rochester

THE FACULTY AND THEIR RESEARCH

R. Betti, Associate Professor; Ph.D., MIT, 1992. Nuclear and mechanical engineering, computational and plasma physics.
N. P. Bigelow, Associate Professor; Ph.D., Cornell, 1989. Experimental quantum optics, studies of laser-cooled and trapped atoms, quantum fluids and gases, Bose-Einstein condensation.
A. Bodek, Professor and Chair; Ph.D., MIT, 1972. Experimental elementary particle physics, proton-antiproton collisions, QCD and structure functions, neutrino physics, tile-fiber calorimetric detectors.
T. G. Castner, Professor Emeritus; Ph.D., Illinois, 1958. Experimental condensed-matter physics, metal-insulator transition.
D. Cline, Professor and Director, Nuclear Structure Research Laboratory; Ph.D., Manchester (England), 1963. Extreme states of nuclei pairing and shape correlations in nuclei.
A. Das, Professor; Ph.D., SUNY at Stony Brook, 1977. Theoretical particle physics, finite temperature field theory, integrable systems and phenomenology.
D. H. Douglass, Professor; Ph.D., MIT, 1959. Condensed-matter physics.
J. H. Eberly, Andrew Carnegie Professor; Ph.D., Stanford, 1962. Theoretical quantum optics, cavity QED, atoms in strong laser fields, adiabatic two-photon optics.
T. Ferbel, Professor; Ph.D., Yale, 1963. Experimental elementary particle physics.
W. J. Forrest, Associate Professor and Director, C. E. Kenneth Mees Observatory; Ph.D., California, San Diego, 1974. Observational infrared astronomy, infrared array detectors.
T. H. Foster, Associate Professor; Ph.D., Rochester, 1990. Biological and medical physics.
A. Frank, Assistant Professor; Ph.D., Washington (Seattle), 1992. Theoretical astrophysics, numerical hydrodynamics and magnetohydrodynamics.
J. B. French, Andrew Carnegie Professor Emeritus; Ph.D., MIT, 1948. Statistical nuclear physics, quantum chaos.
H. W. Fulbright, Professor Emeritus; Ph.D., Washington (St. Louis), 1944. Experimental nuclear physics, radio astronomy of the top quark, phenomenology of strong interactions.
Y. Gao, Associate Professor; Ph.D., Purdue, 1986. Experimental condensed-matter physics.
H. E. Gove, Professor Emeritus; Ph.D., MIT, 1950. Experimental nuclear physics, heavy ions, accelerator mass spectrometry.
C. R. Hagen, Professor; Ph.D., MIT, 1962. Theoretical elementary particle physics; quantum field theory, particularly 2+1 dimensional theories.
H. L. Helfer, Professor Emeritus; Ph.D., Chicago, 1953. Theoretical astrophysics, dense plasma equations of state, production and acceleration of cosmic-ray particles.
R. S. Knox, Professor Emeritus; Ph.D., Rochester, 1958. Theoretical biological physics and condensed-matter physics.
D. S. Koltun, Professor; Ph.D., Princeton, 1961. Theoretical nuclear physics, meson interactions with nuclei, many-body theory, electron scattering.
L. Mandel, Lee A. DuBridge Professor Emeritus; Ph.D., London, 1951. Elementary quantum processes involving single photons and single atoms, locality violations and quantum interference effects.
S. L. Manly, Associate Professor; Ph.D., Columbia, 1989. Experimental relativistic heavy-ion physics, experimental elementary particle physics.
K. S. McFarland, Assistant Professor; Ph.D., Chicago, 1994. Experimental elementary particle physics: properties of top quarks, neutrino physics, electroweak unification.
A. C. Melissinos, Professor; Ph.D., MIT, 1958. Experimental particle physics, high-intensity laser-particle interactions, free-electron lasers, searches for relic gravitational radiation.
D. D. Meyerhofer, Associate Professor; Ph.D., Princeton, 1987. High-intensity laser-matter interaction experiments, plasma physics, quantum optics.
S. Okubo, Professor Emeritus; Ph.D., Rochester, 1958. Theoretical particle physics and mathematical physics.
L. Orr, Assistant Professor; Ph.D., Chicago, 1991. Theoretical elementary particle physics, phenomenology.
J. L. Pipher, Professor; Ph.D., Cornell, 1971. Development of infrared detector arrays for space astronomy, use of arrays for ground-based observations.
S. G. Rajeev, Associate Professor; Ph.D., Syracuse, 1984. Nonperturbative quantum field theory applied to strong interactions.
M. P. Savedoff, Professor Emeritus; Ph.D., Princeton, 1957. Theoretical astrophysics, stellar interiors, interstellar matter, high-energy astrophysics.
Y. Shapir, Associate Professor; Ph.D., Tel-Aviv, 1981. Theoretical condensed-matter physics, statistical mechanics.
A. Simon, Professor; Ph.D., Rochester, 1950. Theoretical plasma physics, controlled thermonuclear fusion.
P. F. Slattery, Professor; Ph.D., Yale, 1967. Experimental elementary particle physics, investigation of QCD via direct photon production, search for new phenomena using high-energy colliders.
R. L. Sproull, Professor Emeritus; Ph.D., Cornell, 1943. Experimental condensed-matter physics.
C. R. Stroud, Professor; Ph.D., Washington (St. Louis), 1969. Theoretical and experimental quantum optics, imaging and control of the states of atomic electrons.
S. L. Teitel, Associate Professor; Ph.D., Cornell, 1981. Statistical and condensed-matter physics.
J. H. Thomas, Professor; Ph.D., Purdue, 1966. Astrophysical fluid dynamics and magnetohydrodynamics, solar physics.
E. H. Thorndike, Professor; Ph.D., Harvard, 1960. Experimental elementary particle physics, weak decays of b quarks.
P. L. Tipton, Associate Professor; Ph.D., Rochester, 1987. Experimental elementary particle physics, production and decay of top and b quarks in proton-antiproton collisions at 1.8 TeV.
H. M. Van Horn, Adjunct Professor; Ph.D., Cornell, 1965. Theoretical astrophysics, degenerate stars.
D. M. Watson, Associate Professor; Ph.D., Berkeley, 1983. Experimental astrophysics, star formation, galactic structure, infrared detector array development.
E. Wolf, Wilson Professor; Ph.D., Bristol (England), 1948. Statistical optics, theory of partial coherence, inverse scattering, diffraction tomography.
F. L. H. Wolfs, Associate Professor; Ph.D., Chicago, 1987. Experimental nuclear physics, relativistic heavy-ion physics.
W. Wu, Assistant Professor; Ph.D., Chicago, 1992. Experimental condensed-matter physics.

RECENT FACULTY PUBLICATIONS

Law, C. K., H. Pu, **N. P. Bigelow,** and **J. H. Eberly.** "Stability signature" in two-species dilute Bose-Einstein condensates. *Phys. Rev. Lett.* 79:3105, 1997.
Seligman, W., et al. **(CCFR Collaboration—A. Bodek).** Improved determination of α_s from neutrino-nucleon scattering. *Phys. Rev. Lett.* 79:1213, 1997.
Apanasevich, L., et al. **(E706 Collaboration—T. Ferbel** and **P. Slattery).** Production of charm at high transverse momentum in 515 GeV/cπ^--nucleon collisions. *Phys. Rev.* D56:1391, 1997.
Park, Y., et al. **(Y. Gao).** Gap-state induced photoluminescence quenching of phenylene vinylene oligomer and its recovery by oxidation. *Phys. Rev. Lett.* 78:3955, 1997.
Gove, H. E., S. J. Mattingly, A. R. David, and L. A. Garza-Valdes. A problematic source of organic contamination of linen. *Nucl. Instrum. Methods Phys. Res.* B123:504, 1997.
Sawicki, D. A., and **R. S. Knox.** Universal relationship between emission and absorption of complex systems: An alternative approach. *Phys. Rev.* A54:4837, 1996.
Ferree, T. C., and **D. S. Koltun.** Inelastic nucleon contributions in (e,e') nuclear response functions. *Phys. Rev.* C55:253, 1997.
Mandel, L. Evidence for the failure of local realism based on the Hardy-Jordan approach. In *Experimental Metaphysics,* p. 135, eds. R. S. Cohen, M. Hoarne and J. Stachel. Lancaster, UK: Kluwer Academic Press, 1997.
Burke, D. L., et al. **(E-144 Collaboration—A. Melissinos and D. D. Meyerhofer).** Positron production in multiphoton light-by-light scattering. *Phys. Rev. Lett.* 79:1626, 1997.
Orr, L. H., T. Stelzer, and W. J. Stirling. Gluon radiation in top-antitop production and decay at the LHC. *Phys. Rev.* D56:446, 1977.
Shapir, Y. Crystalline surface upon a disordered substrate. In *Dynamics of Fluctuating Interfaces and Related Phenomena,* p. 245, eds. Kim, Park, and Khang. World Scientific, 1997.
Alexander, J. P., et al. **(CLEO Collaboration—E. H. Thorndike).** First measurement of the B—>πℓυ and B—>ρ(ω)ℓυ branching fractions. *Phys. Rev. Lett.* 77:5000, 1997.
Satyapal S., et al. **(D. M. Watson, J. L. Pipher,** and **W. J. Forrest).** The intrinsic properties of the stellar clusters in the M82 starburst complex: Propagating star formation? *Astrophys. J.* 483:148, 1997.
Gbur, G., and **E. Wolf.** Sources of arbitrary state of coherence which generate completely coherent fields outside the source. *Opt. Lett.* 22:943, 1997.
Wu, W., J. Williams, and P. W. Adams. Zeeman splitting of the Coulomb anomaly: A tunneling study in two dimensions. *Phys. Rev. Lett.* 77:1139, 1996.

UNIVERSITY OF ROCHESTER

Institute of Optics

Programs of Study

Founded in 1929, the Institute of Optics offers programs of study leading to B.S., M.S., and Ph.D. degrees in optics. Undergraduate study in physics, electrical engineering, optics, or allied fields provides excellent preparation for graduate study in optics. Recipients of the Ph.D. degree in optics are in demand for teaching or research positions at colleges and universities, large and small companies, and government laboratories. The M.S. degree program, which can be completed in nine months (nonthesis option), prepares students for engineering or development positions at industry or government laboratories. Other M.S. program opportunities include an industrial co-op program and a thesis option. Both the M.S. and Ph.D. programs can be pursued part time.

Several specialty options are available in the M.S. program; they include optical communications, electrooptics and nonlinear optics, optical materials, laser engineering, image processing, and optical design and fabrication. These specialties involve four courses in the specialty area following four core courses covering the field of optics more broadly. In addition, students in this program must complete a written review of the current literature in a chosen area. Students may further specialize by carrying out research and writing a thesis in a chosen area instead of taking two of the courses. The M.S. degree is not a prerequisite for the doctorate.

Most entering Ph.D. students receive financial aid, permitting them to take a full load of four courses each semester in the first year. Normally, the first-year curriculum consists of courses in physical optics, electromagnetic theory, geometrical and instrumental optics, quantum mechanics, mathematical methods, radiometry and optical detection, and lasers and laser systems. Students are admitted to candidacy for the Ph.D. after passing a written preliminary examination at the beginning of the second year and an oral qualifying examination (based on a written thesis proposal) in the third year. General requirements for the Ph.D. are one year of full-time residence, 90 semester hours of graduate work (or 60 hours beyond the M.S.), a year of service as a teaching assistant, and completion and defense of a doctoral dissertation. There is no foreign language requirement.

Research Facilities

Facilities for thesis research include laboratories for virtually all phases of optical physics and engineering, including conventional and electronic imaging, microscopy, nonimaging optics, diffractive optics, nonlinear optics, optical communications, optical materials, fiber and guided-wave optics, semiconductor lasers and optical devices, gradient-index optics, quantum optics, and ultrafast optics, among others. Major associated campus laboratories and research centers include the Laboratory for Laser Energetics (LLE), which features the world's most powerful ultraviolet laser; the Center for Optoelectronics and Imaging; the Center for Optics Manufacturing; the Center for Electronic Imaging Systems; and the Center for Visual Science. Computing facilities include scores of networked personal computers and workstations, as well as a CRAY supercomputer located in the LLE.

Financial Aid

Ph.D. students normally receive fellowships providing a full-tuition scholarship and a stipend, which in 1998–99 was $15,000 for twelve months. Usually, students in good standing are supported until completion of the degree. A variety of competitive internal and external fellowships provide opportunities for higher stipends. Financial aid is available for M.S. students in the form of teaching assistantships and partial tuition waivers.

Cost of Study

Graduate tuition for 1998–99 was $21,504.

Living and Housing Costs

The University owns furnished and unfurnished apartments. Many students rent privately owned housing. A register of apartments and houses for rent is maintained by the University's Apartment Office.

Student Group

In 1998, The Institute of Optics had 64 Ph.D. students, 20 full-time M.S. candidates, and 4 part-time M.S. students. In fall 1998, 25 new full-time students entered the program. All of the Institute's 1998 M.S. and Ph.D. recipients obtained jobs in optics.

The University has approximately 5,600 undergraduates and approximately 3,600 graduate students.

Location

Rochester, with a metropolitan area of 600,000 people, specializes in precision industry, much of which is related to optics (Eastman Kodak, Bausch & Lomb, and Xerox being the best known).

The Institute

The Institute of Optics has been a leader in the training of optical scientists and engineers since 1929. The faculty includes 14 full-time professors, 3 professors emeriti, and 7 professors holding joint appointments in other departments and laboratories at the University. Faculty members have been the recipients of honorary degrees, medals, and fellowships in the Optical Society of America, the Society of Photo Optical Instrumentation Engineers, the Institute of Electrical and Electronic Engineers, and the American Physical Society. They have also served as editors or associate editors of a number of journals and as presidents of professional societies. Graduates obtain faculty positions in departments of physics, electrical engineering, and optics at a number of leading universities.

Applying

Requests for application forms should be sent to the Optics Graduate Admissions Committee. Applicants ordinarily have an undergraduate degree in physics or engineering. GRE scores are strongly recommended. Those applying for financial aid must submit completed applications by February 1 for fall entrance. Midyear entrance is strongly discouraged. Students with undergraduate degrees from universities in which English is not the language of instruction, must submit scores on the Test of English as a Foreign Language (TOEFL).

Correspondence and Information

Administrator
Optics Graduate Admissions Committee
University of Rochester
Institute of Optics
Rochester, New York 14627-0186
Telephone: 716-275-7764
E-mail: grad-admissions@optics.rochester.edu
World Wide Web: http://www.optics.rochester.edu

University of Rochester

THE FACULTY AND THEIR RESEARCH

Professors

Dennis G. Hall, Director of the Institute of Optics; Ph.D., Tennessee. Guided-wave optics, novel semiconductor lasers, optical effects in solids.

Govind P. Agrawal, Ph.D., Indian Institute of Technology (Delhi). Semiconductor lasers, solid-state physics, optical communications, laser physics, phase conjugation, optical bistability, nonlinear phenomena.

Robert Boyd, Ph.D., Berkeley. Nonlinear optics, infrared detection and generation.

Joseph H. Eberly, Ph.D., Stanford. Resonant interaction of light with atoms and molecules, multiphoton processes, quantum electrodynamics.

Philippe M. Fauchet, Ph.D., Stanford. Ultrafast measurements, semiconductor nanocrystals, porous silicon.

Nicholas George, Ph.D., Caltech. Electromagnetic theory, physical optics, optical systems, speckle, X-ray optics, pattern recognition.

M. Parker Givens, Emeritus; Ph.D., Cornell. Holography, optical data processing.

Susan Houde-Walter, Ph.D., Rochester. Microoptics, integrated optics, interferometry, holography.

Duncan T. Moore, Ph.D., Rochester. Lens design, automatic phase measurements.

G. Michael Morris, Ph.D., Caltech. Holography, white light optical processing, coherence, electromagnetic wave propagation, diffractive optics.

Carlos R. Stroud Jr., Ph.D., Washington (St. Louis). Quantum optics, short-pulse excitation of atoms and molecules.

Kenneth J. Teegarden, Ph.D., Illinois at Urbana-Champaign. Optical and electronic properties of crystalline and noncrystalline semiconductors and insulators, development of new optical materials.

Brian J. Thompson, Emeritus; Ph.D., Manchester (England). Holography, image processing, coherence, phase microscopy.

Ian A. Walmsley, Ph.D., Rochester. Nonlinear optics, quantum optics, optical probing of fundamental processes in solid-state materials.

Gary Wicks, Ph.D., Cornell. III-V semiconductors: epitaxial growth, optical properties, optical devices.

David Williams, Ph.D., California, San Diego. Sensitivity and resolution of the human visual system to patterns that are modulated in wavelength, space, and time.

Emil Wolf, Ph.D., Bristol (England); D.Sc., Edinburgh. Electromagnetic theory and physical optics, diffraction and theory of partial coherence.

Associate Professors

Thomas G. Brown, Ph.D., Rochester. Guided-wave optics, optical properties of semiconductors, optical communications.

Jay M. Eastman, Ph.D., Rochester. Thin films, optical instrumentation. (part-time)

Stephen D. Jacobs, Ph.D., Rochester. Optical materials.

Wolf Seka, Ph.D., Texas. Lasers.

Assistant Professors

Turan Erdogan, Ph.D., Rochester. Optical fiber devices and communications, semiconductor lasers, integrated optics, applications of holography.

Bryan Stone, Ph.D., Rochester. Design of conventional and unconventional optical systems, aberration theory, design for manufacturing.

SELECTED PUBLICATIONS

Agrawal, G. P. *Fiber-Optic Communication Systems,* 2nd edition. New York: Wiley, 1997.

Essiambre, R.-J., and **G. P. Agrawal.** Soliton communication systems. In *Progress in Optics,* vol. 38, pp. 185–256, ed. E. Wolf. Amsterdam: North-Holland, 1997.

van Tartwijk, G. H. M., and **G. P. Agrawal.** Nonlinear dynamics in the generalized Lorenz-Haken model. *Opt. Commun.* 133:565–77, 1997.

Essiambre, R.-J., and **G. P. Agrawal.** Timing jitter of ultrashort solitons in high-speed communication systems: Part I. General formulation and application to dispersion-decreasing fibers. *J. Opt. Soc. Am. B* 14:314–22, 1997.

Essiambre, R.-J., and **G. P. Agrawal.** Timing jitter of ultrashort solitons in high-speed communication systems: Part II. Control of jitter by periodic phase conjugations. *J. Opt. Soc. Am. B* 14:323–30, 1997.

Law, J. Y., and **G. P. Agrawal.** Effect of spatial hole-burning on gain switching in vertical-cavity surface-emitting lasers. *IEEE J. Quantum Electron.* 33:462–8, 1997.

Marciante, J. R., G. H. M. van Tartwijk, and **G. P. Agrawal.** Spatial feedback effects in narrow-stripe index-guided semiconductor lasers. *IEEE J. Quantum Electron.* 33:469–73, 1997.

Law, J. Y., and **G. P. Agrawal.** Mode-partition noise in vertical-cavity surface-emitting lasers. *IEEE Photon. Technol. Lett.* 9:437–9, 1997.

Bromage, J., et al. **(G. P. Agrawal** and **P. M. Fauchet).** Spatio-temporal shaping of terahertz pulses. *Opt. Lett.* 22:627–9, 1997.

Marciante, J. R., and **G. P. Agrawal.** Spatio-temporal characteristics of filamentation in broad-area semiconductor lasers. *IEEE J. Quantum Electron.* 33:1174–9, 1997.

Maywar, D. N., and **G. P. Agrawal.** Transfer-matrix analysis of optical bistability in DFB semiconductor laser amplifiers with nonuniform gratings. *IEEE J. Quantum Electron.* 33:2029–37, 1997.

Nagasako, E. M., **R. W. Boyd,** and **G. S. Agarwal.** Vacuum-field-induced filamentation in laser-beam propagation. *Phys. Rev. A* 55:1412–5, 1997.

Buckland, E. L., **R. W. Boyd,** and A. F. Evans. Observation of a Raman-induced inter-pulse phase migration in the propagation of an ultrahigh-bit-rate coherent soliton train. *Opt. Lett.* 22:454, 1997.

Buckland, E. L., and **R. W. Boyd.** Measurement of the frequency response of the electrostrictive nonlinearity in optical fibers. *Opt. Lett.* 22:676, 1997.

Bowers, M. W., **R. W. Boyd,** and A. K. Hankla. Brillouin-enhanced four-wave-mixing vector phase conjugate mirror with beam combining capability. *Opt. Lett.* 22:360–2, 1997.

Gehr, R. J., G. L. Fischer, and **R. W. Boyd.** Nonlinear optical response of porous-glass-based composite materials. *J. Opt. Soc. Am. B* 14:2310–4, 1997.

Smith, D. B., G. Fischer, **R. W. Boyd,** and D. A. Gregory. Cancellation of photoinduced absorption in metal nanoparticle composites through a counterintuitive consequence of local field effects. *J. Opt. Soc. Am. B* 14:1625–31, 1997.

Stentz, A. J., and **R. W. Boyd.** Nonlinear optics. In *Handbook of Photonics,* ed. Mool C. Gupta. Boca Raton: CRC Press, 1997.

Brown, T. G., and **D. G. Hall.** Radiative isoelectronic impurities in silicon and silicon-germanium alloys and superlattices. In *Semiconductors and Semimetals,* eds. Willardson and Weber, vol. 49, Light Emission in Silicon: From Physics to Devices, ed. D. J. Lockwood. San Diego: Academic Press, 1997.

Arraf, A., L. Poladian, C. Martijn de Sterke, and **T. G. Brown.** Effective medium approach for contrapropagating waves in nonuniform Bragg gratings. *J. Opt. Soc. Am. A* 14:1137, 1997.

Bieber, A. E., and **T. G. Brown.** Integral coupler/resonator for silicon-based switching and modulation. *Appl. Phys. Lett.* 71:861, 1997.

Bieber, A. E., and **T. G. Brown.** Coupling, switching, and modulation in silicon-based optoelectronic structures. In *Proceedings of the SPIE: Silicon-Based Monolithic and Hybrid Optoelectronic Devices* 3007:12, 1997.

Kreger, S. T., and **T. G. Brown.** Thermal and electronic saturation effects in solid state photon counting. In *Proceedings of the SPIE: Three-Dimensional Microscopy: Image Acquisition and Processing IV* 2984:178, 1997.

Erdogan, T., et al. Integrated-optical Mach-Zehnder add-drop filter fabricated by a single UV-induced grating exposure. *Appl. Opt.* 36:7838–45, 1997.

Erdogan, T. Fiber grating spectra. *J. Lightwave Technol.* 15:1277, 1997.

Erdogan, T. Cladding mode resonances in short and long period fiber grating filters. *J. Opt. Soc. Am. A* 14:1760–73, 1997.

Norton, S. M., **T. Erdogan,** and **G. M. Morris.** Coupled-mode theory of resonant grating filters. *J. Opt. Soc. Am. A* 14:629, 1997.

Zacharias, M., S. J. Atherton, and **P. M. Fauchet.** Defect luminescence in films containing Ge and GeO_2 nanocrystals. *Mater. Res. Soc. Symp. Proc.* 467:379–84, 1997.

Fauchet, P. M., and J. von Behren. The strong visible luminescence in porous silicon: Quantum confinement, not oxide-related defects. *Phys. Status Solid B* 204:R7–8, 1997.

Fauchet, P. M. Porous silicon: Photoluminescence and electroluminescent devices. In *Semiconductors and Semimetals,* eds. Willard and Weber, vol. 49, Light Emission in Silicon: From Physics to Devices, pp. 206–52, ed. D. J. Lockwood. San Diego: Academic Press, 1997.

von Behren, J., E. H. Chimowitz, and **P. M. Fauchet.** Critical behavior and the processing of nanoscale porous materials. *Adv. Mater.* 9:921–6, 1997.

Gardiner, T. A., Ju. V. Vandyshev, G. W. Wicks, and **P. M. Fauchet.** Femtosecond infrared spectroscopy of hot electrons in an In0.53Ga0.47As/In0.52Al0.48As multiple quantum well structure. In *OSA Trends in Optics and Photonics Series,* vol. 13, Ultrafast Electronics and Optoelectronics, pp. 280–3, eds. M. Nuss and J. Bowers. Washington, D.C.: Optical Society of America, 1997.

Zachariasm M., and **P. M. Fauchet.** Blue luminescence in films containing Ge and GeO_2 nanocrystals: The role of defects. *Appl. Phys. Lett.* 71:380–382, 1997.

Fauchet, P. M., L. Tsybeskov, S. P. Duttagupta, and K. D. Hirschman. Stable photoluminescence and electroluminescence from porous silicon. *Thin Solid Films* 297:254–60, 1997.

Tsybeskov, L., K. L. Moore, **P. M. Fauchet,** and **D. G. Hall.** Light emission from intrinsic and doped silicon-rich silicon oxide: From the visible to 1.6 μm. *Mater. Res. Soc. Symp. Proc.* 452:523–8, 1997.

Moore, K. L., L. Tsybeskov, **P. M. Fauchet,** and **D. G. Hall.** Room temperature band-edge luminescence from silicon grains prepared by the recrystallization of mesoporous silicon. *Mater. Res. Soc. Symp. Proc.* 452:517–22, 1997.

George, N. Lensless electronic imaging. *Opt. Commun.* 133:22–6, 1997.

George, N., and S. Radic. Theory for the propagation of short electromagnetic pulses. *Opt. Commun.* 139:1–6, 1997.

Casperson, L. W., **D. G. Hall,** and A. A. Tovar. Sinusoidal-Gaussian beams in complex optical systems. *J. Opt. Soc. Am. A* 14:3341, 1997.

Stuart, H. R., and **D. G. Hall.** The thermodynamic limit to light-trapping in thin planar structures. *J. Opt. Soc. Am. A* 14:3001, 1997.

Jordan, R. H., et al. **(D. G. Hall** and **G. Wicks).** Lasing behavior of circular grating surface emitting semiconductor lasers. *J. Opt. Soc. Am. B* 14:449, 1997.

Sullivan, K. G., and **D. G. Hall.** Enhancement and inhibition of electromagnetic radiation in plane layered media. I. The plane wave spectrum approach to modeling classical effects. *J. Opt. Soc. Am. B* 14:1149, 1997.

Sullivan, K. G., and **D. G. Hall.** Enhancement and inhibition of electromagnetic radiation in plane layered media. II. Enhanced fluorescence in optical waveguide sensors. *J. Opt. Soc. Am. B* 14:1160, 1997.

Kim, S., et al. **(D. G. Hall).** Isoelectronic bound exciton photoluminescence in strained beryllium-doped SiGe epilayers and SiGe/Si superlattices at ambient and elevated hydrostatic pressure. *Phys. Rev. B* 55:7130, 1997.

Tsybeskov, L., et al. **(D. G. Hall** and **P. M. Fauchet).** Room-temperature photoluminescence and electroluminescence from Er-doped silicon-rich silicon oxide. *Appl. Phys. Lett.* 70:1790, 1997.

Peters, P. M., and **S. N. Houde-Walter.** X-ray absorption fine structure determination of the local environment of Er3+ in glass. *Appl. Phys. Lett.* 70(5):541–3, 1997.

Messerschmidt, B., C. H. Hsieh, B. L. McIntyre, and **S. N.**

University of Rochester

Selected Publications (continued)

Houde-Walter. Ionic mobility in an ion exchanged silver-sodium boroaluminosilicate glass for micro-optics. *J. Non-Cryst. Solids* 217:264, 1997.

Messerschmidt, B., et al. **(S. N. Houde-Walter).** Temperature dependence of silver-sodium interdiffusion in micro-optic glasses. *J. Opt. Mater.* 7:165, 1997.

Dogariu, A., et al. **(S. D. Jacobs).** Polarization asymmetry in waves backscattering from highly absorbant random media. *Appl. Opt.* 36:8159–64, 1997.

Jacobs, S. D., H. M. Pollicove, W. I. Kordonski, and D. Golini. Magnetorheological finishing (MRF) in deterministic optics manufacturing. In *Proceedings of the International Conference on Precision Engineering, ICPE '97 (3rd ICMT),* pp. 685–90. Taipei, Taiwan, ROC, 1997.

Jacobs, S. D., and H. M. Pollicove. Update on magnetorheological finishing. In *Progress in Precision Engineering and Nanotechnology,* vol. 2, *Proceedings of the 9th International Precision Engineering Seminar,* pp. 620–3, eds. H. Kunzmann et al. Braunschweig, Germany, 1997.

Jacobs, S. D., et al. Magnetorheological finishing of IR materials. In *Optical Manufacturing and Testing II,* vol. 3134, pp. 258–69, ed. H. P. Stahl. Bellingham, Wash.: SPIE, 1997.

Gillman, B. E., et al. **(S. D. Jacobs).** Application of coolants in deterministic microgrinding of glass. In *Optical Manufacturing and Testing II,* vol. 3134, pp. 198–204, ed. H. P. Stahl. Bellingham, Wash: SPIE, 1997.

Sales, T., and **G. M. Morris.** Diffractive-refractive behavior of kinoform lenses. *Appl. Opt.* 36:253–7, 1997.

Lalanne, P., and **G. M. Morris.** Antireflection behavior of silicon subwavelength periodic structures for visible light. *Nanotechnology* 8:53–6, 1997.

Haidner, H., and **G. M. Morris.** Wavefront Quality of Optimized Diffractive Lenses. *Pure Appl. Opt.* 6:191–202, 1997.

Sales, T., and **G. M. Morris.** On the fundamental limits of optical superresolution. *Opt. Lett.* 22:582–4, 1997.

Stone, B. D., and G. W. Forbes. Differential ray tracing in inhomogeneous media. *J. Opt. Soc. Am. A* 14:2824–36, 1997.

Stone, B. D. Perturbations of optical systems. *J. Opt. Soc. Am. A* 14:2837–49, 1997.

Stone, B. D. Determination of initial ray configurations for asymmetric systems. *J. Opt. Soc. Am. A* 14:3415–29, 1997.

Lasche, J. B., and **B. D. Stone.** Fundamental limits of zoom systems. *Proc. SPIE* 3129:181–92, 1997.

Bromage, J., et al. **(C. R. Stroud Jr., G. Agrawal,** and **P. Fauchet.)** Spatio-temporal shaping of terahertz pulses. *Opt. Lett.* 22:627–9, 1997.

Aronstein, D., and **C. R. Stroud Jr.** Fractional wavefunction revivals in the infinite square well. *Phys. Rev. A* 55:4626–37, 1997.

Corless, J., J. West, J. Bromage, and **C. R. Stroud Jr.** Pulsed single-mode dye laser for coherent control experiments. *Rev. Sci. Instrum.* 68:2259–64, 1997.

Corless, J., and **C. R. Stroud Jr.** Optical mixing of Rydberg angular momenta. *Phys. Rev. Lett.* 79:637–40, 1997.

West, J., and **C. R. Stroud Jr.** Visualization of core-scattering dynamics of Rydberg wave packets. *Opt. Exp.* 1:31–8, 1997.

Noel, M., and **C. R. Stroud Jr.** Shaping an atomic electron wave packet. *Opt. Exp.* 1:176–85, 1997.

Koshel, R. J., and **I. A. Walmsley.** Optimal design of optically side-pumped lasers. *IEEE J. Quantum Electron.* 33:94, 1994.

Wong, V., and **I. A. Walmsley.** Ultrashort pulse characterization from dynamic spectrograms using iterative phase retrieval. *J. Opt. Soc. Am. B* 14:944, 1997.

Grice, W., and **I. A. Walmsley.** Spectral information and distinguishability in type-II downconversion with a broadband pump. *Phys. Rev. A* 56:1627, 1997.

Waxer, L., **I. A. Walmsley,** and W. Vogel. Molecular emission tomography of anharmonic vibrations. *Phys. Rev. A* 56:R2491, 1997.

Wicks, G. W. III-V semiconductor materials. In *Handbook of Photonics.* CRC Press, 1997.

Wamsley, C. C., M. W. Koch, and **G. W. Wicks.** Low threshold 1.3 mm InAsP/GaInAsP lasers grown by solid source molecular beam epitaxy. *J. Cryst. Growth* 175/176:42, 1997.

Roorda, A., and **D. R. Williams.** New directions in imaging the retina. *Opt. Photonics News* 8:23–9, 1997.

Liang, J., **D. R. Williams,** and D. T. Miller. Imaging photoreceptors in the living eye with adaptive optics. In *Basic and Clinical Applications of Vision Science,* The Professor Jay M. Enoch Festschrift Volume, *Documeta Ophthalmologica Proceedings Series 60,* pp. 43–6, ed. V. Lakshminarayanan. Dordercht, the Netherlands: Kluwer Academic Publishers, 1997.

Packer, O. S., and **D. R. Williams.** Photopigment absorptance and directional sensitivity in peripheral primate retina. In *Basic and Clinical Applications of Vision Science,* The Professor Jay M. Enoch Festschrift Volume, *Documeta Ophthalmologica Proceedings Series 60,* pp. 47–50, ed. V. Lakshminarayanan. Dordecht, the Netherlands: Kluwer Academic Publishers, 1997.

Liang, J., and **D. R. Williams.** Aberrations and retinal image quality of the normal human eye. *J. Opt. Soc. Am. A* 14:2873–83, 1997.

Liang, J., **D. R. Williams,** and D. T. Miller. Supernormal vision and high resolution retinal imaging through adaptive optics. *J. Opt. Soc. Am. A* 14:2884–92, 1997.

Wolf, E. Sudarshan's optical researches. *Z. Naturforsch.* 52a:2, 1997.

Wang, W., A. Friberg, and **E. Wolf.** Focusing of partially coherent in systems of large Fresnel numbers. *J. Opt. Soc. Am. A* 14:491–6, 1997.

Habashy, T., A. T. Friberg, and **E. Wolf.** Application of the coherent-mode representation to a class of inverse source problems. *Inverse Probl.* 13:47–61, 1997.

Fischer, D. G., and **E. Wolf.** Theory of diffraction tomography for quasi-homogeneous random objects. *Opt. Commun.* 133:17–21, 1997.

James, D. F. V., and **E. Wolf.** Cross-spectrally pure light and the spectral modulation law. *Opt. Commun.* 138:257–61, 1997.

Visser, T., and **E. Wolf.** Scattering in the presence of field discontinuities at boundaries. *Phys. Lett. A* 234:1–4, 1997.

Wolf, E., T. Shirai, H. Chen, and W. Wang. Coherence filters and their uses part I: Basic theory and examples. *J. Mod. Opt.* 44:1345–53, 1997.

Wolf, E. Far-zone spectral isotropy in weak scattering on spatially random media. *J. Opt. Soc. Am. A* 14:2820–3, 1997.

Devaney, A. J., A. T. Friberg, A. Kumar, and **E. Wolf.** Decrease in spatial coherence of light propagating in free space. *Opt. Lett.* 22:1672–3, 1997.

Gbur, G., and **E. Wolf.** Sources of arbitrary state of coherence which generate completely coherent fields outside the source. *Opt. Lett.* 22:943–5, 1997.

UNIVERSITY OF SOUTH CAROLINA

Department of Physics and Astronomy

Programs of Study

The department offers comprehensive experimental research programs in intermediate-energy nuclear physics; elementary particle physics; and condensed-matter physics, including high-temperature superconductivity and magnetic properties of materials and chemical physics. There is a broad effort in theoretical research, with programs in the foundations of quantum theory, nuclear theory, quantum optics, atomic physics, quantum gravity, quantum electrodynamics, general relativity, cosmology, astrophysics, and critical phenomena.

In addition to the M.S. and Ph.D. in physics, the Master of Arts in Teaching (M.A.T.) in physics and natural science is offered.

The intermediate-energy nuclear physics group performs experiments at accelerator laboratories in the United States and in France using polarized gamma rays to study the properties of the hadronic force and the structure of protons and neutrons. A major effort in double beta decay and the search for cosmic dark matter has installations in the United States, the Commonwealth of Independent States, and Spain. The high-energy physics group participates in experiments at Fermilab on the production and decay of charmed particles and on the detection of neutrinos and neutrino oscillations. The theoretical effort in the foundations of quantum theory is a cooperative venture with Tel-Aviv University, and one of its faculty members holds a joint appointment. The large effort in electron spin resonance is carried out primarily on campus, in collaboration with several other universities in the United States and South America. Neutron diffraction studies of magnetic and ferroelectric samples are carried out at Oak Ridge and Argonne national laboratories.

The remainder of the experimental programs are carried out on campus. They include the investigation of phase transitions, computational physics, electron-spin resonance, superconductivity, magnetism, ferroelectrics, thermal properties, ultrahigh-current phenomena, and coherent transport. In condensed-matter theory there are programs in superconductivity, critical phenomena, and computational physics.

The program in the foundations of quantum theory is coupled with the theoretical efforts in quantum optics and atomic physics. The main thrust uses very simple models to investigate problems of renormalization, dissipation, and relaxation of a physical system coupled to a larger reservoir; potential effects in quantum phenomena; quantum optics; and the development of better techniques in perturbative calculations.

Research Facilities

An eight-story science complex houses an electronics shop, a machine shop, a microscopy center, classrooms, and laboratories. The research equipment includes a novel electron-resonance spectrometer, a large-bore Teslatron (16-T), SQUID susceptometers, and a variety of instrumentation for sensitive high-resolution experiments. Sample fabrication facilities, such as photo and electron lithography facilities, ultrahigh-vacuum and electrodeposition systems for thin films, and furnaces for material preparation, are also available. The high-energy and intermediate-energy nuclear physics programs are carried out at national and international laboratories, as described above.

Financial Aid

Graduate teaching assistantships are available that require 16 hours of work per week and carry a stipend of $12,500 per academic year in 1999–2000. Almost all full-time graduate students receive full graduate assistantships. Additional teaching and research assistantships are available during the summer. A minimum of $1500 is guaranteed during the summer; typically, students earn between $3000 and $4500 during the summer. Beginning with the 1999–2000 academic year, stipends are augmented by a fellowship program, which adds an average of $3000 per academic year to the stipends.

Cost of Study

In 1999–2000, tuition for graduate students who are South Carolina residents is $193 per semester hour; tuition is $404 per semester hour for nonresidents. This rate is reduced to $710 per semester with teaching assistantships for the fall and spring semesters and $181 per semester with teaching assistantships in the summer.

Living and Housing Costs

Costs for rooms on campus were $375 per month for single students in 1998–99. Apartments were available for married students at rents ranging from $402 to $644 per month.

Student Group

There are approximately 27,000 students, including about 10,000 graduate students, at the University. The graduate student body in the physics department numbers between 30 and 40. These students come from many states and countries.

Location

The Columbia metropolitan area, with a population of 472,800, is situated in the center of South Carolina. The climate is moderate, with an average annual temperature of 64°F. Recreational opportunities include camping, swimming, golf, and tennis. Sesquicentennial State Park and ten other state parks are within a 75-mile radius of the city, and Lake Murray, with more than 500 miles of shoreline, is only a few miles northwest of the city.

The University and The Department

The University of South Carolina was founded in 1801 and is located in the center of Columbia, the state capital. The University offers graduate degrees in most of the departments of the Colleges of Liberal Arts and Science and Mathematics and in the Colleges of Business Administration, Education, Engineering, Journalism, Pharmacy, and Public Health. The University's School of Medicine offers the degree of Doctor of Medicine. In addition, graduate professional degrees are offered in accountancy, audiology, business administration, criminal justice, engineering, fine arts, international business studies, librarianship, media arts, music, music education, social work, and speech pathology. The course offerings represent strong traditional curricula at both the undergraduate and graduate levels, with additional courses in the above research areas. The Department of Physics and Astronomy offers a variety of service courses (lower-level courses open to students not majoring in physics), which have total enrollments of more than 2,000 students from other departments and colleges on campus.

Applying

Application forms should be obtained from the Graduate School. Completed applications should be submitted directly to the dean of the Graduate School.

Correspondence and Information

Professor Milind V. Purohit
Department of Physics and Astronomy
University of South Carolina
Columbia, South Carolina 29208
Telephone: 803-777-6996

University of South Carolina

THE FACULTY AND THEIR RESEARCH

Yakir Aharonov, Professor (joint appointment with Tel-Aviv University); Ph.D., Bristol (England). Theoretical physics.
Jeeva S. Anandan, Professor; Ph.D., Pittsburgh. Theoretical physics.
Chi-Kwan Au, Professor; Ph.D., Columbia. Theoretical physics.
Frank T. Avignone III, Professor; Ph.D., Georgia Tech. Nuclear and elementary particle physics.
Gary S. Blanpied, Professor; Ph.D., Texas at Austin. Nuclear physics.
Richard J. Creswick, Associate Professor; Ph.D., Berkeley. Theoretical condensed-matter physics.
Timir Datta, Professor; Ph.D., Tulane. Solid-state physics.
Chaden Djalali, Professor; Ph.D., Paris. Nuclear physics.
Horacio A. Farach, Professor; Ph.D., Buenos Aires. Solid-state physics, magnetic resonance.
Paul G. Huray, Professor; Ph.D., Tennessee. Transuranium elements.
Joseph E. Johnson, Associate Professor; Ph.D., SUNY at Stony Brook. Theoretical physics.
Edwin R. Jones Jr., Professor; Ph.D., Wisconsin. Solid-state physics.
James M. Knight, Professor and Interim Chair; Ph.D., Maryland. Theoretical physics.
Kuniharu Kubodera, Professor; Ph.D., Tokyo. Theoretical nuclear physics.
Milind Kunchur, Assistant Professor; Ph.D., Rutgers. Condensed-matter physics.
Pawel O. Mazur, Associate Professor; Ph.D., Jagiellonian (Krakow). Theoretical physics.
Sanjib R. Mishra, Associate Professor; Ph.D., Columbia. High-energy physics.
Fred Myhrer, Professor; Ph.D., Rochester. Theoretical nuclear physics.
Barry M. Preedom, Professor; Ph.D., Tennessee. Nuclear physics.
Milind V. Purohit, Associate Professor; Ph.D., Caltech. High-energy physics.
Carl Rosenfeld, Professor; Ph.D., Caltech. High-energy physics.
John L. Safko, Professor; Ph.D., North Carolina. Theoretical physics.
David J. Tedeschi, Assistant Professor; Ph.D., Rensselaer. Nuclear physics.
C. Steven Whisnant, Associate Professor; Ph.D., Purdue. Nuclear physics.
Jeffrey R. Wilson, Associate Professor; Ph.D., Purdue. High-energy physics.

A lecture on the foundations of quantum theory.

Detectors used in nuclear physics experiments at the LEGS facility at Brookhaven National Laboratory.

Surface scattering of ions experiment.

THE UNIVERSITY OF TENNESSEE, KNOXVILLE

Department of Physics and Astronomy

Programs of Study

The Department of Physics and Astronomy offers a Master of Science and a Doctor of Philosophy in physics. The M.S. program includes both thesis and nonthesis options, as well as an M.S. in geophysics.

The department offers a challenging program for graduate study. The faculty is concentrated in the following four major research areas that are all well balanced between theory and experiment: elementary particle physics, condensed-matter physics, atomic physics, and nuclear physics. The research effort is strengthened by additional endeavors in astrophysics, biophysics, computational physics, molecular spectroscopy, and textile science. Basic graduate courses cover theoretical physics, classical mechanics, electromagnetic theory, quantum mechanics, and mathematical methods in physics. Further advanced course work is based on the student's chosen area of concentration (especially in the four major research areas given above).

Research Facilities

The department's research facilities include laboratory space in both the Nielsen Physics Building and the Science and Engineering Building. Support services include an electronics shop, machine shop, and use of the University computer center for data analysis and theory work. The department's long-standing partnership with the Oak Ridge National Laboratory allows use of accelerators, reactors, and other major facilities. Beyond local resources, the department enjoys research collaborations with groups at Brookhaven National Laboratory, the Stanford Linear Accelerator Center, the European Center for Nuclear Research (CERN), the CAMD Synchrotron Source at Louisiana State University, and several other institutions.

Financial Aid

The department offers graduate teaching assistantships, research assistantships, and fellowships to help students finance their graduate study. Students must be accepted to the University of Tennessee Graduate School before they can be considered for assistantships. In 1999–2000, teaching assistantships pay a stipend of $9820 for nine months, with a waiver of tuition and fees. Research assistantships offer a similar stipend with a tuition/fee waiver. Other available fellowships include a UT-ORNL Select Graduate Fellowship in Condensed Matter Physics and Science Alliance Fellowships for graduate students in physics. Contact the Graduate School for information on other scholarships and fellowships outside the department.

Cost of Study

In 1999–2000, tuition and fees for full-time students are $1677 per semester for Tennessee residents and $4205 for out-of-state students.

Living and Housing Costs

Estimated costs in 1999–2000, including tuition, are $20,000 for a single student, $25,900 for a married couple, and $29,570 or more for a couple with one child. University housing for married students rents for prices that range from $280 per month for a one-bedroom unfurnished apartment to $350 per month for a three-bedroom furnished apartment. A two-bedroom furnished apartment with all utilities rents for $395 per month.

Student Group

The current enrollment of the University of Tennessee, Knoxville, is 25,612. In 1998–99, there were 91 graduate students in physics. Of these, 15 were from Tennessee, and 37 were international students from fifteen other countries. Twelve were women.

Location

The University is located in the city of Knoxville, with a population of more than 165,000 and metropolitan population of 586,000. The Great Smoky Mountains and many TVA lakes are within easy driving distance.

The University

The University of Tennessee is the official state university and federal land-grant institution of Tennessee. The University offers more than 110 different majors in twelve different colleges leading to bachelor's degrees in 164 fields of study, master's degrees in 76 specialties, and doctorates in 45 specialties.

Applying

All students intending to do graduate work in physics at the University of Tennessee are encouraged to submit Graduate Record Examinations General Test scores. In order to ensure their consideration, all applications for teaching and research assistantships should be submitted by February 1.

Correspondence and Information

Department of Physics and Astronomy
The University of Tennessee
Knoxville, Tennessee 37996-1200
Telephone: 423-974-3342
Fax: 423-974-7843
E-mail: physics@utk.edu
World Wide Web: http://www.phys.utk.edu

University of Tennessee, Knoxville

THE FACULTY AND THEIR RESEARCH

Professor and Head
L. L. Riedinger, Ph.D., Vanderbilt. Experimental nuclear physics.

Professors
F. E. Barnes, Ph.D., Caltech. Theoretical elementary particle physics.
C. R. Bingham, Ph.D., Tennessee. Experimental nuclear physics.
W. E. Blass, Ph.D., Michigan State. Molecular systems and computational physics.
M. Breinig, Ph.D., Oregon. Experimental atomic and molecular physics.
W. M. Bugg, Ph.D., Tennessee. Experimental elementary particle physics.
J. Burgdoerfer, Ph.D., Berlin. Theoretical atomic and molecular physics.
T. A. Callcott, Ph.D., Purdue. Experimental condensed-matter physics.
R. W. Childers, Ph.D., Vanderbilt. Theoretical elementary particle physics.
R. N. Compton, Ph.D., Tennessee. Experimental chemical physics.
K. E. Duckett, Ph.D., Tennessee. Experimental textile science.
A. G. Eguiluz, Ph.D., Brown. Theoretical condensed-matter physics.
S. B. Elston, Ph.D., Massachusetts. Experimental atomic physics.
S. Georghiou, Ph.D., Manchester. Biophysics.
M. W. Guidry, Ph.D., Tennessee. Nuclear physics.
T. Handler, Ph.D., Rutgers. Experimental elementary particle physics.
E. L. Hart, Ph.D., Cornell. Experimental elementary particle physics.
J. H. Macek, Ph.D., RPI. Theoretical atomic physics.
G. D. Mahan, Ph.D., Berkeley. Theoretical condensed-matter physics.
W. Nazarewicz, Ph.D., Warsaw. Theoretical nuclear physics.
L. R. Painter, Ph.D., Tennessee. Experimental liquid-state physics.
D. J. Pegg, Ph.D., New Hampshire. Experimental atomic physics.
E. W. Plummer, Ph.D., Cornell. Experimental condensed-matter physics.
J. J. Quinn, Ph.D., Maryland. Theoretical condensed-matter physics.
I. A. Sellin, Ph.D., Chicago. Experimental atomic physics.
C. C. Shih, Ph.D., Cornell. Theoretical physics.
S. P. Sorensen, Ph.D., Copenhagen. Experimental nuclear physics.
M. R. Strayer, Ph.D., MIT. Theoretical nuclear physics.
J. R. Thompson, Ph.D., Duke. Experimental condensed-matter physics.
B. F. L. Ward, Ph.D., Princeton. Theoretical elementary particle physics.

Associate Professors
G. Canright, Ph.D., Tennessee. Theoretical condensed-matter physics.
T. L. Ferrell, Ph.D., Clemson. Experimental surface physics.
J. C. Levin, Ph.D., Oregon. Experimental elementary particle physics.
S. Y. Shieh, Ph.D., Maryland. Theoretical physics.

Assistant Professors
S. J. Daunt, Ph.D., Queen's at Kingston. Experimental molecular physics.
D. Dean, Ph.D., Vanderbilt. Theoretical nuclear physics.
K. F. Read, Ph.D., Cornell. Experimental nuclear physics.
A. J. Sanders, Ph.D., Tufts. Gravitational physics.
G. Siopsis, Ph.D., Caltech. Theoretical elementary particle physics.
H. H. Weitering, Ph.D., Groningen. Experimental condensed-matter physics.

Research Professors
H. O. Cohn, Ph.D., Indiana. Experimental elementary particle physics.
Y. A. Kamychkov, Ph.D., Moscow. Experimental elementary particle physics.
S. Ovichinnikov, Ph.D., St. Petersburg. Theoretical atomic physics.
N. Thonnard, Ph.D., Kentucky. Resonance ionization spectroscopy.
J. Y. Zhang, Ph.D., Lanzhou. Theoretical nuclear physics.

Research Associate Professors
D. L. McCorkle, Ph.D., Tennessee. Experimental atomic and molecular physics.
L. A. Pinnaduwage, Ph.D., Pittsburgh. Atomic and molecular physics.

Research Assistant Professors
P. G. Datskos, Ph.D., Pittsburgh. Experimental atomic and molecular physics and micro sensors.
Y. V. Efremenko, Ph.D., Russia. Experimental elementary particle physics.
W. Reviol, Ph.D., Germany. Experimental nuclear physics.
L. R. Senesac, Ph.D., Tennessee. Molecular systems and computational physics.
S. A. Yost, Ph.D., Princeton. Theoretical elementary particle physics.

Director of Undergraduate Laboratories
J. E. Parks, Ph.D., Kentucky. Experimental atomic physics.

Instructor
T. Riedinger, M.S., Vanderbilt.

UNIVERSITY OF TEXAS AT AUSTIN

Department of Physics

Programs of Study

The Department of Physics offers programs leading to the Master of Arts, Master of Science in Applied Physics, and Doctor of Philosophy degrees. Requirements for the M.S. and M.A. degrees include 30 semester hours with a minimum of 6 hours in a supporting subject or subjects outside the major program and a thesis.

The Master of Science in Applied Physics requires graduate courses in experimental physics, electromagnetic theory, and quantum mechanics. In addition, supporting work must be in engineering, chemistry, or geology.

For the Ph.D., students must satisfy core course requirements in classical, statistical, and quantum mechanics and electromagnetic theory; show evidence of exposure to modern methods of experimental physics; and pass an oral qualifying examination. Further course work and a dissertation, followed by a final oral examination, is required. For general information and additional requirements, students should consult the Graduate School Catalog.

The Department of Physics has active research groups in nine main areas of current physics research: atomic, molecular, and optical physics; classical physics; condensed-matter physics; nonlinear dynamics; nuclear physics; plasma physics; relativity and cosmology; statistical mechanics and thermodynamics; and elementary particle physics. In most of these fields, both experimental and theoretical work is in progress.

Research Facilities

The Department of Physics occupies an area of more than 190,000 square feet in a modern physics-mathematics-astronomy complex, which includes the Physics Library and five well-equipped technical shops staffed with 26 competent technicians supporting graduate research. A CDC Dual CYBER 170/750 computer system is available on campus, and there is a network of data-acquisition equipment interfaced to the department's DEC VAX-11/780 computer. The research facilities are described more fully in the graduate brochure available from the department.

Financial Aid

Graduate students in the Department of Physics have several possible sources of financial support. Some are employed directly by the department as teaching assistants or graduate assistants, some as research assistants for individual faculty members, and others as physicists for local research organizations. In addition, a limited number of University and federal fellowships are available for students with superior records. The stipends for these positions are comparable to those of other major universities and, where applicable, also include a tuition scholarship for the out-of-state portion of the tuition. Application should be made in the early fall, if at all possible.

Cost of Study

For 1998–99, tuition and required fees for 9 semester hours (a typical course load for graduate students) were $2584 for Texas residents and $6418 for nonresidents and international students. These rates are subject to change.

Living and Housing Costs

University-owned housing is available for both unmarried and married students. During the 1998–99 Long Session, room and meal costs for single graduate students ranged from $4040 to $4823 for a double room and from $5386 to $6169 for a single room. Tax on meals is not included. There is an additional charge of $300 for a private room or connecting bathrooms. There are a limited number of single rooms. The University Apartments offers housing accommodations that ranged in cost from $367 to $540 per month in 1998–99. Rates are subject to change. Private housing, including co-ops, apartments, duplexes, and houses, is also available. There is currently a waiting list for University housing.

Student Group

The University of Texas had an enrollment in 1998–99 of 24,782 men and 24,124 women. The majority of students are Texas residents, but students from all other states and more than 100 countries and U.S. possessions are also in attendance. The University is one of the nation's leading sources of doctors, dentists, scientists, and teachers.

Location

Austin is located in central Texas. It is the state capital and has a population of 632,833. The principal employers are the University, federal and state government agencies, and industrial research laboratories. Austin is a city of many parks and recreational facilities, located in an area of rolling hills and lakes. The climate is moderate with mild winters and warm-to-hot summers.

The University and The Department

The University of Texas is a state-supported institution. In 1998–99, its enrollment was 48,906 at its Austin campus, with 10,326 in its Graduate School and 1,764 faculty members above the rank of instructor. The Department of Physics currently consists of 60 faculty members, 70 nonteaching research personnel, 257 graduate students, and 184 undergraduates majoring in physics. In addition to offering the basic graduate courses, the department has courses and seminars in each area of specialization, as well as frequent colloquia featuring distinguished scientists from other institutions.

Applying

Correspondence concerning admission to the Graduate School should be directed to the Office of Graduate and International Admissions. The Graduate School requires that applicants have a bachelor's degree or the equivalent. Also required for admission is the GRE (Graduate Record Examinations) and the Subject Test in physics. The Test of English as a Foreign Language (TOEFL) with a minimum score of 550 is required for all international students. Applications should be returned by January 15 for fall and summer admission and October 1 for spring admission.

Correspondence and Information

Graduate Coordinator
Department of Physics
University of Texas at Austin
Austin, Texas 78712-1081
Telephone: 512-471-1664

University of Texas at Austin

THE FACULTY AND THEIR RESEARCH

Atomic and Molecular Physics
R. D. Bengtson, Professor; Ph.D., Maryland, 1968. Atomic transition probabilities, Stark broadening.
M. C. Downer, Professor; Ph.D., Harvard, 1983. Condensed-matter physics, atomic physics, femtosecond spectroscopy.
M. Fink, Professor; Ph.D., Karlsruhe (Germany), 1966. Electron diffraction.
L. W. Frommhold, Professor; Dr.Habil., Hamburg (Germany), 1964. Atomic and molecular physics, gas discharge.
D. Heinzen, Associate Professor; Ph.D., MIT, 1988. Ion trapping, photon-ion interactions.
J. W. Keto, Professor; Ph.D., Michigan, 1968. Reactions and radiative processes of excited atoms and molecules.
F. A. Matsen, Professor Emeritus; Ph.D., Princeton, 1940. Quantum mechanics, groups, linear algebra.
C. F. Moore, Professor; Ph.D., Florida State, 1964. High-energy electron collision.
M. Raizen, Associate Professor; Ph.D., Texas at Austin, 1989. Quantum optics, photon-ion interactions.
W. W. Robertson, Professor Emeritus; Ph.D., Texas, 1955. Experimental atomic and molecular physics.
C. W. Scherr, Professor (retired); Ph.D., Chicago, 1954. Theoretical quantum-mechanical studies of high accuracy on simple systems.
G. O. Sitz, Associate Professor; Ph.D., Stanford, 1987. Scattering of molecules from surfaces.
R. E. Wyatt, Professor; Ph.D., Johns Hopkins, 1965. Classical and quantum chaos.

Classical Physics
A. M. Gleeson, Professor; Ph.D., Pennsylvania, 1966. Field theory, underwater acoustics.
T. A. Griffy, Professor; Ph.D., Rice, 1961. Wave propagation, underwater acoustics.
H. L. Swinney, Professor; Ph.D., Johns Hopkins, 1968. Light-scattering studies of hydrodynamic and thermal instabilities.

Condensed-Matter Physics
P. R. Antoniewicz, Professor; Ph.D., Purdue, 1965. Theoretical solid-state physics.
A. L. de Lozanne, Professor; Ph.D., Stanford, 1982. Low-temperature vacuum tunneling microscopy.
F. W. de Wette, Professor Emeritus; Ph.D., Utrecht (Netherlands), 1959. Theoretical solid-state physics, surface dynamics.
M. C. Downer, Professor; Ph.D., Harvard, 1983. Condensed-matter physics, atomic physics, femtosecond spectroscopy.
J. L. Erskine, Professor; Ph.D., Washington (Seattle), 1973. Experimental studies of surface and surface adsorbate phenomena.
J. D. Gavenda, Professor (retired); Ph.D., Brown, 1959. Properties of conduction electrons in metals.
J. Käs, Assistant Professor; Ph.D., Munich Technical. Soft condensed-matter physics in conjunction with cell biology, cell motility, elasticity of filamentous proteins.
L. Kleinman, Professor; Ph.D., Berkeley, 1960. Theoretical studies of thin-metal films.
M. P. Marder, Associate Professor; Ph.D., California, Santa Barbara, 1986. Pattern formation, material science.
J. T. Markert, Associate Professor; Ph.D., Cornell, 1987. Study of physical properties of bulk material, particularly high T_c ceramics.
R. E. Martinez, Assistant Professor; Ph.D., Harvard, 1992. Synthesis and characterization of novel materials, atomic-scale studies of semiconductor surface dynamics.
W. D. McCormick, Professor (retired); Ph.D., Duke, 1959. Experimental low-temperature and solid-state physics, phase transitions.
Q. Niu, Associate Professor; Ph.D., Washington (Seattle), 1985. Field theory of condensed-matter physics, theory of superconductivity.
A. W. Nolle, Professor Emeritus; Ph.D., MIT, 1947. Magnetic resonance relaxation, spectroscopy, luminescence.
C. K. Shih, Associate Professor; Ph.D., Stanford, 1988. Study of surface properties of microelectronic materials.
J. B. Swift, Professor; Ph.D., Illinois at Urbana-Champaign, 1968. Many-body theory, phase transitions.
H. L. Swinney, Professor; Ph.D., Johns Hopkins, 1968. Light-scattering studies of hydrodynamic and thermal instabilities.
J. C. Thompson, Professor Emeritus; Ph.D., Rice, 1956. Transport in liquid metals, amorphous semiconductors, metal-to-nonmetal transition.

Elementary Particle Physics
A. Böhm, Professor; Ph.D., Marburg (Germany), 1966. Particle phenomena—algebraic and group-theoretic methods.
C. B. Chiu, Professor; Ph.D., Berkeley, 1965. Strong interaction physics.
D. Dicus, Professor; Ph.D., UCLA, 1968. Field theory of weak interactions.
J. Distler, Associate Professor; Ph.D., Harvard, 1987. High-energy theory, mathematical physics, string theory.
W. Fischler, Professor; Ph.D., Brussels, 1976. Invisible axion, supersymmetry.
V. Kaplunovsky, Associate Professor; Ph.D., Tel-Aviv, 1983. Phenomenology of string theory.
Y. Ne'eman, Professor; Ph.D., Imperial College (London), 1961. Symmetries in elementary particle physics.
E. C. G. Sudarshan, Professor; Ph.D., Rochester, 1958. Theoretical particle physics.
S. Weinberg, Professor; Ph.D., Princeton, 1957. Theory of strong and weak particle interaction.

High-Energy Physics
K. Lang, Associate Professor; Ph.D., Rochester, 1985. Experimental study of rare decay of the K-meson.
J. L. Ritchie, Associate Professor; Ph.D., Rochester, 1983. Experimental study of rare decay of the K-meson.
R. F. Schwitters, Professor; Ph.D., MIT, 1971. Experimental high-energy physics—detector development and B-physics studies.

Nuclear Physics
W. R. Coker, Professor; Ph.D., Georgia, 1966. Mechanisms of nuclear reactions, three-body final-state problem.
G. W. Hoffmann, Professor; Ph.D., UCLA, 1971. Experimental nuclear physics.
E. V. Ivash, Professor; Ph.D., Michigan, 1952. Theoretical nuclear physics, particularly direct reactions, quantum mechanics.
C. F. Moore, Professor; Ph.D., Florida State, 1964. Experimental nuclear physics.
P. J. Riley, Professor; Ph.D., Alberta, 1962. Nuclear reactions and nuclear structure physics.
T. Udagawa, Professor; Ph.D., Tokyo University of Education, 1962. Theoretical nuclear structure.
S. A. A. Zaidi, Associate Professor; Ph.D., Heidelberg (Germany), 1964. Experimental and theoretical nuclear physics.

Plasma Physics
R. D. Bengtson, Professor; Ph.D., Maryland, 1968. Plasma spectroscopy, experimental plasma physics.
H. Berk, Professor; Ph.D., Princeton, 1964. Theoretical plasma physics, computer simulation of plasmas.
W. E. Drummond, Professor; Ph.D., Stanford, 1958. Theoretical plasma physics.
R. Fitzpatrick, Assistant Professor; Ph.D., Sussex, 1988. Magnetic reconnection and gross plasma instabilities in fusion, terrestrial, and astrophysical contexts.
K. W. Gentle, Professor and Chairman; Ph.D., MIT, 1966. Nonlinear plasma processes.
R. D. Hazeltine, Professor; Ph.D., Michigan, 1968. Theoretical plasma physics.
C. W. Horton Jr., Professor; Ph.D., California, San Diego, 1967. Theoretical plasma physics.
P. J. Morrison, Professor; Ph.D., California, San Diego, 1979. Plasma physics.
M. E. Oakes, Professor; Ph.D., Florida State, 1964. Wave propagation in plasmas with emphasis on resonances.
T. Tajima, Professor; Ph.D., California, Irvine, 1975. Theoretical plasma physics.

Relativity, Cosmology, and Quantum Field Theory
P. Candelas, Professor; D.Phil., Oxford, 1977. General relativity, techniques of quantization in curved space-time.
M. W. Choptuik, Associate Professor; Ph.D., British Columbia, 1986. Computational relativity.
B. S. DeWitt, Professor; Ph.D., Harvard, 1950. Quantum field theory.
C. DeWitt-Morette, Professor; Ph.D., Paris, 1947. Mathematical physics, relativity theory.
W. Fischler, Professor; Ph.D., Brussels, 1976. Cosmology, gravity.
R. A. Matzner, Professor; Ph.D., Maryland, 1967. General cosmology, gravitational radiation.
L. C. Shepley, Associate Professor (retired); Ph.D., Princeton, 1965. Cosmology, interaction of matter with gravitation.
S. Weinberg, Professor; Ph.D., Princeton, 1957. Cosmology, astrophysics.

Statistical Mechanics and Thermodynamics
I. Prigogine, Professor; Ph.D., Brussels, 1941. Statistical mechanics and thermodynamics.
L. E. Reichl, Professor; Ph.D., Denver, 1969. Strong-coupling, nonequilibrium, and quantum statistical mechanics.
W. C. Schieve, Professor; Ph.D., Lehigh, 1959. Nonequilibrium statistical mechanics.
J. S. Turner, Associate Professor; Ph.D., Indiana, 1969. Self-organization in physics, chemistry, and biology.

UNIVERSITY OF VIRGINIA

Department of Physics

Programs of Study

The Department of Physics offers programs leading to the M.A., M.S., and Ph.D. degrees in physics. The primary emphasis is on the Ph.D. program. For an M.S. degree, a student must complete, with satisfactory progress, at least 24 graduate credits in an approved program, write a thesis, and take an examination on the thesis. For the Ph.D. degree, satisfactory performance in an approved course program is required. In addition, students must take a comprehensive examination, write a dissertation, and take the dissertation exam. Doctoral students must spend four semesters in residence at the University.

The department also offers M.S. and Ph.D. degrees in engineering physics in cooperation with the School of Engineering and Applied Science. A Ph.D. in biophysics is available through an interdisciplinary program associated with the physics department and other science departments of the University.

Research Facilities

The physics department has major facilities for atomic, molecular, and optical physics; biophysics; and condensed-matter physics research, including high magnetic fields; lasers; a helium liquefier; low-temperature cryostats, including dilution refrigerators; electron microscopes; photoelectron spectrometers; and electron-scattering devices. Major machine shop and electronics shop facilities are also available. The Institute for Nuclear and Particle Physics supports research programs as well as design work for CEBAF, a 4-GeV electron accelerator. Both the nuclear physics and condensed-matter physics programs have access to facilities such as the PSI Laboratory in Switzerland, Stanford Linear Accelerator Center (SLAC), the Oak Ridge National Laboratory, the Francis Bitter National Magnet Laboratory, and the National High Field Magnet Laboratory. The high-energy physics (HEP) group is currently involved with experiments at Fermi National Accelerator Laboratory and is initiating new experimental programs in Europe at the Frascati National Laboratory (near Rome, Italy) and the European Laboratory for Particle Physics (CERN) in Geneva, Switzerland. The HEP group also has facilities for dedicated computing of 1700 MIPS.

Financial Aid

A number of well-qualified entering students are awarded departmental or University fellowships. For 1999–2000, these fellowships carry stipends of $13,900 to $19,000 for nine months plus remission of tuition. Many other tuition-free assistantships are available and carry stipends of $13,900 for nine months. Students making satisfactory progress are normally supported until the Ph.D. degree program has been completed. Additional support for the summer is generally available through research groups.

Cost of Study

In 1999–2000, tuition and fees are $2460 per semester for Virginia residents and $8303.50 per semester for out-of-state residents. Most students receive fellowships that cover tuition and fees.

Living and Housing Costs

In 1999–2000, estimated expenses for single students are $2330–$2570 for a room in a residence hall, $1700 for personal expenses, and $900 for books and supplies. Housing for married students is available at rents ranging from $454 to $594 per month. For further information, students should write to the Director of Housing at Station 1, Page House. Off-campus housing is also available for married and single graduate students.

Student Group

Enrollment at the University is approximately 18,500, including 5,800 graduate students. The Department of Physics has 75 graduate students.

Location

The University's location in Charlottesville, which, together with Albemarle County, forms a community of about 120,000 people, provides numerous opportunities for a variety of recreational and cultural activities. The nearby Blue Ridge Mountains and the relatively mild but distinctly seasonal weather contribute to the area's reputation as an exceptionally pleasant place to live.

Charlottesville is 110 miles from Washington, D.C., and 70 miles from Richmond. Bus and railway service and direct airline service to Washington, Charlotte, Pittsburgh, Baltimore, Cincinnati, and New York are available.

The University

The University of Virginia, founded in 1819 by Thomas Jefferson, is a coeducational state institution that recognizes the importance of having a student body drawn from throughout the country.

Applying

Applications for admission and financial assistance may be obtained by writing to the Department of Physics. To be eligible for all forms of financial assistance, students should submit completed applications by April 1.

Correspondence and Information

Graduate Advisor
Department of Physics
University of Virginia
McCormick Road
Charlottesville, Virginia 22903

Telephone: 804-924-6317
Fax: 804-924-4576
E-mail: grad-info-request@physics.virginia.edu
World Wide Web: http://www.phys.virginia.edu

University of Virginia

THE FACULTY AND THEIR RESEARCH

Peter B. Arnold, Ph.D., Stanford, 1986: theoretical high-energy physics. Louis A. Bloomfield, Ph.D., Stanford, 1983: experimental atomic and solid-state physics. Arthur S. Brill, Ph.D., Pennsylvania, 1956: experimental biophysics, protons and transition-metal ions. David Brydges, Ph.D., Michigan, 1976: mathematical physics. Vittorio Celli, Dottore in Fisica, Pavia (Italy), 1958: theoretical solid-state physics, surface studies. Sergio Conetti, Dottore in Fisica, Trieste (Italy), 1967: experimental high-energy-particle physics. Bradley B. Cox, Ph.D., Duke, 1967: experimental high-energy-particle physics. Donald G. Crabb, Ph.D., Southampton, 1967; experimental nuclear and particle physics. Donal B. Day, Ph.D., Virginia, 1979: experimental nuclear and particle physics. Bascom S. Deaver Jr., Ph.D., Stanford, 1962: experimental solid-state physics, superconducting devices. Edmond C. Dukes, Ph.D., Michigan, 1984: experimental high-energy-particle physics. Paul Fendley, Ph.D., Harvard, 1990: theoretical condensed matter and high energy. Paul M. Fishbane, Ph.D., Princeton, 1967: theoretical physics, elementary particles. Michael Fowler, Ph.D., Cambridge, 1962: theoretical physics, field theory and solid-state theory. Thomas F. Gallagher, Ph.D., Harvard, 1971: collisions and spectroscopy of atoms and molecules. George B. Hess, Ph.D., Stanford, 1967: experimental solid-state physics, liquid helium, physisorption. Julia W. P. Hsu, Ph.D., Stanford, 1991: experimental solid-state physics, scanning probe microscopy. Pham Q. Hung, Ph.D., UCLA, 1978: theoretical particle physics, cosmology. Robert R. Jones Jr., Ph.D., Virginia, 1990: experimental atomic physics. Eugene B. Kolomeisky, Ph.D., USSR Academy of Sciences, 1988: theoretical condensed matter. Doris Kuhlmann-Wilsdorf, Ph.D., Göttingen, 1947; D.Sc., Witwatersrand (Johannesburg), 1954: theoretical materials science. Mark Lee, Ph.D., Stanford, 1991: experimental condensed-matter physics. Richard A. Lindgren, Ph.D., Yale, 1969: experimental nuclear and particle physics. Ralph C. Minehart, Ph.D., Harvard, 1962: experimental nuclear and particle physics. Kenneth Nelson, Ph.D., Wisconsin, 1986: experimental high-energy-particle physics. Julian V. Noble, Ph.D., Princeton, 1966: theoretical physics, nuclear physics, intermediate-energy physics. Blaine E. Norum, Ph.D., MIT, 1979: experimental nuclear and particle physics. Olivier Pfister, Ph.D., Paris XIII (North), 1993: experimental atomic, molecular, and optical physics. Dinko Počanić, Ph.D., Zagreb (Yugoslavia), 1981: experimental intermediate-energy nuclear and particle physics. S. Joseph Poon, Ph.D., Caltech, 1978: experimental solid-state physics, disordered systems, quasicrystals, superconducting materials. Rogers C. Ritter, Ph.D., Tennessee, 1961: gravitation, precision measurements, medical physics. John Ruvalds, Ph.D., Oregon, 1967: theoretical solid-state physics. Stephen Schnatterly, Ph.D., Illinois, 1965: experimental solid-state physics; soft X-ray and inelastic electron-scattering spectroscopy of solids, atoms, and molecules. Bellave S. Shivaram, Ph.D., Northwestern, 1984: experimental solid-state physics; novel superconductors, ultrasonic measurements. Harry B. Thacker Jr., Ph.D., UCLA, 1973: elementary particle physics and quantum field theory. Stephen T. Thornton, Ph.D., Tennessee, 1967: experimental nuclear physics. Hans J. Weber, Ph.D., Frankfurt, 1965: theoretical nuclear and particle physics.

RESEARCH ACTIVITIES

Theoretical

Condensed Matter. (Celli, Fendley, Fowler, Kolomeisky, Ruvalds). Novel mechanisms for high-temperature superconductivity and Fermi-surface-nesting theory for anomalous properties of high-T_c copper oxides; influence of disorder on superconductor dynamics; structure, dynamics, and optical properties of solid surfaces; gas surface interactions; wave propagation in random media; spin chains; Bethe Ansatz systems; field theoretic models for solid-state systems; theory of macroscopic quantum phenomena; pattern formation; transport in high-temperature superconductors; nonperturbative statistical mechanics; quantum Hall effect; phase transitions and renormalization group methods in statistical physics.

High-Energy Physics. (Arnold, Fendley, Fishbane, Hung, Thacker). Theoretical studies of high-energy physics, including properties of quantum chromodynamics, lattice gauge theory, solvable models and conformal field theory, electroweak interactions, grand unified theories, supersymmetry, high-temperature field theory, and the Very Early Universe.

Nuclear Physics. (Noble, Weber). Structure of light nuclei, electron scattering, and photonuclear reactions; interaction of pions with complex nuclei; quark models of hadrons.

Experimental

Atomic, Molecular, and Optical Physics. (Bloomfield, Gallagher, Jones, Pfister). Laser spectroscopy of atoms, ions, small molecules, and clusters, including photodetachment and photoionization; microwave-optical double resonance; studies of collisions, using spectroscopic techniques; measurement of the effects of strong optical and microwave fields; dynamic evolution of electronic wavepackets; studies of magnetic properties of clusters; development of new techniques in laser spectroscopy; research on optical control of chemical processes.

Biological Physics. (Brill, Ritter). Magnetic and optical properties of transition-metal ions in proteins; development of magnetically driven, MRI, and fluoroscopically guided neurosurgical therapies.

Condensed Matter Physics. (Deaver, Hess, Hsu, Lee, Poon, Schnatterly, Shivaram). Electronic properties of metals and alloys in magnetic fields up to 600 kG, studied via magnetoresistance, Hall effect, and transport in metals; molecular spectroscopy through inelastic tunneling techniques; surface studies by scanning tunneling microscopy; superconducting electronics and devices; inelastic electron-scattering spectroscopy as a probe of plasmons, excitons, interband transitions, and core excitations in solids; soft X-ray emission spectroscopy of solids and surfaces; superconducting and transport properties of disordered and quasi-periodic alloys; high-temperature superconducting materials; properties of physisorbed films; materials with novel symmetry properties; studies of unconventional metals and superconducting systems at very low temperatures using transport, ultrasonic, electromagnetic, and scanning probe measurements; acoustic damping in layered materials; submicron scale optical and structural properties of novel materials via near-field scanning optical microscopy and scanning force microscopy; low-temperature electronic properties and electrodynamic response of novel materials and devices, including superconductors, non-Fermi liquid conductors, and quantum coherent structures.

Gravitational Physics. (Ritter). Use of precision measurements in laboratory experiments testing gravitation.

Nuclear and Particle Physics. (Crabb, Day, Lindgren, Minehart, Norum, Počanić, Thornton, 6 research scientists, 1 principal scientist). Active research programs at various accelerator laboratories in the United States and abroad, with the largest effort in electronuclear physics at the TJNAF electron accelerator (Newport News), the Bates electron accelerator (MIT), LEGS facility at Brookhaven, Amsterdam, Saskatchewan, and SLAC; nuclear structure, nuclear momentum distributions, measurements of the nucleon quark spin distributions at CERN and SLAC, properties of excited nuclei; medium-energy physics, using the intense beams of mesons from the PSI ring accelerator in Switzerland; search for free quarks and various pion-decay modes.

High-Energy Physics. (Cox, Conetti, Dukes, Nelson, Norum, Počanić, 1 research scientist, 1 senior scientist). Currently involved in the analysis of a Fermilab experiment studying hidden Charm and Beauty meson production. Running a set of experiments studying matter-antimatter asymmetry (CP violation) in hyperon decays with HyperCP experiment at Fermilab, kaon decays with the KTeV experiment at Fermilab, and kaon decays at the Frascati National Laboratory in Italy. The group is also preparing an experiment to explore CP violation in Beauty meson decays at the Large Hadron Collider at CERN in Geneva, Switzerland.

Physics Education. (Lindgren, Thornton). An active program to teach physics and physical science to K–12 teachers, including summer workshops and courses throughout the state via satellite television. An outreach program includes a Physics Road Show. Active course developments are under way.

WASHINGTON UNIVERSITY IN ST. LOUIS

Department of Physics

Programs of Study
The Department of Physics offers programs leading to the Ph.D. and M.A. degrees. A minimum of 72 hours is required for the Ph.D., including 36 hours in classroom courses. Candidates must also pass a general qualifying examination and an oral defense of the dissertation research. For the M.A., requirements include 30 hours (at least 24 in classroom courses) and a thesis or final examination. Interdisciplinary studies are facilitated by the McDonnell Center for the Space Sciences, a University-wide center that involves the faculties of the Departments of Physics, Earth and Planetary Sciences, Chemistry, and Engineering.

Research Facilities
Primary experimental equipment includes a Cameca secondary ion mass spectrometer, a scanning electron microscope with an energy-dispersive X-ray detector, a Fourier-transform infrared spectrometer, a VG Isomass 54E mass spectrometer, four high-sensitivity noble gas mass spectrometers, a SQUID acoustomagnetic detection system, six research quality superconducting solenoids, seven Fourier-transform NMR spectrometers, a CTI 1410 closed-cycle helium liquefier, $^3He/^4He$ dilution refrigerators, an X-band–pulsed ESR spectrometer, a JEOL 2000 FX transmission electron microscope with a Gatan 607 energy-loss spectrometer, a Tracor-Northern energy-dispersive X-ray detector, a Perkin-Elmer differential scanning calorimeter, and a differential thermal analyzer. Computer equipment includes a network with a variety of UNIX, MS-DOS, and Macintosh computers. An AppleTalk network is also available. Research computers connected by Ethernet to the departmental system include DEC, Sun, SGI, and IBM workstations as well as other computers. The physics department network is connected to the campuswide network and linked to the Internet and other major networks.

Financial Aid
The department awards a number of teaching and research assistantships. For the 1999–2000 academic year, stipends are $13,680 plus tuition remission. Full or partial fellowship and scholarship stipends range from tuition remission to $19,220 plus tuition remission. Stipends are available for summer support.

Cost of Study
The cost of graduate study at Washington University is comparable to that at other institutions of its type and caliber. For the 1999–2000 academic year, tuition for full-time students is $11,700 per semester. Graduate students enrolled for fewer than 12 units pay $975 per unit.

Living and Housing Costs
Moderately priced rental units may be obtained near the University at average monthly rates of $400 to $800 for one to three bedrooms.

Student Group
Almost half of the 12,035 students at the University are graduate and professional school students. The faculty has 1,991 full-time members. The department has 57 graduate students, 12 of whom are women.

Student Outcomes
Most recent graduates have gone on to postdoctoral research positions at distinguished institutions and laboratories such as Brookhaven National Laboratory, the University of Chicago, the California Institute of Technology, and the Naval Research Laboratory. Former students who completed their postdoctoral research include an assistant professor at Brown University, a research scientist at Dornier Gmbh in Germany, and a staff scientist at MEMC Corporation in St. Peters, Missouri.

Location
The community surrounding the University is both residential and commercial. Entertainment is varied: music lovers can enjoy the St. Louis Symphony, the St. Louis Philharmonic, and many jazz, blues, rock, and dance clubs; theatergoers can attend performances of several repertory groups and musicals at the summer Municipal Opera. Forest Park, which is within walking distance of the campus, contains a golf course, bicycle and running paths, horseback-riding facilities, a fine zoo, the St. Louis Science Center, and the St. Louis Art Museum.

The University
Washington University in St. Louis was founded in 1853 as a private, coeducational institution. In 1904, the University moved to its present 168-acre hilltop campus bordering on the 1,430 acres of Forest Park. Undergraduate programs are offered in arts and science, engineering, business, and fine arts, and graduate programs are offered in all major fields of human inquiry. Twenty Nobel Prize recipients have done all or part of their distinguished work at Washington University. Since 1976, Washington University has placed first in the William Lowell Putnam Mathematical Competition four times and among the top ten all but two times. Graduates often receive such prestigious graduate study awards as Fulbright, Marshall, Beinecke, and Truman scholarships and Mellon, Putnam, National Science Foundation, and NASA graduate fellowships.

Applying
To ensure consideration of a student for admission in September, a completed application, transcript, financial statement, Graduate Record Examinations scores, and three letters of recommendation must be received by January 15. Applications are considered at other times as well. Applicants should have had courses in calculus and physics and should have specialized in physics or a related subject in physical science, engineering, or mathematics.

Correspondence and Information
Graduate Admissions
Department of Physics
Washington University in St. Louis
One Brookings Drive
St. Louis, Missouri 63130-4899

Telephone: 314-935-6250
E-mail: gradinfo@wuphys.wustl.edu
World Wide Web: http://www.physics.wustl.edu/

Washington University in St. Louis

THE FACULTY AND THEIR RESEARCH

Professors
Carl M. Bender, Ph.D., Harvard, 1969. Theoretical physics, mathematical physics, particle physics.
Claude W. Bernard, Ph.D., Harvard, 1976. Theoretical physics, mathematical physics, particle physics.
Thomas Bernatowicz, Ph.D., Washington (St. Louis), 1980. Mass spectrometry, transmission electron microscopy.
Anders E. Carlsson, Ph.D., Harvard, 1981. Condensed-matter theory, biophysics.
John W. Clark, Ph.D., Washington (St. Louis), 1959. Theoretical physics and astrophysics, many-body theory, biophysics.
Mark S. Conradi, Ph.D., Washington (St. Louis), 1977. Experimental magnetic resonance: lung imaging and solid-state systems.
Willem H. Dickhoff, Ph.D., Free University (Amsterdam), 1981. Theoretical physics, many-body theory.
Peter A. Fedders, Ph.D., Harvard, 1965. Solid-state theory.
Michael W. Friedlander, Ph.D., Bristol, 1955. Cosmic rays, astrophysics.
Patrick C. Gibbons, Ph.D., Harvard, 1971. Experimental solid-state physics, electron microscopy, materials science.
Charles M. Hohenberg, Ph.D., Berkeley, 1968. Experimental space science, rare-gas mass spectroscopy.
Martin H. Israel, Ph.D., Caltech, 1968. Cosmic ray astrophysics.
Jonathan I. Katz, Ph.D., Cornell, 1973. Theoretical astrophysics.
Kenneth F. Kelton, Ph.D., Harvard, 1983. Experimental solid-state physics and materials science.
Joseph Klarmann, Emeritus; Ph.D., Rochester, 1958. Cosmic ray astrophysics.
Kazimierz Luszczynski, Ph.D., London, 1959. Solid-state and low-temperature physics, magnetic resonance.
James G. Miller, Ph.D., Washington (St. Louis), 1969. Ultrasonics, biomedical physics, elastic properties of inhomogeneous media.
Richard E. Norberg, Ph.D., Illinois, 1951. Solid-state and low-temperature physics, magnetic resonance.
Michael C. Ogilvie, Emeritus; Ph.D., Brown, 1980. Theoretical physics, mathematical physics, particle physics.
Peter R. Phillips, Emeritus; Ph.D., Stanford, 1961. General relativity and cosmology.
John H. Scandrett, Emeritus; Ph.D., Wisconsin, 1963. Biomedical physics and computer applications.
James S. Schilling, Ph.D., Wisconsin, 1969. Solid-state and high-pressure physics.
J. Ely Shrauner, Ph.D., Chicago, 1963. Theoretical physics, elementary particle theory, high-energy physics, applied physics.
Wai-Mo Suen, Ph.D., Caltech, 1985. Theoretical astrophysics, general relativity, cosmology.
Ronald K. Sundfors, Emeritus; Ph.D., Cornell, 1963. Nuclear acoustic resonance, ultrasonics.
Robert M. Walker, McDonnell Professor; Ph.D., Yale, 1954. Experimental space science, astrophysics, extraterrestrial materials.
Clifford M. Will, Chairman of the Department; Ph.D., Caltech, 1971. Theoretical astrophysics, general relativity.

Visiting Professor
Ramanath Cowsik, Ph.D., Bombay, 1968. Theoretical astrophysics.

Associate Professors
Maarten Golterman, Ph.D., Utrecht (Netherlands), 1986. Nonperturbative quantum field theory, lattice quantum-chromodynamics simulations.
Rodney S. Ruoff, Ph.D., Illinois, 1988. Experimental materials science, nanotechnology, biophysics.

Joint Professor
Shankar Sastry, Ph.D., Toronto, 1974. Materials science and metallurgy, alloys and intermetallic compounds. (Department of Mechanical Engineering)

Joint Associate Professor
Lee G. Sobotka, Ph.D., Berkeley, 1982. Nuclear physics, heavy ion reactions. (Department of Chemistry)

Assistant Professor
James H. Buckley, Ph.D., Chicago, 1994. High-energy astrophysics.

Professors (Courtesy)
Donald P. Ames, Ph.D., Wisconsin–Madison, 1949. Materials research, magnetic resonance.
Charles H. Anderson, Ph.D., Harvard, 1962. Biophysics.
Vijai V. Dixit, Ph.D., Purdue, 1972. Theoretical physics.
Robert Falster, Ph.D., Stanford, 1983. Experimental materials science, semiconductors.
Solomon L. Linder, Ph.D., Washington (St. Louis), 1955. Electrooptics.
Jeffrey E. Mandula, Ph.D., Harvard, 1966. Theoretical physics, particle physics, mathematical physics.
Manfred L. Ristig, Ph.D., Köln (Germany), 1966. Nuclear theory.
Dmitriy Yablonsky, Ph.D., Ukraine, 1973. Radiation physics.

Associate Professors (Courtesy)
Philip B. Fraundorf, Ph.D., Washington (St. Louis), 1980. Space physics, solid-state physics.
Sandor J. Kovacs, M.D., Miami (Florida), 1979; Ph.D., Caltech, 1977. Cardiology, astrophysics.
Samuel A. Wickline, M.D., Hawaii, 1980. Cardiology.

Assistant Professors (Courtesy)
Gregory L. Comer, Ph.D., North Carolina, 1990. General relativity.
Thomas E. Conturo, M.D./Ph.D., Vanderbilt, 1989. Biophysics, magnetic resonance imaging.
Mary M. Leopold, Ph.D., Washington (St. Louis), 1985. Semiconductor physics.
Craig W. Lincoln, Ph.D., Washington (St. Louis). Astrophysics, general relativity.
Ian Redmount, Ph.D., Caltech, 1984. General relativity.

Instructor (Courtesy)
Assen S. Kirov, Ph.D., Ohridsky (Bulgaria), 1993. Radiation physics.

Research Professors
Robert W. Binns, Ph.D., Colorado State, 1969. Astrophysics, medical and health physics.
Ernst Zinner, Ph.D., Washington (St. Louis), 1972. Experimental space science, extraterrestrial materials.

Research Associate Professors
Daniel J. Leopold, Ph.D., Washington (St. Louis), 1983. Chemical physics.
Matt Visser, Ph.D., Berkeley, 1984. Cosmology and field theory.

Research Assistant Professors
Paul L. Hink, Ph.D., Washington (St. Louis). Astrophysics, cosmic rays.
Brian T. Saam, Ph.D., Princeton, 1995. Experimental magnetic resonance, lung imaging.

YALE UNIVERSITY

Graduate School of Arts and Sciences
Department of Physics

Program of Study

The Department of Physics offers a program of study leading to the Ph.D. degree. Students normally take four courses during each of their first three semesters and are required to take a graduate seminar in the first semester. Those who pass their courses with satisfactory grades and who pass the preliminary and qualifying exams are admitted to candidacy for the Ph.D. Dissertation research then becomes the primary activity.

Two 6-hour written exams are given at the beginning of the spring semester. The preliminary exam emphasizes fundamental physics that is normally part of the undergraduate curriculum and is taken after one semester in residence. The qualifying exam, which most students take after three semesters (although it can be taken earlier), is devoted to more advanced physics, with special attention to material at the level of the basic Yale graduate course program. Both exams must be taken by the beginning of the fourth semester.

Formal association with a dissertation adviser normally begins in the fourth semester after the two aforementioned exams have been taken. The adviser can be from a department other than physics, provided that the dissertation topic is deemed suitable for a physics Ph.D.

Approximately two years after passing the qualifying exam, but no later than the end of the fourth year, students take an oral exam centering on a recently published research paper in the field (but not on the topic) of their dissertation research. The final examination is an oral defense of the dissertation. The average time needed to complete all of the Ph.D. requirements has been six years.

Research Facilities

The physics department occupies the Sloane Physics Laboratory, part of the J. W. Gibbs Laboratories, and the Wright Nuclear Structure Laboratory. Research on condensed-matter physics is also done in the Becton Laboratory. Sloane has newly constructed laboratories for research in atomic, molecular, optical, and condensed-matter physics. The theoretical physicists are located in Sloane. The Wright Laboratory contains an Extended Stretch Transuranium (ESTU) 20-megavolt tandem electrostatic accelerator, the most powerful of its kind in the world. Gibbs houses the computers of the high-energy group, which analyze data gathered from experiments at Argonne and Brookhaven National Laboratories, Fermilab, and the Stanford Linear Accelerator Center. Experiments are also done at European accelerators and observations taken at South American astronomical observatories. In addition to the centralized University computer system, each research group has its own appropriate computing facilities. There are four libraries of major pertinence to physics—Kline Science, Astronomy, Mathematics, and Engineering and Applied Science. Research in the Department of Physics focuses most intensely on experimental and theoretical particle physics, experimental and theoretical nuclear physics, experimental and theoretical condensed-matter physics, experimental atomic physics, and astrophysics. There are also interdisciplinary efforts in geophysics, medical physics, chemical physics, and engineering.

Financial Aid

Virtually all entering graduate students in the Department of Physics are offered financial aid for the first three terms in the form of a Yale University Fellowship. This is a combination of stipend, teaching fellowship, tuition, and payment for an Assistantship in Research for the summer following the first year. After the third or fourth semester, when a student has begun dissertation research, full financial support is provided by the student's thesis adviser in the form of an Assistantship in Research. The total support for 1999–2000 is $17,600 for twelve months plus full tuition and health and hospitalization coverage. There are also teaching fellowships available to advanced students.

Cost of Study

After four years, tuition (currently $22,330 per annum) is replaced by an annual continuing registration fee of $460. Purchase of course texts is an additional expense.

Living and Housing Costs

The rents of dormitory rooms for the 1999–2000 academic year range from $2870 for a single room to $4530 for a deluxe single room. Three-bedroom suites, which include a study, are also available. Board plans are offered. The cost for an apartment ranges from $510 to $800 per month. The lease period for graduate housing apartments is usually July 1 through June 30. Off-campus housing in the vicinity of the physics department is plentiful.

Student Group

The total number of students for 1999–2000 is 96, all of whom attend full-time. Of these, about 66 percent are international students, and about 12 percent are women. Students with a strong basic undergraduate physics education, together with some research experience, are prime candidates for admission. Advanced commitment to a particular field is not required.

Location

Yale is located in the center of the city of New Haven (population about 125,000; metropolitan area about 400,000). The city offers an unusually wide variety of activities—especially in theater, music, film, fine arts, sports, and international dining. Frequent rail service to New York City and Boston takes less than 2 hours and about 3 hours, respectively.

The University

Chartered in 1701 as the Collegiate School, Yale was named for Elihu Yale, a London merchant who made a modest donation to help the fledgling school. A medical school was added in 1810. The Department of Philosophy and the Arts was organized in 1847, awarding the first three Ph.D. degrees in the United States in 1861 and becoming the Graduate School in 1892. Women were admitted early in the century to the graduate and professional schools and to Yale College as undergraduates in 1969.

Applying

Application forms are available from the Admissions Office, Yale Graduate School, P.O. Box 208323, New Haven, Connecticut 06520-8323 (telephone: 203-432-2770; e-mail: graduate.admissions@yale.edu). Candidates submitting completed applications and supporting materials before January 2, 2000 will be considered for admission in fall 2000. Applications must be accompanied by an application fee of $65 ($45 for applications received by December 1). Students are required to take the GRE General Test as well as the GRE Subject Test in Physics. Those whose native language is not English must also take the TOEFL; the TSE is recommended. Admission consideration is open to all qualified candidates without regard to race, color, national origin, religion, sex, sexual preference, or handicap.

Correspondence and Information

Director of Graduate Studies
Department of Physics
Yale University
P.O. Box 208120
New Haven, Connecticut 06520-8120
Telephone: 203-432-3607
Fax: 203-432-6175
E-mail: jo-ann.bonnett@yale.edu
World Wide Web: http://www.yale.edu/physics

Yale University

THE FACULTY AND THEIR RESEARCH

Robert K. Adair, Professor Emeritus and Senior Research Scientist; Ph.D., Wisconsin, 1951. Elementary particle physics.
Yoram Alhassid, Professor; Ph.D., Hebrew (Israel), 1979. Nuclear theory.
Thomas Appelquist, Professor; Ph.D., Cornell, 1968. Particle theory.
Charles Baltay, Professor; Ph.D., Yale, 1963. Elementary particle physics.
Sean E. Barrett, Assistant Professor; Ph.D., Illinois, 1992. Condensed-matter physics.
Cornelius Beausang, Assistant Professor; Ph.D., SUNY at Stony Brook, 1987. Nuclear physics.
William R. Bennett Jr., Professor Emeritus; Ph.D., Columbia, 1959. Quantum electronics and laser physics.
Ira B. Bernstein, Professor (joint with Mechanical Engineering); Ph.D., NYU, 1950. Theoretical plasma physics.
Charles K. Bockelman, Professor Emeritus; Ph.D., Wisconsin, 1951. Nuclear physics.
D. Allan Bromley, Professor; Ph.D., Rochester, 1952. Nuclear physics.
Richard Casten, Professor; Ph.D., Yale, 1967. Nuclear physics.
Richard K. Chang, Professor (joint with Applied Physics); Ph.D., Harvard, 1965. Condensed-matter and laser physics.
Alan Chodos, Senior Research Scientist; Ph.D., Cornell, 1970. Particle theory.
Paolo Coppi, Assistant Professor (joint with Astronomy); Ph.D., Caltech, 1990. High-energy astrophysics.
David P. DeMille, Assistant Professor; Ph.D., Berkeley, 1994. Atomic physics.
Satish Dhawan, Senior Research Scientist; Ph.D., Tsukuba (Japan), 1984. Elementary particle physics.
Moshe Gai, Adjunct Professor; Ph.D., SUNY at Stony Brook, 1980. Nuclear physics.
Colin Gay, Assistant Professor; Ph.D., Toronto, 1991. Elementary particle physics.
Kurt E. Gibble, Associate Professor; Ph.D., Colorado, 1990. Atomic physics.
Robert D. Grober, Associate Professor (joint with Applied Physics); Ph.D., Maryland, 1991. Condensed-matter physics.
Martin Gutzwiller, Adjunct Professor; Ph.D., Kansas, 1953. Condensed-matter theory.
John Harris, Professor; Ph.D., SUNY at Stony Brook, 1978. Relativistic heavy-ion physics.
Victor E. Henrich, Professor (joint with Applied Physics); Ph.D., Michigan, 1967. Condensed-matter physics.
Jay L. Hirshfield, Adjunct Professor; Ph.D., MIT, 1960. Beam physics.
Pierre Hohenberg, Adjunct Professor; Ph.D., Harvard, 1962. Condensed-matter theory.
Vernon W. Hughes, Professor Emeritus and Senior Research Scientist; Ph.D., Columbia, 1950. Atomic and particle physics.
H. Richard Hyder, Senior Research Scientist; M.A., Cambridge, 1956. Nuclear physics.
Francesco Iachello, Professor; Ph.D., MIT, 1969. Nuclear theory.
Mark Kasevich, Associate Professor; Ph.D., Stanford, 1992. Atomic physics.
Henry Kasha, Senior Research Scientist; D.Sc., Technion (Israel), 1960. Elementary particle physics.
Martin J. Klein, Professor; Ph.D., MIT, 1948. History of nineteenth- and twentieth-century physics.
Reiner Kruecken, Assistant Professor; Ph.D., Köln (Germany), 1995. Nuclear physics.
Gerd Kunde, Assistant Professor; Ph.D., Frankfurt, 1994. Relativistic heavy-ion physics.
Dimitri Kusnezov, Associate Professor; Ph.D., Princeton, 1988. Nuclear theory.
Samuel W. MacDowell, Professor; Ph.D., Birmingham (England), 1958. Particle theory.
Richard D. Majka, Senior Research Scientist; Ph.D., Yale, 1974. Elementary particle physics.
William J. Marciano, Adjunct Professor; Ph.D., NYU, 1957. Particle theory.
Vincent E. Moncrief, Professor (joint with Mathematics); Ph.D., Maryland, 1972. Gravitation and cosmology.
Gregory Moore, Professor; Ph.D., Harvard, 1985. Particle theory and mathematical physics.
Homer A. Neal Jr., Assistant Professor; Ph.D., Stanford, 1995. Experimental elementary particle physics.
Peter D. M. Parker, Professor; Ph.D., Caltech, 1963. Experimental nuclear physics and nuclear astrophysics.
Erich R. Poppitz, Assistant Professor; Ph.D., Johns Hopkins, 1994. Theoretical elementary particle physics.
Daniel E. Prober, Professor (joint with Applied Physics); Ph.D., Harvard, 1975. Condensed-matter physics.
Karin M. Rabe, Associate Professor (joint with Applied Physics); Ph.D., MIT, 1987. Condensed-matter theory.
Nicholas Read, Professor (joint with Applied Physics); Ph.D., London, 1986. Condensed-matter theory.
Subir Sachdev, Professor; Ph.D., Harvard, 1985. Condensed-matter theory.
Jack Sandweiss, Professor; Ph.D., Berkeley, 1957. Elementary particle physics.
Michael P. Schmidt, Professor; Ph.D., Yale, 1979. Elementary particle physics.
Robert J. Schoelkopf, Assistant Professor; Ph.D., Caltech, 1995. Experimental condensed matter physics.
Ramamurti Shankar, Professor; Ph.D., Berkeley, 1974. Condensed-matter theory and statistical physics.
Samson Shatashvili, Associate Professor; Ph.D., Leningrad, 1985. Particle theory and mathematical physics.
Donald Shirer, Lecturer; Ph.D., Ohio State, 1957. Computational physics.
A. Jean Slaughter, Senior Research Scientist; Ph.D., Yale, 1973. Elementary particle physics.
Jeffrey A. Snyder, Assistant Professor; Ph.D., Yale, 1994. Astrophysics.
Charles M. Sommerfield, Professor; Ph.D., Harvard, 1957. Particle theory.
Katepalli Sreenivasan, Professor (joint with Mechanical Engineering); Ph.D., Indian Institute of Science, 1975. Physics of turbulence.
A. Douglas Stone, Professor (joint with Applied Physics); Ph.D., MIT, 1983. Condensed-matter theory.
John C. Tully, Professor (joint with Chemistry); Ph.D., Chicago, 1968. Theoretical chemical physics.
Robert G. Wheeler, Professor Emeritus (joint with Applied Physics); Ph.D., Yale, 1955. Condensed-matter physics.
Werner P. Wolf, Professor (joint with Applied Physics); D.Phil., Oxford, 1954. Condensed-matter physics.
N. Victor Zamfir, Senior Research Scientist; Ph.D., Institute of Physics, Bucharest, 1984. Nuclear physics.
Michael E. Zeller, Professor; Ph.D., UCLA, 1968. Elementary particle physics.

Academic and Professional Programs in Mathematics

This part of Book 4 consists of one section covering mathematics. The section has a table of contents (listing the program directories, announcements, and in-depth descriptions); program directories, which consist of brief profiles of programs in the relevant fields (and 50-word or 100-word announcements following the profiles, if programs have chosen to include them); Cross-Discipline Announcements, if any programs have chosen to submit such entries; and in-depth descriptions, which are more individualized statements, if programs have chosen to submit them.

Section 7
Mathematical Sciences

This section contains a directory of institutions offering graduate work in mathematical sciences, followed by in-depth entries submitted by institutions that chose to prepare detailed program descriptions. Additional information about programs listed in the directory but not augmented by an in-depth entry may be obtained by writing directly to the dean of a graduate school or chair of a department at the address given in the directory.

For programs offering work in related fields, see all other areas in this book. In Book 2, see Economics and Psychology; in Book 3, see Biological and Biomedical Sciences, Biophysics, Genetics and Developmental Biology, and Pharmacology and Toxicology; in Book 5, see Biochemical Engineering, Bioengineering, and Biotechnology; Computer Science and Information Technology; Electrical and Computer Engineering; Engineering and Applied Sciences; and Industrial Engineering; and in Book 6, see Business Administration and Management, Library and Information Studies, and Public Health.

CONTENTS

CONTENTS

Applied Mathematics

Air Force Institute of Technology, School of Engineering, Department of Mathematics and Statistics, Wright-Patterson AFB, OH 45433-7765. Offers applied mathematics (MS, PhD). Part-time programs available. *Faculty:* 11 full-time (1 woman). Average age 30. In 1998, 2 master's awarded (100% found work related to degree); 1 doctorate awarded (100% found work related to degree). *Degree requirements:* For master's and doctorate, computer language, thesis/dissertation required, foreign language not required. *Entrance requirements:* For master's, GRE General Test (minimum score of 500 on verbal section, 600 on quantitative required), minimum GPA of 3.0, must be military officer or U.S. citizen; for doctorate, GRE General Test (minimum score of 550 on verbal section, 650 on quantitative required), minimum GPA of 3.0, must be military officer or U.S. citizen. *Average time to degree:* Doctorate–3.25 years full-time. Application fee: $0. *Financial aid:* Fellowships, research assistantships available. Aid available to part-time students. Financial aid application deadline: 3/15. *Faculty research:* Semilinear elliptic equations, groundwater modeling, finite extinction time, goodness of fit, finite element analysis. *Unit head:* Alan V. Lair, Head, 937-255-3098, Fax: 937-656-4413, E-mail: alair@afit.af.mil.

American University, College of Arts and Sciences, Department of Mathematics and Statistics, Program in Applied Mathematics, Washington, DC 20016-8001. Offers MA. Part-time and evening/weekend programs available. *Faculty:* 19 full-time (6 women), 5 part-time (3 women). 1 applicants, 100% accepted. *Degree requirements:* For master's, one foreign language required, (computer language can substitute), thesis optional. *Entrance requirements:* For master's, bachelor's degree in mathematics. *Application deadline:* For fall admission, 2/1; for spring admission, 1/1. Application fee: $50. *Financial aid:* Fellowships, teaching assistantships, career-related internships or fieldwork, Federal Work-Study, and institutionally-sponsored loans available. Aid available to part-time students. Financial aid application deadline: 2/1. *Unit head:* Dr. Virginia Stallings, Chair, Department of Mathematics and Statistics, 202-885-3166, Fax: 202-885-3155.

Arizona State University, Graduate College, College of Liberal Arts and Sciences, Department of Mathematics, Tempe, AZ 85287. Offers applied mathematics (MA, PhD); mathematics (MA, MNS, PhD); statistics (MA, PhD). *Faculty:* 95 full-time (22 women), 2 part-time (0 women). *Students:* 67 full-time (20 women), 15 part-time (5 women); includes 6 minority (2 African Americans, 3 Asian Americans or Pacific Islanders, 1 Hispanic American), 37 international. *Degree requirements:* For master's, thesis or alternative required; for doctorate, one foreign language, dissertation required. *Entrance requirements:* For master's and doctorate, GRE General Test. *Application deadline:* For fall admission, 3/1. Application fee: $45. *Unit head:* Dr. Rosemary Renaut, Chair, 480-965-3951.

See in-depth description on page 641.

Auburn University, Graduate School, College of Sciences and Mathematics, Department of Discrete and Statistical Sciences, Auburn, Auburn University, AL 36849-0002. Offers M Prob S, MAM, MS, PhD. *Faculty:* 17 full-time (0 women). *Students:* 12 full-time (6 women), 11 part-time (4 women); includes 4 minority (3 African Americans, 1 Asian American or Pacific Islander), 5 international. 15 applicants, 73% accepted. In 1998, 1 master's, 7 doctorates awarded. *Degree requirements:* For doctorate, dissertation required. *Entrance requirements:* For master's and doctorate, GRE General Test. *Application deadline:* For fall admission, 9/1; for spring admission, 3/1. Applications are processed on a rolling basis. Application fee: $25 ($50 for international students). Tuition, state resident: full-time $2,760; part-time $76 per credit hour. Tuition, nonresident: full-time $8,280; part-time $228 per credit hour. *Financial aid:* Fellowships, teaching assistantships available. Financial aid application deadline: 3/15. *Faculty research:* Discrete mathematics, applied probability, differential equations, cryptography. *Unit head:* Dr. Kevin T. Phelps, Head, 334-844-5111, Fax: 334-844-3611, E-mail: phelpkt@mail.auburn.edu.

Brown University, Graduate School, Division of Applied Mathematics, Providence, RI 02912. Offers Sc M, PhD. *Degree requirements:* For master's, thesis or alternative required, foreign language not required; for doctorate, dissertation, oral exam required. *Entrance requirements:* For master's and doctorate, GRE General Test.

See in-depth description on page 649.

California Institute of Technology, Division of Engineering and Applied Science, Option in Applied Mathematics, Pasadena, CA 91125-0001. Offers PhD. *Faculty:* 8 full-time (0 women). *Students:* 21 full-time (3 women), 11 international. 51 applicants, 8% accepted. In 1998, 5 degrees awarded. *Degree requirements:* For doctorate, dissertation required, foreign language not required. *Entrance requirements:* For doctorate, GRE Subject Test. *Application deadline:* For fall admission, 1/15. Application fee: $0. *Faculty research:* Theoretical and computational fluid mechanics, numerical analysis, ordinary and partial differential equations, linear and nonlinear wave propagation, perturbation and asymptotic methods. *Unit head:* Dr. Oscar Bruno, Executive Officer, 626-395-4548.

See in-depth description on page 651.

California State Polytechnic University, Pomona, Graduate Studies, College of Science, Program in Mathematics, Pomona, CA 91768-2557. Offers applied mathematics (MS); pure mathematics (MS). Part-time programs available. *Students:* 7 full-time (2 women), 26 part-time (11 women); includes 14 minority (9 Asian Americans or Pacific Islanders, 5 Hispanic Americans), 2 international. *Degree requirements:* For master's, thesis or alternative required. *Entrance requirements:* For master's, GRE General Test. *Application deadline:* Applications are processed on a rolling basis. Application fee: $55. Tuition, nonresident: part-time $164 per unit. *Unit head:* Dr. Alan Krinik, Coordinator, 909-869-3479, E-mail: ackrinik@csupomona.edu.

California State University, Fullerton, Graduate Studies, School of Natural Science and Mathematics, Department of Mathematics, Fullerton, CA 92834-9480. Offers applied mathematics (MA); mathematics (MA); mathematics for secondary school teachers (MA). Part-time programs available. *Faculty:* 23 full-time (3 women), 61 part-time. *Students:* 1 full-time (0 women), 56 part-time (26 women); includes 16 minority (7 Asian Americans or Pacific Islanders, 9 Hispanic Americans) *Degree requirements:* For master's, comprehensive exam or project required. *Entrance requirements:* For master's, minimum GPA of 2.5 in last 60 units, major in mathematics or related field. Application fee: $55. Tuition, nonresident: part-time $264 per unit. Required fees: $1,947; $1,281 per year. *Unit head:* Dr. James Friel, Chair, 714-278-3631.

California State University, Long Beach, Graduate Studies, College of Natural Sciences, Department of Mathematics, Long Beach, CA 90840. Offers applied mathematics (MA); mathematics (MA). Part-time programs available. *Faculty:* 20 full-time (1 woman). *Students:* 11 full-time (2 women), 29 part-time (8 women); includes 16 minority (3 African Americans, 10 Asian Americans or Pacific Islanders, 3 Hispanic Americans), 2 international. *Degree requirements:* For master's, comprehensive exam or thesis required. *Application deadline:* For fall admission, 8/1; for spring admission, 12/1. Applications are processed on a rolling basis. Application fee: $55. Electronic applications accepted. Tuition, nonresident: part-time $246 per unit. Required fees: $569 per semester. Tuition and fees vary according to course load. *Unit head:* Dr. Arthur Wayman, Chair, 562-985-4721, Fax: 562-985-8227, E-mail: away@csulb.edu. *Application contact:* Dr. James Stein, Graduate Coordinator, 562-985-5397, Fax: 562-985-8227, E-mail: jimstein@csulb.edu.

California State University, Los Angeles, Graduate Studies, School of Natural and Social Sciences, Department of Mathematics and Computer Science, Los Angeles, CA 90032-8530. Offers mathematics (MS), including applied mathematics, mathematics. Part-time and evening/weekend programs available. *Faculty:* 26 full-time, 59 part-time. *Students:* 15 full-time (8 women), 33 part-time (6 women); includes 32 minority (2 African Americans, 15 Asian Americans

or Pacific Islanders, 15 Hispanic Americans), 4 international. *Degree requirements:* For master's, comprehensive exam or thesis required. *Entrance requirements:* For master's, TOEFL (minimum score of 550 required), previous course work in mathematics. *Application deadline:* For fall admission, 6/30; for spring admission, 2/1. Applications are processed on a rolling basis. Application fee: $55. *Unit head:* Dr. Michael Hoffman, Chair, 323-343-2150.

Case Western Reserve University, School of Graduate Studies, Department of Mathematics, Cleveland, OH 44106. Offers applied mathematics (MS, PhD); mathematics (MS, PhD). Part-time programs available. Terminal master's awarded for partial completion of doctoral program. *Degree requirements:* For master's, thesis (applied mathematics) required; for doctorate, dissertation required. *Entrance requirements:* For master's and doctorate, GRE General Test, TOEFL (minimum score of 550 required). *Faculty research:* Probability theory, differential equations and control theory, differential geometry and topology, Lie groups, functional and harmonic analysis.

Claremont Graduate University, Graduate Programs, Department of Mathematics, Claremont, CA 91711-6163. Offers engineering mathematics (PhD); financial engineering (MS); operations research and statistics (MA, MS); physical applied mathematics (MA, MS); pure mathematics (MA, MS, PhD); scientific computing (MA, MS); systems and control theory (MA, MS). Part-time programs available. *Faculty:* 3 full-time (0 women), 3 part-time (1 woman). *Students:* 12 full-time (8 women), 41 part-time (7 women); includes 17 minority (2 African Americans, 10 Asian Americans or Pacific Islanders, 5 Hispanic Americans), 16 international. Terminal master's awarded for partial completion of doctoral program. *Degree requirements:* For master's, foreign language and thesis not required; for doctorate, 2 foreign languages (computer language can substitute for one), dissertation required. *Entrance requirements:* For master's and doctorate, GRE General Test. *Application deadline:* For fall admission, 2/15 (priority date). Applications are processed on a rolling basis. Application fee: $40. Electronic applications accepted. Tuition: Full-time $20,950; part-time $913 per unit. Required fees: $65 per semester. Tuition and fees vary according to program. *Unit head:* Robert Williamson, Chair, 909-621-8080, Fax: 909-621-8390, E-mail: robert.williamson@cgu.edu. *Application contact:* Mary Solberg, Program Secretary, 909-621-8080, Fax: 909-621-8390, E-mail: math@cgu.edu.

Clark Atlanta University, School of Arts and Sciences, Department of Mathematical Sciences, Atlanta, GA 30314. Offers applied mathematics (MS); computer science (MS). Part-time programs available. *Students:* 11 full-time (2 women), 4 part-time (1 woman); all minorities (all African Americans) *Degree requirements:* For master's, one foreign language (computer language can substitute), thesis required. *Entrance requirements:* For master's, GRE General Test, minimum GPA of 2.5. *Application deadline:* For fall admission, 4/1; for spring admission, 11/1. Applications are processed on a rolling basis. Application fee: $40. *Unit head:* Dr. Michael Bleicher, Chairperson, 404-880-8272. *Application contact:* Michelle Clark-Davis, Graduate Program Assistant, 404-880-8709.

Clemson University, Graduate School, College of Engineering and Science, Department of Mathematical Sciences, Clemson, SC 29634. Offers applied and pure mathematics (MS, PhD); computational mathematics (MS, PhD); management science (PhD); operations research (MS, PhD); statistics (MS, PhD). Part-time programs available. *Students:* 60 full-time (24 women), 1 part-time; includes 3 minority (2 African Americans, 1 Hispanic American), 11 international. *Degree requirements:* For master's, computer language, final project required, thesis optional, foreign language not required; for doctorate, computer language, dissertation, qualifying exams required, foreign language not required. *Entrance requirements:* For master's and doctorate, GRE General Test, TOEFL. *Application deadline:* For fall admission, 6/1. Application fee: $35. *Unit head:* Dr. Robert Fennell, Chair, 864-656-3436, Fax: 864-656-5230, E-mail: mathsci@clemson.edu. *Application contact:* Dr. Douglas Shier, Graduate Coordinator, 864-656-1100, Fax: 864-656-5230, E-mail: shierd@clemson.edu.

Cleveland State University, College of Graduate Studies, College of Arts and Sciences, Department of Mathematics, Program in Applied Mathematics, Cleveland, OH 44115-2440. Offers MS. Part-time programs available. *Degree requirements:* For master's, foreign language and thesis not required. *Application deadline:* For fall admission, 7/15 (priority date). Applications are processed on a rolling basis. Application fee: $25. *Financial aid:* Teaching assistantships, Federal Work-Study, institutionally-sponsored loans, and tuition waivers (full) available. *Application contact:* Dr. S. Allen Broughton, Director, 216-687-4680.

Columbia University, Fu Foundation School of Engineering and Applied Science, Department of Applied Physics and Applied Mathematics, New York, NY 10027. Offers applied physics (MS, PhD), including applied mathematics (PhD), plasma physics (PhD), quantum electronics (PhD), solid state physics (PhD); applied physics and applied mathematics (Eng Sc D); medical physics (MS). Part-time programs available. *Faculty:* 11 full-time (0 women), 4 part-time (0 women). *Students:* 43 full-time (9 women), 16 part-time (7 women); includes 14 minority (2 African Americans, 9 Asian Americans or Pacific Islanders, 3 Hispanic Americans), 27 international. 159 applicants, 18% accepted. In 1998, 28 master's, 7 doctorates awarded (43% entered university research/teaching, 57% found other work related to degree). Terminal master's awarded for partial completion of doctoral program. *Degree requirements:* For master's, foreign language and thesis not required; for doctorate, dissertation, qualifying exam required, foreign language not required. *Entrance requirements:* For master's and doctorate, GRE General Test, GRE Subject Test (strongly recommended), TOEFL. *Application deadline:* For fall admission, 1/5; for spring admission, 10/1. Application fee: $55. *Financial aid:* In 1998–99, 40 students received aid, including 1 fellowship, 31 research assistantships, 4 teaching assistantships; Federal Work-Study and unspecified assistantships also available. Financial aid application deadline: 1/5; financial aid applicants required to submit FAFSA. Total annual research expenditures: $4.7 million. *Unit head:* Dr. Gerald A. Navratil, Chairman, 212-854-4457, E-mail: seasinfo.ap@columbia.edu.

Cornell University, Graduate School, Graduate Fields of Arts and Sciences, Center for Applied Mathematics, Ithaca, NY 14853-0001. Offers PhD. *Faculty:* 84 full-time. *Students:* 35 full-time (10 women); includes 6 minority (1 African American, 5 Hispanic Americans), 11 international. 77 applicants, 21% accepted. In 1998, 5 doctorates awarded. *Degree requirements:* For doctorate, dissertation required. *Entrance requirements:* For doctorate, GRE General Test, TOEFL (minimum score of 550 required). *Application deadline:* For fall admission, 1/15. Application fee: $65. Electronic applications accepted. *Financial aid:* In 1998–99, 35 students received aid, including 12 fellowships with full tuition reimbursements available, 8 research assistantships with full tuition reimbursements available, 15 teaching assistantships with full tuition reimbursements available; institutionally-sponsored loans, scholarships, tuition waivers (full and partial), and unspecified assistantships also available. Financial aid applicants required to submit FAFSA. *Faculty research:* Dynamics, discrete and numerical mathematics, signal and image processing, mathematical biology, mathematical economics and finance. *Unit head:* Director of Graduate Studies, 607-255-4335, Fax: 607-255-9860. *Application contact:* Graduate Field Assistant, 607-255-4335, Fax: 607-255-9860, E-mail: applmath@cam.cornell.edu.

Announcement: The Center for Applied Mathematics is an interdepartmental program with more than 70 faculty members. Students may pursue PhD studies over a broad range of the mathematical sciences and are admitted to the field from a variety of educational backgrounds with strong mathematical components. Students are normally awarded fellowships or teaching or research assistantships.

Cornell University, Graduate School, Graduate Fields of Engineering, Field of Chemical Engineering, Ithaca, NY 14853-0001. Offers advanced materials processing (M Eng, MS, PhD); applied mathematics and computational methods (M Eng, MS, PhD); biochemical engineering (M Eng, MS, PhD); chemical reaction engineering (M Eng, MS, PhD); classical

Applied Mathematics

Cornell University (continued)

and statistical thermodynamics (M Eng, MS, PhD); fluid dynamics, rheology and biorheology (M Eng, MS, PhD); heat and mass transfer (M Eng, MS, PhD); kinetics and catalysis (M Eng, MS, PhD); polymers (M Eng, MS, PhD); surface science (M Eng, MS, PhD). *Faculty:* 18 full-time. *Students:* 71 full-time (17 women); includes 9 minority (1 African American, 7 Asian Americans or Pacific Islanders, 1 Hispanic American), 29 international. *Degree requirements:* For master's, thesis (MS) required; for doctorate, dissertation required, foreign language not required. *Entrance requirements:* For master's and doctorate, GRE General Test, TOEFL (minimum score of 580 required). *Application deadline:* For fall admission, 1/15. Application fee: $65. Electronic applications accepted. *Unit head:* Director of Graduate Studies, 607-255-4550, Fax: 607-255-9166. *Application contact:* Graduate Field Assistant, 607-255-4550, Fax: 607-255-9166, E-mail: dgs@cheme.cornell.edu.

Cornell University, Graduate School, Graduate Fields of Engineering, Field of Operations Research and Industrial Engineering, Ithaca, NY 14853-0001. Offers applied probability and statistics (PhD); manufacturing systems engineering (PhD); mathematical programming (PhD); operations research and industrial engineering (M Eng). *Faculty:* 30 full-time. *Students:* 91 full-time (20 women); includes 22 minority (1 African American, 21 Asian Americans or Pacific Islanders), 36 international. Terminal master's awarded for partial completion of doctoral program. *Degree requirements:* For doctorate, dissertation required, foreign language not required, foreign language not required. *Entrance requirements:* For master's and doctorate, GRE General Test, TOEFL (minimum score of 550 required). *Application deadline:* For fall admission, 1/15. Application fee: $65. Electronic applications accepted. *Unit head:* Director of Graduate Studies, 607-255-9128. *Application contact:* Graduate Field Assistant, 607-255-9128, E-mail: orphd@cornell.edu.

Dalhousie University, Faculty of Graduate Studies, DalTech, Faculty of Engineering, Department of Engineering Mathematics, Halifax, NS B3H 3J5, Canada. Offers M Sc, PhD. *Faculty:* 6 full-time (1 woman), 2 part-time (0 women). *Students:* 8 full-time (1 woman), 1 part-time. Average age 28. 7 applicants, 43% accepted. In 1998, 2 master's awarded (50% found work related to degree, 50% continued full-time study); 1 doctorate awarded (100% entered university research/teaching). *Degree requirements:* For master's and doctorate, thesis/dissertation required, foreign language not required. *Entrance requirements:* For master's and doctorate, TOEFL (minimum score of 580 required). *Application deadline:* For fall admission, 6/1; for winter admission, 10/1; for spring admission, 2/1. Applications are processed on a rolling basis. Application fee: $55. *Financial aid:* In 1998–99, 1 fellowship (averaging $12,000 per year), 1 research assistantship (averaging $3,600 per year), 3 teaching assistantships (averaging $4,800 per year) were awarded.; scholarships also available. *Faculty research:* Piecewise regression and robust statistics, random field theory, dynamical systems, wave loads on offshore structures, digital signal processing. *Unit head:* Dr. W. J. Phillips, Head, 902-494-3288, Fax: 902-423-1801, E-mail: william.phillips@dal.ca. *Application contact:* Shelley Parker, Admissions Coordinator, Graduate Studies and Research, 902-494-1288, Fax: 902-494-3149, E-mail: shelley.parker@dal.ca.

DePaul University, College of Liberal Arts and Sciences, Department of Mathematical Sciences, Program in Applied Mathematics, Chicago, IL 60604-2287. Offers MS. *Students:* 23 full-time (9 women), 20 part-time (8 women); includes 6 minority (3 African Americans, 3 Asian Americans or Pacific Islanders), 4 international. Average age 35. 16 applicants, 100% accepted. In 1998, 18 degrees awarded. *Degree requirements:* For master's, computer language, comprehensive exam required, foreign language and thesis not required. *Application deadline:* Applications are processed on a rolling basis. Application fee: $25. *Unit head:* Dr. Effat Moussa, Director, 312-325-7000 Ext. 1343.

East Carolina University, Graduate School, College of Arts and Sciences, Department of Mathematics, Greenville, NC 27858-4353. Offers applied mathematics (MA); computer science (MS); mathematics (MA, MA Ed). Part-time and evening/weekend programs available. *Faculty:* 15 full-time (4 women). *Students:* 9 full-time (5 women), 23 part-time (12 women); includes 3 minority (2 Asian Americans or Pacific Islanders, 1 Hispanic American), 2 international. *Degree requirements:* For master's, comprehensive exams required. *Entrance requirements:* For master's, GRE General Test, MAT (MA Ed), TOEFL. *Application deadline:* For fall admission, 6/1; for spring admission, 10/15. Applications are processed on a rolling basis. Application fee: $40. Tuition, state resident: full-time $1,012. Tuition, nonresident: full-time $8,578. Required fees: $1,006. Part-time tuition and fees vary according to course load. *Unit head:* Dr. Robert Hursey, Director of Graduate Studies, 252-328-6461, Fax: 252-328-6414, E-mail: hurseyr@mail.ecu.edu. *Application contact:* Dr. Paul D. Tschetter, Senior Associate Dean, 252-328-6012, Fax: 252-328-6071, E-mail: grad@mail.ecu.edu.

École Polytechnique de Montréal, Graduate Programs, Department of Mathematics, Montréal, PQ H3C 3A7, Canada. Offers mathematical method in CA engineering (M Eng, M Sc A, PhD); operational research (M Eng, M Sc A, PhD). Part-time programs available. *Degree requirements:* For master's and doctorate, one foreign language, computer language, thesis/dissertation required. *Entrance requirements:* For master's, minimum GPA of 2.75; for doctorate, minimum GPA of 3.0. *Faculty research:* Statistics and probability, fractal analysis, optimization.

Florida Institute of Technology, Graduate School, College of Science and Liberal Arts, Department of Mathematical Sciences, Program in Applied Mathematics, Melbourne, FL 32901-6975. Offers MS, PhD. Part-time programs available. *Faculty:* 14 full-time (2 women), 1 part-time (0 women). *Students:* 10 full-time (2 women), 16 part-time (7 women); includes 3 minority (2 African Americans, 1 Asian American or Pacific Islander), 7 international. Average age 34. 23 applicants, 83% accepted. In 1998, 2 master's, 1 doctorate awarded. Terminal master's awarded for partial completion of doctoral program. *Degree requirements:* For master's, computer language, comprehensive exam required, thesis optional, foreign language not required; for doctorate, dissertation, comprehensive exam required, foreign language not required. *Entrance requirements:* For master's, minimum GPA of 3.0, proficiency in a computer language; for doctorate, minimum GPA of 3.2. *Application deadline:* Applications are processed on a rolling basis. Application fee: $50. Electronic applications accepted. Tuition: Part-time $575 per credit hour. Required fees: $100. Tuition and fees vary according to campus/location and program. *Financial aid:* In 1998–99, 11 students received aid, including 10 teaching assistantships (averaging $3,290 per year); research assistantships, institutionally-sponsored loans and tuition remissions also available. Financial aid application deadline: 3/1; financial aid applicants required to submit FAFSA. *Faculty research:* Methods of nonlinear analysis, spectral theory of operators, reaction diffusion equations, mathematical modeling. *Application contact:* Carolyn P. Farrior, Associate Dean of Graduate Admissions, 407-674-7118, Fax: 407-723-9468, E-mail: cfarrior@fit.edu.

Florida State University, Graduate Studies, College of Arts and Sciences, Department of Mathematics, Program in Applied Mathematics, Tallahassee, FL 32306. Offers MA, MS, PhD. Part-time programs available. *Faculty:* 10 full-time (0 women), 1 part-time (0 women). *Students:* 12 full-time (6 women), 2 part-time, 6 international. Average age 28. In 1998, 1 master's, 4 doctorates awarded (50% entered university research/teaching, 50% found other work related to degree). Terminal master's awarded for partial completion of doctoral program. *Degree requirements:* For master's, thesis optional, foreign language not required; for doctorate, dissertation required, foreign language not required. *Entrance requirements:* For master's and doctorate, GRE General Test (minimum combined score of 1100 required), minimum GPA of 3.0. *Average time to degree:* Doctorate–5 years full-time. *Application deadline:* For spring admission, 11/22. Applications are processed on a rolling basis. Application fee: $20. Tuition, state resident: part-time $139 per credit hour. Tuition, nonresident: part-time $482 per credit hour. Tuition and fees vary according to program. *Financial aid:* In 1998–99, 2 research assistantships with full tuition reimbursements (averaging $14,000 per year), 10 teaching assistantships with full tuition reimbursements (averaging $14,000 per year) were awarded.; fellowships with full tuition reimbursements, institutionally-sponsored loans also available. Financial aid application deadline: 3/1; financial aid applicants required to submit FAFSA. *Faculty research:* Fluid dynamics, computational methods, partial differential equations, numerical analysis. *Application contact:* Dr. Steven Blumsack, Director of Graduate Studies, 850-644-2488, Fax: 850-644-4053, E-mail: blumsack@math.fsu.edu.

The George Washington University, Columbian School of Arts and Sciences, Department of Mathematics, Program in Applied Mathematics, Washington, DC 20052. Offers MA, MS. Part-time and evening/weekend programs available. *Students:* 1 full-time (0 women), 1 part-time, 1 international. Average age 26. 2 applicants, 50% accepted. *Degree requirements:* For master's, comprehensive exam required, foreign language and thesis not required. *Entrance requirements:* For master's, GRE General Test, GRE Subject Test, interview, minimum GPA of 3.0. *Application deadline:* For fall admission, 6/15. Application fee: $55. Tuition: Full-time $17,328; part-time $722 per credit hour. Required fees: $828; $35 per credit hour. Tuition and fees vary according to campus/location and program. *Financial aid:* Fellowships, teaching assistantships available. Financial aid application deadline: 2/1. *Unit head:* Dr. Hugo Junghenn, Chair, Department of Mathematics, 202-994-6235.

Georgia Institute of Technology, Graduate Studies and Research, College of Sciences, School of Mathematics, Atlanta, GA 30332-0001. Offers algorithms, combinatorics, and optimization (PhD); applied mathematics (MS); mathematics (MS Math, PhD); statistics (MS Stat). Terminal master's awarded for partial completion of doctoral program. *Degree requirements:* For master's, thesis or alternative required, foreign language not required; for doctorate, dissertation required. *Entrance requirements:* For master's and doctorate, GRE General Test, GRE Subject Test, TOEFL (minimum score of 570 required), minimum GPA of 3.0. Electronic applications accepted. *Faculty research:* Dynamical systems, discrete mathematics, probability and statistics, mathematical physics.

Hampton University, Graduate College, Program in Applied Mathematics, Hampton, VA 23668. Offers MS. *Faculty:* 7 full-time (0 women), 1 part-time (0 women). *Students:* 5 full-time (2 women), 1 part-time; includes 5 minority (all African Americans) In 1998, 4 degrees awarded. *Degree requirements:* For master's, thesis optional, foreign language not required. *Entrance requirements:* For master's, GRE General Test (minimum score of 450 on verbal section required). *Application deadline:* For fall admission, 6/1 (priority date); for spring admission, 11/1. Applications are processed on a rolling basis. Application fee: $25. Tuition: Full-time $9,490; part-time $230 per semester hour. Required fees: $60; $35 per semester. Tuition and fees vary according to course load. *Financial aid:* Research assistantships, teaching assistantships, scholarships available. Aid available to part-time students. Financial aid application deadline: 5/1; financial aid applicants required to submit FAFSA. *Unit head:* Dr. Carolyn Morgan, Head, 757-727-5548. *Application contact:* Erika Henderson, Director, Graduate Programs, 757-727-5454, Fax: 757-727-5084.

Harvard University, Graduate School of Arts and Sciences, Division of Engineering and Applied Sciences, Cambridge, MA 02138. Offers applied mathematics (ME, SM, PhD); applied physics (ME, SM, PhD); computer science (ME, SM, PhD); computing technology (PhD); engineering science (ME); engineering sciences (SM, PhD); medical engineering/medical physics (PhD, Sc D), including applied physics (PhD), engineering sciences (PhD), medical engineering/medical physics (Sc D), physics (PhD). *Students:* 143 full-time (31 women); includes 10 minority (1 African American, 9 Asian Americans or Pacific Islanders), 57 international. Terminal master's awarded for partial completion of doctoral program. *Degree requirements:* For master's, foreign language and thesis not required; for doctorate, dissertation required, foreign language not required. *Entrance requirements:* For master's and doctorate, GRE General Test, GRE Subject Test, TOEFL (minimum score of 550 required). Application fee: $60. *Unit head:* Dr. Paul C. Martin, Dean, 617-495-2833. *Application contact:* Office of Admissions and Financial Aid, 617-495-5315.

Hofstra University, College of Liberal Arts and Sciences, Division of Natural Sciences, Mathematics, Engineering, and Computer Science, Department of Mathematics, Hempstead, NY 11549. Offers applied mathematics (MA, MS). Part-time and evening/weekend programs available. *Faculty:* 12 full-time (4 women). *Students:* 2 full-time (1 woman), 12 part-time (3 women), 1 international. Average age 35. In 1998, 2 degrees awarded. *Degree requirements:* For master's, comprehensive exam or oral defense of thesis, proficiency in computer programming required. *Entrance requirements:* For master's, bachelor's degree in mathematics or related field. *Application deadline:* Applications are processed on a rolling basis. Application fee: $40 ($75 for international students). *Financial aid:* In 1998–99, 8 students received aid, including 8 fellowships; teaching assistantships, career-related internships or fieldwork, Federal Work-Study, and tutoring assistantships also available. *Faculty research:* Teacher training, multiparameter stochastic applications, mathematical ecology, algebra, number theory, dynamical systems. Total annual research expenditures: $100,000. *Unit head:* Edward G. Ostling, Chairperson, 516-463-5576, Fax: 516-463-5790, E-mail: matego@hofstra.edu. *Application contact:* Mary Beth Carey, Vice President of Enrollment Services, 516-463-6700, Fax: 516-560-7660, E-mail: hofstra@hofstra.edu.

Howard University, Graduate School of Arts and Sciences, Department of Mathematics, Washington, DC 20059-0002. Offers applied mathematics (MS, PhD); mathematics (MS, PhD). Part-time programs available. *Degree requirements:* For master's, computer language, thesis or alternative, comprehensive exam, qualifying exam required, foreign language not required; for doctorate, 2 foreign languages (computer language can substitute for one), dissertation, comprehensive exam, qualifying exams required. *Entrance requirements:* For master's, GRE General Test, minimum GPA of 3.2 in mathematics; for doctorate, GRE General Test.

Hunter College of the City University of New York, Graduate School, Division of Sciences and Mathematics, Department of Mathematics, New York, NY 10021-5085. Offers applied mathematics (MA); pure mathematics (MA). Part-time and evening/weekend programs available. *Degree requirements:* For master's, one foreign language, computer language, thesis required (for some programs). *Entrance requirements:* For master's, GRE General Test, TOEFL (minimum score of 550 required). Tuition, state resident: full-time $4,350; part-time $185 per credit. Tuition, nonresident: full-time $7,600; part-time $320 per credit. Required fees: $8 per term. *Faculty research:* Data analysis, dynamical systems, computer graphics, topology, statistical decision theory.

Indiana University Bloomington, Graduate School, College of Arts and Sciences, Department of Mathematics, Bloomington, IN 47405. Offers applied mathematics–numerical analysis (MA, PhD); mathematics education (MAT); probability-statistics (MA, PhD). PhD offered through the University Graduate School. *Faculty:* 46 full-time (1 woman). *Students:* 77 full-time (22 women), 26 part-time (5 women); includes 3 minority (2 Asian Americans or Pacific Islanders, 1 Native American), 52 international. Terminal master's awarded for partial completion of doctoral program. *Degree requirements:* For master's, foreign language and thesis not required; for doctorate, dissertation required. *Entrance requirements:* For master's and doctorate, GRE General Test, GRE Subject Test, TOEFL. *Application deadline:* For fall admission, 1/15 (priority date); for spring admission, 9/1 (priority date). Applications are processed on a rolling basis. Application fee: $40. Electronic applications accepted. Tuition, state resident: part-time $161 per credit hour. Tuition, nonresident: part-time $468 per credit hour. Required fees: $360 per year. Tuition and fees vary according to course load and program. *Unit head:* Daniel Maki, Chair, 812-855-2200, Fax: 812-855-0046, E-mail: maki@indiana.edu. *Application contact:* Misty Cummings, Graduate Secretary, 812-855-2645, Fax: 812-855-0046, E-mail: gradmath@indiana.edu.

Indiana University of Pennsylvania, Graduate School, College of Natural Sciences and Mathematics, Department of Mathematics, Program in Applied Mathematics, Indiana, PA 15705-1087. Offers MS. *Students:* 6 full-time (2 women), 3 part-time (2 women), 2 international. Average age 25. 7 applicants, 86% accepted. In 1998, 4 degrees awarded. *Degree requirements:* For master's, thesis optional, foreign language not required. *Entrance requirements:* For master's, TOEFL (minimum score of 500 required). *Application deadline:* For fall admission, 7/1 (priority date); for spring admission, 11/1. Applications are processed on a rolling basis. Application fee: $30. *Financial aid:* Research assistantships, Federal Work-Study available.

Aid available to part-time students. Financial aid application deadline: 3/15. *Unit head:* Dr. Frederick Adkins, Graduate Coordinator, 724-357-3790, E-mail: fadkins@grove.iup.edu.

Indiana University–Purdue University Fort Wayne, School of Arts and Sciences, Department of Mathematical Sciences, Fort Wayne, IN 46805-1499. Offers applied mathematics (MS); mathematics (MS); operations research (MS). Part-time and evening/weekend programs available. *Faculty:* 18 full-time (4 women), 1 (woman) part-time. *Students:* 3 full-time (1 woman), 6 part-time (3 women). *Degree requirements:* For master's, foreign language and thesis not required. *Entrance requirements:* For master's, minimum GPA of 3.0, major or minor in mathematics. *Application deadline:* For fall admission, 5/1 (priority date); for spring admission, 12/1. Applications are processed on a rolling basis. Application fee: $30. *Unit head:* Raymond E. Pippert, Chair, 219-481-6224, Fax: 219-481-6880, E-mail: pippert@cvax.ipfw.indiana.edu. *Application contact:* W. Douglas Weakley, Director of Graduate Studies, 219-481-6238, Fax: 219-481-6880, E-mail: weakley@cvax.ipfw.indiana.edu.

Indiana University–Purdue University Indianapolis, School of Science, Department of Mathematical Sciences, Indianapolis, IN 46202-3216. Offers applied mathematics (MS, PhD); applied statistics (MS); mathematics (MS, PhD). Part-time programs available. *Students:* 7 full-time (2 women), 28 part-time (9 women); includes 2 minority (1 Asian American or Pacific Islander, 1 Native American), 15 international. Terminal master's awarded for partial completion of doctoral program. *Degree requirements:* For master's, thesis optional, foreign language not required; for doctorate, one foreign language, dissertation required. *Entrance requirements:* For master's, TOEFL (minimum score of 570 required); for doctorate, GRE, TOEFL (minimum score of 570 required). *Application deadline:* For fall admission, 2/1 (priority date). Application fee: $25 ($50 for international students). Tuition, state resident: part-time $158 per credit hour. Tuition, nonresident: part-time $455 per credit hour. Required fees: $121 per year. Tuition and fees vary according to course load and degree level. *Unit head:* Eric T. Sawyer, Chair, 317-274-6918, Fax: 317-274-3460. *Application contact:* Yuri Abramovich, Chair, Graduate Committee, 317-274-6927, Fax: 317-274-3460, E-mail: yabramovich@math.iupui.edu.

Iowa State University of Science and Technology, Graduate College, College of Liberal Arts and Sciences, Department of Mathematics, Ames, IA 50011. Offers applied mathematics (MS, PhD); mathematics (MS, PhD); school mathematics (MSM). *Faculty:* 52 full-time. *Students:* 30 full-time (9 women), 21 part-time (7 women); includes 1 minority (Asian American or Pacific Islander), 22 international. *Degree requirements:* For master's, thesis or alternative required; for doctorate, dissertation required. *Entrance requirements:* For master's and doctorate, GRE General Test, TOEFL (minimum score of 550 required). *Application deadline:* For fall admission, 2/1 (priority date); for spring admission, 10/15. Application fee: $20 ($50 for international students). Electronic applications accepted. Tuition, state resident: full-time $3,308. Tuition, nonresident: full-time $9,744. Part-time tuition and fees vary according to course load, campus/location and program. *Unit head:* Dr. Max D. Gunzburger, Chair, 515-294-1752, Fax: 515-294-5454, E-mail: gradmath@iastate.edu.

See in-depth description on page 683.

Kent State University, College of Arts and Sciences, Department of Mathematics and Computer Science, Kent, OH 44242-0001. Offers applied mathematics (MA, MS, PhD); computer science (MA, MS, PhD); pure mathematics (MA, MS, PhD). *Faculty:* 41 full-time. *Students:* 69 full-time (19 women), 60 part-time (23 women); includes 2 minority (both Asian Americans or Pacific Islanders), 78 international. *Degree requirements:* For master's, thesis optional, foreign language not required; for doctorate, dissertation required. *Entrance requirements:* For master's, GRE, minimum GPA of 2.75; for doctorate, GRE, minimum GPA of 3.0. *Application deadline:* For fall admission, 7/12; for spring admission, 11/29. Applications are processed on a rolling basis. Application fee: $30. *Unit head:* Dr. Austin C. Melton, Chairman, 330-672-2430, Fax: 330-672-7824.

Lehigh University, College of Arts and Sciences, Department of Mathematics, Division of Applied Mathematics, Bethlehem, PA 18015-3094. Offers MS, PhD. *Degree requirements:* For master's, comprehensive exam required, foreign language and thesis not required; for doctorate, dissertation, comprehensive and qualifying exams required. *Entrance requirements:* For master's and doctorate, TOEFL (minimum score of 550 required), minimum GPA of 3.0. *Faculty research:* Probability, statistics, differential equations, computational methods, mechanics.

Lehigh University, College of Engineering and Applied Science, Department of Mechanical Engineering and Mechanics, Bethlehem, PA 18015-3094. Offers applied mathematics (MS, PhD); mechanical engineering (M Eng, MS, PhD); mechanics (M Eng, MS, PhD). Part-time programs available. *Faculty:* 29 full-time (0 women). *Students:* 75 full-time (8 women), 11 part-time (1 woman); includes 7 minority (2 African Americans, 5 Hispanic Americans), 43 international. Terminal master's awarded for partial completion of doctoral program. *Degree requirements:* For master's and doctorate, thesis/dissertation required, foreign language not required. *Entrance requirements:* For master's and doctorate, TOEFL (minimum score of 550 required). *Application deadline:* For fall admission, 7/15; for spring admission, 12/1. Applications are processed on a rolling basis. Application fee: $40. *Unit head:* Dr. Charles Smith, Chairman, 610-758-4102, Fax: 610-758-6224, E-mail: crs1@lehigh.edu. *Application contact:* Donna Reiss, Graduate Coordinator, 610-758-4139, Fax: 610-758-6224, E-mail: dmr1@lehigh.edu.

Long Island University, C.W. Post Campus, College of Liberal Arts and Sciences, Department of Mathematics, Brookville, NY 11548-1300. Offers applied mathematics (MS), including classical mathematics, computer mathematics; mathematics and education (MS); mathematics for secondary school teachers (MS). Part-time and evening/weekend programs available. *Faculty:* 14 full-time (3 women). *Students:* 14 full-time (8 women), 18 part-time (9 women). *Degree requirements:* For master's, thesis or alternative, oral presentation required, foreign language not required. *Application deadline:* Applications are processed on a rolling basis. Application fee: $30. Electronic applications accepted. *Unit head:* Dr. Neo Cleopa, Chairman, 516-299-2448, Fax: 516-299-4049, E-mail: ncleopa@phoenix.liunet.edu. *Application contact:* Dr. Shahla Ahdout, Graduate Adviser, 516-299-2448, Fax: 516-299-4049.

Michigan State University, Graduate School, College of Natural Science, Department of Mathematics, East Lansing, MI 48824-1020. Offers applied mathematics (MS, PhD); computational mathematics (MS); mathematics (MA, MAT, MS, PhD); mathematics education (PhD). *Faculty:* 63. *Students:* 92 full-time (26 women), 36 part-time (12 women); includes 9 minority (2 African Americans, 4 Asian Americans or Pacific Islanders, 3 Hispanic Americans), 76 international. Terminal master's awarded for partial completion of doctoral program. *Degree requirements:* For master's, certifying exam required, foreign language and thesis not required; for doctorate, dissertation, exams, seminar required. *Entrance requirements:* For master's, GRE; for doctorate, minimum GPA of 3.0, MS. *Application deadline:* For fall admission, 2/1. Applications are processed on a rolling basis. Application fee: $30 ($40 for international students). *Unit head:* Dr. Peter Lappan, Chairperson, 517-355-9681, Fax: 517-432-1562. *Application contact:* Director of Graduate Studies, 517-353-4650, Fax: 517-432-1562, E-mail: grad@mth.msu.,edu.

Montclair State University, Office of Graduate Studies, College of Science and Mathematics, Department of Mathematics and Computer Science, Program in Computer Science, Upper Montclair, NJ 07043-1624. Offers applied mathematics (MS); applied statistics (MS). Part-time and evening/weekend programs available. *Degree requirements:* For master's, computer language, written comprehensive exam required, foreign language and thesis not required. *Entrance requirements:* For master's, GRE General Test, minimum GPA of 2.67.

Montclair State University, Office of Graduate Studies, College of Science and Mathematics, Department of Mathematics and Computer Science, Programs in Mathematics, Concentration in Pure and Applied Mathematics, Upper Montclair, NJ 07043-1624. Offers MS. Part-time and evening/weekend programs available. *Degree requirements:* For master's, written comprehensive exam required, foreign language and thesis not required. *Entrance requirements:* For master's, GRE General Test, minimum GPA of 2.67.

New Jersey Institute of Technology, Office of Graduate Studies, Department of Mathematical Sciences, Newark, NJ 07102-1982. Offers applied mathematics (MS); mathematical science (PhD). Part-time and evening/weekend programs available. *Degree requirements:* For master's, foreign language and thesis not required; for doctorate, residency required, foreign language and thesis not required. *Entrance requirements:* For master's, GRE General Test (minimum score of 450 on verbal section, 600 on quantitative, 550 on analytical required); for doctorate, GRE General Test (minimum score of 450 on verbal section, 600 on quantitative, 550 on analytical required), minimum graduate GPA of 3.5. Electronic applications accepted. *Faculty research:* Computational methods, probability and statistics, testing-decision theory.

Nicholls State University, Graduate Studies, College of Arts and Sciences, Department of Mathematics, Thibodaux, LA 70310. Offers applied mathematics (MS). Part-time and evening/weekend programs available. *Faculty:* 7 full-time (0 women), 2 part-time (1 woman). *Students:* 4 full-time (1 woman), 5 part-time (3 women); includes 1 minority (African American) *Degree requirements:* For master's, foreign language and thesis not required. *Entrance requirements:* For master's, GRE General Test. *Application deadline:* For fall admission, 6/17 (priority date); for spring admission, 11/15. Applications are processed on a rolling basis. Application fee: $10 ($60 for international students). *Unit head:* Dr. Donald M. Bardwell, Head, College of Arts and Sciences, 504-448-4380, Fax: 504-448-4927, E-mail: math-dmb@nich-nsunet.nich.edu.

North Carolina State University, Graduate School, College of Physical and Mathematical Sciences, Department of Mathematics, Raleigh, NC 27695. Offers applied mathematics (MS, PhD); mathematics (MS, PhD). Part-time programs available. *Faculty:* 64 full-time (4 women), 11 part-time (0 women). *Students:* 104 full-time (46 women), 9 part-time (2 women); includes 14 minority (11 African Americans, 3 Asian Americans or Pacific Islanders), 21 international. Terminal master's awarded for partial completion of doctoral program. *Degree requirements:* For master's, computer language required, thesis optional, foreign language not required; for doctorate, one foreign language, dissertation required. *Entrance requirements:* For master's and doctorate, GRE General Test, GRE Subject Test. *Application deadline:* For fall admission, 4/1 (priority date); for spring admission, 11/25. Applications are processed on a rolling basis. Application fee: $45. *Unit head:* Dr. Robert H. Martin, Head, 919-515-3796, Fax: 919-515-3798, E-mail: rhmartin@math.ncsu.edu. *Application contact:* Dr. Ernest L. Stitzinger, Director of Graduate Programs, 919-515-3258, Fax: 919-515-3798, E-mail: stitz@math.ncsu.edu.

See in-depth description on page 703.

North Dakota State University, Graduate Studies and Research, College of Science and Mathematics, Department of Mathematics, Fargo, ND 58105. Offers applied mathematics (MS, PhD); mathematics (MS, PhD). *Faculty:* 14 full-time (1 woman), 1 part-time (0 women). *Students:* 19 full-time (6 women); includes 2 minority (both Asian Americans or Pacific Islanders), 9 international. *Degree requirements:* For master's, computer language, thesis or alternative required, foreign language not required; for doctorate, one foreign language, computer language, dissertation required. *Entrance requirements:* For master's and doctorate, GRE General Test (combined average 1800 on three sections), TOEFL (minimum score of 525 required; average 590). *Application deadline:* For fall admission, 3/15 (priority date). Applications are processed on a rolling basis. Application fee: $25. *Unit head:* Dr. Dogan Comez, Chair, 701-231-7490, Fax: 701-231-7598.

Northwestern University, The Graduate School, Judd A. and Marjorie Weinberg College of Arts and Sciences, Department of Mathematics, Evanston, IL 60208. Offers applied mathematics (PhD); mathematics (PhD). Admissions and degrees offered through The Graduate School. Part-time programs available. *Faculty:* 36 full-time (5 women). *Students:* 36 full-time (10 women); includes 9 minority (all Asian Americans or Pacific Islanders), 11 international. *Degree requirements:* For doctorate, dissertation, preliminary exam required, foreign language not required. *Entrance requirements:* For doctorate, GRE General Test, GRE Subject Test, TOEFL (minimum score of 600 required). *Application deadline:* For fall admission, 8/30. Application fee: $50 ($55 for international students). *Unit head:* R. Clark Robinson, Chair, 847-491-8035. *Application contact:* Melanie Rubin, Admission Contact, 847-491-8035, Fax: 847-491-8906, E-mail: melanie@math.nwu.edu.

Northwestern University, The Graduate School, Robert R. McCormick School of Engineering and Applied Science, Program in Applied Mathematics, Evanston, IL 60208. Offers MS, PhD. Admissions and degrees offered through The Graduate School. Part-time programs available. *Faculty:* 11 full-time (1 woman), 1 part-time (0 women). *Students:* 37 full-time (10 women); includes 5 minority (3 Asian Americans or Pacific Islanders, 2 Hispanic Americans), 7 international. 27 applicants, 59% accepted. In 1998, 2 master's, 4 doctorates awarded. Terminal master's awarded for partial completion of doctoral program. *Degree requirements:* For master's, foreign language and thesis not required; for doctorate, dissertation required, foreign language not required. *Entrance requirements:* For master's and doctorate, GRE General Test, TOEFL (minimum score of 560 required). *Application deadline:* For fall admission, 8/30. Application fee: $50 ($55 for international students). *Financial aid:* In 1998–99, 6 fellowships with full tuition reimbursements (averaging $11,673 per year), 8 research assistantships with partial tuition reimbursements (averaging $16,285 per year), 13 teaching assistantships with full tuition reimbursements (averaging $12,042 per year) were awarded.; career-related internships or fieldwork, Federal Work-Study, institutionally-sponsored loans, and scholarships also available. Financial aid application deadline: 1/15; financial aid applicants required to submit FAFSA. *Faculty research:* Combustion, interfacial phenomena, nonlinear optics, dynamical systems, scientific computation. Total annual research expenditures: $1.3 million. *Unit head:* Bernard J. Matkowsky, Chair, 847-491-3345. *Application contact:* Edla D'Herckens, Admission Contact, 847-491-3345, Fax: 847-491-2178, E-mail: dherc@elmo.tech.nwu.edu.

See in-depth description on page 709.

Oakland University, Graduate Studies, College of Arts and Sciences, Department of Mathematical Sciences, Program in Industrial Applied Mathematics, Rochester, MI 48309-4401. Offers MS. Part-time and evening/weekend programs available. Average age 44. 4 applicants, 75% accepted. *Degree requirements:* For master's, foreign language and thesis not required. *Entrance requirements:* For master's, minimum GPA of 3.0 for unconditional admission. *Application deadline:* For fall admission, 7/15; for spring admission, 3/15. Application fee: $30. Tuition, state resident: part-time $221 per credit hour. Tuition, nonresident: part-time $488 per credit hour. Required fees: $214 per semester. Part-time tuition and fees vary according to program. *Financial aid:* Federal Work-Study, institutionally-sponsored loans, and tuition waivers (full) available. Financial aid application deadline: 3/1; financial aid applicants required to submit FAFSA. *Unit head:* Holly Johnson, Admission Contact, 847-491-3974, Fax: 847-491-4939, E-mail: h-curry@nwu.edu. *Application contact:* Dr. Kevin Andrews, Coordinator, 248-370-3430.

Oklahoma State University, Graduate College, College of Arts and Sciences, Department of Mathematics, Stillwater, OK 74078. Offers applied mathematics (MS); mathematics (MS, Ed D, PhD). *Faculty:* 24 full-time (2 women), 1 part-time (0 women). *Students:* 20 full-time (5 women), 29 part-time (14 women); includes 5 minority (1 African American, 2 Asian Americans or Pacific Islanders, 2 Native Americans), 17 international. *Degree requirements:* For master's, foreign language and thesis not required; for doctorate, dissertation required. *Entrance requirements:* For master's and doctorate, TOEFL (minimum score of 550 required). *Application deadline:* For fall admission, 6/1 (priority date). Application fee: $25. *Unit head:* Dr. Benny Evans, Head, 405-744-5688.

See in-depth description on page 717.

Old Dominion University, College of Sciences, Department of Mathematics and Statistics, Programs in Computational and Applied Mathematics, Norfolk, VA 23529. Offers applied mathematics (MS, PhD); statistics (MS, PhD). Part-time programs available. *Faculty:* 26

Applied Mathematics

Old Dominion University (continued)

full-time (2 women). *Students:* 19 full-time (8 women), 14 part-time (3 women); includes 2 minority (1 African American, 1 Asian American or Pacific Islander), 13 international. Average age 35. In 1998, 2 master's, 3 doctorates awarded. Terminal master's awarded for partial completion of doctoral program. *Degree requirements:* For master's, comprehensive exam required, foreign language and thesis not required; for doctorate, dissertation, candidacy exam required, foreign language not required. *Entrance requirements:* For master's, GRE General Test, GRE Subject Test, TOEFL, minimum GPA of 3.0 in major, 2.5 overall; for doctorate, GRE General Test (minimum combined score of 1000 required), GRE Subject Test (minimum score of 600 required), TOEFL. *Application deadline:* For fall admission, 7/1. Applications are processed on a rolling basis. Application fee: $30. *Financial aid:* In 1998–99, 20 students received aid, including 15 research assistantships, 1 teaching assistantship; fellowships, grants also available. Financial aid application deadline: 2/15; financial aid applicants required to submit FAFSA. *Faculty research:* Numerical analysis, integral equations, continuum mechanics. *Unit head:* Dr. John J. Swetits, Director, 757-683-3911, E-mail: swetits@math.odu.edu.

Pennsylvania State University University Park Campus, Graduate School, Eberly College of Science, Department of Mathematics, State College, University Park, PA 16802-1503. Offers mathematics (M Ed, MA, D Ed, PhD), including applied mathematics (MA, PhD). *Students:* 52 full-time (12 women), 19 part-time (6 women). *Entrance requirements:* For master's and doctorate, GRE General Test. Application fee: $50. *Unit head:* Dr. Gary L. Mullen, Head, 814-865-7527.

See in-depth description on page 727.

Princeton University, Graduate School, Department of Mathematics, Program in Applied and Computational Mathematics, Princeton, NJ 08544-1019. Offers PhD. *Degree requirements:* For doctorate, dissertation required. *Entrance requirements:* For doctorate, GRE General Test, GRE Subject Test.

Announcement: The program in applied and computational mathematics at Princeton is an interdisciplinary PhD program offering a select group of highly qualified students the opportunity to obtain a thorough knowledge of branches of mathematics indispensable for science and engineering applications, including numerical analysis and other computational methods. Before being admitted to a 3rd year of study, students must sustain the general examination. The general examination is designed as a sequence of interviews with assigned professors, covering 3 areas of applied mathematics and culminating in a seminar on a research topic, delivered toward the end of the 4th semester. The doctoral dissertation may consist of a mathematical contribution to some field of science or engineering or the development or analysis of mathematical or computational methods useful for, inspired by, or relevant to science or engineering. Satisfactory completion of the requirements leads to the PhD degree in applied a nd computational mathematics.

See in-depth description on page 731.

Princeton University, Graduate School, Department of Physics, Princeton, NJ 08544-1019. Offers applied and computational mathematics (PhD); mathematical physics (PhD); physics (PhD); physics and chemical physics (PhD). *Degree requirements:* For doctorate, dissertation required. *Entrance requirements:* For doctorate, GRE General Test, GRE Subject Test.

Princeton University, Graduate School, School of Engineering and Applied Science, Department of Chemical Engineering, Princeton, NJ 08544-1019. Offers applied and computational mathematics (PhD); chemical engineering (M Eng, MSE, PhD); plasma science and technology (MSE, PhD); polymer sciences and materials (MSE, PhD). *Degree requirements:* For master's, thesis required; for doctorate, dissertation, general exam required. *Entrance requirements:* For master's and doctorate, GRE General Test, GRE Subject Test, TOEFL.

Purdue University Calumet, Graduate School, School of Liberal Arts and Sciences, Department of Mathematical Sciences, Hammond, IN 46323-2094. Offers applied mathematics (MS). *Degree requirements:* For master's, foreign language and thesis not required. *Entrance requirements:* For master's, TOEFL.

Rensselaer Polytechnic Institute, Graduate School, School of Science, Department of Mathematical Sciences, Program in Applied Mathematics, Troy, NY 12180-3590. Offers MS. Part-time programs available. *Faculty:* 23 full-time (5 women), 1 (woman) part-time. *Students:* 10 full-time (4 women), 2 part-time (1 woman), 1 international. 11 applicants, 91% accepted. In 1998, 8 degrees awarded. *Degree requirements:* For master's, thesis required (for some programs), foreign language not required. *Entrance requirements:* For master's, GRE General Test, TOEFL (minimum score of 550 required). *Application deadline:* For fall admission, 2/1 (priority date). Applications are processed on a rolling basis. Application fee: $35. *Financial aid:* Fellowships, research assistantships, teaching assistantships, career-related internships or fieldwork and institutionally-sponsored loans available. Financial aid application deadline:2/1. *Faculty research:* Mathematical modeling, differential equations, applications of mathematics in science and engineering, operations research, analysis. Total annual research expenditures: $3.2 million. *Application contact:* Lorraine Pisarczyk, Graduate Coordinator, 518-276-6414, Fax: 518-276-4824, E-mail: pisarl@rpi.edu.

Announcement: At the MS level, the program is designed to prepare students to become practicing applied mathematicians in industry or government. Stresses the construction, analysis, and evaluation of mathematical models of real-world problems and emphasizes related areas of mathematics. Interaction with industry is featured regularly through visiting lecturers and research projects sponsored by industry. At the PhD level, the program interprets applied mathematics in the broadest possible sense. Areas of emphasis include physical mathematics and modeling, differential equations, analysis, scientific computation, mathematical programming and operations research, and applied geometry. Development of expertise in at least 1 field of application is stressed.

Rice University, Graduate Programs, George R. Brown School of Engineering, Department of Computational and Applied Mathematics, Houston, TX 77251-1892. Offers MA, MAM Sc, PhD. Part-time programs available. *Degree requirements:* For master's, thesis required (for some programs), foreign language not required; for doctorate, dissertation required. *Entrance requirements:* For master's and doctorate, GRE General Test, GRE Subject Test, TOEFL (minimum score of 550 required), minimum GPA of 3.0. *Faculty research:* Statistics, operations research, computer science, game theory, numerical analysis.

Rochester Institute of Technology, Part-time and Graduate Admissions, College of Science, Department of Mathematics and Statistics, Rochester, NY 14623-5604. Offers industrial and applied mathematics (MS). *Students:* 2 full-time (1 woman), 1 part-time. 7 applicants, 43% accepted. In 1998, 2 degrees awarded. *Entrance requirements:* For master's, minimum GPA of 3.0. *Application deadline:* For fall admission, 3/1 (priority date). Applications are processed on a rolling basis. Application fee: $40. *Unit head:* Rebecca Hill, Head, 716-475-2498, E-mail: rehsma@rit.edu.

Rutgers, The State University of New Jersey, New Brunswick, Graduate School, Program in Mathematics, New Brunswick, NJ 08903. Offers applied mathematics (MS, PhD); mathematics (MS, PhD). Part-time programs available. *Faculty:* 96 full-time (9 women). *Students:* 63 full-time (10 women), 14 part-time (6 women); includes 7 minority (3 African Americans, 1 Asian American or Pacific Islander, 3 Hispanic Americans), 37 international. Terminal master's awarded for partial completion of doctoral program. *Degree requirements:* For master's, foreign language and thesis not required; for doctorate, dissertation required. *Entrance requirements:* For master's, GRE General Test (minimum combined score of 1200 required), GRE Subject Test (minimum score of 750 required), TOEFL (minimum score of 600 required; 250 for computer-based); for doctorate, GRE General Test (minimum combined score of 1200 required), GRE Subject Test (minimum score of 800 required), TOEFL (minimum score of 600 required; 250 for computer-based). *Application deadline:* For fall admission, 2/1; for spring admission, 11/1. Application fee: $50. *Unit head:* Prof. Peter S. Landweber, Director, 732-445-3864, Fax: 732-445-5530, E-mail: grad-director@math.rutgers.edu.

St. John's University, Graduate School of Arts and Sciences, Department of Mathematics and Computer Science, Jamaica, NY 11439. Offers algebra (MA); analysis (MA); applied mathematics (MA); computer science (MA); geometry-topology (MA); logic and foundations (MA); probability and statistics (MA). Part-time and evening/weekend programs available. *Faculty:* 16 full-time (3 women), 5 part-time (2 women). *Students:* 7 full-time (3 women), 5 part-time (3 women); includes 5 minority (2 African Americans, 1 Asian American or Pacific Islander, 2 Hispanic Americans), 2 international. *Degree requirements:* For master's, comprehensive exam required, thesis optional, comprehensive exam required, thesis optional. *Entrance requirements:* For master's, minimum GPA of 3.0. *Application deadline:* Applications are processed on a rolling basis. Application fee: $40. Tuition: Full-time $13,200; part-time $500 per credit. Required fees: $150; $75 per term. Tuition and fees vary according to degree level and program. *Unit head:* Dr. Charles Traina, Chair, 718-990-6166, E-mail: trainac@stjohns.edu. *Application contact:* Patricia G. Armstrong, Director, Office of Admission, 718-990-2028, Fax: 718-990-2096, E-mail: armstrop@stjohns.edu.

San Diego State University, Graduate and Research Affairs, College of Sciences, Department of Mathematical Sciences, Program in Applied Mathematics, San Diego, CA 92182. Offers MS. Part-time programs available. *Students:* 3 full-time (0 women), 14 part-time (6 women); includes 2 minority (both Hispanic Americans), 4 international. Average age 29. In 1998, 2 degrees awarded. *Degree requirements:* For master's, comprehensive exam required, thesis not required. *Entrance requirements:* For master's, GRE General Test (minimum combined score of 950 required), TOEFL (minimum score of 550 required). *Average time to degree:* Master's–2 years full-time, 4 years part-time. *Application deadline:* For fall admission, 7/1 (priority date); for spring admission, 12/1. Applications are processed on a rolling basis. Application fee: $55. *Faculty research:* Modeling, computational fluid dynamics,biomathematics, thermodynamics. *Unit head:* Brenda Fass-Holmes, Coordinator, Admissions and Student Affairs, 619-594-6317, E-mail: bholmes@mail.sdsu.edu. *Application contact:* Peter Salamon, Graduate Adviser, 619-594-7204, Fax: 619-594-6746, E-mail: salamon.sdsu.edu.

Santa Clara University, School of Engineering, Department of Applied Mathematics, Santa Clara, CA 95053-0001. Offers MSAM. Part-time and evening/weekend programs available. Average age 38. 1 applicants, 0% accepted. In 1998, 4 degrees awarded. *Degree requirements:* For master's, thesis or alternative required, foreign language not required. *Entrance requirements:* For master's, GRE General Test (combined average 1600 on three sections), TOEFL (minimum score of 550 required), minimum GPA of 2.75. *Application deadline:* For fall admission, 6/1; for spring admission, 1/1. Applications are processed on a rolling basis. Application fee: $40. *Financial aid:* Fellowships, research assistantships, teaching assistantships, Federal Work-Study, institutionally-sponsored loans, and scholarships available. Aid available to part-time students. Financial aid application deadline: 2/1; financial aid applicants required to submit CSS PROFILE or FAFSA. *Unit head:* Dr. George Fegan, Chair, 408-554-4061. *Application contact:* Tina Samms, Assistant Director of Graduate Admissions, 408-554-4313, Fax: 408-554-5474, E-mail: engr-grad@scu.edu.

Simon Fraser University, Graduate Studies, Faculty of Science, Department of Mathematics and Statistics, Burnaby, BC V5A 1S6, Canada. Offers applied mathematics (M Sc, PhD); pure mathematics (M Sc, PhD); statistics (M Sc, PhD). *Faculty:* 32 full-time (3 women), 1 part-time (0 women). *Students:* 53 full-time (21 women), 10 part-time (2 women). *Degree requirements:* For master's, thesis required; for doctorate, dissertation, comprehensive exams required. *Entrance requirements:* For master's, GRE Subject Test, TOEFL (minimum score of 570 required), TWE (minimum score of 5 required) or International English Language Test (minimum score of 7.5 required), minimum GPA of 3.0; for doctorate, GRE Subject Test, TOEFL (minimum score of 570 required), TWE (minimum score of 5 required) or International English Language Test (minimum score of 7.5 required), minimum GPA of 3.5. Application fee: $55. *Unit head:* J. Berggren, Chair, 604-291-3331, Fax: 604-291-4947. *Application contact:* Graduate Secretary, 604-291-3801, Fax: 604-291-4947, E-mail: sholmes@sfu.ca.

Southern Methodist University, Dedman College, Department of Mathematics, Dallas, TX 75275. Offers applied mathematics (MS); mathematical sciences (PhD). Part-time programs available. *Faculty:* 16 full-time (1 woman). *Students:* 10 full-time (3 women), 6 part-time (2 women); includes 3 minority (2 African Americans, 1 Asian American or Pacific Islander), 4 international. Average age 29. 42 applicants, 12% accepted. In 1998, 7 master's, 2 doctorates awarded. *Degree requirements:* For master's, thesis optional, foreign language not required; for doctorate, dissertation, oral and written exams required, foreign language not required. *Entrance requirements:* For master's and doctorate, GRE General Test, minimum GPA of 3.0, 18 undergraduate hours in mathematics beyond first and second year calculus. *Application deadline:* For fall admission, 6/30; for spring admission, 11/30. Applications are processed on a rolling basis. Application fee: $50. Tuition: Part-time $686 per credit hour. Required fees: $88 per credit hour. Part-time tuition and fees vary according to course load and program. *Financial aid:* Research assistantships, teaching assistantships available. Financial aid applicants required to submit FAFSA. *Faculty research:* Numerical analysis, scientific computation, biomedical modeling, nonlinear waves, perturbation methods. Total annual research expenditures:$195,000. *Unit head:* Chairman, 214-768-2506. *Application contact:* James Nagy, Director of Graduate Studies, 214-768-4339.

See in-depth description on page 745.

State University of New York at Stony Brook, Graduate School, College of Engineering and Applied Sciences, Department of Applied Mathematics and Statistics, Stony Brook, NY 11794. Offers MS, PhD. *Faculty:* 20 full-time (3 women), 3 part-time (1 woman). *Students:* 68 full-time (27 women), 34 part-time (9 women); includes 18 minority (6 African Americans, 11 Asian Americans or Pacific Islanders, 1 Hispanic American), 55 international. 164 applicants, 51% accepted. In 1998, 20 master's, 14 doctorates awarded. *Degree requirements:* For master's, thesis or alternative required, foreign language not required; for doctorate, dissertation, comprehensive exams required. *Entrance requirements:* For master's and doctorate, GRE General Test, TOEFL. *Application deadline:* For fall admission, 1/15. Application fee: $50. *Financial aid:* In 1998–99, 9 fellowships, 30 research assistantships, 26 teaching assistantships were awarded. *Faculty research:* Biostatistics, combinatorial analysis, differential equations, modeling. Total annual research expenditures: $2.6 million. *Unit head:* Dr. J. Glimm, Chairman, 516-632-8360. *Application contact:* Dr. Woo Jong Kim, Director, 516-632-8360, Fax: 516-632-8490, E-mail: wjkim@ccmail.sunysb.edu.

Stevens Institute of Technology, Graduate School, School of Applied Sciences and Liberal Arts, Department of Mathematical Sciences, Program in Applied Mathematics, Hoboken, NJ 07030. Offers MS, PhD. *Degree requirements:* For master's, thesis optional, foreign language not required; for doctorate, one foreign language, dissertation required. *Entrance requirements:* For master's and doctorate, GRE, TOEFL. Electronic applications accepted.

Temple University, Graduate School, College of Science and Technology, Department of Mathematics, Philadelphia, PA 19122-6096. Offers applied and computational mathematics (MA, PhD); pure mathematics (MA, PhD). Part-time and evening/weekend programs available. *Faculty:* 26 full-time (1 woman). *Students:* 39 (10 women); includes 14 minority (1 African American, 11 Asian Americans or Pacific Islanders, 2 Hispanic Americans) 3 international. Terminal master's awarded for partial completion of doctoral program. *Degree requirements:* For master's, written exam required, thesis optional, foreign language not required; for doctorate, 2 foreign languages, dissertation, oral and written exams required. *Entrance requirements:* For master's and doctorate, GRE General Test (minimum combined score of 1000 required), GRE Subject Test, minimum GPA of 3.0 during previous 2 years, 2.8 overall. *Application deadline:* For fall admission, 2/10 (priority date). Applications are processed on a rolling basis. Application fee: $40. *Unit head:* Dr. Jack Schiller, Chair, 215-204-4650, Fax: 215-204-6433,

E-mail: schiller@euclid.math.temple.edu. *Application contact:* Dr. Eric Grinberg, Graduate Chair, 215-204-7286, Fax: 215-204-6433, E-mail: grinberg@euclid.math.temple.edu.

Towson University, Graduate School, Program in Applied and Industrial Mathematics, Towson, MD 21252-0001. Offers MS. *Students:* 2 full-time, 10 part-time. *Application deadline:* Applications are processed on a rolling basis. Application fee: $40. *Financial aid:* Application deadline: 4/1; *Unit head:* Dr. Raouf Boules, Director, 410-830-3683, Fax: 410-830-4149, E-mail: boules@towson.edu. *Application contact:* Bob Baer, Assistant Director of Graduate School, 410-830-2501, Fax: 410-830-4675, E-mail: petgrad@towson.edu.

Tulane University, Graduate School, Department of Mathematics, New Orleans, LA 70118-5669. Offers applied mathematics (MS); mathematics (MS, PhD); statistics (MS). *Students:* 24 full-time (6 women), 1 part-time; includes 2 minority (1 African American, 1 Asian American or Pacific Islander), 13 international. *Degree requirements:* For doctorate, dissertation required. *Entrance requirements:* For master's, GRE General Test (minimum combined score of 1000 required; average 1200), TOEFL (minimum score of 600 required), TSE (minimum score of 220 required), minimum B average in undergraduate course work; for doctorate, GRE General Test (minimum combined score of 1000 required; average 1200), TOEFL (minimum score of 600 required), TSE (minimum score of 220 required). *Application deadline:* For fall admission, 2/1. Application fee: $45. *Unit head:* Dr. Morris Kalka, Chairman, 504-865-5727.

The University of Akron, Graduate School, Buchtel College of Arts and Sciences, Department of Mathematics and Computer Science, Program in Applied Mathematics, Akron, OH 44325-0001. Offers MS. *Students:* 6 full-time (3 women), 1 part-time, 2 international. Average age 34. In 1998, 4 degrees awarded. *Degree requirements:* For master's, thesis optional, foreign language not required. *Entrance requirements:* For master's, minimum GPA of 2.75. *Average time to degree:* Master's–2 years full-time, 4 years part-time. *Application deadline:* For fall admission, 3/1. Applications are processed on a rolling basis. Application fee: $25 ($50 for international students). Tuition, state resident: part-time $189 per credit. Tuition, nonresident: part-time $353 per credit. Required fees: $7.3 per credit. *Financial aid:* Application deadline: 3/1. *Unit head:* Dr. Gerald Young, Coordinator, 330-972-5731, E-mail: gwyoung@uakron.edu.

The University of Akron, Graduate School, College of Engineering, Program in Engineering-Applied Mathematics, Akron, OH 44325-0001. Offers PhD. *Students:* 2 full-time (0 women), 1 (woman) part-time, 1 international. Average age 25. *Degree requirements:* For doctorate, variable foreign language requirement (computer language can substitute for one), dissertation, candidacy exam, qualifying exam required. *Entrance requirements:* For doctorate, GRE, TOEFL. *Application deadline:* Applications are processed on a rolling basis. Application fee: $25 ($50 for international students). Tuition, state resident: part-time $189 per credit. Tuition, nonresident: part-time $353 per credit. Required fees: $7.3 per credit. *Financial aid:* Application deadline: 3/1. *Unit head:* Dr. S. Graham Kelly, Interim Dean, College of Engineering, 330-972-6978, E-mail: sgraham@uakron.edu.

The University of Alabama, Graduate School, College of Arts and Sciences, Department of Mathematics, Tuscaloosa, AL 35487. Offers applied mathematics (PhD); mathematics (MA); pure mathematics (PhD). *Faculty:* 31 full-time (1 woman). *Students:* 28 full-time (12 women), 1 part-time; includes 2 minority (both African Americans), 12 international. Terminal master's awarded for partial completion of doctoral program. *Degree requirements:* For master's, thesis or alternative required, foreign language not required; for doctorate, one foreign language, dissertation, teaching experience required. *Entrance requirements:* For master's and doctorate, GRE General Test (minimum combined score of 1500 required), TOEFL (minimum score of 550 required), minimum GPA of 3.0. *Application deadline:* For fall admission, 7/6. Applications are processed on a rolling basis. Application fee: $25. Electronic applications accepted. *Unit head:* Wei Shen Hsia, Chairperson, 205-348-5071, Fax: 205-348-7067, E-mail: whsia@gp.as.ua.edu. *Application contact:* Rita Reese, Administrative Specialist, Graduate Advisory Program, 205-348-5074, Fax: 205-348-7067, E-mail: rreese@gp.as.ua.edu.

The University of Alabama at Birmingham, Graduate School, School of Natural Sciences and Mathematics, Department of Mathematics, Birmingham, AL 35294. Offers applied mathematics (PhD); mathematics (MS). *Students:* 18 full-time (6 women), 1 (woman) part-time; includes 4 minority (3 African Americans, 1 Asian American or Pacific Islander), 5 international. Terminal master's awarded for partial completion of doctoral program. *Degree requirements:* For master's, thesis optional; for doctorate, one foreign language (computer language can substitute), dissertation, comprehensive exam required. *Entrance requirements:* For master's and doctorate, GRE General Test. *Application deadline:* Applications are processed on a rolling basis. Application fee: $30 ($60 for international students). Electronic applications accepted. *Unit head:* Dr. Roger T. Lewis, Chairman, 205-934-2154, Fax: 205-934-9025. *Application contact:* Dr. Roger T. Lewis, Chairman, 205-934-2154, Fax: 205-934-9025.

The University of Alabama in Huntsville, School of Graduate Studies, College of Science, Department of Mathematical Sciences, Huntsville, AL 35899. Offers applied mathematics (PhD); mathematics (MA, MS). Part-time and evening/weekend programs available. *Faculty:* 15 full-time (1 woman). *Students:* 17 full-time (8 women), 13 part-time (5 women); includes 2 minority (both African Americans), 6 international. *Degree requirements:* For master's, oral and written exams required, thesis optional, foreign language not required; for doctorate, one foreign language, dissertation, oral and written exams required. *Entrance requirements:* For master's and doctorate, GRE General Test (minimum combined score of 1500 on three sections required), minimum GPA of 3.0. *Application deadline:* For fall admission, 7/24 (priority date); for spring admission, 11/15 (priority date). Applications are processed on a rolling basis. Application fee: $20. Tuition and fees vary according to course load. *Unit head:* Dr. M. H. Chang, Chair, 256-890-6470, Fax: 256-890-6173, E-mail: chang@math.uah.edu.

University of Alberta, Faculty of Graduate Studies and Research, Department of Mathematical Sciences, Edmonton, AB T6G 2E1, Canada. Offers applied mathematics (M Sc, PhD); mathematical finance (M Sc); mathematical physics (M Sc, PhD); mathematics (M Sc, PhD); statistics (M Sc, PhD, Postgraduate Diploma). Part-time programs available. Terminal master's awarded for partial completion of doctoral program. *Degree requirements:* For master's, thesis required (for some programs), foreign language not required; for doctorate, dissertation required, foreign language not required. *Faculty research:* Classical and functional analysis, algebra, differential equations, geometry.

The University of Arizona, Graduate College, Graduate Interdisciplinary Programs, Graduate Interdisciplinary Program in Applied Mathematics, Tucson, AZ 85721. Offers MS, PhD. *Faculty:* 40. *Students:* 35 full-time (9 women), 8 part-time (5 women); includes 5 minority (2 Asian Americans or Pacific Islanders, 2 Hispanic Americans, 1 Native American), 12 international. Average age 27. 59 applicants, 29% accepted. In 1998, 5 master's, 7 doctorates awarded. Terminal master's awarded for partial completion of doctoral program. *Degree requirements:* For master's, computer language required, foreign language and thesis not required; for doctorate, one foreign language, computer language, dissertation required. *Entrance requirements:* For master's and doctorate, GRE, TOEFL (minimum score of 550 required). *Application deadline:* For fall admission, 6/15. Applications are processed on a rolling basis. Application fee: $35. *Financial aid:* Fellowships, research assistantships, teaching assistantships, institutionally-sponsored loans and scholarships available. Financial aid application deadline: 3/1. *Faculty research:* Dynamical systems and chaos, fluid mechanics, partial differential equations, biological applications, optimization and control. *Unit head:* Dr. Michael Tabor, Head, 520-621-4664, Fax: 520-621-8322, E-mail: tabor@math.arizona.edu. *Application contact:* Kathleen Leick, Graduate Secretary, 520-621-2016, Fax: 520-621-8322, E-mail: applmath@ccit.arizona.edu.

See in-depth description on page 753.

University of Arkansas at Little Rock, Graduate School, College of Sciences and Engineering Technology, Department of Mathematics and Statistics, Little Rock, AR 72204-1099. Offers applied mathematics (MS), including applied analysis, mathematical statistics. Part-time and evening/weekend programs available. *Degree requirements:* For master's, computer language, comprehensive exams required, foreign language and thesis not required. *Entrance requirements:* For master's, GRE General Test, GRE Subject Test, minimum GPA of 2.7, previous course work in advanced mathematics.

University of British Columbia, Faculty of Graduate Studies, Institute of Applied Mathematics, Vancouver, BC V6T 1Z2, Canada. Offers M Sc, PhD. *Degree requirements:* For master's, thesis required (for some programs); for doctorate, dissertation, comprehensive exam required. *Entrance requirements:* For master's, TOEFL; for doctorate, TOEFL, master's degree. *Faculty research:* Applied analysis, optimization, mathematical biology, numerical analysis, fluid mechanics.

University of California, Berkeley, Graduate Division, College of Letters and Science, Department of Mathematics, Program in Applied Mathematics, Berkeley, CA 94720-1500. Offers PhD. *Degree requirements:* For doctorate, dissertation, qualifying exam required. *Entrance requirements:* For doctorate, GRE General Test, GRE Subject Test, minimum GPA of 3.0. *Application deadline:* For fall admission, 2/15. Application fee: $40. *Financial aid:* Fellowships, research assistantships, teaching assistantships available. Financial aid application deadline: 12/15. *Unit head:* Janet Johnson, Graduate Admissions, 604-822-4245, E-mail: jjohnson@physic.ubc.ca. *Application contact:* Janet Yonan, Graduate Assistant for Admission, 510-642-0665, Fax: 510-642-8204, E-mail: yonan@math.berkeley.edu.

University of California, Davis, Graduate Studies, Program in Applied Mathematics, Davis, CA 95616. Offers MS, PhD. *Faculty:* 50 full-time (2 women). *Students:* 25 full-time (2 women); includes 7 minority (1 African American, 5 Asian Americans or Pacific Islanders, 1 Hispanic American), 5 international. 27 applicants, 67% accepted. In 1998, 5 master's, 1 doctorate awarded. Terminal master's awarded for partial completion of doctoral program. *Degree requirements:* For master's, thesis required; for doctorate, dissertation required. *Entrance requirements:* For master's, GRE General Test, GRE Subject Test, minimum GPA of 3.0; for doctorate, GRE General Test, GRE Subject Test, master's degree, minimum GPA of 3.0. *Average time to degree:* Master's–2 years full-time; doctorate–5 years full-time. *Application deadline:* For fall admission, 2/15. Application fee: $40. Electronic applications accepted. *Financial aid:* In 1998–99, 5 fellowships with full and partial tuition reimbursements, 8 research assistantships with full and partial tuition reimbursements, 19 teaching assistantships with full and partial tuition reimbursements were awarded.; Federal Work-Study also available. Financial aid application deadline: 1/15; financial aid applicants required to submit FAFSA. *Faculty research:* Mathematical biology, control and optimization, atmospheric sciences, theoretical chemistry, mathematical physics. *Unit head:* Angela Cheer, Chair, 530-752-1912, E-mail: aycheer@ucdavis.edu. *Application contact:* Graduate Coordinator, 530-752-8131, Fax: 530-752-6635, E-mail: gradcord@ucdmath.ucdavis.edu.

University of California, San Diego, Graduate Studies and Research, Department of Mathematics, La Jolla, CA 92093-5003. Offers applied mathematics (MA); mathematics (MA, PhD); statistics (MS). *Faculty:* 54. *Students:* 65 (16 women). *Degree requirements:* For master's, one foreign language required, thesis not required; for doctorate, dissertation required. *Entrance requirements:* For master's and doctorate, GRE General Test, GRE Subject Test. Application fee: $40. *Unit head:* Jeffrey Remmel, Chair, 619-534-2643, E-mail: jremmel@ucsd.edu. *Application contact:* Lois Stewart, Graduate Coordinator, 619-534-6887.

University of California, Santa Barbara, Graduate Division, College of Letters and Science, Division of Math, Life and Physical Science, Department of Mathematics, Program in Applied Mathematics, Santa Barbara, CA 93106. Offers MA. *Faculty:* 31 full-time (2 women). *Students:* 4 full-time (0 women); includes 2 minority (1 Asian American or Pacific Islander, 1 Native American) 4 applicants, 25% accepted. In 1998, 1 degree awarded. *Degree requirements:* For master's, thesis or alternative required, foreign language not required. *Entrance requirements:* For master's, GRE General Test, GRE Subject Test, TOEFL (minimum score of 550 required). *Application deadline:* For fall admission, 5/1. Application fee: $40. Electronic applications accepted. *Financial aid:* Federal Work-Study and institutionally-sponsored loans available. Financial aid application deadline: 1/15; financial aid applicants required to submit FAFSA. *Unit head:* Thomas Sideras, Adviser, 805-893-2179. *Application contact:* Medina Price, Staff Graduate Adviser, 805-893-8192, E-mail: price@math.ucsb.edu.

University of California, Santa Cruz, Graduate Division, Division of Natural Sciences, Department of Mathematics, Santa Cruz, CA 95064. Offers applied mathematics (MA, PhD); mathematics (MA, PhD). *Faculty:* 16 full-time. *Students:* 44 full-time (12 women); includes 8 minority (1 African American, 6 Asian Americans or Pacific Islanders, 1 Hispanic American), 10 international. *Degree requirements:* For doctorate, one foreign language (computer language can substitute), dissertation, qualifying exam required. *Entrance requirements:* For doctorate, GRE General Test, GRE Subject Test. *Application deadline:* For fall admission, 2/1. Application fee: $40. *Unit head:* Dr. Geoffrey Mason, Chairperson, 831-459-2215, E-mail: gem@cats.ucsc.edu. *Application contact:* Graduate Admissions, 831-459-2301.

University of Central Oklahoma, Graduate College, College of Mathematics and Science, Department of Mathematics and Statistics, Edmond, OK 73034-5209. Offers applied mathematical sciences (MS), including computer science, mathematics, mathematics/computer science teaching, statistics. *Accreditation:* NCATE. Part-time programs available. *Faculty:* 11 full-time (3 women), 1 part-time (0 women). *Degree requirements:* For master's, computer language, thesis required, foreign language not required. *Application deadline:* For fall admission, 8/23 (priority date). Applications are processed on a rolling basis. Application fee: $15. *Unit head:* Dr. David Bridge, Chairperson, 405-974-5697. *Application contact:* Dr. James Yates, Adviser, 405-974-5386, Fax: 405-974-3824, E-mail: jyates@aix1.ucok.edu.

University of Chicago, Division of the Physical Sciences, Department of Mathematics, Program in Applied Mathematics, Chicago, IL 60637-1513. Offers SM, PhD. *Degree requirements:* For master's, oral exams required, thesis not required; for doctorate, dissertation, 2 qualifying exams required. *Entrance requirements:* For master's and doctorate, GRE General Test, GRE Subject Test, TOEFL. *Faculty research:* Applied analysis, dynamical systems, theoretical biology, math-physics.

University of Cincinnati, Division of Research and Advanced Studies, McMicken College of Arts and Sciences, Department of Mathematics, Cincinnati, OH 45221-0091. Offers applied mathematics (MS, PhD); mathematics education (MAT); pure mathematics (MS, PhD); statistics (MS, PhD). *Accreditation:* NCATE (one or more programs are accredited). *Faculty:* 38 full-time. *Students:* 69 full-time (41 women), 14 part-time (7 women); includes 6 minority (all Asian Americans or Pacific Islanders), 56 international. *Degree requirements:* For master's, thesis optional, foreign language not required; for doctorate, dissertation, final written exam required. *Entrance requirements:* For master's, TOEFL (minimum score of 520 required). *Application deadline:* For fall admission, 2/1. Application fee: $30. *Unit head:* James Osterburg, Head, 513-556-4054, Fax: 513-556-3417, E-mail: james.osterburg@uc.edu. *Application contact:* Diego Murio, Graduate Program Director, 513-556-4088, Fax: 513-556-3417, E-mail: diego.murio@uc.edu.

University of Colorado at Boulder, Graduate School, College of Arts and Sciences, Department of Applied Mathematics, Boulder, CO 80309. Offers MS, PhD. *Degree requirements:* For master's, thesis or alternative, comprehensive exam required, foreign language not required; for doctorate, dissertation, comprehensive exam required. *Entrance requirements:* For master's and doctorate, GRE General Test, TOEFL.

University of Colorado at Colorado Springs, Graduate School, College of Engineering and Applied Science, Department of Mathematics, Colorado Springs, CO 80933-7150. Offers applied mathematics (MS). Part-time and evening/weekend programs available. *Faculty:* 9 full-time (1 woman). *Students:* 7 full-time (3 women), 7 part-time (2 women); includes 3 minority (1 African American, 1 Asian American or Pacific Islander, 1 Hispanic American) Average age 29. 3 applicants, 67% accepted. In 1998, 9 degrees awarded (100% found work related to degree). *Degree requirements:* For master's, thesis required, foreign language

Applied Mathematics

University of Colorado at Colorado Springs (continued)
not required. *Entrance requirements:* For master's, GRE General Test (minimum combined score of 1200 required), TOEFL (minimum score of 550 required), minimum GPA of 3.0. *Application deadline:* For fall admission, 6/15. Application fee: $40 ($50 for international students). Tuition, state resident: full-time $2,768; part-time $118 per credit. Tuition, nonresident: full-time $10,392; part-time $425 per credit. Required fees: $265; $7.5 per credit. One-time fee: $28. Tuition and fees vary according to program and student level. *Financial aid:* Teaching assistantships available. Financial aid application deadline: 3/1. *Faculty research:* Abelian groups and noncommutative rings, hormone analysis and computer vision, probability and mathematical physics, stochastic dynamics, probability models. Total annual research expenditures: $20,000. *Unit head:* Dr. Jeremy A. Haefner, Chairman, 719-262-3182, Fax: 719-262-3605, E-mail: haefner@vision.uccs.edu. *Application contact:* Rinaldo Schinazi, Graduate Adviser, 719-262-3515, Fax: 719-262-3605, E-mail: schinazi@vision.uccs.edu.

University of Colorado at Denver, Graduate School, College of Liberal Arts and Sciences, Program in Applied Mathematics, Denver, CO 80217-3364. Offers MS, PhD. Part-time and evening/weekend programs available. *Faculty:* 21. *Students:* 11 full-time (2 women), 56 part-time (18 women); includes 9 minority (2 Asian Americans or Pacific Islanders, 5 Hispanic Americans, 2 Native Americans), 7 international. Average age 34. 22 applicants, 91% accepted. In 1998, 11 master's, 3 doctorates awarded. *Degree requirements:* For master's, thesis or alternative required; for doctorate, dissertation required. *Entrance requirements:* For master's, GRE, 30 hours in mathematics; for doctorate, GRE. *Application deadline:* For fall admission, 7/22; for spring admission, 11/1. Applications are processed on a rolling basis. Application fee: $50 ($60 for international students). Electronic applications accepted. Tuition, state resident: part-time $185 per credit hour. Tuition, nonresident: part-time $735 per credit hour. Required fees: $3 per credit hour. $130 per year. One-time fee: $25 part-time. Tuition and fees vary according to program. *Financial aid:* Fellowships, research assistantships, teaching assistantships, Federal Work-Study available. Financial aid application deadline: 3/1; financial aid applicants required to submit FAFSA. Total annual research expenditures: $228,414. *Unit head:* Jan Mandel, Chair, 303-556-4475, Fax: 303-556-8550, E-mail: jmandel@tiger.cudenver.edu. *Application contact:* Debbie Wangerin, Program Assistant, 303-556-2341, Fax: 303-556-8550, E-mail: dwangeri@carbon.cudenver.edu.

University of Dayton, Graduate School, College of Arts and Sciences, Department of Mathematics, Dayton, OH 45469-1300. Offers applied mathematics (MS). Part-time programs available. *Faculty:* 10 full-time (1 woman). *Students:* 5 full-time (2 women), 3 part-time (2 women); includes 5 minority (2 African Americans, 3 Asian Americans or Pacific Islanders) Average age 25. 5 applicants, 80% accepted. In 1998, 2 degrees awarded. *Degree requirements:* For master's, computer language required, foreign language and thesis not required. *Entrance requirements:* For master's, minimum undergraduate GPA of 3.0. *Average time to degree:* Master's–2 years full-time, 4 years part-time. *Application deadline:* For fall admission, 3/1 (priority date). Application fee: $30. Electronic applications accepted. *Financial aid:* In 1998–99, 7 students received aid, including 5 teaching assistantships (averaging $9,700 per year); research assistantships *Faculty research:* Differential equations, integral equations, general topology, measure theory, graph theory. *Unit head:* Dr. Thomas E. Gantner, Chairman, 937-229-2511, Fax: 937-229-2566, E-mail: gantner@udayton.edu. *Application contact:* Dr. Paul Eloe, Graduate Director, 937-229-2016, Fax: 937-229-2566, E-mail: eloe@neelix.udayton.edu.

University of Delaware, College of Arts and Science, Department of Mathematical Sciences, Newark, DE 19716. Offers applied mathematics (MA, MS, PhD); mathematics (MA, MS, PhD). Part-time programs available. *Faculty:* 37. *Students:* 40 full-time (13 women), 1 (woman) part-time; includes 1 minority (African American), 19 international. Terminal master's awarded for partial completion of doctoral program. *Degree requirements:* For master's, thesis required (for some programs), foreign language not required; for doctorate, dissertation, qualifying exam required. *Entrance requirements:* For master's and doctorate, GRE General Test (minimum combined score of 1050 required). *Application deadline:* For fall admission, 3/1 (priority date); for spring admission, 12/15 (priority date). Application fee: $45. *Unit head:* Dr. L. P. Cook, Chair, 302-831-2651, E-mail: cook@math.udel.edu. *Application contact:* Deborah See, Graduate Secretary, 302-831-2654, Fax: 302-831-4511, E-mail: see@math.udel.edu.

See in-depth description on page 761.

University of Denver, Graduate Studies, Faculty of Natural Sciences, Mathematics and Engineering, Department of Mathematics and Computer Science, Denver, CO 80208. Offers applied mathematics (MA, MS); computer science (MS); mathematics and computer science (PhD). Part-time programs available. *Faculty:* 14. *Students:* 56 (16 women); includes 8 minority (1 African American, 6 Asian Americans or Pacific Islanders, 1 Hispanic American) 34 international. Terminal master's awarded for partial completion of doctoral program. *Degree requirements:* For master's, computer language, foreign language, or laboratory experience required, thesis not required; for doctorate, one foreign language (computer language can substitute), dissertation, oral and written exams required. *Entrance requirements:* For master's and doctorate, GRE General Test, TOEFL (minimum score of 550 required). *Application deadline:* Applications are processed on a rolling basis. Application fee: $40 ($45 for international students). *Unit head:* Dr. Joel Cohen, Chairperson, 303-871-3292. *Application contact:* Rick Ball, Graduate Adviser, 303-871-2453.

University of Florida, Graduate School, College of Liberal Arts and Sciences, Department of Mathematics, Gainesville, FL 32611. Offers applied mathematics (MS, PhD); mathematics (MA, MS, PhD); mathematics teaching (MAT, MST). *Accreditation:* NCATE (one or more programs are accredited). Part-time programs available. *Faculty:* 55. *Students:* 74 full-time (13 women), 1 part-time; includes 10 minority (1 African American, 5 Asian Americans or Pacific Islanders, 4 Hispanic Americans), 29 international. Terminal master's awarded for partial completion of doctoral program. *Degree requirements:* For master's, computer language required, thesis optional; for doctorate, dissertation required. *Entrance requirements:* For master's and doctorate, GRE General Test, TOEFL, minimum GPA of 3.0. *Application deadline:* For fall admission, 6/1 (priority date). Applications are processed on a rolling basis. Application fee: $20. Electronic applications accepted. *Unit head:* Dr. Alladi Krishnaswani, Chairman, 352-392-0281 Ext. 227, Fax: 352-392-8357, E-mail: alladi@math.ufl.edu. *Application contact:* Dr. Paul Robinson, Graduate Coordinator, 352-392-0281 Ext. 273, Fax: 352-392-8357, E-mail: plr@math.ufl.edu.

University of Georgia, Graduate School, College of Arts and Sciences, Department of Mathematics, Program in Applied Mathematical Science, Athens, GA 30602. Offers MAMS. *Students:* 10 full-time (5 women), 2 part-time (1 woman); includes 1 minority (African American), 6 international. 17 applicants, 18% accepted. *Degree requirements:* For master's, one foreign language, comprehensive exams, technical report required. *Entrance requirements:* For master's, GRE General Test. *Application deadline:* For fall admission, 7/1 (priority date); for spring admission, 11/15. Application fee: $30. Electronic applications accepted. *Unit head:* Dr. Kenneth D. Johnson, Graduate Coordinator, Department of Mathematics, 706-542-2580, Fax: 706-542-2573, E-mail: grad@math.uga.edu.

University of Georgia, Graduate School, Terry College of Business, Program in Applied Mathematical Science, Athens, GA 30602. Offers MAMS. *Faculty:* 16 full-time (2 women). *Students:* 2 full-time (1 woman), 1 (woman) part-time; includes 1 minority (African American), 2 international. 3 applicants, 33% accepted. In 1998, 1 degree awarded. *Degree requirements:* Foreign language not required. *Application deadline:* For fall admission, 7/1 (priority date); for spring admission, 11/15. Application fee: $30. Electronic applications accepted. *Unit head:* Dr. Ralph E. Steuer, Graduate Coordinator, 706-542-3782, Fax: 706-542-4295, E-mail: rsteuer@cba.uga.edu.

University of Guelph, Faculty of Graduate Studies, College of Physical and Engineering Science, Department of Mathematics and Statistics, Guelph, ON N1G 2W1, Canada. Offers applied mathematics (PhD); applied statistics (PhD); mathematics and statistics (M Sc). Part-time programs available. *Faculty:* 23 full-time (2 women), 3 part-time (1 woman). *Students:* 36 full-time (9 women), 1 part-time, 7 international. *Degree requirements:* For master's, thesis required (for some programs), foreign language not required; for doctorate, dissertation required, foreign language not required. *Entrance requirements:* For master's, minimum B- average during previous 2 years; for doctorate, minimum B average. Application fee: $60. *Expenses:* Tuition and fees charges are reported in Canadian dollars. Tuition, area resident: Full-time $4,725 Canadian dollars; part-time $1,055 Canadian dollars per term. International tuition: $6,999 Canadian dollars full-time. Required fees: $295 Canadian dollars per term. *Unit head:* Dr. J. Mokanski, Chair, 519-824-4120 Ext. 6556, Fax: 519-837-0221, E-mail: chair@msnet.mathstat.uoguelph.ca. *Application contact:* Susan McCormick, Graduate Administrative Assistant, 519-824-4120 Ext. 6553, Fax: 519-837-0221, E-mail: smccormi@msnet.mathstat.uoguelph.ca.

University of Houston, College of Natural Sciences and Mathematics, Department of Mathematics, Houston, TX 77004. Offers applied mathematics (MS); mathematics (MS, PhD). Part-time and evening/weekend programs available. *Faculty:* 41 full-time (2 women). *Students:* 29 full-time (10 women), 20 part-time (4 women); includes 10 minority (5 African Americans, 3 Asian Americans or Pacific Islanders, 1 Hispanic American, 1 Native American), 13 international. *Degree requirements:* For master's, thesis optional, foreign language not required; for doctorate, one foreign language, dissertation required. *Entrance requirements:* For master's, TOEFL (minimum score of 550 required; average 623), minimum GPA of 3.0 in last 60 hours, bachelor's degree in mathematics or related area; for doctorate, GRE General Test (minimum combined score of 1000 required), TOEFL, MS in mathematics or equivalent, minimum GPA of 3.0 in last 60 hours. *Application deadline:* For fall admission, 7/3 (priority date); for spring admission, 12/4. Applications are processed on a rolling basis. Application fee: $25 ($75 for international students). *Unit head:* Dr. Garret Etgen, Chair, 713-743-3510. *Application contact:* Pamela Draughn, Graduate Adviser, 713-743-3517.

See in-depth description on page 767.

University of Illinois at Chicago, Graduate College, College of Liberal Arts and Sciences, Department of Mathematics, Statistics, and Computer Science, Chicago, IL 60607-7128. Offers applied mathematics (MS, DA, PhD); computer science (MS, DA, PhD); probability and statistics (MS, DA, PhD); pure mathematics (MS, DA, PhD); teaching of mathematics (MST). *Faculty:* 69 full-time (4 women). *Students:* 119 full-time (47 women), 30 part-time (12 women). *Degree requirements:* For master's, comprehensive exam required, foreign language and thesis not required; for doctorate, one foreign language, dissertation required. *Entrance requirements:* For master's and doctorate, GRE General Test, TOEFL (minimum score of 550 required), minimum GPA of 3.75 on a 5.0 scale. *Application deadline:* For fall admission, 7/3; for spring admission, 11/8. Application fee: $40 ($50 for international students). *Unit head:* Henri Gillet, Head, 312-996-3044. *Application contact:* David Marker, Director of Graduate Studies, 312-996-3041.

See in-depth description on page 769.

University of Illinois at Urbana–Champaign, Graduate College, College of Liberal Arts and Sciences, Department of Mathematics, Urbana, IL 61801. Offers applied mathematics (MS); mathematics (MS, PhD); teaching of mathematics (MS). *Faculty:* 81 full-time (6 women). *Students:* 159 full-time (40 women); includes 9 minority (1 African American, 7 Asian Americans or Pacific Islanders, 1 Hispanic American), 99 international. *Degree requirements:* For master's, foreign language and thesis not required; for doctorate, dissertation required. *Entrance requirements:* For master's, minimum GPA of 4.0 on a 5.0 scale. *Application deadline:* Applications are processed on a rolling basis. Application fee: $40 ($50 for international students). Tuition, state resident: full-time $4,040. Tuition, nonresident: full-time $11,192. Full-time tuition and fees vary according to program. *Unit head:* Philippe Tondeur, Chair, 217-333-3352. *Application contact:* John W. Gray, Director of Graduate Studies, 217-333-3354, Fax: 217-333-9576, E-mail: gray@math.uiuc.edu.

See in-depth description on page 771.

The University of Iowa, Graduate College, College of Liberal Arts, Program in Applied Mathematical and Computational Sciences, Iowa City, IA 52242-1316. Offers PhD. *Students:* 15 full-time (4 women), 9 part-time (1 woman); includes 3 minority (1 Asian American or Pacific Islander, 2 Hispanic Americans), 18 international. 23 applicants, 57% accepted. In 1998, 1 degree awarded. *Degree requirements:* For doctorate, dissertation, comprehensive exam required. *Entrance requirements:* For doctorate, GRE General Test. *Application deadline:* Applications are processed on a rolling basis. Application fee: $30 ($50 for international students). *Financial aid:* In 1998–99, 2 fellowships, 2 research assistantships, 21 teaching assistantships were awarded. Financial aid applicants required to submit FAFSA. *Unit head:* Herbert W. Hethcote, Chair, 319-335-0790.

University of Kansas, Graduate School, College of Liberal Arts and Sciences, Department of Mathematics, Program in Applied Mathematics and Statistics, Lawrence, KS 66045. Offers MA, PhD. *Degree requirements:* For master's, thesis or alternative required, foreign language not required; for doctorate, dissertation required. *Entrance requirements:* For master's and doctorate, TOEFL (minimum score of 570 required). Application fee: $25. *Financial aid:* Fellowships, research assistantships, teaching assistantships, institutionally-sponsored loans available. Aid available to part-time students. Financial aid application deadline: 2/1. *Application contact:* Daniel Katz, Graduate Director, 785-864-4324.

University of Manitoba, Faculty of Graduate Studies, Faculty of Science, Department of Applied Mathematics, Winnipeg, MB R3T 2N2, Canada. Offers M Sc. *Unit head:* R. S. C. Wong, Head.

University of Maryland, Baltimore County, Graduate School, Department of Mathematics and Statistics, Program in Applied Mathematics, Baltimore, MD 21250-5398. Offers MS, PhD. *Students:* 12 full-time (4 women), 8 part-time (2 women); includes 2 minority (1 African American, 1 Asian American or Pacific Islander), 7 international. 38 applicants, 34% accepted. In 1998, 4 master's, 1 doctorate awarded. *Degree requirements:* For master's, foreign language and thesis not required; for doctorate, dissertation required, foreign language not required. *Entrance requirements:* For master's and doctorate, GRE General Test, GRE Subject Test, TOEFL, minimum GPA of 3.0. *Application deadline:* For fall admission, 2/15. Applications are processed on a rolling basis. Application fee: $45. *Faculty research:* Functional and numerical analysis, computational intelligence, image analysis. *Unit head:* Trudy Lindsey, Director, Graduate Admission and Records, 301-405-4198, Fax: 301-314-9305, E-mail: grschool@deans.umd.edu. *Application contact:* Dr. Nagaraj Neerchal, Director of Graduate Programs, 410-455-2437.

University of Maryland, College Park, Graduate School, College of Computer, Mathematical and Physical Sciences, Department of Mathematics, Applied Mathematics Program, College Park, MD 20742-5045. Offers MA, PhD. *Students:* 46 full-time (19 women), 34 part-time (14 women); includes 20 minority (12 African Americans, 7 Asian Americans or Pacific Islanders, 1 Hispanic American), 21 international. 62 applicants, 34% accepted. In 1998, 12 master's, 10 doctorates awarded. *Degree requirements:* For master's, thesis or alternative, seminar required, foreign language not required; for doctorate, dissertation, exams, seminars required. *Entrance requirements:* For master's, minimum GPA of 3.0. *Application deadline:* Applications are processed on a rolling basis. Application fee: $50 ($70 for international students). Tuition, state resident: part-time $272 per credit hour. Tuition, nonresident: part-time $475 per credit hour. Required fees: $632; $379 per year. *Financial aid:* Fellowships, teaching assistantships available. Financial aid applicants required to submit FAFSA. *Unit head:* Dr. Bruce Kellogg, Director, 301-405-5062, Fax: 301-314-0872. *Application contact:* Trudy Lindsey, Director, Graduate Admission and Records, 301-405-4198, Fax: 301-314-9305, E-mail: grschool@deans.umd.edu.

University of Massachusetts Amherst, Graduate School, College of Natural Sciences and Mathematics, Department of Mathematics and Statistics, Program in Applied Mathematics,

Amherst, MA 01003. Offers MS. *Students:* 8 full-time (3 women), 1 part-time; includes 1 minority (Asian American or Pacific Islander), 3 international. Average age 25. 14 applicants, 57% accepted. In 1998, 1 degree awarded. *Degree requirements:* For master's, foreign language and thesis not required. *Application deadline:* For fall admission, 2/1 (priority date). Applications are processed on a rolling basis. Application fee: $40. Tuition, state resident: full-time $2,640; part-time $165 per credit. Tuition, nonresident: full-time $9,756; part-time $407 per credit. Required fees: $1,221 per term. One-time fee: $110. Full-time tuition and fees vary according to course load, campus/location and reciprocity agreements. *Financial aid:* Fellowships with full tuition reimbursements, research assistantships with full tuition reimbursements, teaching assistantships with full tuition reimbursements, career-related internships or fieldwork, Federal Work-Study, grants, scholarships, traineeships, and unspecified assistantships available. Aid available to part-time students. Financial aid application deadline: 2/1. *Unit head:* Dr. James Humphreys, Director, 413-545-2282, Fax: 413-545-1801, E-mail: jeh@math.umass.edu.

University of Massachusetts Lowell, Graduate School, College of Arts and Sciences, Department of Mathematics, Lowell, MA 01854-2881. Offers applied mathematics (MS); mathematics (MS). Part-time programs available. *Faculty:* 35 full-time (9 women), 2 part-time (0 women). *Students:* 3 full-time (0 women), 40 part-time (16 women); includes 3 minority (all Asian Americans or Pacific Islanders), 1 international. *Degree requirements:* For master's, foreign language and thesis not required. *Entrance requirements:* For master's, GRE General Test. *Application deadline:* For fall admission, 4/1 (priority date); for spring admission, 10/1. Applications are processed on a rolling basis. Application fee: $20 ($35 for international students). *Unit head:* Dr. Kenneth Levasseur, Chair, 978-934-2436, E-mail: kenneth_levasseur@woods.uml.edu. *Application contact:* Dr. James Graham-Eagle, Coordinator, 978-934-2712, E-mail: james_graham-eagle@woods.uml.edu.

The University of Memphis, Graduate School, College of Arts and Sciences, Department of Mathematical Sciences, Memphis, TN 38152. Offers applied mathematics (MS); applied statistics (PhD); computer science (PhD); computer sciences (MS); mathematics (MS, PhD); statistics (MS, PhD). *Faculty:* 35 full-time (3 women), 2 part-time (1 woman). *Students:* 73 full-time (23 women), 37 part-time (9 women); includes 10 minority (5 African Americans, 5 Asian Americans or Pacific Islanders), 77 international. Terminal master's awarded for partial completion of doctoral program. *Degree requirements:* For master's, comprehensive exams required, thesis not required; for doctorate, dissertation, oral exams required. *Entrance requirements:* For master's, GRE General Test, MAT, TOEFL (minimum score of 550 required), minimum GPA of 2.5; for doctorate, GRE General Test, TOEFL (minimum score of 550 required). *Application deadline:* For fall admission, 8/1; for spring admission, 12/1. Applications are processed on a rolling basis. Application fee: $25 ($50 for international students). Tuition, state resident: full-time $3,410; part-time $178 per credit hour. Tuition, nonresident: full-time $8,670; part-time $408 per credit hour. Tuition and fees vary according to program. *Unit head:* Dr. Jerome A. Goldstein, Chairman, 901-678-2482, Fax: 901-678-2480, E-mail: goldstej@msci.memphis.edu. *Application contact:* Dr. Fernanda M. Botelho, Coordinator of Graduate Studies, 901-678-2482, Fax: 901-678-2480, E-mail: lisa@msci.memphis.edu.

University of Minnesota, Duluth, Graduate School, College of Science and Engineering, Department of Mathematics and Statistics, Duluth, MN 55812-2496. Offers applied and computational mathematics (MS). Part-time programs available. *Faculty:* 16 full-time (2 women). *Students:* 13 full-time (6 women), 1 (woman) part-time; includes 9 minority (8 Asian Americans or Pacific Islanders, 1 Hispanic American) Average age 24. 15 applicants, 100% accepted. In 1998, 7 degrees awarded. *Degree requirements:* For master's, thesis or alternative required, foreign language not required. *Entrance requirements:* For master's, GRE General Test (average 750 quantitative), TOEFL (minimum score of 550 required), minimum GPA of 3.0. *Average time to degree:* Master's–2 years full-time, 4 years part-time. *Application deadline:* For fall admission, 3/1 (priority date); for spring admission, 11/15. Applications are processed on a rolling basis. Application fee: $50 ($55 for international students). *Financial aid:* In 1998–99, 1 fellowship (averaging $1,710 per year), 5 research assistantships with full tuition reimbursements (averaging $9,383 per year), 13 teaching assistantships with full tuition reimbursements (averaging $9,383 per year) were awarded.; career-related internships or fieldwork, Federal Work-Study, grants, institutionally-sponsored loans, scholarships, traineeships, and unspecified assistantships also available. Aid available to part-time students. Financial aid application deadline: 3/1. *Faculty research:* Discrete mathematics, diagnostic markers, combinatorics, biostatistics, mathematical modelling and scientific computation. Total annual research expenditures: $453,493. *Unit head:* Dr. John R. Greene, Director of Graduate Studies, 218-726-6328, Fax: 218-726-8399, E-mail: jgreene@d.umn.edu. *Application contact:* Dr. Barry R. James, Admissions Director, 218-726-7998, Fax: 218-726-8399, E-mail: bjames@d.umn.edu.

Announcement: The program in applied mathematics and statistics emphasizes the role of mathematical modeling in science and engineering. It endeavors to prepare graduates for jobs in industry, government, and teaching, as well as for subsequent PhD studies. Within the department are 8 Sun Workstations of various configurations, 12 Silicon Graphics workstations, and a variety of Apple G3 and Intel-based PCs. There is also access to the computing resources of the Minnesota Supercomputer Institute. Faculty research includes graph theory, combinatorics, number theory, scientific computation, dynamical systems, control theory, numerical methods, statistics, biostatistics, and probability.

University of Missouri–Columbia, Graduate School, College of Arts and Sciences, Department of Mathematics, Program in Applied Mathematics, Columbia, MO 65211. Offers MS. *Students:* 9 full-time (3 women), 1 (woman) part-time; includes 1 minority (African American), 2 international. In 1998, 4 degrees awarded. *Degree requirements:* For master's, thesis required, foreign language not required. *Entrance requirements:* For master's, GRE General Test, minimum GPA of 3.0. *Application deadline:* Applications are processed on a rolling basis. Application fee: $30 ($50 for international students). *Financial aid:* Fellowships, research assistantships, teaching assistantships, institutionally-sponsored loans available. *Unit head:* Dr. Nakhle Asmar, Director of Graduate Studies, Department of Mathematics, 573-882-6221.

University of Missouri–Rolla, Graduate School, College of Arts and Sciences, Department of Mathematics and Statistics, Program in Applied Mathematics, Rolla, MO 65409-0910. Offers MS. *Students:* 9 full-time (2 women); includes 1 minority (African American) Average age 28. 10 applicants, 100% accepted. In 1998, 10 degrees awarded. *Degree requirements:* For master's, thesis or alternative required, foreign language not required. *Entrance requirements:* For master's, GRE General Test, GRE Subject Test. *Application deadline:* For fall admission, 7/1. Applications are processed on a rolling basis. Application fee: $25. Electronic applications accepted. *Financial aid:* In 1998–99, 9 teaching assistantships with partial tuition reimbursements (averaging $12,985 per year) were awarded.; fellowships, research assistantships, institutionally-sponsored loans also available. *Faculty research:* Analysis, differential equations, statistics, topological dynamics. *Unit head:* Da Ming Zhu, Principal Graduate Adviser, 816-235-2509, Fax: 816-235-5221, E-mail: zhud@cctr.umkc.edu. *Application contact:* Dr. V. A. Samaranayake, Director of Graduate Studies, 573-341-4658, Fax: 573-341-4741, E-mail: vsam@umr.edu.

University of Missouri–St. Louis, Graduate School, College of Arts and Sciences, Department of Mathematical Sciences, St. Louis, MO 63121-4499. Offers applied mathematics (MA, PhD); computer science (MS). Part-time and evening/weekend programs available. *Faculty:* 20. *Students:* 1 (woman) full-time, 21 part-time (11 women); includes 4 minority (3 African Americans, 1 Asian American or Pacific Islander), 1 international. *Degree requirements:* For master's, thesis optional, foreign language not required; for doctorate, dissertation required, foreign language not required. *Entrance requirements:* For master's, GRE if no BS in computer science; for doctorate, GRE General Test. *Application deadline:* For fall admission, 5/1 (priority date); for spring admission, 12/1. Applications are processed on a rolling basis. Application fee: $25 ($40 for international students). Electronic applications accepted. *Unit head:* Dr. Grant Welland, Director of Graduate Studies, 314-516-5741, Fax: 314-516-5400, E-mail: welland@eads.umsl.edu. *Application contact:* Graduate Admissions, 314-516-5458, Fax: 314-516-6759, E-mail: gradadm@umsl.edu.

The University of Montana–Missoula, Graduate School, College of Arts and Sciences, Department of Mathematical Sciences, Missoula, MT 59812-0002. Offers algebra (MA, PhD); analysis (MA, PhD); applied mathematics (MA, PhD); mathematics (MAT); mathematics education (PhD); operations research (MA, PhD); statistics (MA, PhD). Part-time programs available. *Faculty:* 20 full-time (3 women). *Students:* 25 full-time (11 women), 2 part-time (1 woman); includes 6 minority (5 Asian Americans or Pacific Islanders, 1 Native American) Terminal master's awarded for partial completion of doctoral program. *Degree requirements:* For master's, foreign language and thesis not required; for doctorate, dissertation required. *Entrance requirements:* For master's and doctorate, GRE General Test. *Application deadline:* For fall admission, 3/1 (priority date). Application fee: $45. *Unit head:* Dr. Gloria Hewitt, Chair, 406-243-5311.

University of Nevada, Las Vegas, Graduate College, College of Science, Department of Mathematical Sciences, Las Vegas, NV 89154-9900. Offers applied mathematics (MS); mathematics (MS); pure mathematics (MS); statistics (MS). Part-time programs available. *Faculty:* 27 full-time (4 women). *Students:* 12 full-time (3 women), 5 part-time (1 woman); includes 1 minority (Asian American or Pacific Islander), 2 international. *Degree requirements:* For master's, oral exam required, thesis optional, foreign language not required. *Entrance requirements:* For master's, minimum GPA of 3.0 during previous 2 years, 2.75 overall. *Application deadline:* For fall admission, 6/15 (priority date); for spring admission, 11/15. Applications are processed on a rolling basis. Application fee: $40 ($95 for international students). *Unit head:* Dr. Rohan Dalpadatu, Chair, 702-895-3567. *Application contact:* Graduate College Admissions Evaluator, 702-895-3320.

University of New Hampshire, Graduate School, College of Engineering and Physical Sciences, Department of Mathematics, Durham, NH 03824. Offers applied mathematics (MS); mathematics (MS, MST, PhD); mathematics education (PhD). *Faculty:* 24 full-time. *Students:* 15 full-time (7 women), 9 part-time (6 women), 2 international. Terminal master's awarded for partial completion of doctoral program. *Degree requirements:* For master's, foreign language and thesis not required; for doctorate, 2 foreign languages (computer language can substitute for one), dissertation required. *Application deadline:* For fall admission, 4/1 (priority date). Applications are processed on a rolling basis. Application fee: $50. Tuition, area resident: Full-time $5,750; part-time $319 per credit. Tuition, state resident: full-time $8,625. Tuition, nonresident: full-time $14,640; part-time $598 per credit. Required fees: $224 per semester. Tuition and fees vary according to course load, degree level and program. *Unit head:* Dr. Kenneth I. Appel, Chairperson, 603-862-2673. *Application contact:* Dr. Edward K. Hinson, Graduate Coordinator, 603-862-2688, E-mail: ekh@christa.unh.edu.

University of North Carolina at Charlotte, Graduate School, College of Arts and Sciences, Department of Mathematics, Charlotte, NC 28223-0001. Offers applied mathematics (MS, PhD); applied statistics (MS); mathematics (MA); mathematics education (MA). *Accreditation:* NCATE (one or more programs are accredited). Part-time and evening/weekend programs available. *Faculty:* 43 full-time (6 women). *Students:* 22 full-time (8 women), 24 part-time (14 women); includes 6 minority (2 African Americans, 4 Asian Americans or Pacific Islanders), 16 international. *Degree requirements:* For master's, thesis or written comprehensive exam required; for doctorate, dissertation required. *Entrance requirements:* For master's, GRE General Test or MAT, minimum GPA of 3.0 in undergraduate major, 2.75 overall. *Application deadline:* For fall admission, 7/15; for spring admission, 11/15. Applications are processed on a rolling basis. Application fee: $35. Electronic applications accepted. *Unit head:* Dr. Ram C. Tiwari, Chair, 704-547-4551, Fax: 704-547-6415, E-mail: rtiwari@email.uncc.edu. *Application contact:* Kathy Barringer, Assistant Director of Graduate Admissions, 704-547-3366, Fax: 704-547-3279, E-mail: gradadm@email.uncc.edu.

See in-depth description on page 779.

University of Pittsburgh, Faculty of Arts and Sciences, Department of Mathematics, Program in Applied Mathematics, Pittsburgh, PA 15260. Offers MA, MS. Part-time programs available. *Faculty:* 40 full-time (6 women), 20 part-time (7 women). 103 applicants, 28% accepted. In 1998, 1 degree awarded. *Degree requirements:* For master's, thesis (for some programs), oral comprehensive exam required, foreign language not required. *Entrance requirements:* For master's, GRE General Test, TOEFL (minimum score of 550 required), minimum GPA of 3.0. *Average time to degree:* Master's–2 years full-time, 3 years part-time. *Application deadline:* For fall admission, 2/1 (priority date); for spring admission, 10/1 (priority date). Applications are processed on a rolling basis. Application fee: $30 ($40 for international students). *Financial aid:* Fellowships, research assistantships, teaching assistantships, grants, institutionally-sponsored loans, scholarships, and tuition waivers (partial) available. Financial aid application deadline: 2/1. *Faculty research:* Applied analysis, scientific computing, mathematical biology, discrete mathematics. Total annual research expenditures: $513,200. *Unit head:* Gayle Asburry, Graduate Secretary, 541-346-0992. *Application contact:* Molly Williams, Administrator, 412-624-1175, Fax: 412-624-8397, E-mail: mollyw@vms.cis.pitt.edu.

University of Puerto Rico, Mayagüez Campus, Graduate Studies, College of Arts and Sciences, Department of Mathematics, Mayagüez, PR 00681-5000. Offers applied mathematics (MS); computational sciences (MS); pure mathematics (MS); statistics (MS). Part-time programs available. *Degree requirements:* For master's, one foreign language, comprehensive exam required, thesis optional. *Faculty research:* Automata theory, linear algebra, logic.

University of Rhode Island, Graduate School, College of Business Administration, Kingston, RI 02881. Offers accounting (MS); applied mathematics (PhD); finance (MBA); international business (MBA); international sports management (MBA); management (MBA); management science (MBA), including management information systems, manufacturing; marketing (MBA). *Degree requirements:* For master's and doctorate, foreign language and thesis not required. *Entrance requirements:* For master's and doctorate, GMAT, TOEFL (minimum score of 575 required).

University of Southern California, Graduate School, College of Letters, Arts and Sciences, Department of Mathematics, Program in Applied Mathematics, Los Angeles, CA 90089. Offers MA, MS, PhD. *Students:* 23 full-time (5 women), 7 part-time (1 woman); includes 2 minority (both Asian Americans or Pacific Islanders), 20 international. Average age 29. 27 applicants, 26% accepted. In 1998, 8 master's, 4 doctorates awarded. *Degree requirements:* For doctorate, dissertation required. *Entrance requirements:* For master's and doctorate, GRE General Test. *Application deadline:* For fall admission, 7/1 (priority date); for spring admission, 12/1. Application fee: $55. Tuition: Full-time $22,198; part-time $748 per unit. Required fees: $406. Tuition and fees vary according to program. *Financial aid:* In 1998–99, 6 research assistantships, 22 teaching assistantships were awarded.; fellowships, Federal Work-Study, institutionally-sponsored loans, and scholarships also available. Aid available to part-time students. Financial aid application deadline: 2/15; financial aid applicants required to submit FAFSA. *Unit head:* Dr. Chunming Wang, Head, 213-740-2400.

University of South Florida, Graduate School, College of Arts and Sciences, Department of Mathematics, Tampa, FL 33620-9951. Offers applied mathematics (PhD); mathematics (MA, PhD). Part-time and evening/weekend programs available. *Faculty:* 27 full-time (4 women). *Students:* 39 full-time (11 women), 6 part-time (2 women); includes 3 minority (2 African Americans, 1 Hispanic American), 20 international. Terminal master's awarded for partial completion of doctoral program. *Degree requirements:* For master's, one foreign language required, (computer language can substitute), thesis optional; for doctorate, 2 foreign languages (computer language can substitute for one), dissertation required. *Entrance requirements:* For master's, GRE General Test (minimum score of 650 on quantitative section, 1100 combined required), minimum GPA of 3.0 in mathematics course work (undergraduate), 3.5 in (graduate); for doctorate, GRE General Test (minimum score of 650 on quantitative section, 1100 combined required). *Application deadline:* For fall admission, 6/1; for spring admission, 10/15.

Applied Mathematics

University of South Florida (continued)

Application fee: $20. Electronic applications accepted. Tuition, state resident: part-time $148 per credit hour. Tuition, nonresident: part-time $509 per credit hour. *Unit head:* Marcus McWaters, Chairperson, 813-974-9530, Fax: 813-974-2700, E-mail: marcus@chuma.cas.usf.edu. *Application contact:* India Barnes, Graduate Program Assistant, 813-974-5329, Fax: 813-974-2700, E-mail: ga@math.usf.edu.

University of Tennessee, Knoxville, Graduate School, College of Arts and Sciences, Department of Mathematics, Knoxville, TN 37996. Offers applied mathematics (MS); mathematical ecology (PhD); mathematics (M Math, MS, PhD). Part-time programs available. *Faculty:* 49 full-time (4 women), 3 part-time (1 woman). *Students:* 62 full-time (23 women), 25 part-time (7 women); includes 8 minority (7 African Americans, 1 Asian American or Pacific Islander), 20 international. *Degree requirements:* For master's, thesis or alternative required, foreign language not required; for doctorate, dissertation required. *Entrance requirements:* For master's and doctorate, TOEFL (minimum score of 550 required), minimum GPA of 2.7. *Application deadline:* For fall admission, 2/1 (priority date). Applications are processed on a rolling basis. Application fee: $35. Electronic applications accepted. *Unit head:* Dr. John B. Conway, Head, 423-974-2464, Fax: 423-974-6576, E-mail: gradprogram@novell.math.utk.edu.

University of Tennessee Space Institute, Graduate Programs, Program in Applied Mathematics, Tullahoma, TN 37388-9700. Offers MS. Part-time programs available. *Faculty:* 3 full-time (0 women). *Students:* 4 full-time (3 women), 1 part-time; includes 1 minority (African American) 6 applicants, 83% accepted. In 1998, 1 degree awarded. *Degree requirements:* For master's, thesis required (for some programs), foreign language not required. *Application deadline:* Applications are processed on a rolling basis. Application fee: $35. *Financial aid:* Fellowships, research assistantships, career-related internships or fieldwork, Federal Work-Study, and tuition waivers (partial) available. Financial aid applicants required to submit FAFSA. *Unit head:* Dr. K. C. Reddy, Degree Program Chairman, 931-393-7318, Fax: 931-393-7444, E-mail: kreddy@utsi.edu. *Application contact:* Dr. Edwin M. Gleason, Assistant Dean for Admissions and Student Affairs, 931-393-7432, Fax: 931-393-7346, E-mail: egleason@utsi.edu.

The University of Texas at Austin, Graduate School, Program in Computational and Applied Mathematics, Austin, TX 78712-1111. Offers MA, PhD. *Faculty:* 62 full-time (7 women). *Students:* 24 full-time (5 women); includes 7 minority (4 Asian Americans or Pacific Islanders, 3 Hispanic Americans), 4 international. Average age 28. 58 applicants, 21% accepted. In 1998, 4 master's awarded (0% continued full-time study); 1 doctorate awarded (100% found work related to degree). Terminal master's awarded for partial completion of doctoral program. *Degree requirements:* For master's, computer language required, thesis optional, foreign language not required; for doctorate, computer language, dissertation, 3 area qualifying exams required, foreign language not required. *Average time to degree:* Master's–3 years full-time; doctorate–6 years full-time. *Application deadline:* For fall admission, 2/1. Application fee: $50 ($75 for international students). Electronic applications accepted. *Financial aid:* In 1998–99, 10 fellowships with full and partial tuition reimbursements, 5 research assistantships with full and partial tuition reimbursements (averaging $10,000 per year), 5 teaching assistantships with full and partial tuition reimbursements (averaging $11,000 per year) were awarded. Financial aid application deadline: 2/1. *Unit head:* Clint Dawson, Graduate Adviser, 512-475-8627, E-mail: clint@ticam.utexas.edu. *Application contact:* Kathryn Petro, Graduate Coordinator, 512-471-7386, Fax: 512-471-8694, E-mail: camgrad@ticam.utexas.edu.

The University of Texas at Dallas, School of Natural Sciences and Mathematics, Programs in Mathematical Sciences, Richardson, TX 75083-0688. Offers applied mathematics (MS, PhD); engineering mathematics (MS); mathematical science (MS, PhD); statistics (MS, PhD). Part-time and evening/weekend programs available. *Students:* 22 full-time (7 women), 23 part-time (13 women); includes 6 minority (3 African Americans, 1 Asian American or Pacific Islander, 2 Hispanic Americans), 11 international. *Degree requirements:* For master's, minimum GPA of 3.0 required, thesis optional, foreign language not required; for doctorate, dissertation, minimum GPA of 3.0 required, foreign language not required. *Entrance requirements:* For master's, GRE General Test (minimum score of 500 on verbal section, 550 on quantitative required), TOEFL (minimum score of 550 required), minimum GPA of 3.0 in upper-level course work in field; for doctorate, GRE General Test (minimum score of 550 on verbal section, 650 on quantitative required), TOEFL (minimum score of 550 required), minimum GPA of 3.5 in upper-level course work in field. *Application deadline:* For fall admission, 7/15; for spring admission, 11/15. Applications are processed on a rolling basis. Application fee: $25 ($75 for international students). *Unit head:* Dr. M. Ali Hooshyar, Head, 972-883-2171, Fax: 972-883-6622, E-mail: utdmath@utdallas.edu.

See in-depth description on page 795.

University of Toledo, Graduate School, College of Arts and Sciences, Department of Mathematics, Toledo, OH 43606-3398. Offers applied mathematics (MS); mathematics (MA, MS Ed, PhD); statistics (MS). Part-time programs available. *Degree requirements:* For master's, thesis not required; for doctorate, dissertation required. *Entrance requirements:* For master's and doctorate, GRE General Test, GRE Subject Test. Electronic applications accepted. *Faculty research:* Topology.

University of Victoria, Faculty of Graduate Studies, Faculty of Science, Department of Mathematics and Statistics, Victoria, BC V8W 2Y2, Canada. Offers applied mathematics (M Sc, MA, PhD); pure mathematics (M Sc, MA, PhD); statistics (M Sc, MA). Part-time programs available. *Faculty:* 25 full-time (3 women), 7 part-time (2 women). *Students:* 24 full-time (4 women), 1 part-time, 8 international. *Degree requirements:* For master's, thesis required; for doctorate, one foreign language, dissertation, 3 qualifying exams required. *Application deadline:* For fall admission, 5/31 (priority date). Applications are processed on a rolling basis. Application fee: $50. *Unit head:* Dr. R. Illner, Chair, 250-721-7436, Fax: 250-721-8962. *Application contact:* Dr. J. Phillips, Graduate Adviser, 250-721-7450, Fax: 250-721-8962, E-mail: phillips@math.uvic.ca.

University of Washington, Graduate School, College of Arts and Sciences, Department of Applied Mathematics, Seattle, WA 98195. Offers MS, PhD. *Faculty:* 12 full-time (1 woman), 6 part-time (1 woman). *Students:* 43 full-time (17 women); includes 7 minority (2 African Americans, 2 Asian Americans or Pacific Islanders, 2 Hispanic Americans, 1 Native American), 6 international. Average age 27. 61 applicants, 25% accepted. In 1998, 11 master's awarded (100% found work related to degree); 4 doctorates awarded (100% entered university research/teaching). Terminal master's awarded for partial completion of doctoral program. *Degree requirements:* For master's, computer language required, thesis optional, foreign language not required; for doctorate, computer language, dissertation required, foreign language not required. *Entrance requirements:* For master's, GRE, TOEFL, minimum GPA of 3.0; for doctorate, GRE, TOEFL (minimum score of 500 required), minimum GPA of 3.0. *Average time to degree:* Master's–1 year full-time; doctorate–5 years full-time. *Application deadline:* For fall admission, 2/15. Applications are processed on a rolling basis. Application fee: $50. Tuition, state resident: full-time $5,196; part-time $475 per credit. Tuition, nonresident: full-time $13,485; part-time $1,285 per credit. Required fees: $387; $38 per credit. Tuition and fees vary according to course load. *Financial aid:* In 1998–99, 40 students received aid, including 1 fellowship, 7 research assistantships, 18 teaching assistantships; Federal Work-Study, grants, institutionally-sponsored loans, and tuition waivers (full and partial) also available. Financial aid application deadline: 2/1. *Faculty research:* Mathematical modeling for physical, biological, social, and engineering sciences; development of mathematical methods for analysis, including perturbation, asymptotic, transform, vocational, and numerical methods. *Unit head:* Ka-Kit Tung, Chair, 206-543-5493, Fax: 206-685-1440, E-mail: tung@amath.washington.edu. *Application contact:* Loyce M. Adams, Graduate Coordinator, 206-543-5077, Fax: 206-685-1440, E-mail: adams@amath.washington.edu.

University of Waterloo, Graduate Studies, Faculty of Mathematics, Department of Applied Mathematics, Waterloo, ON N2L 3G1, Canada. Offers M Math, PhD. Part-time programs available. *Faculty:* 20 full-time (4 women), 16 part-time (1 woman). *Students:* 27 full-time (7 women). 26 applicants, 54% accepted. In 1998, 5 master's awarded (% continued full-time study); 2 doctorates awarded. *Degree requirements:* For master's, research paper or thesis required; for doctorate, dissertation required, foreign language not required. *Entrance requirements:* For master's, TOEFL (minimum score of 600 required), honors degree in field, minimum B+ average; for doctorate, TOEFL (minimum score of 600 required), master's degree. *Average time to degree:* Master's–2 years full-time; doctorate–3.5 years full-time. *Application deadline:* For fall admission, 3/31. Applications are processed on a rolling basis. Application fee: $50. *Expenses:* Tuition and fees charges are reported in Canadian dollars. Tuition, state resident: full-time $3,168 Canadian dollars; part-time $792 Canadian dollars per term. Tuition, nonresident: full-time $8,000 Canadian dollars; part-time $2,000 Canadian dollars. Required fees: $45 Canadian dollars per term. Tuition and fees vary according to program. *Financial aid:* In 1998–99, research assistantships (averaging $7,000 per year), teaching assistantships (averaging $10,000 per year) were awarded. *Faculty research:* Differential equations, quantum theory, statistical mechanics, fluid mechanics, relativity, control theory. Total annual research expenditures: $95,890. *Unit head:* Dr. S. Sivaloganathan, Associate Chair, 519-888-4567 Ext. 3248, Fax: 519-746-4319, E-mail: ssivalog@sumathi.uwaterloo.ca. *Application contact:* Helen A. Warren, Graduate Secretary, 519-888-4567 Ext. 3170, Fax: 519-746-4319, E-mail: amgrad@jeeves.uwaterloo.ca.

The University of Western Ontario, Faculty of Graduate Studies, Physical Sciences Division, Department of Applied Mathematics, London, ON N6A 5B8, Canada. Offers M Sc, PhD. *Degree requirements:* For master's, thesis or alternative required, foreign language not required; for doctorate, dissertation required, foreign language not required. *Entrance requirements:* For master's and doctorate, minimum B average. *Faculty research:* Fluid dynamics, mathmatical and computational methods, theoretical physics.

Virginia Commonwealth University, School of Graduate Studies, College of Humanities and Sciences, Department of Mathematical Sciences, Program in Applied Mathematics, Richmond, VA 23284-9005. Offers MS. *Students:* 6 full-time (4 women), 21 part-time (6 women); includes 8 minority (2 African Americans, 6 Asian Americans or Pacific Islanders) *Degree requirements:* Foreign language not required. *Entrance requirements:* For master's, GRE General Test, GRE Subject Test, TOEFL. *Application deadline:* For fall admission, 7/1; for spring admission, 11/15. Applications are processed on a rolling basis. Application fee: $30. Tuition, state resident: full-time $4,031; part-time $224 per credit hour. Tuition, nonresident: full-time $11,946; part-time $664 per credit hour. Required fees: $1,081; $40 per credit hour. Tuition and fees vary according to campus/location and program. *Unit head:* Marilyn F. Bishop, Graduate Program Director, 804-828-1819, Fax: 804-828-7073. *Application contact:* Dr. James A. Wood, Director of Graduate Studies, 804-828-1301, Fax: 804-828-8785, E-mail: jawood@vcu.edu.

Virginia Polytechnic Institute and State University, Graduate School, College of Arts and Sciences, Department of Mathematics, Blacksburg, VA 24061. Offers applied mathematics (MS, PhD); mathematical physics (MS, PhD); pure mathematics (MS, PhD). Part-time programs available. *Faculty:* 55 full-time (5 women). *Students:* 66 full-time (26 women), 81 part-time (45 women); includes 12 minority (10 African Americans, 2 Asian Americans or Pacific Islanders), 14 international. Terminal master's awarded for partial completion of doctoral program. *Degree requirements:* For master's, thesis required (for some programs), foreign language not required; for doctorate, dissertation required. *Entrance requirements:* For master's and doctorate, TOEFL. *Application deadline:* For fall admission, 12/1 (priority date). Applications are processed on a rolling basis. Application fee: $25. *Unit head:* Dr. Robert F. Olin, Head, 540-231-6536, E-mail: olin@math.vt.edu. *Application contact:* Dr. E. L. Green, Graduate Administrator, 540-231-6536.

See in-depth description on page 801.

Washington State University, Graduate School, College of Sciences, Department of Pure and Applied Mathematics, Pullman, WA 99164. Offers MS, DA, PhD. *Faculty:* 31 full-time (4 women), 4 part-time (1 woman). *Students:* 31 full-time (13 women), 1 part-time; includes 2 minority (1 African American, 1 Asian American or Pacific Islander), 7 international. In 1998, 6 master's, 4 doctorates awarded. *Degree requirements:* For master's, thesis or alternative, core exams, oral exam required, foreign language not required; for doctorate, dissertation, core exams, oral exam required. *Entrance requirements:* For master's and doctorate, GRE General Test, GRE Subject Test, TOEFL (minimum score of 600 required), minimum GPA of 3.0. *Average time to degree:* Master's–2 years full-time; doctorate–4 years full-time. *Application deadline:* For fall admission, 3/15 (priority date). Applications are processed on a rolling basis. Application fee: $35. *Financial aid:* In 1998–99, 27 teaching assistantships were awarded.; fellowships, research assistantships, career-related internships or fieldwork, Federal Work-Study, institutionally-sponsored loans, tuition waivers (partial), and teaching associateships also available. Financial aid application deadline: 4/1; financial aid applicants required to submit FAFSA. *Faculty research:* Computational mathematics, operations research, modeling in the natural sciences, applied statistics. Total annual research expenditures: $378,424. *Unit head:* Dr. Valipuram Manoranjan, Chair, 509-335-6868, Fax: 509-335-1188. *Application contact:* Bonnie Collins, Coordinator, 509-335-6868, Fax: 509-335-1188, E-mail: bonnie@wsu.edu.

See in-depth description on page 805.

Wayne State University, Graduate School, College of Science, Department of Mathematics, Program in Applied Mathematics, Detroit, MI 48202. Offers MA, PhD. *Degree requirements:* For doctorate, dissertation required.

Western Michigan University, Graduate College, College of Arts and Sciences, Department of Mathematics and Statistics, Program in Applied Mathematics, Kalamazoo, MI 49008. Offers MS. *Students:* 1 full-time (0 women), 7 part-time (4 women); includes 2 minority (both Asian Americans or Pacific Islanders), 3 international. 5 applicants, 80% accepted. In 1998, 3 degrees awarded. *Degree requirements:* For master's, oral exams required, thesis not required. *Application deadline:* For fall admission, 2/15 (priority date). Applications are processed on a rolling basis. Application fee: $25. *Financial aid:* Fellowships, research assistantships, teaching assistantships, Federal Work-Study available. Financial aid application deadline: 2/15; financial aid applicants required to submit FAFSA. *Application contact:* Paula J. Boodt, Coordinator, Graduate Admissions and Recruitment, 616-387-2000, Fax: 616-387-2355, E-mail: paula.boodt@wmich.edu.

Wichita State University, Graduate School, Fairmount College of Liberal Arts and Sciences, Department of Mathematics and Statistics, Wichita, KS 67260. Offers applied mathematics (PhD); mathematics (MS); statistics (MS). Part-time programs available. *Faculty:* 23 full-time (0 women), 1 part-time (0 women). *Students:* 22 full-time (7 women), 15 part-time (7 women); includes 2 minority (1 African American, 1 Asian American or Pacific Islander), 15 international. *Degree requirements:* For master's, comprehensive exam required, thesis optional, foreign language not required; for doctorate, computer language, dissertation required. *Entrance requirements:* For master's, GRE, TOEFL (minimum score of 550 required); for doctorate, GRE Subject Test, TOEFL (minimum score of 550 required). *Application deadline:* For fall admission, 7/1 (priority date); for spring admission, 1/1. Applications are processed on a rolling basis. Application fee: $25 ($40 for international students). Electronic applications accepted. *Unit head:* Dr. Buma Fridman, Chairperson, 316-978-3985, Fax: 316-978-3748, E-mail: fridman@twsuvm.uc.twsu.edu. *Application contact:* Dr. Ken Miller, Graduate Coordinator, 316-978-3959, Fax: 316-978-3748, E-mail: miller@twsuvm.uc.twsu.edu.

Worcester Polytechnic Institute, Graduate Studies, Department of Mathematical Science, Worcester, MA 01609-2280. Offers applied mathematics (MS); applied statistics (MS); mathematical science (PhD, Certificate); mathematics (MME). Part-time and evening/weekend programs available. *Faculty:* 25 full-time (3 women). *Students:* 17 full-time (8 women), 11 part-time (1 woman); includes 2 minority (1 African American, 1 Asian American or Pacific Islander), 8 international. *Degree requirements:* For master's, thesis optional, foreign language not required; for doctorate, dissertation required, foreign language not required. *Entrance requirements:* For master's, TOEFL (minimum score of 550 required; average 600). *Application deadline:* For fall admission, 2/15 (priority date); for spring admission, 10/15 (priority date). Applications are processed on a rolling basis. Application fee: $50. Electronic applications accepted. *Unit head:* Dr. Homer Walker, Head, 508-831-5316, Fax: 508-831-5824. *Application contact:* Robert Lipton, Graduate Coordinator, 508-831-5321, Fax: 508-831-5824, E-mail: lipton@wpi.edu.

Wright State University, School of Graduate Studies, College of Science and Mathematics, Department of Mathematics and Statistics, Program in Applied Mathematics, Dayton, OH 45435. Offers MS. *Students:* 1 (woman) full-time, 2 part-time, 1 international. Average age 32. 6 applicants, 67% accepted. In 1998, 2 degrees awarded. *Degree requirements:* For master's, comprehensive exams required, foreign language and thesis not required. *Entrance requirements:* For master's, TOEFL (minimum score of 550 required), bachelor's degree in mathematics or related field. *Application deadline:* Applications are processed on a rolling basis. Application fee: $25. *Financial aid:* Fellowships, research assistantships, teaching assistantships, tuition waivers (full and partial) available. Aid available to part-time students. Financial aid application deadline: 2/15; financial aid applicants required to submit FAFSA. *Faculty research:* Control theory, ordinary differential equations, partial differential equations, numerical analysis, mathematical modeling. *Unit head:* Dr. Thomas P. Svobodny, Director, 937-775-2379, Fax: 937-775-3068.

Yale University, Graduate School of Arts and Sciences, Program in Applied Mathematics, New Haven, CT 06520. Offers M Phil, MS, PhD. *Entrance requirements:* For doctorate, GRE General Test. *Application deadline:* For fall admission, 1/4. Application fee: $65. *Financial aid:* Fellowships, research assistantships available. *Application contact:* Graduate Admissions Office, 203-432-2770.

See in-depth description on page 813.

Biometrics

Cornell University, Graduate School, Graduate Fields of Agriculture and Life Sciences, Field of Biometry, Ithaca, NY 14853-0001. Offers MS, PhD. *Faculty:* 13 full-time. *Students:* 11 full-time (6 women); includes 4 minority (all Hispanic Americans), 5 international. 13 applicants, 38% accepted. In 1998, 1 master's, 1 doctorate awarded. Terminal master's awarded for partial completion of doctoral program. *Degree requirements:* For master's and doctorate, thesis/dissertation required, foreign language not required. *Entrance requirements:* For master's and doctorate, GRE General Test, TOEFL (minimum score of 550 required). *Application deadline:* For fall admission, 2/15. Application fee: $65. Electronic applications accepted. *Financial aid:* In 1998–99, 11 students received aid, including 4 fellowships with full tuition reimbursements available, 3 research assistantships with full tuition reimbursements available, 4 teaching assistantships with full tuition reimbursements available; institutionally-sponsored loans, scholarships, tuition waivers (full and partial), and unspecified assistantships also available. Financial aid applicants required to submit FAFSA. *Faculty research:* Environmental, agricultural, and biological statistics; biomathematics; modern nonparametric statistics; statistical genetics; computational statistics. *Unit head:* Director of Graduate Studies, 607-255-1646. *Application contact:* Graduate Field Assistant, 607-255-8066, E-mail: biometrics@cornell.edu.

Louisiana State University Health Science Center, School of Graduate Studies in New Orleans, Department of Biometry and Genetics, Program in Biometry, New Orleans, LA 70112-2223. Offers MS, PhD, MD/PhD. Part-time programs available. *Faculty:* 7 full-time (0 women). *Students:* 10 full-time (6 women), 3 part-time (2 women); includes 7 minority (5 African Americans, 1 Asian American or Pacific Islander, 1 Hispanic American), 3 international. Average age 27. 10 applicants, 80% accepted. In 1998, 1 master's awarded (0% continued full-time study). Terminal master's awarded for partial completion of doctoral program. *Degree requirements:* For master's and doctorate, computer language, thesis/dissertation required, foreign language not required. *Entrance requirements:* For master's and doctorate, GRE General Test (minimum combined score of 1000 required), TOEFL (minimum score of 550 required). *Average time to degree:* Master's–3 years part-time. *Application deadline:* For fall admission, 4/1 (priority date). Applications are processed on a rolling basis. Application fee: $30. *Financial aid:* In 1998–99, 5 students received aid, including 2 research assistantships with tuition reimbursements available; tuition waivers (full) also available. Financial aid application deadline: 4/1. *Faculty research:* Longitudinal data, repeated measures, missing data, generalized estimating equations, multivariate methods. *Application contact:* Dr. William D. Johnson, Professor, 504-568-6152, Fax: 504-568-8500, E-mail: wjohns1@lsumc.edu.

Medical University of South Carolina, College of Graduate Studies, Department of Biometry and Epidemiology, Charleston, SC 29425-0002. Offers biometrics (MS, PhD); biostatistics (MS, PhD); epidemiology (MS, PhD). *Faculty:* 16 part-time (3 women). *Students:* 37 full-time (18 women); includes 1 minority (African American), 8 international. Average age 33. 21 applicants, 67% accepted. In 1998, 6 master's, 7 doctorates awarded. Terminal master's awarded for partial completion of doctoral program. *Degree requirements:* For master's, thesis, research seminar required; for doctorate, dissertation, teaching and research seminar, oral and written exams required. *Entrance requirements:* For master's and doctorate, GRE General Test (minimum combined score of 1650 on three sections required), GRE Subject Test (international applicants), TOEFL, interview. *Application deadline:* Applications are processed on a rolling basis. Application fee: $55. Electronic applications accepted. *Financial aid:* In 1998–99, 9 fellowships were awarded.; research assistantships, teaching assistantships, Federal Work-Study and tuition waivers (partial) also available. Aid available to part-time students. Financial aid application deadline: 4/1; financial aid applicants required to submit FAFSA. *Faculty research:* Statistical modeling, survival analysis, cardiovascular epidemiology, biomathematics, biomedical computing. *Unit head:* Dr. John Dunbar, Interim Chairman, 843-876-1100. *Application contact:* Julie Johnston, Director of Admissions, 843-792-8710, Fax: 843-792-3764.

Mount Sinai School of Medicine of New York University, Graduate School of Biological Sciences, Department of Biomathematical Sciences, New York, NY 10029-6504. Offers PhD, MD/PhD. *Degree requirements:* For doctorate, computer language, dissertation required, foreign language not required. *Entrance requirements:* For doctorate, GRE General Test, GRE Subject Test, TOEFL.

See in-depth description on page 699.

North Carolina State University, Graduate School, College of Physical and Mathematical Sciences, Program in Biomathematics, Raleigh, NC 27695. Offers biomathematics (M Biomath, MS, PhD); ecology (PhD). Part-time programs available. *Faculty:* 12 full-time (3 women), 7 part-time (1 woman). *Students:* 32 full-time (15 women); includes 1 minority (Hispanic American), 5 international. Average age 29. 11 applicants, 45% accepted. In 1998, 1 master's, 2 doctorates awarded. Terminal master's awarded for partial completion of doctoral program. *Degree requirements:* For master's, thesis or alternative required; for doctorate, dissertation required. *Entrance requirements:* For master's and doctorate, GRE General Test, TOEFL. *Application deadline:* For fall admission, 3/1 (priority date); for spring admission, 9/15. Application fee: $45. *Financial aid:* Fellowships, research assistantships, teaching assistantships, career-related internships or fieldwork available. Financial aid application deadline: 3/1. *Faculty research:* Theory and methods of biological modeling, theoretical biology (genetics), applied biology (wildlife). *Unit head:* Dr. Kenneth H. Pollock, Director of Graduate Programs, 919-515-1957, Fax: 919-515-7591, E-mail: pollock@stat.ncsu.edu.

Announcement: Biomathematics is an interdisciplinary program offering master's and PhD degrees in the development, analysis, and application of mathematical models in biology. Requirements are flexible to accommodate students with backgrounds in the biological, mathematical, or physical sciences. Interdisciplinary research is emphasized, and the program has strong ties with biological and mathematical science departments. Research areas include mathematical and statistical methods (dynamical systems, Markov processes, population sampling) and applications in neurobiology, immunology, toxicology, ecology, pharmacology, agricultural and environmental management, and conservation biology. Graduates find positions in universities, government, and industry. Teaching and research assistantships are available. Further information is available on the World Wide Web at http://www2.ncsu.edu/ncsu/pams/stat/dept.html

Oregon State University, Graduate School, College of Science, Department of Statistics, Corvallis, OR 97331. Offers applied statistics (MA, MS, PhD); biometry (MA, MS, PhD); environmental statistics (MA, MS, PhD); mathematical statistics (MA, MS, PhD); operations research (MA, MAIS, MS); statistics (M Agr, MA, MS, PhD). Part-time programs available. *Faculty:* 14 full-time (4 women). *Degree requirements:* For master's, consulting experience required; for doctorate, dissertation, consulting experience required, foreign language not required. *Entrance requirements:* For master's and doctorate, TOEFL (minimum score of 550 required; 213 for computer-based), minimum GPA of 3.0 in last 90 hours. *Application deadline:* For fall admission, 2/15. Applications are processed on a rolling basis. Application fee: $50. *Unit head:* Dr. Robert Smythe, Chair, 541-737-3366. *Application contact:* Dr. Dawn Peters, Director of Graduate Studies, 541-737-1991, Fax: 541-737-3489, E-mail: statoff@stat.orst.edu.

See in-depth description on page 723.

State University of New York at Albany, School of Public Health, Department of Biometry and Statistics, Rensselaer, NY 12144. Offers MS, PhD. *Faculty:* 5 full-time (1 woman). *Students:* 16 full-time (11 women), 10 part-time (4 women); includes 2 minority (1 African American, 1 Hispanic American), 12 international. 21 applicants, 81% accepted. In 1998, 8 master's, 1 doctorate awarded. *Degree requirements:* For doctorate, dissertation required. *Entrance requirements:* For master's and doctorate, GRE General Test. Application fee: $50. Tuition, state resident: full-time $5,100; part-time $213 per credit. Tuition, nonresident: full-time $8,416; part-time $351 per credit. Required fees: $31 per credit. *Unit head:* Dr. Igor Zurbenko, Chair, 518-402-0400.

State University of New York at Buffalo, Graduate School, Graduate Programs in Biomedical Sciences at Roswell Park Cancer Institute, Program in Interdisciplinary Natural and Biomedical Sciences at Roswell Park Cancer Institute, Buffalo, NY 14260. Offers biochemistry (MS); biometry (MS); biophysics (MS); cellular molecular biology (MS); chemistry (MS); epidemiology (MS); immunology (MS); pathology (MS); pharmacology (MS); physiology (MS). Part-time programs available. *Faculty:* 11 full-time (2 women). *Students:* 43 full-time (15 women), 35 part-time (17 women); includes 14 minority (4 African Americans, 8 Asian Americans or Pacific Islanders, 2 Hispanic Americans), 5 international. *Degree requirements:* For master's, thesis, defense of thesis, research project required. *Entrance requirements:* For master's, GRE General Test, TOEFL, TSE (minimum score of 50 required), TWE (minimum score of 4.0 required). *Application deadline:* For fall admission, 6/1 (priority date). Applications are processed on a rolling basis. Application fee: $35. Electronic applications accepted. Tuition, state resident: full-time $5,100; part-time $213 per credit hour. Tuition, nonresident: full-time $8,416; part-time $351 per credit hour. Required fees: $870; $75 per semester. Tuition and fees vary according to course load and program. *Unit head:* Dr. Robert Gregory, Graduate Director, 214-768-3075, Fax: 214-768-2701, E-mail: bgregory@mail.smu.edu. *Application contact:* Craig R. Johnson, Director of Graduate Studies, 716-845-2339, Fax: 716-845-8178, E-mail: rpgradapp@sc3103.med.buffalo.edu.

The University of Alabama at Birmingham, Graduate School, School of Public Health, Department of Biostatistics, Birmingham, AL 35294. Offers biomathematics (MS, PhD); biometry (MPH); biostatistics (MS, PhD). *Students:* 10 full-time (7 women), 4 part-time (1 woman); includes 8 minority (5 African Americans, 3 Asian Americans or Pacific Islanders), 2 international. *Degree requirements:* For master's, thesis, fieldwork, research project required; for doctorate, dissertation, comprehensive exam required. *Entrance requirements:* For master's, GRE General Test (minimum combined score of 1000 required) or MAT, minimum GPA of 3.0; for doctorate, GRE General Test (minimum combined score of 1000 required) or MAT, MPH or MSPH, minimum GPA of 3.0, interview. *Application deadline:* Applications are processed on a rolling basis. Application fee: $30 ($60 for international students). Electronic applications accepted. *Unit head:* Dr. Charles R. Katholi, Interim Chair, 205-934-4905, Fax: 205-975-2540, E-mail: ckatholi@uab.edu. *Application contact:* Nancy O. Pinson, Coordinator of Student Admissions, 205-934-4993, Fax: 205-975-5484.

See in-depth description on page 751.

University of California, Los Angeles, School of Medicine, Graduate Programs in Medicine, Department of Biomathematics, Los Angeles, CA 90095. Offers MS, PhD. *Students:* 15 full-time (6 women); includes 3 minority (1 African American, 2 Asian Americans or Pacific Islanders), 1 international. 10 applicants, 20% accepted. *Degree requirements:* For master's, comprehensive exam or thesis required; for doctorate, dissertation, oral and written qualifying exams required, foreign language not required. *Entrance requirements:* For master's and doctorate, GRE General Test, GRE Subject Test. *Application deadline:* For fall admission, 1/15. Application fee: $40. *Financial aid:* In 1998–99, 15 students received aid, including 14 fellowships, 5 research assistantships, 6 teaching assistantships; Federal Work-Study, institutionally-sponsored loans, scholarships, and tuition waivers (full and partial) also available. Financial aid application deadline: 3/1. *Unit head:* Dr. Eliot Landaw, Chair, 310-825-5554. *Application contact:* Departmental Office, 310-825-5554, E-mail: gradprog@biomath.medsch.ucla.edu.

See in-depth description on page 755.

University of Nebraska–Lincoln, Graduate College, College of Agricultural Sciences and Natural Resources, Department of Biometry, Lincoln, NE 68588. Offers MS. *Faculty:* 6 full-time (2 women). *Students:* 10 full-time (2 women), 2 international. Average age 31. 5 applicants, 80% accepted. In 1998, 10 degrees awarded. *Degree requirements:* For master's, thesis optional, foreign language not required. *Entrance requirements:* For master's, GRE General Test, TOEFL (minimum score of 550 required). *Application deadline:* For fall admission, 6/15; for spring admission, 10/31. Application fee: $35. Electronic applications accepted. *Financial aid:* In 1998–99, 7 research assistantships, 6 teaching assistantships were awarded.; fellowships, Federal Work-Study also available. Aid available to part-time students. Financial aid application deadline: 2/15. *Faculty research:* Design of experiments, linear models, spatial variability, statistical modeling and inference, sampling. *Unit head:* Dr. Anne Parkhurst, Head, 402-472-2903, Fax: 402-472-5179.

University of Southern California, School of Medicine, Graduate Programs in Medicine, Department of Preventive Medicine, Program in Biometry, Los Angeles, CA 90089. Offers

Biometrics–Biostatistics

University of Southern California (continued)
applied biometry/epidemiology (MS); biometry (MS, PhD); epidemiology (PhD); molecular/epidemiology (MS). *Faculty:* 41 full-time (15 women), 4 part-time (3 women). *Students:* 67 full-time (46 women); includes 22 minority (2 African Americans, 18 Asian Americans or Pacific Islanders, 2 Hispanic Americans), 20 international. Average age 30. 38 applicants, 50% accepted. In 1998, 13 master's awarded. Terminal master's awarded for partial completion of doctoral program. *Degree requirements:* For master's and doctorate, computer language, thesis/dissertation required, foreign language not required. *Entrance requirements:* For master's, GRE General Test (minimum combined score of 1000 required), GRE Subject Test, TOEFL, minimum GPA of 3.0; for doctorate, GRE General Test (minimum combined score of 1250 required), GRE Subject Test, TOEFL, minimum GPA of 3.0. *Average time to degree:* Master's–2 years full-time; doctorate–5 years full-time. *Application deadline:* For fall admission, 1/15 (priority date). Applications are processed on a rolling basis. Application fee: $55. *Financial aid:* In 1998–99, 27 students received aid, including 13 research assistantships with tuition reimbursements available (averaging $15,000 per year), 14 teaching assistantships with tuition reimbursements available (averaging $15,000 per year); fellowships, career-related internships or fieldwork, Federal Work-Study, and institutionally-sponsored loans also available. Financial aid application deadline: 4/1. *Faculty research:* Clinical trials in ophthalmology and cancer research, methods of analysis for epidemiological studies, genetic epidemiology. Total annual research expenditures: $1.3 million. *Unit head:* Dr. Stanley P. Azen, Director, 323-442-1810, Fax: 323-442-2993, E-mail: mtrujill@hsc.usc.edu.

Announcement: MS and PhD programs prepare students in applied statistics/epidemiology, with emphasis in health science applications. Research activities include clinical trials, survival analysis, health-care delivery systems, and cancer research. Limited half-time teaching/research assistantships ($20,000–$22,000) available. Interdisciplinary research is encouraged. January 15 deadline for fall. (Telephone: 323-442-1810; WWW: http://www.usc.edu/schools/medicine)

University of Southern California, School of Medicine, Graduate Programs in Medicine, Department of Preventive Medicine, Program in Public Health, Los Angeles, CA 90089. Offers biometry/epidemiology (MPH); health promotion (MPH); preventive nutrition (MPH). *Faculty:* 13 full-time (7 women), 1 part-time (0 women). *Students:* 16 full-time (12 women), 7 part-time (3 women); includes 15 minority (10 Asian Americans or Pacific Islanders, 5 Hispanic Americans), 1 international. *Degree requirements:* For master's, computer language, practicum and final report required, foreign language and thesis not required. *Entrance requirements:* For master's, GRE General Test (minimum combined score of 1000 required), TOEFL, minimum GPA of 3.0. Application fee: $55. Electronic applications accepted. Tuition: Full-time $22,198; part-time $748 per unit. Required fees: $406. *Unit head:* Dr. C. Anderson Johnson, Director, 323-442-2628, Fax: 323-442-2601, E-mail: carljohn@hsc.usc.edu. *Application contact:* Diane T. Rehfeldt, MPH Program Coordinator, 323-442-2580, Fax: 323-442-2601, E-mail: rehfeldt@hsc.usc.edu.

The University of Texas–Houston Health Science Center, Graduate School of Biomedical Sciences, Studies in Biomathematics, Houston, TX 77225-0036. Offers MS, PhD, MD/PhD. *Faculty:* 22 full-time (4 women). *Students:* 2 full-time (1 woman). Average age 27. 2 applicants, 0% accepted. Terminal master's awarded for partial completion of doctoral program. *Degree requirements:* For master's and doctorate, thesis/dissertation required, foreign language not required. *Entrance requirements:* For master's and doctorate, GRE General Test, TOEFL (minimum score of 550 required), TWE (minimum score of 4 required). *Application deadline:* For fall admission, 1/15 (priority date); for spring admission, 11/1. Applications are processed on a rolling basis. Application fee: $10. Electronic applications accepted. *Financial aid:* Fellowships, research assistantships, institutionally-sponsored loans available. Financial aid application deadline: 1/15. *Faculty research:* Clinical trials, radiological modeling, differential modeling of biological processes, radiological and pathological image processing, biomedical statistics. *Unit head:* Dr. Dennis Johnston, Coordinator, 713-792-2617, Fax: 713-792-4262, E-mail: djohnsto@notes.mdacc.tmc.edu. *Application contact:* Anne Baronitis, Director of Admissions, 713-500-9860, Fax: 713-500-9877, E-mail: abaron@gsbs.gs.uth.tmc.edu.

University of Wisconsin–Madison, Graduate School, College of Agricultural and Life Sciences, Biometry Program, Madison, WI 53706-1380. Offers MS.

Biostatistics

Boston University, Graduate School of Arts and Sciences, Program in Biostatistics, Boston, MA 02215. Offers MA, PhD. *Faculty:* 17 full-time (5 women), 2 part-time (0 women). *Students:* 14 full-time (7 women), 17 part-time (12 women); includes 2 minority (both Asian Americans or Pacific Islanders), 8 international. Average age 31. 33 applicants, 36% accepted. In 1998, 6 master's, 1 doctorate awarded. *Degree requirements:* For master's, one foreign language, qualifying exam required, thesis not required; for doctorate, one foreign language, dissertation, qualifying/oral exam required. *Entrance requirements:* For master's and doctorate, GRE General Test, TOEFL (minimum score of 550 required). *Application deadline:* For fall admission, 7/1; for spring admission, 10/15. Applications are processed on a rolling basis. Application fee: $50. Tuition: Full-time $23,770; part-time $743 per credit. Required fees: $220. Tuition and fees vary according to class time, course level, campus/location and program. *Financial aid:* In 1998–99, 9 research assistantships, 1 teaching assistantship were awarded.; fellowships Aid available to part-time students. Financial aid application deadline: 1/15; financial aid applicants required to submit FAFSA. *Faculty research:* Longitudinal analysis. *Unit head:* Ralph B. D'Agostino, Director, 617-353-2767.

Boston University, School of Medicine, School of Public Health, Epidemiology and Biostatistics Department, Boston, MA 02215. Offers biostatistics (MA, MPH, PhD); epidemiology (M Sc, MPH, D Sc). *Accreditation:* CEPH (one or more programs are accredited). *Students:* 92 full-time (56 women), 103 part-time (74 women); includes 44 minority (6 African Americans, 33 Asian Americans or Pacific Islanders, 4 Hispanic Americans, 1 Native American), 17 international. Average age 30. In 1998, 66 master's, 2 doctorates awarded. *Degree requirements:* For master's, foreign language and thesis not required; for doctorate, dissertation, comprehensive written and oral exams required. *Entrance requirements:* For master's, GRE General Test, TOEFL; for doctorate, GRE General Test, MPH or equivalent. *Application deadline:* For fall admission, 4/15; for spring admission, 10/25. Applications are processed on a rolling basis. Application fee: $50. Tuition: Full-time $23,770; part-time $743 per credit. Required fees: $220. *Financial aid:* Career-related internships or fieldwork, Federal Work-Study, and institutionally-sponsored loans available. Aid available to part-time students. *Unit head:* Dr. Adrienne Cupples, Acting Chairman, 617-638-5172. *Application contact:* Barbara St. Onge, Director of Admissions, 617-638-4640, Fax: 617-638-5299, E-mail: sphadmis@bu.edu.

Brown University, Graduate School, Division of Biology and Medicine, Department of Community Health, Program in Biostatistics, Providence, RI 02912. Offers health services research (MS, PhD). *Degree requirements:* For doctorate, dissertation, preliminary exam required, foreign language not required. *Entrance requirements:* For master's and doctorate, GRE General Test. *Application deadline:* For fall admission, 1/2 (priority date). Applications are processed on a rolling basis. Application fee: $60. *Financial aid:* Application deadline: 1/2. *Unit head:* Dr. Constantine Gatsonis, Director, Department of Community Health, 401-863-1106, E-mail: gatsonis@jenny.biomed.brown.edu.

Announcement: The graduate program in the Department of Community Health is designed to provide methodological and subject matter training in the study of the multiplicity of biological, behavioral, and social factors that influence the determinants of disease, its treatment, and its consequences and outcomes, with particular emphasis on health services research. The program offers comprehensive instruction leading to master's and PhD degrees in biostatistics or epidemiology. The program also features an intensive 1-year professional master's degree in each track. For more information on the graduate program, visit the Web site at http://biomed.brown.edu/Medicine_Departments/Commhlth/index.h tml

Case Western Reserve University, School of Medicine, Graduate Programs in Medicine, Department of Epidemiology and Biostatistics, Program in Biostatistics, Cleveland, OH 44106. Offers MS, PhD. Part-time programs available. Terminal master's awarded for partial completion of doctoral program. *Degree requirements:* For master's, exam/practicum required, foreign language and thesis not required; for doctorate, dissertation required, foreign language not required. *Entrance requirements:* For master's and doctorate, GRE General Test, TOEFL (minimum score of 550 required). *Faculty research:* Survey sampling and statistical computing, generalized linear models, statistical modeling, models in breast cancer survival.

Columbia University, Joseph L. Mailman School of Public Health, Division of Biostatistics, New York, NY 10032. Offers MPH, MS, Dr PH, PhD. PhD offered in cooperation with the Graduate School of Arts and Sciences. Part-time programs available. *Students:* 39. In 1998, 7 master's, 1 doctorate awarded. *Degree requirements:* For doctorate, dissertation required, foreign language not required, foreign language not required. *Entrance requirements:* For master's, GRE General Test; for doctorate, GRE General Test, MPH or equivalent (Dr PH). *Average time to degree:* Master's–2 years full-time, 4 years part-time; doctorate–5 years full-time, 7 years part-time. *Application deadline:* For fall admission, 4/1; for spring admission, 10/1. Applications are processed on a rolling basis. Application fee: $60. *Financial aid:* Research assistantships, teaching assistantships, career-related internships or fieldwork and Federal Work-Study available. Financial aid application deadline: 3/15; financial aid applicants required to submit FAFSA. *Faculty research:* Application of statistics in public policy, medical experiments, and legal processing; clinical trial results; statistical methods in epidemiology. *Unit head:* Dr. Bruce Levin, Acting Head, 212-305-9398, Fax: 212-305-9408. *Application contact:* Gerda Cordova, Divisional Administrator, 212-305-9398, Fax: 212-305-9408, E-mail: gb12@columbia.edu.

Drexel University, Graduate School, School of Biomedical Engineering, Science and Health Systems, Philadelphia, PA 19104-2875. Offers biomedical engineering (MS, PhD); biomedical science (MS, PhD); biostatistics (MS); clinical/rehabilitation engineering (MS). *Faculty:* 6 full-time, 4 part-time. *Students:* 32 full-time (12 women), 50 part-time (17 women); includes 13 minority (7 African Americans, 5 Asian Americans or Pacific Islanders, 1 Native American), 34 international. *Degree requirements:* For master's, thesis required (for some programs); for doctorate, dissertation, 1 year of residency, qualifying exam required. *Entrance requirements:* For master's, TOEFL (minimum score of 570 required), minimum GPA of 3.0; for doctorate, TOEFL (minimum score of 570 required), minimum GPA of 3.0, MS. *Application deadline:* For fall admission, 8/21. Applications are processed on a rolling basis. Application fee: $35. Tuition: Full-time $15,795; part-time $585 per credit. Required fees: $375; $67 per term. Tuition and fees vary according to program. *Unit head:* Dr. Banu Onaral, Director, 215-895-2215. *Application contact:* Dr. William Freedman, Graduate Adviser, 215-895-2225.

Emory University, Graduate School of Arts and Sciences, Department of Biostatistics, Atlanta, GA 30322-1100. Offers PhD. *Faculty:* 10 full-time (6 women), 7 part-time (1 woman). *Students:* 18 full-time (10 women); includes 3 minority (2 African Americans, 1 Asian American or Pacific Islander), 6 international. 55 applicants, 18% accepted. In 1998, 2 degrees awarded. *Degree requirements:* For doctorate, dissertation required, foreign language not required. *Entrance requirements:* For doctorate, GRE General Test, TOEFL. *Application deadline:* For fall admission, 1/20 (priority date). Application fee: $45. *Financial aid:* Fellowships, career-related internships or fieldwork and scholarships available. Financial aid application deadline: 1/20. *Faculty research:* Categorical data analysis, probability and stochastic processes, survival data analysis, sample survey design and analysis, statistical computing. *Unit head:* Dr. Vicki Stover Hertzberg, Chair, 404-727-3968, Fax: 404-727-1370. *Application contact:* Dr. Michael Haber, Director of Graduate Studies, 404-727-3968, Fax: 404-727-1370, E-mail: haber@sph.emory.edu.

See in-depth description on page 673.

Emory University, The Rollins School of Public Health, Department of Biostatistics, Atlanta, GA 30322-1100. Offers MPH, MSPH. *Degree requirements:* For master's, thesis (for some programs), practicum required, foreign language not required. *Entrance requirements:* For master's, GRE General Test. *Application deadline:* For fall admission, 2/15 (priority date). Applications are processed on a rolling basis. Application fee: $50. *Financial aid:* Application deadline: 2/15. *Unit head:* Dr. Vicki S. Hertzberg, Chair, 404-727-1881, E-mail: vhertzb@sph.emory.edu. *Application contact:* Marsha Daly, Assistant Director of Academic Programs, 404-727-3968, E-mail: mdaly@sph.emory.edu.

Georgetown University, Graduate School, Programs in Biomedical Sciences, Division of Biostatistics and Epidemiology, Washington, DC 20057. Offers MS. *Entrance requirements:* For master's, GRE General Test, TOEFL (minimum score of 550 required). *Faculty research:* Occupation epidemiology, cancer.

The George Washington University, Columbian School of Arts and Sciences, Department of Statistics, Program in Biostatistics, Washington, DC 20052. Offers MS, PhD. *Faculty:* 8 full-time (2 women), 1 (woman) part-time. *Students:* 4 full-time (2 women), 9 part-time (4 women); includes 2 minority (1 Asian American or Pacific Islander, 1 Hispanic American), 1 international. Average age 32. 26 applicants, 81% accepted. *Degree requirements:* For master's, comprehensive exams required, thesis not required; for doctorate, dissertation, general exam required. *Entrance requirements:* For master's and doctorate, GRE General Test, minimum GPA of 3.0. Application fee: $55. Tuition: Full-time $17,328; part-time $722 per credit hour. Required fees: $828; $35 per credit hour. Tuition and fees vary according to campus/location and program. *Financial aid:* Fellowships, teaching assistantships available. Financial aid application deadline: 2/1. *Unit head:* Dr. John Lachin, Director and Adviser, 301-881-9260.

The George Washington University, School of Public Health and Health Services, Department of Public Health, Track in Epidemiology-Biostatistics, Washington, DC 20052. Offers MPH. *Accreditation:* CEPH. *Students:* 24 full-time (16 women), 49 part-time (34 women); includes 25 minority (14 African Americans, 10 Asian Americans or Pacific Islanders, 1 Hispanic American), 5 international. Average age 30. 68 applicants, 94% accepted. In 1998, 43 degrees awarded. *Degree requirements:* For master's, case study or special project required, thesis not required. *Entrance requirements:* For master's, GMAT, GRE General Test, or MCAT; TOEFL. *Application deadline:* For fall admission, 5/15 (priority date); for spring admission, 11/15. Applications are processed on a rolling basis. Application fee: $55. Tuition: Full-time $17,328; part-time $722 per credit hour. Required fees: $828; $35 per credit hour.

Tuition and fees vary according to campus/location and program. *Unit head:* Dr. Natholyn Harris, Graduate Coordinator, 850-644-4800, Fax: 850-644-0700, E-mail: nharris@mailer.fsu.edu. *Application contact:* Michelle Sparacino, Director of Recruitment, 202-994-2160, Fax: 202-994-3773, E-mail: sphhs-info@gwumc.edu.

Harvard University, School of Public Health, Department of Biostatistics, Boston, MA 02115-6096. Offers SM, SD. Part-time programs available. *Faculty:* 13 full-time (3 women), 30 part-time (9 women). *Students:* 50 full-time (35 women), 1 part-time; includes 14 minority (7 African Americans, 5 Asian Americans or Pacific Islanders, 1 Hispanic American, 1 Native American), 8 international. Average age 29. 89 applicants, 39% accepted. In 1998, 5 master's, 6 doctorates awarded. *Degree requirements:* For doctorate, dissertation, oral and written qualifying exams required. *Entrance requirements:* For master's, GRE, TOEFL (minimum score of 550 required; 220 for computer-based), prior training in mathematics and/or statistics; for doctorate, GRE, TOEFL (minimum score of 550 required; 220 for computer-based)), prior training in mathematics and/or statistics. *Application deadline:* For fall admission, 1/4. Application fee: $60. *Financial aid:* Fellowships, research assistantships, teaching assistantships, Federal Work-Study, grants, scholarships, traineeships, tuition waivers (partial), and unspecified assistantships available. Aid available to part-time students. Financial aid application deadline: 2/12; financial aid applicants required to submit FAFSA. *Faculty research:* Statistical genetics, clinical trials, cancer and AIDS research, environmental and mental health. *Unit head:* Dr. Stephen Lagakos, Chair, 617-432-1056. *Application contact:* Margaret R. Watson, Assistant Director of Admissions, 617-432-1031, Fax: 617-432-2009, E-mail: admisofc@hsph.harvard.edu.

Johns Hopkins University, School of Hygiene and Public Health, Department of Biostatistics, Baltimore, MD 21205-2179. Offers MHS, Sc M, PhD. *Faculty:* 18 full-time, 13 part-time. *Students:* 39 (24 women); includes 4 minority (1 African American, 3 Asian Americans or Pacific Islanders) 14 international. 98 applicants, 34% accepted. In 1998, 9 master's, 2 doctorates awarded. *Degree requirements:* For master's, thesis required (for some programs), foreign language not required; for doctorate, dissertation, 1 year full-time residency, oral and written exams required, foreign language not required. *Entrance requirements:* For master's, GRE General Test, TOEFL (minimum score of 550 required); for doctorate, GRE General Test, TOEFL (minimum score of 580 required). *Application deadline:* For fall admission, 2/1 (priority date). Applications are processed on a rolling basis. Application fee: $60. Electronic applications accepted. Tuition: Full-time $23,660; part-time $493 per unit. Full-time tuition and fees vary according to degree level, campus/location and program. *Financial aid:* Federal Work-Study, institutionally-sponsored loans, scholarships, traineeships, and stipends available. Aid available to part-time students. Financial aid application deadline: 4/15. *Faculty research:* Linear models, environmental statistics, statistical methods, time series analysis, stochastic processes, computer graphics, clinical trials. Total annual research expenditures: $2 million. *Unit head:* Dr. Scott Zeger, Chair, 410-955-3067, E-mail: szeger@jhsph.edu. *Application contact:* Mary Joy Argo, Academic Administrator, 410-955-3067, Fax: 410-955-0958, E-mail: margo@jhsph.edu.

Johns Hopkins University, School of Hygiene and Public Health, Program in Public Health, Baltimore, MD 21218-2699. Offers biochemistry (MPH); biostatistics (MPH); environmental health sciences (MPH); epidemiology (MPH); health policy and management (MPH); international health (MPH); maternal and child health (MPH); mental hygiene (MPH); molecular microbiology and immunology (MPH); population dynamics (MPH). *Accreditation:* CEPH. Part-time and evening/weekend programs available. *Students:* 247 (155 women); includes 60 minority (20 African Americans, 34 Asian Americans or Pacific Islanders, 5 Hispanic Americans, 1 Native American) 48 international. *Degree requirements:* For master's, foreign language and thesis not required. *Entrance requirements:* For master's, GRE General Test, TOEFL (minimum score of 550 required), 2 years of work related experience. *Application deadline:* For fall admission, 2/1 (priority date). Applications are processed on a rolling basis. Application fee: $60. Electronic applications accepted. Tuition: Full-time $23,660; part-time $493 per unit. Full-time tuition and fees vary according to degree level, campus/location and program. *Unit head:* Dr. Miriam Alexander, Director, 410-955-1291, Fax: 410-955-4749. *Application contact:* Lenora Davis, Administrator, 410-955-1291, Fax: 410-955-4749, E-mail: lrdavis@jhsph.edu.

Loma Linda University, School of Public Health, Programs in Biostatistics, Loma Linda, CA 92350. Offers MPH, MSPH. *Students:* 3 full-time (1 woman), 4 part-time (3 women). In 1998, 2 degrees awarded. *Entrance requirements:* For master's, Michigan English Language Assessment Battery (minimum score of 92 required) or TOEFL (minimum score of 600 required). *Application deadline:* Applications are processed on a rolling basis. Application fee: $100. *Financial aid:* Application deadline: 5/15. *Unit head:* Dr. Synnove Knutsen, Chair, 909-824-4590, Fax: 909-824-4087. *Application contact:* Terri Tamayose, Director of Admissions and Academic Records, 909-824-4694, Fax: 909-824-8087, E-mail: ttamayose@sph.llu.edu.

McGill University, Faculty of Graduate Studies and Research, Faculty of Medicine, Department of Epidemiology and Biostatistics, Montréal, PQ H3A 2T5, Canada. Offers community health (M Sc); environmental health (M Sc); epidemiology (M Sc); epidemiology and biostatistics (PhD, Diploma); health care evaluation (M Sc); medical statistics (M Sc); occupational health (M Sc). *Accreditation:* CEPH (one or more programs are accredited). *Faculty:* 35 full-time (7 women), 23 part-time (6 women). *Students:* 49 full-time (33 women), 32 part-time (17 women), 14 international. Average age 30. 86 applicants, 79% accepted. In 1998, 14 master's, 6 doctorates awarded. *Degree requirements:* For master's, thesis optional, foreign language not required; for doctorate, dissertation required, foreign language not required. *Entrance requirements:* For master's, GRE, minimum GPA of 3.0; for doctorate, GRE. *Application deadline:* For fall admission, 3/1. Applications are processed on a rolling basis. Application fee: $60. *Financial aid:* Tuition waivers (full) available. Financial aid application deadline: 2/1. *Faculty research:* Chronic and infectious disease epidemiology, health services research, pharmacoepidemiology. *Unit head:* Dr. G. Theriault, Chair, Graduate Committee, 514-398-6259, Fax: 514-398-4503, E-mail: gtheri@epid.lan.mcgill.ca. *Application contact:* Marlene Abrams, Secretary for Graduate Studies, 514-398-6269, Fax: 514-398-4503, E-mail: marlene@epid.lan.mcgill.ca.

Medical College of Wisconsin, Graduate School of Biomedical Sciences, Division of Biostatistics, Milwaukee, WI 53226-0509. Offers PhD. Part-time programs available. Terminal master's awarded for partial completion of doctoral program. *Degree requirements:* For doctorate, computer language, dissertation required, foreign language not required. *Entrance requirements:* For doctorate, GRE General Test, TOEFL. Electronic applications accepted. *Faculty research:* Survival analysis, spatial statistics, time series, genetic statistics, Bayesian statistics.

See in-depth description on page 693.

Medical University of South Carolina, College of Graduate Studies, Department of Biometry and Epidemiology, Charleston, SC 29425-0002. Offers biometrics (MS, PhD); biostatistics (MS, PhD); epidemiology (MS, PhD). *Faculty:* 16 part-time (3 women). *Students:* 37 full-time (18 women); includes 1 minority (African American), 8 international. Terminal master's awarded for partial completion of doctoral program. *Degree requirements:* For master's, thesis, research seminar required; for doctorate, dissertation, teaching and research seminar, oral and written exams required. *Entrance requirements:* For master's and doctorate, GRE General Test (minimum combined score of 1650 on three sections required), GRE Subject Test (international applicants), TOEFL, interview. *Application deadline:* Applications are processed on a rolling basis. Application fee: $55. Electronic applications accepted. *Unit head:* Dr. John Dunbar, Interim Chairman, 843-876-1100. *Application contact:* Julie Johnston, Director of Admissions, 843-792-8710, Fax: 843-792-3764.

New York Medical College, Graduate School of Health Sciences, Program in Biostatistics and Epidemiology, Valhalla, NY 10595-1691. Offers MPH, MS. Part-time and evening/weekend programs available. *Degree requirements:* For master's, computer language required, foreign language not required. *Entrance requirements:* For master's, TOEFL.

New York Medical College, Graduate School of Health Sciences, Programs in International and Public Health, Valhalla, NY 10595-1691. Offers biostatistics (MPH, MS); emergency medical services (MPH, MS); general public health (MPH); gerontology (MPH); international health (MPH, MS); maternal and child health (MPH). Part-time and evening/weekend programs available. *Degree requirements:* For master's, computer language required, foreign language not required. *Entrance requirements:* For master's, TOEFL.

New York University, Graduate School of Arts and Science, Nelson Institute of Environmental Medicine, Program in Environmental Health Sciences, New York, NY 10012-1019. Offers environmental biology (PhD); environmental carcinogenesis (PhD); environmental epidemiology and biostatistics (PhD); environmental-occupational hygiene (MS); ergonomics and biomechanics (PhD); molecular toxicology (PhD); occupational-environmental hygiene (PhD); systemic toxicology (PhD); toxicology (MS). *Faculty:* 26 full-time (7 women). *Degree requirements:* For master's, thesis or alternative required, foreign language not required; for doctorate, one foreign language, dissertation, oral and written exams required. *Entrance requirements:* For master's and doctorate, GRE General Test, GRE Subject Test, TOEFL, minimum GPA of 3.0; bachelor's degree in biological, physical, or engineering science. *Application deadline:* For fall admission, 8/1; for spring admission, 12/1. Application fee: $60. Tuition: Full-time $17,880; part-time $745 per credit. Required fees: $1,140; $35 per credit. Tuition and fees vary according to course load and program. *Application contact:* Richard Schlesinger, Director of Graduate Studies, 914-885-5281, E-mail: ehs@charlotte.med.nyu.edu.

The Ohio State University, Graduate School, College of Mathematical and Physical Sciences, Department of Statistics, Program in Biostatistics, Columbus, OH 43210. Offers PhD. *Faculty:* 11 full-time. *Students:* 11 full-time (7 women), 2 part-time (1 woman), 8 international. 17 applicants, 6% accepted. In 1998, 1 degree awarded. *Degree requirements:* For doctorate, dissertation required, foreign language not required. *Application deadline:* For fall admission, 8/15. Applications are processed on a rolling basis. Application fee: $30 ($40 for international students). *Financial aid:* Fellowships, research assistantships, teaching assistantships, Federal Work-Study and institutionally-sponsored loans available. Aid available to part-time students. *Unit head:* Saul Blumental, Graduate Studies Committee Chair, 614-292-6071, Fax: 614-292-2096, E-mail: blumenthal.1@osu.edu.

Oregon Health Sciences University, School of Medicine, Department of Public Health and Preventive Medicine, Portland, OR 97201-3098. Offers epidemiology and biostatistics (MPH). Part-time programs available. *Faculty:* 26 part-time (8 women). *Students:* 17 full-time (7 women), 40 part-time (17 women); includes 8 minority (all Asian Americans or Pacific Islanders), 1 international. Average age 27. 106 applicants, 19% accepted. *Degree requirements:* For master's, thesis, fieldwork/internship required, foreign language not required. *Entrance requirements:* For master's, GRE General Test (minimum combined score of 1000 required; average 1200), TOEFL, previous undergraduate course work in statistics. *Average time to degree:* Master's–1.5 years full-time, 3 years part-time. *Application deadline:* For fall admission, 1/16. Applications are processed on a rolling basis. Application fee: $60. *Financial aid:* In 1998–99, 2 research assistantships were awarded.; career-related internships or fieldwork, Federal Work-Study, and institutionally-sponsored loans also available. Aid available to part-time students. Financial aid applicants required to submit FAFSA. *Faculty research:* Health services, health care access, health policy, environmental and occupational health. Total annual research expenditures: $276,453. *Unit head:* Dr. Merwyn R. Greenlick, Professor and Chair, 503-494-8257, Fax: 503-494-4981, E-mail: mitchg@ohsu.edu. *Application contact:* Dr. Katherine J. Riley, Department Administrator, 503-494-2556, Fax: 503-494-4981, E-mail: rileyk@ohsu.edu.

Queen's University at Kingston, Faculty of Medicine, Graduate Programs in Medicine, Department of Community Health and Epidemiology, Kingston, ON K7L 3N6, Canada. Offers biostatistics (M Sc); environmental and occupational health (M Sc); epidemiology (M Sc); general community health (M Sc); health-care systems (M Sc); preventive medicine (M Sc). Part-time programs available. *Students:* 24 full-time (16 women), 13 part-time (10 women). *Degree requirements:* For master's, thesis required, foreign language not required. *Entrance requirements:* For master's, TOEFL (minimum score of 550 required). Application fee: $60. Electronic applications accepted. *Unit head:* Dr. J. L. Pater, Graduate Coordinator, 613-533-2901. *Application contact:* R. E. M. Lees, Graduate Coordinator, 613-533-4954.

San Diego State University, Graduate and Research Affairs, College of Health and Human Services, Graduate School of Public Health, San Diego, CA 92182. Offers environmental health (MPH, MS); epidemiology (MPH, PhD), including biostatistics (MPH); health promotion (MPH); health services administration (MPH); industrial hygiene (MS); toxicology (MS). *Accreditation:* ACEHSA (one or more programs are accredited); CEPH (one or more programs are accredited). Part-time programs available. *Faculty:* 24 full-time (9 women), 20 part-time (7 women). *Students:* 226 full-time (148 women), 128 part-time (92 women); includes 109 minority (9 African Americans, 51 Asian Americans or Pacific Islanders, 46 Hispanic Americans, 3 Native Americans), 6 international. *Degree requirements:* For master's, thesis required (for some programs), foreign language not required; for doctorate, dissertation required, foreign language not required. *Entrance requirements:* For master's, GMAT (health services administration), GRE General Test; for doctorate, GRE General Test. *Application deadline:* For fall admission, 5/15 (priority date); for spring admission, 10/15 (priority date). Applications are processed on a rolling basis. Application fee: $55. *Unit head:* Dr. Kenneth Bart, Director, 619-594-6317. *Application contact:* Brenda Fass-Holmes, Coordinator, Admissions and Student Affairs, 619-594-6317, E-mail: bholmes@mail.sdsu.edu.

Tulane University, School of Public Health and Tropical Medicine, Department of Biostatistics, New Orleans, LA 70118-5669. Offers MS, MSPH, PhD, Sc D. MS and PhD offered through the Graduate School. *Students:* 6 full-time (5 women); includes 1 minority (African American), 3 international. Average age 35. 5 applicants, 80% accepted. In 1998, 6 master's, 1 doctorate awarded. *Degree requirements:* For master's, one foreign language, thesis not required; for doctorate, one foreign language, dissertation, comprehensive exam required. *Entrance requirements:* For master's, GRE General Test (minimum combined score of 1000 required; average 1100), TOEFL (minimum score of 525 required); for doctorate, GRE General Test (minimum combined score of 1000 required; average 1250), TOEFL (minimum score of 525 required). *Application deadline:* For fall admission, 2/1 (priority date). Applications are processed on a rolling basis. Application fee: $45. *Financial aid:* In 1998–99, 2 students received aid, including 1 research assistantship, 1 teaching assistantship; Federal Work-Study also available. Financial aid application deadline: 2/1. *Faculty research:* Clinical trials, measurement, longitudinal analyses. *Unit head:* Dr. Larry Webber, Chairman, 504-588-5164, Fax: 504-584-1706.

The University of Alabama at Birmingham, Graduate School, School of Public Health, Department of Biostatistics, Birmingham, AL 35294. Offers biomathematics (MS, PhD); biometry (MPH); biostatistics (MS, PhD). *Students:* 10 full-time (7 women), 4 part-time (1 woman); includes 8 minority (5 African Americans, 3 Asian Americans or Pacific Islanders), 2 international. 22 applicants, 91% accepted. In 1998, 2 master's, 4 doctorates awarded. *Degree requirements:* For master's, thesis, fieldwork, research project required; for doctorate, dissertation, comprehensive exam required. *Entrance requirements:* For master's, GRE General Test (minimum combined score of 1000 required) or MAT, minimum GPA of 3.0; for doctorate, GRE General Test (minimum combined score of 1000 required) or MAT, MPH or MSPH, minimum GPA of 3.0, interview. *Application deadline:* Applications are processed on a rolling basis. Application fee: $30 ($60 for international students). Electronic applications accepted. *Financial aid:* Fellowships, career-related internships or fieldwork available. *Unit head:* Dr. Charles R. Katholi, Interim Chair, 205-934-4905, Fax: 205-975-2540, E-mail: ckatholi@uab.edu. *Application contact:* Nancy O. Pinson, Coordinator of Student Admissions, 205-934-4993, Fax: 205-975-5484.

See in-depth description on page 751.

Biostatistics

University of California, Berkeley, Graduate Division, School of Public Health, Division of Biostatistics, Berkeley, CA 94720-1500. Offers biostatistics (MPH); epidemiology (PhD); epidemiology/biostatistics (MPH). *Accreditation:* CEPH (one or more programs are accredited). *Faculty:* 5. *Degree requirements:* For master's, oral exam required; for doctorate, dissertation, oral exam required, foreign language not required. *Entrance requirements:* For master's and doctorate, GRE General Test, minimum GPA of 3.0. *Application deadline:* For fall admission, 12/1. Applications are processed on a rolling basis. Application fee: $40. *Financial aid:* Fellowships, research assistantships, teaching assistantships, career-related internships or fieldwork, Federal Work-Study, institutionally-sponsored loans, and tuition waivers (full and partial) available. Financial aid application deadline: 12/1; financial aid applicants required to submit FAFSA. *Unit head:* Dr. Steve Selvin, Head, 510-642-4618. *Application contact:* Bonnie Hutchings, Graduate Assistant, 510-642-3241, Fax: 510-643-5163, E-mail: bjh@stat.berkeley.edu.

University of California, Berkeley, Graduate Division, School of Public Health, Group in Biostatistics, Berkeley, CA 94720-1500. Offers MA, PhD. *Faculty:* 20. *Students:* 22 full-time (14 women); includes 3 minority (1 African American, 2 Asian Americans or Pacific Islanders), 6 international. 48 applicants, 31% accepted. In 1998, 5 master's, 2 doctorates awarded (100% found work related to degree). *Degree requirements:* For master's, oral comprehensive exam required; for doctorate, dissertation, qualifying exam required, foreign language not required. *Entrance requirements:* For master's and doctorate, GRE General Test, minimum GPA of 3.0. *Average time to degree:* Master's–2 years full-time; doctorate–5 years full-time. *Application deadline:* For fall admission, 12/1. Applications are processed on a rolling basis. Application fee: $40. *Financial aid:* Fellowships, research assistantships, teaching assistantships, career-related internships or fieldwork, Federal Work-Study, institutionally-sponsored loans, and tuition waivers (full and partial) available. Financial aid application deadline: 12/1; financial aid applicants required to submit FAFSA. *Faculty research:* Applied statistics, risk research, clinical trials, nonparametrics. *Unit head:* Steve Selvin, Co-Chair, 510-642-4618, E-mail: selvin@stat.berkeley.edu. *Application contact:* Bonnie Hutchings, Graduate Assistant for Admission, 510-642-3241, Fax: 510-643-5163, E-mail: bjh@stat.berkeley.edu.

University of California, Los Angeles, Graduate Division, School of Public Health, Department of Biostatistics, Los Angeles, CA 90095. Offers MS, PhD. *Students:* 44 full-time (29 women); includes 12 minority (1 African American, 10 Asian Americans or Pacific Islanders, 1 Hispanic American), 22 international. 92 applicants, 73% accepted. *Degree requirements:* For master's, comprehensive exam required, foreign language and thesis not required; for doctorate, dissertation, oral and written qualifying exams required, foreign language not required. *Entrance requirements:* For master's, GRE General Test (minimum combined score of 1100 required), minimum GPA of 3.0; for doctorate, GRE General Test (minimum combined score of 1200 required), minimum undergraduate GPA of 3.0. *Application deadline:* For fall admission, 12/15. Application fee: $40. Electronic applications accepted. *Financial aid:* In 1998–99, 37 students received aid; fellowships, research assistantships, teaching assistantships, career-related internships or fieldwork, Federal Work-Study, institutionally-sponsored loans, scholarships, and tuition waivers (full and partial) available. Financial aid application deadline: 3/1. *Unit head:* Dr. William Cumberland, Chair, 310-825-5250. *Application contact:* Departmental Office, 310-267-2186, E-mail: app_bios@admin.ph.ucla.edu.

University of Cincinnati, Division of Research and Advanced Studies, College of Medicine, Graduate Programs in Medicine, Department of Environmental Health, Cincinnati, OH 45267. Offers environmental and industrial hygiene (MS); environmental and occupational medicine (MS); environmental health (PhD); environmental hygiene science and engineering (MS, PhD); epidemiology and biostatistics (MS); occupational safety (MS); toxicology (MS, PhD). *Faculty:* 20 full-time. *Students:* 69 full-time (34 women), 66 part-time (32 women); includes 29 minority (16 African Americans, 12 Asian Americans or Pacific Islanders, 1 Hispanic American), 31 international. Terminal master's awarded for partial completion of doctoral program. *Degree requirements:* For master's, thesis required, foreign language not required; for doctorate, one foreign language, dissertation, qualifying exam required. *Entrance requirements:* For master's, GRE General Test, TOEFL, bachelor's degree in science; for doctorate, GRE General Test, TOEFL. *Application deadline:* For fall admission, 2/1 (priority date). Applications are processed on a rolling basis. Application fee: $30. *Unit head:* Dr. Marshall W. Anderson, Chairman, 513-558-5701, Fax: 513-558-4397, E-mail: marshall.anderson@uc.edu. *Application contact:* Judy Jarrell, Graduate Program Director, 513-558-1729, Fax: 513-558-4397, E-mail: judy.jarrell@uc.edu.

University of Hawaii at Manoa, Graduate Division, College of Health Sciences and Social Welfare, School of Public Health, Honolulu, HI 96822. Offers biostatistics (MPH, MS); community health development and education (MPH, MS); environmental and occupational health (MPH, MS); epidemiology (MPH, MS); health services administration and planning (MPH, MS); maternal and child health (MPH, MS). Part-time programs available. *Faculty:* 23 full-time (7 women). *Students:* 105 full-time (74 women), 67 part-time (39 women); includes 71 minority (3 African Americans, 65 Asian Americans or Pacific Islanders, 2 Hispanic Americans, 1 Native American), 30 international. Terminal master's awarded for partial completion of doctoral program. *Degree requirements:* For master's, thesis required (for some programs); for doctorate, computer language, dissertation required, foreign language not required. *Entrance requirements:* For doctorate, GRE General Test. *Application deadline:* For fall admission, 3/1; for spring admission, 9/1. Application fee: $25 ($50 for international students). *Unit head:* Dr. D. William Wood, Interim Dean, 808-956-8491. *Application contact:* Dr. Jerome Grossman, Graduate Chairperson, 808-956-9500, Fax: 808-956-4585, E-mail: grossman@hawaii.edu.

University of Illinois at Chicago, School of Public Health, Biostatistics Section, Chicago, IL 60607-7128. Offers MS, PhD. *Degree requirements:* For master's, thesis, field practicum required, foreign language not required; for doctorate, dissertation, independent research, internship required, foreign language not required. *Entrance requirements:* For master's and doctorate, GRE General Test (minimum combined score of 1000 required), TOEFL (minimum score of 550 required), minimum GPA of 3.75 on a 5.0 scale. *Application deadline:* For fall admission, 7/3; for spring admission, 11/8. Application fee: $40 ($50 for international students). *Unit head:* Richard Frazier, Advising Assistant, 713-743-3550, Fax: 713-743-3589, E-mail: frazier@uh.edu. *Application contact:* Dr. Sylvia Furner, Director of Graduate Studies, 312-996-6625.

University of Illinois at Chicago, School of Public Health, Program in Epidemiology and Biostatistics, Chicago, IL 60607-7128. Offers MPH, MS, Dr PH, PhD. *Accreditation:* CEPH (one or more programs are accredited). *Degree requirements:* For master's, thesis, field practicum required, foreign language not required; for doctorate, dissertation, independent research, internship required, foreign language not required. *Entrance requirements:* For master's and doctorate, GRE General Test (minimum combined score of 1000 required), TOEFL (minimum score of 550 required), minimum GPA of 3.75 on a 5.0 scale. *Application deadline:* For fall admission, 7/3; for spring admission, 11/8. Application fee: $40 ($50 for international students). *Unit head:* Dr. Paul S. Levy, Director, 312-996-8860. *Application contact:* Dr. Babette Neuberger, Assistant Dean, 312-996-6625.

The University of Iowa, College of Medicine, Graduate Programs in Medicine, Department of Preventive Medicine and Environmental Health, Iowa City, IA 52242-1316. Offers biostatistics (MS, PhD); community health (MS); epidemiology (MS, PhD); industrial hygiene (MS); occupational and environmental health (MS, PhD). Part-time programs available. *Faculty:* 33 full-time (9 women), 10 part-time (3 women). *Students:* 57 full-time (27 women), 62 part-time (34 women); includes 9 minority (5 African Americans, 4 Asian Americans or Pacific Islanders), 29 international. Terminal master's awarded for partial completion of doctoral program. *Degree requirements:* For master's, computer language (biostatistics) required, thesis optional, foreign language not required; for doctorate, dissertation, computer language (biostatistics and epidemiology) required, foreign language not required. *Entrance requirements:* For master's, GRE General Test (minimum combined score of 1050 required), TOEFL (minimum score of 600 required), minimum GPA of 2.7; for doctorate, GRE General Test (minimum combined score of 1050 required), TOEFL (minimum score of 600 required), minimum GPA of 3.0. *Application deadline:* For fall admission, 1/15 (priority date); for spring admission, 10/1. Applications are processed on a rolling basis. Application fee: $30 ($50 for international students). *Unit head:* Dr. James Merchant, Head, 319-335-9833, Fax: 319-335-9772, E-mail: james-merchant@uiowa.edu. *Application contact:* Barbara Scott, Graduate Studies Coordinator, 319-335-8992, Fax: 319-335-9200, E-mail: barbara-scott@uiowa.edu.

University of Michigan, School of Public Health, Department of Biostatistics, Ann Arbor, MI 48109. Offers MPH, MS, PhD. MS and PhD offered through the Horace H. Rackham School of Graduate Studies. *Degree requirements:* For master's, foreign language and thesis not required; for doctorate, oral defense of dissertation, preliminary exam required. *Entrance requirements:* For master's, GRE General Test, MCAT; for doctorate, GRE General Test, MCAT, master's degree. *Faculty research:* Biostatistical methodology, biomedical research.

University of Michigan, School of Public Health, Interdepartmental Program in Clinical Research Design and Statistical Analysis, Ann Arbor, MI 48109. Offers MS. Offered through the Horace H. Rackham School of Graduate Studies. Program admits applicants in odd calendar years. Part-time and evening/weekend programs available. *Degree requirements:* For master's, thesis required, foreign language not required. *Entrance requirements:* For master's, GRE General Test.

University of Minnesota, Twin Cities Campus, School of Public Health, Major in Biostatistics, Minneapolis, MN 55455-0213. Offers MPH, MS, PhD. Part-time programs available. *Faculty:* 12 full-time. *Students:* 18 full-time, 14 part-time; includes 4 minority (all Asian Americans or Pacific Islanders), 13 international. 97 applicants, 62% accepted. In 1998, 17 master's, 1 doctorate awarded. Terminal master's awarded for partial completion of doctoral program. *Degree requirements:* For doctorate, dissertation required, foreign language not required, foreign language not required. *Entrance requirements:* For master's and doctorate, GRE General Test (minimum combined score of 1500 on three sections required), minimum GPA of 3.0. *Application deadline:* For fall admission, 3/1 (priority date). Applications are processed on a rolling basis. Application fee: $50 ($75 for international students). *Financial aid:* Fellowships with partial tuition reimbursements, research assistantships with partial tuition reimbursements, teaching assistantships with partial tuition reimbursements, Federal Work-Study, institutionally-sponsored loans, and traineeships available. *Unit head:* Dr. Anne Goldman, Chair, 612-624-2158, Fax: 612-626-0660, E-mail: goldm003@tc.umn.edu. *Application contact:* Donna Seehausen, Coordinator, 612-624-9185, Fax: 612-626-0660, E-mail: donna@muskie.biostat.umn.edu.

The University of North Carolina at Chapel Hill, Graduate School, School of Public Health, Department of Biostatistics, Chapel Hill, NC 27599. Offers MPH, MS, Dr PH, PhD. Part-time programs available. *Faculty:* 24 full-time (4 women), 39 part-time (14 women). *Students:* 59 full-time (33 women), 49 part-time (20 women); includes 14 minority (3 African Americans, 9 Asian Americans or Pacific Islanders, 2 Hispanic Americans), 32 international. Average age 30. 114 applicants, 53% accepted. In 1998, 16 master's, 6 doctorates awarded. *Degree requirements:* For master's, thesis, major paper, comprehensive exam required, foreign language not required; for doctorate, dissertation, comprehensive exam required, foreign language not required. *Entrance requirements:* For master's and doctorate, GRE General Test (minimum combined score of 1000 required), minimum GPA of 3.0. *Average time to degree:* Master's–2 years full-time, 5 years part-time; doctorate–3 years full-time, 8 years part-time. *Application deadline:* For fall admission, 1/1. Applications are processed on a rolling basis. Application fee: $55. *Financial aid:* In 1998–99, 47 students received aid, including 20 fellowships with tuition reimbursements available, 44 research assistantships with tuition reimbursements available; Federal Work-Study, institutionally-sponsored loans, and unspecified assistantships also available. Financial aid application deadline: 1/1. Total annual research expenditures: $7.9 million. *Unit head:* Dr. Clarence E. Davis, Chair, 919-966-7254, Fax: 919-966-7141, E-mail: ed_davis@unc.edu. *Application contact:* Sra. R. De Costa, Registrar, 919-966-7262, Fax: 919-966-3804, E-mail: decosta@bios.unc.edu.

University of Oklahoma Health Sciences Center, Graduate College, College of Public Health, Program in Biostatistics and Epidemiology, Oklahoma City, OK 73190. Offers biostatistics (MPH, MS, Dr PH, PhD); epidemiology (MPH, MS, Dr PH, PhD). *Accreditation:* CEPH (one or more programs are accredited). Part-time programs available. *Degree requirements:* For master's, computer language, thesis (for some programs), comprehensive exam required, foreign language not required; for doctorate, computer language, dissertation, oral and written comprehensive exam required, foreign language not required. *Entrance requirements:* For master's, TOEFL (minimum score of 550 required); for doctorate, GRE, TOEFL (minimum score of 550 required). *Faculty research:* Statistical methodology, applied statistics, acute and chronic disease epidemiology.

University of Pittsburgh, Graduate School of Public Health, Department of Biostatistics, Pittsburgh, PA 15260. Offers MPH, MS, Dr PH, PhD. Part-time programs available. *Faculty:* 15 full-time (5 women). *Students:* 24 full-time (12 women), 6 part-time (4 women); includes 5 minority (1 African American, 4 Asian Americans or Pacific Islanders), 14 international. 27 applicants, 70% accepted. In 1998, 8 master's, 4 doctorates awarded. Terminal master's awarded for partial completion of doctoral program. *Degree requirements:* For master's, computer language, thesis required, foreign language not required; for doctorate, one foreign language (computer language can substitute), dissertation required. *Entrance requirements:* For master's, GRE General Test (combined average 1160), TOEFL (minimum score of 550 required), previous course work in biology, calculus, and fortran; for doctorate, GRE General Test (minimum combined score of 1200 required), TOEFL (minimum score of 550 required), previous course work in biology, calculus, and fortran. *Average time to degree:* Master's–1.5 years full-time, 2 years part-time; doctorate–3.5 years full-time, 4.5 years part-time. *Application deadline:* For fall admission, 3/30 (priority date); for spring admission, 11/30. Applications are processed on a rolling basis. Application fee: $50 ($60 for international students). *Financial aid:* In 1998–99, 22 students received aid, including 19 research assistantships, 3 teaching assistantships; career-related internships or fieldwork, Federal Work-Study, institutionally-sponsored loans, and tuition waivers (partial) also available. Aid available to part-time students. Financial aid application deadline: 2/28. *Faculty research:* Survival analysis, environmental risk assessment, statistical computing, longitudinal data analysis, experimental design. Total annual research expenditures: $4.3 million. *Unit head:* Dr. Howard E. Rockette, Acting Chairperson, 412-624-3022, Fax: 412-624-2183, E-mail: herbst+@pitt.edu. *Application contact:* Dr. Lisa Weissfeld, Associate Professor, 412-624-3023, Fax: 412-624-2183, E-mail: lweis@vms.cis.pitt.edu.

University of Puerto Rico, Medical Sciences Campus, Graduate School of Public Health, Department of Biostatistics and Epidemiology, Program in Biostatistics, San Juan, PR 00936-5067. Offers MPH. Part-time programs available. *Students:* 10 (7 women). 27 applicants, 44% accepted. In 1998, 13 degrees awarded. *Degree requirements:* For master's, computer language required, foreign language and thesis not required. *Entrance requirements:* For master's, GRE, previous course work in algebra. *Application deadline:* For fall admission, 3/3. Application fee: $15. *Financial aid:* Research assistantships, teaching assistantships, career-related internships or fieldwork, Federal Work-Study, and institutionally-sponsored loans available. Financial aid application deadline: 4/30. *Unit head:* Dr. Gilberto I. Ramos, Coordinator, 787-758-2525 Ext. 1428, Fax: 787-759-6719. *Application contact:* Mayra E. Santiago-Vargas, Counselor, 787-756-5244, Fax: 787-759-6719, E-mail: m_santiago@rcmaxp.upr.clu.edu.

University of Rochester, School of Medicine and Dentistry, Graduate Programs in Medicine and Dentistry, Department of Biostatistics, Rochester, NY 14627-0250. Offers medical statistics (MS); statistics (MA, PhD). *Faculty:* 6. *Students:* 11 full-time (6 women), 8 international. 30 applicants, 37% accepted. In 1998, 3 doctorates awarded. Terminal master's awarded for partial completion of doctoral program. *Degree requirements:* For doctorate, dissertation, qualifying exam required, foreign language not required, foreign language not required. *Entrance requirements:* For master's and doctorate, GRE General Test, TOEFL. *Application deadline:* For fall admission, 2/1. Application fee: $25. *Financial aid:* Fellowships, research assistantships, teaching assistantships, tuition waivers (full and partial) available. Financial aid applica-

598 *Peterson's Graduate Programs in the Physical Sciences, Mathematics, Agricultural Sciences, the Environment & Natural Resources 2000*

tion deadline: 2/1. *Unit head:* Dr. David Oakes, Chair, 716-275-2404. *Application contact:* Patti Kolomic, Administrative Assistant, 716-275-6696, E-mail: kolomic@metro.bst.rochester.edu.

See in-depth description on page 789.

University of South Carolina, Graduate School, School of Public Health, Department of Epidemiology/Biostatistics, Program in Biostatistics, Columbia, SC 29208. Offers MPH, MSPH, Dr PH, PhD. Part-time programs available. *Faculty:* 5 full-time (1 woman). *Students:* 17 full-time (10 women), 9 part-time (4 women); includes 6 minority (4 African Americans, 2 Asian Americans or Pacific Islanders), 7 international. Average age 32. In 1998, 9 master's, 3 doctorates awarded. *Degree requirements:* For master's, thesis (for some programs), practicum (MPH) required, foreign language not required; for doctorate, dissertation required. *Entrance requirements:* For master's and doctorate, GRE General Test. *Application deadline:* Applications are processed on a rolling basis. Application fee: $35. Electronic applications accepted. Tuition, state resident: full-time $4,014; part-time $202 per credit hour. Tuition, nonresident: full-time $8,528; part-time $428 per credit hour. Required fees: $100; $4 per credit hour. Tuition and fees vary according to program. *Financial aid:* Research assistantships, teaching assistantships, traineeships available. *Faculty research:* Bayesian methods, biometric modeling, nonlinear regression, health survey methodology, measurement of health status. *Application contact:* Graduate Director, 803-777-7353, Fax: 803-777-2524.

University of South Florida, Graduate School, College of Public Health, Department of Epidemiology and Biostatistics, Tampa, FL 33620-9951. Offers MPH, MSPH, PhD. *Accreditation:* CEPH (one or more programs are accredited). Part-time and evening/weekend programs available. *Faculty:* 11 full-time (3 women), 3 part-time (1 woman). *Students:* 44 full-time (28 women), 59 part-time (35 women); includes 20 minority (1 African American, 7 Asian Americans or Pacific Islanders, 12 Hispanic Americans), 24 international. 54 applicants, 59% accepted. In 1998, 14 master's, 1 doctorate awarded. *Degree requirements:* For master's and doctorate, thesis/dissertation required, foreign language not required. *Entrance requirements:* For master's, GRE General Test (minimum combined score of 1000 required), TOEFL (minimum score of 550 required), minimum GPA of 3.0 in upper-level course work; for doctorate, GRE General Test (minimum combined score of 1100 required), TOEFL (minimum score of 550 required), minimum GPA of 3.0 in upper-level course work. *Application deadline:* For fall admission, 6/1; for spring admission, 10/15. Applications are processed on a rolling basis. Application fee: $20. Tuition, state resident: part-time $148 per credit hour. Tuition, nonresident: part-time $509 per credit hour. *Financial aid:* In 1998–99, 1 fellowship with full tuition reimbursement (averaging $5,250 per year) was awarded.; research assistantships with full and partial tuition reimbursements, Federal Work-Study and institutionally-sponsored loans also available. Aid available to part-time students. Financial aid applicants required to submit FAFSA. *Faculty research:* Dementia, mental illness, mental health preventative trails, rural health outreach, clinical and administrative studies. *Unit head:* Dr. Thomas J. Mason, Chairperson, 813-974-4860, Fax: 813-974-4719, E-mail: tmason@com1.med.usf.edu. *Application contact:* Magdalene Argiry, Director of Student Services, 813-974-6665, Fax: 813-974-4718, E-mail: margiry@com1.med.usf.edu.

University of Utah, School of Medicine, Graduate Programs in Medicine, Programs in Public Health, Salt Lake City, UT 84112-1107. Offers biostatistics (M Stat); public health (MPH, MSPH). *Accreditation:* CEPH (one or more programs are accredited). Part-time programs available. *Faculty:* 10 full-time (3 women), 23 part-time (4 women). *Students:* 57 full-time (13 women), 33 part-time (11 women); includes 8 minority (2 African Americans, 3 Asian Americans or Pacific Islanders, 3 Hispanic Americans), 4 international. *Degree requirements:* For master's, comprehensive exam, thesis or project (MSPH) required. *Entrance requirements:* For master's, GRE General Test, interview, minimum GPA of 3.0. *Application deadline:* For fall admission, 2/1 (priority date). Applications are processed on a rolling basis. Application fee: $40 ($60 for international students). *Unit head:* Dr. F. Marian Bishop, Director, 801-581-7234, Fax: 801-585-9805, E-mail: mbishop@dfpm.utah.edu. *Application contact:* Dorothy Crockett, Project Coordinator, 801-581-7234, Fax: 801-585-9805, E-mail: dcrockett@dfpm.utah.edu.

University of Vermont, Graduate College, College of Engineering and Mathematics, Department of Mathematics and Statistics, Program in Biostatistics, Burlington, VT 05405-0160. Offers MS. *Degree requirements:* For master's, thesis or alternative required, foreign language not required. *Entrance requirements:* For master's, GRE General Test, TOEFL (minimum score of 550 required).

University of Washington, Graduate School, Interdisciplinary Graduate Program in Quantitative Ecology and Resource Management, Seattle, WA 98195. Offers MS, PhD. *Faculty:* 34 full-time (3 women). *Students:* 18 full-time (12 women), 2 part-time; includes 3 minority (2 Asian Americans or Pacific Islanders, 1 Native American), 2 international. Average age 30. 11 applicants, 27% accepted. In 1998, 1 doctorate awarded (100% found work related to degree). *Degree requirements:* For master's and doctorate, thesis/dissertation required. *Entrance requirements:* For master's and doctorate, GRE General Test (minimum score of 600 on verbal section, 710 on quantitative, 690 on analytical required), TOEFL (minimum score of 500 required), minimum GPA of 3.0. *Application deadline:* For fall admission, 2/1. Application fee: $50. Electronic applications accepted. Tuition, state resident: full-time $5,196; part-time $475 per credit. Tuition, nonresident: full-time $13,485; part-time $1,285 per credit. Required fees: $387; $38 per credit. Tuition and fees vary according to course load. *Financial aid:* In 1998–99, 2 fellowships with full tuition reimbursements (averaging $10,000 per year), 11 research assistantships with full tuition reimbursements (averaging $10,000 per year), 3 teaching assistantships with full tuition reimbursements (averaging $10,000 per year) were awarded.; grants, traineeships, tuition waivers (full), and unspecified assistantships also available. Financial aid applicants required to submit FAFSA. *Faculty research:* Population dynamics, statistical analysis, ecological modeling and systems analysis of aquatic and terrestrial ecosystems. Total annual research expenditures: $1.5 million. *Unit head:* Dr. E. David Ford, Chair, 206-616-9571, Fax: 206-616-9443, E-mail: qerm@cqs.washington.edu. *Application contact:* Joanne Besch, Graduate Assistant, 206-616-9571, Fax: 206-616-9443, E-mail: qerm@cqs.washington.edu.

University of Washington, Graduate School, School of Public Health and Community Medicine, Department of Biostatistics, Seattle, WA 98195. Offers MPH, MS, PhD. *Faculty:* 32 full-time (10 women), 2 part-time (both women). *Students:* 66 full-time (39 women), 3 part-time (1 woman); includes 12 minority (1 African American, 9 Asian Americans or Pacific Islanders, 2 Hispanic Americans), 16 international. 103 applicants, 49% accepted. In 1998, 7 master's awarded (57% entered university research/teaching, 29% found other work related to degree); 3 doctorates awarded (100% entered university research/teaching). Terminal master's awarded for partial completion of doctoral program. *Degree requirements:* For master's and doctorate, computer language, thesis/dissertation, departmental qualifying exams required, foreign language not required. *Entrance requirements:* For master's and doctorate, GRE General Test, TOEFL (minimum score of 580 required), 2 years of advanced calculus, 1 course in linear algebra, 1 course in probability, minimum GPA of 3.0. *Average time to degree:* Master's–2.5 years full-time; doctorate–4.9 years full-time. *Application deadline:* For fall admission, 2/1 (priority date). Applications are processed on a rolling basis. Application fee: $50. Electronic applications accepted. Tuition, state resident: full-time $5,196; part-time $475 per credit. Tuition, nonresident: full-time $13,485; part-time $1,285 per credit. Required fees: $387; $38 per credit. Tuition and fees vary according to course load. *Financial aid:* In 1998–99, 64 students received aid, including 1 fellowship, 40 research assistantships with tuition reimbursements available, 7 teaching assistantships with tuition reimbursements available; career-related internships or fieldwork and traineeships also available. Financial aid application deadline: 2/1. *Faculty research:* Statistical methods for survival data analysis, clinical trials, epidemiological case control and cohort studies, statistical genetics. *Unit head:* Dr. Thomas Fleming, Chair, 206-543-1044. *Application contact:* Alex MacKenzie, Program Coordinator, 206-543-1044, Fax: 206-543-3286, E-mail: alex@biostat.washington.edu.

University of Waterloo, Graduate Studies, Faculty of Mathematics, Department of Statistics and Actuarial Science, Waterloo, ON N2L 3G1, Canada. Offers statistics (PhD); statistics-biostatistics (M Math); statistics-computing (M Math); statistics-finance (M Math). *Faculty:* 29 full-time (6 women), 17 part-time (2 women). *Students:* 43 full-time (22 women), 23 part-time (5 women). *Degree requirements:* For master's, research paper or thesis required; for doctorate, dissertation required, foreign language not required. *Entrance requirements:* For master's, TOEFL (minimum score of 580 required), honors degree in field, minimum B average; for doctorate, TOEFL (minimum score of 580 required), master's degree. *Application deadline:* For fall admission, 3/31 (priority date); for winter admission, 8/31 (priority date); for spring admission, 12/31 (priority date). Applications are processed on a rolling basis. Application fee: $50. *Expenses:* Tuition and fees charges are reported in Canadian dollars. Tuition, state resident: full-time $3,168 Canadian dollars; part-time $792 Canadian dollars per term. Tuition, nonresident: full-time $8,000 Canadian dollars; part-time $2,000 Canadian dollars. Required fees: $45 Canadian dollars per term. Tuition and fees vary according to program. *Unit head:* Dr. M. E. Thompson, Chair, 519-888-4567 Ext. 5543, Fax: 519-746-1875, E-mail: methomps@setosa.uwaterloo.ca. *Application contact:* Dr. W. J. Welch, Graduate Officer, 519-888-4567 Ext. 5545, Fax: 519-746-1875, E-mail: wjwelch@uwaterloo.ca.

The University of Western Ontario, Faculty of Graduate Studies, Biosciences Division, Department of Epidemiology and Biostatistics, London, ON N6A 5B8, Canada. Offers M Sc, PhD. *Accreditation:* CEPH (one or more programs are accredited). Part-time programs available. *Degree requirements:* For master's, thesis required, foreign language not required; for doctorate, comprehensive exam, thesis proposal defense required. *Entrance requirements:* For master's, BA or B Sc honors degree, minimum B+ average in last 10 courses; for doctorate, M Sc or equivalent, minimum B+ average in last 10 courses. *Faculty research:* Chronic disease epidemiology, clinical epidemiology.

Virginia Commonwealth University, School of Graduate Studies, School of Medicine Graduate Programs, Department of Biostatistics, Richmond, VA 23284-9005. Offers MS, PhD. Part-time programs available. *Students:* 18 full-time (13 women), 9 part-time (6 women); includes 4 minority (2 African Americans, 2 Asian Americans or Pacific Islanders), 1 international. In 1998, 1 master's awarded (100% found work related to degree); 3 doctorates awarded (100% found work related to degree). Terminal master's awarded for partial completion of doctoral program. *Degree requirements:* For master's, thesis required, foreign language not required; for doctorate, dissertation, comprehensive oral and written exams required, foreign language not required. *Entrance requirements:* For master's, DAT, GRE General Test, or MCAT; for doctorate, GRE General Test. *Application deadline:* For fall admission, 2/15 (priority date). Application fee: $30. Tuition, state resident: full-time $4,031; part-time $224 per credit hour. Tuition, nonresident: full-time $11,946; part-time $664 per credit hour. Required fees: $1,081; $40 per credit hour. Tuition and fees vary according to campus/location and program. *Financial aid:* Fellowships, teaching assistantships, career-related internships or fieldwork available. *Faculty research:* Health services, linear models, response surfaces, design and analysis of drug/chemical combinations, clinical trials. *Unit head:* Dr. W. Hans Carter, Chair, 804-828-9824, Fax: 804-828-8900. *Application contact:* Russ Boyle, Graduate Program Director, 804-828-9824, Fax: 804-828-8900, E-mail: rmboyle@vcu.edu.

Western Michigan University, Graduate College, College of Arts and Sciences, Department of Mathematics and Statistics, Program in Biostatistics, Kalamazoo, MI 49008. Offers MS. 2 applicants, 50% accepted. In 1998, 4 degrees awarded. *Degree requirements:* For master's, written exams required, thesis not required. *Application deadline:* For fall admission, 2/15 (priority date). Applications are processed on a rolling basis. Application fee: $25. *Financial aid:* Fellowships, research assistantships, teaching assistantships, Federal Work-Study available. Financial aid application deadline: 2/15; financial aid applicants required to submit FAFSA. *Unit head:* Barbara Baily, Director of Graduate Studies, 309-298-1806, Fax: 309-298-2245, E-mail: barb_baily@ccmail.wiu.edu. *Application contact:* Paula J. Boodt, Coordinator, Graduate Admissions and Recruitment, 616-387-2000, Fax: 616-387-2355, E-mail: paula.boodt@wmich.edu.

Yale University, School of Medicine, Department of Epidemiology and Public Health, Division of Biostatistics, New Haven, CT 06520. Offers MPH, MS, PhD. MS and PhD offered through the Graduate School. Part-time programs available. *Faculty:* 7 full-time (2 women), 3 part-time (1 woman). *Students:* 12 full-time (8 women), 3 part-time (1 woman); includes 2 minority (both Hispanic Americans), 7 international. Average age 26. 16 applicants, 63% accepted. In 1998, 4 master's, 2 doctorates awarded. Terminal master's awarded for partial completion of doctoral program. *Degree requirements:* For master's, thesis, internship required, foreign language not required; for doctorate, dissertation, comprehensive exams, residency period required, foreign language not required. *Entrance requirements:* For master's, GMAT, GRE, LSAT, or MCAT; TOEFL, previous undergraduate course work in mathematics and science; for doctorate, GRE General Test (minimum combined score of 1200 required), TOEFL. *Application deadline:* Applications are processed on a rolling basis. Application fee: $60. *Financial aid:* Career-related internships or fieldwork, Federal Work-Study, institutionally-sponsored loans, and scholarships available. Aid available to part-time students. Financial aid application deadline: 4/1. *Faculty research:* Statistical and genetic epidemiology, population models for chronic and infectious diseases, clinical trials, regression methods. *Unit head:* Dr. Robert W. Makuch, Division Head, 203-785-2838, Fax: 203-785-6912, E-mail: robert.makuch@yale.edu. *Application contact:* Maria Z. Dino, Director of Admissions, 203-785-2844, Fax: 203-785-4845, E-mail: maria.dino@yale.edu.

Computational Sciences

California Institute of Technology, Division of Engineering and Applied Science, Option in Computation and Neural Systems, Pasadena, CA 91125-0001. Offers MS, PhD. *Faculty:* 3 full-time (0 women). *Students:* 45 full-time (4 women), 13 international. 84 applicants, 10% accepted. In 1998, 1 master's, 7 doctorates awarded. Terminal master's awarded for partial completion of doctoral program. *Degree requirements:* For doctorate, dissertation, qualifying exam required, foreign language not required, foreign language not required. *Entrance requirements:* For doctorate, GRE General Test. *Application deadline:* For fall admission, 1/15. Application fee: $0. *Financial aid:* Fellowships, research assistantships, teaching assistantships, Federal Work-Study and institutionally-sponsored loans available. Financial aid application deadline: 1/15. *Faculty research:* Biological and artificial computational devices, modeling of sensory processes and learning, theory of collective computation. *Unit head:* Dr. Christof Koch, Executive Officer, 626-395-6855.

Carnegie Mellon University, Graduate School of Industrial Administration, Program in Algorithms, Combinatorics, and Optimization, Pittsburgh, PA 15213-3891. Offers PhD. *Faculty:*

Computational Sciences

Carnegie Mellon University (continued)
4 full-time (0 women). *Degree requirements:* For doctorate, dissertation required, foreign language not required. *Entrance requirements:* For doctorate, GRE General Test. *Application deadline:* For fall admission, 2/1. Application fee: $50. *Financial aid:* Fellowships available. Financial aid application deadline: 5/1. *Application contact:* Jackie Cavendish, Administrative Assistant, 412-268-2301.

Clemson University, Graduate School, College of Engineering and Science, Department of Mathematical Sciences, Clemson, SC 29634. Offers applied and pure mathematics (MS, PhD); computational mathematics (MS, PhD); management science (PhD); operations research (MS, PhD); statistics (MS, PhD). Part-time programs available. *Students:* 60 full-time (24 women), 1 part-time; includes 3 minority (2 African Americans, 1 Hispanic American), 11 international. *Degree requirements:* For master's, computer language, final project required, thesis optional, foreign language not required; for doctorate, computer language, dissertation, qualifying exams required, foreign language not required. *Entrance requirements:* For master's and doctorate, GRE General Test, TOEFL. *Application deadline:* For fall admission, 6/1. Application fee: $35. *Unit head:* Dr. Robert Fennell, Chair, 864-656-3436, Fax: 864-656-5230, E-mail: mathsci@clemson.edu. *Application contact:* Dr. Douglas Shier, Graduate Coordinator, 864-656-1100, Fax: 864-656-5230, E-mail: shierd@clemson.edu.

College of William and Mary, Faculty of Arts and Sciences, Department of Computer Science, Program in Computational Operations Research, Williamsburg, VA 23187-8795. Offers MS. Part-time programs available. *Degree requirements:* For master's, computer language, research project required, thesis optional. *Entrance requirements:* For master's, GRE General Test, minimum GPA of 2.5. *Application deadline:* For fall admission, 3/1 (priority date); for spring admission, 11/1. Applications are processed on a rolling basis. Application fee: $30. *Unit head:* Dr. Georges Fadel, Coordinator, Program in Mechanical Engineering, 864-656-5620, Fax: 864-656-4435. *Application contact:* Vanessa Godwin, Administrative Director, 757-221-3455, Fax: 757-221-1717, E-mail: gradinfo@cs.wm.edu.

Announcement: The College offers a program of study leading to the MS/PhD in computational operations research. Course offerings include linear programming, discrete optimization, networks, deterministic and stochastic models, reliability, decision theory, algorithms, and simulation. Typically fewer than 10 students per course. Students should e-mail cor@cs.wm.edu for brochure and application materials. World Wide Web: http://www.math.wm.edu/~leemis/or.html

Cornell University, Graduate School, Graduate Fields of Engineering, Field of Chemical Engineering, Ithaca, NY 14853-0001. Offers advanced materials processing (M Eng, MS, PhD); applied mathematics and computational methods (M Eng, MS, PhD); biochemical engineering (M Eng, MS, PhD); chemical reaction engineering (M Eng, MS, PhD); classical and statistical thermodynamics (M Eng, MS, PhD); fluid dynamics, rheology and biorheology (M Eng, MS, PhD); heat and mass transfer (M Eng, MS, PhD); kinetics and catalysis (M Eng, MS, PhD); polymers (M Eng, MS, PhD); surface science (M Eng, MS, PhD). *Faculty:* 18 full-time. *Students:* 71 full-time (17 women); includes 9 minority (1 African American, 7 Asian Americans or Pacific Islanders, 1 Hispanic American), 29 international. *Degree requirements:* For master's, thesis (MS) required; for doctorate, dissertation required, foreign language not required. *Entrance requirements:* For master's and doctorate, GRE General Test, TOEFL (minimum score of 580 required). *Application deadline:* For fall admission, 1/15. Application fee: $65. Electronic applications accepted. *Unit head:* Director of Graduate Studies, 607-255-4550, Fax: 607-255-9166. *Application contact:* Graduate Field Assistant, 607-255-4550, Fax: 607-255-9166, E-mail: dgs@cheme.cornell.edu.

Embry-Riddle Aeronautical University, Daytona Beach Campus Graduate Program, Program in Industrial Optimization, Daytona Beach, FL 32114-3900. Offers MSIO. *Faculty:* 2 full-time (1 woman). *Degree requirements:* For master's, thesis optional, foreign language not required. *Entrance requirements:* For master's, TOEFL (minimum score of 550 required). Application fee: $30 ($50 for international students). Tuition: Full-time $8,190; part-time $455 per credit. Required fees: $105 per semester. Tuition and fees vary according to program. *Financial aid:* Application deadline: 4/15; *Faculty research:* Multiple response optimization, risk analysis, statistical process control and improvement, multiple criteria decision making. Total annual research expenditures: $800,000. *Unit head:* Dr. Deborah Osborne, Chair, 904-226-7688, Fax: 904-226-6269, E-mail: osborned@cts.db.erau.edu. *Application contact:* Ginny Tait, Graduate Admissions Specialist, 904-226-6115, Fax: 904-226-6299, E-mail: taitg@cts.db.erau.edu.

See in-depth description on page 671.

George Mason University, Institute for Computational Sciences and Informatics, Fairfax, VA 22030-4444. Offers PhD. Part-time and evening/weekend programs available. *Faculty:* 10 full-time (2 women), 10 part-time (0 women). *Students:* 56 full-time (16 women), 124 part-time (19 women). Average age 30. 52 applicants, 65% accepted. In 1998, 12 degrees awarded (100% found work related to degree). *Degree requirements:* For doctorate, computer language, dissertation required. *Entrance requirements:* For doctorate, GRE General Test, TOEFL (minimum score of 575 required), minimum GPA of 3.0 in last 60 hours. *Average time to degree:* Doctorate–4 years full-time. *Application deadline:* For fall admission, 2/1 (priority date); for spring admission, 11/1 (priority date). Application fee: $30. Tuition, state resident: full-time $4,416; part-time $184 per credit hour. Tuition, nonresident: full-time $12,516; part-time $522 per credit hour. Tuition and fees vary according to program. *Financial aid:* Fellowships, research assistantships, teaching assistantships, career-related internships or fieldwork, Federal Work-Study, institutionally-sponsored loans, and tuition waivers (partial) available. Financial aid application deadline: 2/1; financial aid applicants required to submit FAFSA. *Faculty research:* Space sciences and astrophysics, fluid dynamics, materials modeling and simulation, bioinformatics, global changes and statistics. *Unit head:* Dr. W. Murray Black, Director, 703-993-1999, Fax: 703-993-1993, E-mail: mblack@gmu.edu. *Application contact:* Dr. Peter A. Becker, Graduate Coordinator, 703-993-3619, Fax: 703-993-1980, E-mail: pbecker@science.gmu.edu.

See in-depth description on page 677.

The George Washington University, Columbian School of Arts and Sciences, Program in Computational Sciences, Washington, DC 20052. Offers computational mathematics (MS); computational physics (MS); computational science (MS); computational statistics and stochastic modeling (MS). *Degree requirements:* For master's, thesis or internship required. *Entrance requirements:* For master's, GRE General Test. Application fee: $55. Tuition: Full-time $17,328; part-time $722 per credit hour. Required fees: $828; $35 per credit hour. Tuition and fees vary according to campus/location and program. *Unit head:* Kalvir Dhuga, Director, 202-994-0140, E-mail: compsci@gwu.edu.

Louisiana Tech University, Graduate School, College of Engineering and Science, Department of Physics, Ruston, LA 71272. Offers applied computational analysis and modeling (PhD); physics (MS). Part-time programs available. *Degree requirements:* For master's, computer language, thesis or alternative required, foreign language not required; for doctorate, computer language, dissertation required, foreign language not required. *Entrance requirements:* For master's, GRE General Test (minimum combined score of 1070 required; average 1245), TOEFL (minimum score of 550 required), minimum GPA of 3.0 in last 60 hours; for doctorate, TOEFL (minimum score of 550 required). *Faculty research:* Experimental high energy physics, laser/optics, computational physics, quantum gravity.

Massachusetts Institute of Technology, School of Science, Department of Brain and Cognitive Sciences, Cambridge, MA 02139-4307. Offers cellular/molecular neuroscience (PhD); cognitive neuroscience (PhD); cognitive science (PhD); computational neuroscience (PhD); systems neuroscience (PhD). *Faculty:* 28 full-time. *Students:* 49 full-time (15 women); includes 3 minority (1 African American, 2 Asian Americans or Pacific Islanders), 21 international. *Degree requirements:* For doctorate, dissertation required, foreign language not required. *Entrance requirements:* For doctorate, GRE General Test. *Application deadline:* For fall admission, 1/15. Application fee: $55. *Unit head:* Mriganka Sur, Head, 617-253-8784. *Application contact:* Denise Heintze, Graduate Administrator, 617-253-5742, Fax: 617-258-9216, E-mail: bcsadmiss@wccf.mit.edu.

Memorial University of Newfoundland, School of Graduate Studies, Interdisciplinary Program in Computational Science, St. John's, NF A1C 5S7, Canada. Offers computational science (M Sc); computational science (cooperative) (M Sc). *Students:* 3 full-time (all women). 6 applicants, 67% accepted. *Degree requirements:* For master's, thesis required (for some programs). *Application deadline:* Applications are processed on a rolling basis. Application fee: $40. *Unit head:* Dr. Jolanta Lagowski, Acting Chair, 709-737-2667. *Application contact:* Gail Kenny, Secretary, 709-737-3444, E-mail: gkenny@morgan.ucs.mun.ca.

Michigan State University, Graduate School, College of Natural Science, Department of Mathematics, East Lansing, MI 48824-1020. Offers applied mathematics (MS, PhD); computational mathematics (MS); mathematics (MA, MAT, MS, PhD); mathematics education (PhD). *Faculty:* 63. *Students:* 92 full-time (26 women), 36 part-time (12 women); includes 9 minority (2 African Americans, 4 Asian Americans or Pacific Islanders, 3 Hispanic Americans), 76 international. Terminal master's awarded for partial completion of doctoral program. *Degree requirements:* For master's, certifying exam required, foreign language and thesis not required; for doctorate, dissertation, exams, seminar required. *Entrance requirements:* For master's, GRE; for doctorate, minimum GPA of 3.0, MS. *Application deadline:* For fall admission, 2/1. Applications are processed on a rolling basis. Application fee: $30 ($40 for international students). *Unit head:* Dr. Peter Lappan, Chairperson, 517-355-9681, Fax: 517-432-1562. *Application contact:* Director of Graduate Studies, 517-353-4650, Fax: 517-432-1562, E-mail: grad@mth.msu.,edu.

Michigan State University, Graduate School, College of Natural Science, Department of Statistics and Probability, East Lansing, MI 48824-1020. Offers applied statistics (MS); computational statistics (MS); operations research-statistics (MS); statistics (MA, MS, PhD). Part-time programs available. *Students:* 27 full-time (8 women), 13 part-time (3 women); includes 1 minority (Asian American or Pacific Islander), 33 international. Terminal master's awarded for partial completion of doctoral program. *Degree requirements:* For master's, foreign language and thesis not required; for doctorate, dissertation required. *Entrance requirements:* For master's and doctorate, GRE, TOEFL. *Application deadline:* For fall admission, 1/1 (priority date). Applications are processed on a rolling basis. Application fee: $30 ($40 for international students). *Unit head:* Dr. Habib Salehi, Chairman, 517-353-3391, Fax: 517-432-1405. *Application contact:* James Stapleton, Graduate Program Director, 517-355-9678, Fax: 517-432-1405, E-mail: stapleton@stt.msu.edu.

See in-depth description on page 695.

Michigan Technological University, Graduate School, College of Sciences and Arts, Department of Computer Science, Houghton, MI 49931-1295. Offers computer science (MS); engineering-computational science (PhD). Part-time programs available. *Faculty:* 9 full-time (2 women). *Students:* 5 full-time (all women), 41 part-time (11 women); includes 1 minority (Asian American or Pacific Islander), 33 international. *Degree requirements:* For master's, computer language required, foreign language not required; for doctorate, computer language, dissertation required, foreign language not required. *Entrance requirements:* For master's, GRE General Test (minimum combined score of 1780 on three sections required; average 1998), TOEFL (minimum score of 600 required; average 631); for doctorate, GRE General Test (combined average 2145 on three sections), TOEFL (minimum score of 575 required; average 588). *Application deadline:* For fall admission, 3/15 (priority date). Applications are processed on a rolling basis. Application fee: $30 ($35 for international students). Tuition, state resident: full-time $4,377. Tuition, nonresident: full-time $9,108. Required fees: $126. Tuition and fees vary according to course load. *Unit head:* Dr. Linda Ott, Chair, 906-487-2209, Fax: 906-487-2283, E-mail: linda@mtu.edu. *Application contact:* Dr. Steve Carr, Assistant Professor, 906-487-2950, Fax: 906-487-2283, E-mail: carr@mtu.edu.

Mississippi State University, College of Engineering, Program in Computational Engineering, Mississippi State, MS 39762. Offers MS, PhD. Part-time programs available. *Students:* 29 full-time (5 women), 9 part-time (3 women); includes 17 minority (2 African Americans, 13 Asian Americans or Pacific Islanders, 2 Hispanic Americans), 5 international. Average age 29. 21 applicants, 71% accepted. In 1998, 2 master's, 3 doctorates awarded. *Entrance requirements:* For master's, GRE, TOEFL (minimum score of 550 required), minimum GPA of 2.75. *Application deadline:* For fall admission, 7/1; for spring admission, 11/1. Applications are processed on a rolling basis. *Financial aid:* Federal Work-Study, institutionally-sponsored loans, and unspecified assistantships available. Financial aid applicants required to submit FAFSA. *Faculty research:* 3-D incompressible algorithm, grid generation for fluid applications, simulations of viscous flow, computational methods for internal flows. *Unit head:* Jerry B. Inmon, Director of Admissions, 662-325-2224, Fax: 662-325-7360, E-mail: admit@admissions.msstate.edu. *Application contact:* Jerry B. Inmon, Director of Admissions, 662-325-2224, Fax: 662-325-7360, E-mail: admit@admissions.msstate.edu.

Announcement: The Graduate Program in Computational Engineering (MS and PhD) is an interdisciplinary program designed to educate students in modern computational techniques. The program emphasizes mathematics, numerical analysis, and computer science applied to areas such as computational fluid dynamics, electromagnetics, and heat transfer. See the in-depth description in the computer science section or visit the Web site at http://www.erc.msstate.edu.

Princeton University, Graduate School, Department of Mathematics, Program in Applied and Computational Mathematics, Princeton, NJ 08544-1019. Offers PhD. *Degree requirements:* For doctorate, dissertation required. *Entrance requirements:* For doctorate, GRE General Test, GRE Subject Test.

See in-depth description on page 731.

Princeton University, Graduate School, Department of Physics, Princeton, NJ 08544-1019. Offers applied and computational mathematics (PhD); mathematical physics (PhD); physics (PhD); physics and chemical physics (PhD). *Degree requirements:* For doctorate, dissertation required. *Entrance requirements:* For doctorate, GRE General Test, GRE Subject Test.

Radford University, Graduate College, College of Arts and Sciences, Department of Mathematics and Statistics, Radford, VA 24142. Offers computational science (MS). Part-time programs available. Postbaccalaureate distance learning degree programs offered (minimal on-campus study). *Faculty:* 13 full-time (2 women). *Students:* 13 full-time (5 women); includes 1 minority (Asian American or Pacific Islander), 9 international. Average age 31. 42 applicants, 26% accepted. In 1998, 5 degrees awarded. *Degree requirements:* For master's, thesis (for some programs), comprehensive exam required. *Entrance requirements:* For master's, GMAT, GRE General Test, TOEFL (minimum score of 550 required), minimum GPA of 2.7. *Average time to degree:* Master's–2.1 years full-time. *Application deadline:* For fall admission, 2/15 (priority date); for spring admission, 10/15. Applications are processed on a rolling basis. Application fee: $25. Electronic applications accepted. *Financial aid:* In 1998–99, 7 students received aid, including 7 research assistantships (averaging $5,757 per year); teaching assistantships, career-related internships or fieldwork, Federal Work-Study, grants, institutionally-sponsored loans, and scholarships also available. Financial aid application deadline: 2/1; financial aid applicants required to submit FAFSA. *Unit head:* Dr. David L. Albig, Chair, 540-831-5670, Fax: 540-831-5970, E-mail: dalbig@runet.edu.

Rice University, Graduate Programs, George R. Brown School of Engineering, Department of Computational and Applied Mathematics, Houston, TX 77251-1892. Offers MA, MAM Sc, PhD. Part-time programs available. *Degree requirements:* For master's, thesis required (for some programs), foreign language not required; for doctorate, dissertation required. *Entrance requirements:* For master's and doctorate, GRE General Test, GRE Subject Test, TOEFL (minimum score of 550 required), minimum GPA of 3.0. *Faculty research:* Statistics, operations research, computer science, game theory, numerical analysis.

Stanford University, School of Engineering, Program in Scientific Computing and Computational Mathematics, Stanford, CA 94305-9991. Offers MS, PhD. *Students:* 33 full-time (3 women), 7 part-time (1 woman); includes 11 minority (9 Asian Americans or Pacific Islanders, 2 Hispanic Americans), 17 international. Average age 27. 37 applicants, 38% accepted. In 1998, 10 master's, 7 doctorates awarded. *Degree requirements:* For doctorate, dissertation required. *Entrance requirements:* For master's, GRE General Test, TOEFL; for doctorate, GRE General Test, GRE Subject Test, TOEFL. Application fee: $65 ($80 for international students). Electronic applications accepted. Tuition: Full-time $24,588. Required fees: $152. Part-time tuition and fees vary according to course load. *Financial aid:* Fellowships, research assistantships, institutionally-sponsored loans available. Financial aid application deadline: 2/15. *Unit head:* Dr. Andrew M. Stuart, Director, 650-723-8142, Fax: 650-723-1778, E-mail: stuart@sccm.stanford.edu. *Application contact:* Admissions Coordinator, 650-723-0572.

Temple University, Graduate School, College of Science and Technology, Department of Mathematics, Philadelphia, PA 19122-6096. Offers applied and computational mathematics (MA, PhD); pure mathematics (MA, PhD). Part-time and evening/weekend programs available. *Faculty:* 26 full-time (1 woman). *Students:* 39 (10 women); includes 14 minority (1 African American, 11 Asian Americans or Pacific Islanders, 2 Hispanic Americans) 3 international. Terminal master's awarded for partial completion of doctoral program. *Degree requirements:* For master's, written exam required, thesis optional, foreign language not required; for doctorate, 2 foreign languages, dissertation, oral and written exams required. *Entrance requirements:* For master's and doctorate, GRE General Test (minimum combined score of 1000 required), GRE Subject Test, minimum GPA of 3.0 during previous 2 years, 2.8 overall. *Application deadline:* For fall admission, 2/10 (priority date). Applications are processed on a rolling basis. Application fee: $40. *Unit head:* Dr. Jack Schiller, Chair, 215-204-4650, Fax: 215-204-6433, E-mail: schiller@euclid.math.temple.edu. *Application contact:* Dr. Eric Grinberg, Graduate Chair, 215-204-7286, Fax: 215-204-6433, E-mail: grinberg@euclid.math.temple.edu.

The University of Iowa, Graduate College, College of Liberal Arts, Program in Applied Mathematical and Computational Sciences, Iowa City, IA 52242-1316. Offers PhD. *Students:* 15 full-time (4 women), 9 part-time (1 woman); includes 3 minority (1 Asian American or Pacific Islander, 2 Hispanic Americans), 18 international. 23 applicants, 57% accepted. In 1998, 1 degree awarded. *Degree requirements:* For doctorate, dissertation, comprehensive exam required. *Entrance requirements:* For doctorate, GRE General Test. *Application deadline:* Applications are processed on a rolling basis. Application fee: $30 ($50 for international students). *Financial aid:* In 1998–99, 2 fellowships, 2 research assistantships, 21 teaching assistantships were awarded. Financial aid applicants required to submit FAFSA. *Unit head:* Herbert W. Hethcote, Chair, 319-335-0790.

University of Minnesota, Duluth, Graduate School, College of Science and Engineering, Department of Mathematics and Statistics, Duluth, MN 55812-2496. Offers applied and computational mathematics (MS). Part-time programs available. *Faculty:* 16 full-time (2 women). *Students:* 13 full-time (6 women), 1 (woman) part-time; includes 9 minority (8 Asian Americans or Pacific Islanders, 1 Hispanic American) Average age 24. 15 applicants, 100% accepted. In 1998, 7 degrees awarded. *Degree requirements:* For master's, thesis or alternative required, foreign language not required. *Entrance requirements:* For master's, GRE General Test (average 750 quantitative), TOEFL (minimum score of 550 required), minimum GPA of 3.0. *Average time to degree:* Master's–2 years full-time, 4 years part-time. *Application deadline:* For fall admission, 3/1 (priority date); for spring admission, 11/15. Applications are processed on a rolling basis. Application fee: $50 ($55 for international students). *Financial aid:* In 1998–99, 1 fellowship (averaging $1,710 per year), 5 research assistantships with full tuition reimbursements (averaging $9,383 per year), 13 teaching assistantships with full tuition reimbursements (averaging $9,383 per year) were awarded.; career-related internships or fieldwork, Federal Work-Study, grants, institutionally-sponsored loans, scholarships, traineeships, and unspecified assistantships also available. Aid available to part-time students. Financial aid application deadline: 3/1. *Faculty research:* Discrete mathematics, diagnostic markers, combinatorics, biostatistics, mathematical modelling and scientific computation. Total annual research expenditures: $453,493. *Unit head:* Dr. John R. Greene, Director of Graduate Studies, 218-726-6328, Fax: 218-726-8399, E-mail: jgreene@d.umn.edu. *Application contact:* Dr. Barry R. James, Admissions Director, 218-726-7998, Fax: 218-726-8399, E-mail: bjames@d.umn.edu.

University of Minnesota, Twin Cities Campus, Graduate School, Scientific Computation Program, Minneapolis, MN 55455-0213. Offers MS, PhD. Part-time programs available. *Faculty:* 35 full-time (3 women). *Students:* 6 full-time (2 women), 5 international. 10 applicants, 30% accepted. *Degree requirements:* For master's and doctorate, thesis/dissertation required, foreign language not required. *Entrance requirements:* For doctorate, GRE. *Application deadline:* For fall admission, 1/2 (priority date). Applications are processed on a rolling basis. Application fee: $50 ($55 for international students). *Financial aid:* In 1998–99, 6 students received aid; fellowships, research assistantships, teaching assistantships, career-related internships or fieldwork and Federal Work-Study available. *Faculty research:* Parallel computations, quantum mechanical dynamics, computational materials science, computational fluid dynamics. *Unit head:* Vipin Kumar, Director of Graduate Studies, 612-625-4002, E-mail: kumar@cs.umn.edu. *Application contact:* Georganne E. Tolaas, Graduate Secretary, 612-625-1592, Fax: 612-625-0572, E-mail: scic@cs.umn.edu.

University of Mississippi, Graduate School, School of Engineering, Program in Computational Engineering Science, Oxford, University, MS 38677-9702. Offers MS, PhD. *Students:* 2 full-time (0 women); includes 1 minority (African American), 1 international. *Degree requirements:* For doctorate, dissertation required, foreign language not required, foreign language not required. *Entrance requirements:* For master's, GRE General Test, TOEFL, minimum GPA of 3.0; for doctorate, GRE General Test, TOEFL. *Application deadline:* For fall admission, 8/1. Applications are processed on a rolling basis. Application fee: $0 ($25 for international students). Tuition, state resident: full-time $3,053; part-time $170 per credit hour. Tuition, nonresident: full-time $6,155; part-time $342 per credit hour. Tuition and fees vary according to program. *Financial aid:* Application deadline: 3/1. *Unit head:* Dr. Allie M. Smith, Dean, School of Engineering, 601-232-7407, Fax: 601-232-1287, E-mail: engineer@olemiss.edu.

University of Puerto Rico, Mayagüez Campus, Graduate Studies, College of Arts and Sciences, Department of Mathematics, Mayagüez, PR 00681-5000. Offers applied mathematics (MS); computational sciences (MS); pure mathematics (MS); statistics (MS). Part-time programs available. *Degree requirements:* For master's, one foreign language, comprehensive exam required, thesis optional. *Faculty research:* Automata theory, linear algebra, logic.

University of Saskatchewan, College of Graduate Studies and Research, College of Arts and Sciences, Department of Computational Science, Saskatoon, SK S7N 5A2, Canada. Offers M Sc, PhD. *Degree requirements:* For master's and doctorate, computer language, thesis/dissertation required. *Entrance requirements:* For master's and doctorate, GRE, TOEFL.

The University of Texas at Austin, Graduate School, Program in Computational and Applied Mathematics, Austin, TX 78712-1111. Offers MA, PhD. *Faculty:* 62 full-time (7 women). *Students:* 24 full-time (5 women); includes 7 minority (4 Asian Americans or Pacific Islanders, 3 Hispanic Americans), 4 international. Average age 28. 58 applicants, 21% accepted. In 1998, 4 master's awarded (0% continued full-time study); 1 doctorate awarded (100% found work related to degree). Terminal master's awarded for partial completion of doctoral program. *Degree requirements:* For master's, computer language required, thesis optional, foreign language not required; for doctorate, computer language, dissertation, 3 area qualifying exams required, foreign language not required. *Average time to degree:* Master's–3 years full-time; doctorate–6 years full-time. *Application deadline:* For fall admission, 2/1. Application fee: $50 ($75 for international students). Electronic applications accepted. *Financial aid:* In 1998–99, 10 fellowships with full and partial tuition reimbursements, 5 research assistantships with full and partial tuition reimbursements (averaging $10,000 per year), 5 teaching assistantships with full and partial tuition reimbursements (averaging $11,000 per year) were awarded. Financial aid application deadline: 2/1. *Unit head:* Clint Dawson, Graduate Adviser, 512-475-8627, E-mail: clint@ticam.utexas.edu. *Application contact:* Kathryn Petro, Graduate Coordinator, 512-471-7386, Fax: 512-471-8694, E-mail: camgrad@ticam.utexas.edu.

Western Michigan University, Graduate College, College of Arts and Sciences, Department of Mathematics and Statistics, Program in Computational Mathematics, Kalamazoo, MI 49008. Offers MS. 2 applicants, 50% accepted. *Degree requirements:* For master's, thesis not required. *Application deadline:* For fall admission, 2/15 (priority date). Applications are processed on a rolling basis. Application fee: $25. *Financial aid:* Fellowships, research assistantships, teaching assistantships available. Financial aid application deadline: 2/15; financial aid applicants required to submit FAFSA. *Unit head:* Chris Shankle, Associate Director of Graduate Admissions, 203-837-8244, Fax: 203-837-8338, E-mail: shanklec@wcsu.edu. *Application contact:* Paula J. Boodt, Coordinator, Graduate Admissions and Recruitment, 616-387-2000, Fax: 616-387-2355, E-mail: paula.boodt@wmich.edu.

Mathematics

Adelphi University, Graduate School of Arts and Sciences, Department of Mathematics and Computer Science, Garden City, NY 11530. Offers mathematics (MS, DA). Part-time and evening/weekend programs available. Average age 42. In 1998, 3 degrees awarded. *Degree requirements:* For doctorate, computer language, dissertation required, foreign language not required, foreign language not required. *Application deadline:* Applications are processed on a rolling basis. Application fee: $50. *Financial aid:* Fellowships, teaching assistantships, tuition waivers (full) available. Financial aid application deadline: 3/1. *Unit head:* Dr. David Lubell, Chairperson, 516-877-4480.

Alabama State University, School of Graduate Studies, College of Arts and Sciences, Department of Mathematics, Computers, and Physical Science, Montgomery, AL 36101-0271. Offers mathematics (MS, Ed S). Part-time programs available. *Faculty:* 3 full-time (0 women). *Students:* 11 full-time (4 women), 23 part-time (12 women); includes 26 minority (25 African Americans, 1 Asian American or Pacific Islander) In 1998, 2 master's awarded. *Degree requirements:* For master's, one foreign language (computer language can substitute), thesis, comprehensive exam required; for Ed S, thesis required. *Entrance requirements:* For master's, GRE General Test, GRE Subject Test, Graduate Writing Competency Test (minimum score of 140 required); for Ed S, Graduate Writing Competency Test (minimum score of 140 required), GRE, MAT. *Application deadline:* For fall admission, 7/15; for spring admission, 12/15. Applications are processed on a rolling basis. Application fee: $10. Tuition, state resident: full-time $2,880; part-time $120 per credit. Tuition, nonresident: full-time $5,760; part-time $240 per credit. *Financial aid:* In 1998–99, 1 research assistantship (averaging $9,000 per year) was awarded.; teaching assistantships *Faculty research:* Discrete mathematics, symbolic dynamics, mathematical social sciences. Total annual research expenditures: $25,000. *Unit head:* Dr. Wallace Maryland, Chair, 334-229-4464, Fax: 334-229-4902, E-mail: wmaryl@asunet.alasu.edu. *Application contact:* Dr. Annette Marie Allen, Dean of Graduate Studies, 334-229-4275, Fax: 334-229-4928, E-mail: aallen@asunet.alasu.edu.

American University, College of Arts and Sciences, Department of Mathematics and Statistics, Program in Mathematics, Washington, DC 20016-8001. Offers MA. Part-time and evening/weekend programs available. *Faculty:* 19 full-time (6 women), 5 part-time (3 women). *Students:* 2 full-time (1 woman), 1 (woman) part-time; includes 1 minority (African American), 1 international. 9 applicants, 78% accepted. In 1998, 2 degrees awarded. *Degree requirements:* For master's, one foreign language required, (computer language can substitute), thesis optional. *Entrance requirements:* For master's, BA in mathematics. *Application deadline:* For fall admission, 2/1; for spring admission, 10/1. Application fee: $50. *Financial aid:* Fellowships, teaching assistantships, career-related internships or fieldwork, Federal Work-Study, and institutionally-sponsored loans available. Aid available to part-time students. Financial aid application deadline: 2/1. *Unit head:* Dr. Virginia Stallings, Chair, Department of Mathematics and Statistics, 202-885-3166, Fax: 202-885-3155.

See in-depth description on page 639.

Andrews University, School of Graduate Studies, College of Arts and Sciences, Interdisciplinary Studies in Mathematics and Physical Science Program, Berrien Springs, MI 49104. Offers MS. *Students:* 1 (woman) full-time. *Application deadline:* Applications are processed on a rolling basis. Application fee: $40. *Unit head:* Dr. Robert E. Kingman, Chairman, 616-471-3431.

Angelo State University, Graduate School, College of Sciences, Department of Mathematics, San Angelo, TX 76909. Offers MS. Part-time and evening/weekend programs available. *Faculty:* 6 full-time (1 woman). 2 applicants, 50% accepted. In 1998, 1 degree awarded. *Degree requirements:* For master's, comprehensive exam required, thesis optional, foreign language not required. *Entrance requirements:* For master's, GRE General Test, minimum GPA of 2.5. *Application deadline:* For fall admission, 8/7 (priority date); for spring admission, 1/2. Applications are processed on a rolling basis. Application fee: $25 ($50 for international students). Tuition, state resident: part-time $38 per semester hour. Tuition, nonresident: part-time $249 per semester hour. Required fees: $40 per semester hour. $71 per semester. Tuition and fees vary according to degree level. *Financial aid:* Fellowships, teaching assistantships, Federal Work-Study, tuition waivers (partial), and unspecified assistantships available. Aid available to part-time students. Financial aid application deadline: 8/1. *Unit head:* Dr. Johnny M. Bailey, Head, 915-942-2111.

Appalachian State University, Cratis D. Williams Graduate School, College of Arts and Sciences, Department of Mathematics, Boone, NC 28608. Offers MA. Part-time programs available. *Faculty:* 20 full-time (5 women). *Students:* 7 full-time (3 women), 7 part-time (3 women). 10 applicants, 70% accepted. In 1998, 2 degrees awarded (100% found work related to degree). *Degree requirements:* For master's, one foreign language (computer language can substitute), comprehensive exam required, thesis not required. *Entrance requirements:* For master's, GRE General Test. *Average time to degree:* Master's–2 years full-time, 4 years part-time. *Application deadline:* For fall admission, 7/15 (priority date); for winter admission, 12/5 (priority date). Application fee: $35. *Financial aid:* In 1998–99, 6 students received aid, including 4 research assistantships (averaging $6,500 per year), 2 teaching assistantships (averaging $6,500 per year); fellowships, career-related internships or fieldwork, scholarships, and

Peterson's Graduate Programs in the Physical Sciences, Mathematics, Agricultural Sciences, the Environment & Natural Resources 2000 601

Mathematics

Appalachian State University (continued)
unspecified assistantships also available. Aid available to part-time students. Financial aid application deadline: 7/15. *Faculty research:* Graph theory, differential equations, reverse logic, simulation, register allocation. *Unit head:* Dr. William Bauldry, Chair, 828-262-3050, Fax: 828-265-8617. *Application contact:* Dr. Rudy Curd, Graduate Director, 828-262-2378.

Arizona State University, Graduate College, College of Liberal Arts and Sciences, Department of Mathematics, Tempe, AZ 85287. Offers applied mathematics (MA, PhD); mathematics (MA, MNS, PhD); statistics (MA, PhD). *Faculty:* 95 full-time (22 women), 2 part-time (0 women). *Students:* 67 full-time (20 women), 15 part-time (5 women); includes 6 minority (2 African Americans, 3 Asian Americans or Pacific Islanders, 1 Hispanic American), 37 international. Average age 29. 97 applicants, 85% accepted. In 1998, 10 master's, 9 doctorates awarded. *Degree requirements:* For master's, thesis or alternative required; for doctorate, one foreign language, dissertation required. *Entrance requirements:* For master's and doctorate, GRE General Test. *Application deadline:* For fall admission, 3/1. Application fee: $45. *Faculty research:* Mathematical biology, ordinary and partial differential equations, calculus of variations. *Unit head:* Dr. Rosemary Renaut, Chair, 480-965-3951.

See in-depth description on page 641.

Arkansas State University, Graduate School, College of Arts and Sciences, Department of Computer Science and Mathematics, Jonesboro, State University, AR 72467. Offers computer science (MS); mathematics (MS, MSE). Part-time programs available. *Faculty:* 14 full-time (2 women). *Students:* 11 full-time (1 woman), 12 part-time (6 women), 6 international. Average age 26. In 1998, 12 degrees awarded. *Degree requirements:* For master's, thesis or alternative, comprehensive exam required. *Entrance requirements:* For master's, GRE General Test or MAT, appropriate bachelor's degree. *Application deadline:* For fall admission, 7/1 (priority date); for spring admission, 11/15 (priority date). Applications are processed on a rolling basis. Application fee: $15 ($25 for international students). *Financial aid:* Teaching assistantships available. Aid available to part-time students. Financial aid application deadline: 7/1; financial aid applicants required to submit FAFSA. *Unit head:* Dr. Roger Abernathy, Chair, 870-972-3090, Fax: 870-972-3950, E-mail: raber@caddo.astate.edu.

Auburn University, Graduate School, College of Sciences and Mathematics, Department of Mathematics, Auburn, Auburn University, AL 36849-0002. Offers MAM, MS, PhD. *Faculty:* 39 full-time (3 women). *Students:* 24 full-time (6 women), 23 part-time (6 women). 19 applicants, 21% accepted. In 1998, 5 master's, 5 doctorates awarded. *Degree requirements:* For doctorate, dissertation required. *Entrance requirements:* For master's, GRE General Test, undergraduate mathematics background; for doctorate, GRE General Test, GRE Subject Test. *Application deadline:* For fall admission, 4/15 (priority date). Applications are processed on a rolling basis. Application fee: $25 ($50 for international students). Tuition, state resident: full-time $2,760; part-time $76 per credit hour. Tuition, nonresident: full-time $8,280; part-time $228 per credit hour. *Financial aid:* Fellowships, teaching assistantships, special tuition awards available. *Faculty research:* Pure and applied mathematics. *Unit head:* Dr. George A. Kozlowski, Head, 334-844-4290, Fax: 334-844-6555, E-mail: kozloga@mail.auburn.edu.

Ball State University, Graduate School, College of Sciences and Humanities, Department of Mathematical Sciences, Program in Mathematics, Muncie, IN 47306-1099. Offers mathematics (MA, MS); mathematics education (MAE). *Accreditation:* NCATE (one or more programs are accredited). *Students:* 3 full-time (1 woman), 3 part-time (1 woman). Average age 22. 3 applicants, 67% accepted. In 1998, 4 degrees awarded. *Degree requirements:* Foreign language not required. Application fee: $15 ($25 for international students). *Financial aid:* Research assistantships available. *Unit head:* Charles Parish, Director, 765-285-8645, E-mail: cparish@bsu.edu.

Baylor University, Graduate School, College of Arts and Sciences, Department of Mathematics, Waco, TX 76798. Offers MS. *Students:* 4 full-time (3 women), 1 part-time, 1 international. In 1998, 5 degrees awarded. *Degree requirements:* For master's, computer language, thesis (for some programs), final oral exam required, foreign language not required. *Entrance requirements:* For master's, GRE General Test. *Application deadline:* For fall admission, 8/1. Applications are processed on a rolling basis. Application fee: $25. *Financial aid:* Teaching assistantships, career-related internships or fieldwork, Federal Work-Study, and institutionally-sponsored loans available. Aid available to part-time students. Financial aid application deadline: 5/1. *Faculty research:* Algebra, statistics, probability, applied mathematics, numerical analysis. *Unit head:* Dr. Frank Mathis, Director of Graduate Studies, 254-710-3561, Fax: 254-710-3569, E-mail: frank_mathis@baylor.edu. *Application contact:* Suzanne Keener, Administrative Assistant, 254-710-3588, Fax: 254-710-3870, E-mail: suzanne_keener@baylor.edu.

Boston College, Graduate School of Arts and Sciences, Department of Mathematics, Chestnut Hill, MA 02467-3800. Offers MA, MBA/MA. Part-time programs available. *Faculty:* 25 full-time (4 women). *Students:* 9 full-time (6 women), 7 part-time (4 women); includes 1 African American 12 applicants, 67% accepted. In 1998, 4 degrees awarded. *Degree requirements:* For master's, oral presentation required, thesis optional, foreign language not required. *Entrance requirements:* For master's, GRE General Test. *Application deadline:* For fall admission, 2/1 (priority date). Application fee: $40. *Financial aid:* Fellowships, teaching assistantships, Federal Work-Study and scholarships available. Aid available to part-time students. Financial aid application deadline: 3/15; financial aid applicants required to submit FAFSA. *Faculty research:* Abstract algebra and number theory, topology, probability and statistics, computer science, analysis. *Unit head:* Dr. Richard Jenson, Chairperson, 617-552-3750, E-mail: richard.jenson@bc.edu. *Application contact:* Dr. Ned Rosen, Graduate Program Director, 617-552-3756, E-mail: ned.rosen@bc.edu.

Boston University, Graduate School of Arts and Sciences, Department of Mathematics, Boston, MA 02215. Offers mathematics (MA, PhD); statistics (MA, PhD). *Faculty:* 32 full-time (3 women), 5 part-time (1 woman). *Students:* 58 full-time (22 women), 4 part-time (2 women); includes 5 minority (1 African American, 2 Asian Americans or Pacific Islanders, 2 Hispanic Americans), 31 international. Average age 28. 92 applicants, 32% accepted. In 1998, 7 master's awarded (86% found work related to degree, 14% continued full-time study); 2 doctorates awarded (50% entered university research/teaching, 50% found other work related to degree). Terminal master's awarded for partial completion of doctoral program. *Degree requirements:* For master's, one foreign language, comprehensive exam required, thesis not required; for doctorate, one foreign language, dissertation, oral/qualifying exam required. *Entrance requirements:* For master's and doctorate, GRE General Test, GRE Subject Test, TOEFL (minimum score of 550 required). *Average time to degree:* Master's–2 years full-time; doctorate–5 years full-time. *Application deadline:* For fall admission, 1/15 (priority date); for spring admission, 10/15. Applications are processed on a rolling basis. Application fee: $50. Tuition: Full-time $23,770; part-time $743 per credit. Required fees: $220. Tuition and fees vary according to class time, course level, campus/location and program. *Financial aid:* In 1998–99, 46 students received aid, including 3 fellowships, 11 research assistantships, 23 teaching assistantships; Federal Work-Study and scholarships also available. Aid available to part-time students. Financial aid application deadline: 1/15; financial aid applicants required to submit FAFSA. *Faculty research:* Algebraic and differential geometry, dynamical systems, mathematical biology, number theory, statistics and probability. Total annual research expenditures: $17 million. *Unit head:* Steven Rosenberg, Chairman, 617-353-2560, Fax: 617-353-8100, E-mail: sr@bu.edu. *Application contact:* Dan Abramovich, Director of Graduate Studies, 617-353-9547, Fax: 617-353-8100, E-mail: abrmovic@bu.edu.

Bowling Green State University, Graduate College, College of Arts and Sciences, Department of Mathematics and Statistics, Bowling Green, OH 43403. Offers applied statistics (MS); mathematics (MA, MAT, PhD); mathematics supervision (Ed S); statistics (MA, MAT, PhD). Part-time and evening/weekend programs available. *Faculty:* 22 full-time (1 woman), 7 part-time (0 women). *Students:* 60 full-time (36 women), 14 part-time (9 women). 107 applicants, 57% accepted. In 1998, 22 master's awarded. *Degree requirements:* For master's, thesis or alternative required, foreign language not required; for doctorate, dissertation required, foreign language not required; for Ed S, internship required, foreign language and thesis not required. *Entrance requirements:* For master's, GRE General Test, TOEFL (minimum score of 590 required); for doctorate, GRE General Test, TOEFL (minimum score of 600 required). Application fee: $30. Electronic applications accepted. *Financial aid:* Research assistantships with full tuition reimbursements, teaching assistantships with full tuition reimbursements, Federal Work-Study, institutionally-sponsored loans, and unspecified assistantships available. Financial aid applicants required to submit FAFSA. *Faculty research:* Statistics and probability, algebra, analysis. *Unit head:* Dr. John Hayden, Chair, 419-372-2636. *Application contact:* Dr. Neal Carothers, Graduate Coordinator, 419-372-8317.

See in-depth description on page 645.

Brandeis University, Graduate School of Arts and Sciences, Program in Mathematics, Waltham, MA 02454-9110. Offers PhD. *Faculty:* 15 full-time (1 woman), 1 part-time (0 women). *Students:* 28 full-time (5 women); includes 1 minority (Asian American or Pacific Islander), 32 international. Average age 25. 130 applicants, 20% accepted. In 1998, 5 doctorates awarded (100% entered university research/teaching). *Degree requirements:* For doctorate, 2 foreign languages, dissertation required. *Entrance requirements:* For doctorate, GRE General Test, GRE Subject Test. *Application deadline:* For fall admission, 2/1 (priority date). Application fee: $60. *Financial aid:* Fellowships, research assistantships, teaching assistantships, scholarships available. Financial aid application deadline: 4/15; financial aid applicants required to submit CSS PROFILE or FAFSA. *Faculty research:* Algebra, analysis, number theory, combinatorics, topology. *Unit head:* Dr. Paul Monsky, Chair, 781-736-3051, E-mail: maths@brandeis.edu.

Announcement: Program directed primarily toward PhD in pure mathematics. Benefits from informality, flexibility, and warmth of small department and from intellectual vigor of faculty well known for research accomplishments. Brandeis-Harvard-MIT-Northeastern Colloquium and many joint seminars provide opportunities for contact with other Boston-area mathematicians. Students normally receive full-tuition scholarship and teaching assistantship or fellowship. Contact Professor Jerome Levine, Graduate Adviser, 617-736-3054. E-mail: maths@binah.cc.brandeis.edu.

Brigham Young University, Graduate Studies, College of Physical and Mathematical Sciences, Department of Mathematics, Provo, UT 84602-1001. Offers MA, MS, PhD. Part-time programs available. *Faculty:* 37 full-time (0 women). *Students:* 28 full-time (9 women), 7 part-time (2 women); includes 4 minority (all Asian Americans or Pacific Islanders), 2 international. Average age 23. 25 applicants, 64% accepted. In 1998, 13 master's, 3 doctorates awarded (67% entered university research/teaching, 33% continued full-time study). Terminal master's awarded for partial completion of doctoral program. *Degree requirements:* For master's, thesis (for some programs), project or thesis, written exams required, foreign language not required; for doctorate, 2 foreign languages, dissertation, qualifying exams required. *Entrance requirements:* For master's, GRE General Test, GRE Subject Test, TOEFL (minimum score of 600 required), minimum GPA of 3.0 in last 60 hours; for doctorate, GRE General Test, GRE Subject Test, TOEFL (minimum score of 600 required), undergraduate degree in mathematics or related field. *Average time to degree:* Master's–2 years full-time; doctorate–5 years full-time. *Application deadline:* For fall admission, 3/1 (priority date); for winter admission, 10/1; for spring admission, 11/1. Applications are processed on a rolling basis. Application fee: $30. Tuition: Full-time $3,330; part-time $185 per credit hour. Tuition and fees vary according to program and student's religious affiliation. *Financial aid:* In 1998–99, 35 students received aid, including 3 research assistantships with full tuition reimbursements available (averaging $10,000 per year), 32 teaching assistantships with full tuition reimbursements available (averaging $10,000 per year); fellowships, institutionally-sponsored loans also available. Aid available to part-time students. Financial aid application deadline: 3/1. *Faculty research:* Linear algebra, numerical analysis, partial differential equations, geometrical group theory/topology, algebraic geometry number theory. *Unit head:* Dr. Wayne W. Barrett, Chairman, 801-378-2061, Fax: 801-378-3703, E-mail: wayne@math.byu.edu. *Application contact:* Dr. Tyler J. Jarvis, Chair, Graduate Committee, 801-378-2062, Fax: 801-378-3703, E-mail: gradschool@math.byu.edu.

Brooklyn College of the City University of New York, Division of Graduate Studies, Department of Mathematics, Brooklyn, NY 11210-2889. Offers mathematics (MA, PhD); secondary mathematics education (MA). Part-time and evening/weekend programs available. *Faculty:* 2 full-time (0 women), 2 part-time (1 woman). Average age 30. In 1998, 2 degrees awarded (100% found work related to degree). *Degree requirements:* For master's, thesis or alternative, comprehensive exam (mathematics) required, foreign language not required. *Entrance requirements:* For master's, TOEFL (minimum score of 500 required), minimum GPA of 3.0. *Application deadline:* For fall admission, 3/1; for spring admission, 11/1. Application fee: $40. *Financial aid:* Federal Work-Study, institutionally-sponsored loans, and scholarships available. Aid available to part-time students. Financial aid application deadline: 5/1; financial aid applicants required to submit FAFSA. *Faculty research:* Differential geometry, gauge theory, complex analysis, orthogonal functions. *Unit head:* Dr. George Shapiro, Chairperson, 718-951-5246. *Application contact:* Dr. Kishore Marathe, Graduate Deputy, 718-951-5832, E-mail: kbm@bklyn.edu.

Brown University, Graduate School, Department of Mathematics, Providence, RI 02912. Offers AM, Sc M, PhD. *Faculty:* 19 full-time (2 women). *Students:* 34 full-time (10 women), 21 international. In 1998, 4 master's awarded (25% found work related to degree, 75% continued full-time study); 5 doctorates awarded (100% entered university research/teaching). Terminal master's awarded for partial completion of doctoral program. *Degree requirements:* For master's, one foreign language, thesis not required; for doctorate, 2 foreign languages, dissertation required. *Entrance requirements:* For doctorate, GRE, TOEFL (minimum score of 500 required). *Average time to degree:* Master's–2.5 years full-time; doctorate–5 years full-time. *Application deadline:* For fall admission, 1/2 (priority date). Application fee: $60. *Financial aid:* In 1998–99, 33 students received aid, including 11 fellowships with full tuition reimbursements available (averaging $12,400 per year), 4 research assistantships with full tuition reimbursements available (averaging $12,850 per year), 18 teaching assistantships with full tuition reimbursements available (averaging $12,650 per year); Federal Work-Study, institutionally-sponsored loans, and tuition waivers (full and partial) also available. Financial aid application deadline: 1/2; financial aid applicants required to submit FAFSA. *Faculty research:* Algebraic geometry, number theory, functional analysis, geometry, topology. Total annual research expenditures: $389,878. *Unit head:* Walter Craig, Chairman, 401-863-3319, Fax: 401-863-9471, E-mail: craigw@math.brown.edu. *Application contact:* Thomas Goodwillie, Director of Graduate Studies, 401-863-2590, Fax: 401-863-9471, E-mail: tomg@math.brown.edu.

Bryn Mawr College, Graduate School of Arts and Sciences, Department of Mathematics, Bryn Mawr, PA 19010-2899. Offers MA, PhD. Part-time programs available. *Faculty:* 5. *Students:* 2 full-time (1 woman), 6 part-time (3 women). 6 applicants, 67% accepted. In 1998, 1 master's awarded. *Degree requirements:* For master's, thesis required; for doctorate, dissertation required. *Entrance requirements:* For master's and doctorate, GRE General Test. *Application deadline:* For fall admission, 6/30. Application fee: $40. *Financial aid:* Fellowships, teaching assistantships, Federal Work-Study, institutionally-sponsored loans, unspecified assistantships, and tuition awards available. Aid available to part-time students. Financial aid application deadline: 1/2. *Unit head:* Dr. Victor Donnay, Chairman, 610-526-5348. *Application contact:* Graduate School of Arts and Sciences, 610-526-5072.

Bucknell University, Graduate Studies, College of Arts and Sciences, Department of Mathematics, Lewisburg, PA 17837. Offers MA, MS. *Faculty:* 13 full-time. *Students:* 1 full-time (0 women). *Degree requirements:* For master's, foreign language and thesis not required. *Entrance requirements:* For master's, GRE General Test (minimum combined score of 1000 required), GRE Subject Test, TOEFL (minimum score of 550 required), minimum GPA of 2.8. *Application deadline:* For fall admission, 6/1 (priority date); for spring admission, 12/1 (priority date). Applications are processed on a rolling basis. Application fee: $25. Tuition: Part-time $2,600 per course. Tuition and fees vary according to course load. *Financial aid:* Unspecified assistantships available. Financial aid application deadline: 3/1. *Unit head:* Dr. Allen Schweinsberg, Head, 570-577-1343.

California Institute of Technology, Division of Physics, Mathematics and Astronomy, Department of Mathematics, Pasadena, CA 91125-0001. Offers PhD. *Faculty:* 13. *Students:* 20 full-time (1 woman); includes 1 minority (Hispanic American), 16 international. Average age 25. 101 applicants, 24% accepted. In 1998, 5 degrees awarded. *Degree requirements:* For doctorate, one foreign language, dissertation, candidacy and final exams required. *Entrance requirements:* For doctorate, GRE General Test, GRE Subject Test, TOEFL. *Application deadline:* For fall admission, 1/15. Application fee: $0. *Financial aid:* In 1998–99, 20 students received aid, including fellowships with full tuition reimbursements available (averaging $15,900 per year), 20 teaching assistantships with full tuition reimbursements available (averaging $11,754 per year); research assistantships, Federal Work-Study and institutionally-sponsored loans also available. Financial aid application deadline: 1/15. *Faculty research:* Number theory, combinatorics, differential geometry, dynamical systems, finite groups. *Unit head:* Barry Simon, Executive Officer, 626-395-4330. *Application contact:* G. Lorden, Option Representative, 626-395-4349.

California Polytechnic State University, San Luis Obispo, College of Science and Mathematics, Department of Mathematics, San Luis Obispo, CA 93407. Offers MS. *Faculty:* 34 full-time (4 women), 31 part-time (10 women). *Students:* 5 full-time (4 women), 8 part-time (2 women). 12 applicants, 75% accepted. In 1998, 1 degree awarded. *Degree requirements:* For master's, qualifying exams required, thesis optional. *Entrance requirements:* For master's, minimum GPA of 2.5 in last 90 quarter units. *Application deadline:* For fall admission, 7/1. Applications are processed on a rolling basis. Application fee: $55. Tuition, nonresident: part-time $164 per unit. Required fees: $531 per quarter. *Financial aid:* Career-related internships or fieldwork and Federal Work-Study available. Aid available to part-time students. Financial aid application deadline: 3/2; financial aid applicants required to submit FAFSA. *Unit head:* Dr. Thomas E. Hale, Chair, 805-756-6539, Fax: 805-756-6537, E-mail: thale@calpoly.edu. *Application contact:* Myron Hood, Graduate Coordinator, 805-756-2352, Fax: 805-756-6537, E-mail: mhood@calpoly.edu.

California State Polytechnic University, Pomona, Graduate Studies, College of Science, Program in Mathematics, Pomona, CA 91768-2557. Offers applied mathematics (MS); pure mathematics (MS). Part-time programs available. *Students:* 7 full-time (2 women), 26 part-time (11 women); includes 14 minority (9 Asian Americans or Pacific Islanders, 5 Hispanic Americans), 2 international. Average age 30. 17 applicants, 71% accepted. In 1998, 3 degrees awarded. *Degree requirements:* For master's, thesis or alternative required. *Entrance requirements:* For master's, GRE General Test. *Application deadline:* Applications are processed on a rolling basis. Application fee: $55. Tuition, nonresident: part-time $164 per unit. *Financial aid:* In 1998–99, 3 students received aid. Career-related internships or fieldwork, Federal Work-Study, and institutionally-sponsored loans available. Aid available to part-time students. Financial aid application deadline: 3/2; financial aid applicants required to submit FAFSA. *Unit head:* Dr. Alan Krinik, Coordinator, 909-869-3479, E-mail: ackrinik@csupomona.edu.

California State University, Fresno, Division of Graduate Studies, School of Natural Sciences, Department of Mathematics, Fresno, CA 93740-0057. Offers MA. Part-time programs available. *Faculty:* 9 full-time (3 women). *Students:* 6 full-time (2 women), 4 part-time (2 women); includes 3 minority (1 Asian American or Pacific Islander, 2 Hispanic Americans) Average age 31. 6 applicants, 83% accepted. In 1998, 5 degrees awarded. *Degree requirements:* For master's, thesis or alternative required, foreign language not required. *Entrance requirements:* For master's, GRE General Test, TOEFL (minimum score of 550 required), minimum GPA of 2.5. *Average time to degree:* Master's–3.5 years full-time. *Application deadline:* For fall admission, 8/1 (priority date); for spring admission, 12/1. Applications are processed on a rolling basis. Application fee: $55. Electronic applications accepted. Tuition, nonresident: part-time $246 per unit. Required fees: $1,906; $620 per semester. *Financial aid:* In 1998–99, 5 teaching assistantships were awarded.; fellowships, research assistantships, career-related internships or fieldwork, Federal Work-Study, scholarships, and unspecified assistantships also available. Financial aid application deadline: 3/1; financial aid applicants required to submit FAFSA. *Unit head:* Dr. Robert Arnold, Chair, 559-278-2992, Fax: 559-278-2872, E-mail: robert_arnold@csufresno.edu. *Application contact:* Hugo Sun, Graduate Coordinator, 559-278-4633, Fax: 559-278-2872, E-mail: hugo_sun@csufresno.edu.

Announcement: Master's degree program is designed to provide preparation for high school and junior college teaching, work in industry, and advanced graduate work. Graduate students have access to state-of-the-art computing facilities, including the department's own Mathematica lab.

California State University, Fullerton, Graduate Studies, School of Natural Science and Mathematics, Department of Mathematics, Fullerton, CA 92834-9480. Offers applied mathematics (MA); mathematics (MA); mathematics for secondary school teachers (MA). Part-time programs available. *Faculty:* 23 full-time (3 women), 61 part-time. *Students:* 1 full-time (0 women), 56 part-time (26 women); includes 16 minority (7 Asian Americans or Pacific Islanders, 9 Hispanic Americans) Average age 32. 36 applicants, 86% accepted. In 1998, 20 degrees awarded. *Degree requirements:* For master's, comprehensive exam or project required. *Entrance requirements:* For master's, minimum GPA of 2.5 in last 60 units, major in mathematics or related field. Application fee: $55. Tuition, nonresident: part-time $264 per unit. Required fees: $1,947; $1,281 per year. *Financial aid:* Research assistantships, teaching assistantships, career-related internships or fieldwork, Federal Work-Study, grants, and institutionally-sponsored loans available. Aid available to part-time students. Financial aid application deadline: 3/1. *Unit head:* Dr. James Friel, Chair, 714-278-3631.

California State University, Hayward, Graduate Programs, School of Science, Department of Mathematics and Computer Science, Mathematics Program, Hayward, CA 94542-3000. Offers MS. *Faculty:* 9 full-time (4 women). *Students:* 8 full-time (6 women), 33 part-time (15 women); includes 11 minority (2 African Americans, 8 Asian Americans or Pacific Islanders, 1 Hispanic American), 3 international. 14 applicants, 100% accepted. In 1998, 11 degrees awarded. *Degree requirements:* For master's, comprehensive exam or thesis required. *Entrance requirements:* For master's, minimum GPA of 3.0 in field. Application fee: $55. Tuition, nonresident: part-time $164 per unit. Required fees: $587 per quarter. *Financial aid:* Career-related internships or fieldwork, Federal Work-Study, and institutionally-sponsored loans available. Aid available to part-time students. Financial aid application deadline: 3/1. *Unit head:* Donald L. Wolitzer, Coordinator, 510-885-3467. *Application contact:* Jennifer Rice, Graduate Program Assistant, 510-885-3286, Fax: 510-885-4795, E-mail: gradprograms@csuhayward.edu.

California State University, Long Beach, Graduate Studies, College of Natural Sciences, Department of Mathematics, Long Beach, CA 90840. Offers applied mathematics (MA); mathematics (MA). Part-time programs available. *Faculty:* 20 full-time (1 woman). *Students:* 11 full-time (2 women), 29 part-time (8 women); includes 16 minority (3 African Americans, 10 Asian Americans or Pacific Islanders, 3 Hispanic Americans), 2 international. Average age 32. 31 applicants, 65% accepted. In 1998, 13 degrees awarded. *Degree requirements:* For master's, comprehensive exam or thesis required. *Application deadline:* For fall admission, 8/1; for spring admission, 12/1. Applications are processed on a rolling basis. Application fee: $55. Electronic applications accepted. Tuition, nonresident: part-time $246 per unit. Required fees: $569 per semester. Tuition and fees vary according to course load. *Financial aid:* Teaching assistantships, Federal Work-Study, grants, institutionally-sponsored loans, and traineeships available. Financial aid application deadline: 3/2. *Faculty research:* Algebra, functional analysis, partial differential equations, operator theory, numerical analysis. *Unit head:* Dr. Arthur Wayman, Chair, 562-985-4721, Fax: 562-985-8227, E-mail: away@csulb.edu. *Application contact:* Dr. James Stein, Graduate Coordinator, 562-985-5397, Fax: 562-985-8227, E-mail: jimstein@csulb.edu.

California State University, Los Angeles, Graduate Studies, School of Natural and Social Sciences, Department of Mathematics and Computer Science, Los Angeles, CA 90032-8530. Offers mathematics (MS), including applied mathematics, mathematics. Part-time and evening/weekend programs available. *Faculty:* 26 full-time, 59 part-time. *Students:* 15 full-time (8 women), 33 part-time (6 women); includes 32 minority (2 African Americans, 15 Asian Americans or Pacific Islanders, 15 Hispanic Americans), 4 international. In 1998, 7 degrees awarded. *Degree requirements:* For master's, comprehensive exam or thesis required. *Entrance requirements:* For master's, TOEFL (minimum score of 550 required), previous course work in mathematics. *Application deadline:* For fall admission, 6/30; for spring admission, 2/1. Applications are processed on a rolling basis. Application fee: $55. *Financial aid:* In 1998–99, 12 students received aid; teaching assistantships, Federal Work-Study available. Aid available to part-time students. Financial aid application deadline: 3/1. *Faculty research:* Group theory, functional analysis, convexity theory, ordered geometry. *Unit head:* Dr. Michael Hoffman, Chair, 323-343-2150.

California State University, Northridge, Graduate Studies, College of Science and Mathematics, Department of Mathematics, Northridge, CA 91330. Offers MS. Part-time and evening/weekend programs available. *Faculty:* 57 full-time, 25 part-time. *Students:* 11 full-time (7 women), 36 part-time (13 women); includes 13 minority (3 African Americans, 5 Asian Americans or Pacific Islanders, 5 Hispanic Americans), 4 international. Average age 32. 34 applicants, 76% accepted. In 1998, 5 degrees awarded. *Degree requirements:* For master's, thesis required (for some programs), foreign language not required. *Entrance requirements:* For master's, TOEFL. *Application deadline:* For fall admission, 11/30. Application fee: $55. Tuition, nonresident: part-time $246 per unit. International tuition: $7,874 full-time. Required fees: $1,970. Tuition and fees vary according to course load. *Financial aid:* Teaching assistantships, Federal Work-Study and institutionally-sponsored loans available. Aid available to part-time students. Financial aid application deadline: 3/1. *Unit head:* Dr. Magnhild Lien, Chair, 818-677-2721. *Application contact:* Dr. David Protas, Graduate Coordinator, 818-677-5079.

California State University, Sacramento, Graduate Studies, School of Natural Sciences and Mathematics, Department of Mathematics and Statistics, Sacramento, CA 95819-6048. Offers MA. Part-time programs available. *Degree requirements:* For master's, thesis or alternative, writing proficiency exam required, foreign language not required. *Entrance requirements:* For master's, TOEFL (minimum score of 550 required), minimum GPA of 3.0 in mathematics, 2.5 overall during previous 2 years; BA in mathematics or equivalent. *Application deadline:* For fall admission, 4/15; for spring admission, 11/1. Application fee: $55. *Financial aid:* Research assistantships, teaching assistantships, career-related internships or fieldwork and Federal Work-Study available. Aid available to part-time students. Financial aid application deadline: 3/1. *Unit head:* Dr. Edward Bradley, Chair, 916-278-6534. *Application contact:* Dr. Howard Hamilton, Coordinator, 916-278-6221.

California State University, San Bernardino, Graduate Studies, School of Natural Sciences, Program in Mathematics, San Bernardino, CA 92407-2397. Offers MA. Part-time programs available. *Degree requirements:* For master's, foreign language and thesis not required. *Entrance requirements:* For master's, minor in mathematics. *Faculty research:* Mathematics education, technology in education, algebra, combinatorics, real analysis.

California State University, San Marcos, Program in Mathematical Sciences, San Marcos, CA 92096-0001. Offers MS. Part-time programs available. *Faculty:* 1 full-time (0 women). *Students:* 3 full-time (1 woman), 3 part-time; includes 2 minority (1 African American, 1 Hispanic American) Average age 34. 4 applicants, 50% accepted. In 1998, 1 degree awarded. *Degree requirements:* For master's, thesis optional. *Application deadline:* For fall admission, 4/15 (priority date). Applications are processed on a rolling basis. Application fee: $55. *Financial aid:* Teaching assistantships, career-related internships or fieldwork and Federal Work-Study available. Aid available to part-time students. Financial aid applicants required to submit FAFSA. *Faculty research:* Combinatorics, graph theory, partial differential equations, numerical analysis, computational linear algebra. *Unit head:* Dr. Carolyn R. Mahoney, Director, 760-750-4118, E-mail: cmahoney@csusm.edu.

Carleton University, Faculty of Graduate Studies, Faculty of Science, School of Mathematics and Statistics, Ottawa, ON K1S 5B6, Canada. Offers mathematics (M Sc, PhD). *Faculty:* 29 full-time (4 women). *Students:* 35 full-time (9 women), 5 part-time (2 women). Average age 29. In 1998, 2 master's, 2 doctorates awarded. *Degree requirements:* For master's, thesis optional; for doctorate, dissertation, comprehensive exam required. *Entrance requirements:* For master's, TOEFL (minimum score of 550 required), honors degree; for doctorate, TOEFL (minimum score of 550 required), master's degree. *Average time to degree:* Master's–1.8 years full-time; doctorate–4.7 years full-time. *Application deadline:* For fall admission, 3/1 (priority date). Applications are processed on a rolling basis. Application fee: $35. *Financial aid:* Application deadline: 3/1. *Faculty research:* Pure mathematics, applied mathematics, probability and statistics. Total annual research expenditures: $558,000. *Unit head:* C. W. L. Garner, Associate Director, 613-520-2152, Fax: 613-520-3536, E-mail: cwl_garner@carleton.ca.

Carnegie Mellon University, Mellon College of Science, Department of Mathematical Sciences, Pittsburgh, PA 15213-3891. Offers algorithms, combinatorics, and optimization (PhD); mathematical finance (PhD); mathematical sciences (MS, DA, PhD); pure and applied logic (PhD). Part-time programs available. *Faculty:* 35 full-time (3 women). *Students:* 37 full-time (7 women); includes 1 minority (African American), 25 international. Average age 25. 159 applicants, 18% accepted. In 1998, 6 master's awarded (17% found work related to degree, 83% continued full-time study); 8 doctorates awarded (75% entered university research/teaching, 25% found other work related to degree). Terminal master's awarded for partial completion of doctoral program. *Degree requirements:* For master's, foreign language and thesis not required; for doctorate, dissertation required, foreign language not required. *Entrance requirements:* For master's and doctorate, GRE General Test, GRE Subject Test, TOEFL. *Average time to degree:* Master's–2 years full-time; doctorate–6 years full-time. *Application deadline:* For fall admission, 1/15 (priority date). Application fee: $0. Electronic applications accepted. *Financial aid:* In 1998–99, 36 students received aid, including 4 fellowships with full tuition reimbursements available (averaging $11,925 per year), 4 research assistantships with full tuition reimbursements available (averaging $11,925 per year), 25 teaching assistantships with full tuition reimbursements available (averaging $11,925 per year); scholarships and tuition waivers (full) also available. Financial aid application deadline: 1/15. *Faculty research:* Continuum mechanics, discrete mathematics, applied and computational mathematics. Total annual research expenditures: $1.5 million. *Unit head:* James Greenberg, Head, 412-268-2545, Fax: 412-268-6380, E-mail: greenber@andrew.cmu.edu. *Application contact:* Stella P. Andreoletti, Graduate Coordinator, 412-268-2545, Fax: 412-268-6380, E-mail: sd2e@andrew.cmu.edu.

See in-depth description on page 653.

Case Western Reserve University, School of Graduate Studies, Department of Mathematics, Cleveland, OH 44106. Offers applied mathematics (MS, PhD); mathematics (MS, PhD). Part-time programs available. Terminal master's awarded for partial completion of doctoral program. *Degree requirements:* For master's, thesis (applied mathematics) required; for doctorate, dissertation required. *Entrance requirements:* For master's and doctorate, GRE General Test, TOEFL (minimum score of 550 required). *Faculty research:* Probability theory, differential equations and control theory, differential geometry and topology, Lie groups, functional and harmonic analysis.

Central Connecticut State University, School of Graduate Studies, School of Arts and Sciences, Department of Mathematics, New Britain, CT 06050-4010. Offers MA, MS. Part-time and evening/weekend programs available. *Faculty:* 25 full-time (7 women), 48 part-time (27 women). *Students:* 9 full-time (5 women), 45 part-time (27 women); includes 3 minority (2 African Americans, 1 Asian American or Pacific Islander), 4 international. Average age 37. 76 applicants, 59% accepted. In 1998, 13 degrees awarded. *Degree requirements:* For master's, thesis or alternative, comprehensive exam or special project required. *Entrance requirements:* For master's, TOEFL (minimum score of 550 required), minimum GPA of 2.7. *Application deadline:* For fall admission, 6/1 (priority date); for spring admission, 12/1. Applications are processed on a rolling basis. Application fee: $40. *Financial aid:* Teaching assistantships

Mathematics

Central Connecticut State University (continued)
available. Financial aid application deadline: 3/15; financial aid applicants required to submit FAFSA. *Faculty research:* Statistics, actuarial mathematics, computer systems and engineering, computer programming techniques, operations research. *Unit head:* Dr. William Driscoll, Chair, 860-832-2835.

Central Michigan University, College of Graduate Studies, College of Science and Technology, Department of Mathematics, Mount Pleasant, MI 48859. Offers MA, MAT, PhD. *Faculty:* 28 full-time (7 women). *Students:* 10 full-time (7 women), 16 part-time (4 women), 5 international. Average age 35. In 1998, 4 degrees awarded. *Degree requirements:* For master's, thesis or alternative required, foreign language not required; for doctorate, dissertation required, foreign language not required. *Entrance requirements:* For master's, minimum GPA of 2.5, 20 hours in mathematics; for doctorate, GRE, TOEFL (minimum score of 550 required), minimum GPA of 3.0, 20 hours in mathematics. *Application deadline:* For fall admission, 3/1 (priority date). Applications are processed on a rolling basis. Application fee: $30. Tuition, state resident: part-time $144 per credit hour. Tuition, nonresident: part-time $285 per credit hour. Required fees: $240 per semester. Tuition and fees vary according to degree level and program. *Financial aid:* In 1998–99, 4 fellowships with tuition reimbursements, 1 research assistantship with tuition reimbursement, 20 teaching assistantships with tuition reimbursements were awarded.; career-related internships or fieldwork and Federal Work-Study also available. Financial aid application deadline: 3/7. *Faculty research:* Combinatorics, approximation theory, operations theory, functional analysis, statistics. *Unit head:* Dr. Sidney Graham, Chairperson, 517-774-3596, Fax: 517-774-7106, E-mail: sidney.w.graham@cmich.edu.

Central Missouri State University, School of Graduate Studies, College of Arts and Sciences, Department of Mathematics and Computer Science, Warrensburg, MO 64093. Offers mathematics (MS); mathematics education (MSE). *Accreditation:* NCATE (one or more programs are accredited). Part-time programs available. *Faculty:* 14 full-time (3 women). *Students:* 2 full-time (0 women), 10 part-time (6 women). In 1998, 3 degrees awarded (67% found work related to degree). *Degree requirements:* For master's, thesis (for some programs), comprehensive exam, thesis (MS); comprehensive exam or thesis (MSE) required. *Entrance requirements:* For master's, GRE General Test (MSE), bachelor's degree in mathematics, minimum GPA of 3.0 (MS); minimum GPA of 2.75, teaching certificate (MSE). *Application deadline:* Applications are processed on a rolling basis. Application fee: $25 ($50 for international students). Tuition, state resident: full-time $3,576; part-time $149 per credit hour. Tuition, nonresident: full-time $7,152; part-time $298 per credit hour. Tuition and fees vary according to course load and campus/location. *Financial aid:* In 1998–99, research assistantships with tuition reimbursements (averaging $3,750 per year), 2 teaching assistantships with tuition reimbursements (averaging $3,750 per year) were awarded.; Federal Work-Study, grants, scholarships, and unspecified assistantships also available. Aid available to part-time students. Financial aid application deadline: 3/1; financial aid applicants required to submit FAFSA. *Unit head:* Dr. Edward W. Davenport, Chair, 660-543-4931, Fax: 660-543-8006, E-mail: davenport@cmsu1.cmsu.edu.

Central Washington University, Graduate Studies and Research, College of the Sciences, Department of Mathematics, Ellensburg, WA 98926. Offers MAT. MAT offered during summer only. *Faculty:* 13 full-time (2 women). In 1998, 3 degrees awarded. *Degree requirements:* For master's, thesis or alternative required, foreign language not required. *Entrance requirements:* For master's, minimum GPA of 3.0. Application fee: $35. Tuition, state resident: full-time $4,389; part-time $146 per credit. Tuition, nonresident: full-time $13,365; part-time $446 per credit. Tuition and fees vary according to course load. *Financial aid:* Federal Work-Study available. Financial aid application deadline: 2/15; financial aid applicants required to submit FAFSA. *Unit head:* Dr. Barney Erickson, Chairman, 509-963-2103. *Application contact:* Christie A. Fevergeon, Program Coordinator, Graduate Studies and Research, 509-963-3103, Fax: 509-963-1799, E-mail: masters@cwu.edu.

Chicago State University, Graduate Studies, College of Arts and Sciences, Department of Mathematics, Chicago, IL 60628. Offers MS. *Degree requirements:* For master's, oral exam required, thesis optional, foreign language not required. *Entrance requirements:* For master's, minimum GPA of 2.75.

City College of the City University of New York, Graduate School, College of Liberal Arts and Science, Division of Science, Department of Mathematics, New York, NY 10031-9198. Offers MA. Part-time programs available. *Degree requirements:* For master's, one foreign language required, (computer language can substitute), thesis not required. *Entrance requirements:* For master's, TOEFL (minimum score of 500 required). *Faculty research:* Group theory, number theory, logic, statistics, computational geometry.

Claremont Graduate University, Graduate Programs, Department of Mathematics, Claremont, CA 91711-6163. Offers engineering mathematics (PhD); financial engineering (MS); operations research and statistics (MA, MS); physical applied mathematics (MA, MS); pure mathematics (MA, MS, PhD); scientific computing (MA, MS); systems and control theory (MA, MS). Part-time programs available. *Faculty:* 3 full-time (0 women), 3 part-time (1 woman). *Students:* 12 full-time (8 women), 41 part-time (7 women); includes 17 minority (2 African Americans, 10 Asian Americans or Pacific Islanders, 5 Hispanic Americans), 16 international. Average age 37. In 1998, 13 master's, 3 doctorates awarded. Terminal master's awarded for partial completion of doctoral program. *Degree requirements:* For master's, foreign language and thesis not required; for doctorate, 2 foreign languages (computer language can substitute for one), dissertation required. *Entrance requirements:* For master's and doctorate, GRE General Test. *Application deadline:* For fall admission, 2/15 (priority date). Applications are processed on a rolling basis. Application fee: $40. Electronic applications accepted. Tuition: Full-time $20,950; part-time $913 per unit. Required fees: $65 per semester. Tuition and fees vary according to program. *Financial aid:* Fellowships, research assistantships, career-related internships or fieldwork, Federal Work-Study, institutionally-sponsored loans, and tuition waivers (full and partial) available. Aid available to part-time students. Financial aid application deadline: 2/15; financial aid applicants required to submit FAFSA. *Unit head:* Robert Williamson, Chair, 909-621-8080, Fax: 909-621-8390, E-mail: robert.williamson@cgu.edu. *Application contact:* Mary Solberg, Program Secretary, 909-621-8080, Fax: 909-621-8390, E-mail: math@cgu.edu.

Announcement: Emphasis on industrial applied mathematics, including modeling, numerical analysis, partial differential equations, operations research, statistics, game theory, and financial engineering. Operates leading Mathematics Clinic with industry-sponsored research projects conducted by student teams. Concentrations include physical applied mathematics, scientific computing, systems and control theory, operations research and statistics, and pure mathematics.

Clarkson University, Graduate School, School of Science, Department of Mathematics and Computer Science, Potsdam, NY 13699. Offers computer science (MS); mathematics (MS, PhD). *Faculty:* 15 full-time (2 women), 1 part-time (0 women). *Students:* 17 full-time (9 women); includes 1 minority (Asian American or Pacific Islander), 9 international. Average age 27. 49 applicants, 45% accepted. In 1998, 3 master's, 1 doctorate awarded. Terminal master's awarded for partial completion of doctoral program. *Degree requirements:* For master's, foreign language and thesis not required; for doctorate, dissertation, departmental qualifying exam required, foreign language not required. *Entrance requirements:* For master's, GRE, TOEFL. *Application deadline:* For fall admission, 5/15 (priority date); for spring admission, 10/15 (priority date). Applications are processed on a rolling basis. Application fee: $25 ($35 for international students). Tuition: Part-time $661 per credit hour. Required fees: $215 per semester. *Financial aid:* In 1998–99, 2 research assistantships, 10 teaching assistantships were awarded.; fellowships *Faculty research:* Fiber optics, hydrodynamics, inverse scattering, nonlinear optics, nonlinear waves. Total annual research expenditures: $136,542. *Unit head:* Dr. David L. Powers, Chair, 315-268-2369, Fax: 315-268-6670, E-mail: dpowers@clarkson.edu.

See in-depth description on page 659.

Clemson University, Graduate School, College of Engineering and Science, Department of Mathematical Sciences, Clemson, SC 29634. Offers applied and pure mathematics (MS, PhD); computational mathematics (MS, PhD); management science (PhD); operations research (MS, PhD); statistics (MS, PhD). Part-time programs available. *Students:* 60 full-time (24 women), 1 part-time; includes 3 minority (2 African Americans, 1 Hispanic American), 11 international. Average age 29. 51 applicants, 69% accepted. In 1998, 14 master's, 2 doctorates awarded. *Degree requirements:* For master's, computer language, final project required, thesis optional, foreign language not required; for doctorate, computer language, dissertation, qualifying exams required, foreign language not required. *Entrance requirements:* For master's and doctorate, GRE General Test, TOEFL. *Application deadline:* For fall admission, 6/1. Application fee: $35. *Financial aid:* Fellowships, research assistantships, teaching assistantships available. Financial aid application deadline: 4/15; financial aid applicants required to submit FAFSA. *Faculty research:* Applied and computational analysis, discrete mathematics, mathematical programming statistics. *Unit head:* Dr. Robert Fennell, Chair, 864-656-3436, Fax: 864-656-5230, E-mail: mathsci@clemson.edu. *Application contact:* Dr. Douglas Shier, Graduate Coordinator, 864-656-1100, Fax: 864-656-5230, E-mail: shierd@clemson.edu.

Cleveland State University, College of Graduate Studies, College of Arts and Sciences, Department of Mathematics, Program in Mathematics, Cleveland, OH 44115-2440. Offers MA, MS. *Degree requirements:* For master's, foreign language and thesis not required. *Application deadline:* For fall admission, 7/15 (priority date). Applications are processed on a rolling basis. Application fee: $25. *Unit head:* Sujata Davis, Department Secretary, 508-793-7169. *Application contact:* Dr. John Oprea, Director, 216-687-4680.

Colorado School of Mines, Graduate School, Department of Mathematical and Computer Sciences, Golden, CO 80401-1887. Offers MS, PhD. Part-time programs available. *Faculty:* 18 full-time (2 women), 11 part-time (5 women). *Students:* 12 full-time (3 women), 24 part-time (5 women); includes 2 minority (1 African American, 1 Asian American or Pacific Islander), 16 international. 40 applicants, 68% accepted. In 1998, 13 master's awarded (100% found work related to degree); 3 doctorates awarded (100% found work related to degree). *Degree requirements:* For master's, thesis required, foreign language not required; for doctorate, dissertation, written comprehensive exams required, foreign language not required. *Entrance requirements:* For master's and doctorate, GRE General Test (combined average 1680 on three sections), minimum GPA of 3.0. *Application deadline:* Applications are processed on a rolling basis. Application fee: $40. Electronic applications accepted. *Financial aid:* In 1998–99, 28 students received aid, including 1 fellowship, 9 research assistantships, 10 teaching assistantships; unspecified assistantships also available. Aid available to part-time students. Financial aid applicants required to submit FAFSA. *Faculty research:* Applied statistics, numerical computation, artificial intelligence, linear optimization. Total annual research expenditures: $410,734. *Unit head:* Dr. Graeme Fairweather, Head, 303-273-3860, E-mail: gfairwea@mines.edu. *Application contact:* Willy Hereman, Associate Professor, 303-273-3881, Fax: 303-273-3875, E-mail: whereman@mines.edu.

Colorado State University, Graduate School, College of Natural Sciences, Department of Mathematics, Fort Collins, CO 80523. Offers MS, PhD. *Faculty:* 31 full-time (4 women). *Students:* 34 full-time (14 women), 5 part-time; includes 6 minority (3 Asian Americans or Pacific Islanders, 2 Hispanic Americans, 1 Native American), 7 international. Average age 28. 98 applicants, 27% accepted. In 1998, 11 master's, 2 doctorates awarded. Terminal master's awarded for partial completion of doctoral program. *Degree requirements:* For master's, foreign language and thesis not required; for doctorate, one foreign language, dissertation required. *Entrance requirements:* For master's and doctorate, GRE General Test, TOEFL, minimum GPA of 3.0. *Application deadline:* For fall admission, 3/1 (priority date). Applications are processed on a rolling basis. Application fee: $30. Electronic applications accepted. *Financial aid:* In 1998–99, 4 research assistantships, 30 teaching assistantships were awarded.; fellowships, career-related internships or fieldwork, Federal Work-Study, institutionally-sponsored loans, traineeships, and tuition waivers (partial) also available. Financial aid application deadline: 3/1. *Faculty research:* Applied mathematics, numerical analysis, algebraic geometry, combinatorics. *Application contact:* Secretary to the Graduate Director, 970-491-7925, Fax: 970-491-2161, E-mail: grad_program@math.colostate.edu.

Announcement: Department of Mathematics offers graduate research assistantships with 9 credits of tuition waived per semester and a stipend of $13,500 for the 9-month academic year. These assistantships are funded by the Department of Defense, government labs, and/or industry for research in information fusion using methods of combinatorial optimization and stochastic processes. Preparation for research career with excellent employment opportunities.

Columbia University, Graduate School of Arts and Sciences, Division of Natural Sciences, Department of Mathematics, New York, NY 10027. Offers M Phil, MA, PhD. *Degree requirements:* For master's, written exam required, foreign language and thesis not required; for doctorate, 2 foreign languages, dissertation required. *Entrance requirements:* For master's and doctorate, GRE General Test, TOEFL, major in mathematics. *Faculty research:* Algebra, topology, analysis.

See in-depth description on page 663.

Concordia University, School of Graduate Studies, Faculty of Arts and Science, Department of Mathematics and Statistics, Montréal, PQ H3G 1M8, Canada. Offers mathematics (PhD); mathematics and statistics (M Sc, MA); teaching of mathematics (MTM, Diploma). *Students:* 46 full-time (18 women), 1 part-time. *Degree requirements:* For master's, thesis optional; for doctorate, dissertation, comprehensive exam required. *Entrance requirements:* For master's, honors degree in mathematics or equivalent; for Diploma, Quebec teaching certificate. *Application deadline:* For fall admission, 4/1. Application fee: $50. *Financial aid:* Fellowships, research assistantships, teaching assistantships available. Financial aid application deadline: 2/1. *Faculty research:* Number theory, computational algebra, mathematical physics, differential geometry, dynamical systems and statistics. *Unit head:* Dr. J. Hillel, Chair, 514-848-3234, Fax: 514-848-2831. *Application contact:* Dr. Z. Khalil, Director, 514-848-3250, Fax: 514-848-2831.

Cornell University, Graduate School, Graduate Fields of Arts and Sciences, Field of Mathematics, Ithaca, NY 14853-0001. Offers PhD. *Faculty:* 46 full-time. *Students:* 57 full-time (13 women); includes 4 minority (3 Asian Americans or Pacific Islanders, 1 Native American), 29 international. 173 applicants, 24% accepted. In 1998, 10 doctorates awarded. *Degree requirements:* For doctorate, dissertation, teaching experience required. *Entrance requirements:* For doctorate, GRE General Test, GRE Subject Test, TOEFL (minimum score of 600 required). *Application deadline:* For fall admission, 1/15. Application fee: $65. Electronic applications accepted. *Financial aid:* In 1998–99, 56 students received aid, including 7 fellowships with full tuition reimbursements available, 2 research assistantships with full tuition reimbursements available, 47 teaching assistantships with full tuition reimbursements available; institutionally-sponsored loans, scholarships, tuition waivers (full and partial), and unspecified assistantships also available. Financial aid applicants required to submit FAFSA. *Faculty research:* Analysis, algebra, probability, dynamical systems, Lie theory, logic, topology. *Unit head:* Director of Graduate Studies, 607-255-6757. *Application contact:* Graduate Field Assistant, 607-255-6757, E-mail: gradinfo@math.cornell.edu.

Creighton University, Graduate School, College of Arts and Sciences, Department of Mathematics, Statistics, and Computer Science, Program in Mathematics and Statistics, Omaha, NE 68178-0001. Offers MS. Part-time programs available. *Faculty:* 8 full-time. *Students:* 1 full-time (0 women). In 1998, 3 degrees awarded. *Degree requirements:* For master's, one foreign language required, (computer language can substitute), thesis optional. *Entrance requirements:* For master's, GRE General Test, TOEFL (minimum score of 550 required). *Application deadline:* For fall admission, 3/1. Applications are processed on a rolling basis. Application fee: $30. *Unit head:* Dr. Randall Crist, Director, 402-280-2578. *Application contact:* Dr. Barbara J. Braden, Dean, Graduate School, 402-280-2870, Fax: 402-280-5762.

Dalhousie University, Faculty of Graduate Studies, College of Arts and Science, Faculty of Science, Department of Mathematics and Statistics, Program in Mathematics, Halifax, NS B3H

3J5, Canada. Offers M Sc, PhD. *Faculty:* 17 full-time, 7 part-time. In 1998, 8 master's, 5 doctorates awarded. *Degree requirements:* For master's, thesis required, foreign language not required; for doctorate, dissertation required. *Entrance requirements:* For master's and doctorate, TOEFL (minimum score of 580 required). *Application deadline:* For fall admission, 6/1. Applications are processed on a rolling basis. Application fee: $55. *Financial aid:* In 1998–99, research assistantships (averaging $10,000 per year), teaching assistantships (averaging $2,500 per year) were awarded. *Faculty research:* Applied mathematics, category theory, algebra, analysis, graph theory. *Unit head:* Gerda Cordova, Divisional Administrator, 212-305-9398, Fax: 212-305-9408, E-mail: gb12@columbia.edu. *Application contact:* Dr. P. Keast, Graduate Coordinator, 902-494-7036, Fax: 902-494-5130, E-mail: keast@mscs.dal.ca.

Dartmouth College, School of Arts and Sciences, Department of Mathematics, Hanover, NH 03755. Offers PhD. *Faculty:* 21 full-time (3 women), 3 part-time (0 women). *Students:* 25 full-time (13 women); includes 1 minority (Hispanic American), 2 international. 78 applicants, 19% accepted. In 1998, 1 doctorate awarded (100% entered university research/teaching). *Degree requirements:* For doctorate, dissertation required. *Entrance requirements:* For doctorate, GRE General Test, GRE Subject Test. *Application deadline:* For fall admission, 3/1 (priority date). *Financial aid:* In 1998–99, 25 students received aid, including 16 fellowships with full tuition reimbursements available; research assistantships with full tuition reimbursements available, grants, institutionally-sponsored loans, scholarships, tuition waivers (full and partial), and unspecified assistantships also available. *Unit head:* Dr. Dana Williams, Chairman, 603-646-2421. *Application contact:* Nancy French, Administrative Assistant, 603-646-3722.

See in-depth description on page 665.

Drexel University, Graduate School, College of Arts and Sciences, Department of Mathematics and Computer Science, Program in Mathematics, Philadelphia, PA 19104-2875. Offers MS, PhD. *Students:* 7 full-time (3 women), 16 part-time (6 women); includes 1 minority (Asian American or Pacific Islander), 4 international. 57 applicants, 30% accepted. In 1998, 2 degrees awarded. *Degree requirements:* For master's, thesis not required; for doctorate, dissertation required. *Entrance requirements:* For master's, GRE, TOEFL (minimum score of 570 required), TSE (for teaching assistants); for doctorate, GRE, TOEFL (minimum score of 570 required). *Application deadline:* For fall admission, 8/21. Applications are processed on a rolling basis. Application fee: $35. Tuition: Full-time $15,795; part-time $585 per credit. Required fees: $375; $67 per term. Tuition and fees vary according to program. *Financial aid:* Application deadline: 2/1. *Unit head:* Nancy French, Administrative Assistant, 603-646-3722. *Application contact:* Director of Graduate Admissions, 215-895-6700, Fax: 215-895-5939.

See in-depth description on page 667.

Duke University, Graduate School, Department of Mathematics, Durham, NC 27708-0586. Offers PhD. *Faculty:* 31 full-time, 6 part-time. *Students:* 23 full-time (5 women), 11 international. 57 applicants, 33% accepted. In 1998, 5 doctorates awarded. *Degree requirements:* For doctorate, dissertation required. *Entrance requirements:* For doctorate, GRE General Test, GRE Subject Test. *Application deadline:* For fall admission, 12/31. Application fee: $75. *Financial aid:* Fellowships, research assistantships, teaching assistantships, Federal Work-Study available. Financial aid application deadline: 12/31. *Unit head:* Chadmark L. Schoen, Director of Graduate Studies, 919-660-2825, Fax: 919-660-2821, E-mail: langen@math.duke.edu.

East Carolina University, Graduate School, College of Arts and Sciences, Department of Mathematics, Greenville, NC 27858-4353. Offers applied mathematics (MA); computer science (MS); mathematics (MA, MA Ed). Part-time and evening/weekend programs available. *Faculty:* 15 full-time (4 women). *Students:* 9 full-time (5 women), 23 part-time (12 women); includes 3 minority (2 Asian Americans or Pacific Islanders, 1 Hispanic American), 2 international. Average age 32. 12 applicants, 75% accepted. In 1998, 9 degrees awarded. *Degree requirements:* For master's, comprehensive exams required. *Entrance requirements:* For master's, GRE General Test, MAT (MA Ed), TOEFL. *Application deadline:* For fall admission, 6/1; for spring admission, 10/15. Applications are processed on a rolling basis. Application fee: $40. Tuition, state resident: full-time $1,012. Tuition, nonresident: full-time $8,578. Required fees: $1,006. Part-time tuition and fees vary according to course load. *Financial aid:* Research assistantships with partial tuition reimbursements, teaching assistantships with partial tuition reimbursements available. Financial aid application deadline: 6/1. *Unit head:* Dr. Robert Hursey, Director of Graduate Studies, 252-328-6461, Fax: 252-328-6414, E-mail: hurseyr@mail.ecu.edu. *Application contact:* Dr. Paul D. Tschetter, Senior Associate Dean, 252-328-6012, Fax: 252-328-6071, E-mail: grad@mail.ecu.edu.

Eastern Illinois University, Graduate School, College of Sciences, Department of Mathematics, Charleston, IL 61920-3099. Offers mathematics (MA); mathematics education (MA). *Degree requirements:* For master's, foreign language and thesis not required. *Entrance requirements:* For master's, GRE General Test.

Eastern Kentucky University, The Graduate School, College of Natural and Mathematical Sciences, Department of Mathematics, Statistics and Computer Science, Richmond, KY 40475-3101. Offers mathematical sciences (MS). Part-time programs available. *Students:* 6. In 1998, 5 degrees awarded. *Degree requirements:* For master's, thesis not required. *Entrance requirements:* For master's, GRE General Test, minimum GPA of 2.5. Application fee: $0. *Financial aid:* Research assistantships, teaching assistantships, Federal Work-Study available. Aid available to part-time students. *Unit head:* Dr. Mary Fleming, Chair, 606-622-5942.

Eastern Michigan University, Graduate School, College of Arts and Sciences, Department of Mathematics, Ypsilanti, MI 48197. Offers MA. Evening/weekend programs available. *Faculty:* 31 full-time (11 women). *Students:* 25 full-time, 59 part-time. 97 applicants, 62% accepted. In 1998, 35 degrees awarded. *Degree requirements:* For master's, thesis optional, foreign language not required. *Entrance requirements:* For master's, TOEFL (minimum score of 500 required). *Application deadline:* For fall admission, 5/15; for spring admission, 3/15. Applications are processed on a rolling basis. Application fee: $30. *Financial aid:* Fellowships, teaching assistantships available. Aid available to part-time students. Financial aid application deadline: 3/15; financial aid applicants required to submit FAFSA. *Unit head:* Dr. Donald R. Lick, Head, 734-487-1444. *Application contact:* Dr. Kenneth Shiskowski, Coordinator, 734-487-1444.

Eastern New Mexico University, Graduate School, College of Liberal Arts and Sciences, Department of Mathematical Sciences, Portales, NM 88130. Offers MA. Part-time programs available. *Faculty:* 8 full-time (3 women), 1 part-time (0 women). *Students:* 2 full-time (1 woman), 6 part-time (2 women); includes 1 minority (Hispanic American), 1 international. Average age 33. 5 applicants, 40% accepted. In 1998, 1 degree awarded. *Degree requirements:* For master's, thesis optional, foreign language not required. *Entrance requirements:* For master's, minimum GPA of 2.5. *Application deadline:* Applications are processed on a rolling basis. Application fee: $10. *Financial aid:* In 1998–99, 2 fellowships (averaging $7,200 per year), 5 teaching assistantships (averaging $6,580 per year) were awarded.; research assistantships, career-related internships or fieldwork and Federal Work-Study also available. Aid available to part-time students. Financial aid application deadline: 4/1. *Faculty research:* Applied mathematics, graph theory. *Unit head:* Dr. Douglas Jackson, Graduate Coordinator, 505-562-2367, E-mail: douglas.jackson@enmu.edu.

Eastern Washington University, Graduate School, College of Science, Mathematics and Technology, Department of Mathematics, Cheney, WA 99004-2431. Offers M Ed, MS. *Accreditation:* NCATE. Part-time programs available. *Faculty:* 16 full-time (3 women). *Students:* 6 full-time (3 women), 6 part-time (3 women); includes 1 minority (African American), 1 international. In 1998, 8 degrees awarded. *Degree requirements:* For master's, thesis (for some programs), comprehensive oral exam required. *Entrance requirements:* For master's, GRE General Test, departmental qualifying exam, minimum GPA of 3.0. *Application deadline:* For fall admission, 4/1 (priority date); for spring admission, 1/15. Applications are processed on a rolling basis. Application fee: $35. Tuition, state resident: full-time $4,368. Tuition, nonresident: full-time $13,284. *Financial aid:* Teaching assistantships, Federal Work-Study and institutionally-sponsored loans available. Financial aid application deadline: 2/1. *Unit head:* Dr. Sherry Renga, Chair, 509-359-6225. *Application contact:* Dr. Yves Nievergelt, Adviser, 509-359-2219.

East Tennessee State University, School of Graduate Studies, College of Arts and Sciences, Department of Mathematics, Johnson City, TN 37614-0734. Offers MS. Part-time and evening/weekend programs available. *Degree requirements:* For master's, thesis or alternative, oral and written comprehensive exams required, foreign language not required. *Entrance requirements:* For master's, GRE General Test, TOEFL (minimum score of 550 required). *Faculty research:* Combinatorics, graph theory, complex analysis, statistics, numerical analysis.

École Polytechnique de Montréal, Graduate Programs, Department of Mathematics, Montréal, PQ H3C 3A7, Canada. Offers mathematical method in CA engineering (M Eng, M Sc A, PhD); operational research (M Eng, M Sc A, PhD). Part-time programs available. *Degree requirements:* For master's and doctorate, one foreign language, computer language, thesis/dissertation required. *Entrance requirements:* For master's, minimum GPA of 2.75; for doctorate, minimum GPA of 3.0. *Faculty research:* Statistics and probability, fractal analysis, optimization.

Emory University, Graduate School of Arts and Sciences, Department of Mathematics and Computer Science, Atlanta, GA 30322-1100. Offers mathematics (PhD); mathematics/computer science (MS). *Faculty:* 22 full-time (4 women), 4 part-time (0 women). *Students:* 35 full-time (17 women); includes 4 minority (2 African Americans, 1 Asian American or Pacific Islander, 1 Hispanic American), 16 international. 105 applicants, 28% accepted. In 1998, 13 master's, 4 doctorates awarded. Terminal master's awarded for partial completion of doctoral program. *Degree requirements:* For master's, thesis required; for doctorate, dissertation, comprehensive exams required. *Entrance requirements:* For master's, GRE General Test (combined average 1600 on three sections), TOEFL; for doctorate, GRE General Test (combined average 1800 on three sections), TOEFL. *Application deadline:* For fall admission, 1/20. Application fee: $45. *Financial aid:* Fellowships, teaching assistantships, scholarships available. Financial aid application deadline: 1/20. Total annual research expenditures: $1.1 million. *Unit head:* Dr. Dwight Duffus, Chairman, 404-727-7580, Fax: 404-727-5611. *Application contact:* Ron Gould, Director of Graduate Studies, 404-727-7580, Fax: 404-727-5611, E-mail: dgs@mathcs.emory.edu.

Announcement The department offers a PhD in mathematics and an MS in mathematics or mathematics/computer science. Research specialties in mathematics include algebra, computational algebra, applied math, combinatorics, complex analysis, differential equations, dynamical systems, topology, numerical analysis, and mathematical physics. Full tuition and funding are available in both the math PhD and computer science MS programs. See also the department's computer science announcement in Book 5 of this series.

Emporia State University, School of Graduate Studies, College of Liberal Arts and Sciences, Division of Mathematics and Computer Science, Emporia, KS 66801-5087. Offers mathematics (MS). *Faculty:* 10 full-time (2 women). *Students:* 5 full-time (3 women), 6 part-time (3 women), 1 international. 5 applicants, 80% accepted. In 1998, 1 degree awarded. *Degree requirements:* For master's, comprehensive exam or thesis required. *Entrance requirements:* For master's, TOEFL (minimum score of 550 required). *Application deadline:* For fall admission, 8/15 (priority date). Applications are processed on a rolling basis. Application fee: $30 ($75 for international students). Electronic applications accepted. Tuition, state resident: full-time $2,356; part-time $106 per credit hour. Tuition, nonresident: full-time $6,158; part-time $264 per credit hour. *Financial aid:* In 1998–99, 2 research assistantships (averaging $5,208 per year), 4 teaching assistantships with full tuition reimbursements (averaging $4,876 per year) were awarded.; fellowships, career-related internships or fieldwork, Federal Work-Study, and institutionally-sponsored loans also available. Financial aid application deadline: 3/15; financial aid applicants required to submit FAFSA. *Unit head:* Dr. Larry Scott, Chair, 316-341-5281, E-mail: scottlar@emporia.edu.

Fairleigh Dickinson University, Florham-Madison Campus, Maxwell Becton College of Arts and Sciences, Department of Mathematics, Computer Science and Physics, Madison, NJ 07940-1099. Offers computer science (MS); mathematics (MS). *Faculty:* 5 full-time (0 women), 1 part-time (0 women). *Degree requirements:* For master's, computer language required, foreign language and thesis not required. *Entrance requirements:* For master's, GRE General Test. *Application deadline:* Applications are processed on a rolling basis. Application fee: $35. Tuition: Full-time $9,396; part-time $522 per credit. Required fees: $69 per semester. *Financial aid:* Fellowships, research assistantships, teaching assistantships available. *Unit head:* Dr. Richard Wagner, Chairperson, 973-443-8691.

Fairleigh Dickinson University, Teaneck–Hackensack Campus, University College: Arts, Sciences, and Professional Studies, School of Computer Science and Information Systems, Program in Mathematics, Teaneck, NJ 07666-1914. Offers MS. *Degree requirements:* For master's, computer language required, foreign language and thesis not required. *Entrance requirements:* For master's, GRE General Test. *Faculty research:* Real time computer systems, software design modeling and simulation, parallel processing, pattern recognition, image processing.

Fayetteville State University, Graduate School, Department of Mathematics and Computer Science, Fayetteville, NC 28301-4298. Offers mathematics (MS). Part-time and evening/weekend programs available. *Degree requirements:* For master's, thesis or alternative, comprehensive exams, internship required, foreign language not required. *Entrance requirements:* For master's, GRE General Test.

Florida Atlantic University, Charles E. Schmidt College of Science, Department of Mathematical Science, Boca Raton, FL 33431-0991. Offers MS, MST, PhD. Part-time programs available. *Faculty:* 26 full-time (2 women), 5 part-time (1 woman). *Students:* 20 full-time (11 women), 17 part-time (9 women); includes 3 minority (1 African American, 2 Asian Americans or Pacific Islanders), 4 international. Average age 30. 27 applicants, 67% accepted. In 1998, 13 master's, 1 doctorate awarded (100% entered university research/teaching). Terminal master's awarded for partial completion of doctoral program. *Degree requirements:* For master's, thesis required (for some programs), foreign language not required; for doctorate, dissertation required, foreign language not required. *Entrance requirements:* For master's, GRE General Test (minimum combined score of 1000 required; average 1150), minimum GPA of 3.0; for doctorate, GRE General Test (minimum combined score of 1100 required; average 1220). *Application deadline:* For fall admission, 6/1 (priority date); for spring admission, 10/20 (priority date). Applications are processed on a rolling basis. Application fee: $20. Electronic applications accepted. Tuition, state resident: part-time $148 per credit hour. Tuition, nonresident: part-time $509 per credit hour. *Financial aid:* In 1998–99, 16 students received aid, including teaching assistantships with partial tuition reimbursements available (averaging $11,000 per year); fellowships with partial tuition reimbursements available, Federal Work-Study also available. *Faculty research:* Algebra, analysis, combinatorics, mathematical physics, chaos. Total annual research expenditures: $210,000. *Unit head:* Dr. Heinrich Niederhausen, Chair, 561-297-3341, Fax: 561-297-2436, E-mail: niederha@fau.edu. *Application contact:* Dr. Yuandan Lin, Graduate Adviser, 561-297-3343, Fax: 561-297-2436, E-mail: lin@fau.edu.

Florida International University, College of Arts and Sciences, Department of Mathematics, Miami, FL 33199. Offers mathematical sciences (MS). Part-time and evening/weekend programs available. *Faculty:* 32 full-time (7 women). *Students:* 4 full-time (2 women), 5 part-time (2 women); includes 6 minority (2 Asian Americans or Pacific Islanders, 4 Hispanic Americans) Average age 35. 9 applicants, 22% accepted. In 1998, 4 degrees awarded. *Degree requirements:* For master's, computer language, thesis, project required, foreign language not required. *Entrance requirements:* For master's, GRE General Test (minimum combined score of 1095 required), TOEFL (minimum score of 500 required). *Application deadline:* For fall admission, 4/1 (priority date); for spring admission, 10/1. Applications are processed on a rolling basis. Application fee: $20. Tuition, state resident: part-time $145 per credit hour. Tuition, nonresident: part-time $506 per credit hour. Required fees: $158; $158 per

Mathematics

Florida International University (continued)
year. *Financial aid:* Application deadline: 4/1. *Unit head:* Dr. Enrique Villamor, Chairperson, 305-348-2056, Fax: 305-348-6158, E-mail: villamor@fiu.edu.

Florida State University, Graduate Studies, College of Arts and Sciences, Department of Mathematics, Program in Pure Mathematics, Tallahassee, FL 32306. Offers MA, MS, PhD. Part-time programs available. *Faculty:* 22 full-time (2 women). *Students:* 19 full-time (12 women); includes 3 minority (1 Asian American or Pacific Islander, 2 Hispanic Americans), 6 international. Average age 26. In 1998, 3 doctorates awarded (67% entered university research/teaching, 33% found other work related to degree). Terminal master's awarded for partial completion of doctoral program. *Degree requirements:* For master's, thesis optional, foreign language not required; for doctorate, dissertation required, foreign language not required. *Entrance requirements:* For master's and doctorate, GRE General Test (minimum combined score of 1100 required), minimum GPA of 3.0. *Average time to degree:* Doctorate–5 years full-time. *Application deadline:* For fall admission, 2/1 (priority date); for spring admission, 11/28. Applications are processed on a rolling basis. Application fee: $20. Tuition, state resident: part-time $139 per credit hour. Tuition, nonresident: part-time $482 per credit hour. Tuition and fees vary according to program. *Financial aid:* In 1998–99, 1 fellowship with full tuition reimbursement (averaging $14,000 per year), 2 research assistantships with full tuition reimbursements (averaging $14,000 per year), 16 teaching assistantships with full tuition reimbursements (averaging $14,000 per year) were awarded.; institutionally-sponsored loans also available. Financial aid application deadline: 3/1; financial aid applicants required to submit FAFSA. *Faculty research:* Commutative algebra, ring theory, geometric topology, knot theory, complex and functional analysis. *Unit head:* Carolyn P. Farrior, Associate Dean of Graduate Admissions, 407-674-7118, Fax: 407-723-9468, E-mail: cfarrior@fit.edu. *Application contact:* Dr. Steven Blumsack, Director of Graduate Studies, 850-644-2488, Fax: 850-644-4053, E-mail: blumsack@math.fsu.edu.

George Mason University, College of Arts and Sciences, Department of Mathematical Sciences, Fairfax, VA 22030-4444. Offers mathematics (MS). Evening/weekend programs available. *Faculty:* 28 full-time (5 women), 10 part-time (2 women). *Students:* 4 full-time (1 woman), 20 part-time (5 women); includes 4 minority (2 African Americans, 2 Asian Americans or Pacific Islanders), 1 international. Average age 33. 20 applicants, 65% accepted. In 1998, 3 degrees awarded. *Degree requirements:* For master's, comprehensive oral exam required, thesis optional, foreign language not required. *Entrance requirements:* For master's, minimum GPA of 3.0 in last 60 hours. *Application deadline:* For fall admission, 5/1; for spring admission, 11/1. Application fee: $30. Electronic applications accepted. Tuition, state resident: full-time $4,416; part-time $184 per credit hour. Tuition, nonresident: full-time $12,516; part-time $522 per credit hour. Tuition and fees vary according to program. *Financial aid:* Fellowships, research assistantships, teaching assistantships, career-related internships or fieldwork available. Aid available to part-time students. Financial aid application deadline: 3/1; financial aid applicants required to submit FAFSA. *Unit head:* Robert Sachs, Chair, 703-993-1462, Fax: 703-993-1491, E-mail: rsachs@gmu.edu.

The George Washington University, Columbian School of Arts and Sciences, Department of Mathematics, Program in Mathematics, Washington, DC 20052. Offers MA, PhD. Part-time and evening/weekend programs available. *Students:* 12 full-time (4 women), 10 part-time (2 women); includes 1 minority (Hispanic American), 9 international. Average age 35. 17 applicants, 41% accepted. In 1998, 3 doctorates awarded. Terminal master's awarded for partial completion of doctoral program. *Degree requirements:* For master's, comprehensive exam required, foreign language and thesis not required; for doctorate, dissertation, general exam required. *Entrance requirements:* For master's and doctorate, GRE General Test, GRE Subject Test, interview, minimum GPA of 3.0. Application fee: $55. Tuition: Full-time $17,328; part-time $722 per credit hour. Required fees: $828; $35 per credit hour. Tuition and fees vary according to campus/location and program. *Financial aid:* Fellowships, teaching assistantships available. Financial aid application deadline: 2/1. *Unit head:* Dr. Hugo Junghenn, Chair, Department of Mathematics, 202-994-6235.

Announcement: The GW Department of Mathematics offers programs leading to the MA, MS, and PhD degrees. Faculty members are active in the research areas of algebra, analysis, combinatorics, dynamical systems, ergodic theory, logic, numerical analysis, partial differential equations, knot theory, and topology, offering graduate students the option of specializing in pure or applied mathematics. The library resources at GW and the area's consortium of universities are excellent for advanced study and research. The department's computing facilities offer state-of-the-art mathematical research software. GW's location offers opportunities for contacts with research laboratories and government agencies and a culturally stimulating environment. For additional information, send e-mail to: study@math.gwu.edu or see the World Wide Web site at: http://www.gwu.edu/~math/

Georgia Institute of Technology, Graduate Studies and Research, College of Sciences, School of Mathematics, Atlanta, GA 30332-0001. Offers algorithms, combinatorics, and optimization (PhD); applied mathematics (MS); mathematics (MS Math, PhD); statistics (MS Stat). Terminal master's awarded for partial completion of doctoral program. *Degree requirements:* For master's, thesis or alternative required, foreign language not required; for doctorate, dissertation required. *Entrance requirements:* For master's and doctorate, GRE General Test, GRE Subject Test, TOEFL (minimum score of 570 required), minimum GPA of 3.0. Electronic applications accepted. *Faculty research:* Dynamical systems, discrete mathematics, probability and statistics, mathematical physics.

Georgia Institute of Technology, Graduate Studies and Research, Multidisciplinary Program in Algorithms, Combinatorics, and Optimization, Atlanta, GA 30332-0001. Offers PhD. Offered jointly with the College of Computing, the School of Industrial and Systems Engineering, and the School of Mathematics. *Degree requirements:* For doctorate, dissertation required, foreign language not required. *Entrance requirements:* For doctorate, GRE General Test, GRE Subject Test (computer science or mathematics), TOEFL (minimum score of 590 required; average 615). Electronic applications accepted. *Faculty research:* Complexity, graph minors, combinatorialoptimization, mathematical programming, probabilistic methods.

Georgian Court College, Graduate School, Program in Mathematics, Lakewood, NJ 08701-2697. Offers MA.

Georgia Southern University, Jack N. Averitt College of Graduate Studies, Allen E. Paulson College of Science and Technology, Department of Mathematics and Computer Science, Statesboro, GA 30460. Offers mathematics (MS). Part-time programs available. *Faculty:* 24 full-time (7 women). *Students:* 7 full-time (4 women), 8 part-time (2 women); includes 6 minority (5 African Americans, 1 Asian American or Pacific Islander), 2 international. Average age 30. 19 applicants, 63% accepted. In 1998, 6 degrees awarded. *Degree requirements:* For master's, thesis, terminal exam required. *Entrance requirements:* For master's, GRE, BS in engineering, science, or mathematics, proficiency in a computer programming language, previous course work in calculus, probability, linear algebra. *Average time to degree:* Master's–1.75 years full-time, 1.94 years part-time. *Application deadline:* For fall admission, 7/1 (priority date); for spring admission, 11/15 (priority date). Applications are processed on a rolling basis. Application fee: $0. Electronic applications accepted. *Financial aid:* In 1998–99, 4 students received aid, including 4 research assistantships with partial tuition reimbursements available (averaging $4,900 per year); career-related internships or fieldwork, Federal Work-Study, and unspecified assistantships also available. Aid available to part-time students. Financial aid application deadline: 4/15; financial aid applicants required to submit FAFSA. *Faculty research:* Analysis of numerical, interval, and fuzzy data; approximation theory; computational mathematics; parallel computation; applied statistic and emphasis on biological models. Total annual research expenditures: $19,708. *Unit head:* Dr. Donald Fausett, Chair, 912-681-5132, Fax: 912-681-0654, E-mail: dfausett@gasou.edu. *Application contact:* Dr. John R. Diebolt, Associate Graduate Dean, 912-681-5384, Fax: 912-681-0740, E-mail: gradschool@gasou.edu.

Georgia State University, College of Arts and Sciences, Department of Mathematics and Statistics, Atlanta, GA 30303-3083. Offers mathematics (MA, MS). *Faculty:* 36 full-time (12 women), 1 part-time (0 women). *Students:* 7 full-time (2 women), 12 part-time (6 women); includes 5 minority (1 African American, 3 Asian Americans or Pacific Islanders, 1 Native American), 3 international. 31 applicants, 42% accepted. In 1998, 6 degrees awarded. Application fee: $25. Tuition, state resident: full-time $2,896; part-time $121 per credit hour. Tuition, nonresident: full-time $11,584; part-time $483 per credit hour. Required fees: $468. Tuition and fees vary according to program. *Unit head:* Dr. Jean Bevis, Chair, 404-651-2245, Fax: 404-651-2246, E-mail: jbevis@cs.gsu.edu. *Application contact:* Dr. George Davis, Director of Graduate Studies, 404-651-2245, Fax: 404-651-2246, E-mail: gdavis@cs.gsu.edu.

See in-depth description on page 681.

Graduate School and University Center of the City University of New York, Graduate Studies, Program in Mathematics, New York, NY 10036-8099. Offers PhD. *Faculty:* 43 full-time (2 women). *Students:* 65 full-time (10 women), 3 part-time (1 woman); includes 1 African American, 4 Asian Americans or Pacific Islanders, 2 Hispanic Americans Average age 33. 40 applicants, 80% accepted. In 1998, 5 degrees awarded. *Degree requirements:* For doctorate, dissertation required. *Entrance requirements:* For doctorate, GRE General Test. *Application deadline:* For fall admission, 4/15. Application fee: $40. *Financial aid:* In 1998–99, 36 students received aid, including 31 fellowships; research assistantships, teaching assistantships, career-related internships or fieldwork, Federal Work-Study, institutionally-sponsored loans, and tuition waivers (full and partial) also available. Financial aid application deadline: 2/1; financial aid applicants required to submit FAFSA. *Unit head:* Dr. Josef Dodziuk, Executive Officer, 212-642-2458.

Harvard University, Graduate School of Arts and Sciences, Department of Mathematics, Cambridge, MA 02138. Offers AM, PhD. *Students:* 68 full-time (21 women). 134 applicants, 13% accepted. In 1998, 15 master's, 14 doctorates awarded. *Degree requirements:* For doctorate, dissertation, qualifying exam required. *Entrance requirements:* For master's, GRE General Test, TOEFL (minimum score of 550 required); for doctorate, GRE General Test, GRE Subject Test, TOEFL (minimum score of 550 required). *Application deadline:* For fall admission, 12/15. Application fee: $60. *Financial aid:* Fellowships, research assistantships, teaching assistantships, career-related internships or fieldwork, Federal Work-Study, and institutionally-sponsored loans available. Financial aid application deadline: 12/30. *Unit head:* Dr. Yum-Tong Siu, Chairperson, 617-495-2172. *Application contact:* Office of Admissions and Financial Aid, 617-495-5315.

Howard University, Graduate School of Arts and Sciences, Department of Mathematics, Washington, DC 20059-0002. Offers applied mathematics (MS, PhD); mathematics (MS, PhD). Part-time programs available. *Degree requirements:* For master's, computer language, thesis or alternative, comprehensive exam, qualifying exam required, foreign language not required; for doctorate, 2 foreign languages (computer language can substitute for one), dissertation, comprehensive exam, qualifying exams required. *Entrance requirements:* For master's, GRE General Test, minimum GPA of 3.2 in mathematics; for doctorate, GRE General Test.

Hunter College of the City University of New York, Graduate School, Division of Sciences and Mathematics, Department of Mathematics, New York, NY 10021-5085. Offers applied mathematics (MA); pure mathematics (MA). Part-time and evening/weekend programs available. *Degree requirements:* For master's, one foreign language, computer language, thesis required (for some programs). *Entrance requirements:* For master's, GRE General Test, TOEFL (minimum score of 550 required). Tuition, state resident: full-time $4,350; part-time $185 per credit. Tuition, nonresident: full-time $7,600; part-time $320 per credit. Required fees: $8 per term. *Faculty research:* Data analysis, dynamical systems, computer graphics, topology, statistical decision theory.

Idaho State University, Graduate School, College of Arts and Sciences, Department of Mathematics, Pocatello, ID 83209. Offers mathematics (MS, DA); natural science (MNS). *Degree requirements:* For master's, foreign language and thesis not required; for doctorate, dissertation required, foreign language not required. *Entrance requirements:* For master's and doctorate, GRE General Test, GRE Subject Test. *Faculty research:* Algebra, analysis geometry, statistics,applied mathematics.

Illinois State University, Graduate School, College of Arts and Sciences, Department of Mathematics, Program in Mathematics, Normal, IL 61790-2200. Offers MA, MS. *Students:* 13 full-time (3 women), 17 part-time (14 women); includes 3 minority (all Asian Americans or Pacific Islanders) 9 applicants, 78% accepted. In 1998, 11 degrees awarded. *Degree requirements:* For master's, thesis or alternative required. *Entrance requirements:* For master's, GRE General Test, minimum GPA of 2.8 in last 60 hours. *Application deadline:* Applications are processed on a rolling basis. Application fee: $0. Tuition, state resident: full-time $2,526; part-time $105 per credit hour. Tuition, nonresident: full-time $7,578; part-time $316 per credit hour. Required fees: $1,082; $38 per credit hour. Tuition and fees vary according to course load and program. *Financial aid:* In 1998–99, 3 research assistantships, 10 teaching assistantships were awarded.; tuition waivers (full) and unspecified assistantships also available. Financial aid application deadline: 4/1. *Unit head:* Dr. Lotus Hershberger, Chairperson, Department of Mathematics, 309-438-8781.

Indiana State University, School of Graduate Studies, College of Arts and Sciences, Department of Mathematics, Terre Haute, IN 47809-1401. Offers MA, MS. *Faculty:* 15 full-time (2 women). *Students:* 16 full-time (3 women), 5 part-time (2 women); includes 2 minority (1 African American, 1 Asian American or Pacific Islander), 16 international. Average age 29. 39 applicants, 69% accepted. In 1998, 6 degrees awarded. *Degree requirements:* Foreign language not required. *Average time to degree:* Master's–2 years full-time, 5 years part-time. *Application deadline:* For fall admission, 7/1 (priority date); for spring admission, 11/1 (priority date). Applications are processed on a rolling basis. Application fee: $20. Electronic applications accepted. *Financial aid:* In 1998–99, 6 research assistantships with partial tuition reimbursements were awarded.; teaching assistantships, tuition waivers (partial) also available. Financial aid application deadline: 3/1; financial aid applicants required to submit FAFSA. *Unit head:* Dr. Richard Easton, Chairperson, 812-237-2130.

Indiana University Bloomington, Graduate School, College of Arts and Sciences, Department of Mathematics, Bloomington, IN 47405. Offers applied mathematics–numerical analysis (MA, PhD); mathematics education (MAT); probability-statistics (MA, PhD). PhD offered through the University Graduate School. *Faculty:* 46 full-time (1 woman). *Students:* 77 full-time (22 women), 26 part-time (5 women); includes 3 minority (2 Asian Americans or Pacific Islanders, 1 Native American), 52 international. In 1998, 18 master's, 12 doctorates awarded. Terminal master's awarded for partial completion of doctoral program. *Degree requirements:* For master's, foreign language and thesis not required; for doctorate, dissertation required. *Entrance requirements:* For master's and doctorate, GRE General Test, GRE Subject Test, TOEFL. *Application deadline:* For fall admission, 1/15 (priority date); for spring admission, 9/1 (priority date). Applications are processed on a rolling basis. Application fee: $40. Electronic applications accepted. Tuition, state resident: part-time $161 per credit hour. Tuition, nonresident: part-time $468 per credit hour. Required fees: $360 per year. Tuition and fees vary according to course load and program. *Financial aid:* In 1998–99, 8 fellowships with full tuition reimbursements (averaging $15,000 per year), 101 teaching assistantships with full tuition reimbursements (averaging $12,200 per year) were awarded.; research assistantships, Federal Work-Study also available. Aid available to part-time students. Financial aid application deadline:2/1. *Faculty research:* Topology, geometry, algebra. *Unit head:* Daniel Maki, Chair, 812-855-2200, Fax: 812-855-0046, E-mail: maki@indiana.edu. *Application contact:* Misty Cummings, Graduate Secretary, 812-855-2645, Fax: 812-855-0046, E-mail: gradmath@indiana.edu.

Indiana University of Pennsylvania, Graduate School, College of Natural Sciences and Mathematics, Department of Mathematics, Indiana, PA 15705-1087. Offers applied mathematics (MS); elementary and middle school mathematics education (M Ed); mathematics education (M Ed). Part-time programs available. *Students:* 7 full-time (3 women), 19 part-time (14 women), 2 international. Average age 27. 13 applicants, 85% accepted. In 1998, 20 degrees awarded. *Degree requirements:* For master's, thesis optional, foreign language not required. *Entrance requirements:* For master's, TOEFL (minimum score of 500 required). *Application deadline:* For fall admission, 7/1 (priority date); for spring admission, 11/1. Applications are processed on a rolling basis. Application fee: $30. *Financial aid:* Research assistantships, career-related internships or fieldwork and Federal Work-Study available. Aid available to part-time students. Financial aid application deadline: 3/15. *Unit head:* Dr. Gerald Buriok, Chairperson, 724-357-2608, E-mail: jburiok@grove.iup.edu.

Indiana University–Purdue University Fort Wayne, School of Arts and Sciences, Department of Mathematical Sciences, Fort Wayne, IN 46805-1499. Offers applied mathematics (MS); mathematics (MS); operations research (MS). Part-time and evening/weekend programs available. *Faculty:* 18 full-time (4 women), 1 (woman) part-time. *Students:* 3 full-time (1 woman), 6 part-time (3 women). Average age 25. 3 applicants, 100% accepted. In 1998, 2 degrees awarded. *Degree requirements:* For master's, foreign language and thesis not required. *Entrance requirements:* For master's, minimum GPA of 3.0, major or minor in mathematics. *Average time to degree:* Master's–2 years full-time, 3.5 years part-time. *Application deadline:* For fall admission, 5/1 (priority date); for spring admission, 12/1. Applications are processed on a rolling basis. Application fee: $30. *Financial aid:* In 1998–99, 4 teaching assistantships with partial tuition reimbursements (averaging $6,700 per year) were awarded.; grants and scholarships also available. Financial aid application deadline: 3/1; financial aid applicants required to submit FAFSA. *Faculty research:* Graph theory, biostatistics, statistical design, mathematics education, partial differential equations. *Unit head:* Raymond E. Pippert, Chair, 219-481-6224, Fax: 219-481-6880, E-mail: pippert@cvax.ipfw.indiana.edu. *Application contact:* W. Douglas Weakley, Director of Graduate Studies, 219-481-6238, Fax: 219-481-6880, E-mail: weakley@cvax.ipfw.indiana.edu.

Indiana University–Purdue University Indianapolis, School of Science, Department of Mathematical Sciences, Indianapolis, IN 46202-3216. Offers applied mathematics (MS, PhD); applied statistics (MS); mathematics (MS, PhD). Part-time programs available. *Students:* 7 full-time (2 women), 28 part-time (9 women); includes 2 minority (1 Asian American or Pacific Islander, 1 Native American), 15 international. Average age 32. In 1998, 18 master's awarded. Terminal master's awarded for partial completion of doctoral program. *Degree requirements:* For master's, thesis optional, foreign language not required; for doctorate, one foreign language, dissertation required. *Entrance requirements:* For master's, TOEFL (minimum score of 570 required); for doctorate, GRE, TOEFL (minimum score of 570 required). *Application deadline:* For fall admission, 2/1 (priority date). Application fee: $25 ($50 for international students). Tuition, state resident: part-time $158 per credit hour. Tuition, nonresident: part-time $455 per credit hour. Required fees: $121 per year. Tuition and fees vary according to course load and degree level. *Financial aid:* In 1998–99, 14 students received aid, including 2 research assistantships with tuition reimbursements available (averaging $11,000 per year), 10 teaching assistantships with tuition reimbursements available (averaging $11,000 per year); fellowships with tuition reimbursements available, career-related internships or fieldwork, Federal Work-Study, and tuition waivers (full and partial) also available. Financial aid application deadline:3/1. *Faculty research:* Mathematical physics, analysis, operator theory, functional analysis, integrated systems. *Unit head:* Eric T. Sawyer, Chair, 317-274-6918, Fax: 317-274-3460. *Application contact:* Yuri Abramovich, Chair, Graduate Committee, 317-274-6927, Fax: 317-274-3460, E-mail: yabramovich@math.iupui.edu.

Institute of Paper Science and Technology, Graduate Programs, Program in Physics/Mathematics, Atlanta, GA 30318-5794. Offers MS, PhD. Part-time programs available. Terminal master's awarded for partial completion of doctoral program. *Degree requirements:* For master's, industrial experience, research project required, foreign language and thesis not required; for doctorate, dissertation required, foreign language not required. *Entrance requirements:* For master's and doctorate, GRE (score in 50th percentile or higher required), minimum GPA of 3.0. *Application deadline:* For fall admission, 3/1 (priority date). Application fee: $0. *Financial aid:* Career-related internships or fieldwork and institutionally-sponsored loans available. Financial aid applicants required to submit FAFSA. *Unit head:* John Waterhouse, Acting Director,Fiber and Paper Physics Division, 404-894-1621, Fax: 404-894-4778, E-mail: john.waterhouse@ipst.edu. *Application contact:* Dana Carter, Student Development Counselor, 404-894-5745, Fax: 404-894-4778, E-mail: dana.carter@ipst.edu.

Iowa State University of Science and Technology, Graduate College, College of Liberal Arts and Sciences, Department of Mathematics, Ames, IA 50011. Offers applied mathematics (MS, PhD); mathematics (MS, PhD); school mathematics (MSM). *Faculty:* 52 full-time. *Students:* 30 full-time (9 women), 21 part-time (7 women); includes 1 minority (Asian American or Pacific Islander), 22 international. 67 applicants, 45% accepted. In 1998, 9 master's, 4 doctorates awarded. *Degree requirements:* For master's, thesis or alternative required; for doctorate, dissertation required. *Entrance requirements:* For master's and doctorate, GRE General Test, TOEFL (minimum score of 550 required). *Application deadline:* For fall admission, 2/1 (priority date); for spring admission, 10/15. Application fee: $20 ($50 for international students). Electronic applications accepted. Tuition, state resident: full-time $3,308. Tuition, nonresident: full-time $9,744. Part-time tuition and fees vary according to course load, campus/location and program. *Financial aid:* In 1998–99, 6 research assistantships with partial tuition reimbursements (averaging $11,447 per year), 27 teaching assistantships with partial tuition reimbursements (averaging $11,571 per year) were awarded.; fellowships, scholarships also available. *Unit head:* Dr. Max D. Gunzburger, Chair, 515-294-1752, Fax: 515-294-5454, E-mail: gradmath@iastate.edu.

See in-depth description on page 683.

Jackson State University, Graduate School, School of Science and Technology, Department of Mathematics, Jackson, MS 39217. Offers mathematics (MS); mathematics education (MST). Part-time and evening/weekend programs available. *Faculty:* 20 full-time (4 women). *Students:* 6 full-time (4 women), 1 (woman) part-time; includes 6 minority (all African Americans), 1 international. In 1998, 2 degrees awarded. *Degree requirements:* For master's, thesis (for some programs), comprehensive exam required. *Entrance requirements:* For master's, GRE General Test (minimum combined score of 1000 required), TOEFL (minimum score of 550 required). *Application deadline:* For fall admission, 3/1 (priority date); for spring admission, 10/1. Applications are processed on a rolling basis. Application fee: $20. *Financial aid:* In 1998–99, 6 students received aid. Career-related internships or fieldwork, Federal Work-Study, scholarships, and unspecified assistantships available. Aid available to part-time students. Financial aid application deadline: 3/1; financial aid applicants required to submit FAFSA. *Unit head:* Curtis Gore, Admissions Coordinator, 601-974-5841, Fax: 601-974-6196, E-mail: cgore@ccaix.jsums.edu. *Application contact:* Mae Robinson, Admissions Coordinator, 601-968-2455, Fax: 601-968-8246, E-mail: mrobinson@ccaix.jsums.edu.

Jacksonville State University, College of Graduate Studies and Continuing Education, College of Arts and Sciences, Department of Mathematics, Jacksonville, AL 36265-1602. Offers MS. *Faculty:* 12 full-time (0 women). *Degree requirements:* For master's, thesis optional. *Entrance requirements:* For master's, GRE General Test or MAT. *Application deadline:* Applications are processed on a rolling basis. Application fee: $20. *Financial aid:* Available to part-time students. Application deadline: 4/1. *Unit head:* Dr. Murray L. Kaplan, Director of Graduate Education, 515-294-9304, E-mail: fshn@iastate.edu. *Application contact:* 256-782-5329.

John Carroll University, Graduate School, Department of Mathematics, University Heights, OH 44118-4581. Offers MA, MS. Part-time and evening/weekend programs available. *Faculty:* 16 full-time (3 women). *Students:* 5 full-time (3 women), 32 part-time (21 women); includes 1 minority (Asian American or Pacific Islander), 1 international. Average age 27. 5 applicants, 80% accepted. In 1998, 3 degrees awarded (34% entered university research/teaching, 33% found other work related to degree, 33% continued full-time study). *Degree requirements:* For master's, comprehensive exam, research essay required, foreign language and thesis not required. *Entrance requirements:* For master's, minimum GPA of 2.5, teaching certificate (MA). *Average time to degree:* Master's–2 years full-time, 2.75 years part-time. *Application deadline:* For fall admission, 8/15 (priority date); for spring admission, 1/3. Applications are processed on a rolling basis. Application fee: $25 ($35 for international students). *Financial aid:* In 1998–99, 5 students received aid, including 5 teaching assistantships with full tuition reimbursements available (averaging $8,500 per year); tuition waivers (partial) also available. Financial aid application deadline: 3/1; financial aid applicants required to submit FAFSA. *Faculty research:* Algebraic topology, algebra, differential geometry, combinatorics, Lie groups. *Unit head:* Dr. Dwight M. Olson, Chairperson, 216-397-4351, Fax: 216-397-3033, E-mail: olson@jcvaxa.jcu.edu. *Application contact:* Dr. Douglas A. Norris, Coordinator of Student Services, 216-397-4687, Fax: 216-397-3033, E-mail: norris@jcvaxa.jcu.edu.

Johns Hopkins University, G. W. C. Whiting School of Engineering, Department of Mathematical Sciences, Baltimore, MD 21218-2699. Offers MA, MSE, PhD. *Faculty:* 13 full-time (2 women), 4 part-time (1 woman). *Students:* 30 full-time (9 women), 3 part-time, 13 international. Average age 26. 52 applicants, 58% accepted. In 1998, 6 master's, 3 doctorates awarded. Terminal master's awarded for partial completion of doctoral program. *Degree requirements:* For master's, computer language, thesis required (for some programs), foreign language not required; for doctorate, computer language, dissertation required, foreign language not required. *Entrance requirements:* For master's and doctorate, GRE General Test, GRE Subject Test, TOEFL (minimum score of 560 required). *Average time to degree:* Master's–2 years full-time; doctorate–4 years full-time. *Application deadline:* For fall admission, 1/15 (priority date). Applications are processed on a rolling basis. Application fee: $50. Tuition: Full-time $23,660. Tuition and fees vary according to program. *Financial aid:* In 1998–99, 9 fellowships (averaging $13,230 per year), 10 research assistantships (averaging $13,230 per year), 12 teaching assistantships (averaging $13,230 per year) were awarded.; Federal Work-Study and institutionally-sponsored loans also available. Financial aid application deadline: 1/15. *Faculty research:* Discrete mathematics, probability, optimization, statistics, stochastic processes. Total annual research expenditures: $335,000. *Unit head:* Dr. John C. Wierman, Chair, 410-516-7211, Fax: 410-516-7459, E-mail: wierman@brutus.mts.jhu.edu. *Application contact:* Kay Lutz, Graduate Coordinator, 410-516-7198, Fax: 410-516-7459, E-mail: lutz@jhu.edu.

See in-depth description on page 685.

Johns Hopkins University, Zanvyl Krieger School of Arts and Sciences, Department of Mathematics, Baltimore, MD 21218-2699. Offers MA, PhD. *Faculty:* 19 full-time (1 woman). *Students:* 31 full-time (3 women); includes 1 minority (Asian American or Pacific Islander), 22 international. Average age 26. 35 applicants, 20% accepted. In 1998, 3 master's awarded (% continued full-time study); 2 doctorates awarded. Terminal master's awarded for partial completion of doctoral program. *Degree requirements:* For master's, one foreign language, language and qualifying exams required, thesis not required; for doctorate, one foreign language, dissertation, language and 3 qualifying exams required. *Entrance requirements:* For master's and doctorate, TOEFL (minimum score of 560 required). *Average time to degree:* Master's–2 years full-time; doctorate–5 years full-time. *Application deadline:* For fall admission, 2/14 (priority date). Application fee: $55. Tuition: Full-time $23,660. Tuition and fees vary according to program. *Financial aid:* In 1998–99, 1 fellowship, 30 teaching assistantships were awarded.; Federal Work-Study, institutionally-sponsored loans, and tuition waivers (partial) also available. Financial aid application deadline: 2/15; financial aid applicants required to submit FAFSA. *Faculty research:* Algebraic geometry, number theory, algebraic topology, differential geometry, partial differential equations. Total annual research expenditures:$363,971. *Unit head:* Dr. Steven Zelditch, Chair, 410-516-7397, Fax: 410-516-5549, E-mail: grad@math.jhu.edu. *Application contact:* Phyllis Cook, Graduate Program Assistant, 410-516-7399, Fax: 410-516-5549, E-mail: grad@math.jhu.edu.

Kansas State University, Graduate School, College of Arts and Sciences, Department of Mathematics, Manhattan, KS 66506. Offers MS, PhD. Part-time programs available. *Faculty:* 33 full-time (0 women). *Students:* 45 full-time, 7 part-time (1 woman); includes 2 minority (1 African American, 1 Native American), 18 international. 26 applicants, 46% accepted. In 1998, 14 master's, 1 doctorate awarded (100% entered university research/teaching). Terminal master's awarded for partial completion of doctoral program. *Degree requirements:* For master's, thesis or alternative required, foreign language not required; for doctorate, dissertation required. *Average time to degree:* Master's–4 years full-time; doctorate–7 years full-time. *Application deadline:* For fall admission, 6/1 (priority date); for spring admission, 10/31 (priority date). Applications are processed on a rolling basis. Application fee: $0 ($25 for international students). Electronic applications accepted. *Financial aid:* In 1998–99, 42 students received aid, including 42 teaching assistantships with full tuition reimbursements available (averaging $9,180 per year); Federal Work-Study also available. Aid available to part-time students. Financial aid application deadline: 3/1; financial aid applicants required to submit FAFSA. Total annual research expenditures: $130,000. *Unit head:* Dr. Louis Pigno, Head, 785-532-6750, Fax: 785-532-0546, E-mail: math@math.ksu.edu. *Application contact:* David Surowski, Graduate Coordinator, 785-532-6750, Fax: 785-532-0546.

Kent State University, College of Arts and Sciences, Department of Mathematics and Computer Science, Kent, OH 44242-0001. Offers applied mathematics (MA, MS, PhD); computer science (MA, MS, PhD); pure mathematics (MA, MS, PhD). *Faculty:* 41 full-time. *Students:* 69 full-time (19 women), 60 part-time (23 women); includes 2 minority (both Asian Americans or Pacific Islanders), 78 international. 135 applicants, 76% accepted. In 1998, 14 master's, 9 doctorates awarded. *Degree requirements:* For master's, thesis optional, foreign language not required; for doctorate, dissertation required. *Entrance requirements:* For master's, GRE, minimum GPA of 2.75; for doctorate, GRE, minimum GPA of 3.0. *Application deadline:* For fall admission, 7/12; for spring admission, 11/29. Applications are processed on a rolling basis. Application fee: $30. *Financial aid:* Fellowships, research assistantships, teaching assistantships, Federal Work-Study, institutionally-sponsored loans, and tuition waivers (full) available. Financial aid application deadline: 2/1. *Unit head:* Dr. Austin C. Melton, Chairman, 330-672-2430, Fax: 330-672-7824.

Announcement: Department offers master's and PhD programs in pure mathematics, applied mathematics, statistics, and computer science. PhD areas include numerical, functional, and complex analysis; measure theory; geometric topology; operator theory; ring and group theory; and computer algebra, parallel programming, scientific computing, and networking. For more information, please visit the World Wide Web at http://www.mcs.kent.edu.

Kutztown University of Pennsylvania, College of Graduate Studies and Extended Learning, College of Liberal Arts and Sciences, Program in Mathematics, Kutztown, PA 19530-0730. Offers MA. Part-time and evening/weekend programs available. *Faculty:* 14 full-time (4 women). *Degree requirements:* For master's, comprehensive exam or thesis required. *Entrance requirements:* For master's, GRE General Test, TOEFL, TSE. *Application deadline:* For fall admission, 3/1; for spring admission, 8/1. Application fee: $25. *Financial aid:* Career-related internships or fieldwork, Federal Work-Study, tuition waivers (partial), and unspecified assistantships available. Financial aid application deadline: 3/15; financial aid applicants required to submit FAFSA. *Faculty research:* Operations research. *Unit head:* William Bateman, Chairperson, 610-683-4410, E-mail: bateman@kutztown.edu.

Lakehead University, Graduate Studies and Research, Faculty of Arts and Science, School of Mathematical Sciences, Thunder Bay, ON P7B 5E1, Canada. Offers computer science (M Sc, MA); mathematics and statistics (M Sc, MA). Part-time and evening/weekend programs available. *Degree requirements:* For master's, thesis or alternative required, foreign language not required. *Entrance requirements:* For master's, TOEFL (minimum score of 550 required), minimum B average. *Faculty research:* Numerical analysis, classical analysis, theoretical computer science, abstract harmonic analysis, functional analysis.

Lamar University, College of Graduate Studies, College of Engineering, Department of Mathematics, Beaumont, TX 77710. Offers MS. *Faculty:* 6 full-time (1 woman). *Students:* 2 full-time (0 women), 4 part-time (1 woman). Average age 30. 9 applicants, 100% accepted. In

Mathematics

Lamar University (continued)
1998, 2 degrees awarded. *Degree requirements:* For master's, foreign language and thesis not required. *Entrance requirements:* For master's, GRE General Test (minimum combined score of 900 required), TOEFL (minimum score of 500 required), minimum GPA of 2.5 or 3.0 in last 60 hours of undergraduate course work. *Average time to degree:* Master's–2 years full-time. *Application deadline:* For fall admission, 5/15 (priority date); for spring admission, 10/1 (priority date). Applications are processed on a rolling basis. Application fee: $0. *Financial aid:* In 1998–99, 2 research assistantships, 3 teaching assistantships (averaging $6,000 per year) were awarded.; fellowships Financial aid application deadline: 4/1. *Faculty research:* Complex analysis, functional analysis, wavelets. Total annual research expenditures: $45,000. *Unit head:* Dr. Alec Matheson, Chair, 409-880-8792, Fax: 409-880-8794, E-mail: chair@math.lamar.edu. *Application contact:* Dr. Paul Chiou, Professor, 409-880-8800, Fax: 409-880-8794, E-mail: chiou@math.lamar.edu.

Lehigh University, College of Arts and Sciences, Department of Mathematics, Bethlehem, PA 18015-3094. Offers applied mathematics (MS, PhD); mathematics (MS, PhD); statistics (MS). Part-time programs available. *Students:* 27 full-time (14 women); includes 2 minority (1 African American, 1 Asian American or Pacific Islander), 3 international. Average age 26. 16 applicants, 63% accepted. In 1998, 5 master's, 4 doctorates awarded (100% entered university research/teaching). Terminal master's awarded for partial completion of doctoral program. *Degree requirements:* For master's, comprehensive exam required, foreign language and thesis not required; for doctorate, dissertation, comprehensive and qualifying exams required. *Entrance requirements:* For master's and doctorate, TOEFL (minimum score of 550 required), minimum GPA of 3.0. *Average time to degree:* Master's–2 years full-time; doctorate–6 years full-time, 10 years part-time. *Application deadline:* For fall admission, 7/15; for spring admission, 12/1. Applications are processed on a rolling basis. Application fee: $40. *Financial aid:* In 1998–99, 23 students received aid, including 1 fellowship, 18 teaching assistantships; research assistantships, tuition waivers (full and partial) also available. Financial aid application deadline: 1/15. *Faculty research:* Probability, differential geometry, settheory, algebra, differential equations. *Unit head:* Dr. George E. McCluskey, Chairman, 610-758-3730, Fax: 610-758-6553, E-mail: cgmo@lehigh.edu. *Application contact:* Dr. Vladimir Dobric, Graduate Coordinator, 610-758-3734, Fax: 610-758-6553, E-mail: vd00@lehigh.edu.

Lehman College of the City University of New York, Division of Natural and Social Sciences, Department of Mathematics and Computer Science, Program in Mathematics, Bronx, NY 10468-1589. Offers MA. Part-time and evening/weekend programs available. *Degree requirements:* For master's, one foreign language, computer language, thesis or alternative required. *Application deadline:* For fall admission, 4/1; for spring admission, 11/1. Applications are processed on a rolling basis. Application fee: $40. Tuition, state resident: full-time $4,350; part-time $185 per credit. Tuition, nonresident: full-time $7,600; part-time $320 per credit. *Financial aid:* Federal Work-Study and tuition waivers (full and partial) available. Aid available to part-time students. Financial aid application deadline: 5/15; financial aid applicants required to submit FAFSA. *Unit head:* Charles Berger, Adviser, 718-960-8117, Fax: 718-960-8969.

Long Island University, C.W. Post Campus, College of Liberal Arts and Sciences, Department of Mathematics, Brookville, NY 11548-1300. Offers applied mathematics (MS), including classical mathematics, computer mathematics; mathematics and education (MS); mathematics for secondary school teachers (MS). Part-time and evening/weekend programs available. *Faculty:* 14 full-time (3 women). *Students:* 14 full-time (8 women), 18 part-time (9 women). Average age 25. 20 applicants, 90% accepted. In 1998, 10 degrees awarded (80% found work related to degree, 20% continued full-time study). *Degree requirements:* For master's, thesis or alternative, oral presentation required, foreign language not required. *Average time to degree:* Master's–2 years full-time, 3 years part-time. *Application deadline:* Applications are processed on a rolling basis. Application fee: $30. Electronic applications accepted. *Financial aid:* In 1998–99, 10 students received aid. Career-related internships or fieldwork, Federal Work-Study, institutionally-sponsored loans, tuition waivers (full and partial), and unspecified assistantships available. Aid available to part-time students. Financial aid application deadline: 5/15; financial aid applicants required to submit FAFSA. *Faculty research:* Differential geometry, topological groups, general topology, number theory, analysis and statistics, numerical analysis. *Unit head:* Dr. Neo Cleopa, Chairman, 516-299-2448, Fax: 516-299-4049, E-mail: ncleopa@phoenix.liunet.edu. *Application contact:* Dr. Shahla Ahdout, Graduate Adviser, 516-299-2448, Fax: 516-299-4049.

Louisiana State University and Agricultural and Mechanical College, Graduate School, College of Arts and Sciences, Department of Mathematics, Baton Rouge, LA 70803. Offers MS, PhD. *Faculty:* 41 full-time (1 woman), 1 part-time (0 women). *Students:* 50 full-time (11 women), 6 part-time (3 women); includes 7 minority (4 African Americans, 3 Hispanic Americans), 23 international. Average age 29. 47 applicants, 72% accepted. In 1998, 15 master's, 4 doctorates awarded. Terminal master's awarded for partial completion of doctoral program. *Degree requirements:* For master's, foreign language and thesis not required; for doctorate, 2 foreign languages, dissertation required. *Entrance requirements:* For master's and doctorate, GRE General Test, TOEFL (minimum score of 550 required), minimum GPA of 3.0. *Application deadline:* For fall admission, 1/25 (priority date). Applications are processed on a rolling basis. Application fee: $25. *Financial aid:* In 1998–99, 12 fellowships, 1 research assistantship with partial tuition reimbursement, 34 teaching assistantships with partial tuition reimbursements were awarded.; institutionally-sponsored loans, tuition waivers (full), and unspecified assistantships also available. Financial aid application deadline: 3/1. *Faculty research:* Algebra, graph theory and combinatorics, algebraic topology, analysis and probability, topological algebra. Total annual research expenditures:$465,354. *Unit head:* Dr. James Retherford, Chair, 225-388-1665, Fax: 225-388-4276, E-mail: oncal@math.lsu.edu. *Application contact:* Dr. Len Richardson, Director of Graduate Studies, 225-388-1568, Fax: 225-388-4276, E-mail: rich@math.lsu.edu.

Louisiana Tech University, Graduate School, College of Engineering and Science, Department of Mathematics and Statistics, Ruston, LA 71272. Offers MS. Part-time programs available. *Degree requirements:* For master's, computer language, thesis or alternative required, foreign language not required. *Entrance requirements:* For master's, GRE General Test (minimum combined score of 1070 required; average 1245), TOEFL (minimum score of 550 required), minimum GPA of 3.0 in last 60 hours.

Loyola University Chicago, Graduate School, Department of Mathematical and Computer Sciences, Chicago, IL 60611-2196. Offers computer science (MS); mathematical science (MS). Part-time and evening/weekend programs available. *Degree requirements:* For master's, oral and written comprehensive exams required. *Entrance requirements:* For master's, GRE General Test or TOEFL (minimum score of 550 required), minimum B average. *Faculty research:* Parallel computing, programming language, analysis of algorithms, logic.

See in-depth description on page 689.

Loyola University New Orleans, College of Arts and Sciences, Department of Mathematics and Computer Science, New Orleans, LA 70118-6195. Offers MS. Part-time and evening/weekend programs available. *Faculty:* 6 full-time (1 woman). Average age 37. 2 applicants, 100% accepted. In 1998, 4 degrees awarded. *Degree requirements:* For master's, foreign language and thesis not required. *Entrance requirements:* For master's, documentation of previous work, courses currently being taught, minimum GPA of 3.0 in last 30 hours. *Application deadline:* For fall admission, 8/1 (priority date); for spring admission, 12/1 (priority date). Applications are processed on a rolling basis. Application fee: $20. Electronic applications accepted. *Financial aid:* Tuition waivers (partial) available. Aid available to part-time students. Financial aid application deadline: 5/1; financial aid applicants required to submit FAFSA. *Unit head:* Dr. Bogdan Czejdo, Chair, 504-865-3340, Fax: 504-865-2051, E-mail: czejdo@loyno.edu. *Application contact:* Dr. Antonio Lopez, Adviser, 504-865-3340, Fax: 504-865-2051, E-mail: tlopez@loyno.edu.

Maharishi University of Management, Graduate Studies, Department of Mathematics, Fairfield, IA 52557. Offers MS. *Degree requirements:* For master's, thesis or alternative required, foreign language not required. *Entrance requirements:* For master's, GRE General Test, TOEFL, minimum GPA of 3.0.

Marquette University, Graduate School, College of Arts and Sciences, Department of Mathematics, Statistics, and Computer Science, Milwaukee, WI 53201-1881. Offers algebra (PhD); bio-mathematical modeling (PhD); mathematics (MS); mathematics education (MS); statistics (MS). Part-time programs available. *Faculty:* 24 full-time (3 women). *Students:* 71 full-time (36 women), 28 part-time (10 women); includes 5 minority (2 African Americans, 2 Asian Americans or Pacific Islanders, 1 Hispanic American), 78 international. Average age 30. In 1998, 27 master's, 1 doctorate awarded. Terminal master's awarded for partial completion of doctoral program. *Degree requirements:* For master's, thesis or alternative, comprehensive exam required, foreign language not required; for doctorate, 2 foreign languages, dissertation, comprehensive exam required. *Entrance requirements:* For master's, TOEFL (minimum score of 550 required); for doctorate, TOEFL (minimum score of 550 required), sample of scholarly writing. Application fee: $40. Tuition: Part-time $510 per credit hour. Tuition and fees vary according to program. *Financial aid:* In 1998–99, 2 research assistantships, 20 teaching assistantships were awarded.; Federal Work-Study, institutionally-sponsored loans, scholarships, and tuition waivers (full and partial) also available. Aid available to part-time students. Financial aid application deadline: 2/15. *Faculty research:* Models of physiological systems, mathematical immunology, computational group theory, mathematical logic. Total annual research expenditures: $442,234. *Unit head:* Dr. Douglas Harris, Chairman, 414-288-7573, Fax: 414-288-1578. *Application contact:* Dr. Karl Byleen, Director of Graduate Studies, 414-288-6343.

Marshall University, Graduate College, College of Science, Department of Mathematics, Huntington, WV 25755-2020. Offers MA, MS. *Faculty:* 12 full-time (3 women). In 1998, 6 degrees awarded. *Degree requirements:* For master's, thesis (MS) required. *Entrance requirements:* For master's, GRE General Test (minimum combined score of 1200 required). *Unit head:* Dr. Bruce Ebanks, Chairperson, 304-696-6482, E-mail: ebanks@marshall.edu. *Application contact:* Ken O'Neal, Assistant Vice President, Adult Student Services, 304-746-2500 Ext. 1907, Fax: 304-746-1902, E-mail: oneal@marshall.edu.

Massachusetts Institute of Technology, School of Science, Department of Mathematics, Cambridge, MA 02139-4307. Offers PhD, Sc D. *Faculty:* 52 full-time (1 woman). *Students:* 89 full-time (21 women); includes 6 minority (5 Asian Americans or Pacific Islanders, 1 Hispanic American), 53 international. Average age 25. 272 applicants, 13% accepted. In 1998, 21 doctorates awarded (67% entered university research/teaching, 33% found other work related to degree). *Degree requirements:* For doctorate, one foreign language, dissertation, oral exam required. *Entrance requirements:* For doctorate, GRE General Test, GRE Subject Test, TOEFL. *Average time to degree:* Doctorate–4.8 years full-time. *Application deadline:* For fall admission, 1/15. Application fee: $55. *Financial aid:* In 1998–99, 83 students received aid, including 6 fellowships (averaging $17,149 per year), 10 research assistantships (averaging $14,130 per year), 46 teaching assistantships (averaging $14,130 per year); Federal Work-Study, institutionally-sponsored loans, traineeships, and graduate instructorships also available. Financial aid application deadline: 1/15. *Faculty research:* Analysis, topology, algebraic geometry, logic, Lie theory, combinatorics, fluid dynamics, theoretical computer science. Total annual research expenditures: $2 million. *Unit head:* David A. Vogan, Head, 617-253-6976, Fax: 617-253-4358, E-mail: dept@math.mit.edu. *Application contact:* Linda Okun, Graduate Administrator, 617-253-2689, Fax: 617-253-4358, E-mail: gradofc@math.mit.edu.

McGill University, Faculty of Graduate Studies and Research, Faculty of Science, Department of Mathematics, Montréal, PQ H3A 2T5, Canada. Offers M Sc, MA, PhD. Part-time programs available. *Students:* 64 full-time (20 women), 1 part-time. 94 applicants, 47% accepted. In 1998, 7 master's, 5 doctorates awarded. *Degree requirements:* For master's, thesis required; for doctorate, dissertation required. *Entrance requirements:* For master's, TOEFL (minimum score of 550 required), minimum GPA of 3.0; for doctorate, TOEFL (minimum score of 550 required). *Application deadline:* For fall admission, 3/1 (priority date); for winter admission, 10/1 (priority date). Applications are processed on a rolling basis. Application fee: $60. *Financial aid:* In 1998–99, 52 research assistantships, 59 teaching assistantships were awarded. *Unit head:* G. Schmidt, Chair, 514-398-7373, Fax: 514-398-3899, E-mail: chair@math.mcgill.ca. *Application contact:* W. J. Anderson, Professor, 514-398-7101, Fax: 514-398-3899, E-mail: gradprog@math.mcgill.ca.

McMaster University, School of Graduate Studies, Faculty of Science, Department of Mathematics and Statistics, Hamilton, ON L8S 4M2, Canada. Offers mathematics (PhD); mathematics and statistics (M Sc). Part-time programs available. *Degree requirements:* For master's, thesis or alternative, oral exam required, foreign language not required; for doctorate, dissertation, comprehensive exam required, foreign language not required. *Entrance requirements:* For master's, minimum B+ average in last year of honors degree; for doctorate, minimum B+ average, M Sc in mathematics or statistics. *Faculty research:* Algebra, analysis, applied mathematics, geometry and topology, probability and statistics.

McNeese State University, Graduate School, College of Science, Department of Mathematics, Computer Science, and Statistics, Lake Charles, LA 70609-2495. Offers computer science (MS); mathematics (MS); statistics (MS). Evening/weekend programs available. *Faculty:* 14 full-time (3 women). *Students:* 4 full-time (3 women), 5 part-time (2 women). In 1998, 10 degrees awarded. *Degree requirements:* For master's, computer language, thesis or alternative, written exam required, foreign language not required. *Entrance requirements:* For master's, GRE General Test. *Application deadline:* For fall admission, 7/15 (priority date). Applications are processed on a rolling basis. Application fee: $10 ($25 for international students). *Financial aid:* Teaching assistantships available. Financial aid application deadline: 5/1. *Unit head:* Sid Bradley, Head, 318-475-5788.

Memorial University of Newfoundland, School of Graduate Studies, Department of Mathematics and Statistics, St. John's, NF A1C 5S7, Canada. Offers M Sc, MAS, PhD. Part-time programs available. *Students:* 7 full-time (1 woman), 2 part-time, 7 international. 20 applicants, 10% accepted. In 1998, 1 master's, 1 doctorate awarded. *Degree requirements:* For master's, thesis required (for some programs); for doctorate, dissertation, comprehensive exam required. *Entrance requirements:* For doctorate, MAS or M Sc in mathematics and statistics. *Application deadline:* For fall admission, 1/30. Applications are processed on a rolling basis. Application fee: $40. *Financial aid:* Fellowships, teaching assistantships available. Financial aid application deadline: 1/31. *Faculty research:* Algebra, topology, applied mathematics, mathematical statistics, applied statistics and probability. *Unit head:* Dr. Herbert S. Gaskill, Head, 709-737-8783, Fax: 709-787-3010, E-mail: head@math.mun.ca. *Application contact:* Dr. Wanda Heath, Secretary to Department Head, 709-737-8783, Fax: 709-737-3010, E-mail: mathstat@math.mun.ca.

Miami University, Graduate School, College of Arts and Sciences, Department of Mathematics and Statistics, Program in Mathematics, Oxford, OH 45056. Offers mathematics (MA, MAT, MS); mathematics/operations research (MS); statistics (MS). Part-time programs available. *Faculty:* 20. *Students:* 23 full-time (7 women); includes 1 minority (Asian American or Pacific Islander), 3 international. 67 applicants, 87% accepted. In 1998, 11 degrees awarded. *Degree requirements:* For master's, final exam required, thesis not required. *Entrance requirements:* For master's, minimum undergraduate GPA of 3.0 during previous 2 years or 2.75 overall. *Application deadline:* For fall admission, 3/1 (priority date); for spring admission, 12/1. Applications are processed on a rolling basis. Application fee: $35. *Financial aid:* Fellowships, research assistantships, teaching assistantships, Federal Work-Study and tuition waivers (full) available. Financial aid application deadline: 3/1. *Unit head:* Dr. Sheldon Davis, Director of Graduate Studies, 513-529-3527.

Michigan State University, Graduate School, College of Natural Science, Department of Mathematics, East Lansing, MI 48824-1020. Offers applied mathematics (MS, PhD); computational mathematics (MS); mathematics (MA, MAT, MS, PhD); mathematics education (PhD). *Faculty:* 63. *Students:* 92 full-time (26 women), 36 part-time (12 women); includes 9 minority (2 African Americans, 4 Asian Americans or Pacific Islanders, 3 Hispanic Americans), 76 international. Average age 28. 121 applicants, 38% accepted. In 1998, 14 master's, 11 doctorates awarded. Terminal master's awarded for partial completion of doctoral program. *Degree requirements:* For master's, certifying exam required, foreign language and thesis not required; for doctorate, dissertation, exams, seminar required. *Entrance requirements:* For master's, GRE; for doctorate, minimum GPA of 3.0, MS. *Application deadline:* For fall admission, 2/1. Applications are processed on a rolling basis. Application fee: $30 ($40 for international students). *Financial aid:* In 1998–99, teaching assistantships with tuition reimbursements (averaging $11,289 per year); research assistantships Financial aid applicants required to submit FAFSA. Total annual research expenditures: $346,227. *Unit head:* Dr. Peter Lappan, Chairperson, 517-355-9681, Fax: 517-432-1562. *Application contact:* Director of Graduate Studies, 517-353-4650, Fax: 517-432-1562, E-mail: grad@mth.msu.,edu.

Michigan Technological University, Graduate School, College of Sciences and Arts, Department of Mathematical Sciences, Houghton, MI 49931-1295. Offers MS, PhD. Part-time programs available. *Faculty:* 28 full-time (4 women), 1 part-time (0 women). *Students:* 10 full-time (0 women), 7 part-time (all women); includes 1 minority (African American), 9 international. Average age 29. 29 applicants, 38% accepted. In 1998, 8 master's awarded. *Degree requirements:* For master's, project or thesis required; for doctorate, dissertation required, foreign language not required. *Entrance requirements:* For master's, GRE General Test (combined average 1826 on three sections), TOEFL (minimum score of 550 required; average 588); for doctorate, GRE General Test (combined average 1530 on three sections), TOEFL (minimum score of 550 required). *Average time to degree:* Master's–2.6 years full-time. *Application deadline:* For fall admission, 3/15 (priority date). Applications are processed on a rolling basis. Application fee: $30 ($35 for international students). Tuition, state resident: full-time $4,377. Tuition, nonresident: full-time $9,108. Required fees: $126. Tuition and fees vary according to course load. *Financial aid:* In 1998–99, 1 fellowship (averaging $3,270 per year), 13 teaching assistantships (averaging $9,078 per year) were awarded.; research assistantships, Federal Work-Study and institutionally-sponsored loans also available. Aid available to part-time students. Financial aid application deadline: 4/1; financial aid applicants required to submit FAFSA. *Faculty research:* Combinatorics, statistics and probability, discrete structures, fluid dynamics, mathematical modeling. Total annual research expenditures: $62,582. *Unit head:* Dr. Alphonse H. Baartmans, Head, 906-487-2068, Fax: 906-487-3044, E-mail: baartman@mtu.edu. *Application contact:* Dr. Don Kreher, Director of Graduate Studies, 906-487-3542, Fax: 906-487-3044, E-mail: kreher@mtu.edu.

Middle Tennessee State University, College of Graduate Studies, College of Basic and Applied Sciences, Department of Mathematics, Murfreesboro, TN 37132. Offers mathematics (MS); mathematics education (MST). Part-time programs available. *Faculty:* 21 full-time (4 women). *Students:* 9 full-time (4 women), 19 part-time (15 women). Average age 33. 15 applicants, 40% accepted. In 1998, 4 degrees awarded. *Degree requirements:* For master's, comprehensive exams required, foreign language and thesis not required. *Entrance requirements:* For master's, GRE or MAT (minimum score of 44 required). *Application deadline:* For fall admission, 8/1 (priority date). Applications are processed on a rolling basis. Application fee: $25. Electronic applications accepted. *Financial aid:* Teaching assistantships, institutionally-sponsored loans available. Aid available to part-time students. Financial aid application deadline: 5/1; financial aid applicants required to submit FAFSA. Total annual research expenditures:$7,876. *Unit head:* Dr. Jeff S. Allbritten, Interim Chair, 615-898-2669, Fax: 615-898-5422 Ext. EPHI, E-mail: jallbritten@mtsu.edu.

Minnesota State University, Mankato, College of Graduate Studies, College of Science, Engineering and Technology, Department of Mathematics and Statistics, Program in Computers, Mankato, MN 56002-8400. Offers mathematics: computer science (MS). *Students:* 5 full-time (0 women). *Degree requirements:* For master's, one foreign language, computer language, thesis or alternative, comprehensive exam required. *Entrance requirements:* For master's, GRE General Test, GRE Subject Test, minimum GPA of 3.0 during previous 2 years. *Application deadline:* For fall admission, 7/9 (priority date); for spring admission, 11/27. Applications are processed on a rolling basis. Application fee: $20. *Unit head:* Dr. Lee Cornell, Chairperson, 507-389-2968. *Application contact:* Joni Roberts, Admissions Coordinator, 507-389-2321, Fax: 507-389-5974, E-mail: grad@mankato.msus.edu.

Minnesota State University, Mankato, College of Graduate Studies, College of Science, Engineering and Technology, Department of Mathematics and Statistics, Program in Mathematics, Mankato, MN 56002-8400. Offers MA, MS. *Students:* 4 full-time (2 women), 5 part-time (3 women). Average age 32. In 1998, 1 degree awarded. *Degree requirements:* For master's, one foreign language, computer language, thesis or alternative, comprehensive exam required. *Entrance requirements:* For master's, GRE General Test, minimum GPA of 3.0 during previous 2 years. *Application deadline:* For fall admission, 7/9 (priority date); for spring admission, 11/27. Applications are processed on a rolling basis. Application fee: $20. *Financial aid:* Research assistantships with partial tuition reimbursements, teaching assistantships with partial tuition reimbursements available. Financial aid application deadline: 3/15; financial aid applicants required to submit FAFSA. *Unit head:* Dr. Charles Waters, Coordinator, 507-389-5903. *Application contact:* Joni Roberts, Admissions Coordinator, 507-389-2321, Fax: 507-389-5974, E-mail: grad@mankato.msus.edu.

Mississippi College, Graduate School, College of Arts and Sciences, Department of Mathematics and Computer Science, Clinton, MS 39058. Offers computer science (MS); mathematics (MS). *Faculty:* 12 full-time (6 women), 7 part-time (4 women). *Degree requirements:* For master's. *Entrance requirements:* For master's, minimum GPA of 2.5. *Application deadline:* For fall admission, 8/15 (priority date). Applications are processed on a rolling basis. Application fee: $25 ($75 for international students). *Financial aid:* Application deadline: 4/1. *Unit head:* Dr. Thomas Leavelle, Head, 601-925-3463.

Mississippi College, Graduate School, College of Arts and Sciences, Program in Combined Sciences, Clinton, MS 39058. Offers biology (MCS); chemistry (MCS); mathematics (MCS). *Faculty:* 25 full-time (7 women), 16 part-time (7 women). *Degree requirements:* For master's, thesis or alternative, comprehensive exam required, foreign language not required. *Entrance requirements:* For master's, GRE General Test (minimum combined score of 850 required), minimum GPA of 2.5. *Application deadline:* For fall admission, 8/15 (priority date). Applications are processed on a rolling basis. Application fee: $25 ($75 for international students). *Unit head:* Dr. Ron Howard, Dean, College of Arts and Sciences, 601-925-3327, Fax: 601-925-3499.

Mississippi State University, College of Arts and Sciences, Department of Mathematics and Statistics, Mississippi State, MS 39762. Offers mathematical sciences (PhD); mathematics (MS); statistics (MS). Part-time programs available. *Students:* 29 full-time (14 women), 7 part-time (3 women); includes 15 minority (2 African Americans, 13 Asian Americans or Pacific Islanders), 8 international. Average age 33. 38 applicants, 42% accepted. In 1998, 4 master's, 1 doctorate awarded. Terminal master's awarded for partial completion of doctoral program. *Degree requirements:* For master's, comprehensive oral or written exam required, thesis optional, foreign language not required; for doctorate, one foreign language, computer language, dissertation, comprehensive oral or written exam required. *Entrance requirements:* For master's, TOEFL; for doctorate, GRE, TOEFL. *Application deadline:* For fall admission, 7/1; for spring admission, 11/1. Applications are processed on a rolling basis. Application fee: $25 for international students. *Financial aid:* In 1998–99, 1 fellowship was awarded.; Federal Work-Study, institutionally-sponsored loans, tuition waivers (partial), and unspecified assistantships also available. Financial aid applicants required to submit FAFSA. *Faculty research:* Differential equations, algebra, numerical analysis, functional analysis, applied statistics. *Unit head:* Dr. Shair Ahmad, Head, 662-325-3414, Fax: 662-325-0005, E-mail: office@math.msstate.edu. *Application contact:* Jerry B. Inmon, Director of Admissions, 662-325-2224, Fax: 662-325-7360, E-mail: admit@admissions.msstate.edu.

Montana State University–Bozeman, College of Graduate Studies, College of Letters and Science, Department of Mathematical Sciences, Bozeman, MT 59717. Offers mathematics (MS, PhD); statistics (MS, PhD). Part-time programs available. *Students:* 26 full-time (6 women), 24 part-time (14 women). Average age 31. 23 applicants, 43% accepted. In 1998, 18 master's, 4 doctorates awarded. *Degree requirements:* For master's, computer language, thesis or alternative required, foreign language not required; for doctorate, computer language, dissertation required, foreign language not required. *Entrance requirements:* For master's and doctorate, GRE General Test (minimum score of 420 on verbal section required), TOEFL (minimum score of 580 required). *Application deadline:* For fall admission, 6/1 (priority date); for spring admission, 11/1. Applications are processed on a rolling basis. Application fee: $50. *Financial aid:* In 1998–99, 6 research assistantships with full tuition reimbursements (averaging $10,000 per year), 47 teaching assistantships with full tuition reimbursements (averaging $9,000 per year) were awarded.; institutionally-sponsored loans, scholarships, and tuition waivers (partial) also available. Financial aid application deadline: 3/1; financial aid applicants required to submit FAFSA. *Faculty research:* Mathematical education, numeric analysis, dynamical systems, applied mathematics. Total annual research expenditures: $986,829. *Unit head:* Dr. John R. Lund, Head, 406-994-3601, Fax: 406-994-1789, E-mail: grad@math.montana.edu.

Montclair State University, Office of Graduate Studies, College of Science and Mathematics, Department of Mathematics and Computer Science, Programs in Mathematics, Upper Montclair, NJ 07043-1624. Offers computer science (MS); mathematics education (MS); pure and applied mathematics (MS); statistics (MS). Part-time and evening/weekend programs available. *Degree requirements:* For master's, written comprehensive exam required, foreign language and thesis not required. *Entrance requirements:* For master's, GRE General Test, minimum GPA of 2.67.

Morgan State University, School of Graduate Studies, College of Arts and Sciences, Department of Mathematics, Baltimore, MD 21251. Offers MA. Part-time and evening/weekend programs available. *Degree requirements:* For master's, thesis, comprehensive exam required, foreign language not required. *Faculty research:* Number theory, semigroups, analysis, operations research.

Murray State University, College of Science, Department of Mathematics, Murray, KY 42071-0009. Offers MA, MAT, MS. Part-time programs available. *Students:* 4 full-time (all women), 6 part-time (4 women). 2 applicants, 100% accepted. *Degree requirements:* For master's, thesis required (for some programs), foreign language not required. *Entrance requirements:* For master's, GRE General Test, TOEFL (minimum score of 500 required). *Application deadline:* Applications are processed on a rolling basis. Application fee: $20. *Financial aid:* Research assistantships, teaching assistantships, Federal Work-Study available. Financial aid application deadline: 4/1. *Unit head:* Dr. Gary Jones, Graduate Coordinator, 502-762-3713, Fax: 502-762-2314.

Naval Postgraduate School, Graduate Programs, Department of Mathematics, Monterey, CA 93943. Offers MS, PhD. Program only open to commissioned officers of the United States and friendly nations and selected United States federal civilian employees. Part-time programs available. *Students:* 12 full-time, 1 international. In 1998, 6 master's, 1 doctorate awarded. *Degree requirements:* For master's, computer language, thesis required, foreign language not required; for doctorate, one foreign language, computer language, dissertation required. *Unit head:* Dr. Guillermo Owen, Chairman, 831-656-2206. *Application contact:* Theodore H. Calhoon, Director of Admissions, 831-656-3093, Fax: 831-656-2891, E-mail: tcalhoon@nps.navy.mil.

New Jersey Institute of Technology, Office of Graduate Studies, Department of Mathematical Sciences, Newark, NJ 07102-1982. Offers applied mathematics (MS); mathematical science (PhD). Part-time and evening/weekend programs available. *Degree requirements:* For master's, foreign language and thesis not required; for doctorate, residency required, foreign language and thesis not required. *Entrance requirements:* For master's, GRE General Test (minimum score of 450 on verbal section, 600 on quantitative, 550 on analytical required); for doctorate, GRE General Test (minimum score of 450 on verbal section, 600 on quantitative, 550 on analytical required), minimum graduate GPA of 3.5. Electronic applications accepted. *Faculty research:* Computational methods, probability and statistics, testing-decision theory.

New Mexico Institute of Mining and Technology, Graduate Studies, Department of Mathematics, Socorro, NM 87801. Offers mathematics (MS); operations research (MS). *Faculty:* 10 full-time (1 woman). *Students:* 8 full-time (3 women); includes 1 minority (Hispanic American), 1 international. Average age 30. 9 applicants, 100% accepted. In 1998, 1 degree awarded. *Degree requirements:* For master's, thesis optional, foreign language not required. *Entrance requirements:* For master's, GRE General Test, TOEFL (minimum score of 540 required). *Average time to degree:* Master's–3 years full-time. *Application deadline:* For fall admission, 3/1 (priority date); for spring admission, 6/1. Applications are processed on a rolling basis. Application fee: $16. *Financial aid:* In 1998–99, 1 research assistantship (averaging $9,670 per year), 7 teaching assistantships (averaging $9,670 per year) were awarded.; fellowships, Federal Work-Study and institutionally-sponsored loans also available. Financial aid application deadline: 3/1; financial aid applicants required to submit CSS PROFILE or FAFSA. *Faculty research:* Abstract algebra, applied analysis, probability and statistics, stochastic processes, combinatorics. *Unit head:* Curtis Barefoot, Chairman, 505-835-5393, Fax: 505-835-5366, E-mail: barefoot@nmt.edu. *Application contact:* Dr. David B. Johnson, Dean of Graduate Studies, 505-835-5513, Fax: 505-835-5476, E-mail: graduate@nmt.edu.

New Mexico State University, Graduate School, College of Arts and Sciences, Department of Mathematical Sciences, Las Cruces, NM 88003-8001. Offers MS, PhD. Part-time programs available. *Faculty:* 28 full-time (8 women). *Students:* 23 full-time (5 women), 7 part-time (3 women); includes 2 minority (both Hispanic Americans), 17 international. Average age 33. 24 applicants, 83% accepted. In 1998, 4 master's, 4 doctorates awarded. *Degree requirements:* For master's, final oral exam required, foreign language and thesis not required; for doctorate, one foreign language, dissertation required. *Entrance requirements:* For master's and doctorate, GRE. *Application deadline:* For fall admission, 7/1 (priority date); for spring admission, 11/1. Applications are processed on a rolling basis. Application fee: $15 ($35 for international students). Electronic applications accepted. Tuition, state resident: full-time $2,682; part-time $112 per credit. Tuition, nonresident: full-time $8,376; part-time $349 per credit. Tuition and fees vary according to course load. *Financial aid:* Fellowships, research assistantships, teaching assistantships available. Financial aid application deadline: 3/15. *Faculty research:* Commutative algebra and computational applications, mathematics education, control theory, harmonic analysis and applications, algebraic topology. *Unit head:* Dr. David Finston, Head, 505-646-3901, Fax: 505-646-1064. *Application contact:* Dr. Josefina Alvarez, Professor, 505-646-2717, Fax: 505-646-1064, E-mail: gradcomm@nmsu.edu.

New York University, Graduate School of Arts and Science, Courant Institute of Mathematical Sciences, Department of Mathematics, New York, NY 10012-1019. Offers mathematics (MS, PhD); mathematics and statistics/operations research (MS); mathematics in finance (MS); scientific computing (MS). Part-time and evening/weekend programs available. *Faculty:* 51 full-time (1 woman). *Students:* 110 full-time (19 women), 125 part-time (37 women); includes 21 minority (3 African Americans, 16 Asian Americans or Pacific Islanders, 2 Hispanic Americans), 99 international. Average age 26. 285 applicants, 82% accepted. In 1998, 36 master's, 12 doctorates awarded. *Degree requirements:* For master's, thesis optional, foreign language not required; for doctorate, one foreign language, dissertation, oral and written exams required. *Entrance requirements:* For master's and doctorate, GRE General Test, GRE Subject Test, TOEFL. *Application deadline:* For fall admission, 1/4; for spring admission, 11/1. Application fee: $60. Tuition: Full-time $17,880; part-time $745 per credit. Required fees: $1,140; $35 per credit. Tuition and fees vary according to course load and program. *Financial aid:* Fellowships, research assistantships, teaching assistantships, Federal Work-Study and tuition waivers (full and partial) available. Financial aid application deadline: 1/4; financial aid applicants required to submit FAFSA. *Faculty research:* Partial differential equations, computational science, applied mathematics, geometry and topology, probability and stochastic processes.

Mathematics

New York University (continued)

Unit head: Charles Newman, Chairman, 212-998-3256, Fax: 212-995-4121. *Application contact:* Fedor Bugomolov, Director of Graduate Studies, 212-998-3256, Fax: 212-995-4121, E-mail: admissions@math.nyu.edu.

See in-depth description on page 701.

Nicholls State University, Graduate Studies, College of Arts and Sciences, Department of Mathematics, Thibodaux, LA 70310. Offers applied mathematics (MS). Part-time and evening/weekend programs available. *Faculty:* 7 full-time (0 women), 2 part-time (1 woman). *Students:* 4 full-time (1 woman), 5 part-time (3 women); includes 1 minority (African American) Average age 23. 9 applicants, 100% accepted. In 1998, 5 degrees awarded (100% found work related to degree). *Degree requirements:* For master's, foreign language and thesis not required. *Entrance requirements:* For master's, GRE General Test. *Average time to degree:* Master's–2 years full-time. *Application deadline:* For fall admission, 6/17 (priority date); for spring admission, 11/15. Applications are processed on a rolling basis. Application fee: $10 ($60 for international students). *Financial aid:* In 1998–99, 4 students received aid, including teaching assistantships with tuition reimbursements available (averaging $6,000 per year) Financial aid application deadline: 6/17. *Faculty research:* Operations research, statistics, numerical analysis. *Unit head:* Dr. Donald M. Bardwell, Head, College of Arts and Sciences, 504-448-4380, Fax: 504-448-4927, E-mail: math-dmb@nich-nsunet.nich.edu.

North Carolina Central University, Division of Academic Affairs, College of Arts and Sciences, Department of Mathematics, Durham, NC 27707-3129. Offers MS. Part-time and evening/weekend programs available. *Faculty:* 17 full-time (4 women), 3 part-time (0 women). *Students:* 3 full-time (2 women), 5 part-time (3 women); includes 6 minority (all African Americans) Average age 28. 4 applicants, 100% accepted. In 1998, 1 degree awarded. *Degree requirements:* For master's, one foreign language (computer language can substitute), thesis, comprehensive exam required. *Entrance requirements:* For master's, minimum GPA of 3.0 in major, 2.5 overall. *Application deadline:* For fall admission, 8/1. Application fee: $30. *Financial aid:* Research assistantships, Federal Work-Study and institutionally-sponsored loans available. Aid available to part-time students. Financial aid application deadline: 5/1. *Faculty research:* Structure theorems for Lie algebra, Kleene monoids and semi-groups, theoretical computer science, mathematics education. *Unit head:* Dr. Alade O. Tokuta, Chairperson, 919-560-6315. *Application contact:* Dr. Bernice D. Johnson, Dean, College of Arts and Sciences, 919-560-6368.

North Carolina State University, Graduate School, College of Physical and Mathematical Sciences, Department of Mathematics, Raleigh, NC 27695. Offers applied mathematics (MS, PhD); mathematics (MS, PhD). Part-time programs available. *Faculty:* 64 full-time (4 women), 11 part-time (0 women). *Students:* 104 full-time (46 women), 9 part-time (2 women); includes 14 minority (11 African Americans, 3 Asian Americans or Pacific Islanders), 21 international. Average age 29. 79 applicants, 61% accepted. In 1998, 9 master's, 16 doctorates awarded. Terminal master's awarded for partial completion of doctoral program. *Degree requirements:* For master's, computer language required, thesis optional, foreign language not required; for doctorate, one foreign language, dissertation required. *Entrance requirements:* For master's and doctorate, GRE General Test, GRE Subject Test. *Application deadline:* For fall admission, 4/1 (priority date); for spring admission, 11/25. Applications are processed on a rolling basis. Application fee: $45. *Financial aid:* In 1998–99, 48 research assistantships (averaging $6,039 per year) were awarded.; fellowships, teaching assistantships, career-related internships or fieldwork and institutionally-sponsored loans also available. Financial aid application deadline: 3/1. *Faculty research:* Numerical and applied mathematics, industrial mathematics, algebra including symbolic and Lie, dynamical systems. Total annual research expenditures: $2.7 million. *Unit head:* Dr. Robert H. Martin, Head, 919-515-3796, Fax: 919-515-3798, E-mail: rhmartin@math.ncsu.edu. *Application contact:* Dr. Ernest L. Stitzinger, Director of Graduate Programs, 919-515-3258, Fax: 919-515-3798, E-mail: stitz@math.ncsu.edu.

See in-depth description on page 703.

North Dakota State University, Graduate Studies and Research, College of Science and Mathematics, Department of Mathematics, Fargo, ND 58105. Offers applied mathematics (MS, PhD); mathematics (MS, PhD). *Faculty:* 14 full-time (1 woman), 1 part-time (0 women). *Students:* 19 full-time (6 women); includes 2 minority (both Asian Americans or Pacific Islanders), 9 international. Average age 30. In 1998, 2 master's, 2 doctorates awarded. *Degree requirements:* For master's, computer language, thesis or alternative required, foreign language not required; for doctorate, one foreign language, computer language, dissertation required. *Entrance requirements:* For master's and doctorate, GRE General Test (combined average 1800 on three sections), TOEFL (minimum score of 525 required; average 590). *Average time to degree:* Master's–2.5 years full-time; doctorate–5.5 years full-time. *Application deadline:* For fall admission, 3/15 (priority date). Applications are processed on a rolling basis. Application fee: $25. *Financial aid:* In 1998–99, 17 students received aid, including 15 teaching assistantships; fellowships, research assistantships, Federal Work-Study and institutionally-sponsored loans also available. Aid available to part-time students. Financial aid application deadline: 4/15. *Faculty research:* Differential equations, discrete mathematics, number theory, ergodic theory, algebra. *Unit head:* Dr. Dogan Comez, Chair, 701-231-7490, Fax: 701-231-7598.

Northeastern Illinois University, Graduate College, College of Arts and Sciences, Department of Mathematics, Programs in Mathematics, Chicago, IL 60625-4699. Offers mathematics (MS); mathematics for elementary school teachers (MA). Part-time and evening/weekend programs available. *Faculty:* 14 full-time (4 women). *Students:* 4 full-time (1 woman), 40 part-time (30 women); includes 8 minority (7 Asian Americans or Pacific Islanders, 1 Hispanic American), 1 international. Average age 35. In 1998, 16 degrees awarded. *Degree requirements:* For master's, comprehensive exam, project required, thesis optional, foreign language not required. *Entrance requirements:* For master's, minimum GPA of 2.75, 6 undergraduate courses in mathematics. *Application deadline:* For fall admission, 3/31 (priority date); for spring admission, 9/30. Applications are processed on a rolling basis. Application fee: $0. *Financial aid:* In 1998–99, 26 students received aid, including 1 research assistantship; career-related internships or fieldwork, Federal Work-Study, institutionally-sponsored loans, and tuition waivers (full and partial) also available. Aid available to part-time students. Financial aid applicants required to submit FAFSA. *Faculty research:* Numerical analysis, mathematical biology, operations research, statistics, geometry and mathematics of finance. *Unit head:* Dr. Paul O'Hara, Coordinator, 773-794-2566. *Application contact:* Dr. Mohan K. Sood, Dean of Graduate College, 773-583-4050 Ext. 6143, Fax: 773-794-6670, E-mail: m-sood@neiu.edu.

Northeastern University, College of Arts and Sciences, Department of Mathematics, Boston, MA 02115-5096. Offers mathematics (MAT, MS, PhD); operations management (MS). Part-time and evening/weekend programs available. *Faculty:* 36 full-time (3 women). *Students:* 29 full-time (3 women), 9 part-time (2 women). Average age 31. 65 applicants, 52% accepted. In 1998, 6 master's, 1 doctorate awarded. *Degree requirements:* For doctorate, dissertation, qualifying exams required. *Entrance requirements:* For master's and doctorate, GRE Subject Test, TOEFL. *Application deadline:* For fall admission, 5/15 (priority date). Applications are processed on a rolling basis. Application fee: $50. *Financial aid:* In 1998–99, 5 research assistantships with tuition reimbursements, 28 teaching assistantships with tuition reimbursements were awarded.; Federal Work-Study, institutionally-sponsored loans, tuition waivers (full and partial), and unspecified assistantships also available. Financial aid application deadline: 3/15; financial aid applicants required to submit FAFSA. *Faculty research:* Algebra and singularities, combinatorics, topology, probability and statistics, geometric analysis and partial differential equations. *Unit head:* Dr. Egon Schulte, Chairperson, 617-373-2450, Fax: 617-373-5658, E-mail: mathdept@neu.edu. *Application contact:* Dr. Jerzy Weyman, Graduate Coordinator, 617-373-2450, Fax: 617-373-5658, E-mail: mathdept@neu.edu.

Northern Arizona University, Graduate College, College of Arts and Sciences, Department of Mathematics, Flagstaff, AZ 86011. Offers acturial science (MS); mathematics (MAT, MS); statistics (MS). Part-time programs available. *Faculty:* 24 full-time (2 women). *Students:* 11 full-time (4 women), 8 part-time (4 women); includes 1 minority (Hispanic American) Average age 23. 19 applicants, 53% accepted. In 1998, 16 degrees awarded. *Degree requirements:* For master's, thesis optional, foreign language not required. *Application deadline:* For fall admission, 3/15 (priority date). Applications are processed on a rolling basis. Application fee: $45. *Financial aid:* In 1998–99, 10 teaching assistantships were awarded.; Federal Work-Study and tuition waivers (full and partial) also available. *Faculty research:* Topology, statistics, groups, ring theory, number theory. *Unit head:* Dr. Terry Crites, Chair, 520-523-3481. *Application contact:* Dr. Michael Ratliff, Graduate Coordinator, 520-523-6881, E-mail: grad@math.nau.edu.

Northern Illinois University, Graduate School, College of Liberal Arts and Sciences, Department of Mathematical Sciences, De Kalb, IL 60115-2854. Offers applied probability and statistics (MS); mathematical sciences (PhD); mathematics (MS). Part-time programs available. *Faculty:* 50 full-time (7 women), 6 part-time (1 woman). *Students:* 48 full-time (16 women), 29 part-time (16 women); includes 7 minority (4 African Americans, 2 Asian Americans or Pacific Islanders, 1 Hispanic American), 22 international. Average age 29. 64 applicants, 66% accepted. In 1998, 22 master's, 2 doctorates awarded. Terminal master's awarded for partial completion of doctoral program. *Degree requirements:* For master's, comprehensive exam required, thesis optional, foreign language not required; for doctorate, 2 foreign languages, computer language, candidacy exam, dissertation defense, internship required. *Entrance requirements:* For master's, GRE General Test, TOEFL (minimum score of 550 required; 213 for computer-based), minimum GPA of 2.75; for doctorate, GRE General Test, TOEFL (minimum score of 550 required; 213 for computer-based), minimum GPA of 2.75 (undergraduate), 3.2 (graduate). *Application deadline:* For fall admission, 6/1; for spring admission, 11/1. Applications are processed on a rolling basis. Application fee: $30. *Financial aid:* In 1998–99, 9 research assistantships, 45 teaching assistantships were awarded.; fellowships, career-related internships or fieldwork, Federal Work-Study, tuition waivers (full), and unspecified assistantships also available. Aid available to part-time students. *Unit head:* Dr. William D. Blair, Chair, 815-753-0566. *Application contact:* Dr. Gregory Ammar, Director, Graduate Studies, 815-753-6775.

Northwestern University, The Graduate School, Judd A. and Marjorie Weinberg College of Arts and Sciences, Department of Mathematics, Evanston, IL 60208. Offers applied mathematics (PhD); mathematics (PhD). Admissions and degrees offered through The Graduate School. Part-time programs available. *Faculty:* 36 full-time (5 women). *Students:* 36 full-time (10 women); includes 9 minority (all Asian Americans or Pacific Islanders), 11 international. Average age 22. 102 applicants, 40% accepted. In 1998, 7 degrees awarded. *Degree requirements:* For doctorate, dissertation, preliminary exam required, foreign language not required. *Entrance requirements:* For doctorate, GRE General Test, GRE Subject Test, TOEFL (minimum score of 600 required). *Application deadline:* For fall admission, 8/30. Application fee: $50 ($55 for international students). *Financial aid:* In 1998–99, 7 fellowships with full tuition reimbursements (averaging $11,673 per year), 3 research assistantships with partial tuition reimbursements (averaging $16,285 per year), 18 teaching assistantships with full tuition reimbursements (averaging $12,042 per year) were awarded.; career-related internships or fieldwork, Federal Work-Study, institutionally-sponsored loans, and scholarships also available. Financial aid application deadline: 1/15; financial aid applicants required to submit FAFSA. *Faculty research:* Algebra, algebraic topology, analysis dynamical systems, partial differential equations. Total annual research expenditures: $318,056. *Unit head:* R. Clark Robinson, Chair, 847-491-8035. *Application contact:* Melanie Rubin, Admission Contact, 847-491-8035, Fax: 847-491-8906, E-mail: melanie@math.nwu.edu.

Announcement: The program of study is designed to encourage vigorous study and research in mathematics. The department has strong traditions in algebra, algebraic topology, analysis, applied mathematics, dynamical systems, partial differential equations, and probability theory. All graduate students are eligible for financial support that covers tuition and provides a monthly stipend. In 1998–98, there were about 40 students in the graduate program. For more information, consult the department's Web page at http://www.math.nwu.edu.

Oakland University, Graduate Studies, College of Arts and Sciences, Department of Mathematical Sciences, Rochester, MI 48309-4401. Offers applied mathematical science (PhD); applied statistics (MS, PhD); industrial applied mathematics (MS); mathematics (MA); statistical methods (Certificate). Part-time and evening/weekend programs available. *Faculty:* 25 full-time, 6 part-time. *Students:* 15 full-time (6 women), 35 part-time (14 women); includes 4 minority (3 Asian Americans or Pacific Islanders, 1 Hispanic American), 11 international. 32 applicants, 84% accepted. In 1998, 11 master's, 1 other advanced degree awarded. *Degree requirements:* For master's, foreign language and thesis not required; for doctorate, dissertation required, foreign language not required. *Entrance requirements:* For master's, minimum GPA of 3.0 for unconditional admission; for doctorate, GRE Subject Test, minimum GPA of 3.0 for unconditional admission. *Application deadline:* For fall admission, 7/15; for spring admission, 3/15. Application fee: $30. Tuition, state resident: part-time $221 per credit hour. Tuition, nonresident: part-time $488 per credit hour. Required fees: $214 per semester. Part-time tuition and fees vary according to program. *Financial aid:* Career-related internships or fieldwork, Federal Work-Study, institutionally-sponsored loans, and tuition waivers (full) available. Financial aid application deadline: 3/1; financial aid applicants required to submit FAFSA. *Unit head:* Dr. Marc Lipman, Chair, 248-370-3430. *Application contact:* Dr. Kevin Andrews, Coordinator, 248-370-3430.

The Ohio State University, Graduate School, College of Mathematical and Physical Sciences, Department of Mathematics, Columbus, OH 43210. Offers MS, PhD. *Faculty:* 97 full-time, 10 part-time. *Students:* 105 full-time (24 women), 10 part-time (2 women); includes 4 minority (1 African American, 1 Asian American or Pacific Islander, 1 Hispanic American, 1 Native American), 56 international. 65 applicants, 22% accepted. In 1998, 20 master's, 13 doctorates awarded. *Degree requirements:* For master's, thesis optional, foreign language not required; for doctorate, dissertation required. *Entrance requirements:* For master's and doctorate, GRE General Test, GRE Subject Test. *Application deadline:* For fall admission, 8/15. Applications are processed on a rolling basis. Application fee: $30 ($40 for international students). *Financial aid:* Fellowships, research assistantships, teaching assistantships, Federal Work-Study, institutionally-sponsored loans, and unspecified assistantships available. Aid available to part-time students. *Unit head:* Dr. Ruth Charney, Chairperson, 614-292-4975, Fax: 614-292-1479, E-mail: charney.1@osu.edu.

See in-depth description on page 711.

Ohio University, Graduate Studies, College of Arts and Sciences, Department of Mathematics, Athens, OH 45701-2979. Offers MS, PhD. *Faculty:* 25 full-time (2 women), 7 part-time (2 women). *Students:* 84 full-time (26 women), 24 part-time (13 women); includes 3 minority (all Asian Americans or Pacific Islanders), 78 international. 80 applicants, 75% accepted. In 1998, 45 master's, 3 doctorates awarded. *Degree requirements:* For master's, thesis or alternative required; for doctorate, dissertation, comprehensive exam required. *Entrance requirements:* For master's and doctorate, TOEFL (minimum score of 550 required), minimum GPA of 3.0. *Application deadline:* For fall admission, 3/1 (priority date). Applications are processed on a rolling basis. Application fee: $30. Tuition, state resident: full-time $5,754; part-time $238 per credit hour. Tuition, nonresident: full-time $11,055; part-time $457 per credit hour. Tuition and fees vary according to course load, campus/location and program. *Financial aid:* In 1998–99, 44 students received aid, including 4 fellowships with full tuition reimbursements available (averaging $14,250 per year), 36 teaching assistantships with full tuition reimbursements available (averaging $10,000 per year); Federal Work-Study, institutionally-sponsored loans, and tuition waivers (full and partial) also available. Financial aid application deadline: 3/1. *Faculty research:* Algebra (group and ring theory), functional analysis, topology, differential equations. *Unit head:* Dr. Sergio Lopez-Permouth, Chair, 740-593-1254, Fax: 740-593-9805, E-mail: slopez@bing.math.ohiou.edu. *Application contact:* Dr. M. S. K. Sastry, Admissions Officer, 740-593-1277, Fax: 740-593-9805, E-mail: sastry@bing.math.ohiou.edu.

Announcement: Athens is located in a scenic area of southeastern Ohio. The Mathematics Department offers graduate programs leading to PhD and master's degrees in mathematics, including an MS program with a computer science concentration. In addition to 25 regular faculty members with a history of excellence, flexibility, and accessibility to students, we have several visitors each year. Faculty research interests include algebra, analysis, biomathematics, differential equations, and topology. Ties with applied sciences departments are being developed. Students participate in weekly seminars. Teaching assistantships and fellowships are available. For information visit our home page at http://www.math.ohiou.edu/math/

Oklahoma State University, Graduate College, College of Arts and Sciences, Department of Mathematics, Stillwater, OK 74078. Offers applied mathematics (MS); mathematics (MS, Ed D, PhD). *Faculty:* 24 full-time (2 women), 1 part-time (0 women). *Students:* 20 full-time (5 women), 29 part-time (14 women); includes 5 minority (1 African American, 2 Asian Americans or Pacific Islanders, 2 Native Americans), 17 international. Average age 27. In 1998, 5 master's, 2 doctorates awarded. *Degree requirements:* For master's, foreign language and thesis not required; for doctorate, dissertation required. *Entrance requirements:* For master's and doctorate, TOEFL (minimum score of 550 required). *Application deadline:* For fall admission, 6/1 (priority date). Application fee: $25. *Financial aid:* In 1998–99, 39 students received aid, including 38 teaching assistantships (averaging $13,802 per year); career-related internships or fieldwork, Federal Work-Study, and tuition waivers (partial) also available. Aid available to part-time students. Financial aid application deadline: 3/1. *Unit head:* Dr. Benny Evans, Head, 405-744-5688.

See in-depth description on page 717.

Old Dominion University, College of Sciences, Department of Mathematics and Statistics, Norfolk, VA 23529. Offers computational and applied mathematics (MS, PhD), including applied mathematics, statistics. Part-time programs available. *Faculty:* 26 full-time (2 women). *Students:* 19 full-time (8 women), 14 part-time (3 women); includes 2 minority (1 African American, 1 Asian American or Pacific Islander), 13 international. Average age 33. In 1998, 2 master's, 3 doctorates awarded. Terminal master's awarded for partial completion of doctoral program. *Degree requirements:* For master's, comprehensive exam required, foreign language and thesis not required; for doctorate, dissertation, candidacy exam required, foreign language not required. *Entrance requirements:* For master's, GRE General Test, GRE Subject Test, TOEFL, minimum GPA of 3.0 in major, 2.5 overall; for doctorate, GRE General Test (minimum combined score of 1000 required), GRE Subject Test (minimum score of 600 required), TOEFL. *Application deadline:* For fall admission, 7/1. Applications are processed on a rolling basis. Application fee: $30. *Financial aid:* In 1998–99, 20 students received aid, including 15 research assistantships (averaging $15,861 per year), 1 teaching assistantship (averaging $10,000 per year); fellowships, grants also available. Financial aid application deadline: 2/15; financial aid applicants required to submit FAFSA. *Faculty research:* Numerical analysis, continuum mechanics, integral equations. Total annual research expenditures: $102,588. *Unit head:* Dr. John Tweed, Chair, 757-683-3882, E-mail: tweed@math.odu.edu. *Application contact:* Dr. John J. Swetits, Director, 757-683-3911, E-mail: swetits@math.odu.edu.

See in-depth description on page 721.

Oregon State University, Graduate School, College of Science, Department of Mathematics, Corvallis, OR 97331. Offers MA, MAIS, MS, PhD. *Faculty:* 34 full-time (5 women). *Students:* 40 full-time (14 women), 4 part-time (1 woman); includes 2 minority (1 Asian American or Pacific Islander, 1 Hispanic American), 9 international. Average age 29. In 1998, 17 master's, 1 doctorate awarded. Terminal master's awarded for partial completion of doctoral program. *Degree requirements:* For master's, variable foreign language requirement, thesis or alternative required; for doctorate, one foreign language, dissertation, qualifying exams required. *Entrance requirements:* For master's and doctorate, TOEFL (minimum score of 550 required), minimum GPA of 3.0 in last 90 hours. *Average time to degree:* Master's–2 years full-time. *Application deadline:* For fall admission, 3/1. Applications are processed on a rolling basis. Application fee: $50. *Financial aid:* Research assistantships, teaching assistantships, Federal Work-Study and institutionally-sponsored loans available. Aid available to part-time students. Financial aid application deadline: 2/1. *Unit head:* Dr. John W. Lee, Chair of Graduate Committee, 541-737-2003, Fax: 541-737-0517, E-mail: jwlee@math.orst.edu.

Pennsylvania State University University Park Campus, Graduate School, Eberly College of Science, Department of Mathematics, State College, University Park, PA 16802-1503. Offers mathematics (M Ed, MA, D Ed, PhD), including applied mathematics (MA, PhD). *Students:* 52 full-time (12 women), 19 part-time (6 women). In 1998, 7 master's, 5 doctorates awarded. *Entrance requirements:* For master's and doctorate, GRE General Test. Application fee: $50. *Unit head:* Dr. Gary L. Mullen, Head, 814-865-7527.

See in-depth description on page 727.

Pittsburg State University, Graduate School, College of Arts and Sciences, Department of Mathematics, Pittsburg, KS 66762-5880. Offers MS. *Students:* 3 full-time, 6 part-time. In 1998, 5 degrees awarded. *Degree requirements:* For master's, thesis or alternative required, foreign language not required. Application fee: $0 ($40 for international students). Tuition, state resident: full-time $2,466; part-time $105 per credit hour. Tuition, nonresident: full-time $6,268; part-time $264 per credit hour. *Financial aid:* Teaching assistantships, career-related internships or fieldwork and Federal Work-Study available. *Faculty research:* Operations research, numerical analysis, applied analysis, applied algebra. *Unit head:* Dr. Elwyn Davis, Chairperson, 316-235-4401. *Application contact:* Marvene Darraugh, Administrative Officer, 316-235-4220, Fax: 316-235-4219, E-mail: mdarraug@pittstate.edu.

Polytechnic University, Brooklyn Campus, Department of Applied Mathematics, Major in Mathematics, Brooklyn, NY 11201-2990. Offers MS, PhD. Part-time and evening/weekend programs available. *Faculty:* 16. Average age 33. 10 applicants, 50% accepted. In 1998, 2 master's awarded. *Degree requirements:* For master's, computer language, thesis or alternative required; for doctorate, one foreign language, computer language, dissertation required. *Application deadline:* Applications are processed on a rolling basis. Application fee: $45. Electronic applications accepted. *Financial aid:* Fellowships, research assistantships, teaching assistantships, institutionally-sponsored loans available. Aid available to part-time students. Financial aid applicants required to submit FAFSA. *Faculty research:* Isoperimetric inequalities, problems arising from theoretical physics. Total annual research expenditures: $25,000. *Application contact:* John S. Kerge, Dean of Admissions, 718-260-3200, Fax: 718-260-3446, E-mail: admitme@poly.edu.

Polytechnic University, Farmingdale Campus, Graduate Programs, Department of Applied Mathematics, Major in Mathematics, Farmingdale, NY 11735-3995. Offers MS, PhD. *Degree requirements:* For doctorate, dissertation required. *Application deadline:* Applications are processed on a rolling basis. Application fee: $45. Electronic applications accepted. *Application contact:* John S. Kerge, Dean of Admissions, 718-260-3200, Fax: 718-260-3446, E-mail: admitme@poly.edu.

Portland State University, Graduate Studies, College of Liberal Arts and Sciences, Department of Mathematical Sciences, Portland, OR 97207-0751. Offers mathematical sciences (MA, MAT, MS, MST, PhD); mathematics education (PhD). *Faculty:* 19 full-time (5 women), 17 part-time (8 women). *Students:* 17 full-time (9 women), 20 part-time (11 women); includes 4 minority (3 Asian Americans or Pacific Islanders, 1 Native American), 3 international. Average age 31. 24 applicants, 67% accepted. In 1998, 16 degrees awarded. *Degree requirements:* For master's, variable foreign language requirement, thesis or alternative, exams required; for doctorate, 2 foreign languages, dissertation, exams required. *Entrance requirements:* For master's, TOEFL (minimum score of 550 required), minimum GPA of 3.0 in upper-division course work or 2.75 overall; for doctorate, GRE General Test. *Application deadline:* For fall admission, 4/1; for spring admission, 11/1. Applications are processed on a rolling basis. Application fee: $50. *Financial aid:* In 1998–99, 17 teaching assistantships were awarded.; research assistantships, Federal Work-Study and institutionally-sponsored loans also available. Aid available to part-time students. Financial aid application deadline: 3/1; financial aid applicants required to submit FAFSA. *Faculty research:* Algebra, topology, statistical distribution theory, control theory, statistical robustness. Total annual research expenditures: $254,825. *Unit head:* Dr. Eugene Enneking, Head, 503-725-3621, Fax: 503-725-3661, E-mail: ennekinge@pdx.edu. *Application contact:* John Erdman, Coordinator, 503-725-3621, Fax: 503-725-3661, E-mail: erdman@mth.pdx.edu.

Portland State University, Graduate Studies, Systems Science Program, Portland, OR 97207-0751. Offers systems science/anthropology (PhD); systems science/business administration (PhD); systems science/civil engineering (PhD); systems science/economics (PhD); systems science/engineering management (PhD); systems science/general (PhD); systems science/mathematical sciences (PhD); systems science/mechanical engineering (PhD); systems science/psychology (PhD); systems science/sociology (PhD). *Faculty:* 3 full-time (0 women), 1 part-time (0 women). *Students:* 45 full-time (17 women), 23 part-time (6 women); includes 5 minority (1 African American, 3 Asian Americans or Pacific Islanders, 1 Hispanic American), 12 international. *Degree requirements:* For doctorate, variable foreign language requirement, computer language, dissertation required. *Entrance requirements:* For doctorate, GMAT (score in 75th percentile or higher required), GRE General Test (score in 75th percentile or higher required), TOEFL (minimum score of 575 required), minimum undergraduate GPA of 3.0. *Application deadline:* For fall admission, 2/1; for spring admission, 11/1. Application fee: $50. *Unit head:* Dr. Nancy Perrin, Director, 503-725-4960, E-mail: perrinn@pdx.edu. *Application contact:* Dawn Kuenle, Coordinator, 503-725-4960, E-mail: dawn@sysc.pdx.edu.

Prairie View A&M University, Graduate School, College of Arts and Sciences, Department of Mathematics, Prairie View, TX 77446-0188. Offers MS. *Faculty:* 3 full-time (1 woman), 2 part-time (1 woman). *Students:* 6 full-time (3 women), 19 part-time (15 women); includes 16 minority (all African Americans), 2 international. Average age 30. In 1998, 1 degree awarded (100% found work related to degree). *Degree requirements:* For master's, thesis required, foreign language not required. *Entrance requirements:* For master's, GRE General Test. *Average time to degree:* Master's–2.5 years full-time, 4 years part-time. *Application deadline:* For fall admission, 7/1 (priority date); for spring admission, 11/1. Applications are processed on a rolling basis. Application fee: $10. *Financial aid:* In 1998–99, 5 teaching assistantships were awarded.; Federal Work-Study also available. Financial aid application deadline: 8/1. *Faculty research:* Approximation theory, differential equations, algebraic topology, number theory, complex analysis. *Unit head:* Dr. Evelyn E. Thornton, Head, 409-857-2026, Fax: 409-857-2019. *Application contact:* Dr. G. A. Roberts, Graduate Adviser, 409-857-3807, Fax: 409-857-2019.

Princeton University, Graduate School, Department of Mathematics, Princeton, NJ 08544-1019. Offers applied and computational mathematics (PhD); mathematical physics (PhD); mathematics (PhD). *Degree requirements:* For doctorate, dissertation required. *Entrance requirements:* For doctorate, GRE General Test, GRE Subject Test.

Purdue University, Graduate School, School of Science, Department of Mathematics, West Lafayette, IN 47907. Offers MS, PhD. *Faculty:* 63 full-time (6 women). *Students:* 106 full-time (26 women); includes 1 minority (African American), 73 international. 208 applicants, 44% accepted. In 1998, 24 master's, 15 doctorates awarded. Terminal master's awarded for partial completion of doctoral program. *Degree requirements:* For master's, foreign language and thesis not required; for doctorate, dissertation, oral and written exams required. *Entrance requirements:* For master's and doctorate, TOEFL (minimum score of 570 required). *Average time to degree:* Master's–2 years full-time; doctorate–7 years full-time. *Application deadline:* For fall admission, 3/15. Application fee: $30. Electronic applications accepted. *Financial aid:* In 1998–99, 5 fellowships with partial tuition reimbursements (averaging $15,250 per year), 18 research assistantships with partial tuition reimbursements (averaging $12,400 per year), 83 teaching assistantships with partial tuition reimbursements (averaging $12,500 per year) were awarded. Aid available to part-time students. Financial aid application deadline: 3/15; financial aid applicants required to submit FAFSA. *Faculty research:* Algebra, analysis, topology, differential equations, applied mathematics. Total annual research expenditures: $1.7 million. *Unit head:* Dr. C. C. Cowen, Head, 765-494-1908, Fax: 765-494-0548, E-mail: cowen@math.purdue.edu. *Application contact:* Dr. S. R. Bell, Graduate Committee Chair, 765-494-1961, Fax: 765-494-0548, E-mail: gcomm@math.purdue.edu.

See in-depth description on page 733.

Queens College of the City University of New York, Division of Graduate Studies, Mathematics and Natural Sciences Division, Department of Mathematics, Flushing, NY 11367-1597. Offers MA. Part-time and evening/weekend programs available. *Faculty:* 31 full-time (1 woman). 17 applicants, 94% accepted. In 1998, 6 degrees awarded. *Degree requirements:* For master's, comprehensive exams required, foreign language and thesis not required. *Entrance requirements:* For master's, TOEFL (minimum score of 500 required), minimum GPA of 3.0. *Application deadline:* For fall admission, 4/1; for spring admission, 11/1. Applications are processed on a rolling basis. Application fee: $40. Tuition, state resident: full-time $4,350; part-time $185 per credit. Tuition, nonresident: full-time $7,600; part-time $320 per credit. Required fees: $114; $57 per semester. Tuition and fees vary according to course load and program. *Financial aid:* Career-related internships or fieldwork, Federal Work-Study, institutionally-sponsored loans, tuition waivers (partial), and adjunct lectureships available. Aid available to part-time students. Financial aid application deadline: 4/1; financial aid applicants required to submit FAFSA. *Faculty research:* Topology, differential equations, combinatorics. *Unit head:* Dr. Norman Weiss, Chairperson, 718-997-5800, E-mail: norman_weiss@qc.edu. *Application contact:* Dr. Nick Metas, Graduate Adviser, 718-997-5800, E-mail: nick_metas@qc.edu.

Queen's University at Kingston, School of Graduate Studies and Research, Faculty of Arts and Sciences, Department of Mathematics and Statistics, Kingston, ON K7L 3N6, Canada. Offers mathematics (M Sc, MA, PhD); statistics (M Sc, MA, PhD). Part-time programs available. *Students:* 33 full-time (9 women), 4 part-time (1 woman). In 1998, 14 master's, 4 doctorates awarded. *Degree requirements:* For master's, thesis required, foreign language not required; for doctorate, dissertation, comprehensive exam required. *Entrance requirements:* For master's and doctorate, TOEFL (minimum score of 550 required). *Application deadline:* For fall admission, 2/28 (priority date). Application fee: $60. Electronic applications accepted. *Financial aid:* Fellowships, research assistantships, teaching assistantships, institutionally-sponsored loans available. Financial aid application deadline: 3/1. *Faculty research:* Algebra, analysis, applied mathematics, combinatorics, differential geometry. *Unit head:* Dr. H. E. A. Campbell, Head, 613-533-2428. *Application contact:* Dr. L. B. Jonker, Graduate Coordinator, 613-533-2439.

Rensselaer Polytechnic Institute, Graduate School, School of Science, Department of Mathematical Sciences, Program in Mathematics, Troy, NY 12180-3590. Offers MS, PhD. Part-time programs available. *Faculty:* 23 full-time (5 women), 1 (woman) part-time. *Students:* 34 full-time (10 women), 11 part-time (3 women); includes 4 minority (2 African Americans, 2 Asian Americans or Pacific Islanders), 11 international. 42 applicants, 74% accepted. In 1998, 5 master's, 8 doctorates awarded. *Degree requirements:* For master's, thesis required (for some programs), foreign language not required; for doctorate, dissertation required, foreign language not required. *Entrance requirements:* For master's and doctorate, GRE General Test, TOEFL (minimum score of 550 required). *Application deadline:* For fall admission, 2/1 (priority date). Applications are processed on a rolling basis. Application fee: $35. *Financial aid:* In 1998–99, 45 students received aid; fellowships, research assistantships, teaching assistantships, institutionally-sponsored loans available. Financial aid application deadline:2/1. *Faculty research:* Inverse problems, biomathematics, dynamical systems and their applications, operations research, applied mathematics. *Application contact:* Lorraine Pisarczyk, Graduate Coordinator, 518-276-6414, Fax: 518-276-4824, E-mail: pisarl@rpi.edu.

See in-depth description on page 741.

Mathematics

Rhode Island College, School of Graduate Studies, Faculty of Arts and Sciences, Department of Mathematics, Providence, RI 02908-1924. Offers MA, MAT, CAGS. Evening/weekend programs available. *Faculty:* 24 full-time (5 women). In 1998, 1 degree awarded. *Degree requirements:* For master's, foreign language and thesis not required; for CAGS, thesis required, foreign language not required. *Entrance requirements:* For master's, GRE General Test or MAT. *Application deadline:* For fall admission, 4/1. Applications are processed on a rolling basis. Application fee: $25. Tuition, state resident: part-time $162 per credit. Tuition, nonresident: part-time $328 per credit. Required fees: $18 per credit. One-time fee: $40. Tuition and fees vary according to program and reciprocity agreements. *Financial aid:* Career-related internships or fieldwork available. Financial aid application deadline: 4/1. *Unit head:* Dr. Helen E. Salzberg, Chair, 401-456-8038.

Rice University, Graduate Programs, Wiess School of Natural Sciences, Department of Mathematics, Houston, TX 77251-1892. Offers MA, PhD. *Degree requirements:* For master's, thesis required; for doctorate, dissertation required. *Entrance requirements:* For master's, GRE General Test, TOEFL (minimum score of 550 required), minimum GPA of 3.0; for doctorate, GRE General Test (score in 70th percentile or higher required), minimum GPA of 3.0. *Faculty research:* Geometry, topology.

Roosevelt University, Graduate Division, College of Arts and Sciences, School of Science and Mathematics, Program in Mathematics, Chicago, IL 60605-1394. Offers mathematical sciences (MS), including actuarial science. Part-time and evening/weekend programs available. *Faculty:* 6 full-time (0 women). *Students:* 3 full-time (2 women), 4 part-time (1 woman); includes 1 minority (African American), 1 international. Average age 30. *Degree requirements:* For master's, foreign language and thesis not required. *Application deadline:* For fall admission, 6/1 (priority date). Applications are processed on a rolling basis. Application fee: $25 ($35 for international students). *Financial aid:* Research assistantships, career-related internships or fieldwork and tuition waivers (partial) available. Aid available to part-time students. Financial aid application deadline: 2/15. *Faculty research:* Statistics, mathematics education, finite groups, computers in mathematics. *Unit head:* John Currano, Graduate Adviser, 312-341-3773. *Application contact:* Joanne Canyon-Heller, Coordinator of Graduate Admissions, 312-341-3612, Fax: 312-341-3523, E-mail: applyru@roosevelt.edu.

Rowan University, Graduate Studies, School of Liberal Arts and Sciences, Department of Mathematics, Glassboro, NJ 08028-1701. Offers MA. 8 applicants, 88% accepted. *Application deadline:* For fall admission, 11/1 (priority date); for spring admission, 4/1. Applications are processed on a rolling basis. Application fee: $50. Tuition, state resident: full-time $5,051; part-time $281 per semester hour. Tuition, nonresident: full-time $7,715; part-time $429 per semester hour. Tuition and fees vary according to degree level. *Unit head:* Dr. Gary Itzkowitz, Adviser, 609-256-4845.

Rutgers, The State University of New Jersey, Camden, Graduate School, Program in Mathematics, Camden, NJ 08102-1401. Offers MS. Part-time and evening/weekend programs available. *Faculty:* 8 full-time (0 women), 1 part-time (0 women). *Students:* 3 full-time (2 women), 8 part-time (3 women); includes 2 minority (1 African American, 1 Hispanic American) Average age 24. 13 applicants, 77% accepted. In 1998, 3 degrees awarded (67% found work related to degree, 33% continued full-time study). *Degree requirements:* For master's, comprehensive exam required, thesis optional, foreign language not required. *Entrance requirements:* For master's, GRE General Test. *Average time to degree:* Master's–2 years full-time, 3 years part-time. *Application deadline:* For fall admission, 7/1 (priority date); for spring admission, 12/1. Applications are processed on a rolling basis. Application fee: $50. *Financial aid:* In 1998–99, 6 students received aid, including 3 teaching assistantships with full tuition reimbursements available (averaging $12,000 per year); institutionally-sponsored loans and tuition waivers (partial) also available. Aid available to part-time students. Financial aid application deadline: 3/15; financial aid applicants required to submit FAFSA. *Faculty research:* Differential geometry, automorphic forms, computer simulation, several complex variables, dynamical systems. Total annual research expenditures: $11,000. *Unit head:* Dr. Howard Jacobowitz, Director, 856-225-6538, Fax: 856-225-6495, E-mail: jacobowi@crab.rutgers.edu.

Rutgers, The State University of New Jersey, Newark, Graduate School, Department of Mathematics and Computer Science, Newark, NJ 07102-3192. Offers mathematical sciences (PhD). *Faculty:* 16 full-time (2 women). *Students:* 10 full-time (2 women); includes 5 minority (all Asian Americans or Pacific Islanders) 13 applicants, 54% accepted. *Degree requirements:* For doctorate, dissertation, written qualifying exam required, foreign language not required. *Entrance requirements:* For doctorate, GRE General Test (minimum score of 400 on verbal section, 600 on quantitative, 600 on analytical required; average 420 verbal, 760 quantitative, 660 analytical), TOEFL (minimum score of 560 required; average 600), minimum B average. *Application deadline:* For fall admission, 6/15 (priority date); for spring admission, 12/1. Applications are processed on a rolling basis. Application fee: $40. *Financial aid:* In 1998–99, 7 students received aid, including 1 fellowship with full tuition reimbursement available (averaging $12,000 per year), 6 teaching assistantships with full tuition reimbursements available (averaging $12,136 per year); tuition waivers (full and partial) also available. Financial aid application deadline: 3/1. *Faculty research:* Number theory, automorphic form, low-dimensional topology, Kleinian groups, representation theory. *Unit head:* Ulrich Oertel, Chair, 973-353-5156, Fax: 973-353-5270, E-mail: nwkmath@andromeda.rutgers.edu.

Rutgers, The State University of New Jersey, New Brunswick, Graduate School, Program in Mathematics, New Brunswick, NJ 08903. Offers applied mathematics (MS, PhD); mathematics (MS, PhD). Part-time programs available. *Faculty:* 96 full-time (9 women). *Students:* 63 full-time (10 women), 14 part-time (6 women); includes 7 minority (3 African Americans, 1 Asian American or Pacific Islander, 3 Hispanic Americans), 37 international. 146 applicants, 12% accepted. In 1998, 5 master's, 9 doctorates awarded. Terminal master's awarded for partial completion of doctoral program. *Degree requirements:* For master's, foreign language and thesis not required; for doctorate, dissertation required. *Entrance requirements:* For master's, GRE General Test (minimum combined score of 1200 required), GRE Subject Test (minimum score of 750 required), TOEFL (minimum score of 600 required; 250 for computer-based); for doctorate, GRE General Test (minimum combined score of 1200 required), GRE Subject Test (minimum score of 800 required), TOEFL (minimum score of 600 required; 250 for computer-based). *Average time to degree:* Master's–3 years full-time, 5 years part-time; doctorate–6 years full-time, 10 years part-time. *Application deadline:* For fall admission, 2/1; for spring admission, 11/1. Application fee: $50. *Financial aid:* In 1998–99, 52 students received aid, including 5 fellowships with full tuition reimbursements available (averaging $14,000 per year), 3 research assistantships with full tuition reimbursements available (averaging $12,236 per year), 44 teaching assistantships with full tuition reimbursements available (averaging $12,236 per year); tuition waivers (full) also available. Financial aid application deadline: 2/1; financial aid applicants required to submit FAFSA. *Faculty research:* Logic and set theory, number theory, mathematical physics, control theory, partial differential equations. *Unit head:* Prof. Peter S. Landweber, Director, 732-445-3864, Fax: 732-445-5530, E-mail: grad-director@math.rutgers.edu.

St. Cloud State University, School of Graduate Studies, College of Science and Engineering, Department of Mathematics, St. Cloud, MN 56301-4498. Offers MS. *Faculty:* 18 full-time (7 women). In 1998, 3 degrees awarded. *Degree requirements:* For master's, thesis or alternative required, foreign language not required. *Entrance requirements:* For master's, GRE General Test, minimum GPA of 2.75. Application fee: $20. *Financial aid:* Federal Work-Study and unspecified assistantships available. Financial aid application deadline: 3/1. *Unit head:* Dr. Ralph W. Carr, Chairperson, 320-255-3001, E-mail: mathdept@stcloudstate.edu. *Application contact:* Ann Anderson, Graduate Studies Office, 320-255-2113, Fax: 320-654-5371, E-mail: aeanderson@stcloudstate.edu.

St. John's University, Graduate School of Arts and Sciences, Department of Mathematics and Computer Science, Jamaica, NY 11439. Offers algebra (MA); analysis (MA); applied mathematics (MA); computer science (MA); geometry-topology (MA); logic and foundations (MA); probability and statistics (MA). Part-time and evening/weekend programs available. *Faculty:* 16 full-time (3 women), 5 part-time (2 women). *Students:* 7 full-time (3 women), 5 part-time (3 women); includes 5 minority (2 African Americans, 1 Asian American or Pacific Islander, 2 Hispanic Americans), 2 international. Average age 24. 13 applicants, 100% accepted. In 1998, 1 degree awarded. *Degree requirements:* For master's, comprehensive exam required, thesis optional, comprehensive exam required, thesis optional. *Entrance requirements:* For master's, minimum GPA of 3.0. *Application deadline:* Applications are processed on a rolling basis. Application fee: $40. Tuition: Full-time $13,200; part-time $500 per credit. Required fees: $150; $75 per term. Tuition and fees vary according to degree level and program. *Financial aid:* In 1998–99, 2 research assistantships were awarded.; scholarships also available. Aid available to part-time students. Financial aid application deadline: 3/1; financial aid applicants required to submit FAFSA. *Faculty research:* Development of a computerized metabolicmap. *Unit head:* Dr. Charles Traina, Chair, 718-990-6166, E-mail: trainac@stjohns.edu. *Application contact:* Patricia G. Armstrong, Director, Office of Admission, 718-990-2028, Fax: 718-990-2096, E-mail: armstrop@stjohns.edu.

Saint Louis University, Graduate School, College of Arts and Sciences, Program in Mathematics, St. Louis, MO 63103-2097. Offers MA, MA(R), PhD. *Faculty:* 21 full-time (4 women), 11 part-time (3 women). *Students:* 11 full-time (5 women), 7 part-time (3 women); includes 3 minority (2 African Americans, 1 Asian American or Pacific Islander), 1 international. Average age 33. 19 applicants, 84% accepted. In 1998, 6 master's awarded. *Degree requirements:* For master's, thesis (for some programs), comprehensive oral exam required; for doctorate, dissertation, preliminary exams required. *Entrance requirements:* For master's and doctorate, GRE General Test. *Application deadline:* For fall admission, 7/1; for spring admission, 11/1. Applications are processed on a rolling basis. Application fee: $40. Tuition: Full-time $20,520; part-time $507 per credit hour. Required fees: $38 per term. Tuition and fees vary according to program. *Financial aid:* In 1998–99, 15 students received aid, including 1 fellowship, 14 teaching assistantships Financial aid application deadline: 4/1; financial aid applicants required to submit FAFSA. *Faculty research:* Algebraic and geometric topology, differential geometry, group representation theory, infinite groups. *Unit head:* Dr. T. Christine Stevens, Chairperson, 314-977-2444. *Application contact:* Dr. Marcia Buresch, Assistant Dean of the Graduate School, 314-977-2240, Fax: 314-977-3943, E-mail: bureschm@slu.edu.

Salem State College, Graduate School, Department of Mathematics, Salem, MA 01970-5353. Offers MAT, MS. *Faculty:* 1 part-time (0 women). *Degree requirements:* For master's, foreign language and thesis not required. *Entrance requirements:* For master's, GRE General Test, MAT. *Application deadline:* Applications are processed on a rolling basis. Application fee: $25. Tuition, state resident: part-time $140 per credit hour. Tuition, nonresident: part-time $230 per credit hour. Required fees: $20 per credit hour. *Unit head:* Dr. Arthur J. Rosenthal, Coordinator, 978-542-6392, Fax: 978-542-7175, E-mail: arthur.rosenthal@salem.mass.edu.

Sam Houston State University, College of Arts and Sciences, Division of Mathematical and Information Sciences, Program in Mathematics, Huntsville, TX 77341. Offers M Ed, MA, MS. *Students:* 4 full-time (2 women), 8 part-time (4 women); includes 3 minority (1 African American, 2 Hispanic Americans) Average age 29. In 1998, 5 degrees awarded. *Degree requirements:* For master's, foreign language and thesis not required. *Entrance requirements:* For master's, GRE General Test (minimum combined score of 1000 required), TOEFL (minimum score of 550 required), minimum B average in undergraduate course work. *Application deadline:* For fall admission, 4/30 (priority date). Applications are processed on a rolling basis. Application fee: $15. *Financial aid:* Teaching assistantships, institutionally-sponsored loans available. Aid available to part-time students. *Faculty research:* Approximation theory, nonlinear operator theory, linear algebra, wavelet and fractal theory, quality control. *Application contact:* Dr. Ronald Stoltenberg, Graduate Adviser, 409-294-1589, Fax: 409-294-1882.

San Diego State University, Graduate and Research Affairs, College of Sciences, Department of Mathematical Sciences, San Diego, CA 92182. Offers applied mathematics (MS); computer science (MS); mathematics (MA); mathematics and science education (PhD); statistics (MS). Part-time programs available. *Students:* 83 full-time (27 women), 149 part-time (43 women); includes 68 minority (2 African Americans, 61 Asian Americans or Pacific Islanders, 4 Hispanic Americans, 1 Native American), 64 international. Average age 30. *Degree requirements:* For doctorate, dissertation required. *Entrance requirements:* For master's, GRE General Test (minimum combined score of 950 required), TOEFL (minimum score of 550 required). *Application deadline:* For fall admission, 7/1 (priority date); for spring admission, 12/1. Applications are processed on a rolling basis. Application fee: $55. *Faculty research:* Teacher education in mathematics. Total annual research expenditures: $1.1 million. *Unit head:* John D. Elwin, Chair, 619-594-6191, Fax: 619-594-6746, E-mail: elwin@saturn.sdsu.edu. *Application contact:* Edgar J. Howard, Graduate Coordinator, 619-594-5971, Fax: 619-594-6746, E-mail: ehoward@saturn.sdsu.edu.

San Francisco State University, Graduate Division, College of Science and Engineering, Department of Mathematics, San Francisco, CA 94132-1722. Offers MA. *Faculty:* 7 full-time (2 women). *Students:* 24 (7 women). In 1998, 4 degrees awarded. *Degree requirements:* For master's, oral exam required, thesis optional, foreign language not required. *Entrance requirements:* For master's, minimum GPA of 2.5 in last 60 units. *Application deadline:* For fall admission, 11/30 (priority date). Applications are processed on a rolling basis. Application fee: $55. *Financial aid:* In 1998–99, 8 teaching assistantships were awarded. Financial aid application deadline: 3/1. *Faculty research:* Fuzzy logic, software development, number theory, complex analysis, mathematics education. *Unit head:* Dr. Sheldon Axler, Chair, 415-338-2251, E-mail: axler@sfsu.edu. *Application contact:* Dr. David Meredith, Graduate Coordinator, 415-338-2199, E-mail: meredith@sfsu.edu.

San Jose State University, Graduate Studies, College of Science, Department of Mathematics and Computer Science, San Jose, CA 95192-0001. Offers computer science (MS); mathematics (MA, MS). Part-time and evening/weekend programs available. *Faculty:* 51 full-time (5 women), 3 part-time (0 women). *Students:* 46 full-time (27 women), 101 part-time (46 women); includes 79 minority (1 African American, 75 Asian Americans or Pacific Islanders, 3 Hispanic Americans), 23 international. Average age 31. 365 applicants, 22% accepted. In 1998, 12 degrees awarded. *Degree requirements:* For master's, thesis (for some programs), comprehensive exam required, foreign language not required. *Entrance requirements:* For master's, GRE Subject Test. *Application deadline:* For fall admission, 6/1. Applications are processed on a rolling basis. Application fee: $59. Tuition, nonresident: part-time $246 per unit. Required fees: $1,939; $1,309 per year. *Financial aid:* In 1998–99, 20 teaching assistantships were awarded.; career-related internships or fieldwork and Federal Work-Study also available. Aid available to part-time students. *Faculty research:* Artificial intelligence, algorithms, numerical analysis, software database, number theory. *Unit head:* Dr. Michael Burke, Chair, 408-924-5100, Fax: 408-924-5080. *Application contact:* Dr. John Mitchem, Graduate Adviser, 408-924-5135.

Shippensburg University of Pennsylvania, School of Graduate Studies and Research, College of Arts and Sciences, Department of Mathematics and Computer Science, Shippensburg, PA 17257-2299. Offers computer science (MS); information systems (MS); mathematics (M Ed, MS). Part-time and evening/weekend programs available. *Faculty:* 19 full-time (3 women). *Students:* 19 full-time (7 women), 64 part-time (15 women); includes 3 minority (2 African Americans, 1 Native American), 11 international. Average age 33. In 1998, 45 degrees awarded. *Degree requirements:* For master's, foreign language and thesis not required. *Entrance requirements:* For master's, TOEFL (minimum score of 237 required for computer-based), GRE General Test or minimum GPA of 2.75. *Application deadline:* Applications are processed on a rolling basis. Application fee: $25. Electronic applications accepted. *Financial aid:* Career-related internships or fieldwork, Federal Work-Study, institutionally-sponsored loans, and unspecified assistantships available. Aid available to part-time students. Financial aid application deadline: 3/1; financial aid applicants required to submit FAFSA. *Unit head:* Dr. Fred Nordai, Chairperson, 717-532-1431, Fax: 717-530-4009, E-mail: flnord@ship.edu. *Application contact:* Renee Payne, Assistant Dean of Graduate Studies, 717-532-1213, Fax: 717-530-4038, E-mail: rmpayn@ship.edu.

Simon Fraser University, Graduate Studies, Faculty of Science, Department of Mathematics and Statistics, Burnaby, BC V5A 1S6, Canada. Offers applied mathematics (M Sc, PhD); pure mathematics (M Sc, PhD); statistics (M Sc, PhD). *Faculty:* 32 full-time (3 women), 1 part-time (0 women). *Students:* 53 full-time (21 women), 10 part-time (2 women). Average age 31. In 1998, 6 master's, 4 doctorates awarded. *Degree requirements:* For master's, thesis required; for doctorate, dissertation, comprehensive exams required. *Entrance requirements:* For master's, GRE Subject Test, TOEFL (minimum score of 570 required), TWE (minimum score of 5 required) or International English Language Test (minimum score of 7.5 required), minimum GPA of 3.0; for doctorate, GRE Subject Test, TOEFL (minimum score of 570 required), TWE (minimum score of 5 required) or International English Language Test (minimum score of 7.5 required), minimum GPA of 3.5. Application fee: $55. *Financial aid:* In 1998–99, 14 fellowships were awarded.; research assistantships, teaching assistantships *Faculty research:* Semigroups, lattice-ordered groups, summability, functional analysis, graph theory. *Unit head:* J. Berggren, Chair, 604-291-3331, Fax: 604-291-4947. *Application contact:* Graduate Secretary, 604-291-3801, Fax: 604-291-4947, E-mail: sholmes@sfu.ca.

South Dakota State University, Graduate School, College of Engineering, Department of Mathematics, Brookings, SD 57007. Offers MS. *Degree requirements:* For master's, thesis, oral exam required, foreign language not required. *Entrance requirements:* For master's, TOEFL (minimum score of 550 required). *Faculty research:* Numerical linear algebra, statistics, applied quality number theory, abstract algebra, actuarial mathematics.

Southeast Missouri State University, Graduate School, Department of Mathematics, Cape Girardeau, MO 63701-4799. Offers MNS. *Degree requirements:* For master's, thesis or alternative required, foreign language not required. *Entrance requirements:* For master's, minimum GPA of 3.0 in mathematics.

Southern Connecticut State University, School of Graduate Studies, School of Arts and Sciences, Department of Mathematics, New Haven, CT 06515-1355. Offers MS. Part-time and evening/weekend programs available. *Faculty:* 10 full-time. *Students:* 6 full-time (1 woman), 30 part-time (11 women); includes 1 minority (African American) 55 applicants, 20% accepted. In 1998, 7 degrees awarded. *Degree requirements:* For master's, thesis or alternative required. *Entrance requirements:* For master's, interview. *Application deadline:* For fall admission, 7/15 (priority date). Applications are processed on a rolling basis. Application fee: $40. *Financial aid:* Application deadline: 4/15; *Unit head:* Dr. Leo Kuczynski, Chair, 203-392-5586, Fax: 203-392-6805, E-mail: kuczynski@scsu.ctstateu.edu. *Application contact:* Dr. Martin Hartog, Graduate Coordinator, 203-392-5595, Fax: 203-392-6805, E-mail: hartog@scsu.ctstateu.edu.

Southern Illinois University Carbondale, Graduate School, College of Science, Department of Mathematics, Carbondale, IL 62901-6806. Offers mathematics (MA, MS, PhD); statistics (MS). Part-time programs available. *Faculty:* 31 full-time (2 women). *Students:* 29 full-time (6 women), 10 part-time (5 women); includes 4 minority (2 African Americans, 2 Asian Americans or Pacific Islanders, 13 international. Average age 26. 16 applicants, 94% accepted. In 1998, 8 master's, 2 doctorates awarded. *Degree requirements:* For master's, thesis required, foreign language not required; for doctorate, 2 foreign languages (computer language can substitute for one), dissertation required. *Entrance requirements:* For master's, TOEFL (minimum score of 550 required), minimum GPA of 2.7; for doctorate, TOEFL (minimum score of 550 required), minimum GPA of 3.25. *Application deadline:* Applications are processed on a rolling basis. Application fee: $0. *Financial aid:* In 1998–99, 28 students received aid, including 4 fellowships with full tuition reimbursements available, 2 research assistantships with full tuition reimbursements available, 22 teaching assistantships with full tuition reimbursements available; Federal Work-Study, institutionally-sponsored loans, and tuition waivers (full) also available. Aid available to part-time students. *Faculty research:* Differential equations, combinatorics, probability, algebra, numerical analysis. *Unit head:* Andrew Earnest, Chairperson, 618-453-5302, Fax: 618-453-5300, E-mail: chairman@math.siu.edu. *Application contact:* William T. Patula, Director of Graduate Studies, 618-453-5302, Fax: 618-453-5300, E-mail: wpatula@math.siu.edu.

Southern Illinois University Edwardsville, Graduate Studies and Research, College of Arts and Sciences, Department of Mathematics and Statistics, Edwardsville, IL 62026-0001. Offers MS. Part-time programs available. *Students:* 7 full-time (2 women), 16 part-time (6 women); includes 4 minority (3 African Americans, 1 Asian American or Pacific Islander), 1 international. 7 applicants, 57% accepted. In 1998, 1 degree awarded. *Degree requirements:* For master's, computer language, thesis or alternative, final exam required, foreign language not required. *Entrance requirements:* For master's, TOEFL (minimum score of 550 required), undergraduate major in related area. *Application deadline:* For fall admission, 7/24. Application fee: $25. *Financial aid:* In 1998–99, 1 fellowship with full tuition reimbursement, 10 teaching assistantships with full tuition reimbursements were awarded.; research assistantships with full tuition reimbursements, Federal Work-Study, institutionally-sponsored loans, and unspecified assistantships also available. Aid available to part-time students. *Unit head:* Dr. Nadine Verderber, Acting Chair, 618-650-5985, E-mail: nverder@siue.edu.

Southern Methodist University, Dedman College, Department of Mathematics, Dallas, TX 75275. Offers applied mathematics (MS); mathematical sciences (PhD). Part-time programs available. *Faculty:* 16 full-time (1 woman). *Students:* 10 full-time (3 women), 6 part-time (2 women); includes 3 minority (2 African Americans, 1 Asian American or Pacific Islander), 4 international. Average age 29. 42 applicants, 12% accepted. In 1998, 7 master's, 2 doctorates awarded. *Degree requirements:* For master's, thesis optional, foreign language not required; for doctorate, dissertation, oral and written exams required, foreign language not required. *Entrance requirements:* For master's and doctorate, GRE General Test, minimum GPA of 3.0, 18 undergraduate hours in mathematics beyond first and second year calculus. *Application deadline:* For fall admission, 6/30; for spring admission, 11/30. Applications are processed on a rolling basis. Application fee: $50. Tuition: Part-time $686 per credit hour. Required fees: $88 per credit hour. Part-time tuition and fees vary according to course load and program. *Financial aid:* Research assistantships, teaching assistantships available. Financial aid applicants required to submit FAFSA. *Faculty research:* Numerical analysis, scientific computation, biomedical modeling, nonlinear waves, perturbation methods. Total annual research expenditures:$195,000. *Unit head:* Chairman, 214-768-2506. *Application contact:* James Nagy, Director of Graduate Studies, 214-768-4339.

See in-depth description on page 745.

Southern Oregon University, Graduate Office, School of Sciences, Ashland, OR 97520. Offers environmental education (MA, MS); mathematics/computer science (MA, MS); science (MA, MS). *Degree requirements:* For master's, comprehensive exam (MA) required, thesis optional. *Entrance requirements:* For master's, GRE General Test, minimum GPA of 3.0.

Southern University and Agricultural and Mechanical College, Graduate School, College of Sciences, Department of Mathematics, Baton Rouge, LA 70813. Offers MS. *Faculty:* 16 full-time (4 women). *Students:* 6 full-time (5 women), 9 part-time (6 women); includes 11 minority (all African Americans), 3 international. Average age 25. In 1998, 7 degrees awarded. *Degree requirements:* For master's, thesis optional, foreign language not required. *Entrance requirements:* For master's, GMAT, TOEFL. *Average time to degree:* Master's–2 years full-time, 3 years part-time. *Application deadline:* For fall admission, 6/1 (priority date); for spring admission, 11/1. Applications are processed on a rolling basis. Application fee: $5. *Financial aid:* In 1998–99, 2 research assistantships (averaging $7,000 per year), 1 teaching assistantship (averaging $7,000 per year) were awarded. Financial aid application deadline: 4/15; financial aid applicants required to submit FAFSA. *Unit head:* Dr. Preston Dinkins, Chairperson, 225-771-5180, Fax: 225-771-4762.

Southwest Missouri State University, Graduate College, College of Natural and Applied Sciences, Department of Mathematics, Springfield, MO 65804-0094. Offers MA. Part-time programs available. *Faculty:* 22 full-time (4 women). *Students:* 4 full-time (0 women), 10 part-time (3 women); includes 1 minority (Asian American or Pacific Islander), 3 international. Average age 25. 4 applicants, 100% accepted. In 1998, 1 degree awarded. *Degree requirements:*

For master's, thesis or alternative, comprehensive exam required, foreign language not required. *Entrance requirements:* For master's, GRE General Test, minimum undergraduate GPA of 3.0. *Average time to degree:* Master's–2.5 years full-time, 6 years part-time. *Application deadline:* For fall admission, 8/7 (priority date); for spring admission, 12/17 (priority date). Applications are processed on a rolling basis. Application fee: $25. Electronic applications accepted. *Financial aid:* In 1998–99, research assistantships with tuition reimbursements (averaging $6,000 per year), teaching assistantships with tuition reimbursements (averaging $6,000 per year) were awarded.; Federal Work-Study, scholarships, and unspecified assistantships also available. Financial aid application deadline: 5/1. *Faculty research:* Harmonic analysis, commutative algebra, number theory, K-theory, probability. *Unit head:* Dr. Yungchen Cheng, Head, 417-836-5112, Fax: 417-836-5610, E-mail: yuc471f@mail.smsu.edu.

Southwest Texas State University, Graduate School, School of Science, Department of Mathematics, San Marcos, TX 78666. Offers M Ed, MA, MS. Part-time programs available. *Faculty:* 7 full-time (0 women). *Students:* 8 full-time (4 women), 5 part-time (4 women); includes 3 minority (all Hispanic Americans), 1 international. Average age 32. In 1998, 6 degrees awarded. *Degree requirements:* For master's, thesis (for some programs), comprehensive exam required, foreign language not required. *Entrance requirements:* For master's, GRE General Test (minimum combined score of 900 required), TOEFL (minimum score of 550 required), minimum GPA of 2.75 in last 60 hours. *Application deadline:* For fall admission, 6/15 (priority date); for spring admission, 10/15 (priority date). Applications are processed on a rolling basis. Application fee: $25 ($50 for international students). Tuition, state resident: full-time $684; part-time $38 per semester hour. Tuition, nonresident: full-time $4,572; part-time $254 per semester hour. *Financial aid:* Teaching assistantships, Federal Work-Study and institutionally-sponsored loans available. Aid available to part-time students. Financial aid application deadline: 4/1; financial aid applicants required to submit FAFSA. *Faculty research:* Differential equations, geometric topology, number theory, mathematics education, graph theory. *Unit head:* Dr. Stanley G. Wayment, Chair, 512-245-3555, Fax: 512-245-3425, E-mail: sw05@swt.edu.

Stanford University, School of Engineering, Program in Scientific Computing and Computational Mathematics, Stanford, CA 94305-9991. Offers MS, PhD. *Students:* 33 full-time (3 women), 7 part-time (1 woman); includes 11 minority (9 Asian Americans or Pacific Islanders, 2 Hispanic Americans), 17 international. Average age 27. 37 applicants, 38% accepted. In 1998, 10 master's, 7 doctorates awarded. *Degree requirements:* For doctorate, dissertation required. *Entrance requirements:* For master's, GRE General Test, TOEFL; for doctorate, GRE General Test, GRE Subject Test, TOEFL. Application fee: $65 ($80 for international students). Electronic applications accepted. Tuition: Full-time $24,588. Required fees: $152. Part-time tuition and fees vary according to course load. *Financial aid:* Fellowships, research assistantships, institutionally-sponsored loans available. Financial aid application deadline: 2/15. *Unit head:* Dr. Andrew M. Stuart, Director, 650-723-8142, Fax: 650-723-1778, E-mail: stuart@sccm.stanford.edu. *Application contact:* Admissions Coordinator, 650-723-0572.

Stanford University, School of Humanities and Sciences, Department of Mathematics, Stanford, CA 94305-9991. Offers MAT, MS, PhD. *Faculty:* 32 full-time (1 woman). *Students:* 50 full-time (9 women), 3 part-time (1 woman); includes 5 minority (1 African American, 3 Asian Americans or Pacific Islanders, 1 Hispanic American), 32 international. Average age 26. 159 applicants, 20% accepted. In 1998, 3 master's, 8 doctorates awarded. Terminal master's awarded for partial completion of doctoral program. *Degree requirements:* For master's, foreign language and thesis not required; for doctorate, 2 foreign languages, dissertation, oral exam required. *Entrance requirements:* For master's, GRE General Test, TOEFL; for doctorate, GRE General Test, GRE Subject Test, TOEFL. *Application deadline:* For fall admission, 1/1. Application fee: $65 ($80 for international students). Electronic applications accepted. Tuition: Full-time $23,058. Required fees: $152. Part-time tuition and fees vary according to course load. *Financial aid:* Fellowships, research assistantships, teaching assistantships, Federal Work-Study and institutionally-sponsored loans available. *Unit head:* Leon Simon, Chair, 650-723-2604, Fax: 650-725-4066, E-mail: lms@math.stanford.edu. *Application contact:* Graduate Administrator, 650-723-2601.

State University of New York at Albany, College of Arts and Sciences, Department of Mathematics and Statistics, Albany, NY 12222-0001. Offers mathematics (PhD); secondary teaching (MA); statistics (MA). Evening/weekend programs available. *Faculty:* 29 full-time (2 women), 1 part-time (0 women). *Students:* 31 full-time (11 women), 6 part-time (1 woman); includes 2 minority (both African Americans), 7 international. Average age 25. 33 applicants, 73% accepted. In 1998, 10 master's, 9 doctorates awarded. *Degree requirements:* For master's, foreign language and thesis not required; for doctorate, dissertation required. *Entrance requirements:* For doctorate, GRE General Test, GRE Subject Test. Application fee: $50. Tuition, state resident: full-time $5,100; part-time $213 per credit. Tuition, nonresident: full-time $8,416; part-time $351 per credit. Required fees: $31 per credit. *Financial aid:* Fellowships, research assistantships, teaching assistantships, minority assistantships available. *Unit head:* Timothy Lance, Chair, 518-442-4602.

State University of New York at Binghamton, Graduate School, School of Arts and Sciences, Department of Mathematical Sciences, Binghamton, NY 13902-6000. Offers computer science (MA, PhD); probability and statistics (MA, PhD). *Faculty:* 23 full-time, 9 part-time. *Students:* 44 full-time (16 women), 6 part-time (2 women); includes 1 minority (Asian American or Pacific Islander), 14 international. Average age 29. 31 applicants, 84% accepted. In 1998, 6 master's, 7 doctorates awarded. Terminal master's awarded for partial completion of doctoral program. *Degree requirements:* For master's, thesis or alternative required; for doctorate, dissertation required. *Entrance requirements:* For master's and doctorate, GRE General Test, GRE Subject Test, TOEFL. *Application deadline:* For fall admission, 4/15 (priority date); for spring admission, 11/1. Applications are processed on a rolling basis. Application fee: $50. Electronic applications accepted. Tuition, state resident: full-time $5,100; part-time $213 per credit. Tuition, nonresident: full-time $8,416; part-time $351 per credit. Required fees: $77 per credit. Part-time tuition and fees vary according to course load. *Financial aid:* In 1998–99, 41 students received aid, including 2 fellowships with full tuition reimbursements available (averaging $8,820 per year), 2 research assistantships with full tuition reimbursements available (averaging $6,500 per year), 33 teaching assistantships with full tuition reimbursements available (averaging $6,992 per year); career-related internships or fieldwork, Federal Work-Study, institutionally-sponsored loans, and unspecified assistantships also available. Aid available to part-time students. Financial aid application deadline: 2/15. *Unit head:* Dr. David Hanson, Chairperson, 607-777-2147.

State University of New York at Buffalo, Graduate School, College of Arts and Sciences, Department of Mathematics, Buffalo, NY 14260. Offers MA, PhD. Part-time programs available. *Faculty:* 37 full-time (2 women), 2 part-time (0 women). *Students:* 43 full-time (18 women), 24 part-time (3 women); includes 3 minority (all Asian Americans or Pacific Islanders), 48 international. Average age 29. 85 applicants, 33% accepted. In 1998, 11 master's, 8 doctorates awarded (100% entered university research/teaching). Terminal master's awarded for partial completion of doctoral program. *Degree requirements:* For master's, comprehensive exam, project, or thesis required; for doctorate, one foreign language, dissertation, exams required. *Entrance requirements:* For master's and doctorate, TOEFL (minimum score of 550 required). *Application deadline:* For fall admission, 2/1; for spring admission, 10/15. Applications are processed on a rolling basis. Application fee: $35. Tuition, state resident: full-time $5,100; part-time $213 per credit hour. Tuition, nonresident: full-time $8,416; part-time $351 per credit hour. Required fees: $870; $75 per semester. Tuition and fees vary according to course load and program. *Financial aid:* In 1998–99, 55 students received aid, including 25 teaching assistantships; fellowships, research assistantships, Federal Work-Study, institutionally-sponsored loans, and unspecified assistantships also available. Financial aid application deadline: 2/1; financial aid applicants required to submit FAFSA. *Faculty research:* Applied mathematics, logic, analysis, algebra, topology. Total annual research expenditures: $319,632. *Unit head:* Dr. Jonathan G. Bell, Chairman, 716-829-2148 Ext. 103, Fax: 716-829-2299,

Mathematics

State University of New York at Buffalo (continued)
E-mail: bell@math.buffalo.edu. *Application contact:* Dr. E. Bruce Pitman, Director of Graduate Studies, 716-829-2148 Ext. 109, Fax: 716-829-2299, E-mail: pitman@galileo.math.buffalo.edu.

State University of New York at New Paltz, Graduate School, Faculty of Liberal Arts and Sciences, Department of Mathematics and Computer Science, Program in Mathematics, New Paltz, NY 12561. Offers MA, MAT, MS Ed. *Students:* 1 full-time (0 women), 3 part-time; includes 1 minority (African American) *Degree requirements:* For master's, computer language, comprehensive exam (MS Ed), thesis (MA) required. *Entrance requirements:* For master's, GRE General Test, minimum GPA of 3.0. *Application deadline:* For fall admission, 3/15 (priority date). Applications are processed on a rolling basis. Application fee: $50. *Financial aid:* Teaching assistantships, Federal Work-Study, institutionally-sponsored loans, and tuition waivers (full) available. *Application contact:* H. P. Sankappanavar, Graduate Adviser, 914-257-3535.

State University of New York at Stony Brook, Graduate School, College of Arts and Sciences, Department of Mathematics, Stony Brook, NY 11794. Offers MA, PhD. *Faculty:* 27 full-time (4 women), 11 part-time (3 women). *Students:* 52 full-time (12 women), 25 part-time (8 women); includes 4 minority (all Hispanic Americans), 38 international. 117 applicants, 38% accepted. In 1998, 20 master's, 13 doctorates awarded (100% entered university research/teaching). *Degree requirements:* For master's, foreign language and thesis not required; for doctorate, dissertation required. *Entrance requirements:* For master's and doctorate, GRE General Test, TOEFL. *Application deadline:* For fall admission, 1/15. Application fee: $50. *Financial aid:* In 1998–99, 4 research assistantships, 40 teaching assistantships were awarded.; fellowships *Faculty research:* Real analysis, relativity and mathematical physics, complex analysis, topology, combinatorics. Total annual research expenditures: $659,703. *Unit head:* Dr. Anthony Phillips, Chairman, 516-632-8290. *Application contact:* Dr. Leon Takhtajan, Director, 516-632-8258, Fax: 516-632-7631, E-mail: leontak@math.sunysb.edu.

State University of New York College at Brockport, School of Letters and Sciences, Department of Mathematics, Brockport, NY 14420-2997. Offers MA. Part-time and evening/weekend programs available. *Faculty:* 6 full-time (1 woman). *Students:* 5 full-time (0 women), 6 part-time (3 women). Average age 29. 8 applicants, 75% accepted. *Degree requirements:* For master's, one foreign language (computer language can substitute), comprehensive exam required, thesis not required. *Entrance requirements:* For master's, minimum GPA of 3.0. *Application deadline:* Applications are processed on a rolling basis. Application fee: $50. Tuition, state resident: full-time $5,100; part-time $213 per credit. Tuition, nonresident: full-time $8,416; part-time $351 per credit. Required fees: $464; $25 per credit. *Financial aid:* In 1998–99, 5 students received aid, including 1 fellowship, 3 teaching assistantships; research assistantships, Federal Work-Study and tuition waivers (full) also available. Aid available to part-time students. Financial aid application deadline: 4/1; financial aid applicants required to submit FAFSA. *Faculty research:* Applications of computers, secondary school teacher retraining, complex analysis statistics, combinatorics. *Unit head:* Dr. Charles Sommer, Chairperson, 716-395-2194.

Announcement: Flexible program leading to MA in mathematics. Three required courses in algebra, analysis, and statistics. Four additional elective courses in mathematics or computer science. The remaining 3 courses may be chosen from other departments, including education. Several assistantships, which include a stipend of $6000 and a tuition waiver, are available.

State University of New York College at Potsdam, School of Arts and Sciences, Department of Mathematics, Potsdam, NY 13676. Offers MA. Part-time and evening/weekend programs available. *Faculty:* 5 full-time (1 woman), 1 part-time (0 women). *Students:* 1. 1 applicants, 100% accepted. *Degree requirements:* For master's, comprehensive exam required, foreign language and thesis not required. *Entrance requirements:* For master's, minimum GPA of 2.75 in last 60 hours of undergraduate course work. *Application deadline:* Applications are processed on a rolling basis. Application fee: $50. Tuition, state resident: full-time $5,100; part-time $213 per credit. Tuition, nonresident: full-time $8,416; part-time $351 per credit. Required fees: $285; $11 per credit. Tuition and fees vary according to course load. *Financial aid:* In 1998–99, 1 teaching assistantship with full tuition reimbursement (averaging $3,000 per year) was awarded.; Federal Work-Study also available. Aid available to part-time students. Financial aid application deadline: 3/1. *Unit head:* Dr. Vasily Cateforis, Chairperson, 315-267-2064, Fax: 315-267-3176, E-mail: catefovc@potsdam.edu. *Application contact:* Dr. William Amoriell, Dean of Education and Graduate Studies, 315-267-2515, Fax: 315-267-4802.

Stephen F. Austin State University, Graduate School, College of Sciences and Mathematics, Department of Mathematics and Statistics, Nacogdoches, TX 75962. Offers mathematics (MS); mathematics education (MS); statistics (MS). *Faculty:* 14 full-time (1 woman). *Students:* 11 full-time (5 women), 1 (woman) part-time; includes 1 minority (African American), 5 international. 4 applicants, 100% accepted. In 1998, 4 degrees awarded. *Degree requirements:* For master's, comprehensive exam required, thesis optional, foreign language not required. *Entrance requirements:* For master's, GRE General Test, TOEFL, minimum GPA of 2.8 in last 60 hours, 2.5 overall. *Application deadline:* For fall admission, 8/1 (priority date); for spring admission, 12/15. Applications are processed on a rolling basis. Application fee: $0 ($50 for international students). Tuition, state resident: full-time $1,792. Tuition, nonresident: full-time $6,880. *Financial aid:* Teaching assistantships available. Financial aid application deadline: 3/1. *Faculty research:* Kernel type estimators, fractal mappings, spline curve fitting, robust regression continua theory. *Unit head:* Dr. Jasper Adams, Chair, 409-468-3805.

Stevens Institute of Technology, Graduate School, School of Applied Sciences and Liberal Arts, Department of Mathematical Sciences, Program in Mathematics, Hoboken, NJ 07030. Offers algebra (PhD); analysis (PhD); applied mathematics (PhD); mathematics (MS). *Degree requirements:* For master's, thesis optional, foreign language not required; for doctorate, one foreign language, dissertation required. *Entrance requirements:* For master's and doctorate, GRE, TOEFL. Electronic applications accepted.

Syracuse University, Graduate School, College of Arts and Sciences, Department of Mathematics, Syracuse, NY 13244-0003. Offers mathematics (MS, PhD); mathematics education (MS, PhD). *Faculty:* 35. *Students:* 23 full-time (12 women), 13 part-time (5 women), 13 international. Average age 28. 46 applicants, 50% accepted. In 1998, 5 master's, 2 doctorates awarded. Terminal master's awarded for partial completion of doctoral program. *Degree requirements:* For master's, foreign language and thesis not required; for doctorate, dissertation, qualifying exam required. *Entrance requirements:* For master's and doctorate, GRE General Test, GRE Subject Test, TOEFL. *Application deadline:* Applications are processed on a rolling basis. Application fee: $40. Tuition: Full-time $13,992; part-time $583 per credit hour. *Financial aid:* Fellowships, research assistantships, teaching assistantships, Federal Work-Study and tuition waivers (partial) available. Financial aid application deadline: 3/1. *Faculty research:* Pure mathematics, numerical mathematics, computing statistics. *Unit head:* Douglas Anderson, Chair, 315-443-1472. *Application contact:* Mark Watkins, Graduate Program Director, 315-443-1471.

Tarleton State University, College of Graduate Studies, College of Arts and Sciences, Department of Mathematics and Physics, Stephenville, TX 76402. Offers mathematics (MA). Part-time and evening/weekend programs available. 7 applicants, 57% accepted. In 1998, 1 degree awarded. *Degree requirements:* For master's, thesis (for some programs), comprehensive exam required. *Entrance requirements:* For master's, GRE General Test, minimum GPA of 2.75 during last 60 hours. *Application deadline:* For fall admission, 8/5 (priority date); for spring admission, 12/1. Applications are processed on a rolling basis. Application fee: $25 ($100 for international students). *Financial aid:* In 1998–99, 1 research assistantship (averaging $12,000 per year), 2 teaching assistantships (averaging $12,000 per year) were awarded.; career-related internships or fieldwork and Federal Work-Study also available. Aid available to part-time students. Financial aid application deadline: 5/1; financial aid applicants required to submit FAFSA. *Unit head:* Dr. Joe Cude, Head, 254-968-9168.

Temple University, Graduate School, College of Science and Technology, Department of Mathematics, Philadelphia, PA 19122-6096. Offers applied and computational mathematics (MA, PhD); pure mathematics (MA, PhD). Part-time and evening/weekend programs available. *Faculty:* 26 full-time (1 woman). *Students:* 39 (10 women); includes 14 minority (1 African American, 11 Asian Americans or Pacific Islanders, 2 Hispanic Americans) 3 international. 39 applicants, 67% accepted. In 1998, 5 master's, 3 doctorates awarded. Terminal master's awarded for partial completion of doctoral program. *Degree requirements:* For master's, written exam required, thesis optional, foreign language not required; for doctorate, 2 foreign languages, dissertation, oral and written exams required. *Entrance requirements:* For master's and doctorate, GRE General Test (minimum combined score of 1000 required), GRE Subject Test, minimum GPA of 3.0 during previous 2 years, 2.8 overall. *Application deadline:* For fall admission, 2/10 (priority date). Applications are processed on a rolling basis. Application fee: $40. *Financial aid:* Fellowships, research assistantships, teaching assistantships, Federal Work-Study and institutionally-sponsored loans available. Financial aid application deadline: 4/1. *Faculty research:* Differential geometry, numerical analysis. *Unit head:* Dr. Jack Schiller, Chair, 215-204-4650, Fax: 215-204-6433, E-mail: schiller@euclid.math.temple.edu. *Application contact:* Dr. Eric Grinberg, Graduate Chair, 215-204-7286, Fax: 215-204-6433, E-mail: grinberg@euclid.math.temple.edu.

Announcement: Master's (thesis and nonthesis options) and doctoral programs in pure mathematics, applied and computational mathematics. Flexible tracks with highly favorable faculty-student ratio. Numerous student-faculty seminars. Assistantships and fellowships at competitive levels, with nearly all PhD students receiving support. Faculty research interests include most major fields, with particular strength in harmonic analysis, approximation theory, partial differential equations, number theory, algebra, combinatorics, probability, and statistics. Excellent departmental library and computing facilities. Proximity of several other major universities enhances opportunities for interaction and collaboration. Write to Graduate Chair, Box P, Department of Mathematics.

Tennessee State University, Graduate School, College of Arts and Sciences, Department of Physics and Mathematics, Nashville, TN 37209-1561. Offers mathematics (MS). Part-time and evening/weekend programs available. *Faculty:* 10 full-time (2 women). *Students:* 7 full-time (2 women), 10 part-time (2 women); includes 9 minority (6 African Americans, 1 Hispanic American, 2 Native Americans), 2 international. Average age 23. 8 applicants, 63% accepted. In 1998, 7 degrees awarded. *Degree requirements:* For master's, computer language, thesis, comprehensive exam required, foreign language not required. *Entrance requirements:* For master's, GRE General Test (minimum combined score of 870 required), GRE Subject Test, minimum GPA of 2.5. *Application deadline:* Applications are processed on a rolling basis. Application fee: $15. Tuition, state resident: full-time $2,962; part-time $182 per credit hour. Tuition, nonresident: full-time $7,788; part-time $393 per credit hour. *Financial aid:* In 1998–99, 12 students received aid, including 1 research assistantship (averaging $1,506 per year), 3 teaching assistantships (averaging $8,886 per year); unspecified assistantships also available. Financial aid application deadline: 5/1. *Faculty research:* Chaos theory, semi-coherent light scattering, lattices of topologies, Ramsey Theory, K theory, stochastic processes. Total annual research expenditures: $60,000. *Unit head:* Dr. Vladimir Rosenhaus, Head, 615-963-5811, E-mail: sscheick@picard.tnstate.edu.

Tennessee Technological University, Graduate School, College of Arts and Sciences, Department of Mathematics, Cookeville, TN 38505. Offers MS. Part-time programs available. *Faculty:* 17 full-time (4 women). *Students:* 5 full-time (1 woman), 1 part-time; includes 1 minority (Asian American or Pacific Islander) Average age 27. 10 applicants, 50% accepted. In 1998, 2 degrees awarded. *Degree requirements:* For master's, thesis required, foreign language not required. *Entrance requirements:* For master's, GRE General Test, TOEFL (minimum score of 525 required). *Application deadline:* For fall admission, 3/1 (priority date); for spring admission, 8/1. Application fee: $25 ($30 for international students). Tuition, state resident: part-time $137 per hour. Tuition, nonresident: part-time $361 per hour. Required fees: $17 per hour. Tuition and fees vary according to course load. *Financial aid:* In 1998–99, 5 students received aid, including 4 research assistantships (averaging $6,180 per year), 2 teaching assistantships (averaging $6,180 per year) Financial aid application deadline: 4/1. *Unit head:* Dr. Rafal Ablamowicz, Chairperson, 931-372-3441, Fax: 931-372-6353, E-mail: rablamowicz@tntech.edu. *Application contact:* Dr. Rebecca F. Quattlebaum, Dean of the Graduate School, 931-372-3233, Fax: 931-372-3497, E-mail: rquattlebaum@tntech.edu.

Texas A&M International University, Division of Graduate Studies, Division of Arts and Humanities, Interdisciplinary Programs, Laredo, TX 78041-1900. Offers criminal justice (MAIS); English (MAIS); history (MAIS); mathematics (MAIS); political science (MAIS); psychology (MAIS); sociology (MAIS); Spanish (MAIS). *Degree requirements:* Foreign language not required. *Entrance requirements:* For master's, GRE General Test.

Texas A&M University, College of Science, Department of Mathematics, College Station, TX 77843. Offers MS, PhD. Part-time programs available. *Faculty:* 63 full-time (4 women), 4 part-time (0 women). *Students:* 97 full-time (28 women), 6 part-time (3 women); includes 11 minority (3 African Americans, 2 Asian Americans or Pacific Islanders, 6 Hispanic Americans), 47 international. Average age 27. 121 applicants, 17% accepted. In 1998, 13 master's awarded (23% entered university research/teaching, 46% found other work related to degree, 31% continued full-time study); 8 doctorates awarded (75% entered university research/teaching, 25% found other work related to degree). Terminal master's awarded for partial completion of doctoral program. *Degree requirements:* For master's, thesis optional, foreign language not required; for doctorate, one foreign language, dissertation required. *Entrance requirements:* For master's and doctorate, GRE General Test, TOEFL. *Average time to degree:* Master's–2 years full-time; doctorate–6 years full-time. *Application deadline:* For fall admission, 3/1 (priority date); for spring admission, 8/1. Applications are processed on a rolling basis. Application fee: $50 ($75 for international students). *Financial aid:* In 1998–99, 1 fellowship with partial tuition reimbursement, 10 research assistantships with partial tuition reimbursements, 73 teaching assistantships with partial tuition reimbursements were awarded.; career-related internships or fieldwork, institutionally-sponsored loans, and scholarships also available. Financial aid application deadline: 3/1; financial aid applicants required to submit FAFSA. *Faculty research:* Functional analysis, numerical analysis, algebra, geometry/topology, applied mathematics. *Unit head:* Dr. William Rundell, Head, 409-845-3261, Fax: 409-845-6028. *Application contact:* Monique Stewart, Program Staff Assistant, 409-862-4137, Fax: 409-862-4190, E-mail: gstudies@math.tamu.edu.

See in-depth description on page 749.

Texas A&M University–Commerce, Graduate School, College of Arts and Sciences, Department of Mathematics, Commerce, TX 75429-3011. Offers MA, MS. Part-time programs available. *Faculty:* 6 full-time (0 women). Average age 36. *Degree requirements:* For master's, thesis (for some programs), comprehensive exam required. *Entrance requirements:* For master's, GRE General Test (minimum combined score of 850 required). *Application deadline:* For fall admission, 6/1 (priority date); for spring admission, 11/1 (priority date). Applications are processed on a rolling basis. Application fee: $0 ($25 for international students). Electronic applications accepted. *Financial aid:* In 1998–99, research assistantships (averaging $7,750 per year), teaching assistantships (averaging $7,750 per year) were awarded.; Federal Work-Study, institutionally-sponsored loans, and scholarships also available. Financial aid application deadline: 5/1; financial aid applicants required to submit FAFSA. *Unit head:* Dr. Stuart Anderson, Head, 903-886-5157. *Application contact:* Betty Hunt, Graduate Admissions Adviser, 903-886-5167, Fax: 903-886-5165, E-mail: betty_hunt@tamu_commerce.edu.

Texas A&M University–Corpus Christi, Graduate Programs, College of Science and Technology, Program in Computing and Mathematical Sciences, Corpus Christi, TX 78412-5503. Offers computer science (MS); mathematics (MS). Part-time and evening/weekend programs available. *Degree requirements:* For master's, computer language, thesis required, foreign language not required. *Entrance requirements:* For master's, GRE General Test.

Texas A&M University–Kingsville, College of Graduate Studies, College of Arts and Sciences, Department of Mathematics, Kingsville, TX 78363. Offers MS. Part-time programs available. *Faculty:* 16 full-time (2 women), 1 part-time (0 women). *Students:* 2 full-time (0 women), 5 part-time (1 woman). *Degree requirements:* For master's, thesis or alternative, comprehensive exam required, foreign language not required. *Entrance requirements:* For master's, GRE General Test (minimum combined score of 1000 required), TOEFL (minimum score of 500 required). *Application deadline:* For fall admission, 6/1 (priority date); for spring admission, 11/15. Applications are processed on a rolling basis. Application fee: $15 ($25 for international students). Tuition, state resident: full-time $2,062. Tuition, nonresident: full-time $7,246. *Financial aid:* Teaching assistantships, Federal Work-Study available. Financial aid application deadline: 5/15. *Faculty research:* Complex analysis, multivariate analysis, algebra, numerical analysis, applied statistics. *Unit head:* Dr. Hueytzen Wu, Coordinator, 361-593-3517.

Texas Southern University, Graduate School, College of Arts and Sciences, Department of Mathematics, Houston, TX 77004-4584. Offers MA, MS. *Degree requirements:* For master's, thesis, comprehensive exam required, foreign language not required. *Entrance requirements:* For master's, GRE General Test, TOEFL, minimum GPA of 2.5. *Faculty research:* Statistics, number theory, topology, differential equations, numerical analysis.

Texas Tech University, Graduate School, College of Arts and Sciences, Department of Mathematics, Lubbock, TX 79409. Offers mathematics (MA, MS, PhD); statistics (MS). Part-time programs available. *Faculty:* 39 full-time (4 women), 1 part-time (0 women). *Students:* 67 full-time (24 women), 11 part-time (4 women); includes 6 minority (1 African American, 1 Asian American or Pacific Islander, 4 Hispanic Americans), 13 international. Average age 26. 35 applicants, 63% accepted. In 1998, 18 master's, 7 doctorates awarded. *Degree requirements:* For master's, thesis or alternative required, foreign language not required; for doctorate, dissertation required. *Entrance requirements:* For master's, GRE General Test (combined average 1194); for doctorate, GRE General Test. *Application deadline:* For fall admission, 4/15 (priority date); for spring admission, 11/1 (priority date). Applications are processed on a rolling basis. Application fee: $25 ($50 for international students). Electronic applications accepted. *Financial aid:* In 1998–99, 63 students received aid, including 5 research assistantships (averaging $9,904 per year), 55 teaching assistantships (averaging $11,439 per year); fellowships, Federal Work-Study and institutionally-sponsored loans also available. Aid available to part-time students. Financial aid application deadline: 5/15; financial aid applicants required to submit FAFSA. *Faculty research:* Study of finite semifield planes, computer modeling, analysis for solving VLASOV kinetic equations. Total annual research expenditures: $815,301. *Unit head:* Dr. Ron M. Anderson, Chairman, 806-742-2566, Fax: 806-742-1112.

Texas Woman's University, Graduate School, College of Arts and Sciences, Department of Mathematics and Computer Science, Denton, TX 76204. Offers mathematics (MA, MS). Part-time and evening/weekend programs available. *Faculty:* 14 full-time (7 women), 3 part-time (all women). *Students:* 4 full-time (1 woman), 68 part-time (61 women); includes 14 minority (2 African Americans, 5 Asian Americans or Pacific Islanders, 6 Hispanic Americans, 1 Native American), 6 international. Average age 37. In 1998, 4 degrees awarded. *Degree requirements:* For master's, one foreign language, thesis required. *Entrance requirements:* For master's, GRE General Test (minimum combined score of 700 required), minimum GPA of 3.0. Application fee: $30. *Financial aid:* In 1998–99, 3 research assistantships, 12 teaching assistantships were awarded. Financial aid application deadline: 4/1; financial aid applicants required to submit FAFSA. *Unit head:* Dr. Don Edwards, Chair, 940-898-2166, Fax: 940-898-2179, E-mail: f_edwards@twu.edu.

Truman State University, Graduate School, Division of Mathematics and Computer Science, Program in Mathematics, Kirksville, MO 63501-4221. Offers MA. *Faculty:* 21 full-time (4 women). *Students:* 2 full-time (0 women), 1 international. Average age 24. *Degree requirements:* For master's, comprehensive exam required, foreign language and thesis not required. *Entrance requirements:* For master's, GRE General Test, minimum GPA of 3.0. *Application deadline:* For fall admission, 6/15 (priority date); for spring admission, 11/1. Applications are processed on a rolling basis. Application fee: $0 ($25 for international students). *Financial aid:* In 1998–99, 2 students received aid, including 1 research assistantship, 1 teaching assistantship; Federal Work-Study also available. Financial aid application deadline: 5/1; financial aid applicants required to submit FAFSA. *Unit head:* Dr. Ronald Knight, Head, 660-785-7232, Fax: 660-785-4251, E-mail: mt18@academic.truman.edu. *Application contact:* Peggy Orchard, Graduate Office Secretary, 660-785-4109, Fax: 660-785-7460.

Tufts University, Division of Graduate and Continuing Studies and Research, Graduate School of Arts and Sciences, Department of Mathematics, Medford, MA 02155. Offers MA, MS, PhD. *Faculty:* 21 full-time, 8 part-time. *Students:* 12 (5 women) 6 international. 22 applicants, 50% accepted. In 1998, 2 master's, 1 doctorate awarded. Terminal master's awarded for partial completion of doctoral program. *Degree requirements:* For master's, thesis required; for doctorate, dissertation required. *Entrance requirements:* For master's and doctorate, GRE General Test, GRE Subject Test, TOEFL (minimum score of 550 required). *Application deadline:* For fall admission, 2/15; for spring admission, 10/15. Applications are processed on a rolling basis. Application fee: $50. *Financial aid:* Teaching assistantships with full and partial tuition reimbursements, Federal Work-Study, scholarships, and tuition waivers (partial) available. Financial aid application deadline: 2/15; financial aid applicants required to submit FAFSA. *Unit head:* Richard Weiss, Chair, 617-627-3234, E-mail: mathgrad@tufts.edu. *Application contact:* Fulton Gonzalez, 617-627-3234, E-mail: mathgrad@tufts.edu.

Tulane University, Graduate School, Department of Mathematics, New Orleans, LA 70118-5669. Offers applied mathematics (MS); mathematics (MS, PhD); statistics (MS). *Students:* 24 full-time (6 women), 1 part-time; includes 2 minority (1 African American, 1 Asian American or Pacific Islander), 13 international. 49 applicants, 49% accepted. In 1998, 7 master's, 8 doctorates awarded. *Degree requirements:* For doctorate, dissertation required. *Entrance requirements:* For master's, GRE General Test (minimum combined score of 1000 required; average 1200), TOEFL (minimum score of 600 required), TSE (minimum score of 220 required), minimum B average in undergraduate course work; for doctorate, GRE General Test (minimum combined score of 1000 required; average 1200), TOEFL (minimum score of 600 required), TSE (minimum score of 220 required). *Application deadline:* For fall admission, 2/1. Application fee: $45. *Financial aid:* Fellowships, teaching assistantships, career-related internships or fieldwork, Federal Work-Study, and institutionally-sponsored loans available. Financial aid application deadline: 2/1. *Unit head:* Dr. Morris Kalka, Chairman, 504-865-5727.

Université de Moncton, Faculty of Science, Department of Mathematics and Statistics, Moncton, NB E1A 3E9, Canada. Offers mathematics (M Sc). *Degree requirements:* For master's, computer language, thesis required, foreign language not required. Electronic applications accepted. *Faculty research:* Reliability theory, Bayesian statistics, models in hydrology, theoretical statistics, applied mathematics, analysis and topology, teaching methods in mathematics.

Université de Montréal, Faculty of Graduate Studies, Faculty of Arts and Sciences, Department of Mathematics and Statistics, Montréal, PQ H3C 3J7, Canada. Offers mathematics (M Sc, PhD); statistics (M Sc, PhD). *Faculty:* 57 full-time (7 women). *Students:* 122 full-time (38 women), 2 part-time (1 woman). 38 applicants, 34% accepted. In 1998, 10 master's, 6 doctorates awarded. *Degree requirements:* For master's, thesis required; for doctorate, dissertation, general exam required. *Entrance requirements:* For master's and doctorate, proficiency in French. *Application deadline:* For fall admission, 2/1. Application fee: $30. *Financial aid:* Fellowships, research assistantships, teaching assistantships, monitorships available. Financial aid application deadline: 4/1. *Faculty research:* Pure and applied mathematics, actuarial mathematics. *Unit head:* Sabin Lessard, Chair, 514-343-6710. *Application contact:* Robert Cleroux, Graduate Chairman, 514-343-6987.

Université de Sherbrooke, Faculty of Sciences, Department of Mathematics and Informatics, Sherbrooke, PQ J1K 2R1, Canada. Offers M Sc, PhD. *Degree requirements:* For master's and doctorate, thesis/dissertation required, foreign language not required. *Entrance requirements:* For doctorate, master's degree. *Faculty research:* Measure theory, differential equations, probability, statistics, error control codes.

Université du Québec à Montréal, Graduate Programs, Program in Mathematics, Montréal, PQ H3C 3P8, Canada. Offers M Sc, PhD. Part-time programs available. *Degree requirements:* For master's and doctorate, thesis/dissertation required. *Entrance requirements:* For master's, appropriate bachelor's degree or equivalent and proficiency in French; for doctorate, appropriate master's degree or equivalent and proficiency in French.

Université du Québec à Trois-Rivières, Graduate Programs, Program in Mathematics and Computer Science, Trois-Rivières, PQ G9A 5H7, Canada. Offers M Sc. *Students:* 9 full-time (2 women). 22 applicants, 77% accepted. *Application deadline:* For fall admission, 2/1. Application fee: $30. *Faculty research:* Probability, statistics, scientific calculation. *Unit head:* Dr. Robert La Barre, Director, 819-376-5125 Ext. 3817, Fax: 819-376-5012, E-mail: robert_labarre@uqtr.uquebec.ca. *Application contact:* Suzanne Camirand, Admissions Officer, 819-376-5045 Ext. 2591, Fax: 819-376-5210, E-mail: suzanne_camirand@uqtr.uquebec.ca.

Université Laval, Faculty of Graduate Studies, Faculty of Sciences and Engineering, Department of Mathematics and Statistics, Program in Mathematics, Sainte-Foy, PQ G1K 7P4, Canada. Offers M Sc, PhD. *Students:* 31 full-time (7 women), 10 part-time (2 women). 34 applicants, 68% accepted. In 1998, 8 master's, 5 doctorates awarded. *Application deadline:* For fall admission, 3/1. Application fee: $30. *Unit head:* Charles Cassidy, Director, 418-656-2131 Ext. 2977, Fax: 418-656-2817, E-mail: charles.cassidy@mat.ulaval.ca.

The University of Akron, Graduate School, Buchtel College of Arts and Sciences, Department of Mathematics and Computer Science, Program in Mathematics, Akron, OH 44325-0001. Offers MS. Part-time and evening/weekend programs available. *Students:* 3 full-time (1 woman), 2 part-time (both women). Average age 30. In 1998, 1 degree awarded. *Degree requirements:* For master's, thesis optional, foreign language not required. *Entrance requirements:* For master's, minimum GPA of 2.75. *Average time to degree:* Master's–2 years full-time, 4 years part-time. *Application deadline:* For fall admission, 3/1. Applications are processed on a rolling basis. Application fee: $25 ($50 for international students). Tuition, state resident: part-time $189 per credit. Tuition, nonresident: part-time $353 per credit. Required fees: $7.3 per credit. *Financial aid:* Teaching assistantships with tuition reimbursements available. Financial aid application deadline: 3/1. *Faculty research:* Topology analysis. *Unit head:* Dr. Judith Palagallo, Coordinator, 330-972-7402, E-mail: palagallo@uakron.edu.

The University of Alabama, Graduate School, College of Arts and Sciences, Department of Mathematics, Tuscaloosa, AL 35487. Offers applied mathematics (PhD); mathematics (MA); pure mathematics (PhD). *Faculty:* 31 full-time (1 woman). *Students:* 28 full-time (12 women), 1 part-time; includes 2 minority (both African Americans), 12 international. Average age 27. In 1998, 3 master's awarded (67% found work related to degree, 33% continued full-time study); 1 doctorate awarded (100% entered university research/teaching). Terminal master's awarded for partial completion of doctoral program. *Degree requirements:* For master's, thesis or alternative required, foreign language not required; for doctorate, one foreign language, dissertation, teaching experience required. *Entrance requirements:* For master's and doctorate, GRE General Test (minimum combined score of 1500 required), TOEFL (minimum score of 550 required), minimum GPA of 3.0. *Average time to degree:* Master's–3 years full-time; doctorate–7 years full-time. *Application deadline:* For fall admission, 7/6. Applications are processed on a rolling basis. Application fee: $25. Electronic applications accepted. *Financial aid:* In 1998–99, 29 students received aid, including 1 fellowship, 2 research assistantships, 26 teaching assistantships; Federal Work-Study also available. Financial aid application deadline: 7/14. *Faculty research:* Analysis, topology, algebra, fluid mechanics and system control theory, optimization, stochastic processes. *Unit head:* Wei Shen Hsia, Chairperson, 205-348-5071, Fax: 205-348-7067, E-mail: whsia@gp.as.ua.edu. *Application contact:* Rita Reese, Administrative Specialist, Graduate Advisory Program, 205-348-5074, Fax: 205-348-7067, E-mail: rreese@gp.as.ua.edu.

The University of Alabama at Birmingham, Graduate School, School of Natural Sciences and Mathematics, Department of Mathematics, Birmingham, AL 35294. Offers applied mathematics (PhD); mathematics (MS). *Students:* 18 full-time (6 women), 1 (woman) part-time; includes 4 minority (3 African Americans, 1 Asian American or Pacific Islander), 5 international. 21 applicants, 95% accepted. In 1998, 12 master's, 1 doctorate awarded. Terminal master's awarded for partial completion of doctoral program. *Degree requirements:* For master's, thesis optional; for doctorate, one foreign language (computer language can substitute), dissertation, comprehensive exam required. *Entrance requirements:* For master's and doctorate, GRE General Test. *Application deadline:* Applications are processed on a rolling basis. Application fee: $30 ($60 for international students). Electronic applications accepted. *Financial aid:* In 1998–99, 18 teaching assistantships with tuition reimbursements (averaging $14,000 per year) were awarded.; fellowships, research assistantships, career-related internships or fieldwork, Federal Work-Study, institutionally-sponsored loans, tuition waivers (full and partial), and unspecified assistantships also available. Aid available to part-time students. Financial aid application deadline: 3/31; financial aid applicants required to submit FAFSA. *Faculty research:* Differential equations, topology, mathematical physics, dynamical systems. *Unit head:* Dr. Roger T. Lewis, Chairman, 205-934-2154, Fax: 205-934-9025. *Application contact:* Dr. Roger T. Lewis, Chairman, 205-934-2154, Fax: 205-934-9025.

The University of Alabama in Huntsville, School of Graduate Studies, College of Science, Department of Mathematical Sciences, Huntsville, AL 35899. Offers applied mathematics (PhD); mathematics (MA, MS). Part-time and evening/weekend programs available. *Faculty:* 15 full-time (1 woman). *Students:* 17 full-time (8 women), 13 part-time (5 women); includes 2 minority (both African Americans), 6 international. Average age 31. 17 applicants, 100% accepted. In 1998, 10 master's, 2 doctorates awarded. *Degree requirements:* For master's, oral and written exams required, thesis optional, foreign language not required; for doctorate, one foreign language, dissertation, oral and written exams required. *Entrance requirements:* For master's and doctorate, GRE General Test (minimum combined score of 1500 on three sections required), minimum GPA of 3.0. *Application deadline:* For fall admission, 7/24 (priority date); for spring admission, 11/15 (priority date). Applications are processed on a rolling basis. Application fee: $20. Tuition and fees vary according to course load. *Financial aid:* In 1998–99, 14 students received aid, including 14 teaching assistantships with full and partial tuition reimbursements available (averaging $8,658 per year); fellowships with full and partial tuition reimbursements available, research assistantships with full and partial tuition reimbursements available, career-related internships or fieldwork, Federal Work-Study, grants, institutionally-sponsored loans, scholarships, and tuition waivers (full and partial) also available. Aid available to part-time students. Financial aid application deadline: 4/1; financial aid applicants required to submit FAFSA. *Faculty research:* Statistical modeling, stochastic processes, numerical analysis, combinatorics, fracture mechanics. Total annual research expenditures: $145,329. *Unit head:* Dr. M. H. Chang, Chair, 256-890-6470, Fax: 256-890-6173, E-mail: chang@math.uah.edu.

University of Alaska Fairbanks, Graduate School, College of Science, Engineering and Mathematics, Department of Mathematical Sciences, Fairbanks, AK 99775-7480. Offers computer science (MS); mathematics (MAT, MS, PhD). Part-time programs available. *Faculty:* 23 full-time (3 women), 1 part-time (0 women). *Students:* 8 full-time (3 women), 10 part-time (4 women); includes 2 minority (both Asian Americans or Pacific Islanders), 2 international. Average age 29. 5 applicants, 80% accepted. In 1998, 8 master's awarded. Terminal master's awarded for partial completion of doctoral program. *Degree requirements:* For master's, comprehensive exam, project required; for doctorate, one foreign language (computer language can substitute), dissertation, comprehensive exam required. *Entrance requirements:* For master's and doctorate, GRE General Test, GRE Subject Test, TOEFL (minimum score of 550 required). *Application deadline:* For fall admission, 8/1 (priority date). Application fee: $35. *Financial aid:*

Mathematics

University of Alaska Fairbanks *(continued)*
Research assistantships, teaching assistantships, career-related internships or fieldwork available. Financial aid application deadline: 4/1. *Faculty research:* Numerical analysis, graph theory, statistics, theoretical computer science, algebra topology. *Unit head:* Dr. Clifton Lando, Head, 907-474-7332.

University of Alberta, Faculty of Graduate Studies and Research, Department of Mathematical Sciences, Edmonton, AB T6G 2E1, Canada. Offers applied mathematics (M Sc, PhD); mathematical finance (M Sc); mathematical physics (M Sc, PhD); mathematics (M Sc, PhD); statistics (M Sc, PhD, Postgraduate Diploma). Part-time programs available. Terminal master's awarded for partial completion of doctoral program. *Degree requirements:* For master's, thesis required (for some programs), foreign language not required; for doctorate, dissertation required, foreign language not required. *Faculty research:* Classical and functional analysis, algebra, differential equations, geometry.

The University of Arizona, Graduate College, College of Science, Department of Mathematics, Tucson, AZ 85721. Offers M Ed, MA, MS, PhD. Part-time programs available. *Faculty:* 62. *Students:* 45 full-time (14 women), 11 part-time (3 women); includes 2 minority (1 African American, 1 Asian American or Pacific Islander), 18 international. Average age 30. 44 applicants, 66% accepted. In 1998, 10 master's, 3 doctorates awarded. *Degree requirements:* For master's, computer language required, foreign language and thesis not required; for doctorate, 2 foreign languages (computer language can substitute for one), dissertation required. *Entrance requirements:* For master's and doctorate, GRE (strongly preferred), TOEFL (minimum score of 550 required). Application fee: $35. *Financial aid:* Fellowships, research assistantships, teaching assistantships, scholarships and tuition waivers (full and partial) available. Financial aid application deadline: 3/5. *Faculty research:* Algebra/number theory, computational science, dynamical systems, geometry, analysis. *Unit head:* Dr. Alan Newell, Head, 520-621-2868. *Application contact:* Dr. John Palmer, Chairman, Graduate Committee, 520-621-2068, Fax: 520-621-8322.

University of Arkansas, Graduate School, J. William Fulbright College of Arts and Sciences, Department of Mathematical Sciences, Program in Mathematics, Fayetteville, AR 72701-1201. Offers MS, PhD. *Students:* 24 full-time (9 women), 4 part-time (1 woman); includes 5 minority (4 Asian Americans or Pacific Islanders, 1 Native American), 11 international. 22 applicants, 73% accepted. In 1998, 4 master's, 1 doctorate awarded. *Degree requirements:* For master's, thesis or alternative required, foreign language not required; for doctorate, 2 foreign languages, dissertation required. Application fee: $40 ($50 for international students). Tuition, state resident: full-time $3,186. Tuition, nonresident: full-time $7,560. Required fees: $378. *Financial aid:* Teaching assistantships, career-related internships or fieldwork and Federal Work-Study available. Aid available to part-time students. Financial aid application deadline: 4/1; financial aid applicants required to submit FAFSA. *Unit head:* Dr. Itrel Monroe, Chair of Studies, 501-575-3351, E-mail: gradmath@comp.uark.edu.

University of British Columbia, Faculty of Graduate Studies, Faculty of Science, Department of Mathematics, Vancouver, BC V6T 1Z2, Canada. Offers M Sc, MA, PhD. *Degree requirements:* For doctorate, dissertation, comprehensive exam required. *Entrance requirements:* For master's and doctorate, TOEFL, TSE.

University of Calgary, Faculty of Graduate Studies, Faculty of Science, Department of Mathematics and Statistics, Calgary, AB T2N 1N4, Canada. Offers M Sc, PhD. *Faculty:* 33 full-time (2 women). *Students:* 28 full-time (8 women). Average age 30. 50 applicants, 26% accepted. In 1998, 9 master's, 2 doctorates awarded (100% entered university research/teaching). *Degree requirements:* For doctorate, dissertation, candidacy exam required, foreign language not required, foreign language not required. *Entrance requirements:* For master's, TOEFL (minimum score of 600 required), honours degree in related field; for doctorate, TOEFL (minimum score of 600 required), MA or M Sc. *Average time to degree:* Master's–2.6 years full-time, 4.1 years part-time; doctorate–4.9 years full-time. *Application deadline:* For fall admission, 2/1 (priority date). Applications are processed on a rolling basis. Application fee: $60. *Financial aid:* In 1998–99, 23 students received aid, including 10 research assistantships with partial tuition reimbursements available (averaging $3,920 per year); fellowships, teaching assistantships with partial tuition reimbursements available *Faculty research:* Combinatorics, applied mathematics, statistics, probability, analysis. Total annual research expenditures: $295,850. *Unit head:* E. G. Enns, Head, 403-220-6303, Fax: 403-282-5150, E-mail: enns@math.ucalgary.ca. *Application contact:* Joanne Mellard, Graduate Secretary, 403-220-6299, Fax: 403-282-5150, E-mail: gradapps@math.ucalgary.ca.

University of California, Berkeley, Graduate Division, College of Letters and Science, Department of Mathematics, Berkeley, CA 94720-1500. Offers applied mathematics (PhD); mathematics (MA, PhD, C Phil). *Students:* 168 full-time (35 women); includes 24 minority (6 African Americans, 10 Asian Americans or Pacific Islanders, 7 Hispanic Americans, 1 Native American), 48 international. Average age 23. 325 applicants, 22% accepted. In 1998, 10 master's, 19 doctorates, 20 other advanced degrees awarded. Terminal master's awarded for partial completion of doctoral program. *Degree requirements:* For master's, exam or thesis required; for doctorate, dissertation, qualifying exam required. *Entrance requirements:* For master's and doctorate, GRE General Test, GRE Subject Test, minimum GPA of 3.0. *Average time to degree:* Master's–2 years full-time; doctorate–6 years full-time. *Application deadline:* For fall admission, 1/15. Application fee: $40. *Financial aid:* Fellowships, research assistantships, teaching assistantships, institutionally-sponsored loans available. Financial aid application deadline: 12/15. *Faculty research:* Algebra, analysis, logic, geometry/topology. *Unit head:* Calvin C. Moore, Chair, 510-642-4129. *Application contact:* Janet Yonan, Graduate Assistant for Admission, 510-642-0665, Fax: 510-642-8204, E-mail: yonan@math.berkeley.edu.

University of California, Davis, Graduate Studies, Program in Mathematics, Davis, CA 95616. Offers MA, MAT, PhD. *Faculty:* 28 full-time (4 women). *Students:* 34 full-time (14 women), 1 (woman) part-time; includes 7 minority (1 African American, 5 Asian Americans or Pacific Islanders, 1 Hispanic American), 3 international. 57 applicants, 75% accepted. In 1998, 9 master's, 1 doctorate awarded. Terminal master's awarded for partial completion of doctoral program. *Degree requirements:* For master's, thesis not required; for doctorate, one foreign language, dissertation required. *Entrance requirements:* For master's and doctorate, GRE General Test, GRE Subject Test, minimum GPA of 3.0. *Average time to degree:* Master's–2 years full-time; doctorate–5 years full-time. *Application deadline:* For fall admission, 4/1. Application fee: $40. Electronic applications accepted. *Financial aid:* In 1998–99, 32 students received aid, including 5 fellowships with full and partial tuition reimbursements available, 2 research assistantships with full and partial tuition reimbursements available, 24 teaching assistantships with full and partial tuition reimbursements available; Federal Work-Study, grants, institutionally-sponsored loans, and scholarships also available. Financial aid application deadline: 1/15; financial aid applicants required to submit FAFSA. *Faculty research:* Mathematical physics, geometric topology, probability, partial differential equations, applied mathematics. *Unit head:* John Hunter, Graduate Adviser, 530-752-8131. *Application contact:* Graduate Coordinator, 530-752-8131, Fax: 530-752-6635, E-mail: gradcord@ucdmath.ucdavis.edu.

University of California, Irvine, Office of Research and Graduate Studies, School of Physical Sciences, Department of Mathematics, Irvine, CA 92697. Offers MS, PhD. *Faculty:* 51. *Students:* 50 full-time (13 women), 2 part-time (both women); includes 17 minority (12 Asian Americans or Pacific Islanders, 5 Hispanic Americans), 13 international. 43 applicants, 60% accepted. In 1998, 3 master's, 2 doctorates awarded. Terminal master's awarded for partial completion of doctoral program. *Degree requirements:* For master's, one foreign language required, (computer language can substitute); for doctorate, 2 foreign languages, computer language, dissertation required. *Entrance requirements:* For master's, GRE General Test, GRE Subject Test, TOEFL (minimum score of 550 required), TSE (minimum score of 50 required for teaching assistantships), minimum GPA of 3.0; for doctorate, GRE General Test, GRE Subject Test, TOEFL (minimum score of 550 required), TSE (minimum score of 50

required for teaching assistantships). *Application deadline:* For fall admission, 1/15 (priority date). Applications are processed on a rolling basis. Application fee: $40. Electronic applications accepted. *Financial aid:* Fellowships, research assistantships, teaching assistantships, institutionally-sponsored loans and tuition waivers (full and partial) available. Financial aid application deadline: 3/2; financial aid applicants required to submit FAFSA. *Faculty research:* Algebra and logic, geometry and topology, probability, mathematical physics. *Unit head:* Matthew Foreman, Vice Chair of Graduate Studies, 949-824-5424, Fax: 949-824-7993, E-mail: mforeman@math.uci.edu. *Application contact:* Jennifer Curtis, Graduate Coordinator, 949-824-5544, Fax: 949-824-7993, E-mail: jcurtis@math.uci.edu.

University of California, Los Angeles, Graduate Division, College of Letters and Science, Department of Mathematics, Los Angeles, CA 90095. Offers MA, MAT, PhD. *Students:* 124 full-time (25 women); includes 28 minority (4 African Americans, 22 Asian Americans or Pacific Islanders, 2 Hispanic Americans), 36 international. 170 applicants, 56% accepted. *Degree requirements:* For master's, comprehensive exam, essay required, foreign language and thesis not required; for doctorate, dissertation, oral and written qualifying exams required. *Entrance requirements:* For master's, GRE General Test, GRE Subject Test, minimum GPA of 3.2 in mathematics; for doctorate, GRE General Test, GRE Subject Test, minimum GPA of 3.5 in mathematics. *Application deadline:* For fall admission, 12/15. Application fee: $40. Electronic applications accepted. *Financial aid:* In 1998–99, 117 fellowships, 74 research assistantships were awarded.; teaching assistantships, Federal Work-Study, institutionally-sponsored loans, scholarships, and tuition waivers (full and partial) also available. Financial aid application deadline: 3/1. *Unit head:* Dr. Tony F. C. Chan, Chair, 310-825-4971. *Application contact:* Departmental Office, 310-825-4971, E-mail: chris@math.ucla.edu.

University of California, Riverside, Graduate Division, College of Natural and Agricultural Sciences, Department of Mathematics, Riverside, CA 92521-0102. Offers applied mathematics (MS); mathematics (MS, PhD). Part-time programs available. *Faculty:* 21 full-time (2 women). *Students:* 24 full-time (6 women); includes 5 minority (2 Asian Americans or Pacific Islanders, 2 Hispanic Americans, 1 Native American), 6 international. Average age 30. In 1998, 6 master's, 7 doctorates awarded. Terminal master's awarded for partial completion of doctoral program. *Degree requirements:* For master's, comprehensive exams required, foreign language and thesis not required; for doctorate, dissertation, qualifying exams required, foreign language not required. *Entrance requirements:* For master's and doctorate, GRE General Test (minimum combined score of 1100 required), TOEFL (minimum score of 550 required), minimum GPA of 3.2. *Average time to degree:* Master's–1.7 years full-time; doctorate–6 years full-time. *Application deadline:* For fall admission, 5/1; for winter admission, 9/1; for spring admission, 12/1. Applications are processed on a rolling basis. Application fee: $40. *Financial aid:* In 1998–99, 9 students received aid, including teaching assistantships with full and partial tuition reimbursements available (averaging $13,329 per year); fellowships with tuition reimbursements available, research assistantships, career-related internships or fieldwork, Federal Work-Study, institutionally-sponsored loans, and tuition waivers (full and partial) also available. Financial aid application deadline: 2/1; financial aid applicants required to submit FAFSA. *Faculty research:* Algebraic geometry, commutative algebra, Lie algebra, differential equations, differential geometry. *Unit head:* Dr. Reinhard Schultz, Chair, 909-787-6459, Fax: 909-787-7314, E-mail: schultz@ucrmath.ucr.edu. *Application contact:* Janice Carter, Graduate Program Assistant, 909-787-3113, Fax: 909-787-7314.

University of California, San Diego, Graduate Studies and Research, Department of Mathematics, La Jolla, CA 92093-5003. Offers applied mathematics (MA); mathematics (MA, PhD); statistics (MS). *Faculty:* 54. *Students:* 65 (16 women). 147 applicants, 22% accepted. In 1998, 12 master's, 10 doctorates awarded. *Degree requirements:* For master's, one foreign language required, thesis not required; for doctorate, dissertation required. *Entrance requirements:* For master's and doctorate, GRE General Test, GRE Subject Test. Application fee: $40. *Unit head:* Jeffrey Remmel, Chair, 619-534-2643, E-mail: jremmel@ucsd.edu. *Application contact:* Lois Stewart, Graduate Coordinator, 619-534-6887.

University of California, Santa Barbara, Graduate Division, College of Letters and Science, Division of Math, Life and Physical Science, Department of Mathematics, Program in Mathematics, Santa Barbara, CA 93106. Offers MA, PhD. *Faculty:* 31 full-time (2 women). *Students:* 60 full-time (20 women). In 1998, 11 master's, 4 doctorates awarded. Terminal master's awarded for partial completion of doctoral program. *Degree requirements:* For master's, thesis or alternative required, foreign language not required; for doctorate, one foreign language, dissertation required. *Entrance requirements:* For master's and doctorate, GRE General Test, GRE Subject Test, TOEFL (minimum score of 550 required). *Application deadline:* For fall admission, 5/1. Application fee: $40. Electronic applications accepted. *Financial aid:* Application deadline: 1/15. *Unit head:* Debra Bomar, Graduate Coordinator, 619-534-3293. *Application contact:* Medina Price, Staff Graduate Adviser, 805-893-8192, E-mail: price@math.ucsb.edu.

University of California, Santa Cruz, Graduate Division, Division of Natural Sciences, Department of Mathematics, Santa Cruz, CA 95064. Offers applied mathematics (MA, PhD); mathematics (MA, PhD). *Faculty:* 16 full-time. *Students:* 44 full-time (12 women); includes 8 minority (1 African American, 6 Asian Americans or Pacific Islanders, 1 Hispanic American), 10 international. 35 applicants, 86% accepted. In 1998, 4 master's, 3 doctorates awarded. *Degree requirements:* For doctorate, one foreign language (computer language can substitute), dissertation, qualifying exam required. *Entrance requirements:* For doctorate, GRE General Test, GRE Subject Test. *Application deadline:* For fall admission, 2/1. Application fee: $40. *Financial aid:* Fellowships, research assistantships, teaching assistantships, Federal Work-Study and institutionally-sponsored loans available. Financial aid application deadline: 2/1. *Unit head:* Dr. Geoffrey Mason, Chairperson, 831-459-2215, E-mail: gem@cats.ucsc.edu. *Application contact:* Graduate Admissions, 831-459-2301.

University of Central Arkansas, Graduate School, College of Natural Sciences and Math, Department of Mathematics, Conway, AR 72035-0001. Offers MA. Part-time programs available. *Faculty:* 19 full-time (4 women). *Students:* 7 full-time (5 women), 3 part-time (1 woman). Average age 25. 3 applicants, 100% accepted. In 1998, 3 degrees awarded. *Degree requirements:* For master's, comprehensive exam required, thesis optional, foreign language not required. *Entrance requirements:* For master's, GRE General Test, minimum GPA of 2.7. *Average time to degree:* Master's–2 years full-time, 4 years part-time. *Application deadline:* For fall admission, 3/1 (priority date); for spring admission, 10/1 (priority date). Applications are processed on a rolling basis. Application fee: $25 ($40 for international students). Tuition, state resident: part-time $144 per hour. Tuition, nonresident: part-time $297 per hour. Required fees: $17 per hour. $15 per term. Tuition and fees vary according to program. *Financial aid:* In 1998–99, 10 students received aid, including 3 research assistantships with partial tuition reimbursements available (averaging $8,000 per year), 2 teaching assistantships with partial tuition reimbursements available (averaging $11,000 per year); Federal Work-Study and unspecified assistantships also available. Financial aid application deadline: 2/15. *Unit head:* Dr. Donna Foss, Chair, 501-450-3147, Fax: 501-450-5084, E-mail: donnaf@cc1.mail.edu. *Application contact:* Nancy Gage, Co-Admissions Secretary, 501-450-3124, Fax: 501-450-5339, E-mail: nancyg@ecom.uca.edu.

University of Central Florida, College of Arts and Sciences, Department of Mathematics, Orlando, FL 32816. Offers mathematical science (MS); mathematics (PhD). Part-time and evening/weekend programs available. *Faculty:* 30 full-time, 5 part-time. *Students:* 32 full-time (14 women), 15 part-time (5 women); includes 9 minority (1 African American, 6 Asian Americans or Pacific Islanders, 2 Hispanic Americans), 3 international. Average age 35. 25 applicants, 48% accepted. In 1998, 10 master's, 9 doctorates awarded. *Degree requirements:* For master's, thesis or alternative required, foreign language not required; for doctorate, computer language, dissertation, candidacy exam required, foreign language not required. *Entrance requirements:* For master's, GRE General Test (minimum combined score of 1000 required), TOEFL (minimum score of 550 required; 213 computer-based), minimum GPA of 3.0 in last 60 hours; for doctorate, GRE Subject Test, TOEFL (minimum score of 550 required; 213

computer-based), minimum GPA of 3.0 in last 60 hours or master's qualifying exam. *Application deadline:* For fall admission, 7/15; for spring admission, 12/15. Application fee: $20. Tuition, state resident: full-time $2,054; part-time $137 per credit. Tuition, nonresident: full-time $7,207; part-time $480 per credit. Required fees: $47 per term. *Financial aid:* In 1998–99, 8 fellowships with partial tuition reimbursements (averaging $2,792 per year), 4 research assistantships with partial tuition reimbursements (averaging $3,924 per year), 44 teaching assistantships with partial tuition reimbursements (averaging $5,608 per year) were awarded.; career-related internships or fieldwork, Federal Work-Study, institutionally-sponsored loans, tuition waivers (partial), and unspecified assistantships also available. Financial aid application deadline: 3/1; financial aid applicants required to submit FAFSA. *Faculty research:* Applied mathematics, analysis, approximation theory, graph theory, mathematical statistics. Total annual research expenditures: $20,000. *Unit head:* Dr. J. R. Cannon, Chair, 407-823-2795, Fax: 407-823-6253, E-mail: jcannon@pegasus.cc.ucf.edu. *Application contact:* Dr. David Rollins, Coordinator, 407-823-5239, Fax: 407-823-6253, E-mail: drollins@pegasus.cc.ucf.edu.

See in-depth description on page 759.

University of Central Oklahoma, Graduate College, College of Mathematics and Science, Department of Mathematics and Statistics, Edmond, OK 73034-5209. Offers applied mathematical sciences (MS), including computer science, mathematics, mathematics/computer science teaching, statistics. *Accreditation:* NCATE. Part-time programs available. *Faculty:* 11 full-time (3 women), 1 part-time (0 women). Average age 34. 17 applicants, 100% accepted. In 1998, 8 degrees awarded. *Degree requirements:* For master's, computer language, thesis required, foreign language not required. *Application deadline:* For fall admission, 8/23 (priority date). Applications are processed on a rolling basis. Application fee: $15. *Financial aid:* Federal Work-Study and unspecified assistantships available. Financial aid application deadline: 3/31; financial aid applicants required to submit FAFSA. *Faculty research:* Curvature, FAA, math education. *Unit head:* Dr. David Bridge, Chairperson, 405-974-5697. *Application contact:* Dr. James Yates, Adviser, 405-974-5386, Fax: 405-974-3824, E-mail: jyates@aix1.ucok.edu.

University of Charleston, South Carolina, Graduate School, School of Sciences and Mathematics, Department of Mathematics, Charleston, SC 29424-0001. Offers MS. *Entrance requirements:* For master's, GRE, TOEFL, BS in mathematics or equivalent. *Faculty research:* Algebra and discrete mathematics, dynamical systems, probability and statistics, analysis and topology, applied mathematics.

University of Chicago, Division of the Physical Sciences, Department of Mathematics, Program in Financial Mathematics, Chicago, IL 60637-1513. Offers MS. Part-time and evening/weekend programs available. *Degree requirements:* For master's, foreign language and thesis not required. *Entrance requirements:* For master's, GRE General Test, GRE Subject Test, TOEFL.

University of Cincinnati, Division of Research and Advanced Studies, McMicken College of Arts and Sciences, Department of Mathematics, Cincinnati, OH 45221-0091. Offers applied mathematics (MS, PhD); mathematics education (MAT); pure mathematics (MS, PhD); statistics (MS, PhD). *Accreditation:* NCATE (one or more programs are accredited). *Faculty:* 38 full-time. *Students:* 69 full-time (41 women), 14 part-time (7 women); includes 6 minority (all Asian Americans or Pacific Islanders), 56 international. 27 applicants, 100% accepted. In 1998, 24 master's, 1 doctorate awarded. *Degree requirements:* For master's, thesis optional, foreign language not required; for doctorate, dissertation, final written exam required. *Entrance requirements:* For master's, TOEFL (minimum score of 520 required). *Average time to degree:* Master's–3 years full-time; doctorate–4 years full-time. *Application deadline:* For fall admission, 2/1. Application fee: $30. *Financial aid:* Fellowships, tuition waivers (full) and unspecified assistantships available. Aid available to part-time students. Financial aid application deadline: 3/1. *Faculty research:* Algebra, analysis, differential equations, numerical analysis. Total annual research expenditures: $134,918. *Unit head:* James Osterburg, Head, 513-556-4054, Fax: 513-556-3417, E-mail: james.osterburg@uc.edu. *Application contact:* Diego Murio, Graduate Program Director, 513-556-4088, Fax: 513-556-3417, E-mail: diego.murio@uc.edu.

University of Colorado at Boulder, Graduate School, College of Arts and Sciences, Department of Mathematics, Boulder, CO 80309. Offers MA, PhD. Terminal master's awarded for partial completion of doctoral program. *Degree requirements:* For master's, thesis or alternative, comprehensive exam required, foreign language not required; for doctorate, dissertation, comprehensive exam required. *Entrance requirements:* For master's, minimum undergraduate GPA of 2.75.

University of Connecticut, Graduate School, College of Liberal Arts and Sciences, Field of Mathematics, Storrs, CT 06269. Offers MS, PhD. *Degree requirements:* For doctorate, dissertation required. *Entrance requirements:* For master's and doctorate, GRE General Test, GRE Subject Test.

University of Delaware, College of Arts and Science, Department of Mathematical Sciences, Newark, DE 19716. Offers applied mathematics (MA, MS, PhD); mathematics (MA, MS, PhD). Part-time programs available. *Faculty:* 37. *Students:* 40 full-time (13 women), 1 (woman) part-time; includes 1 minority (African American), 19 international. Average age 25. 77 applicants, 19% accepted. In 1998, 7 master's, 5 doctorates awarded. Terminal master's awarded for partial completion of doctoral program. *Degree requirements:* For master's, thesis required (for some programs), foreign language not required; for doctorate, dissertation, qualifying exam required. *Entrance requirements:* For master's and doctorate, GRE General Test (minimum combined score of 1050 required). *Application deadline:* For fall admission, 3/1 (priority date); for spring admission, 12/15 (priority date). Application fee: $45. *Financial aid:* In 1998–99, 2 fellowships with tuition reimbursements, 1 research assistantship with tuition reimbursement, 35 teaching assistantships with tuition reimbursements were awarded.; career-related internships or fieldwork, institutionally-sponsored loans, scholarships, and tuition waivers (full and partial) also available. Financial aid application deadline: 3/1. *Faculty research:* Scattering theory, inverse problems, fluid dynamics, numerical analysis, combinatorics. *Unit head:* Dr. L. P. Cook, Chair, 302-831-2651, E-mail: cook@math.udel.edu. *Application contact:* Deborah See, Graduate Secretary, 302-831-2654, Fax: 302-831-4511, E-mail: see@math.udel.edu.

See in-depth description on page 761.

University of Denver, Graduate Studies, Faculty of Natural Sciences, Mathematics and Engineering, Department of Mathematics and Computer Science, Denver, CO 80208. Offers applied mathematics (MA, MS); computer science (MS); mathematics and computer science (PhD). Part-time programs available. *Faculty:* 14. *Students:* 56 (16 women); includes 8 minority (1 African American, 6 Asian Americans or Pacific Islanders, 1 Hispanic American) 34 international. 104 applicants, 99% accepted. In 1998, 27 master's, 3 doctorates awarded. Terminal master's awarded for partial completion of doctoral program. *Degree requirements:* For master's, computer language, foreign language, or laboratory experience required, thesis not required; for doctorate, one foreign language (computer language can substitute), dissertation, oral and written exams required. *Entrance requirements:* For master's and doctorate, GRE General Test, TOEFL (minimum score of 550 required). *Application deadline:* Applications are processed on a rolling basis. Application fee: $40 ($45 for international students). *Financial aid:* In 1998–99, 23 students received aid, including 6 fellowships with full and partial tuition reimbursements available (averaging $12,000 per year), 3 research assistantships with full and partial tuition reimbursements available (averaging $11,724 per year), 14 teaching assistantships with full and partial tuition reimbursements available (averaging $11,316 per year); career-related internships or fieldwork, Federal Work-Study, institutionally-sponsored loans, and scholarships also available. Aid available to part-time students. Financial aid application deadline: 3/1; financial aid applicants required to submit FAFSA. *Faculty research:* Real-time software, convex bodies, multidimensional data, parallel computer clusters. Total annual research expenditures: $163,312. *Unit head:* Dr. Joel Cohen, Chairperson, 303-871-3292. *Application contact:* Rick Ball, Graduate Adviser, 303-871-2453.

University of Detroit Mercy, College of Engineering and Science, Department of Mathematics and Computer Science, Detroit, MI 48219-0900. Offers computer science (MSCS); elementary mathematics education (MATM); junior high mathematics education (MATM); mathematics (MA); secondary mathematics education (MATM). Evening/weekend programs available. *Degree requirements:* Foreign language not required. *Entrance requirements:* For master's, minimum GPA of 3.0.

University of Florida, Graduate School, College of Liberal Arts and Sciences, Department of Mathematics, Gainesville, FL 32611. Offers applied mathematics (MS, PhD); mathematics (MA, MS, PhD); mathematics teaching (MAT, MST). *Accreditation:* NCATE (one or more programs are accredited). Part-time programs available. *Faculty:* 55. *Students:* 74 full-time (13 women), 1 part-time; includes 10 minority (1 African American, 5 Asian Americans or Pacific Islanders, 4 Hispanic Americans), 29 international. 113 applicants, 51% accepted. In 1998, 17 master's, 7 doctorates awarded. Terminal master's awarded for partial completion of doctoral program. *Degree requirements:* For master's, computer language required, thesis optional; for doctorate, dissertation required. *Entrance requirements:* For master's and doctorate, GRE General Test, TOEFL, minimum GPA of 3.0. *Application deadline:* For fall admission, 6/1 (priority date). Applications are processed on a rolling basis. Application fee: $20. Electronic applications accepted. *Financial aid:* In 1998–99, 65 students received aid, including 3 fellowships, 11 research assistantships, 58 teaching assistantships; career-related internships or fieldwork and unspecified assistantships also available. Financial aid application deadline: 3/1. *Faculty research:* Combinatorics and number theory, group theory, probability theory, logic, differential geometry and mathematical physics. *Unit head:* Dr. Alladi Krishnaswani, Chairman, 352-392-0281 Ext. 227, Fax: 352-392-8357, E-mail: alladi@math.ufl.edu. *Application contact:* Dr. Paul Robinson, Graduate Coordinator, 352-392-0281 Ext. 273, Fax: 352-392-8357, E-mail: plr@math.ufl.edu.

University of Georgia, Graduate School, College of Arts and Sciences, Department of Mathematics, Athens, GA 30602. Offers applied mathematical science (MAMS); mathematics (MA, PhD). *Faculty:* 34 full-time (3 women). *Students:* 32 full-time (7 women), 3 part-time. 72 applicants, 10% accepted. In 1998, 2 master's, 6 doctorates awarded. *Degree requirements:* For master's; for doctorate, 2 foreign languages, dissertation required. *Entrance requirements:* For master's and doctorate, GRE General Test. *Application deadline:* For fall admission, 7/1 (priority date); for spring admission, 11/15. Application fee: $30. Electronic applications accepted. *Financial aid:* Fellowships, research assistantships, teaching assistantships, unspecified assistantships available. *Unit head:* Dr. Kenneth D. Johnson, Graduate Coordinator, 706-542-2580, Fax: 706-542-2573, E-mail: grad@math.uga.edu.

University of Guelph, Faculty of Graduate Studies, College of Physical and Engineering Science, Department of Mathematics and Statistics, Guelph, ON N1G 2W1, Canada. Offers applied mathematics (PhD); applied statistics (PhD); mathematics and statistics (M Sc). Part-time programs available. *Faculty:* 23 full-time (2 women), 3 part-time (1 woman). *Students:* 36 full-time (9 women), 1 part-time, 7 international. 30 applicants, 33% accepted. In 1998, 7 master's, 3 doctorates awarded (100% found work related to degree). *Degree requirements:* For master's, thesis required (for some programs), foreign language not required; for doctorate, dissertation required, foreign language not required. *Entrance requirements:* For master's, minimum B- average during previous 2 years; for doctorate, minimum B average. *Average time to degree:* Master's–2 years full-time; doctorate–4 years full-time. Application fee: $60. *Expenses:* Tuition and fees charges are reported in Canadian dollars. Tuition, area resident: Full-time $4,725 Canadian dollars; part-time $1,055 Canadian dollars per term. International tuition: $6,999 Canadian dollars full-time. Required fees: $295 Canadian dollars per term. *Financial aid:* In 1998–99, 16 research assistantships, teaching assistantships (averaging $9,500 per year) were awarded.; fellowships, scholarships also available. Financial aid applicants required to submit CSS PROFILE. *Faculty research:* Dynamical systems, mathematical biology, numerical analysis, linear and nonlinear models, reliability and bioassay. Total annual research expenditures: $447,260. *Unit head:* Dr. J. Mokanski, Chair, 519-824-4120 Ext. 6556, Fax: 519-837-0221, E-mail: chair@msnet.mathstat.uoguelph.ca. *Application contact:* Susan McCormick, Graduate Administrative Assistant, 519-824-4120 Ext. 6553, Fax: 519-837-0221, E-mail: smccormi@msnet.mathstat.uoguelph.ca.

University of Hawaii at Manoa, Graduate Division, College of Arts and Sciences, College of Natural Sciences, Department of Mathematics, Honolulu, HI 96822. Offers MA, PhD. Part-time programs available. *Faculty:* 34 full-time (0 women). *Students:* 10 full-time (4 women), 8 part-time (2 women); includes 5 minority (all Asian Americans or Pacific Islanders), 9 international. Average age 27. 24 applicants, 54% accepted. In 1998, 4 master's awarded (50% found work related to degree, 50% continued full-time study); 1 doctorate awarded. Terminal master's awarded for partial completion of doctoral program. *Degree requirements:* For master's, comprehensive exams required, foreign language and thesis not required; for doctorate, 2 foreign languages (computer language can substitute for one), dissertation, comprehensive exams required. *Entrance requirements:* For master's and doctorate, GRE General Test (minimum score of 650 on quantitative section required), TOEFL (minimum score of 500 required), minimum GPA of 3.0. *Average time to degree:* Master's–2.5 years full-time; doctorate–6 years full-time. *Application deadline:* For fall admission, 1/5; for spring admission, 9/1. Applications are processed on a rolling basis. Application fee: $25 ($50 for international students). *Financial aid:* In 1998–99, 1 research assistantship (averaging $16,176 per year), 12 teaching assistantships (averaging $13,134 per year) were awarded.; institutionally-sponsored loans, tuition waivers (full and partial), and unspecified assistantships also available. Aid available to part-time students. Financial aid application deadline: 3/1. *Faculty research:* Analysis, algebra, lattice theory, logic topology, differential geometry. *Unit head:* Dr. Thomas B. Hoover, Chair, 808-956-8792, Fax: 808-956-9139, E-mail: hoover@math.hawaii.edu. *Application contact:* Dr. Edward Bertram, Graduate Chair, 808-956-4677, Fax: 808-956-4659, E-mail: ed@math.hawaii.edu.

University of Houston, College of Natural Sciences and Mathematics, Department of Mathematics, Houston, TX 77004. Offers applied mathematics (MS); mathematics (MS, PhD). Part-time and evening/weekend programs available. *Faculty:* 41 full-time (2 women). *Students:* 29 full-time (10 women), 20 part-time (4 women); includes 10 minority (5 African Americans, 3 Asian Americans or Pacific Islanders, 1 Hispanic American, 1 Native American), 13 international. Average age 33. 60 applicants, 27% accepted. In 1998, 16 master's, 6 doctorates awarded. *Degree requirements:* For master's, thesis optional, foreign language not required; for doctorate, one foreign language, dissertation required. *Entrance requirements:* For master's, TOEFL (minimum score of 550 required; average 623), minimum GPA of 3.0 in last 60 hours, bachelor's degree in mathematics or related area; for doctorate, GRE General Test (minimum combined score of 1000 required), TOEFL, MS in mathematics or equivalent, minimum GPA of 3.0 in last 60 hours. *Application deadline:* For fall admission, 7/3 (priority date); for spring admission, 12/4. Applications are processed on a rolling basis. Application fee: $25 ($75 for international students). *Financial aid:* Fellowships, research assistantships, institutionally-sponsored loans, tuition waivers (partial), and teaching fellowships available. Aid available to part-time students. Financial aid application deadline: 3/15. *Faculty research:* Dynamical systems, scientific computing, partial differential equations, algebra, modern analysis. *Unit head:* Dr. Garret Etgen, Chair, 713-743-3510. *Application contact:* Pamela Draughn, Graduate Adviser, 713-743-3517.

See in-depth description on page 767.

University of Houston–Clear Lake, School of Natural and Applied Sciences, Program in Mathematical Sciences, Houston, TX 77058-1098. Offers MS. *Faculty:* 5 full-time (2 women). *Students:* 1 (woman) full-time, 9 part-time (8 women); includes 1 minority (Hispanic American), 1 international. Average age 32. *Degree requirements:* Foreign language not required. *Entrance requirements:* For master's, GRE General Test. *Application deadline:* Applications are processed on a rolling basis. Application fee: $30 ($70 for international students). *Financial aid:* Research assistantships, teaching assistantships available. Financial aid application deadline: 5/1. *Unit*

Mathematics

University of Houston–Clear Lake (continued)
head: Dr. Martin Spears, Chair, 281-283-3720, Fax: 281-283-3707. *Application contact:* Dr. Robert Ferebee, Associate Dean, 281-283-3700, Fax: 281-283-3707, E-mail: ferebee@uhcl4.cl.uh.edu.

University of Idaho, College of Graduate Studies, College of Letters and Science, Department of Mathematics and Statistics, Program in Mathematics, Moscow, ID 83844-4140. Offers mathematics (MS, PhD); mathematics education (MAT). *Accreditation:* NCATE (one or more programs are accredited). *Faculty:* 23 full-time (5 women), 4 part-time (1 woman). *Students:* 11 full-time (1 woman), 29 part-time (14 women), 5 international. In 1998, 3 master's, 3 doctorates awarded. *Degree requirements:* For master's, foreign language and thesis not required; for doctorate, dissertation required. *Entrance requirements:* For master's, minimum GPA of 2.8; for doctorate, minimum undergraduate GPA of 2.8, 3.0 graduate. *Application deadline:* For fall admission, 8/1; for spring admission, 12/15. Application fee: $35 ($45 for international students). *Financial aid:* In 1998–99, 8 teaching assistantships (averaging $11,009 per year) were awarded. Financial aid application deadline: 2/15. *Faculty research:* Algebra, topology, analysis. *Unit head:* Dr. Erol Barbut, Chair, Department of Mathematics and Statistics, 208-885-6742.

University of Illinois at Chicago, Graduate College, College of Liberal Arts and Sciences, Department of Mathematics, Statistics, and Computer Science, Chicago, IL 60607-7128. Offers applied mathematics (MS, DA, PhD); computer science (MS, DA, PhD); probability and statistics (MS, DA, PhD); pure mathematics (MS, DA, PhD); teaching of mathematics (MST). *Faculty:* 69 full-time (4 women). *Students:* 119 full-time (47 women), 30 part-time (12 women). Average age 27. 121 applicants, 62% accepted. In 1998, 34 master's, 11 doctorates awarded. *Degree requirements:* For master's, comprehensive exam required, foreign language and thesis not required; for doctorate, one foreign language, dissertation required. *Entrance requirements:* For master's and doctorate, GRE General Test, TOEFL (minimum score of 550 required), minimum GPA of 3.75 on a 5.0 scale. *Application deadline:* For fall admission, 7/3; for spring admission, 11/8. Application fee: $40 ($50 for international students). *Financial aid:* In 1998–99, 68 students received aid; fellowships, research assistantships, teaching assistantships, tuition waivers (full) available. *Unit head:* Henri Gillet, Head, 312-996-3044. *Application contact:* David Marker, Director of Graduate Studies, 312-996-3041.

See in-depth description on page 769.

University of Illinois at Urbana–Champaign, Graduate College, College of Liberal Arts and Sciences, Department of Mathematics, Urbana, IL 61801. Offers applied mathematics (MS); mathematics (MS, PhD); teaching of mathematics (MS). *Faculty:* 81 full-time (6 women). *Students:* 159 full-time (40 women); includes 9 minority (1 African American, 7 Asian Americans or Pacific Islanders, 1 Hispanic American), 99 international. 226 applicants, 15% accepted. In 1998, 38 master's, 19 doctorates awarded. *Degree requirements:* For master's, foreign language and thesis not required; for doctorate, dissertation required. *Entrance requirements:* For master's, minimum GPA of 4.0 on a 5.0 scale. *Application deadline:* Applications are processed on a rolling basis. Application fee: $40 ($50 for international students). Tuition, state resident: full-time $4,040. Tuition, nonresident: full-time $11,192. Full-time tuition and fees vary according to program. *Financial aid:* In 1998–99, 9 fellowships, 15 research assistantships, 130 teaching assistantships were awarded.; tuition waivers (full and partial) also available. Financial aid application deadline: 2/15. *Unit head:* Philippe Tondeur, Chair, 217-333-3352. *Application contact:* John W. Gray, Director of Graduate Studies, 217-333-3354, Fax: 217-333-9576, E-mail: gray@math.uiuc.edu.

See in-depth description on page 771.

The University of Iowa, Graduate College, College of Liberal Arts, Department of Mathematics, Iowa City, IA 52242-1316. Offers MS, PhD. *Faculty:* 54 full-time, 1 part-time. *Students:* 40 full-time (7 women), 27 part-time (6 women); includes 14 minority (7 African Americans, 1 Asian American or Pacific Islander, 6 Hispanic Americans), 33 international. 88 applicants, 78% accepted. In 1998, 15 master's, 9 doctorates awarded. *Degree requirements:* For master's, thesis optional; for doctorate, dissertation, comprehensive exam required. *Entrance requirements:* For master's and doctorate, GRE General Test. *Application deadline:* Applications are processed on a rolling basis. Application fee: $30 ($50 for international students). *Financial aid:* In 1998–99, 9 fellowships, 2 research assistantships, 51 teaching assistantships were awarded. Financial aid applicants required to submit FAFSA. *Unit head:* Bor-Luh Lin, Chair, 319-335-0714, Fax: 319-335-0627.

University of Kansas, Graduate School, College of Liberal Arts and Sciences, Department of Mathematics, Program in Mathematics, Lawrence, KS 66045. Offers MA, PhD. *Degree requirements:* For master's, thesis or alternative required, foreign language not required; for doctorate, dissertation required. *Entrance requirements:* For master's and doctorate, TOEFL (minimum score of 570 required). *Financial aid:* Application deadline: 2/1. *Application contact:* Daniel Katz, Graduate Director, 785-864-4324.

University of Kentucky, Graduate School, Graduate School Programs from the College of Arts and Sciences, Program in Mathematics, Lexington, KY 40506-0032. Offers MA, MS, PhD. *Degree requirements:* For master's, comprehensive exam required, thesis optional, foreign language not required; for doctorate, dissertation, comprehensive exam required. *Entrance requirements:* For master's, GRE General Test, minimum undergraduate GPA of 2.5; for doctorate, GRE General Test, minimum graduate GPA of 3.0. *Faculty research:* Numerical analysis, combinatorics, partial differential equations, algebra and number theory, real and complex analysis.

University of Louisville, Graduate School, College of Arts and Sciences, Department of Mathematics, Louisville, KY 40292-0001. Offers MA. Evening/weekend programs available. *Faculty:* 30 full-time (4 women), 13 part-time (6 women). *Students:* 22 full-time (11 women), 11 part-time (9 women); includes 4 minority (2 African Americans, 1 Asian American or Pacific Islander, 1 Hispanic American), 4 international. Average age 31. 27 applicants, 56% accepted. In 1998, 3 degrees awarded. *Degree requirements:* For master's, thesis optional, foreign language not required. *Entrance requirements:* For master's, GRE General Test (minimum combined score of 1150 required). *Application deadline:* Applications are processed on a rolling basis. Application fee: $25. *Financial aid:* In 1998–99, 23 teaching assistantships with full tuition reimbursements (averaging $9,600 per year) were awarded. *Unit head:* Dr. Michael S. Jacobson, Chair, 502-852-6826, Fax: 802-852-7132, E-mail: mikej@louisville.edu. *Application contact:* Dr. Lee M. Larson, Graduate Studies Director, 502-852-6826, Fax: 502-852-7132, E-mail: llarson@louisville.edu.

University of Maine, Graduate School, College of Liberal Arts and Sciences, Department of Mathematics and Statistics, Orono, ME 04469. Offers mathematics (MA). *Faculty:* 15 full-time (1 woman). *Students:* 6 full-time (2 women), 1 international. 5 applicants, 60% accepted. In 1998, 3 degrees awarded. *Degree requirements:* For master's, thesis optional, foreign language not required. *Entrance requirements:* For master's, GRE General Test, GRE Subject Test, TOEFL (minimum score of 550 required). *Application deadline:* For fall admission, 2/1 (priority date); for spring admission, 10/15. Applications are processed on a rolling basis. Application fee: $50. *Financial aid:* In 1998–99, 6 teaching assistantships with tuition reimbursements (averaging $7,936 per year) were awarded.; tuition waivers (full and partial) also available. Financial aid application deadline: 3/1. *Unit head:* Dr. William Bray, Chair, 207-581-3902, Fax: 207-581-4977. *Application contact:* Scott G. Delcourt, Director of the Graduate School, 207-581-3218, Fax: 207-581-3232, E-mail: graduate@maine.edu.

University of Manitoba, Faculty of Graduate Studies, Faculty of Science, Department of Mathematics, Winnipeg, MB R3T 2N2, Canada. Offers M Sc, MA, PhD. *Degree requirements:* For master's, thesis or alternative required; for doctorate, dissertation required. *Unit head:* L. M. Batten, Head.

University of Maryland, College Park, Graduate School, College of Computer, Mathematical and Physical Sciences, Department of Mathematics, Program in Mathematics, College Park, MD 20742-5045. Offers MA, PhD. Postbaccalaureate distance learning degree programs offered. *Students:* 72 full-time (17 women), 29 part-time (7 women); includes 10 minority (4 African Americans, 3 Asian Americans or Pacific Islanders, 3 Hispanic Americans), 43 international. 146 applicants, 36% accepted. In 1998, 12 master's, 14 doctorates awarded. *Degree requirements:* For master's, thesis or alternative required, foreign language not required; for doctorate, dissertation, written exam required. *Entrance requirements:* For master's, minimum GPA of 3.0. *Application deadline:* Applications are processed on a rolling basis. Application fee: $50 ($70 for international students). Tuition, state resident: part-time $272 per credit hour. Tuition, nonresident: part-time $475 per credit hour. Required fees: $632; $379 per year. *Financial aid:* Fellowships, research assistantships, teaching assistantships available. Financial aid applicants required to submit FAFSA. *Unit head:* Trudy Lindsey, Director, Graduate Admission and Records, 301-405-4198, Fax: 301-314-9305, E-mail: grschool@deans.umd.edu. *Application contact:* Trudy Lindsey, Director, Graduate Admission and Records, 301-405-4198, Fax: 301-314-9305, E-mail: grschool@deans.umd.edu.

University of Massachusetts Amherst, Graduate School, College of Natural Sciences and Mathematics, Department of Mathematics and Statistics, Program in Mathematics and Statistics, Amherst, MA 01003. Offers MS, PhD. *Students:* 33 full-time (14 women), 21 part-time (9 women); includes 6 minority (1 African American, 2 Asian Americans or Pacific Islanders, 2 Hispanic Americans, 1 Native American), 23 international. Average age 27. 84 applicants, 44% accepted. In 1998, 12 master's, 8 doctorates awarded. *Degree requirements:* For master's, foreign language and thesis not required; for doctorate, 2 foreign languages, dissertation required. *Application deadline:* For fall admission, 2/1 (priority date); for spring admission, 10/1. Applications are processed on a rolling basis. Application fee: $40. Tuition, state resident: full-time $2,640; part-time $165 per credit. Tuition, nonresident: full-time $9,756; part-time $407 per credit. Required fees: $1,221 per term. One-time fee: $110. Full-time tuition and fees vary according to course load, campus/location and reciprocity agreements. *Financial aid:* Fellowships with full tuition reimbursements, research assistantships with full tuition reimbursements, teaching assistantships with full tuition reimbursements, career-related internships or fieldwork, Federal Work-Study, grants, scholarships, traineeships, and unspecified assistantships available. Aid available to part-time students. Financial aid application deadline: 2/1. *Unit head:* Dr. James Humphreys, Director, 413-545-2282, Fax: 413-545-1801, E-mail: jeh@math.umass.edu.

University of Massachusetts Lowell, Graduate School, College of Arts and Sciences, Department of Mathematics, Lowell, MA 01854-2881. Offers applied mathematics (MS); mathematics (MS). Part-time programs available. *Faculty:* 35 full-time (9 women), 2 part-time (0 women). *Students:* 3 full-time (0 women), 40 part-time (16 women); includes 3 minority (all Asian Americans or Pacific Islanders), 1 international. 26 applicants, 65% accepted. In 1998, 15 degrees awarded. *Degree requirements:* For master's, foreign language and thesis not required. *Entrance requirements:* For master's, GRE General Test. *Application deadline:* For fall admission, 4/1 (priority date); for spring admission, 10/1. Applications are processed on a rolling basis. Application fee: $20 ($35 for international students). *Financial aid:* In 1998–99, 5 teaching assistantships were awarded.; career-related internships or fieldwork, Federal Work-Study, and institutionally-sponsored loans also available. Aid available to part-time students. Financial aid application deadline: 4/1. *Unit head:* Dr. Kenneth Levasseur, Chair, 978-934-2436, E-mail: kenneth_levasseur@woods.uml.edu. *Application contact:* Dr. James Graham-Eagle, Coordinator, 978-934-2712, E-mail: james_graham-eagle@woods.uml.edu.

The University of Memphis, Graduate School, College of Arts and Sciences, Department of Mathematical Sciences, Memphis, TN 38152. Offers applied mathematics (MS); applied statistics (PhD); computer science (PhD); computer sciences (MS); mathematics (MS, PhD); statistics (MS, PhD). *Faculty:* 35 full-time (3 women), 2 part-time (1 woman). *Students:* 73 full-time (23 women), 37 part-time (9 women); includes 10 minority (5 African Americans, 5 Asian Americans or Pacific Islanders), 77 international. Average age 30. 139 applicants, 37% accepted. In 1998, 17 master's, 3 doctorates awarded. Terminal master's awarded for partial completion of doctoral program. *Degree requirements:* For master's, comprehensive exams required, thesis not required; for doctorate, dissertation, oral exams required. *Entrance requirements:* For master's, GRE General Test, MAT, TOEFL (minimum score of 550 required), minimum GPA of 2.5; for doctorate, GRE General Test, TOEFL (minimum score of 550 required). *Application deadline:* For fall admission, 8/1; for spring admission, 12/1. Applications are processed on a rolling basis. Application fee: $25 ($50 for international students). Tuition, state resident: full-time $3,410; part-time $178 per credit hour. Tuition, nonresident: full-time $8,670; part-time $408 per credit hour. Tuition and fees vary according to program. *Financial aid:* In 1998–99, 58 students received aid, including fellowships with full tuition reimbursements available (averaging $17,500 per year), 9 research assistantships with full tuition reimbursements available, 30 teaching assistantships with full tuition reimbursements available; career-related internships or fieldwork and grants also available. *Faculty research:* Differential equations, ergodic theory and dynamics, graph theory and combinations. Total annual research expenditures: $1.1 million. *Unit head:* Dr. Jerome A. Goldstein, Chairman, 901-678-2482, Fax: 901-678-2480, E-mail: goldstej@msci.memphis.edu. *Application contact:* Dr. Fernanda M. Botelho, Coordinator of Graduate Studies, 901-678-2482, Fax: 901-678-2480, E-mail: lisa@msci.memphis.edu.

University of Miami, Graduate School, College of Arts and Sciences, Department of Mathematics and Computer Science, Coral Gables, FL 33124. Offers computer science (MS); mathematics (MS, DA, PhD). Part-time and evening/weekend programs available. *Faculty:* 27. *Students:* 25 full-time (10 women), 18 part-time (4 women); includes 13 minority (3 African Americans, 1 Asian American or Pacific Islander, 9 Hispanic Americans), 14 international. Average age 30. 71 applicants, 75% accepted. In 1998, 7 master's awarded (100% found work related to degree); 1 doctorate awarded (100% entered university research/teaching). Terminal master's awarded for partial completion of doctoral program. *Degree requirements:* For master's, comprehensive exam or project required, foreign language and thesis not required; for doctorate, one foreign language, dissertation, qualifying exams required. *Entrance requirements:* For master's and doctorate, GRE General Test (minimum combined score of 1000 required), TOEFL (minimum score of 550 required), minimum GPA of 3.0. *Average time to degree:* Master's–2 years full-time, 4 years part-time; doctorate–8 years full-time. *Application deadline:* For fall admission, 7/1. Applications are processed on a rolling basis. Application fee: $35. Tuition: Full-time $15,336; part-time $852 per credit. Required fees: $174. Tuition and fees vary according to program. *Financial aid:* In 1998–99, 27 students received aid, including 1 fellowship with tuition reimbursement available, 25 teaching assistantships with tuition reimbursements available; career-related internships or fieldwork and institutionally-sponsored loans also available. Aid available to part-time students. Financial aid application deadline: 3/1. *Unit head:* Dr. Alan Zame, Chairman, 305-284-2348. *Application contact:* Dr. Marvin Mielke, Graduate Adviser, 305-284-2348.

University of Michigan, Horace H. Rackham School of Graduate Studies, College of Literature, Science, and the Arts, Department of Mathematics, Ann Arbor, MI 48109. Offers AM, MS, PhD. Part-time programs available. Terminal master's awarded for partial completion of doctoral program. *Degree requirements:* For master's, foreign language and thesis not required; for doctorate, dissertation, oral defense of dissertation, preliminary exam required. *Entrance requirements:* For master's and doctorate, GRE General Test, GRE Subject Test. *Faculty research:* Algebra, analysis, topology, applied mathematics, geometry.

University of Minnesota, Twin Cities Campus, Graduate School, Institute of Technology, School of Mathematics, Minneapolis, MN 55455-0213. Offers MS, PhD. Part-time programs available. Terminal master's awarded for partial completion of doctoral program. *Degree requirements:* For master's, thesis required (for some programs); for doctorate, dissertation required. *Entrance requirements:* For master's, GRE Subject Test (recommended), TOEFL; for doctorate, GRE Subject Test, TOEFL (minimum score of 600 required). *Faculty research:* Partial and ordinary differential equations, algebra and number theory, geometry, combinatorics, numerical analysis.

University of Mississippi, Graduate School, College of Liberal Arts, Department of Mathematics, Oxford, University, MS 38677-9702. Offers MA, MS, PhD. *Faculty:* 22 full-time (9 women). *Students:* 18 full-time (11 women), 4 part-time (3 women); includes 2 minority (both African Americans), 1 international. In 1998, 7 master's, 1 doctorate awarded. *Degree requirements:* For master's, thesis required (for some programs), foreign language not required; for doctorate, dissertation required, foreign language not required. *Entrance requirements:* For master's, GRE General Test, TOEFL, minimum GPA of 3.0; for doctorate, GRE General Test, TOEFL. *Application deadline:* For fall admission, 8/1. Applications are processed on a rolling basis. Application fee: $0 ($25 for international students). Tuition, state resident: full-time $3,053; part-time $170 per credit hour. Tuition, nonresident: full-time $6,155; part-time $342 per credit hour. Tuition and fees vary according to program. *Financial aid:* Application deadline:3/1. *Unit head:* Dr. Eldon L. Miller, Chairman, 601-232-7401, Fax: 601-232-5491, E-mail: mmmiller@alfred.math.olemiss.edu.

University of Missouri–Columbia, Graduate School, College of Arts and Sciences, Department of Mathematics, Columbia, MO 65211. Offers applied mathematics (MS); mathematics (MA, MST, PhD). *Faculty:* 42 full-time (7 women). *Students:* 28 full-time (8 women), 11 part-time (3 women); includes 2 minority (both African Americans), 17 international. 21 applicants, 86% accepted. In 1998, 6 master's, 4 doctorates awarded. *Degree requirements:* For doctorate, dissertation required, foreign language not required. *Entrance requirements:* For master's and doctorate, GRE General Test, minimum GPA of 3.0. *Application deadline:* Applications are processed on a rolling basis. Application fee: $30 ($50 for international students). *Financial aid:* Fellowships, research assistantships, teaching assistantships, institutionally-sponsored loans available. *Unit head:* Dr. Nakhle Asmar, Director of Graduate Studies, 573-882-6221.

University of Missouri–Kansas City, College of Arts and Sciences, Department of Mathematics and Statistics, Kansas City, MO 64110-2499. Offers MA, MS, PhD. PhD offered through the School of Graduate Studies. Part-time programs available. *Faculty:* 10 full-time (1 woman). *Students:* 1 full-time (0 women), 13 part-time (5 women); includes 1 minority (Hispanic American), 1 international. Average age 33. In 1998, 1 master's awarded. Terminal master's awarded for partial completion of doctoral program. *Degree requirements:* For master's, written exam required, foreign language and thesis not required; for doctorate, 2 foreign languages, dissertation, oral and written exams required. *Entrance requirements:* For master's, bachelor's degree in mathematics, minimum GPA of 3.0; for doctorate, GMAT or GRE General Test (minimum combined score of 1500 on three sections required). *Average time to degree:* Master's–2.5 years full-time. *Application deadline:* For fall admission, 5/1 (priority date). Application fee: $25. *Financial aid:* In 1998–99, 6 students received aid, including 6 teaching assistantships; Federal Work-Study, institutionally-sponsored loans, and tuition waivers (full and partial) also available. Aid available to part-time students. Financial aid application deadline: 4/1. *Faculty research:* Classical real variables, matrix theory, ring theory, linear numerical analysis, point set topology. *Unit head:* Dr. Bruce Wenner, Chairperson, 816-235-2853.

University of Missouri–Rolla, Graduate School, College of Arts and Sciences, Department of Mathematics and Statistics, Program in Mathematics, Rolla, MO 65409-0910. Offers mathematics (PhD); mathematics education (MST). *Students:* 11 full-time (2 women), 7 international. Average age 28. 5 applicants, 40% accepted. *Degree requirements:* For master's, thesis or alternative required, foreign language not required; for doctorate, one foreign language, dissertation required. *Entrance requirements:* For master's and doctorate, GRE General Test, GRE Subject Test. *Application deadline:* For fall admission, 7/1. Applications are processed on a rolling basis. Application fee: $25. Electronic applications accepted. *Financial aid:* In 1998–99, 1 research assistantship with partial tuition reimbursement (averaging $12,985 per year), 10 teaching assistantships with partial tuition reimbursements (averaging $12,985 per year) were awarded.; fellowships, institutionally-sponsored loans also available. *Faculty research:* Analysis, differential equations, topology, statistics. *Unit head:* Marjorie Smith, Executive Secretary, 612-625-5251, Fax: 612-625-2208, E-mail: marjorie.smith@soils.umn.edu. *Application contact:* Dr. V. A. Samaranayake, Director of Graduate Studies, 573-341-4658, Fax: 573-341-4741, E-mail: vsam@umr.edu.

University of Missouri–St. Louis, Graduate School, College of Arts and Sciences, Department of Mathematical Sciences, St. Louis, MO 63121-4499. Offers applied mathematics (MA, PhD); computer science (MS). Part-time and evening/weekend programs available. *Faculty:* 20. *Students:* 1 (woman) full-time, 21 part-time (11 women); includes 4 minority (3 African Americans, 1 Asian American or Pacific Islander), 1 international. In 1998, 4 master's awarded. *Degree requirements:* For master's, thesis optional, foreign language not required; for doctorate, dissertation required, foreign language not required. *Entrance requirements:* For master's, GRE if no BS in computer science; for doctorate, GRE General Test. *Application deadline:* For fall admission, 5/1 (priority date); for spring admission, 12/1. Applications are processed on a rolling basis. Application fee: $25 ($40 for international students). Electronic applications accepted. *Financial aid:* In 1998–99, 6 teaching assistantships with partial tuition reimbursements (averaging $12,000 per year) were awarded. *Faculty research:* Applied mathematics, statistics, algebra, analysis, computer science. Total annual research expenditures: $66,251. *Unit head:* Dr. Grant Welland, Director of Graduate Studies, 314-516-5741, Fax: 314-516-5400, E-mail: welland@eads.umsl.edu. *Application contact:* Graduate Admissions, 314-516-5458, Fax: 314-516-6759, E-mail: gradadm@umsl.edu.

The University of Montana–Missoula, Graduate School, College of Arts and Sciences, Department of Mathematical Sciences, Missoula, MT 59812-0002. Offers algebra (MA, PhD); analysis (MA, PhD); applied mathematics (MA, PhD); mathematics (MAT); mathematics education (PhD); operations research (MA, PhD); statistics (MA, PhD). Part-time programs available. *Faculty:* 20 full-time (3 women). *Students:* 25 full-time (11 women), 2 part-time (1 woman); includes 6 minority (5 Asian Americans or Pacific Islanders, 1 Native American) Average age 28. 11 applicants, 91% accepted. In 1998, 6 master's, 1 doctorate awarded. Terminal master's awarded for partial completion of doctoral program. *Degree requirements:* For master's, foreign language and thesis not required; for doctorate, dissertation required. *Entrance requirements:* For master's and doctorate, GRE General Test. *Application deadline:* For fall admission, 3/1 (priority date). Application fee: $45. *Financial aid:* Teaching assistantships, Federal Work-Study available. Financial aid application deadline: 3/1. *Unit head:* Dr. Gloria Hewitt, Chair, 406-243-5311.

Announcement: Offers MA/PhD programs in algebra, analysis, applied mathematics, mathematics education, operations research, and statistics and an MAT program for secondary school teachers. The PhD program provides advanced training of research mathematics specialists, college mathematics teachers, and other general practitioners of mathematics. The program allows both regular and interdisciplinary thesis work. Teaching assistantships, carrying a tuition waiver and a stipend and normally requiring duties equivalent to teaching 4–6 hours per week, are awarded to qualified graduate students. Contact Department of Mathematical Sciences, University of Montana, Missoula, MT, 59812-1032; telephone: 406-243-5311; e-mail: math@selway.umt.edu; WWW: http://www.umt.edu/math.

University of Nebraska at Omaha, Graduate Studies and Research, College of Arts and Sciences, Department of Mathematics, Omaha, NE 68182. Offers MA, MAT, MS. Part-time programs available. *Faculty:* 9 full-time (2 women). *Students:* 3 full-time (1 woman), 26 part-time (12 women); includes 4 minority (2 African Americans, 2 Asian Americans or Pacific Islanders) Average age 34. 12 applicants, 92% accepted. In 1998, 4 degrees awarded. *Degree requirements:* For master's, thesis (for some programs), comprehensive exams required, foreign language not required. *Entrance requirements:* For master's, minimum GPA of 3.0. *Application deadline:* For fall admission, 7/1 (priority date); for spring admission, 12/1. Applications are processed on a rolling basis. Application fee: $35. Tuition, state resident: part-time $100 per credit hour. Tuition, nonresident: part-time $239 per credit hour. Required fees: $12 per credit hour. $91 per semester. Tuition and fees vary according to course load. *Financial aid:* In 1998–99, 4 students received aid; research assistantships, teaching assistantships, institutionally-sponsored loans and tuition waivers (full) available. Aid available to part-time students. Financial aid application deadline: 3/1; financial aid applicants required to submit FAFSA. *Unit head:* Dr. Margaret Gessaman, Chairperson, 402-554-2838.

University of Nebraska–Lincoln, Graduate College, College of Arts and Sciences, Department of Mathematics and Statistics, Lincoln, NE 68588. Offers M Sc T, MA, MAT, MS, PhD. *Faculty:* 26 full-time (2 women), 3 part-time (0 women). *Students:* 50 full-time (26 women), 4 part-time (1 woman), 14 international. Average age 31. 51 applicants, 43% accepted. In 1998, 8 master's, 4 doctorates awarded. *Degree requirements:* For master's, thesis optional, foreign language not required; for doctorate, dissertation, comprehensive exams required. *Entrance requirements:* For master's and doctorate, GRE General Test, TOEFL (minimum score of 575 required). *Average time to degree:* Doctorate–3.5 years full-time. *Application deadline:* For fall admission, 3/15 (priority date). Applications are processed on a rolling basis. Application fee: $35. Electronic applications accepted. *Financial aid:* In 1998–99, 53 teaching assistantships were awarded.; fellowships, research assistantships, Federal Work-Study also available. Aid available to part-time students. Financial aid application deadline: 2/15. *Faculty research:* Algebra, analysis, combinatorics, differential equations, applied mathematics. *Unit head:* Dr. Jim Lewis, Chair, 402-472-3731, Fax: 402-472-8466.

See in-depth description on page 775.

University of Nevada, Las Vegas, Graduate College, College of Science, Department of Mathematical Sciences, Las Vegas, NV 89154-9900. Offers applied mathematics (MS); mathematics (MS); pure mathematics (MS); statistics (MS). Part-time programs available. *Faculty:* 27 full-time (4 women). *Students:* 12 full-time (3 women), 5 part-time (1 woman); includes 1 minority (Asian American or Pacific Islander), 2 international. 7 applicants, 57% accepted. In 1998, 5 degrees awarded. *Degree requirements:* For master's, oral exam required, thesis optional, foreign language not required. *Entrance requirements:* For master's, minimum GPA of 3.0 during previous 2 years, 2.75 overall. *Application deadline:* For fall admission, 6/15 (priority date); for spring admission, 11/15. Applications are processed on a rolling basis. Application fee: $40 ($95 for international students). *Financial aid:* In 1998–99, 11 teaching assistantships with partial tuition reimbursements (averaging $8,500 per year) were awarded. Financial aid application deadline: 3/1. *Unit head:* Dr. Rohan Dalpadatu, Chair, 702-895-3567. *Application contact:* Graduate College Admissions Evaluator, 702-895-3320.

University of Nevada, Reno, Graduate School, College of Arts and Science, Department of Mathematics, Reno, NV 89557. Offers mathematics (MS); teaching mathematics (MATM). *Degree requirements:* For master's, thesis optional, foreign language not required. *Entrance requirements:* For master's, GRE General Test, TOEFL (minimum score of 500 required), minimum GPA of 2.75. *Faculty research:* Operator algebra, nonlinear systems, differential equations.

University of New Brunswick, School of Graduate Studies, Faculty of Science, Department of Mathematics and Statistics, Fredericton, NB E3B 5A3, Canada. Offers M Sc, PhD. Part-time programs available. *Degree requirements:* For master's, thesis or alternative required; for doctorate, dissertation required. *Entrance requirements:* For master's and doctorate, TOEFL, TWE, minimum GPA of 3.0.

University of New Hampshire, Graduate School, College of Engineering and Physical Sciences, Department of Mathematics, Durham, NH 03824. Offers applied mathematics (MS); mathematics (MS, MST, PhD); mathematics education (PhD). *Faculty:* 24 full-time. *Students:* 15 full-time (7 women), 9 part-time (6 women), 2 international. Average age 28. 28 applicants, 61% accepted. In 1998, 19 master's, 4 doctorates awarded. Terminal master's awarded for partial completion of doctoral program. *Degree requirements:* For master's, foreign language and thesis not required; for doctorate, 2 foreign languages (computer language can substitute for one), dissertation required. *Application deadline:* For fall admission, 4/1 (priority date). Applications are processed on a rolling basis. Application fee: $50. Tuition, area resident: Full-time $5,750; part-time $319 per credit. Tuition, state resident: full-time $8,625. Tuition, nonresident: full-time $14,640; part-time $598 per credit. Required fees: $224 per semester. Tuition and fees vary according to course load, degree level and program. *Financial aid:* In 1998–99, 1 research assistantship, 20 teaching assistantships were awarded.; fellowships, Federal Work-Study, scholarships, and tuition waivers (full and partial) also available. Aid available to part-time students. Financial aid application deadline: 2/15. *Faculty research:* Operator theory, complex analysis, algebra, nonlinear dynamics, statistics. *Unit head:* Dr. Kenneth I. Appel, Chairperson, 603-862-2673. *Application contact:* Dr. Edward K. Hinson, Graduate Coordinator, 603-862-2688, E-mail: ekh@christa.unh.edu.

Announcement: Small classes, friendly atmosphere, great individual attention to students, and an active research faculty are featured. Department brings together pure and applied math, statistics, and math education (PhD work available in all) and provides a broad perspective on mathematical sciences, varied research areas, and interdisciplinary opportunities. MS has applied math and statistics options. Located in beautiful seacoast setting, an hour from mountains and Boston's mathematical and cultural riches. Visit the Web site at http://www.math.unh.edu.

University of New Mexico, Graduate School, College of Arts and Sciences, Department of Mathematics and Statistics, Albuquerque, NM 87131-2039. Offers mathematics (MS, PhD); statistics (MS, PhD). Part-time programs available. *Faculty:* 39 full-time (8 women), 22 part-time (3 women). *Students:* 51 full-time (16 women), 20 part-time (10 women); includes 11 minority (1 African American, 5 Asian Americans or Pacific Islanders, 4 Hispanic Americans, 1 Native American), 15 international. Average age 34. 25 applicants, 80% accepted. In 1998, 6 master's, 7 doctorates awarded. Terminal master's awarded for partial completion of doctoral program. *Degree requirements:* For master's, computer language required, thesis optional, foreign language not required; for doctorate, one foreign language, computer language, dissertation required. *Entrance requirements:* For master's and doctorate, GRE General Test, minimum GPA of 3.0. Application fee: $25. *Financial aid:* In 1998–99, 3 fellowships (averaging $3,122 per year), 9 research assistantships with tuition reimbursements (averaging $4,093 per year), 40 teaching assistantships with tuition reimbursements (averaging $10,526 per year) were awarded.; career-related internships or fieldwork, Federal Work-Study, institutionally-sponsored loans, and tuition waivers (full and partial) also available. Financial aid application deadline: 11/1. *Faculty research:* Pure and applied mathematics, applied statistics, numerical analysis, biostatistics, differential geometry, fluid dynamics, nonparametric curve estimation. Total annual research expenditures: $290,000. *Unit head:* Dr. Ronald M. Schrader, Chair, 505-277-4613, Fax: 505-277-5505, E-mail: schrader@math.unm.edu.

University of New Orleans, Graduate School, College of Sciences, Department of Mathematics, New Orleans, LA 70148. Offers MS. Part-time programs available. *Faculty:* 18 full-time (1 woman). *Students:* 20 full-time (11 women), 4 part-time (2 women); includes 6 minority (5 African Americans, 1 Asian American or Pacific Islander), 12 international. Average age 29. 18 applicants, 83% accepted. In 1998, 11 degrees awarded. *Degree requirements:* For master's, thesis not required. *Entrance requirements:* For master's, BA or BS in mathematics. *Application deadline:* For fall admission, 7/1 (priority date). Applications are processed on a rolling basis. Application fee: $20. Tuition, state resident: full-time $2,362. Tuition, nonresident: full-time $7,888. Part-time tuition and fees vary according to course load. *Financial aid:* Teaching assistantships available. *Faculty research:* Differential equations, combinatorics, statistics, complex analysis, algebra. *Unit head:* Dr. Charles Rees, Chairman, 504-280-6507, Fax: 504-280-5516, E-mail: csrma@uno.edu. *Application contact:* Dr. Lew Lefton, Graduate Coordinator, 504-280-7441, Fax: 504-280-5516, E-mail: lelma@uno.edu.

The University of North Carolina at Chapel Hill, Graduate School, College of Arts and Sciences, Department of Mathematics, Chapel Hill, NC 27599. Offers MA, MS, PhD. *Faculty:* 31 full-time (2 women). *Students:* 45 full-time (15 women); includes 3 minority (1 African American, 2 Hispanic Americans), 12 international. Average age 29. 73 applicants, 27% accepted. In 1998, 1 master's, 9 doctorates awarded. *Degree requirements:* For master's, one foreign language (computer language can substitute), thesis required; for doctorate, 2 foreign languages,

Mathematics

The University of North Carolina at Chapel Hill (continued)
computer language, dissertation, comprehensive exam required. *Entrance requirements:* For master's and doctorate, GRE General Test (minimum combined score of 1000 required), GRE Subject Test, TOEFL, minimum GPA of 3.0. *Application deadline:* For fall admission, 1/1 (priority date). Applications are processed on a rolling basis. Application fee: $55. *Financial aid:* In 1998–99, 7 fellowships with full tuition reimbursements (averaging $14,400 per year), 37 teaching assistantships with full tuition reimbursements were awarded.; research assistantships, unspecified assistantships also available. Financial aid application deadline: 3/1. *Faculty research:* Algebraic geometry, topology, analysis, lie theory, applied math. Total annual research expenditures: $251,982. *Unit head:* Dr. Warren R. Wogen, Chairman, 919-962-1295, Fax: 919-962-2568, E-mail: wrw@math.unc.edu. *Application contact:* Brenda Bethea, Graduate Secretary, 919-962-4178, Fax: 919-962-2568, E-mail: bethea@math.unc.edu.

Announcement: The department, with 31 faculty members and 45–50 graduate students, offers special opportunities for student-faculty interaction in master's and doctoral programs. Faculty includes distinguished, active researchers in most subfields of mathematics, including a strong new group in applied mathematics. Nearby resources are North Carolina State, Duke, and the Research Triangle Park.

University of North Carolina at Charlotte, Graduate School, College of Arts and Sciences, Department of Mathematics, Charlotte, NC 28223-0001. Offers applied mathematics (MS, PhD); applied statistics (MS); mathematics (MA); mathematics education (MA). *Accreditation:* NCATE (one or more programs are accredited). Part-time and evening/weekend programs available. *Faculty:* 43 full-time (6 women). *Students:* 22 full-time (8 women), 24 part-time (14 women); includes 6 minority (2 African Americans, 4 Asian Americans or Pacific Islanders), 16 international. Average age 31. 29 applicants, 97% accepted. In 1998, 8 master's, 1 doctorate awarded. *Degree requirements:* For master's, thesis or written comprehensive exam required; for doctorate, dissertation required. *Entrance requirements:* For master's, GRE General Test or MAT, minimum GPA of 3.0 in undergraduate major, 2.75 overall. *Application deadline:* For fall admission, 7/15; for spring admission, 11/15. Applications are processed on a rolling basis. Application fee: $35. Electronic applications accepted. *Financial aid:* In 1998–99, 1 fellowship (averaging $4,000 per year), 2 research assistantships, 32 teaching assistantships were awarded.; Federal Work-Study also available. Financial aid application deadline:4/1. *Faculty research:* Probability and statistics, analysis. *Unit head:* Dr. Ram C. Tiwari, Chair, 704-547-4551, Fax: 704-547-6415, E-mail: rtiwari@email.uncc.edu. *Application contact:* Kathy Barringer, Assistant Director of Graduate Admissions, 704-547-3366, Fax: 704-547-3279, E-mail: gradadm@email.uncc.edu.

See in-depth description on page 779.

University of North Carolina at Greensboro, Graduate School, College of Arts and Sciences, Department of Mathematics, Greensboro, NC 27412-5001. Offers M Ed, MA. Part-time programs available. *Faculty:* 17 full-time (6 women), 1 part-time (0 women). *Students:* 3 full-time (0 women), 6 part-time (2 women); includes 1 minority (African American), 1 international. 5 applicants, 40% accepted. In 1998, 2 degrees awarded. *Degree requirements:* For master's, thesis (for some programs), comprehensive exam required, foreign language not required. *Entrance requirements:* For master's, GRE General Test, TOEFL. *Application deadline:* For spring admission, 11/1. Applications are processed on a rolling basis. Application fee: $35. *Financial aid:* Research assistantships, teaching assistantships, unspecified assistantships available. *Faculty research:* General and geometric topology, statistics, computer networks, symbolic logic, mathematics education. *Unit head:* Dr. Paul Duvall, Head, 336-334-5836, Fax: 336-334-5949, E-mail: duvallp@uncg.edu. *Application contact:* Dr. James Lynch, Director of Graduate Recruitment, 336-334-4881, Fax: 336-334-4424, E-mail: jmlynch@office.uncg.edu.

University of North Carolina at Wilmington, College of Arts and Sciences, Department of Mathematical Sciences, Wilmington, NC 28403-3201. Offers MA, MS. *Faculty:* 8 full-time (1 woman). *Students:* 3 full-time (0 women), 13 part-time (4 women); includes 5 minority (all Asian Americans or Pacific Islanders) Average age 29. 13 applicants, 69% accepted. In 1998, 11 degrees awarded. *Degree requirements:* For master's, thesis, oral and written comprehensive exams required. *Entrance requirements:* For master's, GRE General Test, GRE Subject Test, minimum B average in undergraduate major. *Application deadline:* For fall admission, 3/15. Applications are processed on a rolling basis. Application fee: $35. *Financial aid:* In 1998–99, 12 teaching assistantships were awarded.; career-related internships or fieldwork and Federal Work-Study also available. Aid available to part-time students. Financial aid application deadline: 3/15. *Unit head:* Dr. Douglas D. Smith, Chairman, 910-962-3290. *Application contact:* Neil F. Hadley, Dean, Graduate School, 910-962-4117, Fax: 910-962-3787, E-mail: hadleyn@uncwil.edu.

University of North Dakota, Graduate School, College of Arts and Sciences, Department of Mathematics, Grand Forks, ND 58202. Offers M Ed, MS. Part-time programs available. *Faculty:* 17 full-time (3 women). *Students:* 8 full-time (3 women), 2 part-time. 5 applicants, 80% accepted. In 1998, 6 degrees awarded. *Degree requirements:* For master's, thesis or alternative required. *Entrance requirements:* For master's, TOEFL (minimum score of 550 required), minimum GPA of 3.0. *Application deadline:* For fall admission, 3/1 (priority date). Applications are processed on a rolling basis. Application fee: $20. *Financial aid:* In 1998–99, 7 students received aid, including 7 teaching assistantships; fellowships, research assistantships, Federal Work-Study, institutionally-sponsored loans, and tuition waivers (full and partial) also available. Financial aid application deadline:3/15. *Unit head:* Dr. Tom Gilsdorf, Chairperson, 701-777-2881, Fax: 701-777-3619, E-mail: gilsdorf@plains.nodak.edu.

University of Northern Colorado, Graduate School, College of Arts and Sciences, Department of Mathematics, Greeley, CO 80639. Offers educational mathematics (MA, PhD); mathematics (MA, PhD). *Accreditation:* NCATE (one or more programs are accredited). *Faculty:* 15 full-time (3 women). *Students:* 17 full-time (9 women), 3 part-time (all women); includes 1 minority (Hispanic American), 6 international. Average age 35. 14 applicants, 64% accepted. In 1998, 22 master's, 1 doctorate awarded. *Degree requirements:* For master's, thesis or alternative, comprehensive exams required; for doctorate, dissertation, comprehensive exams required. *Entrance requirements:* For master's and doctorate, GRE General Test. *Application deadline:* Applications are processed on a rolling basis. Application fee: $35. *Financial aid:* In 1998–99, 16 students received aid, including 8 fellowships, 13 teaching assistantships; research assistantships, unspecified assistantships also available. Financial aid application deadline: 3/1. *Unit head:* Dr. Richard Grassl, Chairperson, 970-351-2820.

University of Northern Iowa, Graduate College, College of Natural Sciences, Department of Mathematics, Cedar Falls, IA 50614. Offers mathematics (MA); mathematics for elementary and middle school (MA). Part-time programs available. *Faculty:* 14 full-time (3 women). *Students:* 3 full-time (0 women), 13 part-time (9 women), 1 international. Average age 33. 9 applicants, 89% accepted. In 1998, 22 degrees awarded. *Degree requirements:* For master's, thesis or alternative required, foreign language not required. *Application deadline:* For fall admission, 8/1 (priority date). Applications are processed on a rolling basis. Application fee: $20 ($30 for international students). Tuition, state resident: full-time $3,308; part-time $184 per hour. Tuition, nonresident: full-time $8,156; part-time $454 per hour. Required fees: $202; $88 per semester. Tuition and fees vary according to course load. *Financial aid:* Career-related internships or fieldwork, Federal Work-Study, scholarships, and tuition waivers (full and partial) available. Aid available to part-time students. Financial aid application deadline: 3/1. *Unit head:* Dr. Joel Haack, Head, 319-273-2631, Fax: 319-273-2546, E-mail: joel.haack@uni.edu.

University of North Florida, College of Arts and Sciences, Department of Mathematics and Statistics, Jacksonville, FL 32224-2645. Offers computer science (MS); mathematical sciences (MS); statistics (MS). Part-time and evening/weekend programs available. *Faculty:* 17 full-time (4 women). *Students:* 7 full-time (3 women), 11 part-time (6 women); includes 2 minority (1 African American, 1 Hispanic American), 3 international. Average age 29. 9 applicants, 100% accepted. In 1998, 2 degrees awarded. *Degree requirements:* For master's, comprehensive exam required, thesis optional, foreign language not required. *Entrance requirements:* For master's, GRE Subject Test, TOEFL (minimum score of 500 required), GRe General Test (minimum combined score of 1000 required) or minimum GPA of 3.0 in last 60 hours. *Application deadline:* For fall admission, 12/31 (priority date). Applications are processed on a rolling basis. Application fee: $20. Electronic applications accepted. *Financial aid:* In 1998–99, 13 students received aid, including 4 teaching assistantships (averaging $3,919 per year); Federal Work-Study and tuition waivers (partial) also available. Aid available to part-time students. Financial aid application deadline: 4/1; financial aid applicants required to submit FAFSA. *Unit head:* Dr. William Caldwell, Chair, 904-620-2653, E-mail: wcaldwell@unf.edu. *Application contact:* Dr. Leonard Lipkin, Coordinator, 904-620-2468, E-mail: llipkin@unf.edu.

University of North Texas, Robert B. Toulouse School of Graduate Studies, College of Arts and Sciences, Department of Mathematics, Denton, TX 76203. Offers MA, MS, PhD. Part-time programs available. *Faculty:* 25 full-time (2 women), 3 part-time (0 women). *Students:* 39 full-time (16 women), 12 part-time (4 women); includes 10 minority (4 African Americans, 2 Asian Americans or Pacific Islanders, 3 Hispanic Americans, 1 Native American), 7 international. Average age 27. In 1998, 7 master's, 1 doctorate awarded. Terminal master's awarded for partial completion of doctoral program. *Degree requirements:* For master's; for doctorate, 2 foreign languages, dissertation required. *Entrance requirements:* For master's and doctorate, GRE General Test (minimum combined score of 1100 required). *Application deadline:* For fall admission, 7/17. Application fee: $25 ($50 for international students). *Financial aid:* Research assistantships, teaching assistantships, Federal Work-Study and institutionally-sponsored loans available. Financial aid application deadline: 6/1. *Faculty research:* Differential equations, descriptive set theory, combinatorics, functional analysis, algebra. *Unit head:* Dr. Neil Brand, Chair, 940-565-2155, Fax: 940-565-4805, E-mail: neal@unt.edu. *Application contact:* Dr. John Ed Allen, Graduate Adviser, 940-565-2155, Fax: 940-565-4805, E-mail: jallen@unt.edu.

University of Notre Dame, Graduate School, College of Science, Department of Mathematics, Notre Dame, IN 46556. Offers MSAM, PhD. *Faculty:* 41 full-time (4 women). *Students:* 27 full-time (6 women), 4 part-time; includes 1 minority (Hispanic American), 16 international. 110 applicants, 25% accepted. In 1998, 10 master's, 6 doctorates awarded (83% entered university research/teaching). Terminal master's awarded for partial completion of doctoral program. *Degree requirements:* For master's, comprehensive exam required, foreign language and thesis not required; for doctorate, one foreign language, dissertation, qualifying exam required. *Entrance requirements:* For master's and doctorate, GRE General Test, GRE Subject Test, TOEFL (minimum score of 600 required; 250 for computer-based)). *Average time to degree:* Master's–2 years full-time; doctorate–5.2 years full-time. *Application deadline:* For fall admission, 2/1 (priority date). Applications are processed on a rolling basis. Application fee: $40. *Financial aid:* In 1998–99, 27 students received aid, including 7 fellowships with full tuition reimbursements available (averaging $16,000 per year), research assistantships with full tuition reimbursements available (averaging $12,500 per year), 20 teaching assistantships with full tuition reimbursements available (averaging $12,500 per year); tuition waivers (full) also available. Financial aid application deadline: 2/1. *Faculty research:* Algebra, analysis, topology, geometry, logic. Total annual research expenditures: $552,000. *Unit head:* Dr. William G. Dwyer, Director of Graduate Studies, 219-631-6571, E-mail: mathgrad@nd.edu. *Application contact:* Dr. Terrence J. Akai, Director of Graduate Admissions, 219-631-7706, Fax: 219-631-4183, E-mail: gradad@nd.edu.

See in-depth description on page 781.

University of Oklahoma, Graduate College, College of Arts and Sciences, Department of Mathematics, Norman, OK 73019-0390. Offers MA, MS, PhD, MBA/MS. Part-time programs available. *Faculty:* 37 full-time (6 women), 8 part-time (2 women). *Students:* 9 full-time (7 women), 29 part-time (11 women); includes 2 minority (1 Asian American or Pacific Islander, 1 Hispanic American), 13 international. 22 applicants, 73% accepted. In 1998, 10 master's, 1 doctorate awarded. Terminal master's awarded for partial completion of doctoral program. *Degree requirements:* For master's, comprehensive exam required, thesis optional, foreign language not required; for doctorate, 2 foreign languages, dissertation, qualifying exam required. *Entrance requirements:* For master's and doctorate, TOEFL (minimum score of 550 required), TSE (minimum score of 210 required). *Application deadline:* For fall admission, 6/1 (priority date). Applications are processed on a rolling basis. Application fee: $25. Tuition, state resident: part-time $86 per credit hour. Tuition, nonresident: part-time $275 per credit hour. Tuition and fees vary according to course level, course load and program. *Financial aid:* In 1998–99, 2 research assistantships, 31 teaching assistantships were awarded.; fellowships, Federal Work-Study and tuition waivers (partial) also available. Aid available to part-time students. *Faculty research:* Algebra, analysis, topology, geometry. *Unit head:* Kevin A. Grasse, Chair, 405-325-2903. *Application contact:* Darryl McCullough, Graduate Liaison, 405-325-6711.

Announcement: The Graduate Mathematics Program at the University of Oklahoma offers students a supportive environment and the opportunity for individual interaction with faculty members involved in broadly diversified research programs. Flexible degree programs allow students to concentrate in pure mathematics, applied mathematics, or research in undergraduate mathematics curriculum and pedagogy. WWW: http:/www.math.ou.edu/.

University of Oregon, Graduate School, College of Arts and Sciences, Department of Mathematics, Eugene, OR 97403. Offers MA, MS, PhD. Part-time programs available. *Faculty:* 28 full-time (3 women), 5 part-time (2 women). *Students:* 46 full-time (16 women), 3 part-time; includes 4 minority (1 Asian American or Pacific Islander, 2 Hispanic Americans, 1 Native American), 9 international. 54 applicants, 30% accepted. In 1998, 14 master's, 2 doctorates awarded. Terminal master's awarded for partial completion of doctoral program. *Degree requirements:* For master's, thesis not required; for doctorate, 2 foreign languages, dissertation required. *Entrance requirements:* For master's and doctorate, GRE General Test, GRE Subject Test, TOEFL (minimum score of 600 required), TSE (minimum score of 50 required). *Application deadline:* For fall admission, 3/1. Application fee: $50. *Financial aid:* In 1998–99, 47 teaching assistantships were awarded.; Federal Work-Study also available. Aid available to part-time students. Financial aid application deadline: 3/1. *Faculty research:* Algebra, topology, analytic geometry, numerical analysis, statistics. *Unit head:* Gary M. Seitz, hEAD, 541-346-4705. *Application contact:* Gayle Asburry, Graduate Secretary, 541-346-0992.

University of Ottawa, School of Graduate Studies and Research, Faculty of Science, Ottawa-Carleton Institute of Mathematics and Statistics, Ottawa, ON K1N 6N5, Canada. Offers M Sc, PhD. Part-time programs available. *Faculty:* 55 full-time, 2 part-time. *Students:* 51 full-time (13 women), 7 part-time (3 women), 12 international. Average age 29. In 1998, 22 master's, 9 doctorates awarded. *Degree requirements:* For master's, thesis optional, foreign language not required; for doctorate, one foreign language, dissertation required. *Entrance requirements:* For master's, honors degree or equivalent, minimum B average; for doctorate, minimum B+ average. *Application deadline:* For fall admission, 3/1 (priority date). Applications are processed on a rolling basis. Application fee: $35. *Financial aid:* Fellowships, research assistantships, teaching assistantships, Federal Work-Study available. Financial aid application deadline: 3/1. *Faculty research:* Pure mathematics, applied mathematics, probability. Total annual research expenditures:$280,000. *Unit head:* David McDonald, Director, 613-562-5800 Ext. 3505, Fax: 613-562-5776, E-mail: dmdsg@uottawa.ca. *Application contact:* David McDonald, Director, 613-562-5800 Ext. 3505, Fax: 613-562-5776, E-mail: dmdsg@uottawa.ca.

University of Pennsylvania, School of Arts and Sciences, Graduate Group in Mathematics, Philadelphia, PA 19104. Offers AM, PhD. Terminal master's awarded for partial completion of doctoral program. *Degree requirements:* For master's, thesis or alternative required; for doctorate, dissertation required. *Entrance requirements:* For master's and doctorate, GRE General Test, GRE Subject Test, TOEFL. *Faculty research:* Geometry-topology, analysis, algebra, logic, combinatorics.

University of Pittsburgh, Faculty of Arts and Sciences, Department of Mathematics, Program in Mathematics, Pittsburgh, PA 15260. Offers MA, MS, PhD. Part-time programs available.

Faculty: 40 full-time (6 women), 20 part-time (7 women). *Students:* 56 full-time (18 women), 20 part-time (6 women); includes 10 minority (7 African Americans, 3 Asian Americans or Pacific Islanders), 30 international. 103 applicants, 28% accepted. In 1998, 7 master's, 6 doctorates awarded. Terminal master's awarded for partial completion of doctoral program. *Degree requirements:* For master's, thesis (for some programs), oral comprehensive exam required, foreign language not required; for doctorate, dissertation, comprehensive and preliminary exams required, foreign language not required. *Entrance requirements:* For master's and doctorate, GRE General Test, TOEFL (minimum score of 550 required), minimum GPA of 3.0. *Average time to degree:* Master's–2 years full-time, 3 years part-time; doctorate–5.5 years full-time, 10 years part-time. *Application deadline:* For fall admission, 2/1 (priority date); for spring admission, 10/1. Applications are processed on a rolling basis. Application fee: $30 ($40 for international students). *Financial aid:* In 1998–99, 63 students received aid, including 3 fellowships with full and partial tuition reimbursements available (averaging $11,600 per year), 6 research assistantships with full and partial tuition reimbursements available (averaging $7,000 per year), 47 teaching assistantships with full and partial tuition reimbursements available (averaging $10,600 per year); grants, institutionally-sponsored loans, scholarships, and tuition waivers (partial) also available. Financial aid application deadline: 2/1. *Faculty research:* Applied analysis, scientific computing, mathematical biology, discrete mathematics. Total annual research expenditures: $513,200. *Unit head:* Sandy Ryan, Graduate Secretary, 541-346-4787, Fax: 541-346-4787. *Application contact:* Molly Williams, Administrator, 412-624-1175, Fax: 412-624-8397, E-mail: mollyw@vms.cis.pitt.edu.

See in-depth description on page 785.

University of Puerto Rico, Mayagüez Campus, Graduate Studies, College of Arts and Sciences, Department of Mathematics, Mayagüez, PR 00681-5000. Offers applied mathematics (MS); computational sciences (MS); pure mathematics (MS); statistics (MS). Part-time programs available. *Degree requirements:* For master's, one foreign language, comprehensive exam required, thesis optional. *Faculty research:* Automata theory, linear algebra, logic.

University of Puerto Rico, Río Piedras, Faculty of Natural Sciences, Department of Mathematics, San Juan, PR 00931. Offers MS. Part-time and evening/weekend programs available. *Students:* 26 full-time (6 women), 10 part-time (4 women); includes 34 minority (all Hispanic Americans), 2 international. Average age 29. In 1998, 3 degrees awarded. *Degree requirements:* For master's, one foreign language, thesis, comprehensive exam required. *Entrance requirements:* For master's, GRE, interview, minimum GPA of 3.0. *Average time to degree:* Master's–6 years full-time. *Application deadline:* For fall admission, 2/1. Application fee: $17. *Financial aid:* Fellowships, research assistantships, teaching assistantships, Federal Work-Study, institutionally-sponsored loans, and tuition waivers (partial) available. Financial aid application deadline: 5/31. *Faculty research:* Investigation of database logistics, cryptograph systems, distribution and spectral theory, Boolean function, differential equations. *Unit head:* Dr. Jorge Punchín, Coordinator, 787-764-0000 Ext. 4676, Fax: 787-281-0651.

University of Regina, Faculty of Graduate Studies and Research, Faculty of Science, Department of Mathematics and Statistics, Regina, SK S4S 0A2, Canada. Offers mathematics (M Sc, MA, PhD); statistics (M Sc, MA). *Faculty:* 20 full-time (3 women). *Students:* 3 full-time (0 women), 3 part-time (1 woman). 14 applicants, 43% accepted. In 1998, 3 degrees awarded. *Degree requirements:* For master's, thesis optional, foreign language not required; for doctorate, variable foreign language requirement, dissertation required. *Entrance requirements:* For master's, TOEFL (minimum score of 550 required); for doctorate, TOEFL. *Application deadline:* Applications are processed on a rolling basis. Application fee: $0. *Expenses:* Tuition and fees charges are reported in Canadian dollars. Tuition, state resident: full-time $1,688 Canadian dollars; part-time $94 Canadian dollars per credit hour. International tuition: $3,375 Canadian dollars full-time. Required fees: $65 Canadian dollars per course. Tuition and fees vary according to course load and program. *Financial aid:* In 1998–99, 1 fellowship, 3 research assistantships, 3 teaching assistantships were awarded.; scholarships also available. Financial aid application deadline: 6/15. *Faculty research:* Pure and applied mathematics, statistics and probability. *Unit head:* Dr. D. Hanson, Head, 306-585-4351, E-mail: denis.hanson@uregina.ca.

University of Rhode Island, Graduate School, College of Arts and Sciences, Department of Mathematics, Kingston, RI 02881. Offers MS, PhD. *Degree requirements:* For master's, thesis optional; for doctorate, dissertation required.

University of Rochester, The College, Arts and Sciences, Department of Mathematics, Rochester, NY 14627-0250. Offers MA, MS, PhD. *Faculty:* 18. *Students:* 18 full-time (5 women), 15 international. 77 applicants, 43% accepted. In 1998, 1 master's, 4 doctorates awarded. Terminal master's awarded for partial completion of doctoral program. *Degree requirements:* For master's, thesis required (for some programs), foreign language not required; for doctorate, dissertation, qualifying exam required, foreign language not required, dissertation, qualifying exam required, foreign language not required. *Entrance requirements:* For master's, GRE General Test; for doctorate, GRE General Test, TOEFL. *Application deadline:* For fall admission, 2/1 (priority date). Application fee: $25. *Financial aid:* Fellowships, research assistantships, teaching assistantships available. Financial aid application deadline: 2/1. *Unit head:* Douglas Ravenel, Chair, 716-275-4411. *Application contact:* Joan Robinson, Graduate Program Secretary, 716-275-4411.

University of Saskatchewan, College of Graduate Studies and Research, College of Arts and Sciences, Department of Mathematics, Saskatoon, SK S7N 5A2, Canada. Offers M Math, MA, PhD. *Degree requirements:* For master's and doctorate, thesis/dissertation required. *Entrance requirements:* For master's, CANTEST (minimum score of 4.5 required) or International English Language Testing System (minimum score of 6 required) or Michigan English Language Assessment Battery (minimum score of 80 required), orTOEFL (minimum score of 550 required; average 560); for doctorate, TOEFL.

University of South Alabama, Graduate School, College of Arts and Sciences, Department of Mathematics, Mobile, AL 36688-0002. Offers MS. Part-time and evening/weekend programs available. *Faculty:* 25 full-time (3 women). *Students:* 4 full-time (2 women), 5 part-time (4 women), 3 international. 12 applicants, 92% accepted. In 1998, 8 degrees awarded. *Degree requirements:* For master's, computer language, written comprehensive exam required, thesis not required. *Entrance requirements:* For master's, GRE, minimum B average. *Application deadline:* For fall admission, 9/1 (priority date). Applications are processed on a rolling basis. Application fee: $25. Tuition, state resident: part-time $116 per semester hour. Tuition, nonresident: part-time $230 per semester hour. Required fees: $121 per semester. Part-time tuition and fees vary according to course load and program. *Financial aid:* In 1998–99, 6 research assistantships were awarded.; fellowships Aid available to part-time students. Financial aid application deadline: 4/1. *Faculty research:* Knot theory, chaos theory. *Unit head:* Dr. Michael Windham, Chairperson, 334-460-6264.

University of South Carolina, Graduate School, College of Science and Mathematics, Department of Mathematics, Columbia, SC 29208. Offers mathematics (MA, MS, PhD); mathematics education (M Math, MAT). MAT offered in cooperation with the College of Education. *Accreditation:* NCATE. Part-time programs available. *Faculty:* 32 full-time (1 woman). *Students:* 45 full-time (13 women), 14 part-time (3 women); includes 3 minority (2 African Americans, 1 Asian American or Pacific Islander), 20 international. Average age 30. 53 applicants, 66% accepted. In 1998, 8 master's, 6 doctorates awarded (100% entered university research/teaching). Terminal master's awarded for partial completion of doctoral program. *Degree requirements:* For master's, thesis required, foreign language not required; for doctorate, one foreign language, computer language, dissertation required. *Entrance requirements:* For master's and doctorate, GRE General Test. *Application deadline:* For fall admission, 7/1 (priority date). Applications are processed on a rolling basis. Application fee: $35. Electronic applications accepted. Tuition, state resident: full-time $4,014; part-time $202 per credit hour. Tuition, nonresident: full-time $8,528; part-time $428 per credit hour. Required fees: $100; $4 per credit hour. Tuition and fees vary according to program. *Financial aid:* In 1998–99, 2 fellowships, 2 research assistantships, 32 teaching assistantships were awarded. Financial aid application deadline: 3/15. *Faculty research:* Applied mathematics, analysis, discrete mathematics, algebra, topology. *Unit head:* Dr. R. M. Stephenson, Chair, 803-777-4224, E-mail: chairman@milo.math.sc.edu. *Application contact:* Dr. Anton R. Schep, Graduate Director, 803-777-4226, Fax: 803-777-3783, E-mail: graddir@milo.math.sc.edu.

University of South Dakota, Graduate School, College of Arts and Sciences, Department of Mathematics, Vermillion, SD 57069-2390. Offers MA, MNS. *Faculty:* 8 full-time (0 women), 1 part-time (0 women). *Students:* 15 full-time (3 women), 2 part-time (both women), 10 international. 11 applicants, 91% accepted. In 1998, 5 degrees awarded. *Degree requirements:* Foreign language not required. *Entrance requirements:* For master's, GRE. *Application deadline:* Applications are processed on a rolling basis. Application fee: $15. *Financial aid:* Teaching assistantships available. *Unit head:* Dr. José Flores, Chair, 605-677-5262.

University of Southern California, Graduate School, College of Letters, Arts and Sciences, Department of Mathematics, Program in Mathematics, Los Angeles, CA 90089. Offers MA, PhD. *Students:* 27 full-time (7 women), 3 part-time; includes 4 minority (1 African American, 2 Asian Americans or Pacific Islanders, 1 Hispanic American), 23 international. Average age 29. 38 applicants, 53% accepted. In 1998, 4 master's, 4 doctorates awarded. *Degree requirements:* For doctorate, dissertation required. *Entrance requirements:* For master's and doctorate, GRE General Test. *Application deadline:* For fall admission, 7/1 (priority date); for spring admission, 12/1. Application fee: $55. Tuition: Full-time $22,198; part-time $748 per unit. Required fees: $406. Tuition and fees vary according to program. *Financial aid:* In 1998–99, 1 research assistantship, 26 teaching assistantships were awarded.; fellowships, Federal Work-Study, institutionally-sponsored loans, and scholarships also available. Aid available to part-time students. Financial aid application deadline: 2/15; financial aid applicants required to submit FAFSA. *Unit head:* Dr. Susan Montgomery, Chairman, Department of Mathematics, 213-740-2400.

See in-depth description on page 793.

University of Southern Mississippi, Graduate School, College of Science and Technology, School of Mathematical Sciences, Department of Mathematics, Hattiesburg, MS 39406-5167. Offers MS. Part-time programs available. *Faculty:* 16 full-time (2 women), 2 part-time (0 women). *Students:* 12 full-time (6 women), 2 part-time (1 woman), 6 international. Average age 25. 29 applicants, 48% accepted. In 1998, 8 degrees awarded. *Degree requirements:* For master's, thesis or alternative, oral/written comprehensive exam required, foreign language not required. *Entrance requirements:* For master's, GRE General Test (minimum combined score of 1000 required), TOEFL (minimum score of 580 required), minimum GPA of 2.75. *Application deadline:* For fall admission, 8/6 (priority date). Applications are processed on a rolling basis. Application fee: $0 ($25 for international students). Tuition, state resident: full-time $2,250; part-time $137 per semester hour. Tuition, nonresident: full-time $3,102; part-time $172 per semester hour. Required fees: $602. *Financial aid:* In 1998–99, 9 teaching assistantships (averaging $7,500 per year) were awarded.; Federal Work-Study and institutionally-sponsored loans also available. Financial aid application deadline: 3/15. *Faculty research:* Dynamical systems, numerical analysis and multigrid methods, random number generation, matrix theory, group theory. *Unit head:* Dr. Wallace C. Pye, Chair, 601-266-4289, Fax: 601-266-5818, E-mail: wallace.pye@usm.edu.

University of South Florida, Graduate School, College of Arts and Sciences, Department of Mathematics, Tampa, FL 33620-9951. Offers applied mathematics (PhD); mathematics (MA, PhD). Part-time and evening/weekend programs available. *Faculty:* 27 full-time (4 women). *Students:* 39 full-time (11 women), 6 part-time (2 women); includes 3 minority (2 African Americans, 1 Hispanic American), 20 international. Average age 31. 60 applicants, 17% accepted. In 1998, 6 master's, 5 doctorates awarded. Terminal master's awarded for partial completion of doctoral program. *Degree requirements:* For master's, one foreign language required, (computer language can substitute), thesis optional; for doctorate, 2 foreign languages (computer language can substitute for one), dissertation required. *Entrance requirements:* For master's, GRE General Test (minimum score of 650 on quantitative section, 1100 combined required), minimum GPA of 3.0 in mathematics course work (undergraduate), 3.5 in (graduate); for doctorate, GRE General Test (minimum score of 650 on quantitative section, 1100 combined required). *Average time to degree:* Master's–2 years full-time, 3 years part-time; doctorate–2 years full-time, 3 years part-time. *Application deadline:* For fall admission, 6/1; for spring admission, 10/15. Application fee: $20. Electronic applications accepted. Tuition, state resident: part-time $148 per credit hour. Tuition, nonresident: part-time $509 per credit hour. *Financial aid:* In 1998–99, 36 students received aid, including 2 fellowships with full tuition reimbursements available (averaging $12,000 per year), 33 teaching assistantships with full tuition reimbursements available (averaging $11,000 per year) *Faculty research:* Approximation theory, differential equations, discrete mathematics, functional analysis topology. *Unit head:* Marcus McWaters, Chairperson, 813-974-9530, Fax: 813-974-2700, E-mail: marcus@chuma.cas.usf.edu. *Application contact:* India Barnes, Graduate Program Assistant, 813-974-5329, Fax: 813-974-2700, E-mail: ga@math.usf.edu.

University of Southwestern Louisiana, Graduate School, College of Sciences, Department of Mathematics, Lafayette, LA 70504. Offers MS, PhD. *Faculty:* 20 full-time (2 women). *Students:* 33 full-time (11 women), 1 part-time; includes 1 minority (African American), 18 international. 38 applicants, 58% accepted. In 1998, 5 master's, 6 doctorates awarded. Terminal master's awarded for partial completion of doctoral program. *Degree requirements:* For master's, thesis or alternative required, foreign language not required; for doctorate, 2 foreign languages (computer language can substitute for one), dissertation required. *Entrance requirements:* For master's, GRE General Test, minimum GPA of 2.75; for doctorate, GRE General Test, minimum GPA of 3.0. *Application deadline:* For fall admission, 5/15. Application fee: $5 ($15 for international students). *Financial aid:* In 1998–99, 2 fellowships with full tuition reimbursements (averaging $15,000 per year), 27 teaching assistantships (averaging $9,370 per year) were awarded.; research assistantships, tuition waivers (full) also available. Financial aid application deadline: 3/1. *Faculty research:* Topology, algebra, applied mathematics, analysis. *Unit head:* Dr. Chiu Yeung Chan, Graduate Coordinator, 318-482-6702.

University of Tennessee, Knoxville, Graduate School, College of Arts and Sciences, Department of Mathematics, Knoxville, TN 37996. Offers applied mathematics (MS); mathematical ecology (PhD); mathematics (M Math, MS, PhD). Part-time programs available. *Faculty:* 49 full-time (4 women), 3 part-time (1 woman). *Students:* 62 full-time (23 women), 25 part-time (7 women); includes 8 minority (7 African Americans, 1 Asian American or Pacific Islander), 20 international. 73 applicants, 74% accepted. In 1998, 16 master's, 4 doctorates awarded. *Degree requirements:* For master's, thesis or alternative required, foreign language not required; for doctorate, dissertation required. *Entrance requirements:* For master's and doctorate, TOEFL (minimum score of 550 required), minimum GPA of 2.7. *Application deadline:* For fall admission, 2/1 (priority date). Applications are processed on a rolling basis. Application fee: $35. Electronic applications accepted. *Financial aid:* In 1998–99, 20 fellowships, 1 research assistantship, 59 teaching assistantships were awarded.; Federal Work-Study, institutionally-sponsored loans, and unspecified assistantships also available. Financial aid application deadline: 2/1; financial aid applicants required to submit FAFSA. *Unit head:* Dr. John B. Conway, Head, 423-974-2464, Fax: 423-974-6576, E-mail: gradprogram@novell.math.utk.edu.

The University of Texas at Arlington, Graduate School, College of Science, Department of Mathematics, Arlington, TX 76019. Offers mathematical sciences (PhD); mathematics (MS). *Faculty:* 23 full-time (0 women), 1 part-time (0 women). *Students:* 30 full-time (11 women), 35 part-time (20 women); includes 12 minority (1 African American, 10 Asian Americans or Pacific Islanders, 1 Hispanic American), 12 international. 18 applicants, 67% accepted. In 1998, 6 master's, 2 doctorates awarded. *Degree requirements:* For master's, computer language, thesis or alternative required, foreign language not required; for doctorate, dissertation required, foreign language not required. *Entrance requirements:* For master's, GRE General Test (minimum combined score of 1000 required); for doctorate, GRE General Test (minimum combined score of 1000 required), 30 hours of graduate course work in mathematics. *Application deadline:* Applications are processed on a rolling basis. Application fee: $25 ($50 for international students).

Mathematics

The University of Texas at Arlington (continued)
Tuition, state resident: full-time $1,368; part-time $76 per semester hour. Tuition, nonresident: full-time $5,454; part-time $303 per semester hour. Required fees: $66 per semester hour. $86 per term. Tuition and fees vary according to course load. *Financial aid:* Teaching assistantships, institutionally-sponsored loans available. *Unit head:* Dr. R. Kannan, Chair, 817-272-3261, Fax: 817-272-5802, E-mail: kannan@uta.edu. *Application contact:* Dr. A. Alan Gillespie, Graduate Adviser, 817-272-3261, Fax: 817-272-5802.

The University of Texas at Austin, Graduate School, College of Natural Sciences, Department of Mathematics, Austin, TX 78712-1111. Offers mathematics (MA, PhD); statistics (MS Stat). *Students:* 97 full-time (26 women), 13 part-time (5 women); includes 6 minority (2 African Americans, 3 Asian Americans or Pacific Islanders, 1 Hispanic American), 36 international. 100 applicants, 43% accepted. In 1998, 19 master's, 10 doctorates awarded. *Entrance requirements:* For master's and doctorate, GRE General Test. *Application deadline:* For fall admission, 2/1. Application fee: $50 ($75 for international students). Electronic applications accepted. *Financial aid:* Fellowships, teaching assistantships available. Financial aid application deadline: 2/1. *Unit head:* Dr. Efraim Armendariz, Chairman, 512-471-0117, E-mail: efraim@math.utexas.edu. *Application contact:* Frank Gerth, Graduate Adviser, 512-471-7711, E-mail: gradadv@math.utexas.edu.

The University of Texas at Dallas, School of Natural Sciences and Mathematics, Programs in Mathematical Sciences, Richardson, TX 75083-0688. Offers applied mathematics (MS, PhD); engineering mathematics (MS); mathematical science (MS, PhD); statistics (MS, PhD). Part-time and evening/weekend programs available. *Students:* 22 full-time (7 women), 23 part-time (13 women); includes 6 minority (3 African Americans, 1 Asian American or Pacific Islander, 2 Hispanic Americans), 11 international. Average age 32. In 1998, 12 master's, 1 doctorate awarded. *Degree requirements:* For master's, minimum GPA of 3.0 required, thesis optional, foreign language not required; for doctorate, dissertation, minimum GPA of 3.0 required, foreign language not required. *Entrance requirements:* For master's, GRE General Test (minimum score of 500 on verbal section, 550 on quantitative required), TOEFL (minimum score of 550 required), minimum GPA of 3.0 in upper-level course work in field; for doctorate, GRE General Test (minimum score of 550 on verbal section, 650 on quantitative required), TOEFL (minimum score of 550 required), minimum GPA of 3.5 in upper-level course work in field. *Application deadline:* For fall admission, 7/15; for spring admission, 11/15. Applications are processed on a rolling basis. Application fee: $25 ($75 for international students). *Financial aid:* Fellowships, research assistantships, teaching assistantships, career-related internships or fieldwork, Federal Work-Study, grants, institutionally-sponsored loans, and scholarships available. Aid available to part-time students. Financial aid application deadline: 4/30; financial aid applicants required to submit FAFSA. *Unit head:* Dr. M. Ali Hooshyar, Head, 972-883-2171, Fax: 972-883-6622, E-mail: utdmath@utdallas.edu.

See in-depth description on page 795.

The University of Texas at El Paso, Graduate School, College of Science, Department of Mathematical Sciences, El Paso, TX 79968-0001. Offers mathematical sciences (MAT, MS); statistics (MS). Part-time and evening/weekend programs available. *Faculty:* 26 full-time (2 women), 11 part-time (4 women). *Students:* 9 full-time (1 woman), 6 part-time (2 women); includes 4 minority (all Hispanic Americans), 6 international. Average age 31. 27 applicants, 19% accepted. In 1998, 6 degrees awarded. *Degree requirements:* For master's, thesis optional, foreign language not required. *Entrance requirements:* For master's, TOEFL (minimum score of 550 required). *Application deadline:* Applications are processed on a rolling basis. Application fee: $15 ($65 for international students). Electronic applications accepted. Tuition, state resident: full-time $2,118. Tuition, nonresident: full-time $7,230. Tuition and fees vary according to program. *Financial aid:* In 1998–99, 10 students received aid, including 1 research assistantship, 9 teaching assistantships; career-related internships or fieldwork, Federal Work-Study, institutionally-sponsored loans, and tuition waivers (partial) also available. Financial aid applicants required to submit FAFSA. *Faculty research:* Biostatistics, combinatorics, functional analysis, numerical solutions of PDE. Total annual research expenditures: $194,676. *Unit head:* Dr. Joe Guthrie, Chairperson, 915-747-5761, Fax: 915-747-6202, E-mail: joe@math.utep.edu. *Application contact:* Susan Jordan, Director, Graduate Student Services, 915-747-5491, Fax: 915-747-5788, E-mail: sjordan@utep.edu.

The University of Texas at San Antonio, College of Sciences and Engineering, Division of Mathematics and Statistics, San Antonio, TX 78249-0617. Offers mathematics (MS), including mathematics education, statistics. Part-time and evening/weekend programs available. *Faculty:* 19 full-time (5 women), 28 part-time (6 women). *Students:* 11 full-time (4 women), 42 part-time (17 women); includes 26 minority (2 African Americans, 6 Asian Americans or Pacific Islanders, 18 Hispanic Americans), 2 international. Average age 34. 17 applicants, 82% accepted. In 1998, 9 degrees awarded. *Degree requirements:* For master's, computer language, comprehensive exam required, foreign language and thesis not required. *Entrance requirements:* For master's, GRE General Test, TOEFL, minimum GPA of 3.0. *Application deadline:* For fall admission, 7/1. Applications are processed on a rolling basis. Application fee: $25. *Financial aid:* Research assistantships, teaching assistantships available. *Unit head:* Dr. Alfonso Castro, Director, 210-458-4451.

The University of Texas at Tyler, Graduate Studies, College of Sciences and Mathematics, Department of Mathematics, Tyler, TX 75799-0001. Offers MA, MS. *Faculty:* 5 full-time (0 women). *Students:* 1 (woman) full-time. In 1998, 42 degrees awarded. *Degree requirements:* For master's, comprehensive exam required. *Entrance requirements:* For master's, GRE General Test (minimum combined score of 1000 required). *Application deadline:* Applications are processed on a rolling basis. Application fee: $0. *Financial aid:* Application deadline: 7/1. *Faculty research:* Graph theory. *Unit head:* Dr. Robert H. Cranford, Chair, 903-566-7403. *Application contact:* Martha D. Wheat, Director of Admissions and Student Records, 903-566-7201, Fax: 903-566-7068.

The University of Texas–Pan American, College of Science and Engineering, Department of Mathematics, Edinburg, TX 78539-2999. Offers MS, MSIS. Part-time and evening/weekend programs available. *Degree requirements:* For master's, thesis or alternative, comprehensive exam required. *Entrance requirements:* For master's, GRE General Test, minimum GPA of 3.0. *Faculty research:* Boundary value problems in differential equations, training of public school teachers in methods of presenting mathematics.

University of the District of Columbia, College of Arts and Sciences, School of Science and Mathematics, Department of Mathematics, Washington, DC 20008-1175. Offers MST. Part-time and evening/weekend programs available. Average age 29. In 1998, 1 degree awarded. *Degree requirements:* For master's, comprehensive exam required, foreign language and thesis not required. *Entrance requirements:* For master's, GRE General Test, writing proficiency exam. *Application deadline:* For fall admission, 6/14 (priority date); for spring admission, 11/15. Applications are processed on a rolling basis. Application fee: $20. *Unit head:* Dr. Lorenzo Hilliard, Chair, 202-274-5153. *Application contact:* 202-274-5011.

University of the Incarnate Word, School of Graduate Studies, College of Arts and Sciences, Program in Mathematics, San Antonio, TX 78209-6397. Offers MAMT, MS, PhD. Part-time and evening/weekend programs available. *Students:* 6 full-time (5 women), 11 part-time (7 women); includes 5 minority (1 African American, 4 Hispanic Americans), 1 international. Average age 27. 25 applicants, 100% accepted. In 1998, 2 degrees awarded (100% found work related to degree). *Degree requirements:* Foreign language not required. *Entrance requirements:* For master's, GRE General Test (minimum combined score of 1200 required), TOEFL (minimum score of 550 required). *Application deadline:* For fall admission, 8/15 (priority date); for spring admission, 12/31. Applications are processed on a rolling basis. Application fee: $20. *Faculty research:* Topology, set theory, mathematics education. Total annual research expenditures: $65,000. *Unit head:* Judith E. Beauford, Assistant Professor of Mathematics, 210-829-3171, Fax: 210-829-3153, E-mail: beauford@universe.uiwtx.edu. *Application contact:* Andrea Cyterski, Director of Admissions, 210-829-6005, Fax: 210-829-3921, E-mail: cyterski@universe.uiwtx.edu.

University of Toledo, Graduate School, College of Arts and Sciences, Department of Mathematics, Toledo, OH 43606-3398. Offers applied mathematics (MS); mathematics (MA, MS Ed, PhD); statistics (MS). Part-time programs available. *Degree requirements:* For master's, thesis not required; for doctorate, dissertation required. *Entrance requirements:* For master's and doctorate, GRE General Test, GRE Subject Test. Electronic applications accepted. *Faculty research:* Topology.

University of Toronto, School of Graduate Studies, Physical Sciences Division, Department of Mathematics, Toronto, ON M5S 1A1, Canada. Offers M Sc, MMF, PhD. Part-time programs available. *Degree requirements:* For master's, research project required, thesis optional; for doctorate, dissertation required.

University of Tulsa, Graduate School, College of Business Administration, Department of Engineering and Technology Management, Tulsa, OK 74104-3189. Offers chemical engineering (METM); computer science (METM); electrical engineering (METM); geological science (METM); mathematics (METM); mechanical engineering (METM); petroleum engineering (METM). Part-time and evening/weekend programs available. *Students:* 3 full-time (1 woman), 1 part-time, 3 international. *Degree requirements:* For master's, foreign language and thesis not required. *Entrance requirements:* For master's, GRE General Test (minimum score of 430 on verbal section, 600 on quantitative required), TOEFL (minimum score of 575 required). *Application deadline:* Applications are processed on a rolling basis. Application fee: $30. Electronic applications accepted. Tuition: Full-time $8,640; part-time $480 per hour. Required fees: $3 per hour. One-time fee: $200 full-time. Tuition and fees vary according to program. *Unit head:* Dr. Richard C. Burgess, Assistant Dean/Director of Graduate Business Studies, 918-631-2242, Fax: 918-631-2142.

University of Tulsa, Graduate School, College of Engineering and Applied Sciences, Department of Mathematical and Computer Sciences, Program in Mathematical Sciences, Tulsa, OK 74104-3189. Offers MS. Part-time programs available. *Students:* 4 full-time (1 woman), 1 (woman) part-time, 1 international. Average age 23. 3 applicants, 100% accepted. In 1998, 1 degree awarded. *Degree requirements:* For master's, computer language required, thesis optional, foreign language not required. *Entrance requirements:* For master's, GRE General Test, TOEFL (minimum score of 550 required), 16 upper level hours in mathematics. *Application deadline:* Applications are processed on a rolling basis. Application fee: $30. Electronic applications accepted. Tuition: Full-time $8,640; part-time $480 per hour. Required fees: $3 per hour. One-time fee: $200 full-time. Tuition and fees vary according to program. *Financial aid:* In 1998–99, 1 fellowship with full and partial tuition reimbursement (averaging $13,200 per year), 2 research assistantships with full and partial tuition reimbursements (averaging $2,120 per year), 3 teaching assistantships with full and partial tuition reimbursements (averaging $6,000 per year) were awarded.; Federal Work-Study and tuition waivers (partial) also available. Financial aid application deadline: 2/1; financial aid applicants required to submit FAFSA. *Unit head:* Dr. Richard A. Redner, Adviser, 918-631-2986, Fax: 918-631-3077.

University of Utah, Graduate School, College of Science, Department of Mathematics, Salt Lake City, UT 84112-1107. Offers M Phil, M Stat, MA, MS, PhD. Part-time programs available. *Faculty:* 46 full-time (1 woman), 24 part-time (4 women). *Students:* 47 full-time (11 women), 22 part-time (8 women), 19 international. Average age 30. In 1998, 9 master's, 7 doctorates awarded. Terminal master's awarded for partial completion of doctoral program. *Degree requirements:* For master's, thesis or alternative, written or oral exam required; for doctorate, dissertation, written and oral exams required. *Entrance requirements:* For master's and doctorate, TOEFL (minimum score of 500 required). *Application deadline:* For fall admission, 3/15. Application fee: $30 ($50 for international students). *Financial aid:* In 1998–99, 50 teaching assistantships were awarded. Financial aid application deadline: 3/15. *Faculty research:* Algebraic geometry, differential geometry, scientific computing, topology, mathematical biology. *Unit head:* James Carlson, Chair, 801-581-7870, Fax: 801-581-4148. *Application contact:* Peter C. Trombi, Director of Graduate Studies, 801-581-8005.

See in-depth description on page 797.

University of Vermont, Graduate College, College of Engineering and Mathematics, Department of Mathematics and Statistics, Program in Mathematics, Burlington, VT 05405-0160. Offers mathematics (MS, PhD); mathematics education (MAT, MST). *Accreditation:* NCATE (one or more programs are accredited). *Degree requirements:* For master's, foreign language and thesis not required; for doctorate, computer language, dissertation required, foreign language not required. *Entrance requirements:* For master's and doctorate, GRE General Test, GRE Subject Test, TOEFL (minimum score of 550 required).

University of Victoria, Faculty of Graduate Studies, Faculty of Science, Department of Mathematics and Statistics, Victoria, BC V8W 2Y2, Canada. Offers applied mathematics (M Sc, MA, PhD); pure mathematics (M Sc, MA, PhD); statistics (M Sc, MA). Part-time programs available. *Faculty:* 25 full-time (3 women), 7 part-time (2 women). *Students:* 24 full-time (4 women), 1 part-time, 8 international. Average age 29. 27 applicants, 63% accepted. In 1998, 4 master's, 1 doctorate awarded. *Degree requirements:* For master's, thesis required; for doctorate, one foreign language, dissertation, 3 qualifying exams required. *Average time to degree:* Master's–2.24 years full-time; doctorate–4.63 years full-time. *Application deadline:* For fall admission, 5/31 (priority date). Applications are processed on a rolling basis. Application fee: $50. *Financial aid:* In 1998–99, 16 students received aid, including 5 fellowships; research assistantships, teaching assistantships, career-related internships or fieldwork, institutionally-sponsored loans, and unspecified assistantships also available. Financial aid application deadline: 2/15. *Faculty research:* Functional analysis and operator theory, applied ordinary and partial differential equations, discrete mathematics and graph theory. Total annual research expenditures: $280,000. *Unit head:* Dr. R. Illner, Chair, 250-721-7436, Fax: 250-721-8962. *Application contact:* Dr. J. Phillips, Graduate Adviser, 250-721-7450, Fax: 250-721-8962, E-mail: phillips@math.uvic.ca.

University of Virginia, College and Graduate School of Arts and Sciences, Department of Mathematics, Program in Mathematics, Charlottesville, VA 22903. Offers MA, MS, PhD. *Faculty:* 34 full-time (4 women), 1 (woman) part-time. *Students:* 37 full-time (15 women), 7 international. Average age 26. 32 applicants, 59% accepted. In 1998, 10 master's, 6 doctorates awarded. *Degree requirements:* For master's, exam required, thesis optional; for doctorate, dissertation, comprehensive exams required. *Entrance requirements:* For master's and doctorate, GRE General Test, GRE Subject Test, TOEFL (minimum score of 600 required). *Application deadline:* For fall admission, 7/15; for spring admission, 12/1. Application fee: $60. *Financial aid:* Fellowships, teaching assistantships, unspecified assistantships available. Financial aid application deadline: 2/1. *Application contact:* Lawrence Thomas, Director, Graduate Admissions, 804-924-4918, Fax: 804-924-3084, E-mail: jar5d@virginia.edu.

University of Washington, Graduate School, College of Arts and Sciences, Department of Mathematics, Seattle, WA 98195. Offers MA, MS, PhD. Part-time programs available. *Faculty:* 54 full-time (4 women), 15 part-time (3 women). *Students:* 76 full-time (19 women), 1 part-time; includes 2 minority (1 Asian American or Pacific Islander, 1 Hispanic American), 23 international. 123 applicants, 49% accepted. In 1998, 6 master's, 6 doctorates awarded. Terminal master's awarded for partial completion of doctoral program. *Degree requirements:* For master's, thesis optional, foreign language not required; for doctorate, 2 foreign languages, dissertation required. *Entrance requirements:* For master's, GRE, TOEFL (minimum score of 500 required), minimum GPA of 3.0; for doctorate, GRE General Test, GRE Subject Test (mathematics), TOEFL (minimum score of 500 required), minimum GPA of 3.0. *Average time to degree:* Master's–2.3 years full-time; doctorate–5.7 years full-time. *Application deadline:* For fall admission, 7/1. Application fee: $50. Electronic applications accepted. Tuition, state resident: full-time $5,196; part-time $475 per credit. Tuition, nonresident: full-time $13,485; part-time $1,285 per credit.

Required fees: $387; $38 per credit. Tuition and fees vary according to course load. *Financial aid:* In 1998–99, 11 fellowships with full tuition reimbursements (averaging $6,138 per year), 66 teaching assistantships with full tuition reimbursements were awarded.; research assistantships with full tuition reimbursements, career-related internships or fieldwork and institutionally-sponsored loans also available. Financial aid application deadline: 2/1. *Faculty research:* Algebraic topology, algebra, analysis, partial differential equations, combinatorics and geometry. *Unit head:* Donald E. Marshall, Chair, 206-543-1151, Fax: 206-543-0397, E-mail: chair@math.washington.edu. *Application contact:* John M. Lee, Graduate Program Coordinator, 206-543-6830, Fax: 206-543-0397, E-mail: grads@math.washington.edu.

University of Washington, Graduate School, Interdisciplinary Graduate Program in Quantitative Ecology and Resource Management, Seattle, WA 98195. Offers MS, PhD. *Faculty:* 34 full-time (3 women). *Students:* 18 full-time (12 women), 2 part-time; includes 3 minority (2 Asian Americans or Pacific Islanders, 1 Native American), 2 international. Average age 30. 11 applicants, 27% accepted. In 1998, 1 doctorate awarded (100% found work related to degree). *Degree requirements:* For master's and doctorate, thesis/dissertation required. *Entrance requirements:* For master's and doctorate, GRE General Test (minimum score of 600 on verbal section, 710 on quantitative, 690 on analytical required), TOEFL (minimum score of 500 required), minimum GPA of 3.0. *Application deadline:* For fall admission, 2/1. Application fee: $50. Electronic applications accepted. Tuition, state resident: full-time $5,196; part-time $475 per credit. Tuition, nonresident: full-time $13,485; part-time $1,285 per credit. Required fees: $387; $38 per credit. Tuition and fees vary according to course load. *Financial aid:* In 1998–99, 2 fellowships with full tuition reimbursements (averaging $10,000 per year), 11 research assistantships with full tuition reimbursements (averaging $10,000 per year), 3 teaching assistantships with full tuition reimbursements (averaging $10,000 per year) were awarded.; grants, traineeships, tuition waivers (full), and unspecified assistantships also available. Financial aid applicants required to submit FAFSA. *Faculty research:* Population dynamics, statistical analysis, ecological modeling and systems analysis of aquatic and terrestrial ecosystems. Total annual research expenditures: $1.5 million. *Unit head:* Dr. E. David Ford, Chair, 206-616-9571, Fax: 206-616-9443, E-mail: qerm@cqs.washington.edu. *Application contact:* Joanne Besch, Graduate Assistant, 206-616-9571, Fax: 206-616-9443, E-mail: qerm@cqs.washington.edu.

University of Waterloo, Graduate Studies, Faculty of Mathematics, Department of Combinatorics/Optimization, Waterloo, ON N2L 3G1, Canada. Offers M Math, PhD. Part-time programs available. *Faculty:* 18 full-time (1 woman), 12 part-time (0 women). *Students:* 25 full-time (5 women). 37 applicants, 51% accepted. In 1998, 8 master's awarded. *Degree requirements:* For master's, research paper or thesis required; for doctorate, dissertation required, foreign language not required. *Entrance requirements:* For master's, GRE General Test (minimum score of 780 required), TOEFL (minimum score of 580 required), honors degree in field, minimum B+ average; for doctorate, GRE General Test (minimum score of 780 required), TOEFL (minimum score of 580 required), master's degree, minimum A average. *Application deadline:* For fall admission, 4/15 (priority date); for spring admission, 12/1. Applications are processed on a rolling basis. Application fee: $50. *Expenses:* Tuition and fees charges are reported in Canadian dollars. Tuition, state resident: full-time $3,168 Canadian dollars; part-time $792 Canadian dollars per term. Tuition, nonresident: full-time $8,000 Canadian dollars; part-time $2,000 Canadian dollars. Required fees: $45 Canadian dollars per term. Tuition and fees vary according to program. *Financial aid:* Research assistantships, teaching assistantships, career-related internships or fieldwork and scholarships available. *Faculty research:* Algebraic and enumerative combinatorics, continuous optimization, cryptography, discrete optimization and graph theory. *Unit head:* Dr. W. H. Cunningham, Chair, 519-888-4567 Ext. 3482, Fax: 519-725-5441, E-mail: combopt@math.uwaterloo.ca. *Application contact:* Dr. C. D. Godsil, Associate Chair, 519-888-4567 Ext. 2696, Fax: 519-725-5441, E-mail: cograd@math.uwaterloo.ca.

University of Waterloo, Graduate Studies, Faculty of Mathematics, Department of Pure Mathematics, Waterloo, ON N2L 3G1, Canada. Offers M Math, PhD. *Faculty:* 18 full-time (1 woman), 10 part-time (1 woman). *Students:* 12 full-time (2 women), 1 (woman) part-time. 18 applicants, 67% accepted. In 1998, 3 doctorates awarded. *Degree requirements:* For master's, thesis required, foreign language not required; for doctorate, one foreign language, dissertation required. *Entrance requirements:* For master's, TOEFL (minimum score of 580 required), honors degree in field, minimum B+ average; for doctorate, TOEFL (minimum score of 580 required), master's degree. *Application deadline:* For fall admission, 2/1 (priority date); for spring admission, 10/1. Applications are processed on a rolling basis. Application fee: $50. *Expenses:* Tuition and fees charges are reported in Canadian dollars. Tuition, state resident: full-time $3,168 Canadian dollars; part-time $792 Canadian dollars per term. Tuition, nonresident: full-time $8,000 Canadian dollars; part-time $2,000 Canadian dollars. Required fees: $45 Canadian dollars per term. Tuition and fees vary according to program. *Financial aid:* In 1998–99, 12 students received aid, including research assistantships with partial tuition reimbursements available (averaging $6,000 per year), teaching assistantships with partial tuition reimbursements available (averaging $12,000 per year); scholarships also available. Financial aid application deadline: 3/1. *Faculty research:* Algebra, algebraic and differential geometry, functional and harmonic analysis, logic and universal algebra, number theory. *Unit head:* Dr. W. Gilbert, Chair, 519-888-4567 Ext. 5558, Fax: 519-725-0160. *Application contact:* Dr. K. Hare, Graduate Officer, 519-888-4567 Ext. 4085, Fax: 519-725-0160, E-mail: kehare@math.uwaterloo.ca.

The University of Western Ontario, Faculty of Graduate Studies, Physical Sciences Division, Department of Mathematics, London, ON N6A 5B8, Canada. Offers MA, PhD. Part-time programs available. Terminal master's awarded for partial completion of doctoral program. *Degree requirements:* For master's, thesis or alternative required, foreign language not required; for doctorate, dissertation, qualifying exam required. *Entrance requirements:* For master's, TOEFL (minimum score of 550 required), minimum B average, honors degree; for doctorate, TOEFL (minimum score of 550 required), master's degree.

University of West Florida, College of Science and Technology, Department of Mathematics and Statistics, Pensacola, FL 32514-5750. Offers mathematics (MA); mathematics education (MAT); statistics (MA). *Accreditation:* NCATE (one or more programs are accredited). Part-time and evening/weekend programs available. *Students:* 8 full-time (3 women), 17 part-time (8 women); includes 8 minority (5 African Americans, 2 Asian Americans or Pacific Islanders, 1 Hispanic American) Average age 34. 13 applicants, 100% accepted. In 1998, 12 degrees awarded. *Degree requirements:* For master's, thesis optional, foreign language not required. *Entrance requirements:* For master's, GRE General Test (minimum combined score of 1000 required), minimum GPA of 3.0. *Application deadline:* For fall admission, 7/19. Application fee: $20. Tuition, state resident: full-time $3,582; part-time $149 per credit hour. Tuition, nonresident: full-time $12,240; part-time $510 per credit hour. *Financial aid:* Fellowships, teaching assistantships, career-related internships or fieldwork and institutionally-sponsored loans available. Aid available to part-time students. *Unit head:* Dr. Rohan Hemasinha, Chairperson, 850-474-2276.

University of Windsor, College of Graduate Studies and Research, Faculty of Science, Mathematics and Statistics, Economics AAV, Windsor, ON N9B 3P4, Canada. Offers mathematics (M Sc, PhD); statistics (M Sc, PhD). Part-time programs available. *Degree requirements:* For master's, thesis required (for some programs); for doctorate, dissertation required. *Entrance requirements:* For master's, GRE, TOEFL (minimum score of 550 required), minimum B average; for doctorate, TOEFL, master's degree. *Faculty research:* Statistics and probability, matrix algebra, functional analysis, mathematical programming.

University of Wisconsin–Madison, Graduate School, College of Letters and Science, Department of Mathematics, Madison, WI 53706-1380. Offers MA, PhD. *Faculty:* 65. *Students:* 116 full-time (26 women), 26 part-time (8 women); includes 52 minority (46 Asian Americans or Pacific Islanders, 6 Hispanic Americans) 204 applicants, 44% accepted. In 1998, 10 master's awarded (20% entered university research/teaching, 20% found other work related to degree, 60% continued full-time study); 24 doctorates awarded. Terminal master's awarded for partial completion of doctoral program. *Degree requirements:* For master's, computer language required, foreign language and thesis not required; for doctorate, one foreign language, dissertation required. *Entrance requirements:* For master's and doctorate, GRE General Test, GRE Subject Test. *Average time to degree:* Master's–2 years full-time; doctorate–6 years full-time. *Application deadline:* For fall admission, 12/31 (priority date). Application fee: $45. Electronic applications accepted. *Financial aid:* In 1998–99, 128 students received aid, including 7 fellowships with full tuition reimbursements available (averaging $13,500 per year), 122 teaching assistantships with full tuition reimbursements available (averaging $10,990 per year); research assistantships, institutionally-sponsored loans also available. Aid available to part-time students. Financial aid application deadline: 12/31. *Faculty research:* Applied mathematics, analysis, algebra, logic, topology. Total annual research expenditures: $2 million. *Unit head:* Alejandro Adem, Chair, 608-263-1161, Fax: 608-263-8891, E-mail: adem@math.wisc.edu. *Application contact:* Sherry M. Lange, Graduate Program Secretary, 608-263-8884, Fax: 608-263-8891, E-mail: lange@math.wisc.edu.

University of Wisconsin–Milwaukee, Graduate School, College of Letters and Sciences, Department of Mathematical Sciences, Milwaukee, WI 53201-0413. Offers mathematics (MS, PhD). *Faculty:* 29 full-time (2 women). *Students:* 38 full-time (12 women), 14 part-time (5 women); includes 5 minority (2 African Americans, 2 Asian Americans or Pacific Islanders, 1 Hispanic American), 24 international. 43 applicants, 51% accepted. In 1998, 3 master's, 9 doctorates awarded. *Degree requirements:* For master's, foreign language and thesis not required; for doctorate, dissertation required. *Application deadline:* For fall admission, 1/1 (priority date); for spring admission, 9/1. Applications are processed on a rolling basis. Application fee: $45 ($75 for international students). *Financial aid:* In 1998–99, 7 fellowships, 35 teaching assistantships were awarded.; research assistantships, career-related internships or fieldwork also available. Aid available to part-time students. Financial aid application deadline: 4/15. *Unit head:* David Schultz, Chair, 414-229-5264.

University of Wyoming, Graduate School, College of Arts and Sciences, Department of Mathematics, Laramie, WY 82071. Offers mathematics (MA, MAT, MS, MST, PhD); mathematics/computer science (PhD). Part-time programs available. *Faculty:* 26 full-time (4 women). *Students:* 14 full-time (5 women), 11 part-time (2 women), 9 international. 12 applicants, 58% accepted. In 1998, 26 master's, 5 doctorates awarded. Terminal master's awarded for partial completion of doctoral program. *Degree requirements:* For master's, thesis or alternative, qualifying exam required, foreign language not required; for doctorate, one foreign language, dissertation, preliminary exam required. *Entrance requirements:* For master's and doctorate, GRE General Test, minimum GPA of 3.0. *Average time to degree:* Master's–2.5 years full-time, 3 years part-time; doctorate–5 years full-time. *Application deadline:* For fall admission, 3/1 (priority date). Applications are processed on a rolling basis. Application fee: $40. Tuition, state resident: full-time $2,520; part-time $140 per credit hour. Tuition, nonresident: full-time $7,790; part-time $433 per credit hour. Required fees: $400; $7 per credit hour. Full-time tuition and fees vary according to course load and program. *Financial aid:* In 1998–99, 2 research assistantships, 19 teaching assistantships were awarded.; institutionally-sponsored loans also available. Financial aid application deadline: 3/1. *Faculty research:* Numerical analysis, classical analysis, mathematical modeling, algebraic combinations. *Unit head:* Dr. Renito Chen, Head, 307-766-4221. *Application contact:* Jeanette Reisenburg, Office Associate, 307-766-6577.

Utah State University, School of Graduate Studies, College of Science, Department of Mathematics and Statistics, Logan, UT 84322. Offers applied statistics (MS); mathematical sciences (PhD); mathematics (M Math, MS). Part-time programs available. *Faculty:* 30 full-time (5 women). *Students:* 16 full-time (5 women), 5 part-time (3 women); includes 2 minority (1 African American, 1 Hispanic American), 6 international. Average age 29. 17 applicants, 24% accepted. In 1998, 3 master's, 2 doctorates awarded. Terminal master's awarded for partial completion of doctoral program. *Degree requirements:* For master's, qualifying exam required, thesis optional, foreign language not required; for doctorate, one foreign language, dissertation, comprehensive exams required. *Entrance requirements:* For master's and doctorate, GRE General Test (score in 40th percentile or higher required), TOEFL (minimum score of 580 required), minimum GPA of 3.0. *Average time to degree:* Master's–2 years full-time; doctorate–5 years full-time. *Application deadline:* For fall admission, 6/15 (priority date); for spring admission, 10/15. Applications are processed on a rolling basis. Application fee: $40. Tuition, state resident: full-time $1,492. Tuition, nonresident: full-time $5,232. Required fees: $434. Tuition and fees vary according to course load. *Financial aid:* In 1998–99, 1 fellowship with partial tuition reimbursement (averaging $12,000 per year), 17 teaching assistantships with partial tuition reimbursements (averaging $14,500 per year) were awarded.; research assistantships with partial tuition reimbursements Aid available to part-time students. Financial aid application deadline: 4/1. *Faculty research:* Differential equations, computational mathematics, dynamical systems, probability and statistics, pure mathematics. *Unit head:* Dr. E. Robert Heal, Head, 435-797-2809, Fax: 435-797-1822. *Application contact:* Dr. Renate Schaaf, Graduate Chairman, 435-797-2821, Fax: 435-797-1822, E-mail: schaaf@sunfs.math.usu.edu.

Vanderbilt University, Graduate School, Department of Mathematics, Nashville, TN 37240-1001. Offers MA, MAT, MS, PhD. *Faculty:* 34 full-time (2 women), 6 part-time (0 women). *Students:* 28 full-time (12 women); includes 2 minority (1 African American, 1 Asian American or Pacific Islander), 8 international. Average age 28. 41 applicants, 56% accepted. In 1998, 6 master's, 10 doctorates awarded. *Degree requirements:* For master's, thesis or alternative required, foreign language not required; for doctorate, dissertation, final and qualifying exams required. *Entrance requirements:* For master's and doctorate, GRE General Test, GRE Subject Test. *Average time to degree:* Master's–2 years full-time; doctorate–5 years full-time. *Application deadline:* For fall admission, 1/15. Application fee: $40. *Financial aid:* In 1998–99, 25 students received aid, including 25 teaching assistantships with full tuition reimbursements available (averaging $13,000 per year); Federal Work-Study and institutionally-sponsored loans also available. Financial aid application deadline: 1/15. *Faculty research:* Algebra, topology, applied mathematics,graph theory, analytical mathematics. *Unit head:* Constantine Tsinakis, Chair, 615-322-6672, Fax: 615-343-0215, E-mail: tsinakis@math.vanderbilt.edu. *Application contact:* John G. Ratcliffe, Director of Graduate Studies, 615-322-6672, Fax: 615-343-0215, E-mail: ratclifj@math.vanderbilt.edu.

Villanova University, Graduate School of Liberal Arts and Sciences, Department of Mathematical Sciences, Program in Mathematical Sciences, Villanova, PA 19085-1699. Offers MA, MS. Part-time and evening/weekend programs available. *Students:* 6 full-time (3 women), 10 part-time (5 women); includes 1 minority (Asian American or Pacific Islander), 1 international. Average age 28. 21 applicants, 90% accepted. In 1998, 8 degrees awarded. *Degree requirements:* Foreign language not required. *Entrance requirements:* For master's, minimum GPA of 3.0. *Application deadline:* For fall admission, 8/1 (priority date); for spring admission, 12/1. Application fee: $40. *Financial aid:* Research assistantships, Federal Work-Study available. Financial aid application deadline: 4/1; financial aid applicants required to submit FAFSA. *Unit head:* Dr. Robert Styer, Chairperson, Department of Mathematical Sciences, 610-519-4850.

Virginia Commonwealth University, School of Graduate Studies, College of Humanities and Sciences, Department of Mathematical Sciences, Richmond, VA 23284-9005. Offers applied mathematics (MS); computer science (MS); mathematics (MS); operations research (MS); statistics (MS, Certificate). *Students:* 14 full-time (5 women), 49 part-time (13 women); includes 24 minority (4 African Americans, 18 Asian Americans or Pacific Islanders, 1 Hispanic American, 1 Native American) Average age 32. In 1998, 20 master's, 5 other advanced degrees awarded. *Degree requirements:* Foreign language not required. *Entrance requirements:* For master's, GRE General Test, GRE Subject Test, TOEFL. *Application deadline:* For fall admission, 7/1; for spring admission, 11/15. Applications are processed on a rolling basis. Application fee: $30. Tuition, state resident: full-time $4,031; part-time $224 per credit hour. Tuition, nonresident: full-time $11,946; part-time $664 per credit hour. Required fees: $1,081; $40 per credit hour. Tuition and fees vary according to campus/location and program. *Financial aid:* Fellowships, research assistantships, teaching assistantships, Federal Work-Study and institutionally-sponsored loans available. Aid available to part-time students. *Unit head:* Dr. Richard Morris,

Mathematics

Virginia Commonwealth University (continued)

Chair, 804-828-1301, Fax: 804-828-8785, E-mail: jrmorris@vcu.edu. *Application contact:* Dr. James A. Wood, Director of Graduate Studies, 804-828-1301, Fax: 804-828-8785, E-mail: jawood@vcu.edu.

Virginia Polytechnic Institute and State University, Graduate School, College of Arts and Sciences, Department of Mathematics, Blacksburg, VA 24061. Offers applied mathematics (MS, PhD); mathematical physics (MS, PhD); pure mathematics (MS, PhD). Part-time programs available. *Faculty:* 55 full-time (5 women). *Students:* 66 full-time (26 women), 81 part-time (45 women); includes 12 minority (10 African Americans, 2 Asian Americans or Pacific Islanders), 14 international. 129 applicants, 69% accepted. In 1998, 16 master's, 9 doctorates awarded. Terminal master's awarded for partial completion of doctoral program. *Degree requirements:* For master's, thesis required (for some programs), foreign language not required; for doctorate, dissertation required. *Entrance requirements:* For master's and doctorate, TOEFL. *Application deadline:* For fall admission, 12/1 (priority date). Applications are processed on a rolling basis. Application fee: $25. *Financial aid:* Fellowships, research assistantships, teaching assistantships, unspecified assistantships available. *Faculty research:* Differential equations, operator theory, numerical analysis, algebra, control theory. *Unit head:* Dr. Robert F. Olin, Head, 540-231-6536, E-mail: olin@math.vt.edu. *Application contact:* Dr. E. L. Green, Graduate Administrator, 540-231-6536.

See in-depth description on page 801.

Virginia State University, School of Graduate Studies and Continuing Education, School of Agriculture, Science and Technology, Department of Mathematics, Petersburg, VA 23806-0001. Offers mathematics (MS); mathematics education (M Ed). *Accreditation:* NCATE (one or more programs are accredited). *Faculty:* 6 full-time (2 women). In 1998, 4 degrees awarded. *Degree requirements:* For master's, thesis required (for some programs). *Application deadline:* For fall admission, 8/15. Applications are processed on a rolling basis. Application fee: $25. Tuition, state resident: full-time $2,306; part-time $106 per credit hour. Tuition, nonresident: full-time $7,824; part-time $346 per credit hour. Required fees: $29 per credit hour. *Financial aid:* Application deadline: 5/1. *Unit head:* Dr. George W. Wimbush, Chair, 804-524-5920. *Application contact:* Dr. Wayne F. Virag, Dean, Graduate Studies and Continuing Education, 804-524-5985, Fax: 804-524-5104, E-mail: wvirag@vsu.edu.

Wake Forest University, Graduate School, Department of Mathematics, Winston-Salem, NC 27109. Offers MA. Part-time programs available. *Faculty:* 16 full-time (1 woman). *Students:* 14 full-time (9 women); includes 3 minority (all Asian Americans or Pacific Islanders) Average age 25. 12 applicants, 83% accepted. In 1998, 7 degrees awarded (100% found work related to degree). *Degree requirements:* For master's, one foreign language (computer language can substitute), thesis required. *Entrance requirements:* For master's, GRE General Test, GRE Subject Test. *Application deadline:* For fall admission, 2/15. Application fee: $25. *Financial aid:* In 1998–99, 12 students received aid, including 3 fellowships, 9 teaching assistantships; scholarships also available. Aid available to part-time students. Financial aid application deadline: 2/15; financial aid applicants required to submit FAFSA. *Faculty research:* Algebra, ring theory, topology, differential equations. *Unit head:* Dr. Ed Allen, Director, 336-758-5354, E-mail: allene@wfu.edu.

Washington State University, Graduate School, College of Sciences, Department of Pure and Applied Mathematics, Pullman, WA 99164. Offers MS, DA, PhD. *Faculty:* 31 full-time (4 women), 4 part-time (1 woman). *Students:* 31 full-time (13 women), 1 part-time; includes 2 minority (1 African American, 1 Asian American or Pacific Islander), 7 international. In 1998, 6 master's, 4 doctorates awarded. *Degree requirements:* For master's, thesis or alternative, core exams, oral exam required, foreign language not required; for doctorate, dissertation, core exams, oral exam required. *Entrance requirements:* For master's and doctorate, GRE General Test, GRE Subject Test, TOEFL (minimum score of 600 required), minimum GPA of 3.0. *Average time to degree:* Master's–2 years full-time; doctorate–4 years full-time. *Application deadline:* For fall admission, 3/15 (priority date). Applications are processed on a rolling basis. Application fee: $35. *Financial aid:* In 1998–99, 27 teaching assistantships were awarded.; fellowships, research assistantships, career-related internships or fieldwork, Federal Work-Study, institutionally-sponsored loans, tuition waivers (partial), and teaching associateships also available. Financial aid application deadline: 4/1; financial aid applicants required to submit FAFSA. *Faculty research:* Computational mathematics, operations research, modeling in the natural sciences, applied statistics. Total annual research expenditures: $378,424. *Unit head:* Dr. Valipuram Manoranjan, Chair, 509-335-6868, Fax: 509-335-1188. *Application contact:* Bonnie Collins, Coordinator, 509-335-6868, Fax: 509-335-1188, E-mail: bonnie@wsu.edu.

See in-depth description on page 805.

Washington University in St. Louis, Graduate School of Arts and Sciences, Department of Mathematics, St. Louis, MO 63130-4899. Offers mathematics (MA, PhD); mathematics education (MAT); statistics (MA, PhD). *Accreditation:* NCATE (one or more programs are accredited). Part-time programs available. *Students:* 26 full-time (7 women), 1 part-time; includes 2 minority (1 African American, 1 Asian American or Pacific Islander), 13 international. 40 applicants, 45% accepted. In 1998, 10 master's, 4 doctorates awarded. Terminal master's awarded for partial completion of doctoral program. *Degree requirements:* For master's, thesis or alternative required; for doctorate, dissertation required. *Entrance requirements:* For master's and doctorate, GRE General Test. *Application deadline:* For fall admission, 1/15 (priority date). Applications are processed on a rolling basis. Application fee: $35. *Financial aid:* Fellowships, research assistantships, teaching assistantships, Federal Work-Study, institutionally-sponsored loans, and tuition waivers (full and partial) available. Aid available to part-time students. Financial aid application deadline: 1/15. *Unit head:* Dr. Edward Wilson, Chairman, 314-935-6760.

Washington University in St. Louis, School of Engineering and Applied Science, Sever Institute of Technology, Department of Systems Science and Mathematics, St. Louis, MO 63130-4899. Offers control engineering (MCE); systems science and mathematics (MS, D Sc); systems science, mathematics, and economics (D Sc). Part-time programs available. *Faculty:* 8 full-time (0 women), 7 part-time (0 women). *Students:* 34 full-time (2 women), 9 part-time; includes 20 minority (19 Asian Americans or Pacific Islanders, 1 Hispanic American), 7 international. Average age 27. 56 applicants, 41% accepted. In 1998, 10 master's, 3 doctorates awarded. Terminal master's awarded for partial completion of doctoral program. *Degree requirements:* For master's, thesis optional, foreign language not required; for doctorate, dissertation, departmental qualifying exam required, foreign language not required. *Entrance requirements:* For master's and doctorate, TOEFL. *Application deadline:* For fall admission, 2/15 (priority date); for spring admission, 10/14. Application fee: $20. *Financial aid:* In 1998–99, 27 students received aid, including 27 research assistantships (averaging $10,000 per year); fellowships, teaching assistantships, career-related internships or fieldwork, Federal Work-Study, and institutionally-sponsored loans also available. Financial aid application deadline: 2/15. *Faculty research:* Linear and nonlinear control systems, robotics and automation, scheduling and transportation systems, computer vision, discrete event dynamical systems. *Unit head:* Dr. I. Norman Katz, Chairman, 314-935-6001, Fax: 314-935-6121, E-mail: katz@zach.wustl.edu. *Application contact:* Sandra Devereaux, Administrative Secretary, 314-935-6001, Fax: 314-935-6121, E-mail: sandra@zach.wustl.edu.

Wayne State University, Graduate School, College of Science, Department of Mathematics, Program in Mathematics, Detroit, MI 48202. Offers MA, PhD. *Degree requirements:* For master's, foreign language and thesis not required; for doctorate, dissertation required.

Wesleyan University, Graduate Programs, Department of Mathematics, Middletown, CT 06459-0260. Offers MA, PhD. Terminal master's awarded for partial completion of doctoral program. *Degree requirements:* For master's, one foreign language, thesis required; for doctorate, 2 foreign languages, dissertation required. *Entrance requirements:* For master's, GRE General Test, GRE Subject Test; for doctorate, GRE Subject Test. *Faculty research:* Topology, analysis.

See in-depth description on page 809.

West Chester University of Pennsylvania, Graduate Studies, College of Arts and Sciences, Department of Mathematics, West Chester, PA 19383. Offers mathematics (M Ed, MA). Part-time and evening/weekend programs available. *Faculty:* 22 part-time. *Students:* 11. Average age 30. *Degree requirements:* For master's, comprehensive exam required, foreign language and thesis not required. *Entrance requirements:* For master's, GRE General Test, interview. *Application deadline:* For fall admission, 4/15 (priority date); for spring admission, 10/15. Applications are processed on a rolling basis. Application fee: $25. Tuition, state resident: full-time $3,780; part-time $210 per credit. Tuition, nonresident: full-time $6,610; part-time $367 per credit. Required fees: $684; $39 per credit. Tuition and fees vary according to course load. *Financial aid:* In 1998–99, 2 research assistantships with full tuition reimbursements (averaging $5,000 per year) were awarded. Aid available to part-time students. Financial aid application deadline: 2/15. *Unit head:* Dr. Frank Milliman, Chair, 610-436-2537. *Application contact:* Dr. John Kerrigan, Graduate Coordinator, 610-436-2351, E-mail: jkerrigan@wcupa.edu.

Western Carolina University, Graduate School, College of Arts and Sciences, Department of Mathematics and Computer Science, Cullowhee, NC 28723. Offers MA Ed, MAT, MS. Part-time and evening/weekend programs available. *Faculty:* 13. *Students:* 10 full-time (4 women), 7 part-time (4 women). 17 applicants, 71% accepted. In 1998, 4 degrees awarded. *Degree requirements:* For master's, comprehensive exam required, thesis optional, foreign language not required. *Entrance requirements:* For master's, GRE General Test, GRE Subject Test (applied mathematics applicants). *Application deadline:* For fall admission, 5/1 (priority date); for spring admission, 10/1 (priority date). Applications are processed on a rolling basis. Application fee: $35. Tuition, state resident: full-time $918. Tuition, nonresident: full-time $8,188. Required fees: $881. *Financial aid:* In 1998–99, 7 students received aid, including 7 research assistantships with full and partial tuition reimbursements available (averaging $5,679 per year); fellowships, teaching assistantships, Federal Work-Study, grants, and institutionally-sponsored loans also available. Financial aid application deadline: 3/15; financial aid applicants required to submit FAFSA. *Unit head:* Harold Williford, Head, 828-227-7245. *Application contact:* Kathleen Owen, Assistant to the Dean, 828-227-7398, Fax: 828-227-7480, E-mail: kowen@wcu.edu.

Western Connecticut State University, Division of Graduate Studies, School of Arts and Sciences, Department of Mathematics and Computer Science, Danbury, CT 06810-6885. Offers mathematics and computer science (MA); theoretical mathematics (MA). Part-time and evening/weekend programs available. In 1998, 3 degrees awarded. *Degree requirements:* For master's, comprehensive exam, thesis, or research project required. *Entrance requirements:* For master's, minimum GPA of 2.5. *Application deadline:* For fall admission, 8/1 (priority date). Applications are processed on a rolling basis. Application fee: $40. *Financial aid:* Fellowships, career-related internships or fieldwork and Federal Work-Study available. Aid available to part-time students. Financial aid application deadline: 5/1; financial aid applicants required to submit FAFSA. *Unit head:* Dr. Josephine Hamer, Chair, 203-837-9347. *Application contact:* Chris Shankle, Associate Director of Graduate Admissions, 203-837-8244, Fax: 203-837-8338, E-mail: shanklec@wcsu.edu.

Western Illinois University, School of Graduate Studies, College of Arts and Sciences, Department of Mathematics, Macomb, IL 61455-1390. Offers MS. Part-time programs available. *Faculty:* 25 full-time (2 women). *Students:* 7 full-time (4 women), 7 part-time (5 women), 5 international. Average age 29. 13 applicants, 54% accepted. In 1998, 5 degrees awarded. *Degree requirements:* For master's, thesis or alternative required, foreign language not required. *Application deadline:* Applications are processed on a rolling basis. Application fee: $0 ($25 for international students). *Financial aid:* In 1998–99, 6 students received aid, including 6 research assistantships with full tuition reimbursements available (averaging $4,880 per year) Financial aid applicants required to submit FAFSA. *Faculty research:* National Council of Teachers of Mathematics standards in geometry and mathematics, mobile computer laboratories, algebra, computational mathematics. *Unit head:* Dr. Iraj Kalantari, Chairperson, 309-298-1054. *Application contact:* Barbara Baily, Director of Graduate Studies, 309-298-1806, Fax: 309-298-2245, E-mail: barb_baily@ccmail.wiu.edu.

Western Kentucky University, Graduate Studies, Ogden College of Science, Technology, and Health, Department of Mathematics, Bowling Green, KY 42101-3576. Offers MA Ed, MS. Part-time programs available. *Faculty:* 15 full-time (3 women). *Students:* 8 full-time (5 women), 5 part-time (3 women); includes 1 minority (African American), 1 international. Average age 26. 6 applicants, 50% accepted. In 1998, 9 degrees awarded. *Degree requirements:* For master's, thesis or alternative, written exam required, foreign language not required, thesis or alternative, written exam required, foreign language not required. *Entrance requirements:* For master's, GRE General Test. *Application deadline:* For fall admission, 8/1 (priority date); for spring admission, 12/1. Applications are processed on a rolling basis. Application fee: $30. Tuition, state resident: full-time $2,590; part-time $140 per hour. Tuition, nonresident: full-time $6,430; part-time $387 per hour. Required fees: $370. *Financial aid:* In 1998–99, 5 research assistantships with partial tuition reimbursements (averaging $6,500 per year), 3 teaching assistantships with partial tuition reimbursements (averaging $6,500 per year) were awarded.; Federal Work-Study, institutionally-sponsored loans, and service awards also available. Aid available to part-time students. Financial aid application deadline: 4/1; financial aid applicants required to submit FAFSA. *Unit head:* Dr. James Porter, Head, 270-745-3651, Fax: 270-745-5385.

Western Michigan University, Graduate College, College of Arts and Sciences, Department of Mathematics and Statistics, Programs in Mathematics, Kalamazoo, MI 49008. Offers mathematics (MA); mathematics education (MA, PhD). *Accreditation:* NCATE (one or more programs are accredited). *Students:* 16 full-time (9 women), 37 part-time (25 women); includes 1 minority (Hispanic American), 5 international. 29 applicants, 62% accepted. In 1998, 43 master's, 6 doctorates awarded. *Degree requirements:* For master's, oral exams required, thesis not required; for doctorate, dissertation, oral exams required. *Entrance requirements:* For doctorate, GRE General Test. *Application deadline:* For fall admission, 2/15 (priority date). Applications are processed on a rolling basis. Application fee: $25. *Financial aid:* Fellowships, research assistantships, teaching assistantships, Federal Work-Study available. Financial aid application deadline: 2/15; financial aid applicants required to submit FAFSA. *Unit head:* Paula J. Boodt, Coordinator, Graduate Admissions and Recruitment, 616-387-2000, Fax: 616-387-2355, E-mail: paula.boodt@wmich.edu. *Application contact:* Paula J. Boodt, Coordinator, Graduate Admissions and Recruitment, 616-387-2000, Fax: 616-387-2355, E-mail: paula.boodt@wmich.edu.

Western Washington University, Graduate School, College of Arts and Sciences, Department of Mathematics, Bellingham, WA 98225-5996. Offers MS. Part-time programs available. *Faculty:* 17. *Students:* 15 full-time (4 women), 4 part-time (1 woman); includes 4 minority (2 African Americans, 2 Hispanic Americans) 18 applicants, 94% accepted. In 1998, 11 degrees awarded. *Degree requirements:* For master's, thesis (for some programs), project required, foreign language not required. *Entrance requirements:* For master's, GRE General Test, TOEFL, minimum GPA of 3.0 in last 60 semester hours or last 90 quarter hours. *Application deadline:* For fall admission, 6/1; for winter admission, 10/1; for spring admission, 2/1. Applications are processed on a rolling basis. Application fee: $35. Tuition, state resident: full-time $3,247; part-time $146 per credit hour. Tuition, nonresident: full-time $13,364; part-time $445 per credit hour. Required fees: $254; $85 per quarter. *Financial aid:* In 1998–99, 16 teaching assistantships with partial tuition reimbursements (averaging $7,563 per year) were awarded.; Federal Work-Study, institutionally-sponsored loans, scholarships, and tuition waivers (partial) also available. Aid available to part-time students. Financial aid application deadline: 2/15; financial aid applicants required to submit FAFSA. *Unit head:* Dr. Tjalling Ypma, Chair, 360-650-3785. *Application contact:* Dr. Edoh Amiran, Graduate Adviser, 360-650-3487.

West Texas A&M University, College of Agriculture, Nursing, and Natural Sciences, Department of Mathematics, Physical Sciences and Engineering Technology, Program in Mathematics, Canyon, TX 79016-0001. Offers MS. Part-time programs available. *Faculty:* 4 full-time (0 women). Average age 34. 1 applicants, 100% accepted. In 1998, 3 degrees awarded. *Degree requirements:* For master's, comprehensive exam required, thesis optional, foreign language not required. *Entrance requirements:* For master's, GRE General Test (combined average 964). *Application deadline:* Applications are processed on a rolling basis. Application fee: $0 ($50 for international students). Electronic applications accepted. Tuition, state resident: full-time $1,152; part-time $48 per credit. Tuition, nonresident: full-time $6,336; part-time $264 per credit. Required fees: $1,063; $531 per semester. *Financial aid:* In 1998–99, research assistantships (averaging $6,500 per year), 2 teaching assistantships (averaging $6,500 per year) were awarded.; Federal Work-Study, grants, institutionally-sponsored loans, scholarships, and tuition waivers (partial) also available. Aid available to part-time students. Financial aid applicants required to submit FAFSA. Total annual research expenditures: $3,600. *Unit head:* Dr. Walter Kauppila, Graduate Admissions Chair, 313-577-2780. *Application contact:* Dr. Randy Combs, Graduate Advisor, 806-651-2531, Fax: 806-651-2544, E-mail: rcombs@mail.wtamu.edu.

West Virginia University, Eberly College of Arts and Sciences, Department of Mathematics, Morgantown, WV 26506. Offers MS, PhD. Part-time programs available. Terminal master's awarded for partial completion of doctoral program. *Degree requirements:* For master's, foreign language and thesis not required; for doctorate, one foreign language, dissertation, comprehensive exam required. *Entrance requirements:* For master's, TOEFL (minimum score of 550 required), minimum GPA of 2.5; for doctorate, GRE, TOEFL (minimum score of 550 required), GRE Subject Test, master's degree in mathematics. *Faculty research:* Combinatorics and graph theory, topology, differential equations, applied and computational mathematics.

Wichita State University, Graduate School, Fairmount College of Liberal Arts and Sciences, Department of Mathematics and Statistics, Wichita, KS 67260. Offers applied mathematics (PhD); mathematics (MS); statistics (MS). Part-time programs available. *Faculty:* 23 full-time (0 women), 1 part-time (0 women). *Students:* 22 full-time (7 women), 15 part-time (7 women); includes 2 minority (1 African American, 1 Asian American or Pacific Islander), 15 international. Average age 35. 19 applicants, 37% accepted. In 1998, 4 master's, 2 doctorates awarded. *Degree requirements:* For master's, comprehensive exam required, thesis optional, foreign language not required; for doctorate, computer language, dissertation required. *Entrance requirements:* For master's, GRE, TOEFL (minimum score of 550 required); for doctorate, GRE Subject Test, TOEFL (minimum score of 550 required). *Application deadline:* For fall admission, 7/1 (priority date); for spring admission, 1/1. Applications are processed on a rolling basis. Application fee: $25 ($40 for international students). Electronic applications accepted. *Financial aid:* In 1998–99, 10 fellowships (averaging $4,000 per year), 4 research assistantships (averaging $5,000 per year), 16 teaching assistantships with full tuition reimbursements (averaging $10,000 per year) were awarded.; Federal Work-Study, institutionally-sponsored loans, and unspecified assistantships also available. Aid available to part-time students. Financial aid application deadline: 4/1; financial aid applicants required to submit FAFSA. *Faculty research:* Partial differential equations, combinatorics, ring theory, minimal surfaces, several complex variables. Total annual research expenditures: $91,665. *Unit head:* Dr. Buma Fridman, Chairperson, 316-978-3985, Fax: 316-978-3748, E-mail: fridman@twsuvm.uc.twsu.edu. *Application contact:* Dr. Ken Miller, Graduate Coordinator, 316-978-3959, Fax: 316-978-3748, E-mail: miller@twsuvm.uc.twsu.edu.

Wilkes University, Graduate Studies, Department of Mathematics, Wilkes-Barre, PA 18766-0002. Offers MS, MS Ed. *Degree requirements:* For master's, thesis or alternative required, foreign language not required. *Entrance requirements:* For master's, GRE.

Winthrop University, College of Arts and Sciences, Department of Mathematics, Rock Hill, SC 29733. Offers M Math. Part-time programs available. *Faculty:* 7 full-time (1 woman). *Students:* 3 full-time (2 women), 5 part-time (3 women); includes 1 minority (African American) Average age 33. In 1998, 2 degrees awarded. *Degree requirements:* For master's, foreign language and thesis not required. *Entrance requirements:* For master's, GRE General Test, minimum GPA of 3.0. *Application deadline:* For fall admission, 7/15 (priority date); for spring admission, 12/1. Applications are processed on a rolling basis. Application fee: $35. Tuition, state resident: full-time $3,928; part-time $164 per semester hour. Tuition, nonresident: full-time $7,060; part-time $294 per semester hour. *Financial aid:* Federal Work-Study, scholarships, and unspecified assistantships available. Aid available to part-time students. Financial aid application deadline: 2/1; financial aid applicants required to submit FAFSA. *Unit head:* Dr. Gary T. Brooks, Chairman, 803-232-2175, E-mail: brooksg@winthrop.edu. *Application contact:* Sharon Johnson, Director of Graduate Studies, 803-323-2204, Fax: 803-323-2292, E-mail: johnsons@winthrop.edu.

Worcester Polytechnic Institute, Graduate Studies, Department of Mathematical Science, Worcester, MA 01609-2280. Offers applied mathematics (MS); applied statistics (MS); mathematical science (PhD, Certificate); mathematics (MME). Part-time and evening/weekend programs available. *Faculty:* 25 full-time (3 women). *Students:* 17 full-time (8 women), 11 part-time (1 woman); includes 2 minority (1 African American, 1 Asian American or Pacific Islander), 8 international. 48 applicants, 90% accepted. In 1998, 12 master's awarded. *Degree requirements:* For master's, thesis optional, foreign language not required; for doctorate, dissertation required, foreign language not required. *Entrance requirements:* For master's, TOEFL (minimum score of 550 required; average 600). *Average time to degree:* Master's–2 years full-time; doctorate–3 years full-time. *Application deadline:* For fall admission, 2/15 (priority date); for spring admission, 10/15 (priority date). Applications are processed on a rolling basis. Application fee: $50. Electronic applications accepted. *Financial aid:* In 1998–99, 11 students received aid, including 2 research assistantships with full tuition reimbursements available (averaging $15,000 per year), 9 teaching assistantships with full tuition reimbursements available (averaging $11,970 per year); fellowships, career-related internships or fieldwork, grants, institutionally-sponsored loans, and scholarships also available. Financial aid application deadline: 2/15; financial aid applicants required to submit FAFSA. *Faculty research:* Computational mathematics, industrial mathematics, scientific computing. Total annual research expenditures: $528,709. *Unit head:* Dr. Homer Walker, Head, 508-831-5316, Fax: 508-831-5824. *Application contact:* Robert Lipton, Graduate Coordinator, 508-831-5321, Fax: 508-831-5824, E-mail: lipton@wpi.edu.

Wright State University, School of Graduate Studies, College of Science and Mathematics, Department of Mathematics and Statistics, Program in Mathematics, Dayton, OH 45435. Offers MS. *Students:* 4 full-time (2 women), 6 part-time (3 women); includes 2 minority (1 African American, 1 Asian American or Pacific Islander), 1 international. Average age 33. 6 applicants, 67% accepted. In 1998, 4 degrees awarded. *Degree requirements:* For master's, comprehensive exams required, foreign language and thesis not required. *Entrance requirements:* For master's, TOEFL (minimum score of 550 required), previous course work in mathematics beyond calculus. Application fee: $25. *Financial aid:* Fellowships, research assistantships, teaching assistantships available. Aid available to part-time students. Financial aid applicants required to submit FAFSA. *Faculty research:* Analysis, algebraic combinatorics, graph theory, operator theory. *Unit head:* Dr. Joanne M. Dombrowski, Director, 937-775-2785, Fax: 937-775-3068.

Yale University, Graduate School of Arts and Sciences, Department of Mathematics, New Haven, CT 06520. Offers MS, PhD. *Faculty:* 38. *Students:* 38 full-time (4 women); includes 1 minority (Hispanic American), 26 international. 92 applicants, 34% accepted. In 1998, 5 degrees awarded. *Degree requirements:* For doctorate, dissertation required. *Entrance requirements:* For doctorate, GRE General Test, GRE Subject Test. *Average time to degree:* Doctorate–5.5 years full-time. *Application deadline:* For fall admission, 1/4. Application fee: $65. *Financial aid:* Fellowships, research assistantships, teaching assistantships, Federal Work-Study and institutionally-sponsored loans available. Aid available to part-time students. *Unit head:* Chair, 203-432-7318. *Application contact:* Admissions Information, 203-432-2770.

York University, Faculty of Graduate Studies, Faculty of Arts, Program in Mathematics and Statistics, Toronto, ON M3J 1P3, Canada. Offers MA, PhD. Part-time programs available. *Degree requirements:* For master's, thesis optional; for doctorate, dissertation, comprehensive exam required.

Youngstown State University, Graduate School, College of Arts and Sciences, Department of Mathematics, Youngstown, OH 44555-0001. Offers MS. Part-time programs available. *Faculty:* 18 full-time (2 women). *Students:* 9 full-time (3 women), 10 part-time (5 women); includes 1 minority (African American), 3 international. 8 applicants, 100% accepted. In 1998, 4 degrees awarded. *Degree requirements:* For master's, computer language, comprehensive exam required, thesis optional, foreign language not required. *Entrance requirements:* For master's, TOEFL (minimum score of 550 required), minimum GPA of 2.7 in computer science and mathematics. *Application deadline:* For fall admission, 8/15 (priority date); for winter admission, 11/15 (priority date); for spring admission, 2/15 (priority date). Applications are processed on a rolling basis. Application fee: $30 ($75 for international students). Tuition, state resident: part-time $97 per credit hour. Tuition, nonresident: part-time $219 per credit hour. Required fees: $21 per credit hour. $41 per quarter. *Financial aid:* In 1998–99, 16 students received aid, including 7 research assistantships with full tuition reimbursements available (averaging $7,500 per year), 3 teaching assistantships with full tuition reimbursements available (averaging $7,500 per year); Federal Work-Study, institutionally-sponsored loans, and scholarships also available. Aid available to part-time students. Financial aid application deadline: 3/1. *Faculty research:* Regression analysis, numerical analysis, statistics, Markov chain, topology and fuzzy sets. *Unit head:* Dr. John J. Buoni, Chair, 330-742-3302. *Application contact:* Dr. Peter J. Kasvinsky, Dean of Graduate Studies, 330-742-3091, Fax: 330-742-1580, E-mail: amgrad03@ysub.ysu.edu.

Statistics

American University, College of Arts and Sciences, Department of Mathematics and Statistics, Program in Statistics, Washington, DC 20016-8001. Offers applied statistics (Certificate); statistics (MA, PhD). Part-time and evening/weekend programs available. *Faculty:* 19 full-time (6 women), 5 part-time (3 women). *Students:* 13 full-time (8 women), 19 part-time (10 women); includes 3 minority (2 African Americans, 1 Asian American or Pacific Islander), 18 international. 31 applicants, 84% accepted. In 1998, 5 master's, 3 doctorates awarded. Terminal master's awarded for partial completion of doctoral program. *Degree requirements:* For master's, one foreign language required, (computer language can substitute), thesis optional; for doctorate, 2 foreign languages (computer language can substitute for one), dissertation, comprehensive exam required. *Application deadline:* For fall admission, 2/1; for spring admission, 10/1. Application fee: $50. *Financial aid:* Fellowships, teaching assistantships, career-related internships or fieldwork, Federal Work-Study, and institutionally-sponsored loans available. Aid available to part-time students. Financial aid application deadline: 2/1. *Faculty research:* Statistical computing; data analysis; random processes; environmental, meteorological, and biological applications. *Unit head:* Dr. Virginia Stallings, Chair, Department of Mathematics and Statistics, 202-885-3166, Fax: 202-885-3155.

American University, College of Arts and Sciences, Department of Mathematics and Statistics, Program in Statistics for Policy Analysis, Washington, DC 20016-8001. Offers MS. Part-time programs available. *Faculty:* 19 full-time (6 women), 5 part-time (3 women). *Students:* 1 full-time (0 women), 3 part-time (all women); includes 2 minority (1 African American, 1 Asian American or Pacific Islander) 3 applicants, 100% accepted. *Degree requirements:* For master's, one foreign language required, (computer language can substitute), thesis optional. *Application deadline:* For fall admission, 2/1; for spring admission, 10/1. Application fee: $50. *Financial aid:* Application deadline: 2/1. *Unit head:* Dr. Virginia Stallings, Chair, Department of Mathematics and Statistics, 202-885-3166, Fax: 202-885-3155.

Arizona State University, Graduate College, College of Liberal Arts and Sciences, Department of Mathematics, Tempe, AZ 85287. Offers applied mathematics (MA, PhD); mathematics (MA, MNS, PhD); statistics (MA, PhD). *Faculty:* 95 full-time (22 women), 2 part-time (0 women). *Students:* 67 full-time (20 women), 15 part-time (5 women); includes 6 minority (2 African Americans, 3 Asian Americans or Pacific Islanders, 1 Hispanic American), 37 international. *Degree requirements:* For master's, thesis or alternative required; for doctorate, one foreign language, dissertation required. *Entrance requirements:* For master's and doctorate, GRE General Test. *Application deadline:* For fall admission, 3/1. Application fee: $45. *Unit head:* Dr. Rosemary Renaut, Chair, 480-965-3951.

See in-depth description on page 641.

Arizona State University, Graduate College, Interdisciplinary Program in Statistics, Tempe, AZ 85287. Offers MS. *Entrance requirements:* For master's, GRE. Application fee: $45. *Faculty research:* Regression, variance components, linear models, biostatistics, decision-theoretic methods. *Unit head:* Dr. Dennis Young, Director, 480-965-5628. *Application contact:* Graduate Secretary, 480-965-2671.

Auburn University, Graduate School, College of Sciences and Mathematics, Department of Discrete and Statistical Sciences, Auburn, Auburn University, AL 36849-0002. Offers M Prob S, MAM, MS, PhD. *Faculty:* 17 full-time (0 women). *Students:* 12 full-time (6 women), 11 part-time (4 women); includes 4 minority (3 African Americans, 1 Asian American or Pacific Islander), 5 international. 15 applicants, 73% accepted. In 1998, 1 master's, 7 doctorates awarded. *Degree requirements:* For doctorate, dissertation required. *Entrance requirements:* For master's and doctorate, GRE General Test. *Application deadline:* For fall admission, 9/1; for spring admission, 3/1. Applications are processed on a rolling basis. Application fee: $25 ($50 for international students). Tuition, state resident: full-time $2,760; part-time $76 per credit hour. Tuition, nonresident: full-time $8,280; part-time $228 per credit hour. *Financial aid:* Fellowships, teaching assistantships available. Financial aid application deadline: 3/15. *Faculty research:* Discrete mathematics, applied probability, differential equations, cryptography. *Unit head:* Dr. Kevin T. Phelps, Head, 334-844-5111, Fax: 334-844-3611, E-mail: phelpkt@mail.auburn.edu.

Ball State University, Graduate School, College of Sciences and Humanities, Department of Mathematical Sciences, Program in Mathematical Statistics, Muncie, IN 47306-1099. Offers MA. *Students:* 1 full-time (0 women), 5 part-time. Average age 36. 2 applicants, 100% accepted. In 1998, 3 degrees awarded. *Degree requirements:* Foreign language not required. Application fee: $15 ($25 for international students). *Financial aid:* Research assistantships available. *Faculty research:* Robust methods. *Unit head:* Mir Ali, Director, 765-285-8670, E-mail: mali@bsu.edu.

Statistics

Baruch College of the City University of New York, Zicklin School of Business, Department of Statistics and Computer Information Systems, Program in Statistics, New York, NY 10010-5585. Offers MBA, MS. Part-time and evening/weekend programs available. *Faculty:* 9 full-time (1 woman), 5 part-time (0 women). *Students:* 1 full-time, 6 part-time. In 1998, 2 degrees awarded. *Degree requirements:* For master's, computer language required, foreign language not required. *Entrance requirements:* For master's, GMAT, GRE General Test (MS), TOEFL (minimum score of 570 required), TWE (minimum score of 4.5 required). *Average time to degree:* Master's–2 years full-time, 4 years part-time. *Application deadline:* For fall admission, 4/1; for spring admission, 11/1. Application fee: $40. *Financial aid:* Research assistantships, career-related internships or fieldwork and Federal Work-Study available. Aid available to part-time students. Financial aid application deadline: 5/3; financial aid applicants required to submit FAFSA. *Unit head:* Gary Clark, Graduate Admissions, 757-594-7993, Fax: 757-594-7333, E-mail: admit@cnu.edu. *Application contact:* Michael S. Wynne, Office of Graduate Admissions, 212-802-2330, Fax: 212-802-2335, E-mail: graduate_admissions@baruch.cuny.edu.

Baylor University, Graduate School, Institute for Graduate Statistics, Waco, TX 76798. Offers MA, PhD. *Faculty:* 7 full-time (1 woman), 4 part-time (1 woman). *Students:* 11 full-time (4 women), 3 part-time (2 women); includes 2 minority (1 Asian American or Pacific Islander, 1 Hispanic American) Average age 24. 38 applicants, 16% accepted. In 1998, 3 master's, 4 doctorates awarded. *Degree requirements:* For doctorate, computer language, dissertation required. *Entrance requirements:* For master's, GRE General Test, 3 semesters of calculus; for doctorate, GRE General Test. *Application deadline:* Applications are processed on a rolling basis. Application fee: $25. *Financial aid:* In 1998–99, 1 fellowship, 5 research assistantships, 7 teaching assistantships were awarded.; institutionally-sponsored loans also available. *Faculty research:* Mathematical statistics, probability theory, biostatistics, linear models, time series. *Unit head:* Dr. Roger E. Kirk, Director, 254-710-1699, Fax: 254-710-3033, E-mail: roger_kirk@baylor.edu. *Application contact:* Suzanne Keener, Administrative Assistant, 254-710-3588, Fax: 254-710-3870, E-mail: suzanne_keener@baylor.edu.

Boston University, Graduate School of Arts and Sciences, Department of Mathematics, Boston, MA 02215. Offers mathematics (MA, PhD); statistics (MA, PhD). *Faculty:* 32 full-time (3 women), 5 part-time (1 woman). *Students:* 58 full-time (22 women), 4 part-time (2 women); includes 5 minority (1 African American, 2 Asian Americans or Pacific Islanders, 2 Hispanic Americans), 31 international. Terminal master's awarded for partial completion of doctoral program. *Degree requirements:* For master's, one foreign language, comprehensive exam required, thesis not required; for doctorate, one foreign language, dissertation, oral/qualifying exam required. *Entrance requirements:* For master's and doctorate, GRE General Test, GRE Subject Test, TOEFL (minimum score of 550 required). *Application deadline:* For fall admission, 1/15 (priority date); for spring admission, 10/15. Applications are processed on a rolling basis. Application fee: $50. Tuition: Full-time $23,770; part-time $743 per credit. Required fees: $220. Tuition and fees vary according to class time, course level, campus/location and program. *Unit head:* Steven Rosenberg, Chairman, 617-353-2560, Fax: 617-353-8100, E-mail: sr@bu.edu. *Application contact:* Dan Abramovich, Director of Graduate Studies, 617-353-9547, Fax: 617-353-8100, E-mail: abrmovic@bu.edu.

Bowling Green State University, Graduate College, College of Arts and Sciences, Department of Mathematics and Statistics, Bowling Green, OH 43403. Offers applied statistics (MS); mathematics (MA, MAT, PhD); mathematics supervision (Ed S); statistics (MA, MAT, PhD). Part-time and evening/weekend programs available. *Faculty:* 22 full-time (1 woman), 7 part-time (0 women). *Students:* 60 full-time (36 women), 14 part-time (9 women). 107 applicants, 57% accepted. In 1998, 22 master's awarded. *Degree requirements:* For master's, thesis or alternative required, foreign language not required; for doctorate, dissertation required, foreign language not required; for Ed S, internship required, foreign language and thesis not required. *Entrance requirements:* For master's, GRE General Test, TOEFL (minimum score of 590 required); for doctorate, GRE General Test, TOEFL (minimum score of 600 required). Application fee: $30. Electronic applications accepted. *Financial aid:* Research assistantships with full tuition reimbursements, teaching assistantships with full tuition reimbursements, Federal Work-Study, institutionally-sponsored loans, and unspecified assistantships available. Financial aid applicants required to submit FAFSA. *Faculty research:* Statistics and probability, algebra, analysis. *Unit head:* Dr. John Hayden, Chair, 419-372-2636. *Application contact:* Dr. Neal Carothers, Graduate Coordinator, 419-372-8317.

See in-depth description on page 645.

Bowling Green State University, Graduate College, College of Business Administration, Department of Applied Statistics and Operations Research, Bowling Green, OH 43403. Offers applied statistics (MS). Part-time programs available. *Faculty:* 8 full-time (3 women). *Students:* 22 full-time (13 women), 2 part-time (1 woman), 11 international. 47 applicants, 64% accepted. In 1998, 16 degrees awarded. *Degree requirements:* For master's, thesis or alternative, comprehensive exam required, foreign language not required. *Entrance requirements:* For master's, GRE General Test, TOEFL (minimum score of 550 required). Application fee: $30. Electronic applications accepted. *Financial aid:* Research assistantships with full tuition reimbursements, teaching assistantships with full tuition reimbursements, career-related internships or fieldwork, institutionally-sponsored loans, and unspecified assistantships available. Financial aid applicants required to submit FAFSA. *Faculty research:* Reliability, linear models, time series, statistical quality control. *Unit head:* Dr. Danny Myers, Chair, 419-372-2363. *Application contact:* Dr. Danny Myers, Chair, 419-372-2363.

Brigham Young University, Graduate Studies, College of Physical and Mathematical Sciences, Department of Statistics, Provo, UT 84602-1001. Offers applied statistics (MS). *Faculty:* 14 full-time (0 women). *Students:* 18 full-time (6 women); includes 1 minority (Asian American or Pacific Islander) Average age 26. 19 applicants, 63% accepted. In 1998, 5 degrees awarded. *Degree requirements:* For master's, computer language, thesis required (for some programs), foreign language not required. *Entrance requirements:* For master's, GRE General Test (minimum combined score of 1700 on three sections required; average 1900), minimum GPA of 3.3 in last 60 hours. *Average time to degree:* Master's–2 years full-time. *Application deadline:* For fall admission, 2/1. Applications are processed on a rolling basis. Application fee: $30. Tuition: Full-time $3,330; part-time $185 per credit hour. Tuition and fees vary according to program and student's religious affiliation. *Financial aid:* In 1998–99, 15 research assistantships with partial tuition reimbursements (averaging $6,400 per year) were awarded.; career-related internships or fieldwork and tuition waivers (partial) also available. Financial aid application deadline: 2/1. *Faculty research:* Statistical education, combining multiple data sets, industrial quality improvement, experimental design, biostatistics. *Unit head:* Dr. Gale Rex Bryce, Chair, 801-378-4505, Fax: 801-378-5722, E-mail: bryceg@byu.edu. *Application contact:* Dr. Gilbert W. Fellingham, Graduate Coordinator, 801-378-2806, Fax: 801-378-5722, E-mail: gwf@byu.edu.

California State University, Fullerton, Graduate Studies, School of Business Administration and Economics, Department of Management Science, Fullerton, CA 92834-9480. Offers management information systems (MS); management science (MBA, MS); operations research (MS); statistics (MS). Part-time and evening/weekend programs available. *Faculty:* 24 full-time (2 women), 16 part-time. *Students:* 7 full-time (6 women), 55 part-time (21 women); includes 19 minority (18 Asian Americans or Pacific Islanders, 1 Hispanic American), 26 international. *Degree requirements:* For master's, computer language, project or thesis required. *Entrance requirements:* For master's, GMAT (minimum score of 950 required), minimum AACSB index of 950. Application fee: $55. Tuition, nonresident: part-time $264 per unit. Required fees: $1,947; $1,281 per year. *Unit head:* Dr. Barry Pasternack, Chair, 714-278-2221.

California State University, Hayward, Graduate Programs, School of Science, Department of Statistics, Hayward, CA 94542-3000. Offers MS. *Faculty:* 5 full-time (1 woman). *Students:* 6 full-time (2 women), 17 part-time (2 women); includes 11 minority (3 African Americans, 7 Asian Americans or Pacific Islanders, 1 Native American), 1 international. 8 applicants, 88% accepted. In 1998, 8 degrees awarded. *Degree requirements:* For master's, comprehensive exam required, foreign language and thesis not required. *Entrance requirements:* For master's, minimum GPA of 2.5 during previous 2 years. Application fee: $55. Tuition, nonresident: part-time $164 per unit. Required fees: $587 per quarter. *Financial aid:* Federal Work-Study and institutionally-sponsored loans available. Aid available to part-time students. Financial aid application deadline: 3/1. *Unit head:* Dr. Julia Norton, Chair, 510-885-3435. *Application contact:* Jennifer Rice, Graduate Program Assistant, 510-885-3286, Fax: 510-885-4795, E-mail: gradprograms@csuhayward.edu.

California State University, Sacramento, Graduate Studies, School of Natural Sciences and Mathematics, Department of Mathematics and Statistics, Sacramento, CA 95819-6048. Offers MA. Part-time programs available. *Degree requirements:* For master's, thesis or alternative, writing proficiency exam required, foreign language not required. *Entrance requirements:* For master's, TOEFL (minimum score of 550 required), minimum GPA of 3.0 in mathematics, 2.5 overall during previous 2 years; BA in mathematics or equivalent. *Application deadline:* For fall admission, 4/15; for spring admission, 11/1. Application fee: $55. *Financial aid:* Research assistantships, teaching assistantships, career-related internships or fieldwork and Federal Work-Study available. Aid available to part-time students. Financial aid application deadline: 3/1. *Unit head:* Dr. Edward Bradley, Chair, 916-278-6534. *Application contact:* Dr. Howard Hamilton, Coordinator, 916-278-6221.

Carnegie Mellon University, College of Humanities and Social Sciences, Department of Statistics, Pittsburgh, PA 15213-3891. Offers mathematical finance (PhD); statistics (MS, PhD), including applied statistics (PhD), computational statistics (PhD), theoretical statistics (PhD). *Faculty:* 19 full-time (5 women). *Students:* 32 full-time (14 women), 6 part-time (2 women); includes 1 minority (Asian American or Pacific Islander), 20 international. Average age 28. In 1998, 2 master's, 1 doctorate awarded (100% found work related to degree). Terminal master's awarded for partial completion of doctoral program. *Degree requirements:* For master's, foreign language and thesis not required; for doctorate, dissertation, oral and written comprehensive exams required. *Entrance requirements:* For master's and doctorate, GRE General Test, TOEFL (minimum score of 550 required). *Application deadline:* For fall admission, 1/15 (priority date). Applications are processed on a rolling basis. Application fee: $25. *Financial aid:* Fellowships, research assistantships, teaching assistantships, career-related internships or fieldwork, Federal Work-Study, institutionally-sponsored loans, traineeships, and tuition waivers (full and partial) available. Aid available to part-time students. Financial aid application deadline: 3/15. *Faculty research:* Stochastic processes, Bayesian statistics, statistical computing, decision theory, psychiatric statistics. Total annual research expenditures: $2.2 million. *Unit head:* Dr. Robert Kass, Head, 412-268-8723, Fax: 412-268-7828.

See in-depth description on page 655.

Case Western Reserve University, School of Graduate Studies, Department of Statistics, Cleveland, OH 44106. Offers MS, PhD. *Degree requirements:* For master's, thesis required (for some programs); for doctorate, dissertation required. *Entrance requirements:* For master's and doctorate, TOEFL (minimum score of 550 required). *Faculty research:* Generalized linear models, asymptotics for restricted MLE Bayesian inference, sample survey theory and methodology, statistical computing, nonparametric inference, projection pursuit, stochastic processes, dynamical systems and chaotic behavior, Bayesian inference, sample survey theory, industrial statistics.

Claremont Graduate University, Graduate Programs, Department of Mathematics, Claremont, CA 91711-6163. Offers engineering mathematics (PhD); financial engineering (MS); operations research and statistics (MA, MS); physical applied mathematics (MA, MS); pure mathematics (MA, MS, PhD); scientific computing (MA, MS); systems and control theory (MA, MS). Part-time programs available. *Faculty:* 3 full-time (0 women), 3 part-time (1 woman). *Students:* 12 full-time (8 women), 41 part-time (7 women); includes 17 minority (2 African Americans, 10 Asian Americans or Pacific Islanders, 5 Hispanic Americans), 16 international. Terminal master's awarded for partial completion of doctoral program. *Degree requirements:* For master's, foreign language and thesis not required; for doctorate, 2 foreign languages (computer language can substitute for one), dissertation required. *Entrance requirements:* For master's and doctorate, GRE General Test. *Application deadline:* For fall admission, 2/15 (priority date). Applications are processed on a rolling basis. Application fee: $40. Electronic applications accepted. Tuition: Full-time $20,950; part-time $913 per unit. Required fees: $65 per semester. Tuition and fees vary according to program. *Unit head:* Robert Williamson, Chair, 909-621-8080, Fax: 909-621-8390, E-mail: robert.williamson@cgu.edu. *Application contact:* Mary Solberg, Program Secretary, 909-621-8080, Fax: 909-621-8390, E-mail: math@cgu.edu.

Clemson University, Graduate School, College of Engineering and Science, Department of Mathematical Sciences, Clemson, SC 29634. Offers applied and pure mathematics (MS, PhD); computational mathematics (MS, PhD); management science (PhD); operations research (MS, PhD); statistics (MS, PhD). Part-time programs available. *Students:* 60 full-time (24 women), 1 part-time; includes 3 minority (2 African Americans, 1 Hispanic American), 11 international. *Degree requirements:* For master's, computer language, final project required, thesis optional, foreign language not required; for doctorate, computer language, dissertation, qualifying exams required, foreign language not required. *Entrance requirements:* For master's and doctorate, GRE General Test, TOEFL. *Application deadline:* For fall admission, 6/1. Application fee: $35. *Unit head:* Dr. Robert Fennell, Chair, 864-656-3436, Fax: 864-656-5230, E-mail: mathsci@clemson.edu. *Application contact:* Dr. Douglas Shier, Graduate Coordinator, 864-656-1100, Fax: 864-656-5230, E-mail: shierd@clemson.edu.

Colorado State University, Graduate School, College of Natural Sciences, Department of Statistics, Fort Collins, CO 80523-0015. Offers MS, PhD. *Faculty:* 12 full-time (1 woman), 5 part-time (1 woman). *Students:* 25 full-time (8 women), 20 part-time (5 women); includes 3 minority (2 Asian Americans or Pacific Islanders, 1 Hispanic American), 8 international. Average age 30. 103 applicants, 48% accepted. In 1998, 4 master's, 5 doctorates awarded. *Degree requirements:* For master's, computer language, project, seminar required, thesis optional, foreign language not required; for doctorate, computer language, dissertation, candidacy exam, preliminary exam, seminar required, foreign language not required. *Entrance requirements:* For master's and doctorate, GRE General Test, TOEFL, minimum GPA of 3.0. *Application deadline:* For fall admission, 2/1 (priority date). Applications are processed on a rolling basis. Application fee: $30. Electronic applications accepted. *Financial aid:* In 1998–99, 3 fellowships, 6 research assistantships, 16 teaching assistantships were awarded.; career-related internships or fieldwork, Federal Work-Study, institutionally-sponsored loans, and traineeships also available. Aid available to part-time students. Financial aid application deadline: 3/15. *Faculty research:* Applied probability, linear models, experimental design, time-series analysis, statistical inference. Total annual research expenditures: $410,000. *Unit head:* Richard A. Davis, Chair, 970-491-5269, Fax: 970-491-7895, E-mail: stats@lamar.colostate.edu. *Application contact:* Graduate Coordinator, 970-491-5269, Fax: 970-491-7895, E-mail: stats@lamar.colostate.edu.

Columbia University, Graduate School of Arts and Sciences, Division of Natural Sciences, Department of Statistics, New York, NY 10027. Offers M Phil, MA, PhD, MD/PhD. Part-time programs available. *Degree requirements:* For master's, foreign language and thesis not required; for doctorate, dissertation, M Phil required, foreign language not required. *Entrance requirements:* For master's and doctorate, GRE General Test, GRE Subject Test, TOEFL.

Concordia University, School of Graduate Studies, Faculty of Arts and Science, Department of Mathematics and Statistics, Montréal, PQ H3G 1M8, Canada. Offers mathematics (PhD); mathematics and statistics (M Sc, MA); teaching of mathematics (MTM, Diploma). *Students:* 46 full-time (18 women), 1 part-time. *Degree requirements:* For master's, thesis optional; for doctorate, dissertation, comprehensive exam required. *Entrance requirements:* For master's, honors degree in mathematics or equivalent; for Diploma, Quebec teaching certificate. *Application deadline:* For fall admission, 4/1. Application fee: $50. *Financial aid:* Fellowships, research assistantships, teaching assistantships available. Financial aid application deadline: 2/1. *Faculty* *research:* Number theory, computational algebra, mathematical physics, differential geometry, dynamical systems and statistics. *Unit head:* Dr. J. Hillel, Chair, 514-848-3234, Fax: 514-848-2831. *Application contact:* Dr. Z. Khalil, Director, 514-848-3250, Fax: 514-848-2831.

Cornell University, Graduate School, Graduate Fields of Agriculture and Life Sciences, Field of Statistics, Ithaca, NY 14853-0001. Offers biometry (MS, PhD); decision theory (MS, PhD); econometrics (MS, PhD); economic and social statistics (MS, PhD); engineering statistics (MS, PhD); experimental design (MS, PhD); mathematical statistics (MS, PhD); probability (MS, PhD); sampling (MS, PhD); statistical computing (MS, PhD); stochastic processes (MS, PhD). *Faculty:* 32 full-time. *Students:* 17 full-time (8 women); includes 1 minority (Asian American or Pacific Islander), 10 international. 107 applicants, 12% accepted. In 1998, 2 master's, 4 doctorates awarded. Terminal master's awarded for partial completion of doctoral program. *Degree requirements:* For master's, thesis required, foreign language not required; for doctorate, dissertation required. *Entrance requirements:* For master's and doctorate, GRE General Test, TOEFL (minimum score of 550 required). *Application deadline:* For fall admission, 3/1. Application fee: $65. Electronic applications accepted. *Financial aid:* In 1998–99, 16 students received aid, including 5 fellowships with full tuition reimbursements available, 1 research assistantship with full tuition reimbursement available, 10 teaching assistantships with full tuition reimbursements available; institutionally-sponsored loans, scholarships, tuition waivers (full and partial), and unspecified assistantships also available. Financial aid applicants required to submit FAFSA. *Faculty research:* Bayes analysis, nonlinear and robust methods, hierarchical and mixed models, survival analysis. *Unit head:* Director of Graduate Studies, 607-255-8066, Fax: 607-255-9801. *Application contact:* Graduate Field Assistant, 607-255-8066, E-mail: csc@cornell.edu.

Cornell University, Graduate School, Graduate Fields of Engineering, Field of Operations Research and Industrial Engineering, Ithaca, NY 14853-0001. Offers applied probability and statistics (PhD); manufacturing systems engineering (PhD); mathematical programming (PhD); operations research and industrial engineering (M Eng). *Faculty:* 30 full-time. *Students:* 91 full-time (20 women); includes 22 minority (1 African American, 21 Asian Americans or Pacific Islanders), 36 international. Terminal master's awarded for partial completion of doctoral program. *Degree requirements:* For doctorate, dissertation required, foreign language not required; foreign language not required. *Entrance requirements:* For master's and doctorate, GRE General Test, TOEFL (minimum score of 550 required). *Application deadline:* For fall admission, 1/15. Application fee: $65. Electronic applications accepted. *Unit head:* Director of Graduate Studies, 607-255-9128. *Application contact:* Graduate Field Assistant, 607-255-9128, E-mail: orphd@cornell.edu.

Creighton University, Graduate School, College of Arts and Sciences, Department of Mathematics, Statistics, and Computer Science, Program in Mathematics and Statistics, Omaha, NE 68178-0001. Offers MS. Part-time programs available. *Faculty:* 8 full-time. *Students:* 1 full-time (0 women). In 1998, 3 degrees awarded. *Degree requirements:* For master's, one foreign language required, (computer language can substitute), thesis optional. *Entrance requirements:* For master's, GRE General Test, TOEFL (minimum score of 550 required). *Application deadline:* For fall admission, 3/1. Applications are processed on a rolling basis. Application fee: $30. *Unit head:* Dr. Randall Crist, Director, 402-280-2578. *Application contact:* Dr. Barbara J. Braden, Dean, Graduate School, 402-280-2870, Fax: 402-280-5762.

Dalhousie University, Faculty of Graduate Studies, College of Arts and Science, Faculty of Science, Department of Mathematics and Statistics, Program in Statistics, Halifax, NS B3H 3J5, Canada. Offers M Sc, PhD. *Faculty:* 7 full-time (0 women). *Students:* 9 full-time (5 women), 1 part-time, 4 international. 20 applicants, 35% accepted. In 1998, 3 degrees awarded (100% found work related to degree). *Degree requirements:* For master's and doctorate, thesis/dissertation, 50 hours of consulting required, foreign language not required. *Entrance requirements:* For master's and doctorate, TOEFL (minimum score of 580 required). *Average time to degree:* Master's–1.5 years full-time; doctorate–3.5 years full-time. *Application deadline:* For fall admission, 6/1. Applications are processed on a rolling basis. Application fee: $55. *Financial aid:* In 1998–99, 10 students received aid, including 5 teaching assistantships with full tuition reimbursements available (averaging $8,000 per year) *Faculty research:* Data analysis, multivariate analysis, robustness, time series. *Unit head:* Graduate Field Assistant, 607-255-4416, E-mail: shh4@cornell.edu. *Application contact:* Dr. B. Smith, Graduate Coordinator, 902-494-2257, Fax: 902-494-5130, E-mail: bsmith@mscs.dal.ca.

Duke University, Graduate School, Institute of Statistics and Decision Sciences, Durham, NC 27708-0586. Offers PhD. Part-time programs available. *Faculty:* 16 full-time. *Students:* 21 full-time (10 women); includes 1 minority (Asian American or Pacific Islander), 12 international. 47 applicants, 40% accepted. *Degree requirements:* For doctorate, dissertation required. *Entrance requirements:* For doctorate, GRE General Test. *Application deadline:* For fall admission, 12/31. Application fee: $75. *Financial aid:* Fellowships, research assistantships, teaching assistantships available. Financial aid application deadline: 12/31. *Unit head:* Dr. Michael Lavine, Director of Graduate Studies, 919-684-8029, Fax: 919-684-8594, E-mail: cjg@stat.duke.edu.

Florida State University, Graduate Studies, College of Arts and Sciences, Department of Statistics, Tallahassee, FL 32306. Offers applied statistics (MS); mathematical statistics (MS, PhD). Part-time programs available. *Faculty:* 12 full-time (1 woman), 3 part-time (1 woman). *Students:* 23 full-time (7 women), 3 part-time (2 women); includes 2 minority (1 African American, 1 Hispanic American), 15 international. Average age 28. 90 applicants, 58% accepted. In 1998, 11 master's awarded (9% entered university research/teaching, 82% found other work related to degree, 9% continued full-time study); 1 doctorate awarded (100% entered university research/teaching). Terminal master's awarded for partial completion of doctoral program. *Degree requirements:* For master's, comprehensive exam for mathematical statistics required, foreign language and thesis not required; for doctorate, dissertation, departmental qualifying exam required, foreign language not required. *Entrance requirements:* For master's, GRE General Test (minimum combined score of 1000 required), course work in calculus, minimum GPA of 3.0; for doctorate, GRE General Test (minimum combined score of 1000 required), minimum GPA of 3.0. *Average time to degree:* Master's–2 years full-time; doctorate–4 years full-time. *Application deadline:* For fall admission, 3/1 (priority date); for spring admission, 7/1 (priority date). Applications are processed on a rolling basis. Application fee: $20. Tuition, state resident: part-time $139 per credit hour. Tuition, nonresident: part-time $482 per credit hour. Tuition and fees vary according to program. *Financial aid:* In 1998–99, 24 students received aid, including 1 fellowship with full tuition reimbursement available (averaging $6,300 per year), 1 research assistantship with full tuition reimbursement available (averaging $8,478 per year), 17 teaching assistantships with full tuition reimbursements available (averaging $10,415 per year); Federal Work-Study, institutionally-sponsored loans, and scholarships also available. Aid available to part-time students. Financial aid application deadline: 2/15; financial aid applicants required to submit FAFSA. *Faculty research:* Statistical inference, probability theory, spatial statistics, nonparametric estimation, automatic target recognition. Total annual research expenditures: $365,148. *Unit head:* Dr. Ian McKeague, Chairman, 850-644-3218, E-mail: info@stat.fsu.edu. *Application contact:* Program Assistant, 850-644-3218, Fax: 850-644-5271, E-mail: info@stat.fsu.edu.

George Mason University, School of Information Technology and Engineering, Department of Applied and Engineering Statistics, Fairfax, VA 22030-4444. Offers statistical science (MS). Part-time and evening/weekend programs available. *Faculty:* 8 full-time (1 woman), 3 part-time (1 woman). *Students:* 3 full-time (2 women), 51 part-time (18 women); includes 11 minority (5 African Americans, 4 Asian Americans or Pacific Islanders, 1 Hispanic American, 1 Native American), 2 international. Average age 36. 40 applicants, 90% accepted. In 1998, 8 degrees awarded. *Degree requirements:* For master's, thesis optional, foreign language not required. *Entrance requirements:* For master's, GMAT or GRE General Test, TOEFL (minimum score of 575 required), previous course work in calculus, probability, and statistics; minimum GPA of 3.0 in last 60 hours. *Application deadline:* For fall admission, 5/1; for spring admission, 11/1. Application fee: $30. Electronic applications accepted. Tuition, state resident:

full-time $4,416; part-time $184 per credit hour. Tuition, nonresident: full-time $12,516; part-time $522 per credit hour. Tuition and fees vary according to program. *Financial aid:* Fellowships, research assistantships, teaching assistantships, career-related internships or fieldwork and Federal Work-Study available. Aid available to part-time students. Financial aid application deadline: 3/1; financial aid applicants required to submit FAFSA. *Faculty research:* Computational statistics, nonparametric function estimation, scientific and statistical visualization, statistical applications to engineering, survey research. Total annual research expenditures: $436,000. *Unit head:* Dr. Edward J. Wegman, Chairperson, 703-993-1691, Fax: 703-993-1734, E-mail: sitegrad@gmu.edu.

The George Washington University, Columbian School of Arts and Sciences, Department of Statistics, Program in Statistics, Washington, DC 20052. Offers applied statistics (MS); mathematical statistics (MS); statistics (PhD). *Students:* 6 full-time (2 women), 15 part-time (3 women); includes 2 minority (1 African American, 1 Asian American or Pacific Islander), 10 international. Average age 31. 27 applicants, 93% accepted. In 1998, 10 master's, 3 doctorates awarded. *Degree requirements:* For master's, comprehensive exam required, thesis not required; for doctorate, computer language, dissertation, general exam required. *Entrance requirements:* For master's and doctorate, GRE General Test, interview, minimum GPA of 3.0. *Application deadline:* For fall admission, 3/15. Application fee: $55. Tuition: Full-time $17,328; part-time $722 per credit hour. Required fees: $828; $35 per credit hour. Tuition and fees vary according to campus/location and program. *Financial aid:* Fellowships, teaching assistantships available. Financial aid application deadline: 2/1. *Unit head:* Dr. Hosam Mahmoud, Chair, Department of Statistics, 202-994-6888.

See in-depth description on page 679.

Georgia Institute of Technology, Graduate Studies and Research, College of Sciences, School of Mathematics, Atlanta, GA 30332-0001. Offers algorithms, combinatorics, and optimization (PhD); applied mathematics (MS); mathematics (MS Math, PhD); statistics (MS Stat). Terminal master's awarded for partial completion of doctoral program. *Degree requirements:* For master's, thesis or alternative required, foreign language not required; for doctorate, dissertation required. *Entrance requirements:* For master's and doctorate, GRE General Test, GRE Subject Test, TOEFL (minimum score of 570 required), minimum GPA of 3.0. Electronic applications accepted. *Faculty research:* Dynamical systems, discrete mathematics, probability and statistics, mathematical physics.

Georgia Institute of Technology, Graduate Studies and Research, Multidisciplinary Program in Statistics, Atlanta, GA 30332-0001. Offers MS Stat. Offered jointly with the School of Industrial and Systems Engineering and the School of Mathematics. Part-time programs available. *Degree requirements:* For master's, computer language required, thesis optional, foreign language not required. *Entrance requirements:* For master's, GRE General Test, TOEFL (minimum score of 550 required), minimum GPA of 3.0. *Faculty research:* Statistical control procedures, statistical modeling of transportation systems.

Harvard University, Graduate School of Arts and Sciences, Department of Statistics, Cambridge, MA 02138. Offers AM, PhD. *Students:* 19 full-time (9 women). 57 applicants, 28% accepted. In 1998, 8 master's, 2 doctorates awarded. Terminal master's awarded for partial completion of doctoral program. *Degree requirements:* For master's, one foreign language required, (computer language can substitute), thesis not required; for doctorate, one foreign language (computer language can substitute), dissertation, exam, qualifying paper required. *Entrance requirements:* For master's and doctorate, GRE General Test, GRE Subject Test (recommended), TOEFL (minimum score of 550 required). *Application deadline:* For fall admission, 12/15. Application fee: $60. *Financial aid:* Fellowships, research assistantships, teaching assistantships, career-related internships or fieldwork, Federal Work-Study, and institutionally-sponsored loans available. Financial aid application deadline: 12/30. *Faculty research:* Interactive graphic analysis of multidimensional data, data analysis, modeling and inference, statistical modeling of U.S. economic time series. *Unit head:* Dr. Carl Morris, Chairperson, 617-495-3812, E-mail: statdept@hustat.harvard.edu. *Application contact:* Office of Admissions and Financial Aid, 617-495-5315.

Announcement: The Department of Statistics offers courses of study in theoretical and applied research leading to the AM and PhD degrees. It encourages applications from students with strong mathematical and computational backgrounds who wish to pursue independent research in statistics. The program offers broad research and training opportunities, partly in collaboration with other university programs in the sciences and medicine. E-mail: statdept@hustat.harvard.edu, World Wide Web: http://fas-www.harvard.edu/~stats/.

Indiana University Bloomington, Graduate School, College of Arts and Sciences, Department of Mathematics, Bloomington, IN 47405. Offers applied mathematics–numerical analysis (MA, PhD); mathematics education (MAT); probability-statistics (MA, PhD). PhD offered through the University Graduate School. *Faculty:* 46 full-time (1 woman). *Students:* 77 full-time (22 women), 26 part-time (5 women); includes 3 minority (2 Asian Americans or Pacific Islanders, 1 Native American), 52 international. Terminal master's awarded for partial completion of doctoral program. *Degree requirements:* For master's, foreign language and thesis not required; for doctorate, dissertation required. *Entrance requirements:* For master's and doctorate, GRE General Test, GRE Subject Test, TOEFL. *Application deadline:* For fall admission, 1/15 (priority date); for spring admission, 9/1 (priority date). Applications are processed on a rolling basis. Application fee: $40. Electronic applications accepted. Tuition, state resident: part-time $161 per credit hour. Tuition, nonresident: part-time $468 per credit hour. Required fees: $360 per year. Tuition and fees vary according to course load and program. *Unit head:* Daniel Maki, Chair, 812-855-2200, Fax: 812-855-0046, E-mail: maki@indiana.edu. *Application contact:* Misty Cummings, Graduate Secretary, 812-855-2645, Fax: 812-855-0046, E-mail: gradmath@indiana.edu.

Indiana University–Purdue University Indianapolis, School of Science, Department of Mathematical Sciences, Indianapolis, IN 46202-3216. Offers applied mathematics (MS, PhD); applied statistics (MS); mathematics (MS, PhD). Part-time programs available. *Students:* 7 full-time (2 women), 28 part-time (9 women); includes 2 minority (1 Asian American or Pacific Islander, 1 Native American), 15 international. Terminal master's awarded for partial completion of doctoral program. *Degree requirements:* For master's, thesis optional, foreign language not required; for doctorate, one foreign language, dissertation required. *Entrance requirements:* For master's, TOEFL (minimum score of 570 required); for doctorate, GRE, TOEFL (minimum score of 570 required). *Application deadline:* For fall admission, 2/1 (priority date). Application fee: $25 ($50 for international students). Tuition, state resident: part-time $158 per credit hour. Tuition, nonresident: part-time $455 per credit hour. Required fees: $121 per year. Tuition and fees vary according to course load and degree level. *Unit head:* Eric T. Sawyer, Chair, 317-274-6918, Fax: 317-274-3460. *Application contact:* Yuri Abramovich, Chair, Graduate Committee, 317-274-6927, Fax: 317-274-3460, E-mail: yabramovich@math.iupui.edu.

Instituto Tecnológico y de Estudios Superiores de Monterrey, Campus Monterrey, Graduate and Research Division, Programs in Engineering, Monterrey, 64849, Mexico. Offers applied statistics (M Eng); artificial intelligence (PhD); automation engineering (M Eng); chemical engineering (M Eng); civil engineering (M Eng); electrical engineering (M Eng); electronic engineering (M Eng); environmental engineering (M Eng); industrial engineering (M Eng, PhD); manufacturing engineering (M Eng); mechanical engineering (M Eng); systems and quality engineering (M Eng). M Eng offered jointly with the University of Waterloo; PhD (industrial engineering) offered jointly with Texas A&M University. Part-time and evening/weekend programs available. Terminal master's awarded for partial completion of doctoral program. *Degree requirements:* For master's and doctorate, one foreign language, computer language, thesis/dissertation required. *Entrance requirements:* For master's, PAEG, TOEFL; for doctorate, GRE, TOEFL, master's in related field. *Faculty research:* Flexible manufacturing cells, materials, statistical methods, environmental prevention, control and evaluation.

Statistics

Iowa State University of Science and Technology, Graduate College, College of Liberal Arts and Sciences, Department of Statistics, Ames, IA 50011. Offers MS, PhD, MBA/MS. *Faculty:* 32 full-time. *Students:* 50 full-time (20 women), 49 part-time (20 women); includes 6 minority (5 Asian Americans or Pacific Islanders, 1 Hispanic American), 47 international. 95 applicants, 57% accepted. In 1998, 33 master's, 10 doctorates awarded. *Degree requirements:* For master's, thesis or alternative required; for doctorate, dissertation required. *Entrance requirements:* For master's and doctorate, GRE General Test, TOEFL (minimum score of 550 required). *Application deadline:* For fall admission, 6/15 (priority date); for spring admission, 11/15. Applications are processed on a rolling basis. Application fee: $20 ($50 for international students). Tuition, state resident: full-time $3,308. Tuition, nonresident: full-time $9,744. Part-time tuition and fees vary according to course load, campus/location and program. *Financial aid:* In 1998–99, 49 research assistantships with partial tuition reimbursements (averaging $10,931 per year), 37 teaching assistantships with partial tuition reimbursements (averaging $11,471 per year) were awarded.; fellowships, scholarships also available. *Unit head:* Dr. Dean L. Isaacson, Head, 515-294-3440, Fax: 515-294-4040, E-mail: statistics@iastate.edu.

Kansas State University, Graduate School, College of Arts and Sciences, Department of Statistics, Manhattan, KS 66506. Offers MS, PhD. Terminal master's awarded for partial completion of doctoral program. *Degree requirements:* For master's, thesis optional, foreign language not required; for doctorate, dissertation required, foreign language not required. *Faculty research:* Data analysis, mathematical statistics, linear models, stochastic processes, nonparametric statistics.

Lakehead University, Graduate Studies and Research, Faculty of Arts and Science, School of Mathematical Sciences, Thunder Bay, ON P7B 5E1, Canada. Offers computer science (M Sc, MA); mathematics and statistics (M Sc, MA). Part-time and evening/weekend programs available. *Degree requirements:* For master's, thesis or alternative required, foreign language not required. *Entrance requirements:* For master's, TOEFL (minimum score of 550 required), minimum B average. *Faculty research:* Numerical analysis, classical analysis, theoretical computer science, abstract harmonic analysis, functional analysis.

Lehigh University, College of Arts and Sciences, Department of Mathematics, Program in Statistics, Bethlehem, PA 18015-3094. Offers MS. *Degree requirements:* For master's, comprehensive exam required, foreign language and thesis not required. *Entrance requirements:* For master's, TOEFL (minimum score of 550 required), minimum GPA of 3.0. *Application deadline:* For fall admission, 7/15; for spring admission, 12/1. Applications are processed on a rolling basis. Application fee: $40. *Financial aid:* Application deadline: 1/15. *Unit head:* Sandy Drane, Coordinator, International Students and Graduate Studies, 409-880-8349, Fax: 409-880-8414, E-mail: dranesl@lub002.lamar.edu. *Application contact:* Dr. Raman Venkataraman, Graduate Coordinator, 610-758-3736, Fax: 610-758-6553, E-mail: rv01@lehigh.edu.

Louisiana State University and Agricultural and Mechanical College, Graduate School, College of Agriculture, Department of Experimental Statistics, Baton Rouge, LA 70803. Offers applied statistics (M App St). Part-time programs available. *Faculty:* 8 full-time (0 women). *Students:* 12 full-time (7 women), 2 part-time (1 woman), 8 international. Average age 32. 2 applicants, 100% accepted. In 1998, 15 degrees awarded. *Degree requirements:* For master's, project required, foreign language and thesis not required. *Entrance requirements:* For master's, GRE General Test, minimum GPA of 3.0. *Application deadline:* For fall admission, 1/25 (priority date). Applications are processed on a rolling basis. Application fee: $25. *Financial aid:* In 1998–99, 9 research assistantships with partial tuition reimbursements, 2 teaching assistantships with partial tuition reimbursements were awarded.; fellowships, career-related internships or fieldwork, institutionally-sponsored loans, and unspecified assistantships also available. Financial aid application deadline: 4/1. *Faculty research:* Linear models, statistical computing, ecological statistics. *Unit head:* Dr. E. Barry Moser, Interim Head, 225-388-8303, Fax: 225-388-8344, E-mail: bmoser@lsu.edu.

Louisiana Tech University, Graduate School, College of Engineering and Science, Department of Mathematics and Statistics, Ruston, LA 71272. Offers MS. Part-time programs available. *Degree requirements:* For master's, computer language, thesis or alternative required, foreign language not required. *Entrance requirements:* For master's, GRE General Test (minimum combined score of 1070 required; average 1245), TOEFL (minimum score of 550 required), minimum GPA of 3.0 in last 60 hours.

Marquette University, Graduate School, College of Arts and Sciences, Department of Mathematics, Statistics, and Computer Science, Milwaukee, WI 53201-1881. Offers algebra (PhD); bio-mathematical modeling (PhD); mathematics (MS); mathematics education (MS); statistics (MS). Part-time programs available. *Faculty:* 24 full-time (3 women). *Students:* 71 full-time (36 women), 28 part-time (10 women); includes 5 minority (2 African Americans, 2 Asian Americans or Pacific Islanders, 1 Hispanic American), 78 international. Terminal master's awarded for partial completion of doctoral program. *Degree requirements:* For master's, thesis or alternative, comprehensive exam required, foreign language not required; for doctorate, 2 foreign languages, dissertation, comprehensive exam required. *Entrance requirements:* For master's, TOEFL (minimum score of 550 required); for doctorate, TOEFL (minimum score of 550 required), sample of scholarly writing. Application fee: $40. Tuition: Part-time $510 per credit hour. Tuition and fees vary according to program. *Unit head:* Dr. Douglas Harris, Chairman, 414-288-7573, Fax: 414-288-1578. *Application contact:* Dr. Karl Byleen, Director of Graduate Studies, 414-288-6343.

McMaster University, School of Graduate Studies, Faculty of Science, Department of Mathematics and Statistics, Hamilton, ON L8S 4M2, Canada. Offers mathematics (PhD); mathematics and statistics (M Sc). Part-time programs available. *Degree requirements:* For master's, thesis or alternative, oral exam required, foreign language not required; for doctorate, dissertation, comprehensive exam required, foreign language not required. *Entrance requirements:* For master's, minimum B+ average in last year of honors degree; for doctorate, minimum B+ average, M Sc in mathematics or statistics. *Faculty research:* Algebra, analysis, applied mathematics, geometry and topology, probability and statistics.

McMaster University, School of Graduate Studies, Program in Statistics, Hamilton, ON L8S 4M2, Canada. Offers applied statistics (M Sc); medical statistics (M Sc); statistical theory (M Sc). *Faculty:* 19 full-time. *Students:* 7 full-time (3 women). In 1998, 8 degrees awarded. *Degree requirements:* For master's, thesis or alternative required, foreign language not required. *Application deadline:* For fall admission, 3/1 (priority date). Applications are processed on a rolling basis. Application fee: $50. *Financial aid:* Fellowships, research assistantships, teaching assistantships available. *Unit head:* Dr. P. D. M. MacDonald, Coordinator, 905-525-9140 Ext. 23423.

McNeese State University, Graduate School, College of Science, Department of Mathematics, Computer Science, and Statistics, Lake Charles, LA 70609-2495. Offers computer science (MS); mathematics (MS); statistics (MS). Evening/weekend programs available. *Faculty:* 14 full-time (3 women). *Students:* 4 full-time (3 women), 5 part-time (2 women). In 1998, 10 degrees awarded. *Degree requirements:* For master's, computer language, thesis or alternative, written exam required, foreign language not required. *Entrance requirements:* For master's, GRE General Test. *Application deadline:* For fall admission, 7/15 (priority date). Applications are processed on a rolling basis. Application fee: $10 ($25 for international students). *Financial aid:* Teaching assistantships available. Financial aid application deadline: 5/1. *Unit head:* Sid Bradley, Head, 318-475-5788.

Memorial University of Newfoundland, School of Graduate Studies, Department of Mathematics and Statistics, St. John's, NF A1C 5S7, Canada. Offers M Sc, MAS, PhD. Part-time programs available. *Students:* 7 full-time (1 woman), 2 part-time, 7 international. 20 applicants, 10% accepted. In 1998, 1 master's, 1 doctorate awarded. *Degree requirements:* For master's, thesis required (for some programs); for doctorate, dissertation, comprehensive exam required. *Entrance requirements:* For doctorate, MAS or M Sc in mathematics and statistics. *Application deadline:* For fall admission, 1/30. Applications are processed on a rolling basis. Application fee: $40. *Financial aid:* Fellowships, teaching assistantships available. Financial aid application deadline:1/31. *Faculty research:* Algebra, topology, applied mathematics, mathematical statistics, applied statistics and probability. *Unit head:* Dr. Herbert S. Gaskill, Head, 709-737-8783, Fax: 709-787-3010, E-mail: head@math.mun.ca. *Application contact:* Dr. Wanda Heath, Secretary to Department Head, 709-737-8783, Fax: 709-737-3010, E-mail: mathstat@math.mun.ca.

Miami University, Graduate School, College of Arts and Sciences, Department of Mathematics and Statistics, Program in Statistics, Oxford, OH 45056. Offers MS. Part-time programs available. *Faculty:* 19. *Students:* 9 full-time (2 women), 1 part-time; includes 1 minority (Asian American or Pacific Islander), 2 international. 14 applicants, 79% accepted. In 1998, 3 degrees awarded. *Degree requirements:* For master's, final exam required, thesis not required. *Entrance requirements:* For master's, minimum undergraduate GPA of 3.0 during previous 2 years or 2.75 overall. *Application deadline:* For fall admission, 3/1 (priority date); for spring admission, 12/15. Applications are processed on a rolling basis. Application fee: $35. *Financial aid:* Fellowships, research assistantships, teaching assistantships, Federal Work-Study and tuition waivers (full) available. Financial aid application deadline: 3/1. *Unit head:* Dr. Sheldon Davis, Director of Graduate Studies, 513-529-3527.

Michigan State University, Graduate School, College of Natural Science, Department of Statistics and Probability, East Lansing, MI 48824-1020. Offers applied statistics (MS); computational statistics (MS); operations research-statistics (MS); statistics (MA, MS, PhD). Part-time programs available. *Students:* 27 full-time (8 women), 13 part-time (3 women); includes 1 minority (Asian American or Pacific Islander), 33 international. Average age 29. 46 applicants, 59% accepted. In 1998, 19 master's, 3 doctorates awarded. Terminal master's awarded for partial completion of doctoral program. *Degree requirements:* For master's, foreign language and thesis not required; for doctorate, dissertation required. *Entrance requirements:* For master's and doctorate, GRE, TOEFL. *Application deadline:* For fall admission, 1/1 (priority date). Applications are processed on a rolling basis. Application fee: $30 ($40 for international students). *Financial aid:* In 1998–99, 24 teaching assistantships with tuition reimbursements (averaging $11,029 per year) were awarded.; fellowships, research assistantships Financial aid application deadline: 1/1; financial aid applicants required to submit FAFSA. *Faculty research:* Weak convergence in statistical inference, stochastic approximation, nonparametrics, sequential procedures, stochastic processes. Total annual research expenditures: $146,031. *Unit head:* Dr. Habib Salehi, Chairman, 517-353-3391, Fax: 517-432-1405. *Application contact:* James Stapleton, Graduate Program Director, 517-355-9678, Fax: 517-432-1405, E-mail: stapleton@stt.msu.edu.

See in-depth description on page 695.

Minnesota State University, Mankato, College of Graduate Studies, College of Science, Engineering and Technology, Department of Mathematics and Statistics, Program in Statistics, Mankato, MN 56002-8400. Offers MS. Average age 32. In 1998, 2 degrees awarded. *Degree requirements:* For master's, one foreign language, computer language, thesis or alternative, comprehensive exam required. *Entrance requirements:* For master's, GRE General Test, minimum GPA of 3.0 during previous 2 years. *Application deadline:* For fall admission, 7/9 (priority date); for spring admission, 11/27. Applications are processed on a rolling basis. Application fee: $20. *Financial aid:* Research assistantships with partial tuition reimbursements, teaching assistantships with partial tuition reimbursements available. Financial aid application deadline: 3/15; financial aid applicants required to submit FAFSA. *Unit head:* Dr. Charles Waters, Coordinator, 507-389-5903. *Application contact:* Joni Roberts, Admissions Coordinator, 507-389-2321, Fax: 507-389-5974, E-mail: grad@mankato.msus.edu.

Mississippi State University, College of Arts and Sciences, Department of Mathematics and Statistics, Mississippi State, MS 39762. Offers mathematical sciences (PhD); mathematics (MS); statistics (MS). Part-time programs available. *Students:* 29 full-time (14 women), 7 part-time (3 women); includes 15 minority (2 African Americans, 13 Asian Americans or Pacific Islanders), 8 international. Average age 33. 38 applicants, 42% accepted. In 1998, 4 master's, 1 doctorate awarded. Terminal master's awarded for partial completion of doctoral program. *Degree requirements:* For master's, comprehensive oral or written exam required, thesis optional, foreign language not required; for doctorate, one foreign language, computer language, dissertation, comprehensive oral or written exam required. *Entrance requirements:* For master's, TOEFL; for doctorate, GRE, TOEFL. *Application deadline:* For fall admission, 7/1; for spring admission, 11/1. Applications are processed on a rolling basis. Application fee: $25 for international students. *Financial aid:* In 1998–99, 1 fellowship was awarded.; Federal Work-Study, institutionally-sponsored loans, tuition waivers (partial), and unspecified assistantships also available. Financial aid applicants required to submit FAFSA. *Faculty research:* Differential equations, algebra, numerical analysis, functional analysis, applied statistics. *Unit head:* Dr. Shair Ahmad, Head, 662-325-3414, Fax: 662-325-0005, E-mail: office@math.msstate.edu. *Application contact:* Jerry B. Inmon, Director of Admissions, 662-325-2224, Fax: 662-325-7360, E-mail: admit@admissions.msstate.edu.

Montana State University–Bozeman, College of Graduate Studies, College of Letters and Science, Department of Mathematical Sciences, Bozeman, MT 59717. Offers mathematics (MS, PhD); statistics (MS, PhD). Part-time programs available. *Students:* 26 full-time (6 women), 24 part-time (14 women). *Degree requirements:* For master's, computer language, thesis or alternative required, foreign language not required; for doctorate, computer language, dissertation required, foreign language not required. *Entrance requirements:* For master's and doctorate, GRE General Test (minimum score of 420 on verbal section required), TOEFL (minimum score of 580 required). *Application deadline:* For fall admission, 6/1 (priority date); for spring admission, 11/1. Applications are processed on a rolling basis. Application fee: $50. *Unit head:* Dr. John R. Lund, Head, 406-994-3601, Fax: 406-994-1789, E-mail: grad@math.montana.edu.

Montclair State University, Office of Graduate Studies, College of Science and Mathematics, Department of Mathematics and Computer Science, Program in Computer Science, Upper Montclair, NJ 07043-1624. Offers applied mathematics (MS); applied statistics (MS). Part-time and evening/weekend programs available. *Degree requirements:* For master's, computer language, written comprehensive exam required, foreign language and thesis not required. *Entrance requirements:* For master's, GRE General Test, minimum GPA of 2.67.

Montclair State University, Office of Graduate Studies, College of Science and Mathematics, Department of Mathematics and Computer Science, Programs in Mathematics, Concentration in Statistics, Upper Montclair, NJ 07043-1624. Offers MS. Part-time and evening/weekend programs available. *Degree requirements:* For master's, written comprehensive exam required, foreign language and thesis not required. *Entrance requirements:* For master's, GRE General Test, minimum GPA of 2.67.

New Mexico State University, Graduate School, College of Business Administration and Economics, Department of Economics and International Business, Las Cruces, NM 88003-8001. Offers economics (MA, MBA, MS); experimental statistics (MS). Part-time programs available. *Faculty:* 22 full-time (4 women). *Students:* 18 full-time (12 women), 11 part-time (7 women); includes 10 minority (1 Asian American or Pacific Islander, 8 Hispanic Americans, 1 Native American), 7 international. *Degree requirements:* For master's, computer language, thesis or alternative required, foreign language not required. *Entrance requirements:* For master's, GMAT, TOEFL, minimum GPA of 3.0. *Application deadline:* For fall admission, 7/1 (priority date); for spring admission, 11/1. Applications are processed on a rolling basis. Application fee: $15 ($35 for international students). Electronic applications accepted. Tuition, state resident: full-time $2,682; part-time $112 per credit. Tuition, nonresident: full-time $8,376; part-time $349 per credit. Tuition and fees vary according to course load. *Unit head:* Dr. Ken Nowotny, Head, 505-646-2113, Fax: 505-646-1915, E-mail: knowotny@nmsu.edu. *Application contact:* Dr. Anthony Popp, Graduate Adviser, 505-646-5198, Fax: 505-646-1915, E-mail: apopp@nmsu.edu.

New York University, Leonard N. Stern School of Business, Department of Statistics and Operations Research, New York, NY 10012-1019. Offers MBA, MS, PhD, APC. *Faculty:* 14 full-time (1 woman), 5 part-time (0 women). *Students:* 40 full-time, 64 part-time. In 1998, 56 master's, 3 doctorates awarded. *Degree requirements:* For master's, computer language required, foreign language and thesis not required; for doctorate, computer language, dissertation required, foreign language not required; for APC, foreign language and thesis not required. *Entrance requirements:* For master's, GMAT, TOEFL (minimum score of 600 required); for doctorate, GMAT. *Average time to degree:* Master's–3 years part-time. *Application deadline:* For fall admission, 3/15. Applications are processed on a rolling basis. Application fee: $75. Tuition: Full-time $27,500. *Financial aid:* Federal Work-Study available. Financial aid application deadline: 1/15; financial aid applicants required to submit FAFSA. *Faculty research:* Time-series modeling, stochastic process and financial modeling, statistical modeling. *Unit head:* Edward Melnick, Chair, 212-998-0440, E-mail: emelnick@stern.nyu.edu. *Application contact:* Mary Miller, Assistant Dean, MBA Admissions and Student Services, 212-998-0600, Fax: 212-995-4231, E-mail: sternmba@stern.nyu.edu.

North Carolina State University, Graduate School, College of Management, Program in Management, Raleigh, NC 27695. Offers biotechnology (MS); computer science (MS); engineering (MS); forest resources management (MS); general business (MS); management information systems (MS); operations research (MS); statistics (MS); telecommunications systems engineering (MS); textile management (MS); total quality management (MS). Part-time programs available. *Faculty:* 40 full-time (9 women), 4 part-time (0 women). *Students:* 48 full-time (15 women), 156 part-time (43 women); includes 33 minority (16 African Americans, 15 Asian Americans or Pacific Islanders, 1 Hispanic American, 1 Native American), 4 international. *Degree requirements:* For master's, computer language required, foreign language and thesis not required. *Entrance requirements:* For master's, GRE or GMAT, TOEFL (minimum score of 550 required), minimum undergraduate GPA of 3.0. *Application deadline:* For fall admission, 6/25; for spring admission, 11/25. Applications are processed on a rolling basis. Application fee: $45. *Unit head:* Dr. Jack W. Wilson, Director of Graduate Programs, 919-515-4327, Fax: 919-515-6943, E-mail: jack_wilson@ncsu.edu. *Application contact:* Dr. Steven G. Allen, Director of Graduate Programs, 919-515-6941, Fax: 919-515-5073, E-mail: steve_allen@ncsu.edu.

North Carolina State University, Graduate School, College of Physical and Mathematical Sciences, Department of Statistics, Raleigh, NC 27695. Offers M Stat, MS, PhD. Part-time programs available. *Faculty:* 50 full-time (12 women), 34 part-time (2 women). *Students:* 138 full-time (67 women), 10 part-time (6 women); includes 9 minority (7 Asian Americans or Pacific Islanders, 1 Hispanic American, 1 Native American), 50 international. Average age 30. 132 applicants, 42% accepted. In 1998, 20 master's, 11 doctorates awarded. *Degree requirements:* For master's, thesis (for some programs), comprehensive exam, final oral exam required, foreign language not required; for doctorate, dissertation, final oral and written exams, written and oral preliminary exams required, foreign language not required. *Entrance requirements:* For master's and doctorate, GRE General Test, TOEFL. *Application deadline:* For fall admission, 3/1; for spring admission, 10/15. Applications are processed on a rolling basis. Application fee: $45. *Financial aid:* In 1998–99, 12 fellowships (averaging $4,599 per year), 111 research assistantships (averaging $6,095 per year), 132 teaching assistantships (averaging $5,459 per year) were awarded.; career-related internships or fieldwork also available. Financial aid application deadline: 3/1. *Faculty research:* Biostatistics; time series; spatial, inference, environmental, industrial, genetics applications; nonlinear models; DOE. Total annual research expenditures: $4.3 million. *Unit head:* Dr. Thomas M. Gerig, Head, 919-515-1901, Fax: 919-515-7591, E-mail: gerig@stat.ncsu.edu. *Application contact:* Dr. Sastry G. Pantula, Director of Graduate Programs, 919-515-1949, Fax: 919-515-7591, E-mail: dsgp@stat.ncsu.edu.

See in-depth description on page 705.

North Dakota State University, Graduate Studies and Research, College of Science and Mathematics, Department of Statistics, Fargo, ND 58105. Offers MS, PhD. *Faculty:* 5 full-time (1 woman). *Students:* 15 full-time (5 women), 4 part-time (3 women); includes 1 minority (African American), 7 international. Average age 24. 10 applicants, 100% accepted. In 1998, 4 master's awarded. *Degree requirements:* For master's and doctorate, computer language, thesis/dissertation required, foreign language not required. *Entrance requirements:* For master's and doctorate, TOEFL (minimum score of 525 required). *Average time to degree:* Master's–2 years full-time; doctorate–3 years full-time. *Application deadline:* Applications are processed on a rolling basis. Application fee: $25. *Financial aid:* In 1998–99, 9 teaching assistantships were awarded.; research assistantships, career-related internships or fieldwork, Federal Work-Study, and institutionally-sponsored loans also available. Financial aid application deadline: 4/15. *Faculty research:* Nonparametric statistics, survival analysis, multivariate analysis, distribution theory, inference modeling, biostatistics. *Unit head:* Dr. Rhonda Magel, Chair, 701-231-7177, Fax: 701-231-8734, E-mail: ndsu-stats@plains.nodak.edu. *Application contact:* Graduate Studies and Research, 701-231-7033.

Northern Arizona University, Graduate College, College of Arts and Sciences, Department of Mathematics, Flagstaff, AZ 86011. Offers acturial science (MS); mathematics (MAT, MS); statistics (MS). Part-time programs available. *Faculty:* 24 full-time (2 women). *Students:* 11 full-time (4 women), 8 part-time (4 women); includes 1 minority (Hispanic American) *Degree requirements:* For master's, thesis optional, foreign language not required. *Application deadline:* For fall admission, 3/15 (priority date). Applications are processed on a rolling basis. Application fee: $45. *Unit head:* Dr. Terry Crites, Chair, 520-523-3481. *Application contact:* Dr. Michael Ratliff, Graduate Coordinator, 520-523-6881, E-mail: grad@math.nau.edu.

Northern Illinois University, Graduate School, College of Liberal Arts and Sciences, Department of Mathematical Sciences, Program in Applied Probability and Statistics, De Kalb, IL 60115-2854. Offers MS. Part-time programs available. *Faculty:* 10 full-time (2 women), 1 part-time (0 women). *Students:* 11 full-time (4 women), 5 international. Average age 29. 16 applicants, 75% accepted. In 1998, 9 degrees awarded. *Degree requirements:* For master's, comprehensive exam required, thesis optional, foreign language not required. *Entrance requirements:* For master's, GRE General Test, TOEFL (minimum score of 550 required; 213 for computer-based), minimum GPA of 2.75. *Application deadline:* For fall admission, 6/1; for spring admission, 11/1. Applications are processed on a rolling basis. Application fee: $30. *Financial aid:* Fellowships, research assistantships, teaching assistantships, career-related internships or fieldwork, Federal Work-Study, tuition waivers (full), and unspecified assistantships available. Aid available to part-time students. *Unit head:* Dr. Mohsen Pourahmadi, Director, Division of Statistics, 815-753-6773. *Application contact:* Dr. Nader Ebrahimi, Director, Graduate Studies, 815-753-6864.

Northwestern University, The Graduate School, Judd A. and Marjorie Weinberg College of Arts and Sciences, Department of Statistics, Evanston, IL 60208. Offers MS, PhD. Admissions and degrees offered through The Graduate School. Part-time programs available. *Faculty:* 7 full-time (0 women). *Students:* 8 full-time (2 women), 3 part-time (1 woman), 8 international. 38 applicants, 68% accepted. In 1998, 1 master's, 1 doctorate awarded. Terminal master's awarded for partial completion of doctoral program. *Degree requirements:* For master's, final exam required, foreign language and thesis not required; for doctorate, dissertation, preliminary exam, final exam required, foreign language not required. *Entrance requirements:* For master's and doctorate, GRE General Test, TOEFL (minimum score of 560 required). *Application deadline:* For fall admission, 8/30. Application fee: $50 ($55 for international students). *Financial aid:* In 1998–99, 3 fellowships with full tuition reimbursements (averaging $11,673 per year), 5 teaching assistantships with full tuition reimbursements (averaging $12,042 per year) were awarded.; research assistantships, career-related internships or fieldwork and institutionally-sponsored loans also available. Financial aid application deadline: 1/15; financial aid applicants required to submit FAFSA. *Faculty research:* Theoretical statistics, applied statistics, computational methods, statistical designs, complex models. *Unit head:* Bruce Spencer, Chair, 847-491-3974, Fax: 847-491-4939. *Application contact:* Holly Johnson, Admission Contact, 847-491-3974, Fax: 847-491-4939, E-mail: h-curry@nwu.edu.

Oakland University, Graduate Studies, College of Arts and Sciences, Department of Mathematical Sciences, Program in Applied Statistics, Rochester, MI 48309-4401. Offers MS, PhD. Part-time and evening/weekend programs available. *Students:* 8 full-time (3 women), 18 part-time (10 women); includes 4 minority (3 Asian Americans or Pacific Islanders, 1 Hispanic American), 6 international. Average age 31. 23 applicants, 78% accepted. In 1998, 9 master's awarded. *Degree requirements:* For master's, foreign language and thesis not required; for doctorate, dissertation required, foreign language not required. *Entrance requirements:* For master's, minimum GPA of 3.0 for unconditional admission; for doctorate, GRE Subject Test, minimum GPA of 3.0 for unconditional admission. *Application deadline:* For fall admission, 7/15; for spring admission, 3/15. Application fee: $30. Tuition, state resident: part-time $221 per credit hour. Tuition, nonresident: part-time $488 per credit hour. Required fees: $214 per semester. Part-time tuition and fees vary according to program. *Financial aid:* Career-related internships or fieldwork and tuition waivers (full) available. Financial aid application deadline: 3/1; financial aid applicants required to submit FAFSA. *Unit head:* Dr. Frances Shipley, Dean of Graduate School, 660-562-1145, E-mail: gradsch@mail.nwmissouri.edu. *Application contact:* Dr. Kevin Andrews, Coordinator, 248-370-3430.

Oakland University, Graduate Studies, College of Arts and Sciences, Department of Mathematical Sciences, Program in Statistical Methods, Rochester, MI 48309-4401. Offers Certificate. *Students:* 1 (woman) full-time, 8 part-time (3 women). Average age 38. 4 applicants, 100% accepted. In 1998, 1 degree awarded. *Application deadline:* For fall admission, 7/15; for spring admission, 3/15. Application fee: $30. Tuition, state resident: part-time $221 per credit hour. Tuition, nonresident: part-time $488 per credit hour. Required fees: $214 per semester. Part-time tuition and fees vary according to program. *Financial aid:* Federal Work-Study, institutionally-sponsored loans, and tuition waivers (full) available. Financial aid application deadline: 3/1; financial aid applicants required to submit FAFSA. *Unit head:* Dr. Kevin Andrews, Coordinator, 248-370-3430. *Application contact:* Dr. Kevin Andrews, Coordinator, 248-370-3430.

The Ohio State University, Graduate School, College of Mathematical and Physical Sciences, Department of Statistics, Columbus, OH 43210. Offers biostatistics (PhD); statistics (M Appl Stat, MS, PhD). *Faculty:* 22 full-time. *Students:* 44 full-time (21 women), 7 part-time (5 women); includes 6 minority (3 African Americans, 3 Asian Americans or Pacific Islanders), 24 international. 116 applicants, 16% accepted. In 1998, 27 master's, 9 doctorates awarded. *Degree requirements:* For master's, thesis optional, foreign language not required; for doctorate, dissertation required, foreign language not required. *Application deadline:* For fall admission, 8/15. Applications are processed on a rolling basis. Application fee: $30 ($40 for international students). *Financial aid:* Fellowships, research assistantships, teaching assistantships, Federal Work-Study and institutionally-sponsored loans available. Aid available to part-time students. *Unit head:* Thomas Santner, Chairman, 614-292-2866, Fax: 614-292-2096, E-mail: santner.1@osu.edu.

See in-depth description on page 713.

Oklahoma State University, Graduate College, College of Arts and Sciences, Department of Statistics, Stillwater, OK 74078. Offers MS, PhD. *Faculty:* 8 full-time (4 women). *Students:* 12 full-time (5 women), 6 part-time (5 women); includes 2 minority (both Native Americans), 3 international. Average age 29. In 1998, 4 master's, 1 doctorate awarded. *Degree requirements:* For doctorate, dissertation required, foreign language not required, foreign language not required. *Entrance requirements:* For master's and doctorate, TOEFL (minimum score of 550 required). *Application deadline:* For fall admission, 7/1 (priority date). Application fee: $25. *Financial aid:* In 1998–99, 11 students received aid, including 11 teaching assistantships (averaging $14,059 per year); Federal Work-Study and tuition waivers (partial) also available. Aid available to part-time students. Financial aid application deadline: 3/1. *Faculty research:* Linear models, sampling methods, ranking and selections procedures, categorical data, multiple comparisons. *Unit head:* Dr. William Warde, Head, 405-744-5684.

Old Dominion University, College of Sciences, Department of Mathematics and Statistics, Programs in Computational and Applied Mathematics, Norfolk, VA 23529. Offers applied mathematics (MS, PhD); statistics (MS, PhD). Part-time programs available. *Faculty:* 26 full-time (2 women). *Students:* 19 full-time (8 women), 14 part-time (3 women); includes 2 minority (1 African American, 1 Asian American or Pacific Islander), 13 international. Average age 35. In 1998, 2 master's, 3 doctorates awarded. Terminal master's awarded for partial completion of doctoral program. *Degree requirements:* For master's, comprehensive exam required, foreign language and thesis not required; for doctorate, dissertation, candidacy exam required, foreign language not required. *Entrance requirements:* For master's, GRE General Test, GRE Subject Test, TOEFL, minimum GPA of 3.0 in major, 2.5 overall; for doctorate, GRE General Test (minimum combined score of 1000 required), GRE Subject Test (minimum score of 600 required), TOEFL. *Application deadline:* For fall admission, 7/1. Applications are processed on a rolling basis. Application fee: $30. *Financial aid:* In 1998–99, 20 students received aid, including 15 research assistantships, 1 teaching assistantship; fellowships, grants also available. Financial aid application deadline: 2/15; financial aid applicants required to submit FAFSA. *Faculty research:* Numerical analysis, integral equations, continuum mechanics. *Unit head:* Dr. John J. Swetits, Director, 757-683-3911, E-mail: swetits@math.odu.edu.

Oregon State University, Graduate School, College of Science, Department of Statistics, Corvallis, OR 97331. Offers applied statistics (MA, MS, PhD); biometry (MA, MS, PhD); environmental statistics (MA, MS, PhD); mathematical statistics (MA, MS, PhD); operations research (MA, MAIS, MS); statistics (M Agr, MA, MS, PhD). Part-time programs available. *Faculty:* 14 full-time (4 women). Average age 30. In 1998, 11 master's, 1 doctorate awarded. *Degree requirements:* For master's, consulting experience required; for doctorate, dissertation, consulting experience required, foreign language not required. *Entrance requirements:* For master's and doctorate, TOEFL (minimum score of 550 required; 213 for computer-based), minimum GPA of 3.0 in last 90 hours. *Application deadline:* For fall admission, 2/15. Applications are processed on a rolling basis. Application fee: $50. *Financial aid:* In 1998–99, 20 research assistantships, 6 teaching assistantships were awarded.; Federal Work-Study and institutionally-sponsored loans also available. Financial aid application deadline: 2/15. *Faculty research:* Analysis of enumerative data, nonparametric statistics, asymptotics, experimental design, generalized regression models, linear model theory, reliability theory, survival analysis, wildlife and general survey methodology. *Unit head:* Dr. Robert Smythe, Chair, 541-737-3366. *Application contact:* Dr. Dawn Peters, Director of Graduate Studies, 541-737-1991, Fax: 541-737-3489, E-mail: statoff@stat.orst.edu.

See in-depth description on page 723.

Pennsylvania State University University Park Campus, Graduate School, Eberly College of Science, Department of Statistics, State College, University Park, PA 16802-1503. Offers MA, MS, PhD. *Students:* 47 full-time (19 women), 17 part-time (10 women). In 1998, 11 master's, 4 doctorates awarded. *Entrance requirements:* For master's and doctorate, GRE General Test. Application fee: $50. *Financial aid:* Fellowships, research assistantships, teaching assistantships, tuition waivers (full) available. *Unit head:* Dr. James L. Rosenberger, Head, 814-865-1348.

Princeton University, Graduate School, School of Engineering and Applied Science, Department of Civil Engineering and Operations Research, Program in Statistics and Operations Research, Princeton, NJ 08544-1019. Offers MSE, PhD. MSE offered jointly with the Department of Electrical Engineering. *Degree requirements:* For master's, thesis required; for doctorate, dissertation, qualifying exam required. *Entrance requirements:* For master's, GRE General Test, GRE Subject Test, bachelor's degree in engineering or science; for doctorate, GRE General Test, GRE Subject Test.

Purdue University, Graduate School, School of Science, Department of Statistics, West Lafayette, IN 47907. Offers applied statistics (MS); statistics (PhD); statistics and computer

Statistics

Purdue University (continued)
science (MS); theoretical statistics (MS). *Faculty:* 24 full-time (4 women). *Students:* 28 full-time (7 women), 25 part-time (8 women); includes 4 minority (1 African American, 3 Asian Americans or Pacific Islanders), 39 international. 103 applicants, 39% accepted. In 1998, 13 master's awarded (23% entered university research/teaching, 54% found other work related to degree, 23% continued full-time study); 5 doctorates awarded (100% found work related to degree). *Degree requirements:* For master's, foreign language and thesis not required; for doctorate, dissertation required, foreign language not required. *Entrance requirements:* For master's and doctorate, GRE, TOEFL (minimum score of 600 required). *Average time to degree:* Master's–2 years full-time; doctorate–5 years full-time. *Application deadline:* For fall admission, 2/1. Application fee: $30. Electronic applications accepted. *Financial aid:* In 1998–99, 2 fellowships with partial tuition reimbursements (averaging $20,000 per year), 8 research assistantships with partial tuition reimbursements (averaging $12,500 per year), 33 teaching assistantships with partial tuition reimbursements (averaging $12,500 per year) were awarded.; career-related internships or fieldwork also available. Aid available to part-time students. Financial aid applicants required to submit FAFSA. *Faculty research:* Decision theory, ranking and selection, wavelets, design of experiments, statistical genetics. *Unit head:* Dr. M. E. Bock, Head, 765-494-3141, Fax: 765-494-0558. *Application contact:* Angie Murphy, Graduate Secretary, 765-494-5794, Fax: 765-494-0558, E-mail: graduate@stat.purdue.edu.

See in-depth description on page 735.

Queen's University at Kingston, School of Graduate Studies and Research, Faculty of Arts and Sciences, Department of Mathematics and Statistics, Kingston, ON K7L 3N6, Canada. Offers mathematics (M Sc, MA, PhD); statistics (M Sc, MA, PhD). Part-time programs available. *Students:* 33 full-time (9 women), 4 part-time (1 woman). In 1998, 14 master's, 4 doctorates awarded. *Degree requirements:* For master's, thesis required, foreign language not required; for doctorate, dissertation, comprehensive exam required. *Entrance requirements:* For master's and doctorate, TOEFL (minimum score of 550 required). *Application deadline:* For fall admission, 2/28 (priority date). Application fee: $60. Electronic applications accepted. *Financial aid:* Fellowships, research assistantships, teaching assistantships, institutionally-sponsored loans available. Financial aid application deadline: 3/1. *Faculty research:* Algebra, analysis, applied mathematics, combinatorics, differential geometry. *Unit head:* Dr. H. E. A. Campbell, Head, 613-533-2428. *Application contact:* Dr. L. B. Jonker, Graduate Coordinator, 613-533-2439.

Rensselaer Polytechnic Institute, Graduate School, School of Engineering, Department of Decision Sciences and Engineering Systems, Program in Operations Research and Statistics, Troy, NY 12180-3590. Offers M Eng, MS, MBA/M Eng. Part-time programs available. *Faculty:* 12 full-time (0 women), 6 part-time (1 woman). *Students:* 21 full-time (8 women), 4 part-time (2 women); includes 5 minority (1 African American, 3 Asian Americans or Pacific Islanders, 1 Hispanic American), 10 international. 17 applicants, 76% accepted. In 1998, 13 degrees awarded. *Degree requirements:* For master's, thesis required (for some programs), foreign language not required. *Entrance requirements:* For master's, GRE General Test, TOEFL (minimum score of 550 required). *Application deadline:* For fall admission, 2/1 (priority date). Applications are processed on a rolling basis. Application fee: $35. *Financial aid:* In 1998–99, 1 fellowship with full tuition reimbursement (averaging $11,000 per year), 1 research assistantship with full tuition reimbursement (averaging $10,600 per year), 3 teaching assistantships with full tuition reimbursements (averaging $10,600 per year) were awarded.; career-related internships or fieldwork and institutionally-sponsored loans also available. Financial aid application deadline: 2/1. *Faculty research:* Manufacturing, MIS, statistical consulting, education services, production, logistics, inventory. Total annual research expenditures: $2 million. *Unit head:* John S. Kerge, Dean of Admissions, 718-260-3200, Fax: 718-260-3446, E-mail: admitme@poly.edu. *Application contact:* Lee Vilardi, Graduate Coordinator, 518-276-6681, Fax: 518-276-8227, E-mail: dsesgr@rpi.edu.

See in-depth description on page 737.

Rice University, Graduate Programs, George R. Brown School of Engineering, Department of Statistics, Houston, TX 77251-1892. Offers M Stat, MA, PhD. *Degree requirements:* For master's, thesis required, foreign language not required; for doctorate, dissertation required. *Entrance requirements:* For master's and doctorate, GRE General Test, GRE Subject Test, TOEFL (minimum score of 550 required), minimum GPA of 3.0.

Rochester Institute of Technology, Part-time and Graduate Admissions, College of Engineering, Center of Quality and Applied Statistics, Rochester, NY 14623-5604. Offers applied statistics (MS); statistical quality (AC). Part-time and evening/weekend programs available. 23 applicants, 65% accepted. In 1998, 26 master's, 2 other advanced degrees awarded. *Degree requirements:* For master's, oral exam required, foreign language and thesis not required. *Entrance requirements:* For master's, TOEFL, previous course work in calculus, minimum GPA of 3.0. *Application deadline:* For fall admission, 3/1 (priority date). Applications are processed on a rolling basis. Application fee: $40. *Financial aid:* Research assistantships available. *Unit head:* Dr. Donald Baker, Director, 716-475-5070, E-mail: ddbcqa@rit.edu.

Rutgers, The State University of New Jersey, New Brunswick, Graduate School, Program in Statistics, New Brunswick, NJ 08903. Offers quality and productivity management (MS); statistics (MS, PhD). Part-time programs available. *Faculty:* 16 full-time (1 woman). *Students:* 51 full-time (28 women), 54 part-time (25 women); includes 20 minority (2 African Americans, 15 Asian Americans or Pacific Islanders, 3 Hispanic Americans), 34 international. Average age 28. 135 applicants, 74% accepted. In 1998, 26 master's, 4 doctorates awarded. Terminal master's awarded for partial completion of doctoral program. *Degree requirements:* For master's, essay, exam required, foreign language and thesis not required; for doctorate, one foreign language (computer language can substitute), dissertation, oral and written exams required. *Entrance requirements:* For master's, GRE General Test; for doctorate, GRE General Test, GRE Subject Test. *Average time to degree:* Master's–2 years full-time, 5 years part-time; doctorate–5 years full-time, 7 years part-time. *Application deadline:* For fall admission, 5/1 (priority date); for spring admission, 12/1 (priority date). Applications are processed on a rolling basis. Application fee: $50. Electronic applications accepted. *Financial aid:* In 1998–99, 11 students received aid, including 3 fellowships with full tuition reimbursements available (averaging $13,000 per year), 10 teaching assistantships with full tuition reimbursements available; research assistantships, career-related internships or fieldwork, Federal Work-Study, and institutionally-sponsored loans also available. Financial aid application deadline: 3/1; financial aid applicants required to submit FAFSA. *Faculty research:* Probability, decision theory, linear models, multivariate statistics, statistical computing. *Unit head:* Dr. Kesar Singh, Director, 732-445-3634, Fax: 732-445-3428, E-mail: kesar@stat.rutgers.edu. *Application contact:* Angela T. Klein, Department Secretary, 732-445-2693, Fax: 732-445-3428, E-mail: aklein@stat.rutgers.edu.

St. John's University, Graduate School of Arts and Sciences, Department of Mathematics and Computer Science, Jamaica, NY 11439. Offers algebra (MA); analysis (MA); applied mathematics (MA); computer science (MA); geometry-topology (MA); logic and foundations (MA); probability and statistics (MA). Part-time and evening/weekend programs available. *Faculty:* 16 full-time (3 women), 5 part-time (2 women). *Students:* 7 full-time (3 women), 5 part-time (3 women); includes 5 minority (2 African Americans, 1 Asian American or Pacific Islander, 2 Hispanic Americans), 2 international. *Degree requirements:* For master's, comprehensive exam required, thesis optional, comprehensive exam required, thesis optional. *Entrance requirements:* For master's, minimum GPA of 3.0. *Application deadline:* Applications are processed on a rolling basis. Application fee: $40. Tuition: Full-time $13,200; part-time $500 per credit. Required fees: $150; $75 per term. Tuition and fees vary according to degree level and program. *Unit head:* Dr. Charles Traina, Chair, 718-990-6166, E-mail: trainac@stjohns.edu. *Application contact:* Patricia G. Armstrong, Director, Office of Admission, 718-990-2028, Fax: 718-990-2096, E-mail: armstrop@stjohns.edu.

San Diego State University, Graduate and Research Affairs, College of Sciences, Department of Mathematical Sciences, Program in Statistics, San Diego, CA 92182. Offers MS. *Students:* 3 full-time (1 woman), 10 part-time (4 women); includes 4 minority (all Asian Americans or Pacific Islanders), 1 international. Average age 30. In 1998, 6 degrees awarded. *Degree requirements:* For master's, comprehensive exam required, foreign language and thesis not required. *Entrance requirements:* For master's, GRE General Test (minimum combined score of 950 required), TOEFL (minimum score of 550 required). *Application deadline:* For fall admission, 7/1 (priority date); for spring admission, 12/1. Applications are processed on a rolling basis. Application fee: $55. *Unit head:* Admissions Office, 902-867-2219, Fax: 902-867-2329, E-mail: admit@stfx.ca. *Application contact:* C. J. Park, Graduate Adviser, 619-594-6171, Fax: 619-594-6746, E-mail: cjpark@saturn.sdsu.edu.

Simon Fraser University, Graduate Studies, Faculty of Science, Department of Mathematics and Statistics, Program in Statistics, Burnaby, BC V5A 1S6, Canada. Offers M Sc, PhD. *Degree requirements:* For master's, thesis required; for doctorate, dissertation, comprehensive exams required. *Entrance requirements:* For master's, GRE Subject Test, TOEFL (minimum score of 570 required), TWE (minimum score of 5 required) or International English Language Test (minimum score of 7.5 required), minimum GPA of 3.0; for doctorate, GRE Subject Test, TOEFL (minimum score of 570 required), TWE (minimum score of 5 required) or International English Language Test (minimum score of 7.5 required), minimum GPA of 3.5. Application fee: $55. *Unit head:* Graduate Coordinator, 408-924-5487. *Application contact:* Graduate Secretary, 604-291-3801, Fax: 604-291-4947.

Southern Illinois University Carbondale, Graduate School, College of Science, Department of Mathematics, Carbondale, IL 62901-6806. Offers mathematics (MA, MS, PhD); statistics (MS). Part-time programs available. *Faculty:* 31 full-time (2 women). *Students:* 29 full-time (6 women), 10 part-time (5 women); includes 4 minority (2 African Americans, 2 Asian Americans or Pacific Islanders), 13 international. *Degree requirements:* For master's, thesis required, foreign language not required; for doctorate, 2 foreign languages (computer language can substitute for one), dissertation required. *Entrance requirements:* For master's, TOEFL (minimum score of 550 required), minimum GPA of 2.7; for doctorate, TOEFL (minimum score of 550 required), minimum GPA of 3.25. *Application deadline:* Applications are processed on a rolling basis. Application fee: $0. *Unit head:* Andrew Earnest, Chairperson, 618-453-5302, Fax: 618-453-5300, E-mail: chairman@math.siu.edu. *Application contact:* William T. Patula, Director of Graduate Studies, 618-453-5302, Fax: 618-453-5300, E-mail: wpatula@math.siu.edu.

Southern Illinois University Edwardsville, Graduate Studies and Research, College of Arts and Sciences, Department of Mathematics and Statistics, Edwardsville, IL 62026-0001. Offers MS. Part-time programs available. *Students:* 7 full-time (2 women), 16 part-time (6 women); includes 4 minority (3 African Americans, 1 Asian American or Pacific Islander), 1 international. 7 applicants, 57% accepted. In 1998, 1 degree awarded. *Degree requirements:* For master's, computer language, thesis or alternative, final exam required, foreign language not required. *Entrance requirements:* For master's, TOEFL (minimum score of 550 required), undergraduate major in related area. *Application deadline:* For fall admission, 7/24. Application fee: $25. *Financial aid:* In 1998–99, 1 fellowship with full tuition reimbursement, 10 teaching assistantships with full tuition reimbursements were awarded.; research assistantships with full tuition reimbursements, Federal Work-Study, institutionally-sponsored loans, and unspecified assistantships also available. Aid available to part-time students. *Unit head:* Dr. Nadine Verderber, Acting Chair, 618-650-5985, E-mail: nverder@siue.edu.

Southern Methodist University, Dedman College, Department of Statistical Science, Dallas, TX 75275. Offers MS, PhD. *Faculty:* 9 full-time (0 women). *Students:* 14 full-time (7 women), 5 part-time (1 woman); includes 6 minority (4 Asian Americans or Pacific Islanders, 2 Hispanic Americans), 6 international. Average age 30. 48 applicants, 83% accepted. In 1998, 10 master's, 2 doctorates awarded. Terminal master's awarded for partial completion of doctoral program. *Degree requirements:* For master's, oral and written exams required, thesis optional, foreign language not required; for doctorate, dissertation, oral and written exams required, foreign language not required. *Entrance requirements:* For master's, GRE General Test, TOEFL (minimum score of 550 required), BS in business, engineering, mathematics, or science; previous course work in linear algebra and advanced calculus; minimum GPA of 3.0; for doctorate, GRE General Test, minimum GPA of 3.0. *Application deadline:* For fall admission, 4/1; for spring admission, 11/30. Application fee: $50. Tuition: Part-time $686 per credit hour. Required fees: $88 per credit hour. Part-time tuition and fees vary according to course load and program. *Financial aid:* Research assistantships, teaching assistantships, tuition waivers (full) available. Financial aid application deadline: 4/30; financial aid applicants required to submit FAFSA. *Faculty research:* Bayesian analysis, nonparametrics, quality control, regression, time series. Total annual research expenditures: $80,000. *Unit head:* Dr. William Schucany, Interim Chair, 214-768-2441. *Application contact:* Rudy Guerra, Graduate Adviser, 214-768-2270.

See in-depth description on page 747.

Stanford University, School of Humanities and Sciences, Department of Statistics, Stanford, CA 94305-9991. Offers MS, PhD. *Faculty:* 13 full-time (0 women). *Students:* 82 full-time (29 women), 8 part-time (2 women); includes 8 minority (7 Asian Americans or Pacific Islanders, 1 Hispanic American), 46 international. Average age 27. 79 applicants, 49% accepted. In 1998, 26 master's awarded (5% entered university research/teaching); 9 doctorates awarded. Terminal master's awarded for partial completion of doctoral program. *Degree requirements:* For master's, computer language required, foreign language not required; for doctorate, computer language, dissertation, oral exam required, foreign language not required. *Entrance requirements:* For master's, GRE General Test, TOEFL; for doctorate, GRE General Test, GRE Subject Test, TOEFL. *Application deadline:* For fall admission, 1/1. Application fee: $65 ($80 for international students). Electronic applications accepted. Tuition: Full-time $23,058. Required fees: $152. Part-time tuition and fees vary according to course load. *Financial aid:* Fellowships, research assistantships, teaching assistantships, institutionally-sponsored loans available. *Unit head:* Brad Efron, Chair, 650-723-2206, Fax: 650-723-3235, E-mail: brad@stat.stanford.edu. *Application contact:* Graduate Administrator, 650-723-2625, Fax: 650-725-8977.

State University of New York at Albany, College of Arts and Sciences, Department of Mathematics and Statistics, Albany, NY 12222-0001. Offers mathematics (PhD); secondary teaching (MA); statistics (MA). Evening/weekend programs available. *Faculty:* 29 full-time (2 women), 1 part-time (0 women). *Students:* 31 full-time (11 women), 6 part-time (1 woman); includes 2 minority (both African Americans), 7 international. Average age 25. 33 applicants, 73% accepted. In 1998, 10 master's, 9 doctorates awarded. *Degree requirements:* For master's, foreign language and thesis not required; for doctorate, dissertation required. *Entrance requirements:* For doctorate, GRE General Test, GRE Subject Test. Application fee: $50. Tuition, state resident: full-time $5,100; part-time $213 per credit. Tuition, nonresident: full-time $8,416; part-time $351 per credit. Required fees: $31 per credit. *Financial aid:* Fellowships, research assistantships, teaching assistantships, minority assistantships available. *Unit head:* Timothy Lance, Chair, 518-442-4602.

State University of New York at Albany, School of Public Health, Department of Biometry and Statistics, Rensselaer, NY 12144. Offers MS, PhD. *Faculty:* 5 full-time (1 woman). *Students:* 16 full-time (11 women), 10 part-time (4 women); includes 2 minority (1 African American, 1 Hispanic American), 12 international. 21 applicants, 81% accepted. In 1998, 8 master's, 1 doctorate awarded. *Degree requirements:* For doctorate, dissertation required. *Entrance requirements:* For master's and doctorate, GRE General Test. Application fee: $50. Tuition, state resident: full-time $5,100; part-time $213 per credit. Tuition, nonresident: full-time $8,416; part-time $351 per credit. Required fees: $31 per credit. *Unit head:* Dr. Igor Zurbenko, Chair, 518-402-0400.

State University of New York at Binghamton, Graduate School, School of Arts and Sciences, Department of Mathematical Sciences, Binghamton, NY 13902-6000. Offers computer science (MA, PhD); probability and statistics (MA, PhD). *Faculty:* 23 full-time, 9 part-time.

Students: 44 full-time (16 women), 6 part-time (2 women); includes 1 minority (Asian American or Pacific Islander), 14 international. Terminal master's awarded for partial completion of doctoral program. *Degree requirements:* For master's, thesis or alternative required; for doctorate, dissertation required. *Entrance requirements:* For master's and doctorate, GRE General Test, GRE Subject Test, TOEFL. *Application deadline:* For fall admission, 4/15 (priority date); for spring admission, 11/1. Applications are processed on a rolling basis. Application fee: $50. Electronic applications accepted. Tuition, state resident: full-time $5,100; part-time $213 per credit. Tuition, nonresident: full-time $8,416; part-time $351 per credit. Required fees: $77 per credit. Part-time tuition and fees vary according to course load. *Unit head:* Dr. David Hanson, Chairperson, 607-777-2147.

State University of New York at Buffalo, Graduate School, School of Medicine and Biomedical Sciences, Graduate Programs in Medicine and Biomedical Sciences, Department of Social and Preventive Medicine, Buffalo, NY 14260. Offers epidemiology (MS); epidemiology and community health (PhD); statistics (MA, PhD). Part-time programs available. *Faculty:* 12 full-time (4 women), 3 part-time (1 woman). *Students:* 19 full-time (16 women), 20 part-time (9 women); includes 7 minority (3 African Americans, 3 Hispanic Americans, 1 Native American), 6 international. *Degree requirements:* For doctorate, dissertation required. *Entrance requirements:* For master's, GRE General Test, TOEFL (minimum score of 550 required); for doctorate, GRE General Test, TOEFL. *Application deadline:* For fall admission, 2/1 (priority date). Applications are processed on a rolling basis. Application fee: $35. Electronic applications accepted. Tuition, state resident: full-time $5,100; part-time $213 per credit hour. Tuition, nonresident: full-time $8,416; part-time $351 per credit hour. Required fees: $870; $75 per semester. *Unit head:* Dr. Maurizio Trevisan, Chairman, 716-829-2975 Ext. 632, Fax: 716-829-2979, E-mail: mtrevisa@buffalo.edu. *Application contact:* Dr. John E. Vena, Director of Graduate Studies, 716-829-2975 Ext. 602, Fax: 716-829-2979, E-mail: jvena@acsu.buffalo.edu.

State University of New York at Buffalo, Graduate School, School of Medicine and Biomedical Sciences, Graduate Programs in Medicine and Biomedical Sciences, Department of Statistics, Buffalo, NY 14260. Offers MA, PhD. *Faculty:* 6 full-time (0 women), 2 part-time (0 women). *Students:* 8 full-time (1 woman), 5 part-time (1 woman), 6 international. Average age 26. In 1998, 5 master's, 1 doctorate awarded. Terminal master's awarded for partial completion of doctoral program. *Degree requirements:* For master's, project required; for doctorate, dissertation required, foreign language not required. *Entrance requirements:* For master's, TOEFL; for doctorate, GRE General Test, TOEFL (minimum score of 550 required). *Application deadline:* For fall admission, 2/1 (priority date). Applications are processed on a rolling basis. Application fee: $35. Tuition, state resident: full-time $5,100; part-time $213 per credit hour. Tuition, nonresident: full-time $8,416; part-time $351 per credit hour. Required fees: $870; $75 per semester. *Financial aid:* In 1998–99, 8 students received aid, including 8 teaching assistantships with full tuition reimbursements available (averaging $9,000 per year); career-related internships or fieldwork, Federal Work-Study, institutionally-sponsored loans, tuition waivers (full), and unspecified assistantships also available. Financial aid application deadline: 2/1; financial aid applicants required to submit FAFSA. *Faculty research:* Statistical inference, Bayesian statistics, optimal sequential design, predictive inference. Total annual research expenditures: $29,203. *Unit head:* Dr. John E. Vena, Director of Graduate Studies, 716-829-2975 Ext. 602, Fax: 716-829-2979, E-mail: jvena@acsu.buffalo.edu. *Application contact:* Dr. John E. Vena, Director of Graduate Studies, 716-829-2975 Ext. 602, Fax: 716-829-2979, E-mail: jvena@acsu.buffalo.edu.

State University of New York at Stony Brook, Graduate School, College of Engineering and Applied Sciences, Department of Applied Mathematics and Statistics, Stony Brook, NY 11794. Offers MS, PhD. *Faculty:* 20 full-time (3 women), 3 part-time (1 woman). *Students:* 68 full-time (27 women), 34 part-time (9 women); includes 18 minority (6 African Americans, 11 Asian Americans or Pacific Islanders, 1 Hispanic American), 55 international. 164 applicants, 51% accepted. In 1998, 20 master's, 14 doctorates awarded. *Degree requirements:* For master's, thesis or alternative required, foreign language not required; for doctorate, dissertation, comprehensive exams required. *Entrance requirements:* For master's and doctorate, GRE General Test, TOEFL. *Application deadline:* For fall admission, 1/15. Application fee: $50. *Financial aid:* In 1998–99, 9 fellowships, 30 research assistantships, 26 teaching assistantships were awarded. *Faculty research:* Biostatistics, combinatorial analysis, differential equations, modeling. Total annual research expenditures: $2.6 million. *Unit head:* Dr. J. Glimm, Chairman, 516-632-8360. *Application contact:* Dr. Woo Jong Kim, Director, 516-632-8360, Fax: 516-632-8490, E-mail: wjkim@ccmail.sunysb.edu.

Stephen F. Austin State University, Graduate School, College of Sciences and Mathematics, Department of Mathematics and Statistics, Nacogdoches, TX 75962. Offers mathematics (MS); mathematics education (MS); statistics (MS). *Faculty:* 14 full-time (1 woman). *Students:* 11 full-time (5 women), 1 (woman) part-time; includes 1 minority (African American), 5 international. 4 applicants, 100% accepted. In 1998, 4 degrees awarded. *Degree requirements:* For master's, comprehensive exam required, thesis optional, foreign language not required. *Entrance requirements:* For master's, GRE General Test, TOEFL, minimum GPA of 2.8 in last 60 hours, 2.5 overall. *Application deadline:* For fall admission, 8/1 (priority date); for spring admission, 12/15. Applications are processed on a rolling basis. Application fee: $0 ($50 for international students). Tuition, state resident: full-time $1,792. Tuition, nonresident: full-time $6,880. *Financial aid:* Teaching assistantships available. Financial aid application deadline: 3/1. *Faculty research:* Kernel type estimators, fractal mappings, spline curve fitting, robust regression continua theory. *Unit head:* Dr. Jasper Adams, Chair, 409-468-3805.

Stevens Institute of Technology, Graduate School, School of Applied Sciences and Liberal Arts, Department of Mathematical Sciences, Program in Applied Statistics, Hoboken, NJ 07030. Offers MS, Certificate. *Degree requirements:* For master's, thesis optional, foreign language not required; for degree, foreign language not required. *Entrance requirements:* For master's, GRE, TOEFL. Electronic applications accepted.

Syracuse University, Graduate School, College of Arts and Sciences, Program in Applied Statistics, Syracuse, NY 13244-0003. Offers MS. *Faculty:* 1 full-time (0 women), 1 part-time (0 women). *Students:* 1 (woman) full-time, 1 part-time, 1 international. Average age 26. 8 applicants, 25% accepted. In 1998, 1 degree awarded. *Entrance requirements:* For master's, GRE. *Application deadline:* Applications are processed on a rolling basis. Application fee: $40. Tuition: Full-time $13,992; part-time $583 per credit hour. *Financial aid:* Application deadline: 3/1. *Unit head:* Daniel Griffith, Director, 315-443-5637.

Syracuse University, Graduate School, School of Management, Program in Managerial Statistics, Syracuse, NY 13244-0003. Offers MBA. *Faculty:* 6. Average age 37. 2 applicants, 50% accepted. *Entrance requirements:* For master's, GMAT. *Application deadline:* For fall admission, 2/1. Application fee: $40. Tuition: Full-time $13,992; part-time $583 per credit hour. *Financial aid:* Application deadline: 3/1. *Unit head:* Chung Chen, Coordinator, 315-443-3747. *Application contact:* Associate Dean, 315-443-3850.

Temple University, Graduate School, School of Business and Management, Department of Statistics, Philadelphia, PA 19122-6096. Offers MS, PhD. Part-time programs available. *Faculty:* 14 full-time (1 woman). *Students:* 43 (20 women); includes 19 minority (1 African American, 18 Asian Americans or Pacific Islanders) 5 international. 45 applicants, 40% accepted. In 1998, 5 master's, 4 doctorates awarded. Terminal master's awarded for partial completion of doctoral program. *Degree requirements:* For master's, comprehensive exam required, foreign language and thesis not required; for doctorate, dissertation, comprehensive and specialty exams required, foreign language not required. *Entrance requirements:* For master's and doctorate, GRE General Test (minimum score of 575 on quantitative section required), TOEFL (minimum score of 575 required), minimum GPA of 3.2 in mathematics during previous 2 years, 2.8 overall. *Application deadline:* For fall admission, 4/15 (priority date). Applications are processed on a rolling basis. Application fee: $40. *Financial aid:* Fellowships, research assistantships, teaching assistantships, institutionally-sponsored loans and tuition waivers (full and partial) available. *Faculty research:* Gibbs sampling, longitudinal data, multiple comparisons, statistical ecology, time series. *Unit head:* Dr. Jagbir Singh, Chairperson, 215-204-8892, Fax: 215-204-1501. *Application contact:* Dr. Francis Hsuan, Director of Graduate Study, 215-204-8105, Fax: 215-204-1501.

Temple University, Graduate School, School of Business and Management, Master's Program in Business Administration, Philadelphia, PA 19122-6096. Offers accounting (MBA, MS); actuarial science (MBA); chemistry (MBA); computer and information sciences (MBA, MS); economics (MBA, MS); finance (MBA, MS); general and strategic management (MBA); healthcare management (MBA, MS), including healthcare financial management (MS), healthcare management (MBA); human resource administration (MBA, MS); international business (MS); international business administration (MBA); legal studies (MBA); management science/operations management (MBA, MS); marketing (MBA, MS); physical distribution (MBA); real estate and urban land studies (MBA, MS); risk management insurance (MBA, MS); statistics (MBA). *Accreditation:* ACEHSA (one or more programs are accredited). Evening/weekend programs available. *Faculty:* 72 full-time (13 women). *Students:* 1,016 (402 women); includes 223 minority (68 African Americans, 138 Asian Americans or Pacific Islanders, 14 Hispanic Americans, 3 Native Americans) 70 international. *Degree requirements:* For master's, foreign language and thesis not required. *Entrance requirements:* For master's, GMAT (average 540), TOEFL (minimum score of 575 required). Application fee: $40. *Unit head:* H. P. Sankappanavar, Graduate Adviser, 914-257-3535. *Application contact:* Linda Whelan, Director, 215-204-7678, Fax: 215-204-8300, E-mail: linda@astro.ocis.temple.edu.

Texas A&M University, College of Science, Department of Statistics, College Station, TX 77843. Offers MS, PhD. Part-time programs available. *Faculty:* 27 full-time (3 women). *Students:* 52 full-time (20 women), 10 part-time (4 women); includes 3 minority (1 African American, 1 Asian American or Pacific Islander, 1 Hispanic American), 40 international. Average age 30. 400 applicants, 13% accepted. In 1998, 9 master's, 9 doctorates awarded. Terminal master's awarded for partial completion of doctoral program. *Degree requirements:* For master's, computer language required, foreign language and thesis not required; for doctorate, dissertation required, foreign language not required. *Entrance requirements:* For master's and doctorate, GRE General Test, TOEFL. *Application deadline:* For fall admission, 3/1 (priority date); for spring admission, 8/1. Applications are processed on a rolling basis. Application fee: $50 ($75 for international students). *Financial aid:* In 1998–99, 40 students received aid, including 2 fellowships, 5 research assistantships, 33 teaching assistantships; career-related internships or fieldwork also available. Financial aid application deadline:3/1. *Faculty research:* Time series, chemometrics, biometrics, smoothing, linear moels. *Unit head:* Dr. James A. Calvin, Head, 409-845-3141, Fax: 409-845-3144. *Application contact:* P. Fred Dahm, Graduate Adviser, 800-826-8009, Fax: 409-845-3144, E-mail: fdahm@stat.tamu.edu.

Texas Tech University, Graduate School, College of Arts and Sciences, Department of Mathematics, Lubbock, TX 79409. Offers mathematics (MA, MS, PhD); statistics (MS). Part-time programs available. *Faculty:* 39 full-time (4 women), 1 part-time (0 women). *Students:* 67 full-time (24 women), 11 part-time (4 women); includes 6 minority (1 African American, 1 Asian American or Pacific Islander, 4 Hispanic Americans), 13 international. *Degree requirements:* For master's, thesis or alternative required, foreign language not required; for doctorate, dissertation required. *Entrance requirements:* For master's, GRE General Test (combined average 1194); for doctorate, GRE General Test. *Application deadline:* For fall admission, 4/15 (priority date); for spring admission, 11/1 (priority date). Applications are processed on a rolling basis. Application fee: $25 ($50 for international students). Electronic applications accepted. *Unit head:* Dr. Ron M. Anderson, Chairman, 806-742-2566, Fax: 806-742-1112.

Tulane University, Graduate School, Department of Mathematics, New Orleans, LA 70118-5669. Offers applied mathematics (MS); mathematics (MS, PhD); statistics (MS). *Students:* 24 full-time (6 women), 1 part-time; includes 2 minority (1 African American, 1 Asian American or Pacific Islander), 13 international. *Degree requirements:* For doctorate, dissertation required. *Entrance requirements:* For master's, GRE General Test (minimum combined score of 1000 required; average 1200), TOEFL (minimum score of 600 required), TSE (minimum score of 220 required), minimum B average in undergraduate course work; for doctorate, GRE General Test (minimum combined score of 1000 required; average 1200), TOEFL (minimum score of 600 required), TSE (minimum score of 220 required). *Application deadline:* For fall admission, 2/1. Application fee: $45. *Unit head:* Dr. Morris Kalka, Chairman, 504-865-5727.

Université de Montréal, Faculty of Graduate Studies, Faculty of Arts and Sciences, Department of Mathematics and Statistics, Montréal, PQ H3C 3J7, Canada. Offers mathematics (M Sc, PhD); statistics (M Sc, PhD). *Faculty:* 57 full-time (7 women). *Students:* 122 full-time (38 women), 2 part-time (1 woman). 38 applicants, 34% accepted. In 1998, 10 master's, 6 doctorates awarded. *Degree requirements:* For master's, thesis required; for doctorate, dissertation, general exam required. *Entrance requirements:* For master's and doctorate, proficiency in French. *Application deadline:* For fall admission, 2/1. Application fee: $30. *Financial aid:* Fellowships, research assistantships, teaching assistantships, monitorships available. Financial aid application deadline: 4/1. *Faculty research:* Pure and applied mathematics, actuarial mathematics. *Unit head:* Sabin Lessard, Chair, 514-343-6710. *Application contact:* Robert Cleroux, Graduate Chairman, 514-343-6987.

Université Laval, Faculty of Graduate Studies, Faculty of Sciences and Engineering, Department of Mathematics and Statistics, Program in Statistics, Sainte-Foy, PQ G1K 7P4, Canada. Offers M Sc. *Students:* 16 full-time (7 women), 1 part-time. 15 applicants, 60% accepted. In 1998, 3 degrees awarded. *Application deadline:* For fall admission, 3/1. Application fee: $30. *Unit head:* Charles Cassidy, Director, 418-656-2131 Ext. 2977, Fax: 418-656-2817, E-mail: charles.cassidy@mat.ulaval.ca.

The University of Akron, Graduate School, Buchtel College of Arts and Sciences, Department of Mathematics and Computer Science, Akron, OH 44325-0001. Offers applied mathematics (MS); computer science (MS); mathematics (MS); statistics (MS). Part-time and evening/weekend programs available. *Faculty:* 29 full-time, 7 part-time. *Students:* 41 full-time (18 women), 24 part-time (7 women); includes 5 minority (1 African American, 4 Asian Americans or Pacific Islanders), 29 international. *Degree requirements:* For master's, thesis optional, foreign language not required. *Entrance requirements:* For master's, minimum GPA of 2.75. *Application deadline:* For fall admission, 3/1. Applications are processed on a rolling basis. Application fee: $25 ($50 for international students). Tuition, state resident: part-time $189 per credit. Tuition, nonresident: part-time $353 per credit. Required fees: $7.3 per credit. *Unit head:* Dr. Phillip Schmidt, Chair, 330-972-7401, E-mail: pschmidt@uakron.edu.

The University of Akron, Graduate School, Buchtel College of Arts and Sciences, Department of Statistics, Akron, OH 44325-0001. Offers MS. Part-time and evening/weekend programs available. *Faculty:* 5 full-time, 2 part-time. *Students:* 9 full-time (6 women), 7 part-time (5 women), 3 international. Average age 32. In 1998, 3 degrees awarded. *Degree requirements:* For master's, thesis optional, foreign language not required. *Entrance requirements:* For master's, minimum GPA of 2.75. *Average time to degree:* Master's–2 years full-time, 4 years part-time. *Application deadline:* For fall admission, 3/1. Applications are processed on a rolling basis. Application fee: $25 ($50 for international students). Tuition, state resident: part-time $189 per credit. Tuition, nonresident: part-time $353 per credit. Required fees: $7.3 per credit. *Financial aid:* In 1998–99, 1 student received aid, including 1 teaching assistantship with full tuition reimbursement available Financial aid application deadline: 3/1. *Faculty research:* Experimental design, sampling biostatistics. *Unit head:* Dr. Chand Midha, Chair, 330-972-7128, E-mail: cmidha@uakron.edu.

The University of Alabama, Graduate School, The Manderson Graduate School of Business, Department of Management Science and Statistics, Program in Applied Statistics, Tuscaloosa, AL 35487. Offers MS, PhD. *Faculty:* 7 full-time (0 women). *Students:* 17 full-time (9 women), 2 part-time; includes 2 minority (1 African American, 1 Asian American or Pacific Islander), 6 international. 9 applicants, 67% accepted. In 1998, 5 master's awarded (80% found work related to degree, 20% continued full-time study); 3 doctorates awarded (67% entered university research/teaching, 33% found other work related to degree). Terminal master's awarded for

Statistics

The University of Alabama (continued)
partial completion of doctoral program. *Degree requirements:* For master's, thesis optional, foreign language not required; for doctorate, dissertation, comprehensive exam required, foreign language not required. *Entrance requirements:* For master's, GMAT or GRE, TOEFL (minimum score of 550 required); for doctorate, GMAT or GRE, TOEFL, undergraduate major in related field. *Average time to degree:* Master's–2 years full-time; doctorate–5 years full-time. *Application deadline:* For fall admission, 7/6. Applications are processed on a rolling basis. Application fee: $25. Electronic applications accepted. *Financial aid:* In 1998–99, 4 fellowships, 1 research assistantship, 9 teaching assistantships were awarded.; career-related internships or fieldwork also available. *Faculty research:* Regression anaylsis, statistical quality control, nonparametric statistics, statistical computing and graphics, data mining. *Unit head:* Brian Gray, Director, 205-348-8912, Fax: 205-348-0560, E-mail: bgray@cba.ua.edu.

University of Alberta, Faculty of Graduate Studies and Research, Department of Mathematical Sciences, Edmonton, AB T6G 2E1, Canada. Offers applied mathematics (M Sc, PhD); mathematical finance (M Sc); mathematical physics (M Sc, PhD); mathematics (M Sc, PhD); statistics (M Sc, PhD, Postgraduate Diploma). Part-time programs available. Terminal master's awarded for partial completion of doctoral program. *Degree requirements:* For master's, thesis required (for some programs), foreign language not required; for doctorate, dissertation required, foreign language not required. *Faculty research:* Classical and functional analysis, algebra, differential equations, geometry.

The University of Arizona, Graduate College, College of Science, Department of Statistics, Tucson, AZ 85721. Offers MS, PhD. Part-time programs available. *Faculty:* 7. *Students:* 1 full-time (0 women), 1 international. Average age 34. *Degree requirements:* For master's, thesis or alternative required, foreign language not required. *Entrance requirements:* For master's, GRE, TOEFL (minimum score of 550 required), minimum GPA of 3.0 in mathematics, 3 semesters of calculus, 6 upper-level units in mathematics; for doctorate, TOEFL (minimum score of 550 required). Application fee: $35. *Financial aid:* Fellowships, research assistantships, teaching assistantships, career-related internships or fieldwork, scholarships, and tuition waivers (partial) available. Financial aid application deadline: 7/1. *Faculty research:* Clinical trials, stochastic processes, extreme value theory, spatial time series, statistical consulting. *Unit head:* Dr. Yashaswini Mittal, Head, 520-621-6208. *Application contact:* Shari Rice, 520-621-6208, Fax: 520-621-1225.

University of Arkansas, Graduate School, J. William Fulbright College of Arts and Sciences, Department of Mathematical Sciences, Program in Statistics, Fayetteville, AR 72701-1201. Offers MS. *Students:* 12 full-time (8 women), 4 international. 14 applicants, 57% accepted. In 1998, 3 degrees awarded. *Degree requirements:* For master's, thesis required, foreign language not required. Application fee: $40 ($50 for international students). Tuition, state resident: full-time $3,186. Tuition, nonresident: full-time $7,560. Required fees: $378. *Financial aid:* Teaching assistantships, career-related internships or fieldwork and Federal Work-Study available. Aid available to part-time students. Financial aid application deadline: 4/1; financial aid applicants required to submit FAFSA. *Unit head:* Dr. Laurie Meaux, Chair of Studies, 501-575-3351, E-mail: gradmath@comp.uark.edu.

University of Arkansas at Little Rock, Graduate School, College of Sciences and Engineering Technology, Department of Mathematics and Statistics, Little Rock, AR 72204-1099. Offers applied mathematics (MS), including applied analysis, mathematical statistics. Part-time and evening/weekend programs available. *Degree requirements:* For master's, computer language, comprehensive exams required, foreign language and thesis not required. *Entrance requirements:* For master's, GRE General Test, GRE Subject Test, minimum GPA of 2.7, previous course work in advanced mathematics.

University of British Columbia, Faculty of Graduate Studies, Faculty of Science, Department of Statistics, Vancouver, BC V6T 1Z2, Canada. Offers M Sc, PhD. Part-time programs available. *Degree requirements:* For master's, thesis required, foreign language not required; for doctorate, dissertation, comprehensive exam required, foreign language not required. *Entrance requirements:* For master's and doctorate, TOEFL (minimum score of 550 required). *Faculty research:* Theoretical, applied, biostatistical, and computational statistics.

University of Calgary, Faculty of Graduate Studies, Faculty of Science, Department of Mathematics and Statistics, Calgary, AB T2N 1N4, Canada. Offers M Sc, PhD. *Faculty:* 33 full-time (2 women). *Students:* 28 full-time (8 women). Average age 30. 50 applicants, 26% accepted. In 1998, 9 master's, 2 doctorates awarded (100% entered university research/teaching). *Degree requirements:* For doctorate, dissertation, candidacy exam required, foreign language not required, foreign language not required. *Entrance requirements:* For master's, TOEFL (minimum score of 600 required), honours degree in related field; for doctorate, TOEFL (minimum score of 600 required), MA or M Sc. *Average time to degree:* Master's–2.6 years full-time, 4.1 years part-time; doctorate–4.9 years full-time. *Application deadline:* For fall admission, 2/1 (priority date). Applications are processed on a rolling basis. Application fee: $60. *Financial aid:* In 1998–99, 23 students received aid, including 10 research assistantships with partial tuition reimbursements available (averaging $3,920 per year); fellowships, teaching assistantships with partial tuition reimbursements available *Faculty research:* Combinatorics, applied mathematics, statistics, probability, analysis. Total annual research expenditures: $295,850. *Unit head:* E. G. Enns, Head, 403-220-6303, Fax: 403-282-5150, E-mail: enns@math.ucalgary.ca. *Application contact:* Joanne Mellard, Graduate Secretary, 403-220-6299, Fax: 403-282-5150, E-mail: gradapps@math.ucalgary.ca.

University of California, Berkeley, Graduate Division, College of Letters and Science, Department of Statistics, Berkeley, CA 94720-1500. Offers MA, PhD. *Students:* 49 full-time (20 women); includes 7 minority (5 Asian Americans or Pacific Islanders, 2 Hispanic Americans), 29 international. 106 applicants, 19% accepted. In 1998, 12 master's, 10 doctorates awarded. *Degree requirements:* For doctorate, dissertation, qualifying exam, written preliminary exam required. *Entrance requirements:* For master's and doctorate, GRE General Test, minimum GPA of 3.0. *Application deadline:* For fall admission, 12/31. Application fee: $40. *Financial aid:* Fellowships, research assistantships, teaching assistantships available. Financial aid application deadline:12/31. *Unit head:* Dr. David Aldous, Chair, 510-642-4272. *Application contact:* Sara Wong, Graduate Assistant for Admission, 510-642-5361, Fax: 510-642-7892, E-mail: sara@stat.berkeley.edu.

University of California, Davis, Graduate Studies, Program in Statistics, Davis, CA 95616. Offers MS, PhD. *Faculty:* 12 full-time (3 women). *Students:* 28 full-time (15 women); includes 9 minority (all Asian Americans or Pacific Islanders), 6 international. Average age 26. 48 applicants, 85% accepted. In 1998, 7 master's, 4 doctorates awarded. *Degree requirements:* For master's, thesis not required; for doctorate, dissertation required. *Entrance requirements:* For master's and doctorate, GRE General Test, TOEFL, minimum GPA of 3.0. Application fee: $40. Electronic applications accepted. *Financial aid:* In 1998–99, 9 fellowships with full and partial tuition reimbursements, 5 research assistantships with full and partial tuition reimbursements, 20 teaching assistantships with full and partial tuition reimbursements were awarded.; Federal Work-Study, grants, and institutionally-sponsored loans also available. Financial aid application deadline: 1/15; financial aid applicants required to submit FAFSA. *Faculty research:* Nonparametric analysis, time series analysis, biostatistics, curve estimation, reliability. *Unit head:* George Roussas, Associate Dean, 530-752-8142. *Application contact:* Wesley Johnson, 530-752-6493.

University of California, Riverside, Graduate Division, College of Natural and Agricultural Sciences, Department of Statistics, Riverside, CA 92521-0102. Offers applied statistics (PhD); statistics (MS). Part-time programs available. *Faculty:* 8 full-time (0 women). *Students:* 19 full-time (8 women), 1 part-time; includes 6 minority (1 African American, 3 Asian Americans or Pacific Islanders, 2 Hispanic Americans), 2 international. Average age 32. In 1998, 2 master's, 2 doctorates awarded. *Degree requirements:* For master's, computer language, comprehensive exams required, foreign language and thesis not required; for doctorate, computer language, dissertation, qualifying exams, 3 quarters of teaching experience required, foreign language not required. *Entrance requirements:* For master's and doctorate, GRE General Test (minimum combined score of 1100 required), TOEFL (minimum score of 550 required), minimum GPA of 3.2. *Average time to degree:* Master's–2.3 years full-time; doctorate–5 years full-time. *Application deadline:* For fall admission, 5/1; for winter admission, 9/1; for spring admission, 12/1. Applications are processed on a rolling basis. Application fee: $40. Electronic applications accepted. *Financial aid:* In 1998–99, 1 fellowship with full and partial tuition reimbursement, 1 research assistantship, 15 teaching assistantships with partial tuition reimbursements were awarded.; career-related internships or fieldwork, Federal Work-Study, institutionally-sponsored loans, and tuition waivers (full and partial) also available. Financial aid application deadline: 2/1; financial aid applicants required to submit FAFSA. *Faculty research:* Design and analysis of experiments, statistical modeling, stochastic models, paired comparisons, statistical design of experiments and linear models. *Unit head:* Robert J. Beaver, Chair, 909-787-3700, Fax: 909-787-3286, E-mail: beaver@ucrac1.ucr.edu. *Application contact:* Peggy Franklin, Graduate Secretary, 909-787-3774, Fax: 909-787-3286.

University of California, San Diego, Graduate Studies and Research, Department of Mathematics, La Jolla, CA 92093-5003. Offers applied mathematics (MA); mathematics (MA, PhD); statistics (MS). *Faculty:* 54. *Students:* 65 (16 women). *Degree requirements:* For master's, one foreign language required, thesis not required; for doctorate, dissertation required. *Entrance requirements:* For master's and doctorate, GRE General Test, GRE Subject Test. Application fee: $40. *Unit head:* Jeffrey Remmel, Chair, 619-534-2643, E-mail: jremmel@ucsd.edu. *Application contact:* Lois Stewart, Graduate Coordinator, 619-534-6887.

University of California, Santa Barbara, Graduate Division, College of Letters and Science, Division of Math, Life and Physical Science, Statistics and Applied Probability Program, Santa Barbara, CA 93106. Offers MA, PhD. *Faculty:* 7 full-time (1 woman). *Students:* 27 full-time (9 women); includes 2 minority (both Asian Americans or Pacific Islanders), 19 international. Average age 24. 63 applicants, 67% accepted. In 1998, 8 master's, 2 doctorates awarded (50% entered university research/teaching, 50% found other work related to degree). Terminal master's awarded for partial completion of doctoral program. *Degree requirements:* For master's, thesis or alternative required, foreign language not required; for doctorate, 2 foreign languages (computer language can substitute for one), dissertation required. *Entrance requirements:* For master's, GRE General Test (minimum combined score of 1200 required; average 1250), TOEFL (minimum score of 550 required); for doctorate, GRE General Test (minimum combined score of 1300 required; average 1350), TOEFL (minimum score of 550 required). *Average time to degree:* Master's–1.67 years full-time; doctorate–5 years full-time. *Application deadline:* For fall admission, 5/1; for spring admission, 2/1. Applications are processed on a rolling basis. Application fee: $40. Electronic applications accepted. *Financial aid:* In 1998–99, 4 fellowships, 20 teaching assistantships were awarded.; research assistantships, Federal Work-Study, institutionally-sponsored loans, and tuition waivers (partial) also available. Financial aid application deadline: 1/15; financial aid applicants required to submit FAFSA. *Faculty research:* Theoretical statistics, applied statistics, stochastic modelling, mathematical finance. *Unit head:* David Hinkley, Chairman, 805-893-8331. *Application contact:* Josianne Merminod, Graduate Program Assistant, Fax: 805-893-2334, E-mail: merminod@pstat.ucsb.edu.

University of Central Florida, College of Arts and Sciences, Program in Statistical Computing, Orlando, FL 32816. Offers MS. Part-time and evening/weekend programs available. *Faculty:* 10 full-time, 1 part-time. *Students:* 11 full-time (5 women), 3 part-time (1 woman); includes 4 minority (3 Asian Americans or Pacific Islanders, 1 Hispanic American), 3 international. Average age 29. 11 applicants, 45% accepted. In 1998, 4 degrees awarded. *Degree requirements:* For master's, computer language, comprehensive exam required, foreign language and thesis not required. *Entrance requirements:* For master's, GRE General Test (minimum combined score of 1000 required), TOEFL (minimum score of 500 required; 173 computer-based), minimum GPA of 3.0 in last 60 hours. *Application deadline:* For fall admission, 7/15; for spring admission, 12/15. Application fee: $20. Tuition, state resident: full-time $2,054; part-time $137 per credit. Tuition, nonresident: full-time $7,207; part-time $480 per credit. Required fees: $47 per term. *Financial aid:* In 1998–99, 14 students received aid, including 2 fellowships with partial tuition reimbursements available (averaging $2,500 per year), 2 research assistantships with partial tuition reimbursements available, teaching assistantships with partial tuition reimbursements available (averaging $4,382 per year); career-related internships or fieldwork, Federal Work-Study, institutionally-sponsored loans, tuition waivers (partial), and unspecified assistantships also available. Financial aid application deadline: 3/1; financial aid applicants required to submit FAFSA. *Faculty research:* Multivariate analysis, quality control, shrinkage estimation. *Unit head:* Dr. David Nickerson, Acting Chair, 407-823-5528, Fax: 407-823-5419. *Application contact:* Dr. James R. Schott, Graduate Coordinator, 407-823-2797, Fax: 407-823-5419, E-mail: schott@eola.cs.ucf.edu.

University of Central Oklahoma, Graduate College, College of Mathematics and Science, Department of Mathematics and Statistics, Edmond, OK 73034-5209. Offers applied mathematical sciences (MS), including computer science, mathematics, mathematics/computer science teaching, statistics. *Accreditation:* NCATE. Part-time programs available. *Faculty:* 11 full-time (3 women), 1 part-time (0 women). Average age 34. 17 applicants, 100% accepted. In 1998, 8 degrees awarded. *Degree requirements:* For master's, computer language, thesis required, foreign language not required. *Application deadline:* For fall admission, 8/23 (priority date). Applications are processed on a rolling basis. Application fee: $15. *Financial aid:* Federal Work-Study and unspecified assistantships available. Financial aid application deadline: 3/31; financial aid applicants required to submit FAFSA. *Faculty research:* Curvature, FAA, math education. *Unit head:* Dr. David Bridge, Chairperson, 405-974-5697. *Application contact:* Dr. James Yates, Adviser, 405-974-5386, Fax: 405-974-3824, E-mail: jyates@aix1.ucok.edu.

University of Chicago, Division of the Physical Sciences, Department of Statistics, Chicago, IL 60637-1513. Offers SM, PhD. Terminal master's awarded for partial completion of doctoral program. *Degree requirements:* For master's, thesis required; for doctorate, dissertation required, foreign language not required. *Entrance requirements:* For master's and doctorate, GRE General Test, GRE Subject Test, TOEFL.

University of Cincinnati, Division of Research and Advanced Studies, McMicken College of Arts and Sciences, Department of Mathematics, Cincinnati, OH 45221-0091. Offers applied mathematics (MS, PhD); mathematics education (MAT); pure mathematics (MS, PhD); statistics (MS, PhD). *Accreditation:* NCATE (one or more programs are accredited). *Faculty:* 38 full-time. *Students:* 69 full-time (41 women), 14 part-time (7 women); includes 6 minority (all Asian Americans or Pacific Islanders), 56 international. *Degree requirements:* For master's, thesis optional, foreign language not required; for doctorate, dissertation, final written exam required. *Entrance requirements:* For master's, TOEFL (minimum score of 520 required). *Application deadline:* For fall admission, 2/1. Application fee: $30. *Unit head:* James Osterburg, Head, 513-556-4054, Fax: 513-556-3417, E-mail: james.osterburg@uc.edu. *Application contact:* Diego Murio, Graduate Program Director, 513-556-4088, Fax: 513-556-3417, E-mail: diego.murio@uc.edu.

University of Connecticut, Graduate School, College of Liberal Arts and Sciences, Field of Statistics, Storrs, CT 06269. Offers MS, PhD. Terminal master's awarded for partial completion of doctoral program. *Degree requirements:* For doctorate, dissertation required, foreign language not required, foreign language not required. *Entrance requirements:* For master's and doctorate, GRE General Test, TOEFL.

University of Florida, Graduate School, College of Liberal Arts and Sciences, Department of Statistics, Gainesville, FL 32611. Offers M Stat, MSTA, PhD. *Faculty:* 33. *Students:* 42 full-time (13 women), 4 part-time (3 women), 21 international. 83 applicants, 72% accepted. In 1998, 5 master's, 4 doctorates awarded. *Degree requirements:* For master's, variable foreign language requirement, computer language, thesis or alternative, comprehensive exam, final oral exam required; for doctorate, variable foreign language requirement, computer language, dissertation required. *Entrance requirements:* For master's and doctorate, GRE General Test (minimum score of 360 on verbal section required), TOEFL (minimum score of 550 required), minimum GPA of 3.0. *Application deadline:* For fall admission, 6/1 (priority date). Applications are processed on a rolling basis. Application fee: $20. Electronic applications accepted. *Financial aid:* In 1998–99, 40 students received aid, including 1 fellowship, 24 research assistantships, 13 teaching assistantships; unspecified assistantships also available. Financial aid application deadline: 2/1. *Faculty research:* Categorical data, time series, Bayesian analysis, nonparametrics, sampling. *Unit head:* Dr. Ronald Randles, Chair, 352-392-1941 Ext. 213, Fax: 352-392-5175, E-mail: rrandles@stat.ufl.edu. *Application contact:* Dr. James Booth, Graduate Coordinator, 352-392-1941, Fax: 352-392-5175, E-mail: jbooth@stat.ufl.edu.

University of Georgia, Graduate School, College of Arts and Sciences, Department of Statistics, Athens, GA 30602. Offers applied mathematical science (MAMS); statistics (MS, PhD). *Faculty:* 19 full-time (5 women). *Students:* 35 full-time, 3 part-time; includes 3 minority (1 African American, 1 Asian American or Pacific Islander, 1 Native American), 21 international. 47 applicants, 47% accepted. In 1998, 13 master's, 4 doctorates awarded. *Degree requirements:* For master's, thesis (for some programs), technical report (MAMS) required, foreign language not required; for doctorate, one foreign language (computer language can substitute), dissertation required. *Entrance requirements:* For master's and doctorate, GRE General Test. *Application deadline:* For fall admission, 7/1 (priority date); for spring admission, 11/15. Application fee: $30. Electronic applications accepted. *Financial aid:* Fellowships, research assistantships, teaching assistantships, unspecified assistantships available. *Unit head:* Dr. Jaxk H. Reeves, Graduate Coordinator, 706-542-5232, Fax: 706-542-3391, E-mail: jaxk@stat.uga.edu.

See in-depth description on page 763.

University of Guelph, Faculty of Graduate Studies, College of Physical and Engineering Science, Department of Mathematics and Statistics, Guelph, ON N1G 2W1, Canada. Offers applied mathematics (PhD); applied statistics (PhD); mathematics and statistics (M Sc). Part-time programs available. *Faculty:* 23 full-time (2 women), 3 part-time (1 woman). *Students:* 36 full-time (9 women), 1 part-time, 7 international. 30 applicants, 33% accepted. In 1998, 7 master's, 3 doctorates awarded (100% found work related to degree). *Degree requirements:* For master's, thesis required (for some programs), foreign language not required; for doctorate, dissertation required, foreign language not required. *Entrance requirements:* For master's, minimum B- average during previous 2 years; for doctorate, minimum B average. *Average time to degree:* Master's–2 years full-time; doctorate–4 years full-time. Application fee: $60. *Expenses:* Tuition and fees charges are reported in Canadian dollars. Tuition, area resident: Full-time $4,725 Canadian dollars; part-time $1,055 Canadian dollars per term. International tuition: $6,999 Canadian dollars full-time. Required fees: $295 Canadian dollars per term. *Financial aid:* In 1998–99, 16 research assistantships, teaching assistantships (averaging $9,500 per year) were awarded.; fellowships, scholarships also available. Financial aid applicants required to submit CSS PROFILE. *Faculty research:* Dynamical systems, mathematical biology, numerical analysis, linear and nonlinear models, reliability and bioassay. Total annual research expenditures:$447,260. *Unit head:* Dr. J. Mokanski, Chair, 519-824-4120 Ext. 6556, Fax: 519-837-0221, E-mail: chair@msnet.mathstat.uoguelph.ca. *Application contact:* Susan McCormick, Graduate Administrative Assistant, 519-824-4120 Ext. 6553, Fax: 519-837-0221, E-mail: smccormi@msnet.mathstat.uoguelph.ca.

University of Houston, College of Business Administration, Program in Statistics and Operations Research, Houston, TX 77004. Offers MBA, PhD. Part-time and evening/weekend programs available. *Faculty:* 6 full-time (0 women), 1 part-time (0 women). In 1998, 1 degree awarded. *Degree requirements:* For master's, computer language required, foreign language and thesis not required; for doctorate, computer language, dissertation, comprehensive exam required, foreign language not required. *Entrance requirements:* For master's, GMAT (average 590), TOEFL (minimum score of 620 required); for doctorate, GMAT or GRE. *Average time to degree:* Master's–2 years full-time, 3.5 years part-time; doctorate–4.5 years full-time. *Application deadline:* For fall admission, 5/1; for spring admission, 10/1. Applications are processed on a rolling basis. Application fee: $50 ($125 for international students). *Financial aid:* Research assistantships, teaching assistantships, career-related internships or fieldwork and Federal Work-Study available. Aid available to part-time students. Financial aid application deadline: 3/1; financial aid applicants required to submit FAFSA. *Unit head:* Dr. Dennis Adams, Chair, 713-743-4747. *Application contact:* 713-743-4900, Fax: 713-743-4942, E-mail: oss@cba.uh.edu.

University of Houston–Clear Lake, School of Natural and Applied Sciences, Program in Statistics, Houston, TX 77058-1098. Offers MS. *Faculty:* 3 full-time (0 women), 2 part-time (0 women). *Students:* 2 full-time (1 woman), 12 part-time (3 women); includes 2 minority (1 Asian American or Pacific Islander, 1 Hispanic American), 3 international. *Degree requirements:* Foreign language not required. *Entrance requirements:* For master's, GRE General Test. *Application deadline:* Applications are processed on a rolling basis. Application fee: $30 ($70 for international students). *Financial aid:* Research assistantships, teaching assistantships available. Financial aid application deadline: 5/1. *Unit head:* Dr. Raj Chhikara, Chair, 281-283-3850, Fax: 281-283-3707. *Application contact:* Dr. Robert Ferebee, Associate Dean, 281-283-3700, Fax: 281-283-3707, E-mail: ferebee@uhcl4.cl.uh.edu.

University of Idaho, College of Graduate Studies, College of Letters and Science, Department of Mathematics and Statistics, Program in Statistics, Moscow, ID 83844-4140. Offers MS. *Faculty:* 5 full-time (0 women), 1 (woman) part-time. *Students:* 3 full-time (2 women), 2 part-time, 1 international. In 1998, 4 degrees awarded. *Degree requirements:* For master's, foreign language and thesis not required. *Entrance requirements:* For master's, minimum GPA of 2.8. *Application deadline:* For fall admission, 8/1; for spring admission, 12/15. Application fee: $35 ($45 for international students). *Financial aid:* In 1998–99, 5 teaching assistantships (averaging $8,558 per year) were awarded. Financial aid application deadline: 2/15. *Unit head:* Dr. Al R. Manson, Chair, 208-885-2929.

University of Illinois at Chicago, Graduate College, College of Liberal Arts and Sciences, Department of Mathematics, Statistics, and Computer Science, Chicago, IL 60607-7128. Offers applied mathematics (MS, DA, PhD); computer science (MS, DA, PhD); probability and statistics (MS, DA, PhD); pure mathematics (MS, DA, PhD); teaching of mathematics (MST). *Faculty:* 69 full-time (4 women). *Students:* 119 full-time (47 women), 30 part-time (12 women). *Degree requirements:* For master's, comprehensive exam required, foreign language and thesis not required; for doctorate, one foreign language, dissertation required. *Entrance requirements:* For master's and doctorate, GRE General Test, TOEFL (minimum score of 550 required), minimum GPA of 3.75 on a 5.0 scale. *Application deadline:* For fall admission, 7/3; for spring admission, 11/8. Application fee: $40 ($50 for international students). *Unit head:* Henri Gillet, Head, 312-996-3044. *Application contact:* David Marker, Director of Graduate Studies, 312-996-3041.

See in-depth description on page 769.

University of Illinois at Urbana–Champaign, Graduate College, College of Liberal Arts and Sciences, Department of Statistics, Urbana, IL 61801. Offers MS, PhD. *Faculty:* 9 full-time (0 women), 1 part-time (0 women). *Students:* 19 full-time (13 women), 8 international. 93 applicants, 5% accepted. In 1998, 8 master's, 5 doctorates awarded. Terminal master's awarded for partial completion of doctoral program. *Degree requirements:* For master's, foreign language and thesis not required; for doctorate, dissertation required, foreign language not required. *Entrance requirements:* For master's, TOEFL. *Application deadline:* Applications are processed on a rolling basis. Application fee: $40 ($50 for international students). Tuition, state resident: full-time $4,040. Tuition, nonresident: full-time $11,192. Full-time tuition and fees vary according to program. *Financial aid:* Fellowships, research assistantships, teaching assistantships, tuition waivers (full) available. Financial aid application deadline: 2/15. *Faculty research:* Statistical decision theory, sequential analysis, computer-aided stochastic modeling. *Unit head:* Adam Martinsek, Chair, 217-333-2167. *Application contact:* Ditlev Monrad, Director of Graduate Studies, 217-333-6408, Fax: 217-244-7190, E-mail: monrad@stat.uiuc.edu.

The University of Iowa, Graduate College, College of Liberal Arts, Department of Statistics, Iowa City, IA 52242-1316. Offers MS, PhD. *Faculty:* 16 full-time, 5 part-time. *Students:* 37 full-time (11 women), 20 part-time (6 women); includes 2 minority (both Asian Americans or Pacific Islanders), 35 international. 107 applicants, 77% accepted. In 1998, 24 master's, 3 doctorates awarded. *Degree requirements:* For master's, thesis optional; for doctorate, dissertation, comprehensive exam required. *Entrance requirements:* For master's and doctorate, GRE General Test. *Application deadline:* Applications are processed on a rolling basis. Application fee: $30 ($50 for international students). *Financial aid:* In 1998–99, 1 fellowship, 12 research assistantships, 35 teaching assistantships were awarded. Financial aid applicants required to submit FAFSA. *Unit head:* James D. Broffitt, Chair, 319-335-0712, Fax: 319-335-3017.

University of Kansas, Graduate School, College of Liberal Arts and Sciences, Department of Mathematics, Program in Applied Mathematics and Statistics, Lawrence, KS 66045. Offers MA, PhD. *Degree requirements:* For master's, thesis or alternative required, foreign language not required; for doctorate, dissertation required. *Entrance requirements:* For master's and doctorate, TOEFL (minimum score of 570 required). Application fee: $25. *Financial aid:* Fellowships, research assistantships, teaching assistantships, institutionally-sponsored loans available. Aid available to part-time students. Financial aid application deadline: 2/1. *Application contact:* Daniel Katz, Graduate Director, 785-864-4324.

University of Kentucky, Graduate School, Graduate School Programs from the College of Arts and Sciences, Program in Statistics, Lexington, KY 40506-0032. Offers MS, PhD. *Degree requirements:* For master's, comprehensive exam required, thesis optional, foreign language not required; for doctorate, dissertation, comprehensive exam required, foreign language not required. *Entrance requirements:* For master's, GRE General Test, minimum undergraduate GPA of 2.5; for doctorate, GRE General Test, minimum graduate GPA of 3.0. *Faculty research:* Computer intensive statistical inference, biostatistics, mathematical and applied statistics, applied probability.

University of Manitoba, Faculty of Graduate Studies, Faculty of Science, Department of Statistics, Winnipeg, MB R3T 2N2, Canada. Offers M Sc, PhD. *Degree requirements:* For master's, thesis or alternative required, foreign language not required; for doctorate, dissertation required. *Unit head:* L. K. Chan, Head.

University of Maryland, Baltimore County, Graduate School, Department of Mathematics and Statistics, Program in Statistics, Baltimore, MD 21250-5398. Offers MS, PhD. *Students:* 15 full-time (4 women), 6 part-time (2 women); includes 2 minority (both Asian Americans or Pacific Islanders), 10 international. 30 applicants, 47% accepted. In 1998, 5 master's, 3 doctorates awarded. *Degree requirements:* For master's, foreign language and thesis not required; for doctorate, dissertation required, foreign language not required. *Entrance requirements:* For master's and doctorate, GRE General Test, GRE Subject Test, TOEFL, minimum GPA of 3.0. *Application deadline:* For fall admission, 2/15. Applications are processed on a rolling basis. Application fee: $45. *Financial aid:* Fellowships, research assistantships, teaching assistantships available. *Unit head:* Trudy Lindsey, Director, Graduate Admission and Records, 301-405-4198, Fax: 301-314-9305, E-mail: grschool@deans.umd.edu. *Application contact:* Dr. Nagaraj Neerchal, Director of Graduate Programs, 410-455-2437.

University of Maryland, College Park, Graduate School, College of Computer, Mathematical and Physical Sciences, Department of Mathematics, Program in Mathematical Statistics, College Park, MD 20742-5045. Offers MA, PhD. *Students:* 10 full-time (3 women), 12 part-time (6 women); includes 2 minority (1 Asian American or Pacific Islander, 1 Hispanic American), 12 international. 31 applicants, 35% accepted. In 1998, 5 master's, 4 doctorates awarded. *Degree requirements:* For master's, thesis or comprehensive exams required, thesis optional, foreign language not required; for doctorate, dissertation, written and oral exams required. *Entrance requirements:* For master's, minimum GPA of 3.0. *Application deadline:* Applications are processed on a rolling basis. Application fee: $50 ($70 for international students). Tuition, state resident: part-time $272 per credit hour. Tuition, nonresident: part-time $475 per credit hour. Required fees: $632; $379 per year. *Financial aid:* Fellowships, research assistantships, teaching assistantships available. Financial aid applicants required to submit FAFSA. *Faculty research:* Statistics and probability, stochastic processes. *Unit head:* Dr. Paul J. Smith, Director, 301-405-5061. *Application contact:* Trudy Lindsey, Director, Graduate Admission and Records, 301-405-4198, Fax: 301-314-9305, E-mail: grschool@deans.umd.edu.

University of Massachusetts Amherst, Graduate School, College of Natural Sciences and Mathematics, Department of Mathematics and Statistics, Program in Mathematics and Statistics, Amherst, MA 01003. Offers MS, PhD. *Students:* 33 full-time (14 women), 21 part-time (9 women); includes 6 minority (1 African American, 2 Asian Americans or Pacific Islanders, 2 Hispanic Americans, 1 Native American), 23 international. Average age 27. 84 applicants, 44% accepted. In 1998, 12 master's, 8 doctorates awarded. *Degree requirements:* For master's, foreign language and thesis not required; for doctorate, 2 foreign languages, dissertation required. *Application deadline:* For fall admission, 2/1 (priority date); for spring admission, 10/1. Applications are processed on a rolling basis. Application fee: $40. Tuition, state resident: full-time $2,640; part-time $165 per credit. Tuition, nonresident: full-time $9,756; part-time $407 per credit. Required fees: $1,221 per term. One-time fee: $110. Full-time tuition and fees vary according to course load, campus/location and reciprocity agreements. *Financial aid:* Fellowships with full tuition reimbursements, research assistantships with full tuition reimbursements, teaching assistantships with full tuition reimbursements, career-related internships or fieldwork, Federal Work-Study, grants, scholarships, traineeships, and unspecified assistantships available. Aid available to part-time students. Financial aid application deadline: 2/1. *Unit head:* Dr. James Humphreys, Director, 413-545-2282, Fax: 413-545-1801, E-mail: jeh@math.umass.edu.

The University of Memphis, Graduate School, College of Arts and Sciences, Department of Mathematical Sciences, Memphis, TN 38152. Offers applied mathematics (MS); applied statistics (PhD); computer science (PhD); computer sciences (MS); mathematics (MS, PhD); statistics (MS, PhD). *Faculty:* 35 full-time (3 women), 2 part-time (1 woman). *Students:* 73 full-time (23 women), 37 part-time (9 women); includes 10 minority (5 African Americans, 5 Asian Americans or Pacific Islanders), 77 international. Terminal master's awarded for partial completion of doctoral program. *Degree requirements:* For master's, comprehensive exams required, thesis not required; for doctorate, dissertation, oral exams required. *Entrance requirements:* For master's, GRE General Test, MAT, TOEFL (minimum score of 550 required), minimum GPA of 2.5; for doctorate, GRE General Test, TOEFL (minimum score of 550 required). *Application deadline:* For fall admission, 8/1; for spring admission, 12/1. Applications are processed on a rolling basis. Application fee: $25 ($50 for international students). Tuition, state resident: full-time $3,410; part-time $178 per credit hour. Tuition, nonresident: full-time $8,670; part-time $408 per credit hour. Tuition and fees vary according to program. *Unit head:* Dr. Jerome A. Goldstein, Chairman, 901-678-2482, Fax: 901-678-2480, E-mail: goldstej@msci.memphis.edu. *Application contact:* Dr. Fernanda M. Botelho, Coordinator of Graduate Studies, 901-678-2482, Fax: 901-678-2480, E-mail: lisa@msci.memphis.edu.

University of Michigan, Horace H. Rackham School of Graduate Studies, College of Literature, Science, and the Arts, Department of Statistics, Ann Arbor, MI 48109. Offers applied statistics (AM); statistics (AM, PhD). *Faculty:* 12 full-time (2 women). *Students:* 68 full-time (25 women); includes 4 minority (1 African American, 2 Asian Americans or Pacific Islanders, 1 Hispanic American), 47 international. Average age 28. 111 applicants, 63% accepted. In 1998, 16 master's awarded (19% entered university research/teaching, 50% found other work related to degree, 31% continued full-time study); 3 doctorates awarded (67% entered university research/teaching, 33% found other work related to degree). Terminal master's awarded for partial completion of doctoral program. *Degree requirements:* For master's, foreign language and thesis not required; for doctorate, one foreign language (computer language can substitute), dissertation, oral defense of dissertation, preliminary exam required. *Entrance requirements:* For master's and doctorate, GRE General Test, GRE Subject Test (mathematics), TOEFL (minimum score of 560 required). *Average time to degree:* Master's–2 years full-time, 4.5 years part-time; doctorate–4.5 years full-time, 7 years part-time. *Application deadline:* For fall admission, 2/15 (priority date). Applications are processed on a rolling basis. Application fee:

Statistics

University of Michigan (continued)
$55. Electronic applications accepted. *Financial aid:* In 1998–99, 45 students received aid, including 4 fellowships with partial tuition reimbursements available, 6 research assistantships with partial tuition reimbursements available, 34 teaching assistantships with full tuition reimbursements available (averaging $11,330 per year); career-related internships or fieldwork, Federal Work-Study, institutionally-sponsored loans, and scholarships also available. Aid available to part-time students. *Faculty research:* Sequential analysis, Bayesian statistics, multivariate analysis. *Unit head:* Vijayan Nair, Chair, 734-763-3519, Fax: 734-763-4676, E-mail: vnn@umich.edu. *Application contact:* Julian Faraway, Graduate Chairman, 734-763-5238, Fax: 734-763-4676, E-mail: stat-admission@umich.edu.

University of Minnesota, Twin Cities Campus, Graduate School, College of Liberal Arts, School of Statistics, Minneapolis, MN 55455-0213. Offers MS, PhD. Part-time programs available. *Faculty:* 17 full-time (2 women), 3 part-time (0 women). *Students:* 48 full-time (17 women), 2 part-time; includes 4 minority (2 African Americans, 2 Asian Americans or Pacific Islanders), 30 international. Average age 24. 78 applicants, 69% accepted. In 1998, 9 master's awarded (44% found work related to degree, 56% continued full-time study); 7 doctorates awarded (86% entered university research/teaching, 14% found other work related to degree). Terminal master's awarded for partial completion of doctoral program. *Degree requirements:* For master's, foreign language and thesis not required; for doctorate, dissertation required, foreign language not required. *Entrance requirements:* For master's and doctorate, GRE General Test (average 750 quantitative), TOEFL (minimum score of 550 required). *Average time to degree:* Master's–2 years full-time; doctorate–6 years full-time. *Application deadline:* For fall admission, 6/15; for spring admission, 10/15. Application fee: $50 ($55 for international students). Electronic applications accepted. *Financial aid:* In 1998–99, 44 students received aid, including 4 fellowships with tuition reimbursements available, 10 research assistantships with tuition reimbursements available, 25 teaching assistantships with tuition reimbursements available; grants and tuition waivers (full and partial) also available. Financial aid application deadline: 2/7. *Faculty research:* Data analysis, statistical computing, experimental design, probability theory, Bayesian inference, multivariate analysis. Total annual research expenditures: $290,399. *Unit head:* Seymour Geisser, Director, 612-625-8046, Fax: 612-624-8868, E-mail: geisser@stat.umn.edu. *Application contact:* Mary Hildre, Principal Secretary, 612-625-7300, Fax: 612-624-8868, E-mail: mary@stat.umn.edu.

University of Missouri–Columbia, Graduate School, College of Arts and Sciences, Department of Statistics, Columbia, MO 65211. Offers MA, PhD. *Faculty:* 12 full-time (0 women). *Students:* 18 full-time (11 women), 8 part-time (2 women); includes 2 minority (1 African American, 1 Asian American or Pacific Islander), 14 international. 9 applicants, 67% accepted. In 1998, 3 master's, 6 doctorates awarded. *Degree requirements:* For master's, thesis not required; for doctorate, dissertation required. *Entrance requirements:* For master's and doctorate, GRE General Test, minimum GPA of 3.0. *Application deadline:* For fall admission, 2/15 (priority date). Applications are processed on a rolling basis. Application fee: $30 ($50 for international students). *Financial aid:* Research assistantships, teaching assistantships, institutionally-sponsored loans and tuition waivers (full and partial) available. *Unit head:* Dr. Joe Cavanaugh, Director of Graduate Studies, 573-882-4491.

University of Missouri–Kansas City, College of Arts and Sciences, Department of Mathematics and Statistics, Kansas City, MO 64110-2499. Offers MA, MS, PhD. PhD offered through the School of Graduate Studies. Part-time programs available. *Faculty:* 10 full-time (1 woman). *Students:* 1 full-time (0 women), 13 part-time (5 women); includes 1 minority (Hispanic American), 1 international. Average age 33. In 1998, 1 master's awarded. Terminal master's awarded for partial completion of doctoral program. *Degree requirements:* For master's, written exam required, foreign language and thesis not required; for doctorate, 2 foreign languages, dissertation, oral and written exams required. *Entrance requirements:* For master's, bachelor's degree in mathematics, minimum GPA of 3.0; for doctorate, GMAT or GRE General Test (minimum combined score of 1500 on three sections required). *Average time to degree:* Master's–2.5 years full-time. *Application deadline:* For fall admission, 5/1 (priority date). Application fee: $25. *Financial aid:* In 1998–99, 6 students received aid, including 6 teaching assistantships; Federal Work-Study, institutionally-sponsored loans, and tuition waivers (full and partial) also available. Aid available to part-time students. Financial aid application deadline: 4/1. *Faculty research:* Classical real variables, matrix theory, ring theory, linear numerical analysis, point set topology. *Unit head:* Dr. Bruce Wenner, Chairperson, 816-235-2853.

The University of Montana–Missoula, Graduate School, College of Arts and Sciences, Department of Mathematical Sciences, Missoula, MT 59812-0002. Offers algebra (MA, PhD); analysis (MA, PhD); applied mathematics (MA, PhD); mathematics (MAT); mathematics education (PhD); operations research (MA, PhD); statistics (MA, PhD). Part-time programs available. *Faculty:* 20 full-time (3 women). *Students:* 25 full-time (11 women), 2 part-time (1 woman); includes 6 minority (5 Asian Americans or Pacific Islanders, 1 Native American) Terminal master's awarded for partial completion of doctoral program. *Degree requirements:* For master's, foreign language and thesis not required; for doctorate, dissertation required. *Entrance requirements:* For master's and doctorate, GRE General Test. *Application deadline:* For fall admission, 3/1 (priority date). Application fee: $45. *Unit head:* Dr. Gloria Hewitt, Chair, 406-243-5311.

University of Nebraska–Lincoln, Graduate College, College of Arts and Sciences, Department of Mathematics and Statistics, Lincoln, NE 68588. Offers M Sc T, MA, MAT, MS, PhD. *Faculty:* 26 full-time (2 women), 3 part-time (0 women). *Students:* 50 full-time (26 women), 4 part-time (1 woman), 14 international. Average age 31. 51 applicants, 43% accepted. In 1998, 8 master's, 4 doctorates awarded. *Degree requirements:* For master's, thesis optional, foreign language not required; for doctorate, dissertation, comprehensive exams required. *Entrance requirements:* For master's and doctorate, GRE General Test, TOEFL (minimum score of 575 required). *Average time to degree:* Doctorate–3.5 years full-time. *Application deadline:* For fall admission, 3/15 (priority date). Applications are processed on a rolling basis. Application fee: $35. Electronic applications accepted. *Financial aid:* In 1998–99, 53 teaching assistantships were awarded.; fellowships, research assistantships, Federal Work-Study also available. Aid available to part-time students. Financial aid application deadline: 2/15. *Faculty research:* Algebra, analysis, combinatorics, differential equations, applied mathematics. *Unit head:* Dr. Jim Lewis, Chair, 402-472-3731, Fax: 402-472-8466.

See in-depth description on page 775.

University of Nevada, Las Vegas, Graduate College, College of Science, Department of Mathematical Sciences, Las Vegas, NV 89154-9900. Offers applied mathematics (MS); mathematics (MS); pure mathematics (MS); statistics (MS). Part-time programs available. *Faculty:* 27 full-time (4 women). *Students:* 12 full-time (3 women), 5 part-time (1 woman); includes 1 minority (Asian American or Pacific Islander), 2 international. *Degree requirements:* For master's, oral exam required, thesis optional, foreign language not required. *Entrance requirements:* For master's, minimum GPA of 3.0 during previous 2 years, 2.75 overall. *Application deadline:* For fall admission, 6/15 (priority date); for spring admission, 11/15. Applications are processed on a rolling basis. Application fee: $40 ($95 for international students). *Unit head:* Dr. Rohan Dalpadatu, Chair, 702-895-3567. *Application contact:* Graduate College Admissions Evaluator, 702-895-3320.

University of Nevada, Reno, Graduate School, M. C. Fleischmann College of Agriculture, Department of Applied Economics and Statistics, Reno, NV 89557. Offers resource and applied economics (MS). *Degree requirements:* For master's, thesis optional, foreign language not required. *Entrance requirements:* For master's, GRE, TOEFL (minimum score of 500 required), minimum GPA of 2.75.

University of New Brunswick, School of Graduate Studies, Faculty of Science, Department of Mathematics and Statistics, Fredericton, NB E3B 5A3, Canada. Offers M Sc, PhD. Part-time programs available. *Degree requirements:* For master's, thesis or alternative required; for doctorate, dissertation required. *Entrance requirements:* For master's and doctorate, TOEFL, TWE, minimum GPA of 3.0.

University of New Mexico, Graduate School, College of Arts and Sciences, Department of Mathematics and Statistics, Albuquerque, NM 87131-2039. Offers mathematics (MS, PhD); statistics (MS, PhD). Part-time programs available. *Faculty:* 39 full-time (8 women), 22 part-time (3 women). *Students:* 51 full-time (16 women), 20 part-time (10 women); includes 11 minority (1 African American, 5 Asian Americans or Pacific Islanders, 4 Hispanic Americans, 1 Native American), 15 international. Average age 34. 25 applicants, 80% accepted. In 1998, 6 master's, 7 doctorates awarded. Terminal master's awarded for partial completion of doctoral program. *Degree requirements:* For master's, computer language required, thesis optional, foreign language not required; for doctorate, one foreign language, computer language, dissertation required. *Entrance requirements:* For master's and doctorate, GRE General Test, minimum GPA of 3.0. Application fee: $25. *Financial aid:* In 1998–99, 3 fellowships (averaging $3,122 per year), 9 research assistantships with tuition reimbursements (averaging $4,093 per year), 40 teaching assistantships with tuition reimbursements (averaging $10,526 per year) were awarded.; career-related internships or fieldwork, Federal Work-Study, institutionally-sponsored loans, and tuition waivers (full and partial) also available. Financial aid application deadline: 11/1. *Faculty research:* Pure and applied mathematics, applied statistics, numerical analysis, biostatistics, differential geometry, fluid dynamics, nonparametric curve estimation. Total annual research expenditures: $290,000. *Unit head:* Dr. Ronald M. Schrader, Chair, 505-277-4613, Fax: 505-277-5505, E-mail: schrader@math.unm.edu.

The University of North Carolina at Chapel Hill, Graduate School, College of Arts and Sciences, Department of Statistics, Chapel Hill, NC 27599. Offers MS, PhD. *Faculty:* 13 full-time (1 woman). *Students:* 21 full-time (8 women), 8 part-time; includes 3 minority (2 Asian Americans or Pacific Islanders, 1 Hispanic American), 14 international. 48 applicants, 23% accepted. In 1998, 1 master's, 5 doctorates awarded. *Degree requirements:* For master's, comprehensive exam, essay, or thesis required; for doctorate, dissertation, comprehensive exam required, foreign language not required. *Entrance requirements:* For master's, GRE General Test (minimum combined score of 1000 required), GRE Subject Test, TOEFL, minimum GPA of 3.0; for doctorate, GRE General Test (minimum combined score of 1000 required), GRE Subject Test, minimum GPA of 3.0. *Application deadline:* For fall admission, 1/1 (priority date). Applications are processed on a rolling basis. Application fee: $55. *Financial aid:* In 1998–99, 2 fellowships, 14 teaching assistantships were awarded.; research assistantships Financial aid application deadline: 3/1. *Unit head:* Prof. Douglas G. Kelly, Chairman, 919-962-9609, Fax: 919-962-1279, E-mail: kelly@stat.unc.edu. *Application contact:* Prof. Chuanshu Ji, Director of Admissions, 919-962-3917, Fax: 919-962-1279, E-mail: cji@stat.unc.edu.

University of North Carolina at Charlotte, Graduate School, College of Arts and Sciences, Department of Mathematics, Charlotte, NC 28223-0001. Offers applied mathematics (MS, PhD); applied statistics (MS); mathematics (MA); mathematics education (MA). *Accreditation:* NCATE (one or more programs are accredited). Part-time and evening/weekend programs available. *Faculty:* 43 full-time (6 women). *Students:* 22 full-time (8 women), 24 part-time (14 women); includes 6 minority (2 African Americans, 4 Asian Americans or Pacific Islanders), 16 international. *Degree requirements:* For master's, thesis or written comprehensive exam required; for doctorate, dissertation required. *Entrance requirements:* For master's, GRE General Test or MAT, minimum GPA of 3.0 in undergraduate major, 2.75 overall. *Application deadline:* For fall admission, 7/15; for spring admission, 11/15. Applications are processed on a rolling basis. Application fee: $35. Electronic applications accepted. *Unit head:* Dr. Ram C. Tiwari, Chair, 704-547-4551, Fax: 704-547-6415, E-mail: rtiwari@email.uncc.edu. *Application contact:* Kathy Barringer, Assistant Director of Graduate Admissions, 704-547-3366, Fax: 704-547-3279, E-mail: gradadm@email.uncc.edu.

See in-depth description on page 779.

University of North Florida, College of Arts and Sciences, Department of Mathematics and Statistics, Jacksonville, FL 32224-2645. Offers computer science (MS); mathematical sciences (MS); statistics (MS). Part-time and evening/weekend programs available. *Faculty:* 17 full-time (4 women). *Students:* 7 full-time (3 women), 11 part-time (6 women); includes 2 minority (1 African American, 1 Hispanic American), 3 international. Average age 29. 9 applicants, 100% accepted. In 1998, 2 degrees awarded. *Degree requirements:* For master's, comprehensive exam required, thesis optional, foreign language not required. *Entrance requirements:* For master's, GRE Subject Test, TOEFL (minimum score of 500 required), GRe General Test (minimum combined score of 1000 required) or minimum GPA of 3.0 in last 60 hours. *Application deadline:* For fall admission, 12/31 (priority date). Applications are processed on a rolling basis. Application fee: $20. Electronic applications accepted. *Financial aid:* In 1998–99, 13 students received aid, including 4 teaching assistantships (averaging $3,919 per year); Federal Work-Study and tuition waivers (partial) also available. Aid available to part-time students. Financial aid application deadline: 4/1; financial aid applicants required to submit FAFSA. *Unit head:* Dr. William Caldwell, Chair, 904-620-2653, E-mail: wcaldwell@unf.edu. *Application contact:* Dr. Leonard Lipkin, Coordinator, 904-620-2468, E-mail: llipkin@unf.edu.

University of Ottawa, School of Graduate Studies and Research, Faculty of Science, Ottawa-Carleton Institute of Mathematics and Statistics, Ottawa, ON K1N 6N5, Canada. Offers M Sc, PhD. Part-time programs available. *Faculty:* 55 full-time, 2 part-time. *Students:* 51 full-time (13 women), 7 part-time (3 women), 12 international. Average age 29. In 1998, 22 master's, 9 doctorates awarded. *Degree requirements:* For master's, thesis optional, foreign language not required; for doctorate, one foreign language, dissertation required. *Entrance requirements:* For master's, honors degree or equivalent, minimum B average; for doctorate, minimum B+ average. *Application deadline:* For fall admission, 3/1 (priority date). Applications are processed on a rolling basis. Application fee: $35. *Financial aid:* Fellowships, research assistantships, teaching assistantships, Federal Work-Study available. Financial aid application deadline: 3/1. *Faculty research:* Pure mathematics, applied mathematics, probability. Total annual research expenditures: $280,000. *Unit head:* David McDonald, Director, 613-562-5800 Ext. 3505, Fax: 613-562-5776, E-mail: dmdsg@uottawa.ca. *Application contact:* David McDonald, Director, 613-562-5800 Ext. 3505, Fax: 613-562-5776, E-mail: dmdsg@uottawa.ca.

University of Pennsylvania, Wharton School, Department of Statistics, Philadelphia, PA 19104. Offers AM, PhD. *Faculty:* 17 full-time (2 women). *Students:* 19 full-time (4 women); includes 1 minority (Asian American or Pacific Islander), 16 international. Average age 26. 80 applicants, 9% accepted. In 1998, 6 master's awarded (0% continued full-time study); 5 doctorates awarded (40% entered university research/teaching, 60% found other work related to degree). Terminal master's awarded for partial completion of doctoral program. *Degree requirements:* For master's, thesis not required; for doctorate, dissertation required. *Entrance requirements:* For master's and doctorate, GRE. *Average time to degree:* Master's–2 years full-time; doctorate–5 years full-time. *Application deadline:* For fall admission, 1/15. Application fee: $65. *Financial aid:* In 1998–99, 19 students received aid, including 2 research assistantships with full tuition reimbursements available (averaging $15,000 per year), 17 teaching assistantships with full tuition reimbursements available (averaging $14,750 per year); fellowships Financial aid application deadline: 11/15. *Faculty research:* Nonparametric function estimation, analysis of algorithms, time series analysis, observational studies, inference. Total annual research expenditures: $101,000. *Unit head:* Dr. Paul Shaman, Chairman, 215-898-8749, Fax: 215-898-1280, E-mail: shaman@stat.wharton.upenn.edu. *Application contact:* Dr. Paul R. Rosenbaum, Coordinator, 215-898-3120, Fax: 215-898-1280, E-mail: rosenbaum@stat.wharton.upenn.edu.

University of Pittsburgh, Faculty of Arts and Sciences, Department of Statistics, Pittsburgh, PA 15260. Offers applied statistics (MA, MS); statistics (MA, MS, PhD). Part-time programs available. *Faculty:* 40 full-time (6 women), 20 part-time (7 women). *Students:* 26 full-time (8 women), 6 part-time (2 women), 23 international. 61 applicants, 43% accepted. In 1998, 4 master's, 2 doctorates awarded. Terminal master's awarded for partial completion of doctoral program. *Degree requirements:* For master's, thesis (for some programs), written comprehensive exam required, foreign language not required; for doctorate, dissertation, oral and written comprehensive exam required, foreign language not required. *Entrance requirements:* For master's, GRE General Test, TOEFL (minimum score of 550 required); for doctorate, TOEFL (minimum score of 550 required). *Average time to degree:* Master's–1.5 years full-time, 3 years part-time; doctorate–5 years full-time. *Application deadline:* For fall admission, 3/1 (priority date); for spring admission, 10/1 (priority date). Applications are processed on a rolling basis. Application fee: $30 ($40 for international students). *Financial aid:* In 1998–99, 19 students received aid, including 1 fellowship (averaging $10,650 per year), 3 research assistantships (averaging $5,300 per year), 15 teaching assistantships (averaging $10,600 per year); career-related internships or fieldwork, Federal Work-Study, grants, institutionally-sponsored loans, scholarships, and tuition waivers (full and partial) also available. Financial aid application deadline: 2/1; financial aid applicants required to submit FAFSA. *Faculty research:* Multivariate statistics, time series, reliability, meta-analysis, linear and nonlinear regression modelling. Total annual research expenditures: $250,000. *Unit head:* Allan R. Sampson, Chairman, 412-624-8372, Fax: 412-648-8814, E-mail: asampson@stat.pitt.edu. *Application contact:* Leon J. Gleser, Director of Graduate Studies, 412-624-3925, Fax: 412-648-8814, E-mail: ljg@stat.pitt.edu.

University of Puerto Rico, Mayagüez Campus, Graduate Studies, College of Arts and Sciences, Department of Mathematics, Mayagüez, PR 00681-5000. Offers applied mathematics (MS); computational sciences (MS); pure mathematics (MS); statistics (MS). Part-time programs available. *Degree requirements:* For master's, one foreign language, comprehensive exam required, thesis optional. *Faculty research:* Automata theory, linear algebra, logic.

University of Regina, Faculty of Graduate Studies and Research, Faculty of Science, Department of Mathematics and Statistics, Regina, SK S4S 0A2, Canada. Offers mathematics (M Sc, MA, PhD); statistics (M Sc, MA). *Faculty:* 20 full-time (3 women). *Students:* 3 full-time (0 women), 3 part-time (1 woman). 14 applicants, 43% accepted. In 1998, 3 degrees awarded. *Degree requirements:* For master's, thesis optional, foreign language not required; for doctorate, variable foreign language requirement, dissertation required. *Entrance requirements:* For master's, TOEFL (minimum score of 550 required); for doctorate, TOEFL. *Application deadline:* Applications are processed on a rolling basis. Application fee: $0. *Expenses:* Tuition and fees charges are reported in Canadian dollars. Tuition, state resident: full-time $1,688 Canadian dollars; part-time $94 Canadian dollars per credit hour. International tuition: $3,375 Canadian dollars full-time. Required fees: $65 Canadian dollars per course. Tuition and fees vary according to course load and program. *Financial aid:* In 1998–99, 1 fellowship, 3 research assistantships, 3 teaching assistantships were awarded.; scholarships also available. Financial aid application deadline: 6/15. *Faculty research:* Pure and applied mathematics, statistics and probability. *Unit head:* Dr. D. Hanson, Head, 306-585-4351, E-mail: denis.hanson@uregina.ca.

University of Rhode Island, Graduate School, College of Arts and Sciences, Department of Computer Science and Statistics, Kingston, RI 02881. Offers MS, PhD. *Degree requirements:* For master's, thesis optional; for doctorate, dissertation required. *Entrance requirements:* For master's, GRE Subject Test.

University of Rochester, School of Medicine and Dentistry, Graduate Programs in Medicine and Dentistry, Department of Biostatistics, Rochester, NY 14627-0250. Offers medical statistics (MS); statistics (MA, PhD). *Faculty:* 6. *Students:* 11 full-time (6 women), 8 international. 30 applicants, 37% accepted. In 1998, 3 doctorates awarded. Terminal master's awarded for partial completion of doctoral program. *Degree requirements:* For doctorate, dissertation, qualifying exam required, foreign language not required, foreign language not required. *Entrance requirements:* For master's and doctorate, GRE General Test, TOEFL. *Application deadline:* For fall admission, 2/1. Application fee: $25. *Financial aid:* Fellowships, research assistantships, teaching assistantships, tuition waivers (full and partial) available. Financial aid application deadline: 2/1. *Unit head:* Dr. David Oakes, Chair, 716-275-2404. *Application contact:* Patti Kolomic, Administrative Assistant, 716-275-6696, E-mail: kolomic@metro.bst.rochester.edu.

See in-depth description on page 789.

University of South Carolina, Graduate School, College of Science and Mathematics, Department of Statistics, Columbia, SC 29208. Offers MIS, MS, PhD. Part-time programs available. *Faculty:* 10 full-time (1 woman), 2 part-time (0 women). *Students:* 22 full-time (10 women), 6 part-time (4 women); includes 5 minority (2 African Americans, 1 Asian American or Pacific Islander, 1 Hispanic American, 1 Native American), 6 international. Average age 31. 49 applicants, 49% accepted. In 1998, 8 master's, 4 doctorates awarded (100% entered university research/teaching). Terminal master's awarded for partial completion of doctoral program. *Degree requirements:* For master's, thesis required, foreign language not required; for doctorate, computer language, dissertation required, foreign language not required. *Entrance requirements:* For master's and doctorate, GRE General Test (minimum combined score of 1050 required). *Application deadline:* For fall admission, 3/1 (priority date). Applications are processed on a rolling basis. Application fee: $35. Electronic applications accepted. Tuition, state resident: full-time $4,014; part-time $202 per credit hour. Tuition, nonresident: full-time $8,528; part-time $428 per credit hour. Required fees: $100; $4 per credit hour. Tuition and fees vary according to program. *Financial aid:* In 1998–99, 18 students received aid, including 1 fellowship, 4 research assistantships, 15 teaching assistantships; career-related internships or fieldwork also available. *Faculty research:* Reliability and quality control, multiple comparisons, environmetrics, statistics computing. Total annual research expenditures: $175,000. *Unit head:* Dr. William J. Padgett, Chair, 803-777-5070, Fax: 803-777-4048, E-mail: padgett@stat.sc.edu. *Application contact:* Dr. Don Edwards, Graduate Director, 803-777-7800, Fax: 803-777-4048, E-mail: edwards@stat.sc.edu.

University of Southern California, Graduate School, College of Letters, Arts and Sciences, Department of Mathematics, Program in Statistics, Los Angeles, CA 90089. Offers MS. *Students:* 3 full-time (1 woman), 2 international. Average age 30. 11 applicants, 45% accepted. In 1998, 1 degree awarded. *Degree requirements:* For master's, thesis required. *Entrance requirements:* For master's, GRE General Test. *Application deadline:* For fall admission, 7/1 (priority date); for spring admission, 12/1. Application fee: $55. Tuition: Full-time $22,198; part-time $748 per unit. Required fees: $406. Tuition and fees vary according to program. *Financial aid:* In 1998–99, 1 fellowship, 1 research assistantship, 2 teaching assistantships were awarded.; Federal Work-Study and institutionally-sponsored loans also available. Aid available to part-time students. Financial aid application deadline: 2/15; financial aid applicants required to submit FAFSA. *Unit head:* Dr. Simon Tavaré, Chair, 213-740-2400.

University of Tennessee, Knoxville, Graduate School, College of Business Administration, Department of Statistics, Knoxville, TN 37996. Offers industrial statistics (MS); statistics (MS). Part-time programs available. *Faculty:* 11 full-time (2 women), 1 part-time (0 women). *Students:* 17 full-time (8 women), 3 part-time (2 women); includes 2 minority (1 African American, 1 Asian American or Pacific Islander), 5 international. 28 applicants, 50% accepted. In 1998, 7 degrees awarded. *Degree requirements:* For master's, thesis or alternative required, foreign language not required. *Entrance requirements:* For master's, GMAT or GRE General Test, TOEFL (minimum score of 550 required), minimum GPA of 2.7. *Application deadline:* For fall admission, 2/1 (priority date). Applications are processed on a rolling basis. Application fee: $35. Electronic applications accepted. *Financial aid:* Fellowships, teaching assistantships, career-related internships or fieldwork, Federal Work-Study, institutionally-sponsored loans, and unspecified assistantships available. Financial aid application deadline: 2/1; financial aid applicants required to submit FAFSA. *Unit head:* Dr. Robert Mee, Head, 423-974-2556, Fax: 423-974-2490, E-mail: rmee@utk.edu. *Application contact:* Dr. Esteban Walker, Graduate Representative, 423-974-1640, E-mail: ewalker@utk.edu.

University of Tennessee, Knoxville, Graduate School, College of Business Administration, Program in Business Administration, Knoxville, TN 37996. Offers accounting (PhD); economics (MBA); entrepreneurship/new venture analysis (MBA); environmental management (MBA); executive business administration (MBA); finance (MBA, PhD); forest industries management (MBA); global business (MBA); logistics and transportation (MBA, PhD); management (MBA, PhD); manufacturing management (MBA); marketing (MBA, PhD); professional business administration (MBA); statistics (MBA, PhD). Postbaccalaureate distance learning degree programs offered. *Faculty:* 51 full-time (6 women). *Students:* 278 full-time (72 women), 17 part-time (2 women); includes 24 minority (13 African Americans, 5 Asian Americans or Pacific Islanders, 2 Hispanic Americans, 4 Native Americans), 47 international. *Degree requirements:* For master's, computer language, thesis or alternative required, foreign language not required; for doctorate, computer language, dissertation required, foreign language not required. *Entrance requirements:* For master's and doctorate, GMAT, TOEFL (minimum score of 550 required), minimum GPA of 2.7. *Application deadline:* For fall admission, 2/1 (priority date). Application fee: $35. Electronic applications accepted. *Unit head:* Dr. Gary Dicer, Director, 423-974-5033, Fax: 423-974-3826, E-mail: gdicer@utk.edu. *Application contact:* Donna Potts, Graduate Representative, 423-974-5033, Fax: 423-974-3826, E-mail: dpotts@utk.edu.

The University of Texas at Austin, Graduate School, College of Natural Sciences, Department of Mathematics, Program in Statistics, Austin, TX 78712-1111. Offers MS Stat. *Students:* 18 (10 women) 6 international. 23 applicants, 70% accepted. In 1998, 9 degrees awarded. *Entrance requirements:* For master's, GRE General Test. *Application deadline:* For fall admission, 2/1. Application fee: $50 ($75 for international students). *Financial aid:* Fellowships available. Financial aid application deadline: 2/1. *Unit head:* Mary Ann Rankin, Head, 512-471-3285. *Application contact:* Dr. Peter John, Graduate Adviser, 512-471-5139.

The University of Texas at Dallas, School of Natural Sciences and Mathematics, Programs in Mathematical Sciences, Richardson, TX 75083-0688. Offers applied mathematics (MS, PhD); engineering mathematics (MS); mathematical science (MS, PhD); statistics (MS, PhD). Part-time and evening/weekend programs available. *Students:* 22 full-time (7 women), 23 part-time (13 women); includes 6 minority (3 African Americans, 1 Asian American or Pacific Islander, 2 Hispanic Americans), 11 international. *Degree requirements:* For master's, minimum GPA of 3.0 required, thesis optional, foreign language not required; for doctorate, dissertation, minimum GPA of 3.0 required, foreign language not required. *Entrance requirements:* For master's, GRE General Test (minimum score of 500 on verbal section, 550 on quantitative required), TOEFL (minimum score of 550 required), minimum GPA of 3.0 in upper-level course work in field; for doctorate, GRE General Test (minimum score of 550 on verbal section, 650 on quantitative required), TOEFL (minimum score of 550 required), minimum GPA of 3.5 in upper-level course work in field. *Application deadline:* For fall admission, 7/15; for spring admission, 11/15. Applications are processed on a rolling basis. Application fee: $25 ($75 for international students). *Unit head:* Dr. M. Ali Hooshyar, Head, 972-883-2171, Fax: 972-883-6622, E-mail: utdmath@utdallas.edu.

See in-depth description on page 795.

The University of Texas at El Paso, Graduate School, College of Science, Department of Mathematical Sciences, El Paso, TX 79968-0001. Offers mathematical sciences (MAT, MS); statistics (MS). Part-time and evening/weekend programs available. *Faculty:* 26 full-time (2 women), 11 part-time (4 women). *Students:* 9 full-time (1 woman), 6 part-time (2 women); includes 4 minority (all Hispanic Americans), 6 international. *Degree requirements:* For master's, thesis optional, foreign language not required. *Entrance requirements:* For master's, TOEFL (minimum score of 550 required). *Application deadline:* Applications are processed on a rolling basis. Application fee: $15 ($65 for international students). Electronic applications accepted. Tuition, state resident: full-time $2,118. Tuition, nonresident: full-time $7,230. Tuition and fees vary according to program. *Unit head:* Dr. Joe Guthrie, Chairperson, 915-747-5761, Fax: 915-747-6202, E-mail: joe@math.utep.edu. *Application contact:* Susan Jordan, Director, Graduate Student Services, 915-747-5491, Fax: 915-747-5788, E-mail: sjordan@utep.edu.

The University of Texas at San Antonio, College of Sciences and Engineering, Division of Mathematics and Statistics, San Antonio, TX 78249-0617. Offers mathematics (MS), including mathematics education, statistics. Part-time and evening/weekend programs available. *Faculty:* 19 full-time (5 women), 28 part-time (6 women). *Students:* 11 full-time (4 women), 42 part-time (17 women); includes 26 minority (2 African Americans, 6 Asian Americans or Pacific Islanders, 18 Hispanic Americans), 2 international. *Degree requirements:* For master's, computer language, comprehensive exam required, foreign language and thesis not required. *Entrance requirements:* For master's, GRE General Test, TOEFL, minimum GPA of 3.0. *Application deadline:* For fall admission, 7/1. Applications are processed on a rolling basis. Application fee: $25. *Unit head:* Dr. Alfonso Castro, Director, 210-458-4451.

University of Toledo, Graduate School, College of Arts and Sciences, Department of Mathematics, Toledo, OH 43606-3398. Offers applied mathematics (MS); mathematics (MA, MS Ed, PhD); statistics (MS). Part-time programs available. *Degree requirements:* For master's, thesis not required; for doctorate, dissertation required. *Entrance requirements:* For master's and doctorate, GRE General Test, GRE Subject Test. Electronic applications accepted. *Faculty research:* Topology.

University of Toronto, School of Graduate Studies, Physical Sciences Division, Department of Statistics, Toronto, ON M5S 1A1, Canada. Offers M Sc, PhD. Part-time programs available. *Degree requirements:* For master's, thesis not required; for doctorate, dissertation required.

University of Utah, Graduate School, Interdepartmental Program in Statistics, Salt Lake City, UT 84112-1107. Offers M Stat. Part-time programs available. *Students:* 4 full-time (2 women), 11 part-time (6 women), 4 international. Average age 33. In 1998, 2 degrees awarded. *Degree requirements:* For master's, comprehensive exam, projects required, foreign language and thesis not required. *Entrance requirements:* For master's, TOEFL (minimum score of 500 required), minimum GPA of 3.0, previous course work in calculus, matrix theory, statistics. *Application deadline:* For fall admission, 7/1. Application fee: $30 ($50 for international students). *Financial aid:* Career-related internships or fieldwork available. *Faculty research:* Biostatistics, management, economics, educational psychology, mathematics. *Unit head:* David Mason, Chair, University Statistics Committee, 801-581-6830.

University of Vermont, Graduate College, College of Engineering and Mathematics, Department of Mathematics and Statistics, Program in Statistics, Burlington, VT 05405-0160. Offers MS. *Degree requirements:* Foreign language not required. *Entrance requirements:* For master's, GRE General Test, TOEFL (minimum score of 550 required). *Faculty research:* Applied statistics.

University of Victoria, Faculty of Graduate Studies, Faculty of Science, Department of Mathematics and Statistics, Victoria, BC V8W 2Y2, Canada. Offers applied mathematics (M Sc, MA, PhD); pure mathematics (M Sc, MA, PhD); statistics (M Sc, MA). Part-time programs available. *Faculty:* 25 full-time (3 women), 7 part-time (2 women). *Students:* 24 full-time (4 women), 1 part-time, 8 international. Average age 29. 27 applicants, 63% accepted. In 1998, 4 master's, 1 doctorate awarded. *Degree requirements:* For master's, thesis required; for doctorate, one foreign language, dissertation, 3 qualifying exams required. *Average time to degree:* Master's–2.24 years full-time; doctorate–4.63 years full-time. *Application deadline:* For fall admission, 5/31 (priority date). Applications are processed on a rolling basis. Application fee: $50. *Financial aid:* In 1998–99, 16 students received aid, including 5 fellowships; research assistantships, teaching assistantships, career-related internships or fieldwork, institutionally-sponsored loans, and unspecified assistantships also available. Financial aid application deadline: 2/15. *Faculty research:* Functional analysis and operator theory, applied ordinary and partial differential equations, discrete mathematics and graph theory. Total annual research expenditures: $280,000. *Unit head:* Dr. R. Illner, Chair, 250-721-7436, Fax: 250-721-8962. *Application contact:* Dr. J. Phillips, Graduate Adviser, 250-721-7450, Fax: 250-721-8962, E-mail: phillips@math.uvic.ca.

University of Virginia, College and Graduate School of Arts and Sciences, Department of Mathematics, Division of Statistics, Charlottesville, VA 22903. Offers MS, PhD. *Faculty:* 7 full-time (2 women). *Students:* 12 full-time (6 women), 1 (woman) part-time; includes 2 minority (1 African American, 1 Hispanic American), 6 international. Average age 27. 12 applicants, 50% accepted. In 1998, 3 master's, 1 doctorate awarded. *Degree requirements:* For master's,

Statistics

University of Virginia (continued)
thesis required; for doctorate, dissertation required. *Entrance requirements:* For master's and doctorate, GRE General Test, GRE Subject Test. *Application deadline:* For fall admission, 7/15; for spring admission, 12/1. Applications are processed on a rolling basis. Application fee: $60. *Financial aid:* Application deadline: 2/1. *Unit head:* Donald Richards, Chairman, 804-924-3222. *Application contact:* Duane J. Osheim, Associate Dean, 804-924-7184, E-mail: grad-as@virginia.edu.

University of Washington, Graduate School, College of Arts and Sciences, Department of Statistics, Seattle, WA 98195. Offers MS, PhD. Terminal master's awarded for partial completion of doctoral program. *Degree requirements:* For master's, computer language required, thesis optional, foreign language not required; for doctorate, one foreign language, computer language, dissertation required. *Entrance requirements:* For master's and doctorate, GRE General Test (minimum combined score of 1500 on quantitative and analytical sections required), TOEFL (minimum score of 580 required), minimum GPA of 3.0. Tuition, state resident: full-time $5,196; part-time $475 per credit. Tuition, nonresident: full-time $13,485; part-time $1,285 per credit. Required fees: $387; $38 per credit. Tuition and fees vary according to course load. *Faculty research:* Mathematical statistics, stochastic modeling, spatial statistics, statistical computing.

University of Waterloo, Graduate Studies, Faculty of Mathematics, Department of Statistics and Actuarial Science, Waterloo, ON N2L 3G1, Canada. Offers statistics (PhD); statistics-biostatistics (M Math); statistics-computing (M Math); statistics-finance (M Math). *Faculty:* 29 full-time (6 women), 17 part-time (2 women). *Students:* 43 full-time (22 women), 23 part-time (5 women). In 1998, 12 master's, 4 doctorates awarded. *Degree requirements:* For master's, research paper or thesis required; for doctorate, dissertation required, foreign language not required. *Entrance requirements:* For master's, TOEFL (minimum score of 580 required), honors degree in field, minimum B average; for doctorate, TOEFL (minimum score of 580 required), master's degree. *Application deadline:* For fall admission, 3/31 (priority date); for winter admission, 8/31 (priority date); for spring admission, 12/31 (priority date). Applications are processed on a rolling basis. Application fee: $50. *Expenses:* Tuition and fees charges are reported in Canadian dollars. Tuition, state resident: full-time $3,168 Canadian dollars; part-time $792 Canadian dollars per term. Tuition, nonresident: full-time $8,000 Canadian dollars; part-time $2,000 Canadian dollars. Required fees: $45 Canadian dollars per term. Tuition and fees vary according to program. *Financial aid:* Research assistantships, teaching assistantships, career-related internships or fieldwork and scholarships available. Financial aid application deadline: 2/28. *Faculty research:* Biometry, multivariate analysis, risk theory, inference, stochastic processes, quantitative finance. *Unit head:* Dr. M. E. Thompson, Chair, 519-888-4567 Ext. 5543, Fax: 519-746-1875, E-mail: methomps@setosa.uwaterloo.ca. *Application contact:* Dr. W. J. Welch, Graduate Officer, 519-888-4567 Ext. 5545, Fax: 519-746-1875, E-mail: wjwelch@uwaterloo.ca.

The University of Western Ontario, Faculty of Graduate Studies, Physical Sciences Division, Department of Statistical and Actuarial Sciences, London, ON N6A 5B8, Canada. Offers M Sc, PhD.

University of West Florida, College of Science and Technology, Department of Mathematics and Statistics, Pensacola, FL 32514-5750. Offers mathematics (MA); mathematics education (MAT); statistics (MA). *Accreditation:* NCATE (one or more programs are accredited). Part-time and evening/weekend programs available. *Students:* 8 full-time (3 women), 17 part-time (8 women); includes 8 minority (5 African Americans, 2 Asian Americans or Pacific Islanders, 1 Hispanic American) Average age 34. 13 applicants, 100% accepted. In 1998, 12 degrees awarded. *Degree requirements:* For master's, thesis optional, foreign language not required. *Entrance requirements:* For master's, GRE General Test (minimum combined score of 1000 required), minimum GPA of 3.0. *Application deadline:* For fall admission, 7/19. Application fee: $20. Tuition, state resident: full-time $3,582; part-time $149 per credit hour. Tuition, nonresident: full-time $12,240; part-time $510 per credit hour. *Financial aid:* Fellowships, teaching assistantships, career-related internships or fieldwork and institutionally-sponsored loans available. Aid available to part-time students. *Unit head:* Dr. Rohan Hemasinha, Chairperson, 850-474-2276.

University of Windsor, College of Graduate Studies and Research, Faculty of Science, Mathematics and Statistics, Economics AAV, Windsor, ON N9B 3P4, Canada. Offers mathematics (M Sc, PhD); statistics (M Sc, PhD). Part-time programs available. *Degree requirements:* For master's, thesis required (for some programs); for doctorate, dissertation required. *Entrance requirements:* For master's, GRE, TOEFL (minimum score of 550 required), minimum B average; for doctorate, TOEFL, master's degree. *Faculty research:* Statistics and probability, matrix algebra, functional analysis, mathematical programming.

University of Wisconsin–Madison, Graduate School, College of Letters and Science, Department of Statistics, Madison, WI 53706-1380. Offers MS, PhD. Part-time programs available. *Faculty:* 13 full-time (1 woman), 10 part-time (0 women). *Students:* 78 full-time (32 women), 61 international. Average age 27. 154 applicants, 75% accepted. In 1998, 9 master's awarded (22% entered university research/teaching, 22% found other work related to degree, 33% continued full-time study); 8 doctorates awarded (50% entered university research/teaching, 50% found other work related to degree). *Degree requirements:* For master's, exam required, foreign language and thesis not required; for doctorate, dissertation required, foreign language not required. *Entrance requirements:* For master's and doctorate, GRE, TOEFL (minimum score of 590 required). *Average time to degree:* Master's–2 years full-time; doctorate–4.5 years full-time. *Application deadline:* For fall admission, 12/15 (priority date); for spring admission, 10/1. Applications are processed on a rolling basis. Application fee: $45. Electronic applications accepted. *Financial aid:* In 1998–99, 59 students received aid, including 20 research assistantships (averaging $14,592 per year), 27 teaching assistantships (averaging $10,314 per year); fellowships, career-related internships or fieldwork and institutionally-sponsored loans also available. Aid available to part-time students. Financial aid application deadline: 12/15. *Faculty research:* Biostatistics, bootstrap and other resampling theory and methods, linear and nonlinear models, nonparametrics, stochastic processes. Total annual research expenditures: $398,155. *Unit head:* Gregory Reinsel, Chair, 608-262-3720, Fax: 608-262-0032, E-mail: office@stat.wisc.edu. *Application contact:* Jude Grudzina, Program Assistant, 608-262-2598, Fax: 608-262-0032, E-mail: jzg@stat.wisc.edu.

University of Wyoming, Graduate School, College of Arts and Sciences, Department of Statistics, Laramie, WY 82071. Offers MS, PhD. *Faculty:* 7 full-time (1 woman). *Students:* 12 full-time (3 women), 6 part-time (4 women), 2 international. Average age 33. 12 applicants, 50% accepted. In 1998, 4 master's awarded (0% continued full-time study); 1 doctorate awarded (100% found work related to degree). Terminal master's awarded for partial completion of doctoral program. *Degree requirements:* For master's and doctorate, thesis/dissertation required, thesis/dissertation required. *Entrance requirements:* For master's, GMAT, GRE General Test, minimum GPA of 3.0; for doctorate, GRE General Test, minimum GPA of 3.0. *Average time to degree:* Master's–3 years full-time; doctorate–4 years full-time. *Application deadline:* For fall admission, 3/5 (priority date). Applications are processed on a rolling basis. Application fee: $40. Electronic applications accepted. Tuition, state resident: full-time $2,520; part-time $140 per credit hour. Tuition, nonresident: full-time $7,790; part-time $433 per credit hour. Required fees: $400; $7 per credit hour. Full-time tuition and fees vary according to course load and program. *Financial aid:* In 1998–99, 4 research assistantships, 9 teaching assistantships were awarded.; Federal Work-Study and institutionally-sponsored loans also available. Financial aid application deadline: 3/1. *Faculty research:* Mining impacts, biotic integrity. Total annual research expenditures: $25,000. *Unit head:* Dr. Stephen Bieber, Head, 307-766-4229, Fax: 307-766-3927, E-mail: barbr@uwyo.edu.

Utah State University, School of Graduate Studies, College of Science, Department of Mathematics and Statistics, Program in Applied Statistics, Logan, UT 84322. Offers MS. 10 applicants, 30% accepted. In 1998, 5 degrees awarded. *Degree requirements:* For master's, qualifying exam required, thesis optional, foreign language not required. *Entrance requirements:*

For master's, GRE General Test (score in 40th percentile or higher required), TOEFL (minimum score of 580 required), minimum GPA of 3.0. *Application deadline:* For fall admission, 6/15 (priority date); for spring admission, 10/15. Applications are processed on a rolling basis. Application fee: $40. Tuition, state resident: full-time $1,492. Tuition, nonresident: full-time $5,232. Required fees: $434. Tuition and fees vary according to course load. *Financial aid:* Fellowships, research assistantships, teaching assistantships available. Aid available to part-time students. Financial aid application deadline: 4/1. *Unit head:* Suzanne S. Stoker, Senior Secretary, 435-797-2459, Fax: 435-797-1871. *Application contact:* Dr. Renate Schaaf, Graduate Chairman, 435-797-2821, Fax: 435-797-1822, E-mail: schaaf@sunfs.math.usu.edu.

Villanova University, Graduate School of Liberal Arts and Sciences, Department of Mathematical Sciences, Program in Applied Statistics, Villanova, PA 19085-1699. Offers MS. Part-time and evening/weekend programs available. *Students:* 4 full-time (2 women), 19 part-time (7 women), 1 international. Average age 33. 10 applicants, 80% accepted. In 1998, 16 degrees awarded. *Degree requirements:* For master's, comprehensive exam required, foreign language and thesis not required. *Entrance requirements:* For master's, minimum GPA of 3.0. *Application deadline:* For fall admission, 8/1 (priority date); for spring admission, 12/1. Application fee: $40. *Financial aid:* Research assistantships, Federal Work-Study available. Financial aid application deadline: 4/1; financial aid applicants required to submit FAFSA. *Unit head:* Dr. Robert Styer, Chairperson, Department of Mathematical Sciences, 610-519-4850.

Virginia Commonwealth University, School of Graduate Studies, College of Humanities and Sciences, Department of Mathematical Sciences, Program in Statistics, Richmond, VA 23284-9005. Offers MS, Certificate. In 1998, 5 degrees awarded. *Degree requirements:* Foreign language not required. *Entrance requirements:* For master's, GRE General Test, GRE Subject Test, TOEFL. *Application deadline:* For fall admission, 7/1; for spring admission, 11/15. Applications are processed on a rolling basis. Application fee: $30. Tuition, state resident: full-time $4,031; part-time $224 per credit hour. Tuition, nonresident: full-time $11,946; part-time $664 per credit hour. Required fees: $1,081; $40 per credit hour. Tuition and fees vary according to campus/location and program. *Unit head:* Andrew Lacatell, Assistant Director, 804-828-7202, Fax: 804-828-0503, E-mail: adlacate@vcu.edu. *Application contact:* Dr. James A. Wood, Director of Graduate Studies, 804-828-1301, Fax: 804-828-8785, E-mail: jawood@vcu.edu.

Virginia Polytechnic Institute and State University, Graduate School, College of Arts and Sciences, Department of Statistics, Blacksburg, VA 24061. Offers MS, PhD. *Faculty:* 20 full-time (4 women). *Students:* 37 full-time (16 women), 5 part-time (1 woman); includes 5 minority (4 Asian Americans or Pacific Islanders, 1 Hispanic American), 13 international. 41 applicants, 61% accepted. In 1998, 20 master's, 5 doctorates awarded. *Degree requirements:* For master's, computer language, qualifying exam required, thesis optional, foreign language not required; for doctorate, computer language, dissertation, preliminary exam required, foreign language not required. *Entrance requirements:* For master's and doctorate, TOEFL (minimum score of 600 required). *Application deadline:* For fall admission, 12/1 (priority date). Applications are processed on a rolling basis. Application fee: $25. *Financial aid:* Fellowships, research assistantships, teaching assistantships, institutionally-sponsored loans and unspecified assistantships available. Financial aid application deadline:4/1. *Faculty research:* Design and sampling theory, computing and simulation, nonparametric statistics, robust and multivariate methods, biostatistics quality. *Unit head:* Dr. Marvin Lentner, Head, 540-231-5657.

See in-depth description on page 803.

Washington University in St. Louis, Graduate School of Arts and Sciences, Department of Mathematics, St. Louis, MO 63130-4899. Offers mathematics (MA, PhD); mathematics education (MAT); statistics (MA, PhD). *Accreditation:* NCATE (one or more programs are accredited). Part-time programs available. *Students:* 26 full-time (7 women), 1 part-time; includes 2 minority (1 African American, 1 Asian American or Pacific Islander), 13 international. Terminal master's awarded for partial completion of doctoral program. *Degree requirements:* For master's, thesis or alternative required; for doctorate, dissertation required. *Entrance requirements:* For master's and doctorate, GRE General Test. *Application deadline:* For fall admission, 1/15 (priority date). Applications are processed on a rolling basis. Application fee: $35. *Unit head:* Dr. Edward Wilson, Chairman, 314-935-6760.

Wayne State University, Graduate School, College of Science, Department of Mathematics, Program in Statistics, Detroit, MI 48202. Offers MA, PhD. *Degree requirements:* For master's, foreign language and thesis not required; for doctorate, dissertation required.

Western Michigan University, Graduate College, College of Arts and Sciences, Department of Mathematics and Statistics, Program in Statistics, Kalamazoo, MI 49008. Offers MS, PhD. *Students:* 11 full-time (2 women), 21 part-time (7 women); includes 2 minority (both Asian Americans or Pacific Islanders), 9 international. 29 applicants, 59% accepted. In 1998, 12 master's awarded. *Degree requirements:* For master's, oral exams required, thesis not required; for doctorate, dissertation required. *Entrance requirements:* For doctorate, GRE General Test. *Application deadline:* For fall admission, 2/15 (priority date). Applications are processed on a rolling basis. Application fee: $25. *Financial aid:* Fellowships, research assistantships, teaching assistantships, Federal Work-Study available. Financial aid application deadline: 2/15; financial aid applicants required to submit FAFSA. *Application contact:* Paula J. Boodt, Coordinator, Graduate Admissions and Recruitment, 616-387-2000, Fax: 616-387-2355, E-mail: paula.boodt@wmich.edu.

West Virginia University, Eberly College of Arts and Sciences, Department of Statistics, Morgantown, WV 26506. Offers MS. *Degree requirements:* For master's, computer language, thesis, comprehensive exams required, foreign language not required. *Entrance requirements:* For master's, TOEFL (minimum score of 550 required), minimum GPA of 3.0. *Faculty research:* Linear models, multivariate analysis, categorical data analysis, statistical computing, experimental design.

Wichita State University, Graduate School, Fairmount College of Liberal Arts and Sciences, Department of Mathematics and Statistics, Wichita, KS 67260. Offers applied mathematics (PhD); mathematics (MS); statistics (MS). Part-time programs available. *Faculty:* 23 full-time (0 women), 1 part-time (0 women). *Students:* 22 full-time (7 women), 15 part-time (7 women); includes 2 minority (1 African American, 1 Asian American or Pacific Islander), 15 international. Average age 35. 19 applicants, 37% accepted. In 1998, 4 master's, 2 doctorates awarded. *Degree requirements:* For master's, comprehensive exam required, thesis optional, foreign language not required; for doctorate, computer language, dissertation required. *Entrance requirements:* For master's, GRE, TOEFL (minimum score of 550 required); for doctorate, GRE Subject Test, TOEFL (minimum score of 550 required). *Application deadline:* For fall admission, 7/1 (priority date); for spring admission, 1/1. Applications are processed on a rolling basis. Application fee: $25 ($40 for international students). Electronic applications accepted. *Financial aid:* In 1998–99, 10 fellowships (averaging $4,000 per year), 4 research assistantships (averaging $5,000 per year), 16 teaching assistantships with full tuition reimbursements (averaging $10,000 per year) were awarded; Federal Work-Study, institutionally-sponsored loans, and unspecified assistantships also available. Aid available to part-time students. Financial aid application deadline: 4/1; financial aid applicants required to submit FAFSA. *Faculty research:* Partial differential equations, combinatorics, ring theory, minimal surfaces, several complex variables. Total annual research expenditures: $91,665. *Unit head:* Dr. Buma Fridman, Chairperson, 316-978-3985, Fax: 316-978-3748, E-mail: fridman@twsuvm.uc.twsu.edu. *Application contact:* Dr. Ken Miller, Graduate Coordinator, 316-978-3959, Fax: 316-978-3748, E-mail: miller@twsuvm.uc.twsu.edu.

Worcester Polytechnic Institute, Graduate Studies, Department of Mathematical Science, Worcester, MA 01609-2280. Offers applied mathematics (MS); applied statistics (MS); mathematical science (PhD, Certificate); mathematics (MME). Part-time and evening/weekend programs available. *Faculty:* 25 full-time (3 women). *Students:* 17 full-time (8 women), 11 part-time (1 woman); includes 2 minority (1 African American, 1 Asian American or Pacific Islander), 8 international. *Degree requirements:* For master's, thesis optional, foreign language not required;

for doctorate, dissertation required, foreign language not required. *Entrance requirements:* For master's, TOEFL (minimum score of 550 required; average 600). *Application deadline:* For fall admission, 2/15 (priority date); for spring admission, 10/15 (priority date). Applications are processed on a rolling basis. Application fee: $50. Electronic applications accepted. *Unit head:* Dr. Homer Walker, Head, 508-831-5316, Fax: 508-831-5824, E-mail: lipton@wpi.edu.

Wright State University, School of Graduate Studies, College of Science and Mathematics, Department of Mathematics and Statistics, Program in Applied Statistics, Dayton, OH 45435. Offers MS. *Students:* 4 full-time (1 woman), 5 part-time (2 women); includes 1 minority (Native American), 1 international. Average age 30. 11 applicants, 64% accepted. In 1998, 7 degrees awarded. *Degree requirements:* For master's, computer language, comprehensive exams required, foreign language and thesis not required. *Entrance requirements:* For master's, TOEFL (minimum score of 550 required), 1 year of course work in calculus and matrix algebra, previous course work in computer programming and statistics. Application fee: $25. *Financial aid:* Fellowships, research assistantships, teaching assistantships available. Aid available to part-time students. Financial aid applicants required to submit FAFSA. *Faculty research:* Reliability theory, stochastic process, nonparametric statistics, design of experiments, multivariate statistics. *Unit head:* Dr. Barbara L. Mann, Director, 937-775-4204, Fax: 937-775-3068, E-mail: bmann@nova.wright.edu.

Yale University, Graduate School of Arts and Sciences, Department of Statistics, New Haven, CT 06520. Offers MS, PhD. *Faculty:* 6. *Students:* 17 full-time (8 women), 2 part-time (1 woman), 12 international. 54 applicants, 19% accepted. In 1998, 1 degree awarded. Terminal master's awarded for partial completion of doctoral program. *Degree requirements:* For master's, foreign language and thesis not required; for doctorate, dissertation required, foreign language not required. *Entrance requirements:* For doctorate, GRE General Test, GRE Subject Test. *Average time to degree:* Doctorate–6.3 years full-time. *Application deadline:* For fall admission, 1/4. Application fee: $65. *Financial aid:* Fellowships, research assistantships, teaching assistantships, Federal Work-Study and institutionally-sponsored loans available. Aid available to part-time students. *Unit head:* Chair, 203-432-0666. *Application contact:* Admissions Information, 203-432-2770.

York University, Faculty of Graduate Studies, Faculty of Arts, Program in Mathematics and Statistics, Toronto, ON M3J 1P3, Canada. Offers MA, PhD. Part-time programs available. *Degree requirements:* For master's, thesis optional; for doctorate, dissertation, comprehensive exam required.

Cross-Discipline Announcements

Boston College, The Graduate School of the Wallace E. Carroll School of Management, Chestnut Hill, MA 02467-3800.

Boston College's MBA Program and BC's master's program in mathematics offer a dual-degree program that allows students to simultaneously obtain an MBA and an MA in mathematics. See in-depth description in Book 6.

The George Washington University, School of Public Health and Health Services, Department of Public Health, Washington, DC 20052.

MPH Program offers specialty track in epidemiology-biostatistics. MS and PhD in epidemiology and in biostatistics offered in collaboration with Statistics Department and GW Biostatistics Center. Field experience and research opportunities in nation's capital, including the National Cancer Institute. Evening and late afternoon classes available. See in-depth description in Book 6 or visit the Web site at http://www.gwumc.edu/sphhs

Northeastern University, College of Computer Science, Boston, MA 02115-5096.

The College of Computer Science offers programs leading to the MS and PhD degrees. The MS program prepares students for challenging technical positions in the software industry. The PhD program equips its graduates with the depth of knowledge and experience needed to conduct advanced research in either academia or industry.

Northwestern University, The Graduate School, Robert R. McCormick School of Engineering and Applied Science, Department of Industrial Engineering and Management Sciences, Evanston, IL 60208.

The department offers master's and doctoral programs in applied probability, economics and production (including manufacturing engineering), logistics, optimization (mathematical programming), organization theory, statistics and decision analysis, and systems analysis and design. For further information, see in-depth description in Book 5, Industrial Engineering section.

The Ohio State University, Graduate School, College of Engineering, Department of Civil and Environmental Engineering and Geodetic Science, Program in Geodetic Science and Surveying, Columbus, OH 43210.

Geodetic science uses advanced mathematical and statistical tools, GPS, and altimetry to solve problems related to Earth's gravity field, satellite orbits, Earth rotation, movements of Earth's crust, satellite positioning for mapping, analysis of digital and photographic images, computer-assisted mapping, and GIS. Master's and PhD. WWW: http://www-ceg.eng.ohio-state.edu.

Stanford University, School of Engineering, Program in Scientific Computing and Computational Mathematics, Stanford, CA 94305-9991.

Studies in SCCM focus on applied mathematics, numerical analysis, and scientific computing. It is an interdisciplinary program with a mathematics and numerical analysis core, a firm foundation in an application area, and coverage of important issues in computer science. For more information, see the in-depth description in Volume 5, Section 8.

Virginia Commonwealth University, School of Graduate Studies, School of Medicine Graduate Programs, Department of Human Genetics, Richmond, VA 23284-9005.

Human quantitative genetics applies mathematical and biostatistical models to problems in the genetics of human populations. Genetic linkage and segregation analyses of disease are increasingly important tools in biomedical research. Linear structural equation modeling of physical and behavioral traits is used to study their development and biological and cultural inheritance.

Wayne State University, Graduate School, College of Science, Department of Computer Science, Detroit, MI 48202.

The department offers challenging programs leading to master's and PhD degrees. State-of-the-art learning environments are provided for students of widely varying backgrounds, covering a broad range of interests and emphasizing artificial intelligence, computational modeling of biological systems, computer graphics, data mining, database systems, image and video computing, multimedia information systems, natural language processing, neural networks, numerical analysis, parallel and distributed systems, pattern recognition, and software engineering.

AMERICAN UNIVERSITY

Department of Mathematics and Statistics

Programs of Study

The M.S. in statistics program has two tracks: mathematical statistics and applied statistics. The applied statistics track places special emphasis on statistical applications and methodology training. The mathematical statistics track provides a theoretical framework for the development of analytic and computational techniques and contains the prerequisites for pursuing a Ph.D. in statistics. The M.S. in statistics for policy analysis program provides technical statistical training together with the fundamentals of policy analysis necessary for evaluating and analyzing a broad range of public policy issues. Students studying for an M.A. in mathematics choose between theoretical study in pure mathematics and a more applied curriculum appropriate to professions such as economics, physics, or management. Students may take up to 6 semester hours of courses in a field of application such as statistics, computer science, economics, or physics.

The Ph.D. program in mathematics education is based on a curriculum of mathematical sciences, including statistics and computer science. Practical training and innovative research are combined to address critical issues in mathematics education and enable graduates to work in a research, classroom, supervisory, or administrative setting. The Ph.D. in statistics program leads to the forefront of statistical theory. This training enables students to be productive researchers in the field.

Research Facilities

The Bender Library and Learning Resources Center houses more than 700,000 volumes and 3,000 periodical titles as well as extensive microform collections and a nonprint media center. In addition, more than fourteen indexes in compact disc format are searchable using library microcomputers. Graduate students have unlimited borrowing privileges at six college and university libraries in the Washington Research Library Consortium, all accessible through the online catalog. Dozens of other research collections, including the Library of Congress, are readily available locally. The department houses a computer laboratory with SPARC and NeXT workstations. Software includes SAS, SYSTAT, ISP, S-Plus, Mathematica, MatLab, Pascal, FORTRAN, and C. Several additional University computer laboratories are also available 24 hours a day with access to an IBM mainframe. The department LAN is connected through the University fiber-optic network. Access to a Cray supercomputer may be arranged. A newly renovated classroom is equipped with fifteen Pentium machines for teaching.

Financial Aid

Fellowships, scholarships, and graduate assistantships are available to full-time students. Special opportunity grants for minority group members parallel the regular honor awards and take the form of assistantships and scholarships. Research and teaching fellowships provide stipends plus tuition. Graduate assistantships provide up to 18 credit hours of tuition remission per year. Well-qualified students often teach as lecturers or instructors for the department. Part-time work, loans, and deferred-payment programs are also available.

Cost of Study

For the 1999–2000 academic year, tuition is $721 per credit hour.

Living and Housing Costs

Although many graduate students live off campus, the University provides graduate dormitory rooms and apartments. The Off-Campus Housing Office maintains a referral file of rooms and apartments. Housing costs in Washington, D.C., are comparable to those in other major metropolitan areas.

Student Group

Fifty-eight graduate students in the Department of Mathematics and Statistics form a cosmopolitan international group. Almost half are women; many are minority students as well as international students.

Student Outcomes

Alumni have obtained excellent jobs in government, academia, and business, including research laboratories and consulting firms. American University's emphasis on experiential education outside the classroom may prove a stepping stone to a future career. Graduates of the University's programs have pursued doctoral studies, entered academic and policy-oriented careers, become professionals in their areas of expertise, or found employment in private industry in the United States and around the world. Because so many international students study in the department, alumni work all over the globe and provide an excellent network for job placement. The department boasts a high completion rate. A total of 18 Ph.D.'s and 29 master's degrees have been awarded over the last five years.

Location

The national capital area offers students access to an unparalleled variety of educational, governmental, and cultural resources that enrich the student's degree program with opportunities for practical applications of theoretical studies. Opportunities for research, internships, cooperative educational placements, and part-time jobs are plentiful. Local bus and rail transportation from the campus provides easy access to sites in the greater metropolitan area. Ties between faculty and both private and public research teams allow students opportunities for field experience through internships such as with the National Institutes of Health, the Environmental Protection Agency, and the World Bank.

The University and The Department

American University was founded as a Methodist institution, chartered by Congress in 1893, and intended originally for graduate study only. The University is located on an 84-acre site in a residential area of northwest Washington. As a member of the Consortium of Universities of the Washington area, American University can offer its degree candidates the option of taking courses at other consortium universities for residence credit. American's distinguished faculty attracts internationally renowned guests and specialists. The department sponsors a colloquia series that is regularly attended by faculty members and graduate students. The strong faculty-student relationships fostered in the department create a supportive and friendly learning environment. The department includes 18 full-time faculty members, 6 of whom are women, and 5 full-time instructors.

Applying

Admission to graduate programs requires a degree in mathematics, statistics, or a directly related field from an accredited college or university with at least a 3.0 cumulative GPA (on a 4.0 scale) for the last 60 credit hours of undergraduate work. Applicants need to submit an application, a $50 application fee, a personal statement, and two letters of recommendation. GRE scores are recommended, and international students must submit TOEFL scores. Applications should be received by February 1 to be considered for priority financial aid.

Correspondence and Information

To contact faculty members and for specific program information:

Department of Mathematics and Statistics
College of Arts and Sciences
American University
4400 Massachusetts Avenue, NW
Washington, D.C. 20016-8050

Telephone: 202-885-3120
E-mail: mathstat@american.edu
World Wide Web: http://www.american.edu/
    academic.depts/cas/~mathstat/

For an application and University catalog:

Graduate Admissions Office
American University
4400 Massachusetts Avenue, NW
Washington, D.C. 20016-8001

Telephone: 202-885-6000
E-mail: afa@america.edu

American University

THE FACULTY AND THEIR RESEARCH

Austin M. Barron, Associate Professor; Ph.D., Purdue. Decision theory, nonparametric statistics.
Stephen D. Casey, Associate Professor; Ph.D., Maryland. Harmonic and complex analysis, geometry.
I-Lok Chang, Associate Professor; Ph.D., Cornell. Complex variables, numerical analysis.
Mary Christman, Assistant Professor; Ph.D., George Washington. Sequential estimation, sampling, biometry.
Olga Cordero-Braña, Assistant Professor; Ph.D., Utah. Clustering methods classification, mixture models, robust methods.
Lawrence Crone, Associate Professor; Ph.D., Catholic University. Complex analysis and function theory, computer graphics.
David S. Crosby, Professor; Ph.D., Arizona. Probability, meteorology, environmental statistics.
Ali Enayat, Associate Professor; Ph.D., Wisconsin. Mathematical logic, set theory, model theory.
Nancy Flournoy, Professor; Ph.D., Washington (Seattle). Biostatistics, response-driven experimental designs.
Mary W. Gray, Professor; Ph.D., Kansas; J.D., American. Algebra, statistics and the law, regulatory statistics, computer law.
Jeffrey Hakim, Associate Professor; Ph.D., Columbia. Number theory, harmonic analysis.
Richard Holzsager, Professor; Ph.D., Harvard. Concurrent language design, statistical computing, algebraic topology.
Robert W. Jernigan, Professor; Ph.D., South Florida. Statistical computing, mathematical ecology and evolution, environmental statistics.
Dan Kalman, Assistant Professor; Ph.D., Wisconsin. Numerical analysis, linear algebra, mathematics education.
Nathan Mantel, Research Professor; M.S., American. Biometrics, biostatistics, cancer research.
John P. Nolan, Associate Professor; Ph.D., Virginia. Probability theory, stochastic process, genetics.
Scott Parker, Professor; Ph.D., Columbia. Scaling, nonparametric methods, statistical applications to social science research.
Hanna Sandler, Associate Professor; Ph.D., Columbia. Hyperbolic geometry and complex analysis.
Virginia Stallings, Associate Professor and Chair; Ph.D., Southern Mississippi. Mathematics education.

Instructors
Katie Ambruso, Ph.D. candidate (math education), American.
Mary Donahue, Ph.D. candidate (math education), American.
Katia Foret, Ph.D. candidate (math education), American.
Hasan Hamdan, Ph.D. candidate (statistics), American.

Distinguished Adjunct Professors
T. Hoy Booker, Ph.D., American. Retired Assistant Professor, Gallaudet University.
William Lese Jr., Ph.D., Delaware. Retired Scientific and Technical Advisor for United States Central Command.
Eugene Mignogna, Ph.D., American. Senior Vice President, Analytic Services Inc., Arlington, Virginia.
Richard Morris, M.S., Texas Tech. Branch Chief of Technology, McDonnell Douglas Aerospace, Arlington, Virginia.
James Mosimann, M.S., Johns Hopkins. Office of Scientific Integrity, National Institutes of Health.
Antoinette Rizzi, J.D., George Washington. National Law Center, private practice.
John Sullivan, M.S., Naval Postgraduate School. Vice President of RVJ International, Inc., Arlington, Virginia.

Recent Doctoral Dissertations in Mathematics Education
"A Comparison of Problem-Solving Abilities Between Reform Calculus Students and Traditional Calculus Students," Maria Brunett.
"The Effects of Student Self-Assessment on Academic Performance and Students' Attitudes in College Mathematics," Carol Tascione.
"A Comparison of Male and Female Students' Mathematics Course Work and How It Affects Their Income," Maureen McShea.
"Quality Control in Education," Charles Pierre.
"An Investigation of the Behavior of Calculus Students Work Collaborative in an InterActive Software Environment," Angela Hare.

Recent Doctoral Dissertations in Statistics
"Sequential Designs for Opposing Failure Functions," Wenpu Li.
"The Geometric Up-and-Down Design," Misrak Gezmu.
"Approximation of Multivariate Stable Densities," Husein Abdul-Hamid.
"Robustness of Bioequivalence Procedures Under Box-Cox Alternatives," Weizheng Xiao.
"Influence on Smoothness in Penalized Likelihood Regression for Binary Data," Julie O'Connell.
"Distribution of Errors and Methods of Inference for Automated DNA Sequencing," Gregory Alexander.

Recent Master's Projects in Statistics
"Genetic Data Analysis: DNA Profiling" and "Markov Chains in Neural Networks," Robert Baran.
"Time Series Analysis," Hippolyte Fofack.
"Comparing Methods for the Analysis of Longitudinal Data of Richard Jones with Nan Daird and Jin Ware," Marlar Phyer.
"Statistical Methods Used for Testing Periodicity of Extinction in the Geologic Past," Elena Randou.
"A Study of Ratio Estimators From a Systematic Sample," Hasan Hamdan.
"Development of an Alternate Market Composite Index Through Adaptive Sampling of Securities on the American Stock Exchange," Kenton Davis.
"Forecasting Turning Points in Economic Time Series Data," Susan Popowitz.
"Random Algorithms," Fairouz Makhlouf.

Recent Master's Project in Statistical Computing
"Poverty Measurements and Computation," Shaohua Chen.

Recent Master's Projects in Mathematics
"Ramsey's Theorem and a Combinatorial Approach to Determining Bounds for Ramsey Numbers," Blair Jones.
"A Look at Coding Theory," Betsy Andersen.
"X + Y = Z — Q.E.D.?: A Discussion of Fermat's Last Theorem," John Beyers.
"Using Permutation Polynomials in Cryptography," Katia Foret.
"Multichannel Deconvolution: A Computational Study," Matthew Fivash.
"Multidimensional Shannon Sampling," Chris Organ.

Senior graduate students and Professor Nancy Flournoy (far right) gather around guest speakers Professor E. Lehmann and J. Shaffer (front center) after a student colloquium.

ARIZONA STATE UNIVERSITY

Department of Mathematics

Programs of Study

The Department of Mathematics offers graduate study leading to the Ph.D. and the M.A. degrees in many areas of mathematics. In particular, the department has strengths in algebra, analysis, computational mathematics, control and system science, differential equations, discrete mathematics, dynamical systems and chaos, mathematical biology, mathematics education, number theory, and statistics.

The Ph.D. program is intended for the student with superior mathematical ability and emphasizes the development of creative scholarship and breadth and depth in background knowledge. A doctoral student must take certain advanced courses during his or her first year and take two qualifying examinations. After successful completion of the qualifying examinations, each student must take written and oral comprehensive exams covering more advanced material. A reading knowledge of a foreign language is also required. After the examinations are passed, a dissertation that constitutes an original contribution to the discipline must be written.

The master's program offers students with a bachelor's degree in mathematics or related fields an opportunity to broaden their knowledge by undertaking course work at the graduate level. A master's degree student must pass two written examinations and complete a thesis. Precise requirements differ as to the area of study. Written examinations for the master's and Ph.D. programs are highly integrated. Exams passed at the appropriate level in the master's program may fulfill Ph.D. examination requirements.

The department also participates in the Master of Science degree in statistics and the Master of Natural Science (M.N.S.) degree for interdisciplinary study, for which a thesis is not required. In collaboration with the College of Education, the Department of Mathematics offers a new option for the M.N.S. that leads to high school certification.

Research Facilities

There are 59 faculty members in the department, and their research interests cover most aspects of mathematics, including education. The Daniel E. Noble Science Library, a member of the Center for Research Libraries, has a very good holding of mathematical texts and journals; its operations are fully computerized to aid in literature searches.

The central Computing Services facilities are offered at no charge to the University community for use in academic pursuits. The department has an advanced computing facility built around a network of high-performance UNIX workstations (HP, Sun, and Silicon Graphics) that feature state-of-the-art graphics and numerous scientific packages. The University also has several clusters of high-performance UNIX workstations, a Silicon Graphics Power Challenge Supercomputer with six processors, and access to electronic mail for all students.

Financial Aid

Financial assistance for graduate students is available through teaching and research assistantships. The department also has a few in-state and out-of-state tuition waivers available. Currently, seventy teaching assistantships are assigned each semester. Research assistantships are usually reserved for advanced students. Teaching and research assistants must enroll for a minimum of 6 semester hours of graduate credit their first semester, and 9 semester hours each subsequent semester. They receive scholarships covering nonresident tuition but must pay the usual registration fee each semester. A Ph.D. student may expect to be supported for up to five years, a master's degree student for up to five semesters. Effective January 1, 1999, the assistantship stipend for the academic year is $14,650 for an entry-level doctoral student and $13,650 for a master's student.

Cost of Study

Arizona residents registered for 7 or more semester hours are considered full-time students for fee payment purposes and pay registration and tuition fees of $1044 per semester in 1999–2000. Out-of-state students pay an additional $377 per credit hour. Part-time students (6 hours or fewer) pay $110 per credit hour (in-state students) or $487 per credit hour (out-of-state students).

Living and Housing Costs

The room and board charges for University housing, available for graduate students, range between $2830 and $3455 per year. A large number of privately owned apartments are available in the community. Students living off campus typically pay between $500 and $700 per month for food and rent. The University Residence Life Office can supply additional information.

Student Group

The University currently has more than 1,913 faculty members and 45,463 students, of whom 10,604 are graduate students. There are 100 students enrolled in the graduate programs offered by the Department of Mathematics.

Location

The state of Arizona is famous worldwide for its great natural beauty, from Monument Valley and the Grand Canyon in the north to the Sonoran Desert in the south. The University is centrally located in Tempe, one of several neighboring cities occupying the wide expanse of the Salt River Valley (known locally as the Valley of the Sun). The population of Tempe is close to 150,000, and the city combines the advantages of a moderate-sized, university-oriented community with the cultural and technical resources of a major metropolitan area. Phoenix is home to major electronics and aerospace industries, to the mutual benefit of the company and the University.

The University

Arizona State University was founded in 1885 as a training college for teachers in what was then the sparsely populated Arizona Territory. Following the rapid growth of the Phoenix metropolitan area, the institution became Arizona State College in 1945 and Arizona State University in 1958. In 1994, the University gained Research I status.

The University is noted for its attractive campus. There are extensive recreational facilities, and the University offers both a rich cultural heritage and a diverse student population.

Applying

Application forms for admission and financial support, as well as additional information about the department and its programs, can be obtained from the address given below. All applicants must submit a completed application form and transcripts of academic records to the Graduate College of the University. GRE General Test scores are required. They must also submit to the graduate secretary of the Department of Mathematics at least three letters of recommendation from persons who are familiar with their qualifications to pursue graduate study in mathematics. Application materials may be submitted at any time. To be considered for teaching assistantships, applications must be received by March 1. Late applicants will be considered only if there are vacancies.

Correspondence and Information

Dr. Dieter Armbruster
Director of Graduate Studies
Department of Mathematics
Arizona State University
Tempe, Arizona 85287-1804

Telephone: 602-965-3951
E-mail: grad@math.la.asu.edu
World Wide Web: http://math.la.asu.edu/

Arizona State University

THE FACULTY AND THEIR RESEARCH

Dieter Armbruster, Professor; Ph.D., Tübingen (Germany), 1984. Bifurcations, dynamical systems.
Steven Baer, Associate Professor; Ph.D., Illinois at Chicago, 1984. Bifurcation analysis, numerical methods, neurobiology.
Hélène Barcelo, Associate Professor; Ph.D., California, San Diego, 1988. Algebraic combinatorics.
Douglas Blount, Associate Professor; Ph.D., Wisconsin–Madison, 1987. Probability theory.
Andrew Bremner, Professor; Ph.D., Cambridge, 1978. Number theory.
Joaquin Bustoz, Professor; Ph.D., Arizona State, 1967. Classical analysis.
Marilyn P. Carlson, Assistant Professor; Ph.D., Kansas, 1995. Mathematics education.
Nancy Childress, Assistant Professor; Ph.D., Ohio State, 1985. Number theory, arithmetic geometry.
Andrzej Czygrinow, Assistant Professor; Ph.D., Emory, 1998. Discrete mathematics.
Michael Driscoll, Associate Professor; Ph.D., Arizona, 1971. Statistics.
Genghua Fan, Associate Professor; Ph.D., Waterloo, 1988. Graph theory.
Frank D. Farmer, Associate Professor; Ph.D., Washington (Seattle), 1970. Combinatorial algebraic topology.
Alan Feldstein, Professor; Ph.D., UCLA, 1964. Numerical analysis, computer science, applied mathematics.
Carl Gardner, Associate Professor; Ph.D., MIT, 1981. Computational fluid dynamics, semiconductor analysis and simulation.
Anne Gelb, Assistant Professor; Ph.D., Brown, 1996. Numerical analysis.
Matthew J. Hassett, Associate Professor; Ph.D., Rutgers, 1966. Mathematics of finance.
Jon Helton, Professor; Ph.D., Texas at Austin, 1970. Analysis, summability, application of mathematics to the biological sciences.
Frank C. Hoppensteadt, Professor; Ph.D., Wisconsin–Madison, 1965. Differential equations, mathematical biology.
Glenn Hurlbert, Associate Professor; Ph.D., Rutgers, 1990. Discrete mathematics.
Edwin Ihrig, Professor; Ph.D., Toronto, 1974. General relativity.
Zdzislaw Jackiewicz, Professor; Ph.D., Gdansk (Poland), 1980. Numerical analysis.
Don Jones, Assistant Professor; Ph.D., California, Irvine, 1992. Partial differential equations.
John Jones, Associate Professor; Ph.D., Harvard, 1987. Arithmetic geometry, Iwasawa theory.
Kevin Kadell, Professor; Ph.D., Penn State, 1979. Algebraic combinatorics, classical analysis.
Steven Kaliszewski, Assistant Professor; Ph.D., Dartmouth, 1994. Operator algebras.
Matthias Kawski, Professor; Ph.D., Colorado at Boulder, 1986. Control theory, differential geometry, analysis.
Henry Kierstead, Professor; Ph.D., California, San Diego, 1979. Discrete mathematics.
Eric Kostelich, Associate Professor; Ph.D., Maryland, 1985. Differential equations, dynamical systems.
Yang Kuang, Associate Professor; Ph.D., Alberta, 1988. Dynamical systems, mathematical biology, differential equations.
Hendrik Kuiper, Professor; Ph.D., Wisconsin–Madison, 1971. Partial differential equations, numerical analysis.
Lynn Kurtz, Associate Professor; Ph.D., Utah, 1964. Functional analysis.
Philip Leonard, Professor; Ph.D., Penn State, 1968. Algebra, number theory.
Sharon Lohr, Associate Professor; Ph.D., Wisconsin–Madison, 1987. Statistics.
Juan Lopez, Associate Professor; Ph.D., Monash (Australia), 1985. Computational mathematics, fluid dynamics.
Alex Mahalov, Assistant Professor; Ph.D., Cornell, 1991. Applied mathematics, fluid dynamics.
Joan H. McCarter, Associate Professor; M.A., Arizona, 1958. Mathematics education.
John McDonald, Professor; Ph.D., Rutgers, 1969. Convexity, complex analysis.
Hans Mittelmann, Professor; Ph.D., Darmstadt (Germany), 1973. Numerical analysis, scientific computing.
J. Douglas Moore, Associate Professor; Ph.D., Syracuse, 1969. Algebra, automata theory.
Basil Nicolaenko, Professor; Ph.D., Michigan, 1968. Nonlinear partial differential equations, infinite dimensional dynamical systems.
Sergey Nikitin, Assistant Professor; Ph.D., Moscow, 1987. Control theory, dynamical systems.
Kathryn Prewitt, Assistant Professor; Ph.D., California, Davis, 1991. Statistics.
John Quigg, Associate Professor; Ph.D., Drexel, 1979. Operator algebras.
Rosemary Renaut, Professor; Ph.D., Cambridge, 1985. Numerical analysis, computational mathematics.
Christian Ringhofer, Professor; Ph.D., Vienna, 1981. Numerical analysis.
Hal Smith, Professor; Ph.D., Iowa, 1976. Differential equations, dynamical systems, mathematical biology.
Harvey Smith, Professor; Ph.D., Pennsylvania, 1964. Functional analysis, mathematical modeling.
John Spielberg, Associate Professor; Ph.D., Berkeley, 1985. Operator algebras.
Sergei Suslov, Assistant Professor; Ph.D., Kurchatov Institute (Moscow), 1986. Classical analysis, mathematical physics.
Alvin Swimmer, Associate Professor; Ph.D., Berkeley, 1963. Geometry, tensor analysis, Grassmann algebra, geometric design.
Tom Taylor, Associate Professor; Ph.D., Harvard, 1983. Nonlinear control theory, stochastic processes, filtering, dynamical systems.
Horst Thieme, Professor; Ph.D., Münster (Germany), 1976. Differential equations, mathematical modeling.
William Trotter, Regents Professor; Ph.D., Alabama, 1969. Combinatorics, graph theory.
James Turner, Associate Professor; Ph.D., Carnegie-Mellon, 1986. Computational math.
Neil Weiss, Professor; Ph.D., UCLA, 1970. Probability theory, statistics and probability education.
Bruno Welfert, Associate Professor; Ph.D., California, San Diego, 1990. Numerical analysis.
Dennis L. Young, Professor; Ph.D., Purdue, 1970. Statistics.
Michelle Zandieh, Assistant Professor; Ph.D., Oregon, 1997. Mathematics education.
Yijun Zuo, Assistant Professor; Ph.D., Texas at Dallas, 1998. Statistics.

Recent Doctoral Dissertations

"On Path Decompositions of Graphs." Lirong Yan (Adviser: Genghua Fan). 1998
"Robust Multivariate Analysis: Principal Components Analysis and Discriminant Analysis." Kang Hong (Adviser: Dennis Young). 1998
"A Finite Element Solver for the Navier-Stokes Equations using a Preconditioned Adaptive BiCGstab(L) Method." Leigh J. Little (Advisers: Hans Mittelmann and Bruno Welfert). 1998
"The Dynamics of Queues of Re-entrant Manufacturing Systems." Ivonne Diaz Rivera (Adviser: Dieter Armbruster). 1997
"Characterization of Non-Uniformly Spaced Discrete-Time Signals from Their Fourier Phase." Andrew Siefker (Adviser: John McDonald). 1997
"Actions of Inverse Semigroups in C*-Algebras." Nandor Sieben (Adviser: John Quigg). 1997
"Nonlinear Parabolic Systems and Attractions." Dung Le (Advisers: Hendrik Kuiper and Basil Nicolaenko). 1997
"Numerical Methods for Problems in Computational Aeroacoustics." Jodi Mead (Adviser: Rosemary Renaut). 1998
"Theoretical and Numerical Evaluation of Convergence Acceleration for the Stokes Problem." Xiaohong Ding (Adviser: Rosemary Renaut). 1998
"Analysis of Chemo-Stat Models with Distinct Removal Rates." Bingtuan Li (Adviser: Yang Kuang). 1998

Recent Master's Theses

"Some New Z-cyclic Triplewhist Tournaments." Lauree Attinger (Adviser: Philip Leonard). 1998
"On the Stability of Reentrant Manufacturing Systems." Danielle Hanson (Adviser: Tom Taylor). 1998
"Relaxation Oscillators and Bursters Coupled to Passive Cables." Katherine Zaremba (Adviser: Steve Baer). 1998
"Effects of Random Motility on Steady State Concentrations of a Microbial Population in a Flow Reactor." Anthony Smith (Adviser: Hal Smith). 1998
"Dynamo Action Forced by Periodic Velocity Fields." Mark Nelson (Adviser: Dieter Armbruster). 1998
"Single Resource Plant Competition." Christian Miller (Adviser: Hal Smith). 1998
"A Survey of Techniques in Cryptanalysis." Brandon Baldock (Adviser: John Jones). 1998
"Modeling and Control of a Polluted Water Environment with a Single Population." Natalia Navarova (Adviser: Horst Thieme). 1998
"Modularity in the Lattice of F_4." Mariana Maris (Adviser: Helene Barcelo). 1997

Recent Applied Projects in Statistics

"Kmenta and Maximum Likelihood Cross-Sectional Pooling with Time Series: Asymptotic Results and Small-Sample Comparisons." Liming Chen (Adviser: Sharon Lohr). 1998
"An Overview of Random Number Generation." Xiaowen Liao (Adviser: Michael F. Driscoll). 1997
"Sorting and Shading Proximity Matrices." Jon K. Ruterman (Adviser: Michael F. Driscoll). 1996
"Robust Analysis of Variance: High Breakdown F Tests in the One-Way ANOVA Model." Jackie Hui (Adviser: Dennis Young). 1996

SELECTED PUBLICATIONS

Oprea, I., P. Chossat, and **D. Armbruster.** Simulating the kinematic dynamo forced by heteroclinic convective velocity fields. *Theor. Comp. Fluid Dynamics* 9(314):293–309, 1997.

Armbruster, D., A. Palacios, E. J. Kostelich, and E. Stone. Analyzing the dynamics of cellular flames. *Physica D* 132–61, 1996.

Wu, H.-Y., and **S. M. Baer.** Analysis of an excitable dendritic spine with an activity-dependent stem conductance. *J. Math. Biol.* 36:569–92, 1998.

Baer, S. M., J. Rinzel, and H. Carrillo. Analysis of an autonomous phase model for neuronal parabolic bursting. *J. Math. Biol.* 33:309–33, 1995.

Barcelo, H., and **E. Ihrig.** Modular elements in the lattice L(A) when A is a real reflection arrangement. Discrete Math. 193:61–8, 1998.

Barcelo, H., and A. Goupil. Nonbroken circuits of reflection groups and their factorization in D_n. *Israel J. of Math.* 91(1–3):285–306, 1995.

Bremner, A. Some special curves of genus 5. *Acta Arithmetica* LXXIX.1:41–51, 1997.

Bremner, A. Some interesting curves of genus 2 to 7. *J. Number Theory* 67:277–90, 1997.

Bustoz, J., and **S. K. Suslov.** Basic analog of Fourier Series on a q-quadratic grid. *Methods Appl. Anal.* 5(1):1–38, 1998.

Childress, N., and D. Grant. Formal groups of twisted multiplative groups and L-series. *Proc. Symp. Pure Math.* 58.2:89–102, 1995.

Childress, N. λ-invariants and Γ-transforms. *Manu. Math.* 64:359–75, 1989.

Driscoll, M. F., and B. Krasnicka. An accessible proof of Craig's theorem in the general case. *Am. Stat.* 49:59–62, 1995.

Driscoll, M. F. Generalized intraclass matrices and equi-probable orderings. *Sankhya B* 55:103–10, 1993.

Fan, G. Proofs of two minimum circuit cover conjectures. *J. Combinator. Theory Ser. B* 74:353–67, 1998.

Fan, G. Extensions of flow theorems. *J. Combinator. Theory Ser. B* 69:10–24, 1197.

Feldstein, A., and P. Turner. Overflow and underflow in multiplication and division. *Appl. Num. Math.* 21:221–39, 1996.

Feldstein, A., and A. Iserles. Embedding of delay equations into an infinite-dimensional ODE system. *J. Diff. Equat.* 117:127, 1995.

Hoppensteadt, F. *An Introduction to the Mathematics of Neurons: Modeling in the Frequency Domain.* Second Edition. New York: Cambridge University Press, 1997.

Hoppensteadt, F., and E. Izhikevich. *Weakly Connected Neural Networks.* Springer, 1997.

Hurlbert, G., T. Clarke, and R. Hochberg. Pebbling in diameter two graphs and products of paths. *J. Graph Theory* 25:119–28, 1997.

Hurlbert, G., C. Mitchell, and K. Patterson. On the existence of De Bruijn tori with 2X2 windows. *J. Comb. Theor. (A)* 76:213–30, 1996.

Jackiewicz, Z., K. Burrage, and **R. Renaut.** The performance of preconditioned waveform relaxation techniques for pseudospectral methods. *Num. Meth. Partial Diff. Equat.* 12:245–63, 1996.

Jackiewicz, Z., K. Burrage, S. P. Norsett, and **R. Renaut.** Preconditioning waveform relaxation iterations for differential systems. *BIT* 36:54–76, 1996.

Jacobowitz, R., and J. F. Ronderos. Comparative pullout strength of tapped and utapped pilot holes for bicortical anterior certical screws. *Spine* 22:167–70, 1997.

Jacobowitz, R., and P. J. Apostolides. Lumbar discectomy/microdiscectomy: the gold standard. *Clin. Neurosurg.* 43:228–38, 1996.

Jones, D., and S. Shkoller. Persistence of invariant manifolds for nonlinear PDEs. *Stud. Appl. Math.* 102:27–67, 1999.

Jones, D., A. Poje, and L. Margolin. Resolution effects and enslaved finite difference schemes for a double gyre, shallow water model. *J. Theor. Comp. Fluid Dynamics 9:269–80, 1997.*

Jones, J. and D. Roberts. Timing Analysis of Targeted Hunter Searches. *Springer Lecture Notes in Computer Science.* 1423:412–23, 1998.

Jones, J. Plater's p-adic orthogonality relation for Abelian varieties. *Houston J. Math.* 21:261–82, 1995.

Echterhoff, S., **S. Kaliszewski,** and I. Raeburn. Crossed products by dual coactions of groups and homogeneous spaces. *J. Operator. Theory* 39:151–76, 1998.

Kawski, M. Homogeneous stabilizing feedback laws. *Contr. Theory Adv. Tech.* 6:497–516, 1990.

Kawski, M. Control variations with an increasing number of switchings. *Bull. Am. Math. Soc.* 18:149–52, 1988.

Kierstead, H. On-line coloring k-colorable graphs. *Israel J. Math.,* in press.

Kierstead, H., S. G. Penrice, and W. T. Trotter. On-line graph coloring and recursive graph theory. *SIAM J. Discrete Math.* 7:27–89, 1994.

Kostelich, E. J., et al. Unstable dimension variability: A source of nonhyperbolicity in chaotic systems. *Physica D* 109:81–90, 1997.

Kostelich, E. J. The analysis of chaotic time series data. *Syst. Control Lett.* 31:313–9, 1997.

Kuang, Y., and E. Beretta. Global qualitative analysis of a ratio-dependent predator-prey system. *J. Math. Biol.* 36:389–406, 1998.

Cooke, K., **Y. Kuang,** and B. Li. Analysis of an antiviral immune response model with time delays. *Can. Appl. Math. Q.* 6:321–54, 1998.

Kuiper, H., and A. Castro. On the number of radially symmetric solutions to Dirichlet problems with jumping nonlinearities of superlinear order. *TAMS,* in press.

Arizona State University

Selected Publications (continued)

Kuiper, H. Positive invariance and asymptotic stability of solutions to certain Riccati equations. *Dynamics Stability Syst.* 9:331–44, 1994.

Leonard, P., and N. J. Finizio. More ZCPS-Wh(v) and several new infinite classes of Z-cyclic whist tournaments. *Discrete Appl. Math.* 85:193–202, 1998.

Leonard, P. Some new Z-cyclic whist tournaments. *Utilitas Mathematica* 49:223–32, 1996.

Lohr, S. *Sampling: Design and Analysis.* Pacific Grove, CA: Duxbury Press, 1999.

Lohr, S., and M. Divan. A comparison of confidence intervals for variance components with unbalanced data. *J. Stat. Comput. Simul.* 58:83–97, 1997.

Lopez, J. M. Characteristics of endwall and sidewall boundary layers in a rotating cylinder with a differentially rotating endwall. *J. Fluid Mech.* 359:49079, 1998.

Lopez, J. M., and J. Shen. An efficient spectral-projection method for the Navier-Stokes equations in cylindrical geometries. I. Axisymmetric cases. *J. Comput. Phys.* 139:308–26, 1998.

Babin, A., **A. Mahalov,** and **B. Nicolaenko.** Global regularity and integrability of 3D euler and Navier-Stokes equations for uniformly rotating fluids. *Asympt. Anal.* 15(2):103–50, 1997.

Mahalov, A., S. Leibovich, and E. S. Titi. Invariant helical subspaces for the Navier-Stokes equations. *Arch. Ratio. Mech. Anal.* 112:193–222, 1990.

McDonald, J., and N. Weiss. *A Course in Real Analysis.* Academic Press, 1999.

McDonald, J. An extreme absolutely continuous RP-measure. *Proc. Am. Math. Soc.* 109(3):731–8, 1990.

Mittelmann, H. D., and J. P. Berrut. Matrices for the direct determination of the barycentric weights of rational interpolation. *J. Comp. Appl. Math.* 78:355–70, 1997.

Mittelmann, H. D., J. C. Butcher, and Z. Jackiewicz. Nonlinear optimization approach to construction of general linear methods. *J. Comp. Appl. Math.* 81:181–96, 1997.

Nicolaenko, B., A. Babin, and **A. Mahalov.** On the nonlinear baroclinic waves and the adjustment of pancake dynamics in atmospheric flows. *Theor. Comp. Fluid Dynamics* 215–35, 1998.

Nicolaenko, B., A. Eden, C. Foias, and R. Temam. Exponential attractors for dissipative evolution equations, *RAM Series,* vol. 38, New York: John Wiley & Sons, 1994.

Nikitin, S. Control of manufacturing systems with re-entrant lines. *Math. Mod. Meth. Appl. Sci.* 6:195–215, 1996.

Nikitin, S. Decoupling normalizing transformations and local stabilization of nonlinear systems. *Mathematica Bohemica* 121:225–48, 1996.

Quigg, J. Crossed product duality for partial C*-automorphisms. *Rocky Mountain J. Math.* 28:1067–88, 1998.

Quigg, J., and S. Kaliszewski. Imprimitivity for C*-coactions of non-amenable groups. *Math. Proc. Cambridge Philos. Soc.* 123:101–18, 1998.

Quigg, J., S. Kaliszewski, and I. Raeburn. Duality of restriction and induction for C*-coactions. *Trans. Am. Math. Soc.* 349:2085–113, 1997.

Jeltsch, R., **R. A. Renaut,** and J. H. Smit. An accuracy barrier for stable three-time level difference schemes for hyperbolic equations. ETH Research Report #95–01, Seminar für Angewandte Mathematik, Zürich. *IMA J. Numer. Anal.,* 1998.

Renaut, R. A. A parallel multisplitting solution of the least squares problem. *Numer. Linear Alg. Appl.* 4(4), 1:21, 1997.

Smith, H., S. B. Hsu, and P. Waltman. Competitive exclusion and coexistence for competitive systems on ordered Banach spaces. *Trans. Am. Math. Soc.* 348:4083–94, 1996.

Smith, H., and P. Waltman. The theory of the chemostat. Cambridge University Press, 1995.

Spielberg, J., R. J. Archbald, and D. W. B. Somerset. Upper multiplicity and bounded trace ideals in C*-algebras. *J. Functional Anal.* 146:430–63, 1997.

Spielberg, J., and M. Laca. Purely infinite C*-algebras from boundary actions of discrete groups. *J. reine angew. Math.* 480:125–39, 1996.

Suslov, S. K. Multiparameter Ramanujan-type q-beta integrals. *Ramanujan J.* 2(3):351–69, 1998.

Swimmer, A. The completion of Grassmann's Natur-Wissenschaftliche Methode. In *Hermann Günther Graßmann (1809-1877): Visionary Mathematician, Scientist and Neohumanist Scholar,* pp. 265–80, ed. G. Schubring. Amsterdam, the Netherlands: Kluwer Academic Publishers.

Thieme, H. Positive perturbations of dual and integrated semigroups. *Adv. Math. Sci. Appl.* 6:445–507, 1996.

Thieme, H., and C. Castillo-Chavez. How may infection-age-dependent infectivity affect the dynamics of HIV/AIDS? *SIAM J. Appl. Math.* 53:1447–79, 1993.

Zandieh, M. The role of a formal definition in nine students' concept image of derivative. *Proc. Twentieth Annu. Meeting PME-NA (North American Chapter of the International Group for the Psychology of Mathematics Education),* pp. 136–41, 1998.

Zandieh, M. A theoretical framework for analyzing student understanding of the concept of derivative. Research in *Collegiate Mathematics Education, Conference Board of the Mathematical Sciences, Issues in Mathematics Education, American Mathematical Society,* in press.

BOWLING GREEN STATE UNIVERSITY

Department of Mathematics and Statistics

Programs of Study

The Department of Mathematics and Statistics offers a full range of graduate degrees. Degree options at the master's level include the M.A., with concentrations in pure mathematics, scientific computation, and probability and statistics, and the M.S. in applied statistics. The department also offers a Master of Arts in Teaching (M.A.T.) in mathematics for those interested in teaching at the secondary level or at two- and four-year colleges. M.A.T. course work is tailored to the individual and may be supplemented by an internship or other field experience. The master's degree programs are two-year programs of study, but well-qualified students can complete a degree in three semesters. All programs are offered with a thesis option and a comprehensive examination option.

The Ph.D. program combines advanced study with individual research; a dissertation consisting of original research is required. Strong research areas include probability and statistics, algebra, analysis, and scientific computation. The research environment is further enhanced by the department's active program of seminars and colloquia. Weekly seminars are conducted in algebra, analysis, mathematics education, scientific computation, and statistics. The department has 26 full-time faculty members, all of whom have Ph.D. degrees. The department hosts several distinguished visiting scholars each year, including a Lukacs Distinguished Professor in Probability and Statistics. In addition to working with advanced graduate students, the Lukacs Professor organizes the Annual Lukacs Symposium, which attracts leading statisticians from around the world.

As part of the department's continuing commitment to quality instruction, all students are given opportunities for a variety of training and mentoring experiences that are designed to enhance their effectiveness both as students and as teachers.

Research Facilities

Faculty member and graduate student offices are located in the Mathematical Sciences Building, which also houses the Frank C. Ogg Science Library and the Scientific Computing Laboratory. The Science Library, in addition to its extensive holdings, maintains subscriptions to approximately 400 journals, both paper and electronic, in mathematics and statistics. Further, the interlibrary OhioLink program provides access to the holdings of all other state-funded university libraries in Ohio. The Scientific Computing Laboratory offers microcomputer access with fast Internet connections and a wealth of software, UNIX/X11 access, and a full-time staff to provide assistance to users. Additional computing resources include a network of UNIX workstations that are maintained by the department and available to students at all times. The University also maintains several systems for student use, including a four-processor SGI Power Challenge, a DEC Alpha 2100 5/250, a DEC Vax 6620, two IBM mainframes, and various graphics workstations. Each graduate student office is furnished with a microcomputer with network access.

Financial Aid

The department provides approximately fifty teaching assistantships, with stipends that range from $9200 to $10,500 for the academic year, and one nonservice fellowship of $13,300 for the calendar year. Instructional and nonresident fees are waived. The department also provides summer support through a variety of fellowships and assistantships that range from $1330 to $2600. In addition, all new students are encouraged to accept Summer Fellowships of $1500 for an initial six-week summer program.

Teaching assistants serve as instructors for small individual classes that consist of about 30 students. This involves five or six contact hours per week with undergraduate students. The University's Statistical Consulting Center also provides consultantships for graduate assistants with appropriate backgrounds. These positions provide valuable experience for those preparing for careers in statistics. The stipends offered by the Statistical Consulting Center are the same amount as those awarded to teaching assistants. For further information, students should consult the department's Web site (address below).

Cost of Study

Tuition and most fees are covered by the assistantship package, except for a one-time admission fee of $15, a registration fee of $8, and a refundable legal services fee of $5. Students are also required to have adequate health insurance, which may be purchased through the University at a nominal fee. Students must purchase their own books and pay any applicable thesis or dissertation fees.

Living and Housing Costs

As a small town, Bowling Green offers a modest cost of living. Most graduate students choose to live off campus. The city of Bowling Green offers a wide variety of rental housing, with prices beginning at $150 and averaging $350 per month. A limited number of rooms in on-campus residence halls are set aside for graduate students.

Student Group

There are currently 50 full-time graduate students in the department. Of these, 25 are international students, 29 are women, 35 are in the master's programs, and 15 are in the Ph.D. program.

Student Outcomes

Bowling Green State University (BGSU) graduates enjoy a very high placement rate. At the Ph.D. level, for instance, 38 students have graduated since 1990; of the 35 respondents to a recent survey of graduates, all report that they are meaningfully employed in academic or industrial research positions.

Location

Bowling Green is a peaceful semirural community in historic northwest Ohio. Founded in 1833, the city's early growth was greatly influenced by the prosperous oil-boom era of the late 1800s, evident today through downtown Bowling Green's stately architecture. Bowling Green is conveniently located on Interstate 75, just 20 miles south of Toledo, Ohio, and 90 miles south of Detroit, Michigan. The average temperature in August is 71.1°F (21.7°C); the average temperature in January is 25.5°F (-3.6°C).

The University

Established in 1910 as a teacher-training college, BGSU attained full university status in 1935 and has since grown into a multidimensional institution that offers approximately 200 different degree programs from the bachelor's through doctoral levels. The intellectual climate—in the University generally and in the department particularly—combines the warmth and collegiality of a liberal arts atmosphere with the resources and opportunities of a research institution.

Applying

The application (for both admission and financial assistance) consists of completed application and financial disclosure forms, which are available by request; a brief personal statement that indicates the applicant's goals and academic interests; three letters of reference; two copies of official transcripts from each institution attended; test scores on the GRE General Test; a $30 check or money order made payable to the Graduate College, Bowling Green State University; and, if the applicant's native language is not English, test scores on the TOEFL or MELAB. The deadline for applications is March 1. Late applications are considered if positions are still available. Full instructions for applying, along with an online application form, can be found at the department's Web site. Application materials may also be requested via e-mail (address below).

Correspondence and Information

Graduate Coordinator
Department of Mathematics and Statistics
Bowling Green State University
Bowling Green, Ohio 43403-0221

Telephone: 419-372-2637
Fax: 419-372-6092
E-mail: carother@bgnet.bgsu.edu
World Wide Web: http://www.bgsu.edu/departments/math/

Bowling Green State University

THE FACULTY AND THEIR RESEARCH

James H. Albert, Professor; Ph.D., Purdue. Mathematical statistics, decision theory, Bayesian analysis.
Curtis Bennett, Associate Professor; Ph.D., Chicago. Algebra, combinatorics.
Josef Blass, Professor; Ph.D., Michigan. Number theory, mathematical modeling.
Neal Carothers, Professor and Chair; Ph.D., Ohio State. Functional analysis, Banach space theory, real analysis.
Kit Chan, Associate Professor; Ph.D., Michigan. Functional analysis, function theory.
Hanfeng Chen, Associate Professor; Ph.D., Wisconsin–Madison. Transformed data analysis, statistical process control, finite mixture models.
So-Hsiang Chou, Professor; Ph.D., Pittsburgh. Numerical analysis, fluid mechanics.
Humphrey S. Fong, Associate Professor; Ph.D., Ohio State. Probability, real analysis.
John T. Gresser, Associate Professor; Ph.D., Wisconsin–Milwaukee. Complex analysis.
Arjun K. Gupta, Distinguished University Professor; Ph.D., Purdue. Multivariate statistical analysis, analysis of categorical data, applied statistics.
John L. Hayden, Professor; Ph.D., Michigan State. Group theory, combinatorics.
Corneliu Hoffman, Assistant Professor; Ph.D., USC. Representations of finite groups, inverse Galois problems.
W. Charles Holland, Distinguished Research Professor; Ph.D., Tulane. Ordered group theory.
Alexander Izzo, Associate Professor; Ph.D., Berkeley. Complex analysis, functional analysis.
Stephen H. McCleary, Professor; Ph.D., Wisconsin. Ordered groups.
David E. Meel, Assistant Professor; Ed.D., Pittsburgh. Mathematics education.
Barbara E. Moses, Associate Professor; Ph.D., Indiana. Mathematics education, problem solving.
Truc T. Nguyen, Professor; Ph.D., Pittsburgh. Mathematical statistics.
Edsel A. Peña, Professor; Ph.D., Florida State. Mathematical statistics, inference in stochastic processes, survival analysis and reliability, nonparametrics.
Steven M. Seubert, Associate Professor and Graduate Coordinator; Ph.D., Virginia. Functional analysis, operator theory.
Sergey Shpectorov, Associate Professor; Ph.D., Moscow State. Groups and geometries.
Tong Sun, Assistant Professor; Ph.D., Texas A&M. Numerical analysis, partial differential equations.
Gábor Székely, Professor; Ph.D., Eötvös Loránd (Budapest). Probability and statistics.
J. Gordon Wade, Associate Professor; Ph.D., Brown. Numerical analysis, inverse problems.
Waldemar C. Weber, Associate Professor; Ph.D., Illinois. Geometry.
Craig L. Zirbel, Assistant Professor; Ph.D., Princeton. Probability, stochastic processes.

Mathematical Sciences Building.

SELECTED PUBLICATIONS

Albert, J. H. Bayesian testing and estimation of association in a two-way contingency table. *J. Am. Stat. Assoc.* 92:685–93, 1997.

Albert, J. H. Bayesian selection of log-linear modes. *Can. J. Stat.* 24:327–47, 1996.

Albert, J. H., and S. Chib. Bayesian residual analysis for binary response regression models. *Biometrika* 82:747–59, 1995.

Bennett, C. D. Twin trees and IL-gons. *Trans. Am. Math. Soc.* 349(5):1305–8, 1997.

Bennett, C. D. Affine L-buildings I. *Proc. London Math. Soc.* 68(3):541–76, 1994.

Bennett, C. D. Imaginary roots of a Kac-Moody lie algebra whose reflections preserve root multiplicities. *J. Algebra* 158(1):244–67, 1993.

Blass, J., P. Blass, and S. Klasa. Alexandre Grothendieck's EGAV; Part VII(a): Axiomatization of some geometric results Part a. *Ulam Q.* 3(1):54–7, 1995.

Blass, J., P. Blass, and J. Kolibal. Open problems: Electronic Scottish Cafe. *Ulam Q.* 2(1), 1993.

Blass, J., P. Blass, and J. Lary. Some questions on unique factorization. *Ulam Q.* 2(1), 1993.

Carothers, N. L., S. Dilworth, and D. Sobecki. Splittings of Banach spaces induced by Clifford algebras. *Proc. Am. Math. Soc.,* in press.

Carothers, N. L. *Real Analysis.* New York: Cambridge University Press, in press.

Carothers, N. L., S. Dilworth, and C. Lennard. On a localization of the UKK property. In *Proceedings of the International Conference on the Interaction Between Functional Analysis, Harmonic Analysis and Probability Theory.* New York: Marcel Dekker, 1995.

Chan, K. Hypercyclicity of the operator algebra for a separable Hilbert space. *J. Operator Theory,* in press.

Chan, K., and Z. Cuckovic. C*-algebras generated by a subnormal operator. *Trans. Am. Math. Soc.* 351:1445–60, 1999.

Chan, K., and **S. M. Seubert.** Reducing subspaces of compressed analytic Toeplitz operators on the Hardy space. H_2 *Integral Equations Operator Theory* 28:147–57, 1997.

Al-Amiri, H., and **K. Chan** et al. (**J. Gresser** and **S. Seubert**). Integral operators on certain subclasses of univalent functions. *Rev. Roum. Math. Pures Appl.* 40:339–48, 1995.

Al-Amiri, H., and **K. Chan** et al. (**J. Gresser** and **S. Seubert**). Starlikeness of certain analytic functions. *Math. Cluj* 36:73–9, 1994.

Chen, H. Asymptotic analysis of a class of process capability indices. *Statistics* 30:149–62, 1997.

Chen, H., and S. Kotz. An asymptotic distribution of Wright's capability index sensitive to skewness. *J. Stat. Comput. Sim.* 55:147–58, 1996.

Chen, H. Tests following transformations. *Ann. Stat.* 23(5):1587–93, 1995.

Chou, S.-H., D. Y. Kwak, and P. S. Vassilevski. Mixed covolume methods for elliptic problems on triangular grids. *SIAM J. Numerical Anal.* 35(5):1850–1861, 1998.

Chou, S.-H., and D. Y. Kwak. A covolume method based on rotated bilinears for the generalized Stokes problem. *SIAM J. Numerical Anal.* 35(2):497–507, 1998.

Chou, S.-H. Analysis and convergence of a covolume method for the generalized Stokes problem. *Math. Comput.* 217(66):85–104, 1997.

Gresser, J. *A Maple Approach to Calculus.* Englewood Cliffs, N.J.: Prentice Hall Publishing Company, 1998.

Gupta, A. K., T. T. Nguyen, and W. B. Zeng. Characterization of multivariate distributions through a functional equation of their characteristic functions. *J. Stat. Plann. Inference* 63:187–201, 1997.

Chen, J., and **A. K. Gupta.** Testing and locating variance change points with applications to stochastic prices. *J. Am. Stat. Assoc.* 92:739–42, 1997.

Gupta, A. K., and D. Song. Characterization of p-generalized normality. *J. Multivariate Anal.* 60:61–71, 1997.

Gupta, A. K., and D. Song, L_p-norm uniform distribution. *Proc. Am. Math. Soc.* 125:595–601, 1997.

Hayden, J. L. Generalized Hadamard matrices. *Designs Codes Cryptogr.* 12:69–73, 1997.

Dey, P., and **J. L. Hayden.** On symmetric incidence matrices of projective planes. *Designs Codes Cryptogr.* 6:179–88, 1995.

Hayden, J. L., and T. VanAken. Character theory and idempotents in affine difference sets. *Congressus Numerantium* 12:185–90, 1995.

Holland, W. C. Varieties and universal words for automorphism groups of orders. In *Advances in Algebra and Model Theory,* pp. 135–47, eds. M. Droste and R. Göbel. Amsterdam: Gordon and Breach Science Publishers, 1997.

Holland, W. C., and N. Ya. Medvedev. A very large class of small varieties of lattice-ordered groups. *Commun. Algebra* 22(2):551–78, 1994.

Holland, W. C. Partial orders of the group of automorphisms of the real line: Proceedings of the Malcev Conference, Novosibirsk 1989. *Contemp. Math.* 131(1):197–207, 1992.

Izzo, A. A characterization of C(K) among the uniform algebras containing A(K). *Indiana University Math. J.* 46:771–88, 1997.

Izzo, A. Failure of polynomial approximation on polynomially convex subsets of the sphere. *Bull. London Math. Soc.* 28:393–7, 1996.

Izzo, A. Uniform algebras generated by holomorphic and pluriharmonic functions on strictly pseudoconvex domains. *Pacific J. Math.* 171:429–36, 1995.

Ball, R., and **S. H. McCleary.** Tyings in lattice-ordered permutation groups. *Algebra Universalis* 37:24–69, 1997.

Ball, R., and **S. H. McCleary.** The closure of a lattice-ordered permutation group. *Algebra Universalis* 37:342–73, 1997.

Darnel, M., M. Giraudet, and **S. H. McCleary.** Uniqueness of the group operation on the lattice of order-automorphisms of the real line. *Algebra Universalis* 33:419–27, 1995.

Meel, D. E. Honor students' calculus understandings: Comparing Calculus and Mathematica and traditional calculus students. In *Research in Collegiate Mathematics Education III,* pp. 163–215, eds. A. H. Schoenfeld, J. Kaput, and E. Dubinsky. Providence, R.I.: American Mathematical Society, 1998.

Meel, D. E. Calculator-available assessments: The why, what, and how. *Educ. Assess.* 4(3):149–75, 1997.

Meel, D. E. A mis-generalization in calculus: Searching for the origins. In *Proceedings of the Nineteenth Annual Meeting of the North American Chapter of the International Group for the Psychology of Mathematics Education,* pp. 23–9, eds. J. A. Dossey, J. O. Swafford, M. Parmantie, and A. E. Dossey. Columbus, Ohio: ERIC Clearinghouse for Science, Mathematics, and Environmental Education, 1997.

Moses, B. E. Beyond problem solving: Problem posing. In *Problem Posing: Reflections and Applications,* eds. S. Brown and M. Walter. Mahwah, N.J.: Lawrence Erlbaum Associates, 1993.

Moses, B. E. IDEAS: Mathematics and music. *Arithmetic Teacher* 40(4):215–25, 1992.

Moses, B. E. Developing spatial thinking in the middle grades. *Arithmetic Teacher* 37(6):59–63, 1990.

Nguyen, T. T. Characterization of normal distributions supporting goodness-of-fit tests based on sample skewness and sample kurtosis. *Metrika* 48:21–30, 1998.

Nguyen, T. T. Conditional distributions and characterizations of multivariate stable distribution. *J. Multivariate Anal.* 53:181–93, 1995.

Peña, E. A. Smooth goodness-of-fit tests for composite hypothesis in hazard-based models. *Ann. Stat.* 26:1935–71, 1998.

Peña, E. A. Smooth goodness-of-fit tests for the baseline hazard in Cox's proportional hazards model. *J. Am. Stat. Assoc.* 93:673–92, 1998.

Baltazar-Aban, I., and **E. A. Peña.** Properties of hazard-based residuals and implication in model diagnosis. *J. Am. Stat. Assoc.* 90:185–97, 1995.

Cheng, R., and **S. M. Seubert.** Weakly outer polynomials. *Mich. J. Math.* 41:235–46, 1994.

Bowling Green State University

Selected Publications (continued)

Ivanov, A., and **S. Shpectorov.** The universal non-abelian representation of the Peterson type geometry related to J-4. *J. Algebra* 191:541–67, 1997.

Ivanov, A., D. Pasechnik, and **S. Shpectorov.** Non-abelian embeddings of some sporadic geometries. *J. Algebra* 181:523–57, 1996.

Del Fra, A., A. Pasini, and **S. Shpectorov.** Geometries with bi-affine and bi-linear diagrams. *Eur. J. Combinatorics* 16:439–59, 1995.

Rao, C. R., and **G. Székely.** *Statistics for the 21st Century.* New York: Dekker, 1999.

Székely, G. *Contests in Higher Mathematics,* pp. 1–570. New York: Springer, 1996.

Ruzsa, I. Z., and **G. Székely.** *Algebraic Probability Theory.* New York: Wiley, 1988.

Filippova, D. V., and **J. G. Wade.** A preconditioner for regularized inverse problems. *SIAM J. Sci. Computation,* in press.

Wade, J. G., and P. S. Vassilevski. A comparison of multilevel methods for total variation regularization. *Elec. Trans. Numerical Anal.* 6:225–70, 1997.

Wade, J. G., and C. R. Vogel. Analysis of costate discretizations in parameter estimation for linear evolution equations. *SIAM J. Control Optimization* 33(1):227–54, 1995.

Zirbel, C. L. Translation and dispersion of mass by isotropic Brownian flows. *Stochastic Processes Appl.* 70:1–29, 1997.

Zirbel, C. L. Mean occupation times of continuous one-dimensional Markov processes. *Stochastic Processes Appl.* 69:161–78, 1997.

Cinlar, E., and **C. L. Zirbel.** Dispersion of particle systems in Brownian flows. *Adv. Appl. Probability* 28:53–74, 1996.

BROWN UNIVERSITY

Division of Applied Mathematics

Programs of Study	The Division of Applied Mathematics offers graduate programs leading to the Ph.D. and Sc.M. degrees.
	The emphasis of the Ph.D. program is on both thesis research and obtaining a solid foundation for future work. Course programs are designed to suit each individual's needs. Admission to Ph.D. candidacy is based on a preliminary examination designed individually for each student in light of his or her interests. Research interests of the faculty can be gauged from the list on the reverse of this page and include partial differential equations and dynamical systems, control theory (including stochastic control), probability and statistics, numerical analysis and scientific computation, continuum and fluid mechanics, computer vision, image reconstruction and speech recognition, and pattern theory. A wide spectrum of graduate courses is offered, reflecting the broad interests of the faculty in the different areas of applied mathematics. Relevant courses are also offered by the Departments of Mathematics, Physics, Computer Sciences, Economics, Geological Sciences, Linguistics, and Psychology and the Divisions of Engineering and of Biology and Medicine.
	The Sc.M. program does not require a thesis, and students with sound preparation usually complete it in one year.
Research Facilities	The University's science library houses an outstanding collection in mathematics and its applications. The Computer Center is equipped with an IBM mainframe computer, and the University maintains access to supercomputer installations and other facilities. Within the Division, the Center for Intelligent Control Systems maintains computing and imaging equipment, and the Center for Fluid Mechanics, Turbulence and Computation has a network of Sun and SGI workstations with equipment for video recording and a state-of-the-art IBM SP2 parallel computer with twenty-four processors. All computer systems on campus are interconnected by a high-speed network.
Financial Aid	Fellowships, scholarships, and research and teaching assistantships, which cover tuition and living expenses, are available for qualified full-time graduate students. Exceptional candidates receive guaranteed support for four years, provided that they make satisfactory progress toward the degree. Summer support can usually be arranged.
Cost of Study	Tuition fees for full-time students are $24,624 per year in 1999–2000. Teaching assistants and research assistants are not charged for tuition.
Living and Housing Costs	The cost of living in Providence is somewhat lower than the national average. Housing for graduate students in Miller Hall is available at $4470 for the 1999–2000 academic year. Numerous off-campus apartments are available for students to rent.
Student Group	Brown University has approximately 5,600 undergraduates and 1,300 graduate students. The Division of Applied Mathematics has about 50 full-time graduate students, of whom about 40 receive financial support from the University. A number of other students hold outside fellowships.
Location	Brown University is located on a hill overlooking Providence, the capital of Rhode Island and one of America's oldest cities. The proximity of Providence to the excellent beaches and ocean ports of Rhode Island and Massachusetts provides considerable recreational opportunities. Numerous nearby ski facilities are available for winter recreation. The libraries, theaters, museums, and historic sites in Providence and Newport offer an abundance of cultural resources. In addition, Providence is only an hour from Boston and 4 hours from New York City by auto or train.
The University and The Division	Brown University was founded in 1764 in Warren, Rhode Island, as Rhode Island College. It is the seventh-oldest college in America and the third-oldest in New England. In 1770, the College was moved to College Hill, high above the city of Providence, where it has remained ever since. The name was changed to Brown University in 1804 in honor of Nicholas Brown, son of one of the founders of the College. The University awarded its first Doctor of Philosophy degree in 1889. The University attracts many distinguished lecturers both in the sciences and in the arts. Brown is a member of the Ivy League and participates in all intercollegiate sports.
	Brown has the oldest tradition and one of the strongest programs in applied mathematics of all universities in the country. Based on a wartime program instituted in 1942, the Division of Applied Mathematics at Brown was established in 1946 as a center of graduate education and fundamental research. It includes several research centers, has cooperative programs with many other universities, and attracts many scientific visitors.
Applying	Applications for admission to the Graduate School and for financial aid may be obtained by writing directly to the Admissions Office, Graduate School. The bulletin of the Graduate School may also be requested from the Admissions Office.
Correspondence and Information	Professor Chi-Wang Shu, Chair Division of Applied Mathematics Brown University Providence, Rhode Island 02912

Brown University

THE FACULTY AND THEIR RESEARCH

Frederic E. Bisshopp, Professor of Applied Mathematics; Ph.D., Chicago. Asymptotics, nonlinear wave propagation, fluid mechanics.

Constantine M. Dafermos, Professor of Applied Mathematics and Alumni-Alumnae University Professor; Ph.D., Johns Hopkins. Continuum mechanics, differential equations.

Philip J. Davis, Emeritus Professor of Applied Mathematics; Ph.D., Harvard. Numerical analysis, approximation theory.

Paul G. Dupuis, Professor of Applied Mathematics; Ph.D., Brown. Stochastic control and probability theory.

Peter L. Falb, Professor of Applied Mathematics; Ph.D., Harvard. Control and stability theory.

Wendell H. Fleming, Emeritus Professor of Applied Mathematics and Mathematics; Ph.D., Wisconsin. Stochastic differential equations, stochastic control theory.

Walter F. Freiberger, Professor of Applied Mathematics and of Medical Science and Chair of the Executive Committee of the Center for Statistical Sciences; Ph.D., Cambridge. Statistics, biostatistics.

Constantine Gatsonis, Associate Professor of Medical Science and Applied Mathematics; Ph.D., Cornell. Bayesian statistical inference, biostatistics.

Stuart Geman, Professor of Applied Mathematics, James Manning Professor; Ph.D., MIT. Probability and statistics, natural and computer vision.

Basilis Gidas, Professor of Applied Mathematics; Ph.D., Michigan. Mathematical physics, nonlinear partial differential equations, artificial intelligence.

David Gottlieb, Professor of Applied Mathematics and Ford Foundation Professor; Ph.D., Tel-Aviv. Numerical methods, scientific computation.

Ulf Grenander, Emeritus Professor of Applied Mathematics; Ph.D., Stockholm. Probability and statistics, pattern theory.

Yan Guo, Assistant Professor of Applied Mathematics, Manning Assistant Professor, and Sloan Research Fellow; Ph.D., Brown. Partial differential equations.

Gyorgy Haller, Associate Professor of Applied Mathematics and Sloan Research Fellow; Ph.D., Caltech. Nonlinear dynamical systems and chaos, partial differential equations.

Jan S. Hesthaven, Assistant Professor of Applied Mathematics; Ph.D., Denmark Technical. Numerical analysis, spectral and high-order methods, scientific computing, computational electromagnetics, optics, and fluid dynamics.

Din-Yu Hsieh, Professor of Applied Mathematics; Ph.D., Caltech. Fluid mechanics, mathematical physics.

Christopher K. R. T. Jones, Professor of Applied Mathematics; Ph.D., Wisconsin. Differential equations, dynamical systems.

George Em Karniadakis, Professor of Applied Mathematics; Ph.D., MIT. Computational fluid dynamics, scientific computing, turbulence modeling.

Harold J. Kushner, Professor of Applied Mathematics and Engineering, L. Herbert Ballou University Professor, and Director of the Lefschetz Center for Dynamical Systems; Ph.D., Wisconsin. Stochastic control and stability, operations research.

John Mallet-Paret, Professor of Applied Mathematics and Chair of the Graduate Program of Applied Mathematics; Ph.D., Minnesota. Ordinary and functional differential equations.

Martin Maxey, Professor of Applied Mathematics and Engineering and Director of the Center for Fluid Mechanics, Turbulence and Computation; Ph.D., Cambridge. Dynamics of two-phase flow, turbulence, turbulent mixing and dispersion of particles or bubbles.

Donald E. McClure, Professor of Applied Mathematics; Ph.D., Brown. Pattern analysis, image processing, mathematical statistics.

David Mumford, University Professor; Ph.D., Harvard. Pattern theory, biological and computer vision.

Chi-Wang Shu, Professor of Applied Mathematics and Chair of the Division; Ph.D., UCLA. Numerical analysis, scientific computation, computational physics.

Lawrence Sirovich, Emeritus Professor of Applied Mathematics; Ph.D., Johns Hopkins. Gasdynamics, perturbation methods, mathematical biology.

Walter Strauss, Professor of Mathematics and Applied Mathematics and L. Herbert Ballou University Professor; Ph.D., MIT. Nonlinear waves, scattering theory, partial differential equations.

Chau-Hsing Su, Professor of Applied Mathematics; Ph.D., Princeton. Fluid mechanics, mathematical physics.

CALIFORNIA INSTITUTE OF TECHNOLOGY

Applied Mathematics Program

Program of Study	An interdisciplinary program of study in applied mathematics that leads to the Ph.D. degree is offered by the Institute. In addition to various basic and advanced courses taught by the applied mathematics faculty, broad selections are available in mathematics, physics, engineering, and other areas. During the course of their studies, students are expected to obtain sufficient training in an allied field (e.g., physics, biology, engineering, etc.) and to ultimately perform thesis research in applied mathematics relevant to that field. A subject minor in applied computation is offered jointly with the computer science option.

The Institute requirements for a Ph.D. specify three academic years of study after the bachelor's degree. The first year usually consists of a full program of four or five courses. An oral candidacy examination is given at the beginning of the second term of the second year to assess the student's readiness for research. After this the emphasis is on research and thesis work. |
| **Research Facilities** | The Institute library facilities are excellent and are supplemented by specialized departmental libraries that cater to specific needs. Remote consoles for easy online access to various computers are located throughout the campus. The applied mathematics group has access to a variety of massively parallel supercomputers on campus. Additional access to SGI/Cray supercomputers and a massively parallel SGI/Cray T3D is also available through JPL. In addition, the applied mathematics group has a local network of Sun, SGI, and PC workstations that support scientific computation. The local applied mathematics network is connected to campuswide and national networks.

Strong interactions with applied mathematics and computing programs at Rice University, Los Alamos National Laboratory, and Argonne National Laboratory exist as a result of the NSF Center for Research in Parallel Computing, of which Caltech is a major component. |
| **Financial Aid** | Teaching or research assistantships are available for qualified students. The assistantships include tuition scholarships and carry cash stipends ranging from $11,187 per academic year for first-year graduate students to $14,607 for advanced students in 1999–2000. The duties involved may include grading, teaching, and research, but they permit the holder to carry a full schedule of graduate study. A number of assistantships are available for research in the summer months.

In addition, Institute fellowships in applied mathematics are awarded; they carry stipends at least comparable to those mentioned above. Additional sources of support common at Caltech include NSF and Hertz fellowships. |
| **Cost of Study** | Tuition for 1999–2000 is $19,260 for the academic year, including health fees. |
| **Living and Housing Costs** | Single students may find on-campus housing in dormitory or apartment-style accommodations that range in price from $347 to $466 per month. Married students may find on-campus housing in apartment-style accommodations that range in price from $725 to $840 per month. More detailed information can be found on the Web at http://www.caltech.edu/~cabs/housing/index.html.

Married students can also find attractive accommodations in one of the apartment buildings located in the vicinity of the campus. The Housing Office maintains and rents single-family houses and apartments at costs considerably below competitive market value. Early application for these is advised, as demand exceeds supply. |
| **Student Group** | Caltech has approximately 900 undergraduate students and about 1,100 graduate students. There are about 25 graduate students in applied mathematics, all of whom are receiving financial support of some kind. Admission to graduate study in applied mathematics is highly competitive; only about 5 to 7 new students can be admitted each year. |
| **Student Outcomes** | Graduates typically go on to postdoctoral research appointments followed by academic careers in teaching and research; alternatively, graduates seek research careers in government or private industry. |
| **Location** | Pasadena is a city of approximately 140,000 inhabitants, located just northeast of Los Angeles at the foot of the San Gabriel Mountains. The city contains both residential and light industrial areas. Caltech is located in the center of a residential area but is within a few blocks of shopping facilities. Most of the cultural activities of the large metropolitan area may be reached in an hour or less by car.

Recreational facilities abound. Hiking, camping, bicycling, and (occasionally) skiing are immediately at hand in the mountains; the Pacific Ocean is an hour or two away by car; and on a weekend any part of southern California can be explored. |
| **The Institute** | Throughout its history, Caltech has maintained a small, select student body and a faculty that is unusually active in research. The staff currently numbers 2,300, including postdoctoral fellows; of this number, more than 275 are professorial.

There is a strong emphasis on fundamental studies in science and engineering, with a minimum of specialization. There is also considerable emphasis on humanistic studies. The humanities have always played an essential role in the undergraduate curriculum, and undergraduates are permitted to major in these areas.

There are approximately 19,000 Institute alumni scattered all over the world, many eminent in their fields of science and engineering. Twenty-six of them have received Nobel Prizes.

Musical and dramatic events are presented on campus throughout the year. |
| **Applying** | Students are admitted only at the beginning of the fall term, and applications should be received by January 15. Only full-time Ph.D. candidates are accepted. All applicants are urged to take the Graduate Record Examinations General Test as well as the GRE mathematics Subject Test. Applicants from other countries are required to take the TOEFL exam. Application forms for admission and financial assistance may be obtained from the graduate office. The application may also be downloaded from the World Wide Web at http://www.caltech.edu/~gradofc/. |
| **Correspondence and Information** | Dean of Graduate Studies
California Institute of Technology
Pasadena, California 91125 |

California Institute of Technology

THE FACULTY AND THEIR RESEARCH

The core members of the faculty most concerned with teaching, advising, and supervising the research of students in applied mathematics are listed below.

Oscar P. Bruno, Professor of Applied Mathematics; Ph.D., NYU (Courant), 1989. Partial differential equations, materials and microstructure, electrodynamics, computational physics.

Donald S. Cohen, Charles Lee Powell Professor of Applied Mathematics; Ph.D., NYU (Courant), 1962. Perturbation theory, bifurcation theory, diffusive systems.

Joel N. Franklin, Professor of Applied Mathematics; Ph.D., Stanford, 1953. Mathematical programming, ill-posed problems, numerical analysis, stochastic processes, computer algorithms.

Thomas Y. Hou, Professor of Applied Mathematics; Ph.D., UCLA, 1987. Numerical analysis, computational fluid dynamics, homogenization, vortex dynamics, dispersive waves.

Herbert B. Keller, Professor of Applied Mathematics; Ph.D., NYU (Courant), 1954. Numerical analysis, bifurcation theory, large-scale scientific computing.

Daniel I. Meiron, Professor of Applied Mathematics; Sc.D., MIT, 1981. Computational physics, large-scale scientific computing.

Philip G. Saffman, Theodore von Kármán Professor of Applied Mathematics and Aeronautics, Emeritus; Ph.D., Cambridge, 1956. Theoretical and computational fluid mechanics.

Gerald B. Whitham, Charles Lee Powell Professor of Applied Mathematics, Emeritus; Ph.D., Manchester, 1953. Fluid mechanics, wave propagation, nonlinear problems.

In addition, the following faculty members outside the core Applied Mathematics faculty have also been involved with teaching, advising, and supervising the research of students in applied mathematics.

Yaser S. Abu-Mostafa, Professor of Electrical Engineering and Computer Science; Ph.D., Caltech, 1983. Learning theory, neural networks, information theory, computational complexity, pattern recognition.

K. Mani Chandy, Professor of Computer Science; Ph.D., MIT, 1969. Parallel programs, concurrency, algorithms, performance modeling.

Noel R. Corngold, Professor of Applied Physics; Ph.D., Harvard, 1954. Statistical mechanics; theory of particle transport in gases, liquids, and plasmas.

Michael C. Cross, Professor of Theoretical Physics; Ph.D., Cambridge, 1975. Spatiotemporal chaos in complex systems, fluid dynamics and turbulence, nonequilibrium statistical mechanics.

James K. Knowles, Professor of Applied Mechanics, Emeritus; Ph.D., MIT, 1957. Mathematical problems in solid mechanics.

Anthony Leonard, Professor of Aeronautics; Ph.D., Stanford, 1963. Computational and theoretical fluid mechanics, fluid turbulence, fluid-structure interaction.

Richard M. Murray, Associate Professor of Mechanical Engineering; Ph.D., Berkeley, 1991. Nonlinear control of mechanical systems, robotic manipulation.

Dale I. Pullin, Professor of Aeronautics; Ph.D., Imperial College (London), 1974. Computational and theoretical fluid mechanics, compressible and incompressible flow, computational applied mathematics.

Zhen-Gang Wang, Associate Professor of Chemical Engineering; Ph.D., Chicago, 1987. Statistical mechanics, structures, phase transitions and dynamics of complex fluids.

Stephen R. Wiggins, Professor of Applied Mechanics; Ph.D., Cornell, 1985. Nonlinear dynamical systems, chaotic phenomena.

RESEARCH ACTIVITIES

Because mathematics is applied by most scientists in almost all disciplines at Caltech, significant research by applied mathematics students is encouraged in all areas. Areas in which research has been particularly strong include fluid dynamics, materials science, elasticity, dynamics, numerical analysis, ordinary and partial differential equations, integral equations, linear and nonlinear wave propagation, water waves, bifurcation theory, perturbation and asymptotic methods, stability theory, computational fluid mechanics, stochastic processes, variational methods, large-scale scientific computing, applications of parallel processing, computational relativity, and other related branches of analysis. The department has many visitors, from senior scientists to postdoctoral research fellows, who specialize in these and other topics for varying periods.

CARNEGIE MELLON UNIVERSITY

Mellon College of Science
Department of Mathematical Sciences

Programs of Study

The Department of Mathematical Sciences offers programs leading to the degrees of Master of Science in mathematical sciences and Master of Science in computational finance; Ph.D. and D.A. in mathematical sciences; Ph.D. in algorithms, combinatorics, and optimization; Ph.D. in pure and applied logic; and Ph.D. in mathematical finance.

The master's degree programs involve rather strict course requirements; a master's thesis or a research project is optional. The usual time taken in residence to complete the master's is two years, although unusually well-qualified students can meet all requirements within one year.

The first requirement for the doctoral degrees is completion of a set of core courses at an appropriate level. After this, the emphasis is on preparation for research. After passing a qualifying examination that measures competence in the proposed research area, the student begins serious research. The differences between Ph.D. and D.A. theses is that the Ph.D. thesis must consist of original publishable research in depth; the D.A. thesis is a scholarly publishable work that need not report new results.

The research of the department is mainly specialized in several areas of applied mathematics, in combinatorics, and in logic. Greater breadth in course offerings and in research areas is available through cooperation with the Department of Computer Science, the Department of Statistics, and the operations research and finance groups in the Graduate School of Industrial Administration. The department houses the Center for Nonlinear Analysis, which is funded by the National Science Foundation and the Department of Defense to perform basic research on mathematical issues arising in such areas as materials science, stochastic modeling, and continuum mechanics.

Research Facilities

The University offers outstanding computational facilities, including easy access to powerful networked workstations and to the CRAY Y-MP of the Pittsburgh Supercomputer Center. In addition, the department is well equipped with workstations.

Financial Aid

The most common mode of support for students is through teaching assistantships, with approximately 35 students so supported. Advanced students may obtain research assistantships. The number available varies, but is on the order of ten. Both forms of assistantship include a tuition waiver and a stipend competitive with other institutions.

Cost of Study

Tuition and fees for the academic year 1999–2000 are $22,100.

Living and Housing Costs

Pittsburgh provides an attractive and reasonably priced living environment. There is no on-campus housing, but the Off-Campus Housing Office assists students in finding suitable accommodations. Most graduate students choose to live in nearby rooms and apartments, which are readily available.

Student Group

CMU has about 4,600 undergraduates and 2,700 graduate students. The Department of Mathematical Sciences graduate program includes 37 students in 1999–2000. A total of twenty-six Ph.D.'s and thirty-seven master's degrees have been awarded in the past five years.

Location

Pittsburgh is in a large metropolitan area with a population of 2.3 million people. It has been rated by the *Rand-McNally Places Rated Almanac* as the nation's most livable city. Pittsburgh is the headquarters for fifteen Fortune 500 corporations, and there is a large concentration of research laboratories in the area. Carnegie Mellon is located in Oakland, the cultural and civic center of Pittsburgh. The campus occupies 90 acres and adjoins Schenley Park, the largest city park. The city's cultural and recreational opportunities are truly outstanding.

The University

Carnegie Mellon is the result of a 1967 merger of the Carnegie Institute of Technology, founded by Andrew Carnegie and known primarily for preparing engineers, and the Mellon Institute, founded by A. W. and R. B. Mellon, which carried out pure and applied research in conjunction with local industry. By carefully selecting areas of research concentration and encouraging interdisciplinary programs, Carnegie Mellon maintains a research program that rivals those of universities many times its size. Thus, the University gives graduate students both the advantages of a wide range of opportunities for research and the comparative intimacy of a small university. In addition to the seven colleges—the Carnegie Institute of Technology, the Mellon College of Science, the College of Fine Arts, the College of the Humanities and Social Sciences, the School of Urban and Public Affairs, the Graduate School of Industrial Administration, and the School of Computer Science—the interdisciplinary centers on campus, including the Center for Nonlinear Analysis, the Robotics Institute, the Engineering Design Research Center, and the Magnetic Materials Research Group, further enrich the opportunities for research collaboration. Since several of these colleges and research centers draw heavily upon mathematics, it is an excellent environment for mathematical research. The research activities of the University are complemented by those of the University Teaching Center, whose programs are open to graduate students and can be helpful to the beginning instructor.

Applying

Completed applications and credentials for graduate study in mathematical sciences should be submitted by January 15 for decision by mid-April. In addition to the application form, transcripts from all college-level institutions attended, three letters of recommendation, and an official report of the applicant's scores on the General Test and the Subject Test in mathematics of the Graduate Record Examinations are required. An official report on the Test of English as a Foreign Language (TOEFL) is also required for applicants whose native language is not English. A full description of procedures and programs is given in the booklet *Carnegie Mellon Graduate Studies in Mathematical Sciences,* which will be sent on request. This booklet is also available on the department's Web site (address below).

Correspondence and Information

Graduate Applications Committee
Department of Mathematical Sciences
Carnegie Mellon University
Pittsburgh, Pennsylvania 15213

Telephone: 412-268-2545
World Wide Web: http://www.math.cmu.edu

Carnegie Mellon University

THE FACULTY AND THEIR RESEARCH

Peter B. Andrews, Professor; Ph.D., Princeton, 1964. Mathematical logic, automated theorem proving.

Egon Balas, Professor; D.Sc.Ec., Brussels, 1967; D.U., Paris, 1968. Disjunctive programming, combinatorial optimization, algorithmic methods for optimization.

Tom Bohman, Assistant Professor; Ph.D., Rutgers, 1996. Extremal combinatorics, discrete probability, cellular automata.

Charles V. Coffman, Professor; Ph.D., Johns Hopkins, 1963. Ordinary and partial differential equations, functional analysis.

Gerard P. Cornuejols, Professor; Ph.D., Cornell, 1974. Integer and combinatorial programming.

James W. Cummings, Assistant Professor; Ph.D., Cambridge, 1998. Set theory and mathematical logic.

Irene M. Fonseca, Professor; Ph.D., Minnesota, 1985. Partial differential equations, elastic crystals, phase transformations.

Alan M. Frieze, Professor; Ph.D., London, 1975. Combinatorial optimization, random graphs, computational complexity.

James M. Greenberg, Professor and Head; Ph.D., Brown, 1966. Nonlinear hyperbolic equations, free boundary problems, viscoelastic models.

Rami Grossberg, Associate Professor; Ph.D., Hebrew (Jerusalem), 1986. Mathematical logic, model theory, set theory.

Morton E. Gurtin, Professor; Ph.D., Brown, 1961. Continuum mechanics, population dynamics, variational calculus, partial differential equations.

David C. Heath, Professor; Ph.D., Illinois, 1967. Probability theory and mathematical finance.

William J. Hrusa, Professor; Ph.D., Brown, 1982. Partial differential equations, integrodifferential equations.

Anthony J. Kearsley, Assistant Professor; Ph.D., Rice, 1996. Optimization, partial differential equations.

David Kinderlehrer, Professor; Ph.D., Berkeley, 1968. Nonlinear partial differential equations, calculus of variations, liquid crystal theory.

John P. Lehoczky, Professor; Ph.D., Stanford, 1969. Stochastic control, with applications to finance manufacturing and queueing.

Wen-Ching Lien, Richard Duffin Visiting Assistant Professor; Ph.D., Stanford, 1998. Hyperbolic partial differential equations.

Richard C. MacCamy, Professor Emeritus; Ph.D., Berkeley, 1956. Integral equations, integrodifferential equations, nonlinear and degenerate models, partial differential equations.

Victor J. Mizel, Professor; Ph.D., MIT, 1955. Calculus of variations, stochastic control problems, hereditary phenomena.

R. A. Nicolaides, Professor; Ph.D., London, 1972. Numerical solution of partial differential equations, computational fluid dynamics, phase transitions.

Walter Noll, Professor Emeritus; Ph.D., Indiana, 1954. Axiomatic foundations of physical theories, continuum mechanics and thermodynamics, theory of relativity.

David R. Owen, Professor; Ph.D., Brown, 1968. Plastic and viscoelastic materials, foundations of classical thermodynamics.

Agoston Pisztora, Assistant Professor; Ph.D., ETH Zürich, 1993. Probability theory and phase transitions.

Jack Schaeffer, Associate Professor; Ph.D., Indiana, 1983. Nonlinear partial differential equations, Poisson-Vlasov and Maxwell-Vlasov systems.

Juan Jorge Schäffer, Professor; Dr.sc.techn., Swiss Federal Institute of Technology, 1956; Dr.phil., Zürich, 1956. Functional analysis, ordinary and functional differential equations.

Ernest Schimmerling, Assistant Professor; Ph.D., UCLA, 1992. Mathematical logic and set theory.

Dana S. Scott, University Professor of Computer Science and Mathematical Logic and Philosophy; Ph.D., Princeton, 1958. Logic, model theory, automata, modal and intuitionistic logic, semantics of programming languages.

Robert F. Sekerka, Professor of Physics and Mathematics; Ph.D., Harvard, 1965. Morphological stability of phase transitions.

Steven S. Shreve, Professor; Ph.D., Illinois, 1977. Optimization in the presence of uncertainty, control of diffusion processes.

Richard Statman, Professor; Ph.D., Stanford, 1974. Computation, symbolic computation, lambda calculus and combinatory algebra.

Shlomo Ta'Asan, Associate Professor; Ph.D., Weizmann (Israel), 1985. Multigrid methods, computational fluid dynamics, optimization.

Luc C. Tartar, Professor; Ph.D., Paris VI (Curie), 1971. Nonlinear functional analysis, nonlinear partial differential equations.

Lubos Thoma, Zeev Nehari Visiting Assistant Professor; Ph.D., Emory, 1996. Combinatorics, Ramsey theory, quantum groups.

Gerald L. Thompson, IBM Professor of Systems and Operations Research; Ph.D., Michigan, 1953. Mathematical programming, combinatorial optimization, large-scale linear programming, large-scale network algorithms.

Suzanne E. Tourville, Zeev Nehari Visiting Assistant Professor; Ph.D., Washington (St. Louis), 1997. Harmonic analysis and Navier-Stokes equations.

Reha Tütüncü, Zeev Nehari Visiting Professor; Ph.D., Cornell, 1996. Optimization, mathematical finance, computational mathematics.

Russell C. Walker, Senior Lecturer and Associate Department Head; D.A., Carnegie Mellon, 1972. Mathematical exposition.

Noel J. Walkington, Associate Professor, Ph.D., Texas, 1988. Numerical analysis, nonlinear partial differential equations, acoustic equations.

William O. Williams, Professor; Ph.D., Brown, 1967. General laws of mechanics and thermodynamics, phase transitions, viscoplasticity, biological mechanics.

Oswald Wyler, Professor Emeritus; Dr.sc.math., Swiss Federal Institute of Technology, 1950. Theory of categories, categorical logic, quasitopoi.

Doctoral Theses Since 1996

Polynomial Separation Procedures and Facet Determination for Inequalities of the Traveling Salesman Polytope

The Smyth Completion: A Common Topological Foundation for Denotational Semantics and Complexity Analysis

Variational and Measure Theoretic Techniques for Material Equilibria

On Some Problems of Hypergraphs

Applications of the Covolume Method in Computational Electromagnetics

Numerical Solution of a Nonconvex Optimization Problem Modeling Martensitic Microstructure

Laminations in Linearized Elasticity and a Lusin Type Theorem for Sobolev Spaces

On Some Problems Related to Linear Elasticity, Optimal Design and Homogenisation

Heavy Traffic Limits of Queues with Due Dates

Analysis of Artificial Boundary Conditions for Black-Scholes Equations

Spurious Fields in Computational Electromagnetics

Structure and Applications of Totally Decomposable Metrics

Unique Global Solvability for Initial-Boundary Value Problems in One-Dimensional Nonlinear Thermoviscoelasticity with Phase Transitions

Liquid Diffusion Couple in a Microgravity Environment

Valuation of Exotic Options Under Shortselling Constraints

Applications of a Dynamic Programming Approach to the Traveling Salesman Problem

Dependence Relations in Nonelementary Classes

A Unifying Credit Model

Numerical Methods for the Shallow Water-Equations

Dependent Types in Practical Programming

CARNEGIE MELLON UNIVERSITY

Department of Statistics

Programs of Study

Statisticians apply rigorous thinking and modern computational methods to help scientists, engineers, computer scientists, and policymakers draw reliable inferences from quantitative information. The program at Carnegie Mellon prepares students for such work by providing them with collaborative experience while they master technical skills based on a solid conceptual foundation. The faculty members are all very active in research and professional endeavors yet put a high priority on graduate training. The moderate size of the department and its congenial and supportive environment foster close working relationships between the faculty and students. The outstanding success of the department's graduates, when they take positions in industry, government, and academic institutions, may be attributed to their unusual abilities, the state-of-the-art training given to them, and the dedication they develop during their studies.

In pursuing graduate degrees, students follow programs that may be tailored to suit individual interests. The master's degree program trains students in applied statistics by imparting knowledge of the theory and practice of statistics. Requirements are satisfactory completion of course work and a written comprehensive examination. There is no thesis requirement. Students complete the program in 1, 1½, or 2 years, depending on their previous preparation.

The Ph.D. program is structured to prepare students for careers in university teaching and research and for industrial and government positions that involve consulting and research in new statistical methods. Doctoral candidates first complete the requirements for the M.S. in statistics. They then typically complete another year of courses in probability and statistics. A written Ph.D. comprehensive examination and an oral thesis proposal presentation and defense are required. Proficiency in the use of the computer is required. There are no foreign language requirements.

The department also offers three cross-disciplinary Ph.D. programs. The first is in psychiatric and mental health statistics and is sponsored jointly with the Department of Psychiatry in the School of Medicine at the University of Pittsburgh. The second leads to a Ph.D. in statistics and public policy and is sponsored jointly with the H. John Heinz III School of Public Policy and Management. The third is a joint program with the Center for Automated Learning and Discovery. Students can obtain additional information by visiting the Web site.

Research Facilities

The computational resources available to students at Carnegie Mellon are unsurpassed and are a major strength of the program. The Department of Statistics operates its own computer facilities, which provide students with experience using advanced graphics workstations. There are more than forty such computers, consisting of color HP UNIX workstations sharing a large disk file system with a capacity of more than 1 million megabytes (MB). About half of the workstations are configured with more than 100 MB each of RAM, including two workstations with 768 MB each of RAM. There are also several personal computers, Macintosh computers, and laser printers. The workstations are interconnected by a departmental Ethernet network, which, in turn, is connected to University and worldwide networks. The department also has a graphics laboratory with equipment for producing computer-animated videotapes and for digitizing video images.

Financial Aid

The department attempts to provide financial aid for all of its students, both master's and Ph.D. candidates. Tuition scholarships are usually granted in conjunction with graduate assistantships, which currently offer a stipend of $10,980 for nine months in return for duties as teaching or research assistants. Students who receive both tuition scholarships and graduate assistantships are expected to maintain a full course load and devote effort primarily to their studies and assigned duties. These duties require, on average, no more than 10 hours per week. Exceptionally well qualified candidates may qualify for a fellowship that pays tuition and a stipend and requires no assistantship duties.

Cost of Study

The tuition fee for full-time graduate students in 1999–2000 is $22,100 per academic year.

Living and Housing Costs

Pittsburgh has attractive, reasonably priced neighborhoods where students attending Carnegie Mellon University can live comfortably.

Student Group

Carnegie Mellon University has 4,823 undergraduate and 2,809 graduate students. The teaching faculty numbers approximately 620. During 1998–99, there were 41 full-time students in the graduate program; 31 were working toward a Ph.D. degree. Roughly 60 percent of the statistics graduate students are U.S. citizens and one third are women. Graduate students in statistics have diverse backgrounds, with typical preparation being an undergraduate program in mathematics or in engineering, science, economics, or management. All had outstanding undergraduate records, and many have won nationally competitive fellowships.

Location

Located in a metropolitan area of more than 2 million people, Pittsburgh is the headquarters of many of the nation's largest corporations. There is an unusually large concentration of research laboratories in the area. Carnegie Mellon is located in Oakland, the cultural center of the city. The campus is within walking distance of museums and libraries and is close to the many cultural and sports activities of the city.

The University

One of the leading universities in the country, Carnegie Mellon has long been devoted to liberal professional education. Five colleges—the Carnegie Institute of Technology, the College of Fine Arts, the College of Humanities and Social Sciences, the Mellon College of Science, and the School of Computer Science—offer both undergraduate and graduate programs. The Graduate School of Industrial Administration and the H. John Heinz III School of Public Policy and Management offer graduate programs only.

Applying

The application deadline is January 15 and students are encouraged to apply even earlier, if possible. A course in probability and statistics at the level of DeGroot's *Probability and Statistics* is highly desirable, but excellence and promise always balance a lack of formal preparation. The General Test of the Graduate Record Examinations is required of all applicants. International applicants are also required to take the TOEFL and the Test of Spoken English and should further document their ability to speak English, if possible.

Correspondence and Information

Department of Statistics
Carnegie Mellon University
Pittsburgh, Pennsylvania 15213-3890
Telephone: 412-268-8588
Fax: 412-268-7828
E-mail: admissions@stat.cmu.edu
World Wide Web: http://www.stat.cmu.edu/www/cmu-stats/GSS/

Carnegie Mellon University

THE FACULTY AND THEIR RESEARCH

Ngai Hang Chan, Professor of Statistics; Ph.D., Maryland, 1985. Time-series analysis, asymptotics, parametric inference, econometrics, finance.

Bernie Devlin, Adjunct Senior Research Scientist; Ph.D., Penn State, 1986. Statistical genetics, genetic epidemiology, genomics.

George T. Duncan, Professor of Statistics (primary appointment with the H. John Heinz III School of Public Policy and Management); Ph.D., Minnesota, 1970. Confidentiality of databases, mediation and negotiation, Bayesian decision making.

Douglas Dunn, Professor of Industrial Administration and Statistics and Dean, Graduate School of Industrial Administration; Ph.D., Michigan, 1970. Time-series analysis, forecasting, data mining, statistical computing.

William F. Eddy, Professor of Statistics; Ph.D., Yale, 1976. Neuroimaging, data mining, visualization.

Stephen E. Fienberg, Maurice Falk University Professor of Statistics and Social Science; Ph.D., Harvard, 1968. Categorical data, criminal justice statistics, disclosure limitation, federal statistics, multivariate data analysis, statistical inference.

Christopher R. Genovese, Assistant Professor of Statistics; Ph.D., Berkeley, 1994. Statistical inverse problems, magnetic resonance imaging, inference from spatio-temporal processes, model selection, functional inference.

Joel B. Greenhouse, Professor of Statistics and Associate Dean for Academic Affairs, College of Humanities and Social Sciences; Ph.D., Michigan, 1982. Methodology, biostatistics, psychiatric statistics.

Brian W. Junker, Associate Professor of Statistics; Ph.D., Illinois, 1988. Mixture and hierarchical models for multivariate discrete measures, nonparametric and semiparametric inference for latent variables, applications in education, psychology, the social sciences, and biostatistics.

Joseph B. Kadane, Leonard J. Savage Professor of Statistics and Social Science (joint appointment with Department of Social and Decision Sciences and with the Graduate School of Industrial Administration); Ph.D., Stanford, 1966. Statistical inference, econometrics, statistical methods in social sciences, sequential problems, statistics and the law, clinical trials.

Robert E. Kass, Professor and Head of Statistics; Ph.D., Chicago, 1980. Bayesian inference, statistics in cognitive neuroscience.

Nicole Lazar, Assistant Professor of Statistics; Ph.D., Chicago, 1996. Likelihood ratio statistics and tests, mixture models, applications to social science and psychological data.

John P. Lehoczky, Thomas Lord Professor of Statistics and Mathematics; Ph.D., Stanford, 1969. Stochastic processes with applications in real-time computer systems, computational finance, biostatistics.

Kathryn Roeder, Professor of Statistics; Ph.D., Penn State, 1988. Semiparametric inference, mixture models, and statistical models in genetics and molecular biology.

Mark J. Schervish, Professor of Statistics; Ph.D., Illinois at Urbana-Champaign, 1979. Statistical computing, foundations of statistics, multivariate analysis, statistical methods in engineering.

Teddy Seidenfeld, Herbert A. Simon Professor of Philosophy and Statistics (primary appointment in Department of Philosophy); Ph.D., Columbia, 1976. Foundations of statistical inference and decision theory.

Isabella Verdinelli, Senior Research Scientist in Statistics; Ph.D., Carnegie Mellon, 1996. Bayesian design of experiments, reliability and designs, Bayes factor, nonparametric Bayesian statistics.

Pantelis K. Vlachos, Research Scientist in Statistics; Ph.D., Connecticut, 1996. Bayesian inference, biostatistics.

Larry A. Wasserman, Professor of Statistics; Ph.D., Toronto, 1988. Nonparametric inference, mixture models, causality, model selection.

Carnegie Mellon University

SELECTED PUBLICATIONS

Chan, N. H., J. B. Kadane, and T. Jiang. On the time series analysis of the diurnal cycle of small scale turbulence. *Environmetrics,* in press.

Chan, N. H., and W. Palma. State space modeling of long-memory time series. *Ann. Stat.,* in press.

Chan, N. H., J. B. Kadane, R. Miller, and W. Palma. Predictions of tropical sea level anomaly by an improved Kalman filter. *J. Phys. Oceanogr.* 26:1286–303, 1996.

Chan, N. H., and N. C. Terrin. Inference for unstable long-memory processes with applications to fractional unit root autoregressions. *Ann. Statist.* 23:1662–83, 1995.

Devlin, B., S. E. Fienberg, D. Resnick, and K. Roeder, eds. *Intelligence, Genes and Success: Scientists Respond to The Bell Curve.* New York: Springer-Verlag, 1997.

Devlin, B., M. Daniels, and K. Roeder. On the heritability of IQ. *Nature* 388:468–71, July 1997.

Devlin, B., N. Risch, and K. Roeder. Disequilibrium mapping: Composite likelihood for pairwise disequilibrium. *Genomics* 36:1–16, 1996.

Duncan, G. T. Data for health: Privacy and access standards for a health-care information infrastructure. In *Health Care and Information Ethics: Protecting Fundamental Human Rights,* pp. 299–339, ed. A. R. Chapman. Sheed and Ward, 1997.

Duncan, G. T., and S. Kaufman. Who should manage information and private conflicts? Institutional design for third-party mechanisms. *Int. J. Conflict Manage.* 7:21–44, 1996.

Duncan, G. T., R. Krishnan, and S. Mukherjee. Inference channel detection in multilevel relational databases: A graph-based approach. *J. Organiz. Comput.* 5:123–38, 1995.

Duncan, G. T., T. B. Jabine, and V. A. de Wolf. *Private Lives and Public Policies: Confidentiality and Accessibility of Government Statistics.* Washington, D.C.: National Academy Press, 1993.

Duncan, G. T., W. Gorr, and J. Szczypula. Bayesian forecasting for seemingly unrelated time-series data: Application to local government forecasting. *Manage. Sci.* 39:275–93, 1993.

Dunn, D. M., and J. M. Landwehr. Analyzing clustering effects across time. *JASA* 75:8–15, 1980.

Cleveland, W. S., D. M. Dunn, and I. J. Terpenning. SABL—A resistant seasonal adjustment procedure with graphical methods for interpretation and diagnosis. In *Seasonal Analysis of Economic Time Series,* pp. 201–31, ed. Arnold Zellner. U.S. Department of Commerce, Bureau of the Consensus, Washington, D.C., 1978.

Davis, E. G., D. M. Dunn, and W. H. Williams. Ambiguities in the cross-section analysis of per share financial data. *J. Finance* 28:1241–8, 1973.

Dunn, D. M., W. Spivey, W. Allen, and W. H. Williams. Analysis and prediction of telephone demand in local geographical areas. *Bell J. Econ. Manage. Sci.* 2:561–76, 1971.

Mockus, J., et al. (W. F. Eddy). *Bayesian Heuristic Approach to Discrete and Global Optimization.* Algorithms, visualization, software, and applications. Dordrecht: Kluwer Academic Publishers, 1997.

Goddard, N. H., et al. (W. F. Eddy and C.R. Genovese). Online analysis of functional MRI datasets on parallel platforms. *J. Supercomputing* 11:295–318, 1997.

Noll, D. C., F. E. Boada, and W. F. Eddy. A spectral approach to analyzing slice selection in planar imaging: Optimization for through-plane interpolation. *Magn. Reson. Med.* 38:151–60, 1997.

Eddy, W. F., M. Fitzgerald, and D. C. Noll. Improved image registration using Fourier interpolation. *Magn. Reson. Med.* 36(6): 923–31, 1997.

Qian, S., and W. F. Eddy. An algorithm for isotonic regression on ordered rectangular grids. *J. Comp. Graph. Stat.* 5(3):225–35, 1996.

Just, M. A., et al. (W. F. Eddy). Brain activation modulated by sentence comprehension. *Science* 274:114–6, 1996.

Eddy, W. F., et al. (C. R. Genovese). Functional imaging analysis software—computational olio. In *Proceedings in Computational Statistics,* pp. 39–49, ed. A. Prat. Heidelberg: Physica-Verlag, 1996.

Eddy, W. F., and A. Mockus. Discovering, describing, and understanding spatial-temporal patterns of disease using dynamic graphics. In *Proceedings of the 25th Public Health Conference on Records and Statistics,* pp. 14–17, 1995.

Eddy, W. F., and M. J. Schervish. How many comparisons does Quicksort use? *J. Algorithms* 19:402–31, 1995.

Fienberg, S. E., and J. Tanur. Reconsidering the fundamental contributions of Fisher and Neyman on experimentation and sampling. *Int. Statist. Rev.,* in press.

Fienberg, S. E. Ethics and the expert witness: Statistics on trial. *J. Roy. Statist. Soc. Series A* 160:321–31, 1997.

Fienberg, S. E., U. Makov, and A. Sanil. A Bayesian approach to data disclosure: Optimal intruder behavior for continuous data. *J. Official Stat.* 13:75-89, 1997.

Fienberg, S. E., and M. O. Finkelstein. Bayesian statistics and the law. In *Bayesian Statistics* 5:129–46. eds. J. M. Bernardo, J. O. Berger, A. P. Dawid, and A. F. M. Smith. Oxford University Press, 1996.

Fienberg, S. E., U. Makov, and R. J. Steele. Statistical notions of data disclosure avoidance and their relationship to traditional statistical methodology: Data swapping and loglinear models. In *Proceedings of the U.S. Bureau of the Census Twelfth Annual Research Conference,* 1996.

Darroch, J. N., S. E. Fienberg, G. F. V. Gloneck, and B. W. Junker. A three-sample multiple-recapture approach to population estimation with heterogeneous catchability. *JASA* 88:1137–48, 1993.

Meyer, M. M., and S. E. Fienberg, eds. *Assessing Evaluation Studies: The Case of Bilingual Education Strategies.* National Academy Press, 1992.

Genovese, C. R., D. C. Noll, and W. F. Eddy. Estimating test-retest reliability in functional MR Imaging I: Statistical methodology. *Magn. Reson. Med.* 38:497–507, 1997.

Genovese, C. R., and P. B. Stark. Data reduction and statistical inconsistency in linear inverse problems. *Phys. Earth Planet. Int.* 98:143–62, 1996.

Genovese, C. R., P. B. Stark, and M. J. Thompson. Uncertainties for two-dimensional models of solar rotation from helioseismic eigenfrequency splitting. *Astrophys. J.* 443:843–54, 1995.

Greenhouse, J. B., and N. P. Silliman. Applications of a mixture survival model with covariates to the analysis of a depression prevention trial. *Stat. Med.* 15:2077–94, 1996.

Greenhouse, J., and L. Wasserman. A practical robust method for Bayesian model selection: A case study in the analysis of clinical trials. In *Bayesian Robustness: Proceedings of the Workshop on Bayesian Robustness.* eds. J. O. Berger, B. Betro, E. Moreno, et al. IMS Lecture Notes—Monograph Series, Volume 29, Institute of Mathematical Statistics. 1996.

Pauler, D. K., M. D. Esocbar, J. A. Sweeney, and J. Greenhouse. Mixture models for eye-tracking data: A case study. *Stat. Med.* 15:1365–76, 1996.

Kamlet, M. S., et al. (J. B. Greenhouse). Cost-utility analysis of maintenance treatment for recurrent depression. *Controlled Clin. Trials: Design Methods Anal.* 16:17–40, 1995.

Junker, B. W., and J. L. Ellis. A characterization of monotone unidimensional latent variable models. *Ann. Stat.* 25:1327–43, 1997.

Hemker, B. T., K. Sijtsma, I. W. Molenaar, and B. W. Junker. Stochastic ordering using the latent trait and the sum score in polytomous IRT models. *Psychometrika* 62:331–47, 1997.

Huguenard, B., et al. (B. W. Junker and R. E. Kass). Working memory failure in phone-based interaction. ACM *Transactions on Computer-Human Interaction* 4:67–102, 1997.

Kadane, J. B., and L. J. Wolfson. Experiences in elicitation. *J. Roy. Statist. Soc., Series D,* in press.

Daponte, B. O., J. B. Kadane, and L. J. Wolfson. Bayesian demography: Projecting the Iraqi Kurdish population, 1977-1990. *JASA* 92: 1256–67, 1997.

Berry, S., and J. B. Kadane. Optimal Bayesian randomization. *J. Roy. Statist. Soc., Series B* 59(4):813–9, 1997.

Wolfson, L. J., J. B. Kadane, and M. J. Small. Bayesian environmental policy decisions: Two case studies. *Ecological Applications* 6(4): 1056–66, 1996.

Carnegie Mellon University

Selected Publications (continued)

Kadane, J. B., and L. Wasserman. Symmetric, coherent, Choquet capacities. *Ann. Stat.* 24:1250–64, 1996.

Kadane, J. B., and D. A. Schum. *A Probabilistic Analysis of the Sacco and Vanzetti Evidence.* New York: J. Wiley & Sons, 1996.

Kadane, J. B., ed. *Bayesian Methods and Ethics in a Clinical Trial Design.* New York: John Wiley & Sons, 1996.

Kadane, J. B., and A. O'Hagan. Using finitely additive probability: Uniform distributions on the natural numbers. *JASA* 90:626–31, 1995.

Meyer, M. M., and J. B. Kadane. Evaluation of a reconstruction of the adjusted 1990 census for Florida. *J. Off. Stat.* 13(2):103–12, 1995.

Meyer, M. M., and J. B. Kadane. Reconstructing the adjusted census for Florida: A case study in data snooping. *J. Comput. Graph. Stat.* 1:287–300, 1992.

Kadane, J. B., M. J. Schervish, and T. Seidenfeld. Statistical implications of finitely additive probability. In *Bayesian Inference and Decision Techniques,* pp. 59–76, eds. P. K. Goel and A. Zellner. Amsterdam: North Holland, 1986.

Kass, R. E., and P. W. Vos. *Geometrical Foundations of Asymptotic Inference.* New York: J. Wiley & Sons, 1997.

Kass, R. E., and L. Wasserman. The selection of prior distributions by formal rules. *JASA* 91:1343–70, 1996.

Kass, R. E., and A. E. Raftery. Bayes factors. *JASA* 90:773–95, 1995.

Lazar, N., and P. A. Mykland. An evaluation of the power and conditionality properties of empirical likelihood. *Biometrika,* in press.

Bostrom, J., C. Crawford-Swent, N. Lazar, and D. Helmer. Learning needs of hospitalized and recently discharged patients. *Patient Ed. Counsel.* 23:83–9, 1994.

Lazar, N. Examination of the validity of the selection process for officer candidates—1987–88. COM(1)-0612, Department of Behavioral Sciences, Israel Defense Forces (Research Report, Classified), 1990.

Lehoczky, J. Simulation methods for option pricing. In *Mathematics of Derivative Securities,* pp. 528–44, eds. M. A. Dempster and S.R. Plisha. Cambridge University Press, 1997.

Lehoczky, J. Real-time queueing network theory. *Proc. Real-Time Systems Symposium,* pp. 58–67, 1997.

Lehoczky, J. Using real-time queueing theory to control lateness in real-time systems. *Perform. Eval. Rev.* 25:158–68, 1997.

Rao, S., A. Strojwas, J. Lehoczky, and M. Schervish. Monitoring multistage integrated circuit fabrication processes. *IEEE Trans. Semiconduc. Manufact.* 495–505, 1996.

Carroll, R. C., K. Roeder, and L. Wasserman. Flexible measurement error models. *Biometrics,* in press.

Roeder, K., and L. Wasserman. Practical Bayesian density estimation using mixtures of normals. *JASA* 92:894–902, 1997.

Lindsay, B. G., and K. Roeder. Moment-based oscillation properties of mixture models. *Ann. Stat.* 25:378–86, 1997.

Roeder, K., R. G. Carroll, and B. G. Lindsay. A nonparametric maximum likelihood approach to case-control studies with errors in covariables. *JASA* 91:722–32, 1996.

Barron, A., M. Schervish, and L. Wasserman. The consistency of posterior distributions in nonparametric problems. *Ann. Stat.,* in press.

Schervish, M. J. P-values: What they are and what they are not. *Am. Statist.* 50:203–6, 1996.

Schervish, M. J. *Theory of Statistics.* New York: Springer-Verlag, 1995.

Schervish, M. J., and T. Seidenfeld. An approach to consensus and certainty with increasing evidence. *J. Stat. Plann. Infer.* 25:401–14, 1990.

Heron, T., T. Seidenfeld, and L. Wasserman. Divisive conditioning: Further results on dilation. *Phil. Sci.,* in press.

Seidenfeld, T., M. J. Schervish, and J. Kadane. A representation of partially ordered preferences. *Ann. Stat.* 23:2168–217, 1995.

Seidenfeld, T., and L. Wasserman. Dilation for sets of probabilities. *Ann. Stat.* 21:1139–54, 1993.

Seidenfeld, T. R. A. Fisher's fiducial argument and Bayes' theorem. *Stat. Sci.* 7:358–68, 1992.

Seidenfeld, T., J. B. Kadane, and M. J. Schervish. On the shared preferences of two Bayesian decision makers. *J. Phil.* 86:225–44, 1989.

Verdinelli, I., and L. A. Wasserman. Bayesian goodness of fit testing using infinite dimensional exponential families. *Ann. Stat.,* in press.

Verdinelli, I. Bayesian design for the normal linear model with unknown error variance. Technical Report #647. Department of Statistics, Carnegie Mellon University, 1996.

Verdinelli, I., and L. A. Wasserman. Bayes factors, nuisance parameters, and imprecise tests. In *Bayesian Statistics,* 5:765–71, eds. J. M. Bernardo, J. O. Berger, A. P. Dawid, and A. F. M. Smith, Oxford: Claredon Press, 1996.

Chaloner, K., and I. Verdinelli. Bayesian experimental design: A review. *Stat. Sci.* 10:237–304, 1995.

Verdinelli, I., and L. A. Wasserman. Computing Bayes factors by using a generalization of the Savage-Dickey density ratio. *JASA* 90:614–8, 1995.

Vlachos, P. K., and A. E. Gelfand. Nonparametric Bayesian clinical trials design for continuous patient response. In press.

Dey, D. K., A. E. Gelfand, T. B. Swartz, and P. K. Vlachos. A simulation-intensive approach for checking hierarchical models. In press.

Vlachos, P. K., and A. E. Gelfand. Issues in the Bayesian design of clinical trials with multiple categorical endpoints. In *Proceed. ASA Sec. Bayesian Stat. Sci.* 1–6, 1995.

Robins, J., and L. Wasserman. On the impossibility of inferring causation from association without background knowledge. In press.

CLARKSON UNIVERSITY

Department of Mathematics and Computer Science

Programs of Study
The Department of Mathematics and Computer Science of Clarkson University offers graduate programs leading to the M.S. and Ph.D. degrees in mathematics and the M.S. degree in computer science. Students interested in advanced studies in computer science may do research toward the Ph.D. degree in mathematics in any of various areas of computer science that have a definite mathematical content. The regular course load for a full-time student, including research credit toward an M.S. or Ph.D. degree, varies from 18 to 30 credit hours per calendar year. Thirty credit hours are required for an M.S. degree, and 90 credit hours are required for a Ph.D. degree. Most students complete their Ph.D. in four to six years. The atmosphere in the department is friendly and informal. Class sizes are small, promoting greater individual attention. Information concerning the department and the graduate program can be obtained from the department Web site, which is listed below.

Research Facilities
Clarkson's Science Center houses the School of Science and is conveniently located next door to the modern Educational Resources Center, which houses Clarkson's library and computer center. The library has substantial holdings of books and journals in mathematics and computer science, which are supplemented by interlibrary loan arrangements and computerized bibliographic database services. The main campus computing environment is based on more than 200 IBM RS/6000 Power Stations. The computing environment within the department is provided by a network of Sun SPARCstations. All major machines on campus are linked by an Ethernet network that is connected to worldwide networks.

Financial Aid
A few teaching and research assistantships are offered each year to qualified U.S. and international applicants. All students are considered for financial assistance, which is awarded on a merit basis. Assistantships carry a stipend of $15,200 for the 1999–2000 academic year as well as a full tuition waiver. Higher stipends may be available for exceptionally well-qualified students. Teaching assistantships typically require 4 contact hours of service per week under the supervision of a professor. Research assistantships require 40 hours of service per week, which includes classroom and research duties. International students who do not receive full support must secure a guarantee of adequate financial support before an I-20 is provided to them. Tuition-paying students may receive a partial tuition scholarship in return for some service to the department. International students who are interested in teaching assistantships are encouraged to submit a Test of Spoken English (TSE) score in addition to the required TOEFL.

Cost of Study
Tuition for the 1999–2000 academic year is $661 per credit hour. There is also a health and recreation fee of $215 per year.

Living and Housing Costs
Clarkson stipends can adequately cover a single student's living expenses in Potsdam. Many off-campus apartments are available within walking distance of the campus at reasonable monthly rents. For questions concerning housing, students are advised to contact Residence Life.

Student Group
In 1998–99, the total number of graduate students in the Department of Mathematics and Computer Science was 18, of whom 15 were full-time students. Typically, two or three M.S. and one or two Ph.D. degrees are awarded annually, with about the same number of openings available each year for new applicants. The graduate student population is about an equal mix of domestic and international students and of men and women.

Student Outcomes
Recent Clarkson mathematics Ph.D. graduates have found employment at such places as Los Alamos National Labs; the University of Rochester Optics Center; Corning Science and Technology Laboratory; Array Systems Computing, Inc.; and Princess Sumaya University College for Technology.

Location
Clarkson University is located in the picturesque village of Potsdam, which has a population of 10,000, on the Raquette River in upstate New York near the Canadian border. There is local bus service throughout the village. Lake Placid, the Adirondacks, and the cities of Montreal and Ottawa are all within a 2-hour drive. Clarkson's membership in the Associated Colleges of the St. Lawrence Valley—a consortium that includes the State University of New York College at Potsdam and St. Lawrence University in Canton, which is 11 miles away—contributes to the area's vigorous educational and cultural atmosphere. Potsdam enjoys approximately three months of each of the four seasons. The temperature fluctuates considerably over the year, with winter lows of -10°F (-23°C) and summer highs of 80°F (27°C).

The University
Clarkson University is an independent, coeducational university located in Potsdam, New York, in the foothills of the Adirondack Mountains. It is attended by approximately 2,400 undergraduate and 370 graduate students. Nationally recognized for its strong technical and scientific programs, Clarkson is distinguished by three major characteristics: the excellence of the faculty and student body, the professional orientation of the curricula, and the friendliness of the people. In recent years, the development of a number of outstanding research programs in engineering, mathematics, chemistry, physics, biology, business, and the social sciences has attracted many notable researchers to Clarkson and has brought the University millions of dollars in research grants from some of the nation's major federal agencies and private institutions. Clarkson has a popular International Student Organization as well as Chinese, Indian, Muslim, and other international student groups. More information for international students can be obtained by contacting Ms. Mary Theis, International Student Adviser, Clarkson University, Box 5645, Potsdam, New York 13699-5645 (E-mail: theism@clarkson.edu).

Applying
Applications for admission and financial aid should be submitted to the address listed below no later than March 15 for fall enrollment and October 15 for spring enrollment. GRE scores are required. International students for whom English is not the native language are required to submit a TOEFL score of at least 550. At the time of orientation, all entering international students take an English placement test. Students who test below the acceptable score (as determined by the ESL coordinator) are required to enroll in a one- or two-semester course in English as a second language.

Correspondence and Information
Graduate Coordinator
School of Science
Clarkson University
Potsdam, New York 13699-5802
Telephone: 315-268-3802
E-mail: caslertc@clarkson.edu
World Wide Web: http://www.clarkson.edu/~mcs

Clarkson University

THE FACULTY AND THEIR RESEARCH

R. Croos-Dabrera, Assistant Professor; Ph.D., Minnesota, 1994. Generalized linear models, regression and statistical graphics.

K. Dempsey, Research Assistant Professor; Ph.D., Auckland, 1978, UCLA, 1993. Computational nonlinear dynamics, educational software.

R. Dobrow, Assistant Professor; Ph.D., Johns Hopkins, 1994. Random trees, Poisson approximation, Markov chains, self-organizing structures.

M. Felland, Instructor; M.S., Chicago, 1979. Nonlinear partial differential equations, applied mathematics.

A. S. Fokas, Professor; Ph.D., Caltech, 1979; M.D., Miami (Florida), 1986. Exactly solvable nonlinear equations, symmetries, inverse scattering in multidimensions, Painlevé equations.

S. Fulton, Associate Professor; Ph.D., Colorado State, 1984. Computational mathematics, multigrid and spectral methods, atmospheric modeling.

M. L. Glasser, Professor; Ph.D., Carnegie-Mellon, 1962. Statistical mechanics, Ising and vertex models for phase transitions, lattice sums and special functions.

A. J. Jerri, Associate Professor; Ph.D., Oregon State, 1967. Integral and discrete transforms, sampling expansions, Gibbs phenomena, modified iterative methods for nonlinear problems, operational sum methods.

D. J. Kaup, Professor; Ph.D., Maryland, 1967. Applied mathematics, mathematical physics, solitons, nonlinear optics and plasma physics.

C. Lynch, Assistant Professor; Ph.D., Boston University, 1994. Automated deduction, mathematical logic, efficient algorithms, software verification.

J. Lynch, Professor; Ph.D., Colorado, 1977. Finite-model theory, mathematical logic, and combinatorics in the study of computational complexity.

A. Maciel, Assistant Professor; Ph.D., McGill, 1995. Complexity theory, Boolean circuits, algebraic theory of automata, proof complexity.

D. Powers, Professor and Chair; Ph.D., Pittsburgh, 1966. Graph theory and applications, algebraic graph theory, relations between matrices/graphs, control theory.

J. Searleman, Instructor; M.S., SUNY at Stony Brook, 1976. Artificial intelligence, expert systems, distributed artificial intelligence.

R. Sipcić, Assistant Professor; Ph.D., MIT, 1998. Applied mathematics, nonlinear evolution equations in water waves, nonlinear dynamics, fluid dynamics.

C. T. Tamon, Assistant Professor; Ph.D., Calgary, 1996. Computational learning theory, complexity theory, machine learning.

C. Xenophontos, Assistant Professor; Ph.D., Maryland, 1996. Finite-element method; applications to boundary layers, singular perturbations, and nonsmooth domains.

Recent Ph.D. Dissertations

Ali Al Jarrah, 1998. Bessel integrals and sums: Old and new.
Taras Lakoba, 1997. Perturbations and stability of solitary waves in nonlinear optics.
Qiming Liu, 1996. Generalized conditional symmetries, asymptotic integrability and integrable surfaces.
Sergey Burtsev, 1995. The novel integrable equations of nonlinear optics and inverse scattering transform.
Anwar Saleh, 1994. Self-adaptive multilevel methods for fluid flow problems.
Yimin Kang, 1994. Analysis and applications of combined numerical methods for systems of differential equations.

SELECTED PUBLICATIONS

Cook, R. D., and **R. Croos-Dabrera.** Partial residual plots in generalized linear models. *J. Am. Stat. Assoc.* 93:442, 1998.

Quinn, D. D., C. B. Clemons, and **K. M. Dempsey.** The singular nature of rotating circular rings with symmetry. *4th International Symposium on Fluid-Structure Interactions, Aeroelasticity, Flow-Induced Vibration and Noise at the ASME International Mechanical Engineering Congress and Exposition in Dallas, Texas.* 53-1:299–306, 1997.

Dempsey, K. M. Dynamic nonlinear forcing of elastic rings. *Proc. Roy. Soc. London A* 452:1927–43, 1996.

Dempsey, K. M., and I. Gladwell. Numerical instability in the breathing-mode dynamics of elastic rings. *Appl. Num. Math.* 20:211–20, 1996.

Fokas, A. S., and B. Pelloni. The solution of certain IBV problems for the linearized KdV equation. *Proc. Roy. Soc. London A* 454:645–57, 1998.

Fokas, A. S., and S. Tanveer. A Hele-Shaw problem and the second Painleve transcendent. *Math. Proc. Camb. Phil. Soc.* 124:169–91, 1998.

Fokas, A. S. Integrability: From d'Alembert to Lax. In *Recent Advances in PDE's and Applications (in honor of P. Lax and L. Nirenberg),* p. 54, eds. R. Spigler and S. Venakedes. AMA, 1998.

Bressloff, P., and **A. S. Fokas.** Dendrites and IBV problems for the continuous and discrete heat equations. In *Symmetries and Integrability of Difference Equations,* eds. P. Clarkson and F. Nijhoff. Cambridge: Cambridge University Press, 1998.

Fokas, A. S. Lax pairs and a new spectral method for linear and integrable nonlinear PDE's. *Selecta Math.* 4:31–68, 1998.

Fokas, A. S., and Q. M. Liu. Linear superpositions in nonlinear wave equations. *Methods Applications Anal.* 4:156–61, 1997.

Fokas, A. S. A unified transform method for solving linear and certain nonlinear PDE's. *Proc. Roy. Soc. London A* 453:1411–43, 1997.

Fokas, A. S., R. H. J. Grimshaw, and D. E. Pelinovsky. On the asymptotic integrability of a higher-order evolution equation describing internal waves in a deep fluid. *J. Math. Phys.* 37:3415–21, 1996.

Fokas, A. S., and I. M. Gelfand. Surfaces on Lie groups, on Lie algebras, and their integrability. *Comm. Math. Phys.* 177:203, 1996.

Liu, Q. M., and **A. S. Fokas.** Exact interaction of solitary waves for certain non-integrable equations. *J. Math. Phys.* 37:324–45, 1996.

Fokas, A. S., and T. Bountis. Order and the ubiquitous occurrence of chaos. *Physica A* 228:236–44, 1996.

Fokas, A. S., and Q. M. Liu. Asymptotic integrability of water waves. *Phys. Rev. Lett.* 77:2347, 1996.

Fokas, A. S., I. M. Gelfand, and Y. Kurylev. Inversion method for magnetoencephalography. *Inverse Problems* 12:9, 1996.

Fokas, A. S. On a new class of physically important integrable equations. *Physica D* 87:145, 1995.

Fokas, A. S. The Korteweg-de Vries equation and beyond. *Acta Applicandae Mathematicae* 39:295–305, 1995.

Fulton, S. R. A comparison of multilevel adaptive methods for hurricane track prediction. *Elec. Trans. Num. Anal.* 6:120–32, 1997.

Fulton, S. R., W. H. Schubert, and S. A. Hausman. Dynamical adjustment of mesoscale convective anvils. *Monthly Weather Rev.* 123:3215–26, 1995.

Fulton, S. R. Can Maple help in teaching calculus with limited time and staff? In *Maple V: Mathematics and Its Application,* pp. 63–70, ed. R. J. Lopez. Boston: Birkhauser, 1994.

Fulton, S. R. A semi-implicit spectral method for the anelastic equations. *J. Comp. Phys.* 106:299–305, 1993.

Fulton, S. R. Multigrid solution of nonlinear balance equations in meteorology. *Comm. Appl. Num. Methods* 8:695–706, 1992.

Glasser, M. L., and A. A. Al-Jarrah. Some Sosine-Gegenbauer integrals. *Fractional Calculus Appl. Analysis* 1:271, 1998.

Mattis, D. C., and **M. L. Glasser.** The uses of quantum field theory in diffusion-limited reactions. *Rev. Modern Phys.* 70:979, 1998.

Fernandez, D. J., **M. L. Glasser,** and L. M. Nieto. New isospectral oscillator potentials. *Phys. Lett. A* 240:15, 1998.

Glasser, M. L., and V. Kowalenko. A method for evaluating Laplace transforms and other integrals. *Integral Transforms Special Funct.* 5:161, 1997.

Cadilhe, A., **M. L. Glasser,** and V. Privman. Exact solutions of low-dimensional reaction-diffusion systems. *Int. J. Modern Phys. B* 11:109, 1997.

Drumheller, D. M., and **M. L. Glasser.** Detection of chi-square fluctuating targets in arbitrary clutter. *IEEE Trans. Aerospace Elect. Syst.* 33:784, 1997.

Davies, K. T. R., **M. L. Glasser,** V. Protopopescu, and F. Tabakin. The mathematics of principal value integrals and applications to nuclear physics, transport theory, and condensed matter physics. *Math. Models Methods Appl. Sci.* 6:833, 1996.

Privman, V., A. Cadilhe, and **M. L. Glasser.** Anisotropic diffusion-limited reactions with coagulation and annihilation. *Phys. Rev. E* 53:739, 1996.

Privman, V., A. Cadilhe, and **M. L. Glasser.** Exact solutions of anisotropic diffusion-limited reactions with coagulation and annihilation. *J. Stat. Phys.* 81:881, 1995.

Kowalenko, V., and **M. L. Glasser.** Extensions and results from a method for evaluating fractional integrals. *Integral Transforms Special Funct.* 3:135, 1995.

Glasser, M. L. Exchange corrections to the static Lindhard screening functions. *Phys. Rev. B: Condens. Matter* 51:7283, 1995.

Glasser, M. L., and A. J. Guttmann. Lattice green function (at 0) for the 4D hypercubic lattice. *J. Phys. A* 27:7011, 1994.

Glasser, M. L., and K. T. R. Davies. Boundary effects on vortex flow. *Revista Tecnica* 17:51, 1994.

Shegelski, M., D. J. W. Geldart, **M. L. Glasser,** and D. Neilson. Nonlocal exchange contributions to the free energy of inhomogeneous many-fermion systems III. *Can. J. Phys.* 72:14, 1994.

Glasser, M. L., D. J. W. Geldart, and E. Dunlap. Non-local exchange contribution to the free energy of inhomogeneous many-fermion systems, II. *Can. J. Phys.* 72:7, 1994.

Glasser, M. L., and E. Montoldi. Some integrals involving Bessel functions. *J. Math. Analysis Appl.* 183:577, 1994.

Jerri, A. J. *Introduction to Integral Equations with Applications,* 2nd ed. New York: John Wiley and Sons, 1999.

Jerri, A. J. *The Gibbs Phenomenon in Fourier Analysis, Splines and Wavelet Approximations.* Dordrecht: Kluwer Academic, 1998.

Jerri, A. J., and R. L. Herman. The solution of the Poisson-Boltzmann equation between two spheres: Modified iterative method. *J. Sci. Computing* 11:2, 127–53, 1996.

Jerri, A. J., and R. L. Herman. The Poisson-Boltzmann equation and other boundary value problems: Modified iterative methods. *Trends Chem. Eng.* 3:103–13, 1996.

Jerri, A. J. *Linear Difference Equations with Discrete Transform Methods.* Dordrecht: Kluwer Academic, 1996.

Jerri, A. J. *Integral and Discrete Transforms with Applications and Error Analysis.* New York: Marcel Dekker, 1992.

Lakoba, T. I., J. Yang, **D. J. Kaup,** and B. A. Malomed. Conditions for stationary pulse propagation in the strong dispersion management regime. *Opt. Commun.* 149:366–75, 1998.

Kaup, D. J., T. I. Lakoba, and Y. Matsuno. Complete integrability of the Benjamin-Ono equation by means of action-angle variables. *Phys. Lett. A* 238:123–33, 1998.

Gerdjikov, V. S., et al. **(D. J. Kaup).** Stability and quasi-equidistant propagation of NLS soliton trains. *Phys. Lett. A* 241:323–8, 1998.

Lakoba, T. I., and **D. J. Kaup.** On the shape of the stationary pulse in the strong dispersion management region. *Electron. Lett.* 34:1124–6, 1998.

Kaup, D. J., and B. A. Malomed. Gap solitons in asymmetric dual-core nonlinear optical fibers. *JOSA B* 15:2838–46, 1998.

Lakoba, T. I., and **D. J. Kaup.** Hermite-Gaussian expansion for pulse propagation in strongly dispersion managed fibers. *Phys. Rev. E* 58:6728–41, 1998.

Kaup, D. J., B. A. Malomed, and J. Yang. Inter-channel pulse collision in a wavelength division-multiplexed system with strong dispersion management. *Opt. Lett.* 23:1600–2, 1998.

Ibragimov, E., A. Struthers, and **D. J. Kaup.** Soliton pulse compression in the theory of optical parametric amplification. *Opt. Commun.* 152:101–7, 1998.

Kaup, D. J., and Y. Matsuno. The inverse scattering transform for the Benjamin-Ono equation. *Stud. Appl. Math.* 101:73–98, 1998.

Kaup, D. J., and G. E. Thomas. Stationary operating density profiles in a crossed-field amplifier. *J. Plasma Phys.* 59:259–76, 1998.

Kaup, D. J., T. I. Lakoba, and B. A. Malomed. Asymmetric solitons in mismatched dual-core optical fibers. *JOSA B* 14:1199–206, 1997.

Clarkson University

Selected Publications (continued)

Kaup, D. J., and G. E. Thomas. Density profiles and current flow in a crossed-field amplifier. *J. Plasma Phys.* 58:145–61, 1997.

Matsuno, Y., and **D. J. Kaup**. Linear stability of multiple internal solitary waves in fluids of great depth. *Phys. Lett. A* 228:176–81, 1997.

Kaup, D. J., and B. A. Malomed. Solitons in nonlinear fiber couplers with two orthogonal polarizations. *Phys. Rev. E* 55:6107–20, 1997.

Matsuno, Y., and **D. J. Kaup**. Initial value problem of the linearized Benjamin-Ono equation and its applications. *J. Math. Phys.* 38:5198–224, 1997.

Lakoba, T. I., and **D. J. Kaup**. Stability of solitons in nonlinear fiber couplers with two orthogonal polarizations. *Phys. Rev. E* 56:4791–802, 1997.

Kaup, D. J., and T. I. Lakoba. Perturbation theory for the Manakov soliton and its application to pulse propagation in randomly birefringent fibers. *Phys. Rev. E* 56:6147–65, 1997.

Kaup, D. J., and G. E. Thomas. Variational principle for cross-field devices. *J. Plasma Phys.* 57:765–84, 1997.

Burtsev, S., and **D. J. Kaup**. Effective control of a soliton by the sliding-frequency guided filters. *JOSA B* 14:627–35, 1997.

Steudel, H., R. Meinel, and **D. J. Kaup**. Solutions of degenerate two-photon propagation from Backlund transformations. *J. Mod. Opt.* 44:287–303, 1997.

Kaup, D. J., and T. I. Lakoba. Variational method: How it can generate false instabilities. *J. Math. Phys.* 37:3442, 1996.

Kaup, D. J., A. E. Kozhekin, and V. I. Rupasov. Stimulated Raman scattering by a point-like medium—Classical and quantum treatments. *Phys. Rev. A* 53:573–85, 1996.

Kaup, D. J., and T. I. Lakoba. The squared eigenfunctions of the massive thirring model in laboratory coordinates. *J. Math. Phys.* 37:308–23, 1996.

Kaup, D. J., and G. E. Thomas. Creation of a resonant diocotron mode. *Phys. Plasmas* 3:771–80, 1996.

Kaup, D. J., and V. I. Rupasov. Exactly solvable 1D model of resonance energy transfer. *J. Phys. A* 29:2149–62, 1996.

Kaup, D. J., and V. I. Rupasov. Exactly solvable 3D model of resonance energy transfer. *J. Phys. A* 29:6911–23, 1996.

Steudel, H., and **D. J. Kaup**. Degenerate two-photon propagation and the oscillating two-stream instability: General solution for amplitude-modulated pulses. *J. Mod. Opt.* 43:1851–66, 1996.

Antani, S. N., **D. J. Kaup**, and N. N. Rao. Excitation of upper-hybrid waves from O-mode electromagnetic waves via density gradient in the ionosphere. *J. Geophys. Res.* 101:27035–41, 1996.

Karlsson, M., **D. J. Kaup**, and B. A. Malomed. Interactions between polarized soliton pulses in optical fibers: Exact solutions. *Phys. Rev. E* 54:5802–8, 1996.

Gerdjikov, V. S., **D. J. Kaup**, I. M. Uzunov, and E. G. Evstatiev. Asymptotic behavior of N-soliton trains of the nonlinear Schrödinger equation. *Phys. Rev. Lett.* 77:3943–6, 1996.

Burtsev, S., **D. J. Kaup**, and B. A. Malomed. Optimum reshaping of an optical soliton by a nonlinear amplifier. *JOSA B* 13:888, 1996.

Kaup, D. J., and B. A. Malomed. Tails and decay of a Raman-driven pulse in a nonlinear optical fiber. *JOSA B* 12:1656–62, 1995.

Kaup, D. J., and B. A. Malomed. The variational principle for nonlinear waves with dissipative terms. *Physica D* 87:155–9, 1995.

Burtsev, S., **D. J. Kaup**, and B. A. Malomed. Interaction of a soliton with a strong inhomogeneity in a nonlinear fiber. *Phys. Rev. E* 52:4474–81, 1995.

Lynch, C. Local simplification. *Information Computation* 142:102–26, 1998.

Lynch, C., and P. Strogova. SOUR graphs for efficient completion. *Discrete Math. Theor. Comput. Sci.* 2:1–25, 1998.

Lynch, C. Oriented equational logic programming is complete. *J. Symbolic Computation* 23:1, 24–45, 1997.

Lynch, C., and W. Snyder. Redundancy criteria for constrained completion. *Theor. Comput. Sci.* 142:2, 141–77, 1995.

Lynch, C., L. Bachmain, H. Ganzinger, and W. Snyder. Basic paramodulation. *Information Computation* 121:2, 172–92, 1995.

Lynch, J. Convergence laws for random graphs. In *Logic Colloquium 1995, Lecture Notes in Logic*, vol. 11, pp. 115–33, eds. J. Makowsky and E. Ravve. New York: Springer-Verlag, 1998.

Lynch, J. Pebble games in model theory. Structures in Logic and Computer Science. In *Lecture Notes in Computer Science*, vol. 1261, pp. 66–83, eds. J. Mycielski, G. Rozenberg, and A. Salomaa. New York: Springer-Verlag, 1997.

Lynch, J., editor (with R. Boppana). *Logic and Random Structures, DIMACS Series in Discrete Mathematics and Theoretical Computer Science*, vol. 33. American Mathematical Society, 1997.

Lynch, J. Infinitary logics and very sparse random graphs. *J. Symbolic Logic* 62:609–23, 1997.

Lynch, J. On the threshold of chaos in random Boolean cellular automata. *Random Struct. Algorithms* 6:239–60, 1995.

Lynch, J. A relation between complexity and entropy. *Ulam Q.* 3:7–14, 1995.

Lynch, J. An extension of 0-1 laws. *Random Struct. Algorithms* 5:155–72, 1994.

Lynch, J. Random resource allocation graphs and the probability of deadlock. *SIAM J. Discrete Math.* 7:458–73, 1994.

Lynch, J. A phase transition in random Boolean networks. In *Artificial Life IV*, pp. 236–45, eds. R. A. Brooks and P. Maes. Cambridge: MIT Press, 1994.

Maciel, A., and D. Therien. Threshold circuits of small majority-depth. *Information Computation* 146:55–83, 1998.

Maciel, A., and T. Pitassi. Towards lower bounds for bounded-depth Frege proofs with modular connectives. In *Proof Complexity and Feasible Arithmetics, DIMACS Series in Discrete Mathematics and Theoretical Computer Science*, vol. 39, pp. 195–227, eds. P. Beame and S. Buss. American Mathematical Society, 1998.

Beigel, R., and **A. Maciel**. Upper and lower bounds for some depth-3 circuit classes. *Computational Complexity* 6:235–55, 1997.

Maciel, A., and D. Therien. Threshold circuits for iterated multiplication: Using AC^0 for free. In *Proceedings of the 10th Annual Symposium on Theoretical Aspects of Computer Science V (STACS 93), Lecture Notes in Computer Science*, vol. 665, pp. 545–54. New York: Springer-Verlag, 1993.

Powers, D. L. *Boundary Value Problems*, 4th ed. Boston: Harcourt Academic, 1999.

Sipcic, R. Generalized long wave evolution equations. MIT thesis, 1998.

Lukas, S. K., **R. Sipcic**, and H. A. Stone. An integral equation solution for the steady-state current at a periodic array of surface microelectrodes. *SIAM J. Appl. Math.* 57:6, 1997.

Bshouty, N. H., **C. Tamon**, and D. K. Wilson. On learning decision trees with large output domains. *Algorithmica* 20:77–100, 1998.

Bergadano, F., N. H. Bshouty, **C. Tamon**, and S. Varricchio. On learning branching programs and small depth circuits. In *Third European Conference on Computational Learning Theory, Jerusalem, Israel, March 17–19*. ps, 1997.

Bshouty, N. H., **C. Tamon**, and D. K. Wilson. Learning matrix functions over rings. In *Third European Conference on Computational Learning Theory, Jerusalem, Israel, March 17–19*. ps, 1997.

Bshouty, N. H., **C. Tamon**, and D. K. Wilson. On learning width two branching programs. In *Proc. 9th ACM Conference on Computational Learning Theory*. ps, 1996.

Bshouty, N. H., and **C. Tamon**. On the Fourier spectrum of monotone functions. *J. Assoc. Comp. Mach.* 43(4):747–70, 1996.

Bshouty, N. H., et al **(C. Tamon)**. Oracles and queries that are sufficient for exact learning. *J. Comput. System Sci.* 52(3):421–33, 1996.

Xenophontos, C. The hp finite element method for singularly perturbed problems in non-smooth domains. *Num. Methods PDEs* 15(1):63–90, 1999.

Xenophontos, C. Finite element computations for the Reissner-Mindlin plate model. *Commun. Num. Methods Eng.* 14:1119–31, 1998.

Xenophontos, C. The h-p finite element method for singularly perturbed problems in smooth domains. *Math. Models Methods Appl. Sci.* 2(8): 299–326, 1998.

Schwab, C., M. Suri, and **C. Xenophontos**. The h-p finite element method for problems in mechanics with boundary layers. *Comput. Methods Appl. Mech. Eng.* 2(3/4):311–34, 1998.

Schwab, C., M. Suri, and **C. Xenophontos**. Boundary layer approximation by spectral h-p methods. *Houston J. Math. Spec. Issue ICOSAHOM '95 Conference*, pp. 501–8, eds. A. V. Ilin and L. R. Scott, 1996.

COLUMBIA UNIVERSITY

Graduate School of Arts and Sciences
Department of Mathematics

Programs of Study

The Department of Mathematics offers programs leading to the degrees of Doctor of Philosophy and Master of Arts.

The Ph.D. program is an intensive course of study designed for the full-time student planning a career in research and teaching at the university level or in basic research in a nonacademic setting. Admission is limited and selective. Applicants should present an undergraduate major in mathematics from a college with strong mathematics offerings. In the first year, students must pass written qualifying examinations in areas chosen from a first-year core curriculum, which offers courses in modern geometry, arithmetic and algebraic geometry, complex analysis, analysis and probability, groups and representations, and algebraic topology. Most of the formal course work is completed in the second year, when an oral examination in two selected topics must be passed. Also required is a reading knowledge of two languages, chosen from French, German, and Russian. The third and fourth years are devoted to seminars and the preparation of a dissertation. Students are required to serve as teaching assistants for three years beginning with the second year of study. A number of students are selected for NSF funding and are exempt from one or two years of teaching duties.

The master's degree requires 36 hours of part- or full-time course work. Students are required to take courses in each of four core areas: algebra, analysis, geometry-topology, and applications of mathematics. After completion of the M.A. program, students have the opportunity to transfer to the doctoral program after evaluation and recommendation by a department faculty committee. Within its M.A. program, the department also offers a track with specialization in the mathematics of finance.

There are allied graduate programs available in mathematical statistics and in computer science.

Research Facilities

The mathematics and statistics departments are housed in a comfortable building containing an excellent Mathematics Library, computing facilities, graduate student offices, lounge for tea and conversation, and numerous seminar and lecture rooms.

Financial Aid

The department has a broad fellowship program designed to enable qualified students to achieve the Ph.D. degree in the shortest practicable time. Each student admitted to the Ph.D. program is appointed a fellow in the Department of Mathematics for the duration of his or her doctoral candidacy, up to a total of four years. A fellow receives a stipend of $15,000 for the 1999–2000 nine-month academic year and is exempt from payment of tuition and fees. An additional $3000 of NSF summer support is available to a number of selected students. Financial aid is generally not available to M.A. students.

A fellow in the Department of Mathematics may hold a fellowship from a source outside Columbia University. When not prohibited by the terms of the outside fellowship, the University supplements the outside stipend to bring it up to the level of the University fellowship. Candidates for admission are urged to apply for fellowships for which they are eligible (e.g., National Science Foundation, New York State Regents).

Cost of Study

All students admitted to the Ph.D. program become fellows in the department and are exempt from fees, as explained above.

Living and Housing Costs

Students in the program have managed to live comfortably in the University neighborhood on their fellowship stipends.

Student Group

The Ph.D. program in mathematics has an enrollment of approximately 40 students. Normally, 8 to 12 students enter each year. While students come from all over the world, they have always been socially as well as scientifically cohesive and mutually supportive.

Location

New York City is America's major center of culture. Columbia University's remarkably pleasant and sheltered campus, near the Hudson River and Riverside Park, is situated within 20 minutes of Lincoln Center, Broadway theaters, Greenwich Village, and major museums. Most department members live within a short walk of the University.

The University

Since receiving its charter from King George II in 1754, Columbia University has played an eminent role in American education. In addition to its various faculties and professional schools (such as Engineering, Law, and Medicine), the University has close ties with nearby museums, schools of music and theology, the United Nations, and the city government.

Applying

The application deadline is mid-January; however, applicants of unusual merit are considered beyond the application deadline. Applicants who expect to be in the New York vicinity are encouraged to arrange a department visit and interview.

Correspondence and Information

For information on the department and program:
Chairman
Department of Mathematics
Mail Code 4406
Columbia University
New York, New York 10027
Telephone: 212-854-4112
World Wide Web: http://www.math.columbia.edu

For applications:
Graduate School of Arts and Sciences
Office of Student Affairs
Mail Code 4304
107 Low Memorial Library
Columbia University
New York, New York 10027
Telephone: 212-854-4737

Columbia University

THE FACULTY AND THEIR RESEARCH

Hyman Bass, Professor; Ph.D., Chicago, 1959. Algebraic K theory, group theory.
David A. Bayer, Professor; Ph.D., Harvard, 1982. Algebraic geometry.
Joan Birman, Professor; Ph.D., NYU, 1968. Low-dimensional topology, knot theory.
Lev Borisov, Ritt Assistant Professor; Ph.D., Michigan, 1996. Algebraic geometry.
Frederik Denef, VIGRE Assistant Professor; Ph.D., Institut voor Theoretische Fysica, Leuven (Belgium), 1999. String theory.
Bjorn Engquist, Professor; Ph.D., Uppsala (Sweden), 1975. Numerical analysis, scientific computing, applied differential equations.
Michael Faux, VIGRE Assistant Professor; Ph.D., Pennsylvania, 1994. String theory.
Robert Friedman, Professor; Ph.D., Harvard, 1981. Algebraic geometry.
Patrick X. Gallagher, Professor; Ph.D., Princeton, 1959. Analytic number theory, group theory.
Dorian Goldfeld, Professor and Chair; Ph.D., Columbia, 1969. Number theory.
Brian Greene, Professor; Ph.D., Oxford, 1987. Mathematical physics, string theory.
Richard Hamilton, Professor; Ph.D., Princeton, 1966. Differential geometry.
Hervé Jacquet, Professor; Dr.Sci.Math., Paris, 1967. Representation theory, automorphic functions.
Troels Jorgensen, Professor; Cand.Scient., Copenhagen, 1970. Hyperbolic geometry, complex analysis.
Yakov Kanter, Ritt Assistant Professor; Ph.D., Cornell, 1997. Geometry/physics.
Ioannis Karatzas, Professor; Ph.D., Columbia, 1980. Probability, mathematical finance.
Igor Krichever, Professor; Ph.D., Moscow State, 1972. Integrable systems, algebraic geometry.
Masatake Kuranishi, Professor; Ph.D., Nagoya (Japan), 1952. Partial differential equations.
John Loftin, Ritt Assistant Professor; Ph.D., Harvard, 1999. Differential geometry, Teichmuller theory.
Zhiqin Lu, Ritt Assistant Professor; Ph.D., NYU, 1997. Differential geometry.
Brian Mangum, Assistant Professor; Ph.D., California, Santa Barbara, 1996. Topology.
John W. Morgan, Professor; Ph.D., Rice, 1969. Geometric topology, manifold theory.
Tahl Nowik, Ritt Assistant Professor; Ph.D., Hebrew (Jerusalem), 1996. Three-dimensional manifolds.
Patricia Pacelli, Assistant Professor; Ph.D., Boston, 1996. Number theory.
Duong H. Phong, Professor; Ph.D., Princeton, 1977. Analysis.
Henry C. Pinkham, Professor; Ph.D., Harvard, 1974. Algebraic geometry.
Sorin Popescu, Ritt Assistant Professor; Ph.D., Saarland (Germany), 1993. Algebraic geometry.
Wei-Dong Ruan, Ritt Assistant Professor; Ph.D., Harvard, 1995. Differential geometry.
Mikhail Smirnov, Ritt Assistant Professor; Ph.D., Princeton, 1995. Differential and integral geometry.
Michael Thaddeus, Associate Professor; Ph.D., Oxford, 1992. Algebraic geometry.
Peter Woit, Director of Instruction; Ph.D., Princeton, 1985. Mathematical physics, topology.
Jared Wunsch, VIGRE Assistant Professor; Ph.D., Harvard, 1998. Microlocal analysis and partial differential equations, differential geometry.
Chia-Fu Yu, Ritt Assistant Professor; Ph.D., Pennsylvania, 1999. Arithmetic algebraic geometry.
Douglas Zare, VIGRE Assistant Professor; Ph.D., Caltech, 1999. Topology, combinatorics.
Shouwu Zhang, Professor; Ph.D., Columbia, 1991. Number theory, arithmetic algebraic geometry.

DARTMOUTH COLLEGE
Department of Mathematics

Program of Study

The Dartmouth Ph.D. program in mathematics is designed to develop mathematicians highly qualified for both teaching and research at the college or university level or for research in the mathematical sciences in industry or government. Students earn a master's degree as part of becoming a candidate for the Ph.D. degree but should not apply to study only for a master's degree.

During the first six terms (eighteen months) of residence, the student develops a strong basic knowledge of algebra, analysis, applied mathematics, topology, and a fifth area of mathematics chosen by the student. Areas recently chosen for this fifth area include combinatorics, geometry, logic, number theory, probability, and statistics. Rather than using traditional qualifying exams, the department requires that 2 faculty members certify that the student knows the material on the departmental syllabus in each of the five areas. This certification may be based on a formal oral exam, course work, informal discussions, supervised independent study, seminar presentations, informal oral exams, or any means that seems appropriate. Students and faculty usually find a formal oral exam to be the most efficient route to certification.

After completion of at least eight graduate courses and certification, students are awarded the master's degree and, subject to departmental approval, are admitted to candidacy for the Ph.D. degree. This normally occurs during the second year of graduate study. After admission to candidacy, the student chooses a thesis adviser and thesis area and begins in-depth study of the chosen area. Normally, the thesis is completed during the fourth year of graduate study, although it is not uncommon to use a fifth year. The typical thesis consists of publishable original work. Areas recently chosen for thesis research include algebra, analysis, applied mathematics, combinatorics, computer science, geometry, logic, number theory, set theory, and topology. Students continue taking courses according to their interests and demonstrate competence in two foreign languages while doing their thesis research.

Dartmouth is committed to helping its graduate students develop as teachers by providing examples of effective teaching, by instruction in a graduate course on teaching mathematics, and by provision of carefully chosen opportunities to gain real teaching experience. These opportunities begin as tutorial or discussion leader positions for courses taught by senior faculty. They culminate in the third and fourth years, after completion of the graduate course, in the opportunity to teach one course for one term each year. The first of these courses is normally a section of a multisection course supervised by a senior faculty member, and the second is chosen to fit the interests and needs of the students and the department.

Research Facilities

In Bradley Hall, the department has well-equipped offices and a lounge for graduate students, an outstanding research library, faculty offices, classrooms, lounges, and computer facilities. The department also uses Choate House, a historic building that provides additional office, laboratory, and seminar space for faculty members and graduate students, and a wing of Sudikoff Laboratory for Computational Sciences for those who need exceptionally fast access to exceptionally fast computers. The campus has a high-performance central computing environment with parallel computer servers and tools, in addition to a mail server, file servers, and the online catalog. The department has its own network of UNIX workstations, including a laboratory with two Digital Equipment alpha workstations and a network of Macintosh computers for research and teaching. Students may purchase Apple Macintosh and other personal computers at a discount through the College.

Financial Aid

Students receive a full tuition scholarship and the Dartmouth College teaching fellowship, for which the stipend in 1999–2000 is $1278 per month. This stipend continues for twelve months per year through the fourth year and may be renewable for a fifth year as well. Duties involve 8–12 hours per week for two terms in each of the first two years and about 20 hours per week for one term in each of the last two years.

Cost of Study

With the exception of textbooks, all costs of study are covered by the scholarship.

Living and Housing Costs

Students find that $1278 per month suffices comfortably for living in College housing, renting local apartments, or sharing a rented house with other students. A married student whose spouse does not work or hold a similar fellowship can maintain a spartan life in College-owned married student housing.

Student Group

Dartmouth attracts and admits students from colleges and universities of all types. More than 40 percent are women, the percentage of married students has varied from 5 to 35, 1 or 2 often are not recent graduates, and 1 or 2 often are not from North America. The department has 29 graduate students, and it offers an effective placement program for its Ph.D. graduates. Recipients of the Ph.D. degree from Dartmouth have found employment at a broad cross section of academic institutions, including Ivy League institutions, major state universities, and outstanding four-year liberal arts colleges. Some are now working as research mathematicians in industry and government as well.

Location

Dartmouth is in a small town that has an unusual metropolitan flavor. There are adequate shopping facilities but no large cities nearby. Hiking, boating, fishing, swimming, ski touring, and Alpine skiing are all available in the immediate area. A car is a pleasant luxury, but many students find it unnecessary.

The College

Dartmouth has about 4,000 undergraduate students, who are among the most talented and best motivated in the nation. There are under 1,000 graduate students in the College (arts and sciences faculty) and in associated professional schools in engineering, medicine, and business. With a faculty–graduate student ratio higher than 1:1, the department is a friendly place where student-faculty interaction is encouraged.

Applying

Application forms are available from the department. Applicants should send to the address below a completed application form, an undergraduate transcript, and three letters of recommendation that describe their mathematical background and ability, estimate their potential as teachers, and compare them with a peer group of the recommender's choice. Applicants must take both the General Test and Subject Test of the Graduate Record Examinations and have the official scores sent to the department. All sections of the TOEFL, including the Test of Spoken English, are required of applicants whose native language is not English. Applicants whose files are complete by February 15 receive first consideration.

Correspondence and Information

Graduate Admissions Committee Chair
Ph.D. Program in Mathematics
Department of Mathematics
6188 Bradley Hall
Dartmouth College
Hanover, New Hampshire 03755-3551
Telephone: 603-646-3722 or 603-646-2415
E-mail: mathphd@dartmouth.edu
World Wide Web: http://www.math.dartmouth.edu/

Dartmouth College

THE FACULTY AND THEIR RESEARCH

Professors

Martin Arkowitz, Ph.D., Cornell, 1960. Algebraic topology and differential geometry. Provides thesis supervision in these areas.

James E. Baumgartner, Ph.D., Berkeley, 1970. Set theory, general topology, and mathematical logic. Currently working with combinatorial set theory, theory of forcing, reflection principles obtained from large cardinals, and consistency questions in general topology. Provides thesis supervision in all areas listed above.

Thomas Bickel, Ph.D., Michigan, 1965. Finite groups, permutation groups, and representation theory. Provides thesis supervision in group theory and related topics in algebra and combinatorial mathematics.

Kenneth P. Bogart, Ph.D., Caltech, 1968. Combinatorial mathematics and algebra and their applications. Current research in ordered sets, the theory of generating functions, algebraic coding theory, and database design. Provides thesis supervision in algebra, combinatorics, and their applications.

Carolyn Gordon, Ph.D., Washington (St. Louis), 1979. Geometry. Provides thesis supervision in differential geometry.

Marcia Groszek, Ph.D., Harvard, 1981. Logic. Provides thesis supervision in logic.

Donald L. Kreider, Ph.D., MIT, 1959. Logic and computer science. Provides thesis supervision in logic and related areas.

Charles Dwight Lahr, Ph.D., Syracuse, 1971. Analysis, especially functional analysis. Provides thesis supervision in functional analysis.

Thomas R. Shemanske, Ph.D., Rochester, 1979. Number theory and modular forms. Currently interested in Hilbert/Siegel modular forms and theta series. Provides thesis supervision in number theory and related areas of mathematics.

Dorothy Wallace, Ph.D., California, San Diego, 1982. Number theory, especially analytic number theory. Provides thesis supervision in number theory.

David L. Webb, Ph.D., Cornell, 1983. Algebraic K theory. Provides thesis supervision in algebra.

Dana P. Williams, Department Chair; Ph.D., Berkeley, 1979. Analysis. Provides thesis supervision in analysis.

Associate Professors

Dennis Healy Jr., Ph.D., California, San Diego, 1986. Analysis. Provides thesis supervision in analysis.

Daniel Rockmore, Ph.D., Harvard, 1989. Representation theory, fast transforms, group theoretic transforms, dynamical systems, signal processing, data analysis. Provides thesis supervision in analysis and representation theory.

Assistant Professors

Rosa Orellana, Ph.D., California, San Diego, 1999. Finite dimensional representations of braid groups of type B, algebraic combinatorics. Provides thesis supervision in combinatorics.

John Trout, Ph.D., Penn State, 1995. Analysis. Functional analysis, operator algebras and noncommutative topology/geometry. Provides thesis supervision in analysis.

John Wesley Young Research Instructors

The JWY Research Instructorship is a two-year visiting position; the people involved and their fields thus change from year to year.

Douglas Drinen, Ph.D., Arizona State, 1999. Analysis.

John Mackey, Ph.D., Hawaii, 1994. Combinatorics/graphs, statistics, probability.

Eran Makover, Ph.D., Hebrew (Jerusalem), 1998. Spectral geometry of Reimann surfaces, combinatorics.

Jindrich Zapletal, Ph.D., Penn State, 1995. Logic, set theory, topology.

Visiting and Adjunct Faculty

Denis Devlin, Adjunct Associate Professor of Mathematics and Computer Science and Director of Computing, Department of Mathematics; Ph.D., Dartmouth, 1980.

Claudia Henrion, Visiting Scholar in Mathematics; Ph.D., Dartmouth, 1985.

DREXEL UNIVERSITY

College of Arts and Sciences
Programs in Mathematics

Programs of Study

Drexel University's College of Arts and Sciences offers distinctive programs in mathematics, with concentrations in applied mathematics, statistics and operations research, scientific computing, and industrial mathematics. Studies in these areas lead to M.S. and Ph.D. degrees. Both full-time and part-time programs are available; full-time students can usually complete the M.S. in two years. A minimum of 45 quarter credits is required.

In the M.S. program in mathematics, areas of emphasis include applied mathematics, combinatorics, computer algebra, differential equations, functional analysis, mathematical biology, numerical analysis, operations research, parallel computation, population dynamics, probability and statistics, scientific computation, special functions, and theory of algorithms. The Ph.D. is awarded for academic achievement and the proven ability to carry out independent research rather than for the completion of a prescribed course of study. The equivalent of four or five years beyond the B.S. degree is usually necessary for the Ph.D.; candidates must write and defend an original dissertation.

Students with strong backgrounds in both mathematics and computer science are encouraged to pursue the dual M.S. in mathematics and computer science. Typically, this requires an additional half year of study beyond the time required for an M.S. degree in one field. The degrees are awarded simultaneously upon completion of the program.

Research Facilities

A department-wide local area network, MCSNET, is the cornerstone for the computing facilities in the Department of Mathematics and Computer Science. MCSNET directly supports the administrative, instructional, and research activities of the department and provides access to centralized resources operated by Drexel's Office of Computing Services; resources operated by other Drexel departments, making possible joint instructional and research efforts; remote resources via the Internet; and the Pennsylvania Education Network (PrepNET) via a T3 connection. The departmental research computers are connected to the campus backbone at 100 megabits per second and are also on the vBNS via a campus OCS ATM connection.

Student-oriented departmental facilities include an E3000 computer server with an E150 file server, twenty-five lab machines (Suns, PC/NTs, and Macs), and a tutorial area with a PC/NT and two Macs. Research-specific facilities include various Sun workstations, an SGI workstation, NT and Linus workstations and servers, and X-terminals. General faculty/departmental facilities include a Sun MP630 SPARC10; OSs, including Solaris 2.x, Windows NT, Windows 95, MacOS, and Iris; Linus languages, including C, C++, Pascal, Fortran, Lisp, Java, and others; and databases, including Oracle packages, Nag Fortran library, Matlab, Maple, and Network Linda.

The Laboratory for Geometric and Intelligent Computation includes a heterogeneous network of Intel/Windows NT–based CAD/CAE graphics workstations (five P-IIs 300 and 400 MHz) and Unix graphics workstations (Solaris SPARC, Solaris x86, and Linix) and servers (one Ultra 30, two Ultra 2s, and one P-II 226) as well as a Bridgeport VMC 600 Vertical Machining Center (four-axis).

The Drexel Hagerty Library, which has more than 480,000 volumes, has approximately 120,000 in the science and technology section.

Financial Aid

A significant number of teaching and research assistantships are available. A teaching assistant position includes a teaching stipend and a tuition stipend. For 1998–99, teaching stipends averaged $10,000 per academic year. The tuition stipend includes tuition remission of up to 27 credits for the academic year.

Cost of Study

Tuition varies with the program of study. For 1999–2000, tuition for mathematics students is $585 per credit hour. The general University fee is $125 per term for full-time students and $67 per term for part-time students.

Living and Housing Costs

Accommodations for single students are available in University residence halls. Ample housing is also available in the neighborhood bordering campus. For the nine-month academic year, transportation and living expenses for a single student are estimated at $11,450.

Student Group

The University has a total enrollment of 9,590 students, including 2,785 at the graduate level. Approximately 30 graduate students are enrolled in the mathematics programs. Evening course offerings are sufficient to offer a robust degree program for part-time evening students.

The Philadelphia/Delaware Valley area is part of a technological corridor with a wealth of companies that hire Drexel graduates. The graduate student body is a diverse mixture of part-time students with full-time industry jobs, mathematics teachers, students from other countries, and full-time students with interests in advanced graduate study. Job opportunities for Drexel graduates exist not only in the Delaware Valley but throughout the country and the world.

Location

As a part of the University City area of west Philadelphia, Drexel is conveniently located within minutes of downtown Philadelphia, a great cultural, educational, and industrial center. From campus, New York City and Washington, D.C., are easily reached by train, bus, or car. Amtrak's 30th Street Station, a hub for national and local transportation, is located within three blocks of the University.

The University

Founded in 1891, Drexel University is a private institution offering undergraduate and graduate programs in arts and sciences, business and administration, design arts, engineering, and information studies. The University operates on an academic calendar of four terms per year.

Applying

Graduate students may apply with the intention of enrolling in any of Drexel's four terms (these begin in January, March, June, and September; application deadlines vary accordingly). Transcripts and letters of recommendation are required. For assistantship consideration, students must submit their application by February 1.

Correspondence and Information

For further information and an application form, students should contact:

Office of Graduate Admissions, Box P
Drexel University
Philadelphia, Pennsylvania 19104
Telephone: 215-895-6700
E-mail: admissions-grad@post.drexel.edu

Drexel University

THE FACULTY AND THEIR RESEARCH

Loren N. Argabright, Professor; Ph.D., Washington (Seattle), 1963. Functional analysis, wavelets, abstract harmonic analysis and the theory of group representations.

Robert P. Boyer, Professor and Associate Department Head; Ph.D., Pennsylvania, 1978. Functional analysis, C* algebras and the theory of group representations.

Robert C. Busby, Professor; Ph.D., Pennsylvania, 1969. Functional analysis, C* algebras and group representations, computer science.

Bruce W. Char, Professor; Ph.D., Berkeley, 1980. Symbolic mathematical computation, algorithms and systems for computer algebra, automatic scientific programming, parallel and distributed computation.

William M. Y. Goh, Associate Professor; Ph.D., Ohio State, 1987. Number theory, approximation theory and special functions, combinatorial enumeration, asymptotic analysis.

Herman Gollwitzer, Associate Professor; Ph.D., Minnesota, 1967. Applied mathematics, differential equations, data analysis, user interface design, visualization and scientific computing.

William J. Gordon, Professor; Ph.D., Brown, 1965. Numerical analysis, multivariate interpolation and approximation, numerical solution of partial differential equations, computer graphics.

Lloyd G. Greenwald, Assistant Professor; Ph.D., Brown. Time-critical planning and scheduling, robotics, resource-bounded reasoning, sequential decision making, reinforcement learning, medical informatics.

Nira Herrmann, Associate Professor and Department Head; Ph.D., Stanford, 1976. Mathematical and applied statistics, early decision problems, expert systems in statistics, computer science, computer science education, multivariate analysis, biostatistics.

Thomas T. Hewett, Professor; Ph.D., Illinois at Urbana-Champaign. Applied cognitive psychology, human-computer interaction, scientific problem-solving environments, networked engineering design, instructional computing.

Jeremy R. Johnson, Assistant Professor; Ph.D., Ohio State, 1991. Computer algebra, parallel computation, algebraic algorithms, scientific computing.

Bernard Kolman, Professor; Ph.D., Pennsylvania, 1965. Lie algebras; theory, applications, and computational techniques, operations research.

Yagati N. Lakshman, Assistant Professor; Ph.D., Rensselaer, 1990. Computational algebra, design and analysis of algorithms, symbolic computation systems.

Spiros Mancoridis, Assistant Professor; Ph.D., Toronto, 1996. Software engineering.

Charles J. Mode, Professor; Ph.D., California, Davis, 1956. Probability and statistics, biostatistics, epidemiology, mathematical demography, data analysis, computer-intensive methods.

Ljubomir Perkovic, Assistant Professor; Ph.D., Carnegie Mellon. Graph theory and algorithms, combinatorial optimization, probabilistic methods, theoretical computer science.

Ronald K. Perline, Associate Professor; Ph.D., Berkeley, 1984. Applied mathematics, numerical analysis, symbolic computation, differential geometry, mathematical physics.

Marci A. Perlstadt, Associate Professor; Ph.D., Berkeley, 1978. Applied mathematics, special functions, numerical analysis of function reconstruction, signal processing, combinatorics.

Jeffrey L. Popyack, Associate Professor; Ph.D., Virginia, 1982. Operations research, stochastic optimization, computational methods for Markov decision processes, artificial intelligence, computer science education.

William Regli, Assistant Professor; Ph.D., Maryland, 1995. Solid modeling, intelligent design and manufacturing.

Chris Rorres, Professor; Ph.D., NYU (Courant), 1969. Applied mathematics, scattering theory, mathematical modeling in biological sciences, dynamical systems.

Eric Schmutz, Associate Professor; Ph.D., Pennsylvania, 1988. Probability, algorithms, discrete mathematics.

Li Sheng, Assistant Professor; Ph.D., Rutgers. Discrete optimization, probabilistic methods in combinatorics, operations research, graph theory and its application in molecular biology, social sciences and communication networks, biostatistics.

Justin Smith, Associate Professor; Ph.D., NYU (Courant), 1976. Computer science; parallel algorithms, artificial intelligence, computer vision.

Chunguang Sun, Assistant Professor; Ph.D., Penn State. Parallel and distributed computing, graph algorithms, numerical linear algebra, design and implementation of programming languages.

Jet Wimp, Professor; Ph.D., Edinburgh, 1968. Applied mathematics, special functions, approximation theory, numerical techniques, asymptotic analysis.

Stanley Zietz, Associate Professor; Ph.D., Berkeley, 1977. Population dynamics, applied mathematics, mathematical biology, biophysics, image analysis.

SELECTED PUBLICATIONS

Boyer, R. P. The product expansion for sin *x*. *Int. J. Math. Educ. Sci. Technol.* 27:774–6, 1996.

Boyer, R. P. Generalized characters of U(∞). In *Algebraic Methods in Operator Theory,* eds. R. Curto and P. Jorgensen. Birkhauser, 1994.

Boyer, R. P. Representation theory of infinite dimensional unitary groups. *Contemp. Math.* 145:381–91, 1993.

Boyer, R. P. Characters and factor representations of the unitary group of the CAR algebra. *J. Operator Theory* 30:315–28, 1993.

Boyer, R. P. Characters and factor representations of the infinite dimensional classical groups. *J. Operator Theory* 28:281–307, 1992.

Busby, R. C., and W. Fair. Quadratic operator equations and periodic operator continued fractions. *J. Comput. Appl. Math.* 54(3):377–87, 1994.

Pickens, G. T., **R. C. Busby,** and **C. J. Mode.** Computerization of a population projection model based on generalized age-dependent branching processes: A connection with the Leslie matrix. *Math. Biosci.* 64:91–7, 1983.

Char, B. W., Y. N. Lakshman, and **J. Johnson.** Software components for symbolic mathematical computation. In *Proceedings of the 1998 International Symposium on Symbolic and Algebraic Computation,* pp. 46–53. ACM Press, 1998.

Char, B. W., J. Johnson, D. Saunders, and A. Wack. Some experiments with parallel bignum arithmetic. In *First International Symposium on Parallel Symbolic Computation,* pp. 94–103, ed. Hoon Hong. World Scientific, 1994.

Char, B. W. Progress report on a system for general-purpose parallel symbolic algebraic computation. In *Proceedings of the 1990 International Symposium on Symbolic and Algebraic Computation,* eds. S. Watanabe and M. Nagata. ACM Press, 1990.

Mutrie, M., R. H. Bartels, and **B. W. Char.** An approach for floating-point error analysis using computer algebra. In *Proceedings of the International Symposium on Symbolic and Algebraic Computation,* pp. 284–93. Association for Computing Machinery, 1992.

Char, B. W. Computer algebra tools for program manipulation. In *Automatic Differentiation of Algorithms,* eds. A. Griewank and G. F. Corliss. SIAM, 1991.

Goh, W. M. Y. Plancherel-rotach asymptotics for the Charlier polynomials. *Constructive Approximation* 14:151–68, 1998.

Goh, W. M. Y., E. Schmutz, and **J. Wimp.** On some recursive triangular systems. *Ann. Numer. Math.* 4(1–4):343–50, 1997.

Goh, W. M. Y., and **J. Wimp.** The zero distribution of the Tricomi-Carlitz polynomials. *Comput. Math. Appl.* 33(1/2):119–27, 1997.

Goh, W. M. Y., and **E. Schmutz.** The number of distinct part sizes in a random integer partition. *J. Combinatorial Theory* Series A 69(1):149–58, 1995.

Goh, W. M. Y., and **E. Schmutz.** Unlabeled trees: Distribution of the maximum degree. *Random Struct. Algorithms* 5(3):411–40, 1994.

Goh, W. M. Y., and **J. Wimp.** Asymptotics for the moments of singular distributions. *J. Approximation Theory* 74(3):301–34, 1993.

Goh, W. M. Y., and **E. Schmutz.** Random matrices and Brownian motion. *Combinatorics Probability Comput.* 2:157–80, 1993.

Goh, W. M. Y., and **E. Schmutz.** Gap-free set partitions. *Random Struct. Algorithms* 3(1):9–18, 1992.

Goh, W. M. Y., and **E. Schmutz.** The expected order of a random permutation. *Bull. London Math. Soc.* 23:34–42, 1991.

Greenwald, L., and T. Dean. A conditional scheduling approach to designing real-time systems. *Fourth International Conference on AI Planning Systems,* 1998.

Greenwald, L., and T. Dean. Tradeoffs in the design of on-line systems. *AAAI-97 Workshop on On-Line Search,* working notes, 1997.

Greenwald, L., and T. Dean. Package routing in transportation networks with fixed vehicle schedules. *Networks* 27:81–93, 1996.

Greenwald, L., and T. Dean, Solving time-critical decision-making problems with predictable computational demands. *Second International Conference on AI Planning Systems,* 1994.

Hewett, T. T., and B. Adelson. Psychological science and analogical reminding in the design of artifacts. *Behav. Res. Methods Instruments Comput.* 30:314–9, 1998.

Hewett, T. T. Cognitive factors in design: Basic phenomena in human memory and problem solving. In *CHI 98 Summary,* pp. 117–8, eds. C. M. Karat and A. Lund. New York: Association for Computing Machinery, 1998.

Hewett, T. T. Towards a generic strategy for empirical evaluation of interactive computing systems. In *Human Factors Perspectives on Human-Computer Interaction,* pp. 167–71, eds. G. Perlman, G. K. Green, and M. Wolgalter. Santa Monica, Calif.: Human Factors and Ergonomics Society, 1995.

Johnson, J., and R. W. Johnson. Automatic generation and implementation of FFT algorithms. In *State-of-the-Art FFT—Algorithms, Implementations, and Software,* SIAM Conference on Parallel Processing for Scientific Computing, 1999.

Johnson, J., et al. **(T. T. Hewett).** Virtual office hours using TechTalk, a web-based mathematical collaboration tool. In *Proceedings of 3rd Annual Conference on Integrating Technology into Computer Science Education,* pp. 130–3. New York: ACM Press, 1998.

Caviness, B. F., and **J. Johnson** (eds.). Quantifier elimination and cylindrical algebraic decomposition. In *Texts and Monographs in Symbolic Computation.* Springer-Verlag, 1998.

Johnson, J., Y. N. Lakshman, and **B. Char.** Software components using symbolic computation for problem solving environments. In *Proceedings of the 1998 International Symposium on Symbolic and Algebraic Computation,* pp. 46–53, ed. Oliver Gloor. ACM Press, 1998.

Johnson, J., and W. Krandick. Polynomial real root isolation using approximate arithmetic. In *Proceedings of the ACM-SIGSAM 1997 International Symposium on Symbolic and Algebraic Computation,* pp. 225–32, ed. W. K"uchlin. ACM Press, 1997.

Johnson, J., R. W. Johnson, and L. Auslander. Multidimensional Cooley-Tukey algorithms revisited. *Adv. Appl. Math.* 17:477–519, 1996.

Mancoridis, S., et al. Using automatic clustering to produce high-level system organizations of source code. In *IEEE Proceedings of the 1998 International Workshop on Program Understanding,* Ischia, Italy, 1998.

Mancoridis, S., and R. C. Holt. Algorithms for managing the evolution of software design. In *ACM/IEEE Proceedings of the 1998 International Conference on Software Engineering and Knowledge Engineering,* San Francisco, California, 1998.

Mancoridis, S. ISF: A visual formalism for specifying interconnection styles for software design. *Int. J. Software Eng. Knowledge Eng.,* 1998.

Fahmy, H., R. C. Holt, and **S. Mancoridis.** Repairing software style using graph grammars. In *IBM Proceedings of the Seventh Centre for Advanced Studies Conference,* Toronto, Ontario, Canada, 1997.

Mancoridis, S. Customizable notations for software design. In *ACM/IEEE Proceedings of the 1997 International Conference on Software Engineering and Knowledge Engineering,* Madrid, Spain, 1997.

Mancoridis, S., and R. C. Holt. Recovering the structure of software systems using tube graph interconnection clustering. In *IEEE Proceedings of the 1996 International Conference on Software Maintenance,* Monterey, California, 1996.

Mancoridis, S. Toward a generic framework for computing subsystem interfaces. In *ACM Proceedings of the Second International Workshop on Software Architecture,* San Francisco, California, 1996; *ACM SIGSOFT Software Eng. Notes* (22)1:42–56, 1997.

Mancoridis, S., and R. C. Holt. Extending programming environments to support architectural design. In *IEEE Proceedings of the Seventh International Workshop on Computer-Aided Software Engineering,* Toronto, Canada, 1995.

Mode, C. J. Threshold parameters for a simple stochastic partnership model of sexually transmitted diseases formulated as a two-type CMJ process. *IMA J. Math. Appl. Med. Biol.* 14(4):251–60, 1997.

Drexel University

Selected Publications (continued)

Mode, C. J. An extension of a Galton-Watson process to a two-sex density dependent model. In *Branching Processes,* ed. C. C. Heyde. *Proceedings of the First World Congress,* Varna, Bulgaria, September 5–12, 1993; *Lecture Notes in Statistics,* vol. 99, pp. 152–168. New York: Springer-Verlag, 1995.

Ringel, E. I., and **C. J. Mode.** A stochastic analysis of state transitions in an air-space management system. *Operations Res.* 42(2):262–73, 1994.

Perkovic, L., and B. Reed. Edge coloring regular graphs of high degree. *Discrete Math.* 165/166:567–78, 1997.

Dyer, M., et al. **(L. Perkovic).** A mildly exponential time algorithm for approximating the number of solutions to a multidimensional knapsack problem. *Combinatorics Probability Comput.* 2:271–84, 1993.

Kam, M., **C. Rorres,** W. Chang, and X. Zhu. Performance and geometric interpretation for design fusion with memory. *IEEE Trans. Syst. Man Cybernetics* 29:52–62, 1999.

Rorres, C., and D. G. Romano. Finding the center of a circular starting line in an ancient Greek stadium. *SIAM Rev.* 39:745–54, 1997.

Seliktar, M., and **C. Rorres.** The flow of hot water from a distant hot-water tank. *SIAM Rev.* 36:474–9, 1994.

Kam, M., W. Chang, and **C. Rorres.** Systems of random mappings with a common fixed point. *Int. J. Syst. Sci.* 23:2113–9, 1992.

Schmutz, E., and J. Hansen. Near optimum bounded degree spanning trees. World Wide Web: http://www.mcs.drexel.edu/eschmutz/PS/bdspt.ps

Schmutz, E., and J. Hansen. How random is the characteristic polynomial of a random matrix? *Math. Proc. Cambridge Philos. Soc.* 114(3):507–16, 1993.

Roberts, F. S., and **L. Sheng.** Phylogeny numbers. *Discrete Appl. Math.* 87:213–28, 1998.

Roberts, F. S., and **L. Sheng.** Phylogeny graphs of arbitrary digraphs. In *Mathematical Hierarchies in Biology,* pp. 233–8, eds. B. Mirkin, F. R. McMorris, F. S. Roberts, and A. Rzhetsky. Providence, R.I.: American Mathematical Society, 1997.

Roberts, F. S., and **L. Sheng.** Threshold role assignments. *Congressus Numerantium* 123:135–48, 1997.

Roberts, F. S., and **L. Sheng.** Role primitive indifference graphs and role assignments on w-fan graphs. *Congressus Numerantium* 121:65–75, 1996.

Zhang, X. S., and **L. Sheng.** Some useful numerical examples in discussion on continuity of solutions of parametric linear programming. In *Proceedings of APORS'91,* pp. 501–8. Peking University Press, 1992.

Smith, J. Iterating the cobar construction. *Mem. Am. Math. Soc.* 524, 1994.

Smith, J. *The Design and Analysis of Parallel Algorithms.* Oxford: Oxford University Press, XVIII, 1993.

Smith, J. Topological realizations of chain complexes. II: The rational case. *Pacific J. Math.* 138(1):169–208, 1989.

Sun, C. Parallel solution of sparse linear least squares problems on distributed-memory multiprocessors. *Parallel Comput.* 23:2075–93, 1997.

Sun, C. Parallel sparse orthogonal factorization on distributed-memory multiprocessors. *SIAM J. Sci. Comput.* 17:666–85, 1996.

Pothen, A., and **C. Sun.** A mapping algorithm for parallel sparse Cholesky factorization. *SIAM J. Sci. Comput.* 14:1253–7, 1993.

Wimp, J. The umbral calculus and identities for hypergeometric functions with special arguments. In *Mathematical Essays in Honor of Gian-Carlo Rota's 65th Birthday,* eds. B. E. Sagan et al. Boston, Mass.: Birkhauser, 1998; *Prog. Math.* 161:439–57, 1998.

Wimp, J., P. McCabe, and J. N. L. Connor. Computation of Jacobi functions of the second kind for use in nearside-farside scattering theory. *J. Comput. Appl. Math.* 82(1–2):447–64, 1997.

Kiesel, H., and **J. Wimp.** A note on Koornwinder's polynomials with weight function $(1-x)^\alpha (1+x)^\beta+ M\delta (x+1)+ N\delta (x-1)$. *Numerical Algorithms* 11(1–4):229–41, 1996.

Wimp, J., and H. Kiesel. Non-linear recurrence relations and some derived orthogonal polynomials. *Ann. Numer. Math.* 2(1–4):169–80, 1995.

Wimp, J., C. Rorres, and R. F. Wayland. Acoustic impulse responses for nonuniform media. *J. Computational Appl. Math.* 142:89–107, 1992.

EMBRY-RIDDLE AERONAUTICAL UNIVERSITY

Office of Graduate Programs and Research
Department of Computing and Mathematics
Program in Industrial Optimization

Programs of Study	Embry-Riddle Aeronautical University's Master of Science in industrial optimization (MSIO) degree program is designed to provide recent engineering and science graduates, as well as midcareer engineers and scientists, an opportunity to develop skills in optimization, statistics, and quality that can be applied to product and process design and improvement. Engineers and scientists who complete this program can assume key positions in engineering and scientific research. The MSIO degree program achieves its purpose by the extensive use of case studies that enable the students to gain practical skills in analyzing and solving current aviation/aerospace problems that require the application of optimization tools and/or statistics. Application software and teams are used, enabling students to solve problems in an environment that simulates process and product design and improvement organizations. MSIO students have the opportunity to strengthen and expand discipline-specific skills by taking several courses in their field of expertise (engineering, computer science, business, or human factors) while developing the mathematical foundation necessary to solve complex application problems within their field. The curriculum includes required courses in mathematical foundations, optimization, mathematical programming and decision making, and statistical quality analysis. The MSIO program offers students three program options: a thesis option that requires 30 credit hours, a research project option that requires 33 credit hours, and a course-only option that requires 36 credit hours. For the thesis option, 6 credit hours of specified electives and a 6-credit-hour thesis are required. For the research project option, 12 credit hours of specified electives and a 3-credit-hour research report are required. For the course-only option, 18 credit hours of specified electives are required, and a department-administered comprehensive exam must be satisfactorily completed prior to graduation.
Research Facilities	MSIO students have access to a state-of-the-art graphics and computing laboratory that consists of ten SGI 02s and four SGI Indys with many modern graphics features. Commercial software is available to perform many tasks in statistics, computation, and visualization. The department also has a variety of flight simulators as well as an on-campus Flight Safety Simulation Center. The Airway Science Simulation Laboratory contains many tools for simulating the National Airspace System, including weather, air traffic control, and several pilot–human factors interactions. A rapid prototyping laboratory is available as well as a laboratory devoted to real-time simulations and processes. Multiple PC laboratories, most at the Pentium level, are available at central locations across the campus.
Financial Aid	Embry-Riddle makes every effort, within the limitations of the financial resources available, to ensure that no qualified student is denied the opportunity to obtain an education because of inadequate funds. However, the primary responsibility for financing an education must be assumed by the student. A number of graduate assistantships that provide a stipend and a tuition waiver are available on a competitive basis each year. Other financial aid programs are Federal Stafford Student Loans, short-term loans, scholarship and fellowship programs, and the Embry-Riddle Student Employment Program (available on the Daytona Beach Campus). All graduate programs are approved for Veterans Administration education benefits.
Cost of Study	In 1999–2000, tuition costs are $455 per credit hour. Books and supplies cost approximately $300 per semester.
Living and Housing Costs	Some on-campus housing is available to graduate students. The cost of a standard double-occupancy room is $1400 per semester. Off-campus housing is reasonably priced. Single students who share rental and utility expenses can expect yearly off-campus room and board expenses of $4000. Married students should expect a higher average for yearly expenses.
Student Group	The graduate programs currently enroll 250 students on the Daytona Beach Campus. The College of Career Education enrolls more than 3,000 students in off-campus graduate degree programs, and the Center for Distance Learning enrolls an additional 900 students. On the Daytona Beach Campus, 40 percent are international students, 20 percent are women, and 11 percent are members of minority groups. More than 10 percent of the campus-based graduate students are employed full-time.
Location	The Daytona Beach Campus is adjacent to the Daytona Beach International Airport and 10 minutes from the Daytona beaches. Within an hour's drive are Disney World and EPCOT Center, the Kennedy Space Center, Sea World, and St. Augustine.
The University	The University comprises the eastern campus at Daytona Beach, a western campus in Prescott, Arizona, and the Extended Campus for off-campus programs. Within the field of aviation, Embry-Riddle Aeronautical University has built a reputation for the high quality of instruction in its programs since its founding in 1926.
Applying	Applicants must possess an earned baccalaureate degree in engineering or science or the equivalent. The minimum undergraduate cumulative GPA is 2.5 on a 4.0 scale and a cumulative GPA of 3.0 in the senior year. Applications from U.S. citizens and permanent residents should be received at least thirty days prior to the first day of the term in which the student plans to enroll. International students should submit all of their documents at least ninety days prior to the first day of the term in which they plan to enroll.
Correspondence and Information	Graduate Admissions Embry-Riddle Aeronautical University 600 South Clyde Morris Boulevard Daytona Beach, Florida 32114-3900 Telephone: 904-226-6115 800-388-3728 (toll-free) Fax: 904-226-7050 E-mail: admit@db.erau.edu World Wide Web: http://www.db.erau.edu

Embry-Riddle Aeronautical University
THE FACULTY AND THEIR RESEARCH
David G. Caraballo, Assistant Professor; Ph.D., Princeton.
John H. George, Professor; Ph.D., Alabama.
Deborah M. Osborne, Associate Professor; Ph.D., Central Florida.
David L. Ross, Associate Professor; M.A., Kentucky.
John R. Watret, Associate Professor; Ph.D., Texas A&M.

The research interests of the faculty include multivariate optimization, statistical process control, experimental design, operations research, decision theory, statistics, mathematical modeling, scientific computing and visualization, product design, aviation/aerospace applications of optimization techniques, and quality control and improvement. Faculty members receive recognition for the quality of their research by regularly obtaining competitive grants from agencies such as the Federal Aviation Administration, the Naval Research Laboratory, the Department of Energy, and the National Aeronautics and Space Administration.

EMORY UNIVERSITY

Graduate School of Arts and Sciences
Rollins School of Public Health
Department of Biostatistics

Programs of Study	Biostatistics is the science that applies statistical theory and methods to the solution of problems in the biological and health sciences. The Department of Biostatistics at Emory University offers programs of study leading to the Master of Science and Doctor of Philosophy degrees in biostatistics through the Graduate School of Arts and Sciences. In addition, the department offers study leading to the Master of Public Health and the Master of Science in Public Health degrees in biostatistics through the Rollins School of Public Health. The programs are designed for individuals with a strong background in the mathematical sciences and an interest in the biological or health sciences. Graduates have pursued a wide variety of career options in academia; federal, state, and local government; health agencies; health insurance organizations; the pharmaceutical industry; and other public and private research organizations.
	The research activities of the faculty members are diverse and include studies of national and international scope on the mathematical modeling of infectious diseases, including work on AIDS; estimation of vaccine efficacy; the design, management, and analysis of clinical trials; sample survey design and analysis; breast cancer epidemiology; reproductive epidemiology; aging and quality of life; statistics of vector-borne and parasitic diseases; statistical genetics; discrete multivariate analysis; linear models; categorical data analysis; probability; stochastic processes; statistical computing; and survival analysis. The Department of Biostatistics is situated within a rich environment of collaborative institutes. Many active research and employment opportunities for students are available at the Rollins School of Public Health, the Medical School, the neighboring Centers for Disease Control and Prevention (CDC)—the federal institute responsible for disease surveillance and control; the Carter Center; the American Cancer Society; the Georgia Department of Human Resources; and local health departments. The department coordinates the activities of the Biostatistics Consulting Center, which serves as a resource for advice on the design, conduct, and analysis of studies in the health sciences. Students may get hands-on experience in practical biostatistical problems through working with faculty members on real-life consulting problems.
	Biostatistics students are required to complete a core curriculum that consists of graduate courses in biostatistics. Advanced course work and research are tailored to the experience, training, area of concentration, and degree objective of each student. The M.S., M.S.P.H., and M.P.H. programs usually include four semesters of course work and generally take two years to complete. The Ph.D. degree program normally requires four calendar years to complete, including four to six semesters of course work.
Research Facilities	The Department of Biostatistics conducts active research programs in biostatistics, categorical data analysis, complex sample survey methods, and methods for infectious disease epidemiology. The Rollins School of Public Health is equipped with state-of-the-art computers and numerous microcomputers. A network of mainframe computers is accessible to the School through high-speed telecommunications lines. Extensive analytical research laboratories are housed in the School and at the CDC. Health sciences libraries are conveniently located at Emory University, the national headquarters of the American Cancer Society, and the CDC.
Financial Aid	Qualified Ph.D. students are supported by nationally competitive graduate school fellowships that include full tuition coverage and a stipend. Research assistantships may be available to M.S.P.H. and M.P.H. students. Financial aid information is available through the Office of Financial Aid.
Cost of Study	Tuition for M.S. and Ph.D. students in 1999–2000 is $11,385 per semester for full-time study or $949 per credit hour. For M.S.P.H. and M.P.H. students, the cost is $7500 per semester for full-time students or $655 per credit hour. The student activity and athletic fees total $150 per semester. In addition, the cost of books and supplies averages $1000 per year.
Living and Housing Costs	Living expenses for a single person are estimated to be $12,500 per year. Interested students may obtain information regarding University and off-campus housing by contacting the Housing Office.
Student Group	Emory University has a total enrollment of about 11,000 students. Enrollments in the various schools of the University are restricted in order to maintain a favorable balance between resources, faculty members, and students. There are approximately 6,000 students in the undergraduate college and 5,000 in the eight graduate and professional schools. The student body represents all areas of the United States and 105 nations.
Location	The Atlanta metropolitan area has a population of nearly 3 million. It is the academic center in the Southeast: there are eight major universities in the metropolitan area. Atlanta is green the year round, with numerous parks and a temperate climate. Professional, athletic, cultural, and recreational activities are available throughout the year. Atlanta is one of the leading convention centers in the United States, and the city is served by one of the busiest airports in the world, providing convenient access to national and international destinations. Atlanta was the site of the 1996 Summer Olympics.
The University and The School	Emory University ranks among the twenty-five most distinguished centers for higher education in the United States. The heavily wooded 631-acre campus features a blend of traditional and contemporary architecture. A main corridor through the campus incorporates the expanding health sciences complex with the headquarters of the CDC and the American Cancer Society. Within a short drive from the main campus are a variety of affiliated resources, such as the Georgia Mental Health Institute, the Georgia Department of Human Resources, the Carter Center of Emory University, and Grady Memorial Hospital.
	The Rollins School of Public Health has six academic departments, which offer M.P.H. and M.S.P.H. degrees—Behavioral Sciences and Health Education, Biostatistics, Environmental/Occupational Health, Epidemiology, Health Policy and Management, and International Health.
	The Rollins School of Public Health is ranked ninth in the nation by public health deans, faculty members, and administrators of accredited graduate programs of public health. Research strengths in the School make it the second-highest-ranked school at Emory in terms of research funding.
Applying	Minimum requirements for admission include a baccalaureate degree from an accredited college or university and satisfactory performance on the GRE. Prerequisites for the M.P.H., M.S.P.H., M.S., and Ph.D. program include at least two semesters of calculus and one semester of linear algebra. International students whose schooling has not been in English must submit a TOEFL score. Application forms for admission to the M.S./Ph.D. program may be obtained from the Graduate School of Arts and Sciences, Emory University, Atlanta, Georgia 30322. Admissions information on the M.S.P.H. and M.P.H. degrees can be obtained from the Office of Admissions, Rollins School of Public Health, Emory University, Atlanta, Georgia 30322.
Correspondence and Information	Marsha Ann Daly, Assistant Director of Academic Programs Department of Biostatistics Rollins School of Public Health Emory University 1518 Clifton Road, NE Atlanta, Georgia 30322 Telephone: 404-727-3968 E-mail: mdaly@sph.emory.edu World Wide Web: http://www.sph.emory.edu/hpbios.html

Emory University

THE FACULTY AND THEIR RESEARCH

Huiman X. Barnhart, Associate Professor; Ph.D., Pittsburgh, 1992. Analysis for repeated measures, categorical data analysis, clinical trials. Dr. Barnhart's research interests include developing models for categorical and continuous data with repeated measures. She has investigated models for multivariate random length data with applications in clinical trials, multinomial models for ordinal data, Markov models for HIV-infected children, goodness-of-fit tests for GEE modeling, and small-sample performance of the proportional odds model for correlated ordinal data fitted with GEE. She is currently involved in Emory Bypass and Angioplasty Trial and Pallidotomy for Parkinson's Disease Trial.

Donna J. Brogan, Professor; Ph.D., Iowa State, 1967. Sample survey design and analysis, breast cancer epidemiology. Dr. Brogan's interests focus on the theory and application of sample surveys. Federally funded surveys she has designed and/or conducted in Georgia include prevalence of hypertension among adults, prevalence of mental disorders among adults and children, quality of life among older persons, particularly older persons on dialysis, and prevalence of risk factors for breast cancer. Dr. Brogan conducts courses and workshops on specialized techniques for analyzing data from complex sample surveys. Current interests include comparison of random digit dialing sampling to area probability sampling, methods for estimation of epidemiological parameters such as relative risk and odds ratios using sample survey data, and survey integration.

Michael J. Haber, Professor; Ph.D., Hebrew (Jerusalem), 1976. Categorical data analysis, models of infectious diseases. Dr. Haber conducts research in categorical data analysis and statistical methods for the analysis of infectious disease data. In categorical data analysis, Dr. Haber generalizes existing models and develops new methods for investigating particular types of data. He also explores the properties of methods for 2x2 tables and developed an exact unconditional test for comparing two proportions. In the area of analyzing infectious disease data, Dr. Haber, in collaboration with Drs. Longini and Halloran, develops methods for estimation of transmission probabilities and for evaluating the efficacy and effectiveness of vaccines. These methods are applied to data on influenza, measles, mumps, and AIDS.

M. Elizabeth Halloran, Professor; M.D., Berlin, 1983; D.Sc., Harvard, 1989. Causal inference, epidemiologic methods for infectious disease, Bayesian methods, vaccine evaluation. Her research interests encompass methodological problems in studying and evaluating effects of interventions against infectious disease, especially vector-borne and parasitic diseases. Dr. Halloran draws on Bayesian methods and paradigms of causal inference. She has also worked on spatial mapping and inference for phylogenetic trees.

John J. Hanfelt, Assistant Professor; Ph.D., Johns Hopkins, 1994. Dr. Hanfelt's research interests are in the design and analysis of family-based case-control studies, longitudinal data analysis, and the theory of estimating functions and approximate likelihood inference.

Vicki Stover Hertzberg, Associate Professor and Chair, Department of Biostatistics; Ph.D., Washington (Seattle), 1980. Categorical data analysis, clinical trials, reproductive epidemiology. Dr. Hertzberg's research interests include categorical data analysis, especially for clustered binary data, as result from a variety of clinical trials in reproductive epidemiology studies. She works especially closely with neurologists involved in stroke research.

Andrzej S. Kosinski, Assistant Professor; Ph.D., Washington (Seattle), 1990. Linear models, cardiovascular clinical trials, statistical computing, survival analysis. Dr. Kosinski's interests are in undue influence of groups of observations on the estimation process and in diagnostic procedures to detect such influence. His work involves cardiovascular clinical trials, including the Emory Angioplasty-Surgery Trial (EAST).

Ira M. Longini Jr., Professor; Ph.D., Minnesota, 1977. Stochastic processes, models of infectious diseases. Dr. Longini's research interests are in the area of stochastic processes applied to epidemiological problems. He has specialized in the mathematical and statistical theory of epidemics—a process that involves constructing and analyzing mathematical models of infectious disease transmission and the analysis of infectious disease data based on these models. This work has been carried out jointly with other faculty members and collaborators at other universities and at the CDC. Dr. Longini has worked extensively on the analysis of epidemics of influenza, dengue fever, rhinovirus, rotavirus, measles, and HIV.

Robert H. Lyles, Assistant Professor, Ph.D., North Carolina at Chapel Hill, 1996. Longitudinal data analysis, prediction of random effects, measurement error models. Dr. Lyles' research has investigated applications in the areas of occupational and HIV epidemiology.

Amita K. Manatunga, Associate Professor; Ph.D., Rochester, 1990. Multivariate survival analysis, frailty models, categorical data analysis, longitudinal data. Dr. Manatunga's research interests focus on theory and application of survival data analysis. She has worked on multivariate survival data where the interest centers on estimating the covariate effects as well as the correlation between outcomes of survival times. She is interested in developing statistical methodologies based on frailty models and their application in genetics. Dr. Manatunga also has worked closely with medical researchers in the fields of hypertension and pharmacology. She is the biostatistician at the General Clinical Research Center of Emory University.

Lance A. Waller, Associate Professor; Ph.D., Cornell, 1992. Spatial statistics, point process models, environmental statistics. Dr. Waller's research interests involve statistical analysis of spatial patterns in public health data. Past investigations include development of statistical tests of spatial clustering in disease incidence data and implementation of spatial and space-time Markov random field models for maps of disease rates. He is currently investigating statistical methods to analyze environmental exposure, demographic, and disease incidence data linked through geographic information systems (GISs).

Adjunct Faculty

Carol A. Gotway Crawford, Mathematical Statistician, National Center for Environmental Health, Biometry Branch, Centers for Disease Control and Prevention; Ph.D., Iowa State, 1989. Spatial prediction and mapping, geostatistics, time series analysis, mixed model applications.

Owen J. Devine, Chief, Risk Assessment and Communication Section, Radiation Studies Branch, National Center for Environmental Health, Centers for Disease Control and Prevention; Ph.D., Emory, 1992. Use of stochastic methods in environmental health risk assessment, mapping of health effects of environmental exposure, methods for addressing uncertainty in environmental exposure, the planning and analysis of environmental epidemiologic studies.

John M. Karon, Mathematical Statistician, National Center for HIV, STD, and TB Prevention, Division of HIV/AIDS Prevention: Surveillance and Epidemiology, Centers for Disease Control and Prevention; Ph.D., Stanford, 1968. Epidemiologic methods, HIV/AIDS modeling, clinical trials.

Lillian S. Lin, Mathematical Statistician, National Center for HIV, STD, and TB Prevention, Division of HIV/AIDS Prevention: Surveillance and Epidemiology, Centers for Disease Control and Prevention; Ph.D., Washington (Seattle), 1990. Cluster-randomized studies, social and behavioral sciences applied to HIV/AIDS prevention.

Philip H. Rhodes, Mathematical Statistician, Division of Sexually Transmitted Disease Prevention, Centers for Disease Control and Prevention; Ph.D., Emory, 1992. Survival analysis, models for infectious disease data.

Glen A. Satten, Mathematical Statistician, Division of HIV/AIDS, Center for Infectious Diseases, Centers for Disease Control and Prevention; Ph.D., Harvard, 1985. Stochastic processes, HIV/AIDS modeling.

Donna F. Stroup, Associate Director for Science, Epidemiology Program Office, Centers for Disease Control and Prevention; Ph.D., Princeton, 1980. Stopping rules for stochastic approximations, disease surveillance, Bayesian approaches to detecting aberrations in public health surveillance data, ethical issues in public health.

Fengzhu Sun, Assistant Professor, Department of Genetics, Emory University School of Medicine; Ph.D., USC, 1994. Stochastic modeling of biological processes, computational biology, statistical genetics.

G. David Williamson, Assistant Director for Science, Division of Prevention Research and Analytic Methods, Epidemiology Program Office, Centers for Disease Control and Prevention; Ph.D., Emory, 1987. Methods for disease surveillance, epidemiologic studies.

John M. Williamson, Mathematical Statistician, National Center for HIV, STD, and TB Prevention, Division of HIV/AIDS Prevention: Surveillance and Epidemiology, Centers for Disease Control and Prevention; Sc.D., Harvard, 1993. Clustered correlated data, Interrater agreement, HIV/AIDS modeling.

Associate Faculty

Lisa K. Elon, Associate; M.P.H., Emory, 1997. Sample survey analysis, retrospective cohort study of industrial mercury exposure.

Michael J. Lynn, Senior Associate; M.S., Mississippi State, 1976. Clinical trials, statistical applications in ophthalmic research, statistical computing.

Claudine C. Manning, Associate; M.S., Virginia Commonwealth, 1998. Data management, clinical trials, statistical analysis.

Azhar Nizam, Senior Associate; M.S., South Carolina, 1987. Statistical education.

Rebecca H. Zhang, Senior Associate; M.S., Florida State, 1994. Data management, statistical analyses.

SELECTED PUBLICATIONS

Barnhart, H. X., and **J. M. Williamson.** Goodness-of-fit tests for GEE modeling with binary response. *Biometrics,* in press.

Wolf, S. L., and **H. X. Barnhart** et al. The effect of Tai Chi Quan and computerized balance training on postural stability in older subjects. *Phys. Ther.,* in press.

Albert, P. S., D. Follman, and **H. X. Barnhart.** A generalized estimating equation approach for modeling random-length binary vector data. *Biometrics* 53:1116–24, 1997.

Wolf, S. L., and **H. X. Barnhart** et al. Reducing frailty and falls in older persons: An investigation of Tai Chi and computerized balance training. *J. Am. Geriatr. Soc.* 44(5):489–97, 1996.

Barnhart, H. X., et al. Natural history of HIV disease in perinatally infected children: An analysis from the Pediatric Spectrum of Disease Project. *Pediatrics* 97:710–6, 1996.

Barnhart, H. X., and A. R. Sampson. Multiple population models for multivariate random-length data with applications in clinical trials. *Biometrics* 51(1):195–204, 1995.

Barnhart, H. X., and A. R. Sampson. Overview of multinomial models for ordinal data. *Commun. Stat.* 23(12):3395–416, 1994.

Barnhart, H. X. Models for multivariate random length data with applications in clinical trials. *Drug Information J.* 27:1147–57, 1993.

Brogan, D. J. Software for analysis of sample surveys: Misuses of standard packages. Invited chapter in *Encyclopedia of Biostatistics,* editors-in-chief P. Armitage and T. Colton. New York: John Wiley, in press.

Brinton, L., et al. **(D. J. Brogan).** Ethnicity and variation in breast cancer incidence. *Int. J. Cancer,* in press.

Frank, E., **D. J. Brogan,** and M. Schiffman. Prevalence and correlates of harassment among U.S. women physicians. *Arch. Intern. Med.,* in press.

Frank, E., and **D. J. Brogan** et al. Health-related behaviors of U.S. Women Physicians versus other U.S. women. *Arch. Intern. Med.,* in press.

Weiss, H., et al. **(D. J. Brogan).** Prenatal and perinatal risk factors for breast cancer in young women. *Epidemiology* 8(2):181–7, 1997.

Kutner, N., **D. J. Brogan,** and B. Fielding. Physical and psychosocial resource variables related to long-term survival in older dialysis patients. *Geriatr. Nephrol. Urol.* 7:23–9, 1997.

Malilay, J., D. Flanders, and **D. Brogan.** A modified cluster sampling method for post-disaster rapid needs assessment. *Bull. World Health Organ.* 74(4):399–405, 1996.

Weiss, H., et al. **(D. Brogan).** Epidemiology of in situ and invasive breast cancer in women aged under 45. *Br. J. Cancer* 73:1298–305, 1996.

Brogan, D., E. Flagg, M. Deming, and R. Waldman. Increasing the accuracy of the expanded programme on immunization's cluster survey design. *Ann. Epidemiol.* 4:302–11, 1994.

Goodman, S. H., **D. J. Brogan,** M. E. Lynch, and B. Fielding. Social and emotional competence in children of depressed mothers. *Child Dev.* 64:516–31, 1993.

Adams, M. M., and **D. J. Brogan** et al. Smoking, pregnancy, and source of prenatal care: Results from the Pregnancy Risk Assessment Monitoring System. *Obstet. Gynecol.* 80:738–44, 1992.

Brogan, D. J., N. Kutner, and E. Flagg. Survival differences among older dialysis patients in the Southeast. *Am. J. Kidney Dis.* 20(4):376–87, 1992.

Brogan, D. J., D. Lakatos, and E. Lakatos. Hypertension control in the U.S.: Not as bad as it seems? *Am. J. Epidemiol.* 124(5):738–45, 1986.

Slome, C., **D. J. Brogan,** S. Eyres, and W. Lednar. *Basic Epidemiological Methods and Biostatistics: A Workbook.* Belmont, Calif.: Wadsworth, 1983.

Browne, P. C., L. H. Hamner, and **W. S. Clark.** Ultrasound fetal growth curves from an indigent obstetrical population in Atlanta, Georgia: I. Singleton pregnancies. *Am. J. Perinatol.* 9:467–76, 1992.

Clark, W. S. Modeling infectious disease transmission probabilities from distinct contacts and its application to the human immunodeficiency virus. Ph.D. dissertation, Emory, 1990.

Haber, M. J. Estimation of the population effectiveness of vaccination. *Stat. Med.* 16:601–10, 1997.

Haber, M. J., W. A. Orenstein, **M. E. Halloran,** and **I. M. Longini.** The effect of disease prior to an outbreak on estimation of vaccine efficacy following the outbreak. *Am. J. Epidemiol.* 141:980–90, 1995.

Haber, M. J., L. Watelet, and **M. E. Halloran.** On individual and population effectiveness of vaccination. *Int. J. Epidemiol.* 24:1249–60, 1995.

Haber, M., I. M. Longini, and **M. E. Halloran.** Measures of the effects of vaccination in a randomly mixing population. *Int. J. Epidemiol.* 20:300–10, 1991.

Haber, M., I. M. Longini, and G. A. Cotsonis. Models for the statistical analysis of infectious data. *Biometrics* 44:163–73, 1988.

Haber, M., and M. B. Brown. Maximum likelihood methods for log-linear models when expected frequencies are subject to linear constraints. *J. Am. Stat. Assoc.* 81:477–82, 1986.

Haber, M. J. Testing for pairwise independence. *Biometrics* 42:429–35, 1986.

Haber, M. J. Maximum likelihood methods for linear and log-linear models in categorical data. *Comput. Stat. Data Anal.* 3:1–10, 1985.

Haber, M. J. Log-linear models for linked loci. *Biometrics* 40:189–98, 1984.

Haber, M. J. Testing for independence in intraclass contingency tables. *Biometrics* 38:93–103, 1982.

Golm, G. T., **M. E. Halloran,** and **I. M. Longini.** Semiparametric models for mismeasured exposure information in vaccine trials. *Statistics Med.,* in press.

Halloran, M. E., C. J. Struchiner, and **I. M. Longini.** Study designs for different efficacy and effectiveness aspects of vaccination. *Am. J. Epidemiol.* 146:789–803, 1997.

Halloran, M. E., M. Haber, I. M. Longini, and C. J. Struchiner. Estimation and interpretation of vaccine efficacy under frailty mixing models. *Am. J. Epidemiol.* 144:1–14, 1996.

Halloran, M. E., and C. J. Struchiner. Causal inference for interventions in infectious diseases. *Epidemiology* 6:142–51, 1995.

Hanfelt, J. J. Optimal multi-stage designs for a phase II trial that permits one dose escalation. *Statistics Med.,* in press.

Hanfelt, J. J., and K.-Y. Liang. Inference for odds ratio regression models with sparse dependent data. *Biometrics* 54:136–47, 1998.

Hanfelt, J. J. Statistical approaches to experimental design and data analysis of in vivo studies. *Breast Cancer Res. Treatment* 46:279–302, 1997.

Hanfelt, J. J., and K.-Y. Liang. Approximate likelihoods for generalized linear errors-in-variables models. *J. R. Stat. Soc. B* 59:627–37, 1997.

Liang, K.-Y., C. A. Rohde, and **J. J. Hanfelt.** Instrumental variable estimation and estimating functions. *Statistica Applicata* 8:43–58, 1996.

Hanfelt, J. J., and K.-Y Liang. Approximate likelihood ratios for general estimating functions. *Biometrics* 82:461–77, 1995.

Liang, K.-Y., and **J.J. Hanfelt.** On the use of the quasi-likelihood method in tautological experiments. *Biometrics* 50:872–80, 1994.

Hertzberg, V. S. Simulation evaluation of three models for correlated binary data with covariates specific to each binary observation. *Commun. Stat.* 26:375–96, 1997.

Rosenman, K., et al. **(V. S. Hertzberg).** Silicosis among foundry workers: Implication for the need to revise the OSHA standard. *Am. J. Epidemiol.* 144:890–900, 1996.

Reilly, M. J., et al. **(V. S. Hertzberg).** Ocular effects of exposure to triethylamine in a foundry sand core cold box operation. *Occup. Environ. Med.* 52:337–43, 1995.

Hertzberg, V. S. Utilization 2: Special datasets. *Stat. Med.* 14:693, 1995.

Hertzberg, V. S., C. Rice, S. Pinney, and D. Linz. Occupational epidemiology in the era of TQM: Challenges for the future. In *1994 Proceedings of the Epidemiology Section, American Statistical Association.*

Hertzberg, V. S., G. K. Lemasters, K. Hansen, and H. M. Zenick. Statistical issues in risk assessment of reproductive outcomes with chemical mixtures. *Environ. Health Perspect.* 90:171–5, 1991.

Hertzberg, V. S., and L. D. Fisher. A model for variability in arteriographic reading. *Statistics Med.* 5:619–27, 1986.

Stiger, T. R., **A. S. Kosinski, H. X. Barnhart,** and D. G. Kleinbaum. ANOVA for repeated ordinal data with small sample size? A comparison of ANOVA, MANOVA, WLS and GEE methods by simulation. In *Communications in Statistics—Simulation and Computation,* in press.

Cecil, M. C., and **A. S. Kosinski** et al. The importance of work-up (verification) bias correction in assessing the accuracy of SPECT thallium-201 testing for the diagnosis of coronary artery disease. *J. Clin. Epidemiol.* 49(7):735–42, 1996.

Waksman, R., and **A. S. Kosinski** et al. Relation of lumen size to restenosis after percutaneous transluminal coronary balloon angioplasty. Lovastain Restenosis Trial Group. *Am. J. Cardiol.* 78(2):221–4, 1996.

Treasure, C. B., et al. **(A. S. Kosinski).** Beneficial effects of cholesterol-lowering therapy on the coronary endothelium in patients with coronary artery disease. *N. Engl. J. Med.* 332(8):481–7, 1995.

Weintraub, W. S., et al. **(A. S. Kosinski).** A comparison of the costs of and quality of life after coronary angioplasty versus coronary surgery for multivessel coronary artery disease: Results from the Emory Angioplasty vs Surgery Trial (EAST). *Circulation* 92(10):2831–40, 1995.

Flanders, W. D., C. D. Drews, and **A. S. Kosinski.** Use of two data

Emory University

Selected Publications (continued)

sources to estimate odds ratios in case-control studies with a differential misclassification is present across two strata. *Epidemiology* 6(2):152–6, 1995.

King III, S. B., et al. **(A. S. Kosinski** and **H. X. Barnhart).** A randomized trial comparing coronary angioplasty with coronary bypass surgery: Emory Angioplasty Versus Surgery Trial (EAST). *N. Engl. J. Med.* 331(16):1044–50, 1994.

Weintraub, W. S., et al. **(A. S. Kosinski).** Lack of effect of lovastatin on restenosis after coronary angioplasty. *N. Engl. J. Med.* 331(20):1331–7, 1994.

Weintraub, W. S., **A. S. Kosinski,** C. L. Brown III, and S. B. King III. Can restenosis be predicted after coronary angiography from clinical variables? *JACC* 21(1):6–14, 1993.

Drews, C. D., W. D. Flanders, and **A. S. Kosinski.** Use of two data sources to estimate odds ratios in case-controlled studies. *Epidemiology* 4:327–35, 1993.

Cain, K. C., R. A. Kronmal, and **A. S. Kosinski.** Analyzing the relationship between change in a risk factor and risk of disease. *Stat. Med.* 11:783–97, 1992.

Durham, L. K., et al. **(I. M. Longini, M. E. Halloran,** and **A. Nizam).** Estimation of vaccine efficacy in the presence of waning: Application to cholera vaccines. *Am. J. Epidemiol.*, in press.

Longini, I. M., S. Datta, and M. E. Halloran. Measuring vaccine efficacy for both susceptibility to infection and reduction in infectiousness for prophylactic HIV-1 vaccines. *J. Acquired Immun. Defic. Syndromes Hum. Retrovirol.* 13:440–7, 1996.

Longini, I. M., and M. E. Halloran. A frailty mixture model for estimating vaccine efficacy. *Appl. Stat.* 45:165–73, 1996.

Longini, I. M., and M. E. Halloran. AIDS: Modeling epidemic control. Letter to the editor. *Science* 267:1250–1, 1995.

Longini, I. M., M. E. Halloran, and M. J. Haber. Estimation of vaccine efficacy from epidemics of acute infectious agents under vaccine-related heterogeneity. *Math. Biosci.* 117:271–81, 1993.

Longini, I. M., W. S. Clark, and J. M. Karon. Effect of routine use of therapy in slowing the clinical course of human immunodeficiency virus infection in a population-based cohort. *Am. J. Epidemiol.* 137:1229–40, 1993.

Longini, I. M., M. E. Halloran, M. Haber, and R. T. Chen. Methods for estimating vaccine efficacy from outbreaks of acute infectious agents. *Stat. Med.* 12:249–63, 1993.

Longini, I. M., R. H. Byers, N. A. Hessol, and W. Y. Tan. Estimating the stage-specific numbers of HIV infection using a Markov model and back-calculation. *Stat. Med.* 11:831–43, 1992.

Longini, I. M., W. S. Clark, L. I. Gardner, and J. F. Brundage. The dynamics of CD4+ T-lymphocyte decline in HIV-infected individuals: A Markov modeling approach. *J. AIDS* 4:1141–7, 1991.

Longini, I. M., and W. S. Clark et al. Statistical analysis of the stages of HIV infection using a Markov model. *Stat. Med.* 8:831–43, 1989.

Longini, I. M. A mathematical model for predicting the geographic spread of new infectious agents. *Math. Biosci.* 90:367–83, 1988.

Longini, I. M., J. S. Koopman, M. J. Haber, and G. A. Cotsonis. Statistical inference on risk-specific household and community transmission parameters for infectious diseases. *Am. J. Epidemiol.* 128:845–9, 1988.

Lyles, R. H., et al. Prognostic value of HIV RNA in the natural history of *Pneumocystis carinii* pneumonia, cytomegalovirus, and *Mycobacterium avium* complex disease. *AIDS*, in press.

Lyles, R. H., et al. Adjusting for measurement error to assess health effects of variability in biomarkers. *Statistics Med.*, in press.

Lyles, R. H., and J. Xu. Classifying individuals based on predictors of random effects. *Statistics Med.* 18:35–52, 1999.

Lyles, R. H., and L. L. Kupper. AUMVU estimators for the population mean and variance based on random effects models for lognormal data. *Commun. Statistics-Theory Methods* 27:795–818, 1998.

Lyles, R. H., and L. L. Kupper. A detailed evaluation of adjustment methods for multiplicative measurement error in multiple linear regression, with applications in occupational epidemiology. *Biometrics* 53:1008–25, 1997.

Stein, D. S., **(R. H. Lyles),** et al. Predicting clinical progression or death in subjects with early stage HIV infection: A comparative

analysis of quantification of HIVRNA, soluble TNF type II receptors, neopterin, and b_2-microglobulin. *J. Infect. Dis.* 176:1161–7, 1997.

Lyles, R. H., L. L. Kupper, and S. M. Rappaport. On prediction of lognormal-scale mean exposure levels in epidemiologic studies, *J. Agricultural, Biol., Environ. Stats.* 2:417–39, 1997.

Lyles, R. H., and L. L. Kupper. On strategies for comparing occupational exposure data to limits. *Am. Indust. Hyg. Assoc.* 57:6–15, 1996.

Lyles, R. H., and L. E. Chambless. Effects of model misspecification in the estimation of variance components and intraclass correlation for paired data, *Statistics Med.* 14:1693–706, 1995.

Rappaport, S. M., R. H. Lyles, and L. L. Kupper. An exposure-assessment strategy accounting for within- and between-worker sources of variability. *Ann. Occ. Hygiene* 39(4):469–95, 1995.

Chen, M.-H., A. K. Manatunga, and C. J. Williams. Heritability estimates from human twin data by incorporating historical prior information. *Biometrics*, in press.

Manatunga, A. K., and D. Oakes. A measure for bivariate frailty distribution. *J. Multivar. Analysis* 56:60–74, 1996.

Oakes, D., and A. K. Manatunga. Fisher information for a bivariate extreme value distribution. *Biometrika* 79:827–32, 1992.

Oakes, D., and A. K. Manatunga. A new representation of Cox's score statistic and its variance. *Stat. Probab. Lett.* 4:107–10, 1992.

Rhodes, P., M. E. Halloran, and I. M. Longini. Counting process models for infectious disease data: Distinguishing exposure to infection from susceptibility. *J. R. Stat. Soc. B* 58:751–62, 1997.

Satten, G. A., and I. M. Longini. Markov chains with measurement error: Estimating the "true" course of a marker on HIV disease progression (with discussion). *Appl. Stat.* 45:275–309, 1996.

Satten, G. A., and I. M. Longini. Estimation of incidence of HIV infection using cross-sectional marker surveys. *Biometrics* 50:675–88, 1994.

Satten, G. A., T. D. Mastro, and I. M. Longini. Estimating the heterosexual transmission probability of HIV-1 in Thailand. *Stat. Med.* 13:2097–106, 1994.

Yu, C., L. A. Waller, and D. Zelterman. A discrete distribution for use in twin studies. *Biometrics* 54:546–57, 1998.

Waller, L. A., and R. B. McMaster. Incorporating indirect standardization in tests for disease clustering in a GIS environment. *Geog. Systems* 4:327–42, 1997.

Waller, L. A., T. A. Louis, and B. P. Carlin. Bayes methods for combining disease and exposure data in assessing environmental justice. *Environ. Ecol. Statistics* 4:267–81, 1997.

Waller, L. A., and D. Zelterman. Log-linear modeling with the negative multinomial distribution. *Biometrics* 53:971–82, 1997.

Waller, L. A., B. P. Carlin, and H. Xia. Structuring correlation within hierarchical spatio-temporal models for disease rates. *In Modeling Longitudinal and Spatially Correlated Data: Lecture Notes in Statistics 122,* pp. 309–19, eds. T. G. Gregoire, D. R. Brillinger, P. J. Diggle, E. Russek-Cohen, W. G. Warren, and R. D. Wolfinger. New York: Springer Verlag, 1997.

Waller, L. A., B. P. Carlin, H. Xia, and A. Gelfand. Hierarchical spatio-temporal mapping of disease rates. *J. Am. Stat. Assoc.* 92:607–17, 1997.

Xia, H., B. P. Carlin, and L. A. Waller. Hierarchical models for mapping Ohio lung cancer rates. *Environmetrics* 8:107–20, 1997.

Lawson, A. B., and L. A. Waller. A review of point pattern methods for spatial modeling of events around sources of pollution. *Environmetrics* 7:471–88, 1996.

Waller, L. A., Does the characteristic function numerically distinguish distributions? *Am. Statistician* 49:150–2, 1995.

Waller, L. A., and G. M. Jacquez. Disease models implicit in statistical tests of disease clustering. *Epidemiology* 6:584–90, 1995.

Williamson, G. D., and M. J. Haber. Models for three-dimensional contingency tables with completely and partially cross-classified data. *Biometrics* 50:194–203, 1994.

Williamson, J. M., and A. K. Manatunga. Assessing interrater agreement from dependent data. *Biometrics* 53(2):707–14, 1997.

GEORGE MASON UNIVERSITY

Institute for Computational Sciences and Informatics

Program of Study

The Institute for Computational Sciences and Informatics (CSI) offers a doctoral program in the broad area of computational sciences. It focuses on graduate student training leading to a Ph.D. in computational sciences and informatics. Computational sciences is defined as the systematic development and application of computational methodologies and computational techniques to understand, model, and simulate phenomena in the natural sciences and engineering. Informatics is defined as the systematic development and application of computing systems to computational techniques, analysis of data, modeling, and database search. The doctoral program provides interdisciplinary research opportunities in several computational areas, including astrophysics, material science, biology, chemistry, fluid dynamics, applied mathematics, physics, space sciences, statistics, and earth systems and global change.

The doctoral program combines three intellectual elements: core computational science topics; computational intensive courses in specific scientific areas; and research leading to the dissertation. Entering students have a bachelor's degree in mathematics, engineering, computer science, or a natural science. The doctoral program is designed to be completed in four to five years and includes 12 hours of core computational courses (scientific computing, databases, visualization), 12 hours from courses in one of the science areas, 12 hours in electives from science courses, 12 hours from computational topics, and 24 hours in dissertation research.

Multidisciplinary graduate research is conducted at CSI. The Institute's research activities reflect the recognized role of computation as part of a triad with theory and experiment to generate new knowledge and a better understanding of nature. The Institute maintains several active and well-attended weekly seminar series that ensure frequent communication with scientists from other institutions. Participation in national and international meetings is encouraged.

Research Facilities

The CSI Computing Facility houses a massively parallel computer, the Intel Paragon, with 61 nodes, 1 gigabyte RAM, and a high-performance symmetric multiprocessor computer, the Silicon Graphics Origin 2000, with 16 nodes and 4 gigabytes RAM. There is also a Silicon Graphics cluster consisting of 24 workstations (O2 and octane) and a Microsoft Windows NT Cluster using 12 Pentium Pro and Pentium machines, which can be accessed from X-Windows platforms. In addition, there are several research computer platforms available to advanced students actively pursuing research in collaboration with faculty members. General University facilities are available to CSI students. CSI program information can be accessed on the World Wide Web (http://www.science.gmu.edu).

Financial Aid

A limited number of highly competitive research assistantships are available carrying a full tuition waiver and a stipend. The 1998–99 stipend was about $11,500 for the fiscal year. Assistantships in research, fellowships, and student loans are available. Further information can be obtained from CSI.

Cost of Study

Full-time students take at least 9 credit hours per semester. In 1998–99, out-of-state tuition was $521 per credit hour, and in-state tuition was $181 per credit hour.

Living and Housing Costs

Approximately 3,000 students live on campus in six residential areas. Most graduate students prefer off-campus housing. Estimated costs per year are $3200–$4000 for room, $1500–$1800 for board, and $600 for books and supplies. Further information can be obtained by calling the Office of Housing at 703-993-2720.

Student Group

The total number of doctoral students at CSI is currently 180. Full-time students number about 56, and the remainder are part-time students. A wide variety of age groups and academic, ethnic, and national backgrounds are represented among these students.

Location

George Mason University and the surrounding community together provide an ideal environment for learning and research. The campus is located 15 miles from Washington, D.C., on 583 wooded acres in Fairfax, northern Virginia. The setting combines the quietness of a residential suburban area with access to Fairfax County's high-technology firms; to Washington, D.C.'s libraries, galleries, museums, and national and federal laboratories; and to Virginia's historical sites. The Patriot Center and the Performing Arts Center house continuous community activities and recreational events. The 2,000-seat Concert Hall is host to full-scale music, dance, opera, and theater of the most renowned productions. The Sports and Recreational Complex and the three student unions available on campus also offer a variety of recreational activities.

The University and The Institute

In the last decade, George Mason University has emerged as a major academic institution offering nationally recognized programs in advanced technology and science, among others. From its origins in 1957, George Mason has grown into a medium-sized state university in northern Virginia with innovative programs that have attracted a faculty of world-renowned scholars and teachers. In 1979, George Mason received doctoral status approval. CSI, founded in 1991, is a dynamic and forward-looking institute with a strong commitment to develop a diverse and innovative research curriculum.

Applying

A bachelor's degree in mathematics, engineering, computer science, or any natural science with a minimum GPA of 3.0 is needed to apply. The GRE is required. A TOEFL score of 575 is required for international students. All international transcripts must be evaluated by a U.S. evaluation service. These are listed in the Application for Admission. Applications should be received by March 1 for the fall semester and by November 1 for the spring semester. Applications requesting financial support should be received by February 1 for the fall semester, and GRE scores are part of the consideration for financial support.

Correspondence and Information

Office of the Graduate Coordinator
CSI/Institute for Computational Sciences and Informatics
George Mason University
Fairfax, Virginia 22030-4444
Telephone: 703-993-1990
Fax: 703-993-1980
E-mail: pbecker@science.gmu.edu

George Mason University

THE FACULTY AND THEIR RESEARCH

Director
W. Murray Black, Professor; Ph.D., Penn State, 1971. Microwave engineering and processing of advanced ceramics.

CSI Full-time Faculty
Peter Becker, Associate Professor; Ph.D., Colorado, 1987. Astrophysics.
Avrama Blackwell, Associate Professor; Ph.D., Pennsylvania, 1988. Bioengineering.
Estela Blaisten-Barojas, Professor; Ph.D., Paris VI (Curie), 1974. Computational molecular physics and condensed-matter physics.
Tarek A. El-Ghazawi, Associate Professor; Ph.D., New Mexico State, 1988. Computer architecture.
James E. Gentle, Professor; Ph.D., Texas A&M, 1973. Computational statistics.
Menas Kafatos, Professor; Ph.D., MIT, 1972. Astrophysics and space sciences.
Rainald Löhner, Associate Professor; Ph.D., Swansea (Wales), 1984. Computational fluid dynamics.
George S. Michaels, Associate Professor; Ph.D., Florida, 1985. Molecular biology and bioinformatics.
Jagadish Shukla, Professor and Director of the Center for Ocean and Land Atmospheric Studies; Ph.D., MIT, 1967. Meteorology and global change.
John Wallin, Associate Professor; Ph.D., Iowa State, 1989. Astronomy and astrophysics.

CSI Part-time Faculty
Jim Beall, Adjunct Professor; Ph.D., Maryland, 1979. Astrophysics and space sciences.
John Guillory, Senior Contract Professor; Ph.D., Berkeley, 1970. Plasma science.
Steven Hanna, Research Professor; Ph.D., Penn State, 1967.
Paul Hertz, Senior Contract Associate Professor; Ph.D., Harvard, 1983. Astrophysics, statistical astronomy.
Lawrence Hunter, Senior Contract Professor; Ph.D., Yale, 1989. Machine learning and molecular biology.
Leonid M. Ozernoy, Senior Contract Professor; Ph.D., Shternberg Astronomical Institute (Moscow), 1966. Astrophysics and space sciences.
Dimitris Papaconstantopoulos, Senior Contract Professor; Ph.D., London, 1967. Solid-state physics.
Jeff Solka, Contract Assistant Professor; Ph.D., George Mason, 1995. Computational statistics.
Valery Soyfer, Professor; Ph.D., Byelorussia State (Minsk), 1974. Molecular biology.
Lev Titarchuk, Research Professor; Ph.D., Space Research Institute (Moscow), 1972.
Edward J. Wegman, Dunn Professor; Ph.D., Iowa, 1968. Computational statistics.
Kent Wood, Senior Contract Professor; Ph.D., MIT, 1973. Astrophysics and space sciences.

CSI Program Faculty in Other Departments and Institutes
Daniel Carr, Professor; Ph.D., Stanford, 1973. Applied and engineering statistics.
Peter H. Ceperly, Associate Professor; Ph.D., Stanford, 1973. Electrical and computer engineering.
Stephen Davis, Associate Professor; Ph.D., Yale, 1976. Quantum chemistry and spectroscopy.
Peter J. Denning, Professor; Ph.D., MIT, 1968. Computer sciences.
Maria Dworzecka, Professor; Ph.D., Warsaw (Poland), 1969. Nuclear and computational physics.
Robert Ehrlich, Professor; Ph.D., Columbia, 1964. Physics.
Robert Ellsworth, Professor; Ph.D., Rochester, 1965. High-energy particle physics.
John C. Evans, Associate Professor; Ph.D., Michigan, 1966. Physics.
Gregory D. Foster, Associate Professor; Ph.D., California, Davis, 1985. Environmental chemistry.
Barry Haack, Professor; Ph.D., Michigan, 1977. Geography.
R. Chris Jones, Associate Professor; Ph.D., Wisconsin, 1980. Environmental biology.
Ittai Kan, Associate Professor; Ph.D., Illinois, 1984. Dynamical systems.
Larry Kerschberg, Professor; Ph.D., Case Western Reserve, 1969. Software engineering and intelligent databases.
B. Joseph Lieb, Professor; Ph.D., William and Mary, 1971. Experimental nuclear physics.
Jeng-Eng Lin, Associate Professor; Ph.D., Brown, 1976. Partial differential equations and neural networks.
Andrzej S. Manitius, Professor; Ph.D., Warsaw Technical, 1968. Control theory and dynamics.
John J. Miller, Associate Professor; Ph.D., Stanford, 1974. Statistics.
Harold Morowitz, Robinson Professor; Ph.D., Yale, 1951. Biology.
George W. Mushrush, Professor; Ph.D., George Washington, 1968. Fuels chemistry.
Stephen G. Nash, Associate Professor; Ph.D., Stanford, 1982. Operations research.
Eugene Norris, Associate Professor; Ph.D., Florida, 1969. Computer science.
David Rine, Professor; Ph.D., Iowa, 1970. Computer science.
Robert L. Sachs, Associate Professor; Ph.D., NYU (Courant), 1970. Nonlinear partial differential equations.
Stephen H. Saperstone, Professor; Ph.D., Maryland, 1970. Ordinary differential equations.
Indubala Satija, Professor; Ph.D., Columbia, 1983. Nonlinear dynamics.
Timothy D. Sauer, Associate Professor; Ph.D., Berkeley, 1982. Chaos and dynamical systems.
Arun Sood, Professor; Ph.D., Carnegie-Mellon, 1971. Computer science.
Mark Spikell, Professor; Ph.D., Boston University, 1972. Education.
Daniele Struppa, Professor; Ph.D., Maryland, 1981. Complex analysis.
Clifton Sutton, Assistant Professor; Ph.D., Stanford, 1987. Statistics.
Mark R. Walbridge, Assistant Professor; Ph.D., North Carolina, 1986. Biology.
Pearl Wang, Associate Professor; Ph.D., Wisconsin, 1980. Computer sciences.
Harry Wechsler, Professor; Ph.D., California, Irvine, 1975. Computer vision.
James D. Willett, Professor; Ph.D., MIT, 1965. Biochemistry.
Kent Wood, Adjunct Professor; Ph.D., MIT, 1973. Astrophysics and space sciences.
Stanley M. Zoltek, Associate Professor; Ph.D., SUNY at Stony Brook, 1976. Differential geometry.

CSI Affiliate Faculty
David P. Bacon, Affiliate Professor; Ph.D., Dartmouth, 1982. Atmospheric physics.
Alex Belenki, Affiliate Associate Professor; Ph.D., Levedev Institute (Moscow), 1975. Computational materials sciences and metallurgy.
Zafer Boybeyi, Affiliate Assistant Professor; Ph.D., North Carolina, 1993. Meteorology, atmospheric physics.
Joseph Feldman, Affiliate Professor; Ph.D., Rutgers, 1965. Condensed-matter physics.
Bruce Gaber, Affiliate Professor; Ph.D., USC, 1968. Biochemistry.
David George, Affiliate Associate Professor; Ph.D., Temple, 1985. Bioinformatics and computer science.
Patrick M. Gillevet, Affiliate Associate Professor; Ph.D., Manitoba, 1982. Molecular biology.
Randy Jost, Affiliate Associate Professor; Ph.D., Missouri–Columbia, 1988. Computational fluid dynamics.
Micah Krichevsky, Affiliate Professor; Ph.D., Illinois, 1958. Bacteriology.
Byungkook Lee, Affiliate Associate Professor; Ph.D., Cornell, 1967. Physical chemistry.
James Olds, Affiliate Associate Professor; Ph.D., Michigan, 1987. Neuroscience.
Ross Overbeek, Affiliate Professor; Ph.D., Penn State, 1971. Computational sciences and bioinformatics.
Adrian E. Roitberg, Affiliate Assistant Professor; Ph.D., Illinois at Chicago, 1992. Physical chemistry.
A. Ananthakrishna Sarma, Affiliate Professor; Ph.D., Colorado State, 1986. Atmospheric science.
Michael Summers, Adjunct Associate Professor; Ph.D., Caltech, 1985. Atmospheric physics.
Edward Szuszczewicz, Affiliate Associate Professor; Ph.D., 1969, St. Louis. Space sciences.
Derek A. Tidman, Affiliate Professor; Ph.D., London, 1956. Plasma physics.

THE GEORGE WASHINGTON UNIVERSITY

Programs in Statistics and Biostatistics

Programs of Study

The Department of Statistics offers graduate programs leading to the M.S. and Ph.D. degrees in statistics; the M.S. and Ph.D. degrees in biostatistics; and the M.S. degree in engineering and industrial statistics.

The degree of Master of Science in statistics has two options: mathematical statistics and applied statistics. The M.S. in biostatistics is offered jointly with the School of Public Health and Health Services, and the M.S. in engineering and industrial statistics is offered jointly with the Department of Operations Research. The master's programs are designed primarily to provide professional degrees for those seeking careers as statisticians in government or industry or as biostatisticians. No thesis is required.

The Ph.D. degree programs provide students with additional training to engage in research and teaching at the university level. The Ph.D. degree program in biostatistics is offered jointly with the School of Public Health and Health Services.

Part-time study toward either master's or Ph.D. degrees is possible. Students enrolled part-time are required to maintain a course load of 6 hours per semester.

Research Facilities

In addition to an extensive collection of statistical journals at the Gelman Library, George Washington University (GWU) students have online access to the collected holdings of the Washington Research Library Consortium, which comprises eight local universities. The department and the University maintain an array of modern computing equipment, both stand-alone and mainframe. The Biostatistics Center, administered by the department, serves as the statistical center for several large-scale medical research programs. A unit of the Biostatistics Center provides statistical support to research activities of the GWU Medical Center. Biostatistics students can gain consulting experience in cooperation with the Biostatistics Center or the center's Medical Center Unit.

Financial Aid

A limited number of teaching assistantships, research assistantships, and fellowships are available to entering graduate students. Teaching assistants received 18 semester hours of tuition credit per year in addition to (in 1998–99) a salary and a stipend of $10,800. Their duties include assisting faculty members with undergraduate instruction or statistical consultation at the Computer Information and Resource Center. Research assistants generally work with faculty members at the Biostatistics Center or the Medical Center Unit. Student loan programs are available.

Cost of Study

The tuition fee for graduate study was $680 per credit hour for 1998–99. In addition, all students were required to pay a University fee of $34.50 per credit hour.

Living and Housing Costs

Many graduate students live in nearby rooms and apartments. The University's location on a main subway line gives quick access to campus from lower-cost areas in Virginia and Maryland as well as the District of Columbia.

Student Group

The graduate and professional enrollment at the University is approximately 11,000. There are about 40 students enrolled in the department's graduate programs, of whom more than half are doctoral students.

Location

The University is located in downtown Washington, D.C., a city rich in architectural and historical treasures. The campus is 10 minutes' walk from the John F. Kennedy Center for the Performing Arts and is equally close to the White House. A multitude of museums, libraries, restaurants, and cultural and historic attractions are easily accessible from the University. Nearby recreational opportunities include Rock Creek Park, the C&O Canal, the Chesapeake Bay, and the Blue Ridge Mountains.

Washington is the center of statistical and biostatistical activity for the federal government, including the Bureau of the Census, the Bureau of Labor Statistics, the National Institutes of Health, and the Food and Drug Administration. The Washington Statistical Society is the largest chapter of the American Statistical Association and offers a wide variety of seminars and short courses.

The University and The Department

The George Washington University a private, nonsectarian institution, has just celebrated its 175th anniversary. A comprehensive university, it offers professional training in law, medicine, engineering, business, and education in addition to a full range of undergraduate and graduate studies. The Department of Statistics, founded in 1935, is the oldest statistics department in an arts and sciences college in the United States. The Biostatistics Center, founded in 1972, is known worldwide for its work in clinical trials.

Applying

Applications for financial assistance should be received by February 1. For admission without financial aid, fall semester deadlines are March 1 for the Ph.D. programs and May 1 for the master's programs; the spring semester deadline is October 1. For admission to all graduate programs, the Graduate Record Examinations General Test is required. International applicants for financial aid are required to take the TOEFL and the Test of Spoken English.

Correspondence and Information

For application forms and a
University Bulletin:
Columbian School of Arts and
Sciences
The George Washington University
Washington, D.C. 20052
Telephone: 202-994-6210

For information about statistics
programs:
Chair
Department of Statistics
The George Washington University
Washington, D.C. 20052
Telephone: 202-994-6888
E-mail: statp1@gwu.edu
World Wide Web: http://www.gwu.
edu/~stat/

For information about biostatistics
programs:
Ava Flores
School of Public Health and Health
Services
Ross Hall
The George Washington University
Washington, D.C. 20052
Telephone: 202-994-2632
E-mail: sphasf@gwumc.edu
World Wide Web: http://www.bsc.
gwu.edu

The George Washington University

THE FACULTY AND THEIR RESEARCH

Raymond Bain, Research Professor of Statistics and Biostatistics; Ph.D., Emory, 1981. Design and analysis of clinical trials.
Predictors of progression from impaired glucose tolerance to NIDDM: An analysis of six prospective studies. *Diabetes,* 1997. With coauthors.
Nonparametric tests of stochastic ordering for multiple longitudinal measures. *J. Biopharm. Stat.,* 1995. With Rosenberger and Lachin.
Sudip Bose, Associate Professor of Statistics; Ph.D., Purdue, 1990. Bayesian statistics, Bayesian robustness, genetic statistics.
Nondependence of the predictive distribution on the population size. *Stat. Prob. Lett.,* 1996. With Kedem.
Maximin efficiency-robust tests and some extensions. *J. Stat. Plann. Inference,* 1995. With Slud.
Bayesian robustness with mixture classes of priors. *Ann. Stat.,* 1994.
Efstathia Bura, Assistant Professor of Statistics; Ph.D., Minnesota, 1996. Regression and regression graphics, multivariate analysis, nonparametrics.
Testing the adequacy of regression functions. *Biometrika,* 1997. With Cook.
Dimension reduction via parametric regression. L_1-*Stat. Proc. Rel. Top.,* 1997.
Joseph L. Gastwirth, Professor of Statistics and Economics; Ph.D., Columbia, 1963. Nonparametric and robust statistical inference; applications in law, economics, and public policy.
Diagnostic Test Methodology in the Design and Analysis of Judge–Jury Agreement. *Jurimetrics,* 1998. With Sinclair.
Statistical evidence in discrimination cases. *J. R. Stat. Soc. A,* 1997.
Statistical Reasoning in Law and Public Policy. Orlando: Academic Press, 1988.
Samuel W. Greenhouse, Professor Emeritus of Statistics; Ph.D., George Washington, 1959. Biostatistics, clinical trials, epidemiologic methods.
Some reflections on the beginnings and developments of statistics at the NIH. *Stat. Sci.,* 1998.
The joint asymptotic distribution of the maximum likelihood and the Mantel-Haenszel estimators of the common odds ratio in k 2x2 tables. *Modelling Prediction,* 1996. With Gastwirth.
Angiographic findings and outcomes in diabetic patients treated with thrombolytic therapy for acute myocardial infarctions. *J. Am. Coll. Cardiol.,* 1996. With coauthors.
David A. Grier, Assistant Professor of Statistics; Ph.D., Washington (Seattle), 1986. History and sociology of computing, mathematics, and technology.
Henry Wallace and the Start of Statistical Computing. *Chance,* 1999.
The Math Tables Project: The Reluctant Start of the Computing Era. *Annals of the History of Computing,* 1998.
Politics, Control, and Computer Networks: The Chinese Student Lobby of 1989. *Communications of the ACM,* 1998.
Arthur D. Kirsch, Professor Emeritus of Statistics and Psychology; Ph.D., Purdue, 1957. Survey research, experimental design, statistics in public policy.
Giving and volunteering in the United States. *Ind. Sector,* 1997. With coauthors.
From belief to commitment. *Ind. Sector,* 1993. With coauthors.
John M. Lachin, Professor of Statistics and Biostatistics and Director of the Biostatistics Center; Sc.D., Pittsburgh, 1972. Statistical methods for clinical trials, repeated measures with incomplete observations, survival analysis.
Group sequential monitoring of distribution-free analyses of repeated measures. *Stat. Med.,* 1997.
Sequential monitoring of survival data with the Wilcoxon statistic. *Biometrics,* 1995. With Lan and Rosenberger.
Martingales without tears. *Lifetime Data Anal.,* 1995. With Lan.
Zhaohai Li, Associate Professor of Statistics and Biostatistics; Ph.D., Columbia, 1989.
Establishing the nadir of the body mass index–mortality relationship. A case study. *J. Am. Stat. Assoc.,* 1997. With Durazo-Arvizu, McGee, and Cooper.
A random effects model for meta-analysis of multiple quantitative sibpair linkage studies. *Genet. Epidemiol.,* 1996. With Rao.
Hubert Lilliefors, Professor of Statistics; Ph.D., George Washington, 1964. Simulation, goodness-of-fit tests.
It's time to stop. In *Computer Science and Statistics, Proceedings of the 19th Symposium on the Interface,* 1988.
Kolmogorov-Smirnov and Anderson-Darling statistics with parameters estimated by linear combination of order statistics and some robustness properties. In *Colloquia Mathematica Societatis Janos Bolyai,* 1987.
Hosam Mahmoud, Professor of Statistics; Ph.D., Ohio State, 1983. Analysis of algorithms, design of combinatorial and randomized algorithms, random structures.
On rotations in fringe-balanced binary trees. *Inf. Proc. Lett.,* 1998.
On tree-growing search strategies. *Ann. Appl. Prob.,* 1997. With Lent.
On the distribution for the duration of a randomized leader election algorithm. *Ann. Appl. Prob.,* 1996. With Szpankowski and Fill.
Reza Modarres, Associate Professor of Statistics; Ph.D., American, 1990. Computer-intensive methods, statistical computing, Monte Carlo Risk Analysis.
A hybrid test of symmetry. *Appl. Stat.,* 1998. With Gastwirth.
A modified test for symmetry. *Stat. Prob. Lett.,* 1996. With Gastwirth.
Bootstrap power of the generalized correlation coefficient. *Stats. Comput.,* 1996.
Tapan K. Nayak, Professor of Statistics; Ph.D., Pittsburgh, 1983. Software reliability, diversity analysis, inference.
Estimating the number of components of a system of superimposed renewal processes. *Sankhya Ser. A,* 1995. With Dewanji and Sen.
Sequential unbiased estimation of the number of classes in a population. *Stat. Sinica,* 1994. With Christman.
Pitman nearness comparison of some estimators of population variance. *Am. Stat.,* 1994.
James Rochon, Associate Research Professor of Statistics and Biostatistics; Ph.D., North Carolina, 1985. Statistical methods for clinical trials, repeated measures.
Application of the GEE procedure for sample size calculations in repeated measures experiments. *Stat. Med.,* 1998.
Analyzing bivariate repeated measures for discrete and continuous outcome variables. *Biometrics,* 1996.
Accounting for covariates observed post randomization for discrete and continuous repeated measures data. *J. R. Stat. Soc. B,* 1996.
Nozer D. Singpurwalla, Professor of Operations Research and of Statistics; Ph.D., NYU, 1968. Reliability theory, Bayesian inference, and foundational issues.
Unification of software reliability models by self-exciting point processes. *Adv. Appl. Prob.,* 1997. With Chen.
A Bayesian assessment of network reliability. *SIAM Rev.,* 1997. With Lynn and Smith.
Burn-in makes us feel good. *Stat. Sci.,* 1997. With Lynn.
Blaza Toman, Associate Professor of Statistics; Ph.D., Ohio State, 1987. Optimal design of experiments, Bayesian statistics.
Bayesian Sample Size Calculation For The Binomial Experiment. *J. Stat. Planning* and *INFELENCE,* 1999. With Katsis.
The U.S. versus Marine Shale Processors: Statistical issues. *Environmetrics,* 1997. With Gastwirth.
Bayes experimental design for multiple hypothesis testing. *J. Am. Stat. Assoc.,* 1996.

GEORGIA STATE UNIVERSITY

College of Arts and Sciences
Department of Mathematics and Statistics

Programs of Study

The Department of Mathematics and Statistics offers programs leading to the degrees of Master of Arts (M.A.), Master of Science (M.S.), and Master of Arts for Teachers (M.A.T.). All degrees require 36 semester hours of study. The M.A. and M.S. degrees in mathematics may be earned with a concentration in computer information systems, computer science, statistics, or statistics with an allied field. Both thesis and nonthesis options are available. The M.A.T. degree is a nonthesis degree. All graduate degrees require a general examination.

Research Facilities

The departmental local area network consists of 130 machines, each of which is connected via Ethernet to the University Net, and includes thirty-two UNIX machines, eighty-five Pentium PCs, thirteen Pentium II PCs, and twenty Macintosh machines. In addition, there are six laboratories, including two smaller labs. University-wide large-scale computing is offered via an Amdahl 5995-500 that uses IBM's MVS/XA operating system and a Unisys 2200/500, which supports the library. A Silicon Graphics Power Challenge L provides support for research and instructional use. A Sun SPARCserver 1000 supports UNIX-based e-mail services. More than 100 network fileservers provide access to centrally supplied software, support e-mail (GroupWise), and provide services to more than 4,000 microcomputer workstations, including more than 450 workstations in open and instructional labs.

Financial Aid

Normally, research assistantships that pay up to $3000 per semester, laboratory assistantships, teaching assistantships, and tuition waivers are available. Students working on specific research programs are also often supported by extramural funds.

Cost of Study

For current tuition figures, please visit the University's Web site at http://www.gsu.edu.

Living and Housing Costs

Georgia State University has a nonresidential campus located in downtown Atlanta at the center of a network of highways and rapid-transit services that extend throughout the greater metropolitan area. This transportation network makes it possible to live anywhere in the metropolitan area and get to downtown easily. The cost of living in Atlanta is moderate compared with that in other centers in the United States. Dormitory housing is available at the Georgia State Village, which is a short distance from Georgia State's downtown campus.

Student Group

Georgia State University is a public institution with more than 24,000 students. Its graduate student population of more than 7,000 is one of the largest in the Southeast. The average age of graduate students is 33. Students from 113 countries and all fifty states attend the University.

Location

The University is located in the heart of Atlanta's central business district. The city is a rapidly growing metropolitan area characterized by a spectacular skyline and a culturally diverse population. Atlanta's Hartsfield International Airport is one of the world's largest and busiest, making the city easily accessible from anywhere in the world. The climate is moderate, with a mean July temperature of 23°C and a mean January temperature of 10°C. Atlanta is located in the foothills of the southern Appalachian mountain range and is close to both the Great Smoky Mountains and the Atlantic and Gulf coasts.

The University

Georgia State University is responsive to students' career goals and provides educational and research programs that are relevant to the practical needs of both the students and the community. The University offers nearly fifty undergraduate and graduate programs covering some 200 fields of study through its five colleges—Arts and Sciences, Business Administration, Education, Health and Human Services, and Law—and the School of Policy Studies.

Applying

Application materials may be obtained from the department or from the Office of Graduate Studies of the College of Arts and Sciences. Applicants must submit the Application for Graduate Study and the University information forms, a $25 application fee, official copies of transcripts from each institution attended, General Test scores on the Graduate Record Examinations, and a list of references. Applicants may obtain additional information about the Department of Mathematics and Statistics by contacting the Director of Graduate Studies or by viewing the Web page, listed below.

Correspondence and Information

Director of Graduate Studies
Department of Mathematics and Computer Science
Georgia State University
University Plaza
Atlanta, Georgia 30303-3083

Telephone: 404-651-2253
Fax: 404-651-2246
E-mail: matgjd@langate.gsu.edu
World Wide Web: http://www.cs.gsu.edu

Georgia State University

THE FACULTY AND THEIR RESEARCH

Margo P. Alexander, Instructor; Ph.D., Georgia State, 1993. Mathematics education.
Mihaly Bakonyi, Assistant Professor; Ph.D., William and Mary, 1992. Linear algebra, operator theory.
Jean H. Bevis, Professor; Ph.D., Florida, 1965. Linear algebra.
Guantao Chen, Assistant Professor; Ph.D., Memphis State, 1991. Combinations and graph theory.
Susmita Datta, Assistant Professor; Ph.D., Georgia, 1995. Statistical genetics, infectious disease modeling, survival analysis.
George J. Davis, Associate Professor; Ph.D., New Mexico, 1979. Numerical analysis.
Lifeng Ding, Associate Professor; Ph.D., Georgia, 1990. Operator theory.
Gayla S. Domke, Associate Professor; Ph.D., Clemson, 1988. Graph theory.
Ed Dubinsky, Professor; Ph.D., Michigan, 1962. Mathematics education, functional analysis.
Carolyn A. Eschenbach, Associate Professor; Ph.D., Clemson, 1987. Linear algebra, matrix analysis.
Frank J. Hall, Professor; Ph.D., North Carolina State, 1973. Matrix analysis, linear algebra.
Johannes Hattingh, Assistant Professor; Ph.D., Rand Afrikaans, 1989. Graph theory, algorithmic graph theory.
Yu-Sheng Hsu, Associate Professor; Ph.D., Purdue, 1975. Mathematical statistics, econometrics, biostatistics.
Zhongshan Li, Assistant Professor; Ph.D., North Carolina State, 1990. Matrix theory.
Michael J. Meyer, Associate Professor; Ph.D., Oregon, 1988. Banach algebras, Banach spaces.
Valerie A. Miller, Assistant Professor; Ph.D., South Carolina, 1985. Numerical analysis, mathematical visualization.
Vadim Olshevsky, Assistant Professor; Ph.D., Voronezh (Russia), 1989. Operator theory, fast algorithms, numerical accuracy of computations, structured matrices, rational interpolation, signal processing.
Victor Patrangenaru, Assistant Professor; Ph.D., Indiana, 1988; Ph.D., Haifa, 1994. Statistics, mathematics.
Ronald F. Patterson, Associate Professor; Ph.D., South Carolina, 1984. Probability theory.
Draga Vidakovic, Assistant Professor; Ph.D., Purdue, 1993. Mathematics education.
Joseph J. Walker, Associate Professor; Ph.D., North Carolina at Chapel Hill, 1976. Multivariate analysis, distribution theory, computational statistics.

RESEARCH ACTIVITIES

Combinatorics and graph theory: Variations of colorings, independence and domination in graphs, ranks of graphs, graph algorithms, applications of combinatorics in VLSI design and software engineering, optimization methods.

Differential geometry and topology: Homogeneous spaces, general relativity, Riemannian geometry, harmonic maps, Lie groups.

Functional analysis: Non-selfadjoint operator algebras, ideals, norms on Banach algebras, operators on Banach spaces, dilation theory, operator-valued analytic functions, interpolation, Frechet spaces.

Matrix theory: Matrix completions and factorizations, generalized inverses of matrices, integer matrices, LU-factorizations of matrices, qualitative matrix analysis, sign pattern matrices, structured matrices, consimilarity of matrices, combinatorial matrix theory.

Mathematics education: Visualization of mathematical concepts, technology in the classroom, theories of learning, curriculum development, innovative pedagogy, cooperative learning, alternative assessment, teacher education.

Numerical analysis: Numerical analysis and numerical linear algebra, parallel implementation of techniques in numerical analysis and numerical linear algebra, fast algorithms, numerical accuracy, signal processing.

Statistics: Distribution theory, multivariate analysis, econometrics, biostatistics, computational statistics, estimation under order restrictions, multiple comparisons of response rates, applied statistics, probability, limit theorems for dependent and independent random variables, statistical genetics, infectious disease modeling, survival analysis, large sample theory, bootstrap, directional and shape analysis.

Human-computer interaction: Hypermedia, multimedia, computer-supported cooperative work, visual representations of concepts and processes in mathematics, applications of fractals in mathematical visualization, visualization methods for data analysis and teaching, medical imaging.

Parallel computation: Parallel algorithms and data structures, parallel compilation.

IOWA STATE UNIVERSITY

Department of Mathematics

Programs of Study

The department offers programs leading to the Ph.D. in mathematics or applied mathematics, the M.S. in mathematics or applied mathematics, and the Master of School Mathematics. All the graduate programs have considerable flexibility to suit individual needs. The faculty has strong, active research groups in algebra, applied mathematics, combinatorics, computational mathematics, control theory, functional analysis, logic, mathematical biology, numerical analysis, partial differential equations, and stochastic processes. A large portion of the faculty members are engaged in interdisciplinary research.

The M.S. degree in mathematics or applied mathematics requires 30 credits, including four courses (12 credits) in core areas (chosen from algebra, analysis, or applied mathematics). The program may be taken either with a thesis or with a creative component (a formal mathematics paper) option. Typically, students earn an M.S. degree in two years of graduate study. The Master of School Mathematics degree is intended for in-service secondary mathematics teachers.

The Ph.D. degree in mathematics or applied mathematics requires 72 credits. The credits must include 54 credits of course work with 18 of those in core courses. Doctoral degree students must also pass written qualifying exams and an oral preliminary exam. Each student must do an original piece of mathematical research that is described in a thesis and pass a final oral examination on the thesis. Typically, students earn a Ph.D. degree in four to six years of graduate study.

Research Facilities

The Department of Mathematics is located in Carver Hall—a modern, air-conditioned, centrally located facility. The Mathematics Reading Room, conveniently located in the department, has extensive holdings and current issues of many research journals. Excellent computing facilities are available for students and faculty, including DEC, SGI, and Sun workstations; Macintoshes; and Gateway machines.

Financial Aid

Teaching assistantships are available to support most of the students admitted to a degree program. Teaching assistants normally teach no more than three courses per academic year, do some paper grading for a faculty member, or work in a helproom. The starting stipend for the 1999–2000 academic year is $11,900. Exceptional applications will be considered for additional awards to supplement the assistantship stipend. Research and teaching assistantships are also available for summer support.

Cost of Study

Teaching assistants currently pay $1584 per year in tuition. Full tuition scholarships are available for some well qualified students.

Living and Housing Costs

Private and University housing in a variety of price ranges is available in the immediate campus area, as well as in areas served by the city bus system. The yearly cost of living is estimated at $6200.

Student Group

The Department of Mathematics has more than 50 graduate students. The total University enrollment is approximately 25,000 students.

Student Outcomes

In recent years, many M.S. students have continued in Ph.D. programs at Iowa State or other schools. Other students have found positions teaching junior college or with firms such as Texas Instruments, Ricoh Industries, IBM, the National Security Association, and insurance companies.

Iowa State's Ph.D. students have typically found jobs teaching mathematics at four-year colleges or universities. Others have been successful in finding jobs in the private sector at companies such as Lockheed Martin, World Precision Instruments, Exxon, Boeing Aerospace, Bell Labs, and Western Geophysical.

Location

The University is situated on a 1,000-acre tract in Ames, Iowa (population, 50,000), 35 miles north of the state capital of Des Moines. Ames is at the crossroads of three major highways: running north and south, I-35, and running east and west, U.S. 30 and (30 miles to the south) I-80. The city offers a calendar of social, cultural, and athletic activities that surpasses that of many much larger metropolitan areas. Students, faculty members, and Ames residents are a cosmopolitan group, representing more than 100 countries. The city maintains more than 700 acres of woods, streams, and open meadows as parks, and the general atmosphere of Ames is relaxed and friendly.

The University

Iowa State was chartered in 1858 and became the land-grant institution for the state of Iowa after the passage of the Morrill Act. Graduate study was offered almost as soon as classes began in 1868, and the first graduate degree was conferred in 1877.

Students interested in applying are invited to write the Graduate Coordinator at the address below for appropriate forms and application information. All applicants must supply GRE General Test scores. All international applicants must supply TOEFL scores, as well as GRE General Test and GRE Mathematics Subject Test scores. International students awarded assistantships must pass a speaking test upon arrival to receive the full stipend. To receive full consideration for financial support, applications should be completed by February 1. However, late applications will be considered.

Correspondence and Information

Professor Janet Peterson, Graduate Coordinator
Department of Mathematics
Iowa State University
Ames, Iowa 50011-2064
Telephone: 515-294-8171 or 1752
Fax: 515-294-5454
E-mail: gradmath@iastate.edu
World Wide Web: http://www.math.iastate.edu/

Iowa State University

THE FACULTY AND THEIR RESEARCH
R. Alexander, Ph.D., Berkeley. Numerical analysis.
D. Ashlock, Ph.D., Caltech. Discrete mathematics, graph theory, artificial life.
K. Athreya, Ph.D., Stanford. Stochastic processes.
C. Bergman, Ph.D., Berkeley. Universal algebra, logic, analysis of algorithms.
B. Cain, Ph.D. Wisconsin. Linear algebra.
P. Colwell, Ph.D., Minnesota. Complex analysis.
J. Cornette, Ph.D., Texas. Biomathematics, biomolecular structures.
R. Dahiya, Ph.D., India. Delay and advanced differential equations, transform theory.
D. D'Alessandro, Ph.D., California, Santa Barbara; Ph.D., Universita 'degli Studi di Pavoda, Italy. Control theory.
Q. Du, Ph.D., Carnegie Mellon. Numerical analysis, applied mathematics, parallel computing.
O. Emanouvilov, Ph.D., Moscow State. Partial differential equations, control theory.
J. Evans, Ph.D., Adelaide (Australia). Nonequilibrium statistical mechanics.
A. Fink, Ph.D., Iowa State. Inequalities, differential equations.
A. Gautesen, Ph.D., Northwestern. Development of asymptotic methods for direct and inverse scattering problems.
R. Gregorac, Ph.D., Iowa. Algebra, group theory, geometry.
M. Gunzburger, Ph.D., NYU. Numerical analysis, finite element methods, computational fluids and control, superconductivity.
S. Hansen, Ph.D., Wisconsin–Madison. Analysis, control theory.
K. Heimes, Ph.D., Nebraska. Free-boundary problems.
I. Hentzel, Ph.D., Iowa. Computer algorithms, deterministic and probabilistic for processing algebraic identities.
L. Hogben, Ph.D., Yale. Nonassociative rings.
L. S. Hou, Ph.D., Carnegie Mellon. Numerical analysis, control theory, partial differential equations, fluids.
E. Johnston, Ph.D., Illinois. Complex analysis, geometric function theory, faber series expansions on simply connected sets.
F. Keinert, Ph.D., Oregon State. Numerical analysis, wavelets.
B. Keller, Ph.D., Western Michigan. Mathematics education, collegiate mathematics education.
W. Kliemann, Ph.D., Bremen (Germany). Stochastic and deterministic system theory, applications in mechanical and electrical engineering.
H. Levine, Ph.D., Cornell. Ill-posed problems, eigen value problems, systems of reaction-diffusion equations, chemotoxis.
G. Lieberman, Ph.D., Stanford. Elliptic partial differential equations.
G. Luecke, Ph.D., Caltech. Parallel algorithms.
R. Maddux, Ph.D., Berkeley. Logic.
J. Murdock, Ph.D., NYU. Dynamical systems, perturbation theory, averaging and normal forms.
E. Peake, Ph.D., New Mexico State. Algebra.
J. Peters, Ph.D., Minnesota. Operator theory, operator algebras.
J. Peterson, Ph.D., Tennessee, Knoxville. Numerical analysis, finite element methods, superconductivity, computational fluids.
D. Pigozzi, Ph.D., Berkeley. Logic.
Y. Poon, Ph.D., UCLA. Operator algebra, matrix theory.
P. Sacks, Ph.D., Wisconsin. Partial differential equations, inverse problems.
T. Seppalainen, Ph.D., Minnesota. Probability theory, large deviation theory, statistical mechanics, scaling limits of interacting processes.
S. Sethuraman, Ph.D., NYU. Stochastic analysis.
M. Smiley, Ph.D., Michigan. Partial differential equations, dynamical systems.
J. Smith, Ph.D., Cambridge (England). Combinatorics, algebra and information theory, applications in computer science, physics, biology.
R. Smith, Ph.D., Montana State. Numerical analysis, applied mathematics, parameter estimation, control theory.
S. Song, Ph.D., Ohio State. Combinatorics.
M. Tidriri, Ph.D., Paris IX (Dauphine). Mathematical physics, numerical analysis, scientific computing.
R. Tondra, Ph.D., Michigan State. Manifold theory.
B. Wagner, Ph.D., Berkeley. Operator algebras.
X. Wang, Ph.D., Indiana. Partial differential equations, Navier-Stokes equations.
A. Weerasinghe, Ph.D., Minnesota. Stochastic processes.
S. Willson, Ph.D., Michigan. Fractals, differential topology.
J. Wilson, Ph.D., Wisconsin. Special functions.
F. Wright, Ph.D., Northwestern. Integration theory.

JOHNS HOPKINS UNIVERSITY

Department of Mathematical Sciences

Programs of Study

The Department of Mathematical Sciences offers programs in statistics/probability/stochastic processes, discrete mathematics, and operations research/optimization/decision science leading to the M.A., M.S.E., and Ph.D. degrees. These programs are supported by a strong curriculum in computational and applied mathematics, including matrix and numerical analysis. A graduate program may emphasize one of the primary areas or may be more diversified in the mathematical sciences. Research specializations for the doctoral dissertation may be selected from an area represented in the department or may be interdisciplinary and involve allied faculty members in other departments.

Fields represented in the department include probability, stochastic processes, mathematical statistics, statistical inference, applied statistics, operations research, continuous and discrete optimization, numerical optimization, computer modeling, game theory, numerical analysis, matrix analysis, graph theory, graph algorithms, and combinatorics. Closely allied departments include Biostatistics, which offers programs involving the application of statistics in the life sciences; and Geography and Environmental Engineering, which offers programs involving the application of operations research to public-sector planning and policy analysis. Close liaisons are also maintained with the Departments of Computer Science and Mathematics and with the Johns Hopkins Applied Physics Laboratory.

Master's degree programs require students to take eight to ten 1-semester graduate courses in a coherent program. Doctoral degree programs include, in addition, a program of original research and its clear exposition in a written dissertation worthy of publication as a significant contribution to knowledge.

Research Facilities

The University's Milton S. Eisenhower Library, on the Homewood campus, one of the nation's foremost research facilities, has more than 2 million volumes, general stack access, a highly qualified staff, capability for computerized literature searches, ample photocopying facilities, and study carrels for graduate students. The facilities of Homewood Academic Computing's three time-sharing systems, workstations, and terminals are available to students for research and instruction. Terminals for access are available in the department. The department maintains a variety of personal computers, terminals and printers, a reference collection of books and journals, and a lounge for use by the faculty and graduate students. Office space is provided for full-time resident graduate students.

Financial Aid

Full tuition and an academic-year stipend are awarded competitively to Ph.D. candidates. The stipend level depends on the source, which may be a fellowship, teaching assistantship, or research assistantship. The minimum nine-month stipend for 1999–2000 is $13,500. In addition, summer employment opportunities are usually available through the University or in the Baltimore-Washington area.

Cost of Study

Tuition for 1999–2000 is $23,660; first-year students also pay a matriculation fee of $500.

Living and Housing Costs

Nearby off-campus accommodations, ranging from simple efficiencies to spacious apartments with French windows and marble steps, are available in five University-owned security apartment buildings. Current rents, including furnishings and utilities, vary from $250 to $700 per month for single students and from $500 to $1500 for married students. Other off-campus housing is also available nearby. General assistance is provided by the University's Housing Office. The campus cafeterias and other neighborhood eating establishments offer a variety of culinary attractions at reasonable prices.

Student Group

The University enrolls approximately 3,500 undergraduates and 1,500 graduate students in the School of Arts and Sciences and the School of Engineering. There are 35 undergraduates and 39 Ph.D. candidates in the Department of Mathematical Sciences. Among the graduate students, about one third are international students and about one third are women. Formal graduate classes at Hopkins are often quite small, and students and their research advisers usually have close working relationships.

Student Outcomes

Doctoral graduates follow a number of career paths. A majority obtain academic positions, but significant numbers are employed in government agencies and laboratories and in industry.

Location

The historic 140-acre Homewood campus is located in one of the finest residential neighborhoods in the northern section of Baltimore. Adjacent to the campus is the Baltimore Museum of Art, and short distances away are the Peabody Conservatory of Music, Walters Art Gallery, Joseph Meyerhoff Symphony Hall, Morris Mechanic Theater, Center Stage, Oriole Park at Camden Yards, Pimlico Race Course (site of the Preakness), and the acclaimed downtown Inner Harbor, home of the National Aquarium, Maryland Science Center, and many fine restaurants and shops.

Washington, D.C., just an hour away, offers an international atmosphere abundant with cultural and recreational opportunities, such as the Kennedy Center, the Smithsonian Institution, and the Library of Congress.

The University and The Department

Privately endowed, Johns Hopkins University was founded in 1876 as a graduate and research institution offering collegiate preparation. The faculty members seek a balance between their commitment to scholarship and research and their commitment to teaching. In addition to the School of Arts and Sciences and the School of Engineering at the Homewood campus, the University has several other divisions. In East Baltimore, contiguous with the renowned Johns Hopkins Hospital, are the School of Medicine and the School of Hygiene and Public Health. (The University provides a free shuttle between the Homewood, Peabody, and East Baltimore campuses.) The School of Advanced International Studies is located in Washington, D.C.; this school also has a center for foreign studies in Bologna, Italy. The Johns Hopkins Applied Physics Laboratory, noted for contributions to applied sciences in a variety of fields, lies midway between Baltimore and Washington. The Peabody Institute, a leading professional school of music affiliated with Johns Hopkins, is located near the Homewood campus. The Homewood campus is also the location of the scientific research facility for the Space Telescope, an instrument placed in orbit around the earth in 1990. The Athletic Center, on the Homewood campus, is available to students and the faculty seven days a week.

Applying

Application materials for admission and financial assistance are available from the department, along with further information on programs and facilities. Completed applications, letters of recommendation, transcripts, and GRE scores (the General Test plus the Subject Test in mathematics) are due by January 15 for initial decisions. International students whose native language is not English must also provide official TOEFL score reports at this time.

Correspondence and Information

Graduate Admissions Coordinator
Department of Mathematical Sciences
Johns Hopkins University
Baltimore, Maryland 21218-2682
Telephone: 410-516-7198
Fax: 410-516-7459

Johns Hopkins University

THE FACULTY AND THEIR RESEARCH

Members of the primary department faculty are listed below. In addition, jointly appointed or visiting faculty members join the department each year.

Cheng Cheng, Assistant Professor; Ph.D., Texas A&M, 1993. Nonparametric statistics, applied probability.

Lenore Cowen, Assistant Professor; Ph.D., MIT, 1993. Discrete mathematics, combinatorics, graph algorithms.

James A. Fill, Professor; Ph.D., Chicago, 1980. Probability, stochastic processes, random structures, algorithms.

Alan J. Goldman, Professor; Ph.D., Princeton, 1956. Operations research, game theory, optimization, graph theory.

Leslie Hall, Associate Professor; Ph.D., MIT, 1989. Combinatorial optimization, integer programming.

Shih-Ping Han, Professor; Ph.D., Wisconsin, 1974. Parallel optimization, mathematical programming.

Lancelot F. James, Assistant Professor; Ph.D., SUNY at Buffalo, 1995. Statistics, bootstrap.

Daniel Q. Naiman, Professor; Ph.D., Illinois at Urbana-Champaign, 1982. Statistics, probability, geometry.

Jong-Shi Pang, Professor; Ph.D., Stanford, 1976. Mathematical programming, network equilibrium, computational finance, computational economics, engineering optimization.

Carey E. Priebe, Assistant Professor; Ph.D., George Mason, 1993. Statistics, nonparametric estimation, image analysis.

Edward R. Scheinerman, Professor; Ph.D., Princeton, 1984. Discrete mathematics, graph theory, partially ordered sets, random methods.

John C. Wierman, Professor and Chair; Ph.D., Washington (Seattle), 1976. Probability, stochastic processes, statistics, random graphs.

Colin Wu, Associate Professor; Ph.D., Berkeley, 1990. Statistics, semiparametric models, nonparametric smoothing techniques.

RESEARCH ACTIVITIES

Recent research projects of the department faculty and graduate students include:

Empirical and quantile processes.
Multisample nonparametric comparison.
Perfect sampling using Markov chain Monte Carlo.
Self-organizing data structures.
Network programming models of ecosystem development.
Partially ordered sets.
Simultaneous statistical inference.
Regression and analysis of variance models.
Nonlinear methods in multivariate analysis.
Numerical methods in nonlinear programming.
Probabilistic analysis of algorithms.
Critical values in bond, site, and mixed percolation models.
Optimal location of obnoxious and mesometric facilities.

Numerical analysis and algorithms.
The linear complementarity problem.
Finite-dimensional variational inequalities.
Theory of intersection graphs.
Robust estimation of Rayleigh distribution parameters.
Rates of convergence of Markov chains.
Scheduling theory.
Random graphs.
Optimization in network design.
Algorithms for network optimization.
Smoothing techniques and nonparametric regression.
Statistical image analysis.
Semiparametric estimation and testing.

MATHEMATICAL SCIENCES LECTURE SERIES

The Department of Mathematical Sciences hosts a weeklong, research-level lecture series during some summers. A distinguished mathematical scientist delivers the lectures, and the conference is attended by advanced graduate students and researchers. The conference is sponsored by the department, the Johns Hopkins University Press, and federal agencies. Recent speakers and topics have been Carsten Thomassen (graphs on surfaces), 1993; Ulf Grenander (statistical analysis of patterns and images), 1991; W. T. Trotter (partially ordered sets), 1990; Arthur P. Veinott Jr. (lattice programming), 1989; Robert C. Thompson (matrix spectral inequalities), 1988; Richard Karp (probabilistic analysis of algorithms), 1987; Peter C. Fishburn (nonlinear utility theory), 1986; Charles R. Johnson (combinatorial aspects of matrix theory), 1985; A. N. Shiryayev (inference for diffusion processes), 1984; Peter J. Bickel (adaptive statistical inference), 1983; Ralph L. Disney (queuing networks and applications), 1982; Darwin Klingman (network flows), 1981.

WEEKLY SEMINAR SERIES

Each week during the academic year, the Mathematical Sciences department hosts a Thursday afternoon seminar series. Faculty members or invited guests present a lecture on their current research. While it is a public forum, the seminar series is designed to give students the opportunity to explore areas of interest with the faculty and help students decide what they wish to pursue.

THE ACHESON J. DUNCAN LECTURE IN MATHEMATICAL SCIENCES

Created in 1986 through funding by an anonymous donor, the endowment supports an annual lecture and visit by a distinguished mathematical scholar. The lectureship honors the late Professor Emeritus Acheson J. Duncan, who was a faculty member for twenty-five years. Dr. Duncan is internationally recognized for his contributions in quality control and industrial statistics. Past participants have included Dr. Rudolph Beran, University of California at Berkeley; Dr. Peter Ney, University of Wisconsin–Madison; Dr. Persi Diaconis, Harvard University; Dr. David J. Aldous, University of California at Berkeley; Dr. Michael Saks, Rutgers University; Dr. Rick Durett, Cornell University; and Dr. David Pollard, Yale University.

THE ACHESON J. DUNCAN FUND FOR EXCELLENCE IN RESEARCH AND STATISTICS

This fund is used to support statistical research by faculty members. It was created in 1986 through funding by an anonymous donor to honor the late Professor Emeritus Acheson J. Duncan, who was a faculty member for twenty-five years. Dr. Duncan is internationally recognized for his contributions in quality control and industrial statistics.

RECENT DISSERTATION TOPICS AND INITIAL EMPLOYMENT POSITIONS

"Linear Smoothing Methods with Longitudinal Dependent Variable," Chin-Tsang Chiang (1998). Assistant Professor, Department of Statistics, Tunghai University, Taiwan.

"Posets, Graphs, and Matrices," Donniell Fishkind (1998). University of Southern Maine.

"Random Walks on Wreath Products of Groups and Markov Chains on Related Homogenous Spaces," Clyde H. Schoolfield Jr. (1998). Visiting Assistant Professor, Department of Mathematics, Duke University.

"Complementarity Problems in Robotics," Grace Lo (1997). Associate, ICF Kaiser International, Inc., Fairfax, Virginia.

"Stochastic Approximation Algorithms: Theory and Application," Nathan Kleinman (1996). Teacher, Brigham Young University, Provo, Utah.

"Facility Location with Forbidden Regions," Glenn Sabin (1996). Consultant, ZS Associates, Princeton, NJ.

"Advancing the Resampling Paradigm," Dominic Lee (1996). Defense Science Organization, Singapore.

"Random Intersection Graphs," Karen Singer (1995). Assistant Professor, School of Mathematics, University of Minnesota.

"Interior Point Algorithms for Constrained Systems of Equations," Tao Wang (1995). TransQuest Information Solutions, Atlanta, Georgia.

"Markov Chain Analysis of Some Self-organizing Schemes for Lists and Trees," Robert Dobrow (1994). Postdoctoral Research Associateship, National Institute of Standards and Technology, Gaithersburg, MD; Assistant Professor, Division of Mathematics, Truman State University.

"An Algorithmic Analysis of Multiquadratic and Semidefinite Programming Problems," Motakuri Ramana (1994). Postdoctoral Fellow, Rutgers Center for Operations Research, New Brunswick, NJ.

"Large Derivations of U-Empirical Probability Measures and Statistical Functionals," Wenyang Wang (1994). University of Texas at Dallas.

"The Grassmann Manifold and Statistics," Onn Chan (1992). Department of Mathematics, National University of Singapore.

"Algorithms for the Nonlinear Complementarity Problem: The NE/SQP Method and Extensions," Steven Gabriel (1992). Consultant, Arthur D. Little, Inc., Washington, D.C.

"Topics in Matrix Analysis," Dennis I. Merino (1992). Department of Mathematics, Southeastern Louisiana University.

"AB Percolation," Martin J. Appel (1991). Eliezer Naddor Fellowship, Department of Mathematics, Cornell University; Assistant Professor, Department of Statistics and Actuarial Science, University of Iowa.

"Vehicle Routing on Acyclic Networks," Ingrid K. Busch (1991). Oak Ridge National Laboratory, Oak Ridge, TN.

"Preparation Cost Structures in Inspection Games," Alan J. Kosansky (1991). Operations Research Analyst, Rohm and Haas, Philadelphia, PA.

"Nonsmooth Optimization: Algorithms and Applications," Narayan Rangaraj (1991). Department of Mechanical Engineering, Indian Institute of Technology, Powai, Bombay.

"Sequencing Jobs for a Machine Subject to Weardown," Steven J. Steinsaltz (1991). Assistant Professor, Department of Mathematics and Statistics, Trenton State College.

"Generalized Perfect Graphs," Ann N. Trenk (1991). Eliezer Naddor Fellowship, Department of Mathematics and Computer Science, Dartmouth College; Assistant Professor, Department of Mathematics, Wellesley College.

Johns Hopkins University

SELECTED PUBLICATIONS

Cheng, C., and Y. L. Tong. Concentration order on a metric space, with some statistical applications. *Stat. Probability Lett.,* in press.

Cheng, C. A Berry-Esseen type theorem of quantile density estimators. *Stat. Probability Lett.* 39:255–62, 1998.

Cheng, C., and E. Parzen. Unified estimators of smooth quantile and quantile density functions. *J. Stat. Plann. Inference* 59:291–307, 1997.

Cheng, C., G. M. Maggiora, M. Lajiness, and M. A. Johnson. Four association coefficients for relating molecular similarity measures. *J. Chem. Info. Sys. Comp. Sci.* 36:909–15, 1996.

Cheng C. Uniform consistency of generalized kernel estimators of quantile density. *Ann. Stat.* 23:2285–91, 1995.

Cheng, C. The Bernstein polynomial estimator of a smooth quantile function. *Stat. Probability Lett.* 24:321–330, 1995.

Cheng, C., and M. A. Johnson. Relative aggregation and random quadrat sampling. *Computing Science and Statistics,* pp. 81–5, ed. J. Sall, 1994.

Cowen, L., and C. Priebe. Randomized nonlinear projections uncover high-dimensional structure. *Adv. Appl. Math.* 19:319–31, 1997.

Cowen, L., and R. Mathar. The offset problem. *Combinatorics Probability Computing* 6:159–64, 1997.

Cowen, L., W. Goddard, and E. Jesurum. Defected coloring revisited. *J. Graph Theory* 24(3):205–19, 1997.

Cowen, L., W. Goddard, and E. Jesurum. Coloring with defect. *Proceedings of the Eighth ACM-SIAM Symposium on Discrete Algorithms (SODA),* January 1997, pp. 548–57.

Berger, B., and **L. Cowen.** Scheduling with concurrency-based constraints. *J. Algorithms* 18:98–123, 1995.

Awerbuch, B., B. Berger, **L. Cowen,** and D. Peleg. Low diameter graph decomposition is in NC. *Random Struct. Algorithms* 5(3):442–52, 1994.

Dobrow, R. P., and **J. A. Fill.** Total path length for random recursive trees. *Combinatorics Probability Computing,* in press.

Fill, J. A., and D. E. Fishkind. The Moore-Penrose generalized inverse for sums of matrices. *SIAM J. Matrix Analysis App.,* in press.

Fill, J. A., D. E. Fishkind, and **E. R. Scheinerman.** Affine isomorphism for partially ordered sets. *Order,* in press.

Fill, J. A. The move-to-front rule: a case study for two perfect sampling algorithms. *Probability Eng. Informational Sci.* 12:283–302, 1998.

Fill, J. A. An interruptible algorithm for perfect sampling via Markov chains. Refereed extended abstract. *Proceedings of the Twenty-Ninth Annual ACM Symposium on the Theory of Computing,* pp. 688–95, 1997. *Ann. Appl. Probability* 8:131–62, 1998.

Dobrow, R. P., and **J. A. Fill.** The number of m-ary search trees on n keys. *Combinatorics Probability Computing,* 6:435–53, 1997.

Dette, H., **J. A. Fill,** J. Pittman, and W. J. Studden. Wall and Siegmund duality relations for birth and death chains with reflecting barrier. Article invited to special issue in honor of 70th birthday of Murray Rosenblatt. *J. Theoret. Probability* 10:349–74, 1997.

Dobrow, R. P., and **J. A. Fill.** Multiway trees of maximum and minimum probability under the random permutation model. *Combinatorics Probability Computing* 5:351–71, 1996.

Fill, J. A., H. Mahmoud, and W. Szpankowski. On the distribution for the duration of a randomized leader election algorithm. *Ann. Appl. Probability* 6:1260–83, 1996.

Fill, J. A. Limits and rates of convergence for the distribution of search cost under the move-to-front rule. *Theor. Comp. Sci. A* 164:185–206, 1996.

Fill, J. A., and L. Holst. On the distribution of search cost for the move-to-front rule. *Random Struct. Algorithms* 8:179–86, 1996.

Fill, J. A. An exact formula for the move-to-front rule for self-organizing lists. *J. Theor. Probability* 9:113–60, 1996.

Fill, J. A. On the distribution for binary search trees under the random permutation model. *Random Struct. Algorithms* 8:1–25, 1996.

Dobrow, R. P., and **J. A. Fill.** On the Markov chain for the move-to-root for binary search trees. *Ann. Appl. Probability* 5:1–19, 1995.

Dobrow, R. P., and **J. A. Fill.** Rates of convergence for the move-to-root Markov chain for binary search trees. *Ann. Appl. Probability* 5:20–36, 1995.

Dobrow, R. P., and **J. A. Fill.** The move-to-front rule for self-organizing lists with Markov dependent requests. Refereed article, pp. 57–80 in *Discrete Probability and Algorithms* (eds. D. Aldous, P. Diaconis, J. Spencer, and J. M. Steele), *IMA Volumes in Mathematics and its Applications,* 72, Springer-Verlag, 1995.

Ramana, M. K., and **A. J. Goldman.** Some geometrical results in semidefinite programming. *J. Global Optimization* 7:33–50, 1995.

Steinsaltz, S. J., and **A. J. Goldman.** Characterizing connectivity families. *Bull. Inst. Combinatorics Applications* 13:83–90, 1995.

McCarty, P. L., and **A. J. Goldman.** Ranking hazardous-waste sites for remedial action. National Research Council, National Academy Press, 1994.

Benjamin, A. T., and **A. J. Goldman.** Localization of optimal strategies in certain games. *Nav. Res. Logistics* 41:669–76, 1994.

Hall, L. A. Approximability of flow-shop scheduling. *Math. Programming B* 82:175–90, 1998.

Hall, L. A., and V. Strusevich. An openshop scheduling problem with a non-bottleneck machine. *Oper. Res. Lett.* 21:11–8, 1997.

Hall, L. A., D. B. Shmoys, and J. Wein. Scheduling to minimize average completion time: off-line and on-line algorithms. *Math. Operations Res.* 22:513–44, 1997.

Hall, L. A. Experience with a cutting plane algorithm for the capacitated spanning tree problem. *INFORMS J. Comput.* 8:219–34, 1996.

Hall, L. A., and M. X. Goemans. The strongest facets of the acyclic subgraph polytope are unknown. *Integer Programming and Combinatorial Optimization Proceedings of the 5th International IPCO Conference.* eds. W. H. Cuggingham, S. T. McCormick, and M. Queyranne. pp. 415–29, 1996.

Hall, L. A. A polynomial approximation scheme for a constrained flow-shop scheduling problem. *Math. Operations Res.* 19:68–85, 1994.

Han, S. P. On the validity of a nonlinear programming method for solving minimax problems. *J. Optimiz. Theory Appl.,* in press.

Han, S. P. Least squares solution of linear inequalities, MRC Technical Report 2141. *Math. Programming,* in press.

Han, S. P. Some parallel decomposition algorithms for convex programs. *Math. Programming,* in press.

James, L. F. A study of a class of weighted bootstraps for censored data. *Ann. of Stat.* 25:1595–1621, 1997.

Naiman, D. Q., and R. Stone. A homological characterization of Q-matrices. *Math. Operations Res.* 23:463–78, 1998.

Naiman, D. Q., and H. P. Wynn. Abstract tubes and improved inclusion-exclusion identities and inequalities. *Ann. Stat.* 25:1954–83, 1997.

Naiman, D. Q., and H. P. Wynn. Independence number and the complexity of famililes of sets. *Discrete Math.,* in press.

Naiman, D. Q., and Onn Chan. Some simple U-statistic tests for uniformity on certain homogeneous spaces. *J. Multivariate Analysis,* 54:210–26, 1995.

Lee, D. S., and **D. Q. Naiman.** A hybrid estimator for the cumulative probability of detection of surveillance radars. *IEEE Trans on Aerospace and Electronic Systems,* 32:476–80, 1995.

Chou, C. C., K. F. Ng, and **J. S. Pang.** Minimizing and stationary sequences of optimization problems. *SIAM J. Control Optimization* 36:1908–36, 1998.

Christensen, P. W., A. Klarbring, **J. S. Pang,** and N. Stromberg. Formulation and comparison of algorithms for frictional contact problems. *Int. J. Numerical Methods Eng.* 42:145–73, 1998.

Fukushima, M., and **J. S. Pang.** Some feasibility issues in mathematical programs with equilibrium constraints. *SIAM J. Optimization* 8:673–81, 1998.

Johns Hopkins University

Selected Publications (continued)

Klarbring, A., and **J. S. Pang.** Existence of solutions to discrete semicoercive frictional contact problems. *SIAM J. Optimization* 8:414–42, 1998.

Lewis, A. S., and **J. S. Pang.** Error bounds for convex inequality systems. In *Generalized Convexity, Generalized Monotonicity: Recent Results*, eds. J. P. Crouzeix, J.-E. Martinez-Legaz, and M. Volle, *Refereed Proceedings of the Fifth Symposium on Generalized Convexity*, pp. 75–110. Luminy-Marseille: Kluwer Academic Publishers, 1998.

Fukushima, M., Z. Q. Luo, and **J. S. Pang.** A globally convergent sequential quadratic programming algorithm for mathematical programs with equilibrium constraints. *Computational Optimization Applications* 10:1–31, 1998.

Ferris, M. C., and **J. S. Pang,** eds. *Variational and Complementarity Problems: State of the Art.* Philadelphia: SIAM Publications, 1997.

Pang, J. S. Error bounds in mathematical programming. *Math. Programming* B79:299–332, 1997.

Ferris, M. C., and **J. S. Pang.** Engineering and economic applications of complementarity problems. *SIAM Rev.* 39:669–713, 1997.

Trinkle, J. C., **J. S. Pang,** S. Sudarsky, and G. Lo. On dynamic multi-rigid-body contact problems with Coulomb friction. *Z. Angew. Mathematik Mechanik* 77:267–79, 1997.

Pang, J. S., and D. Ralph. Piecewise smoothness, local invertibility, and parametric analysis of normal maps. *Math. Operations Res.* 21:401–26, 1996.

Luo, Z. Q., **J. S. Pang,** and D. Ralph. *Mathematical Programs With Equilibrium Constraints.* Cambridge: Cambridge University Press, 1996.

Friedman, H. S., and **C. E. Priebe.** Smoothing bandwidth selection for response latency estimation. *J. Neurosci. Methods,* in press.

Lee, D. S., and **C. E. Priebe.** Exact mean and mean squared error of the smoothed bootstrap mean integrated squared error estimator. *Computational Stat.,* in press.

Friedman, H. S., and **C. E. Priebe.** Estimating stimulus response latency. *J. Neurosci. Math.,* in press.

Soka, J. L., et al. **(C. E. Priebe).** Mixture structure analysis using the Akaike Information Criterion and the bootstrap. *Stat. Computing* 8:177–88, 1998.

Marchette, D. J., R. A. Lorey, and **C. E. Priebe.** An analysis of local feature extraction in digital mammography. *Pattern Recognition Lett.* 30:1547–54, 1997.

Priebe, C. E., D. J. Marchette, and G. W. Rogers. Segmentation of random fields via borrowed strength density estimation. *IEEE Transaction on Pattern Analysis and Machine Intelligence* 19:494–9, 1997.

Priebe, C. E., D. J. Marchette, and G. W. Rogers. Semiparametric nonhomogeneity analysis. *J. Stat. Plan. Inference* 59:45–60, 1997.

Cowen, L. J. and **C. E. Priebe.** Randomized non-linear projections uncover high-dimensional structure. *Adv. App. Math.* 9:319–31, 1997.

Poston, W. L., E. J. Wegman, **C. E. Priebe,** and J. L. Solka. A deterministic method for robust estimation of multivariate location and shape. *J. Comput. Graph. Stat.* 6:300–13, 1997.

Priebe, C. E. Nonhomogeneity analysis using borrowed strength, *J. Am. Stat. Assoc.* 91:1497–503, 1996.

Marchette, D. J., **C. E. Priebe,** G. W. Rogers, and J. L. Solka. Filtered kernel density estimation. *Computational Stat.* 11:95–112, 1996.

Priebe, C. E., T. Olson, and D.M. Healy. A spatial scan statistic for stochastic scan partitions. *J. Am. Stat. Assoc.* 92(440):1476–84, 1997.

Rogers, G. W., J. L. Solka, and **C. E. Priebe.** A PDP approach to localized fractal dimension computation with segmentation boundaries.*Simulation* 65:26–36, 1995.

Lorey, R. A., **C. E. Priebe,** et al. Mammographic computer assisted diagnosis using computational statistics pattern recognition. *Real-Time Imaging* 1:95–104, 1995.

Priebe, C. E. Adaptive mixtures. *J. Am. Stat. Assoc.* 89(427):796–806, 1994.

Priebe, C. E., et al. The application of fractal analysis to mammographic tissue classification. *Cancer Lett.* 77:183–9, 1994.

Poston, W. L., G. W. Rogers, **C. E. Priebe,** and J. L. Solka. A qualitative analysis of the resistive grid kernel estimator. *Pattern Recognition Lett.* 15:219–25, 1994.

Fiduccia, C., **E. R. Scheinerman,** A. Trenk, and J. Zito. Dot product representations of graphs. *Discrete Math.* 81:113–38, 1998.

Scheinerman. E. R., and P. Tanenbaum. Unshrinkable minimal elements in sphere representations of partially ordered sets. *Order* 14:59–66, 1997.

Scheinerman, E. R., M. Jacobson, and G. Levin. On fractional Ramsey numbers. *Discrete Mathematics* 176:159–75, 1997.

Scheinerman, E. R., and D. Ullman. *Fractional Graph Theory: A Rational Approach to the Theory of Graphs.* New York: Wiley, 1997.

Scheinerman, E. R. *Invitation to Dynamical Systems.* Englewood Cliffs, N.J.: Prentice Hall, 1996.

Scheinerman, E. R., A. Trenk, and D. Ullman. On point-halfspace graphs. *J. Graph Theory* 20:19–35, 1995.

Scheinerman, E. R., and H. Wilf. The rectilinear crossing number of a complete graph and Sylvester's "Four Point Problem." *Am. Math. Monthly* 101:939–43, 1994.

Wierman, J. C. Substitution method critical probability bounds for the square lattice site percolation model. *Combinatorics Prob. Computing* 4:181–8, 1995.

Wierman, J. C., T. Luczak, and B. Pittel. The structure of a random graph at the point of the phase transition. *Trans. Am. Math. Soc.* 341:721–48, 1995.

Wierman, J. C. Equality of directional critical exponents in multiparameter percolation models. *J. Phys. A: Math. Gen.* 27:1851–8, 1995.

Wu, C. O., C.-T. Chiang, and D. R. Hoover. Asymptotic confidence regions for kernel smoothing of a varying-coefficient model with longtitudinal data. *J. Am. Stat. Assoc.* 93:1388–402, 1998.

Hoover, D. R., J. Rice, **C. O. Wu,** and L. P. Lang. Non parametric smoothing estimates of time-varying coefficient models with longitudinal data. *Biometricka* 85:809–22, 1998.

Wu, C. O. A cross-validation bandwidth choice for kernel density estimates with selection biased data. *J. Multivariate Analysis,* 61:38–60, 1997.

Wu, C. O. The effects of kernel choices in density estimation with biased data. *Stat. Prob. Lett.,* 34:373–83, 1997.

Wu, C. O., and A. Q. Mao. Minimax kernels for density estimation with biased data. *Ann. Inst. Stat. Math.* 48:451–67, 1996.

Wu, C. O. Kernel smoothing of nonparametric maximum likelihood estimates for biased sampling models. *Math. Meth. Stat.* 5:275–98, 1996.

Wu, C. O. Estimating the real parameter in a two-sample proportional odds model. *Ann. Stat.* 23:376–95, 1995.

Wu, C. O. Minimax density estimation with length biased data. *Math. Methods Stat.* 4:56–80, 1995.

LOYOLA UNIVERSITY CHICAGO

Department of Mathematical and Computer Sciences
Mathematical Science Program

Programs of Study

The Department of Mathematical and Computer Sciences at Loyola University offers a flexible program of study leading to the M.S. degree. Courses of study include concentrations in pure mathematics, probability and statistics, operations research (including financial mathematics), and computer science. The program in mathematical sciences leads to careers in industry, teaching, or further graduate education in mathematics or another discipline. Typical employment opportunities include jobs in computer software engineering, statistics (pharmaceutical companies), finance (pricing of contingent claims and trading strategies), operations research (optimization of business strategies and operations), and actuarial science (insurance and pension companies). Loyola University offers a rigorous course of study to introduce students to new modes of inquiry and to deepen their understanding and awareness of fundamental results and applications of mathematical science. To accommodate part-time students, most classes are offered during the evening and on Saturday. Students may be admitted to the graduate program with backgrounds in areas other than mathematical science, such as engineering, chemistry, physics, or economics.

A minimum of seven 3-credit, 400-level graduate courses and two approved 300-level undergraduate courses are required. Examples of courses to be offered include probability, stochastic processes, design of experiments, real analysis, algebra, applied mathematics, topics in operations research, system performance evaluation, simulation and modeling, algebraic coding theory, financial mathematics, cryptography, and algorithms and complexity. Some computer science courses that the student may take in the M.S. program require proficiency in a high-level computer language such as Java or C/C++. A fully prepared student can expect to finish the program in three semesters. Students who require prerequisite course work can expect to finish in two years.

The department also offers a certificate program in actuarial science, which prepares students to pass actuarial exams at the advanced level.

Research Facilities

The department has more than forty Sun Workstations and seventy Pentium PC's using Windows NT. These are all networked with the University computer system and the Internet. The department runs its own Gopher and World Wide Web servers, which offer information about the department, courses offered, and faculty research (http://www.math.luc.edu/). A variety of programming languages is available, including Ada, C/C++, Haskell, Java, Lisp, ML, Pascal, Perl, Prolog, S+, Sather, Scheme, and Tcl/Tk. Installed UNIX software includes FrameMaker, Gopher, IslandWrite, Mathematica, Mosaic, Netscape, SoftWindows, Tex/LaTex, XEmacs, Xess (a spreadsheet), and others. The departmental computers are also connected to the University network and have access to Loyola's larger machines, which include an IBM 3081D mainframe and an IBM RS/6000. Dial-up access is also available. Loyola's Sullivan Library contains an excellent collection of books in mathematics, computer science, and statistics and receives most major national and international journals in these areas.

Financial Aid

The Department of Mathematical and Computer Sciences currently offers teaching and research assistantships for highly qualified students. Graduate assistants receive a nine-month stipend of $10,600 and full tuition remission. Applications for assistantships should be completed no later than February 1 for the fall semester or November 1 for the spring semester.

Cost of Study

Tuition in 1999–2000 for a 3-hour graduate course is $1500. The University services and programs fee is $58. Increases should be expected for future years.

Living and Housing Costs

There are two campus residence halls that are exclusively for graduate students. Rooms and apartments are available in the campus neighborhood as well as throughout the Chicago area at widely varying costs.

Student Group

The department has programs in mathematical science and computer science. Between the two programs, there are about 155 graduate students, with 120 studying full-time. It is an international group, with students coming from the United States, Canada, Europe, and Asia. Approximately 50 students graduate each year, and the majority of these take positions in industry, research institutes, high schools, and colleges. Other graduates continue their studies toward a Ph.D. degree.

Location

The department is located at the Lake Shore Campus of the University, on the north side of Chicago directly on the shore of Lake Michigan. The University has an active theater program and a museum of medieval art and sponsors many cultural events. The Chicago area has a large concentration of universities and colleges and is home to many world-renowned museums such as the Art Institute, the Museum of Science and Industry, and the Field Museum of Natural History. Chicago has a wide diversity of ethnic groups, including large Chinese, Polish, Russian, Greek, and Hispanic populations.

The University and The Department

Loyola University of Chicago was founded by the Society of Jesus in 1870 and is committed to the Jesuit tradition of education. Loyola is a Carnegie Doctoral I institution and enrolls 13,800 students. The University offers bachelor's degrees in forty-two fields, master's degrees in forty fields, and doctoral degrees in thirty-two fields. In fall 1998, there were 5,700 students enrolled in graduate and professional programs at the University. The department offers undergraduate and graduate degrees in computer science, mathematics, and statistics.

Applying

Applicants are expected to possess a bachelor's degree in mathematics or a related area from an accredited institution and to have earned a B average in undergraduate course work. The following courses (or their equivalent) are prerequisites: calculus I–III, ordinary differential equations, introductory statistics, and linear algebra. The pure mathematics concentration also requires prerequisites in real analysis and abstract algebra. It is strongly recommended that students have received course credit in structured programming or the equivalent. Applicants are required to submit three letters of recommendation and transcripts of previous undergraduate and graduate work. Applicants must take the GRE General Test. The Graduate School requires a minimum undergraduate GPA of 3.0 for admission, and international students must submit TOEFL scores (at least 550, paper-based; 213, computer-based). Students may apply to be admitted for fall, spring, or summer sessions. Loyola University is an equal opportunity educator and employer.

Correspondence and Information

For applications for admission and for financial aid:
Office of the Graduate School
Loyola University Chicago
6525 North Sheridan Road
Chicago, Illinois 60626
Telephone: 773-508-3396

For specific information concerning the program:
Graduate Program Director
Department of Mathematical and Computer Sciences
Loyola University Chicago
6525 North Sheridan Road
Chicago, Illinois 60626
Telephone: 773-508-3570
E-mail: info@math.luc.edu
World Wide Web: http://www.math.luc.edu/

Loyola University Chicago

THE FACULTY AND THEIR RESEARCH

E. N. Barron, Professor; Ph.D., Northwestern.
Martin Buntinas, Professor; Ph.D., IIT.
Christopher Colby, Assistant Professor; Ph.D., Carnegie Mellon.
John Del Greco, Associate Professor; Ph.D., Purdue.
Peter Lars Dordal, Associate Professor; Ph.D., Harvard.
Stephen Doty, Professor; Ph.D., Notre Dame.
Gerald Funk, Associate Professor; Ph.D., Michigan State.
Anthony Giaquinto, Associate Professor; Ph.D., Pennsylvania.
Ronald Greenberg, Associate Professor; Ph.D., MIT.
Michael Handel, Visiting Professor; Ph.D., Berkeley.
Andrew N. Harrington, Associate Professor; Ph.D., Stanford.
Christine Haught, Associate Professor; Ph.D., Cornell.
William Cary Huffman, Professor; Ph.D., Caltech.
Anne Peters Hupert, Associate Professor; Ph.D., Chicago.
Radha Jagadeesan, Associate Professor; Ph.D., Cornell.
Robert Jensen, Professor; Ph.D., Northwestern.
Konstantin Läufer, Associate Professor; Ph.D., NYU.
Satya Lokam, Assistant Professor; Ph.D., Chicago.
Richard J. Lucas, Professor; Ph.D., Illinois at Chicago.
Richard J. Maher, Associate Professor; Ph.D., Northwestern.
Joseph Mayne, Associate Professor; Ph.D., IIT.
Anne Leggett McDonald, Associate Professor; Ph.D., Yale.
Gerard McDonald, Associate Professor; Ph.D., SUNY at Stony Brook.
Timothy O'Brien, Assistant Professor; Ph.D., North Carolina State.
Alan Saleski, Associate Professor; Ph.D., Berkeley.
Chandra Sekharan, Associate Professor; Ph.D., Clemson.
J. Richard VandeVelde, S.J., Associate Professor; Ph.D., Chicago.
Changyou Wang, Assistant Professor; Ph.D., Rice.

The research interests of the faculty include analysis, functional analysis, partial differential equations, game theory, logic, abstract algebra, coding theory, probability, finance theory, statistics, control theory, operations research, and topology. Faculty members receive recognition for the quality of their research by regularly obtaining competitive grants from agencies such as the National Science Foundation, the Air Force Office of Scientific Research, and the National Security Agency.

SELECTED PUBLICATIONS

Barron, E. N., R. Jensen, and W. Liu. Explicit solution of some first-order PDE's. *J. Dynam. Control. Syst.* 3:149–64, 1997.

Barron, E. N., R. Jensen, and W. Liu. Optimal control of the blowup time of a diffusion. *Math. Methods Model. Appl. Sci.* 6:665–87, 1996.

Barron, E. N., and W. Liu. Optimal control of blowup time. *SIAM J. Control Optimiz.* 34:102–23, 1996.

Barron, E. N., and W. Liu. Semicontinuous viscosity solutions for Hamilton Jacobi equations and the L-infinity control problem. *Appl. Math. Optimiz.* 34:325–60, 1996.

Barron, E. N. A verification theorem and application to the linear quadratic regulator for minimax control problems. *J. Math. Anal. Appl.* 182:516–39, 1994.

Barron, E. N. Averaging in Lagrange and minimax problems of optimal control. *SIAM J. Control Optimiz.* 31:1630–52, 1993.

Barron, E. N., J. L. Menaldi, and **R. Jensen.** Optimal control and differential games with measures. *Nonlinear Anal. Theory Meth. Appl.* 21:241–68, 1993.

Barron, E. N. The Bellman equation for control of the running max of a diffusion and applications to look back options. *Appl. Anal.* 48:205–22, 1993.

Barron, E. N., and R. Jensen. Total risk aversion and the pricing of options. *Appl. Math. Optimiz.* 23:51–76, 1991.

Barron, E. N. Differential games with maximum cost. *Nonlinear Anal. Theory Meth. Appl.* 14:971–89, 1990.

Buntinas, M. Strong summability in Fréchet spaces with applications to Fourier series. *J. Approx. Theory* 68:56–73, 1992.

Buntinas, M., and N. Tanovic-Miller. Absolute boundedness and absolute convergence in sequence spaces. *Proc. Am. Math. Soc.* 111:967–79, 1991.

Buntinas, M., and N. Tanovic-Miller. Strong boundedness and strong convergenece in sequence spaces. *Can. J. Math.* 43:960–74, 1991.

Buntinas, M., and N. Tanovic-Miller. New integrability classes and L1 convergence for even trigonometric series II. Conference on Approximation Theory, Kecskemet, Hungary. *Colloq. Math. Soc. Janos Bolyai* 58:103–25, 1991.

Buntinas, M., and N. Tanovic-Miller. Integrability classes and summability. Conference on Summability Interpolation and Approximation, Tel Aviv, Israel. *Israel Math. Conference Proc.* 4:75–88, 1991.

del Greco, J., and L. L. Gardner. A note on D-Y and Y-D graphs. *J. Combinatorial Math. Combinatorial Computing* 19:259–72, 1995.

del Greco, J., C. R. Coullard, and D. K. Wagner. Uncovering generalized-network structure in matrices. *Discrete Appl. Math.* 46:191–220, 1993.

del Greco, J., C. R. Coullard, and D. K. Wagner. Recognizing a class of bicircular matroids. *Discrete Appl. Math.* 43:197–215, 1993.

del Greco, J., C. R. Coullard, and D. K. Wagner. Representations of bicurcular matroids. *Discrete Appl. Math.* 32:223–40, 1992.

del Greco, J. Characterizing bias matroids. *Discrete Math.* 103:153–9, 1992.

Doty, S. Resolutions of *B* modules. *Indag. Math.* 5:267–83, 1994.

Doty, S., and G. Walker. Modular symmetric functions and irreducible modular representations of general linear groups. *J. Pure Appl. Algebra* 82:1–26, 1992.

Doty, S., and G. Walker. The composition factors of $F_p[x_1,x_2,x_3]$ as a *GL* module. *J. Algebra* 147:411–41, 1992.

Doty, S. The symmetric algebra and representations of general linear groups. *Proc. of the Hyderabad Conf. on Algebraic Groups,* pp. 123–50, ed. S. Ramanan. Madras: Manoj Prokashan, 1991.

Funk, G., J. Savitz, L. Bardygula-Nonn, and A. Simpson. Survival of smaller sport caught Chinook, *Oncorhynchus tshawytscha* (Walbaum), and Coho *Oncorhynchus kisutch* (Walbaum), salmon from Lake Michigan and its management implications. *Fisheries Manage. Ecol.* 2:11–6, 1995.

Funk, G., J. Savitz, and L. Bardygula-Nonn. Returns of caged-released Chinook and Coho salmon in Illinois harbors of Lake Michigan. *North Am. J. Fisheries Manage.* 13:550–7, 1993.

Giaquinto, A., and T. J. Hodges. Nonstandard solutions of the quantum Yang-Baxter equation. *Lett. Math. Phys.* 44:67–75, 1998.

Giaquinto, A., and M. Gerstenhaber. Boundary solutions of the quantum Yang-Baxter equation and solutions in three dimensions. *Lett. Math. Phys.* 44:131–41, 1998.

Giaquinto, A., and J. J. Zhang. Quantum Weyl algebras. *J. Algebra* 176:861–81, 1995.

Handel, M. The forcing partial order on the three times punctured disk. *Ergodic Theory Dynam. Syst.* 17:593–610, 1997.

Handel, M., and M. Bestvina. Train tracks for surface homeomorphisms. *Topology* 32:109–40, 1995.

Handel, M., and M. Bestvina. Train tracks and automorphisms of free groups. *Ann. Math.* 135:1–51, 1992.

Haught, C. A., and R. G. Downey. Embedding lattices into the wtt-degrees below 0'. *J. Symbolic Logic* 59:1360–82, 1994.

Haught, C. A., and R. Shore. Undecidability and initial segments of the (r.e.)tt-degrees. *J. Symbolic Logic* 55:987–1006, 1990.

Huffman, W. C. The equivalence of two cyclic objects on pq elements. *Discrete Math.* 154:103–27, 1996.

Huffman, W. C., V. Job, and V. S. Pless. Multipliers and generalized multipliers of cyclic codes and cyclic objects. *J. Combinatorial Theory, Series A* 62:183–215, 1993.

Huffman, W. C. On extremal self-dual ternary codes of lengths 28 to 40. *IEEE Trans. Information Theory* IT-38:1395–1400, 1992.

Huffman, W. C. On extremal self-dual quaternary codes of lengths 18 to 28, II. *IEEE Trans. Information Theory* IT-37:1206–16, 1991.

Jagadeesan, R., V. A. Saraswat, and V. Gupta. Computing with continuous change. *Sci. Comput. Programming* 30:3–49, 1998.

Jagadeesan, R., V. Gupta, and V. A. Saraswat. Default timed concurrent constraint programming. *Proc. 22nd Annual ACM SIGPLAN-SIGACT Symp. Principles Programming Lang.* January 1995.

Jagadeesan, R., and L. Jagadeesan. True concurrency and causality—a dataflow analysis of the n-calculus. *Proc. Fourth Int. Conf. Algebraic Methodology Software Technol., Lecture notes in computer science,* 936. July 1995.

Jagadeesan, R., D. Bobrow, V. Gupta, and V. Saraswat. Programming in hybrid concurrent constraint languages. Proceedings of the workshop on hybrid systems and autonomous control. *Lecture notes in computer science,* 999, 1995.

Jagadeesan, R, V. Saraswat, and V. Gupta. Foundations of timed concurrent constraint programming. *Proc. 9th Annual IEEE Symp. Logic Comput. Sci.* July 1994.

Jagadeesan, R., V. Gupta, and V. Saraswat. Programming in timed concurrent constraint languages. In *"Constraint Programming," NATO Advanced Science Institute Series,* Series F: Computer and System Sciences. 131(4.4):367–413, 1994.

Jensen, R. R., E. N. Barron, and W. Liu. Optimal control of the blow-up time of a diffusion. *Math. Methods Modeling Appl. Sci.* 6:665–87, 1996.

Jensen, R. R., E. N. Barron, and **W. Liu.** A Hopf type formula for $u_t + H(u, Du) = O$. *J. Differential Equations* 126:48–61, 1996.

Jensen, R. R., and **E. N. Barron.** Relaxed minimax control. *SIAM J. Control Optimiz.* 33:1028–39, 1995.

Jensen, R. R. Uniqueness of Lipschitz extensions: Minimizing the sup-norm of the gradient. *Arch. Rational Mechanics Anal.* 123:51–74, 1993.

Läufer, K., and M. Odersky. Putting type annotations to work. *Proc. 23rd ACM Symp. Principles Programming Languages (POPL),* St. Petersburg, January 1996.

Läufer, K. A framework for higher-order functions in C++. *Proc. USENIX Conf. Object-Oriented Technologies (COOTS),* Monterey, California, 1995.

Läufer, K. Interactive Web applications based on finite state machines. *Proc. Symp. Information Syst. Anal. Synthesis (ISAS),* Baden-Baden, Germany, August 1995.

Läufer, K., and M. Odersky. Extending the Hindley/Milner system

Loyola University Chicago

Selected Publications (continued)

with existential and universal polymorphism. Presented at the *Workshop on Advances in Type Systems for Computing (ATSC),* Cambridge, August 1995.

Läufer, K., and M. Odersky. Polymorphic type inference and abstract data types. *ACM Transactions on Programming Languages,* September 1994.

Läufer, K. Combining type classes and existential types. *Proc. XX Latin Am. Conf. (PANEL),* Mexico, 1994.

Lokam, S. Remarks on graph complexity. In *Proc. 18th Conf. Found. Software Technol. Theor. Computer Sci.,* 1998.

Lokam, S. Spectral methods for matrix rigidity with applications to size-depth tradeoffs and communication complexity. In *Proc. 36th IEEE. Symp. Found. Computer Sci.,* 1995.

Lucas, R. An inverse problem for scattering by an ellipsoidal boss. *J. Acoust. Soc. Am.* 95:2645–50, 1995.

Lucas, R., and G. Dassios. An inverse problem in low frequency scattering by an ellipsoidally embossed surface. *Wave Motion* 20:33–9, 1994.

Lucas, R. An inverse problem in low frequency scattering by a rigid ellipsoid. *J. Acoust. Soc. Am.* 95:2330–3, 1994.

Lucas, R., and J. V. Mallow. Multiple resonances in the double flash effect. *J. Opt. Soc. Am.* A9:2105–10, 1992.

Lucas, R., N. E. Berger, and V. Twersky. Polydisperse scattering theory and comparisons with data for red blood cells. *J. Acoust. Soc. Am.* 89:1394–401, 1991.

Maher, R. Step by step proofs and small group work in first courses in algebra and analysis. *PRIMUS* 4, 1994.

Maher, R. Precalculus and calculus students: What can we do for them right now? *PRIMUS* 1, 1991.

Mayne, J. H. Centralizing automorphisms of Lie ideals in prime rings. *Canad. Math. Bull.* 35:510–4, 1992.

O'Brien, T. E., and H. Dette. A new class of optimal criteria for regression models. *Biometrika,* in press.

O'Brien, T. E., and J. O. Rawlings. A non-sequential design procedure for parameter estimation and model discrimination in nonlinear regression models. *J. Stat. Plann. Inference* 55:77–93, 1996.

O'Brien, T. E. A note on quadratic design for nonlinear regression models. *Biometrika* 79:847–9, 1992.

Sekharan, C., D. Chen, D. T. Lee, and R. Sridhar. Solving the all-pair shortest path query problem on interval and circular-arc graphs. *Networks* 31:4, 1998.

Sekharan, C. Efficient algorithms for shortest distance queries in special classes of polygons. *Theor. Computer Sci.* 140:291–300, 1995.

Sekharan, C., S. T. Hedetniemi, and T. Wimmer. Enumeration techniques for certain *k*-terminal families of graphs. *J. Combinatorics, Information Syst. Sci.* 19:131–48, 1994.

Sekharan, C. MasPaWS—A massively parallel war simulator. *Proc. Winter Simulation Conf.* pp. 744–51, December 1994.

Sekharan, C., and S. Hannenhalli. Efficient algorithms for computing matching and chromatic polynomials in series-parallel graphs. *J. Combinatorial Math. Combinatorial Computing* 15:19–32, 1994.

Sekharan, C., R. Sridhar, and D. Joshi. The *k*-neighbor, *r*-domination problem on interval graphs. *Eur. J. Operational Res.* 79:352–68, 1994.

Sekharan, C., V. S. Lakshmanan, and M. Medidi. Efficient parallel algorithms for finding chordless cycles in graphs. *Parallel Processing Lett.* 3:165–70, 1993.

Sekharan, C., and A. Jain. An efficient parallel algorithm for min-cost flow on directed series-parallel networks. *Proc. 7th Int. Parallel Processing Symp.* pp. 188–92, 1993.

VandeVelde, R. J., and D. Perrine. Of men and merigolds: Counting the Quaterthienyls. *J. Chem. Educ.* 69, 1992.

Wang, C. Minimality, perturbation of singularities for some p-harmonic maps. *Indiana U. Math. J.* 47:725–40, 1998.

Wang, C., F. H. Lin, and R. Hardt. On the singularity of p-harmonic maps. *Commun. Pure Appl. Math.* 50:399–447, 1997.

Wang, C. Bubbling phenomena of certain Palais-Smale sequences to general targets. *Houston J. Math.* 22:559–90, 1996.

MEDICAL COLLEGE OF WISCONSIN

Graduate School of Biomedical Sciences
Division of Biostatistics

Program of Study

The Division of Biostatistics offers a program leading to the Ph.D. The program is designed for students with strong undergraduate preparation in mathematics and trains students in biostatistical methodology, theory, and practice. Emphasis is placed on sound theoretical understanding of statistical principles, research in the development of applied methodology, and collaborative research with biomedical scientists and clinicians. In addition, students gain substantial training and experience in statistical computing and in the use of software packages. Courses in the program are offered in collaboration with the Department of Mathematics at the University of Wisconsin–Milwaukee. The degree requirements, including the dissertation research, are typically completed in five years beyond a bachelor's degree that includes strong mathematical preparation.

Faculty members are engaged in a number of collaborative research projects at the International Bone Marrow Transplant Registry, the General Clinical Research Center, the Center for AIDS Intervention Research, and the Cancer Center, as well as specific projects in genetics, medical imaging, clinical trials, and pharmacologic modeling. Students participate in these projects under faculty supervision. Dissertation research topics in statistical methodology often evolve from such participation, and students usually become coauthors on medically oriented papers arising from these projects.

Research Facilities

The Division of Biostatistics is located in the Health Policy Institute of the Medical College of Wisconsin (MCW). The Medical College has extensive research laboratories and facilities available for faculty and student use. The Division has an up-to-date network of Hewlett-Packard workstations, PCs, Macintoshes, and peripherals. This network is linked with the campus backbone, providing direct access to the Internet. The Division's network is equipped with all leading statistical software and tools needed for the development of statistical methodology. The MCW libraries' holdings are among the largest health sciences collections in the Midwest, with more than 234,000 volumes and subscriptions to 2,172 journals. The libraries operate the "Medical Information Network," a remote-access computer network that includes the full MEDLINE database along with other medical science databases. The libraries also provide access to several bibliographic databases on compact disc workstations as well as the Internet and the World Wide Web. Students also have access to the University of Wisconsin–Milwaukee's extensive library, and the Division maintains its own library of statistical journals, books, and monographs.

The Epidemiologic Data Service provides access to national data on health and health care and special clinical data sets collected locally (the Medical College is a repository for the National Center for Health Statistics). The Biostatistics Consulting Service provides students with extensive experience in biomedical research.

Financial Aid

Students are supported by fellowships and research assistantships. Each of these includes tuition and a stipend. The stipend for 1999–2000 is $15,000. The research assistantships provide students with the opportunity to gain experience in statistical consulting.

Cost of Study

Tuition is $9135 per year. Tuition and health insurance are included in the fellowships and research assistantships.

Living and Housing Costs

Many rental units are available in pleasant residential neighborhoods surrounding the Medical College. Housing costs began at about $500 per month for a married couple or 2 students sharing an apartment. The usual stipend supports a modest standard of living.

Student Group

There are 216 degree-seeking graduate students, 690 residents and fellows, 807 medical students, and 495 M.P.H. students at the Medical College. A low student-faculty ratio fosters individual attention and a close working relationship between students and faculty members. Graduates pursue academic positions and jobs in government and industry.

Location

Milwaukee has long been noted for its old-world image. Its many ethnic traditions, especially from Middle Europe, give the city this distinction. Cultural opportunities are numerous and include museums, concert halls, art centers, and theaters. Milwaukee has a well-administered government, a low crime rate, and excellent schools. It borders Lake Michigan and lies within commuting distance of 200 inland lakes. Outdoor activities may be pursued year-round.

The College

The College was established in 1913 as the Marquette University School of Medicine. It was reorganized in 1967 as an independent corporation and renamed the Medical College of Wisconsin in 1970. There are 834 full-time faculty and 42 visiting faculty members; they are assisted by more than 1,700 physicians who practice in the Milwaukee community and participate actively in the College's teaching programs. MCW is one of seven organizations working in partnership on the Milwaukee Regional Medical Complex (MRMC) campus. Most physicians who staff the clinics and hospitals are full-time faculty physicians of MCW. Other MRMC member organizations include the Froedtert Memorial Lutheran Hospital, Children's Hospital of Wisconsin, the Blood Center of Southeastern Wisconsin, Curative Rehabilitation Services, and the Milwaukee County Mental Health Complex. Annually, these organizations admit nearly 45,000 patients and record nearly 860,000 outpatient and emergency visits. The graduate programs of the biochemistry, bioethics, cellular biology, epidemiology, microbiology, pathology, pharmacology, toxicology, and physiology departments are closely coordinated, and full-time students in any department may enroll in graduate courses in other departments and in programs of the University of Wisconsin–Milwaukee and Marquette University without any increase in basic tuition.

Applying

Prerequisites for admission to the program include the baccalaureate degree, satisfactory GRE scores on the General Test, and adequate preparation in mathematics. A complete description of the graduate program and application forms may be obtained by writing to the graduate program director at the address given below. Complete application materials should be submitted by February 15.

Correspondence and Information

Dr. Varghese George
Graduate Program Director
Division of Biostatistics
Medical College of Wisconsin
P.O. Box 26509
Milwaukee, Wisconsin 53226-0509
Telephone: 414-456-8280
Fax: 414-266-8481
E-mail: george@biostat.mcw.edu
World Wide Web: http://www.biostat.mcw.edu/

Send Completed Applications to:
Graduate Admissions
Graduate School of Biomedical Sciences
Medical College of Wisconsin
P.O. Box 26509
Milwaukee, Wisconsin 53226-0509
Telephone: 414-456-8218
E-mail: gradschool@post.its.mcw.edu
World Wide Web: http://www.mcw.edu/gradschool/

Medical College of Wisconsin

THE FACULTY AND THEIR RESEARCH

Professor and Head of the Division of Biostatistics

John P. Klein, Ph.D., Missouri–Columbia. Survival analysis, dependent competing risks theory, methods for dynamic interpretation of time dependent covariates, probabilistic models for cancer and the metastatic process, graphical association models for longitudinal data, and techniques for the design and analysis of clinical trials. Research methods have been applied to transplant data and data from the Framingham Heart Study and the Danish Breast Cancer Cooperative Group. Professor Klein also serves as the Statistical Director of the International Bone Marrow Transplant Registry at the Medical College. He is an elected member of the International Statistical Institute.
Klein, J. P., and M. L. Moeschberger. Survival analysis: techniques for censored and truncated data. *Springer-Verlag*, 1997.
Keiding, N., P. K. Anderson, and **J. P. Klein.** The role of Frailty models and accelerated failure time models in describing heterogeneity due to omitted covariates. *Stat. Med.* 16:215–24, 1997.
Anderson, P. K., **J. P. Klein,** K. M. Knudsen, and R. T. Palacios. Estimation of variance in Cox's regression model with shared gamma frailties. *Biometrics* 53:1475–84, 1997.

Associate Professors

Varghese George, Ph.D., Missouri–Columbia. Statistical genetics, genetic epidemiology, likelihood inference, regression modeling, health policy research, and general biostatistical and epidemiological methods. In the area of statistical genetics, research areas include ascertainment sampling, association, and linkage. Collaborative research projects include renal transplant recurrent diseases, pediatric asthma, genetics of ischemic heart disease, early discharge and neonatal readmission, genetics of cardioprotection, and genetics of hypertension.
George, V., et al. Linkage and association analyses of alcoholism using a regression-based transmission/disequilibrium test. *Genet. Epidemiol.,* in press.
George, V., W. D. Johnson, A. Shahane, and T. G. Nick. Testing for treatment effect in the presence of regression toward the mean. *Biometrics* 53:101–10, 1997.
Shahane, A., **V. George,** and W. D. Johnson. Effect of bivariate regression toward the mean in uncontrolled clinical trials. *Commun. Stat. Theory Methods* 24:2165–81, 1995.

Raymond G. Hoffmann, Ph.D., Johns Hopkins. Linear and nonlinear time series, GLM models for sexual behavior data, methods for identifying changes in fMRI images of the brain, statistical methods in epidemiology, analysis of spatial patterns of disease. Collaborative projects include AIDS prevention trials, fMRI neuroimaging of cocaine addiction, and evaluation of the process of breast cancer treatment. Dr. Hoffmann is the Publications Officer of the Statistics in Epidemiology Section of the ASA and is its newsletter editor.
Bloom, A., **R. G. Hoffmann,** and E. A. Stein. An activation detection procedure for drug-induced changes in functional MRI signal using a pharmacokinetic model. *Human Brain Mapping,* in press.
Kelly, J. A., **R. G. Hoffmann,** D. Rompa, and M. Gray. Protease inhibitor combination therapies and perceptions of gay men regarding AIDS severity and the need to maintain safer sex. *AIDS* 12:91–5, 1998.
Nattinger, A. B., **R. G. Hoffmann,** A. Howell-Pelz, and J. S. Goodwin. Effect of Nancy Reagan's mastectomy on choice of surgery for breast cancer by U.S. women. *J. Am. Med. Assoc.* 279:762–6, 1998.

Purushottam (Prakash) W. Laud, Ph.D., Missouri–Columbia. Development of Bayesian statistical methods of applications in the biomedical sciences; Bayesian inference and model selection in linear, generalized linear, hierarchical, bioassay, and survival methods; Markov chain Monte Carlo methods; and statistical models and inference for T-cell receptor diversity. Dr. Laud also serves as the Director of the Statistical core of the Spinal Cord Injury Model Center at the College.
Laud, P. W., and J. G. Ibrahim. Predictive specification of prior model probabilities in variable selection. *Biometrika* 83:267–74, 1996.
Damien, P., **P. W. Laud,** and A. F. M. Smith. Implementation of Bayesian nonparametric inference bases on beta processes. *Scand. J. Stat.* 23:27–36, 1996.
Laud, P. W., A. F. M. Smith, and P. Damien. Monte Carlo methods for approximating a posterior hazard rate process. *Stat. Comput.* 6:77–83, 1996.

Timothy L. McAuliffe, Ph.D., UCLA. Epidemiological methods, clinical trials, group-randomized trials, and space-time clustering. Dr. McAuliffe also serves as Director of the Quantitative Models and Analysis Core of the AIDS Intervention Research at the Medical College, and he is involved in collaborative research with the Cancer Center at the College.
Nattinger, A. B., **T. L. McAuliffe,** and M. M. Schapira. Generalizability of the surveillance, epidemiology, and end results registry population: Factors relevant to epidemiologic and health-care research. *J. Clin. Epidemiol.* 50:939–45, 1997.
Kelly, J. A., et al. **(T. L. McAuliffe).** Randomised, controlled, community-level HIV-prevention intervention for sexual-risk behaviour among homosexual men in U.S. cities. *Lancet* 350:1500–5, 1997.
Witt, P. L., et al. **(T. L. McAuliffe).** Phase 1/1B Study of polyadenylic-polyuridylic acid in patients with advanced malignancies: clinical and biologic effect. *J. Interferon. Cytokine Res.* 16: 632–5, 1996.

Assistant Professor

Mei-Jie Zhang, Ph.D., Florida State. Survival analysis, inference for stochastic processes, nonlinear models. As a biostatistician for the International Bone Marrow Transplant Registry at the Medical College, Dr. Zhang is interested in developing statistical models and methodology for analyzing complex transplant data.
Schieke, T. H., and **M. J. Zhang.** Cumulative regression function tests for regression models for longitudinal data. *Ann. Stat.* 26:1328–55, 1998.
Zhang, M. J., et al. Long-term follow-up of adults with acute lymphoblastic leukemia in a first remission treated with chemotherapy or bone marrow transplant. *Ann. Intern. Med.* 123:428–31, 1995.
McKeague, I. W., and **M. J. Zhang.** Identification of nonlinear time series from first order cumulative characteristics. *Ann. Stat.* 22:495–514, 1994.

Adjunct Faculty

Jay Beder, Associate Professor; Ph.D., George Washington. Gaussian processes, factorial experiments, categorical data analysis, clustering.
Jugal Ghorai, Professor; Ph.D., Purdue. Nonparametric estimation, density and survival function estimation, censored data analysis.
Eric Key, Associate Professor; Ph.D., Cornell. Probability theory and stochastic processes, ergodic theory.
Malgorzata Klosek, Associate Professor; Ph.D., Northwestern. Stochastic processes and applications, asymptotic expansions.
Tom O'Bryan, Associate Professor; Ph.D., Michigan State. Empirical Bayes, decision theory.
Andrew Soms, Associate Professor; Ph.D., Wisconsin–Madison. Reliability, statistical computing.
Gilbert Walter, Professor; Ph.D., Wisconsin–Madison. Sampling, mixing distributions with orthogonal functions, wavelets.

MICHIGAN STATE UNIVERSITY

Programs in Statistics and Probability

Programs of Study

The Department of Statistics and Probability offers programs leading to the Doctor of Philosophy (Ph.D.) degree in statistics and to Master of Science (M.S.) degrees with majors in statistics, operations research, applied statistics, and computational statistics.

The emphasis of the doctoral degree is on the attainment of a sound background in theoretical probability and statistics. A doctoral student may choose to emphasize and perform dissertation research in either probability theory or mathematical statistics. For admission, a student should have a strong record of performance in mathematics and statistics, with at least one year each of analysis and of probability and mathematical statistics.

The master's programs require 30 semester hours of approved course work, primarily in probability and statistics and mathematics. All four M.S. degrees mix theory with applications. The applied statistics degree requires courses at a lower theoretical level but requires 36 semester hours. The operations research and computational statistics degrees require courses in management and computer science. For admission, a student should have at least two courses at the junior level in mathematics. Previous probability or statistics courses are not required.

Research Facilities

The Department of Statistics and Probability is housed in Wells Hall, a modern air-conditioned office and classroom building. The departments of Mathematics and Computer Science share the same building. Assistants are assigned two per office. Computer facilities are available on the same floors for student use for e-mail, word processing, and computations. The Grove Mathematics Library in Wells Hall has 41,000 volumes and subscribes to 340 mathematical and statistical periodicals.

Financial Aid

The department provides financial support for approximately 20 students through consulting, research, and teaching assistantships and fellowships. Beginning assistants are usually assigned as teaching assistants, conducting recitation classes for large lectures, or as graders. In the 1999–2000 academic year, the stipend varies from $10,500 to $11,600 for the nine-month academic year, depending upon the student's level. Almost all assistants receive summer support. Assistants receive free tuition for 6 credits for fall and spring and 4 for the summer, pay the in-state rate for additional credits, and receive health insurance. Decisions on assistantship offers are made in early March, based upon grade records, recommendations, and GRE scores. Visits are encouraged.

Cost of Study

The 1999–2000 fees and tuition for graduate study are approximately $275 plus $220 per credit hour for Michigan residents and $430 per credit hour for out-of-state students. A normal credit load is 6 to 9 credits.

Living and Housing Costs

For the fall-spring academic year, a room in the Owen Graduate Dormitory costs $3640 (including $560 toward meal costs). University apartments rent for approximately $390 to $420 per month for one bedroom and $430 to $475 for two bedrooms. Off-campus rooms and apartments are available at similar or higher rates.

Student Group

The University has a total enrollment of approximately 40,000, including 6,500 graduate students. The department has approximately 35 master's and 20 doctoral students. Approximately 40 percent of the student body are women and 75 percent are international students.

Location

The University occupies approximately 2,000 beautifully landscaped acres in East Lansing, a residential community of 25,000 in addition to on-campus students. The state capital in Lansing, a city of 110,000, is 5 miles away. Detroit is 90 miles away. Recreational facilities for both summer and winter are nearby.

The University and The Department

Michigan State University, founded in 1855, is one of the eleven members of the "Big Ten" and ranks among the top fifteen in enrollment in the nation. All of its many cultural and recreational facilities are available to graduate students. The department was founded in 1955 and was one of the first departments of statistics. In forty years, it has produced 127 Ph.D. and 419 M.S. degrees.

The department conducts classes for approximately 1,300 undergraduates and 250 graduate students each semester. Its Statistical Consulting Service, staffed by a director and two senior-level graduate assistants, provides help to faculty members and graduate student users of statistics for the entire University. Collaboration with Michigan State's medical school provides good practical experience for faculty members and students. Seminars on probability, finance, and statistics are active. A weekly colloquium features distinguished speakers from around the world reporting on the most recent research. The department will continue to host outstanding scholars for visits lasting from one week to one year. Many courses employ computers for analysis and simulations.

Applying

Applicants should have completed a minimum of 6 semester hours in mathematics beyond calculus (more extensive course work, including a course in analysis, is preferred). Scores on the Graduate Record Examinations (GRE) are not required, but are desirable. A "short-form" unofficial application provides a quick turn-around evaluation for domestic students. Women and members of minority groups are particularly encouraged to apply. Telephone and e-mail inquiries and visits are encouraged.

Correspondence and Information

Graduate Director
Department of Statistics and Probability
Michigan State University
East Lansing, Michigan 48824
Telephone: 517-355-9589
Fax: 517-432-1405
E-mail: sparks@stt.msu.edu
World Wide Web: http://www.stt.msu.edu

Michigan State University

THE FACULTY AND THEIR RESEARCH

Roy V. Erickson, Professor; Ph.D., Michigan, 1968. Limit theorems.

Vaclav Fabian, Professor; R.N.Dr., Charles (Czechoslovakia), 1953. Asymptotic theory, stochastic approximation, vague convergence.

Dorian Feldman, Professor; Ph.D., Berkeley, 1961. Decision theoretic orderings of experiments.

Martin Fox, Professor; Ph.D., Berkeley, 1959. Game theory, admissibility.

Joseph C. Gardiner, Professor; Ph.D., North Carolina, 1978. Biostatistics, sequential methods, nonparametric statistics.

Dennis Gilliland, Professor; Ph.D., Michigan State, 1966. Compound and empirical Bayes theory, design of experiments, applications.

James F. Hannan, Professor; Ph.D., North Carolina, 1953. Compound decision theory, asymptotic theory.

Marianne Huebner, Assistant Professor; Ph.D., USC, 1993. Stochastic differential equations, parametric estimation, asymptotic theory.

Hira Lal Koul, Professor; Ph.D., Berkeley, 1967. Nonparametric and semiparametric inference, survival analysis, long-range analysis.

Raoul LePage, Professor; Ph.D., Minnesota, 1967. Stable processes, resampling theory, mathematical finance.

Shlomo Levental, Associate Professor; Ph.D., Wisconsin, 1986. Empirical processes, mathematical finance.

V. Mandrekar, Professor; Ph.D., Michigan State, 1965. Measures on function spaces, Markov fields, stochastic stability, signal analysis.

Vincent Melfi, Assistant Professor; Ph.D., Michigan, 1991. Markov chains, renewal theory, sequential allocations.

Connie Page, Professor; Ph.D., Michigan, 1972. Sequential allocation, statistical methods for auditing.

R. V. Ramamoorthi, Associate Professor; Ph.D., Indian Statistical Institute, 1981. Foundations, Bayesian inference, comparison of experiments.

Habib Salehi, Professor; Ph.D., Indiana, 1965. Prediction theory, time series analysis, stochastic analysis.

Anatoli Skorohod, Professor; Ph.D., Moscow State, 1957; Doctor of Mathematics, Institute for Mathematics (Kiev), 1962. Member of the Academy of Sciences of the Ukraine. Limit theorems for stochastic processes, stochastic dynamical systems.

James Stapleton, Professor; Ph.D., Purdue, 1957. Linear and log-linear models.

Yimen Xiao, Assistant Professor; Ph.D., Ohio State, 1995. Stochastic processes.

Lijian Yang, Assistant Professor; Ph.D., North Carolina, 1995. Time series, density estimation.

Michigan State University

SELECTED PUBLICATIONS

Erickson, R. V. Robust estimation of the location of a vertical tangent in distribution. *Ann. Stat.* 24(3), 1996.

Erickson, R. V., V. Fabian, and J. Marik. An optimum design for estimating the first derivative. *Ann. Stat.* 23(4):1234–47, 1995.

Erickson, R. V. Lipschitz smoothness and covergence with applications to the central limit theorem for summation processes. *Ann. Prob.* 9:831–51, 1981.

Erickson R. V., M. P. Quine, and N. C. Weber. Explicit bounds for the departure from normality of sums of dependent random variables. *Acta Math. Acad. Sci. Hungaricae* 34, 1979.

Fabian, V., and J. Dippon. Stochastic approximation of global minimum point. *J. Stat. Plan. Infer.* 41:327–47, 1994.

Fabian, V. Polynomial estimation of regression functions with the supremum norm. *Ann. Stat.* 16:1345–68, 1988.

Fabian, V., and J. Hannan. *Introduction to Probability and Mathematical Statistics.* New York: Wiley, 1985.

Feldman, D., and **M. Fox.** *Probability: The Mathematics of Uncertainty.* Marcel Dekker, Inc., 1991.

Feldman, D., and F. Osterreicher. Divergenzen Von Wahrscheinlichkeitsverteilungen—Integralgeometrisch Betrachtet. *ACTA Math. Sci. Hung.* 37:329–37, 1981.

Feldman, D., and **M. Fox.** Three simple inductive proofs in probability and statistics. *Am. Stat.* 34:50–1, 1980.

Feldman, D., and **M. Fox.** Estimation of the parameter n in the binomial distribution. *J. Am. Stat. Assoc.* 63:150–8, 1968.

Fox, M., and R. E. Odeh. *Sample Size Choice—Charts for Experiments with Linear Models,* 2nd ed. Marcel Dekker, Inc., 1991.

Fox, M. An inadmissible best invariant estimate: the i.i.d. case. *Ann. Stat.* 9:1127–9, 1981.

Fox, M. Duels with possibly asymetric goals. *Zastosowania Matematyski* XVII:15–25, 1980.

Gardiner, J., et al. Confidence intervals for cost-effectiveness ratios. *Med. Decision Making* 15:254–63, 1995.

Gardiner, J., et al. Cost effectiveness analysis in heart disease. Part III, ischemia, congestive heart failure, and arrhythmias. *Prog. Cardiovasc. Dis.* 37(5):307–46, 1995.

Gardiner, J., and G. Aras. Fixed diameter confidence ellipsoids in time-sequential models. *Seq. Anal.* 14(1):29–39, 1995.

Gardiner, J., Z. Wang, and **R. V. Ramamoorthi.** Identifiability in an interval censorship model. *Stat. Prob. Lett.* 21:215–21, 1994.

Gilliland, D. *Experiences in Statistics,* pp. 1–104. Kendall/Hunt Publishing Company, 1990.

Gilliland, D., and K. L. D. Gunawardena. Binary image classification. *Proc 21st Symp. Interface,* 1989.

Gilliland, D., and R. Karunamuni. On empirical Bayes with sequential component. *Ann. Inst. Stat. Math.* 40:187–93, 1988.

Gilliland, D. On the Probability of Reversal in Contested Elections. *Statistics and the Law,* pp. 391–416, eds. DeGroot, Fienberg, and Kadan. New York: Wiley, 1986.

Hannan, J., and Y. Nogami. Bounds for the difference of two integrals of a bounded function in terms of extensions of Levy metric. *Proceedings of the Fifth Japan-USSR Symposium of Probability Theory,* eds. Prokhorov and Wantanabe, 1987.

Hannan, J., and **V. Fabian.** Local asymptotic behavior of densities. *Stat. Decision* 5:105–38, 1987.

Hannan, J. Multivariate normal maximum likelihood estimation. *Am. Stat.* 39(4), 1985.

Hannan, J., and **D. Gilliland.** Identification of the ordered bivariate normal distribution by minimum variate. *J. Am. Stat. Assoc.* 75:651–65, 1980.

Huebner, M., and B. Rozovskii. On asymptotic properties of maximum likelihood estimators for parabolic stochastic PDE's. *Prob. Theory Rel. Field.* 103:143–63, 1995.

Huebner, M., R. Khasminskii, and B. Rozovskii. Two examples of parameter estimation. In *Stochastic Processes,* eds. Cambanis, Ghosh, Karandikar, and Sen. 1993.

Koul, H. L. Bahadur representations for GM-estimates in auto-regression models. *J. Stoch. Proc. Appl.* 57:167–89, 1995.

Koul, H. L. Auto-regression quantiles and related rank-score processes. *Ann. Stat.* 23:670–89, 1995.

Koul, H. L. Minimum distance estimation of the center of symmetry with randomly censored data. *Metrika* 42:79–97, 1995.

Koul, H. L. Regression quantiles and related processes under long range dependent errors. *J. Mult. Anal.* 51:317–8, 1994.

LePage R., and K. Podgórski. Resampling permutations in regression without second moments. *J. Multivar. Anal.* 57:119–41, 1996.

LePage, R., and K. Podgórski. Giving the boot, block and shuffle to statistics. *Sci. Comp. Auto.* 10:29–34, 1994.

LePage, R. Bootstrapping signs. In *Exploring the Limits of Bootstrap,* eds. L. Billard and R. LePage. 1990.

Levental, S., and A. V. Skorokhod. Necessary and sufficient conditions for absence of arbitrage with tame portfolios. *Ann. Appl. Prob.* (5):906–25, 1995.

Levental, S., and J. Bae. Uniform CLT for Markov chains and its invariance principle: A Martingale approach. *J. Theoret. Prob.* (8):549–570, 1995.

Levental, S. Uniform CLT for Markov chains with discrete state space. *Stoch. Process. Appl.* (30):245–53, 1990.

Levental, S., and **H. L. Koul.** Weak convergence in explosive autoregression. *Ann. Stat.* (17):1784–94, 1989.

Mandrekar, V. *Mathematical Work of Norbert Wiener.* American Mathematical Society, 1995.

Mandrekar, V., and A. Makagon. Remarks on AC-continuity and the spectral representation of stationary $S\alpha S$ sequences. *Ullam Quart.* 2, 1994.

Mandrekar, V., and L. Gawarecki. Girsanov type theorem for anticipative shifts. *Birkhauser* 301–16, 1994.

Mandrekar, V., and R. Khasminskii. On stability of stochastic evolution equations. *Birkhauser* 185–98, 1992.

Page, C., D. Kreling, and E. Matsumara. Comparison of mean per unit and ratio estimators under a simple applications motivated model. *Stat. Prob. Lett.* 17:97–104, 1993.

Page, C. Computing science and statistics. *Proceedings of the 22nd Symposium on the Interface.* Springer-Verlag, 1992.

Page, C. Allocation proportional to coefficient of variation when estimating the product of parameters. *J. Am. Stat. Assoc.* 85:1134–9, 1990.

Page, C. Sequential designs for estimating the product of parameters. *Comm. Stat.: Seq. Anal.* 6:351–71, 1987.

Ramamoorthi, R. V. On Bayes sufficiency and separation of strongly convex sets. *Proc. Am. Math. Soc.* 111:239–45, 1991.

Ramamoorthi, R. V. Sufficiency, ancillarity and independence in invariant models. *J. Stat. Plan. Inferen.* 26:59–63, 1990.

Ramamoorthi, R. V. Equivalence of behavioural and randomised equivariant rules. *Stat. Decis.* 7:96–104, 1989.

Ramamoorthi, R. V., and K. K. Roy. A note on weakly dominated experiments. *Sankhya Ser. A* 49:128–9, 1986.

Salehi, H., F. Hoppensteadt, and **A. Skorokhod.** Randomly perturbed Voltera integral equations and some applications. *Stoch. Stoch. Rep.* 51:89–125, 1995.

Salehi, H., A. Makagon, and A. G. Miamee. Continuous time periodically correlated processes: Spectrum and prediction. *Stoch. Process. Appl.* 49:277–95, 1994.

Salehi, H., and **A. Skorokhod.** On asymptotic behavior of solutions of the wave equations perturbed by a fast Markov process. *Ulam Quart.* 2:40–56, 1994.

Salehi, H., P. Brockwell, and R. Davis. Transfer-function models with non-stationary input. In *New Directions in Time Series Analysis Part I,* vol. 45, pp. 65–74. Springer-Verlag, 1992.

Skorokhod, A. V., and **H. Salehi.** An averaging principle for dynamical systems in Hilbert space with Markov random perturbation. *Stoch. Process. Appl.* 61:85–108, 1996.

Michigan State University

Selected Publications (continued)

Skorokhod, A. V., and J. Jacod. Jumping filtration and Martingales with finite variation. *Lect. Notes Math* 1583, 1994.

Skorokhod, A. V., E. B. Dynkin, and S. E. Kuznetsov. Branching measure-valued processes. *Prob. Theory Rel. Fields* (99):55–96, 1994.

Skorokhod, A. V. Infinite systems of randomly interacting particles. *Random Oper. Stoch. Eq.* (1)N1:1–13, 1993.

Stapleton, J. *Linear Statistical Models.* New York: Wiley and Sons, 1995.

Stapleton, J., R. Khasminskii, and N. B. Lazarova. Some procedures for state estimation of a hidden Markov chain with 2 states. *Proc. Purdue Conf. Decision Theory* 477–87, 1993.

Stapleton, J., and G. J. Wallace. Analysis of auditory comprehensive performance in severely aphasic individuals. *Arch. Phys. Med. Rehab.* 72:674–8, 1991.

Stapleton, J., and **J. Gardiner.** Simulation study on the performance of bounded length confidence intervals for quantiles with censored data. *Commun. Stat. Sim. Comp.* 19(2):419–32, 1990.

Xiao, Y. Local time and related properties of multi-dimensional iterated Brownian motion. *J. Theor. Probability* 11:383–408, 1998.

Xiao, Y. Weak dimension of the image of fractional Brownian motion. *Stat. Probability Lett.* 33:379–87, 1997.

Xiao, Y. Fractal measures of the sets associated to Gaussian random fields. In *Trends in Probabilities and Related Analysis: Proceedings of the Symposium on Analysis and Probability 1996,* pp. 311–24, eds. N. Kôno and N.-R. Shieh. World Scientific, 1997.

Xiao, Y. Dimension results for Gaussian vector fields and index-α stable fields. *Ann. Probability* 23:273–91, 1995.

MOUNT SINAI SCHOOL OF MEDICINE OF NEW YORK UNIVERSITY

Department of Biomathematical Sciences

Program of Study

The Department of Biomathematical Sciences seeks to train future leaders of theoretical research in the quantitative biology of the twenty-first century. Students who enter this program will have extraordinary opportunities to develop careers at the forefront of the biological revolution. Areas of faculty expertise span the biomathematical sciences, with emphasis on macromolecular structure and function, physiology, epidemiology, and statistics.

All entering students take a core curriculum that includes molecular and cell biology and physiology, mathematical methods and modeling, numerical and computational methods, and statistics. In the first and second years, students are oriented to the research opportunities available in the department and the School by participating on a rotating basis in circumscribed research projects with each of several faculty members. First-year and second-year students also participate in a seminar program and a journal club. In addition to the core curriculum, students choose advanced courses in accord with their interests. These may include appropriate courses given at the Courant Institute of Mathematical Sciences of New York University or at other graduate institutions in Manhattan. As students become increasingly involved in the research program, each develops a dissertation proposal. After passing a written proficiency examination in biomathematical sciences and giving a satisfactory oral presentation of the dissertation proposal, the student devotes full time to research in close consultation with his or her chosen adviser. The progress of each student is overseen at all stages by a committee of 3 advisers, who ensure that the program is carefully tailored to individual needs and interests. The usual time needed to complete all requirements for a Ph.D. degree is four to five years.

The department's extensive links with other basic science and clinical units in the medical school provide ample opportunities to develop collaborative research projects with experimental groups. In addition, the department maintains close ties with other institutions in the New York area that have active research programs in mathematical biology. These include the Courant Institute of Mathematical Sciences of New York University, the Applied Mathematics Department at SUNY at Stony Brook, the Cold Spring Harbor Laboratory, and the Institute for Discrete Mathematics and Computer Science at Rutgers University.

A combined M.D./Ph.D. program also is available.

Research Facilities

The department's modern and well-equipped computing resources include a twelve-processor SGI Power Challenge XL, several quad-processor SGI Origin 200 systems, and O2 graphical workstations. There are numerous Sun Ultra10 and Sparc workstations, plus Pentium II and III desktops and iMacs, all with Internet access. The department also remains up-to-date with the latest mathematical and statistical software, including Matlab, Mathematica, Maple, MathCad, SAS, Splus, Stat-Xact, and others. Sequence analysis is available through the GCG package as well as through specialized programs developed by the department. C^{++} and Fortran programming are supported on Solaris, Irix, and WinNT platforms.

Financial Aid

Students are supported to a common stipend level using Mount Sinai fellowships, graduate assistantships and traineeships, and departmental research grant funds. For the 1999–2000 year, students receive tuition, a stipend of $22,000 per annum, and a book/travel allowance of $300 per annum.

Cost of Study

The cost of study usually is met by financial aid awards, as described above.

Living and Housing Costs

Student housing is available for all students at a wide range of costs. Housing is available in dormitories and other buildings owned by the School of Medicine.

Student Group

The biomathematical sciences subarea maintains a low student-faculty ratio to preserve a productive and congenial atmosphere in which students receive close faculty guidance.

Student Outcomes

Five students have graduated since 1994. All have received postdoctoral fellowships in university research laboratories. One of these fellowships, awarded in 1995, was from the NIH.

Location

The Mount Sinai School of Medicine adjoins Central Park on the Upper East Side of Manhattan. Several important medical and scientific institutions are nearby, including the New York Academy of Medicine and the New York Academy of Sciences. Students can attend meetings, symposia, and conferences at these centers. Students also have access to several major specialty libraries in the area. Discounted tickets and free passes to many theater, concert, and dance performances and other cultural events are also available to students.

The School

The School of Medicine was founded in 1963 as part of the Mount Sinai Medical Center, a major medical research center. The biomedical sciences doctoral program is affiliated with New York University. The biomathematical sciences subarea was added to this doctoral program in 1988.

Applying

The department seeks to attract students with strong research potential. Because of the interdisciplinary nature of the program, students with a wide variety of majors are encouraged to apply. Academic background should include sound training in mathematics and/or computer science, plus at least one year each of physics, biology, and chemistry and a course in organic chemistry. In some cases, prerequisites can be made up after admission.

If an applicant is interested in biomathematics but would like to explore other areas before committing to a program, Mount Sinai offers a flexible entry option.

All applicants to the doctoral program must submit Graduate Record Examinations scores, TOEFL scores if their native language is not English, official transcripts of undergraduate and any previous graduate work, and letters of recommendation. Application is made directly to the Graduate School of the Mount Sinai School of Medicine.

Correspondence and Information

Director of Graduate Studies
Department of Biomathematical Sciences
Box 1023
Mount Sinai School of Medicine
1 Gustave Levy Place
New York, New York 10029

Mount Sinai School of Medicine

THE FACULTY AND THEIR RESEARCH

Craig J. Benham, Professor and Acting Chairman; Ph.D. (mathematics), Princeton, 1972. Topological properties of biomolecules and their relationships to energetics, structure, and function, with emphasis on nucleic acids.

Gary Benson, Assistant Professor; Ph.D. (computer science), Maryland, 1992. Algorithm development for molecular sequence analysis.

Agnes Berger, Professorial Lecturer; Ph.D. (mathematics), Budapest, 1939. Statistical methods for studying chronic diseases, late-onset genetic diseases.

Carol Bodian, Assistant Professor; Dr.P.H. (biostatistics), Columbia, 1983. Biostatistics for clinical research, cancer epidemiology.

Richard Everson, Assistant Professor; Ph.D. (mathematics), Leeds (England), 1988. Image analysis and medical imaging, neural modeling, computational and numerical analysis.

Warren Hirsch, Professorial Lecturer; Ph.D. (mathematics), NYU, 1952. Epidemiology of infectious diseases, theoretical immunology, mathematical physiology of the kidney.

Bruce Knight, Adjunct Professor; B.A. (physics and mathematics), Dartmouth, 1952. Biophysics, dynamics of the visual system.

Wendy Lou, Assistant Professor; Ph.D. (biostatistics), Toronto, 1994. Biostatistics and clinical applications, epidemiology.

John Mandeli, Research Associate Professor; Ph.D. (statistics), Cornell, 1978. Design and analysis of clinical experiments, combinatorial problems in experimental design.

Michiel Noordewier, Associate Professor; Ph.D. (computer science), Wisconsin, 1990. Genomic sequence analysis, computational drug discovery.

Ahmet Omurtag, Research Assistant; Ph.D. candidate (mechanical engineering), Columbia. Theoretical and computational fluid dynamics, with applications in biology.

Shalom R. Rackovsky, Associate Professor; Ph.D. (chemical physics), MIT, 1972. Theory of protein structures and interactions.

Henry Sacks, Professor; M.D., Ph.D. (microbiology), Albany Medical College, 1971. Clinical epidemiology, including meta-analysis, decision analysis, clinical trials methodology, and AIDS epidemiology.

Harold Scheraga, Adjunct Professor; Ph.D. (physical chemistry), Duke, 1946. Theory of protein conformation and the mechanisms of folding, chemistry of blood clotting, structure of water and dilute aqueous solutions.

Lawrence Sirovich, Professor; Ph.D. (fluid mechanics), Johns Hopkins, 1960. Mathematical methods applied to large data sets and image analysis, fluid mechanics, dynamical systems.

Istvan Sugar, Associate Professor; Ph.D. (biophysics), Eötvös Loránd (Budapest), 1973. Theory of magnetic resonance, theoretical membrane biophysics.

Sylvan Wallenstein, Associate Professor; Ph.D. (statistics), Rutgers, 1971. Biostatistics, with applications to epidemiology, clustering, clinical trials, and experimental design.

NEW YORK UNIVERSITY

Courant Institute of Mathematical Sciences
Department of Mathematics

Program of Study

The graduate program offers a balanced array of options, with special focus on mathematical analysis and on applications of mathematics in the broadest sense. It includes computational applied mathematics and cross relations with the University's other science departments. The program of study leads to the M.S. and Ph.D. degrees. It is possible to earn both degrees by part-time study, but most students in the Ph.D. program are full-time.

In addition to the standard M.S. degree, special career-oriented programs are available in financial mathematics, scientific computing, and statistics and operations research. The M.S. degree can be completed in the equivalent of three or four terms of full-time study. Doctoral students obtain the M.S. degree as they fulfill the requirements for the Ph.D. Students must earn 72 course and research points for the Ph.D., but no specific courses are required. One requirement is the Written Comprehensive Examination, often taken during the first year of full-time study. A second requirement is the Oral Preliminary Examination, which serves as the threshold between course work and thesis research. Thereafter, students engage in research under the supervision of a faculty adviser, leading to the writing and defense of a doctoral dissertation. Students are encouraged from the outset to participate in the Institute's extensive research activities and to use its sophisticated computing environment.

The department occupies a leading position in applied mathematics, differential equations, geometry/topology, probability, and scientific computing. In applied mathematics, the department's activities go beyond differential equations and numerical analysis to encompass many topics not commonly found in a mathematics department, including atmosphere/ocean science, computational fluid dynamics, financial mathematics, materials science, mathematical physiology, neural science, plasma physics, and statistical physics.

The department has been successful in helping its Ph.D. graduates find desirable positions at universities or in nonacademic employment.

Research Facilities

The Courant Institute Library, located in the same building as the department, has one of the nation's most complete mathematics collections; it receives more than 280 journals and holds more than 65,000 volumes. Students have access to MathSciNet and Web of Science (Science Citation Index) and an increasing number of electronic journals. The Institute's computer network is fully equipped with scientific software; X-terminals are available in public locations and in every graduate student office. The Courant Applied Mathematics Laboratory comprises an experimental facility in fluid mechanics and other applied areas, coupled with a visualization and simulation facility.

Financial Aid

Fellowships and assistantships are awarded to students who intend to engage in full-time Ph.D. study; they cover tuition and, in 1999–2000, provide a stipend of $16,000 for the nine-month academic year. Some summer positions associated with Courant Institute research projects are available to assistants with computational skills. Because the department is unable to support all of its full-time students, applicants should apply for other support as well. Federally funded low-interest loans are available to qualified U.S. citizens on the basis of need.

Cost of Study

In 1999–2000, tuition is calculated at $745 per point. Associated fees are calculated at $178 for the first point in fall 1999, $192 for the first point in spring 2000, and $35 per point thereafter in both terms. A full-time program of study normally consists of 24 points per year (four 3-point courses each term).

Living and Housing Costs

University housing for graduate students is limited. It consists mainly of shared studio apartments in buildings adjacent to Warren Weaver Hall and shared suites in residence halls within walking distance of the University. University housing rents in the 1998–99 academic year ranged from $6310 to $10,020.

Student Group

In 1998–99, the department had more than 240 graduate students. About half were full-time students.

Location

New York City is a world capital for art, music, and drama and for the financial and communications industries. NYU is located at Washington Square in Greenwich Village, just north of SoHo and Tribeca in a residential neighborhood consisting of apartments, lofts, art galleries, theaters, restaurants, and shops.

The University and The Institute

New York University, founded in 1831, enrolls about 50,000 students and is one of the major private universities in the country. Its various schools offer a wide range of undergraduate, graduate, and professional degrees. Among its internationally known divisions is the Courant Institute of Mathematical Sciences. Named for its founder, Richard Courant, the Institute combines research in the mathematical sciences with advanced training at the graduate and postdoctoral levels. Its activities are supported by the University, government, industry, and private foundations and individuals. The graduate program in mathematics is conducted by the faculty of the Courant Institute. The mathematics department ranks among leading departments in the country and is the only highly distinguished department to have made applications a focal concern of its programs. Eleven members of the Courant Institute faculty are members of the National Academy of Sciences.

Applying

The graduate program is open to students with strong mathematical interests, regardless of their undergraduate major. They are expected to have a knowledge of the elements of mathematical analysis. Applications for admission are evaluated throughout the year, but a major annual review of applications for financial aid occurs in February, and most awards for the succeeding academic year are made by early March. Financial aid applications must include GRE scores on both the General and Subject tests and must be received by January 4. The application deadline for general admission to the Ph.D. program is April 15; for the M.S. program it is July 15.

Correspondence and Information

For program and financial aid information:
Fellowship Committee
Courant Institute
New York University
251 Mercer Street
New York, New York 10012
Telephone: 212-998-3256
E-mail: admissions@math.nyu.edu

For application forms and a Graduate School bulletin:
Graduate Enrollment Services
Graduate School of Arts and Science
New York University
P.O. Box 907, Cooper Station
New York, New York 10276-0907
Telephone: 212-998-8050

New York University

THE FACULTY AND THEIR RESEARCH

Professors
Marco M. Avellaneda, Ph.D. Applied mathematics, mathematical modeling in finance, probability.
Simeon M. Berman, Ph.D. Stochastic processes, probability, statistical applications.
Fedor A. Bogomolov, Ph.D. Algebraic geometry and related problems in algebra, topology, number theory.
Sylvain E. Cappell, Ph.D. Algebraic and geometric topology, symplectic and algebraic geometry.
Jeff Cheeger, Ph.D. Differential geometry and its connections with topology and analysis.
W. Stephen Childress, Ph.D. Fluid dynamics, magnetohydrodynamics, asymptotic methods.
Percy A. Deift, Ph.D. Spectral theory and inverse spectral theory, integrable systems, Riemann-Hilbert problems.
Weinan E, Ph.D. Applied mathematics, partial differential equations, numerical analysis.
Harold M. Edwards, Ph.D. Algebra, number theory, history of mathematics.
Paul R. Garabedian, Ph.D. Complex analysis, computational fluid dynamics, plasma physics.
Jonathan Goodman, Ph.D. Fluid dynamics, computational physics, computational finance.
Leslie Greengard, Ph.D. Applied and computational mathematics, partial differential equations, computational chemistry, mathematical biology.
Frederick P. Greenleaf, Ph.D. Noncommutative harmonic analysis, Lie groups and group representations, invariant partial differential operators.
Mikhael Gromov, Ph.D. Riemannian manifolds, symplectic manifolds, infinite groups.
Eliezer Hameiri, Ph.D. Applied mathematics, magnetohydrodynamics, plasma physics.
Melvin Hausner, Ph.D. Combinatorics, geometry, nonstandard analysis.
Helmut Hofer, Ph.D. Symplectic geometry, dynamical systems, partial differential equations.
Robert V. Kohn, Ph.D. Nonlinear partial differential equations, materials science, mathematical finance.
Fang-Hua Lin, Ph.D. Partial differential equations, geometric measure theory.
Andrew J. Majda, Ph.D. Modern applied mathematics, atmosphere/ocean science, partial differential equations.
Henry P. McKean, Ph.D. Probability, partial differential equations, complex function theory.
David W. McLaughlin, Ph.D. Applied mathematics, nonlinear wave equations, visual neural science.
Charles M. Newman, Ph.D. Probability theory, statistical physics, stochastic models.
Albert B. J. Novikoff, Ph.D. Analysis, history of mathematics, pedagogy.
Jerome K. Percus, Ph.D. Chemical physics, mathematical biology.
Charles S. Peskin, Ph.D. Mathematics and computing in medicine and biology, cardiac fluid dynamics, biomolecular motors, neurophysiology.
Richard M. Pollack, Ph.D. Real algebraic geometry, discrete geometry, computational geometry.
John Rinzel, Ph.D. Computational neuroscience, nonlinear dynamics of neurons and neural circuits, sensory processing.
Jacob T. Schwartz, Ph.D. Robotics, computational geometry, analysis of algorithms.
Jalal M. I. Shatah, Ph.D. Partial differential equations, dynamical systems, analysis.
Michael Shelley, Ph.D. Applied mathematics and modeling, visual neuroscience, fluid dynamics, computational physics and neuroscience.
Joel H. Spencer, Ph.D. Discrete mathematics, theoretical computer science.
Srinivasa S. R. Varadhan, Ph.D. Probability theory, stochastic processes, partial differential equations.
Harold Weitzner, Ph.D. Plasma physics, fluid dynamics, differential equations.
Olof Widlund, Phil.Dr. Numerical analysis, partial differential equations, parallel computing.
Zhouping Xin, Ph.D. Partial differential equations, numerical analysis.
Horng-tzer Yau, Ph.D. Probability theory, statistical mechanics, quantum mechanics.
Lai-Sang Young, Ph.D. Dynamical systems and ergodic theory.

Associate Professors
Tobias H. Colding, Ph.D. Differential geometry, geometric analysis, partial differential equations, low-dimensional topology.
Malcolm Goldman, Ph.D. Probability and statistics, functional analysis.
Daniel Tranchina, Ph.D. Mathematical modeling in visual neuroscience, intercellular and extracellular recording from retinal neurons.

Assistant Professors
Yu Chen, Ph.D. Numerical scattering theory, ill-posed problems, scientific computing.
David M. Holland, Ph.D. Ocean modeling, ocean circulation theory, ocean-climate interactions.
David J. Muraki, Ph.D. Asymptotic modeling and analysis, nonlinear waves and dynamics, meteorological fluid dynamics.
Esteban G. Tabak, Ph.D. Dynamics of the atmosphere and ocean, energy transfer in systems with many degrees of freedom.

Affiliated Professors
Tamar Schlick, Ph.D.
Eero Simoncelli, Ph.D.
Alan Sokal, Ph.D.
George Zaslavsky, Ph.D.

NORTH CAROLINA STATE UNIVERSITY

Department of Mathematics

Programs of Study	The Department of Mathematics offers programs leading to the M.S. and Ph.D. in mathematics and applied mathematics. Within the program in applied mathematics, students may concentrate in computational mathematics. The programs are flexible and meet the needs of students with a wide variety of interests and career plans. The department includes active research groups in algebra, including ring theory, Lie theory, and symbolic computation; linear algebra; numerical analysis and optimization; control theory; probability; ordinary differential equations and dynamical systems; partial differential equations; mathematical physics; and topology. The M.S. degree requires nine courses and a project. For the M.S. degree in mathematics, there is a four-course core of courses in analysis, algebra, linear algebra or matrix theory, and topology or manifolds. For the M.S. degree in applied mathematics, the core includes courses in analysis and numerical analysis and two courses selected from matrix theory, ODEs, PDEs, probability, linear programming, and control theory. Both degrees require the study of one or two fields in some depth and allow up to three courses outside the mathematics department. The Ph.D. degrees require a six-course core with some flexibility. The qualifying examination is based on three 2-course sequences selected by the student from ten possibilities, including analysis, algebra, linear algebra and Lie algebras, matrix theory, topology, differential geometry, ODEs, PDEs, probability, numerical analysis, and control. Graduate students in the Department of Mathematics benefit from a nationally recognized program of training in university-level teaching. Students interested in applications of mathematics can participate in the Industrial Applied Mathematics Program, whose joint research endeavors pair members of the mathematics department with industrial and governmental partners. This program was described in an article in the June 1996 *SIAM News*.
Research Facilities	In addition to the Department of Mathematics' workstation laboratories, students and faculty members have access to high-performance computing and visualization equipment at the North Carolina Supercomputing Center (NCSC) in Research Triangle Park. NCSC currently operates a CRAY T916, a 32-node CRAY T3D, and a 36-node CRAY T3E and has a well-equipped visualization laboratory. The North Carolina State University (NCSU) libraries contain nearly 2.5 million volumes and receive more than 18,000 periodicals. By arrangement with the nearby University of North Carolina at Chapel Hill and Duke University libraries, virtually all mathematics journals are received by at least one of the area universities. The Center for Research in Scientific Computation, which is housed in the Department of Mathematics and is directed by University Professor of Mathematics H. T. Banks, serves as the University's focal point for research in computational science, engineering, and mathematics. The center's activities include the Industrial Applied Mathematics Program and the two-week Industrial Mathematics Modeling Workshop for Graduate Students, which brings students from around the country to NCSU each August.
Financial Aid	Most first-year graduate students are supported by teaching assistantships, which pay $12,300 per academic year. TAs teach two recitation sections or one course per semester. Summer grading and teaching positions pay an additional $1900 to $2800. Some first-year students receive fellowships or research assistantships. Supported students receive free tuition and free health insurance. They pay only student fees.
Cost of Study	In 1998–99, tuition for full-time graduate students was $714 per semester for North Carolina residents and an additional $4493 per semester for nonresidents. Fees were $424 per semester. Graduate students who are U.S. citizens or permanent residents normally become North Carolina residents after one year.
Living and Housing Costs	E. S. King Village on campus has 295 graduate student apartments; two-bedroom apartments rent for $345 per month. Most students live in off-campus apartments, usually within walking distance of campus or along free University bus routes. Off-campus two-bedroom apartments rent for $400 to $750 per month.
Student Group	Of 94 mathematics graduate students in spring 1998, 32 were women, 16 were international, and 5 were part-time. Forty were teaching assistants, 11 were fully supported by various fellowships, and 19 were research assistants. Nine additional students were partially supported. About 25 were in M.S. programs, and the rest were in Ph.D. programs.
Student Outcomes	Fifteen Ph.D. students graduated from May 1997 to May 1998. Three accepted tenure-track positions in academia, 5 took postdoctoral positions at academic and scientific organizations, and 7 applied mathematics graduates took industrial jobs, some of which were at national laboratories. M.S. students have readily found employment, with about half going into industry and half going into teaching (high school through four-year college) or working for governmental agencies. A full list may be found on the department's Web site at http://www.math.ncsu.edu/index.html/grad/brochure/phd1990.html.
Location	The Research Triangle region, which includes Raleigh, Durham, and Chapel Hill, is a vibrant metropolitan area of more than 1 million in rolling, wooded central North Carolina. In 1994, *Money* magazine named the Triangle the best place to live in the U.S. In addition to NCSU, the region is home to the University of North Carolina at Chapel Hill and Duke University. In the center of the region is Research Triangle Park, the location of more than seventy public, nonprofit, and corporate research centers. Recreational opportunities include water sports on numerous lakes and hiking in Umstead State Park and on the 38-mile Raleigh Greenway. Major cultural attractions include the North Carolina Museum of Art and North Carolina Symphony Orchestra in Raleigh, the capital of North Carolina; the American Dance Festival in Durham; and Playmakers Theater in Chapel Hill. Ocean beaches and mountain recreation areas are within a 2½- to 4-hour drive.
The University	North Carolina State University, founded in 1887, is a major research university that is deeply rooted in the land-grant tradition. Its research and education programs emphasize science and technology. One of the two flagship public universities of North Carolina, NCSU has more than 27,000 students, including more than 5,000 graduate students. Its main campus of 623 acres is just west of downtown Raleigh. An adjacent expansion campus of 1,000 acres houses science and engineering research centers, as well as cooperating private and governmental research efforts.
Applying	Application forms may be obtained from the Department of Mathematics or the Graduate School. The application form should be submitted together with the required fee, two sets of transcripts, letters of recommendation, and scores on the General Test of the Graduate Record Examinations (GRE). It is recommended that applicants also take the GRE test in advanced mathematics. Students whose native language is not English may be required to submit TOEFL scores. For fullest consideration, applications for the fall semester should be submitted by February 1.
Correspondence and Information	Janet Early Graduate Program Secretary Department of Mathematics North Carolina State University Raleigh, North Carolina 27695-8205 Telephone: 919-513-2301 Fax: 919-513-1991 E-mail: early@math.ncsu.edu

North Carolina State University

THE FACULTY AND THEIR RESEARCH

H. T. Banks, University Professor; Ph.D., Purdue, 1967. Control and parameter estimation for PDEs, applications to biology and engineering.
John W. Bishir, Professor; Ph.D., North Carolina State, 1961. Mathematical modeling in the biological sciences.
J. David Brown, Assistant Professor; Ph.D., Texas, 1985. General relativity, quantum gravity, mechanics, astrophysics.
Ernest E. Burniston, Professor; Ph.D., London, 1962. Applications of complex analysis to physical problems.
Stephen L. Campbell, Professor; Ph.D., Northwestern, 1972. Implicit systems of ordinary differential equations.
Richard E. Chandler, Professor; Ph.D., Florida State, 1963. General topology, especially Hausdorff compactifications.
Harvey J. Charlton, Assistant Professor; Ph.D., Virginia Tech, 1966. Curriculum development in applied mathematics.
Moody T. Chu, Professor; Ph.D., Michigan State, 1982. Numerical methods for ODEs, numerical linear algebra.
Ethelbert N. Chukwu, Professor; Ph.D., Case Western Reserve, 1972. Functional differential equations, applications to economics.
Lung O. Chung, Professor; Ph.D., UCLA, 1974. Ring theory, complex analysis.
Jo-Ann D. Cohen, Professor; Ph.D., Duke, 1976. Topological algebra, ring theory.
J. M. A. Danby, Professor; Ph.D., Manchester, 1953. Celestial mechanics.
Joseph C. Dunn, Professor; Ph.D., Adelphi, 1967. Nonlinear optimization, optimal control.
Gary D. Faulkner, Associate Professor; Ph.D., Georgia Tech, 1976. Analysis, functional analysis, topology.
Amassa Fauntleroy, Professor; Ph.D., Northwestern, 1970. Algebraic geometry, complex differential geometry, algebra.
Ben G. Fitzpatrick, Associate Professor; Ph.D., Brown, 1988. Control and parameter estimation for PDE models in biology and mechanics.
Jean-Pierre Fouque, Associate Professor; Ph.D., Paris VI (Curie), 1979. Probability theory, random media, financial mathematics.
John E. Franke, Associate Professor; Ph.D., Northwestern, 1973. Dynamical systems, applications to population biology.
Ronald O. Fulp, Professor; Ph.D., Auburn, 1965. Geometry of fiber bundles, mathematical physics.
Dennis E. Garoutte, Associate Professor; Ph.D., Montana State, 1967. Complex analysis.
Pierre A. Gremaud, Assistant Professor; Ph.D., Lausanne Federal Polytechnic, 1991. Numerical analysis for PDEs.
Robert E. Hartwig, Professor; Ph.D., Adelaide (Australia), 1966. Matrix theory, cryptography, error-correcting codes.
Aloysius G. Helminck, Associate Professor; Ph.D., Utrecht (Netherlands), 1985. Algebraic groups, finite groups, representation theory.
Pavel Hitczenko, Associate Professor; Ph.D., Warsaw, 1987. Probability.
Hoon Hong, Associate Professor; Ph.D., Ohio State, 1990. Symbolic computation, computer algebra, polynomial equations.
Ilse Ipsen, Associate Professor; Ph.D., Penn State, 1983. Numerical linear algebra.
Kazufumi Ito, Professor; Ph.D., Washington (St. Louis), 1981. Optimal control and inverse problems for PDEs.
Naihuan Jing, Associate Professor; Ph.D., Yale, 1989. Representational theory, quantum groups, infinite-dimensional Lie algebras.
Erich Kaltofen, Professor; Ph.D., Rensselaer, 1982. Computational algebra, symbolic manipulation systems.
Carl T. Kelley, Professor; Ph.D., Purdue, 1976. Nonlinear equations, multilevel methods, optimization.
Arkady Kheyfets, Associate Professor; Ph.D., Texas, 1986. General relativity, quantum gravity, cosmology.
Kwangil Koh, Professor; Ph.D., North Carolina, 1964. Ring theory, topological algebra.
Thomas Lada, Associate Professor; Ph.D., Notre Dame, 1974. Algebraic topology, homotopy theory, cohomology operations.
Dana May Latch, Associate Professor; Ph.D., CUNY, 1971. Automated theorem proving, functional programming languages, category theory.
Zhilin Li, Assistant Professor; Ph.D., Washington (Seattle), 1994. Numerical analysis, physical problems involving interfaces.
Xiao-Biao Lin, Associate Professor: Ph.D., Brown, 1985. Dynamical systems, bifurcations, singular perturbations.
Sharon R. Lubkin, Assistant Professor of Mathematics and Statistics; Ph.D., Cornell, 1992. Mathematical biology, mechanical aspects of pattern formation.
Jiang Luh, Professor; Ph.D., Michigan, 1963. Rings, modules.
Joe A. Marlin, Professor; Ph.D., North Carolina State, 1965. Ordinary differential equations.
Robert H. Martin Jr., Professor; Ph.D., Georgia Tech, 1970. ODEs, parabolic and elliptic PDEs.
William M. McEneaney, Assistant Professor; Ph.D., Brown, 1993. Control theory, game theory, applications to aerospace engineering and finance.
Carl D. Meyer Jr., Professor; Ph.D., Colorado State, 1968. Matrix theory, Markov chains, scientific computing.
Kailash C. Misra, Professor; Ph.D., Rutgers, 1982. Representations of Lie algebras, quantum groups, vertex operator algebras.
Larry K. Norris, Associate Professor; Ph.D., North Carolina State, 1980. General relativity, gauge theories, generalized symplectic geometry.
Lavon B. Page, Associate Professor; Ph.D., Virginia, 1968. Analysis of networks.
C. V. Pao, Professor; Ph.D., Pittsburgh, 1968. Parabolic systems with delay, reaction-diffusion systems, transport theory.
Sandra O. Paur, Assistant Professor; Ph.D., Indiana, 1973. Geometric measure theory.
Elmor L. Peterson, Professor; Ph.D., Carnegie Mellon, 1964. Convex analysis, geometric programming.
Mohan S. Putcha, Professor; Ph.D., California, Santa Barbara, 1973. Semigroups, algebraic groups, algebraic geometry.
Robert T. Ramsey, Associate Professor, Ph.D., Miami (Florida), 1967. Topology.
Jesus Rodriguez, Associate Professor; Ph.D., Maryland, 1980. Ordinary differential equations, difference equations.
Nicholas J. Rose, Professor (Emeritus); Ph.D., NYU (Courant), 1956. Control theory, differential equations, matrix theory.
Stephen Schecter, Professor; Ph.D., Berkeley, 1975. Bifurcations, systems of conservation laws.
Jeffrey S. Scroggs, Associate Professor; Ph.D., Illinois, 1988. Numerical analysis, scientific computing.
James F. Selgrade, Professor; Ph.D., Wisconsin, 1973. Dynamical systems, applications to biomathematics.
Frederick H. Semazzi, Associate Professor; Ph.D., Nairobi (Kenya), 1983. Numerical climate modeling and weather prediction.
Michael Shearer, Professor; D.Phil., Oxford, 1976. Hyperbolic PDEs, systems of conservation laws, mechanics.
Charles E. Siewert, Professor; Ph.D., Michigan, 1965. Reactor analysis, neutron transport, computational methods.
Robert Silber, Associate Professor; Ph.D., Clemson, 1968. Combinatorial games, calculus of variations, optimal control.
Jack W. Silverstein, Professor; Ph.D., Brown, 1975. Spectral properties of random matrices.
Michael F. Singer, Professor; Ph.D., Berkeley, 1974. Algebraic theory of differential equations, computer algebra.
Ralph C. Smith, Associate Professor; Ph.D., Montana State, 1990. Smart material systems, numerical analysis, control, PDEs.
Ernest L. Stitzinger, Professor; Ph.D., Pittsburgh, 1969. Lie algebras, group theory.
Hien T. Tran, Associate Professor; Ph.D., Rensselaer, 1986. Scientific computing, identification and control of infinite-dimensional systems.
Robert E. White, Professor; Ph.D., Massachusetts, 1973. Parallel computing, PDEs.

NORTH CAROLINA STATE UNIVERSITY

NC STATE UNIVERSITY

Department of Statistics

Programs of Study

The Department of Statistics offers programs of study leading to the Master of Statistics (M.Stat.) degree, the Master of Science (M.Sc.) degree in statistics, and the Doctor of Philosophy (Ph.D.). Optional concentrations are available at the master's level in biomedical, environmental, and industrial statistics and statistical genetics. In addition to its degree programs in statistics, the department also offers programs of study in biomathematics leading to the Ph.D., M.Sc., and Master of Biomathematics degrees. For students entering with all the prerequisites, M.Stat. and M.Sc. in statistics programs require a minimum of 34 semester hours. Included are courses on statistical methods, statistical theory, linear models, sampling, experimental design, the analysis of categorical and censored data, supervised consulting, and courses from other statistical and supporting areas. Students pursuing the M.Sc. degree take 6 hours of research in place of 6 hours of electives. All master's students must pass the departmental Basic Examination, which is normally taken at the beginning of the student's second year. A final oral examination is also a requirement and is usually taken at the end of the student's second year.

Admission to the Ph.D. program is granted to those who have been admitted to the master's program and have passed the Basic Comprehensive Examination at the Ph.D. level. Requirements for the degree vary with the background of the student. However, all students are required to take courses on measure theory, advanced probability, advanced inference, and supervised consulting, in addition to statistics and supporting electives. The student must pass both a preliminary written and oral examination, prepare a dissertation describing independent and original research, and defend the dissertation in a final oral examination. A minimum of two years beyond the master's degree is commonly required to obtain the Ph.D. degree. Flexible co-major programs at the master's and Ph.D. level with other departments can also be arranged.

A large faculty with varied interests provides an education blending theory, methods, and practice. Areas of specialization include time series, econometrics, ecology, statistical genetics, biomathematics, biostatistics, linear and nonlinear models, design of experiments, sampling, probability, environmental applications, statistical process and quality control, statistical computing, nonparametric regression and inference, stochastic processes, and statistical inference.

Research Facilities

Students in the program have access to the departmental library, the D. H. Hill Library, and various other libraries at North Carolina State (NCSU), UNC–Chapel Hill, and Duke University. Computers and computing play a key role in the department. Departmental computational facilities include the Statistics Instructional Computing Laboratory (SICL) with approximately thirty-five Sun Workstations organized in a classroom setting with networked printer availability. SICL is also a part of the campus Athena computing realm, which provides network services including e-mail, Usenet, World Wide Web browsers, and an increasingly large library of software. This network is made up of more than 1,000 UNIX computers and allows the users to log in remotely into any machine and access their own files along with the same suite of software packages. Students also have access to the Statistics Research Computing Information System (SRCIS), a facility maintained for use by statistics graduate students. SRCIS is a UNIX-based/AFS distributed computing network with high-end Sun servers and several Sun Workstations. Personal computers and high-resolution printers are also available. SRCIS is connected via Ethernet to the campus fiber-optic network. Available software packages and languages include SAS, C, Splus, IMSL, maple, matlab, FORTRAN, and Pascal, as well as many others. Academic research accounts are available on a CRAY Y-MP 8E/4128 at the North Carolina Supercomputing Center (NCSC).

Financial Aid

Graduate teaching and research assistantships, industrial traineeships, VIGRE traineeships, and fellowships are awarded each year on a competitive basis. Fellowships are provided through the department's Gertrude M. Cox Fellowship Fund. The stipend for teaching assistantships in 1998–99 was $11,500 for nine months. Graduate industrial traineeships from Glaxo-Wellcome, Becton Dickinson, the Chemical Industry Institute of Toxicology, Nortel, and other local industries are also available. Several faculty members appoint students to research assistantships, normally in the second or later years of study. Special aid programs are also available for applicants from minority groups. Those students receiving assistantships or fellowships receive health insurance coverage and certain amounts of in-state and out-of-state tuition.

Cost of Study

Annual tuition costs are about $2370 for in-state and $11,536 for out-of-state students.

Living and Housing Costs

A large number of apartments are available within walking distance of the campus or along a bus route. A two-bedroom apartment can be rented for about $650 a month. NCSU also offers a graduate dormitory and married student housing. Raleigh residents enjoy a moderate cost of living.

Student Group

The department has 150 graduate students, of whom 50 percent are women, 70 percent are U.S. citizens, and more than half are pursuing Ph.D. degrees as their ultimate goal. Last year, more than 100 students received financial assistance in the form of teaching and research assistantships, industrial traineeships, and fellowships. Students with varied backgrounds, including agriculture, biology, engineering, forestry, mathematics, and psychology, who have an interest in the practice of statistics and the theory behind the applications of statistics join the program.

Student Outcomes

Recent graduates are currently employed as statisticians, biostatisticians, and data analysts at various pharmaceutical, market research, and semiconductor research companies; clinical research organizations; and government agencies in the Research Triangle Park and across the country. Companies employing graduates include Glaxo Wellcome, Becton Dickinson, SAS Institute, Abbott Labs, Price Waterhouse, GE, Quintiles, Pratt & Whitney, United Airlines, Merck, Nortel, Eli Lilly, and Ciba. Doctoral degree graduates are also working at various universities.

Location

Raleigh, the state capital, is located in the rolling terrain of the North Carolina Piedmont, halfway between the unspoiled beaches of the Outer Banks and the Appalachian Mountains. Raleigh is located just minutes from the Research Triangle Park, which houses more than 100 top technology companies. Raleigh is the home of several colleges; the North Carolina Symphony; museums of art, history, and natural science; and a variety of cultural and recreational activities. Golf, tennis, swimming, boating, fishing, and hiking and an extensive park and greenway system are all available. Raleigh maintains the friendliness of small-town living while providing the diversity of a big city.

The University

NCSU has been a national center for research in science and technology since 1887. The department was founded in 1941 by Gertrude M. Cox, who established a tradition of excellence. Building on her vision, the department has maintained its applied orientation while providing a solid foundation in statistical theory. More than 800 students have received master's and doctoral degrees from the department. The department is a part of the College of Physical and Mathematical Sciences. Several faculty members have joint appointments with the College of Agriculture and Life Sciences.

Applying

A completed application and application fee must be received by March 1 for fall admission and by October 15 for spring in order to receive higher priority for financial aid. Graduate School deadlines are June 25 for fall and November 25 for spring. Different deadlines for international students are detailed in materials sent by the Graduate School. Graduate Record Examinations (GRE) General Test scores are required of all applicants. Test of English as a Foreign Language (TOEFL) scores are required of certain applicants.

Correspondence and Information

Dr. Sastry G. Pantula, Director of Graduate Programs
Department of Statistics, Box 8203
North Carolina State University
Raleigh, North Carolina 27695-8203

Telephone: 919-515-2528
Fax: 919-515-7591
E-mail: dsgp@stat.ncsu.edu
World Wide Web: http://www.stat.ncsu.edu

North Carolina State University

THE FACULTY AND THEIR RESEARCH

Professors

Roger L. Berger, Ph.D., Purdue. Decision theory, theory of hypothesis testing, ordered parameters, bioequivalence.
Bibhuti B. Bhattacharyya, Ph.D., London School of Economics. Large sample theory, nonlinear regression and optimization, spatial processes.
Peter Bloomfield, Ph.D., Imperial College (London). Time series, statistical computing, environmental statistics, statistics in finance.
Dennis D. Boos, Ph.D., Florida State. Robust and nonparametric methods, generalized score tests, resampling methods.
Cavell Brownie, Ph.D., Cornell. Survival rates, biological statistics, spatial analysis of agricultural data.
Marie Davidian, Ph.D., North Carolina at Chapel Hill. Nonlinear regression, heteroscedastic models, clinical trials, longitudinal models.
David A. Dickey, Ph.D., Iowa State. Time series, stochastic processes, statistical methods, econometrics.
E. Jacqueline Dietz, Ph.D., Connecticut. Statistics education, nonparametric multivariate statistics.
Stephen P. Ellner, Ph.D., Cornell. Theoretical and mathematical population biology, nonlinear dynamics.
Thomas M. Gerig, Department Head; Ph.D., North Carolina at Chapel Hill. Multivariate analysis, biometrical collaborative studies.
Francis G. Giesbrecht, Ph.D., Iowa State. Experimental design, variance components, mixed models.
Thomas Johnson, Ph.D., North Carolina State. Econometrics, dynamic models, total quality management.
Jye-Chyi Lu, Ph.D., Wisconsin–Madison. Reliability, censored data analysis, industrial statistics, ordered statistics.
John F. Monahan, Ph.D., Carnegie-Mellon. Statistical computing, Bayesian inference, time series.
Douglas W. Nychka, Ph.D., Wisconsin. Nonparametric regression, statistical computing, spatial statistics, spatial-temporal modeling.
Sastry G. Pantula, Director of Graduate Programs; Ph.D., Iowa State. Time series, mixed linear and nonlinear models, spatial statistics.
Kenneth H. Pollock, Director of Graduate Programs for Biomathematics; Ph.D., Cornell. Sampling, statistical ecology, wildlife and fisheries statistics.
Don L. Ridgeway, Ph.D., Rochester. Algebraic statistical mechanics.
Daniel L. Solomon, Associate Dean; Ph.D., Florida State. Bayesian inference, mathematical ecology, statistics education.
Leonard A. Stefanski, Ph.D., North Carolina at Chapel Hill. Measurement error models, simulation and resampling methods, environmental statistics.
William H. Swallow, Director of Undergraduate Programs; Ph.D., Cornell. Linear models, experimental design, regression diagnostics, group testing.
Anastasios "Butch" Tsiatis, Ph.D., Berkeley. Biostatistics, survival analysis, statistical inference.
John L. Wasik, Ed.D., Florida State. Experimental design, multivariate methods, sample survey methodology.
Bruce S. Weir, William Neal Reynolds Professor; Ph.D., North Carolina State. Population and statistical genetics, DNA profile matching.
Zhao-Bang Zeng, Research Professor; Ph.D., Edinburgh. Statistical and quantitative genetics, statistical methods of gene mapping.

Associate Professors

Marcia L. Gumpertz, Ph.D., North Carolina State. Repeated measures, spatial statistics, environmental and agricultural statistics.
Jacqueline M. Hughes-Oliver, Ph.D., North Carolina State. Group testing, nonlinear models, industrial and spatial statistics.
Thomas B. Kepler, Ph.D., Brandeis. Theoretical biology, immunology and microbiology, dynamical systems.
Thomas W. Reiland, Ph.D., Florida State. Mathematical programming, nonsmooth optimization, operations research.
Charles E. Smith, Ph.D., Chicago. Biomathematics, biomedical applications, stochastic processes.
Jeffrey L. Thorne, Ph.D., Washington (Seattle). DNA and protein sequence analysis, molecular evolution, genetics.

Assistant Professors

Tonya Balan, Ph.D., North Carolina State. Statistical computing, SAS, spatial statistics.
Tim Elston, Ph.D., Georgia Tech. Biophysics, biomathematics, bioinformatics.
Montserrat Fuentes, Ph.D., Chicago. Spatial statistics, statistical computing, environmental statistics.
Sujit K. Ghosh, Ph.D., Connecticut. Survival analysis, statistical computing, spatial statistics, Bayesian inference.
Sharon Lubkin, Ph.D., Cornell. Biomathematics, scientific computing.
Spencer Muse, Ph.D., North Carolina State. Statistical genetics, bioinformatics.
Daowen Zhang, Ph.D., Michigan. Clinical trials, biostatistics, semiparametric and nonparametric regression.

Associate Faculty in Statistics

William R. Atchley, Professor of Genetics; Ph.D., Kansas. Quantitative and population genetics, biostatistics.
Ted H. Emigh, Associate Professor of Genetics; Ph.D., Iowa State. Genetic statistics, linear models, design of experiments.
Major M. Goodman, Distinguished University Professor and William Neal Reynolds Professor; Professor of Crop Science; Ph.D., North Carolina State. Numerical taxonomy, quantitative genetics.
Alastair R. Hall, Professor of Economics; Ph.D., Warwick (England). Econometrics, time series, generalized estimating equations.
Moon W. Suh, Professor of Textiles; Ph.D., North Carolina State. Industrial statistics, operations research.

Recent Doctoral Dissertations

Asymptotics and applications of local Lyapunov exponents. Barbara A. Bailey, 1996.
The effect of measurement error on two-sample tests. Cathleen F. Barrows, 1996.
Probabilistic and statistical modeling for geometric structure of nonwoven fabrics. Heuiju Chun, 1998.
Confidence bands for nonparametric curve estimates. David Jesse Cummins, 1997.
Simulation extrapolation methods for heteroscedastic measurement error models with replicate measurements. Viswanath Devanarayan, 1996.
Quality of service modeling for wide area network. Paritosh Dixit, 1998.
Development and adaptations of data-driven nonparametric goodness-of-fit tests for a regression function. D. Bruce Elsheimer, 1995.
Estimation and hypothesis testing in nonstationary time series using frequency domain. Barry Evans, 1998.
Estimating population parameters using multiple frame and capture-recapture methodology. Dawn Haines, 1997.
Adjustment for carryover in crossover designs: Use of weighted estimation and hypothesis testing as an alternative to classical two-stage procedures. Judith Jayawickrama, 1997.
Estimation of percentiles using group testing when the underlying response variable is continuous. Jeffrey Jonkman, 1998.
Semi-nonparametric likelihood estimation in a nonlinear mixed effects model for group risk crop insurance. Alan Philip Ker, 1996.
4^N fractional factorial designs by pseudo-factors. Dongwoo Kim, 1997.
Unit root tests in nonstationary time series. Taiyeong Lee, 1998.
Characterizing the structure of genetic population. Yi-Ju Li, 1996.
Approximations for skewed probability densities based on Laguerre series and biological applications. Te-Hsin Lung, 1998.
Models for testing variance parameters equal to zero in a random coefficient regression model. Jane Elizabeth Morgan, 1996.
Statistical inference for heterogeneous random fields. Jeffrey Andrew Royle, 1996.
Uniformly more powerful one-sided tests for hypothesis about linear inequalities with unknown covariance. Khalil Georges Saikali, 1996.
Exact unconditional tests for discrete data. Kurex Sidik, 1998.
Random coefficient models for degradation and spatially correlated count data. Cheng Su, 1996.
Testing for trends and causality in time series data. Hongguang Sun, 1997.
Survival analysis for telemetry data in animal studies. Kuenhi Tsai, 1996.
The cubic ternary complex model: a heuristic for classifying equilibrium pharmacological models and for understanding efficacy and apparent affinity in these models. Jack M. Weiss, 1996.
Generalized estimating equations for spatially correlated data. Chi-Tsung Wu, 1998.
Multiresolution analysis of random processes with application on numerical model evaluations. Jun Zhai, 1998.
Inference for correlated categorical data. Jie Zhang, 1996.
Integrating resource types, access conditions, and preference differences into models for use and nonuse values: the case of marine debris control. Xiaolong Zhang, 1996.

North Carolina State University

SELECTED PUBLICATIONS

Hsu, J. C., and **R. L. Berger.** Stepwise confidence intervals without multiplicity adjustment for dose response and toxicity studies. *J. Am. Stat. Assoc.,* in press.

Berger, R. L., and **D. D. Boos.** Confidence limits for the onset and duration of treatment effect. *Biometrical J.,* in press.

Berger, R. L. Likelihood ratio tests and intersection-union tests. In *Advances in Statistical Decision Theory and Applications,* pp. 225–37, eds. S. Panchapakesan and N. Balakrishnan. Boston: Birkhauser, 1997.

Berger, R. L., and J. C. Hsu. Bioequivalence trials, intersection-union tests, and equivalence confidence sets (with discussion). *Stat. Sci.* 11:283–319, 1996.

Casella, G., and **R. L. Berger.** *Statistical Inference.* Belmont, Calif.: Duxbury Press, 1990.

Khalil, T. M., **B. B. Bhattacharyya,** and G. D. Richardson. Gauss-Newton estimates of parameters for a spatial autoregression model. *Stat. Prob. Lett.* 28:173–9, 1996.

Bloomfield, P., J. A. Royle, L. H. Steinberg, and Q. Yang. Accounting for meteorological effects in measuring urban ozone levels and trends. *Atmos. Environ.* 30:3067–77, 1996.

Lund, R., H. Hurd, **P. Bloomfield,** and R. Smith. Climatological time series with periodic correlation. *J. Climate* 8:2787–809, 1995.

Bloomfield, P., and W. L. Stieger. *Least Absolute Deviations. Theory, Applications, and Algorithms.* Boston: Birkhauser, 1983.

Bloomfield, P. *Fourier Analysis of Time Series: An Introduction.* New York: John Wiley & Sons, 1976.

Boos, D. D., and **J. M. Hughes-Oliver.** Applications of Basu's theorem. *Am. Stat.* 52:218–21, 1998.

Boos, D. D. Bartlett's test. *Encyclopedia Biostatistics* 1:252–3, 1998.

Zhang, J., and **D. D. Boos.** Mantel-Haenszel test statistics for correlated binary data. *Biometrics* 53:1185–98, 1997.

Brownie, C., and **M. L. Gumpertz.** Validity of spatial analyses for large field trials. *J. Agric. Biol. Environ. Stat.* 2:1–23, 1997.

Etchison, T., **C. Brownie,** and **S. G. Pantula.** A portmanteau test for spatial ARMA models. *Biometrics* 51:1536–42, 1995.

Brownie, C., and **D. D. Boos.** Type I error robustness of ANOVA and ANOVA on ranks when the number of treatments is large. *Biometrics* 50:542–9, 1994.

Higgins, K. M., **M. Davidian,** G. Chew, and H. Burge. The effect of serial dilution error on calibration inference for immunoassay. *Biometrics* 54:336–48, 1998.

Zeng, Q., and **M. Davidian.** Bootstrap adjusted calibration confidence intervals for immunoassay. *J. Am. Stat. Assoc.* 92:278–90, 1997.

Davidian, M., and D. Giltinan. *Nonlinear Models for Repeated Measurement Data.* London: Chapman and Hall, 1995.

Steel, R. G. D., J. H. Torrie, and **D. A. Dickey.** *Principles and Procedures of Statistics,* 3rd ed. New York: McGraw-Hill, 1997.

Akdi, Y., and **D. A. Dickey.** Periodograms of unit root time series: Distributions and tests. *Commun. Stat.* 27:69–87, 1997.

Bowerman, B. L., R. T. O'Connell, and **D. A. Dickey.** *Linear Statistical Models: An Applied Approach.* New York: Duxbury, 1986.

Brocklebank, J. C., and **D. A. Dickey.** *The SAS System for Forecasting Time Series.* Cary, N.C.: SAS Institute, 1986.

Dietz, E. J. Journal of statistics education. In *Encyclopedia of Statistical Sciences,* update volume 2, pp. 349–50. New York: John Wiley & Sons, 1998.

Felder, R. M., et al. **(E. J. Dietz).** A longitudinal study of engineering student performance and retention: III. Gender differences in student performance and attitudes. *J. Eng. Educ.* 84:151–64, 1995.

Dietz, E. J. A cooperative learning activity on methods of selecting a sample. *Am. Statistician* 47:104–8, 1993.

Fuentes, M., S. Doney, and D. Glover. Spatial-temporal structure of ocean color data in the North Atlantic. In *Statistics for the Atmosphere,* in press.

LeGrange, J. D., et al. **(M. Fuentes).** The dependence of the electro-optical properties of polymer dispersed liquid crystals on the photopolymerization process. *J. Appl. Phys.* 81(9), 1997.

Gizlice, Z., T. E. Carter Jr., **T. M. Gerig,** and J. W. Burton. Genetic diversity patterns in North American public soybean cultivars. *Crop Sci.* 36:753–65, 1996.

Jones, M. G., and **T. M. Gerig.** Ability grouping and classroom interactions. *J. Classroom Interact.* 29:27–34, 1994.

Ghosh, S. K., and A. E. Gelfand. Latent waiting time models for bivariate event times with censoring. *Sankhya B* 60:31–47, 1999.

Ghosh, S. K., and A. E. Gelfand. A latent risk approach for modeling individual level data consisting of multiple event times. *J. Stat. Res.* 32:23–39, 1998.

Gelfand, A. E., and **S. K. Ghosh.** Model choice: A minimum posterior predictive loss approach. *Biometrika* 85:1–11, 1998.

Gelfand, A. E., **S. K. Ghosh,** J. R. Knight, and C. F. Sirmans. Spatio-temporal modeling of residential sales data. *J. Business Econ. Stat.* 16:312–21, 1998.

Gumpertz, M. L., C. T. Wu, and J. M. Pye. Logistic regression for southern pine beetle outbreaks with spatial and temporal autocorrelation. *Institute of Statistics Mimeo Series #2513.* Raleigh, N.C., 1999.

Gumpertz, M. L., and **S. G. Pantula.** Random coefficient regression. In *Encyclopedia of Statistical Science,* update volume 2, pp. 581–8, eds. S. Kotz, C. Read, and D. Banks. New York: John Wiley & Sons, 1998.

Gumpertz, M. L., J. Graham, and J. B. Ristaino. Autologistic model of spatial pattern of Phytophthora epidemic in bell pepper: Effects of soil variables on disease presence. *J. Agric. Biol. Environ. Stat.* 2:131–56, 1997.

Gumpertz, M. L., and G. P. Y. Clarke. Two stage mixed model analysis using expected value transformations. *S. Afr. Stat. J.* 30:91–117, 1996.

Hughes-Oliver, J. M. Optimal designs for nonlinear models with correlated errors. In *New Developments and Applications in Experimental Design.* In press.

Hughes-Oliver, J. M., J. C. Lu, J. C. Davis, and R. S. Gyurcsik. Achieving uniformity in a semi-conductor fabrication process using spatial modeling. *J. Am. Stat. Assoc.* 93:36–45, 1998.

Hughes-Oliver, J. M., G. Gonzalez-Farias, **J. C. Lu,** and D. Chen. Parametric nonstationary correlation models. *Stat. Prob. Lett.* 40:267–78, 1998.

Hughes-Oliver, J. M., and **W. Swallow.** A two-stage adaptive group-testing procedure for estimating small proportions. *J. Am. Stat. Assoc.* 89:982–93, 1994.

Li, C. S., and **J. C. Lu** et al. A multivariate zero-inflated Poisson distribution and its inferences. *Technometrics* 41:29–38, 1999.

Lu, J. C., and C. Unal. Bayesian analyses of censored data from industrial experiments, part II: Process characterization and optimization. *Trans. Indian Assoc. Productivity Quality Reliability (IAPQR)* 23:1–23, 1998.

Chen, D., **J. C. Lu, J. M. Hughes-Oliver,** and C. S. Li. The asymptotics of maximum likelihood estimation for the bivariate exponential of Marshall and Olkin based on mixed bivariate censored data. *Metrika* 48:109–25, 1998.

Liu, S., **J. C. Lu,** D. W. Kolpin, and W. Q. Meeker. Analysis of environmental data with censored observations. *Environ. Sci. Technol.* 31:3358–62, 1997.

Lu, J. C. A new plan for life-testing two-component parallel systems. *Stat. Prob. Lett.* 34:19–32, 1997.

Lu, J. C., J. Park, and Q. Yang. Statistical inference of a time-to-failure distribution from linear degradation data. *Technometrics* 39:391–400, 1997.

Monahan, J., and A. Genz. Stochastic integration rules for infinite regions. *SIAM J. Sci. Comput.* 19:426–39, 1998.

Monahan, J., and A. Genz. Radial-spherical integration methods for Bayesian integration. *J. Am. Stat. Assoc.* 92:664–74, 1997.

Monahan, J., D. Hoium, A. Riordan, and K. Keeter. Severe thunderstorm and tornado warnings at Raleigh, North Carolina. *Bull. Am. Meteorol. Assoc.* 78:2559–75, 1997.

Thomas, G. H., et al. **(S. V. Muse).** Intragenic duplication and divergence in the spectrin superfamily of proteins. *Mol. Biol. Evol.,* in press.

Muse, S. V. Modeling the molecular evolution of HIV sequences. In *Molecular Evolution of HIV,* ed. K. A. Crandall. In press.

Lin, Q., E. S. Buckler IV, **S. V. Muse,** and J. C. Walker. Molecular evolution of type one serine/threonine protein phosphotases. *Mol. Phylo. Evol.,* in press.

North Carolina State University

Selected Publications (continued)

Muse, S. V. Rates and patterns of nucleotide substitution in plants. In *Plant Molecular Evolution,* eds. B. S. Gaut and J. J. Doyle. In press.

Muse, S. V., and B. S. Gaut. Comparing patterns of nucleotide substitution rates among chloroplast loci using the relative ratio test. *Genetics* 146:393–9, 1997.

Gaut, B. S., L. G. Clark, J. F. Wendel, and S. V. Muse. Comparisons of the molecular evolutionary process at rbcL and ndhF in the grass family (Poaceae). *Mol. Biol. Evol.* 14:769–77, 1997.

O'Connell, M., and D. Nychka et al. Syringe grading based on extracted features from high dimensional friction data. *J. Am. Stat. Assoc.* 90:1171–8, 1996.

Nychka, D. Smoothing splines as locally weighted averages. *Ann. Stat.* 23:1175–97, 1995.

Sun, H., and S. G. Pantula. Testing for trends in correlated data. *Stat. Prob. Lett.* 41:87–95, 1999.

Park, Y. J., and S. G. Pantula. Variance estimators in the Chu-White test for structural change. *Commun. Stat.-Simulation* 27:1019–29, 1998.

Rawlings, J. O., S. G. Pantula, and D. A. Dickey. *Applied Regression Analysis: A Research Tool.* New York: Springer, 1998.

Ramos, R. Q., and S. G. Pantula. Estimation of nonlinear random coefficient models. *Stat. Prob. Lett.* 24:49–56, 1995.

Pollock, K. H., and J. M. Hoenig. Change-in-ratio estimators. In *Encyclopedia of Statistics,* update volume 2, pp. 109–12, 1998.

Pollock, K. H., J. D. Nichols, C. Brownie, and J. E. Hines. Statistical inference for capture-recapture experiments. *Wildlife Soc. Monogr.* 107, 1997.

Pollock, K. H., C. M. Jones, and T. L. Brown. Angler surveys and their application to fisheries management. In *American Fisheries Society Special Publication 25.* Bethesda, Md.: 1994.

Smith, C. E., P. Lansky, and T. H. Lung. Cycle-time and residence-time density approximations in a stochastic model for circulatory transport. *Bull. Math. Biol.* 59:1–22, 1997.

Smith, C. E., and J. C. Liu. Serial dependency in neural spike trains. *J. Soc. Instrum. Control Eng.* 34:901–6, 1995.

Solomon, D. L., B. Trumbo, and P. Vellman. Electronic publications in statistics: Ready or not, here they come. *Am. Statistician* 48:191–6, 1994.

Solomon, D. L. Invited comment: Statistical consulting as scholarship. *Am. Statistician* 46:299–300, 1992.

Carroll, R. J., and L. A. Stefanski. Asymptotic theory for the SIMEX estimator in measurement error models. In *Advances in Statistical Decision Theory and Applications,* eds. S. Panchapakesan and N. Balakrishnan. Berlin: Birkhauser, 1997.

Carroll, R. J., D. Ruppert, and L. A. Stefanski. *Measurement Error in Nonlinear Models.* London: Chapman Hall, 1995.

Stefanski, L. A., and J. R. Cook. Simulation-extrapolation: The measurement error jackknife. *J. Am. Stat. Assoc.* 90:1247–56, 1995.

Stefanski, L. A., and J. S. Buzas. Instrumental variable estimation in binary regression models. *J. Am. Stat. Assoc.* 90:541–50, 1995.

Kianifard, F., and W. H. Swallow. A review of the development and application of recursive residuals in linear models. *J. Am. Stat. Assoc.* 91:391–400, 1996.

Swallow, W. H., and F. Kianifard. Using robust scale estimates in detecting multiple outliers in linear regression. *Biometrics* 52:545–56, 1996.

Chen, C. L., and W. H. Swallow. Sensitivity analysis of variable-size group testing and its related continuous models. *Biometrical J.* 2:173–81, 1995.

Goldman, N., J. L. Thorne, and D. T. Jones. Assessing the impact of secondary structure and solvent accessibility on protein evolution. *Genetics* 149:445–58, 1998.

Lio, P., N. Goldman, J. L. Thorne, and D. T. Jones. PASSML: Combining protein secondary structure prediction and evolutionary inference. *Bioinformatics* 14:726–33, 1998.

Thorne, J. L., and G. A. Churchill. Estimation and reliability of molecular sequence alignments. *Biometrics* 51:100–13, 1995.

Hu, P., A. A. Tsiatis, and M. Davidian. Estimating the parameters in the Cox model when covariate variables are measured with error. *Biometrics* 54:1407–19, 1998.

Scharfstein, D. O., and A. A. Tsiatis. The use of simulation and bootstrap in information-based group sequential studies. *Statistician* Med. 17:75–87, 1998.

Tsiatis, A. A. Competing risks. *Encyclopedia of Biostatistics.* 1998.

Tsiatis, A. A. Interim analysis of censored data. *Encyclopedia of Biostatistics.* 1998.

Scharfstein, D. O., and A. A. Tsiatis. Semiparametric efficiency and its implication on the design and analysis of group sequential studies. *J. Am. Stat. Assoc.* 92:1342–50, 1997.

Shoemaker, J., I. Painter, and B. S. Weir. A Bayesian characterization of Hardy-Weinberg disequilibrium. *Genetics* 149:2079–88, 1998.

Monks, S. A., N. L. Kaplan, and B. S. Weir. A comparative study of sibship tests of linkage and/or association. *Am. J. Hum. Genet.* 63:1507–16, 1998.

Nielsen, D., M. G. Ehm, and B. S. Weir. Detecting marker-disease association by testing for Hardy-Weinberg disequilibrium at a marker locus. *Am. J. Hum. Genet.* 63:1531–40, 1998.

Evett, I. W., and B. S. Weir. *Interpreting DNA Evidence.* Sunderland, Mass.: Sinauer, 1998.

Weir, B. S. *Genetic Data Analysis II.* Sunderland, Mass.: Sinauer, 1996.

Weir, B. S. *Genetic Data Analysis.* Sunderland, Mass.: Sinauer, 1990.

Jiang, C., and Z.-B. Zeng. Mapping quantitative trait loci with dominant and missing markers in various crosses from two inbred lines. *Genetica* 101:47–58, 1997.

Kao, C.-H., and Z.-B. Zeng. General formulae for obtaining the MLEs and the asymptotic variance-covariance matrix in mapping quantitative trait loci when using the EM algorithm. *Biometrics* 53:653–65, 1997.

True, J. R., et al. (Z.-B. Zeng). Quantitative genetic analysis of divergence in male secondary sexual traits between *Drosophila simulans* and *Drosophila mauritiana. Evolution* 51:816–32, 1997.

Doerge, R. W., Z.-B. Zeng, and B. S. Weir. Statistical issues in the search for genes affecting quantitative traits in experimental populations. *Stat. Sci.* 12:195–219, 1997.

Lin, X., and D. Zhang. Inference in generalized additive mixed models using smoothing splines. *J. Roy. Stat. Soc.* Series B, in press.

Sowers, M. F., D. Zhang, and C. A. Janney. Postpartum weight retention pattern in lactating women with a short inter-pregnancy interval. *J. Maternal-Fetal Med.,* in press.

Sowers, M. F., and D. Zhang et al. Calciotrophic hormone levels in postpartum women. *Am. J. Clin. Nutr.,* in press.

Zhang, D., X. Lin, J. Raz, and M. Sowers. Semiparametric stochastic mixed models for longitudinal data. *J. Am. Stat. Assoc.* 93:710–9, 1998.

Janney, C. A., D. Zhang, and M. F. Sowers. Lactation and postpartum weight retention. *Am. J. Clin. Nutr.* 66:1116–24, 1997.

NORTHWESTERN UNIVERSITY

Program in Applied Mathematics

Programs of Study
Graduate programs leading to the M.S. and Ph.D. degrees in applied mathematics are offered by the Department of Engineering Sciences and Applied Mathematics. Qualified students with backgrounds in engineering, mathematics, or natural science are eligible for admission to these programs. Study plans are drawn up to meet the needs of the individual student; they encompass courses in mathematical methods and in one or more fields of science or engineering, where significant applications of mathematics are made.

A student can obtain the M.S. degree in one academic year of full-time study. This entails the successful completion of an approved program of courses, followed by an examination relative to the work. No thesis is required for the M.S. degree. The Ph.D. program takes a minimum of three years beyond the B.S. degree. For the Ph.D. degree, the student must achieve a distinguished record in an approved program of courses and pass both a preliminary and a qualifying examination in the general research area to be followed in the doctoral dissertation. A final examination on the doctoral dissertation is required upon its completion.

Research Facilities
The department maintains a number of UNIX workstations for graduate student research, and computational time is available both on computers maintained on campus and at the National Supercomputer Centers. All of Northwestern's buildings have high-speed fiber-optic network connections to the Internet for convenient access to such facilities (through the vBNS, the very high-speed Backbone Network Service). In addition, the University has a number of laboratories with workstation-class machines available for classroom work and computers that provide access to electronic mail, Usenet, the World Wide Web, and various other networked information servers.

Financial Aid
Students who have been accepted for graduate study toward the Ph.D. in applied mathematics are eligible for various forms of financial support. University scholarships and fellowships as well as teaching and research assistantships cover tuition costs and provide a monthly stipend for living expenses. Some students may also qualify for a University loan. All full-time students are entitled to the benefits of the University Health Service as well as hospitalization and surgical insurance coverage.

Cost of Study
Tuition totals $21,798 for the academic year 1999–2000, with varying rates applicable during the summer quarter.

Living and Housing Costs
A variety of housing is available in the area. In addition to University-owned dwellings, there are apartments and rooms to be rented in the surrounding community. Costs vary according to the type of housing and the location.

Student Group
Graduate students in the applied mathematics program come from all parts of the United States and from various other countries. There are 35–40 students in the program.

Student Outcomes
Graduates have been successfully placed in industry, government, and academic positions, both postdoctoral and tenure track. Recent postdoctoral placements include Cambridge, Harvard, Princeton, and Stanford Universities. Recent tenure-track positions include Colgate University, Courant Institute, and the Universities of Delaware, Maryland, and Washington. Graduates have recently obtained corporate and government placements at NIH, NIST, IBM, Naval Research Lab, 3M Corporation, Argonne National Lab, Los Alamos National Lab, and Merrill Lynch.

Location
The main campus of the University is located in the residential suburb of Evanston, immediately north of Chicago. It occupies some 170 acres, partly bounded by a mile of Lake Michigan shoreline. This location provides the combined advantages of a lovely suburban community and the many cultural opportunities of Metropolitan Chicago. The University maintains its own beach and sailing club for use by students, faculty, and staff.

The University
Northwestern University was founded in 1851 and is a privately supported school in the Big Ten. It is a coeducational institution that offers a full range of educational opportunities. Research awards at the University exceeded $170 million last year.

Applying
Northwestern University operates on the quarter system. It is usual practice for new students to enter at the beginning of the fall quarter. Admissions applications that request financial aid should be completed by January 31. Application forms can be requested directly through e-mail at gradapp@nwu.edu.

Correspondence and Information
Director of Applied Mathematics
Department of Engineering Sciences and Applied Mathematics
McCormick School of Engineering and Applied Science
Northwestern University
Evanston, Illinois 60208-3125
Telephone: 847-491-5397
Fax: 847-491-2178
World Wide Web: http://www.esam.nwu.edu

Northwestern University

THE FACULTY AND THEIR RESEARCH

Jan D. Achenbach, Ph.D., Stanford. Theoretical and applied mechanics.
Alvin Bayliss, Ph.D., NYU (Courant). Numerical analysis, scientific computations.
David Chopp, Ph.D., Berkeley. Numerical methods for PDEs, evolution of fronts, scientific computing.
Stephen H. Davis, Ph.D., Rensselaer. Hydrodynamic stability, interfacial phenomena, phase-change phenomena.
William L. Kath, Ph.D., Caltech. Wave propagation and optics.
Gregory G. Luther, Ph.D., Rochester. Nonlinear optics.
Moshe Matalon, Ph.D., Cornell. Combustion theory, chemically reacting flows.
Bernard J. Matkowsky, Ph.D., NYU (Courant). Bifurcation and stability, combustion, pattern formation, nonlinear dynamics.
Michael J. Miksis, Ph.D., NYU (Courant). Interfacial phenomena, multiphase flow, scientific computations.
Toshio Mura, Ph.D., Tokyo. Micromechanics.
W. Edward Olmstead, Ph.D., Northwestern. Reaction-diffusion theory, shear localization effects, blow-up phenomena.
Edward L. Reiss, Ph.D., NYU. Bifurcation analysis, elastic buckling and hydrodynamic stability.
Hermann Riecke, Ph.D., Bayreuth (Germany). Extended dynamical systems, pattern formation.
Mary Silber, Ph.D., Berkeley. Dynamical systems, symmetry-breaking bifurcations, pattern formation.
Vladimir A. Volpert, Ph.D., USSR Academy of Sciences. Dynamical systems, pattern formation, combustion, reaction-diffusion systems.

Selected Recent Doctoral Dissertations

"Asymptotic analysis of random wave selections," Rachel A. Kuske.
"Morphological instability and the effect of elastic stresses," Brian J. Spencer.
"Premixed flame propagation in closed tubes," Jennifer Levin McGreevy.
"A class of integral equations which model explosion phenomena," Catherine A. Roberts.
"Bifurcation analysis of multimode instabilities in class B lasers," Thomas W. Carr.
"Numerical studies of nonlinear optical pulse propagation," Cheryl V. Hile.
"Thermal effects in rapid directional solidification," Douglas A. Huntley.
"Adaptive pseudo-spectral methods with applications to sheer band formation in viscoplastic materials," Dawn A. L. Crumpler.
"Domain structures and their stability," David Raitt.
"Stability of two-layer fluid flow in an inclined channel," Burt S. Tilley.
"Numerical solution of free boundary problems with surface tension at low Reynolds number," T.-M. Tsai.
"Interaction of a dislocation with an imperfectly bonded anchor in an anisotrophic bimaterial," Tom A. Homulka.
"Pulse propagation in nonlinear optical fibers using phase-sensitive amplifiers," J. Nathan Kutz.
"Shear stabilization of morphological instability during directional solidification," Timothy P. Schulze.
"Shear-diffusion mixing of passive scalars and vorticity in monopoles and dipoles," Joseph F. Lingevitch.
"The dynamics of thin liquid films," Michael P. Ida.
"Filtration combustion with applications to smoldering and combustion synthesis of materials," Daniel A. Schult.
"Soliton dynamics in optical fibers," Anne Niculae.

THE OHIO STATE UNIVERSITY

Department of Mathematics

Programs of Study

The Department of Mathematics offers programs leading to the M.S. and Ph.D. degrees. Courses of study are available in all of the principal branches of mathematics: algebra, analysis, applied mathematics, combinatorics, geometry, logic, group theory, number theory, probability, ergodic theory, representation theory, and topology.

Research Facilities

The Ohio State libraries have more than 4 million volumes and are served by a campuswide automated circulation system. In addition to the main library, there are eighteen departmental libraries. The Science and Engineering Library serves the College of Mathematics and Physical Sciences and the College of Engineering. This library contains more than 350,000 volumes and currently receives more than 2,750 serial titles. Students have ready access to microcomputers and the University mainframes. Academic Technology Services is a research and service facility that serves all departments, offering short-term seminars and noncredit courses directed to the needs of faculty and staff members and graduate students.

Financial Aid

Complete financial assistance is offered to nearly every mathematics graduate student attending Ohio State, in the form of fellowships and/or teaching associateships. Both forms of support carry a stipend plus total waiver of all regular tuition and fees. In 1999–2000, stipends for entering graduate students range from $13,000 to $15,000 for a nine-month appointment. The work load of teaching associates involves 6 hours per week of classroom contact, plus preparation and grading. Each new graduate student at Ohio State is also encouraged to accept an initial Head Start Summer Fellowship, which carries a stipend of $2450 in 1999. The majority of continuing students receive summer-quarter support in the form of either fellowships or research associate or teaching associate appointments. Graduate teaching assistant positions are renewable depending on the progress of the student.

Cost of Study

In 1999–2000, tuition for full-time graduate study is $1824 per quarter for Ohio residents and $4724 for nonresidents.

Living and Housing Costs

Convenient housing is located on and near the Columbus campus. Two dormitories house graduate students exclusively, at a cost of $281 per person per month. Ohio State maintains an apartment complex for married students; monthly rents range from $385 for a one-bedroom unit to $505 for a two-bedroom unit, including gas and water. The Off-Campus Student Center keeps files of available off-campus housing as a free service.

Student Group

The Department of Mathematics has approximately 100 graduate students, representing approximately twenty states and fifteen countries. Over the past four years, the department has averaged fifteen Ph.D. degrees and fourteen M.S. degrees. Most Ph.D. recipients seek and find employment in academic institutions, whereas M.S. recipients are employed, for the most part, by business, industry, or government. The department is also home to the International Mathematics Research Institute, at the Ohio State University.

Location

Columbus is centrally located in the eastern half of the country, 316 miles from Chicago, 555 miles from New York City, 560 miles from Atlanta, and 404 miles from St. Louis. The Columbus metropolitan area has approximately 1.25 million residents. It is the only major population center in Ohio to have gained residents since 1970. Columbus has a wide variety of fine restaurants and cultural activities. The city supports its own art museum and symphony orchestra and is home to one of the premier zoos in the nation. Temperatures average 73.5°F in August and 30.1°F in January. The average annual precipitation is 36.29 inches.

The University

The Ohio State University, comprising seventeen colleges, nine schools, four regional campuses, and the Graduate School, is the principal center for graduate and professional study in Ohio and one of the leading institutions of higher education in the United States. Approximately 48,500 students are enrolled in the University, more than 13,000 of them pursuing graduate or professional degrees. Each year the University attracts a large number of visiting scholars (about 40 in mathematics) who contribute to the intellectual vigor of the Ohio State community. Many Ohio State faculty members play important roles as consultants to federal and state government bodies and to private enterprise.

Applying

Candidates for graduate admission to Ohio State must send an application form (applications for fellowships or teaching associateships may be made on the same form) along with all college transcripts to the Ohio State Admissions Office, 1800 Cannon Drive, Columbus, Ohio 43210-1174. In addition, applicants must forward to the address below three letters of recommendation, an autobiography, and scores on the GRE General Test (required of all fellowship nominees). Candidates for admission to the graduate program in mathematics must also submit a GRE Subject Test score.

Applicants from non-English-speaking countries must take the TOEFL. Applications for fellowships must be completed by January 15.

Correspondence and Information

Yung-Chen Lu, Director
The Ohio State University
231 West 18th Avenue
Columbus, Ohio 43210-1174

Telephone: 614-292-6274
Fax: 614-292-1479
E-mail: bonace@math.ohio-state.edu (Re: graduate applications)
World Wide Web: http://www.math.ohio-state.edu

The Ohio State University

THE FACULTY AND THEIR RESEARCH

Algebra
Harry Allen, Ph.D., Yale.
Robert Brown, Ph.D., Chicago.
Joseph Ferrar, Ph.D., Yale.
Daniel Shapiro, Ph.D., Berkeley.

Algebraic Geometry
Roy Joshua, Ph.D., Northwestern.
Andras Nemethi, Ph.D., Romanian Academy.

Analysis
Zita Divis, Ph.D., Heidelberg (Germany).
Gerald Edgar, Ph.D., Harvard.
Boris Mityagin, Ph.D., Moscow.
Paul Nevai, Ph.D., Szeged (Hungary).

Applied Mathematics
Gregory Baker, Ph.D., Caltech.
George Majda, Ph.D., NYU (Courant).
Edward Overman, Ph.D., Arizona.
Bjorn Sandstede, Ph.D., Stuttgart (Germany).
Saleh Tanveer, Ph.D., Caltech.
David Terman, Ph.D., Minnesota.

Combinatorics
Thomas Dowling, Ph.D., North Carolina.
Stephen Milne, Ph.D., Caltech.
Dijen Ray-Chaudhuri, Ph.D., North Carolina.
Neil Robertson, Ph.D., Waterloo.
Akos Seress, Ph.D., Ohio State.

Complex Variables
Bodgan Baishanski, Ph.D., Belgrade.
Francis Carroll, Ph.D., Purdue.
Jeffery McNeal, Ph.D., Purdue.

Differential Geometry
Andrzej Derdzinski, Ph.D., Wroclaw (Poland).
Fangyang Zheng, Ph.D., Harvard.

Ergodic Theory and Probability
Vitaly Bergelson, Ph.D., Hebrew (Jerusalem).
Neil Falkner, Ph.D., British Columbia.
Alexander Leibman, Ph.D., Technion (Israel).
Peter March, Ph.D., Minnesota.
Robin Pemantle, Ph.D., MIT.
Boris Pittel, Ph.D., Leningrad.
Michel Talagrand, Ph.D., Paris.

Group Theory
Koichiro Harada, Ph.D., Tokyo.
Surinder Sehgal, Ph.D., Notre Dame.

Ronald Solomon, Ph.D., Yale.
Sia Wong, Ph.D., Monash (Australia).

Harmonic Analysis and Representation Theory
Luis Casian, Ph.D., MIT.
Yuval Flicker, Ph.D., Cambridge.
Wenzhi Luo, Ph.D., Rutgers.
Henri Moscovici, Ph.D., Bucharest.
Steve Rallis, Ph.D., MIT.
Robert Stanton, Ph.D., Cornell.

Logic
Timothy Carlson, Ph.D., Minnesota.
Randall Dougherty, Ph.D., Berkeley.
Harvey Friedman, Ph.D., MIT.
Chris Miller, Ph.D., Illinois at Urbana-Champaign.

Mathematical Physics
Alexander Dynin, Ph.D., Moscow.
Ulrich Gerlach, Ph.D., Princeton.
Yuji Kodama, Ph.D., Clarkson.

Number Theory
Avner Ash, Ph.D., Harvard.
Robert Gold, Ph.D., MIT.
David Goss, Ph.D., Harvard.
John Hsia, Ph.D., MIT.
Manohar Madan, Ph.D., Göttingen (Germany).
Alayne Parson, Ph.D., Illinois at Chicago.
Paul Ponomarev, Ph.D., Yale.
Alice Silverberg, Ph.D., Princeton.
Warren Sinnott, Ph.D., Stanford.

Operator Theory
Ilya Zakharevich, Ph.D., Moscow State.

System/Control Theory
Bostwick Wyman, Ph.D., Berkeley.

Topology
Dan Burghelea, Ph.D., Romanian Academy.
Ruth Charney, Ph.D., Princeton.
Michael Davis, Ph.D., Princeton.
Zbigniew Fiedorowicz, Ph.D., Chicago.
Henry Glover, Ph.D., Michigan.
John Philip Huneke, Ph.D., Wesleyan.
Yuan Lou, Ph.D., Minnesota.
Yung-Chen Lu, Ph.D., Berkeley.
Crichton Ogle, Ph.D., Brandeis.

THE OHIO STATE UNIVERSITY

Department of Statistics

Programs of Study

The emphasis of The Ohio State University's Department of Statistics is on obtaining innovative solutions to real-world problems and in theoretical research stimulated by and directed at these problems. Interdisciplinary research with scientists in other fields is encouraged and valued. The major thrust of the published research of the faculty members is the development and analysis of statistical methodology motivated by issues that arise in fields of application. The broad range of statistical interests of the faculty members and the extensive course offerings give graduates a great variety of professional opportunities.

The Master of Applied Statistics (M.A.S.) program provides a professional, terminal degree that prepares students to apply statistical or biostatistical methodology. The core of the Master of Science (M.S.) program coincides with the first year of the Ph.D. programs, but the requirements are flexible enough for the M.S. to be either a terminal degree preparing the student for a career in applied statistics or a stepping-stone to one of the Ph.D. degrees. The M.A.S. and nonthesis M.S. degrees require 50 quarter credits of course work, including a course in statistical consulting, and a written examination. The thesis M.S. option requires fewer courses and an oral thesis defense. Either master's degree usually takes two years to complete.

Both the statistics and biostatistics Ph.D. degrees require a mathematical statistics sequence and an applied sequence that includes linear model theory, followed by measure theoretic probability and inference sequences (including Bayesian analysis). The selection of advanced topics courses differs for the two degrees. All Ph.D. candidates acquire consulting experience either by working for the department's Statistical Consulting Service or as research assistants on projects in a subject area such as engineering, the social sciences, or the biological and medical sciences. A two-part qualifying examination is given at the beginning of a student's second and third years of study. The general examination, consisting of written and oral portions, covers material related to the expected thesis topic. There is an oral thesis defense. The entire degree typically takes six years to complete.

Entering M.A.S. students should have completed courses in mathematics through advanced calculus and matrix algebra, while entering M.S. and Ph.D. students should have classroom experience in linear algebra and two semesters of real analysis. An academic background that includes an introductory statistics course and some computer programming is also helpful. Minor deficiencies can be made up after matriculation.

Research Facilities

The department has a dedicated UNIX research computing environment, with twenty-seven Hewlett-Packard workstations. Graduate students have access to the departmental system from two graduate student computing rooms that contain seven workstations and four X-terminals. The department also operates a graphics lab with a Silicon Graphics computer. Macintoshes are available in some graduate student offices, the department's Macintosh lab, and at other campus locations maintained by the University's Academic Computing Services (ACS). Graduate students also have access to other computing and graphics facilities of the ACS. All major statistical packages are available between the University and departmental systems. The department has a direct link to the Ohio Supercomputer Center, which operates a CRAY Supercomputer.

The Science and Engineering Library, which serves the mathematics and statistics departments, is located near the department and allows 24-hour access to the collection. The University library has a computerized catalog and circulation system, and computerized searches of all major bibliographic databases are available.

Financial Aid

Most entering graduate students in the M.A.S., M.S., and Ph.D. programs have either a half-time Teaching Associateship (TA) or a University Fellowship. Both forms of aid pay a stipend and give full exemption from tuition and fees. The stipend is $11,500 per academic year for 1999–2000. Entering teaching associates and fellows are encouraged to accept an initial Early Start Summer Fellowship, which carried a stipend of $2800 in 1999. The department awards a few one-time grants that supplement the TA or University Fellowship stipend. Students making satisfactory progress toward their degree generally receive continued support. Advanced students often work as research associates on faculty projects either in the department or in other departments on campus or hold internships in the Columbus area.

Cost of Study

The 1998–99 academic-year tuition for Ohio residents was $5472 and for nonresidents was $14,172.

Living and Housing Costs

In 1998–99, a single room in the graduate dormitory was $291 per month, and University apartments for married students cost $375 or $480 for one or two bedrooms, respectively. A meal ticket (nineteen meals per week) was $820 a quarter in 1998–99. Convenient off-campus housing is priced comparably or slightly lower.

Student Group

There are typically about 80 graduate students in the department. About 60 percent are in the Ph.D. program, approximately 50 percent are international students, and about 50 percent are women. Most students are enrolled full-time.

Student Outcomes

Ph.D. graduates in statistics and biostatistics work in many different academic, government, and industrial institutions. Recent graduates in academia are employed in either statistics or public health departments of major state universities or in mathematics departments of smaller liberal arts colleges. In industry, they are employed in independent research organizations and research divisions of major industrial and pharmaceutical firms. In government, they work in both federal and state agencies. Master's graduates are in great demand in business, industry, and government.

Location

Columbus is the capital of Ohio, with a population exceeding 1.37 million in its metropolitan area. There is a great diversity of shopping and restaurants available. Cultural activities, both with visiting artists and indigenous organizations, run the full gamut of tastes. The employment base is widely diversified, ranging from heavy industry to light manufacturing and from corporate headquarters, including insurance companies, to research organizations.

The University

The Ohio State University was founded in 1870 as a land-grant college. It now enrolls about 50,000 students. Graduate student enrollment exceeds 10,000. Statistics is one of six departments in the College of Mathematical and Physical Sciences.

Applying

Application materials and information may be obtained from the department. Applications requesting financial support should be complete by January 15. GRE General Test scores are required; students from non-English-speaking countries must also submit TOEFL scores.

Correspondence and Information

Graduate Committee Chairperson
Department of Statistics
The Ohio State University
1958 Neil Avenue
Columbus, Ohio 43210-1247
Telephone: 614-292-2866
Fax: 614-292-2096
E-mail: statgradinfo@stat.ohio-state.edu
World Wide Web: http://www.stat.ohio-state.edu

The Ohio State University

THE FACULTY AND THEIR RESEARCH

Mark Berliner, Professor; Ph.D., Purdue, 1980. Bayesian and robust Bayesian theory and applications, geophysical statistics, dynamical systems and chaos, image analysis.

Saul Blumenthal, Professor; Ph.D., Cornell, 1962. Estimating sample size with truncated data, burn-in to improve reliability; superimposed renewal processes, estimating ordered parameters.

Michael Browne, Professor (joint appointment with Department of Psychology); Ph.D., South Africa, 1969. Multivariate analysis, modeling multivariate psychological data, asymptotic distribution theory.

Noel A. Cressie, Professor; Ph.D., Princeton, 1975. Statistical modeling and analysis of spatiotemporal data and analysis of discrete data, with special emphasis on goodness-of-fit testing; applications in areas such as remote sensing of the earth's protective ozone layer, prediction of regional and global climate, and ambient-air pollution modeling.

Douglas E. Critchlow, Associate Professor; Ph.D., Harvard, 1984. Analyzing data in ranking form, statistical issues in DNA research, inference for evolutionary trees, nonparametric statistics, group theoretic methods in statistics.

Angela M. Dean, Professor; Ph.D., Southampton, 1975. Design of factorial experiments, crossover designs, mixture experiments, group testing.

Hani Doss, Professor; Ph.D., Stanford, 1982. Bayesian analysis, especially Markov chain Monte Carlo methods for Bayesian computation; survival analysis, particularly bootstrap methods for censored data and Bayesian nonparametric approaches.

Michael A. Fligner, Professor; Ph.D., Connecticut, 1974. Nonparametrics and probability models for rank data, capture-recapture methods, statistical techniques related to wildlife management.

Prem K. Goel, Professor; Ph.D., Carnegie Mellon, 1971. Bayesian modeling and decision support systems, Bayesian networks and value of information, combining information and microdata simulation, comparison of experiments, interdisciplinary research in engineering and medicine, pattern recognition, small-area estimation, spatial analysis.

Jason C. Hsu, Professor; Ph.D., Purdue, 1977. Multiple comparisons and statistical computing, multiple comparisons in the general linear model, bioequivalence inference, graphical representation of multiple-comparison methods, human factors.

Mark E. Irwin, Assistant Professor; Ph.D., Chicago, 1994. Analysis of genetic pedigree data, survival data analysis.

Stanley Lemeshow, Professor (joint appointment with the School of Public Health); Ph.D., UCLA, 1976. Application of statistical methods to the areas of medicine, epidemiology, and health services; development of predictive models of outcome of patients entering general medical/surgical intensive care units; textbooks in the areas of logistic regression, sampling, sample size, and survival analysis.

Shili Lin, Associate Professor; Ph.D., Washington (Seattle), 1993. Monte Carlo methods, statistical analysis.

Steven N. MacEachern, Associate Professor; Ph.D., Minnesota, 1988. Bayesian theory and practice: nonparametric and semiparametric Bayesian modeling, Bayesian computational methods, inference for dynamical systems.

H. N. Nagaraja, Professor; Ph.D., Iowa State, 1980. Order and record statistics, stochastic modeling, heart rate variability, biostatistical applications.

William I. Notz, Professor; Ph.D., Cornell, 1978. Optimal design of experiments, designs for comparing treatments with a control, weighing designs, designs for regression, computer experiments, designs robust to missing data.

Omer Ozturk, Assistant Professor (Marion campus); Ph.D., Penn State, 1994. Robust estimation, testing and nonparametric inference.

Dennis K. Pearl, Professor; Ph.D., Berkeley, 1981. Probabilistic modeling of biological phenomena, including nucleotide sequence data, phylogenetics, and AIDS data; simulation-based estimation for high-dimensional models.

Mario Peruggia, Associate Professor; Ph.D., Carnegie Mellon, 1990. Iterated function systems, computational and graphical methods for statistical analysis, Bayesian inference, graphical displays of multiple comparison confidence intervals.

Nandini Raghavan, Assistant Professor; Ph.D., Illinois at Urbana-Champaign, 1993. Spatial statistics and applications to materials science, nonparametric function estimation, statistical computing and Monte Carlo methods, Bayesian inference, pattern recognition.

Thomas J. Santner, Professor and Chairman; Ph.D., Purdue, 1973. Statistical applications, especially in biomechanics and imaging; selection and screening; Bayesian methods.

Xiaotong Shen, Associate Professor; Ph.D., Chicago, 1991. Likelihood methods, semiparametric and nonparametric inferences, statistical applications to atmospheric science, signal processing, neural networks.

Elizabeth A. Stasny, Professor; Ph.D., Carnegie Mellon, 1983. Modeling missing data, especially from sample surveys; assessing fairness of jurors in death-penalty cases and response bias in reports of rape and domestic violence.

Joseph A. Verducci, Professor; Ph.D., Stanford, 1982. Multivariate analysis; modeling random objects, such as random graphs and pairs of permutations, and applying these models; inferring evolutionary paths of DNA sequences.

Douglas A. Wolfe, Professor; Ph.D., Iowa, 1969. Nonparametric procedures for ranked-set samples, rank-based tests for the presence of interaction, nonparametric inference under restricted parameter configurations.

Cockins Hall, home of the Department of Statistics.

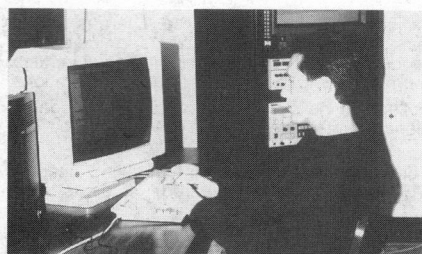

The department's systems administrator in the Dynamic Graphics Lab.

Professors Dean and Notz discuss a research problem with a Ph.D. student.

The Ohio State University

SELECTED PUBLICATIONS

McMillan, N. J., and **L. M. Berliner.** Hierarchical image reconstruction using Markov random fields. In *Bayesian Statistics V,* pp. 675–83, eds. J. M. Bernardo et al. Oxford University Press, 1996.

Berliner, L. M. Testing a precise null hypothesis by combining experiments. *Probab. Math. Stat.* 15:73–83, 1995.

Berliner, L. M. Statistics, probability, and chaos. *Stat. Sci.* 7:69–122 (with discussion), 1992.

Berliner, L. M. Likelihood and Bayesian prediction for chaotic systems. *J. Am. Stat. Assoc.* 86:938–52, 1991.

Blumenthal, S., and R. C. Dahiya. Estimation of sample size with grouped data. *J. Stat. Plann. Inference.* 44:95–115, 1995.

Blumenthal, S. Subset estimators of the largest mean. In *Design of Experiments—Ranking and Selection—Essays in Honor of Robert E. Bechhofer,* pp. 251–68, eds. T. J. Santner and A. C. Tamhane. New York: Marcel Dekker, 1994.

Blumenthal, S. New approximations for the event count distribution for superimposed renewal processes at the time origin with application to the reliability of new series systems. *Oper. Res.* 41:409–18, 1993.

Zhou, X. H., and **S. Blumenthal.** Two stage reliability tests for new series systems. *J. Stat. Plann. Inference* 33:345–66, 1992.

Browne, M. W. Structured latent curve models. In *Multivariate Analysis: Future Directions,* pp. 171–97, eds. C. M. Cuadras and C. R. Rao, vol. 7, North Holland Series in Statistics & Probability. Amsterdam: North Holland, 1993.

Browne, M. W., and S. H. C. Du Toit. Automated fitting of nonstandard models. *Multivar. Behav. Res.* 27:269–300, 1992.

Browne, M. W., and R. Cudeck. Alternative ways of assessing model fit. *Sociol. Meth. Res.* 21:230–58, 1992.

Browne, M. W. Circumplex models for correlation matrices. *Psychometrika* 57:469–97, 1992.

Cressie, N. A., and J. J. Majure. Spatio-temporal statistical modeling of livestock waste in streams. *J. Agricultural Biol. Environ. Stat.* 2:24–47, 1997.

Huang, H. C., and **N. A. Cressie.** Spatio-temporal prediction of snow water equivalent using the Kalman filter. *Computational Stat. Data Anal.* 22:159–75, 1996.

Helterbrand, J. D., **N. A. Cressie,** and J. L. Davidson. A statistical approach to identifying closed object boundaries in images. *Adv. Appl. Probab.* 26:831–54, 1994.

Cressie, N. A. *Statistics for Spatial Data,* revised edition. New York: John Wiley & Sons, 1993.

Read, T. R. C., and **N. A. Cressie.** *Goodness-of-Fit Testing For Discrete Multivariate Data.* New York: Springer-Verlag, 1988.

Critchlow, D. E., D. K. Pearl, and C. Qian. The triples distance for rooted bifurcating phylogenetic trees. *Systematic Biol.* 45:323–34, 1996.

Huh, M. -H., et al. **(D. E. Critchlow** and **J. S. Verducci).** A symmetric analysis of paired rankings with application to temporal patterns of hormonal concentration. *Biometrics* 51:1361–71, 1995.

Critchlow, D. E., and **M. A. Fligner.** Ranking models with item covariates. In *Probability Models and Statistical Analyses for Ranking Data,* pp. 1–19. New York: Springer-Verlag, 1993.

Critchlow, D. E. *Metric Methods for Analyzing Partially Ranked Data,* vol. 34, Lecture Notes in Statistics. New York: Springer-Verlag, 1985.

Dean, A. M., and D. T. Voss. *Design and Analysis of Experiments.* New York: Springer-Verlag, 1999.

Dean, A. M., and **D. A. Wolfe.** Nonparametric analysis of experiments. In *Handbook of Statistics,* volume 13, pp. 707–58, eds. S. Ghosh and C. R. Rao, 1996.

Kao, L. -J., P. Yates, S. M. Lewis, and **A. M. Dean.** Theoretical optimal designs for estimating given sets of contrasts. *Statistica Sinica* 5:593–8, 1995.

Lewis, S. M., **A. M. Dean,** P. Prescott, and N. R. Draper. Mixture designs for q components in othogonal blocks. *J. Roy. Stat. Soc.* 56:457–68, 1994.

Dean, A. M. Designing factorial experiments—a survey of the use of generalized cyclic designs. In *Design of Experiments with Application to Engineering and Physical Science,* pp. 479–515, ed. S. Ghosh. New York: Marcel Dekker, 1990.

Doss, H., F. Huffer, and K. Lawson. Bayesian nonparametric estimation via Gibbs sampling for coherent systems with redundancy. *Ann. Stat.* 25:1109–39, 1997.

Athreya, K. B., **H. Doss,** and J. Sethuraman. On the convergence of the Markov chain simulation method. *Ann. Stat.* 24:69–100, 1996.

Doss, H. Bayesian nonparametric estimation for incomplete data via successive substitution sampling. *Ann. Stat.* 22:1763–86, 1994.

Burr, D., and **H. Doss.** Confidence bands for the median survival time as a function of the covariates in the Cox model. *J. Am. Stat. Assoc.* 88:1330–40, 1993.

Doss, H., and R. D. Gill. An elementary approach to weak convergence for quantile processes, with applications to censored survival data. *J. Am. Stat. Assoc.* 87:869–77, 1992.

Fligner, M., and **J. Verducci,** eds. *Probability Models and Statistical Analyses for Ranking Data.* New York: Springer-Verlag, 1993.

Fligner, M., and **J. Verducci.** Posterior probabilities for a consensus ordering. *Psychometrika* 55:53–63, 1990.

McCord, M., D. Hidalgo, M. O'Kelley, and **P. K. Goel.** Value of traffic assignment and flow prediction in multiattribute network design: Framework, issues, and preliminary results. *Transportation Res. Rec.* 1607:171–7, 1997.

Matkovic, V., et al. **(P. K. Goel).** Leptin is inversely related to age at menarche in human females. *J. Clin Endocrinol. Metab.* 82:3239–45, 1997.

Goel, P. K., and P. Palettas. Predictive modeling for fatigue crack propagation via linearizing time transformations. In *Reliability and Maintenance of Complex Systems,* pp. 51–67, ed. S. Ozekici. Dordrecht, Netherlands: Kluwer Publications NATO ASI Series, 1996.

Goel, P. K., and M. L. R. Padilla. Generalized Hellinger transforms as information measures. Proceedings of the ASA Section on Bayesian Statistical Science, 1994.

Goel, P. K., and P. Hall. On the average difference between concommitants and order statistics. *Ann. Probab.* 22:126–44, 1994.

Hsu, J. C., and B. L. Nelson. Multiple comparisons in the general linear model. *J. Computational Graphical Stat.* 7:23–41, 1998.

Berger, R. L., and **J. C. Hsu.** Bioequivalence trials, intersection-union tests, and equivalence confidence sets. *Stat. Sci.* 11:283–315, 1996.

Hsu, J. C. *Multiple Comparisons: Theory and Methods.* London: Chapman and Hall, 1996.

Hayter, A., and **J. C. Hsu.** On the relationship between stepwise decision procedures and confidence sets. *J. Am. Stat. Assoc.* 89:128–36, 1994.

Hsu, J., and **M. Peruggia.** Graphical representation of Tukey's multiple comparison method. *J. Comput. Graph. Stat.* 3:143–61, 1994.

Irwin, M., N. Cox, and A. Kong. Sequential imputation for multilocus analysis. *Proc. Natl. Acad. Sci. U.S.A.* 91:11684–8, 1994.

Kong, A., M. Frigge, **M. Irwin,** and N. Cox. Importance sampling (I): Computing multimodel p-values in linkage analysis. *Am. J. Hum. Genet.* 51:1413–29, 1992.

Kan, L., B. Wiggs, **M. Irwin,** and I. Yee. Acute respiratory health effects in asthmatic and non-asthmatic children associated with short term exposure to air pollutants. *Can. J. Stat.* 18:373–7, 1990.

Sadovnick, A. D., **M. E. Irwin,** P. A. Baird, and B. L. Beattie. Genetic studies on an Alzheimer clinic population. *Genet. Epidemiol.* 6:663, 1989.

Lemeshow, S., et al. Illustration of analysis taking into account complex survey considerations: The association between wine consumption and dementia in the Paquid study. *Am. J. Epidemiol.* 148:298–306, 1998.

Groeger, J. S., and **S. Lemeshow** et al. Multicenter outcome study of cancer patients admitted to the intensive care unit: A probability of mortality model. *J. Clin. Oncol.* 16:761–70, 1998.

Le Gall, J.-R., et al. **(S. Lemeshow).** The logistic organ dysfunction system: A new way to assess organ dysfunction in the intensive care unit. *J. Am. Med. Assoc.* 276:802–10, 1996.

Lemeshow, S., and J.-R. Le Gall. Modeling the severity of illness of ICU patients: A systems update. *J. Am. Med. Assoc.* 272:1049–55, 1994.

The Ohio State University

Selected Publications (continued)

Lin, S. Multipoint linkage analysis via Metropolis jumping kernels. *Biometrics* 52:1417–27, 1996.

Lin, S. Monte Carlo methods in genetic analysis. In *Genetic Mapping and DNA Sequencing. IMA Volumes in Mathematics and its Applications,* pp. 15–38, eds. T. P. Speed and M. S. Waterman. New York: Springer-Verlag, 1996.

Lin, S., and T. P. Speed. A note on the combination of estimates of a recombination fraction. *Ann. Hum. Genet.* 60:251–7, 1996.

Lin, S. A scheme for constructing an irreducible Markov chain for pedigree data. *Biometrics* 51:318–22, 1995.

Bush, C. A., and **S. N. MacEachern.** A semiparametric Bayesian model for randomized block designs. *Biometrika* 83:275–86, 1996.

MacEachern, S. N., and **L. M. Berliner.** Asymptotic inference for dynamical systems observed with errors. *J. Stat. Plann. Inference* 46:277–92, 1995.

MacEachern, S. N., W. I. Notz, D. C. Whittinghill, and Y. Zhu. Robustness to the unavailability of data in the general linear model, with applications. *J. Stat. Plann. Inference* 48:207–13, 1995.

MacEachern, S. N., and **L. M. Berliner.** Subsampling the Gibbs sampler. *Am. Statistician* 48:188–90, 1994.

MacEachern, S. N. Estimating normal means with a conjugate style Dirichlet process prior. *Commun. Stat.: Simulation Computation* 23:727–41, 1994.

MacEachern, S. N. A characterization of some conjugate prior distributions for exponential families. *Scandinavian J. Stat.* 20:77–82, 1993.

David, H. A., and **H. N. Nagaraja.** Concomitants of order statistics. In *Handbook of Statistics,* vol. 16, *Order Statistics and Their Applications,* pp. 487–513, eds. C. R. Rao and N. Balakrishnan. Amsterdam: Elsevier, 1998.

Arnold, B. C., N. Balakrishnan, and **H. N. Nagaraja.** *Records.* New York: John Wiley & Sons, 1998.

Berntson, G. G., et al. **(H. N. Nagaraja).** Heart rate variability: Origins, methods, and interpretive caveats. *Psychophysiology* 3:623–48, 1997.

Nagaraja, H. N. Tukey's linear sensitivity and order statistics. *Ann. Inst. Stat. Math.* 46:757–68, 1994.

Arnold, B. C., N. Balakrishnan, and **H. N. Nagaraja.** *A First Course in Order Statistics.* New York: John Wiley & Sons, 1992.

Kao, L. -J., **W. I. Notz,** and **A. M. Dean.** Efficient block designs for estimating conditional main effects. *J. Indian Soc. Agric. Stat., Special Golden Jubilee Issue,* in press.

Chang, Y. -J., and **W. I. Notz.** Model robust designs. In *Handbook of Statistics,* vol. 13, pp. 1055–98, eds. S. Ghosh and C. R. Rao. Amsterdam: Elsevier Science B. V., 1996.

Chang, Y. J., and **W. I. Notz.** Some optimal nested row-column designs. *Statistica Sinica* 4:249–63, 1994.

Notz, W. I., D. C. Whittinghill, and Y. Zhu. Robustness to the unavailability of data in block designs. *Metrika* 41:263–75, 1994.

Ozturk, O., and T. P. Hettmansperger. Generalized Cramer-von Mises distance estimator. *Biometrika* 84:283–94, 1997.

Ozturk, O., and T. P. Hettmansperger. Almost fully efficient and robust simultaneous estimator of location and scale parameters: A minimum distance approach. *Stat. Prob. Lett.* 29:233–44, 1996.

Maa, J. -F., **D. K. Pearl,** and **R. Bartoszynski.** Reducing multidimensional two-sample data to one-dimensional interpoint distances. *Ann. Stat.* 24:1069–74, 1996.

Peng, N., **D. K. Pearl,** W. Chan, and **R. Bartoszynski.** Linear birth and death processes under the influence of disasters with time-dependent killing probabilities. *Stoch. Proc. Appl.* 45:243–58, 1993.

Pearl, D. K., and D. Fairley. Using strength of opinion to test for nonresponse bias in sample surveys. *Sankhya* 53:340–51, 1991.

Pearl, D. K. A stochastic model of the ultraviolet induction of skin cancer. In *Proceedings of the Second International Conference on Mathematical Population Dynamics,* pp. 435–67, eds. O. Arino, D. E. Axelrod, and M. Kimmel. New York: Marcel Dekker, 1990.

Peruggia, M., and **T. J. Santner.** Bayesian analysis of time evolution of earthquake. *J. Am. Stat. Assoc.* 91:1209–18, 1996.

Peruggia, M., T. J. Santner, Y. Y. Ho, and N. McMillan. A hierarchical Bayesian analysis of circular data with autoregressive errors: Modeling the mechanical properties of cortical bone. In *Statistical Decision Theory and Related Topics,* vol. V, pp. 201–20. New York: Springer-Verlag, 1994.

Peruggia, M. *Discrete Iterated Function Systems.* Wellesley: AK Peters, 1993.

Peruggia, M., F. Schoen, and M. G. Speranza. Queue predictors for stochastic traffic flows control. In *Lecture Notes in Control and Information Sciences—Stochastic Programming,* vol. 76, pp. 88–94. Berlin: Springer-Verlag, 1986.

Raghavan, N., and D. D. Cox. Analysis of the posterior for spline estimators in logistic regression. *J. Stat. Plann. Inference* 71:117–36, 1998.

Raghavan, N., and D. D. Cox. Adaptive mixture importance sampling. *J. Stat. Computing Simulation* 60:237–59, 1998.

Bechhofer, R., **T. J. Santner,** and D. Goldsman. *Design and Analysis of Experiments for Statistical Selection, Screening and Multiple Comparisons.* New York: John Wiley & Sons, 1995.

Pan, G. H., and **T. J. Santner.** Subset selection in two-factor experiments using randomization restricted designs. *J. Stat. Plann. Inference* 62:417–30, 1997.

Santner, T. J., and D. Duffy. *The Statistical Analysis of Discrete Data.* New York: Springer-Verlag, 1989.

Shen, X. On methods of sieves and penalization. *Ann. Stat.* 25:2555–91, 1997.

Shen, X., and W. H. Wong. Convergence rate of sieve estimates. *Ann. Stat.* 22:580–615, 1994.

Shen, X. Comments on exploring regression structure with graphics. *Test* 2:50–3, 1993.

Shen, X., M. Stein, and P. Styer. Application of a simple regression model to acid rain data. *Can. J. Stat.* 21:331–46, 1993.

Stasny, E. A., B. G. Toomey, and R. J. First. Estimating the rate of rural homelessness: A study of non-urban Ohio. *Survey Methodology* 20:87–94, 1994.

Stasny, E. A. Comment on small area estimation: An appraisal, by M. Ghosh and J. N. K. Rao. *Stat. Sci.* 9:87–9, 1994.

Stasny, E. A., P. K. Goel, and D. J. Rumsey. County estimates of wheat production. *Survey Methodology* 17:211–25, 1991.

Stasny, E. A. Hierarchical models for the probabilities of a survey classification and nonresponse. *J. Am. Stat. Assoc.* 86:296–303, 1991.

Joe, H., and **J. Verducci.** Multivariate majorization by positive combinations. In *Stochastic Inequalities,* pp. 159–81, eds. M. Shaked and Y. L. Tong. IMS Lecture Notes—Monograph Series, vol. 22, 1992.

Verducci, J., M. Mack, and M. DeGroot. On estimating the kappa measure of multiple rater agreement in the case of a rare diagnosis. *J. Multivar. Anal.* 27:512–35, 1988; reprinted in *Multivariate Statistics and Probability: Essays in Memory of Paruchuri R. Krishnaiah,* pp. 539–62, ed. M. M. Rao. Boston: Academic Press, 1989.

Hollander, M., and **D. A. Wolfe.** *Nonparametric Statistical Methods,* 2nd edition. New York: John Wiley & Sons, 1999.

Lim, D., and **D. A. Wolfe.** Nonparametric tests for comparing umbrella pattern treatment effects with a control in a randomized block design. *Biometrics* 53:410–8, 1997.

Pan, G., and **D. A. Wolfe.** Test for qualitative interaction of clinical significance. *Stat. Med.* 16:1645–52, 1997.

Pan, G., and **D. A. Wolfe.** Comparing groups with umbrella orderings. *J. Am. Stat. Assoc.* 91:311–7, 1996.

OKLAHOMA STATE UNIVERSITY

Department of Mathematics

Programs of Study

The Department of Mathematics offers programs leading to the Master of Science and Doctor of Philosophy degrees. There are two Master of Science degree options, pure mathematics and applied mathematics, each requiring 32 credit hours of graduate course work in mathematics and/or related subjects. Students must pass a written comprehensive exam covering core courses of the appropriate option and write a thesis, a report, or a creative component. Students with a good background in mathematics should expect to complete all requirements within two years. The Doctor of Philosophy program accepts only students with superior records in their graduate or undergraduate study. There are two options in the doctoral program: the mathematics research option and the mathematics education option. The research option is designed to prepare students for faculty positions at major research universities. The mathematics education option is a blend of traditional foundational course work in mathematics and work in mathematics education and is designed to prepare students for positions in which mathematics teaching and educational concerns are a primary focus. A minimum of 90 credit hours of graduate credit beyond the bachelor's degree is required for each option, with 24 hours credited for a thesis. Students must pass a written comprehensive exam covering core courses and embark on a study of a chosen area of mathematics, pass an oral qualifying examination, and complete the foreign language requirement. The most important requirement is the preparation of an acceptable thesis, which must demonstrate the candidate's ability to do independent, original work in mathematics or mathematics education. A well-prepared, motivated student should expect to complete all requirements within five to six years.

Research Facilities

The department operates a network of Sun microcomputer workstations, personal computers, and X-terminals with several file servers. These facilities are available for use by graduate students and are conveniently located. Through this network, access to the University Computer Center is available. The department also houses current issues of important mathematics journals in a reading room. This makes about 100 journals available in a very convenient location. Electronic access is available for the Math Reviews, tables of contents of many journals, and the library catalog.

Financial Aid

Teaching assistantships are available to qualified students, with appointments covering the fall and spring semesters (renewed each year based on satisfactory progress). Students without prior teaching experience do not teach in their first year and are provided with training to enhance their instructional skills. Subsequently, students normally have 5–6 hours of instructional duties per week. Some reduction in teaching is available to doctoral candidates making good progress toward their degree. Stipends are $10,600 for master's students and $11,100 for doctoral students with subsequent increases. Some summer appointments are available.

Cost of Study

Tuition is reduced to the in-state level for all assistants, with full tuition waivers given to some exceptional incoming students. In-state tuition and fees are approximately $96 per credit hour. Nonresidents pay an additional $175 per credit hour.

Living and Housing Costs

On-campus housing is available in a residence hall and in an apartment complex. It is recommended that prospective students contact the Office of Residential Life (telephone: 405-744-5592; e-mail: reslife@okway.okstate.edu; World Wide Web: http://www.reslife.okstate.edu) for information. Most students live in apartment complexes in the surrounding community, which cost $300 and up per month.

Student Group

Of the current student body of about 45 students, 35 percent are women and 40 percent are international students. Almost all are full-time students on teaching assistantships. The department seeks highly motivated students without regard to race, color, national origin, religion, sex, or handicap.

Student Outcomes

The department has been very successful in having all its recent doctoral students obtain positions in higher education institutions across the country. Master's students have placed very well in industry, community colleges, and schools. Some master's students have gone on to pursue doctoral degrees.

Location

Stillwater, a small city of about 40,000, is a safe, friendly, and lively community. The cost of living is relatively low, and affordable housing is plentiful. The city offers most of the cultural and recreational opportunities of a college town and is just an hour's drive from Oklahoma City and Tulsa.

The University

Oklahoma State University, a comprehensive research university with more than 20,000 students and almost 1,000 faculty members, is located on a scenic campus in Stillwater, Oklahoma. Founded in 1890, the University has developed an international reputation for excellence in teaching and research, especially in the basic and applied sciences. Students come to OSU from fifty states and more than fifty countries. The Graduate College has about 4,000 students.

Applying

An application package may be obtained from the Mathematics Department. Applicants should plan to have three letters of recommendation sent to the department. GRE scores are not required, but they are strongly recommended. The Graduate Committee in the Mathematics Department begins deliberations in late January and continues the process until March. It is recommended that applicants read the departmental World Wide Web page for a detailed description.

Correspondence and Information

Director of Graduate Studies
Department of Mathematics
Oklahoma State University
Stillwater, Oklahoma 74078-1058
E-mail: graddir@math.okstate.edu
World Wide Web: http://www.math.okstate.edu/grad/welcome2.html

Oklahoma State University

THE FACULTY AND THEIR RESEARCH
RESEARCH ACTIVITIES

Algebraic Geometry: three-dimensional algebraic varieties, birational geometry, degenerations of surfaces, geometry of resolutions, birational geometry of projective spaces; enumerative geometry, interaction of algebraic geometry with theoretical physics; complex holomorphic vector bundles over algebraic varieties, intersection theory on the moduli space of curves.

Analysis: functional analysis, geometry of Banach spaces; approximation theory, numerical analysis, optimization; several complex variables, convexity properties of pseudoconvex domains; harmonic analysis, random Fourier series, boundary behavior of harmonic and analytic functions; Riemann surfaces.

Lie Groups: representation theory of semisimple and reductive Lie groups, analysis and geometry of homogeneous spaces, symmetry and groups of transformations, algebraic aspects of the study of Lie groups and arithmetic groups.

Mathematics Education: school mathematics curriculum, professional development of mathematics teachers, technology in the classroom and applications in the curriculum, mathematics reform issues, equity and minority issues, early intervention testing programs.

Number Theory: L-functions of algebraic varieties over finite fields and cohomological techniques, automorphic representations and L-functions, analytic number theory and the distribution of zeros of the Riemann zeta function, algebraic number theory and cubic extensions of number fields, algebraic groups over algebraic number fields and geometric invariant theory.

Topology: structure and classification of compact 3-manifolds; normal, incompressible, and Heegaard surfaces; algorithms and computation in low-dimensional topology; relations with combinatorial and geometric group theory; structure of noncompact 3-manifolds; covering spaces of 3-manifolds; Casson invariants, Floer homology, symplectic topology, dynamical systems; topology of locally symmetric spaces and applications in number theory, automorphic forms, algebraic geometry, and analysis.

Alan Adolphson, Regents Professor; Ph.D., Princeton, 1973. Number theory, arithmetical algebraic geometry.
Douglas Aichele, Professor; Ed.D., Missouri, 1969. Mathematics education.
Dale Alspach, Regents Professor; Ph.D., Ohio State, 1976. Functional analysis, Banach space theory.
Leticia Barchini, Associate Professor; Ph.D., National University (Argentina), 1987. Representations of Lie groups.
Dennis Bertholf, Professor; Ph.D., New Mexico State, 1968. Abelian group theory, mathematics education.
Birne Binegar, Associate Professor; Ph.D., UCLA, 1982. Representations of Lie groups and Lie algebras, mathematical physics.
Hermann Burchard, Professor; Ph.D., Purdue, 1968. Approximation theory, numerical analysis.
Jen-Tseh Chang, Associate Professor; Ph.D., Harvard, 1985. Representations of Lie groups, D-modules.
James Choike, Professor; Ph.D., Wayne State, 1970. Complex analysis, mathematics education.
James Cogdell, Professor; Ph.D., Yale, 1981. Number theory, automorphic forms.
J. Brian Conrey, Professor; Ph.D., Michigan, 1980. Number theory, automorphic forms.
Bruce Crauder, Professor; Ph.D., Columbia, 1981. Algebraic geometry.
Benny Evans, Professor; Ph.D., Michigan, 1971. Topology of low-dimensional manifolds, mathematics education.
Carel Faber, Associate Professor; Ph.D., Amsterdam, 1988. Algebraic geometry.
Amit Ghosh, Professor; Ph.D., Nottingham, 1981. Number theory, automorphic forms.
William Jaco, G. B. Kerr Professor; Ph.D., Wisconsin, 1968. Topology of low-dimensional manifolds.
Sheldon Katz, Professor; Ph.D., Princeton, 1980. Algebraic geometry, mathematical physics.
Marvin Keener, Professor; Ph.D., Missouri, 1970. Ordinary differential equations.
Weiping Li, Assistant Professor; Ph.D., Michigan State, 1992. Low-dimensional topology, gauge theory, differential geometry.
Lisa Mantini, Associate Professor; Ph.D., Harvard, 1983. Representations of Lie groups, integral geometry.
Mark McConnell, Associate Professor; Ph.D., Brown, 1987. Algebraic topology, locally symmetric spaces.
J. Robert Myers, Associate Professor; Ph.D., Rice, 1977. Topology of low-dimensional manifolds.
Alan Noell, Associate Professor; Ph.D., Princeton, 1983. Several complex variables.
Wayne Powell, Professor; Ph.D., Tulane, 1978. Universal algebra, automata theory.
Zhenbo Qin, Associate Professor; Ph.D., Columbia, 1990. Algebraic geometry.
David Ullrich, Professor; Ph.D., Wisconsin, 1986. Harmonic analysis.
David Witte, Associate Professor; Ph.D., Chicago, 1985. Lie groups and ergodic theory, graph theory, finite groups.
John Wolfe, Professor; Ph.D., Berkeley, 1971. Functional analysis, mathematics education.
David J. Wright, Associate Professor; Ph.D., Harvard, 1982. Algebraic number theory, Riemann surfaces.
Akihiko Yukie, Associate Professor; Ph.D., Harvard, 1986. Number theory, arithmetic algebraic groups.
Roger Zierau, Associate Professor; Ph.D., Berkeley, 1985. Representations of Lie groups.

Oklahoma State University

SELECTED PUBLICATIONS

Adolphson, A., and S. Sperber. A remark on local cohomology. *J. Algebra* 206(2):555–67, 1998.

Adolphson, A., and S. Sperber. On twisted de Rham cohomology. *Nagoya Math. J.* 146:55–81, 1997.

Adolphson, A., and S. Sperber. On the zeta function of a complete intersection. *Ann. Sci. Ecole Norm. Sup. (4)* 29(3), 1996.

Adolphson, A., and B. Dwork. Contiguity relations for generalized hypergeometric functions. *Trans. Am. Math. Soc.* 347(2), 1995.

Adolphson, A. Hypergeometric functions and rings generated by monomials. *Duke Math. J.* 73(2), 1994.

Adolphson, A., and S. Sperber. Exponential sums and Newton polyhedra: cohomology and estimates. *Ann. Math. (2)* 130(2), 1989.

Aichele, D. B., et al. *Geometry—Explorations and Applications.* Boston: Houghton Mifflin/McDougal Littell, 1997.

Aichele, D. B., and S. Gay. Middle school students' understanding of number sense related to percent. Sch. Sci. Mathematics 97(1):27–36, January 1997.

Aichele, D. B., editor. *Professional Development for Teachers of Mathematics—1994 Yearbook,* Reston, Va: NCTM, 1994.

Alspach, D. E. Tensor products and independent sums of L_p-spaces, $1<p<\infty$. *Mem. Amer. Math. Soc.,* in press.

Alspach, D. E. Operators on $C(w^\infty)$ which do not preserve $C(w^\infty)$. *Fundam. Math.* 153(1):81–98, 1997.

Alspach, D. E. Level sets and the uniqueness of measures. *J. London Math. Soc. (2)* 48(2), 1993.

Alspach, D. E., and S. Argyros. Complexity of weakly null sequences. *Dissertationes Math.* (Rozprawy Mat.) 321, 1992.

Barchini, L., and **R. Zierau.** Square integrable harmonic forms and representation theory. *Duke Math. J.* 92(3):645–64, 1998.

Barchini, L., S. G. Gindikin, and H. W. Wong. The geometry of flag manifold and holomorphic extension of Szegö kernels for SU(p,q). *Pacific J. Math.* 179(2):201–20, 1997.

Barchini, L., S. G. Gindikin, and H. W. Wong. Determinant functions and the geometry of the flag manifold for SU (p, q). *J. Lie Theory* 6(2):191–206, 1996.

Barchini, L., M. G. Eastwood, and A. R. Gover. An integral operator into Dolbeault cohomology. *J. Funct. Anal.* 137(2):364–80, 1996.

Barchini, L. Szegö kernels associated with Zuckerman modules. *J. Funct. Anal.* 131(1):145–82, 1995.

Binegar, B., and **R. Zierau.** A singular representation of E_6. *Trans. Am. Math. Soc.* 341(2), 1994.

Binegar, B., and **R. Zierau.** Unitarization of a singular representation of SO$_{(p,q)}$. *Comm. Math. Phys.* 138(2), 1991.

Binegar, B. Cohomology and deformations of Lie superalgebras. *Lett. Math. Phys.* 12, 1987.

Burchard, H. G., and J. Lei. Coordinate order of approximation by functional-based approximation operators. *J. Approx. Theory* 82(2), 1995.

Burchard, H. G., J. A. Ayers, W. H. Frey, and N. S. Sapidis. Approximation with aesthetic constraints. Designing fair curves and surfaces. In *Geometric Design Publishing,* pp. 3–28. Philadelphia: SIAM, 1994.

Burchard, H. G. Discrete curves and curvature constraints. In *Curves and Surfaces II,* ed. L. L. Schumaker et el. Boston: AKPeters, 1994.

Chang, J.-T. Large components of principal series and characteristic cycles. *Proc. Am. Math. Soc.,* in press.

Chang, J.-T., and **J. W. Cogdell.** n-homology of generic representations for GL(N). *Proc. Am. Math. Soc.,* in press.

Chang, J.-T. Characteristic cycles of discrete series for R-rank one groups. *Trans. Am. Math. Soc.* 341(2), 1994.

Chang, J.-T. Asymptotics and characteristic cycles for representations of complex groups. *Compositio Math.* 88(3), 1993.

Chang, J.-T. Characteristic cycles of holomorphic discrete series. *Trans. Am. Math. Soc.* 334(1), 1992.

Cogdell, J. W., and I. I. Piatetski-Shapiro. Stability of gamma factors for SO($2n+1$). *Manuscripta Math.* 95(4):437–61, 1998.

Cogdell, J. W., and I. I. A converse theorem for GL$_4$. *Math. Res. Lett.* 3(1):67–76, 1996.

Cogdell, J. W., and I. I. Piatetski-Shapiro. Unitarity and functoriality. *Geom. Funct. Anal.* 5(2), 1995.

Cogdell, J. W., and I. I. Piatetski-Shapiro. Converse theorems for GL$_n$. *Inst. Hautes tudes Sci. Pub. Math.,* number 79, 1994.

Conrey, J. B., A. Ghosh, and S. M. Gonek. Simple zeros of the Riemann zeta-function. *Proc. London Math. Soc.* 76(3):497–522, 1998.

Conrey, J. B., and **A. Ghosh.** A conjecture for the sixth power moment of the Riemann zeta-function. *Int. Math. Res. Notices* 15:775–80, 1998.

Conrey, J. B., W. Duke, and D. W. Farmer. The distribution of the eigenvalues of Hecke operators. *Acta. Arith.* 78(4):405–9, 1997.

Conrey, J. B., E. Fransen, R. Klein, and C. Scott. Mean values of Dedekind sums. *J. Number Theory* 56(2), 1996.

Conrey, J. B., and D. W. Farmer. An extension of Hecke's converse theorem. *Internat. Math. Res. Notices,* number 9, 1995.

Conrey, J. B. A note on the fourth power moment of the Riemann zeta-function. In *Progressive Mathematics,* p. 138. Boston: Birkhäuser Boston, 1996; *Anal. Number Theory* 1:225–30, 1995.

Conrey, J. B., and **A. Ghosh.** Turán inequalities and zeros of Dirichlet series associated with certain cusp forms. *Trans. Am. Math. Soc.* 342(1):407–19, 1994.

Crauder, B., and R. Miranda. Quantum cohomology of rational surfaces. In *The Moduli Space of Curves* (Texel Island, 1994) *Progr. Math.,* 129. Boston: Birkhäuser Boston, 1995.

Crauder, B., and D. R. Morrison. Minimal models and degenerations of surfaces with Kodaira number zero. *Trans. Am. Math. Soc.* 343(2), 1994.

Crauder, B., and **S. Katz.** Cremona transformers and Hartshorne's conjecture. *Am. J. Math.* 113(2), 1991.

Crauder, B. Degenerations of minimal ruled surfaces. *Ark. Mat.* 28(2), 1990.

Evans, B., and J. Johnson. *Linear Algebra with MAPLE.* John Wiley and Sons, 1994.

Evans, B. DERIVE in linear algebra. In *Proceedings of the Fifth International Conference on Technology in Collegiate Mathematics,* 1993.

Evans, B., and J. Johnson. *Discovering Calculus with DERIVE.* John Wiley and Sons, 1992.

Evans, B. The long annulus theorem. *Canad. Math. Bull.* 29(3), 1986.

Faber, C. Intersection-theoretical computations on $\overline{M}_g$. In *Parameter Spaces,* pp. 71–81. Warsaw: Banach Center Publishing, 1994; *Polish Acad. Sci. Warsaw* 36, 1996.

Aluffi, P., and **C. Faber.** A remark on the Chern class of a tensor product. *Manuscripta Math.* 88(1):85–6, 1995.

Aluffi, P., and **C. Faber.** Linear orbits of d-tuples of points in $\mathbf{P}^1$. *J. Reine Angew. Math.* 445:205–20, 1993.

Faber, C. Chow rings of moduli spaces of curves. II. Some results on the Chow ring of $\overline{M}_4$. *Ann. Math.* (2) 132(3):421–49, 1990.

Faber, C. Chow rings of moduli spaces of curves. I. The Chow ring of M_3. *Ann. Math* (2) 132(2):331–419, 1990.

Jaco, W., and J. L. Tollefson. Algorithms for the complete decomposition of a closed 3-manifold. *Illinois J. Math.* 39(3), 1995.

Jaco, W., and J. H. Rubinstein. PL equivariant surgery and invariant decompositions of 3-manifolds. *Adv. Math.* 73(2), 1989.

Jaco, W., and J. H. Rubinstein. PL minimal surfaces in 3-manifolds. *J. Differential Geom.,* number 3, 1988.

Jaco, W. Lectures on three-manifold topology. *CBMS Regional Conference Series in Mathematics,* 43. Providence, Rhode Island: American Mathematical Society, 1980.

Katz, S., Z. Qin, and Y. Ruan. Enumeration of nodal genus-2 plane curves with fixed complex structure. *J. Algebraic Geom.* 7(3):569–87, 1998.

Katz, S., P. Mayr, and C. Vafa. Mirror symmetry and exact solution of 4D $N=2$ gauge theories. I. *Adv. Theor. Math. Phys.* 1(1):53–114, 1997.

Katz, S., and C. Vafa. Matter from geometry. *Nucl. Phys. B* 497(1–2):146–54, 1997.

Berglund, P., S. Katz, A. Klemm, and P. Mayr. New Higgs transitions between dual N = 2 string models. *Nucl. Phys. B* 483(1–2):209–28, 1997.

Berglund, P., and **S. Katz.** Mirror symmetry constructions: A review. Mirror symmetry, II, 87–113. *AMS/IP Stud. Adv. Math. 1,* Providence, RI: American Mathematical Society, 1997.

Oklahoma State University

Selected Publications (continued)

Katz, S. Gromov-Witten invariants via algebraic geometry. S-duality and mirror symmetry (Trieste, 1995). *Nucl. Phys. B. Proc. Suppl.* 46:108–15, 1996.

Li, W. Singular connections and Riemann theta functions. *Topol. Appl.* 90(1–3):149–63, 1998.

Li, W. Casson-Lin's invariant and Floer homology. *J. Knot Theory Ramifications* 6(6):851–77, 1997.

Li, W. Floer homology for connected sums of homology 3-spheres. *J. Differential Geom.* 40(1), 1994.

Lorch, J. D., and **L. A. Mantini.** Inversion of an integral transform and ladder representations of U(1,q). In *Representation Theory and Harmonic Analysis* (Cincinnati, Ohio, 1994); *Contemp. Math.,* 191; *Am. Math. Soc.* Providence, Rhode Island, 1995.

Mantini, L. A. An L^2-cohomology construction of unitary highest weight modules for U(p,q). *Trans. Am. Math. Soc.* 323(2), 1991.

Mantini, L. A. An L^2-cohomology construction of negative spin mass zero equations for U(p,q). *Math. Anal. Appl.* 136(2), 1988.

Mantini, L. A. An L^2-cohomology analogue of the Penrose transform for the oscillator representation. In *Integral Geometry* (Brunswick, Maine, 1984); *Contemp. Math.,* 63; *Am. Math. Soc.* Providence, Rhode Island, 1987.

Ash, A., and **M. McConnell.** Cohomology at infinity and the well-rounded retract for general linear groups. *Duke Math. J.* 90(3):549–76, 1997.

MacPherson, R., and **M. McConnell.** Explicit reduction theory for Siegel modular threefolds. *Invent. Math.* 111(3), 1993.

Ash, A., and **M. McConnell.** Mod p cohomology of SL(n,Z). *Topology* 31(2), 1992.

Ash, A., and **M. McConnell.** Experimental indications of three-dimensional Galois representations from the cohomology of SL(3,Z). *Exp. Math.* 1(3), 1992.

Myers, R. Compactifying sufficiently regular covering spaces of compact 3-manifolds. *Proc. Am. Math. Soc.,* in press.

Myers, R. On covering translations and homeotopy groups of contractible open n-manifolds. *Proc. Am. Math. Soc.,* in press.

Myers, R. Contractible open 3-manifolds which non-trivially cover only non-compact 3-manifolds. *Topology* 38(1):85–94, 1999.

Myers, R. Attaching boundary planes to irreducible open 3-manifolds.*Q. J. Math. Oxford Ser.* 48(191):363–404, 1997.

Myers, R. Excellent 1-manifolds in compact 3-manifolds. *Topology Appl.* 49(2), 1993.

Myers, R. On mapping class groups of contractible open 3-manifolds.*Trans. Am. Math. Soc.* 335(1), 1993.

Noell, A. Local and global plurisubharmonic defining functions. *Pacific J. Math.* 176(2):421–6, 1996.

Noell, A. Peak functions for pseudoconvex domains in C^n. In *Several Complex Variables* (Stockholm, 1987/1988); *Math. Notes,* 38. Princeton: Princeton University Press, 1993.

Noell, A. Local versus global convexity of pseudoconvex domains. In *Several Complex Variables and Complex Geometry,* part 1 (Santa Cruz, Calif., 1989); *Proc. Sympos. Pure Math.,* 52, part 1; *Am. Math. Soc.* Providence, Rhode Island, 1991.

Noell, A. Interpolation from curves in pseudoconvex bouderies. *Michigan Math. J.* 37(2), 1990.

Cherri, M., and **W. B. Powell.** Free products of lattice ordered modules. *Algebra Universalis* 36(3):379–91, 1996.

Cherri, M., and **W. B. Powell.** Strong amalgamations of lattice ordered groups and modules. *Int. J. Math. Math. Sci.* 16(1), 1993.

Powell, W. B. Total orders on free groups and monoids. In *Words,*

Languages and Combinatorics (Kyoto, 1990). River Edge, New Jersey: World Scientific Publishing, 1992.

Qin, Z., and Y. Ruan. Quantum cohomology of projective bundles over P^n. *Trans. Am. Math. Soc.* 350(9):3615–38, 1998.

Li, W. and **Z. Qin.** Extensions of vector bundles and rationality of certain moduli spaces of stable bundles. *J. Reine Angew. Math.* 475:209–20, 1996.

Friedman, R., and **Z. Qin.** On complex surfaces diffeomorphic to rational surfaces. *Invent. Math.* 120(1), 1995.

Qin, Z. On smooth structures of potential surfaces of general type homeomorphic to rational surfaces. *Invent. Math.* 113(1), 1993.

Choe, B. R., W. Ramey, and **D. Ullrich.** Bloch-to-BMOA pullbacks on the disk. *Proc. Am. Math. Soc.* 125(10):2987–96, 1997.

Stegenga, D. A., and **D. C. Ullrich.** Superharmonic functions in Hölder domains. *Rocky Mtn. J. Math.* 25(4), 1995.

Ullrich, D. C. Radial divergence in BMOA. *Proc. London Math. Soc. (3)* 68(1), 1994.

Ullrich, D. C. Recurrence for lacunary cosine series. In *The Madison Symposium on Complex Analysis* (Madison, Wisc., 1991); *Contemp. Math.,* 137; *Am. Math. Soc.* Providence, Rhode Island, 1992.

Witte, D., A. Yukie, and R. Zierau. Prehomogeneous vector spaces and ergodic theory. II. *Trans. Am. Math. Soc.,* in press.

Witte, D. Superrigid subgroups of solvable Lie groups. *Proc. Am. Math. Soc.* 125(11):3433–8, 1997.

Witte, D. Archimedean superrigidity of solvable S-arithmetic groups. *J. Algebra* 187(1):268–88, 1997.

Witte, D. Superrigidity of lattices in solvable Lie groups. *Invent. Math.* 122(1), 1995.

Dunham, D., D. S. Jungreis, and **D. Witte.** Infinite Hamiltonian paths in Cayley digraphs of hyperbolic symmetry groups. *Discrete Math.* 143(1–3), 1995.

Wright, D. J., and **A. Yukie.** Prehomogeneous vector spaces and field extensions. *Invent. Math.* 110(2), 1992.

Wright D. J. Twists of the Iwasawa-Tate zeta function. *Math. Z.* 200(2), 1989.

Wright D. J. Distribution of discriminants of abelian extensions. *Proc. London Math. Soc. (3)* 58(1), 1989.

Yukie, A. Prehomogeneous vector spaces and ergodic theory. III. *J. Number Theory* 70(2):160–83, 1998.

Yukie, A. On Shintani zeta functions for GL(2). *Trans. Am. Math. Soc.* 12:5067–94, 1998.

Yukie, A. Prehomogeneous vector spaces and ergodic theory. I. *Duke Math. J.* 90(1):123–47, 1997.

Yukie, A. Prehomogeneous vector spaces and field extensions. III. *J. Number Theory* 67(1):115–37, 1997.

Kable, A. C., and **A. Yukie.** Prehomogeneous vector spaces and field extensions. II. *Invent. Math.* 130(2):315–44, 1997.

Yukie, A. Shintani zeta functions. *London Mathematical Society Lecture Note Series,* 183. Cambridge: Cambridge University Press, 1993.

Wolf, J. A., and **R. Zierau.** Cayley transforms and orbit structure in complex flag manifolds. *Transformation Groups* 2(4):391–405, 1997.

Dunne, E. G., and **R. Zierau.** The automorphism groups of complex homogeneous spaces. *Math. Ann.* 307(3):489–503, 1997.

Wolf, J. A., and **R. Zierau.** Riemannian exponential maps and decompositions of reductive Lie groups. In *Topics in Geometry,* 349–53, *Progr. Nonlinear Differential Equations Appl.* 20, Boston: Birkhäuser, 1996.

OLD DOMINION UNIVERSITY

Department of Mathematics and Statistics

Programs of Study	The department offers a graduate program (entitled Computational and Applied Mathematics) leading to the M.S. and Ph.D. degrees, with options in applied mathematics and statistics.
	Master's students must complete a total of 30 credit hours of course work. Up to 6 of these credits may be chosen from a field of application in which the student applies analytical and numerical techniques to another discipline. The program is flexible and may vary considerably, depending on the student's interests and career goals. A master's thesis is not required.
	The Ph.D. program requires a minimum of 24 credit hours beyond the master's degree and exclusive of doctoral dissertation work. A foreign language is not required.
	In applied mathematics, students choose from courses in ordinary and partial differential equations, biomathematics, complex and real analysis, optimization techniques, numerical analysis, continuum mechanics, integral equations, transform methods, numerical fluid dynamics, tensor analysis, calculus of variations, and singular perturbation methods.
	The statistics curriculum offers courses in sampling theory, design and analysis of experiments, regression and analysis of variance, stochastic models, nonparametric methods, reliability and life testing, linear models, multivariate analysis, time-series analysis, statistical inference, and probability theory. All students in the statistics option are required to complete a modeling project.
	In a recent ranking of institutions worldwide, based on total publication pages in the primary statistics journals during 1980–1986, Old Dominion's statistics group ranked first in Virginia. Among institutions in the southern region of the United States, ODU's program was ranked sixth-best based on publications in the *Annals of Statistics* and ninth-best when judged by publications in all nine journals surveyed for the study.
Research Facilities	Faculty research is currently being supported through grants from the National Science Foundation, the U.S. Army Research Office, the Air Force Office of Scientific Research, and the National Aeronautics and Space Administration.
	ODU's computer center operates a CDC CYBER 930-931 and an IBM 3090 with VM/XA-SP and MVS/SP operating systems. The department also owns several IBM microcomputers for student and faculty member use and also has a Sun network.
	The University library holdings of more than a million items are accessible through a computer output microfiche catalog located in each academic department. The library has a comprehensive collection of periodicals and books in support of the graduate curriculum and research in mathematics, statistics, and related areas. The library offers computer-assisted searches of more than 100 indexing and abstracting services. Interlibrary loan services are conducted on line and are available to graduate students.
Financial Aid	Departmental graduate assistantships offer stipends ranging up to $10,000. Nonresidents of Virginia who hold assistantships pay resident tuition. Tuition is waived for doctoral students who have a master's degree and are graduate assistants. In addition, a number of teaching and research positions are available for financial support of graduate assistants during the summer months.
	There are occasional opportunities for graduate students to participate in joint research projects at NASA Langley Research Center. NASA Fellowships carry stipends of $12,000 and provide for payment of tuition, fees, and some additional expenses.
Cost of Study	Tuition for the academic year 1998–99 was $180 per semester hour for Virginia residents and $477 per semester hour for nonresidents. All holders of assistantships qualify for resident status.
Living and Housing Costs	Off-campus apartments are available, starting at about $300 per month for a furnished one-bedroom apartment. The area also offers opportunities for shared housing arrangements.
Student Group	The University enrolls approximately 15,000 students; graduate students account for a quarter of the enrollment. There are about 50 graduate students in applied mathematics and statistics.
Student Outcomes	Of the recent graduates of the doctoral program, most hold teaching positions at colleges and universities across the United States. The remainder are employed in private industry.
Location	Norfolk, in eastern Virginia, is among the most rapidly growing urban areas along the Atlantic seaboard. The city is located in one of the most favored climatic regions of the United States. Proximity to the ocean and Gulf Stream moderates the summer's heat, and winter temperatures usually approximate those in northern Florida.
	The University's 146-acre campus lies within the seven-city Hampton Roads metropolitan area that is nationally known for its historical, recreational, cultural, educational, and military facilities. The many points of interest include Virginia Beach; the Chesapeake Bay; the historic towns of Williamsburg, Jamestown, and Yorktown; commercial and naval shipping and shipbuilding facilities; and the NASA-Langley Research Center. The area supports a full schedule of cultural events, including theater, opera, ballet, dance, art exhibitions, symphony and popular music concerts, and lecture series.
The University	Old Dominion University is a coeducational, state-supported public institution. ODU is organized into six academic colleges: Business Administration, Arts and Letters, Education, Engineering, Sciences, and Health Sciences. The University currently offers forty-seven master's programs and thirteen doctoral programs.
Applying	Applicants to the master's program should have a bachelor's degree in either mathematics, statistics, computer science, or an application area with a strong mathematics component (such as physics or engineering). Undergraduate mathematics preparation should include course work in linear algebra, advanced calculus, differential equations, probability, and numerical methods.
	Applicants to the Ph.D. program are normally students who have earned a master's degree in mathematics or statistics or a related application area. However, students with a strong undergraduate degree may apply for admission directly into the Ph.D. program.
Correspondence and Information	Graduate Program Director Department of Mathematics and Statistics Old Dominion University Norfolk, Virginia 23529 Telephone: 804-683-3887

Old Dominion University

THE FACULTY AND THEIR RESEARCH

Applied Mathematics
John Adam, Ph.D., London. Mathematical biology, astrophysical magnetohydrodynamics, mathematical modeling.
Przemck Bogacki, Ph.D., SMU. Numerical solution of initial value problems for ordinary differential equations, including implementation for parallel processing.
Charlie H. Cooke, Ph.D., North Carolina State. Differential equations, numerical fluid mechanics, finite-element methods.
J. Mark Dorrepaal, Ph.D., Toronto. Stokes flow, transform methods, asymptotic analysis.
John H. Heinbockel, Ph.D., North Carolina State. Differential equations, systems analysis–optimization, numerical methods, mathematical modeling, integral transforms, tensor analysis, solar energy.
Fang Hu, Ph.D., Florida State. Computational fluids with an emphasis in turbulent mixing.
Hideaki Kaneko, Ph.D., Clemson. Numerical solution of integral equations, fixed-point theory, approximation theory.
John E. Kroll, Ph.D., Yale. Geophysical fluid dynamics, oceanography.
David G. Lasseigne, Ph.D., Northwestern. Combustion theory, application of integral equations.
Wu Li, Ph.D., Penn State. Approximation theory, optimization theory.
Gordon Melrose, Ph.D., Old Dominion. Singular integral equations, special functions, fracture mechanics.
Richard D. Noren, Ph.D., Virginia Tech. Volterra integral equations.
Constance Schober, Ph.D., Arizona. Dynamical systems, chaos.
John Swetits, Ph.D., Lehigh. Approximation theory, functional analysis.
John Tweed, Ph.D., Glasgow. Integral equations, transform techniques, elasticity and fracture mechanics.
Stanley E. Weinstein, Ph.D., Michigan State. Numerical analysis and approximation.
Philip R. Wohl, Ph.D., Cornell. Asymptotic analysis, differential equations, fluid dynamics, mathematical biology.

Statistics
N. Rao Chaganty, Ph.D., Florida State. Applied probability, reliability.
Ram C. Dahiya, Ph.D., Wisconsin. Statistical methodology and inference, biostatistics, applied statistics.
Michael J. Doviak, Ph.D., Florida. Applied statistics.
Larry D. Lee, Ph.D., Missouri. Statistical inference, reliability.
John P. Morgan, Ph.D., North Carolina. Design of experiments.
Dayanand N. Naik, Ph.D., Pittsburgh. Linear models.

OREGON STATE UNIVERSITY

College of Science
Department of Statistics

Programs of Study
The department offers graduate work leading to the M.S. and Ph.D. degrees. Major fields are applied statistics, environmental statistics, mathematical statistics, and operations research (M.S. only). Students can concentrate on theory or applications, and programs can be tailored to emphasize such areas of interest as ecology, engineering, forestry, mathematics, or oceanography.

An M.S. candidate in statistics must pass written comprehensive exams in both mathematical statistics and applied statistics. A thesis or research paper is optional. M.S. candidates in operations research must pass the written comprehensive exam in either mathematical statistics or applied statistics; in addition, a thesis or research project is required. All students must gain consulting and teaching experience. Prerequisites for admission are multivariable calculus, linear algebra, and an undergraduate sequence in mathematical statistics, but some applicants without the usual prerequisites may be admitted on a provisional basis. A student can normally complete the M.S. program in five quarters.

To enter the Ph.D. program, a student must have the equivalent of an M.S. degree and must pass the department's M.S. comprehensive examinations. A Ph.D. candidate takes one or two years of advanced course work. Current research areas in the department include analysis of enumerative data, nonparametric statistics, asymptotics, experimental design, generalized regression models, linear model theory, reliability theory, sampling methodology, environmental statistics, survival analysis, and wildlife and general survey methodology. A student can normally complete the Ph.D. degree program in two to five years.

Research Facilities
The department is located in Kidder Hall, which is adjacent to the University library and the University Computing Services Center. In addition to these University facilities, the department maintains its own library and its own computer systems. The departmental library contains approximately 700 volumes of research and reference works and subscribes to most of the major journals in statistics and operations research. The departmental computer system consists of an expanding network of Sun Workstations and personal computers.

Financial Aid
In 1999–2000, assistantships carry stipends ranging from $3159 to $13,344 per academic year, depending on the qualifications of the applicant and the source of funds. Depending upon the terms of the appointment, graduate assistants are required to spend 8 to 20 hours per week assisting in teaching or departmental research. Tuition is waived for graduate assistants, but fees of approximately $300 per term must be paid. Summer aid is also available.

Cost of Study
In 1999–2000, tuition and fees for graduate students are estimated at $2069 per term for residents and $3517 per term for nonresidents. International students must obtain financial clearance from the Graduate School.

Living and Housing Costs
Single students may obtain room and board in University residence halls for approximately $5065 per academic year. Residence hall housing is also available during the summer term. The University maintains a number of furnished apartments for married students. Rents for off-campus housing vary considerably but are considered reasonable by national standards. Additional information is available from the University's Department of Housing.

Student Group
The Department of Statistics, which has an active student statistical association, has about 30 graduate students. In the past three years, the average number of degrees awarded annually has been fifteen M.S. and three Ph.D. degrees. Enrollment in the University is about 14,600 students, of whom approximately 3,000 are graduate students.

Student Outcomes
Graduates have a variety of employment opportunities. All students this past year have been successful in finding employment. Employers of recent M.S. graduates include EPA, University of Nebraska Medical Center, Fred Hutchinson Cancer Center, Hewlett-Packard, and SAS. Employers of recent Ph.D. graduates include IBM, Proctor and Gamble, National Institutes of Health, St. Jude Children's Research Hospital, U.S.D.A. Forest Service, New England Research Institute, Oregon Department of Transportation (ODOT), and the University of Otago, New Zealand.

Location
The city of Corvallis, an attractive community with a population of 49,000, is situated in the Willamette Valley between Portland and Eugene. An hour to the west is the Pacific Ocean; an hour to the east, the Cascade Mountains. The region offers numerous recreational opportunities, including camping, fishing, hiking, hunting, and skiing. A variety of cultural activities are offered in Corvallis, Eugene, and Portland, and the famous Oregon Shakespearean Festival is in Ashland. The area has a temperate climate with generally mild winters and sunny summers with moderate temperatures.

The University and The Department
Oregon State offers a variety of programs in its various schools and colleges: Agricultural Sciences, Business, Engineering, Forestry, Health and Physical Education, Home Economics, Liberal Arts, Oceanography, Pharmacy, Science, and Veterinary Medicine. The University started as a land-grant institution in 1868 and in 1971 was also designated a sea-grant institution.

A statistical consulting and computer service was initiated at Oregon State in 1947, and ten years later the Department of Statistics was established. The first M.S. degree was awarded in 1962 and the first Ph.D. degree in 1969. The University has an active Survey Research Center, established in 1973.

Applying
Application forms for graduate study at OSU are available from the Department of Statistics and through the Office of Admissions. Two copies of the completed form, a $50 nonrefundable application fee, official (sealed) transcripts of work completed at other institutions, and a letter indicating the applicant's particular field of interest should be sent to the Office of Admissions. A third copy of the completed application form, three letters of reference, additional transcripts, GRE scores (optional, but recommended for students requesting financial assistance), and a copy of the applicant's letter of interest should be sent to the Department of Statistics.

Applications for admission to the Department of Statistics are considered at any time, but applicants desiring financial aid should apply by February 15.

Correspondence and Information
Director of Graduate Studies
Department of Statistics
Oregon State University
44 Kidder Hall
Corvallis, Oregon 97331-4606
Telephone: 541-737-3366
E-mail: statoff@stat.orst.edu
World Wide Web: http://www.orst.edu/dept/statistics/

Oregon State University

THE FACULTY AND THEIR RESEARCH

Jeffrey L. Arthur, Professor; Ph.D., Purdue, 1977. Mathematical programming and applications, network optimization, societal impacts of operations research.

David S. Birkes, Associate Professor; Ph.D., Washington (Seattle), 1969. Linear models, mathematical statistics.

H. Daniel Brunk, Professor Emeritus; Ph.D., Rice, 1944. Fellow of IMS and ASA; elected member of ISI. Probability, mathematical statistics.

David A. Butler, Professor; Ph.D., Stanford, 1975. Machine vision, applications of operations research to forestry, reliability theory and applications.

Lyle D. Calvin, Professor Emeritus; Ph.D., North Carolina State, 1953. Fellow of ASA and AAAS; elected member of ISI. Sampling methods, experimental design.

Virginia Lesser, Assistant Professor; Ph.D., North Carolina, 1992. Sampling methodology, environmental statistics.

Paul A. Murtaugh, Associate Professor; Ph.D., Washington (Seattle), 1989. Statistical ecology, biostatistics, survival analysis.

W. Scott Overton, Professor Emeritus; Ph.D., North Carolina State, 1964. Statistical ecology, systems ecology.

Cliff Pereira, Research Associate; Ph.D., Oregon State, 1985. Biological applications of statistics, linear models, experimental design.

Dawn Peters, Associate Professor; Ph.D., Florida, 1988. Nonparametric statistics, asymptotics.

Donald A. Pierce, Professor Emeritus; Ph.D., Oklahoma State, 1965. Fellow of IMS and ASA; elected member of ISI. Theory of inference, asymptotics, applied statistics, enumerative data, generalized regression models, survival data.

Fred L. Ramsey, Professor; Ph.D., Iowa State, 1964. Elected member of ISI; fellow of ASA. Wildlife survey methods, biometry, statistical ecology, time series analysis, stochastic processes.

Kenneth E. Rowe, Professor Emeritus; Ph.D., Iowa State, 1966. Statistical computing, design and analysis of experiments.

Daniel W. Schafer, Professor; Ph.D., Chicago, 1982. Regression analysis, generalized linear models.

Justus F. Seely, Professor; Ph.D., Iowa State, 1969. Fellow of IMS and ASA; elected member of ISI. Linear models.

Robert T. Smythe, Professor and Chair; Ph.D., Stanford, 1969. Fellow of IMS and ASA; elected member of ISI. Stochastic processes, biostatistics.

David R. Thomas, Professor Emeritus; Ph.D., Iowa State, 1965. Applied statistics, resampling methods, tolerance intervals, survival analysis.

N. Scott Urquhart, Professor; Ph.D., Colorado State, 1965. Fellow of ASA. Applied linear models, environmental statistics.

Edward C. Waymire, Professor; Ph.D., Arizona, 1976. Fellow of IMS. Random fields and spatial statistics with applications in geophysics, hydrology.

Oregon State University

SELECTED PUBLICATIONS

Arthur, J. L., M. T. Hachey, K. Sahr, and A. R. Kiester. Finding all optimal solutions to the reserve site selection problem: Formulation and computational analysis. *Env. Ecol. Stat.* 4(2):153–65, 1997.

Arthur, J. L., and D. J. Nalle. Clarification on the use of linear programming and GIS for land-use modeling. *Int. J. Geo. Inform. Sci.* 11(4):397–402, 1997.

Lang, A., and **J. L. Arthur**. Parameter approximation for phase-type distributions. In *Matrix-Analytic Methods in Stochastic Models*, pp. 151–206, eds. S. Chakravarty and A. S. Alfa, New York: Marcel Dekker, 1996.

Van Leeuwen, D. M., J. F. Seely, and **D. Birkes**. Sufficient conditions for orthogonal designs in mixed linear models. *J. Stat. Plann. Infer.* 73:373–89, 1998.

Seely, J. F., **D. Birkes**, and Y. Lee. Characterizing sums of squares by their distributions. *Amer. Stat.* 51:55–8, 1997.

Li, Y., **D. Birkes**, and D. R. Thomas. The residual likelihood ratio test for the variance ratio in a linear model with two variance components. *Biomet. J.* 38:961–72, 1996.

Brunner, C. C., et al. **(D. A. Butler)**. The interaction of sawing and edging operations on red alder finger-joint cut-stock production. *Forest Prod. J.* 47(7/8):75–82, 1997.

Brunner, C. C., et al. **(D. A. Butler)**. The effects of edging severity on cut-stock production from red alder lumber. *Forest Prod. J.* 46(7/8):56–61, 1996.

Brunner, C. C., A. G. Maristany, and **D. A. Butler**. Wood species identification by spectral reflectance. *Forest Prod. J.* 46(2):82–5, 1996.

Lesser, V. M., and W. D. Kalsbeek. A comparison of periodic survey designs employing multi-stage sampling. *Environ. Ecol. Stat.* 4:117–30, 1997.

Ormrod, D., **V. M. Lesser**, D. Olszyk and D. Tingey. Douglas-fir needle pigment response to climate change and correlations with seedling growth. *Plant Physiol.* 114:90, 1997.

Ramsey, F. L., and **V. M. Lesser**. Conditional and unconditional estimators of population size. *Environ. Ecol. Stat.* 2(3):181–90, 1995.

Murtaugh, P. A., and D. L. Phillips. Temporal correlation of classifications in remote sensing. *J. Agr. Biol. Environ. Stat.* 3:1–12, 1998.

Murtaugh, P. A., and D. R. Derryberry. Models of connectance in food webs. *Biometrics* 54:54–61, 1998.

Murtaugh, P. A., and J. P. Kollath. Variation of trophic fractions and connectance in food webs. *Ecology* 78:1382–7, 1997.

Bailey, G. S., et al. **(C. Pereira)**. Molecular dosimetry in fish: Quantitative target organ DNA adduction and hepatocarcinogenicity for four aflatoxins by two exposure routes in rainbow trout. *Mutat. Res.* 339:233–44, 1998.

Contreras-Sanchez, W. M., C. B. Schreck, M. S. Fitzpatrick, and **C. B. Pereira**. Effects of stress on the reproductive behavior of rainbow trout (Oncorhynchus mykiss). *Biol. Reprod.* 58:439–47, 1998.

Rodriguez-Saona, L. E., P. E. Wrolstad, and **C. Pereira**. Modeling the contribution of sugars, ascorbic acid, chlorogenic acid and amino acids to non-enzymatic browning of potato chips. *J. Food Sci.* 62:1001–5, 1997.

Pierce, D. A., and **D. Peters**. Higher order asymptotics and the likelihood principle: One-parameter models. *Biometrika* 81(1):1–10, 1994.

Pierce, D. A., and **D. Peters**. Practical use of higher-order asymptotics for multiparameter exponential families (with discussion). *JRSSB* 54(3):701–37, 1992.

Peters, D. An adaptive multivariate signed-rank test for the one-sample location problem. *J. Nonparametric Stat.* 1:157–63, 1991.

Ramsey, F. L., and **D. W. Schafer**. *The Statistical Sleuth*. Duxbury Press, 1997.

Ramsey, F. L., M. McCracken, M. Drut, and J. Crawford. Habitat association studies of the northern spotted owl, sage grouse and flammulated owl. *Case Studies in Biometry* (Chapter 10), eds, N. Lange et al. International Biometrics Society, 1994.

Ramsey, F. L., J. M. Scott, S. Mountainspring, and C. B. Kepler. Forest bird communities of the Hawaiian Islands: Their dynamics, ecology and conservation. *Stud. Avian Biol.* 9:325, 1986.

Schafer, D. W., and K. G. Purdy. Likelihood Analysis for Errors-in-Variables Regression with Replicate Measurement. *Biometrika* 83:813–24, 1996.

Schafer, D. W. Likelihood analysis for probit regression with measurement error. *Biometrika* 80:899–904, 1993.

Pierce, D. A., D. O. Stram, M. Vaeth, and **D. W. Schafer**. The errors-in-variables problem: considerations provided by radiation dose-response analyses of the A-bomb survivor data. *JASA* 87:351–9, 1992.

Seely, J. F., D. Birkes, and Y. Lee. Characterizing sums of squares by their distributions. *Amer. Stat.* 51(1):55–8, 1997.

Lee, Y., and **J. F. Seely**. Computing the Wald interval for a variance ratio. *Biometrics* 52(4):1486–91, 1996.

Saleh, A. A., Y. Lee, and **J. F. Seely**. Recovery of inter-block information: Extensions in a two variance component model. *Comm. Stat.: Theory Meth.* 25(9):2189–200, 1996.

Mahmoud, H., and **R. T. Smythe**. Probabilistic analysis of multiple quick select. *Algorithmica* 22:569–84, 1998.

Smythe, R. T., H. Mahmoud, and M. Regnier. Analysis of Boyer-Moor-Horspool string-matching heuristic. *Random Struct. Algorithms* 10:169–86, 1997.

Smythe, R. T., K. Fung, and D. Krewski. A comparison of tests for trend with historical controls in carcinogen bioassay. *Can. J. Stat.* 24:431–54, 1997.

Cordy, C. B., and **D. R. Thomas**. Deconvolution of a distribution function. *JASA*, in press.

Li, Y., D. Birkes, and **D. R. Thomas**. The residual likelihood ratio test for the variance ratio in a linear model with two variance components. *Biomet. J.*, 1996.

Limam, M., and **D. R. Thomas**. Simultaneous tolerance intervals for the linear regression models. *JASA* 83(403):801–4, 1988.

Urquhart, N. S., S. G. Paulsen, and D. P. Larsen. Monitoring for regional and policy-relevant trends over time. *Ecol. Appl.* 8:246–57, 1998.

Van Leeuwen, D. M., L. W. Murray, and **N. S. Urquhart**. A mixed model with both fixed and random trend components across time. *J. Agricultural, Biol. Environ. Stat.* 1:435–53, 1996.

Clason, D. L., J. N. Corgan, C. M. Cryder-Wilson, and **N. S. Urquhart**. Mixture fraction and linkage analysis for hybrid onions. *Case Studies in Biometry*, pp. 145–56, eds. N. Long et al. New York: John Wiley and Sons, 1994.

Ossiander, M., **E. Waymire**, and Q. Zhang. Some width function asymptotics for weighted trees. *Ann. Applied. Prob.* 7(4):972–95, 1997.

Waymire, E., and S. Williams. A cascade decomposition theory with applications to Markov and exchangeable cascades. *Trans. AMS* 348(2):585–632, 1996.

She, Z. S., and **E. Waymire**. Quantized energy cascase and log-Poisson statistics in fully developed turbulence. *Phys. Rev. Lett.* 74(2):262–5, 1995.

PENNSYLVANIA STATE UNIVERSITY

Department of Mathematics

Programs of Study	The Department of Mathematics offers Ph.D., D.Ed., M.A., and M.Ed. degree programs. A wide range of faculty interests provides a broad spectrum of areas of specialization in which students may choose their course work and research topics. There are several areas of mathematics in which Penn State has groups of world-class researchers on faculty. These areas include the theory of operator algebras, K-theory, and related areas; dynamical systems, ergodic theory, and related areas; number theory and arithmetical algebraic geometry; differential geometry, algebraic geometry, and Lie groups; set theory and mathematical logic; numerical analysis; and applied mathematics. The Pritchard Fluid Mechanics Laboratory provides a unique opportunity for students specializing in applied mathematics to carry out mathematical research starting from experimental grounds. In addition, the University has recently founded three research centers within the Department of Mathematics: the Center for Dynamical Systems, the Center for Geometry and Mathematical Physics, and the Center for Computational Mathematics and Applications. In a typical year, the department admits about 20 students, almost all to the Ph.D. program. All doctoral students are required to pass three qualifying examinations. The qualifying examinations are in the areas of analysis, algebra, and topology/geometry unless a student chooses to enroll in the Applied Mathematics Option or the Logic and Foundations Option. For the Applied Mathematics Option, the qualifying examinations are in the areas of analysis, numerical analysis, and partial differential equations, and for the Logic and Foundations Option, the areas are analysis, algebra, and logic and foundations. Among other requirements for the Ph.D. are at least eleven 3-credit graduate courses, reading knowledge in one foreign language, passing a comprehensive examination, writing a thesis, and passing a final oral examination based on the thesis. The length of time it takes students to complete their Ph.D. degree is typically between 5½ and six years.
Research Facilities	The Department of Mathematics is housed in McAllister Building, a large four-story structure located in the heart of the Penn State campus. The Mathematics Library is conveniently located on the first floor of McAllister Building. It is a first-rate library, containing more than 45,000 volumes and receiving almost 600 mathematical journals and serials. The library also subscribes to *MathSci*, the Web-based edition of *Math Reviews*. The department maintains a network of nearly 150 Sun Workstations, together with specialized machines to support very high speed computation, high-resolution three-dimensional visualization, and specialized software. The network is readily accessible to graduate students, with workstations in graduate student offices. Supported software includes TeX, MACSYMA, Maple, Mathematica, Matlab, and more specialized packages such as Pari, GAP, and DSLIB. The network has an excellent Internet connection via a fiber-optic link to the Penn State data backbone. Through it, faculty members and graduate students access Penn State's 50-node SP-2 parallel computer and the national supercomputer centers.
Financial Aid	Most of the graduate students are supported by teaching assistantships. In addition to the tuition waiver, the expected stipend for a half-time teaching assistantship is $11,500 (for ten months) prior to admittance to candidacy, after which time it increases to $12,300. A half-time assistantship requires the student to teach 3 hours per week in the first year and 4½ hours per week in subsequent years. The other sources of support are Curry Fellowships, which are awarded to incoming doctoral students based on their performance in Ph.D. qualifying examinations taken upon arrival in August and that carry a stipend of $14,400 for ten months, and various Graduate School and Eberly College of Science fellowships. These fellowships give students one or two semesters free of teaching. Summer teaching assistantships are also available to many students.
Cost of Study	Students holding any of the fellowships or assistantships described above receive a tuition waiver (in 1998–99, $3267 per semester for Pennsylvania residents and $6750 per semester for nonresidents).
Living and Housing Costs	For a single student, a room in a University residence hall and board are available for about $2000 per semester. For married students, 358 family units are available, with monthly rates that range from $325 to $485. The town of State College also provides attractive and reasonably priced off-campus living within walking distance of campus.
Student Group	As of September 1998, the department has 70 mathematics graduate students. Of these, 63 are doctoral students, with the remaining 7 students seeking a master's degree. Sixty-two percent are international students from all over the world. Teaching assistantships are provided for 68 students. Currently in the program is 1 recipient of the NSF Graduate Research Fellowship and 1 recipient of the Sloan Doctoral Dissertation Fellowship for the 1998–99 academic year.
Student Outcomes	In spite of the very difficult job market in mathematics in general over the past years, graduates have been successfully placed in academic positions and industry. Recent academic placements include tenure-track and postdoctoral positions at Princeton, MSRI, Caltech, UCLA, Dartmouth, SUNY, Purdue, Rutgers, University of Minnesota, University of Pennsylvania, and University of Georgia. Corporate placements include (Bellcore) Lucent Technologies; Parametric Technology Corporation; Electronic Digital System; HRB Systems; Micro Strategy, Inc.; and CVC International.
Location	The University Park Campus of Penn State is in the town of State College—a metropolitan area of more than 100,000 people in the center of the commonwealth. Located in a rural and scenic part of the Appalachian Mountains, it is only 3 to 4 hours from Pittsburgh, Philadelphia, and Washington, D.C. Various cultural, educational, and athletic activities are available throughout the year.
The University	Founded in 1855, Penn State is the land-grant university of Pennsylvania. It is one of the largest universities in the country, with twenty-three campuses. The University Park Campus is the center of most of the graduate studies at the University. University enrollment is approximately 70,000, including 60,000 undergraduates and 10,000 graduate students. The graduate faculty has about 1,800 members. Enrollment at the University Park Campus is about 39,000.
Applying	Application forms must be obtained from the Department of Mathematics. Applicants must submit one copy of the application form (white original) and a $40 nonrefundable fee to Graduate Enrollment Services. The pink copy of the application form, transcripts, test scores (GRE and TOEFL, if applicable), visa application (if applicable), three letters of recommendation, and a brief description of junior, senior, and graduate-level mathematics courses that the applicant will have completed upon entering graduate school must be sent to the Department of Mathematics by February 1. A minimum TOEFL score of 550 is required for all applicants whose native language is not English.
Correspondence and Information	Director of Graduate Studies Department of Mathematics Pennsylvania State University University Park, Pennsylvania 16802 Telephone: 814-865-7529 E-mail: gradstudies@math.psu.edu World Wide Web: http://www.math.psu.edu/Grad/

Pennsylvania State University

THE FACULTY AND THEIR RESEARCH

Joel H. Anderson, Professor of Mathematics; Ph.D., Indiana, 1971. Operator algebras.

George E. Andrews, Evan Pugh Professor of Mathematics; Ph.D., Pennsylvania, 1964. Number theory, partitions.

Steve Armentrout, Professor of Mathematics; Ph.D., Texas at Austin, 1956. Topology.

Douglas N. Arnold, Distinguished Professor of Mathematics; Ph.D., Chicago, 1979. Numerical analysis, differential equations, mechanics.

Augustin Banyaga, Professor of Mathematics; Ph.D., Geneva, 1976. Symplectic, contact geometry and topology, geometry of gauge fields, especially the Seiberg-Witten theory.

Jesse Barlow, Professor of Mathematics and Computer Science and Engineering; Ph.D., Northwestern, 1981. Numerical linear algebra, concurrent scientific computing, accuracy of computation.

Paul F. Baum, Evan Pugh Professor of Mathematics; Ph.D., Princeton, 1963. Topology and operator algebras.

Andrew Belmonte, Assistant Professor of Mathematics; Ph.D., Princeton, 1994. Experimental fluid dynamics and nonlinear dynamics.

Leonid Berlyand, Assistant Professor of Mathematics and Materials Science; Ph.D., Kharkov (Russia), 1984. Partial differential equations and applications in materials science, homogenization theory, mathematical physics.

W. Dale Brownawell, Distinguished Professor of Mathematics; Ph.D., Cornell, 1970. Number theory, transcendence.

Jean-Luc Brylinski, Eberly Family Professor of Mathematics; Paris Sud, 1981. Geometry, topology, mathematical physics.

Ranee Kathryn Brylinski, Professor of Mathematics; Ph.D., MIT, 1981. Geometry, Lie groups, mathematical physics.

Dmitri Burago, Associate Professor of Mathematics; Ph.D., St. Petersburg (Russia), 1992. Differential and Riemannian geometry.

Maria-Carme Calderer, Professor of Mathematics; Ph.D., Heriot-Watt (Edinburgh), 1980. Differential equations, continuum mechanics.

Wenwu Cao, Associate Professor of Mathematics and Materials Science, Ph.D., Penn State, 1987. Applied mathematics, computer simulations, materials sciences.

Min Chen, Assistant Professor of Mathematics; Ph.D., Indiana, 1991. Numerical analysis, applied mathematics.

Frank R. Deutsch, Professor of Mathematics; Ph.D., Brown, 1966. Approximation theory in Banach and Hilbert spaces.

Dmitry Dolgopyat, Assistant Professor of Mathematics; Ph.D., Princeton, 1997. Dynamical systems.

Charles F. Doran, S. Chowla Research Postdoctoral Fellow; Ph.D., Harvard, 1999. Algebraic and complex geometry, number theory, mathematics of string theory.

Alexander N. Dranishnikov, Professor of Mathematics; Ph.D., Moscow State, 1983; Doctor of Science, Steklov Mathematical Institute, 1987. Geometric topology, geometric group theory, dimension theory and cohomological dimension.

Edward Formanek, Professor of Mathematics; Ph.D., Rice, 1970. Algebra, ring theory.

Moses Glasner, Associate Professor of Mathematics; Ph.D., UCLA, 1966. Potential theory, complex variables and differential geometry.

Dima Grigoriev, Professor of Mathematics and Computer Science and Engineering; Ph.D., Russian Academy of Science, 1979. Computational complexity.

Diane M. Henderson, Associate Professor of Mathematics; Ph.D., California, San Diego, 1989. Fluid dynamics, applied mathematics.

Nigel Higson, Professor of Mathematics; Ph.D., Dalhousie, 1986. Operator algebras and K-theory.

Robert P. Hunter, Professor of Mathematics; Ph.D., LSU, 1958. Transformation groups, abstract semigroups.

Jon T. Jacobsen, S. Chowla Research Postdoctoral Fellow; Ph.D., Utah, 1999. Nonlinear analysis, differential equations, geometry.

Donald G. James, Professor of Mathematics; Ph.D., MIT, 1963. Algebra and number theory, quadratic forms.

Kevin James, S. Chowla Research Assistant Professor; Ph.D., Georgia, 1997. Number theory.

Thomas J. Jech, Professor of Mathematics; Ph.D., Prague, 1966. Set theory.

Anatole Katok, Raymond N. Shibley Professor of Mathematics; Ph.D., Moscow State, 1968. Dynamical systems, ergodic theory and differential geometry.

Svetlana Katok, Professor of Mathematics; Ph.D., Maryland, 1983. Automorphic forms, analysis on manifolds, dynamical systems.

Gerard Lallement, Professor of Mathematics; Doctorat es Mathematiques, Paris, 1966. Algebraic and combinatorial semigroup theory.

Joseph M. Lambert, Associate Professor of Mathematics and Computer Science and Engineering; Ph.D., Purdue, 1970. Approximation theory in Banach spaces, computational methods in numerical analysis.

Mark Levi, Professor of Mathematics; Ph.D., NYU (Courant), 1978. Dynamical systems and their applications in physics and engineering.

L. C. Li, Associate Professor of Mathematics; Ph.D., NYU (Courant), 1983. Differential equations, completely integrable Hamiltonian systems.

W. C. Winnie Li, Professor of Mathematics; Ph.D., Berkeley, 1974. Automorphic forms, representation theory, number theory, algebra and combinatorics.

Jenny Xiaoe Li, Assistant Professor of Mathematics and Economics; Ph.D., Cornell, 1993. Mathematical economics, mathematical finance, computational economics.

Chun Liu, Assistant Professor of Mathematics; Ph.D., NYU (Courant), 1995. Partial differential equations, calculus of variations, applied mathematics.

Richard B. Mansfield, Associate Professor of Mathematics; Ph.D., Stanford, 1970. Mathematical logic.

Peter H. Maserick, Professor of Mathematics; Ph.D., Maryland, 1960. Harmonic analysis on semigroups.

Gary L. Mullen, Professor of Mathematics; Ph.D., Penn State, 1974. Number theory and combinatorics.

Florence Newberger, S. Chowla Research Assistant Professor; Ph.D., Maryland, 1998. Ergodic theory on negatively curved manifolds.

Victor Nistor, Professor of Mathematics; Ph.D., Berkeley, 1992. Operator algebras and topology.

Adrian Ocneanu, Professor of Mathematics; Ph.D., Warwick (England), 1983. Operator algebras.

Ken Ono, Assistant Professor of Mathematics; Ph.D., UCLA, 1993. Number theory, modular forms, partitions.

Yakov Pesin, Professor of Mathematics; Ph.D., Moscow State, 1979. Dynamical systems and ergodic theory.

John Roe, Professor of Mathematics; D.Phil., Oxford, 1984. Index theory, coarse geometry, C*-algebras, topology.

Dmitry Roytenberg, S. Chowla Research Assistant Professor; Ph.D., Berkeley, 1999. Symplectic and Poisson geometry, representation theory, deformation theory, supermanifolds, mathematical physics.

Jie Shen, Associate Professor of Mathematics; Ph.D., Paris Sud, 1987. Numerical analysis, applied mathematics.

David A. Sibley, Associate Professor of Mathematics; Ph.D., Caltech, 1972. Algebra, group theory.

Stephen G. Simpson, Professor of Mathematics; Ph.D., MIT, 1971. Mathematical logic, foundations of mathematics.

Gregory Swiatek, Professor of Mathematics; Ph.D., Warsaw, 1987. Dynamical systems.

Simon J. Tavener, Associate Professor of Mathematics; Ph.D., Oxford, 1986. Computational and experimental fluid dynamics.

Arkady Tempelman, Professor of Mathematics and Statistics; Ph.D., Vilnius, 1975. Ergodic theory, statistics.

Boris Tsygan, Professor of Mathematics; Ph.D., Moscow State, 1987. Cyclic homology, K-theory, Riemann-Roch and index theorems, algebraic topology and quantum groups.

Leonid N. Vaserstein, Professor of Mathematics; Ph.D., Moscow State, 1969. Algebraic K-theory.

Robert C. Vaughan, Professor of Mathematics; Ph.D., London, 1970. Analytic number theory.

Roger P. Ware, Professor of Mathematics; Ph.D., California, Santa Barbara, 1970. Algebraic theory of quadratic forms and infinite Galois theory.

William C. Waterhouse, Professor of Mathematics; Ph.D., Harvard, 1968. Algebra, number theory, affine group schemes, history of mathematics.

Howard Weiss, Associate Professor of Mathematics; Ph.D., Maryland, 1986. Dynamical systems.

Jinchao Xu, Professor of Mathematics; Ph.D., Cornell, 1989. Applied mathematics, numerical analysis.

Ping Xu, Associate Professor of Mathematics; Ph.D., Berkeley, 1990. Symplectic geometry and mathematical physics.

Yuri Zarhin, Professor of Mathematics; Ph.D., Leningrad (Russia), 1986. Algebraic geometry.

SELECTED PUBLICATIONS

Andrews, G., F. J. Dyson, and D. R. Hickerson. Partitions and indefinite quadratic forms. *Invent. Math.* 91:391–407, 1988.

Andrews, G., and F. G. Garvan. Dyson's crank of a partition. *Bull. Am. Math. Soc.* 18:167–71, 1988.

Andrews, G. The fifth and seventh order mock theta functions. *Trans. Am. Math. Soc.* 293(1):113–34, 1986.

Arnold, D. N., and R. Falk. A uniformly accurate finite element method for the Reissner-Mindlin plate. *SIAM J. Numer. Anal.* 26:1276–90, 1989.

Arnold, D. N., and F. Brezzi. Mixed and nonconforming finite element methods: Implementation, postprocessing and error estimates. *Math. Mod. Numer. Anal.* 19:7–32, 1985.

Arnold, D. N., F. Brezzi, and M. Fortin. A stable finite element for the Stokes equations. *Calcolo* 21:337–44, 1984.

Banyaga, A. The structure of classical diffeomorphism groups. In *Mathematics and Its Applications,* vol. 400. Dordrecht: Kluwer Academic Publishers, 1997.

Banyaga, A., R. de la Llave, and E. Wayne. Cohomology equations and commutators of germs of contact diffeomorphisms. *Trans. Am. Math. Soc.* 312(2):755–78, 1989.

Banyaga, A. Sur la structure du groupe des diffeomorphismes qui preservent une forme symplectique. *Comment. Math. Helv.* 53:174–227, 1978.

Baum, P., A. Connes, and **N. Higson.** Classifying space for proper actions and K-theory of group C* algebras. In *C*-Algebras: 1943–1993 A Fifty Year Celebration, Contemporary Mathematics,* 167:241–91, ed. R. Doran. Providence: AMS, 1994.

Baum, P., and R. Douglas. K homology and index theory. *Proc. Symp. Pure Math.,* 38:117–73. Providence: AMS, 1982.

Baum, P., W. Fulton, and R. MacPherson. Riemann-Roch for singular varieties. *Publ. Math. IHES.* 45:101–67, 1975.

Belmonte, A., H. Eisenberg, and E. Moses. From flutter to tumble: Inertial drag and Froude similarity in falling paper. *Phys. Rev. Lett.* 81:345–8, 1998.

Flesselles, J.-M., **A. Belmonte,** and V. G'asp'ar. Dispersion relation for waves in the Belousov-Zhabotinsky reaction. *J. R. Chem. Soc. Faraday Trans.* 94:851–6, 1998.

Belmonte, A. Buoyant plumes and internal waves: Two experiments in turbulent convection. In *Turbulence at Ultra-High Rayleigh and Reynolds Numbers: A Status Report,* eds. R. J. Donnelly and K. R. Sreenivasan. New York: Springer, 1998.

Berlyand, L. V., and J. Wehr. Nongaussian limiting behavior of the percolation threshold in a large system. *Commun. Math. Phys.,* in press.

Berlyand, L. V., and J. Xin. Large time asymptotics of solution of a model combustion system with critical nonlinearity. *Nonlinearity* 8:161–78, 1995.

Berlyand, L. V., and S. M. Kozlov. Asymptotics for homogenized moduli for elastic chessboard composite. *Arch. Ration. Mechanics Anal.* 118:95–112, 1992.

Brownawell, D. Bounds for the degrees in the Nullstellensatz. *Ann. Math.* 126:577–91, 1987.

Beukers, F., **D. Brownawell,** and G. Heckman. Siegel normality. *Ann. Math.* 127:279–308, 1987.

Brownawell, D., and D. W. Masser. Multiplicity estimates for analytic functions 1. *J. Reine Angew. Math.* 314:200–16, 1980.

Brylinski, J. L. Loop spaces, characteristic classes and geometric quantization. In *Progress Math.,* vol. 107. Boston: Birkhaüser, 1993.

Brylinski, J. L. A differential complex for Poisson manifolds. *J. Diff. Geom.* 28:93–114, 1988.

Brylinski, J. L., and M. Kashiwara. Kazhdan-Lusztig conjecture and holonomic systems. *Invent. Math.* 64:387–410, 1981.

Brylinski, R., and B. Kostant. Lagrangian models of minimal representations of E6, E7 and E8. In *Gelfand Festschrift, PM,* 131:13–63. Boston: Birkhaüser, 1995.

Brylinski, R., and B. Kostant. Nilpotent orbits, normality, and Hamiltonian group actions. *J. Am. Math. Soc.* 7:269–98, 1994.

Brylinski, R. Limits of weight spaces, Lusztig's q-analogs, and fiberings of adjoint orbits. *J. Am. Math. Soc.* 2:517–33, 1989.

Burago, D., S. Ferleger, and A. Kononenko. Uniform estimates for the number of collisions in semi-dispersing billiards. *Ann. Math.,* in press.

Burago, D., and S. Ivanov. Riemannian Tori without conjugate points are flat. *Geom. Funct. Anal.* 3(4):259–69, 1994.

Burago, D. Periodic metrics. In *Progress in Nonlinear Differential Equations,* pp. 90–5, ed. H. Brezis. Boston: Birkhaüser, 1993.

Calderer, M. C., and B. Mukherjee. On Poiseuille flow of liquid crystals. *Liq. Cryst.* 22:121–36, 1997.

Calderer, M. C., and B. Mukherjee. Chevron patterns in liquid crystal flows. *Physica D* 98:201–24, 1996.

Calderer, M. C. Radial motions of viscoelastic shells. *J. Diff. Eq.* 63:289–305, 1986.

Cao, W., and L. E. Cross. Theory of tetragonal twin structure in ferroelectric perovskite with first order phase transition. *Phys. Rev. B* 44:5–12, 1991.

Cao, W., and G. R. Barsch. Landau-Ginzburg model of interface boundaries in improper ferroelastic perovskites of D4h symmetry. *Phys. Rev. B* 41:4334–48, 1990.

Cao, W., and J. A. Krumhansl. Continuum theory of 4mm-2mm proper ferroelastic transition under inhomogeneous stress. *Phys. Rev. B* 42:4334–40, 1990.

Chen, M., et al. **(J. Shen).** The incremental unknowns-multilevel scheme for the simulation of turbulent channel flows. In *Proceedings of 1996 Summer Program, Center for Turbulence Research,* pp. 291–308. NASA Ames/Stanford University, 1996.

Chen, M., and R. Temam. Incremental unknowns in finite differences: Condition number of the matrix. *SIAM J. Matrix Anal. Appl.* 14(2):432–55, 1993.

Chen, M., and R. Temam. Incremental unknowns for solving partial differential equations. *Numer. Math.* 59:255–71, 1991.

Deutsch, F., and H. Hundal. The rate of convergence for the method of alternating projections II. *J. Math. Anal. Applic.* 205:381–405, 1997.

Deutsch, F. The angle between subspaces of a Hilbert space. In *Recent Developments in Approximation Theory,* pp. 107–30, ed. S. P. Singh. Boston: Kluwer Academic Publishers, 1995.

Deutsch, F., and H. Hundal. The rate of convergence of Dykstra's cyclic projections algorithm: The polyhedral case. *Numer. Funct. Anal. Optimiz.* 15:537–65, 1994.

Dolgopyat, D. On decay of correlations in Anosov flows. *Ann. Math.,* in press.

Dolgopyat, D. Bounded orbits of Anosov flows. *Duke J. Math.* 87:87–114, 1997.

Dolgopyat, D., and V. Sidorov. Multifractal properties of sets of zeroes of Brownian paths. *Fundam. Math.* 147:157–71, 1995.

Higson, N., and G. Kasparov. Operator K-theory for groups which act properly and isometrically on Hilbert space. *ERA Am. Math. Soc.* 3:131–42, 1997.

Higson, N., and **J. Roe.** On the coarse Baum-Connes conjecture. In *Proceedings of the 1993 Oberwolfach Conference on the Novikov Conjecture. London Math. Soc. Lecture Notes* 227:227–54, 1995.

Connes, A., and **N. Higson.** Déformations, morphismes asymptotiques et K-théorie bivariante. *Comptes Rendus Acad. Sci. Paris* 311:101–6, 1990.

James, D., and C. Maclachlan. Fuchsian subgroups of Bianchi groups. *Trans. Am. Math. Soc.* 348:1989–2002, 1996.

James, D. The number of embeddings of quadratic S-lattices. In *K-theory and Algebraic Geometry: Connections with Quadratic Forms and Division Algebras, Proc. Sympos. Pure Math.,* 58.2:265–74. Providence: AMS, 1995.

James, D. Integral sums of squares in algebraic number fields. *Am. J. Math.* 113:129–46, 1991.

Jech, T. Multiple forcing. In *Cambridge Tracts in Mathematics.* Cambridge: Cambridge University Press, 1986.

Pennsylvania State University

Selected Publications (continued)

Jech, T. *Set Theory.* New York: Academic Press, 1978.

Jech, T. Non-provability of Souslin's hypothesis. *Commentationes Mathematicae Universitatis Carolinae* 8:291–305, 1967.

Katok, A., and B. Hasselblatt. *Introduction to the Modern Theory of Smooth Dynamical Systems.* Cambridge: Cambridge University Press, 1995.

Katok, A., and J.-M. Strelcyn. Smooth maps with singularities, invariant manifolds, entropy and billiards. In *Springer Lecture Notes in Math.,* vol. 1222. New York: Springer-Verlag, 1986.

Katok, A. Entropy and closed geodesics. *Erg. Th. Dynam. Sys.* 2(3-4):339–66, 1982.

Katok, S., and P. Sarnak. Heegner points, cycles and Maass forms. *Israel J. Math.* 84(1-2):193–227, 1993.

Katok, S. *Fuchsian Groups.* Chicago: University of Chicago Press, 1992.

Katok, S. Closed geodesics, periods and arithmetic of modular forms. *Invent. Math.* 80:469–80, 1985.

Li, L. C. The SVD flows on generic symplectic leaves are completely integrable. *Adv. Math.* 128:82–118, 1997.

Li, L. C. On the complete integrability of some Lax equations on a periodic lattice. *Trans. Am. Math. Soc.* 349:331–72, 1997.

Li, L. C. Long time behaviour of an infinite particle system. *Commun. Math. Phys.* 110:617–23, 1987.

Li, W. *Number Theory with Applications.* Singapore: World Scientific, 1996.

Li, W. Character sums and abelian Ramanujan graphs. *J. Number Theory* 41:199–214, 1992.

Gerardin, P., and **W. Li.** Degree two monomial representations of local Weil groups. *J. Reine Angew. Math.* 394:1–30, 1989.

Liu, C., M. C. Calderer, and K. Voss. Radical configurations of smectic A materials and focal conics. *Phys. D* 124:11–22, 1998.

Liu, C., and F.-H. Lin. Nonlinear dissipative systems modeling the flow of liquid crystals. *Commun. Pure Appl. Math.* XLVIII:501–37, 1995.

Cohen, S. D., **G. Mullen,** and P. J. S. Shiue. The difference between permutation polynomials over finite fields. *Proc. Am. Math. Soc.* 123:2011–5, 1995.

Laywine, C. F., **G. Mullen,** and G. Whittle. D-dimensional hypercubes and the Euler and MacNeish conjectures. *Monatsh. Math.* 119:223–38, 1995.

Nistor, V. Cyclic cohomology of crossed products by algebraic groups. *Invent. Math.* 112:615–38, 1993.

Nistor, V. A bivariant Chern-Connes character. *Ann. Math.* 138:555–90, 1993.

Nistor, V. Group cohomology and the cyclic cohomology of crossed products. *Invent. Math.* 99:411–24, 1990.

Kohnen, W., and **K. Ono.** Indivisibility of class numbers of imaginary quadratic fields and orders of Tate-Shafarevich groups of elliptic curves with complex multiplication. *Invent. Math.,* in press.

Ono, K., and C. Skinner. Fourier coefficients of half integral weight modular forms modulo 1. *Ann. Math.* 147:451–68, 1998.

Ono, K., and K. Soundararajan. Ramanujan's ternary quadratic form. *Invent. Math.* 130:415–54, 1997.

Pesin, Y. Dimensionlike characterizations for invariant sets of the dynamical systems. *Russ. Math. Surveys* 43(4):111–51, 1988.

Pesin, Y. Characteristic Lyapunov exponents and smooth ergodic theory. *Russ. Math. Surveys* 32(4):506–15, 1977.

Pesin, Y. Geodesic flows on closed Riemannian manifolds without focal points. *Math. USSR Izvestija* 11(6):1195–228, 1977.

Shen, J. On error estimates of penalty method for unsteady Navier-Stokes equations. *SIAM J. Numer. Anal.* 32:386–403, 1995.

Shen, J. Efficient spectral Galerkin method II. Direct solvers of the second order and fourth order equations by using Chebyshev polynomials. *SIAM J. Sci. Comput.* 16:74–87, 1995.

Shen, J. Hopf bifurcation of the unsteady regularized driven cavity flows. *J. Comput. Phys.* 95:228–45, 1991.

Simpson, S. G. On the strength of König's duality theorem for countable bipartite graphs. *J. Symbolic Logic* 59:113–23, 1994.

Simpson, S. G. Partial realizations of Hilbert's program. *J. Symbolic Logic* 53:349–63, 1988.

Simpson, S. G., editor. Logic and combinatorics. In *Contemporary Mathematics,* vol. 65. Providence: AMS, 1987.

Graczyk, J., and **G. Swiatek.** Induced expansion for quadratic polynomials. *Ann. Scient. Éc. Norm. Sup.* 29:399–482, 1996.

Graczyk, J., and **G. Swiatek.** Critical circle maps near bifurcation. *Commun. Math. Phys.* 176:227–60, 1996.

Swiatek, G. Rational rotation numbers for maps of the circle. *Commun. Math. Phys.* 119:109–28, 1988.

Ware, R. Valuation rings and rigid elements in fields. *Can. J. Math.* 33:1338–55, 1981.

Knebusch, M., A. Rosenberg, and **R. Ware.** Structure of Witt rings and quotients of abelian group rings. *Am. J. Math.* 94:119–55, 1972.

Ware, R. Endomorphism rings of projective modules. *Trans. Am. Math. Soc.* 155:233-56, 1971.

Waterhouse, W. A counterexample for Germain. *Am. Math. Monthly* 101:140–50, 1994.

Waterhouse, W. Composition of norm-type forms. *J. Reine Angew. Math.* 353:85–97, 1984.

Waterhouse, W. Introduction to affine group schemes. *Graduate Texts Math.,* vol. 66. New York: Springer-Verlag, 1979.

Knieper, G., and **H. Weiss.** An example of a surface with positive curvature and positive topological entropy. *J. Diff. Geom.* 39:229–49, 1994.

Weiss, H. Non-smooth geodesic flows and the earthquake flow on Teichmuller space. *Erg. Theory Dynam. Sys.* 9:571–86, 1989.

Knieper, G., and **H. Weiss.** Differentiability of measure theoretic entropy I. *Invent. Math.* 95:579–89, 1989.

Xu, J. An auxiliary space preconditioning technique with applications to unstructured grids. *Computing* 56:215–35, 1996.

Xu, J. Iterative methods by space decomposition and subspace correction. *SIAM Rev.* 34(4):581–613, 1992.

Bramble, J., J. Pasciak, and **J. Xu.** Parallel multilevel preconditioners. *Math. Comp.* 55(191):1–22, 1990.

Xu, P. Noncommutative Poisson algebras. *Am. J. Math.* 116:101–25, 1994.

Xu, P., and A. Weinstein. Classical solutions of the quantum Yang-Baxter equations. *Commun. Math. Phys.* 148:309–43, 1992.

Xu, P. Morita equivalence of Poisson manifolds. *Commun. Math. Phys.* 142:493–509, 1991.

Silverberg, A., and **Y. Zarhin.** Semistable reduction and torsion subgroups of abelian varieties. *Annales de l'Institut Fourier* 45:403–20, 1995.

Silverberg, A., and **Y. Zarhin.** Connectedness results for l-adic representations associated to abelian varieties. *Compositio Math.* 97:273–84, 1995.

Zarhin, Y. A finiteness theorem for unpolarized Abelian varieties over number fields with prescribed places of bad reduction. *Invent. Math.* 79:309–21, 1985.

PRINCETON UNIVERSITY

Program in Applied and Computational Mathematics

Program of Study	Situated physically and intellectually between the mathematics department and the sciences and engineering, the program offers a small number of highly qualified students the opportunity to obtain a thorough knowledge of the branches of mathematics that are indispensable for applications in science and engineering, with emphasis on the use of computers in numerical analysis as well as less traditional computations.
	The general examination, designed as a sequence of interviews with assigned professors, covers three subject areas of applied mathematics and culminates in a seminar on a research topic. The seminar is delivered toward the end of the fourth semester.
	The doctoral dissertation may consist of a mathematical contribution to some field of science or engineering or to the development or analysis of mathematical or computational methods that are useful for, inspired by, or relevant to science or engineering.
	Satisfactory completion of the requirements leads to the degree of Doctor of Philosophy (Ph.D.) in applied and computational mathematics.
Research Facilities	Computing facilities located in Fine Hall include SGI high-performance workstations, Personal IRISes, Indigo IIs, Crimsons, Sun SPARCstations, X terminals, Apple Power Macintoshes, color graphic capabilities, and color and black and white laser printers. Access to supercomputers and high-level workstations is available to students at the discretion of their advisers. In addition, there are numerous public workstation clusters throughout the campus.
	The library system at Princeton University has more than 12 million holdings throughout the campus. In addition to Firestone Library, the main library, there are eight special science branch libraries: Fine Hall, Engineering, Astrophysics, Biology, Chemistry, Geology, Population Research, and Plasma Physics. Fine Hall Library supports the teaching and research of the mathematics and physics departments with 900 journal subscriptions, more than 50,000 monographs, more than 50,0000 bound journals, pamphlets, and theses. Princeton subscribes to selective e-journals (140 e-journals in mathematics and physics).
Financial Aid	The type of financial support awarded to a student is determined by the program and the graduate school. Two principal sources of graduate student financial support are University-sponsored fellowships and service awards. Service awards consist of assistantships in research and teaching assistantships. Such awards cover tuition and provide academic year stipends, with additional summer support available. The average stipend for the academic year 1999–2000 is $14,000. Applicants are also encouraged to apply for support from external agencies and programs.
Cost of Study	See the financial aid section above.
Living and Housing Costs	Estimated 1999–2000 costs for rooms at the Graduate College range from $2312 to $4027 for the academic year of thirty-five weeks. Several meal plans are available and are priced from $2529 to $3638. University apartments for married students rent for $485 to $755 per month. Accommodations are also available in the surrounding community.
Student Group	Princeton University has 1,800 graduate students, 4,600 undergraduates, and 993 faculty members. The program enrollment is between 15 and 22 students. A wide variety of academic, ethnic, and national backgrounds are represented among the students.
Student Outcomes	Examples of recent graduate placement are two postdoctoral fellowships, IMA, University of Minnesota; a Wylie Instructorship, University of Utah; two research associates, Courant Institute of Mathematical Sciences, NYU; a research staff member for a management firm; a principal at a technical science consulting firm; a research staff member, Los Alamos National Laboratory; an associate, J. P. Morgan; and a program manager, Microsoft. Since 1995, 3 students have received NSF Mathematical Sciences Postdoctoral Fellowships.
Location	Princeton University and the surrounding community provide an exciting and rich environment for study and research. Centrally located on the Northeast Corridor, Princeton is easily accessible by bus, train, and highway. Convenient air service is provided by the international airports in Newark, New York, and Philadelphia. Numerous major corporations maintain their research and corporate offices in the surrounding area. The Institute for Advanced Study, Rutgers University, the Educational Testing Center, the Gallup Organization, AT&T Laboratories, Bell Labs Innovations/Lucent Technologies, NEC Siemens, and the *Wall Street Journal* are a few neighboring institutions.
	The town of Princeton, a charming university community, offers its residents a repertory theater, orchestras, ballet, chamber music, choral groups, art galleries, cinemas, shops, and restaurants. Additional cultural and sporting events are just a short distance away in New York City and Philadelphia.
The University	Princeton University was founded in 1746 as the College of New Jersey. The name was changed in 1896 to Princeton University at the 150th anniversary of its founding. The Graduate School was formally established in 1900 and is presently the home of more than 1,800 graduate students who are engaged in the study of arts and sciences, engineering, architecture, and public affairs.
Applying	Application procedures are set forth in the *Application and Guide to Graduate Admission,* which is available upon request from the Office of Graduate Admissions, Princeton University, P. O. Box 270, Princeton, New Jersey 08544-0270. The deadline for applying is traditionally the first week in January for the academic year that starts the following September. Applications are considered without regard to sex, race, creed, color, national origin, religion, age, or handicap.
Correspondence and Information	Director of Graduate Studies Program in Applied and Computational Mathematics Princeton University 204 Fine Hall, Washington Road Princeton, New Jersey 08544-1000 Telephone: 609-258-3008

Princeton University

THE FACULTY AND THEIR RESEARCH

Ingrid Daubechies (Director). Wavelets, signal processing, image reconstruction.
René Carmona. Stochastic processes and PDEs, signal processing, image analysis.
Philip J. Holmes. Dynamical systems, nonlinear mechanics of fluids and solids.
Yannis G. Kevrekidis. Computational nonlinear dynamics, numerical bifurcation theory.
Paul D. Seymour. Graph and matroid theory, discrete optimization.
H. Mete Soner. Nonlinear partial differential equations, stochastic optimal control, financial engineering.
Sergio Verdu. Information theory, communication theory.

Associated Faculty

Dilip Abreu. Dynamic games, bargaining.
Yacine Ait-Sahalia. Derivative pricing, interest rate models, nonparametric methods.
Michael Aizenman. Probability theory, statistical physics.
Demetrios Christodoulou. Partial differential equations, general relativity, fluid dynamics.
Erhan Cinlar. Random phenomena in engineering, optimal control of stochastic processes.
Francis A. Dahlen. Seismic wave propagation, mechanics of mountain building.
Bradley W. Dickinson. Linear and nonlinear system theory, estimation theory and random processes, signal processing.
David P. Dobkin. Computer graphics, analysis of algorithms, computational geometry.
Christodoulos A. Floudas. Local and global optimization, process control, process design.
John Hopfield. Biological computation, neural networks, dynamics.
Sergiu Klainerman. Partial differential equations, general relativity.
John A. Krommes. Nonlinear theories of plasma turbulence and transport.
Simon A. Levin. Spatial heterogeneity and problems of scale; evolutionary, mathematical, and theoretical ecology.
Elliott Lieb. Mathematical physics, analysis.
Luigi Martinelli. Computational fluid dynamics.
H. Vincent Poor. Statistical signal processing, signal detection and estimation, multiple-access digital communications.
Jean-Herve Prevost. Computational solid mechanics, porous media, finite elements methods.
Herschel A. Rabitz. Quantum mechanics, collision theory, nonlinear systems.
Yakov G. Sinai. Dynamical systems, phase transition, statistical mechanics.
Burton H. Singer. Stochastic processes and statistical methods in biology, epidemiology, and social sciences.
Salvatore Torquato. Random heterogeneous media, statistical mechanics, image science.
Robert J. Vanderbei. Constrained optimization, probability theory, and stochastic control.
Michael D. Woodford. Mathematical economics, economic dynamics.

The program in applied and computational mathematics shares Fine Hall with the mathematics department.

PURDUE UNIVERSITY

Department of Mathematics

Programs of Study	The Department of Mathematics offers programs leading to the degrees of Master of Science and Doctor of Philosophy. There are several programs leading to the Master of Science degree, some of which prepare the student to seek nonacademic employment; others prepare the student to continue to the Ph.D. degree. The interdisciplinary Computational Science and Engineering Program gives students the opportunity to study mathematics and computing in a multidisciplinary environment. The Master of Science and CS&E degree programs each require 30 hours of course work. Another master's degree program, the Computational Finance Program, requires 35 hours of course work.
	There are no required oral or written examinations, and a thesis is not required. A student with a half-time teaching assistantship normally takes two years to complete the master's degree program.
	Among the requirements for the Ph.D. are a minimum of 42 hours of graduate work, reading knowledge in one foreign language, passing written qualifying examinations and an oral specialty examination, writing a thesis, and passing a final oral examination based on the thesis. A student with a half-time teaching assistantship would require a minimum of four years to complete the Ph.D. program, and most students spend five or six years in the program.
Research Facilities	The Mathematics Library, located in the Mathematical Sciences Building, features an outstanding collection of research journals and reference materials in pure and applied mathematics. The department maintains a network of more than sixty Sun Workstations, several high-performance scientific computing and graphics workstations, and equipment for high-quality graphics output. Supported software includes TEX, Macaulay, MACSYMA, Maple, Mathematica, and MATLAB. University facilities for research computing include an Intel Paragon parallel supercomputer.
Financial Aid	Beginning graduate students who intend to work toward the Ph.D. degree and who supply application material by February 1 will be considered for fellowships. Andrews Fellowships provide a tax-free, twelve-month stipend of $16,680 and are renewable for a second year. The department also makes nominations for Master's and Doctoral Graduate Opportunities Fellowships, which also provide a tax-free, twelve-month stipend of $16,680 and which are renewable for one year contingent upon satisfactory progress. Final selection for Graduate Opportunity Fellowships is made by University committees. All three of these fellowships are supplemented by $819, paid in twelve monthly payments, to purchase medical insurance. A limited number of department fellowships are available each year.
	A number of graduate teaching assistantships are available with stipends ranging from $11,500 to $15,500 per academic year (1999–2000), depending on duties. Half-time positions are available in the summer for assistants who perform satisfactorily in course work and assistantship duties.
	For advanced students, research fellowships are available for both the summer and the academic year.
Cost of Study	Students holding any of the fellowships or assistantships described above receive remission of tuition and fees (in 1999–2000, $1812 per semester for Indiana residents and $6124 per semester for nonresidents), except for $320 each semester and $160 for the summer session.
Living and Housing Costs	Unmarried students may live in one of two graduate dormitories. The minimum cost is $8.15 per day for a double room and $10.75 per day for a single room. The University operates 1,300 apartments for married students. Monthly rates range from $322 to $409, depending on the type of accommodations. These rates normally include heat, gas, water, and electricity, but not telephone.
Student Group	Purdue has approximately 30,000 undergraduate students and 6,500 graduate students. There are 106 graduate students in mathematics, nearly all of whom receive financial support.
Student Outcomes	The majority of Ph.D. program graduates seek and obtain academic positions. In recent years, these included positions at such universities as Michigan, Minnesota, Brigham Young (Hawaii), Wayne State, Seoul National University, National Chiao Tung University, Penn State (Berks Campus), Courant Institute, New Mexico State University, and Rice. Some positions are tenure track, while others are postdoctoral. A few Ph.D. students in pure and applied mathematics have obtained positions in industry or the government at INTEL and the National Security Agency or on Wall Street. Many master's program students continue on to the Ph.D. program, while others enter industry or the government.
Location	Purdue's main campus is located on 650 acres in the city of West Lafayette, Indiana, across the Wabash River from Lafayette. The population of the two cities exceeds 70,000. Amtrak and major bus lines serve the Greater Lafayette area. Two airlines, Northwest Airlink and United Express, operate out of the Purdue Airport. Purdue is 60 miles northwest of Indianapolis, the state capital, and 126 miles southeast of Chicago. The West Lafayette campus offers a wide variety of cultural and recreational opportunities for graduate students and their families.
The University	During the past decade, Purdue has ranked high among American universities in awarding the Doctor of Philosophy degree. The Graduate School is nationally recognized as being in the top category for the competence of its faculty and the quality of its graduates in the broad life science area, engineering, and basic physical sciences and mathematics.
Applying	Application forms may be obtained by writing to the Mathematics Graduate Office. There is a $30 application fee. Completed applications for assistantships beginning in the fall semester should be received before March 15. Assistantships are usually not available in the spring semester. Completed applications for fellowships should be received by February 1. Applicants should arrange to take the General Test and the Subject Test in Mathematics of the Graduate Record Examinations so that scores are received by the department before February 1. A minimum TOEFL score of 570 is required for all applicants whose native language is not English. An official score report not more than two years old must be submitted. Purdue does not discriminate against qualified handicapped persons in any of its programs or activities.
	Purdue is an Equal Opportunity/Equal Access university.
Correspondence and Information	Graduate Committee Chairman Department of Mathematics 1395 Mathematical Sciences Building Purdue University West Lafayette, Indiana 47907-1395
	Telephone: 765-494-1961 Fax: 765-494-0548 E-mail: gcomm@math.purdue.edu World Wide Web: http://www.math.purdue.edu/

Purdue University

THE FACULTY AND THEIR RESEARCH

S. Abhyankar, Professor; Ph.D., Harvard, 1955. Algebraic geometry.
C. D. Aliprantis, Professor; Ph.D., Caltech, 1973. Functional analysis, mathematical economics.
D. Arapura, Professor; Ph.D., Columbia, 1985. Algebraic geometry.
S. Archava, Research Assistant Professor; Ph.D., UCLA, 1999. Algebraic geometry.
L. Avramov, Professor; Ph.D., Moscow State, 1975. Commutative algebra.
R. Bañuelos, Professor; Ph.D., UCLA, 1984. Probability and its applications to harmonic analysis, partial differential equations, spectral theory and geometry.
P. Bauman, Professor; Ph.D., Minnesota, 1982. Partial differential equations, applied mathematics.
J. Becker, Professor; Ph.D., Michigan, 1964. Algebraic topology.
S. Bell, Professor; Ph.D., MIT, 1980. Several complex variables.
E. Belogay, Research Assistant Professor; Ph.D., Georgia Tech, 1998. Applied analysis, wavelets, algorithms.
M. Benjamin, Associate Professor; Ph.D., Moscow, 1971. Group representations.
L. Berkovitz, Professor; Ph.D., Chicago, 1951. Control theory.
D. Boyd, Research Assistant Professor; Ph.D., Illinois, 1998. Complex variables.
L. de Branges, Professor; Ph.D., Cornell, 1957. Number theory, complex analysis, operator theory, functional analysis.
J. Brown, Professor; Ph.D., Michigan, 1979. Complex variables.
L. Brown, Professor; Ph.D., Harvard, 1968. Operator algebras, operator theory.
Z. Cai, Associate Professor; Ph.D., Colorado, 1990. Numerical analysis, applied mathematics.
D. Catlin, Professor; Ph.D., Princeton, 1978. Several complex variables.
C. Cowen, Professor; Ph.D., Berkeley, 1976. Operator theory, complex analysis, linear algebra.
J. Cushman, Professor; Ph.D., Iowa State, 1978. Applied mathematics.
M. Dadarlat, Associate Professor; Ph.D., UCLA, 1991. Operator algebras.
B. Davis, Professor; Ph.D., Illinois, 1968. Probability.
H. Donnelly, Professor; Ph.D., Berkeley, 1974. Differential geometry.
J. Douglas, Professor; Ph.D., Rice, 1952. Computational modeling, numerical analysis.
D. Drasin, Professor; Ph.D., Cornell, 1966. Complex variables, potential theory.
D. Dugger, Research Assistant Professor; Ph.D., MIT, 1999. Algebraic topology.
A. Eremenko, Professor; Ph.D., Rostov (USSR), 1979. Complex analysis, dynamical systems.
Z. Feng, Assistant Professor; Ph.D., Arizona State, 1994. Mathematical biology, applied mathematics.
A. Gabrielov, Professor; Ph.D., Moscow State, 1973. Real algebraic and analytic geometry.
N. Garofalo, Professor; Ph.D., Minnesota, 1987. Partial differential equations, harmonic analysis.
W. Gautschi, Professor; Ph.D., Basel (Switzerland), 1953. Numerical analysis.
D. Goldberg, Associate Professor; Ph.D., Maryland, 1991. Representation theory.
D. Gottlieb, Professor; Ph.D., UCLA, 1962. Algebraic topology, mathematical physics.
S. Gupta, Professor; Ph.D., North Carolina, 1956. Statistics.
G. Harel, Professor; Ph.D., Ben-Gurion (Israel), 1985. Mathematics education.
W. Heinzer, Professor; Ph.D., Florida State, 1966. Commutative algebra.
R. Hunt, Professor; Ph.D., Washington (St. Louis), 1965. Harmonic analysis.
I. Kontoyiannis, Assistant Professor; Ph.D., Stanford, 1998. Probability, stochastic processes.
L. Lempert, Professor; Ph.D., Eötvös Loránd Tudományegyetem (Budapest), 1979. Complex analysis.
J. Lipman, Professor; Ph.D., Harvard, 1965. Algebraic geometry.
L. Lipshitz, Professor; Ph.D., Princeton, 1972. Logic, algebra.
B. Lucier, Professor; Ph.D., Chicago, 1981. Numerical analysis, wavelets.
J. Ma, Associate Professor; Ph.D., Minnesota, 1992. Probability.
K. Matsuki, Associate Professor; Ph.D., Columbia, 1988. Algebraic geometry.
J. McClure, Professor; Ph.D., Chicago, 1978. Topology.
F. Milner, Professor; Ph.D., Chicago, 1983. Numerical analysis, applied mathematics.
T. Moh, Professor; Ph.D., Purdue, 1969. Algebraic geometry.
C. Neugebauer, Professor; Ph.D., Ohio State, 1954. Harmonic analysis.
L. Ni, Research Assistant Professor; Ph.D., California, Irvine, 1998. Global analysis, analysis on manifolds.
R. Penney, Professor; Ph.D., MIT, 1971. Group representations, harmonic analysis, several complex variables.
D. Phillips, Professor; Ph.D., Minnesota, 1981. Partial differential equations.
J. Price, Professor; Ph.D., Pennsylvania, 1956. Orthogonal expansions.
P. Protter, Professor; Ph.D., California, San Diego, 1975. Probability.
J. Rice, Professor; Ph.D., Caltech, 1959. Applied mathematics, numerical analysis.
H. Rubin, Professor; Ph.D., Chicago, 1948. Statistics.
J. E. Rubin, Professor; Ph.D., Stanford, 1955. Logic, set theory.
A. Sa Barreto, Associate Professor; Ph.D., MIT, 1988. Partial differential equations.
S. Samuels, Professor; Ph.D., Stanford, 1964. Probability theory and applications.
J. Santos, Associate Professor; Ph.D., Chicago, 1983. Numerical analysis, applied mathematics.
F. Shahidi, Professor; Ph.D., Johns Hopkins, 1975. Automorphic forms.
Q. Shen, Research Assistant Professor; Ph.D., Penn State, 1998. Applied mathematics.
B. Shipley, Assistant Professor; Ph.D., MIT, 1995. Algebraic topology.
J. Smith, Associate Professor; Ph.D., MIT, 1981. Algebraic topology.
W. Studden, Professor; Ph.D., Stanford, 1962. Probability and statistics.
J. Thurber, Professor; Ph.D., NYU, 1961. Applied mathematics.
Y. L. Tong, Professor; Ph.D., Johns Hopkins, 1970. Complex manifolds.
J. Wang, Professor; Ph.D., Cornell, 1966. Lie groups.
S. Weingram, Associate Professor; Ph.D., Princeton, 1962. Algebraic topology.
A. Weitsman, Professor; Ph.D., Syracuse, 1968. Complex variables.
V. Weston, Professor; Ph.D., Toronto, 1956. Applied mathematics, inverse problems.
C. Wilkerson, Professor; Ph.D., Rice, 1970. Algebraic topology.
L.- M. Yeh, Visiting Associate Professor; Ph.D., Purdue, 1994. Applied mathematics.
S. K. Yeung, Associate Professor; Ph.D., Columbia, 1989. Differential geometry, complex manifolds.
N. K., Yip, Assistant Professor; Ph.D., Princeton, 1996. Partial differential equations.
E. Zachmanoglou, Professor; Ph.D., Berkeley, 1962. Partial differential equations.

PURDUE UNIVERSITY

Department of Statistics

Programs of Study	The Master of Science programs with emphases in applied statistics, statistics and computer science, or in computational finance serve students' interests in careers as statisticians or operations analysts in industry and government. These degree programs do not require a thesis and are usually completed in two years. Students in the programs are encouraged to participate in the department's consulting service.
	The Doctor of Philosophy program in statistics prepares students for careers in university teaching and research or in government or industrial research. Students take a three-semester core program in probability and theoretical and applied statistics in preparation for general examinations. Specialized study and thesis research in the student's chosen area follows. Students are encouraged to strengthen their training through advanced courses and participation in statistical consulting. Completion of the Ph.D. program normally takes four or five years.
Research Facilities	The Department of Statistics is housed in the Mathematical Sciences Building along with the Department of Mathematics. This building contains faculty and graduate student offices, seminar rooms, classrooms, the Mathematical Sciences Library, and the Computing Center. The library contains 57,000 volumes and subscribes to 550 journals in mathematics and related fields.
	The Department of Statistics has a network of IBM RS/6000 servers and workstations and Pentium Pro PCs. Access is available through departmental computers to an Intel Paragon supercomputer. Graduate students can access the departmental IBM RS/6000 servers using X terminals in their offices, through one of the X terminals or PCs in one of the statistics labs or elsewhere on campus, through dial-up access, or from anywhere on the Internet. Statistical software packages maintained on departmental computers include SAS, SPSS, BMDP, S-Plus, Mathematica, Maple, and Matlab. Other software packages are available through the Purdue University Computing Center (PUCC). The Statistics Department Instructional Computer Laboratory contains Pentium PCs equipped with CD-ROM drives.
	The equipment is maintained by PUCC, a full-time Computer Systems Administrator, a Web master, and two part-time Assistant Computer Systems Administrators.
Financial Aid	Most students have half-time teaching assistantships. For 1999–2000, most have a minimum stipend of $13,000 for the fall and spring semesters, plus reduction of tuition and fees to approximately $320 per semester. Purdue University fellowships are available to entering students on a competitive basis; the fellowship stipend for 1999–2000 is $20,000 for one year, with tuition and fees reduced as above. The fellowships may be renewed for one year for students with good records. Summer assistantships are also available.
Cost of Study	In 1999–2000, tuition is $3624 per year for Indiana residents and $12,248 per year for out-of-state students. Students with assistantships and fellowships pay $640 per year.
Living and Housing Costs	Dormitory rooms in University-supervised graduate residences range from $280 to $530 per month in 1999–2000. Meals in the campus cafeterias are served al a carte and therefore the prices per month vary. The cost of one- or two-bedroom unfurnished apartments in Married Student Housing ranges from $402 to $505 per month. Off-campus rates are comparable.
Student Group	Purdue University has about 6,000 graduate students. The Department of Statistics has about 65 graduate students, with about 30 working toward the Ph.D. About one third are female and about two thirds are international students. Many of the American students begin graduate work immediately after the B.S. Some enter after the M.S., and a few have some work experience.
	The Graduate Student Organization (GSO) is a group concerned with the input and opinions of graduate students on matters such as department policy, course requirements, and new course creation. All students admitted to the department are automatically members. The organization also serves as a social group, introducing new members to each other and to previous members related to Purdue University and the immediate area.
Location	Purdue University is the principal institution in West Lafayette, Indiana, which has a population of 26,000. In the larger Lafayette–West Lafayette area (population, 130,000), there are several other large organizations. Although Lafayette is an industrial town, it retains the atmosphere of an agricultural county seat. However, there are shopping malls, restaurants of note, two hospitals, and two large municipal parks. The Purdue University Airport (LAF) is served by United Airlines and Northwest Airlines. Community groups present plays, operettas, and musical programs several times each year, and the University offers musical, dramatic, and athletic events that may be attended by the general public. Several state parks are close to Lafayette.
The University and The Department	Purdue University, the land-grant college of Indiana, has achieved international recognition in the areas of agriculture, engineering, and science. The West Lafayette campus of Purdue enrolls about 36,000 students. Purdue University is an Equal Opportunity/Affirmative Action employer.
	The Department of Statistics is one of the seven departments that constitute Purdue's School of Science. The department's faculty members interact with other faculty members and graduate students through teaching, research, and a statistical consulting service. The faculty quality has been consistently ranked among the top ten statistics departments in the country by the National Research Council Surveys.
Applying	Application materials and information may be obtained from the department. An applicant's mathematical training should include linear algebra and advanced calculus; probability and mathematical statistics are desirable.
	Applications for Purdue University fellowships should be received before February 1. Other applications are considered at any time, although the availability of assistantships becomes limited after mid-April.
Correspondence and Information	Department of Statistics 1399 Mathematical Sciences Building Purdue University West Lafayette, Indiana 47907-1399 Telephone: 765-494-5794 E-mail: graduate@stat.purdue.edu World Wide Web: http://www.stat.purdue.edu

Purdue University

THE FACULTY AND THEIR RESEARCH

Mary Ellen Bock, Head (Illinois at Urbana-Champaign). Function estimation using wavelets, statistical computing, genome analysis.
Tony Cai (Cornell). Nonparametric function estimation, statistical decision theory.
Bruce Craig (Wisconsin–Madison). Markov chain Monte Carlo methods, Bayesian analysis, statistical computing.
Anirban DasGupta (Indian Statistical Institute). Decision theory, mathematical statistics, applied probability.
Burgess Davis (Illinois at Urbana-Champaign). Probability.
Rebecca Doerge (North Carolina State). Statistical issues in quantitative genetics, resampling methods, regression.
Jayanta K. Ghosh (Calcutta). Bayesian analysis, asymptotics, stochastic modeling.
Chong Gu (Wisconsin). Statistical computing, nonparametric estimation.
Shanti S. Gupta (North Carolina). Selection and ranking, decision theory, reliability, order statistics.
Ioannis Kontoyiannis (Stanford). Probability theory, stochastics processes, information theory, data compression, nonparametrics.
Thomas Kuczek (Purdue). Experimental design, response surface alternatives to Taguchi, probability models in biology.
Steven P. Lalley (Stanford). Ergodic theory, probability, and applications to dynamical systems and geometry.
George P. McCabe (Columbia). Applied statistics, biostatistics, linear models.
David S. Moore (Cornell). Statistical education, applied statistics.
Philip Protter (California, San Diego). Probability theory: stochastic integration and differential equations; finance theory; numerical analysis of SDEs; weak convergence.
Herman Rubin (Chicago). Mathematical statistics, probability theory, numerical methods, robustness, decision theory.
Stephen M. Samuels (Stanford). Probability theory and applications, dynamic optimization, disclosure risk assessment for microdata.
Thomas Sellke (Stanford). Sequential analysis, probability theory.
Katy Simonsen (Cornell). Statistical genetics, coalescent models, linkage analysis.
William J. Studden (Stanford). Optimal designs, spline smoothing, canonical moments.

RECENT PUBLICATIONS

Bock, M. E., and G. Pliego. Using a Daubechie wavelet in nonparametric regression. *Am. Stat. Assoc. Stat. Comp. Stat. Graphics Newslett.* 3(2):27–34, 1992.

Cai, T., and D. Brown. Wavelet shrinkage for nonequispaced samples. *Ann. Stat.,* 26:1783–99, 1998.

Craig, B., et al. Analysis of aerial survey on Florida manatee using Markov Chain Monte Carlo. *Biometrics* 53:129–46, 1997.

DasGupta, A., and W. E. Strawderman. All estimates with a given risk, Ricati differential equations, and a new proof of a theorem of Brown. *Ann. Stat.* 25:1208–21, 1997.

Davis, B., and D. McDonald. An elementary proof of the Local Central Limit Theorem. *J. Theor. Probability* 8:693–701, 1995.

Doerge, R., Z. -B. Zeng, and B. S. Weir. Statistical issues in the search for genes affecting quantitative traits in experimental populations. *Stat. Sci.* 12(3):195–219, 1997.

Ghosh, J. K., and B. Clarke. Convergence of posterior given sample mean. *Ann. Stat.* 23:2116–44, 1995.

Gu, C. Smoothing spline density estimation: Conditional distribution. *Stat. Sin.* 5:709–26, 1995.

Gupta, S. S., and K. J. Miescke. Bayesian look ahead one-stage sampling allocations for selection of the best population. *J. Stat. Plann. Inf.* 54:229–44, 1996.

Kontoyiannis, I. Asymptotic recurrence and waiting times for stationary processes. *J. Theoretical Probabability* 11:795–811, 1998.

Kuczek, T., and T. C. K. Chan. The rate-normal model for tumor drug resistance. *Cancer Chemo. Pharm.* 30:355–9, 1992.

Lalley, S. P. Falconer's formula for the Hausdorff dimension of a self-afine set in R^2. *Ergodic Theory Dynamical Syst.* 15:77–97, 1995.

McCabe, G. P., et al. Dietary calcium, protein, and phosphorous are related to bone mineral density and content in young women. *Am. J. Clin. Nutr.* 68:749–54, 1998.

Moore, D. S. Statistics among the liberal arts. *J. Am. Stats. Assoc.* 93:1253–9, 1998.

Protter, P., and J. Jacod. Asymptotic error distributions for the Euler method for stochastic differential equations. *Ann. Probability* 26:267–307, 1998.

Rubin, H., and **K. S. Song.** Exact computation of the asymptotic efficiency of maximum likelihood estimators of discontinuous signal in a Gaussian white noise. *Ann. Stat.* 23:732–9, 1995.

Samuels, S. M. A Bayesian species-sampling-inspired approach to the uniques problem in microdata disclosure risk assessment. *J. Official Stats.* 14:1998.

Sellke, T., and **S. P. Lalley.** Hyperbolic branching Brownian motion. *Probability Theory Related Fields* 108:171–92, 1997.

Simonsen, K., and G. A. Churchill. A Markov chain model of coalescence with recombination. *Theoretical Popul. Biol.* 52:43–59, 1997.

Studden, W. J., and H. Dette. *The Theory of Canonical Moments.* New York: John Wiley & Sons, 1997.

Graduate students after a successful GSO meeting.

RENSSELAER POLYTECHNIC INSTITUTE

Department of Decision Sciences and Engineering Systems

Programs of Study

Rensselaer recognized the need for a new endeavor in decision sciences by forming a unique interdisciplinary department, Decision Sciences and Engineering Systems (DSES), within the Schools of Engineering, Management, and Science. The objectives of the department are to conduct research that leads to a better understanding of how information technology and quantitative analysis and modeling can support individuals, groups, and organizations in problem solving and decision making and to prepare engineers to design, develop, and implement complex decision support systems. In order to accomplish these objectives, knowledge from disciplines such as systems and industrial engineering, statistics, probability, operations research, information systems, artificial intelligence, computer science, and economics must be extended and integrated. The department combines degree programs in industrial and management engineering, manufacturing systems engineering, and operations research and statistics.

Concentrations available through DSES master's programs include data mining, financial engineering, information systems, management, quality engineering, service systems, simulation, systems engineering, systems modeling, and transportation systems. The Master of Science program requires 30–33 credit hours, including required and elective courses. Among the required courses is a 6-credit-hour master's project or thesis. The M.Eng. program is a nonthesis degree intended for professional practice. A student with an accredited B.S. or its equivalent can typically complete this 30–33 credit program in one year.

The Master of Science and Master of Engineering program in operations research and statistics focus on mathematical modeling and statistical techniques applicable to a wide range of practical problems connected with business, economic, social, and engineering systems. Students learn the theories, methodologies, and applications that underlie a range of analytical and optimization approaches. The program requires 30–33 credit hours, which may include 6 credit hours of a research project.

The Master of Science and Professional Master of Engineering programs in manufacturing systems engineering require 30–33 credit hours of study and focus on manufacturing issues, with concentrations in manufacturing quality systems, manufacturing systems modeling, manufacturing processes and technology, manufacturing information systems, and management systems. The program prepares students to deal with problems related to product design for manufacturability, operations analysis, the design of integrated manufacturing systems (planning, scheduling, and control), financial, organizational, and strategic management issues, and many elements of automation.

The Doctor of Philosophy program in decision sciences and engineering systems requires 90 credit hours of graduate studies (60 credits after a master's degree) with specialization either in industrial engineering, information systems, manufacturing systems engineering, operations research, or statistics. In addition to the course work, the program includes a qualifying examination, concentration area requirements, a candidacy examination, and a dissertation requirement.

Research Facilities

The DSES department has two strategic research thrusts: intelligent manufacturing and service systems, and data mining and decision support. The department is located in the George M. Low Center for Industrial Innovation, which also houses the Center for Advanced Technology in Automation, Robotics and Manufacturing; Center for Integrated Electronics and Electronics Manufacturing; and Rensselaer's Electronic Agile Manufacturing Research Institute. This proximity provides a symbiotic environment conducive to excellence in research. Other resources include an advanced computer graphics facility, a general industrial engineering laboratory, a teaching factory emulation laboratory, and an artificial intelligence facility.

Financial Aid

Financial aid is available in the form of teaching assistantships and scholarships. The stipend for assistantships ranged up to $10,980 for the 1999–2000 academic year. Tuition waivers may also be granted. Outstanding students may qualify for University-supported Rensselaer Scholar Fellowships, which carry a stipend of $15,000 and a full tuition scholarship. Low-interest, deferred-repayment graduate loans are also available for U.S. citizens with demonstrated need.

Cost of Study

Tuition for 1999–2000 is $665 per credit hour. Other fees amount to approximately $535 per semester. Books and supplies cost about $1700 per year.

Living and Housing Costs

The cost of rooms for single students in residence halls or apartments ranges from $3356 to $5298 for the 1999–2000 academic year. Family student housing apartments, with monthly rents of $592 to $720, are available.

Student Group

There are about 4,300 undergraduates and 1,750 graduate students representing all fifty states and more than eighty countries at Rensselaer.

Student Outcomes

Eighty-eight percent of Rensselaer's 1998 graduate students were hired after graduation with starting salaries that averaged $56,259 for master's degree recipients and $57,000–$75,000 for doctoral degree recipients.

Location

Rensselaer is situated on a scenic 260-acre hillside campus in Troy, New York, across the Hudson River from the state capital of Albany. Troy's central Northeast location provides students with a supportive, active, medium-sized community in which to live; an easy commute to Boston, New York, and Montreal; and some of the country's finest outdoor recreation sites, including Lake George, Lake Placid, and the Adirondack, Catskill, Berkshire, and Green mountains. The Capital Region has one of the largest concentrations of academic institutions in the United States. Sixty thousand students attend fourteen area colleges and benefit from shared activities and courses.

The University

Founded in 1824 and the first American college to award degrees in engineering and science, Rensselaer Polytechnic Institute today is accredited by the Middle States Association of Colleges and Schools and is a private, nonsectarian, coeducational university. Rensselaer has five schools—Architecture, Engineering, Management, Science, and Humanities and Social Sciences. The School of Engineering ranks among the top twenty engineering schools nationally by the *U.S. News & World Report* survey and is ranked in the top ten by practicing engineers.

Applying

Admissions applications and all supporting credentials should be submitted well in advance of the preferred semester of entry. GRE General Test scores are required. The application fee is $35. Since the first departmental awards are made in February and March for the next full academic year, applicants requesting financial aid are encouraged to submit all required credentials by February 1 to ensure consideration.

Correspondence and Information

For written information about graduate study:

Student Operations Coordinator
Department of Decision Sciences
   and Engineering Systems
Rensselaer Polytechnic Institute
110 8th Street
Troy, New York 12180-3590
Telephone: 518-276-6681
E-mail: dses@rpi.edu
World Wide Web: http://www.rpi.edu/dept/
   dses/www/homepage.html

For applications and admissions information:

Director of Graduate Academic and Enrollment
   Services, Graduate Center
Rensselaer Polytechnic Institute
110 8th Street
Troy, New York 12180-3590
Telephone: 518-276-6789
E-mail: grad-services@rpi.edu
World Wide Web: http://www.rpi.edu/dept/dses/www/

Rensselaer Polytechnic Institute

THE FACULTY AND THEIR RESEARCH

J. L. Adler, (civil engineering); Ph.D., California at Irvine. Intelligent transportation systems, traveler information systems, driver behavior models, network algorithms, knowledge-based systems.

D. Berg, Institute Professor; Ph.D., Yale. Management of technological organizations, innovation, policy, manufacturing strategy, robotics, policy issues of research and development in the service sector.

R. J. Burke, Associate Professor; Ph.D., Massachusetts. Total quality management, industrial statistics, production management and process improvement, process reengineering.

J. G. Ecker, Professor; Ph.D., Michigan. Mathematical programming, multiobjective programming, geometric programming, mathematical programming applications, ellipsoid algorithms.

M J. Embrechts, Associate Professor; Ph.D., Virginia Tech. Neural networks, mathematical programming, artificial intelligence, systems engineering, computational cybernetics, data analysis.

R. J. Graves, Professor; Ph.D., SUNY at Buffalo. Manufacturing systems modeling and analysis, facilities planning and material handling system design, scheduling systems, concurrent engineering and design for manufacture, continuous flow manufacturing systems design.

J. Haddock, Professor; Ph.D., Purdue. Simulation, manufacturing/production and robotics and financial systems.

S. S. Heragu, Associate Professor and Director of Undergraduate Program; Ph.D., Manitoba. Artificial intelligence, cellular manufacturing, expert systems, facility design, flexible manufacturing systems, group technology, manufacturing systems, mathematical programming, operations research, plant layout, process planning, production and operations management.

C. Hsu, Professor and Director of Doctoral Program; Ph.D., Ohio State. Large-scale information systems, database and knowledge-based systems, computerized manufacturing, probabilistic programming and scheduling.

G. List, Professor; Ph.D., Pennsylvania. Real-time control of transportation network operations; multiobjective routing, scheduling, and fleet sizing; operations planning; hazardous materials logistics.

C. J. Malmborg, Professor and Acting Chair; Ph.D., Georgia Tech. Applied mathematical modeling, facility design, materials handling, material flow systems, manufacturing systems modeling and analysis, vehicle routing and scheduling.

M. Raghavachari, Professor; Ph.D., Berkeley. Statistical inference, quality control, multivariate methods, scheduling problems.

N. Shang, Assistant Professor; Ph.D., Berkeley. Computational statistics, statistical inference, design of experiments, data analysis.

G. R. Simons, Professor; Ph.D., Rensselaer. Managerial policy and organization.

P. Sullo, Associate Professor; Ph.D., Florida State. Reliability, life testing, and quality assurance; biostatistics; policy and risk analysis.

J. M. Tien, Professor and Acting Dean, School of Engineering; Ph.D., MIT. Systems modeling, queuing theory, public policy and decision analysis, computer performance evaluation, information and decision support systems, expert systems, computational cybernetics.

W. A. Wallace, Professor; Ph.D., Rensselaer. Public management and systems, decision support systems, expert systems.

J. W. Wilkinson, Professor Emeritus; Ph.D., North Carolina. Applied statistics, design of experiments, regression modeling, data analysis, statistical quality control.

T. R. Willemain, Associate Professor; Ph.D., MIT. Probabilistic modeling, data analysis, forecasting.

Research and Adjunct Faculty

W. J. Foley, Clinical Associate Professor; Ph.D., Rensselaer. Engineering design, computer simulation modeling, health applications of operations research, health-care policy analysis.

M. Grabowski, Research Associate Professor; Ph.D., Rensselaer. Management information systems, expert systems.

M. Kupferschmid, Adjunct Associate Professor; Ph.D., Rensselaer; PE. Mathematical programming, algorithm performance evaluation, engineering applications.

D. Sandhu, Adjunct Associate Professor; Ph.D., Toronto. Stochastic models in operations research, complex queuing networks and their applications to communication and manufacturing systems.

P. Witbeck, Adjunct Lecturer, DSES; M.S., Rensselaer. Industrial safety and hygiene.

Affiliated Faculty

A. A. Desrochers, Professor; Ph.D., Purdue. Nonlinear systems, robotics, control of automated manufacturing systems.

F. Dicesare, Professor Emeritus; Ph.D., Carnegie Mellon. Mathematical modeling, information systems, microprocessor applications.

W. R. Franklin, Associate Professor; Ph.D., Harvard. Computational geometry, graphics, CAD, cartography, parallel algorithms, large databases, expert systems.

D. H. Goldenberg, Associate Professor; Ph.D., Florida. Corporation finance and investment.

D. A. Grivas, Professor; Ph.D., Purdue. Geostochastics, applications of probability to the description of soil behavior, statistical analysis of soil parameters, numerical methods in geotechnical engineering, reliability analysis of soil structures and foundations.

J. E. Mitchell, Associate Professor; Ph.D., Cornell. Mathematical programming, combinatorics, nonlinear programming.

J. R. Norsworthy, Professor; Ph.D., Virginia. Economics of productivity, productivity measurements, industrial economics.

A. S. Paulson, Professor; Ph.D., Virginia Tech. Risk management, financial models, multivariate statistics, time series and forecasting, survival data analysis.

Major Research Activities

Material flow systems: design of automated guided vehicle systems, material flow system design, cellular manufacturing systems, vehicle routing and scheduling, automated storage and retrieval systems.

Flexible assembly systems: concurrent engineering, flow-line scheduling, workstation-based assembly system design.

Quality systems: multivariable control charting, nonparametric process control methods, experimental design methods for quality systems, reliability engineering, statistical computing.

Manufacturing and service facility design: modeling the relationship between product, facility, and logistical system design; development of imbedded design algorithms; forecasting models and decision support systems; storage systems modeling.

Modeling: modeling science, simulation, queuing, optimization, stochastic programming, neural networks, computational intelligence.

Information systems: knowledge/expert systems, decision support systems, performance evaluation, multicriteria decision making.

Management systems: management of technological organizations, management information/organizational systems, disaster management, health management/policy, project management, public systems and transportation management.

Rensselaer Polytechnic Institute

SELECTED PUBLICATIONS

Berg, D., et al. Key success factors affecting choice in an emergent technology base. In *Proceedings of the Portland International Conference on Management of Engineering and Technology,* p. 221, Portland, Oregon, July 27–31, 1997.

Berg, D., and E. Alef. *The Learning Factory.* University Press, 1996.

Berg, D., S. T. Walsh, R. L. Boylan, and A. Paulson. The dynamic nature of core capabilities in the semiconductor silicon industry. *IAMOT,* 1996.

Haberle, K., **R. J. Burke,** and **R. J. Graves.** A note on measuring parallelism in concurrent engineering. *Int. J. Production Res.,* in press.

Burke, R. J., J. M. Tien, and P. D. Santos. A retrospective multi-period sampling approach. In *Proceedings of the 1997 IEEE International Conference on Systems, Man and Cybernetics,* pp. 1781–6, Orlando, Florida, October 1997.

Kewley, R. Jr., **M. J. Embrechts,** and C. M. Breneman. Neural network analysis for data strip mining problems. In *Intelligent Engineering Systems Through Artificial Neural Networks,* vol. 8, pp. 391–6. New York: ASME Press, 1998.

Embrechts, M. J., R. Kewley Jr., and C. M. Breneman. Computationally intelligent data mining for the automated discovery of novel pharmaceuticals. In *Intelligent Engineering Systems Through Artificial Neural Networks,* vol. 8, pp. 397–403. New York: ASME Press, 1998.

Embrechts, M. J., and C. Breneman. Data mining with neural networks for the prediction and understanding of molecular properties. In *Proceedings of the 215th American Chemical Society National Meeting,* Dallas, Texas, March 29, 1998.

Embrechts, M. J., and R. H. Kewley. Fuzzy genetic decision optimization for positioning of military combat units. In *Proceedings of the IEEE International Conference on Systems, Man and Cybernetics,* October 1998.

Embrechts, M. J. A hitchhiker's guide to backpropagation. In *Intelligent Engineering Systems Through Artificial Neural Networks,* vol. 7, pp. 1037–43. New York: ASME Press, 1997.

Embrechts, M. J. Neural networks for data mining. In *Intelligent Engineering Systems Through Artificial Neural Networks,* vol. 7, pp. 741–6, eds. C. H. Dagli et al. New York: ASME Press, 1997.

Embrechts, M. J., and S. Benedek. Identification of nuclear power plant transients with neural networks. In *Proceedings of SMC'97,* pp. 912–7, Orlando, Florida, October 12–15, 1997.

Embrechts, M. J., M. J. Luetzelschwab, F. DiCesare, and M. C. Mattina. Neural networks for embedded control designs applied to the smarter car. In *Emergent Computing Methods in Engineering Design: Applications of Genetic Algorithms and Neural Networks,* pp. 136–49, eds. D. Grierson and P. Hajela. Springer Verlag, 1996.

Embrechts, M. J., and S. Benedek. Rapid identification of nuclear power plant transients with artificial neural networks via Fourier transformed signals. In *Intelligent Engineering Systems Through Artificial Neural Networks, Volume 6: Smart Engineering Systems: Neural Networks, Fuzzy Logic and Evolutionary Programming,* pp. 903–8, eds. C. Dagli et al. New York: ASME Press, 1996.

Embrechts, M. J., V. Sankaran, R. P. Kraft, and D. L. Millard. IMAGINET: A novel probabilistic neural network for rapid multi-scale image classification. In *Intelligent Engineering Systems Through Artificial Neural Networks, Volume 6: Smart Engineering Systems: Neural Networks, Fuzzy Logic and Evolutionary Programming,* pp. 431–6, eds. C. Dagli et al. New York: ASME Press, 1996.

Embrechts, M. J., and S. Goel. Qualification of shape characteristics by using neural nets. In *Intelligent Engineering Systems Through Artificial Neural Networks, Volume 6: Smart Engineering Systems: Neural Networks, Fuzzy Logic and Evolutionary Programming,* pp. 459–66, eds. C. Dagli et al. New York: ASME Press, 1996.

Foley, W. R., et al. Taking charge: The role of nursing administrators in removing restraints. *J. Nurs. Administration* 27(3):42–8, 1997.

Grabowski, M. R., et al. Using system simulation to model the impact of human error in a maritime system. *Safety Sci.* 30:235–47, 1998.

Grabowski, M. R., and K. Roberts. Risk mitigation in large scale systems: Lessons from high reliability organizations. *California Manage. Rev.* 39(4):1–11, 1997.

Grabowski, M. R. Safety brokering: Seven lessons learned for maritime safety. In *Proceedings of the Marine Safety Council,* pp. 43–52, summer 1997.

Grabowski, M. R. Safety brokering: Borrowing lessons learned for maritime safety. In *Proceedings of the Marine Safety Council* 54:3. Washington, D.C.: U.S. Coast Guard, 1997.

Grabowski, M. R., T. Fowler, and J. Harrald. Overview of the Prince William Sound risk assessment project. In *Proceedings of the Institute of Marine Engineers Conference,* London, May 17–18, 1997.

Grabowski, M. R., et al. *Prince William Sound Risk Assessment Final Report.* Cleveland, Ohio: BP Oil Shipping Company, U.S.A., 1996.

Subbu, R., A. C. Sanderson, C. Hocaoglu, and **R. J. Graves.** Evolutionary intelligent agents for distributed virtual design. *Production Plann. Control,* in press.

Haberle, K., and **R. J. Graves.** Cycle time estimation for printed circuit board assemblies. In *IEEE Transactions on Components, Packaging and Manufacturing Technology,* in press.

Agrawal, A., and **R. J. Graves.** A distributed systems model for estimation of printed circuit board fabrication costs. *Production Plann. Control,* in press.

Graves, R. J., et al. (eds.). J. S. Kochhar agile manufacturing layout design. In *Progress in Material Handling Research: 1998,* pp. 281–96. Ann Arbor, Mich.: Braun-Brumfield, Inc., 1999.

Graves, R. J. A retrospective view of recent research literature in material handling. In *Progress in Material Handling Research: 1999,* eds. L. F. McGinnis, D. Medeiros, R. E. Ward, and M. E. Wilhelm. Material Handling Institute, 1999.

Graves, R. J., and C. Lucarelli. Bibliography on material handling. *Material Handling Industry,* vol. 7, 1999.

Graves, R. J., et al. (eds.). *Progress in Material Handling Research.* Ann Arbor, Mich.: Material Handling Institute, Braun-Brumfield, Inc., 1998.

Graves, R. J., S. S. Heragu, and **C. J. Malmborg** (eds.). Design and planning integration in cellular manufacturing systems. *Ann. Operations Res.* (special issue) vol. 77, 1998.

Graves, R. J., and L. Bunde. The multi-line palletizer material flow problem: Cost analysis. In *Proceedings of the 1998 Material Handling Research Colloquium,* Phoenix, Arizona, June 1998.

Graves, R. J., and L. Bunde. Extension of the multi-line palletizer material flow problem: Cost analysis. In *Proceedings of the International Material Handling Research Colloquium* (CD-ROM), Phoenix, Arizona, June 1998.

Graves, R. J., and R. J. Milne. A new method for order release. *Int. J. Production Plann. Control* 8(4):332–42, 1997.

Graves, R. J., A. Agrawal, and K. Haberle. Estimating tools to support multi-path agility in electronics manufacturing. *IEEE CPMT Trans.* 19(1):48–56, 1996.

Taylor, G. D., J. R. English, and **R. J. Graves.** The compatibility of product quality and process flexibility. *Quality Eng.* 7(4):813–30, 1995.

Chen, J., and **S. S. Heragu.** Step-wise decomposition approaches for large scale cell formation problems. *Eur. J. Operational Res.* 113(1):64–79, 1999.

Heragu, S. S. Formation problems. *Eur. J. Operational Res.* 113(1):64–79, 1999.

Heragu, S. S., E. Chow, and F. Malik. Review of factory programs—Factory CAD, FactoryFLOW and FactoryPLAN. *IIE Trans.* 30(4):409–10, 1998.

Heragu, S. S., and J. Chen. Optimal solution of cellular manufacturing system design: Bender's decomposition approach. *Eur. J. Operational Res.* 107(1), 1998.

Kochhar, J. S., B. L. Foster, and **S. S. Heragu.** HOPE: A genetic algorithm for the unequal area layout problem. *Comput. Operations Res.* 25(8):583–94, 1998.

Kochhar, J. S., and **S. S. Heragu.** MULTI-HOPE: A tool for multiple floor layout problems. *Int. J. Production Res.* 36(12):3421–35, 1998.

Heragu, S. S., and S. Rajagopalan. Advances in discrete material handling systems design. *Sadhana* 24(2):281–92, 1997.

Heragu, S. S., and S. R Kakuturi. Grouping and placement of machine cells. *IIE Trans.* 29(7):561–71, 1997.

Heragu, S. S., and S. K. Kakuturi. An interactive program for machine grouping and layout. In *Manufacturing Decision Support Systems, Chapman and Hall Series on Manufacturing Systems,* chap. 9, pp. 180–203, eds. H. R. Parsaei, S. Kolli, and T. R. Hanley. London: Chapman and Hall, 1997.

Rensselaer Polytechnic Institute

Selected Publications (continued)

Heragu, S. S., and A. Kusiak. Machine layout problem in flexible manufacturing systems. *Operations Res.* 36(2):258–68, 1988.

Hsu, C., and S. Pant. An integrated framework for strategic information systems planning and development. *Information Resources Manage. J.* 12(1):15–25, 1998.

Hsu, C., and H. Kung. Software maintenance: A case study. In *Proceedings of the 1998 International Conference on Software Maintenance*, Washington, D.C., November 1998.

Hsu, C., and O. Schaefer. An information architecture for integrating real time process control into enterprise management. In *Manufacturing Systems Engineering Series: Integrated Product, Process and Enterprise Design*, pp. 45–63, ed. B. Wang. London: Chapman and Hall, 1997.

Hsu, C., and L. Yee. A visualization architecture for enterprise information. In *CODATA Euro-American Workshop on Visualization of Information and Data*, Paris, France, June 24–25, 1997.

Babin, G., and **C. Hsu.** Decomposition of knowledge for concurrent processing. *IEEE Trans. Knowledge Data Eng.* 8:758–72, 1996.

Cheung, W., and **C. Hsu.** The model-assisted global query system for multiple databases in distributed enterprises. *ACM Trans. Information Syst.* 14:421–70, 1996.

Hsu, C. *Enterprise Integration and Modeling.* Norwell, Mass.: Kluwer Academic Publishers, 1996.

Hsu, C., Y. Tao, M. Bouziane, and G Babin. Paradigm translations in integrated manufacturing information using a meta-model: The TSER approach. *J. Information Syst. Eng.* 1:325–52, 1993.

Hsu, C., M. Bouziane, L. Rattner, and L. Yee. Information resources management in heterogeneous distributed environments: A metadatabase approach. *IEEE Trans. Software Eng.* 17:604–25, 1991.

Malmborg, C. J. Empirical approximation of volume distance distributions for line layout problems. *Int. J. Production Res.* 37(2):375–92, 1999.

Bukhari, F., **C. J. Malmborg,** and C. McDermott. Predicting volume distance performance for layout problems with static distance functions. *Int. J. Production Res.* 36(9):2339–54, 1998.

Malmborg, C. J., and K. Al-Tassan. Analysis of storage assignment policies in less than unit load warehousing systems. *Int. J. Production Res.* 36(12):3459–75, 1998.

Malmborg, C. J., G. D. Taylor, and D. B. Pratt. *Progress in Material Handling Practice: 1995, 1996, and 1997.* Charlotte, N.C.: Material Handling Institute Press, 1998.

Malmborg, C. J., and F. Bukhari. Material flow analysis and volume distance sampling in heuristic layout procedures. *Int. J. Production Res.* 35(7):2045–63, 1997.

Malmborg, C. J., and K. Al-Tassan. Approximating work cycle times in warehousing systems. *Int. J. Ind. Eng.* 4(1):14–23, 1997.

Malmborg, C. J. An integrated materials handling model for machine location in existing facilities. *Int. J. Production Res.* 34(4):1145–59, 1996.

Malmborg, C. J. An integrated storage system evaluation model. *Appl. Math. Modeling* 20(5):359–70, 1996.

Malmborg, C. J. A genetic algorithm for service level based vehicle scheduling. *Eur. J. Operational Res.* 93(2):121–34, 1996.

Malmborg, C. J. Storage assignment policy tradeoffs. *Int. J. Production Res.* 34(2):363–78, 1996.

Mendonca, D., and **M. Raghavachari.** Comparing efficacy of ranking methods for multiple round-robin tournaments. *Eur. J. Operational Res.*, in press.

Rajendra Prasad, V., and **M. Raghavachari.** Optimal allocation of interchangeable components in a series-parallel system. *IEEE Trans. Reliability* 47:255–60, 1998.

Raghavachari, M., A. Srinivasan, and P. Sullo. Poisson mixture yield models for integrated circuits: A critical review. *Microelectronics Reliability* 37:565–80, 1997.

Liu, W., and **M. Raghavachari.** The target mean problem for an arbitrary quality characteristic distribution. *Int. J. Production Res.* 35:1713–27, 1997.

Raghavachari, M., U. Al-Turki, and J. Mittenthal. The single machine absolute deviation early-tardy problem with random completion times. *Naval Res. Logistics* 43:573–87, 1996.

Mittenthal, J., **M. Raghavachari,** and A. Rana. A class of single machine central tendency-dispersion bicriteria problems. *J. Operational Res. Soc.* 47:1355–65, 1996.

Shang, N., and N. Holland. Studies on genotoxicity of molybdenum salts in human cells in vitro and in mice in vivo. *Environ. Mol. Mutagen.* 32:251–9, 1998.

Shang, N., and N. Holland. Micronuclei in lymphocytes and exfoliated buccal cells of postmenopausal women with dietary changes in folate. *Mutat. Res.* 417:101–14, 1998.

Shang, N., and L. Zhang. Benzene metabolites induce the loss and long arm deletion of chromosomes 5 and 7 in human lymphocytes. *Leukemia Res.* 22:105–13, 1998.

Shang, N., and L. Zhang. Micronuclei and developmental abnormalities in 4-day mouse embryos after paternal treatment with acrylamide. *Environ. Mol. Mutagen.* 31:206–17, 1998.

Tien, J. M., and Y. Lee. Strategic parameter-driven routing models for multi-destination traffic in telecommunication networks. In *Proceedings of the 1997 IEEE International Conference on Systems, Man and Cybernetics,* pp. 3325–30, Orlando, Florida, October 1997.

Tien, J. M., A. Goyal, and P. Voss. Integrating uncertainty considerations in learning engineering economy. *Eng. Economist* 42(3):249–57, 1997.

Tien, J. M., and R. M. Kandadai. A knowledge-base generating hierarchical controller. *IEEE Trans. Neural Networks* 8(6):1531–41, 1997.

Tein, J. M., and **D. Berg.** Systems engineering in the growing service economy. *IEEE Trans. Syst. Man Cybern.* 25(5):721–6, May 1995.

Wallace, W. A., and G. Beroggi. *Operational Risk Management: The Integration of Decision Communications, and Multimedia Technologies.* Norwell, Mass.: Kluwer Academic Publishers, 1998.

Wallace, W. A., K. Carley, R. Cohn, and L. Waisel. The Pothole Lake fire: An analysis of emotion in a successful emergency response. *Safety Sci.* 30:183–207, 1998.

Wallace, W. A., and G. Beroggi. *Operational Risk Management.* Norwell, Mass.: Kluwer Academic Publishers, 1998.

Wallace, W. A., Y. Ikeda, and G Beroggi. Supporting multi-group emergency management with multimedia. *Safety Sci.* 30:223–34, 1998.

Wallace, W. A., D. Litynski, and **M. Grabowski.** The relationship between three dimensional imaging and group decision-making: An exploratory study. *IEEE Trans. Syst. Man Cybern.* 27(4):402–11, 1997.

Wallace, W. A., and G. Beroggi. The effects of reasoning logics on real-time decision-making. *IEEE Trans. Syst. Man Cybern.* 27(6):743–9, 1997.

Wallace, W. A., et al. The use of visual modeling in designing a manufacturing process for advanced composite structures. *IEEE Trans. Eng. Manage.* 42(3):1–10, 1995.

Wallace, W. A., and G. Beroggi. Operational control of the transportation of hazardous materials: An assessment of alternative decision models. *Manage. Sci.* 41(12):1962–77, 1995.

Wallace, W. A. (ed.). *Ethics in Modeling.* Oxford: Pergamon Press, 1994.

Park, D., and **T. R. Willemain.** Jackknife-after-jackknife. *Am. Stat.,* in press.

Willemain, T. R., W. Kroner, and J. Stark-Martin. Rensselaer's West Bend Mutual Study: Using advanced office technology to increase productivity. In *Building Evaluation Techniques.* New York: McGraw Hill, 1996.

Willemain, T. R., and G. C. Runger. Statistical process control using run sums. *J. Stat. Computation Simulation* 61:361–78.

Runger, G., and **T. R. Willemain.** Using partial ranking information in the design of small-sample comparisons. *J. Stat. Computation Simulation* 54:75–86, 1996.

RENSSELAER POLYTECHNIC INSTITUTE

Department of Mathematical Sciences

Programs of Study

The Department of Mathematical Sciences offers graduate studies leading to the Master of Science and the Doctor of Philosophy. The program of study may be selected to emphasize either mathematics or applied mathematics.

The interests of most faculty members center on applied mathematics and analysis. Applied mathematics is interpreted in the broadest possible sense, with particular emphasis on mathematical modeling; methods of applied mathematics, differential equations, and functional analysis; applications of mathematics in the physical sciences, biological sciences, and engineering; applied geometry; numerical analysis and computer science; and mathematical programming and operations research.

While specific course requirements are minimal, every doctoral program in mathematics includes advanced courses in several fundamental areas of mathematics. In addition, doctoral candidates must pass a written preliminary examination covering basic mathematical topics, pass an oral qualifying examination based on the contents of three graduate courses, pass an oral candidacy examination in their field of proposed research, and present and defend an acceptable thesis containing the results of their own research. The Ph.D. program is normally completed within about four years, and the M.S. program in two years or less.

Research Facilities

In addition to the mathematics collection in the main library, there is also a department reference collection. The department operates, jointly with the Department of Computer Science, a computational facility that houses a network of Sun Workstations, two Sequent multiprocessor computers, a hypercube, and a MasPar computer for parallel computation. Graduate students are expected to utilize the computer facilities for performance of course assignments and for computation necessary to their research.

Research is supported by such state-of-the-art facilities as the Rensselaer Libraries, whose electronic information systems provide access to collections, databases, and Internet resources from campus and remote terminals; the Rensselaer Computing System, which permeates the campus with a coherent array of advanced workstations, a shared toolkit of applications for interactive learning and research, and high-speed Internet connectivity; a visualization laboratory for scientific computation; and a high-performance computing facility that includes a 36-node SP2 parallel computer.

Financial Aid

Rensselaer Scholar and Graduate School Fellowships, competitive across the University, provide stipends of up to $15,000. These fellowships also include a full tuition and fees scholarship. Graduate assistantships, involving teaching, research, or some combination of these, provide stipends ranging up to $12,000 for the academic year, plus tuition for up to 21 credits per academic year. Special research fellowships and assistantships are available within the department to enable highly qualified graduate students to work in selected areas. These range up to $12,000 for the academic year. Additional summer support is generally available to students who have passed the preliminary examination. Full or partial tuition scholarships, low-interest loans, and part-time work are also available.

Cost of Study

Tuition for 1999–2000 is $665 per credit hour. Other fees amount to approximately $535 per semester. Books and supplies cost about $1700 per year.

Living and Housing Costs

The cost of rooms for single students in residence halls or apartments ranges from $3356 to $5298 for the 1999–2000 academic year. Family student housing, with a monthly rent of $592 to $720, is available.

Student Group

There are about 4,300 undergraduates and 1,750 graduate students representing all fifty states and more than eighty countries at Rensselaer.

Student Outcomes

Eighty-eight percent of Rensselaer's 1998 graduate students were hired after graduation, with starting salaries that averaged $56,259 for master's degree recipients and $57,000 to $75,000 for doctoral degree recipients.

Location

Rensselaer is situated on a scenic 260-acre hillside campus in Troy, New York, across the Hudson River from the state capital of Albany. Troy's central Northeast location provides students with a supportive, active, medium-sized community in which to live and an easy commute to Boston, New York, Montreal, and some of the country's finest outdoor recreation sites, including Lake George, Lake Placid, and the Adirondack, Catskill, Berkshire, and Green Mountains. The Capital Region has one of the largest concentrations of academic institutions in the United States. Sixty thousand students attend fourteen area colleges and benefit from shared activities and courses.

The University

Founded in 1824 and the first American college to award degrees in engineering and science, Rensselaer Polytechnic Institute today is accredited by the Middle States Association of Colleges and Schools and is a private, nonsectarian, coeducational university. Rensselaer's five schools—Architecture, Engineering, Management, Science, and Humanities and Social Sciences—offer a total of ninety-eight graduate degrees in forty-seven fields.

Applying

Students with quite varied backgrounds are welcomed into the program. While many of the entering graduate students have an undergraduate major in mathematics, the department welcomes students who have majored in such other areas as physics, engineering, management, and computer science and who are particularly concerned with the applications of mathematics to these fields. The GRE General Test is required and the Subject Test is desirable, particularly when requesting financial support.

Admissions applications and all supporting credentials should be submitted well in advance of the preferred semester of entry to allow sufficient time for departmental review and processing. The application fee is $35. Since the first departmental awards are made in February and March for the next full academic year, applicants requesting financial aid are encouraged to submit all required credentials by February 1 to ensure consideration. Entrance in the spring term is possible.

Correspondence and Information

For written information about graduate study:
Department of Mathematical Sciences
Graduate Admissions Committee
Rensselaer Polytechnic Institute
110 8th Street
Troy, New York 12180-3590
Telephone: 518-276-6414
E-mail: math-program@rpi.edu
World Wide Web: http://www.math.rpi.edu/index/html

For application and admissions information:
Director of Graduate Academic and Enrollment
   Services, Graduate Center
Rensselaer Polytechnic Institute
110 8th Street
Troy, New York 12180-3590
Telephone: 518-276-6789
E-mail: grad-services@rpi.edu
World Wide Web: http://www.rpi.edu

Rensselaer Polytechnic Institute

THE FACULTY AND THEIR RESEARCH

Professors
W. E. Boyce (Emeritus), Ph.D., Carnegie Mellon. Applied mathematics, random differential equations.
M. Cheney, Ph.D., Indiana. Applied mathematics, analysis, differential equations, mathematical physics, inverse problems.
D. A. Drew, Ph.D, Rensselaer. Applied mathematics, fluid mechanics, multiphase flow, semiconductor device modeling.
J. G. Ecker, Ph.D., Michigan. Mathematical programming and operations research.
B. A. Fleishman (Emeritus), Ph.D., NYU. Free boundary problems, precollege education.
G. J. Habetler, D.Sc., Carnegie Tech. Functional analysis, numerical analysis.
I. H. Herron, Ph.D., Johns Hopkins. Applied mathematics, stability of fluid flows.
M. H. Holmes, Ph.D., UCLA. Applied mathematics, mathematical physiology.
D. Isaacson, Ph.D., NYU. Mathematical physics, numerical analysis, biomedical computer imaging.
A. K. Kapila, Ph.D, Cornell. Applied mathematics, reactive fluid mechanics, combustion.
M. Levi, Ph.D., NYU. Dynamical systems, applied analysis, nonlinear ordinary differential equations.
E. H. Luchins (Emeritus), Ph.D., Oregon. Mathematics education, math psychology, history and philosophy of math.
H. W. McLaughlin II, Ph.D., Maryland College Park. Geometric modeling.
J. R. McLaughlin, Ph.D., California, Riverside. Differential equations, inverse problems, optimization.
V. Roytburd, Ph.D., Berkeley. Applied mathematics, analysis, partial differential equations.
L. A. Rubenfeld; Ph.D., NYU. Applied mathematics, mathematics and science education.
W. L. Siegmann, Ph.D., MIT. Applied mathematics, wave propagation.

Associate Professors
S. L. Cole, Ph.D., UCLA. Applied mathematics, asymptotic analysis, fluid dynamics.
G. Kovacic, Ph.D., Caltech. Applied dynamical systems, Hamiltonian dynamics, bifurcations and perturbation theory.
C. C. Lim, Ph.D., Brown. Applied mathematics, dynamical systems, theory, combinatorics.
J. E. Mitchell, Ph.D., Cornell. Mathematical programming, combinatorial optimization, operations research.
B. R. Piper, Ph.D., Utah. Computer-aided geometric design, applied geometry.
D. W. Schwendeman, Ph.D., Caltech. Scientific computing, wave propagation.

Assistant Professor
K. Bennett, Ph.D., Wisconsin–Madison. Mathematical programming, neural nets, operations research.
T. Yu, Ph.D., Stanford. Wavelets, subdivision curves and surfaces, signal and image reconstruction.

Joint Appointments with Computer Science
Professors
J. E. Flaherty, Ph.D., Polytechnic. Applied mathematics, numerical analysis.
E. H. Rogers, Ph.D., Carnegie Mellon. VLSI architectures, computer applications.

SELECTED PUBLICATIONS

Bennett, K. P., and E. Bredensteiner. Multicategory classification by support vector machines. *Comp. Optimiz. Applicat,* in press.

Bennett, K. P., and A. Demiriz. Semi-supervised support vector machines. *Advances in Neural Information Processing Systems 11,* Denver, Colorado, 1998, to appear.

Bennett, K. P., and J. Blue. Hybrid extreme point Tabu search. *Eur. J. Operat. Res.* 106:676–88, 1998.

Boyce, W. E. Differential equations in the Information Age. *Differential Equations for the Next Millennium.* ed. M. J. Kallaher, *Mathematical Association of America Notes,* to appear.

Boyce, W. E., and J. E. Ecker. The computer-oriented calculus course at Rensselaer Polytechnic Institute. *College Math. J.* 26:45–50, 1995.

Cheney, M., D. Isaacson, and J. C. Newell. Electrical Impedance Tomography. *SIAM Review 40* 85–101, 1999.

Cheney, M. Inverse boundary-value problems. *Am. Sci.* 85:448–55, 1997.

Cheney, M., and D. Isaacson. Inverse problems for a perturbed dissipative half-space. *Inv. Problems* 11:865–88, 1995.

Cole, S. L., and T. D. Strayer. Low-speed two-dimensional free surface flow past a body. *J. Fluid Mech.* 245:437–47, 1992.

Cole, S. L. A simple example from Flat Ship Theory. *J. Fluid Mech.* 189:301–10, 1988.

Drew, D. A., and S. L. Passman. *Theory of Multicomponent Fluids.* Springer-Verlag, 1998.

Drew, D. A., et al. The interaction of background ocean air bubbles with a surface ship. *Int. J. Numerical Meth. In Fluids* 28:571–600, 1998.

Drew, D. A., and H. Mandyam. Effective media theory using nearest neighbor pair distributions. Particulate Flows: Processing and Rehology, IMA Volumes In Mathematics and its Applications. eds. D. A. Drew, D. D. Joseph, and S. L. Passman. Springer-Verlag: 1998.

Ecker, J. G. *Studio Calculus.* Harper Collins College Publishers: New York, 1996.

Ecker, J. G., and J. H. Song. Optimizing a linear function over an efficient set. *J. Optimiz. Theory Applic.* 83(4), 1994.

Ecker, J. G., M. Kupferschmid, and S. P. Marin. Robot trajectory planning by nonlinear programming. *SIAM J. Sci. Stat. Comp.* 15(6):1401–12, 1994.

Flaherty, J. E., S. Adjerid, and I. Babuska. A posteriori error estimation for the finite element method-of-line solution of parabolic problems. *Math Models Meths. Appl. Sci,* to appear.

Flaherty, J. E., et al. Additive Schwarz algorithms for solving hp-version finite element systems on triangular meshes. *SIAM J. Numer. Anal.,* submitted.

Flaherty, J. E., et al. Parallel structures and dynamic load balancing for adaptive finite element computation. *Appl. Numer. Maths* 26:241–63, 1998.

Fleishman, B. A., and P. David. A discontinuous nonlinear problem: Stability and convergence of iterates in a finite number of steps. *Applicable Anal.* 23:139–57, 1986.

Fleishman, B. A., E. H. Luchins, and L. Rubenfeld. The RPI report: Appraisal of the New York State Mathematics Program. *NYS Math. Teacher J.* 35:121–7, 1985.

Habetler, G. J., and C. N. Haddad. Stability of piecewise linear generalized Volterra discrete diffusion systems with patches. *App. Math. Lett.* 12:95–9, 1997.

Habetler, G. J., and B. Szanc. Existence and uniqueness of solutions for the generalized complementary problem. *J. Optimiz. Theory Applic.* 84:103–16, 1995.

Habetler, G. J., et al. Stability analysis of higher-order time-domain paraxial equations. *J. Ac. Soc. Am.* 93:1335–46, 1993.

Herron, I. H. Spectral problems in the stability of forced solitary waves. *App. Math. Lett.* 12:19–22, 1999.

Herron, I. H., and P. R. Dwarka. The modulation equations for the asymptotic suction velocity profile and the Ekman boundary layer. *Stud. App. Math.* 96:163–81, 1996.

Herron, I. H. A simple criterion for exchange of stabilities in a model of Langmuir circulations. *Eur. J. Mech. B/Fluids* 15:771–9, 1996.

Holmes, M. H., and M. A. Haider. Indentation of a think compressible elastic layer: Approximate analytic and numerical solutions for rigid flat indenters. *J. Mech. Phys. Solids* 43:1199–219, 1995.

Holmes, M. H., J. Bell, and S. J. Bolanowski. The structure and function of pacinian corpuscles: A review. *Prog. Neurobio.* 42:79–128, 1994.

Holmes, M. H. Model of the dynamics of receptor potential in a mechanoreceptor. *J. Biosci.* 110:139–74, 1992.

Kapila, A. K., et al. Two-phase modeling of deflagration-to-detonation transition in granular materials. *Phys. Fluids* 11:378–402, 1999.

Kapila, A. K., and M. Short. Blowup in semilinear parabolic equations with weak diffusion. *Comb. Theory Model.* 2:283–91, 1998.

Kapila, A. K., et al. Two-phase modeling of DDT: Structure of the velocity relaxation zone. *Phys. Fluids* 9:3885–97, 1997.

Kovacic, G., R. Camassa, and S. K. Tin. A Melnikov method for homoclinic orbits with many pulses. *Arch. Rat. Mech. Anal.* 143:105–93, 1998.

Kovacic, G., et al. Homoclinic orbits and chaos in a second-harmonic generating optical cavity. *Phys. Lett. A* 233:203–8, 1997.

Kovacic, G., and T. J. Kaper. Multi-bump orbits homoclinic to resonance bands. *Trans. AMS* 348:3835–87, 1996.

Levi, M. A new randomness-generating mechanism in forced relaxation oscillations. *Physica D,* to appear.

Levi, M. Shadowing property of geodesics in Hedlund's metric. *Ergodyn. Theory Dynam. Sys.* 17:187–203, 1997.

Levi, M., and H. Broer. Geometrical aspects of stability theory for Hill's equations. *Arch. Rat. Mech. Anal.* 131:225–40, 1995.

Lim, C. C. Mean field theory and coherent structures for point vortices on the plane. *Phys. Fluids* 11(5):1201–7, 1999.

Lim, C. C. A long range spherical model for the Helmholtz vortex gas and the 2-D Euler equation, submitted.

Lim, C. C. Relative equilibria of symmetric N-body problems on a sphere: Inverse and direct results. *Comm. Pure Appl. Math.* LI:341–71, 1998.

Luchins, E. H. Preparation for college mathematics teaching: The West Point model from a visiting professor's perspective. *Report of the Committee on Preparation of College Teachers,* 1993.

Luchins, E. H., and A. S. Luchins. Task complexity and order effect in computer presentations of water-jar problems. *J. Gen. Psych.* 118(1):45–72, 1991.

Mitchell, J. E., P. O. Paradalos, and M. G. C. Resende. Interior point methods for combinatorial optimization. *Combinator. Optimiz.* Vol. 1, 1998.

Mitchell, J. E., and B. Borchers. Solving real-world linear ordering problems using a primal-dual interior point cutting plane method. *Ann. Op. Res.* 62:253–76, 1996.

Mitchell, J. E. An interior point column generation method for linear programming using shifted barriers. *SIAM J. Optimiz.* 4:423–40, 1994.

McLaughlin, H. W. Algorithms for geometric modeling. *Comp. Mech. Eng.* 5(3):38–41, 1986.

McLaughlin, H. W. Discrete curves: A definition of shape. *Computer Aided Geometric Design,* to appear.

McLaughlin, J. R., Y. Y. Lu, and J. Huang. Local orthogonal transformation and one-way methods for acoustic wave guides. *Wave Motion,* to appear.

McLaughlin, J. R. Inverse problems: Recovery of BF coefficients from nodes. *Inv. Problems* 14:245–73, 1998.

McLaughlin, J. R., and S. Wang. Recovery of a vertically stratified seabed in shallow water. Mathematical and Numerical Aspects of Wave Propagation. *SIAM,* 1998.

Piper, B. R., and C. Labenski. Fill in regions. *Computing Suppl.* 13, 1998.

Piper, B. R., and C. Labenski. Coils. *Computer Aided Geometric Design* Vol. 13, July, 1996.

Piper, B. R., and J. A. Roulier. Prescribing the length of rational B'ezier curves. *Computer Aided Geometric Design* Vol. 13, February, 1996.

Roythburd, V., and M. Frankel. On dynamics of exothermic interfaces. *Contemporary Math.,* submitted.

Roythburd, V., M. Frankel, and G. Sivashinsky. Complex dynamics generated by a sharp interface model of self-propagating high-temperature synthesis. *Comb. Theory Model.* 2:479–96, 1998.

Roythburd, V., et al. Finite-dimensional dynamical system modeling thermal instabilities. *Physica D,* 1997.

Rubenfeld, L. A., et al. A notebook of ideas on problems for courses I-II-III mathematics sequence. *New York State Department of Education Report.*

Rubenfeld, L. A., E. H. Luchins, and B. Fleishman. The RPI report on the New York State High School Mathematics Curriculum: Courses I-II-III. *New York State Mathematics Teachers J.* 35(3), 1985.

Rensselaer Polytechnic Institute

Selected Publications (continued)

Schwendeman, D. W. A higher order Godunov method for the hyperbolic equations modeling shock dynamics. *Proc. Royal Soc. London* A455:1215–33, 1999

Schwendeman, D. W., J. D. Cole, and S. Triantafillou. Optimization of conical wings in hypersonic flow. *J. Theoret. Comput. Aerodyn.* 12:219–32, 1998.

Schwendeman, D. W. A front dynamics approach to curvature-dependent flow. *SIAM J. App. Math.* 56:1523–8, 1996.

Siegmann, W. L., et al. Nonlinear pulse propagation in shallow-water environments with attending and dispersive sediments. *J. Acoust. Soc. Am.* 104:1356–62, 1998.

Siegmann, W. L., M. Badiey, and K. Bongiovanni. Analysis and model/data comparison of broadband acoustic propagation at the Atlantic Generating Station (AGS) site. *J. Acoust. Soc. Am.* 101:1921–35, 1997.

Siegmann, W. L., R. J. Cederberg, and W. M. Carey. Modal analysis of geoacoustic influences on shallow-water propagation. *IEEE J. Ocean Eng.* 22:237–44, 1997.

Yu, T. P.-Y. Hermite subdivision schemes: Classification, analysis and conjectures. 1999.

Yu, T. P.-Y., and D. L. Donoho. Nonlinear wavelet transform based on median-interpolation. *SIAM J. Math. Anal.,* 1998

Yu, T. P.-Y., and T. N. Goodman. Interpolation of median. *Adv. Computat. Math.,* 1998.

SOUTHERN METHODIST UNIVERSITY

Department of Mathematics

Programs of Study

The Master of Science degree in computational and applied mathematics at Southern Methodist University (SMU) requires eleven graduate courses, which can include up to three courses outside of mathematics. A comprehensive exam is given at the end of the student's last semester of course work. Courses taken for the M.S. degree prepare students for industrial employment or for further graduate work in computational and applied mathematics, engineering, and related disciplines.

The Doctor of Philosophy program in computational and applied mathematics has flexible course requirements but must include the equivalent of 54 semester hours of graduate course credit (excluding dissertation) beyond the bachelor's degree and at least 6 semester hours of dissertation. The Ph.D. qualifying examination consists of written examinations and a written paper. The examinations are based on individualized concentration courses in applied mathematics, numerical analysis, and scientific computation, and the paper is usually based on a reading course with a faculty member.

Research Facilities

The Department of Mathematics at SMU has a network of DEC Alpha servers and workstations (running Digital UNIX) and several IBM-compatible networked Pentium personal computers. Graduate student offices have X-terminals to access the UNIX machines as well as Pentium PCs. In addition, graduate students have access to several DEC Alpha servers in the University's Bradfield Computing Center as well as to a multiprocessor DEC Alpha server and Alpha server cluster located in the University's School of Engineering and Applied Sciences.

Mathematical software available to graduate students includes matlab, maple, Mathematica, NAG, IMSL, and a Lapack.

The SMU libraries, which contain more than 2.9 million volumes, comprise the largest private research library in the Southwest and rank third within the region in total volumes. The Science and Engineering Library has holdings of more than 900,000 volumes in the areas of sciences and engineering. The Electronic Reference Center provides online access to PONI (an online catalog of all holdings) and to the Internet.

Financial Aid

Teaching assistantships, which consist of a stipend and waiver of all tuition and fees, are readily available. The typical stipend is between $10,000 and $12,000, although outstanding candidates are eligible for a Dean's Award, which can increase the stipend to as much as $15,000.

Cost of Study

In 1998–99, tuition and fees for full-time graduate study were $13,474 for students without a teaching assistantship. Students with a teaching assistantship or with a tuition waiver fellowship do not pay tuition and fees.

Living and Housing Costs

The Office of Housing and Residence Life operates four residence halls designated primarily for graduate students, including three apartment buildings. Costs for these range from $400 to $500 per month; costs for off-campus housing are comparable.

Meals are available in campus cafeterias, and many restaurants and coffee shops are within easy walking distance of campus.

Student Group

Approximately 3,800 graduate and professional students are currently enrolled in Southern Methodist University. There are approximately 16 graduate students in the Computational and Applied Mathematics program, with about 30 percent working on a Ph.D. and 90 percent receiving financial aid in the form of a teaching assistantship. Approximately 30 percent are women, and 30 percent are international students.

Student Outcomes

In recent years, graduates of the M.S. program have obtained jobs at companies such as Buck Consultants, E-Systems, IBM, Nortel, Raytheon, and Texas Instruments. Job titles of some recent graduates include Analytical Services Engineer, Actuarial Assistant, Education Specialist, Technical Staff Engineer, and Software Systems Engineer.

Recent Ph.D. graduates have taken academic positions at Colorado State, Louisiana Tech, Northern Illinois, Oakland, Old Dominion, the Universities of Arkansas and Southern Mississippi, and the United States Air Force Academy and industrial positions at Arthur Andersen, BNR, Raytheon, and Texas Instruments.

Location

SMU's tree-lined, 164-acre campus is located in University Park, a residential area just 5 miles north of downtown Dallas. Neighborhood shops, restaurants, coffee shops, and banks are within easy walking distance of campus. Students who live in University Park or in the neighboring suburb of Highland Park may enroll their children in the Highland Park Independent School District, regarded as one of the best public school systems in the nation. Dallas offers a range of recreational, sports, entertainment, and cultural opportunities. The Dallas–Fort Worth International Airport is serviced by most major international airlines, with direct flights to most major cities in the U.S. and to cities in Canada, Europe, Asia, and Latin America. The Dallas–Fort Worth metroplex is one of the nation's fastest-growing areas and offers a diversified economy with many postgraduate job opportunities at a variety of high-tech companies.

The University and The Department

Southern Methodist University is a private, nonprofit, coeducational institution that was founded in 1911. SMU enrolls approximately 9,000 students and is nonsectarian in its teaching.

The Department of Mathematics is part of the Dedman College of Arts and Sciences. The graduate program has ties to the University's graduate programs in computer science, electrical engineering, mechanical engineering, and statistics.

Applying

Application materials and information may be obtained from the department by mail or electronically through the department's World Wide Web page, listed below. An applicant should have a strong background in mathematics, particularly in calculus, differential equations, numerical methods, and linear algebra. In addition, previous course experience in physics, engineering, and/or computer science is useful. Applications are considered at any time, although to receive full consideration for financial aid, applications must be submitted by March 1.

Correspondence and Information

Department of Mathematics
P.O. Box 750156
Southern Methodist University
Dallas, Texas 75275-0156

Telephone: 214-768-2506
Fax: 214-768-2355
E-mail: math@mail.smu.edu
World Wide Web: http://www.smu.edu/~math

Southern Methodist University

THE FACULTY AND THEIR RESEARCH

Kirk Brattkus, Associate Professor; Ph.D., Northwestern, 1988. Solidification, continuum theories of phase transformations, hydrodynamic stability.

Thomas Carr, Assistant Professor; Ph.D., Northwestern, 1993. Asymptotic and perturbation methods; bifurcation theory and dynamical systems theory applied to coupled oscillators, laser instabilities, and Josephson-junctions.

Zhangxin Chen, Assistant Professor; Ph.D., Purdue, 1991. Finite element method, multigrid methods, numerical solution of partial differential equations, oil reservoir simulation, semiconductor design.

Robert Davis, Associate Professor; Ph.D., Tulane, 1967. Universal algebra, logic, combinatorics, history of mathematics.

Warren Ferguson, Professor; Ph.D., Caltech, 1975. Computer arithmetic; numerical analysis; scientific computation as applied to injection lasers, special functions, and partial differential equations.

Ian Gladwell, Professor and Department Chair; Ph.D., Manchester, 1970. Mathematical software, numerical analysis (ordinary and partial differential equations, boundary value problems), parallel computation. Editor, *IMA Journal of Numerical Analysis, Computing Reviews,* and *Parallel and Distributed Computing Practices;* coeditor (with J. Cash), *Computational Ordinary Differential Equations,* Oxford University Press, 1992.

Richard Haberman, Professor; Ph.D., MIT, 1971. Nonlinear phenomena (shock and dispersive waves, solitons, dynamical systems), asymptotic and perturbation methods for ordinary and partial differential equations. Author, *Elementary Applied Partial Differential Equations (with Fourier Series and Boundary Value Problems),* Prentice Hall, 1998; coauthor (with S. Campbell), *Introduction to Differential Equations with Boundary Value Problems,* Houghton-Mifflin, 1996.

Mogens Melander, Associate Professor; Ph.D., Denmark Technical, 1983. Mathematical modeling, scientific computation, fluid dynamics, vortex dynamics turbulence.

Montie Monzingo, Associate Professor; Ph.D., 1966, Oklahoma. Abstract algebra and number theory, mathematical education.

James Nagy, Associate Professor and Graduate Advisor; Ph.D., North Carolina State, 1991. Numerical linear algebra, scientific computation, numerical solutions to discrete ill-posed problems in signal and image processing.

George W. Reddien, Professor; Ph.D., Georgia Tech, 1971. Numerical analysis, numerical bifurcation theory, boundary-value problems. Former managing editor, *SIAM Journal on Numerical Analysis.*

Douglas Reinelt, Professor and Undergraduate Advisor; Ph.D., Caltech, 1983. Scientific computation and perturbation analysis of free surface fluid problems, including fluid dynamics of bubbles and thin films, coating flows, and foam rheology.

Lawrence F. Shampine, Professor and Betty Clements Chair in Applied Mathematics; Ph.D., Caltech, 1964. Numerical analysis and computation (ordinary differential equations and mathematical software in Fortran, matlab, and maple). Coauthor (with R. Allen and S. Pruess), *Fundamentals of Numerical Computing,* J. Wiley & Sons, 1997; author, *Numerical Solution of Ordinary Differential Equations,* Chapman & Hall, 1994.

Johannes Tausch, Assistant Professor; Ph.D., Colorado State, 1995. Numerical approximation and fast methods for boundary integral equations, with applications to computational electromagnetics.

Richard Williams, Professor; Ph.D., Vanderbilt, 1965. Topology, real and complex analysis.

SOUTHERN METHODIST UNIVERSITY

Department of Statistical Science

Programs of Study

Professional statisticians, particularly those with graduate degrees, are in demand now and will continue to be offered challenging, rewarding career opportunities in the future. The Department of Statistical Science in the Dedman College of Humanities and Sciences at Southern Methodist University (SMU) has earned a reputation for excellence in preparing today's graduate students to become tomorrow's leading statisticians. It offers small classes taught by a full-time faculty of distinguished scholars, researchers, and consultants as well innovative hands-on learning experiences.

Each student in the Department of Statistical Science must pass through one or both of two phases of development. The first phase, culminating with the awarding of a Master of Science (M.S.) degree, emphasizes breadth and fundamental knowledge of a wide variety of statistical theories and applications. The second phase stresses depth, and its successful completion results in the awarding of the Doctor of Philosophy (Ph.D.) degree.

The emphasis in the master's program is on developing a fundamental breadth in both theory and applications. It generally requires two years of study beyond the baccalaureate degree. The goal of the Department of Statistical Science is for the M.S. candidate to be able to apply statistical thinking, principles, and methods in a variety of situations that may be faced upon graduation. With this in mind, the M.S. curriculum stresses applied courses and encourages the student to become knowledgeable in as many different methodologies as possible, as well as becoming adept with a variety of statistical software. Experience in the practice of statistical consulting earns course credit.

The doctoral phase of the graduate program consists of advanced courses that are required of all doctoral candidates and specialized courses in the field of intended dissertation research. Students in the doctoral phase of the program need not select an area of intended research until completion of the Ph.D. written examination, but they are encouraged to limit possible areas at the beginning of the third year so they can choose course work most closely related to their likely research area(s).

Research Facilities

Because computers have become indispensable tools in statistical analysis, the Department of Statistical Science has its own computer lab, where graduate students can complete course assignments, conduct research projects, and perform consulting assignments. The department has several SUN Workstations, an SGI graphics workstation, and more than twenty personal computers. These are connected to the University's network of computers and to state, regional, national, and international networks. These networks provide access to e-mail, national supercomputer centers, worldwide library collections, specialized databases, and the World Wide Web. Computers in the lab have the latest statistical software, including S-plus, SAS, SPSS, and IMSL, as well as a wide variety of graphic and word processing programs.

SMU's Science and Engineering Library in the Fondren Library Center has one of the most extensive collections of statistical literature in the Southwest, including more than 150 statistical and mathematical journals and all major abstracting services. Students have open-stack access. The Don Owen Library, located within the department, has more than 500 key reference books on statistics and a collection of more than twenty statistics journals.

Financial Aid

The Department of Statistical Science offers an outstanding array of teaching and research assistantships and fellowships that are awarded on the basis of academic achievement. Most full-time graduate students in the department receive teaching assistantships, which include tuition, fees, and a competitive monthly stipend. Teaching assistants conduct first-year laboratory sections in statistics or carry out some equivalent function. Outstanding candidates also are eligible for a Dean's award that provides additional assistance and summer research support, which results in a stipend of as much as $15,000.

Cost of Study

In 1998–99, tuition and fees for full-time graduate study were $13,474 for students without a teaching assistantship. Students with a teaching assistantship or with a tuition waiver fellowship do not pay tuition and fees.

Living and Housing Costs

For 1998–99, the cost of on-campus housing was $2000 per person (double occupancy) per semester. Married student housing (one-bedroom apartment) was $4000 per academic year. Other on-campus room plans are available. Board costs between $1000 and $1450 per semester.

Student Group

Of the approximately 9,500 students enrolled at SMU, about 4,000 are graduate students in the humanities, sciences, social sciences, business, arts, engineering, theology, and law. Students come from all states and many other countries.

Location

SMU is located in University Park, a residential area just 5 miles north of downtown Dallas. Beyond the campus, the Dallas area provides an abundance of affordable housing, outstanding schools, shopping, public transportation, and cultural and entertainment opportunities.

The University

Established in 1911 by the United Methodist Church, SMU is a nonsectarian institution dedicated to academic excellence and freedom of inquiry. It has six undergraduate, graduate, and professional schools.

Applying

Students of proven ability with undergraduate preparation in appropriate fields are eligible to apply. For application materials, students should contact the department at the address below.

Correspondence and Information

Department of Statistical Science
Southern Methodist University
P.O. Box 750332
Dallas, Texas 75275-0332
Telephone: 214-768-2441
Fax: 214-768-4035
E-mail: stat@mail.smu.edu
World Wide Web: http://www.smu.edu/~statistics/

Southern Methodist University

THE FACULTY AND THEIR RESEARCH

U. Narayan Bhat, Ph.D., Western Australia, 1964. Queueing theory, applied probability, stochastic processes.

William F. Christensen, Ph.D., Iowa State, 1999. Multivariate analysis, spatial statistics, nonparametric methods, resampling methods, reliability, statistical computing, analysis of environmental data, survey sampling.

Henry L. Gray, C. F. Frensley Professor of Mathematical Sciences; Ph.D., Texas, 1966. Time series, spectral estimation, prediction and forecasting, robust procedures for estimation and testing, distribution theory, integral transform theory, multivariate outlier detection, testing for trend, mixture models.

Rudy Guerra, Ph.D., Berkeley, 1991. General applied statistics with an emphasis in the biosciences and methodology, biostatistics, genetics.

Richard Gunst, Ph.D., SMU, 1972. Regression analysis, linear models, statistical design and analysis of industrial experiments, statistical methods for modeling dynamic spatiotemporal environmental processes.

Roberto Gutierrez, Ph.D., Texas A&M, 1995. Smoothing and nonparametric regression, measurement error models, semiparametrics, mixture models.

Harold J. Hietala, Ph.D., UCLA, 1973. Nonparametric statistics, robust estimation, anthropological statistics.

Chandrakant H. Kapadia, Ph.D., Oklahoma State, 1961. General methods, survey sampling theory, statistical inference, design and analysis of experiments, linear models.

Campbell B. Read, Professor Emeritus; Ph.D., North Carolina, 1969. Sequential analysis, properties of statistical distributions, medical applications, categorical data analysis, history of science, ecological statistics.

Steve Sain, Ph.D., Rice, 1994. Nonparametric function estimation, statistical computing, graphics and visualization, classification and outlier testing, data mining, environmental statistics, biostatistics.

William R. Schucany, Ph.D., SMU, 1970. Data analysis with applications in legal evidence, medical research, and survey sampling of business records; nonparametric curve estimation, local linear and kernels, and adaptive bandwidths; resampling methodology, including jackknife, bootstrap, and randomization tests.

Wayne A. Woodward, Ph.D., Texas Tech, 1974. Time-series analysis, robust estimation, statistical analysis of data related to climate change, multivariate outlier detection, testing for trend, mixture models.

TEXAS A&M UNIVERSITY

Department of Mathematics

Programs of Study

The Department of Mathematics offers both an M.S. (thesis and nonthesis) and a Ph.D. degree in mathematics. The M.S. program includes, in addition to a traditional track, the following options: applied mathematics, business/industrial mathematics, computational mathematics, mathematical finance, and mathematics teaching. Students seeking a Ph.D. receive broad exposure to graduate-level mathematics and pursue an area of specialization in their mathematical research.

Research Facilities

The Department of Mathematics is host to the Center for Approximation Theory and has strong ties to the interdisciplinary faculty members in Material Science Engineering and the Institute for Scientific Computation. The department has a 32-node Intel Paragon supercomputer and an extensive network of Sun and NeXT Workstations and X-station terminals.

Financial Aid

The majority of the graduate students in the Department of Mathematics receive financial support in the form of graduate assistantships throughout their graduate career. These assistantships are nine-month or, in some cases, twelve-month appointments with beginning stipends of $1500 per month. Highly qualified applicants may also be awarded fellowships offered through the Department of Mathematics, the Office of Graduate Studies, and other campus programs.

Cost of Study

In 1998–99, in-state tuition and fees were $1260.73 for 9 credit hours per fall and spring semester. Graduate students who have assistantships are granted out-of-state tuition waivers that allow them to pay in-state tuition and fees. Students can also expect to pay about $200 per semester for miscellaneous items.

Living and Housing Costs

Living costs vary depending on the kind of housing in which students choose to live. The average cost of a one-bedroom apartment in the Bryan/College Station area is $450 per month. Students can receive more information on available housing by contacting the Off-Campus Housing Center at 409-845-1741.

Student Group

The Department of Mathematics has approximately 100 graduate students; they are fairly evenly split between those pursuing an M.S. degree and those pursuing a Ph.D. degree. International students comprise about 40 percent of the graduate students. Approximately 85 of the graduate students are supported by the department; the others receive private funding or fellowships.

Student Outcomes

Virtually all Ph.D. and M.S. graduates obtain employment after graduation. The jobs range from tenure-track and postdoctoral academic positions at such institutions as the University of Nevada, Las Vegas; Princeton; Duke; and St. Thomas University to positions in business and industry with such companies as E Systems, Andersen Consulting, Schlumberger, Mobil, and IBM.

Location

Texas A&M University is located in College Station. The local population, excluding students but including the adjacent city of Bryan, exceeds 110,000. Bryan/College Station is located centrally among three of the country's ten largest cities—Dallas, Houston, and San Antonio.

The University

Established in 1876, Texas A&M University was the first public college in the state of Texas. It is one of a few universities holding land-grant, sea-grant, and space-grant designations. Texas A&M is the only university to be ranked nationally among the top ten in each of these areas: total enrollment, enrollment of National Merit Finalists, value of research, and endowment.

Applying

Applications for admission are accepted at any time. To apply, students must submit an application form, official transcripts, official GRE scores (international applicants also need to submit official TOEFL scores), and three letters of recommendation. Those seeking financial assistance are strongly urged to take the GRE Subject Test in mathematics as well as the required General Test.

Correspondence and Information

Graduate Programs Office
Department of Mathematics
Texas A&M University
College Station, Texas 77843-3368
Telephone: 409-862-4137
E-mail: gstudies@math.tamu.edu
World Wide Web: http://www.math.tamu.edu

Texas A&M University

THE FACULTY AND THEIR RESEARCH

G. D. Allen, Professor; Ph.D., Wisconsin–Madison, 1971. Applied mathematics.
L. Anderson, Assistant Professor; Ph.D., MIT, 1994. Manifolds and cell complexes.
D. L. Barrow, Associate Professor; Ph.D., Michigan, 1973. Partial differential equations.
G. A. Battle III, Professor; Ph.D., Duke, 1977. Mathematical physics.
G. R. Blakley, Professor; Ph.D., Maryland, 1960. Cryptography.
H. P. Boas, Professor; Ph.D., MIT, 1980. Several complex variables.
A. Boggess, Professor and Associate Head for Operations; Ph.D., Rice, 1979. Several complex variables.
I. Borosh, Professor; Ph.D., Weizmann (Israel), 1966. Number theory.
J. Bramble, Distinguished Professor; Ph.D., Maryland, 1958. Numerical analysis.
J. Bryant, Professor; Ph.D., Rice, 1965. Pattern recognition.
H.-D. Cao, Associate Professor; Ph.D., Princeton, 1986. Differential geometry.
G. Chen, Professor; Ph.D., Wisconsin, 1977. Control theory.
C. K. Chui, Distinguished Professor; Ph.D., Wisconsin, 1967. Approximation theory.
P. Daripa, Associate Professor; Ph.D., Brown, 1985. Fluid dynamics.
R. D. DeBlassie, Associate Professor; Ph.D., MIT, 1984. Probability.
D. C. Dobson, Associate Professor; Ph.D., Rice, 1990. Partial differential equations.
R. Douglas, Distinguished Professor and Provost; Ph.D., LSU, 1962. Functional analysis.
K. Dykema, Assistant Professor; Ph.D., Berkeley, 1993. Operator theory.
T. Erdelyi, Associate Professor; Ph.D., South Carolina, 1989. Approximation theory.
R. Ewing, Distinguished Professor and Dean, College of Science; Ph.D., Texas, 1974. Scientific computation.
S. A. Fulling, Professor; Ph.D., Princeton, 1972. Mathematical physics.
S. C. Geller, Professor; Ph.D., Cornell, 1975. Algebraic K-theory.
R. A. Gustafson, Associate Professor; Ph.D., Yale, 1979. Group representations.
D. J. Harfiel, Professor; Ph.D., Houston, 1969. Matrix theory.
D. A. Hensley, Professor; Ph.D., Minnesota, 1974. Number theory.
A. M. Hobbs, Professor; Ph.D., Waterloo, 1971. Graph theory.
W. B. Johnson, Distinguished Professor and Owen Chair; Ph.D., Iowa State, 1969. Functional analysis.
T. R. Kiffe, Associate Professor; Ph.D., Wisconsin, 1975. Integral equations.
H. E. Lacey, Professor; Ph.D., New Mexico State, 1963. Banach spaces.
D. R. Larson, Professor; Ph.D., Berkeley, 1976. Operator theory.
R. Lazarov, Professor; Ph.D., Moscow State, 1972. Numerical analysis.
R. Letzter, Associate Professor; Ph.D, Virginia Tech, 1986. Quantum algebra.
D. R. Lewis, Professor; Ph.D., LSU, 1970. Functional analysis.
P. Lima-Filho, Associate Professor; Ph.D., SUNY at Stony Brook, 1989. Algebraic geometry/topology.
B. Lowe, Associate Professor; Ph.D., NYU (Courant), 1986. Applied mathematics.
C. J. Maxson, Professor; Ph.D., Buffalo, 1967. Near rings.
J. McCammond, Assistant Professor; Ph.D., Berkeley, 1991. Group theory.
J. J. Morgan, Associate Professor and Associate Head for Undergraduate Studies; Ph.D., Houston, 1986. Partial differential equations.
F. J. Narcowich, Professor; Ph.D., Princeton, 1972. Mathematical physics.
P. Nelson, Professor of Computer Science and Mathematics; Ph.D., Mexico, 1969. Numerical analysis.
J. Pasciak, Professor; Ph.D., Cornell, 1977. Numerical analysis.
C. M. Pearcy Jr., Professor; Ph.D., Rice, 1960. Functional analysis.
W. L. Perry, Professor and Associate Provost; Ph.D., Illinois, 1972. Integral equations.
M. S. Pilant, Professor; Ph.D., NYU (Courant), 1982. Partial differential equations.
G. Pisier, Distinguished Professor and Owen Chair; Paris VII, 1977. Functional analysis.
J. T. Pitts, Professor; Ph.D., Princeton, 1974. Geometric analysis.
A. Poltoratski, Assistant Professor; Ph.D., Caltech, 1995. Functions of a complex variable.
H. W. Pu, Professor; Ph.D., Ohio State, 1964. Classical analysis.
M. H. Rahe, Associate Professor; Ph.D., Stanford, 1976. Ergodic theory.
K. R. Rajagopal, Professor of Mechanical Engineering and Mathematics; Ph.D., Minnesota, 1978. Continuum mechanics.
W. Rundell, Professor and Department Head; Ph.D., Glasgow, 1974. Partial differential equations.
D. Sanchez, Professor; Ph.D., Michigan, 1964. Ordinary differential equations.
J. F. Schielack, Associate Professor; Ph.D., Texas A&M, 1988. Math education.
V. P. Schielack Jr., Associate Professor; Ph.D., Texas, 1982. Math education.
T. Schlumprecht, Associate Professor; Ph.D., Munich, 1988. Functional analysis.
N. Sivakumar, Associate Professor; Ph.D., Alberta, 1990. Approximation theory.
J. Slattery, Professor of Chemical Engineering and Mathematics; Ph.D., Wisconsin, 1959. Transport theory.
K. C. Smith, Professor; Ph.D., Wisconsin, 1969. Near rings.
R. R. Smith, Professor; Ph.D., Oxford, 1975. Operator theory.
M. Stecher, Associate Professor; Ph.D., Indiana, 1973. Partial differential equations.
P. F. Stiller, Professor; Ph.D., Princeton, 1977. Algebraic geometry.
E. J. Straube, Professor; Ph.D., E.T.H., 1983. Several complex variables.
S. D. Taliaferro, Associate Professor; Ph.D., Stanford, 1976. Partial differential equations.
R. Thomas, Assistant Professor; Ph.D., Cornell, 1994. Operations research/combinatorics.
L. B. Treybig, Professor; Ph.D., Texas, 1958. Topology.
T. I. Vogel, Associate Professor; Ph.D., Stanford, 1981. Partial differential equations.
J. R. Walton, Professor and Associate Head for Graduate Studies; Ph.D., Indiana, 1973. Solid mechanics.
J. D. Ward, Professor; Ph.D., Purdue, 1973. Approximation theory.
C. Yan, Assistant Professor; Ph.D., MIT, 1997. Combinatorics.
P. B. Yasskin, Associate Professor; Ph.D., Maryland, 1979. Mathematical physics.
X. Zhang, Assistant Professor; Ph.D., NYU (Courant), 1991. Numerical analysis.
J. Zhou, Associate Professor; Ph.D., Penn State, 1986. Control theory.
M. Ziane, Assistant Professor; Ph.D., Indiana, 1997. Partial differential equations.
J. Zinn, Professor; Ph.D., Wisconsin, 1972. Probability.

THE UNIVERSITY OF ALABAMA AT BIRMINGHAM

Graduate School
Department of Biostatistics

Programs of Study

The Department of Biostatistics, through the University of Alabama at Birmingham (UAB) Graduate School, offers the M.S. and Ph.D. degrees in biostatistics. These programs provide a balance between theory and application of statistics, as applied to biomedical research. The educational objective is to produce research-oriented scientists who are able to advance statistical and modeling theory through the extension of existing statistical theory and the adaptation of existing methodology to handle new problems. These program graduates are also able to work effectively as members of the interdisciplinary research teams required for good, modern, scientific investigation. Quality statistical collaboration is critical for increasing knowledge in most applications fields today.

Through the School of Public Health, the department offers the M.P.H. degree in biometry. This is a professional degree rather than a research degree and is less suitable for candidates who intend to complete both a master's and a Ph.D. The curriculum for the M.P.H. requires core courses in a number of other public health disciplines, such as epidemiology and health behavior, in addition to biostatistics course work. The program is intended primarily for individuals who wish to acquire an M.P.H. with an emphasis in applied database management and use of computer-based statistical, analytical applications in addition to some basic exposure to statistical theory and methodology rather than for those seeking a more in-depth concentration in statistical theory and methodology.

Currently, there are 10 faculty members with primary appointments in the department and 4 emeritus and adjunct professors. In addition to their teaching commitments, faculty members conduct research in statistical methodology and applications and in the modeling of biological systems and participate in research grant proposals in other disciplines.

Research Facilities

The new Ryals School of Public Health Building houses the Department of Biostatistics. Two computer laboratories with advanced personal computers and extensive software are available for student use 24 hours per day. The laboratories are serviced by a Novell 3.12 file server and provide Internet access. Biostatistics students have secure disk storage space and individual e-mail addresses.

UAB's nationally recognized research facilities include the Comprehensive Cancer Center, the General Clinical Research Center, the Center for Aging, the Burn Center, the Cardiovascular Research and Training Center, the AIDS Research Center, the Nephrology and Diabetes Research and Training Centers, the Arthritis and Musculoskeletal Diseases Center, the Pediatric Pulmonary Center, the Injury Center, the Deep South Occupational Health and Safety Educational Resource Center, and the Center for Health Promotion and Disease Prevention.

The Lister Hill Library of the Health Sciences is the largest biomedical library in Alabama and houses 318,102 volumes and 2,436 periodical subscriptions. The Mervyn H. Sterne Library has nearly 1.3 million holdings and 2,511 periodical subscriptions.

Financial Aid

The Department of Biostatistics currently offers two fellowships from the School of Public Health and one from the UAB Graduate School. Each pays an $11,000 stipend and remission of 48 credit hours of tuition per year. Through the Graduate School, the Comprehensive Minority Faculty and Student Development Program offers four years of support to members of minority groups who are enrolled in doctoral programs. Under the Academic Common Market Agreement, qualified students from Arkansas, Florida, Kentucky, Maryland, Mississippi, Tennessee, Texas, Virginia, and West Virginia can enter the program at the in-state tuition rate. Full- or part-time jobs as statistical analysts are frequently available on campus.

Cost of Study

Tuition is $102 per credit hour for Alabama residents and $204 for nonresidents. Fees include a $9 per-credit-hour resource learning fee, a $23 student services fee, a $37 quarterly fee, and a processing fee of $25 for international students or $5 for U.S. students. Estimated tuition and fees for full-time students are $1530 per quarter for Alabama residents and $2755 for nonresidents, with $571 per year for individual hospitalization insurance. Fees are subject to change on a quarterly basis. Book expenses add approximately $350 per quarter.

Living and Housing Costs

Birmingham offers a variety of housing choices, ranging from the large, older homes near UAB to modern apartment complexes with pools and tennis courts. Commuting times average less than 30 minutes from a number of surrounding communities. A limited number of apartments are available on campus. Monthly costs for a single student average about $400 for housing and $450 for food.

Student Group

The total enrollment of the University of Alabama at Birmingham is more than 16,000, of whom 11,800 are in undergraduate programs and more than 4,000 in graduate and professional school programs. Approximately 400 students are enrolled in programs housed in the School of Public Health. Of these, 53 percent are women, 35 percent are members of minority groups, and 12 percent are international students. The Department of Biostatistics has approximately 20 students in its master's and Ph.D. programs.

Student Outcomes

Nationally, there are more jobs available for individuals with graduate degrees in biometry and biostatistics than there are qualified individuals to fill them. Depending upon their education experience and interests, graduates from the department's program are typically able to choose from employment opportunities available in national, state, or local public health agencies; research institutions or foundations; pharmaceutical or other industrial corporations; and academic institutions.

Location

Located in the southern foothills of the Appalachian chain and surrounded by state parks, lakes, and rivers, Birmingham's attractions include a symphony orchestra, dance and theater groups, a chamber music society, a museum of art, a botanical garden, a zoo, and sports. The white sand beaches of the Gulf of Mexico and the Great Smoky Mountains are only 5 hours away.

The University

UAB is one of the top research universities in the country, receives more than $220 million in training and research grants annually, and ranks fifteenth in funds received from the National Institutes of Health. UAB's three major academic units—the undergraduate programs, the Medical Center, and the Graduate School—contain a total of twelve schools. The Medical Center comprises six health professional schools and the University of Alabama Hospitals and Clinics. The campus encompasses a seventy-block area on Birmingham's Southside.

Applying

Requirements include the completion of the three components of the Graduate Record Examinations General Test (scores of at least 500 in each section are preferred), linear algebra, and a full calculus sequence. TOEFL scores of at least 600 are required of all international students whose native language is not English. There are nonrefundable applications fees of $35 for U.S. citizens and permanent residents and $60 for others. Applications should be filed by April 1 for fall admission, and financial aid applications should be submitted by February 15.

Correspondence and Information

Katharine A. Kirk, Ph.D.
Professor and Director of the Graduate Program
Department of Biostatistics
Room 327J, Ryals Building
The University of Alabama at Birmingham
1665 University Boulevard
University Station
Birmingham, Alabama 35294-0022

Telephone: 205-975-5048
Fax: 205-975-2540
E-mail: kkirk@uab.edu

The University of Alabama at Birmingham

THE FACULTY AND THEIR RESEARCH

Alfred A. Bartolucci, Professor; Ph.D., SUNY at Buffalo. Clinical trials, survival analysis, Bayesian statistics.

Charles R. Katholi, Professor and Interim Chair; Ph.D., Adelphi. Computationally intensive statistical methods, applied numerical analysis, mathematical models of biological systems.

Katharine A. Kirk, Professor and Director of the Graduate Program; Ph.D., Alabama at Birmingham. Multivariate analysis, general and generalized linear models, categorical data analysis.

Karan P. Singh, Professor; Ph.D., Memphis State. Cancer modeling, logistic models, risk assessment, survival analysis, AIDS research.

Irene M. Trawinski, Associate Professor; Ph.D., Virginia Tech. Multivariate analysis, mathematical statistics, probability.

O. Dale Williams, Professor; Ph.D., North Carolina. Public health education, cardiovascular disease epidemiology, clinical trials.

Adjunct Faculty

Seng-jaw Soong, Adjunct Professor; Ph.D., Alabama at Birmingham. Biometry, cancer clinical trials.

Emeritus Faculty

Edwin L. Bradley Jr., Professor Emeritus; Ph.D., Florida. Mathematical statistics, research consulting, nonlinear estimation.

David C. Hurst, Professor Emeritus; Ph.D., North Carolina State. Design of experiments, variance components, discrete multivariate models.

Malcolm E. Turner, Professor Emeritus; Ph.D., North Carolina State. Biological models, scientific inference, distribution theory.

THE UNIVERSITY Of
ARIZONA
TUCSON ARIZONA®

THE UNIVERSITY OF ARIZONA

Department of Mathematics
and Program in Applied Mathematics

Programs of Study

The Department of Mathematics at the University of Arizona offers a broad spectrum of graduate courses and seminars in algebra, analysis, applied mathematics, geometry, mathematical physics, number theory, probability, and statistics that lead to the degrees of Master of Arts, Master of Science, and Doctor of Philosophy with majors in mathematics.

In addition, the interdisciplinary Program in Applied Mathematics offers courses of study leading to the degrees of Master of Science and Doctor of Philosophy with majors in applied mathematics.

Each of the master's degree programs (M.A. and M.S.) that is offered by the Department of Mathematics requires course work outside the department, a master's thesis, and a computer programming examination as well as substantial course work in mathematics. Both master's degrees can serve as a basis for further study toward a Ph.D. degree. Highly flexible options in pure and applications-oriented mathematics are offered in the Ph.D. program in mathematics. Completion of substantial course work in mathematics and outside the department is required in order to enhance the ability to communicate mathematical concepts to professionals in other fields. Study toward the Ph.D. culminates with a dissertation presenting the student's original research.

The Program in Applied Mathematics offers courses of study leading to the Master of Science and Doctor of Philosophy degrees. It supports and encourages research in many areas of mathematical, physical, biological, and engineering sciences in which the use and development of mathematical methods and modeling techniques play a central role. Students entering the program are expected to have a strong background in mathematics, including advanced calculus, complex variables, and differential equations. However, entry into the program is not restricted to students who have an undergraduate mathematics major. Courses of study in the program are flexible and individually designed. In the first year, students take a sequence of core courses offered in conjunction with the Department of Mathematics that includes numerical analysis, principles of analysis, and methods of applied mathematics. In addition, students attend a series of weekly case studies and research tutorial groups in which they learn about current research opportunities. In subsequent years, students are able to choose from a broad variety of courses suited to their evolving research interests. For the Doctor of Philosophy degree, a dissertation is required. This dissertation is expected to contain original contributions by the student to the solution of a mathematical problem in a scientific discipline or to the development of applicable mathematical methods and modeling techniques.

The faculty members of the program (listed on the reverse side of this page) are actively involved in the supervision and teaching of program graduate students. The departmental affiliations of the faculty in this list give an indication of the breadth of research activities. In addition, the program has a substantial body of affiliate members who are involved in research with a strong applied mathematics component and who are potential research advisers. The combined network of members and affiliate members creates an unusually broad base of interdisciplinary research opportunities in applied mathematics. A list of affiliate members is available upon request.

Research Facilities

The Department of Mathematics occupies a seven-story building in which most seminars and graduate courses are held. The department maintains an extensive computing system, including a network of Sun and Intel/Linux workstations available to graduate students in both mathematics and applied mathematics. The Mathematics Reading Room contains about 5,000 volumes and displays the latest issues of major mathematical research journals. The applied mathematics program has an experimental laboratory for advanced mathematical modeling courses and research.

The Science Library houses an extensive collection of research journals and a large circulating collection of mathematics books and monographs. It subscribes to MathSciNet and an increasing number of full-text electronic journals on line. The University Computer Center has a wide variety of computing facilities, which are available to members of the University community.

Financial Aid

Teaching assistantships are available for qualified graduate students. The stipends in 1999–2000 range from $13,474 to $14,797 for teaching 4 class hours per semester. Out-of-state tuition is waived, but a registration fee of $1004 is required for each semester. Fellowships are available on a highly competitive basis.

Cost of Study

Full-time students who are Arizona residents are required to pay registration fees of $1044 per semester in 1999–2000. Full-time out-of-state students pay registration fees plus tuition of up to $4320 each semester. Part-time students pay proportionately.

Living and Housing Costs

University-maintained off-campus housing is available for married students. Single graduate students may live in the dormitories. Meals are available on campus. Excluding registration/tuition fees, the minimum cost for an academic year for a student living on campus has been estimated to be $10,360 for the current year.

Student Group

The University of Arizona has more than 35,000 students, including more than 7,000 graduate students. Total enrollment in the mathematics and applied mathematics graduate programs is about 160, of whom more than one fifth are women. Most students receive financial aid. Many recent graduates hold positions in universities, national research laboratories, or industry.

Location

The Tucson metropolitan area has a population of 800,000. It is located in a valley surrounded by mountain ranges, some of which rise 7,000 feet above the city. The Mexican border is 65 miles south of the University. The climate and surroundings lend themselves to outdoor recreational activities. Classical music concerts, theater, skiing, and mountain hiking are all readily available.

The University and The Department

The state-supported University of Arizona, founded in 1885, is located in the center of Tucson. The Department of Mathematics has a professional staff of about 60, who maintain a high level of research activity.

Applying

Application should be made to only one of the two programs at any one time. Forms are available from the addresses below. GRE scores should be submitted to the appropriate program. International students must ensure that their complete applications for admission and financial aid are received by February 1. Applications from U.S. students can be accepted somewhat later.

Correspondence and Information

Graduate Committee
Department of Mathematics
The University of Arizona
Tucson, Arizona 85721-0089

Telephone: 520-621-2068
WWW: http://www.math.arizona.edu/

Graduate Committee
Program in Applied Mathematics
The University of Arizona
Tucson, Arizona 85721-0089

Telephone 520-621-2016
E-mail: applmath@u.arizona.edu
WWW: http://w3.arizona.edu/~applmath/

The University of Arizona

THE FACULTY

DEPARTMENT OF MATHEMATICS

Professors. Hermann Flaschka (head), John Brillhart, Jim M. Cushing, John L. Denny (emeritus), Nicholas M. Ercolani, William G. Faris, Paul Fife (emeritus), David Gay, W. M. Greenlee, Helmut Groemer (emeritus), Larry C. Grove, Deborah Hughes Hallet, Thomas G. Kennedy, George L. Lamb (emeritus), C. David Levermore, David O. Lomen, John S. Lomont (emeritus), David Lovelock, Henry B. Mann (emeritus), Warren May, William G. McCallum, Yashaswini D. Mittal, Jerome V. Moloney, Donald E. Myers, Alan C. Newell, John N. Palmer, Adrian Patrascioiu, Yves Pomeau, Alwyn C. Scott, Timothy W. Secomb, Moshe Shaked, Daniel Stein, Arthur H. Steinbrenner (emeritus), Frederick W. Stevenson, Michael Tabor, Elias Toubassi, William Y. Velez, Stephen S. Willoughby, Vladimir Zakharov.

Associate Professors. Bruce J. Bayly, Moysey Brio, Marta Civil, William E. Conway, Carl L. DeVito, Samuel Evens, Leonid Friedlander, Oma Hamara, Minhyong Kim, Theodore W. Laetsch, Jiang-Hua Lu, Daniel Madden, Robert S. Maier, Douglas M. Pickrell, Marek Rychlik, Dinesh S. Thakur, Richard B. Thompson, Douglas Ulmer, Joseph Watkins, Jan Wehr, Maciej P. Wojtkowski, Bruce Wood, A. Larry Wright, Xue Xin.

Assistant Professors. Robert Beals, Gregory Eyink, Alain Goriely, Lucas Hsu, Joceline Lega, Juan Restrepo.

Lecturers. Robert C. Dillon (emeritus), John L. Leonard, Stephen D. Tellman.

Research Activities

Algebra and Number Theory. Algebraic function fields, algebraic number theory, arithmetical algebraic geometry, associative algebras, combinatorics, Galois theory, geometry of numbers, infinite Abelian groups, number theory and computational algorithms, representations of finite groups, ring theory, theory of equations, computational group theory, theoretical computer science.

Fluid Dynamics. Aerodynamics, computational fluid mechanics, hydrodynamics, soil mechanics.

Geometry. Symplectic and Poisson manifolds, Abelian varieties, algebraic geometry of dynamical systems, differential geometry and analysis on manifolds, Lie theory.

Mathematical Biology and Chemistry. Mathematical ecology, nonlinear diffusion, population dynamics.

Mathematical Physics. Nonlinear waves and solitons, quantum mechanics and operator theory, quantum optics, relativity and classical field theory, statistical mechanics and quantum field theory.

Nonlinear and Computational Analysis. Approximation theory, bifurcation theory, calculus of variations, convexity, eigenvalue problems, smooth ergodic theory, integral equations, linear and nonlinear functional analysis, numerical methods, ordinary and partial differential equations, singular perturbations. Special emphasis is placed on the nonlinear phenomena encountered in physical and engineering structures.

Probability and Statistics. Probability, random matrices, statistics, stochastic processes.

PROGRAM IN APPLIED MATHEMATICS

Key to abbreviations: A.M.E.—Aerospace and Mechanical Engineering; A.R.L.—Arizona Research Laboratory; E.C.E.—Electrical and Computer Engineering; E.E.B.—Ecology and Evolutionary Biology; L.P.L.—Lunar and Planetary Laboratory; S.I.E.—Systems and Industrial Engineering.

W. D. Arnett (Physics). Computational physics, astrophysics.

T. F. Balsa (A.M.E.). Aerodynamics, linear and nonlinear hydrodynamic stability, fluid mechanics.

B. R. Barrett (Physics). Nuclear many-body theory, structure finite nuclei, interacting boson model.

H. H. Barrett (Radiology). Inverse problems in medicine.

J. C. Baygents (Chemical Engineering). Fluid mechanics, colloidal phenomena and bioseparations.

M. Brio (Mathematics). Numerical solution of partial differential equations.

W. J. Cocke (Astronomy). Turbulence theory, general relativity, cosmology, nature of the redshift.

J. M. Cushing (Mathematics). Differential equations, integral equations, population dynamics and ecology.

W. J. Dallas (Radiology). Medical image acquisition, processing and display of images.

P. J. Downey (Computer Science). Analysis of algorithms, scheduling theory, computer performance modeling.

N. M. Ercolani (Mathematics). Applications of algebraic geometry, nonlinear analysis.

G. L. Eyink (Mathematics). Mathematical physics, fluid mechanics, turbulence, dynamical systems, equilibrium and nonequilibrium statistical physics.

W. G. Faris (Mathematics). Operator theory, quantum mechanics, probability, statistical mechanics.

H. Flaschka (Mathematics). Nonlinear waves, dynamical systems.

L. Friedlander (Mathematics). Spectral geometry, spectrum of differential operators and geometry of manifolds, analytic torsion-system design.

J. B. Goldberg (S.I.E.). Mathematics programming applications in production systems design.

R. T. Goldstein (Physics). Condensed-matter theory, nonlinear dynamics, pattern formation, fluid dynamics, experimental and theoretical biological physics.

A. Goriely (Mathematics). Dynamical systems (pure and applied), dynamics of elastic.

T. G. Kennedy (Mathematics). Statistical mechanics, condensed matter theory.

E. J. Kerschen (A.M.E.). Aeroacoustics, fluid mechanics, singular perturbations.

J. Lega (Mathematics). Nonlinear dynamics (pattern formation, envelope equations, weak turbulence) and applications to hydrodynamics, optics, and biology.

C. D. Levermore (Mathematics). Partial differential equations, numerical analysis.

J. I. Lunine (Planetary Science). Theoretical studies of outer solar system bodies.

M. W. Marcellin (E.C.E.). Digital communication/data storage systems, data compression, digital signal/image processing.

J. V. Moloney (Mathematics). Nonlinear optics, instability and chaos in lasers.

D. E. Myers (Mathematics). Geostatistics.

S. P. Neuman (Hydrology). Subsurface hydrology and underground transport, computer simulation.

M. F. Neuts (S.I.E.). Numerical methods in probability and stochastic models.

A. C. Newell (Mathematics and A.R.L.). Nonlinear processes, waves, cooperative phenomena, numerical analysis.

J. N. Palmer (Mathematics). Solvable models in statistical mechanics and field theory.

J. Restrepo (Mathematics) Geophysical fluid dynamics, large-scale computing and numerical analysis, nonlinear waves.

W. M. Schaffer (E.E.B.). Nonlinear dynamics, ecology, epidemiology.

A. C. Scott (Mathematics). Nonlinear dynamics (solitons, chaos).

T. W. Secomb (Physiology). Fluid mechanics, microcirculation, blood rheology.

M. Shaked (Mathematics). Applied probability, reliability theory, statistics.

M. Tabor (Applied Mathematics). Nonlinear dynamics, chaos, solitons, fluid mechanics.

H. S. Tharp (E.C.E.). Control systems.

L. P. Tolbert (Neurobiology). Developmental neurobiology.

T. C. Wallace (Geosciences). Computational seismology.

J. C. Watkins (Mathematics). Probability theory and stochastic processes, particularly limit theorems and models of random processes in biology and physics.

J. Wehr (Mathematics). Mathematical physics, probability, differential equations.

A. Winfree (E.E.B.). Theoretical biology, reaction-diffusion waves.

M. P. Wojtkowski (Mathematics). Dynamical systems.

J. X. Xin (Mathematics). Nonlinear partial differential equations, homogenization and its applications in fluids and geology.

A list of Affiliate Members is available upon request.

UNIVERSITY OF CALIFORNIA, LOS ANGELES

School of Medicine
Department of Biomathematics

Programs of Study

The Department of Biomathematics offers a graduate program leading to the Master of Science and Doctor of Philosophy degrees in biomathematics. The goal of the doctoral program is to train creative, fully independent investigators who can initiate research in both applied mathematics and their chosen biomedical specialty. The department's orientation is away from abstract modeling and toward theoretical and applied research vital to the advancement of current biomedical frontiers. This is reflected in a curriculum providing doctoral-level competence in a biomedical specialty; substantial training in applied mathematics, statistics, and computing; and appropriate biomathematics courses and research experience. A low student-faculty ratio permits close and frequent contact between students and faculty throughout the training and research years.

Entering students come from a variety of backgrounds in mathematics, biology, the physical sciences, and computer science. Some of the students are enrolled in the UCLA M.D./Ph.D. program. Doctoral students generally use the first two years to take the core sequence and electives in biomathematics, to broaden their backgrounds in biology and mathematics, and to begin directed individual study or research. Comprehensive examinations in biomathematics are taken after this period, generally followed by the choice of a major field and dissertation area. Individualized programs permit students to select graduate courses in applied mathematics, biomathematics, and statistics appropriate to their area of research and to choose among diverse biomedical specialties. At present, approved fields of special emphasis for which courses of study and qualifying examinations have been developed include genetics, physiology, neurosciences, pharmacology, immunology, and molecular biology. Other major fields can be added to the list by petition. The expected time for completion of the Ph.D. degree is five to six years.

The master's program can be a step to further graduate work in biomathematics, but it also can be adapted to the needs of researchers desiring supplemental biomathematical training or of individuals wishing to provide methodologic support to biomedical researchers. The M.S. program requires at least five graduate biomathematics courses and either a thesis or comprehensive examination plan. The master's degree can be completed in one or two years.

Research Facilities

The department is situated in the Center for the Health Sciences, close to UCLA's rich research and educational resources in the School of Medicine and in the Departments of Mathematics, Biology, Computer Science, Engineering, Chemistry, and Physics. The department has for many years housed multidisciplinary research programs comprising innovative modeling, statistical, and computing methods directed to many areas of biomedical research. It was the original home of the BMDP statistical programs and has an active consulting clinic for biomedical researchers. Computers within the department and graduate student offices include Macintosh units, Pentium PCs, and UNIX-based workstations. A Silicon Graphics IRIS Indigo is available for high-end graphics application. Nearby are terminals to UCLA's supercomputing resources (SP/2 cluster) and access to networked SUN computers and University-wide supercomputing. The Biomedical Library is one of the finest libraries of its kind in the country, and nearby are the Engineering and Mathematical Sciences Library and other subject libraries of the renowned nineteen-branch University Library. The department maintains a small library with selected titles in mathematical biology and statistics.

Financial Aid

The department maintains its own NIGMS Systems and Integrative Biology Training Grant for eligible students. Tuition, fees, some supplies, and travel to scientific meetings are paid for by the grant. Each trainee also receives a yearly cost-of-living allowance, which is set at $11,748 for 1999–2000. Supplementation is also possible from unrestricted funds, a teaching associate position, research assistantships, consulting, UCLA fellowships, and other merit-based funds. These additional sources of support and nonresident tuition waivers are available to exceptionally well qualified international students as well.

Cost of Study

The 1998–99 registration and other fees were $4555.50 per year, and nonresident tuition fees were $9384 per year. Domestic students may attain residency status after one year. The University's fee proposal is subject to change based on state budget decisions. Any fee increase would be reflected in bills for winter and spring terms.

Living and Housing Costs

The estimated cost of living varies. (The cost of living is in addition to the cost of study.) For additional housing information, students can go to the Web site (http://www.housing.ucla.edu/housing/housing.htm).

Student Group

Currently about 20 graduate students are enrolled in the department's program. About a fifth of the students are international. The departmental NIH predoctoral training grant supports 6 students. Most other students are also receiving financial support and/or are employed on campus in the area of their research. Many graduates hold tenure-track appointments at leading universities, research appointments at the National Institutes of Health, or in industry.

Location

UCLA's 411 acres are cradled in rolling green hills just 5 miles inland from the ocean, in one of the most attractive areas of southern California. The campus is bordered on the north by the protected wilderness of the Santa Monica Mountains and at its southern gate by Westwood Village, one of the entertainment magnets of Los Angeles.

The University

UCLA is one of America's most prestigious and influential public universities, serving more than 33,000 students. The Department of Biomathematics is one of ten basic science departments in the School of Medicine. The medical school, regarded by many to be among the best in the nation, is situated on the south side of the UCLA campus, just adjacent to the Life Sciences Building and the Court of Sciences. For more information, students can visit the University's Web site (http://www.ucla.edu).

Applying

Most students enter in the fall quarter, but applications for winter or spring quarter entry are considered. However, it is advantageous for candidates applying for financial support to initiate the application by the middle of January for decisions for the following fall. The department expects applicants for direct admission to the doctoral program to submit scores on the General Test of the Graduate Record Examinations and on one GRE Subject Test of the student's choice. Inquiries are welcome from students early in their undergraduate training. The department supports minority recruitment.

Correspondence and Information

Admissions Committee Chair
Department of Biomathematics
UCLA School of Medicine
Los Angeles, California 90095-1766

Telephone: 310-825-5554
Fax: 310-825-8685
E-mail: gradprog@biomath.medsch.ucla.edu
World Wide Web: http://www.biomath.medsch.ucla.edu/

University of California, Los Angeles

THE FACULTY AND THEIR RESEARCH

A. A. Afifi, Professor of Biostatistics and Biomathematics; Ph.D. (statistics), Berkeley, 1965. Multivariate statistical analysis, with applications to biomedical and public health problems.

Wilfrid J. Dixon, Professor of Biomathematics, Biostatistics, and Psychiatry (Emeritus); Ph.D. (statistics), Princeton, 1944. Statistical computation, statistical theory, biological applications, data analysis, psychiatric research.

Janet D. Elashoff, Adjunct Professor of Biomathematics; Ph.D. (statistics), Harvard, 1966. Design and analysis of clinical trials and evaluations of robustness of standard statistical techniques.

Robert M. Elashoff, Professor of Biomathematics and Biostatistics; Chair of Biostatistics; Ph.D. (statistics), Harvard, 1963. Markov renewal models in survival analysis, random coefficient regression models.

Eli Engel, Adjunct Associate Professor of Biomathematics; M.D., Buffalo, 1951; Ph.D. (physiology), UCLA, 1975. Mechanisms for acid neutralization in gastric mucus, facilitated transport of oxygen, theory of intracellular microelectrodes.

Alan B. Forsythe, Adjunct Professor of Biomathematics and Dentistry; Ph.D. (biometry), Yale, 1967. Methods development in robust regression and hypothesis testing, design and analysis of clinical and epidemiological studies, computer systems design.

Sanjiv Gambhir, Assistant Professor of Molecular and Medical Pharmacology and Biomathematics; affiliated with the CRUMP Institute for Biological Imaging; Ph.D. (biomathematics), UCLA, 1990; M.D., UCLA, 1993. Positron emission tomography (PET), deterministic modeling, medical imaging, neural networks, imaging gene expression, and nuclear medicine.

Karim F. Hirji, Associate Professor-In-Residence of Biomathematics; Ph.D. (biostatistics), Harvard, 1986. Exact statistical methods for categorical data.

Sung-Cheng (Henry) Huang, Professor of Medical Pharmacology and Biomathematics; D.Sc. (electrical engineering), Washington (St. Louis), 1973. Positron emission computed tomography and physiological modeling.

Donald J. Jenden, Professor of Pharmacology and Biomathematics (Emeritus); M.B.,B.S. (pharmacology and therapeutics), Westminster (London), 1950. Pharmacokinetic modeling, chemical pharmacology, analysis of GC/MS data, neuropharmacology.

Robert I. Jennrich, Professor of Mathematics, Biomathematics, and Biostatistics (Emeritus); Ph.D. (mathematics), UCLA, 1960. Statistical methodology, computational algorithms, nonlinear regression, factor analysis, compartment analysis.

Timothy D. Johnson, Assistant Adjunct Professor of Biomathematics; Ph.D. (biostatistics), UCLA, 1997. Exact statistical methods, Markov models, longitudinal data analysis.

Elliot M. Landaw, Professor and Chair of Biomathematics; M.D., Chicago, 1972; Ph.D. (biomathematics), UCLA, 1980. Identifiability and optimal experiment design for compartmental models; nonlinear regression; modeling/estimation applications in pharmacokinetics, ligand-receptor analysis, transport, and pediatrics.

Kenneth L. Lange, Professor of Biomathematics; Ph.D. (mathematics), MIT, 1971. Statistical and mathematical methods for human genetics and population growth, image reconstruction algorithms.

Carol M. Newton, Professor of Biomathematics and Radiation Oncology; Ph.D. (physics and mathematics), Stanford, 1956; M.D., Chicago, 1960. Simulation; cellular models for hematopoiesis, cancer treatment strategies, optimization; interactive graphics for modeling; model-based exploration of complex data structures (pedigrees).

Michael E. Phelps, Norton Simon Professor; Chair, Department of Molecular and Medical Pharmacology; Professor of Biomathematics; Chief, Division of Nuclear Medicine; Director, CRUMP Institute for Biological Imaging; and Associate Director, Laboratory of Structural Biology and Molecular Medicine; Ph.D. (nuclear chemistry), Washington (St. Louis), 1970. Positron emission tomography (PET), tracer kinetic modeling of biochemical and pharmacokinetic processes; biological imaging of human disease.

Nathaniel Schenker, Associate Professor of Biostatistics and Biomathematics; Ph.D. (statistics), Chicago, 1985. Missing data, sampling, U.S. census, statistics in cancer and AIDS research.

Janet S. Sinsheimer, Assistant Professor in Residence of Biomathematics and Biostatistics; Ph.D. (biomathematics), UCLA, 1994. Statistical models of molecular evolution and genetics.

University of California, Los Angeles

SELECTED PUBLICATIONS

Leung, K. M., and **R. M. Elashoff.** A three-state disease model with application to AIDS and melanoma. *J. Lifetime Anal.* 1996.

Leung, K. M., **R. M. Elashoff,** and **A. A. Afifi.** On censoring. *Am. J. Public Health Mono.* 1996.

Leung, K. M., and **R. M. Elashoff.** Generalized linear mixed-effects models with finite-support random-effects distribution: A maximum-penalized likelihood approach. *Biometr. J.* 1995.

Leung, K. M., and **R. M. Elashoff.** Estimation of generalized linear mixed-effects models with finite-support random-effects distribution via Gibbs sampling. *Biometr. J.* 1995.

Wanek, L. A., and **R. M. Elashoff** et al. Application of multistage Markov modeling to malignant melanoma progression. *Cancer* 73(2):336–43, 1994.

Livingston, E. H., and **E. Engel.** Modeling of the gastric gel mucus layer: Application to the measured pH gradient. *J. Clin. Gastroenterol.* 21:S120–4, 1995.

Engel, E., P. H. Guth, Y. Nishizaki, and J. D. Kaunitz. Barrier function of the gastric mucus gel. *Am. J. Physiol.* (Gastrointest. Liver Physiol. 32) 269:G994–9, 1995.

Livingston, E. H., J. Miller, and **E. Engel.** Bicarbonate diffusion through mucus. *Am. J. Physiol.* (Gastrointest. Liver Physiol. 32) 269:G453–7, 1995.

Engel, E., A. Peskoff, G. L. Kauffman, and M. I. Grossman. Analysis of hydrogen ion concentration in the gastric gel mucus layer. *Am. J. Physiol.* (Gastrointest. Liver Physiol. 10) 247:G321–38, 1984.

Engel, E., V. Barcilon, and R. S. Eisenberg. The interpretation of current-voltage relations recorded from a spherical cell with a single microelectrode. *Biophys. J.* 12(4):384–403, 1972.

Eisenberg, R. S., and **E. Engel.** The spatial variation of membrane potential near a small source of current in a spherical cell. *J. Gen. Physiol.* 55(6):736–57, 1970.

Hathout, G. M., R. K. Gopi, P. Bandettini, and **S. S. Gambhir.** The lag of cerebral hemodynamics with rapidly alternating periodic stimulation: Modeling for functional MRI. *Magnet. Res. Imaging* 17(1):9–20, 1999.

Gambhir, S. S., et al. Imaging adenoviral-directed reporter gene expression in living animals with positron emission tomography (PET). *Proc. Natl. Acad. Sci. U.S.A.* 96(5):2333–8, 1999.

Pan, D., et al. **(S. S. Gambhir** and **M. E. Phelps).** Rapid synthesis of a 5′-fluorineated oligodeoxynucleotide: A model antisense probe for use in imaging with positron emission tomography (PET). *Bioorg. Med. Chem. Lett.* 8:1317–20, 1998.

Gambhir, S. S. Clinical positron imaging and the transition toward an online electronic journal. *Clin. Pos. Imag.* 1(1):71–9, 1998.

Silverman, D. H. S., et al. **(S. S. Gambhir** and **M. E. Phelps).** Evaluating tumor biology and oncologic disease with positron emission tomography (PET). *J. Sem. Rad. Oncol.* 8(3):183–96, 1998.

Gambhir, S. S., et al. **(M. E. Phelps).** Imaging of adenoviral-directed herpes simplex virus type I thymidine kinase gene expression in mice with ganciclovir. *J. Nucl. Med.* 39:2003–11, 1998. (cover article)

Scott, W., J. Shepherd, and **S. S. Gambhir.** Cost-effectiveness of FDG-PET for staging non–small cell lung cancer (NSCLC): A decision analysis. *Ann. Thorac. Surg.* 66(6):1876–83, 1998. Discussion. 1883–85 (lead article).

Eisneberg, L., D. Dirks, and **J. Gornbein.** Subjective judgments of speech clarity measured by paired comparisons and category rating. *Ear Hear.,* July-August 1997.

Gratt, B., et al. **(J. Gornbein).** Thermographic assessment of craniomandibular disorders: Diagnostic interpretation versus temperature measurement analysis *J. Orofacial Pain* 8(3):278–88, 1994.

Buyalos, R., et al. **(J. Gornbein).** The influence of LH and insulin on sex steroids and sex hormone-binding globulin in polycystic ovarian syndrome. *Fertil. Steril.* 60(4):626–33, October 1993.

Martin, F. C., et al. **(J. Gornbein).** Production of IL-1 by microglia in response to substance P: Role for a nonclassical NK-1 receptor. *J. Neuroimmunol.* 42(1):53–60, January 1993.

Gornbein, J., C. Lazaro, and R. J. A. Little. Incomplete data in repeated measures analysis. *Stat. Meth. Med. Res.* 1(3), December 1992.

Gornbein, J. Program 5V—expanded repeated measures analysis. *BMDP Commun.,* Spring 1988.

Gornbein, J. Introducing 5V—incomplete repeated measures ANOVA with alternative covariance matrix structures. *BMDP Commun.,* Winter 1988.

Hirji, K. F., S. E. Vollset, I. M. Reis, and **A. A. Afifi.** Exact tests for interaction in several 2*2 tables. *J. Comp. Graph. Stat.* 5:209–24, 1996.

Hirji, K. F. Exact analysis for paired binary data. *Biometrics* 50:964–74, 1994.

Hirji, K. F., M. L. Tang, S. E. Vollset, and **R. M. Elashoff.** Efficient power computation for exact and mid-P tests for the common odds ratio in several 2*2 tables. *Stat. Med.* 13:1539–49, 1994.

Ngowi, J. A., R. Redding-Lallinger, and **K. F. Hirji.** An assessment of the use of anthropometric measures for predicting low birth weight. *J. Tropical Pediat.* 39:356–60, 1993.

Hirji, K. F. Computing exact distributions for polytomous response data. *J. Am. Stat. Assoc.* 87:487–92, 1992.

Mhalu, F., and **K. F. Hirji** et al. A cross-sectional study of a program for HIV infection control among public house workers. *J. Acq. Immun. Defic. Synd.* 4:290–6, 1991.

Hirji K. F., C. R. Mehta, and N. R. Patel. Exact inference for matched case-control studies. *Biometrics* 44:803–14, 1988.

Hirji, K. F., C. R. Mehta, and N. R. Patel. Computing distributions for exact logistic regression. *J. Am. Stat. Assoc.* 82:1110–7, 1987.

Huang, S. C., and Y. Zhou. Spatially-coordinated regression for image-wise model fitting to dynamic PET data for generating parametric images. *IEEE Trans. Nucl. Sci.,* 1998.

Stout, D., and **S. C. Huang** et al. **(M. E. Phelps).** Effects of plasma large neutral amino acid on cerebral FDOPA uptake. *J. Cereb. Blood Flow* 18:43–51, 1998.

Wu, H. M., and **S. C. Huang** et al. **(M. E. Phelps).** Factor analysis for derivation of input function from dynamic FDG PET studies in small hearts. *J. Nucl. Med.* 37:1717–22, 1996.

Barrio, J. R., and **S. C. Huang** et al. **(M. E. Phelps).** Radiofluorinated L-m-Tyrosines: new in-vivo probes for central dopamine biochemistry. *J. Cereb. Blood Flow and Metabol.* 16:667–78, 1996.

Lin, K. P., and **S. C. Huang** et al. **(M. E. Phelps).** Automated image registration of FDOPA PET studies. *Phys. Med. Biol.* 41:2775–88, 1996.

Ng, C. K., **S. C. Huang,** H. R. Schelbert, and D. B. Buxton. Validation of a model for [1-11C]acetate as a tracer of cardiac oxidative metabolism. *Am. J. Physiol.* 266:H1304–15, 1994.

Huang, S. C., et al. **(M. E. Phelps).** Kinetics and modeling of 6-[F-18]fluoro-L-DOPA in human positron emission tomographic studies. *J. Cereb. Blood Flow Metab.* 11:898–913, 1991

Jamshidian, M., and **R. I. Jennrich.** Acceleration of the EM algorithm using quasi-Newton methods. *J. Royal Stat. Soc. B* 59:569–87.

Chen, J. S., and **R. I. Jennrich.** The signed root deviance profile and confidence intervals in maximum likelihood analysis. *J. Am. Stat. Assoc.,* pp. 993–8, 1996.

Chen, J. S., and **R. I. Jennrich.** Transformations for improving linearization confidence intervals in nonlinear regression. *J. Am. Stat. Assoc.,* pp. 1271–6, 1995.

Jennrich, R. I. *An Introduction to Computational Statistics: Regression Analysis.* Englewood Cliffs, New Jersey: Prentice Hall, 1995.

Chen, J. S., and **R. I. Jennrich.** Diagnostics for linearization confidence intervals in nonlinear regression. *J. Am. Stat. Assoc.,* pp. 1068–74, 1995.

Jamshidian, M., and **R. I. Jennrich.** Conjugate gradient acceleration of the EM algorithm. *J. Am. Stat. Assoc.,* pp. 221–8, 1993.

Jamshidian, M., and **R. I. Jennrich.** Conjugate gradient methods in confirmatory factor analysis. *Comp. Stat. Data Anal.,* pp. 247–63, 1992.

University of California, Los Angeles

Selected Publications (continued)

Walker, W. L., **E. M. Landaw,** R. E. Dickerson, and D. S. Goodsell. Estimation of the DNA sequence discriminatory ability of hairpin-linked lexitropsins. *Proc. Natl. Acad. Sci. U.S.A.,* in press.

Liu, W. V., **E. M. Landaw,** and J. R. Froines. Comparison of the dynamic behavior of compartmental models for lead distribution in the human body. *Occupat. Hyg.* 1:293–304, 1995.

Landaw, E. M. Model-based adaptive control for cancer chemotherapy with suramin. In *Proceedings of the Simulation in Health Sciences Conferences,* pp. 93–8, eds. J. G. Anderson and M. Katzper. San Diego: Society for Computer Simulation, 1994.

Cho, A. K., et al. **(E. M. Landaw).** A pharmacokinetic study of phenylcyclohexyldiethylamine (PCDE) an analog of phencyclidine. *Drug Metab. Dispos.* 21:125–32, 1993.

Marino, A. T., J. J. Distefano III, and **E. M. Landaw.** DIMSUM: an expert system for multiexponential model discrimination. *Am. J. Physiol.* (Endocrinol. Metab. 25) 262:E546–56, 1992.

Landaw, E. M., and J. J. DiStefano III. Multiexponential, multicompartmental modeling. Part 2—Data analysis and statistical considerations. *Am. J. Physiol.* (Regulatory, Integrative and Comparative Physiology 15) 246:R665–77, 1984.

Landaw, E. M. Optimal multicompartmental sampling designs for parameter estimation-practical aspects of the identification problem. *Math. Comp. Simul.* 24:525–30, 1982.

Lange, K. *Numerical Analysis for Statisticians.* New York: Springer, 1999.

Fan, R., and **K. Lange.** Models for haplotype evolution in a nonstationary population. *Theor. Popul. Biol.* 53:184–98, 1998.

Lange, K. *Mathematical and Statistical Methods for Genetic Analysis.* New York: Springer, 1997.

Feesler, J. A., E. P. Ficaro, N. H. Clinthome, and **K. Lange.** Grouped-coordinate ascent algorithms for penalized likelihood transmission image reconstruction. *IEEE Trans. Med. Imaging* 16:166–75, 1997.

Becker, M. P., I. Yang, and **K. Lange.** EM algorithms without missing data. *Stat. Methods Med. Res.* 6:3738, 1997.

Sobel, E., and **K. Lange.** Descent graphs in pedigree analysis: Applications to haplotyping, location scores, and marker sharing statistics. *Am. J. Human Genetics* 59:717–25, 1996.

Lange, K., and J. A. Fessler. Globally convergent algorithms for maximum a posteriori transmission tomography. *IEEE Trans. Image. Process.* 4:1430–8, 1995.

Lange, K., M. Boehnke, D. R. Cox, and K. L. Lunetta. Statistical methods for polyploid radiation hybrid mapping. *Genome Res.* 5:136–50, 1995.

Lange, K. A stochastic model for genetic linkage equilibrium. *Theor. Pop. Biol.* 44:129–48, 1993.

Lange, K. Match probabilities in racially admixed populations. *Am. J. Human Genet.* 52:305–11, 1993.

Lange, K., and **J. S. Sinsheimer.** Normal/independent distributors and their application in robust regression. *J. Comp. Graph. Stat.* 2:175–98, 1993.

Lange, K., and M. Boehnke. Bayesian methods and optimal experimental design for gene mapping by radiation hybrids. *Ann. Human Genet.* 56:119–44, 1992.

Lange, K., and **J. S. Sinsheimer.** Calculation of genetic identity coefficients. *Ann. Human Genet.* 56:339–46, 1992.

Newton, C. M. An interactive graphics system for real-time investigation and multivariate data portrayal for complex pedigree data systems. *Comp. Biomed. Res.* 26:327–43, 1993.

Newton, C. M. Exploring categorical and scalar data interactions: Another graphical approach. *Proc. Am. Stat. Assoc. Meet. (Section on Statistical Graphics),* pp. 49–54, Boston, Mass., August 1992.

Newton, C. M. Conference retrospective: An appropriate modeling infrastructure for cancer research. *Bull. Math. Biol.* 48(3/4):443–52, 1986.

Bailey, J. N, M. A. Suchard, S. L. Smalley, and **J. S. Sinsheimer.** Search for a gene by environment interaction: GXE hunt. *Genet. Epidemiol.,* in press.

Schadt, E. E., **J. S. Sinsheimer,** and **K. Lange.** Computational advances in maximum likelihood methods for molecular phylogeny. *Genome Res.* 8:222–33, 1998.

Weeks, D. E. and **J. S. Sinsheimer.** Consanguinity and relative pair methods for linkage analysis. *Am. J. Human Genetics* 62:728–31, 1998.

Chitnavis, J., and **J. S. Sinsheimer** et al. Genetic influences in end-stage osteoarthritis. Sibling risks of hip and knee replacement for idiopathic osteoarthritis. *J. Bone Joint Surg.* 79:660–4, 1997.

Sinsheimer, J. S., J. A. Lake, and R. J. A. Little. Inference for phylogenies under a hybrid parsimony method: Evolutionary-symmetric transversion parsimony. *Biometrics* 53:23–38, 1997.

Sinsheimer, J. S., J. A. Lake, and R. J. A. Little. Bayesian hypothesis testing of four-taxon topologies using molecular sequence data. *Biometrics* 52:190–203, 1996.

UNIVERSITY OF CENTRAL FLORIDA

Department of Mathematics

Programs of Study

The Department of Mathematics of the University of Central Florida (UCF) offers high-quality graduate programs leading to the M.S. degree in mathematical science and the Ph.D. degree in mathematics, with emphasis on applied and industrial mathematics. Graduate students in these programs work with a congenial faculty of international stature.

The M.S. program requires 30 credit hours of approved course work, including a 3-credit-hour thesis or 36 credit hours of approved course work and a written examination. The 75-credit-hour Ph.D. program is based on a required core of 18 credit hours in the foundations of mathematics. Each student, in conjunction with an Advisory Committee, plans an individual program designed to create an outstanding background in the general area of applied mathematics and expertise in the area of the student's research. To further this development, the student is expected to enroll in a minimum of 6 credit hours, and is strongly encouraged to take 12 credit hours, in a single related area of mathematical application, such as physics, computer science, statistics, economics, electrical engineering, or mechanical engineering.

The doctoral student is expected to pass a written qualifying examination and an oral candidacy examination, as well as to conduct a major piece of publishable research and write and defend a dissertation.

The curriculum and research opportunities have been designed to develop experts in several areas of faculty expertise, including applied analysis, differential equations, methods of mathematical physics, probability and mathematical statistics, numerical analysis, approximation theory, wavelets, nonlinear dynamics, fluid mechanics, wave propagation, abstract algebra, algebraic geometry, and combinatorics and graph theory.

Research Facilities

Graduate students have access to Sun IPC and Sun SPARC II Workstations in the department. Also available are a DEC MPP 1200 parallel processor and a Harris Nighthawk NH-3800 processor within the Computer Science Department, IBM RS/6000 model 580 and IBM 4381 model T92 processors within the Computer Services Department, an ES/9000 model 740 with three vectors at the Northeast Regional Data Center, and access via the Internet to worldwide computer facilities. Additional computing facilities include UNIX workstations, Apple Macintosh labs, and PC labs scattered around the campus and interconnected via a Novell network.

The department sponsors numerous colloquia and a visiting scholars program throughout the year.

Financial Aid

Graduate teaching assistantships, which carry a basic nine-month stipend of $9000 ($10,000 with a master's degree in mathematics) and a partial tuition waiver, are available for qualified applicants. Stipend enhancements, ranging from $1000 to $5000, and maximum allowable tuition waivers are available for outstanding applicants.

Cost of Study

Fees for 1999–2000 are estimated at $140 per credit hour for Florida residents and $480 per credit hour for nonresidents, plus required University fees. Graduate teaching assistants normally take 6 to 9 credit hours per semester.

Living and Housing Costs

Off-campus privately owned housing is available for graduate students. A room in a shared apartment can be rented for less than $400 per month. A one-bedroom apartment can be rented for $550 per month. The meal plan is $850 to $1000 per semester.

Student Group

The University has approximately 29,500 students, including almost 5,000 graduate students.

Location

Orlando is located approximately 50 miles from the Atlantic coast and 100 miles from the Gulf of Mexico. The greater Orlando metropolitan area has a population of about 1.4 million. Students at UCF enjoy the climate and recreational resources that draw millions of visitors to the area each year. In addition, a vigorous economy with a large high-technology component provides special work and research opportunities for students.

The University

The University of Central Florida is a member of Florida's State University System. It is one of Florida's fastest-growing universities. Situated in one of the most rapidly developing areas in the nation, the campus is located on 1,227 acres on the east side of Orlando. Adjacent to the University is Florida's most highly rated research park.

Applying

Application must be made on a form available upon request from Graduate Admissions, University of Central Florida, P.O. Box 160112, Orlando, Florida 32816-0112. A $20 application fee, official transcripts from a SUS-approved college, and GRE General Test scores are required of all applicants. TOEFL scores are required for international students.

Application for assistantships should be made by March 1 for the fall semester and by October 1 for the spring semester. Assistantship applications require three reference letters. Late applications are given consideration if additional openings become available. All qualified students, especially women and minorities, are strongly encouraged to apply.

Correspondence and Information

Graduate Program Coordinator
Department of Mathematics
University of Central Florida
P.O. Box 161364
Orlando, Florida 32816-1364
Telephone: 407-823-5239
Fax: 407-823-6253
E-mail: math@pegasus.cc.ucf.edu
World Wide Web: http://www.cas.ucf.edu/mathematics/

University of Central Florida

THE FACULTY AND THEIR RESEARCH

L. C. Andrews, Professor; Ph.D. (mathematical mechanics), Michigan State, 1970. Wave propagation in random media, mathematical optics, special functions.

J. M. Anthony, Associate Professor; Ph.D. (mathematics), North Carolina State, 1969. Analysis.

L. H. Armstrong, Professor; Ph.D. (mathematics education), Florida State, 1973. Mathematics education.

R. C. Brigham, Professor; Ph.D. (mathematics), NYU, 1970. Graph theory and combinatorics.

J. R. Cannon, Professor; Ph.D. (mathematics), Rice, 1962. Differential and integral equations, numerical analysis, inverse and ill-posed problems, free-boundary problems.

R. M. Caron, Associate Professor; Ph.D. (mathematics), LSU, 1972. Graph theory and combinatorics, coding theory.

S. R. Choudhury, Associate Professor; Ph.D. (applied mathematics), Cornell, 1985. Numerical analysis, computational mathematics, nonlinear waves, nonlinear dynamics and chaos.

T. L. Clarke, Faculty Associate; Ph.D. (applied mathematics), Miami (Florida), 1982. Applied mathematics.

L. Debnath, Professor; Ph.D. (pure mathematics), Calcutta, 1965; Ph.D. (applied mathematics), London, 1967. Integral transforms, fluid dynamics, continuum mechanics, nonlinear waves, applied partial differential equations.

M. N. Heinzer, Associate Professor; Ph.D. (mathematics), Florida State, 1968. Algebra.

P. J. Hilton, Distinguished Professor; D.Phil. (pure mathematics), Oxford, 1950; Ph.D., Cambridge, 1952. Abstract algebra, group theory, algebraic topology, homological algebra, number theory.

C. Y. Hopen, Assistant Professor; Ph.D. (applied mathematics), Washington (Seattle), 1996. Pulse propagation, laser-satellite communications, special functions and perturbation methods.

R. C. Jones, Assistant Professor; Ph.D. (mathematics), Case Western Reserve, 1966. Approximation theory.

A. J. Kassab, Associate Professor; Ph.D. (mechanical engineering), Florida, 1989. Numerical fluid dynamics, numerical and computational mathematics, boundary-element method.

A. Katsevich, Assistant Professor; Ph.D. (mathematics), Kansas State, 1994. Applied mathematics, tomography, the radon transform, pseudodifferential operators, asymptotic expansions, ill-posed and inverse problems, numerical analysis, geophysics, statistics, image processing, signal analysis.

X. Li, Associate Professor; Ph.D. (mathematics), South Florida, 1989. Analysis, approximation theory, special functions.

H. M. Martin, Assistant Professor; Ph.D. (mathematics), LSU, 1993. Commutative algebra, algebraic geometry.

P. Mikusinski, Professor; Ph.D. (mathematics), Polish Academy of Sciences, 1983. Generalized functions, measure theory, numerical and computational mathematics.

R. N. Mohapatra, Professor; Ph.D. (mathematics), Jabalpur (India), 1968. Classical analysis, approximation theory and splines.

D. W. Nicholson, Professor; Ph.D. (mechanical engineering), Yale, 1971. Solid mechanics, finite-element theory, numerical and computational mathematics.

M. Y. Pensky, Assistant Professor; Ph.D. (statistics), Moscow, 1988. Theoretical statistics, Bayesian analysis.

R. L. Phillips, Professor; Ph.D. (electrical engineering), Arizona State, 1966. Wave propagation, math modeling.

R. E. Pyle, Instructor; M.S. (mathematics), Central Florida, 1991. Mathematics education.

C. P. Rautenstrauch, Associate Professor; Ph.D. (mathematics), Auburn, 1967. Classical analysis, approximation theory.

G. D. Richardson, Professor; Ph.D. (mathematics), 1969, Ph.D. (statistics), 1985, North Carolina State. Mathematical statistics, asymptotic results in the area of parameter estimation, convergence spaces.

R. S. Rodriguez, Associate Professor; Ph.D. (mathematics), Tennessee, 1968. Complex analysis, approximation theory.

D. K. Rollins, Associate Professor; Ph.D. (applied mathematics), Caltech, 1986. Fluid dynamics, nonlinear dynamics.

F. L. Salzmann, Assistant Professor; Ph.D. (mathematics), Auburn, 1970. Fractal geometry.

H. Sherwood, Professor; Ph.D. (mathematics), Arizona, 1966. Nondeterministic analysis, doubly stochastic measures, functional equations.

B. K. Shivamoggi, Professor; Ph.D. (engineering science), Colorado, 1978. Fluid dynamics, plasma physics, nonlinear dynamics, stochastic processes.

M. D. Taylor, Professor; Ph.D. (mathematics), Florida State, 1969. Multiply stochastic hypermatrices, generalized functions.

A. Tovbis, Assistant Professor; Ph.D. (mathematics), Voronezh (Russia), 1985. Nonlinear dynamical systems, perturbation, asymptotic and numerical methods, differential equations, applied and industrial mathematics.

K. Vajravelu, Professor; Ph.D. (mathematics), Indian Institute of Technology, 1979. Applied partial differential equations, fluid mechanics, heat and mass transfer.

A. I. Zayed, Professor; Ph.D. (mathematics), Wisconsin–Milwaukee, 1979. Sampling theory, wavelets, function transforms, generalized functions.

UNIVERSITY OF DELAWARE

Department of Mathematical Sciences

Programs of Study	The Department of Mathematical Sciences offers master's and Ph.D. programs in mathematics and applied mathematics. Students receive instruction in a broad range of courses and may specialize in many areas of mathematics. Strong departmental research groups exist in analysis, applied mathematics, partial differential equations, combinatorics, inverse problems, topology, probability and statistics, and numerical analysis. Master's programs normally require two years for completion, while the Ph.D. usually takes four to five years. Internship programs with industry and government are available in an NSF-sponsored industrial mathematics program.
Research Facilities	The University libraries contain 2 million volumes and documents and subscribe to 24,000 periodicals and serials. The University library belongs to the Association of Research Libraries.
	The University Information Technologies Department provides e-mail and network access via two Sun Ultra Enterprise 4000 servers. The mathematical sciences department has its own network of Sun Workstations, two Sun Workstation classrooms, a microcomputer laboratory, and a Silicon Graphics Origin 2000 parallel computer.
	The department fosters an active research environment, with numerous seminars and colloquia and many national and international visitors.
Financial Aid	Graduate assistantships and fellowships are available on a competitive basis. Teaching assistantships in 1999–2000 range from $12,867.75 to $16,112.25 plus tuition remission for nine months, which includes two semesters and a winter session. Additional summer session stipends are also often available. At present, most full-time students receive some financial support. Some research assistantships and fellowships in industrial mathematics (NSF-GIG) are also available, as are a limited number of Unidel fellowships.
Cost of Study	Course fees for full-time students in 1999–2000 are $4462 per academic year for residents of Delaware and $12,862 per academic year for out-of-state students. Fees for the summer sessions and for part-time students are $298 per credit for Delaware residents and $689 per credit for nonresidents. The graduation fee is $35 for the master's degree and $95 for the Ph.D.
Living and Housing Costs	While prices vary widely throughout the area, average monthly rent for a one-bedroom apartment is $465 plus utilities.
Student Group	There are approximately 40 full-time graduate students in the Department of Mathematical Sciences. About one quarter of these are international students.
Location	The University is located in Newark, Delaware, a pleasant college community of about 30,000 people. Newark is 14 miles southwest of Wilmington and halfway between Philadelphia and Baltimore. It offers the advantages of a small community yet is within easy driving distance of Philadelphia, New York, Baltimore, and Washington, D.C. It is also close to the recreational areas on the Atlantic Ocean and Chesapeake Bay.
The University	The University of Delaware grew out of a small academy founded in 1743. It has been a degree-granting institution since 1834. In 1867, an act of the Delaware General Assembly made the University a part of the nationwide system of land-grant colleges and universities. Delaware College and the Women's College, an affiliate, were combined under the name of the University of Delaware in 1921. In 1950, the Graduate College was organized to administer the existing graduate programs and to develop new ones. In the past fifteen years, the University has greatly expanded the scope of its educational endeavors. In 1976, the University was named a sea-grant college. In 1985, it was one of the first six universities to receive an NSF grant for an Engineering Research Center.
Applying	Application forms may be obtained from the address below. Completed applications, including letters of recommendation, a $45 application fee, GRE General Test scores, and transcripts of previous work, should be submitted as early as possible but no later than March 1 to be considered for financial aid for the fall semester.
Correspondence and Information	Coordinator of Graduate Studies Department of Mathematical Sciences University of Delaware Newark, Delaware 19716 Telephone: 302-831-2346 E-mail: see@math.udel.edu World Wide Web: http://www.math.udel.edu

University of Delaware

THE FACULTY AND THEIR RESEARCH

Thomas S. Angell, Professor; Ph.D., Michigan. Optimal control theory, differential equations.
Willard E. Baxter, Professor Emeritus; Ph.D., Pennsylvania. Algebra.
David P. Bellamy, Professor; Ph.D., Michigan State. Topology.
John G. Bergman, Associate Professor; Ph.D., Illinois at Urbana-Champaign. Functional analysis, probability.
Richard J. Braun, Assistant Professor; Ph.D., Northwestern. Perturbation and computational methods.
Jinfa Cai, Assistant Professor; Ph.D., Pittsburgh. Mathematics education.
David L. Colton, Unidel Professor; Ph.D., D.Sc., Edinburgh. Partial differential equations, integral equations.
L. Pamela Cook-Ioannidis, Professor and Chair; Ph.D., Cornell. Applied mathematics, perturbation theory, transonic flow.
Richard J. Crouse, Associate Professor; Ph.D., Delaware. Mathematics education.
Gary L. Ebert, Professor; Ph.D., Wisconsin–Madison. Combinatorics.
David A. Edwards, Assistant Professor; Ph.D., Caltech. Applied math.
Paul P. Eggermont, Associate Professor; Ph.D., SUNY at Buffalo. Numerical analysis, integral equations, image reconstruction.
Robert P. Gilbert, Unidel Chair Professor; Ph.D., Carnegie Mellon. Integral and differential equations, function theory.
David J. Hallenbeck, Professor; Ph.D., SUNY at Albany. Function theory.
George C. Hsiao, Professor; Ph.D., Carnegie Mellon. Differential and integral equations, perturbation theory, fluid dynamics.
Judy A. Kennedy, Professor; Ph.D., Auburn. Topology and dynamical systems.
Vincent N. LaRiccia, Associate Professor; Ph.D., Texas A&M. Mathematical statistics.
Felix Lazebnik, Professor; Ph.D., Pennsylvania. Graph theory, combinatorics, algebra.
Yuk J. Leung, Associate Professor; Ph.D., Michigan. Function theory.
Wenbo Li, Associate Professor; Ph.D., Wisconsin–Madison. Probability theory, stochastic processes, statistics.
Richard J. Libera, Professor Emeritus; Ph.D., Rutgers. Function theory.
Albert E. Livingston, Professor and Associate Chairman; Ph.D., Rutgers. Function theory.
Walter K. Mallory, Assistant Professor; Ph.D., Rutgers. Mathematical logic, fuzzy set theory.
David M. Mason, Professor; Ph.D., Washington (Seattle). Probability, statistics.
Peter Monk, Professor; Ph.D., Rutgers. Numerical analysis.
M. Zuhair Nashed, Professor; Ph.D., Michigan. Numerical analysis, functional analysis, integral equations, optimization and approximation theory.
David Olagunju, Associate Professor; Ph.D., Northwestern. Applied mathematics.
Petr Plechac, Assistant Professor; CSC (Ph.D.), Charles (Prague). Scientific computing and numerical analysis.
Georgia B. Pyrros, Instructor; M.S., McMaster. Nuclear physics.
Rakesh, Associate Professor; Ph.D., Cornell. Partial differential equations.
Lidia Rejtö, Associate Professor; Ph.D., Eötvös Loránd (Budapest). Probability and statistics.
David P. Roselle, Professor and President of the University; Ph.D., Duke. Combinatorics.
Lillian M. Russell, Instructor; M.S., Delaware. Statistics.
Renate Scheidler, Assistant Professor; Ph.D., Manitoba. Cryptography.
Gilberto Schleiniger, Associate Professor; Ph.D., UCLA. Scientific computing, numerical analysis.
Clifford W. Sloyer, Professor; Ph.D., Lehigh. Topology, mathematics education.
Ivar Stakgold, Professor Emeritus; Ph.D., Harvard. Nonlinear boundary-value problems.
Robert M. Stark, Professor; Ph.D., Delaware. Applied probability, operations research, civil engineering systems.
Richard J. Weinacht, Professor; Ph.D., Maryland. Partial differential equations.
Ronald H. Wenger, Associate Professor; Ph.D., Michigan State. Algebra, mathematics education.
Qing Xiang, Assistant Professor; Ph.D., Ohio State. Combinatorics.
Shangyou Zhang, Associate Professor; Ph.D., Penn State. Numerical analysis and scientific computation.

Joint Appointments with Other Departments
Morris W. Brooks, Ph.D., Harvard. Computer-based instruction.
Bobby F. Caviness, Ph.D., Carnegie Mellon. Computer algebra.
Kathleen Hollowell, Ed.D., Boston University. Mathematics education.
William B. Moody, Ed.D., Maryland. Mathematics education.
Richard S. Sacher, Ph.D., Stanford. Scientific computing, operations research.
David Saunders, Ph.D., Wisconsin–Madison. Computer algebra.
Leonard W. Schwartz, Ph.D., Stanford. Fluid mechanics.

Adjunct Faculty and Their Affiliations
Steven P. Bailey, DuPont Company. Design of experiments, Bayesian inference.
Spencer Free. Consultant in biostatistics.
Alan Jeffrey, University of Newcastle-upon-Tyne. Wave propagation.
Rainer Kress, University of Göttingen. Integral equations, scattering theory.
James M. Lucas. Response surface methodology and quality control.
Donald W. Marquardt. Nonlinear estimation, biased estimation, spectrum estimation.
Lassi Paivarinta, University of Oulu (Finland).
Charles G. Pfeifer, DuPont Company. Group testing, applied statistics.
Darryl Pregibon, Bell Laboratories. Expert systems, regression.
Gary Roach, University of Strathclyde. Operator theory, scattering theory.
Malcolm Taylor. U.S. Army Ballistics Research Laboratory.
Dana Ullery, DuPont Company. Applied statistics.

UNIVERSITY OF GEORGIA

Department of Statistics

Programs of Study

The Department of Statistics offers graduate degree programs leading to the Master of Science in statistics, Master of Applied Mathematical Sciences, and Doctor of Philosophy in statistics.

The Doctor of Philosophy degree in statistics is a research degree designed to prepare students to work on the frontiers in the discipline of statistics. This program prepares students for careers in research and teaching as well as for leadership roles in industry, business, and government, where statistical methodology and unusual statistical applications are required.

The Master of Science (M.S.) degree program offers two options: one in applied statistics and the other in mathematical statistics. In both options, preparation of an M.S. thesis is optional. The thesis option requires a minimum of 27 semester hours of graduate credit, exclusive of the thesis. The nonthesis option requires 33 semester hours.

The Master of Applied Mathematical Sciences (M.A.M.S.) requires 33 semester hours of graduate-level courses and one or two technical reports (in lieu of a thesis) prepared either as part of a regular course or in a special seminar. Specialization is possible in applied mathematics, operations research, or computer science and statistical analysis. The program is designed for students who seek broad training in applied quantitative methods as preparation for professional employment in business, government, or industry.

Research Facilities

The department currently has a Sun Microsystems Enterprise 4000 server that provides application, file, and Internet services to the computers in the department, which include fourteen Sun Microsystems UNIX workstations and twenty-one Pentium PCs. There is a graduate lab that contains eight Sun workstations and four PentiumPro machines. In addition, there are sixty-two PentiumPro computers for introductory statistical courses, and thirty-one Pentium class PCs running on a single Pentium II processor Dell 4100 server for advanced statistics classes.

Students can acquire experience in statistical and computational computing through the Statistical Computing Service, which is operated by the department. Valuable experience with actual problems can be gained through the cooperative program that exists between the department and several universities, research institutes, and research organizations. The Cohen Reading Room, located in the Statistics Building, provides students with access to a variety of statistical information through books and journals. Also nearby is the Science Library, which has an extensive collection in the mathematical sciences and subscribes to all of the major statistical journals. Access to the GALIN system, which enables students to quickly look up library references via computer terminals, is also available.

Financial Aid

Teaching and research assistantships are available for qualified applicants. The 1999–2000 stipends are $11,133 and $11,867 for master's and doctoral students, respectively. Graduate students are also eligible for a number of National Science Foundation grants and University graduate assistantships awarded in the Graduate School on a University-wide, competitive basis. A limited number of out-of-state tuition waivers are also available. Graduate students achieve teaching experience through a structured program of teaching assignments, in which initial assignments of a laboratory-assistance nature lead to actual teaching responsibilities.

Cost of Study

In 1998–99, the rate for state residents for 12 semester hours or more was $1465 per semester; the nonresident rate for 12 semester hours or more was $4930. The rates for 1999–2000 have not been determined, but it is anticipated that they will be 4–6 percent higher than the 1998–99 rates. Tuition fees are prorated for fewer than 12 semester hours. Tuition fees for students on assistantships are waived.

Living and Housing Costs

Housing is available for married students in apartments on campus. There are also residence halls reserved exclusively for graduate students. Off-campus housing and apartments are also available. A realistic budget for a single person living on campus is approximately $4000 per semester in 1999–2000.

Student Group

The total University enrollment for the fall of 1999 is estimated to be 30,500 students, including 7,000 graduate students. The graduate student body in all degree programs in the Department of Statistics consists of about 40 students.

Location

The city of Athens is a typical college town with a population of approximately 85,000. Athens is about 65 miles from Atlanta, and it is only a few hours' drive from the mountains to the north and the Atlantic coast to the east.

The University

The University of Georgia, the first chartered state university in the United States, was founded in 1785. It contains thirteen schools and colleges. The campus covers 3,500 acres and has its own transit system.

Applying

Admission is possible in both semesters, but fall admission is preferable. Applicants seeking financial assistance should apply before February 15. Applications must include a completed application form, three letters of recommendation, official transcripts, and GRE General Test scores.

Correspondence and Information

Graduate Coordinator
Department of Statistics
University of Georgia
Athens, Georgia 30602-1952

Telephone: 706-542-5232
Fax: 706-542-3391
E-mail: dept@stat.uga.edu
World Wide Web: http://www.stat.uga.edu

University of Georgia

THE FACULTY AND THEIR RESEARCH

Jonathan Arnold, Adjunct Associate Professor; Ph.D., Yale, 1982. Statistical genetics, statistical analysis of DNA sequences, discrete multivariate analysis, applied probability models in genetics.

Rolf E. Bargmann, Professor Emeritus; Ph.D., North Carolina, 1957. Multivariate analysis, statistical computation.

Ishwar V. Basawa, Professor; Ph.D., Sheffield (England), 1971. Inference in stochastic processes, time series, asymptotics, inference for spatial point processes and random fields.

Julie Bérubé, Assistant Professor; Ph.D., Michigan, 1997. Statistical quality assurance, optimal experimental designs, robust statistical analysis.

Lynne Billard, University Professor; Ph.D., New South Wales (Australia), 1969. Epidemic processes, AIDS, sequential analysis, time series.

Ralph A. Bradley, Research Professor Emeritus; Ph.D., North Carolina, 1949. Design of experiments, nonparametric statistics, multivariate analysis.

Hubert J. Chen, Professor; Ph.D., Rochester, 1974. Ranking and selection, multiple-comparison procedures, hypothesis testing, stock market analysis.

A. Clifford Cohen, Professor Emeritus; Ph.D., Michigan, 1941. Truncated and censored sampling, statistical quality control.

Jem Corcoran, Assistant Professor; Ph.D., Colorado State, 1998. Statistical computing and algorithms, Markov chain simulations, Gibbes sampling.

Gauri Sankar Datta, Associate Professor; Ph.D., Florida, 1990. Statistical inference, linear models, survey sampling, Bayesian inference, generalized linear models.

Somnath Datta, Professor; Ph.D., Michigan State, 1988. Compound decision, empirical Bayes, bootstrap, density estimation, asymptotics.

Christine A. Franklin, Temporary Instructor; M.A., North Carolina at Greensboro, 1980. Statistical education, computing.

Daniel B. Hall, Assistant Professor; Ph.D., Northwestern, 1994. Generalized linear models, longitudinal data analysis, categorical data analysis.

Kermit Hutcheson, Professor; Ph.D., Virginia Tech, 1970. Ecological diversity, multinomial-type distributions.

Carl F. Kossack, Professor Emeritus; Ph.D., Michigan, 1939. Classification techniques, sample survey.

Robert B. Lund, Associate Professor; Ph.D., North Carolina, 1993. Time series, applied probability, density estimation, statistics in climatology.

Nancy I. Lyons, Associate Professor; Ph.D., North Carolina State, 1975. Inference in ecological models, sample survey, statistical computation.

William P. McCormick, Professor and Assistant Head; Ph.D., Stanford, 1978. Extreme value theory, Gaussian processes, time series, resampling.

Mary C. Meyer, Assistant Professor; Ph.D., Michigan, 1996. Regression analysis, statistical smoothing techniques, function estimation.

Broderick Oluyede, Assistant Professor; Ph.D., Bowling Green State, 1991. Categorical data analysis, order-restricted statistical inference, large sample theory, statistical computation.

Stephen L. Rathbun, Associate Professor; Ph.D., Iowa State, 1990. Environmental statistics, spatial statistics, inference for spatial processes.

Jaxk H. Reeves, Associate Professor; Ph.D., Berkeley, 1982. Statistical consulting, statistical phylogenetics, ranking and selection.

Lynne Seymour, Assistant Professor; Ph.D., North Carolina, 1993. Periodic time series, random field models, pseudo-likelihood estimation.

Leonard R. Shenton, Professor Emeritus; Ph.D., Edinburgh, 1940. Estimation and asymptotic series.

Jill E. Smith, Temporary Instructor; M.S., Texas Tech, 1993. Biostatistics, categorical data analysis, and epidemiology.

Tharuvai N. Sriram, Associate Professor; Ph.D., Michigan State, 1986. Sequential estimation, branching processes, bootstrap, adaptive designs, large sample theory.

Robert L. Taylor, Professor and Head; Ph.D., Florida State, 1971. Laws of large numbers, stochastic convergence and density estimation.

Anand N. Vidyashankar, Assistant Professor; Ph.D., Iowa State, 1994. Statistical toxicology, longitudinal data analysis, survival analysis, response-adaptive designs and clinical trials.

SELECTED PUBLICATIONS

Bargmann, R. E. Identification of virtual clusters by interactive use of a personal computer. In *Recent Developments of Statistics and the Applications,* pp. 209–25. Ohio State University and Korea University, 1989.

Bargmann, R. E. A single union-intersection statistic for testing internal independence. In *Proceedings of the Indian Statistical Institute, Golden Jubilee, Sankhya,* pp. 20–32, 1984.

Bargmann, R. E., and E. Halfon. Efficient algorithms for statistical estimation in compartmental analysis. *Ecol. Modelling* 3:211–26, 1977.

Posten, H. O., and **R. E. Bargmann.** Power of the likelihood-ratio test of the general linear hypothesis in multivariate analysis. *Biometrika* 51:467–80, 1964.

Bargmann, R. E. Signifikanzuntersuchungen der Einfachen Struktur in der Faktorenanalyse. *Mitteilungsblatt f.d. Math. Statistik* (precursor of *Metrika)* 1–24, 1955.

Basawa, I. V., V. P. Godambe, and **R. L. Taylor.** Selected Proceedings of the Symposium on Estimating Functions. *IMS Lecture Notes* 32, 1997.

Hwang, S., and **I. V. Basawa.** Asymptotic optimal inference for a class of nonlinear time series models. *Stoch. Proc. Appl.* 46:91–113, 1993.

Basawa, I. V., et al. **(W. P. McCormick** and **J. H. Reeves).** Bootstrapping unstable first-order autoregressive processes. *Ann. Stat.* 19:1098–101, 1991.

Basawa, I. V. Asymptotic distributions of prediction errors and related tests of fit for non-stationary processes. *Ann. Stat.* 15:46–58, 1987.

Basawa, I. V., and D. J. Scott. *Asymptotic Optimal Inference for Non-ergodic Models.* New York: Springer-Verlag, 1983.

Basawa, I. V. Efficient conditional tests for mixture experiments with applications to the birth and branching processes. *Biometrika* 68:153–65, 1981.

Basawa, I. V., and B. L. S. Prakasa Rao. *Statistical Inference for Stochastic Processes.* London: Academic Press, 1980.

Bérubé, J., and V. N. Nair. Exploiting the inherent structure in robust parameter design experiments. *Statistica Sin.,* in press.

Bérubé, J., and G. P. H. Styan. Decomposable three-way layouts. *J. Stat. Plann. Inference* 36:311–22, 1993.

Bérubé, J., and G. P. H. Styan. On certain inequalities for average efficiency factors associated with the three-way layout of experimental design. In *Data Analysis and Statistical Inference, Festschrift in Honour of Friedhelm Eicker,* eds. S. Schach and G. Trenkler, 1992.

Worsley, K. J., G. P. H. Styan, and **J. Bérubé.** Genstat ANOVA efficiency factors and canonical efficiency factors for non-orthogonal designs. *Genstat Newslett.* 26:22, 1991.

Dai, Y., and **L. Billard.** A space-time bilinear model and its identification. *J. Time Ser. Anal.* 19:657–79, 1998.

Billard, L. A voyage of discovery. *J. Am. Stat. Assoc.* 92:1–12, 1997.

Billard, L., and Z. Zhao. Multiple stage nonhomogeneous Markov models for the AIDS epidemic. *J. R. Stat. Soc. B* 56:673–86, 1994.

Meshkani, M. R., and **L. Billard.** Empirical Bayes estimators and some of their properties for the transition probability matrix of a finite Markov chain. *Biometrika* 79:185–93, 1992.

Medley, G. F., **L. Billard,** D. R. Cox, and R. M. Anderson. The distribution of the incubation period for the acquired immunodeficiency syndrome (AIDS). *Proc. R. Soc. Ser. B* 233:367–77, 1988.

Bradley, R. A., and R. L. Anderson. The Biometric Society and biometrics: Contributions to experimental design. In *Advances in Biometry: 50 Years of the Biometric Society,* pp. 25–50, eds. P. Armitage and H. A. David, 1996.

Stewart, F. P., and **R. A. Bradley.** Interblock information in multidimensional block designs. *Can. J. Stat.* 21:295–302, 1993.

Bradley, R. A. The statistics profession—some questions for the future. In *Proceedings of the ISI 49th Session,* pp. 49–66, 1993.

Stewart, F. P., and **R. A. Bradley.** Some partially variance balanced structurally incomplete row-column designs. *Commun. Stat. Theory Methods* 20:2451–65, 1991.

Bradley, R. A., and F. P. Stewart. Interblock analysis of designs with multiple blocking criteria. *J. Am. Stat. Assoc.* 86:792–7, 1991.

Chen, H. J., and S. Y. Chen. A nearly optimal confidence interval for the largest normal mean. *Commun. Stat. Simulation Computation* 28(1), 1999.

Chen, H. J., and S. F. Wu. Multiple comparison procedures with the average for scale families: Normal and exponential populations. *Commun. Stat.* 28(1), 1999.

Chen, H. J., and S. F. Wu. Multiple comparison procedures with the average for exponential location parameters. *Computational Stat. Data Anal.* 26:461–84, 1998.

Chen, H. J., and S. F. Wu. Multiple comparisons with the average for normal distributions. *Am. J. Math. Manage. Sci.* 18(1 & 2):193–218, 1998.

Chen, H. J., and S. Y. Chen. Single-stage analysis of variance under heteroscedasticity. *Commun. Stat. Simulation Computation* 27(3): 641–66, 1998.

Cohen, A. C. The role of order statistics in estimating threshold parameters. In *Order Statistics and Their Applications—A Volume in the Series Handbook of Statistics,* pp. 283–314, eds. N. Balakrishnan and C. R. Rao. Amsterdam: Elsevier Science Publishers, 1998.

Cohen, A. C. *Truncated and Censored Samples—Theory and Applications.* Marcel Dekker, Inc., 1991.

Cohen, A. C., and N. Balakrishnan. *Order Statistics and Inference: Estimation Methods.* Boston: Academic Press, 1990.

Cohen, A. C., and B. J. Whitten. *Parameter Estimation in Reliability and Life Span Models.* Marcel Dekker, Inc., 1988.

Cohen, A. C. Simplified estimators for the normal distribution when samples are singly censored or truncated. *Technometrics* 1:217–37, 1959.

Foss, S. G., R. L. Tweedie, and **J. N. Corcoran.** Simulating the invariant measures of Markov chains using backward coupling at regeneration times. *Probability Eng. Informational Sci.,* in press.

Datta, G. On priors providing frequentist validity for Bayesian inference for multiple parametric functions. *Biometrika* 83:287–98, 1996.

Datta, G., and M. Ghosh. On the invariance of noninformative priors. *Ann. Stat.* 24:141–59, 1996.

Datta, G., and M. Ghosh. Some remarks on noninformative priors. *J. Am. Stat. Assoc.* 90:1357–63, 1995.

Datta, G., and J. K. Ghosh. On priors providing frequentist validity for Bayesian inference. *Biometrika* 82:37–45, 1995.

Datta, G., and M. Ghosh. Bayesian prediction in linear models: Applications to small area estimation. *Ann. Stat.* 19:1748–70, 1991.

Datta, S., and **W. P. McCormick.** Some continuous Edgeworth expansions for Markov chains with applications to bootstrap. *J. Multivar. Anal.* 52:83–106, 1995.

Datta, S., and **W. P. McCormick.** Bootstrap inference for a first order autoregression with positive innovations. *J. Am. Stat. Assoc.* 90:1289–300, 1995.

Datta, S. Some nonasymptotic bounds for L_1 density estimation using kernels. *Ann. Stat.* 20:1658–67, 1992.

Datta, S. On the consistency of posterior mixtures and its application. *Ann. Stat.* 19:338–53, 1991.

Datta, S. Asymptotic optimality of Bayes compound estimators in compact exponential families. *Ann. Stat.* 19:354–65, 1991.

Franklin, C. *Instructor's and Student Solution Manuals* to accompany *Introductory Statistics,* 4th ed., by N. Weiss, 1994, 1996.

Franklin, C. *Instructor's and Student Solution Manuals* to accompany *Introduction to Probability and Its Applications,* 2nd ed., by R. Scheaffer, 1995.

Franklin, C. Testbank to accompany *A Course in Business Statistics,* 4th ed., by W. Mendenhall and R. Beaver. Wadsworth, 1995.

Franklin, C. *Instructor's and Student Solution Manuals* to accompany *Probability and Statistics for Engineers,* 4th ed., by R. Scheaffer and J. McClave. Wadsworth, 1994.

Franklin, C. *Instructor's and Student Solution Manuals* to accompany *An Introduction to Statistical Methods and Data Analysis* by L. Ott. Wadsworth, 1993.

Hall, D. B. On GEE-based regression estimators under first moment misspecification. *Commun. Stat. Theory Methods* 28(4), 1999.

Hall, D. B., R. F. Woolson, W. R. Clarke, and M. F. Jones. Cochran-Mantel-Haenszel techniques: Applications involving epidemiologic survey data. In *Handbook of Statistics,* vol. 17, 1999.

Hall, D. B., and T. A. Severini. Extended generalized estimating equations for clustered data. *J. Am. Stat. Soc.* 99:1365–75, 1998.

Hall, D. B. The Iowa Persian Gulf Study Group. Self-reported illness and health status among Gulf War veterans: A population-based study. *J. Am. Med. Assoc.* 277:238–45, 1997.

Davis, C. S., and **D. B. Hall.** A computer program for regression analysis of ordered categorical repeated measurements. *Comput. Methods Programs Biomed.* 51:153–69, 1996.

Hutcheson, K., and N. I. Lyons. A significance test for Morisita's index of dispersion and the moments when the population is negative

University of Georgia

Selected Publications (continued)

binomial and Poisson. In *Proceedings Symposium on Estimation and Analysis of Insect Populations*, vol. 55, pp. 335–46. Laramie, Wyo.: Springer-Verlag, 1989.

Hutcheson, K., and N. I. Lyons. The mean and variance of the likelihood ratio criterion for the multinomial distribution. *Metrika* 26:57–61, 1979 (Zblt. Math. 396, No. 62034).

Sugg, M. N., and **K. Hutcheson.** Gauss-Krawtchouk quadrature approximations for moments of multinomial type distributions. *Biometrika* 63(2):395–400, 1976.

Hutcheson, K. A test for comparing diversities based on the Shannon formula. *J. Theor. Biol.* 29:151–4, 1970.

Lund, R., and **L. Seymour.** Assessing temperature anomalies: A control chart approach. *Environmetrics,* in press.

Lund, R., W. J. Padgett, and **L. Seymour.** A control chart for a general Gaussian process. *J. Stat. Plann. Inference* 70:19–34, 1998.

Lund, R. B., S. Meyn, and R. L. Tweedie. Computable exponential convergence rates for stochastically ordered Markov processes. *Ann. Appl. Probability* 6:218–37, 1996.

Lund, R. B., and R. L. Tweedie. Geometric convergence rates of stochastically ordered Markov chains. *Math. Operations Res.* 21:182–94, 1996.

Lund, R. B., H. Hurd, P. Bloomfield, and R. L. Smith. Climatological time series with periodic correlation. *J. Climate* 11:2787–809, 1995.

Lund, R. B. The annual arrival cycle of Atlantic tropical cyclones. *J. Appl. Stat.* 21:195–204, 1994.

Lund, R. B. A dam with seasonal input. *J. Appl. Probability* 31:526–41, 1994.

Lyons, N. I., and **K. Hutcheson.** Generation of ordered multinomial frequencies. *Appl. Stat.* 45:387–98, 1996.

Lyons, N. I., K. Hutcheson, and M. N. Sugg. A small sample study of the moments and distribution of the log likelihood ratio statistics. *Metrika* 36:195–207, 1989.

Lyons, N. I., and **K. Hutcheson.** Distributional properties of the number of moves index of diversity. *Biometrics* 44:131–40, 1988.

Lyons, N. I., and **K. Hutcheson.** Estimation of Simpson's diversity when counts follow a Poisson distribution. *Biometrics* 42(1):171–6, 1986.

McCormick, W. P., and H. C. Ho. Asymptotic distribution of sum and maximum for Gaussian processes. *J. Appl. Probability,* in press.

McCormick, W. P., and **S. Datta.** Inference for the tail parameters of a linear process with heavy tailed innovations. *J. Inst. Stat. Math.* 50:337–59, 1998.

McCormick, W. P., S. Datta, and G. Mathew. Nonlinear autoregression with positive innovations. *Aust. New Zealand J. Stat.* 40:229–39, 1998.

McCormick, W. P. Extremes for shot noise processes with heavy tailed amplitudes. *J. Appl. Probability* 34:643–56, 1997.

McCormick, W. P., and Y. S. Park. An analysis of poisson moving average processes. *Probability Eng. Informational Sci.* 11:487–507, 1997.

McCormick, W. P., N. I. Lyons, and **K. Hutcheson.** Distributional properties of Jaccard's index of similarity. *Commun. Stat.* 21:51–68, 1992.

Meyer, M. C. A comparison of nonparametric shape-constrained bioassay estimators. *Stat. Probability Lett.,* in press.

Meyer, M. C. An extension of the mixed primal-dual bases algorithm to the case of more constraints than dimensions. *J. Stat. Plann. Inference,* in press.

Meyer, M. C. Determination of sample size in the generalized linear model. In *Proceedings, Computing Science and Statistics,* vol. 30.

Meyer, M. C. Choosing a smoothing parameter by minimizing an estimate of the risk for shape constrained smoothing splines. In *Proceedings, Computing Science and Statistics,* vol. 29, pp. 62–6.

Meyer, M. C., and E. F. Meyer. Solid-liquid phase behavior of nonadecylcyclohexane and nonadecylbenzene. *J. Chem. Eng. Data* 28:148–50, 1983.

Oluyede, B. A comparative study of tests of positive association in ordinal discrete data. *Comput. Sci. Stat.* 16(2):565–72, 1997.

Oluyede, B. Dependence functions and frailties. *Biometrical J.* 36(6):1–16, 1996.

Oluyede, B. A modified chi-square test of independence against a class of ordered alternatives in an RxC contingency table. *Can. J. Stat.* 22(1):75–87, 1994.

Oluyede, B. A family of bivariate binomial distribution generated by extreme bivariate Bernoulli distributions. *Commun. Stat.* 23(5):1531–47, 1994.

Oluyede, B. A modified chi-square test for testing the equality of two multinomial populations against an order restricted alternative. *Commun. Stat.* 22(4):1133–51, 1993.

Rathbun, S. L. Estimation of Poisson intensity using partially observed concomitant variables. *Biometrics* 52:226–42, 1996.

Rathbun, S. L. Asymptotic properties of the maximum likelihood estimator for spatio-temporal point processes. *J. Stat. Plann. Inference* 51:55–74, 1996.

Rathbun, S. L., and N. Cressie. Asymptotic properties of estimators for the parameters of spatial inhomogeneous Poisson processes. *Adv. Appl. Probability* 26:122–54, 1994.

Rathbun, S. L., and N. Cressie. Space-time survival point processes: Longleaf pines in southern Georgia. *J. Am. Stat. Assoc.* 89:1164–74, 1994.

Platt, W. J., G. W. Evans, and **S. L. Rathbun.** The population dynamics of a long-lived conifer *(Pinus palustris). Am. Naturalist* 131:491–525, 1988.

Reeves, J. H., E. M. Hillson, and C. A. McMillan. A statistical signalling model for use in surveillance of adverse drug reaction data. *Stat. Med.* 17:262–8, 1997.

Reeves, J. H., and E. M. Hillson. A lag-adjusted model for postmarketing surveillance of adverse drug event reports. *Drug Information J.* 29:1583–99, 1995.

Reeves, J. H. Heterogeneity in the substitution process of amino acid sites of proteins coded for by mitochondrial DNA. *J. Mol. Evol.* 35:17–31, 1992.

Wright, D. H., and **J. H. Reeves.** On the meaning and measurement of nestedness in species assemblages. *Oecologia* 92:416–28, 1992.

Seymour, L., and C. Ji. Approximate Bayes model selection procedures for Gibbs-Markov random fields. *J. Stat. Plann. Inference, Special Issue on Spatial Statistics,* 51:75–97, 1996.

Ji, C., and **L. Seymour.** A consistent model selection procedure for Markov random fields based on penalized pseudolikelihood. *Ann. Appl. Probability* 6:423–43, 1996.

Etemadi, N., **T. N. Sriram,** and **A. N. Vidyashankar.** Convergence of harmonic moments with applications to sequential estimation in linear regression. *J. Stat. Plan. Inference,* in press.

Sriram, T. N., and **S. Datta.** A modified bootstrap for branching processes with immigration. *Stoch. Proc. Appl.* 56:275–94, 1995.

Sriram, T. N. Invalidity of bootstrap for critical branching processes with immigration. *Ann. Stat.* 22:1013–23, 1994.

Sriram, T. N. An improved sequential procedure for estimating the regression parameter in regression models with symmetric errors. *Ann. Stat.* 20:1441–53, 1992.

Sriram, T. N., I. V. Basawa, and R. M. Huggins. Sequential estimation for branching processes with immigration. *Ann. Stat.* 19:2232–43, 1991.

Sriram, T. N. Sequential estimation of the mean of a first order stationary autoregressive process. *Ann. Stat.* 15:1079–90, 1987.

Taylor, R. L., A. Bozognia, and R. F. Patterson. Chung type strong laws for arrays of random elements and bootstrapping. *Stoch. Anal. Appl.* 15:651–69, 1997.

Taylor, R. L., and T. C. Hu. On the strong law for arrays and the bootstrap mean and variance. *Int. J. Math. Math. Sci.* 20:375–82, 1997.

Taylor, R. L., and H. Inoue. Laws of large numbers for random sets. In *Random Sets: Theory and Applications. IMA Volumes in Mathematics and Its Applications* 97:347–60, 1997.

Taylor, R. L., J. Hoffmann-Jorgensen, and K. L. Su. The law of large numbers and the Ito-Nisio theorem for vector valued random fields. *J. Theor. Probability* 10:145–83, 1997.

Basu, A., S. Sarkar, and **A. N. Vidyashankar.** Minimum negative exponential disparity estimation for parametric models. *J. Stat. Plann. Inference,* in press.

Athreya, K. B., and **A. N. Vidyashankar.** Large deviation rates for supercritical and critical branching processes. In *Proceedings of IMA Workshop on Classical and Modern Branching Processes.* New York: Springer-Verlag, 1995.

Athreya, K. B., and **A. N. Vidyashankar.** Large deviation rates for branching processes-2, the multitype case. *Ann. Appl. Probability* 5(2):566–76, 1995.

Athreya, K. B., and **A. N. Vidyashankar.** Large deviation rates for branching processes, stochastic processes. In *A Festschrift in Honour of Kallianpur,* pp. 5–9, eds. Cambanis, Ghosh, and Karandikar. New York: Springer-Verlag, 1994.

UNIVERSITY OF HOUSTON

Department of Mathematics

Programs of Study	The Department of Mathematics offers programs leading to the Doctor of Philosophy and Master of Science degrees in mathematics and the Master of Science in Applied Mathematics. Candidates for the M.S. degree may elect either the thesis or nonthesis option. The thesis option requires a minimum of 24 hours of course work and the successful completion and defense of a thesis. The nonthesis option requires 36 hours, including a tutorial project. In both options, at least 15 hours must be taken in core courses in analysis, algebra, and topology. Candidates for the Ph.D. degree must demonstrate proficiency in a foreign language and pass a comprehensive preliminary examination in mathematics. Ph.D. candidates must also present and orally defend a dissertation representing significant original research. At least one year of continuous full-time residence at the University of Houston, after the attainment of the equivalent of the M.S. degree, is required for the Ph.D.
	The degree of Master of Science in Applied Mathematics requires 36 hours of course work, including a tutorial project. Eighteen hours must be taken in core courses in applied analysis, numerical analysis, and probability and statistics. Admission to the degree program requires a baccalaureate degree in a field related to mathematics and a substantial background in undergraduate mathematics.
	The College of Natural Sciences and Mathematics is beginning an interdisciplinary Ph.D. program offering a computational science option to Department of Mathematics students.
	The Department of Mathematics publishes the *Houston Journal of Mathematics.* The department is the home of several research institutes, including two centers funded by the National Science Foundation (NSF) Grand Challenge Program. The department is a member of the Texas Center for Computational and Information Science, which fosters research, education, and interaction with industry and national laboratories in the field of large-scale scientific computing. The Institute for Theoretical and Engineering Science offers an interdisciplinary program in nonlinear dynamics and scientific computing. The Keck Center for Computational Biology also offers educational programs in a multidisciplinary effort involving faculty members and students from the University of Houston, Rice University, and the Baylor College of Medicine.
Research Facilities	The department occupies the entire sixth floor of the Philip G. Hoffman Building. The department has its own computing facilities, including IBM, Sun, Silicon Graphics, and DEC high-performance workstations and more than forty X-window terminals. Every graduate student office contains at least one X-window terminal or workstation. The University provides a diverse computing environment, ranging from an IBM SP-2 supercomputer to a multimedia computer laboratory containing thirty-five SGI workstations. Network access to worldwide computing facilities is excellent. The University library contains more than a million volumes. Journal subscriptions in mathematical sciences number more than 300. The library facilities of other Houston-area universities are available.
Financial Aid	Teaching fellowships are available to most full-time graduate students in mathematics. In 1998–99, stipends ranged from $11,200 to $11,550 for nine months. Nine hours of tuition are waived for students holding teaching fellowships. Support for summer study is usually available. The College of Natural Sciences and Mathematics awards two $15,000 Texaco Graduate Fellowships annually, and the University awards the Ehrhardt/Cullen Graduate Scholarship, a $7000 supplement based on merit. Financial aid in the form of work-study programs and student loans is also available. Most fellowships are awarded in the spring for the following academic year; however, late applications are considered if positions are still available.
Cost of Study	Full-time graduate students who are residents of Texas pay $1058.50 in tuition and fees for 9 semester hours; nonresidents pay $2678.50. Students holding teaching fellowships pay the Texas-resident tuition and fees for hours above 9. For students holding teaching fellowships, 9 hours of tuition are waived and only fees ($482.50 per semester) must be paid.
Living and Housing Costs	Dormitory rates for single students, including room and board, range from $4240 to $4850 per academic year. University-owned housing for single graduate students ranges in price from $1381.50 to $1499 per semester. On-campus housing (Cambridge Oaks) for married students, seniors, and graduates rents for $252 to $1625 per month. Off-campus apartment rates range upward from $375 per month.
Student Group	Enrollment at the University is 32,296 students, including 5,824 graduate students. The Department of Mathematics has 50 graduate students, of whom 30 attend full-time. Approximately half of the graduate students in the department are pursuing the Ph.D. degree.
Student Outcomes	The Department of Mathematics graduates 3 to 5 Ph.D. students and 10 to 15 M.S. students each year. Recent Ph.D. graduates are pursuing postdoctoral appointments at the Courant Institute and Purdue University and at the Universities of Texas at Austin and Alberta and at N.I.S.T. Others hold tenure-track positions at universities and colleges and research positions at IBM, Texas Medical Center, and other companies. Recent M.S. graduates are in Ph.D. programs around the country, in teaching positions at community colleges, and working in industry.
Location	Houston is the nation's fourth-largest city and the largest city in the South. Cultural and recreational activities are plentiful. The city has parks, theaters, museums, a symphony orchestra, and opera and ballet companies. The area has collegiate and professional teams in baseball, football, basketball, and other sports. Houston is a center for medical, aerospace, and geophysical research and offers opportunities for employment in highly technical fields.
The University	The University of Houston was founded in 1927 and became a state-supported university in 1963. It is now the third-largest university in Texas. The campus is located 3 miles from the downtown area of Houston and is easily accessible by automobile or public transportation. The College of Natural Sciences and Mathematics and the Department of Mathematics are committed to high standards of research and teaching in all areas of mathematics.
Applying	Consideration for admission is given to students in good standing who expect to receive a baccalaureate degree in mathematics or a closely related area prior to entrance. A GPA of 3.0 for the last 60 hours is required, and GRE General Test scores are required and are used in admissions decisions. International students from non-English-speaking countries must score at least 550 on the TOEFL. International students applying for a teaching fellowship must also score at least 50 on the TSE. Students should submit application material directly to the Department of Mathematics three months prior to the date of proposed entrance. Teaching fellowship applicants should complete their files by March 15 to ensure full consideration.
Correspondence and Information	Director of Graduate Studies Department of Mathematics University of Houston 4800 Calhoun Road Houston, Texas 77204-3476 Telephone: 713-743-3500 E-mail: pamela@math.uh.edu World Wide Web: http://www.math.uh.edu

University of Houston

THE FACULTY AND THEIR RESEARCH

Neal R. Amundson, Cullen Professor and member of National Academy of Sciences and American Academy of Arts and Science; Ph.D., Minnesota, 1945. Applied mathematics.

James F. G. Auchmuty, Professor; Ph.D., Chicago, 1970. Applied mathematics, variational methods and optimization theory.

Joseph G. Baldwin, Associate Professor; Dr.rer.nat., Göttingen (Germany), 1963. Probability.

David Bao, Professor; Ph.D., Berkeley, 1983. Differential geometry.

David P. Blecher, Associate Professor; Ph.D., Edinburgh, 1988. Operator algebras and operator theory.

E. Andrew Boyd, Adjunct Associate Professor; Ph.D., MIT, 1988. Operations research.

Dennison R. Brown, Professor; Ph.D., LSU, 1963. Topological semigroups.

Suncica Canic, Associate Professor; Ph.D., SUNY at Stony Brook, 1992. Nonlinear partial differential equations, applied mathematics.

S. S. Chern, Distinguished Visiting Professor; Ph.D., Hamburg, 1936. Differential geometry.

Howard Cook, Professor; Ph.D., Texas, 1962. Point-set topology.

Edward Dean, Associate Professor; Ph.D., Rice, 1985. Numerical analysis.

Henry P. Decell, Professor; Ph.D., LSU, 1963. Applied mathematics.

Garret J. Etgen, Professor and Chairman of the Department; Ph.D., North Carolina at Chapel Hill, 1964. Ordinary differential equations.

Siemion Fajtlowicz, Professor; Ph.D., Wroclaw (Poland), 1967. Graph theory, universal algebra.

Michael J. Field, Professor; Ph.D., Warwick (England), 1970. Dynamical systems, bifurcation theory, and symmetry.

William E. Fitzgibbon, Professor; Ph.D., Vanderbilt, 1972. Partial differential equations, applied mathematics, mathematical biology.

Michael Friedberg, Professor; Ph.D., LSU, 1965. Topological algebra, topological semigroups, uniquely divisible semigroups.

Roland Glowinski, Cullen Professor, Director of Center for Advanced Scientific Computation and member of French Academy of Science; Thèse d'État, Paris, 1970. Numerical analysis, applied mathematics.

Martin Golubitsky, Cullen Professor, Director of Institute for Theoretical Engineering and Science, and Fellow of American Association for the Advancement of Science; Ph.D., MIT, 1970. Bifurcation theory, nonlinear dynamics, symmetry.

John T. Hardy, Associate Professor; Ph.D., LSU, 1965. Number theory.

Jutta Hausen, Professor; Ph.D., Frankfurt, 1967. Abelian groups and module theory.

Andrew V. Ilin, Adjunct Associate Professor; Ph.D., Leningrad State (Russia), 1986. Applied mathematics.

Shanyu Ji, Associate Professor; Ph.D., Johns Hopkins, 1988. Complex analysis, differential geometry.

Gordon G. Johnson, Professor; Ph.D., Tennessee, 1964. Analysis.

Johnny A. Johnson, Professor; Ph.D., California, Riverside, 1968. Algebra.

Lennart Johnsson, Cullen Professor; Ph.D., Chalmers Institute of Technology, 1970. Scientific computation.

Klaus Kaiser, Professor and Managing Editor of *Houston Journal of Mathematics*; Ph.D., Bonn, 1966. Model theory, logic programming.

Hideo Kawarada, Adjunct Professor; Ph.D., Tokyo, 1965. Numerical analysis and partial differential equations.

Barbara L. Keyfitz, Professor and Fellow of American Association for the Advancement of Science; Ph.D., NYU, 1970. Nonlinear partial differential equations, applied mathematics.

Yuri Kuznetsov, Professor; Ph.D., Academy of Sciences of the USSR, 1969. Computational mathematics.

Andrew S. Lelek, Professor; Ph.D., Wroclaw (Poland), 1959. Set-theoretic topology, continua theory.

Ian Melbourne, Professor; Ph.D., Warwick (England), 1987. Equivariant dynamical systems, bifurcation theory.

Christopher B. Murray, Assistant Professor; Ph.D., Texas, 1964. Analysis, statistics.

Matthew J. O'Malley, Professor; Ph.D., Florida State, 1967. Algebra.

Tsorng-Whay Pan, Assistant Professor; Ph.D., Minnesota, 1990. Scientific computation.

Vern I. Paulsen, Professor; Ph.D., Michigan, 1977. Operator algebras and operator theory.

Jacques Périaux, Adjunct Professor; Ph.D., Paris VI, 1979. Computational mathematics.

Burnis C. Peters, Associate Professor; Ph.D., Texas A&M, 1973. Mathematical statistics.

Olivier Pironneau, Adjunct Professor; Thèse d'État, Paris VI, 1976. Numerical analysis, partial differential equations.

Min Ru, Associate Professor; Ph.D., Notre Dame, 1990. Complex analysis, differential geometry.

Richard Sanders, Associate Professor; Ph.D., UCLA, 1981. Numerical solutions of partial differential equations.

Ridgway Scott, M.D. Anderson Professor and Director of Texas Center for Advanced Molecular Computation; Ph.D., MIT, 1973. Numerical solution of partial differential equations, scientific computation.

James W. Stepp, Professor; Ph.D., Kentucky, 1968. Topological semigroups.

Charles T. Tucker, Associate Professor; Ph.D., Texas, 1966. Functional analysis.

David H. Wagner, Associate Professor; Ph.D., Michigan, 1980. Nonlinear partial differential equations.

Philip W. Walker, Associate Professor; Ph.D., Georgia, 1969. Ordinary differential equations.

Lewis T. Wheeler, Professor; Ph.D., Caltech, 1969. Applied mathematics, partial differential equations.

Mary F. Wheeler, Affiliated Senior Scientist; Ph.D., Rice, 1971. Numerical solution of partial differential equations.

Clifton T. Whyburn, Associate Professor; Ph.D., North Carolina at Chapel Hill, 1964. Analytic number theory.

Tiee-Jian Wu, Associate Professor; Ph.D., Indiana, 1982. Nonparametric statistics.

RECENT BOOKS BY FACULTY MEMBERS

Bao, D., S. S. Chern, and Z. Shen, eds. *Finsler Geometry.* Providence: AMS, 1996.

Cook, H., et al. **(A. Lelek),** eds. *Continua: With the Houston Problem Book.* New York: Dekker, 1995.

Bristeau, M. O., et al, eds. **(W. Fitzgibbon, J. Périaux,** and **M. F. Wheeler).** *Computational Science for the 21st Century.* Chichester, England: John Wiley & Sons, 1997.

Field, M. J., and **M. Golubitsky.** *Symmetry and Chaos: a Search for Pattern in Mathematics, Art and Nature.* Oxford: Oxford University Press, 1992.

Field, M. *Symmetry Breaking for Compact Lie Groups.* Providence: AMS, 1996.

Field, M. *Lectures on Bifurcations, Dynamics and Symmetry.* Pitman, 1996.

Fitzgibbon, W. E., and **M. F. Wheeler,** eds. *Computational Methods in Geosciences* (vol. I), *Modeling and Analysis of Diffusive and Advective Processes in Geosciences* (vol. II), and *Wave Propagation and Inversion* (vol. III). Philadelphia: SIAM, 1992.

Glowinski, R., and A. Lichnewsky, eds. *Computing Methods in Applied Sciences and Engineering.* Philadelphia: SIAM, 1990.

Glowinski, R., and **Y. A. Kuznetsov** et al, eds. **(J. Périaux).** *Domain Decomposition Methods for Partial Differential Equations.* Philadelphia: SIAM, 1991.

Abgrall, R., J.-A. Désidéri, **R. Glowinski,** M. Mallet, and **J. Périaux,** eds. *Hypersonic Flows for Reentry Problems,* vol. III. Heidelberg: Springer, 1993.

Stewart, I. N., and **M. Golubitsky.** *Fearful Symmetry: Is God a Geometer.* London: Basil Blackwell, 1992.

Ilin, A. V., and **L. R. Scott,** eds. *ICOSAHOM.95: Proceedings of the Third International Conference on Spectral and High Order Methods. Houston J. Math.,* 1996.

Douglas, R. G., and **V. I. Paulsen.** *Hilbert Modules over Function Algebras.* Harlow, England: Pitman, 1989.

Quarteroni, A., **J. Périaux, Y. A. Kuznetsov,** and O. B. Widlund, eds. *Domain Decomposition Methods in Science and Engineering.* Providence: AMS, 1994.

Brenner, S. C., and **L. R. Scott.** *The Mathematical Theory of Finite Element Methods.* New York: Springer, 1993.

UIC

UNIVERSITY OF ILLINOIS AT CHICAGO

Department of Mathematics, Statistics, and Computer Science

Programs of Study

The department, which ranks in the top thirty-five research mathematics departments nationwide, offers a wide variety of programs of study leading to degrees at the master's and doctoral levels.

The Master of Science (M.S.) degree program in mathematics is designed to lay foundations for doctoral work and also to prepare students for careers in business, government, and industry. The M.S. degree can be earned with a concentration in pure mathematics, computer science, applied mathematics, or probability and statistics. The department has programs in each of these four areas leading to the Ph.D. degree. The Master of Science in Teaching (M.S.T.) in mathematics and the Doctor of Arts (D.A.) degree programs are designed for teaching at various levels.

Students in the M.S. program have the option of passing a cumulative exam or writing a thesis. Students from other institutions seeking admission to the department's doctoral program must complete the work equivalent to that of the department's M.S. program. They may be required to pass a departmental exam to fully satisfy this requirement.

Two written preliminary exams must be passed and a minor course sequence must be successfully completed for the Ph.D. degree. The Ph.D. dissertation is expected to be a significant contribution to original mathematical research.

The M.S.T. program is designed to strengthen the preparation and background of secondary school and primary school teachers. The program is arranged on an individual basis and has no thesis requirement. Students who are teaching can complete it through evening and summer courses.

The D.A. program is designed to prepare students for instruction at two- and four-year colleges. It includes study and research in methodology and techniques for successful teaching of college mathematics. A dissertation is required.

Research Facilities

The University Library houses more than 1.5 million volumes and specialized collections. The Mathematics Library, located in the department, has more than 20,000 volumes and maintains more than 240 journals. In addition, students have access to the library resources of nearby institutions and the University of Illinois at Urbana-Champaign.

The University offers state-of-the-art computing facilities and Internet access. Resources include an IBM mainframe, a Convex mini-supercomputer, and an extensive network of UNIX workstations and PCs.

The department operates a diverse computing environment with UNIX workstations and PCs available for graduate student use. Graduate students have access to the department's Laboratory for Advanced Computing for research-related programming, supercomputers through specific departmental courses, and a statistical laboratory for research in statistics.

Financial Aid

The department awards a large number of teaching assistantships, some research assistantships, and a few tuition and fee waivers. Some summer support is available. The 1999–2000 stipend for the full-time, nine-month teaching assistantship (4–6 contact hours per week) is approximately $12,020. The campus awards a limited number of University fellowships for graduate study, with a 1999–2000 stipend of $14,000.

Cost of Study

Semester tuition and fees for 1999–2000 are $2538 for Illinois residents and $5856 for all others. Tuition and the service fee are waived for those holding teaching assistantships or fellowships as well as for those on tuition and fee waivers.

Living and Housing Costs

Some of UIC's residence halls are exclusively for graduate students. Rooms and apartments are available near campus and throughout the city at widely varying costs. The campus is easily accessible by public transportation.

Student Group

Approximately 25,000 students are enrolled at UIC, nearly 5,000 of whom are graduate students. They come from all parts of Illinois and the United States as well as from many other countries. The department has about 180 full-time students, of whom approximately 65 are in the doctoral program.

Location

UIC is located just west of the Loop, Chicago's downtown center, which is 5 minutes away by public transportation. Adjacent to campus are the Jane Addams's Hull House and two historic landmark residential areas. The city is well-known for its concerts, theater, galleries and museums, parks, ethnic restaurants, and lakefront recreation. There are other distinguished institutions of higher learning in the metropolitan area, which, along with UIC, contribute to an exciting atmosphere for the study of mathematics.

The University

UIC is the largest institution of higher learning in the Chicago area, and it is grouped in the top 100 research universities in the United States. The University offers bachelor's degrees in ninety-eight fields, master's degrees in seventy-nine, and doctoral degrees in forty-six.

Applying

Applicants are required to take the GRE General Test and a Subject Test in mathematics or computer science. The department requires three letters of recommendation and at least a B average in mathematics beyond calculus. Applications for fall admission should be submitted no later than March 20 for consideration for a fall teaching assistantship or research assistantship. Students wishing to be considered for a University Fellowship should submit their application materials no later than January 15. Study may also begin in the spring or summer semesters.

Correspondence and Information

Director of Graduate Studies
Department of Mathematics, Statistics, and Computer Science (Mail Code 249)
University of Illinois at Chicago
851 South Morgan Street
Chicago, Illinois 60607-7045

Telephone: 312-996-3041
Fax: 312-996-1491
E-mail: kdueball@uic.edu
World Wide Web: http://www.math.uic.edu

University of Illinois at Chicago

THE FACULTY AND THEIR RESEARCH

Algebra
A. O. L. Atkin, Ph.D. (emeritus), Cambridge, 1952. Modular forms, number theory.
Daniel Bernstein, Ph.D., Berkeley, 1995. Number theory.
Paul Brown, Ph.D., Berkeley, 1997. Polygons of finite groups.
Paul Fong, Ph.D., Harvard, 1959. Group theory, representation theory of finite groups.
Richard G. Larson, Ph.D., Chicago, 1965. Hopf algebras, application of computers to algebra, algorithms.
David E. Radford, Ph.D., North Carolina at Chapel Hill, 1970. Hopf algebras, algebraic groups.
Mark A. Ronan, Ph.D., Oregon, 1978. Buildings, geometries of finite groups.
Fredrick L. Smith, Ph.D., Ohio State, 1972. Group theory.
Stephen D. Smith, D.Phil., Oxford, 1973. Finite groups, representation theory.
Bhama Srinivasan, Ph.D., Manchester, 1960. Representation theory of finite and algebraic groups.
Jeremy Teitelbaum, Ph.D., Harvard, 1986. Number theory.
Yuri Tschinkel, Ph.D., MIT, 1992. Arithmetic algebraic geometry.

Analysis
Herbert J. Alexander, Ph.D., Berkeley, 1968. Several complex variables, function algebras.
Calixto P. Calderon, Ph.D., Buenos Aires, 1969. Harmonic analysis, differentiation theory.
Shmuel Friedland, D.Sc., Technion (Israel), 1971. Matrix theory and its applications.
Melvin L. Heard, Ph.D., Purdue, 1967. Integrodifferential equations.
Nets Katz, Ph.D., Pennsylvania, 1993. Harmonic analysis.
Jeff E. Lewis, Ph.D., Rice, 1966. Partial differential equations, microlocal analysis.
Charles S. C. Lin, Ph.D., Berkeley, 1967. Operator theory, perturbation theory, functional analysis.
Howard A. Masur, Ph.D., Minnesota, 1974. Quasiconformal mappings, Teichmuller spaces.
Yoram Sagher, Ph.D., Chicago, 1967. Harmonic analysis, interpolation theory.
Zbigniew Slodkowski, D.Sc., Warsaw, 1981. Several complex variables.
W. F. Stinespring, Ph.D., Chicago, 1957. Abstract analysis and operator algebra.
David S. Tartakoff, Ph.D., Berkeley, 1969. Partial differential equations, several complex variables.

Applied Mathematics
Eugene M. Barston, Ph.D., Stanford, 1964. Stability theory, fluid dynamics, plasma dynamics.
Neil E. Berger, Ph.D., NYU, 1968. Applied elasticity, fluid dynamics.
Susan Friedlander, Ph.D., Princeton, 1972. Geophysical and fluid dynamics.
Floyd B. Hanson, Ph.D., Brown, 1968. Numerical methods, asymptotic methods, stochastic bioeconomics.
Charles Knessl, Ph.D., Northwestern, 1986. Stochastic models, perturbation methods, queuing theory.
Alexander Lipton, Ph.D., Moscow State, 1982. Mathematical physics.
G. V. Ramanathan, Ph.D., Princeton, 1965. Statistical mechanics, critical phenomena.
Charles Tier, Ph.D., NYU, 1976. Analysis of stochastic models, queuing theory.

Computer Science and Combinatorics
Robert Grossman, Ph.D., Princeton, 1985. Applications of computers to analysis, symbolic computation.
Jeffrey S. Leon, Ph.D., Caltech, 1971. Computer methods in group theory and combinatorics, algorithms.
Glenn Manacher, Ph.D., Carnegie Tech, 1961. Algorithms, complexity, computer language design.
Uri N. Peled, Ph.D., Waterloo, 1976. Optimization, combinatorial algorithms, computational complexity.
Vera Pless, Ph.D., Northwestern, 1957. Coding theory, combinatorics.
Gyorgy Turan, Ph.D., Attila József (Hungary), 1982. Complexity theory, logic, combinatorics.

Geometry and Topology
A. K. Bousfield, Ph.D., MIT, 1966. Algebraic topology, homotopy theory.
Marc Culler, Ph.D., Berkeley, 1978. Low-dimensional topology, group theory.
Lawrence Ein, Ph.D., Berkeley, 1981. Algebraic geometry.
Henri Gillet, Ph.D., Harvard, 1978. Algebraic K-theory, algebraic geometry.
Brayton I. Gray, Ph.D., Chicago, 1965. Homotopy theory, cobordism theory.
James L. Heitsch, Ph.D., Chicago, 1971. Differential topology, theory of foliations.
Steven Hurder, Ph.D., Illinois at Urbana-Champaign, 1980. Differential topology, theory of foliations.
Louis Kauffman, Ph.D., Princeton, 1972. Differential topology, knot theory of singularities.
Anatoly S. Libgober, Ph.D., Tel-Aviv, 1977. Topology of varieties, theory of singularities.
Peter Shalen, Ph.D., Harvard, 1972. Low-dimensional topology, group theory.
Martin C. Tangora, Ph.D., Northwestern, 1966. Algebraic topology, homotopy theory.
John W. Wood, Ph.D., Berkeley, 1968. Differential topology, topology of varieties.
Stephen S.-T. Yau, Ph.D., SUNY at Stony Brook, 1976. Complex geometry, singularities of complex algebraic varieties.

Logic and Universal Algebra
John T. Baldwin, Ph.D., Simon Fraser, 1971. Model theory, universal algebra.
Joel D. Berman, Ph.D., Washington (Seattle), 1970. Lattice theory, universal algebra.
Willem J. Blok, Ph.D., Amsterdam, 1976. Algebraic logic, universal algebra, nonclassical logics.
William A. Howard, Ph.D., Chicago, 1956. Foundations of mathematics, proof theory.
Olivier Lessmann, Ph.D., Carnegie Mellon, 1998. Model theory.
David Marker, Ph.D., Yale, 1983. Model theory and applications to algebra.

Mathematics Education
Steven L. Jordan, Ph.D., Berkeley, 1970. Education, computer graphics, computational geometry.
David A. Page, M.A., Illinois, 1950. Elementary mathematics education.
Philip Wagreich, Ph.D., Columbia, 1966. Algebraic geometry, discrete groups, mathematics education.
A. I. Weinzweig, Ph.D., Harvard, 1957. Teaching and learning of mathematics, microcomputers in education.

Probability and Statistics
Emad El-Neweihi, Ph.D., Florida State, 1973. Reliability theory, probability, stochastic processes.
Nasrollah Etemadi, Ph.D., Minnesota, 1974. Probability theory, stochastic processes.
A. Hedayat, Ph.D., Cornell, 1969. Optimal designs, sampling theory, linear models, discrete optimization.
Dibyen Majumdar, Ph.D., Indian Statistical Institute, 1981. Optimal designs, linear models.
Klaus J. Miescke, Dr.rer.nat., Heidelberg, 1972. Statistics, decision theory, selection procedures.
T. E. S. Raghavan, Ph.D., Indian Statistical Institute, 1966. Game theory, optimization methods in matrices, statistics.

UNIVERSITY OF ILLINOIS AT URBANA–CHAMPAIGN

Department of Mathematics

Programs of Study
The department offers the Ph.D. in mathematics and the Master of Science in mathematics, applied mathematics (with several options, including actuarial science), or the teaching of mathematics.

The doctoral program is designed to be completed within three or four years after a master's degree or four to six years after a bachelor's degree, depending on the level of preparation. The department offers Ph.D. training in many areas, including algebra, analysis, combinatorics and optimization, differential equations and applications, geometry and topology, logic, number theory, and probability. Degree requirements include passing a comprehensive examination, acquiring a reading knowledge of two foreign languages, passing the preliminary examination, and writing and defending a thesis.

The Department of Mathematics has a harmonious working relation with the Departments of Statistics, Computer Science, and Physics and with engineering. It is possible to write an applied mathematics Ph.D. thesis largely under the direction of a faculty member from another department.

Research Facilities
The Mathematics Library is among the best in the world. It contains more than 90,000 volumes and subscribes to more than 900 periodicals in mathematics. It is in Altgeld Hall, the landmark Romanesque building that houses the department. Computer facilities available to graduate students include a group of Sun Workstations in Altgeld Hall and many Macintosh and DOS machines. The campus has very large computing facilities for those who need them. All students who have financial aid have assigned office space.

Financial Aid
The department offers about thirty new graduate teaching assistantships each year. The stipend is more than $13,500 for the 1999–2000 school year. The appointment includes a waiver of all tuition and some fees. The department also offers several full fellowships each year. More than 75 percent of the graduate students have full support, including almost all of the doctoral students. About 10 percent of the students with financial support have full fellowships; others have partial fellowships. Research assistantships are available for some advanced students.

Cost of Study
For 1999–2000, estimated tuition and fees are $5064 for residents of Illinois and $11,940 for nonresidents.

Living and Housing Costs
Students can live for a year in Champaign-Urbana on $10,000. An average one-bedroom apartment costs about $400 per month. The University offers accommodations for graduate students in two graduate dormitories, and the minimum charge for room and board in the 1998–99 academic year was $5542.

Student Group
The Department of Mathematics has 176 graduate students. Of these, 156 are in the doctoral program, 50 are women, and 116 are international students.

Location
Urbana-Champaign has a population of about 100,000. The area offers rich recreational and cultural programs. The four-theater Krannert Center for the Performing Arts offers a variety of concerts, operas, plays, and other theatrical events. Assembly Hall is an arena for events such as basketball games, ice shows, and rock concerts. There are superb facilities for graduate students to take part in team and individual sports. The University has the World Heritage Museum, the Krannert Art Museum, and the Natural History Museum and schedules many lectures by distinguished visitors in different fields in the arts, humanities, and sciences. There are more than thirty movie screens in the two cities, and the University also shows films of special interest.

The University
The University of Illinois has three locations, the original campus in Champaign-Urbana, the Chicago campus, and the Springfield campus. The Urbana-Champaign campus, with 25,000 undergraduate and 10,000 graduate students, has long been a major center for research and scholarship. It is particularly strong in the physical sciences, as well as mathematics, engineering, the biological sciences, and agriculture. The faculty and students in the department form a major mathematical community.

Applying
A bachelor's degree from an accredited institution is required for admission to graduate study. The completed application consists of the application form, three letters of recommendation, and transcripts describing college work. GRE scores are not absolutely necessary but are strongly advised, particularly the Subject Test in mathematics. The department realizes that this may not be possible for international students. International students must pass the Test of Spoken English with a score of 50 or higher to be considered for a teaching assistantship.

Correspondence and Information
John Gray
Director of Graduate Studies
Department of Mathematics
University of Illinois at Urbana-Champaign
1409 West Green Street
Urbana, Illinois 61801
Telephone: 217-333-3354 or 5749
Fax: 217-333-9576
E-mail: gray@math.uiuc.edu

University of Illinois at Urbana-Champaign

THE FACULTY AND THEIR RESEARCH

Actuarial Science
R. Gorvett, Ph.D.: actuarial science. E. Portnoy, Ph.D.: actuarial science, especially statistical methods in graduation and estimation of survival models.

Algebra
N. Boston, Ph.D.: algebraic number theory, group theory. D. Bowman, Ph.D.: number theory, hypergeometric functions. E. Dade, Ph.D.: representation theory, finite groups, ring theory. L. L. Dornhoff, Ph.D.: computer-aided instruction, switching and automata theory, algebraic coding theory, finite groups. S. Dutta, Ph.D.: commutative ring theory, homological algebra. E. G. Evans, Ph.D.: commutative algebra, algebraic geometry, homological algebra, polynomials in several variables. R. M. Fossum, Ph.D.: commutative algebra. D. R. Grayson, Ph.D.: K theory, L functions, algebraic geometry, algebraic groups. P. A. Griffith, Ph.D.: commutative algebra, polynomials in several variables, homological algebra, ring theory. S. Ivanov, Ph.D.: combinatorial group theory. G. J. Janusz, Ph.D.: representation theory, finite groups, cyclotomic fields, ring theory. L. R. McCulloh, Ph.D.: algebraic number theory, Galois module structure. R. R. Rao, Ph.D.: reductive groups and their representations, probability theory. D. J. S. Robinson, Ph.D.: infinite groups, homological algebra, combinatorial group theory. J. J. Rotman, Ph.D.: homological algebra, combinatorics, group theory. M. Suzuki, Ph.D.: finite groups, representation theory, algebraic groups, partial order structures. S. V. Ullom, Ph.D.: algebraic number theory, Galois module problems, representation theory, ideal class groups, p-extensions of number fields.

Analysis
I. D. Berg, Ph.D.: operator theory, spectral theory, almost periodic functions, manifolds with boundary. D. L. Burkholder, Ph.D.: probability theory, stochastic processes, functional analysis, Fourier analysis. J. P. D'Angelo, Ph.D.: several complex variables, partial differential equations, differential geometry, algebraic geometry. A. Hinkkanen, Ph.D.: conformal and quasiconformal mappings, potential theory, approximation theory, value distributions, differential equations, complex analytic dynamics, singular integral operators. M. Junge, Ph.D.: local theory of Banach spaces. R. P. Kaufman, Ph.D.: classical analysis, complex function theory, Hausdorff measure, spectral theory. R. Laugesen, Ph.D.: analysis and mathematical physics. P. A. Loeb, Ph.D.: nonstandard analysis, potential theory, compactification. H. P. Lotz, Ph.D.: Banach spaces, Banach lattices, positive operators. J. B. Miles, Ph.D.: entire and meromorphic functions, complex function theory, classical analysis. H. A. Porta, Ph.D.: functional analysis. Zhong-jin Ruan, Ph.D.: operator algebra. D. R. Sherbert, Ph.D.: functional analysis. A. Tumanov, M.S.: complex analysis. J. J. Uhl Jr., Ph.D.: vector measures, Banach spaces, functional analysis, measure theory. J.-M. Wu, Ph.D.: potential theory, conformal mapping, exceptional sets, complex function theory.

Applied Mathematics
M. Bergvelt, Ph.D.: mathematical physics, completely integrable systems, soliton equations. R. L. Jerrard, Ph.D.: nonlinear partial differential equations. L. McLinden, Ph.D.: nonlinear optimization, variational inequalities, nonlinear analysis, convex analysis and duality. R. G. Muncaster, Ph.D.: theory of elasticity, kinetic theory of gases, invariant manifolds, mathematical modeling. J. I. Palmore, Ph.D.: dynamical systems.

Combinatorics and Computer Science
Z. Füredi, Ph.D.: combinatorics, theory of finite sets with applications in geometry, designs, computer science. B. Reznick, Ph.D.: combinatorial methods in algebra, analysis, number theory, and geometry. A. Kostochka, Ph.D.: combinatorics. P. M. Weichsel, Ph.D.: algebraic graph theory, graph theory, combinatorial group theory, combinatorics. D. West, Ph.D.: combinatorics, graph theory, computational complexity, algorithms.

Geometry and Topology
S. B. Alexander, Ph.D.: differential geometry, global analysis. M. Ando, Ph.D.: stable homotopy theory and algebra geometry. A. Babakhanian, Ph.D.: algebraic geometry, homological algebra, ordinary differential equations. Steven Bradlow, Ph.D.: differential geometry, gauge theory, holomorphic vector bundles. R. F. Craggs, Ph.D.: geometric topology, PL topology, combinatorial group theory. G. K. Francis, Ph.D.: descriptive topology, topological design, differential topology, dynamical systems. J. W. Gray, Ph.D.: category theory, with applications in theoretical computer science—data types, denotational and algebraic semantics of programming languages, models of the lambda calculus. W. J. Haboush, Ph.D.: algebraic geometry. W. R. G. Haken, Ph.D.: low-dimensional topology, algorithms. E. M. Lerman, Ph.D.: group actions, stratified symplectic spaces and reduction. R. McCarthy, Ph.D.: algebraic topology and algebraic K-theory. I. Nikolaev, Ph.D.: differential geometry and generalized Riemann spaces in connection with Gromov's compactness theorem. J. Sullivan, Ph.D.: geometry. S. Tolman, Ph.D.: geometry, topology. P. Tondeur, Ph.D.: differential geometry, foliation theory, fiber spaces, differentiable manifolds.

Logic
C. W. Henson, Ph.D.: geometry of Banach spaces, nonstandard analysis, computational complexity, decision problems. C. G. Jockusch, Ph.D.: recursion theory and its connections with model theory and combinatorics. P. E. Schupp, Ph.D.: combinatorial group theory, decision problems, automata theory and formal language theory, computational complexity. A. Pillay, Ph.D.: model theory (stability theory, O-minimality) and connections with algebra, especially groups and differential algebra. L. van den Dries, Ph.D.: model theory, applications of model theory to algebra and analysis, definability theory.

Number Theory
B. C. Berndt, Ph.D.: analytic number theory, classical analysis, Gauss sums, Ramanujan's work. H. G. Diamond, Ph.D.: analytic number theory, distribution of primes, arithmetic functions, sieve methods. A. Hildebrand, Ph.D.: analytic number theory, probabilistic number theory, arithmetic functions. K. B. Stolarsky, Ph.D.: analytic number theory, combinatorics, zeros of polynomials, exponential polynomials, geometrical extremal problems.

Probability
C. D'Oleans-Dade (Adjunct); Ph.D.: probability theory, stochastic processes. D. Monrad, Ph.D.: Levy processes, Gaussian processes, Markov processes, stochastic processes. W. V. Philipp, Ph.D.: probability limit theorems, probability theory, stochastic processes, probabilistic number theory. R. Song, Ph.D.: probability. R. Sowers, Ph.D.: probability.

University of Illinois at Urbana-Champaign

SELECTED PUBLICATIONS

Alexander, S. B., I. D. Berg, and R. L. Bishop. Geometric curvature bounds in Riemannian manifolds with boundary. *Trans. Am. Math. Soc.* 339:703–16, 1993.

Alexander, S. B., and R. J. Currier. Nonnegatively curved hypersurfaces of hyperbolic space and subharmonic functions. *J. London Math. Soc.* 41(2):347–60, 1990.

Berg, I. D., and K. R. Davidson. Almost commuting matrices and a quantitative version of the Brown-Douglas-Fillmore theorem. *Acta Mathematican* 166:121–61, 1991.

Berg, I. D., T. Peck, and H. Porta. There is no continuous projection from the measurable functions on the square onto the measurable functions on the interval. *Israel J. Math.* 14:199–204, 1973.

Bergvelt, M. J., and A. P. E. ten Kroode. Partitions, vertex operator constructions and multi-component KP equations. *Pacific J. Math.,* in press.

Adams, M. R., and **M. J. Bergvelt.** The Krichever map, vector bundles over algebraic curves and Heisenberg algebras. *Comm. Math. Phys.* 154:265–305, 1993.

Berndt, B. C. *Ramanujan's Notebooks, Part IV.* New York: Springer-Verlag, 1994.

Berndt, B. C. *Ramanujan's Notebooks, Part III.* New York: Springer-Verlag, 1991.

Boston, N., H. W. Lensbra Jr., and K. A. Ribet. Quotients of group rings arising from two-dimensional representations. *C. R. Acad. Sci. Paris* 312(I):323–28, 1991.

Boston, N. Explicit deformation of Galois representations. *Inventiones Mathematicae* 103:181–96, 1991.

Bowman, D. A new generalization of Davison's theorem. *Fibonacci Quart.* 26:40–45, 1988.

Bradlow, S. B. Special metrics and stability for holomorphic bundles with global sections. *J. Diff. Geom.* 33:162–214, 1991.

Bradlow, S. B., and G. Daskalopoulos. Moduli of stable pairs for holomorphic bundles over Riemann surfaces. *Int. J. Math.* 2:477–513, 1991.

Burkholder, D. L. A geometrical characterization of Banach spaces in which Martingale difference sequences are unconditional. *Ann. Probab.* 9:997–1011, 1981.

Burkholder, D. L. Martingale transforms. *Ann. Math. Stat.* 37:1494–504, 1966.

Craggs, R. Links in 3-manifolds as obstructions in free reduction problems. *Topol. Applns.* 49:15–53, 1993.

Craggs, R. Free Heegaard diagrams and extended Nielson transformations II. *Illinois J. Math.* 23:101–27, 1979.

Dade, E. C. Counting characters in blocks, I. *Inventiones Mathematicae* 109:187–210, 1992.

Dade, E. C. Clifford theory for group-graded rings. *J. Reine Angew. Mathematik* 369:40–86, 1986.

Diamond, H., H. Halberstam, and H. E. Richert. A boundary value problem for a pair of differential delay equations related to sieve theory II. *J. Number Theory* 45:129–85, 1993.

Diamond, H., and J. Steinig. An elementary proof of the prime number theorem with a remainder term. *Inventiones Mathematicae* 11:199–258, 1970.

Dornhoff, L., and F. E. Hohn. *Applied Modern Algebra.* Macmillan, 1978.

Dornhoff, L. *Group Representation Theory.* Marcel Dekker, 1972.

Dutta, S. P. Syzygies and homological conjectures. *Proceedings of Microprogram,* June 15–July 2, 1987, eds. M. Hochster, C. Huneke, and J. D. Sally. New York: Springer-Verlag, 1989.

Dutta, S. P., M. Hochster, and J. E. Mclaughlin. Modules of finite projective dimension with negative intersection multiplicities. *Inventiones Mathematicae* 79:253–91, 1985.

Fossum, R. M. One dimensional formal group actions. *Contemp. Math. Am. Math. Soc.* 88:227–397, 1989.

Fossum, R. M. The divisor class group of a Krull domain. In *Ergebnisse der Mathematik und ihrer Grenzebiete.* Berlin, Heidelberg, and New York: Springer-Verlag, 1973.

Francis, G. K. *A Topological Picturebook.* New York: Springer-Verlag, 1987.

Francis, G. K. The folded ribbon theorem, a contribution to the study of immersed circles. *Trans. Am. Math. Soc.* 141:271–303, 1969.

Frankl, P., and **Z. Furedi.** Beyond the Erdös-Ko-Rado theorem. *J. Combinatorial Theory A* 56:182–94, 1991.

Furedi, Z. Matchings and covers in hypergraphs. *Graphs and Combinatorics* 4:115–206, 1988.

Gray, J. W. The integration of logical and algebraic types. In *Proc. Int. Workshop on Categorical Methods in Computer Science with Aspects from Topology, Lecture Notes in Computer Science,* vol. 393, pp. 16–36. New York: Springer-Verlag, 1989.

Gray, J. W. Enriched algebras, spectra and homotopy limits. In *Category Theory Applied to Algebra, Logic and Topology, Proc. Conference Gummersbach 1981, Lecture Notes in Mathematics,* vol. 962, pp. 82–99. New York: Springer-Verlag, 1982.

Grayson, D. R. Weight filtrations in algebraic K-theory. In *Motives, Proceedings of the Summer Research Conference on Motives in Seattle, 1991, Proceedings of Symposia in Pure Mathematics,* vol. 55, part 1, pp. 207–38. American Mathematical Society, 1994.

Gillet, H., and **D. R. Grayson.** The loop space of Q-construction. *Illinois J. Math.* 31:574–97, 1987.

Compton, K., and **W. Henson.** A uniform method for proving lower bounds on the computational complexity of logical decision problems. *Ann. Pure Appl. Logic* 36:207–24, 1987.

Henson, W., and L. A. Rubel. Some applications of Nevanlinna theory to mathematical logic: Identities of exponential functions. *Trans. Am. Math. Soc.* 282:1–32, 1984; 294:381, 1986.

Hildebrand, A., and G. Tenenbaum. On a class of differential-difference equations arising in number theory. *J. d'Analyse Math.* 67:145–79, 1993.

Hildebrand, A. The prime number theorem via the large sieve. *Mathematika* 33:23–30, 1986.

Hinkkanen, A. A sharp form of Nevanlinna's second fundamental theorem. *Inventiones Mathematicae* 108:549–74, 1992.

Hinkkanen, A. The structure of certain quasi-symmetric groups. *Memoirs Am. Math. Soc.* 83(422):87, 1990.

Ivanov, S. V. The free burnside groups of sufficiently large exponents. *Intl. J. Alg. Comput.* 4(1–2):1–312, 1994.

Ivanov, S. V., and A. Yu. Ol'Shanski. Some applications of graded diagrams in combinatorial group theory. Lecture notes, *London Math. Soc.* 160:258–308, 1991.

Jerrard, R. L. Fully nonlinear phase field equations and generalized mean curvature motion. *Comm. Partial Differential Equations* 20:233–65, 1995.

Jockusch, C., and R. A. Shore. Pseudo-jump operators II: Transfinite iterations, hierarchies, and minimal covers. *J. Symbol. Logic* 49:1205–36, 1984.

Jockusch, C. Ramsey's theorem and recursion theory. *J. Symbol. Logic* 37:268–80, 1972.

Laugesen, R. Eigenvalues of the Laplacian on inhomogeneous membranes. *Am. J. Math.,* in press.

Ashbaugh, M., and **R. Laugesen.** Fundamental tones and buckling loads of clamped plates. *Ann. della Scuola Normale Superiore di Pisa* 23:383–402, 1996.

Lerman, E. M., and R. Sjamaar. Stratified symplectic spaces and reduction. *Ann. Math.* 134:375–422, 1991.

Loeb, P. A reduction technique for limite theorems in analysis and probability theory. *Arlov Matematik* 20(1):25–43, 1992.

Loeb, P. Conversion from nonstandard to standard measure spaces and applications in probability theory. *Trans. Am. Math. Soc.* 211:113–22, 1974.

Dundas, B., and **R. McCarthy.** Stable K-theory and topological Hochschild homology. *Ann. Math.,* in press.

McCarthy, R. The cyclic homology of an exact category. *J. Pure Appl. Math.* 93:251–96, 1994.

University of Illinois at Urbana-Champaign

Selected Publications (continued)

McCulloh, L. R. Galois module structure of abelian extensions. *J. Reine Angew. Math.* 375/376:259–306, 1987.

McCulloh, L. R. A class number formula for elementary-abelian-group rings. *J. Algebra* 68(2):443–52, 1981.

Hayman, W. K., and **J. Miles.** On the growth of a meromorphic function and its derivatives. *Complex Variables Theory Applns.* 12:245–60, 1989.

Miles, J. Some examples of the dependence of the Nevanlinna deficiency upon the choice of origin. *Proc. London Math. Soc.* 47(3):145–76, 1983.

Berestovskii, V., and **I. G. Nikolaev.** Multidimensional generalized Riemannian spaces. In *Encyclopaedia of Mathematical Sciences, Geometry IV,* vol. 70, pp. 165–243. Berlin and Heidelberg: Springer-Verlag, 1994.

Nikolaev, I. G. Closure of the set of classical Riemannian manifolds. *J. Soviet Math.* 55:2100–2114, 1991.

Palmore, J. A relation between Newton's method and successive approximations for quadratic irrationals. In *From Topology to Computation: Proceedings of the Smalefest,* pp. 254–59, eds. M. Hirsch, J. Marsden, and M. Shub. New York: Springer, 1993.

Herring, C., and **J. Palmore.** Computer arithmetic, chaos and fractals. *Physica D* 42(1–3):99–110, 1990.

Pillay, A. Differential algebraic groups and the number of countable differentially closed fields. In *Model Theory of Fields,* Lecture Notes in Logic 5. Springer-Verlag, 1996.

Pillay, A. *Geometric Stability Theory.* Oxford University Press, 1996.

Pillay, A., and E. Hrushovski. Definable subgroups of algebraic groups over finite fields. *J. Reine Angew. Mathematik* 462:69–91, 1995.

Pillay, A. The geometry of forking and groups of finite Morley rank. *J. Symbol. Logic* 60, 1995.

Pillay, A. Model theory, differential algebra, and number theory. In *Proceedings of the International Congress of Mathematicians '94.* Birkhauser Verlag, 1995.

Pillay, A., and E. Hrushovski. Groups definable in local fields and pseudofinite fields. *Israel J. Math.* 85:203–62, 1994.

Portnoy, E. *Bivariate Schuette Graduation, Actuarial Research Clearing House,* vol. 1, pp. 127–34, 1994.

Portnoy, E. Crossover in mortality rates by sex. *Trans. Soc. Actuaries* 38:229–41, 1986.

Reznick, B. Sums of even powers of real linear forms. *Memoirs Am. Math. Soc.* 96(463), March 1992.

Reznick, B. Forms derived from the arithmetic-geometric inequality. *Math. Ann.* 283:431–64, 1989.

Robinson, D. J. S. The algorithmic theory of polycyclic-by-finite groups. *J. Algebra* 142:118–49, 1991.

Robinson, D. J. S. The vanishing of certain homology and cohomology groups. *J. Pure Appl. Algebra* 7:145–67, 1976.

Rotman, J., and P. Weichsel. Simple Lie algebras and graphs. *J. Algebra* 169:775–90, 1994.

Rotman, J. The Grothendieck group of torsion-free abelian groups of finite rank. *Proc. London Math. Soc.* 13(3):724–32, 1963.

Effros, G., and **Z.-J. Ruan.** On approximation properties for operator spaces. *Intl. J. Math.* 1:163–87, 1990.

Ruan, Z.-J. Subspaces of C*-algebras. *J. Funct. Anal.* 76:217–30, 1988.

Muller, D., and **P. E. Schupp.** Simulating alternating automata by nondeterministic automata. *Theoret. Comp. Sci.,* in press.

Lynden, R. C., and **P. E. Schupp.** Combinatorial group theory. In *Ergebnisse der Mathematik,* vol. 89. New York: Springer-Verlag, 1977.

Brown, J. W., and **D. Sherbert.** *Linear Algebra with Business Applications,* 2nd edition. New York: McGraw-Hill, 1993.

Bartel, R. G., and **D. Sherbert.** *Introduction to Real Analysis,* 2nd edition. New York: Wiley, 1992.

Chen, Z.-Q., and **R. Song.** Intrinsic ultracontractivity and conditional gauge for symmetric stable processes. *J. Funct. Analysis* 150:204–38, 1997.

Song, R., and X. Y. Zhou. A remark on diffusion of directed polymers in random environments. *J. Stat. Phys.* 85(1–2):277–89, 1996.

Sowers, R. Blowup for the heat equation with a noise term. *Probability Theory and Related Fields* 97:287–320, 1993.

Stolarsky, K. B. Singularities of Bessel-zeta functions, and Hawkins' polynomials. *Mathematika* 32:96–103, 1985.

Stolarsky, K. B. Sums of distances between points on a sphere II. *Proc. Am. Math. Soc.* 41:575–82, 1973.

Kusner, R., and **J. Sullivan.** M'obius Energies for Knots and Links, Surfaces and Submanifolds. In *Geometric Topology,* pp. 570–604, ed. Kazez. International Press, 1996.

Hsu, L., R. Kusner, and **J. Sullivan.** Minimizing the squared mean curvature integral for surfaces in space forms. *Exp. Math.* 1(3):191–207, 1992.

Maeda, Y., **P. Tondeur,** and S. Rosenberg. Global analysis in modern mathematics. In *The Palais Festival Volume,* pp. 171–217. Publish or Perish, Inc., 1993.

Kamber, F. W., and **P. Tondeur.** Characteristic invariants of foliated bundles. *Manuscripta Mathematica* 11:51–89, 1974.

Tumanov, A. Connections and propagation of analyticity for CR functions. *Duke Math J.* 73:1–24, 1994.

Tumanov, A. Extension of CR functions into a wedge from a manifold of finite type. *Math USSR Sbornik* 64:129–40, 1989.

Boston, N., and **S. V. Ullom.** Representations related to CM elliptic curves. *Math. Proc. Camb. Phil. Soc.* 1113:71–85, 1993.

Ullom, S. V. Class groups of cyclotomic fields and group rings. *J. London Math. Soc.* 17(2):231–39, 1978.

van den Dries, L., A. Macintyre, and D. Marker. The elementary theory of restricted analytic fields with exponentiation. *Ann. Math.* 140:183–205, 1994.

Denef, J., and **L. van den Dries.** P-adic and real subanalytic sets. *Ann. Math.* 128:79–138, 1988.

Scheinerman, and **D. B. West.** The interval number of a planar graph—three intervals suffice. *J. Combinatorial Theory B* 35:224–39, 1983.

West, D. B. A symmetric chain decomposition of L(4,n). *Europ. J. Combinatorics* 1:379–83, 1980.

Lewis, J. L., and **J.-M. Wu.** On conjectures of Arakelyan and Littlewood. *J. d'Analyse Math.* 50:259–83, 1988.

Hayman, W. K., and **J.-M. Wu.** Level sets of univalent functions. *Comment. Math. Helvetici* 56:361–403, 1981.

UNIVERSITY OF NEBRASKA–LINCOLN

Department of Mathematics and Statistics

Programs of Study

The department's programs provide a congenial and supportive atmosphere for learning and lead to the M.S., M.A., M.A. for teachers, and Ph.D. degrees, with particular strengths in applied mathematics and differential equations; commutative algebra, algebraic geometry, and coding theory; discrete and experimental mathematics (combinatorics, semigroup theory, geometric group theory); operator algebras and related areas; and statistics (survey sampling, Bayesian statistics, biostatistics). Department faculty members and graduate students are also involved in interdisciplinary work with biometry, chemistry, computer science, the Gallup Center for Survey Research, geology, electrical engineering, and the Teachers College.

In addition to academic work, graduate students are presented with unusual opportunities for professional development. A strong commitment to mathematics and science curricular reform, as evidenced by the department's "Math Across the Curriculum" NSF grant, prepares students for the full range of academic employment. Graduate students have leading roles in departmental curricular reform, receive support for attending professional conferences and job seeking, and serve on faculty hiring committees. Experienced graduate teaching assistants often are given full responsibility for teaching classes of their own (not just assisting a professor), and the department actively solicits graduate student concerns via its Graduate Student Advisory Board.

The master's degrees require 36 credits and a comprehensive exam and can include minors inside or outside the department; they typically take two years to complete. The Ph.D. requires 90 credits, a qualifying exam (covering master's-level material), a comprehensive exam in preparation for beginning research, a language (math) or research tool (statistics) requirement, an original thesis, and an oral thesis defense.

Research Facilities

Departmental offices are in Oldfather Hall, with additional first-year graduate student offices in a nearby building. The mathematics library is excellent and is conveniently located within the department. The department also has an Internet-connected computer lab with 24-hour access, and every graduate student office has Internet access. All graduate students and faculty members have accounts on the departmental computer network, which supports an array of mathematical software in addition to student and faculty member Web pages, Web browsers, e-mail, document preparation programs such as TeX, and online access to library holdings and the American Mathematical Society's Mathematical Reviews. Additional facilities include a classroom computer lab of Internet-connected NeXTstep workstations and an adjacent high-tech classroom with substantial computer and video capabilities.

Financial Aid

Most graduate students have graduate teaching assistantships, with stipends depending on experience and duties. The 2000–01 academic year stipend for first-year teaching assistants will range from $12,000 to $15,000, plus a full tuition waiver. The $12,000 stipend will involve 4 contact hours per week and a weekly time commitment of 13 to 14 hours, including preparation, grading, and consultation. Summer appointments, which pay an additional $2200 to $3300, are usually available, and 10 or more students are awarded research or fellowship support each summer.

Cost of Study

Teaching assistants receive tuition waivers valued at $2300 for residents and $5675 for nonresidents. Student fees of about $240 are charged to all students.

Living and Housing Costs

With Lincoln's low cost of living, a student is well able to live on a teaching assistantship. Current typical housing costs are $250–$460 for one-bedroom apartments and $350–$600 for two-bedroom apartments and duplexes. A small graduate student dormitory is also available; room and board for single rooms in the graduate student dormitory for the 1999–2000 academic year are $4870.

Student Group

The department supports between 55 and 60 full-time graduate students; half are women.

Student Outcomes

Due in part to the attention given to students' overall preparation, students have done well in the job market. Areas of employment of recent master's students include the armed forces, education (both secondary and college level), and business, at companies such as Hormel, Cerner Corp., Meredith Corp., Gallup, and Anderson Consulting. Employment offers for Ph.D.'s since 1996 include an NSF postdoctoral fellowship at RPI; assistant professorships at the University of Texas at Arlington, the U.S. Air Force Academy, Virginia Commonwealth University, Jordan University of Science and Technology, West Texas A&M, University of South Dakota, Concordia College, and Shippensburg University; postdoctoral instructorships at Duke University, Central Michigan University, and the University of Texas at Austin; data analyst at National Indemnity in Omaha; and research scientist at Telecommunications Advancement Organization in Japan.

Location

The University is located in Lincoln, the state capital, on an attractive campus near downtown. Bike trails provide easy access to most of the city; daytime bus service is available and free to all University of Nebraska–Lincoln (UNL) students. Lincoln has many parks, theaters, museums, and performance spaces; venues such as The Zoo Bar (1993 W. C. Handy "Blues Club of the Year" winner) make the music scene notably active.

The University and The Department

The University of Nebraska–Lincoln is the flagship research university of the Nebraska University system. The University was founded in 1869, and in 1896 it established the first graduate college west of the Mississippi. The current total enrollment is 21,959, and graduate enrollment is 4,404. The Department of Mathematics and Statistics recently celebrated the 100th anniversary of the awarding of its first Ph.D. degree. University facilities host world-class theater, music, and dance and include the internationally recognized Sheldon Art Gallery, which also houses two film series specializing in independent and foreign film.

Applying

A completed application includes a $35 application fee, an application form, official transcripts from all prior college- or university-level work, three letters of reference, and a letter of intent discussing interests and goals. A minimum TOEFL score of 550 and the GRE are required for international students. There is no separate application for financial aid. Students should request application materials at the address below or apply online via a link from the departmental graduate program Web site, which is listed below. E-mail inquiries are welcomed.

Correspondence and Information

Graduate Committee Chair
Department of Mathematics and Statistics
University of Nebraska–Lincoln
Lincoln, Nebraska 68588-0323

Telephone: 402-472-3731
Fax: 402-472-8466
E-mail: gc@math.unl.edu
World Wide Web: http://www.math.unl.edu/Dept/Info/Grad

University of Nebraska–Lincoln

THE FACULTY AND THEIR RESEARCH

Mark Brittenham, Visiting Assistant Professor; Ph.D., Cornell, 1990. Topology.

Trent Buskirk, Assistant Professor; Ph.D., Arizona State, 1999. Survey sampling.

Leo Chouinard, Associate Professor; Ph.D., Princeton, 1975. Algebra, combinatorics.

Steve Cohn, Associate Professor; Ph.D., NYU (Courant), 1989. Partial differential equations, applied math.

Bo Deng, Associate Professor; Ph.D., Michigan State, 1987. Chaotic theory and applications, bifurcation theory, mathematical biology, neural networks.

Allan Donsig, Assistant Professor; Ph.D., Texas A&M, 1993. Operator algebras and operator theory.

Steven Dunbar, Professor; Ph.D., Minnesota, 1981. Applied mathematics, dynamical systems.

Lynn Erbe, Visiting Professor; Ph.D., Nebraska, 1968. Differential equations.

Brian Harbourne, Professor; Ph.D., MIT, 1982. Algebraic geometry, commutative algebra.

Susan Hermiller, Assistant Professor; Ph.D., Cornell, 1992. Geometric group theory.

Gwendolen Hines, Assistant Professor; Ph.D., Georgia Tech, 1993. Dynamical systems, delay equations, partial differential equations.

David Jaffe, Associate Professor; Ph.D., Berkeley, 1987. Algebraic geometry, coding theory.

Gerald Johnson, Professor; Ph.D., Minnesota, 1968. Analysis.

Earl Kramer, Professor; Ph.D., Michigan, 1969. Combinatorics, design theory, abstract and mathematical art.

Partha Lahiri, Professor; Ph.D., Florida, 1986. Survey sampling, inference.

Glenn Ledder, Associate Professor; Ph.D., Rensselaer, 1990. Applied mathematics: mathematical modeling, asymptotics, and integral equations; applications to problems in diffusion, groundwater flow, and combustion.

Jim Lewis, Professor; Ph.D., LSU, 1971. Commutative algebra, mathematics education.

David Logan, Professor; Ph.D., Ohio State, 1970. Applied mathematics, partial differential equations.

Tapabrata Maiti, Assistant Professor; Ph.D., Indian Statistical Institute (Calcutta), 1996. Survey sampling, Bayesian statistics.

Tom Marley, Associate Professor; Ph.D., Purdue, 1989. Commutative algebra: cohomology theory of modules; Hilbert function theory.

John Meakin, Professor; Ph.D., Monash (Australia), 1969. Semigroups, combinatorial group theory.

Walter Mientka, Professor; Ph.D., Colorado, 1955. Number theory.

Dan Nettleton, Assistant Professor; Ph.D., Iowa, 1996. Statistical genetics, order-restricted inference, asymptotic distribution theory.

Lisa Orlandi-Korner, Visiting Assistant Professor; Ph.D., Cornell, 1998. Geometric group theory.

John Orr, Associate Professor; Ph.D., London, 1989. Operator theory, operator algebras, instructional technology.

Allan Peterson, Professor; Ph.D., Tennessee, 1968. Difference equations and differential equations.

David Pitts, Professor; Ph.D., Berkeley, 1986. Functional analysis, operator algebras, nest algebras, commutative subspace lattices, noncommutative function theory.

Jamie Radcliffe, Assistant Professor; Ph.D., Cambridge, 1989. Combinatorics: extremal set systems, random methods, geometry of convex bodies.

Mohammad Rammaha, Associate Professor; Ph.D., Indiana, 1985. Partial differential equations and analysis, hyperbolic and parabolic PDEs and applications.

Richard Rebarber, Professor; Ph.D., Wisconsin, 1984. Control theory, partial differential equations, stability.

Thomas Shores, Professor; Ph.D., Kansas, 1968. Numerical analysis and applied mathematics: sinc methods, numerical solutions of differential equations, solute transport in porous media, inverse problems.

David Skoug, Professor; Ph.D., Minnesota, 1966. Integration in function space, Wiener and Feynman integrals.

Melvin Thornton, Professor; Ph.D., Illinois, 1965. Algebraic topology, point set topology, semigroups, mathematics education.

Robert Tortora, Adjunct Professor; Ph.D., Bowling Green, 1975. Survey research.

Judy Walker, Assistant Professor; Ph.D., Illinois at Urbana-Champaign, 1996. Algebraic geometry and coding theory.

Mark Walker, Assistant Professor; Ph.D., Illinois at Urbana-Champaign, 1996. Algebraic K-theory, algebraic geometry, commutative algebra.

Roger Wiegand, Professor; Ph.D., Washington (Seattle), 1967. Commutative algebra, representation theory, algebraic geometry.

Sylvia Wiegand, Professor; Ph.D., Wisconsin–Madison, 1972. Commutative algebra, ring theory.

Gordon Woodward, Associate Professor; Ph.D., Maryland, 1971. Harmonic analysis, operator theory.

University of Nebraska–Lincoln

SELECTED PUBLICATIONS

Brittenham, M., and Y.-Q. Wu. The classification of Dehn surgeries on 2-bridge knots. *Comm. Anal. Geom.,* in press.

Brittenham, M., and R. Roberts. When incompressible tori meet essential laminations. *Pacific J. Math.,* in press.

Brittenham, M. Essential laminations, exceptional Seifert-fibered spaces, and Dehn filling. *J. Knot Theory Ramifications* 7:425–32, 1998.

Brittenham, M., R. Naimi, and R. Roberts. Graph manifolds and taut foliations. *J. Diff. Geom.* 45:446–70, 1997.

Brittenham, M. Essential laminations in Seifert-fibered spaces. *Topology* 32:61–85, 1993.

Buskirk, T. D. Nonparametric density estimation using complex survey data. *Am. Stat. Assoc. Proc. Survey Methodology Sect.,* in press.

Cohn, S., J. D. Logan, and **T. Shores.** Stability of traveling waves for a solute transport problem in porous media. *Can. Appl. Math. Q.* 4:243–63, 1996.

Cohn, S., and **J. D. Logan.** Mathematical analysis of a reactive-diffusive model of the dispersal of a chemical tracer with nonlinear convection. *Math. Models Methods Appl. Sci.* 5(1):29–46, 1995.

Cohn, S. Global existence for the nonresonant Schrodinger equation in two space dimensions. *Can. Appl. Math. Q.* 2(5):257–82, 1994.

Chow, S.-N., **B. Deng,** and M. Friedman. Heteroclinic loop bifurcations with nongeneric parameters. *SIAM J. Appl. Math.,* in press.

Deng, B. Glucose-induced period-doubling cascade in the electrical activity of pancreatic beta-cells. *J. Math. Biol.* 38:21–78, 1999.

Deng, B. Constructing Lorenz type attractors through singular perturbations. *Int. J. Bif. Chaos* 5:1633–42, 1995.

Deng, B. Constructing homoclinic orbits and chaotic attractors. *Int. J. Bif. Chaos* 4:823–41, 1994.

Deng, B. Homoclinic twisting bifurcations and cusp horseshoe maps. *J. Dynam. Diff. Equations* 5:417–67, 1993.

Donsig, A. P. Dilations of limit algebras and interpolating spectrum. *Pacific J. Math.* 184:75–93, 1998.

Davidson, K. R., **A. P. Donsig,** and T. D. Hudson. Norm-closed bimodules of nest algebras. *J. Operator Theory* 39:59–87, 1998.

Donsig, A. P., and S. C. Power. Homology for operator algebras IV: On the regular classification of limits of 4-cycle algebras. *J. Funct. Anal.* 150:240–87, 1997.

Donsig, A. P., and S. C. Power. The failure of approximate inner conjugacy for standard diagonals in regular limit algebras. *Can. Math. Bull.* 39:420–8, 1996.

Donsig, A. P., and T. D. Hudson. The lattice of ideals of a triangular AF algebra. *J. Funct. Anal.* 138:1–39, 1996.

Anderson, J., D. Stephens, and **S. Dunbar.** Saltatory search: A theoretical analysis. *Behav. Ecol.,* in press.

Dunbar, S. The average distance between points in geometric figures. *Coll. Math. J.,* May 1997.

Dunbar, S. A geometric approach to a nonlinear boundary layer problem arising in physical oceanography. *SIAM J. Math. Anal.* 24(2):444–65, 1993.

Erbe, L., and **A. Peterson.** Green's functions and comparison theorems for differential equations on measure chains. *Dynam. Continuous Discrete Impulsive Syst.* 6:121–37, 1999.

Erbe, L., and M. Tang. Uniqueness theorems for positive radial solutions of quasilinear elliptic equations in a ball. *J. Diff. Equations* 138:351–79, 1997.

Harbourne, B. The ideal generation problem for fat points. *J. Pure Appl. Algebra,* in press.

Harbourne, B. Free resolutions of fat point ideals on P^2. *J. Pure Appl. Algebra* 125:213–34, 1998.

Harbourne, B. Birational models of rational surfaces. *J. Algebra* 190:145–62, 1997.

Harbourne, B. Anticanonical rational surfaces. *Trans. AMS* 349:1191–208, 1997.

Harbourne, B. Rational surfaces with $K^2 > 0$. *Proc. AMS* 124:727–33, 1996.

Hermiller, S., and J. Meier. Artin groups, rewriting systems, and three-manifolds. *J. Pure Appl. Algebra* 136:141–56, 1999.

Hermiller, S. M., X. H. Kramer, and R. C. Laubenbacher. Monomial orderings and Gröbner bases for the commutator ideal of a free algebra. *J. Symbolic Computation* 27:133–41, 1999.

Hermiller, S., and J. Meier. Tame combings, almost convexity, and rewriting systems for groups. *Math. Z.* 225:263–76, 1997.

Hermiller, S., and J. Meier. Algorithms and geometry for graph products of groups. *J. Algebra* 171:230–57, 1995.

Hermiller, S. M. Rewriting systems for Coxeter groups. *J. Pure Appl. Algebra* 92:137–48, 1994.

Carvalho, A. N., and **G. Hines.** Lower semicontinuity of local unstable manifolds for gradient systems. *J. Dynam. Syst.,* in press.

Gedeon, T., and **G. Hines.** Upper semicontinuity of Morse sets of a discretization of a delay-differential equation. *J. Differ. Equations* 151(1):36–78, 1999.

Hines, G. Upper semicontinuity of the attractor with respect to parameter dependent delays. *J. Differ. Equations* 123(1):56–92, 1995.

Hines, G. On the perturbation of the kernel for delay systems with continuous kernel. *Appl. Anal.* 56(3/4):243–63, 1995.

Jaffe, D. B., and V. D. Tonchev. Computing linear codes and unitals. *Designs Codes Cryptography,* in press.

Jaffe, D. B. A brief tour of split linear programming. In *Proc. AAECC 12,* Springer Lecture Notes in Computer Science 1255:164–173, 1997.

Jaffe, D. B. Coherent functors, with application to torsion in the Picard group. *Trans. AMS* 349:481–527, 1997.

Jaffe, D. B., and D. Ruberman. A sextic surface cannot have 66 nodes. *J. Algebra Geom.* 6:151–68, 1997.

Guralnick, R., **D. B. Jaffe,** W. Raskind, and **R. Wiegand.** On the Picard group: Torsion and the kernel induced by a faithfully flat map. *J. Algebra* 183:420–55, 1996.

De Facio, B., **G. W. Johnson,** and M. Lapidus. Feynman's operational calculus and evolution equations. *Acta Appl. Math.,* in press.

Albeverio, S., **G. W. Johnson,** and Z. M. Ma. The analytic operator-valued Feynman integral via additive functionals of Brownian motion. *Acta Appl. Math.* 42:267–95, 1996.

Johnson, G. W., and G. Kallianpur. Homogeneous chaos, p-forms, scaling and the Feynman integral. *Trans. AMS* 340:503–48, 1993.

Kramer, E. S., D. L. Kreher, and R. A. Mathon. On Steiner 3-wise balanced designs of order 17. *J. Combinatorial Designs* 5:125–45, 1997.

Kramer, E. S. t-wise balanced designs. Chapter in *The CRC Handbook of Combinatorial Designs,* pp. 1–753, eds. C. J. Colbourn and J. H. Dinitz. CRC Press, 1996.

Brualdi, R. A., et al. (**E. S. Kramer**). On a matrix partition conjecture. *J. Combinatorial Theory* Series A, 69:333–46, 1995.

Arora, V., **P. Lahiri,** and K. Mukherjee. Empirical Bayes estimation of finite population means from complex surveys. *J. Am. Stat. Assoc.,* in press.

Datta, G. S., and **P. Lahiri.** Robust hierarchical Bayes estimation of small area characteristics in presence of covariates and outliers. *J. Multivar. Anal.* 54(2):310–28, 1995.

Rao, J. N. K., and **P. Lahiri.** Robust estimation of mean square error of small area estimators. *J. Am. Stat. Assoc.* 90:758–66, 1995.

Ledder, G., and J.-J. Ren. On Cramer-Von Mises tests of goodness of fit with censored data. *Commun. Stat. Simul. Comput.,* in press.

Ledder, G., and **J. D. Logan.** Traveling waves for a nonequilibrium, two-site nonlinear sorption model. *Appl. Math. Modeling* 19:270–7, 1995.

Ledder, G. Analytical solution of a near-equidiffusional flame problem. *IMA. J. Appl. Math.* 52:201–20, 1994.

Logan, J. D. Weighted-L^2 stability of traveling waves in a porous medium. *Commun. Appl. Nonl. Anal.* 4:55–62, 1997.

Logan, J. D. Solute transport in porous media with scale-dependent dispersion and periodic boundary conditions. *J. Hydrol.* 184:261–76, 1996.

Logan, J. D. *Introduction to Nonlinear Partial Differential Equations.* New York: Wiley-Interscience, 1994.

Datta, G. S., D. Bannmo, and **T. Maiti.** A nested error regression model for multivariate hierarchical Bayes estimation of small area means. *Sankhya Ser. A* 60:344–62, 1998.

Maiti, T. Hierarchical Bayes estimation of mortality rates for disease mapping. *J. Stat. Plann. Inference* 69:339–48, 1998.

Ghosh, M., and **T. Maiti.** Discussion of the paper by D. Pfeffermann, C. J. Skinner, H. Goldstein, D. J. Holmes and J. Rasbash. *J. Roy. Stat. Soc. Ser. B,* 1998.

Ghosh, M., D.-H. Kim, and **T. Maiti.** Hierarchical Bayesian analysis of longitudinal data. *Sankhya Ser. B* 59:326–34, 1997.

Chaudhuri, A., and **T. Maiti.** Variance estimation in model assisted survey sampling. *Comm. Stat. Theory Methods* 23:1203–14, 1994.

Marley, T. Finitely graded local cohomology and the depths of graded algebras. *Proc. Am. Math. Soc.* 123:3601–7, 1995.

Marley, T. Depth formulas for certain graded ring associated to an ideal. *Nagoya Math. J.* 133:57–69, 1994.

University of Nebraska–Lincoln

Selected Publications (continued)

Birget, J.-C., S. Margolis, and **J. Meakin**. On the word problem for tensor products and amalgams of semigroups. *Int. J. Algebra Comput.*, in press.

Birget, J.-C., S. Margolis, **J. Meakin,** and P. Weil. PSPACE complete problems for subgroups of free groups and finite inverse automata. *Theor. Comput. Sci.*, in press.

Cherubini, A., **J. Meakin**, and B. Piochi. Amalgams of free inverse semigroups. *Semigroup Forum* 54:199–220, 1997.

Meakin, J., and M. Sapir. The word problem in the variety of inverse semigroups with abelian covers. *J. London Math. Soc.* 53:79–98, 1996.

Haataja, S., S. Margolis, and **J. Meakin**. Bass-Serre theory of groupoids and the structure of full regular semigroup amalgams. *J. Algebra* 183:38–54, 1996.

Nettleton, D. Testing for ordered means in a variation of the normal mixture model. *J. Stat. Plann. Inference,* in press.

Nettleton, D. Order restricted hypothesis testing in a variation of the normal mixture model. *Can. J. Stat.,* in press.

Nettleton, D. Convergence properties of the EM algorithm for constrained parameter spaces. *Can. J. Stat.,* in press.

Nettleton, D. Investigating home court advantage. *J. Stat. Educ.* 6:n2, 1998.

Nettleton, D., and J. Praestgaard. Interval mapping of quantitative trait loci through order restricted inference. *Biometrics* 54:74–87, 1998.

Orlandi-Korner, L. The Bieri-Neumann-Strebel invariant of $P\Sigma_n$. *Proc. Am. Math. Soc.,* in press.

Orr, J. L., and **D. R. Pitts**. Factorization of triangular operators and ideals through the diagonal. *Proc. Edinburgh Math. Soc.* 40:227–41, 1997.

Davidson, K. R., **J. L. Orr,** and **D. R. Pitts**. Connectedness of the invertibles in certain nest algebras. *Can. Math. Bull.* 38:412–20, 1995.

Orr, J. L. Triangular algebras and ideals of nest algebras. *Mem. Am. Math. Soc.* 562(117), 1995.

Davidson, K. R., and **J. L. Orr**. The invertibles are connected in infinite multiplicity nest algebras. *Bull. London Math. Soc.* 27:155–61, 1995.

Davidson, K. R., and **J. L. Orr**. The Jacobson radical of a CSL algebra. *Trans. Am. Math. Soc.* 334(2):925–47, 1994.

Orr, J. L. The maximal ideals of a nest algebra. *J. Funct. Analysis* 124(1):119–34, 1994.

Orr, J. L. An estimate on the norm of the product of infinite block operator matrices. *J. Combinatorial Theory Ser. A* 63(2):195–209, 1993.

Ahlbrandt, C., and **A. Peterson**. *Discrete Hamiltonian Systems: Difference Equations, Continued Fractions, and Riccati Equations.* Kluwer Academic Publishers, 1996.

Peterson, A. *Sturmian theory and oscillation of a third order linear difference equation, Boundary Value Problems for Functional Differential Equations,* pp. 261–7, ed. J. Henderson. World Scientific Publishing Co., 1995.

Kelley, W., and **A. Peterson**. *Difference Equations: An Introduction with Applications.* Academic Press, 1991.

Davidson, K. R., and **D. R. Pitts**. Invariant subspaces and hyper-reflexivity for free semigroup algebras. *Proc. London Math. Soc.* 78:401–30, 1999.

Davidson, K. R., and **D. R. Pitts**. The algebraic structure of non-commutative analytic toeplitz algebras. *Math. Ann.* 311:275–303, 1998.

Davidson, K. R., and **D. R. Pitts**. Nevanlinna-Pick interpolation for non-commutative analytic Toeplitz algebras. *Integral Equations Operator Theory* 31:321–37, 1998.

Radcliffe, A. J., and Zs. Szaniszlo. Extremal cases of the Ahlswede-Cai inequality. *JCTA* 76:108–20, 1996.

Leader, I. B., and **A. J. Radcliffe**. Littlewood-Offord inequalities for sums of random variables. *SIAM J. Discrete Math.* 7:90–101, 1994.

Cao, C., E. S. Titi, and **M. A. Rammaha**. The Navier-Stokes equations on the rotating 2-D sphere: Gevrey regularity and asymptotic degrees of freedom. *Z. Angew. Math. Phys.,* in press.

Cao, C., E. S. Titi, and **M. A. Rammaha**. Gevrey regularity of solutions for nonlinear analytic parabolic equations on the sphere. *J. Dynam. Differ. Equations,* in press.

Rammaha, M. A. A note on nonlinear wave equation in two and three space dimensions. *Comm. Partial Differ. Equations* 22:799–810, 1997.

Avalos, G., I. Lasiecka, and **R. Rebarber**. Lack of time-delay robustness for stabilization of a structural acoustics model. *SIAM J. Control Optimiz.,* in press.

Rebarber, R., and S. Townley. Generalized sampled-data feedback control of distributed parameter systems. *Syst. Control Lett.* 34:229–40, 1998.

Rebarber, R., and S. Townley. Robustness with respect to delays for exponential stability of distributed parameter systems. *SIAM J. Control Optimiz.* 37:230–44, 1998.

Logemann, H., and **R. Rebarber**. PDEs with distributed control and delay in the loop: Transfer function poles, exponential modes and robustness of stability. *Eur. J. Control* 4:333–44, 1998.

Rebarber, R., and H. Zwart. Open loop stabilizability of infinite-dimensional systems. *Math. Control Signals Syst.* 11:129–60, 1998.

Mueller, J., and **T. Shores**. Uniqueness and numerical recovery of a potential on the real line. *Inverse Problems,* in press.

Shores, T., and C. Tiahrt. Subspace projection variants on Newton's method. *Comput. Math. Appl.* 27:7–17, 1994.

Park, C., **D. Skoug**, H. Zwart, and D. Storvick. Relationships among the first variation, the convolution product, and the Fourier-Feynman transform. *Rocky Mtn. J. Math.* 28:1447–68, 1998.

Park, C., **D. Skoug**, and H. Zwart. Integration by parts formulas involving analytic Feynman integrals. *Panam. Math. J.* 8:1–11, 1998.

Park, C., and **D. Skoug**. Linear transformations of multi-parameter Wiener integrals. *Panam. Math. J.* 7:15–25, 1997.

Huffman, T., C. Park, and **D. Skoug**. Generalized transforms and convolutions. *Int. J. Math. Math. Sci.* 20:19–32, 1997.

Huffman, T., C. Park, and **D. Skoug**. Convolution and Fourier-Feynman transforms. *Rocky Mtn. J. Math.* 27:827–41, 1997.

Voloch, J.-F., and **J. Walker**. Codes over rings from curves of higher genus. *IEEE Trans. Inform. Theory,* in press.

Boston, N., and **J. Walker**. Two-groups with few conjugacy classes. *Proc. Edinburgh Math. Soc.,* in press.

Walker, J. Algebraic geometric codes over rings. *J. Pure Appl. Algebra,* in press.

Walker, J. The Nordstrom Robinson code is algebraic geometric. *IEEE Trans. Inf. Theory* 43:1588–93, 1997.

Walker, J. A new approach to the main conjecture on algebraic-geometric MDS codes. *Des. Codes Cryptogr.* 9:115–20, 1996.

Walker, M. Weight zero motivic cohomology and the general linear group of a simplicial ring. *J. Pure Appl. Algebra,* in press.

Walker, M. Adams operations for bivariant K-theory and a filtration using projective lines. *K-theory,* in press.

Walker, M. The primitive topology of a scheme. *J. Algebra* 201:656–85, 1998.

Rotthaus, C., D. Weston, and **R. Wiegand**. Indecomposable Gorenstein modules of odd rank. *J. Algebra* 214:122–7, 1999.

Wiegand, R. Local rings of finite Cohen-Macaulay type. *J. Algebra* 203:156–68, 1998.

Huneke, C., and **R. Wiegand**. Tensor products of modules, rigidity, and local cohomology. *Math. Scand.* 81:161–83, 1997.

Colliot-Thélène, J.-L., R. Guralnick, and **R. Wiegand**. Multiplicative groups of fields modulo products of subfields. *J. Pure Appl. Algebra* 106:233–62, 1996.

Huneke, C., and **R. Wiegand**. Tensor products of modules and the rigidity of Tor. *Math. Ann.* 299:449–76, 1994.

Heinzer, W., C. Rotthaus, and **S. Wiegand**. Approximating discrete valuation rings by regular local rings,}. *Proc. Am. Math. Soc.,* in press.

Rotthaus, C., W. Heinzer, and **S. Wiegand**. Noetherian domains inside a homomorphic image of a completion. *J. Algebra,* in press.

Li, A., and **S. Wiegand**. Prime ideals in two-dimensional domains over the integers. *J. Pure Appl. Algebra* 130:313–24, 1998.

Heinzer, W., and **S. Wiegand**. Prime ideals in polynomial rings over one-dimensional domains. *Trans. Am. Math. Soc.* 347(2):639–50, 1995.

Abhyankar, S., W. Heinzer, and **S. Wiegand**. On the compositum of two power series rings. *Proc. Am. Math. Soc.* 112(3):629–36, 1991.

UNIVERSITY OF NORTH CAROLINA AT CHARLOTTE

Department of Mathematics

Programs of Study

The Department of Mathematics offers programs that lead to the M.S. and Ph.D. in applied mathematics, the M.S. in applied statistics, and the M.A. in mathematics and math education. These programs are designed to develop advanced skills, knowledge, and critical-thinking abilities that are directly applicable to a wide variety of positions in industry, business, government, and teaching at the secondary school, community college, and/or university level. The department has active research programs in commutative algebra; theory and simulation of combustion phenomena; computational fluid dynamics and electromagnetics; numerical analysis; dynamical systems; operator algebras, Banach space geometry, and wavelets; partial differential equations and mathematical physics; probability and stochastic processes; and statistics.

The M.S. degrees in applied mathematics and statistics require nine and ten courses, respectively, and a project. The programs follow a rigorously structured framework of analytical and applied subjects. The M.A. in mathematics requires ten courses and offers a good deal of flexibility to a student who wants a broad background of pure and applied courses. The M.A. in mathematics education is primarily designed for secondary school teachers who are interested in professional growth and graduate certification. It requires ten courses, with at least six in mathematics and the other four chosen from mathematics, mathematics education, and/or education. All master's programs require a comprehensive oral exam. Completion of a thesis is optional for all master's programs.

After their first year, students in the Ph.D. program are required to pass a preliminary exam based on a yearlong advanced real analysis sequence and a yearlong basic course sequence in an applied area of their choice. By the end of their third year, Ph.D. students are expected to pass a qualifying exam for admission to candidacy; the qualifying exam is based on advanced topics in their area of specialization. In addition, Ph.D. students are required to pass a foreign language reading proficiency exam and complete a two- to three-course interdisciplinary minor. The latter can often be coordinated via the department's external consulting unit, the Office of Statistics and Applied Mathematics. Finally, Ph.D. students are required to complete a Ph.D. dissertation that comprises a substantial and original contribution to their area of study.

Research Facilities

The Department of Mathematics provides state-of-the-art computing facilities in its two UNIX workstation labs, which house thirty-five Sun workstations (with nine additional Silicon Graphics workstations in the department). Three PC labs with 105 Pentium PCs are housed in the recently completed Fretwell building, the new home of the Department of Mathematics. All graduate student and faculty member offices are equipped with either a PC or a workstation. In addition, for computationally intensive projects, faculty members and students have fast access to the North Carolina Supercomputing Center's CRAY T916, 32-node CRAY T3E, and visualization facilities. The J. Murrey Atkins University Library contains 750,000 bound volumes (including 13,000 monograph holdings in mathematics, computer science, and statistics) as well as more than 200 mathematics research journals and more than 1 million units in microfilm. The J. Murrey Atkins Library is the final phase of a three-year expansion project that has added more than 11,000 square feet for its holding and reading areas and upgraded its information-searching capabilities.

Financial Aid

Most students accepted into mathematics graduate programs are supported by teaching assistantships, which pay $9200 for master's students and start at $11,500 for Ph.D. students. Assistantships for advanced Ph.D. students pay $12,500. A limited number of fellowship awards can be applied to supplement the above stipends for especially qualified students. Some students are supported by project-specific externally funded research assistantships, with stipends starting at $12,000. Virtually all out-of-state teaching and research assistants receive waivers for their out-of-state tuition, and a few in-state tuition waivers are available for especially qualified North Carolina residents.

Cost of Study

Tuition and academic fees for 1999–2000 are $919 per semester for North Carolina residents and $4554 for nonresidents. Graduate students who are U.S. citizens or permanent residents normally become residents of North Carolina after their first year.

Living and Housing Costs

Typical room and board expenses for students living off campus are about $1500 per semester. Off-campus rents average about $600 per month for a two- to four-bedroom apartment. A limited amount of on-campus housing is available with somewhat lower rents.

Student Group

Of 25 mathematics graduate students in spring 1999, 8 were women, 14 were international, and 2 were part-time. Twenty-one were teaching assistants, 2 held research assistantships, and 3 held stipend increases from fellowship sources. In mathematics education, there were 2 full-time students with teaching assistantships, 1 of whom was a woman; 1 was an international student. In addition, there were 20 part-time math education students already working in area high schools.

Location

The city of Charlotte is the hub of a dynamic and growing metropolitan area in terms of economic and cultural development. The city features two major sports franchises, an internationally renowned symphony orchestra, Opera Carolina, and the North Carolina Dance Theater. Specialty shops, galleries, and restaurants reflect the tastes and culture of an ethnically diverse multinational community. Recreational opportunities include biking, boating, and fishing at and around nearby Lake Norman, Lake Lure, and Mountain Island Lake. Many parks and uptown areas host yearly festivals. Mountain recreation areas and ocean beaches are within a 2½- to 4½-hour drive.

The University

The University of North Carolina (UNC) at Charlotte is located in the largest urban center in the Carolinas. Its campus occupies 1,000 wooded acres in the University City area, which also includes University Place, University Hospital, and University Research Park, the nation's sixth-largest university-affiliated research park. The Research Park has more than 11,000 employees and a number of large firms, including AT&T, IBM, Duke Power, Nations Bank, First Union, and the *Wall Street Journal*. The University maintains many professional contacts with several of the firms, and graduate students are very often involved. Of the University's 16,000 students who represent forty-six states and sixty-five countries, almost 2,700 are graduate students. UNC Charlotte is known for its academic excellence and is distinguished by its commitment to scholarly activities and teaching accomplishments.

Applying

Application forms may be obtained from the Department of Mathematics or the Graduate School. All students must take the General Test of the Graduate Record Examinations (GRE). The Subject Test is recommended but not required. International applicants must take the TOEFL and score above 550 or have received a degree from an American institution. For full consideration for financial support, applicants for the fall semester should submit all materials by January 15.

Correspondence and Information

Joel Avrin
Graduate Coordinator
Department of Mathematics
University of North Carolina at Charlotte
Charlotte, North Carolina 28223-0001

Telephone: 704-547-4929
Fax: 704-510-6415
E-mail: jdavrin@email.uncc.edu

University of North Carolina at Charlotte

THE FACULTY AND THEIR RESEARCH

Robert Anderson, Associate Professor; Ph.D., Minnesota, 1972. Probability.
Joel Avrin, Professor; Ph.D., Berkeley, 1982. Partial differential equations and mathematical physics.
Charles Burnap, Associate Professor; Ph.D., Harvard, 1976. Mathematical physics.
Wei Cai, Associate Professor; Ph.D., Brown, 1989. Computational fluid dynamics and electromagnetics.
Zongwu Cai, Assistant Professor; Ph.D., California, Davis, 1995. Statistics.
Vic Cifarelli, Assistant Professor; Ph.D., Purdue, 1988. Mathematics education.
Xingde Dai, Associate Professor; Ph.D., Texas A&M, 1990. Operator algebras.
Yunan Diao, Associate Professor; Ph.D., Florida State, 1990. Topology.
Eimear Goggin, Assistant Professor; Ph.D., Wisconsin, 1988. Probability.
Kim Harris, Associate Professor; Ph.D., Georgia, 1985. Mathematics education.
Evan Houston, Professor; Ph.D., Texas at Austin, 1973. Commutative algebra.
Phillip Johnson, Associate Professor; Ph.D., Vanderbilt, 1968. Mathematics education.
John Kawczak, Assistant Professor; Ph.D., Western Ontario, 1998. Statistics.
Mohammad Kazemi, Associate Professor; Ph.D., Michigan, 1982. Control theory.
Michael Kilbanov, Professor; Ph.D., Ural State (Russia), 1977. Inverse problems.
Alan Lambert, Professor; Ph.D., Michigan, 1970. Operator theory.
Thomas G. Lucas, Associate Professor; Ph.D., Missouri, 1983. Commutative algebra.
Thomas R. Lucas, Professor; Ph.D., Georgia Tech, 1970. Numerical analysis.
Stanislav Molchanov, Professor; Ph.D., Moscow State, 1967. Probability/mathematical physics.
Hae-Soo Oh, Associate Professor; Ph.D., Michigan, 1980. Numerical analysis.
Alexander Papadopoulos, Professor; Ph.D., Virginia Tech, 1972. Statistics.
Joseph Quinn, Professor; Ph.D., Michigan State, 1970. Stochastic processes.
Harold Reiter, Associate Professor; Ph.D., Clemson, 1969. Combinatorics.
Franz Rothe, Associate Professor; Ph.D., Tübingen (Germany), 1975. Partial differential equations.
David C. Royster, Associate Professor; Ph.D., LSU, 1978. Differential topology.
Adalira Saenz-Ludlow, Assistant Professor; Ph.D., Florida State, 1990. Mathematics education.
Douglas Shafer, Professor; Ph.D., North Carolina at Chapel Hill, 1978. Dynamical systems.
Isaac Sonin, Professor; Ph.D., Moscow State, 1971. Probability/operations research.
Nicholas Stavrakas, Professor; Ph.D., Clemson, 1973. Convexity.
Yanqing Sun, Assistant Professor; Ph.D., Florida State, 1992. Statistics.
Boris Vainberg, Professor; Ph.D., Moscow State, 1963. Partial differential equations and mathematical physics.
Barnet Weinstock, Professor; Ph.D., MIT, 1966. Several complex variables.
Volker Wihstutz, Professor; Ph.D., Bremen (Germany), 1975. Stochastic dynamical systems.
Alexander Yushkevich, Professor; Ph.D., Moscow State, 1956. Probability/operations research.
Zhi-Yi Zhang, Associate Professor; Ph.D., Rutgers, 1990. Statistics.
You-Lan Zhu, Professor; Ph.D., Qinghau (China), 1963. Computational fluid dynamics.

UNIVERSITY OF NOTRE DAME

Graduate Studies in Mathematics

Program of Study

The purpose of the graduate program in mathematics is to give students the opportunity to develop into educated and creative mathematicians. In most instances, the doctoral program starts with two years of basic training, including supervised teaching experience and introductory and advanced course work in the fundamentals of algebra, analysis, geometry, and topology. This is followed by thesis work done in close association with one or more members of the faculty. Limited enrollment and the presence of several active groups of research mathematicians provide thesis opportunities in many areas of algebra, algebraic geometry, applied mathematics, complex analysis, differential geometry, logic, partial differential equations, and topology.

Research Facilities

Every effort is made to enable students to avail themselves of the opportunities provided by the excellent mathematics faculty at Notre Dame. The Department of Mathematics has its own building with all modern facilities, including a comprehensive research library of 27,000 volumes that subscribes to 300 current journals. All graduate students have comfortable offices (two to an office). Students are ensured a stimulating and challenging intellectual experience.

Financial Aid

In 1999–2000, all new students receive a twelve-month stipend of at least $16,000 and have no teaching duties the first year. Then they become teaching assistants with a stipend of at least $15,600 and begin the three stages of supervised teaching provided by the department. A teaching assistant usually starts by doing tutorial work in freshman and sophomore calculus courses (4 classroom hours per week); this is followed by a variety of duties in advanced undergraduate courses; the final, lecturing stage involves independent teaching in the classroom. All doctoral students in mathematics also receive a full tuition fellowship. Support is available for citizens and noncitizens.

Cost of Study

Virtually all graduate students in mathematics are supported by fellowships or assistantships, which include tuition scholarships.

Living and Housing Costs

University housing includes two-bedroom apartments for single men and women, four-bedroom town houses for single men and women, and two- and four-bedroom apartments for married students at rents that ranged from $300 to $600 per month in 1998–99. Comfortable and attractive off-campus rooms normally cost between $200 and $400 per month. Other expenses are lower than in most metropolitan areas.

Student Group

The carefully selected men and women who make up the student body of the University come from every state in the Union and sixty-six countries. There are about 30 graduate students working for their doctorate in mathematics. The faculty-student ratio is greater than 1:1.

Location

The University is just north of South Bend, a pleasant Midwestern city with a population of about 110,000. The Notre Dame campus is exceptionally rich in active cultural programs, and the wide variety of cultural, educational, and recreational facilities of Chicago and Lake Michigan are less than 2 hours away by car.

The University

Founded in 1842, the University of Notre Dame has a 1,250-acre campus. Much of the campus is heavily wooded, and two delightful lakes lie entirely within it. Total enrollment is about 10,000; approximately one fifth of these are graduate students. The University is proud of its tradition as a Catholic university with a profound commitment to intellectual freedom in every area of contemporary thought. The students and faculty represent a rich diversity of religious, racial, and ethnic backgrounds.

Applying

All applicants are required to take the General Test of the Graduate Record Examinations and are urged to take the Subject Test in mathematics. Application for these tests should be made to Educational Testing Service in Princeton, New Jersey 08541, or at 1947 Center Street, Berkeley, California 94704. The application fee is $40 for all applications submitted after December 1. The fee for applications submitted by December 1 for the following fall semester is $25. The application deadline for students who wish to be considered for financial aid is February 1. All applicants are considered without regard to race, sex, or religious affiliation.

Correspondence and Information

Director of Graduate Studies
Department of Mathematics
University of Notre Dame
Room 370, CCMB
Notre Dame, Indiana 46556-5683
Telephone: 219-631-7245
Fax: 219-631-6579

University of Notre Dame

THE FACULTY AND THEIR RESEARCH

Algebra
Mario Borelli, Ph.D., Indiana. Algebraic geometry, computer graphics.
Matthew Dyer, Ph.D., Sydney. Representation theory, algebraic groups.
Samuel R. Evens, Ph.D., MIT. Geometry of Lie groups and homogeneous spaces and representation theory.
Alexander J. Hahn, Ph.D., Notre Dame. Linear groups, theory of algebra, quadratic forms.
George McNinch, Ph.D., Oregon. Representation theory, algebraic groups.
Barth Pollak, Ph.D., Princeton. Quadratic forms, orthogonal groups, composition algebras.
Warren J. Wong, Ph.D., Harvard. Theory of finite groups and their representations.

Algebraic Geometry
Karen Chandler, Ph.D., Harvard. Castelnuovo theory, zero-dimensional schemes.
Juan C. Migliore, Ph.D., Brown. Algebraic curves, liaison theory.
Andrew Sommese, Ph.D., Princeton. Numerical analysis of polynomial systems, adjunction theory.

Applied Mathematics
Mark Alber, Ph.D., Pennsylvania. Dynamical systems and nonlinear partial differential equations.
Amarjit S. Budhiraja, Ph.D., North Carolina. Stochastic analysis.
Leonid Faybusovich, Ph.D., Harvard. Differential dynamical systems.
Brian C. Hall, Ph.D., Cornell. Stochastic analysis.
Bei Hu, Ph.D., Minnesota. Nonlinear partial differential equations.
Florian Jarre, Ph.D., Würzburg (Germany). Optimization, numerical analysis and applications.
Gerard Misiolek, Ph.D., SUNY at Stony Brook. Global analysis, geometric mechanics and partial differential equations.
Joachim Rosenthal, Ph.D., Arizona State. Geometric control theory.

Complex Analysis
Jeffrey A. Diller, Ph.D., Michigan. Several complex variables.
Dennis M. Snow, Ph.D., Notre Dame. Homogeneous complex manifolds, group actions.
Pit-Mann Wong, Ph.D., Notre Dame. Several complex variables.

Differential Geometry
Jianguo Cao, Ph.D., Pennsylvania. Manifolds of nonpositive curvature.
Alan Howard, Ph.D., Brown. Complex manifolds.
Xiaobo Liu, Ph.D., Pennsylvania. Differential geometry.
Brian Smyth, Ph.D., Brown. Differential geometry.
Frederico J. Xavier, Ph.D., Rochester. Differential geometry.

Logic
Steven A. Buechler, Ph.D., Maryland. Model theory.
Peter Cholak, Ph.D., Wisconsin. Recursion theory.
Julia Knight, Ph.D., Berkeley. Model theory.
Sergei Starchenko, Ph.D., Novosibirsk (Russia). Model theory.

Partial Differential Equations
Qing Han, Ph.D., NYU (Courant). Partial differential equations, geometric measure theory, analysis in differential geometry.
A. Alexandrou Himonas, Ph.D., Purdue. Partial differential equations.
Mei-Chi Shaw, Ph.D., Princeton. Partial differential equations and several complex variables.
Nancy K. Stanton, Ph.D., MIT. Differential geometry, complex manifolds.

Topology
Francis X. Connolly, Ph.D., Rochester. Differential and algebraic topology.
John E. Derwent, Ph.D., Notre Dame. Differential and algebraic topology.
William G. Dwyer, Ph.D., MIT. Algebraic topology.
Liviu Nicolaescu, Ph.D., Michigan State. Gauge theory.
Stephan A. Stolz, Ph.D., Mainz (Germany). Algebraic topology and differential geometry.
Laurence R. Taylor, Ph.D., Berkeley. Geometric and algebraic topology.
E. Bruce Williams, Ph.D., MIT. Geometric topology, homotopy theory.

SELECTED PUBLICATIONS

Alber, M. S., G. G. Luther, and J. E. Marsden. Energy dependent Schrodinger operators and complex Hamiltonian systems on Riemann surfaces. *Nonlinearity* 10:223–42, 1997.

Alber, M. S., and J. E. Marsden. Semi-classical monodromy and the spherical pendulum as a complex Hamiltonian system. *Fields Inst. Commun.* 8:1–18, 1996.

Alber, M. S., R. Camassa, D. D. Holm, and J. E. Marsden. On umbilic geodesics and soliton solutions of nonlinear PDE's. *Proc. Roy. Soc. London A* 450:677–92, 1995.

Borelli, M. Variedades casi-proyectivas y divisoriales. *Publicationes del Institutio de Matematicas de la Universidad Nacional Interamericana,* Lima, Peru, in press.

Borelli, M. The cohomology of divisorial schemes. *Pacific J. Math.* 37:1–7, 1971.

Borelli, M. Affine complements of divisors. *Pacific J. Math.* 31:595–605, 1969.

Budhiraja, A., and P. Dupuis. Simple necessary and sufficient conditions for the stability of constrained processes. *SIAM J. Appl. Math., Technical Report LCDS 97-15,* in press.

Budhiraja, A., and H. J. Kushner. Robustness of nonlinear filters over the infinite time interval. *SIAM J. Control Opt.* 36(5):1618–37, 1998.

Budhiraja, A., and D. Ocone. Exponential stability of discrete time filters without signal ergodicity. *Syst. Control Lett.* 30:185–93, 1997.

Buechler, S. Vaught's conjecture for superstable theories of finite rank. *Ann. Pure Appl. Logic,* in press.

Buechler, S. Lascar strong types in some simple theories. *J. Symbol. Logic,* in press.

Buechler, S. *Essential Stability Theory, Perspectives in Mathematical Logic.* New York: Springer-Verlag, 1996.

Cao, J., and I. Benjamin. Examples of simply-connected Lionville manifolds with positive spectrum. *J. Differential Application* 6:31–50, 1996.

Calabi, E., and **J. Cao.** Simple closed geodesics on convex surfaces. *J. Differential Geom.* 36:517–49, 1993.

Cao, J. The existence of generalized isothermal coordinates for higher dimensional Riemannian manifolds. *Trans. Am. Math. Soc.* 324:31–50, 1991.

Chandler, K. A. Higher infinitesimal neighbourhoods. *J. Algebra,* in press.

Chandler, K. A. Regularity of the powers of an ideal. *Commun. Algebra* 25(12):3773–6, 1997.

Chandler, K. A. Geometry of dots and ropes. *Trans. Am. Math. Soc.* 347(3):767–84, 1995.

Cholak, P. The dense simple sets are orbit complete for simple sets. *Ann. Pure Appl. Logic* 94:37–44, 1998.

Cholak, P. Automorphisms of the lattice of recursively enumerable sets. *Mem. Am. Math. Soc.* 113(541), 1995.

Cholak, P., and R. Downey. Permutations and presentations. *Proc. Am. Math. Soc.* 122:1237–49, 1994.

Connolly, F. X., and D. Anderson. Finiteness obstructions to cocompact actions on S^m x $\hat{A}^n$. *Comment. Math. Helvetici* 68:85–110, 1993.

Connolly, F. X., and T. Kozniewski. Examples of lack of rigidity in crystallographic groups. In *Lecture Notes in Mathematics–Algebraic Topology,* Poznan, 1989, vol. 1474, pp. 139–45. Berlin/Heidelberg: Springer-Verlag, 1991.

Connolly, F. X., and T. Kozniewski. Rigidity and crystallographic groups I. *Inventiones Math.* 99:25–48, 1990.

Derwent, J. E. A note on numerable covers. *Proc. Am. Math. Soc.* 19:1130–2, 1968.

Derwent, J. E. Inverses for fiber spaces. *Proc. Am. Math. Soc.* 19:1491–4, 1968.

Derwent, J. E. Handle decompositions of manifolds. *J. Math. Mech.* 15:329–46, 1966.

Diller, J., and D. Barrett. A new construction of Riemann surfaces with corona. *J. Geom. Anal.,* in press.

Diller, J. Contraction properties of the Poincare series operator. *Mich. Math. J.* 43:519–38, 1996.

Diller, J., and D. Barrett. Dynamics of birational maps of C^2. *Indiana Univ. Math. J.* 45:721–72, 1996.

Dwyer, W. G., and C. W. Wilkerson. The elementary geometric structure of compact Lie groups. *Bull. London Math. Soc.* 30:337–64, 1998.

Dwyer, W. G., S. Stolz, and **L. R. Taylor.** On the dimension of infinite covers. *Proc. Am. Math. Soc.* 124:2235–9, 1996.

Dwyer, W. G. Transfer maps for fibrations. *Math. Proc. Cambridge Philos. Soc.* 120:221–35, 1996.

Dwyer, W. G., and J. Spalinski. Homotopy theories and model categories. In *Handbook of Algebraic Topology,* pp. 73–126, ed. I. M. James. Amsterdam: Elsevier, 1995.

Dyer, M. J. Representation theories from coxeter groups. *Can. Math. Soc. Conf. Proc.* 16:105–39, 1995.

Dyer, M. J. Bruhat intervals, polyhedral cones and Kazhdan-Lusztig-Stanley polynomials. *Math. Z.* 215:223–36, 1994.

Dyer, M. J. The nil Hecke ring and Deodhar's conjecture on Bruhat intervals. *Inventiones Math.* III:571–4, 1993.

Evens, S., and J.-H. Lu. Poisson harmonic forms, Kostant harmonic forms, and the S1-equivariant cohomology of K/T. *Adv. Math.* 142:171–220, 1999.

Evens, S., and I. Mirkovic. Fourier transform and the Iwahori-Matsumoto involution. *Duke Math. J.* 86:435–64, 1997.

Evens, S. On Springer representations and the Zuckerman functor. *Pacific J. Math.* 180:221–8, 1997.

Faybusovich, L. Semi definite programming: A path-following algorithm for a linear-quadratic functional. *SIAM J. Optimization* 6(4):1007–24, 1996.

Faybusovich, L. A Hamiltonian structure for generalized affine-scaling vector fields. *J. Nonlinear Sci.* 5:11–28, 1995.

Faybusovich, L. On a matrix generalization of affine-scaling vector fields. *SIAM J. Matrix Anal. Applications* 16(3):886–97, 1995.

Hahn, A. J. The elements of the orthogonal group Ω_n (V) as products of commutators of symmetries. *J. Algebra* 184:927–44, 1996.

Hahn, A. J. Quadratic algebras, Clifford algebras and arithmetic Witt groups. In *UNIVERSITEXT Series.* Berlin and New York: Springer-Verlag, 1994.

Hahn, A. J., and O. T. O'Meara. The classical groups and K-theory. In *Grundlehren der Mathematik,* vol. 291. Berlin and New York: Springer-Verlag, 1989.

Hall, B. C., and B. K. Driver. Yang-Mills theory and the Segal-Bargmann transform. *Commun. Math. Phys.* 201:249–90, 1999.

Hall, B. C., and A. N. Sengupta. The Segal-Bargmann transform for path-groups. *J. Funct. Anal.* 152:220–54, 1998.

Hall, B. C. The Segal-Bargmann "coherent state" transform for compact Lie groups. *J. Funct. Anal.* 122:103–51, 1994.

Han, Q., and F.-H. Lin. Nodal sets of solutions of parabolic equations. *Commun. Pure Appl. Math.,* pp. 1219–38, 1994.

Han, Q., and F.-H. Lin. On the geometric measure of nodal sets of solutions. *J. Partial Differential Equations* 7:111–31, 1994.

Arrieta, J., J. Hale, and **Q. Han.** Eigenvalue problems for nonsmoothly perturbed domains. *J. Differential Equations* 91:24–52, 1991.

Cordaro, P. D., and **A. A. Himonas.** Global analytic hypoellipticity for sums of squares of vector fields. *Trans. Am. Math. Soc.* 350(12):4993–5001, 1998.

Himonas, A. A., and G. Misiolek. The Cauchy problem for shallow water type equations. *Commun. Partial Differential Equations* 23(1&2):123–39, 1998.

Hanges, N., and **A. A. Himonas.** Singular solutions for a class of Grusin type operators. *Proc. AMS* 1245:1549–57, 1996.

Howard, A., and **P.-M. Wong** (eds.). Contributions to several complex variables: In honor of Wilhelm Stoll. In *Aspects of Mathematics,* vol. E9. Braunschweig/Wiesbaden: Vieweg, 1986.

Howard, A. Finiteness theorems for meromorphic maps. In *Seminar Berichte aus dem Fachbereich Mathematik und Informatik, Fernuniversität Hagen,* pp. 119–91, 1984.

Howard, A., and **A. J. Sommese.** On the theorem of DeFranchis. *Ann. Scuola Norm. Supp. Pisa* 10(3):429–36, 1983.

Friedman, A., and **B. Hu.** Head-media interaction in magnetic recording. *Arch. Ration. Mech. Anal.* 140:79–101, 1997.

Friedman, A., and **B. Hu.** A non-stationary multi-scale oscillating free boundary for the laplace and heat equation. *J. Differential Equations* 137(1):119–65, 1997.

University of Notre Dame

Selected Publications (continued)

Hu, B., and H.-M. Yin. The profile near blowup time for solutions of the heat equation with a nonlinear boundary condition. *Trans. Am. Math. Soc.* 346(1):117–35, 1994.

Jarre, F., M. Kocvara, and J. Zowe. Optimal truss design by interior-point methods. *SIAM J. Optimization* 8(4):1084–107, 1998.

Freund, R. W., and **F. Jarre.** A QMR-based interior-point algorithm for solving linear programs. *Math. Programming Ser. B* 76:183–210, 1997.

Jarre, F. On the convergence of the method of analytic centers when applied to convex quadratic programs. *Math. Programming* 49:341–58, 1991.

Knight, J. F. True approximations and models of arithmetic. *Logic Colloquium '97,* in press.

Knight, J. F. Coding a family of sets. *Ann. Pure Appl. Logic* 94:127–42, 1998.

Knight, J. F., and B. Luense. Control theory, modal logic, and games. In *Hybrid Systems IV,* pp. 160–73, eds. Antsaklis et al., 1997.

Heintze, E., and **X. Liu.** Homogeneity of infinite dimensional isoparametric submanifolds. *Ann. Math.* 149:149–81, 1999.

Heintze, E., and **X. Liu.** A splitting theorem for isoparametric submanifolds in Hilbert space. *J. Differential Geom.* 45:319–35, 1997.

Liu, X. Volume minimizing cycles in compact Lie groups. *Am. J. Math.* 117:1203–48, 1995.

McNinch, G. Dimensional criteria for semisimplicity of representations. *Proc. London Math. Soc.* 76:95–149, 1998.

McNinch, G. Semisimplicity in positive characteristics. In *Proceedings of the NATO/ASI on Representations of Algebraic and Related Finite Groups.* Isaac Newton Institute Group, 1997.

McNinch, G. Dimensional criteria for semisimplicity of representations. Ph.D. Thesis, University of Oregon, 1996.

Migliore, J. Introduction to liaison theory and deficiency modules. In *Progress in Mathematics,* vol. 165. Boston: Birkhäuser, 1998.

Migliore, J., and C. Peterson. A construction of codimension three arithmetically Gorenstein subschemes of projective space. *Trans. Am. Math. Soc.* 349:3803–21, 1997.

Martin, H., and **J. Migliore.** Submodules of the deficiency modules and an extension of Dubreil's theorem. *J. London Math. Soc.* 56:463–76, 1997.

Misiolek, G. The exponential map on the free loop space is Fredholm. *Geom. Funct. Anal.* 7:954–69, 1997.

Misiolek, G. Conjugate points in $D_\mu(T^2)$. *Proc. Am. Math. Soc.* 124:977–82, 1996.

Nicolaescu, L. Adiabatic limits of the Seiberg-Witten equations on Seifert manifolds. *Commun. Anal. Geom.* 6:301–62, 1998.

Nicolaescu, L. Generalized symplectic geometries and the index of families of elliptic problems. *Mem. Am. Math. Soc.* 128(609), 1997.

Nicolaescu, L. The spectral flow, the Maslov index and decompositions of manifolds. *Duke Univ. J.* 80:485–534, 1995.

Pollak, B. Orthogonal groups over global fields of characteristic 2. *J. Algebra* 15:589–95, 1970.

Pollak, B. Orthogonal groups of R $((\pi))$. *Am. J. Math.* 90:214–30, 1968.

Pollak, B. Generation of local integral orthogonal groups in characteristic 2. *Can. J. Math.* 20:1178–91, 1968.

Helton, W., **J. Rosenthal,** and X. Wang. Matrix extensions and eigenvalue completions, the generic case. *Trans. Am. Math. Soc.* 349(8):3401–8, 1997.

Rosenthal, J., J. M. Schumacher, and E. V. York. On behaviors and convolutional codes. *IEEE Trans. Inform. Theory* 42(6):1881–91, 1996.

Rosenthal, J., J. M. Schumacher, and J. C. Willems. Generic eigenvalue assignment by memoryless real output feedback. *Syst. Control Lett.* 26:253–60, 1995.

Michel, J., and **M.-C. Shaw.** Subelliptic estimates for the $\bar\partial$-Neumann operator on piecewise smooth strictly pseudoconvex domains. *Duke Math. J.,* in press.

Michel, J., and **M.-C. Shaw.** C∞-regularity of solutions of the tangential CR-equations on weakly pseudoconvex manifolds. *Math. Ann.,* in press.

Shaw, M.-C. Homotopy formulas for $\bar\partial_b$ in CR manifolds with mixed Levi signatures. *Math. Z.* 224:113–36, 1997.

Smyth, B., and **F. Xavier.** Real solvability of the equation $\partial 2/z\ \omega = pg$ and the topology of isolated umbilics. *J. Geom. Anal.,* in press.

Smyth, B., and **F. Xavier.** Injectivity of local diffeomorphisms from nearly spectral conditions. *J. Differential Equations* 130:406–14, 1996.

Smyth, B., and **F. Xavier.** A sharp geometric estimate for the index of an umbilic on a smooth surface. *Bull. London Math. Soc.* 24:176–80, 1992.

Snow, D. M. Compact complex homogeneous manifolds with large automorphism groups. *Inventiones Math.* 134:139–44, 1998.

Snow, D. M., and L. Manivel. A Borel-Weil theorem for holomorphic forms. *Compositio Math.* 103:351–65, 1996.

Snow, D. M. The nef value of homogeneous line bundles and related vanishing theorems. *Forum Math.* 7:385–92, 1995.

Lanteri, A., M. Palleschi, and **A. J. Sommese.** On the discriminant locus of an ample and spanned line bundle. *J. Reine Angew. Math.* 477:199–219, 1996.

Beltrametti, M., and **A. J. Sommese.** The adjunction theory of complex projective varieties. In *Expositions in Mathematics* 16:398+xxi pages. Berlin: Walter De Gruyter, 1995.

Morgan, A., **A. J. Sommese,** and C. Wampler. A product-decomposition bound for Bezout numbers. *SIAM J. Numer. Anal.* 32:1308–25, 1995.

Stanton, N. K. Spectral invariants of pseudoconformal manifolds. *Proc. Symp. Pure Math.* 54(2):551–7, 1993.

Stanton, N. K. The Riemann mapping non-theorem. *Math. Intelligencer* 14:32–6, 1992.

Stanton, N. K. A normal form for rigid hypersurfaces in C^2. *Am. J. Math.* 113:877–910, 1991.

Stolz, S. A conjecture concerning positive Ricci curvature and the Witten genus. *Math. Ann.* 304:785–800, 1996.

Stolz, S. Simply connected manifolds of positive scalar curvature. *Ann. Math.* 136:511–40, 1992.

Stolz, S., and M. Kreck. Some homeomorphic but not diffeomorphic homogeneous 7-manifolds with positive sectional curvature. *J. Differential Geom.* 3:465–86, 1991.

Taylor, L. R. An invariant of smooth 4-manifolds. *Geom. Topol.* 1:71–89, 1997. Also available on line (http://www.maths.warwick.ac.uk/gt/GTVol1/paper6.abs.html).

Hughes, B., **L. R. Taylor,** and **B. Williams.** Rigidity of fibrations over nonpositively curved manifolds. *Topology* 34:565–74, 1995.

Weiss, M., and **B. Williams.** Assembly, Novikov, conjectures, index theorems and rigidity. *Proceedings of the 1993 Oberwolfach Meeting on Novikov Conjectures,* pp. 332–52. Cambridge: Cambridge University Press, 1995.

Wong, P.-M. Holomorphic curves into spaces of constant curvature. In *Complex Geometry,* eds. G. Komatsu and Y. Sakane. New York: Marcel Dekker, 1992.

Wong, P.-M. Diophantine approximation and the theory of holomorphic curves. In *Proceedings of the Symposium on Value Distribution Theory in Several Complex Variables, Notre Dame Mathematics Lectures,* vol. 12, pp. 115–56, ed. W. Stoll, 1992.

Ru, M., and **P.-M. Wong.** Integral points of P^n-{2n+1 hyperplanes in general position}. *Inventiones Math.* 106:195–216, 1991.

Wong, W. J. Bilinear and quadratic maps, and some p-groups of class 2. *J. Algebra* 163(2):516–37, 1994.

Wong, W. J. Rank 1 preservers on the unitary Lie ring. *J. Aust. Math. Soc.* (Series A) 49:399–417, 1990.

Wong, W. J. Powers of a prime dividing binomial coefficients. *Am. Math. Monthly* 96:513–7, 1989.

Xavier, F. J. On the structure of complete simply connected embedded minimal surfaces. *J. Geom. Anal.* 3(5):513–27, 1993.

Xavier, F. J. Invertibility of Bass-Connell-Wright polynomial maps. *Math. Ann.* 295:163–6, 1993.

Xavier, F. J., and **B. Smyth.** A sharp geometric estimate for the index of an umbilic on a smooth surface. *Bull. London Math. Soc.* 24:176–80, 1992.

UNIVERSITY OF PITTSBURGH

Department of Mathematics

Programs of Study

The Department of Mathematics offers programs leading to the Master of Arts, Master of Science, and Doctor of Philosophy degrees in mathematics.

The degrees of Master of Arts (M.A.) and Master of Science (M.S.) require a B average and 24 credits (30 for the M.A. and M.S. in applied mathematics). Joint master's degrees offered in conjunction with other departments require 45 credits. Students are also required to pass an oral examination (M.A.) or to write a master's-level thesis (M.S.). The M.A. and M.S. degrees can be completed in the equivalent of two years of full-time study.

To receive a Doctor of Philosophy (Ph.D.) degree, the student must maintain a B average over 72 credit hours of course work and pass departmental preliminary and comprehensive examinations. Furthermore, the student is required to write a dissertation embodying a substantial piece of original mathematical research and to defend the thesis in a public oral examination. The well-prepared, full-time student can finish the Ph.D. in five years. In exceptional cases, an additional year may be needed.

The department has an active and broadly based research faculty working in diverse areas of pure and applied mathematics, including algebra and combinatorics, foundations, analysis, mathematical biology, ordinary and partial differential equations, mathematical physics and differential geometry, numerical analysis and scientific computing, mathematical finance, and topology.

Research Facilities

A large, well-equipped Mathematics Library with a sophisticated online catalog provides immediate access to the many other University of Pittsburgh libraries as well as to libraries in the Pittsburgh area and various global databases.

All students have access to workstations and personal computers in the University's outstanding computer facilities. There are direct connections to the Pittsburgh Supercomputing Center's state-of-the-art supercomputers and strong support for scientific computing. All computers are equipped with current symbolic computing programs such as maple and Mathematica.

Financial Aid

Teaching assistantships, teaching fellowships, research assistantships, and Mellon Fellowships are available. All of these include full tuition scholarships.

Currently, teaching assistants and fellows receive a two-term living stipend between $10,600 and $11,030 and health-care benefits. These amounts may be increased due to an annual cost of living adjustment.

Research assistantships depend upon the availability of grants funded by the government and private agencies. The current two-term research assistant stipend ranges from $8650 to $11,120.

Mellon Fellowships are awarded competitively by the University to exceptionally strong second- or third-year students. They currently include a stipend of $14,000 for two terms.

Cost of Study

The 1998–99 single-term tuition and fees for full-time study were $4239 for Pennsylvania residents and $8484 for out-of-state residents.

Living and Housing Costs

Pittsburgh offers a large choice of accommodations in apartments and houses. Monthly rents range from $400 to $500. Most residences are also within easy walking or biking distance of the campus.

Student Group

The University of Pittsburgh has about 24,000 undergraduates and 10,000 graduate students drawn from fifty-two states and U.S. territories and from 107 countries. The Department of Mathematics' graduate student body currently consists of about 60 full-time and 20 part-time students from the U.S. and a variety of other countries, including China, Romania, Turkey, and Jordan, and from the continent of Africa.

Student Outcomes

Recent graduates have received academic positions at various universities, such as the University of California, Davis; Boston University; Bryn Mawr College; and King Fahd University, Saudi Arabia. Other graduates have secured jobs in industry with such companies as USF&G, Computer Sciences Corporation, Information Technologists, Wolfram, and CommTech Corporation.

Location

The Department of Mathematics is located on the 132-acre Oakland campus of the University. A large park borders one side of the campus. Many of Pittsburgh's cultural attractions, including museums and botanical gardens, are an easy walk from the department. Downtown Pittsburgh is 3 miles west of the campus and is easily reached by bus or car.

The University

The University of Pittsburgh is an internationally recognized center of learning and research and is strong in the arts, sciences, and professions. It is a member of AAU, an association of the sixty leading research institutions in the United States. The University is world-renowned in several areas, particularly in philosophy and medical research. Past discoveries have included the polio vaccine, planetary systems outside the solar system, and the soliton.

Applying

Applicants should have a bachelor's degree in mathematics or a closely related field, a minimum quality point average (QPA) of 3.0 (on a 4.0 scale) in all undergraduate subjects, and a minimum QPA of 3.25 in the mathematics curriculum. It is desirable that the applicant's undergraduate background include courses in calculus, linear and abstract algebra, differential equations, and real and complex analysis. It is also strongly suggested that applicants provide their scores on the GRE General Test and, if possible, on the GRE Subject Test in mathematics. Applicants whose native language is not English are required to obtain a paper-based total score of at least 550 or a computer-based total score of at least 213 on the Test of English as a Foreign Language (TOEFL). Applications may be submitted at any time but, for fall admission, should be received by the beginning of February. Three letters of recommendation are required.

Correspondence and Information

Graduate Studies Administrator
Department of Mathematics
University of Pittsburgh
Pittsburgh, Pennsylvania 15260

Telephone: 412-624-1175
Fax: 412-624-8397
E-mail: mollyw@vms.cis.pitt.edu
World Wide Web: http://www.math.pitt.edu/

University of Pittsburgh

THE FACULTY AND THEIR RESEARCH

Mihai Anitescu, Assistant Professor; Ph.D., Iowa, 1997. Numerical optimization, multibody dynamics, numerical analysis.

Elayne Arrington, Lecturer; Ph.D., Cincinnati, 1974. Pedagogy.

Florencio G. Asenjo, Professor; Ph.D., La Plata (Argentina), 1956. Antinomic mathematical systems, nonclassical set theories.

Frank H. Beatrous Jr., Professor; Ph.D., Tulane, 1978. Several complex variables.

Jacob Burbea, Professor; Ph.D., Stanford, 1971. Several complex variables.

Gunduz Caginalp, Professor; Ph.D., Cornell, 1978. Nonlinear differential equations, mathematical finance.

John Chadam, Professor and Department Chairman; Ph.D., MIT, 1965. Nonlinear partial differential equations, mathematical finance.

Chong-Yun Chao, Professor; Ph.D., Michigan, 1961. Algebra and combinatorics.

Xinfu Chen, Associate Professor; Ph.D., Minnesota, 1991. Nonlinear ordinary and partial differential equations, phase transitions, free boundaries, singular perturbations, dynamical systems, geometric measures, industrial problems.

Carson C. Chow, Assistant Professor; Ph.D., MIT, 1992. Applied mathematics, biological mathematics, nonlinear dynamics.

Henry B. Cohen, Associate Professor; Ph.D., New Mexico State, 1963. Functional analysis.

Gregory M. Constantine, Professor; Ph.D., Illinois at Chicago, 1990. Combinatorial theory, discrete nonlinear optimization, extremal graph theory, matrix theory.

G. Bard Ermentrout, Professor; Ph.D., Chicago, 1979. Dynamical systems, nonlinear differential and integral equations, mathematical biology, neuroscience.

Charles A. Hall, Emeritus; Ph.D., Pittsburgh, 1964. Computational approximation theory, finite-element methodology, computational fluid and structural mechanics, scientific computing, numerical analysis.

Stuart P. Hastings, Professor; Ph.D., MIT, 1964. Nonlinear ordinary differential equations.

Robert W. Heath, Professor; Ph.D., North Carolina, 1959. Analytic topology.

Delma J. Hebert Jr., Emeritus; Ph.D., Texas, 1967. Probability theory, wavelet and fractal image processing, pattern formation in nonlinear stochastic partial differential equations, high-level programming languages, simplicial grid computations, automatic image and pattern analysis, simulation of stochastic reaction diffusion systems.

Ka-Sing Lau, Professor; Ph.D., Washington (Seattle), 1972. Functional analysis with application to statistics.

William J. Layton, Professor; Ph.D., Tennessee, 1980. Numerical analysis of partial differential equations, scientific computing, computational fluid dynamics, finite-element analysis, parallel and self-adaptive algorithms.

Christopher J. Lennard, Associate Professor; Ph.D., Kent State, 1988. Functional analysis, inequalities, operator theory, Banach spaces.

Juan J. Manfredi, Professor; Ph.D., Washington (St. Louis), 1986. Partial differential equations.

Martin J. Marsden, Emeritus; Ph.D., Wisconsin, 1968. Spline functions, approximation theory, numerical analysis.

J. Bryce McLeod, Professor; D.Phil., Oxford, 1958; FRS. Linear and nonlinear partial and ordinary differential equations.

Thomas A. Metzger, Associate Professor; Ph.D., Purdue, 1971. Riemann surfaces, Fuchsian groups and automorphic forms, iteration of rational maps.

Beverly K. Michael, Senior Lecturer; Ph.D., Pittsburgh, 1976. Pedagogy.

Yibiao Pan, Associate Professor; Ph.D., Princeton, 1989. Harmonic analysis.

Thomas A. Porsching, Emeritus; Ph.D., Carnegie Tech, 1964. Numerical analysis and scientific computing, computational fluid dynamics, network theory.

John R. Porter, Emeritus; Ph.D., Texas, 1965. Mathematical physics.

Patrick J. Rabier, Professor; Ph.D., Paris, 1977. Nonlinear functional analysis, nonlinear mechanics, partial differential equations, bifurcation theory, singular ordinary differential equations, degree theory.

Werner C. Rheinboldt, Emeritus; Ph.D., Freiburg (Germany), 1955. Numerical analysis and scientific computing.

Frank G. Slaughter Jr., Emeritus; Ph.D., Duke, 1966. Analytic topology.

George A. J. Sparling, Associate Professor; Ph.D., London, 1975. Twistor theory, geometry.

Alan Thompson, Emeritus; Ph.D., London, 1962. Mathematical physics.

William C. Troy, Professor; Ph.D., SUNY at Buffalo, 1974. Nonlinear ordinary and partial differential equations.

Glen Whitehead, Associate Professor; Ph.D., USC, 1971. Graph theory, combinatorial designs and algorithms.

Ivan Yotov, Assistant Professor; Ph.D., Rice, 1996. Numerical analysis, numerical solution of partial differential equations, large-scale parallel scientific computing, porous media.

SELECTED PUBLICATIONS

Anitescu, M., G. Lesaja, and F. A. Potra. An infeasible-interior-point predictor-corrector algorithm for the P_*-geometric LCP. *Appl. Math. Optimization* 36:203–28, 1997.

Moulin, P., **M. Anitescu,** K. O. Kortanek, and F. A. Potra. The role of linear semi-infinite programming in signal-adapted QMF bank design. *IEEE J. Signal Processing* 45:2160–74, 1997.

Anitescu, M., and F. A. Potra. Formulating dynamic multi-rigid-body contact problems with friction as solvable linear complementarity problems. *Nonlinear Dynam.* 14:231–47, 1997.

Asenjo, F. G. Antinomicity and the axiom of choice: A chapter in antinomic mathematics. In *Logic and Logical Philosophy,* vol. 4, pp. 41–83. Torun, Poland: Nicolas Copernicus University Press, 1996.

Asenjo, F. G. Continua without sets. In *Logic and Logical Philosophy,* vol. 1, pp. 95–128. Torun, Poland: Nicolas Copernicus University Press, 1993.

Caginalp, G., and W. Xie. A mathematical analysis of the phase field alloy model. *Arch. Ration. Mech. Anal.,* in press.

Caginalp, G. Length scales in phase transition models: Phase field, Cahn-Hilliard and blow-up problems. In *Fields Institute Communications,* vol. 5, *Pattern Formation: Symmetry Methods and Applications,* pp. 67–83. Providence, R.I.: American Math Society, 1996.

Caginalp, G., and D. Balenovich. Trend based asset flow in technical analysis and securities marketing. *Psychol. Marketing* 53:407–44, 1996.

Caginalp, G. A renormalization group calculation of anomalous exponents for nonlinear diffusion. *Phys. Rev. E* 53:66–73, 1996.

Chadam, J., and Y. Qin. Spatial decay estimates for flow in a porous medium. *SIAM J. Math. Anal.,* in press.

Chadam, J., X. Chen, R. Gianni, and R. Ricci. A reaction infiltration problem: Classical solutions. *Proc. R. Soc. Edinburgh,* in press.

Chadam, J., and Y. Qin. Reactive flow in a porous medium. *Dynam. Continuous Discrete Impulsive Syst.* 1:145–61, 1996.

Qin, Y., and **J. Chadam.** Nonlinear convective stability of a fluid with temperature-dependent viscosity and inertial drag. *Stud. Appl. Math.* 96:273–88, 1996.

Chao, C.-Y. On the classification of toughness of generalized permutation star-graphs. *Czechoslovak Math. J.* 47:431–52, 1997.

Chao, C.-Y. A critical graph. *Discrete Math.* 172:3–7, 1997.

Chao, C.-Y., Z.-Y. Guo, and N.-Z. Li. On q-graphs. *Discrete Math.* 172:9–16, 1997.

Chao, C.-Y. Polynomials over finite fields which commute with a permutation polynomial. *J. Algebra* 163:295–311, 1994.

Chen, X. Existence, uniqueness, and asymptotic stability of traveling waves in nonlocal evolution equations. *Adv. Diff. Eq.* 2:125–60, 1997.

Chen, X., D. Hilhorst, and E. Logak. Asymptotic behavior of solutions of an Allen-Cahn equation with a local term. *Nonlinear Anal. Theor. Methods Appl.* 28:1283–98, 1997.

Chen, X. Lorenz equations, Part II: Rotated homoclinic orbits and chaotic trajectories. *Discrete Continuous Dynam. Syst.* 2:121–40, 1996.

Chen, X., and M. Kowalczyk. Existence of equilibria for Cahn-Hilliard equation via local minimizers of perimeter. *Commun. Partial Differ. Eq.* 21:1207–33, 1996.

White, J. A., et al. **(C. C. Chow).** Synchronization and oscillatory dynamics in heterogeneous, mutually inhibited neurons. *J. Comp. Neurol.* 5:5–16, 1998.

Lauk, M., **C. C. Chow,** A. E. Pavlik, and J. J. Collins. Human balance out of equilibrium: Nonequilibrium statistical mechanics in posture control. *Phys. Rev. Lett.* 80:413–6, 1998.

Chow, C. C., and J. A. White. Spontaneous action potentials due to channel fluctuations. *Biophys. J.* 71:3013–21, 1996.

Chow, C. C., and T. Hwa. Defect-mediated stability: An effective hydrodynamic theory of spatiotemporal chaos. *Physica D* 84:494–512, 1995.

Constantine, G., and L. N. Xue. Aliasing in the absence of within group interactions. *J. Stat. Plann. Inference,* in press.

Constantine, G., and L. N. Xue. Aliasing in the case of a separation of factors. *J. Stat. Plann. Inference,* in press.

Ren, L., and **B. Ermentrout.** Monotonicity of phaselocked solutions in chains and arrays of nearest-neighbor coupled oscillators. *SIAM J. Math. Anal.* 29:208–34, 1998.

Rinzel, J., D. Terman, X. J. Wang, and **B. Ermentrout.** Propagating activity patterns in large-scale inhibitory neuronal networks. *Science* 279:1351–5, 1998.

Ermentrout, G. B., and N. Kopell. Fine structure of neural spiking and synchronization in the presence of conduction delays. *Proc. Natl. Acad. Sci. U.S.A.* 95:1259–64, 1998.

Harris, A. E., **G. B. Ermentrout,** and S. L. Small. A model of ocular dominance column development by competition for trophic factor. *Proc. Natl. Acad. Sci. U.S.A.* 94:9944–9, 1997.

Hall, C. A., and **T. A. Porsching.** A characteristics-like method for thermally expandable flow on unstructured triangular grids. *Int. J. Numer. Methods Fluids* 22:731–54, 1996.

Hastings, S. P., M. K. Kwong, and **W. C. Troy.** The existence of multibump solutions of a Ginzburg-Landau type model of superconductors. *Eur. J. Appl. Math.* 7:559–74, 1996.

Hastings, S. P., and **J. B. McLeod.** An oscillatory differential equation. *Methods Appl. Anal.* 3:432–46, 1996.

Hebert, D. J. A branching random walk model for diffusion-reaction-convection. *Adv. Math.* 125:121–53, 1997.

Ho, A., and **K.-S. Lau.** On the discount sum of Bernoulli random variables. *J. Stat. Plann. Inference,* in press.

Fan, A., and **K.-S. Lau.** Asymptotic behavior of multiperiodic functions. *J. Fourier Anal. Appl.,* in press.

Lau, K.-S. A weighted Tauberian theorem. *J. Fourier Anal. Appl.* 2:397–406, 1996.

Lau, K.-S., M. F. Ma, and J. R. Wang. On some sharp regularity estimations of L^2-scaling functions. *SIAM J. Math. Anal.* 27:835–64, 1996.

Axelsson, O., and **W. Layton.** A two-level method for the discretization of nonlinear boundary value problems. *SIAM J. Numer. Anal.* 33:2359–74, 1996.

Layton, W., and B. Polman. Oscillation absorption finite element methods. *SIAM J. Sci. Comput.* 17:1328–46, 1996.

Layton, W., A. Sunmonu, and N. L. Troyani. A mathematical model of side ledge position in aluminum reduction cells. In *Numerical Methods in Engineering Simulation,* pp. 385–94, eds. Cerrolaza, Gajardo, and Brebbia. Boston: Computational Mechanics Publications, 1996.

Ervin, V., **W. Layton,** and J. Maubach. A posteriori error estimation for a two-level finite element method for the Navier-Stokes equations. *Numer. Methods Partial Differ. Eq.* 12:333–46, 1996.

Dowling, P. N., **C. J. Lennard,** and B. Turett. Asymptotically isometric copies of c_0 in Banach spaces. *J. Math. Anal. Appl.,* in press.

Kicey, C. J., and **C. J. Lennard.** Unique reconstruction of band-limited signals by a Mallat-Zhong wavelet transform algorithm. *J. Fourier Anal. Appl.* 3:63–82, 1997.

Dowling, P. N., **C. J. Lennard,** and B. Turett. Reflexivity and the fixed point property for nonexpansive maps. *J. Math. Anal. Appl.* 200:653–62, 1996.

Manfredi, J., and E. Villamor. Mappings with integrable dilatation in higher dimensions. *Bull. Am. Math. Soc.* 32:235–40, 1995.

Lindqvist, P., and **J. Manfredi.** The Harnack inequality for infinte-harmonic functions. *Electron. J. Diff. Eq.* 4:1–5, 1995.

Koskela, P., **J. Manfredi,** and E. Villamor. Regularity theory and traces for A-harmonic functions. *Trans. AMS* 348:755–66, 1995.

Manfredi, J., and V. Vespri. η-Harmonic morphisms are Mobius transformations. *Mich. J. Math.* 41:135–42, 1994.

McLeod, J. B., and K. R. Rajagopal. Inhomogeneous deformations between intersecting planes. *Arch. Ration. Mech. Anal.,* in press.

McLeod, J. B. The Stokes and Krasovskii conjectures for the wave of greatest height. *Stud. Appl. Math.,* in press.

McLeod, J. B., S. V. Raghavan, and **W. C. Troy.** A singular

University of Pittsburgh

Selected Publications (continued)

perturbation problem arising from the Kuramoto-Sivashinsky equation. *Diff. Integral Eq.* 10:1–36, 1997.

Friesecke, G., and **J. B. McLeod.** Dynamics as a mechanism preventing the formation of finer and finer microstructure. *Arch. Ration. Mech. Anal.* 133:199–247, 1996.

Michael, B. *A Graphing Calculation Workbook: Explorations Using the TI-82 & TI-83.* New York: John Wiley & Sons, 1998.

Kime, L., et al. **(B. Michael).** *Explorations in College Algebra.* New York: John Wiley & Sons, 1998.

Hickey, M., and **B. Michael.** *Instructors Manual: Explorations in College Algebra.* New York: John Wiley & Sons, 1998.

Fan, D., and **Y. Pan.** Singular integral operators with rough kernels supported by subvarieties. *Am. J. Math.,* in press.

Pan, Y. L^p-improving properties for some measures supported on curves. *Math. Scand.* 78:121–32, 1996.

Fan, D., and **Y. Pan.** Oscillatory integrals and atoms on the unit sphere. *Manuscripta Math.* 89:179–92, 1996.

Pan, Y. Oscillatory singular integrals on L^p and Hardy spaces. *Proc. AMS* 124:2821–5, 1996.

Chou, S.-H., and **T. A. Porsching.** A note on the restarted CG method and reduced space additive correction. *Comput. Math. Appl.* 35:129–36, 1998.

Porsching, T. A., C. A. Hall, and T. Bennett. Minimax approximation of optical profiles. *SIAM J. Appl. Math.,* in press.

Porsching, T. A., and **C. A. Hall.** Computationally directed axisymmetric aspheric figuring (after N. J. Brown). *Appl. Opt.* 35:4463–70, 1996.

Rabier, P. J. Ehresmann fibrations and Palais-Smale conditions for morphisms of Finsler manifolds. *Ann. Math.,* in press.

Rabier, P. J., and **W. C. Rheinboldt.** Classical and generalized solutions of time-dependent linear DAEs. *Linear Alg. Appl.* 245:259–93, 1996.

Rabier, P. J., and **W. C. Rheinboldt.** Time-dependent linear DAEs with discontinuous inputs. *Linear Alg. Appl.* 247:1–29, 1996.

Rabier, P. J., and **W. C. Rheinboldt.** Discontinuous solutions of semilinear DAE's. Part I: Distribution solutions. *Nonlinear Anal.* 27:1241–56, 1996.

Rabier, P. J., and **W. C. Rheinboldt.** Discontinuous solutions of semilinear DAE's. Part II: P-consistency. *Nonlinear Anal.* 27:1257–80, 1996.

Liu, J. L., and **W. C. Rheinboldt.** A posteriori finite element error estimators for parametrized nonlinear boundary problems. *Numer. Funct. Anal. Optimiz.* 17:605–37, 1996.

Sparling, G. A. J. Inversion for the Radon line transform in higher dimensions. *Phil. Trans. R. Soc. London,* in press.

Peletier, L. A., and **W. C. Troy.** Spatial patterns described by the extended Fisher-Kolmogorov equation: Periodic solutions. *SIAM J. Math. Anal.,* in press.

Peletier, L. A., and **W. C. Troy.** Multibump periodic travelling wave solutions of a model of suspension bridges. *Proc. R. Soc. Edinburgh,* in press.

Peletier, L. A., and **W. C. Troy.** Chaotic spatial patterns described by the extended Fisher-Kolmogorov equation. *J. Diff. Eq.* 129:458–508, 1996.

Peletier, L. A., and **W. C. Troy.** A topological shooting method and the existence of kinks in the Extended Fisher-Kolmogorov equation. *Topol. Methods Nonlinear Anal.* 6:331–55, 1996.

Read, R. C., and **E. G. Whitehead Jr.** Chromatic polynomials of homeomorphism classes of graphs. *Research Report CORR 97-08,* Faculty of Mathematics, University of Waterloo, 1997.

Guo, Z. Y., and **E. G. Whitehead Jr.** Chromaticity of a family of K_4 homeomorphs. *Discrete Math.* 172:53–8, 1997.

Arbogast, T., et al. **(I. Yotov).** Enhanced cell-centered finite differences for elliptic equations on general geometry. *SIAM J. Sci. Comp.* 19:404–25, 1998.

Yotov, I. A mixed finite element discretization on non-matching multiblock grids for a degenerate parabolic equation arising in porous media flow. *East-West J. Num. Math.* 5:211–30, 1997.

Arbogast, T., and **I. Yotov.** A non-mortar mixed finite element method for elliptic problems on non-matching multiblock grids. *Comp. Methods Appl. Mech. Eng.* 149:255–65, 1997.

Arbogast, T., M. F. Wheeler, and **I. Yotov.** Mixed finite elements for elliptic problems with tensor coefficients as cell-centered finite differences. *SIAM J. Num. Anal.* 34:828–52, 1997.

UNIVERSITY OF ROCHESTER

Department of Biostatistics
Program in Statistics

Programs of Study

The Department of Biostatistics in the School of Medicine and Dentistry offers graduate programs leading to the M.A. and Ph.D. degrees in statistics and the M.S. degree in medical statistics. A joint M.A. program in mathematics and statistics is also available. The department interprets the term "statistics" very broadly, with specialization available in theoretical and applied probability, statistical theory and analysis, and biostatistics. The department cooperates closely with the Program in Statistics in the College (Arts and Science), the Departments of Mathematics and Computer Science, and various clinical and basic science departments in the Medical School. Students have opportunities for supervised teaching and statistical consulting experience. The department gives individual attention to each student through intensive advising, extensive small seminars, and research collaboration. Prior to receiving their degrees, many Ph.D. students have had several publications based on research done in collaboration with faculty members in biostatistics/statistics and in various medical departments. Ph.D. program graduates have found employment at Bowman Gray School of Medicine, Carnegie Mellon, Case Western Reserve, Harvard, Emory, Johns Hopkins, Lehigh, Rochester, RIT, Rutgers, ten state universities, and numerous industrial concerns. M.A. and M.S. graduates are in various academic programs and in industrial, government, research, and consulting positions.

The M.S. program in medical statistics is primarily intended for students who wish to follow careers in the pharmaceutical industry or other health-related professions. The M.S. degree requires one or two years of study, depending upon preparation, and includes an applied project.

Entering Ph.D. students need undergraduate preparation in mathematics, including mathematical analysis (advanced calculus) and linear algebra and a year of probability and statistics. The prerequisites for the M.S. program in medical statistics are somewhat less stringent. Minor deficiencies can be made up after matriculation. Normally, doctoral students are initially considered M.A. candidates; this nonthesis degree can be completed in three or four semesters or, in some cases, in one calendar year. The degree prepares a student for doctoral studies or for professional employment. Ph.D. studies consist of additional specialized courses and seminars and supervised research leading to a dissertation. There is no foreign language requirement.

Research Facilities

The department is located in the Medical Center. Computing facilities include networks of Windows-based computers and Sun Workstations. The department library contains an excellent selection of current texts and major journals. The nearby Carlson Library holds a more extensive collection. Office space is available for teaching and research assistants.

Financial Aid

In 1999–2000, a well-qualified beginning graduate student may receive up to $16,500 for the year (including summer). A teaching assistant's duties may include teaching recitation sections, assisting on consulting projects, computer programming, or grading tests and papers. Advanced students may be supported as research assistants or instructors. Traineeships in cancer and environmental health biostatistics funded by the National Institutes of Health are also available for U.S. citizens and permanent residents and cover both stipend and tuition.

Cost of Study

In 1999–2000, anticipated tuition is $22,579 per year but is waived for students receiving support. Basic single health coverage is provided without charge through the University Health Service.

Living and Housing Costs

Apartments are available in six University-operated facilities near the campus. In 1999–2000, a single person pays $322 to $666 per month, depending on the type of accommodation desired. The cost for a married couple with or without children is between $544 and $665. The Community Living Information Center maintains a file of private rooms and apartments that are available in the area.

Student Group

In 1998–99, there were 11 full-time graduate students in the department from the United States, Europe, and Asia. Several had completed master's degrees at Rochester or elsewhere.

Location

Located on the south shore of Lake Ontario, a short drive from the Finger Lakes area, Rochester is a cultural center for upstate New York. The more than 700,000 residents of the Rochester metropolitan area enjoy the year-round activities of the University-owned Memorial Art Gallery, the cinematic and photographic offerings of George Eastman House, and the events at the University's Eastman Theatre, where concerts are given by the Rochester Philharmonic Orchestra and by students and faculty of the University's Eastman School of Music. Known as the photographic and optical capital of the world, Rochester is the home of many highly technological industries. Sailing, skiing, and camping facilities abound.

The University

The University of Rochester, founded in 1850, is a medium-sized coeducational private university. It has developed into a major center for graduate education in recent times. A survey conducted by the American Council on Education gave the highest possible rating to the University's graduate programs in nine of the thirteen fields evaluated. There are 4,600 undergraduates and 3,300 graduate students. The main campus is along the Genesee River at the edge of the city, where a riverside path for bicyclists and strollers and a launching dock for canoeists are available. The medical campus is adjacent to the main campus, and the Eastman School of Music is downtown.

Applying

Applications requesting financial support should be submitted by February 1. GRE General Test scores are required; students from non-English-speaking countries must also submit TOEFL scores.

Correspondence and Information

Pattie Kolomic
Department of Biostatistics
University of Rochester, Box 630
Rochester, New York 14642
Telephone: 716-275-6696
E-mail: grad_info@bst.rochester.edu

University of Rochester

THE FACULTY AND THEIR RESEARCH

Several of the faculty members listed below have primary appointments in the Program in Statistics in the College (Arts and Sciences) or the Graduate School of Management.

Professors
Christopher Cox, Ph.D., Illinois at Urbana-Champaign. Biostatistics, generalized linear models, applications in toxicology and psychiatry.
K. Ruben Gabriel (Emeritus), Ph.D., Hebrew (Jerusalem). Data analysis, multivariate analysis, graphics.
W. J. Hall (Part-Time), Ph.D., North Carolina. Large-sample theory, sequential analysis, robust inference, technology assessment.
Julian Keilson (Emeritus), Ph.D., Harvard. Probability theory, stochastic processes, congestion theory.
G. S. Mudholkar, Ph.D., North Carolina. Statistical theory, multivariate analysis, robust methods.
David Oakes, Chair; Ph.D., London. Survival analysis, medical statistics, semiparametric inference.
P. S. R. S. Rao, Ph.D., Harvard. Sampling theory, variance components, linear models, bootstrap.

Associate Professors
John Kolassa, Ph.D., Chicago. Biostatistics, series expansion techniques, asymptotics.
Michael McDermott, Ph.D., Rochester. Order-restricted inference, biostatistics, applications in neurologic disease.
Richard Raubertas, Ph.D., Wisconsin–Madison. Biostatistics, spatial statistics.

Assistant Professors
Heng Li, Ph.D., Harvard. Measurement theory, linear models.
Derick Peterson, Ph.D., Berkeley. Biostatistics, smoothing, interval censored data, model selection.
Hongwei Zhao, D.Sc., Harvard. Survival analysis, semi-parametric theory, quality of life data.

Research Assistant Professor
Vladimir Dragalin, Ph.D., Steklov Institute of Mathematics (Moscow). Sequential analysis, many hypothesis testing, selection problem, change point problem.

Instructor
Luc Miller Watelet, Ph.D., Washington (Seattle). Survival analysis.

Research projects, many federally funded, in which the department's faculty members are major participants include:
Studies of Suicide and Depression in the Elderly.
Effects of Ultrafine Particles on Lung Function.
Studies of Exposures to Environmental Pollutants in Normal and Asthmatic Subjects.
Clustering and Trends in Disease Incidence Data.
Statistical Analysis of Multiple Event Time Data.
Nonparametric Analysis of Censored Data.
Correlates of Alzheimer's Disease.
Epidemiologic Study of Tourette's Syndrome.
Clinical and Genetic Studies of Facioscapulohumeral Muscular Dystrophy.
Child Development Study in the Seychelle Islands.
Multicenter Automatic Defibrillator Implantation Trial (MADIT-II).
Long QT Syndrome Longitudinal and Genetic Study.
Small Sample Biostatistical Inference.
Secondary Inferences in Cardiovascular Clinical Trials.
Angina in Primary Care.
Earlier Versus Later Levodopa in Parkinson's Disease.
Thrombogenic Factors and Recurrent Cardiac Events.
Neurocognitive Function, HIV Load, and Surrogate Markers.

The Charles L. Odoroff Library, housed in the Department of Biostatistics, contains a large selection of current texts and journals and is also used as a conference room for departmental meetings.

SELECTED PUBLICATIONS

Chen, S., **C. Cox**, and L. Cui. A more flexible regression-to-the-mean model with possible stratification. *Biometrics* 54:939–47, 1998.

Cox, C. The delta method. In *Encyclopedia of Biostatistics*, eds. P. Armitage and T. Colton. New York: John Wiley, in press.

Cox, C. Nonlinear quasi-likelihood models: Applications to continuous proportions. *Comp. Stat. Data Anal.* 21:449–61, 1996.

Cox, C., D. O. Marsh, G. J. Myers, and T. W. Clarkson. Analysis of data on delayed development from the 1971–1972 outbreak of methylmercury poisoning in Iraq: Assessment of influential points. *Neurotoxicology* 16:727–30, 1995.

Cox, C. Location-scale cumulative odds models for ordinal data: A generalized nonlinear model approach. *Stat. Med.* 14:1191–203, 1995.

Cox, C., and G. Ma. Asymptotic confidence bands for generalized nonlinear regression models. *Biometrics* 51:142–50, 1995.

Cox, C. Statistical issues for animal studies of developmental neurotoxicity. In *Neurobehavioral Toxicity*, pp. 93–101, eds. B. Weiss and J. L. O'Donoghue. New York: Raven Press, 1994.

Cox, C., et al. A test for teratological effects of power frequency magnetic fields on chick embryos. *IEEE Trans. Biomed. Eng.* 40:605–10, 1993.

Cox, C. A GLM approach to quantal response models for mixtures. *Biometrics* 48:911–28, 1992.

Chen, S., and **C. Cox**. Use of baseline data for estimation of treatment effects in the presence of regression to the mean. *Biometrics* 48:593–8, 1992.

Dragalin, V. The design and analysis of 2-CUSUM procedure. *Commun. Statist.-Comput. Simul.* 26:67–81, 1997.

Dragalin, V. Sequential change point problem. *Econ. Quality Control* 12:95–122, 1997.

Dragalin, V. A simple and effective scanning rule for a multi-channel system. *Metrika* 43:165–82, 1996.

Dragalin, V. Retrospective change point problem. *Econ. Quality Control* 11:3–21, 1996.

Dragalin, V. An optimal sequential selection procedure. *Comm. Statist.-Theor. Methods* 24:29–443, 1995.

Dragalin, V. Optimal CUSUM envelope for monitoring the mean of normal distribution. *Econ. Quality Control* 9:185–202, 1994.

Dragalin, V. Optimality of generalized CUSUM procedure in quickest detection problem. In *Proceedings of Steklov Math. Institute: "Statistics and Control of Stochastic Processes,"* vol. 202, pp. 132–48, 1993.

Dragalin, V., and A. A. Novikov. Asymptotic expansions for 2-SPRT. *Lect. Notes Math.* 1299:366–75, 1988.

Dragalin, V., and A. A. Novikov. Asymptotic solution of the Kiefer-Weiss problem for process with independent increments. *Theory Probab. Appl.* 32:617–27, 1987.

Hall, W. J. The distribution of Brownian motion on linear stopping boundaries. *Sequential Anal.* 16:345–52, 1997.

Moss, A. J., and **W. J. Hall** et al. Improved survival with an implanted defibrillator in patients with coronary disease at high risk for ventricular arrhythmia. *N. Engl. J. Med.* 335:1933–40, 1996.

Choi, S., **W. J. Hall**, and A. Schick. Asymptotically uniformly most powerful tests in parametric and semiparametric models. *Ann. Stat.* 24:841–61, 1996.

Hall, W. J., and D. J. Mathiason. On large-sample estimation and testing in parametric models. *Int. Stat. Rev.* 58:77–97, 1990.

Dalal, S. R., and **W. J. Hall**. Approximating priors by mixtures of natural conjugate priors. *J. R. Stat. Soc. B* 45:278–86, 1983.

Begun, J. M., **W. J. Hall**, W.-M. Huang, and J. A. Wellner. Information and asymptotic efficiency in parametric-nonparametric models. *Ann. Stat.* 12:432–52, 1983.

Lambert, D., and **W. J. Hall**. Asymptotic lognormality of P-values. *Ann. Stat.* 10:44–64, 1982.

Hall, W. J., and J. A. Wellner. Simultaneous confidence bands for a survival curve from censored data. *Biometrika* 67:133–43, 1980.

Hall, W. J. Embedding submartingales in Wiener processes with drift, with applications in sequential analysis. *J. Appl. Probab.* 6:612–32, 1969.

Hall, W. J., R. A. Wijsman, and J. K. Ghosh. The relationship between sufficiency and invariance, with applications in sequential analysis. *Ann. Math. Stat.* 36:575–614, 1965.

Kolassa, J. E. Uniformity of double saddlepoint conditional probability approximations. *J. Multivariate Anal.*, in press.

Kolassa, J. E. Confidence intervals for parameters lying in a random polygon. *Can. J. Stat.*, in press.

Kolassa, J. E., and M. A. Tanner. Approximate Monte Carlo conditional inference in exponential families. In *Proceedings of the Symposium on the Interface*, vol. 28, Interface Foundation of North America, Fairfax Station, Virginia, in press.

Katz, P. R., J. Karuza, **J. E. Kolassa**, and A. Hutson. Medical practice with nursing home residents: Results from the National Physician Activities Census. *J. Am. Geriatrics Soc.* 45:911–17, 1997.

Kolassa, J. E. *Series Approximation Methods in Statistics*, second edition. New York: Springer-Verlag, 1997.

Kolassa, J. E. Infinite parameter estimates in logistic regression. *Scand. J. Stat.* 24:523–30, 1997.

Kolassa, J. E. Higher-order approximations to conditional distribution functions. *Ann. Stat.* 24:353–65, 1996.

Kolassa, J. E., and M. A. Tanner. Approximate conditional inference in exponential families via the Gibbs Sampler. *J. Am. Stat. Assoc.* 89:697–702, 1994.

Kolassa, J. E. Confidence intervals for thermodynamic constants. *Geochim. Cosmochim. Acta* 55:3543–52, 1992.

Kolassa, J. E., and P. McCullagh. Edgeworth series for lattice distributions. *Ann. Stat.* 18:981–5, 1990.

Li, H. The resolution of some paradoxes related to reliability and validity (with discussion). *J. Educ. Behav. Stat.*, in press.

Li, H., and H. Wainer. Toward a coherent view of reliability in test theory. *J. Educational Behav. Stat.* 22:479–85, 1997.

Li, H., and H. Stern. Bayesian inference for nested designs based on Jeffreys' Prior. *Am. Stat.* 51:219–24, 1997.

Li, H. A unifying expression for the maximal reliability of a linear composite. *Psychometrika* 62:245–49, 1997.

Li, H., R. Rosenthal, and D. B. Rubin. Reliability of measurement in psychology: From Spearman-Brown to maximal reliability. *Psychol. Methods* 1:98–107, 1996.

McDermott, M. P. Generalized orthogonal contrast tests for homogeneity of ordered means. *Can. J. Stat.*, in press.

Zou, K. H., and **M. P. McDermott**. Higher-moment approaches to approximate interval estimation for a certain intraclass coefficient. *Stat. Med.*, in press.

Wang, Y., and **M. P. McDermott**. Conditional likelihood ratio rest for a nonnegative normal mean vector. *J. Am. Stat. Assoc.* 93:380–6, 1998.

Wang, Y., and **M. P. McDermott**. A conditional test for a nonnegative mean vector based on a Hotelling's T2-type statistic. *J. Mult. Anal.* 66:64–70, 1998.

McDermott, M. P. The FSH-DY Group. A prospective, quantitative study of the natural history of facioscapulohumeral muscular dystrophy (FSHD): Implications for therapeutic trials. *Neurology* 48:38–46, 1997.

McDermott, M. P., et al. Factors predictive of the need for levodopa therapy in early, untreated Parkinson's disease. *Arch. Neurol.* 52:565–70, 1995.

McDermott, M. P., and G. S. Mudholkar. A simple approach to testing homogeneity of order constrained means. *J. Am. Stat. Assoc.* 88:1371–9, 1993.

Mudholkar, G. S., and A. D. Hutson. Some refinements of the quasi-quantiles. *Stat. Probab. Lett.* 32:67–74, 1997.

Mudholkar, G. S., D. K. Srivastava, and G. D. Kollia. A generalization of the Weibull distribution with application to the analysis of survival data. *J. Am. Stat. Assoc.* 91:1575–83, 1996.

Mudholkar, G. S., and A. D. Hutson. The exponentiated Weibull Family: Some properties and a flood data application. *Commun. Stat. Theory Methods* 25:3059–83, 1996.

Mudholkar, G. S., D. K. Srivastava, and M. Freimer. Exponentiated Weibull family: A reanalysis of the Bus failure data. *Technometrics* 37:436–45, 1995.

Mudholkar, G. S., M. P. McDermott, and A. Mudholkar. Robust finite-intersection tests for homogeneity of ordered variances. *J. Stat. Plann. Inf.* 43:185–95, 1995.

Larsson, L. G., J. Baum, **G. S. Mudholkar**, and G. Kollia. Hypermobility—asset or liability: A joint specific analysis. *N. Engl. J. Med.* 329:1079–83, 1993.

Mudholkar, G. S., M. P. McDermott, and J. Aumont. Testing homogeneity of ordered variances. *Metrika* 40:271–81, 1993.

Srivastava, D. K., **G. S. Mudholkar**, and A. Mudholkar. Assessing the significance of difference between two quick estimates of location. *J. Appl. Stat.* 19:405–16, 1992.

Freimer, M., G. Kollia, **G. S. Mudholkar**, and C. T. Lin. Extremes,

University of Rochester

Selected Publications (continued)

extremes spacings and outliers in the Tukey and Weibull families. *Commun. Stat. Theory Methods* 18:4261–74, 1989.

Mudholkar, G. S., and **M. P. McDermott.** A class of tests for equality of ordered means. *Biometrika* 76:161–8, 1989.

Freimer, M., **G. S. Mudholkar,** G. Kollia, and C. T. Lin. A study of generalized Tukey-lambda family. *Commun. Stat. Theory Methods* 17:3547–67, 1988.

Mudholkar, G. S., and M. Freimer. A structure theorem for the polars of unitarily invariant norms. *Proc. Am. Math. Soc.* 95:331–8, 1985.

Freimer, M., and **G. S. Mudholkar.** A class of generalizations of Holder's inequality. In *Inequalities in Statistics and Probability,* vol. 5, pp. 59–68, ed. Y. L. Tong. IMS Monograph, 1984.

Oakes, D. Direct calculation of the information matrix via the EM algorithm. *J. R. Stat. Soc. B,* in press.

Manatunga, A. K., and **D. Oakes.** Parametric analysis of matched pairs survival data. *Lifetime Data Anal.,* in press.

Lin, D. Y., **D. Oakes,** and Z. Ying. Additive hazards regression with current status data. *Biometrika* 85:289–98, 1998.

Oakes, D., and J.-H. Jeong. Frailty models and rank tests. *Lifetime Data Anal.* 4:209–28, 1998.

Oakes, D. Model based and or marginal analysis of multiple event time data. In *Proceedings of the First Seattle Symposium in Biostatistics: Survival Analysis,* pp. 84–98, eds. D. Y. Lin and T. R. Fleming. New York: Springer, 1997.

Emond, M. J., J. Ritz, and **D. Oakes.** Bias in GEE estimates of population average parameters from longitudinal data. *Commun. Stat. Theory Methods* 26:15–32, 1997.

Manatunga, A. K., and **D. Oakes.** A measure of association for bivariate frailty distributions. *J. Mult. Anal.* 56:60–74, 1996.

Oakes, D. Multiple time scales in survival analysis. *Lifetime Data Anal.* 1:7–20, 1995.

Oakes, D. Multivariate survival distributions. *Nonparametric Stat.* 3:343–54, 1994.

Oakes, D., and L. Cui. A note on semiparametric inference for modulated renewal processes. *Biometrika* 81:83–90, 1994.

Oakes, D., et al. **(M. P. McDermott).** The Multicenter Diltiazem Post-Infarction Trial Research Group. Use of compliance measures in an analysis of the effect of diltiazem on mortality and reinfarction after myocardial infarction. *J. Am. Stat. Assoc.* 88:44–9, 1993.

Oakes, D. The Parkinson Study Group. Effects of tocopherol and deprenyl on the progression of disability in early Parkinson's disease. *N. Engl. J. Med.* 328:176–83, 1993.

Oakes, D. Bivariate survival models induced by frailties. *J. Am. Stat. Assoc.* 84:487–93, 1989.

Cox, D. R., and **D. Oakes.** *Analysis of Survival Data.* London: Chapman and Hall, 1984.

van der Laan, M. J., N. P. Jewell, and **D. R. Peterson.** Efficient estimation of the lifetime and disease onset distribution. *Biometrika* 84:539–54, 1997.

Poduri, S. R. S. Rao, and C. E. Heckler. Variance components of the three-stage nested designs. *J. Stat. Plann. Inf.,* in press.

Poduri, S. R. S. Rao. *Variance Components Estimation: Mixed Models, Methodologies and Applications.* London and New York: Chapman and Hall, 1997.

Poduri, S. R. S. Rao, W. G. Cochran, and J. Kaplan. ANOVA and MINQUE type estimators for the one-way random effects model. *J. Am. Stat. Assoc.* 76:89–97, 1981.

Poduri, S. R. S. Rao. Theory of the Minque—a review. *Sankhya* Series B 39:201–10, 1977

Poduri, S. R. S. Rao. On the two-phase ratio estimator in finite populations. *J. Am. Stat. Assoc.* 70:839–45, 1975.

Poduri, S. R. S. Rao. Jack-knifing the ratio estimator. *Sankhya* Series C 36:8497, 1974.

Poduri, S. R. S. Rao, and J. N. K. Rao. Small sample results for ratio estimators. *Biometrika* 58:625–30, 1971.

Poduri, S. R. S. Rao. On three procedures of sampling from finite populations. *Biometrika* 55:438–40, 1968.

Rodewald, L. E., et al. **(R. F. Raubertas).** Health insurance for low-income working families: Effect on the provision of immunizations to preschool-age children. *Arch. Pediatrics Adolescent Med.* 151:798–803, 1997.

Raubertas, R. F. Statistical considerations in caries models: Reaction paper. *Adv. Dental Res.* 9:285–9, 1995.

Sarkar, I. C., G. S. Mudholkar, and **R. F. Raubertas.** An approximation to the distribution of the resultant from a Fisher distribution. *Commun. Stat. Simul. Comp.* 24:227–41, 1995.

Raubertas, R. F., L. E. Rodewald, S. G. Humiston, and P. G. Szilagyi. ROC curves for classification trees. *Med. Decis. Making* 14:169–74, 1994.

Humiston, S. G., et al. **(R. F. Raubertas).** Decision rules for predicting vaccination status of preschool-age emergency department patients. *J. Pediatr.* 123:887–92, 1993.

Raubertas, R. F. The envelope probability plot as a goodness-of-fit test. *Commun. Stat. Simul. Comp.* 21:189–202, 1992.

Raubertas, R. F. Spatial and temporal analysis of disease occurrence for detection of clustering. *Biometrics* 44:1121–9, 1988.

Zhao, H., and A. A. Tsiatis. Efficient estimation of the distribution of quality adjusted survival time. *Biometrics,* in press.

Zhao, H., and A. A. Tsiatis. Estimating mean quality adjusted lifetime with censored data. *Sankhya,* in press.

Zhao, H., and A. A. Tsiatis. A consistent estimator for the distribution of quality adjusted survival times. *Biometrika* 84:339–48, 1997.

UNIVERSITY OF SOUTHERN CALIFORNIA

Department of Mathematics

Programs of Study	The department offers degree programs leading to the Master of Arts in mathematics, applied mathematics, and mathematical finance; the Master of Science in applied mathematics and statistics; and the Doctor of Philosophy in mathematics and applied mathematics.
	Introductory graduate courses are offered in algebra, real analysis, complex analysis, numerical analysis, linear and nonlinear functional analysis, algebraic topology, combinatorics, differential geometry, ordinary differential equations, partial differential equations, control theory, applied mathematics, probability, and statistics. Advanced courses in these and related areas, leading to research topics, are also offered.
	The Ph.D. degree can normally be completed within four years. Candidates must take a written prequalifying exam in algebra or analysis by the end of their second semester and two written qualifying exams, as well as an oral exam, by the end of their fifth semester. Once these exams have been successfully completed, independent research is begun under the direction of a senior faculty member. The student must write an acceptable dissertation that exhibits original and independent research. A reading knowledge of two languages, other than English, in which there is a significant body of research in mathematics is required.
	The M.A. degree program normally requires three semesters of graduate study; it is completed either by passing written comprehensive examinations or by writing a thesis. In both the M.S. in applied mathematics and the M.S. in statistics, the degree is completed by carrying out a practicum (research project) in a selected area. The M.S. in statistics also has statistical consulting as a requirement.
Research Facilities	All graduate assistants are provided with office space in the mathematics building. Seaver Science Library contains more than 200,000 books and current subscriptions to about 350 journals of mathematical interest (3,000 journals in all fields). Facilities of the UCLA and Caltech libraries are also available through interlibrary loan, as well as the facilities of the Research Libraries Group, a corporation of major universities and research institutions of which USC is a member. A variety of computing facilities is available for academic and research purposes on the main campus and in the department. Also within the Department of Mathematics is the Center for Applied Mathematical Sciences, an interdisciplinary research group with interests in the application of mathematics to problems in engineering and the sciences.
Financial Aid	Almost all of the department's graduate students are supported by assistantships or fellowships for the duration of their study. About twenty-five teaching assistantships and two fellowships are available for new graduate students each year. These assistantships carry a stipend of $14,000 for the 1999–2000 academic year, tuition remission for up to 12 units per semester during the academic year (9 units is a normal load), and tuition remission for 12 units the following summer. In addition, summer teaching assistantships are available at stipends of $3500. The C. W. Trigg Fellowship is available for the applicant best demonstrating mathematical problem-solving ability, and several summer research assistantships are available for Ph.D. students who have completed the Ph.D. qualifying exam. A limited number of University fellowships, research assistantships, and tuition fellowships are also available. California residents are strongly urged to apply for California State Graduate Fellowships, even if they expect to receive other financial aid.
Cost of Study	For 1999–2000, the tuition for full-time graduate students is $11,099 for 15 to 18 units or $748 per unit for students taking fewer than 15 units. Fees (e.g., student health services) are $160 per semester. A one-time publication fee of $113 is charged for microfilming and binding the thesis.
Living and Housing Costs	In 1999–2000, monthly rates for graduate student family housing vary between $625 and $750 for a one-bedroom apartment and $785 to $900 for a two-bedroom apartment. Monthly rates for single graduate student housing vary from $260 for a two-bedroom suite (2 students per unit) to $800 for a one-bedroom single. There are also many privately owned apartments available in the area.
Student Group	There are currently about 70 graduate students in the department (working with about 40 faculty members); approximately 15 percent are women, and 60 percent are international students. The total University enrollment is about 28,000, of whom about 13,000 are graduate students.
Location	The main campus of USC is located near the center of Los Angeles and its varied cultural attractions. It takes only a few minutes to reach the Music Center, the Art Museum, Dodger Stadium, and Hollywood. The campus is within an hour's drive of mountains, deserts, and beaches and within only a few hours' drive of Mexico or the Sierra Nevada. Shuttle-bus service is available to and from the campuses of UCLA and Caltech.
The University	Founded in 1880, USC is the oldest major independent, coeducational, nonsectarian university in the West. There are 105 buildings on its 150 urban acres. More graduate and professional degrees than bachelor's degrees have been awarded by USC each year since 1960.
Applying	Although applications for admission and financial aid are considered at all times, they should be submitted by February 1 to ensure consideration for the following academic year. Scores on the General Test of the Graduate Record Examinations (GRE), as well as transcripts and three letters of recommendation, are required for admission to all programs. Scores on the GRE Subject Test in mathematics are required for admission to the Ph.D. program. International applicants who are applying for a teaching assistantship are advised to take the TSE and TOEFL. Applicants to the Ph.D. and M.A. programs in mathematics must have taken full-year sequences at the undergraduate level in real analysis and algebra; admission in special standing may be feasible while remedying deficiencies, but this delays progress. Applicants for the M.S. in applied mathematics and statistics programs should have a substantial undergraduate background in mathematics, which includes one semester of real analysis or advanced calculus and one semester of linear algebra.
Correspondence and Information	Graduate Vice-Chair Department of Mathematics University of Southern California Los Angeles, California 90089-1113 Telephone: 213-740-8168 E-mail: lburge@math.usc.edu World Wide Web: http://www.usc.edu/dept/math/

University of Southern California

THE FACULTY AND THEIR RESEARCH

Kenneth Alexander, Professor; Ph.D., MIT. Probability.
Henry A. Antosiewicz, Professor; Ph.D., Vienna. Differential equations, applications to finance.
Richard Arratia, Professor; Ph.D., Wisconsin–Madison. Probability, combinatorics.
Peter Baxendale, Professor; Ph.D., Warwick (England). Probability.
Edward K. Blum, Professor; Ph.D., Columbia. Numerical analysis, mathematical neuroscience.
Francis Bonahon, Professor; Ph.D., Paris. Geometry, topology.
Ronald E. Bruck, Professor; Ph.D., Chicago. Nonlinear functional analysis.
Larry Goldstein, Professor; Ph.D., California, San Diego. Statistics.
Solomon Golomb, Professor; Ph.D., Harvard. Combinatorial analysis, number theory.
Robert M. Guralnick, Professor; Ph.D., UCLA. Group theory, representation theory, matrix theory.
Eugene Gutkin, Professor; Ph.D., Brandeis. Dynamical systems, mathematical physics.
Nicolai T. A. Haydn, Associate Professor; Ph.D., Warwick (England). Ergodic theory, dynamical systems.
Sheldon Kamienny, Professor; Ph.D., Harvard. Algebraic geometry.
Igor Kukavica, Associate Professor; Ph.D., Indiana. Partial differential equations.
P. Vijay Kumar, Professor; Ph.D., USC. Algebraic coding theory, algebraic geometry.
Chung-Chieh (Jay) Kuo, Associate Professor; Ph.D., MIT. Signal and image processing, parallel computing and numerical analysis.
Charles P. Lanski, Professor; Ph.D., Chicago. Noncommutative ring theory.
M. Susan Montgomery, Professor; Ph.D., Chicago. Noncommutative rings, Hopf algebra.
Robert Penner, Professor; Ph.D., MIT. Geometry, topology.
Pavel Pevzner, Professor; Ph.D., Moscow Institute of Physics and Technology. Computational molecular biology.
Wlodek Proskurowski, Professor; Ph.D., Royal Institute of Technology (Stockholm). Numerical analysis, scientific computing.
Wayne Raskind, Associate Professor; Ph.D., Cambridge. Algebraic K-theory, number theory.
John E. Rolph, Professor; Ph.D., Berkeley. Statistics.
I. Gary Rosen, Professor; Ph.D., Brown. Applied mathematics.
Boris Rozovskii, Professor; Ph.D., Moscow State. Applied mathematics, stochastic processes, partial differential equations.
Robert J. Sacker, Professor; Ph.D., NYU. Differential equations and dynamical systems.
Alan Schumitzky, Professor; Ph.D., Cornell. Applied mathematics.
Simon Tavaré, Professor; Ph.D., Sheffield (England). Applied probability, statistics, molecular evolution.
Zdenek Vorel, Professor; Ph.D., Czechoslovak Academy of Sciences. Ordinary and functional differential equations.
Chunming Wang, Associate Professor; Ph.D., Brown. Control theory.
Michael S. Waterman, Professor; Ph.D., Michigan State. Applied mathematics, statistics, molecular biology.
Paul Yang, Professor; Ph.D., Berkeley. Differential geometry.

Emeritus Professors

Theodore E. Harris. Probability.
Donald E. Hyers. Integral equations, functional analysis.
B. Andreas Troesch. Numerical analysis, applied mathematics.
Paul A. White. Mathematical education.

THE UNIVERSITY OF TEXAS AT DALLAS

Mathematical Sciences

Programs of Study

The mathematical sciences department at the University of Texas at Dallas offers the Master of Science degree in four specializations: applied mathematics, engineering mathematics, mathematics, and statistics. The Doctor of Philosophy degree is offered in applied mathematics and in statistics. The program has major research faculty and thrusts in the latter two areas. The degree programs are designed to prepare graduates for careers in mathematical sciences or in related fields for which these disciplines provide indispensable foundations and tools. There is no language requirement.

The Master of Science degree requires 33–36 semester hours of course work, consisting of core courses and approved electives. The student may choose a thesis plan or a nonthesis plan. In the thesis plan, the thesis replaces 6 semester hours of course work.

The Ph.D. program is tailored to the student, who arranges a course program with the guidance and approval of the graduate adviser. Adjustments can be made as the student's interests develop and a specific dissertation topic is chosen. Approximately 39 hours of core courses and 18–24 hours of elective courses are required for a typical degree program. After completion of about two years of course work, the student must undertake and pass a Ph.D. qualifying examination in order to continue in the program. The program culminates in the preparation of a dissertation, which must be approved by the graduate program. The topic may be in mathematical sciences exclusively or may involve considerable work in an area of application. Typical areas of concentrations within applied mathematics include, but are not restricted to, applied analysis, relativity theory, differential equations, scattering theory, systems theory, control theory, signal processing, and differential geometry. In the area of statistics, concentrations are offered in mathematical statistics, applied statistics, statistical computing, probability, stochastic processes, linear models, time series analysis, statistical classification, multivariate analysis, robust statistics, statistical inference, and asymptotic theory.

In addition to a wide range of courses in mathematics and statistics, the mathematical sciences program offers a unique selection of courses that consider theoretical and computational aspects of engineering and scientific problems.

Research Facilities

The program occupies spacious quarters in the modern Computer and Engineering Science building. Faculty members and graduate students in mathematical sciences have access to state-of-the-art scientific workstations and supercomputers. Faculty offices are equipped with Sun SPARCstations or X-terminals, and all teaching assistant offices are equipped with X-terminals, connected via Ethernet to mathematical sciences' three Sun SPARCserver 10's. Two of the SPARCserver 10's are servers for the X-terminals, while the third is configured for large computational projects. Mathematical sciences students also have direct access to the mathematical sciences computer room, which has additional Sun SPARCstations and X-terminals. A large collection of mathematical and statistical software is maintained on the SPARCserver 10's for research and educational use. This software includes Matlab, S, and Mathematica, among others. Mathematical Sciences also has access via the Academic Computer Center to Silicon Graphics graphics workstations and the University of Texas system CRAY Y-MP supercomputer.

Financial Aid

Teaching assistantships are available for full-time graduate students in mathematical sciences. In 1998–99, the stipends were $9900 for nine months. Support for summer study is usually available. The stipends were $3300 for summer 1998. UT Dallas has also developed a comprehensive program of grants, scholarships, loans, and employment opportunities to assist students in meeting the cost of their education.

Cost of Study

Nonresidents holding teaching assistantships are eligible to pay tuition at the lower rate applicable to Texas residents. The rates for 1999–2000 for a 9-hour course load are $1372.60 for Texas residents and $3289.60 for nonresidents. In past years, the University has provided additional financial assistance to teaching assistants in an amount that covers much of the nonresident tuition cost. It is anticipated that this will continue.

Living and Housing Costs

Students in the program typically live in a nearby apartment complex that offers comfortable accommodations at attractive rates. In spring 1999, monthly rates were $370 for efficiency, $404–$544 for one-bedroom, and $680–$736 for two-bedroom apartments, some including washer and dryer.

Student Group

The total enrollment at the University is 8,942, including 3,910 graduate students. The mathematical sciences program has 17 master's students and 21 Ph.D. candidates, some of whom attend part-time while employed full-time with companies in the Dallas area.

Student Outcomes

The most recent 5 Ph.D. graduates of the program have secured employment in both industrial and academic positions. Of the program's 2 most recent Ph.D. students in applied mathematics, 1 is now employed by Convex Computer Corporation (a manufacturer of high-end computers), and the other has joined the faculty at Virginia Tech. In statistics, the 2 most recent Ph.D. graduates have joined the faculties of the Universities of Houston and Oklahoma, and a third has joined the research staff of BNR, a telecommunications firm.

Location

UT Dallas is located in Richardson, a quiet suburb of North Dallas, which is easily accessible to the more than 800 high-technology companies located in the Dallas–Fort Worth area. Many of these companies are located within 10 miles of UT Dallas, providing graduates with numerous career opportunities. The Dallas metropolitan area also offers a wide range of cultural, social, and sports activities.

The University and The Program

The University of Texas at Dallas was created in 1969 when the privately funded Southwest Center for Advanced Studies was transferred to the state of Texas. In 1972 the Program in Mathematical Sciences was introduced and in 1975 became part of the School of Natural Sciences and Mathematics. Research at the graduate level has continued to represent a major thrust of the University and of the program.

Applying

Applications are considered at any time until vacancies are filled. For consideration for teaching assistantships, the deadline of January 15 is set for first-round consideration. Applicants should arrange for GRE scores and (for international students) TOEFL scores to be included as early as possible in the application materials. Applications not complete before March 15 receive relatively late consideration for teaching assistantships.

Correspondence and Information

Head
Mathematical Sciences
The University of Texas at Dallas
P.O. Box 830688, MS EC35
Richardson, Texas 75083-0688
Telephone: 972-883-2161
Fax: 972-883-6622
E-mail: utdmath@utdallas.edu

The University of Texas at Dallas

THE FACULTY AND THEIR RESEARCH

Larry P. Ammann, Professor; Ph.D., Florida State, 1976. Robust multivariate statistical methods, signal processing, statistical computing, applied probability, remote sensing.

Michael Baron, Assistant Professor; Ph.D., Maryland, 1995. Mathematical statistics, sequential analysis, change-point problems, applications in semiconductor manufacturing, psychology, actuarial science.

Tiberiu Constantinescu, Assistant Professor; Ph.D., Bucharest, 1989. Functional analysis, operator theory, linear and multilinear algebra, matrix theory, combinatorics, system theory and control.

M. Ali Hooshyar, Professor; Ph.D., Indiana, 1970. Scattering theory, inverse scattering theory with geophysical and optical applications, fission.

Raimund Ober, Associate Professor; Ph.D., Cambridge, 1987. Systems and control, system identification, model reduction, robust control.

Istvan Ozsvath, Professor; Ph.D., Hamburg, 1960. Relativistic cosmology, differential geometry.

Viswanath Ramakrishna, Assistant Professor; Ph.D., Washington (St. Louis), 1991. Control, optimization, computation, applications in material and molecular sciences.

Ivor Robinson, Professor; B.A., Cambridge, 1947. General relativity theory, particularly exact solutions to Einstein's equations of gravitation.

Robert Serfling, Professor; Ph.D., North Carolina, 1967. Probability theory, statistical inference, robust and nonparametric methods, asymptotic theory, stochastic processes.

Janos Turi, Professor, Ph.D., Virginia Tech, 1986. Functional differential equations, integral equations, approximation theory, optimal control theory, numerical analysis, applied functional analysis.

John Van Ness, Professor; Ph.D., Brown, 1964. Robust linear models, statistical classification, multivariate analysis, applications of statistics to the physical and medical sciences.

John Wiorkowski, Professor; Ph.D., Chicago, 1972. Statistical time series, forecasting, applied statistics, regression analysis, multivariate techniques.

SELECTED PUBLICATIONS

Ammann, L., E. M. Dowling, and R. D. DeGroat. A TQR-iteration based adaptive SVD for real-time angle and frequency tracking. *IEEE Trans. Signal Processing* 42:914–26, 1994.

Ammann, L. Robust singular value decompositions: A new approach to projection pursuit. *J. Am. Stat. Assoc.* 88:504–14, 1993.

Baron, M., and A. L. Rukhin. Asymptotic behavior of confidence regions in the change-point problem. *J. Stat. Plann. Inference* 58:263–82, 1997.

Baron, M. On the first passage time for waiting processes. *Theory Probab. Appl.* 41:328–34, 1996.

Constantinescu, T., A. H. Sayed, and T. Kailath. Displacement structures and maximum entropy. *IEEE Trans. IT* 43:1074–80, 1997.

Constantinescu, T., *Schur Parameters, Factorization and Dilation Problems.* Birkhäuser, 1996.

Hooshyar, M. A., T. H. Lam, and M. Ravazy. Inverse problem of the wave equation and the Schwinger approximation. *J. Acous. Soc. Am.*, submitted.

Hooshyar, M. A. Variation principles and the one-dimensional profile reconstruction. *J. Opt. Soc. Am.* 15:1867–76, 1998.

Ober, R., and J. Sefton. Properties of optimally robust controllers. *Intern. J. Control* 59:1191–1210, 1994.

Ober, R., and J. Sefton. Hankel norm approximation and control systems. *Linear Algebra Applications* 205/206:1081–1120, 1994.

Ozsvath, I., and E. Schucking. The world viewed from outside. *J. Geometry Phys.* 24:303–333, 1998.

Ozsvath, I. The finite rotating universe revisited. *Class Quantum Gravity* 14:A291–7, 1997.

Ozsvath, I., and E. L. Schucking. Isometric embedding for homogeneous compact 3-manifold. *GRG* 28, 1996.

Ramakrishna, V. Local solvability of degenerate, overdetermined systems—a control-theoretic perspective. *J. Differential Equations,* in press.

Ramakrishna, V. Controlled invariance for singular distributions. *SIAM J. Control Optimization* 32:790–807, 1994.

Robinson, I. On the Bel-Robinson tensor. *Classical Quantum Gravity,* in press.

Robinson, I., and I. Trautman. The conformal geometry of complex quadrics and the fractional-linear form of Mobius transformations. *J. Math. Phys.* 34:5391, 1993.

Serfling, R. Robust and nonparametric estimation via a generalized L-statistics: theory, applications, and perspectives. *Proc. Int. Conference IISA 1998,* in press.

Serfling, R., and T. Christofides. U-statistics on a lattice of i.i.d. random variables. *Stat. Probab. Lett.* 40:293–303, 1998.

Serfling, R. *Approximation Theorems of Mathematical Statistics.* Wiley, 1980.

Turi, J., and T. Hagen. A semigroup approach to a class of semilinear parabolic differential equations. *J. Nonlinear Analysis, Theory, Methods, Appl.* 34:17–35, 1998.

Turi, J., and F. Hartung. On differentiality of solutions with respect to parameters in state-dependent delay equations. *J. Differential Equations* 135:192–237, 1997.

Van Ness, J., and C. L. Cheng. *Statistical Regression with Measurement Error.* Edward Arnold Publishers, London, 1999.

Van Ness, J., and Z. Chen. Characterization of nearest and farthest neighbor algorithms by clustering admissibility conditions. *Pattern Recognition,* 1998.

Van Ness, J. and J. Yang. Robust discriminant analysis: Training data breakdown point. *J. Stat. Plann. Inference* 1:67–84, 1998.

Wiorkowski, J. A lightly annotated bibliography of the publications of the American Statistical Association. *Am. Statistician* 44:106–13, 1990.

Wiorkowski, J. Fitting of growth curves over time when the data are obtained from a single realization. *J. Forecasting* 7:259–72, 1988.

UNIVERSITY OF UTAH

Department of Mathematics

Programs of Study

The Department of Mathematics offers programs leading to the degrees of Doctor of Philosophy, Master of Arts, and Master of Science in mathematics.

The master's degree requires 30 hours of course work beyond certain basic prerequisites. The candidate for the M.A. degree must satisfy the standard proficiency requirement in one foreign language; a further requirement is an expository thesis of good quality or an approved two-semester graduate course sequence.

The doctoral degree carries a minimum course requirement designed to prepare the student to pass a written preliminary examination in the basic fields of mathematics. An oral examination, with emphasis on the candidate's area of specialization, is also required. A dissertation describing independent and original work is required. The Department of Mathematics stresses excellence in research. A master's degree is not a requirement for the Ph.D.

Research Facilities

The Mathematics Branch Library collection in theoretical mathematics consists of 190 journal subscriptions, 15,000 bound journals, and 12,000 books. In addition, the Marriott Library collection includes numerous books and journals of interest to mathematics researchers and scholars. There are extensive interactive computing and computer graphics facilities available in the department.

Financial Aid

Approximately 65 percent of the mathematics graduate students are supported by fellowships. There are teaching fellowships that grant from $13,000 to $14,100 plus state-resident tuition and fees. In most cases, nonresident tuition is also waived. Application for University research fellowships of $10,000 can be made through the Research Committee Office, 120 Park, at the University.

The normal teaching load for a teaching assistant and teaching fellow is the equivalent of one 4-hour section each semester. Summer teaching is available.

Cost of Study

For 1999–2000, tuition is $1131.10 per semester for Utah residents and $3405.80 per semester for nonresidents (10 credit hours). (Tuition rates may change without notice.) All resident tuition fees are waived for teaching assistants and fellows (except for a small computer fee), and, in most cases, nonresident tuition is also waived.

Living and Housing Costs

A wide variety of housing is offered by the University on or near the campus. The cost of a single room is $2500 per academic year and board is about $1800 per semester for a single student. University Village, for married students, is operated by the University. One-, two-, and three-bedroom apartments range from $340 to $680 per month, including heat, hot water, electricity, range, and refrigerator. (These rates may change without notice.) There is a waiting period of about eight to twelve months for the University's married student housing. Privately owned housing near the campus is also available.

Student Group

The University's total enrollment is currently 25,215. The Department of Mathematics has 75 graduate students; 40 receive financial support.

Student Outcomes

Graduates typically go on to postdoctoral research appointments followed by academic careers in teaching and research, or careers in government and industry. In the past two years, 20 graduates took positions at various universities, including MIT, Colorado, Brown, Minnesota, Tufts, Mittag-Leffler, Leeds, and California, San Diego.

Location

The Salt Lake City metropolitan area has a population of about 1 million and is the cultural, economic, and educational center of the Intermountain West. The Utah Symphony and Ballet West are located in Salt Lake City. The Delta Center is the home of the Utah Jazz basketball team. Climate and geography combine in the Salt Lake environs to provide ideal conditions for outdoor sports. Some of the world's best skiing is available less than an hour's drive from the University campus.

The University and The Department

The University of Utah is a state-supported coeducational public institution. Founded in 1850, it is the oldest state university west of the Missouri River.

In the last five years, the Department of Mathematics has awarded 85 graduate degrees. In recent years, the Graduate School has been awarding about 205 doctoral degrees per year. The University faculty has 1,392 members.

Applying

Admission to graduate status requires that students hold a bachelor's degree or its equivalent and that they show promise for success in graduate work. Applicants are urged to take the mathematics Subject Test of the Graduate Record Examinations.

Students are normally admitted at the beginning of the autumn term. It is desirable that applications for teaching fellowships, as well as for other financial grants, be submitted as early as possible. All applications received before March 1 will automatically be considered for fellowships.

Correspondence and Information

Graduate Fellowship Committee
Attention: Graduate Secretary
Department of Mathematics
155 S 1400 E, Room 233
University of Utah
Salt Lake City, Utah 84112-0090
World Wide Web: http://www.math.utah.edu

University of Utah

THE FACULTY AND THEIR RESEARCH

Distinguished Professors
Paul Fife, Ph.D., NYU, 1959. Applied mathematics.
János Kollár, Ph.D., Brandeis, 1984. Algebraic geometry.

Professors
P. W. Alfeld, Ph.D., Dundee (Scotland), 1977. Numerical analysis.
M. Bestvina, Ph.D., Tennessee, 1984. Topology.
R. M. Brooks, Ph.D., LSU, 1963. Topological algebras.
J. A. Carlson, Ph.D., Princeton, 1971. Algebraic geometry.
A. V. Cherkaev, Ph.D., St. Petersburg Technical (Russia), 1979. Applied math.
C. H. Clemens, Ph.D., Berkeley, 1966. Algebraic geometry.
W. J. Coles, Ph.D., Duke, 1954. Ordinary differential equations.
S. N. Ethier, Ph.D., Wisconsin–Madison, 1975. Probability and statistics.
A. L. Fogelson, Ph.D., NYU, 1982. Computational fluids.
E. S. Folias, Ph.D., Caltech, 1963. Applied mathematics, elasticity.
S. M. Gersten, Ph.D., Cambridge, 1965. Algebra.
L. C. Glaser, Ph.D., Wisconsin–Madison, 1964. Geometric topology.
K. M. Golden, Ph.D., NYU, 1984. Applied math.
F. I. Gross, Ph.D., Caltech, 1964. Algebra.
G. B. Gustafson, Ph.D., Arizona State, 1968. Ordinary differential equations.
H. Hecht, Ph.D., Columbia, 1974. Lie groups.
L. Horvath, Ph.D., Szeged (Hungary), 1982. Probability, statistics.
M. Kapovich, Ph.D., Soviet Academy of Science, 1988. Geometry.
J. P. Keener, Ph.D., Caltech, 1972. Applied mathematics.
N. J. Korevaar, Ph.D., Stanford, 1981. Partial differential equations.
J. D. Mason, Ph.D., California, Riverside, 1968. Probability.
D. Milicic, Ph.D., Zagreb (Yugoslavia), 1973. Lie groups.
G. Milton, Ph.D., Cornell, 1985. Materials science.
H. G. Othmer, Ph.D., Minnesota, 1969. Applied mathematics.
P. C. Roberts, Ph.D., McGill, 1974. Commutative algebra, algebraic geometry.
H. Rossi, Ph.D., MIT, 1960. Complex analysis.
G. Savin, Ph.D., Harvard, 1988. Group representation.
K. Schmitt, Ph.D., Nebraska, 1967. Differential equations.
J. L. Taylor, Ph.D., LSU, 1964. Abstract analysis.
D. Toledo, Ph.D., Cornell, 1972. Algebraic and differential geometry.
A. E. Treibergs, Ph.D., Stanford, 1980. Differential geometry.
P. C. Trombi, Ph.D., Illinois at Urbana–Champaign, 1970. Lie groups.
D. H. Tucker, Ph.D., Texas, 1958. Differential equations, functional analysis.

Emeritus Professors
C. E. Burgess, Ph.D., Texas, 1951. Topology.
E. A. Davis, Ph.D., Berkeley, 1951. Mathematical economics, teacher training.
C. H. Wilcox, Ph.D., Harvard, 1955. Applied mathematics, scattering theory.
J. E. Wolfe, Ph.D., Harvard, 1948. Geometric integration theory.

Visiting Faculty: S. Mori, Ph.D., Kyoto (Japan), 1978: algebraic geometry.

Associate Professors
F. Adler, Ph.D., Cornell, 1991. Mathematical biology.
A. Bertram, Ph.D., UCLA, 1989. Algebraic geometry and physics.
D. Khoshnevisan, Ph.D., Berkeley, 1989. Probability.
B. Kleiner, Ph.D., Berkeley, 1990. Differential geometry.
M. Lewis, D.Phil., Oxford, 1990. Mathematical biology.
N. Smale, Ph.D., Berkeley, 1987. Differential geometry.
J. Zhu, Ph.D., NYU (Courant), 1989. Computational fluid dynamics.

Assistant Professors
A. Balk, Ph.D., Moscow Institute of Physics, 1988. Nonlinear phenomena.
R. Morelli, Ph.D., Harvard, 1989. Algebraic geometry.
W. Niziol, Ph.D., Chicago, 1991. Arithmetical algebraic geometry.

Adjunct Professors: M. J. Egger, Ph.D., Stanford, 1979: statistics. J. C. Reading, Ph.D., Stanford, 1970: statistics. **Adjunct Associate Professors:** N. Beebe, Ph.D., Florida, 1972: numerical analysis. D. H. Clark, Ed.D., Brigham Young, 1974: secondary foundations and instruction. C. Johnson, Ph.D., Utah, 1990: cardiovascular research. J. Johnson, Ph.D., Brandeis, 1989: automorphic forms. L. C. Lewis, Ph.D., Indiana, 1969: complex analysis. A. D. Roberts, Ph.D., McGill, 1972: analysis. **Adjunct Assistant Professors:** S. Foresti, Ph.D., Pavia (Italy), 1987: scientific computing. M. Pernice, Ph.D., Colorado, 1986: scientific computing.

Research Professor
R. Horn, Ph.D., Stanford, 1967. Matrix analysis.

Instructors
P. Belkale, Ph.D., Chicago, 1999: algebraic geometry. X. Chen, Ph.D., Case Western Reserve, 1997: probability/statistics. K. Glasner, Ph.D., Chicago, 1998: applied mathematics. I. Grigorescy, Ph.D., NYU (Courant), 1997: probability/statistics. V. Guirardel, Ph.D., Universite Paul Sabatier, 1998: geometric group theory. C. Hacon, Ph.D., UCLA, 1998: algebraic geometry. B. Li, Ph.D., Arizona State, 1998: ordinary differential equations. G. Muic, Ph.D., Zagreb (Croatia), 1997: representation theory. J. Raquepas, Ph.D., Montana State, 1997: mathematical biology. A. Singh, Ph.D., Michigan, 1998: commutative algebras. K. Solna, Ph.D., Stanford, 1997: partial differential equations. K. Whyte, Ph.D., Chicago, 1998: geometric group theory.

SELECTED PUBLICATIONS

Adler, F. R. *Modeling the Dynamics of Life: Calculus and Probability for Life Scientists.* Pacific Grove, Calif.: Brooks/Cole Publishing Co., 1998.

Adler, F. R. A model of self-thinning through local competition. *Proc. Natl. Acad. Sci. U.S.A.* 93:9980–4, 1996.

Alfeld, P. W., and L. L. Schumaker. Non-existence of Star-supported spline bases. In press.

Alfeld, P. W., M. Neamtu, and L. L. Schumaker. Bernstein-Bezier polynomials on spheres and sphere-like surfaces. *CAGD J.* 13:333–49, 1996.

Balk, A., and T. Yoshikawa. The growth of fingers and bubbles in the strongly nonlinear regime of the Richtmyer-Meshkov instability. *Phys. Lett. A* 251:184–90, 1999.

Balk, A. New conservation laws for the interaction of nonlinear waves. *SIAM Rev.* 39:68–94, 1997.

Bertram, A. Quantum Schubert calculus. *Adv. Math.* 128(2):289–305, 1997.

Bertram, A. Stable pairs and log flips. In *AMS Proceedings of Symposia in Pure Math* 62(1):185–201, 1997.

Bestvina, M. Local homological properties of boundaries of groups. *Mich. Math. J.* 43:123–39, 1996.

Bestvina, M., and M. Feighn. Stable actions of groups on real trees. *Inventiones Math.* 121:287–321, 1995.

Brooks, R. M. Analytic structure in the spectra of certain uF-algebras. *Math. Annalen* 240:27–33, 1979.

Brooks, R. M. On the spectrum of an inverse limit of holomorphic function algebras. *Adv. Math.* 19:238–44, 1976.

Carlson, J. A., D. Allcock, and D. Toledo. Complex hyperbolic structures for moduli of cubic surfaces. *C. R. Acad. Sci. Paris Ser. I* 326:49–54, 1998.

Carlson, J. A., and D. Toledo. On fundamental groups of class seven surfaces. *Bull. London Math. Soc.* 29(1):98–102, 1997.

Cherkaev, A. V., and T. Burns. Optimal distribution of multimaterial composites for tortioned beams. *Struct. Optimization* 13(1):1–4, 1997.

Cherkaev, A. V., and G. W. Milton. Which elasticity tensors are realizable? *J. Eng. Mater. Technol.* 117:483–93, 1995.

Clemens, C. H., and H. P. Kley. Counting curves which move with threefolds. *J. Alg. Geom.,* in press.

Clemens, C. H. The infinitesimal Abel-Jacobi mapping and moving the 0(2)+0(-4) curve. *Duke Math. J.* 59:233–40, 1989.

Coles, W. J., and M. K. Kinyon. Some oscillation results for second order matrix differential equations. *Rocky Mtn. J. Math.* 1:19–36, 1994.

Coles, W. J. Oscillation for self-adjoint second order matrix differential equations. *Diff. Integral Eq.* 1(4):195–204, 1991.

Ethier, S. N., A. D. Barbour, and R. C. Griffiths. A transition function expansion for a diffusion model with selection. *Ann. Appl. Prob.,* in press.

Ethier, S. N., and T. G. Kurtz. Coupling and ergodic theorems for Fleming-Viot processes. *Ann. Prob.* 26:533–61, 1998.

Fife, P. C. Pattern formation in gradient systems. In *Handbook for Dynamical Systems, Vol. 3, Applications,* eds. B. Fiedler and N. Kopell, in press.

Fife, P. C., and C. Charach. Solidification fronts and solute trapping in a binary alloy. *SIAM J. Appl. Math.* 58:1826–51, 1998.

Fogelson, A. L., and N. T. Wang. Platelet dense granule centralization and the persistence of ADP secretion. *Am. J. Physiol.,* in press.

Fogelson, A. L., and R. Dillon. Optimal smoothing in function transport particle methods for diffusion problems. *J. Comput. Phys.* 109:155–63, 1993.

Folias, E. S. Boundary layer effects of interfaminar stresses adjacent to a hole in a laminated composite plate. *Int. J. Solids Struct.* 29(2):171–86, 1992.

Folias, E. S., and J. Walker. Effect of stress waves on cracked laminated composite plate: Part 1. *Int. J. Solids Struct.* 29(2):145–70, 1992.

Gersten, S. M., and D. Allcock. A homological characterization of hyperbolic groups. *Inventiones Math.* 135(3):723–42, 1999.

Gersten, S. M. Cohomological lower bounds for isoperimetric functions on groups. *Topology* 37:1031–72, 1998.

Glaser, L. C., and T. B. Rushing (eds.). Geometric topology. In *Proceedings of the Geometric Topology Conference,* Park City, Utah, February 1974, vol. 438, Lectures in Mathematics, p. 459. New York: Springer-Verlag, 1975.

Glaser, L. C. On tame Cantor sets in spheres having the same projection in each direction. *Pacific J. Math.* 60:87–102, 1975.

Golden, K. M., et al. Inverse electromagnetic scattering models for sea ice. *IEEE Trans. Geosci. Remote Sensing,* in press.

Golden, K. M. Critical behavior of transport in lattice and continuum percolation models. *Phys. Rev. Lett.* 78:3935–8, 1997.

Gross, F. I. Odd order Hall subgroups of the classical linear groups. *Math Zeit.* 220:317–36, 1995.

Gross, F. I. Hall subgroups of order not divisible by 3. *Rocky Mtn. J. Math.* 23:569–91, 1993.

Gustafson, G. G., and H. Gingold. Uniqueness for nth order de la Vallée-Poussin boundary value problems. *Applicable Anal.* 20(3–4):201–20, 1995.

Gustafson, G. G., and J. Ridenhour. Solutions branching in linear differential equations. *JDE* 101(2):373–87, 1993.

Hecht, H. On Casselman's compatibility theorem for n-homology, in "Reductive Lie Groups." In *Proceedings of Cordoba Conference.* Birkhauser, 1997.

Hecht, H., and J. L. Taylor. A comparison theorem for n-homology. *Composition Mathematica* 86:189–207, 1993.

Horvath, L., and M. Csorgo. *Limit Theorems in Change-Point Analysis.* New York: John Wiley & Sons, 1997.

Horvath, L., and M. Csorgo. *Weighted Approximations in Probability and Statistics.* New York: John Wiley & Sons, 1993.

Kapovich, M., and B. Leeb. Quasi-isometries preserve the geometric decomposition of Haken manifolds. *Inventiones Math.* 128(2):393–416, 1997.

Kapovich, M., and J. Millson. On the deformation theory of representations of fundamental groups of compact hyperbolic 3-manifolds. *Topology* 35:(N4)1085–106, 1996.

Keener, J. P. The effect of gap junctional distribution on difibrillation. *Chaos* 8:175–87, 1998.

Keener, J. P., and K. Bogar. A numerical method for the solution of the bidomain equations in cardiac tissue. *Chaos* 8:234–41, 1998.

Khoshnevisan, D., and K. Burdzy. Brownian motion in a Brownian crack. *Ann. Appl. Prob.* (8)3:708–48, 1998.

Khoshnevisan, D., and Z. Shi. Chung's law for integrated Brownian motion. *Trans. Am. Math. Soc.* 350(10):4253–6, 1998.

Kleiner, B., and D. Burago. Separated nets in Euclidean space and Jacobians of biLipschitz maps. *GAFA* 8:273–82, 1998.

Kleiner, B., and B. Leeb. Rigidity of quasi-isometries for symmetric spaces and Euclidean buildings. *C. R. Acad. Sci. Paris Ser. I Math* 324(6):639–43, 1997.

Kollár, J. *Rational Curves on Algebraic Varieties.* New York: Springer-Verlag, 1996.

Kollár, J. *Shafarevich Maps and Automorphic Forms.* Princeton, N.J.: Princeton University Press, 1995.

Korevaar, N. J., and R. M. Schoen. Harmonic maps to non-locally compact spaces. *Comm. Anal. Geom.* 5(2):333–87, 1997.

Korevaar, N. J., and R. Kusner. The global structure of constant mean curvature surfaces. *Inventiones Math.* 114:311–32, 1993.

Lewis, M. A. Spread rate for a nonlinear stochastic invasion. *J. Math. Biol.,* in press.

University of Utah

Selected Publications (continued)

Lewis, M. A., and P. R. Moorcroft. Crabtree: Analysis of coyote (*Canis latrans*) home ranges using a mechanistic home range model. *Ecology,* in press.

Mason, J. D., and T. Burns. A structural equations approach to combining data sets. Accepted as a paper for *International Congress of Sociologists,* 1994.

Mason, J. D., and Z. J. Jurek. *Operator-Limit Distribution in Probability Theory.* New York: John Wiley & Sons, 1993.

McLaughlin, R. M., and J. C. Bronski. Scalar intermittency and the ground state of periodic Schrödinger equations. *Phys. Fluids* 9:181–90, 1997.

McLaughlin, R. M., and A. J. Majda. An explicit example with non-Gaussian probability distribution for nontrivial scalar mean and fluctuation. *Phys. Fluids* 8(2):536–47, 1996.

Milicic, D., and P. Pandzic. Equivariant derived categories, Zuckerman functors and localization, in "Geometry and Representation Theory of Real and *p*-adic Lie Groups," in *Progress in Mathematics,* vol. 158, pp. 209–42, eds. J. Tirao, D. Vogan, and J. A. Wolfe. Boston: Birkhäuser, 1997.

Milicic, D., and P. Pandzic. On degeneration of the spectral sequence for the composition of Zuckerman functors. *Glasnik Maternativcki* 32(52):179–99, 1997.

Milton, G. W., L. C. Botten, and R. C. McPhedran. Perfectly conducting lamellar gratings: Babinet's principle and circuit models. *J. Mod. Opt.* 42:2453–73, 1995.

Milton, G. W., and A. B. Movchan. A correspondence between plane elasticity and the two-dimensional real and complex dielectric equations in anisotropic media. *Proc. Roy. Soc. London* 450:293–317, 1995.

Morelli, R. *The Birational Geometry of Toric Varieties,* in press.

Morelli, R. Pick's theorem and the Todd class of a toric variety. *Adv. Math.* 100(2):183–231, 1993.

Niziol, W. Crystalline conjecture via K-theory. *Ann. Sci. Ecole Norm. Supp.* 31:659–81, 1998.

Niziol, W. On the image of *p*-adic regulators. *Inventiones Math.* 127:375–400, 1997.

Othmer, H. G., and A. Stevens. Aggregation, blowup and collapse: The ABC's of generalized taxis. *SIAM J. Appl. Math.* 57:1044–81, 1997.

Othmer, H. G., and J. Dallon. A discrete cell model with adaptive signalling. In *Dynamics of Cell and Tissue Motion,* pp. 195–7, eds. W. Alt, A. Deutsch, and G. Dunn. Boston: Birkhauser-Verlag, 1997.

Roberts, P. C. Recent developments on Serre's multiplicity conjectures: Gabber's proof of the nonnegativity conjecture. *l'Enseignement Mathématique* 44:305–24, 1998.

Roberts, P. C. Multiplicities and Chern classes in local algebra. In *Cambridge Tracts in Mathematics,* p. 133. Cambridge University Press, 1998.

Rossi, H., and C. Patton. Unitary structures on cohomology. *TAMS* 290, 1985.

Rossi, H. LeBrun's nonrealizability theorem in higher dimensions. *Duke Math. J.* 52:457–525, 1985.

Savin, G., and B. Gross. The dual pair PGL_3 x G_2. *Can. Math. Bull.* 40:376–84, 1997.

Savin, G., J. S. Huang, and P. Pandzic. New dual pair correspondences. *Duke Math. J.* 82:447–71, 1996.

Schmitt, K., and V. K. Le. On variational inequalities associated with Navier-Stokes problems: Some bifurcation problems. *Elect. J. Diff. Eq.* 137–48, 1998.

Schmitt, K. On boundary value problems for quasilinear elliptic equations. *Fields Inst. Commun.* 21:419–27, 1998.

Smale, N. Singular homology area minimizing surfaces of codimension one in Riemannian manifolds. *Inventiones Math.* 135:145–83, 1999.

Smale, N. A construction of homologically area minimizing hypersurfaces with higher dimensional singular sets. *I.H.E.S.* preprint, 1997. To appear in *Trans. AMS.*

Taylor, J. L., and H. Hecht. Geometry and representation theory of real and p-adic Lie groups. In *Progress in Mathematics,* vol. 158, eds. J. Tirao, D. Vogan, and J. A. Wolfe. Boston: Birkhauser, 1997.

Taylor, J. L., and H. Hecht. A comparison theorem for n-homology. *Compositio Math* 86:189–207, 1993.

Toledo, D., and J. Carlson. On fundamental groups of class VII surfaces. *Bull. London Math. Soc.,* in press.

Toledo, D., and J. Carlson. Quadratic presentations and nilpotent Kahler groups. *J. Geom. Anal.* 5:359–77, 1995.

Treibergs, A. E., and H. Chan. Nonpositively curved surface in R3. Preprint, 1999.

Treibergs, A. E., Z.-C. Han, L.-F. Tam, and T. Wan. Harmonic maps from the complex plane into surfaces with nonpositive curvature. *Comm. Anal. Geom.* 3:85–114, 1995.

Trombi, P. C. Uniform asymptotics for real reductive Lie groups. *Pacific J. Math.* 146:131–99, 1990.

Trombi, P. C. Invariant harmonic analysis on split rank one groups with applications. *Pacific J. Math.* 100:80–102, 1982.

Tucker, D. H., and J. F. Gold. A new vector product. In *Proceedings of the 10th National Conference on Undergraduate Research.* 1996.

Tucker, D. H., and D. T. M. Ha. Concerning differential type operators: A preliminary report. In *Proceedings, International Conference on Analysis and Mechanics of Continuous Media,* Ho Chi Minh City, December 27–29, 1995.

Wilcox, C. H., and G. B. Gustafson. *Advanced Engineering Mathematics.* New York: Springer-Verlag, 1998.

Wilcox, C. H. Examples of cylindrical shock wave conversion by focusing. *Rocky Mtn. J. Math.* 22:761–75, 1992.

Zhu, J., X. Chen, and T. Hou. An efficient boundary integral method for the Mullins-Sekerka problem. *J. Computational Phys.* 127:246–67, 1996.

Zhu, J., C. Durney, W. Sui, and D. Christensen. A general formulation for connecting sources and passive lumped-circuit elements across multiple 3D FDTD cell. *IEEE Microwave Guided Wave Lett.* 6(2):85–7, 1996.

VIRGINIA POLYTECHNIC INSTITUTE AND STATE UNIVERSITY

Department of Mathematics

Programs of Study	The department offers programs of study in pure and applied mathematics and in mathematical physics leading to the M.S. and Ph.D. degrees. The department has a history of active interdisciplinary interactions in both pure and applied mathematics. These programs prepare students for careers in teaching, research, industry, and government service.
	The M.S. degree requires 30 semester hours of graduate credit and is usually completed in two years. Candidates may choose the thesis, nonthesis, or interdisciplinary options.
	The Ph.D. degree program emphasizes a strong foundation in fundamental areas of mathematics as well as specialized study in selected research areas. Requirements include a thesis, successful performance on preliminary exams, and a final oral exam and thesis defense. Students generally need an additional three years beyond the M.S. to earn the Ph.D.
Research Facilities	The University Library has extensive holdings in all areas of mathematics and related disciplines. The department's computer network consists of UNIX systems and personal computers, including a multiprocessor Sun server. Graduate students have free and easy access to all computing facilities.
	Three special research centers are affiliated with the department: the Interdisciplinary Center for Applied Mathematics (ICAM), the Center for Transport Theory and Mathematical Physics (CTTMP), and the Center for Mathematical Computation (CMC). Each provides special facilities and support for graduate students.
Financial Aid	Graduate teaching and research assistantships are offered to most students. Beginning stipends range from $1085 to $1335 (monthly), with amounts up to $1500 for advanced students. Assistantships include full tuition waivers. Some summer support is usually available.
Cost of Study	The 1998–99 tuition and fees for full-time graduate students were $2376 for residents and $3492 for nonresidents per semester. Students on assistantships pay only $385 in fees.
Living and Housing Costs	On-campus housing for graduate students is very limited. Most students live off campus, where housing is plentiful, high-quality, and inexpensive. A town bus system provides transportation directly to campus. (The cost of this service is included in the student fees.)
Student Group	The mathematics department has approximately 80 graduate students, of whom one third are women. About 90 percent have assistantships, and about 40 percent are in the Ph.D. program.
Student Outcomes	Graduates at both the M.S. and Ph.D. levels have been very successful in obtaining teaching and research positions in colleges and universities and positions in business, industry, and the government. Past graduates hold a range of professional positions, including college/university faculty member, research laboratory staff member, consultant to major corporations (Boeing, Martin Marietta), programmer/computer scientist, operations research analyst, software instructor (Cray Research), actuary, research engineer (NASA), statistician (Census Bureau), and research manager (Bell Atlantic).
Location	Virginia Tech is located in Blacksburg, a town of about 30,000, situated on a plateau between the Blue Ridge and Allegheny mountains in southwest Virginia. The area is noted for its beauty and high quality of life. Opportunities for outdoor activities such as hiking, canoeing, bicycling, and skiing abound.
The University and The Department	Virginia Tech has an enrollment of more than 24,000, including almost 4,000 graduate students. The University has been known for many years as a center of science and engineering. The mathematics department, in particular, is increasingly gaining recognition for the high quality of its research and graduate programs.
Applying	Application forms for admission and financial aid are supplied upon request by the mathematics department and the Graduate School Admissions Office. Applicants are required to take the GRE General Test, and those whose native language is not English must submit TOEFL scores. While applications are accepted at any time during the year, decisions on admission and financial aid are customarily made in January and February for the following fall term. Consequently, completed applications should reach the department by February 1 to receive the fullest consideration.
Correspondence and Information	Chairman, Graduate Admissions Committee Department of Mathematics Virginia Polytechnic Institute and State University Blacksburg, Virginia 24061-0123 Telephone: 540-231-6536 E-mail: info@math.vt.edu World Wide Web: http://www.math.vt.edu

Virginia Polytechnic Institute and State University

THE FACULTY AND THEIR RESEARCH

Hatcher Professor of Mathematics
J. A. Burns, Ph.D., Oklahoma. Applied mathematics, control theory.

Professors
J. T. Arnold, Ph.D., Florida State. Commutative rings.
J. A. Ball, Ph.D., Virginia. Operator theory, systems theory.
C. A. Beattie, Ph.D., Johns Hopkins. Functional analysis and numerical analysis.
M. B. Boisen, Ph.D., Nebraska. Mathematical crystallography, commutative rings.
E. A. Brown, Ph.D., LSU. Number theory, history of mathematics.
M. V. Day, Ph.D., Colorado. Stochastic processes, probability.
W. J. Floyd, Ph.D., Princeton. Topology and geometric group theory.
E. L. Green, Ph.D., Brandeis. Representation theory of rings and algebras.
W. Greenberg, Ph.D., Harvard. Mathematical physics, statistical mechanics.
G. A. Hagedorn, Ph.D., Princeton. Mathematical physics.
K. D. Hannsgen, Ph.D., Wisconsin. Volterra equations, control theory.
T. L. Herdman, Ph.D., Oklahoma. Applied mathematics, functional differential equations.
J. R. Holub, Ph.D., LSU. Functional analysis.
L. W. Johnson, Ph.D., Michigan State. Numerical analysis.
J. U. Kim, Ph.D., Brown. Nonlinear partial differential equations.
M. Klaus, Ph.D., Zurich. Mathematical physics.
W. E. Kohler, Ph.D., RPI. Applied mathematics.
P. A. Linnell, Ph.D., Cambridge. Group rings.
R. A. McCoy, Ph.D., Iowa State. General topology.
R. F. Olin, Ph.D., Indiana. Operator theory, functional analysis.
C. J. Parry, Ph.D., Michigan State. Number theory.
C. W. Patty, Ph.D., Georgia. Topology.
C. L. Prather, Ph.D., Northwestern. Complex analysis.
F. S. Quinn, Ph.D., Princeton. Topology of manifolds.
M. Renardy, Dr.rer.nat., Stuttgart. Nonlinear partial differential equations, fluid mechanics.
Y. Renardy, Ph.D., Western Australia. Fluid mechanics.
R. D. Riess, Ph.D., Iowa State. Numerical analysis.
R. C. Rogers, Ph.D., Maryland. Partial differential equations, continuum mechanics.
J. F. Rossi, Ph.D., Hawaii. Complex analysis.
D. L. Russell, Ph.D., Minnesota. Ordinary differential equations, partial differential equations, systems theory.
J. K. Shaw, Ph.D., Kentucky. Complex analysis, differential equations.
R. L. Snider, Ph.D., Miami (Florida). Ring theory.
S. Sun, Ph.D., Wisconsin. Partial differential equations.
J. E. Thomson, Ph.D., North Carolina. Operator theory.
L. T. Watson, Ph.D., Michigan. Numerical analysis, nonlinear programming, mathematical software, fluid mechanics, image processing, parallel computation.
R. L. Wheeler, Ph.D., Wisconsin. Integrodifferential equations, control theory.

Associate Professors
R. S. Crittenden, Ph.D., North Carolina. Ring theory.
D. Gao, Ph.D., Tsing Hua (Beijing). Partial differential equations.
P. E. Haskell, Ph.D., Brown. Index theory.
B.B. King, Ph.D., Clemson. Computational control.
T. Lin, Ph.D., Wyoming. Numerical analysis, large-scale numerical simulation.
M. A. Murray, Ph.D., Yale. Harmonic analysis.
B. E. Reed, Ph.D., Georgia. Nonassociative algebras.
C. J. Ribbens, Ph.D., Purdue. Numerical analysis, parallel and vector computing, mathematical software.
J. E. Shockley, Ph.D., North Carolina. Number theory.

Assistant Professors
J. Borggaard, Ph.D., Virginia Tech. Optimal design.
G. Letzter, Ph.D., Chicago. Representation theory of quantum groups.
G. Lloyd, Ph.D., Michigan. Mathematics education.
C. McMillan, Ph.D., Virginia. Control theory.
J. K. Washenberger, Ph.D., Iowa State. Analysis, functional analysis.

VIRGINIA POLYTECHNIC INSTITUTE AND STATE UNIVERSITY

Department of Statistics

Programs of Study

The Department of Statistics offers thesis and nonthesis Master of Science degrees and a Doctor of Philosophy degree. Both M.S. programs require 30 semester hours of credit. The nonthesis program requires 26 semester hours of course work within the department. In the thesis program there is no fixed departmental credit hour requirement, and the thesis may count for 6 to 10 semester hours of credit. The master's degree can be obtained in sixteen months of graduate study. First-year core courses for both programs include Probability and Distribution Theory, Statistical Inference, Linear Models Theory, Applied Statistics, and Experimental Design and Analysis. Additional courses may be taken in statistics and mathematics or in approved areas of application. Each student participates in statistical consulting activities for at least one semester. For the Ph.D. program, students must complete a minimum of 90 credit hours of graduate study, including at least 54 semester hours of course work. Core courses (beyond the first-year core courses) are Measure and Probability and Advanced Statistical Inference. Students are expected to complete at least two semesters of courses in two areas of concentration, chosen in conjunction with the Advisory Committee. A field of application may be selected in place of one area of concentration. Each student participates for three semesters in specialized professional training in statistical consulting and/or teaching. Students with no previous graduate training in statistics can expect to complete the Ph.D. program in four to five years.

Research Facilities

The department has excellent facilities for classwork, consulting, and research. There are two graduate computing laboratories. One contains a variety of Macintosh and IBM PC-clone computers and numerous software packages, including SAS, MINITAB, NCSS, SYSTAT, JMP, SPSS, Design Expert, StatXact, Splus, and the IMSL Math and Statistics libraries. The lab also has a variety of laser and color inkjet printers and scanners. Many language compilers are also available, including Fortran, Basic, and Pascal. A second laboratory contains twenty Sun Workstations, along with laser printers. The department also maintains an undergraduate computing laboratory. The University library has an extensive collection of statistical publications, including complete files of most statistical journals. The department maintains a small library containing reference books, recent issues of major journals, and a large reprint file. The department operates the University's Statistical Consulting Center, through which faculty members and students work with members of other departments in various research activities.

Financial Aid

Graduate assistantships, with stipends for the 1998–99 academic year of $1050 to $1255 per month for nine months, are available to highly qualified applicants. Responsibilities include 20 hours per week of grading, consulting, teaching, and/or special assignments, and graduate assistants must carry between 9 and 12 credits per semester. In-state tuition is paid for students on assistantships, and some financial aid is available in the summer. Limited scholarships for minority students are available.

Cost of Study

The 1998–99 instructional fee (tuition) for full-time graduate students was $2061 per semester for Virginia residents and for nonresidents who hold graduate assistantships paying more than $4000 per year. Nonresidents who do not hold such assistantships paid an additional $1305 per semester. All students paid a comprehensive fee of $384.50 per semester that included health services, student activities, athletics, and bus service.

Living and Housing Costs

Privately owned housing (both rooms and apartments) is available both in the town of Blacksburg and in the surrounding area at varying rents. Limited graduate student housing is also available on the campus of Virginia Tech.

Student Group

The current graduate enrollment in the department is approximately 50. Students have previously studied at many different universities in various countries. Graduates of the department have never experienced difficulty in obtaining excellent academic, industrial, and government positions. Salaries for professional statisticians are appreciably higher than those offered after similar training in most other fields of science.

Location

The University is located in Blacksburg, a town of about 40,000 people in scenic southwestern Virginia. The 2,300-acre campus lies on a plain between the Blue Ridge and Allegheny mountains. The area is noted for its beauty and recreational opportunities. Boating, swimming, camping, and fishing facilities are available at nearby Claytor Lake State Park. Also nearby are Mountain Lake, the Blue Ridge Parkway, the Roanoke and Shenandoah valleys, Jefferson National Forest, and the Appalachian Trail. Roanoke, 38 miles to the east, is easily reached via four-lane highways. Commercial air service is provided through Roanoke.

The University and The Department

Founded in 1872, Virginia Tech, with approximately 26,000 students, now has the largest resident enrollment in the state. Master's degree programs are offered in sixty fields and Ph.D. programs in forty.

The Department of Statistics is one of the oldest in the nation. The Statistical Laboratory was organized in 1948, and the department was established the following year. The department's reputation for significant research in modern statistical theory and methodology is supported by an impressive list of publications and research grants. With a faculty–graduate student ratio of approximately 1:3, there are ample opportunities for individual attention. An undergraduate curriculum is also offered.

Applying

Admission to the Graduate School normally requires a minimum cumulative grade point average of 3.0 (on a 4.0 scale) for the equivalent of the last two years of undergraduate study. Exceptions may be made upon recommendation of the department; substantial evidence of ability to succeed in graduate work must be presented. Prospective applicants are urged to take the GRE General Test. The department encourages applications from students in fields other than mathematics and statistics, although mathematical training at least through advanced calculus and matrix algebra is desirable. Matrix algebra may be taken after enrollment, but advanced calculus should be completed before the start of the first academic year. Applications for admission should be forwarded to the Graduate School office. A complete application consists of an application form, two official and up-to-date transcripts of the student's undergraduate and graduate records, at least three letters of recommendation, and a $25 application fee. Students desiring to apply for financial aid should so indicate to the dean of the Graduate School when applying for admission. Applications for financial aid should be received before January 31; awards are announced in late February and early March. Later applications will be considered if vacancies occur or new positions are made available.

Correspondence and Information

For application forms and a graduate catalog:

Graduate School
Virginia Polytechnic Institute
   and State University
Blacksburg, Virginia 24061-0325
Telephone: 540-231-6691

For more information about the department:

Dr. Jesse Arnold, Graduate Program Administrator
Department of Statistics
Virginia Polytechnic Institute
   and State University
Blacksburg, Virginia 24061-0439
Telephone: 540-231-5366
E-mail: jca@vt.edu
World Wide Web: http://www.cas.vt.edu/statistics/

Virginia Polytechnic Institute and State University

THE FACULTY AND THEIR RESEARCH

Christine Anderson-Cook, Assistant Professor; Ph.D., Waterloo, 1994. Teaching: linear models, response surface analysis, engineering statistics. Research areas: industrial statistics, directional data, experimental design.

Jesse C. Arnold, Professor; Ph.D., Florida State, 1967. Teaching: nonparametric statistics, inference, sampling. Research areas: estimation, sampling, nutrition. Other: Graduate Administrator.

Jeffrey B. Birch, Associate Professor; Ph.D., Washington (Seattle), 1977. Teaching: statistical methods, regression, bioassay, exploratory and robust analysis. Research areas: robust procedures, Monte Carlo methods, regression analysis. Other activities: consulting in biostatistics; associate editor, *Biometrics*.

Hegang Chen, Assistant Professor; Ph.D., Illinois at Chicago, 1993. Teaching: linear models, experimental design. Research areas: experimental design. Other: consultant for engineering, biological, and health sciences.

Clint W. Coakley, Assistant Professor; Ph.D., Penn State, 1991. Teaching: nonparametric methods. Research areas: nonparametric methods, robust regression. Other: Undergraduate Coordinator.

Robert Foutz, Professor; Ph.D., Ohio State, 1974. Teaching: time series, statistical inference. Research areas: time series, large sample theory, statistical inference. Other: consulting.

Klaus H. Hinkelmann, Professor; Ph.D., Iowa State, 1963. Teaching: experimental design, linear models, analysis of variance, genetic statistics, statistical methods. Research areas: experimental design, genetic statistics. Other: consulting; interdepartmental genetics program; editor, *Biometrics*.

Golde I. Holtzman, Associate Professor; Ph.D., North Carolina State, 1980. Teaching: biostatistics. Research areas: biomathematics, mathematical ecology, population dynamics.

Donald R. Jensen, Professor; Ph.D., Iowa State, 1962. Teaching: probability and distribution theory, mathematical statistics, multivariate analysis. Research areas: multivariate analysis, large sample theory, simultaneous inference, process control.

John P. Lawrence, Assistant Professor; Ph.D., Ohio State, 1996. Teaching: computational statistics, simulation, engineering statistics. Research areas: multidimensional tests, stochastic modeling.

Marvin Lentner, Professor and Department Head; Ph.D., Kansas State, 1967. Teaching: statistical methods, experimental design. Research areas: experimental design. Other: consultant, College of Agriculture and Life Sciences.

Anya M. McGuirk, Assistant Professor of Agricultural Economics and Statistics; Ph.D., Cornell, 1988. Teaching: econometrics.

Marion R. Reynolds Jr., Professor of Statistics and Forestry; Ph.D., Stanford, 1972. Teaching: sequential analysis, quality control, statistical inference, probability and distribution theory, engineering statistics. Research areas: sequential analysis, statistical process control, mathematical modeling in natural resource problems. Other: consultant, Department of Forestry and Wildlife.

Timothy J. Robinson, Visiting Assistant Professor; Ph.D., Virginia Tech, 1997. Teaching: statistical methods, biological statistics. Research areas: regression, linear models, smoothing. Other: consulting.

Robert S. Schulman, Associate Professor; Ph.D., North Carolina at Chapel Hill, 1974. Teaching: statistics for social sciences, applied statistics. Research areas: test theory, psychometric methods. Other: consultant for research in social sciences.

Eric P. Smith, Professor and Director, Statistical Consulting Center; Ph.D., Washington (Seattle), 1982. Teaching: statistical methods, biometry, multivariate methods. Research areas: multivariate analysis, multivariate graphics, biological sampling, modeling. Other: consultant for Anaerobe Laboratory and Center for Environmental Studies.

George R. Terrell, Associate Professor; Ph.D., Rice, 1978. Teaching: mathematical statistics, probability, statistical computing. Research areas: nonparametric density estimation, multivariate nonparametric methods, projection pursuit methods. Other: consulting.

Keying Ye, Associate Professor; Ph.D., Purdue, 1990. Teaching: mathematical statistics, Bayesian statistics. Research areas: Bayesian inference, statistical decision theory, sequential analysis.

Selected Publications

Anderson-Cook, C. M. An extension to modeling cylindrical variables. *Stat. Prob. Lett.* 35:215–23, 1997.

Chen, H., C. Y. Suen, and C. F. J. Wu. Some identities on q^{n-m} designs with application to minimum aberration designs. *Ann. Stat.* 25:1176–88, 1997.

Hinkelmann, K. H., and J. Jo. Linear trend-free Box-Behnken designs. *J. Stat. Plann. Inf.* 72:347–54, 1998.

Jensen, D. R. Conditioning and concentration of principal components. *Aust. J. Stat.* 39:93–104, 1997.

Lee, H., and **R. V. Foutz.** A new spectral model for binary or categorical-valued time series data. *J. Stat. Comput. Sim.* 58:217–35, 1997.

Reynolds, M. R. Jr., and Z. G. Stoumbos. The SPRT chart for monitoring a proportion. *IIE Trans.* 30:545–61, 1998.

Smith, E. P. Randomization methods and the analysis of multivariate ecological data. *Environmetrics* 9:37–51.

Recent Dissertations

"Outlier Resistant Model Robust Regression," Christopher A. Assaid (1997).

"Optimal Experimental Design for Poisson Impaired Reproduction Studies," Jennifer Huffman (1998).

"Construction and Analysis of Linear Trend-free Factorial Designs Under a General Cost Structure," Ki Ho Kim (1997).

"A New Method for Comparing Experiments and Measuring Information," Patricia Kitchin (1997).

"Fisher Information Test of Normality," Yew Haur Lee (1998).

"Measurement Error in Designed Experiments for Second Order Models," Angela R. McMahan (1997).

"Dual Model Robust Regression," Timothy J. Robinson (1997).

"Analysis of Zero Heavy Data Using a Mixture Model Approach," Shin Cheng Wang (1998).

WASHINGTON STATE UNIVERSITY

College of Sciences
Department of Pure and Applied Mathematics

Programs of Study	The Department of Pure and Applied Mathematics offers graduate programs leading to the M.S., Ph.D., and Ph.D with teaching emphasis, as well as an M.S. in applied mathematics tailored to industrial employment. Courses of study are available in all of the principal branches of mathematics with special emphases in the applied areas of operations research, computational mathematics, applied statistics, and mathematical modeling as well as in the more traditional fields of number theory, finite geometry, general topology, algebra, and analysis. The Ph.D. program combines the more traditional orientations usually associated with university teaching and research with options specifically directed toward careers in industry and government. The Ph.D. with teaching emphasis program is designed to prepare exceptionally well qualified teachers of undergraduate mathematics. The degree program is distinguished from that of the traditional Ph.D. by a greater emphasis on breadth of course work and a critical, historical, or expository thesis.
Research Facilities	All mathematics faculty members and graduate students are housed in the recently remodeled Neill Hall. These modern and spacious facilities include offices, seminar rooms, classrooms, consulting rooms, a student computer laboratory, a remote viewing astronomy room, and computing facilities. An outstanding collection of mathematics books and journals are housed in the nearby Owen Science and Engineering Library. The department has several RISC-based computers used for instruction and research. The instruction and research labs are equipped with high-resolution graphics terminals and laser printers in addition to Apple and IBM-compatible microcomputers. All faculty and graduate student offices have access to the department's computer resources as well as the IBM 3090 mainframe and minicomputers located in the University's Computing Service Center.
Financial Aid	More than 90 percent of the mathematics graduate students are supported by teaching assistantships; stipends ranged from $9877 to $10,485 for the 1998–99 academic year. Normal duties are 20 hours per week teaching classes or assisting a faculty member. Summer teaching assignments for an additional stipend are usually available as are a few annual research assistantships for advanced students. Federal and state-supported work-study and loan programs are also available. Three special scholarships are granted each year: the Distinguished TA, the Abelson, and the Hacker, which carry stipends of $5000, $3000, and $2000, respectively.
Cost of Study	Tuition for full-time study (more than 6 credit hours) is $2566 per semester for Washington residents and $6433 for nonresidents. Part-time and summer students pay on a per-credit-hour basis. There are tuition waivers for teaching and research assistants.
Living and Housing Costs	The University maintains a residence center strictly for graduate students as well as a wide variety of single-student and family apartments. University-owned apartments rent from $270 to $362 per month, including utilities; room and board at the graduate center are about $4320 to $5020 per academic year. Private apartments are readily available at slightly higher rates.
Student Group	Washington State University has an enrollment of approximately 16,000, including more than 2,000 graduate students; about 40 of the latter are in mathematics. The mathematics graduate students come from many areas of the United States and several other countries, and about a dozen complete an advanced degree each year.
Student Outcomes	Recent recipients of advanced degrees have taken positions in academic institutions, in the private sector, and in governmental agencies. The academic appointments include teaching and research at both comprehensive universities and four-year liberal arts colleges. The nonacademic positions include systems analyst, actuary, program manager, senior scientist, research mathematician, reliability analyst, and computer consultant.
Location	Pullman, a city of about 25,000, is located in the heart of the Palouse region in southeastern Washington. It is a rich agricultural area that enjoys clean air and a generally dry, "continental" climate. The area offers easy access to outdoor recreational opportunities such as fishing, hiking, camping, sailing, skiing, and white-water rafting in three states—Washington, Idaho, and Oregon. The on-campus activities both at WSU and at the University of Idaho (8 miles away) contribute greatly to the cultural, athletic, and scientific life of the area.
The University and the Department	The University was founded in 1890 and was the first land-grant institution to establish a chapter of Phi Beta Kappa. Today, the core of the Pullman campus covers nearly 600 acres, and some 100 major buildings house the faculty members and students associated with the more than fifty academic disciplines. Mathematics is the largest department in the Division of Sciences, with a faculty of 40. Master's degrees were first awarded in 1912, and more than 100 mathematics Ph.D.'s have been hooded since 1960.
Applying	Requests for information or applications for admission and financial support should be directed to the department. Completed applications and other necessary credentials should be submitted as early as possible, preferably by February 1 for fall admission. Applicants are required to take the Graduate Record Examinations General Test and are advised to take the Subject Test in mathematics. Also required are copies of transcripts of all previous college work and three letters of recommendation. TOEFL scores must be submitted to the Office of Admissions by all students whose native language is not English.
Correspondence and Information	Graduate Committee Department of Pure and Applied Mathematics Washington State University Pullman, Washington 99164-3113 Telephone: 509-335-6868

Washington State University

THE FACULTY AND THEIR RESEARCH

Algebra and Number Theory
J. H. Jordan, Ph.D., Colorado, 1962. Number theory, elementary and computer education, combinatorial geometry.
D. Ng, Ph.D., Oregon State, 1973. Algebra.
W. A. Webb, Ph.D., Penn State, 1968. Number theory, fair division problems, combinatorics, cryptography.

Analysis
S. C. Cooper, Ph.D., Colorado State, 1988. Approximation theory.
D. W. DeTemple, Ph.D., Stanford, 1970. Combinatorics, graph theory, analysis, elementary geometry, mathematics education.
R. A. Johnson, Ph.D., Iowa, 1964. Measure theory and integration, real functions.
J. E. Kucera, Ph.D., Czechoslovak Academy of Sciences, 1966. Functional analysis, distributions.

Applied Analysis
J. A. Cochran, Ph.D., Stanford, 1964. Differential and integral equations, electromagnetics, special functions, operator theory, asymptotics.
A. Y. Khapalov, Ph.D., Russian Academy of Sciences, 1982. Linear and semilinear partial differential equation.
H. Yin, Ph.D., Washington State, 1968. Applied partial differential equations.

Astronomy
J. A. Brown, Ph.D., Texas at Austin, 1986. Astronomy, high-resolution stellar spectroscopy.
J. H. Lutz, Ph.D., Illinois, 1971. Astronomy, planetary nebulae.

Modeling
R. H. Dillon, Ph.D., Utah, 1993. Numerical analysis, modeling biological processes.
R. S. Gomulkiewicz, Ph.D., California, Davis, 1989. Theoretical population biology.
T. P. LoFaro, Ph.D. Boston University, 1993. Dynamical systems, biomathematics.
V. S. Manoranjan, Ph.D., Dundee (Scotland), 1982. Mathematical modeling, biomathematics, numerical analysis, nonlinear waves.
E. F. Pate, Ph.D., RPI, 1976. Mathematical modeling, biomathematics.
M. F. Schumaker, Ph.D., Texas at Austin, 1987. Mathematical modeling, biomathematics.
D. J. Wollkind, Ph.D., RPI, 1968. Continuum mechanics, asymptotic methods, stability techniques and mathematical modeling.

Numerical Analysis and Operations Research
K. A. Ariyawansa, Ph.D., Toronto, 1983. Mathematical programming and optimization, high-performance computing, operations research, applied statistical inference.
A. Genz, Ph.D., Kent (England), 1976. Numerical analysis, numerical integration, scientific computing.
R. B. Mifflin, Ph.D., Berkeley, 1971. Operations research, nonsmooth optimization.
C. B. Millham, Ph.D., Iowa State, 1962. Mathematical and scientific visualization and imaging.
J. L. Nazareth, Ph.D., Berkeley, 1973. Operations research, optimization, numerical analysis.
D. S. Watkins, Ph.D., Calgary, 1974. Numerical analysis, scientific computing.

Probability and Applied Statistics
M. A. Jacroux, Ph.D., Oregon State, 1976. Experimental design, optimal experimental design, estimation in linear and nonlinear models.
V. K. Jandhyala, Ph.D., Western Ontario, 1986. Statistical inference, stochastic processes.
H. Li, Ph.D., Arizona, 1994. Stochastic orderings, statistical theory of reliability, stochastic convexity, probabilistic modeling.

Topology and Geometry
M. Hudelson, Ph.D., Washington (Seattle), 1995. Combinatorics, discrete geometry.
M. J. Kallaher, Ph.D., Syracuse, 1967. Algebra, projective geometry, finite geometries.
D. C. Kent, Ph.D., New Mexico, 1963. General topology.

Thesis Titles and Current Positions of Recent Graduates
M. Burke. *A Model of the Initial Stages of Plant Naturalizations.* Postdoctoral Associate, Woods Hole Marine Institute.
R. Drake. *A Dynamically Adaptive Method and Spectrum Enveloping Technique.* Research Scientist, SANDIA Laboratory.
M. Olmos-Gomez. *Analytical and Numerical Solutions of Diffusion Problems with Convection/Reaction.* Professor of Mathematics, University of Guadalajara, Mexico.
B. E. Peterson. *Integer Polyhedra and the Perfect Box.* Assistant Professor of Mathematics, Oregon State University.
L. E. Stephenson. *Weakly Nonlinear Stability Analyses of Turing Pattern Formation in the CIMA/Starch Reaction Diffusion Model System.* Senior Engineer/Scientist, United Defense LP.

SELECTED PUBLICATIONS

Ariyawansa, K. A. Line search termination criteria for collinear scaling algorithms for minimizing a class of convex functions. *Numerische Mathematik,* in press.

Ariyawansa, K. A. An upper bound suitable for parallel processing for the objective function in a class of stochastic optimization problems. In *The Impact of Emerging Technologies on Computer Science and Operations Research,* pp. 1–25, eds. S. G. Nash and A. Sofer. Kluwer, 1995.

Ariyawansa, K. A. On the existence and uniqueness of maximizers of two likelihood functions. *Statistische Hefte* 35:139–50, 1994.

Brown, J. A., G. Wallerstein, and D. Zucker. High resolution CCD spectra of stars in globular clusters, IX. The "young" clusters Ruprecht 106 and Pal 12. *Astron. J.,* in press.

Whitmer, J. C., B. Beck-Winchatz, **J. A. Brown,** and G. Wallerstein. Star No. 1412 in M4, a post-AGB star with low carbon and enhanced TiO. *Publ. Astron. Soc. Pac.* 107:127, 1994.

Cochran, J., A. D. Klemm, A. J. Gilks, D. Rhodes. Pair-correlation functions of hard spheres from Green's functions. To appear.

Cochran, J., and Z. Y. Cai. Mode bifurcation in corrugated waveguides. In *Mathematical and Numerical Aspects of Wave Propagation Phenomena,* pp. 651–9, eds. G. Cohen, L. Halpern, and P. Joly. Philadelphia: SIAM, 1991.

Cochran, J., and L. M. Ciasullo. Accelerating the convergence of Chebyshev series. In *Asymptotic and Computational Analysis,* pp. 95–136, ed. R. Wong. New York: Marcel Dekker, 1990.

Jones, W. B., W. J. Thron, and **S. C. Cooper.** Separate convergence for log-normal modified S-fractions. *Continued Fractions and Orthogonal Functions: Theory and Applications, Proceedings,* Loen, Norway, 1992. In *Lecture Notes in Pure and Applied Mathematics,* pp. 101–13, eds. S. Clement Cooper and W. J. Thron, Marcel Dekker, 1993.

Cochran, L., and **S. C. Cooper.** Orthogonal Laurent polynomials on the real line. *Continued Fractions and Orthogonal Functions: Theory and Applications, Proceedings,* Loen, Norway, 1992. In *Lecture Notes in Pure and Applied Mathematics,* pp. 47–100, eds. S. C. Cooper and W. J. Thron, Marcel Dekker, 1993.

Jones, W. B., W. J. Thron, and **S. C. Cooper.** Asymptotics of orthogonal L-polynomials for log-normal distributions. *Const. Approx.* 8:59–67, 1992.

Ambeek, C. J., **D. W. DeTemple,** K. McAvaney, and J. M. Robertson. When are chordal graphs also partition graphs? *Australasian J. Combinatorics* 16:285–93, 1997.

DeTemple, D. W., and C. T. Long. *Mathematical Reasoning for Elementary School Teachers.* Reading: Addison-Wesley, 1996.

DeTemple, D. The geometry of circumscribing polygons of minimal perimeter. *J. Geom.* 49:72–89, 1994.

Dillon, R., L. Fauci, A. Fogelson, and D. Gaver. Modeling biofilm processes using the immersed boundary method. *J. Comput. Phys.* 129:57–73, 1996.

Dillon, R., L. Fauci, and D. Gaver. A microscale model of bacterial swimming, chemotaxis, and substrate transport. *J. Theor. Biol.* 177:325–40, 1995.

Genz, A., and J. Monahan. Stochastic integration rules for infinite regions. *SIAM J. Sci. Com.* 19:426–39, 1998.

Genz, A., and B. Keister. Fully symmetric interpolatory rules for multiple integrals over infinite regions. *J. Comp. Appl. Math.* 71:299–309, 1996.

Genz, A. Numerical computation of multivariate normal probabilities. *J. Comp. Graph. Stat.* 1:141–50, 1992.

Holt, R. D., and **R. Gomulkiewicz.** The evolution of species' niches: a population dynamic perspective. In *Case Studies in Mathematical Modeling: Ecology, Physiology, and Cell Biology,* pp. 25–50, eds. H. G. Othmer, F. R. Adler, M. A. Lewis, and J. C. Dalton. New York: Prentice-Hall, 1997.

Gomulkiewicz, R., and J. H. Beder. The selection gradient of an infinite-dimensional trait. *SIAM J. Appl. Math.* 56:509–23, 1996.

Gomulkiewicz, R., and R. D. Holt. When does evolution by natural selection prevent extinction? *Evolution* 49:201–7, 1995.

Hudelson, M., V. K. Klee, and D. Larman. Largest j-simplices in

d-cubes: the Hadamard maximum determinant problem and some of its relatives. *Linear Alg. Appl.* 241-3:519–98, 1996.

Jacroux, M. A note on the determination and construction of E-optimal block designs in the presence of linear trends. *Sankhya B,* in press.

Jacroux, M. On the determination and construction of E-optimal block designs in the presence of linear trends. *J. Stat. Plann. Inf.,* in press.

Jacroux, M., and F. Githinji. On the determination and construction of optimal designs for comparing a set of test treatments with a set of controls in the presence of linear trends. *J. Stat. Plann. Inf.* 66:161–74, 1998.

Jandhyala, V. K., and S. B. Fotopoulos. Capturing the distributional behavior of the maximum likelihood estimate of a change-point. *Biometrika,* in press.

Jandhyala, V. K., and I. B. MacNeill. Iterated partial sum sequences of regression residuals and tests for change-points with continuity constraints. *J. R. Stat. Soc. B* 59:147–56, 1997.

Jandhyala, V. K., and P. L. Jian. Eigenvalues of a Fredholm integral operator and applications to problems of statistical inference. *J. Int. Equat. Appl.* 8:413–27, 1996.

Wilczynski, W., and **R. Johnson.** Pseudocontinuous functions. In *Proceedings of the Banach Center Semester in Real Analysis,* to appear.

Wilczynski, W., and **R. Johnson.** Finite products of Borel measures. In *Supplemento ai Rendiconti del Circolo Matematico di Palermo Serv. II,* pp. 141–8, 1992.

Wajch, E., W. Wilczynski, and **R. Johnson.** Metric spaces and multiplication of Borel sets. *Rocky Mtn. J. Math.* 22:1341–7, 1992.

Peterson, B. E., and **J. Jordan.** Integer hexahedron topologically equivalent to a perfect box. *Am. Math. Monthly* 102(1):41–5, 1995.

Peterson, B. E., and **J. Jordan.** Almost regular integer Fibonacci pentagons. *Rocky Mtn. J. Math.* 23(1):243–7, 1993.

Jordan, J. Almost regular integer hexagons. *J. Geom.* 39:116–9, 1990.

Kallaher, M. Translation planes. In *Handbook of Geometry,* ed. F. Buckenhout, 1994 (an invited review chapter).

Hanson, J., and **M. Kallaher.** Finite Bol quasifields are nearfields. *Utilitas Math.* 37:45–64, 1990.

Kent, D., and P. Brock. Approach spaces, limit tower spaces, and probabilistic convergence spaces. *Applied Categorical Structures* 5:1–12, 1997.

Kent, D., and D. Liu. Ordered compactifications and families of maps. *Int. J. Math. Math. Sci.* 20:105–10, 1997.

Kent, D., and G. Richardson. Diagonal Cauchy spaces. *Bull. Austral. Math. Soc.* 54:255–65, 1996.

Khapalov, A. Exponential decay for the one-dimensional wave equation with integral pointwise damping. *Math. Methods Appl. Sci.* 20:1171–83. 1997.

Khapalov, A. Exact controllability of second-order hyperbolic equations under impulse controls. *Applicable Analysis* 63:223–8, 1996.

Khapalov, A. Interior point control and observation for the wave equation. *Abst. Appl. Anal.,* 1:219–35, 1996.

Khapalov, A. Some aspects of the asymptotic behavior of the solutions of the semi-linear heat equation and approximate controllability. *J. Math. Anal. Appl.* 194:858–82, 1995.

Bosch, C., T. Gilsdorf, and **J. Kucera.** Remarks on the uniform boundedness principle. *Pittman Res. Notes* No. 316, New York, 1994.

Bosch, C., and **J. Kucera.** On regularity of inductive limits. *Czech. Math. J.* 45:120, 1995.

McKennon, K., and **J. Kucera.** Quasi-incomplete regular LB-space. *Int. J. Math.* 16(4):675–8, 1993.

Li, H., M. Scarsini, and M. Shaked. Linkages: A tool for the construction of multivariate distribution with given multivariate marginals. *J. Multivariate Anal.* 56:200–41, 1996.

Washington State University

Selected Publications (continued)

Li, H., and M. Shaked. On the first passage times for Markov processes with monotone convex transition kernels. *Stochastic Processes Applications* 58:205–16, 1995.

Li, H., and M. Shaked. Stochastic convexity and concavity of Markov processes. *Math. Operations Res.* 19:477–93, 1994.

LoFaro, T. Period-adding bifurcations in a one-parameter family of interval maps. *Math. Comput. Modelling* 24:27–41, 1996.

Kopell, N., E. Marder, S. Hooper, and **T. LoFaro.** Subharmonic coordination in networks of neurons with slow conductances. *Neural Computation* January(6):69–84, 1994.

Kopell, N., E. Marder, S. Hooper, and **T. LoFaro.** The effects of i_h currents on bursting patterns of pairs of coupled neurons. In *Computation in Neurons and Neural Systems,* ed. F. A. Eeckman. Boston: Kluwer Academic Publishers, 1994.

Lutz, J. The type la supernova 1989B in NGC 6327 (M66), ed. L. A. Wells. *Astron. J.* 1994.

Lutz, J. Observational parameters: Definitions and limits in planetary nebulae, vol. 19, eds. R. Weinberger and A. Acker. Dordrecht: Kluwer, 1993.

Manoranjan, V. S., and M. Olmos-Gomez. A two-step Jacobi type iterative method. *Comp. Math. Appl.* 34:1–9, 1997.

Manoranjan, V. S., and T. B. Stauffer. Exact solution for contaminant Langmuir sorption. *Water Resources Res.* 32:749–52, 1996.

Drake, R., and **V. S. Manoranjan.** A dynamic mesh adaption technique. *Int. Num. Meth. Eng. J.* 39:939–49, 1996.

Mifflin, R., D. Sun, and L. Qi. Quasi-Newton bundle-type methods for nondifferentiable optimization. *SIAM J. Optimization,* in press.

Mifflin, R. A quasi-second-order proximal bundle algorithm. *Math. Programming* 73:51–72, 1996.

Mifflin, R., and J. L. Nazareth. The least prior deviation update. *Math. Programming* 65:247–61, 1995.

Millham, C. Using gapped Hermite cubics for obtaining a mathematical representation of a given point file. *Adv. Eng. Software,* 1993.

Meyer, A., and **C. Millham.** Modified Hermite quintic curves and applications. *Computer-Aided Design,* 1992.

Zheng, J. L., and **C. Millham.** Detecting and tracing planar section curves of free-form surfaces. *Comp. Graph.,* 1992.

Kolda, T. G., D. P. O'Leary, and **J. L. Nazareth.** BFGS with update skipping and varying memory. *SIAM J. Optimization,* in press.

Nazareth, J. L. A framework for interior methods of linear programming. In *Optimization Methods and Software,* 5:227–34, 1995.

Nazareth, J. L. *The Newton-Cauchy Framework: A Unified Approach to Unconstrained Nonlinear Minimization,* LNCS 769. Berlin and New York: Springer-Verlag, 1994.

Pate, E., K. Franks-Skiba, and R. Cooke. Depletion of phosphate in active muscle fibers probes actmyosin states within the powerstroke. *Biophys. J.* 74:369–80, 1998.

Cuda, G., **E. Pate,** R. Cooke, and J. R. Sellers. In vitro actin filament sliding velocities produced by mixtures of different types of myosin. *Biophys. J.* 72:1767–79, 1997.

Pate, E. Mathematical modeling of muscle crossbridge mechanics. In *The Art of Mathematical Modeling: Case Studies in Ecology, Physiology, and Biofluids,* pp. 221-254, eds. H. G. Othmer, F. R. Adler, M. A. Lewis, and J. C. Dalton. Berlin: Springer-Verlag, 1996.

McGill, P., and **M. F. Schumaker.** Boundary conditions for single-ion diffusion. *Biophys. J.* 71:1723–42, 1996.

Schumaker, M. F., and P. McGill. Orientation independence of single-vacancy and single-ion permeability ratios. *Biophys. J.* 69:84–93, 1995.

Lark, E., C. K. Omoto, and **M. F. Schumaker.** Functional multiplicity of motor molecules revealed by a simple kinetic analysis. *Biophys. J.* 67:1134–40, 1994.

Benner, P., H. Fassbender, and **D. S. Watkins.** Two connections between the SR and HR eigenvalue algorithms. *Linear Alg. Appl.* 272:17–32, 1998.

Watkins, D. S. Unitary orthogonalization processes. *J. Comp. Appl. Math.* 86:335–45, 1997.

Watkins, D. S. The transmission of shifts and shift blurring in the QR algorithm. *Linear Alg. Appl.* 241-3:877–96, 1996.

Webb, W. How to cut a cake fairly using a minimal number of cuts. *Dis. Appl. Math.* 74:183–90, 1997.

Webb, W., and J. Robertson. Near exact and envy-free cube division. *Ars Combinatorics* 45:97–108, 1997.

Kimball, W., and **W. Webb.** Some congruences for generalized binomial coefficients. *Rocky Mtn. J. Math.* 25:1079–85, 1995.

Stephenson, L. E., and **D. J. Wollkind.** Weakly nonlinear stability analyses of one-dimensional Turing pattern formation in activator-inhibitor/immobilizer model systems. *J. Math. Biol.* 33:771–815, 1995.

Wollkind, D., V. S. Manoranjan, and L. Zhang. Weakly nonlinear stability analyses of prototype reaction-diffusion model equations. *SIAM Rev.* 36:176–214, 1994.

Zhang, L., and **D. Wollkind.** The effect of suspended particles on Rayleigh-Bénard convection II. A nonlinear stability analysis of a thermal disequilibrium model. *Math. Comput. Modelling* 19:43–74, 1994.

Yin, H. On Maxwell's equations in an electromagnetic field with temperature effects. *SIAM J. Math. Anal.* 29:637–51, 1998.

Yin, H., S. Ding, and Y. Tao. A chemical diffusion process with reaction taking place at a free boundary. *Can. Appl. Math. Q.* 5:49–74, 1998.

WESLEYAN UNIVERSITY

Department of Mathematics

Programs of Study

The Department of Mathematics offers a program of courses and research leading to the degrees of Master of Arts and Doctor of Philosophy both in mathematics and in computer science.

The Ph.D. degree in mathematics demands breadth of knowledge, intensive specialization in one field, original contribution to that field, and expository skill. First-year courses are designed to provide a strong foundation in algebra, analysis, and topology or in computer science. Written preliminary examinations are normally taken by the middle of the second year. During the second year, the student continues with a variety of courses, sampling areas of possible concentration. By the start of the third year, the student chooses a specialty and begins research work under the guidance of a thesis adviser. Also required is the ability to read mathematics in at least two of the following languages: French, German, and Russian. The usual time required for completion of all requirements for a Ph.D., including the dissertation, is four to five years. A similar set of requirements is in place for the Ph.D. program in computer science.

After passing the preliminary examinations, most Ph.D. candidates teach one course per year, typically a small section (fewer than 20 students) of calculus or linear algebra.

The M.A. degree is designed to ensure basic knowledge and the capacity for sustained scholarly study; requirements are six semester courses at the graduate level and the writing and oral presentation of a thesis. The thesis requires (at least) independent search and study of the literature.

Students are also involved in a variety of departmental activities, including seminars and colloquia. The small size of the program contributes to an atmosphere of informality and accessibility. During 1998–99, graduate students had an active role in arranging outside visits and colloquia.

The emphasis at Wesleyan is in pure mathematics and theoretical computer science, and most Wesleyan Ph.D.'s have chosen academic careers.

Research Facilities

The department is housed in the Science Center, where all graduate students and faculty members have offices. Computer facilities are available for both learning and research purposes. The Science Library collection has about 120,000 volumes, with extensive mathematics holdings; there are more than 200 subscriptions to mathematics journals, and approximately 60 new mathematics books arrive each month. The proximity of students and faculty and the daily gatherings at teatime are also key elements of the research environment.

Financial Aid

Each applicant for admission is automatically considered for appointment to an assistantship. For the 1999–2000 academic year, the stipend is $12,241, plus a dependency allowance when appropriate. All students in good standing are given financial support for the duration of their studies. Approximately $4080 more is usually available for the student who wishes to remain on campus to study during the summer. Costs of tuition and health fees are borne by the University.

Cost of Study

The only academic costs to the student are books and other educational materials.

Living and Housing Costs

The University provides some subsidized housing and assists in finding private housing. The academic-year cost of a single student's housing (a private room in a 2- or 4-person house, with common kitchen and living area) is about $3310.

Student Group

The number of graduate students in mathematics ranges from 18 to 24, with an entering class of 4 to 8 each year. There have always been both male and female students, graduates of small colleges and large universities, and U.S. and international students, including, in recent years, students from China, Germany, Hungary, Korea, Mexico, Peru, and Yugoslavia.

All of the department's recent Ph.D. recipients have obtained academic employment. Some of these have subsequently taken positions as industrial mathematicians.

Location

Middletown, Connecticut, is a small city of 40,000 on the Connecticut River, about 19 miles southeast of Hartford and 25 miles northeast of New Haven, midway between New York and Boston. The University provides many cultural and recreational opportunities, supplemented by those in the countryside and in larger cities nearby. Several members of the mathematical community are actively involved in sports, including distance running, golf, handball, hiking, softball, squash, table tennis, volleyball, and cycling.

The University

Founded in 1831, Wesleyan is an independent coeducational institution of liberal arts and sciences, with Ph.D. programs in biology, chemistry, ethnomusicology, mathematics, and physics and master's programs in a number of departments. Current enrollments show about 2,800 undergraduates and 145 graduate students.

Applying

No specific courses are required for admission, but it is expected that the equivalent of an undergraduate major in mathematics will have been completed. The complete application consists of the application form, transcripts of all previous academic work at or beyond the college level, letters of recommendation from three college instructors familiar with the applicant's mathematical ability and performance, and GRE scores (if available). Applications should be submitted by February 15 in order to receive adequate consideration, but requests for admission from outstanding candidates are welcome at any time. Preference is given to Ph.D. candidates. A visit to the campus is strongly recommended for its value in determining the suitability of the program for the applicant.

Correspondence and Information

Graduate Education Committee
Department of Mathematics
Wesleyan University
Middletown, Connecticut 06459-0128

Telephone: 860-685-2620
E-mail: nprocyk@wesleyan.edu

Wesleyan University

THE FACULTY AND THEIR RESEARCH

Professors
W. Wistar Comfort, Ph.D., Washington (Seattle). Point-set topology, ultrafilters, set theory, topological groups.
Ethan M. Coven, Ph.D., Yale. Dynamical systems.
Adam Fieldsteel, Ph.D., Berkeley. Ergodic theory.
Anthony W. Hager, Ph.D., Penn State. Lattice-ordered algebraic structures, general and categorical topology.
F. E. J. Linton, Ph.D., Columbia. Categorical algebra, functorial semantics, topoi.
James D. Reid, Ph.D., Washington (Seattle). Abelian groups, module theory.
Lewis C. Robertson, Ph.D., UCLA. Lie groups, topological groups, representation theory.
Rae Michael Shortt, Ph.D., MIT. Measure theory.
Carol Wood, Ph.D., Yale. Mathematical logic, applications of model theory to algebra.

Associate Professors
Karen Collins, Ph.D., MIT. Combinatorics.
Philip H. Scowcroft, Ph.D., Cornell. Foundations of mathematics, model-theoretic algebra.

Associate Professors of Computer Science
Daniel Dougherty Jr., Ph.D., Maryland. Logic, theoretical computer science.
James Lipton, Ph.D., Cornell. Logic and computation, logic programming, type theory, linear logic.
Michael Rice, Ph.D., Wesleyan. Parallel computing, formal specification methods.

Faculty-student conferences, daily gatherings at teatime, and discussions in graduate students' offices are key ingredients of the research environment in the Department of Mathematics.

SELECTED PUBLICATIONS

Collins, K. L. Chromatic difference sequences, to appear.

Collins, K. L. The number of Hamiltonian paths in a rectangular grid, to appear.

Collins, K. L. Factoring distance matrix polynomials. *Disc. Math.* 122:103–12, 1993.

Collins, K. L. Planar lattices are lexicographically shellable. *Order* 8:375–81, 1992.

Comfort, W. W., S. Hernandez, and F. J. Trigos-Arrieta. Relating a locally compact Abelian group to its Bohr compactification. *Adv. Math.* 120:322–44, 1996.

Comfort, W. W. Topological groups. In *Handbook of General Topology*, pp. 1143–263, eds. K. Kunen and J. Vaughan. Amsterdam: North-Holland Publishing Co., Inc., 1984.

Comfort, W. W., and L. C. Robertson. Proper pseudocompact extensions of compact Abelian group topologies. *Proc. Am. Math. Soc.* 86:173–8, 1982.

Comfort, W. W., and **A. W. Hager.** Cardinality of k-complete Boolean algebras. *Pacific J. Math.* 40:541–5, 1972.

Comfort, W. W., and K. A. Ross. Pseudocompactness and uniform continuity in topological groups. *Pacific J. Math.* 16:483–96, 1966.

Coven, E. M., and A. M. Blokh. Sharkovskii type of cycles. *Bull. London Math. Soc.* 28, 1996.

Coven, E. M., L. S. Block, and A. M. Blokh. Zero entropy permutations. *Internat. J. Bifurcations Chaos Appl. Sci. Eng.* 5:1331–7, 1995.

Coven, E. M., J. Ashley, and W. Geller. Entropy of semipatterns or how to connect the dots to minimize entropy. *Proc. Am. Math. Soc.* 113:1115–21, 1991.

Coven, E. M., I. Kan, and J. Yorke. Pseudo-orbit shadowing in the family of tent maps. *Trans. Am. Math. Soc.* 308:227–41, 1988.

Dougherty, D., and P. Johann. A combinatory logic approach to higher-order E-unification. *Theoret. Comp. Sci.*, to appear.

Dougherty, D., F. Otto, and P. Narendran. Some independence results for equational unification. In *Proceedings of the Sixth International Conference on Rewriting Techniques Applications,* Kaiserlauten, Germany, 1995.

Dougherty, D., and R. Subrahmanyam. Equality between functionals in the presence of coproducts. In *Proceedings of the Tenth IEEE Symposium on Logic in Computer Science,* San Diego, 1995.

Dougherty, D. Higher-order unification via combinators. *Theoret. Comp. Sci.* 114:273–98, 1993.

Fieldsteel, A., A. del Junco, and D. J. Rudolph. α-equivalence: A refinement of Kakutani equivalence. *Ergod. Th. Dynam. Sys.*, in press.

Fieldsteel, A. A topological formulation of restricted orbit equivalence.Preprint.

Fieldsteel, A., and D. J. Rudolph. An ergodic transformation with trivial Kakutani centralizer. *Ergod. Th. Dynam. Sys.* 12:459–78, 1992.

Fieldsteel, A., and D. J. Rudolph. Stability of m-equivalence to the weak Pinsker property. *Ergod. Th. Dynam. Sys.* 10:119–29, 1990.

Hager, A. W., and J. Martinez. Functorial rings of quotients II. *Forum Math.*, in press.

Hager, A. W., and J. Martinez. Maximum monoreflections. *Appl. Category Theory*, in press.

Hager, A. W., and A. Kizanis. Certain extensions and factorization of alpha-complete homomorphisms in archimedean lattice-ordered groups. Submitted.

Hager, A. W., and R. N. Ball. Algebraic extensions of an archimedean lattice-ordered group I. *J. Pure Appl. Alg.* 85:1–20, 1993.

Linton, F. E. J., and O. Acuña-Ortega. Finiteness and decidability. In *Proc. L.M.S. Sheaf Theory Symposium* (Durham, 1977), Springer Lecture Notes in Mathematics, vol. 753, 1979.

Linton, F. E. J. Multilinear Yoneda lemmas: Toccata, fugue, and fantasia on themes by Eilenberg-Kelly and Yoneda. In *Reports of the Midwest Category Seminar V,* Springer Lecture Notes in Mathematics, vol. 195, pp. 209–29, 1971.

Linton, F. E. J. Relative functorial semantics: Adjointness results. In *Category Theory, Homology Theory and Its Applications III,* Proceedings of the Conference at The Battelle Memorial Institute, 1968, Springer Lecture Notes in Mathematics, vol. 99, pp. 384–418, 1969.

Linton, F. E. J. Some aspects of equational categories. In *Proceedings of the Conference on Categorical Algebra* (La Jolla, June 7–15, 1965), pp. 84–94. Berlin: Springer, 1966.

Lipton, J., and M. O'Donnell. Some intuitions behind realizability semantics for constructive logic: Tableaux and L\"auchli countermodels." *Ann. Pure Appl. Logic,* vol. 81, pp. 187–239, Elsevier North-Holland, 1996.

Lipton, J., P. Freyd, and S. Finkelstein. Logic programming in tau-categories. In *Computer Science Logic '94,* Lecture Notes in Computer Science, vol. 933, pp. 249–63. Springer, 1995.

Lipton, J., and J. Chirimar. Provability in TBLL (the Tensor Bang Fragment of Linear Logic). In *Computer Science Logic,* Proceedings of CSL '91, Bern, Lecture Notes in Computer Science, vol. 613, pp. 53–67. Springer-Verlag, 1992.

Reid, J. D., and K. M. Rangaswamy. Common extensions of finitely additive measures and a characterization of cotorsion abelian groups. In *Proceedings Curaçao,* pp. 231–39. Marcel Dekker, 1993.

Reid, J. D., and G. P. Niedzwecki. Abelian groups projective over their endomorphism rings. *J. Algebra* 139–49, 1993.

Reid, J. D. Warfield duality and irreducible groups. *Contemp. Math. Am. Math. Soc.* 361–70, 1992.

Reid, J. D. Some groups of exponent p. *Bull. Irish Math. Soc.* 55–62, 1991.

Rice, M., and S. Seidman. Using architectural style to support software understanding and reuse. *WISR8—Eighth Annual Workshop on Software Reuse,* Ohio State University, Columbus, Ohio, March 23–26, 1997.

Rice, M. Reflexive objects in topological categories. *Math. Struct. Comput. Sci.* 6:1–12, 1996.

Rice, M. Covering spaces, boundary sets, and interconnection networks. Papers on general topology and applications, Eighth Summer Conference, Queens College, June 1992, *Annals of the New York Academy of Sciences,* 728:210–26, 1994.

Rice, M. D., and S. B. Seidman. A formal model for module interconnection languages. *IEEE Trans. Software Eng.* 20(1):88–101, 1994.

Robertson, L. C., et al. (**W. W. Comfort** and **A. W. Hager**). Epsilon spaces. *Rocky Mtn. J. Math.*, in press.

Robertson, L. C., and **W. W. Comfort.** Extremal phenomena in certain classes of totally bounded groups. *Dissert. Math.* CCLXXII, 1988.

Robertson, L. C., and **W. W. Comfort.** Images and quotients of So(3, ℝ). *Rocky Mtn. J. Math.* 17:1–13, 1987.

Robertson, L. C., R. M. Shortt, and S. Landry. Dice with fair sums. *Am. Math. Monthly* 95:316–38, 1988.

Scowcroft, P. H. Cross-sections for p-adically closed fields. *J. Algebra* 183:913–28, 1996.

Scowcroft, P. H., and A. Macintyre. On the elimination of imaginaries from certain valued fields. *Ann. Pure Appl. Logic* 61:241–76, 1993.

Scowcroft, P. H. A new model for intuitionistic analysis. *Ann. Pure Appl. Logic* 47:145–65, 1990.

Scowcroft, P. H., and L. van den Dries. On the structure of semialgebraic sets over p-adic fields. *J. Symbol. Logic* 53:1138–64, 1988.

Scowcroft, P. H. A transfer theorem in constructive real algebra. *Ann. Pure Appl. Logic* 40:29–87, 1988.

Shortt, R. M. Strassen's theorem for vector measures. *Proc. Am. Math. Soc.* 122:811–20, 1994.

Shortt, R. M., and M. Droste. Bounded Petri nets of finite dimension

Wesleyan University

Selected Publications (continued)

have only finitely many reachable markings. *Bull. Europ. Assoc. Theoret. Comp. Sci.* 48:172–75, 1992.

Shortt, R. M., and K. P. S. Bhaskara Rao. Group-valued charges: Common extensions and the Chinese remainder property. *Proc. Am. Math. Soc.* 113:965–72, 1991.

Shortt, R. M. Extensions of group-valued set functions. *Periodica Mathematica Hungarica* 33:35–44, 1996.

Wood, C., and M. Messmer. Hasse fields of finite invariant. *J. Symbol. Logic,* to appear.

Wood, C., and D. Saracino. Partially homogeneous partially ordered sets. *J. Combinatorial Theory A* 62:216–24, 1993.

Wood, C., G. Cherlin, and D. Saracino. On homogeneous nilpotent groups and rings. *Proc. Am. Math. Soc.* 119:1289–306, 1993.

Wood, C., and D. Saracino. Homogeneous finite rings in characteristic 2^n. *Ann. Pure Appl. Logic* 40:11–28, 1988.

YALE UNIVERSITY

Applied Mathematics Program

Program of Study
Yale University's graduate program in applied mathematics begins in fall 1999. The program will offer M.S., M.Phil., and Ph.D. degrees.

Research Facilities
The program draws on the general resources at Yale as well as computing resources of the participating faculty members.

Financial Aid
Most Ph.D. students receive financial aid in the form of fellowships or research assistantships. For 1999–2000, assistantship stipends are $13,000 for nine months. Financial aid includes tuition in addition to the stipend. Students may supplement their income with teaching assistantships.

Cost of Study
Tuition for the two-semester academic year is $23,330 in 1999–2000.

Living and Housing Costs
During the 1999–2000 academic year, the cost of living is approximately $12,875 for a single student and $19,980 for a married student. A wide range of privately owned accommodations is available within an easy commuting distance.

Student Group
Twenty students are expected to participate in the Ph.D. and M.Phil. programs, and about 8 are expected to participate in the M.S. program in the steady state.

Location
A small Yankee town of 136,000 people lies outside the Yale campus. New Haven dates back to 1638, and in the midst of a busy urban center, several areas of the city retain the atmosphere of earlier days. The city has a rich cultural life, independent of that provided by the University. Furthermore, there is hourly train service to New York City, which is only 75 miles away.

The University and The Program
Yale was established in 1701 and today is one of the leading universities in the world. It draws students from every part of the United States and from many other countries. Yale has a number of faculty members in the mathematical sciences departments (Mathematics, Computer Science, and Statistics) as well as in the engineering department who are interested in applied mathematics. The Applied Mathematics Program will be a selective interdisciplinary program that will run side by side with the more traditional programs within each discipline.

Applying
An applicant should have a B.S. or B.A. degree prior to matriculation. No specific major is required, but candidates should possess an appropriate level of mathematical sophistication.

Correspondence and Information
Graduate Admissions
Applied Mathematics Program
Yale University
P.O. Box 208236
New Haven, Connecticut 06520-8236
Telephone: 203-432-2770

Yale University

THE FACULTY AND THEIR RESEARCH

James Aspnes, Associate Professor; Ph.D., Carnegie Mellon, 1992. Randomized, distributed, online algorithms.

Andrew Baron, Professor; Ph.D., Stanford, 1985. Statistical information theory, probability limit theorems, function estimation, neural networks.

Richard W. Beals, Professor; Ph.D., Yale, 1964. Differential operators, partial differential equations, real and complex function theory, scattering theory.

Donald Brown, Professor and Member, American Academy of Arts and Sciences; Ph.D., Stevens, 1969. Mathematical economics.

Joseph Chang, Associate Professor; Ph.D., Stanford, 1989. Probability, random walks, sequential analysis, pattern recognition, and machine learning.

Ronald R. Coifman, Professor; Ph.D., Geneva, 1965. Nonlinear analysis, scattering theory, real and complex analysis, singular integrals, numerical analysis.

Eric V. Denardo, Professor; Ph.D., Northwestern, 1965. Optimization, decisions under uncertainty, operations management, telecommunications.

Stanley C. Eisenstat, Professor; Ph.D., Stanford, 1972. Numerical linear and nonlinear algebra, direct and iterative methods for solving sparse linear systems, eigenvalue problems, parallel computing.

Michael J. Fischer, Professor; Ph.D., Harvard, 1968. Cryptography and computer security, distributed systems and protocols, communication networks, analysis of algorithms and data structures, complexity theory.

John Hartigan, Professor; Ph.D., Princeton, 1962. Foundations of probability and statistics, Bayes theory, classification, statistical computing, graphical methods.

Nicolas Hengartner, Assistant Professor; Ph.D., Berkeley, 1993. Semiparametric inference, geophysics, census data.

Roger Howe, Professor; Ph.D., Berkeley, 1969. Representation theory, automorphic forms, harmonic analysis, invariant theory.

Peter Jones, Professor; Ph.D., UCLA, 1978. Real, complex, and Fourier analysis; singular integrals; potential theory; dynamical systems.

Ravi Kannan, Professor; Ph.D., Cornell, 1980. Mathematical algorithms, theoretical computer science.

Laszlo Lovasz, Professor; Ph.D., Eötvös Loránd (Budapest), 1971. Combinatorial optimization, discrete mathematics, randomized algorithms, complexity theory.

Steven Orszag, Professor; Ph.D., Princeton, 1966. Applied mathematics, fluid dynamics, numerical analysis: materials science, electronics manufacturing, mathematical biology.

David Pollard, Professor; Ph.D., Australian National, 1976. Weak convergence and empirical processes, stochastic processes, asymptotics, semiparametrics, econometrics.

Vladimir Rokhlin, Professor; Ph.D., Rice, 1983. Numerical scattering theory, elliptic partial differential equations, numerical solution of integral equations.

Herbert Scarf, Professor; Ph.D., Princeton, 1954. General equilibrium theory, game theory, mathematical methods.

Martin H. Schultz, Professor of Computer Science; Ph.D., Harvard, 1965. Numerical analysis, scientific computing, parallel computation.

Mitchell Smooke, Professor; Ph.D., Harvard, 1978. Computational combustion, numerical solution of ordinary and partial differential equations, scattering theory, chemical vapor deposition.

Katepalli Sreenivasan, Professor; Ph.D., Indian Institute of Science, 1975. Fluid turbulence, dynamical behavior of liquids, gases, and soft matter.

Marten Wegkamp, Assistant Professor; Ph.D., Leiden (Netherlands), 1996. Theory of empirical processes, bootstrap.

Steven Zucker, Professor of Computer Science and Electrical Engineering; Ph.D., Drexel, 1975. Computational vision, computational neuroscience, robotics, psychophysics.

Academic and Professional Programs in the Agricultural Sciences

This part of Book 4 consists of one section covering the agricultural sciences. The section has a table of contents (listing the program directories, announcements, and in-depth descriptions); program directories, which consist of brief profiles of the programs in the relevant fields (and 50-word or 100-word announcements following the profiles, if the programs have chosen to include them); Cross-Discipline Announcements, if any programs have chosen to submit such entries; and in-depth descriptions, which are more individualized statements, if programs have chosen to submit them.

Section 8
Agricultural and Food Sciences

This section contains a directory of institutions offering graduate work in agricultural and food sciences, followed by in-depth entries submitted by institutions that chose to prepare detailed program descriptions. Additional information about programs listed in the directory but not augmented by an in-depth entry may be obtained by writing directly to the dean of a graduate school or chair of a department at the address given in the directory.

For programs offering related work, see also in this book Natural Resources. In Book 2, see Architecture (Landscape Architecture) and Economics (Agricultural Economics and Agribusiness); in Book 3, see Biological and Biomedical Sciences; Botany and Plant Sciences; Ecology, Environmental Biology, and Evolutionary Biology; Entomology; Genetics and Developmental Biology; Nutrition; Pathology; Physiology; and Zoology; in Book 5, see Agricultural Engineering and Bioengineering, Biomedical Engineering, and Biotechnology; and in Book 6, see Education (Agricultural Education) and Veterinary Medicine and Sciences.

CONTENTS

Agricultural Sciences—General

Alabama Agricultural and Mechanical University, School of Graduate Studies, School of Agricultural and Environmental Sciences, Normal, AL 35762-1357. Offers MS, MURP, PhD. Part-time and evening/weekend programs available. *Faculty:* 29 full-time (6 women). *Students:* 45 full-time (13 women), 59 part-time (30 women); includes 76 minority (74 African Americans, 1 Hispanic American, 1 Native American), 20 international. In 1998, 25 master's, 2 doctorates awarded (100% entered university research/teaching). Terminal master's awarded for partial completion of doctoral program. *Degree requirements:* For doctorate, one foreign language, computer language, dissertation required, foreign language not required. *Entrance requirements:* For master's, GRE General Test; for doctorate, GRE General Test (minimum combined score of 1000 required), MS. *Average time to degree:* Master's–2.5 years full-time, 4 years part-time; doctorate–4.2 years full-time, 8 years part-time. *Application deadline:* For fall admission, 5/1. Application fee: $15 ($20 for international students). Tuition, state resident: full-time $1,932. Tuition, nonresident: full-time $3,864. Tuition and fees vary according to course load. *Financial aid:* Fellowships, research assistantships, teaching assistantships, career-related internships or fieldwork and Federal Work-Study available. Aid available to part-time students. Financial aid application deadline: 4/1. *Faculty research:* Remote sensing, environmental pollutants, food biotechnology, plant growth. Total annual research expenditures: $2.5 million. *Unit head:* Dr. James W. Shuford, Dean, 256-851-5783, Fax: 256-851-5906.

Alcorn State University, School of Graduate Studies, School of Agriculture and Applied Science, Lorman, MS 39096-9402. Offers agricultural economics (MS Ag); agronomy (MS Ag); animal science (MS Ag). *Degree requirements:* For master's, thesis optional, foreign language not required. *Faculty research:* Aquatic systems, dairy herd improvement, fruit production, alternative farming practices.

Arkansas State University, Graduate School, College of Agriculture, Jonesboro, State University, AR 72467. Offers agricultural education (MSA, SCCT); agriculture (MSA); vocational-technical administration (MS, SCCT). Part-time programs available. *Faculty:* 14 full-time (3 women). *Students:* 7 full-time (6 women), 22 part-time (8 women), 1 international. Average age 31. In 1998, 8 master's, 1 other advanced degree awarded. *Degree requirements:* For master's, thesis or alternative, comprehensive exam required; for SCCT, comprehensive exam required, thesis not required. *Entrance requirements:* For master's, GRE General Test or MAT, appropriate bachelor's degree; for SCCT, GRE General Test or MAT, interview, master's degree. *Application deadline:* For fall admission, 7/1 (priority date); for spring admission, 11/15 (priority date). Applications are processed on a rolling basis. Application fee: $15 ($25 for international students). *Financial aid:* Teaching assistantships available. Aid available to part-time students. Financial aid application deadline: 7/1; financial aid applicants required to submit FAFSA. *Unit head:* Dr. Keith Rogers, Dean, 870-972-2085, Fax: 870-972-3885, E-mail: krogers@creek.astate.edu.

Auburn University, Graduate School, College of Agriculture, Auburn, Auburn University, AL 36849-0002. Offers M Ag, M Aq, MS, PhD. Part-time programs available. *Faculty:* 163 full-time (13 women). *Students:* 113 full-time (43 women), 114 part-time (26 women); includes 8 minority (4 African Americans, 2 Asian Americans or Pacific Islanders, 1 Hispanic American, 1 Native American), 75 international. 76 applicants, 45% accepted. In 1998, 47 master's, 20 doctorates awarded. *Degree requirements:* For master's, thesis (MS) required; for doctorate, dissertation required. *Entrance requirements:* For master's, GRE General Test; for doctorate, GRE General Test (minimum score of 400 on each section required). *Application deadline:* For fall admission, 9/1; for spring admission, 3/1. Applications are processed on a rolling basis. Application fee: $25 ($50 for international students). Tuition, state resident: full-time $2,760; part-time $76 per credit hour. Tuition, nonresident: full-time $8,280; part-time $228 per credit hour. *Financial aid:* Fellowships, research assistantships, teaching assistantships, Federal Work-Study available. Aid available to part-time students. Financial aid application deadline: 3/15. *Unit head:* Dr. Luther Waters, Dean, 334-844-2237. *Application contact:* Dr. John F. Pritchett, Dean of the Graduate School, 334-844-4700.

Brigham Young University, Graduate Studies, College of Biological and Agricultural Sciences, Provo, UT 84602-1001. Offers MS, PhD. Part-time programs available. *Faculty:* 92 full-time (7 women), 7 part-time (3 women). *Students:* 131 full-time (45 women), 8 part-time (2 women); includes 10 minority (3 Asian Americans or Pacific Islanders, 6 Hispanic Americans, 1 Native American), 14 international. Average age 27. 140 applicants, 30% accepted. In 1998, 33 master's, 4 doctorates awarded. Terminal master's awarded for partial completion of doctoral program. *Degree requirements:* For doctorate, dissertation required. *Entrance requirements:* For master's and doctorate, GRE General Test. *Application deadline:* Applications are processed on a rolling basis. Application fee: $30. Electronic applications accepted. Tuition: Full-time $3,330; part-time $185 per credit hour. Tuition and fees vary according to program and student's religious affiliation. *Financial aid:* In 1998–99, 104 students received aid; fellowships, research assistantships, teaching assistantships, career-related internships or fieldwork, institutionally-sponsored loans, scholarships, tuition waivers (partial), and tuition awards available. Aid available to part-time students. *Unit head:* Dr. R. Kent Crookston, Dean, 801-378-2007, Fax: 801-378-7499.

California Polytechnic State University, San Luis Obispo, College of Agriculture, San Luis Obispo, CA 93407. Offers MS. Part-time programs available. *Faculty:* 5 full-time (1 woman), 2 part-time (1 woman). *Students:* 46 full-time (26 women), 34 part-time (18 women), 8 international. 55 applicants, 76% accepted. In 1998, 34 degrees awarded. *Degree requirements:* For master's, thesis, oral and written comprehensive exams required, foreign language not required. *Entrance requirements:* For master's, TOEFL (minimum score of 550 required), TWE (minimum score of 4.5 required), minimum GPA of 2.50 in last 90 quarter units. *Application deadline:* For fall admission, 8/15 (priority date); for spring admission, 2/1. Applications are processed on a rolling basis. Application fee: $55. Tuition, nonresident: part-time $164 per unit. Required fees: $531 per quarter. *Financial aid:* Fellowships, research assistantships, teaching assistantships, career-related internships or fieldwork, Federal Work-Study, and institutionally-sponsored loans available. Aid available to part-time students. Financial aid application deadline: 3/2; financial aid applicants required to submit FAFSA. *Faculty research:* Soils, food processing, forestry, dairy products development, irrigation. *Unit head:* Glen Casey, Graduate Coordinator, 805-756-2161, Fax: 805-756-6577, E-mail: gcasey@calpoly.edu. *Application contact:* Linda Madrigal, Admissions Evaluator, 805-756-2311.

California State Polytechnic University, Pomona, Graduate Studies, College of Agriculture, Pomona, CA 91768-2557. Offers agricultural science (MS); animal science (MS); foods and nutrition (MS). Part-time programs available. *Faculty:* 24. *Students:* 17 full-time (13 women), 49 part-time (35 women); includes 25 minority (4 African Americans, 11 Asian Americans or Pacific Islanders, 10 Hispanic Americans), 8 international. Average age 31. 36 applicants, 47% accepted. In 1998, 8 degrees awarded. *Degree requirements:* For master's, thesis or alternative required. *Application deadline:* Applications are processed on a rolling basis. Application fee: $55. Tuition, nonresident: part-time $164 per unit. *Financial aid:* In 1998–99, 11 students received aid. Career-related internships or fieldwork, Federal Work-Study, and institutionally-sponsored loans available. Aid available to part-time students. Financial aid application deadline: 3/2; financial aid applicants required to submit FAFSA. *Faculty research:* Equine nutrition, physiology, and reproduction; leadership development; bioartificial pancreas; plant science; ruminant and human nutrition. *Unit head:* Dr. Wayne R. Bidlack, Dean, 909-869-2200, E-mail: wrbidlack@csupomona.edu.

California State University, Chico, Graduate School, School of Agriculture, Chico, CA 95929-0722. Offers MS. In 1998, 1 degree awarded. *Degree requirements:* For master's, thesis or alternative, oral exam required, foreign language not required. *Financial aid:* Fellowships, teaching assistantships available. *Unit head:* Thomas E. Dickinson, Dean, 530-898-5844.

California State University, Fresno, Division of Graduate Studies, School of Agricultural Sciences and Technology, Fresno, CA 93740-0057. Offers MS. Part-time and evening/weekend programs available. *Faculty:* 42 full-time (11 women). *Students:* 19 full-time (7 women), 32 part-time (16 women); includes 11 minority (4 Asian Americans or Pacific Islanders, 5 Hispanic Americans, 2 Native Americans), 7 international. Average age 31. 43 applicants, 81% accepted. In 1998, 7 degrees awarded. *Degree requirements:* Foreign language not required. *Entrance requirements:* For master's, GRE General Test, TOEFL (minimum score of 550 required). *Average time to degree:* Master's–3.5 years full-time. *Application deadline:* For fall admission, 6/1 (priority date); for spring admission, 11/1. Applications are processed on a rolling basis. Application fee: $55. Electronic applications accepted. Tuition, nonresident: part-time $246 per unit. Required fees: $1,906; $620 per semester. *Financial aid:* In 1998–99, 1 fellowship was awarded.; career-related internships or fieldwork, Federal Work-Study, and scholarships also available. Aid available to part-time students. Financial aid application deadline: 3/1; financial aid applicants required to submit FAFSA. *Unit head:* Dr. Daniel P. Bartell, Dean, 559-278-2061, Fax: 559-278-4496, E-mail: daniel_bartell@csufresno.edu.

Central Missouri State University, School of Graduate Studies, College of Applied Sciences and Technology, Department of Agriculture, Warrensburg, MO 64093. Offers agricultural technology (MS). Part-time programs available. *Faculty:* 5 full-time (0 women). *Students:* 4 full-time (2 women), 5 part-time, 1 international. In 1998, 1 degree awarded (100% found work related to degree). *Degree requirements:* For master's, comprehensive exam, research project prepared for publishing required, thesis not required. *Entrance requirements:* For master's, minimum GPA of 2.5. *Application deadline:* For fall admission, 6/30 (priority date). Applications are processed on a rolling basis. Application fee: $25 ($50 for international students). Tuition, state resident: full-time $3,576; part-time $149 per credit hour. Tuition, nonresident: full-time $7,152; part-time $298 per credit hour. Tuition and fees vary according to course load and campus/location. *Financial aid:* In 1998–99, research assistantships with tuition reimbursements (averaging $3,750 per year), 4 teaching assistantships with tuition reimbursements (averaging $3,750 per year) were awarded.; Federal Work-Study, grants, scholarships, and unspecified assistantships also available. Aid available to part-time students. Financial aid application deadline: 3/1; financial aid applicants required to submit FAFSA. *Unit head:* Dr. Fred Worman, Chair, 660-543-4240, Fax: 660-543-8031, E-mail: worman@cmsu1.cmsu.edu.

Clemson University, Graduate School, College of Agriculture, Forestry and Life Sciences, Clemson, SC 29634. Offers M Ag, M Ag Ed, M Engr, MFR, MS, PhD. Part-time programs available. *Faculty:* 251 full-time (27 women), 11 part-time (3 women). *Students:* 476 full-time (216 women), 181 part-time (81 women); includes 22 minority (15 African Americans, 3 Asian Americans or Pacific Islanders, 3 Hispanic Americans, 1 Native American), 186 international. 746 applicants, 37% accepted. In 1998, 149 master's, 56 doctorates awarded. *Degree requirements:* For doctorate, dissertation required. *Entrance requirements:* For master's and doctorate, GRE General Test, TOEFL. *Application deadline:* Applications are processed on a rolling basis. Application fee: $35. Electronic applications accepted. *Financial aid:* Fellowships, research assistantships, teaching assistantships, career-related internships or fieldwork, Federal Work-Study, grants, institutionally-sponsored loans, and unspecified assistantships available. Financial aid applicants required to submit FAFSA. *Unit head:* Dr. William Wehrenberg, Dean, 864-656-3013, Fax: 864-656-1286, E-mail: bwhrnbr@clemson.edu.

See in-depth description on page 843.

Colorado State University, Graduate School, College of Agricultural Sciences, Fort Collins, CO 80523-0015. Offers M Agr, MS, PhD. Part-time programs available. *Faculty:* 110. *Students:* 142 full-time (62 women), 64 part-time (29 women); includes 3 minority (1 African American, 1 Asian American or Pacific Islander, 1 Hispanic American), 58 international. Average age 32. 226 applicants, 49% accepted. In 1998, 55 master's, 16 doctorates awarded. *Degree requirements:* For master's, thesis required (for some programs); for doctorate, dissertation required. *Entrance requirements:* For master's and doctorate, GRE General Test, TOEFL, minimum GPA of 3.0. *Application deadline:* For fall admission, 2/1 (priority date). Applications are processed on a rolling basis. Application fee: $30. Electronic applications accepted. *Financial aid:* In 1998–99, 4 fellowships, 60 research assistantships, 23 teaching assistantships were awarded.; career-related internships or fieldwork, Federal Work-Study, institutionally-sponsored loans, and traineeships also available. Aid available to part-time students. *Faculty research:* Systems methodology, biotechnology, plant and animal breeding, water management, plant protection. Total annual research expenditures: $5.1 million. *Unit head:* James C. Heird, Associate Dean, 970-491-6272, Fax: 970-491-4895, E-mail: jheird@ceres.agsci.colostate.edu.

Dalhousie University, Faculty of Graduate Studies, Nova Scotia Agricultural College, Halifax, NS B3H 3J5, Canada. Offers M Sc. Part-time programs available. *Faculty:* 33 full-time (4 women), 14 part-time (1 woman). *Students:* 23 full-time (15 women), 17 part-time (8 women). 26 applicants, 77% accepted. In 1998, 8 degrees awarded (13% entered university research/teaching, 75% found other work related to degree, 12% continued full-time study). *Degree requirements:* For master's, thesis, candidacy exam required. *Entrance requirements:* For master's, TOEFL (minimum score of 580 required), minimum GPA of 3.0. *Average time to degree:* Master's–2.7 years full-time, 3 years part-time. *Application deadline:* For fall admission, 6/1; for winter admission, 10/1; for spring admission, 12/1. Applications are processed on a rolling basis. Application fee: $55. *Financial aid:* In 1998–99, 22 students received aid, including research assistantships (averaging $13,500 per year), teaching assistantships (averaging $900 per year); career-related internships or fieldwork also available. *Faculty research:* Biology, soil science, animal science, plant science, environmental science, biotechnology. Total annual research expenditures: $1.5 million. *Unit head:* Dr. Bruce Gray, Vice Principal, Academic, 902-893-6030, Fax: 902-897-9399, E-mail: bgray@cadmin.nsac.ns.ca. *Application contact:* Jill Rogers-Langille, Graduate Coordinator, 902-893-6360, Fax: 902-897-9399, E-mail: jrogers-langille@cadmin.nsac.ns.ca.

Illinois State University, Graduate School, College of Applied Science and Technology, Department of Agriculture, Normal, IL 61790-2200. Offers agribusiness (MS). *Faculty:* 12 full-time (2 women). *Students:* 8 full-time (2 women), 10 part-time (1 woman), 10 international. 2 applicants, 100% accepted. In 1998, 2 degrees awarded. *Degree requirements:* For master's, thesis optional. *Entrance requirements:* For master's, GRE General Test, minimum GPA of 3.0 in last 60 hours. *Application deadline:* Applications are processed on a rolling basis. Application fee: $0. Tuition, state resident: full-time $2,526; part-time $105 per credit hour. Tuition, nonresident: full-time $7,578; part-time $316 per credit hour. Required fees: $1,082; $38 per credit hour. Tuition and fees vary according to course load and program. *Financial aid:* Research assistantships, teaching assistantships, tuition waivers (full) and unspecified assistantships available. Financial aid application deadline: 4/1. *Faculty research:* Commercial aquaculture, compost, evaluation of swine waste as a feedstuff and soil amendment. Total annual research expenditures: $578,901. *Unit head:* Dr. J. R. Winter, Chairperson, 309-438-5654.

Instituto Tecnológico y de Estudios Superiores de Monterrey, Campus Monterrey, Graduate and Research Division, Program in Agriculture, Monterrey, 64849, Mexico. Offers agricultural parasitology (PhD); agricultural sciences (MS); farming productivity (MS); food processing engineering (MS); phytopathology (MS). Part-time programs available. *Degree requirements:* For master's and doctorate, thesis/dissertation required. *Entrance requirements:* For master's, PAEG, TOEFL; for doctorate, GMAT or GRE, TOEFL, master's in related field. *Faculty research:* Animal embryos and reproduction, crop entomology, tropical agriculture, agricultural productivity, induced mutation in oleaginous plants.

Iowa State University of Science and Technology, Graduate College, College of Agriculture, Ames, IA 50011. Offers M Ag, MS, PhD. Part-time programs available. Postbaccalaureate distance learning degree programs offered (minimal on-campus study). *Faculty:* 242 full-time, 20 part-time. *Students:* 444 full-time (160 women), 187 part-time (54 women); includes 23 minority (11 African Americans, 5 Asian Americans or Pacific Islanders, 6 Hispanic Americans,

1 Native American), 205 international. 346 applicants, 34% accepted. In 1998, 84 master's, 53 doctorates awarded. *Degree requirements:* For doctorate, dissertation required. *Entrance requirements:* For master's and doctorate, TOEFL. *Application deadline:* Applications are processed on a rolling basis. Application fee: $20 ($50 for international students). Electronic applications accepted. Tuition, state resident: full-time $3,308. Tuition, nonresident: full-time $9,744. Part-time tuition and fees vary according to course load, campus/location and program. *Financial aid:* In 1998–99, 319 research assistantships with partial tuition reimbursements (averaging $9,059 per year), 26 teaching assistantships with partial tuition reimbursements (averaging $9,762 per year) were awarded.; fellowships, Federal Work-Study and scholarships also available. Aid available to part-time students. *Unit head:* Dr. David G. Topel, Dean, 515-294-2518, Fax: 515-294-6800, E-mail: dtopel@iastate.edu.

Iowa State University of Science and Technology, Graduate College, Interdisciplinary Programs, Program in Professional Agriculture, Ames, IA 50011. Offers M Ag. Postbaccalaureate distance learning degree programs offered (minimal on-campus study). 5 applicants, 20% accepted. In 1998, 5 degrees awarded. *Degree requirements:* For master's, thesis or alternative required. *Entrance requirements:* For master's, TOEFL. Application fee: $20 ($50 for international students). Electronic applications accepted. Tuition, state resident: full-time $3,308. Tuition, nonresident: full-time $9,744. Part-time tuition and fees vary according to course load, campus/location and program. *Unit head:* Dr. W. Wade Miller, Supervisory Committee Chair, 515-294-0895, E-mail: proaginfo@iastate.edu.

Kansas State University, Graduate School, College of Agriculture, Manhattan, KS 66506. Offers MAB, MS, PhD. Part-time programs available. Postbaccalaureate distance learning degree programs offered (minimal on-campus study). Terminal master's awarded for partial completion of doctoral program. Electronic applications accepted.

Louisiana State University and Agricultural and Mechanical College, Graduate School, College of Agriculture, Baton Rouge, LA 70803. Offers M App St, MS, MSBAE, PhD. Part-time programs available. *Faculty:* 225 full-time (32 women), 3 part-time (0 women). *Students:* 345 full-time (140 women), 170 part-time (76 women); includes 33 minority (17 African Americans, 6 Asian Americans or Pacific Islanders, 7 Hispanic Americans, 3 Native Americans), 157 international. Average age 33. 265 applicants, 51% accepted. In 1998, 85 master's, 49 doctorates awarded. Terminal master's awarded for partial completion of doctoral program. *Degree requirements:* For doctorate, dissertation required, foreign language not required. *Entrance requirements:* For master's and doctorate, GRE General Test, minimum GPA of 3.0. *Application deadline:* Applications are processed on a rolling basis. Application fee: $25. *Financial aid:* In 1998–99, 10 fellowships, 229 research assistantships with partial tuition reimbursements, 20 teaching assistantships with partial tuition reimbursements were awarded.; career-related internships or fieldwork, Federal Work-Study, institutionally-sponsored loans, tuition waivers (full), and unspecified assistantships also available. Aid available to part-time students. *Faculty research:* Biotechnology, resource economics and marketing, aquaculture, food science and technology. *Unit head:* Dr. Kenneth Koonce, Dean, 225-388-2362, Fax: 225-388-2526, E-mail: kkoonce@agctr.lsu.edu.

McGill University, Faculty of Graduate Studies and Research, Faculty of Agricultural and Environmental Sciences, Montréal, PQ H3A 2T5, Canada. Offers M Sc, M Sc A, PhD, Certificate, MBA/M Sc. Part-time programs available. *Faculty:* 92 full-time (17 women), 59 part-time (14 women). *Students:* 385 full-time (173 women), 115 international. Average age 28. 193 applicants, 52% accepted. In 1998, 75 master's, 37 doctorates awarded. *Degree requirements:* For doctorate, dissertation required; for Certificate, thesis not required. *Entrance requirements:* For master's, TOEFL; for doctorate, TOEFL, M Sc; for Certificate, TOEFL (minimum score of 550 required), minimum GPA of 3.0, B Sc in biological sciences. *Application deadline:* For fall admission, 1/1 (priority date); for winter admission, 5/1 (priority date); for spring admission, 9/1 (priority date). Applications are processed on a rolling basis. Application fee: $60. *Financial aid:* Fellowships, research assistantships, teaching assistantships, career-related internships or fieldwork, institutionally-sponsored loans, scholarships, and tuition waivers available. *Faculty research:* Agriculture, environmental, food sciences, nutrition and molecular biology, biosystems and agricultural engineering. Total annual research expenditures: $9.4 million. *Unit head:* Dr. Deborah J. Buszard, Dean, 514-398-7707, Fax: 514-398-7766. *Application contact:* 514-398-7708, Fax: 514-398-7968, E-mail: grad@macdonald.mcgill.ca.

Michigan State University, Graduate School, College of Agriculture and Natural Resources, East Lansing, MI 48824-1020. Offers MS, PhD. Part-time and evening/weekend programs available. Postbaccalaureate distance learning degree programs offered. *Faculty:* 261. *Students:* 313 full-time (130 women), 346 part-time (160 women); includes 69 minority (30 African Americans, 18 Asian Americans or Pacific Islanders, 20 Hispanic Americans, 1 Native American), 227 international. Average age 30. In 1998, 141 master's, 62 doctorates awarded. Terminal master's awarded for partial completion of doctoral program. *Degree requirements:* For doctorate, dissertation required. *Entrance requirements:* For master's and doctorate, GRE. *Application deadline:* Applications are processed on a rolling basis. Application fee: $30 ($40 for international students). Electronic applications accepted. *Financial aid:* In 1998–99, 409 research assistantships (averaging $10,603 per year), 38 teaching assistantships with tuition reimbursements (averaging $10,570 per year) were awarded.; fellowships, career-related internships or fieldwork, Federal Work-Study, institutionally-sponsored loans, and tuition waivers (partial) also available. Aid available to part-time students. Financial aid applicants required to submit FAFSA. *Faculty research:* Plant science, animal sciences, forestry, fisheries and wildlife, recreation and tourism, packaging. Total annual research expenditures: $50.4 million. *Unit head:* Dr. William Taylor, Acting Dean, 517-355-0232.

Mississippi State University, College of Agriculture and Life Sciences, Mississippi State, MS 39762. Offers MABM, MS, PhD. Part-time programs available. *Students:* 200 full-time (84 women), 109 part-time (42 women); includes 87 minority (16 African Americans, 54 Asian Americans or Pacific Islanders, 16 Hispanic Americans, 1 Native American), 37 international. Average age 31. 138 applicants, 67% accepted. In 1998, 55 master's, 35 doctorates awarded. Terminal master's awarded for partial completion of doctoral program. *Degree requirements:* For doctorate, dissertation required, foreign language not required. *Entrance requirements:* For master's and doctorate, TOEFL. *Application deadline:* For fall admission, 7/1; for spring admission, 11/1. Applications are processed on a rolling basis. Application fee: $25 for international students. *Financial aid:* Research assistantships, teaching assistantships, career-related internships or fieldwork, Federal Work-Study, institutionally-sponsored loans, scholarships, tuition waivers (partial), and unspecified assistantships available. Financial aid applicants required to submit FAFSA. *Unit head:* Dr. Bill Fox, Dean, 662-325-2110. *Application contact:* Jerry B. Inmon, Director of Admissions, 662-325-2224, Fax: 662-325-7360, E-mail: admit@admissions.msstate.edu.

Montana State University–Bozeman, College of Graduate Studies, College of Agriculture, Bozeman, MT 59717. Offers MS, PhD. Part-time programs available. *Students:* 40 full-time (15 women), 70 part-time (24 women); includes 3 minority (2 Asian Americans or Pacific Islanders, 1 Native American) Average age 30. 70 applicants, 59% accepted. In 1998, 21 master's, 6 doctorates awarded. Terminal master's awarded for partial completion of doctoral program. *Degree requirements:* For doctorate, dissertation required, foreign language not required, foreign language not required. *Entrance requirements:* For master's and doctorate, GRE General Test, TOEFL (minimum score of 550 required). *Application deadline:* For fall admission, 6/1 (priority date); for spring admission, 11/1. Applications are processed on a rolling basis. Application fee: $50. *Financial aid:* Fellowships, research assistantships, teaching assistantships, career-related internships or fieldwork and tuition waivers (full and partial) available. Financial aid application deadline: 3/1; financial aid applicants required to submit FAFSA. *Faculty research:* Rule based automated classification program, licensing MSUSTAT, stock growers research, biosciences. Total annual research expenditures: $9.4 million. *Unit head:* Dr. Sharron Quisenberry, Dean, 406-994-3681, Fax: 406-994-6579.

Murray State University, College of Industry and Technology, Department of Agriculture, Murray, KY 42071-0009. Offers MS. Part-time programs available. *Students:* 24 full-time (5 women), 24 part-time (6 women), 4 international. 18 applicants, 100% accepted. *Degree requirements:* Foreign language not required. *Entrance requirements:* For master's, GRE General Test, TOEFL (minimum score of 600 required). *Application deadline:* Applications are processed on a rolling basis. Application fee: $20. *Financial aid:* Research assistantships, teaching assistantships, Federal Work-Study available. Financial aid application deadline: 4/1. *Unit head:* Dr. John Mikulcik, Graduate Coordinator, 502-762-6929, Fax: 502-762-3441.

New Mexico State University, Graduate School, College of Agriculture and Home Economics, Las Cruces, NM 88003-8001. Offers M Ag, MA, MS, PhD. Part-time and evening/weekend programs available. *Faculty:* 85 full-time (21 women), 1 part-time (0 women). *Students:* 139 full-time (64 women), 93 part-time (48 women); includes 40 minority (1 Asian American or Pacific Islander, 36 Hispanic Americans, 3 Native Americans), 51 international. Average age 33. 152 applicants, 48% accepted. In 1998, 69 master's, 15 doctorates awarded. *Degree requirements:* For doctorate, dissertation required, foreign language not required. *Application deadline:* For spring admission, 11/1. Applications are processed on a rolling basis. Application fee: $15 ($35 for international students). Electronic applications accepted. Tuition, state resident: full-time $2,682; part-time $112 per credit. Tuition, nonresident: full-time $8,376; part-time $349 per credit. Tuition and fees vary according to course load. *Financial aid:* Research assistantships, teaching assistantships, career-related internships or fieldwork and Federal Work-Study available. Aid available to part-time students. Financial aid application deadline: 3/1. *Faculty research:* Biological control, competitiveness in agricultural business, family social issues, management of natural resources, plant and animal improvement. *Unit head:* Dr. Jerry Schickedanz, Interim Dean, 505-646-1806, Fax: 505-646-5975, E-mail: agdean@nmsu.edu. *Application contact:* Donald Lindsey, Interim Associate Dean and Director of Academic Programs, 505-646-1807, Fax: 505-646-5975, E-mail: dlindsey@taipan.nmsu.edu.

North Carolina Agricultural and Technical State University, Graduate School, School of Agriculture, Greensboro, NC 27411. Offers MS. Part-time and evening/weekend programs available. *Faculty:* 17 full-time (3 women). *Students:* 27 full-time (11 women), 49 part-time (33 women); includes 60 minority (57 African Americans, 2 Asian Americans or Pacific Islanders, 1 Hispanic American), 3 international. Average age 32. 55 applicants, 78% accepted. In 1998, 15 degrees awarded. *Degree requirements:* For master's, comprehensive exam, qualifying exam required. *Entrance requirements:* For master's, GRE General Test. *Application deadline:* For fall admission, 6/1 (priority date); for spring admission, 12/1. Applications are processed on a rolling basis. Application fee: $35. *Financial aid:* Fellowships, research assistantships, teaching assistantships, career-related internships or fieldwork available. Financial aid application deadline: 6/1. *Faculty research:* Aid for small farmers, agricultural technology, housing, food science, nutrition. *Unit head:* Dr. Daniel Godfrey, Dean, 336-334-7979, Fax: 336-334-7580, E-mail: danield@aurora.ncat.edu.

North Carolina State University, Graduate School, College of Agriculture and Life Sciences, Raleigh, NC 27695. Offers M Ag, M Econ, M Ed, M Soc, M Tox, MA, MAWB, MBAE, MLS, MS, MSA, Ed D, PhD. Part-time programs available. *Faculty:* 454 full-time (55 women), 235 part-time (21 women). *Students:* 599 full-time (287 women), 184 part-time (87 women); includes 61 minority (29 African Americans, 16 Asian Americans or Pacific Islanders, 13 Hispanic Americans, 3 Native Americans), 139 international. Average age 32. 721 applicants, 26% accepted. In 1998, 115 master's, 66 doctorates awarded. Application fee: $45. *Financial aid:* In 1998–99, 34 fellowships (averaging $5,272 per year), 392 research assistantships (averaging $5,079 per year), 56 teaching assistantships (averaging $5,453 per year) were awarded.; career-related internships or fieldwork, Federal Work-Study, institutionally-sponsored loans, traineeships, and tuition waivers (partial) also available. Aid available to part-time students. Total annual research expenditures: $150.1 million. *Unit head:* Dr. James L. Oblinger, Interim Dean, 919-515-2668, Fax: 919-515-6980, E-mail: james_oblinger@ncsu.edu. *Application contact:* Bee Smith, Administrative Assistant, 919-515-2668, Fax: 919-515-6980, E-mail: bee_smithncsu.edu.

See in-depth description on page 849.

North Dakota State University, Graduate Studies and Research, College of Agriculture, Fargo, ND 58105. Offers MS, PhD. Part-time programs available. *Faculty:* 136. *Students:* 117 full-time (49 women), 13 part-time (5 women); includes 9 minority (5 Asian Americans or Pacific Islanders, 3 Hispanic Americans, 1 Native American), 23 international. In 1998, 37 master's, 14 doctorates awarded. *Degree requirements:* For doctorate, dissertation required, foreign language not required. *Entrance requirements:* For master's and doctorate, TOEFL. *Application deadline:* Applications are processed on a rolling basis. Application fee: $25. Electronic applications accepted. *Financial aid:* Fellowships with full tuition reimbursements, research assistantships with full tuition reimbursements, teaching assistantships with full tuition reimbursements, career-related internships or fieldwork, Federal Work-Study, and institutionally-sponsored loans available. Aid available to part-time students. *Faculty research:* Horticulture and forestry, plant and wheat breeding, diseases of insects, animal and range sciences, soil science, veterinary medicine. *Unit head:* Dr. Glen Statler, Interim Associate Dean and Director of Academic Programs, 701-231-8790, Fax: 701-231-8520, E-mail: gstatler@ndsuext.nodak.edu.

Northwest Missouri State University, Graduate School, College of Arts and Sciences, Department of Agriculture, Maryville, MO 64468-6001. Offers agriculture (MS); teaching secondary agriculture education (MS Ed). Part-time programs available. *Faculty:* 11 full-time (1 woman). *Students:* 5 full-time (2 women), 3 part-time (2 women); includes 1 minority (Asian American or Pacific Islander), 2 international. 3 applicants, 100% accepted. In 1998, 5 degrees awarded. *Degree requirements:* For master's, thesis (for some programs), comprehensive exam required, foreign language not required. *Entrance requirements:* For master's, GRE General Test (minimum score of 300 on each section required), TOEFL (minimum score of 550 required), minimum undergraduate GPA of 2.5, writing sample. *Application deadline:* Applications are processed on a rolling basis. Application fee: $0 ($50 for international students). *Financial aid:* In 1998–99, 2 research assistantships, 1 teaching assistantship were awarded.; unspecified assistantships also available. Financial aid application deadline: 3/1. *Unit head:* Dr. Arley Larson, Chairperson, 660-562-1161. *Application contact:* Dr. Frances Shipley, Dean of Graduate School, 660-562-1145, E-mail: gradsch@mail.nwmissouri.edu.

Nova Scotia Agricultural College, Research and Graduate Studies, Truro, NS B2N 5E3, Canada. Offers agriculture (M Sc), including animal behavior, animal genetics, animal management, animal nutrition, animal technology, botany, crop breeding, crop management, crop physiology, ecology, environmental microbiology, food science, geology, nutrient management, pest management, physiology, plant biotechnology, plant pathology, soil chemistry, soil fertility, soil physics, waste management. Part-time programs available. *Faculty:* 33 full-time (4 women), 14 part-time (1 woman). *Students:* 23 full-time (15 women), 17 part-time (8 women). 26 applicants, 77% accepted. In 1998, 8 degrees awarded (12% entered university research/teaching, 75% found other work related to degree, 13% continued full-time study). *Degree requirements:* For master's, thesis, candidacy exam required. *Entrance requirements:* For master's, TOEFL (minimum score of 580 required), minimum GPA of 3.0. *Average time to degree:* Master's–2.7 years full-time, 3 years part-time. *Application deadline:* For fall admission, 6/1; for winter admission, 10/1; for spring admission, 2/1. Applications are processed on a rolling basis. Application fee: $55. *Financial aid:* In 1998–99, 22 students received aid, including research assistantships (averaging $13,500 per year), teaching assistantships (averaging $900 per year); career-related internships or fieldwork also available. *Faculty research:* Organogenesis, somatic embryogenesis, composting, sustainable agriculture, ecotoxicology, nutrient metabolism, plant and animal nutrition, physiology genetics and production, biological resistance weed control, cell biology, DNA technology, waste management. Total annual research expenditures: $1.5 million. *Unit head:* Jill L. Rogers-Langille, Coordinator, 902-893-6360, Fax: 902-897-9399, E-mail: jrogers-langille@cadmin.nsac.ns.ca. *Application contact:* Kari Duff, Assistant, 902-893-6502, Fax: 902-897-9399, E-mail: kduff@cadmin.nsac.ns.ca.

The Ohio State University, Graduate School, College of Food, Agricultural, and Environmental Sciences, Columbus, OH 43210. Offers MS, PhD. Part-time programs available. *Faculty:* 223

Agricultural Sciences—General

The Ohio State University *(continued)*
full-time, 77 part-time. *Students:* 344 full-time (154 women), 97 part-time (51 women); includes 30 minority (20 African Americans, 4 Asian Americans or Pacific Islanders, 6 Hispanic Americans), 153 international. 509 applicants, 30% accepted. In 1998, 101 master's, 37 doctorates awarded. *Degree requirements:* For doctorate, dissertation required, foreign language not required, foreign language not required. *Application deadline:* For fall admission, 8/15. Applications are processed on a rolling basis. Application fee: $30 ($40 for international students). *Financial aid:* Fellowships, research assistantships, teaching assistantships, career-related internships or fieldwork, Federal Work-Study, institutionally-sponsored loans, and unspecified assistantships available. Aid available to part-time students. *Unit head:* Bobby Moser, Dean, 614-292-6891, Fax: 614-292-1218, E-mail: moser.2@osu.edu.

Oklahoma State University, Graduate College, College of Agricultural Sciences and Natural Resources, Stillwater, OK 74078. Offers M Ag, M Bio E, MS, Ed D, PhD. Part-time programs available. *Faculty:* 196 full-time (20 women), 3 part-time (0 women). *Students:* 202 full-time (58 women), 209 part-time (70 women); includes 39 minority (9 African Americans, 6 Asian Americans or Pacific Islanders, 7 Hispanic Americans, 17 Native Americans), 135 international. Average age 30. In 1998, 75 master's, 34 doctorates awarded. *Degree requirements:* For doctorate, dissertation required. *Entrance requirements:* For master's and doctorate, TOEFL (minimum score of 550 required). Application fee: $25. *Financial aid:* In 1998–99, 245 students received aid, including 212 research assistantships (averaging $12,633 per year), 28 teaching assistantships (averaging $12,257 per year); fellowships, career-related internships or fieldwork, Federal Work-Study, and tuition waivers (partial) also available. Aid available to part-time students. Financial aid application deadline: 3/1. *Unit head:* Dr. Samuel S. Curl, Dean, 405-744-5398.

Oregon State University, Graduate School, College of Agricultural Sciences, Corvallis, OR 97331. Offers M Ag, M Agr, MA, MAIS, MAT, MS, PhD. Part-time programs available. *Faculty:* 365 full-time (73 women), 121 part-time (58 women). *Students:* 290 full-time (135 women), 18 part-time (6 women); includes 16 minority (2 African Americans, 5 Asian Americans or Pacific Islanders, 7 Hispanic Americans, 2 Native Americans), 114 international. Average age 31. In 1998, 55 master's, 36 doctorates awarded. Terminal master's awarded for partial completion of doctoral program. *Degree requirements:* For doctorate, dissertation required. *Entrance requirements:* For master's and doctorate, GRE, TOEFL, minimum GPA of 3.0 in last 90 hours. Application fee: $50. *Financial aid:* Fellowships, research assistantships, teaching assistantships, career-related internships or fieldwork, Federal Work-Study, and institutionally-sponsored loans available. Aid available to part-time students. Financial aid application deadline: 2/1. *Faculty research:* Fish and wildlife biology, food science, soil/water/plant relationships, natural resources, animal biochemistry. *Unit head:* Dr. Thayne R. Dutson, Dean, 541-737-2331, Fax: 541-737-4574, E-mail: thayne.dutson@orst.edu. *Application contact:* Dr. Michael J. Burke, Associate Dean, 541-737-2211, Fax: 541-737-2256, E-mail: mike.burke@orst.edu.

See in-depth description on page 851.

Pennsylvania State University University Park Campus, Graduate School, College of Agricultural Sciences, State College, University Park, PA 16802-1503. Offers M Agr, M Ed, MFR, MS, D Ed, PhD. *Students:* 196 full-time (79 women), 93 part-time (28 women). *Entrance requirements:* For master's and doctorate, GRE General Test. Application fee: $50. *Unit head:* Dr. Robert D. Steele, Dean, 814-865-2541.

See in-depth description on page 853.

Prairie View A&M University, Graduate School, College of Agriculture, Nutrition and Human Ecology, Department of Agriculture, Nutrition and Human Ecology, Prairie View, TX 77446-0188. Offers animal science (MS); human sciences (MS); soil science (MS). *Students:* 19 full-time (14 women), 12 part-time (9 women); includes 25 minority (all African Americans), 4 international. In 1998, 19 degrees awarded. *Degree requirements:* For master's, thesis required, foreign language not required. *Entrance requirements:* For master's, GRE General Test. *Average time to degree:* Master's—1.5 years full-time, 2.5 years part-time. *Application deadline:* For fall admission, 7/1 (priority date); for spring admission, 11/1. Applications are processed on a rolling basis. Application fee: $10. *Financial aid:* Career-related internships or fieldwork, Federal Work-Study, and institutionally-sponsored loans available. Financial aid application deadline: 8/1. *Faculty research:* Environmental quality, toxic metals, marketing goat products, stocking density in poultry. *Unit head:* Dr. Cecil L. Strickland, Interim Head, 409-857-2812, Fax: 409-857-2811.

Purdue University, Graduate School, School of Agriculture, West Lafayette, IN 47907. Offers EMBA, M Agr, MS, MSF, PhD. Part-time programs available. *Faculty:* 236. *Students:* 363 full-time (136 women), 73 part-time (26 women); includes 24 minority (8 African Americans, 8 Asian Americans or Pacific Islanders, 6 Hispanic Americans, 2 Native Americans), 193 international. 522 applicants, 30% accepted. In 1998, 79 master's, 52 doctorates awarded. *Degree requirements:* For doctorate, dissertation required. *Entrance requirements:* For master's, TOEFL (minimum score of 550 required); for doctorate, TOEFL. Application fee: $30. Electronic applications accepted. *Financial aid:* Fellowships, research assistantships, teaching assistantships, career-related internships or fieldwork and tuition waivers (partial) available. Aid available to part-time students. Financial aid applicants required to submit FAFSA. *Unit head:* Dr. Victor L. Lechtenberg, Dean, 765-494-8392.

Sam Houston State University, College of Education and Applied Science, Department of Agricultural Sciences, Huntsville, TX 77341. Offers agricultural business (MS); agricultural education (M Ed); agricultural mechanization (MS); agriculture (MS); vocational education (M Ed, MS). Part-time and evening/weekend programs available. *Students:* 12 full-time (6 women), 13 part-time (1 woman). Average age 28. In 1998, 6 degrees awarded (100% found work related to degree). *Degree requirements:* For master's, thesis optional, foreign language not required. *Entrance requirements:* For master's, GRE General Test (minimum combined score of 800 required), minimum GPA of 2.5. *Application deadline:* For fall admission, 5/1. Application fee: $15. *Financial aid:* Teaching assistantships, career-related internships or fieldwork available. Financial aid application deadline: 5/1. *Faculty research:* Legumes in pastures, fire ant control, plasma cholesterol in swine, obesity/lean in swine, water management. Total annual research expenditures: $80,000. *Unit head:* Dr. Robert A. Lane, Chair, 409-294-1225, Fax: 409-294-1232, E-mail: agr_ral@shsu.edu.

South Dakota State University, Graduate School, College of Agriculture and Biological Sciences, Brookings, SD 57007. Offers MS, PhD. Part-time programs available. *Degree requirements:* For master's, thesis, oral exam required, foreign language not required; for doctorate, dissertation, preliminary oral and written exams required. *Entrance requirements:* For master's and doctorate, TOEFL.

Southern Illinois University Carbondale, Graduate School, College of Agriculture, Carbondale, IL 62901-6806. Offers MS, MBA/MS. Part-time programs available. *Faculty:* 50 full-time (7 women), 1 (woman) part-time. *Students:* 87 full-time (37 women), 34 part-time (17 women). 100 applicants, 36% accepted. In 1998, 23 degrees awarded. *Degree requirements:* Foreign language not required. *Entrance requirements:* For master's, TOEFL (minimum score of 550 required), minimum GPA of 2.7. *Application deadline:* Applications are processed on a rolling basis. Application fee: $0. *Financial aid:* In 1998–99, 35 students received aid, including 31 research assistantships; fellowships, teaching assistantships, career-related internships or fieldwork, Federal Work-Study, institutionally-sponsored loans, and tuition waivers (full) also available. Aid available to part-time students. *Faculty research:* Production and studies in crops, animal nutrition, agribusiness economics and management, forest biology and ecology, microcomputers in agriculture. *Unit head:* James McGuire, Dean.

Southern University and Agricultural and Mechanical College, Graduate School, College of Agricultural, Family and Consumer Sciences, Baton Rouge, LA 70813. Offers urban forestry (MS). *Faculty:* 4 full-time (2 women), 3 part-time (0 women). *Students:* 6 full-time (1 woman), 2 part-time (1 woman); includes 3 minority (all African Americans) 8 applicants, 100% accepted. *Degree requirements:* For master's, thesis required, foreign language not required. *Entrance requirements:* For master's, GRE, TOEFL, minimum GPA of 3.0. *Application deadline:* For fall admission, 6/1 (priority date); for spring admission, 11/1 (priority date). Applications are processed on a rolling basis. Application fee: $5. *Financial aid:* In 1998–99, 5 research assistantships (averaging $5,897 per year), 1 teaching assistantship (averaging $5,897 per year) were awarded. Financial aid application deadline: 4/15; financial aid applicants required to submit FAFSA. *Unit head:* Dr. Kirkland E. Mellad, Interim Dean.

Tarleton State University, College of Graduate Studies, College of Agriculture, Stephenville, TX 76402. Offers MS. Part-time and evening/weekend programs available. Postbaccalaureate distance learning degree programs offered (minimal on-campus study). *Faculty:* 18 full-time (2 women). *Students:* 11 full-time (1 woman), 15 part-time (4 women), 1 international. 11 applicants, 91% accepted. In 1998, 9 degrees awarded. *Degree requirements:* For master's, thesis (for some programs), comprehensive exam required. *Entrance requirements:* For master's, GRE General Test, minimum GPA of 2.75 during previous 60 hours. *Application deadline:* For fall admission, 8/5 (priority date); for spring admission, 12/1. Applications are processed on a rolling basis. Application fee: $25 ($100 for international students). *Financial aid:* In 1998–99, 5 research assistantships (averaging $12,000 per year), 4 teaching assistantships (averaging $12,000 per year) were awarded.; career-related internships or fieldwork, Federal Work-Study, and institutionally-sponsored loans also available. Aid available to part-time students. Financial aid application deadline: 5/1; financial aid applicants required to submit FAFSA. *Unit head:* Don Knotts, Acting Dean, 254-968-9227.

Tennessee State University, Graduate School, School of Agriculture and Family Services, Nashville, TN 37209-1561. Offers MS. Part-time and evening/weekend programs available. *Faculty:* 8 full-time (5 women), 5 part-time (1 woman). *Students:* 10 full-time (8 women), 21 part-time (7 women); includes 24 minority (22 African Americans, 1 Asian American or Pacific Islander, 1 Hispanic American), 1 international. Average age 35. 14 applicants, 64% accepted. In 1998, 6 degrees awarded. *Degree requirements:* For master's, thesis required, foreign language not required. *Entrance requirements:* For master's, GRE General Test, GRE Subject Test, MAT. *Application deadline:* Applications are processed on a rolling basis. Application fee: $15. Electronic applications accepted. Tuition, state resident: full-time $2,962; part-time $182 per credit hour. Tuition, nonresident: full-time $7,788; part-time $393 per credit hour. *Financial aid:* In 1998–99, 2 research assistantships (averaging $5,924 per year), 1 teaching assistantship (averaging $2,962 per year) were awarded. *Faculty research:* Small farm economics, ornamental horticulture, beef cattle production, rural elderly. *Unit head:* Dr. Troy Wakefield, Dean, 615-963-7620, E-mail: twakefield@picard.tnstate.edu.

Texas A&M University, College of Agriculture and Life Sciences, College Station, TX 77843. Offers M Agr, M Ed, M Eng, MAB, MS, DE, Ed D, PhD. Part-time programs available. *Faculty:* 322 full-time (37 women), 20 part-time (5 women). *Students:* 1,136 (561 women); includes 74 minority (10 African Americans, 21 Asian Americans or Pacific Islanders, 41 Hispanic Americans, 2 Native Americans) 296 international. Average age 29. 1129 applicants, 38% accepted. In 1998, 149 master's, 83 doctorates awarded. *Entrance requirements:* For master's and doctorate, GRE General Test, TOEFL. *Application deadline:* Applications are processed on a rolling basis. Application fee: $50 ($75 for international students). Electronic applications accepted. *Financial aid:* Fellowships, research assistantships, teaching assistantships, career-related internships or fieldwork, Federal Work-Study, grants, institutionally-sponsored loans, scholarships, tuition waivers (partial), and unspecified assistantships available. Aid available to part-time students. Financial aid applicants required to submit FAFSA. *Unit head:* Dr. Edward A. Hiler, Dean, 409-845-4747.

Texas A&M University–Commerce, Graduate School, College of Arts and Sciences, Department of Agriculture, Commerce, TX 75429-3011. Offers agricultural education (M Ed, MS); agricultural sciences (M Ed, MS). Part-time programs available. *Faculty:* 5 full-time (1 woman), 1 part-time (0 women). *Students:* 5 full-time (3 women), 8 part-time (2 women). Average age 36. In 1998, 3 degrees awarded. *Degree requirements:* For master's, thesis (for some programs), comprehensive exam required. *Entrance requirements:* For master's, GRE General Test (minimum combined score of 850 required). *Application deadline:* For fall admission, 6/1 (priority date); for spring admission, 11/1 (priority date). Applications are processed on a rolling basis. Application fee: $0 ($25 for international students). Electronic applications accepted. *Financial aid:* In 1998–99, research assistantships (averaging $7,750 per year), teaching assistantships (averaging $7,750 per year) were awarded.; Federal Work-Study, institutionally-sponsored loans, and scholarships also available. Financial aid application deadline: 5/1; financial aid applicants required to submit FAFSA. *Faculty research:* Soil conservation. Total annual research expenditures: $252,270. *Unit head:* Dr. Donald Cawthon, Head, 903-886-5358. *Application contact:* Betty Hunt, Graduate Admissions Adviser, 903-886-5167, Fax: 903-886-5165, E-mail: betty_hunt@tamu_commerce.edu.

Texas A&M University–Kingsville, College of Graduate Studies, College of Agriculture and Home Economics, Kingsville, TX 78363. Offers MS, PhD. Part-time and evening/weekend programs available. *Faculty:* 12 full-time (5 women), 13 part-time (2 women). *Students:* 53 full-time (23 women), 41 part-time (20 women). In 1998, 24 degrees awarded. *Degree requirements:* For master's, thesis or alternative, comprehensive exam required, foreign language not required; for doctorate, one foreign language, dissertation, comprehensive exam required. *Entrance requirements:* For master's, GRE General Test (minimum combined score of 800 required), TOEFL (minimum score of 525 required), minimum GPA of 3.0; for doctorate, GRE General Test (minimum combined score of 1000 required), minimum GPA of 3.5. *Application deadline:* For fall admission, 6/1; for spring admission, 11/15. Applications are processed on a rolling basis. Application fee: $15 ($25 for international students). Tuition, state resident: full-time $2,062. Tuition, nonresident: full-time $7,246. *Financial aid:* Fellowships, research assistantships, teaching assistantships, career-related internships or fieldwork and Federal Work-Study available. Aid available to part-time students. Financial aid application deadline: 5/15. *Faculty research:* Mesquite cloning; genesis of soil salinity; dove management; bone development; egg, meat, and milk consumption versus price. *Unit head:* Dr. Charles DeYoung, Dean, 361-593-3712. *Application contact:* Dr. James D. Arnold, Graduate Coordinator, 361-593-3711.

Texas Tech University, Graduate School, College of Agricultural Sciences and Natural Resources, Lubbock, TX 79409. Offers M Agr, MLA, MS, PhD, JD/MS. Part-time and evening/weekend programs available. *Faculty:* 56 full-time (6 women), 1 part-time (0 women). *Students:* 153 full-time (47 women), 45 part-time (10 women); includes 4 minority (2 Asian Americans or Pacific Islanders, 2 Hispanic Americans), 31 international. Average age 29. 118 applicants, 47% accepted. In 1998, 48 master's, 10 doctorates awarded. *Degree requirements:* For doctorate, dissertation required, foreign language not required. *Entrance requirements:* For master's, GRE General Test (combined average 987); for doctorate, GRE General Test. *Application deadline:* For fall admission, 4/15 (priority date); for spring admission, 11/1 (priority date). Applications are processed on a rolling basis. Application fee: $25 ($50 for international students). Electronic applications accepted. *Financial aid:* In 1998–99, 107 students received aid, including 95 research assistantships, 8 teaching assistantships; fellowships, career-related internships or fieldwork, Federal Work-Study, and institutionally-sponsored loans also available. Aid available to part-time students. Financial aid application deadline: 5/15; financial aid applicants required to submit FAFSA. Total annual research expenditures: $8.4 million. *Unit head:* Dr. John R. Abernathy, Dean, 806-742-2808, Fax: 806-742-2836.

Tuskegee University, Graduate Programs, College of Agricultural, Environmental and Natural Sciences, Department of Agricultural Sciences, Tuskegee, AL 36088. Offers agricultural economics (MS); animal and poultry sciences (MS); environmental sciences (MS); soil sciences and management (MS). *Faculty:* 17 full-time (4 women), 2 part-time (1 woman). *Students:* 25 full-time (15 women), 15 part-time (7 women); includes 38 minority (35 African Americans, 2 Asian Americans or Pacific Islanders, 1 Native American) Average age 24. In 1998, 9 degrees awarded. *Degree requirements:* For master's, computer language, thesis required, foreign language not required. *Entrance requirements:* For master's, GRE General Test. *Application deadline:* For fall admission, 7/15. Applications are processed on a rolling basis. Application fee: $25 ($35 for international students). *Financial aid:* In 1998–99, 5 fellowships, 4 research assistantships were awarded. Financial aid application deadline: 4/15. *Unit head:* Dr. P. K. Biswas, Head, 334-727-8632.

Université Laval, Faculty of Graduate Studies, Faculty of Agricultural and Food Sciences, Sainte-Foy, PQ G1K 7P4, Canada. Offers M Sc, PhD, Diploma. *Students:* 281 full-time (129 women), 65 part-time (34 women), 96 international. Average age 30. 186 applicants, 55% accepted. In 1998, 69 master's, 18 doctorates awarded. *Application deadline:* For fall admission, 3/1. Application fee: $30. *Unit head:* Jean-Claude Dufour, Dean, 418-656-2131 Ext. 3496, Fax: 418-656-7821, E-mail: jean-claude.dufour@eac.ulaval.ca.

University of Alberta, Faculty of Graduate Studies and Research, Department of Agricultural, Food and Nutritional Science, Edmonton, AB T6G 2E1, Canada. Offers M Ag, M Eng, M Sc, PhD, MBA/M Ag. *Degree requirements:* For master's and doctorate, thesis/dissertation required, foreign language not required. *Faculty research:* Animal science, food scieence, nutrition and metabolism, bioresource engineering, plant science and range management.

The University of Arizona, Graduate College, College of Agriculture, Tucson, AZ 85721. Offers M Ag Ed, MHE Ed, ML Arch, MS, PhD. Part-time programs available. *Faculty:* 248. *Students:* 364 full-time (161 women), 146 part-time (66 women). Average age 35. In 1998, 70 master's, 34 doctorates awarded. *Degree requirements:* For doctorate, dissertation required. *Entrance requirements:* For master's and doctorate, TOEFL (minimum score of 550 required). *Application deadline:* Applications are processed on a rolling basis. Application fee: $35. *Financial aid:* Fellowships, research assistantships, teaching assistantships, career-related internships or fieldwork, Federal Work-Study, institutionally-sponsored loans, scholarships, and tuition waivers (full and partial) available. *Unit head:* Dr. Eugene G. Sander, Dean, 520-621-7621, Fax: 520-621-7196. *Application contact:* Dr. W. David Shoup, Associate Dean, 520-621-3613.

See in-depth description on page 857.

University of Arkansas, Graduate School, Dale Bumpers College of Agricultural, Food and Life Sciences, Fayetteville, AR 72701-1201. Offers MAT, MS, PhD. *Faculty:* 146 full-time (16 women), 5 part-time (0 women). *Students:* 226 full-time (104 women), 30 part-time (8 women); includes 25 minority (12 African Americans, 9 Asian Americans or Pacific Islanders, 3 Hispanic Americans, 1 Native American), 78 international. 175 applicants, 64% accepted. In 1998, 54 master's, 24 doctorates awarded. *Degree requirements:* For doctorate, dissertation required. Application fee: $40 ($50 for international students). Tuition, state resident: full-time $3,186. Tuition, nonresident: full-time $7,560. Required fees: $378. *Financial aid:* In 1998–99, 153 research assistantships, 18 teaching assistantships were awarded.; fellowships, career-related internships or fieldwork, Federal Work-Study, scholarships, and unspecified assistantships also available. Aid available to part-time students. Financial aid application deadline: 4/1; financial aid applicants required to submit FAFSA. *Unit head:* Dr. C. J. Scifres, Dean, 501-575-2252.

University of British Columbia, Faculty of Graduate Studies, Faculty of Agricultural Sciences, Vancouver, BC V6T 1Z2, Canada. Offers M Sc, MA, MASLA, MLA, PhD. Part-time programs available. *Entrance requirements:* For master's and doctorate, TOEFL.

University of California, Davis, Graduate Studies, Program in International Agricultural Development, Davis, CA 95616. Offers MS. *Faculty:* 82 full-time (11 women). *Students:* 30 full-time (19 women); includes 1 minority (Native American), 6 international. Average age 29. 34 applicants, 76% accepted. In 1998, 11 degrees awarded. *Degree requirements:* For master's, thesis optional. *Entrance requirements:* For master's, GRE General Test, minimum GPA of 3.0. *Application deadline:* For fall admission, 1/15. Application fee: $40. Electronic applications accepted. *Financial aid:* In 1998–99, 8 fellowships with full and partial tuition reimbursements, 12 research assistantships with full and partial tuition reimbursements, 8 teaching assistantships with full and partial tuition reimbursements were awarded.; Federal Work-Study, grants, and scholarships also available. Financial aid application deadline: 1/15; financial aid applicants required to submit FAFSA. *Faculty research:* Aspects of agricultural, environmental and social sciences on agriculture and related issues in developing countries. *Unit head:* Graduate Adviser, 530-752-1926, Fax: 530-752-5660. *Application contact:* Judy Erwin, Graduate Assistant, 530-752-1926, Fax: 530-752-5660, E-mail: gjerwin@ucdavis.edu.

University of Connecticut, Graduate School, College of Agriculture and Natural Resources, Storrs, CT 06269. Offers MS, PhD. *Degree requirements:* For doctorate, dissertation required.

University of Delaware, College of Agriculture and Natural Resources, Newark, DE 19716. Offers MS, PhD. Part-time programs available. *Degree requirements:* For master's and doctorate, thesis/dissertation required, foreign language not required. *Entrance requirements:* For master's and doctorate, GRE General Test. Electronic applications accepted.

University of Florida, Graduate School, College of Agriculture, Gainesville, FL 32611. Offers M Ag, MAB, ME, MFAS, MFRC, MS, MST, PhD, Engr, JD/MFRC, JD/MS, JD/PhD. Part-time programs available. *Faculty:* 727. *Students:* 501 full-time (200 women), 169 part-time (73 women); includes 75 minority (17 African Americans, 22 Asian Americans or Pacific Islanders, 36 Hispanic Americans), 210 international. 608 applicants, 48% accepted. In 1998, 129 master's, 50 doctorates awarded. *Degree requirements:* For doctorate, dissertation required. *Entrance requirements:* For master's and doctorate, GRE General Test. *Application deadline:* Applications are processed on a rolling basis. Application fee: $20. Electronic applications accepted. *Financial aid:* In 1998–99, 390 students received aid, including 30 fellowships, 290 research assistantships, 45 teaching assistantships; career-related internships or fieldwork, Federal Work-Study, institutionally-sponsored loans, and unspecified assistantships also available. Aid available to part-time students. *Unit head:* Dr. Jimmy Cheek, Dean, 352-392-1961, Fax: 352-392-8988, E-mail: jgc@gnv.ifas.ufl.edu. *Application contact:* Dr. Rachel Shireman, Assistant Dean for Academic Programs, 352-392-2251, Fax: 352-392-8988, E-mail: rbs@gnv.ifas.ufl.edu.

University of Georgia, Graduate School, College of Agricultural and Environmental Sciences, Athens, GA 30602. Offers MA Ext, MAE, MPPPM, MS, PhD. *Faculty:* 236 full-time (22 women). *Students:* 268 full-time (115 women), 50 part-time (17 women). 323 applicants, 34% accepted. In 1998, 57 master's, 46 doctorates awarded. *Degree requirements:* For doctorate, dissertation required, foreign language not required. *Entrance requirements:* For master's and doctorate, GRE General Test. *Application deadline:* For fall admission, 7/1 (priority date); for spring admission, 11/15. Application fee: $30. Electronic applications accepted. *Financial aid:* Fellowships, research assistantships, teaching assistantships, career-related internships or fieldwork and unspecified assistantships available. *Unit head:* Dr. Gale A. Buchanan, Dean, 706-542-3924, Fax: 706-542-0803.

University of Guelph, Faculty of Graduate Studies, Ontario Agricultural College, Guelph, ON N1G 2W1, Canada. Offers M Sc, MLA, PhD. Part-time programs available. *Students:* 401 full-time (185 women), 74 part-time (27 women). In 1998, 116 master's, 35 doctorates awarded. *Degree requirements:* For doctorate, dissertation required. Application fee: $60. *Expenses:* Tuition and fees charges are reported in Canadian dollars. Tuition, area resident: Full-time $4,725 Canadian dollars; part-time $1,055 Canadian dollars per term. International tuition: $6,999 Canadian dollars full-time. Required fees: $295 Canadian dollars per term. *Financial aid:* Fellowships, research assistantships, teaching assistantships, scholarships and unspecified assistantships available. Aid available to part-time students. *Unit head:* Dr. R. J. McLaughlin, Dean, 519-824-4120 Ext. 2285, E-mail: mclaughl@oac.uoguelph.ca.

University of Hawaii at Manoa, Graduate Division, College of Tropical Agriculture and Human Resources, Honolulu, HI 96822. Offers MS, PhD. Part-time programs available. *Faculty:* 219 full-time (34 women). *Students:* 78 full-time (37 women), 49 part-time (20 women); includes 1 African American, 15 Asian Americans or Pacific Islanders, 61 international. 132 applicants, 43% accepted. In 1998, 18 master's, 12 doctorates awarded. *Degree requirements:* For doctorate, dissertation required, foreign language not required. *Entrance requirements:* For doctorate, GRE. *Application deadline:* For fall admission, 3/1; for spring admission, 9/1. Application fee: $25 ($50 for international students). *Financial aid:* In 1998–99, 53 research assistantships (averaging $15,556 per year), 13 teaching assistantships (averaging $13,028 per year) were awarded.; fellowships, career-related internships or fieldwork, Federal Work-Study, institutionally-sponsored loans, tuition waivers (full and partial), and unspecified assistantships also available. *Unit head:* Dr. Charles Laughlin, Dean, 808-956-8234, Fax: 808-956-9105, E-mail: ta_deanl@avax.ctahr.hawaii.edu.

See in-depth description on page 861.

University of Idaho, College of Graduate Studies, College of Agriculture, Moscow, ID 83844-4140. Offers M Engr, MS, PhD. *Faculty:* 99 full-time (21 women), 4 part-time (2 women). *Students:* 101 full-time (41 women), 81 part-time (27 women); includes 4 minority (2 African Americans, 2 Asian Americans or Pacific Islanders), 38 international. In 1998, 37 master's, 12 doctorates awarded. *Degree requirements:* For doctorate, dissertation required, foreign language not required. *Application deadline:* For fall admission, 8/1; for spring admission, 12/15. Application fee: $35 ($45 for international students). *Financial aid:* Research assistantships, teaching assistantships, career-related internships or fieldwork and Federal Work-Study available. Aid available to part-time students. Financial aid application deadline: 2/15. *Unit head:* Dr. Larry Branen, Dean, 208-885-6681.

University of Illinois at Urbana–Champaign, Graduate College, College of Agricultural, Consumer and Environmental Sciences, Urbana, IL 61801. Offers AM, MS, PhD, MD/PhD. *Faculty:* 241 full-time (58 women). *Students:* 503 full-time (214 women); includes 44 minority (17 African Americans, 16 Asian Americans or Pacific Islanders, 8 Hispanic Americans, 3 Native Americans), 163 international. 358 applicants, 26% accepted. In 1998, 140 master's, 54 doctorates awarded. *Degree requirements:* For doctorate, dissertation required. *Entrance requirements:* For master's, minimum GPA of 4.0 on a 5.0 scale. *Application deadline:* Applications are processed on a rolling basis. Application fee: $40 ($50 for international students). Tuition, state resident: full-time $4,040. Tuition, nonresident: full-time $11,192. Full-time tuition and fees vary according to program. *Financial aid:* In 1998–99, 21 fellowships, 396 research assistantships, 53 teaching assistantships were awarded.; career-related internships or fieldwork and tuition waivers (full and partial) also available. Financial aid application deadline: 2/15. *Unit head:* David L. Chicoine, Dean, 217-333-0460. *Application contact:* Wesley D. Seitz, Director of Graduate Studies, 217-333-6313, Fax: 217-333-5538, E-mail: w-seitz@uiuc.edu.

University of Kentucky, Graduate School, Graduate School Programs from the College of Agriculture, Lexington, KY 40506-0032. Offers MS, MS Ag, MSFOR, PhD. Part-time programs available. Terminal master's awarded for partial completion of doctoral program. *Degree requirements:* For master's, comprehensive exam required; for doctorate, comprehensive exam required. *Entrance requirements:* For master's and doctorate, GRE General Test.

University of Maine, Graduate School, College of Natural Sciences, Forestry, and Agriculture, Orono, ME 04469. Offers MF, MPS, MS, MWC, PhD. *Accreditation:* SAF (one or more programs are accredited). Part-time and evening/weekend programs available. *Students:* 288 (148 women). *Degree requirements:* For doctorate, dissertation required. *Entrance requirements:* For master's and doctorate, GRE General Test, TOEFL (minimum score of 550 required). *Application deadline:* For fall admission, 2/1 (priority date); for spring admission, 10/15. Applications are processed on a rolling basis. Application fee: $50. *Financial aid:* Fellowships, research assistantships, teaching assistantships, career-related internships or fieldwork, Federal Work-Study, grants, institutionally-sponsored loans, scholarships, tuition waivers (full and partial), and unspecified assistantships available. Aid available to part-time students. Financial aid application deadline: 3/1. *Unit head:* Dr. G. Bruce Wiersma, Dean, 207-581-3202, Fax: 207-581-3207. *Application contact:* Scott G. Delcourt, Director of the Graduate School, 207-581-3218, Fax: 207-581-3232, E-mail: graduate@maine.edu.

University of Manitoba, Faculty of Graduate Studies, Faculty of Agriculture, Winnipeg, MB R3T 2N2, Canada. Offers M Sc, PhD. *Degree requirements:* For master's, thesis or alternative required, foreign language not required; for doctorate, dissertation required. *Unit head:* J. I. Elliot, Dean.

University of Maryland, College Park, Graduate School, College of Agriculture and Natural Resources, College Park, MD 20742-5045. Offers MS, PhD. Part-time and evening/weekend programs available. *Faculty:* 352 full-time (128 women), 39 part-time (22 women). *Students:* 123 full-time (68 women), 96 part-time (55 women); includes 29 minority (13 African Americans, 14 Asian Americans or Pacific Islanders, 2 Hispanic Americans), 76 international. 317 applicants, 28% accepted. In 1998, 31 master's, 17 doctorates awarded. *Degree requirements:* For doctorate, dissertation required. *Entrance requirements:* For master's, minimum GPA of 3.0. *Application deadline:* Applications are processed on a rolling basis. Application fee: $50 ($70 for international students). Tuition, state resident: part-time $272 per credit hour. Tuition, nonresident: part-time $475 per credit hour. Required fees: $632; $379 per year. *Financial aid:* In 1998–99, 5 fellowships with full tuition reimbursements (averaging $15,310 per year), 111 research assistantships with tuition reimbursements (averaging $13,450 per year), 48 teaching assistantships with tuition reimbursements (averaging $10,874 per year) were awarded.; career-related internships or fieldwork, Federal Work-Study, grants, and scholarships also available. Aid available to part-time students. Financial aid applicants required to submit FAFSA. Total annual research expenditures: $4.1 million. *Unit head:* Dr. Thomas Fretz, Dean, 301-405-4685, Fax: 301-314-9146. *Application contact:* Trudy Lindsey, Director, Graduate Admission and Records, 301-405-4198, Fax: 301-314-9305, E-mail: grschool@deans.umd.edu.

University of Minnesota, Twin Cities Campus, Graduate School, College of Agricultural, Food, and Environmental Sciences, Minneapolis, MN 55455-0213. Offers M Ag, M Ed, MA, MBAE, MS, MSBAE, Ed D, PhD. Part-time and evening/weekend programs available. *Degree requirements:* For doctorate, dissertation required.

University of Missouri–Columbia, Graduate School, College of Agriculture, Columbia, MO 65211. Offers MS, PhD, MD/MS, MD/PhD. Part-time programs available. *Faculty:* 133 full-time (13 women), 4 part-time (1 woman). *Students:* 133 full-time (51 women), 92 part-time (35 women); includes 14 minority (11 African Americans, 2 Asian Americans or Pacific Islanders, 1 Hispanic American), 93 international. 66 applicants, 53% accepted. In 1998, 29 master's, 24 doctorates awarded. *Degree requirements:* For doctorate, dissertation required. *Entrance requirements:* For master's and doctorate, GRE General Test, minimum GPA of 3.0. *Application deadline:* Applications are processed on a rolling basis. Application fee: $30 ($50 for international students). *Financial aid:* Fellowships, research assistantships, teaching assistantships, institutionally-sponsored loans available. *Unit head:* Dr. Thomas T. Payne, Dean, 573-882-3846.

University of Nebraska–Lincoln, Graduate College, College of Agricultural Sciences and Natural Resources, Lincoln, NE 68588. Offers MS, PhD. *Faculty:* 207 full-time (21 women), 6 part-time (0 women). *Students:* 242 full-time (86 women), 135 part-time (46 women); includes 13 minority (6 African Americans, 3 Asian Americans or Pacific Islanders, 4 Hispanic Americans), 158 international. Average age 31. 205 applicants, 42% accepted. In 1998, 86 master's, 46 doctorates awarded. *Degree requirements:* For doctorate, dissertation, comprehensive exams required. *Entrance requirements:* For master's and doctorate, TOEFL. *Average time to degree:* Doctorate–3.9 years full-time. Application fee: $35. Electronic applications accepted. *Financial aid:* In 1998–99, 40 fellowships, 236 research assistantships, 31 teaching assistantships were awarded.; career-related internships or fieldwork and Federal Work-Study also available. Aid available to part-time students. Financial aid application deadline: 2/15. *Faculty research:* Environmental sciences, animal sciences, human resources and family sciences, plant breeding and genetics, food and nutrition. *Unit head:* Dr. Donald M. Edwards, Dean, 402-472-2201.

University of Nevada, Reno, Graduate School, M. C. Fleischmann College of Agriculture, Reno, NV 89557. Offers MS, PhD. *Degree requirements:* For master's, thesis optional, foreign language not required; for doctorate, dissertation required. *Entrance requirements:* For master's, GRE, TOEFL (minimum score of 500 required), minimum GPA of 2.75; for doctorate, TOEFL (minimum score of 500 required), minimum GPA of 3.0.

University of New Hampshire, Graduate School, College of Life Sciences and Agriculture, Durham, NH 03824. Offers MAOE, MS, PhD. Part-time programs available. *Faculty:* 135 full-time. *Students:* 145 full-time (85 women), 132 part-time (73 women); includes 8 minority (5 Asian Americans or Pacific Islanders, 3 Hispanic Americans), 34 international. Average age 34. 279 applicants, 41% accepted. In 1998, 47 master's, 17 doctorates awarded. Terminal master's awarded for partial completion of doctoral program. *Degree requirements:* For doctorate, dissertation required, foreign language not required. *Application deadline:* Applications are processed on a rolling basis. Application fee: $50. Tuition, area resident: Full-time $5,750; part-time $319 per credit. Tuition, state resident: full-time $8,625. Tuition, nonresident: full-time $14,640; part-time $598 per credit. Required fees: $224 per semester. Tuition and fees vary according to course load, degree level and program. *Financial aid:* In 1998–99, 9 fellowships, 70 research assistantships, 78 teaching assistantships were awarded.; career-related internships or fieldwork, Federal Work-Study, scholarships, and tuition waivers (full and partial) also available. Aid available to part-time students. Financial aid application deadline: 2/15. *Unit head:* Dr. William Mautz, Interim Dean, 603-862-1450.

University of Puerto Rico, Mayagüez Campus, Graduate Studies, College of Agricultural Sciences, Mayagüez, PR 00681-5000. Offers MS. Part-time programs available. *Degree requirements:* For master's, thesis, comprehensive exam required, foreign language not required.

University of Saskatchewan, College of Graduate Studies and Research, College of Agriculture, Saskatoon, SK S7N 5A2, Canada. Offers M Ag, M Sc, MA, PhD. Part-time programs available. *Degree requirements:* For master's and doctorate, thesis/dissertation required. *Entrance requirements:* For master's, CANTEST (minimum score of 4.5 required) or International English Language Testing System (minimum score of 6 required) or Michigan English Language Assessment Battery (minimum score of 80 required), orTOEFL (minimum score of 550 required; average 560); for doctorate, TOEFL.

University of Tennessee, Knoxville, Graduate School, College of Agricultural Sciences and Natural Resources, Knoxville, TN 37996. Offers MS, PhD. Part-time programs available. Postbaccalaureate distance learning degree programs offered (minimal on-campus study). *Faculty:* 115 full-time (12 women). *Students:* 128 full-time (51 women), 90 part-time (31 women); includes 11 minority (7 African Americans, 3 Asian Americans or Pacific Islanders, 1 Hispanic American), 30 international. 172 applicants, 52% accepted. In 1998, 55 master's, 9 doctorates awarded. *Degree requirements:* For master's, thesis required (for some programs), foreign language not required; for doctorate, dissertation required, foreign language not required. *Entrance requirements:* For master's and doctorate, TOEFL (minimum score of 550 required), minimum GPA of 2.7. *Application deadline:* For fall admission, 2/1 (priority date). Applications are processed on a rolling basis. Application fee: $35. Electronic applications accepted. *Financial aid:* In 1998–99, 1 fellowship with full tuition reimbursement, 104 research assistantships with full tuition reimbursements, 23 teaching assistantships with full tuition reimbursements were awarded.; career-related internships or fieldwork, Federal Work-Study, institutionally-sponsored loans, and unspecified assistantships also available. Financial aid application deadline: 2/1; financial aid applicants required to submit FAFSA. *Unit head:* Dr. John Riley, Dean, 423-974-7303.

University of Vermont, Graduate College, College of Agriculture and Life Sciences, Burlington, VT 05405-0160. Offers M Ext Ed, MAT, MS, MST, PhD. Part-time programs available. *Degree requirements:* For doctorate, dissertation required. *Entrance requirements:* For master's and doctorate, GRE General Test, TOEFL (minimum score of 550 required).

University of Wisconsin–Madison, Graduate School, College of Agricultural and Life Sciences, Madison, WI 53706-1380. Offers MA, MBA, MS, PhD. MBA (agribusiness) offered jointly with the School of Business. Part-time programs available. Electronic applications accepted.

University of Wisconsin–Platteville, School of Graduate Studies, College of Business, Industry, Life Science, and Agriculture, Program in Agricultural Industries, Platteville, WI 53818-3099. Offers MS. Part-time programs available. *Degree requirements:* For master's, thesis or alternative, comprehensive exam required, foreign language not required. *Entrance requirements:* For master's, TOEFL (minimum score of 500 required). Electronic applications accepted.

University of Wisconsin–River Falls, School of Graduate and Professional Studies, College of Agriculture, Food, and Environmental Sciences, River Falls, WI 54022-5001. Offers MS. *Students:* 3 (2 women). *Degree requirements:* For master's, thesis required, foreign language not required. *Application deadline:* For fall admission, 3/1. Application fee: $45. Tuition, state resident: full-time $3,892. Tuition, nonresident: full-time $12,250. *Financial aid:* Research assistantships, Federal Work-Study available. Financial aid application deadline: 3/1; financial aid applicants required to submit FAFSA. *Unit head:* Gary E. Rohde, Dean, 715-425-3841, E-mail: gary.e.rohde@uwrf.edu. *Application contact:* Graduate Admissions, 715-425-3843.

University of Wyoming, Graduate School, College of Agriculture, Laramie, WY 82071. Offers MS, PhD. Part-time programs available. *Faculty:* 84. *Students:* 96 full-time (46 women), 47 part-time (24 women); includes 2 minority (1 African American, 1 Asian American or Pacific Islander), 24 international. 107 applicants, 38% accepted. In 1998, 28 master's, 12 doctorates awarded. Terminal master's awarded for partial completion of doctoral program. *Degree requirements:* For doctorate, dissertation required, dissertation required, foreign language not required. *Entrance requirements:* For master's and doctorate, GRE General Test, minimum GPA of 3.0. *Average time to degree:* Master's–2.25 years full-time; doctorate–4 years full-time. *Application deadline:* Applications are processed on a rolling basis. Application fee: $40. Electronic applications accepted. Tuition, state resident: full-time $2,520; part-time $140 per credit hour. Tuition, nonresident: full-time $7,790; part-time $433 per credit hour. Required fees: $400; $7 per credit hour. Full-time tuition and fees vary according to course load and program. *Financial aid:* In 1998–99, 3 fellowships, 15 research assistantships, 32 teaching assistantships were awarded.; career-related internships or fieldwork, Federal Work-Study, institutionally-sponsored loans, and tuition waivers (partial) also available. Financial aid application deadline: 3/1. *Faculty research:* Nutrition, molecular biology, animal science, plant science. *Unit head:* Steven Horn, Dean, 307-766-4133.

Utah State University, School of Graduate Studies, College of Agriculture, Logan, UT 84322. Offers MA, MCED, MS, MSS, PhD. Part-time programs available. Postbaccalaureate distance learning degree programs offered (minimal on-campus study). *Students:* 38 full-time (13 women), 22 part-time (6 women); includes 1 minority (African American), 14 international. Average age 30. 67 applicants, 45% accepted. In 1998, 10 master's, 4 doctorates awarded. Terminal master's awarded for partial completion of doctoral program. *Degree requirements:* For doctorate, dissertation required, foreign language not required, foreign language not required. *Entrance requirements:* For master's and doctorate, GRE General Test (score in 40th percentile or higher required), TOEFL (minimum score of 550 required), minimum GPA of 3.0. *Application deadline:* For spring admission, 10/15. Applications are processed on a rolling basis. Application fee: $40. Tuition, state resident: full-time $1,492. Tuition, nonresident: full-time $5,232. Required fees: $434. Tuition and fees vary according to course load. *Financial aid:* Fellowships, research assistantships, teaching assistantships, career-related internships or fieldwork, Federal Work-Study, institutionally-sponsored loans, scholarships, and tuition waivers (full and partial) available. Aid available to part-time students. *Unit head:* Dr. Rodney Brown, Dean, 435-797-2215.

Virginia Polytechnic Institute and State University, Graduate School, College of Agriculture and Life Sciences, Blacksburg, VA 24061. Offers MS, PhD. Part-time programs available. *Students:* 203 full-time (85 women), 68 part-time (32 women); includes 23 minority (12 African Americans, 5 Asian Americans or Pacific Islanders, 6 Hispanic Americans), 63 international. 269 applicants, 41% accepted. In 1998, 43 master's, 27 doctorates awarded. *Entrance requirements:* For master's and doctorate, TOEFL. *Application deadline:* For fall admission, 12/1 (priority date). Applications are processed on a rolling basis. Application fee: $25. *Financial aid:* Fellowships, research assistantships, teaching assistantships, career-related internships or fieldwork, Federal Work-Study, institutionally-sponsored loans, tuition waivers (full and partial), and unspecified assistantships available. Aid available to part-time students. Financial aid application deadline: 4/1. *Unit head:* Dr. L. A. Swiger, Dean, 540-231-4152.

Washington State University, Graduate School, College of Agriculture and Home Economics, Pullman, WA 99164. Offers MA, MS, PhD. Part-time programs available. *Students:* 238 full-time (113 women), 44 part-time (26 women); includes 23 minority (4 African Americans, 11 Asian Americans or Pacific Islanders, 7 Hispanic Americans, 1 Native American), 94 international. In 1998, 48 master's, 19 doctorates awarded. Terminal master's awarded for partial completion of doctoral program. *Degree requirements:* For master's, oral exam required; for doctorate, dissertation, oral exam required, foreign language not required. *Entrance requirements:* For master's and doctorate, minimum GPA of 3.0. *Average time to degree:* Master's–2 years full-time; doctorate–4 years full-time. *Application deadline:* Applications are processed on a rolling basis. Application fee: $35. Electronic applications accepted. *Financial aid:* In 1998–99, 10 fellowships, 107 research assistantships, 50 teaching assistantships were awarded.; career-related internships or fieldwork, Federal Work-Study, institutionally-sponsored loans, tuition waivers (partial), unspecified assistantships, and staff assistantships, teaching associateships also available. Financial aid application deadline: 4/1; financial aid applicants required to submit FAFSA. Total annual research expenditures: $25 million. *Unit head:* Dr. James Zuiches, Dean, 509-335-4561.

Western Kentucky University, Graduate Studies, Ogden College of Science, Technology, and Health, Department of Agriculture, Bowling Green, KY 42101-3576. Offers MA Ed, MS. Part-time and evening/weekend programs available. *Faculty:* 12 full-time (1 woman). *Students:* 5 full-time (2 women), 14 part-time (4 women); includes 1 minority (African American), 2 international. Average age 27. 14 applicants, 57% accepted. In 1998, 6 degrees awarded. *Degree requirements:* For master's, thesis or alternative, comprehensive exam required. *Entrance requirements:* For master's, GRE General Test. *Application deadline:* For fall admission, 8/1 (priority date); for spring admission, 12/1. Applications are processed on a rolling basis. Application fee: $30. Tuition, state resident: full-time $2,590; part-time $140 per hour. Tuition, nonresident: full-time $6,430; part-time $387 per hour. Required fees: $370. *Financial aid:* In 1998–99, 2 research assistantships with partial tuition reimbursements (averaging $3,800 per year), 1 teaching assistantship with partial tuition reimbursement (averaging $3,800 per year) were awarded.; Federal Work-Study, institutionally-sponsored loans, and service awards also available. Aid available to part-time students. Financial aid application deadline: 4/1; financial aid applicants required to submit FAFSA. *Faculty research:* Forage and environmental science. *Unit head:* Dr. Jenks Britt, Head, 270-745-5960, Fax: 270-745-5972.

West Texas A&M University, College of Agriculture, Nursing, and Natural Sciences, Division of Agriculture, Canyon, TX 79016-0001. Offers agricultural business and economics (MS); agriculture (MS); animal science (MS); plant science (MS). Part-time programs available. *Faculty:* 10 full-time (0 women), 13 part-time (1 woman). *Students:* 17 full-time (7 women), 24 part-time (2 women); includes 1 minority (African American), 4 international. Average age 34. 5 applicants, 20% accepted. In 1998, 5 degrees awarded. *Degree requirements:* For master's, comprehensive exam required, thesis optional, foreign language not required. *Entrance requirements:* For master's, GRE General Test (minimum combined score of 950 required; average 964). *Average time to degree:* Master's–3 years full-time, 6 years part-time. *Application deadline:* Applications are processed on a rolling basis. Application fee: $0 ($50 for international students). Electronic applications accepted. Tuition, state resident: full-time $1,152; part-time $48 per credit. Tuition, nonresident: full-time $6,336; part-time $264 per credit. Required fees: $1,063; $531 per semester. *Financial aid:* In 1998–99, research assistantships with tuition reimbursements (averaging $6,500 per year), 16 teaching assistantships with tuition reimbursements (averaging $6,500 per year) were awarded.; Federal Work-Study, grants, institutionally-sponsored loans, scholarships, traineeships, and tuition waivers (partial) also available. Aid available to part-time students. Financial aid applicants required to submit FAFSA. *Faculty research:* Pest management. Total annual research expenditures: $1.4 million. *Unit head:* Dr. Donald Topliff, Head, 806-651-2550, Fax: 806-651-2938, E-mail: dtopliff@mail.wtamu.edu.

West Virginia University, College of Agriculture, Forestry and Consumer Sciences, Morgantown, WV 26506. Offers M Agr, MS, MSF, PhD. Part-time programs available. *Entrance requirements:* For master's and doctorate, TOEFL (minimum score of 550 required). *Faculty research:* Production agriculture and forestry, forage production, reproductive physiology, marketing, land reclamation, resource economics.

Agronomy and Soil Sciences

Alabama Agricultural and Mechanical University, School of Graduate Studies, School of Agricultural and Environmental Sciences, Department of Plant, Soil and Animal Sciences, Normal, AL 35762-1357. Offers animal sciences (MS); environmental science (MS); plant and soil science (PhD). Evening/weekend programs available. *Faculty:* 12 full-time (1 woman). *Students:* 11 full-time (6 women), 29 part-time (4 women); includes 28 minority (27 African Americans, 1 Asian American or Pacific Islander), 12 international. In 1998, 2 master's awarded (100% found work related to degree); 1 doctorate awarded (100% entered university research/teaching). Terminal master's awarded for partial completion of doctoral program. *Degree requirements:* For master's, thesis required, foreign language not required; for doctorate, one foreign language, computer language, dissertation required. *Entrance requirements:* For master's, GRE General Test, BS in agriculture; for doctorate, GRE General Test (minimum combined score of 1000 required), MS. *Average time to degree:* Master's–3 years full-time; doctorate–7 years full-time. *Application deadline:* For fall admission, 5/1. Applications are processed on a rolling basis. Application fee: $15 ($20 for international students). Tuition, state resident: full-time $1,932. Tuition, nonresident: full-time $3,864. Tuition and fees vary according to course load. *Financial aid:* In 1998–99, 1 fellowship with tuition reimbursement (averaging $18,000 per year), 9 research assistantships with tuition reimbursements (averaging $9,000 per year) were awarded.; career-related internships or fieldwork and Federal Work-Study also available. Financial aid application deadline: 4/1. *Faculty research:* Plant breeding, cytogenetics, crop production, soil chemistry and fertility, remote sensing. *Unit head:* Dr. Govind Sharma, Chair, 256-851-5462.

Agronomy and Soil Sciences

Alcorn State University, School of Graduate Studies, School of Agriculture and Applied Science, Lorman, MS 39096-9402. Offers agricultural economics (MS Ag); agronomy (MS Ag); animal science (MS Ag). *Degree requirements:* For master's, thesis optional, foreign language not required. *Faculty research:* Aquatic systems, dairy herd improvement, fruit production, alternative farming practices.

Auburn University, Graduate School, College of Agriculture, Department of Agronomy and Soils, Auburn, Auburn University, AL 36849-0002. Offers M Ag, MS, PhD. Part-time programs available. *Faculty:* 25 full-time (2 women). *Students:* 20 full-time (7 women), 14 part-time (1 woman), 13 international. 7 applicants, 100% accepted. In 1998, 8 master's, 3 doctorates awarded. *Degree requirements:* For master's, thesis (MS) required; for doctorate, dissertation required, foreign language not required. *Entrance requirements:* For master's, GRE General Test; for doctorate, GRE General Test (minimum score of 400 on each section required). *Application deadline:* For fall admission, 9/1; for spring admission, 3/1. Applications are processed on a rolling basis. Application fee: $25 ($50 for international students). Tuition, state resident: full-time $2,760; part-time $76 per credit hour. Tuition, nonresident: full-time $8,280; part-time $228 per credit hour. *Financial aid:* Research assistantships, teaching assistantships, Federal Work-Study available. Aid available to part-time students. Financial aid application deadline: 3/15. *Faculty research:* Plant breeding and genetics; weed science; crop production; soil fertility and plant nutrition; soil genesis,morphology, and classification. *Unit head:* Dr. Joseph T. Touchton, Head, 334-844-4100, E-mail: jtouchto@ag.auburn.edu. *Application contact:* Dr. John F. Pritchett, Dean of the Graduate School, 334-844-4700.

Brigham Young University, Graduate Studies, College of Biological and Agricultural Sciences, Department of Agronomy and Horticulture, Provo, UT 84602-1001. Offers agronomy (MS); horticulture (MS). *Faculty:* 10 full-time (0 women). *Students:* 7 full-time (2 women), 1 international. Average age 25. 7 applicants, 57% accepted. In 1998, 7 degrees awarded (43% found work related to degree, 29% continued full-time study). *Degree requirements:* For master's, thesis optional, foreign language not required. *Entrance requirements:* For master's, GRE General Test (minimum combined score of 1400 required; average 1447), minimum GPA of 3.0 during previous 2 years. *Average time to degree:* Master's–2 years full-time, 4 years part-time. *Application deadline:* For fall admission, 2/15. Applications are processed on a rolling basis. Application fee: $30. Tuition: Full-time $3,330; part-time $185 per credit hour. Tuition and fees vary according to program and student's religious affiliation. *Financial aid:* In 1998–99, 2 research assistantships with partial tuition reimbursements, 5 teaching assistantships with partial tuition reimbursements were awarded.; institutionally-sponsored loans, scholarships, and tuition waivers (partial) also available. Financial aid application deadline: 3/1. *Faculty research:* Iron nutrition in plants–mode of uptake, photosynthesis, forage quality, seed physiology/modeling, cytogenetics, molecular genetics. Total annual research expenditures: $35,000. *Unit head:* Dr. Von D. Jolley, Chair, 801-378-2760 Ext. 2491, Fax: 801-378-7499, E-mail: von_jolley@byu.edu.

Clemson University, Graduate School, College of Agriculture, Forestry and Life Sciences, School of Natural Resources, Faculty of Soils and Land Use, Clemson, SC 29634. Offers MS. Offered in cooperation with the Department of Agronomy. *Degree requirements:* For master's, thesis required, foreign language not required. *Entrance requirements:* For master's, GRE General Test, TOEFL. Application fee: $35. *Financial aid:* Applicants required to submit FAFSA. *Unit head:* Dr. Ralph Franklin, Chair, 864-656-3511, Fax: 864-656-3443, E-mail: soils@clemson.edu.

Clemson University, Graduate School, College of Agriculture, Forestry and Life Sciences, School of Plant, Statistical and Ecological Sciences, Department of Agronomy, Clemson, SC 29634. Offers MS, PhD. Offered in cooperation with the Faculty of Soils and Land Use. Part-time programs available. *Students:* 10 full-time (4 women), 2 part-time, 5 international. Average age 24. 4 applicants, 50% accepted. In 1998, 8 master's awarded. *Degree requirements:* For master's and doctorate, thesis/dissertation required, foreign language not required. *Entrance requirements:* For master's and doctorate, GRE General Test, TOEFL. *Application deadline:* For fall admission, 6/1. Application fee: $35. *Financial aid:* Research assistantships, career-related internships or fieldwork available. Financial aid applicants required to submit FAFSA. *Faculty research:* Soil: physical, chemical, and biological processes; plant genetics and breeding; livestock systems; weed science; environmental science. *Unit head:* Dr. Doyce Graham, Chair, 864-656-3511, Fax: 864-656-3443, E-mail: dgraham@clemson.edu. *Application contact:* Dr. R. E. Franklin, Coordinator, 864-656-3511, E-mail: rfrnkln@clemson.edu.

Colorado State University, Graduate School, College of Agricultural Sciences, Department of Soil and Crop Sciences, Fort Collins, CO 80523-0015. Offers crop science (MS, PhD); plant genetics (MS, PhD); soil science (MS, PhD). Part-time programs available. *Faculty:* 20 full-time (3 women). *Students:* 19 full-time (6 women), 12 part-time (3 women); includes 1 minority (Hispanic American), 12 international. Average age 34. 25 applicants, 56% accepted. In 1998, 6 master's, 6 doctorates awarded. *Degree requirements:* For master's, one foreign language, computer language, thesis required (for some programs); for doctorate, one foreign language, computer language, dissertation required. *Entrance requirements:* For master's, GRE General Test, TOEFL (minimum score of 550 required), minimum GPA of 3.0, appropriate bachelor's degree; for doctorate, GRE General Test, TOEFL (minimum score of 550 required), minimum GPA of 3.0, appropriate master's degree. *Application deadline:* For fall admission, 2/1 (priority date). Applications are processed on a rolling basis. Application fee: $30. Electronic applications accepted. *Financial aid:* In 1998–99, 1 fellowship, 9 research assistantships, 1 teaching assistantship were awarded.; career-related internships or fieldwork and traineeships also available. *Faculty research:* Water quality, soil fertility, soil/plant ecosystems, plant breeding, crop physiology. Total annual research expenditures: $2 million. *Unit head:* Dr. James S. Quick, Head, 970-491-6517, Fax: 970-491-0564. *Application contact:* Dr. Dan M. Smith, 970-491-6371, Fax: 970-491-0564, E-mail: dsmith@ceres.agsci.colostate.edu.

Cornell University, Graduate School, Graduate Fields of Agriculture and Life Sciences, Field of Soil, Crop, and Atmospheric Sciences, Ithaca, NY 14853. Offers agronomy (MPS, MS, PhD); atmospheric sciences (MPS, MS, PhD); environmental management (MPS); field crop science (MPS, MS, PhD); soil science (MPS, MS, PhD). *Faculty:* 44 full-time. *Students:* 42 full-time (14 women); includes 1 minority (Hispanic American), 21 international. 54 applicants, 24% accepted. In 1998, 8 master's, 11 doctorates awarded. Terminal master's awarded for partial completion of doctoral program. *Degree requirements:* For master's, thesis (MS), project paper (MPS) required; for doctorate, dissertation required, foreign language not required. *Entrance requirements:* For master's and doctorate, GRE General Test, TOEFL (minimum score of 550 required). *Application deadline:* For fall admission, 2/1. Application fee: $65. Electronic applications accepted. *Financial aid:* In 1998–99, 34 students received aid, including 5 fellowships with full tuition reimbursements available, 24 research assistantships with full tuition reimbursements available, 5 teaching assistantships with full tuition reimbursements available; institutionally-sponsored loans, scholarships, tuition waivers (full and partial), and unspecified assistantships also available. Financial aid applicants required to submit FAFSA. *Faculty research:* Environmental modeling, soil chemistry, international agriculture, weather and climate, crop physiology. *Unit head:* Director of Graduate Studies, 607-255-5457, Fax: 607-255-8615. *Application contact:* Graduate Field Assistant, 607-255-5457, E-mail: scas_grad_field@cornell.edu.

Announcement: Research covers wide spectrum of specializations. Soil science: agricultural management, environmental protection/interactions, and physics/chemistry of natural ecosystems. Environmental information science. Crop science: sustainable production, tropical cropping systems, seed science, plant responses to environmental stresses, and cell physiology/molecular biology. Atmospheric science: atmospheric and climate dynamics, statistical and applied climatology, boundary-layer meteorology and hydrology, atmospheric turbulence, planetary atmospheric dynamics, and upper atmospheric physics.

Cornell University, Graduate School, Graduate Fields of Agriculture and Life Sciences, Field of Vegetable Crops, Ithaca, NY 14853-0001. Offers MPS, MS, PhD. *Faculty:* 15 full-time. *Students:* 11 full-time (3 women), 7 international. 4 applicants, 0% accepted. In 1998, 1 doctorate awarded. Terminal master's awarded for partial completion of doctoral program. *Degree requirements:* For master's, thesis (MS), project paper (MPS) required; for doctorate, dissertation, teaching experience required, foreign language not required. *Entrance requirements:* For master's, TOEFL (minimum score of 550 required); for doctorate, GRE General Test, TOEFL (minimum score of 550 required). *Application deadline:* Applications are processed on a rolling basis. Application fee: $65. Electronic applications accepted. *Financial aid:* In 1998–99, 8 students received aid, including 6 research assistantships with full tuition reimbursements available, 2 teaching assistantships with full tuition reimbursements available; fellowships with full tuition reimbursements available, institutionally-sponsored loans and tuition waivers (full and partial) also available. Financial aid applicants required to submit FAFSA. *Faculty research:* Vegetable nutrition and physiology, post-harvest physiology and storage, new technologies including genetic, sustainable vegetable production, weed management and IPM. *Unit head:* Director of Graduate Studies, 607-255-4568, Fax: 607-255-0599. *Application contact:* Graduate Field Assistant, 607-255-4568, E-mail: cah8@cornell.edu.

Iowa State University of Science and Technology, Graduate College, College of Agriculture, Department of Agronomy, Ames, IA 50011. Offers agricultural meteorology (MS, PhD); agronomy (MS); crop production and physiology (MS, PhD); plant breeding (MS, PhD); soil science (MS, PhD). *Faculty:* 72 full-time, 8 part-time. *Students:* 111 full-time (34 women), 61 part-time (16 women); includes 4 minority (2 African Americans, 2 Hispanic Americans), 60 international. 61 applicants, 54% accepted. In 1998, 18 master's, 15 doctorates awarded. *Degree requirements:* For master's, thesis or alternative required; for doctorate, dissertation required. *Entrance requirements:* For master's and doctorate, TOEFL. *Application deadline:* For fall admission, 6/15 (priority date); for spring admission, 11/15 (priority date). Applications are processed on a rolling basis. Application fee: $20 ($50 for international students). Electronic applications accepted. Tuition, state resident: full-time $3,308. Tuition, nonresident: full-time $9,744. Part-time tuition and fees vary according to course load, campus/location and program. *Financial aid:* In 1998–99, 91 research assistantships with partial tuition reimbursements (averaging $9,340 per year), 1 teaching assistantship with partial tuition reimbursement (averaging $10,800 per year) were awarded.; fellowships, scholarships also available. *Unit head:* Dr. Tom E. Loynachan, Interim Head, 515-294-7636, Fax: 515-294-3163.

Kansas State University, Graduate School, College of Agriculture, Department of Agronomy, Manhattan, KS 66506. Offers crop science (MS, PhD); range management (MS, PhD); soil science (MS, PhD); weed science (MS, PhD). Part-time programs available. *Faculty:* 51 full-time (2 women). *Students:* 51 full-time (11 women), 5 part-time (2 women); includes 17 minority (6 African Americans, 10 Asian Americans or Pacific Islanders, 1 Hispanic American) 21 applicants, 24% accepted. In 1998, 13 master's awarded (77% found work related to degree, 23% continued full-time study); 9 doctorates awarded (33% entered university research/teaching, 67% found other work related to degree). Terminal master's awarded for partial completion of doctoral program. *Degree requirements:* For master's, thesis optional, foreign language not required; for doctorate, dissertation required, foreign language not required. *Entrance requirements:* For master's and doctorate, TOEFL (minimum score of 550 required). *Average time to degree:* Master's–2 years full-time, 3 years part-time; doctorate–4 years full-time, 5 years part-time. *Application deadline:* Applications are processed on a rolling basis. Application fee: $0 ($25 for international students). Electronic applications accepted. *Financial aid:* In 1998–99, 37 students received aid, including 2 fellowships (averaging $20,000 per year), 35 research assistantships (averaging $14,245 per year); teaching assistantships, institutionally-sponsored loans also available. Aid available to part-time students. Financial aid application deadline: 3/1; financial aid applicants required to submit FAFSA. Total annual research expenditures: $5.9 million. *Unit head:* Dr. David B. Mengel, Head, 785-532-6101, Fax: 785-532-6094. *Application contact:* Dr. Richard L. Vanderlip, Graduate Coordinator, 785-532-7249, E-mail: vanderrl@ksu.edu.

Louisiana State University and Agricultural and Mechanical College, Graduate School, College of Agriculture, Department of Agronomy, Baton Rouge, LA 70803. Offers MS, PhD. Part-time programs available. *Faculty:* 32 full-time (1 woman), 1 part-time (0 women). *Students:* 29 full-time (7 women), 5 part-time, 21 international. Average age 33. 21 applicants, 57% accepted. In 1998, 7 master's, 1 doctorate awarded. *Degree requirements:* For master's, thesis or alternative required, foreign language not required; for doctorate, dissertation required, foreign language not required. *Entrance requirements:* For master's and doctorate, GRE General Test (minimum combined score of 1000 required), TOEFL (minimum score of 550 required), minimum GPA of 3.0. *Application deadline:* For fall admission, 1/25 (priority date). Applications are processed on a rolling basis. Application fee: $25. *Financial aid:* In 1998–99, 25 research assistantships with partial tuition reimbursements (averaging $9,900 per year) were awarded.; fellowships, teaching assistantships with partial tuition reimbursements, tuition waivers (full) also available. *Faculty research:* Crop production, resource management, environmental studies, soil science, plant genetics. *Unit head:* Dr. F. A. Martin, Head, 225-388-2110, Fax: 225-388-1403, E-mail: fmartin@agctr.lsu.edu.

McGill University, Faculty of Graduate Studies and Research, Faculty of Agricultural and Environmental Sciences, Department of Agricultural and Biosystems Engineering, Montréal, PQ H3A 2T5, Canada. Offers computer applications (M Sc, M Sc A, PhD); food engineering (M Sc, M Sc A, PhD); grain drying (M Sc, M Sc A, PhD); irrigation and drainage (M Sc, M Sc A, PhD); machinery (M Sc, M Sc A, PhD); pollution control (M Sc, M Sc A, PhD); postharvest (M Sc, M Sc A, PhD); soil dynamics (M Sc, M Sc A, PhD); structure and environment (M Sc, M Sc A, PhD); vegetable and fruit storage (M Sc, M Sc A, PhD). Part-time programs available. *Faculty:* 12 full-time (2 women). *Students:* 52 full-time (9 women), 15 international. *Degree requirements:* For master's and doctorate, thesis/dissertation required. *Entrance requirements:* For master's, TOEFL (minimum score of 550 required), minimum GPA of 3.0; for doctorate, TOEFL (minimum score of 550 required), M Sc. *Application deadline:* For fall admission, 1/1 (priority date); for winter admission, 5/1 (priority date); for spring admission, 9/1 (priority date). Applications are processed on a rolling basis. Application fee: $60. *Unit head:* Dr. G. S. V. Raghavan, Chair, 514-398-7773, Fax: 514-398-8387, E-mail: raghavan@agreng.lan.mcgill.ca. *Application contact:* 514-398-7708, Fax: 514-398-7968, E-mail: grad@macdonald.mcgill.ca.

McGill University, Faculty of Graduate Studies and Research, Faculty of Agricultural and Environmental Sciences, Department of Natural Resource Sciences, Montréal, PQ H3A 2T5, Canada. Offers agrometeorology (M Sc, PhD); entomology (M Sc, PhD); forest science (M Sc, PhD); microbiology (M Sc, PhD); soil science (M Sc, PhD); wildlife biology (M Sc, PhD). *Faculty:* 18 full-time (1 woman), 26 part-time (3 women). *Students:* 83 full-time (35 women), 10 international. *Degree requirements:* For master's and doctorate, thesis/dissertation required. *Entrance requirements:* For master's, TOEFL (minimum score of 550 required), minimum GPA of 3.0; for doctorate, TOEFL (minimum score of 550 required), M Sc. *Application deadline:* For fall admission, 1/1 (priority date); for winter admission, 5/1 (priority date); for spring admission, 9/1 (priority date). Applications are processed on a rolling basis. Application fee: $60. *Unit head:* Dr. W. H. Hendershot, Chair, 514-398-7942, Fax: 514-398-7990, E-mail: chair@nrs.mcgill.ca. *Application contact:* 514-398-7708, Fax: 514-398-7968, E-mail: grad@macdonald.mcgill.ca.

Michigan State University, Graduate School, College of Agriculture and Natural Resources, Department of Crop and Soil Sciences, East Lansing, MI 48824-1020. Offers crop and soil science-environmental toxicology (PhD); crop science (MS, PhD); plant breeding and genetics-crop and soil sciences (MS, PhD); soil science (MS, PhD). *Faculty:* 33. *Students:* 41 full-time (14 women), 45 part-time (16 women); includes 8 minority (5 African Americans, 3 Hispanic Americans), 28 international. Average age 30. 48 applicants, 27% accepted. In 1998, 13 master's, 7 doctorates awarded. *Degree requirements:* For doctorate, dissertation, comprehensive exam required. *Entrance requirements:* For master's, GRE; for doctorate, GRE General Test. *Application deadline:* Applications are processed on a rolling basis. Application fee: $30 ($40 for international students). *Financial aid:* In 1998–99, 75 research assistantships (averaging $10,562 per year) were awarded.; teaching assistantships Financial aid applicants required to submit FAFSA. Total annual research expenditures: $1.8 million. *Unit head:* Dr. Boyd G. Ellis,

Agronomy and Soil Sciences

Michigan State University (continued)
Chairperson, 517-355-0271, Fax: 517-353-5174. *Application contact:* Dr. Taylor Johnston, Coordinator, 517-355-2234, E-mail: johnsto4@pilot.msu.edu.

Mississippi State University, College of Agriculture and Life Sciences, Department of Plant and Soil Sciences, Mississippi State, MS 39762. Offers agronomy (MS, PhD); horticulture (MS, PhD); weed science (MS, PhD). Part-time programs available. *Students:* 56 full-time (15 women), 37 part-time (4 women); includes 21 minority (4 African Americans, 14 Asian Americans or Pacific Islanders, 3 Hispanic Americans), 19 international. Average age 34. 27 applicants, 56% accepted. In 1998, 16 master's, 19 doctorates awarded. *Degree requirements:* For master's, thesis, comprehensive oral or written exam required, foreign language not required; for doctorate, computer language, dissertation, comprehensive oral or written exam required, foreign language not required. *Entrance requirements:* For master's and doctorate, TOEFL. *Application deadline:* For fall admission, 7/1; for spring admission, 11/1. Applications are processed on a rolling basis. Application fee: $25 for international students. *Financial aid:* Career-related internships or fieldwork, Federal Work-Study, institutionally-sponsored loans, and unspecified assistantships available. Financial aid applicants required to submit FAFSA. *Faculty research:* Metabolism, morphology, growth regulators, biotechnology, stress physiology, weed physiology, soil sciences/conservation, breeding genetics. Total annual research expenditures: $4 million. *Unit head:* Dr. Richard Mullenax, Head, 662-325-2311, Fax: 662-325-8742, E-mail: mullenax@pss.msstate.edu. *Application contact:* Jerry B. Inmon, Director of Admissions, 662-325-2224, Fax: 662-325-7360, E-mail: admit@admissions.msstate.edu.

New Mexico State University, Graduate School, College of Agriculture and Home Economics, Department of Agronomy and Horticulture, Las Cruces, NM 88003-8001. Offers general agronomy (MS, PhD); horticulture (MS). Part-time programs available. *Faculty:* 24 full-time (3 women). *Students:* 39 full-time (13 women), 20 part-time (2 women); includes 3 minority (all Hispanic Americans), 31 international. Average age 37. 34 applicants, 41% accepted. In 1998, 9 master's, 10 doctorates awarded. *Degree requirements:* For master's, thesis required, foreign language not required; for doctorate, one foreign language, dissertation required. *Entrance requirements:* For master's, minimum GPA of 3.0; for doctorate, minimum GPA of 3.3. *Application deadline:* For fall admission, 7/1 (priority date); for spring admission, 11/1. Applications are processed on a rolling basis. Application fee: $15 ($35 for international students). Electronic applications accepted. Tuition, state resident: full-time $2,682; part-time $112 per credit. Tuition, nonresident: full-time $8,376; part-time $349 per credit. Tuition and fees vary according to course load. *Financial aid:* Research assistantships, teaching assistantships, career-related internships or fieldwork and Federal Work-Study available. Aid available to part-time students. Financial aid application deadline: 3/1. *Faculty research:* Plant breeding and genetics, molecular biology, plant physiology, soil science and environmental remediation, urban horticulture. *Unit head:* Dr. James T. Fisher, Head, 505-646-3406, Fax: 505-646-6041, E-mail: jtfisher@nmsu.edu.

North Carolina State University, Graduate School, College of Agriculture and Life Sciences, Department of Crop Science, Raleigh, NC 27695. Offers M Ag, MS, PhD. Part-time programs available. *Faculty:* 59 full-time (3 women), 28 part-time (2 women). *Students:* 51 full-time (17 women), 12 part-time (4 women), 17 international. Average age 32. 20 applicants, 35% accepted. In 1998, 9 master's, 14 doctorates awarded. Terminal master's awarded for partial completion of doctoral program. *Degree requirements:* For master's, thesis (MS) required; for doctorate, dissertation required, foreign language not required. *Entrance requirements:* For master's and doctorate, GRE. *Application deadline:* For fall admission, 6/25; for spring admission, 11/25. Application fee: $45. *Financial aid:* In 1998–99, 1 fellowship (averaging $5,630 per year), 36 research assistantships (averaging $5,361 per year) were awarded.; career-related internships or fieldwork, Federal Work-Study, and institutionally-sponsored loans also available. Aid available to part-time students. Financial aid application deadline: 6/25. *Faculty research:* Crop breeding and genetics, application of biotechnology to crop improvement, plant physiology, crop physiology and management, agroecology. Total annual research expenditures: $11.8 million. *Unit head:* Dr. H. Thomas Stalker, Interim Head, 919-515-2647, Fax: 919-515-7959, E-mail: tom_stalker@ncsu.edu. *Application contact:* Dr. David A. Danehower, Interim Director of Graduate Programs, 919-515-3667, Fax: 919-515-7959, E-mail: david_danehower@ncsu.edu.

North Carolina State University, Graduate School, College of Agriculture and Life Sciences, Department of Soil Science, Raleigh, NC 27695. Offers M Ag, MS, PhD. Part-time programs available. *Faculty:* 34 full-time (1 woman), 15 part-time (0 women). *Students:* 23 full-time (5 women), 18 part-time (8 women); includes 3 minority (1 Asian American or Pacific Islander, 1 Hispanic American, 1 Native American), 11 international. Average age 35. 24 applicants, 58% accepted. In 1998, 4 master's, 3 doctorates awarded. *Degree requirements:* For master's and doctorate, thesis/dissertation required. *Entrance requirements:* For master's and doctorate, minimum GPA of 3.0. *Application deadline:* For fall admission, 6/25; for spring admission, 11/25. Application fee: $45. *Financial aid:* In 1998–99, 24 research assistantships (averaging $7,394 per year) were awarded.; fellowships, Federal Work-Study and institutionally-sponsored loans also available. Aid available to part-time students. Financial aid application deadline: 6/25. *Faculty research:* Soil fertility, soil management, soil-environmental relations, chemical and physical properties of soils, nutrient and water management. Total annual research expenditures: $6.7 million. *Unit head:* Dr. John Havlin, Head, 919-515-2655, Fax: 919-515-2167, E-mail: havlin@ncsu.edu. *Application contact:* Dr. C. David Raper, Director of Graduate Programs, 919-515-2644, Fax: 919-515-2167, E-mail: david_raper@ncsu.edu.

North Dakota State University, Graduate Studies and Research, College of Agriculture, Department of Soil Sciences, Fargo, ND 58105. Offers natural resources management (MS); soil sciences (MS, PhD). Part-time programs available. *Faculty:* 12 full-time (0 women). *Students:* 5 full-time (2 women), 4 part-time (1 woman). Average age 23. 2 applicants, 100% accepted. In 1998, 2 master's awarded (100% found work related to degree). *Degree requirements:* For master's and doctorate, thesis/dissertation, classroom teaching required, foreign language not required. *Entrance requirements:* For master's, GRE General Test, TOEFL (minimum score of 525 required); for doctorate, GRE General Test, TOEFL. *Average time to degree:* Master's–3 years full-time, 5 years part-time. *Application deadline:* Applications are processed on a rolling basis. Application fee: $25. *Financial aid:* In 1998–99, 5 research assistantships with full tuition reimbursements (averaging $10,800 per year) were awarded.; Federal Work-Study and institutionally-sponsored loans also available. Financial aid application deadline: 3/15. *Faculty research:* Microclimate, nitrogen management, landscape studies, water quality, soil management. *Unit head:* Dr. Lynn Brun, Chair, 701-231-8903, Fax: 701-231-7861, E-mail: lbrun@ndsuext.nodak.edu.

Nova Scotia Agricultural College, Research and Graduate Studies, Truro, NS B2N 5E3, Canada. Offers agriculture (M Sc), including animal behavior, animal genetics, animal management, animal nutrition, animal technology, botany, crop breeding, crop management, crop physiology, ecology, environmental microbiology, food science, geology, nutrient management, pest management, physiology, plant biotechnology, plant pathology, soil chemistry, soil fertility, soil physics, waste management. Part-time programs available. *Faculty:* 33 full-time (4 women), 14 part-time (1 woman). *Students:* 23 full-time (15 women), 17 part-time (8 women). *Degree requirements:* For master's, thesis, candidacy exam required. *Entrance requirements:* For master's, TOEFL (minimum score of 580 required), minimum GPA of 3.0. *Application deadline:* For fall admission, 6/1; for winter admission, 10/1; for spring admission, 2/1. Applications are processed on a rolling basis. Application fee: $55. *Unit head:* Jill L. Rogers-Langille, Coordinator, 902-893-6360, Fax: 902-897-9399, E-mail: jrogers-langille@cadmin.nsac.ns.ca. *Application contact:* Kari Duff, Assistant, 902-893-6502, Fax: 902-897-9399, E-mail: kduff@cadmin.nsac.ns.ca.

The Ohio State University, Graduate School, College of Food, Agricultural, and Environmental Sciences, Program in Soil Science, Columbus, OH 43210. Offers MS, PhD. *Faculty:* 13 full-time, 8 part-time. *Students:* 16 full-time (5 women), 5 part-time (3 women); includes 1 minority (African American), 5 international. 9 applicants, 67% accepted. In 1998, 1 master's awarded. *Degree requirements:* For doctorate, dissertation required, foreign language not required, foreign language not required. *Application deadline:* For fall admission, 8/15. Applications are processed on a rolling basis. Application fee: $30 ($40 for international students). *Unit head:* Donald J. Eckert, Graduate Studies Chairperson, 614-292-9048, Fax: 614-292-7162, E-mail: eckert.1@osu.edu.

Oklahoma State University, Graduate College, College of Agricultural Sciences and Natural Resources, Department of Plant and Soil Sciences, Stillwater, OK 74078. Offers agronomy (M Ag, MS, PhD); crop science (PhD); soil science (PhD). *Faculty:* 30 full-time (1 woman), 1 part-time (0 women). *Students:* 31 full-time (9 women), 29 part-time (10 women); includes 5 minority (1 African American, 4 Native Americans), 11 international. Average age 30. In 1998, 10 master's, 1 doctorate awarded. *Degree requirements:* For master's and doctorate, thesis/dissertation required. *Entrance requirements:* For master's and doctorate, TOEFL (minimum score of 550 required). *Application deadline:* For fall admission, 6/1 (priority date). Application fee: $25. *Financial aid:* In 1998–99, 40 students received aid, including 38 research assistantships (averaging $13,574 per year), 2 teaching assistantships (averaging $14,070 per year); career-related internships or fieldwork, Federal Work-Study, and tuition waivers (partial) also available. Aid available to part-time students. Financial aid application deadline: 3/1. *Faculty research:* Crop science, weed science, rangeland ecology and management, biotechnology, breeding and genetics. *Unit head:* Dr. Robert L. Westerman, Head, 405-744-6425.

Oregon State University, Graduate School, College of Agricultural Sciences, Department of Crop and Soil Science, Program in Crop Science, Corvallis, OR 97331. Offers M Agr, MAIS, MS, PhD. Part-time programs available. *Students:* 26 full-time (10 women), 2 part-time, 21 international. Average age 32. In 1998, 6 doctorates awarded. *Degree requirements:* For master's, thesis, thesis (MS) required, foreign language not required; for doctorate, variable foreign language requirement, dissertation required. *Entrance requirements:* For master's and doctorate, GRE, TOEFL (minimum score of 550 required), minimum GPA of 3.0 in last 90 hours. *Application deadline:* For fall admission, 3/1. Applications are processed on a rolling basis. Application fee: $50. *Financial aid:* Fellowships, research assistantships, teaching assistantships, career-related internships or fieldwork, Federal Work-Study, and institutionally-sponsored loans available. Aid available to part-time students. Financial aid application deadline: 2/1. *Faculty research:* Cereal and new crops breeding and genetics; weed science; seed technology and production; potato, new crops, and general crop production; plant physiology. *Unit head:* Dr. M. S. K. Sastry, Admissions Officer, 740-593-1277, Fax: 740-593-9805, E-mail: sastry@bing.math.ohiou.edu. *Application contact:* Dr. Alvin Mosely, Associate Professor, 541-737-5835, Fax: 541-737-1589, E-mail: mosley@css.orst.edu.

Oregon State University, Graduate School, College of Agricultural Sciences, Department of Crop and Soil Science, Program in Soil Science, Corvallis, OR 97331. Offers M Agr, MAIS, MS, PhD. Part-time programs available. *Students:* 28 full-time (12 women), 1 part-time; includes 3 minority (2 Asian Americans or Pacific Islanders, 1 Native American), 5 international. Average age 30. In 1998, 4 master's, 3 doctorates awarded. *Degree requirements:* For master's, thesis, thesis (MS required, foreign language not required; for doctorate, variable foreign language requirement, dissertation required. *Entrance requirements:* For master's and doctorate, GRE, TOEFL (minimum score of 550 required), minimum GPA of 3.0 in last 90 hours. *Application deadline:* For fall admission, 3/1. Applications are processed on a rolling basis. Application fee: $50. *Financial aid:* Fellowships, research assistantships, teaching assistantships, career-related internships or fieldwork, Federal Work-Study, and institutionally-sponsored loans available. Aid available to part-time students. Financial aid application deadline: 2/1. *Faculty research:* Soil physics, chemistry, biology, fertility, and genesis. *Unit head:* Charlotte Vickers, Advising Specialist, 541-737-1941, Fax: 541-737-3590, E-mail: vickersc@ccmail.orst.edu. *Application contact:* Dr. Neil Christensen, Professor, 541-737-5733, Fax: 541-737-5725, E-mail: christen@css.orst.edu.

Pennsylvania State University University Park Campus, Graduate School, College of Agricultural Sciences, Department of Agronomy, Program in Agronomy, State College, University Park, PA 16802-1503. Offers M Agr, MS, PhD. *Students:* 6 full-time (4 women), 5 part-time (2 women). In 1998, 3 master's awarded. *Entrance requirements:* For master's and doctorate, GRE General Test. Application fee: $50. *Unit head:* Dr. S. L. Fales, Chair, 814-865-6541.

Pennsylvania State University University Park Campus, Graduate School, College of Agricultural Sciences, Department of Agronomy, Program in Soil Science, State College, University Park, PA 16802-1503. Offers M Agr, MS, PhD. *Students:* 9 full-time (1 woman), 9 part-time (3 women). In 1998, 8 master's, 2 doctorates awarded. *Entrance requirements:* For master's and doctorate, GRE General Test. Application fee: $50. *Unit head:* Dr. Gary Petersen, Chair, 814-865-6541.

Prairie View A&M University, Graduate School, College of Agriculture, Nutrition and Human Ecology, Department of Agriculture, Nutrition and Human Ecology, Prairie View, TX 77446-0188. Offers animal science (MS); human sciences (MS); soil science (MS). *Students:* 19 full-time (14 women), 12 part-time (9 women); includes 25 minority (all African Americans), 4 international. *Degree requirements:* For master's, thesis required, foreign language not required. *Entrance requirements:* For master's, GRE General Test. *Application deadline:* For fall admission, 7/1 (priority date); for spring admission, 11/1. Applications are processed on a rolling basis. Application fee: $10. *Unit head:* Dr. Cecil L. Strickland, Interim Head, 409-857-2812, Fax: 409-857-2811.

Purdue University, Graduate School, School of Agriculture, Department of Agronomy, West Lafayette, IN 47907. Offers MS, PhD. Part-time programs available. *Faculty:* 35 full-time (3 women). *Students:* 49 full-time (12 women), 20 part-time (4 women); includes 3 minority (1 African American, 1 Asian American or Pacific Islander, 1 Native American), 32 international. 44 applicants, 20% accepted. In 1998, 13 master's, 12 doctorates awarded. *Degree requirements:* For doctorate, dissertation required. *Entrance requirements:* For master's and doctorate, TOEFL (minimum score of 550 required). Application fee: $30. Electronic applications accepted. *Financial aid:* Fellowships, research assistantships, teaching assistantships available. Aid available to part-time students. Financial aid applicants required to submit FAFSA. *Faculty research:* Plant genetics and breeding, crop physiology and ecology, agricultural meteorology, soil microbiology. Total annual research expenditures: $7.5 million. *Unit head:* Dr. W. W. McFee, Head, 765-494-4774, Fax: 765-496-1368.

South Dakota State University, Graduate School, College of Agriculture and Biological Sciences, Department of Plant Science, Program in Agronomy, Brookings, SD 57007. Offers MS, PhD. *Degree requirements:* For master's, thesis, oral exam required, foreign language not required; for doctorate, dissertation, preliminary oral and written exams required. *Entrance requirements:* For master's and doctorate, GRE General Test, TOEFL (minimum score of 525 required). *Faculty research:* Breeding/genetics, weed science, soil science, production agronomy, molecular biology.

Southern Illinois University Carbondale, Graduate School, College of Agriculture, Department of Plant, Soil, and General Agriculture, Carbondale, IL 62901-6806. Offers horticultural science (MS); plant and soil science (MS). *Faculty:* 19 full-time (1 woman), 1 (woman) part-time. *Students:* 25 full-time (9 women), 13 part-time (5 women). 16 applicants, 13% accepted. In 1998, 8 degrees awarded. *Degree requirements:* For master's, thesis required, foreign language not required. *Entrance requirements:* For master's, TOEFL (minimum score of 550 required), minimum GPA of 2.7. *Application deadline:* Applications are processed on a rolling basis. Application fee: $0. *Financial aid:* In 1998–99, 22 students received aid, including 16 research assistantships with full tuition reimbursements available, 6 teaching assistantships with full tuition reimbursements available; fellowships with full tuition reimbursements available, Federal Work-Study, institutionally-sponsored loans, and tuition waivers (full) also available. Aid available to part-time students. *Faculty research:* Herbicides, fertilizers, agriculture education, landscape design, plant breeding. Total annual research expenditures: $2 million. *Unit head:* Donald Stucky, Chairperson, 618-453-2496.

Texas A&M University, College of Agriculture and Life Sciences, Department of Soil and Crop Sciences, College Station, TX 77843. Offers agricultural chemistry (M Agr); agronomy (M Agr, MS, PhD); food science and technology (M Agr, MS, PhD); genetics (MS, PhD); plant breeding (MS, PhD); plant physiology and plant biotechnology (MS, PhD); soil science (MS, PhD). *Faculty:* 36 full-time (1 woman), 2 part-time (0 women). *Students:* 94 full-time (30 women), 31 part-time (11 women); includes 2 minority (1 Asian American or Pacific Islander, 1 Hispanic American), 50 international. Average age 31. 28 applicants, 79% accepted. In 1998, 15 master's awarded (80% found work related to degree, 20% continued full-time study); 13 doctorates awarded (15% entered university research/teaching, 85% found other work related to degree). *Degree requirements:* For master's and doctorate, thesis/dissertation required, foreign language not required. *Entrance requirements:* For master's and doctorate, GRE General Test, TOEFL. *Average time to degree:* Master's–2.5 years full-time, 4 years part-time; doctorate–3.5 years full-time, 6 years part-time. *Application deadline:* For fall admission, 3/1 (priority date); for spring admission, 8/1. Applications are processed on a rolling basis. Application fee: $50 ($75 for international students). *Financial aid:* In 1998–99, 9 fellowships (averaging $13,500 per year), 42 research assistantships (averaging $13,500 per year), 13 teaching assistantships (averaging $13,500 per year) were awarded.; career-related internships or fieldwork, Federal Work-Study, and institutionally-sponsored loans also available. *Faculty research:* Soil and crop management, turfgrass science, weed science, cereal chemistry, food protein chemistry. Total annual research expenditures: $6.5 million. *Unit head:* Dr. Edward C. A. Runge, Head, 409-845-3341. *Application contact:* Murray H. Milford, Graduate Adviser, 409-845-3341.

Texas A&M University–Kingsville, College of Graduate Studies, College of Agriculture and Home Economics, Program in Plant and Soil Sciences, Kingsville, TX 78363. Offers MS. *Faculty:* 2 full-time (0 women), 3 part-time (0 women). *Students:* 8 full-time (4 women), 2 part-time (1 woman). *Degree requirements:* For master's, thesis or alternative, comprehensive exam required, foreign language not required. *Entrance requirements:* For master's, GRE General Test (minimum combined score of 800 required), TOEFL (minimum score of 525 required), minimum GPA of 3.0. *Application deadline:* For fall admission, 6/1; for spring admission, 11/15. Applications are processed on a rolling basis. Application fee: $15 ($25 for international students). Tuition, state resident: full-time $2,062. Tuition, nonresident: full-time $7,246. *Financial aid:* Fellowships, research assistantships, teaching assistantships available. Financial aid application deadline: 5/15. *Unit head:* Graduate Coordinator, 361-593-3711.

Texas Tech University, Graduate School, College of Agricultural Sciences and Natural Resources, Department of Plant and Soil Science, Lubbock, TX 79409. Offers agronomy (PhD); crop science (MS); entomology (MS); horticulture (MS); plant and soil science (M Agr); soil science (MS). Part-time programs available. *Faculty:* 13 full-time (2 women), 1 part-time (0 women). *Students:* 35 full-time (14 women), 22 part-time (4 women); includes 1 minority (Asian American or Pacific Islander), 11 international. Average age 31. 15 applicants, 60% accepted. In 1998, 8 master's, 5 doctorates awarded. *Degree requirements:* For master's, foreign language and thesis not required; for doctorate, dissertation required. *Entrance requirements:* For master's, GRE General Test (combined average 1005); for doctorate, GRE General Test. *Application deadline:* For fall admission, 4/15 (priority date); for spring admission, 11/1 (priority date). Applications are processed on a rolling basis. Application fee: $25 ($50 for international students). Electronic applications accepted. *Financial aid:* In 1998–99, 30 students received aid, including 19 research assistantships (averaging $9,990 per year), 3 teaching assistantships (averaging $10,125 per year); fellowships, Federal Work-Study and institutionally-sponsored loans also available. Aid available to part-time students. Financial aid application deadline: 5/15; financial aid applicants required to submit FAFSA. *Faculty research:* Molecular and cellular biology of plant stress, physiology/genetics of cotton and sorghum production in semiarid conditions, biology of red fire ants. Total annual research expenditures: $1.3 million. *Unit head:* Dr. Dick L. Auld, Chair, 806-742-2837, Fax: 806-742-0775.

Tuskegee University, Graduate Programs, College of Agricultural, Environmental and Natural Sciences, Department of Agricultural Sciences, Program in Soil Sciences and Management, Tuskegee, AL 36088. Offers MS. *Faculty:* 13 full-time (1 woman), 2 part-time (1 woman). *Students:* 4 full-time (2 women), 6 part-time (2 women); includes 9 minority (8 African Americans, 1 Native American) Average age 24. In 1998, 3 degrees awarded. *Degree requirements:* For master's, computer language, thesis required, foreign language not required. *Entrance requirements:* For master's, GRE General Test. *Application deadline:* For fall admission, 7/15. Applications are processed on a rolling basis. Application fee: $25 ($35 for international students). *Financial aid:* Application deadline: 4/15. *Unit head:* Dr. P. K. Biswas, Head, Department of Agricultural Sciences, 334-727-8632.

Université Laval, Faculty of Graduate Studies, Faculty of Agricultural and Food Sciences, Department of Soils and Agricultural Engineering, Program in Soils, Sainte-Foy, PQ G1K 7P4, Canada. Offers M Sc, PhD. *Students:* 24 full-time (9 women), 7 part-time (2 women). 10 applicants, 60% accepted. In 1998, 7 master's, 3 doctorates awarded. *Application deadline:* For fall admission, 3/1. Application fee: $30. *Unit head:* Antoine Karam, Director, 418-656-2131 Ext. 7420, Fax: 418-656-3723, E-mail: antoine.karam@sls.ulaval.ca.

University of Alberta, Faculty of Graduate Studies and Research, Department of Renewable Resources, Edmonton, AB T6G 2E1, Canada. Offers agroforestry (M Ag, M Sc, MF); conservation biology (M Sc, PhD); forest biology and management (M Sc, PhD); land reclamation and remediation (M Sc, PhD); protected areas and wildlands management (M Sc, PhD); soil science (M Ag, M Sc, PhD); water and land resources (M Ag, M Sc, PhD); wildlife ecology and management (M Sc, PhD). *Degree requirements:* For doctorate, dissertation required.

The University of Arizona, Graduate College, College of Agriculture, Department of Soil, Water and Environmental Science, Tucson, AZ 85721. Offers MS, PhD. *Faculty:* 17. *Students:* 74 full-time (31 women), 28 part-time (9 women); includes 8 minority (1 African American, 3 Asian Americans or Pacific Islanders, 3 Hispanic Americans, 1 Native American), 33 international. Average age 32. 58 applicants, 60% accepted. In 1998, 14 master's, 5 doctorates awarded. *Degree requirements:* For master's, thesis required, foreign language not required; for doctorate, one foreign language, computer language, dissertation required. *Entrance requirements:* For master's and doctorate, TOEFL (minimum score of 550 required). *Application deadline:* For fall admission, 3/1. Applications are processed on a rolling basis. Application fee: $35. *Financial aid:* Research assistantships, teaching assistantships, Federal Work-Study, institutionally-sponsored loans, scholarships, and tuition waivers (full and partial) available. Financial aid application deadline: 5/1. *Faculty research:* Plant production, environmental microbiology, contaminant flow and transport. *Unit head:* Dr. Peter Wierenga, Head, 520-621-7228. *Application contact:* Dr. Mark Brusseau, Graduate Admissions Coordinator, 520-621-3228, Fax: 520-621-1647.

University of Arkansas, Graduate School, Dale Bumpers College of Agricultural, Food and Life Sciences, Department of Crop, Soil and Environmental Sciences, Fayetteville, AR 72701-1201. Offers agronomy (MS, PhD). *Faculty:* 34 full-time (0 women), 1 part-time (0 women). *Students:* 48 full-time (17 women), 7 part-time (2 women); includes 6 minority (3 African Americans, 1 Asian American or Pacific Islander, 1 Hispanic American, 1 Native American), 16 international. 17 applicants, 71% accepted. In 1998, 10 master's, 8 doctorates awarded. *Degree requirements:* For master's, thesis optional, foreign language not required; for doctorate, variable foreign language requirement, dissertation required. Application fee: $40 ($50 for international students). Tuition, state resident: full-time $3,186. Tuition, nonresident: full-time $7,560. Required fees: $378. *Financial aid:* In 1998–99, 36 research assistantships, 1 teaching assistantship were awarded.; career-related internships or fieldwork and Federal Work-Study also available. Aid available to part-time students. Financial aid application deadline: 4/1; financial aid applicants required to submit FAFSA. *Unit head:* Dr. James Barrentine, Chair, 501-575-2347, E-mail: gfry@comp.uark.edu.

University of British Columbia, Faculty of Graduate Studies, Faculty of Agricultural Sciences, Department of Soil Science, Vancouver, BC V6T 1Z2, Canada. Offers M Sc, PhD. *Degree requirements:* For doctorate, dissertation, comprehensive exam required. *Entrance requirements:* For master's and doctorate, TOEFL. *Faculty research:* Soil and water conservation, soil genesis and classification, land use and land classification, forest soils, soil fertility.

University of California, Davis, Graduate Studies, Program in Agronomy, Davis, CA 95616. Offers MS. *Faculty:* 28 full-time (4 women). *Students:* 10 full-time (5 women); includes 1 minority (Hispanic American), 3 international. Average age 25. 11 applicants, 55% accepted. In 1998, 1 degree awarded. *Degree requirements:* For master's, thesis optional. *Entrance requirements:* For master's, GRE General Test, minimum GPA of 3.0. *Average time to degree:* Master's–2 years full-time. Application fee: $40. Electronic applications accepted. *Financial aid:* In 1998–99, 2 fellowships with full and partial tuition reimbursements, 4 research assistantships with full and partial tuition reimbursements, 1 teaching assistantship with full and partial tuition reimbursement were awarded. Financial aid application deadline: 1/15; financial aid applicants required to submit FAFSA. *Faculty research:* Production, quantitative agronomy, breeding and genetics, physiology. *Unit head:* James Hill, Chairperson, 530-752-1715. *Application contact:* Garda Johnson, Program Assistant, 530-752-1715, Fax: 530-752-4361, E-mail: gljohnson@ucdavis.edu.

University of California, Davis, Graduate Studies, Program in Soil Science, Davis, CA 95616. Offers MS, PhD. *Faculty:* 30 full-time (3 women). *Students:* 30 full-time (16 women); includes 1 minority (Asian American or Pacific Islander), 10 international. Average age 28. 26 applicants, 38% accepted. In 1998, 2 master's awarded (100% found work related to degree); 5 doctorates awarded. Terminal master's awarded for partial completion of doctoral program. *Degree requirements:* For master's, computer language required, thesis optional; for doctorate, computer language, dissertation required. *Entrance requirements:* For master's, minimum GPA of 3.3; for doctorate, GRE, minimum GPA of 3.3. *Application deadline:* For fall admission, 1/15. Applications are processed on a rolling basis. Application fee: $40. Electronic applications accepted. *Financial aid:* In 1998–99, 1 fellowship with full and partial tuition reimbursement, 23 research assistantships with full and partial tuition reimbursements, 3 teaching assistantships with full and partial tuition reimbursements were awarded.; career-related internships or fieldwork, Federal Work-Study, and institutionally-sponsored loans also available. Aid available to part-time students. Financial aid application deadline: 1/15; financial aid applicants required to submit FAFSA. *Faculty research:* Rhizosphere ecology, soil transport processes, biogeochemical cycling, sustainable agriculture. Total annual research expenditures: $3 million. *Unit head:* Robert Zasoski, Graduate Adviser, 530-752-1669, Fax: 530-752-5262. *Application contact:* Diane Swindall, Academic Adviser, 530-752-1669, Fax: 530-752-5262, E-mail: dgswindall@ucdavis.edu.

University of California, Riverside, Graduate Division, College of Natural and Agricultural Sciences, Department of Environmental Sciences, Riverside, CA 92521-0102. Offers soil science (MS, PhD). Part-time programs available. *Faculty:* 22 full-time (3 women). *Students:* 23 full-time (8 women); includes 2 minority (1 Asian American or Pacific Islander, 1 Hispanic American), 4 international. Average age 31. In 1998, 7 master's, 4 doctorates awarded. Terminal master's awarded for partial completion of doctoral program. *Degree requirements:* For master's, thesis required, foreign language not required; for doctorate, dissertation, oral and written qualifying exams required, foreign language not required. *Entrance requirements:* For master's and doctorate, GRE General Test (minimum combined score of 1100 required), TOEFL (minimum score of 550 required), bachelor's degree in natural and physical sciences, engineering, or economics, minimum GPA of 3.2. *Average time to degree:* Master's–2.7 years full-time; doctorate–4.3 years full-time. *Application deadline:* For fall admission, 5/1; for winter admission, 9/1; for spring admission, 12/1. Applications are processed on a rolling basis. Application fee: $40. Electronic applications accepted. *Financial aid:* Fellowships, research assistantships, teaching assistantships, career-related internships or fieldwork, Federal Work-Study, institutionally-sponsored loans, and tuition waivers (full and partial) available. Financial aid application deadline: 2/1; financial aid applicants required to submit FAFSA. *Faculty research:* Soil chemistry, soil physics, soil mineralogy, soil microbiology and biochemistry, soil morphology. *Unit head:* Dr. Lanny J. Lund, Chair, 909-787-5116, Fax: 909-787-4652, E-mail: ljlund@ucrac1.ucr.edu. *Application contact:* Mari Ridgeway, Student Affairs Officer, 909-787-5103, Fax: 909-787-3993, E-mail: marir@ucrac1.ucr.edu.

University of Connecticut, Graduate School, College of Agriculture and Natural Resources, Field of Plant Science, Storrs, CT 06269. Offers plant and soil sciences (MS, PhD). *Degree requirements:* For doctorate, dissertation required. *Entrance requirements:* For master's and doctorate, GRE General Test, GRE Subject Test.

University of Delaware, College of Agriculture and Natural Resources, Department of Plant and Soil Sciences, Newark, DE 19716. Offers MS, PhD. *Degree requirements:* For master's and doctorate, thesis/dissertation required, foreign language not required. *Entrance requirements:* For master's and doctorate, GRE General Test. *Faculty research:* Soil chemistry, plant and cell tissue culture, plant breeding and genetics, soil physics, soil biochemistry, plant molecular biology, soil microbiology.

University of Florida, Graduate School, College of Agriculture, Department of Agronomy, Gainesville, FL 32611. Offers MS, PhD. *Faculty:* 53. *Students:* 25 full-time (12 women), 6 part-time (2 women); includes 2 minority (1 Asian American or Pacific Islander, 1 Hispanic American), 12 international. 36 applicants, 56% accepted. In 1998, 3 master's, 3 doctorates awarded. *Degree requirements:* For master's, thesis optional; for doctorate, dissertation required. *Entrance requirements:* For master's and doctorate, GRE General Test (minimum combined score of 1000 required), minimum GPA of 3.0. *Application deadline:* For fall admission, 6/1 (priority date). Applications are processed on a rolling basis. Application fee: $20. Electronic applications accepted. *Financial aid:* In 1998–99, 16 research assistantships were awarded.; fellowships, teaching assistantships, career-related internships or fieldwork, institutionally-sponsored loans, and unspecified assistantships also available. *Faculty research:* Genetics and plant breeding, aquatic and terrestrial weed science, plant physiology, molecular biology, forage and crop production. *Unit head:* Dr. J. M. Bennett, Chair, 352-392-1811, Fax: 352-392-1840, E-mail: jmbt@gnv.ifas.ufl.edu. *Application contact:* Dr. D. S. Wofford, Graduate Coordinator, 352-392-1823, Fax: 352-392-7248, E-mail: dsw@gnv.ifas.ufl.edu.

University of Florida, Graduate School, College of Agriculture, Department of Soil and Water Science, Gainesville, FL 32611. Offers M Ag, MS, PhD. Part-time programs available. *Faculty:* 48. *Students:* 30 full-time (7 women), 13 part-time (1 woman); includes 5 minority (4 Asian Americans or Pacific Islanders, 1 Hispanic American), 19 international. 39 applicants, 64% accepted. In 1998, 9 master's, 5 doctorates awarded. Terminal master's awarded for partial completion of doctoral program. *Degree requirements:* For master's, thesis optional; for doctorate, dissertation required. *Entrance requirements:* For master's and doctorate, GRE General Test, minimum GPA of 3.0. *Application deadline:* For fall admission, 6/1 (priority date); for spring admission, 10/1. Applications are processed on a rolling basis. Application fee: $20. Electronic applications accepted. *Financial aid:* In 1998–99, 33 students received aid, including 27 research assistantships, 2 teaching assistantships; fellowships, career-related internships or fieldwork, Federal Work-Study, institutionally-sponsored loans, and unspecified assistantships also available. Aid available to part-time students. *Faculty research:* Environmental fate and transport of pesticides, conservation, wetlands, land application of nonhazardous waste, soil/water agrochemical management. *Unit head:* Dr. Randy Brown, Chair, 352-392-1804, Fax: 352-392-3399, E-mail: rbb@gnv.ifas.ufl.edu. *Application contact:* Dr. K. Ramesh Reddy, Graduate Coordinator, 352-392-1804, Fax: 352-392-3399, E-mail: krr @gnv.ifas.ufl.edu.

University of Georgia, Graduate School, College of Agricultural and Environmental Sciences, Department of Crop and Soil Sciences, Athens, GA 30602. Offers agronomy (MS, PhD); plant protection and pest management (MPPPM). *Faculty:* 38 full-time (2 women). *Students:* 31 full-time (10 women), 5 part-time (3 women), 15 international. 25 applicants, 28% accepted. In 1998, 1 master's, 11 doctorates awarded. *Degree requirements:* For master's, thesis (MS) required; for doctorate, one foreign language (computer language can substitute), dissertation required. *Entrance requirements:* For master's and doctorate, GRE General Test. *Applica-*

Agronomy and Soil Sciences

University of Georgia (continued)

tion deadline: For fall admission, 7/1 (priority date); for spring admission, 11/15. Application fee: $30. Electronic applications accepted. *Financial aid:* Fellowships, research assistantships, teaching assistantships, unspecified assistantships available. *Unit head:* Dr. David E. Radcliffe, Graduate Coordinator, 706-542-2461, Fax: 706-542-0914.

University of Guelph, Faculty of Graduate Studies, Ontario Agricultural College, Department of Land Resource Science, Guelph, ON N1G 2W1, Canada. Offers atmospheric science (M Sc, PhD); land science (M Sc, PhD). Part-time programs available. *Faculty:* 17 full-time (1 woman), 3 part-time (0 women). *Students:* 42 full-time (19 women), 11 part-time (2 women), 9 international. 23 applicants, 30% accepted. In 1998, 6 master's awarded (67% found work related to degree, 33% continued full-time study); 4 doctorates awarded (50% entered university research/teaching, 50% found other work related to degree). *Degree requirements:* For master's and doctorate, thesis/dissertation required. *Entrance requirements:* For master's, minimum B-average during previous 2 years. *Average time to degree:* Master's–2.5 years full-time; doctorate–3.5 years full-time. *Application deadline:* Applications are processed on a rolling basis. Application fee: $60. *Expenses:* Tuition and fees charges are reported in Canadian dollars. Tuition, area resident: Full-time $4,725 Canadian dollars; part-time $1,055 Canadian dollars per term. International tuition: $6,999 Canadian dollars full-time. Required fees: $295 Canadian dollars per term. *Financial aid:* In 1998–99, 40 research assistantships (averaging $16,500 per year), 15 teaching assistantships (averaging $3,800 per year) were awarded.; fellowships, scholarships also available. *Faculty research:* Soil science, environmental earth science, land resource management. Total annual research expenditures: $2.1 million. *Unit head:* Dr. T. J. Gillespie, Chairman, 519-824-4120 Ext. 2447, Fax: 519-824-5730, E-mail: tgillesp@lrs.uoguelph.ca. *Application contact:* Dr. W. Chesworth, Graduate Coordinator, 519-824-4120 Ext. 2457, Fax: 519-824-5730, E-mail: wcheswor@lrs.uoguelph.ca.

University of Hawaii at Manoa, Graduate Division, College of Tropical Agriculture and Human Resources, Department of Agronomy and Soil Sciences, Honolulu, HI 96822. Offers MS, PhD. *Faculty:* 19 full-time (3 women). *Students:* 12 full-time (1 woman), 4 part-time; all minorities (3 African Americans, 12 Asian Americans or Pacific Islanders, 1 Native American), 7 international. 20 applicants, 35% accepted. In 1998, 2 master's, 4 doctorates awarded. *Degree requirements:* For master's and doctorate, thesis/dissertation required, foreign language not required. *Entrance requirements:* For master's and doctorate, GRE, TOEFL (minimum score of 520 required). *Application deadline:* For fall admission, 3/1; for spring admission, 9/1. Applications are processed on a rolling basis. Application fee: $25 ($50 for international students). *Financial aid:* In 1998–99, 15 students received aid, including 6 research assistantships (averaging $15,364 per year), 2 teaching assistantships (averaging $13,041 per year) *Faculty research:* Plant/soil microorganism interaction, management of organic wastes, phosphorus decision support system. *Unit head:* Dr. Samir A. El-Swarfy, Chair, 808-956-8708. *Application contact:* Dr. Mitiku Habte, Graduate Chair, 808-956-6906, Fax: 808-956-6539, E-mail: mitiku@hawaii.edu.

University of Idaho, College of Graduate Studies, College of Agriculture, Department of Plant, Soil, and Entomological Sciences, Program in Soil Science, Moscow, ID 83844-4140. Offers MS, PhD. *Students:* 6 full-time (3 women), 7 part-time (2 women); includes 1 minority (Asian American or Pacific Islander) In 1998, 4 master's, 2 doctorates awarded. *Degree requirements:* For doctorate, dissertation required, foreign language not required, foreign language not required. *Entrance requirements:* For master's, minimum GPA of 3.0; for doctorate, GRE, minimum GPA of 3.0. *Application deadline:* For fall admission, 8/1; for spring admission, 12/15. Application fee: $35 ($45 for international students). *Financial aid:* Application deadline: 2/15. *Unit head:* Dr. Denny V. Naylor, Acting Head, 208-885-6276. *Application contact:* Dr. Matthew J. Morra, Chairman, Graduate Admissions Committee, 208-885-6315.

University of Illinois at Urbana–Champaign, Graduate College, College of Agricultural, Consumer and Environmental Sciences, Department of Crop Sciences, Urbana, IL 61801. Offers MS, PhD. *Faculty:* 72 full-time (6 women). *Students:* 69 full-time (23 women); includes 1 minority (African American), 25 international. 32 applicants, 16% accepted. In 1998, 25 master's, 6 doctorates awarded. *Degree requirements:* For master's, thesis, comprehensive exam required; for doctorate, dissertation, comprehensive exam required, foreign language not required. *Entrance requirements:* For master's, minimum GPA of 4.0 on a 5.0 scale. *Application deadline:* Applications are processed on a rolling basis. Application fee: $40 ($50 for international students). Tuition, state resident: full-time $4,040. Tuition, nonresident: full-time $11,192. Full-time tuition and fees vary according to program. *Financial aid:* In 1998–99, 57 research assistantships were awarded.; fellowships, teaching assistantships, tuition waivers (full and partial) also available. Financial aid application deadline: 2/15. *Faculty research:* Plant breeding and genetics, molecular biology, crop production, plant physiology, weed science. *Unit head:* Gary H. Heichel, Head, 217-333-9480. *Application contact:* John W. Dudley, Director of Graduate Studies, 217-333-9480, Fax: 217-333-9817, E-mail: jdudley@uiuc.edu.

University of Kentucky, Graduate School, Graduate School Programs from the College of Agriculture, Program in Crop Science, Lexington, KY 40506-0032. Offers MS, MS Ag, PhD. *Degree requirements:* For master's, comprehensive exam required, thesis optional, foreign language not required; for doctorate, dissertation required, foreign language not required. *Entrance requirements:* For master's, GRE General Test, minimum GPA of 2.5; for doctorate, GRE General Test, minimum GPA of 3.0. *Faculty research:* Crop physiology, crop ecology, crop management, crop breeding and genetics, weed science.

University of Kentucky, Graduate School, Graduate School Programs from the College of Agriculture, Program in Plant and Soil Science, Lexington, KY 40506-0032. Offers MS. *Degree requirements:* For master's, comprehensive exam required, thesis optional, foreign language not required. *Entrance requirements:* For master's, GRE General Test, minimum undergraduate GPA of 2.5, minimum graduate GPA of 3.0.

University of Kentucky, Graduate School, Graduate School Programs from the College of Agriculture, Program in Soil Science, Lexington, KY 40506-0032. Offers PhD. *Degree requirements:* For doctorate, dissertation, comprehensive exam required, foreign language not required. *Entrance requirements:* For doctorate, GRE General Test, minimum graduate GPA of 3.0. *Faculty research:* Soil fertility and plant nutrition, soil chemistry and physics, soil genesis and morphology, soil management and conservation, water and environmental quality.

University of Maine, Graduate School, College of Natural Sciences, Forestry, and Agriculture, Department of Plant, Soil, and Environmental Sciences, Orono, ME 04469. Offers biological sciences (PhD); ecology and environmental sciences (MS, PhD); forest resources (PhD); plant science (PhD); plant, soil, and environmental sciences (MS); resource utilization (MS). *Students:* 11 (6 women). 10 applicants, 40% accepted. In 1998, 3 degrees awarded. *Entrance requirements:* For master's and doctorate, GRE General Test, TOEFL (minimum score of 550 required). Application fee: $50. *Financial aid:* In 1998–99, 9 research assistantships with tuition reimbursements (averaging $8,000 per year) were awarded.; teaching assistantships, grants, tuition waivers (full and partial), and unspecified assistantships also available. *Unit head:* Dr. Ivan Fernandez, Chair. *Application contact:* Mary Fernandez, 207-581-2938, Fax: 207-581-2999, E-mail: fern@maine.maine.edu.

University of Manitoba, Faculty of Graduate Studies, Faculty of Agriculture, Department of Soil Science, Winnipeg, MB R3T 2N2, Canada. Offers M Sc, PhD. *Degree requirements:* For master's, thesis required, foreign language not required; for doctorate, dissertation required. *Unit head:* G. J. Racz, Head.

University of Maryland, College Park, Graduate School, College of Agriculture and Natural Resources, Department of Natural Resource Sciences and Landscape Architecture, Program in Agronomy, College Park, MD 20742-5045. Offers MS, PhD. *Students:* 16 full-time (8 women), 14 part-time (5 women); includes 7 minority (4 African Americans, 3 Asian Americans or Pacific Islanders), 5 international. 31 applicants, 35% accepted. In 1998, 6 master's, 3 doctorates awarded. *Degree requirements:* For master's, thesis or alternative required, foreign language not required; for doctorate, dissertation, written and oral exams required. *Entrance requirements:* For master's, GRE General Test, TOEFL, minimum GPA of 3.0; for doctorate, GRE General Test, TOEFL, MS degree in related area. *Application deadline:* Applications are processed on a rolling basis. Application fee: $50 ($70 for international students). Tuition, state resident: part-time $272 per credit hour. Tuition, nonresident: part-time $475 per credit hour. Required fees: $632; $379 per year. *Financial aid:* Fellowships, research assistantships, teaching assistantships, career-related internships or fieldwork available. Financial aid applicants required to submit FAFSA. *Faculty research:* Cereal crop production, soil and water conservation, turf management, x-ray defraction. *Unit head:* Mary Fernandez, 207-581-2938, Fax: 207-581-2999, E-mail: fern@maine.maine.edu. *Application contact:* Trudy Lindsey, Director, Graduate Admission and Records, 301-405-4198, Fax: 301-314-9305, E-mail: grschool@deans.umd.edu.

University of Massachusetts Amherst, Graduate School, College of Food and Natural Resources, Department of Plant and Soil Sciences, Amherst, MA 01003. Offers plant science (PhD); soil science (MS, PhD). *Faculty:* 21 full-time (3 women). *Students:* 19 full-time (8 women), 20 part-time (8 women), 17 international. Average age 34. 22 applicants, 32% accepted. In 1998, 8 master's, 5 doctorates awarded. Terminal master's awarded for partial completion of doctoral program. *Degree requirements:* For master's, thesis optional, foreign language not required; for doctorate, dissertation required, foreign language not required. *Entrance requirements:* For master's and doctorate, GRE General Test. *Application deadline:* For fall admission, 2/1 (priority date); for spring admission, 10/1. Applications are processed on a rolling basis. Application fee: $40. Tuition, state resident: full-time $2,640; part-time $165 per credit. Tuition, nonresident: full-time $9,756; part-time $407 per credit. Required fees: $1,221 per term. One-time fee: $110. Full-time tuition and fees vary according to course load, campus/location and reciprocity agreements. *Financial aid:* In 1998–99, 25 research assistantships with full tuition reimbursements (averaging $7,652 per year), 15 teaching assistantships with full tuition reimbursements (averaging $5,124 per year) were awarded.; fellowships with full tuition reimbursements, career-related internships or fieldwork, Federal Work-Study, grants, scholarships, traineeships, and unspecified assistantships also available. Aid available to part-time students. Financial aid application deadline: 2/1. *Unit head:* Dr. William J. Bramlage, Director, 413-545-2242, Fax: 413-545-3075, E-mail: bramlage@pssci.umass.edu.

University of Minnesota, Twin Cities Campus, Graduate School, College of Agricultural, Food, and Environmental Sciences, Department of Soil, Water, and Climate, Minneapolis, MN 55455-0213. Offers MS, PhD. *Degree requirements:* For master's, thesis or alternative required, foreign language not required; for doctorate, dissertation required, foreign language not required. *Entrance requirements:* For master's and doctorate, GRE General Test (minimum combined score of 1650 on three sections required), minimum GPA of 3.0. Electronic applications accepted. *Faculty research:* Soil water and atmospheric resources, soil physical management, agricultural chemicals and their management, plant nutrient management, biological nitrogen fixation.

University of Missouri–Columbia, Graduate School, College of Agriculture, Program in Agronomy, Columbia, MO 65211. Offers MS, PhD. *Faculty:* 19 full-time (1 woman), 1 part-time (0 women). *Students:* 20 full-time (7 women), 8 part-time (2 women), 9 international. 5 applicants, 80% accepted. In 1998, 3 master's, 1 doctorate awarded. Terminal master's awarded for partial completion of doctoral program. *Degree requirements:* For master's and doctorate, thesis/dissertation required. *Entrance requirements:* For master's and doctorate, GRE General Test, minimum GPA of 3.0. *Application deadline:* For fall admission, 5/1 (priority date). Applications are processed on a rolling basis. Application fee: $30 ($50 for international students). *Financial aid:* Research assistantships, teaching assistantships, institutionally-sponsored loans available. *Unit head:* Dr. Robert Sharp, Director of Graduate Studies, 573-882-1841.

University of Missouri–Columbia, Graduate School, School of Natural Resources, Department of Soil and Atmospheric Sciences, Columbia, MO 65211. Offers MS, PhD. *Faculty:* 9 full-time (1 woman). *Students:* 7 full-time (3 women), 9 part-time (2 women); includes 2 minority (1 Asian American or Pacific Islander, 1 Hispanic American), 5 international. 3 applicants, 67% accepted. In 1998, 7 master's, 3 doctorates awarded. Terminal master's awarded for partial completion of doctoral program. *Degree requirements:* For master's and doctorate, thesis/dissertation required, foreign language not required. *Entrance requirements:* For master's and doctorate, GRE General Test, minimum GPA of 3.0. *Application deadline:* Applications are processed on a rolling basis. Application fee: $30 ($50 for international students). *Financial aid:* Research assistantships, teaching assistantships, grants and institutionally-sponsored loans available. *Unit head:* Dr. Steve Anderson, Director of Graduate Studies, 573-882-6303.

University of Nebraska–Lincoln, Graduate College, College of Agricultural Sciences and Natural Resources, Department of Agronomy, Lincoln, NE 68588. Offers MS, PhD. *Faculty:* 39 full-time (1 woman), 2 part-time (0 women). *Students:* 59 full-time (20 women), 43 part-time (12 women); includes 2 minority (1 African American, 1 Hispanic American), 49 international. Average age 33. 48 applicants, 50% accepted. In 1998, 21 master's, 20 doctorates awarded. *Degree requirements:* For master's, thesis required, foreign language not required; for doctorate, dissertation, comprehensive exams required, foreign language not required. *Entrance requirements:* For master's and doctorate, TOEFL (minimum score of 500 required). *Average time to degree:* Doctorate–4.3 years part-time. *Application deadline:* For fall admission, 3/1 (priority date). Applications are processed on a rolling basis. Application fee: $35. Electronic applications accepted. *Financial aid:* In 1998–99, 10 fellowships, 41 research assistantships, 2 teaching assistantships were awarded.; Federal Work-Study also available. Aid available to part-time students. Financial aid application deadline: 2/15. *Faculty research:* Crop physiology and production, plant breeding and genetics, range and forage management, soil and water science, weed science. *Unit head:* Dr. Kenneth Cassman, Head, 402-472-1555, Fax: 402-472-7904.

University of New Hampshire, Graduate School, College of Life Sciences and Agriculture, Graduate Programs in the Biological Sciences and Natural Resources, Durham, NH 03824. Offers animal and nutritional sciences (MS, PhD); biochemistry and molecular biology (MS, PhD); biology (MS); genetics (MS, PhD); microbiology (MS, PhD); natural resources (MS, PhD), including environmental conservation (MS), forestry (MS), natural resources (PhD), soil science (MS), water resources management (MS), wildlife (MS); plant biology (MS, PhD); zoology (MS, PhD). Part-time programs available. *Faculty:* 129 full-time. *Students:* 127 full-time (74 women), 111 part-time (56 women); includes 6 minority (4 Asian Americans or Pacific Islanders, 2 Hispanic Americans), 31 international. Terminal master's awarded for partial completion of doctoral program. *Degree requirements:* For doctorate, dissertation required, foreign language not required. *Entrance requirements:* For master's, GRE General Test. *Application deadline:* Applications are processed on a rolling basis. Application fee: $50. Tuition, area resident: Full-time $5,750; part-time $319 per credit. Tuition, state resident: full-time $8,625. Tuition, nonresident: full-time $14,640; part-time $598 per credit. Required fees: $224 per semester. Tuition and fees vary according to course load, degree level and program. *Unit head:* Dr. William Mautz, Interim Dean, College of Life Sciences and Agriculture, 603-862-1450.

University of New Hampshire, Graduate School, College of Life Sciences and Agriculture, Graduate Programs in the Biological Sciences and Natural Resources, Department of Natural Resources, Option in Soil Science, Durham, NH 03824. Offers MS. Part-time programs available. Average age 32. 2 applicants, 50% accepted. In 1998, 1 degree awarded. *Degree requirements:* For master's, thesis or alternative required, foreign language not required. *Entrance requirements:* For master's, GRE General Test. *Application deadline:* For fall admission, 4/1 (priority date). Applications are processed on a rolling basis. Application fee: $50. Tuition, area resident: Full-time $5,750; part-time $319 per credit. Tuition, state resident: full-time $8,625. Tuition, nonresident: full-time $14,640; part-time $598 per credit. Required fees: $224 per semester. Tuition and fees vary according to course load, degree level and program. *Financial aid:* In 1998–99, 1 research assistantship was awarded.; teaching assistantships, career-related internships or fieldwork, Federal Work-Study, scholarships, and tuition waivers (full and partial) also available. Aid available to part-time students. Financial aid application deadline: 2/15. *Faculty research:* Soil chemistry, soil classification, soil microbiology, forest soils. *Application contact:* Dr. Robert Harter, Graduate Coordinator, 603-862-3944.

University of Puerto Rico, Mayagüez Campus, Graduate Studies, College of Agricultural Sciences, Department of Agronomy, Mayagüez, PR 00681-5000. Offers crops (MS); soils (MS). Part-time programs available. *Degree requirements:* For master's, thesis, comprehensive exam required, foreign language not required. *Faculty research:* Soil physics and chemistry, soil management, plant physiology, ecology, plant breeding.

University of Puerto Rico, Mayagüez Campus, Graduate Studies, College of Agricultural Sciences, Department of Crop Protection, Mayagüez, PR 00681-5000. Offers MS. Part-time programs available. *Degree requirements:* For master's, thesis, comprehensive exam required, foreign language not required. *Faculty research:* Nematology, virology, plant pathology, weed control, peas and soybean seed diseases.

University of Saskatchewan, College of Graduate Studies and Research, College of Agriculture, Department of Soil Science, Saskatoon, SK S7N 5A2, Canada. Offers M Sc, PhD. *Degree requirements:* For master's and doctorate, thesis/dissertation required. *Entrance requirements:* For master's, CANTEST (minimum score of 4.5 required) or International English Language Testing System (minimum score of 6 required) or Michigan English Language Assessment Battery (minimum score of 80 required), orTOEFL (minimum score of 550 required; average 560); for doctorate, TOEFL.

University of Tennessee, Knoxville, Graduate School, College of Agricultural Sciences and Natural Resources, Department of Plant and Soil Sciences, Knoxville, TN 37996. Offers crop physiology and ecology (MS, PhD); plant breeding and genetics (MS, PhD); soil science (MS, PhD). Part-time programs available. *Faculty:* 19 full-time (1 woman). *Students:* 22 full-time (10 women), 12 part-time (4 women), 3 international. 16 applicants, 63% accepted. In 1998, 7 master's, 4 doctorates awarded. *Degree requirements:* For master's, thesis or alternative required, foreign language not required; for doctorate, dissertation required, foreign language not required. *Entrance requirements:* For master's and doctorate, GRE General Test, TOEFL (minimum score of 550 required), minimum GPA of 2.7. *Application deadline:* For fall admission, 2/1 (priority date). Applications are processed on a rolling basis. Application fee: $35. Electronic applications accepted. *Financial aid:* In 1998–99, 20 research assistantships, 1 teaching assistantship were awarded.; fellowships, career-related internships or fieldwork, Federal Work-Study, and institutionally-sponsored loans also available. Financial aid application deadline: 2/1; financial aid applicants required to submit FAFSA. *Unit head:* Dr. Fred L. Allen, Head, 423-974-7101, Fax: 423-974-7997, E-mail: allenf@utk.edu. *Application contact:* Dr. Mike Essington, Graduate Representative, 423-974-8818, E-mail: messington@utk.edu.

University of Vermont, Graduate College, College of Agriculture and Life Sciences, Department of Plant and Soil Science, Burlington, VT 05405-0160. Offers MS, PhD. *Degree requirements:* For master's, thesis required, foreign language not required; for doctorate, dissertation required. *Entrance requirements:* For master's and doctorate, GRE General Test, TOEFL (minimum score of 550 required). *Faculty research:* Soil chemistry, plant nutrition.

University of Wisconsin–Madison, Graduate School, College of Agricultural and Life Sciences, Department of Agronomy, Madison, WI 53706-1380. Offers MS, PhD. *Degree requirements:* For master's, thesis or alternative required; for doctorate, dissertation required. *Entrance requirements:* For master's and doctorate, GRE. *Faculty research:* Plant breeding and genetics, plant molecular biology and physiology, cropping systems and management, weed science.

University of Wisconsin–Madison, Graduate School, College of Agricultural and Life Sciences, Department of Soil Science, Madison, WI 53706-1380. Offers MS, PhD. *Degree requirements:* For master's and doctorate, thesis/dissertation required, foreign language not required. *Entrance requirements:* For master's and doctorate, GRE General Test. Electronic applications accepted. *Faculty research:* Physical chemistry of soil colloids/surfaces, forest biogeochemistry, soil-plant-atmosphere interactions, organic byproducts recycling, microbial metabolism in soil.

University of Wyoming, Graduate School, College of Agriculture, Department of Plant, Soil, and Insect Sciences, Program in Agronomy, Laramie, WY 82071. Offers agronomy (MS, PhD); plant pathology (MS). *Faculty:* 14. *Students:* 8 full-time (3 women), 5 part-time (2 women), 2 international. 4 applicants, 50% accepted. In 1998, 1 master's awarded (100% found work related to degree). *Degree requirements:* For master's, thesis required, foreign language not required; for doctorate, dissertation required, dissertation required. *Entrance requirements:* For master's and doctorate, GRE General Test, minimum GPA of 3.0. *Application deadline:* For fall admission, 6/1 (priority date). Applications are processed on a rolling basis. Application fee: $40. Tuition, state resident: full-time $2,520; part-time $140 per credit hour. Tuition, nonresident: full-time $7,790; part-time $433 per credit hour. Required fees: $400; $7 per credit hour. Full-time tuition and fees vary according to course load and program. *Financial aid:* Research assistantships available. Financial aid application deadline: 3/1. *Faculty research:* Plant biology, molecular biology/physiology/morphology, production, genetics/breeding, weed control. *Unit head:* Dr. Ron Delaney, Head, Department of Plant, Soil, and Insect Sciences, 307-766-3103, Fax: 307-766-5549, E-mail: rdelaney@uwyo.edu.

Utah State University, School of Graduate Studies, College of Agriculture, Department of Plants, Soils, and Biometeorology, Logan, UT 84322. Offers biometeorology (MS, PhD); ecology (MS, PhD); plant science (MS, PhD); soil science (MS, PhD). Part-time programs available. *Faculty:* 28 full-time (3 women), 15 part-time (0 women). *Students:* 16 full-time (4 women), 12 part-time (2 women); includes 1 minority (African American), 7 international. Average age 33. 17 applicants, 65% accepted. In 1998, 3 master's, 2 doctorates awarded. Terminal master's awarded for partial completion of doctoral program. *Degree requirements:* For master's and doctorate, thesis/dissertation required, foreign language not required. *Entrance requirements:* For master's, GRE General Test (score in 40th percentile or higher required), TOEFL (minimum score of 550 required), BS in plant science, biological science, or related field, minimum GPA of 3.0; for doctorate, GRE General Test (score in 40th percentile or higher required), TOEFL (minimum score of 550 required), minimum GPA of 3.0. *Application deadline:* For fall admission, 6/15 (priority date); for spring admission, 10/15. Applications are processed on a rolling basis. Application fee: $40. Tuition, state resident: full-time $1,492. Tuition, nonresident: full-time $5,232. Required fees: $434. Tuition and fees vary according to course load. *Financial aid:* In 1998–99, 1 fellowship with partial tuition reimbursement (averaging $12,000 per year), 25 research assistantships with partial tuition reimbursements (averaging $12,000 per year), 4 teaching assistantships with partial tuition reimbursements were awarded.; Federal Work-Study, institutionally-sponsored loans, and tuition waivers (full and partial) also available. Aid available to part-time students. Financial aid application deadline: 4/15. *Faculty research:* Plant physiology and developmental biology; plant improvement through breeding and biotechnology, soil, plant, water, and nutrient relationships; agronomic and landscape management; adaptations to weather. *Unit head:* Dr. V. Philip Rasmussen, Head, 435-797-3394, Fax: 435-797-3376, E-mail: soilcomp@cc.usu.edu. *Application contact:* Dr. John G. Carman, Graduate Student Coordinator, 435-797-2238, Fax: 435-797-3376, E-mail: jcarm@mendel.usu.edu.

Virginia Polytechnic Institute and State University, Graduate School, College of Agriculture and Life Sciences, Department of Crop and Soil Environmental Sciences, Blacksburg, VA 24061. Offers MS, PhD. *Students:* 37 full-time (15 women), 8 part-time (3 women); includes 5 minority (3 African Americans, 2 Hispanic Americans), 6 international. 38 applicants, 47% accepted. In 1998, 9 master's, 5 doctorates awarded. *Entrance requirements:* For master's and doctorate, TOEFL. *Application deadline:* For fall admission, 12/1 (priority date). Applications are processed on a rolling basis. Application fee: $25. *Financial aid:* Fellowships, research assistantships, teaching assistantships, unspecified assistantships available. Financial aid application deadline: 4/1. *Unit head:* Dr. Jack Hall, Head, 540-231-6305, E-mail: jrhall3@vt.edu.

Washington State University, Graduate School, College of Agriculture and Home Economics, Department of Soil and Crop Sciences, Program in Crop Sciences, Pullman, WA 99164. Offers MS, PhD. *Faculty:* 16 full-time (2 women). *Students:* 14 full-time (3 women), 1 part-time; includes 1 minority (Asian American or Pacific Islander), 5 international. In 1998, 1 doctorate awarded. *Degree requirements:* For master's, oral exam required, thesis optional, foreign language not required; for doctorate, dissertation, oral exam required, foreign language not required. *Entrance requirements:* For master's and doctorate, minimum GPA of 3.0. *Average time to degree:* Master's–2 years full-time; doctorate–5 years full-time. *Application deadline:* For fall admission, 3/1 (priority date); for spring admission, 8/1. Applications are processed on a rolling basis. Application fee: $35. *Financial aid:* In 1998–99, 4 research assistantships, 1 teaching assistantship were awarded.; fellowships, career-related internships or fieldwork, Federal Work-Study, institutionally-sponsored loans, tuition waivers (partial), and teaching associateships also available. Financial aid application deadline: 4/1; financial aid applicants required to submit FAFSA. *Unit head:* Dr. Thomas Lumpkin, Chairman, Department of Soil and Crop Sciences, 509-335-3471, Fax: 509-335-8674.

Washington State University, Graduate School, College of Agriculture and Home Economics, Department of Soil and Crop Sciences, Program in Soil Sciences, Pullman, WA 99164. Offers MS, PhD. *Faculty:* 17 full-time (0 women). *Students:* 12 full-time (5 women), 2 part-time (both women), 4 international. In 1998, 3 master's, 1 doctorate awarded. *Degree requirements:* For master's, oral exam required, thesis optional, foreign language not required; for doctorate, dissertation, oral exam required, foreign language not required. *Entrance requirements:* For master's and doctorate, minimum GPA of 3.0. *Average time to degree:* Doctorate–4 years full-time. *Application deadline:* For fall admission, 3/1 (priority date); for spring admission, 8/1. Applications are processed on a rolling basis. Application fee: $35. *Financial aid:* In 1998–99, 7 research assistantships, 3 teaching assistantships were awarded.; career-related internships or fieldwork, Federal Work-Study, institutionally-sponsored loans, tuition waivers (partial), and teaching associateships also available. Financial aid application deadline: 4/1; financial aid applicants required to submit FAFSA. *Unit head:* Dr. Thomas Lumpkin, Chairman, Department of Soil and Crop Sciences, 509-335-3471, Fax: 509-335-8674.

West Virginia University, College of Agriculture, Forestry and Consumer Sciences, Division of Plant and Soil Sciences, Morgantown, WV 26506. Offers MS, PhD. *Degree requirements:* For master's, thesis required, foreign language not required; for doctorate, dissertation, comprehensive exam required, foreign language not required. *Entrance requirements:* For master's, GRE, TOEFL (minimum score of 550 required), minimum GPA of 2.5; for doctorate, GRE General Test (minimum combined score of 1300 required), TOEFL (minimum score of 550 required), minimum GPA of 3.0. *Faculty research:* Water quality, reclamation of disturbedland, crop production, pest control, environmental protection.

Animal Sciences

Alabama Agricultural and Mechanical University, School of Graduate Studies, School of Agricultural and Environmental Sciences, Department of Plant, Soil and Animal Sciences, Normal, AL 35762-1357. Offers animal sciences (MS); environmental science (MS); plant and soil science (PhD). Evening/weekend programs available. *Faculty:* 12 full-time (1 woman). *Students:* 11 full-time (6 women), 29 part-time (4 women); includes 28 minority (27 African Americans, 1 Asian American or Pacific Islander), 12 international. Terminal master's awarded for partial completion of doctoral program. *Degree requirements:* For master's, thesis required, foreign language not required; for doctorate, one foreign language, computer language, dissertation required. *Entrance requirements:* For master's, GRE General Test, BS in agriculture; for doctorate, GRE General Test (minimum combined score of 1000 required), MS. *Application deadline:* For fall admission, 5/1. Applications are processed on a rolling basis. Application fee: $15 ($20 for international students). Tuition, state resident: full-time $1,932. Tuition, nonresident: full-time $3,864. Tuition and fees vary according to course load. *Unit head:* Dr. Govind Sharma, Chair, 256-851-5462.

Alcorn State University, School of Graduate Studies, School of Agriculture and Applied Science, Lorman, MS 39096-9402. Offers agricultural economics (MS Ag); agronomy (MS Ag); animal science (MS Ag). *Degree requirements:* For master's, thesis optional, foreign language not required. *Faculty research:* Aquatic systems, dairy herd improvement, fruit production, alternative farming practices.

Angelo State University, Graduate School, College of Sciences, Department of Agriculture, San Angelo, TX 76909. Offers animal science (MS). Part-time and evening/weekend programs available. *Faculty:* 6 full-time (0 women), 11 part-time (0 women). *Students:* 20 full-time (6 women), 7 part-time (3 women); includes 1 minority (Native American) *Degree requirements:* For master's, thesis, comprehensive exam required, foreign language not required. *Entrance requirements:* For master's, GRE General Test, minimum GPA of 2.5. *Application deadline:* For fall admission, 8/7 (priority date); for spring admission, 1/2. Applications are processed on a rolling basis. Application fee: $25 ($50 for international students). Tuition, state resident: part-time $38 per semester hour. Tuition, nonresident: part-time $249 per semester hour. Required fees: $40 per semester hour. $71 per semester. Tuition and fees vary according to degree level. *Unit head:* Dr. Donald Shelby, Head, 915-942-2027.

Auburn University, Graduate School, College of Agriculture, Department of Animal and Dairy Sciences, Auburn, Auburn University, AL 36849-0002. Offers M Ag, MS, PhD. Part-time programs available. *Faculty:* 25 full-time (3 women). *Students:* 10 full-time (6 women), 6 part-time (3 women), 5 international. 8 applicants, 38% accepted. In 1998, 7 master's awarded. *Degree requirements:* For master's, thesis (MS) required; for doctorate, dissertation required, foreign language not required. *Entrance requirements:* For master's, GRE General Test; for doctorate, GRE General Test (minimum score of 400 on each section required). *Application deadline:* For fall admission, 9/1; for spring admission, 3/1. Applications are processed on a rolling basis. Application fee: $25 ($50 for international students). Tuition, state resident: full-time $2,760; part-time $76 per credit hour. Tuition, nonresident: full-time $8,280; part-time $228 per credit hour. *Financial aid:* Research assistantships, teaching assistantships, Federal Work-Study available. Aid available to part-time students. Financial aid application deadline: 3/15. *Faculty research:* Animal breeding and genetics, animal biochemistry and nutrition, physiology of reproduction, animal production. *Unit head:* Dr. James Floyd, Interim Head,

Animal Sciences

Auburn University (continued)

334-844-4160. *Application contact:* Dr. John F. Pritchett, Dean of the Graduate School, 334-844-4700.

Auburn University, Graduate School, College of Agriculture, Department of Poultry Science, Auburn, Auburn University, AL 36849-0002. Offers M Ag, MS, PhD. Part-time programs available. *Faculty:* 13 full-time (0 women). *Students:* 6 full-time (1 woman), 13 part-time (4 women), 9 international. 4 applicants, 50% accepted. In 1998, 5 master's awarded. *Degree requirements:* For master's, thesis (MS) required; for doctorate, dissertation, computer language or statistics course work required, foreign language not required. *Entrance requirements:* For master's, GRE General Test; for doctorate, GRE General Test (minimum score of 400 on each section required), MS. *Application deadline:* For fall admission, 9/1; for spring admission, 3/1. Applications are processed on a rolling basis. Application fee: $25 ($50 for international students). Tuition, state resident: full-time $2,760; part-time $76 per credit hour. Tuition, nonresident: full-time $8,280; part-time $228 per credit hour. *Financial aid:* Research assistantships, Federal Work-Study available. Aid available to part-time students. Financial aid application deadline: 3/15. *Faculty research:* Poultry nutrition, poultry breeding, poultry physiology, poultry diseases and parasites, processing/food science. *Unit head:* Dr. Robert Brewer, Head, 334-844-4133, E-mail: rbrewer@ag.auburn.edu. *Application contact:* Dr. John F. Pritchett, Dean of the Graduate School, 334-844-4700.

Brigham Young University, Graduate Studies, College of Biological and Agricultural Sciences, Department of Animal Science, Provo, UT 84602-1001. Offers MS. *Faculty:* 9 full-time (1 woman). *Students:* 13 full-time (4 women), 1 international. Average age 24. 8 applicants, 38% accepted. In 1998, 2 degrees awarded (50% entered university research/teaching, 50% continued full-time study). *Degree requirements:* For master's, thesis required. *Entrance requirements:* For master's, GRE General Test, minimum GPA of 3.0 during previous 2 years. *Average time to degree:* Master's–2 years full-time. *Application deadline:* For fall admission, 2/28; for spring admission, 2/20. Application fee: $30. Tuition: Full-time $3,330; part-time $185 per credit hour. Tuition and fees vary according to program and student's religious affiliation. *Financial aid:* In 1998–99, 13 students received aid, including 2 fellowships with tuition reimbursements available (averaging $10,500 per year), 2 research assistantships with partial tuition reimbursements available (averaging $1,600 per year), 2 teaching assistantships (averaging $1,600 per year); career-related internships or fieldwork and institutionally-sponsored loans also available. Financial aid application deadline: 3/23. *Faculty research:* Alternate feedstuffs, follicular development, equine reproduction, pathogenity of disease, gene mapping. Total annual research expenditures: $398,000. *Unit head:* Dr. Richard N. Thwaits, Chair, 801-378-4294, Fax: 801-378-4211, E-mail: richard_thwaits@byu.edu. *Application contact:* Love Cheri Myers, Department Secretary, 801-378-4294, Fax: 801-378-4211, E-mail: lcmyers@byu.edu.

California State Polytechnic University, Pomona, Graduate Studies, College of Agriculture, Pomona, CA 91768-2557. Offers agricultural science (MS); animal science (MS); foods and nutrition (MS). Part-time programs available. *Faculty:* 24. *Students:* 17 full-time (13 women), 49 part-time (35 women); includes 25 minority (4 African Americans, 11 Asian Americans or Pacific Islanders, 10 Hispanic Americans), 8 international. *Degree requirements:* For master's, thesis or alternative required. *Application deadline:* Applications are processed on a rolling basis. Application fee: $55. Tuition, nonresident: part-time $164 per unit. *Unit head:* Dr. Wayne R. Bidlack, Dean, 909-869-2200, E-mail: wrbidlack@csupomona.edu.

California State University, Fresno, Division of Graduate Studies, School of Agricultural Sciences and Technology, Department of Animal Science and Agricultural Education, Fresno, CA 93740-0057. Offers agriculture (MS), including animal science. Part-time and evening/weekend programs available. *Faculty:* 8 full-time (1 woman). *Students:* 1 full-time (0 women), 2 part-time (1 woman). Average age 31. 3 applicants, 100% accepted. In 1998, 1 degree awarded. *Degree requirements:* For master's, thesis required, foreign language not required. *Entrance requirements:* For master's, GRE General Test, TOEFL (minimum score of 550 required), minimum GPA of 3.0 in last 60 hours. *Average time to degree:* Master's–3.5 years full-time. *Application deadline:* For fall admission, 6/1 (priority date); for spring admission, 11/1. Applications are processed on a rolling basis. Application fee: $55. Electronic applications accepted. Tuition, nonresident: part-time $246 per unit. Required fees: $1,906; $620 per semester. *Financial aid:* Fellowships, career-related internships or fieldwork, Federal Work-Study, and scholarships available. Aid available to part-time students. Financial aid application deadline: 3/1; financial aid applicants required to submit FAFSA. *Faculty research:* Horse nutrition, animal health and welfare, electronic monitoring. *Unit head:* Dr. Arthur A. Parham, Chair, 559-278-2971, Fax: 559-278-4101, E-mail: arthur_parham@csufresno.edu.

Clemson University, Graduate School, College of Agriculture, Forestry and Life Sciences, Interdepartmental Program in Agriculture, Clemson, SC 29634. Offers agricultural economics (M Ag); agricultural mechanization and business (M Ag); animal industries (M Ag); plant health (M Ag). Part-time programs available. *Students:* 1 (woman) full-time, 1 part-time. *Degree requirements:* For master's, thesis not required. *Entrance requirements:* For master's, GRE General Test, TOEFL, work experience. *Application deadline:* For fall admission, 6/1. Application fee: $35. Electronic applications accepted. *Unit head:* Dave Alverson, Coordinator, 864-656-3136, Fax: 864-656-4960, E-mail: dalverson@clemson.edu.

Clemson University, Graduate School, College of Agriculture, Forestry and Life Sciences, School of Animal, Biomedical and Biological Sciences, Department of Animal, Dairy and Veterinary Sciences, Program in Animal and Food Industries, Clemson, SC 29634. Offers MS. Offered in cooperation with the Departments of Food Science and Poultry Science. *Students:* 10 full-time (5 women), 5 part-time (2 women), 2 international. 20 applicants, 45% accepted. In 1998, 13 degrees awarded. *Degree requirements:* For master's, thesis required. *Entrance requirements:* For master's, GRE General Test, TOEFL. *Application deadline:* For fall admission, 6/1. Applications are processed on a rolling basis. Application fee: $35. Electronic applications accepted. *Financial aid:* Fellowships with partial tuition reimbursements, research assistantships with partial tuition reimbursements, teaching assistantships with partial tuition reimbursements available. Financial aid applicants required to submit FAFSA. *Unit head:* Dr. Donald M. Hendricks, Coordinator, 864-656-5687, Fax: 864-656-3131.

Clemson University, Graduate School, College of Agriculture, Forestry and Life Sciences, School of Animal, Biomedical and Biological Sciences, Department of Poultry Science, Clemson, SC 29634. Offers animal and food industries (MS); animal physiology (MS, PhD); nutrition (MS, PhD). MS (animal and food industries) offered in cooperation with the Department of Animal, Dairy and Veterinary Sciences and the Department of Food Science. *Degree requirements:* For doctorate, dissertation required. *Entrance requirements:* For master's and doctorate, GRE General Test, TOEFL. *Application deadline:* For fall admission, 6/1. Application fee: $35. *Financial aid:* Applicants required to submit FAFSA. *Unit head:* Dr. Thomas R. Scott, Director, 864-656-3163, Fax: 864-656-7396, E-mail: trscott@clemson.edu.

Colorado State University, Graduate School, College of Agricultural Sciences, Department of Animal Sciences, Fort Collins, CO 80523-0015. Offers animal breeding and genetics (MS, PhD); animal nutrition (MS, PhD); animal reproduction (MS, PhD); animal sciences (M Agr); livestock handling (MS, PhD); meats (MS, PhD); production management (MS, PhD). *Faculty:* 23 full-time (3 women), 3 part-time (1 woman). *Students:* 36 full-time (16 women), 8 part-time (3 women), 7 international. Average age 28. 55 applicants, 38% accepted. In 1998, 11 master's, 1 doctorate awarded. *Degree requirements:* For master's, thesis, publishable paper required, foreign language not required; for doctorate, dissertation, 2 publishable papers required, foreign language not required. *Entrance requirements:* For master's and doctorate, GRE General Test, TOEFL (minimum score of 550 required), minimum GPA of 3.0. *Application deadline:* For fall admission, 2/1 (priority date). Applications are processed on a rolling basis. Application fee: $30. Electronic applications accepted. *Financial aid:* In 1998–99, 26 research assistantships were awarded.; fellowships, teaching assistantships, traineeships also available. *Faculty research:* Efficiency, food safety, beef management. Total annual research expenditures: $2 million. *Unit head:* David R. Ames, Head, 970-491-7803, Fax: 970-491-5326.

Cornell University, Graduate School, Graduate Fields of Agriculture and Life Sciences, Field of Animal Breeding, Ithaca, NY 14853-0001. Offers animal breeding (MS, PhD); animal genetics (MS, PhD). *Faculty:* 8 full-time. *Students:* 10 full-time (3 women), 5 international. 4 applicants, 50% accepted. In 1998, 1 doctorate awarded. Terminal master's awarded for partial completion of doctoral program. *Degree requirements:* For master's and doctorate, thesis/dissertation, teaching experience required, foreign language not required. *Entrance requirements:* For master's and doctorate, TOEFL (minimum score of 550 required). *Application deadline:* Applications are processed on a rolling basis. Application fee: $65. Electronic applications accepted. *Financial aid:* In 1998–99, 6 students received aid, including 1 fellowship with full tuition reimbursement available, 1 research assistantship with full tuition reimbursement available, 4 teaching assistantships with full tuition reimbursements available; institutionally-sponsored loans, scholarships, tuition waivers (full and partial), and unspecified assistantships also available. Financial aid applicants required to submit FAFSA. *Unit head:* Director of Graduate Studies, 607-255-4416, Fax: 607-255-9829. *Application contact:* Graduate Field Assistant, 607-255-4416, Fax: 607-255-9829, E-mail: shh4@cornell.edu.

Cornell University, Graduate School, Graduate Fields of Agriculture and Life Sciences, Field of Animal Science, Ithaca, NY 14853-0001. Offers animal nutrition (MPS, MS, PhD); animal science (MPS, MS, PhD); physiology of reproduction (MPS, MS, PhD). *Faculty:* 38 full-time. *Students:* 41 full-time (18 women); includes 3 minority (2 Asian Americans or Pacific Islanders, 1 Hispanic American), 22 international. 47 applicants, 38% accepted. In 1998, 14 master's, 6 doctorates awarded. *Degree requirements:* For master's, teaching experience, thesis (MS) required; for doctorate, dissertation, teaching experience required, foreign language not required. *Entrance requirements:* For master's and doctorate, GRE General Test, TOEFL (minimum score of 550 required). *Application deadline:* Applications are processed on a rolling basis. Application fee: $65. Electronic applications accepted. *Financial aid:* In 1998–99, 34 students received aid, including 7 fellowships with full tuition reimbursements available, 18 research assistantships with full tuition reimbursements available, 9 teaching assistantships with full tuition reimbursements available; institutionally-sponsored loans, scholarships, tuition waivers (full and partial), and unspecified assistantships also available. Financial aid applicants required to submit FAFSA. *Faculty research:* Meat science and muscle biology, animal growth and development, dairy science. *Unit head:* Director of Graduate Studies, 607-255-4416, Fax: 607-255-9829. *Application contact:* Graduate Field Assistant, 607-255-4416, E-mail: shh4@cornell.edu.

Iowa State University of Science and Technology, Graduate College, College of Agriculture, Department of Animal Science, Ames, IA 50011. Offers MS, PhD. *Faculty:* 56 full-time, 2 part-time. *Students:* 74 full-time (23 women), 23 part-time (3 women); includes 2 minority (1 African American, 1 Hispanic American), 34 international. 57 applicants, 39% accepted. In 1998, 13 master's, 5 doctorates awarded. *Degree requirements:* For master's, thesis required (for some programs); for doctorate, dissertation required. *Entrance requirements:* For master's and doctorate, GRE General Test, TOEFL. *Application deadline:* For fall admission, 6/15 (priority date); for spring admission, 11/15 (priority date). Application fee: $20 ($50 for international students). Electronic applications accepted. Tuition, state resident: full-time $3,308. Tuition, nonresident: full-time $9,744. Part-time tuition and fees vary according to course load, campus/location and program. *Financial aid:* In 1998–99, 64 research assistantships with partial tuition reimbursements (averaging $8,930 per year), 2 teaching assistantships with partial tuition reimbursements (averaging $8,775 per year) were awarded.; fellowships, scholarships also available. *Faculty research:* Animal breeding, animal nutrition, meat science, muscle biology, nutritional physiology. *Unit head:* Dr. Dennis N. Marple, Head, 515-294-2160, Fax: 515-294-6994, E-mail: ansci@iastatae.edu. *Application contact:* Dr. Joe Sebranek, 515-294-2160.

Kansas State University, Graduate School, College of Agriculture, Department of Animal Sciences and Industry, Manhattan, KS 66506. Offers animal nutrition (MS, PhD); animal reproduction (MS, PhD); animal sciences and industry (MS, PhD); genetics (MS, PhD); meat science (MS, PhD). *Faculty:* 44 full-time (4 women). *Students:* 73 (20 women). *Degree requirements:* For master's and doctorate, thesis/dissertation required, foreign language not required. Application fee: $0 ($25 for international students). *Financial aid:* Research assistantships, teaching assistantships available. *Unit head:* Jack G. Riley, Head, 785-532-6533, Fax: 785-532-7059, E-mail: jriley@oz.oznet.ksu.edu. *Application contact:* J. Ernest Minton, Graduate Coordinator, 785-532-1238, Fax: 785-532-7059, E-mail: eminton@oz.oznet.ksu.edu.

Louisiana State University and Agricultural and Mechanical College, Graduate School, College of Agriculture, Department of Animal Science, Baton Rouge, LA 70803. Offers MS, PhD. Part-time programs available. *Faculty:* 17 full-time (0 women), 1 part-time (0 women). *Students:* 30 full-time (16 women), 12 part-time (3 women); includes 2 minority (1 Hispanic American, 1 Native American), 5 international. Average age 28. 23 applicants, 70% accepted. In 1998, 2 master's, 2 doctorates awarded. Terminal master's awarded for partial completion of doctoral program. *Degree requirements:* For master's and doctorate, thesis/dissertation required, foreign language not required. *Entrance requirements:* For master's and doctorate, GRE General Test, minimum GPA of 3.0. *Application deadline:* For fall admission, 1/25 (priority date). Applications are processed on a rolling basis. Application fee: $25. *Financial aid:* In 1998–99, 18 research assistantships with partial tuition reimbursements, 4 teaching assistantships with partial tuition reimbursements were awarded.; fellowships, Federal Work-Study and institutionally-sponsored loans also available. Aid available to part-time students. *Faculty research:* Breeding and genetics, nutrition, reproduction, meats, biotechnology. *Unit head:* Dr. Paul E. Humes, Head, 225-388-3241, Fax: 225-388-3279, E-mail: phumes@agctr.lsu.edu. *Application contact:* D. L. Thompson, Graduate Coordinator, 225-388-3445, Fax: 225-388-3279, E-mail: dthompson@agctr.lsu.edu.

Louisiana State University and Agricultural and Mechanical College, Graduate School, College of Agriculture, Department of Dairy Science, Baton Rouge, LA 70803. Offers MS, PhD. *Faculty:* 7 full-time (1 woman). *Students:* 10 full-time (3 women); includes 1 minority (Asian American or Pacific Islander), 7 international. Average age 30. 2 applicants, 50% accepted. In 1998, 1 master's, 2 doctorates awarded. *Degree requirements:* For master's, thesis required, foreign language not required; for doctorate, dissertation required. *Entrance requirements:* For master's and doctorate, GRE General Test, minimum GPA of 3.0. *Application deadline:* For fall admission, 1/25 (priority date). Applications are processed on a rolling basis. Application fee: $25. *Financial aid:* In 1998–99, 8 research assistantships with partial tuition reimbursements, 1 teaching assistantship with partial tuition reimbursement were awarded.; fellowships, unspecified assistantships also available. *Faculty research:* Nutrition physiology, genetics, dairy foods technology, dairy management, dairy microbiology. *Unit head:* Dr. Bruce Jenny, Head, 225-388-4411, Fax: 225-388-4008, E-mail: bjenny@agctr.lsu.edu. *Application contact:* Dr. J. D. Roussel, Graduate Adviser, 225-388-4411, Fax: 225-388-4008.

McGill University, Faculty of Graduate Studies and Research, Faculty of Agricultural and Environmental Sciences, Department of Animal Science, Montréal, PQ H3A 2T5, Canada. Offers M Sc, M Sc A, PhD. *Faculty:* 14 full-time (0 women), 9 part-time (3 women). *Students:* 34 full-time (17 women), 4 international. Average age 28. 12 applicants, 58% accepted. In 1998, 7 master's, 6 doctorates awarded. *Degree requirements:* For master's, thesis required (for some programs); for doctorate, dissertation required. *Entrance requirements:* For master's, TOEFL (minimum score of 550 required), minimum GPA of 3.0; for doctorate, TOEFL (minimum score of 550 required), M Sc. *Average time to degree:* Master's–3 years full-time; doctorate–5 years full-time. *Application deadline:* For fall admission, 1/1 (priority date); for winter admission, 5/1 (priority date); for spring admission, 9/1 (priority date). Applications are processed on a rolling basis. Application fee: $60. *Financial aid:* In 1998–99, 20 research assistantships with full tuition reimbursements (averaging $12,000 per year), 13 teaching assistantships (averaging $400 per year) were awarded.; fellowships, institutionally-sponsored loans, scholarships, and tuition waivers (full) also available. *Faculty research:* Animal nutrition, genetics, embryo transfer, DNA fingerprinting, dairy, milk recording, biochemistry. Total annual research expenditures: $867,743. *Unit head:* X. Zhao, Chair, 514-398-7794, Fax: 514-398-7964, E-mail: zhao@agradm.lan.mcgill.ca. *Application contact:* 514-398-7708, Fax: 514-398-7968, E-mail: grad@macdonald.mcgill.ca.

Michigan State University, Graduate School, College of Agriculture and Natural Resources, Department of Animal Science, East Lansing, MI 48824-1020. Offers MS, PhD. *Faculty:* 41. *Students:* 22 full-time (9 women), 46 part-time (27 women); includes 11 minority (3 African Americans, 1 Asian American or Pacific Islander, 7 Hispanic Americans), 16 international. Average age 27. 38 applicants, 37% accepted. In 1998, 10 master's, 3 doctorates awarded. *Degree requirements:* For doctorate, dissertation required. *Entrance requirements:* For master's and doctorate, GRE, TOEFL. *Application deadline:* Applications are processed on a rolling basis. Application fee: $30 ($40 for international students). *Financial aid:* In 1998–99, 49 research assistantships (averaging $10,325 per year) were awarded. Financial aid application deadline: 4/15; financial aid applicants required to submit FAFSA. Total annual research expenditures: $91,000. *Unit head:* Dr. Maynard Hogberg, Chairperson, 517-355-8383. *Application contact:* 517-355-8383.

Mississippi State University, College of Agriculture and Life Sciences, Department of Poultry Science, Mississippi State, MS 39762. Offers MS. *Students:* 4 full-time (1 woman), 2 part-time; includes 2 minority (both Asian Americans or Pacific Islanders), 1 international. Average age 28. 2 applicants, 100% accepted. *Degree requirements:* For master's, thesis required, foreign language not required. *Entrance requirements:* For master's, TOEFL. *Application deadline:* For fall admission, 7/1; for spring admission, 11/1. Applications are processed on a rolling basis. Application fee: $25 for international students. *Financial aid:* Federal Work-Study, institutionally-sponsored loans, scholarships, and unspecified assistantships available. Financial aid applicants required to submit FAFSA. *Faculty research:* Physiology, nutrition management, food science. Total annual research expenditures: $733,168. *Unit head:* Dr. G. Wallace Morgan, Head, 662-325-3416, Fax: 662-325-8292, E-mail: wmorgan@poultry.msstate.edu. *Application contact:* Jerry B. Inmon, Director of Admissions, 662-325-2224, Fax: 662-325-7360, E-mail: admit@admissions.msstate.edu.

Montana State University–Bozeman, College of Graduate Studies, College of Agriculture, Department of Animal and Range Sciences, Bozeman, MT 59717. Offers MS. Part-time programs available. *Students:* 8 full-time (0 women), 8 part-time (4 women). Average age 27. 8 applicants, 88% accepted. In 1998, 5 degrees awarded. *Degree requirements:* For master's, thesis or alternative required, foreign language not required. *Entrance requirements:* For master's, GRE General Test, TOEFL (minimum score of 550 required). *Application deadline:* For fall admission, 6/1 (priority date); for spring admission, 11/1. Applications are processed on a rolling basis. Application fee: $50. *Financial aid:* In 1998–99, 8 research assistantships (averaging $10,000 per year), 1 teaching assistantship (averaging $10,000 per year) were awarded.; career-related internships or fieldwork also available. Financial aid application deadline: 3/1; financial aid applicants required to submit FAFSA. *Faculty research:* Reclamation research, animal genetics/breeding, animal nutrition, reproductive physiology, rangeland resources. Total annual research expenditures: $1.1 million. *Unit head:* Dr. Peter Burfening, Head, 406-994-3721, Fax: 409-994-5589, E-mail: uaspb@montana.edu.

New Mexico State University, Graduate School, College of Agriculture and Home Economics, Department of Animal and Range Sciences, Las Cruces, NM 88003-8001. Offers animal science (M Ag, MS, PhD); range science (M Ag, MS, PhD). Part-time programs available. *Faculty:* 17 full-time (1 woman). *Students:* 29 full-time (8 women), 6 part-time (1 woman); includes 5 minority (3 Hispanic Americans, 2 Native Americans), 7 international. Average age 30. 35 applicants, 63% accepted. In 1998, 7 master's, 5 doctorates awarded. *Degree requirements:* For master's, thesis, seminar required, foreign language not required; for doctorate, dissertation, research tool required, foreign language not required. *Entrance requirements:* For master's, minimum GPA of 3.0 in last 60 hours of undergraduate course work (MS); for doctorate, minimum graduate GPA of 3.2. *Application deadline:* For fall admission, 7/1 (priority date); for spring admission, 11/1. Applications are processed on a rolling basis. Application fee: $15 ($35 for international students). Electronic applications accepted. Tuition, state resident: full-time $2,682; part-time $112 per credit. Tuition, nonresident: full-time $8,376; part-time $349 per credit. Tuition and fees vary according to course load. *Financial aid:* Research assistantships, teaching assistantships, Federal Work-Study available. Aid available to part-time students. Financial aid application deadline: 3/1. *Faculty research:* Reproductive physiology, ruminant nutrition, nutrition toxicology, range ecology, wildland hydrology. *Unit head:* Dr. Bobby J. Rankin, Head, 505-646-2514, Fax: 505-646-5441, E-mail: brankin@nmsu.edu.

North Carolina State University, Graduate School, College of Agriculture and Life Sciences, Department of Animal Science, Raleigh, NC 27695. Offers M Ag, MS, PhD. *Faculty:* 31 full-time (3 women), 24 part-time (2 women). *Students:* 21 full-time (5 women), 6 part-time (5 women); includes 1 minority (Hispanic American), 6 international. Average age 29. 32 applicants, 25% accepted. In 1998, 6 master's awarded. *Degree requirements:* For master's, thesis required (for some programs); for doctorate, dissertation required, foreign language not required. *Entrance requirements:* For master's and doctorate, GRE, minimum GPA of 3.0. *Application deadline:* For fall admission, 6/25; for spring admission, 11/25. Application fee: $45. *Financial aid:* In 1998–99, 20 research assistantships (averaging $4,994 per year), 1 teaching assistantship (averaging $9,008 per year) were awarded. Financial aid application deadline: 4/1. *Faculty research:* Energy utilization, puberty and reproduction, genetics of disease resistance, mineral nutrition and transgenics. Total annual research expenditures: $10.2 million. *Unit head:* Dr. Kenneth L. Esbenshade, Head, 919-515-2755, Fax: 919-515-6884, E-mail: ken_esbenshade@ncsu.edu. *Application contact:* Dr. Eugene J. Eisen, Director of Graduate Programs, 919-515-4017, Fax: 919-515-7780, E-mail: gene_eisen@ncsu.edu.

North Carolina State University, Graduate School, College of Agriculture and Life Sciences, Department of Poultry Science, Raleigh, NC 27695. Offers MS. Part-time programs available. *Faculty:* 23 full-time (1 woman), 11 part-time (0 women). *Students:* 7 full-time (4 women), 2 part-time, 2 international. Average age 28. 3 applicants, 67% accepted. In 1998, 3 degrees awarded. *Degree requirements:* For master's, thesis required, foreign language not required. *Application deadline:* For fall admission, 6/25; for spring admission, 11/25. Applications are processed on a rolling basis. Application fee: $45. *Financial aid:* In 1998–99, 1 teaching assistantship (averaging $5,505 per year) was awarded.; fellowships, research assistantships, career-related internships or fieldwork and institutionally-sponsored loans also available. *Faculty research:* Reproductive physiology, nutrition, toxicology, immunology, molecular biology. Total annual research expenditures: $5.5 million. *Unit head:* Dr. Gerald B. Havenstein, Head, 919-515-5555, Fax: 919-515-2625, E-mail: gerald_havenstein@ncsu.edu. *Application contact:* Dr. Thomas D. Siopes, Director of Graduate Programs, 919-515-5535, Fax: 919-515-2625, E-mail: tom_s@poultry.poulsci.ncsu.edu.

North Dakota State University, Graduate Studies and Research, College of Agriculture, Department of Animal and Range Sciences, Fargo, ND 58105. Offers animal science (MS, PhD); natural resources management (MS); range science (MS, PhD). *Faculty:* 23 full-time (2 women), 3 part-time (1 woman). *Students:* 23 full-time (7 women), 3 part-time, 2 international. Average age 24. 19 applicants, 100% accepted. *Degree requirements:* For master's and doctorate, thesis/dissertation required, foreign language not required. *Entrance requirements:* For master's and doctorate, GRE General Test, TOEFL (minimum score of 525 required). *Application deadline:* Applications are processed on a rolling basis. Application fee: $25. *Financial aid:* In 1998–99, 21 students received aid, including 20 research assistantships with tuition reimbursements available (averaging $9,200 per year); fellowships, teaching assistantships, Federal Work-Study and institutionally-sponsored loans also available. Financial aid application deadline: 3/15. *Faculty research:* Reproduction, nutrition, meat and muscle biology, breeding/genetics. *Unit head:* Jerrold L. Dodd, Chair, 701-231-7658, Fax: 701-231-7590.

Nova Scotia Agricultural College, Research and Graduate Studies, Truro, NS B2N 5E3, Canada. Offers agriculture (M Sc), including animal behavior, animal genetics, animal management, animal nutrition, animal technology, botany, crop breeding, crop management, crop physiology, ecology, environmental microbiology, food science, geology, nutrient management, pest management, physiology, plant biotechnology, plant pathology, soil chemistry, soil fertility, soil physics, waste management. Part-time programs available. *Faculty:* 33 full-time (4 women), 14 part-time (1 woman). *Students:* 23 full-time (15 women), 17 part-time (8 women). *Degree requirements:* For master's, thesis, candidacy exam required. *Entrance requirements:* For master's, TOEFL (minimum score of 580 required), minimum GPA of 3.0. *Application deadline:* For fall admission, 6/1; for winter admission, 10/1; for spring admission, 2/1. Applications are processed on a rolling basis. Application fee: $55. *Unit head:* Jill L. Rogers-Langille, Coordinator, 902-893-6360, Fax: 902-897-9399, E-mail: jrogers-langille@cadmin.nsac.ns.ca. *Application contact:* Kari Duff, Assistant, 902-893-6502, Fax: 902-897-9399, E-mail: kduff@cadmin.nsac.ns.ca.

Oklahoma State University, Graduate College, College of Agricultural Sciences and Natural Resources, Department of Animal Sciences, Stillwater, OK 74078. Offers animal breeding (PhD); animal nutrition (PhD); animal sciences (M Ag, MS); food science (MS, PhD). *Faculty:* 29 full-time (1 woman). *Students:* 41 full-time (11 women), 44 part-time (16 women); includes 11 minority (1 African American, 2 Asian Americans or Pacific Islanders, 3 Hispanic Americans, 5 Native Americans), 19 international. Average age 29. In 1998, 15 master's, 4 doctorates awarded. *Degree requirements:* For master's, thesis required, foreign language not required; for doctorate, dissertation required. *Entrance requirements:* For master's and doctorate, TOEFL (minimum score of 550 required). *Application deadline:* For fall admission, 6/1 (priority date). Application fee: $25. *Financial aid:* In 1998–99, 50 students received aid, including 42 research assistantships (averaging $10,609 per year), 7 teaching assistantships (averaging $11,477 per year); career-related internships or fieldwork, Federal Work-Study, and tuition waivers (partial) also available. Aid available to part-time students. Financial aid application deadline: 3/1. *Faculty research:* Quantitative trait loci identification for economical traits in swing/beef; quantitative genetic selection in farm animals; waste management strategies in livestock; endocrine control of reproductive processes in farm animals; cholesterol synthesis, inhibition, and reduction; food safety research for E. Coli and Listeria. *Unit head:* Donald G. Wagner, Head, 405-744-6062.

Oregon State University, Graduate School, College of Agricultural Sciences, Department of Animal Sciences, Program in Poultry Science, Corvallis, OR 97331. Offers M Agr, MAIS, MS, PhD. *Faculty:* 17 full-time (1 woman). *Students:* 2 full-time (1 woman). Average age 31. Terminal master's awarded for partial completion of doctoral program. *Degree requirements:* For master's, thesis (MS) required; for doctorate, dissertation required, foreign language not required. *Entrance requirements:* For master's and doctorate, GRE General Test, TOEFL (minimum score of 550 required), minimum GPA of 3.0 in last 90 hours. *Application deadline:* For fall admission, 3/1. Applications are processed on a rolling basis. Application fee: $50. *Financial aid:* Fellowships, research assistantships, career-related internships or fieldwork, Federal Work-Study, and institutionally-sponsored loans available. Aid available to part-time students. Financial aid application deadline: 2/1. *Faculty research:* Reproductive physiology, nutrition, genetics management. *Unit head:* James R. Males, Head, Department of Animal Sciences, 541-737-3431, Fax: 541-737-4174, E-mail: malesj@ccmail.orst.edu.

Pennsylvania State University University Park Campus, Graduate School, College of Agricultural Sciences, Department of Dairy and Animal Science, State College, University Park, PA 16802-1503. Offers animal science (M Agr, MS, PhD). *Students:* 14 full-time (6 women), 7 part-time (2 women). In 1998, 1 master's, 2 doctorates awarded. *Entrance requirements:* For master's and doctorate, GRE General Test. Application fee: $50. *Unit head:* Dr. Terry Etherton, Head, 814-863-3665. *Application contact:* Dr. Craig R. Baumrucker, Co-Graduate Officer, 814-863-3664.

Prairie View A&M University, Graduate School, College of Agriculture, Nutrition and Human Ecology, Department of Agriculture, Nutrition and Human Ecology, Prairie View, TX 77446-0188. Offers animal science (MS); human sciences (MS); soil science (MS). *Students:* 19 full-time (14 women), 12 part-time (9 women); includes 25 minority (all African Americans), 4 international. *Degree requirements:* For master's, thesis required, foreign language not required. *Entrance requirements:* For master's, GRE General Test. *Application deadline:* For fall admission, 7/1 (priority date); for spring admission, 11/1. Applications are processed on a rolling basis. Application fee: $10. *Unit head:* Dr. Cecil L. Strickland, Interim Head, 409-857-2812, Fax: 409-857-2811.

Purdue University, Graduate School, School of Agriculture, Department of Animal Sciences, West Lafayette, IN 47907. Offers MS, PhD. Part-time programs available. *Faculty:* 31 full-time (2 women), 6 part-time (3 women). *Students:* 37 full-time (20 women), 12 part-time (4 women); includes 2 minority (1 African American, 1 Hispanic American), 13 international. 53 applicants, 49% accepted. In 1998, 10 master's, 3 doctorates awarded. *Degree requirements:* For master's, thesis optional, foreign language not required; for doctorate, dissertation required, foreign language not required. *Entrance requirements:* For master's and doctorate, GRE General Test, TOEFL (minimum score of 550 required), TWE. *Application deadline:* For fall admission, 4/15 (priority date); for spring admission, 10/15. Applications are processed on a rolling basis. Application fee: $30. Electronic applications accepted. *Financial aid:* In 1998–99, 35 students received aid, including 29 research assistantships, 2 teaching assistantships; fellowships Aid available to part-time students. Financial aid applicants required to submit FAFSA. *Faculty research:* Genetics, meat science, nutrition, management, ethology. Total annual research expenditures: $3 million. *Unit head:* Dr. J. D. Armstrong, Head, 765-494-4809, Fax: 765-494-9346. *Application contact:* C. Carmony, Graduate Secretary, 765-494-2649, Fax: 765-494-6816, E-mail: grad@ansc.purdue.edu.

Rutgers, The State University of New Jersey, New Brunswick, Graduate School, Program in Animal Sciences, New Brunswick, NJ 08903. Offers endocrine control of growth and metabolism (MS, PhD); nutrition of ruminant and nonruminant animals (MS, PhD); reproductive endocrinology and neuroendocrinology (MS, PhD). Part-time programs available. *Faculty:* 15 full-time (5 women), 14 part-time (2 women). *Students:* 15 full-time (11 women), 6 part-time (3 women); includes 3 minority (1 Asian American or Pacific Islander, 2 Hispanic Americans), 4 international. Average age 23. 18 applicants, 39% accepted. In 1998, 2 master's, 3 doctorates awarded (100% found work related to degree). Terminal master's awarded for partial completion of doctoral program. *Degree requirements:* For master's and doctorate, thesis/dissertation required, foreign language not required. *Entrance requirements:* For master's and doctorate, GRE General Test, GRE Subject Test. *Application deadline:* For fall admission, 5/1 (priority date). Applications are processed on a rolling basis. Application fee: $50. *Financial aid:* In 1998–99, 16 students received aid, including 3 research assistantships with full tuition reimbursements available, 13 teaching assistantships with full tuition reimbursements available; fellowships with full tuition reimbursements available Aid available to part-time students. Financial aid application deadline: 3/1; financial aid applicants required to submit FAFSA. *Unit head:* Henry John-Alder, Director, 732-932-3229.

South Dakota State University, Graduate School, College of Agriculture and Biological Sciences, Department of Animal Science and Range Science, Brookings, SD 57007. Offers animal science (MS, PhD). *Degree requirements:* For master's, thesis, oral exam required, foreign language not required; for doctorate, dissertation, preliminary oral and written exams required. *Entrance requirements:* For master's and doctorate, TOEFL (minimum score of 550 required). *Faculty research:* Ruminant and nonruminant nutrition, meat science, reproductive physiology, range utilization, ecology genetics.

South Dakota State University, Graduate School, College of Agriculture and Biological Sciences, Department of Dairy Science, Brookings, SD 57007. Offers MS, PhD. *Degree requirements:* For master's, thesis, oral exam required, foreign language not required; for doctorate, dissertation, preliminary oral and written exams required. *Entrance requirements:* For master's and doctorate, TOEFL (minimum score of 525 required). *Faculty research:* Dairy cattle nutrition, energy metabolism, lowfat cheese technology, food safety, sensory evaluation of dairy products.

Animal Sciences

Southern Illinois University Carbondale, Graduate School, College of Agriculture, Department of Animal Science, Food and Nutrition, Program in Animal Science, Carbondale, IL 62901-6806. Offers MS. *Faculty:* 7 full-time (1 woman), 2 part-time (0 women). *Students:* 12 full-time (6 women), 4 part-time (all women), 2 international. Average age 29. 10 applicants, 80% accepted. In 1998, 6 degrees awarded. *Degree requirements:* For master's, thesis required, foreign language not required. *Entrance requirements:* For master's, TOEFL (minimum score of 550 required), minimum GPA of 2.7. *Application deadline:* Applications are processed on a rolling basis. Application fee: $0. *Financial aid:* In 1998–99, 9 students received aid; fellowships with full tuition reimbursements available, research assistantships with full tuition reimbursements available, teaching assistantships with full tuition reimbursements available, career-related internships or fieldwork, Federal Work-Study, institutionally-sponsored loans, and tuition waivers (full) available. Aid available to part-time students. *Faculty research:* Nutrition, reproductive physiology, animal biotechnology, phytoestrogens and animal reproduction. Total annual research expenditures: $300,000. *Unit head:* Dr. Robert Arthor, Chair, Department of Animal Science, Food and Nutrition, 618-453-2329, Fax: 618-453-5231.

Sul Ross State University, Division of Range Animal Science, Program in Animal Science, Alpine, TX 79832. Offers M Ag, MS. Part-time programs available. *Degree requirements:* For master's, thesis required (for some programs), foreign language not required. *Entrance requirements:* For master's, GRE General Test (minimum combined score of 850 required), minimum GPA of 2.5 in last 60 hours of undergraduate work. *Faculty research:* Reproductive physiology, meat processing, animal nutrition, equine foot and motion studies, Spanish goat and Barbido sheep studies.

Texas A&M University, College of Agriculture and Life Sciences, Department of Animal Science, College Station, TX 77843. Offers animal breeding (MS, PhD); animal science (M Agr, MS, PhD); dairy science (M Agr, MS); food science and technology (MS, PhD); genetics (MS, PhD); nutrition (MS, PhD); physiology of reproduction (MS, PhD). *Faculty:* 48 full-time (10 women), 5 part-time (3 women). *Students:* 190 full-time (109 women), 5 part-time (3 women); includes 11 minority (4 Asian Americans or Pacific Islanders, 6 Hispanic Americans, 1 Native American), 37 international. Average age 26. 172 applicants, 24% accepted. In 1998, 32 master's, 17 doctorates awarded (60% entered university research/teaching, 40% found other work related to degree). *Degree requirements:* For master's and doctorate, thesis/dissertation required, foreign language not required. *Entrance requirements:* For master's and doctorate, GRE General Test, TOEFL. *Average time to degree:* Master's–2 years full-time; doctorate–4 years full-time. *Application deadline:* For fall admission, 2/1 (priority date); for spring admission, 10/1 (priority date). Applications are processed on a rolling basis. Application fee: $50 ($75 for international students). *Financial aid:* In 1998–99, 5 fellowships (averaging $12,000 per year), 39 research assistantships (averaging $11,250 per year), 33 teaching assistantships (averaging $11,250 per year) were awarded.; career-related internships or fieldwork, Federal Work-Study, institutionally-sponsored loans, and scholarships also available. Financial aid application deadline: 2/1; financial aid applicants required to submit FAFSA. *Faculty research:* Genetic engineering/gene markers, dietary effects on colon cancer, biotechnology. *Unit head:* Dr. Bryan H. Johnson, Head, 409-845-1541. *Application contact:* Ronnie Edwards, Graduate Adviser, 409-845-1542, Fax: 409-845-6433, E-mail: r-edwards@tamu.edu.

Texas A&M University, College of Agriculture and Life Sciences, Department of Poultry Science, College Station, TX 77843. Offers M Agr, MS, PhD. Part-time programs available. *Faculty:* 13 full-time (1 woman). *Students:* 21 full-time (9 women), 7 part-time (3 women); includes 4 minority (1 African American, 3 Hispanic Americans), 4 international. Average age 29. In 1998, 4 master's awarded (100% found work related to degree); 3 doctorates awarded (67% entered university research/teaching, 33% found other work related to degree). Terminal master's awarded for partial completion of doctoral program. *Degree requirements:* For master's, thesis required (for some programs); for doctorate, dissertation required. *Entrance requirements:* For master's and doctorate, GRE General Test (minimum combined score of 1000 required), TOEFL (minimum score of 550 required). *Average time to degree:* Master's–2 years full-time; doctorate–6 years full-time. Application fee: $50 ($75 for international students). Electronic applications accepted. *Financial aid:* In 1998–99, 23 students received aid, including 3 fellowships (averaging $12,000 per year), 20 research assistantships (averaging $12,000 per year); teaching assistantships, unspecified assistantships also available. Financial aid application deadline: 4/1; financial aid applicants required to submit FAFSA. *Faculty research:* Poultry genetics and breeding, poultry nutrition and feeding, avian physiology, game bird management, poultry product development. *Unit head:* Dr. Clarence Creger, Head, 409-845-1931, Fax: 409-845-1921, E-mail: dcreger@poultry.tamu.edu. *Application contact:* Roy Fanguy, Graduate Adviser, 409-845-1931, Fax: 409-845-1921.

Texas A&M University–Kingsville, College of Graduate Studies, College of Agriculture and Home Economics, Program in Animal Sciences, Kingsville, TX 78363. Offers MS. *Faculty:* 2 full-time (1 woman), 1 part-time (0 women). *Students:* 7 full-time (3 women), 4 part-time. *Degree requirements:* For master's, thesis or alternative, comprehensive exam required, foreign language not required. *Entrance requirements:* For master's, GRE General Test (minimum combined score of 800 required), TOEFL (minimum score of 525 required), minimum GPA of 3.0. *Application deadline:* For fall admission, 6/1; for spring admission, 11/15. Applications are processed on a rolling basis. Application fee: $15 ($25 for international students). Tuition, state resident: full-time $2,062. Tuition, nonresident: full-time $7,246. *Financial aid:* Application deadline: 5/15. *Unit head:* Graduate Coordinator, 361-593-3711.

Texas Tech University, Graduate School, College of Agricultural Sciences and Natural Resources, Department of Animal Science and Food Technology, Lubbock, TX 79409. Offers animal breeding (MS); animal nutrition (MS); animal science (MS, PhD); animal science and food technology (M Agr); food technology (MS); meat science (MS). Part-time programs available. *Faculty:* 10 full-time (2 women). *Students:* 47 full-time (14 women), 8 part-time (4 women); includes 1 minority (Hispanic American), 8 international. Average age 28. 37 applicants, 51% accepted. In 1998, 11 master's, 5 doctorates awarded. *Degree requirements:* For master's, thesis, internship (M Agr) required, foreign language not required; for doctorate, dissertation required. *Entrance requirements:* For master's, GRE General Test (combined average 958); for doctorate, GRE General Test. *Application deadline:* For fall admission, 4/15 (priority date); for spring admission, 11/1 (priority date). Applications are processed on a rolling basis. Application fee: $25 ($50 for international students). Electronic applications accepted. *Financial aid:* In 1998–99, 31 research assistantships (averaging $6,672 per year), 6 teaching assistantships (averaging $6,362 per year) were awarded.; fellowships, Federal Work-Study and institutionally-sponsored loans also available. Aid available to part-time students. Financial aid application deadline: 5/15; financial aid applicants required to submit FAFSA. *Faculty research:* Animal growth composition and product acceptability, animal nutrition and utilization, animal physiology and adaptation to stress. Total annual research expenditures: $1.2 million. *Unit head:* Dr. Kevin R. Pond, Chairman, 806-742-2513, Fax: 806-742-0898.

Tuskegee University, Graduate Programs, College of Agricultural, Environmental and Natural Sciences, Department of Agricultural Sciences, Program in Animal and Poultry Sciences, Tuskegee, AL 36088. Offers MS. *Faculty:* 13 full-time (1 woman), 2 part-time (1 woman). *Students:* 3 full-time (all women), 2 part-time (both women); includes 4 minority (all African Americans) In 1998, 1 degree awarded. *Degree requirements:* For master's, computer language, thesis required, foreign language not required. *Entrance requirements:* For master's, GRE General Test. *Application deadline:* For fall admission, 7/15. Applications are processed on a rolling basis. Application fee: $25 ($35 for international students). *Financial aid:* Application deadline: 4/15. *Unit head:* Dr. P. K. Biswas, Head, Department of Agricultural Sciences, 334-727-8632.

Université Laval, Faculty of Graduate Studies, Faculty of Agricultural and Food Sciences, Department of Animal Sciences, Sainte-Foy, PQ G1K 7P4, Canada. Offers M Sc, PhD. *Students:* 43 full-time (15 women), 14 part-time (8 women). 17 applicants, 59% accepted. In 1998, 6 master's, 3 doctorates awarded. *Application deadline:* For fall admission, 3/1. Applica-

tion fee: $30. *Unit head:* Jean-Paul Laforest, Director, 418-656-2131 Ext. 2596, Fax: 418-656-3766, E-mail: jean-paul.laforest@san.ulaval.ca.

The University of Arizona, Graduate College, College of Agriculture, Department of Animal Sciences, Tucson, AZ 85721. Offers MS. PhD. Part-time programs available. *Faculty:* 21 full-time (1 woman). *Students:* 3 full-time (1 woman), 4 part-time; includes 1 minority (Hispanic American), 3 international. Average age 30. 12 applicants, 17% accepted. In 1998, 5 master's, 3 doctorates awarded. *Degree requirements:* For master's and doctorate, thesis/dissertation required, foreign language not required. *Entrance requirements:* For master's, GRE Subject Test, TOEFL (minimum score of 550 required); for doctorate, GRE Subject Test (biology or chemistry recommended), TOEFL (minimum score of 550 required). *Application deadline:* For fall admission, 8/1. Applications are processed on a rolling basis. Application fee: $45. *Financial aid:* Fellowships, research assistantships, teaching assistantships, institutionally-sponsored loans, scholarships, and tuition waivers (partial) available. *Faculty research:* Nutrition of beef and dairy cattle, reproduction and breeding, muscle growth and function, animal stress, meat science. *Unit head:* Dr. Roy L. Ax, Head, 520-621-1322. *Application contact:* Cheryl McCauley, Administrative Assistant, 520-621-1322, Fax: 520-621-9435.

University of Arkansas, Graduate School, Dale Bumpers College of Agricultural, Food and Life Sciences, Department of Animal Science, Fayetteville, AR 72701-1201. Offers MS, PhD. *Faculty:* 25 full-time (1 woman), 2 part-time (0 women). *Students:* 21 full-time (11 women), 7 part-time (3 women). 18 applicants, 67% accepted. In 1998, 1 doctorate awarded. *Degree requirements:* For master's, thesis required, foreign language not required; for doctorate, variable foreign language requirement, dissertation required. Application fee: $40 ($50 for international students). Tuition, state resident: full-time $3,186. Tuition, nonresident: full-time $7,560. Required fees: $378. *Financial aid:* In 1998–99, 17 research assistantships were awarded.; teaching assistantships, career-related internships or fieldwork and Federal Work-Study also available. Aid available to part-time students. Financial aid application deadline: 4/1; financial aid applicants required to submit FAFSA. *Unit head:* Dr. Keith Lusby, Chair, 501-575-4351. *Application contact:* Dr. Wayne Kellogg, Graduage Coordinator, E-mail: wkellogg@comp.uark.edu.

University of Arkansas, Graduate School, Dale Bumpers College of Agricultural, Food and Life Sciences, Department of Poultry Science, Fayetteville, AR 72701-1201. Offers MS, PhD. *Students:* 32 full-time (17 women), 5 part-time; includes 5 minority (4 Asian Americans or Pacific Islanders, 1 Hispanic American), 21 international. 19 applicants, 79% accepted. In 1998, 5 master's, 3 doctorates awarded. *Degree requirements:* For master's, thesis required, foreign language not required; for doctorate, variable foreign language requirement, dissertation required. Application fee: $40 ($50 for international students). Tuition, state resident: full-time $3,186. Tuition, nonresident: full-time $7,560. Required fees: $378. *Financial aid:* In 1998–99, 28 research assistantships were awarded.; teaching assistantships, career-related internships or fieldwork and Federal Work-Study also available. Aid available to part-time students. Financial aid application deadline: 4/1; financial aid applicants required to submit FAFSA. *Unit head:* James H. Denton, Head, 501-575-4952, E-mail: mslavik@comp.uark.edu.

University of British Columbia, Faculty of Graduate Studies, Faculty of Agricultural Sciences, Department of Animal Science, Vancouver, BC V6T 1Z2, Canada. Offers M Sc, PhD. Part-time programs available. Terminal master's awarded for partial completion of doctoral program. *Degree requirements:* For master's and doctorate, thesis/dissertation, research paper required, foreign language not required. *Entrance requirements:* For master's and doctorate, TOEFL (minimum score of 550 required). *Faculty research:* Aquaculture, nutrition and metabolism, animal production, animal behaviour and welfare, reproductive physiology, animal genetics.

University of California, Davis, Graduate Studies, Program in Animal Science, Davis, CA 95616. Offers MAM, MS. *Faculty:* 31 full-time (4 women). *Students:* 25 full-time (20 women); includes 3 minority (2 Asian Americans or Pacific Islanders, 1 Hispanic American), 6 international. 52 applicants, 38% accepted. In 1998, 14 degrees awarded. *Degree requirements:* For master's, thesis optional. *Entrance requirements:* For master's, GRE General Test, minimum GPA of 3.0. *Application deadline:* For fall admission, 1/15 (priority date). Application fee: $40. Electronic applications accepted. *Financial aid:* In 1998–99, 7 fellowships with full and partial tuition reimbursements, 3 research assistantships with full and partial tuition reimbursements, 14 teaching assistantships with full and partial tuition reimbursements were awarded. Financial aid application deadline: 1/15; financial aid applicants required to submit FAFSA. *Faculty research:* Genetics, nutrition, physiology and behavior in domestic and aquatic animals. *Unit head:* Edward O. Price, Chair, 530-752-1682. *Application contact:* Lynn Boosembark, Advising Assistant, 530-752-2382, Fax: 530-752-0175, E-mail: ansgradinf@asmail.ucdavis.edu.

University of Connecticut, Graduate School, College of Agriculture and Natural Resources, Department of Animal Science, Storrs, CT 06269. Offers MS, PhD. *Degree requirements:* For doctorate, dissertation required. *Entrance requirements:* For master's and doctorate, GRE General Test, GRE Subject Test, TOEFL.

University of Florida, Graduate School, College of Agriculture, Department of Animal Sciences, Gainesville, FL 32611. Offers M Ag, MS, PhD. *Faculty:* 68. *Students:* 33 full-time (12 women), 14 part-time (9 women); includes 5 minority (2 Asian Americans or Pacific Islanders, 3 Hispanic Americans), 13 international. 50 applicants, 54% accepted. In 1998, 10 master's, 2 doctorates awarded. *Degree requirements:* For master's, thesis optional; for doctorate, dissertation required. *Entrance requirements:* For master's and doctorate, GRE General Test, minimum GPA of 3.0. *Application deadline:* For fall admission, 6/1 (priority date). Applications are processed on a rolling basis. Application fee: $20. Electronic applications accepted. *Financial aid:* In 1998–99, 32 students received aid, including 1 fellowship, 25 research assistantships, 2 teaching assistantships *Faculty research:* Meat science, breeding and genetics, animal physiology, molecular biology, animal nutrition. Total annual research expenditures: $4.1 million. *Unit head:* Dr. F. G. Hembry, Chair, 352-392-1911, Fax: 352-392-7652, E-mail: hembry@animal.ufl.edu. *Application contact:* Dr. Henry Herbert Head, Graduate Coordinator, 352-392-5590, Fax: 352-392-7652, E-mail: head@dps.ufl.edu.

University of Florida, Graduate School, College of Agriculture, Department of Dairy and Poultry Science, Gainesville, FL 32611. Offers M Ag, MS. *Faculty:* 48. *Students:* 24 full-time (7 women), 4 part-time (2 women); includes 4 minority (1 Asian American or Pacific Islander, 3 Hispanic Americans), 12 international. 7 applicants, 57% accepted. In 1998, 6 master's awarded. *Degree requirements:* For master's, thesis optional. *Entrance requirements:* For master's, GRE General Test (minimum combined score of 1000 required), minimum GPA of 3.0. *Application deadline:* For fall admission, 6/1 (priority date). Applications are processed on a rolling basis. Application fee: $20. Electronic applications accepted. *Financial aid:* In 1998–99, 1 fellowship, 14 research assistantships were awarded.; teaching assistantships *Faculty research:* Environment, biochemistry, animal science, food science, nutrition. *Unit head:* Dr. Roger P. Natzke, Chair, 352-392-1981, Fax: 352-392-5595, E-mail: rpn@gnv.ifas.ufl.edu. *Application contact:* Dr. Henry Herbert Head, Graduate Coordinator, 352-392-5590, Fax: 352-392-7652, E-mail: head@dps.ufl.edu.

University of Georgia, Graduate School, College of Agricultural and Environmental Sciences, Department of Animal and Dairy Sciences, Athens, GA 30602. Offers animal and dairy science (PhD); animal science (MS); dairy science (MS). *Faculty:* 28 full-time (1 woman). *Students:* 22 full-time (8 women), 3 part-time; includes 1 minority (Asian American or Pacific Islander), 12 international. 29 applicants, 41% accepted. In 1998, 5 master's, 1 doctorate awarded. *Degree requirements:* For master's, thesis required, foreign language not required; for doctorate, one foreign language (computer language can substitute), dissertation required. *Entrance requirements:* For master's and doctorate, GRE General Test. *Application deadline:* For fall admission, 7/1 (priority date); for spring admission, 11/15. Application fee: $30. Electronic applications accepted. *Financial aid:* Fellowships, research assistantships, teaching assistantships, unspecified assistantships available. *Unit head:* Dr. George Rampacek, Graduate Coordinator, 706-542-0953, Fax: 706-542-0399.

University of Georgia, Graduate School, College of Agricultural and Environmental Sciences, Department of Poultry Science, Program in Animal Nutrition, Athens, GA 30602. Offers PhD. *Students:* 1 full-time (0 women). 3 applicants, 0% accepted. *Degree requirements:* For doctorate, one foreign language (computer language can substitute), dissertation required. *Entrance requirements:* For doctorate, GRE General Test. *Application deadline:* For fall admission, 7/1 (priority date); for spring admission, 11/15. Application fee: $30. Electronic applications accepted. *Financial aid:* Fellowships, research assistantships, teaching assistantships, unspecified assistantships available. *Unit head:* Dr. Gene M. Pesti, Graduate Coordinator, 706-542-1347, Fax: 706-542-1827, E-mail: gpesti@arches.uga.edu.

University of Guelph, Faculty of Graduate Studies, Ontario Agricultural College, Department of Animal and Poultry Science, Guelph, ON N1G 2W1, Canada. Offers animal science (M Sc, PhD); poultry science (M Sc, PhD). *Faculty:* 34 full-time (2 women), 1 (woman) part-time. *Students:* 73 full-time (27 women), 9 part-time (3 women), 27 international. In 1998, 16 master's, 8 doctorates awarded. *Degree requirements:* For master's, thesis required (for some programs); for doctorate, dissertation required. *Entrance requirements:* For master's, minimum B- average during previous 2 years; for doctorate, minimum B average. *Application deadline:* Applications are processed on a rolling basis. Application fee: $60. *Expenses:* Tuition and fees charges are reported in Canadian dollars. Tuition, area resident: Full-time $4,725 Canadian dollars; part-time $1,055 Canadian dollars per term. International tuition: $6,999 Canadian dollars full-time. Required fees: $295 Canadian dollars per term. *Financial aid:* Fellowships, research assistantships, teaching assistantships available. *Faculty research:* Animal breeding and genetics (quantitative or molecular), animal nutrition (monogastric or ruminant), animal physiology (environmental, reproductive or behavioral), growth and metabolism (meat science). Total annual research expenditures: $5 million. *Unit head:* Dr. Ann M. Gibbins, Chair, 519-824-4120 Ext. 2251, E-mail: agibbins@aps.uoguelph.ca. *Application contact:* Dr. T. Smith, Graduate Coordinator, 519-824-4120 Ext. 3746, E-mail: tsmith@aps.uoguelph.ca.

University of Hawaii at Manoa, Graduate Division, College of Tropical Agriculture and Human Resources, Department of Animal Sciences, Honolulu, HI 96822. Offers MS. *Faculty:* 18 full-time (2 women). *Students:* 10 full-time (8 women), 2 part-time (1 woman); includes 6 minority (5 Asian Americans or Pacific Islanders, 1 Hispanic American), 2 international. Average age 26. 9 applicants, 89% accepted. In 1998, 2 degrees awarded (33% found work related to degree, 67% continued full-time study). *Entrance requirements:* For master's, GRE. *Average time to degree:* Master's–2.5 years full-time. *Application deadline:* For fall admission, 3/1; for spring admission, 9/1. Application fee: $25 ($50 for international students). *Financial aid:* In 1998–99, 2 research assistantships (averaging $14,958 per year), 1 teaching assistantship (averaging $12,786 per year) were awarded.; tuition waivers (full and partial) also available. *Faculty research:* Reproduction, nutrition, growth regulation and modulation, livestock management, meat science. Total annual research expenditures: $200,000. *Unit head:* Dr. Douglas Vincent, Chairperson, 808-956-8356, Fax: 808-956-4883, E-mail: vincent@hawaii.edu. *Application contact:* Dr. Richard Early, Graduate Field Chairperson, 808-956-8356, Fax: 808-956-4883, E-mail: rearly@hawaii.edu.

University of Idaho, College of Graduate Studies, College of Agriculture, Department of Animal and Veterinary Science, Moscow, ID 83844-4140. Offers animal physiology (PhD); veterinary science (MS). *Faculty:* 12 full-time (1 woman). *Students:* 18 full-time (6 women), 4 part-time (all women), 5 international. In 1998, 4 master's awarded. *Degree requirements:* For doctorate, dissertation required, foreign language not required. *Entrance requirements:* For master's, GRE General Test, minimum GPA of 2.8; for doctorate, minimum undergraduate GPA of 2.8, 3.0 graduate. *Application deadline:* For fall admission, 8/1; for spring admission, 12/15. Application fee: $35 ($45 for international students). *Financial aid:* In 1998–99, 5 research assistantships (averaging $11,178 per year) were awarded.; teaching assistantships Financial aid application deadline: 2/15. *Faculty research:* Agribusiness, range-livestock management. *Unit head:* Dr. Richard A. Battaglia, Head, 208-885-6345.

University of Illinois at Urbana–Champaign, Graduate College, College of Agricultural, Consumer and Environmental Sciences, Department of Animal Sciences, Urbana, IL 61801. Offers MS, PhD. *Faculty:* 46 full-time (2 women). *Students:* 97 full-time (32 women); includes 8 minority (2 African Americans, 3 Asian Americans or Pacific Islanders, 2 Hispanic Americans, 1 Native American), 16 international. 58 applicants, 29% accepted. In 1998, 22 master's, 13 doctorates awarded. *Degree requirements:* For master's, foreign language and thesis not required; for doctorate, dissertation required. *Entrance requirements:* For master's, minimum GPA of 4.0 on a 5.0 scale. *Application deadline:* Applications are processed on a rolling basis. Application fee: $40 ($50 for international students). Tuition, state resident: full-time $4,040. Tuition, nonresident: full-time $11,192. Full-time tuition and fees vary according to program. *Financial aid:* Fellowships, research assistantships, teaching assistantships, tuition waivers (full and partial) available. Financial aid application deadline: 2/15. *Unit head:* R. A. Easter, Head, 217-333-3462. *Application contact:* Bryan White, Director of Graduate Studies, 217-333-2091, E-mail: b-white2@uiuc.edu.

University of Kentucky, Graduate School, Graduate School Programs from the College of Agriculture, Program in Animal Sciences, Lexington, KY 40506-0032. Offers MS, PhD. Terminal master's awarded for partial completion of doctoral program. *Degree requirements:* For master's, comprehensive exam required, thesis optional, foreign language not required; for doctorate, dissertation, comprehensive exam required, foreign language not required. *Entrance requirements:* For master's, GRE General Test, minimum undergraduate GPA of 2.5; for doctorate, GRE General Test, minimum graduate GPA of 3.0. *Faculty research:* Nutrition of horses, cattle, swine, poultry, and sheep; physiology of reproduction and lactation; food science; microbiology.

University of Maine, Graduate School, College of Natural Sciences, Forestry, and Agriculture, Department of Biosystems Science and Engineering, Program in Animal Sciences, Orono, ME 04469. Offers MPS, MS. *Students:* 1 (woman) 2 applicants, 50% accepted. *Degree requirements:* For master's, computer language, thesis required, foreign language not required. *Entrance requirements:* For master's, GRE General Test (minimum combined score of 1000 required), TOEFL (minimum score of 550 required), BS in animal sciences or related area. *Application deadline:* For fall admission, 2/1 (priority date); for spring admission, 10/15. Applications are processed on a rolling basis. Application fee: $50. *Financial aid:* Application deadline: 3/1. *Unit head:* Scott G. Delcourt, Director of the Graduate School, 207-581-3218, Fax: 207-581-3232, E-mail: graduate@maine.edu. *Application contact:* Scott G. Delcourt, Director of the Graduate School, 207-581-3218, Fax: 207-581-3232, E-mail: graduate@maine.edu.

University of Manitoba, Faculty of Graduate Studies, Faculty of Agriculture, Department of Animal Science, Winnipeg, MB R3T 2N2, Canada. Offers M Sc, PhD. *Degree requirements:* For master's, thesis required, foreign language not required; for doctorate, dissertation required. *Unit head:* R. J. Parker, Head.

University of Maryland, College Park, Graduate School, College of Agriculture and Natural Resources, Department of Animal and Avian Sciences, Program in Animal Sciences, College Park, MD 20742-5045. Offers MS, PhD. *Students:* 32 full-time (21 women), 13 part-time (8 women); includes 4 minority (2 African Americans, 2 Asian Americans or Pacific Islanders), 8 international. In 1998, 5 master's, 1 doctorate awarded. *Degree requirements:* For master's, thesis or alternative, oral exam or written comprehensive exam required, foreign language not required; for doctorate, dissertation, publication in journal, 2 semesters of teaching experience required. *Entrance requirements:* For master's, GRE General Test, minimum GPA of 3.0; for doctorate, GRE General Test. *Application deadline:* Applications are processed on a rolling basis. Application fee: $50 ($70 for international students). Tuition, state resident: part-time $272 per credit hour. Tuition, nonresident: part-time $475 per credit hour. Required fees: $632; $379 per year. *Financial aid:* Fellowships, research assistantships, teaching assistantships available. Financial aid applicants required to submit FAFSA. *Faculty research:* Animal physiology, pathology, virology, immunology, cell and molecular biology, DNA, radioactivity. *Unit head:* Scott G. Delcourt, Director of the Graduate School, 207-581-3218, Fax: 207-581-3232, E-mail: graduate@maine.edu. *Application contact:* Trudy Lindsey, Director, Graduate Admission and Records, 301-405-4198, Fax: 301-314-9305, E-mail: grschool@deans.umd.edu.

University of Maryland, College Park, Graduate School, College of Agriculture and Natural Resources, Department of Animal and Avian Sciences, Program in Poultry Science, College Park, MD 20742-5045. Offers MS, PhD. *Students:* 3 full-time (1 woman); includes 1 minority (Asian American or Pacific Islander), 2 international. In 1998, 3 master's, 1 doctorate awarded. *Degree requirements:* For master's, thesis, annual seminar required; for doctorate, dissertation, annual seminar, qualifying/oral exam required. *Entrance requirements:* For master's, GRE General Test, minimum GPA of 3.0; for doctorate, GRE General Test. *Application deadline:* Applications are processed on a rolling basis. Application fee: $50 ($70 for international students). Tuition, state resident: part-time $272 per credit hour. Tuition, nonresident: part-time $475 per credit hour. Required fees: $632; $379 per year. *Financial aid:* Fellowships, research assistantships, teaching assistantships available. Financial aid applicants required to submit FAFSA. *Faculty research:* Amino acids, atomic absorption, histology and histochemistry, tissue culture. *Unit head:* Trudy Lindsey, Director, Graduate Admission and Records, 301-405-4198, Fax: 301-314-9305, E-mail: grschool@deans.umd.edu. *Application contact:* Trudy Lindsey, Director, Graduate Admission and Records, 301-405-4198, Fax: 301-314-9305, E-mail: grschool@deans.umd.edu.

University of Massachusetts Amherst, Graduate School, College of Food and Natural Resources, Department of Veterinary and Animal Sciences, Amherst, MA 01003. Offers mammalian and avian biology (MS, PhD). Part-time programs available. *Faculty:* 13 full-time (3 women). *Students:* 7 full-time (4 women), 16 part-time (8 women); includes 2 minority (1 African American, 1 Hispanic American), 11 international. Average age 31. 19 applicants, 68% accepted. In 1998, 4 master's, 3 doctorates awarded. Terminal master's awarded for partial completion of doctoral program. *Degree requirements:* For master's, thesis or alternative required, foreign language not required; for doctorate, dissertation required, foreign language not required. *Entrance requirements:* For master's and doctorate, GRE General Test. *Application deadline:* For fall admission, 2/1 (priority date); for spring admission, 10/1. Applications are processed on a rolling basis. Application fee: $40. Tuition, state resident: full-time $2,640; part-time $165 per credit. Tuition, nonresident: full-time $9,756; part-time $407 per credit. Required fees: $1,221 per term. One-time fee: $110. Full-time tuition and fees vary according to course load, campus/location and reciprocity agreements. *Financial aid:* In 1998–99, 34 research assistantships with full tuition reimbursements (averaging $9,044 per year), 6 teaching assistantships with full tuition reimbursements (averaging $6,665 per year) were awarded.; fellowships with full tuition reimbursements, career-related internships or fieldwork, Federal Work-Study, grants, scholarships, traineeships, and unspecified assistantships also available. Aid available to part-time students. Financial aid application deadline: 2/1. *Unit head:* Dr. Robert Duby, Director, 413-545-2312, Fax: 413-545-6326, E-mail: duby@vasci.umass.edu.

University of Minnesota, Twin Cities Campus, Graduate School, College of Agricultural, Food, and Environmental Sciences, Department of Animal Science, Minneapolis, MN 55455-0213. Offers MS, PhD. Part-time programs available. *Faculty:* 35 full-time (2 women). *Students:* 45 full-time (13 women), 6 part-time (3 women), 24 international. 54 applicants, 46% accepted. In 1998, 4 master's, 1 doctorate awarded. *Degree requirements:* For master's and doctorate, thesis/dissertation required, foreign language not required. *Financial aid:* In 1998–99, 1 fellowship, 32 research assistantships were awarded. *Faculty research:* Animal physiology, growth biology, animal nutrition, genetics, animal production systems. *Unit head:* Dr. F. Abel Ponce de León, Head, 612-624-1205, Fax: 612-625-5789, E-mail: apl@tc.umn.edu. *Application contact:* Kimberly A. Reno, Principal Secretary, 612-624-3491, Fax: 612-625-1283, E-mail: renox001@tc.umn.edu.

University of Missouri–Columbia, Graduate School, College of Agriculture, Department of Animal Sciences, Columbia, MO 65211. Offers MS, PhD. *Faculty:* 33 full-time (1 woman). *Students:* 35 full-time (13 women), 16 part-time (7 women); includes 2 minority (both African Americans), 15 international. 3 applicants, 33% accepted. In 1998, 9 master's, 7 doctorates awarded. Terminal master's awarded for partial completion of doctoral program. *Degree requirements:* For doctorate, dissertation required, foreign language not required. *Entrance requirements:* For master's and doctorate, GRE General Test, minimum GPA of 3.0. *Application deadline:* Applications are processed on a rolling basis. Application fee: $30 ($50 for international students). *Financial aid:* Research assistantships, teaching assistantships, institutionally-sponsored loans available. *Unit head:* Dr. Bill Lamberson, Director of Graduate Studies, 573-882-8234.

University of Nebraska–Lincoln, Graduate College, College of Agricultural Sciences and Natural Resources, Department of Animal Science, Lincoln, NE 68588. Offers MS, PhD. *Faculty:* 36 full-time (3 women), 1 part-time (0 women). *Students:* 50 full-time (14 women), 24 part-time (5 women), 21 international. Average age 29. 44 applicants, 52% accepted. In 1998, 18 master's, 12 doctorates awarded. *Degree requirements:* For master's, thesis required, foreign language not required; for doctorate, dissertation, comprehensive exams required. *Entrance requirements:* For master's and doctorate, GRE General Test, TOEFL (minimum score of 525 required). *Average time to degree:* Doctorate–4 years full-time. *Application deadline:* For fall admission, 3/1 (priority date). Applications are processed on a rolling basis. Application fee: $35. Electronic applications accepted. *Financial aid:* In 1998–99, 5 fellowships, 46 research assistantships, 17 teaching assistantships were awarded.; Federal Work-Study also available. Aid available to part-time students. Financial aid application deadline: 2/15. *Faculty research:* Animal breeding and genetics, meat and poultry products, nonruminant and ruminant nutrition, physiology. Total annual research expenditures: $390,809. *Unit head:* Dr. Roger Mandigo, Head, 402-472-3571, Fax: 402-472-6362.

University of Nevada, Reno, Graduate School, M. C. Fleischmann College of Agriculture, Program in Animal Science, Reno, NV 89557. Offers MS. *Degree requirements:* For master's, thesis optional, foreign language not required. *Entrance requirements:* For master's, GRE, TOEFL (minimum score of 500 required), minimum GPA of 2.75. *Faculty research:* Sperm fertility, embryo development, ruminant utilization of forages.

University of New Hampshire, Graduate School, College of Life Sciences and Agriculture, Graduate Programs in the Biological Sciences and Natural Resources, Department of Animal and Nutritional Sciences, Durham, NH 03824. Offers MS, PhD. Part-time programs available. *Faculty:* 18 full-time. *Students:* 14 full-time (12 women), 8 part-time (6 women), 1 international. Average age 32. 23 applicants, 65% accepted. In 1998, 4 master's, 2 doctorates awarded. Terminal master's awarded for partial completion of doctoral program. *Degree requirements:* For master's and doctorate, thesis/dissertation required, foreign language not required. *Entrance requirements:* For master's and doctorate, GRE General Test. *Application deadline:* For fall admission, 4/1 (priority date). Applications are processed on a rolling basis. Application fee: $50. Tuition, area resident: Full-time $5,750; part-time $319 per credit. Tuition, state resident: full-time $8,625. Tuition, nonresident: full-time $14,640; part-time $598 per credit. Required fees: $224 per semester. Tuition and fees vary according to course load, degree level and program. *Financial aid:* In 1998–99, 6 research assistantships, 9 teaching assistantships were awarded.; fellowships, career-related internships or fieldwork, Federal Work-Study, scholarships, and tuition waivers (full and partial) also available. Aid available to part-time students. Financial aid application deadline: 2/15. *Faculty research:* Diseases, nutrition, parasites, cell biology, animal breeding. *Unit head:* Dr. William E. Berndtson, Chairperson, 603-862-2553. *Application contact:* Dr. Robert Taylor, Graduate Studies, 603-862-2178.

University of Puerto Rico, Mayagüez Campus, Graduate Studies, College of Agricultural Sciences, Department of Animal Industry, Mayagüez, PR 00681-5000. Offers MS. Part-time programs available. *Degree requirements:* For master's, thesis, comprehensive exam required, foreign language not required. *Faculty research:* Swine production and nutrition, poultry production, dairy science and technology, microbiology.

Animal Sciences–Aquaculture

University of Rhode Island, Graduate School, College of Resource Development, Department of Fisheries, Aquaculture and Pathology, Kingston, RI 02881. Offers animal science (MS).

University of Saskatchewan, College of Graduate Studies and Research, College of Agriculture, Department of Animal and Poultry Science, Saskatoon, SK S7N 5A2, Canada. Offers M Sc, PhD. *Degree requirements:* For master's and doctorate, thesis/dissertation required. *Entrance requirements:* For master's, CANTEST (minimum score of 4.5 required) or International English Language Testing System (minimum score of 6 required) or Michigan English Language Assessment Battery (minimum score of 80 required), orTOEFL (minimum score of 550 required; average 560); for doctorate, TOEFL.

University of Tennessee, Knoxville, Graduate School, College of Agricultural Sciences and Natural Resources, Department of Animal Science, Knoxville, TN 37996. Offers animal anatomy (PhD); breeding (MS, PhD); management (MS, PhD); nutrition (MS, PhD); physiology (MS, PhD). Part-time programs available. *Faculty:* 19 full-time (2 women). *Students:* 26 full-time (15 women), 8 part-time (4 women); includes 3 minority (1 African American, 1 Asian American or Pacific Islander, 1 Hispanic American), 6 international. 25 applicants, 68% accepted. In 1998, 5 master's, 2 doctorates awarded. *Degree requirements:* For master's and doctorate, thesis/dissertation required, foreign language not required. *Entrance requirements:* For master's and doctorate, GRE General Test, TOEFL (minimum score of 550 required), minimum GPA of 2.7. *Application deadline:* For fall admission, 2/1 (priority date). Applications are processed on a rolling basis. Application fee: $35. Electronic applications accepted. *Financial aid:* In 1998–99, 17 research assistantships, 6 teaching assistantships were awarded.; fellowships, career-related internships or fieldwork, Federal Work-Study, institutionally-sponsored loans, and unspecified assistantships also available. Financial aid application deadline: 2/1; financial aid applicants required to submit FAFSA. *Unit head:* Dr. Kelly Robbins, Head, 423-974-7286, Fax: 423-974-7297, E-mail: krobbins@utk.edu. *Application contact:* Dr. James Godkin, Graduate Representative, E-mail: jgodkin@utk.edu.

University of Vermont, Graduate College, College of Agriculture and Life Sciences, Department of Animal Sciences, Burlington, VT 05405-0160. Offers MS, PhD. *Degree requirements:* For master's, thesis required, foreign language not required; for doctorate, dissertation required. *Entrance requirements:* For master's and doctorate, GRE General Test, TOEFL (minimum score of 550 required). *Faculty research:* Animal nutrition, dairy production.

University of Wisconsin–Madison, Graduate School, College of Agricultural and Life Sciences, Department of Animal Sciences, Madison, WI 53706-1380. Offers MS, PhD. *Degree requirements:* For doctorate, dissertation required. Electronic applications accepted.

University of Wisconsin–Madison, Graduate School, College of Agricultural and Life Sciences, Department of Dairy Science, Madison, WI 53706-1380. Offers MS, PhD. Part-time programs available. *Degree requirements:* For master's, thesis required (for some programs), foreign language not required; for doctorate, dissertation required, foreign language not required. *Entrance requirements:* For master's and doctorate, GRE General Test (score in 50th percentile or higher required), TOEFL (minimum score of 550 required). Electronic applications accepted. *Faculty research:* Genetics, nutrition, lactation, reproduction, management of dairy cattle.

University of Wyoming, Graduate School, College of Agriculture, Department of Animal Sciences, Program in Animal Sciences, Laramie, WY 82071. Offers MS, PhD. *Degree requirements:* For master's, thesis required, foreign language not required; for doctorate, dissertation required, dissertation required. *Entrance requirements:* For master's, GRE General Test (minimum combined score of 900 required; average 1000), minimum GPA of 3.0; for doctorate, GRE General Test (minimum combined score of 1000 required), minimum GPA of 3.0. Tuition, state resident: full-time $2,520; part-time $140 per credit hour. Tuition, nonresident: full-time $7,790; part-time $433 per credit hour. Required fees: $400; $7 per credit hour. Full-time tuition and fees vary according to course load and program.

Utah State University, School of Graduate Studies, College of Agriculture, Department of Animal, Dairy and Veterinary Sciences, Logan, UT 84322. Offers animal science (MS, PhD); bioveterinary science (MS, PhD); dairy science (MS). Part-time programs available. *Faculty:* 20 full-time (2 women). *Students:* 18 full-time (7 women), 7 part-time (4 women), 7 international. Average age 25. 25 applicants, 48% accepted. In 1998, 2 master's awarded. *Degree requirements:* For master's, thesis required (for some programs), foreign language not required; for doctorate, dissertation required, foreign language not required. *Entrance requirements:* For master's and doctorate, GRE General Test (score in 40th percentile or higher required), TOEFL (minimum score of 550 required), minimum GPA of 3.0. *Application deadline:* For fall admission, 5/15 (priority date); for spring admission, 10/15. Applications are processed on a rolling basis. Application fee: $40. Tuition, state resident: full-time $1,492. Tuition, nonresident: full-time $5,232. Required fees: $434. Tuition and fees vary according to course load. *Financial aid:* In 1998–99, 18 research assistantships with partial tuition reimbursements, 3 teaching assistantships with partial tuition reimbursements were awarded.; fellowships with partial tuition reimbursements, career-related internships or fieldwork, Federal Work-Study, institutionally-sponsored loans, scholarships, and tuition waivers (partial) also available. Financial aid application deadline: 4/1. *Faculty research:* Monoclonal antibodies, antiviral chemotherapy, management systems, biotechnology, rumen fermentation manipulation. *Unit head:* Dr. Mark C. Healey, Head, 435-797-2162, Fax: 435-797-2118, E-mail: mchealey@cc.usu.edu. *Application contact:* Dr. Jeffrey L. Walters, Graduate Program Coordinator, 435-797-2161, Fax: 435-797-2118, E-mail: jwalters@cc.usu.edu.

Virginia Polytechnic Institute and State University, Graduate School, College of Agriculture and Life Sciences, Department of Animal and Poultry Science, Blacksburg, VA 24061. Offers animal science (MS, PhD); poultry science (MS, PhD), including behavior, genetics, management, nutrition, physiology. Part-time programs available. *Faculty:* 21 full-time (1 woman). *Students:* 30 full-time (17 women), 4 part-time (3 women); includes 4 minority (1 African American, 2 Asian Americans or Pacific Islanders, 1 Hispanic American), 6 international. 34 applicants, 41% accepted. In 1998, 5 master's, 2 doctorates awarded. *Degree requirements:* For master's, thesis required (for some programs); for doctorate, dissertation required. *Entrance requirements:* For master's and doctorate, GRE, TOEFL. *Application deadline:* For fall admission, 12/1 (priority date). Applications are processed on a rolling basis. Application fee: $25. *Financial aid:* In 1998–99, 13 research assistantships, 4 teaching assistantships were awarded.; fellowships, tuition waivers (partial) and unspecified assistantships also available. Aid available to part-time students. Financial aid application deadline: 4/1. *Faculty research:* Quantitative genetics of cattle and sheep, swine nutrition and management, use of nontraditional foodstuffs, uterine physiology of swine, protein metabolism. *Unit head:* Dr. Gary Minish, Head, 540-231-6311, E-mail: minish@vt.edu. *Application contact:* Dr. D. R. Notter, Professor, 540-231-5135.

Virginia Polytechnic Institute and State University, Graduate School, College of Agriculture and Life Sciences, Department of Dairy Science, Blacksburg, VA 24061. Offers MS, PhD. *Faculty:* 18 full-time (1 woman). *Students:* 12 full-time (6 women), 4 part-time (1 woman); includes 1 minority (Hispanic American), 3 international. 11 applicants, 73% accepted. In 1998, 4 master's, 1 doctorate awarded. *Degree requirements:* For master's and doctorate, thesis/dissertation required, foreign language not required. *Entrance requirements:* For master's and doctorate, TOEFL. *Application deadline:* For fall admission, 12/1 (priority date). Applications are processed on a rolling basis. Application fee: $25. *Financial aid:* In 1998–99, 3 fellowships were awarded.; research assistantships, teaching assistantships, unspecified assistantships also available. Financial aid application deadline: 4/1. *Faculty research:* Genetics, nutrition, reproduction, lactation. *Unit head:* Dr. William E. Vinson, Head, 540-231-6331. *Application contact:* Dr. William M. Etgen, 540-231-4771.

Washington State University, Graduate School, College of Agriculture and Home Economics, Department of Animal Sciences, Pullman, WA 99164. Offers animal sciences (MS, PhD); nutrition (PhD). *Faculty:* 21 full-time (3 women). *Students:* 32 full-time (13 women), 6 part-time (1 woman); includes 4 minority (1 African American, 3 Asian Americans or Pacific Islanders), 10 international. In 1998, 4 doctorates awarded. *Degree requirements:* For master's and doctorate, thesis/dissertation, oral exam required, foreign language not required. *Entrance requirements:* For master's and doctorate, GRE General Test, minimum GPA of 3.0. *Average time to degree:* Master's–2 years full-time; doctorate–4 years full-time. *Application deadline:* For fall admission, 3/1 (priority date). Applications are processed on a rolling basis. Application fee: $35. *Financial aid:* In 1998–99, 12 research assistantships, 8 teaching assistantships were awarded.; fellowships, career-related internships or fieldwork, Federal Work-Study, institutionally-sponsored loans, tuition waivers (partial), and teaching associateships also available. Financial aid application deadline: 4/1; financial aid applicants required to submit FAFSA. *Faculty research:* Reproduction, genetics. Total annual research expenditures: $634,534. *Unit head:* Dr. Raymond Wright, Chair, 509-335-5523.

West Texas A&M University, College of Agriculture, Nursing, and Natural Sciences, Division of Agriculture, Emphasis in Animal Science, Canyon, TX 79016-0001. Offers MS. Part-time programs available. *Faculty:* 3 full-time (0 women), 4 part-time (1 woman). *Students:* 5 full-time (1 woman), 7 part-time (2 women). Average age 34. *Degree requirements:* For master's, comprehensive exam required, thesis optional, foreign language not required. *Entrance requirements:* For master's, GRE General Test (minimum combined score of 950 required; average 964). *Application deadline:* Applications are processed on a rolling basis. Application fee: $0 ($50 for international students). Electronic applications accepted. Tuition, state resident: full-time $1,152; part-time $48 per credit. Tuition, nonresident: full-time $6,336; part-time $264 per credit. Required fees: $1,063; $531 per semester. *Financial aid:* In 1998–99, research assistantships (averaging $6,500 per year), 10 teaching assistantships (averaging $6,500 per year) were awarded.; Federal Work-Study, grants, institutionally-sponsored loans, scholarships, traineeships, and tuition waivers (partial) also available. Aid available to part-time students. *Faculty research:* Nutrition, animal breeding, meat science, reproduction physiology. *Unit head:* Sally Elmore, Graduate Coordinator, 360-650-3646. *Application contact:* Dr. Ted Montgomery, Graduate Adviser, 806-651-2560, Fax: 806-651-2938, E-mail: tmontgomery@mail.wtamu.edu.

West Virginia University, College of Agriculture, Forestry and Consumer Sciences, Division of Animal and Veterinary Sciences, Program in Animal and Food Sciences, Morgantown, WV 26506. Offers agricultural sciences (PhD). *Degree requirements:* For doctorate, dissertation, oral and written exams required, foreign language not required. *Entrance requirements:* For doctorate, TOEFL (minimum score of 550 required). *Faculty research:* Ruminant nutrition, metabolism, forage utilization, physiology, reproduction.

West Virginia University, College of Agriculture, Forestry and Consumer Sciences, Division of Animal and Veterinary Sciences, Program in Animal and Veterinary Sciences, Morgantown, WV 26506. Offers MS. Part-time programs available. *Degree requirements:* For master's, thesis, oral and written exams required, foreign language not required. *Entrance requirements:* For master's, TOEFL (minimum score of 550 required), minimum GPA of 2.5. *Faculty research:* Animal nutrition, reproductive physiology, food science.

West Virginia University, Eberly College of Arts and Sciences, Department of Biology, Morgantown, WV 26506. Offers biology (MS), including animal behavior, cellular and molecular biology, environmental ecology, plant ecology, plant systematics, population genetics; cellular and molecular biology (PhD); environmental plant biology (PhD); plant ecology (PhD). Terminal master's awarded for partial completion of doctoral program. *Degree requirements:* For master's, thesis, final exam required, foreign language not required; for doctorate, dissertation, preliminary and final exams required, foreign language not required. *Entrance requirements:* For master's, GRE General Test (score in 50th percentile or higher required), GRE Subject Test (score in 50th percentile or higher required), TOEFL (minimum score of 600 required), minimum GPA of 3.0; for doctorate, GRE General Test (minimum combined score of 1100 required), GRE Subject Test (score in 50th percentile or higher required), TOEFL (minimum score of 600 required), minimum GPA of 3.0. *Faculty research:* Environmental biology, genetic engineering, developmental biology, global change, biodiversity.

Aquaculture

Auburn University, Graduate School, College of Agriculture, Department of Fisheries and Allied Aquacultures, Auburn, Auburn University, AL 36849-0002. Offers M Aq, MS, PhD. Part-time programs available. *Faculty:* 20 full-time (0 women). *Students:* 37 full-time (10 women), 37 part-time (7 women); includes 4 minority (2 Asian Americans or Pacific Islanders, 1 Hispanic American, 1 Native American), 21 international. 26 applicants, 38% accepted. In 1998, 15 master's, 13 doctorates awarded. *Degree requirements:* For master's, thesis (MS) required; for doctorate, 2 foreign languages (computer language can substitute for one), dissertation required. *Entrance requirements:* For master's, GRE General Test; for doctorate, GRE General Test (minimum score of 400 on each section required). *Application deadline:* For fall admission, 9/1; for spring admission, 3/1. Applications are processed on a rolling basis. Application fee: $25 ($50 for international students). Tuition, state resident: full-time $2,760; part-time $76 per credit hour. Tuition, nonresident: full-time $8,280; part-time $228 per credit hour. *Financial aid:* Fellowships, research assistantships, teaching assistantships, Federal Work-Study available. Aid available to part-time students. Financial aid application deadline: 3/15. *Faculty research:* Channel catfish production; aquatic animal health; community and population ecology; pond management; production hatching, breeding and genetics. Total annual research expenditures: $8 million. *Unit head:* Dr. John W. Jensen, Head, 334-844-4786. *Application contact:* Dr. John F. Pritchett, Dean of the Graduate School, 334-844-4700.

Clemson University, Graduate School, College of Agriculture, Forestry and Life Sciences, School of Natural Resources, Department of Aquaculture, Fisheries and Wildlife, Clemson, SC 29634. Offers MS. *Students:* 19 full-time (7 women), 4 part-time (1 woman); includes 3 minority (1 African American, 1 Hispanic American, 1 Native American), 3 international. Average age 25. 46 applicants, 7% accepted. In 1998, 10 degrees awarded. *Degree requirements:* For master's, thesis required, foreign language not required. *Entrance requirements:* For master's, GRE General Test, TOEFL, minimum undergraduate GPA of 3.0. *Application deadline:* For fall admission, 6/1. Application fee: $35. *Financial aid:* In 1998–99, 16 research assistantships were awarded.; fellowships, teaching assistantships, career-related internships or fieldwork also available. Financial aid applicants required to submit FAFSA. *Faculty research:* Intensive freshwater culture systems, conservation biology, stream management, applied wildlife management. *Unit head:* Dr. John R. Sweeney, Chair, 864-656-3117, Fax: 864-656-5332, E-mail: jrswny@clemson.edu.

Memorial University of Newfoundland, School of Graduate Studies, Interdisciplinary Program in Aquaculture, St. John's, NF A1C 5S7, Canada. Offers M Sc. *Students:* 17 full-time (12 women), 6 part-time (1 woman), 4 international. 5 applicants, 20% accepted. In 1998, 2 degrees awarded. *Entrance requirements:* For master's, honors B Sc, diploma in aquaculture from the Marine Institute of Memorial University of Newfoundland. *Application deadline:* Applications are processed on a rolling basis. Application fee: $40. *Financial aid:* Fellowships, research assistantships, teaching assistantships available. *Faculty research:* Marine fish larval biology, fin fish nutrition, shellfish culture, fin fish virology, fin fish reproductive biology. *Unit head:* Dr. Joe Brown, Chair, 709-737-3252, Fax: 709-737-3220, E-mail: jabrown@morgan.ucs.mun.ca. *Application contact:* Gail Kenny, Secretary, 709-737-3444, E-mail: gkenny@morgan.ucs.mun.ca.

University of Florida, Graduate School, College of Agriculture, Department of Fisheries and Aquatic Science, Gainesville, FL 32611. Offers MFAS, MS, PhD. *Faculty:* 23. *Students:* 26 full-time (8 women), 12 part-time (5 women); includes 2 minority (both Hispanic Americans), 3 international. 34 applicants, 35% accepted. In 1998, 11 master's awarded. *Degree requirements:* For master's, thesis optional, foreign language not required; for doctorate, dissertation required, foreign language not required. *Entrance requirements:* For master's and doctorate, GRE General Test, TOEFL, minimum GPA of 3.0. *Application deadline:* For fall admission, 6/1. Applications are processed on a rolling basis. Application fee: $20. Electronic applications accepted. *Financial aid:* In 1998–99, 1 fellowship, 21 research assistantships were awarded.; unspecified assistantships also available. *Unit head:* Dr. Wallis H. Clark, Chair, 352-392-9617, Fax: 352-846-1088, E-mail: faa@gnv.ifas.ufl.edu. *Application contact:* Dr. Ed Philips, Graduate Coordinator, 352-392-9617 Ext. 248, Fax: 352-846-1088, E-mail: ejph@gnv.ifas.ufl.edu.

University of Guelph, Faculty of Graduate Studies, Program in Aquaculture, Guelph, ON N1G 2W1, Canada. Offers M Sc. *Faculty:* 14 full-time (3 women). *Students:* 2 full-time (1 woman). Average age 24. 8 applicants, 25% accepted. In 1998, 5 degrees awarded. *Degree requirements:* For master's, thesis not required. *Entrance requirements:* For master's, minimum B- average during previous 2 years. *Application deadline:* For fall admission, 5/31 (priority date). Applications are processed on a rolling basis. Application fee: $60. *Expenses:* Tuition and fees charges are reported in Canadian dollars. Tuition, area resident: Full-time $4,725 Canadian dollars; part-time $1,055 Canadian dollars per term. International tuition: $6,999 Canadian dollars full-time. Required fees: $295 Canadian dollars per term. *Financial aid:* Teaching assistantships, career-related internships or fieldwork available. *Faculty research:* Protein and amino acid metabolism, genetics, gamete cryogenics, pathology, epidemiology. *Unit head:* R. Moccia, Co-Coordinator, 519-824-4120 Ext. 6216, Fax: 519-767-0573, E-mail: rmoccia@aps.uoguelph.ca.

University of Rhode Island, Graduate School, College of Resource Development, Department of Fisheries, Aquaculture and Pathology, Kingston, RI 02881. Offers animal science (MS).

Virginia Polytechnic Institute and State University, Graduate School, College of Natural Resources, Department of Fisheries and Wildlife Sciences, Blacksburg, VA 24061. Offers aquaculture (MS, PhD); conservation biology (MS, PhD); fisheries science (MS, PhD); wildlife science (MS, PhD). *Faculty:* 21 full-time (2 women). *Students:* 43 full-time (14 women), 7 part-time (2 women); includes 2 minority (both African Americans), 4 international. *Degree requirements:* For master's and doctorate, thesis/dissertation required. *Entrance requirements:* For master's and doctorate, GRE General Test, TOEFL, minimum GPA of 3.0. *Application deadline:* For fall admission, 12/1 (priority date). Applications are processed on a rolling basis. Application fee: $25. *Unit head:* Dr. Brian R. Murphy, Head, 540-231-5573, Fax: 540-231-7580, E-mail: murphybr@vt.edu.

Food Science and Technology

Alabama Agricultural and Mechanical University, School of Graduate Studies, School of Agricultural and Environmental Sciences, Department of Family and Consumer Sciences, Normal, AL 35762-1357. Offers family and consumer sciences (MS); food science (MS, PhD). Part-time and evening/weekend programs available. *Faculty:* 7 full-time (3 women). *Students:* 9 full-time (all women); all minorities (8 African Americans, 1 Asian American or Pacific Islander) *Degree requirements:* For master's, comprehensive exam required, thesis optional, foreign language not required; for doctorate, one foreign language, computer language, dissertation required. *Entrance requirements:* For master's, GRE General Test; for doctorate, GRE General Test (minimum combined score of 1000 required), MS. *Application deadline:* For fall admission, 5/1. Application fee: $15 ($20 for international students). Tuition, state resident: full-time $1,932. Tuition, nonresident: full-time $3,864. Tuition and fees vary according to course load. *Unit head:* Dr. Bernice Richardson, Chair, 256-851-5455, Fax: 256-851-5433.

Auburn University, Graduate School, School of Human Sciences, Department of Nutrition and Food Science, Auburn, Auburn University, AL 36849-0002. Offers MACT, MS, PhD. Part-time programs available. *Faculty:* 15 full-time. *Students:* 17 full-time (13 women), 19 part-time (12 women); includes 1 minority (Asian American or Pacific Islander), 9 international. 27 applicants, 59% accepted. In 1998, 4 master's, 3 doctorates awarded. *Degree requirements:* For master's, thesis (MS) required; for doctorate, dissertation required. *Entrance requirements:* For master's, GRE General Test; for doctorate, GRE General Test (minimum score of 400 on each section required). *Application deadline:* For fall admission, 9/1; for spring admission, 3/1. Applications are processed on a rolling basis. Application fee: $25 ($50 for international students). Tuition, state resident: full-time $2,760; part-time $76 per credit hour. Tuition, nonresident: full-time $8,280; part-time $228 per credit hour. *Financial aid:* Research assistantships, teaching assistantships, career-related internships or fieldwork and Federal Work-Study available. Aid available to part-time students. Financial aid application deadline: 3/15. *Faculty research:* Food quality and safety, diet, food supply, physical activity in maintenance of health, prevention of selected chronic disease states. *Unit head:* Dr. Cheng-i Wei, Head, 334-844-4261. *Application contact:* Dr. John F. Pritchett, Dean of the Graduate School, 334-844-4700.

Brigham Young University, Graduate Studies, College of Biological and Agricultural Sciences, Department of Food Science and Nutrition, Provo, UT 84602-1001. Offers food science (MS); molecular biology (MS); nutrition (MS). Part-time programs available. *Faculty:* 12 full-time (4 women), 4 part-time (3 women). *Students:* 11 full-time (3 women), 1 international. Average age 27. 12 applicants, 25% accepted. In 1998, 5 degrees awarded (40% entered university research/teaching, 60% continued full-time study). *Degree requirements:* For master's, thesis required, foreign language not required. *Entrance requirements:* For master's, GRE General Test, minimum GPA of 3.0 during previous 2 years. *Average time to degree:* Master's–2 years full-time. *Application deadline:* For fall admission, 2/1. Application fee: $30. Tuition: Full-time $3,330; part-time $185 per credit hour. Tuition and fees vary according to program and student's religious affiliation. *Financial aid:* In 1998–99, 10 students received aid, including 6 research assistantships, 4 teaching assistantships; career-related internships or fieldwork and institutionally-sponsored loans also available. Financial aid application deadline: 3/23. *Faculty research:* Dairy foods, lipid oxidation, food processes, magnesium and selenium nutrition, nutrient effect on gene expression. Total annual research expenditures: $460,000. *Unit head:* Dr. Lynn V. Ogden, Chair, 801-378-3912, Fax: 801-378-8714, E-mail: lynn_ogden@byu.edu. *Application contact:* Dr. Clayton S. Huber, Graduate Coordinator, 801-378-6038, Fax: 801-378-8714, E-mail: clayton_huber@byu.edu.

California State Polytechnic University, Pomona, Graduate Studies, College of Agriculture, Pomona, CA 91768-2557. Offers agricultural science (MS); animal science (MS); foods and nutrition (MS). Part-time programs available. *Faculty:* 24. *Students:* 17 full-time (13 women), 49 part-time (35 women); includes 25 minority (4 African Americans, 11 Asian Americans or Pacific Islanders, 10 Hispanic Americans), 8 international. *Degree requirements:* For master's, thesis or alternative required. *Application deadline:* Applications are processed on a rolling basis. Application fee: $55. Tuition, nonresident: part-time $164 per unit. *Unit head:* Dr. Wayne R. Bidlack, Dean, 909-869-2200, E-mail: wrbidlack@csupomona.edu.

California State University, Fresno, Division of Graduate Studies, School of Agricultural Sciences and Technology, Department of Enology, Food Science, and Nutrition, Fresno, CA 93740-0057. Offers agriculture (MS), including agricultural chemistry, food science and nutrition. Part-time programs available. *Faculty:* 6 full-time (3 women). *Students:* 3 full-time (1 woman), 8 part-time (all women); includes 1 minority (Native American) Average age 31. 18 applicants, 83% accepted. In 1998, 2 degrees awarded. *Degree requirements:* For master's, thesis required, foreign language not required. *Entrance requirements:* For master's, GRE General Test, TOEFL (minimum score of 550 required), minimum GPA of 3.0 in last 60 hours. *Average time to degree:* Master's–3.5 years full-time. *Application deadline:* For fall admission, 6/1 (priority date); for spring admission, 11/1. Applications are processed on a rolling basis. Application fee: $55. Electronic applications accepted. Tuition, nonresident: part-time $246 per unit. Required fees: $1,906; $620 per semester. *Financial aid:* Fellowships, career-related internships or fieldwork, Federal Work-Study, and scholarships available. Financial aid application deadline: 3/1; financial aid applicants required to submit FAFSA. *Faculty research:* Liquid foods, agro-ecosystems, pruning evaluations, characterization of juice concentrates, evaluation of root systems. *Unit head:* Dr. Marie Dunford, Chair, 559-278-2164, Fax: 559-278-7623, E-mail: marie_dunford@csufresno.edu. *Application contact:* Dr. Sandra Witte, Graduate Coordinator, 559-278-2164, Fax: 559-278-7623, E-mail: sandra_witte@csufresno.edu.

Chapman University, Graduate Studies, Program in Food Science and Nutrition, Orange, CA 92866. Offers MS. *Faculty:* 2 full-time (1 woman). *Students:* 27. In 1998, 6 degrees awarded. *Degree requirements:* For master's, thesis or alternative required, foreign language not required. *Entrance requirements:* For master's, GRE General Test (minimum combined score of 900 required), minimum GPA of 3.0 (undergraduate). *Application deadline:* Applications are processed on a rolling basis. Application fee: $40. *Financial aid:* Application deadline: 3/1. *Unit head:* Dr. Fredric Caporaso, Chair, 714-997-6638.

Clemson University, Graduate School, College of Agriculture, Forestry and Life Sciences, School of Animal, Biomedical and Biological Sciences, Department of Animal, Dairy and Veterinary Sciences, Clemson, SC 29634. Offers animal and food industries (MS); animal physiology (MS, PhD); food technology (PhD); genetics (MS, PhD); nutrition (MS, PhD). *Students:* 32 full-time (23 women), 19 part-time (12 women), 6 international. *Degree requirements:* For doctorate, dissertation required. *Entrance requirements:* For master's and doctorate, GRE General Test, TOEFL. *Application deadline:* Applications are processed on a rolling basis. Application fee: $35. Electronic applications accepted. *Unit head:* Dr. George Skelley, Chair, 864-656-3428, Fax: 864-656-3131, E-mail: gsklly@clemson.edu.

Clemson University, Graduate School, College of Agriculture, Forestry and Life Sciences, School of Applied Science and Agribusiness, Department of Food Science, Program in Food Technology, Clemson, SC 29634. Offers PhD. *Students:* 15 full-time (8 women), 4 part-time (1 woman); includes 1 minority (African American), 10 international. 6 applicants, 17% accepted. In 1998, 1 degree awarded. *Degree requirements:* For doctorate, dissertation required, foreign language not required. *Entrance requirements:* For doctorate, GRE General Test, TOEFL. *Application deadline:* For fall admission, 6/1. Application fee: $35. *Financial aid:* Applicants required to submit FAFSA. *Unit head:* Dr. R. L. Thomas, Graduate Coordinator, 864-656-5697, Fax: 864-656-0331, E-mail: rthms@clemson.edu.

Colorado State University, Graduate School, College of Applied Human Sciences, Department of Food Science and Human Nutrition, Fort Collins, CO 80523-0015. Offers food science (MS, PhD); nutrition (MS, PhD). Part-time programs available. *Faculty:* 13 full-time (6 women), 19 part-time (6 women). *Students:* 30 full-time (28 women), 21 part-time (18 women); includes 8 minority (5 African Americans, 1 Asian American or Pacific Islander, 2 Hispanic Americans), 6 international. Average age 31. 89 applicants, 55% accepted. In 1998, 15 master's, 9 doctorates awarded. *Degree requirements:* For master's, thesis optional, foreign language not required; for doctorate, dissertation required, foreign language not required. *Entrance requirements:* For master's and doctorate, GRE General Test, TOEFL (minimum score of 550 required; 213 for computer-based), minimum GPA of 3.0. *Application deadline:* For fall admission, 2/1 (priority date); for spring admission, 9/1 (priority date). Applications are processed on a rolling basis. Application fee: $30. Electronic applications accepted. *Financial aid:* In 1998–99, 3 fellowships, 12 research assistantships, 12 teaching assistantships were awarded.; career-related internships or fieldwork, Federal Work-Study, and traineeships also available. *Faculty research:* Exercise and energy metabolism, nutrition education, lipid metabolism, eicosanoids, tool product development. Total annual research expenditures: $760,000. *Unit head:* Pat Kendall, Head, 970-491-5093, Fax: 970-491-3875, E-mail: kendall@cahs.colostate.edu. *Application contact:* Irene Lewus, Coordinator, 970-491-6535, Fax: 970-491-3875, E-mail: lewus@cahs.colostate.edu.

Cornell University, Graduate School, Graduate Fields of Agriculture and Life Sciences, Field of Food Science and Technology, Ithaca, NY 14853-0001. Offers dairy science (MPS, MS, PhD); food chemistry (MPS, MS, PhD); food engineering (MPS, MS, PhD); food microbiology (MPS, MS, PhD); food processing waste technology (MPS, MS, PhD); food science (MFS, MPS, MS, PhD); international food science (MPS, MS, PhD); sensory evaluation (MPS, MS, PhD). *Faculty:* 41 full-time. *Students:* 69 full-time (34 women); includes 7 minority (1 African American, 6 Asian Americans or Pacific Islanders), 44 international. 107 applicants, 39% accepted. In 1998, 25 master's, 6 doctorates awarded. *Degree requirements:* For master's, thesis (MS), teaching experience required; for doctorate, dissertation, teaching experience required, foreign language not required. *Entrance requirements:* For master's and doctorate, GRE General Test, TOEFL (minimum score of 550 required). *Application deadline:* For fall admission, 1/15. Application fee: $65. Electronic applications accepted. *Financial aid:* In 1998–99, 44 students received aid, including 6 fellowships with full tuition reimbursements available, 24 research assistantships with full tuition reimbursements available, 14 teaching assistantships with full tuition reimbursements available; institutionally-sponsored loans, scholarships, tuition waivers (full and partial), and unspecified assistantships also available. Financial aid applicants required to submit FAFSA. *Faculty research:* Food biotechnology, food safety/toxicology, sensory science/flavor chemistry, food packaging. *Unit head:* Director of Graduate Studies, 607-255-7637. *Application contact:* Graduate Field Assistant, 607-255-7637, E-mail: tjf2@cornell.edu.

Dalhousie University, Faculty of Graduate Studies, DalTech, Faculty of Engineering, Department of Food Science and Technology, Halifax, NS B3H 3J5, Canada. Offers M Sc, PhD. *Faculty:* 5 full-time (0 women), 2 part-time (0 women). *Students:* 19 full-time (8 women), 5

Food Science and Technology

Dalhousie University (continued)

international. 12 applicants, 67% accepted. In 1998, 2 master's awarded (100% found work related to degree); 1 doctorate awarded (100% entered university research/teaching). *Degree requirements:* For master's and doctorate, thesis/dissertation required, foreign language not required. *Entrance requirements:* For master's and doctorate, TOEFL (minimum score of 580 required). *Application deadline:* For fall admission, 6/1; for winter admission, 10/1; for spring admission, 2/1. Application fee: $55. *Financial aid:* Fellowships, research assistantships, teaching assistantships, scholarships and unspecified assistantships available. *Faculty research:* Food microbiology, food safety/HALLP, rheology and rheometry, food processing, seafood processing. *Unit head:* Dr. Tom Gill, Head, 902-494-6030, Fax: 902-420-0219, E-mail: elizabeth.macdonald@dal.ca. *Application contact:* Shelley Parker, Admissions Coordinator, Graduate Studies and Research, 902-494-1288, Fax: 902-494-3149, E-mail: shelley.parker@dal.ca.

Drexel University, Graduate School, College of Arts and Sciences, Department of Bioscience and Biotechnology, Program in Nutrition and Food Sciences, Philadelphia, PA 19104-2875. Offers food science (MS); nutrition science (PhD). Part-time programs available. *Students:* 7 full-time (all women), 18 part-time (15 women); includes 1 minority (Hispanic American), 9 international. Average age 32. 36 applicants, 58% accepted. In 1998, 7 degrees awarded. Terminal master's awarded for partial completion of doctoral program. *Degree requirements:* For master's and doctorate, thesis/dissertation required, foreign language not required. *Entrance requirements:* For master's and doctorate, GRE General Test, TOEFL (minimum score of 570 required). *Application deadline:* For fall admission, 8/21. Applications are processed on a rolling basis. Application fee: $35. Tuition: Full-time $15,795; part-time $585 per credit. Required fees: $375; $67 per term. Tuition and fees vary according to program. *Financial aid:* In 1998–99, 5 teaching assistantships were awarded.; research assistantships, Federal Work-Study and unspecified assistantships also available. Financial aid application deadline: 2/1. *Faculty research:* Metabolism of lipids, W-3 fatty acids, obesity, diabetes and heart disease, mineral metabolism. *Unit head:* Dr. Stanley Segall, Head, 215-895-2416, Fax: 215-895-2421. *Application contact:* Director of Graduate Admissions, 215-895-6700, Fax: 215-895-5939.

Florida State University, Graduate Studies, College of Human Sciences, Department of Nutrition, Food, and Exercise Sciences, Tallahassee, FL 32306. Offers exercise science (MS, PhD), including exercise physiology, motor learning and control; nutrition and food science (PhD); nutrition and food sciences (MS), including clinical nutrition, food science, nutrition and sport, nutrition science, nutrition, education and health promotion. *Faculty:* 13 full-time (9 women). *Students:* 49 full-time (30 women), 32 part-time (15 women); includes 9 minority (3 African Americans, 3 Asian Americans or Pacific Islanders, 3 Hispanic Americans), 11 international. 143 applicants, 55% accepted. In 1998, 21 master's awarded (100% found work related to degree); 1 doctorate awarded. *Degree requirements:* For master's, thesis optional, foreign language not required; for doctorate, dissertation required, foreign language not required. *Entrance requirements:* For master's and doctorate, GRE General Test (minimum combined score of 1000 required), minimum GPA of 3.0. Application fee: $20. Tuition, state resident: part-time $139 per credit hour. Tuition, nonresident: part-time $482 per credit hour. Tuition and fees vary according to program. *Financial aid:* In 1998–99, 24 students received aid, including 2 fellowships (averaging $10,000 per year), 3 research assistantships with partial tuition reimbursements available (averaging $8,000 per year), 19 teaching assistantships with partial tuition reimbursements available (averaging $8,000 per year); Federal Work-Study and unspecified assistantships also available. Financial aid applicants required to submit FAFSA. *Faculty research:* Nutrition and exercise, vitamin A deficiency, protein biochemistry, cardiovascular responses to exercises, physiological effects of cigarette smoking related to health and wellness. *Unit head:* Dr. Robert Moffatt, Chair, 850-644-1828, Fax: 850-644-0700, E-mail: rmoffatt@mailer.fsu.edu. *Application contact:* Dr. Natholyn Harris, Graduate Coordinator, 850-644-4800, Fax: 850-644-0700, E-mail: nharris@mailer.fsu.edu.

Framingham State College, Graduate Programs, Department of Chemistry and Food Science, Framingham, MA 01701-9101. Offers food science and nutrition science (MS). Part-time and evening/weekend programs available. *Faculty:* 2 full-time, 2 part-time. *Students:* 23 full-time, 24 part-time. In 1998, 12 degrees awarded. *Degree requirements:* For master's, foreign language and thesis not required. *Entrance requirements:* For master's, GRE General Test. *Unit head:* Dr. Suzanne Neubauer, Chair, 508-626-4754. *Application contact:* 508-626-4550.

Announcement: The MS program in food science and nutrition science focuses on analytical food chemistry, nutritional biochemistry, basic food processing technology, chemical and microbiological food safety, and food formulation. Thesis and nonthesis options exist for full- and part-time study, using up-to-date laboratory facilities, instrumentation, and food pilot plant capabilities. E-mail: crussel@frc.mass.edu; WWW: http://www.framingham.edu

Illinois Institute of Technology, Graduate College, Armour College of Engineering and Sciences, Department of Food Safety and Technology, Chicago, IL 60616-3793. Offers MS. Part-time and evening/weekend programs available. *Students:* 2 full-time (0 women), 2 part-time (1 woman), 2 international. 6 applicants, 67% accepted. In 1998, 1 degree awarded. *Degree requirements:* For master's, thesis (for some programs), comprehensive exam, project required, foreign language not required. *Entrance requirements:* For master's, GRE General Test (minimum combined score of 1400 on three sections required), TOEFL (minimum score of 550 required), undergraduate GPA of 3.0 required. *Application deadline:* For fall admission, 8/1 (priority date); for spring admission, 11/1. Applications are processed on a rolling basis. Application fee: $30. Electronic applications accepted. *Financial aid:* In 1998–99, 2 research assistantships were awarded.; fellowships, teaching assistantships, career-related internships or fieldwork, Federal Work-Study, and institutionally-sponsored loans also available. Financial aid application deadline: 3/1. *Faculty research:* Food science, microbiology, food preservation, food processing. Total annual research expenditures: $2.5 million. *Unit head:* Dr. Charles Sizer, Director, National Center for Food Safety and Technology, 708-563-1576, Fax: 708-563-1873, E-mail: sizerc@alpha1.ais.iit.edu. *Application contact:* Dr. S. Mohammad Shahidehpour, Dean of Graduate College, 312-567-3024, Fax: 312-567-7517, E-mail: grad@minna.cns.iit.edu.

Iowa State University of Science and Technology, Graduate College, College of Family and Consumer Sciences, Department of Food Science and Human Nutrition, Ames, IA 50011. Offers food science and technology (MS, PhD); nutrition (MS, PhD). *Faculty:* 28 full-time. *Students:* 47 full-time (33 women), 18 part-time (12 women); includes 1 minority (Asian American or Pacific Islander), 30 international. Average age 28. 92 applicants, 20% accepted. In 1998, 4 master's, 2 doctorates awarded. *Degree requirements:* For master's and doctorate, thesis/dissertation required. *Entrance requirements:* For master's and doctorate, GRE General Test, TOEFL (minimum score of 550 required). *Application deadline:* For fall admission, 1/31 (priority date); for spring admission, 9/1. Application fee: $20 ($50 for international students). Electronic applications accepted. Tuition, state resident: full-time $3,308. Tuition, nonresident: full-time $9,744. Part-time tuition and fees vary according to course load, campus/location and program. *Financial aid:* In 1998–99, 45 research assistantships with partial tuition reimbursements (averaging $9,859 per year) were awarded.; fellowships, teaching assistantships, scholarships also available. *Unit head:* Dr. Diane F. Birt, Chair, 515-294-3011, Fax: 515-294-8181, E-mail: fshn@iastate.edu. *Application contact:* Dr. Murray L. Kaplan, Director of Graduate Education, 515-294-9304, E-mail: fshn@iastate.edu.

See in-depth description on page 845.

Kansas State University, Graduate School, College of Agriculture, Department of Grain Science and Industry, Manhattan, KS 66506. Offers MS, PhD. Part-time programs available. *Faculty:* 16 full-time (3 women). *Students:* 54 full-time (19 women), 8 part-time (4 women); includes 1 minority (Hispanic American), 41 international. Average age 32. 22 applicants, 64% accepted. In 1998, 6 master's, 14 doctorates awarded. Terminal master's awarded for partial completion of doctoral program. *Degree requirements:* For master's and doctorate, thesis/dissertation required, foreign language not required. *Application deadline:* For fall admission, 3/11 (priority date); for spring admission, 4/1. Application fee: $0 ($25 for international students). *Financial aid:* In 1998–99, 44 research assistantships, 1 teaching assistantship were awarded.; Federal Work-Study also available. *Faculty research:* Polymers, milling/feed flour processing, nutrition. *Unit head:* Brendan J. Donnelly, Head, 785-532-6161. *Application contact:* Carol Klopfenstein, Graduate Coordinator, 785-532-6161.

Announcement: Grain science students specialize in cereal chemistry, bakery science, extrusion technology, milling science, feed production, grain processing and utilization, or grain storage. Department facilities include a pilot-scale commercial flour mill, feed processing center, extrusion research center, and bakery, along with other laboratory facilities. Assistantships are available. Contact the Graduate Coordinator, 785-532-6161.

Kansas State University, Graduate School, College of Human Ecology, Department of Foods and Nutrition, Manhattan, KS 66506. Offers food science (MS, PhD); nutrition (MS, PhD). Part-time programs available. *Faculty:* 8 full-time (4 women), 3 part-time (1 woman). *Students:* 20 full-time (11 women), 4 part-time (2 women); includes 3 minority (1 African American, 2 Asian Americans or Pacific Islanders), 13 international. Average age 27. 19 applicants, 37% accepted. In 1998, 2 master's awarded (50% found work related to degree, 50% continued full-time study); 4 doctorates awarded (100% found work related to degree). *Degree requirements:* For master's, thesis or alternative required, foreign language not required; for doctorate, dissertation required, foreign language not required. *Entrance requirements:* For master's and doctorate, GRE General Test (minimum combined score of 1000 required). *Average time to degree:* Master's–2 years full-time; doctorate–3 years full-time. *Application deadline:* For fall admission, 6/1; for spring admission, 11/1. Applications are processed on a rolling basis. Application fee: $0 ($25 for international students). Electronic applications accepted. *Financial aid:* In 1998–99, 15 research assistantships, 3 teaching assistantships were awarded.; career-related internships or fieldwork, Federal Work-Study, and tuition waivers (full) also available. *Faculty research:* Lipid soluble vitamins, dietary fiber, nutrition for young adults and the elderly, nutrition and exercise, sensory analysis. Total annual research expenditures: $800,000. *Unit head:* Mary Clarke, Interim Head, 785-532-5508, Fax: 785-532-3132, E-mail: clarke@humec.ksu.edu. *Application contact:* Sung Koo, Professor, 785-532-5508, Fax: 785-532-3132, E-mail: janetkay@ksu.edu.

Kansas State University, Graduate School, Food Science Program, Manhattan, KS 66506. Offers MS, PhD. Postbaccalaureate distance learning degree programs offered (minimal on-campus study). *Faculty:* 34 full-time (7 women), 2 part-time (both women). *Students:* 60 full-time (30 women), 9 part-time (all women); includes 3 minority (1 Asian American or Pacific Islander, 2 Hispanic Americans), 42 international. Average age 30. 165 applicants, 13% accepted. In 1998, 9 master's, 4 doctorates awarded. *Degree requirements:* For master's and doctorate, thesis/dissertation required, foreign language not required. *Entrance requirements:* For master's and doctorate, GRE General Test (minimum combined score of 1000 required), TOEFL (minimum score of 550 required). *Application deadline:* Applications are processed on a rolling basis. Application fee: $0 ($25 for international students). *Financial aid:* In 1998–99, 18 research assistantships, 2 teaching assistantships were awarded.; institutionally-sponsored loans also available. *Faculty research:* Food safety, food microbiology, sensory evaluation, food chemistry, food processing and engineering. *Unit head:* Ike Jeon, Chair, 785-532-1211, Fax: 785-532-5681, E-mail: ijeon@0z.0znet.ksu.edu.

Louisiana State University and Agricultural and Mechanical College, Graduate School, College of Agriculture, Department of Food Science, Baton Rouge, LA 70803. Offers MS, PhD. Part-time programs available. *Faculty:* 20 full-time (7 women). *Students:* 25 full-time (11 women), 7 part-time (4 women); includes 1 minority (African American), 22 international. Average age 31. 51 applicants, 43% accepted. In 1998, 2 master's, 8 doctorates awarded. *Degree requirements:* For master's and doctorate, thesis/dissertation required, foreign language not required. *Entrance requirements:* For master's and doctorate, GRE General Test (minimum combined score of 1000 required), minimum GPA of 3.0. *Average time to degree:* Master's–2 years full-time, 5 years part-time; doctorate–3 years full-time, 7 years part-time. *Application deadline:* For fall admission, 1/25 (priority date). Applications are processed on a rolling basis. Application fee: $25. *Financial aid:* In 1998–99, 19 research assistantships with partial tuition reimbursements (averaging $7,875 per year) were awarded.; fellowships, teaching assistantships with partial tuition reimbursements, institutionally-sponsored loans also available. Financial aid application deadline: 4/1. *Faculty research:* Food toxicology, food microbiology, food quality, food safety, food processing, by-product utilization, food and drug law. Total annual research expenditures: $660,000. *Unit head:* Dr. Douglas L. Park, Head, 225-388-5206, Fax: 225-388-5300, E-mail: dpark@lsu.edu. *Application contact:* Dr. Leslie C. Plhak, Graduate Adviser, 225-388-5206, Fax: 225-388-5300, E-mail: lplhak@unixl.sncc.lsu.edu.

McGill University, Faculty of Graduate Studies and Research, Faculty of Agricultural and Environmental Sciences, Department of Food Science and Agricultural Chemistry, Montréal, PQ H3A 2T5, Canada. Offers M Sc, PhD. *Faculty:* 9 full-time (0 women), 1 part-time (0 women). *Students:* 69 full-time (35 women), 21 international. Average age 27. 26 applicants, 38% accepted. In 1998, 8 master's, 7 doctorates awarded. *Degree requirements:* For master's and doctorate, thesis/dissertation required. *Entrance requirements:* For master's, TOEFL (minimum score of 550 required), B Sc in related discipline, minimum GPA of 3.0; for doctorate, TOEFL (minimum score of 550 required), M Sc. *Application deadline:* For fall admission, 1/1 (priority date); for winter admission, 5/1 (priority date); for spring admission, 9/1 (priority date). Applications are processed on a rolling basis. Application fee: $60. *Financial aid:* Research assistantships, teaching assistantships, institutionally-sponsored loans available. *Faculty research:* Food processing, food biotechnology/enzymology, food microbiology/packaging, food analysis, food chemistry/biochemistry. Total annual research expenditures: $1.1 million. *Unit head:* I. Alli, Chair, 514-398-7920, Fax: 514-398-7977, E-mail: alli@mcgill.ca. *Application contact:* 514-398-7708, Fax: 514-398-7968, E-mail: grad@macdonald.mcgill.ca.

Memorial University of Newfoundland, School of Graduate Studies, Department of Biochemistry, St. John's, NF A1C 5S7, Canada. Offers biochemistry (M Sc, PhD); food science (M Sc, PhD). Part-time programs available. *Students:* 19 full-time (5 women), 1 part-time, 12 international. 28 applicants, 4% accepted. In 1998, 3 master's, 1 doctorate awarded. *Degree requirements:* For master's, thesis required; for doctorate, dissertation, comprehensive exam required. *Entrance requirements:* For master's, 2nd class degree in related field; for doctorate, M Sc. Application fee: $40. *Financial aid:* Fellowships, research assistantships, teaching assistantships available. *Faculty research:* Toxicology, cell and molecular biology, food engineering, marine biotechnology, lipid biology. Total annual research expenditures: $1.1 million. *Unit head:* Dr. John Brosnan, Head, 709-737-8530, E-mail: jbrosnan@morgan.ucs.mun.ca. *Application contact:* Dr. John Robinson, Graduate Officer, 709-737-8545, Fax: 709-737-2422, E-mail: johnro@morgan.ucs.mun.ca.

Michigan State University, Graduate School, College of Human Ecology, Department of Food Science and Human Nutrition, East Lansing, MI 48824-1020. Offers food science (MS, PhD); human nutrition (MS, PhD). *Faculty:* 14. *Students:* 46 full-time (36 women), 36 part-time (25 women); includes 11 minority (6 African Americans, 5 Asian Americans or Pacific Islanders), 39 international. Average age 29. 155 applicants, 28% accepted. In 1998, 13 master's, 9 doctorates awarded. Terminal master's awarded for partial completion of doctoral program. *Degree requirements:* For master's, thesis optional, foreign language not required; for doctorate, dissertation required, foreign language not required. *Entrance requirements:* For master's, GRE, minimum GPA of 3.0 in last 2 years of undergraduate course work; for doctorate, GRE, minimum GPA of 3.0 (MS). *Application deadline:* For fall admission, 1/15 (priority date). Applications are processed on a rolling basis. Application fee: $30 ($40 for international students). *Financial aid:* In 1998–99, 47 research assistantships with tuition reimbursements (averaging $10,347 per year), 4 teaching assistantships with tuition reimbursements (averaging $10,075 per year) were awarded.; fellowships Financial aid application deadline: 1/15; financial aid applicants required to submit FAFSA. Total annual research expenditures: $553,000. *Unit head:* Dr. Mark A. Uebersax, Interim Chairperson, 517-355-8474, Fax: 517-353-8963, E-mail:

uebersax@pilot.msu.edu. *Application contact:* Dr. John E. Linz, Director of Graduate Studies, 517-353-9624, Fax: 517-353-8963, E-mail: jlinz@pilot.msu.edu.

Mississippi State University, College of Agriculture and Life Sciences, Department of Food Science and Technology, Mississippi State, MS 39762. Offers MS, PhD. *Students:* 23 full-time (11 women), 20 part-time (9 women); includes 23 minority (2 African Americans, 20 Asian Americans or Pacific Islanders, 1 Hispanic American), 8 international. Average age 32. 21 applicants, 71% accepted. In 1998, 10 master's, 6 doctorates awarded. *Degree requirements:* For master's and doctorate, thesis/dissertation, comprehensive oral or written exam required, foreign language not required. *Entrance requirements:* For master's, GRE General Test (minimum combined score of 800 required), TOEFL (minimum score of 550 required), minimum GPA of 2.8; for doctorate, GRE General Test (minimum combined score of 800 required), TOEFL (minimum score of 550 required), minimum GPA of 3.0. *Application deadline:* For fall admission, 7/1; for spring admission, 11/1. Applications are processed on a rolling basis. Application fee: $25 for international students. *Financial aid:* Federal Work-Study, institutionally-sponsored loans, and unspecified assistantships available. Financial aid applicants required to submit FAFSA. *Faculty research:* Food preservation, food chemistry, food processing, product development. Total annual research expenditures: $1.2 million. *Unit head:* Dr. Charles H. White, Head, 662-325-3200, Fax: 662-325-8728, E-mail: chwhite@ra.msstate.edu. *Application contact:* Jerry B. Inmon, Director of Admissions, 662-325-2224, Fax: 662-325-7360, E-mail: admit@admissions.msstate.edu.

North Carolina State University, Graduate School, College of Agriculture and Life Sciences, Department of Food Science, Raleigh, NC 27695. Offers M Ag, MS, PhD. *Faculty:* 29 full-time (3 women), 17 part-time (1 woman). *Students:* 43 full-time (26 women), 12 part-time (9 women); includes 8 minority (6 African Americans, 1 Asian American or Pacific Islander, 1 Hispanic American), 10 international. Average age 29. 95 applicants, 20% accepted. In 1998, 17 master's, 7 doctorates awarded. *Degree requirements:* For master's, thesis required (for some programs), foreign language not required; for doctorate, dissertation required, foreign language not required. *Application deadline:* For fall admission, 6/25; for spring admission, 11/25. Applications are processed on a rolling basis. Application fee: $45. *Financial aid:* In 1998–99, 2 fellowships (averaging $6,381 per year), 44 research assistantships (averaging $4,549 per year), 2 teaching assistantships (averaging $5,505 per year) were awarded.; Federal Work-Study also available. *Faculty research:* Food safety, value-added food products, environmental quality, nutrition and health, biotechnology. Total annual research expenditures: $6.3 million. *Unit head:* Dr. Kenneth R. Swartzel, Head, 919-515-7435, Fax: 919-515-4694, E-mail: ken_swartzel@ncsu.edu. *Application contact:* Dr. Jonathan C. Allen, Director of Graduate Programs, 919-513-2257, Fax: 919-515-7124, E-mail: jon_allen@ncsu.edu.

North Dakota State University, Graduate Studies and Research, College of Agriculture, Department of Cereal Science, Fargo, ND 58105. Offers MS, PhD. *Faculty:* 5 full-time (1 woman), 6 part-time (1 woman). *Students:* 9 full-time (5 women), 6 part-time (4 women), 7 international. 3 applicants, 33% accepted. In 1998, 1 master's awarded (100% found work related to degree); 1 doctorate awarded. *Degree requirements:* For master's and doctorate, thesis/dissertation required, foreign language not required. *Entrance requirements:* For master's and doctorate, TOEFL (minimum score of 600 required). *Average time to degree:* Master's–2.5 years full-time; doctorate–3.5 years full-time. *Application deadline:* Applications are processed on a rolling basis. Application fee: $25. *Financial aid:* Fellowships, research assistantships, career-related internships or fieldwork, Federal Work-Study, and institutionally-sponsored loans available. Financial aid application deadline: 4/15. *Faculty research:* Cereal proteins, cereal carbohydrates, electrophoresis, bioprocessing, fermentation. *Unit head:* Dr. Dennis T. Gordon, Chair, 701-231-7711, Fax: 701-231-7723, E-mail: dgordon@plains.nodak.edu. *Application contact:* Dr. Khalil Khan, Graduate Coordinator, 701-231-7711, Fax: 701-231-7723.

North Dakota State University, Graduate Studies and Research, College of Human Development and Education, Department of Food and Nutrition, Fargo, ND 58105. Offers cellular and molecular biology (PhD); food and nutrition (MS). *Faculty:* 7 full-time (5 women). *Students:* 11 full-time (7 women); includes 5 minority (all Asian Americans or Pacific Islanders), 2 international. Average age 26. In 1998, 4 degrees awarded. *Degree requirements:* For master's, thesis or alternative required, foreign language not required. *Entrance requirements:* For master's, TOEFL (minimum score of 525 required), minimum GPA of 3.0; for doctorate, TOEFL. *Application deadline:* Applications are processed on a rolling basis. Application fee: $25. *Financial aid:* In 1998–99, 6 research assistantships with full tuition reimbursements (averaging $4,647 per year), 3 teaching assistantships with full tuition reimbursements (averaging $4,666 per year) were awarded.; fellowships, Federal Work-Study and institutionally-sponsored loans also available. Aid available to part-time students. Financial aid application deadline: 4/15. *Faculty research:* Lipids, fiber, protein, nutrition education, sensory evaluation. *Unit head:* Dr. Theresa Nicklas, Chair, 701-231-7475, Fax: 701-231-7174, E-mail: nicklas@badlands.nodak.edu.

Nova Scotia Agricultural College, Research and Graduate Studies, Truro, NS B2N 5E3, Canada. Offers agriculture (M Sc), including animal behavior, animal genetics, animal management, animal nutrition, animal technology, botany, crop breeding, crop management, crop physiology, ecology, environmental microbiology, food science, geology, nutrient management, pest management, physiology, plant biotechnology, plant pathology, soil chemistry, soil fertility, soil physics, waste management. Part-time programs available. *Faculty:* 33 full-time (4 women), 14 part-time (1 woman). *Students:* 23 full-time (15 women), 17 part-time (8 women). *Degree requirements:* For master's, thesis, candidacy exam required. *Entrance requirements:* For master's, TOEFL (minimum score of 580 required), minimum GPA of 3.0. *Application deadline:* For fall admission, 6/1; for winter admission, 10/1; for spring admission, 2/1. Applications are processed on a rolling basis. Application fee: $55. *Unit head:* Jill L. Rogers-Langille, Coordinator, 902-893-6360, Fax: 902-897-9399, E-mail: jrogers-langille@cadmin.nsac.ns.ca. *Application contact:* Kari Duff, Assistant, 902-893-6502, Fax: 902-897-9399, E-mail: kduff@cadmin.nsac.ns.ca.

The Ohio State University, Graduate School, College of Food, Agricultural, and Environmental Sciences, Program in Food Science and Nutrition, Columbus, OH 43210. Offers MS, PhD. *Faculty:* 17 full-time, 8 part-time. *Students:* 54 full-time (34 women), 7 part-time (5 women); includes 8 minority (5 African Americans, 3 Asian Americans or Pacific Islanders), 29 international. 120 applicants, 16% accepted. In 1998, 13 master's, 6 doctorates awarded. *Degree requirements:* For master's, thesis optional, foreign language not required; for doctorate, dissertation required, foreign language not required. *Entrance requirements:* For master's and doctorate, GRE General Test. *Application deadline:* For fall admission, 8/15. Applications are processed on a rolling basis. Application fee: $30 ($40 for international students). *Financial aid:* Fellowships, research assistantships, Federal Work-Study and institutionally-sponsored loans available. Aid available to part-time students. *Unit head:* Grady Chism, Graduate Studies Committee Chair, 614-292-7719, Fax: 614-292-0218, E-mail: chism.2@osu.edu.

Oklahoma State University, Graduate College, College of Agricultural Sciences and Natural Resources, Department of Animal Sciences, Program in Food Science, Stillwater, OK 74078. Offers MS, PhD. *Students:* 4 full-time (2 women), 2 part-time (1 woman); includes 1 minority (African American), 2 international. Average age 31. In 1998, 5 master's awarded. *Degree requirements:* For master's and doctorate, thesis/dissertation required, foreign language not required. *Entrance requirements:* For master's and doctorate, TOEFL (minimum score of 550 required). *Application deadline:* For fall admission, 6/1 (priority date). Application fee: $25. *Financial aid:* Research assistantships, teaching assistantships, career-related internships or fieldwork, Federal Work-Study, and tuition waivers (partial) available. Aid available to part-time students. Financial aid application deadline: 3/1. *Unit head:* Gerald Fitch, Coordinator, 405-744-6065.

Oregon State University, Graduate School, College of Agricultural Sciences, Department of Food Science and Technology, Corvallis, OR 97331. Offers M Agr, MAIS, MS, PhD. *Faculty:* 17 full-time (2 women). *Students:* 28 full-time (19 women), 3 part-time (1 woman); includes 1 minority (Asian American or Pacific Islander), 21 international. Average age 28. In 1998, 4 master's, 3 doctorates awarded. *Degree requirements:* For master's, thesis (MS) required; for doctorate, dissertation required, foreign language not required. *Entrance requirements:* For master's and doctorate, GRE General Test, TOEFL (minimum score of 550 required), minimum GPA of 3.0 in last 90 hours. *Application deadline:* For fall admission, 3/1. Applications are processed on a rolling basis. Application fee: $50. *Financial aid:* Fellowships, research assistantships, teaching assistantships, career-related internships or fieldwork, Federal Work-Study, and institutionally-sponsored loans available. Aid available to part-time students. Financial aid application deadline: 2/1. *Faculty research:* Diet, cancer, and anticarcinogenesis; sensory analysis; chemistry and biochemistry. *Unit head:* Dr. Daniel F. Farkas, Head, 541-737-3131, Fax: 541-737-1877, E-mail: farkasd@bcc.orst.edu. *Application contact:* Jan Carlson, Academic Programs Secretary, 541-737-6486, Fax: 541-737-1877, E-mail: carlsonj@bcc.orst.edu.

Announcement: The Graduate Field of Food Science and Technology at Oregon State University comprises the following areas of study: food chemistry, food microbiology, food biotechnology, enology and brewing, flavor chemistry, sensory evaluation, food process engineering, and dairy, fruit, vegetable, and marine products processing. Web address: http://osu.orst.edu/dept/foodsci.

Pennsylvania State University University Park Campus, Graduate School, College of Agricultural Sciences, Department of Food Science, State College, University Park, PA 16802-1503. Offers MS, PhD. *Students:* 22 full-time (9 women), 10 part-time (3 women). In 1998, 13 master's, 4 doctorates awarded. *Entrance requirements:* For master's and doctorate, GRE General Test. Application fee: $50. *Unit head:* Dr. Donald B. Thompson, Head, 814-863-2950. *Application contact:* Dr. M. Sigman-Grant, Chair, 814-865-5444.

Purdue University, Graduate School, School of Agriculture, Department of Food Science, West Lafayette, IN 47907. Offers MS, PhD. Part-time programs available. *Faculty:* 15 full-time (2 women). *Students:* 41 full-time (17 women), 8 part-time (7 women); includes 1 minority (African American), 30 international. Average age 25. 56 applicants, 18% accepted. In 1998, 6 master's, 6 doctorates awarded. *Degree requirements:* For master's, thesis required (for some programs), foreign language not required; for doctorate, dissertation required, foreign language not required. *Entrance requirements:* For master's and doctorate, GRE General Test (minimum score of 400 on each section, 1100 combined required), TOEFL (minimum score of 575 required). *Application deadline:* For fall admission, 5/1 (priority date); for spring admission, 10/1. Applications are processed on a rolling basis. Application fee: $30. Electronic applications accepted. *Financial aid:* In 1998–99, 4 fellowships (averaging $17,000 per year), 33 research assistantships (averaging $13,000 per year), 1 teaching assistantship (averaging $13,000 per year) were awarded.; career-related internships or fieldwork also available. Aid available to part-time students. Financial aid application deadline: 4/1; financial aid applicants required to submit FAFSA. *Faculty research:* Processing, technology, microbiology, chemistry of foods, carbohydrate chemistry. *Unit head:* Dr. P. E. Nelson, Head, 765-494-8256, Fax: 765-494-7953. *Application contact:* Dr. S. S. Nielsen, Graduate Committee Chair, 765-494-8328, Fax: 765-494-7953, E-mail: nielsens@foodsci.purdue.edu.

Purdue University, Graduate School, School of Consumer and Family Sciences, Department of Foods and Nutrition, West Lafayette, IN 47907. Offers food sciences (MS, PhD); nutrition (MS, PhD). *Faculty:* 15 full-time (8 women), 2 part-time (0 women). *Students:* 29 full-time (24 women), 7 part-time (6 women); includes 5 minority (3 African Americans, 1 Hispanic American, 1 Native American), 15 international. 58 applicants, 40% accepted. In 1998, 6 master's, 1 doctorate awarded. *Degree requirements:* For master's and doctorate, thesis/dissertation required. *Entrance requirements:* For master's, GRE General Test (minimum combined score of 1000 required), TOEFL (minimum score of 600 required); for doctorate, GRE General Test (minimum combined score of 1000 required), TOEFL (minimum score of 550 required). *Application deadline:* Applications are processed on a rolling basis. Application fee: $30. Electronic applications accepted. *Financial aid:* Fellowships, research assistantships, teaching assistantships available. Aid available to part-time students. Financial aid applicants required to submit FAFSA. *Faculty research:* Nutrient requirements, nutrient metabolism, nutrition and disease prevention. *Unit head:* Dr. C. M. Weaver, Head, 765-494-8237, Fax: 765-494-0674. *Application contact:* Dawn Haan, Graduate Secretary, 765-494-8231, Fax: 765-494-0674.

Rutgers, The State University of New Jersey, New Brunswick, Graduate School, Program in Food Science, New Brunswick, NJ 08903. Offers M Phil, MS, PhD. Part-time and evening/weekend programs available. Postbaccalaureate distance learning degree programs offered (minimal on-campus study). *Faculty:* 24 full-time (2 women). *Students:* 55 full-time (28 women), 61 part-time (32 women); includes 20 minority (4 African Americans, 14 Asian Americans or Pacific Islanders, 2 Hispanic Americans), 54 international. Average age 25. 114 applicants, 39% accepted. In 1998, 13 master's awarded (100% found work related to degree); 4 doctorates awarded. *Degree requirements:* For master's, thesis required (for some programs), foreign language not required; for doctorate, dissertation required, foreign language not required. *Entrance requirements:* For master's and doctorate, GRE General Test (minimum combined score of 1100 required; average 1250). *Average time to degree:* Master's–3 years full-time, 5 years part-time; doctorate–5 years full-time, 7 years part-time. *Application deadline:* For fall admission, 5/1 (priority date); for spring admission, 11/1. Applications are processed on a rolling basis. Application fee: $50. *Financial aid:* In 1998–99, 40 students received aid, including 3 fellowships with tuition reimbursements available (averaging $15,000 per year), 33 research assistantships with tuition reimbursements available (averaging $14,000 per year), 4 teaching assistantships with tuition reimbursements available (averaging $12,236 per year); Federal Work-Study and tuition waivers (full) also available. Financial aid application deadline: 3/1; financial aid applicants required to submit FAFSA. *Faculty research:* Flavor analysis, food chemistry, food engineering, food biochemistry, mass spectrometry. Total annual research expenditures: $5 million. *Unit head:* Dr. Joseph D. Rosen, Director, 732-932-9611 Ext. 215, Fax: 732-932-6776, E-mail: jrosen@aesop.rutgers.edu. *Application contact:* Mary Toglia, Graduate Secretary, 732-932-9611 Ext. 207, Fax: 732-932-6776, E-mail: toglia@aesop.rutgers.edu.

See in-depth description on page 855.

Texas A&M University, College of Agriculture and Life Sciences, Department of Animal Science, Intercollegiate Faculty of Food Science and Technology, College Station, TX 77843. Offers MS, PhD. *Faculty:* 17 full-time (5 women). *Students:* 46 full-time (29 women); includes 4 minority (1 African American, 2 Asian Americans or Pacific Islanders, 1 Hispanic American), 24 international. Average age 28. 54 applicants, 26% accepted. In 1998, 9 master's, 2 doctorates awarded. *Degree requirements:* For master's and doctorate, thesis/dissertation required, foreign language not required. *Entrance requirements:* For master's and doctorate, GRE General Test, TOEFL. *Average time to degree:* Master's–2 years full-time; doctorate–4 years full-time. *Application deadline:* For fall admission, 2/1 (priority date); for spring admission, 10/1 (priority date). Applications are processed on a rolling basis. Application fee: $35 ($75 for international students). *Financial aid:* In 1998–99, 3 fellowships (averaging $12,000 per year), 9 research assistantships (averaging $11,250 per year), 7 teaching assistantships (averaging $11,250 per year) were awarded.; career-related internships or fieldwork and scholarships also available. *Faculty research:* Food safety, microbiology, product development. *Unit head:* Al Wagner, Chair, 409-845-1044, Fax: 409-845-0727. *Application contact:* Al Wagner, Chair, 409-845-1044, Fax: 409-845-0727.

Texas Tech University, Graduate School, College of Agricultural Sciences and Natural Resources, Department of Animal Science and Food Technology, Lubbock, TX 79409. Offers animal breeding (MS); animal nutrition (MS); animal science (MS, PhD); animal science and food technology (M Agr); food technology (MS); meat science (MS). Part-time programs available. *Faculty:* 10 full-time (2 women). *Students:* 47 full-time (14 women), 8 part-time (4 women); includes 1 minority (Hispanic American), 8 international. Average age 28. 37 applicants, 51% accepted. In 1998, 11 master's, 5 doctorates awarded. *Degree requirements:* For master's, thesis, internship (M Agr) required, foreign language not required; for doctorate, dissertation required. *Entrance requirements:* For master's, GRE General Test (combined average 958); for doctorate, GRE General Test. *Application deadline:* For fall admission, 4/15 (priority

Food Science and Technology

Texas Tech University (continued)

date); for spring admission, 11/1 (priority date). Applications are processed on a rolling basis. Application fee: $25 ($50 for international students). Electronic applications accepted. *Financial aid:* In 1998–99, 31 research assistantships (averaging $6,672 per year), 6 teaching assistantships (averaging $6,362 per year) were awarded.; fellowships, Federal Work-Study and institutionally-sponsored loans also available. Aid available to part-time students. Financial aid application deadline: 5/15; financial aid applicants required to submit FAFSA. *Faculty research:* Animal growth composition and product acceptability, animal nutrition and utilization, animal physiology and adaptation to stress. Total annual research expenditures: $1.2 million. *Unit head:* Dr. Kevin R. Pond, Chairman, 806-742-2513, Fax: 806-742-0898.

Texas Woman's University, Graduate School, College of Health Sciences, Department of Nutrition and Food Sciences, Denton, TX 76204. Offers food science (MS); institutional administration (MS); nutrition (MS, PhD); nutrition/dietetic internship (MS). Part-time and evening/weekend programs available. *Faculty:* 14 full-time (11 women), 4 part-time (all women). *Students:* 67 full-time (63 women), 105 part-time (100 women); includes 30 minority (5 African Americans, 11 Asian Americans or Pacific Islanders, 13 Hispanic Americans, 1 Native American), 9 international. Average age 31. 57 applicants, 82% accepted. In 1998, 35 master's, 4 doctorates awarded (33% entered university research/teaching, 67% found other work related to degree). *Degree requirements:* For master's, thesis required (for some programs), foreign language not required; for doctorate, dissertation, statistics, qualifying exam required, dissertation, statistics, qualifying exam required. *Entrance requirements:* For master's, GRE General Test (minimum combined score of 700 required), minimum GPA of 3.0; for doctorate, GRE General Test (minimum combined score of 900 required), minimum GPA of 3.0. *Application deadline:* Applications are processed on a rolling basis. Application fee: $30. *Financial aid:* In 1998–99, 18 research assistantships, 17 teaching assistantships were awarded.; career-related internships or fieldwork, Federal Work-Study, institutionally-sponsored loans, and scholarships also available. Aid available to part-time students. Financial aid application deadline: 4/1. *Faculty research:* Obesity, nutrition and cancer, mineral metabolism, renal disease. Total annual research expenditures: $290,458. *Unit head:* Dr. Carolyn Bednar, Chair, 940-898-2636, Fax: 940-898-2634.

Tuskegee University, Graduate Programs, College of Agricultural, Environmental and Natural Sciences, Department of Food and Nutritional Sciences, Tuskegee, AL 36088. Offers MS. *Faculty:* 4 full-time (3 women). *Students:* 7 full-time (6 women), 6 part-time (5 women); includes 12 minority (11 African Americans, 1 Asian American or Pacific Islander), 1 international. Average age 24. In 1998, 9 degrees awarded. *Degree requirements:* For master's, computer language, thesis required, foreign language not required. *Entrance requirements:* For master's, GRE General Test. *Application deadline:* For fall admission, 7/15. Applications are processed on a rolling basis. Application fee: $25 ($35 for international students). *Financial aid:* Application deadline: 4/15. *Unit head:* Dr. Walter A. Hill, Dean, College of Agricultural, Environmental and Natural Sciences, 334-727-8157.

Universidad de las Américas–Puebla, Division of Graduate Studies, School of Engineering, Program in Chemical Engineering, Cholula, 72820, Mexico. Offers chemical engineering (MS); food technology (MS). Part-time and evening/weekend programs available. *Faculty:* 10 full-time (0 women), 2 part-time (0 women). *Students:* 31 full-time (20 women), 20 part-time (1 woman); all minorities (all Hispanic Americans) *Degree requirements:* For master's, one foreign language, computer language, thesis required. *Application deadline:* For fall admission, 7/16. Applications are processed on a rolling basis. Application fee: $0. *Unit head:* Dr. Rene Reyes, Coordinator, 22-29-21-26, Fax: 22-29-20-32, E-mail: rreyes@mail.udlap.mx. *Application contact:* Mauricio Villegas, Chair of Admissions Office, 22-29-20-17, Fax: 22-29-20-18, E-mail: admision@mail.udlap.mx.

Université de Moncton, School of Nutrition and Family Studies, Moncton, NB E1A 3E9, Canada. Offers family studies (M Sc); foods/nutrition (M Sc). Part-time programs available. *Faculty:* 5 full-time (4 women). *Students:* 15 full-time (14 women); includes 1 African American *Degree requirements:* For master's, one foreign language, thesis required. *Entrance requirements:* For master's, previous course work in statistics. *Application deadline:* For fall admission, 6/15 (priority date). Applications are processed on a rolling basis. Application fee: $30. *Unit head:* Lita Villalon, Director, 506-858-4003, Fax: 506-858-4540, E-mail: villall@umoncton.ca.

Université Laval, Faculty of Graduate Studies, Faculty of Agricultural and Food Sciences, Department of Food Sciences and Nutrition, Program in Food Sciences and Technology, Sainte-Foy, PQ G1K 7P4, Canada. Offers M Sc, PhD. *Students:* 63 full-time (35 women), 9 part-time (5 women). 29 applicants, 41% accepted. In 1998, 15 master's, 3 doctorates awarded. *Application deadline:* For fall admission, 3/1. Application fee: $30. *Unit head:* Jean-Christophe Vuillemard, Director, 418-656-2131 Ext. 5968, Fax: 418-656-3353, E-mail: sta@sta.ulaval.ca.

The University of Akron, Graduate School, College of Fine and Applied Arts, School of Family and Consumer Sciences, Program in Food Science, Akron, OH 44325-0001. Offers MA. *Students:* 1 (woman) full-time, 3 part-time (all women); includes 1 minority (Asian American or Pacific Islander) Average age 32. In 1998, 1 degree awarded. *Degree requirements:* For master's, thesis or alternative required, foreign language not required. *Entrance requirements:* For master's, GRE General Test, minimum GPA of 2.75. *Average time to degree:* Master's–2 years full-time, 4 years part-time. *Application deadline:* For fall admission, 8/15. Applications are processed on a rolling basis. Application fee: $25 ($50 for international students). Tuition, state resident: part-time $189 per credit. Tuition, nonresident: part-time $353 per credit. Required fees: $7.3 per credit. *Financial aid:* Application deadline: 3/1. *Unit head:* Dr. Donna Gaboury, Associate Professor, 330-972-7725, E-mail: gaboury@uakron.edu. *Application contact:* Dr. Virginia Gunn, Graduate Adviser, 330-972-7729, E-mail: vgunn@uakron.edu.

University of Arkansas, Graduate School, Dale Bumpers College of Agricultural, Food and Life Sciences, Department of Food Science, Fayetteville, AR 72701-1201. Offers MS, PhD. *Faculty:* 6 full-time (0 women). *Students:* 31 full-time (20 women), 1 part-time; includes 3 minority (1 African American, 2 Asian Americans or Pacific Islanders), 10 international. 32 applicants, 50% accepted. In 1998, 5 master's, 2 doctorates awarded. *Degree requirements:* For master's and doctorate, thesis/dissertation required, foreign language not required. Application fee: $40 ($50 for international students). Tuition, state resident: full-time $3,186. Tuition, nonresident: full-time $7,560. Required fees: $378. *Financial aid:* In 1998–99, 23 research assistantships, 1 teaching assistantship were awarded.; career-related internships or fieldwork, Federal Work-Study, scholarships, and unspecified assistantships also available. Aid available to part-time students. Financial aid application deadline: 4/1; financial aid applicants required to submit FAFSA. *Unit head:* Dr. Terry Siebenmorgen, Head, 501-575-4605. *Application contact:* Navam Hettiarachchy, Graduate Coordinator, E-mail: nhettiar@comp.uark.edu.

University of British Columbia, Faculty of Graduate Studies, Faculty of Agricultural Sciences, Department of Food Science, Vancouver, BC V6T 1Z2, Canada. Offers M Sc, PhD. *Degree requirements:* For master's, thesis required; for doctorate, dissertation, comprehensive exam required. *Entrance requirements:* For master's and doctorate, TOEFL (minimum score of 570 required). *Faculty research:* Food chemistry, physical and structural bromatology, environmental bromatology, food process science, food toxicology.

University of California, Davis, Graduate Studies, Program in Food Science, Davis, CA 95616. Offers MS, PhD. *Students:* 70 full-time (38 women); includes 9 minority (8 Asian Americans or Pacific Islanders, 1 Hispanic American), 29 international. 109 applicants, 32% accepted. In 1998, 6 master's, 6 doctorates awarded. *Degree requirements:* For master's, thesis optional; for doctorate, dissertation required. *Entrance requirements:* For master's and doctorate, GRE General Test, minimum GPA of 3.0. *Application deadline:* For fall admission, 1/15. Application fee: $40. Electronic applications accepted. *Financial aid:* In 1998–99, 21 fellowships with full and partial tuition reimbursements, 27 research assistantships with full and partial tuition reimbursements, 11 teaching assistantships with full and partial tuition reimbursements were awarded.; Federal Work-Study, grants, and scholarships also available. Financial aid application deadline: 1/15; financial aid applicants required to submit FAFSA. *Unit head:* Dana Ogrydziak, Graduate Adviser, 530-752-1415.

University of Delaware, College of Agriculture and Natural Resources, Department of Animal and Food Sciences, Newark, DE 19716. Offers animal sciences (MS, PhD); food sciences (MS). Part-time programs available. *Faculty:* 20 full-time (4 women). *Students:* 26 full-time (17 women), 4 part-time (2 women), 11 international. 20 applicants, 30% accepted. In 1998, 6 master's, 1 doctorate awarded. *Degree requirements:* For master's and doctorate, thesis/dissertation required, foreign language not required. *Entrance requirements:* For master's and doctorate, GRE General Test, TOEFL. *Application deadline:* For fall admission, 7/1 (priority date); for spring admission, 12/1. Applications are processed on a rolling basis. Application fee: $45. *Financial aid:* In 1998–99, 1 fellowship with full tuition reimbursement (averaging $15,000 per year), 8 research assistantships with full tuition reimbursements (averaging $13,775 per year), 6 teaching assistantships with full tuition reimbursements (averaging $9,473 per year) were awarded.; scholarships and tuition waivers also available. *Faculty research:* Food chemistry, food microbiology, process engineering technology, packaging, food analysis, microbial genetics, molecular endocrinology, growth physiology, avian immunology and virology, monogastric nutrition, avian geomics. Total annual research expenditures: $1.3 million. *Unit head:* Dr. John K. Rosenberger, Chairman, 302-831-2524, Fax: 302-831-2822, E-mail: john.rosenberger@mvs.udel.edu. *Application contact:* Dr. Jack Gelb, Graduate Program Coordinator, 302-831-2524, Fax: 302-831-2822, E-mail: jgelb@udel.edu.

University of Florida, Graduate School, College of Agriculture, Department of Food Science and Human Nutrition, Gainesville, FL 32611. Offers M Ag, MS, PhD. *Faculty:* 38. *Students:* 61 full-time (33 women), 12 part-time (9 women); includes 16 minority (3 African Americans, 5 Asian Americans or Pacific Islanders, 8 Hispanic Americans), 14 international. 90 applicants, 48% accepted. In 1998, 22 master's, 4 doctorates awarded. *Degree requirements:* For master's, thesis optional; for doctorate, dissertation required. *Entrance requirements:* For master's and doctorate, GRE General Test, TOEFL, minimum GPA of 3.0. *Application deadline:* For fall admission, 6/1 (priority date). Applications are processed on a rolling basis. Application fee: $20. Electronic applications accepted. *Financial aid:* In 1998–99, 37 students received aid, including 9 fellowships, 25 research assistantships, 8 teaching assistantships; career-related internships or fieldwork also available. *Faculty research:* Pesticide research, nutritional biochemistry and microbiology, food safety and toxicology assessment and dietetics, food chemistry. *Unit head:* Dr. Douglas L. Archer, Chair, 352-392-1991 Ext. 102, Fax: 352-392-9467, E-mail: dlar@gnv.ifas.ufl.edu. *Application contact:* Dr. Robert P. Bates, Graduate Coordinator, 352-392-1991, Fax: 352-392-9467, E-mail: rpb@gnv.ifas.ufl.edu.

See in-depth description on page 859.

University of Georgia, Graduate School, College of Agricultural and Environmental Sciences, Department of Food Science, Athens, GA 30602. Offers MS, PhD. *Faculty:* 22 full-time (4 women). *Students:* 64 full-time (29 women), 8 part-time (5 women); includes 5 minority (3 African Americans, 2 Asian Americans or Pacific Islanders), 50 international. 55 applicants, 35% accepted. In 1998, 16 master's, 8 doctorates awarded. *Degree requirements:* For master's, thesis required, foreign language not required; for doctorate, one foreign language (computer language can substitute), dissertation required. *Entrance requirements:* For master's and doctorate, GRE General Test. *Application deadline:* For fall admission, 7/1 (priority date); for spring admission, 11/15. Application fee: $30. Electronic applications accepted. *Financial aid:* Fellowships, research assistantships, teaching assistantships, unspecified assistantships available. *Unit head:* Dr. Philip E. Koehler, Graduate Coordinator, 706-542-2286, Fax: 706-542-1050, E-mail: pkoehler@arches.uga.edu.

Announcement: Graduates with degrees in other fields are often attracted to food science because of the challenge of feeding humankind and the vocational opportunities open to those with advanced degrees. Programs can be tailored to allow individuals to best utilize prior training. Modern facilities and a faculty trained in fundamental science disciplines as well as food technology allow preparation for any career objective.

University of Guelph, Faculty of Graduate Studies, Ontario Agricultural College, Department of Food Science, Guelph, ON N1G 2W1, Canada. Offers M Sc, PhD. *Faculty:* 18 full-time (1 woman). *Students:* 66 full-time (36 women), 10 part-time (5 women), 8 international. 58 applicants, 38% accepted. In 1998, 15 master's, 8 doctorates awarded. *Degree requirements:* For master's and doctorate, thesis/dissertation required. *Entrance requirements:* For master's, minimum B- average during previous 2 years; for doctorate, minimum B average. Application fee: $60. *Expenses:* Tuition and fees charges are reported in Canadian dollars. Tuition, area resident: Full-time $4,725 Canadian dollars; part-time $1,055 Canadian dollars per term. International tuition: $6,999 Canadian dollars full-time. Required fees: $295 Canadian dollars per term. *Financial aid:* In 1998–99, 40 research assistantships (averaging $12,000 per year), 14 teaching assistantships (averaging $3,744 per year) were awarded. *Faculty research:* Food chemistry, food microbiology, foodprocessing, preservative and utilization. *Unit head:* Dr. R. Yada, Chair, 519-824-4120 Ext. 8915, E-mail: ryada@uoguelph.ca. *Application contact:* Dr. R. Lencki, Graduate Coordinator, 519-824-4120 Ext. 4327, E-mail: rlencki@foodsci.uoguelph.ca.

University of Guelph, Faculty of Graduate Studies, Program in Food Safety and Quality Assurance, Guelph, ON N1G 2W1, Canada. Offers M Sc. Part-time programs available. *Faculty:* 25 full-time (4 women). *Students:* 17 full-time (8 women), 4 part-time (2 women), 3 international. In 1998, 6 degrees awarded (100% found work related to degree). *Degree requirements:* For master's, thesis not required. *Average time to degree:* Master's–2 years full-time, 3 years part-time. Application fee: $60. *Expenses:* Tuition and fees charges are reported in Canadian dollars. Tuition, area resident: Full-time $4,725 Canadian dollars; part-time $1,055 Canadian dollars per term. International tuition: $6,999 Canadian dollars full-time. Required fees: $295 Canadian dollars per term. *Financial aid:* In 1998–99, 2 students received aid, including 1 teaching assistantship (averaging $3,744 per year); scholarships also available. *Faculty research:* Food microbiology, food chemistry, food engineering, food processing, veterinary microbiology, epidemiology, risk analysis. Total annual research expenditures: $2 million. *Unit head:* Dr. M. W. Griffiths, Chair, 519-824-4120 Ext. 2269, Fax: 519-824-6631, E-mail: mgriffit@uoguelph.ca. *Application contact:* M. Walmsley, Graduate Student Secretary, 519-824-4120 Ext. 6983, Fax: 519-824-6631, E-mail: mwalmsle@foodsci.uoguelph.ca.

University of Hawaii at Manoa, Graduate Division, College of Tropical Agriculture and Human Resources, Department of Food Science and Human Nutrition, Program in Food Science, Honolulu, HI 96822. Offers MS. *Students:* 3 full-time (2 women); includes 1 Asian American or Pacific Islander, 2 international. Average age 27. 5 applicants, 0% accepted. *Entrance requirements:* For master's, GRE General Test. *Application deadline:* For fall admission, 3/1; for spring admission, 9/1. Application fee: $25 ($50 for international students). *Financial aid:* Research assistantships, teaching assistantships available. *Faculty research:* Biochemistry of natural products, sensory evaluation, food processing, food chemistry, food safety. *Unit head:* Dr. Rachel Novotny, Graduate Chairperson, 808-956-8236, Fax: 808-956-4024, E-mail: novotny@hawaii.edu.

University of Idaho, College of Graduate Studies, College of Agriculture, Department of Food Science and Toxicology, Moscow, ID 83844-4140. Offers food science (MS). *Faculty:* 7 full-time (3 women). *Students:* 4 full-time (2 women), 3 part-time (1 woman), 1 international. In 1998, 2 degrees awarded. *Degree requirements:* Foreign language not required. *Entrance requirements:* For master's, minimum GPA of 2.8. *Application deadline:* For fall admission, 8/1; for spring admission, 12/15. Application fee: $35 ($45 for international students). *Financial aid:* In 1998–99, 2 research assistantships (averaging $9,694 per year) were awarded.; teaching assistantships Financial aid application deadline: 2/15. *Unit head:* Dr. Jerry H. Exon, Head, 208-885-7081.

University of Illinois at Urbana–Champaign, Graduate College, College of Agricultural, Consumer and Environmental Sciences, Department of Food Science and Human Nutrition,

Urbana, IL 61801. Offers MS, PhD, MD/PhD. *Faculty:* 23 full-time (7 women). *Students:* 44 full-time (22 women); includes 4 minority (all Asian Americans or Pacific Islanders), 20 international. 64 applicants, 13% accepted. In 1998, 28 master's, 9 doctorates awarded. *Degree requirements:* For master's, foreign language and thesis not required; for doctorate, dissertation required. *Entrance requirements:* For master's, minimum GPA of 4.0 on a 5.0 scale. *Application deadline:* Applications are processed on a rolling basis. Application fee: $40 ($50 for international students). Tuition, state resident: full-time $4,040. Tuition, nonresident: full-time $11,192. Full-time tuition and fees vary according to program. *Financial aid:* Fellowships, research assistantships, teaching assistantships, tuition waivers (full and partial) available. Financial aid application deadline: 2/15. Total annual research expenditures: $4.4 million. *Unit head:* Dr. Bruce M. Chassy, Head, 217-244-4498. *Application contact:* Dr. William Artz, Graduate Admissions Coordinator, 217-333-9328, E-mail: w-artz@uiuc.edu.

Announcement: Excellent graduate research programs are available in food science and human nutrition (MS, MS/RD, PhD, PhD/MD, PhD/RD), including food analysis, food and flavor chemistry, food processing/engineering, packaging, food microbiology, biotechnology, and all aspects of human nutrition, from community and clinical nutrition to nutritional biochemistry. For information, contact 217-333-0521, e-mail: kmc@uiuc.edu.

University of Kentucky, Graduate School, College of Human Environmental Sciences, Program in Nutrition and Food Science, Lexington, KY 40506-0032. Offers MS. *Degree requirements:* For master's, comprehensive exam required, thesis optional, foreign language not required. *Entrance requirements:* For master's, GRE General Test, minimum undergraduate GPA of 2.5.

University of Maine, Graduate School, College of Natural Sciences, Forestry, and Agriculture, Department of Food Science and Human Nutrition, Orono, ME 04469. Offers food and nutritional sciences (PhD); food science and human nutrition (MS). Part-time programs available. *Faculty:* 4 full-time (1 woman). *Students:* 34 (28 women). Average age 23. 48 applicants, 25% accepted. In 1998, 2 master's awarded (100% found work related to degree). *Degree requirements:* For master's and doctorate, thesis/dissertation required, foreign language not required. *Entrance requirements:* For master's, GRE General Test (minimum combined score of 1000 required), TOEFL (minimum score of 550 required), minimum GPA of 3.0; for doctorate, GRE General Test, TOEFL (minimum score of 550 required). *Application deadline:* For fall admission, 2/1 (priority date); for spring admission, 10/15. Applications are processed on a rolling basis. Application fee: $50. *Financial aid:* In 1998–99, 9 research assistantships with tuition reimbursements (averaging $8,200 per year), 4 teaching assistantships with tuition reimbursements (averaging $8,200 per year) were awarded.; scholarships and tuition waivers (full and partial) also available. Financial aid application deadline: 3/1. *Faculty research:* Product development of fruit and vegetables, lipid oxidation in fish and meat, analytical methods development, metabolism of potato glycoalkaloids, seafood quality. *Unit head:* Rod Bushway, Chair, 207-581-1625, Fax: 207-581-1636. *Application contact:* Scott G. Delcourt, Director of the Graduate School, 207-581-3218, Fax: 207-581-3232, E-mail: graduate@maine.edu.

University of Manitoba, Faculty of Graduate Studies, Faculty of Agriculture, Department of Food Science, Winnipeg, MB R3T 2N2, Canada. Offers M Sc. *Degree requirements:* For master's, thesis required, foreign language not required. *Unit head:* W. Bushuk, Head.

University of Maryland, College Park, Graduate School, College of Agriculture and Natural Resources, Department of Human Nutrition and Food Science, Program in Food Science, College Park, MD 20742-5045. Offers MS, PhD. *Students:* 7 full-time (4 women), 8 part-time (4 women); includes 3 minority (1 African American, 2 Asian Americans or Pacific Islanders), 4 international. 30 applicants, 27% accepted. In 1998, 1 master's, 1 doctorate awarded. *Degree requirements:* For master's, thesis or alternative, comprehensive exam, research-based thesis or equivalent paper required, foreign language not required; for doctorate, dissertation, candidacy exam, assist in teaching 1 course, research paper required, foreign language not required. *Entrance requirements:* For master's, GRE General Test (minimum combined score of 1500 on three sections required), TOEFL (minimum score of 550 required), minimum GPA of 3.0, professional experience; for doctorate, GRE General Test (minimum combined score of 1500 on three sections required), TOEFL (minimum score of 550 required), minimum GPA of 3.0. *Application deadline:* For fall admission, 4/1. Applications are processed on a rolling basis. Application fee: $50 ($70 for international students). Tuition, state resident: part-time $272 per credit hour. Tuition, nonresident: part-time $475 per credit hour. Required fees: $632; $379 per year. *Financial aid:* Fellowships, research assistantships, teaching assistantships available. Financial aid applicants required to submit FAFSA. *Faculty research:* Food chemistry, engineering, microbiology, and processing technology; quality assurance; membrane separations, rheology and texture measurement. *Unit head:* Dr. George Bean, Director, 301-405-4521, Fax: 301-405-7980. *Application contact:* Trudy Lindsey, Director, Graduate Admission and Records, 301-405-4198, Fax: 301-314-9305, E-mail: grschool@deans.umd.edu.

University of Maryland, College Park, Graduate School, College of Agriculture and Natural Resources, Department of Human Nutrition and Food Science, Program in Human Nutrition and Food Science, College Park, MD 20742-5045. Offers MS, PhD. *Students:* 2 full-time (both women), 3 part-time (all women); includes 1 minority (Asian American or Pacific Islander), 3 international. In 1998, 2 master's, 2 doctorates awarded. *Degree requirements:* For master's, comprehensive exam, research-based thesis or equivalent paper required; for doctorate, dissertation, candidacy exam required, foreign language not required. *Entrance requirements:* For master's and doctorate, GRE General Test (minimum combined score of 1500 on three sections required), TOEFL, minimum GPA of 3.0. *Application deadline:* Applications are processed on a rolling basis. Application fee: $50 ($70 for international students). Tuition, state resident: part-time $272 per credit hour. Tuition, nonresident: part-time $475 per credit hour. Required fees: $632; $379 per year. *Financial aid:* Fellowships, research assistantships, teaching assistantships, Federal Work-Study and tuition waivers (full) available. Financial aid applicants required to submit FAFSA. *Unit head:* Scott G. Delcourt, Director of the Graduate School, 207-581-3218, Fax: 207-581-3232, E-mail: graduate@maine.edu. *Application contact:* Trudy Lindsey, Director, Graduate Admission and Records, 301-405-4198, Fax: 301-314-9305, E-mail: grschool@deans.umd.edu.

University of Massachusetts Amherst, Graduate School, College of Food and Natural Resources, Department of Food Science, Amherst, MA 01003. Offers MS, PhD. Part-time programs available. *Faculty:* 12 full-time (1 woman). *Students:* 15 full-time (8 women), 24 part-time (9 women); includes 1 minority (African American), 28 international. Average age 28. 73 applicants, 29% accepted. In 1998, 6 master's awarded. Terminal master's awarded for partial completion of doctoral program. *Degree requirements:* For master's, thesis or alternative required, foreign language not required; for doctorate, computer language, dissertation required, foreign language not required. *Entrance requirements:* For master's and doctorate, GRE General Test. *Application deadline:* For fall admission, 2/1 (priority date); for spring admission, 10/1. Applications are processed on a rolling basis. Application fee: $40. Tuition, state resident: full-time $2,640; part-time $165 per credit. Tuition, nonresident: full-time $9,756; part-time $407 per credit. Required fees: $1,221 per term. One-time fee: $110. Full-time tuition and fees vary according to course load, campus/location and reciprocity agreements. *Financial aid:* In 1998–99, 2 fellowships with full tuition reimbursements (averaging $16,565 per year), 34 research assistantships with full tuition reimbursements (averaging $7,607 per year), 9 teaching assistantships with full tuition reimbursements (averaging $6,811 per year) were awarded.; career-related internships or fieldwork, Federal Work-Study, grants, scholarships, traineeships, and unspecified assistantships also available. Aid available to part-time students. Financial aid application deadline: 2/1. *Unit head:* Dr. Fergus Clydesdale, Head, 413-545-2277, Fax: 413-545-1262, E-mail: fergc@foodsci.umass.edu.

University of Minnesota, Twin Cities Campus, Graduate School, College of Agricultural, Food, and Environmental Sciences, Department of Food Science and Nutrition, Program in Food Science, Minneapolis, MN 55455-0213. Offers MS, PhD. Part-time programs available. *Faculty:* 28 full-time (7 women). *Students:* 62; includes 3 minority (1 African American, 1 Asian American or Pacific Islander, 1 Hispanic American), 17 international. In 1998, 10 master's, 5 doctorates awarded. Terminal master's awarded for partial completion of doctoral program. *Degree requirements:* For master's, thesis required (for some programs), foreign language not required; for doctorate, dissertation required, foreign language not required. *Entrance requirements:* For master's, GRE General Test (combined average 1692 on three sections), TOEFL (minimum score of 550 required; 213 for computer-based), previous course work in general chemistry, organic chemistry, calculus, and physics; for doctorate, GRE General Test (combined average 1780 on three sections), TOEFL (minimum score of 550 required; 213 for computer-based), previous course work in general chemistry, organic chemistry, calculus, and physics. *Average time to degree:* Master's–2.5 years full-time; doctorate–5 years full-time. *Application deadline:* For fall admission, 3/15 (priority date); for spring admission, 9/15 (priority date). Applications are processed on a rolling basis. Application fee: $50 ($55 for international students). Electronic applications accepted. *Financial aid:* In 1998–99, 1 fellowship with full tuition reimbursement (averaging $13,300 per year), 36 research assistantships with full and partial tuition reimbursements (averaging $13,300 per year) were awarded.; teaching assistantships, career-related internships or fieldwork, Federal Work-Study, institutionally-sponsored loans, and scholarships also available. Aid available to part-time students. *Faculty research:* Food chemistry, food microbiology, foodtechnology, grain science, dairy science. Total annual research expenditures: $2.7 million. *Unit head:* Dr. Gary Reineccius, Director of Graduate Studies, 612-624-3201, Fax: 612-625-5272, E-mail: garein@che2.che.umn.edu. *Application contact:* Susan J.A. Punchochar, Student Services Coordinator, 612-624-6753, Fax: 612-625-5272, E-mail: spuncoch@che2.che.umn.edu.

University of Missouri–Columbia, Graduate School, College of Agriculture, Department of Food Science and Human Nutrition, Columbia, MO 65211. Offers food science (MS, PhD); foods and food systems management (MS); human nutrition (MS). *Faculty:* 13 full-time (4 women), 1 part-time (0 women). *Students:* 15 full-time (9 women), 11 part-time (7 women); includes 3 minority (1 African American, 2 Asian Americans or Pacific Islanders), 18 international. 21 applicants, 52% accepted. In 1998, 8 master's, 1 doctorate awarded. Terminal master's awarded for partial completion of doctoral program. *Degree requirements:* For doctorate, dissertation required, foreign language not required. *Entrance requirements:* For master's and doctorate, GRE General Test, minimum GPA of 3.0. *Application deadline:* For fall admission, 8/1 (priority date). Applications are processed on a rolling basis. Application fee: $30 ($50 for international students). *Financial aid:* Research assistantships, teaching assistantships, institutionally-sponsored loans available. *Unit head:* Dr. Robert Marshall, Director of Graduate Studies, 573-882-4113. *Application contact:* Dr. Robert Marshall, Director of Graduate Studies, 573-882-4113.

University of Missouri–Columbia, Graduate School, College of Human Environmental Science, Department of Human Nutrition, Foods, Food System Management, and Exercise Physiology, Columbia, MO 65211. Offers exercise physiology (PhD); exercise science (MA); food science (MS, PhD); foods and food systems management (MS); human nutrition (MS). *Faculty:* 11 full-time (4 women). *Students:* 2 full-time (both women), 3 part-time (all women). 2 applicants, 0% accepted. In 1998, 3 master's, 4 doctorates awarded. *Degree requirements:* For doctorate, dissertation required. *Entrance requirements:* For master's and doctorate, GRE General Test, TOEFL, minimum GPA of 3.0. *Application deadline:* Applications are processed on a rolling basis. Application fee: $30 ($50 for international students). *Financial aid:* Fellowships, research assistantships, teaching assistantships, institutionally-sponsored loans available. *Unit head:* Dr. Richard P. Dowdy, Director of Graduate Studies, 573-882-7014.

University of Nebraska–Lincoln, Graduate College, College of Agricultural Sciences and Natural Resources, Department of Food Science and Technology, Lincoln, NE 68588. Offers MS, PhD. *Faculty:* 11 full-time (2 women), 1 part-time (0 women). *Students:* 34 full-time (18 women), 12 part-time (7 women); includes 7 minority (3 African Americans, 2 Asian Americans or Pacific Islanders, 2 Hispanic Americans), 26 international. Average age 31. 29 applicants, 24% accepted. In 1998, 8 master's, 4 doctorates awarded. *Degree requirements:* For master's, thesis optional, foreign language not required; for doctorate, dissertation, comprehensive exams required. *Entrance requirements:* For master's and doctorate, GRE General Test, TOEFL (minimum score of 550 required). *Average time to degree:* Doctorate–4.2 years full-time. *Application deadline:* For fall admission, 3/1 (priority date). Applications are processed on a rolling basis. Application fee: $35. Electronic applications accepted. *Financial aid:* In 1998–99, 5 fellowships, 23 research assistantships were awarded.; teaching assistantships, Federal Work-Study also available. Aid available to part-time students. Financial aid application deadline: 2/15. *Faculty research:* Food chemistry, microbiology, processing, engineering, and biotechnology. *Unit head:* Dr. Stephen Taylor, Head, 402-472-2831, Fax: 402-472-1693, E-mail: staylor2@unl.edu.

University of Puerto Rico, Mayagüez Campus, Graduate Studies, College of Agricultural Sciences, Department of Food Technology, Mayagüez, PR 00681-5000. Offers MS. *Degree requirements:* For master's, thesis, comprehensive exam required, foreign language not required. *Entrance requirements:* For master's, minimum GPA of 2.5. *Faculty research:* Food microbiology, food science, seafood technology, food engineering and packaging, fermentation.

University of Rhode Island, Graduate School, College of Resource Development, Department of Food Science and Nutrition, Kingston, RI 02881. Offers food and nutrition science (MS, PhD); food science and technology, nutrition and dietetics (MS, PhD). *Entrance requirements:* For master's and doctorate, GRE General Test, TOEFL.

University of Saskatchewan, College of Graduate Studies and Research, College of Agriculture, Department of Applied Microbiology and Food Science, Saskatoon, SK S7N 5A2, Canada. Offers M Sc, PhD. *Degree requirements:* For master's and doctorate, thesis/dissertation required. *Entrance requirements:* For master's, CANTEST (minimum score of 4.5 required) or International English Language Testing System (minimum score of 6 required) or Michigan English Language Assessment Battery (minimum score of 80 required), orTOEFL (minimum score of 550 required; average 560); for doctorate, TOEFL.

The University of Tennessee at Martin, Graduate Studies, School of Agriculture and Human Environment, Department of Human Environmental Sciences, Martin, TN 38238-1000. Offers child development and family relations (MSHES); food science and nutrition (MSHES). Part-time programs available. *Faculty:* 6 full-time (5 women), 1 (woman) part-time. *Students:* 25 (24 women); includes 5 minority (all African Americans) *Degree requirements:* For master's, thesis optional, foreign language not required. *Entrance requirements:* For master's, GRE General Test (minimum combined score of 650 required), minimum GPA of 2.5. *Application deadline:* For fall admission, 7/1 (priority date). Applications are processed on a rolling basis. Application fee: $25 ($50 for international students). *Unit head:* Dr. Lisa LeBleu, Coordinator, 901-587-7116, E-mail: llebleu@utm.edu.

University of Tennessee, Knoxville, Graduate School, College of Agricultural Sciences and Natural Resources, Department of Food Science and Technology, Knoxville, TN 37996. Offers food science and technology (MS, PhD), including food chemistry (PhD), food microbiology (PhD), food processing (PhD), sensory evaluation of foods (PhD). Part-time programs available. *Faculty:* 8 full-time (4 women). *Students:* 11 full-time (4 women), 14 part-time (8 women); includes 1 minority (Asian American or Pacific Islander), 10 international. 33 applicants, 21% accepted. In 1998, 5 master's, 1 doctorate awarded. *Degree requirements:* For master's, thesis or alternative required, foreign language not required; for doctorate, dissertation required, foreign language not required. *Entrance requirements:* For master's and doctorate, GRE General Test, TOEFL (minimum score of 550 required), minimum GPA of 2.7. *Application deadline:* For fall admission, 2/1 (priority date). Applications are processed on a rolling basis. Application fee: $35. Electronic applications accepted. *Financial aid:* In 1998–99, 10 research assistantships, 3 teaching assistantships were awarded.; fellowships, career-related internships or fieldwork, Federal Work-Study, institutionally-sponsored loans, and unspecified assistantships also available. Financial aid application deadline: 2/1; financial aid applicants required to submit FAFSA. *Unit head:* Dr. Clark Brekke, Head, 423-974-7331, Fax: 423-974-7332, E-mail:

University of Tennessee, Knoxville (continued)

cbrekke@utk.edu. *Application contact:* Dr. David Golden, Graduate Representative, 423-974-7247, E-mail: dgolden@utk.edu.

University of Wisconsin–Madison, Graduate School, College of Agricultural and Life Sciences, Department of Food Science, Madison, WI 53706-1380. Offers MS, PhD. Part-time programs available. *Faculty:* 12 full-time (1 woman). *Students:* 62 full-time (35 women), 5 part-time (2 women). 61 applicants, 16% accepted. In 1998, 13 master's, 7 doctorates awarded. *Degree requirements:* For master's and doctorate, thesis/dissertation required, foreign language not required. *Entrance requirements:* For master's and doctorate, GRE General Test (minimum combined score of 1600 on three sections required), TOEFL (minimum score of 550 required). *Average time to degree:* Master's–2.5 years full-time; doctorate–3.5 years full-time. *Application deadline:* For fall admission, 6/15 (priority date); for winter admission, 11/15 (priority date); for spring admission, 5/5 (priority date). Applications are processed on a rolling basis. Application fee: $45. Electronic applications accepted. *Financial aid:* In 1998–99, 32 students received aid, including 29 research assistantships with full tuition reimbursements available (averaging $15,500 per year), 3 teaching assistantships with full tuition reimbursements available (averaging $10,900 per year); fellowships, scholarships also available. *Faculty research:* Food chemistry, food engineering, food microbiology, food processing. Total annual research expenditures: $715,888. *Unit head:* Dr. James L. Steele, Chair, 608-263-2008, Fax: 608-262-6872, E-mail: jlsteele@facstaff.wisc.edu.

University of Wisconsin–Stout, Graduate Studies, College of Human Development, Program in Food Science and Nutrition, Menomonie, WI 54751. Offers MS. Part-time programs available. *Students:* 15 full-time (all women), 8 part-time (6 women), 5 international. 14 applicants, 57% accepted. In 1998, 6 degrees awarded. *Degree requirements:* For master's, thesis required, foreign language not required. *Application deadline:* Applications are processed on a rolling basis. Application fee: $45. *Financial aid:* In 1998–99, 3 research assistantships, 1 teaching assistantship were awarded.; Federal Work-Study and tuition waivers (full and partial) also available. Aid available to part-time students. Financial aid application deadline: 4/1; financial aid applicants required to submit FAFSA. *Unit head:* Dr. Barbara Knoub, Director, 715-232-1994.

University of Wyoming, Graduate School, College of Agriculture, Department of Animal Sciences, Program in Food Science and Human Nutrition, Laramie, WY 82071. Offers MS. *Faculty:* 7 full-time (1 woman). *Students:* 6 full-time (4 women), 1 (woman) part-time. 2 applicants, 0% accepted. In 1998, 3 degrees awarded. *Degree requirements:* For master's, thesis required, foreign language not required. *Entrance requirements:* For master's, GRE General Test (minimum combined score of 900 required; average 1000), minimum GPA of 3.0. *Application deadline:* For fall admission, 6/1 (priority date). Applications are processed on a rolling basis. Application fee: $40. Tuition, state resident: full-time $2,520; part-time $140 per credit hour. Tuition, nonresident: full-time $7,790; part-time $433 per credit hour. Required fees: $400; $7 per credit hour. Full-time tuition and fees vary according to course load and program. *Financial aid:* In 1998–99, 5 research assistantships were awarded.; career-related internships or fieldwork, Federal Work-Study, and institutionally-sponsored loans also available. Financial aid application deadline: 3/1. *Faculty research:* Protein and lipid metabolism, food microbiology, food safety, meat science. *Unit head:* Daniel Rule, Coordinator, 307-766-3404, Fax: 307-766-2355.

Utah State University, School of Graduate Studies, College of Family Life, Department of Nutrition and Food Sciences, Logan, UT 84322. Offers molecular biology (MS, PhD); nutrition and food sciences (MS, PhD). *Faculty:* 17 full-time (7 women), 2 part-time (0 women). *Students:* 19 full-time (10 women), 17 part-time (9 women); includes 2 minority (1 Asian American or Pacific Islander, 1 Hispanic American), 17 international. Average age 27. 47 applicants, 17% accepted. In 1998, 5 master's, 6 doctorates awarded. *Degree requirements:* For master's, thesis required, foreign language not required; for doctorate, computer language, dissertation, teaching experience required, foreign language not required. *Entrance requirements:* For master's and doctorate, GRE General Test (score in 40th percentile or higher required), TOEFL (minimum score of 550 required), minimum GPA of 3.0, previous course work in chemistry. *Application deadline:* For fall admission, 6/15 (priority date); for spring admission, 10/15. Applications are processed on a rolling basis. Application fee: $40. Tuition, state resident: full-time $1,492. Tuition, nonresident: full-time $5,232. Required fees: $434. Tuition and fees vary according to course load. *Financial aid:* In 1998–99, 22 research assistantships with partial tuition reimbursements were awarded.; fellowships with partial tuition reimbursements, teaching assistantships with partial tuition reimbursements, Federal Work-Study, institutionally-sponsored loans, and tuition waivers (full and partial) also available. *Faculty research:* Mineral balance, meat microbiology and nitrate interactions, milk ultrafiltration, lactic culture, milk coagulation. *Unit head:* Ann Sorenson, Head, 435-797-2102, Fax: 435-797-2379. *Application contact:* Carolyn Glover, Receptionist, 435-797-2126, Fax: 435-797-2379.

Virginia Polytechnic Institute and State University, Graduate School, College of Agriculture and Life Sciences, Department of Food Science and Technology, Blacksburg, VA 24061. Offers MS, PhD. Part-time programs available. *Faculty:* 14 full-time. *Students:* 20 full-time (11 women), 7 part-time (2 women); includes 3 minority (1 African American, 1 Asian American or Pacific Islander, 1 Hispanic American), 1 international. 35 applicants, 49% accepted. In 1998, 2 master's awarded. *Degree requirements:* For master's and doctorate, thesis/dissertation required, foreign language not required. *Entrance requirements:* For master's and doctorate, GRE General Test (minimum combined score of 1000 required), TOEFL (minimum score of 570 required). *Application deadline:* For fall admission, 12/1 (priority date). Applications are processed on a rolling basis. Application fee: $25. *Financial aid:* In 1998–99, 3 fellowships, 13 research assistantships, 1 teaching assistantship were awarded.; career-related internships or fieldwork and unspecified assistantships also available. Financial aid application deadline: 4/1. *Faculty research:* Food microbiology, food chemistry, food processing, engineering, muscle foods. *Unit head:* Dr. Cameron R. Hackney, Head, 540-231-6805, E-mail: hackneyc@vt.edu.

Announcement: The Department of Food Science and Technology at Virginia Tech has 2 IFT-approved undergraduate options, an M.S. program, and a Ph.D. program. Most graduate students are admitted from the principle supporting disciplines of biology, microbiology, biochemistry, chemistry, animal science, horticulture, and process engineering. Research and outreach (extension) programs are strongly related, and applied research is stressed to solve problems directly affecting the food industry. Food safety (including produce, fruits, dairy, poultry, and meats HACCP), seafood technology, sensory, processing technology, packaging technology, muscle biology, dairy processing, enology, and wine chemistry are the principle research areas. Assistantships that include tuition remission, including out-of-state tuition, are available.

Washington State University, Graduate School, College of Agriculture and Home Economics, Department of Food Science and Human Nutrition, Program in Food Science, Pullman, WA 99164. Offers MS, PhD. *Faculty:* 19 full-time (12 women). *Students:* 31 full-time (14 women), 5 part-time (all women); includes 4 minority (3 Asian Americans or Pacific Islanders, 1 Hispanic American), 19 international. In 1998, 5 master's awarded. *Degree requirements:* For master's and doctorate, thesis/dissertation, oral exam required, foreign language not required. *Entrance requirements:* For master's and doctorate, GRE General Test, minimum GPA of 3.0. *Average time to degree:* Master's–2 years full-time. *Application deadline:* For fall admission, 3/1 (priority date). Applications are processed on a rolling basis. Application fee: $35. *Financial aid:* In 1998–99, 12 research assistantships, 3 teaching assistantships were awarded.; fellowships, career-related internships or fieldwork, Federal Work-Study, institutionally-sponsored loans, tuition waivers (partial), and unspecified assistantships also available. Financial aid application deadline: 4/1; financial aid applicants required to submit FAFSA. *Unit head:* Dr. Alan McCurdy, Chair, Department of Food Science and Human Nutrition, 509-335-9103, Fax: 509-335-4815.

Wayne State University, Graduate School, College of Science, Department of Nutrition and Food Science, Detroit, MI 48202. Offers MA, MS, PhD. Terminal master's awarded for partial completion of doctoral program. *Degree requirements:* For master's, thesis required (for some programs), foreign language not required; for doctorate, dissertation required, foreign language not required. *Entrance requirements:* For master's and doctorate, GRE General Test, minimum GPA of 3.0. *Faculty research:* Nutrition and cancer, obesity and diabetes, mineral metabolism, food microbiology, lipoprotein metabolism.

West Virginia University, College of Agriculture, Forestry and Consumer Sciences, Division of Animal and Veterinary Sciences, Program in Animal and Food Sciences, Morgantown, WV 26506. Offers agricultural sciences (PhD). *Degree requirements:* For doctorate, dissertation, oral and written exams required, foreign language not required. *Entrance requirements:* For doctorate, TOEFL (minimum score of 550 required). *Faculty research:* Ruminant nutrition, metabolism, forage utilization, physiology, reproduction.

Horticulture

Auburn University, Graduate School, College of Agriculture, Department of Horticulture, Auburn, Auburn University, AL 36849-0002. Offers M Ag, MS, PhD. Part-time programs available. *Faculty:* 17 full-time (1 woman). *Students:* 7 full-time (1 woman), 14 part-time (8 women); includes 1 minority (African American), 2 international. 7 applicants, 71% accepted. In 1998, 4 master's, 1 doctorate awarded. *Degree requirements:* For master's, thesis (MS) required; for doctorate, dissertation required. *Entrance requirements:* For master's, GRE General Test; for doctorate, GRE General Test (minimum score of 400 on each section required). *Application deadline:* For fall admission, 9/1; for spring admission, 3/1. Applications are processed on a rolling basis. Application fee: $25 ($50 for international students). Tuition, state resident: full-time $2,760; part-time $76 per credit hour. Tuition, nonresident: full-time $8,280; part-time $228 per credit hour. *Financial aid:* Research assistantships, teaching assistantships, Federal Work-Study available. Aid available to part-time students. Financial aid application deadline: 3/15. *Faculty research:* Environmental regulators, water quality, weed control, growth regulators, plasticulture. *Unit head:* Dr. W. Alfred Dozier, Chair, 334-844-4862. *Application contact:* Dr. John F. Pritchett, Dean of the Graduate School, 334-844-4700.

Brigham Young University, Graduate Studies, College of Biological and Agricultural Sciences, Department of Agronomy and Horticulture, Provo, UT 84602-1001. Offers agronomy (MS); horticulture (MS). *Faculty:* 10 full-time (0 women). *Students:* 7 full-time (2 women), 1 international. Average age 25. 7 applicants, 57% accepted. In 1998, 7 degrees awarded (43% found work related to degree, 29% continued full-time study). *Degree requirements:* For master's, thesis optional, foreign language not required. *Entrance requirements:* For master's, GRE General Test (minimum combined score of 1400 required; average 1447), minimum GPA of 3.0 during previous 2 years. *Average time to degree:* Master's–2 years full-time, 4 years part-time. *Application deadline:* For fall admission, 2/15. Applications are processed on a rolling basis. Application fee: $30. Tuition: Full-time $3,330; part-time $185 per credit hour. Tuition and fees vary according to program and student's religious affiliation. *Financial aid:* In 1998–99, 2 research assistantships with partial tuition reimbursements, 5 teaching assistantships with partial tuition reimbursements were awarded.; institutionally-sponsored loans, scholarships, and tuition waivers (partial) also available. Financial aid application deadline: 3/1. *Faculty research:* Iron nutrition in plants–mode of uptake, photosynthesis, forage quality, seed physiology/modeling, cytogenetics, molecular genetics. Total annual research expenditures: $35,000. *Unit head:* Dr. Von D. Jolley, Chair, 801-378-2760 Ext. 2491, Fax: 801-378-7499, E-mail: von_jolley@byu.edu.

Clemson University, Graduate School, College of Agriculture, Forestry and Life Sciences, School of Plant, Statistical and Ecological Sciences, Department of Horticulture, Clemson, SC 29634. Offers genetics (PhD); horticulture (MS); plant physiology (PhD). Part-time programs available. *Students:* 9 full-time (4 women), 3 part-time (1 woman), 3 international. Average age 30. 15 applicants, 27% accepted. In 1998, 8 degrees awarded. *Degree requirements:* For master's and doctorate, thesis/dissertation required, foreign language not required. *Entrance requirements:* For master's, GRE General Test, TOEFL, minimum undergraduate GPA of 3.0; for doctorate, GRE General Test, TOEFL, minimum graduate GPA of 3.0. *Application deadline:* For fall admission, 6/1. Application fee: $35. *Financial aid:* Fellowships, research assistantships, teaching assistantships available. Financial aid applicants required to submit FAFSA. *Faculty research:* Molecular biology, tissue culture, plant breeding, plant cultural systems. *Unit head:* Dr. Calvin L. Shoulties, Chair, 864-656-7592, Fax: 864-656-4960. *Application contact:* Dr. W. Vance Baird, Coordinator, 864-656-4953, Fax: 864-656-4960, E-mail: vbaird@clemson.edu.

Colorado State University, Graduate School, College of Agricultural Sciences, Department of Horticulture and Landscape Architecture, Fort Collins, CO 80523-0015. Offers floriculture (M Agr, MS, PhD); horticultural food crops (M Agr, MS, PhD); nursery and landscape management (M Agr, MS, PhD); plant genetics (MS, PhD); plant physiology (MS, PhD); turf management (M Agr, MS, PhD). Part-time programs available. *Faculty:* 9 full-time (2 women), 2 part-time (0 women). *Students:* 16 full-time (9 women), 9 part-time (3 women), 14 international. Average age 33. 35 applicants, 34% accepted. In 1998, 4 master's, 1 doctorate awarded. *Degree requirements:* For master's, thesis optional, foreign language not required; for doctorate, dissertation required, foreign language not required. *Entrance requirements:* For master's and doctorate, GRE General Test, TOEFL, minimum GPA of 3.0. *Application deadline:* For fall admission, 2/1 (priority date). Applications are processed on a rolling basis. Application fee: $30. Electronic applications accepted. *Financial aid:* In 1998–99, 5 teaching assistantships were awarded.; fellowships, research assistantships, career-related internships or fieldwork, Federal Work-Study, institutionally-sponsored loans, and traineeships also available. Total annual research expenditures: $600,000. *Unit head:* Dr. Stephen J. Wallner, Head, 970-491-7018, Fax: 970-491-7745. *Application contact:* Judith A. Croissant, Administrative Assistant III, 970-491-7018, Fax: 970-491-7745, E-mail: jcroissa@ceres.agsci.colostate.edu.

Cornell University, Graduate School, Graduate Fields of Agriculture and Life Sciences, Field of Floriculture and Ornamental Horticulture, Ithaca, NY 14853-0001. Offers controlled environmental horticulture (MPS, MS, PhD); floriculture crop production (MPS, MS, PhD); horticultural physiology (MS, PhD); horticulture physiology (MPS); landscape horticulture (MPS, MS, PhD); nursery crop production (MPS, MS, PhD); nutrition of horticultural crops (MPS, MS, PhD); plant materials and horticultural taxonomy (MPS, MS, PhD); plant propagation (MPS, MS, PhD); turfgrass science (MPS, MS, PhD); urban horticulture (MPS, MS, PhD); weed science (MPS, MS, PhD). *Faculty:* 11 full-time. *Students:* 28 full-time (10 women); includes 1 minority (Asian American or Pacific Islander), 9 international. 23 applicants, 52% accepted. In 1998, 6 master's, 2 doctorates awarded. *Degree requirements:* For master's, teaching experience, thesis (MS) required; for doctorate, dissertation, teaching experience required, foreign language not required. *Entrance requirements:* For master's and doctorate, GRE General Test, TOEFL (minimum score of 550 required). *Application deadline:* For fall admission, 1/15.

Application fee: $65. Electronic applications accepted. *Financial aid:* In 1998–99, 15 students received aid, including 1 fellowship with full tuition reimbursement available, 10 research assistantships with full tuition reimbursements available, 4 teaching assistantships with full tuition reimbursements available; institutionally-sponsored loans, scholarships, tuition waivers (full and partial), and unspecified assistantships also available. Financial aid applicants required to submit FAFSA. *Faculty research:* Plant selection/plant materials, greenhouse management, greenhouse crop production, urban landscape management, turfgrass management, bulb and herbaceous crop management. *Unit head:* Director of Graduate Studies, 607-255-3134. *Application contact:* Graduate Field Assistant, 607-255-3134, Fax: 607-255-9998, E-mail: fohgrad@cornell.edu.

Cornell University, Graduate School, Graduate Fields of Agriculture and Life Sciences, Field of Pomology, Ithaca, NY 14853-0001. Offers MPS, MS, PhD. *Faculty:* 13 full-time. *Students:* 11 full-time (5 women), 6 international. 7 applicants, 57% accepted. In 1998, 3 master's awarded. *Degree requirements:* For master's, thesis (MS), project paper (MPS) required; for doctorate, dissertation required, foreign language not required. *Entrance requirements:* For master's and doctorate, GRE General Test, TOEFL (minimum score of 550 required). *Application deadline:* Applications are processed on a rolling basis. Application fee: $65. Electronic applications accepted. *Financial aid:* In 1998–99, 5 research assistantships with full tuition reimbursements, 4 teaching assistantships with full tuition reimbursements were awarded.; fellowships with full tuition reimbursements, institutionally-sponsored loans, scholarships, tuition waivers (full and partial), and unspecified assistantships also available. Financial aid applicants required to submit FAFSA. *Faculty research:* Fruit breeding and biotechnology, fruit crop physiology, orchard management, orchard ecology and IPM, post-harvest physiology. *Unit head:* Director of Graduate Studies, 607-255-4568, Fax: 607-255-0544. *Application contact:* Graduate Field Assistant, 607-255-4568, Fax: 607-255-0599, E-mail: cah8@cornell.edu.

Cornell University, Graduate School, Graduate Fields of Agriculture and Life Sciences, Field of Vegetable Crops, Ithaca, NY 14853-0001. Offers MPS, MS, PhD. *Faculty:* 15 full-time. *Students:* 11 full-time (3 women), 7 international. 4 applicants, 0% accepted. In 1998, 1 doctorate awarded. Terminal master's awarded for partial completion of doctoral program. *Degree requirements:* For master's, thesis (MS), project paper (MPS) required; for doctorate, dissertation, teaching experience required, foreign language not required. *Entrance requirements:* For master's, TOEFL (minimum score of 550 required); for doctorate, GRE General Test, TOEFL (minimum score of 550 required). *Application deadline:* Applications are processed on a rolling basis. Application fee: $65. Electronic applications accepted. *Financial aid:* In 1998–99, 8 students received aid, including 6 research assistantships with full tuition reimbursements available, 2 teaching assistantships with full tuition reimbursements available; fellowships with full tuition reimbursements available, institutionally-sponsored loans and tuition waivers (full and partial) also available. Financial aid applicants required to submit FAFSA. *Faculty research:* Vegetable nutrition and physiology, post-harvest physiology and storage, new technologies including genetic, sustainable vegetable production, weed management and IPM. *Unit head:* Director of Graduate Studies, 607-255-4568, Fax: 607-255-0599. *Application contact:* Graduate Field Assistant, 607-255-4568, E-mail: cah8@cornell.edu.

Iowa State University of Science and Technology, Graduate College, College of Agriculture, Department of Horticulture, Ames, IA 50011. Offers MS, PhD. *Faculty:* 17 full-time. *Students:* 12 full-time (7 women), 3 part-time (1 woman); includes 3 minority (2 Asian Americans or Pacific Islanders, 1 Native American), 3 international. 32 applicants, 28% accepted. In 1998, 3 master's, 1 doctorate awarded. *Degree requirements:* For master's, thesis or alternative required; for doctorate, dissertation required. *Entrance requirements:* For master's and doctorate, GRE General Test, TOEFL. *Application deadline:* For fall admission, 3/1 (priority date); for spring admission, 10/1. Applications are processed on a rolling basis. Application fee: $20 ($50 for international students). Electronic applications accepted. Tuition, state resident: full-time $3,308. Tuition, nonresident: full-time $9,744. Part-time tuition and fees vary according to course load, campus/location and program. *Financial aid:* In 1998–99, research assistantships with partial tuition reimbursements (averaging $8,775 per year); fellowships, teaching assistantships, scholarships also available. *Unit head:* Dr. Michael H. Chaplin, Head, 515-294-3718, E-mail: hortgrad@iastate.edu. *Application contact:* Dr. William R. Graves, Director of Graduate Education, 515-294-2751, E-mail: hortgrad@iastate.edu.

Kansas State University, Graduate School, College of Agriculture, Department of Horticulture, Forestry and Recreation Resources, Manhattan, KS 66506. Offers horticulture (MS, PhD). *Degree requirements:* For master's and doctorate, thesis/dissertation required, foreign language not required. *Entrance requirements:* For master's and doctorate, GRE General Test (minimum combined score of 1500 on three sections required). Electronic applications accepted. *Faculty research:* Environmental stress, molecular genetics, cold tolerance, turfgrass, horticultural therapy.

Louisiana State University and Agricultural and Mechanical College, Graduate School, College of Agriculture, Department of Horticulture, Baton Rouge, LA 70803. Offers MS, PhD. Part-time programs available. *Faculty:* 9 full-time (0 women). *Students:* 10 full-time (5 women), 9 part-time (1 woman), 8 international. Average age 31. 8 applicants, 38% accepted. Terminal master's awarded for partial completion of doctoral program. *Degree requirements:* For master's, thesis required (for some programs), foreign language not required; for doctorate, dissertation required, foreign language not required. *Entrance requirements:* For master's and doctorate, GRE General Test (minimum combined score of 1000 required), minimum GPA of 3.0. *Application deadline:* For fall admission, 7/1 (priority date). Applications are processed on a rolling basis. Application fee: $25. *Financial aid:* In 1998–99, 9 research assistantships with partial tuition reimbursements (averaging $9,583 per year) were awarded.; fellowships, teaching assistantships with partial tuition reimbursements, Federal Work-Study and unspecified assistantships also available. Financial aid application deadline: 4/15. *Faculty research:* Plant breeding, stress physiology, postharvest physiology, biotechnology. *Unit head:* Dr. C. P. Hegwood, Acting Head, 225-388-2158, Fax: 225-388-1068, E-mail: chegwood@agctr.lsu.edu. *Application contact:* Dr. Paul Wilson, Graduate Coordinator, 225-388-1025, Fax: 225-388-1068, E-mail: pwilson@agctr.lsu.edu.

Michigan State University, Graduate School, College of Agriculture and Natural Resources, Department of Horticulture, East Lansing, MI 48824-1020. Offers horticulture (MS, PhD); plant breeding and genetics-horticulture (MS, PhD). *Faculty:* 27. *Students:* 18 full-time (6 women), 27 part-time (15 women); includes 5 minority (4 Asian Americans or Pacific Islanders, 1 Hispanic American), 15 international. Average age 29. 47 applicants, 17% accepted. In 1998, 2 master's, 5 doctorates awarded. *Degree requirements:* For doctorate, dissertation required. *Entrance requirements:* For master's and doctorate, GRE, TOEFL (minimum score of 580 required), minimum GPA of 3.0. *Application deadline:* Applications are processed on a rolling basis. Application fee: $30 ($40 for international students). *Financial aid:* In 1998–99, 36 research assistantships with tuition reimbursements (averaging $10,257 per year), 1 teaching assistantship with tuition reimbursement (averaging $9,036 per year) were awarded. Financial aid application deadline: 3/1; financial aid applicants required to submit FAFSA. Total annual research expenditures: $686,900. *Unit head:* Dr. Wayne Loescher, Chairperson, 517-355-5191, Fax: 517-353-0890.

New Mexico State University, Graduate School, College of Agriculture and Home Economics, Department of Agronomy and Horticulture, Las Cruces, NM 88003-8001. Offers general agronomy (MS, PhD); horticulture (MS). Part-time programs available. *Faculty:* 24 full-time (3 women). *Students:* 39 full-time (13 women), 20 part-time (2 women); includes 3 minority (all Hispanic Americans), 31 international. Average age 37. 34 applicants, 41% accepted. In 1998, 9 master's, 10 doctorates awarded. *Degree requirements:* For master's, thesis required, foreign language not required; for doctorate, one foreign language, dissertation required. *Entrance requirements:* For master's, minimum GPA of 3.0; for doctorate, minimum GPA of 3.3. *Application deadline:* For fall admission, 7/1 (priority date); for spring admission, 11/1. Applications are processed on a rolling basis. Application fee: $15 ($35 for international students). Electronic applications accepted. Tuition, state resident: full-time $2,682; part-time $112 per credit. Tuition, nonresident: full-time $8,376; part-time $349 per credit. Tuition and fees vary according to course load. *Financial aid:* Research assistantships, teaching assistantships, career-related internships or fieldwork and Federal Work-Study available. Aid available to part-time students. Financial aid application deadline: 3/1. *Faculty research:* Plant breeding and genetics, molecular biology, plant physiology, soil science and environmental remediation, urban horticulture. *Unit head:* Dr. James T. Fisher, Head, 505-646-3406, Fax: 505-646-6041, E-mail: jtfisher@nmsu.edu.

North Carolina State University, Graduate School, College of Agriculture and Life Sciences, Department of Horticultural Science, Raleigh, NC 27695. Offers M Ag, MS, PhD. *Faculty:* 39 full-time (6 women), 18 part-time (2 women). *Students:* 33 full-time (10 women), 8 part-time (3 women); includes 1 minority (Asian American or Pacific Islander), 13 international. Average age 33. 28 applicants, 43% accepted. In 1998, 4 master's, 3 doctorates awarded. Terminal master's awarded for partial completion of doctoral program. *Degree requirements:* For master's and doctorate, thesis/dissertation required, foreign language not required. *Entrance requirements:* For master's and doctorate, GRE General Test, bachelor's degree in agriculture or biology, minimum GPA of 3.0. *Application deadline:* For fall admission, 6/25; for spring admission, 11/25. Applications are processed on a rolling basis. Application fee: $45. *Financial aid:* In 1998–99, 1 fellowship (averaging $6,084 per year), 22 research assistantships (averaging $4,171 per year), 7 teaching assistantships (averaging $5,991 per year) were awarded. Financial aid application deadline: 6/25. *Faculty research:* Plant physiology breeding and genetics, tissue culture, herbicide, physiology, nutrition. Total annual research expenditures: $9 million. *Unit head:* Thomas J. Monaco, Head, 919-515-1187, Fax: 919-515-7747, E-mail: tom_monaco@ncsu.edu. *Application contact:* Dr. Stuart L. Warren, Director of Graduate Programs, 919-515-1193, Fax: 919-515-2505, E-mail: stu_warren@ncsu.edu.

North Dakota State University, Graduate Studies and Research, College of Agriculture, Department of Plant Sciences, Fargo, ND 58105. Offers crop and weed sciences (MS); horticulture (MS); natural resources management (MS); plant sciences (PhD). Part-time programs available. *Faculty:* 33 full-time (1 woman), 15 part-time (1 woman). *Students:* 24 full-time (10 women), 7 part-time (3 women), 11 international. *Degree requirements:* For master's and doctorate, thesis/dissertation required, foreign language not required. *Entrance requirements:* For master's and doctorate, TOEFL (minimum score of 525 required). *Application deadline:* Applications are processed on a rolling basis. Application fee: $25. Electronic applications accepted. *Unit head:* Dr. Al Schneiter, Chair, 701-231-7971, Fax: 701-231-8474, E-mail: aschneit@plains.nodak.edu.

The Ohio State University, Graduate School, College of Food, Agricultural, and Environmental Sciences, Department of Horticulture and Crop Science, Columbus, OH 43210. Offers MS, PhD. *Faculty:* 38 full-time, 8 part-time. *Students:* 21 full-time (10 women), 2 part-time (1 woman); includes 2 minority (both Hispanic Americans), 7 international. 61 applicants, 26% accepted. In 1998, 3 master's, 1 doctorate awarded. *Degree requirements:* For master's, thesis optional, foreign language not required; for doctorate, dissertation required, foreign language not required. *Entrance requirements:* For master's and doctorate, GRE General Test. *Application deadline:* For fall admission, 8/15. Applications are processed on a rolling basis. Application fee: $30 ($40 for international students). *Financial aid:* Fellowships, research assistantships, teaching assistantships, Federal Work-Study and institutionally-sponsored loans available. Aid available to part-time students. *Unit head:* A. Raymond Miller, Chair, 614-292-2001, Fax: 614-292-7162, E-mail: miller.5@osu.edu.

Oklahoma State University, Graduate College, College of Agricultural Sciences and Natural Resources, Department of Horticulture and Landscape Architecture, Stillwater, OK 74078. Offers M Ag, MS. *Faculty:* 19 full-time (1 woman), 1 part-time (0 women). *Students:* 1 full-time (0 women), 8 part-time (3 women), 3 international. Average age 31. In 1998, 3 degrees awarded. *Degree requirements:* For master's, thesis or alternative required, foreign language not required. *Entrance requirements:* For master's, TOEFL (minimum score of 550 required). *Application deadline:* For fall admission, 6/1 (priority date). Application fee: $25. *Financial aid:* In 1998–99, 9 students received aid, including 9 research assistantships (averaging $12,617 per year); career-related internships or fieldwork, Federal Work-Study, and tuition waivers (partial) also available. Aid available to part-time students. Financial aid application deadline: 3/1. *Faculty research:* Stress and postharvest physiology; water utilization and runoff; ipm systems and nursery, turf, floriculture, vegetable, net and fruit produces and natural resources, food extraction, and processing; public garden management. *Unit head:* Dale M. Maronek, Head, 405-744-5414.

Oregon State University, Graduate School, College of Agricultural Sciences, Department of Horticulture, Corvallis, OR 97331. Offers M Ag, MAIS, MS, PhD. *Faculty:* 40 full-time (6 women). *Students:* 25 full-time (11 women), 2 part-time (1 woman), 18 international. Average age 32. In 1998, 4 master's, 2 doctorates awarded. *Degree requirements:* For master's, thesis (MS) required; for doctorate, dissertation required, foreign language not required. *Entrance requirements:* For master's and doctorate, GRE General Test, TOEFL (minimum score of 550 required), minimum GPA of 3.0 in last 90 hours. *Application deadline:* For fall admission, 3/1. Applications are processed on a rolling basis. Application fee: $50. *Financial aid:* Research assistantships, teaching assistantships, career-related internships or fieldwork, Federal Work-Study, and institutionally-sponsored loans available. Aid available to part-time students. Financial aid application deadline: 2/1. *Unit head:* Charles Boyer, Head, 541-737-3695, Fax: 541-737-3479, E-mail: boyerc@bcc.orst.edu. *Application contact:* Machteld Mok, Graduate Coordinator, 541-737-5456.

Pennsylvania State University University Park Campus, Graduate School, College of Agricultural Sciences, Department of Horticulture, State College, University Park, PA 16802-1503. Offers M Agr, MS, PhD. *Students:* 21 full-time (10 women), 4 part-time (2 women). In 1998, 3 master's, 4 doctorates awarded. *Entrance requirements:* For master's and doctorate, GRE General Test. Application fee: $50. *Unit head:* Dr. Dennis Decoteau, Head, 814-865-2572. *Application contact:* Dr. Kathleen Evensen, Chair, 814-863-2189.

Purdue University, Graduate School, School of Agriculture, Department of Horticulture and Landscape Architecture, West Lafayette, IN 47907. Offers horticulture (M Agr, MS, PhD). Part-time programs available. *Faculty:* 20 full-time (1 woman). *Students:* 39 full-time (15 women), 2 part-time (1 woman); includes 3 minority (2 Asian Americans or Pacific Islanders, 1 Hispanic American), 18 international. 53 applicants, 15% accepted. In 1998, 4 master's awarded (50% found work related to degree, 50% continued full-time study); 2 doctorates awarded. Terminal master's awarded for partial completion of doctoral program. *Degree requirements:* For doctorate, dissertation required, foreign language not required, foreign language not required. *Entrance requirements:* For master's and doctorate, TOEFL (minimum score of 550 required). *Average time to degree:* Master's–2.5 years full-time; doctorate–3.5 years full-time. *Application deadline:* For fall admission, 8/1. Applications are processed on a rolling basis. Application fee: $30. Electronic applications accepted. *Financial aid:* In 1998–99, 26 research assistantships with tuition reimbursements (averaging $14,000 per year), 4 teaching assistantships with tuition reimbursements (averaging $14,000 per year) were awarded.; fellowships Aid available to part-time students. Financial aid applicants required to submit FAFSA. *Faculty research:* Plant physiology, plant genetics and breeding, plant molecular biology and cell physiology, environmental and production horticulture. *Unit head:* Dr. E. N. Ashworth, Head, 765-494-1306, Fax: 765-494-0391, E-mail: ashworth@hort.purdue.edu. *Application contact:* Dr. P. M. Hasegawa, Graduate Committee Chair, 765-494-1315, Fax: 765-494-0391.

Rutgers, The State University of New Jersey, New Brunswick, Graduate School, Program in Plant Biology, New Brunswick, NJ 08903. Offers horticulture (MS, PhD); molecular biology and biochemistry (MS, PhD); pathology (MS, PhD); plant ecology (MS, PhD); plant genetics (PhD); plant physiology (MS, PhD); production and management (MS); structure and plant groups (MS, PhD). Part-time programs available. *Faculty:* 64 full-time (8 women), 1 part-time (0 women). *Students:* 48 full-time (19 women), 7 part-time (1 woman); includes 5 minority (2 African Americans, 3 Asian Americans or Pacific Islanders), 26 international. Terminal master's awarded for partial completion of doctoral program. *Degree requirements:* For master's and doctorate, thesis/dissertation required, foreign language not required. *Entrance requirements:*

Horticulture

Rutgers, The State University of New Jersey, New Brunswick (continued)

For master's and doctorate, GRE General Test, GRE Subject Test (recommended). *Application deadline:* For fall admission, 6/1. Application fee: $50. Electronic applications accepted. *Unit head:* Dr. Thomas Leustek, Director, 732-932-8165 Ext. 326, Fax: 732-932-9377, E-mail: leustek@aesop.rutgers.edu. *Application contact:* Barbara Mulder, Administrative Assistant, 732-932-9375 Ext. 358, Fax: 732-932-9377, E-mail: plantbio@aesop.rutgers.edu.

Southern Illinois University Carbondale, Graduate School, College of Agriculture, Department of Plant, Soil, and General Agriculture, Carbondale, IL 62901-6806. Offers horticultural science (MS); plant and soil science (MS). *Faculty:* 19 full-time (1 woman), 1 (woman) part-time. *Students:* 25 full-time (9 women), 13 part-time (5 women). *Degree requirements:* For master's, thesis required, foreign language not required. *Entrance requirements:* For master's, TOEFL (minimum score of 550 required), minimum GPA of 2.7. *Application deadline:* Applications are processed on a rolling basis. Application fee: $0. *Unit head:* Donald Stucky, Chairperson, 618-453-2496.

Texas A&M University, College of Agriculture and Life Sciences, Department of Horticultural Sciences, College Station, TX 77843. Offers horticulture (PhD); horticulture and floriculture (M Agr, MS). *Faculty:* 19 full-time (2 women). *Students:* 21 full-time (10 women), 10 part-time (2 women); includes 4 minority (1 Asian American or Pacific Islander, 3 Hispanic Americans), 15 international. Average age 29. 28 applicants, 43% accepted. In 1998, 13 master's, 6 doctorates awarded. *Degree requirements:* For master's, thesis required (for some programs), foreign language not required; for doctorate, dissertation required, foreign language not required. *Entrance requirements:* For master's and doctorate, GRE General Test, TOEFL. Application fee: $50 ($75 for international students). *Financial aid:* In 1998–99, 30 students received aid, including 1 fellowship, 17 research assistantships, 13 teaching assistantships; career-related internships or fieldwork and tuition waivers (partial) also available. Financial aid application deadline: 4/1. *Faculty research:* Plant breeding, molecular biology, plant nutrition, postharvest physiology. *Unit head:* Dr. Sam Cotner, Head, 409-845-0139, Fax: 409-845-0627, E-mail: dwreed@tamu.edu.

Texas Tech University, Graduate School, College of Agricultural Sciences and Natural Resources, Department of Plant and Soil Science, Lubbock, TX 79409. Offers agronomy (PhD); crop science (MS); entomology (MS); horticulture (MS); plant and soil science (M Agr); soil science (MS). Part-time programs available. *Faculty:* 13 full-time (2 women), 1 part-time (0 women). *Students:* 35 full-time (14 women), 22 part-time (4 women); includes 1 minority (Asian American or Pacific Islander), 11 international. *Degree requirements:* For master's, foreign language and thesis not required; for doctorate, dissertation required. *Entrance requirements:* For master's, GRE General Test (combined average 1005); for doctorate, GRE General Test. *Application deadline:* For fall admission, 4/15 (priority date); for spring admission, 11/1 (priority date). Applications are processed on a rolling basis. Application fee: $25 ($50 for international students). Electronic applications accepted. *Unit head:* Dr. Dick L. Auld, Chair, 806-742-2837, Fax: 806-742-0775.

University of Arkansas, Graduate School, Dale Bumpers College of Agricultural, Food and Life Sciences, Department of Horticulture, Fayetteville, AR 72701-1201. Offers MS. *Faculty:* 9 full-time (0 women). *Students:* 7 full-time (4 women), 1 part-time. 9 applicants, 44% accepted. In 1998, 3 degrees awarded. *Degree requirements:* For master's, thesis required, foreign language not required. Application fee: $40 ($50 for international students). Tuition, state resident: full-time $3,186. Tuition, nonresident: full-time $7,560. Required fees: $378. *Financial aid:* Fellowships, research assistantships, teaching assistantships, career-related internships or fieldwork and Federal Work-Study available. Aid available to part-time students. Financial aid application deadline: 4/1; financial aid applicants required to submit FAFSA. *Unit head:* Dr. Stephen Myers, Head, 501-575-2603. *Application contact:* Dr. J. Brad Murphy, Graduate Coordinator, 501-575-2446, E-mail: jbmurph@comp.uark.edu.

University of California, Davis, Graduate Studies, Programs in the Biological Sciences, Program in Horticulture, Davis, CA 95616. Offers MS. *Faculty:* 52 full-time (8 women). *Students:* 33 full-time (15 women); includes 1 minority (Asian American or Pacific Islander), 12 international. 28 applicants, 61% accepted. In 1998, 11 degrees awarded. *Degree requirements:* For master's, thesis optional. *Entrance requirements:* For master's, GRE General Test. *Application deadline:* For fall admission, 4/1. Applications are processed on a rolling basis. Application fee: $40. Electronic applications accepted. *Financial aid:* In 1998–99, 10 fellowships, 10 research assistantships, 3 teaching assistantships were awarded.; career-related internships or fieldwork, Federal Work-Study, and tuition waivers (full and partial) also available. Financial aid application deadline: 1/15; financial aid applicants required to submit FAFSA. *Faculty research:* Postharvest physiology, mineral nutrition, crop improvement, plant growth and development. *Unit head:* M. Andrew Walker, Chairperson, 530-752-0902, Fax: 530-752-0382, E-mail: awalker@ucdavis.edu. *Application contact:* Lisa Brown, Graduate Group Secretary, 530-752-7738, Fax: 530-752-1819, E-mail: lfbrown@ucdavis.edu.

University of Delaware, College of Agriculture and Natural Resources, Longwood Graduate Program in Public Horticulture Administration, Newark, DE 19716. Offers MS. *Faculty:* 1 full-time (0 women). *Students:* 11 full-time (7 women). Average age 27. 31 applicants, 19% accepted. In 1998, 3 degrees awarded. *Degree requirements:* For master's, thesis, internship required, foreign language not required. *Entrance requirements:* For master's, GRE General Test. *Application deadline:* For fall admission, 11/30. Application fee: $45. *Financial aid:* Fellowships, career-related internships or fieldwork available. *Unit head:* Dr. James E. Swasey, Coordinator, 302-831-2517, Fax: 302-831-3651, E-mail: james.swasey@mvs.udel.edu.

University of Florida, Graduate School, College of Agriculture, Program in Environmental Horticulture, Gainesville, FL 32611. Offers MS, PhD. *Faculty:* 35. *Students:* 13 full-time (4 women), 11 part-time (8 women); includes 2 minority (both Hispanic Americans), 4 international. 23 applicants, 57% accepted. In 1998, 7 master's, 2 doctorates awarded. *Degree requirements:* For master's, thesis optional; for doctorate, dissertation required. *Entrance requirements:* For master's, GRE General Test (minimum combined score of 1000 required), minimum GPA of 3.0; for doctorate, GRE General Test, minimum GPA of 3.0. *Application deadline:* For fall admission, 6/1 (priority date); for spring admission, 11/1. Applications are processed on a rolling basis. Application fee: $20. Electronic applications accepted. *Financial aid:* In 1998–99, 14 students received aid, including 6 research assistantships, 2 teaching assistantships; fellowships, unspecified assistantships also available. Financial aid application deadline: 6/1. *Faculty research:* Production and genetics, landscape horticulture, turf grass, foliage, floriculture. *Unit head:* Dr. T. Nell, Chair, 352-392-1831, Fax: 352-392-3870, E-mail: tan@gnv.ifas.ufl.edu. *Application contact:* Michael E. Kane, Graduate Coordinator, 352-392-7937, Fax: 352-392-3870, E-mail: mek@gnv.ifas.ufl.edu.

University of Florida, Graduate School, College of Agriculture, Program in Horticultural Sciences, Fruit and Vegetable Crops, Gainesville, FL 32611. Offers fruit crops (MS, PhD); vegetable crops and crop science (MS, PhD). *Faculty:* 81. *Students:* 35 full-time (12 women), 17 part-time (4 women); includes 3 minority (1 Asian American or Pacific Islander, 2 Hispanic Americans), 26 international. 66 applicants, 27% accepted. In 1998, 12 master's, 5 doctorates awarded. *Degree requirements:* For master's, thesis optional; for doctorate, dissertation required. *Entrance requirements:* For master's and doctorate, GRE General Test (minimum combined score of 1000 required), minimum GPA of 3.0. *Application deadline:* For fall admission, 6/1 (priority date). Applications are processed on a rolling basis. Application fee: $20. Electronic applications accepted. *Financial aid:* In 1998–99, 26 students received aid, including 1 fellowship, 22 research assistantships; teaching assistantships, institutionally-sponsored loans also available. Financial aid application deadline: 6/1. *Faculty research:* Genetics, plant nutrition, stress physiology, biotechnology, postharvest physiology. *Unit head:* Dr. D. J. Cantliffe, Chair, 352-392-1928, Fax: 352-392-6479, E-mail: djc@gnv.ifas.ufl.edu. *Application contact:* Dr. Donald J. Huber, Graduate Coordinator, 352-392-1928 Ext. 214, Fax: 352-392-6479, E-mail: djh@gnv.ifas.ufl.edu.

University of Georgia, Graduate School, College of Agricultural and Environmental Sciences, Department of Horticulture, Athens, GA 30602. Offers horticulture (MS, PhD); plant protection and pest management (MPPPM). *Faculty:* 21 full-time (4 women). *Students:* 18 full-time (8 women), 4 part-time (1 woman). 16 applicants, 25% accepted. In 1998, 4 master's, 5 doctorates awarded. *Degree requirements:* For master's, thesis (MS) required; for doctorate, one foreign language (computer language can substitute), dissertation required. *Entrance requirements:* For master's and doctorate, GRE General Test. *Application deadline:* For fall admission, 7/1 (priority date); for spring admission, 11/15. Application fee: $30. Electronic applications accepted. *Financial aid:* Fellowships, research assistantships, teaching assistantships, unspecified assistantships available. *Unit head:* Dr. Hazel Y. Wetzstein, Graduate Coordinator, 706-542-2471, Fax: 706-542-0624, E-mail: hywetz@arches.uga.edu.

University of Guelph, Faculty of Graduate Studies, Ontario Agricultural College, Department of Plant Agriculture, Guelph, ON N1G 2W1, Canada. Offers M Sc, PhD. *Faculty:* 27 full-time (3 women), 2 part-time (1 woman). *Students:* 82 full-time (33 women), 9 part-time (2 women), 16 international. 36 applicants, 47% accepted. In 1998, 11 master's, 4 doctorates awarded. *Degree requirements:* For master's and doctorate, thesis/dissertation required. *Entrance requirements:* For master's, minimum B- average during previous 2 years; for doctorate, minimum B average. *Average time to degree:* Master's–2.5 years full-time; doctorate–5 years full-time. Application fee: $60. *Expenses:* Tuition and fees charges are reported in Canadian dollars. Tuition, area resident: Full-time $4,725 Canadian dollars; part-time $1,055 Canadian dollars per term. International tuition: $6,999 Canadian dollars full-time. Required fees: $295 Canadian dollars per term. *Financial aid:* In 1998–99, 27 students received aid, including fellowships (averaging $3,555 Canadian dollars per year), research assistantships (averaging $13,662 Canadian dollars per year), teaching assistantships (averaging $2,117 Canadian dollars per year) *Faculty research:* Plant physiology, biochemistry, taxonomy, morphology, genetics, production, ecology, breeding and biotechnology. Total annual research expenditures: $6.6 million. *Unit head:* Dr. C. J. Swanton, Chair, 519-824-4120 Ext. 3386, Fax: 519-763-8933. *Application contact:* Dr. J. A. Sullivan, Graduate Coordinator, 519-842-4120 Ext. 2792, Fax: 519-767-0755, E-mail: asullivan@evbhort.uoguelph.ca.

University of Hawaii at Manoa, Graduate Division, College of Tropical Agriculture and Human Resources, Department of Horticulture, Honolulu, HI 96822. Offers MS, PhD. *Faculty:* 32 full-time (5 women). *Students:* 14 full-time (7 women), 9 part-time (4 women); includes 1 minority (Asian American or Pacific Islander), 15 international. 19 applicants, 37% accepted. In 1998, 2 master's awarded. *Degree requirements:* For master's, thesis required (for some programs), foreign language not required; for doctorate, dissertation required, foreign language not required. *Entrance requirements:* For doctorate, GRE. *Application deadline:* For fall admission, 3/1; for spring admission, 9/1. Application fee: $25 ($50 for international students). *Financial aid:* In 1998–99, 10 research assistantships (averaging $15,933 per year), 1 teaching assistantship (averaging $12,786 per year) were awarded.; tuition waivers (full and partial) also available. *Faculty research:* Genetics and breeding; physiology, culture, and management; weed science; turfgrass and landscape; sensory evaluation. *Unit head:* Dr. Harry C. Bittenbender, Chairman, 808-956-8389, Fax: 808-956-3894, E-mail: hcbitt@hawaii.edu. *Application contact:* Robert E. Paull, Chairman, 808-956-5900, Fax: 808-956-3894, E-mail: paull@hawaii.edu.

University of Maine, Graduate School, College of Natural Sciences, Forestry, and Agriculture, Department of Biosystems Science and Engineering, Program in Horticulture, Orono, ME 04469. Offers MS. *Faculty:* 5 full-time (0 women). *Students:* 2 (both women) 2 applicants, 50% accepted. In 1998, 1 degree awarded. *Degree requirements:* Foreign language not required. *Entrance requirements:* For master's, GRE General Test, TOEFL (minimum score of 550 required). *Application deadline:* For fall admission, 2/1 (priority date); for spring admission, 10/15. Applications are processed on a rolling basis. Application fee: $50. *Financial aid:* Research assistantships with tuition reimbursements, teaching assistantships with tuition reimbursements, tuition waivers (full and partial) available. Financial aid application deadline: 3/1. *Application contact:* Scott G. Delcourt, Director of the Graduate School, 207-581-3218, Fax: 207-581-3232, E-mail: graduate@maine.edu.

University of Manitoba, Faculty of Graduate Studies, Faculty of Agriculture, Department of Plant Science, Winnipeg, MB R3T 2N2, Canada. Offers horticulture (M Sc, PhD). *Degree requirements:* For master's, thesis required, foreign language not required; for doctorate, dissertation required. *Unit head:* I. N. Morrison, Head.

University of Maryland, College Park, Graduate School, College of Agriculture and Natural Resources, Department of Natural Resource Sciences and Landscape Architecture, Program in Horticulture, College Park, MD 20742-5045. Offers MS, PhD. *Students:* 7 full-time (3 women), 9 part-time (7 women), 7 international. 22 applicants, 18% accepted. In 1998, 3 master's, 1 doctorate awarded. *Degree requirements:* For master's, thesis or alternative, oral exam required, foreign language not required; for doctorate, dissertation, oral exam required. *Entrance requirements:* For master's, GRE General Test, minimum GPA of 3.0; for doctorate, GRE General Test. *Application deadline:* Applications are processed on a rolling basis. Application fee: $50 ($70 for international students). Tuition, state resident: part-time $272 per credit hour. Tuition, nonresident: part-time $475 per credit hour. Required fees: $632; $379 per year. *Financial aid:* Fellowships, research assistantships, teaching assistantships, career-related internships or fieldwork available. Financial aid applicants required to submit FAFSA. *Faculty research:* Mineral nutrition, genetics and breeding, chemical growth, histochemistry, postharvest physiology, chromatography, spectrophotometry. *Unit head:* Scott G. Delcourt, Director of the Graduate School, 207-581-3218, Fax: 207-581-3232, E-mail: graduate@maine.edu. *Application contact:* Trudy Lindsey, Director, Graduate Admission and Records, 301-405-4198, Fax: 301-314-9305, E-mail: grschool@deans.umd.edu.

University of Minnesota, Twin Cities Campus, Graduate School, College of Agricultural, Food, and Environmental Sciences, Department of Horticultural Science, Minneapolis, MN 55455-0213. Offers M Ag, MS, PhD. Part-time programs available. *Faculty:* 25 full-time (5 women). *Students:* 21 full-time (13 women), 4 part-time (2 women). 8 applicants, 38% accepted. In 1998, 3 master's, 1 doctorate awarded. *Degree requirements:* For doctorate, dissertation required, foreign language not required, foreign language not required. *Entrance requirements:* For master's and doctorate, GRE General Test (minimum score of 500 on verbal section, 550 on quantitative, 500 on analytical required; average 585 verbal, 630 quantitative, 655 analytical), TOEFL (minimum score of 555 required; average 570). *Average time to degree:* Master's–2.5 years full-time, 4.5 years part-time; doctorate–4 years full-time, 6 years part-time. *Application deadline:* For fall admission, 7/15; for spring admission, 12/15. Applications are processed on a rolling basis. Application fee: $40 ($50 for international students). *Financial aid:* In 1998–99, 17 students received aid, including 17 research assistantships; fellowships, career-related internships or fieldwork and Federal Work-Study also available. Aid available to part-time students. Financial aid application deadline: 1/15. *Faculty research:* Plant growth and development, biotechnology, sustainable cropping systems, breeding and genetics, environmental stress, restoration ecology. Total annual research expenditures: $287,866. *Unit head:* Dr. Gary M. Gardner, Head, 612-624-3606, Fax: 612-624-4941, E-mail: ggardner@maroon.tc.umn.edu. *Application contact:* Dr. James J. Luby, Director of Graduate Studies, 612-624-3453, Fax: 612-624-4941, E-mail: lubyx001@maroon.tc.umn.edu.

University of Missouri–Columbia, Graduate School, College of Agriculture, Program in Horticulture, Columbia, MO 65211. Offers MS, PhD. *Faculty:* 7 full-time (2 women). *Students:* 3 full-time (all women), 2 part-time (1 woman); includes 1 minority (African American), 1 international. 1 applicants, 100% accepted. *Degree requirements:* For master's, thesis required, foreign language not required; for doctorate, dissertation required. *Entrance requirements:* For master's and doctorate, GRE General Test, minimum GPA of 3.0. *Application deadline:* Applications are processed on a rolling basis. Application fee: $30 ($50 for international students). *Financial aid:* Research assistantships, teaching assistantships, institutionally-sponsored loans available. *Unit head:* Dr. Robert Sharp, Director of Graduate Studies, 573-882-1841.

University of Nebraska–Lincoln, Graduate College, College of Agricultural Sciences and Natural Resources, Department of Horticulture, Lincoln, NE 68588. Offers MS. *Faculty:* 17 full-time (2 women), 1 part-time (0 women). *Students:* 8 full-time (3 women), 5 part-time (all women), 4 international. Average age 32. 7 applicants, 71% accepted. In 1998, 5 degrees awarded. *Degree requirements:* For master's, thesis optional, foreign language not required. *Entrance requirements:* For master's, GRE General Test, TOEFL (minimum score of 550 required). *Application deadline:* For fall admission, 5/1; for spring admission, 10/1. Application fee: $35. Electronic applications accepted. *Financial aid:* In 1998–99, 2 fellowships, 3 research assistantships, 2 teaching assistantships were awarded.; Federal Work-Study also available. Aid available to part-time students. Financial aid application deadline: 2/15. *Faculty research:* Horticultural crops: production, management, cultural, and ecological aspects; tissue and cell culture; plant nutrition and anatomy; postharvest physiology and ecology. *Unit head:* Dr. David Lewis, Head, 402-472-2854.

University of Nebraska–Lincoln, Graduate College, College of Agricultural Sciences and Natural Resources, Interdepartmental Area of Horticulture and Forestry, Lincoln, NE 68588. Offers PhD. *Students:* 9 full-time (0 women), 4 part-time (1 woman), 10 international. Average age 32. 7 applicants, 29% accepted. In 1998, 1 degree awarded. *Degree requirements:* For doctorate, dissertation, comprehensive exams required, foreign language not required. *Entrance requirements:* For doctorate, GRE General Test, TOEFL (minimum score of 550 required). *Average time to degree:* Doctorate–2.6 years full-time. *Application deadline:* For fall admission, 5/1; for spring admission, 10/1. Application fee: $35. Electronic applications accepted. *Financial aid:* Fellowships, research assistantships, teaching assistantships, Federal Work-Study available. Aid available to part-time students. Financial aid application deadline: 2/15. *Faculty research:* Plant breeding and genetics, tissue and cell culture, plant anatomy and nutrition, urban landscapes, turf grass science. *Unit head:* Dr. Ellen T. Paparozzi, Graduate Committee Chair, 402-472-1129.

University of Puerto Rico, Mayagüez Campus, Graduate Studies, College of Agricultural Sciences, Department of Horticulture, Mayagüez, PR 00681-5000. Offers MS. Part-time programs available. *Degree requirements:* For master's, thesis, comprehensive exam required, foreign language not required. *Faculty research:* Growth regulators, floriculture, starchy crops, coffee and fruit technology.

University of Saskatchewan, College of Graduate Studies and Research, College of Agriculture, Department of Horticulture Science, Saskatoon, SK S7N 5C8, Canada. Offers M Sc, PhD. *Degree requirements:* For master's and doctorate, thesis/dissertation required. *Entrance requirements:* For master's, CANTEST (minimum score of 4.5 required) or International English Language Testing System (minimum score of 6 required) or Michigan English Language Assessment Battery (minimum score of 80 required), orTOEFL (minimum score of 550 required; average 560); for doctorate, TOEFL.

University of Tennessee, Knoxville, Graduate School, College of Agricultural Sciences and Natural Resources, Department of Ornamental Horticulture and Landscape Design, Knoxville, TN 37996. Offers floriculture (MS); landscape design (MS); public horticulture (MS); turfgrass (MS); woody ornamentals (MS). Part-time programs available. *Faculty:* 12 full-time (2 women). *Students:* 7 full-time (4 women), 5 part-time (3 women), 1 international. 10 applicants, 40% accepted. In 1998, 4 degrees awarded. *Degree requirements:* For master's, thesis or alternative required, foreign language not required. *Entrance requirements:* For master's, TOEFL (minimum score of 550 required), minimum GPA of 2.7. *Application deadline:* For fall admission, 2/1 (priority date). Applications are processed on a rolling basis. Application fee: $35. Electronic applications accepted. *Financial aid:* In 1998–99, 5 research assistantships, 2 teaching assistantships were awarded.; fellowships, career-related internships or fieldwork, Federal Work-Study, institutionally-sponsored loans, and unspecified assistantships also available. Financial aid application deadline: 2/1; financial aid applicants required to submit FAFSA. *Unit head:* Dr. Mary Lewnes Albrecht, Head, 423-974-7324, Fax: 423-947-1947, E-mail: mlalbrecht@utk.edu. *Application contact:* Dr. Robert Augé, Graduate Representative, E-mail: auge@utk.edu.

University of Washington, Graduate School, College of Forest Resources, Seattle, WA 98195. Offers forest economics (MS, PhD); forest ecosystem analysis (MS, PhD); forest engineering/forest hydrology (MS, PhD); forest products marketing (MS, PhD); forest soils (MS, PhD); pulp and paper science (MS, PhD); quantitative resource management (MS, PhD); silviculture (MFR); silviculture and forest protection (MS, PhD); social sciences (MS, PhD); urban horticulture (MFR, MS, PhD); wildlife science (MS, PhD). *Faculty:* 47 full-time (4 women), 16 part-time (2 women). *Students:* 161 full-time (65 women), 16 part-time (5 women); includes 15 minority (1 African American, 10 Asian Americans or Pacific Islanders, 1 Hispanic American, 3 Native Americans), 9 international. *Degree requirements:* For master's, thesis required (for some programs), foreign language not required; for doctorate, dissertation required, foreign language not required. *Entrance requirements:* For master's and doctorate, TOEFL (minimum score of 500 required), minimum GPA of 3.0. *Application deadline:* For fall admission, 2/1 (priority date); for winter admission, 11/1; for spring admission, 2/1. Applications are processed on a rolling basis. Application fee: $50. Electronic applications accepted. Tuition, state resident: full-time $5,196; part-time $475 per credit. Tuition, nonresident: full-time $13,485; part-time $1,285 per credit. Required fees: $387; $38 per credit. Tuition and fees vary according to course load. *Unit head:* Dr. David B. Thorud, Dean, 206-685-1928, Fax: 206-685-0790. *Application contact:* Michelle Trudeau, Student Services Manager, 206-616-1533, Fax: 206-685-0790, E-mail: michtru@u.washington.edu.

University of Wisconsin–Madison, Graduate School, College of Agricultural and Life Sciences, Department of Horticulture, Madison, WI 53706-1380. Offers horticulture (MS, PhD); plant breeding and plant genetics (MS, PhD). Part-time programs available. *Entrance requirements:* For master's and doctorate, minimum GPA of 3.0. Electronic applications accepted. *Faculty research:* Biotechnology, crop breeding/genetics, environmental physiology, crop management, cytogenetics.

Virginia Polytechnic Institute and State University, Graduate School, College of Agriculture and Life Sciences, Department of Horticulture, Blacksburg, VA 24061. Offers MS, PhD. *Students:* 16 full-time (7 women), 25 part-time (14 women); includes 3 minority (2 African Americans, 1 Hispanic American), 4 international. 15 applicants, 13% accepted. In 1998, 3 master's, 1 doctorate awarded. *Entrance requirements:* For master's and doctorate, TOEFL. *Application deadline:* For fall admission, 12/1 (priority date). Applications are processed on a rolling basis. Application fee: $25. *Financial aid:* Research assistantships, teaching assistantships, unspecified assistantships available. Financial aid application deadline: 4/1. *Unit head:* Dr. R. D. Wright, Head, 540-231-5451, E-mail: wrightr@vt.edu.

Washington State University, Graduate School, College of Agriculture and Home Economics, Department of Horticulture and Landscape Architecture, Pullman, WA 99164. Offers horticulture (MS, PhD). Part-time programs available. *Faculty:* 26 full-time (3 women). *Students:* 18 full-time (6 women), 6 part-time (3 women); includes 1 minority (Asian American or Pacific Islander), 10 international. Average age 31. In 1998, 3 master's, 3 doctorates awarded. *Degree requirements:* For master's and doctorate, thesis/dissertation, oral exam required, foreign language not required. *Entrance requirements:* For master's and doctorate, GRE General Test, minimum GPA of 3.0. *Average time to degree:* Master's–2 years full-time; doctorate–4 years full-time. *Application deadline:* For fall admission, 3/1 (priority date); for spring admission, 7/1. Applications are processed on a rolling basis. Application fee: $35. Electronic applications accepted. *Financial aid:* In 1998–99, 9 research assistantships, 4 teaching assistantships were awarded.; career-related internships or fieldwork, Federal Work-Study, institutionally-sponsored loans, and tuition waivers (partial) also available. Financial aid application deadline: 4/1; financial aid applicants required to submit FAFSA. *Faculty research:* Post-harvest physiology, genetics/plant breeding, molecular biology. Total annual research expenditures: $1.7 million. *Unit head:* Dr. William Hendrix, Chair, 509-335-9502, Fax: 509-335-8690. *Application contact:* Lisa Washburn, Coordinator, 509-335-9504, Fax: 509-335-8690, E-mail: washburn@wsu.edu.

Cross-Discipline Announcements

Purdue University, Graduate School, Interdisciplinary Program in Plant Biology, West Lafayette, IN 47907.

The Plant Biology Program (PBP) is an integrated PhD program administered by a diverse 48-member faculty from the Departments of Agronomy, Biochemistry, Biology, Botany and Plant Pathology, Chemistry, Horticulture and Landscape Architecture, and Medicinal Chemistry and Molecular Pharmacology. PBP provides the opportunity for students to specialize in one of 4 areas of emphasis: biochemistry and molecular biology, cell and developmental biology, ecology evolution and systematics, and physiology. See in-depth description in Botany and Plant Sciences section of Book 3.

University of Kentucky, Graduate School, Graduate School Programs from the College of Agriculture, Department of Plant Pathology, Lexington, KY 40506-0032.

The Plant Pathology Department excels in virology, mycology, and molecular biology, and has a strong tradition of mentoring. Students are trained broadly and appropriately to enhance prospects for their intended careers. Thus, the department maintains an outstanding record of placing its graduates in academia, biotechnology, extension, and research institutions.

Yale University, School of Forestry and Environmental Studies, New Haven, CT 06520.

The School of Forestry and Environmental Studies, Yale University, offers graduate study at the master's and doctoral levels in environmental and natural resource management and science. The programs and faculty are multidisciplinary and emphasize the social sciences (policy, economics, sociology) and natural sciences (ecology, hydrology, soil science), among others.

CLEMSON UNIVERSITY

College of Agriculture, Forestry and Life Sciences

Programs of Study

Clemson University's College of Agriculture, Forestry and Life Sciences offers programs leading to the Master of Science and Doctor of Philosophy degrees and three professional degrees: the Master of Agricultural Education, Master of Agriculture, and Master of Zoology. The College has graduate programs that offer opportunities for basic research and the application of knowledge in the following areas: agricultural economics, including community and rural development and applied natural resource economics; agricultural education; agricultural mechanization and business; agronomy; animal and food industries; animal physiology; animal science; applied economics; aquaculture, fisheries, and wildlife biology; biochemistry; botany; dairy science; entomology; environmental sciences; environmental toxicology; experimental statistics; food science; food technology; forest resources; genetics; horticulture; microbiology; nutrition; plant pathology; integrated pest management; plant physiology; poultry science; and zoology. Excellent opportunities exist to become involved in biotechnology applications to agricultural production and processing systems in many departments within the College. A biosystems engineering program is jointly administered with the College of Engineering and Science.

Research Facilities

The departments are well equipped for both basic and applied research in science and engineering. Library facilities and resources make Clemson one of the most important research institutions in the Southeast. The catalog and circulation system is computerized, and the library is linked by computer to more than 5,000 other libraries. Computer resources are excellent. Satellite terminals and microcomputers located across the campus and in the departments, both on the main campus and in four Research and Education Centers, provide ready access to mainframe computers for statistical applications, word processing programs, and library resources, including online access to commercial databases. The excellent spirit of cooperation at Clemson minimizes the effects of departmental boundaries and enhances the opportunities for interdisciplinary graduate education.

Financial Aid

Graduate students may apply for grants, loans, fellowships, scholarships, and assistantships. Teaching and research assistantships are awarded by the departments on a competitive basis and are usually one-half time, requiring 20 hours of work per week. A minimum enrollment is required for appointment as a department graduate assistant. During the academic year, students enrolled in a doctoral program or a thesis option master's program must enroll in at least 12 credit hours each semester. Students enrolled in a master's program not requiring a thesis must enroll in 9 credit hours each semester. Minimum enrollment in the summer session is 3 credit hours per session irrespective of the degree objective.

Cost of Study

Resident graduate students are required to pay $130 per semester hour up to 11 hours and $1577 for 12 or more semester hours. Nonresidents pay $264 per semester hour up to 11 hours and $3226 for 12 or more semester hours. Graduate assistants pay a flat fee of $493 per semester and $165 for each summer session. All fees are subject to change.

Living and Housing Costs

The cost of living in the Clemson area is quite modest. Residence halls and apartments located on the main campus provide excellent accommodations at economical rates for graduate and undergraduate students. Privately owned housing in the surrounding community accommodates the majority of graduate students, both married and single. The International Services Office assists international students or visiting scholars in finding housing in the community as well as on campus. The University offers three economical board plans and also provides meals on a cash basis in two student dining halls.

Student Group

The student body of the College of Agriculture, Forestry and Life Sciences comprises about 520 graduate and 2,000 undergraduate students. Enrollments at the undergraduate and graduate levels have been increasing in recent years. Graduate students come from all parts of the United States and a number of other countries. Growth in the number of international students is anticipated.

Location

Clemson University is located in the northwestern corner of South Carolina, in the foothills of the Blue Ridge Mountains. The campus abuts Lake Hartwell and is a little more than 2 hours' driving time from Atlanta, Georgia; Charlotte, North Carolina; and Great Smoky Mountains National Park. This beautiful, scenic area provides an excellent environment for outdoor recreation, including boating, fishing, skiing, hunting, swimming, sailing, bicycling, camping, and hiking. The Clemson campus, with its Performing Arts Center, offers a wide variety of entertainment, including lectures, films, plays, and concerts—rock, jazz, and classical. Students also enjoy participating in or watching University-sponsored intramural and intercollegiate athletics.

The University

Clemson University, founded in 1889, is a state-supported coeducational land-grant institution. The 1,400-acre main campus is surrounded by 20,860 acres of University farms and woodlands devoted to research. Enrollment is approximately 16,500, including 3,800 graduate students. The University employs approximately 4,300 persons on a full-time basis, approximately 1,220 of whom hold academic rank.

Applying

For admission to a graduate program in the College, applicants must have a baccalaureate degree and must submit transcripts of all prior college work, letters of recommendation, and scores on the General Test of the Graduate Record Examinations. Applicants must also meet departmental requirements for course work in specific fields. A statement of the applicant's research and career interests is desirable. In addition to applying for admission to the College of Agriculture, Forestry and Life Sciences, students interested in financial aid must submit a financial aid application to the University. While there are no fixed deadlines, students are urged to submit their applications as early as possible. Additional information can be obtained from individual departments or the address below.

Correspondence and Information

Dr. William B. Wehrenberg
Dean
College of Agriculture, Forestry and Life Sciences
101 Barre Hall, Box 340303
Clemson University
Clemson, South Carolina 29634-0303
Telephone: 864-656-3013
Fax: 864-656-1286

Clemson University

DEPARTMENTS AND DEGREE PROGRAMS

All of the campus addresses given below are at Clemson University, Clemson, South Carolina 29634.

Agricultural and Applied Economics (M.S. in agricultural and applied economics; thesis option and nonthesis agribusiness option): Dr. G. J. Wells, Chair; 220 Barre Hall. Graduate faculty: 26. The thesis M.S. program provides broad training in agricultural and applied economics, economic theory, and research methodology and is designed for students planning to pursue a Ph.D. degree or a career in research. The nonthesis M.S. program provides practical training in economics and business and in a particular technical area and is designed to provide additional technical skills for business-oriented students and additional business skills for students with technical backgrounds.

Agricultural and Biological Engineering (M.S., M.Eng., and Ph.D. in biosystems engineering): Dr. J. C. Hayes, Chair; 201 McAdams Hall. Graduate faculty: 14. Programs offered in biotechnology, sensors and instrumentation, power and machinery, soil and water resources, aquaculture engineering, computers and instrumentation, structures, tillage energy, precision agriculture, waste management, and agricultural mechanization and business.

Agricultural Education (M.Ag.Ed. and Ed.D.): Dr. T. R. Scott, Acting Chair; 109 Barre Hall. Graduate faculty: 3. Programs emphasize planning, learning theory, technology transfer, teaching methods, and evaluation in the agricultural industry, and extension and occupational education for youth and adults. A minor in related technical fields is encouraged.

Agronomy (M.S. and Ph.D. in agronomy; Ph.D. in genetics): Dr. W. D. Graham, Chair; 277 Poole Ag Center. Graduate faculty: 17. Programs specialize in agroecology, soil chemistry, soil physics, soil fertility, soil microbiology, pedology, crop physiology, field crop and forage management, plant breeding and genetics, weed science, and waste management.

Animal and Veterinary Sciences (M.S. and Ph.D. in animal physiology; M.S. and Ph.D. in nutrition; M.S. in animal and food industries; Ph.D. in genetics and food technology): Dr. D. M. Henricks, Chair; 130 Poole Ag Center. Graduate faculty: 16. Students may specialize in nutrition, physiology, meat and dairy products, or genetics at the Ph.D. level and in breeding and genetics, meat science and muscle biology, animal management, ruminant nutrition, reproductive physiology, mycotoxicology, and dairy products at the master's level.

Applied Economics (Ph.D. in applied economics); a cooperative program with the Department of Economics: Dr. G. J. Wells, Program Administrator, 220 Barre Hall. Graduate faculty: 43. The Ph.D. program emphasizes economic theory and quantitative and qualitative research methods to analyze problems in economic development, environmental and resource economics, regional analysis, agricultural marketing, production economics, finance, industrial organization, international trade, and public policy.

Aquaculture, Fisheries and Wildlife (M.S. in aquaculture, fisheries, and wildlife biology and Ph.D. in fisheries and wildlife science): Dr. J. R. Sweeney, Chair; G-08 Lehotsky Hall. Graduate faculty: 11. Programs emphasize relationships between animals and their changing environments and production of aquatic organisms. Concentrations are offered in aquaculture, uplands and wetlands wildlife biology, conservation biology, and freshwar and marine fisheries science.

Biological Sciences (M.S. and Ph.D. in biochemistry, genetics, and zoology; M.S. in botany; nonthesis M.S. in zoology; Ph.D. in plant physiology): Dr. T. M. McInnis, Chair; 132 Long Hall. Graduate faculty: 23. Studies span the spectrum of biology, ranging from molecular and cellular biology through organismal biology to ecology, evolution, and population biology.

Entomology (M.S. and Ph.D. in entomology): Dr. P. M. Horton, Chair; 112 Long Hall. Graduate faculty: 24. Programs emphasize basic and applied environmental entomology (concerning insects and their relatives). Areas of specialization include aquatic arthropod diversity, crop insect management, insect genetics and biotechnology, medical and veterinary entomology, and urban entomology.

Environmental Toxicology (M.S. and Ph.D. in environmental toxicology): Dr. J. H. Rodgers, Chair; 509 Westinghouse Rd., P.O. Box 709, Pendleton, South Carolina 29670. Graduate faculty: 12. Program emphasizes basic and applied toxicology in aquatic, analytical, biochemical, and behavioral toxicology; environmental chemistry; and ecotoxicology. Research emphasizes fate and effects of materials on aquatic and terrestrial wildlife resources.

Experimental Statistics (Advanced degrees are not awarded, but a minor is offered at the M.S. and Ph.D. levels): Dr. H. S. Hill Jr., Chair; F-148 Poole Ag Center. Graduate faculty: 6. Experimental statistics and statistical services.

Food Science (Ph.D. in food technology; M.S. and Ph.D. in nutrition; M.S. in animal and food industries): Dr. S. F. Barefoot, Acting Chair; 224 Poole Ag Center. Graduate faculty: 9. Studies are offered in food biochemistry/chemistry, microbiology, product evaluation/development, food engineering, food proteins, muscle foods, food packaging, membrane technology (ultrafiltration), and human nutrition.

Forest Resources (M.F.R., M.S., and Ph.D. in forest resources): Dr. B. Allen Dunn, Interim Chair; 261 Lehotsky Hall, Graduate faculty: 28. Programs emphasize management, use, and stewardship of forest resources. Research emphasizes ecological forest management, forested wetlands, forest products, pest problems of intensive forest management, forest nursery practices, wildlife management, remote sensing and GIS, forest economics, tree physiology, and urban forestry.

Horticulture (M.S. in horticulture; Ph.D. in plant physiology; Ph.D. in genetics): Dr. T. Whitwell, Acting Chair; E-142 Poole Ag Center. Graduate faculty: 19. Programs are offered in floriculture, vegetable crops, ornamental horticulture, fruit crops, turfgrass management, physiology, production, cultural practices, genetics and breeding, biotechnology, postharvest physiology, and molecular biology.

Microbiology and Molecular Medicine (M.S. and Ph.D. in microbiology): Dr. S. S. Hayasaka, Chair; 124 Long Hall. Graduate faculty: 16. Programs emphasize medical microbiology, molecular medicine, food safety, and bioremediation.

Plant Pathology and Physiology (M.S. and Ph.D. in plant pathology; Ph.D. in genetics): Dr. C. L. Schoulties, Acting Chair; 118 Long Hall. Graduate faculty: 16. Research programs emphasize plant physiology, molecular genetics, virology, nematology, and certain plant diseases caused by fungi and bacteria. Research may include in-depth study of pathogen biology of important crop diseases.

Poultry Science (M.S. and Ph.D. in animal physiology; M.S. and Ph.D. in nutrition; M.S. in animal and food industries): Graduate faculty: 7. Students may specialize in immunology, nutrition, pathology, physiology, or products and processing and may receive an M.S. degree in comprehensive animal and food industries.

INTERDEPARTMENTAL GRADUATE PROGRAMS

Agriculture (M.Ag.): Dr. D. R. Alverson, Coordinator; 112 Long Hall. This graduate program leads to a professional, nonthesis degree. Concentrations are offered in animal industries, plant health, and agricultural mechanization and business.

Animal and Food Industries (M.S.): Dr. C. E. Thompson, Coordinator; 156 Poole Ag Center. Students may concentrate in animal science, dairy science, food science, or poultry science.

Animal Physiology (M.S. and Ph.D.): Dr. J. R. Diehl, Coordinator; 149 Poole Ag Center. The program includes graduate programs developed and offered by faculty in the Departments of Animal and Veterinary Sciences; Aquaculture, Fisheries and Wildlife; Biological Sciences; Environmental Toxicology; and Food Science. Studies emphasize physiological processes, particularly those relating to reproduction, endocrinology, digestion, and environmental factors.

Food Technology (Ph.D.): Dr. R. L. Thomas, Coordinator; 216 Poole Ag Center. Faculty are from Animal and Veterinary Sciences, Agricultural Engineering, Food Science, Horticulture, Microbiology and Molecular Medicine, and Packaging Science. Students may conduct research in food science and technology or in the chemistry, microbiology, or engineering of different food commodities.

Genetics (M.S. and Ph.D.): Dr. W. V. Baird, Acting Chair; 178 Poole Ag Center. Graduate faculty: 27. Faculty direct research emphasis areas that include animal, plant, molecular, microbial, biometrical, and environmental bioremediation genetics.

Nutrition (M.S. and Ph.D.): Dr. D. V. Maurice, Coordinator; 137 Poole Ag Center. Graduate programs are directed by faculty in the Departments of Animal and Veterinary Sciences and Food Science. Subject areas involve use of human, laboratory animal, or domestic animal models.

Plant Physiology (Ph.D.): Dr. N. D. Camper, Coordinator; B10 Long Hall. Dissertation projects are available in such areas as plant tissue and cell culture, host-parasite relationships, physiology related to fruiting and yield, postharvest physiology, plant metabolism, algae and fungal physiology, physiological ecology, and various aspects of stress physiology. Participating departments include Crop and Soil Environmental Science, Horticulture, Plant Pathology and Physiology, Biological Sciences (Botany and Biochemistry), and Forest Resources.

IOWA STATE UNIVERSITY

Department of Food Science and Human Nutrition

Programs of Study

The Department of Food Science and Human Nutrition is jointly administered by the Colleges of Agriculture and of Family and Consumer Sciences. The department offers M.S. and Ph.D. degrees in food science and technology and in nutrition. Graduate work in meat science is offered as a co-major with the Department of Animal Science. The department participates in the interdepartmental majors of molecular, cellular, and developmental biology and of toxicology. The graduate programs provide breadth of knowledge and perspective in food chemistry, food safety, fermentation, food engineering, commodity processing technology, food microbiology, nutritional science, basic and clinical human nutrition, community nutrition, and education. Current research areas include physicochemical characteristics of proteins, carbohydrates, and lipids; food safety and toxicology; nutritional effects on carcinogenesis; nutritive quality of food; chemical and microbiological changes in foods during processing and storage; processing commodities to nonfood products; and nutritional science with an emphasis on molecular, cellular, metabolic, community, and educational approaches to improve health. Programs of Study (POS) are developed by the graduate student and major professor with the POS committee. M.S. students take 30 credits, with approximately 20 in course work, and write a thesis. Ph.D. students take 70 credits of course work, including M.S. credits, with approximately 40 course credits, and defend a dissertation. All graduate students are required to complete a teaching function.

Research Facilities

The department is housed in the Food Sciences Building, the Human Nutritional Sciences Building, and MacKay Hall. The Center for Crop Utilization Research (CCUR) and the Center for Designing Foods to Improve Nutrition (HNC) are affiliated with the department. The research budget is in excess of $7.6 million, with more than $4.3 million in external funding. The Meat Laboratory houses a Department of Energy project linear accelerator irradiation facility. CCUR has more than 14,000 square feet of pilot plants with extruders (food and nonfood), mills, grinders, fermenters, retorts, supercritical fluid extraction systems, and a countercurrent solvent extractor. The HNC opened in 1992, and contains state-of-the-art animal-care and diet-making facilities; sensory evaluation and food analysis laboratories; a Finnegan ICP-MS for complete mineral analyses; Fisons Optima GC-C-IRMS with breath gas manifold and elemental analyzer interfaces; Fisons Trio GC-MS with EI and CI; toxicology, cell culture, and other analytical instrumentation; TOBEC and DEXA for assessment of human body composition and energy metabolism; and facilities for large-scale human feeding trials.

Financial Aid

Research assistantships are available for most students from faculty research grants and the Experiment Station. All students on at least quarter-time assistantships are assessed as in-state residents. Students with half-time assistantships receive 50 percent tuition scholarships.

Cost of Study

In 1998–99, graduate fees for a semester of full-time study totaled $1524 for state residents and $2159 for nonresidents.

Living and Housing Costs

The University provides housing facilities for single and married graduate students. Costs for 1998–99 ranged from $2680 per semester for double-occupancy residence halls to $365 to $411 per month for University student apartments. The Off-Campus Center assists students seeking rooms, apartments, or duplexes in Ames or in surrounding communities.

Student Group

There are approximately 60 graduate students in the department. About 60 percent are food science majors, 34 percent are nutrition majors, and the balance are in toxicology. There are 30 percent men and 70 percent women. Ninety percent are research assistants. Sixty percent are international students. There are 250 undergraduates in the department.

Student Outcomes

Nearly all graduates find employment upon or soon after graduation in postdoctoral positions, academic positions, federal laboratories (such as the USDA, DOE, and FDA), state laboratories, or the food industry. Employment examples for 1998 graduates include General Mills, GPC, Red Star Yeast, McCormick, Burnes-Philp-Tones, ConAgra, Pillsbury, Pepsi, and U.S. and international academic institutions.

Location

The University is situated on a 1,000-acre tract in Ames, Iowa (population 50,000). It is located 35 miles north of Des Moines (population 500,000), the state capital, on I-35 and U.S. Highway 30, near I-80. The city offers social, cultural, and athletic events that surpass those of some metropolitan areas. The Ames-University community is cosmopolitan, representing more than 100 countries. The city maintains more than 700 acres of parks. The atmosphere is relaxed and friendly.

The University

Iowa State University (ISU) was chartered in 1858 and is the land-grant institution in Iowa. The first graduate degree was conferred in 1877. George Washington Carver was one of the early graduates. Currently, the enrollment is approximately 25,000, including 4,500 graduate students.

Applying

A baccalaureate degree in food science/technology, nutrition or other physical or biological science, or engineering that is substantially equivalent to those at Iowa State is a prerequisite to major work. Applications for fall semester admission and assistantships should be completed by April 1 for consideration. For admission to other terms, materials should be completed sixty days before the beginning of the next term for U.S. citizens and ninety days for international applicants. Application materials can be obtained by writing to the address below or to the Graduate Admissions Office, Alumni Hall, ISU, Ames, Iowa 50011. Application fees are $50 for domestic students, $20 for international students, and $50 for international nonimmigrants. The department requires the scores of the General Test of the Graduate Record Examinations, three letters of reference, transcripts of previous academic work, and a statement of purpose.

Correspondence and Information

Dr. Murray L. Kaplan, Director of Graduate Education
Department of Food Science and Human Nutrition
2312 Food Sciences Building
Iowa State University
Ames, Iowa 50011
Telephone: 515-294-6442
Fax: 515-294-8181
E-mail: bmalchow@iastate.edu
World Wide Web: http://www.ag.iastate.edu/departments/foodsci/FoodSci.html

Iowa State University

THE FACULTY AND THEIR RESEARCH

L. Alekel, Assistant Professor; Ph.D., Illinois, 1993. Relationship of body composition, physical activity, and nutrient intake to bone mineral density and osteoporotic risk in women; effect of the menopausal transition and reproductive function/menstrual dysfunction on bone and body composition; assessment of nutritional status and body composition in health and disease.

D. F. Birt, Professor and Chairman; Ph.D., Purdue, 1975. Identifying and studying mechanisms for cancer prevention by novel dietary constituents, studying mechanisms for cancer enhancement by overeating and obesity.

T. Boylston, Assistant Professor; Ph.D., Michigan State, 1988. Effects of processing and storage on the lipid and flavor composition of foods.

C. Ford, Associate Professor; Ph.D., Iowa, 1981. Genetic engineering of glucoamylase, structure-function relationships of cloned gene product, recovery and purification of fusion proteins.

B. A. Glatz, University Professor; Ph.D., Wisconsin, 1975. Production of antimicrobials (acids, bacteriocins) by beneficial microorganisms, reduction of *E. coli* in fresh apples and cider.

E. G. Hammond, University Professor; Ph.D., Minnesota, 1953. Analysis, stability, structure, metabolism, and utilization of fats, oils, and lipids; flavor and odor perception and identification; production and flavor of healthful dairy products; fermentations.

S. Hendrich, Professor; Ph.D., Berkeley, 1985. Food toxicology, influence of bioavailability of phytochemicals and naturally occurring toxicants on their biological effects.

J. Jane, Professor; Ph.D., Iowa State, 1984. Biosynthesis of starch and chemical, physical, and enzymatic modification of starch; internal starch granule structures; industrial utilization; biodegradable plastics.

L. A. Johnson, Professor; Ph.D., Kansas State, 1978. Value-added processing of cereals and legumes, especially corn and soybeans; extraction, separation; food and industrial product applications of vegetable and unconventional protein sources; processes for fabricated foods.

M. L. Kaplan, Professor; Ph.D., CUNY, 1972. Diet and endocrine interactions in the regulation of biosynthetic and oxidative processes of carbohydrate; lipid and energy metabolism during postnatal development in adipose tissue, muscle, and liver.

D. S. Lewis, Associate Professor; Ph.D., Michigan State, 1978. Nutritional regulation of growth and development, effect of breast and formula feeding on hepatic and adipose tissue metabolism.

J. A. Love, Associate Professor; Ph.D., Michigan State, 1973. Lipid oxidation in meats, functional properties of plant proteins, sensory evaluation methodology.

M. H. Love, Associate Professor; Ph.D., Michigan State, 1975. Nutrient retention in processed foods, physicochemical determinants of texture in processed vegetables.

G. S. Marquis, Assistant Professor; Ph.D., Cornell, 1996. Infant and child nutrition in the domestic and international setting, with an emphasis on the interactions among breast-feeding, dietary intakes, morbidity, and growth.

P. A. Murphy, Professor; Ph.D., Michigan State, 1979. Soy isoflavone analysis and health benefits, fumonisin toxicology, soy storage proteins.

D. J. Myers, Associate Professor; Ph.D., Iowa State, 1984. Utilization of legume and cereal proteins in nonfood and food applications and their functionality.

Z. Nikolov, Professor; Ph.D., Iowa State, 1986. Bioprocessing of transgenic crops for production of recombinant proteins.

M. J. Oakland, Associate Professor; Ph.D., Iowa State, 1985. Nutrition education and community nutrition, including nutrition/health status of elderly and children with disabilities.

D. G. Olson, Professor; Ph.D., Iowa State, 1975. Meat and poultry irradiation, product and process development, exports, safety and shelf-life enhancement.

F. C. Parrish Jr., University Professor; Ph.D., Missouri, 1965. Chemistry and structure of postmortem muscle, meat proteins, meat tenderness, meat nutritive value, sensory evaluation.

A. L. Pometto III, Professor; Ph.D., Idaho, 1987. Microbial degradation of degradable plastics, bioconversion of agricultural commodities into alternative products via fermentation, development of novel bioreactors, strain development of industrially important microorganisms for enhanced production, production of enzymes of the food industry, bioremediation of food industrial wastes, bioremediation of contaminated soil and water systems.

K. J. Prusa, Professor; Ph.D., Kansas State, 1983. Preharvest treatment of pigs for the improvement of pork quality and safety.

M. Reddy, Assistant Professor; Ph.D., Texas A&M, 1987. Isolation of highly bioavailable iron compounds in meat and human milk, assessment of iron status and oxidative stress induced by iron overload.

C. Reitmeier, Associate Professor; Ph.D., Iowa State, 1988. Quality attributes of small fruit, irradiation of fruit, production of textile fibers from soy protein, utilization of soybeans for human food.

E. Schafer, Professor; Ph.D., Iowa State, 1980. Public health nutrition issues in the Iowa population, nutrition programs, nutritional status assessment.

K. L. Schalinske, Assistant Professor; Ph.D., Wisconsin, 1992. Regulation of iron homeostasis and folate/methyl group metabolism relevant to health and disease.

J. G. Sebranek, University Professor; Ph.D., Wisconsin, 1974. Meat processing and preservation; influence of additives, new technology, and processing techniques on quality.

R. Serfass, Professor; Ph.D., Wisconsin, 1975. Nutrition and metabolism, stable isotopes.

P. J. White, Professor; Ph.D., Iowa State, 1981. Oxidation of edible oils and their sensory and chemical changes, uses of antioxidants in oils, lipid-carbohydrate interactions, starch structure and function, genetic variation of fatty acid composition in corn and soybeans and of starch structure in corn.

W. S. White, Assistant Professor; Ph.D., Cornell, 1990. Bioavailability and metabolism of beta-carotene and other carotenoids, health protective effects of carotenoids, mechanisms of intestinal lipid absorption.

L. A. Wilson, Professor; Ph.D., California, Davis, 1975. Flavor chemistry; food quality evaluation; improving thermal processes for foods; commodities: soybeans, soyfoods, spices, and their use as ingredients.

Courtesy Faculty

C. R. Hurburgh Jr., Professor; Ph.D., Iowa State, 1981. Quality characteristics of corn and soybeans, engineering-economic modeling of grain processing, value-added grains.

J. A. Olson, Distinguished Professor; Ph.D., Harvard, 1952. Nutrition metabolism, function, toxicology of vitamin A and carotenoids.

Iowa State University

SELECTED PUBLICATIONS

Arjmandi, B. H., et al. **(L. Alekel).** The role of soy protein with normal or reduced isoflavone content in reversing bone loss induced by ovarian hormone deficiency in rats. *Am. J. Clin. Nutr.* 68(Suppl): 1358S–63S, 1998.

Birt, D., and **S. Hendrich.** Principles of experimental nutrition in cancer research. In *Nutritional Oncology,* pp. 117–24, eds. D. Heber and G. L. Blackburn. San Diego: Academic Press, 1999.

Yaktine, A. L., et al. **(D. F. Birt).** Dietary energy restriction in the Sencar mouse: Elevation of glucocorticoid hormone levels but no change in distribution of glucocorticoid receptor in epidermal cells. *Mol. Carcinog.* 21:62–9, 1998.

Birt, D. F., et al. Inhibition of ultraviolet light induced skin carcinogenesis in SKH-1 mice by apigenin, a plant flavonoid. *Anticancer Res.* 17:85–92, 1997.

Lin, H., **T. D. Boylston,** L. O. Luedecke, and T. D. Shultz. Factors affecting the conjugated linoleic acid content of cheddar cheese. *J. Agric. Food Chem.* 46:801–7, 1998.

Boylston, T. D., et al. Volatile lipid oxidation products of Wagyu and domestic breeds of beef. *J. Agric. Food Chem. 4* 44:1091–5, 1996.

Fang, T.-Y., and **C. Ford.** Protein engineering of *Aspergillus awamori* glucoamylase to increase its pH optimum. *Protein Eng.* 11:383–8, 1998.

Liu, H.-L., P. M. Coutinho, **C. Ford,** and P. J. Reilly. Mutations to alter *Aspergillus awamori* glucoamylase selectivity III. N20C/A27C, A27P, S30P, K108R, K108M, G137A, 311–4 loop, Y312W, and S436P. *Protein Eng.* 11:383–98, 1998.

Gu, Z., D. A. Rickert, **B. A. Glatz,** and C. E. Glatz. Feasibility of propionic acid production by extractive fermentation. *Lait,* in press.

Rickert, D. A., C. E. Glatz, and **B. A. Glatz.** Improved organic acid production by calcium alginate-immobilized propionibacteria. *Enzyme Microb. Technol.* 22:409–14, 1998.

Tekin, A., and **E. G. Hammond.** Factors affecting the electrical resistivity of soybean oil. *J. Am. Oil Chem. Soc.* 75:737–40, 1998.

Kao, J.-W., X. Wu, **E. G. Hammond,** and **P. J. White.** The impact of furanoid fatty acids and 3-methylnonane-2,4-dione on the flavor of oxidized soybean oil. *J. Am. Oil Chem. Soc.* 75:831–5, 1998.

Hendrich, S., et al. **(P. A. Murphy).** Human bioavailability of soy bean isoflavones: Influences of diet, dose, time and gut microflora. In *Functional Foods,* ACS Monograph, pp. 150–6, ed. T. Shibamoto. Washington, D.C.: ACS Books, 1998.

Hopmans, E. C., **S. Hendrich,** and **P. A. Murphy.** Excretion of fumonisin B1, hydrolyzed fumonisin B1 and fumonisin B1-fructose adduct in rats. *J. Agric. Food Chem.* 45:2618–25, 1997.

Hurburgh, C. R., Jr. U.S. soybean quality related to costs and benefits of soybean cleaning. *Appl. Eng. Agric.* 12(3):379–82, 1996.

Hurburgh, C. R., Jr., J. Buresch, and G. Rippke. Aspiration cleaning of soybeans. *Appl. Eng. Agric.* 12(5):585–6, 1996.

Radosavljevic, M., **J. Jane,** and **L. A. Johnson.** Isolation of amaranth starch by diluted alkaline-protease treatment. *Cereal Chem.* 75(20):212–6, 1998.

Wang, K. S., and **J. Jane.** Quantitative analysis of debranched amylopectin by HPAEC-PAD with a post-column enzyme reactor. *J. Liq. Chromatogr.* 20:297–310, 1997.

Lu, T.-J., **J. Jane,** and P. Keeling. Temperature effect on the amylose retrogradation rate and crystalline structure. *Carbohydr. Polym.* 33:19–26, 1997.

Johnson, L. A. Recovery, refining, converting and stabilizing edible fats and oils. In *Lipid Chemistry,* ed. C. Akoh. New York: Marcel Dekker, 1998.

Zhou, X., and **M. L. Kaplan.** Soluble amylose corn starch is more digestible than soluble amylopectin potato starch in rats. *J. Nutr.* 127:1349–56, 1997.

Oh, S. S., and **M. L. Kaplan.** Early treatment of obese (ob/ob) mice with triiodothyronine increases oxidative metabolism in muscle but not in brown adipose tissue or liver. *J. Nutr.* 125:112–24, 1995.

Wilson, T., et al. **(D. S. Lewis).** Surprising atherosclerosis promoting effect of reservatrol in hypercholesterolemic rabbits. *Life Sci.* 59:15–21, 1996.

McGill, H. C. Jr., et al. **(D. S. Lewis).** Early determinants of adult metabolic regulation: Effects of infant nutrition on adult lipid and lipoprotein metabolism. *Nutr. Rev.* 54:S31–40, 1996.

Love, J. Animal fats. In *Bailey's Industrial Oil and Fat Products,* 5th ed., chap. 1, ed. Y. H. Hui. New York: John Wiley and Sons, 1995.

Lee, C. C., **J. A. Love,** and **L. A. Johnson.** Sensory and physical properties of cakes with bovine plasma products substituted for egg. *Cereal Chem.* 70:18–21, 1993.

Kopper-Arguedas, G. Y., and **M. H. Love.** Determinacion de la estabilidad del coco (*Cocos nucifera L.*) rallado deshiratado segun el pardeamiento no-enzimatico. *Reviteca* 6:1–9, 1997.

Marquis, G. S., et al. Recognizing the reversible nature of child-feeding decisions. Breastfeeding, weaning, and relactation patterns in a shanty town community of Lima, Peru. *Soc. Sci. Med.* 47:645–56, 1998.

Marquis, G. S., et al. Human milk or animal protein foods improve linear growth of Peruvian toddlers on marginal diets. *Am. J. Clin. Nutr.* 66:1102–9, 1997.

Zhang, Y., et al. **(P. A. Murphy,** and **S. Hendrich).** Daidzein and genistein glucuronides in vitro are weakly estrogenic and activate human natural killer cells in nutritionally relevant concentrations. *J. Nutr.,* in press.

Song, T., K. Barua, G. Buseman, and **P. A. Murphy.** Soy isoflavone analysis: quality control and new internal standard. *J. Am. Diet. Assoc.* 68:1474S–9S, 1998.

Wu, S., **D. J. Myers,** and **L. A. Johnson.** Effects of maize hybrid and meal drying conditions on yield and yield and quality of extracted zein. *Cereal Chem.* 74(3):268–73, 1997.

Wu, S., **D. J. Myers,** and **L. A. Johnson.** Factors affecting yield and composition of zein extracted from commercial corn gluten meal. *Cereal Chem.* 74(3):258–63, 1997.

Kusnadi, A. R., et al. **(Z. L. Nikolov).** Processing of transgenic corn and its effect on the recovery of -glucuronidase. *Biotechnol. Bioeng.* 60:44–52, 1998.

Evangelista, R. L., A. R. Kusnadi, J. Howard, and **Z. L. Nikolov.** Process and economic evaluation of the recovery of recombinant beta-glucuronidase from transgenic corn. *Biotechnol. Prog.* 14:607–14, 1998.

Clark, M. P., **M. J. Oakland,** and M. J. Brotherson. Nutrition screening for children with special health care needs. *Child. Health Care* 27(4):231–45, 1998.

Brotherson, M. J., and **M. J. Oakland,** et al. Quality of life issues for family who make the decision to use a feeding tube with their child with disabilities. *J. Assoc. Persons Severe Handicaps* 20(5):202–12, 1995.

Olson, D. G. Irradiation of food: Scientific status summary. *J. Food Technol.* 52(1):56–62, 1998.

Fox, J. A., and **D. G. Olson.** Market trials of irradiated chicken. *Radiat. Phys. Chem.* 52:63–6, 1998.

Olson, J. A. Carotenoids. In *Modern Nutrition in Health and Disease,* 9th ed., pp. 525–42, eds. M. E. Shils, **J. A. Olson,** M. Shike, and A. C. Ross. Baltimore: Williams and Wilkins, 1999.

Olson, J. A. Metabolism, kinetics, and genetic variation in humans. In *IARC Handbooks on Cancer Prevention,* vol. 3, pp. 31–9, ed. H. Vainio. Lyon: IARC Press, 1998.

Huff-Lonergan, E. J., **F. C. Parrish Jr.,** and **D. G. Olson.** Proteolysis of specific muscle proteins by :-calpain at low pH and temperature is similar to degradation in postmortem bovine muscle. *J. Anim. Sci.* 74:993–1008, 1996.

Huff-Lonergan, E. J., T. Mitsuhashi, **F. C. Parrish Jr.,** and R. M. Robson. Sodium dodecyl sulfate-polyacrylamide gel electrophoresis and western blotting comparisons of purified myofibrils and whole muscle preparations for evaluating titin and nebulin in postmortem bovine muscle. *J. Anim. Sci.* 74:779–85, 1996.

Pometto III, A. L., et al. Potential of agricultural by-products in the bioremediation of fuel spills. *J. Ind. Microbiol. Biotechnol.* 20:369–72, 1998.

Lee, J., **A. L. Pometto III,** A. Demirci, and P. Hinz. Media evaluation in microbial fermentations for enzyme production. *J. Agric. Food Chem.* 46:4775–8, 1998.

Stadler, K. J., et al. **(K. J. Prusa).** Effects of preslaughter management on the quality of carcasses from porcine stress syndrome heterozygous market hogs. *J. Anim. Sci.* 76:2435–43, 1998.

Prusa, K. J. Pork quality issues in the future. In *Proceedings of the First Roche International Swine Conference.* September 28, Edinburgh, Scotland, 1998.

Hurrell R. F., et al. **(M. B. Reddy).** A comparison of iron absorption in adults and infants consuming identical infant formulas. *Br. J. Nutr.* 79:31–6, 1998.

Reddy, M. B., and J. D. Cook. The effect of calcium intake on nonheme iron absorption from a complete diet. *Am. J. Clin. Nutr.* 65:1820–5, 1997.

Torres-Penaranda, A. V., et al. **(C. A. Reitmeier** and **L. A. Wilson).** Sensory characteristics of soymilk and tofu made from lipoxygenase-free and normal soybeans. *J. Food Sci.* 63(6):1084–7, 1998.

Iowa State University

Selected Publications (continued)

Gladon, R. J., et al. **(C. A. Reitmeier** and **D. G. Olson).** Irradiation of horticultural crops at Iowa State University. *HortScience* 32(4):582–5, 1997.

Yu, L., **C. A. Reitmeier,** and **M. H. Love.** Effects of electron beam irradiation on texture and pectin content of strawberries. *J. Food Sci.* 61:844–6, 1996.

Schafer, E., M. K. Vogel, S. Viegas, and C. Hausafus. Volunteer peer counselors increase breastfeeding duration among rural low-income women. *Birth: Issues Perinat. Care* 25(2):101–6, 1998.

Schafer, E., and P. Anderson. Heart*Style: A worksite nutrition education program in a rural setting. *J. Nutr. Educ.* 29:62–5, 1997.

Schalinske, K. L., and R. D. Steele. Methotrexate alters carbon flow through the hepatic folate-dependent one-carbon pool in rats. *Carcinogenesis* 17:1695–700, 1996.

Schalinske, K. L., and R. S. Eisenstein. Phosphorylation and activation of both iron regulatory proteins 1 and 2 in HL-60 cells. *J. Biol. Chem.* 271:7168–76, 1996.

Nanke, K. E., **J. G. Sebranek,** and **D. G. Olson.** Color characteristics of irradiated vacuum-packaged pork, beef, and turkey. *J. Food Sci.* 63:1001–6, 1998.

DeFreitas, Z., **J. G. Sebranek, D. G. Olson,** and J. M. Carr. Carrageenan effects of salt-soluble meat proteins in model systems. *J. Food Sci.* 62:539–43, 1997.

Zhao, Y., and **J. G. Sebranek.** Technology for meat-grinding systems to improve removal of hard particles from ground meat. *Meat Sci.* 45:389, 1997.

Luong, E., R. S. Houk, and **R. E. Serfass.** Chromatographic isolation of molybdenum from human blood plasma and determination by inductively coupled plasma mass spectrometry with isotope dilution. *J. Anal. Atomic Spectrom.* 12:703–8, 1997.

Fomon, S. J., and **R. E. Serfass.** Erythrocyte incorporation of iron is similar in infants fed formulas fortified with 12 mg/L or 8 mg/L of iron. *J. Nutr.* 127:83–8, 1997.

Stromer, M. H., R. Wang, and T. W. Huiatt. Integrin expression in developing smooth muscle cells. *J. Histochem. Cytochem.* 46:119–25, 1998.

Ho, C.-Y., **M. H. Stromer,** G. Rouse, and R. M. Robson. Effects of electrical stimulation and postmortem storage on changes in titan, nebulin, desmin, troponin-T, and muscle ultrastructure in *Bos indicus* crossbred cattle. *J. Anim. Sci.* 75:366–76, 1997.

King, J. M., et al. **(P. J. White).** Oxidative and flavor lipoxygenase-free soybeans. *J. Am. Oil Chem. Soc.* 75:1121–6, 1998.

Krieger, K. M., L. M. Pollak, T. J. Brumm, and **P. J. White.** Effects of pollination method on starch thermal properties of corn hybrids grown in two locations. *Cereal Chem.* 75:656–9, 1998.

Liang, Y., **W. S. White,** L. Yao, and **R. E. Serfass.** Use of high-precision gas isotope ratio mass spectrometry to determine natural abundance 13C in lutein isolated from C3 and C4 plant sources. *J. Chromatogr. A* 800:51–8, 1998.

Paetau, I., D. Chen, N. M.-Y. Goh, and **W. S. White.** Interactions of the postprandial appearance of beta-carotene and canthaxanthin in plasma triacylglycerol-rich lipoproteins in humans. *Am. J. Clin. Nutr.* 66:1133–43, 1997.

Bai, Y., **L. A. Wilson,** and **B. A. Glatz.** Quality of commercial shelf-stable soymilk products. *J. Food Prot.* 61(9):1161–4, 1998.

Fuentes-Granados, R., M. P. Widrlechner, and **L. A. Wilson.** An overview of agastache research. *J. Herb Spices Med. Plants* 6:69–97, 1998.

Ke, J., and **E. S. Wurtele.** Structure of the CAC1 gene and in situ characterization of its expression: The *Arabidopsis thaliana* gene coding for the biotin-containing subunit of the plastidic acetyl-CoA carboxylase. *Plant Physiol.* 113:357–65, 1997.

NORTH CAROLINA STATE UNIVERSITY

College of Agriculture and Life Sciences

Programs of Study

The College of Agriculture and Life Sciences offers both the Master of Science and the Doctor of Philosophy degrees in animal science, biochemistry, biological and agricultural engineering, biomathematics, botany, crop science, entomology, food science, genetics, horticultural science, immunology, microbiology, nutrition, physiology, plant pathology, soil science, toxicology, and zoology. Master of Science degrees are offered in agricultural and resource economics and in rural sociology, and the Ph.D. is offered in economics and in sociology. Master of Science degrees are also offered in agricultural and extension education, ecology, natural resources administration (soil science option), poultry science, and wildlife biology. All of these degrees require a thesis or dissertation. Nonthesis master's degrees are available in most departments. Minors are offered in several interdisciplinary programs as well as in the various departments.

Each graduate student's program is planned with an advisory committee of graduate faculty members. Graduate education is the final stage in the development of intellectual independence, and emphasis is placed upon the student's scholarly development through formal course work, seminars, research, and independent investigation. All doctoral students are required to take preliminary written and oral examinations, conducted by their advisory committees, at least one semester prior to the completion of degree requirements and scheduling of the final oral examination. When research is completed, both M.S. and Ph.D. candidates are required to pass an oral final examination in which they defend their theses and dissertations, respectively.

Research Facilities

The College of Agriculture and Life Sciences is well equipped and provides extensive facilities for laboratory and field research. Included are sophisticated computing facilities; a 180-acre Biology Field Laboratory with a 20-acre pond and modern laboratories; a Center for Electron Microscopy; a biotechnology 500- and 360-MHz NMR facility; a circular dichroism facility; molecular graphics facilities; hybridoma and DNA synthesis facilities; a molecular genetics center; the Highlands Biological Station; a Pesticide Residue Research Laboratory; a Reproductive Physiology Research Laboratory; a turfgrass field laboratory; a Phytotron, maintained in cooperation with the Southeastern Plant Environmental Laboratories; a cell and molecular imaging facility; a transgenic plant greenhouse; a biological resources building (animal facility); and sixteen outlying research facilities distributed throughout the state. NASA has established the Specialized Center of Research and Training (NSCORT) in gravitational biology, based in the Department of Botany. Animal research facilities for cattle, swine, sheep, and poultry are outstanding and include capabilities for intensive metabolism studies; laboratory animal facilities are being expanded. In addition, a variety of resources are made available through the University's participation in the Organization for Tropical Studies.

Financial Aid

Each department in the College of Agriculture and Life Sciences awards graduate research assistantships, graduate teaching assistantships, or both. Stipends for the 1999–2000 academic year range from $10,000 to $20,000 per year for half-time appointments. In some fields, fellowships or scholarships are available on a competitive basis. Several programs have received funding for graduate students through national competition. For example, training grants from NSF/DOE/USDA and from NASA have provided funding in the plant sciences (botany, crop science, forestry, and genetics), and USDA National Needs Graduate Fellowships have been awarded in the areas of agricultural economics, biological and agricultural engineering, food science and nutrition, genetics, plant biotechnology, and water science. There are numerous opportunities for employment of students' spouses within the University and the Research Triangle community.

Cost of Study

In 1998–99, tuition and fees for a full program of study were $1185 per semester for residents of North Carolina and $5768 for nonresidents. Students granted graduate assistantships normally receive out-of-state tuition remission and are charged in-state costs. All new graduate student stipend holders are provided tuition remission (the difference between out-of-state and in-state tuition) and in-state tuition awards, subject to eligibility requirements. All graduate students who are appointed to a graduate teaching or research assistantship, a fellowship, or any combination of the three who earn $3000 or more per semester or $8000 on a twelve-month appointment (amounts to be updated periodically) and who meet the eligibility requirements are provided with health insurance at no cost. Students should contact the Graduate School for additional information on eligibility requirements and other conditions.

Living and Housing Costs

Housing facilities are available on campus and in the community. Accommodations in the graduate dormitory cost $1450 per semester for double occupancy in 1999–2000. Apartments for married students rent for $385 to $455 per month.

Student Group

In 1998–99, the University enrolled 27,960 students, including 5,101 graduate students; 783 graduate students are in the College of Agriculture and Life Sciences. Approximately 175 graduate degrees are awarded annually in the College. The Graduate Student Association plays an active role in matters relating to graduate education.

Student Outcomes

Graduates have been successful finding employment in a variety of settings from business, government, education, and nonprofit organizations to human services. A 1998 survey of graduates revealed that most of the respondents were employed in their field. Sample job titles include food chemist, postdoctoral fellow, economist, environmental engineer, reproductive physiologist, clinical researcher, agronomist, research and development manager, and assistant professor. A career services office for the College assists graduates in locating positions in their field of study.

Location

Raleigh is a cosmopolitan city of more than 276,000 residents. It forms one corner of the Research Triangle, a community of three major universities, the National Humanities Center, numerous colleges and junior colleges, and more than twenty research laboratories, public and private. The presence of these educational institutions and research centers creates a stimulating environment.

The University

North Carolina State University has served as a major center for scientific and technological education and research since its founding in 1887. Many of the graduate faculty members are nationally and internationally known for their research.

Applying

Application and reference forms may be obtained by: 1) downloading the forms via the Web at http://www2.acs.ncsu.edu/grad/admission.htm; 2) requesting them online at shiela_thomas@ncsu.edu; or 3) writing or visiting the Dean of the Graduate School, 104 Peele Hall, Box 7102, North Carolina State University, Raleigh, North Carolina 27695-7102. Applications for admission must be returned according to instructions and must include two official transcripts from all colleges and universities previously attended. Scores on the Graduate Record Examinations are required by many of the departments.

Correspondence and Information

Inquiries may be sent directly to the department or program of interest (listed on the reverse of this page) or to the address below.

Associate Dean and Director of Academic Programs
College of Agriculture and Life Sciences
North Carolina State University, Box 7642
Raleigh, North Carolina 27695-7642

E-mail: cals_programs@ncsu.edu
World Wide Web: http://www.cals.ncsu.edu (College of Agriculture and Life Sciences)
http://www.acs.ncsu.edu/cgi-bin/mail_gradschool (Graduate School)

North Carolina State University

FACULTY HEADS AND RESEARCH AREAS

Students writing to a department head or program coordinator should include the name of the department or program and the University, followed by the box number (given below), Raleigh, North Carolina 27695.

Department Heads

Agricultural and Extension Education: Dr. R. W. Shearon, Box 7607. E-mail: rshearon@amaroq.ces.ncsu.edu
Agricultural and Resource Economics: Dr. J. A. Brandt, Box 8109. E-mail: jon_brandt@ncsu.edu
Animal Science: Dr. K. L. Esbenshade, Box 7621. E-mail: ken_esbenshade@ncsu.edu
Biochemistry: Dr. D. T. Brown, Box 7622. E-mail: dennis_brown@ncsu.edu
Biological and Agricultural Engineering: Dr. D. B. Beasley, Box 7625. E-mail: beasley@eos.ncsu.edu
Botany: Dr. E. Davies, Box 7612. E-mail: eric_davies@ncsu.edu
Crop Science: Dr. H. Thomas Stalker, Box 7620. E-mail: tom_stalker@ncsu.edu
Entomology: Dr. J. D. Harper, Box 7613. E-mail: james_harper@ncsu.edu
Food Science: Dr. K. R. Swartzel, Box 7624. E-mail: ken_swartzel@ncsu.edu
Genetics: Dr. S. E. Curtis, Box 7614. E-mail: securtis@ncsu.edu
Horticultural Science: Dr. T. J. Monaco, Box 7609. E-mail: tom_monaco@ncsu.edu
Microbiology: Dr. H. M. Hassan, Box 7615. E-mail: hmhassan@mbio.ncsu.edu
Plant Pathology: Dr. O. W. Barnett, Box 7616. E-mail: ow_barnett@ncsu.edu
Poultry Science: Dr. G. B. Havenstein, Box 7608. E-mail: gerald_havenstein@ncsu.edu
Sociology and Anthropology: Dr. W. B. Clifford, Box 8107. E-mail: william_clifford@ncsu.edu
Soil Science: Dr. J. L. Havlin, Box 7619. E-mail: john_havlin@ncsu.edu
Toxicology: Dr. G. W. Winston, Box 7633. E-mail: gary_winston@ncsu.edu
Zoology: Dr. T. L. Grove, Box 7617. E-mail: thurman_grove@ncsu.edu

Departmental Research Activities

Agricultural and Extension Education: agricultural education foundations; program development; teaching effectiveness; delivery of extension programs; instructional methodology and technology; instructional message design; leadership and career development; mentoring; needs assessment; organizational development; personality type; program evaluation; visual literacy; volunteerism and community development; strategic planning; distance education.
Agricultural and Resource Economics: agricultural and food policy; international trade; agricultural price and market analysis; farm management/production economics; natural resource economics; developmental economics; econometrics.
Animal Science: animal breeding and genetics; animal nutrition; biotechnology; reproductive physiology; livestock production relating to beef and dairy cattle, swine, and sheep.
Biochemistry: structure, function, and cell-specific regulation of expression of proteins and nucleic acids; molecular biology; biophysical structure (NMR, CD, fluorescence) and biochemistry of DNA and RNA; molecular biology/bioinorganic chemistry of metalloproteins; hormonal mechanisms of gene expression; RNA processing and control of translation; plant biochemistry/molecular biology; lipid metabolism; enzyme immobilization; antibody and other protein structure-function relationships; autoimmunity; computational chemistry and molecular graphics.
Biological and Agricultural Engineering: bioinstrumentation; biomechanics; bioprocessing and materials handling; biosystems modeling; energy conservation and alternative fuels; environmental control in agricultural structures; human engineering; mechanization; microprocessor applications; waste management; water management and hydrology.
Botany: molecular biology, cell biology, and physiology of development; calcium, the cytoskeleton, and signal transduction; biochemistry of crown gall; physiological ecology of freshwater, marine, and terrestrial plants; community ecology; wetland plants; plant systematics; ultrastructure.
Crop Science: crop breeding and genetics; crop physiology, management, and ecology; weed science; turf management; forage physiology and management; agroecology; integrated pest management; plant chemistry and biochemistry; extension.
Entomology: agricultural entomology; apiculture; behavior; biochemistry and physiology; biocontrol; ecology; forest entomology; host-plant resistance; medical and veterinary entomology; molecular biology; modeling; pathology; pest management; population dynamics; soil entomology; systematics; systems analysis; toxicology; urban entomology.
Food Science: food chemistry/biochemistry; food microbiology; food engineering; nutrition; red meats, poultry, seafoods, dairy, and plant products processing; aseptic processing; food biotechnology.
Genetics: molecular, biochemical, developmental, and microbial genetics; evolution; plant and animal improvement; quantitative and population genetics.
Horticultural Science: cultural practices for fruits, vegetables, woody ornamental, and floricultural crops; growth and developmental physiology; weed science; postharvest physiology; plant breeding and genetics; tissue culture; molecular biology; nutrition.
Microbiology: molecular biology; microbial genetics; microbial physiology; immunology; virology; nitrogen fixation; bacterial metabolism; microbial diversity; bioremediation; biotechnology; membrane structure and function; pathogenic bacteriology; yeast biology.
Plant Pathology: management and control of plant diseases and nematodes by cultural, biological, and chemical methods; molecular biology; investigation of the basic biology and ecology of plant pathogens through use of new biotechnologies; epidemiology; air pollution effects on plants. (Web site: http://www.cals.ncsu.edu/plantpath/)
Poultry Science: nutrition; physiology; toxicology; microbiology; immunology; biotechnology; diseases, management, and environment, using layer- and meat-type chickens, turkeys, and coturnix quail as experimental animals.
Sociology/Rural Sociology: rural communities and change; demographic analysis; rural health; labor markets and rural restructuring; sociology of agriculture; technology assessment and transfer; environment and natural resources.
Soil Science: soil fertility, chemistry, and physics; mineralogy; soil genesis; soil microbiology; environmental management; tropical soil management; plant nutrition; waste management.
Toxicology: xenobiotic-metabolizing enzymes; absorption and distribution of xenobiotics; toxicokinetics; genetic toxicology; biochemistry of resistance to toxicants; nutritional toxicology; mycotoxins; tumor promotion; neurotoxicology; aquatic toxicology.
Zoology: animal diversity; terrestrial, aquatic, and population ecology; physiology; development; cell biology; biorhythms; behavior; reproduction; fisheries and wildlife biology; conservation biology; aquaculture; mathematical biology.

Interdisciplinary Program Coordinators

Biotechnology: Dr. M. A. Conkling, Box 7614. E-mail: mark_conkling@ncsu.edu
Immunology: Dr. W. Tompkins, Box 8401. E-mail: wayne_tompkins@ncsu.edu
Nutrition: Dr. J. C. Allen, Box 7624. E-mail: nutrition_program@ncsu.edu
Physiology: Dr. J. E. Gadsby, Box 8401. E-mail: john_gadsby@ncsu.edu
Plant Physiology: Dr. T. W. Rufty, Box 7620. E-mail: tom_rufty@ncsu.edu

Program Research Activities

Biotechnology: recombinant DNA; cell fusion; embryo manipulation and transfer; tissue culture; molecular biology; immobilized enzymes and cells; fermentation; genetics and development; physiology and biochemistry; monoclonal antibodies; biophysical analysis of protein and nucleic acid structure.
Immunology: cell and molecular biology; hybridoma technology; T and B lymphocytes; macrophage; cytokines; infectious diseases; recombinant DNA; immunotoxicology; immunodeficiency; mucosal immunology; vaccines.
Nutrition: experimental animal and poultry nutrition; nutritional biochemistry.
Physiology: physiology of vertebrates and invertebrates, including cellular, neural, cardiovascular, pulmonary, gastrointestinal, environmental, lactational, and reproductive physiology; approaches range from whole animal studies to the cellular and molecular level.
Plant Physiology: photosynthesis; nitrogen metabolism; plant-pathogen interactions; molecular biology and biochemistry; nutrition; tissue culture; protoplast fusion; stress physiology.

OREGON STATE UNIVERSITY

College of Agricultural Sciences

Programs of Study

Master of Science and Doctor of Philosophy degrees are offered in agricultural and resource economics, agricultural education, animal science, bioresource engineering, botany and plant pathology, crop science, economics, fisheries science, entomology, food science and technology, genetics, horticulture, microbiology, molecular and cellular biology, plant physiology, rangeland resources, soil science, statistics, toxicology, and wildlife science. Master's degrees are on both thesis and nonthesis bases. Doctor of Philosophy degrees require a dissertation. Minors are offered in several interdisciplinary programs as well as in the various departments.

Research Facilities

The College of Agricultural Sciences consists of fourteen academic departments (four of which are shared with the College of Science). It is a partner with eight other colleges and with a dozen multidisciplinary centers. The diversity of Oregon's climate, soils, crops, and animals requires site-specific research. Research is conducted at Corvallis and on some 25,000 acres of research plots at ten branches at fourteen sites statewide. Research is supported in other units such as the Center for Gene Research and Biotechnology, the Environmental Health Sciences Center, and the Western Rural Development Center. In addition, departments have extensive facilities for laboratory and field research.

Financial Aid

Graduate research and teaching assistantships are offered on a competitive basis by most departments in the College of Agricultural Sciences. Stipends for the 1998–99 academic year ranged from $9000 to $15,000 per year for half-time appointments. In addition, graduate assistantships include a tuition waiver. In some fields, fellowships or scholarships are also available.

Cost of Study

In 1998–99, tuition and fees for a full program of graduate study were $2066 per term for residents of Oregon and $3514 for nonresidents.

Living and Housing Costs

Housing facilities are available on campus and in the community. Two residence halls, West International House and The College Inn, are available for U.S. citizens and international students who are 21 years of age and older. The cost of room (single occupancy) and board (thirteen meals per week) is $5064 per academic year. Rent for student family housing apartments starts at about $375 per month. Rental housing in Corvallis and nearby rural areas is reasonably priced.

Student Group

Annual enrollment at OSU is 14,618, including 2,620 graduate students; 47 percent are women. Approximately 305 graduate students are studying in the College of Agricultural Sciences.

Location

Situated on the Willamette River, between the mountains of the Coast Range and the Cascades, Corvallis, population 46,000, is the home of Oregon State University. Corvallis is 85 miles south of Portland, 50 miles east of the Pacific Ocean, and 85 miles west of the crest of the Cascades. Outdoor recreation is a favorite pastime of area residents and visitors. The climate is mild—average daytime temperatures in winter are in the 40s, and summer temperatures usually range from the low 50s at night to the low 80s during the day. Summers are dry and sunny.

The University

Oregon State University is recognized for its excellent academic programs in agriculture, engineering, oceanography, and the biological sciences. As a land-grant, sea-grant, and space-grant university, OSU embodies a special responsibility for education and research and desires to enable people to develop and utilize human, land, atmospheric, and oceanic resources. The 400-acre campus is beautifully landscaped with trees, flowering shrubs, and pleasant lawns.

Applying

Application forms are available from individual departments of the College of Agricultural Sciences or the Admissions Office of Oregon State University. A $50 application fee is required of all applicants. Interested students may apply at any time, but applications received early in the calendar year, prior to departmental deadlines, are most competitive. Scores on the General Test of the Graduate Record Examinations, and often a relevant Subject Test score, are required by many departments. A TOEFL score of at least 550 is required of all applicants whose primary language is not English.

Correspondence and Information

For general information, interested students may contact the office listed below. Students may wish to contact individual departments for more specific information.

M. J. Burke, Associate Dean
College of Agricultural Sciences
137 Strand Agriculture Hall
Oregon State University
Corvallis, Oregon 97331-2202
Telephone: 541-737-2211
Fax: 541-737-2256
E-mail: casstudy@orst.edu
World Wide Web: http://www.orst.edu/dept/agric/agrsci.htm

Oregon State University

DEPARTMENT HEADS AND RESEARCH AREAS

All campus addresses are at Oregon State University, Corvallis, Oregon 97331. A telephone number for each department head, chairperson, or director follows in parentheses; the area code in each case is 541. Departmental areas of concentration follow department head information. This listing also includes listings for interdepartmental programs of interest.

Agricultural and Resource Economics
William Boggess, Head, Ballard Extension Hall 217 (737-2942).
Food markets and trade; resource and environmental economics; production economics; economics of development (M.S. only).

Agricultural Chemistry
Ian Tinsley, Chairperson, Agricultural and Life Sciences Building 1007 (737-1789).
Molecular and cell biology; toxicology and environmental toxicology; biochemistry; chemistry; physics.

Animal Sciences
James Males, Head, Withycombe Hall 112 (737-3431).
Nutrition and management of beef cattle, especially winter nutrition of beef cows and utilization of high-fiber and nontraditional feedstuffs.

Bioresource Engineering
James A. Moore, Head, Gilmore Hall 116 (737-2041).
Bioprocess engineering (bioconversion, bioseparation, food quality preservation, food engineering); water resource and quality (watershed analysis, hydrologic systems modeling, groundwater monitoring and modeling, irrigation management); biological systems modeling; remote sensing and geographic information systems; livestock waste management; environmental quality.

Botany and Plant Pathology
Stella M. Coakley, Chairperson, Cordley Hall 2082 (737-3451).
Ecology, genetics; molecular and cellular biology; mycology; nematology; plant physiology; structural botany, systematics.

Crop and Soil Science
Sheldon L. Ladd, Head, Crop Science Building 109 (737-2821).
Cereal breeding and genetics; cereal production; forage and pasture management; new crops; oilseed crop breeding and genetics; seed physiology and production; seed technology; weed science; environmental soil science; soil chemistry; soil fertility; soil genesis and morphology; soil microbiology; soil physics; soil quality; wetland soils.

Entomology
Paul C. Jepson, Chairperson, Cordley Hall 2046 (737-4733).
Acarology; agricultural entomology; apiculture; aquatic entomology; biological control; forest entomology; insect biochemistry and physiology; integrated pest management; insect biosystematics; pollination biology.

Fisheries and Wildlife
Erik Fritzell, Head, Nash Hall 104 (737-4531).
Interaction of wildlife with land uses; migratory waterfowl; upland game birds; forest bird communities; endangered species; marine and freshwater fish populations; fish systematics; stream ecology; modeling aquatic ecosystems; conservation biology.

Food Science and Technology
Daniel F. Farkas, Head, Wiegand Hall 100 (737-3131).
Food chemistry/biochemistry (carbohydrates, enzymes, flavors, lipids, pigments, and proteins); food microbiology; food toxicology; food processing; seafood processing; sensory evaluation; enology and beverage technology.

Genetics
L. Walter Ream, Director, Agricultural and Life Sciences Building 3021 (737-3799).
Applied genetics in the areas of plant and animal improvement; molecular biology.

Horticulture
Charles D. Boyer, Head, Agricultural and Life Sciences Building 4017 (737-5475).
Physiology and biochemistry; genetics; breeding; culture and management of fruit, vegetable, or ornamental crops.

Microbiology
JoAnn Leong, Chairperson, Nash Hall 220 (737-4441).
Microbial physiology and genetics; industrial fermentation and biotransformation processes; food, dairy, soil, freshwater, and marine microbiology; immunology; pathogenic microbiology, including bacteria and viruses.

Molecular and Cellular Biology
Daniel J. Arp, Director, Agricultural and Life Sciences Building 3021 (737-3799).
Drug design; nitrogen metabolism; oncogenes; yeast genetics; developmental biology; immunology; environmental stress; viruses; hormones; membrane biogenesis; enzyme mechanisms; DNA repair; structure of nucleic acids and proteins; gene expression; plant evolution; DNA replication; host-microbe interactions; genetic engineering.

Plant Physiology
Patrick J. Breen, Director, Agricultural and Life Sciences Building 4017 (737-5475).
Regulation of plant growth and development; metabolism; stress physiology; molecular biology; whole-plant and environmental physiology; ecophysiology.

Rangeland Resources
William C. Krueger, Head, Strand Hall 202 (737-3341).
Range ecology; physiology of range plants; range nutrition; range improvement; range watershed management; agroforestry; riparian ecology of rangeland resources.

Statistics
Robert Smythe, Chair, Kidder Hall 44 (737-3366).
Statistics; biostatistics; environmental statistics; mathematical statistics; operations research.

Toxicology
Donald R. Buhler, Director, Agricultural and Life Sciences Building 1158 (737-2363).
Analytical, aquatic, biochemical, comparative, environmental, food, and general toxicology.

PENNSTATE

PENNSYLVANIA STATE UNIVERSITY

College of Agricultural Sciences

Programs of Study	Penn State's College of Agricultural Sciences is internationally recognized for its contributions to research, commitment to teaching, and cooperative extension education programs. Graduate programs in the College lead to Master of Science and Doctor of Philosophy degrees and to a variety of graduate professional degrees, including the Master of Agriculture. Degrees may be earned in departmental and interdepartmental programs within the College and in interdisciplinary programs with other colleges in the University.
	The College has or cooperates in graduate programs with opportunities for study in applied and basic research and the practical application of knowledge in twenty-five areas: agricultural and biological engineering, agricultural economics, agricultural education, agronomy, animal science, demography, ecology, entomology, environmental pollution control, extension education, food science, forest resources, genetics, horticulture, integrative bioscience, materials, nutrition, operations research, pathobiology, physiology, plant pathology, plant physiology, rural sociology, soil science, and wildlife and fisheries science.
	As part of its role as a land-grant institution, the College offers resident education and carries out research and extension education programs across the state on contemporary societal issues. These activities complement and support graduate programs.
Research Facilities	In addition to sharing the general resources of the University—libraries with about 3.3 million cataloged volumes, computation centers for instruction and research, and several research institutes of special interest to students in agricultural sciences—graduate students in the College have a wealth of specialized research and educational facilities available to them. The College also participates in Penn State's Biotechnology Institute and the Life Sciences Consortium.
	The College has about 12,000 acres of research forests and farms, including the Russell E. Larson Agricultural Research Center at Rock Springs and the Experimental Forest at Stone Valley. There are specialized teaching and research facilities for livestock (dairy and beef cattle, sheep, swine, horses, and deer) and about 10,500 domestic poultry. Other resources include the Center for Economic and Community Development, the Dairy Breeding Research Center, wood products laboratories, the Mushroom Research Center, the Pesticide Research Laboratory, the Cooperative Wetlands Center, the Fish and Wildlife Cooperative Research Unit, the Center for Professional Personnel Development in Vocational Education, greenhouses, the Center for Food Manufacturing, field research plots, and well-equipped research and computer laboratories.
Financial Aid	Graduate students may apply for grants, loans, fellowships, scholarships, assistantships, part-time work, work-study positions, and special minority student awards. Teaching and research assistantships awarded by departments are usually half-time appointments for which students receive a stipend and a grant-in-aid for tuition; most require 20 hours of work a week, allowing students to register for 8 to 11 credits a semester. Students may contact individual departments, the Graduate School, the College, and the Office of Student Aid for more information. The majority of graduate students receive some form of financial assistance.
Cost of Study	In 1998–99, tuition for full-time study (12 or more graduate credits) was $3267 per semester for Pennsylvania residents and $6730 for non-Pennsylvanians. Tuition for fewer than 12 credits a semester was calculated at $276 per credit for Pennsylvanians and $561 for non-Pennsylvanians.
Living and Housing Costs	The cost of living at the University Park Campus and in surrounding areas is modest. The University offers some on-campus housing. One-, two-, and four-bedroom apartments are located within easy walking distance of classrooms and laboratories. Single and double rooms are also available in campus dormitories. Graduate students may purchase University food services. For those who prefer off-campus housing, private homes and apartment complexes in town and in nearby communities offer a choice of accommodations at a wide range of prices.
Student Group	About 3,000 undergraduate and 490 graduate students are enrolled in the College. Approximately 65 percent of the graduate students are men. Twenty-five percent are international students, who represent a wide range of cultural, racial, geographic, and educational backgrounds. The College actively recruits students from minority groups. About 75 percent of the students have an urban or other nonfarm background.
Location	State College is the center of a standard metropolitan statistical area of more than 100,000 residents and is the major cultural center of central Pennsylvania. The town has a collegiate atmosphere with many interesting shops, restaurants, theaters, and bookstores. It is within a 5-hour drive of New York, Washington, and Philadelphia and has bus and air commuting services to all major cities. The Centre Area Transit Authority operates frequent buses from residential areas to the town and the University. The University and the community sponsor cultural, athletic, professional, and scholarly events. There are excellent recreational opportunities on campus and in the surrounding open countryside and mountain forests.
The University	Founded in 1855, Penn State is the land-grant university of Pennsylvania. It is one of the largest universities in the country, with twenty-two campuses. The University Park Campus is the center of most of the graduate studies at the University.
	University enrollment is approximately 70,000, including 60,000 undergraduates and 10,000 graduate students. There are about 700 U.S. minority-group graduate students. The graduate faculty has about 1,800 members. Enrollment at the University Park Campus is about 39,000.
Applying	For admission to a graduate program in the College, applicants must have a baccalaureate degree and must submit transcripts of all prior college work. Applicants must also meet program requirements for course work in specific fields and for the minimum grade point average to be admitted as regular degree candidates. Most programs also require letters of recommendation, statements of applicants' research and career interests, and scores on the Graduate Record Examinations or on an approved equivalent test. Financial aid application deadlines vary; the earliest is January 31 for entrance in the following fall.
Correspondence and Information	Further information can be obtained from individual programs or the addresses below.

Dr. Paul A. Backman
Associate Dean for Research and
   Graduate Education
College of Agricultural Sciences
201 Agricultural Administration Building
Pennsylvania State University
University Park, Pennsylvania 16802
Telephone: 814-865-5410
E-mail: pbackman@psu.edu

Dr. William L. Henson
Coordinator of Graduate Student Recruitment
College of Agricultural Sciences
101 Agricultural Administration Building
Pennsylvania State University
University Park, Pennsylvania 16802
Telephone: 814-865-7521
E-mail: wlh3@psu.edu

Pennsylvania State University

DEPARTMENT HEADS AND GRADUATE PROGRAMS

Agricultural Economics (Ph.D., M.S., M.Agr.): Dr. D. Blandford, Head; 103 Armsby Building. Graduate faculty: 26. Programs emphasize economic theory and analytical techniques in agribusiness, resource and environmental economics, production economics, agricultural marketing, rural development, agricultural policy, and international agricultural trade and development.

Agricultural Education (Ph.D., D.Ed., M.S., M.Ed.): Dr. Blannie E. Bowen, Head; 323 Agricultural Administration Building. Graduate faculty: 22. Programs are designed to prepare teachers and extension and other nonformal education personnel in core areas, including educational processes, communications and leadership development, program development and evaluation, research, and administration/supervision for advanced positions in youth and family education, international education, and agricultural education.

Agricultural and Biological Engineering (Ph.D., M.S.): Dr. Roy E. Young, Head; 250 Agricultural Engineering Building. Graduate faculty: 19. Programs are offered in soil and water management and conservation, geographic information systems, environmental protection, waste management, food engineering, properties of biological materials, particulate mechanics, systems engineering, wood engineering, horticultural engineering, building environmental control, agricultural structures, microclimate modifications, safety engineering, and machinery systems.

Agronomy (Ph.D., M.S., M.Agr.): Dr. S. L. Fales, Head; 116 Agricultural Sciences and Industries Building. Graduate faculty: 44. Studies emphasize efficiency in the production of agronomic crops, effective management of turfgrass communities, improvements in the quality and quantity of feed available for animals, understanding of the basic soil-plant-animal-climate complex, and improvements in the overall quality of the environment. Students may specialize in crop science, turfgrass science, or environmental quality.

Animal Science (Ph.D., M.S., M.Agr.): Dr. T. D. Etherton, Head; 324 Henning Building. Graduate faculty: 27. Students specialize in animal management; breeding and genetics; meat science; metabolism; nutrition of various species; physiology and endocrinology of reproduction, growth, or lactation; or transgenic biology.

Entomology (Ph.D., M.S., M.Agr.): Dr. J. L. Frazier, Head; 501 Agricultural Sciences and Industries Building. Graduate faculty: 20. Studies are offered in integrated pest management, population biology, ecology and biodiversity, modeling and artificial intelligence, insect-plant interactions, environmental and developmental regulation of genes, and environmental quality.

Extension Education (M.Agr., M.Ed.): Dr. Blannie E. Bowen, Chair; 323 Agricultural Administration Building. Graduate faculty: 23. Students are prepared to develop, evaluate, and administer cooperative extension and other nonformal education programs relating to agriculture, youth development, family living, international extension, or community development.

Food Science (Ph.D., M.S.): Dr. D. B. Thompson, Head; 111 Borland Laboratory. Graduate faculty: 18. Studies are offered in food chemistry, microbiology, nutrition and food engineering. Students can specialize in several commodity or discipline areas.

Forest Resources (Ph.D., M.S., M.Agr., M.F.R.): Dr. L. A. Nielsen, Director; 113 Ferguson Building. Graduate faculty: 20. The program includes two major areas: wood products covers the manufacturing and marketing of solid wood and composite products for consumer goods and construction, and forest science covers a diverse set of disciplines including forest biology, forest management, urban forestry, watershed hydrology, and ecosystem management.

Horticulture (Ph.D., M.S., M.Agr.): Dr. D. R. Decoteau, Head; 103 Tyson Building. Graduate faculty: 23. Programs are offered in the commodity areas of floriculture, olericulture, ornamental horticulture, and pomology. Students may also specialize in molecular biology, genetics and breeding, nutrition, physiology, postharvest physiology, propagation, and ecophysiology.

Pathobiology (Ph.D., M.S.): Dr. A. Catharine Ross, Head; 115 Henning Building. Graduate faculty: 20. Programs emphasize immunology, toxicology, microbiology, veterinary pathology, nutrition, and physiology as related to diseases of domestic animals and their biomedical implications in animals and humans.

Plant Pathology (Ph.D., M.S., M.Agr.): Dr. E. L. Stewart, Head; 211 Buckhout Laboratory. Graduate faculty: 26. Studies on biology of host-pathogen and host-environmental stress interactions, including ecology, genetics, molecular evolution, physiology, and pollution effects; mycology and mushroom science; etiology and control of diseases of agricultural, amenity, and forest species.

Poultry Science (Ph.D., M.S.): Dr. R. Michael Hulet, Interim Head; 213 Henning Building. Graduate faculty: 10. Programs emphasize avian skeletal and connective tissue biology, endocrine regulation of growth and development, operations research, nutrient waste management, and environmental effects in meat and egg production.

Rural Sociology (Ph.D., M.S., M.Agr.): Dr. D. Blandford, Head; 103 Armsby Building. Graduate faculty: 15. Studies focus on the sociology of communities, community and economic development in both developed and developing societies, leadership, demography, health, environment and natural resources, the sociology of agriculture, and social science research methods.

Soil Science (Ph.D., M.S., M.Agr.) Dr. S. L. Fales, Head; 116 Agricultural Sciences and Industries Building. Graduate faculty: 20. Studies emphasize the basic soil sciences, including genesis, classification, morphology, mapping, physics, and chemistry applications in geographic information systems, environmental chemistry, remote sensing, and resource inventory, assessment, and management.

Wildlife and Fisheries Science (Ph.D., M.S., M.Agr., M.F.R.): Dr. L. A. Nielsen, Director; 113 Ferguson Building. Graduate faculty: 10. Programs are offered in the biology and management of birds, mammals, and fish and their environment; the study of successional stages, land uses, and management of habitats; studies of recreational, aesthetic, and socioeconomic values of wildlife; and biodiversity and ecosystem management.

INTERCOLLEGE GRADUATE PROGRAMS THAT INCLUDE COLLEGE OF AGRICULTURAL SCIENCES FACULTY

Demography (Dual-title Ph.D., M.S.): Dr. G. F. DeJong, Director; 601 Oswald Tower. Graduate faculty: 32. Part of the Population Research Institute, this program allows students to earn a dual-title master's or doctoral degree in demography and either agricultural economics or rural sociology. Students develop expertise and skills in demographic theories, methodologies, and policy implications.

Ecology (Ph.D., M.S.): Dr. R. H. Yahner, Chair; 107 Ferguson Building. Graduate faculty: 54. Program emphasizes the properties of ecosystems by focusing attention on interactions of single organisms, populations, and communities with their environment. The program is designed to give students an understanding of ecological theory and research.

Environmental Pollution Control (M.S., M.E.P.C., M.Eng.): Dr. H. A. Elliott, Chair; 207 ASI Building. Graduate faculty: 39. The program deals with control of air and water pollution and the disposal of solid waste. Options in air, water, and solid/hazardous waste are available.

Genetics (Ph.D., M.S.): Dr. G. F. Barbato, Chair; 226 Henning Building. Graduate faculty: 68. Programs include molecular, biochemical, physiological, cellular, behavioral, developmental, pharmacological, population, and evolutionary genetics; genetic engineering; and breeding plants and animals.

Integrative Biosciences (Ph.D.): Dr. C. R. Matthews and Dr. J. S. Bond, Co-Directors; 517 Wartik Lab. Graduate faculty: 200, including faculty members at the College of Medicine at Hershey and the Sigfried and Janet Weis Center for Research in Danville, Pennsylvania. Program provides options in biomolecular transport dynamics, cell and developmental biology, chemical biology, cellular and molecular mechanisms of toxicity, immunobiology, ecological and molecular plant physiology, molecular medicine, neurosciences, and nutrition sciences to promote interdisciplinary research in the life sciences.

Materials (Ph.D., M.S.): Dr. R. N. Pangborn, Chair; 117 Hammond Building. Graduate faculty: 113. Programs include structure, properties, processing, and behavior of solid materials. Options offered are materials science and materials engineering.

Nutrition (Ph.D., M.S., M.Ed.): Dr. J. A. Milner, Director; S-126 Henderson Building. Graduate faculty: 49. Programs include human and animal nutrition sciences; public health, community, and clinical nutrition; and nutrition education. Supporting courses in allied fields include food, poultry, dairy and animal sciences; physiology; biochemistry; gerontology; exercise science; and social sciences.

Operations Research (Dual-Title Ph.D., M.S., M.A.): Dr. M. J. Chandra, Chair; 207 Hammond Building. Graduate faculty: 40. This option enables students to learn and use the tools, techniques, and methodology of operations research while maintaining a close association with areas of application, including agricultural economics, entomology, forest resources, and poultry science.

Physiology (Ph.D., M.S.): Dr. D. R. Deaver, Chair; 324 Henning Building. Graduate faculty: 34. Programs include areas of animal science, biochemistry, molecular biology, bioengineering, biology, exercise science, nutrition, poultry science, and veterinary science.

Plant Physiology (Ph.D., M.S.): Dr. E. J. Pell, Chair; 321 Buckhout Lab. Graduate faculty: 36. Faculty members are competent to prepare candidates in almost all subfields of modern plant physiology from the molecular and biochemical to the whole plant, including studies of cyanobacteria, algae, plant tissue and cell culture, and higher plants.

RUTGERS, THE STATE UNIVERSITY OF NEW JERSEY, NEW BRUNSWICK

Program in Food Science

Program of Study	The graduate Program in Food Science is among the top three food science programs in the nation. Areas of specialization include basic studies in physiological, chemical, and microbiological changes in foods; chemistry of fats and oils; flavor chemistry, including isolation and identification of food flavors; chemistry of food proteins; nutritional aspects of food products; food enzymology; food toxicology; food rheology and fluid mechanics; biophysical properties of foods; food extrusion; energy conservation in processing; theoretical aspects of food packaging; food functionality and properties; food colors; food emulsions; sensory attributes of food; biotechnology; fermentations; food pathogens; and food safety. The program offers the Master of Science and Doctor of Philosophy degrees. Candidates with bachelor's degrees in food science, chemistry, biochemistry, microbiology, or engineering are encouraged to apply. Both a thesis option and a nonthesis option are available to M.S. candidates.
	The program offers students the opportunity to study in a part of the country that is rich in resources for learning and research. More than a third of the 100 major food companies in the United States have headquarters, manufacturing, or research facilities in New Jersey. An industrial advisory board, which includes senior executives of major food companies, provides an additional dimension to program activities. The Center for Advanced Food Technology (CAFT), one of New Jersey's high-technology centers, provides a valuable complement to the goals and objectives of the food science graduate program. CAFT research projects, funded by the University, private industry, the state, and federal government, provide support for research assistantships.
	Because there are no residence requirements for degrees, students may matriculate on a part-time basis. Most food science graduate courses are taught in the late afternoon and evening.
Research Facilities	The program is housed in the Food Science Building on the Cook College campus. The building has six levels with 80,000 square feet of floor space, including classrooms, teaching and research laboratories, and pilot plants. An additional 32,000 square feet of pilot plant, laboratories, and offices for CAFT are also available. State-of-the-art equipment includes a tandem MS-MS and three other mass spectrometers; UV, visible, fluorescence, phosphorescence, and IR spectrometers; two differential scanning calorimeters; gas and liquid chromatographs; a temperature-controlled research microscope; and three rheometers. The sophisticated instrumentation rivals that of many chemistry departments. Students have access to the University's Center for Computer and Information Services, which is among the strongest and most innovative computer facilities in the country. In addition, microcomputers are available for student use. Rutgers' library system, with its holdings of almost 3 million volumes, ranks among the top twenty-five public research libraries in the nation.
Financial Aid	In 1998–99, teaching and research assistantships provided annual stipends beginning at $12,136 plus remission of tuition. Fellowships supported by federal, state, and private funds provide annual stipends of up to $15,000 and usually include tuition remission.
Cost of Study	For 1998–99, tuition for New Jersey residents was $3246 per semester for full-time enrollment and $267.60 per credit for part-time enrollment. Tuition for nonresident students was $4760 per semester for full-time enrollment and $395 per credit for part-time enrollment. Student fees were $367 per semester for full-time enrollment and $107 per semester for part-time enrollment. The application fee was $50.
Living and Housing Costs	In 1998–99, single-student dormitory housing cost from $2121 to $2422 per semester. Apartments for married students rented for $563 to $716 per month. Dining facilities provided various meal plans ranging in cost from $395 to $1145 per semester.
Student Group	There are nearly 5,000 students participating in more than sixty graduate programs in the Graduate School–New Brunswick. Approximately 125 graduate students are enrolled in the Program in Food Science.
Student Outcomes	A recent survey found that in the past ten years every Ph.D. graduate of the program was employed upon graduation. Most graduates secure positions with large American food companies.
Location	The New Brunswick area campuses of Rutgers are located in central New Jersey, on the periphery of the state's urban section. The surrounding area is diverse in character and offers numerous recreational and cultural activities. Close by are New York City, Philadelphia, the Jersey shore, and the Pocono Mountains.
The University	Chartered as Queens College in 1766, Rutgers was the eighth institution of higher education founded in Colonial America. In 1825, the name was changed to Rutgers in honor of Colonel Henry Rutgers, a veteran of the Revolutionary War. Graduate instruction began at Rutgers in 1876. A graduate faculty was organized in 1932, and the Graduate School was formally established in 1952. Rutgers is a member of the Association of American Universities and is one of the nation's largest state university systems, with an enrollment at the New Brunswick, Newark, and Camden campuses of approximately 48,000 students.
Applying	A bachelor's degree in science with at least a B average in academic work is required for admission. The Admissions Committee also considers scores on the General Test of the Graduate Record Examinations, and letters of recommendation. TOEFL scores are required of students from countries in which English is not the native language. Candidates are generally expected to have completed one year of organic chemistry, physics, and calculus. Biochemistry, microbiology, nutrition, physical chemistry, and statistics are recommended. Applications for the fall term must be submitted before May 1; for international students, before April 1. The application deadlines for the spring term are December 1 for domestic students and November 1 for international students.
Correspondence and Information	For program information: Graduate Director Program in Food Science Rutgers, The State University of New Jersey Cook Campus 65 Dudley Road New Brunswick, New Jersey 08901-8520 Telephone: 908-932-9611 Ext. 207 or 215	For applications: Office of Graduate and Professional Admissions 18 Bishop Place, P.O. Box 5053 Rutgers, The State University of New Jersey New Brunswick, New Jersey 08903 Telephone: 908-932-7711

Rutgers, The State University of New Jersey, New Brunswick

THE FACULTY AND THEIR RESEARCH

George M. Carman, Ph.D., Massachusetts. Biochemistry; membranes; phospholipids; enzymes.
Henryk Daun, Sc.D., Gdansk Polytechnic (Poland). Chemistry of food colors; thermal degradation of foods.
Chaim Frenkel, Ph.D., Washington State. Postharvest biology; chilling stress; oxygen signal transduction.
Michael A. Gallo, Ph.D., Albany Medical College. Food additives; toxicology.
Thomas G. Hartman, Ph.D., Rutgers. Food chemistry; mass spectrometry; chromatography; infrared spectroscopy; toxicology.
Chi-Tang Ho, Ph.D., Washington (St. Louis). Flavor chemistry; antioxidants; natural product chemistry.
Mukund Karwe, Ph.D., Rutgers. Numerical simulation of extrusion processes; heat transfer; instrumentation of extruders; fluid mechanics.
Jozef Kokini, Ph.D., Carnegie Mellon. Food rheology; fluid mechanics; biophysical properties of foods; food extrusion.
Paul A. Lachance, Ph.D., Ottawa. Nutrition (obesity, toxicology); nutritional aspects of food processing; food fortification.
Tung-Ching Lee, Ph.D., California, Davis. Food chemistry; biotechnological applications in food processing; seafood technology; nutritional and safety evaluation of food processing.
Thomas Leustek, Ph.D., Rutgers. Sulfur metabolism; molecular genetics and biochemistry.
Richard D. Ludescher, Ph.D., Oregon. Protein chemistry and physical chemistry; muscle biophysics; luminescence spectroscopy.
Karl R. Matthews, Ph.D., Kentucky. Pathogenesis and reservoirs of food-borne pathogens.
Thomas J. Montville, Ph.D., MIT. Physiological and metabolic studies on food-related bacteria; fermentation characteristics of lactobacillus species; bacteriocins; food safety.
Joseph D. Rosen, Ph.D., Rutgers. Food chemistry; analytical toxicology; mass spectrometry.
Robert T. Rosen, Ph.D., Rutgers. Analytical and food chemistry; mass spectrometry; instrumental analysis; natural products chemistry; chromatography.
Donald W. Schaffner, Ph.D., Georgia. Mathematical modeling of microbial growth; rapid methods in food microbiology.
Karen M. Schaich, Sc.D., MIT. Lipid chemistry; lipid oxidation; oxidative degradation of biological materials; antioxidants; free radical reactions; ESR spectroscopy.
Myron Solberg, Ph.D., MIT. Synthesis and regulating mechanisms of microbes.
Beverly J. Tepper, Ph.D., Tufts. Sensory evaluation of food; taste preferences and nutrition; taste in disease.
Shaw S. Wang, Ph.D., Rutgers. Biochemical engineering; extrusion; starch technology.
Robert R. Wolfe, Ph.D., Purdue. Food-quality inspection; applied machine vision; unit operations.
Kit Yam, Ph.D., Michigan State. Food packaging; controlled/modified packaging; packaging development.
Chung S. Yang, Ph.D., Cornell. Cancer prevention by dietary constituents; molecular and cellular mechanisms of carcinogenesis.

Adjunct Members
Gail V. Civille, B.S., Mount Saint Vincent. Sensory evaluation; methodology.
Dennis R. Heldman, Ph.D., Michigan State. Use of food product composition to predict thermophysical properties.
Alangaram Ramalingam, Ph.D., Cornell. Food process modeling and synthesis, separation, and purification.
Israel Saguy, D.Sc., Technion (Israel). Food processing; frying; kinetics modeling; shelf-life simulation optimization.

THE UNIVERSITY OF ARIZONA

College of Agriculture

Programs of Study

The College of Agriculture offers graduate studies leading to both the Master of Science and the Doctor of Philosophy degrees, with majors in a large number of disciplines. In addition, a Master of Agricultural Education is available. Graduate and professional education programs prepare students for a wide range of career opportunities in the agricultural sciences, renewable natural resources, and family and consumer resources. The various curricula offer professional preparation for careers in research, business, government, public service agencies, retail and service industries, human health institutions, financial institutions, youth development agencies, conservation and environmental organizations, farming and ranching, and research and extension.

Research Facilities

Modern research and teaching facilities are housed in six major buildings on the main campus. Laboratories are designed for biochemical, molecular, and cellular research activities, and greenhouses and field study facilities are close by. The College operates eleven agricultural centers in nine locations across the state.

Financial Aid

The various schools and departments in the College offer a variety of student support programs. Students should contact the departments for specific information.

Cost of Study

The 1998–99 registration fee for Arizona residents enrolled for 7 or more credits was $1081 per semester. Nonresident tuition was $3807 for 10 credits. Students who receive any graduate assistantships or associateships must enroll in a minimum of 10 credits per semester. All costs are subject to change.

Living and Housing Costs

University housing is available to graduate and undergraduate students at Christopher City Apartments. Residents may be single or married, with or without children. The complex of 354 ground-level apartments features furnished or unfurnished studio, one-bedroom, two-bedroom, and three-bedroom apartments; a community center, which has study rooms, recreation rooms, and a computer room; swimming and wading pools; a preschool; a playground; and spacious grounds. Rent includes the cost of water, gas, and electricity. For information, students can write to Christopher City Apartments, 3401 North Columbus Boulevard, Tucson, Arizona 85712 (telephone: 520-327-5918; fax: 520-322-5881).

Student Group

The University of Arizona has an enrollment of 34,000 students, including about 8,000 graduate students, and more than 2,000 faculty members. There are about 500 graduate students in the College of Agriculture.

Location

The University of Arizona is located in Tucson, a city of 450,000 in a metropolitan area of 600,000. Tucson is in the Sonoran Desert, 65 miles from the Mexican border, at an elevation of 2,400 feet. The area offers a wide variety of recreational and sightseeing opportunities, including the Grand Canyon, the Desert Museum, and Saguaro and Organ Pipe national monuments. Tucson is also a cultural center with museums, art galleries, and the Tucson Symphony Orchestra.

The University and The College

The University of Arizona, founded in 1885, is the land-grant university in Arizona and is rated among the top twenty state universities in research expenditures by the National Science Foundation. The University is a member of the prestigious Association of American Universities. The College of Agriculture, one of fourteen colleges in the University, is housed in six buildings on a 300-acre University campus.

Applying

Applicants are expected to have a B average in undergraduate work with an appropriate academic background. An application for admission includes letters of recommendation and an official transcript of credit. Scores on standardized tests may be required. Students should check with the appropriate department for specific information.

Correspondence and Information

Dr. David E. Cox
Associate Dean and Director of Academic Programs
College of Agriculture
P.O. Box 210036
The University of Arizona
Tucson, Arizona 85721-0036
Telephone: 520-621-3612
Fax: 520-621-8662
E-mail: dcox@ag.arizona.edu
World Wide Web: http://ag.arizona.edu

The University of Arizona

HEADS OF DEPARTMENTS/SCHOOLS AND AREAS OF RESEARCH CONCENTRATION

Agricultural and Biosystems Engineering
Donald C. Slack, Head (telephone: 520-621-1607; e-mail: slackd@u.arizona.edu; Web site: http://ag.arizona.edu/ABE/).
Biological/biomedical systems, water quality, irrigation, electronic applications, machinery and processing, energy, international technologies.

Agricultural and Resource Economics
Dennis Cory, Head (telephone: 520-621-2581; e-mail: dcory@ag.arizona.edu; Web site: http://ag.arizona.edu/arec/)
Natural resources and the environment, economic development, agribusiness economics.

Agricultural Education
Roger Huber, Head (telephone: 520-621-1523; e-mail: rhuber@ag.arizona.edu; Web site: http://ag.arizona.edu/AED/aedhome.html).
Teacher education, extension education, agricultural technology management, vocational education, leadership development.

Animal Sciences
Roy L. Ax, Head (telephone: 520-621-7623; e-mail: royax@ag.arizona.edu; Web site: http://ag.arizona.edu/ANS/anshome.html).
Ruminant nutrition, reproduction, thermal adaptation, molecular and population genetics.

Entomology
Bruce E. Tabashnik, Head (telephone: 520-621-1511; e-mail:brucet@ag.arizona.edu; Web site: http://www.ag.arizona.edu/ENTO/entohome.html).
Applied insect ecology; behavioral ecology; biochemical toxicology; biological control; caste determination; chemical ecology; crop loss assessment; evolution; flight, migration, and dispersal; insect behavior, insect pest management; insect physiology; insect systematics; natural products chemistry; pesticide resistance management; reproductive biology; social insect biology.

School of Family and Consumer Resources
Rodney M. Cate, Director (telephone: 520-621-1075; e-mail: rcate@ag.arizona.edu; Web site: http://www.ag.arizona.edu/FCR).
Family studies (FS): adolescent development, close relationships, family problems; transitions. Retail Consumer Studies (RCS): consumer theory, strategic retail management, international consumption retailing, nonstore and service retailing, consumer studies.

Nutritional Sciences
Fred Wolfe, Head (master's program) (telephone: 520-621-1186 or 1187; e-mail: bquinn@ag.arizona.edu; Web site: http://ag.arizona.edu/NSC/nschome.html).
Human nutrition (dietetics), nutritional education, health and wellness.

Darrel Goll, interdisciplinary Ph.D. program (telephone: 520-621-5630; e-mail: nusc@ag.arizona.edu; Web site http://ag.arizona.edu/NSC/nschome.htm).
Human nutrition (dietetics), nutritional biochemistry.

Pathobiology
Charles R. Sterling, Head Veterinary Science and Microbiology (telephone: 520-621-4580; e-mail: csterlin@u.arizona.edu; Web site: http://microvet.arizona.edu/).
Molecular pathogenesis, immunology, genetics, and ecology of bacterial, viral, and parasitic diseases; infectious diseases of aquaculture systems; pathophysiology, pathogenesis, and diagnostic pathology of animal diseases and their interrelations with animal and human health.

Plant Pathology
Merritt R. Nelson, Head (telephone: 520-621-1828; e-mail: mrnelson@ag.arizona.edu; Web site: http://www.ag.arizona.edu/PLP/).
Plant, microorganism interactions that result in disease or beneficial effects on plants.

Plant Sciences
Robert T. Leonard, Head (telephone: 520-621-1945; e-mail: plshead@ag.arizona.edu; Web site: http://www.ag.arizona.edu/PLS/).
Plant development, physiology, cell biology, crop production, genetics, and plant breeding.

School of Renewable Natural Resources (SRNR)
C. P. Patrick Reid, Director; Mary E. Soltero, Academic Advisor (telephone: 520-621-7260; e-mail: mes@ag.arizona.edu; Web site: http://www.srnr.arizona.edu/).
Rangeland management, renewable natural resource studies, watershed hydrology management, wildlife and fisheries science and landscape assessment and analysis.

Soil, Water and Environmental Science
Peter J. Wierenga, Head (telephone: 520-621-7228; e-mail: wierenga@ag.arizona.edu; Web site: http://ag.arizona.edu/SWES/).
Soil physics, soil morphology, soil chemistry, water quality, bioremediation, contaminant transport, environmental chemistry, environmental microbiology, environmental biology, microclimatology, remote sensing, soil fertility and plant nutrition, aquaculture.

UNIVERSITY OF FLORIDA

Institute of Food and Agricultural Sciences

Programs of Study

The Institute of Food and Agricultural Sciences (IFAS) offers graduate study in many areas of concentration in the College of Agriculture and School of Forest Resources and Conservation. Thesis and nonthesis master's programs are available. The degree of Doctor of Philosophy is offered in twelve areas of study. About 345 faculty members have specific appointments in teaching; they and many other faculty members are involved in teaching and directing graduate research in the Programs of Agricultural Education and Communication, Agricultural and Biological Engineering (Agricultural Operations Management), Agronomy, Animal Science, Botany, Dairy and Poultry Sciences, Entomology and Nematology, Environmental Horticulture, Fisheries and Aquatic Sciences, Food and Resource Economics, Food Science and Human Nutrition, Horticultural Sciences, Microbiology and Cell Science, Plant Molecular and Cellular Biology, Plant Pathology, Soil and Water Science, and Wildlife Ecology and Conservation and in the College of Veterinary Medicine and the School of Forest Resources and Conservation. Most of the faculty members have joint appointments in research or extension, a significant asset to the teaching program.

Interdisciplinary programs among the departments in IFAS and with other University departments provide the student with an excellent combination of educational programs. An example of this is the plant molecular and cellular biology degree program. The graduate student plans his or her program with the advice and assistance of a supervisory committee.

Research Facilities

The Institute's academic units have well-equipped laboratories, animal facilities, greenhouses, field plots and field laboratories, and other facilities for study and research. Opportunities for specialized work are available through the thirteen agricultural research and educational centers located throughout the state. The College of Agriculture participates in other research programs, such as those of the Center for Tropical Agriculture, the Center for Latin American Studies, the Florida Water Resources Research Center, the Center for Biomass Energy Systems, and the Florida Sea Grant College Program. In addition, departments have cooperative projects with state and federal agencies that support graduate student research, as well as grant support from private and commercial organizations.

Students and faculty members have access to computing facilities and services provided by the Northeast Regional Data Center located on campus. The center's facilities are used for instructional, administrative, and research computing; in addition, numerous personal computers are available in departments and in University support centers. The University of Florida libraries have more than 3.2 million cataloged volumes and receive about 24,000 periodicals. The Central Science Library houses materials for agriculture, as well as chemistry, engineering, and the biological sciences.

Financial Aid

Qualified graduate students in every department are eligible for a limited number of fellowships, assistantships, and other awards. One-third-time assistantships provide stipends of $9000 to $13,000 or more for twelve months and require $13\frac{1}{3}$ hours per week in research or teaching. A limited number of fellowships ($15,000) and half-time assistantships are available for doctoral students; these assistantships provide higher stipends and require assigned duties amounting to 20 hours per week. Stipend rates vary from department to department. Financial assistance is awarded on a competitive basis; undergraduate academic records, GRE scores, and letters of recommendation are important criteria. Waivers of 95 percent of the nonresident tuition and 80 percent of in-state fees are available for most students on assistantships or fellowships.

Cost of Study

In 1998–99, registration fees were $137.75 per credit hour for graduate-level instruction. Nonresidents paid 481.31 per credit hour. Certain undergraduate courses may be counted toward graduate degree requirements.

Living and Housing Costs

The University of Florida operates six apartment villages that are available as married student housing. Most single graduate students live in apartments in the area surrounding the University campus, as do many married students.

Student Group

There are more than 700 graduate students enrolled for advanced degrees in the College of Agriculture, Department of Agricultural Engineering, and School of Forest Resources and Conservation. About 300 graduate students are enrolled in the Ph.D. program. They come from most of the states in the nation and many countries of the world. The graduate students have diverse educational backgrounds and academic interests.

Location

The University of Florida is located in Gainesville, a city with an urban population of approximately 130,000, excluding University of Florida students. Situated in north-central Florida, midway between the Atlantic Ocean and the Gulf of Mexico, the city is known as a center for agriculture and small industry. Gainesville offers a moderate climate and many other advantages to students. A golf course is within easy reach of campus, and swimming and boating facilities are available at nearby springs and rivers. The lakes in the vicinity abound in freshwater fish, and the Atlantic Ocean and the Gulf of Mexico are within 65 to 70 miles. Nearly every religious denomination is represented in the Gainesville area.

The University

The University of Florida is a land-grant university with an enrollment of more than 40,000. Graduate study has had a phenomenal growth; in the fall term 1998, nearly 7,000 graduate students were enrolled in more than ninety fields.

The academic year consists of two semesters and two short summer terms. The semesters begin in late August and early January. The two summer terms begin in early May and late June.

Applying

Application for admission must be made to the director of admissions as soon as possible within one year before the beginning of the desired term of admission. A bachelor's degree from an accredited college, an average of B or better for the last two years of the baccalaureate program, and satisfactory scores on the GRE General Test are required for admission. Application forms may be obtained from the director of admissions. Applications for financial aid should be directed to the department in which the student's interest lies.

Correspondence and Information

Rachel Shireman, Assistant Dean
College of Agriculture
2014 McCarty
University of Florida
Gainesville, Florida 32611-0270
Telephone: 352-392-2251
E-mail: rbs@gnv.ifas.ufl.edu

Director of Admissions
Registrar's Office
University of Florida
222 Criser
Gainesville, Florida 32611

University of Florida

DEPARTMENT CHAIRS AND AREAS OF FOCUS

All graduate coordinators' campus addresses are at the University of Florida, Gainesville, Florida 32611.

Agricultural and Biological Engineering (M.S., M.Eng., Ph.D., and Eng.) Dr. C. D. Baird, Chair. The technical management program includes management of biological and environmental systems, business, production, and technical sales and safety. Engineering programs include environmental design, soil and water engineering, postharvest technology and food processing, power and machinery, and information technologies and system sciences. (Graduate Coordinator: Dr. K. V. Chau, Box 110570; e-mail: khe@agen.ufl.edu)

Agricultural Education and Communication (M.S., M.Ag.) Dr. E. W. Osborne, Chair. Primary areas of focus are leadership and human resource development, opinion formation and organizational communication, program development and evaluation, teaching and learning. (Graduate Coordinator: Dr. M. T. Baker, Box 110540; e-mail: mtb@gnv.ifas.ufl.edu)

Agronomy (M.S., Ph.D.) Dr. J. M. Bennett, Chair. Areas of focus include crop ecology, nutrition, physiology, and production; weed science, genetics, cytogenetics, and plant breeding. (Graduate Coordinator: Dr. D. S. Wofford, Box 110300; e-mail: dsw@gnv.ifas.ufl.edu)

Animal Science (M.Ag., M.S., Ph.D.) Dr. F. G. Hembry, Chair. Areas of focus include animal nutrition, meats, animal physiology, and breeding and genetics. (Graduate Coordinator: Dr. H. H. Head, Box 110920; e-mail: head@dps.ufl.edu)

Botany (M.Ag., M.S., Ph.D.) Dr. P. A. Jones, Chair. Areas of focus include ecology and physiology/biochemistry. (Graduate Coordinator: Dr. A. C. Harmon, Box 118526)

Dairy and Poultry Sciences (M.Ag., M.S., and Ph.D. offered through the Animal Science Department) Dr. R. P. Natzke, Chair. Specialization may be in dairy or poultry production. Areas of focus include physiology, nutrition, genetics, biotechnology, management, and product development. (Graduate Coordinator: Dr. H. H. Head, Box 110920; e-mail: head@dps.ufl.edu)

Entomology and Nematology (M.S., Ph.D.) Dr. J. L. Capinera, Chair. Faculty members are located on the Gainesville campus and at fourteen research and education centers statewide. There is close affiliation with two USDA labs and the Florida Division of Plant Industry lab located on campus. Areas of focus include biological control, pest management, genetics, ecology, physiology, toxicology, systematics and taxonomy, medical and veterinary entomology, urban entomology, and nematology. (Graduate Coordinator: Dr. G. C. Smart Jr., Box 110620; e-mail: gcs@gnv.ifas.ufl.edu)

Family, Youth and Community Sciences (Advanced degrees are not presently awarded, but a master's program is planned for the future.) Dr. N. Torres, Chair. Areas of focus include family decision making, family stress and coping, and nutrition and food safety. (Graduate Coordinator: Dr. N. Torres, Box 110310; e-mail: nit@gnv.ifas.ufl.edu)

Fisheries and Aquatic Sciences (M.S., M.F.A.S., Ph.D.) Dr. W. H. Clark, Chair. Areas of focus include management of inland waters, dynamics of Florida's coastal marine environment, and aquaculture. (Graduate Coordinator: Dr. E. J. Phlips, Box 110600; e-mail: ejph@gnv.ifas.ufl.edu)

Food and Resource Economics (M.S., Master of Agribusiness, Ph.D.) Dr. John Gordon, Chair. Areas of focus include agricultural business management, marketing, production, economic development, econometrics, and resource and environmental economics. (Graduate Coordinator: Dr. T. H. Spreen, Box 110240; e-mail: spreen@fred.ifas.ufl.edu)

Food Science and Human Nutrition (M.S., Ph.D.) Dr. Douglas Archer, Chair. Specializations are in food science or nutritional sciences. Areas of focus are nutritional biochemistry, nutrient function, assessment and metabolism, dietetics, food chemistry, sensory analysis, food safety, seafood technology, citrus processing, and pesticide analysis. (Graduate Coordinator: Dr. R. P. Bates, Box 110370; e-mail: rpb@gnv.ifas.ufl.edu)

Horticultural Sciences (M.S., Ph.D.) Dr. D. J. Cantliffe, Chair of Horticultural Science; Dr. T. A. Nell, Chair of Environmental Horticulture. Specializations are in vegetable crops, fruit crops, or environmental horticulture. Areas of focus include crop or seed physiology and biochemistry, crop breeding and genetics, crop production and management, landscape horticulture, postharvest physiology biochemistry, handling, environmental science, and taxonomy. Opportunities exist to conduct research at one of the UF/IFAS Research Centers in other parts of the state. (Graduate Coordinators: Dr. D. J. Huber [Horticultural Science], Box 110690; e-mail: djh@gnv.ifas.ufl.edu. Dr. M. E. Kane [Environmental Horticulture], Box 110670; e-mail: mek@gnv.ifas.ufl.edu)

Microbiology and Cell Science (M.S., Ph.D.) Dr. E. M. Hoffman, Chair. Areas of focus include anaerobic metabolism, biomass conversion, membrane and cell-wall chemistry, genetics, immunology, virology, and cell ultrastructure. (Graduate Coordinator: Dr. F. C. Davis, Box 110700; e-mail: fdavis@micro.ifas.ufl.edu)

Plant Pathology (M.S., Ph.D.) Dr. G. N. Agrios, Chair. Areas of focus include fungal, bacterial, or viral plant pathology; diagnostics; control and biochemistry of host-pathogens; epidemiology; etiology; genetics of host-pathogen systems; soil microbiology; and taxonomy. (Graduate Coordinator: Dr. F. W. Zettler, Box 110680; e-mail: fwz@gnv.ifas.ufl.edu)

School of Forest Resources and Conservation (M.S., M.F.R.C. [non-thesis], Ph.D.) Dr. W. H. Smith, Director. Areas of focus include agroforestry, biometrics, ecology, economics, ecotourism, environmental education, genetics, management, pathology, physiology, and silviculture. (Graduate Coordinator: Dr. H. L. Gholz, Box 110410; e-mail: hlg@nervm.nerdc.ufl.edu)

Soil and Water Science (M.S., Ph.D.) Dr. R. B. Brown, Chair. Areas of focus include land application of nonhazardous waste, pedology, rhizosphere dynamics, remediation of contaminated water, soils and aquifers, soil, water and agrichemical management, wetlands, and aquatic systems. (Graduate Coordinator: Dr. J. B. Sartain, Box 110510; e-mail: jbs@gnv.ifas.ufl.edu)

Veterinary Medical Sciences (M.S., Ph.D.) Dr. C. H. Courtney, Associate Dean. Major areas of concentration are large and small animal clinical sciences, physiological sciences, infectious diseases, and experimental pathology. (Graduate Coordinator: Dr. C. H. Courtney, Box J125, JHMHC; e-mail: chc@vetmed1.vetmed.ufl.edu)

Wildlife Ecology and Conservation (M.S., Ph.D.) Dr. N. Frazer, Chair. Areas of focus include wildlife biology and management, conservation biology, landscape ecology and restoration, urban wildlife relations, tropical conservation, and conservation education. (Graduate Coordinator: Dr. G. Tanner, Box 110430; e-mail: gwt@gnv.ifas.ufl.edu)

Research Centers. The Citrus Research and Education Center at Lake Alfred has the largest off-campus graduate program. Nine disciplinary departments are represented by 39 faculty members. All aspects of citrus research are emphasized. (Dr. H. Browning, Director; telephone: 813-956-1151)

INTERDEPARTMENTAL GRADUATE PROGRAM

Plant Molecular and Cell Biology (M.S., Ph.D.) Dr. R. R. Schmidt, Director. Areas of focus include plant biochemical, molecular, or physiological genetics; regulation of gene expression; metabolism; growth and development; genome structure/function; host/pathogen interaction; and plant biotechnology. (Graduate Coordinator: Dr. L. C. Hannah, Box 110690; e-mail: hannah@icbr.ifas.ufl.edu)

INTERDISCIPLINARY GRADUATE STUDIES

Center for Tropical Agriculture. A certificate program or a minor is offered in this interdisciplinary program. (Dean's Office, Box 110270; e-mail: rbs@gnv.ifas.ufl.edu)

Agroforestry. A specialization or a minor is available. (E-mail: pkn@gnv.ifas.ufl.edu)

Animal Molecular and Cell Biology. Specialization is available. (Graduate Coordinator: R. C. Simmen, Box 110920; telephone: 352-392-2185)

Hydrologic Sciences. Specialization is available. (E-mail: pscr@gnv.ifas.ufl.edu)

Center for Environmental and Human Toxicology. Specialization is available. (Director, Box 110885)

UNIVERSITY OF HAWAII AT MANOA

College of Tropical Agriculture and Human Resources

Programs of Study

The College of Tropical Agriculture and Human Resources (CTAHR) is known nationally and internationally as a leader in tropical agriculture. The College belongs to the nationwide network of land-grant universities, and CTAHR's tripartite mission is visible in its separate but interacting programs in teaching, research, and public service. The last two functions are administered through the Hawaii Institute for Tropical Agriculture and Human Resources (HITAHR), which is an integral part of the College. CTAHR offers the M.S. and Ph.D. degrees in the following graduate programs: Agricultural and Resource Economics, Agronomy and Soil Science, Botanical Sciences (Plant Physiology), Botanical Sciences (Plant Pathology), Entomology, and Horticulture. CTAHR also offers the M.S. degree in Biosystems Engineering, Animal Sciences, Food Science, and Nutritional Sciences programs. Three of the College's graduate programs in tropical agriculture—Agronomy and Soil Science, Entomology, and Horticulture— have been recognized as distinctive programs by WICHE, the Western Interstate Commission for Higher Education; qualified graduate students from participating states (Alaska, Arizona, Colorado, Idaho, Montana, Nevada, New Mexico, Oregon, Utah, Washington, and Wyoming) may enroll in these Western Regional Graduate Programs at resident tuition rates.

Upon acceptance, the student and his or her adviser develop a program of study that generally includes required and elective courses and seminars, written and oral examinations, and original research guided by a major professor. At the master's level, both Plan A (thesis) and Plan B (nonthesis) programs are offered.

Research Facilities

CTAHR shares in the use of general University facilities, including the libraries, which offer extensive collections and information services, and the computing center, which provides a full range of computers, from individual computers to large mainframes. It jointly sponsors, with the Pacific Biomedical Research Center, the Biotechnology–Molecular Biology Instrumentation Facility for the benefit of researchers throughout the University of Hawaii. The College's facilities include a microcomputer laboratory, several research stations, and specialized laboratories with state-of-the-art equipment, all of which support research and instruction in the agricultural sciences. On-campus affiliations with the Hawaii Institute of Marine Biology, Water Research Center, East-West Center, Harold L. Lyon Arboretum, Sea Grant College Program, and Hawaii Natural Energy Institute extend CTAHR's resources. The College also is affiliated closely with off-campus institutions, such as the Bernice P. Bishop Museum, USDA/ARS Tropical Fruit and Vegetable Research Laboratory, Hawaiian Sugar Planter's Association, U.S. Geological Survey, National Marine Fisheries Service, and Hawaii State Department of Agriculture.

Financial Aid

Students may contact individual departments (listed on the reverse of this page), the Graduate Division (2540 Maile Way, Spalding Hall, Honolulu, Hawaii 96822), or the Financial Aids Office (2600 Campus Road, Honolulu, Hawaii 96822) for information on grants, fellowships, assistantships, scholarships, tuition waivers, loans, work-study programs, and job opportunities. Graduate assistantships start at $14,382 per year for M.S. candidates and $15,552 per year for Ph.D. candidates for eleven-month half-time appointments.

Cost of Study

In 1999–2000, tuition for full-time study (12 or more credit hours) is $2074.70 per semester for residents of Hawaii and $5038.70 for nonresidents. Part-time graduate students are assessed $219.30 per credit hour for Hawaii residents and $466.30 for nonresidents.

Living and Housing Costs

Dormitory rooms and apartments, ranging from approximately $934 to $1704 per person per semester, are available to single and married graduate students. These accommodations are on campus within walking distance of classrooms and laboratories. Meal plans are available through the University food service for $700 to $1065 a semester. Most graduate students elect to live off campus in shared apartments and houses, the costs of which vary widely.

Student Group

There are 4,514 graduate students at Manoa. The College's 125 graduate students come from throughout the United States and many countries, as well as from Hawaii, and represent a diversity of educational, cultural, and academic backgrounds.

Location

The University of Hawaii is located in Manoa Valley, a residential section close to the heart of Metropolitan Honolulu, the capital of the state of Hawaii. The campus is a short distance from the center of the commercial, cultural, and political life of Hawaii, and a variety of recreational, athletic, and social activities are available to students throughout the year. Hawaii's population is diverse, and its climate moderate and tropical. Hawaii provides CTAHR with a living laboratory that cannot be duplicated elsewhere: a full range of the soils and climates found throughout the world; tropical plants, animals, and organisms; and a location as the gateway to Asia and the Pacific Basin.

The University

The University of Hawaii at Manoa was founded in 1907 as a land-grant college of agriculture and mechanic arts. Today, it is a major comprehensive research institution with 17,365 students and offers course work leading to bachelor's degrees in eighty-eight fields of study, master's degrees in eighty-seven, doctorates in fifty-three, first professional degrees in law and medicine, and a number of certificates. It is accredited by the Accrediting Commission for Senior Colleges and Universities of the Western Association of Schools and Colleges.

Applying

The deadline for receipt of applications, transcripts, GRE scores, and letters of recommendation is March 1 for the following fall semester and September 1 for the following spring semester. The deadline for international students is January 15 and August 1 for fall and spring semesters, respectively. International students must submit Test of English as a Foreign Language (TOEFL) scores in addition to the items mentioned above. Information regarding the program, admission criteria, and financial assistance is available from the individual departments (the names and addresses of the departmental chairs are listed on the reverse side). Additional information may be obtained from the individual departments or from Dr. Iwaoka.

Correspondence and Information

Dr. Wayne Iwaoka, Interim Associate Dean for Academic Affairs
College of Tropical Agriculture and Human Resources
University of Hawaii
3050 Maile Way, Gil 211
Honolulu, Hawaii 96822
E-mail: iwaokaw@avax.ctahr.hawaii.edu
World Wide Web: http://www.ctahr.hawaii.edu

University of Hawaii at Manoa

THE FACULTY

The addresses at which the department chairs may be contacted are given in parentheses for each chair; the street address should be preceded by the name of the department and the University.

Department of Agricultural and Resource Economics
S. A. El-Swaify, Interim Chair (3050 Maile Way, Honolulu, Hawaii 96822).

Richard L. Bowen, Ph.D., Colorado State, 1982. Chauncey Ching, Ph.D., California, Davis, 1967. Linda J. Cox, Ph.D., Texas A&M, 1982. Carol A. Ferguson, Ph.D., Cornell, 1985. Peter V. Garrod, Ph.D., Berkeley, 1972. Chennat Gopalakrishnan, Ph.D., Montana State, 1967. Stuart T. Nakamoto, Ph.D., Hawaii, 1986. Gary R. Vieth, Ph.D., Oregon State, 1976. Hiroshi Yamauchi, Ph.D., Berkeley, 1968. John Yanagida, Ph.D., Illinois, 1978.

Department of Biosystems Engineering
Charles M. Kinoshita, Interim Chair (3050 Maile Way, Gil 111, Honolulu, Hawaii 96822).

Loren D. Gautz, Ph.D., California, Davis, 1990. Charles M. Kinoshita, Ph.D., Berkeley, 1980. Pin Sun Leung, Ph.D., Hawaii, 1977. Tung Liang, Ph.D., North Carolina State, 1967. Scott Q. Turn, Ph.D., California, Davis, 1994. Jaw-Kai Wang, Ph.D., Michigan State, 1958. Michael R. Williamson, Ph.D., Hawaii, 1986. I-Pai Wu, Ph.D., Purdue, 1963. Ping-Yi Yang, Ph.D., Oklahoma State, 1972.

Department of Agronomy and Soil Science
S. A. El-Swaify, Interim Chair (1910 East-West Road, Sherman 101, Honolulu, Hawaii 96822).

I. Scott Campbell, Ph.D., Florida, 1980. Ramon de la Peña, Ph.D., Hawaii, 1969. Samir A. El-Swaify, Ph.D., California, Davis, 1964. Carl I. Evensen, Ph.D., Hawaii, 1989. James H. Fownes, Ph.D., Wisconsin, 1985. Mitiku Habte, Ph.D., Cornell, 1976. Nguyen V. Hue, Ph.D., Auburn, 1981. Rollin Jones, Ph.D., Arizona, 1971. Susan M. Miyasaka, Ph.D., Cornell, 1988. Phillip S. Motooka, Ph.D., North Carolina State, 1973. Paul W. Singleton, Ph.D., Hawaii, 1982. Burton J. Smith, Ph.D., Florida, 1978. Goro Uehara, Ph.D., Michigan State, 1959. Russell Yost, Ph.D., North Carolina, 1977.

Department of Animal Science
Douglas L. Vincent, Interim Chair (1800 East-West Road, Henke 118, Honolulu, Hawaii 96822).
Richard Early, Chair of Graduate Faculty (1800 East-West Road, Henke 106, Honolulu, Hawaii 96822).

Shannon K. Atkinson, Ph.D., Murdoch, 1985. William C. Bergin, D.V.M., Kansas State, 1967. James A. Brock, D.V.M., Washington State, 1977. Christopher Brown, Ph.D., Delaware, 1984. Brent A. Buckley, Ph.D., Nebraska, 1985. James R. Carpenter, Ph.D., Cornell, 1976. Richard J. Early, Ph.D., Wisconsin, 1982. E. Gordon Grau, Ph.D., Delaware, 1978. Karim P. Jeraj, B.V.Sc., Nairobi, 1969. Yong-Soo Kim, Ph.D., California, Davis, 1988. Bradley R. LeaMaster, Ph.D., Hawaii, 1991. Chin Nyean Lee, Ph.D., Wisconsin, 1984. Spencer R. Malecha, Ph.D., Hawaii, 1971. Douglas L. Vincent, Ph.D., Illinois, 1983. Charles W. Weems, Ph.D., West Virginia, 1975. Halina Zaleski, Ph.D., Guelph, 1992.

Department of Entomology
Donald P. Schmitt, Interim Chair (3050 Maile Way, Gilmore 310, Honolulu, Hawaii 96822).
Stephen Saul, Chair of Graduate Faculty (3050 Maile Way, Gilmore 310, Honolulu, Hawaii 96822).

Lorna Arita-Tsutsumi, Ph.D., Hawaii, 1983. Rosemary G. Gillespie, Ph.D., Tennessee, 1986. M. Lee Goff, Ph.D., Hawaii, 1977. J. Kenneth Grace, Ph.D., Berkeley, 1986. Arnold Hara, Ph.D., California, Davis, 1982. Marshall W. Johnson, Ph.D., California, Riverside, 1979. Vincent P. Jones, Ph.D., California, Riverside, 1983. Kenneth Kaneshiro, Ph.D., Hawaii, 1968. Ronald F. L. Mau, Ph.D., Hawaii, 1975. Susan D. McCombs, Ph.D., Hawaii, 1992. Russell H. Messing, Ph.D., Oregon State, 1986. George K. Roderick, Ph.D., Berkeley, 1987. Stephen Saul, Ph.D., Rochester, 1970. Josef Seifert, Ph.D., Prague Institute of Chemical Technology, 1973. Julian R. Yates, Ph.D., Hawaii, 1988.

Department of Food Science and Human Nutrition
Douglas L. Vincent, Interim Chair (1800 East-West Road, Henke 224, Honolulu, Hawaii 96822).
Rachel Novotny, Chair of Graduate Programs (1800 East-West Road, Henke 224, Honolulu, Hawaii 96822).

Dian Dooley, Ph.D., Wisconsin, 1988. Michael Dunn, Ph.D., Penn State, 1985. Karen Glanz, Ph.D., Michigan, 1979. Ronald K. Hetzler, Ph.D., Southern Illinois, 1988. William D. Hiller, M.D., Thomas Jefferson, 1981. Aurora S. Hodgson, Ph.D., Massachusetts, 1978. Alvin Huang, Ph.D., Wisconsin, 1985. Wayne Iwaoka, Ph.D., Illinois, 1973. James H. Moy, Ph.D., Rutgers, 1965. Wai-Kip Nip, Ph.D., Texas A&M, 1969. Rachel Novotny, Ph.D., Cornell, 1986. Anne C. Shovic, Ph.D., Washington State, 1982. C. Alan Titchenal, Ph.D., California, Davis, 1986.

Cooperating Graduate Faculty: Harry Ako, Ph.D., Washington State, 1973. James Carpenter, Ph.D., Cornell, 1976. Catherine Cavaletto, M.S., Hawaii, 1968. Richard Early, Ph.D., Wisconsin, 1981. Dan Galanis, Ph.D., Cornell, 1994. Jean Hankin, Dr.P.H., Berkeley, 1966. Sophia Kathariou, Ph.D., Berkeley, 1981. David Lally, Ph.D., Hawaii, 1973. Qingxiao Li, Ph.D., California, Davis, 1990. Josef Seifert, Diploma, Prague Institute of Chemical Technology, 1973. Chung-Shih Tang, Ph.D., Berkeley, 1967. Thomas Vogt, M.D., California, San Francisco, 1971. Carol Waslien, Ph.D., Berkeley, 1968. Charles Weems, Ph.D., West Virginia, 1975. Ping-Yi Yang, Ph.D., Oklahoma State, 1972.

Department of Horticulture
David L. Hensley, Interim Chair (3190 Maile Way, St. John 102, Honolulu, Hawaii 96822).
Robert Paull, Chair of Graduate Programs (3190 Maile Way, St. John 516, Honolulu, Hawaii 96822).

H. C. Bittenbender, Ph.D., Michigan State, 1977. James L. Brewbaker, Ph.D., Cornell, 1952. Catherine G. Cavaletto, M.S., Hawaii, 1968. C. L. Chia, Ph.D., Cornell, 1975. Richard A. Criley, Ph.D., UCLA, 1968. Joseph DeFrank, Ph.D., Michigan State, 1983. Kent D. Fleming, Ph.D., Massachusetts, 1991. Sheldon C. Furutani, Ph.D., Michigan State, 1982. John M. Halloran, Ph.D., Michigan State, 1983. David L. Hensley, Ph.D., Purdue, 1978. Kent D. Kobayashi, Ph.D., Oregon State, 1981. Bernard A. Kratky, Ph.D., Purdue, 1971. Adelheid R. Kuehnle, Ph.D., Cornell, 1988. John T. Kunisaki, M.S., Hawaii, 1964. Richard M. Manshardt, Ph.D., Florida, 1980. Mike A. Nagao, Ph.D., Massachusetts, 1975. Roy K. Nishimoto, Ph.D., Purdue, 1970. Robert E. Paull, Ph.D., Berkeley, 1974. Yoneo Sagawa, Ph.D., Connecticut, 1956. William S. Sakai, Ph.D., Hawaii, 1970. Terry T. Sekioka, Ph.D., Minnesota, 1969. Michael J. Tanabe, Ph.D., Hawaii, 1976. Kenneth Y. Takeda, Ph.D., Hawaii, 1974. Hector R. Valenzuela, Ph.D., Florida, 1990.

Department of Plant Molecular Physiology
Charles M. Kinoshita, Interim Chair (3190 Maile Way, St. John 503, Honolulu, Hawaii 96822).

Dulal Borthakur, Ph.D., East Anglia (England), 1987. John E. Bowen, Ph.D., Maryland, 1965. David Christopher, Ph.D., Arizona, 1989. H. Michael Harrington, Ph.D., Ohio, 1978. John I. Stiles, Ph.D., Cornell, 1976. Harry Yamamoto, Ph.D., California, Davis, 1962.

Department of Plant Pathology
Donald P. Schmitt, Interim Chair (3190 Maile Way, Honolulu, Hawaii 96822).

Anne M. Alvarez, Ph.D., Berkeley, 1972. John J. Cho, Ph.D., Berkeley, 1974. Stephen A. Ferreira, Ph.D., California, Davis, 1974. John S. Hu, Ph.D., Cornell, 1987. Wen-hsiung Ko, Ph.D., Michigan State, 1966. Scot C. Nelson, Ph.D., North Carolina State, 1992. Wayne T. Nishijima, Ph.D., Wisconsin, 1977. Jeri J. Ooka, Ph.D., Minnesota, 1975. Kenneth G. Rohrbach, Ph.D., Colorado, 1967. Donald P. Schmitt, Ph.D., Iowa State, 1971. Brent S. Sipes, Ph.D., North Carolina State, 1991. Eduardo E. Trujillo, Ph.D., Berkeley, 1962. Janice Y. Uchida, Ph.D., Hawaii, 1984.

University of Hawaii at Manoa

SELECTED PUBLICATIONS

Qin, J. G., A. W. Fast, and **H. Ako.** Growth performance of diploid and triploid Chinese catfish *Clarias fuscus. Aquaculture* 166:247–58, 1998.

Tamaru, C. S., **H. Ako,** and R. Paguirigan. Essential fatty acid profiles of maturation feeds used in freshwater ornamental fish culture. *Hydrobiologia* 358:265–8, 1997.

Fukui, H., **A. M. Alvarez,** and R. Fukui. Differential susceptibility of *anthurium cultivars* to bacterial blight in foliar and systemic infection phases. *Plant Disease* 82:800–6, 1998.

Bittenbender, H. C., N. V. Hue, K. Fleming, and H. Brown. Sustainability of organic fertilization of macadamia with macadamia husk-manure compost. *Commun. Soil Sci. Plant Analysis* 29(3–4):490–19, 1998.

You, Z., X. Gao, M. M. Ho, and **D. Borthakur.** A stomatin-like protein encoded by the *slp* gene of *Rhizobium etli* is required for nodulation competitiveness on the common bean. *Microbiology* 144:2619–27, 1998.

Parveen, N., D. T. Webb, and **D. Borthakur.** The symbiotic phenotypes of exopolysaccharide-defective mutants of *Rhizobium* sp. strain TAL1145 do not differ on determinate- and indeterminate-nodulating tree legumes. *Microbiology* 43:1959–67, 1997.

Britten, P., ed. *The Nutrition Idea Book: Innovative Strategies and Resources for Nutrition Education.* Minneapolis: Society for Nutrition Education Foundation, 1997.

Chakravorty, U., J. Roumassett, and K. P. Tse. Endogenous substitution of energy resources and global warming. *J. Polit. Econ.* 105(6):1201–34, 1997.

Cho, J. J., D. M. Custer, S. H. Brommonschenkel, and S. D. Tanksley. Conventional breeding: Host-plant resistance and the use of molecular markers to develop resistance to tomato spotted wilt virus in vegetables. *Acta Hortic.* 431:367–78, 1996.

Christopher, D. A., and P. H. Hoffer. DET1 represses a chloroplast blue light-responsive promoter in a developmental and tissue-specific manner in *Arabidopsis thaliana. Plant J.* 14:1–11, 1998.

Hoffer, P. H., and **D. A. Christopher.** Structure and blue light–responsive transcription of a chloroplast *psbD* promoter from *Arabidopsis thaliana. Plant Physiol.* 115:213–22, 1997.

Christopher, D. A., X. Li, M. Kim, and J. E. Mullet. Involvement of protein kinase and extra-plastidic serine/threonine protein phosphatases in signaling pathways regulating plastid transcription and the *psbD* blue light-responsive promoter in barley *(Hordeum vulgare* L.). *Plant Physiol.* 113:1273–82, 1997.

Criley, R. A., and **W. S. Sakai.** *Heliconia wagneriana* is a short day plant. *HortScience* 32:1044–5, 1997.

Dooley, D. A. Integrating ethics into a pre-professional curriculum: Nutrition education for dietetics/health professionals. *J. Coll. Sci. Teaching,* in press.

Dooley, D. A., R. Novotny, and **P. J. Britten.** Integrating research into the undergraduate nutrition curriculum: Improving shoppers' awareness and understanding of NUTRITION FACTS labels. *J. Nutr. Educ.* 30(4):225–31, 1998.

Dooley, D. A., R. Novotny and **P. J. Britten.** Integrating research into the undergraduate nutrition curriculum: Improving shoppers' awareness and understanding of NUTRITION FACTS labels. *J. Nutr. Educ.,* in press.

Dunn, M. A., S. L. Too, and M. Y. B. Liew. Characterization of a novel protein in chick intestine that exhibits calcium-binding activity, and regulation by dietary calcium, aluminum and vitamin D. *J. Nutr.* 125:2916–24, 1995.

Shell, T. M., **R. J. Early, J. R. Carpenter, D. L. Vincent,** and **B. A. Buckley.** Prepartum nutrition and solar radiation in beef cattle: I. Relationship of body fluid compartments, packed cell volume, plasma urea nitrogen, and estrogens to prenatal development. *J. Anim. Sci.* 73:1289–1302, 1995.

El-Swaify, S. A., and D. Yakowitz. Multiple objective decision making for land, water and environmental management. *Proceedings of the 1st International Conference on MODSS.* 1:3–7, 1998.

Evensen, C. I. Cover crops for coffee orchards in Hawaii. *Proceedings of the 2nd Annual Meeting of the Hawaiian Coffee Association,* July 25–26, 1997.

Evensen, C. I. Natural resources conservation programs in Hawaii. *Hawaiian Agriculture Environ. Quality Newsletter* 6:147, 1998.

Evensen, C. I., R. V. Osgood, and **S. A. El-Swaify.** Small grain cover crops in Hawaii for erosion and weed control. *J. Soil Water Conservation* 53(3):292, 1998.

Wan, Y., R. A. Fox, and **C. I. Evensen.** Phosphorus sorption by marine sediments and soils in Pearl Harbor basin, Hawaii. *J. Soil Water Conservation* 53(2):183, 1998.

Herbert, D. A., **J. H. Fownes,** and P. M. Vitousek. Hurricane damage to a Hawaiian forest: Nutrient supply rate affects resistance and resilience. *Ecology* 80(3):908–20, 1999.

Gautz, L. D., and C. Wong. Device for opening and closing magenta vessels for micropropagation. *HortTechnology* 3(3):340–2, 1993.

Goff, M. L., and B. H. Win. Estimation of postmortem interval based on colony development time for *Anoplolepsis longipes* (Hymenoptera: Formicidae). *J. Forensic Sci.* 42:1176–9, 1997.

Malla, P. B., and **C. Gopalakrishnan.** Residential water demand in a fast-growing metropolis: The case of Honolulu, Hawaii. *Int. J. Water Res. Dev.* 13(1):35–51, 1997.

Grace, J. K., D. M. Ewart, and C. H. M. Tome. Termite resistance of wood species grown in Hawaii. *Forest Prod. J.* 46(10):57–60, 1996.

Shelton, T. G., and **J. K. Grace.** Suggestion of an environmental influence on intercolony agonism of Formosan subterranean termites *(Isoptera: Rhinotermitidae). Environ. Entomol.* 26:632–7, 1997.

Habte, M., and B. N. Byappanahalli. Influence of pre-storage drying conditions and duration of storage on the effectiveness of root innoculum of glomus aggregation. *J. Plant Nutr.* 21:1375–89, 1998.

Hu, J. S., D. M. Sether, X. P. Liu, M. Wang, F. Zee, and D. E. Ullman. Use of a tissue blotting immunoassay to examine the distribution of pineapple closterovirus in Hawaii. *Plant Disease* 81:1150–4, 1997.

Sether, D. M., D. E. Ullman, and **J. S. Hu.** Transmission of pineapple mealybug wilt-associated virus by two species of mealybugs *(Dysmicoccus spp.). Phytopathology* 88:1224–30, 1998.

Huang, A. S., and J. Hollyer. Manufacturing of acridity-free raw flour from Aracea tubers. U.S. Patent, 464,646, 1996.

Iwaoka, W. T., P. Britten, and F. M. Dong. The changing face of food science education. *Trends Food Sci. Technol.* 7:105–12, 1996.

Johnson, M. W., and B. E. Tabashnik. Enhanced biological control through pesticide selectivity. In *Handbook of Biological Control,* eds. T. W. Fisher, T. S. Bellows, L. E. Caltagirone, D. L. Dahlsten, C. Huffaker, and G. Gordh. Academic Press: in press.

Jones, R. C., C. J. Babcock, and W. B. Knowlton. Estimation of the total amorphous content of Hawaiian soils by the Rietveld method. *Soil Sci. Soc. Am. J.,* in press.

Jones, V. P., C. H. M. Tome, and L. C. Caprio. Life tables for the koa seedworm *(Lepidoptera: Tortricidae)* based on degree-day demography. *Environ. Entomol.* 26: 1291–8, 1997.

Kim, Y. H., and **Y. S. Kim.** Effects of active immunization against clenbuterol on the growth-promoting effect of clenbuterol in rats. *J. Anim. Sci.* 75:446–53, 1997.

Teng, H., **C. M. Kinoshita,** S. M. Masutani, and J. Zhou. Entropy generation in multicomponent reacting flows. *J. Energy Resources Tech.* 120:226–32, 1998.

Kinoshita, C. M., S. Q. Turn, R. P. Overend, and R. L. Bain. Power generation potential of biomass gasification systems, *J. Energy Eng.* 123(3):88–99, 1997.

Kuanprasert, N., **A. R. Kuehnle,** and **C. S. Tang.** Floral fragrance compounds of some Anthurium species and hybrids. *Phytochemistry* 49(2):521–8, 1998.

Wang, K. H., **A. R. Kuehnle,** and **B. S. Sipes.** In vitro screening for burrowing nematode, *Radopholus citrophilus,* tolerance and resistance in commercial Anthurium hybrids. *In Vitro Cell Dev. Biol.* 33:205–8, 1997.

Weems, Y. S., et al. **(B. R. LeaMaster, D. L. Vincent,** and **C. W. Weems).** PGE1 or PGE2 not LH regulates section of progesterone in vitro by the 88–90 day ovine corpus luteum of pregnancy. *Prostaglandins* 53:337–53, 1997.

LeaMaster, B. R., W. A. Walsh, **J. A. Brock,** and R. S. Fujioka. Cold

University of Hawaii at Manoa

Selected Publications (continued)

stress induced changes in the aerobic heterotrophic gastrointestinal tract bacterial flora of red tilapia. *J. Fish Biol.* 50:770–80, 1997.

Lee, C. N., T. Z. Huang, and A. B. Sagayaga. Conception rate in dairy cattle is affected by the number of semen straws thawed for breeding. *J. Dairy Sci.* 80(Suppl. 1):151, 1997.

Leung, P. S., and W. Miklius. Demand for nutrition vs. demand for tastes. *Appl. Econ. Lett.* 4(5):291–5, 1997.

Sharma, K. R., **P. S. Leung,** and **H. M. Zaleski.** Production economics of the swine industry in Hawaii. *Swine Health Prod.* 5:103–10, 1997.

Liang, T., P. N. Walker, and M. A. Khan. GIS technology applied to environmental control energy analysis: An example. *Comput. Electronics Agric.* 7:231–47, 1992.

Luis, S., **R. M. Manshardt,** et al. Pathogen-derived resistance provides papaya with effective protection against papaya ringspot virus. *Mol. Breeding* 3:161–8, 1997.

Messing, R. H., L. M. Klungness, and E. B. Jang. Effects of wind on movement of *Diachasmimorpha longicaudata,* a parasitoid of tephritid fruit flies, in a laboratory flight tunnel. *Entomologia Experimentalis et Applicata* 82:147–52, 1997.

Ma, Z. and **S. C. Miyasaka.** Oxalate exudation by taro in response to aluminum. *Plant Physiol.* 118:861–5, 1998.

Hill, S., R. Abaidoo, and **S. C. Miyasaka.** Effects of sodium chloride on early growth and nutrient accumulation in taro. *Horticultural Sci.* 33:1153–6, 1998.

Nishimoto, R. K., and L. B. McCarty. Fluctuating temperature and light influence seed germination of goosegrass *(Eleusine indica). Weed Sci.,* in press.

Novotny, R., J. S. Han, and I. Biernacke. Motivators and barriers to consuming calcium-rich foods among Asian adolescents in Hawaii. *J. Nutr. Educ.,* in press.

Novotny, R., J. Davis, P. Ross, and R. D. Wasnich. Adiposity and blood pressure in a multiethnic population of women in Hawaii. *Ethnicity Health* 3(3):167–71, 1998.

Novotny, R., J. Davis, P. Ross, and R. D. Wasnich. Adolescent milk consumption, menarche, birth weight and ethnicity influence height of women in Hawaii. *J. Am. Dietet. Assoc.* 96(8):802–4, 1996.

Su, W. W., B. J. He, H. Liang, and **S. M. Sun.** A perfusion air-lift bioreactor for high density plant cell cultivation and secreted protein production. *J. Biotechnol.* 50:225–33, 1996.

Uchida, J. Y. Diseases of orchids in Hawaii. *Plant Disease* 78:220–4, 1994.

Ogoshi, R. M., G. Y. Tsuji, **G. Uehara,** and N.P. Kefford. Simulation of best management practices of soy bean production. *Soil and Crop Manage.* 2:1998.

Valenzuela, H. R., B. Kratky, and **J. Cho.** Lettuce production guidelines for Hawaii. *CTAHR Res. Ext. Ser.* 164, 1996.

Vieth, G. R., and P. Suppapanya. An evaluation of selected decision models: A case of crop choice in Northern Thailand. *J. Agric. Appl. Econ.* 28(2):381–91, 1996.

Meenan, R. T., et al. **(T. M. Vogt).** Cost effectiveness of a hospital-based smoking-cessation program. *Med. Care* 36:670–8, 1998.

Vogt, T. M., et al. The medical care system and prevention: The need for a new paradigm. *HMO Pract.* 12:5–13, 1998.

Wang, J. K. A systematic approach to physical aquaculture water management. *Bull. Natl. Inst. Aquacult. Suppl.* 1:89–96, 1994.

Weems, Y. S., et al. **(C. W. Weems).** Effect of luteinizing hormone (LH), PGE2, 8-Epi-PGE1, 8-Epi-PGE2, trichosantin, and pregnancy specific protein B (PSPB) on secretion of progesterone in vitro by corpora lutea (CL) from nonpregnant and pregnant cows. *Prostaglandins* 55:27–42, 1998.

Weems, Y. S., et al. **(C. W. Weems).** Effect of luteinizing hormone (LH), PGE2, 8-Epi-PGE1, 8-Epi-PGE2, trichosantin and pregnancy specific protein B (PSPB), on secretion of prostaglandin (PG) E (PGE) of F2a (PGF2A) in vitro by corpora lutea (CL) from nonpregnant and pregnant cows. *Prostaglandins* 55:359–76, 1998.

Wu, I. P. An assessment of hydraulic design of micro-irrigation systems. *Agric. Water Manage.* 32:275–84, 1997.

Bugos, R. C., A. D. Hieber, and **H. Y. Yamamoto.** Xanthophyll-cycle enzymes are members of the lipocalin family, the first identified from plants. *J. Biol. Chem.* 273:15321–4, 1998.

Bugos, R. C., and **H. Y. Yamamoto.** Molecular cloning of violaxanthin de-epoxidase from romaine lettuce and expression in *Escherichia coli. Proc. Natl. Acad. Sci. U.S.A.* 93:6320–5, 1996.

Monhanty, N., and **H. Y. Yamamoto.** Induction of two types of non-photochemical chlorophyll fluorescence quenching in carbon-assimilating intact spinach chloroplasts: The effects of ascorbate, de-epoxidation and dibucaine. *Plant Sci.* 115:267–75, 1996.

Yanagida, J. F., and X. Tian. An empirical analysis of competitive advantage in rice and wheat for selected Asia-Pacific countries. *Asian Econ. Rev.* 38(3):451–66, 1996.

Zhou, D., **J. F. Yanagida, U. Chakravorty,** and **P. S. Leung.** Estimating economic impacts from tourism: CGE and IO techniques. *Ann. Tourism Res.* 24(1):76–89, 1996.

Yang, P. Y., Z. Q. Zhang, and B. G. Jeong. Simultaneous removal of carbon and nitrogen using an entrapped-mixed-microbial-cell process. *Water Res.* 31(10):2617–25, 1997.

Academic and Professional Programs in the Environment and Natural Resources

This part of Book 4 consists of two sections covering the environment and natural resources. Each section has a table of contents (listing the program directories, announcements, and in-depth descriptions); program directories, which consist of brief profiles of the programs in the relevant fields (and 50-word or 100-word announcements following the profiles, if the programs have chosen to include them); Cross-Discipline Announcements, if any programs have chosen to submit such entries; and in-depth descriptions, which are more individualized statements, if programs have chosen to submit them.

Section 9
Environmental Sciences and Management

This section contains a directory of institutions offering graduate work in environmental sciences and management, followed by in-depth entries submitted by institutions that chose to prepare detailed program descriptions. Additional information about programs listed in the directory but not augmented by an in-depth entry may be obtained by writing directly to the dean of a graduate school or chair of a department at the address given in the directory.

For programs offering related work, see also in this book Natural Resources; in Book 2, see Political Science and International Affairs and Public, Regional, and Industrial Affairs; in Book 3, see Ecology, Environmental Biology, and Evolutionary Biology; and in Book 5, see Management of Engineering and Technology.

CONTENTS

Environmental Policy and Resource Management

Adelphi University, Graduate School of Arts and Sciences, Department of Earth Sciences, Garden City, NY 11530. Offers earth sciences (MS); environmental management (Certificate). Part-time and evening/weekend programs available. *Degree requirements:* For master's, computer language required, thesis optional, foreign language not required. *Application deadline:* Applications are processed on a rolling basis. Application fee: $50. *Unit head:* Dr. Anthony Cok, Chairperson, 516-877-4170.

Air Force Institute of Technology, School of Engineering, Department of Engineering and Environmental Management, Wright-Patterson AFB, OH 45433-7765. Offers MS. Part-time programs available. *Faculty:* 7 full-time (0 women). *Students:* 35 full-time, 1 part-time. *Degree requirements:* For master's, thesis required, foreign language not required. *Entrance requirements:* For master's, GRE General Test (minimum score of 500 on verbal section, 600 on quantitative required), minimum GPA of 3.0, must be military officer or U.S. citizen. *Average time to degree:* Master's–1.5 years full-time. Application fee: $0. *Faculty research:* Groundwater contaminant modeling/remediation, system dynamics modeling, landfill performance. *Unit head:* Lt. Col. Steven T. Lofgren, Head, 937-255-2998, E-mail: slofgren@afit.af.mil.

American University, College of Arts and Sciences, Department of Biology, Environmental Studies Program, Washington, DC 20016-8001. Offers MA, MS. *Faculty:* 8 full-time (3 women). *Students:* 7 full-time (6 women), 1 part-time; includes 2 minority (both African Americans), 2 international. 11 applicants, 82% accepted. In 1998, 5 degrees awarded. *Degree requirements:* For master's, comprehensive written exam, tool of research exam required. *Entrance requirements:* For master's, GRE General Test, GRE Subject Test, TOEFL, minimum GPA of 3.0. *Application deadline:* For fall admission, 2/1; for spring admission, 10/1. Application fee: $50. *Financial aid:* Application deadline: 2/1. *Unit head:* Dr. Daniel Fong, Chair, Department of Biology, 202-885-2178.

See in-depth description on page 887.

American University, School of International Service, Washington, DC 20016-8001. Offers comparative and regional studies (MA); development management (MS); environmental policy (MA); international communication (MA); international development (MA); international development management (Certificate); international economic policy (MA); international peace and conflict resolution (MA); international politics (MA); international relations (PhD); U.S. foreign policy (MA). Part-time and evening/weekend programs available. *Faculty:* 50 full-time (17 women), 9 part-time (3 women). *Students:* 328 full-time (201 women), 281 part-time (158 women); includes 127 minority (46 African Americans, 40 Asian Americans or Pacific Islanders, 41 Hispanic Americans), 118 international. Terminal master's awarded for partial completion of doctoral program. *Degree requirements:* For master's, one foreign language, computer language, thesis or alternative, comprehensive exam required; for doctorate, one foreign language, computer language, dissertation, comprehensive exams required. *Entrance requirements:* For master's and doctorate, GRE General Test, TOEFL (minimum score of 600 required), 24 credits in related social sciences. *Application deadline:* For fall admission, 1/15 (priority date); for spring admission, 10/1 (priority date). Applications are processed on a rolling basis. Application fee: $50. *Unit head:* Dr. Louis W. Goodman, Dean, 202-885-1603. *Application contact:* Graduate Office, 202-885-1690.

Antioch New England Graduate School, Graduate School, Department of Environmental Studies, Program in Resource Management and Administration, Keene, NH 03431-3516. Offers MS. *Faculty:* 3 full-time (1 woman), 22 part-time (8 women). *Students:* 30 full-time (11 women), 9 part-time (4 women). Average age 31. 22 applicants, 64% accepted. In 1998, 18 degrees awarded. *Degree requirements:* For master's, practicum required, thesis optional, foreign language not required. *Entrance requirements:* For master's, interview, previous undergraduate course work in science. *Application deadline:* For fall admission, 8/1; for spring admission, 12/1. Applications are processed on a rolling basis. Application fee: $40. Tuition: Full-time $12,600. Full-time tuition and fees vary according to course load, degree level, program and student level. *Financial aid:* In 1998–99, 25 students received aid, including 3 fellowships (averaging $1,000 per year), 2 teaching assistantships (averaging $1,600 per year); career-related internships or fieldwork and Federal Work-Study also available. Financial aid applicants required to submit FAFSA. *Faculty research:* Waste management, land use. *Unit head:* Michael Simpson, Director, 603-357-3122 Ext. 252, Fax: 603-357-0718, E-mail: msimpson@antiochne.edu. *Application contact:* Robbie P. Hertneky, Director of Admissions, 603-357-6265, Fax: 603-357-0718, E-mail: rhertneky@antiochne.edu.

Announcement: The Resource Management and Administration Program provides practice-oriented training in environmental policy, science, and organizational management. The program prepares individuals for leadership in organizations that manage, conserve, and restore natural systems and trains professionals to understand the substance of environmental issues while working effectively to implement change within organizational settings.

Antioch University Seattle, Graduate Programs, Program in Management, Program in Environment and Community, Seattle, WA 98121-1814. Offers MS. Evening/weekend programs available. *Application deadline:* For fall admission, 8/15; for spring admission, 2/3. Applications are processed on a rolling basis. Application fee: $50. *Financial aid:* Application deadline: 6/15. *Unit head:* Graduate Studies Adviser, 202-885-2766. *Application contact:* Steve Bangs, Director of Admissions and Enrollment Services, 206-441-5352 Ext. 5200.

Bard College, Graduate School of Environmental Studies, Annandale-on-Hudson, NY 12504. Offers MSES. Offered during summer only. *Faculty:* 5 full-time (2 women), 9 part-time (1 woman). *Students:* 45 full-time (21 women); includes 5 minority (2 Asian Americans or Pacific Islanders, 1 Hispanic American, 2 Native Americans), 1 international. Average age 30. 40 applicants, 48% accepted. In 1998, 7 degrees awarded. *Degree requirements:* For master's, thesis required, foreign language not required. *Entrance requirements:* For master's, resumé, interview, published materials. *Average time to degree:* Master's–4 years full-time. *Application deadline:* For fall admission, 2/1 (priority date). Applications are processed on a rolling basis. Application fee: $45. *Financial aid:* Fellowships, career-related internships or fieldwork and scholarships available. Financial aid application deadline: 3/1; financial aid applicants required to submit FAFSA. *Faculty research:* Environmental ethics, environmental economics, environmental impact assessment, cultural ecology, wetland ecology and management. *Unit head:* Joanne Fox-Przeworski, Director, 914-758-7067, Fax: 914-758-7636, E-mail: jfp@bard.edu. *Application contact:* Gloria Cestero-Hurd, Coordinator, 914-758-7073, Fax: 914-758-7636, E-mail: gch@bard.edu.

Baylor University, Graduate School, College of Arts and Sciences, Department of Environmental Studies, Waco, TX 76798. Offers MES, MS. *Students:* 15 full-time (7 women), 2 part-time (1 woman), 4 international. In 1998, 7 degrees awarded. *Degree requirements:* For master's, thesis required, foreign language not required. *Entrance requirements:* For master's, GRE General Test, minimum GPA of 3.0 in major, 2.7 overall. *Application deadline:* For fall admission, 8/1 (priority date); for spring admission, 1/1. Applications are processed on a rolling basis. Application fee: $25. *Financial aid:* Research assistantships, teaching assistantships, career-related internships or fieldwork, Federal Work-Study, and institutionally-sponsored loans available. *Faculty research:* Renewable energy/waste management policies, Third World environmental problem solving, ecotourism. *Unit head:* Dr. Dudley J. Burton, Chair, 254-710-3405, Fax: 254-710-3409, E-mail: dudley_burton@baylor.edu. *Application contact:* Suzanne Keener, Administrative Assistant, 254-710-3588, Fax: 254-710-3870, E-mail: suzanne_keener@baylor.edu.

Bemidji State University, Graduate Studies, Division of Social and Natural Sciences, Center for Environmental Studies, Bemidji, MN 56601-2699. Offers MS. Part-time programs available. *Faculty:* 3 part-time (0 women). *Students:* 4 full-time (2 women), 12 part-time (2 women). Average age 28. In 1998, 1 degree awarded. *Degree requirements:* For master's, thesis or alternative required, thesis or alternative required. *Entrance requirements:* For master's, GRE General Test (minimum combined score of 1410 on three sections required). *Application deadline:* For fall admission, 5/1. Application fee: $20. *Financial aid:* In 1998–99, 1 research assistantship with partial tuition reimbursement (averaging $5,500 per year) was awarded.; career-related internships or fieldwork and Federal Work-Study also available. Aid available to part-time students. Financial aid application deadline: 5/1. *Unit head:* Dr. Steven Spigarelli, Director, 218-755-2910, Fax: 218-755-4107, E-mail: saspigarelli@vax1.bemidji.msus.edu. *Application contact:* Dr. Steven Spigarelli, Director, 218-755-2910, Fax: 218-755-4107, E-mail: saspigarelli@vax1.bemidji.msus.edu.

Boise State University, Graduate College, College of Social Science and Public Affairs, Program in Public Policy and Administration, Boise, ID 83725. Offers environmental and natural resources policy and administration (MPA); general public administration (MPA); state and local government policy and administration (MPA). *Accreditation:* NASPAA. Part-time programs available. *Faculty:* 9 full-time (1 woman), 8 part-time (2 women). *Students:* 17 full-time (8 women), 35 part-time (17 women). *Degree requirements:* For master's, directed research project, internship, oral and written comprehensive exam required, thesis not required. *Entrance requirements:* For master's, GRE General Test (minimum combined score of 1000 required), TOEFL (minimum score of 550 required), minimum GPA of 3.0. *Application deadline:* For fall admission, 7/23 (priority date); for spring admission, 11/24. Applications are processed on a rolling basis. Application fee: $20 ($30 for international students). Electronic applications accepted. *Unit head:* Dr. James D. Weatherby, Chair, 208-426-1476, Fax: 208-426-4370, E-mail: bmeyer@boisestate.edu.

Boston University, Graduate School of Arts and Sciences, Department of International Relations, Boston, MA 02215. Offers African studies (Certificate); international relations (MA); international relations and communication (MA); international relations and resource and environmental management (MA). *Faculty:* 18 full-time (1 woman), 2 part-time (0 women). *Students:* 49 full-time (31 women), 11 part-time (5 women); includes 4 minority (2 Asian Americans or Pacific Islanders, 1 Hispanic American, 1 Native American), 22 international. *Degree requirements:* For master's, one foreign language, thesis, comprehensive exam required. *Entrance requirements:* For master's, GRE General Test, TOEFL (minimum score of 600 required); for Certificate, GRE General Test, TOEFL (minimum score of 550 required). *Application deadline:* For fall admission, 4/15; for spring admission, 10/15. Applications are processed on a rolling basis. Application fee: $50. Tuition: Full-time $23,770; part-time $743 per credit. Required fees: $220. Tuition and fees vary according to class time, course level, campus/location and program. *Unit head:* Dr. Erik Goldstein, Chairman, 617-353-9280, Fax: 617-353-9290, E-mail: goldstee@bu.edu. *Application contact:* Graduate Program Administrator.

Boston University, Graduate School of Arts and Sciences, Program in Energy and Environmental Studies, Boston, MA 02215. Offers energy and environmental analysis (MA); environmental remote sensing and geographic information systems (MA); international relations and resource and environmental management (MA); resource science (MA). Part-time programs available. *Faculty:* 9 full-time (1 woman), 1 part-time (0 women). *Students:* 9 full-time (7 women), 2 part-time (1 woman), 4 international. Average age 27. 106 applicants, 58% accepted. In 1998, 15 degrees awarded. *Degree requirements:* For master's, one foreign language, research paper required. *Entrance requirements:* For master's, GRE General Test, TOEFL (minimum score of 550 required). *Application deadline:* For fall admission, 7/1; for spring admission, 11/15. Applications are processed on a rolling basis. Application fee: $50. Tuition: Full-time $23,770; part-time $743 per credit. Required fees: $220. Tuition and fees vary according to class time, course level, campus/location and program. *Financial aid:* In 1998–99, 5 students received aid, including 1 fellowship, 3 research assistantships; career-related internships or fieldwork and Federal Work-Study also available. Aid available to part-time students. Financial aid application deadline: 1/15; financial aid applicants required to submit FAFSA. *Faculty research:* Modeling and systems analysis, policy analysis and evaluation. *Unit head:* Cutler J. Cleveland, Director, 617-353-7552, Fax: 617-353-5986, E-mail: cutler@bu.edu. *Application contact:* Alo Roy, Administrative Assistant, 617-353-3083, Fax: 617-353-5986, E-mail: alpana@bu.edu.

Brown University, Graduate School, Center for Environmental Studies, Providence, RI 02912. Offers AM. Part-time programs available. *Faculty:* 5 full-time (1 woman), 2 part-time (both women). *Students:* 9 full-time (6 women), 12 part-time (7 women); includes 4 minority (1 African American, 3 Asian Americans or Pacific Islanders), 3 international. Average age 29. 43 applicants, 63% accepted. In 1998, 6 degrees awarded (66% found work related to degree, 17% continued full-time study). *Degree requirements:* For master's, thesis required, foreign language not required. *Entrance requirements:* For master's, GRE, writing sample. *Average time to degree:* Master's–2 years full-time, 3 years part-time. *Application deadline:* For fall admission, 1/2 (priority date). Applications are processed on a rolling basis. Application fee: $60. *Financial aid:* In 1998–99, 7 students received aid, including 2 teaching assistantships with full tuition reimbursements available (averaging $10,500 per year); career-related internships or fieldwork, Federal Work-Study, and tuition waivers (partial) also available. Financial aid application deadline: 1/2; financial aid applicants required to submit FAFSA. *Faculty research:* Solid waste management, risk management policy (environmental health), resource management policy (water/fisheries), climate change, acid rain. *Unit head:* Harold Ward, Director, 401-863-3449, Fax: 401-863-3503, E-mail: harold_ward@brown.edu. *Application contact:* Patricia-Ann Caton, Administrative Manager, 401-863-3449, Fax: 401-863-3503, E-mail: patti_caton@brown.edu.

California State University, Fullerton, Graduate Studies, School of Humanities and Social Sciences, Program in Environmental Studies, Fullerton, CA 92834-9480. Offers environmental education and communication (MS); environmental policy and planning (MS); environmental sciences (MS); technological studies (MS). Part-time programs available. *Students:* 2 full-time (1 woman), 102 part-time (53 women); includes 21 minority (1 African American, 11 Asian Americans or Pacific Islanders, 8 Hispanic Americans, 1 Native American), 11 international. Average age 33. 54 applicants, 70% accepted. In 1998, 35 degrees awarded. *Degree requirements:* For master's, thesis required, foreign language not required. *Entrance requirements:* For master's, minimum GPA of 2.5 in last 60 units. Application fee: $55. Tuition, nonresident: part-time $264 per unit. Required fees: $1,947; $1,281 per year. *Financial aid:* Career-related internships or fieldwork, Federal Work-Study, grants, and institutionally-sponsored loans available. Aid available to part-time students. Financial aid application deadline: 3/1. *Unit head:* Dr. Stewart Long, Acting Chair, 714-278-2228.

Carleton University, Faculty of Graduate Studies, Faculty of Arts and Social Sciences, Department of Geography and Environmental Studies, Ottawa, ON K1S 5B6, Canada. Offers MA, PhD. *Faculty:* 21 full-time (6 women). *Students:* 43 full-time (25 women), 18 part-time (3 women). Average age 33. In 1998, 17 master's, 1 doctorate awarded. *Degree requirements:* For master's, thesis, seminar required; for doctorate, dissertation, 2 comprehensive exams required. *Entrance requirements:* For master's, TOEFL (minimum score of 550 required), honors degree; for doctorate, TOEFL (minimum score of 550 required), master's degree in geography. *Average time to degree:* Master's–2.4 years full-time, 4.1 years part-time; doctorate–2.7 years full-time. *Application deadline:* For fall admission, 3/1 (priority date). Applications are processed on a rolling basis. Application fee: $35. *Financial aid:* Application deadline: 3/1. *Faculty research:* Geography of societal change (global political economy, environment, feminist geographies), geography of environmental change. Total annual research expenditures: $496,000. *Unit head:* J. Kenneth Torrance, Chair, 613-520-2561, Fax: 613-520-4301, E-mail: ken_torrance@carleton.ca. *Application contact:* Hazel Anderson, Graduate Secretary, 613-520-2561, Fax: 613-520-4301, E-mail: hazel_anderson@carleton.ca.

Central Washington University, Graduate Studies and Research, College of the Sciences, Program in Resource Management, Ellensburg, WA 98926. Offers MS. *Faculty:* 23 full-time (7 women). *Students:* 26 full-time (11 women), 12 part-time (7 women); includes 8 minority (1 Asian American or Pacific Islander, 1 Hispanic American, 6 Native Americans) 21 applicants, 76% accepted. In 1998, 7 degrees awarded. *Degree requirements:* For master's, thesis, internship required, foreign language not required. *Entrance requirements:* For master's, minimum GPA of 3.0. *Application deadline:* For fall admission, 4/1 (priority date); for spring admission, 1/1. Applications are processed on a rolling basis. Application fee: $35. Tuition, state resident: full-time $4,389; part-time $146 per credit. Tuition, nonresident: full-time $13,365; part-time $446 per credit. Tuition and fees vary according to course load. *Financial aid:* In 1998–99, 2 research assistantships with partial tuition reimbursements (averaging $6,470 per year), 7 teaching assistantships with partial tuition reimbursements (averaging $6,470 per year) were awarded.; career-related internships or fieldwork and Federal Work-Study also available. Financial aid application deadline: 2/15; financial aid applicants required to submit FAFSA. *Unit head:* Dr. Morris Uebelacker, Director, 509-963-1188. *Application contact:* Christie A. Fevergeon, Program Coordinator, Graduate Studies and Research, 509-963-3103, Fax: 509-963-1799, E-mail: masters@cwu.edu.

Clark University, Graduate School, Environmental Science and Policy Program, Worcester, MA 01610-1477. Offers MA. Part-time programs available. *Students:* 8 (6 women). In 1998, 4 degrees awarded. *Degree requirements:* For master's, thesis required. *Entrance requirements:* For master's, GRE General Test, TOEFL (minimum score of 575 required). *Application deadline:* For fall admission, 2/15. Application fee: $40. *Financial aid:* Fellowships, research assistantships, teaching assistantships, career-related internships or fieldwork available. *Faculty research:* Water resources, environmental management, natural and man-made hazards, health risks, public health policy, hazard management, energy and environmental systems analysis, technology and environmental assessment, global climate change. *Unit head:* Dr. Halina Brown, Director, 508-793-7655. *Application contact:* Marcia V. Szugda, Administrative Assistant, 508-793-7655, Fax: 508-793-8861.

College of the Atlantic, Program in Human Ecology, Bar Harbor, ME 04609-1198. Offers M Phil. *Degree requirements:* For master's, thesis required, foreign language not required. *Faculty research:* Conservation of endangered species, public policy/community planning, environmental education, history, philosophy.

Colorado State University, Graduate School, College of Natural Resources, Department of Natural Resource Recreation and Tourism, Fort Collins, CO 80523-0015. Offers commercial recreation and tourism (MS); human dimensions in natural resources (PhD); recreation resource management (MS, PhD); resource interpretation (MS). *Faculty:* 7 full-time (2 women). *Students:* 43; includes 4 minority (3 Asian Americans or Pacific Islanders, 1 Hispanic American), 4 international. Average age 34. 76 applicants, 22% accepted. In 1998, 6 master's, 2 doctorates awarded. *Degree requirements:* For master's, thesis or alternative required, foreign language not required; for doctorate, dissertation required, dissertation required. *Entrance requirements:* For master's, GRE General Test (minimum combined score of 1000 required), TOEFL (minimum score of 550 required), minimum GPA of 3.0; for doctorate, GRE General Test (minimum combined score of 1000 required), TOEFL, minimum GPA of 3.0. *Application deadline:* For fall admission, 2/1 (priority date). Applications are processed on a rolling basis. Application fee: $30. Electronic applications accepted. *Financial aid:* In 1998–99, 5 research assistantships, 8 teaching assistantships were awarded.; fellowships, career-related internships or fieldwork, Federal Work-Study, and traineeships also available. Aid available to part-time students. Financial aid application deadline: 2/1; financial aid applicants required to submit FAFSA. *Faculty research:* International tourism, wilderness preservation, resource interpretation, human dimensions in natural resources, protected areas management. Total annual research expenditures: $600,000. *Unit head:* Michael J. Manfredo, Chair, 970-491-6591, Fax: 970-491-2255. *Application contact:* Jerry Vaske, Graduate Program Administrator, 970-491-2360, Fax: 970-491-2255, E-mail: jerryv@cnr.colostate.edu.

Cornell University, Graduate School, Graduate Fields of Agriculture and Life Sciences, Field of Natural Resources, Ithaca, NY 14853-0001. Offers aquatic science (MPS, MS, PhD); environmental management (MPS); fishery science (MPS, MS, PhD); forest science (MPS, MS, PhD); resource policy and management (MPS, MS, PhD); wildlife science (MPS, MS, PhD). *Faculty:* 24 full-time. *Students:* 58 full-time (24 women); includes 5 minority (1 African American, 1 Asian American or Pacific Islander, 2 Hispanic Americans, 1 Native American), 11 international. Terminal master's awarded for partial completion of doctoral program. *Degree requirements:* For master's, thesis (MS), project paper (MPS) required; for doctorate, dissertation required, foreign language not required. *Entrance requirements:* For master's and doctorate, GRE General Test, TOEFL (minimum score of 550 required). *Application deadline:* Applications are processed on a rolling basis. Application fee: $65. Electronic applications accepted. *Unit head:* Director of Graduate Studies, 607-255-2807, Fax: 607-255-0349. *Application contact:* Graduate Field Assistant, 607-255-2807, E-mail: nrgrad@cornell.edu.

Dalhousie University, Faculty of Graduate Studies, Faculty of Management, School for Resource and Environmental Studies, Halifax, NS B3H 3J5, Canada. Offers MES. Part-time programs available. *Faculty:* 5 full-time, 25 part-time. *Students:* 44 full-time (33 women), 8 part-time (4 women), 2 international. Average age 25. 70 applicants, 50% accepted. In 1998, 15 degrees awarded. *Degree requirements:* For master's, thesis required, foreign language not required. *Entrance requirements:* For master's, TOEFL (minimum score of 580 required), honors degree. *Application deadline:* For fall admission, 2/15. Applications are processed on a rolling basis. Application fee: $55. *Financial aid:* In 1998–99, 15 fellowships (averaging $9,000 per year), 5 teaching assistantships were awarded. Financial aid application deadline: 2/1. *Faculty research:* Resource management and ecology, aboriginal resource rights, management of toxic substances, environmental impact assessment, forest management, policy, coastal zone management. *Unit head:* Dr. Peter Duinker, Director, 902-494-7100, Fax: 902-494-3728, E-mail: peter.duinker@dal.ca. *Application contact:* Dr. Karen Beazley, Graduate Coordinator, 902-494-3632, Fax: 902-494-3728, E-mail: karen.beazley@dal.ca.

Duke University, Graduate School, Department of Environment, Durham, NC 27708-0586. Offers natural resource economics/policy (AM, PhD); natural resource science/ecology (AM, PhD); natural resource systems science (AM, PhD). Part-time programs available. *Faculty:* 39 full-time, 14 part-time. *Students:* 69 full-time, 1 part-time; includes 5 minority (3 African Americans, 1 Asian American or Pacific Islander, 1 Hispanic American), 17 international. Terminal master's awarded for partial completion of doctoral program. *Degree requirements:* For doctorate, dissertation required, foreign language not required. *Entrance requirements:* For master's and doctorate, GRE General Test. *Application deadline:* For fall admission, 12/31. Application fee: $75. *Unit head:* Kenneth Knoerr, Director of Graduate Studies, 919-613-8002, Fax: 919-684-8741, E-mail: nettleto@acpub.duke.edu.

Duke University, Nicholas School of the Environment, Durham, NC 27708-0328. Offers coastal environmental management (MEM); environmental science and policy (PhD); environmental toxicology, chemistry, and risk assessment (MEM); forest resource management (MF); resource ecology (MEM); resource economics and policy (MEM); water and air resources (MEM). PhD offered through the Graduate School. *Accreditation:* SAF (one or more programs are accredited). Part-time programs available. *Faculty:* 61 full-time (10 women), 23 part-time (3 women). *Students:* 228 full-time (136 women); includes 7 minority (2 African Americans, 4 Asian Americans or Pacific Islanders, 1 Hispanic American), 24 international. Average age 25. 400 applicants, 63% accepted. In 1998, 116 master's, 10 doctorates awarded. Terminal master's awarded for partial completion of doctoral program. *Degree requirements:* For master's, thesis required (for some programs), foreign language not required; for doctor-

ate, dissertation required, foreign language not required. *Entrance requirements:* For master's, GRE General Test, TOEFL, previous course work in biology or ecology, calculus, statistics, and microeconomics; computer familiarity with word processing and data analysis; for doctorate, GRE General Test, TOEFL. *Average time to degree:* Master's–2 years full-time, 3 years part-time; doctorate–5 years full-time, 8 years part-time. *Application deadline:* For fall admission, 2/1; for spring admission, 10/15. Applications are processed on a rolling basis. Application fee: $75. *Financial aid:* In 1998–99, 29 fellowships (averaging $11,500 per year), 53 research assistantships (averaging $2,600 per year), 15 teaching assistantships (averaging $6,000 per year) were awarded.; career-related internships or fieldwork, Federal Work-Study, institutionally-sponsored loans, scholarships, and unspecified assistantships also available. Financial aid application deadline: 2/1; financial aid applicants required to submit FAFSA. *Faculty research:* Ecosystem management, conservation ecology, earth systems, risk assessment. *Unit head:* Dr. Norman L. Christensen, Dean, 919-613-8004, Fax: 919-684-8741. *Application contact:* Bertie S. Belvin, Associate Dean for Academic Services, 919-613-8070, Fax: 919-684-8741, E-mail: envadm@duke.edu.

Announcement: Interdisciplinary focus of Resource Economics and Policy Program provides excellent background for careers with a broad spectrum of employers. Opportunities for specialization in environmental management, forestry, international development, coastal and marine resources, water and air resources, environmental health. Concurrent degrees available: MBA, JD in environmental law, AM in public policy, MA in Teaching. Fellowships for qualified students. See in-depth description in the Natural Resources section of this volume.

Duquesne University, Bayer School of Natural and Environmental Sciences, Environmental Science and Management Program, Pittsburgh, PA 15282-0001. Offers environmental management (Certificate); environmental science (Certificate); environmental science and management (MS). Part-time and evening/weekend programs available. Postbaccalaureate distance learning degree programs offered (no on-campus study). *Faculty:* 6 full-time (1 woman), 20 part-time (3 women). *Students:* 32 full-time (19 women), 70 part-time (26 women); includes 3 minority (2 African Americans, 1 Asian American or Pacific Islander), 4 international. Average age 31. 73 applicants, 84% accepted. In 1998, 26 degrees awarded (85% found work related to degree, 15% continued full-time study). *Degree requirements:* For master's, thesis or internship required. *Entrance requirements:* For master's, GRE General Test, TOEFL, previous course work in chemistry, biology, calculus, statistics. *Average time to degree:* Master's–2 years full-time, 3.25 years part-time. *Application deadline:* For fall admission, 4/1 (priority date); for spring admission, 10/1 (priority date). Applications are processed on a rolling basis. Application fee: $40. Tuition: Part-time $511 per credit. Required fees: $46 per credit. $50 per year. One-time fee: $125 part-time. Tuition and fees vary according to program. *Financial aid:* In 1998–99, 1 fellowship with tuition reimbursement (averaging $13,500 per year) was awarded.; career-related internships or fieldwork, scholarships, and tuition waivers (partial) also available. Financial aid application deadline: 5/15; financial aid applicants required to submit FAFSA. *Faculty research:* Sustainable development, environmental analytical chemistry, environmental ecology, environmental microbiology, environmental management systems. Total annual research expenditures: $170,000. *Unit head:* Dr. Daniel Donnelly, Director, 412-396-4367, Fax: 412-396-4881. *Application contact:* Amy Johnson, Assistant to the Dean, Graduate Student Administrator, 412-396-6339, Fax: 412-396-4881, E-mail: gradinfo@duq.edu.

See in-depth description on page 889.

The Evergreen State College, Graduate Programs, Program in Environmental Studies, Olympia, WA 98505. Offers MES. Part-time and evening/weekend programs available. *Faculty:* 6 full-time (2 women), 5 part-time (3 women). *Students:* 99 (54 women); includes 7 minority (1 African American, 2 Asian Americans or Pacific Islanders, 2 Hispanic Americans, 2 Native Americans) 3 international. Average age 42. 72 applicants, 70% accepted. In 1998, 28 degrees awarded (100% found work related to degree). *Degree requirements:* For master's, thesis required, foreign language not required. *Entrance requirements:* For master's, GRE, minimum undergraduate GPA of 3.0; BA/BS major in biological, physical, or social science. *Average time to degree:* Master's–2 years full-time, 3 years part-time. *Application deadline:* For fall admission, 2/15 (priority date). Applications are processed on a rolling basis. Application fee: $35. *Financial aid:* In 1998–99, 25 students received aid, including 12 fellowships (averaging $1,500 per year), 4 research assistantships (averaging $1,000 per year); Federal Work-Study, institutionally-sponsored loans, tuition waivers (partial), and unspecified assistantships also available. Aid available to part-time students. Financial aid application deadline: 2/15; financial aid applicants required to submit FAFSA. *Faculty research:* Land and water policy, sustainability, international-domestic relations, canopy studies. *Unit head:* Dr. John Perkins, Director, 360-866-6000 Ext. 6503, Fax: 360-866-6794, E-mail: perkinsj@elwha.evergreen.edu. *Application contact:* Bonita Evans, Coordinator, 360-866-6000 Ext. 6707, Fax: 360-866-6794, E-mail: evansb@evergreen.edu.

See in-depth description on page 893.

Fairleigh Dickinson University, Teaneck–Hackensack Campus, University College: Arts, Sciences, and Professional Studies, Department of Systems Science, Teaneck, NJ 07666-1914. Offers computer engineering (MS); environmental studies (MS). *Degree requirements:* For master's, foreign language and thesis not required. *Entrance requirements:* For master's, GRE General Test.

Florida Institute of Technology, Graduate School, College of Engineering, Division of Marine and Environmental Systems, Program in Environmental Resource Management, Melbourne, FL 32901-6975. Offers MS. Part-time programs available. *Students:* 3 full-time (1 woman), 8 part-time (7 women); includes 2 minority (both Hispanic Americans), 1 international. Average age 25. 16 applicants, 81% accepted. In 1998, 4 degrees awarded. *Degree requirements:* For master's, internship required, foreign language and thesis not required. *Entrance requirements:* For master's, GRE General Test (minimum combined score of 1050 required; average 1250), minimum GPA of 3.0. *Application deadline:* Applications are processed on a rolling basis. Application fee: $50. Electronic applications accepted. Tuition: Part-time $575 per credit hour. Required fees: $100. Tuition and fees vary according to campus/location and program. *Financial aid:* Research assistantships, teaching assistantships, career-related internships or fieldwork and tuition remissions available. Financial aid application deadline: 3/1; financial aid applicants required to submit FAFSA. *Faculty research:* Coastal management issues, environmental policy, land use, impacts of growth, managing aquatic resources. *Unit head:* Bjorn Lamborn, Graduate Coordinator, 561-297-3304, Fax: 561-297-2662, E-mail: lamborn@acc.fau.edu. *Application contact:* Carolyn P. Farrior, Associate Dean of Graduate Admissions, 407-674-7118, Fax: 407-723-9468, E-mail: cfarrior@fit.edu.

Florida International University, College of Arts and Sciences, Department of Environmental Studies, Miami, FL 33199. Offers biological management (MS); energy (MS); pollution (MS). *Faculty:* 5 full-time (1 woman), 4 part-time (0 women). *Students:* 9 full-time (5 women), 16 part-time (7 women); includes 7 minority (1 African American, 1 Asian American or Pacific Islander, 5 Hispanic Americans), 4 international. Average age 32. 23 applicants, 43% accepted. *Degree requirements:* For master's, thesis required. *Entrance requirements:* For master's, GRE General Test (minimum combined score of 1000 required), TOEFL (minimum score of 500 required), minimum GPA of 3.0. *Application deadline:* For fall admission, 4/1; for spring admission, 10/30. Application fee: $20. Tuition, state resident: part-time $145 per credit hour. Tuition, nonresident: part-time $506 per credit hour. Required fees: $158; $158 per year. *Financial aid:* Research assistantships, teaching assistantships available. Financial aid application deadline: 4/1. *Unit head:* Dr. David Bray, Chairperson, 305-348-1930, Fax: 305-348-3137, E-mail: brayd@fiu.edu.

Friends University, Graduate Programs, College of Arts and Sciences, Program in Environmental Studies, Wichita, KS 67213. Offers MSES. Evening/weekend programs available. *Faculty:* 9. *Students:* 13. *Degree requirements:* Foreign language not required. *Application deadline:* Applications are processed on a rolling basis. Application fee: $45. *Unit head:*

Environmental Policy and Resource Management

Friends University (continued)
Dr. Alan Maccarone, Director, 800-794-6945 Ext. 5890. *Application contact:* Director of Graduate Admissions, 800-794-6945 Ext. 5583.

George Mason University, College of Arts and Sciences, Department of Biology, Master's Program in Biology, Fairfax, VA 22030-4444. Offers bioinformatics (MS); ecology, systematics and evolution (MS); environmental science and public policy (MS); interpretive biology (MS); molecular, microbial, and cellular biology (MS); organismal biology (MS). Part-time programs available. *Faculty:* 32 full-time (11 women), 26 part-time (16 women). *Students:* 1 full-time (0 women), 63 part-time (34 women); includes 6 minority (4 African Americans, 1 Asian American or Pacific Islander, 1 Hispanic American), 2 international. *Degree requirements:* For master's, thesis or alternative required, foreign language not required. *Entrance requirements:* For master's, GRE General Test (minimum combined score of 1100 required), GRE Subject Test, bachelor's degree in biology or equivalent. *Application deadline:* For fall admission, 5/1; for spring admission, 11/1. Application fee: $30. Electronic applications accepted. Tuition, state resident: full-time $4,416; part-time $184 per credit hour. Tuition, nonresident: full-time $12,516; part-time $522 per credit hour. Tuition and fees vary according to program. *Unit head:* Dr. George E. Andrykovitch, Director, 703-993-1027, Fax: 703-993-1046.

George Mason University, College of Arts and Sciences, Department of Biology, Program in Environmental Science and Public Policy, Fairfax, VA 22030-4444. Offers PhD. Part-time programs available. *Faculty:* 32 full-time (11 women), 26 part-time (16 women). *Students:* 10 full-time (3 women), 93 part-time (49 women); includes 11 minority (4 African Americans, 3 Asian Americans or Pacific Islanders, 4 Hispanic Americans), 10 international. Average age 39. 33 applicants, 73% accepted. In 1998, 6 degrees awarded. *Degree requirements:* For doctorate, dissertation, internship required, foreign language not required. *Entrance requirements:* For doctorate, GRE General Test, GRE Subject Test. *Application deadline:* For fall admission, 5/1; for spring admission, 11/1. Application fee: $30. Electronic applications accepted. Tuition, state resident: full-time $4,416; part-time $184 per credit hour. Tuition, nonresident: full-time $12,516; part-time $522 per credit hour. Tuition and fees vary according to program. *Financial aid:* Fellowships, research assistantships, teaching assistantships available. Aid available to part-time students. Financial aid application deadline: 3/1; financial aid applicants required to submit FAFSA. *Unit head:* Dr. Robert Jonas, Director, 703-993-1030, Fax: 703-993-1046.

The George Washington University, Columbian School of Arts and Sciences, Interdisciplinary Programs in Public Policy, Program in Environmental and Resource Policy, Washington, DC 20052. Offers MA. *Students:* 8 full-time (3 women), 10 part-time (7 women), 6 international. Average age 26. 33 applicants, 79% accepted. In 1998, 9 degrees awarded. *Degree requirements:* For master's, comprehensive exam, project required, foreign language and thesis not required. *Entrance requirements:* For master's, GRE General Test, minimum GPA of 3.0. *Application deadline:* For fall admission, 6/15. Application fee: $55. Tuition: Full-time $17,328; part-time $722 per credit hour. Required fees: $828; $35 per credit hour. Tuition and fees vary according to campus/location and program. *Financial aid:* In 1998–99, 3 students received aid, including 3 fellowships; Federal Work-Study and institutionally-sponsored loans also available. Financial aid application deadline: 2/1. *Unit head:* Dr. Henry C. Merchant, Academic Director, 202-994-7123.

Hardin-Simmons University, Graduate School, Program in Environmental Management, Abilene, TX 79698-0001. Offers MS. Part-time programs available. *Faculty:* 7 full-time (1 woman). *Students:* 1 full-time (0 women), 18 part-time (3 women). Average age 30. 12 applicants, 83% accepted. In 1998, 7 degrees awarded. *Degree requirements:* For master's, thesis or alternative, internship required, foreign language not required. *Entrance requirements:* For master's, minimum undergraduate GPA of 3.0 in major, 2.7 overall. *Application deadline:* For fall admission, 8/15 (priority date); for spring admission, 1/5 (priority date). Applications are processed on a rolling basis. Application fee: $25 ($100 for international students). Tuition: Full-time $5,400; part-time $300 per credit. Required fees: $630; $50 per semester. Tuition and fees vary according to program. *Financial aid:* In 1998–99, 15 students received aid, including 4 fellowships with partial tuition reimbursements available (averaging $750 per year); career-related internships or fieldwork, Federal Work-Study, grants, scholarships, and tuition waivers (full and partial) also available. Aid available to part-time students. Financial aid application deadline: 3/15; financial aid applicants required to submit FAFSA. *Faculty research:* Water quality. *Unit head:* Dr. Gary Stanlake, Director, 915-670-1394, Fax: 915-670-1391, E-mail: gstanlake@hsutx.edu. *Application contact:* Dr. Dan McAlexander, Dean of Graduate Studies, 915-670-1298, Fax: 915-670-1564, E-mail: gradoffice@hsutx.edu.

Illinois Institute of Technology, Graduate College, Stuart School of Business, Program in Environmental Management, Chicago, IL 60616-3793. Offers MS, JD/MS, MBA/MS. Part-time and evening/weekend programs available. *Degree requirements:* For master's, foreign language and thesis not required. *Entrance requirements:* For master's, GRE or GMAT, TOEFL (minimum score of 550 required). *Application deadline:* For fall admission, 8/1; for spring admission, 4/15. Applications are processed on a rolling basis. Application fee: $30. *Financial aid:* Application deadline: 3/1. *Unit head:* George Nassos, Director, 312-567-6500, Fax: 312-906-6549, E-mail: degrees@stuart.iit.edu. *Application contact:* George Nassos, Director, 312-567-6500, Fax: 312-906-6549, E-mail: degrees@stuart.iit.edu.

See in-depth description on page 897.

Kansas State University, Graduate School, College of Architecture, Planning and Design, Department of Landscape Architecture/Regional and Community Planning, Manhattan, KS 66506. Offers environmental planning and management (MA). Part-time and evening/weekend programs available. Postbaccalaureate distance learning degree programs offered (minimal on-campus study). *Degree requirements:* Foreign language not required. Electronic applications accepted.

Lamar University, College of Graduate Studies, College of Engineering, Department of Civil Engineering, Program in Environmental Studies, Beaumont, TX 77710. Offers MS. Part-time programs available. *Faculty:* 5 full-time (0 women). *Students:* 7 full-time (2 women), 3 part-time (2 women); includes 1 minority (Hispanic American), 4 international. Average age 28. In 1998, 3 degrees awarded (100% found work related to degree). *Degree requirements:* For master's, thesis optional, foreign language not required. *Entrance requirements:* For master's, GRE General Test (minimum combined score of 950 required), TOEFL (minimum score of 525 required). *Average time to degree:* Master's–1.5 years full-time, 3 years part-time. *Application deadline:* For fall admission, 5/15 (priority date); for spring admission, 10/1 (priority date). Applications are processed on a rolling basis. Application fee: $0. *Financial aid:* In 1998–99, 1 fellowship was awarded. Financial aid application deadline: 4/1. *Faculty research:* Coastal engineering, lake hydrodynamics, contamination transport. *Unit head:* Jane Peterson, Secretary, 785-532-1603, Fax: 785-532-6806, E-mail: graduate@phys.ksu.edu. *Application contact:* Sandy Drane, Coordinator, International Students and Graduate Studies, 409-880-8349, Fax: 409-880-8414, E-mail: dranesl@lub002.lamar.edu.

Lesley College, Graduate School of Arts and Social Sciences, Cambridge, MA 02138-2790. Offers clinical mental health counseling (MA), including expressive therapies counseling, holistic counseling, school and community counseling; counseling psychology (MA, CAGS), including school counseling (MA); creative arts in learning (M Ed, CAGS), including individually designed (M Ed, MA, MA), multicultural education (M Ed, MA), storytelling (M Ed), theater studies (M Ed); ecological literacy (MS); environmental education (MS); expressive therapies (MA, CAGS), including art therapy (MA), dance therapy (MA), individually designed (M Ed, MA, MA), mental health counseling (MA), music therapy (MA); independent studies (M Ed); independent study (MA); intercultural relations (MA, CAGS), including development project administration (MA), individually designed (M Ed, MA, MA), intercultural conflict resolution (MA), intercultural health and human services (MA), intercultural training and consulting (MA), international education exchange (MA), international student adv ising (MA), managing culturally diverse human resources (MA), multicultural education (M Ed, MA); interdisciplinary studies (MA). MS (environmental education) offered jointly with the Audubon Society Expedition Institute. Part-time and evening/weekend programs available. Postbaccalaureate distance learning degree programs offered (minimal on-campus study). *Faculty:* 26 full-time (15 women), 343 part-time (226 women). *Students:* 175 full-time (145 women), 1,819 part-time (1,670 women); includes 190 minority (87 African Americans, 44 Asian Americans or Pacific Islanders, 42 Hispanic Americans, 17 Native Americans), 164 international. *Degree requirements:* For master's, internship, practicum, thesis (expressive therapies) required; for CAGS, thesis, internship (counseling psychology, expressive therapies) required. *Entrance requirements:* For master's, TOEFL (minimum score of 550 required), MAT (counseling psychology), interview; for CAGS, interview, master's degree. *Application deadline:* Applications are processed on a rolling basis. Application fee: $45. *Unit head:* Dr. Martha B. McKenna, Dean, 617-349-8467, Fax: 617-349-8366. *Application contact:* Maxine Lentz, Dean of Admissions and Enrollment Planning, 800-999-1959, Fax: 617-349-8366.

Long Island University, C.W. Post Campus, College of Liberal Arts and Sciences, Program in Environmental Studies, Brookville, NY 11548-1300. Offers environmental management (MS); environmental science (MS). Part-time and evening/weekend programs available. *Faculty:* 17 full-time (4 women), 4 part-time (1 woman). *Students:* 3 full-time (0 women), 25 part-time (8 women). Average age 30. 19 applicants, 84% accepted. In 1998, 5 degrees awarded. *Degree requirements:* For master's, internship or thesis required. *Entrance requirements:* For master's, GRE General Test (minimum score of 500 on each section required), 1 year of course work in general chemistry, 1 year of course work in biology or geology, 1 semester in organic chemistry, computer proficiency. *Application deadline:* Applications are processed on a rolling basis. Application fee: $30. Electronic applications accepted. *Financial aid:* In 1998–99, 3 teaching assistantships were awarded.; career-related internships or fieldwork, institutionally-sponsored loans, and unspecified assistantships also available. Aid available to part-time students. Financial aid application deadline: 5/15; financial aid applicants required to submit FAFSA. *Faculty research:* Symbiotic algae, local marine organisms, coastal processes, applied petrophysics, global tectonics, paleomagnetism. *Unit head:* Dr. Margaret Boorstein, Chair, Department of Earth and Environmental Science, 516-299-2318, Fax: 516-299-3945, E-mail: maboorst@eagle.liunet.edu. *Application contact:* Dr. Lillian Hess, Graduate Director, 516-299-2428, Fax: 516-299-3945.

Longwood College, Graduate Programs, Department of Natural Sciences, Farmville, VA 23909-1800. Offers MS. Part-time programs available. *Degree requirements:* For master's, thesis required. *Entrance requirements:* For master's, minimum GPA of 2.5.

Louisiana State University and Agricultural and Mechanical College, Graduate School, Center for Coastal, Energy and Environmental Resources, Institute for Environmental Studies, Baton Rouge, LA 70803. Offers environmental planning and management (MS); environmental toxicology (MS). *Faculty:* 12 full-time (3 women). *Students:* 28 full-time (14 women), 25 part-time (10 women); includes 3 minority (1 African American, 2 Hispanic Americans), 8 international. Average age 32. 38 applicants, 55% accepted. In 1998, 13 degrees awarded. *Degree requirements:* For master's, thesis required (for some programs), foreign language not required. *Entrance requirements:* For master's, GRE General Test, minimum GPA of 3.0. *Application deadline:* For fall admission, 1/25 (priority date). Applications are processed on a rolling basis. Application fee: $25. *Financial aid:* In 1998–99, 1 fellowship, 1 research assistantship with partial tuition reimbursement, 1 teaching assistantship with partial tuition reimbursement were awarded.; career-related internships or fieldwork and unspecified assistantships also available. *Faculty research:* Fates and movement of pollutants, neurobiotic metabolism, application of cellular toxicity/mutagenicity testing. *Unit head:* Dr. Michael Wascom, Director, 225-388-8521, Fax: 225-388-4286, E-mail: coewas@lsu.edu. *Application contact:* Dr. Ralph J. Portier, Graduate Adviser, 225-388-8522, E-mail: rportie@lsu.edu.

Michigan State University, Graduate School, College of Agriculture and Natural Resources, Department of Resource Development, East Lansing, MI 48824-1020. Offers resource development (MS, PhD); resource development-urban studies (MS, PhD). *Faculty:* 16. *Students:* 19 full-time (11 women), 33 part-time (15 women); includes 6 minority (3 African Americans, 2 Asian Americans or Pacific Islanders, 1 Native American), 10 international. Average age 35. 45 applicants, 44% accepted. In 1998, 16 master's, 12 doctorates awarded. *Degree requirements:* For doctorate, dissertation required. *Entrance requirements:* For master's, GRE General Test, minimum GPA of 3.0; for doctorate, GRE General Test, masters. *Application deadline:* Applications are processed on a rolling basis. Application fee: $30 ($40 for international students). *Financial aid:* In 1998–99, 8 research assistantships with tuition reimbursements (averaging $10,367 per year), 6 teaching assistantships with tuition reimbursements (averaging $10,098 per year) were awarded. Total annual research expenditures: $395,000. *Unit head:* Dr. Cynthia Fridgen, Chairperson, 517-355-3421, Fax: 517-353-8994, E-mail: 2233fri@msu.edu.

Michigan Technological University, Graduate School, College of Sciences and Arts, Department of Social Sciences, Program in Environmental Policy, Houghton, MI 49931-1295. Offers MS. Part-time programs available. *Faculty:* 16 full-time (5 women), 1 part-time (0 women). *Students:* 4 full-time (all women), 4 part-time; includes 1 minority (Native American) Average age 25. In 1998, 2 degrees awarded. *Degree requirements:* For master's, thesis or alternative, fieldwork required, foreign language not required. *Entrance requirements:* For master's, GRE General Test, TOEFL. *Average time to degree:* Master's–2.3 years full-time. *Application deadline:* For fall admission, 3/1 (priority date). Applications are processed on a rolling basis. Application fee: $30 ($35 for international students). Tuition, state resident: full-time $4,377. Tuition, nonresident: full-time $9,108. Required fees: $126. Tuition and fees vary according to course load. *Financial aid:* In 1998–99, 2 research assistantships (averaging $10,792 per year), 3 teaching assistantships (averaging $4,403 per year) were awarded.; fellowships, career-related internships or fieldwork, Federal Work-Study, and institutionally-sponsored loans also available. Aid available to part-time students. Financial aid application deadline: 3/1; financial aid applicants required to submit FAFSA. *Faculty research:* Citizen participation, pollution prevention, natural resource policy, energy policy, environmental history. *Application contact:* Dr. Bradley Baltensperger, Director, 906-487-2113, Fax: 906-487-2468, E-mail: brad@mtu.edu.

Montclair State University, Office of Graduate Studies, College of Science and Mathematics, Department of Earth and Environmental Studies, Upper Montclair, NJ 07043-1624. Offers environmental studies (MS), including environmental education, environmental health, environmental management, environmental science; geoscience (MS). Part-time and evening/weekend programs available. *Degree requirements:* For master's, comprehensive exam required. *Entrance requirements:* For master's, GRE General Test.

Monterey Institute of International Studies, Graduate School of International Policy Studies, Program in International Environmental Policy Studies, Monterey, CA 93940-2691. Offers international environmental policy (MA), including international environmental policy/English for non-native speakers, international environmental policy/French, international environmental policy/German, international environmental policy/Japanese, international environmental policy/Mandarin, international environmental policy/Russian, international environmental policy/Spanish. *Faculty:* 15 full-time (7 women), 22 part-time (7 women). *Students:* 47 full-time (29 women), 1 part-time; includes 1 minority (Asian American or Pacific Islander), 8 international. Average age 26. 42 applicants, 90% accepted. In 1998, 19 degrees awarded. *Degree requirements:* For master's. *Entrance requirements:* For master's, TOEFL (minimum score of 550 required), minimum GPA of 3.0, proficiency in a foreign language. *Average time to degree:* Master's–2 years full-time. *Application deadline:* For fall admission, 8/1 (priority date); for spring admission, 12/1. Applications are processed on a rolling basis. Application fee: $50. Tuition: Full-time $18,750; part-time $785 per credit. Required fees: $25 per semester. *Financial aid:* Career-related internships or fieldwork, Federal Work-Study, and institutionally-sponsored loans available. Financial aid application deadline: 3/15; financial aid applicants required to submit FAFSA. *Unit head:* Dr. Jackson Davis, Head, 831-647-6418, Fax: 831-647-4199. *Application contact:* 831-647-4123, Fax: 831-647-6405, E-mail: admit@miis.edu.

Announcement: Interdisciplinary options for the MA in international environmental policy include using electives to expand area studies expertise or acquiring management expertise by taking courses in the international management or international public administration programs. Call 831-647-4123. See in-depth description in this volume.

See in-depth description on page 901.

The Naropa University, Graduate Programs, Program in Environmental Leadership, Boulder, CO 80302-6697. Offers MA. *Faculty:* 2 full-time (1 woman), 9 part-time. *Students:* 17 full-time (6 women), 9 part-time (7 women); includes 2 minority (1 Asian American or Pacific Islander, 1 Hispanic American) Average age 33. 17 applicants, 76% accepted. In 1998, 3 degrees awarded. *Degree requirements:* For master's, thesis required, foreign language not required. *Entrance requirements:* For master's, interview. *Application deadline:* For fall admission, 2/1 (priority date); for spring admission, 11/1 (priority date). Applications are processed on a rolling basis. Application fee: $50. *Financial aid:* In 1998–99, 8 students received aid. Federal Work-Study, scholarships, and tuition waivers (partial) available. Aid available to part-time students. Financial aid application deadline: 3/1; financial aid applicants required to submit FAFSA. *Unit head:* Dr. Anne Parker, Chair, 303-245-4613. *Application contact:* Susan Boyle, Director of Admissions, 303-546-3572, Fax: 303-546-3583, E-mail: admissions@naropa.edu.

National University, Graduate Studies, School of Business and Technology, Department of Technology, La Jolla, CA 92037-1011. Offers e-commerce (MBA, MS); electronic engineering (MS); engineering management (MS); environmental management (MBA, MS); industrial engineering management (MS); software engineering (MS); technology management (MBA, MS); telecommunication systems management (MS). Part-time and evening/weekend programs available. Postbaccalaureate distance learning degree programs offered (minimal on-campus study). *Faculty:* 12 full-time, 125 part-time. *Students:* 305 (79 women); includes 122 minority (34 African Americans, 69 Asian Americans or Pacific Islanders, 17 Hispanic Americans, 2 Native Americans) 53 international. *Degree requirements:* For master's, foreign language and thesis not required. *Entrance requirements:* For master's, interview, minimum GPA of 2.5. *Application deadline:* Applications are processed on a rolling basis. Application fee: $60 ($100 for international students). Tuition: Full-time $7,830; part-time $870 per course. One-time fee: $60. Tuition and fees vary according to campus/location. *Unit head:* Dr. Leonid Preiser, Chair, 858-642-8425, Fax: 858-642-8716, E-mail: lpreiser@nu.edu. *Application contact:* Nancy Rohland, Director of Enrollment Management, 858-642-8180, Fax: 858-642-8709, E-mail: nrohland@nu.edu.

New Jersey Institute of Technology, Office of Graduate Studies, Department of Humanities and Social Sciences, Program in Environmental Policy Studies, Newark, NJ 07102-1982. Offers MS. Part-time and evening/weekend programs available. *Degree requirements:* For master's, project or thesis required. *Entrance requirements:* For master's, GRE General Test (minimum score of 450 on verbal section, 600 on quantitative, 550 on analytical required). Electronic applications accepted. *Faculty research:* Technology transfer, global sustainability, environmental policy, technology policy, professional ethics.

New Mexico Highlands University, Graduate Office, College of Arts and Sciences, Department of Life Sciences, Las Vegas, NM 87701. Offers biology (MS); environmental science and management (MS). Part-time programs available. *Faculty:* 9 full-time (2 women). *Students:* 11 full-time (6 women), 8 part-time (3 women); includes 13 minority (1 African American, 1 Asian American or Pacific Islander, 11 Hispanic Americans), 2 international. *Degree requirements:* For master's, thesis or alternative required, foreign language not required. *Entrance requirements:* For master's, minimum undergraduate GPA of 3.0. *Application deadline:* For fall admission, 8/1 (priority date). Applications are processed on a rolling basis. Application fee: $15. Tuition, state resident: full-time $1,988; part-time $83 per credit hour. Tuition, nonresident: full-time $8,034; part-time $83 per credit hour. Tuition and fees vary according to course load. *Unit head:* Dr. Maureen Romine, Chair, 505-454-3264, Fax: 505-454-3063, E-mail: romine_m@merlin.nmhu.edu. *Application contact:* Dr. Glen W. Davidson, Provost, 505-454-3311, Fax: 505-454-3558, E-mail: glendavidson@venus.nmhu.edu.

New York Institute of Technology, Graduate Division, School of Engineering and Technology, Program in Energy Management, Old Westbury, NY 11568-8000. Offers energy management (MS); energy technology (Certificate); environmental management (Certificate). Part-time and evening/weekend programs available. Postbaccalaureate distance learning degree programs offered. *Students:* 14 full-time (2 women), 130 part-time (27 women); includes 57 minority (35 African Americans, 9 Asian Americans or Pacific Islanders, 13 Hispanic Americans), 6 international. *Degree requirements:* For master's, thesis or alternative, oral or written comprehensive exam required, foreign language not required; for degree, foreign language not required. *Entrance requirements:* For master's, minimum QPA of 2.85. *Application deadline:* For fall admission, 8/1. Applications are processed on a rolling basis. Application fee: $50. Electronic applications accepted. *Unit head:* Dr. Robert Amundsen, Chair, 516-686-7578. *Application contact:* Glenn Berman, Executive Director of Admissions, 516-686-7519, Fax: 516-626-0419, E-mail: gberman@iris.nyit.edu.

North Carolina State University, Graduate School, College of Management, Program in Management, Raleigh, NC 27695. Offers biotechnology (MS); computer science (MS); engineering (MS); forest resources management (MS); general business (MS); management information systems (MS); operations research (MS); statistics (MS); telecommunications systems engineering (MS); textile management (MS); total quality management (MS). Part-time programs available. *Faculty:* 40 full-time (9 women), 4 part-time (0 women). *Students:* 48 full-time (15 women), 156 part-time (43 women); includes 33 minority (16 African Americans, 15 Asian Americans or Pacific Islanders, 1 Hispanic American, 1 Native American), 4 international. *Degree requirements:* For master's, computer language required, foreign language and thesis not required. *Entrance requirements:* For master's, GRE or GMAT, TOEFL (minimum score of 550 required), minimum undergraduate GPA of 3.0. *Application deadline:* For fall admission, 6/25; for spring admission, 11/25. Applications are processed on a rolling basis. Application fee: $45. *Unit head:* Dr. Jack W. Wilson, Director of Graduate Programs, 919-515-4327, Fax: 919-515-6943, E-mail: jack_wilson@ncsu.edu. *Application contact:* Dr. Steven G. Allen, Director of Graduate Programs, 919-515-6941, Fax: 919-515-5073, E-mail: steve_allen@ncsu.edu.

North Dakota State University, Graduate Studies and Research, Interdisciplinary Program in Natural Resources Management, Fargo, ND 58105. Offers MS. Part-time programs available. *Faculty:* 16 full-time (1 woman). *Students:* 11 full-time (3 women), 1 (woman) part-time, 2 international. Average age 28. 10 applicants, 80% accepted. *Degree requirements:* For master's, thesis required, foreign language not required. *Entrance requirements:* For master's, TOEFL (minimum score of 525 required). *Average time to degree:* Master's–2 years full-time, 5 years part-time. *Application deadline:* Applications are processed on a rolling basis. Application fee: $25. *Financial aid:* In 1998–99, 10 students received aid; research assistantships with full tuition reimbursements available, teaching assistantships with full tuition reimbursements available available. Aid available to part-time students. Financial aid application deadline: 3/15. *Faculty research:* Natural resources economics, wetlands issues, wildlife, prairie ecology, range management. Total annual research expenditures: $500,000. *Unit head:* Dr. Carolyn E. Grygiel, Director, 701-231-8180, Fax: 701-231-7590, E-mail: grygiel@prairie.nodak.edu.

Northeastern Illinois University, Graduate College, College of Arts and Sciences, Department of Geography, Environmental Studies and Economics, Program in Geography and Environmental Studies, Chicago, IL 60625-4699. Offers MA. Part-time and evening/weekend programs available. *Faculty:* 8 full-time (1 woman), 2 part-time (0 women). *Students:* 2 full-time (both women), 22 part-time (11 women); includes 1 minority (African American) Average age 34. In 1998, 12 degrees awarded. *Degree requirements:* For master's, oral or written comprehensive exams required, thesis optional, foreign language not required. *Entrance requirements:* For master's, undergraduate minor in geography or environmental studies, minimum GPA of 2.75. *Application deadline:* For fall admission, 3/31 (priority date); for spring admission, 9/30. Applications are processed on a rolling basis. Application fee: $0. *Financial aid:* In 1998–99, 19 students received aid, including 3 research assistantships; career-related internships or fieldwork, Federal Work-Study, institutionally-sponsored loans, and tuition waivers (full and partial) also available. Aid available to part-time students. Financial aid applicants required to submit FAFSA. *Faculty research:* Segregation and urbanization of minority groups in the Chicago area, scale dependence and parameterization in nonpoint source pollution modeling, ecological land classification and mapping, ecosystem restoration, soil-vegetation relationships, soil morphology and soil mapping, assessment of impacts on the management of urban runoff and urban nonpoint source pollution, potential landfill sites in Cook County. *Unit head:* Dr. E. Howenstine, Graduate Adviser, 773-794-2617. *Application contact:* Dr. Mohan K. Sood, Dean of Graduate College, 773-583-4050 Ext. 6143, Fax: 773-794-6670, E-mail: m-sood@neiu.edu.

Nova Scotia Agricultural College, Research and Graduate Studies, Truro, NS B2N 5E3, Canada. Offers agriculture (M Sc), including animal behavior, animal genetics, animal management, animal nutrition, animal technology, botany, crop breeding, crop management, crop physiology, ecology, environmental microbiology, food science, geology, nutrient management, pest management, physiology, plant biotechnology, plant pathology, soil chemistry, soil fertility, soil physics, waste management. Part-time programs available. *Faculty:* 33 full-time (4 women), 14 part-time (1 woman). *Students:* 23 full-time (15 women), 17 part-time (8 women). *Degree requirements:* For master's, thesis, candidacy exam required. *Entrance requirements:* For master's, TOEFL (minimum score of 580 required), minimum GPA of 3.0. *Application deadline:* For fall admission, 6/1; for winter admission, 10/1; for spring admission, 2/1. Applications are processed on a rolling basis. Application fee: $55. *Unit head:* Jill L. Rogers-Langille, Coordinator, 902-893-6360, Fax: 902-897-9399, E-mail: jrogers-langille@cadmin.nsac.ns.ca. *Application contact:* Kari Duff, Assistant, 902-893-6502, Fax: 902-897-9399, E-mail: kduff@cadmin.nsac.ns.ca.

Ohio University, Graduate Studies, College of Arts and Sciences, Program in Environmental Studies, Athens, OH 45701-2979. Offers MS. Part-time programs available. *Students:* 19 full-time (11 women), 10 part-time (5 women), 6 international. Average age 28. 34 applicants, 47% accepted. In 1998, 7 degrees awarded. *Degree requirements:* For master's, thesis, oral and written exams required, foreign language not required. *Entrance requirements:* For master's, GRE, TOEFL (average 600), minimum GPA of 3.0. *Application deadline:* For fall admission, 3/1 (priority date). Application fee: $30. Tuition, state resident: full-time $5,754; part-time $238 per credit hour. Tuition, nonresident: full-time $11,055; part-time $457 per credit hour. Tuition and fees vary according to course load, campus/location and program. *Financial aid:* In 1998–99, 20 students received aid, including 5 teaching assistantships with tuition reimbursements available (averaging $8,000 per year); research assistantships with tuition reimbursements available, career-related internships or fieldwork, Federal Work-Study, institutionally-sponsored loans, and tuition waivers (full) also available. Financial aid application deadline: 4/1. *Faculty research:* Stress tolerance of plants, acid mine drainage, environmental policy, effects of pesticides on animal health, sustainable forest products. *Unit head:* Dr. Gene Mapes, Director, 740-593-9358, Fax: 740-593-0482, E-mail: gmapes1@ohiou.edu.

Oregon Graduate Institute of Science and Technology, Graduate Studies, Department of Environmental Science and Engineering, Portland, OR 97291-1000. Offers ecosystem management and restoration (MS); environmental science (MS, PhD); environmental systems management (MS). Part-time programs available. *Faculty:* 9 full-time (1 woman). *Students:* 20 full-time (11 women), 4 part-time, 1 international. Terminal master's awarded for partial completion of doctoral program. *Degree requirements:* For master's, thesis optional, foreign language not required; for doctorate, comprehensive exam, oral defense of dissertation required. *Entrance requirements:* For master's, GRE General Test (strongly recommended), TOEFL (minimum score of 600 required); for doctorate, GRE General Test, TOEFL (minimum score of 600 required). Application fee: $50. Electronic applications accepted. *Unit head:* Dr. James F. Pankow, Head, 503-690-1196, Fax: 503-690-1273, E-mail: pankow@ese.ogi.edu. *Application contact:* Director of Admissions, 800-685-2423, Fax: 503-690-1285, E-mail: admissions@admin.ogi.edu.

See in-depth description on page 903.

Oregon State University, Graduate School, College of Oceanic and Atmospheric Sciences, Program in Marine Resource Management, Corvallis, OR 97331. Offers MA, MS. *Students:* 23 full-time (14 women), 1 (woman) part-time; includes 1 minority (Asian American or Pacific Islander), 3 international. Average age 28. In 1998, 7 degrees awarded. *Degree requirements:* For master's, thesis optional, foreign language not required. *Entrance requirements:* For master's, GRE General Test, TOEFL (minimum score of 550 required), minimum GPA of 3.0 in last 90 hours. *Application deadline:* For fall admission, 2/1 (priority date). Applications are processed on a rolling basis. Application fee: $50. *Financial aid:* Fellowships, research assistantships, teaching assistantships, career-related internships or fieldwork, Federal Work-Study, and institutionally-sponsored loans available. Aid available to part-time students. Financial aid application deadline: 2/1. *Faculty research:* Ocean and coastal resources, fisheries resources, marine pollution, marine recreation and tourism. *Unit head:* Jim W. Good, Coordinator, 541-737-1340, Fax: 541-737-2064, E-mail: good@oce.orst.edu. *Application contact:* Irma Delson, Assistant Director, Student Services, 541-737-5190, Fax: 541-737-2064, E-mail: student_adviser@oce.orst.edu.

Announcement: The College invites students with social science degrees and basic science backgrounds to apply for the graduate Program in Marine Resource Management. This intensive multidisciplinary program trains students for careers in planning, development, conservation, protection, and management of marine and coastal ecosystems and natural resources. See description under Marine Sciences and Oceanography in this volume.

Pennsylvania State University University Park Campus, Graduate School, College of Health and Human Development, Department of Man-Environment Relations, State College, University Park, PA 16802-1503. Offers M Ed, MS, D Ed, PhD. *Students:* 18 full-time (8 women), 7 part-time (2 women). *Entrance requirements:* For master's and doctorate, GRE General Test. Application fee: $50. *Unit head:* Dr. William P. Andrew, Professor in Charge, 814-863-0272.

Pennsylvania State University University Park Campus, Graduate School, Intercollege Graduate Programs, Intercollege Program in Environmental Pollution Control, State College, University Park, PA 16802-1503. Offers M Eng, MEPC, MS. *Students:* 22 full-time (9 women), 12 part-time (3 women). In 1998, 25 degrees awarded. *Entrance requirements:* For master's, GRE General Test, TOEFL (minimum score of 560 required). *Application deadline:* For fall admission, 6/1. Application fee: $50. *Unit head:* Dr. Herschel A. Elliott, Professor in Charge, 814-865-1417, Fax: 814-863-0109.

Portland State University, Graduate Studies, College of Liberal Arts and Sciences, Interdisciplinary Program in Environmental Sciences and Resources, Portland, OR 97207-0751. Offers environmental management (MEM); environmental sciences/biology (PhD); environmental sciences/chemistry (PhD); environmental sciences/civil engineering (PhD); environmental sciences/economics (PhD); environmental sciences/geography (PhD); environmental sciences/geology (PhD); environmental sciences/physics (PhD); environmental studies (MS). Part-time programs available. *Faculty:* 7 full-time (1 woman). *Students:* 38 full-time (11 women), 20 part-time (5 women); includes 4 minority (2 Asian Americans or Pacific Islanders, 1 Hispanic American, 1 Native American), 12 international. *Degree requirements:* For doctorate, variable foreign language requirement, computer language, dissertation, oral and qualifying exams required. *Entrance requirements:* For doctorate, TOEFL (minimum score of 550 required), minimum GPA of 3.0 in upper-division course work or 2.75 overall. *Application deadline:* For fall admission, 4/1 (priority date). Applications are processed on a rolling basis. Application fee: $50. *Unit head:* Dr. James R. Pratt, Director, 503-725-4209, Fax: 503-725-3888, E-mail: prattja@pdx.edu. *Application contact:* Betty Knudson, Coordinator, 503-725-4209, Fax: 503-725-3888, E-mail: envir@pdx.edu.

See in-depth description on page 907.

Environmental Policy and Resource Management

Prescott College, Graduate Programs, Program in Environmental Studies, Prescott, AZ 86301-2990. Offers agroecology (MA); ecopsychology (MA); environmental education (MA); environmental studies (MA); sustainability (MA). MA (environmental education) offered jointly with Teton Science School. Postbaccalaureate distance learning degree programs offered (minimal on-campus study). *Degree requirements:* For master's, thesis, fieldwork or internship, practicum required, foreign language not required.

Princeton University, Graduate School, School of Engineering and Applied Science, Department of Mechanical and Aerospace Engineering, Princeton, NJ 08544-1019. Offers applied physics (M Eng, MSE, PhD); computational methods (M Eng, MSE); dynamics and control systems (M Eng, MSE, PhD); energy and environmental policy (M Eng, MSE, PhD); energy conversion, propulsion, and combustion (M Eng, MSE, PhD); flight science and technology (M Eng, MSE, PhD); fluid mechanics (M Eng, MSE, PhD). *Faculty:* 26 full-time (2 women). *Students:* 46 full-time (6 women); includes 5 minority (4 Asian Americans or Pacific Islanders, 1 Hispanic American), 17 international. *Degree requirements:* For master's and doctorate, thesis/dissertation required, foreign language not required. *Entrance requirements:* For master's and doctorate, GRE General Test. *Application deadline:* For fall admission, 1/3. Electronic applications accepted. *Unit head:* Prof. Richard B. Miles, Director of Graduate Studies, 609-258-4683, Fax: 609-258-6109, E-mail: maegrad@princeton.edu. *Application contact:* Etta Recke, Graduate Administrator, 609-258-4683, Fax: 609-258-6109, E-mail: etta@princeton.edu.

Rensselaer at Hartford, Lally School of Management and Technology, Program in Environmental Management and Policy, Hartford, CT 06120-2991. Offers MS. *Degree requirements:* For master's, foreign language and thesis not required. *Entrance requirements:* For master's, TOEFL (minimum score of 570 required).

Rensselaer Polytechnic Institute, Graduate School, Lally School of Management and Technology, Program in Environmental Management and Policy, Troy, NY 12180-3590. Offers MS, PhD. Part-time and evening/weekend programs available. *Faculty:* 36 full-time (5 women), 5 part-time (0 women). *Students:* 21 full-time (11 women), 6 part-time (2 women); includes 4 minority (1 African American, 2 Asian Americans or Pacific Islanders, 1 Hispanic American), 8 international. 23 applicants, 96% accepted. In 1998, 8 master's awarded. *Degree requirements:* For master's, computer language, practicum required, foreign language and thesis not required; for doctorate, computer language, dissertation required, foreign language not required. *Entrance requirements:* For master's, GRE General Test, TOEFL (minimum score of 550 required); for doctorate, GMAT or GRE General Test, TOEFL (minimum score of 550 required). *Application deadline:* For fall admission, 2/1 (priority date). Applications are processed on a rolling basis. Application fee: $35. *Financial aid:* In 1998–99, 22 students received aid, including 10 research assistantships, 1 teaching assistantship; fellowships, career-related internships or fieldwork, institutionally-sponsored loans, scholarships, and tuition waivers (full and partial) also available. Financial aid application deadline: 2/1. *Faculty research:* Corporate environmental management and strategy, strategic implications of new policy development, environmental communications/auditing/performance standards. Total annual research expenditures: $2,500. *Unit head:* Dr. Bruce W. Piasecki, Director, 518-276-2705. *Application contact:* JoAnn Drost, Student Coordinator/Office Manager, 518-276-6565, Fax: 518-276-6783, E-mail: drostj@rpi.edu.

See in-depth description on page 911.

Rensselaer Polytechnic Institute, Graduate School, School of Humanities and Social Sciences, Department of Economics, Interdisciplinary Program in Ecological Economics, Troy, NY 12180-3590. Offers PhD. Part-time and evening/weekend programs available. *Faculty:* 7 full-time (2 women). *Students:* 17 full-time (12 women), 6 part-time (1 woman), 10 international. 27 applicants, 30% accepted. In 1998, 1 degree awarded. *Degree requirements:* For doctorate, dissertation required, foreign language not required. *Entrance requirements:* For doctorate, GMAT or GRE General Test, TOEFL (minimum score of 550 required). *Application deadline:* For fall admission, 2/1 (priority date). Applications are processed on a rolling basis. Application fee: $35. *Financial aid:* In 1998–99, 10 students received aid, including 1 fellowship (averaging $11,000 per year), 6 teaching assistantships (averaging $9,800 per year); institutionally-sponsored loans and tuition waivers (full and partial) also available. Financial aid application deadline: 2/1. *Faculty research:* Sustainable development, natural resource economics, cost-benefit analysis, social economics. Total annual research expenditures: $50,000. *Unit head:* Lorraine Pisarczyk, Graduate Coordinator, 518-276-6414, Fax: 518-276-4824, E-mail: pisarl@rpi.edu. *Application contact:* Kathy Keenan, Administrative Secretary, 518-276-8088, Fax: 518-276-2235, E-mail: keenak@rpi.edu.

Announcement: The Economics Department at Rensselaer offers an interdisciplinary PhD in ecological economics and an MS in economics. The focus is the relationship between economic systems, social systems, and the natural world. Faculty members include prominent ecological economists whose research interests include biodiversity valuation, cost-benefit analysis, discursive ethics, evolutionary economics, Ghandian economics, input-output analysis, regional economics, and sustainable development. Interests of other Rensselaer faculty members participating in the PhD program include environmental ethics, environmental justice, fresh water ecology, and population and development. Teaching and research assistantships and fellowships are available. For an application, contact Kathy Keenan, 518-276-8088, fax: 518-276-2235, e-mail: keenak@rpi.edu, WWW: http://www.rpi.edu/dept/economics/.

Rensselaer Polytechnic Institute, Graduate School, School of Humanities and Social Sciences, Program in Ecological Economics, Values, and Policy, Troy, NY 12180-3590. Offers new 9/1/1999 (MS). *Faculty:* 10 full-time (3 women). *Entrance requirements:* For master's, TOEFL. *Application deadline:* For fall admission, 2/1 (priority date). Applications are processed on a rolling basis. Application fee: $35. *Financial aid:* Fellowships, research assistantships, teaching assistantships available. Financial aid application deadline: 2/1. *Faculty research:* Environmental politics, environmental ethics, technological change, environment and culture. *Unit head:* Dr. Steve Breyman, Director, 518-276-8515.

See in-depth description on page 909.

Rochester Institute of Technology, Part-time and Graduate Admissions, College of Applied Science and Technology, Department of Environmental Management, Rochester, NY 14623-5604. Offers MS. *Students:* 3 full-time (0 women), 29 part-time (13 women); includes 2 minority (both Hispanic Americans), 2 international. 28 applicants, 43% accepted. *Entrance requirements:* For master's, minimum GPA of 3.0. *Application deadline:* For fall admission, 3/1 (priority date). Applications are processed on a rolling basis. Application fee: $40. Electronic applications accepted. *Unit head:* John Morelli, Chair, 716-475-7213, E-mail: jxmctp@rit.edu.

St. Cloud State University, School of Graduate Studies, College of Science and Engineering, Department of Environmental and Technological Studies, St. Cloud, MN 56301-4498. Offers MS. *Faculty:* 7 full-time (1 woman), 2 part-time (0 women). In 1998, 2 degrees awarded. *Degree requirements:* For master's, thesis or alternative required, foreign language not required. *Entrance requirements:* For master's, GRE General Test, minimum GPA of 2.75. Application fee: $20. *Financial aid:* Federal Work-Study and unspecified assistantships available. Financial aid application deadline: 3/1. *Unit head:* Dr. Anthony Schwaller, Chairperson, 320-255-3235, Fax: 320-654-5122, E-mail: ets@stclousstate.edu. *Application contact:* Ann Anderson, Graduate Studies Office, 320-255-2113, Fax: 320-654-5371, E-mail: aeanderson@stcloudstate.edu.

Saint Joseph's University, Erivan K. Haub School of Business, Programs in Graduate Business, Program in Environmental Protection and Safety Management, Philadelphia, PA 19131-1395. Offers environmental protection and safety management (MS); public safety (MS). Part-time and evening/weekend programs available. *Faculty:* 2 full-time (0 women), 9 part-time (3 women). Average age 35. 25 applicants, 80% accepted. In 1998, 20 degrees awarded. *Degree requirements:* For master's, foreign language and thesis not required. *Entrance requirements:* For master's, GMAT (minimum score of 450 required), TOEFL (minimum score of 550 required; 213 on computer-based), interview. *Average time to degree:* Master's–3 years part-time. *Application deadline:* For fall admission, 7/15 (priority date); for spring admission, 11/15. Applications are processed on a rolling basis. Application fee: $35. *Financial aid:* Unspecified assistantships available. Financial aid application deadline: 5/1. *Faculty research:* Occupational safety, health disaster/emergency. *Unit head:* Dr. Vincent P. McNally, Director, 610-660-1641, Fax: 610-660-2903, E-mail: vmcnally@sju.edu.

Saint Mary-of-the-Woods College, Interdisciplinary Program in Earth Literacy, Saint Mary-of-the-Woods, IN 47876. Offers MA. Part-time programs available. Postbaccalaureate distance learning degree programs offered (minimal on-campus study). *Faculty:* 6 part-time (all women). 9 applicants, 100% accepted. *Degree requirements:* For master's, thesis or alternative, qualifying exam required. *Application deadline:* Applications are processed on a rolling basis. Application fee: $35. Tuition: Part-time $315 per credit hour. Required fees: $65 per term. *Financial aid:* Career-related internships or fieldwork available. *Faculty research:* Ecology, phipeology, art, spirituality. *Unit head:* Mary Lou Dolan, Director, 812-535-5160, Fax: 812-535-5127, E-mail: mldolan@smwc.edu.

Samford University, Howard College of Arts and Sciences, Program in Environmental Management, Birmingham, AL 35229-0002. Offers MSEM, JD/MSEM. Part-time and evening/weekend programs available. *Faculty:* 3 full-time (0 women), 6 part-time (0 women). *Students:* 14 full-time (8 women), 26 part-time (8 women); includes 7 minority (all African Americans) Average age 30. 19 applicants, 95% accepted. In 1998, 37 degrees awarded. *Degree requirements:* For master's, foreign language and thesis not required. *Entrance requirements:* For master's, GRE General Test (minimum combined score of 1000 required) or MAT (minimum score of 50 required), minimum GPA of 2.5, 3 years of work experience. *Application deadline:* For fall admission, 8/30; for spring admission, 1/2. Application fee: $25. Tuition: Part-time $351 per credit. Tuition and fees vary according to degree level and program. *Unit head:* Dr. Ron Hunsinger, Head, 205-870-2944, Fax: 205-870-2479.

San Francisco State University, Graduate Division, College of Behavioral and Social Sciences, Department of Geography and Human Environmental Studies, San Francisco, CA 94132-1722. Offers geography (MA), including environmental planning, resource management. Part-time programs available. *Faculty:* 10 full-time (3 women). *Students:* 48 (23 women). *Degree requirements:* For master's, thesis, exam required, foreign language not required. *Entrance requirements:* For master's, minimum GPA of 2.5 in last 60 units. *Application deadline:* For fall admission, 11/30 (priority date). Applications are processed on a rolling basis. Application fee: $55. *Unit head:* Dr. Nancy Wilkinson, Chair, 415-338-2049. *Application contact:* Dr. Barbara Holzman, Associate Professor, 415-338-7506, E-mail: bholzman@sfsu.edu.

San Jose State University, Graduate Studies, College of Social Sciences, Department of Environmental Studies, San Jose, CA 95192-0001. Offers MS. Part-time programs available. *Faculty:* 4 full-time (0 women), 3 part-time (0 women). *Students:* 14 full-time (9 women), 19 part-time (14 women); includes 2 minority (1 Asian American or Pacific Islander, 1 Hispanic American), 2 international. Average age 33. 35 applicants, 63% accepted. In 1998, 4 degrees awarded. *Degree requirements:* For master's, thesis or alternative, comprehensive exam required, foreign language not required. *Entrance requirements:* For master's, minimum GPA of 3.0. *Application deadline:* For fall admission, 6/1. Applications are processed on a rolling basis. Application fee: $59. Tuition, nonresident: part-time $246 per unit. Required fees: $1,939; $1,309 per year. *Financial aid:* In 1998–99, 2 teaching assistantships were awarded.; career-related internships or fieldwork, Federal Work-Study, and institutionally-sponsored loans also available. Aid available to part-time students. *Faculty research:* Remote sensing, land use/land cover mapping. *Unit head:* Dr. Lynne Trulio, Acting Chair, 408-924-5450, Fax: 408-924-5477. *Application contact:* Graduate Coordinator, 408-924-5487.

Shippensburg University of Pennsylvania, School of Graduate Studies and Research, College of Arts and Sciences, Department of Geography and Earth Science, Shippensburg, PA 17257-2299. Offers geoenvironmental studies (MS). Part-time and evening/weekend programs available. *Faculty:* 11 full-time (3 women), 1 part-time (0 women). *Students:* 33 full-time (13 women), 16 part-time (8 women). Average age 28. In 1998, 19 degrees awarded. *Degree requirements:* For master's, internship or thesis, comprehensive written exam required. *Entrance requirements:* For master's, TOEFL (minimum score of 237 required for computer-based), GRE General Test or minimum GPA of 2.75, 12 credit hours of geography or earth sciences. *Application deadline:* Applications are processed on a rolling basis. Application fee: $25. Electronic applications accepted. *Financial aid:* Career-related internships or fieldwork, Federal Work-Study, institutionally-sponsored loans, and unspecified assistantships available. Aid available to part-time students. Financial aid application deadline: 3/1; financial aid applicants required to submit FAFSA. *Unit head:* Dr. John E. Benhart, Chairperson, 717-532-1685, Fax: 717-530-4029, E-mail: jebenh@ship.edu. *Application contact:* Renee Payne, Assistant Dean of Graduate Studies, 717-532-1213, Fax: 717-530-4038, E-mail: rmpayn@ship.edu.

Simon Fraser University, Graduate Studies, Faculty of Applied Science, School of Resource and Environmental Management, Burnaby, BC V5A 1S6, Canada. Offers MRM, PhD, MBA/MRM. *Faculty:* 10 full-time (2 women). *Students:* 82 full-time (43 women), 8 part-time (5 women). Average age 33. In 1998, 14 master's awarded. *Degree requirements:* For master's, thesis or alternative required; for doctorate, dissertation, comprehensive exam required. *Entrance requirements:* For master's, TOEFL (minimum score of 570 required), TWE (minimum score of 5 required), or International English Language Test (minimum score of 7.5 required), minimum GPA of 3.0; for doctorate, TOEFL (minimum score of 570 required), TWE (minimum score of 5 required), or International English Language Test (minimum score of 7.5 required), minimum GPA of 3.5. Application fee: $55. *Financial aid:* In 1998–99, 27 fellowships were awarded. *Faculty research:* Management of resources, environmental law, resource economics, regional planning, public policy analysis. *Unit head:* F. Gobas, Director, 604-291-4659, Fax: 604-291-4968. *Application contact:* Graduate Secretary, 604-291-3074, Fax: 604-291-4968, E-mail: reminfo@sfu.ca.

Slippery Rock University of Pennsylvania, Graduate School, College of Health and Human Services, Department of Parks, Recreation, and Environmental Education, Slippery Rock, PA 16057. Offers environmental education (M Ed); resource management (MS); sustainable systems (MS). Part-time and evening/weekend programs available. *Faculty:* 16 full-time (8 women). *Students:* 29 full-time (12 women), 19 part-time (12 women); includes 3 minority (1 African American, 2 Hispanic Americans), 3 international. *Degree requirements:* For master's, comprehensive exams required, thesis optional, foreign language not required. *Entrance requirements:* For master's, GRE General Test (minimum combined score of 1350 on three sections), minimum GPA of 2.75. *Application deadline:* For fall admission, 7/1 (priority date); for spring admission, 11/1. Applications are processed on a rolling basis. Application fee: $25. Electronic applications accepted. *Unit head:* Dr. William Shiner, Graduate Coordinator, 724-738-2068. *Application contact:* Carla Hradisky-Coffelt, Interim Director of Graduate Admissions and Recruitment, 724-738-2051, Fax: 724-738-2908.

Southwest Missouri State University, Graduate College, College of Natural and Applied Sciences, Department of Geography, Geology, and Planning, Springfield, MO 65804-0094. Offers resource planning (MS). Part-time and evening/weekend programs available. *Faculty:* 19 full-time (1 woman). *Students:* 10 full-time (3 women), 9 part-time (3 women); includes 2 minority (both Native Americans) Average age 30. 14 applicants, 93% accepted. In 1998, 4 degrees awarded (100% found work related to degree). *Degree requirements:* For master's, thesis, comprehensive exam required, foreign language not required. *Entrance requirements:* For master's, GRE General Test (minimum score of 400 on verbal section, 475 on quantitative required; average 450 verbal, 475 quantitative), minimum undergraduate GPA of 3.0. *Application deadline:* For fall admission, 8/7 (priority date); for spring admission, 12/17 (priority date). Applications are processed on a rolling basis. Application fee: $25. Electronic applications accepted. *Financial aid:* In 1998–99, research assistantships with tuition reimbursements (averaging $6,000 per year), teaching assistantships with tuition reimbursements (averaging $6,000 per year) were awarded.; career-related internships or fieldwork, Federal Work-Study, and unspecified assistantships also available. Financial aid application deadline: 4/15. *Faculty research:* Water resources, small town planning, recreation and open space planning. *Unit* *head:* Dr. Yongwei Zhang, Acting Head, 417-836-5800, Fax: 417-836-6934. *Application contact:* Dr. Dimitri Ionnides, Graduate Adviser, 417-836-5800, Fax: 417-836-6934, E-mail: dii608f@mail.smsu.edu.

Southwest Texas State University, Graduate School, School of Liberal Arts, Department of Geography and Planning, Program in Resource and Environmental Studies, San Marcos, TX 78666. Offers MAG. Part-time and evening/weekend programs available. *Students:* 9 full-time (7 women), 24 part-time (10 women). Average age 32. In 1998, 16 degrees awarded. *Degree requirements:* For master's, comprehensive exam, internship or thesis required. *Entrance requirements:* For master's, GRE General Test (minimum combined score of 900 required), TOEFL (minimum score of 550 required), minimum GPA of 2.75 in last 60 hours. *Application deadline:* For fall admission, 6/15 (priority date); for spring admission, 10/15 (priority date). Applications are processed on a rolling basis. Application fee: $25 ($50 for international students). Tuition, state resident: full-time $684; part-time $38 per semester hour. Tuition, nonresident: full-time $4,572; part-time $254 per semester hour. *Financial aid:* Research assistantships, teaching assistantships, career-related internships or fieldwork, Federal Work-Study, institutionally-sponsored loans, and scholarships available. Aid available to part-time students. Financial aid application deadline: 4/1; financial aid applicants required to submit FAFSA. *Unit head:* Dr. Fred Shelley, Graduate Adviser, 512-245-8704, Fax: 512-245-8353, E-mail: fs03@swt.edu.

Stanford University, School of Earth Sciences, Earth Systems Program, Stanford, CA 94305-9991. Offers MS. Students admitted at the undergraduate level. *Students:* 15 full-time (10 women), 1 (woman) part-time; includes 3 minority (1 African American, 1 Asian American or Pacific Islander, 1 Hispanic American) Average age 23. In 1998, 12 degrees awarded. Application fee: $65 ($80 for international students). Electronic applications accepted. Tuition: Full-time $23,058. Required fees: $152. Part-time tuition and fees vary according to course load. *Unit head:* Joan Roughgarden, Director, 650-723-4961, Fax: 650-725-0958, E-mail: rough@pangea.stanford.edu.

State University of New York at Albany, College of Arts and Sciences, Department of Biological Sciences, Program in Biodiversity, Conservation, and Policy, Albany, NY 12222-0001. Offers MS. *Degree requirements:* For master's, one foreign language required. *Entrance requirements:* For master's, GRE General Test. Application fee: $50. Tuition, state resident: full-time $5,100; part-time $213 per credit. Tuition, nonresident: full-time $8,416; part-time $351 per credit. Required fees: $31 per credit. *Unit head:* Dr. Jon Jacklet, Chair, Department of Biological Sciences, 518-442-4300.

State University of New York College of Environmental Science and Forestry, Faculty of Forestry, Syracuse, NY 13210-2779. Offers agronomy and soil sciences management (MPS, MS, PhD); forest resources management (MPS, MS, PhD); forestry (MPS, MS, PhD); natural resources management (MPS, MS, PhD). Part-time programs available. *Faculty:* 24 full-time (2 women). *Students:* 55 full-time (17 women), 32 part-time (10 women); includes 5 minority (2 African Americans, 2 Hispanic Americans, 1 Native American), 21 international. Average age 31. 60 applicants, 83% accepted. In 1998, 16 master's, 3 doctorates awarded. Terminal master's awarded for partial completion of doctoral program. *Degree requirements:* For master's, thesis or alternative required, foreign language not required; for doctorate, dissertation required. *Entrance requirements:* For master's and doctorate, GRE General Test. *Application deadline:* For fall admission, 4/15 (priority date); for spring admission, 11/15. Applications are processed on a rolling basis. Application fee: $50. *Financial aid:* In 1998–99, 7 fellowships with tuition reimbursements, 17 research assistantships with tuition reimbursements, 21 teaching assistantships with tuition reimbursements were awarded.; career-related internships or fieldwork and Federal Work-Study also available. Aid available to part-time students. *Faculty research:* Silviculture recreation management, tree improvement, operations management, economics. Total annual research expenditures: $1.5 million. *Unit head:* Dr. William Bentley, Chair, 315-470-6536, Fax: 315-470-6535, E-mail: wbentley@csf.edu. *Application contact:* Dr. Robert H. Frey, Dean, Instruction and Graduate Studies, 315-470-6599, Fax: 315-470-6978, E-mail: esfgrad@esf.edu.

Texas Tech University, Graduate School, College of Architecture, Program in Land-Use Planning, Management, and Design, Lubbock, TX 79409. Offers community planning and design (PhD); environmental/natural resource planning and management (PhD); historic preservation (PhD); public policy administration (PhD). *Students:* 7 full-time (4 women), 4 part-time (1 woman), 5 international. Average age 36. 11 applicants, 36% accepted. *Degree requirements:* For doctorate, dissertation required. *Entrance requirements:* For doctorate, GRE General Test (combined average 1170). *Application deadline:* For fall admission, 4/15 (priority date); for spring admission, 11/1 (priority date). Applications are processed on a rolling basis. Application fee: $25 ($50 for international students). Electronic applications accepted. *Financial aid:* Fellowships, research assistantships, career-related internships or fieldwork, Federal Work-Study, and institutionally-sponsored loans available. Aid available to part-time students. Financial aid application deadline: 5/15; financial aid applicants required to submit FAFSA. *Faculty research:* Wildlife biology, environmental engineering, desertification, arid and semiarid land. Total annual research expenditures: $162,296. *Unit head:* Dr. Michael A. Jones, Coordinator, 806-742-2781, Fax: 806-742-2855.

Trent University, Graduate Studies, Program in Watershed Ecosystems, Program in Environmental and Resource Studies, Peterborough, ON K9J 7B8, Canada. Offers M Sc, PhD. *Degree requirements:* For master's and doctorate, thesis/dissertation required, foreign language not required. *Entrance requirements:* For master's, honours degree; for doctorate, master's degree. *Application deadline:* For fall admission, 2/1 (priority date). Applications are processed on a rolling basis. Application fee: $45. *Financial aid:* Fellowships, research assistantships, teaching assistantships, career-related internships or fieldwork available. *Faculty research:* Environmental biogeochemistry, aquatic organic contaminants, fisheries, wetland ecology, renewable resource management. *Unit head:* Dr. M. Fox, Chair, 705-748-1273, E-mail: mfox@trentu.ca. *Application contact:* Graduate Studies Officer, 705-748-1245, Fax: 705-748-1587.

Troy State University, Graduate School, College of Arts and Sciences, Program in Environmental Analysis and Management, Troy, AL 36082. Offers MS. Part-time and evening/weekend programs available. *Degree requirements:* For master's, thesis, comprehensive exam required, foreign language not required. *Entrance requirements:* For master's, GRE General Test, MAT, minimum GPA of 2.5. Electronic applications accepted.

Tufts University, Division of Graduate and Continuing Studies and Research, Graduate School of Arts and Sciences, College of Engineering, Department of Civil and Environmental Engineering, Medford, MA 02155. Offers civil engineering (MS, PhD), including geotechnical engineering, structural engineering; environmental engineering (MS, PhD), including environmental engineering and environmental sciences, environmental geotechnology, environmental health, environmental science and management, hazardous materials management, water resources engineering. Part-time programs available. *Faculty:* 13 full-time, 10 part-time. *Students:* 99 (47 women); includes 21 minority (5 African Americans, 7 Asian Americans or Pacific Islanders, 9 Hispanic Americans) 16 international. Terminal master's awarded for partial completion of doctoral program. *Degree requirements:* For master's, thesis or alternative required, foreign language not required; for doctorate, dissertation required, foreign language not required. *Entrance requirements:* For master's and doctorate, GRE General Test, TOEFL (minimum score of 550 required). *Application deadline:* For fall admission, 2/15; for spring admission, 10/15. Applications are processed on a rolling basis. Application fee: $50. *Unit head:* Dr. Stephen Levine, Chair, 617-627-3211, Fax: 617-627-3994. *Application contact:* Linfield Brown, 617-627-3211, Fax: 617-627-3994.

Tufts University, Division of Graduate and Continuing Studies and Research, Graduate School of Arts and Sciences, Department of Urban and Environmental Policy, Medford, MA 02155. Offers community development (MA); environmental policy (MA); health and human welfare (MA); housing policy (MA); international environment/development policy (MA); public policy and citizen participation (MA). Part-time programs available. *Faculty:* 7 full-time, 12 part-time. *Students:* 99 (68 women); includes 16 minority (7 African Americans, 7 Asian Americans or Pacific Islanders, 2 Hispanic Americans) 12 international. 126 applicants, 86% accepted. In 1998, 43 degrees awarded. *Degree requirements:* For master's, thesis, internship required. *Entrance requirements:* For master's, GRE General Test, TOEFL (minimum score of 550 required). *Application deadline:* For fall admission, 2/15. Applications are processed on a rolling basis. Application fee: $50. *Financial aid:* Fellowships with full and partial tuition reimbursements, teaching assistantships with full and partial tuition reimbursements, career-related internships or fieldwork, Federal Work-Study, scholarships, and tuition waivers (partial) available. Aid available to part-time students. Financial aid application deadline: 2/15; financial aid applicants required to submit FAFSA. *Unit head:* Rachel Bratt, Chair, 617-627-3394, Fax: 617-627-3377.

Tufts University, Division of Graduate and Continuing Studies and Research, Professional and Continuing Studies, Community Environmental Studies Program, Medford, MA 02155. Offers Certificate. Part-time and evening/weekend programs available. Average age 34. 7 applicants, 100% accepted. In 1998, 4 degrees awarded. *Average time to degree:* 1 year part-time. *Application deadline:* For fall admission, 8/15 (priority date); for spring admission, 12/12. Applications are processed on a rolling basis. Application fee: $40. *Financial aid:* Career-related internships or fieldwork available. Aid available to part-time students. Financial aid application deadline: 5/1; financial aid applicants required to submit FAFSA. *Unit head:* Bob Baer, Assistant Director of Graduate School, 410-830-2501, Fax: 410-830-4675, E-mail: petgrad@towson.edu. *Application contact:* Bob Baer, Assistant Director of Graduate School, 410-830-2501, Fax: 410-830-4675, E-mail: petgrad@towson.edu.

Tufts University, Division of Graduate and Continuing Studies and Research, Professional and Continuing Studies, Environmental Management Program, Medford, MA 02155. Offers Certificate. Part-time and evening/weekend programs available. Average age 26. 1 applicants, 100% accepted. In 1998, 3 degrees awarded. *Average time to degree:* 1 year part-time. *Application deadline:* For fall admission, 8/15 (priority date); for spring admission, 12/12. Applications are processed on a rolling basis. Application fee: $40. *Financial aid:* Available to part-time students. Application deadline: 5/1;

Universidad del Turabo, Graduate Programs, Program in Science and Technology, Turabo, PR 00778-3030. Offers environmental studies (MES). *Degree requirements:* For master's, thesis not required. *Entrance requirements:* For master's, GRE, PAEG, interview.

Universidad Metropolitana, School of Environmental Affairs, Program in Environmental Management, Río Piedras, PR 00928-1150. Offers MS. *Faculty:* 1 full-time (0 women), 15 part-time (1 woman). *Students:* 120 full-time; all minorities (all Hispanic Americans) 68 applicants, 84% accepted. In 1998, 6 degrees awarded. *Degree requirements:* For master's, thesis required, foreign language not required. *Entrance requirements:* For master's, PAEG (score in 60th percentile or higher required), interview. *Average time to degree:* Master's–1.5 years full-time, 3 years part-time. *Application deadline:* Applications are processed on a rolling basis. Application fee: $25. *Unit head:* Dr. Carlos Padin, Head, School of Environmental Affairs, 787-766-1717 Ext. 6410.

Université de Montréal, Faculty of Graduate Studies, Programs in Environmental Protection, Montréal, PQ H3C 3J7, Canada. Offers DESS. 24 applicants, 71% accepted. In 1998, 13 degrees awarded. *Degree requirements:* For DESS, thesis not required. Application fee: $30. *Unit head:* Joseph Zayed, Director, 514-343-6134.

Université du Québec à Chicoutimi, Graduate Programs, Program in Renewable Resources, Chicoutimi, PQ G7H 2B1, Canada. Offers M Sc. Part-time programs available. *Degree requirements:* For master's, thesis required. *Entrance requirements:* For master's, appropriate bachelor's degree, proficiency in French.

Université du Québec à Rimouski, Graduate Programs, Program in Management of Marine Resources, Rimouski, PQ G5L 3A1, Canada. Offers M Sc. Part-time programs available. *Degree requirements:* For master's, thesis not required. *Entrance requirements:* For master's, appropriate bachelor's degree, proficiency in French.

University of Alaska Fairbanks, Graduate School, College of Natural Resource Development and Management, School of Agriculture and Land Resources Management, Fairbanks, AK 99775-7480. Offers natural resources management (MS). Part-time programs available. *Faculty:* 24 full-time (4 women), 4 part-time (3 women). *Students:* 15 full-time (9 women), 8 part-time (4 women); includes 1 minority (Native American), 3 international. Average age 32. 18 applicants, 61% accepted. In 1998, 4 degrees awarded. *Degree requirements:* For master's, thesis (for some programs), comprehensive exams required, foreign language not required. *Entrance requirements:* For master's, GRE General Test, TOEFL (minimum score of 550 required). *Application deadline:* For fall admission, 8/1. Applications are processed on a rolling basis. Application fee: $35. *Financial aid:* Research assistantships, teaching assistantships, career-related internships or fieldwork available. *Faculty research:* Conservation biology, soil/water conservation, land use policy and planning in the arctic and subarctic, forest ecosystem management, subarctic agricultural production. *Unit head:* Dr. Fred Husby, Acting Director, 907-474-7083. *Application contact:* Barbara Pierson, Recruitment Coordinator, 907-474-5276.

University of Alberta, Faculty of Graduate Studies and Research, Department of Economics, Edmonton, AB T6G 2E1, Canada. Offers economics (MA, PhD); economics and finance (MA); environmental and natural resource economics (PhD). Part-time programs available. Terminal master's awarded for partial completion of doctoral program. *Degree requirements:* For master's, foreign language and thesis not required; for doctorate, dissertation required, foreign language not required. *Entrance requirements:* For master's and doctorate, GRE, TOEFL (minimum score of 550 required). *Faculty research:* Public finance, international trade, industrial organization, Pacific Rim economics, monetary economics.

The University of Arizona, Graduate College, Graduate Interdisciplinary Programs, Graduate Interdisciplinary Program in Planning, Tucson, AZ 85721. Offers MS. *Accreditation:* ACSP. *Faculty:* 38. *Students:* 24 full-time (10 women), 11 part-time (5 women); includes 3 minority (all Hispanic Americans), 4 international. Average age 32. 36 applicants, 69% accepted. In 1998, 12 degrees awarded. *Degree requirements:* For master's, thesis or alternative required, foreign language not required. *Entrance requirements:* For master's, GRE General Test, TOEFL, minimum B average. Application fee: $35. *Financial aid:* Research assistantships, teaching assistantships, career-related internships or fieldwork, Federal Work-Study, scholarships, and tuition waivers (partial) available. Financial aid application deadline: 3/15. *Faculty research:* Environmental analysis, regional planning, land development, regional development, arid lands. *Unit head:* Ken Clark, Chairman, 520-621-6752, Fax: 520-621-8700, E-mail: clarkkn@ccit.arizona.edu. *Application contact:* Karen Young, Coordinator, 520-621-9597, Fax: 520-621-8700, E-mail: youngkl@ccit.arizona.edu.

University of British Columbia, Faculty of Graduate Studies, Program in Resource Management and Environmental Studies, Vancouver, BC V6T 1Z2, Canada. Offers M Sc, MA, PhD. *Degree requirements:* For master's, thesis required; for doctorate, dissertation, comprehensive exam required. *Entrance requirements:* For master's and doctorate, TOEFL (minimum score of 600 required). *Faculty research:* Land management, water resources, energy, environmental assessment, risk evaluation.

University of Calgary, Faculty of Graduate Studies, Program in Resources and the Environment, Calgary, AB T2N 1N4, Canada. Offers M Sc, MA, PhD. *Students:* 22 full-time (12 women). 10 applicants, 60% accepted. In 1998, 2 degrees awarded. *Degree requirements:* For master's, thesis required, foreign language not required; for doctorate, dissertation, written and oral candidacy exam required, foreign language not required. *Entrance requirements:* For master's, TOEFL (minimum score of 550 required). *Average time to degree:* Master's–2 years full-time. *Application deadline:* For fall admission, 4/30; for winter admission, 9/15; for spring admission, 1/31. Applications are processed on a rolling basis. Application fee: $60. *Financial aid:* In 1998–99, 7 students received aid, including 4 research assistantships (averag-

Environmental Policy and Resource Management

University of Calgary (continued)

ing $3,920 per year), 4 teaching assistantships (averaging $5,344 per year) Financial aid application deadline: 2/1. *Unit head:* Dr. Richard D. Revel, Director, 403-220-3622, Fax: 403-284-4399, E-mail: revel@ucalgary.ca. *Application contact:* Pauline Fisk, Administrative Assistant, 403-220-7209, Fax: 403-284-4399, E-mail: pfisk@ucalgary.ca.

University of California, Berkeley, Graduate Division, College of Natural Resources, Department of Environmental Science, Policy, and Management, Berkeley, CA 94720-1500. Offers environmental science, policy, and management (MS, PhD); forestry (MF); range management (MS). *Faculty:* 67 full-time (15 women), 2 part-time (1 woman). *Students:* 183 full-time (88 women); includes 12 minority (9 Asian Americans or Pacific Islanders, 3 Hispanic Americans), 21 international. 294 applicants, 19% accepted. In 1998, 15 master's, 14 doctorates awarded (80% entered university research/teaching, 20% found other work related to degree). *Degree requirements:* For doctorate, dissertation, qualifying exam required. *Entrance requirements:* For master's and doctorate, GRE General Test, minimum GPA of 3.0. *Average time to degree:* Master's–2 years full-time; doctorate–5 years full-time. *Application deadline:* For fall admission, 12/15. Application fee: $40. Electronic applications accepted. *Financial aid:* Application deadline: 12/15; *Faculty research:* Biology and ecology of insects; ecosystem function and environmental issues of soils; plant health/interactions from molecular to ecosystem levels; range management and ecology; forest and resource policy, sustainability, and management. *Unit head:* Dr. James W. Bartolome, Chair, 510-642-7945, Fax: 510-643-5438, E-mail: jwbart@nature.berkeley.edu. *Application contact:* Sue Jennison, Student Affairs Officer, 510-642-6410, Fax: 510-643-5438, E-mail: espmgradproginfo@nature.berkeley.edu.

See in-depth description on page 919.

University of California, Berkeley, Graduate Division, Group in Energy and Resources, Berkeley, CA 94720-1500. Offers MA, MS, PhD. *Students:* 50 full-time (22 women); includes 3 minority (1 Asian American or Pacific Islander, 1 Hispanic American, 1 Native American), 9 international. 59 applicants, 32% accepted. In 1998, 14 master's, 4 doctorates awarded. *Degree requirements:* For master's, project or thesis required; for doctorate, dissertation, qualifying exam required. *Entrance requirements:* For master's and doctorate, GRE General Test, minimum GPA of 3.0. *Application deadline:* For fall admission, 1/5. Application fee: $40. *Financial aid:* Application deadline: 1/5. *Faculty research:* Technical, economic, environmental, and institutional aspects of energy conservation in residential and commercial buildings; international patterns of energy use; renewable energy sources and barriers to their potential contribution to energy supplies; assessment of conventional and nonconventional valuation of energy and environmental resources pricing. *Unit head:* Per Peterson, Chair, 510-642-1640. *Application contact:* Kate Blake, Student Affairs Officer, 510-642-1750, Fax: 510-642-1085, E-mail: kblake2@socrates.berkeley.edu.

University of California, Irvine, Office of Research and Graduate Studies, School of Social Ecology, Department of Environmental Analysis and Design, Irvine, CA 92697. Offers environmental analysis and design (PhD); environmental health science and policy (MS, PhD); social ecology (MA, PhD). *Faculty:* 11 full-time (5 women). *Students:* 57 full-time (39 women); includes 17 minority (1 African American, 9 Asian Americans or Pacific Islanders, 6 Hispanic Americans, 1 Native American), 2 international. 46 applicants, 61% accepted. In 1998, 4 doctorates awarded. Terminal master's awarded for partial completion of doctoral program. *Degree requirements:* For master's, thesis required; for doctorate, dissertation, research project required. *Entrance requirements:* For master's, GRE General Test, minimum GPA of 3.0; for doctorate, GRE General Test. *Application deadline:* For fall admission, 1/15 (priority date). Applications are processed on a rolling basis. Application fee: $40. Electronic applications accepted. *Financial aid:* Fellowships, research assistantships, teaching assistantships, institutionally-sponsored loans and tuition waivers (full and partial) available. Financial aid application deadline: 3/2; financial aid applicants required to submit FAFSA. *Faculty research:* Effects of environmental stressors, environmental pollution, biology and politics of water pollution, potential impacts of natural disasters, risk management. *Unit head:* John Whiteley, Acting Chair, 949-824-5576. *Application contact:* Jeanne Haynes, Office of Student Affairs, 949-824-5917.

University of California, Santa Barbara, Graduate Division, School of Environmental Science and Management, Santa Barbara, CA 93106. Offers MESM. *Entrance requirements:* For master's, GRE, TOEFL (minimum score of 550 required). *Application deadline:* For fall admission, 3/1 (priority date). Application fee: $40. *Financial aid:* Fellowships, research assistantships, teaching assistantships, Federal Work-Study and institutionally-sponsored loans available. Financial aid applicants required to submit FAFSA. *Unit head:* Jeff Dozier, Dean, 805-893-7363, E-mail: info@bren.ucsb.edu. *Application contact:* Laura Haston, Assistant Dean of Students, 805-893-7363, E-mail: laura@esm.ucsb.edu.

See in-depth description on page 921.

University of California, Santa Cruz, Graduate Division, Division of Social Sciences, Program in Environmental Studies, Santa Cruz, CA 95064. Offers PhD. *Faculty:* 10 full-time. *Students:* 35 full-time (15 women); includes 4 minority (1 Asian American or Pacific Islander, 3 Hispanic Americans), 3 international. 58 applicants, 22% accepted. *Degree requirements:* For doctorate, dissertation, qualifying exam required. *Entrance requirements:* For doctorate, GRE General Test. *Application deadline:* For fall admission, 1/7. Application fee: $40. *Financial aid:* Fellowships, research assistantships, teaching assistantships, career-related internships or fieldwork, Federal Work-Study, and institutionally-sponsored loans available. Financial aid application deadline: 1/7. *Faculty research:* Political economy and sustainability, conservation biology, agroecology. *Unit head:* David Goodman, Chairperson, 831-459-4561. *Application contact:* Graduate Admissions, 831-459-2301.

University of Chicago, The Irving B. Harris Graduate School of Public Policy Studies, Chicago, IL 60637-1513. Offers environmental science and policy (MS); public policy studies (AM, MPP, PhD). Part-time programs available. *Faculty:* 23 full-time (3 women), 5 part-time (1 woman). *Students:* 148 full-time, 7 part-time; includes 38 minority (11 African Americans, 19 Asian Americans or Pacific Islanders, 8 Hispanic Americans), 44 international. Terminal master's awarded for partial completion of doctoral program. *Degree requirements:* For master's, foreign language and thesis not required; for doctorate, dissertation required, foreign language not required. *Entrance requirements:* For master's and doctorate, GMAT or GRE General Test, TOEFL. *Application deadline:* For fall admission, 1/15 (priority date). Applications are processed on a rolling basis. Application fee: $50. *Unit head:* Dr. Robert T. Michael, Dean, 773-702-9623, E-mail: r-michael@uchicago.edu. *Application contact:* Ellen Cohen, Director of Admission, 773-702-8401, Fax: 773-702-0926, E-mail: eb-cohen@uchicago.edu.

University of Connecticut, Graduate School, College of Agriculture and Natural Resources, Field of Natural Resources: Land, Water, and Air, Storrs, CT 06269. Offers MS. *Entrance requirements:* For master's, GRE General Test, GRE Subject Test, TOEFL. *Faculty research:* Natural resource management, forest management, forest protection, water resources, biometeorology.

University of Delaware, College of Human Resources, Education and Public Policy, Center for Energy and Environmental Policy, Newark, DE 19716. Offers environmental and energy policy (MS, PhD); urban affairs and public policy (MA, PhD), including energy and environmental policy (MA), technology, environment and society (PhD). *Faculty:* 10 full-time (3 women), 2 part-time (0 women). *Students:* 43 full-time (15 women), 17 part-time (8 women); includes 11 minority (4 African Americans, 2 Asian Americans or Pacific Islanders, 3 Hispanic Americans, 2 Native Americans), 27 international. 110 applicants, 12% accepted. *Degree requirements:* For master's, analytical paper or thesis required; for doctorate, dissertation required, foreign language not required. *Entrance requirements:* For master's, GRE General Test (minimum combined score of 1100 required), TOEFL (minimum score of 580 required), minimum GPA of 3.0; for doctorate, GRE General Test (minimum combined score of 1100 required), TOEFL (minimum score of 600 required), minimum GPA of 3.5. *Application deadline:* For fall admission, 12/1 (priority date); for spring admission, 3/1. Application fee: $45. *Financial aid:* In 1998–99, 39 students received aid, including 12 fellowships with tuition reimbursements available, 26 research assistantships with tuition reimbursements available; career-related internships or fieldwork and Federal Work-Study also available. Financial aid application deadline: 3/1. *Faculty research:* Sustainable development, renewable energy, climate change, environmental policy, environmental justice. Total annual research expenditures: $590,000. *Unit head:* Dr. John Byrne, Director, 302-831-8405, Fax: 302-831-3098, E-mail: jbbyrne@strauss.udel.edu. *Application contact:* Patricia Grimes, Staff Assistant, 302-831-8405, Fax: 302-831-3098, E-mail: patricia.grimes@mus.udel.edu.

See in-depth description on page 923.

University of Denver, University College, Denver, CO 80208. Offers applied communication (MSS); computer information systems (MCIS); environmental policy and management (MEPM); healthcare systems (MHS); liberal studies (MLS); library and information services (MLIS); public health (MPH); technology management (MoTM); telecommunications (MTEL). Part-time and evening/weekend programs available. Postbaccalaureate distance learning degree programs offered (no on-campus study). *Faculty:* 1 (woman) full-time, 553 part-time (181 women). *Students:* 1,529 (804 women); includes 189 minority (67 African Americans, 33 Asian Americans or Pacific Islanders, 75 Hispanic Americans, 14 Native Americans) 61 international. *Entrance requirements:* For master's, minimum undergraduate GPA of 3.0. *Application deadline:* For fall admission, 8/10; for spring admission, 2/22. Applications are processed on a rolling basis. Application fee: $25. *Unit head:* Peter Warren, Dean, 303-871-3268, Fax: 303-871-4047, E-mail: pwarren@du.edu. *Application contact:* Bryan Ehrlich, Admission Coordinator, 303-871-3969, Fax: 303-871-3303, E-mail: behrlich@du.edu.

The University of Findlay, College of Science, Natural Science Division, Findlay, OH 45840-3653. Offers environmental management (MSEM). *Degree requirements:* For master's, cumulative project required. *Entrance requirements:* For master's, GMAT.

University of Guelph, Faculty of Graduate Studies, Ontario Agricultural College, Department of Environmental Biology, Guelph, ON N1G 2W1, Canada. Offers environmental management (M Sc, PhD); plant protection (M Sc, PhD). *Faculty:* 21 full-time (2 women), 6 part-time (0 women). *Students:* 57 full-time (39 women), 10 part-time (2 women), 8 international. *Degree requirements:* For master's and doctorate, thesis/dissertation required. *Entrance requirements:* For master's, minimum B- average during previous 2 years; for doctorate, minimum B average. *Application deadline:* Applications are processed on a rolling basis. Application fee: $60. *Expenses:* Tuition and fees charges are reported in Canadian dollars. Tuition, area resident: Full-time $4,725 Canadian dollars; part-time $1,055 Canadian dollars per term. International tuition: $6,999 Canadian dollars full-time. Required fees: $295 Canadian dollars per term. *Unit head:* Dr. M. K. Sears, Chair, 519-824-4120 Ext. 3921, Fax: 519-837-0442, E-mail: msears@evbhort.uoguelph.ca. *Application contact:* Dr. G. J. Boland, Admissions Coordinator, 519-824-4120 Ext. 2755, Fax: 519-837-0442, E-mail: gboland@evbhort.uoguelph.ca.

University of Guelph, Faculty of Graduate Studies, Program in Resource and Environmental Economics, Guelph, ON N1G 2W1, Canada. Offers PhD. Offered in cooperation with the Department of Agricultural Economics and Business and the Department of Economics. *Faculty:* 18 full-time (1 woman). *Students:* 11 full-time (4 women). 15 applicants, 33% accepted. In 1998, 1 degree awarded. *Degree requirements:* For doctorate, dissertation required. *Entrance requirements:* For doctorate, minimum A- average. *Application deadline:* For fall admission, 3/1 (priority date). Application fee: $60. *Expenses:* Tuition and fees charges are reported in Canadian dollars. Tuition, area resident: Full-time $4,725 Canadian dollars; part-time $1,055 Canadian dollars per term. International tuition: $6,999 Canadian dollars full-time. Required fees: $295 Canadian dollars per term. *Financial aid:* In 1998–99, 3 fellowships, 7 teaching assistantships were awarded.; bursaries also available. Financial aid application deadline: 2/1. *Faculty research:* Regulation and taxation of polluting industries, enforcement, contingent valuation, nonpoint source pollution, petroleum economics. *Unit head:* Dr. A. Sadanand, Graduate Coordinator, 519-824-4120 Ext. 8947, Fax: 519-763-8497, E-mail: asha@css.uoguelph.ca.

University of Hawaii at Manoa, Graduate Division, College of Arts and Sciences, College of Social Sciences, Department of Urban and Regional Planning, Honolulu, HI 96822. Offers community planning and social policy (MURP); environmental planning and management (MURP); land use and infrastructure planning (MURP); urban and regional planning in Asia and Pacific (MURP). *Accreditation:* ACSP. *Faculty:* 26 full-time (6 women). *Students:* 31 full-time (16 women), 29 part-time (9 women); includes 22 minority (21 Asian Americans or Pacific Islanders, 1 Hispanic American), 12 international. *Entrance requirements:* For master's, GRE, TOEFL, minimum GPA of 3.0. *Application deadline:* For fall admission, 2/1; for spring admission, 9/1. Application fee: $25 ($50 for international students). *Unit head:* Karl Kim, Chairperson, 808-956-7381, Fax: 808-956-6870.

University of Houston–Clear Lake, School of Business and Public Administration, Program in General Business, Houston, TX 77058-1098. Offers administration of health services (MS); environmental management (MS); healthcare administration (MHA); human resource management (MA); public management (MA). *Accreditation:* ACEHSA (one or more programs are accredited). *Faculty:* 15. *Students:* 28 full-time (20 women), 60 part-time (24 women); includes 14 minority (3 African Americans, 5 Asian Americans or Pacific Islanders, 6 Hispanic Americans), 3 international. *Degree requirements:* For master's, thesis optional, foreign language not required. *Entrance requirements:* For master's, GMAT (average 510). *Application deadline:* For fall admission, 8/1; for spring admission, 12/1. Applications are processed on a rolling basis. Application fee: $30 ($70 for international students). Electronic applications accepted. *Unit head:* Dr. Richard Allison, Chair, 281-283-3251. *Application contact:* Dr. Sue Neeley, Associate Dean, 281-283-3110.

University of Idaho, College of Graduate Studies, College of Forestry, Wildlife, and Range Sciences, Department of Resource Recreation and Tourism, Moscow, ID 83844-4140. Offers MS, PhD. *Faculty:* 8 full-time (0 women). *Students:* 11 full-time (3 women), 6 part-time (2 women); includes 2 minority (1 African American, 1 Native American), 1 international. In 1998, 6 degrees awarded. *Degree requirements:* For doctorate, dissertation required, foreign language not required, foreign language not required. *Entrance requirements:* For master's, minimum GPA of 2.8; for doctorate, minimum undergraduate GPA of 2.8, 3.0 graduate. *Application deadline:* For fall admission, 8/1; for spring admission, 12/15. Application fee: $35 ($45 for international students). *Financial aid:* In 1998–99, 4 research assistantships (averaging $7,672 per year), 7 teaching assistantships (averaging $7,162 per year) were awarded. Financial aid application deadline: 2/15. *Unit head:* Dr. John D. Hunt, Head, 208-885-7911.

University of Illinois at Springfield, Graduate Programs, College of Public Affairs and Administration, Program in Environmental Studies, Springfield, IL 62794-9243. Offers MA. *Faculty:* 6 full-time (0 women), 1 part-time (0 women). *Students:* 22 full-time (13 women), 52 part-time (32 women); includes 4 minority (2 African Americans, 1 Asian American or Pacific Islander, 1 Hispanic American), 4 international. Average age 31. 35 applicants, 54% accepted. In 1998, 13 degrees awarded. *Degree requirements:* For master's, thesis or alternative required, foreign language not required. *Entrance requirements:* For master's, GRE General Test, minimum GPA of 3.0. *Application deadline:* Applications are processed on a rolling basis. Application fee: $0. *Financial aid:* In 1998–99, 26 students received aid, including 3 research assistantships with full and partial tuition reimbursements available; career-related internships or fieldwork, Federal Work-Study, grants, tuition waivers (partial), and unspecified assistantships also available. Financial aid application deadline: 6/1; financial aid applicants required to submit FAFSA. *Faculty research:* Population ecology and evolution, transportation and energy resource planning, environmental economics, environmental policies, risk assessment. *Unit head:* Malcolm Levin, Chair, 217-206-6720.

University of Maine, Graduate School, College of Natural Sciences, Forestry, and Agriculture, Program in Resource Utilization, Orono, ME 04469. Offers MS. *Faculty:* 10 full-time (1 woman).

Students: 3 (1 woman). Average age 26. 1 applicants, 100% accepted. In 1998, 3 degrees awarded. *Degree requirements:* For master's, thesis required, foreign language not required. *Entrance requirements:* For master's, GRE General Test, TOEFL (minimum score of 550 required). *Application deadline:* For fall admission, 2/1 (priority date); for spring admission, 10/15. Applications are processed on a rolling basis. Application fee: $50. *Financial aid:* Research assistantships, teaching assistantships, career-related internships or fieldwork, Federal Work-Study, institutionally-sponsored loans, scholarships, and tuition waivers (full and partial) available. Financial aid application deadline: 3/1. *Faculty research:* Waste utilities, wildlife evaluation, tourism and recreation economics. *Unit head:* Scott G. Delcourt, Director of the Graduate School, 207-581-3218, Fax: 207-581-3232, E-mail: graduate@maine.edu. *Application contact:* Scott G. Delcourt, Director of the Graduate School, 207-581-3218, Fax: 207-581-3232, E-mail: graduate@maine.edu.

University of Manitoba, Faculty of Graduate Studies, Natural Resources Institute, Winnipeg, MB R3T 2N2, Canada. Offers natural resources management (MNRM). *Unit head:* F. Berkes, Director and Chair, Graduate Committee.

University of Maryland, College Park, Graduate School, College of Life Sciences, Program in Sustainable Development and Conservation Biology, College Park, MD 20742-5045. Offers MS. *Students:* 23 full-time (17 women), 15 part-time (9 women); includes 3 minority (2 Hispanic Americans, 1 Native American), 4 international. 70 applicants, 43% accepted. In 1998, 11 degrees awarded. *Degree requirements:* For master's, internship, scholarly paper required, foreign language and thesis not required. *Entrance requirements:* For master's, GRE General Test, minimum GPA of 3.0. *Application deadline:* Applications are processed on a rolling basis. Application fee: $50 ($70 for international students). Tuition, state resident: part-time $272 per credit hour. Tuition, nonresident: part-time $475 per credit hour. Required fees: $632; $379 per year. *Financial aid:* Fellowships, research assistantships, teaching assistantships available. Financial aid applicants required to submit FAFSA. *Faculty research:* Biodiversity, global change, conservation. *Unit head:* Dr. David W. Inouye, Acting Director, 301-405-7409. *Application contact:* Trudy Lindsey, Director, Graduate Admission and Records, 301-405-4198, Fax: 301-314-9305, E-mail: grschool@deans.umd.edu.

University of Maryland University College, Graduate School of Management and Technology, Program in Environmental Management, College Park, MD 20742-1600. Offers MS. Offered evenings and weekends only. Part-time and evening/weekend programs available. Postbaccalaureate distance learning degree programs offered (no on-campus study). 16 applicants, 100% accepted. In 1998, 3 degrees awarded. *Degree requirements:* For master's, thesis or alternative required, foreign language not required. *Entrance requirements:* For master's, BS/BA in social science, physical science, engineering; 6 semester hours in biology and chemistry; 1 year of experience in field. *Application deadline:* Applications are processed on a rolling basis. Application fee: $50. Electronic applications accepted. Tuition, state resident: full-time $5,058; part-time $281 per credit. Tuition, nonresident: full-time $6,876; part-time $382 per credit. Tuition and fees vary according to program. *Financial aid:* Federal Work-Study, grants, and scholarships available. Aid available to part-time students. Financial aid application deadline: 6/1; financial aid applicants required to submit FAFSA. *Unit head:* John Aje, Director, 301-985-7200, Fax: 301-985-4611, E-mail: jaje@nova.umuc.edu. *Application contact:* Coordinator, Graduate Admissions, 301-985-7155, Fax: 301-985-7175, E-mail: gradinfo@nova.umuc.edu.

University of Michigan, School of Natural Resources and Environment, Program in Natural Resource Economics, Ann Arbor, MI 48109. Offers PhD, MS/AM. Offered through the Horace H. Rackham School of Graduate Studies; MS/AM offered jointly with the Interdepartmental Program in Russian and East EuropeanStudies. *Degree requirements:* For doctorate, oral defense of dissertation, preliminary exam required. *Entrance requirements:* For doctorate, GRE General Test, TOEFL, master's degree.

University of Minnesota, Twin Cities Campus, Graduate School, Hubert H. Humphrey Institute of Public Affairs, Program in Science, Technology, and Environmental Policy, Minneapolis, MN 55455-0213. Offers MS. *Degree requirements:* For master's, thesis, internship or equivalent work experience required, foreign language not required. *Entrance requirements:* For master's, GRE General Test, TOEFL (minimum score of 600 required), undergraduate training in the biological or physical sciences or engineering. *Application deadline:* For fall admission, 1/15 (priority date). Applications are processed on a rolling basis. Application fee: $50 ($55 for international students). Electronic applications accepted. *Financial aid:* Fellowships, research assistantships, teaching assistantships, career-related internships or fieldwork, scholarships, and tuition waivers (full and partial) available. Financial aid application deadline: 1/15. *Faculty research:* Economics, history, philosophy, and politics of science and technology; organization and management of science and technology. *Unit head:* Helen Lum, Administrative Associate II, 734-764-4260, Fax: 734-763-7863, E-mail: helenlum@engin.umich.edu. *Application contact:* Lynda Wilson, Director of Admissions, 612-626-7229, Fax: 612-625-6351, E-mail: admissions@hhh.umn.edu.

University of Missouri–St. Louis, Graduate School, College of Arts and Sciences, Department of Biology, St. Louis, MO 63121-4499. Offers biology (MS, PhD), including animal behavior (MS), biochemistry, biotechnology (MS), conservation biology (MS), development (MS), ecology (MS), environmental studies (PhD), evolution (MS), genetics (MS), molecular biology and biotechnology (PhD), molecular/cellular biology (MS), physiology (MS), plant systematics, population biology (MS), tropical biology (MS); biotechnology (Certificate); tropical biology and conservation (Certificate). Part-time programs available. *Faculty:* 47. *Students:* 20 full-time (12 women), 73 part-time (47 women); includes 18 minority (3 African Americans, 4 Asian Americans or Pacific Islanders, 11 Hispanic Americans), 22 international. *Degree requirements:* For master's, thesis or alternative required, foreign language not required; for doctorate, one foreign language, dissertation, 1 semester of teaching experience required. *Entrance requirements:* For doctorate, GRE General Test. *Application deadline:* For fall admission, 7/1 (priority date); for spring admission, 11/1 (priority date). Applications are processed on a rolling basis. Application fee: $25 ($40 for international students). Electronic applications accepted. *Unit head:* Director of Graduate Studies, 314-516-6203, Fax: 314-516-6233, E-mail: icte@umsl.edu. *Application contact:* Graduate Admissions, 314-516-5458, Fax: 314-516-6759, E-mail: gradadm@umsl.edu.

The University of Montana–Missoula, Graduate School, College of Arts and Sciences, Program in Environmental Studies (EVST), Missoula, MT 59812-0002. Offers MS, JD/MS. Part-time programs available. *Faculty:* 3 full-time (1 woman), 5 part-time (0 women). *Students:* 61 full-time (31 women), 26 part-time (10 women); includes 4 minority (1 African American, 3 Native Americans), 5 international. Average age 28. 151 applicants, 46% accepted. In 1998, 30 degrees awarded. *Degree requirements:* For master's, portfolio, professional paper, or thesis required. *Entrance requirements:* For master's, GRE General Test (minimum score of 500 on verbal section required). *Average time to degree:* Master's–2.2 years full-time, 3 years part-time. *Application deadline:* For fall admission, 2/15. Application fee: $45. *Financial aid:* In 1998–99, 9 teaching assistantships with tuition reimbursements (averaging $6,900 per year) were awarded.; career-related internships or fieldwork and Federal Work-Study also available. Aid available to part-time students. Financial aid application deadline: 3/1. *Faculty research:* Conservation and pollution biology, applied ecology. *Unit head:* Tom M. Roy, Director, 406-243-6273, E-mail: tomroy@selway.umt.edu. *Application contact:* Tom M. Roy, Director, 406-243-6273, E-mail: tomroy@selway.umt.edu.

Announcement: An interdisciplinary graduate program leading to a master's degree, the Environmental Studies Program accepts students from all disciplines. Emphasis is upon activism, with strengths in environmental science, policy-law, education, public-land ecosystem management, water issues, and environmental thought and writing. For more information, application, and in-depth description of the program, contact 406-243-6273 (E-mail: evst@selway.umt.edu, World Wide Web: http://www.umt.edu/evst).

The University of Montana–Missoula, Graduate School, School of Forestry, Program in Ecosystem Management, Missoula, MT 59812-0002. Offers MEM. *Students:* 3 full-time (all women), 1 part-time. Average age 23. In 1998, 1 degree awarded. *Degree requirements:* For master's, foreign language and thesis not required. *Entrance requirements:* For master's, GRE General Test (minimum combined score of 1540 on three sections required). *Application deadline:* For fall admission, 1/31. Application fee: $45. *Financial aid:* Application deadline: 3/1. *Unit head:* Dr. Don Potts, Associate Dean, 406-243-5521.

University of Nevada, Reno, Graduate School, Interdisciplinary Program in Land Use Planning, Reno, NV 89557. Offers MS. Offered through the College of Arts and Science, the College of Engineering, and the College of Agriculture. *Degree requirements:* For master's, thesis required, foreign language not required. *Entrance requirements:* For master's, GRE General Test, TOEFL (minimum score of 500 required), minimum GPA of 3.0.

University of New Hampshire, Graduate School, College of Life Sciences and Agriculture, Department of Resource Economics and Development, Durham, NH 03824. Offers resource administration and management (MS); resource economics (MS). Part-time programs available. *Faculty:* 6 full-time. *Students:* 12 full-time (6 women), 4 part-time (1 woman); includes 1 minority (Asian American or Pacific Islander), 3 international. Average age 32. 13 applicants, 92% accepted. In 1998, 3 degrees awarded. *Degree requirements:* For master's, thesis or alternative required, foreign language not required. *Entrance requirements:* For master's, GRE General Test. *Application deadline:* For fall admission, 4/1 (priority date). Applications are processed on a rolling basis. Application fee: $50. Tuition, area resident: Full-time $5,750; part-time $319 per credit. Tuition, state resident: full-time $8,625. Tuition, nonresident: full-time $14,640; part-time $598 per credit. Required fees: $224 per semester. Tuition and fees vary according to course load, degree level and program. *Financial aid:* In 1998–99, 4 research assistantships, 3 teaching assistantships were awarded.; career-related internships or fieldwork, Federal Work-Study, scholarships, and tuition waivers (full and partial) also available. Aid available to part-time students. Financial aid application deadline: 2/15. *Unit head:* Dr. Bruce E. Lindsay, Chairperson, 603-862-3923. *Application contact:* Doug Morris, Graduate Coordinator, 603-862-3233.

University of New Hampshire, Graduate School, College of Life Sciences and Agriculture, Graduate Programs in the Biological Sciences and Natural Resources, Durham, NH 03824. Offers animal and nutritional sciences (MS, PhD); biochemistry and molecular biology (MS, PhD); biology (MS); genetics (MS, PhD); microbiology (MS, PhD); natural resources (MS, PhD), including environmental conservation (MS), forestry (MS), natural resources (PhD), soil science (MS), water resources management (MS), wildlife (MS); plant biology (MS, PhD); zoology (MS, PhD). Part-time programs available. *Faculty:* 129 full-time. *Students:* 127 full-time (74 women), 111 part-time (56 women); includes 6 minority (4 Asian Americans or Pacific Islanders, 2 Hispanic Americans), 31 international. Terminal master's awarded for partial completion of doctoral program. *Degree requirements:* For doctorate, dissertation required, foreign language not required. *Entrance requirements:* For master's, GRE General Test. *Application deadline:* Applications are processed on a rolling basis. Application fee: $50. Tuition, area resident: Full-time $5,750; part-time $319 per credit. Tuition, state resident: full-time $8,625. Tuition, nonresident: full-time $14,640; part-time $598 per credit. Required fees: $224 per semester. Tuition and fees vary according to course load, degree level and program. *Unit head:* Dr. William Mautz, Interim Dean, College of Life Sciences and Agriculture, 603-862-1450.

University of New Hampshire, Graduate School, College of Life Sciences and Agriculture, Graduate Programs in the Biological Sciences and Natural Resources, Department of Natural Resources, Option in Environmental Conservation, Durham, NH 03824. Offers MS. *Students:* 9 full-time (6 women), 7 part-time (3 women). Average age 32. 22 applicants, 45% accepted. In 1998, 6 degrees awarded. *Degree requirements:* For master's, thesis or alternative required, foreign language not required. *Entrance requirements:* For master's, GRE General Test. *Application deadline:* For fall admission, 3/15. Application fee: $50. Tuition, area resident: Full-time $5,750; part-time $319 per credit. Tuition, state resident: full-time $8,625. Tuition, nonresident: full-time $14,640; part-time $598 per credit. Required fees: $224 per semester. Tuition and fees vary according to course load, degree level and program. *Financial aid:* In 1998–99, 5 research assistantships, 3 teaching assistantships were awarded.; Federal Work-Study, scholarships, and tuition waivers (full and partial) also available. Financial aid application deadline: 2/15. *Unit head:* Dr. David Lambert, Director of Graduate Studies, 702-784-1675, E-mail: davel@unr.edu. *Application contact:* Dr. Robert Harter, Graduate Coordinator, 603-862-3944.

University of New Hampshire, Graduate School, College of Life Sciences and Agriculture, Graduate Programs in the Biological Sciences and Natural Resources, Department of Natural Resources, Option in Water Resources Management, Durham, NH 03824. Offers MS. *Students:* 3 full-time (2 women), 7 part-time (4 women), 1 international. Average age 28. 11 applicants, 27% accepted. In 1998, 4 degrees awarded. *Degree requirements:* For master's, thesis or alternative required, foreign language not required. *Entrance requirements:* For master's, GRE General Test. *Application deadline:* For fall admission, 4/1. Application fee: $50. Tuition, area resident: Full-time $5,750; part-time $319 per credit. Tuition, state resident: full-time $8,625. Tuition, nonresident: full-time $14,640; part-time $598 per credit. Required fees: $224 per semester. Tuition and fees vary according to course load, degree level and program. *Financial aid:* In 1998–99, 3 research assistantships were awarded.; teaching assistantships, Federal Work-Study, scholarships, and tuition waivers (full and partial) also available. Financial aid application deadline: 2/15. *Application contact:* Dr. Robert Harter, Graduate Coordinator, 603-862-3944.

University of Oregon, Graduate School, College of Arts and Sciences, Interdisciplinary Program in Environmental Studies, Eugene, OR 97403. Offers MA, MS, JD/MS. *Faculty:* 1 part-time (0 women). *Students:* 13 full-time (8 women), 4 part-time; includes 1 minority (Asian American or Pacific Islander), 1 international. Average age 30. 71 applicants, 7% accepted. In 1998, 7 degrees awarded. *Degree requirements:* For master's, thesis required, foreign language not required. *Entrance requirements:* For master's, GRE General Test (minimum combined score of 1100 required; average 1868 on three sections), TOEFL. *Average time to degree:* Master's–3 years full-time, 5 years part-time. *Application deadline:* For fall admission, 1/15. Application fee: $50. *Financial aid:* Teaching assistantships, career-related internships or fieldwork and Federal Work-Study available. *Unit head:* Daniel Udovic, Director, 541-346-5006, Fax: 541-346-5954, E-mail: udovic@oregon.uoregon.edu. *Application contact:* Jacqueline Willoughby, Graduate Secretary, 541-346-5006, Fax: 541-346-5954, E-mail: jacwill@oregon.uoregon.edu.

Announcement: The Environmental Studies Program is supported by a full range of graduate-level courses offered by over 80 faculty members in many disciplines. The program offers a flexible, explicitly interdisciplinary, largely student-designed program that attracts exceptionally strong students, many of whom have nonacademic environmental experience (employment, volunteer work, internships, Peace Corps). Visit the Web site at http://darkwing.uoregon.edu/~ecostudy.

University of Rhode Island, Graduate School, College of Arts and Sciences, Department of Marine Affairs, Kingston, RI 02881. Offers MA, MMA.

See in-depth description on page 925.

University of Rhode Island, Graduate School, College of Resource Development, Department of Environmental and Natural Resource Economics, Kingston, RI 02881. Offers resource economics and marine resources (MS, PhD). *Degree requirements:* For master's, thesis optional; for doctorate, dissertation required. *Entrance requirements:* For master's and doctorate, GRE General Test, TOEFL.

Environmental Policy and Resource Management

University of St. Thomas, Graduate Studies, Graduate School of Business, Day MBA Program, St. Paul, MN 55105-1096. Offers accounting (MBA); environmental management (MBA); finance (MBA); financial services management (MBA); franchise management (MBA); government contracts (MBA); health care management (MBA); human resource management (MBA); information management (MBA); insurance and risk management (MBA); management (MBA); manufacturing systems (MBA); marketing (MBA); nonprofit management (MBA); sports and entertainment management (MBA); venture management (MBA). *Faculty:* 13 full-time (4 women), 4 part-time (0 women). *Students:* 63 full-time (24 women), 10 part-time (4 women); includes 4 minority (2 African Americans, 2 Asian Americans or Pacific Islanders), 6 international. *Degree requirements:* For master's, computer language required, foreign language and thesis not required. *Entrance requirements:* For master's, GMAT (score in 50th percentile or higher required). *Application deadline:* For fall admission, 5/1 (priority date). Applications are processed on a rolling basis. Application fee: $30. Tuition: Full-time $16,155; part-time $497 per credit. Tuition and fees vary according to program and student level. *Unit head:* Martha Ballard, Director of Faculty and Student Services, 651-962-4226, Fax: 651-962-4260, E-mail: mbballard@stthomas.edu. *Application contact:* Jim O'Connor, Program Services Manager, 651-962-4233, Fax: 651-962-4260, E-mail: jdconner@stthomas.edu.

University of St. Thomas, Graduate Studies, Graduate School of Business, Evening MBA Program, St. Paul, MN 55105-1096. Offers accounting (MBA, Certificate); environmental management (MBA); finance (MBA); financial services management (MBA); franchise management (MBA, Certificate); government contracts (MBA, Certificate); health care management (MBA, Certificate); human resource management (MBA, Certificate); information management (MBA); insurance and risk management (MBA); management (MBA); manufacturing systems (MBA); marketing (MBA); nonprofit management (MBA, Certificate); sports and entertainment management (MBA); venture management (MBA, Certificate). Part-time and evening/weekend programs available. *Faculty:* 19 full-time (4 women), 93 part-time (20 women). *Students:* 45 full-time (23 women), 1,791 part-time (710 women); includes 72 minority (20 African Americans, 34 Asian Americans or Pacific Islanders, 14 Hispanic Americans, 4 Native Americans), 47 international. *Degree requirements:* For master's, computer language required, foreign language and thesis not required. *Entrance requirements:* For master's, GMAT (score in 50th percentile or higher required). *Application deadline:* For fall admission, 8/1 (priority date); for spring admission, 12/1. Applications are processed on a rolling basis. Application fee: $30. Tuition: Part-time $437 per credit. Tuition and fees vary according to degree level, program and student level. *Unit head:* Dr. Stanford Nyquist, MBA Director, 651-962-4242. *Application contact:* Martha Ballard, Director of Faculty and Student Services, 651-962-4226, Fax: 651-962-4260, E-mail: mbballard@stthomas.edu.

University of San Diego, College of Arts and Sciences, Program in Marine and Environmental Studies, San Diego, CA 92110-2492. Offers marine science (MS). Part-time programs available. *Faculty:* 5 full-time (3 women), 9 part-time (3 women). *Students:* 30 (15 women); includes 4 minority (1 Asian American or Pacific Islander, 2 Hispanic Americans, 1 Native American) 2 international. Average age 25. 23 applicants, 70% accepted. In 1998, 7 degrees awarded. *Degree requirements:* For master's, thesis required, foreign language not required. *Entrance requirements:* For master's, GRE, TOEFL (minimum score of 580 required), TWE (minimum score of 4.5 required), minimum GPA of 3.0, undergraduate major in science. *Application deadline:* For fall admission, 5/1 (priority date). Applications are processed on a rolling basis. Application fee: $45. Tuition: Part-time $630 per unit. Tuition and fees vary according to degree level. *Financial aid:* Fellowships with partial tuition reimbursements, teaching assistantships with partial tuition reimbursements, career-related internships or fieldwork, Federal Work-Study, institutionally-sponsored loans, tuition waivers (partial), and unspecified assistantships available. Aid available to part-time students. Financial aid application deadline: 5/1; financial aid applicants required to submit FAFSA. *Faculty research:* Marine ecology; paleoclimatology; geochemistry; functional morphology; marine zoology of mammals, birds and turtles. *Unit head:* Dr. Hugh I. Ellis, Director, 619-260-4075, Fax: 619-260-6804, E-mail: ellis@acusd.edu. *Application contact:* Mary Jane Tiernan, Director of Graduate Admissions, 619-260-4524, Fax: 619-260-4158, E-mail: grads@acusd.edu.

University of San Francisco, College of Arts and Sciences, Program in Environmental Management, San Francisco, CA 94117-1080. Offers MS. Evening/weekend programs available. *Faculty:* 4 full-time (1 woman), 11 part-time (2 women). *Students:* 40 full-time (20 women), 22 part-time (9 women); includes 15 minority (2 African Americans, 8 Asian Americans or Pacific Islanders, 3 Hispanic Americans, 2 Native Americans), 2 international. Average age 33. 61 applicants, 90% accepted. In 1998, 24 degrees awarded. *Degree requirements:* For master's, thesis required, foreign language not required. *Entrance requirements:* For master's, 3 semesters of chemistry, minimum GPA of 2.7, work experience in environmental field. *Application deadline:* For fall admission, 3/1 (priority date). Applications are processed on a rolling basis. Application fee: $40 ($50 for international students). Tuition: Full-time $12,618; part-time $701 per unit. Tuition and fees vary according to course load, degree level, campus/location and program. *Financial aid:* In 1998–99, 20 students received aid; teaching assistantships, career-related internships or fieldwork available. Financial aid application deadline: 3/2. *Faculty research:* Problems of environmental managers, water quality, hazardous materials, environmental health. *Unit head:* Dr. R. James Brown, Director, 415-422-6553, Fax: 415-422-2346.

University of South Carolina, Graduate School, School of the Environment, Program in Earth and Environmental Resources Management, Columbia, SC 29208. Offers MEERM. Part-time programs available. Postbaccalaureate distance learning degree programs offered (no on-campus study). *Faculty:* 125 full-time (23 women). *Students:* 20 full-time (11 women), 21 part-time (6 women); includes 3 minority (all African Americans), 3 international. Average age 31. 24 applicants, 42% accepted. In 1998, 10 degrees awarded. *Degree requirements:* For master's, thesis optional, foreign language not required. *Entrance requirements:* For master's, GRE General Test, TOEFL. *Average time to degree:* Master's–2 years full-time, 4 years part-time. *Application deadline:* For fall admission, 7/15 (priority date); for spring admission, 11/15. Applications are processed on a rolling basis. Application fee: $35. Electronic applications accepted. Tuition, state resident: full-time $4,014; part-time $202 per credit hour. Tuition, nonresident: full-time $8,528; part-time $428 per credit hour. Required fees: $100; $4 per credit hour. Tuition and fees vary according to program. *Financial aid:* In 1998–99, 9 students received aid, including 1 fellowship with partial tuition reimbursement available, 8 research assistantships with partial tuition reimbursements available, 3 teaching assistantships with partial tuition reimbursements available; career-related internships or fieldwork and grants also available. *Faculty research:* Hydrology, sustainable development, environmental geology and biology, energy/environmental resources management. *Application contact:* Dr. M. Jerry Bartholomew, Program/Graduate Director, 803-777-1325, Fax: 803-777-5715, E-mail: meerm@environ.sc.edu.

University of Tennessee, Knoxville, Graduate School, College of Arts and Sciences, Department of Sociology, Knoxville, TN 37996. Offers criminology (MA, PhD); energy, environment, and resource policy (MA, PhD); political economy (MA, PhD). Part-time programs available. *Faculty:* 15 full-time (2 women), 1 (woman) part-time. *Students:* 31 full-time (19 women), 26 part-time (13 women); includes 4 minority (3 African Americans, 1 Native American), 4 international. *Degree requirements:* For master's, thesis or alternative required, foreign language not required; for doctorate, dissertation required, foreign language not required. *Entrance requirements:* For master's, GRE General Test, TOEFL (minimum score of 550 required), minimum GPA of 3.0; for doctorate, GRE General Test, TOEFL (minimum score of 550 required), minimum GPA of 3.5. *Application deadline:* For fall admission, 2/1 (priority date). Applications are processed on a rolling basis. Application fee: $35. Electronic applications accepted. *Unit head:* Dr. Suzanne Kurth, Head, 423-974-6021, Fax: 423-974-7013, E-mail: skurth@utk.edu. *Application contact:* Dr. Robert G. Perrin, Graduate Representative, 423-974-7032, E-mail: rgperrin@utk.edu.

University of Tennessee, Knoxville, Graduate School, College of Business Administration, Program in Business Administration, Knoxville, TN 37996. Offers accounting (PhD); economics (MBA); entrepreneurship/new venture analysis (MBA); environmental management (MBA); executive business administration (MBA); finance (MBA, PhD); forest industries management (MBA); global business (MBA); logistics and transportation (MBA, PhD); management (MBA, PhD); manufacturing management (MBA); marketing (MBA, PhD); professional business administration (MBA); statistics (MBA, PhD). Postbaccalaureate distance learning degree programs offered. *Faculty:* 51 full-time (6 women). *Students:* 278 full-time (72 women), 17 part-time (2 women); includes 24 minority (13 African Americans, 5 Asian Americans or Pacific Islanders, 2 Hispanic Americans, 4 Native Americans), 47 international. *Degree requirements:* For master's, computer language, thesis or alternative required, foreign language not required; for doctorate, computer language, dissertation required, foreign language not required. *Entrance requirements:* For master's and doctorate, GMAT, TOEFL (minimum score of 550 required), minimum GPA of 2.7. *Application deadline:* For fall admission, 2/1 (priority date). Application fee: $35. Electronic applications accepted. *Unit head:* Dr. Gary Dicer, Director, 423-974-5033, Fax: 423-974-3826, E-mail: gdicer@utk.edu. *Application contact:* Donna Potts, Graduate Representative, 423-974-5033, Fax: 423-974-3826, E-mail: dpotts@utk.edu.

University of Toronto, School of Graduate Studies, Life Sciences Division, Collaborative Program in Environmental Studies, Toronto, ON M5S 1A1, Canada. Offers M Sc, M Sc F, MA. *Degree requirements:* For master's, thesis required (for some programs).

University of Vermont, Graduate College, School of Natural Resources, Program in Natural Resources Planning, Burlington, VT 05405-0160. Offers MS, PhD. *Degree requirements:* For master's, thesis or alternative required, foreign language not required; for doctorate, dissertation required. *Entrance requirements:* For master's and doctorate, GRE General Test, TOEFL (minimum score of 550 required).

University of Washington, Graduate School, College of Forest Resources, Seattle, WA 98195. Offers forest economics (MS, PhD); forest ecosystem analysis (MS, PhD); forest engineering/forest hydrology (MS, PhD); forest products marketing (MS, PhD); forest soils (MS, PhD); pulp and paper science (MS, PhD); quantitative resource management (MS, PhD); silviculture (MFR); silviculture and forest protection (MS, PhD); social sciences (MS, PhD); urban horticulture (MFR, MS, PhD); wildlife science (MS, PhD). *Faculty:* 47 full-time (4 women), 16 part-time (2 women). *Students:* 161 full-time (65 women), 16 part-time (5 women); includes 15 minority (1 African American, 10 Asian Americans or Pacific Islanders, 1 Hispanic American, 3 Native Americans), 9 international. *Degree requirements:* For master's, thesis required (for some programs), foreign language not required; for doctorate, dissertation required, foreign language not required. *Entrance requirements:* For master's and doctorate, GRE, TOEFL (minimum score of 500 required), minimum GPA of 3.0. *Application deadline:* For fall admission, 2/1 (priority date); for winter admission, 11/1; for spring admission, 2/1. Applications are processed on a rolling basis. Application fee: $50. Electronic applications accepted. Tuition, state resident: full-time $5,196; part-time $475 per credit. Tuition, nonresident: full-time $13,485; part-time $1,285 per credit. Required fees: $387; $38 per credit. Tuition and fees vary according to course load. *Unit head:* Dr. David B. Thorud, Dean, 206-685-1928, Fax: 206-685-0790. *Application contact:* Michelle Trudeau, Student Services Manager, 206-616-1533, Fax: 206-685-0790, E-mail: michtru@u.washington.edu.

University of Washington, Graduate School, Interdisciplinary Graduate Program in Quantitative Ecology and Resource Management, Seattle, WA 98195. Offers MS, PhD. *Faculty:* 34 full-time (3 women). *Students:* 18 full-time (12 women), 2 part-time; includes 3 minority (2 Asian Americans or Pacific Islanders, 1 Native American), 2 international. Average age 30. 11 applicants, 27% accepted. In 1998, 1 doctorate awarded (100% found work related to degree). *Degree requirements:* For master's and doctorate, thesis/dissertation required. *Entrance requirements:* For master's and doctorate, GRE General Test (minimum score of 600 on verbal section, 710 on quantitative, 690 on analytical required), TOEFL (minimum score of 500 required), minimum GPA of 3.0. *Application deadline:* For fall admission, 2/1. Application fee: $50. Electronic applications accepted. Tuition, state resident: full-time $5,196; part-time $475 per credit. Tuition, nonresident: full-time $13,485; part-time $1,285 per credit. Required fees: $387; $38 per credit. Tuition and fees vary according to course load. *Financial aid:* In 1998–99, 2 fellowships with full tuition reimbursements (averaging $10,000 per year), 11 research assistantships with full tuition reimbursements (averaging $10,000 per year), 3 teaching assistantships with full tuition reimbursements (averaging $10,000 per year) were awarded.; grants, traineeships, tuition waivers (full), and unspecified assistantships also available. Financial aid applicants required to submit FAFSA. *Faculty research:* Population dynamics, statistical analysis, ecological modeling and systems analysis of aquatic and terrestrial ecosystems. Total annual research expenditures: $1.5 million. *Unit head:* Dr. E. David Ford, Chair, 206-616-9571, Fax: 206-616-9443, E-mail: qerm@cqs.washington.edu. *Application contact:* Joanne Besch, Graduate Assistant, 206-616-9571, Fax: 206-616-9443, E-mail: qerm@cqs.washington.edu.

Announcement: Application of statistical, mathematical, and decision sciences to terrestrial and marine ecology, natural resource management, and biometrical and mathematical biology problems. MS and PhD program designed for students interested in contemporary ecological or resource management problems from a quantitative perspective. For more information, contact Quantitative Ecology and Resource Management, University of Washington, Box 351720, Seattle, WA 98195-1720; 206-616-9571; e-mail: qerm@cqs.washington.edu; WWW: http://weber.u.washington.edu/~qerm

University of Waterloo, Graduate Studies, Faculty of Environmental Studies, Program in Environment and Resource Studies, Waterloo, ON N2L 3G1, Canada. Offers MES. Part-time programs available. *Faculty:* 9 full-time (2 women), 8 part-time (2 women). *Students:* 17 full-time (8 women), 5 part-time (4 women). 37 applicants, 19% accepted. In 1998, 7 degrees awarded. *Degree requirements:* For master's, thesis required, foreign language not required. *Entrance requirements:* For master's, TOEFL (minimum score of 600 required), honors degree, minimum B average. *Application deadline:* For fall admission, 1/31. Application fee: $50. *Expenses:* Tuition and fees charges are reported in Canadian dollars. Tuition, state resident: full-time $3,168 Canadian dollars; part-time $792 Canadian dollars per term. Tuition, nonresident: full-time $8,000 Canadian dollars; part-time $2,000 Canadian dollars. Required fees: $45 Canadian dollars per term. Tuition and fees vary according to program. *Financial aid:* In 1998–99, 1 research assistantship (averaging $4,950 per year), 13 teaching assistantships (averaging $10,298 per year) were awarded.; scholarships also available. *Faculty research:* Sustainable development, water conservation, native issues, environmental assessment. *Unit head:* Dr. James E. Robinson, Chair, 519-888-4567 Ext. 2706, Fax: 519-746-0292, E-mail: jrobin@watserv1.uwaterloo.ca. *Application contact:* Dr. Robert Gibson, Graduate Officer, 519-888-4567 Ext. 3407, Fax: 519-746-0292, E-mail: rbgibson@watserv1.uwaterloo.ca.

University of Waterloo, Graduate Studies, Faculty of Environmental Studies, Program in Local Economic Development, Waterloo, ON N2L 3G1, Canada. Offers MAES. Part-time programs available. *Faculty:* 12 full-time (3 women), 1 part-time (0 women). *Students:* 8 full-time (4 women), 14 part-time (7 women). Average age 31. 19 applicants, 47% accepted. In 1998, 5 degrees awarded. *Degree requirements:* For master's, research paper required, foreign language and thesis not required. *Entrance requirements:* For master's, TOEFL (minimum score of 600 required) or alternative test of English, honors degree in related field, minimum B average. *Application deadline:* For fall admission, 3/1 (priority date). Applications are processed on a rolling basis. Application fee: $50. *Expenses:* Tuition and fees charges are reported in Canadian dollars. Tuition, state resident: full-time $3,168 Canadian dollars; part-time $792 Canadian dollars per term. Tuition, nonresident: full-time $8,000 Canadian dollars; part-time $2,000 Canadian dollars. Required fees: $45 Canadian dollars per term. Tuition and fees vary according to program. *Financial aid:* In 1998–99, 6 research assistantships were awarded.; career-related internships or fieldwork, institutionally-sponsored loans, and scholarships also available. Aid available to part-time students. *Faculty research:* Urban and regional economics, regional economic development, strategic planning, environmental economics, economic geography. *Unit head:* Dr. T. Rutherford, Graduate Officer, 519-888-4567 Ext. 3068, Fax: 519-746-2031, E-mail: trutherf@watserv1.uwaterloo.ca. *Application contact:* Lori McConnell,

Assistant to the Associate Dean, Graduate Studies and Research, 519-888-4567 Ext. 6574, Fax: 519-746-2031, E-mail: lmcconne@fes.uwaterloo.ca.

University of West Florida, College of Science and Technology, Department of Biology, Specialization in Coastal Zone Studies, Pensacola, FL 32514-5750. Offers biology (MS). Part-time programs available. *Students:* 2 full-time (both women), 11 part-time (4 women), 1 international. Average age 27. In 1998, 1 degree awarded. *Degree requirements:* For master's, thesis or alternative required, foreign language not required. *Entrance requirements:* For master's, GRE General Test (minimum combined score of 1000 required). *Application deadline:* For fall admission, 7/19. Applications are processed on a rolling basis. Application fee: $20. Tuition, state resident: full-time $3,582; part-time $149 per credit hour. Tuition, nonresident: full-time $12,240; part-time $510 per credit hour. *Unit head:* Dr. J. Riehm, Chairperson, Department of Biology, 850-474-2748.

University of Wisconsin–Green Bay, Graduate Studies, Track in Environmental Science and Policy, Green Bay, WI 54311-7001. Offers MS. Part-time programs available. *Students:* 8 full-time (2 women), 31 part-time (8 women); includes 1 minority (Native American), 8 international. Average age 32. In 1998, 17 degrees awarded. *Degree requirements:* For master's, thesis required, foreign language not required. *Entrance requirements:* For master's, GRE General Test, minimum GPA of 3.0. *Application deadline:* For fall admission, 8/1; for spring admission, 11/1. Applications are processed on a rolling basis. Application fee: $45. Tuition, state resident: full-time $3,510; part-time $195 per credit. Tuition, nonresident: full-time $11,868; part-time $660 per credit. Required fees: $277 per semester. *Financial aid:* In 1998–99, 3 research assistantships, 9 teaching assistantships were awarded.; career-related internships or fieldwork, Federal Work-Study, and institutionally-sponsored loans also available. Financial aid application deadline: 7/15; financial aid applicants required to submit FAFSA. *Faculty research:* Bald eagle, parasitic population of domestic and wild animals, resource recovery, anaerobic digestion of organic waste. *Unit head:* Dr. John Stoll, Coordinator, 920-465-2358, E-mail: stollj@uwgb.edu.

University of Wisconsin–Madison, Graduate School, College of Agricultural and Life Sciences, School of Natural Resources, Recreation Resources Management Program, Madison, WI 53706-1380. Offers MS.

University of Wisconsin–Madison, Graduate School, Institute for Environmental Studies, Land Resources Program, Madison, WI 53706-1380. Offers MS, PhD. Part-time programs available. *Students:* 73 full-time (31 women), 31 part-time (14 women); includes 10 minority (1 African American, 1 Asian American or Pacific Islander, 4 Hispanic Americans, 4 Native Americans), 15 international. 89 applicants, 47% accepted. In 1998, 15 master's, 6 doctorates awarded. *Degree requirements:* For master's and doctorate, thesis/dissertation required, foreign language not required. *Entrance requirements:* For master's and doctorate, GRE General Test. *Application deadline:* For fall admission, 2/15; for spring admission, 10/15. Application fee: $45. Electronic applications accepted. *Financial aid:* In 1998–99, 48 students received aid, including 9 fellowships with full tuition reimbursements available, 13 research assistantships with full tuition reimbursements available, 10 teaching assistantships with full tuition reimbursements available; career-related internships or fieldwork, Federal Work-Study, grants, traineeships, and unspecified assistantships also available. Financial aid application deadline: 1/2; financial aid applicants required to submit FAFSA. *Faculty research:* Land use issues, soil science/watershed management, geographic information systems, environmental law/justice, waste management. *Unit head:* Kenneth W. Potter, Chair, 608-263-1796, Fax: 608-262-2273, E-mail: iesgrad@macc.wisc.edu. *Application contact:* Jim E. Miller, Clerical Assistant, 608-263-1796, Fax: 608-262-2273, E-mail: jemiller@facstaff.wisc.edu.

Vermont Law School, Law School, Environmental Law Center, South Royalton, VT 05068-0096. Offers LL M, MSEL, JD/MSEL. Part-time programs available. *Faculty:* 10 full-time (3 women), 8 part-time (4 women). *Students:* 39 full-time (20 women); includes 7 minority (1 African American, 1 Asian American or Pacific Islander, 2 Hispanic Americans, 3 Native Americans), 1 international. Average age 28. 72 applicants, 76% accepted. In 1998, 60 degrees awarded (5% entered university research/teaching, 90% found other work related to degree, 5% continued full-time study). *Degree requirements:* For master's, foreign language and thesis not required. *Entrance requirements:* For master's, GRE General Test (average 544 verbal, 640 quantitative, 679 analytical) or LSAT, TOEFL. *Average time to degree:* Master's–1 year full-time, 3 years part-time. *Application deadline:* For fall admission, 2/15 (priority date). Applications are processed on a rolling basis. Application fee: $50. Tuition: Full-time $20,200. Required fees: $75. *Financial aid:* In 1998–99, 36 students received aid, including 2 fellowships with full tuition reimbursements available (averaging $7,000 per year); career-related internships or fieldwork, Federal Work-Study, grants, institutionally-sponsored loans, and tuition waivers (partial) also available. Aid available to part-time students. Financial aid application deadline: 2/15; financial aid applicants required to submit FAFSA. *Faculty research:* Environment and technology; takings; international environmental law; interaction among science, law, and environmental policy; air pollution; cultural resources protection; law of ecosystems; endangered species. Total annual research expenditures: $52,000. *Unit head:* Karin Sheldon, Director, 802-763-8303 Ext. 2201, Fax: 802-763-2490, E-mail: elcinfo@vermontlaw.edu. *Application contact:* Shari Young, Assistant Director, 802-763-8303 Ext. 2201, Fax: 802-763-2940, E-mail: elcinfo@vermontlaw.edu.

Virginia Commonwealth University, School of Graduate Studies, Center for Environmental Studies, Richmond, VA 23284-9005. Offers environmental communication (MIS); environmental health (MIS); environmental planning (MIS); environmental sciences (MIS). Average age 33. *Entrance requirements:* For master's, GRE General Test. Application fee: $30. Tuition, state resident: full-time $4,031; part-time $224 per credit hour. Tuition, nonresident: full-time $11,946; part-time $664 per credit hour. Required fees: $1,081; $40 per credit hour. Tuition and fees vary according to campus/location and program. *Unit head:* Greg Garman, Director, 804-828-7202, Fax: 804-828-0503, E-mail: gcgarman@vcu.edu. *Application contact:* Andrew Lacatell, Assistant Director, 804-828-7202, Fax: 804-828-0503, E-mail: adlacate@vcu.edu.

Webster University, College of Arts and Sciences, Department of Science, St. Louis, MO 63119-3194. Offers environmental management (MS); nurse anesthesia (MS). Postbaccalaureate distance learning degree programs offered. *Students:* 19 full-time (12 women), 2 part-time (1 woman). *Unit head:* Joyce Bork, Chair, 314-961-2660 Ext. 7524. *Application contact:* Dr. Beth Russell, Director of Graduate Admissions, 314-968-7089, Fax: 314-968-7166, E-mail: russelmb@webster.edu.

West Virginia University, College of Agriculture, Forestry and Consumer Sciences, Division of Resource Management, Program in Natural Resource Economics, Morgantown, WV 26506. Offers PhD. Part-time programs available. *Degree requirements:* For doctorate, dissertation required. *Entrance requirements:* For doctorate, GRE General Test (minimum combined score of 1100 required), TOEFL (minimum score of 550 required).

Announcement: Specialized MS and PhD degree programs with emphasis in environmental and natural resource economics and policy. An accomplished faculty combines expertise in resource, environmental, energy, agricultural, and regional and Third World development economics. Graduate research assistantships are available on a competitive basis ($9396 for MS, $11,040 for PhD, plus waiver of tuition and most fees). A special feature of the program is the opportunity to combine economic analysis with strong skills in spatial econometrics and GIS applications. Division computer facilities include PC labs as well as a research lab with DEC and Sun Workstations.

York University, Faculty of Graduate Studies, Faculty of Environmental Studies, Toronto, ON M3J 1P3, Canada. Offers MES, PhD, MES/LL B, MES/MA. Part-time programs available. *Degree requirements:* For master's, thesis optional; for doctorate, dissertation, research seminar required.

See in-depth description on page 929.

Environmental Sciences

Alabama Agricultural and Mechanical University, School of Graduate Studies, School of Agricultural and Environmental Sciences, Department of Plant, Soil and Animal Sciences, Normal, AL 35762-1357. Offers animal sciences (MS); environmental science (MS); plant and soil science (PhD). Evening/weekend programs available. *Faculty:* 12 full-time (1 woman). *Students:* 11 full-time (6 women), 29 part-time (4 women); includes 28 minority (27 African Americans, 1 Asian American or Pacific Islander), 12 international. Terminal master's awarded for partial completion of doctoral program. *Degree requirements:* For master's, thesis required, foreign language not required; for doctorate, one foreign language, computer language, dissertation required. *Entrance requirements:* For master's, GRE General Test, BS in agriculture; for doctorate, GRE General Test (minimum combined score of 1000 required), MS. *Application deadline:* For fall admission, 5/1. Applications are processed on a rolling basis. Application fee: $15 ($20 for international students). Tuition, state resident: full-time $1,932. Tuition, nonresident: full-time $3,864. Tuition and fees vary according to course load. *Unit head:* Dr. Govind Sharma, Chair, 256-851-5462.

Alaska Pacific University, Graduate Programs, Environmental Science Department, Anchorage, AK 99508-4672. Offers MSES. Part-time programs available. *Degree requirements:* For master's, thesis, comprehensive exam required, foreign language not required. *Entrance requirements:* For master's, GRE General Test, minimum GPA of 3.0, resume. *Faculty research:* Animal-plant interactions, public attitudes towards native and wildlife, species-area relationships, conservation biology, forest canopy ecology.

American University, College of Arts and Sciences, Department of Biology, Environmental Studies Program, Washington, DC 20016-8001. Offers MA, MS. *Faculty:* 8 full-time (3 women). *Students:* 7 full-time (6 women), 1 part-time; includes 2 minority (both African Americans), 2 international. 11 applicants, 82% accepted. In 1998, 5 degrees awarded. *Degree requirements:* For master's, comprehensive written exam, tool of research exam required. *Entrance requirements:* For master's, GRE General Test, GRE Subject Test, TOEFL, minimum GPA of 3.0. *Application deadline:* For fall admission, 2/1; for spring admission, 10/1. Application fee: $50. *Financial aid:* Application deadline: 2/1. *Unit head:* Dr. Daniel Fong, Chair, Department of Biology, 202-885-2178.

See in-depth description on page 887.

Antioch New England Graduate School, Graduate School, Department of Environmental Studies, Doctoral Program in Environmental Studies, Keene, NH 03431-3516. Offers PhD. *Faculty:* 4 full-time (2 women), 1 (woman) part-time. *Students:* 31 full-time (19 women). Average age 41. 16 applicants, 88% accepted. *Degree requirements:* For doctorate, dissertation, practicum required, foreign language not required. *Entrance requirements:* For doctorate, GRE General Test, GRE Subject Test, interview. *Application deadline:* For fall admission, 1/28. Application fee: $75. Tuition: Full-time $15,500. Full-time tuition and fees vary according to student level. *Financial aid:* In 1998–99, 12 students received aid, including 2 fellowships (averaging $1,000 per year); career-related internships or fieldwork and Federal Work-Study also available. *Faculty research:* Environmental history, green politics, ecopsychology. *Unit head:* Dr. Mitchell Thomashow, Director, 603-357-3122 Ext. 235, Fax: 603-357-0718, E-mail: mthomashow@antiochne.edu. *Application contact:* Robbie P. Hertneky, Director of Admissions, 603-357-6265, Fax: 603-357-0718, E-mail: rhertneky@antiochne.edu.

Announcement: The Doctoral Program in Environmental Studies is for those committed to scholarly excellence who wish to design, implement, and evaluate research regarding crucial environmental issues. The program cultivates a dynamic learning community of environmental scholars and practitioners who combine scope and vision with depth and precision, conceptualizing and implementing research strategies and designs that contribute to solving and anticipating regional, national, and global environmental problems.

Arkansas State University, Graduate School, College of Arts and Sciences, Department of Biological Sciences, Jonesboro, State University, AR 72467. Offers biology (MS); biology education (MSE, SCCT); environmental sciences (PhD). *Accreditation:* NCATE (one or more programs are accredited). Part-time programs available. *Faculty:* 17 full-time (3 women). *Students:* 7 full-time (4 women), 30 part-time (12 women); includes 2 minority (1 Asian American or Pacific Islander, 1 Native American), 1 international. *Degree requirements:* For master's, thesis (for some programs), comprehensive exam required; for doctorate, dissertation, comprehensive exam required; for SCCT, comprehensive exam required, thesis not required. *Entrance requirements:* For master's, GRE General Test, appropriate bachelor's degree; for doctorate, GRE General Test, interview, master's degree; for SCCT, GRE General Test or MAT, interview, master's degree. *Application deadline:* For fall admission, 7/1 (priority date); for spring admission, 11/15 (priority date). Applications are processed on a rolling basis. Application fee: $15 ($25 for international students). *Unit head:* Dr. Roger Buchanan, Chair, 870-972-3082, Fax: 870-972-2638, E-mail: rbuck@navajo.astate.edu.

Bard College, Graduate School of Environmental Studies, Annandale-on-Hudson, NY 12504. Offers MSES. Offered during summer only. *Faculty:* 5 full-time (2 women), 9 part-time (1 woman). *Students:* 45 full-time (21 women); includes 5 minority (2 Asian Americans or Pacific Islanders, 1 Hispanic American, 2 Native Americans), 1 international. Average age 30. 40 applicants, 48% accepted. In 1998, 7 degrees awarded. *Degree requirements:* For master's, thesis required, foreign language not required. *Entrance requirements:* For master's, resumé, interview, published materials. *Average time to degree:* Master's–4 years full-time. *Application deadline:* For fall admission, 2/1 (priority date). Applications are processed on a rolling basis. Application fee: $45. *Financial aid:* Fellowships, career-related internships or fieldwork and scholarships available. Financial aid application deadline: 3/1; financial aid applicants required to submit FAFSA. *Faculty research:* Environmental ethics, environmental economics, environmental impact assessment, cultural ecology, wetland ecology and management. *Unit head:* Joanne Fox-Przeworski, Director, 914-758-7067, Fax: 914-758-7636, E-mail: jfp@bard.edu. *Application contact:* Gloria Cestero-Hurd, Coordinator, 914-758-7073, Fax: 914-758-7636, E-mail: gch@bard.edu.

Announcement: Bard College offers a summer graduate degree program that leads to the Master of Science in Environmental Studies. Program provides interdisciplinary training with equal emphasis placed on natural and social sciences. Students develop understanding of key ecological and natural resource concepts and the ability to become effective environmental professionals. Teaching team includes a broad range of professional experts—lawyers, anthropologists, geologists, and economists—to create a truly extraordinary program. MSES degree is appropriate for careers in such areas as government, environmental research, international

Environmental Sciences

Bard College (continued)
development, education, resource management, business, and public planning. Graduates are prepared to pursue a PhD. Course work offered during summer months in two 4-week sessions. Students can complete degree requirements, including courses and thesis, in 3 summers. The program is intensive, demanding, and exciting. In 2001, Bard will begin a master's degree prog ram during the academic year as part of its new Center for Environmental Policy (CEP). The Center is dedicated to teaching, research, and public service. For an application to GSES, contact 914-758-7073, fax: 914-758-7636, e-mail: gch@bard.edu

California State University, Fullerton, Graduate Studies, School of Humanities and Social Sciences, Program in Environmental Studies, Fullerton, CA 92834-9480. Offers environmental education and communication (MS); environmental policy and planning (MS); environmental sciences (MS); technological studies (MS). Part-time programs available. *Students:* 2 full-time (1 woman), 102 part-time (53 women); includes 21 minority (1 African American, 11 Asian Americans or Pacific Islanders, 8 Hispanic Americans, 1 Native American), 11 international. *Degree requirements:* For master's, thesis required, foreign language not required. *Entrance requirements:* For master's, minimum GPA of 2.5 in last 60 units. Application fee: $55. Tuition, nonresident: part-time $264 per unit. Required fees: $1,947; $1,281 per year. *Unit head:* Dr. Stewart Long, Acting Chair, 714-278-2228.

Christopher Newport University, Graduate Studies, Department of Biology, Chemistry and Environmental Science, Newport News, VA 23606-2998. Offers environmental science (MS). Part-time and evening/weekend programs available. *Faculty:* 7 full-time (2 women). *Students:* 5 full-time (2 women), 20 part-time (6 women). Average age 34. *Degree requirements:* For master's, thesis, comprehensive exam required, foreign language not required. *Entrance requirements:* For master's, GRE General Test, minimum GPA of 3.0. *Application deadline:* For fall admission, 7/1 (priority date); for spring admission, 12/15. Applications are processed on a rolling basis. Application fee: $40. Electronic applications accepted. Tuition, state resident: part-time $145 per credit hour. Tuition, nonresident: part-time $351 per credit hour. Required fees: $20 per year. *Financial aid:* In 1998–99, 3 research assistantships with full tuition reimbursements (averaging $2,500 per year) were awarded.; career-related internships or fieldwork and Federal Work-Study also available. Aid available to part-time students. Financial aid application deadline: 3/1; financial aid applicants required to submit FAFSA. *Faculty research:* Wetlands ecology and restoration, aquatic ecology, wetlands mitigation, greenhouse gases. *Unit head:* Dr. James Reed, Coordinator, 757-594-7307, Fax: 757-594-7919, E-mail: reed@cnu.edu. *Application contact:* Gary Clark, Graduate Admissions, 757-594-7993, Fax: 757-594-7333, E-mail: admit@cnu.edu.

City College of the City University of New York, Graduate School, College of Liberal Arts and Science, Division of Science, Department of Earth and Atmospheric Sciences, New York, NY 10031-9198. Offers earth and environmental science (PhD); earth systems science (MA). PhD offered through the Graduate School and University Center of the City University of New York. *Degree requirements:* For master's, thesis, comprehensive exam required, foreign language not required. *Entrance requirements:* For master's, TOEFL (minimum score of 500 required), appropriate bachelor's degree. *Faculty research:* Water resources, high-temperature geochemistry, sedimentary basin analysis, tectonics.

Clemson University, Graduate School, College of Agriculture, Forestry and Life Sciences, School of Applied Science and Agribusiness, Department of Environmental Toxicology, Clemson, SC 29634. Offers MS, PhD. *Students:* 26 full-time (10 women), 7 part-time (6 women); includes 2 minority (both African Americans), 4 international. Average age 25. 40 applicants, 38% accepted. In 1998, 17 master's, 5 doctorates awarded. *Degree requirements:* For master's, thesis required; for doctorate, dissertation required. *Entrance requirements:* For master's and doctorate, GRE General Test, TOEFL. *Application deadline:* For fall admission, 6/1. Application fee: $35. *Financial aid:* Fellowships, research assistantships, teaching assistantships, career-related internships or fieldwork, Federal Work-Study, and institutionally-sponsored loans available. Financial aid applicants required to submit FAFSA. *Faculty research:* Biochemical toxicology, analytical toxicology, ecological risk assessment, wildlife toxicology, mathematical modeling. Total annual research expenditures: $3 million. *Unit head:* Dr. Steve Klaine, Chair, 864-646-2377, Fax: 864-646-2277, E-mail: sklaine@clemson.edu.

Cleveland State University, College of Graduate Studies, College of Arts and Sciences, Department of Biological, Geological and Environmental Sciences, Cleveland, OH 44115-2440. Offers MS, PhD. Part-time programs available. *Faculty:* 18 full-time (3 women). *Students:* 3 full-time (2 women), 45 part-time (25 women); includes 5 minority (3 African Americans, 2 Asian Americans or Pacific Islanders), 9 international. Average age 32. 30 applicants, 30% accepted. In 1998, 5 master's, 5 doctorates awarded. Terminal master's awarded for partial completion of doctoral program. *Degree requirements:* For doctorate, dissertation required, foreign language not required, foreign language not required. *Entrance requirements:* For master's and doctorate, GRE General Test, GRE Subject Test. *Application deadline:* For fall admission, 9/1 (priority date). Applications are processed on a rolling basis. Application fee: $25. *Financial aid:* In 1998–99, 12 research assistantships, 15 teaching assistantships were awarded.; institutionally-sponsored loans and unspecified assistantships also available. *Faculty research:* Physiology, biochemistry/neurochemistry, immunology, taxonomic botany, molecular parasitology. *Unit head:* Dr. Michael Gates, Interim Chairperson, 216-687-3917, Fax: 216-687-6972, E-mail: gates@biology.csuohio.edu. *Application contact:* Director, 216-687-2440.

College of Staten Island of the City University of New York, Graduate Programs, Program in Environmental Science, Staten Island, NY 10314-6600. Offers MA. Part-time and evening/weekend programs available. *Faculty:* 12 full-time (2 women), 2 part-time (0 women). *Students:* 3 full-time (0 women), 15 part-time (10 women); includes 4 minority (2 African Americans, 2 Asian Americans or Pacific Islanders) Average age 34. 14 applicants, 64% accepted. In 1998, 2 degrees awarded (50% found work related to degree, 50% continued full-time study). *Degree requirements:* For master's, thesis required, foreign language not required. *Entrance requirements:* For master's, GRE General Test, TOEFL, 1 year of course work in chemistry, physics, calculus, and ecology. *Average time to degree:* Master's–3.5 years part-time. *Application deadline:* For fall admission, 8/15 (priority date); for spring admission, 1/15. Applications are processed on a rolling basis. Application fee: $40. Tuition, state resident: full-time $4,350; part-time $185 per credit. Tuition, nonresident: full-time $7,600; part-time $320 per credit. Required fees: $53; $27 per term. *Financial aid:* In 1998–99, 1 research assistantship, 3 teaching assistantships were awarded.; fellowships, career-related internships or fieldwork and Federal Work-Study also available. Aid available to part-time students. *Faculty research:* Environmental pollution, epidemiology, forest and wetlands ecology, vertebrate ecology, microbial ecology and toxicology, geohydrology. Total annual research expenditures: $50,000. *Unit head:* Dr. John Oppenheimer, Director, 718-982-3921, Fax: 713-982-3923, E-mail: oppenheimer@postbox.csi.cuny.edu. *Application contact:* Earl Teasley, Director of Admissions, 718-982-2010, Fax: 718-982-2500.

Colorado School of Mines, Graduate School, Division of Environmental Science and Engineering, Golden, CO 80401-1887. Offers MS, PhD. Part-time programs available. *Faculty:* 8 full-time (1 woman), 8 part-time (1 woman). *Students:* 50 full-time (13 women), 27 part-time (10 women); includes 2 minority (1 African American, 1 Hispanic American), 17 international. 92 applicants, 72% accepted. In 1998, 33 master's awarded (100% found work related to degree); 2 doctorates awarded (100% found work related to degree). *Degree requirements:* For master's, thesis required (for some programs), foreign language not required; for doctorate, dissertation, comprehensive exam required, foreign language not required. *Entrance requirements:* For master's and doctorate, GRE General Test (combined average 1660 on three sections), minimum GPA of 3.0. *Application deadline:* Applications are processed on a rolling basis. Application fee: $40. Electronic applications accepted. *Financial aid:* In 1998–99, 56 students received aid, including 6 fellowships, 12 research assistantships, 9 teaching assistantships; unspecified assistantships also available. Aid available to part-time students. Financial aid applicants required to submit FAFSA. *Faculty research:* Treatment of water and wastes, environmental law–policy and practice, natural environment systems, hazardous waste management, environmental data analysis. Total annual research expenditures: $505,431. *Unit head:* Dr. Philippe Ross, Head, 303-273-3473, Fax: 303-273-3413, E-mail: pross@mines.edu. *Application contact:* Juanita Chuven, Administrative Assistant, 303-273-3427, Fax: 303-273-3413, E-mail: jchuven@mines.edu.

Colorado State University, Graduate School, College of Engineering, Department of Civil Engineering, Specialization in Water Resources, Hydrologic and Environmental Sciences, Fort Collins, CO 80523-0015. Offers MS, PhD. Part-time programs available. *Faculty:* 5 full-time (1 woman). In 1998, 7 master's, 6 doctorates awarded. Terminal master's awarded for partial completion of doctoral program. *Degree requirements:* For master's, thesis or alternative required, foreign language not required; for doctorate, dissertation required, foreign language not required. *Entrance requirements:* For master's and doctorate, GRE General Test, TOEFL (minimum score of 550 required; 213 for computer-based), minimum GPA of 3.0. *Average time to degree:* Master's–2 years full-time, 5 years part-time; doctorate–4 years full-time. *Application deadline:* For fall admission, 3/1 (priority date); for spring admission, 8/1 (priority date). Applications are processed on a rolling basis. Application fee: $30. Electronic applications accepted. *Financial aid:* Fellowships, research assistantships, teaching assistantships, Federal Work-Study and institutionally-sponsored loans available. *Faculty research:* Flood prediction, stochastic hydrology, drought analysis, watershed modeling, groundwater quality and contamination, drainage, flow through porous media, conjunctive use, numerical modeling. Total annual research expenditures: $600,000. *Unit head:* James W. Warner, Leader, 970-491-8381, Fax: 970-491-7727, E-mail: warner@engr.colostate.edu. *Application contact:* Laurie Howard, Student Adviser, 970-491-5844, Fax: 970-491-7727, E-mail: lhoward@engr.colostate.edu.

Columbus State University, Graduate Studies, College of Science, Program in Environmental Science, Columbus, GA 31907-5645. Offers MS. *Faculty:* 4 full-time (0 women). *Students:* 12 full-time (5 women), 18 part-time (10 women); includes 9 minority (6 African Americans, 1 Asian American or Pacific Islander, 2 Hispanic Americans), 1 international. 19 applicants, 58% accepted. In 1998, 2 degrees awarded. *Degree requirements:* For master's, thesis required, foreign language not required. *Entrance requirements:* For master's, GRE General Test (minimum combined score of 800 required), MAT (minimum score of 44 required). *Average time to degree:* Master's–1.5 years full-time, 3 years part-time. *Application deadline:* For fall admission, 8/4 (priority date); for spring admission, 12/17. Application fee: $20. *Financial aid:* Application deadline: 6/4. *Unit head:* Dr. James Gore, Program Director, 706-568-2067. *Application contact:* Katie Thornton, Graduate Admissions, 706-568-2279, Fax: 706-568-2462, E-mail: thornton_katie@colstate.edu.

Drexel University, Graduate School, School of Environmental Science, Engineering and Policy, Philadelphia, PA 19104-2875. Offers environmental engineering (MS, PhD); environmental science (MS, PhD). Part-time and evening/weekend programs available. *Faculty:* 7 full-time, 7 part-time. *Students:* 17 full-time (11 women), 50 part-time (20 women); includes 4 minority (all Asian Americans or Pacific Islanders), 12 international. Average age 30. 101 applicants, 60% accepted. In 1998, 29 master's awarded. Terminal master's awarded for partial completion of doctoral program. *Degree requirements:* For master's, thesis optional; for doctorate, dissertation required. *Entrance requirements:* For master's, TOEFL (minimum score of 570 required), minimum GPA of 3.0; for doctorate, TOEFL (minimum score of 570 required), minimum GPA of 3.0, MS. *Application deadline:* For fall admission, 8/21. Applications are processed on a rolling basis. Application fee: $35. Tuition: Full-time $15,795; part-time $585 per credit. Required fees: $375; $67 per term. Tuition and fees vary according to program. *Financial aid:* In 1998–99, 8 research assistantships, 3 teaching assistantships were awarded.; career-related internships or fieldwork and unspecified assistantships also available. Financial aid application deadline: 2/1. *Faculty research:* Environmental health, water quality and resources, hazardous-waste disposal, environmental chemistry. *Unit head:* Dr. Michael Gealt, Director, 215-895-2265. *Application contact:* Director of Graduate Admissions, 215-895-6700, Fax: 215-895-5939.

Announcement: The School of Environmental Science, Engineering and Policy of Drexel University awards the BS, MS, and PhD in environmental engineering and the MS and PhD in environmental science. Both part-time study and a nonthesis option are available for the MS program. Research and teaching assistantships are available on a very limited basis. Drexel's programs have existed since 1967 and have more than 800 graduates. Visit the Web site at http://www.coas.drexel.edu/environ/.

Duke University, Graduate School, Department of Environment, Durham, NC 27708-0586. Offers natural resource economics/policy (AM, PhD); natural resource science/ecology (AM, PhD); natural resource systems science (AM, PhD). Part-time programs available. *Faculty:* 39 full-time, 14 part-time. *Students:* 69 full-time, 1 part-time; includes 5 minority (3 African Americans, 1 Asian American or Pacific Islander, 1 Hispanic American), 17 international. 126 applicants, 24% accepted. In 1998, 4 master's, 10 doctorates awarded. Terminal master's awarded for partial completion of doctoral program. *Degree requirements:* For doctorate, dissertation required, foreign language not required. *Entrance requirements:* For master's and doctorate, GRE General Test. *Application deadline:* For fall admission, 12/31. Application fee: $75. *Financial aid:* Fellowships, research assistantships, teaching assistantships, Federal Work-Study available. Financial aid application deadline: 12/31. *Unit head:* Kenneth Knoerr, Director of Graduate Studies, 919-613-8002, Fax: 919-684-8741, E-mail: nettleto@acpub.duke.edu.

Duke University, Nicholas School of the Environment, Durham, NC 27708-0328. Offers coastal environmental management (MEM); environmental science and policy (PhD); environmental toxicology, chemistry, and risk assessment (MEM); forest resource management (MF); resource ecology (MEM); resource economics and policy (MEM); water and air resources (MEM). PhD offered through the Graduate School. *Accreditation:* SAF (one or more programs are accredited). Part-time programs available. *Faculty:* 61 full-time (10 women), 23 part-time (3 women). *Students:* 228 full-time (136 women); includes 7 minority (2 African Americans, 4 Asian Americans or Pacific Islanders, 1 Hispanic American), 24 international. Average age 25. 400 applicants, 63% accepted. In 1998, 116 master's, 10 doctorates awarded. Terminal master's awarded for partial completion of doctoral program. *Degree requirements:* For master's, thesis required (for some programs), foreign language not required; for doctorate, dissertation required, foreign language not required. *Entrance requirements:* For master's, GRE General Test, TOEFL, previous course work in biology or ecology, calculus, statistics, and microeconomics; computer familiarity with word processing and data analysis; for doctorate, GRE General Test, TOEFL. *Average time to degree:* Master's–2 years full-time, 3 years part-time; doctorate–5 years full-time, 8 years part-time. *Application deadline:* For fall admission, 2/1; for spring admission, 10/15. Applications are processed on a rolling basis. Application fee: $75. *Financial aid:* In 1998–99, 29 fellowships (averaging $11,500 per year), 53 research assistantships (averaging $2,600 per year), 15 teaching assistantships (averaging $6,000 per year) were awarded.; career-related internships or fieldwork, Federal Work-Study, institutionally-sponsored loans, scholarships, and unspecified assistantships also available. Financial aid application deadline: 2/1; financial aid applicants required to submit FAFSA. *Faculty research:* Ecosystem management, conservation ecology, earth systems, risk assessment. *Unit head:* Dr. Norman L. Christensen, Dean, 919-613-8004, Fax: 919-684-8741. *Application contact:* Bertie S. Belvin, Associate Dean for Academic Services, 919-613-8070, Fax: 919-684-8741, E-mail: envadm@duke.edu.

Duquesne University, Bayer School of Natural and Environmental Sciences, Environmental Science and Management Program, Pittsburgh, PA 15282-0001. Offers environmental management (Certificate); environmental science (Certificate); environmental science and management (MS). Part-time and evening/weekend programs available. Postbaccalaureate distance learning degree programs offered (no on-campus study). *Faculty:* 6 full-time (1 woman), 20 part-time (3 women). *Students:* 32 full-time (19 women), 70 part-time (26 women); includes 3 minority (2 African Americans, 1 Asian American or Pacific Islander), 4 international. Average age 31. 73 applicants, 84% accepted. In 1998, 26 degrees awarded (85% found work related to degree, 15% continued full-time study). *Degree requirements:* For master's, thesis or internship required. *Entrance requirements:* For master's, GRE General Test, TOEFL, previous course work in chemistry, biology, calculus, statistics. *Average time to degree:* Master's–2 years full-time, 3.25 years part-time. *Application deadline:* For fall admission, 4/1 (priority date); for spring admission, 10/1 (priority date). Applications are processed on a rolling basis. Application fee: $40. Tuition: Part-time $511 per credit. Required fees: $46 per credit. $50 per year. One-time fee: $125 part-time. Tuition and fees vary according to program. *Financial aid:* In 1998–99, 1 fellowship with tuition reimbursement (averaging $13,500 per year) was awarded.; career-related internships or fieldwork, scholarships, and tuition waivers (partial) also available. Financial aid application deadline: 5/15; financial aid applicants required to submit FAFSA. *Faculty research:* Sustainable development, environmental analytical chemistry, environmental ecology, environmental microbiology, environmental management systems. Total annual research expenditures: $170,000. *Unit head:* Dr. Daniel Donnelly, Director, 412-396-4367, Fax: 412-396-4881. *Application contact:* Amy Johnson, Assistant to the Dean, Graduate Student Administrator, 412-396-6339, Fax: 412-396-4881, E-mail: gradinfo@duq.edu.

See in-depth description on page 889.

Florida Atlantic University, Charles E. Schmidt College of Science, Environmental Sciences Program, Boca Raton, FL 33431-0991. Offers MS. *Faculty:* 23 part-time (4 women). Average age 48. *Degree requirements:* For master's, thesis required, foreign language not required. *Entrance requirements:* For master's, GRE General Test (minimum combined score of 1000 required). *Application deadline:* For fall admission, 6/1. Application fee: $20. Tuition, state resident: part-time $148 per credit hour. Tuition, nonresident: part-time $509 per credit hour. *Financial aid:* Career-related internships or fieldwork and Federal Work-Study available. *Faculty research:* Tropical and terrestrial ecology, coastal/marine/wetlands ecology, hydrogeology, tropical botany. *Unit head:* Dr. Dan Austin, Director, 561-297-3327, Fax: 561-297-2749, E-mail: daustin@fau.edu.

Florida Institute of Technology, Graduate School, College of Engineering, Division of Marine and Environmental Systems, Program in Environmental Science, Melbourne, FL 32901-6975. Offers MS, PhD. Part-time programs available. *Faculty:* 4 full-time (0 women), 1 part-time (0 women). *Students:* 3 full-time (2 women), 9 part-time (4 women); includes 1 minority (Asian American or Pacific Islander), 2 international. Average age 33. 28 applicants, 54% accepted. In 1998, 5 master's awarded. *Degree requirements:* For master's, comprehensive exam required, thesis optional, foreign language not required; for doctorate, one foreign language, dissertation, comprehensive and departmental qualifying exams required. *Entrance requirements:* For master's, GRE General Test (minimum combined score of 1050 required; average 1250), minimum GPA of 3.0; for doctorate, GRE General Test (minimum combined score of 1050 required; average 1300), minimum GPA of 3.2. *Application deadline:* Applications are processed on a rolling basis. Application fee: $50. Electronic applications accepted. Tuition: Part-time $575 per credit hour. Required fees: $100. Tuition and fees vary according to campus/location and program. *Financial aid:* In 1998–99, 6 students received aid, including 2 research assistantships (averaging $2,850 per year), 3 teaching assistantships (averaging $3,025 per year); career-related internships or fieldwork and tuition remissions also available. Financial aid application deadline: 3/1; financial aid applicants required to submit FAFSA. *Faculty research:* Remote sensing, aquatic systems, pollution abatement, environmental analysis, marine policy, solid and hazardous resource management. *Unit head:* Dr. John G. Windsor, Chair, 407-674-7300, Fax: 407-674-7212, E-mail: jwindsor@marine.fit.edu. *Application contact:* Carolyn P. Farrior, Associate Dean of Graduate Admissions, 407-674-7118, Fax: 407-723-9468, E-mail: cfarrior@fit.edu.

See in-depth description on page 895.

Florida International University, College of Arts and Sciences, Department of Environmental Studies, Miami, FL 33199. Offers biological management (MS); energy (MS); pollution (MS). *Faculty:* 5 full-time (1 woman), 4 part-time (0 women). *Students:* 9 full-time (5 women), 16 part-time (7 women); includes 7 minority (1 African American, 1 Asian American or Pacific Islander, 5 Hispanic Americans), 4 international. Average age 32. 23 applicants, 43% accepted. *Degree requirements:* For master's, thesis required. *Entrance requirements:* For master's, GRE General Test (minimum combined score of 1000 required), TOEFL (minimum score of 500 required), minimum GPA of 3.0. *Application deadline:* For fall admission, 4/1; for spring admission, 10/30. Application fee: $20. Tuition, state resident: part-time $145 per credit hour. Tuition, nonresident: part-time $506 per credit hour. Required fees: $158; $158 per year. *Financial aid:* Research assistantships, teaching assistantships available. Financial aid application deadline: 4/1. *Unit head:* Dr. David Bray, Chairperson, 305-348-1930, Fax: 305-348-3137, E-mail: brayd@fiu.edu.

Announcement: The Department of Environmental Studies at Florida International University is an interdisciplinary academic unit in the College of Arts and Sciences. It offers a 36-credit-hour MS degree. Students specialize in one of 3 areas: energy, pollution, or biological management. Faculty research interests include energy policy, ecotourism, conservation biology, toxicology, demography, restoration ecology, and environmental education. The department has 12 core faculty members and 25 affiliated faculty members from other units, such as engineering, chemistry, philosophy, biology, and sociology, and maintains research ties to a number of institutions on and off campus. Graduate teaching and research assistantships are available.

George Mason University, College of Arts and Sciences, Department of Biology, Master's Program in Biology, Fairfax, VA 22030-4444. Offers bioinformatics (MS); ecology, systematics and evolution (MS); environmental science and public policy (MS); interpretive biology (MS); molecular, microbial, and cellular biology (MS); organismal biology (MS). Part-time programs available. *Faculty:* 32 full-time (11 women), 26 part-time (16 women). *Students:* 1 full-time (0 women), 63 part-time (34 women); includes 6 minority (4 African Americans, 1 Asian American or Pacific Islander, 1 Hispanic American), 2 international. *Degree requirements:* For master's, thesis or alternative required, foreign language not required. *Entrance requirements:* For master's, GRE General Test (minimum combined score of 1100 required), GRE Subject Test, bachelor's degree in biology or equivalent. *Application deadline:* For fall admission, 5/1; for spring admission, 11/1. Application fee: $30. Electronic applications accepted. Tuition, state resident: full-time $4,416; part-time $184 per credit hour. Tuition, nonresident: full-time $12,516; part-time $522 per credit hour. Tuition and fees vary according to program. *Unit head:* Dr. George E. Andrykovitch, Director, 703-993-1027, Fax: 703-993-1046.

George Mason University, College of Arts and Sciences, Department of Biology, Program in Environmental Science and Public Policy, Fairfax, VA 22030-4444. Offers PhD. Part-time programs available. *Faculty:* 32 full-time (11 women), 26 part-time (16 women). *Students:* 10 full-time (3 women), 93 part-time (49 women); includes 11 minority (4 African Americans, 3 Asian Americans or Pacific Islanders, 4 Hispanic Americans), 10 international. Average age 39. 33 applicants, 73% accepted. In 1998, 6 degrees awarded. *Degree requirements:* For doctorate, dissertation, internship required, foreign language not required. *Entrance requirements:* For doctorate, GRE General Test, GRE Subject Test. *Application deadline:* For fall admission, 5/1; for spring admission, 11/1. Application fee: $30. Electronic applications accepted. Tuition, state resident: full-time $4,416; part-time $184 per credit hour. Tuition, nonresident: full-time $12,516; part-time $522 per credit hour. Tuition and fees vary according to program. *Financial aid:* Fellowships, research assistantships, teaching assistantships available. Aid available to part-time students. Financial aid application deadline: 3/1; financial aid applicants required to submit FAFSA. *Unit head:* Dr. Robert Jonas, Director, 703-993-1030, Fax: 703-993-1046.

Graduate School and University Center of the City University of New York, Graduate Studies, Program in Earth and Environmental Sciences, New York, NY 10036-8099. Offers PhD. *Faculty:* 36 full-time (5 women). *Students:* 46 full-time (16 women), 9 part-time (2 women); includes 3 African Americans, 1 Asian American or Pacific Islander, 2 Hispanic Americans Average age 37. 44 applicants, 82% accepted. In 1998, 3 degrees awarded. *Degree requirements:* For doctorate, one foreign language (computer language can substitute), dissertation, comprehensive exam required. *Entrance requirements:* For doctorate, GRE General Test. *Application deadline:* For fall admission, 4/15. Application fee: $40. *Financial aid:* In 1998–99, 25 students received aid, including 13 fellowships, 1 teaching assistantship; research assistantships, career-related internships or fieldwork, Federal Work-Study, institutionally-sponsored loans, and tuition waivers (full and partial) also available. Financial aid application deadline: 2/1; financial aid applicants required to submit FAFSA. *Unit head:* Dr. Frederick Shaw, Executive Officer, 212-642-2202.

Harvard University, School of Public Health, Department of Environmental Health, Boston, MA 02115-6096. Offers environmental epidemiology (SM, DPH, SD); environmental health (SM); environmental science and engineering (SM, SD); occupational health (MOH, SM, DPH, SD); physiology (SD). *Accreditation:* CEPH. Part-time programs available. *Faculty:* 23 full-time (5 women), 31 part-time (4 women). *Students:* 75 full-time (38 women), 6 part-time (4 women); includes 8 minority (2 African Americans, 6 Asian Americans or Pacific Islanders), 34 international. *Degree requirements:* For master's, thesis not required; for doctorate, dissertation, qualifying exam required. *Entrance requirements:* For master's, GRE, TOEFL (minimum score of 550 required; 220 for computer-based); for doctorate, GRE, TOEFL (minimum score of 550 required; 220 for computer-based)). *Application deadline:* For fall admission, 1/4. Application fee: $60. *Unit head:* Dr. Joseph D. Brain, Chairman, 617-432-1272. *Application contact:* Margaret R. Watson, Assistant Director of Admissions, 617-432-1031, Fax: 617-432-2009, E-mail: admisofc@hsph.harvard.edu.

Humboldt State University, Graduate Studies, College of Natural Resources and Sciences, Program in Environmental Systems, Arcata, CA 95521-8299. Offers MS. *Faculty:* 11 full-time (2 women), 4 part-time (1 woman). *Students:* 32 full-time (11 women), 20 part-time (3 women); includes 5 minority (1 Asian American or Pacific Islander, 3 Hispanic Americans, 1 Native American), 2 international. Average age 31. 29 applicants, 72% accepted. In 1998, 20 degrees awarded. *Degree requirements:* For master's, computer language, thesis required, foreign language not required. *Entrance requirements:* For master's, GRE, TOEFL (minimum score of 550 required), appropriate bachelor's degree, minimum GPA of 2.5. *Application deadline:* Applications are processed on a rolling basis. Application fee: $55. *Financial aid:* Application deadline: 3/1. *Faculty research:* Mathematical modeling, international development technology, geology, environmental resources engineering. *Unit head:* Dr. Roland Lamberson, Coordinator, 707-826-4346.

Indiana University Bloomington, School of Public and Environmental Affairs, Environmental Science Programs, Bloomington, IN 47405. Offers MSES, PhD, JD/MSES, MSES/MA, MSES/MPA, MSES/MS. MSES/MA offered jointly with the Department of Biology; MSES/MS offered jointly with the Department of Geological Sciences. Part-time programs available. *Students:* 106 full-time (61 women), 32 part-time (14 women); includes 8 minority (5 Asian Americans or Pacific Islanders, 3 Hispanic Americans), 14 international. Average age 25. 150 applicants, 75% accepted. In 1998, 66 degrees awarded. Terminal master's awarded for partial completion of doctoral program. *Degree requirements:* For master's, foreign language and thesis not required; for doctorate, computer language, dissertation required, foreign language not required. *Entrance requirements:* For master's, GRE General Test, LSAT (JD/MSES); for doctorate, GRE General Test. *Application deadline:* For fall admission, 2/1 (priority date). Applications are processed on a rolling basis. Application fee: $40. Tuition, state resident: part-time $194 per credit hour. Tuition, nonresident: part-time $527 per credit hour. Required fees: $360 per year. *Financial aid:* Fellowships, research assistantships, teaching assistantships, career-related internships or fieldwork, Federal Work-Study, institutionally-sponsored loans, and minority fellowships, Peace Corps assistantships available. Financial aid application deadline: 2/1; financial aid applicants required to submit FAFSA. *Faculty research:* Applied ecology, environmental chemistry, hazardous materials management, water resources. *Application contact:* Charles A. Johnson, Coordinator of Student Recruitment, 800-765-7755, Fax: 812-855-7802, E-mail: speainfo@indiana.edu.

See in-depth description on page 899.

Jackson State University, Graduate School, School of Science and Technology, Department of Biology, Jackson, MS 39217. Offers biology education (MST); environmental science (MS, PhD). Part-time and evening/weekend programs available. *Faculty:* 9 full-time (1 woman), 2 part-time (1 woman). *Students:* 47 full-time (30 women), 37 part-time (18 women); includes 71 minority (67 African Americans, 2 Asian Americans or Pacific Islanders, 1 Hispanic American, 1 Native American), 8 international. *Degree requirements:* For master's, comprehensive exam, thesis (alternative accepted for MST) required; for doctorate, dissertation, comprehensive exam required. *Entrance requirements:* For master's, GRE General Test (minimum combined score of 1000 required), TOEFL (minimum score of 550 required); for doctorate, MAT (minimum score of 45 required). *Application deadline:* For fall admission, 3/1 (priority date); for spring admission, 10/1. Applications are processed on a rolling basis. Application fee: $20. *Unit head:* Dr. Mark Hardy, Acting Chair, 601-968-2586, Fax: 601-974-5853, E-mail: mhardy@ccaix.jsums.edu. *Application contact:* Curtis Gore, Admissions Coordinator, 601-974-5841, Fax: 601-974-6196, E-mail: cgore@ccaix.jsums.edu.

Lehigh University, College of Arts and Sciences, Department of Earth and Environmental Sciences, Bethlehem, PA 18015-3094. Offers environmental science (MS, PhD); geological sciences (MS, PhD). *Students:* 25 full-time (14 women); includes 1 minority (Hispanic American), 2 international. Average age 28. 33 applicants, 30% accepted. In 1998, 6 master's, 1 doctorate awarded (100% entered university research/teaching). *Degree requirements:* For master's, thesis required, foreign language not required; for doctorate, dissertation, language at the discretion of the PhD committee required. *Entrance requirements:* For master's and doctorate, GRE General Test (score in 75th percentile or higher required), TOEFL (minimum score of 550 required). *Average time to degree:* Master's–2 years full-time; doctorate–4.5 years full-time. *Application deadline:* For fall admission, 7/15; for spring admission, 12/1. Applications are processed on a rolling basis. Application fee: $40. *Financial aid:* In 1998–99, 3 fellowships, 4 research assistantships, 8 teaching assistantships were awarded.; Federal Work-Study, institutionally-sponsored loans, and tuition waivers (full and partial) also available. Financial aid application deadline: 1/15. *Faculty research:* Tectonics, surficial processes, aquatic ecology. Total annual research expenditures: $1.5 million. *Unit head:* Dr. Peter Zeitler, Chairman, 610-758-3667, Fax: 610-758-3677, E-mail: pkz0@lehigh.edu. *Application contact:* Dr. Donald Morris, Graduate Coordinator, 610-758-5831, Fax: 610-758-3677, E-mail: dpmz0@lehigh.edu.

Long Island University, C.W. Post Campus, College of Liberal Arts and Sciences, Program in Environmental Studies, Brookville, NY 11548-1300. Offers environmental management (MS); environmental science (MS). Part-time and evening/weekend programs available. *Faculty:* 17 full-time (4 women), 4 part-time (1 woman). *Students:* 3 full-time (0 women), 25 part-time (8 women). *Degree requirements:* For master's, internship or thesis required. *Entrance requirements:* For master's, GRE General Test (minimum score of 500 on each section required), 1 year of course work in general chemistry, 1 year of course work in biology or geology, 1 semester in organic chemistry, computer proficiency. *Application deadline:* Applications are processed on a rolling basis. Application fee: $30. Electronic applications accepted. *Unit head:* Dr. Margaret Boorstein, Chair, Department of Earth and Environmental Science, 516-299-2318, Fax: 516-299-3945, E-mail: maboorst@eagle.liunet.edu. *Application contact:* Dr. Lillian Hess, Graduate Director, 516-299-2428, Fax: 516-299-3945.

Louisiana State University and Agricultural and Mechanical College, Graduate School, College of Agriculture, School of Forestry, Wildlife, and Fisheries, Baton Rouge, LA 70803. Offers fisheries (MS); forestry (MS, PhD); wildlife (MS); wildlife and fisheries science (PhD). *Faculty:* 31 full-time (0 women). *Students:* 79 full-time (21 women), 22 part-time (4 women); includes 3 minority (2 Asian Americans or Pacific Islanders, 1 Hispanic American), 31 international. *Degree requirements:* For master's and doctorate, thesis/dissertation required, foreign language not required. *Entrance requirements:* For master's, GRE General Test (minimum combined score of 1000 required), minimum GPA of 3.0; for doctorate, GRE General Test (minimum combined score of 1100 required), MS, minimum GPA of 3.0. *Application deadline:* For fall admission, 1/25 (priority date). Applications are processed on a rolling basis. Applica-

Environmental Sciences

Louisiana State University and Agricultural and Mechanical College (continued)

tion fee: $25. *Unit head:* Dr. Norman E. Linnartz, Interim Director, 225-388-4131, Fax: 225-388-4227, E-mail: nelinn@lsu.edu. *Application contact:* Dr. D. Allen Rutherford, Coordinator of Graduate Studies, 225-388-4187, Fax: 225-388-4144, E-mail: druther@lsu.edu.

Loyola Marymount University, Graduate Division, College of Science and Engineering, Department of Civil Engineering and Environmental Science, Program in Environmental Science, Los Angeles, CA 90045-8350. Offers MS. Part-time and evening/weekend programs available. *Faculty:* 36 full-time (8 women), 19 part-time (6 women). *Students:* 1 full-time (0 women), 13 part-time (6 women); includes 5 minority (all Asian Americans or Pacific Islanders) 11 applicants, 18% accepted. In 1998, 1 degree awarded. *Degree requirements:* For master's, computer language, comprehensive exam required, foreign language and thesis not required. *Entrance requirements:* For master's, TOEFL (minimum score of 550 required). Application fee: $35. Tuition: Part-time $525 per unit. Required fees: $143; $14 per semester. Tuition and fees vary according to program. *Financial aid:* In 1998–99, 6 students received aid. Federal Work-Study and grants available. Aid available to part-time students. Financial aid application deadline: 3/2; financial aid applicants required to submit FAFSA. *Unit head:* Dr. James E. Foxworthy, Professor, 310-338-2828. *Application contact:* Dr. James E. Foxworthy, Professor, 310-338-2828.

Marshall University, Graduate College, Graduate School of Information, Technology and Engineering, Program in Environmental Science, Huntington, WV 25755-2020. Offers MS. Part-time and evening/weekend programs available. *Students:* 6 full-time (4 women), 34 part-time (6 women); includes 1 minority (Hispanic American) Average age 37. In 1998, 11 degrees awarded. *Degree requirements:* For master's, final project, oral exam required. *Entrance requirements:* For master's, GRE General Test, minimum GPA of 2.5, previous course work in calculus. *Financial aid:* Tuition waivers (full) available. Aid available to part-time students. Financial aid application deadline: 8/1; financial aid applicants required to submit FAFSA. *Unit head:* Dr. F. William Kroesser, Director, 304-746-2045, E-mail: wkroesser@marshall.edu.

McNeese State University, Graduate School, College of Science, Department of Biological and Environmental Sciences, Lake Charles, LA 70609-2495. Offers biology (MS); environmental sciences (MS). Evening/weekend programs available. *Faculty:* 16 full-time (2 women). *Students:* 8 full-time (2 women), 9 part-time (3 women). In 1998, 1 degree awarded. *Degree requirements:* For master's, thesis or alternative required, foreign language not required. *Entrance requirements:* For master's, GRE General Test. *Application deadline:* For fall admission, 7/15 (priority date). Applications are processed on a rolling basis. Application fee: $10 ($25 for international students). *Financial aid:* Application deadline: 5/1. *Unit head:* Dr. Robert Maples, Head, 318-475-5674.

Medical University of South Carolina, College of Graduate Studies, Program in Environmental Studies, Charleston, SC 29425-0002. Offers MS. *Students:* 55 full-time (24 women), 18 part-time (6 women); includes 1 minority (Native American), 1 international. Average age 29. 46 applicants, 74% accepted. In 1998, 15 degrees awarded. *Degree requirements:* For master's, thesis, research seminar required. *Entrance requirements:* For master's, GRE General Test (minimum combined score of 1650 on three sections required), GRE Subject Test (international applicants), TOEFL, interview. *Application deadline:* Applications are processed on a rolling basis. Application fee: $55. Electronic applications accepted. *Financial aid:* In 1998–99, 24 students received aid. Federal Work-Study available. Aid available to part-time students. Financial aid application deadline: 4/1; financial aid applicants required to submit FAFSA. *Unit head:* Eberhard Voit, Director, 843-876-1122, Fax: 843-953-8140. *Application contact:* Dodie Weise, Administrative Assistant, 843-876-1144, Fax: 843-876-1146.

Memorial University of Newfoundland, School of Graduate Studies, Interdisciplinary Program in Environmental Science, St. John's, NF A1C 5S7, Canada. Offers M Env Sc, M Sc. *Students:* 29 full-time (17 women), 6 part-time (3 women). 24 applicants, 42% accepted. In 1998, 8 degrees awarded. *Degree requirements:* For master's, thesis (M Sc) required. *Entrance requirements:* For master's, honors B Sc or 2nd class B Eng. *Application deadline:* For fall admission, 7/2; for winter admission, 11/1; for spring admission, 2/1. Application fee: $40. *Financial aid:* Fellowships, research assistantships, teaching assistantships available. Financial aid application deadline: 3/1. *Unit head:* Dr. Niall Gogan, Chair, 709-737-8253, Fax: 709-737-2589, E-mail: ngogan@morgan.ucs.mun.ca. *Application contact:* Gail Kenny, Secretary, 709-737-3444, E-mail: gkenny@morgan.ucs.mun.ca.

Miami University, Graduate School, Institute of Environmental Sciences, Oxford, OH 45056. Offers M En S. Part-time programs available. *Faculty:* 17. *Students:* 35 full-time (21 women), 33 part-time (17 women); includes 4 minority (3 African Americans, 1 Asian American or Pacific Islander), 5 international. 83 applicants, 72% accepted. In 1998, 24 degrees awarded. *Degree requirements:* For master's, thesis, final exam required. *Entrance requirements:* For master's, minimum undergraduate GPA of 3.0 during previous 2 years or 2.75 overall. *Application deadline:* For fall admission, 2/1. Application fee: $35. *Financial aid:* Fellowships, research assistantships, teaching assistantships, career-related internships or fieldwork, Federal Work-Study, and tuition waivers (full) available. *Unit head:* Dr. Gene Willeke, Director, 513-529-5811.

Michigan State University, Graduate School, College of Natural Science, Department of Geological Sciences, East Lansing, MI 48824-1020. Offers environmental geosciences (MS, PhD); geological sciences (MA, MS, PhD). Part-time programs available. *Faculty:* 15 full-time (2 women), 7 part-time (2 women). *Students:* 33 full-time (15 women), 4 part-time (2 women); includes 1 minority (Asian American or Pacific Islander), 2 international. *Degree requirements:* For master's, thesis required (for some programs), foreign language not required; for doctorate, dissertation required, foreign language not required. *Entrance requirements:* For master's and doctorate, GRE General Test, TOEFL. *Application deadline:* For fall admission, 6/1; for spring admission, 11/1. Applications are processed on a rolling basis. Application fee: $30 ($40 for international students). Electronic applications accepted. *Unit head:* Dr. Thomas Vogel, Chairperson, 517-355-4626, Fax: 517-353-8787, E-mail: geosci@pilot.msu.edu.

Minnesota State University, Mankato, College of Graduate Studies, College of Science, Engineering and Technology, Department of Biological Sciences, Program in Environmental Science, Mankato, MN 56002-8400. Offers ecology (MS); economic and political systems (MS); human ecosystems (MS); physical science (MS); technology (MS). *Faculty:* 1 (woman) full-time. *Students:* 2 full-time (1 woman), 4 part-time (1 woman). Average age 31. In 1998, 5 degrees awarded. *Degree requirements:* For master's, one foreign language, thesis or alternative, comprehensive exam required. *Entrance requirements:* For master's, minimum GPA of 3.0 during previous 2 years. *Application deadline:* For fall admission, 7/9 (priority date); for spring admission, 11/27. Applications are processed on a rolling basis. Application fee: $3. *Financial aid:* Research assistantships with partial tuition reimbursements, teaching assistantships with partial tuition reimbursements, career-related internships or fieldwork, Federal Work-Study, and institutionally-sponsored loans available. Financial aid application deadline: 3/15; financial aid applicants required to submit FAFSA. *Unit head:* Dr. Beth Proctor, Graduate Coordinator, 507-389-5697. *Application contact:* Joni Roberts, Admissions Coordinator, 507-389-2321, Fax: 507-389-5974, E-mail: grad@mankato.msus.edu.

Montana State University–Bozeman, College of Graduate Studies, College of Agriculture, Department of Land Resources and Environmental Sciences, Bozeman, MT 59717. Offers MS, PhD. Part-time programs available. *Faculty:* 19 full-time (0 women). *Students:* 7 full-time (2 women), 14 part-time (5 women). Average age 32. 19 applicants, 100% accepted. In 1998, 7 master's, 3 doctorates awarded. Terminal master's awarded for partial completion of doctoral program. *Degree requirements:* For master's, thesis or alternative required, foreign language not required; for doctorate, dissertation required, foreign language not required. *Entrance requirements:* For master's and doctorate, GRE General Test, TOEFL (minimum score of 550 required). *Application deadline:* For fall admission, 6/1 (priority date); for spring admission, 11/1. Applications are processed on a rolling basis. Application fee: $50. *Financial aid:* In 1998–99, 1 fellowship with full tuition reimbursement (averaging $15,000 per year), 23 research assistantships with full and partial tuition reimbursements (averaging $12,000 per year), 2 teaching assistantships with full tuition reimbursements (averaging $10,000 per year) were awarded.; tuition waivers (full and partial) also available. Financial aid application deadline: 3/1. *Faculty research:* Agronomic characteristics, plant breeding/genetics, groundwater quality, irrigation, soil/water conservation. Total annual research expenditures: $2 million. *Unit head:* Dr. Jeffrey S. Jacobsen, Head, 406-994-7060, Fax: 406-994-3933, E-mail: jefj@montana.edu.

Montclair State University, Office of Graduate Studies, College of Science and Mathematics, Department of Earth and Environmental Studies, Upper Montclair, NJ 07043-1624. Offers environmental studies (MS), including environmental education, environmental health, environmental management, environmental science; geoscience (MS). Part-time and evening/weekend programs available. *Degree requirements:* For master's, comprehensive exam required. *Entrance requirements:* For master's, GRE General Test.

New Jersey Institute of Technology, Office of Graduate Studies, Department of Chemical Engineering, Chemistry and Environmental Science, Program in Environmental Science, Newark, NJ 07102-1982. Offers MS, PhD. *Degree requirements:* For doctorate, dissertation, residency required, foreign language not required, foreign language not required. *Entrance requirements:* For master's, GRE General Test (minimum score of 450 on verbal section, 600 on quantitative, 550 on analytical required); for doctorate, GRE General Test (minimum score of 450 on verbal section, 600 on quantitative, 550 on analytical required), minimum graduate GPA of 3.5.

New Mexico Highlands University, Graduate Office, College of Arts and Sciences, Department of Life Sciences, Las Vegas, NM 87701. Offers biology (MS); environmental science and management (MS). Part-time programs available. *Faculty:* 9 full-time (2 women). *Students:* 11 full-time (6 women), 8 part-time (3 women); includes 13 minority (1 African American, 1 Asian American or Pacific Islander, 11 Hispanic Americans), 2 international. *Degree requirements:* For master's, thesis or alternative required, foreign language not required. *Entrance requirements:* For master's, minimum undergraduate GPA of 3.0. *Application deadline:* For fall admission, 8/1 (priority date). Applications are processed on a rolling basis. Application fee: $15. Tuition, state resident: full-time $1,988; part-time $83 per credit hour. Tuition, nonresident: full-time $8,034; part-time $83 per credit hour. Tuition and fees vary according to course load. *Unit head:* Dr. Maureen Romine, Chair, 505-454-3264, Fax: 505-454-3063, E-mail: romine_m@merlin.nmhu.edu. *Application contact:* Dr. Glen W. Davidson, Provost, 505-454-3311, Fax: 505-454-3558, E-mail: glendavidson@venus.nmhu.edu.

New Mexico Institute of Mining and Technology, Graduate Studies, Department of Chemistry, Socorro, NM 87801. Offers biochemistry (MS); chemistry (MS); environmental chemistry (PhD); explosives technology and atmospheric chemistry (PhD). *Faculty:* 7 full-time (1 woman). *Students:* 13 full-time (3 women); includes 1 minority (Hispanic American), 7 international. *Degree requirements:* For master's and doctorate, thesis/dissertation required, foreign language not required. *Entrance requirements:* For master's, GRE General Test, TOEFL (minimum score of 540 required); for doctorate, GRE General Test, GRE Subject Test, TOEFL (minimum score of 540 required). *Application deadline:* For fall admission, 3/1 (priority date); for spring admission, 6/1. Applications are processed on a rolling basis. Application fee: $16. *Unit head:* Dr. Lawrence Werbelow, Chairman, 505-835-5263, Fax: 505-835-5364, E-mail: werbelow@jupiter.nmt.edu. *Application contact:* Dr. David B. Johnson, Dean of Graduate Studies, 505-835-5513, Fax: 505-835-5476, E-mail: graduate@nmt.edu.

Nova Southeastern University, Oceanographic Center, Fort Lauderdale, FL 33314-7721. Offers coastal-zone management (MS); marine biology (MS); marine environmental science (MS); oceanography (PhD). Part-time and evening/weekend programs available. *Students:* 13 full-time (9 women), 59 part-time (30 women); includes 5 minority (1 Asian American or Pacific Islander, 3 Hispanic Americans, 1 Native American), 2 international. *Degree requirements:* For master's, thesis optional, foreign language not required; for doctorate, dissertation, departmental qualifying exam required. *Entrance requirements:* For master's, GRE General Test (minimum combined score of 1000 required); for doctorate, GRE General Test (minimum combined score of 1100 required), master's degree. *Application deadline:* Applications are processed on a rolling basis. Application fee: $50. Tuition: Part-time $417 per credit hour. Required fees: $50 per semester. Tuition and fees vary according to degree level and program. *Unit head:* Dr. Julian P. McCreary, Dean, 954-920-1909, Fax: 954-947-8559, E-mail: jay@ocean.nova.edu. *Application contact:* Dr. Richard Dodge, Associate Dean, 954-920-1909, Fax: 954-947-8559, E-mail: dodge@ocean.nova.edu.

Oakland University, Graduate Studies, College of Arts and Sciences, Department of Chemistry, Rochester, MI 48309-4401. Offers chemistry (MS, PhD); health and environmental chemistry (PhD). *Faculty:* 15 full-time. *Students:* 8 full-time (5 women), 5 part-time (2 women); includes 2 minority (both Asian Americans or Pacific Islanders), 5 international. *Degree requirements:* For master's and doctorate, thesis/dissertation required, foreign language not required. *Entrance requirements:* For master's, minimum GPA of 3.0 for unconditional admission; for doctorate, GRE Subject Test, minimum GPA of 3.0 for unconditional admission. *Application deadline:* For fall admission, 7/15; for spring admission, 3/15. Application fee: $30. Tuition, state resident: part-time $221 per credit hour. Tuition, nonresident: part-time $488 per credit hour. Required fees: $214 per semester. Part-time tuition and fees vary according to program. *Unit head:* Dr. Michael Sevilla, Chair, 248-370-2328. *Application contact:* Dr. Arthur W. Bull, Coordinator, 248-370-2320.

The Ohio State University, Graduate School, College of Engineering, Program in Environmental Science, Columbus, OH 43210. Offers MS, PhD. *Faculty:* 78 full-time, 10 part-time. *Students:* 63 full-time (28 women), 12 part-time (6 women); includes 4 minority (1 African American, 2 Asian Americans or Pacific Islanders, 1 Hispanic American), 28 international. 109 applicants, 24% accepted. In 1998, 7 master's, 7 doctorates awarded. *Degree requirements:* For master's, one foreign language required, (computer language can substitute), thesis optional; for doctorate, one foreign language (computer language can substitute), dissertation required. *Entrance requirements:* For master's and doctorate, GRE General Test, GRE Subject Test (biology). *Application deadline:* For fall admission, 8/15. Applications are processed on a rolling basis. Application fee: $30 ($40 for international students). *Financial aid:* Fellowships, research assistantships, teaching assistantships, Federal Work-Study and institutionally-sponsored loans available. Aid available to part-time students. *Unit head:* Audeen W. Fentimen, Director, 614-292-7930, E-mail: fentimen.1@osu.edu.

Oklahoma State University, Graduate College, Program in Environmental Sciences, Stillwater, OK 74078. Offers MS, PhD. *Students:* 1 (woman) full-time, 4 part-time (all women); includes 1 minority (African American) Average age 40. In 1998, 14 master's, 4 doctorates awarded. *Degree requirements:* For master's and doctorate, thesis/dissertation required. *Entrance requirements:* For master's and doctorate, GRE, TOEFL (minimum score of 575 required). *Application deadline:* For fall admission, 7/1 (priority date). Application fee: $25. *Financial aid:* Research assistantships, teaching assistantships, tuition waivers (partial) available. Aid available to part-time students. Financial aid application deadline: 3/1. *Unit head:* Dr. Edward Knobbe, Director, 405-744-9995.

Oregon Graduate Institute of Science and Technology, Graduate Studies, Department of Environmental Science and Engineering, Portland, OR 97291-1000. Offers ecosystem management and restoration (MS); environmental science (MS, PhD); environmental systems management (MS). Part-time programs available. *Faculty:* 9 full-time (1 woman). *Students:* 20 full-time (11 women), 4 part-time, 1 international. Average age 28. 74 applicants, 18% accepted. In 1998, 13 master's, 3 doctorates awarded. Terminal master's awarded for partial completion of doctoral program. *Degree requirements:* For master's, thesis optional, foreign language not required; for doctorate, comprehensive exam, oral defense of dissertation required. *Entrance requirements:* For master's, GRE General Test (strongly recommended), TOEFL (minimum score of 600 required); for doctorate, GRE General Test, TOEFL (minimum score of 600 required). *Average time to degree:* Master's–1.5 years full-time; doctorate–5 years full-time. Application fee: $50. Electronic applications accepted. *Financial aid:* In 1998–99, 20 students received aid, including 11 research assistantships; fellowships, teaching assistantships, Federal Work-Study and scholarships also available. Financial aid application deadline: 2/15. *Faculty research:* Air and water science, hydrogeology, estuarine and coastal modeling, environmental microbiology, contaminant transport, ecosystems. *Unit head:* Dr. James F. Pankow, Head, 503-690-1196, Fax: 503-690-1273, E-mail: pankow@ese.ogi.edu. *Application contact:* Director of Admissions, 800-685-2423, Fax: 503-690-1285, E-mail: admissions@admin.ogi.edu.

Announcement: The Institute offers new interdisciplinary educational programs in environmental systems management (an 18-month MS program) and ecosystem management and restoration (a 12-month MS program). For further information about the department, please visit the Web site at http://www.ese.ogi.edu/.

See in-depth description on page 903.

Pace University, Dyson College of Arts and Sciences, Program in Environmental Science, New York, NY 10038. Offers MS. *Faculty:* 7 full-time, 7 part-time. *Students:* 2 full-time (0 women), 10 part-time (4 women). Average age 29. 13 applicants, 85% accepted. *Degree requirements:* Foreign language not required. *Entrance requirements:* For master's, GRE. *Application deadline:* For fall admission, 7/31 (priority date); for spring admission, 11/30. Applications are processed on a rolling basis. Application fee: $60. Electronic applications accepted. *Unit head:* Dr. David Rahni, Coordinator, 914-773-3665. *Application contact:* Lois Rich, Associate Director, 914-422-4283, Fax: 914-442-4287, E-mail: gradwp@pace.edu.

See in-depth description on page 905.

Pennsylvania State University Great Valley School of Graduate Professional Studies, Graduate Studies and Continuing Education, Intercollege Graduate Programs, Program in Environmental Pollution Control, Malvern, PA 19355-1488. Offers MEPC. Application fee: $50. *Unit head:* Dr. Lily Sehayek, Adviser, 610-648-3243. *Application contact:* 610-648-3242, Fax: 610-889-1334.

Pennsylvania State University Harrisburg Campus of the Capital College, Graduate Center, School of Science, Engineering and Technology, Program in Environmental Pollution Control, Middletown, PA 17057-4898. Offers M Eng, MEPC, MS. Evening/weekend programs available. *Students:* 8 full-time (4 women), 32 part-time (12 women). Average age 33. In 1998, 14 degrees awarded. *Degree requirements:* For master's, thesis required, foreign language not required. *Entrance requirements:* For master's, GRE General Test, TOEFL (minimum score of 560 required), minimum GPA of 2.75. *Application deadline:* For fall admission, 7/26. Application fee: $50. *Unit head:* Dr. Scott Huebner, Coordinator, 717-948-6127.

Pennsylvania State University University Park Campus, Graduate School, Intercollege Graduate Programs, Intercollege Program in Environmental Pollution Control, State College, University Park, PA 16802-1503. Offers M Eng, MEPC, MS. *Students:* 22 full-time (9 women), 12 part-time (3 women). In 1998, 25 degrees awarded. *Entrance requirements:* For master's, GRE General Test, TOEFL (minimum score of 560 required). *Application deadline:* For fall admission, 6/1. Application fee: $50. *Unit head:* Dr. Herschel A. Elliott, Professor in Charge, 814-865-1417, Fax: 814-863-0109.

Polytechnic University, Brooklyn Campus, Department of Humanities and Social Sciences, Major in Environment Behavior Studies, Brooklyn, NY 11201-2990. Offers MS. Part-time and evening/weekend programs available. *Degree requirements:* For master's, thesis not required. *Application deadline:* Applications are processed on a rolling basis. Application fee: $45. Electronic applications accepted. *Unit head:* Dr. M. Sigman-Grant, Chair, 814-865-5444. *Application contact:* John S. Kerge, Dean of Admissions, 718-260-3200, Fax: 718-260-3446, E-mail: admitme@poly.edu.

Portland State University, Graduate Studies, College of Liberal Arts and Sciences, Interdisciplinary Program in Environmental Sciences and Resources, Portland, OR 97207-0751. Offers environmental management (MEM); environmental sciences/biology (PhD); environmental sciences/chemistry (PhD); environmental sciences/civil engineering (PhD); environmental sciences/economics (PhD); environmental sciences/geography (PhD); environmental sciences/geology (PhD); environmental sciences/physics (PhD); environmental studies (MS). Part-time programs available. *Faculty:* 7 full-time (1 woman). *Students:* 38 full-time (11 women), 20 part-time (5 women); includes 4 minority (2 Asian Americans or Pacific Islanders, 1 Hispanic American, 1 Native American), 12 international. Average age 35. 48 applicants, 52% accepted. In 1998, 8 degrees awarded. *Degree requirements:* For doctorate, variable foreign language requirement, computer language, dissertation, oral and qualifying exams required. *Entrance requirements:* For doctorate, TOEFL (minimum score of 550 required), minimum GPA of 3.0 in upper-division course work or 2.75 overall. *Application deadline:* For fall admission, 4/1 (priority date). Applications are processed on a rolling basis. Application fee: $50. *Financial aid:* In 1998–99, 1 research assistantship, 4 teaching assistantships were awarded.; Federal Work-Study and institutionally-sponsored loans also available. Aid available to part-time students. Financial aid application deadline: 3/1; financial aid applicants required to submit FAFSA. *Faculty research:* Environmental aspects of biology, chemistry, civil engineering, geology, physics. Total annual research expenditures: $159,571. *Unit head:* Dr. James R. Pratt, Director, 503-725-4209, Fax: 503-725-3888, E-mail: prattja@pdx.edu. *Application contact:* Betty Knudson, Coordinator, 503-725-4209, Fax: 503-725-3888, E-mail: envir@pdx.edu.

See in-depth description on page 907.

Rensselaer Polytechnic Institute, Graduate School, School of Science, Department of Earth and Environmental Sciences, Troy, NY 12180-3590. Offers environmental chemistry (MS, PhD); geochemistry (MS, PhD); geology (MS, PhD); geophysics (MS, PhD); hydrogeology (MS); petrology (MS, PhD); planetary geology (MS, PhD); tectonics (MS, PhD). Part-time programs available. *Faculty:* 7 full-time (0 women), 2 part-time (0 women). *Students:* 19 full-time (8 women), 1 (woman) part-time; includes 2 minority (1 African American, 1 Native American) 20 applicants, 75% accepted. In 1998, 6 master's, 2 doctorates awarded. *Degree requirements:* For master's, thesis required (for some programs); for doctorate, dissertation required. *Entrance requirements:* For master's and doctorate, GRE General Test, TOEFL (minimum score of 550 required). *Application deadline:* For fall admission, 2/1 (priority date). Applications are processed on a rolling basis. Application fee: $35. *Financial aid:* In 1998–99, 9 research assistantships with partial tuition reimbursements (averaging $10,500 per year), 4 teaching assistantships with partial tuition reimbursements (averaging $10,500 per year) were awarded.; fellowships, career-related internships or fieldwork, institutionally-sponsored loans, and tuition waivers (partial) also available. Financial aid application deadline: 2/1. *Faculty research:* Groundwater modeling, asteroid chemistry, mantel geochemistry, contaminant geochemistry, seismology, GPS geodesy, remote sensing. Total annual research expenditures: $1.8 million. *Unit head:* Dr. Robert McCaffrey, Chair, 518-276-6474, Fax: 518-276-6680, E-mail: ees@rpi.edu. *Application contact:* Dr. Steven Roecker, Associate Professor, 518-276-6474, Fax: 518-276-6680, E-mail: ees@rpi.edu.

Rice University, Graduate Programs, George R. Brown School of Engineering, Department of Environmental Science and Engineering, Houston, TX 77251-1892. Offers environmental engineering (MEE, MES, MS, PhD); environmental science (MEE, MES, MS, PhD). Part-time programs available. *Degree requirements:* For master's, thesis required (for some programs), foreign language not required; for doctorate, dissertation required, foreign language not required. *Entrance requirements:* For master's and doctorate, GRE General Test, GRE Subject Test, TOEFL (minimum score of 550 required), minimum GPA of 3.0. *Faculty research:* Biology and chemistry of groundwater, pollutant fate in groundwater systems, water quality monitoring, urban storm water runoff.

Rutgers, The State University of New Jersey, New Brunswick, Graduate School, Program in Environmental Sciences, New Brunswick, NJ 08903. Offers air resources (MS, PhD); aquatic biology (MS, PhD); aquatic chemistry (MS, PhD); chemistry and physics of aerosol and hydrosol systems (MS, PhD); environmental chemistry (MS, PhD); environmental microbiology (MS, PhD); environmental toxicology (MS, PhD); exposure assessment (PhD); water and wastewater treatment (MS, PhD); water resources (MS, PhD). Part-time and evening/weekend programs available. *Faculty:* 33 full-time (7 women), 36 part-time (6 women). *Students:* 42 full-time (16 women), 92 part-time (30 women); includes 22 minority (17 Asian Americans or Pacific Islanders, 5 Hispanic Americans), 31 international. Average age 26. 122 applicants, 39% accepted. In 1998, 27 master's, 16 doctorates awarded. Terminal master's awarded for partial completion of doctoral program. *Degree requirements:* For master's, thesis or alternative, oral final exam required, foreign language not required; for doctorate, dissertation, thesis defense, qualifying exam required, foreign language not required. *Entrance requirements:* For master's and doctorate, GRE General Test (minimum score of 500 on verbal section, 600 on quantitative required), TOEFL (minimum score of 590 required). *Application deadline:* For fall admission, 3/1; for spring admission, 11/1. Applications are processed on a rolling basis. Application fee: $50. *Financial aid:* In 1998–99, 1 fellowship (averaging $3,000 per year), 15 research assistantships with full tuition reimbursements (averaging $13,956 per year), 4 teaching assistantships with full tuition reimbursements (averaging $12,136 per year) were awarded.; career-related internships or fieldwork and Federal Work-Study also available. Financial aid application deadline: 3/1; financial aid applicants required to submit FAFSA. *Faculty research:* Atmospheric sciences; biological waste treatment; contaminant fate and transport; exposure assessment; air, soil and water quality. *Unit head:* Dr. Peter F. Strom, Director, 732-932-8078, Fax: 732-932-8644, E-mail: strom@aesop.rutgers.edu. *Application contact:* Paul J. Lioy, Graduate Admissions Committee, 732-932-0150, Fax: 732-445-0116, E-mail: plioy@eohsi.rutgers.edu.

See in-depth description on page 913.

South Dakota School of Mines and Technology, Graduate Division, Joint PhD Program in Atmospheric, Environmental, and Water Resources, Rapid City, SD 57701-3995. Offers PhD. *Students:* 15 full-time (5 women), 9 international. Average age 47. *Degree requirements:* For doctorate, dissertation required. *Entrance requirements:* For doctorate, GRE General Test, GRE Subject Test, TOEFL (minimum score of 520 required), TWE. *Application deadline:* For fall admission, 6/15 (priority date); for spring admission, 10/15. Applications are processed on a rolling basis. Application fee: $15. Electronic applications accepted. Tuition, state resident: part-time $89 per hour. Tuition, nonresident: part-time $261 per hour. Part-time tuition and fees vary according to program. *Financial aid:* In 1998–99, 2 students received aid, including 1 research assistantship, 1 teaching assistantship *Unit head:* Admissions Office, 902-867-2219, Fax: 902-867-2329, E-mail: admit@stfx.ca. *Application contact:* Brenda Brown, Secretary, 800-454-8162 Ext. 2493, Fax: 605-394-5360, E-mail: graduate_admissions@silver.sdmt.edu.

South Dakota State University, Graduate School, College of Engineering, Joint PhD Program in Atmospheric, Environmental, and Water Resources, Brookings, SD 57007. Offers PhD. Offered jointly with the South Dakota School of Mines and Technology. *Degree requirements:* For doctorate, dissertation, preliminary oral and written exams required. *Entrance requirements:* For doctorate, GRE General Test, GRE Subject Test, TOEFL. *Faculty research:* Use of fabric-reinforced soil wall for internal abutment bridge, end treatment performance evaluation of water and wastewater treatment.

Southern Illinois University Edwardsville, Graduate Studies and Research, College of Arts and Sciences, Program in Environmental Sciences, Edwardsville, IL 62026-0001. Offers MS. *Students:* 9 full-time (6 women), 40 part-time (20 women); includes 3 minority (2 African Americans, 1 Native American), 3 international. 26 applicants, 73% accepted. In 1998, 22 degrees awarded. *Degree requirements:* For master's, thesis or alternative, final exam, oral exam required, foreign language not required. *Entrance requirements:* For master's, GRE General Test, TOEFL (minimum score of 550 required). *Application deadline:* For fall admission, 7/24. Application fee: $25. *Financial aid:* In 1998–99, 1 research assistantship with full tuition reimbursement was awarded.; fellowships with full tuition reimbursements, teaching assistantships with full tuition reimbursements, career-related internships or fieldwork, Federal Work-Study, institutionally-sponsored loans, and unspecified assistantships also available. Aid available to part-time students. *Unit head:* Dr. James Houpis, Graduate Director, 618-650-5786, E-mail: jhoupis@siue.edu.

Southern University and Agricultural and Mechanical College, Graduate School, College of Sciences, Department of Chemistry, Baton Rouge, LA 70813. Offers analytical chemistry (MS); biochemistry (MS); environmental sciences (MS); inorganic chemistry (MS); organic chemistry (MS); physical chemistry (MS). *Faculty:* 9 full-time (2 women), 3 part-time (2 women). *Students:* 4 full-time (3 women), 20 part-time (12 women); includes 19 minority (all African Americans), 4 international. *Degree requirements:* For master's, thesis required, foreign language not required. *Entrance requirements:* For master's, GMAT or GRE General Test, TOEFL. *Application deadline:* For fall admission, 6/1 (priority date); for spring admission, 11/1. Applications are processed on a rolling basis. Application fee: $5. *Unit head:* Dr. Robert Harvey Miller, Chairman, 225-771-3990, Fax: 225-771-3992.

Stanford University, School of Earth Sciences, Department of Geological and Environmental Sciences, Stanford, CA 94305-9991. Offers MS, PhD, Eng. *Faculty:* 20 full-time (3 women). *Students:* 72 full-time (23 women), 19 part-time (3 women); includes 7 minority (2 African Americans, 2 Asian Americans or Pacific Islanders, 2 Hispanic Americans, 1 Native American), 29 international. Average age 28. 94 applicants, 36% accepted. In 1998, 6 master's, 18 doctorates awarded. Terminal master's awarded for partial completion of doctoral program. *Degree requirements:* For master's and doctorate, thesis/dissertation required; for Eng, computer language, thesis required, foreign language not required. *Entrance requirements:* For master's, doctorate, and Eng, GRE General Test, TOEFL. *Application deadline:* For fall admission, 1/15. Application fee: $65 ($80 for international students). Tuition: Full-time $23,058. Required fees: $152. Part-time tuition and fees vary according to course load. *Financial aid:* Fellowships, research assistantships, teaching assistantships, Federal Work-Study and institutionally-sponsored loans available. Aid available to part-time students. Financial aid application deadline: 1/15. *Unit head:* Gail Mahood, Chair, 650-723-1429, Fax: 650-725-0979, E-mail: gail@pangea.stanford.edu. *Application contact:* Graduate Admissions Coordinator, 650-725-0574.

Stanford University, School of Earth Sciences, Earth Systems Program, Stanford, CA 94305-9991. Offers MS. Students admitted at the undergraduate level. *Students:* 15 full-time (10 women), 1 (woman) part-time; includes 3 minority (1 African American, 1 Asian American or Pacific Islander, 1 Hispanic American) Average age 23. In 1998, 12 degrees awarded. Application fee: $65 ($80 for international students). Electronic applications accepted. Tuition: Full-time $23,058. Required fees: $152. Part-time tuition and fees vary according to course load. *Unit head:* Joan Roughgarden, Director, 650-723-4961, Fax: 650-725-0958, E-mail: rough@pangea.stanford.edu.

State University of New York at Stony Brook, Graduate School, Marine Sciences Research Center, Program in Marine Environmental Sciences, Stony Brook, NY 11794. Offers MS. Evening/weekend programs available. *Faculty:* 19 full-time (6 women), 1 (woman) part-time. *Students:* 58 full-time (35 women), 8 part-time (7 women); includes 3 minority (1 African American, 1 Asian American or Pacific Islander, 1 Hispanic American), 9 international. Average age 24. 54 applicants, 54% accepted. In 1998, 24 degrees awarded. *Degree requirements:* For master's, thesis, written comprehensive exam required, foreign language not required. *Entrance requirements:* For master's, GRE General Test, TOEFL (minimum score of 550 required), minimum GPA of 3.0. *Application deadline:* For fall admission, 1/15. Application fee: $50. *Financial aid:* Fellowships, research assistantships, teaching assistantships available. *Application contact:* Dr. Henry Bokuniewicz, Director, 516-632-8681, Fax: 516-632-8200, E-mail: hbokuniewicz@ccmail.sunysb.edu.

State University of New York College of Environmental Science and Forestry, Faculty of Environmental Science, Syracuse, NY 13210-2779. Offers MPS, MS, PhD. Part-time programs available. *Faculty:* 10 full-time (6 women), 2 part-time (both women). *Students:* 46 full-time (26 women), 25 part-time (11 women); includes 6 minority (2 African Americans, 4

Environmental Sciences

State University of New York College of Environmental Science and Forestry (continued)
Hispanic Americans), 13 international. Average age 29. 69 applicants, 77% accepted. In 1998, 12 master's, 1 doctorate awarded. Terminal master's awarded for partial completion of doctoral program. *Degree requirements:* For master's, thesis or alternative required; for doctorate, dissertation required. *Entrance requirements:* For master's and doctorate, GRE General Test (minimum combined score of 1800 on three sections required), minimum GPA of 3.0. *Application deadline:* For fall admission, 4/15 (priority date); for spring admission, 11/15. Applications are processed on a rolling basis. Application fee: $50. *Financial aid:* In 1998–99, 8 fellowships with tuition reimbursements, 6 research assistantships with tuition reimbursements, 12 teaching assistantships with tuition reimbursements were awarded.; career-related internships or fieldwork and Federal Work-Study also available. Aid available to part-time students. *Faculty research:* Environmental education/communications, water resources, land resources, waste management. Total annual research expenditures: $135,297. *Unit head:* Dr. Richard Smardon, Chairperson, 315-470-6636, Fax: 315-470-6915, E-mail: rsmardon@mailbox.syr.edu. *Application contact:* Dr. Robert H. Frey, Dean, Instruction and Graduate Studies, 315-470-6599, Fax: 315-470-6978, E-mail: esfgrad@esf.edu.

See in-depth description on page 917.

Stephen F. Austin State University, Graduate School, College of Sciences and Mathematics, Department of Environmental Science, Nacogdoches, TX 75962. Offers MS. *Students:* 20 full-time (11 women), 3 part-time; includes 4 minority (3 African Americans, 1 Hispanic American), 1 international. 13 applicants, 77% accepted. *Degree requirements:* For master's, comprehensive exam required. *Entrance requirements:* For master's, GRE General Test, TOEFL, minimum GPA of 2.8 in last 60 hours, 2.5 overall. *Application deadline:* For fall admission, 8/1 (priority date); for spring admission, 12/15. Applications are processed on a rolling basis. Application fee: $0 ($50 for international students). Tuition, state resident: full-time $1,792. Tuition, nonresident: full-time $6,880. *Financial aid:* In 1998–99, research assistantships (averaging $6,750 per year) Financial aid application deadline: 3/1. *Unit head:* Dr. Jack I. McCullough, Director, 409-468-4582.

Tarleton State University, College of Graduate Studies, College of Arts and Sciences, Program in Environmental Science, Stephenville, TX 76402. Offers MS. Part-time and evening/weekend programs available. 2 applicants, 50% accepted. In 1998, 2 degrees awarded. *Degree requirements:* For master's, comprehensive exam required, thesis optional. *Entrance requirements:* For master's, GRE General Test, minimum GPA of 2.75. *Application deadline:* For fall admission, 8/5 (priority date); for spring admission, 12/1. Applications are processed on a rolling basis. Application fee: $25 ($100 for international students). *Financial aid:* Research assistantships, teaching assistantships, career-related internships or fieldwork and Federal Work-Study available. Aid available to part-time students. Financial aid application deadline: 5/1; financial aid applicants required to submit FAFSA. *Unit head:* Dr. Hugh Jeffes, Head, 254-968-9863.

Tennessee Technological University, Graduate School, College of Arts and Sciences, Department of Environmental Sciences, Cookeville, TN 38505. Offers PhD. *Students:* 5 full-time (0 women), 1 (woman) part-time. 21 applicants, 62% accepted. *Degree requirements:* For doctorate, one foreign language (computer language can substitute), dissertation required. *Entrance requirements:* For doctorate, GRE Subject Test, TOEFL (minimum score of 525 required). *Application deadline:* For fall admission, 3/1 (priority date); for spring admission, 8/1. Application fee: $25 ($30 for international students). Electronic applications accepted. Tuition, state resident: part-time $137 per hour. Tuition, nonresident: part-time $361 per hour. Required fees: $17 per hour. Tuition and fees vary according to course load. *Financial aid:* In 1998–99, 6 research assistantships (averaging $1,000 per year) were awarded.; fellowships, teaching assistantships Financial aid application deadline: 4/1. *Unit head:* Dr. Dale Ensor, Director, 931-372-3493, Fax: 931-372-3434, E-mail: densor@tntech.edu. *Application contact:* Dr. Rebecca F. Quattlebaum, Dean of the Graduate School, 931-372-3233, Fax: 931-372-3497, E-mail: rquattlebaum@tntech.edu.

Texas A&M University–Corpus Christi, Graduate Programs, College of Science and Technology, Program in Sciences, Corpus Christi, TX 78412-5503. Offers biology (MS); environmental sciences (MS); mariculture (MS). Part-time and evening/weekend programs available. *Degree requirements:* For master's, thesis required (for some programs), foreign language not required. *Entrance requirements:* For master's, GRE General Test.

Texas Christian University, Add Ran College of Arts and Sciences, Department of Biology, Program in Environmental Sciences, Fort Worth, TX 76129-0002. Offers MS. Part-time and evening/weekend programs available. *Students:* 15 (8 women); includes 2 minority (both Asian Americans or Pacific Islanders) 2 international. 14 applicants, 71% accepted. In 1998, 4 degrees awarded. *Degree requirements:* For master's, thesis optional, foreign language not required. *Entrance requirements:* For master's, GRE General Test (minimum combined score of 1000 required), GRE Subject Test, TOEFL (minimum score of 550 required), 1 year of biology and chemistry; 1 semester of calculus, government, and physical geology. *Application deadline:* For fall admission, 3/1; for spring admission, 12/1. Applications are processed on a rolling basis. Application fee: $0. *Financial aid:* Unspecified assistantships available. Financial aid application deadline: 3/1. *Unit head:* Dr. Leo Newland, Director, 817-257-7271.

Tufts University, Division of Graduate and Continuing Studies and Research, Graduate School of Arts and Sciences, College of Engineering, Department of Civil and Environmental Engineering, Medford, MA 02155. Offers civil engineering (MS, PhD), including geotechnical engineering, structural engineering; environmental engineering (MS, PhD), including environmental engineering and environmental sciences, environmental geotechnology, environmental health, environmental science and management, hazardous materials management, water resources engineering. Part-time programs available. *Faculty:* 13 full-time, 10 part-time. *Students:* 99 (47 women); includes 21 minority (5 African Americans, 7 Asian Americans or Pacific Islanders, 9 Hispanic Americans) 16 international. Terminal master's awarded for partial completion of doctoral program. *Degree requirements:* For master's, thesis or alternative required, foreign language not required; for doctorate, dissertation required, foreign language not required. *Entrance requirements:* For master's and doctorate, GRE General Test, TOEFL (minimum score of 550 required). *Application deadline:* For fall admission, 2/15; for spring admission, 10/15. Applications are processed on a rolling basis. Application fee: $50. *Unit head:* Dr. Stephen Levine, Chair, 617-627-3211, Fax: 617-627-3994. *Application contact:* Linfield Brown, 617-627-3211, Fax: 617-627-3994.

Tuskegee University, Graduate Programs, College of Agricultural, Environmental and Natural Sciences, Department of Agricultural Sciences, Program in Environmental Sciences, Tuskegee, AL 36088. Offers MS. *Faculty:* 13 full-time (1 woman), 2 part-time (1 woman). *Students:* 8 full-time (5 women), 7 part-time (3 women); all minorities (14 African Americans, 1 Asian American or Pacific Islander) Average age 24. In 1998, 2 degrees awarded. *Degree requirements:* For master's, computer language, thesis required, foreign language not required. *Entrance requirements:* For master's, GRE General Test. *Application deadline:* For fall admission, 7/15. Applications are processed on a rolling basis. Application fee: $25 ($35 for international students). *Financial aid:* Application deadline: 4/15. *Unit head:* Dr. P. K. Biswas, Head, Department of Agricultural Sciences, 334-727-8632.

Université de Sherbrooke, Faculty of Sciences, Diplôme de gestion de l'environement, Sherbrooke, PQ J1K 2R1, Canada. Offers Diploma. Postbaccalaureate distance learning degree programs offered (no on-campus study). *Degree requirements:* For degree.

Université de Sherbrooke, Faculty of Sciences, Program in the Environment, Sherbrooke, PQ J1K 2R1, Canada. Offers M Env. *Degree requirements:* For master's, thesis required, foreign language not required.

Université du Québec à Montréal, Graduate Programs, Program in Environmental Sciences, Montréal, PQ H3C 3P8, Canada. Offers M Sc, PhD. Part-time programs available. *Degree requirements:* For master's, research report required, thesis not required; for doctorate, dissertation required. *Entrance requirements:* For master's, appropriate bachelor's degree or equivalent and proficiency in French; for doctorate, appropriate master's degree or equivalent and proficiency in French.

Université du Québec à Trois-Rivières, Graduate Programs, Program in Environmental Sciences, Trois-Rivières, PQ G9A 5H7, Canada. Offers M Sc. Part-time programs available. *Students:* 24 full-time (12 women). 17 applicants, 41% accepted. In 1998, 5 degrees awarded. *Degree requirements:* For master's, thesis required. *Entrance requirements:* For master's, appropriate bachelor's degree, proficiency in French. *Application deadline:* For fall admission, 2/1. Application fee: $30. *Financial aid:* Fellowships, research assistantships, teaching assistantships available. *Faculty research:* Aquatic communities. *Unit head:* Marco Rodriguez, Director, 819-376-5053 Ext. 3363, Fax: 819-376-5012, E-mail: marco_rodriguez@uqtr.uquebec.ca. *Application contact:* Suzanne Camirand, Admissions Officer, 819-376-5045 Ext. 2591, Fax: 819-376-5210, E-mail: suzanne_camirand@uqtr.uquebec.ca.

The University of Akron, Graduate School, Buchtel College of Arts and Sciences, Department of Geology, Program in Environmental Geology, Akron, OH 44325-0001. Offers MS. *Students:* 8 full-time (3 women); includes 1 minority (African American) Average age 28. In 1998, 4 degrees awarded. *Degree requirements:* For master's, thesis required, foreign language not required. *Entrance requirements:* For master's, minimum GPA of 2.75. *Average time to degree:* Master's–2 years full-time, 4 years part-time. *Application deadline:* For fall admission, 3/1. Applications are processed on a rolling basis. Application fee: $25 ($50 for international students). Tuition, state resident: part-time $189 per credit. Tuition, nonresident: part-time $353 per credit. Required fees: $7.3 per credit. *Unit head:* Dr. David McConnell, Director of Graduate Studies, 330-972-8047, E-mail: mcconnell@uakron.edu.

The University of Alabama in Huntsville, School of Graduate Studies, College of Science, Department of Atmospheric and Environmental Science, Huntsville, AL 35899. Offers MS, PhD. Part-time and evening/weekend programs available. *Faculty:* 6 full-time (0 women), 2 part-time (0 women). *Students:* 24 full-time (5 women), 5 part-time; includes 2 minority (1 Asian American or Pacific Islander, 1 Hispanic American), 10 international. Average age 31. 9 applicants, 100% accepted. In 1998, 2 master's, 4 doctorates awarded. *Degree requirements:* For master's, oral and written exams required, thesis optional, foreign language not required; for doctorate, dissertation, oral and written exams required, foreign language not required. *Entrance requirements:* For master's and doctorate, GRE General Test (minimum combined score of 1650 on three sections required), minimum GPA of 3.0. *Application deadline:* For fall admission, 7/24 (priority date); for spring admission, 11/15 (priority date). Applications are processed on a rolling basis. Application fee: $20. Tuition and fees vary according to course load. *Financial aid:* In 1998–99, 22 students received aid, including 21 research assistantships with full and partial tuition reimbursements available (averaging $11,248 per year), 1 teaching assistantship with full and partial tuition reimbursement available (averaging $9,450 per year); fellowships with full and partial tuition reimbursements available, career-related internships or fieldwork, Federal Work-Study, grants, institutionally-sponsored loans, scholarships, and tuition waivers (full and partial) also available. Aid available to part-time students. Financial aid application deadline: 4/1; financial aid applicants required to submit FAFSA. *Faculty research:* Air pollution, climate dynamics, severe storms, remote sensing, satellite meteorology, statistical climatology. *Unit head:* Dr. Ronald Welch, Chair, 256-922-5754, Fax: 256-922-5755, E-mail: ron.welch@atmos.uah.edu.

University of Alaska Anchorage, School of Engineering, Program in Environmental Quality Engineering, Anchorage, AK 99508-8060. Offers MS. Part-time and evening/weekend programs available. *Students:* 3 full-time (0 women), 8 part-time (2 women); includes 3 minority (all Asian Americans or Pacific Islanders) 4 applicants, 75% accepted. In 1998, 13 degrees awarded. *Degree requirements:* For master's, computer language required, foreign language not required. *Entrance requirements:* For master's, GRE General Test, BS in engineering. *Application deadline:* For fall admission, 5/1 (priority date). Applications are processed on a rolling basis. Application fee: $45. *Financial aid:* In 1998–99, 2 research assistantships were awarded.; Federal Work-Study and traineeships also available. Aid available to part-time students. Financial aid application deadline: 4/1; financial aid applicants required to submit FAFSA. *Faculty research:* Wastewater treatment, environmental regulations, water resources management, justification of public facilities, rural sanitation, biological treatment process. *Unit head:* Dr. John Oloffson, Chair, 907-786-1075, Fax: 907-786-1079. *Application contact:* Cecile Mitchell, Director for Enrollment Services, 907-786-1558.

University of Alaska Anchorage, School of Engineering, Program in Environmental Quality Science, Anchorage, AK 99508-8060. Offers MS. *Students:* 7 full-time (2 women), 15 part-time (9 women); includes 2 minority (1 Hispanic American, 1 Native American) 13 applicants, 92% accepted. *Degree requirements:* For master's, computer language required, foreign language not required. *Entrance requirements:* For master's, GRE General Test, BS in engineering or scientific field. *Application deadline:* For fall admission, 5/1 (priority date). Applications are processed on a rolling basis. Application fee: $45. *Financial aid:* Research assistantships, Federal Work-Study available. Aid available to part-time students. Financial aid application deadline: 4/1; financial aid applicants required to submit FAFSA. *Faculty research:* Waste water treatment, environmental regulations, water resources management, justification of public facilities, rural sanitation, biological treatment process. *Unit head:* Dr. John Oloffson, Chair, 907-786-1075, Fax: 907-786-1079. *Application contact:* Cecile Mitchell, Director for Enrollment Services, 907-786-1558.

University of Alaska Fairbanks, Graduate School, College of Science, Engineering and Mathematics, Department of Civil Engineering, Fairbanks, AK 99775-7480. Offers arctic engineering (MS); civil engineering (MCE, MS); environmental quality engineering (MS); environmental quality science (MS). *Faculty:* 8 full-time (1 woman), 3 part-time (0 women). *Students:* 9 full-time (5 women), 6 part-time (3 women), 2 international. *Degree requirements:* For master's, thesis or alternative, comprehensive exam required, foreign language not required. *Entrance requirements:* For master's, GRE General Test, TOEFL (minimum score of 550 required). *Application deadline:* For fall admission, 8/1. Applications are processed on a rolling basis. Application fee: $35. *Unit head:* Dr. Lufti Raad, Head, 907-474-7241.

University of Alberta, Faculty of Graduate Studies and Research, Department of Civil and Environmental Engineering, Edmonton, AB T6G 2E1, Canada. Offers construction engineering and management (M Eng, M Sc, PhD); environmental engineering (M Eng, M Sc, PhD); environmental science (M Sc, PhD); geoenvironmental engineering (M Eng, M Sc, PhD); geotechnical engineering (M Sc); geotechnical engineering (M Eng, PhD); mining engineering (M Eng, M Sc, PhD); petroleum engineering (M Eng, M Sc, PhD); structural engineering (M Eng, M Sc, PhD); water resources (M Eng, M Sc, PhD). Part-time programs available. *Degree requirements:* For master's, thesis required (for some programs), foreign language not required; for doctorate, dissertation required, foreign language not required. *Faculty research:* Mining.

The University of Arizona, Graduate College, College of Agriculture, Department of Soil, Water and Environmental Science, Tucson, AZ 85721. Offers MS, PhD. *Faculty:* 17. *Students:* 74 full-time (31 women), 28 part-time (9 women); includes 8 minority (1 African American, 3 Asian Americans or Pacific Islanders, 3 Hispanic Americans, 1 Native American), 33 international. Average age 32. 58 applicants, 60% accepted. In 1998, 14 master's, 5 doctorates awarded. *Degree requirements:* For master's, thesis required, foreign language not required; for doctorate, one foreign language, computer language, dissertation required. *Entrance requirements:* For master's and doctorate, TOEFL (minimum score of 550 required). *Application deadline:* For fall admission, 3/1. Applications are processed on a rolling basis. Application fee: $35. *Financial aid:* Research assistantships, teaching assistantships, Federal Work-Study, institutionally-sponsored loans, scholarships, and tuition waivers (full and partial) available. Financial aid application deadline: 5/1. *Faculty research:* Plant production, environmental microbiology, contaminant flow and transport. *Unit head:* Dr. Peter Wierenga, Head, 520-621-7228. *Application contact:* Dr. Mark Brusseau, Graduate Admissions Coordinator, 520-621-3228, Fax: 520-621-1647.

The University of Arizona, Graduate College, Graduate Interdisciplinary Programs, Graduate Interdisciplinary Program in Arid Land Resource Sciences, Tucson, AZ 85721. Offers PhD. *Faculty:* 42. *Students:* 10 full-time (4 women), 15 part-time (8 women); includes 3 minority (1 African American, 1 Hispanic American, 1 Native American), 6 international. Average age 42. 3 applicants, 33% accepted. In 1998, 3 degrees awarded. *Degree requirements:* For doctorate, dissertation required. *Entrance requirements:* For doctorate, TOEFL (minimum score of 550 required). Application fee: $35. *Financial aid:* Fellowships, scholarships available. *Unit head:* Dr. Joseph Hoffman, Director, 520-621-7896, Fax: 520-621-3816, E-mail: jjhoff@ccit.arizona.edu. *Application contact:* Carmen Ortiz Henley, Graduate Secretary, 520-621-7896, Fax: 520-621-3816, E-mail: chenley@ag.arizona.edu.

University of California, Berkeley, Graduate Division, College of Natural Resources, Department of Environmental Science, Policy, and Management, Berkeley, CA 94720-1500. Offers environmental science, policy, and management (MS, PhD); forestry (MF); range management (MS). *Faculty:* 67 full-time (15 women), 2 part-time (1 woman). *Students:* 183 full-time (88 women); includes 12 minority (9 Asian Americans or Pacific Islanders, 3 Hispanic Americans), 21 international. 294 applicants, 19% accepted. In 1998, 15 master's, 14 doctorates awarded (80% entered university research/teaching, 20% found other work related to degree). *Degree requirements:* For doctorate, dissertation, qualifying exam required. *Entrance requirements:* For master's and doctorate, GRE General Test, minimum GPA of 3.0. *Average time to degree:* Master's–2 years full-time; doctorate–5 years full-time. *Application deadline:* For fall admission, 12/15. Application fee: $40. Electronic applications accepted. *Financial aid:* Application deadline: 12/15; *Faculty research:* Biology and ecology of insects; ecosystem function and environmental issues of soils; plant health/interactions from molecular to ecosystem levels; range management and ecology; forest and resource policy, sustainability, and management. *Unit head:* Dr. James W. Bartolome, Chair, 510-642-7945, Fax: 510-643-5438, E-mail: jwbart@nature.berkeley.edu. *Application contact:* Sue Jennison, Student Affairs Officer, 510-642-6410, Fax: 510-643-5438, E-mail: espmgradproginfo@nature.berkeley.edu.

See in-depth description on page 919.

University of California, Berkeley, Graduate Division, College of Natural Resources, Group in Agricultural and Environmental Chemistry, Berkeley, CA 94720-1500. Offers MS, PhD. *Students:* 11 full-time (7 women). 3 applicants, 33% accepted. Terminal master's awarded for partial completion of doctoral program. *Degree requirements:* For master's, exam or thesis required; for doctorate, dissertation, qualifying exam, seminar presentation required. *Entrance requirements:* For master's and doctorate, GRE General Test, minimum GPA of 3.0. *Application deadline:* For fall admission, 1/5. Application fee: $40. *Financial aid:* Research assistantships, Federal Work-Study and institutionally-sponsored loans available. Financial aid application deadline: 1/5. *Unit head:* Dr. Isao Kubo, Chair, 510-642-5167. *Application contact:* Jennifer Vorih, Graduate Assistant for Admission, 510-642-5167, Fax: 510-642-4995, E-mail: pmb.stud@nature.berkeley.edu.

University of California, Davis, Graduate Studies, Program in Soil Science, Davis, CA 95616. Offers MS, PhD. *Faculty:* 30 full-time (3 women). *Students:* 30 full-time (16 women); includes 1 minority (Asian American or Pacific Islander), 10 international. Average age 28. 26 applicants, 38% accepted. In 1998, 2 master's awarded (100% found work related to degree); 5 doctorates awarded. Terminal master's awarded for partial completion of doctoral program. *Degree requirements:* For master's, computer language required, thesis optional; for doctorate, computer language, dissertation required. *Entrance requirements:* For master's, minimum GPA of 3.3; for doctorate, GRE, minimum GPA of 3.3. *Application deadline:* For fall admission, 1/15. Applications are processed on a rolling basis. Application fee: $40. Electronic applications accepted. *Financial aid:* In 1998–99, 1 fellowship with full and partial tuition reimbursement, 23 research assistantships with full and partial tuition reimbursements, 3 teaching assistantships with full and partial tuition reimbursements were awarded.; career-related internships or fieldwork, Federal Work-Study, and institutionally-sponsored loans also available. Aid available to part-time students. Financial aid application deadline: 1/15; financial aid applicants required to submit FAFSA. *Faculty research:* Rhizosphere ecology, soil transport processes, biogeochemical cycling, sustainable agriculture. Total annual research expenditures: $3 million. *Unit head:* Robert Zasoski, Graduate Adviser, 530-752-1669, Fax: 530-752-5262. *Application contact:* Diane Swindall, Academic Adviser, 530-752-1669, Fax: 530-752-5262, E-mail: dgswindall@ucdavis.edu.

Announcement: Soils are essential parts of managed and natural ecosystems. At Davis, learning and research experience emphasize the role of soils in the fate and transport of pollutants and nutrients, remediation and restoration, sustainable agriculture, nutrient cycling, soil-plant-water interrelationships, microbial ecology, geochemistry, and soil genesis and morphology. Visit us at http://lawr.ucdavis.edu/gradprg.htm

University of California, Los Angeles, Graduate Division, School of Public Health, Program in Environmental Science and Engineering, Los Angeles, CA 90095. Offers D Env. *Students:* 37 full-time (16 women); includes 6 minority (1 African American, 4 Asian Americans or Pacific Islanders, 1 Hispanic American), 6 international. 24 applicants, 33% accepted. *Degree requirements:* For doctorate, dissertation, oral and written qualifying exams required, foreign language not required. *Entrance requirements:* For doctorate, GRE General Test (minimum combined score of 1200 required), minimum undergraduate GPA of 3.0, master's degree or equivalent in a natural science, engineering, or public health. *Application deadline:* For fall admission, 12/15. Application fee: $40. Electronic applications accepted. *Financial aid:* In 1998–99, 32 students received aid, including 26 fellowships, 26 research assistantships, 4 teaching assistantships; institutionally-sponsored loans, scholarships, and tuition waivers (full and partial) also available. Financial aid application deadline: 3/1. *Faculty research:* Toxic and hazardous substances, air and water pollution, risk assessment/management, water resources, marine science. *Unit head:* Dr. Richard F. Ambrose, Director, 310-825-9901. *Application contact:* Departmental Office, 310-825-9901, E-mail: app_ese@admin.ph.ucla.edu.

University of California, Riverside, Graduate Division, College of Natural and Agricultural Sciences, Department of Environmental Sciences, Riverside, CA 92521-0102. Offers soil science (MS, PhD). Part-time programs available. *Faculty:* 22 full-time (3 women). *Students:* 23 full-time (8 women); includes 2 minority (1 Asian American or Pacific Islander, 1 Hispanic American), 4 international. Average age 31. In 1998, 7 master's, 4 doctorates awarded. Terminal master's awarded for partial completion of doctoral program. *Degree requirements:* For master's, thesis required, foreign language not required; for doctorate, dissertation, oral and written qualifying exams required, foreign language not required. *Entrance requirements:* For master's and doctorate, GRE General Test (minimum combined score of 1100 required), TOEFL (minimum score of 550 required), bachelor's degree in natural and physical sciences, engineering, or economics, minimum GPA of 3.2. *Average time to degree:* Master's–2.7 years full-time; doctorate–4.3 years full-time. *Application deadline:* For fall admission, 5/1; for winter admission, 9/1; for spring admission, 12/1. Applications are processed on a rolling basis. Application fee: $40. Electronic applications accepted. *Financial aid:* Fellowships, research assistantships, teaching assistantships, career-related internships or fieldwork, Federal Work-Study, institutionally-sponsored loans, and tuition waivers (full and partial) available. Financial aid application deadline: 2/1; financial aid applicants required to submit FAFSA. *Faculty research:* Soil chemistry, soil physics, soil mineralogy, soil microbiology and biochemistry, soil morphology. *Unit head:* Dr. Lanny J. Lund, Chair, 909-787-5116, Fax: 909-787-4652, E-mail: ljlund@ucrac1.ucr.edu. *Application contact:* Mari Ridgeway, Student Affairs Officer, 909-787-5103, Fax: 909-787-3993, E-mail: marir@ucrac1.ucr.edu.

University of California, Santa Barbara, Graduate Division, School of Environmental Science and Management, Santa Barbara, CA 93106. Offers MESM. *Entrance requirements:* For master's, GRE, TOEFL (minimum score of 550 required). *Application deadline:* For fall admission, 3/1 (priority date). Application fee: $40. *Financial aid:* Fellowships, research assistantships, teaching assistantships, Federal Work-Study and institutionally-sponsored loans available. Financial aid applicants required to submit FAFSA. *Unit head:* Jeff Dozier, Dean, 805-893-7363, E-mail: info@bren.ucsb.edu. *Application contact:* Laura Haston, Assistant Dean of Students, 805-893-7363, E-mail: laura@esm.ucsb.edu.

See in-depth description on page 921.

University of Charleston, South Carolina, Graduate School, School of Sciences and Mathematics, Program in Environmental Studies, Charleston, SC 29424-0001. Offers MS. Offered jointly with the Medical University of South Carolina. *Entrance requirements:* For master's, GRE, TOEFL.

University of Chicago, The Irving B. Harris Graduate School of Public Policy Studies, Chicago, IL 60637-1513. Offers environmental science and policy (MS); public policy studies (AM, MPP, PhD). Part-time programs available. *Faculty:* 23 full-time (3 women), 5 part-time (1 woman). *Students:* 148 full-time, 7 part-time; includes 38 minority (11 African Americans, 19 Asian Americans or Pacific Islanders, 8 Hispanic Americans), 44 international. Terminal master's awarded for partial completion of doctoral program. *Degree requirements:* For master's, foreign language and thesis not required; for doctorate, dissertation required, foreign language not required. *Entrance requirements:* For master's and doctorate, GMAT or GRE General Test, TOEFL. *Application deadline:* For fall admission, 1/15 (priority date). Applications are processed on a rolling basis. Application fee: $50. *Unit head:* Dr. Robert T. Michael, Dean, 773-702-9623, E-mail: r-michael@uchicago.edu. *Application contact:* Ellen Cohen, Director of Admission, 773-702-8401, Fax: 773-702-0926, E-mail: eb-cohen@uchicago.edu.

University of Cincinnati, Division of Research and Advanced Studies, College of Engineering, Department of Civil and Environmental Engineering, Program in Environmental Sciences, Cincinnati, OH 45221-0091. Offers MS, PhD. *Students:* 19 full-time (12 women), 8 part-time (4 women); includes 2 minority (1 Asian American or Pacific Islander, 1 Hispanic American), 7 international. In 1998, 13 master's, 1 doctorate awarded. *Degree requirements:* For master's, thesis or alternative required, foreign language not required; for doctorate, one foreign language (computer language can substitute), dissertation required. *Entrance requirements:* For master's and doctorate, GRE General Test, TOEFL. *Average time to degree:* Master's–3.3 years full-time; doctorate–9.8 years full-time. *Application deadline:* For fall admission, 2/1 (priority date). Application fee: $40. *Financial aid:* Fellowships, tuition waivers (full) and unspecified assistantships available. Aid available to part-time students. Financial aid application deadline: 2/1. *Unit head:* Dr. Frank Pinski, Head, Department of Physics, 513-556-0511, Fax: 513-556-3425, E-mail: frank.pinski@uc.edu. *Application contact:* Frank Weisgerber, Graduate Program Director, 513-556-3673, Fax: 513-556-2599, E-mail: fweisger@boss.cee.uc.edu.

University of Colorado at Denver, Graduate School, College of Liberal Arts and Sciences, Program in Environmental Science, Denver, CO 80217-3364. Offers MS. Part-time and evening/weekend programs available. *Students:* 6 full-time (3 women), 21 part-time (13 women); includes 1 minority (African American), 3 international. Average age 30. 21 applicants, 86% accepted. In 1998, 14 degrees awarded. *Degree requirements:* For master's, thesis or alternative required. *Entrance requirements:* For master's, GRE General Test. *Application deadline:* For fall admission, 4/1; for spring admission, 10/1. Applications are processed on a rolling basis. Application fee: $50 ($60 for international students). Electronic applications accepted. Tuition, state resident: part-time $185 per credit hour. Tuition, nonresident: part-time $735 per credit hour. Required fees: $3 per credit hour. $130 per year. One-time fee: $25 part-time. Tuition and fees vary according to program. *Financial aid:* Research assistantships, teaching assistantships, Federal Work-Study available. Financial aid application deadline: 3/1; financial aid applicants required to submit FAFSA. Total annual research expenditures: $47,565. *Unit head:* Willard Chappell, Director, 303-556-3460, Fax: 303-556-4292. *Application contact:* Rosemary Wormington, Administrative Assistant, 303-556-4520, Fax: 303-556-4292.

University of Guam, Graduate School and Research, College of Arts and Sciences, Program in Environmental Science, Mangilao, GU 96923. Offers MS. Part-time programs available. *Faculty:* 19 full-time (1 woman). *Students:* 4 full-time (1 woman), 10 part-time (6 women); includes 9 minority (all Asian Americans or Pacific Islanders), 1 international. In 1998, 3 degrees awarded (100% found work related to degree). *Degree requirements:* For master's, thesis required, foreign language not required. *Entrance requirements:* For master's, GRE General Test (minimum combined score of 900 required), TOEFL (minimum score of 550 required). *Average time to degree:* Master's–5 years part-time. *Application deadline:* For fall admission, 6/11; for spring admission, 11/16. Applications are processed on a rolling basis. Application fee: $39 ($67 for international students). Tuition, state resident: part-time $99 per credit hour. Tuition, nonresident: part-time $246 per credit hour. Required fees: $170 per semester. Tuition and fees vary according to course load. *Financial aid:* In 1998–99, 10 students received aid, including 4 research assistantships with tuition reimbursements available; career-related internships or fieldwork, institutionally-sponsored loans, and unspecified assistantships also available. *Faculty research:* Water resources, ecology, karst formations, hydrogeology, meterology. *Unit head:* Dr. Gary Denton, Chair, 671-735-2690, Fax: 671-734-8890, E-mail: gdenton@uog9.uog.edu.

University of Houston–Clear Lake, School of Natural and Applied Sciences, Program in Environmental Science, Houston, TX 77058-1098. Offers MS. *Faculty:* 8 full-time (2 women), 3 part-time (0 women). *Students:* 15 full-time (6 women), 51 part-time (20 women); includes 9 minority (3 African Americans, 1 Asian American or Pacific Islander, 4 Hispanic Americans, 1 Native American), 3 international. *Degree requirements:* Foreign language not required. *Entrance requirements:* For master's, GRE General Test. *Application deadline:* Applications are processed on a rolling basis. Application fee: $30 ($70 for international students). *Financial aid:* Research assistantships, teaching assistantships available. Financial aid application deadline: 5/1. *Unit head:* Dr. Dennis Casserly, Chair, 281-283-3770, Fax: 281-283-3707, E-mail: casserly@uhcl4.cl.uh.edu. *Application contact:* Dr. Robert Ferebee, Associate Dean, 281-283-3700, Fax: 281-283-3707, E-mail: ferebee@uhcl4.cl.uh.edu.

University of Idaho, College of Graduate Studies, College of Engineering, Program in Environmental Science, Moscow, ID 83844-4140. Offers MS. *Students:* 11 full-time (6 women), 11 part-time (5 women). In 1998, 5 degrees awarded. *Application deadline:* For fall admission, 8/1; for spring admission, 12/15. Applications are processed on a rolling basis. Application fee: $35 ($45 for international students). *Financial aid:* Research assistantships, teaching assistantships available. Financial aid application deadline: 2/15. *Unit head:* Margrit von Braun, Director, 208-885-6113.

University of Illinois at Urbana–Champaign, Graduate College, College of Agricultural, Consumer and Environmental Sciences, Department of Natural Resources and Environmental Science, Urbana, IL 61801. Offers MS, PhD. *Faculty:* 11 full-time (1 woman). *Students:* 112 full-time (42 women); includes 5 minority (1 African American, 1 Asian American or Pacific Islander, 3 Hispanic Americans), 25 international. 32 applicants, 78% accepted. In 1998, 17 master's, 9 doctorates awarded. *Degree requirements:* For master's and doctorate, thesis/dissertation required, foreign language not required. *Entrance requirements:* For master's, minimum GPA of 4.0 on a 5.0 scale. *Application deadline:* Applications are processed on a rolling basis. Application fee: $40 ($50 for international students). Tuition, state resident: full-time $4,040. Tuition, nonresident: full-time $11,192. Full-time tuition and fees vary according to program. *Financial aid:* Fellowships, research assistantships, teaching assistantships, tuition waivers (full and partial) available. Financial aid application deadline: 2/15. *Unit head:* Gary L. Rolfe, Head, 217-333-2770. *Application contact:* John A. Juvik, Director of Graduate Studies, 217-333-1966, Fax: 217-244-3219, E-mail: j-juvik@uiuc.edu.

University of Illinois at Urbana–Champaign, Graduate College, College of Engineering, Department of Civil and Environmental Engineering, Program in Environmental Engineering and Environmental Science, Urbana, IL 61801. Offers environmental engineering (MS, PhD); environmental science (MS, PhD). *Faculty:* 10 full-time. *Students:* 65 full-time (27 women);

Environmental Sciences

University of Illinois at Urbana–Champaign (continued)
includes 7 minority (5 Asian Americans or Pacific Islanders, 2 Hispanic Americans), 23 international. *Degree requirements:* For master's, thesis or alternative required, foreign language not required; for doctorate, dissertation required, foreign language not required. *Application deadline:* Applications are processed on a rolling basis. Application fee: $40 ($50 for international students). Tuition, state resident: full-time $4,616. Tuition, nonresident: full-time $11,768. Full-time tuition and fees vary according to course load. *Unit head:* V. L. Snoeyink, Coordinator, 217-333-4700. *Application contact:* Dr. Frederick V. Lawrence, Director of Graduate Studies, 217-333-6928, Fax: 217-333-9464, E-mail: flawrenc@uiuc.edu.

University of Kansas, Graduate School, School of Engineering, Department of Civil and Environmental Engineering, Lawrence, KS 66045. Offers civil engineering (MS, DE, PhD); environmental engineering (MS, PhD); environmental science (MS, PhD); water resources engineering (MS); water resources science (MS). *Faculty:* 20 full-time (0 women). *Students:* 23 full-time (6 women), 80 part-time (15 women); includes 9 minority (1 African American, 3 Asian Americans or Pacific Islanders, 4 Hispanic Americans, 1 Native American), 29 international. *Degree requirements:* For master's, thesis or alternative, exam required, foreign language not required; for doctorate, dissertation, comprehensive exam required. *Entrance requirements:* For master's and doctorate, Michigan English Language Assessment Battery, TOEFL, minimum GPA of 3.0. *Application deadline:* For fall admission, 7/1. Application fee: $30 ($45 for international students). *Unit head:* Steve McCabe, Chair, 785-864-3766. *Application contact:* David Parr, Graduate Director.

University of Maine, Graduate School, College of Natural Sciences, Forestry, and Agriculture, Department of Biological Sciences, Program in Ecology and Environmental Science, Orono, ME 04469. Offers MS, PhD. Part-time programs available. *Students:* 39 (23 women). 72 applicants, 26% accepted. In 1998, 4 master's awarded. *Degree requirements:* For doctorate, dissertation required. *Entrance requirements:* For master's and doctorate, GRE General Test, TOEFL (minimum score of 550 required). *Application deadline:* For fall admission, 2/1 (priority date); for spring admission, 10/15. Applications are processed on a rolling basis. Application fee: $50. *Financial aid:* Fellowships, research assistantships, teaching assistantships, career-related internships or fieldwork, Federal Work-Study, institutionally-sponsored loans, and tuition waivers (full) available. Financial aid application deadline: 3/1. *Unit head:* Dr. Chris Cronan, Chair, 207-581-3236. *Application contact:* Scott G. Delcourt, Director of the Graduate School, 207-581-3218, Fax: 207-581-3232, E-mail: graduate@maine.edu.

University of Maine, Graduate School, College of Natural Sciences, Forestry, and Agriculture, Department of Plant, Soil, and Environmental Sciences, Orono, ME 04469. Offers biological sciences (PhD); ecology and environmental sciences (MS, PhD); forest resources (PhD); plant science (PhD); plant, soil, and environmental sciences (MS); resource utilization (MS). *Students:* 11 (6 women). *Entrance requirements:* For master's and doctorate, GRE General Test, TOEFL (minimum score of 550 required). Application fee: $50. *Unit head:* Dr. Ivan Fernandez, Chair. *Application contact:* Mary Fernandez, 207-581-2938, Fax: 207-581-2999, E-mail: fern@maine.edu.

University of Maryland, Graduate School, Program in Marine-Estuarine-Environmental Sciences (an intercampus, interdisciplinary program), Baltimore, MD 21201-1627. Offers MS, PhD. *Faculty:* 5 full-time (1 woman). *Students:* 4 (1 woman) 1 international. 4 applicants, 75% accepted. In 1998, 2 degrees awarded. *Degree requirements:* For master's, thesis required; for doctorate, dissertation, comprehensive exam, proposal defense required. *Entrance requirements:* For master's and doctorate, minimum GPA of 3.0. *Application deadline:* For fall admission, 3/1; for spring admission, 11/1. Application fee: $50. *Financial aid:* Research assistantships, teaching assistantships available. *Unit head:* Dr. Kennedy T. Paynter, Director, 301-405-6938.

University of Maryland, Baltimore County, Graduate School, Program in Marine-Estuarine-Environmental Sciences (an intercampus, interdisciplinary program), Baltimore, MD 21250-5398. Offers MS, PhD. *Faculty:* 15. *Students:* 8 full-time (6 women), 2 part-time (both women); includes 1 minority (Hispanic American), 1 international. 12 applicants, 33% accepted. In 1998, 1 doctorate awarded. *Degree requirements:* For master's, thesis required, foreign language not required; for doctorate, dissertation, comprehensive exam, proposal defense required, foreign language not required. *Entrance requirements:* For master's and doctorate, GRE General Test, TOEFL, minimum GPA of 3.0. *Application deadline:* For fall admission, 3/1; for spring admission, 11/1. Applications are processed on a rolling basis. Application fee: $45. Electronic applications accepted. *Financial aid:* Fellowships, research assistantships with tuition reimbursements, teaching assistantships with tuition reimbursements, career-related internships or fieldwork available. *Unit head:* Dr. Kennedy T. Paynter, Director, 301-405-6938, Fax: 301-314-4139, E-mail: mees@mees.umd.edu. *Application contact:* Dr. Kennedy T. Paynter, Director, 301-405-6938, Fax: 301-314-4139, E-mail: mees@mees.umd.edu.

University of Maryland, College Park, Graduate School, College of Life Sciences, Program in Marine-Estuarine-Environmental Sciences (an intercampus, interdisciplinary program), College Park, MD 20742-5045. Offers MS, PhD. Part-time programs available. *Faculty:* 138. *Students:* 219 (104 women); includes 14 minority (3 African Americans, 5 Asian Americans or Pacific Islanders, 5 Hispanic Americans, 1 Native American) 45 international. 243 applicants, 37% accepted. In 1998, 16 master's, 17 doctorates awarded. Terminal master's awarded for partial completion of doctoral program. *Degree requirements:* For master's, thesis required; for doctorate, dissertation, comprehensive exam, proposal defense required. *Entrance requirements:* For master's and doctorate, GRE General Test, minimum GPA of 3.0. *Application deadline:* For fall admission, 3/1; for spring admission, 11/1. Applications are processed on a rolling basis. Application fee: $70. Electronic applications accepted. Tuition, state resident: part-time $272 per credit hour. Tuition, nonresident: part-time $475 per credit hour. Required fees: $632; $379 per year. *Financial aid:* In 1998–99, 1 fellowship with full tuition reimbursement (averaging $5,000 per year), 3 teaching assistantships with tuition reimbursements (averaging $12,903 per year) were awarded.; research assistantships, Federal Work-Study, grants, and scholarships also available. Aid available to part-time students. Financial aid applicants required to submit FAFSA. *Faculty research:* Marine and estuarine organisms, terrestrial and freshwater ecology, remote environmental sensing. *Unit head:* Dr. Kennedy T. Paynter, Director, 301-405-6938, Fax: 301-314-4139, E-mail: mees@mees.umd.edu. *Application contact:* 301-405-6938, Fax: 301-314-4139, E-mail: meesgrad@mees.umd.edu.

University of Massachusetts Boston, Graduate Studies, College of Arts and Sciences, Faculty of Sciences, Program in Environmental, Coastal and Ocean Sciences, Boston, MA 02125-3393. Offers environmental biology (PhD); environmental sciences (MS); environmental, coastal and ocean sciences (PhD). *Degree requirements:* For master's and doctorate, thesis/dissertation, comprehensive exams required, foreign language not required. *Entrance requirements:* For master's and doctorate, GRE General Test, minimum GPA of 2.75.

University of Massachusetts Lowell, Graduate School, College of Arts and Sciences, Department of Chemistry, Lowell, MA 01854-2881. Offers biochemistry (PhD); chemistry (MS, PhD); environmental studies (PhD); polymer sciences (MS, PhD). PhD (biochemistry) offered jointly with the Department of Biological Sciences. *Faculty:* 24 full-time (2 women). *Students:* 36 full-time (11 women), 35 part-time (23 women); includes 12 minority (all Asian Americans or Pacific Islanders), 32 international. Terminal master's awarded for partial completion of doctoral program. *Degree requirements:* For master's, thesis required, foreign language not required; for doctorate, 2 foreign languages, computer language, dissertation required. *Entrance requirements:* For master's and doctorate, GRE General Test. *Application deadline:* For fall admission, 4/1 (priority date); for spring admission, 10/1. Applications are processed on a rolling basis. Application fee: $20 ($35 for international students). *Unit head:* Dr. Edwin Johngen, Chair, 978-934-3663. *Application contact:* Dr. Melissa McDonald, Coordinator, 978-934-3683, E-mail: melissa_mcdonald@woods.uml.edu.

University of Massachusetts Lowell, Graduate School, James B. Francis College of Engineering, Department of Civil Engineering, Program in Environmental Studies, Lowell, MA 01854-2881. Offers MS Eng. Part-time programs available. *Faculty:* 13 full-time. *Students:* 6 full-time (1 woman), 59 part-time (20 women); includes 7 minority (all African Americans), 1 international. 71 applicants, 49% accepted. *Degree requirements:* For master's, thesis optional, foreign language not required. *Entrance requirements:* For master's, GRE General Test. *Application deadline:* For fall admission, 4/1 (priority date); for spring admission, 10/1. Applications are processed on a rolling basis. Application fee: $20 ($35 for international students). *Financial aid:* Teaching assistantships, career-related internships or fieldwork available. Financial aid application deadline: 4/1. *Faculty research:* Remote sensing of air pollutants, atmospheric deposition of toxic metals, contaminant transport in groundwater, soil remediation. *Application contact:* Dr. Burton Segall, Graduate Coordinator, 978-934-2288, E-mail: burton_segall@woods.uml.edu.

The University of Montana–Missoula, Graduate School, College of Arts and Sciences, Program in Environmental Studies (EVST), Missoula, MT 59812-0002. Offers MS, JD/MS. Part-time programs available. *Faculty:* 3 full-time (1 woman), 5 part-time (0 women). *Students:* 61 full-time (31 women), 26 part-time (10 women); includes 4 minority (1 African American, 3 Native Americans), 5 international. Average age 28. 151 applicants, 46% accepted. In 1998, 30 degrees awarded. *Degree requirements:* For master's, portfolio, professional paper, or thesis required. *Entrance requirements:* For master's, GRE General Test (minimum score of 500 on verbal section required). *Average time to degree:* Master's–2.2 years full-time, 3 years part-time. *Application deadline:* For fall admission, 2/15. Application fee: $45. *Financial aid:* In 1998–99, 9 teaching assistantships with tuition reimbursements (averaging $6,900 per year) were awarded.; career-related internships or fieldwork and Federal Work-Study also available. Aid available to part-time students. Financial aid application deadline: 3/1. *Faculty research:* Conservation and pollution biology, applied ecology. *Unit head:* Tom M. Roy, Director, 406-243-6273, E-mail: tomroy@selway.umt.edu. *Application contact:* Tom M. Roy, Director, 406-243-6273, E-mail: tomroy@selway.umt.edu.

University of Nevada, Las Vegas, Graduate College, Greenspun College of Urban Affairs, Department of Environmental Studies, Las Vegas, NV 89154-9900. Offers environmental sciences (MS). *Faculty:* 11 full-time (2 women). *Students:* 5 full-time (4 women), 7 part-time (4 women); includes 1 minority (Asian American or Pacific Islander), 1 international. 17 applicants, 47% accepted. *Degree requirements:* For master's, comprehensive exam required. *Entrance requirements:* For master's, GRE General Test, minimum GPA of 3.0 during previous 2 years, 2.75 overall. *Application deadline:* For fall admission, 6/15; for spring admission, 11/15. Application fee: $40 ($95 for international students). *Financial aid:* In 1998–99, 2 teaching assistantships with partial tuition reimbursements (averaging $8,500 per year) were awarded.; research assistantships Financial aid application deadline: 3/1. *Unit head:* Dr. Helen Neill, Interim Chair, 702-895-4440.

University of Nevada, Reno, Graduate School, Center for Environmental Sciences and Engineering, Graduate Program in Environmental Sciences and Health, Reno, NV 89557. Offers MS, PhD. *Degree requirements:* For master's and doctorate, thesis/dissertation required. *Entrance requirements:* For master's, GRE General Test (minimum combined score of 1000 required), TOEFL (minimum score of 600 required), minimum GPA of 2.75; for doctorate, GRE General Test (minimum combined score of 1000 required), TOEFL (minimum score of 600 required), minimum GPA of 3.0.

University of Nevada, Reno, Graduate School, M. C. Fleischmann College of Agriculture, Department of Environmental and Resource Sciences, Reno, NV 89557. Offers environmental and natural resource science (MS). *Degree requirements:* For master's, thesis optional, foreign language not required. *Entrance requirements:* For master's, GRE, TOEFL (minimum score of 500 required), minimum GPA of 2.75. *Faculty research:* Range management, plant physiology, remote sensing, soils, wildlife.

University of New Haven, Graduate School, College of Arts and Sciences, Program in Environmental Sciences, West Haven, CT 06516-1916. Offers MS. Part-time and evening/weekend programs available. *Students:* 10 full-time (7 women), 53 part-time (21 women); includes 5 minority (1 Asian American or Pacific Islander, 4 Hispanic Americans) 33 applicants, 61% accepted. In 1998, 20 degrees awarded. *Degree requirements:* For master's, thesis or alternative required, foreign language not required. *Application deadline:* Applications are processed on a rolling basis. Application fee: $50. *Financial aid:* Career-related internships or fieldwork and Federal Work-Study available. Aid available to part-time students. Financial aid application deadline: 5/1; financial aid applicants required to submit FAFSA. *Faculty research:* Mapping and assessing geological and living resources in Long Island Sound, geology, San Salvador Island, Bahamas. *Unit head:* Dr. Roman Zajac, Coordinator, 203-932-7114.

The University of North Carolina at Chapel Hill, Graduate School, School of Public Health, Department of Environmental Sciences and Engineering, Chapel Hill, NC 27599. Offers environmental engineering (MSEE); environmental sciences and engineering (MS, PhD); public health (MPH, MSPH). *Accreditation:* ABET (one or more programs are accredited). *Faculty:* 36 full-time (5 women), 31 part-time (5 women). *Students:* 99 full-time (45 women), 63 part-time (27 women); includes 13 minority (5 African Americans, 4 Asian Americans or Pacific Islanders, 3 Hispanic Americans, 1 Native American), 31 international. Average age 28. 208 applicants, 53% accepted. In 1998, 20 master's, 15 doctorates awarded. Terminal master's awarded for partial completion of doctoral program. *Degree requirements:* For master's, research paper, comprehensive exam required; for doctorate, dissertation, comprehensive exam required, foreign language not required. *Entrance requirements:* For master's and doctorate, GRE General Test (minimum combined score of 1000 required), minimum GPA of 3.0. *Application deadline:* For fall admission, 1/1 (priority date); for spring admission, 9/15. Applications are processed on a rolling basis. Application fee: $55. *Financial aid:* In 1998–99, 81 students received aid, including 14 fellowships with tuition reimbursements available (averaging $14,000 per year), 48 research assistantships with tuition reimbursements available (averaging $17,000 per year), 6 teaching assistantships with tuition reimbursements available (averaging $12,133 per year); career-related internships or fieldwork, Federal Work-Study, and traineeships also available. Aid available to part-time students. Financial aid application deadline: 1/1. *Faculty research:* Air, radiation and industrial hygiene, aquatic and atmospheric sciences, environmental health sciences, environmental management and policy, water resources engineering. Total annual research expenditures: $6.5 million. *Unit head:* Dr. Donald Fox, Chair, 919-966-1024, Fax: 919-966-7911, E-mail: don_fox@unc.edu. *Application contact:* Nikki Bryant, Assistant Registrar, 919-966-3844, Fax: 919-966-7911.

University of Northern Iowa, Graduate College, College of Natural Sciences, Program in Environmental Science/Technology, Cedar Falls, IA 50614. Offers MS. *Students:* 9 full-time (4 women), 8 international. Average age 33. 10 applicants, 50% accepted. In 1998, 3 degrees awarded. *Degree requirements:* For master's, thesis or alternative required, foreign language not required. *Application deadline:* For fall admission, 8/1 (priority date). Applications are processed on a rolling basis. Application fee: $20 ($30 for international students). Tuition, state resident: full-time $3,308; part-time $184 per hour. Tuition, nonresident: full-time $8,156; part-time $454 per hour. Required fees: $202; $88 per semester. Tuition and fees vary according to course load. *Financial aid:* Application deadline: 3/1. *Unit head:* Dr. Edward Brown, Head, 319-273-2645, Fax: 319-273-5815, E-mail: ed.brown@uni.edu.

University of North Texas, Robert B. Toulouse School of Graduate Studies, College of Arts and Sciences, Department of Biological Sciences, Program in Environmental Science, Denton, TX 76203. Offers MS, PhD. *Faculty:* 6 full-time (1 woman), 2 part-time (0 women). *Students:* 32 full-time (16 women), 39 part-time (16 women); includes 5 minority (1 Asian American or Pacific Islander, 4 Hispanic Americans), 7 international. In 1998, 15 master's awarded. *Degree requirements:* For master's, oral defense of thesis required; for doctorate, dissertation, oral and written comprehensive exams required. *Entrance requirements:* For master's, GRE General Test (minimum score of 400 on each section, 1000 combined required), minimum GPA of 3.0; for doctorate, GRE General Test (minimum combined score of 1000 required), minimum GPA of 3.0. *Application deadline:* For fall admission, 7/17. Application fee: $25 ($50 for international students). *Unit head:* Dr. Kenneth L. Dickson, Director, 940-565-2694.

University of Oklahoma, Graduate College, College of Engineering, School of Civil Engineering and Environmental Science, Program in Environmental Science, Norman, OK 73019-0390. Offers air (M Env Sc); environmental science (PhD); groundwater management (M Env Sc); hazardous solid waste (M Env Sc); occupational safety and health (M Env Sc); process design (M Env Sc); water quality resources (M Env Sc). Part-time and evening/weekend programs available. *Students:* 10 full-time (3 women), 24 part-time (14 women); includes 3 minority (1 African American, 1 Hispanic American, 1 Native American), 6 international. Average age 28. 27 applicants, 78% accepted. In 1998, 15 master's, 1 doctorate awarded. Terminal master's awarded for partial completion of doctoral program. *Degree requirements:* For master's, comprehensive and oral exams required, foreign language and thesis not required; for doctorate, dissertation, comprehensive, oral, and qualifying exams required. *Entrance requirements:* For master's, GRE General Test, TOEFL (minimum score of 575 required), minimum GPA of 3.0; for doctorate, GRE General Test, TOEFL (minimum score of 575 required), minimum graduate GPA of 3.5. *Application deadline:* For fall admission, 4/1 (priority date). Applications are processed on a rolling basis. Application fee: $25. Tuition, state resident: part-time $86 per credit hour. Tuition, nonresident: part-time $275 per credit hour. Tuition and fees vary according to course level, course load and program. *Financial aid:* Fellowships, research assistantships, teaching assistantships available. Financial aid application deadline: 3/1. *Faculty research:* Industrial/hazardous wastes, soils and materials. *Unit head:* Dr. Jeffrey Falzarano, Graduate Coordinator, 504-280-7184, Fax: 504-280-5542, E-mail: jmfna@uno.edu. *Application contact:* Robert C. Knox, Graduate Liaison, 405-325-4256, Fax: 405-325-7508.

University of Rochester, School of Medicine and Dentistry, Graduate Programs in Medicine and Dentistry, Department of Environmental Medicine, Program in Environmental Studies and Industrial Hygiene, Rochester, NY 14627-0250. Offers MS. Part-time programs available. *Students:* 6 full-time (2 women), 11 part-time (5 women); includes 1 minority (African American) 3 applicants, 100% accepted. In 1998, 12 degrees awarded. *Degree requirements:* Foreign language not required. *Entrance requirements:* For master's, GRE General Test. *Application deadline:* For fall admission, 2/1. Application fee: $25. *Financial aid:* Application deadline: 2/1. *Unit head:* Dr. Victor Laties, Director, 716-275-4453. *Application contact:* Joyce Morgan, Graduate Program Secretary, 716-275-6702.

University of Tennessee at Chattanooga, Graduate Division, College of Arts and Sciences, Department of Biological and Environmental Sciences, Program in Environmental Sciences, Chattanooga, TN 37403-2598. Offers MS. *Faculty:* 5 full-time (1 woman). *Students:* 19 full-time (10 women), 20 part-time (11 women); includes 1 minority (African American), 1 international. Average age 37. 9 applicants, 89% accepted. *Degree requirements:* For master's, minimum GPA of 3.0 required, thesis optional. *Entrance requirements:* For master's, GRE General Test, minimum undergraduate GPA of 2.75. *Application deadline:* Applications are processed on a rolling basis. Application fee: $25. *Financial aid:* Application deadline: 4/1. *Unit head:* Dr. Gary Litchford, Coordinator, 423-755-4324, Fax: 423-785-2285, E-mail: gary-litchford@utc.edu. *Application contact:* Dr. Deborah E. Arfken, Assistant Provost for Graduate Studies, 423-755-4667, Fax: 423-755-4478, E-mail: deborah-arfken@utc.edu.

The University of Texas at Arlington, Graduate School, Program in Environmental Science and Engineering, Arlington, TX 76019. Offers MS. *Students:* 6 full-time (1 woman), 5 part-time (4 women), 7 international. 24 applicants, 58% accepted. In 1998, 2 degrees awarded. *Application deadline:* Applications are processed on a rolling basis. Application fee: $25 ($50 for international students). Tuition, state resident: full-time $1,368; part-time $76 per semester hour. Tuition, nonresident: full-time $5,454; part-time $303 per semester hour. Required fees: $66 per semester hour. $86 per term. Tuition and fees vary according to course load. *Unit head:* Dr. John S. Wickham, Head, 817-272-2332, Fax: 817-272-2628, E-mail: wickham@uta.edu.

The University of Texas at El Paso, Graduate School, Interdisciplinary Program in Environmental Science and Engineering, El Paso, TX 79968-0001. Offers PhD. *Students:* 9 full-time (4 women), 12 part-time (4 women); includes 8 minority (1 Asian American or Pacific Islander, 7 Hispanic Americans), 5 international. Average age 39. 10 applicants, 80% accepted. *Degree requirements:* For doctorate, dissertation required. *Entrance requirements:* For doctorate, GRE General Test, TOEFL (minimum score of 550 required). *Application deadline:* Applications are processed on a rolling basis. Application fee: $15 ($65 for international students). Tuition, state resident: full-time $2,790. Tuition, nonresident: full-time $7,710. *Financial aid:* Fellowships, research assistantships, teaching assistantships, Federal Work-Study, institutionally-sponsored loans, and tuition waivers (partial) available. Financial aid applicants required to submit FAFSA. *Unit head:* Dr. Charles Groat, Director, 915-747-5954. *Application contact:* Susan Jordan, Director, Graduate Student Services, 915-747-5491, Fax: 915-747-5788, E-mail: sjordan@utep.edu.

The University of Texas at San Antonio, College of Sciences and Engineering, Division of Earth and Physical Sciences, San Antonio, TX 78249-0617. Offers chemistry (MS); environmental sciences (MS); geology (MS). *Faculty:* 22 full-time (1 woman), 27 part-time (6 women). *Students:* 22 full-time (11 women), 83 part-time (29 women); includes 27 minority (2 African Americans, 6 Asian Americans or Pacific Islanders, 19 Hispanic Americans), 6 international. Average age 34. 30 applicants, 67% accepted. In 1998, 25 degrees awarded. *Entrance requirements:* For master's, GRE General Test. *Application deadline:* For fall admission, 7/1. Applications are processed on a rolling basis. Application fee: $25. *Financial aid:* Research assistantships, teaching assistantships available. *Unit head:* Dr. Weldon Hammond, Interim Director, 210-458-4455.

Announcement: Graduate studies in chemistry, geology, and environmental sciences. Programs are designed to help prepare students for careers in industry, research, and teaching or professional training. Research concentrations include lanthanide chemistry, morphology development in polymers, mechanisms of organic reactions, organic synthesis, natural-products synthesis, environmental and materials chemistry, geochemistry, molecular dynamics, inorganic, laser-active ions, bioremediation, geomicrobiology, mineralogy, hydrogeology, and geographical information research system. Equipment includes mass spectrometers, 90-MHz NMR equipment, high-pressure liquid chromatograph, IR spectrometers, UV-visible and A-A spectrophotometers. Nine-month teaching assistantships with stipends up to $8937 are available. Graduate tuition stipends are available.

University of Toronto, School of Graduate Studies, Life Sciences Division, Collaborative Program in Environmental Studies, Toronto, ON M5S 1A1, Canada. Offers M Sc, M Sc F, MA. *Degree requirements:* For master's, thesis required (for some programs).

University of Virginia, College and Graduate School of Arts and Sciences, Department of Environmental Sciences, Charlottesville, VA 22903. Offers MA, MS, PhD. *Faculty:* 32 full-time (5 women), 2 part-time (both women). *Students:* 75 full-time (33 women); includes 2 minority (1 African American, 1 Asian American or Pacific Islander), 7 international. Average age 28. 62 applicants, 45% accepted. In 1998, 9 master's, 11 doctorates awarded. *Degree requirements:* For master's and doctorate, thesis/dissertation required, foreign language not required. *Entrance requirements:* For master's and doctorate, GRE General Test, GRE Subject Test. *Application deadline:* For fall admission, 7/15; for spring admission, 12/1. Applications are processed on a rolling basis. Application fee: $60. *Financial aid:* Application deadline: 2/1. *Unit head:* James N. Galloway, Chairman, 804-924-7761. *Application contact:* Duane J. Osheim, Associate Dean, 804-924-7184, E-mail: grad-a-s@virginia.edu.

See in-depth description on page 927.

The University of Western Ontario, Faculty of Graduate Studies, Biosciences Division, Department of Plant Sciences, London, ON N6A 5B8, Canada. Offers plant and environmental sciences (M Sc); plant sciences (M Sc, PhD). *Degree requirements:* For master's and doctorate, thesis/dissertation required, foreign language not required. *Faculty research:* Ecology systematics, plant biochemistryand physiology, yeast genetics.

University of Wisconsin–Green Bay, Graduate Studies, Track in Environmental Science and Policy, Green Bay, WI 54311-7001. Offers MS. Part-time programs available. *Students:* 8 full-time (2 women), 31 part-time (8 women); includes 1 minority (Native American), 8 international. Average age 32. In 1998, 17 degrees awarded. *Degree requirements:* For master's, thesis required, foreign language not required. *Entrance requirements:* For master's, GRE General Test, minimum GPA of 3.0. *Application deadline:* For fall admission, 8/1; for spring admission, 11/1. Applications are processed on a rolling basis. Application fee: $45. Tuition, state resident: full-time $3,510; part-time $195 per credit. Tuition, nonresident: full-time $11,868; part-time $660 per credit. Required fees: $277 per semester. *Financial aid:* In 1998–99, 3 research assistantships, 9 teaching assistantships were awarded.; career-related internships or fieldwork, Federal Work-Study, and institutionally-sponsored loans also available. Financial aid application deadline: 7/15; financial aid applicants required to submit FAFSA. *Faculty research:* Bald eagle, parasitic population of domestic and wild animals, resource recovery, anaerobic digestion of organic waste. *Unit head:* Dr. John Stoll, Coordinator, 920-465-2358, E-mail: stollj@uwgb.edu.

University of Wisconsin–Madison, Graduate School, Institute for Environmental Studies, Environmental Monitoring Program, Madison, WI 53706-1380. Offers MS, PhD. Part-time programs available. *Students:* 20 full-time (5 women), 6 part-time (1 woman); includes 2 minority (both Hispanic Americans), 4 international. 27 applicants, 22% accepted. In 1998, 4 master's awarded. *Degree requirements:* For master's and doctorate, computer language, thesis/dissertation required, foreign language not required. *Entrance requirements:* For master's and doctorate, GRE General Test. *Application deadline:* For fall admission, 2/15; for spring admission, 10/15. Application fee: $45. Electronic applications accepted. *Financial aid:* In 1998–99, 20 students received aid, including 1 fellowship with full tuition reimbursement available, 10 research assistantships with full tuition reimbursements available, 1 teaching assistantship with full tuition reimbursement available; career-related internships or fieldwork, Federal Work-Study, grants, and unspecified assistantships also available. Financial aid application deadline: 1/2; financial aid applicants required to submit FAFSA. *Faculty research:* Remote sensing, geographic information systems, climate modeling, natural resource management. *Unit head:* Thomas M. Lillesand, Chair, 608-263-1796, Fax: 608-262-2273, E-mail: iesgrad@macc.wisc.edu. *Application contact:* Jim E. Miller, Clerical Assistant, 608-263-1796, Fax: 608-262-2273, E-mail: jemiller@facstaff.wisc.edu.

Virginia Commonwealth University, School of Graduate Studies, Center for Environmental Studies, Richmond, VA 23284-9005. Offers environmental communication (MIS); environmental health (MIS); environmental planning (MIS); environmental sciences (MIS). *Entrance requirements:* For master's, GRE General Test. Application fee: $30. Tuition, state resident: full-time $4,031; part-time $224 per credit hour. Tuition, nonresident: full-time $11,946; part-time $664 per credit hour. Required fees: $1,081; $40 per credit hour. Tuition and fees vary according to campus/location and program. *Unit head:* Greg Garman, Director, 804-828-7202, Fax: 804-828-0503, E-mail: gcgarman@vcu.edu. *Application contact:* Andrew Lacatell, Assistant Director, 804-828-7202, Fax: 804-828-0503, E-mail: adlacate@vcu.edu.

Virginia Polytechnic Institute and State University, Graduate School, College of Engineering, Department of Civil and Environmental Engineering, Program in Environmental Sciences and Engineering, Blacksburg, VA 24061. Offers MS, PhD. *Students:* 13 full-time (3 women), 17 part-time (6 women); includes 2 minority (both Asian Americans or Pacific Islanders), 4 international. 75 applicants, 24% accepted. In 1998, 10 master's awarded. *Degree requirements:* For master's, thesis required, foreign language not required; for doctorate, dissertation required. *Entrance requirements:* For master's and doctorate, GRE General Test (minimum score of 400 on each section required), TOEFL (minimum score of 600 required). *Application deadline:* For fall admission, 12/1 (priority date). Applications are processed on a rolling basis. Application fee: $25. *Financial aid:* Fellowships, research assistantships, teaching assistantships, unspecified assistantships available. Financial aid application deadline: 4/1. *Unit head:* Dr. John T. Novak, Chairman, 540-231-6635.

Washington State University, Graduate School, College of Sciences, Program in Environmental Science and Regional Planning, Concentration in Environmental Science, Pullman, WA 99164. Offers MS, PhD. *Faculty:* 4 full-time (0 women), 2 part-time (0 women). *Students:* 24 full-time (12 women), 4 part-time (2 women); includes 1 minority (Hispanic American), 3 international. In 1998, 28 degrees awarded. *Degree requirements:* For master's, oral exam required, thesis optional, foreign language not required; for doctorate, dissertation, oral exam required, foreign language not required. *Entrance requirements:* For master's and doctorate, GRE General Test, minimum GPA of 3.0. *Average time to degree:* Master's–2 years full-time. *Application deadline:* For fall admission, 3/1 (priority date). Applications are processed on a rolling basis. Application fee: $35. *Financial aid:* In 1998–99, 2 research assistantships, 12 teaching assistantships were awarded.; Federal Work-Study, institutionally-sponsored loans, tuition waivers (partial), and teaching associateships also available. Financial aid application deadline: 4/1; financial aid applicants required to submit FAFSA. *Unit head:* Dr. William Budd, Chair, Program in Environmental Science and Regional Planning, 509-335-5538.

Announcement: Specialization options in the MS and PhD degree programs include agricultural ecology, biological science, environmental education, environmental quality control, environmental systems, hazardous waste management, human ecology, and natural resource management. Specializations in the MRP and PhD degree programs include land-use planning, ecological planning, geographic analysis and assessment, and planning and environmental policy. Excellent facilities for research and instruction are available for student use within the program and through cooperating faculty in the Colleges of Sciences, Liberal Arts, Engineering and Architecture, and Agriculture and Home Economics. Students electing the environmental education option can work concurrently to obtain certification for teaching in endorsement areas appropriate to their interests.

Washington University in St. Louis, Graduate School of Arts and Sciences, Program in Environmental Science, St. Louis, MO 63130-4899. Offers MA. *Students:* 2 full-time (0 women). 2 applicants, 100% accepted. *Entrance requirements:* For master's, GRE General Test. *Application deadline:* Applications are processed on a rolling basis. Application fee: $35. *Financial aid:* Fellowships, teaching assistantships, Federal Work-Study, institutionally-sponsored loans, and tuition waivers (full and partial) available. Financial aid application deadline: 1/15. *Unit head:* Dr. Everett Shock, Chairperson, 314-935-4258.

Western Connecticut State University, Division of Graduate Studies, School of Arts and Sciences, Department of Biological and Environmental Sciences, Danbury, CT 06810-6885. Offers MA. Part-time and evening/weekend programs available. *Students:* 1 full-time (0 women), 10 part-time (5 women); includes 1 minority (Asian American or Pacific Islander) In 1998, 5 degrees awarded. *Degree requirements:* For master's, comprehensive exam or thesis required. *Entrance requirements:* For master's, minimum GPA of 2.5. *Application deadline:* For fall admission, 8/1 (priority date). Applications are processed on a rolling basis. Application fee: $40. *Financial aid:* Fellowships, career-related internships or fieldwork and Federal Work-Study available. Aid available to part-time students. Financial aid application deadline: 5/1; financial aid applicants required to submit FAFSA. *Unit head:* Dr. Howard Russock, Chair, 203-837-8798. *Application contact:* Chris Shankle, Associate Director of Graduate Admissions, 203-837-8244, Fax: 203-837-8338, E-mail: shanklec@wcsu.edu.

Western Washington University, Graduate School, Huxley College of Environmental Studies, Center for Environmental Science, Bellingham, WA 98225-5996. Offers MS. Part-time programs available. *Faculty:* 23. *Students:* 19 full-time (8 women), 7 part-time (4 women); includes 1 minority (Native American) 39 applicants, 56% accepted. In 1998, 9 degrees awarded. *Degree requirements:* For master's, thesis required, foreign language not required. *Entrance requirements:* For master's, GRE General Test, TOEFL, minimum GPA of 3.0 in last 60

Environmental Sciences–Cross-Discipline Announcements

Western Washington University (continued)
semester hours or last 90 quarter hours. *Application deadline:* For fall admission, 2/1. Application fee: $35. Tuition, state resident: full-time $3,247; part-time $146 per credit hour. Tuition, nonresident: full-time $13,364; part-time $445 per credit hour. Required fees: $254; $85 per quarter. *Financial aid:* In 1998–99, 7 teaching assistantships with partial tuition reimbursements (averaging $7,563 per year) were awarded.; Federal Work-Study, institutionally-sponsored loans, and scholarships also available. Aid available to part-time students. Financial aid application deadline: 2/15; financial aid applicants required to submit FAFSA. *Unit head:* Dr. John Hardy, Director, 360-650-2844. *Application contact:* Sally Elmore, Graduate Coordinator, 360-650-3646.

West Texas A&M University, College of Agriculture, Nursing, and Natural Sciences, Department of Life, Earth, and Environmental Sciences, Program in Environmental Science, Canyon, TX 79016-0001. Offers MS. Part-time programs available. *Faculty:* 1 full-time (0 women), 7 part-time (1 woman). *Students:* 3 full-time (2 women), 16 part-time (6 women); includes 3 minority (2 Hispanic Americans, 1 Native American) Average age 34. 5 applicants, 0% accepted. In 1998, 1 degree awarded. *Degree requirements:* For master's, comprehensive exam required, thesis optional, foreign language not required. *Entrance requirements:* For master's, GRE General Test (minimum combined score of 950 required; average 964). *Average time to degree:* Master's–3 years full-time, 6 years part-time. *Application deadline:* Applications are processed on a rolling basis. Application fee: $0 ($50 for international students). Electronic applications accepted. Tuition, state resident: full-time $1,152; part-time $48 per credit. Tuition, nonresident: full-time $6,336; part-time $264 per credit. Required fees: $1,063; $531 per semester. *Financial aid:* In 1998–99, 2 teaching assistantships (averaging $6,500 per year) were awarded.; Federal Work-Study, institutionally-sponsored loans, and tuition waivers (partial) also available. Aid available to part-time students. Financial aid applicants required to submit FAFSA. *Application contact:* Dr. David Parker, Graduate Advisor, 806-651-2581, E-mail: dparker@mail.wtamu.edu.

Wichita State University, Graduate School, Fairmount College of Liberal Arts and Sciences, Program in Environmental Science, Wichita, KS 67260. Offers MS. *Students:* 1 (woman) full-time, 7 part-time (2 women). Average age 35. 11 applicants, 45% accepted. In 1998, 1 degree awarded. *Entrance requirements:* For master's, GRE, TOEFL (minimum score of 550 required), minimum GPA of 2.75. Application fee: $25 ($40 for international students). *Financial aid:* Research assistantships, teaching assistantships available. Financial aid application deadline: 4/1. *Unit head:* Dr. Michael Lydy, Coordinator, 316-978-3111, Fax: 316-978-3772, E-mail: lydy@wsuhub.uc.twsu.edu.

Wright State University, School of Graduate Studies, College of Science and Mathematics, Department of Biological Sciences, Dayton, OH 45435. Offers biological sciences (MS); environmental sciences (MS). *Students:* 30 full-time (14 women), 14 part-time (8 women); includes 5 minority (2 African Americans, 1 Asian American or Pacific Islander, 1 Hispanic American, 1 Native American), 3 international. *Degree requirements:* For master's, thesis optional, foreign language not required. *Entrance requirements:* For master's, TOEFL (minimum score of 550 required). Application fee: $25. *Unit head:* Dr. Michele Wheatly, Chair, 937-775-2655, Fax: 937-775-3320. *Application contact:* Dr. David L. Goldstein, Director, 937-775-3430, Fax: 937-775-3320.

Wright State University, School of Graduate Studies, College of Science and Mathematics, Department of Chemistry, Dayton, OH 45435. Offers chemistry (MS); environmental sciences (MS). Part-time and evening/weekend programs available. *Students:* 22 full-time (14 women), 5 part-time (1 woman); includes 1 minority (Hispanic American), 6 international. *Degree requirements:* For master's, oral defense of thesis, seminar required. *Entrance requirements:* For master's, TOEFL (minimum score of 600 required). *Application deadline:* For fall admission, 6/1 (priority date). Applications are processed on a rolling basis. Application fee: $25. *Unit head:* Dr. M. Paul Servé, Chair, 937-775-2855, Fax: 937-775-2717. *Application contact:* Dr. Paul G. Seybold, Chair, Graduate Studies Committee, 937-775-2407, Fax: 937-775-2717.

Wright State University, School of Graduate Studies, College of Science and Mathematics, Department of Geological Sciences, Program in Geological Sciences, Dayton, OH 45435. Offers environmental geology (MS); environmental sciences (MS); geological sciences (MS); geophysics (MS); hydrogeology (MS); petroleum geology (MS). Part-time programs available. *Students:* 32 full-time (14 women), 9 part-time (2 women), 1 international. *Degree requirements:* For master's, computer language, thesis required, foreign language not required. *Entrance requirements:* For master's, TOEFL (minimum score of 550 required). Application fee: $25. *Unit head:* Dr. Dennis Burns, Graduate Coordinator, 316-978-3120, Fax: 316-978-3431, E-mail: burns@twsuvm.uc.twsu.edu. *Application contact:* Deborah L. Cowles, Assistant to Chair, 937-775-3455, Fax: 937-775-3462.

Yale University, Graduate School of Arts and Sciences, Department of Forestry and Environmental Studies, New Haven, CT 06520. Offers environmental sciences (PhD); forestry (PhD). *Faculty:* 39 full-time (9 women). *Students:* 44 full-time (25 women); includes 3 minority (2 Asian Americans or Pacific Islanders, 1 Hispanic American), 13 international. 60 applicants, 12% accepted. In 1998, 5 degrees awarded. *Degree requirements:* For doctorate, dissertation required, foreign language not required. *Entrance requirements:* For doctorate, GRE General Test. *Average time to degree:* Doctorate–6.4 years full-time. *Application deadline:* For fall admission, 1/4. Application fee: $65. *Financial aid:* Fellowships, Federal Work-Study and institutionally-sponsored loans available. Aid available to part-time students. *Unit head:* Dean, School of Forestry and Environmental Studies, 203-432-5109. *Application contact:* Admissions Information, 203-432-2770.

Yale University, School of Forestry and Environmental Studies, New Haven, CT 06520. Offers MES, MF, MFS, DFES, PhD, JD/MES, MBA/MES, MES/MA, MES/MPH, MF/MA. *Accreditation:* SAF (one or more programs are accredited). Part-time programs available. *Faculty:* 27 full-time, 10 part-time. *Students:* 282 full-time, 10 part-time; includes 20 minority (2 African Americans, 10 Asian Americans or Pacific Islanders, 8 Hispanic Americans), 42 international. Average age 28. 392 applicants, 55% accepted. In 1998, 104 master's, 7 doctorates awarded. Terminal master's awarded for partial completion of doctoral program. *Degree requirements:* For master's, thesis not required; for doctorate, dissertation required. *Entrance requirements:* For master's and doctorate, GRE General Test. *Average time to degree:* Master's–2 years full-time, 4 years part-time. *Application deadline:* For fall admission, 2/1. Application fee: $0. *Financial aid:* In 1998–99, 135 students received aid. Career-related internships or fieldwork available. Aid available to part-time students. Financial aid application deadline: 2/1; financial aid applicants required to submit FAFSA. *Faculty research:* Ecosystem science and management, coastal and watershed systems, environmental policy and management, social ecology and community development, conservation biology. *Unit head:* Dr. James Gustave Speth, Dean, 203-432-5109, Fax: 203-432-5942. *Application contact:* Daniel C. Esty, Director of Admissions and Associate Dean, 203-432-5100, Fax: 203-432-5942, E-mail: fesinfo@yale.edu.

Cross-Discipline Announcements

Carnegie Mellon University, Carnegie Institute of Technology, Department of Engineering and Public Policy, Pittsburgh, PA 15213-3891.

PhD program addresses policy problems in which technical details are critically important by using tools of engineering, science, and the social sciences. Carnegie Mellon offers excellent environment for interdisciplinary research. Program requires equivalent of undergraduate degree in engineering, physical science, or mathematics. See in-depth description in the Engineering and Applied Sciences volume of this series. Write to Victoria Massimino, Coordinator of Graduate Recruiting.

The George Washington University, School of Business and Public Management, Department of Public Administration, Washington, DC 20052.

The George Washington University's Master of Public Administration (MPA) program is known for its exceptional faculty, distinctive curricular approaches, and well-established links with business, government, and nonprofit organizations. Located 4 blocks from the White House and 6 subway stops from the US Congress, The George Washington University MPA program places graduates in think tanks, policy advocacy and lobbying organizations, national associations, nonprofit organizations, businesses, and international organizations as well as local, state, and federal government agencies. Students can begin or enhance their career with an MPA or PhD in public administration from The George Washington University School of Business and Public Management.

Georgia Institute of Technology, Graduate Studies and Research, College of Architecture, Program in City Planning, Atlanta, GA 30332-0001.

The environmental specialization prepares students to address issues associated with land use, urban growth, and environmental quality. Emphasis is placed on environmental impacts of urbanization, techniques for assessing those impacts and policies, programs for enhancing environmental quality, and the use of computer technology. Please see in-depth description in Book 2, Section 25: Public, Regional, and Industrial Affairs.

Massachusetts Institute of Technology, School of Engineering, Division of Bioengineering and Environmental Health, Cambridge, MA 02139-4307.

Program provides opportunities for specialization in molecular toxicology, including studies in environmental carcinogenesis; metabolism of foreign compounds; molecular dosimetry; genetic toxicology; molecular aspects of interactions of mutagens, carcinogens, and anticancer drugs with nucleic acids and proteins; and pathogenesis and molecular aspects of infectious disease. See in-depth description in the Pharmacology and Toxicology section of Book 3 of this series.

Tufts University, School of Nutrition Science and Policy, Medford, MA 02155.

Concentration in Agriculture, Food, and Environment within the Social Science Program of the School of Nutrition Science and Policy emphasizes policy aspects of the interconnections of food production and supply with environmental constraints and problems. The program draws on interdisciplinary domestic and international expertise at Tufts. Students receive an MS or PhD from the School of Nutrition Science and Policy and interact with students and faculty members at the Tufts Department of Urban and Environmental Policy through a collaborative arrangement. MS includes a field internship and directed research project. For further information, see in-depth description in Book 3, Biological Sciences, in the Nutrition section.

University of Minnesota, Twin Cities Campus, Graduate School, Hubert H. Humphrey Institute of Public Affairs, Program in Science, Technology, and Environmental Policy, Minneapolis, MN 55455-0213.

The MS program provides an understanding of scientific and technological processes, products, and mechanisms of support and the resultant economic, social, and environmental impacts needed for making sound public-sector decisions about scientific and technological investment and infrastructure. Students should have undergraduate training in the biological/physical sciences or engineering. For information, contact 612-626-7229, e-mail: admissions@hhh.umn.edu

AMERICAN UNIVERSITY

Environmental Studies Program

AMERICAN UNIVERSITY
W A S H I N G T O N , D C

Programs of Study

The Environmental Studies Program offers both an M.S. and an M.A. degree. Both degrees are rigorous, interdisciplinary programs of study with courses drawn from the College of Arts and Sciences, the School of International Service, and the School of Public Affairs. The course of study is designed to provide the student with a basic understanding of the scientific, social, and policy processes that shape the environment. The M.S. and M.A. programs accommodate the training needs of established professionals in the environmental field as well as recent college graduates. The programs can serve as terminal degrees themselves or as stepping stones for further graduate work toward a Ph.D. in environmental studies or related disciplines. In addition to meeting the minimum University requirements for graduate study, students of both programs must have completed one year of calculus and one year of laboratory science (biology, chemistry, geology, or physics). A year of economics is recommended. Graduates of the 35-credit M.S. Environmental Science Program have a rigorous multidisciplinary science foundation and courses in environmental policy and specialize in toxicology, conservation biology, or earth and atmospheric science. All students participate in an environmental research seminar and practicum that provides an opportunity to establish links between policy and science in an applied context. The 38-credit M.A. Environmental Policy Program is a solid multidisciplinary program that covers a wide range of topics, including environmental toxicology, conservation biology, environmental economics, and domestic and international environmental policy.

Research Facilities

The Bender Library and Learning Resources Center houses more than 700,000 volumes and 3,000 periodical titles as well as extensive microform collections and a nonprint media center. Graduate students have unlimited borrowing privileges at six other college and university libraries in the Washington Research Library Consortium, all of which are accessible through the online catalog. Microcomputer resources are extensive and can be used 24 hours a day at various campus locations. Research opportunities in the Washington area through internships, cooperative education, and work-study programs may be available at sites such as the World Wildlife Fund, the Nature Conservancy, the Environmental Protection Agency, and the Wilderness Society. The Environmental Protection Agency, the National Geographic Society, the Worldwatch Institute, the Smithsonian Institution, the National Institutes of Health, the Library of Congress, the World Bank, the International Monetary Fund, the libraries of more than 140 embassies, and the headquarters of many environmental organizations and public research institutes are all located in Washington, D.C.

Financial Aid

Fellowships, scholarships, and graduate assistantships are available to full-time students. Special opportunity grants for minority group members parallel the regular honor awards and take the form of assistantships and scholarships. Research and teaching fellowships provide stipends plus tuition. Graduate assistantships provide up to 18 credit hours of tuition remission per year.

Cost of Study

For the 1999–2000 academic year, tuition is $721 per credit hour.

Living and Housing Costs

Although many graduate students live off campus, the University provides graduate dormitory rooms and apartments. The Off-Campus Housing Office maintains a referral file of rooms and apartments. Housing costs in Washington, D.C., are comparable to those in other major metropolitan areas.

Student Group

The diversity of the University's students extends beyond racial and ethnic lines to include students of varying ages, nationalities, and experiences. Small class sizes allow for interaction among students and between students and professors. Many graduate students work and attend classes part-time, which enables them to begin to integrate professional experiences and interests into their programs of study.

Student Outcomes

American University's emphasis on experiential education outside the classroom may prove a stepping stone to a future career. Graduates of the M.S. program are prepared for employment in natural resource fields dealing with basic and applied scientific interests. Graduates of the M.A. program find employment in environmental and policy fields.

Location

The national capital area offers students access to an unparalleled variety of educational, governmental, and cultural resources that enrich the student's degree program with opportunities for practical applications of theoretical studies. Local bus and rail transportation from the campus provides easy access to sites in the greater metropolitan area.

The University

American University was founded as a Methodist institution and was chartered by Congress in 1893. Originally, the University was intended for graduate study only. The University is located on an 84-acre site in a residential area of northwest Washington, D.C. As a member of the Consortium of Universities of the Washington Area, American University can offer its degree candidates the option of taking courses at other consortium universities for residence credit.

Applying

Applications for admission should be submitted prior to February 1 if the student is also applying for financial aid. Deadlines vary for different fields of study, but early application is always encouraged. The application fee is $50.

Correspondence and Information

To contact faculty members:
Environmental Studies Program
College of Arts and Sciences
American University
Hurst Hall 101
4400 Massachusetts Avenue, NW
Washington, D.C. 20016-8007

Telephone: 202-885-2178
E-mail: environ@american.edu
World Wide Web:
  http://www.american.edu/academic.depts/cas/

For an application and University Catalog:
Graduate Admissions Office
American University
4400 Massachusetts Avenue, NW
Washington, D.C. 20016-8001

Telephone: 202-885-6000
E-mail: afa@american.edu

American University

THE FACULTY AND THEIR RESEARCH

Madeline Adamczeski, Ph.D., California, Santa Cruz. Natural products chemistry from aquatic invertebrates and plants. Co-inventor of two U.S. patents related to antitumor, antibiotic, and anthelminthic amino acid-derived oxazole and e-caprolactam natural products and synthetic analogs thereof, isolated from marine sponge.

William Banta, Ph.D., USC. Zoology of aquatic invertebrates, especially the Bryozoa and the biological and chemical assessment of water quality; electron microscopy and analysis of organic contaminants in fresh water. Author, *The Bryozoa of the Galapagos*.

Robin Broad, Head of the International Development Program's master's concentration in environment and development; Ph.D., Princeton. Co-author, *Plundering Paradise: The Struggle for the Environment in the Philippines*, which is a case study of the political economy of natural resource degradation in the Third World.

Albert Cheh, Ph.D., Berkeley. Mechanisms by which environmental carcinogens damage DNA, determination of the kinds of mutations caused by these compounds, and identification of the byproducts of water chlorination.

Mary Christman, Ph.D., George Washington. Sampling designs, biometry, environmental statistics, spatial modeling, population models, and oceanography. Author, *Efficiency of Some Sampling Designs for Spatially Clustered Populations*.

David Culver, Ph.D., Yale. Karst, environmental problems associated with water quality, and the ecology and evolution of the invertebrates that inhabit the underground waters of karst. Author, *Cave Life, Adaptation and Natural Selection in Caves*, and more than 100 articles.

Daniel Fong, Director of the Environmental Studies Program; Ph.D., Northwestern. Ecology, genetics, and evolution of organisms found in groundwater habitats. Author, *Madison Cave Isopod Recovery Plan* and papers in such journals as *Annual Review of Ecology and Systematics, Evolution,* and *Hydrobiologia*.

James Girard, Ph.D., Penn State. Environmental analysis by mass spectrometry and chromatography and in analytical chemistry.

Robin Hahnel, Ph.D., American. Environmental justice and policy, combining carbon taxes with sequestration subsidies as a more equitable policy approach to combat global warming.

Robert Jernigan, Ph.D., South Florida. Computational statistical methods applicable to the study of ecological systems and evolutionary biology.

Richard Kay, Ph.D., Arkansas. Photons and their interaction with atoms, and parenthetically, in their role in lasers.

Boian Koulov, Ph.D., Institute of Geography of the Bulgarian Academy of Science. Political-environmental and human geography and U.S.S.R./East European Studies. Author, *Reconstructing the Balkans: A Geography of New Southeast Europe*.

Harvey Lieber, Ph.D., Columbia. Environmental quality management. Previously served as Executive Secretary of Administrator's Toxic Substances Committee of the U.S. Environmental Protection Agency. Author, *Federalism and Clean Waters: The 1972 Water Pollution Control Act*.

George Loeb, Ph.D., Cornell. Interaction of organisms with surfaces and in water quality analysis of pollutants. Author of more than forty peer-reviewed papers and inventor of several U.S. patents.

Mieke Meurs, Ph.D., Massachusetts. Environmental problems in the transforming economies of Eastern Europe and in industrialized market economies. Author of a number of articles in such journals as *Soviet Studies, World Development,* and *Review of Radical Political Economy*.

Howard Reiss, Ph.D., Maryland. Fundamental theory of the interaction of extremely strong electromagnetic fields with matter and the implications of these theories for the interactions of very strong lasers with nuclear, atomic, and solid-state systems with applications for the disposal of radioactive wastes.

Catherine Schaeff, Ph.D., Queens. Behavior, ecology, and population genetics of endangered species, especially marine mammals. Author, *Comparison of North and South Atlantic Right Whale (Eubalaena) Genetic Variability Using DNA Fingerprinting*, which has been used in designing recovery plans for the endangered North American right whale.

Romeo Segnan, Ph.D., Carnegie Institute of Technology. Magnetism and materials science; use of the Mössbauer technique to measure the properties of many iron- and lead-rich alloys.

Russell Stone, Ph.D., Princeton. Environmental sociology and environmental attitudes, including resident reactions to the environmental crisis at Love Canal and environmental perceptions in Taiwan.

Paul Wapner, Ph.D., Princeton. Global environmental politics and social movements. Author, *Environmental Activism and World Civil Politics* and articles in *World Politics* and *Politics and the Life Sciences*.

Water quality analysis class field trip.

DUQUESNE UNIVERSITY

Bayer School of Natural and Environmental Sciences
Environmental Science and Management Program

Program of Study

The Environmental Science and Management Program is a program of graduate study in environmental science and management that leads to the M.S. degree. Joint programs with the Graduate School of Business and School of Law offer programs of graduate study leading to the M.B.A./M.S.–ESM and J.D./M.S.–ESM degrees. Five-year B.S./M.S.–ESM programs are available in chemistry, biology, and microbiology, as is a fast-track one-year option for full-time M.S. students. Two professional certificates are also offered for those students wishing to acquire professional knowledge in environmental sciences or environmental studies.

The 42-credit Environmental Science and Management Program curriculum emphasizes a strong foundation in environmental sciences, the necessary training in business and behavioral sciences, and an introduction to public policy and law. Practice in writing and related communication skills is integrated throughout the program. The two internships, in industry and in a regulatory agency, provide valuable practical experience; however, in certain cases, students may elect to write a thesis instead. Students who attend full time (e.g., three courses a semester) should be able to complete the requirements within two full years (four semesters plus two summers for the internships). Graduate students must maintain a letter grade average of at least a B (3.0 QPA).

Students who wish to pursue the joint degree programs must apply to both schools: to the Graduate School of Business and the Environmental Science and Management program for the M.B.A./M.S.–ESM and to the School of Law and the Environmental Science and Management program for the J.D./M.S.–ESM.

Research Facilities

The Environmental Science and Management Program is housed in the newly renovated Fisher Hall, which is Duquesne's first energy star building. The newly opened Bayer Learning Center houses classrooms and seminar rooms. The Gumberg Library contains more than 100,000 square feet of space with a collection of more than 549,373 volumes, 4,305 journal titles, and an extensive microprint and audiovisual collection.

Financial Aid

A limited number of partial teaching and research assistantships are available for graduate students.

Cost of Study

Tuition in 1998–99 was $525 per credit. This included a $39 per credit University fee.

Living and Housing Costs

There are a limited number of on-campus dormitory rooms available to graduate students. Room and board in a double room cost approximately $6000 per academic year. Living costs for off-campus housing are very reasonable compared with those in other urban areas of the United States.

Student Group

Duquesne University has a total enrollment of more than 9,000 students in its ten schools. With 200 students and 45 faculty members in the graduate program in the Bayer School of Natural and Environmental Sciences, the University offers graduate students a highly personalized learning and advising environment.

Most students pursuing the M.S. degree in environmental science and management have a Bachelor of Science degree in biology or chemistry. The certificate in environmental sciences is normally for students with a B.S. or B.A. degree in the natural sciences or engineering. A bachelor's degree in business or social sciences is generally required for the certificate of environmental studies.

Student Outcomes

The M.S. degree in environmental science and management provides the skills required for today's professionals in industry, regulatory agencies, and academe who must deal with increasingly complex environmental issues. Graduates have been hired by such companies as PPG, Fisher Scientific, and Bayer Corporation.

Location

Duquesne University is located on a bluff overlooking the city of Pittsburgh. This location offers ready access to the many cultural, social, and entertainment attractions of the city. Within walking distance of the campus are Heinz Hall for the Performing Arts (home of the symphony, opera, ballet, theater, and other musical and cultural institutions), the Civic Arena (center for indoor sporting events and various exhibitions, concerts, and conventions), the Three Rivers Stadium (for outdoor sporting events), and Market Square (entertainment and nightlife center). The libraries, museums, art galleries, and music hall of the Carnegie Institute in the Oakland area are easily accessible by public transportation (routes pass immediately adjacent to the campus) or by private automobile. As the third-largest center for corporate headquarters and one of the twenty largest metropolitan areas in the United States, Pittsburgh also offers many professional career opportunities for its residents.

The University

Founded in 1878 by the Fathers and Brothers of the Congregation of the Holy Ghost, Duquesne University has provided the opportunity for an education to students from many backgrounds, without regard to sex, race, creed, color, or national or ethnic origins. In the past twenty-five years, the University has undergone a dramatic physical transformation, from a makeshift physical plant occupying approximately 12 acres to a modern, highly functional educational facility that is located on its own 40-acre hilltop overlooking downtown Pittsburgh.

Applying

Applications for admission to graduate study should be submitted no later than sixty days prior to the beginning of the semester in which admission is desired. All applications require an application form, including the nonrefundable application fee, official transcripts of previous undergraduate and graduate work, two letters of recommendation from persons who are familiar with the applicant's past academic progress, an official report of GRE aptitude test scores (this requirements is waived for applicants who have completed their previous formal education five or more years prior to the date of application), and an official score report indicating satisfactory performance on TOEFL examination (applicable to international students only.) Application forms are available by writing to or calling the Bayer School of Natural and Environment Sciences Graduate Office at 412-396-4900.

Correspondence and Information

Program Director
Environmental Science and Management Program
331 Fisher Hall
Duquesne University
Pittsburgh, Pennsylvania 15282

Telephone: 412-396-4367
Fax: 412-396-4091
World Wide Web: http://www.science.duq.edu

Duquesne University

THE FACULTY AND THEIR RESEARCH

Course instruction is provided by Duquesne faculty members, adjunct faculty members, and guest lecturers from industry and regulatory agencies.

J. Douglas Bricker, Associate Professor of Pharmacology-Toxicology and Associate Dean, School of Pharmacy; Ph.D., Duquesne. Study of the biochemical mechanisms related to the pharmacological and toxicological actions of drugs and chemicals.

Daniel K. Donnelly, Director, Environmental Science and Management Program; M.B.A., Maryland; Ph.D., George Mason. Board of Directors, Pennsylvania Environmental Council; Advisory Board, Environmental City Network. Leadership and organizational behaviors.

Frederick W. Fochtman, Associate Professor of Pharmacology and Chairman, Department of Pharmacology-Toxicology; Ph.D., Duquesne. Diplomate of the American Board of Toxicology and the American Board of Forensic Toxicology. Pharmacology/toxicology, pharmaceutical chemistry.

James F. Frain, Senior Consultant; M.A., Pittsburgh. Record systems to comply with environmental regulations and corporate guidelines.

W. Peter Geissler, B.S., Duke. Writing, importance and principles of efficient writing.

W. Michael Griffin, Adjunct Professor; Ph.D., Rhode Island. Commercial biotechnology, research and development.

Cynthia L. Harter, Assistant Professor of Economics and Associate Director, Business School's Study Abroad Program; Ph.D., Purdue. Natural resources and environmental economics, econometrics, economic education.

Bruce M. Herschlag, J.D., North Carolina. Assistant Counsel to the Commonwealth of Pennsylvania, Department of Environmental Protection. Water management, mining, solid waste, and bankruptcy areas of the law.

John Holveck, M.B.A., Pittsburgh; Ph.D., Duquesne. Philosophy, business consulting, writing.

Stanley J. Kabala, Adjunct Research Professor; Ph.D., Pittsburgh. U.S. and international environmental issues, environmental management in international business.

Paul M. King, J.D., Pittsburgh. Corporate Director of Environment, Health and Safety for PPG Industries, Inc., and Chair of its Environmental Affairs Committee; President, Air and Waste Management Association; Chairman, Board of Directors, Pennsylvania Environmental Council.

H. M. (Skip) Kingston, Professor of Chemistry; Ph.D., American. Separation science, chromatography microwave energy application, instrument development, standard reference materials development and certification, analytical and environmental test-method development, laboratory automation: expert systems and robotics.

Barbara M. Manner, Associate Professor of Earth Science and Science Education; Ph.D., Akron. Secondary education and geology, environmental hydrogeology.

Robert J. O'Gara, M.A., Duquesne. Former Director of Public Relations and Manager of Communications, Koppers Company. Liberal studies, public relations.

Robert J. Oltmanns, M.E.R., Pittsburgh. Energy resources, public relations.

Joseph P. Pezze, M.S., Pittsburgh. Environmental Protection Manager for Air Quality, Southwest Regional Office.

Mary Beth Pfohl, J.D., Villanova. Partner, Jones, Day, Reavis & Pogue; member, American Bar Association, Pennsylvania Bar Association, New Jersey State Bar Association. Environmental law.

Charles T. Rubin, Associate Professor of Political Science and Graduate Faculty of the Graduate Center for Social and Public Policy; Ph.D., Boston College. Public policy, political thought, environmental problems, technology and politics, ethics and public policy.

Kyle W. Selcer, Associate Professor of Biological Sciences; Ph.D., Texas Tech. Evolutionary ecology, comparative endocrinology, environmental toxicants that disrupt the endocrine system, role of steroids in reproduction of reptiles and amphibians, new drugs for the treatment of estrogen-dependent breast cancer.

John F. Stolz, Associate Professor of Biology; Ph.D., Boston University. Board of Directors, Pittsburgh Voyager. Microbial ecology, abundance and distribution of microbial species in stratified microbial ecosystems, function of prokaryotes in biogeochemical cycles, physiology and biochemistry of magnetogenic bacteria and green sulfur bacteria.

Cheryl Terai, J.D., Arkansas. Partner, Kirkpatrick & Lockhart LLP; member, American Bar Association (Natural Resources Law Section), Pennsylvania Bar Association (Environmental, Mineral and Natural Resources Section), and Allegheny County Bar Association (Environmental Law Section). Environmental law.

John W. Ubinger Jr., J.D., Notre Dame. Member, Steering Committee of the PennACCORD Center of Environmental Dispute Resolution; Director and Secretary, Pennsylvania Environmental Council; member, Allegheny County Health Department Air Pollution Control Advisory Committee. Environmental law.

James H. Vines, M.S., Missouri. Retired Corporate Senior Vice President, Health, Safety, and Environment, Bayer Corporation; member, American Institute of Chemical Engineers; member, North American Membrane Society.

Robert Volkmar, M.S., West Virginia. Corporate Manager of Environmental Affairs, Aristech Chemical Corporation; Chairman, Western Pennsylvania Section, Air and Waste Management Association.

Dietrich A. Weyel, Sc.D., Pittsburgh. President, Occupational Health Consultants, Inc. Technological studies of aerosols and vapors: engineering applications and risk assessments.

Thomas A. Zordan, Ph.D., Louisville. Physical chemistry: risk assessment techniques for environmentally sensitive projects.

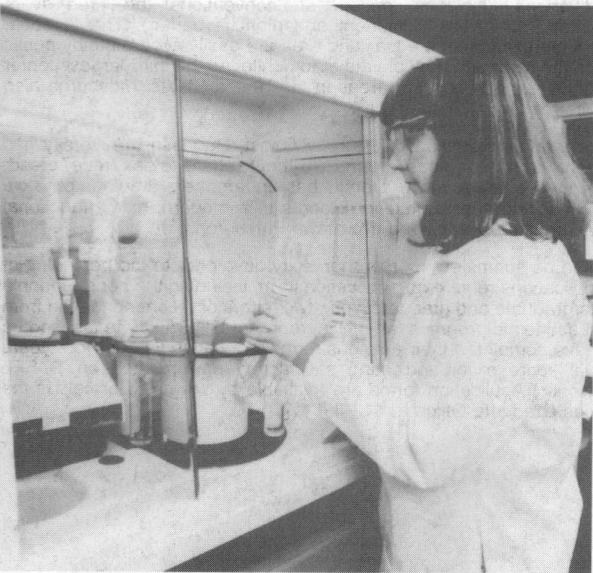

An ESM student performing environmental analyses.

The Academic Walk at Duquesne University.

SELECTED PUBLICATIONS

King, P. Global warming: A primer. *Environ. Managers* 12:19–20, 1997

Kingston, H. M. S., D. Huo, and Y. Lu. Accuracy in species analysis: Speciated isotope dilution mass spectrometry (SIDMS) exemplified by the evaluation of chromium species. *Spectrochim. Acta. Part B,* in press.

Kingston, H. M. S., and S. Haswell, eds. *Microwave Enhanced Chemistry: Fundamentals, Sample Preparation, and Applications.* Washington, D.C.: American Chemical Society, 1997.

Walter, P. J., S. Chalk, E. Lorentzen, and H. M. S. Kingston. A review of overview of microwave assisted sample preparation. In *Microwave Enhanced Chemistry: Fundamentals, Sample Preparation, and Applications,* chapter 2, pp. 55–223. Washington, D.C.: American Chemical Society, 1997.

Kingston, H. M. S., et al. Environmental microwave sample preparation: Fundamentals, methods, and applications. In *Microwave Enhanced Chemistry: Fundamentals, Sample Preparation, and Applications,* chapter 3, pp. 223–340. Washington, D.C.: American Chemical Society, 1997.

Chalk, S., K. McQullin, J. Brown, and H. M. S. Kingston. SamplePrep web: The Analytical Sample Preparation and Microwave Chemistry Research Center. In *Microwave Enhanced Chemistry: Fundamentals, Sample Preparation, and Applications,* chapter 15, pp. 667–93. Washington, D.C.: American Chemical Society, 1997.

Kingston, H. M. S., P. J. Walter, G. W. Engelhart, and P. J. Parsons. Chemical laboratory microwave safety. In *Microwave Enhanced Chemistry: Fundamentals, Sample Preparation, and Applications,* chapter 16, pp. 697–745. Washington, D.C.: American Chemical Society, 1997.

Kingston, H. M. S., P. J. Walter, S. Chalk, and D. Huo. SamplePrep Web™. World Wide Web: http://sampleprep.duq.edu/sampleprep/. January 22, 1998.

Kingston, H. M. S., D. Link, and P. J. Walter. Method 3015A, microwave assisted acid leach of aqueous samples and extracts. In *Solid Waste Manual 846, Update IV.* Washington, D.C.: U.S. Government Printing Office, 1998.

Kingston, H. M. S., D. Link, and P. J. Walter. Method 3051A, microwave assisted acid dissolution of sediments, sludges, soils, oils. In *Solid Waste Manual 846, Update IV.* Washington, D.C.: U.S. Government Printing Office, 1998.

Kingston, H. M. S., H. Boylan, and P. J. Walter. Method 7473, direct mercury analysis: Field and laboratory validation for EPA method 7473. In *Solid Waste Manual 846, Update IV.* Washington, D.C.: U.S. Government Printing Office, 1998.

Jiang, W., S. J. Chalk, and H. M. S. Kingston. Ozone degradation of residual carbon in biological samples using microwave irradiation. *Analyst* 122:211–5, 1997.

Lu, Y., D. Huo, and H. M. S. Kingston. Determination of analytical biases and chemical mechanisms in the analysis of Cr(VI) using EPA protocols.

Link, D. D., P. J. Walter, and H. M. S. Kingston. Development and validation of the new EPA microwave-assisted leach method 3051A.

Walter, P. J., and H. M. S. Kingston. Total microwave sample preparation: Integration of all sample preparation steps.

Boylan, H., P. J. Walter, and H. M. S. Kingston. Direct mercury analysis: Field and laboratory validation for EPA method 7473.

Manner, B. A 'real world' project in an environmental geoscience class. Presented at the Regional Meetings of the National Science Teacher's Association, Pittsburgh, Pennsylvania, October 31, 1997.

Selcer, K. W., and J. W. Clemens. Androgen effects and receptors in subavian species. In *Encyclopedia of Reproduction.* San Diego: Academic Press, in press.

Palmer, B. D., D. L. Pieto, L. K. Huth, and K. W. Selcer. Vitellogenin as a biomarker for xenobiotic estrogens in an amphibian model system. *Environ. Toxicol. Chem.* 17:30–6, 1998.

Selcer, K. W., P. K. Li, and P. Hedge. Inhibition of estrone sulfatase and breast cancer cell proliferation by nonsteroidal (p-O-sulfamoyl)-N-alkanoyl tyramines. *Cancer Res.* 57:1–6, 1997.

Palmer, B. D., and K. W. Selcer. Vitellogenin as a biomarker for xenobiotic estrogens. In *Environmental Toxicology and Risk Assessment: Biomarkers and Risk Assessment,* vol. 5, ASTM STP 1306, pp. 3–22, eds. D. A. Bengtson and D. S. Henshel. West Conshohocken, Penn.: American Society for Testing and Materials, 1996.

Selcer, K. W., S. Jagannathan, and P. K. Li. Inhibition of placental estrone sulfatase activity and MCF-7 breast cancer cell proliferation by estrone-3-amino derivatives. *J. Steroid Biochem. Mol. Biol.* 59:83–91, 1996.

Selcer, K. W., and P. K. Li. Estrogenicity, antiestrogenicity, and estrone sulfatase inhibition of estrone-3-amine and estrone-3-thiol. *J. Steroid Biochem. Mol. Biol.* 52:281–6, 1995.

Selcer, K. W., and B. D. Palmer. Estrogen downregulation of albumin and a 170 kDa protein in the turtle *Trachemys scripta. Gen. Comp. Endocrinol.* 97:340–52, 1995.

Stolz, J. F. The structure of microbial mats and biofilms. In *Microbial Sediments,* eds. R. Riding and S. Awramik. Berlin: Springer-Verlag, in press.

Oremland, R. S., and J. F. Stolz. Dissimilatory reduction of selenate and arsenate in nature. In *Environmental Metal-Microbe Interaction,* ed. D. R. Lovley. New York: Plenum Press, in press.

Stolz, J. F., et al. Differential cytochrome content and reductase activity in *Geospirillum barnesii* strain SeS3. *Arch. Microbiol.* 167:1–5, 1997.

THE EVERGREEN STATE COLLEGE

Graduate Program in Environmental Studies

Program of Study	The Evergreen State College (TESC) instituted an integrated, interdisciplinary course of study in 1984 leading to the degree of Master of Environmental Studies (M.E.S.). Students interested in the application of technical and management aspects of environmental studies gain the background and working skills necessary to solve a broad range of environmental problems and prepare to enter a wide variety of career areas.
	The 72-quarter-hour program can be completed in two years by full-time students and in as little as three years by part-time students. The program is composed of three distinct components. The first is a core sequence of four programs: Political, Economic, and Ecological Processes; Population, Energy, and Resources; Case Studies: Environmental Assessment Policy and Management; and Quantitative Analysis and Research Methods. Each of these programs is 8 quarter hours and is offered by an interdisciplinary team of social and natural scientists. The second component is the creation of an individual program through the selection of regular electives offered by the College, as well as opportunities for internships for credit and "Individual Learning Contracts." The electives that are offered include pesticides, wetlands ecology, environmental policy, environmental philosophy and ethics, environmental health, urban ecology, forest ecology, environmental economics, ecological principles and methods, hydrology, and salmonid ecology. The third component of the program is a thesis that consists of applied research and analysis in the form of an individual or small-group project. Full-time students carry out the parts of this plan concurrently, while part-time students complete components consecutively.
	All students entering the program are expected to have had course work and/or work-related experience in both the social and natural sciences. Evergreen prides itself on its active, interdisciplinary, action-oriented teaching methods. Faculty members also pursue a variety of additional relevant research and professional interests. The faculty members advise students on electives, thesis work, and professional development.
Research Facilities	The College's research facilities include chemical and biological laboratory facilities, an organic farm, 700 acres of second-growth forest, 3,000 feet of undeveloped marine shoreline, and a variety of computers with a full range of software, including GIS capability.
	The College's location in the state capital provides extensive research opportunities within state government. TESC library and the nearby Washington State library provide needed reference materials. Students can make use of local and regional agencies and communities as sites to carry out research activities. The program will help coordinate such work. Evergreen is the site of the Editorial Office for *Environmental Practice,* a peer-reviewed professional journal published by Oxford University Press for the National Association of Environmental Professionals.
Financial Aid	Program financial aid is available. Sources of support include fellowships, program assistantships, work-study positions, employment with the College, paid internships, and participation in contract research. In addition, the M.E.S. program assists students in finding external funding sources and locating part-time employment with public and private agencies. Students should also check with TESC's Financial Aid Office and file a financial aid form by February 15 for priority consideration.
Cost of Study	Full-time tuition for Washington State residents was $1405 per quarter in 1998–99 or $140.50 per quarter hour for part-time students. Nonresident tuition was $4265 per quarter or $426.50 per quarter hour. Fees are subject to change.
Living and Housing Costs	An estimated $4800 covers room and board for a single person living on or off campus during the nine-month academic year. Most graduate students live in or near Olympia in rental units or in apartments adjacent to campus.
Student Group	Approximately 40 students enroll each fall quarter. Total program size is currently about 100 students. A cooperative spirit within the student group is emphasized primarily through seminars and group assignments. Another 80 graduate students in Evergreen's M.P.A. program share some space and faculty members with the M.E.S. program.
Student Outcomes	More than half of the program alumni are employed in the public sector, predominantly in state government agencies. Almost a quarter work in the private sector, and others work in positions in education or nongovernmental organizations or are pursuing further study. Most graduates are employed in positions that are degree related. The Assistant Director for Student Services assists students in their professional development planning.
Location	Olympia lies at the southern end of Puget Sound, equidistant from the Cascade Range, the Pacific Ocean, and the Olympic Mountains. Train, bus, and highway connections provide easy access to metropolitan Seattle and Portland. Evergreen serves as a cultural and intellectual focus for Washington's capital city of Olympia. The city and surrounding area have a population of 100,000, with excellent outdoor recreation opportunities nearby.
The College	The Evergreen State College opened in 1971. Its national reputation for innovative curricular design and academic excellence have drawn a diverse faculty, staff, and student body to the 1,000-acre campus, which is located 7 miles northwest of Olympia. The most distinctive feature of the curriculum is the concept of interdisciplinary instruction carried out in coordinated study programs for a quarter or longer. This results in the student having both a single and a multifaceted academic commitment at the same time. This concept of study is the essence of the core component of the M.E.S. program.
	Evergreen has the usual recreational and athletic facilities on campus, including those for tennis, swimming, racquetball, basketball, and soccer. The College's beach on Puget Sound is the focus for water recreation, and the Cascade and Olympic Mountains provide excellent hiking, climbing, and skiing.
Applying	Admission is normally granted for the fall quarter so that the student can begin the core sequence. Application forms and a catalog are available from TESC's Office of Admissions. Questions about the program should be sent to the Program Coordinator.
Correspondence and Information	Program Coordinator Graduate Program in Environmental Studies The Evergreen State College Olympia, Washington 98505 Telephone: 360-866-6000 Ext. 6707 E-mail: mes@elwha.evergreen.edu World Wide Web: http://www.evergreen.edu

The Evergreen State College

THE FACULTY

Shown below are the areas of interest in teaching and study of each faculty member.

Natural Science

Sharon Anthony. Environmental chemistry.
Michael Beug. Chemistry, mycology.
Frederica Bowcutt. Botany, restoration ecology, natural history.
Paul Butler. Geology, hydrology.
Richard Cellarius. Plant biology, biophysics, environmental policy. (Emeritus)
Gerardo Chin-Leo. Biology, marine studies.
Robert Cole. Physics, energy studies.
Steven Herman. Field biology, ornithology.
Robert Knapp. Physics, energy systems.
Patricia Labine. Ecological agriculture.
David Milne. Marine ecology.
Nalini Nadkarni. Forest ecology.
John Perkins. Biology, history of technology and environment, editor of *Environmental Practice*.
Oscar Soule. Ecology.
Brian Spence. Biology, fisheries.
James Stroh. Geology.
Kenneth Tabbutt. Geology.
Gabriel Tucker. Forest ecology, silviculture.
Jude Van Buren. Epidemiology, environmental health.
Alfred Wiedemann. Biology, botany.

Social Science

Jovanna Brown. Native American issues, water and land rights.
Carolyn Dobbs. Environmental planning, community organization.
Peter Dorman. Political economy.
Russell Fox. Community planning and development.
Martha Henderson. Cultural geography, human ecology, public lands management.
Carol Minugh. Native American community-based environmental studies.
Ralph Murphy. Environmental economics, natural resource policy.
Lin Nelson. Environmental health and advocacy.
Thomas Rainey. History, political economy.
Matthew Smith. Political science, environmental politics.
Linda Moon Stumpff. Natural resource policy.
Gregory Weeks. Managerial and natural resource economics.
Theodore Whitesell. Geography.
Tom Womeldorff. Environmental economics.

Contributing Adjunct Faculty

Stephen L. Beck. Environmental philosophy and ethics.
John Calambokidis. Marine mammal ecology.
Nina Carter. Environmental management.
Jeffrey Cederholm. Fisheries biology.
Jean MacGregor. Environmental education.
Robert Plotnikoff. Aquatic ecology.
Meredith Savage. Wetlands ecology and restoration.
Betty Tabbutt. Environmental policy.

An M.E.S. student presents his candidacy paper to fellow students and faculty members.

Every year, M.E.S. students organize the Rachel Carson forum to publicly debate an environmental issue.

Students have opportunities to study in the field, here, with a forest ecologist.

FLORIDA INSTITUTE OF TECHNOLOGY

College of Engineering, Division of Marine and Environmental Systems
Programs in Environmental Sciences
and Environmental Resource Management

Programs of Study

Florida Institute of Technology offers programs of study leading to Master of Science and Doctor of Philosophy degrees in environmental sciences and to the M.S. degree in environmental resource management. These programs are designed to prepare students for careers in industry, government, colleges and universities, or consulting firms. Emphasis is on the application of scientific principles to the maintenance and wise use of man's environment. The environmental science curriculum provides a thorough background in the biological and chemical fundamentals of natural systems and water and wastewater treatment systems. The principal areas of emphasis in environmental science are related to freshwater and estuarine problems in areas such as eutrophication, toxic wastes, aquatic ecology, and hydrology; to groundwater contamination problems from sources such as septic tanks, landfills, and underground storage tanks; to air pollution, such as air quality monitoring and impacts of air pollutants on natural systems; to marine waste policy; to waste stabilization and waste utilization; and to nuclear-waste management and site remediation, environmental and marine remote sensing, and real-time spectral monitoring of environmental systems using in situ sensors, aircraft, and ships as well as satellites and meteorology.

The Division also offers an M.S. program in coastal zone management and M.S. and Ph.D. programs in the marine sciences of biological, chemical, and physical oceanography, with specializations in geophysical remote sensing of the environment and in ocean engineering. A highly interdisciplinary education is emphasized in this program.

Master's degree requirements consist of 30 semester hours of required and elective courses, including 6 semester hours of thesis research work or internship or 33 semester hours (nonthesis) of courses. Ph.D. students must complete a minimum of 81 semester hours beyond the bachelor's degree or 48 semester hours beyond the master's degree. Interested students should see the full-page entry for Florida Tech's Graduate School in *Peterson's Guide to Graduate and Professional Programs: An Overview,* Book 1 of the Guides to Graduate Study, or write for more information on the doctoral program.

Graduate student research most frequently involves work on current environmental problems and may be funded by federal, state, and local agencies and industries. Research opportunities and internships are also available at nearby government agencies, research organizations, and private industry.

Research Facilities

The programs offer extensive facilities for instruction and research, such as an advanced remote sensing lab, satellite data reception, and environmental optics lab as part of the Florida Tech Marine and Environmental Optics Remote Sensing Center and the Geographical Information System (GIS) Laboratory. The environmental analysis laboratory is equipped with such standard water analysis equipment as balances, ovens, muffle furnaces, a chemical oxygen-demand apparatus, a macro-Kjeldahl apparatus, pH meters, and spectrophotometers. Analytical instruments provided for advanced study include an ion chromatograph, a gas chromatograph, a total organic carbon analyzer, an atomic absorption spectrophotometer, and an auto analyzer. Advanced instrumental analysis is also available at the nearby Brevard Teaching and Research Labs.

Financial Aid

Graduate teaching and research assistantships are available to a limited number of qualified students. For 1999–2000, typical financial support ranges from $16,000 upward, including stipend and tuition, per academic year for approximately half-time duties. Stipend-only assistantships are sometimes awarded for less time commitment. Students with internships may receive an hourly salary.

Cost of Study

Tuition is $575 per graduate semester hour in 1999–2000. New students must pay an entrance deposit of $300, which is deducted from the first semester's tuition charge.

Living and Housing Costs

Room and board on campus cost approximately $2400 per semester in 1999–2000. On-campus housing (dormitories and apartments) is available for full-time single and married graduate students, but priority for dormitory rooms is given to undergraduate students. Many apartment complexes and rental houses are available near the campus.

Student Group

Graduate students constitute more than one quarter of the approximately 4,000 students on the Melbourne campus. They come from all parts of the United States and from many other countries.

Student Outcomes

Graduates of the program obtain positions in places such as the Florida Department of Environmental Protection; St. John's River Water Management District; Brevard County; Sarasota County; Volusia County; South Florida Water Management District; U.S. Army Corps of Engineers; National Park Service; Lockheed Martin; NASA; Dynamac; Bionetics; Jordan, Jones and Goulding, Inc.; Brevard Teaching and Research Labs; Florida Groundwater Services; Harris Corp.; and Walt Disney World.

Location

Melbourne is located on the east coast of Florida. The climate is extremely pleasant, and opportunities for outdoor recreation abound. The John F. Kennedy Space Center and Disney World/EPCOT Center are nearby and the Atlantic beaches are within 3 miles of campus.

The Institute

Florida Institute of Technology was founded in 1958 by a group of scientists and engineers pioneering America's space program at Cape Canaveral. The environmental remote sensing program utilizes the technology developed by the space program. Florida Tech has rapidly developed into a residential institution and is the only independent technological university in the Southeast. It is supported by the community and industry and is the recipient of many research grants and contracts, a number of which provide financial support for graduate students. The campus covers 175 acres and includes a beautiful botanical garden and an internationally known collection of palm trees.

Applying

Forms and instructions for applying for admission and assistantships are sent on request. Admission is possible at the beginning of any semester, but admission in the fall semester is recommended. It is advantageous to apply early. Entering students are expected to have had courses in general chemistry, organic chemistry, analytical chemistry, calculus, physics, and biology as well as a year or more of advanced science courses. The GRE General Test is required for admission.

Correspondence and Information

Dr. John G. Windsor Jr., Program Chair
Environmental Sciences Program
Florida Institute of Technology
Melbourne, Florida 32901
Telephone: 407-674-8096
Fax: 407-984-8461
E-mail: dmes@marine.fit.edu
World Wide Web: http://www.fit.edu/AcadRes/dmes

Graduate Admissions Office
Florida Institute of Technology
Melbourne, Florida 32901
Telephone: 407-674-8027
800-944-4348 (toll-free)
Fax: 407-723-9468
World Wide Web: http://www.fit.edu

Florida Institute of Technology

THE FACULTY AND RESEARCH AREAS

Ballard M. Barker, Associate Professor; Ph.D., Oklahoma.
Thomas V. Belanger, Professor; Ph.D., Florida.
Charles R. Bostater, Associate Professor; Ph.D., Delaware.
Iver W. Duedall, Professor; Ph.D., Dalhousie.
Howell H. Heck, Associate Professor; Ph.D., Arkansas.
G. A. Maul, Professor; Ph.D., Miami.
Mark B. Moldwin, Assistant Professor; Ph.D., Boston University.
Randall W. Parkinson, Associate Professor; Ph.D., Miami (Florida).
Hamid K. Rassoul, Associate Professor; Ph.D., Texas at Dallas.
Chih-Shin Shieh, Senior Research Scientist; Ph.D., Florida Tech.
John H. Trefry, Professor; Ph.D., Texas A&M.
John G. Windsor Jr., Professor and Program Chair, Environmental Sciences; Ph.D., William and Mary.

Adjunct Faculty

Joseph Angelo, Ph.D. Science Application, Inc.
Michael F. Helmstetter, Ph.D. Brevard Teaching and Research Laboratory.
Brian E. LaPointe, Ph.D. Harbor Branch Oceanographic Institution.
Robert W. Virnstein, Ph.D. St. John's River Water Management District.

RESEARCH INTERESTS

Within the broad discipline of environmental science are areas of specialization that focus on physical, biological, or chemical issues of natural and man-made systems. Because of the interdisciplinary nature of environmental sciences, the department offers programs that link the following major areas in an integrated systems approach, focusing on quantitative techniques.

Environmental Biology. Aquatic ecology, eutrophication of lakes, water quality indicator organisms, microbiology of wastewater treatment, wetlands systems, limnology, environmental planning, and impact statements.

Environmental Chemistry. Chemistry of natural waters, wetlands, nutrient cycling, nitrogen transformations, biogeochemical mass balance modeling, toxic organics in natural waters and water supplies, decomposition, management models for water quality control, non-point-source pollution, and waste treatment.

Environmental Modeling. Specialized environmental climatological environmental systems, theoretical studies and numerical modeling of coastal processes, water quality modeling and toxic chemical modeling, and hazard assessments of chemicals in the environment.

Environmental Resource Management. Recycling and reuse of waste materials. Applied management practicums in internship opportunities are offered, such as EIS development and review, policy analysis, and natural resource management in developing countries.

Global Change. Global temperature change and sea level rise, carbon flux, and ozone depletion.

Remote Sensing and Real-time Optical Spectral Monitoring. Environmental remote sensing utilizing optical and microwave radiometry based on aircraft and ships and in estuarine, coastal, and inland waters and satellite altimetry. The program maintains a Marine and Environmental Optics Remote Sensing Center with an image processing/remote sensing laboratory and an environmental optics laboratory.

Sustainable Development. Population control, wise use of resources, and environmental economics, with a special focus on islands.

Waste Management. Scientific aspects of waste management methodologies, including marine, estuarine, and freshwater systems; waste interactions with biological, chemical, and physical systems; trace contaminant analyses; ocean pollutant studies; plastics recycling; and incineration ash stabilization and utilization in artificial reef construction.

RESEARCH ACTIVITIES

Aeration of mosquito-control impoundments to improve water quality, to eliminate fish kills, and to enable potential aquaculture use.
Air quality monitoring.
Artificial reef construction impacts.
Benthic oxygen demand in Florida lakes.
Effects of urban stormwater runoff on water quality in the Indian River Lagoon system.
Groundwater/surface water interactions in Florida water bodies.
Impact of septic tank leachate on the Indian River Lagoon.
Importance of groundwater seepage in East Lake Tohopekaliga (part of a water management district).
Indian River Lagoon circulation patterns.
In situ optical monitoring of water, wastewater, and coastal systems.
Investigation of oxygen budgets in the Everglades.
Light limitation of sea grass distribution.
The littoral zone of Lake Okeechobee as a source of phosphorus in open waters of the lake.
Marine waste policy.
Nutrient-enhanced coastal ocean productivity.
Phytoplankton population distributions in the upper and middle St. Johns River.
Plastics and other wastes in the ocean.
Real-time optical spectral monitoring.
Recycled plastic utilization in marine environments.
Remote sensing.
Sebastian Inlet biological studies.
Stabilization of ash waste.
Trace metals in the upper St. Johns River and their land use relationships.
Waste utilization.
Water quality characteristics of agricultural pumpage in the upper St. Johns River.
Water quality modeling; modeling the fate, transport, and distribution of chemicals in the environment, coupled with physical-optical models in marine systems.

ILLINOIS INSTITUTE OF TECHNOLOGY

Stuart School of Business
Environmental Management Program

Program of Study

The Stuart School of Business offers an M.S. in environmental management (EM). Two dual degrees are also offered: the M.B.A./M.S. in environmental management and a J.D./M.S. in environmental management offered with IIT's Chicago-Kent College of Law.

The Environmental Management Program is an interdisciplinary program integrating business, law, and science to manage environmental affairs. To create this program, the Stuart School of Business joined forces with IIT's top-ranked programs in environmental engineering and environmental law. The program provides the knowledge and skills to plan, manage, and communicate environmental strategies by balancing and integrating economic, legal, technical, business, and regulatory dimensions. Courses are offered in environmental law and regulation, environmental risk assessment and management, industrial ecology, air and water pollution control, solid and hazardous waste management, industrial health and safety, environmental and OSHA monitoring and compliance, financial and managerial accounting, organizational behavior, managerial economics, managerial finance, marketing, operations management, and international business.

The program prepares students for management-level positions in the growing environmental products and services industry and at government agencies, many corporations, nonprofit organizations, public utilities, and consulting firms.

The M.S. curriculum consists of fourteen to sixteen quarter courses, including eleven required core courses, one elective course, two capstone courses, and two courses that may be required, depending on the student's knowledge of science and mathematics. The degree can be completed in as few as four quarters of study. Students may take up to six years to complete the program. Courses are offered once a week, in the evenings, at IIT's Downtown Chicago Campus.

Research Facilities

The Downtown Campus Information Center is an open-stack collection of more than 500,000 volumes, including the business holdings of the Stuart Business Library, the Chicago-Kent Law Library with its large holdings in environmental law, and the Library of International Relations, a depository for numerous government agencies, international organizations, and the United Nations (UN). UN Environmental Program documents and environmental treaties and protocols are available to students. Stuart students have access to IIT's full library system, including its extensive holdings in environmental science and, using the Illinet Online library catalog, can obtain access to materials and books in hundreds of Illinois libraries.

Stuart's Downtown Campus is equipped with two computer labs offering a total of seventy student workstations linked to the Internet and networked with IIT libraries, including the Downtown Campus Information Center's CD-ROM databases. The labs provide access to a wide range of software and resources through a Windows interface. Computer skills workshops are offered throughout the year.

Financial Aid

Partial tuition scholarships of 25 percent to 50 percent are offered on a merit basis to full-time students. A variety of government-supported loans are available for qualified U.S. residents enrolled in at least two courses per quarter. IIT alumni receive a one-third reduction in tuition in one course per quarter. A tuition installment plan is available and, for students whose employers offer tuition reimbursement, a tuition deferment plan is available.

Cost of Study

Tuition for 1999–2000 is $1800 per course.

Living and Housing Costs

Stuart's downtown Chicago location makes it easily accessible by public transportation from most locations in the metropolitan area. Full-time students may live in apartment housing on IIT's Main Campus.

Student Group

In 1998, of the nearly 700 students enrolled in Stuart School programs, 10 percent were in the EM Program. About 90 percent of students in the EM Program are working professionals. Their average age is 33, and 40 percent are women.

Student Outcomes

Students and recent graduates work at a range of organizations, including Amoco, Argonne National Laboratory, the Chicago Department of the Environment, R.R. Donnelly, IT Corporation, the Environmental Protection Agency, the Metropolitan Water Reclamation District, Motorola, and Waste Management, Inc.

Location

The Stuart School of Business is located in IIT's state-of-the-art Downtown Chicago Campus, in Chicago's financial and business center. Chicago offers a rich variety of recreation and culture, ranging from professional basketball to the Lyric Opera. The shoreline of Lake Michigan features beaches, parks, and splendid scenery.

The Institute and The School

Illinois Institute of Technology is a private university established in 1890. IIT's Stuart School of Business has focused on unique industry-responsive master's programs. The EM Program was established in 1995 with the assistance of leaders from Chicago's environmental law and consulting firms, corporations, and environmental agencies who now serve as its advisory board. Stuart also offers M.S. degrees in financial markets and trading, operations and technology management, and marketing communication, along with the M.B.A. and Ph.D. in management science. The Stuart School of Business is accredited by AACSB–The International Association for Management Education.

Applying

Admission to the EM Program is based on a profile combination of GPA, GMAT or GRE test scores, professional goals, work experience, and letters of recommendation. Applicants from non-English-speaking countries must also submit TOEFL scores. Applications are accepted throughout the year, and students may enter the program in any quarter. Stuart follows an academic calendar of four quarters, beginning in August, November, February, and May. To ensure full consideration, early submission of applications is encouraged.

Correspondence and Information

Stuart School of Business
Illinois Institute of Technology
565 West Adams Street
Chicago, Illinois 60661-3691

Telephone: 312-906-6543
Fax: 312-906-6549
E-mail: degrees@stuart.iit.edu
World Wide Web: http://www.stuart.iit.edu

Illinois Institute of Technology

THE FACULTY AND THEIR RESEARCH

M. Zia Hassan, Dean and Professor; Ph.D., IIT. Effective organizations, strategic and quality issues in organizations.

Paul R. Anderson, Associate Professor; Ph.D. (environmental engineering), Washington (Seattle). Aquatic surface chemistry, physical and chemical treatment processes, characteristics and fate of particulates in aquatic environments.

Hamid Arastoopour, Professor and Chair of the Department of Chemical and Environmental Engineering; Ph.D. (gas engineering), IIT. Multiphase flow and fluidization, flow through porous media, environmental issues in energy, materials processing and recycling.

Martin L. Bariff, Associate Professor; Ph.D. (accountancy), Illinois at Urbana-Champaign. Impact of information technology on business strategy, work group design, human decision making.

Christopher M. Barlow, Assistant Professor; Ph.D. (organizational behavior), Case Western Reserve. Cross-functional teamwork, with a particular emphasis on integrating technical and business perspectives.

James Berry, Adjunct Professor; Ph.D. (biology), Utah; J.D., IIT. Environmental and energy law.

John F. O. Bilson, Associate Professor; Ph.D., (economics) Chicago. Foreign exchange, the futures markets, international economics.

James P. Butler, Adjunct Professor; Ph.D. (environmental health science), NYU. Development of risk-based approaches for deriving environmental cleanup criteria.

Eve M. Caudill, Assistant Professor; Ph.D. (marketing), Illinois at Urbana-Champaign. Consumer behavior.

William J. Franek, Adjunct Professor; Ph.D. (environmental engineering), Illinois at Chicago. Sources and control of volatile organic compounds, receptor modeling of air pollution.

Martin E. Ginn, Associate Professor; Ph.D. (industrial engineering and management science), Northwestern. Creativity management, new product development.

Joel Goldhar, Professor; D.B.A. (business administration), George Washington. Computer-integrated manufacturing, impacts of technology on business strategy.

W. Clayton Hall, Associate Professor; Ph.D. (economics), Illinois at Urbana-Champaign. Public sector financial, economic, and industrial relations issues.

Gary M. Hutter, Adjunct Professor; Ph.D. (environmental and occupational health studies), Illinois at Chicago. Environmental engineering and safety.

Syed A. Imam, Assistant Professor; Ph.D. (operations management), IIT. Implementation and management of manufacturing systems, quality management.

Kamyar Jabbari, Lecturer; M.B.A. (finance), Chicago. Project financing, international banking, independent power production.

Nasrin R. Khallili, Assistant Professor; Ph.D. (environmental engineering), IIT. Characterizing and modeling atmospheric sources of toxic organic chemicals, removal of organic pollutants from industrial gas streams, development of two-phase receptor modeling for industrial emissions.

Thomas W. Knowles, Professor; Ph.D., Chicago. Mathematical and computer modeling.

George D. Kraft, Associate Professor; Ph.D. (electrical engineering), Case Tech. Use of leading-edge technologies in enhancing the corporate information environment.

Henry R. Linden, Professor; Ph.D. (chemical engineering), IIT. Energy policy analysis, with specialization in energy economics and forecasting; industrial ecology; global climate change; energy technology development; energy/environment/economics interrelationships.

George P. Nassos, Adjunct Professor; Ph.D. (chemical engineering), Northwestern. Process-engineered fuel, waste minimization, environmental strategy.

Ali K. Oskouie, Adjunct Professor; Ph.D. (environmental engineering), IIT. Fine particle technology in air and water pollution.

Paul R. Prabhaker, Associate Professor; Ph.D. (marketing), Rochester. Marketing research and strategy, marketing implications of newer manufacturing technologies.

David P. Quinn, Assistant Professor; Ph.D. (finance), Yale. Incentives for innovation, energy markets, bankruptcy in emerging markets, market microstructure, investments.

Nick T. Thomopoulos, Professor; Ph.D. (industrial engineering), IIT. Forecasting, inventory, assembly line systems.

Khairy A. Tourk, Associate Professor; Ph.D. (economics), Berkeley. Fossil-energy policy research and international product development, energy economics and systems analysis, international trade and finance.

John R. Twombly, Clinical Assistant Professor; Ph.D. (accounting), Chicago. Managerial accounting, finance.

Richard J. Vamos, Adjunct Professor; Ph.D. (environmental engineering), IIT. Air and water pollution monitoring and control.

INDIANA UNIVERSITY BLOOMINGTON

School of Public and Environmental Affairs
Environmental Science Graduate Programs

Programs of Study	The primary objective of the environmental science graduate programs offered by the School of Public and Environmental Affairs (SPEA) is to train professionals who combine an environmental science specialization with the administrative skills necessary for applying this knowledge in broader policy-making settings. The two-year, professional Master of Science in Environmental Science (M.S.E.S.) program combines core courses in environmental science, management, and policy with a concentration area. Concentration areas include applied ecology, environmental chemistry, hazardous materials management, and water resources. To integrate this academic training with a practical framework, students are required to complete an internship or significant research project. Program flexibility allows students to design individualized concentrations tailored to their career goals.
	Joint-degree programs are offered with SPEA's Master of Public Affairs (M.P.A.) program; the Indiana University biology, geography, and geology departments; and the Indiana University Schools of Law and Journalism.
	Ph.D. programs in environmental science, public affairs, and public policy are also available. The doctoral program in Environmental Science at SPEA is designed to provide a rigorous, interdisciplinary education. The main objectives of the program are to further understanding of the nature and management of natural and human environments; encourage advanced research and scientific analysis of environmental events, issues, and problems; and provide an opportunity for students and faculty members to engage in collaborative environmental research.
	SPEA is a top-ranked professional school committed to teaching, applied research, and technical assistance. The School is recognized for its interdisciplinary faculty and research in both the natural and the social sciences.
Research Facilities	The research facilities and equipment available in the School of Public and Environmental Affairs are excellent. Equipment includes two programmable environmental chambers, three UV-visible spectrophotometers, an atomic absorption spectrophotometer with graphic furnace and flame atomization, six gas chromatographs, an ion chromatograph, an autoanalyzer, an organic carbon analyzer, three mass spectrometers, an inductively coupled plasma analyzer, a CHN thermal analyzer, a portable photosynthesis analyzer, and anaerobic chamber, a phase contrast/epifluorescent microscope, a 2.5 liter bacterial fermentor, a high-end compound research microscope (DM) with camera attachments, two stereo microscopes, a rotary microtome, a cryostat, an Nd:YAG pumped dye laser system, and an adiabatic bomb calorimeter. SPEA also has excellent terrestrial and aquatic field sampling equipment and instruments, a sixteen-foot research boat, cartographic equipment and map files, and aerial photographic and photo interpretation equipment.
	Libraries on the Bloomington campus house more than 5 million volumes, and another 2.3 million are available through the University's seven other campuses.
Financial Aid	Departmental assistance for qualified students is awarded on a competitive basis and is determined by merit. Awards include teaching and research assistantships. SPEA also dedicates awards to qualified returning Peace Corps or AmeriCorps volunteers. Students may apply for need-based aid through the University's Office of Student Financial Assistance.
Cost of Study	In-state residents paid $180 per credit hour and out-of-state residents paid $488 per credit hour for the master's programs in 1998–99. Other academic fees, services, and supplies total between $400 and $500 a year.
Living and Housing Costs	On-campus room and board for single graduate students during the 1998–99 academic year ranged from $3900 to $5775. The 1,500 on-campus housing units for married students ranged in monthly rent from $442 for an efficiency to $884 for a furnished three-bedroom apartment. A variety of off-campus housing is available near the University. Rents are generally inexpensive, with the average two-bedroom unit renting for $500 to $650 per month.
Student Group	Approximately 100 students are enrolled in the M.S.E.S. program, with 67 students pursuing the joint M.P.A./M.S.E.S. program, and 37 students enrolled in the Ph.D. programs in environmental science. About one tenth of these students are international, more than one half are women, and more than one tenth are members of minority groups. In addition, about 45 graduate students are returned Peace Corps volunteers.
Student Outcomes	SPEA maintains an outstanding placement record, which is attributed to a well-rounded curriculum, national prestige, and strong alumni support. The SPEA Placement and Internship Office is staffed with professionals who assist graduate students in obtaining permanent employment and internship experiences. Samples of recent placements include the U.S. Fish and Wildlife Service, U.S. Environmental Protection Agency, Radian Corporation, World Wildlife Federation, ICF Kaiser Environmental, and Upjohn Company.
Location	Bloomington, a college town of 60,000 people, was chosen as one of the top ten college towns in America for its "rich mixture of atmospherics and academia" by Edward Fiske, former education editor of the *New York Times*. It is a culturally vibrant community settled among southern Indiana's rolling hills just 45 miles south of Indianapolis, the state capital. Mild winters and warm summers are ideal for outdoor recreation in the two state forests, one national forest, and three state parks that surround Bloomington.
The University and The School	Established in 1820, Indiana University has more than 7,000 graduate students and more than 36,000 students total enrolled on the Bloomington campus. Fifty-five academic departments are ranked in the top twenty in the country, including SPEA, music, business, biology, foreign languages, political science, and chemistry. Attractions include nearly 1,000 musical performances each year, including eight full-length operas and professional Broadway plays; the IU Art Museum, designed by I. M. Pei, with more than 30,000 art objects; fifty campus and community volunteer agencies; more than 500 student clubs and organizations; two indoor student recreational facilities; and Big Ten sports.
	SPEA, founded in 1972, was the first school to combine public management, policy, and administration with the environmental sciences.
Applying	Applications must include the SPEA Admission and Financial Aid application form, transcripts, GRE General Test scores, and three letters of recommendation. Priority is given to applications received by February 1. School visits are encouraged.

Correspondence and Information	For master's programs:
	Graduate Programs Office
	SPEA 260
	Indiana University
	Bloomington, Indiana 47405
	Telephone: 812-855-2840
	    800-765-7755 (toll-free in U.S. only)
	E-mail: speainfo@indiana.edu
	World Wide Web: http://www.indiana.edu/~speaweb
		For doctoral programs:
		Ph.D. Programs Office
		SPEA 441
		Indiana University
		Bloomington, Indiana 47405
		Telephone: 812-855-2457
		    800-765-7755 (toll-free in U.S. only)

Indiana University Bloomington

THE FACULTY AND THEIR RESEARCH

Robert Agranoff, Ph.D., Pittsburgh, 1967. Human services administration, intergovernmental relations and management, community development.

David B. Audretsch, Ph.D., Wisconsin, 1980. Economic development.

Matthew Auer, Ph.D., Yale, 1996. International and comparative environmental policy, politics of foreign aid.

Debera Backhus, Ph.D., MIT, 1990. Environmental processes affecting fate and transport of organic contaminants, hazardous waste site remediation strategies.

Randall Baker, Ph.D., London, 1968. International environmental policy, environmental management in the tropics, the civil service in transitional economies.

A. James Barnes, J.D., Harvard, 1967. Environmental law/policy, ethics.

R. Richard Bauer, M.P.A., Washington, 1981. Environmental management, quality management, transformational leadership, interpersonal relations management.

Lisa Bingham, J.D., Connecticut, 1979. Alternative dispute resolution, public law, labor law.

Charles F. Bonser, D.B.A., Indiana, 1965. Executive leadership, economic development, public finance, business economics and forecasting.

Lynton K. Caldwell, Ph.D., Chicago, 1943. International environmental law/policy for science and technology.

Laku Chidambaram, Ph.D., Indiana, 1989. Information systems, international business, computer-mediated groupwork.

Christopher B. Craft, Ph.D., North Carolina State, 1987. Wetlands ecology and restoration, ecological succession theory.

Jon P. Gant, Ph.D., Carnegie Mellon, 1998. Organizational strategies for sharing and processing information, spatial organization and performance of industries, design and implementation of geographic information systems.

David Good, Ph.D., Pennsylvania, 1985. Quantitative policy modeling, productivity measurement in public and regulated industries, urban policy analysis.

Kirtsen Grönbjerg, Ph.D., Chicago, 1974. Nonprofit funding and management.

Hendrik Haitjema, Ph.D., Minnesota, 1982. Groundwater hydrology, groundwater flow modeling, soil mechanics.

Diane Henshel, Ph.D., Washington (St. Louis), 1987. Effects of dioxins and other pollutants on neural embryonic development.

Ronald Hites, Ph.D., MIT, 1968. Organic environmental chemistry, PCBs, dioxins, pesticides.

Jack W. Hopkins, Ph.D., Florida, 1966. Public administration, international administration and development, public policy, environmental policy in Latin America.

Craig Johnson, Ph.D., SUNY at Albany, 1993. Public financial management, public budgeting and finance, capital markets and institutions.

Herbert J. Kiesling, Ph.D., Harvard, 1966. Public finance, social and public choice, economics, philosophy.

Robert S. Kravchuk, Ph.D., Syracuse, 1989. Public budgeting and financial management, political economy of former socialist economies in transition.

Kerry Krutilla, Ph.D., Duke, 1988. Environmental regulation, trade and the environment, sustainable development, natural resource management, energy policy.

Eugene B. McGregor Jr., Ph.D., Syracuse, 1969. Public administration, human resource management, policy analysis.

Vicky J. Meretsky, Ph.D., Arizona, 1995. Conservation biology, ecosystem ecology, applied ecology.

John L. Mikesell, Ph.D., Illinois, 1969. Public finance and budgeting, taxation, fiscal administration.

Theodore Miller, Ph.D., Iowa, 1970. Statistical analysis.

Emilio Moran, Ph.D., Florida, 1975. Tropical ecosystem ecology, Amazon Basin, secondary successional forests, human ecology.

E. Philip Morgan, Ph.D., Syracuse, 1970. International economic development, international and comparative public administration.

Patrick O'Meara, Ph.D., Indiana, 1970. Political development; international politics with focus on African public policy; ethics and the public sector.

Clinton V. Oster Jr., Ph.D., Harvard, 1977. Business/government regulations, transportation policy, aviation safety.

David F. Parkhurst, Ph.D., Wisconsin, 1970. Applied statistics and mathematical modeling, physiological plan ecology, risk and decision analysis.

Roger B. Parks, Ph.D., Indiana, 1979. Policy analysis, urban policy and management, intergovernmental management.

D. Jeanne Patterson, D.B.A., Indiana, 1967. Financial management, government accounting.

James L. Perry, Ph.D., Syracuse, 1974. Public management, human resource management, national and community service.

Flynn Picardal, Ph.D., Arizona, 1992. Bioremediation, environmental microbiology.

Maureen Pirog, Ph.D., Pennsylvania, 1981. Child support enforcement, adolescent parenting, poverty, policy analytic methods.

Orville Powell, M.P.A., Penn State, 1963. Public administration.

J. C. Randolph, Ph.D., Carleton (Ottawa), 1972. Forest ecology, ecological aspects of global environmental change, applications of GIS and remote sensing to natural resources management.

David Reingold, Ph.D., Chicago, 1996. Urban policy, community and economic development, and social welfare policy.

Rafael Reuveny, Ph.D., Indiana, 1997. Political science, business, economics.

Edwardo L. Rhodes, Ph.D., Carnegie-Mellon, 1978. Management science, natural resources and environmental policy, university performance evaluation and measurement.

Kenneth R. Richards, J.D./Ph.D., Pennsylvania, 1997. Environmental policy implementation, global climate change economics, integration of technology development and environmental policy.

Marc A. Rodwin, Ph.D., Brandeis, 1991, J.D., Virginia, 1982. Health policy, health law.

Barry M. Rubin, Ph.D., Wisconsin, 1977. Urban and regional planning, analytical methods.

Richard S. Rubin, Ph.D., Cornell, 1973. Public sector labor-management relations.

Philip J. Rutledge, LL.D., Indiana, 1980. International development, public administration, employment policy.

John W. Ryan, Ph.D., Indiana, 1959. Comparative public policy analysis, comparative university organization/policy, general public administration.

Roy W. Shin, Ph.D., Minnesota, 1960. Political economy, international economic development and trade.

Philip S. Stevens, Ph.D., Harvard, 1990. Atmospheric chemistry, kinetics and mechanisms.

Ming Tai-Seale, Ph.D., UCLA, 1995. Health economics, health services research, physician behavior, managed care.

Mary Tschirhart, Ph.D., Michigan, 1993. Public and nonprofit management, organizational behavior and theory.

Frank J. Vilardo, Dr.P.H., North Carolina, 1971. Health administration and policy, public safety policy.

Gerry Wedig, Ph.D., Harvard, 1987. Economics.

Jeffrey R. White, Ph.D., Syracuse, 1984. Environmental biogeochemistry, aquatic chemistry, limnology.

Daniel E. Willard, Ph.D., California at Davis, 1966. Wetlands ecology and regulation, natural history, environmental policy.

York Y. Wilbern, Ph.D., Texas, 1943. Public policy and administration, urban government.

Charles R. Wise, Ph.D., Indiana, 1972. Public law, U.S. Congress, democratic transitions, and public management.

Lois R. Wise, Ph.D., Indiana, 1982. Employment policy, human resource management, public/private sector management reform.

C. Kurt Zorn, Ph.D., Syracuse, 1981. Public finance, applied economics, transportation safety.

MONTEREY INSTITUTE OF INTERNATIONAL STUDIES

M.A. in International Environmental Policy Studies

Programs of Study
The Master of Arts in International Environmental Policy (M.A.I.E.P.) responds to the growing need for policymakers to address environmental issues in government, intergovernmental organizations, nonprofit issue-oriented groups, and business. The curriculum includes courses in policy analysis, environmental law and organizations, environmental and resource economics, and data analysis. Admission to this degree does not assume prior environmental studies, and one of the core courses surveys the scientific foundations of international environmental policy; this course may be waived for those with prior study in environmental science.

Electives include courses on energy, sustainable development, comparative national environmental policy, and the export of environmental hazards. Other electives may be chosen from any of the courses offered by the Graduate School of International Policy Studies, from advanced languages classes beyond those required, or from courses in the Graduate School of International Business.

The Monterey Bay region is a world-renowned center of marine environmental research, and the M.A.I.E.P. curriculum includes courses on the state of the oceans and oceans policy.

Like all degrees in the Graduate School of International Policy Studies, the two-year M.A.I.E.P. includes an advanced foreign language component that emphasizes integrating the language and professional studies. While the base language of instruction at the Institute is English, selected policy courses are offered in other languages when staffing permits. Languages offered for nonnative speakers are Arabic, English, French, German, Japanese, Mandarin Chinese, Russian, and Spanish. Students without at least four semesters of instruction in the foreign language they intend to use as part of their graduate studies may gain this proficiency through the Institute's Summer Intensive Language program, either before entering the degree program or in the summer between the first and second years.

Internships provide relevant work experience and are an important bridge to a career. The Graduate School of International Policy Studies has an internship coordinator to help students identify appropriate internship opportunities. Recent locations where internships were undertaken in the environmental field include the White House Environmental Office, the International Environmental Affairs Bureau of the National Oceans and Atmospheric Administration in Washington, D.C., the United Nations Institute for Training and Research in Geneva, the Rainforest Action Network in San Francisco, the Monterey Bay National Marine Sanctuary in Monterey, and the Charles Darwin Foundation, Galapagos Islands, Ecuador.

Research Facilities
The Monterey Institute's specialized international library has a collection of 68,000 carefully selected volumes and 550 periodical titles, about one third in languages other than English, and offers CD-ROM workstations. DOS-based and Macintosh microcomputer laboratories are available for course-related computing; they also offer workshops and individualized assistance.

Internships and research opportunities are available through the Institute's centers for Russian and Eurasian studies, for nonproliferation studies, for East Asian studies, and for international trade. Internships and advanced language study are also available through the Institute's summer programs in China, France, Germany, Mexico, and Russia.

Financial Aid
The Institute makes every effort to provide need-based, federally funded financial aid to U.S. citizens and eligible noncitizens. Approximately three quarters of the students receive some form of aid, usually a combination of grants, loans, and work opportunities. In addition, the Institute awards competitive merit-based scholarships to both U.S. citizens and international students. Scholarships are awarded to former participants of university-accredited study abroad programs, overseas volunteer programs, high school exchange programs, Concordia Language Villages, the Japanese Exchange and Teaching (JET) program, and the U.S. Peace Corps. Scholarships are also awarded in recognition of the academic achievements of international students, international employment experience, and Phi Beta Kappa membership. Minority scholarships are available to U.S. citizens.

Cost of Study
Fees for 1999–2000 are $9375 per semester (two semesters per academic year).

Living and Housing Costs
In 1999–2000, the average amount for off-campus housing is $465 per month, typically in a room in a nearby private house or a shared apartment. Total housing and living expenses are estimated at $7680 for the nine-month academic year.

Student Group
About half of the Institute's 800 students represent more than fifty countries, and almost all U.S. students have lived, worked, or studied abroad. Students share a multidisciplinary experience in course work and social activities. Monterey alumni form a worldwide network for professional and social contacts.

Location
The Monterey Institute is situated in one of the most spectacular natural environments in the world. The Monterey Peninsula is 130 miles south of San Francisco on California's central coast, surrounded by ocean and mountains; it has a population of 100,000. The area combines a variety of rich cultural resources and recreational activities.

The Institute
Founded in 1955, the Monterey Institute has maintained its character as a tightly knit cosmopolitan community. Its relatively small size creates a sense of intimacy and cohesion between students and faculty members, who encourage lively classroom interaction. The Institute is accredited by the Western Association of Schools and Colleges.

Applying
Applicants to the master's programs in the Graduate School of International Policy Studies must have a U.S. bachelor's degree or the equivalent, with a minimum grade point average of 3.0 on a 4.0 scale. Application may be made at any time, provided it is received at least one month prior to the applicant's proposed semester of enrollment, or three months in advance for international students residing in their home countries. There is no application deadline for most forms of financial aid; however, applications for California grants and fellowships (residents only) or for Monterey Institute scholarships must be submitted by the published March deadline. Nonnative English speakers must submit a minimum TOEFL score of 550 or enhance their language skills at the Institute's Intensive English as a Second Language Program. Other entering students ordinarily must have completed a minimum of two years of recent university courses in their second language to meet the Institute's entrance requirements. Students may develop or enhance language skills at the Institute's Summer Intensive Language Program.

Correspondence and Information
Admissions Office
Monterey Institute of International Studies
425 Van Buren Street
Monterey, California 93940
Telephone: 831-647-4123
  800-824-7235 (toll-free within the United States)
Fax: 831-647-6405
E-mail: admit@miis.edu
World Wide Web: http://www.miis.edu

Monterey Institute of International Studies

THE FACULTY AND THEIR RESEARCH

The faculty is made up of 65 full-time members who bring to the Institute a combination of superior academic credentials and professional experience in their respective fields; it is augmented by 70 part-time members who offer special professional expertise in the areas of business, government, languages, and education. The student-faculty ratio is 12:1, but the size of classes varies widely by program. Although primary emphasis is placed on teaching, faculty members are expected and encouraged to maintain research agendas and to publish or consult in their fields. The full-time faculty members of the Graduate School of International Policy Studies are listed below.

Jackson Davis, Professor and International Environmental Policy Program Head; Ph.D. (biology), Oregon. Dr. Davis holds a joint appointment at the Monterey Institute and as professor of biology and environmental studies, University of California, Santa Cruz. He has held postdoctoral appointments in neuroscience at the University of Oregon, Stanford, and the National Institutes of Health, and he is the author of dozens of scientific works on marine biology. For more than a decade, Dr. Davis has been an adviser to governments of Pacific island nations on international marine policy issues. He is currently Scientific Advisor and Delegate of the Republic of Nauru to the London Dumping Convention, U.N. Maritime Organization, London; South Pacific Forum, U.N. Alliance of Small Island States; U.N. Group of 77; and Framework Convention on Climate Change. He is the director of the Monterey Institute's Project OCEANS, a computerized policy and scientific data bank on the state of the marine environment.

Laura Strohm, Assistant Professor; Ph.D. (international environmental policy), Tufts (Fletcher). Dr. Strohm has taught at the School of Public and Environmental Affairs, Indiana University. She has worked for the U.S. Soil Conservation Service and was a researcher for the International Union for the Conservation of Nature in Geneva, Switzerland.

Steven J. Baker, Provost and Associate Professor; Ph.D. (political science), UCLA. Dr. Baker also has an M.Sc. from the London School of Economics and was a Fulbright Fellow in Rome. He was a research associate in the Peace Studies Program at Cornell and in the Program for Science and International Affairs at Harvard. He has been a consultant to the RAND Corporation and was foreign policy adviser to Senate Majority Leader Robert C. Byrd. Dr. Baker has taught at the University of Texas and at the Institute for International Studies and Training in Fujinomiya, Japan.

Tsuneo Akaha, Professor and Director, Center for East Asian Studies; Ph.D. (political science), USC. A native of Japan, Dr. Akaha has undergraduate degrees from Oregon State University and Waseda University in Tokyo. He has been a professor in the Department of Political Science at Bowling Green State University, where he was Director of the Asian Studies Program. He was also a Senior Fulbright Fellow at Seikei University in Tokyo and Tokyo University.

Jan Knippers Black, Associate Professor; Ph.D. (international studies), American. Dr. Black was previously a research professor in the Division of Public Administration, University of New Mexico. She has held visiting positions with George Mason University and with the University of Pittsburgh's Semester-at-Sea Program.

Stephen Garrett, Professor; Ph.D. (political science), Virginia. Dr. Garrett has previously taught at the University of Virginia and the American University of Beirut. He spent academic year 1978–79 in Bangkok, Thailand, as a senior lecturer on a Fulbright Fellowship and was appointed to the Gordon Paul Smith Chair of International Policy Studies in 1988–89.

Gil Gunderson, Associate Professor; Ph.D., Berkeley. Dr. Gunderson has taught at California State University at Northridge, the University of Guam, Boston University (in Germany), and the American University of Beirut. He served as a Peace Corps volunteer in Nigeria. He did field research for his dissertation in Botswana and has served as a consultant to the governments of Northern Nigeria and Qatar.

Nuket Kardam, Associate Professor and M.P.A. Program Head; Ph.D. (political science), Michigan State. Dr. Kardam previously taught at Pomona College. She has served as a consultant to the UN office in Vienna, Division for Advancement of Women; for UNICEF on projects on women's education and employment in Turkey; and for the World Bank.

Edward J. Laurance, Professor and Associate Director, Program for Nonproliferation Studies; Ph.D. (international relations), Pennsylvania. Dr. Laurance taught at the Naval Postgraduate School and was a visiting professor at the University of California, Davis. He has served as a special assistant to the Chief, Arms Transfer Division, the U.S. Arms Control and Disarmament Agency and has testified twice before Congress on U.S. arms transfer policy. He was the study director for the Rockefeller Foundation's Arms Trade Project and is a consultant to the United Nation's Department of Disarmament Affairs. He is codirector of the Institute's International Missile Proliferation Project.

Beryl Levinger, Distinguished Professor of Nonprofit Management; Ph.D. (educational planning), Alabama. Dr. Levinger did her undergraduate studies at Cornell University, and she has previously taught at Teachers College, Columbia University. Until 1992, Dr. Levinger was president of AFS Intercultural Programs, the world's largest private educational exchange program. Before going to AFS, she served as the deputy executive director of CARE, the world's largest private international relief and development organization. Dr. Levinger has served on U.S. delegations to the Organization of Economic Cooperation and Development and has undertaken studies for UNESCO and USAID.

E. Philip Morgan, Dean; Ph.D. (political science), Syracuse. International public administration, African development management, comparative public policy. Dean Morgan was a faculty member and director of undergraduate programs of the School of Public and Environmental Affairs at Indiana University. He served as associate dean of Indiana University's international programs and was director of Indiana University's overseas study program. He was a Fulbright Lecturer at the Institute of Development Management, University of Botswana. In 1992–93, he was coordinator of the World Bank's Regional Research Program on Indigenous Institutions and Management Practices in Africa. Dean Morgan has published widely in the areas of program and project management, comparative civil service systems and reforms, and the linkages between development policy formation and the instruments of policy action. He serves on the editorial advisory boards of several journals (e.g., *Public Administration and Development (UK)* and the *Journal of African Public Policy*) and publishing firms specializing in international development policy and management. (E-mail: pmorgan@miis.edu)

Robert McCleery, Professor; Ph.D. (economics), Stanford. International economics, trade, Asia and Latin America. International experiences include consulting for the Institute for Developing Economics in Tokyo, the International Center for Economic Growth in Osak, and USAID in Jakarta. Before coming to the Monterey Institute, Professor McCleery was a visiting associate professor at Claremont McKenna and an associate professor at Kobe University's Research Institute for Economics and Business Administration. In addition, he has served as a post-doctoral researcher at Stanford and as a research associate for the East-West Center Development Policy Program. Among his many published articles, he has authored *The Dynamics of Integration in the Americas: A Look at the Political Economy of NAFTA Expansion, Relevance of Asian Development Experiences to African Development Problems, Economic Policy Reform: A Latin American Perspective,* and *On Continuing Economic Growth in Developing Asia: Is Human Resource Development the Key to the "Pacific Century?".*

William Potter, Professor and Director, Center for Russian and Eurasian Studies and the Center for Nonproliferation Studies; Ph.D. (political science), Michigan. Dr. Potter has worked for the Center of International and Strategic Affairs at UCLA.

Moyara de Moraes Ruehsen, Assistant Professor; Ph.D. (international economics and Middle Eastern studies), Johns Hopkins. Dr. Ruehsen has taught at the University of California, Berkeley, University of San Francisco, Johns Hopkins University, and the Foreign Service Institute. She was a Fulbright scholar in Bahrain.

Glynn Wood, Professor; Ph.D. (political science), MIT. Dr. Wood has an M.A. in journalism from Stanford, was previously on the faculty of American University in Washington, D.C., and for two years was Dean of the School of Government and Public Administration there. He has been actively involved with the South Asia Division of the State Department's Foreign Service Institute as consultant and lecturer. He served with USIA as a cultural affairs officer with postings to Beirut, Kabul, and Bangalore, India. His primary research interests have focused on South Asia.

OREGON GRADUATE INSTITUTE OF SCIENCE & TECHNOLOGY

Department of Environmental Science and Engineering

Programs of Study	The Department of Environmental Science and Engineering offers graduate study leading to the degrees of Master of Science (M.S.) (nonthesis and thesis) and Doctor of Philosophy (Ph.D.). The nonthesis M.S. program can be completed in twelve months, and the Environmental Systems Management (ESM) program can be completed in eighteen months. Students are accepted into the M.S. thesis option on a space-available basis, and the program takes approximately two years to complete. The Ph.D. program is research-oriented and generally takes four to five years to complete.
	The department currently consists of 9 full-time faculty members. The department's low student-faculty ratio (about 2.5:1) allows for close interaction with faculty members and personal attention from research advisers. Faculty members are very active in grant-supported research in the areas listed below, and the courses they teach are highly relevant to modern environmental science and engineering. The department offers interdisciplinary educational programs that successfully prepare graduates for work in industry or government or for the pursuit of further work in academia. The ESM program combines training in environmental science with innovative instruction in the management of technology. The newest educational program, Ecosystem Management and Restoration, integrates rigorous environmental science principles, laboratory and field applications, modeling, toxicology, project management, and policy/regulation into a cohesive curriculum.
	The areas in which the department has notable concentrations of expertise include groundwater hydrology and geochemistry, aquatic chemistry of organic and inorganic pollutants, estuarine and coastal hydrodynamics, environmental microbiology, trace organic analysis of air and water, and nutrient cycling in soils, water, and watersheds. In each area, the department strives to maintain a balance between the pursuit of new knowledge about the environment and the development of practical tools for solving recognized environmental problems.
Research Facilities	The department operates modern, well-equipped laboratories. A partial list of the equipment available for student use includes gas chromatograph/mass spectrometers; high-resolution mass spectrometers; state-of-the-art capillary gas chromatographs with flame ionization, electron capture, thermal conductivity, and photoionization detectors; high-pressure/high-performance liquid chromatographs; and ion chromatographs. Students and faculty members have access to a wide variety of computers that are interconnected through a campuswide local area network. This makes available powerful facilities for scientific computing, online text and document processing, and national and international electronic mail communications. Access to supercomputers is available through NorthWestNet.
	Two research centers are housed in the department. The Center for Groundwater Research (CGR) is a multidisciplinary group of scientists that conducts research on important issues related to groundwater quality and quantity. CGR operates a variety of large experimental aquifers, unlike any in the world, in which contaminant migration in groundwater can be studied in a completely controlled environment at very nearly field scale. The Center for Coastal and Land-Margin Research is dedicated to regional scale and interdisciplinary research and its applications to ecosystems at the margins of the land and the sea. Advanced modeling and scientific visualization techniques are used to integrate process-oriented research on the physics, chemistry, and biology of land-margin ecosystems.
Financial Aid	Tuition scholarships, research assistantships, and teaching assistantships are available on a competitive basis for M.S. and Ph.D. students. The Institute provides guidance for students who wish to secure external fellowships or student loans.
Cost of Study	Tuition for 1999–2000 is $4465 per academic quarter (full-time) or $495 per credit hour (part-time). The total tuition cost of the one-year nonthesis M.S. degree is $17,860. Books cost approximately $500 for one year. Because the M.S. degree can be completed in one year, students can enter the workforce quickly, lose less work income, and gain more valuable work experience.
Living and Housing Costs	A variety of off-campus housing is available nearby. All graduate students live off campus, and most share rent with other students. Monthly rent for off-campus apartments ranges from $550 to $850.
Student Group	The department currently has 20 full-time students (11 women), 4 part-time students, and 1 international student pursuing M.S. and Ph.D. degrees. The department attracts students from across the United States, Europe, East Asia, and India. Students enjoy a high degree of interdisciplinary professional and social interaction.
Student Outcomes	Recent graduates have been highly successful in finding employment. To date, the M.S. program has 150 graduates, most of whom work at the various major environmental firms throughout the country and at government agencies. Most of the 34 Ph.D. graduates are now faculty members; scientists at laboratories of the Environmental Protection Agency, U.S. Geological Survey, and Department of Energy; or environmental program managers at private, state, federal, and international agencies.
Location	The Oregon Graduate Institute (OGI) is located in the beautiful Pacific Northwest, which provides a very enjoyable setting for study. OGI is 12 miles west of downtown Portland and just 60 miles from the famous Oregon coast or from excellent downhill and cross-country skiing on Mount Hood. World-class windsurfing in the scenic Columbia River Gorge is also an easy drive from the campus. Olympic Mountains National Park is within a day's drive. Mount Rainier National Park, Crater Lake National Park, the rugged desert country of eastern Oregon, and the breathtaking redwood forests of northern California are at driving distances ranging from a few hours to one day.
The Institute	OGI is a private, graduate-only technical university dedicated to contemporary scientific research and education. Founded in 1963, OGI combines the vigorous research emphasis of a large university with the personal interaction and collaborative characteristics of a small research institution.
	The graduate enrollment is more than 350, including both part-time and full-time degree-seeking students. In addition to environmental science and engineering, degree programs are offered in computer science and engineering, electrical and computer engineering, materials science and engineering, biochemistry and molecular biology, management in science and technology, and computational finance.
Applying	M.S. applications are considered year-round, but applications received before June 15 are given priority consideration. Ph.D. applications should be received by February 15. Required admissions materials for M.S. and Ph.D. applicants include three letters of recommendation, transcripts, and a statement of purpose. The GRE general test is required for Ph.D. applicants and is highly recommended for M.S. applicants. The OGI institutional code for the GRE is 4592. Applicants whose native language is not English must submit a minimum TOEFL score of 600. The TOEFL requirement may be waived if the student has previously received a degree in the United States.
Correspondence and Information	Admissions Office of Academic and Student Services Oregon Graduate Institute P.O. Box 91000 Portland, Oregon 97291-1000 Telephone: 503-748-1027 800-685-2423 (toll-free) E-mail: admissions@admin.ogi.edu World Wide Web: http://www.ogi.edu http://www.ese.ogi.edu/

Oregon Graduate Institute of Science & Technology

THE FACULTY AND THEIR RESEARCH

James F. Pankow, Professor and Department Head; Ph.D., Caltech, 1978. Physical and analytical chemistry of trace organics and metals in natural water and the atmosphere, fates of organic and inorganic compounds in the environment.

António M. Baptista, Associate Professor; Ph.D., MIT, 1987. Integrated analysis of estuarine and coastal processes, land-water interactions, numerical modeling, and scientific visualization.

Robert L. Doneker, Assistant Professor; Ph.D., Cornell, 1989. Development of decision support systems and simulation models for water resource systems.

James J. Huntzicker, Professor (part-time), Senior Vice President, and Provost; Ph.D., Berkeley, 1968. Atmospheric chemistry, gas to particle conversion, carbonaceous and sulfate aerosols, urban air pollution, instrument development.

Wesley M. Jarrell, Professor; Ph.D., Oregon State, 1977. Bioavailability of nutrient and non-nutrient elements in soils, biogeochemical cycles in natural and distributed ecosystems, development and function of plant root systems, restoration of terrestrial and aquatic ecosystems.

David A. Jay, Associate Professor; Ph.D., Washington (Seattle), 1987. Circulation and transport in stratified estuarine waters and the role of physical processes in coastal ecosystems (through observational and theoretical studies); specific interests include tides, waves, turbulence, and mixing.

Richard L. Johnson, Associate Professor; Ph.D., Oregon Graduate Center, 1985. Physical and chemical behavior of organic contaminants in the air, soil, and water; groundwater transport; fate and modeling of contaminants in porous media.

Reinhold A. Rasmussen, Professor; Ph.D., Washington (St. Louis), 1964. Measurement of trace gases, including the chlorofluorocarbons and their replacement HCFCs and HFCs, methane, nitrous oxide, carbon monoxide, hydrogen, carbonyl sulfide, and the C_2-C_{15} hydrocarbons, both biogenic isoprene-terpenoids and anthropogenic air toxic emissions of other VOCs, and their roles in stratospheric ozone destruction, greenhouse effect, and regional ozone formation.

Patricia L. Toccalino, Assistant Professor; Ph.D., Oregon Graduate Institute of Science and Technology, 1992. Hydrocarbon biodegradation in soil and water, transport processes, human and ecological risk assessments.

Paul G. Tratnyek, Assistant Professor; Ph.D., Colorado School of Mines, 1987. Kinetics of reactions that degrade organic pollutants in the natural environment and in remediation or waste-treatment technologies; chemical, microbiological, and photochemical oxidation-reduction reactions of pesticides, phenols, and chlorinated hydrocarbons.

The OGI campus and Science Park share a beautiful natural setting.

A pilot-scale project using a permeable barrier containing surfactant-modified zeolite (SMZ) to remediate groundwater contamination. The permeable barrier is in a synthetic aquifer at the Large Experimental Aquifer Program (LEAP) site at OGI.

PACE UNIVERSITY

Dyson College of Arts and Sciences
Master of Science in Environmental Science

Program of Study	The Departments of Biological Sciences and of Chemistry and Physical Sciences offer the Master of Science in Environmental Science degree program. This 39-credit multidisciplinary program responds to the need for professionals with the strong academic background and practical scientific skills required to address the environmental challenges facing the global community.
Research Facilities	Extensive library facilities are available at Pace University. Holdings total approximately 825,000 volumes and 4,000 serial publications. The Dyson Hall of Science in Pleasantville, New York, is a modern facility of nearly 20,000 square feet, which includes environmental instrumentation and aquatic ecology laboratories. Laboratory and field equipment for ecological research includes a research boat. An FT-NMR and an HPLC, GC-M5 are available for analytical research. Biomolecular instrumentation includes DGGE and PCR technology, a fluorescence microscope, and higher temperature incubators. The use of computer hardware, software, and state-of-the-art instrumentation is an integral and necessary component of this degree program. Molecular and environmental modeling, data acquisition, manipulation, data reduction, and analysis representations are essential tools in most, if not all, of the courses in the program. Currently, there are eighty mainframe terminals (3170/3270), 200 IBM microcomputers (486 and Pentium IIs), and thirty-five Macintosh microcomputers available to the students, faculty, and staff in the computer labs and classrooms of the New York and Westchester campuses. An IBM RISC 6000 running AIX is connected to the Pace network.
Financial Aid	A number of graduate scholarships are available. Awards are made on the basis of outstanding academic performance, as indicated by the applicant's previous college record and standardized test scores. In addition, several deferred payment plans and loan programs are available. For further information, students should contact the Financial Aid Office, Pace University, Bedford Road, Pleasantville, New York 10573 (telephone: 914-773-3751).
Cost of Study	Tuition for graduate courses is $545 per credit for 1999–2000.
Living and Housing Costs	Dormitory rooms cost $4720 for a double room and $5350 for a single room for the 1999–2000 academic year. A variety of housing is available in the area for students who choose to live off campus.
Student Group	The M.S. in Environmental Science Program seeks to enroll highly motivated individuals who wish to pursue graduate education to advance their careers or who wish to enter such fields as environmental research (at nonprofit foundations, corporations, government research centers, and universities), environmental services (testing, analysis, field assessment, mitigation, waste management, reduction, and transportation), and environmental management systems (policy implementation, monitoring, compliance, enforcement, and industrial hygiene).
Location	The suburban Pleasantville/Briarcliff Campus in Westchester County, New York, is accessible by car, bus, and commuter railroad. It is surrounded by towns and villages that have gifted resident artisans, local musical and theatrical groups, and rural museums. New York City is easily accessible from Pleasantville by bus, train, or car.
The University	Founded in 1906, Pace University is a private, nonsectarian, coeducational institution. It has multiple campuses in Manhattan and Westchester County, New York. In 1948, Pace Institute became Pace College; in 1973 the New York Board of Regents approved a charter change to designate Pace a university.
Applying	Admission to the M.S. in Environmental Science Program requires satisfactory completion of a baccalaureate degree from an accredited institution. An undergraduate major in science is not required, but preparation should include one year of course work in each of the following areas: general biology, general chemistry, organic chemistry, physics, and calculus. One semester in statistics is also encouraged. A completed application includes two letters of reference, an essay, official college transcripts, and an official score report indicating satisfactory performance on the GRE General Test.
	Applications are processed throughout the year. Applicants are urged to submit all materials by August 1 for the fall semester, December 1 for the spring semester, and May 1 for the summer sessions.
Correspondence and Information	Master of Science in Environmental Science Office of Graduate Admission Pace University 1 Martine Avenue White Plains, New York 10606 Telephone: 914-422-4283 Fax: 914-422-4287 E-mail: gradwp@pace.edu World Wide Web: http://www.pace.edu/dyson/environment/masters.htm

Pace University

THE FACULTY

Carl Candiloro, Professor of Biological Sciences; Ph.D., St. John's (New York). Biotechnology.
James Cannon, Professor of Physics; Ph.D., Fordham. Energy.
Robert Chapman, Associate Professor of Philosophy; Ph.D., Fordham. Environmental ethics.
David N. Rahni, Professor of Chemistry and Physical Sciences; Ph.D., New Orleans. Environmental chemistry.
Anthony Salotto, Professor and Chair of Chemistry and Physical Sciences; Ph.D., NYU. Environmental chromatography.
Ellen Weiser, Professor of Chemistry and Physical Sciences; Ph.D., CUNY Graduate School. Environmental biochemistry.

PORTLAND STATE UNIVERSITY

Program in Environmental Sciences and Resources

Programs of Study
The Program in Environmental Sciences and Resources (ESR) focuses on basic problems in environmental science and environmental management. The program combines training in disciplinary areas with education in environmental science and management that is directed towards significant problems. Students may also participate in a joint campus graduate program with Oregon State University and the University of Oregon.

The program offers master's degrees in environmental science (M.S.), environmental management (M.E.M.), and environmental education (M.S.T.) and the Ph.D. degree in environmental sciences and resources, in cooperation with the departments of biology, chemistry, civil engineering, economics, geography, geology, and physics. Individual departments also offer discipline-oriented master's degrees. ESR also offers a graduate certificate in hydrology.

All students in the program take core courses in environmental sciences and resources, attend ESR seminars, and are required to develop a knowledge of statistics. In addition, departments provide further courses and guidance. An appropriate course of study is developed by the student and the adviser and is approved by the student advisory committee.

The program is recommended for students interested in science-related careers in environmental, energy, and resource-related fields in government, industry, and educational institutions.

Research Facilities
Research laboratories and offices are located in several buildings on the downtown Portland State campus. Laboratories are equipped with a wide variety of special instruments interfaced with laboratory microcomputers. Some labs include Sun workstation networks with GIS and environmental modeling capabilities. Facilities include greenhouses, electron microscopes, ultracentrifuges, liquid scintillation counters, spectrophotometers, NMR spectrometers, gas chromatograph and HPLC equipment, growth facilities for animals and microorganisms and biotechnology research, and equipment for DNA analysis and sequencing. Specialty equipment includes X-ray diffractometers, atomic absorption spectrometers, field geophysical instrumentation, a BET surface area analyzer, instrumentation for trace-element analysis, a ballistic compressor for research on corrosive environments, equipment for studies at low temperatures, instrumentation for studying the temperature control and behavioral response of animals, neurophysiological instrumentation, and biophysical instrumentation for pharmacological and toxicological studies on biomembranes at the molecular level. Field ecosystem sampling and monitoring equipment includes flow and field meters, TDR instruments, GPS units, and total surveying stations. Support facilities include minicomputers and several local area networks, as well as machine and electronic shops staffed by highly qualified personnel experienced in the design, fabrication, and repair of research instruments.

Financial Aid
Graduate teaching and research assistantships are available. These carry a stipend and a tuition waiver. The stipend range is $6000 to $12,000, depending upon the academic accomplishment of the applicant and the type of assistantship.

Cost of Study
For 1998–99, tuition and fees for full-time graduate students were $1729 per term for Oregon residents and $2873 per term for nonresidents, but this cost is offset by tuition waivers for teaching assistants and research assistants.

Living and Housing Costs
Living costs for a single student, excluding tuition and books, are estimated at $8845 for twelve months. Books and supplies are estimated at $695. University housing is available and includes a mix of studio and one- and two-bedroom units.

Student Group
Portland State University enrolls approximately 15,000 students, of whom nearly 4,000 are in various graduate programs. The current enrollment in the Program in Environmental Sciences and Resources includes 35 master's and 42 doctoral students. More than 65 Ph.D. degrees have been granted over the past twenty years. The student group is diverse and includes full-time and part-time students, which includes students drawn from the local professional community.

Student Outcomes
Graduates are employed in a wide variety of academic, government, and private-sector positions ranging from environmental consulting to science positions in agencies, colleges, and universities.

Location
The center of the largest metropolitan area in Oregon (with a population of 1.4 million), Portland is the center for high-technology (mostly microelectronic) industries in the state, and it is becoming a hub of trade and cultural exchange for countries of the Pacific Rim. Downtown Portland offers a variety of theaters, symphony concerts, ballet, and opera, as well as fine restaurants and city cafés, all within walking distance of the University. Mount St. Helens, Mount Hood, and ocean beaches are all within a 70-mile radius and offer excellent skiing, climbing, hiking, and other outdoor activities.

The University
Portland State University, located in the fifty-block university district, has more than forty academic departments and more than 750 faculty members. The major buildings on campus have been constructed since the University received its charter as a degree-granting institution in 1955.

Applying
Master's degree students should obtain application materials from the ESR program office, which can also supply information about advisers and project and research opportunities. Ph.D. students can obtain specific departmental requirements and information by contacting the department with which they wish to be affiliated (Biology, Chemistry, Civil Engineering, Economics, Geography, Geology, or Physics) at the address below. The department will review the application and make recommendations for admission.

Correspondence and Information
For application materials and general information aboout the program:

Director
Environmental Sciences and Resources (ESR)
Portland State University
P.O. Box 751
Portland, Oregon 97207-0751
Telephone: 503-725-4980
         800-547-8887 Ext. 4980 (toll-free)
Fax: 503-725-3888
E-mail: envir@pdx.edu
World Wide Web: http://www.esr.pdx.edu

Portland State University

THE FACULTY AND AREAS OF RESEARCH

Environmental Sciences and Resources (Telephone: 503-725-4980)

*James R. Pratt, Professor and Director. Microbial ecology, use of microbial communities as environmental monitors, protozoology.

Nancy J. Bowers, Adjunct Assistant Professor. Molecular systematics and evolution, freshwater fish ecology and systematics.

*William Fish, Associate Professor. Water and sediment quality chemistry, fate and transport of contaminants in aqueous environments.

*Roy W. Koch, Professor. Hydrologic modeling and water resources management.

Joseph Maser, Adjunct Assistant Professor. Wetland ecology, impact assessment.

Rudi Nussbaum, Professor Emeritus. Health effects of low doses of ionizing radiation.

*Song Qian, Assistant Professor. Environmental statistics, water quality modeling and management.

*Yangdong Pan, Assistant Professor. Stream ecology, biological indicators, ecology of freshwater algae.

Martha Shearer, Research Associate. Global environmental change, atmospheric physics and chemistry.

Shanru Wang, Research Associate. Interaction of contaminants with membranes.

*J. Alan Yeakley, Assistant Professor. Soil moisture in heterogeneous terrain, riparian nutrient flux, watershed analysis.

Biology (Telephone: 503-725-3851)
Environmental biology group

David Boone, Professor. Microbial ecology of oxygen-free environments, methane-producing prokaryotes.

Clyde L. Calvin, Professor Emeritus. Morphology, systematics and evolution of parasitic angiosperms.

M. Carol Carter, Assistant Professor. Genetic diversity within and between natural and exotic populations of plants, fungi, and insects.

Robert L. Millette, Professor. Regulation of viral and cellular gene expression by herpes simplex viruses.

Yijun Pang, Adjunct Assistant Professor. Emerging infectious diseases, molecular microbiology.

*Richard R. Petersen, Professor. Aquatic ecology and limnology, planktonic primary productivity.

Anna Louise Reysenbach, Assistant Professor. Microbial ecology of extreme environments, such as hot springs.

John G. Rueter, Professor. Trace metal nutrition and toxicity in aquatic plants, cyanobacterial physiology.

Trygve P. Steen, Professor. Developmental biology, environmental biology of old growth forests.

*Mark D. Sytsma, Adjunct Assistant Professor. Lake management, management of nonindigenous species.

Mary L. Taylor, Professor Emeritus. Microbiology, detoxification of heavy metals.

Carol Wilson, Assistant Professor. Plant systematics and evolution.

Organismal biology group

Stanley S. Hillman, Professor and Chair. Environmental physiology of amphibians and reptiles.

Larry I. Crawshaw, Professor. Temperature regulation: comparative physiology, ethanol effects, genetic basis.

Deborah Duffield, Professor. Comparative cytogenetic, protein, and DNA analysis of population structure in whales and dolphins.

*Richard B. Forbes, Professor. Ecological studies of terrestrial vertebrates, especially mammals.

Curt Gamperl, Assistant Professor. Environmental effects on cardiac and performance physiology in fishes and amphibians.

Lester J. Newman, Professor. Polytene chromosome analysis of the marine midges, *Telmatogeton* and *Paraclunio*.

Leonard Simpson, Professor Emeritus. Invertebrate zoology, comparative physiology of invertebrates.

Robert O. Tinnin, Professor. Structure of urban woodland vegetation, ecology of plant parasites.

Randy D. Zelick, Professor. Neural basis of animal behavior.

Chemistry (Telephone: 503-725-3811)

David McClure, Professor and Chair. Computational chemistry.

Dean Atkinson, Assistant Professor. Chemical kinetics and atmospheric monitoring, cavity ring-down spectroscopy.

Dennis W. Barnum, Professor. Geochemical processes in natural waters and soils.

Gary L. Gard, Professor. New environmentally compatible fluorinated material with improved properties.

Bryant A. Gilbert, Assistant Professor. Molecular mechanisms in signal transduction and inhibitor design.

Thomas M. Hard, Research Associate. Atmospheric chemistry, photochemical kinetics of tropospheric free radicals.

Dirk Iwata-Reuyl, Assistant Professor. Chemistry and enzymology of RNA modification.

*Jie Lin, Assistant Professor. Near-IR spectroscopy, laser-induced fluorescence spectroscopy and environmental applications.

*Robert J. O'Brien, Professor. Chemistry of free radicals in clean and polluted air.

David H. Peyton, Associate Professor. Biological structural interactions using NMR.

Carl C. Wamser, Professor. Solar energy conversion by artificial photosynthesis, photochemistry of polymeric porphyrins.

Mingdi Yan, Assistant Professor. Organic chemistry/materials science, use of organic and polymeric materials for molecular recognition.

Center for Science Education (Telephone: 503-725-4243)

*Marian Dresner, Assistant Professor. Environmental education.

Linda A. George, Assistant Professor. Atmospheric chemistry, transformations of nitrogen oxide species in the troposphere.

Julie Smith, Assistant Professor. Environmental education and science through community partnerships.

Civil Engineering (Telephone: 503-725-4282)

Franz N. Rad, Professor and Chair. Behavior of reinforced concrete structures.

Manouchehr Gorji, Associate Professor. Fiber-reinforced metal matrix composite materials.

B. Kent Lall, Professor. Traffic flow, analysis of traffic stream variables.

Shu-Guang Li, Assistant Professor. Simulation modeling of groundwater contamination.

Wendelin H. Mueller, Professor. Behavior of transmission structures.

Trevor D. Smith, Professor. Behavior of earth dams, dam collapse.

Scott A. Wells, Professor. Environmental fluid mechanics, surface water quality and hydrodynamic modeling.

Economics (Telephone: 503-725-3915)

Patricia Koss, Assistant Professor. Environmental regulation and policy design, antitrust legislation, energy conservation.

Geography (Telephone: 503-725-3916)

Daniel Johnson, Professor and Chair. Climatology.

*Teresa Bulman, Associate Professor. Water resource management, geography education.

*Joseph Poracsky, Associate Professor. Cartography, remote sensing, urban forestry.

Ric Vrana, Assistant Professor. Spatial analysis, geographic information systems.

Geology (Telephone: 503-725-3022)

Ansel G. Johnson, Professor and Chair. Field geophysics and groundwater.

Scott F. Burns, Associate Professor. Landslides, environmental geology (radon, soil radionuclides, heavy metals, trace elements in soils), soil geomorphology.

Sherry Cady, Assistant Professor. Biogeochemistry and astropaleobiology, biogenic signatures, ancient microbial ecosystems.

*Kenneth M. Cruikshank, Assistant Professor. Geomechanics, application of physical processes to geological phenomena.

*Michael L. Cummings, Professor. Relations among volcanism, sedimentation, regional structure, and hydrothermal activity.

*Curt D. Peterson, Associate Professor. Coastal and fluvial sediment budgets and quaternary stratigraphy.

Martin Streck, Assistant Professor. Igneous petrology and volcanology, evolution and eruption of magmas using field-based chemical and mineralogical data.

David G. Taylor, Adjunct Associate Professor. Mesozoic marine invertebrate faunas.

Physics (Telephone: 503-725-3812)

Erik Bodegom, Professor and Chair. Cryogenics, STM, chaos.

Jonathan J. Abramson, Professor. Molecular mechanisms of muscle action.

Carl G. Bachhuber, Associate Professor Emeritus. Physics of simple biological systems.

Laird C. Brodie, Professor Emeritus. Heat transfer and nucleation of cryogens.

John Dash, Professor Emeritus. Low-temperature nuclear reaction.

Donald G. Howard, Professor. Mossbauer spectroscopy, solid-state physics.

*M. Aslam Khan Khalil, Professor. Global environmental change, atmospheric physics and chemistry, global biogeochemical cycles.

Pui-Tak (Peter) Leung, Associate Professor. Surface physics, molecular fluorescence, optical sensing, near-field optics, optothermal processing.

Gertrude F. Rempfer, Professor Emerita. Electron optics, photoelectron microscopy.

Jack S. Semura, Professor. Thermodynamics, first-order liquid-vapor phase transitions.

*Pavel K. Smejtek, Professor. Adsorption of toxic chemicals on membranes, physicochemical origins of toxicity in membranes, scanning tunneling microscopy.

Jack C. Straton, Assistant Professor. Modern optics, electron microscopy, computational physics, and many-body theory.

Makoto Takeo, Professor Emeritus. Physical behavior of disperse systems.

*Master's program advisers

RENSSELAER POLYTECHNIC INSTITUTE

Ecological Economics, Values and Policy Program

Programs of Study

The professional Master of Science in Ecological Economics, Values and Policy (EEVP) Program is a 30- or 45-credit joint offering of the Departments of Economics and Science and Technology Studies. The program builds on Rensselaer's internationally recognized expertise and course offerings in the economic, political, social, cultural, and ethical implications and interactions of science, technology, environment, and society. A student can choose to add 15 credit hours of science and/or engineering to earn the equivalent of a minor in environmental science or engineering, for which a Certificate in Multidisciplinary Environmental Studies is awarded. EEVP is aimed at recent graduates and midcareer professionals in state and local government, secondary education, business, and the nonprofit sector who are looking to upgrade their skills, advance their careers, and solve pressing problems.

Research Facilities

Research is supported by Folsom Library, other Rensselaer libraries, and the Environmental Education Center. The Departments of Economics and Science and Technology Studies have extensive holdings, including books, periodicals, journals, videos, CD-ROMs, and serials, that are directly pertinent to the program. Rensselaer was listed as the fifth "most wired" campus in the U.S. in a recent survey. Dorm rooms have Internet connections, and there are numerous UNIX, Sun, Windows, and Mac workstations and PCs available for student use in several computer labs. There are also midsize and mainframe computers available at the Vorhees Computing Center. Rensselaer's award-winning Web presence gives EEVP students opportunities to learn HTML, Java, and other languages and skills necessary to design and create Web pages. Rensselaer has state-of-the-art science and engineering laboratories available in Walker Laboratory, the Jonsson Engineering Center, the Materials Research Center, the Center for Industrial Innovation, the Science Center, the Fresh Water Institute, and Cogswell Laboratory.

Financial Aid

Financial aid is available in the form of tuition scholarships, research and teaching assistantships, and Rensselaer Scholar fellowships, which carry stipends of $15,000 and a full tuition scholarship. Low-interest, deferred repayment graduate loans are also available to U.S. citizens with demonstrated need.

Cost of Study

Tuition for 1999–2000 is $665 per credit hour. Other fees amount to approximately $535 per semester. Books and supplies cost about $1700 per year.

Living and Housing Costs

The cost of rooms for single students in residence halls or apartments ranges from $3356 to $5298 for the 1999–2000 academic year. Family student housing, with a monthly rent of $592 to $720, is available.

Student Group

There are about 4,300 undergraduates and 1,750 graduate students representing all fifty states and more than eighty countries at Rensselaer.

Student Outcomes

Eighty-eight percent of Rensselaer's 1998 graduate students were hired after graduation, with starting salaries that averaged $56,259 for master's degree recipients and $57,000 to $75,000 for doctoral degree recipients.

Location

Rensselaer is situated on a scenic 260-acre hillside campus in Troy, New York, across the Hudson River from Albany. Troy's location provides students with a medium-sized community in which to live; an easy commute to Boston, New York, and Montreal; and some of the country's finest outdoor recreation sites, including Lake George, Lake Placid, and the Adirondack, Catskill, Berkshire, and Green Mountains. The Capital Region has one of the largest concentrations of academic institutions in the United States. Sixty thousands students attend fourteen area colleges and benefit from shared activities and courses.

The University

Founded in 1824 and the first American college to award degrees in engineering and science, Rensselaer today is accredited by the Middle States Association of Colleges and Schools and is a private, nonsectarian, coeducational university. Rensselaer has five schools—Architecture, Engineering, Management, Science, and Humanities and Social Sciences—that offer a total of ninety-eight graduate degrees in forty-seven fields.

Applying

Applications and all supporting credentials should be submitted well in advance of the preferred semester of entry to allow sufficient time for departmental review and processing. The application fee is $35. Since the first departmental awards are made in February and March for the next full academic year, applicants requesting aid are encouraged to submit all required credentials by February 1 to ensure consideration.

Correspondence and Information

For written information about graduate work:
Professor Steve Breyman, Director
Ecological Economics, Values and Policy Program
Department of Science and Technology Studies
Rensselaer Polytechnic Institute
110 8th Street
Troy, New York 12180-3590
Telephone: 518-276-8515
E-mail: breyms@rpi.edu
World Wide Web: http://www.rpi.edu/dept/sts/eevp

For applications and admissions information:
Director of Graduate Academic and Enrollment
    Services, Graduate Center
Rensselaer Polytechnic Institute
110 8th Street
Troy, New York 12180-3590
Telephone: 518-276-6789
E-mail: grad-services@rpi.edu
World Wide Web: http://www.rpi.edu

Rensselaer Polytechnic Institute

THE FACULTY AND THEIR RESEARCH

Steve Breyman, Assistant Professor of Political Science and Director of the Ecological Economics, Values and Policy Program; Ph.D., California, Santa Barbara. Environmentalism, environmental politics and policy, political economy.

Kim Fortun, Assistant Professor of Anthropology; Ph.D., Rice. Environment and culture, environment and health, globalization, Third World politics.

John Gowdy, Professor and Chair, Department of Economics; Ph.D., West Virginia. Ecological economics, technological change, environmental theory and policy, ecological valuation, evolutionary models.

David Hess, Professor of Anthropology and Director, Science and Society Program; Ph.D., Cornell. Medicine and society, theory, culture and society.

Linda Layne, Associate Professor of Anthropology; Ph.D., Cambridge. Environment and health, medicine, culture and society.

Sabine O'Hara, Assistant Professor and Graduate Director, Department of Economics; Ph.D., Göttingen (Germany). Ecological economics, social valuation.

Sal Restivo, Professor; Ph.D., Michigan State. Sociology of mind, mathematics, and physics; sociology of science and knowledge.

John Schumacher, Professor and Chair, Department of Science and Technology Studies; D.Phil., Oxford. Nature of inquiry, environmental ethics and philosophy, design.

Langdon Winner, Professor of Political Science and Graduate Director, Department of Science and Technology Studies; Ph.D., Berkeley. Political, technological, and environmental theory; design; political economy.

Edward J. Woodhouse, Associate Professor of Political Science; Ph.D., Yale. Decision making; science, technology, and environmental policy.

Selected Faculty Publications

Breyman, S. *Movement Genesis.*
   Why Movements Matter.
Fortun, K. *Advocating Bhopal.*
Gowdy, J. *Evolutionary Economics.*
Hess, D. *Can Bacteria Cause Cancer?*
   Science Studies: An Advanced Introduction.
   Science and Technology in a Multicultural World.
Layne, L. *Motherhood Lost: The Cultural Construction of Pregnancy Loss.*
   Home and Homeland.
   Knowledge and Society: Science, Technology, and Culture.
O'Hara, S. *Economics for Environmentalists.*
Restivo, S. *The Sociology of Mind.*
Schumacher, J. *Human Posture: The Nature of Inquiry.*
Winner, L. *Autonomous Technology.*
   The Whale and the Reactor.
Woodhouse, E. J. *Averting Catastrophe.*
   The Policy-Making Process.
   The Demise of Nuclear Power?

RENSSELAER POLYTECHNIC INSTITUTE

Program in Environmental Management and Policy

Program of Study	The Program in Environmental Management and Policy (EMAP) is a 45-credit Master of Science degree dedicated to training environmental managers. Established in 1991 within the Lally School of Management and Technology, EMAP explores the intersection between managerial practice, environmental technology, and public policy. As an applied program, EMAP combines course work in the technical dimensions of environmental strategy, with instruction in the planning, decision making, and regulatory skills required for effective policymaking and implementation in both the private and public sectors.
	The EMAP program is multidisciplinary, growing out of Rensselaer's long history of programs in environmental studies, the Freshwater Institute, research in groundwater systems, and Rensselaer's pioneering work in environmental engineering. This foundation, combined with course work in management and policy and four core integrative courses, allows students to focus on technical competencies and the managerial skills necessary for developing successful environmental strategy and implementing policy. Student research may include internships at a quarterly practitioner journal called *Corporate Environmental Strategy: The Journal of Environmental Leadership.*
	The aim of the program is to produce graduates with the dual competencies required to undertake a professional role in business, government or other organizations concerned with the environment, energy, and issues of sustainable development. The intent is to apply technical expertise and managerial training to find solutions to environmental problems in an efficient and cost-effective manner.
	The EMAP program draws on faculty members and courses from the Schools of Architecture, Engineering, Management and Technology, Science, and Social Science. Students are attracted from a broad range of disciplines. Doctoral work in environmental management is administered through the Lally School of Management and Technology.
Research Facilities	Research is supported by such state-of-the-art facilities as the computing facilities in the Center for Industrial Innovation; the Rensselaer libraries, whose library system allows access to collections, databases, and Internet resources from campus terminals; the Rensselaer Computing System, which permeates the campus with a coherent array of advanced workstations, a shared toolkit of applications for interactive learning and research, and high-speed Internet connectivity; a visualization laboratory for scientific computation; and a high-performance computing facility that includes a 36-node SP2 parallel computer.
Financial Aid	Financial aid is available in the form of tuition scholarships. Outstanding students may qualify for University-supported Rensselaer Scholar fellowships, which carry stipends of $15,000 and a full tuition scholarship. Low-interest, deferred-repayment graduate loans are also available to U.S. citizens with demonstrated need.
Cost of Study	Tuition for 1999–2000 is $665 per credit hour. Other fees amount to approximately $535 per semester. Books and supplies cost about $1700 per year.
Living and Housing Costs	The cost of rooms for single students in residence halls or apartments ranges from $3356 to $5298 for the 1999–2000 academic year. Family student housing, with monthly rents of $592 to $720, is available.
Student Group	There are about 4,300 undergraduate and 1,750 graduate students representing fifty states and more than eighty countries at Rensselaer.
Student Outcomes	Eighty-eight percent of Rensselaer's 1998 graduate students were hired after graduation with starting salaries that averaged $56,259 for master's degree recipients and $57,000–$75,000 for doctoral degree recipients.
Location	Rensselaer is situated on a scenic 260-acre hillside campus in Troy, New York, across the Hudson River from the state capital of Albany. Troy's central Northeast location provides students with a supportive, active, medium-sized community in which to live; an easy commute to Boston, New York, and Montreal; and some of the country's finest outdoor recreation sites, including Lake George, Lake Placid, and the Adirondack, Catskill, Berkshire, and Green Mountains. The Capital Region has one of the largest concentrations of academic institutions in the United States. Sixty thousand students attend fourteen area colleges and benefit from shared activities and courses.
The University	Founded in 1824 and the first American college to award degrees in engineering and science, Rensselaer Polytechnic Institute today is accredited by the Middle States Association of Colleges and Schools and is a private, nonsectarian, coeducational university. Rensselaer has five schools—Architecture, Engineering, Management, Science, and Humanities and Social Sciences—that offer a total of ninety-eight graduate degrees in forty-seven fields.
Applying	Admissions applications and all supporting credentials should be submitted well in advance of the preferred semester of entry to allow sufficient time for departmental review and processing. GRE General Test scores are required. The application fee is $35. Since the first departmental awards are made in February and March for the next full academic year, applicants requesting financial aid are encouraged to submit all required credentials by February 1 to ensure consideration.
Correspondence and Information	For written information about graduate work: Assistant to the Director Environmental Management and Policy Room 2502, Russell Sage Hall Rensselaer Polytechnic Institute 110 8th Street Troy, New York 12180-3590 Telephone: 518-276-6562 World Wide Web: http://lallyschool.rpi.edu/academic/masters/emp.html For applications and admissions information: Director of Graduate Academic Enrollment Services, Graduate Center Rensselaer Polytechnic Institute 110 8th Street Troy, New York 12180-3590 Telephone: 518-276-6789 E-mail: grad-services@rpi.edu World Wide Web: http://www.rpi.edu

Rensselaer Polytechnic Institute

THE FACULTY AND THEIR RESEARCH

Bruce W. Piasecki, Associate Professor and Director of the Program; Ph.D., Cornell. Utility-based environmental strategy, development of case work in corporate environmental leadership, business strategies to combat global warming and other regulatory demands.

Charles W. Boylen, Professor and Director of the Fresh Water Institute; Ph.D., Wisconsin–Madison. Microbial and ecological bacteriological systems.

Lenore S. Clesceri, Associate Professor; Ph.D., Wisconsin–Madison. Microbial ecology, biotransformation and biodegradation of natural polymers and pesticides, biotechnology.

Nicholas L. Clesceri, Professor; Ph.D., Wisconsin–Madison. Water pollution and control.

Henry L. Ehrlich, Professor; Ph.D., Wisconsin–Madison. Environmental biochemistry and geomicrobiological systems.

John M. Gowdy, Associate Professor; Ph.D., West Virginia. Ecological economics, productivity and technological change, environmental theory and policy, evolutionary models of economic change.

E. Bruce Nauman, Professor; Ph.D., Leeds (England). Performance plastics, recycling and recovery of mixed plastics streams.

John R. Norsworthy, Professor; Ph.D., Virginia. Productivity and technological change, environmental effects in manufacturing and service industries.

William A. Wallace, Professor; Ph.D., Rensselaer. Modeling, analytical approach to planning the response to technological disasters.

Bruce Watson, Professor; Ph.D., MIT. Geology, earth and environmental sciences.

Donald Watson, Professor; M.Env.Des., Yale. Energy and environmental architecture and lighting research.

Thomas F. Zimmie, Associate Professor; Ph.D., Connecticut. Soil mechanics and foundations, geotechnical engineering, ground water hydrology, sedimentation, flow through porous media, soil porosimetry, triaxial soil testing, rural sanitation and water supply.

Adjunct Faculty

David Hopkins, J.D., Albany Law. Environmental management.
Kevin Jones, M.P.A., SUNY at Albany. Managing energy issues.
Frank Mendelson, M.S., Rensselaer. Environmental strategy.
Peter Skinner, M.S. candidate, Rensselaer. Managing environmental technologies.

Selected Faculty Publications

Fletcher, K. A., **F. J. Mendelson,** and **B. W. Piasecki.** *Environmental Management and Business Strategy: Leadership Skills for the 21st Century.*

Medelson, F. J. Practicum Coordinator and Executive Editor, *Journal of Corporate Environmental Strategy.*

Nauman, E. B. *Introductory Systems Analysis for Process Engineers.*

Piasecki, B. W. Editor, *Journal of Corporate Environmental Strategy.*
Environmental Management and Business Strategy: Leadership Skills for the 21st Century.
Beyond Dumping, America's Future in Toxic Waste Management.
In Search of Environmental Excellence: Moving Beyond Blame.
Corporate Environmental Strategy: The Avalanche of Change Since Bhopal.

Skinner, P. N. *The Road to Love Canal.*

Wallace, W. A. Editor, *Advances in Applied Business Strategy.*
Operational Routing and Scheduling of Hazardous Materials Transportation: Methodic Approaches, Computer Implementation, Experimental Evaluation.

Watson, D. Editor, *Energy Design Handbook.*
Climatic Building Design.

THE STATE UNIVERSITY OF NEW JERSEY
RUTGERS

RUTGERS, THE STATE UNIVERSITY OF NEW JERSEY, NEW BRUNSWICK

Department of Environmental Sciences

Programs of Study

The Department of Environmental Sciences offers a program of study that leads to the degrees of Master of Science and Doctor of Philosophy. Options are provided in pollution prevention and remediation, atmospheric science, and general environmental science. A Ph.D. option in exposure assessment is offered jointly with the graduate program in public health, in conjunction with the Department of Environmental and Community Medicine at the University of Medicine and Dentistry of New Jersey–Robert Wood Johnson Medical School (UMDNJ–RWJMS). A Ph.D. option in environmental toxicology is offered jointly with the Graduate Program in Toxicology at Rutgers University. Within these options, possibilities exist for a wide range of specializations, including environmental biology, environmental chemistry, bioremediation, modeling of ground and surface water movement and pollution, atmospheric measurement and modeling, climate modeling and data analysis, contaminant transport and fate, human exposure and risk, soil physics, chemistry and microbiology, water and wastewater treatment, and water resources as well as for exploring policy aspects of environmental issues. All students are assigned an initial faculty adviser, which may be changed in response to changes in the student's interests.

The M.S. program offers two plans. Plan A requires 24 credits of course work, 6 credits of research, and a comprehensive oral exam, including the defense of a research thesis. Plan B requires 30 credits of course work, submission of an acceptable critical essay, and a comprehensive oral exam. The Ph.D. program requires 48 credits of course work, 24 credits of research, and the successful completion and defense of a research dissertation. Admission to candidacy for the Ph.D. degree is through a qualifying exam that is normally taken when the student has completed a major portion of the course requirements. Ph.D. students must present two seminars, while M.S. students must present one seminar. All students take two courses in fundamental concepts of environmental science. The M.S. degree is typically completed in two years, the Ph.D. degree in four years.

Research Facilities

Research is conducted in modern laboratories on the Cook Campus of Rutgers University, including those in the Department of Environmental Sciences, the Biotechnology Center for Agriculture and the Environment in Foran Hall, and the Institute for Marine and Coastal Sciences and at the Environmental and Occupational Health Sciences Institute (EOHSI) on the Busch Campus. A state-of-the-art computer lab is available for student use within the department, and machine shop, electronics shop, and glassblowing facilities are available on the New Brunswick campuses. There is a wide variety of research equipment in individual research groups, including several GC-MS systems, GCs, HPLCs, atomic absorption spectrometers, a computational laboratory equipped with Pentium-based and networked workstations, a differential scanning calorimeter, an X-ray diffractometer, a scintillation counter, a differential mobility analyzer, Dionix ion chromatographs, and walk-in environmental chambers.

The Institute of Marine and Coastal Sciences operates the Rutgers Marine Field Station in Tuckerton, New Jersey, which includes 48-foot and 30-foot research vessels. Instrumental facilities include mass spectrometers, atomic absorption spectrometers, ICP/MS, and a Shimadzu high-temperature catalysis DOC analyzer.

The Biotech Center possesses several quadrupole GC-MS instruments, an LC-MS, several GCs and HPLCs, an FPLC, a 30-liter fermenter, ABI 373 and 377 automated DNA sequencers, PCR instrumentation, anaerobe chambers, radioactive gas analyzer, a MIDI fatty acid analyzer, cold and warm rooms, a phosphorimager, gel scanners, and photographic dark rooms.

The Environmental and Occupational Health Sciences Institute houses a major analytical facility that is easily utilized by and fully accessible to faculty and staff members and students of the graduate program in environmental sciences. Equipment includes ICP-MS, flame and graphite furnace AAS, and HPLC-MS; a scanning fluorescence spectrometer; a GC-MS; a Fourier transform infrared spectrometer; and a stable isotope GC-MS.

Financial Aid

Financial support at Rutgers ranges from grants that cover tuition charges to awards that pay for all educational and living expenses. Limited financial aid in the form of teaching assistantships is awarded by application to the department. Graduate assistantships are available through research grants and contracts obtained by members of the graduate faculty. Outstanding students are recommended for Rutgers Excellence Fellowships. Many other University-based fellowship programs are available. More information is available via the department's Web site (address below).

Cost of Study

In 1998–99, the yearly tuition and fees for full-time students were $7292 for New Jersey residents and $10,320 for nonresidents.

Living and Housing Costs

Housing for graduate students is available on all Rutgers campuses. Single graduate students may be accommodated near the department in furnished residence halls on the Douglas Campus or in furnished apartments on Cook Campus. Starkey Apartments on Cook Campus house 4 students in single-bedroom accommodations with shared full kitchens and bathrooms. Graduate families are housed in efficiency and one- and two-bedroom units on the Busch Campus. Additional information is available from the Division of Housing at 732-445-2215 (single) or 732-445-3222 (family). Accommodations are also available in the surrounding community.

Student Group

The faculty seeks students who are committed to excellence in studying environmental problems that are local, national, or global in scope. Of the approximately 200 students in the program, typically 40 percent are women and 30 percent are international students. One quarter of the full-time Ph.D. students receive financial aid. M.S. and Ph.D. students are about equal in number. About 60 percent of the students attend part-time.

Location

New Brunswick (population 42,000) is located in central New Jersey approximately 33 miles south of New York City, 16 miles north of Princeton, and 60 miles from Philadelphia. Frequent buses and trains near the College Avenue Campus serve these and other cities. Libraries, theaters, concert halls, museums, galleries, and other cultural and educational resources of the New York–Philadelphia region are readily accessible.

The University and The Department

Rutgers is a colonial college, a land-grant institution, and a state university. Chartered in 1766 as Queen's College, it opened its doors in 1771. Its name was changed in 1825 in honor of a revolutionary war veteran, Colonel Henry Rutgers. Cook College originated as the New Jersey Agricultural Experiment Station in 1880, and its academic programs have special emphasis on the environment. The Department of Environmental Sciences celebrated its 75th anniversary in 1996.

Applying

The backgrounds of successful applicants vary greatly. All applicants are expected to have earned an undergraduate degree in a science or engineering discipline with an appropriate background in biology, chemistry, and mathematics. Accepted applicants with a deficiency in any of these areas will correct it during their first year of graduate study.

Admission materials are available from the Office of Graduate and Professional Admissions, 18 Bishop Place, New Brunswick, New Jersey 08903. Materials are also available on line at the University's Web site (address below). Deadlines are March 1 for fall admission and November 1 for spring admission.

Correspondence and Information

Environmental Sciences Graduate Program
Department of Environmental Sciences
Rutgers, The State University of New Jersey
14 College Farm Road
New Brunswick, New Jersey 08901-8551
Telephone: 732-932-9185
World Wide Web: http://www.envsci.rutgers.edu

Rutgers, The State University of New Jersey, New Brunswick

THE FACULTY AND THEIR RESEARCH

Graduate Faculty

Alan Appleby, Professor of Radiation Science; Ph.D., Durham. Radiation chemistry, radiation interactions at the molecular level.

Roni Avissar, Professor of Meteorology; Ph.D., Hebrew (Jerusalem). Micrometerology, boundary-layer meteorology, air-sea interactions, numerical modeling.

Baruch Boxer, Professor of Human Ecology; Ph.D., Chicago. Problems of integrating scientific information and knowledge with policy and regulation.

Joanna Burger, Professor of Biology; Ph.D., Minnesota. Behavioral ecology, ecotoxicology, ecological risk.

Marcos Cheney, Assistant Professor of Environmental Sciences; Ph.D., California, Davis. Quantitation of abiotic degradation of xenobiotics on mineral surfaces using microcalorimetry and spectroscopy, physical/chemical properties of soil surfaces in relation to contaminant behavior.

Keith R. Cooper, Professor of Toxicology; Ph.D., Rhode Island. Xenobiotic metabolism and diseases of aquatic animals, animal models.

Robert M. Cowan, Assistant Professor of Environmental Sciences; Ph.D., SUNY at Buffalo. Environmental engineering, biological treatment, bioremediation, process modeling.

Joan G. Ehrenfeld, Associate Professor of Ecology; Ph.D., CUNY. Wetland, soil, and ecosystems ecology and pollution impacts.

Steven J. Eisenreich, Professor of Environmental Sciences; Ph.D., Wisconsin–Madison. Environmental organic chemistry, atmosphere-water and -land exchange of toxic organic compounds.

Karen Erstfeld, Assistant Professor of Environmental Sciences; Ph.D., Michigan. Public health, risk assessment, environmental chemistry, ecotoxicology.

Melvin S. Finstein, Professor of Environmental Sciences; Ph.D., Berkeley. Pollution microbiology, waste-treatment composting as a controlled system.

Susan E. Ford, Assistant Research Professor of Oyster Culture; Ph.D., Duke. Invertebrate pathology/parasitology, genetics and resistance.

Jennifer Francis, Assistant Research Professor of Marine and Coastal Sciences; Ph.D., Washington (Seattle). Polar meteorology, remote sensing.

Michael A. Gallo, Professor of Environmental and Community Medicine; Ph.D., Albany Medical College. Food additives, phototoxins, dermatotoxicology.

Emil J. Genetelli, Professor of Environmental Sciences; Ph.D., Rutgers. Biological wastewater treatment process.

Daniel Gimenez, Assistant Professor of Environmental Sciences; Ph.D., Minnesota. Soil structure, water movement and solute transport through soils, soil quality.

William Goldfarb, Professor of Environmental Sciences; Ph.D., Columbia. Environmental, water resources, and hazardous substances law and policy.

Fred Grassle, Director, Institute of Marine and Coastal Sciences; Ph.D., Duke. Ecology of marine bottom-dwelling organisms.

Max M. Haggblom, Research Assistant Professor, Center for Agricultural Molecular Biology; Ph.D., Helsinki. Environmental and applied microbiology, biodegradation, and bioremediation.

Robert P. Harnack, Professor of Meteorology; Ph.D., Maryland. Synoptic and climatic aspects of meteorology.

Sidney A. Katz, Professor of Chemistry; Ph.D., Pennsylvania. Environmental, nutritional, and toxicological aspects of trace elements.

Stanley E. Katz, Research Professor of Microbiology; Ph.D., Rutgers. Antibiotic residues in tissues and soils.

Kathleen I. Keating, Professor of Environmental Sciences; Ph.D., Yale. Trace-element nutrition, plankton community structure, defined media for zooplankton and phytoplankton, allelochemistry, biogeochemistry.

David S. Kosson, Associate Professor of Chemical Engineering; Ph.D., Rutgers. Microbial degradation of hazardous wastes and remediation.

Uta Krogmann, Assistant Professor of Environmental Sciences; Ph.D., Technical (Germany). Solid-waste management and engineering: collection systems, waste analyses, recycling, waste minimization, anaerobic digestion, composting, land application.

Jerome J. Kukor, Assistant Professor of Environmental Sciences; Ph.D., Michigan. Physiology and biochemistry of microbial degradation of xenobiotics.

Paul J. Lioy, Professor of Environmental and Community Medicine; Ph.D., Rutgers. Human exposure to pollutants, air pollution, industrial hygiene, risk assessment.

James R. Miller, Professor of Marine and Coastal Sciences; Ph.D., Maryland. Climate modeling, climate change, earth system science.

George H. Nieswand, Professor of Environmental Systems Engineering; Ph.D., Rutgers. Environmental systems analysis.

Clare E. Reimers, Associate Professor of Marine and Coastal Sciences; Ph.D., Oregon State. Marine carbon cycle/sedimentary geochemistry.

John R. Reinfelder, Assistant Professor of Environmental Sciences; Ph.D., SUNY at Stony Brook. Trace-metal biogeochemistry of aquatic systems, phytoplankton ecology.

David A. Robinson, Professor of Geography; Ph.D., Columbia. Climate and climate change, snow dynamics.

Alan Robock, Professor of Environmental Sciences; Ph.D., MIT. Climate modeling and data analysis, soil moisture.

Robert M. Sherrell, Assistant Professor of Marine and Coastal Sciences; Ph.D., MIT. Marine geochemistry of trace metals and natural radionuclides.

Georgiy L. Stenchikov, Professor; Ph.D., Moscow Physical Technical Institute. Climate and mesoscale modeling.

Peter F. Strom, Associate Professor of Environmental Sciences; Ph.D., Rutgers. Biological treatment, hazardous wastes.

Gary L. Taghon, Associate Professor of Marine and Coastal Sciences; Ph.D., Washington (Seattle). Marine ecology.

Robert L. Tate III, Professor of Soils and Crops; Ph.D., Wisconsin. Soil microbiology.

Paul E. Thomas, Professor of Chemical Biology; Ph.D., Ohio. Metabolism of drugs and environmental chemicals.

Barbara Turpin, Assistant Professor of Environmental Sciences; Ph.D., Oregon Graduate Institute. Air pollution, chemistry and physics of aerosols.

Christopher G. Uchrin, Professor of Environmental Sciences; Ph.D., Michigan. Math modeling of contamination transport in surface and groundwaters.

Judith S. Weis, Professor of Biological Sciences; Ph.D., NYU. Effects of environmental stressors on estuarine organisms.

Clifford P. Weisel, Associate Professor of Environmental and Community Medicine; Ph.D., Rhode Island. Measurement of environmental pollutants and biomarkers to assess human exposure.

Lily Y. Young, Professor of Environmental Sciences; Ph.D., Harvard. Anaerobic microbial metabolism of contaminants, microbial ecology.

Junfeng Zhang, Assistant Professor of Environmental and Community Medicine; Ph.D., Rutgers/UMDNJ. Air pollution, exposure assessment, atmospheric chemistry, and greenhouse gases.

Gerben J. Zylstra, Associate Professor of Biochemistry and Microbiology; Ph.D., Michigan. Genetics and physiology of microbial aromatic hydrocarbon degradation.

Associate and Adjunct Graduate Faculty

John W. Baum, Senior Scientist, Brookhaven National Laboratory; Ph.D., Michigan. Radiological physics, bioeffects and risks of radiations.

Brian Buckley, Administrative Director Laboratories, EOHSI; Ph.D., North Carolina State. Analytical chemistry of environmental samples.

Edward A. Christman, Assistant Clinical Professor, Columbia University; Ph.D., Rutgers. Radiation science/protection, occupational health/safety.

Nancy L. Fiedler, Associate Professor of Environmental and Community Medicine; Ph.D., Bowling Green State. Neurobehavioral health effects, human exposure to hazardous substances.

Natalie Freeman, Adjunct Assistant Professor of Environmental and Community Medicine, UMDNJ–RWJMS; Ph.D., Rutgers. Nonoccupational exposure of adults/children, questionnaire development.

Elan J. Gandsman, Director of Health and Safety, Yale University; Ph.D., Tel-Aviv (Israel). Health physics, radiation safety, occupational health.

Panos Georgopoulos, Assistant Professor of Environmental and Community Health; Ph.D., Caltech. Environmental modeling.

Francis J. Haughey, Professor Emeritus of Radiation Science; Ph.D., Rutgers. Radiation, aerosol, and health physics; environmental radioactivity.

Robert Hordon, Associate Professor of Geography; Ph.D., Columbia. Ground and surface water hydrology, water quality.

Joseph V. Hunter, Professor Emeritus of Environmental Sciences; Ph.D., Rutgers. Source, fate, and detection of water and soil pollutants.

Howard Kipen, Assistant Professor of Environmental and Community Medicine; M.D., California, San Francisco. Occupational health.

Richard Lathrop, Assistant Professor of Environmental Resources; Ph.D., Wisconsin–Madison. Remote sensing and spatial modeling of ecosystems.

Norberto J. Palleroni, Research Professor, Center for Agricultural Molecular Biology, CC; Ph.D., Buenos Aires. Taxonomic and phylogenetic studies of environmentally important bacteria.

Nathan M. Reiss, Professor Emeritus of Meteorology; Ph.D., NYU. Air pollution meteorology, physical meteorology.

Mark Robson, Clinical Assistant Professor of Community Medicine, UMDNJ–RWJMS; Ph.D., Rutgers. Public health, risk assessment, pesticide exposure.

Theodore B. Shelton, Extension Specialist in Water Resources Management; Ph.D., Rutgers. Water quality.

K. David Steidley, Chief Physicist, St. Barnabas Medical Center; Ph.D., Rutgers. Medical physics, biophysics, health physics, computers in medicine.

Alan Stern, Research Scientist, NJDEP and Energy; Ph.D., Columbia. Population exposures to metals in the environment.

Arthur C. Upton, Professor of Environmental and Community Medicine, UMDNJ–RWJMS; Ph.D., Michigan. Biological effects and risks of radiation.

Wesley R. Van Pelt, President, Wesley R. Van Pelt Associates, Inc.; Ph.D., NYU. Health physics, industrial hygiene, environmental radioactivity.

Sam C. Wainwright, Assistant Professor of Marine and Coastal Sciences; Ph.D., Georgia. Ecology of marine organisms.

Stephen M. Waldow, Clinical Assistant Professor and Director of Radiation Research, Cooper Hospital; Ph.D., SUNY at Buffalo. Radiation biology.

George Winnett, Professor Emeritus of Environmental Sciences; M.A., NYU. Pesticide residue and pollution research.

Rutgers, The State University of New Jersey, New Brunswick

SELECTED PUBLICATIONS

Kim, I. S., et al. **(A. Appleby).** Trapping of radioactive inert gas radon on an oxide glass: Scintillating glass fiber bundle method. *J. Porous Mater.* 4:51–7, 1997.

Kim, I. S., et al. **(A. Appleby** and **E. A. Christman).** A new approach to monitoring radon and radon progeny using a glass scintillator in a fiber optic bundle structure. *Nucl. Instrum. Methods Phys. Res. Sect. A* 356:537–43, 1995.

Avissar, R., E. W. Eloranta, K. Gurer, and G. J. Tripoli. An evaluation of the large-eddy simulation option of the regional atmospheric modeling system in simulating a convective boundary layer: A FIFE case study. *J. Atmos. Sci.* 55(7):1109–30, 1998.

Avissar, R., and T. Schmidt. An evaluation of the scale at which ground-surface heat flux patchiness affects the convective boundary layer using a large-eddy simulation model. *J. Atmos. Sci.* 55(16):2666–89, 1998.

Avissar, R. Which type of soil-vegetation-atmosphere transfer scheme is needed for general circulation models: A proposal for a higher-order scheme. *J. Hydrol.* 212:136–54, 1998.

Burger, J., and M. Gochfeld. Risk, mercury levels, and birds: Relating adverse laboratory effects to field monitoring. *Environ. Res.* 75:1776–82, 1997.

Burger, J., and M. Gochfeld. Lead and behavioral development: Parental compensation for behaviorally impaired chicks. *Pharm. Biochem. Behav.* 55:339–49, 1996.

Nasser, A., G. Sposito, and **M. Cheney.** Mechanochimical transformation of 2,4-D on manganese dioxide. *Colloid Surface Sci.,* in press.

Cheney, M., et al. Atrazine dealkylation on manganese dioxide. *Colloid Surface Sci.* 137:267–73, 1998.

Cheney, M., G. Sposito, A. McGrath, and R. Criddle. Abiotic degradation of 2,4-D (dichlorophenoxyacetic acid) on synthetic birnessite: A calorespirometric method. *Colloids Surfaces A: Physicochem. Eng. Aspects* 107:131–40, 1996.

Schiager, K. J., et al. **(E. A. Christman).** Consensus radiation protection practices for academic research institutions. *Health Phys.* (71)6:960–5, 1996.

Christman, E. A., and **E. J. Gandsman.** Radiation safety as part of a comprehensive university occupational health and safety program. *Health Phys.* 66(5):581–4, 1994.

Nacci, D., et al. **(K. R. Cooper).** A fish embryonic EROD bioassay. *Environ. Toxicol. Chem.* 17:2481–6, 1998.

Kim, Y.-C., and **K. R. Cooper.** Interactions of 2,3,7,8-tetrachlorodibenzopdioxin (TCDD) and 3,3',4,4'5-petachlorobiphenyl (PCB126) for producing lethal and sublethal effects in the Japanese medaka embryos and larvae. *Chemosphere* 36:409–18, 1998.

McGrath, L. F., **K. R. Cooper,** P. Georgopoulos, and **M. Gallo.** Alternative models for lowdose-response analysis of biochemical and immunological endpoints for tetrachlorodibenzo-p-dioxin. *Regul. Toxicol. Pharmacol.* 21:382–96, 1995.

Joshi, J. A., and **R. M. Cowan** et al. **(P. F. Strom** and **M. S. Finstein).** Gaseous ammonia removal in biofilters: Effect of biofilter media on products of nitrification. *ICES SAE Technical Paper #981613.* Warrendale, Pennsylvania: SAE, Inc., 1998.

Hogan, J. A., and **R. M. Cowan** et al. **(P. F. Strom** and **M. S. Finstein).** On development of advanced life support systems maximally reliant on biological systems. *SAE (Society of Automotive Engineers) Technical Paper 981535, 28th International Conference on Environmental Systems (ICES),* 1998.

Grady, C. P. L., Jr., **R. M. Cowan,** and S. M. Sock. Biotreatability kinetics: A critical component in the scale up of wastewater treatment systems. *Biotechnol. Sustainable Environ.* 54:307–21, 1997.

Cowan, R. M., and K. Park. Biodegradation of the gasoline oxygenates MTBE, ETBE, TAME, TBA, and TAA by aerobic mixed cultures. *Proc. 28th Mid-Atlantic Ind. Waste Conf., SUNY at Buffalo, Buffalo, New York,* pp. 523–30. Lancaster, Pennsylvania: Technomic Publishing Company, 1996.

Kourtev, P., **J. G. Ehrenfeld,** and W. Huang. Effects of exotic plant species on soil properties in hardwood forests of New Jersey. *Water, Air, Soil Pollut.* 105:493–501, 1998.

Ehrenfeld, J. G., et al. Live and dead roots in forest soil horizons: Contrasting effects on nitrogen dynamics. *Ecology* 78:348–62, 1997.

Zhang, H., and **S. J. Eisenreich** et al. Evidence for the increased gaseous PCB fluxes to Lake Michigan from Chicago. *Environ. Sci. Technol.,* in press.

Jeremiason, J. J., and **S. J. Eisenreich** et al. Biogeochemical cycling of atmospherically-derived PCBs in lakes of variable trophic status: A paired lake experiment. *Limnol. Oceanogr.,* in press.

Jeremiason, J. J., **S. J. Eisenreich,** J. E. Baker, and B. J. Eadie. PCB decline in settling particles and benthic recycling of PCBs and PAHs in Lake Superior. *Environ. Sci. Technol.* 32(21):3249–56, 1998.

Erstfeld, K. M., and C.-Y. Chen. Comparative supercritical fluid and soxhlet extraction methods for the determination of chlorothalonil in cranberry bog soils. *J. Agric. Food Chem.* 46:499–503, 1998.

Erstfeld, K. M., and S. S. Park. Dynamics of chlordane under nonconstant exposure conditions: A numerical bioaccumulation model. *Bull. Environ. Contam. Toxicol.* 58:364–71, 1997.

Fiedler, N., et al. **(H. Kipen).** Neuropsychological effects of a residential mercury exposure. *Environ. Health Perspect.,* in press.

Fiedler, N., **H. Kipen,** K. Kelly-McNeil, and R. Fenske. Long-term use of organophosphates and neuropsychological performance. *Am. J. Ind. Med.* 32:487–96, 1997.

Fiedler, N., **H. Kipen,** B. Natelson, and J. Ottenweller. Chemical sensitivities and the Gulf War: Department of veterans affairs research center in basic and clinical science studies of environmental hazards. *Regul. Toxicol. Pharmacol.* 24:S129–38, 1996.

Cook, T., et al. **(S. Ford** and **J. Miller).** The relationship between increasing sea-surface temperature and the northward spread of *Perkinsus Marinus* (Dermo) disease epizootics in oysters. *Estuarine, Coastal Shelf Sci.* 46:587–97, 1998.

Gish, T. J., **D. Giménez,** and W. J. Rawls. Impacts of roots on groundwater quality. *Plant Soil* 200:47–54, 1998.

Rawls, W. J., **D. Giménez,** and R. Grossman. Use of soil texture, bulk density, and slope of the water retention curve to predict saturated hydraulic conductivity. *Trans. ASAE* 41:983–8, 1998.

Giménez, D., R. R. Allmaras, D. R. Huggins, and E. A. Nater. Prediction of saturated hydraulic conductivity-porosity dependence using fractals. *Soil Sci. Soc. Am. J.* 61:1285–92, 1997.

Plater, Z., R. Abrams, **W. Goldfarb,** and R. Graham. *Environmental Law and Policy: Nature, Law, and Society,* 2nd edition. St. Paul: West Publishing Co., 1998.

Goldfarb, W. *Water Law,* 2nd edition. Chelsea, Michigan: Lewis Publishers, Inc., 1989.

Knight, V. K., L. J. Kerkhof, and **M. M. Häggblom.** Community analysis of sulfidogenic 2-bromophenol dehalogenating and phenol degrading consortia. *FEMS Microbiol. Ecol.,* in press.

Häggblom, M. M., and P. W. Milligan. Anaerobic degradation of halogenated pesticides: Influence of alternate electron acceptors. In *Soil Biochemistry,* Vol. 10, eds. J.-M. Bollag and G. Stotzky, in press.

Häggblom, M. M. Reductive dehalogenation by a sulfate-reducing consortium. *FEMS Microbiol. Ecol.* 26:35–41, 1998.

Harnack, R. P., et al. Investigation of upper-air conditions occurring with heavy summer rain in Utah, USA. *Int. J. Climate,* in press.

Harnack, R. P., et al. Investigation of upper-air conditions occurring with severe wind events in Utah. *Weather For.* 12:282–93, 1997.

Hordon, R. M., K. D. Lawrence, and S. M. Lawrence. Water demand estimation on a state-by-state basis. In *Advances in Business and Management Forecasting,* Vol. 2, pp. 101–12, eds. K. D. Lawrence, M. Guerts, and J. B. Guerard. Greenwich, Connecticut: JAI Press, Inc., 1998.

Lawrence, K. D., S. M. Lawrence, **R. M. Hordon,** and Z. Jin. A multicriteria network model for water supply planning in northern New Jersey. In *Applications of Management Science,* Vol. 9, pp. 243–9, eds. K. D. Lawrence and G. R. Reeves. Greenwich, Connecticut: JAI Press, Inc., 1996.

Jenniss, S. W., **S. A. Katz,** and R. W. Lynch. *Applications of Atomic Spectrometry to Regulatory Compliance Monitoring, 2nd edition.* New York: John Wiley & Sons, 1997.

Sikovec, M., M. Franko, F. G. Cruz, and **S. A. Katz.** Thermal lens spectrometric determination of hexavalent chromium. *Anal. Chim. Acta* 330:245–50, 1996.

Rutgers, The State University of New Jersey, New Brunswick

Selected Publications (continued)

Keating, K. I., and P. B. Caffrey. A selenium deficiency induced by zinc deprivation. *Proc. Natl. Acad. Sci. U.S.A.* 86:6436–40, 1989.

Keating, K. I. Allelopathic influence on blue-green algae bloom sequence in a eutrophic lake. *Science* 196:885–7, 1977.

Krogmann, U. Effects of season and population density on source-separated waste composts. *Waste Manage. Res.* 16:1–15, 1999.

Park, J., Y.-M. Chen, **J. J. Kukor,** and L. M. Abriola. Substrate concentration-dependent regulation of toluene degradation activities of *Ralstonia pickettii* PKO1 under low substrate conditions: Laboratory column experiments. *Environ. Sci. Technol.,* in press.

Kukor, J. J. In situ bioremediation of fuel hydrocarbons and chlorinated solvents in suboxic aquifer environments: What controls microbial activity? In *Environmental Technology '99,* in press.

Olsen, R. H., **J. J. Kukor,** A. M. Byrne, and G. R. Johnson. Evidence for the evolution of a single component phenol/cresol hydroxylase from a multicomponent toluene monooxygenase. *J. Ind. Microbiol. Biotechnol.* 19:360–8, 1997.

Russell, G. L., **J. R. Miller,** and D. Rind. A coupled atmosphere-ocean model for transient climate change studies. *Atmos.-Ocean* 33:683–730, 1995.

Van Blarcum, S., **J. R. Miller,** and G. L. Russell. High latitude river runoff in a doubled CO_2 climate. *Climatic Change* 30:7–26, 1995.

Reinfelder, J. R., and S. I. Chang. Speciation and microalgal bioavailability of inorganic silver. *Environ. Sci. Technol.,* in press.

Reinfelder, J. R., et al. Assimilation efficiencies and turnover rates of trace elements in marine bivalves: A comparison of oysters, clams and mussels. *Marine Biol.* 129:443–52, 1997.

Tortell, P. D., **J. R. Reinfelder,** and F. M. M. Morel. Bicarbonate utilization in coastal diatom blooms. *Nature* 390:243–4, 1997.

Clark, M., et al. **(D. A. Robinson).** Atmospheric controls on Eurasian snow extent. *Int. J. Climatic* 19:27–40, 1999.

Frei, A., and **D. A. Robinson.** Evaluation of snow extent and its variability in the Atmospheric Model Intercomparison Project. *J. Geophys. Res.-Atmos.* 103:8859–71, 1998.

D'Arrigo, R. D., G. C. Jacoby, M. Free, and **A. Robock.** Northern Hemisphere annual to decadal temperature variability for the past three centuries: Tree-ring and model estimates. *Climatic Change,* in press.

Vinnikov, K. Y., and **A. Robock** et al. Satellite remote sensing of soil moisture in Illinois, U.S.A. *J. Geophys. Res.* 104:4145–68, 1999.

Mao, J., and **A. Robock.** Surface air temperature simulations by AMIP general circulation models: Volcanic and ENSO signals and systematic errors. *J. Climate* 11:1538–52, 1998.

Steidley, K. D. Use of radiochromic dosimetry film for HDR brachytherapy quality assurance. *Med. Dosim.* 23(1):37–8, 1998.

Kirchner, I., and **G. L. Stenchikov** et al. **(A. Robock).** Climate model simulation of winter warming and summer cooling following the 1991 Mount Pinatubo volcanic eruption. *J. Geophys. Res.,* in press.

Stenchikov, G. L., et al. **(A. Robock).** Radiative forcing from the 1991 Mount Pinatubo volcanic eruption. *J. Geophys. Res.* 103:13837–57, 1998.

Dickerson, R. R., et al. **(G. L. Stenchikov).** The impact of aerosols on solar ultraviolet radiation and photochemical smog. *Science* 278:827–30, 1997.

Laor, Y., **P. F. Strom,** and W. J. Farmer. Bioavailability of phenanthrene sorbed to mineral-associated humic acid. *Water Res.* 33:1719–29, 1999.

Chung, J.-C., and **P. F. Strom.** Filamentous bacteria and protozoa found in the rotating biological contactor. *J. Environ. Sci. Health* A32:671–86, 1997.

Strom, P. F., and **M. S. Finstein.** *New Jersey's Manual on Composting Leaves and Management of Other Yard Trimmings.* New Jersey Department of Environmental Protection, 1995.

Tso, S.-F., and **G. L. Taghon.** Factors affecting predation by *Cyclidium sp.* and *Euplotes sp.* on PAH-degrading and non-degrading bacteria. *Microbial Ecol.* 37:3–12, 1999.

Krasnow, L. D., and **G. L. Taghon.** Rates of tube building and sediment particle size selection during tube construction by the crustacean *Leptochelia dubia. Estuaries* 20:534–46, 1997.

Fisk, A. C., S. L. Murphy, and **R. L. Tate III.** Microscopic observations of bacterial sorption in soil cores. *Biol. Fertil. Soils* 28:111–6, 1999.

Kelly, J. J., and **R. L. Tate III.** Use of BIOLOG for the analysis of microbial communities from zinc contaminated soils. *J. Environ. Qual.* 27:600–8, 1998.

Tate, R. L. III. *Soil Microbiology.* New York: John Wiley and Sons, 1995.

Turpin, B. J., et al. Secondary formation and the Smoky Mountain organic aerosol: An examination of aerosol polarity and functional group composition during SEAVS. *Environ. Sci. Technol.* 32:604–13, 1998.

Turpin, B. J., and J. J. Huntzicker. Identification of secondary organic aerosol episodes and quantitation of primary and secondary organic aerosol concentrations during SCAQS. *Atmos. Environ.* 29:3527–44, 1995.

Bartone, D. M., and **C. G. Uchrin.** Comparison of pollutant removal efficiency for two residential storm water basins. Accepted by *J. Environ. Eng. ASCE.*

Shaffer, K. L., and **C. G. Uchrin.** Uptake of methyl tertiary butyl ether (MTBE) by groundwater solids. *Bull. Environ. Contam. Toxicol.* 59:744–9, 1997.

Fischer, D., and **C. G. Uchrin.** Laboratory simulation of VOC entry into residence basements from soil gas. *Environ. Sci. Technol.* 30:2598–603, 1996.

Weis, J. S., P. Weis, and T. Proctor. The extent of benthic impacts of CCA-treated wood structures in Atlantic Coast estuaries. *Arch. Environ. Contam. Toxicol.* 34:313–22, 1998.

Zhou, T., and **J. S. Weis.** Swimming behavior and predator avoidance in three populations of *Fundulus heteroclitus* larvae after embryonic and/or larval exposure to methylmercury. *Aquat. Toxicol.* 43:131–48, 1998.

Kim, H., and **C. P. Weisel.** Dermal absorption of dichloro- and trichloroacetic acids from chlorinated water. *J. Exposure Anal. Environ. Epidemiol.* 8:555–75, 1998.

Chen, W. J., and **C. P. Weisel.** Halogenated DBP concentrations in a distribution system. *J. Am. Water Works Assoc.* 90:151–63, 1998.

Weisel, C. P., R. Yu, A. Roy, and **P. Georgopoulos.** Biomarkers of environmental benzene exposure. *Environ. Health Perspect.* 104:1141–6, 1996.

Boyle, A. W., C. D. Phelps, and **L. Y. Young.** Isolation from estuarine sediments of a desulfovibrio strain which can grow on lactate coupled to the reductive dehalogenation of 2,4,6-tribromophenol. *Appl. Environ. Microbiol.,* in press.

Phelps, C. D., L. J. Kerkhof, and **L. Y. Young.** Molecular characterization of a sulfate-reducing consortium which mineralizes benzene. *FEMS Microbiol. Ecol.* 27:269–79, 1998.

Van Schie, P. M., and **L. Y. Young.** Isolation and characterization of phenol-degrading denitrifying bacteria. *Appl. Environ. Microbiol.* 64:2432–8, 1998.

Zhang, J., et al. Monoxide from cookstoves in developing countries: 1. Emission factors. *Chemosphere,* in press.

Zhang, J., et al. Effects of air pollution on adults' respiratory health in three Chinese cities. *Arch. Environ. Health,* in press.

Hibbert, R., et al. **(J. Zhang).** High lead exposures resulting from pottery production in a village in Michoacan State, Mexico. *J. Exposure Anal. Environ. Epidemiol.,* in press.

Kieboom, J., J. J. Dennis, J. A. M. de Bont, and **G. J. Zylstra.** Identification and molecular characterization of an efflux pump involved in *Pseudomonas putida* S12 solvent tolerance. *J. Biol. Chem.* 273:85–91, 1998.

Zylstra, G. J., and E. Kim. Aromatic hydrocarbon degradation by *Sphingomonas yanoikuyae* B1. *J. Ind. Microbiol. Biotechnol.* 19:408–14, 1997.

STATE UNIVERSITY OF NEW YORK COLLEGE OF ENVIRONMENTAL SCIENCE AND FORESTRY

Graduate Program in Environmental Science

Programs of Study

The Graduate Program in Environmental Science offers the M.P.S., M.S., and Ph.D. degrees through the Faculty of Environmental Studies and with involvement of the Faculties of Environmental and Forest Biology, Chemistry, Forestry, Environmental and Resource Engineering, and Landscape Architecture. The following areas are available for graduate study: environmental policy and democratic process, environmental and community land planning, environmental systems and risk management, and water and wetland resources. More information on these areas is available on the reverse of this page.

The Master of Professional Studies (M.P.S.) degree is intended to be a terminal degree. The M.P.S. is offered in all options. This degree requires the successful completion of a minimum of 39 credits at the graduate level. Each student's study plan must be approved by the student's major professor, steering committee, and faculty chair. In addition, individual programs may require an integrative experience, such as an internship, team project, or paper.

The M.S. is intended for students seeking education in a scientific, professional, or technological field. The degree programs provides an introduction to research and related scholarly and professional activities. The M.S. degree requires a minimum of 36 credits of work designed expressly for graduate students. This program also requires completion of a satisfactory thesis and an oral examination.

The Ph.D. is intended for students seeking the highest level of education in a scientific, professional, or technological field. This degree is reserved for students who not only demonstrate the ability to do course work in an outstanding manner but can also make a definite contribution in original research. The Ph.D. requires the completion of at least 60 graduate credits beyond the bachelor's degree. A preliminary examination may be required to assist in the development of a student's program of study. An examination for admission to candidacy, a dissertation, and an oral defense of the dissertation are also required.

Research Facilities

The research programs of the College and the Graduate Program in Environmental Science have attracted worldwide sponsors who provide support of more than $7 million annually. Research facilities include Randolph G. Pack Environmental Institute, a social science laboratory, a computer visualization lab, a geographical modeling laboratory, and remote-sensing/photogrammetry equipment. The College maintains more than 25,000 acres of land with diverse environmental conditions at nine regional campuses and experiment stations. The Faculty of Environmental Studies includes the administrator of the Great Lakes Research Consortium, with links to twelve New York State universities.

Financial Aid

Assistantships are awarded to students whose education and experience enable them to assist in instruction and research. In 1999–2000, stipends range from $8000 to $15,000 per year, plus tuition scholarship. Special fellowships are offered in several programs, including Randolph G. Pack Environmental Institute Research Awards and the Great Lakes Research Consortium Assistantships.

Cost of Study

In 1998–99 graduate tuition for New York State residents was $2550 per semester. Nonresident tuition was $4208 per semester. All graduate students pay fees of approximately $243 per year.

Living and Housing Costs

Accommodations and food services are available through Syracuse University. For a single student, apartments ranged in cost from $1845 to $3375 per semester in 1998–99; for married students, apartments ranged in cost from $590 to $690 per month. Meals are available on the Syracuse University campus for $730 to $1235 per semester depending on the meal contract chosen.

Student Group

There are approximately 80 graduate students in the program and 40 in residence on campus. Forty percent of these students are women, and one third are married. Approximately 65 percent have been awarded teaching or research assistantships. There is an active graduate student association on campus as well as numerous professional and special interest groups. Graduate students come from throughout the United States and many countries.

Location

The main campus of the College of Environmental Science and Forestry is in Syracuse, New York, and is adjacent to Syracuse University. The city has a growing metropolitan area of nearly 500,000 people, with diversified industry and commerce. There are many cultural and recreational opportunities, including a symphony orchestra, opera, several museums, theaters, and historic sites. Major transportation networks are easily accessible from Syracuse.

The College

The College of Environmental Science and Forestry is a specialized center of the State University of New York. Because of its location, and through long tradition, the College maintains a special relationship with Syracuse University. This relationship provides students with the opportunity to study in a small college environment while having access to the cultural, social, and athletic opportunities available at a large university.

Applying

All applicants must provide a transcript of all previous academic work, supporting letters of recommendation, and scores on the General Test of the Graduate Record Examinations. A statement of educational objectives must also be submitted. There is a $50 application fee.

Students should direct requests for further information on particular programs to the graduate director. For application material and general information, students should contact the addresses below.

Correspondence and Information

Dr. Robert H. Frey
Dean of Instruction and Graduate Studies
State University of New York
College of Environmental Science
  and Forestry
227 Bray Hall
1 Forestry Drive
Syracuse, New York 13210
Telephone: 315-470-6599
Fax: 315-470-6978
E-mail: esfgrad@esf.edu
World Wide Web: http://www.esf.edu

Dr. Richard C. Smardon
Graduate Director and Chair of
  Environmental Studies
State University of New York
College of Environmental Science
  and Forestry
106/107 Marshall Hall
1 Forestry Drive
Syracuse, New York 13210
Telephone: 315-470-6576
Fax: 315-470-6915
E-mail: rsmardon@mailbox.syr.edu
World Wide Web: http://www.esf.edu/es

State University of New York College of Environmental Science and Forestry

THE FACULTY AND THEIR RESEARCH

Environmental Policy & Democratic Process

The focus of this study area is on developing new understanding of public participation in environmental decision making, against the backdrop of environmental policy making and program implementation. Particular attention is given to the variety of organizations involved in participation, which generally are the institutions and agencies of government, citizen-based nongovernmental organizations, and the business or industrial sector; the availability and utility of environmental information for these groups; and the participation and integration of all informed stakeholders into environmental decision making. The tripartite scheme of organizations, information, and participation frames student programs of study and suggests important directions for student and faculty research efforts.

John Felleman, Coordinator. Environmental information policy. (E-mail: felleman@esf.edu; World Wide Web: http://www.esf.edu/es)
William Bently. Resource management. (E-mail: wbentley@esf.edu)
Donald Floyd. Natural resources policy and management. (E-mail: dfloyd@mailbox.syr.edu)
Sara Keith. Environmental policy and politics. (E-mail: sekeith@mailbox.syr.edu)
Robert Malsheimer. Environmental law and policy. (E-mail: rwmalmsh@mailbox.syr.edu)
Mark Meisner. Environmental discourse and communication. (E-mail: mmeisner@esf.edu)
Susan Senecah. Environmental interest groups/communication process. (E-mail: ssenecah@mailbox.syr.edu)
Richard Smardon. Landscape and environmental planning. (E-mail: rsmardon@mailbox.syr.edu)

Environmental & Community Land Planning

Environmental and community planning is concerned with orderly, efficient, equitable, and aesthetic development of land with special concern for the state of the natural environment, the physical character of communities, and decision making at state, county, and local levels of government. Planning balances competing demands on land and environment brought about by expanding urban and rural development, and enhancing viable natural and cultural resources is an important planning perspective. Another perspective involves the guiding of private and public development processes within a pluralistic political environment in order to promote sustainable communities while at the same time respecting fiscal, environmental, and legal constraints.

Allen Lewis, Coordinator. Community land planning, GIS. (E-mail: arlewis@mailbox.syr.edu)
Emanual Carter. Community planning and design.
Cheryl Doble. Community planning and participation design. (E-mail: csdoble@mailbox.syr.edu)
Miklos Gratzer. Wildlife and recreation management.
Richard Hawks. Community planning and GIS. (E-mail: rshawk@mailbox.syr.edu)
Scott Shannon. Urban analysis and design. (E-mail: ssshanno@mailbox.syr.edu)

Environmental Systems & Risk Management

The environmental systems and risk management study area focuses on problems in environmental and natural resource policy in which technical issues are of central importance. The program is designed for graduate students with a science or engineering background. Current research includes spatial model construction, ecosystems modeling, development of model assessment and selection criteria, environmental risk assessment, use of technical information by regulatory agencies, land use forecasting for public policy decision making, and water resource assessment and planning. The environmental systems and risk management areas of study provide a unique opportunity to study interdisciplinary problems.

Charles Hall, Co-Coordinator. Systems ecology. (E-mail: chall@mailbox.syr.edu)
Brenda Nordenstam, Co-Coordinator. Environmental risk communication. (E-mail: bjnorden@mailbox.syr.edu)
James Hassett. Environmental modeling. (E-mail: jphassett@mailbox.syr.edu)
Lee Herrington. Computers, GIS, micrometeorology. (E-mail: lpherrin@mailbox.syr.edu)
David Johnson. Environmental chemistry. (E-mail: wljohnso@mailbox.syr.edu)
Chuck Kroll. Environmental modeling. (E-mail: cnkroll@mailbox.syr.edu)
Valerie Luzadis. Economic valuation and modeling. (E-mail: vluzadis@mailbox.syr.edu)
Myron Mitchell. Biogeochemistry, nutrient cycling. (E-mail: mitchell@mailbox.syr.edu)
Tsutomu Nakatsugawa. Toxicology, health impacts. (E-mail: tnakatsu@mailbox.syr.edu)

Water & Wetland Resources

The water and wetland resources area of study develops an understanding of technical, social, and institutional aspects of water resources management, mitigation, and restoration. Individual students may emphasize scientific or social subject areas, but all study in both areas. Scientific aspects include the basic physical, chemical, and biological interactions occurring in water resource systems. The social aspects are concerned with planning, regulation, law and institutions, and management of water and wetland resources. Water serves as the focus of graduate study in water and related land resources management and water pollution and water quality control.

Richard Smardon, Coordinator. Wetland assessment, water resource planning, and Great Lakes policy. (E-mail: rsmardon@mailbox.syr.edu)
Guy Baldassarre. Waterfowl ecology. (E-mail: gabaldas@mailbox.syr.edu)
Peter Black. Water and related land resources. (E-mail: peblack@mailbox.syr.edu)
James Hassett. Hydrology and modeling. (E-mail: jhassett@mailbox.syr.edu)
Chuck Kroll. Hydrology and modeling. (E-mail: cnkroll@mailbox.syr.edu)
Donald Leopold. Wetland ecology. (E-mail: dendro@mailbox.syr.edu)

Student working on GIS.

Group student problem solving.

UNIVERSITY OF CALIFORNIA, BERKELEY

Department of Environmental Science, Policy, and Management

Programs of Study

The Department of Environmental Science, Policy, and Management (ESPM) offers both the M.S. and Ph.D. degrees in environmental science, policy, and management. The degree programs address current and future anthropogenic environmental problems of major social and political impact that are based in the biological and physical sciences. Two general kinds of education are needed to produce people qualified to address these hybrid problems: 1) broadly based interdisciplinary education, and 2) disciplinary education in relevant fields supplemented with exposure to cross-disciplinary communication and problem solving. The program integrates the biological, social, and physical sciences to provide advanced education in basic and applied environmental sciences, develops critical analytical abilities, and fosters the capacity to conduct research into the structure and function of ecosystems at molecular through ecosystem levels and their interlinked human social systems.

The program in ESPM requires that a student complete three core courses and course work in the following four areas: disciplinary emphasis, area of specialization, research methods, and breadth requirement, in addition to the dissertation. Working with a Graduate Advisor and a Guiding Committee, the student designs a program that fulfills the program requirements and meets the student's individual needs. The Ph.D. requires approximately five years to complete.

The research areas in ESPM vary widely but include biology and ecology of insects; ecosystem function and environmental issues of the atmosphere; soil, water, and plant health/interactions from molecular to ecosystem levels; wildlife ecology, conservation, and management; forest and resource policy, sustainability, and management; range management and ecology; and social distributions of power and resources affecting environmental dynamics and their social consequences.

Research Facilities

Departmental facilities offer state-of-the-art instrumentation and laboratories, insectary buildings, controlled environment chambers, extensive greenhouse space, and field plots at the Oxford Tract (on campus) and are available to support graduate student research and education. Field facilities available include the 3,500-acre Blodgett Forest, Whitaker's Forest (with giant sequoia stands adjacent to King's Canyon National Park), and Russell Reservation, which is located 13 miles east of the campus. Students may conduct research at any of several University of California Field Stations located throughout the state.

The University library system includes more than 8 million volumes, 90,000 current serial publications, 400,000 maps, and hundreds of thousands of government documents. The Bioscience and Natural Resources Library branch houses more than 450,000 volumes and subscribes to more than 8,300 journals, including government publications from the United States and other countries.

Financial Aid

ESPM makes every effort to support entering and continuing students from a variety of funding sources, including University Fellowships, Departmentally Restricted Fellowships, Graduate Student Research (GSR) Assistantships and Graduate Student Instructor (GSI) positions. The stipend for the fellowships and GSR assistantships is approximately $11,490 for ten months, and a waiver is included for fees ($4408.50 per year) and, if necessary, a nonresident tuition waiver ($10,323 per year) is provided. Offers of financial support are made at the time ESPM makes formal offers of admission.

Cost of Study

If an applicant does not receive financial support from the department, the cost for graduate study in 2000–2001 will be $4408.50 per year for fees and, when necessary, an additional $10,323 per year for nonresident tuition. Books and supplies may cost an additional $825 per year.

Living and Housing Costs

Berkeley graduate students live in both University and community housing. The cost of University housing varies from $624 to $676 per month for a studio in a residence hall to $401 to $645 per month for apartments in married student housing. Those students seeking community housing may find that the cost varies from $650 to $950 for a studio and from $750 to $1100 for a one-bedroom apartment.

Student Group

ESPM has 200 full-time graduate students in the program who come from a wide variety of academic, cultural, and national backgrounds. The student group consists of 52 percent men and 48 percent women, of whom approximately 11 percent are international students.

Student Outcomes

ESPM has been monitoring initial employment for graduates for several years and has found that 32 percent accept postdoctoral fellowships, 28 percent secure academic (tenure and non-tenure track) positions, 17 percent are employed by nongovernmental organizations, 13 percent accept positions with government agencies, and 10 percent pursue careers in consulting, industry, or research.

Location

Berkeley is a large and complex institution surrounded by wooded rolling hills and by the city of Berkeley, where the population is 106,500. The San Francisco Bay Area offers culture, entertainment, and natural beauty. All of northern California, with its great variety of cultural and recreational opportunities, is within easy reach.

The University

The University of California, Berkeley, was founded in 1868. Berkeley's faculty includes 7 Nobel laureates, 118 members of the National Academy of Sciences, and 69 members of the National Academy of Engineering. In national surveys, Berkeley's academic departments consistently rank among the top five in the country. The Department of Environmental Science, Policy, and Management is the largest of four academic departments in the College of Natural Resources, with 74 faculty members and affiliates, 200 graduate students, and 260 undergraduate students.

Applying

Applicants must submit a Graduate Division application form postmarked by December 15, 1999, to be considered for admission for fall 2000. ESPM accepts applications for the fall semester only. The Graduate Division application is available by contacting the department or may be downloaded from the Graduate Division Home Page (http://amber.berkeley.edu:5900/). A nonrefundable fee of $40 is required at the time of submission.

Correspondence and Information

Graduate Student Services Office
Department of Environmental Science, Policy, and Management
145 Mulford Hall #3114
University of California, Berkeley
Berkeley, California 94720-3114

Telephone: 510-642-6410
Fax: 510-643-5438
E-mail: espmgradproginfo@nature.berkeley.edu
World Wide Web: http://www.cnr.Berkeley.edu/departments/espm/grad/

University of California, Berkeley

THE FACULTY AND THEIR RESEARCH

Barbara Allen-Díaz, Associate Professor, Division of Ecosystem Science. Rangeland ecology and management.
Miguel A. Altieri, Associate Professor, Division of Insect Biology. Biological control, agroecology.
Ronald G. Amundson, Professor, Division of Ecosystem Science. Pedology and isotope biogeochemistry.
Dennis Baldocchi, Acting Associate Professor, Division of Ecosystem Science. Biometeorology, biosphere-atmosphere trace gas fluxes.
Reginald H. Barrett, Professor, Division of Ecosystem Science, Wildlife biology and management.
James W. Bartolome, Professor and ESPM Chair, Division of Ecosystem Science. Rangeland ecology and management.
John J. Battles, Assistant Professor, Division of Ecosystem Science. Forest community ecology.
Frank C. Beall, Professor, Division of Forest Science. Forest products and wood technology.
Steven R. Beissinger, Associate Professor, Division of Ecosystem Science. Conservation biology.
Tracy L. Benning, Assistant Professor, Division of Ecosystem Science. Landscape ecology.
Peter Berck, Professor, Division of Resource Institutions, Policy, and Management. Natural resources and applied microeconomics.
Gregory S. Biging, Professor, Division of Ecosystem Science. Forest biometrics and remote sensing.
Alexander Borst, Acting Associate Professor, Division of Insect Biology. Neural image processing.
Thomas D. Bruns, Associate Professor, Division of Ecosystem Science. Fungal molecular evolution and ecology.
Claudia J. Carr, Associate Professor, Division of Resource Institutions, Policy, and Management. International/rural resource development.
John E. Casida, Professor, Division of Insect Biology. Pesticide chemistry and toxicology.
Ignacio H. Chapela, Assistant Professor, Division of Ecosystem Science. Microbial ecology.
Donald L. Dahlsten, Professor, Division of Insect Biology. Forest entomology, biological control.
Howell V. Daly, Professor of the Graduate School, Division of Insect Biology. Systematic entomology.
Alain de Janvry, Professor, Division of Resource Institutions, Policy, and Management. International rural economic development.
Richard S. Dodd, Associate Professor, Division of Forest Science. Wood formation by plant systematics/evolution.
Harvey E. Doner, Professor, Division of Ecosystem Science. Soil chemistry, trace elements, elemental associations/distributions.
Sally K. Fairfax, Professor, Division of Resource Institutions, Policy, and Management. Conservation policy/public land administration,
Mary K. Firestone, Professor, Division of Ecosystem Science. Soil microbiology, nutrient cycling.
Louise P. Fortmann, Professor, Division of Resource Institutions, Policy, and Management. Natural resource sociology.
Gordon W. Frankie, Professor, Division of Insect Biology. Urban entomology.
Inez Y. Fung, Professor, Division of Ecosystem Science. Climate change, biogeochemical cycles.
Paul L. Gersper, Associate Professor, Division of Forest Science. Soil-plant relationships, land use.
Wayne M. Getz, Professor, Division of Insect Biology. Insect olfaction, resource and wildlife management.
Masoud Ghodrati, Assistant Professor, Division of Ecosystem Science. Soil physics.
Gregory S. Gilbert, Assistant Professor, Division of Ecosystem Science. Plant disease ecology.
Rosemary Gillespie, Associate Professor, Division of Insect Biology. Evolution, conservation, Pacific islands.
J. Keith Gilless, Associate Professor, Division of Resource Institutions, Policy, and Management. Forest economics.
Allen H. Goldstein, Assistant Professor, Division of Ecosystem Science. Biogeochemistry, atmospheric chemistry.
Peng Gong, Associate Professor, Division of Ecosystem Science. Remote sensing and GIS.
Andrew P. Gutierrez, Professor, Division of Ecosystem Science. Systems ecology, biological control.
W. Michael Hanemann, Professor, Division of Resource Institutions, Policy, and Management. Environmental economics and policy.
John Harte, Professor, Division of Ecosystem Science. Global change, ecosystem ecology, biodiversity.
Oenes C. Huisman, Associate Professor, Division of Insect Biology. Fungal ecology, pathogen physiology.
Lynn Huntsinger, Associate Professor, Division of Ecosystem Science. Rangeland ecology and conservation.
Judith E. Innes, Professor, Division of Resource Institutions, Policy, and Management. Social policy analysis.
Nina Maggi Kelly, Adjunct Assistant Professor, Division of Ecosystem Science. GIS/remote sensing, wetlands, coastal management.
Isao Kubo, Professor, Division of Insect Biology. Natural products chemistry.
Robert S. Lane, Professor, Division of Insect Biology. Parasitology, tick biology.
Steven E. Lindow, Professor, Division of Insect Biology. Microbial ecology, epidemiology of bacterial plant diseases.
Joe R. McBride, Professor, Division of Forest Science. Forest ecology.
John G. McColl, Professor, Division of Ecosystem Science. Soil science: nutrient cycling, forest soils.
Dale R. McCullough, Professor, Division of Ecosystem Science. Wildlife biology and management.
Carolyn Merchant, Professor, Division of Resource Institutions, Policy, and Management. Environmental history, philosophy, ethics.
Adina M. Merenlender, Adjunct Assistant Professor, Division of Ecosystem Science. Ecology, conservation biology, landscape ecology.
Nicholas J. Mills, Associate Professor, Division of Insect Biology. Biological control.
Katharine Milton, Professor, Division of Insect Biology. Tropical ecology of human/nonhuman primates, diet, parasite-host interactions.
T. N. Narasimhan, Professor, Division of Ecosystem Science. Groundwater in relation to ecosystems/environment, water policy.
Kevin L. O'Hara, Associate Professor, Division of Forest Science. Stand dynamics, silviculture, forest management.
Kate O'Neill, Assistant Professor, Division of Resource Institutions, Policy, and Management. International environmental politics/political economy.
George F. Oster, Professor, Division of Insect Biology. Mathematical ecology.
Nancy L. Peluso, Associate Professor, Division of Resource Institutions, Policy, and Management. Environmental sociology/resource policy.
Jerry A. Powell, Professor of the Graduate School, Division of Insect Biology. Systematic entomology.
Alexander H. Purcell, Professor, Division of Insect Biology. Insect vectors of plant pathogens.
Ye Qi, Assistant Professor, Division of Resource Institutions, Policy, and Management. Ecosystem modeling and management.
Vincent H. Resh, Professor, Division of Insect Biology. Aquatic ecology.
George Roderick, Assistant Professor, Division of Insect Biology. Population biology and genetics, evolution.
Jeffrey M. Romm, Professor, Division of Resource Institutions, Policy, and Management. Natural resource and environmental policy.
Elisabeth Sadoulet, Associate Professor, Division of Resource Institutions, Policy, and Management. International economic development.
Whendee L. Silver, Assistant Professor, Division of Ecosystem Science. Ecosystem ecology.
Felix A. H. Sperling, Assistant Professor, Division of Insect Biology. Arthropod systematics.
Garrison Sposito, Professor, Division of Ecosystem Science. Soil physical chemistry.
Mark A. Tanouye, Professor, Division of Insect Biology. Insect neurophysiology.
Loy E. Volkman, Professor, Division of Insect Biology. Baculovirus pathogenesis and host interactions.
Stephen C. Welter, Associate Professor, Division of Insect Biology. Agriculture entomology/plant-insect interactions
Lee C. Wensel, Professor, Division of Forest Science. Sampling inventory, mensuration.
W. Wayne Wilcox, Professor, Division of Forest Science. Biodeterioration.
Carroll B. Williams, Adjunct Professor, Division of Forest Science. Forest pest management.
David L. Wood, Professor of the Graduate School, Division of Insect Biology. Forest entomology/chemical ecology.

UNIVERSITY OF CALIFORNIA, SANTA BARBARA

Donald Bren School of Environmental Science and Management

Programs of Study

The Master of Environmental Science and Management (M.E.S.M.) is a professional degree intended for students who are going to enter or reenter the workforce after graduation. The two-year master's program of study includes a set of core courses that provide significant graduate-level training in both science and management. Students are also trained in statistics, mathematics, and computation. The curriculum is rigorous in its quantitative and analytical approach and challenges students to become complex problem solvers. Beyond the core courses, each master's student selects an area in which to specialize and creates, with faculty guidance, an individual program of study that is appropriate for that specialization given the student's background, interests, and goals. The most unique aspect of the Bren School master's program is the three-quarter capstone Group Project that serves as a master's thesis. Students work in teams of 5 to 7 to address a current problem in environmental policy or management for which effective solutions require application of scientific research and analysis in a policy or management context. Students are strongly encouraged to collaborate with outside entities (industry, government, NGOs) to produce projects that are useful to applicable real-life clients.

The Ph.D. program aims to preserve the University of California, Santa Barbara's (UCSB) mission of training high-caliber future research professors while simultaneously meeting the urgent need for highly trained personnel in the public and private sectors. The cornerstone of the doctoral degree is an original piece of research in environmental science and/or management. The requirements for the Ph.D. are highly individualized. Students, in conjunction with their doctoral committee, design a course of study that enables them to become experts and high-level researchers in a particular area of specialization. The program is designed to accommodate a wide range of Ph.D. students and their interests, from those who are highly focused in a particular discipline to those who are strongly interdisciplinary and whose research integrates the component disciplines. Admission to the Ph.D. program is highly competitive and dependent upon acceptance by a faculty sponsor with compatible research interests. A master's degree is not required for admission. Ph.D. students may choose to enrich their program of study by participating in the University's new Graduate Program in Management Practice to gain a sound and essential introduction to the fundamentals of business management.

Research Facilities

Currently, there are research laboratories housed within the School for the disciplines of environmental microbiology and biogeochemistry. The new Donald Bren Building, in which the School of Environmental Science and Management will be housed, is due to be completed in 2001 and will provide fully integrated environmental laboratories. The student computing facility contains thirty workstations for student use and teaching.

Financial Aid

For exceptional master's applicants, the School makes awards of $3000 to $7000 per year for student support in the form of teaching assistant (TA) positions and stipends. Sponsoring professors usually provide graduate student research assistant support for their Ph.D. students, who may also be eligible for campus-based fellowships. Loans and other federally based support are available through the Financial Aid Office.

Cost of Study

Graduate student expenses for 1998–99 were $16,300 for California residents and $25,200 for nonresidents. The figures include housing, food, books and supplies, personal expenses, transportation, and fees.

Living and Housing Costs

There is a high demand for rental housing in the Santa Barbara area, and per-month prices range from $550 for a studio and $990 for a two-bedroom apartment to $1873 for a three-bedroom house (these costs are averages only).

Student Group

Students at the School range from those who arrive straight from their undergraduate training to those who have spent years working in such varied fields as engineering, ecology, and human resources.

Student Outcomes

The Bren School operates its own career development program, which is committed to helping students develop the necessary job search and career development skills needed for successful transition into rewarding environmental careers after graduation. With the Bren School's interdisciplinary approach and strong career development program, students find employment and develop successful careers in a variety of environmental positions and organizations. Graduates work for consulting firms, corporations, governments, universities, and nonprofit organizations. Some recent graduates are working in the following positions: environmental scientist, planner, researcher, environmental policy analyst, junior environmental engineer, environmental consultant, senior engineer, assistant project manager, and project scientist.

Location

The School is located on the California coast about 100 miles north of the Los Angeles metropolitan area and 10 miles west of Santa Barbara. The campus is surrounded by extraordinary natural beauty and is blessed with a mild, Mediterranean climate. Santa Barbara is the ideal setting for the study of environmental science and management.

The School

The Donald Bren School of Environmental Science and Management is a professional school aimed at training graduate students in rigorous, interdisciplinary approaches to environmental problem solving. The School was renamed the Donald Bren School of Environmental Science and Management in December 1997 in honor of a major gift from the Donald Bren Foundation. The School's faculty members are recognized leaders or rising new stars in their disciplinary fields and also dedicated to innovative, interdisciplinary research and teaching. The School graduated its first class of professional master's students in June 1998 and initiated a research-oriented Ph.D. program in fall 1998.

The mission of the Bren School is to produce professionals with outstanding training in environmental science and management who will devote their skills to the diagnosis, assessment, mitigation, prevention, and remediation of environmental problems of today and in the future. The Bren School's goal is to produce a graduate who understands the environment from an integrated natural and social science perspective and has an appreciation and understanding of the interrelationship of business and economics, law and public policy, and science; has rigorous training in quantitative and analytical approaches to problem solving; has skills in modern technological tools and applications; and understands societal and institutional frameworks.

The purpose of the Bren gift is to support this mission by transforming the School into a multicampus interdisciplinary program. The Bren School takes advantage of the great academic strengths of the UC system by coupling Santa Barbara's extraordinary strength in natural sciences with the expertise in law, public policy, and business management that exists at other UC campuses. The Bren School's curriculum is designed to take advantage of other campuses' courses and faculty members for regular offerings that are part of the School's degree programs.

Applying

Prospective students may apply electronically (http://www.graddiv.ucsb.edu/admissions/adm_index.html) or contact the School for an application form. They should be prepared to submit a statement of purpose, three letters of recommendation, two copies of official transcripts for all tertiary-level institutions, an application fee (currently $40), official GRE scores, recent TOEFL scores for nonnative English speakers, and a resume. Applications are normally accepted for the fall only; the application deadline is February 1 for primary consideration and for consideration for School-based financial support. Applications are accepted until May 1, space permitting. Ph.D. students who wish to be considered in the campuswide fellowship competition must have their applications completed by December 15.

Correspondence and Information

Donald Bren School of Environmental Science and Management
4670 Physical Sciences North
University of California, Santa Barbara
Santa Barbara, California 93106-5131

Telephone: 805-893-7611
Fax: 805-893-7612
E-mail: info@bren.ucsb.edu
World Wide Web: http://www.bren.ucsb.edu

University of California, Santa Barbara

THE FACULTY AND THEIR RESEARCH

The Bren School is currently engaged in an extensive campaign of faculty recruitment and will appoint approximately 17 full-time faculty members by the year 2001. Many additional faculty members will hold joint appointments between the School and other UCSB departments. More than 20 affiliated faculty members from other departments and campuses further diversify and strengthen the Bren School's teaching, research, and curriculum development.

Jeff Dozier, Dean; Ph.D., Michigan, 1973. Snow science, hydrology, hydrochemistry of alpine regions, remote sensing.
Dennis Aigner, Bren Associate Dean (UC Irvine); Ph.D., Berkeley, 1963. Environmental management.
John Dwyer, Bren Associate Dean (UC Berkeley); Ph.D., Caltech, 1978. Environmental law.
*Frank Davis, Professor; Ph.D., Johns Hopkins, 1982. Terrestrial biogeography, plant ecology, conservation biology.
Magali Delmas, Assistant Professor; Ph.D., Graduate School of Management (Paris), 1996. Environmental policy and management.
Thomas Dunne, Professor; Ph.D., Johns Hopkins, 1969. Geomorphology and hydrology.
James Frew, Assistant Professor; Ph.D., California, Santa Barbara, 1990. Information science.
Patricia Holden, Assistant Professor; Ph.D., Berkeley, 1995. Environmental microbiology, bioremediation.
Arturo Keller, Assistant Professor; Ph.D., Stanford, 1997. Biogeochemistry, fate and transport of pollutants in the environment.
Bruce Kendall, Assistant Professor; Ph.D., Arizona, 1996. Population ecology, conservation biology, metapopulation dynamics.
*Charles D. Kolstad, Professor; Ph.D., Stanford, 1982. Environmental economics, climate.
Natalie Mahowald, Assistant Professor; Ph.D., MIT, 1996. Atmospheric transport, atmospheric chemistry, biogeochemistry.
*John Melack, Professor; Ph.D., Duke, 1976. Limnology, ecology, biogeochemistry, remote sensing.
*David Siegel, Professor; Ph.D., USC, 1988. Optical oceanography, ocean color remote sensing.

Joint appointment with at least one other UCSB department.

UNIVERSITY OF DELAWARE

Center for Energy and Environmental Policy

Programs of Study	The Center for Energy and Environmental Policy (CEEP), under the auspices of the Graduate College of Human Resources, Education and Public Policy (CHEP) at the University of Delaware, provides graduate instruction and conducts interdisciplinary research in the areas of energy policy, environmental policy, and sustainability development. Collaborative research and exchange agreements to foster international research and graduate study have been established with Asian, African, Latin American, and European universities and research institutes. CEEP is composed of an internationally diverse faculty and graduate student body with backgrounds in political science, economics, sociology, geography, philosophy, urban planning, environmental studies, history, anthropology, and engineering.
	CEEP offers M.A. and Ph.D. programs of study in urban affairs and public policy, with specializations in the following areas: comparative energy and environmental policy; environmental justice; conservation and renewable energy policy; integrated resource planning; and technology, environment, and society. The M.A. degree includes 36 credit hours of graduate work, of which 15 are in the core curriculum and at least 12 are in an area of specialization. The Ph.D. program has three components: a 15-credit-hour core curriculum, the development of a research area and the dissertation proposal involving at least 27 credit hours, and the writing of the dissertation. In addition, two new programs of study are supported: a Master of Energy and Environmental Policy (M.E.E.P.) and a Ph.D. in Energy and Environmental Policy (Ph.D./E.E.P.). The new degrees offer in-depth study in the fields of sustainable development, energy policy, the political economy of energy and the environment, disasters research, and environmental policy. The M.E.E.P. includes 36 credits, of which 15 credits are electives; the Ph.D./E.E.P. includes 45 credits, of which 24 credits are electives. CEEP also supports a specialization in environmental and energy management in the 42-credit Master of Public Administration (M.P.A.) program.
	Opportunities exist for students to participate in research projects on such topics as socioeconomic impacts of global climate change, economic and environmental evaluation of renewable energy options (especially photovoltaic technology), environmental ethics, impacts of the Clean Air Act Amendments of 1990, development of a sustainability index, sustainable urban development strategies, energy and poverty issues, integrated resource planning and demand-side management in developing countries, and water conservation planning and policy. Students have obtained paid internships with the World Bank, UNDP, overseas research institutes, U.S. senators' offices, federal and state government agencies, and nonprofit organizations.
Research Facilities	University Libraries contain more than 2 million books and journals and serve as a depository library for U.S. government publications. The University maintains a computerized online catalog, accessible via a campus computer network, the Internet, and telephone and computer modem from anywhere in the world. The University's computing services include microcomputer laboratories, UNIX multiworkstation and time-sharing facilities, and an IBM vector processing time-sharing service.
Financial Aid	Nearly three quarters of CEEP graduate students receive financial awards. University and minority fellowships, tuition scholarships, and research assistantships are awarded on the basis of merit. Awards are made only to full-time students in good academic standing. It is current CEEP policy that students admitted to the Ph.D. program in research areas related to ongoing Center activity are awarded full assistantships covering tuition (up to $12,750 per year) and stipend ($11,000 in 1999–2000). Funding may be provided for four years, depending upon academic performance. Students admitted to the M.A. program may receive research stipends during their first year of study and full assistantships in their second year.
Cost of Study	In 1999–2000, graduate tuition is $4380 per year for full-time resident students and $12,750 per year for full-time nonresident students. Full-time matriculated students are automatically assessed nonrefundable fees for health ($282) and student-sponsored activities ($100).
Living and Housing Costs	The University's Office of Housing and Residence Life offers graduate students a number of housing options. Single graduate student housing rates range from $320 to $640. Family housing rates range from $620 to $715. The cost includes all utilities and local telephone service. Students who are seeking accommodations in adjacent residential areas within walking or commuting distance should contact the Off-Campus Housing Office for a list of rooms, apartments, and houses to rent or share. Further information can be obtained from the Office of Housing and Conference Services (telephone: 302-831-2491).
Student Group	Enrollment at the University in 1998–99 included 15,629 undergraduate students, 3,250 graduate students, and 2,287 students in the Division of Continuing Education. Currently, the University offers eighty different programs leading to a master's degree and forty programs leading to a doctoral degree through forty-six departments in its seven instructional colleges. Fall 1999 graduate enrollment in CEEP includes 27 Ph.D. and 30 M.A. students.
Location	The main campus of the University is located in the residential community of Newark. Newark is a suburban community of 30,000, located midway between Philadelphia and Baltimore and within 2 hours by train of New York City and Washington, D.C. Newark lies a short distance from the Delaware and Chesapeake bays and from Delaware's ocean beaches.
The University	The University is a comprehensive land- and sea-grant institution of higher education. Opened in 1743, the Newark campus currently consists of 991 acres and a $499-million physical plant with 318 buildings, including classrooms, laboratories, athletic complexes, and student activity centers. Other land holdings include a 405-acre Marine Studies Complex and a 347-acre Agricultural Substation. The University's distinguished faculty includes internationally recognized researchers, artists, authors, and teachers. In 1999 there are thirty-nine named professorships. The University community includes 915 faculty members, 69 postdoctoral fellows, 967 research staff, 913 salaried staff, and 481 hourly employees.
Applying	For the M.A. and M.E.E.P. degrees, the successful candidate for admission must have an undergraduate GPA above 3.0 (on a 4.0 scale). A combined GRE score above 1100 (math and verbal portions) is normally expected. Admission to the Ph.D. program requires a master's degree with at least a 3.5 GPA. A combined GRE score above 1150 (math and verbal portions) is normally expected. Complete applications contain three letters of recommendation, a 1,000-word statement of the applicant's research interest, academic transcript(s), and GRE scores. For students whose first language is not English, a demonstrated proficiency in English is required. This may be judged on the basis of a TOEFL score of at least 550. Ph.D. students are expected to have TOEFL scores above 600. Most students are admitted for the fall semester. A completed admission application and all credentials should be submitted by March 1 to guarantee consideration for financial aid.
Correspondence and Information	Dr. John Byrne, Director Center for Energy and Environmental Policy College of Human Resources, Education and Public Policy University of Delaware Newark, Delaware 19716
	Telephone: 302-831-8405 Fax: 302-831-3098 E-mail: jbbyrne@udel.edu World Wide Web: http://www.udel.edu/ceep

University of Delaware

THE FACULTY AND THEIR RESEARCH

Core Faculty

John M. Byrne, Professor, Graduate School of Urban Affairs and Public Policy, and Director of the Center for Energy and Environmental Policy (CEEP); Ph.D., Delaware, 1980. Technology, environment and society, political economy, sustainable development, environmental justice.

Paul T. Durbin, Professor, Department of Philosophy and CEEP Senior Policy Fellow; Ph.D., Aquinas Institute, 1966. Technology and society, philosophy of science, environmental ethics.

Yda Schreuder, Associate Professor, Department of Geography, and CEEP Senior Policy Fellow; Ph.D., Wisconsin–Madison, 1982. Global resources, development, and environment; sustainable development and growth management.

Richard T. Sylves, Professor, Department of Political Science and International Relations and College of Human Resources, Education and Public Policy; CEEP Senior Policy Fellow; and Director, Energy and Environmental Policy Program; Ph.D., Illinois, 1976. Environmental policy, emergency response management, energy policy.

Young-Doo Wang, Associate Professor, Graduate School of Urban Affairs and Public Policy, and CEEP Associate Director; Ph.D., Delaware, 1980. Energy and environmental policy, economic analysis of alternative energy options, econometric applications.

Adjunct Faculty

Cesar Cuello, Professor of Social Sciences, Instituto Tecnologico de Costa Rica, and CEEP Policy Fellow; Ph.D., Delaware, 1997. Sustainable development; philosophy of science, technology, and society; environmental philosophy.

J. Barry Cullingworth, Professor of Land Use Planning and Oxford and CEEP Senior Policy Fellow; Oxford, 1974; MRTPI, FRSA. Environmental planning, land-use policy, urban management.

Steven M. Hoffman, Professor and Director, Environmental Studies Program, St. Thomas (Minnesota), and CEEP Senior Policy Fellow; Ph.D., Delaware, 1986. Technology and society, political economy, energy and environmental policy.

Jong-dall Kim, Associate Professor and Director, Research Institute for Energy, Environment, and Economy, Kyungpuk National University (Korea), and CEEP Policy Fellow; Ph.D., Delaware, 1991. Energy and environmental policy analysis, sustainable development, integrated resource planning.

Cecilia Martinez, Assistant Professor, Metropolitan State (Minnesota); Research Fellow, American Indian Research and Policy Institute; and CEEP Policy Fellow; Ph.D., Delaware, 1990. Technology, environment and society, political economy, energy and environmental policy.

UNIVERSITY OF RHODE ISLAND

Department of Marine Affairs

Programs of Study	The Department of Marine Affairs offers master's degrees and a Ph.D. in marine affairs for those with interests in the policy and management of ocean and coastal environments. Courses and research opportunities are available in coastal management, fisheries management, marine ecosystem management, maritime transportation and ports, national and international ocean policy, and marine human ecology. Within the instructional program of the University of Rhode Island (URI), there are more than 150 graduate-level courses in eighteen marine and environmental topic areas. Many are directly pertinent to the research and instructional programs of the Department of Marine Affairs.
	The Master of Arts (M.A.) in marine affairs is a two-year degree for recent college graduates. The Master of Marine Affairs (M.M.A.) is a one-year degree for those with five or more years of significant experience in the field or those who already have a relevant graduate degree. The M.M.A./J.D. joint-degree program between the University of Rhode Island and Roger Williams University Law School allows the completion of law and marine affairs degrees in less than four years.
	The Ph.D. in marine affairs is for highly motivated individuals holding a master's degree in a related field who wish to complete advanced research pertinent to careers in ocean and coastal management, in academic research, and in teaching.
Research Facilities	The Department of Marine Affairs faculty and students occupy facilities in the colonial village of Kingston. The main offices house a library of trade magazines and newsletters as well as a computer laboratory that is devoted to student use. The University libraries, located on both the Kingston and Narragansett Bay campuses, have particular emphasis in marine topics and hold approximately 1 million bound volumes and the equivalent of 1 million volumes in microform. A geographic information system (GIS) laboratory is also available on campus. Other specialized units at URI that are related to marine affairs include the Coastal Partnership, the Coastal Institute, the Sea Grant Program, and the Coastal Resources Center.
Financial Aid	A limited number of competitive, partial graduate assistantships are available for M.A. students in their second year of study. Assistantships provide tuition waivers and a stipend. Highly qualified Ph.D. candidates are offered full graduate assistantships for the first two years of study. Research projects in the department and allied units at the University provide employment for students as well. In addition, marine affairs students may compete for a small number of University-wide tuition waivers and scholarships. Student loans and Federal Work-Study Program positions are also available. The University strongly encourages application for financial assistance from members of minority and underrepresented groups.
Cost of Study	In 1999–2000, the annual estimated cost of tuition for full-time graduate study is $4054 for Rhode Island residents, $5824 for regional students, and $10,630 for nonresidents. Full-time graduate student fees total $1342.
Living and Housing Costs	There are approximately 140 unfurnished apartments available on campus for graduate students. There is a long waiting list for these apartments. As the University is located in a summer resort area, most students live off-campus in September-to-June (off-season) rentals. Monthly rents generally range from $600 to $1200, depending on size and location. Year-round and summer housing are more expensive.
Student Group	The University of Rhode Island has approximately 17,000 students on three campuses—Kingston, Narragansett, and Providence. The Kingston campus, where the programs are located, has 13,000 students. There are about 3,700 graduate students. Each year there are about 60 graduate students in residence in the marine affairs program. To date, the department has enrolled students from more than forty-five nations. While most of the M.A. students are full-time, many of the M.M.A. students are already employed and study on a part-time basis.
Student Outcomes	For marine affairs graduates, the National Oceanic and Atmospheric Administration (NOAA) is a prominent employer; however, graduates have joined the USEPA, the U.S. Department of the Interior, the National Science Foundation (NSF), the U.S. Agency for International Development (USAID), the United States Coast Guard (USCG), and research groups such as Resources for the Future. State departments of the environment or coastal management as well as local planning agencies seek marine affairs graduates. Nongovernmental organizations at the national (World Wildlife Fund, Conservation International, Center for Marine Conservation), regional (Save the Bay, Chesapeake Bay Foundation), and local levels employ students from the program. Consulting and engineering firms (Bechtel, Arthur D. Little, and CH2M Hill) as well as ports have also attracted graduates. International students, often sent by their governments, return to their home countries or to an international organization such as the United Nations with significant advancements in their responsibilities.
Location	The main campus of the University is situated in Kingston, Rhode Island, a suburban/rural environment close to the ocean and about 30 miles south of Providence. The Bay campus is located in Narragansett on the west shore of Narragansett Bay and just a few miles from the main campus.
The University	The University of Rhode Island is a medium-sized, land-grant, state university. Because of its location near the ocean and Narragansett Bay, URI has developed strong marine and environmental programs. The small size of the state of Rhode Island and the excellence of the University's marine affairs programs means that students come into frequent contact with government officials at all levels and are often involved with officials in research projects, internships, and classroom experiences.
Applying	The primary application deadline is April 15 for fall and summer admission, but applications are accepted until July 15 on a space-available basis. International applications for the fall semester are due in the Department of Marine Affairs by February 1. Admission for all programs is based on the applicant's undergraduate academic record, current GRE scores, a specific statement of purpose, and letters of recommendation. The GRE requirement is waived for applicants for the M.M.A. degree program.
Correspondence and Information	Graduate Program Department of Marine Affairs Washburn Hall University of Rhode Island Kingston, Rhode Island 02881-0817 Telephone: 401-874-2596 Fax: 401-874-2156 E-mail: smyette@uri.edu World Wide Web: http://www.uri.edu/artsci/maf

University of Rhode Island

THE FACULTY AND THEIR RESEARCH

Lewis Alexander, Professor Emeritus; Ph.D. (geography), Clark. International maritime boundaries, marine jurisdictional issues, international fisheries.

Richard Burroughs, Professor and Chair; Ph.D. (oceanography), MIT/Woods Hole Oceanographic. Marine environmental policy formulation, implementation, and evaluation; ecosystem management; marine pollution; science and public policy; estuaries.

Christopher Dyer, Assistant Professor; Ph.D. (anthropology), Arizona State. Fisheries management, coastal disasters and hazards, implications of climatic change for coastal communities, maritime anthropology.

William R. Gordon, Associate Professor; Ph.D. (environmental planning), Texas A&M. Environmental law and planning, environmental impact assessment and auditing, coastal and water resources management (U.S. and international), program and policy evaluation, artificial reef planning and management, marine recreational fisheries, GIS/LIS applications.

Timothy Hennessey, Professor of Political Science and Marine Affairs; Ph.D. (political science), North Carolina. Role of science in marine policy, adaptive management of estuarine ecosystems, fishery management policy, program evaluation of natural resource and coastal management systems.

Lawrence Juda, Professor; Ph.D. (political science/international relations), Columbia. International and national ocean law, policy, and institutions; ocean governance and management systems and their evolution; international fishery problems; maritime policy.

Gerald H. Krausse, Associate Professor; Ph.D. (geography), Pittsburgh. Island ecosystem management, sustainable tourism, and marine park management; urban waterfront development and community participation.

Bruce Marti, Professor; Ph.D. (geography), Florida. Economic geography, transportation geography, maritime transport, port planning and development.

Dennis W. Nixon, Professor; J.D., Cincinnati. Admiralty law, with particular reference to research and fishing vessels; fisheries law and management; coastal zone law; marine pollution law; marine insurance.

John Poggie, Professor of Anthropology and Marine Affairs; Ph.D. (anthropology), Minnesota. Maritime anthropology, fishing communities, and human maritime adaptations.

Richard Pollnac, Professor of Anthropology and Marine Affairs; Ph.D. (anthropology), Missouri. Human adaptation to the marine environment.

Niels West, Professor; Ph.D. (geography), Rutgers. Environmental impact assessment, coastal demography, marine recreation and tourism, marine affairs as a discipline.

UNIVERSITY OF VIRGINIA

Department of Environmental Sciences

Programs of Study	The Department of Environmental Sciences (EVSC) is an academic department that offers instruction and conducts research in the areas of ecology, geosciences, hydrology, and atmospheric sciences. This unique juxtaposition of several sciences in one department fosters cooperation and exchange among traditional disciplines that share similar methodological and philosophical problems. The research endeavors of both the faculty and graduate students, whether disciplinary or interdisciplinary, deal largely with problems of fundamental scientific interest. Research fields include environmental biogeochemistry, coastal processes, hydrogeology, catchment hydrology, microbial ecology, wetlands ecology, terrestrial ecology, boundary-layer meteorology, atmospheric chemistry, and climatology. Initiatives involving groups of faculty members in contaminant hydrogeology, global environmental change, and coastal ecosystems encompass a number of graduate research opportunities.
	The department offers two graduate degree programs: the Master of Science (M.S.) and the Doctor of Philosophy (Ph.D.). The M.S. program emphasizes research in addition to fundamental course work. A degree candidate must complete a minimum of 24 credit hours of course work, including one course from each of the four core-areas of the department (ecology, hydrology, geosciences, and atmospheric sciences). The Ph.D. degree program emphasizes original research and independent study. The degree candidate is required to complete the four core area courses, one 700-level course in an area outside of their area of specialization, and a minimum of 54 credit hours, including thesis research. Thesis committees are usually interdisciplinary and are composed according to the type of research to be conducted. Ph.D. candidates must pass a written and oral comprehensive examination administered by their dissertation committee within four semesters of entering the program.
Research Facilities	Departmental facilities include field vehicles; boats; a machine and electronics shop; environmental chambers; analytical chemistry laboratories with extensive instrumentation; greenhouse facilities; state-of-the-art computers, including a computational hydrology laboratory; a GIS facility; NAFAX and FAA weather information; and GOES-Tap satellite receiver. Departmental field facilities include the Pace/Steger teaching/research site. Major interdisciplinary research initiatives with off-site research stations include the Virginia Coast Reserve/Long-Term Ecological Research (VCR/LTER) studies of marsh and barrier island ecosystems on Virginia's Eastern Shore. Blandy Experimental Farm and the Orland E. White Arboretum are the focus of ecological research near Front Royal, Virginia. The Program of Interdisciplinary Research in Contaminant Hydrogeology (PIRCH), which includes EVSC and engineering faculty members and students, conducts research on hydrogeochemical and microbial processes in the subsurface. The Shenandoah Watershed Study (SWAS) investigates catchment biogeochemical and hydrological processes in the Blue Ridge region. An active research group focuses on the study of global environmental change.
Financial Aid	All students who complete applications by January 15 are considered for financial aid that is awarded on the basis of background and merit. Fellowships are awarded to the most academically qualified students. Teaching assistants teach laboratory sections of undergraduate and graduate courses. Research assistantships are available through individual professor's research projects; potential advisers should be contacted directly. At present, 98 percent of graduate students receive financial support. A full stipend is $10,000 to $12,000 for nine months; most students receive an additional $3000 to $4000 summer research stipend. Most entering students are awarded a full-tuition fellowship. Small grants to support research and travel to professional meetings are routinely awarded.
Cost of Study	Tuition, depending on course load, ranges between $1925 and $4911 per academic year for Virginia residents and $5510 and $16,598 per academic year for out-of-state students. Students with financial awards receive partial or complete tuition fellowships.
Living and Housing Costs	A variety of affordable housing options exist, from small apartments near grounds to houses in the country. Most students live off grounds in shared apartments or houses. The rent for an individual in a shared arrangement ranges from $250 to $350, excluding utilities. Living alone costs $350 to $500. Most graduate students are able to meet their living expenses with their stipends.
Student Group	Currently, there are 86 students enrolled; 44 are in M.S. programs, and 42 are in Ph.D. programs. Students choose at least one area of specialization in their graduate programs. There are 30 students in ecology, 30 in geosciences, 12 in hydrology, and 14 in atmospheric sciences. Thirty-five percent of the students are women. Students come from a wide range of scientific backgrounds, including geology, chemistry, biology, physics, and engineering. Occasional students have completed nonscience undergraduate degrees and have prepared for graduate study through continuing education.
Student Outcomes	EVSC maintains an exceptional placement record largely due to the rigorous interdisciplinary training program, with an emphasis on research, and the reputation and connections of departmental faculty members. Ph.D. students find employment in universities and colleges, federal laboratories and agencies, and research institutes. M.S. students find employment in federal and state laboratories and agencies, foundations, and private industry. Examples include USGS, NASA, NOAA, EPA, and DOE national laboratories.
Location	The University grounds are located in Charlottesville, beside the foothills of the Blue Ridge Mountains in central Virginia. The University is 110 miles from Washington, D.C., with its varied cultural and scholarly resources; moments from the mountains; a 2-hour drive from the Chesapeake Bay; and 4 hours from the Atlantic Ocean.
The University and The Department	The University of Virginia was founded in 1819 by Thomas Jefferson. The original buildings, designed by Jefferson, represent one of the great achievements of American architecture and help to make the grounds of the University of Virginia one of the most attractive campuses in the United States. The total University enrollment is 20,000, with 10,000 students in the College of Arts and Sciences. EVSC, founded in 1970, is among the oldest and most well-known interdisciplinary environmental sciences programs in the country.
Applying	To apply for admission, students should submit to the Graduate School of Arts and Sciences by January 15: an application, an official transcript of their entire college record, results of the Graduate Record Examinations (only the verbal and quantitative aptitude tests), and at least two letters of recommendation. Other information indicative of the applicant's academic and research abilities should be included. Direct contact with faculty members with similar interests is essential. A personal interview is recommended.
Correspondence and Information	Graduate Admissions Chair Department of Environmental Sciences Clark Hall University of Virginia Charlottesville, Virginia 22903 Telephone: 804-924-7761 Fax: 804-982-2137 World Wide Web: http://www.evsc.virginia.edu

University of Virginia

THE FACULTY AND THEIR RESEARCH

John D. Albertson, Assistant Professor; Ph.D., California, Davis, 1996. Hydrology: surface hydrology, surface-atmosphere interactions, turbulent flow and transport, evaporation.

Robert E. Davis, Associate Professor; Ph.D., Delaware, 1988. Atmospheric sciences: synoptic and applied climatology, statistical climatology, climate impact assessment, climate change.

Robert Dolan, Professor; Ph.D., LSU, 1965. Geosciences: coastal processes and geomorphology, coastal hazards, shoreline erosion, barrier island dynamics.

Howard E. Epstein, Assistant Professor; Ph.D., Colorado State, 1997. Ecology: plant community and ecosystem dynamics in grasslands, shrublands, and tundra; remote sensing, modeling, and geographic information systems.

Jose Fuentes, Assistant Professor; Ph.D., Guelph, 1991. Atmospheric sciences: deposition of ozone, micrometerology, atmospheric chemistry, troposphere/biosphere interactions.

James N. Galloway, Professor and Chairman; Ph.D., California, San Diego, 1972. Atmospheric sciences: global atmospheric geochemistry, atmosphere-limnologic interrelationships, acid rain in small watersheds.

Bruce P. Hayden, Professor; Ph.D., Chicago, 1968. Atmospheric sciences: dynamic climatology and bioclimatology, marine biogeography, ecology of coastal plants and animals, coastal processes, geomorphology.

Janet S. Herman, Professor and Director, Program of Interdisciplinary Research in Contaminant Hydrogeology; Ph.D., Penn State, 1982. Geosciences: aqueous geochemistry, water-rock interactions, karst.

George M. Hornberger, Ernest H. Ern Professor; Ph.D., Stanford, 1970. Hydrology: numerical analysis, groundwater flow.

Alan D. Howard, Professor; Ph.D., John Hopkins, 1970. Geosciences:fluvial geomorphology, simulation modeling of landscape evolution, Martian geomorphology, groundwater sapping.

Deborah Lawrence, Assistant Professor; Ph.D., Duke, 1998. Ecology:botany, tropical rainforests, ecosystem function, sustainability of managed and natural ecosystems.

Stephen A. Macko, Professor; Ph.D., Texas at Austin, 1981. Geosciences: biogeochemistry, marine organic geochemistry, stable isotope geochemistry.

Michael E. Mann, Assistant Professor; Ph.D., Yale, 1998. Atmospheric sciences: climatology, paleoclimatology, climate modeling, statistical climatology, time-series methods.

Karen J. McGlathery, Assistant Professor; Ph.D., Cornell, 1992. Ecology: nutrient and grazing influences on seagrass community dynamics, aquatic ecology, seagrasses, microalgae, nutrient fluxes.

Aaron L. Mills, Professor; Ph.D., Cornell, 1975. Ecology: microbial ecology, microbial transformation of groundwater pollutants, bacterial transport through porous media.

Wallace E. Reed, Associate Professor; Ph.D., Chicago, 1967. Atmospheric sciences: urban systems, location theory, land-use modeling, air quality.

William F. Ruddiman, Professor; Ph.D., Columbia, 1969. Geosciences:marine geology, paleoclimatology, paleoceanography.

Herman H. Shugart, Corcoran Professor and Director, Global Environmental Change; Ph.D., Georgia, 1970. Ecology: global change, systems ecology, forest ecosystem analysis and dynamics, ornithology.

David E. Smith, Associate Professor and Associate Chairman; Ph.D., Texas A&M, 1982. Ecology: biological oceanography, marine ecology, invertebrate zoology, ecology of blue-water plankton.

Thomas M. Smith, Associate Professor; Ph.D., Tennessee, 1981. Ecology: theoretical ecology, vegetation modeling, global ecology.

Patricia L. Wiberg, Associate Professor; Ph.D., Washington (Seattle), 1987. Geosciences: sediment transport, oceanography, geological fluid mechanics.

Joseph C. Zieman, Professor; Ph.D., Miami, 1970. Ecology: marine ecology, production and trophic utilization ecology of seagrass meadows, mangrove and reef ecosystems.

Research Faculty

Peter Berg, Research Assistant Professor; Ph.D., Denmark Technical, 1988. Ecology: modeling of transport by diffusion, convection, and radiation; nitrogen transformations; water movement in soils.

Linda K. Blum, Research Associate Professor; Ph.D., Cornell, 1980. Ecology: productivity and community structure in estuarine systems, microbe-plant interactions, microbial community structure and processes.

Michael A. Bowers, Research Associate Professor and Resident Coordinator, Blandy Experimental Farm; Ph.D., Arizona, 1984. Ecology: foraging behavior, habitat selection, conservation biology, and plant-herbivore interactions.

Arthur J. Bulger, Research Assistant Professor; Ph.D., Connecticut, 1978. Ecology: physiological ecology of fishes.

B. Jack Cosby, Research Professor; Ph.D., Virginia, 1982. Hydrology:limnology, biogeochemistry, quantitative analysis of environmental data, simulation modeling.

Paul Desanker, Research Assistant Professor; Ph.D., Michigan Tech, 1992. Ecology: modeling of vegetation dynamics, land cover, and land use change in Central and Southern Africa.

William Emanuel, Research Associate Professor; Ph.D., Oklahoma State, 1975. Ecology: global biogeochemistry and environmental change, terrestrial ecology, ecosystem modeling and analysis.

George D. Emmitt, Research Associate Professor; Ph.D., Virginia, 1975. Atmospheric sciences: laser atmospheric wind sounder instrument, fugitive dust emission.

R. Michael Erwin, Research Professor and Wildlife Biologist, Patuxent Wildlife Center, Biological Resources Division, U.S. Geological Survey; Ph.D., Maryland, 1975. Ecology: conservation ecology.

Michael Garstang, Professor Emeritus and Research Professor; Ph.D., Florida State, 1964. Atmospheric sciences: tropical marine and continental meteorology, convective storms, trace gas and aerosol transports, experimental meteorology.

H. Grant Goodell, Research Professor; Ph.D., Northwestern, 1958. Geosciences: sedimentation, marine geology, marine affairs, field hydrogeology, hydrogeology, radionuclides in groundwater, salt-water intrusion.

Christopher Justice, Research Professor; Ph.D., Reading (United Kingdom), 1977. Ecology.

William C. Keene, Research Associate Professor; M.S., Virginia, 1978. Atmospheric sciences: multiphase tropospheric chemistry, atmosphere/biosphere interactions, measurements techniques.

Patrick J. Michaels, Research Professor and State Climatologist; Ph.D., Wisconsin, 1979. Atmospheric sciences: ecological and mesoscale climatology, climate change.

Jennie L. Moody, Research Assistant Professor; Ph.D., Michigan, 1986. Atmospheric sciences: long-range atmospheric transport and trajectory modeling, acid deposition modeling and precipitation chemistry, chemical climatology.

John H. Porter, Research Assistant Professor; Ph.D., Virginia, 1988. Ecology: mammalian dispersal; population, community, and landscape ecology; multivariate statistics; remote-sensing and GIS.

G. Carlton Ray, Research Professor; Ph.D., Columbia, 1960. Ecology: marine ecology, conservation and management, marine mammalogy, coastal ecological processes.

Robert J. Swap, Research Assistant Professor; Ph.D., Virginia, 1996. Atmospheric sciences: tropospheric aerosol and trace gas transport and characterization, atmosphere-biosphere interactions, experimental/observational atmospheric science.

Affiliated Faculty

Ralph O. Allen, Professor (Department of Chemistry); Ph.D., Wisconsin–Madison, 1970. Geosciences: trace-element geochemistry, hazardous waste management.

Henry M. Wilber, B. F. D. Runk Professor and Director, Mountain Lake Biological Station (Department of Biology); Ph.D., Michigan, 1971. Ecology: population biology and community ecology, ecological genetics.

YORK UNIVERSITY

Faculty of Environmental Studies

Program of Study

The twenty-first century will pose diverse and complex challenges to those exploring problems and issues in natural, social, built, and organizational environments. The Faculty of Environmental Studies (FES) attempts to meet these challenges through graduate programs that lead to the degrees of Master in Environmental Studies (M.E.S.) and Doctor of Philosophy (Ph.D.) in environmental studies.

The M.E.S. program is individualized and flexible; students investigate a broad range of areas that encompass natural, built, social, and organizational environments. It attracts candidates from a wide array of backgrounds, including many who are in midcareer. Through a plan of study, each student combines an integration of theory and practice with the opportunity to identify and explore problems from varied yet interconnected perspectives. The program may be pursued in a variety of ways, including joint arrangements with other organizations and programs. These include association with the Canadian Institute of Planners, integration of environmental studies and law through the joint M.E.S./LL.B. program offered through FES and Osgoode Hall Law School, or individually arranged concurrent degree programs with other graduate programs at York University.

The doctoral program offers a research Ph.D. degree. At this level, the nature of environmental studies is expressed in terms of the research of faculty members as delineated by two fields of research specialization: Nature, Culture, and Society, which is concerned with the philosophical and ethical characteristics of the relationships between human society and the totality of nature, of which humans are a part, and Environments, Institutions, and Interventions, which focuses on the relationships between human institutional frameworks and the social and cultural construction of human environments. Doctoral students enter the program in September and are required to be full-time and in residence for the first twelve months.

The key to understanding the faculty's approach is its comprehensive and dynamic perspective on "environment." Environment is seen as the sum total of interacting factors and circumstances that surround, influence, and direct the growth and behaviour of individual beings, groups, species, communities, and organizations. For the faculty, the overall objective of environmental studies is to promote an appreciation of the complexity and diversity of relationships within and among environmental systems, an understanding of the processes of environmental change, and the search for more effective means of managing human activities and the built environment. Environmental studies, therefore, means more than studying environments; it also means thinking, learning, and acting environmentally.

Research Facilities

Research facilities include the York University Libraries; fourteen research units at York University, including the Centre for Feminist Research, the Centre for Health Studies, the Centre for Refugee Studies, the Centre for Research on Latin America & the Caribbean, and the Institute for Social Research; both PC and MAC computing facilities for students; and a Resources Centre in the Leonard G. Lumbers Building. Information on the holdings of the York Libraries are available on *Yorkline*, an automated online catalogue. Graduate students may also borrow directly from the nineteen member institutions of the Ontario Council of University Libraries.

Financial Aid

Graduate assistantships are awarded on a competitive basis to students in the master's program; teaching assistantships are awarded to students in the Ph.D. program. Also available from York University on a competitive basis are entrance scholarships, Graduate Fellowship for Academic Distinction, and bursaries for visa students. Qualifying students from Canada may apply for SSHRC, NSRC, and OGS.

Cost of Study

Tuition for full-time study for 1999–2000 is Can$5070.93 per year for Canadian residents and Can$10,836.30 per year for international students. Students register for three terms each year.

Living and Housing Costs

On-campus, furnished housing is available for graduate students in the form of bachelor, one-bedroom, and two-bedroom apartments that range in cost from Can$561 each month to Can$918 each month. Estimates for cost of living for a graduate student in Toronto, including tuition, housing, and books, are approximately Can$18,000 per year for Canadian residents and Can$30,000 per year for Visa students.

Student Group

Approximately 280 students are registered in the master's program and 30 students are registered in the Ph.D. program. The wide range of areas of concentration of students in these programs can be seen by visiting the FES home page on the Internet (http://www.yorku.ca/faculty/fes).

Student Outcomes

Graduates from the M.E.S. program, which is currently in its thirtieth year, have held such positions as chief, Environmental Information Section, Statistics Canada, Ottawa; vice president, Operations and Human Resources, Sunnybrook Health Science Centre, Toronto; in-house counsel/senior policy analyst, Environmental Commissioner of Ontario, Toronto; director, SDRI, and professor, Sustainable Development Research Institute, University of British Columbia, Vancouver; and senior planning and coordination officer, United Nations Development Program, New York.

Location

York University is located at the northern edge of the city of Toronto, Canada's largest urban area.

The University and The Program

One of the first environmental studies faculties to be established in North America, York University's Faculty of Environmental Studies (FES) was created in 1968 to meet the demand for new and more appropriate responses to environmental problems and issues. The largest graduate program in environmental studies in Canada, FES offers those interested in earning the Master of Environmental Studies or the Ph.D. in environmental studies an opportunity to pursue their own interests, build on past experience, and explore ideas from a variety of perspectives. FES aims to provide educational experiences in which students have opportunities to acquire the knowledge and develop the skills they need to act in creative and innovative ways in an ever-changing world.

Applying

Applications to the M.E.S. or Ph.D. program in environmental studies at York University for admission in September should be submitted by March 1; applications received by January 2 are reviewed for early consideration. To be considered for admission to the M.E.S. program, applicants must normally have an undergraduate degree from a recognized university with not less than a B (second class) standing. The normal admission standard for the Ph.D. program is a master's degree from a recognized university.

Correspondence and Information

Information and application materials for either graduate program may be obtained by contacting the University at the address below.

Joanne Nonnekes, Coordinator of External Relations
Faculty of Environmental Studies
York University
4700 Keele Street
Toronto, Ontario M3J 1P3
Canada
Telephone: 416-736-5252
Fax: 416-736-5679
E-mail: fesinfo@yorku.ca
World Wide Web: http://www.yorku.ca/faculty/fes

York University

THE FACULTY AND THEIR RESEARCH

Dean

Peter A. Victor, Ph.D. (economics), British Columbia. Environmental economics.

Professors

David V. J. Bell, Ph.D. (political science), Harvard. Political linguistics, political culture, environmental policy, politics of sustainability.

Gerald P. Daly, Ph.D. (urban studies), Cambridge; MCIP, AICP. Urban/regional planning, housing, homelessness, social policy.

William C. Found, Ph.D. (geography), Florida. Agricultural land use, integrated rural planning/development, international development, program implementation.

Bryn Greer-Wootten, Ph.D. (geography and planning), McGill. Resource management and policy, epistemology, waste management.

H. Peter M. Homenuck, Ph.D. (geography), Cincinnati; MCIP. Social impact assessment, social planning, Native-Canadian relations, public consultation, strategic planning.

Reg Lang, Ed.D. (adult education), Toronto; MCIP. Planning and strategic change processes, planning/management and personality types, applied ethics, learning style and self-directed learning.

Edward S. Spence, Ph.D. (geography), Alberta; MCIP. International development, resource management, environmental policy/planning.

Gerda R. Wekerle, Ph.D. (sociology), Northwestern. Gender and environments, social and urban policy and planning, qualitative research methods, urban politics, housing, violence against women, safe cities.

Paul F. Wilkinson, Ph.D. (geography), Toronto. Resource/environmental management, recreation/tourism, international development.

Associate Professors

Audrey M. Armour, Ph.D. (urban and regional planning), Waterloo; MCIP. Conflict management, environmental/social impact assessment, environmental/urban planning, integrated resource planning/management, public participation, facility siting processes.

Mora D. F. P. Campbell, Ph.D. (philosophy), Waterloo. Environmental thought/ethics, agricultural ethics, philosophy of technology, ecofeminism, philosophy of time, temporal studies.

Howard E. Daugherty, Ph.D. (biogeography), UCLA. Human disturbance of tropical ecosystems, ecodevelopment, natural resource policy/management, biological conservation, international development.

Gene Desfor, Ph.D. (regional science), Pennsylvania. Urban development, growth, and decline; Third World transformations.

Roger Keil, D.Phil. (political science), Frankfurt. Urban internationalization, spatial/political and urban theory, world city formation, urban ecology and politics, environmental policy and politics, cultural studies, planning and politics.

Bonnie Lee Kettel, Ph.D. (social anthropology), Illinois. International development, gender and development, indigenous resource management, politics/policy, arid/semi-arid regions.

Robert G. Macdonald, Ph.D. (physics and physical chemistry), Toronto. Energy policy/conservation, renewable energy, international development, action research, sustainable development.

Lewis Molot, Ph.D. (oceanography), Alaska. Water quality, biogeochemistry, the effect of climate change on UV and nutrient cycling in northern forests.

G. Peter Penz, D.Phil. (social studies), Oxford. Socio-environmental politics, justice, and development ethics; indigenous peoples in the Third World; environmental refugees; basic needs; human rights; advocacy and social movements; south Asia.

Patricia E. Perkins, Ph.D. (economics), Toronto. International trade and environment; ecological economics; community economic development; debt, poverty, and environmental degradation; women, ecology, and economics.

Rebecca L. Peterson, Ph.D. (psychology), Claremont. Women and environments, environment and behavior, work environments, health.

Barbara L. Rahder, Ph.D. (urban and regional planning), Toronto; MCIP. Urban/community planning/development; social equity, diversity, and change; women and environments; housing and community services; urban design; violence prevention; participatory planning.

Brent M. Rutherford, Ph.D. (political science), Northwestern. Program/policy evaluation and analysis, quantitative methods.

L. Anders Sandberg, Ph.D. (geography), McGill. Environmental/forest policy; political economy; environmental/professional history; alternative economic development; Canada, Maritimes, and Scandinavia.

Assistant Professors

Deborah Barndt, Ph.D. (sociology), Michigan State. Popular education and social movements; media analysis; participatory research/education/action; cultural production; community development; women, globalization, and food.

Carmela Canzonieri, M.L.A. (landscape architecture), Harvard. Design and planning of urban and regional environments, cultural and agricultural landscapes, restoration ecology, land ethics and landscape stewardship.

Leesa K. Fawcett, M.E.S. Human/animal relationships; environmental education; biological conservation and natural history; ecofeminism; women, science, and technology.

Femida Handy, Ph.D. (environmental studies), York. Environmental/ecological economics, nonprofit sector, environmental organizations.

Ilan Kapoor, Ph.D. (political science), Toronto. Socioenvironmental issues/problems in developing countries; new social movements (especially environmental, feminist, and ethnic) and radical democracy; new critiques of development (ecological, postmodern, post-Marxist, feminist, non-Western, and postcolonial); participatory approaches to environmental policy making and planning.

Raymond A. Rogers, Ph.D. (environmental studies), York. Economic and natural world relationships, conservation and development, social theory and the environmental crisis, cultural studies.

Catriona A. H. Sandilands, Ph.D. (sociology), York. Nature and environment in social and political theory; feminism, gender, and sexuality; environmental politics and environmental movements; psychoanalysis; radical democracy and postmodernism.

Grant Sheng, Ph.D. (computer science), Wageningen (the Netherlands). Computer modelling/simulation; ecological modelling; nuclear/toxic waste disposal; risk analysis; computer technology, culture, and society; facility siting processes.

Joint Appointment Professors

M. Brock Fenton, Ph.D. (zoology), Toronto. Animal behaviour, ecology, and evolution; biology and ecology of bats; echolocation; bioethics; conservation.

Elinor Melville, Ph.D. (anthropology), Michigan. Environmental history, grazing in semi-arid lands, European expansion, colonial political economies, development.

R. L. Liora Salter, M.A. (communication studies), Simon Fraser; FRSC. Communications; law, science, and technology policy standards; regulation and public policy.

Joseph W. Sheridan, Ph.D. (intercultural/international education), Alberta. Environmental education, environmental thought and First Nations tradition, folk culture, media technology and oral cultures, homelessness.

Joan Steigerwald, M.A. (science and religion), Manitoba. Environmental thought; nature and culture; epistemology and experimental techniques; science, literature, and aesthetics; representation; narrative and historical thought.

SELECTED PUBLICATIONS

Armour, A., and M. Cox. Public participation: Does it really affect decision-makers' decisions? *IAP J.,* 1996.

Armour, A. Risk assessment in environmental policy making. *Policy Stud. Rev.* 12(3–4):178–96, 1993.

Armour, A., S. Cohen, and D. Hurley. Coping with impacts: An approach to assessing community vitality. *Network. Newslett. Board Commun. Psych., Austral. Psych. Soc.* 8(3):1–14, 1993.

Barndt, D. Para cambiar esta casa: Educacion popular bajo los Sandinistas. (Spanish edition of "To change this house"). *INIEP, Nicaraguan Inst. Popular Res. Ed.,* 1995.

Barndt, D. To change this house: Popular education under the Sandinistas. Toronto: Between the Lines, the Jesuit Centre and Doris Marshall Institute for Education and Action, 1991.

Barndt, D. *English at Work: Teacher's Guide.* American edition adapted by the Centre for Workforce Education, Laubach Literacy International. Syracuse: New Readers Press, 1991.

Bell, D., R. Keil, and G. R. Wekerle. *Local Places in the Age of the Global City.* Montreal: Black Rose Books, 1996.

Bell, D., R. Keil, and G. R. Wekerle. *Human Society and the Natural World: Perspectives on Sustainable Futures.* North York: Faculty of Environmental Studies, York University, 1994.

Bell, D., and F. Fletcher et al. *Reaching the Voter: Constituency Campaigning in Canada. Royal Commission on Electoral Reform and Party Financing, Vol. 20.* Toronto: Dundern Press, 1993.

Campbell, M. Cy-borg temporarily. In *Philosophy in the Service of Things: Devices, Focal Practices, and the Quality of Life,* eds. E. Higgs, A. Light, D. Strong, and J. Tatum. Chicago: University of Chicago Press, 1998.

Campbell, M. Dirt in our mouths and hunger in our bellies: Metaphor, theory, and the systems approaches to sustainable agriculture and food security. *J. Agric. Human Values* 15(1), 1998.

Campbell, M. Beyond the terms of the contract: Mothers and farmers. *J. Agr. Environ. Ethics* 7(2):205–20, 1994.

Campbell, M. Time waits for no beast: The dis-integration of nature. *Alternatives,* pp. 22–27, Summer 1993.

Canzonieri, C. Massachusetts turnpike study. In *Studio Work: 1989–1990,* p. 67. Cambridge, Mass.: Harvard, 1990.

Daly, G. *Homeless: Policies, Strategies and Lives on the Street.* London and New York: Routledge, 1996.

Daly, G. People in the street. In *Images of the Street: Representation, Experience and Control in Public Space,* ed. N. Fyfe. London and New York: Routledge, 1996.

Daly, G. Charity begins at home: The role of the third sector. In *Critical Perspectives on Homelessness,* eds. M. J. Huth and T. Wright. Greenwood Press, 1996.

Daugherty, H. *Analisis del Marco Legal Instructional/Politico para el Manejo del Recurso Agua en Venezuela.* Toronto: DELCAN International Corporation, 1993.

Daugherty, H., ed. *Perfil Ambiental de Honduras* Washington: Development Alternatives, Inc., 1990.

Desfor, G., and R. Keil. (Ähnlichkeiten und Differenzen bei der Umsetzung gesellschaftlicher Anspruche auf der städtischen Ebene in lokal spezifische Policy—Die Beispiele Toronto und Los Angeles. In *Zivilgesellschaftliche Zukünfte - Gestaltungsmöglichkeiten einer zivilen Gesellschaft.* Eds. H. Heinelt and K. M. Schmals, 1997

Desfor, G., C. Robinson, and D. LaFramboise. Remediation of a contaminated site owned by Ontario hydro in Markham. *Canadian Standards Association Case Study.* Toronto: Canadian Standards Association, 1997.

Desfor, G., and R. Keil. Making local environmental policy in Los Angeles. *Cities* 23(3):303-13, 1996.

Fawcett, L. Unsettling possibilities: Natural history, oppressions and feminism. In *Human Society and the Natural World: Perspectives on Sustainable Futures,* eds. D. V. J. Bell, R. Keil, and G. Wekerle. North York: Faculty of Environmental Studies, York University, 1994.

Fawcett, L., and S. Staniforth. *Metamorphosis for Environmental Education: A Care Course Guide for Primary/Elementary Teacher Training.* Vancouver: The Commonwealth of Learning, 1994.

Fawcett, L., and S. Staniforth. *Environmental Education Syllabus for Inservice Primary and Elementary Teacher Training.* Vancouver: The Commonwealth of Learning, 1993.

Found, W. Agriculture in a world of subsidies. In *Organization of Canadian Space Economy,* pp. 155–68, ed. J. N. H. Britton. Montreal and Kingston: McGill-Queen's University Press, 1996.

Found, W. The field of rural planning, and its relation to the Ciamis, Jasinga-Leusoiliang, and Rawa Sragi case studies. In *Working with People: Indonesian Experiences with Community-Based Development,* pp. 1–5, eds. H. Poerbo, F. Carden, W. Found, and L. Grenier. Bandung and Toronto: University Consortium on the Environment, University of Toronto Press, 1995.

Found, W., J. Bater, S. Martopo, and M. Soerjani. Implications of the Bali experience for sustainable development. In *Bali: Balancing Environment, Economy and Culture,* pp. 613–33, eds. S. Martopo and B. Mitchell. Waterloo: University of Waterloo, 1995.

Handy, F., and E. Katz. The wage differential between nonprofit institutions and corporations: Getting more by paying less? *J. Comp. Econ.* 26, 1998.

Handy, F. Co-existence of nonprofits, for profits, and public sector institutions. *Ann. Public Coop. Econ.* 68(2), June 1997.

Handy, F. Defining who is a volunteer: Conceptual and empirical considerations. *Nonprofit Volun. Sector Quarter.* 25(3), 1996.

Homenuck, P. Social and political changes in the relationship between first nations and Canadian society. In *Human Society and the Natural World: Perspectives on Sustainable Futures,* pp. 12–13, eds. D. V. J. Bell, R. Keil, and G. Wekerle. North York: Faculty of Environmental Studies, York University, 1994.

Homenuck, P. Environmental values in the workplace and marketplace. *Total Qual. Rev.* July 1994.

Keil, R., and D. V. J. Bell et al. *Local Places in the Age of the Global City.* Montreal: Black Rose Books, 1996.

Keil, R. World city formation, local places and sustainability. In *Local Places in the Age of the Global City,* eds. R. Keil, G. R. Wekerle, and D. V. J. Bell. Montreal: Black Rose Books, 1996.

Keil, R. The environmental problematic in world cities. In *World Cities in a World-System,* eds. P. L. Knox and P. J. Taylor. New York: Cambridge University Press, 1995.

Kettel, B. Women, environment and development: From Rio to Beijing. *Political Ecology: Global and Local,* eds. In R. Keil, D.V.J. Bell, L. Fawcett, and P. Penz. London/New York: Routledge, in press.

Kettel, B. Women, health and the environment. Special Issue on "Women and Health Policy in Developing Countries." In *Soc. Sci. Med.* 42(10):1367–79, 1996.

Kettel, B. Key pathways for science and technology for sustainable and equitable development. In *Missing Links: Gender Equity in Science Technology for Development. United Nations Commission on Science and Technology for Development.* Ottawa: International Research Developmental Research Centre, 1995.

Kettel, B. Gender and environments: Lessons from WEDNET. In *EnGENDERing Wealth and Well-being,* eds. R. Blumburg et al. Boulder: Westview, 1995.

Lang, R. Type flexibility in processes of strategic planning and change. In *Developing Leaders: Research and Applications in Psychological Type and Leadership Development,* eds. C. Fitzgerald and L. K. Kirby. Palo Alto, Calif.: Consulting Psychologists Press, 1996.

Lang, R. An equity-based approach to waste management facility siting. In *Planning Ethics: A Reader in Planning Philosophy, Practice and Education,* ed. S. Hendler. New Brunswick, New Jersey: Centre for Urban Policy Research, 1995.

Lang, R. Urban ecosystem: From concept to application. In *Human Society and the Natural World: Perspectives on Sustainable Futures,* eds. D. V. J. Bell, R. Keil, and G. Wekerle. North York: Faculty of Environmental Studies, York University, 1994.

Macdonald, R. Energy strategies for sustainable futures. In *Human Society and the Natural World: Perspectives on Sustainable Futures,* pp. 12–13, eds. D. V. J. Bell, R. Keil, and G. Wekerle. North York: Faculty of Environmental Studies, York University, 1994.

York University

Selected Publications (continued)

Molot, L., and P. J. Dillon. Photolytic regulation of dissolved organic carbon in northern lakes. *Global Biogeochem. Cycles* 11:357–65, 1997.

Molot, L., and P. J. Dillon. Long term phosphorus budgets and an examination of the steady state mass balance model. *Water Res.* 30(10): 2237–80, 1997.

Molot, L., P.J. Dillon, and M. Futter. The effect of El Niño-related drought on the recovery of acidified lakes. *Int. J. Environ. Monitor. Audit.,* 1997.

Penz, P., and J. Drydyk. International Economic Justice and Exploitation, pp. 71–78. Conclusion: Globalizing Socialism, pp. 271–90. In *Global Justice, Global Democracy,* Halifax: Fernwood Press, 1997.

Penz, P. Development-induced Displacement: Overview, pp. 1-3. The Ethics of Development-induced Displacement, pp. 37-41. In *Refuge* 16(3), 1997

Penz, P. Environmental victims and state sovereignty: A normative analysis. *Social Justice* 23(4):41–61, 1996.

Perkins, P. E. Introduction. In *Special Issue on Women, Ecology and Economics, Ecological Economics,* February 1997.

Perkins, P. E. Trade liberalization, the natural environment, and cities. In *Local Places in the Age of the Global City,* eds. R. Keil, G. Wekerle, and D. V. J. Bell. Montreal: Black Rose Books, 1996.

Perkins, P. E. Building communities to limit trade: Following the example of women's initiatives. *Alternatives* 22(1), January/February 1996.

Peterson, R. Women, environments and health: Overview and strategic directions for research and action. In *International Perspectives in Environment and Health,* eds. Shahi et al. New York: Springer, 1996.

Rahder, B. Victims No Longer: Participatory Planning with a Diversity of Women at Risk of Abuse. *J. Plan. Ed. Res.* 19(1), 1999.

Rahder, B. Women and planning: Education for social change. *Planning Practice and Research* 13(3):247–65, 1998.

Rahder, B. Women plan Toronto: Grassroots participation in re-shaping the city. In *Possible Urban Worlds: Urban Strategies at the End of the 20th Century,* pp. 100–3, eds. R. Wolff et al. Basel: Birkehauser, 1998.

Rogers, R. *The Oceans are Emptying: Fish Wars and Sustainability.* Montreal: Black Rose Books, 1995.

Rogers, R. *Nature and the Crisis of Modernity: A Critique of Contemporary Discourse on Managing the Earth.* Montreal: Black Rose Books, 1994.

Rogers, R. Political economy and natural community: The case of Canada's east coast fishery. In *Issues in Sustainability: Human Society and the Natural World,* eds. D. V. J. Bell, R. Keil, and G. R. Wekerle. North York: Faculty of Environmental Studies, York University, 1994.

Rutherford, B., and G. Wekerle. The mobility of capital and the immobility of female labour: Responses to economic restructuring. In *The Power of Geography: How Territory Shapes Social Life,* eds. J. Wolch and M. Dear. London: Unwin and Hyman, 1989.

Rutherford, B., and G. Wekerle. Single parents in the suburbs: Journey-to-work and access to transportation. *J. Special. Transport. Plan. Practice* III(3), Summer, 1989.

Rutherford, B., and G. Wekerle. Captive rider, captive labour: Spatial constraints and women's unemployment. *Urban Geog.* 9(2), 1988.

Sandberg, A., and S. Sörlin (eds.). *Sustainability—The Challenge: People, Power, and the Environment.* Montreal: Black Rose Books, 1998.

Sandberg, A., and R. Janzen. Good work, productivity and sustainability in Canadian forestry. *Econ. Ind. Democracy* 19:119–35, 1998.

Sandberg, A., ed. *Trouble in the Woods: Forest Policy and Social Conflict in Nova Scotia and New Brunswick.* Frederiction: Acadiensis, 1992.

Sandilands, C. *The Good-Natured Feminist: Ecofeminism and Democracy.* Minneapolis: University of Minnesota Press, 1999.

Sandilands, C. Domestic politics: Multiculturalism, wilderness and the desire for Canada. *Space Culture,* fall 1999.

Sandilands, C. Sex at the limit. In *Discourses of the Environment,* ed. E. Darier. Oxford: Blackwell, 1998.

Sheng, G., Y. Sheng, M. Shoukri, and P. Wood. A modification to the SIMPLE method for buoyancy-driven flows. *Numerical Heat Trans.* B(33):65–78, 1998.

Sheng, G., and J. Toth. Enhancing nuclear waste disposal safety by exploiting regional groundwater flow: The Recharge Area concept. *Hydrogeol. J.* 4(4):4–25, 1996.

Sheng, G., M. S. Elzas, T. I. Oren, and B. T. Cronhjort. Model validation: A systemic and systematic approach. *Reliability Eng. Syst. Safety* 42:247–59, 1993.

Spence, E., and W. C. Found. The drainage act 1975: Its evolution and possible impacts. *Can. Water Resour. J.* 2(2), 1977.

Spence, E., W. C. Found, and A. R. Hill. A study of the impacts on agricultural land drainage in Ontario. *J. Soil Water Conserv.* 31(1), 1976.

Victor, P., and E. F. Schumacher. *The Encyclopedia of Conservation and Environmentalism,* ed. R. Paehlke. New York: Garland Publishing Inc., 1995.

Victor, P., J. Hanna, and A. Kubursi. How strong is weak sustainability? *Economic Appliquée,* tome XLVIII(2):75–94, 1995.

Victor, P. Indicators of sustainable development: some lessons from capital theory. *J. Ecol. Econ.* 4:191–213, 1991.

Evans, P., and **G. Wekerle,** eds. *Women and the Canadian Welfare State.* Toronto: University of Toronto Press, 1997.

Wekerle, G., D. V. J. Bell, and R. Keil, eds. *Local Places in the Age of the Global City.* Montreal: Black Rose Books, 1996.

Wekerle, G., and Carolyn Whitzman. *Safe Cities: Guidelines for Planning, Design and Management.* New York: Van Nostrand Reinhard, 1995.

Wilkinson, P. *Tourism Policy and Planning: Case Studies from the Commonwealth Caribbean.* Elmsford, New York: Cognizant Communications, 1997.

Wilkinson, P. Jamaican tourism: From dependency theory to a world-economy perspective. In *Island Tourism,* eds. D. G. Lockhart and D. Drakikis-Smith. London: Mansell, 1997.

Wilkinson, P. The tourist area cycle of evolution: Graphical images of the Commonwealth Caribbean. In *Practicing Responsible Tourism: Case Studies in Tourism Planning, Policy and Development,* eds. L.C. Harrison and W. Husbands. Toronto: Wiley, 1996.

Section 10
Natural Resources

This section contains a directory of institutions offering graduate work in natural resources, followed by in-depth entries submitted by institutions that chose to prepare detailed program descriptions. Additional information about programs listed in the directory but not augmented by an in-depth entry may be obtained by writing directly to the dean of a graduate school or chair of a department at the address given in the directory.

For programs offering related work, see also in this book Environmental Sciences and Management and Meteorology and Atmospheric Sciences; in Book 2, see Architecture (Landscape Architecture) and Public, Regional, and Industrial Affairs; in Book 3, see Biological and Biomedical Sciences; Botany and Plant Sciences; Ecology, Environmental Biology, and Evolutionary Biology; Entomology; Genetics and Developmental Biology; Nutrition; Pathology; Pharmacology and Toxicology; Physiology; and Zoology; in Book 5, see Agricultural Engineering; Civil and Environmental Engineering; Geological, Mineral/Mining, and Petroleum Engineering; Management of Engineering and Technology; and Ocean Engineering; and in Book 6, see Veterinary Medicine and Sciences.

CONTENTS

Fish, Game, and Wildlife Management

Auburn University, Graduate School, College of Agriculture, Department of Fisheries and Allied Aquacultures, Auburn, Auburn University, AL 36849-0002. Offers M Aq, MS, PhD. Part-time programs available. *Faculty:* 20 full-time (0 women). *Students:* 37 full-time (10 women), 37 part-time (7 women); includes 4 minority (2 Asian Americans or Pacific Islanders, 1 Hispanic American, 1 Native American), 21 international. 26 applicants, 38% accepted. In 1998, 15 master's, 13 doctorates awarded. *Degree requirements:* For master's, thesis (MS) required; for doctorate, 2 foreign languages (computer language can substitute for one), dissertation required. *Entrance requirements:* For master's, GRE General Test; for doctorate, GRE General Test (minimum score of 400 on each section required). *Application deadline:* For fall admission, 9/1; for spring admission, 3/1. Applications are processed on a rolling basis. Application fee: $25 ($50 for international students). Tuition, state resident: full-time $2,760; part-time $76 per credit hour. Tuition, nonresident: full-time $8,280; part-time $228 per credit hour. *Financial aid:* Fellowships, research assistantships, teaching assistantships, Federal Work-Study available. Aid available to part-time students. Financial aid application deadline: 3/15. *Faculty research:* Channel catfish production; aquatic animal health; community and population ecology; pond management; production hatching, breeding and genetics. Total annual research expenditures: $8 million. *Unit head:* Dr. John W. Jensen, Head, 334-844-4786. *Application contact:* Dr. John F. Pritchett, Dean of the Graduate School, 334-844-4700.

Auburn University, Graduate School, College of Sciences and Mathematics, Department of Zoology and Wildlife Science, Program in Wildlife Science, Auburn, Auburn University, AL 36849-0002. Offers MS, PhD. Part-time programs available. *Students:* 1 (woman) full-time, 9 part-time (2 women), 1 international. 11 applicants, 18% accepted. In 1998, 7 master's awarded. *Degree requirements:* For master's, thesis required, foreign language not required; for doctorate, dissertation required. *Entrance requirements:* For master's, GRE General Test; for doctorate, GRE General Test (minimum score of 500 on each section required), GRE Subject Test (minimum score of 600 required). *Application deadline:* For fall admission, 2/1 (priority date). Applications are processed on a rolling basis. Application fee: $25 ($50 for international students). Tuition, state resident: full-time $2,760; part-time $76 per credit hour. Tuition, nonresident: full-time $8,280; part-time $228 per credit hour. *Financial aid:* Research assistantships, teaching assistantships, Federal Work-Study available. Aid available to part-time students. Financial aid application deadline: 2/1. *Faculty research:* Wildlife habitat, game management, endangered species, physiology and nutrition, habitat analysis. *Unit head:* Dr. John F. Pritchett, Dean of the Graduate School, 334-844-4700. *Application contact:* Dr. John F. Pritchett, Dean of the Graduate School, 334-844-4700.

Brigham Young University, Graduate Studies, College of Biological and Agricultural Sciences, Department of Botany and Range Science, Provo, UT 84602-1001. Offers biological science education (MS); botany (MS, PhD); range science (MS); wildlife and range resources (MS, PhD). *Faculty:* 17 full-time (1 woman). *Students:* 32 full-time (14 women); includes 3 minority (1 Asian American or Pacific Islander, 2 Hispanic Americans), 3 international. *Degree requirements:* For master's and doctorate, thesis/dissertation required. *Entrance requirements:* For master's, GRE General Test (minimum combined score of 1100 required), minimum GPA of 3.2 during previous 2 years; for doctorate, GRE General Test (minimum combined score of 1100 required). *Application deadline:* For fall admission, 2/15; for winter admission, 9/15. Applications are processed on a rolling basis. Application fee: $30. Tuition: Full-time $3,330; part-time $185 per credit hour. Tuition and fees vary according to program and student's religious affiliation. *Unit head:* Dr. Bruce A. Roundy, Chair, 801-378-2582, Fax: 801-378-7499. *Application contact:* Rex G. Cates, Graduate Coordinator, 801-378-4281, Fax: 801-378-7499.

Brigham Young University, Graduate Studies, College of Biological and Agricultural Sciences, Department of Zoology, Provo, UT 84602-1001. Offers biological science education (MS); molecular biology (MS, PhD); wildlife and range resources (MS, PhD); zoology (MS, PhD). Part-time programs available. *Faculty:* 31 full-time (0 women), 3 part-time (0 women). *Students:* 47 full-time (16 women), 7 part-time (2 women); includes 6 minority (1 Asian American or Pacific Islander, 4 Hispanic Americans, 1 Native American), 6 international. *Degree requirements:* For master's and doctorate, thesis/dissertation required, foreign language not required. *Entrance requirements:* For master's, GRE General Test (minimum combined score of 1600 on three sections required), minimum GPA of 3.0 during previous 2 years; for doctorate, GRE General Test (minimum combined score of 1600 on three sections required). *Application deadline:* For fall admission, 2/1 (priority date). Application fee: $30. Electronic applications accepted. Tuition: Full-time $3,330; part-time $185 per credit hour. Tuition and fees vary according to program and student's religious affiliation. *Unit head:* Dr. John D. Bell, Chair, 801-378-2006, Fax: 801-378-7423, E-mail: jdb32@email.byu.edu. *Application contact:* Dr. R. Ward Rhees, Graduate Coordinator, 801-378-2158, Fax: 801-378-7423, E-mail: ward_rhees@byu.edu.

Clemson University, Graduate School, College of Agriculture, Forestry and Life Sciences, School of Natural Resources, Department of Aquaculture, Fisheries and Wildlife, Clemson, SC 29634. Offers MS. *Students:* 19 full-time (7 women), 4 part-time (1 woman); includes 3 minority (1 African American, 1 Hispanic American, 1 Native American), 3 international. Average age 25. 46 applicants, 7% accepted. In 1998, 10 degrees awarded. *Degree requirements:* For master's, thesis required, foreign language not required. *Entrance requirements:* For master's, GRE General Test, TOEFL, minimum undergraduate GPA of 3.0. *Application deadline:* For fall admission, 6/1. Application fee: $35. *Financial aid:* In 1998–99, 16 research assistantships were awarded.; fellowships, teaching assistantships, career-related internships or fieldwork also available. Financial aid applicants required to submit FAFSA. *Faculty research:* Intensive freshwater culture systems, conservation biology, stream management, applied wildlife management. *Unit head:* Dr. John R. Sweeney, Chair, 864-656-3117, Fax: 864-656-5332, E-mail: jrswny@clemson.edu.

Colorado State University, Graduate School, College of Natural Resources, Department of Fishery and Wildlife Biology, Fort Collins, CO 80523-0015. Offers MS, PhD. Part-time programs available. *Faculty:* 16 full-time (1 woman), 2 part-time (0 women). *Students:* 23 full-time (13 women), 8 part-time (5 women); includes 1 minority (Native American), 1 international. Average age 30. 91 applicants, 12% accepted. In 1998, 14 master's, 5 doctorates awarded. *Degree requirements:* For master's, thesis or alternative required, foreign language not required; for doctorate, one foreign language (computer language can substitute), dissertation required. *Entrance requirements:* For master's, GRE General Test (minimum combined score of 1200 required), TOEFL (minimum score of 550 required), minimum GPA of 3.0, BA or BS in related field; for doctorate, GRE General Test (minimum combined score of 1200 required), TOEFL (minimum score of 550 required), minimum GPA of 3.0, MS in related field. *Application deadline:* For fall admission, 2/15 (priority date). Application fee: $30. Electronic applications accepted. *Financial aid:* In 1998–99, 1 fellowship, 18 research assistantships, 6 teaching assistantships were awarded.; career-related internships or fieldwork, Federal Work-Study, institutionally-sponsored loans, and traineeships also available. Financial aid application deadline: 2/15. *Faculty research:* Conservation biology, aquatic ecology, animal behavior, population modeling, habitat evaluation and management. *Unit head:* Randall Robinette, Head, 970-491-1410, Fax: 970-491-5091, E-mail: fwb@cnr.colostate.edu. *Application contact:* Graduate Affairs Secretary, 970-491-5020, Fax: 970-491-5091, E-mail: fwb@cnr.colostate.edu.

Cornell University, Graduate School, Graduate Fields of Agriculture and Life Sciences, Field of Natural Resources, Ithaca, NY 14853-0001. Offers aquatic science (MPS, MS, PhD); environmental management (MPS); fishery science (MPS, MS, PhD); forest science (MPS, MS, PhD); resource policy and management (MPS, MS, PhD); wildlife science (MPS, MS, PhD). *Faculty:* 24 full-time. *Students:* 58 full-time (24 women); includes 5 minority (1 African American, 1 Asian American or Pacific Islander, 2 Hispanic Americans, 1 Native American), 11 international. Terminal master's awarded for partial completion of doctoral program. *Degree requirements:* For master's, thesis (MS), project paper (MPS) required; for doctorate, dissertation required, foreign language not required. *Entrance requirements:* For master's and doctorate, GRE General Test, TOEFL (minimum score of 550 required). *Application deadline:* Applications are processed on a rolling basis. Application fee: $65. Electronic applications accepted. *Unit head:* Director of Graduate Studies, 607-255-2807, Fax: 607-255-0349. *Application contact:* Graduate Field Assistant, 607-255-2807, E-mail: nrgrad@cornell.edu.

Frostburg State University, Graduate School, School of Natural and Social Sciences, Department of Biology, Program in Fisheries and Wildlife Management, Frostburg, MD 21532-1099. Offers MS. Part-time and evening/weekend programs available. *Faculty:* 11. *Students:* 9 full-time (3 women), 13 part-time (4 women); includes 1 minority (Hispanic American) Average age 29. *Degree requirements:* For master's, thesis required, foreign language not required. *Entrance requirements:* For master's, GRE General Test (minimum combined score of 1000 required), resume. *Application deadline:* For fall admission, 7/15 (priority date). Applications are processed on a rolling basis. Application fee: $30. Tuition, state resident: full-time $3,132; part-time $174 per credit hour. Tuition, nonresident: full-time $3,636; part-time $202 per credit hour. *Financial aid:* In 1998–99, 3 research assistantships with full tuition reimbursements (averaging $5,000 per year) were awarded.; Federal Work-Study also available. Financial aid application deadline: 4/1; financial aid applicants required to submit FAFSA. *Faculty research:* Evolution and systematics of freshwater fishes, biochemical mechanisms of temperature adaptation in freshwater fishes, wildlife and fish parasitology, biology of freshwater invertebrates, remote sensing, GIS, spatial modeling. *Unit head:* Dr. Gwen Brewer, Coordinator, 301-687-4166. *Application contact:* Robert E. Smith, Assistant Dean for Graduate Services, 301-687-7053, Fax: 301-687-4597, E-mail: rsmith@frostburg.edu.

Iowa State University of Science and Technology, Graduate College, College of Agriculture, Department of Animal Ecology, Ames, IA 50011. Offers animal ecology (MS, PhD); fisheries biology (MS, PhD); wildlife biology (MS, PhD). *Faculty:* 14 full-time, 3 part-time. *Students:* 32 full-time (10 women), 8 part-time (3 women); includes 2 minority (1 African American, 1 Asian American or Pacific Islander), 1 international. *Degree requirements:* For master's and doctorate, thesis/dissertation required. *Entrance requirements:* For master's and doctorate, GRE General Test, TOEFL. *Application deadline:* For fall admission, 6/15 (priority date); for spring admission, 11/15 (priority date). Application fee: $20 ($50 for international students). Electronic applications accepted. Tuition, state resident: full-time $3,308. Tuition, nonresident: full-time $9,744. Part-time tuition and fees vary according to course load, campus/location and program. *Unit head:* Dr. Bruce W. Menzel, Chair, 515-294-6148, Fax: 515-294-7874, E-mail: aecgradm@iastate.edu.

Louisiana State University and Agricultural and Mechanical College, Graduate School, College of Agriculture, School of Forestry, Wildlife, and Fisheries, Baton Rouge, LA 70803. Offers fisheries (MS); forestry (MS, PhD); wildlife (MS); wildlife and fisheries science (PhD). *Faculty:* 31 full-time (0 women). *Students:* 79 full-time (21 women), 22 part-time (4 women); includes 3 minority (2 Asian Americans or Pacific Islanders, 1 Hispanic American), 31 international. Average age 30. 58 applicants, 38% accepted. In 1998, 19 master's, 6 doctorates awarded (100% found work related to degree). *Degree requirements:* For master's and doctorate, thesis/dissertation required, foreign language not required. *Entrance requirements:* For master's, GRE General Test (minimum combined score of 1000 required), minimum GPA of 3.0; for doctorate, GRE General Test (minimum combined score of 1100 required), MS, minimum GPA of 3.0. *Application deadline:* For fall admission, 1/25 (priority date). Applications are processed on a rolling basis. Application fee: $25. *Financial aid:* In 1998–99, 3 fellowships, 61 research assistantships with partial tuition reimbursements, 2 teaching assistantships with partial tuition reimbursements were awarded.; Federal Work-Study also available. Financial aid application deadline: 4/15. *Faculty research:* Forest biology and management, aquaculture, fisheries biology and ecology, upland and wetlands wildlife. *Unit head:* Dr. Norman E. Linnartz, Interim Director, 225-388-4131, Fax: 225-388-4227, E-mail: nelinn@lsu.edu. *Application contact:* Dr. D. Allen Rutherford, Coordinator of Graduate Studies, 225-388-4187, Fax: 225-388-4144, E-mail: druther@lsu.edu.

McGill University, Faculty of Graduate Studies and Research, Faculty of Agricultural and Environmental Sciences, Department of Natural Resource Sciences, Montréal, PQ H3A 2T5, Canada. Offers agrometeorology (M Sc, PhD); entomology (M Sc, PhD); forest science (M Sc, PhD); microbiology (M Sc, PhD); soil science (M Sc, PhD); wildlife biology (M Sc, PhD). *Faculty:* 18 full-time (1 woman), 26 part-time (3 women). *Students:* 83 full-time (35 women), 10 international. *Degree requirements:* For master's and doctorate, thesis/dissertation required. *Entrance requirements:* For master's, TOEFL (minimum score of 550 required), minimum GPA of 3.0; for doctorate, TOEFL (minimum score of 550 required), M Sc. *Application deadline:* For fall admission, 1/1 (priority date); for winter admission, 5/1 (priority date); for spring admission, 9/1 (priority date). Applications are processed on a rolling basis. Application fee: $60. *Unit head:* Dr. W. H. Hendershot, Chair, 514-398-7942, Fax: 514-398-7990, E-mail: chair@nrs.mcgill.ca. *Application contact:* 514-398-7708, Fax: 514-398-7968, E-mail: grad@macdonald.mcgill.ca.

Memorial University of Newfoundland, School of Graduate Studies, Interdisciplinary Program in Marine Studies, St. John's, NF A1C 5S7, Canada. Offers fisheries resource management (MMS). *Students:* 2 full-time (1 woman), 10 part-time (2 women). Application fee: $40. *Unit head:* Dr. Peter Fisher, Chair, 709-778-0461, E-mail: pfisher@gill.ifmt.nf.ca.

Michigan State University, Graduate School, College of Agriculture and Natural Resources, Department of Fisheries and Wildlife, East Lansing, MI 48824-1020. Offers fisheries and wildlife (MS, PhD), including environmental toxicology (PhD). *Faculty:* 23. *Students:* 31 full-time (11 women), 40 part-time (26 women); includes 4 minority (1 African American, 1 Asian American or Pacific Islander, 2 Hispanic Americans), 6 international. Average age 28. 75 applicants, 27% accepted. In 1998, 10 master's, 5 doctorates awarded. *Degree requirements:* For doctorate, dissertation required. *Entrance requirements:* For master's and doctorate, GRE, TOEFL, minimum GPA of 3.0. *Application deadline:* Applications are processed on a rolling basis. Application fee: $30 ($40 for international students). *Financial aid:* In 1998–99, 52 research assistantships (averaging $10,282 per year), 5 teaching assistantships (averaging $9,576 per year) were awarded. Financial aid application deadline: 2/1; financial aid applicants required to submit FAFSA. *Faculty research:* Ecosystem management and modeling, white-tailed deer, human dimensions, fish and wildlife population dynamics. Total annual research expenditures: $878,000. *Unit head:* Dr. Thomas G. Coon, Acting Chair, 517-355-4478, Fax: 517-432-1699. *Application contact:* Graduate Program Director, 517-353-3707, Fax: 517-432-1699.

Mississippi State University, College of Forest Resources, Department of Wildlife and Fisheries, Mississippi State, MS 39762. Offers wildlife ecology (MS). *Students:* 30 full-time (6 women), 8 part-time (2 women); includes 1 minority (Asian American or Pacific Islander), 2 international. Average age 28. 14 applicants, 21% accepted. In 1998, 11 degrees awarded (100% entered university research/teaching). *Degree requirements:* For master's, thesis, comprehensive oral or written exam required, foreign language not required. *Entrance requirements:* For master's, GRE General Test, TOEFL (minimum score of 550 required), minimum GPA of 3.0 in last 60 undergraduate credits. *Application deadline:* For fall admission, 7/1; for spring admission, 11/1. Applications are processed on a rolling basis. Application fee: $25 for international students. *Financial aid:* Federal Work-Study, institutionally-sponsored loans, and unspecified assistantships available. Financial aid applicants required to submit FAFSA. *Faculty research:* Aquaculture, fisheries, wildlife management, wildlife ecology, human dimensions. Total annual research expenditures: $2.2 million. *Unit head:* Dr. Bruce D. Leopold, Interim Head, 662-325-3830, Fax: 662-325-8726, E-mail: bleopold@admissions.msstate.edu.

Montana State University–Bozeman, College of Graduate Studies, College of Letters and Science, Department of Biology, Bozeman, MT 59717. Offers biological sciences (MS, PhD);

fish and wildlife biology (PhD); fish and wildlife management (MS). Part-time programs available. *Students:* 23 full-time (7 women), 41 part-time (13 women); includes 2 minority (1 African American, 1 Native American) *Degree requirements:* For master's, thesis or alternative required, foreign language not required; for doctorate, dissertation required, foreign language not required. *Entrance requirements:* For master's and doctorate, GRE General Test (minimum combined score of 1100 required), TOEFL (minimum score of 550 required), minimum GPA of 3.0. *Application deadline:* For fall admission, 6/1 (priority date); for spring admission, 11/1. Applications are processed on a rolling basis. Application fee: $50. *Unit head:* Dr. Ernest Vyse, Interim Head, 406-994-4548, Fax: 406-994-3190, E-mail: biology@montana.edu.

New Mexico State University, Graduate School, College of Agriculture and Home Economics, Department of Fishery and Wildlife Sciences, Las Cruces, NM 88003-8001. Offers wildlife science (MS). Part-time programs available. *Faculty:* 5 full-time (0 women). *Students:* 19 full-time (9 women), 9 part-time (3 women); includes 4 minority (all Hispanic Americans), 1 international. Average age 31. 39 applicants, 18% accepted. In 1998, 10 degrees awarded. *Degree requirements:* For master's, thesis, research methods course required, foreign language not required. *Entrance requirements:* For master's, GRE General Test, minimum GPA of 3.0. *Application deadline:* For fall admission, 4/1 (priority date); for spring admission, 11/1. Applications are processed on a rolling basis. Application fee: $15 ($35 for international students). Electronic applications accepted. Tuition, state resident: full-time $2,682; part-time $112 per credit. Tuition, nonresident: full-time $8,376; part-time $349 per credit. Tuition and fees vary according to course load. *Financial aid:* Research assistantships, teaching assistantships, career-related internships or fieldwork and Federal Work-Study available. Aid available to part-time students. Financial aid application deadline: 3/1. *Faculty research:* Ecosystems analyses, landscape and wildlife ecology, wildlife and fish population dynamics, management models, wildlife and fish habitat relationships. *Unit head:* Dr. Donald Caccamise, Acting Head, 505-646-1544, Fax: 505-646-1281, E-mail: dcaccami@nmsu.edu.

North Carolina State University, Graduate School, College of Forest Resources, Program in Fisheries and Wildlife Management, Raleigh, NC 27695. Offers MS. *Faculty:* 16 full-time (0 women), 1 part-time (0 women). *Students:* 2 full-time (1 woman), 1 (woman) part-time. Average age 27. 6 applicants, 33% accepted. In 1998, 1 degree awarded. *Degree requirements:* Foreign language not required. *Entrance requirements:* For master's, GRE General Test, TOEFL (minimum score of 550 required). Application fee: $45. *Unit head:* Dr. Ben A. Bergmann, Director of Graduate Programs, 919-515-7563, Fax: 919-515-8149, E-mail: bergmann@cfr.cfr.ncsu.edu.

Oregon State University, Graduate School, College of Agricultural Sciences, Department of Fisheries and Wildlife, Program in Fisheries Science, Corvallis, OR 97331. Offers M Agr, MAIS, MS, PhD. Part-time programs available. *Faculty:* 13 full-time (3 women), 12 part-time (0 women). *Students:* 39 full-time (13 women), 5 part-time (2 women); includes 3 minority (1 African American, 2 Hispanic Americans), 11 international. Average age 32. In 1998, 6 master's, 3 doctorates awarded. *Degree requirements:* For master's, thesis (MS) required; for doctorate, dissertation required, foreign language not required. *Entrance requirements:* For master's and doctorate, GRE, TOEFL (minimum score of 550 required), minimum GPA of 3.0 in last 90 hours. *Average time to degree:* Master's–3 years full-time. *Application deadline:* For fall admission, 3/15; for spring admission, 12/15. Applications are processed on a rolling basis. Application fee: $50. *Financial aid:* Fellowships, research assistantships, teaching assistantships, career-related internships or fieldwork, Federal Work-Study, and institutionally-sponsored loans available. Aid available to part-time students. Financial aid application deadline: 2/1. *Faculty research:* Fisheries ecology, fish toxicology, stream ecology, quantitative analyses of marine and freshwater fish populations. *Unit head:* Dr. Michael J. Burke, Associate Dean, 541-737-2211, Fax: 541-737-2256, E-mail: mike.burke@orst.edu. *Application contact:* Charlotte Vickers, Advising Specialist, 541-737-1941, Fax: 541-737-3590, E-mail: vickersc@ccmail.orst.edu.

Oregon State University, Graduate School, College of Agricultural Sciences, Department of Fisheries and Wildlife, Program in Wildlife Science, Corvallis, OR 97331. Offers MAIS, MS, PhD. *Faculty:* 11 full-time (0 women), 16 part-time (2 women). *Students:* 29 full-time (13 women), 1 part-time; includes 1 minority (Hispanic American), 1 international. Average age 31. In 1998, 13 master's, 1 doctorate awarded. *Degree requirements:* For master's, thesis (MS) required; for doctorate, dissertation required, foreign language not required. *Entrance requirements:* For master's and doctorate, GRE, TOEFL (minimum score of 550 required), minimum GPA of 3.0 in last 90 hours. *Average time to degree:* Master's–3 years full-time. Application fee: $50. *Financial aid:* Fellowships, research assistantships, teaching assistantships, career-related internships or fieldwork, Federal Work-Study, and institutionally-sponsored loans available. Financial aid application deadline: 2/1. *Unit head:* Dr. John J. Swetits, Director, 757-683-3911, E-mail: swetits@math.odu.edu. *Application contact:* Charlotte Vickers, Advising Specialist, 541-737-1941, Fax: 541-737-3590, E-mail: vickersc@ccmail.orst.edu.

Pennsylvania State University University Park Campus, Graduate School, College of Agricultural Sciences, School of Forest Resources, Program in Wildlife and Fisheries Sciences, State College, University Park, PA 16802-1503. Offers M Agr, MFR, MS, PhD. *Students:* 9 full-time (3 women), 3 part-time. *Entrance requirements:* For master's and doctorate, GRE General Test. Application fee: $50. *Unit head:* Dr. David R. DeWalle, Chair, 814-863-3532.

South Dakota State University, Graduate School, College of Agriculture and Biological Sciences, Department of Wildlife and Fisheries Sciences, Brookings, SD 57007. Offers biological sciences (PhD); wildlife and fisheries sciences (MS). *Degree requirements:* For master's, thesis, oral exam required, foreign language not required; for doctorate, dissertation, preliminary oral and written exams required. *Entrance requirements:* For master's, GRE, TOEFL (minimum score of 500 required); for doctorate, TOEFL. *Faculty research:* Agriculture interactions, wetland conservation, biostress.

Sul Ross State University, Division of Range Animal Science, Program in Range and Wildlife Management, Alpine, TX 79832. Offers M Ag, MS. Part-time programs available. *Degree requirements:* For master's, thesis required (for some programs), foreign language not required. *Entrance requirements:* For master's, GRE General Test (minimum combined score of 850 required), minimum GPA of 2.5 in last 60 hours of undergraduate work.

Tennessee Technological University, Graduate School, College of Arts and Sciences, Department of Biology, Cookeville, TN 38505. Offers environmental biology (MS); fish, game, and wildlife management (MS). Part-time programs available. *Faculty:* 22 full-time (2 women). *Students:* 28 full-time (11 women), 12 part-time (3 women); includes 3 minority (2 Asian Americans or Pacific Islanders, 1 Hispanic American) *Degree requirements:* For master's, thesis required, foreign language not required. *Entrance requirements:* For master's, GRE General Test, TOEFL (minimum score of 525 required). *Application deadline:* For fall admission, 3/1 (priority date); for spring admission, 8/1. Application fee: $25 ($30 for international students). Tuition, state resident: part-time $137 per hour. Tuition, nonresident: part-time $361 per hour. Required fees: $17 per hour. Tuition and fees vary according to course load. *Unit head:* Dr. Daniel Combs, Interim Chairperson, 931-372-3134, Fax: 931-372-6257, E-mail: dcombs@tntech.edu. *Application contact:* Dr. Rebecca F. Quattlebaum, Dean of the Graduate School, 931-372-3233, Fax: 931-372-3497, E-mail: rquattlebaum@tntech.edu.

Texas A&M University, College of Agriculture and Life Sciences, Department of Wildlife and Fisheries Sciences, College Station, TX 77843. Offers M Agr, MS, PhD. *Faculty:* 28 full-time (2 women), 1 part-time (0 women). *Students:* 119 full-time (53 women), 47 part-time (20 women); includes 14 minority (1 Asian American or Pacific Islander, 12 Hispanic Americans, 1 Native American), 28 international. Average age 31. 129 applicants, 34% accepted. In 1998, 12 master's, 14 doctorates awarded. Terminal master's awarded for partial completion of doctoral program. *Degree requirements:* For master's and doctorate, thesis/dissertation, final oral defense required, foreign language not required. *Entrance requirements:* For master's and doctorate, GRE General Test (minimum score of 450 on each section, 1050 combined required), TOEFL (minimum score of 550 required). *Average time to degree:* Master's–2.5 years full-time, 4 years part-time; doctorate–4.5 years full-time, 6 years part-time. *Application deadline:* Applications are processed on a rolling basis. Application fee: $50 ($75 for international students). Electronic applications accepted. *Financial aid:* In 1998–99, 119 students received aid, including 11 fellowships (averaging $13,500 per year), 37 research assistantships (averaging $11,700 per year), 31 teaching assistantships (averaging $11,700 per year); career-related internships or fieldwork, grants, institutionally-sponsored loans, and scholarships also available. Financial aid application deadline: 3/1; financial aid applicants required to submit FAFSA. *Faculty research:* Wildlife ecology and management, fisheries ecology and management, aquaculture, biological inventories and museum collections, biosystematics and genome analysis. Total annual research expenditures: $1.3 million. *Unit head:* Dr. Robert D. Brown, Head, 409-845-5777, Fax: 409-845-3786, E-mail: r-brown@tamu.edu. *Application contact:* Janice Crenshaw, Senior Academic Adviser I, 409-845-5777, Fax: 409-845-3786, E-mail: j-crenshaw@tamu.edu.

Texas A&M University–Kingsville, College of Graduate Studies, College of Agriculture and Home Economics, Program in Range and Wildlife Management, Kingsville, TX 78363. Offers MS. *Faculty:* 1 full-time (0 women), 7 part-time (0 women). *Students:* 20 full-time (3 women), 12 part-time (3 women). *Degree requirements:* For master's, thesis or alternative, comprehensive exam required, foreign language not required. *Entrance requirements:* For master's, GRE General Test (minimum combined score of 800 required), TOEFL (minimum score of 525 required), minimum GPA of 3.0. *Application deadline:* For fall admission, 6/1; for spring admission, 11/15. Applications are processed on a rolling basis. Application fee: $15 ($25 for international students). Tuition, state resident: full-time $2,062. Tuition, nonresident: full-time $7,246. *Financial aid:* Fellowships, research assistantships available. Financial aid application deadline: 5/15. *Unit head:* Graduate Coordinator, 361-593-3711.

Texas A&M University–Kingsville, College of Graduate Studies, College of Agriculture and Home Economics, Program in Wildlife Science, Kingsville, TX 78363. Offers PhD. *Students:* 5 full-time (2 women), 1 part-time. *Degree requirements:* For doctorate, one foreign language, dissertation, comprehensive exam required. *Entrance requirements:* For doctorate, GRE General Test (minimum combined score of 1000 required), minimum GPA of 3.5. *Application deadline:* For fall admission, 6/1; for spring admission, 11/15. Applications are processed on a rolling basis. Application fee: $15 ($25 for international students). Tuition, state resident: full-time $2,062. Tuition, nonresident: full-time $7,246. *Financial aid:* Application deadline: 5/15. *Unit head:* Dr. Fred Guthery, Head, 361-593-3711.

Texas Tech University, Graduate School, College of Agricultural Sciences and Natural Resources, Department of Range, Wildlife, and Fisheries Management, Lubbock, TX 79409. Offers fishery science (MS, PhD); range science (MS, PhD); wildlife science (MS, PhD). Part-time programs available. *Faculty:* 13 full-time (0 women). *Students:* 33 full-time (7 women), 6 part-time (1 woman); includes 2 minority (1 Asian American or Pacific Islander, 1 Hispanic American), 6 international. Average age 29. 19 applicants, 26% accepted. In 1998, 10 master's awarded. *Degree requirements:* For master's, thesis required, foreign language not required; for doctorate, dissertation required. *Entrance requirements:* For master's, GRE General Test (combined average 1012); for doctorate, GRE General Test. *Application deadline:* For fall admission, 4/15 (priority date); for spring admission, 11/1 (priority date). Applications are processed on a rolling basis. Application fee: $25 ($50 for international students). Electronic applications accepted. *Financial aid:* In 1998–99, 24 students received aid, including 21 research assistantships (averaging $8,448 per year), 5 teaching assistantships (averaging $8,020 per year); fellowships, Federal Work-Study and institutionally-sponsored loans also available. Aid available to part-time students. Financial aid application deadline: 5/15; financial aid applicants required to submit FAFSA. *Faculty research:* Use of fire on range lands, waterfowl, upland game birds and playa lakes in the southern Great Plains, reproductive physiology in fisheries. Total annual research expenditures: $1.5 million. *Unit head:* Dr. Phillip J. Zwank, Chairman, 806-742-2841, Fax: 806-742-2280.

Université du Québec à Rimouski, Graduate Programs, Program in Wildlife Resources Management, Rimouski, PQ G5L 3A1, Canada. Offers M Sc, Diploma. *Degree requirements:* For master's and Diploma, thesis not required. *Entrance requirements:* For degree, appropriate bachelor's degree, proficiency in French.

University of Alaska Fairbanks, Graduate School, College of Science, Engineering and Mathematics, Department of Biology and Wildlife, Program in Wildlife Biology and Management, Fairbanks, AK 99775-7480. Offers MS, PhD. Part-time programs available. *Students:* 9 full-time (4 women), 5 part-time (2 women); includes 1 minority (African American) Average age 32. 27 applicants, 19% accepted. In 1998, 2 master's, 2 doctorates awarded. *Degree requirements:* For master's, thesis, comprehensive exam required, foreign language not required; for doctorate, one foreign language (computer language can substitute), dissertation, comprehensive exam required. *Entrance requirements:* For master's and doctorate, GRE General Test, GRE Subject Test, TOEFL (minimum score of 550 required). *Application deadline:* For fall admission, 8/1. Applications are processed on a rolling basis. Application fee: $35. *Financial aid:* Fellowships, research assistantships, teaching assistantships, career-related internships or fieldwork available. Financial aid application deadline: 3/1. *Faculty research:* Wildlife ecology. *Unit head:* Dr. Ed Murphy, Acting Dean, College of Science, Engineering and Mathematics, 907-474-7941.

University of Alaska Fairbanks, Graduate School, School of Fisheries and Ocean Sciences, Program in Fisheries, Fairbanks, AK 99775-7480. Offers MS, PhD. *Faculty:* 7 full-time (0 women). *Students:* 33 full-time (13 women), 17 part-time (4 women); includes 5 minority (4 Asian Americans or Pacific Islanders, 1 Native American), 10 international. Average age 33. 47 applicants, 77% accepted. In 1998, 6 master's, 1 doctorate awarded. *Degree requirements:* For master's, thesis, comprehensive exam required, foreign language not required; for doctorate, one foreign language (computer language can substitute), dissertation, comprehensive exam required. *Entrance requirements:* For master's and doctorate, GRE General Test, TOEFL (minimum score of 550 required). *Application deadline:* For fall admission, 3/1 (priority date). Applications are processed on a rolling basis. Application fee: $35. *Financial aid:* Research assistantships available. *Faculty research:* Marine stock reconstruction, oil spill research on marine life. *Unit head:* Dr. Tom Shirley, Associate Dean, School of Fisheries and Ocean Sciences, 907-474-7531.

The University of Arizona, Graduate College, College of Agriculture, School of Renewable Natural Resources, Division of Wildlife and Fisheries Science, Tucson, AZ 85721. Offers MS, PhD. *Students:* 23 full-time (11 women), 26 part-time (13 women); includes 6 minority (4 Hispanic Americans, 2 Native Americans), 5 international. Average age 32. 15 applicants, 40% accepted. In 1998, 7 master's, 4 doctorates awarded. *Degree requirements:* For master's, computer language, thesis required, foreign language not required; for doctorate, one foreign language (computer language can substitute), dissertation required. *Entrance requirements:* For master's and doctorate, GRE General Test, GRE Subject Test (biology), TOEFL (minimum score of 550 required), minimum GPA of 3.0. *Application deadline:* For fall admission, 8/1. Applications are processed on a rolling basis. Application fee: $35. *Financial aid:* Fellowships, research assistantships, teaching assistantships, career-related internships or fieldwork available. *Faculty research:* Short-term effects of artificial oases on Arizona wildlife, elk response to cattle in northern Arizona, effect of reservoir operation on tailwaters. *Unit head:* Dr. Bill Shaw, Head, 520-621-7265. *Application contact:* Mary E. Soltero, Administrative Assistant, 520-621-7260, Fax: 520-621-8801.

University of Florida, Graduate School, College of Agriculture, Department of Wildlife Ecology, Gainesville, FL 32611. Offers MS, PhD. *Faculty:* 34. *Students:* 51 full-time (21 women), 35 part-time (15 women); includes 7 minority (3 African Americans, 4 Hispanic Americans), 12 international. 65 applicants, 29% accepted. In 1998, 11 master's, 7 doctorates awarded. *Degree requirements:* For master's, thesis optional; for doctorate, dissertation required. *Entrance requirements:* For master's and doctorate, GRE General Test (minimum combined score of 1200 required), minimum GPA of 3.3. *Application deadline:* For fall admission, 6/1 (priority date); for spring admission, 12/1. Applications are processed on a rolling basis. Application fee: $20. Electronic applications accepted. *Financial aid:* In 1998–99, 46 students received

Fish, Game, and Wildlife Management

University of Florida (continued)
aid, including 6 fellowships, 26 research assistantships, 9 teaching assistantships; institutionally-sponsored loans also available. *Faculty research:* Wildlife biology and management, tropical ecology and conservation, conservation biology, landscape ecology and restoration, conservation education. *Unit head:* Dr. Nat Frazer, Chair, 352-846-0552, E-mail: gwt@gnv.ifas.ufl.edu.

University of Idaho, College of Graduate Studies, College of Forestry, Wildlife, and Range Sciences, Department of Fish and Wildlife Resources, Program in Fishery Resources, Moscow, ID 83844-4140. Offers fishery management (MS); fishery resources (PhD). *Faculty:* 2 full-time (both women). *Students:* 15 full-time (6 women), 17 part-time (5 women); includes 1 minority (Native American) In 1998, 4 degrees awarded. *Degree requirements:* For doctorate, dissertation required, foreign language not required, foreign language not required. *Entrance requirements:* For master's, minimum GPA of 2.8; for doctorate, minimum undergraduate GPA of 2.8, 3.0 graduate. *Application deadline:* For fall admission, 8/1; for spring admission, 12/15. Application fee: $35 ($45 for international students). *Financial aid:* In 1998–99, 12 research assistantships (averaging $11,866 per year) were awarded. Financial aid application deadline: 2/15. *Unit head:* Dr. George W. LaBar, Head, Department of Fish and Wildlife Resources, 208-885-6434.

University of Idaho, College of Graduate Studies, College of Forestry, Wildlife, and Range Sciences, Department of Fish and Wildlife Resources, Program in Wildlife Resources, Moscow, ID 83844-4140. Offers MS, PhD. *Faculty:* 11 full-time (2 women), 1 part-time (0 women). *Students:* 19 full-time (7 women), 8 part-time (3 women); includes 2 minority (both Asian Americans or Pacific Islanders), 2 international. In 1998, 4 degrees awarded. *Degree requirements:* For doctorate, dissertation required, foreign language not required, foreign language not required. *Entrance requirements:* For master's, minimum GPA of 2.8; for doctorate, minimum undergraduate GPA of 2.8, 3.0 graduate. *Application deadline:* For fall admission, 8/1; for spring admission, 12/15. Application fee: $35 ($45 for international students). *Financial aid:* In 1998–99, 20 research assistantships (averaging $12,878 per year), 7 teaching assistantships (averaging $11,820 per year) were awarded. Financial aid application deadline: 2/15. *Unit head:* Dr. George W. LaBar, Head, Department of Fish and Wildlife Resources, 208-885-6434.

University of Idaho, College of Graduate Studies, College of Forestry, Wildlife, and Range Sciences, Program in Forestry, Wildlife, and Range Sciences, Moscow, ID 83844-4140. Offers PhD. *Faculty:* 3 full-time (0 women). *Students:* 28 full-time (6 women), 32 part-time (9 women); includes 3 minority (1 African American, 1 Asian American or Pacific Islander, 1 Native American), 12 international. In 1998, 4 degrees awarded. *Degree requirements:* For doctorate, dissertation required, foreign language not required. *Entrance requirements:* For doctorate, minimum undergraduate GPA of 2.8, 3.0 graduate. *Application deadline:* For fall admission, 8/1; for spring admission, 12/15. Application fee: $35 ($45 for international students). *Financial aid:* Fellowships, research assistantships, teaching assistantships available. Financial aid application deadline: 2/15. *Application contact:* Dr. Ali Moslemi, Graduate Coordinator, 208-885-6126.

University of Maine, Graduate School, College of Natural Sciences, Forestry, and Agriculture, Department of Wildlife Ecology, Orono, ME 04469. Offers wildlife conservation (MWC); wildlife ecology (MS, PhD). Part-time programs available. *Faculty:* 6 full-time (0 women). *Students:* 16 (8 women). Average age 26. 62 applicants, 8% accepted. In 1998, 1 master's, 3 doctorates awarded. *Degree requirements:* For master's, computer language, thesis required (for some programs), foreign language not required; for doctorate, one foreign language, computer language, dissertation required. *Entrance requirements:* For master's and doctorate, GRE General Test, GRE Subject Test (biology), TOEFL (minimum score of 550 required). *Application deadline:* For fall admission, 2/1 (priority date); for spring admission, 10/15. Applications are processed on a rolling basis. Application fee: $50. *Financial aid:* In 1998–99, 1 fellowship with tuition reimbursement (averaging $11,250 per year), 10 research assistantships with tuition reimbursements (averaging $7,650 per year), 3 teaching assistantships with tuition reimbursements (averaging $7,800 per year) were awarded.; career-related internships or fieldwork, Federal Work-Study, institutionally-sponsored loans, and tuition waivers (full and partial) also available. Financial aid application deadline: 3/1. *Faculty research:* Integration of wildlife and forest management, population dynamics, behavior, physiology and nutrition, wetland ecology and influence of environmental disturbances. *Unit head:* Dr. James Gilbert, Chair, 207-581-2866, Fax: 207-581-2858. *Application contact:* Scott G. Delcourt, Director of the Graduate School, 207-581-3218, Fax: 207-581-3232, E-mail: graduate@maine.edu.

University of Massachusetts Amherst, Graduate School, College of Food and Natural Resources, Department of Forestry and Wildlife Management, Program in Wildlife and Fisheries Conservation, Amherst, MA 01003. Offers MS, PhD. Part-time programs available. *Faculty:* 25 full-time (3 women). *Students:* 30 full-time (12 women), 46 part-time (24 women); includes 2 minority (1 African American, 1 Asian American or Pacific Islander), 6 international. Average age 31. 70 applicants, 27% accepted. In 1998, 17 master's, 1 doctorate awarded. Terminal master's awarded for partial completion of doctoral program. *Degree requirements:* For master's, thesis optional, foreign language not required; for doctorate, variable foreign language requirement, dissertation required. *Entrance requirements:* For master's and doctorate, GRE General Test. *Application deadline:* For fall admission, 2/1 (priority date); for spring admission, 10/1. Applications are processed on a rolling basis. Application fee: $40. Tuition, state resident: full-time $2,640; part-time $165 per credit. Tuition, nonresident: full-time $9,756; part-time $407 per credit. Required fees: $1,221 per term. One-time fee: $110. Full-time tuition and fees vary according to course load, campus/location and reciprocity agreements. *Financial aid:* Fellowships with full tuition reimbursements, research assistantships with full tuition reimbursements, teaching assistantships with full tuition reimbursements, career-related internships or fieldwork, Federal Work-Study, grants, scholarships, traineeships, and unspecified assistantships available. Aid available to part-time students. Financial aid application deadline: 2/1. *Unit head:* Dr. Todd K. Fuller, Director, 413-545-2665, Fax: 413-545-4358, E-mail: tkfuller@forwild.umass.edu.

University of Miami, Graduate School, Rosenstiel School of Marine and Atmospheric Science, Division of Marine Biology and Fisheries, Miami, FL 33149. Offers MA, MS, PhD. *Faculty:* 19 full-time (4 women), 1 (woman) part-time. *Students:* 44 full-time (17 women), 5 part-time (3 women); includes 4 minority (2 African Americans, 1 Hispanic American, 1 Native American), 15 international. Average age 28. 111 applicants, 13% accepted. In 1998, 2 doctorates awarded. Terminal master's awarded for partial completion of doctoral program. *Degree requirements:* For master's and doctorate, thesis/dissertation required. *Entrance requirements:* For master's and doctorate, GRE General Test (score in 75th percentile or higher required), GRE Subject Test, TOEFL (minimum score of 550 required). *Average time to degree:* Master's–3 years full-time; doctorate–6 years full-time. *Application deadline:* For fall admission, 2/1 (priority date). Applications are processed on a rolling basis. Application fee: $35. Electronic applications accepted. Tuition: Full-time $15,336; part-time $852 per credit. Required fees: $174. Tuition and fees vary according to program. *Financial aid:* In 1998–99, 43 students received aid, including 6 fellowships with tuition reimbursements available, 36 research assistantships with tuition reimbursements available (averaging $17,000 per year), 1 teaching assistantship with tuition reimbursement available (averaging $17,000 per year); institutionally-sponsored loans also available. Financial aid application deadline: 2/1. *Faculty research:* Biochemistry, physiology, plankton, coral, fisheries biology. Total annual research expenditures: $5 million. *Unit head:* Dr. Samuel Snedaker, Chairmain, 305-361-4176. *Application contact:* Dr. Frank Millero, Associate Dean, 305-361-4155, Fax: 305-361-4771, E-mail: gso@rsmas.miami.edu.

University of Minnesota, Twin Cities Campus, Graduate School, College of Natural Resources, Department of Fisheries and Wildlife, Minneapolis, MN 55455-0213. Offers conservation biology (MS, PhD); fisheries (MS, PhD); wildlife conservation (MS, PhD). *Faculty:* 13 full-time (2 women), 21 part-time (0 women). *Students:* 35 full-time (12 women), 2 part-time (1 woman); includes 2 minority (1 Asian American or Pacific Islander, 1 Native American), 3 international. 78 applicants, 19% accepted. In 1998, 9 master's awarded (11% entered university research/teaching, 66% found other work related to degree, 11% continued full-time study); 1 doctorate awarded (100% entered university research/teaching). *Degree requirements:* For doctorate, dissertation required. *Entrance requirements:* For master's and doctorate, GRE. *Application deadline:* For fall admission, 1/15 (priority date). Application fee: $50 ($55 for international students). *Financial aid:* In 1998–99, 30 students received aid, including 4 fellowships with full tuition reimbursements available (averaging $12,000 per year), 25 research assistantships with full and partial tuition reimbursements available, 1 teaching assistantship with full and partial tuition reimbursement available Financial aid application deadline: 1/15. *Faculty research:* Management, ecology, physiology, genetics, and computer modeling of fish and wildlife. *Unit head:* Dr. Ira R. Adelman, Head, 612-624-3600. *Application contact:* Kathleen Walter, Assistant for Graduate Studies, 612-624-2748, Fax: 612-624-8701, E-mail: kwalter@forestry.umn.edu.

University of Missouri–Columbia, Graduate School, School of Natural Resources, Program in Fisheries and Wildlife, Columbia, MO 65211. Offers MS, PhD. *Students:* 19 full-time (12 women), 30 part-time (8 women); includes 2 minority (both Hispanic Americans), 3 international. 26 applicants, 15% accepted. In 1998, 6 master's awarded. *Degree requirements:* For doctorate, dissertation required. *Entrance requirements:* For master's and doctorate, GRE General Test, minimum GPA of 3.0. *Application deadline:* Applications are processed on a rolling basis. Application fee: $30 ($50 for international students). *Financial aid:* Research assistantships, teaching assistantships, grants and institutionally-sponsored loans available. *Unit head:* Dr. Ron Drobeny, Director of Graduate Studies, 573-882-3436.

The University of Montana–Missoula, Graduate School, School of Forestry, Program in Fish and Wildlife Biology, Missoula, MT 59812-0002. Offers MS, PhD. *Faculty:* 5 full-time (0 women), 10 part-time (0 women). *Students:* 17 full-time (7 women), 9 part-time (1 woman); includes 3 minority (2 Asian Americans or Pacific Islanders, 1 Native American) Average age 23. 71 applicants, 11% accepted. In 1998, 5 master's, 4 doctorates awarded. *Degree requirements:* For master's and doctorate, thesis/dissertation required, foreign language not required. *Entrance requirements:* For master's, GRE General Test (minimum combined score of 1540 on three sections required), GRE Subject Test; for doctorate, GRE General Test. *Application deadline:* For fall admission, 1/31. Application fee: $45. *Financial aid:* Teaching assistantships, career-related internships or fieldwork, Federal Work-Study, and institutionally-sponsored loans available. Financial aid application deadline: 3/1. *Faculty research:* Wildlife management, wetland ecology, wildlife habitat selection, population and behavioral ecology, predation and big-game management. *Unit head:* Dr. Daniel Pletscher, Chair, 406-243-5272. *Application contact:* Dr. Les Marcum, Graduate Committee Chair, 406-243-6237.

University of New Hampshire, Graduate School, College of Life Sciences and Agriculture, Graduate Programs in the Biological Sciences and Natural Resources, Durham, NH 03824. Offers animal and nutritional sciences (MS, PhD); biochemistry and molecular biology (MS, PhD); biology (MS); genetics (MS, PhD); microbiology (MS, PhD); natural resources (MS, PhD), including environmental conservation (MS), forestry (MS), natural resources (PhD), soil science (MS), water resources management (MS), wildlife (MS); plant biology (MS, PhD); zoology (MS, PhD). Part-time programs available. *Faculty:* 129 full-time. *Students:* 127 full-time (74 women), 111 part-time (56 women); includes 6 minority (4 Asian Americans or Pacific Islanders, 2 Hispanic Americans), 31 international. Terminal master's awarded for partial completion of doctoral program. *Degree requirements:* For doctorate, dissertation required, foreign language not required. *Entrance requirements:* For master's, GRE General Test. *Application deadline:* Applications are processed on a rolling basis. Application fee: $50. Tuition, area resident: Full-time $5,750; part-time $319 per credit. Tuition, state resident: full-time $8,625. Tuition, nonresident: full-time $14,640; part-time $598 per credit. Required fees: $224 per semester. Tuition and fees vary according to course load, degree level and program. *Unit head:* Dr. William Mautz, Interim Dean, College of Life Sciences and Agriculture, 603-862-1450.

University of New Hampshire, Graduate School, College of Life Sciences and Agriculture, Graduate Programs in the Biological Sciences and Natural Resources, Department of Natural Resources, Option in Wildlife, Durham, NH 03824. Offers MS. Part-time programs available. *Students:* 6 full-time (4 women), 3 part-time. Average age 26. 16 applicants, 31% accepted. In 1998, 1 degree awarded. *Degree requirements:* For master's, thesis or alternative required, foreign language not required. *Entrance requirements:* For master's, GRE General Test. *Application deadline:* For fall admission, 4/1 (priority date). Applications are processed on a rolling basis. Application fee: $50. Tuition, area resident: Full-time $5,750; part-time $319 per credit. Tuition, state resident: full-time $8,625. Tuition, nonresident: full-time $14,640; part-time $598 per credit. Required fees: $224 per semester. Tuition and fees vary according to course load, degree level and program. *Financial aid:* In 1998–99, 1 fellowship, 3 research assistantships, 3 teaching assistantships were awarded.; career-related internships or fieldwork, Federal Work-Study, scholarships, and tuition waivers (full and partial) also available. Aid available to part-time students. Financial aid application deadline: 2/15. *Faculty research:* Habitat evaluation and management, nutrition and physiology, land use planning. *Application contact:* Dr. Robert Harter, Graduate Coordinator, 603-862-3944.

University of North Dakota, Graduate School, College of Arts and Sciences, Department of Biology, Grand Forks, ND 58202. Offers botany (MS, DA, PhD); ecology (MS, DA, PhD); entomology (MS, DA, PhD); environmental biology (MS, DA, PhD); fisheries/wildlife (MS, DA, PhD); genetics (MS, DA, PhD); zoology (MS, DA, PhD). *Faculty:* 18 full-time (3 women). *Students:* 16 full-time (5 women). Terminal master's awarded for partial completion of doctoral program. *Degree requirements:* For master's and doctorate, thesis/dissertation required. *Entrance requirements:* For master's, GRE General Test, GRE Subject Test, TOEFL (minimum score of 550 required), minimum GPA of 3.0; for doctorate, GRE General Test, GRE Subject Test, TOEFL (minimum score of 550 required), minimum GPA of 3.5. *Application deadline:* For fall admission, 3/1 (priority date). Applications are processed on a rolling basis. Application fee: $20. *Unit head:* Dr. Jeff Lang, Director, 701-777-2621, Fax: 701-777-2623, E-mail: jlang@badlands.nodak.edu.

University of Rhode Island, Graduate School, College of Resource Development, Department of Fisheries, Aquaculture and Pathology, Kingston, RI 02881. Offers animal science (MS).

University of Tennessee, Knoxville, Graduate School, College of Agricultural Sciences and Natural Resources, Department of Forestry, Wildlife, and Fisheries, Program in Wildlife and Fisheries Science, Knoxville, TN 37996. Offers MS. *Students:* 13 full-time (5 women), 9 part-time (3 women); includes 1 minority (African American), 2 international. 33 applicants, 36% accepted. In 1998, 6 degrees awarded. *Degree requirements:* For master's, thesis required, foreign language not required. *Entrance requirements:* For master's, GRE General Test, TOEFL (minimum score of 550 required), minimum GPA of 2.7. *Application deadline:* For fall admission, 2/1 (priority date). Applications are processed on a rolling basis. Application fee: $35. Electronic applications accepted. *Financial aid:* Application deadline: 2/1; *Application contact:* Dr. Richard Strange, Graduate Representative, E-mail: rstrange@utk.edu.

University of Vermont, Graduate College, School of Natural Resources, Program in Wildlife and Fisheries Biology, Burlington, VT 05405-0160. Offers MS. *Degree requirements:* For master's, thesis required. *Entrance requirements:* For master's, GRE General Test, TOEFL (minimum score of 550 required).

University of Washington, Graduate School, College of Forest Resources, Seattle, WA 98195. Offers forest economics (MS, PhD); forest ecosystem analysis (MS, PhD); forest engineering/forest hydrology (MS, PhD); forest products marketing (MS, PhD); forest soils (MS, PhD); pulp and paper science (MS, PhD); quantitative resource management (MS, PhD); silviculture (MFR); silviculture and forest protection (MS, PhD); social sciences (MS, PhD); urban horticulture (MFR, MS, PhD); wildlife science (MS, PhD). *Faculty:* 47 full-time (4 women), 16 part-time (2 women). *Students:* 161 full-time (65 women), 16 part-time (5 women); includes

15 minority (1 African American, 10 Asian Americans or Pacific Islanders, 1 Hispanic American, 3 Native Americans), 9 international. *Degree requirements:* For master's, thesis required (for some programs), foreign language not required; for doctorate, dissertation required, foreign language not required. *Entrance requirements:* For master's and doctorate, GRE, TOEFL (minimum score of 500 required), minimum GPA of 3.0. *Application deadline:* For fall admission, 2/1 (priority date); for winter admission, 11/1; for spring admission, 2/1. Applications are processed on a rolling basis. Application fee: $50. Electronic applications accepted. Tuition, state resident: full-time $5,196; part-time $475 per credit. Tuition, nonresident: full-time $13,485; part-time $1,285 per credit. Required fees: $387; $38 per credit. Tuition and fees vary according to course load. *Unit head:* Dr. David B. Thorud, Dean, 206-685-1928, Fax: 206-685-0790. *Application contact:* Michelle Trudeau, Student Services Manager, 206-616-1533, Fax: 206-685-0790, E-mail: michtru@u.washington.edu.

See in-depth description on page 963.

University of Washington, Graduate School, College of Ocean and Fishery Sciences, School of Fisheries, Seattle, WA 98195. Offers MS, PhD. *Faculty:* 34 full-time (6 women). *Students:* 85 full-time (32 women), 31 part-time (11 women); includes 9 minority (2 African Americans, 2 Asian Americans or Pacific Islanders, 5 Hispanic Americans), 19 international. 139 applicants, 19% accepted. In 1998, 22 master's, 9 doctorates awarded. *Degree requirements:* For master's and doctorate, thesis/dissertation required, foreign language not required. *Entrance requirements:* For master's and doctorate, GRE General Test (minimum combined score of 1100 required), TOEFL (minimum score of 580 required, 237 for computer based), minimum GPA of 3.0. *Average time to degree:* Master's–3 years full-time, 5 years part-time; doctorate–5 years full-time, 8 years part-time. *Application deadline:* For fall admission, 1/5. Application fee: $50. Tuition, state resident: full-time $5,196; part-time $475 per credit. Tuition, nonresident: full-time $13,485; part-time $1,285 per credit. Required fees: $387; $38 per credit. Tuition and fees vary according to course load. *Financial aid:* In 1998–99, 100 students received aid, including 2 fellowships with tuition reimbursements available, 57 research assistantships with tuition reimbursements available, 16 teaching assistantships with tuition reimbursements available; career-related internships or fieldwork, Federal Work-Study, institutionally-sponsored loans, and tuition waivers (full and partial) also available. Aid available to part-time students. *Faculty research:* Fish and shellfish ecology, fisheries management, aquatic ecology, conservation biology. Total annual research expenditures: $6 million. *Unit head:* Dr. David Armstrong, Director, 206-543-4270, Fax: 206-685-7471, E-mail: daa@fish.washington.edu. *Application contact:* Lin Murdock, Student Servivces Coordinator, 206-543-7457, Fax: 206-616-9758, E-mail: graduates@fish.washington.edu.

Utah State University, School of Graduate Studies, College of Natural Resources, Department of Fisheries and Wildlife, Logan, UT 84322. Offers fisheries and wildlife (MS, PhD); fisheries biology (MS, PhD); wildlife biology (MS, PhD). *Faculty:* 21 full-time (1 woman). *Students:* 44 full-time (26 women), 23 part-time (11 women); includes 3 minority (2 Asian Americans or Pacific Islanders, 1 Hispanic American), 6 international. Average age 27. 69 applicants, 22% accepted. In 1998, 18 master's, 3 doctorates awarded. *Degree requirements:* For master's, thesis required (for some programs), foreign language not required; for doctorate, dissertation required, foreign language not required. *Entrance requirements:* For master's and doctorate, GRE General Test (score in 40th percentile or higher required), TOEFL (minimum score of 550 required), minimum GPA of 3.0. *Average time to degree:* Master's–2.5 years full-time; doctorate–6 years full-time. *Application deadline:* For fall admission, 2/15 (priority date); for spring admission, 10/15. Applications are processed on a rolling basis. Application fee: $40. Tuition, state resident: full-time $1,492. Tuition, nonresident: full-time $5,232. Required fees: $434. Tuition and fees vary according to course load. *Financial aid:* In 1998–99, 5 fellowships with partial tuition reimbursements, 47 research assistantships with partial tuition reimbursements, 6 teaching assistantships with partial tuition reimbursements were awarded.; career-related internships or fieldwork, Federal Work-Study, and institutionally-sponsored loans also available. Aid available to part-time students. Financial aid application deadline: 2/1. *Faculty research:* Behavior, population ecology, habitat, conservation biology, restoration. Total annual research expenditures: $3 million. *Unit head:* Dr. Raymond D. Dueser, Head, 435-797-2463, Fax: 435-797-1871, E-mail: fishnwlf@cc.usu.edu. *Application contact:* Suzanne S. Stoker, Senior Secretary, 435-797-2459, Fax: 435-797-1871.

Virginia Polytechnic Institute and State University, Graduate School, College of Natural Resources, Department of Fisheries and Wildlife Sciences, Blacksburg, VA 24061. Offers aquaculture (MS, PhD); conservation biology (MS, PhD); fisheries science (MS, PhD); wildlife science (MS, PhD). *Faculty:* 21 full-time (2 women). *Students:* 43 full-time (14 women), 7 part-time (2 women); includes 2 minority (both African Americans), 4 international. 66 applicants, 12% accepted. In 1998, 10 master's, 3 doctorates awarded. *Degree requirements:* For master's and doctorate, thesis/dissertation required. *Entrance requirements:* For master's and doctorate, GRE General Test, TOEFL, minimum GPA of 3.0. *Application deadline:* For fall admission, 12/1 (priority date). Applications are processed on a rolling basis. Application fee: $25. *Financial aid:* Fellowships, research assistantships, teaching assistantships, Federal Work-Study and tuition waivers (full) available. Financial aid application deadline: 4/1. *Faculty research:* Fisheries management, wildlife management, wildlife toxicology and physiology, endangered species, computer applications. *Unit head:* Dr. Brian R. Murphy, Head, 540-231-5573, Fax: 540-231-7580, E-mail: murphybr@vt.edu.

West Virginia University, College of Agriculture, Forestry and Consumer Sciences, Division of Forestry, Program in Wildlife and Fisheries Resources, Morgantown, WV 26506. Offers MS. Part-time programs available. *Degree requirements:* For master's, thesis required (for some programs), foreign language not required. *Entrance requirements:* For master's, GRE, TOEFL (minimum score of 550 required), minimum GPA of 3.0. *Faculty research:* Managing habitat for game, nongame, and fish.

Forestry

Auburn University, Graduate School, School of Forestry, Auburn, Auburn University, AL 36849-0002. Offers MF, MS, PhD. Part-time programs available. *Faculty:* 27 full-time (3 women). *Students:* 34 full-time (9 women), 9 part-time (1 woman); includes 2 minority (both African Americans), 7 international. 22 applicants, 41% accepted. In 1998, 10 master's, 4 doctorates awarded. *Degree requirements:* For master's, oral exam (MF), thesis (MS) required; for doctorate, dissertation required, foreign language not required. *Entrance requirements:* For master's and doctorate, GRE General Test (minimum score of 450 on verbal section, 550 on quantitative required). *Application deadline:* For fall admission, 9/1; for spring admission, 3/1. Applications are processed on a rolling basis. Application fee: $25 ($50 for international students). Tuition, state resident: full-time $2,760; part-time $76 per credit hour. Tuition, nonresident: full-time $8,280; part-time $228 per credit hour. *Financial aid:* Fellowships, research assistantships, teaching assistantships, Federal Work-Study available. Aid available to part-time students. Financial aid application deadline: 3/15. *Faculty research:* Forest nursery management, silviculture and vegetation management, biological processes and ecological relationships, growth and yield of plantations and natural stands, urban forestry, forest taxation, law and policy. *Unit head:* Richard W. Brinker, Dean, 334-844-1007, Fax: 334-844-1084, E-mail: brinker@forestry.auburn.edu. *Application contact:* Dr. John F. Pritchett, Dean of the Graduate School, 334-844-4700, E-mail: hatchlb@mail.auburn.edu.

Clemson University, Graduate School, College of Agriculture, Forestry and Life Sciences, School of Natural Resources, Department of Forest Resources, Clemson, SC 29634. Offers MFR, MS, PhD. Part-time programs available. *Students:* 26 full-time (4 women), 16 part-time (6 women), 6 international. Average age 25. 19 applicants, 47% accepted. In 1998, 17 master's, 4 doctorates awarded. *Degree requirements:* For master's and doctorate, thesis/dissertation required, foreign language not required. *Entrance requirements:* For master's, GRE General Test, TOEFL, minimum B average in last 2 years of undergraduate course work; for doctorate, GRE General Test, TOEFL, minimum B average in graduate course work. *Application deadline:* For fall admission, 3/1 (priority date); for spring admission, 10/1. Application fee: $35. *Financial aid:* Fellowships, research assistantships, teaching assistantships available. Financial aid application deadline: 5/1; financial aid applicants required to submit FAFSA. *Faculty research:* Wetlands management, wood technology, forest management, silviculture, economics. *Unit head:* Dr. Thomas Wooten, Interim Chair, 864-656-3303, Fax: 864-656-3304. *Application contact:* Dr. Allan Marsinko, Coordinator, 864-656-4829, Fax: 864-656-3304, E-mail: amrsnk@clemson.edu.

Colorado State University, Graduate School, College of Natural Resources, Department of Forest Sciences, Fort Collins, CO 80523-0015. Offers forestry (MF, MS, PhD). Part-time programs available. *Faculty:* 16 full-time (1 woman), 22 part-time (5 women). *Students:* 49; includes 7 minority (2 African Americans, 3 Asian Americans or Pacific Islanders, 1 Hispanic American, 1 Native American), 7 international. Average age 31. 52 applicants, 44% accepted. In 1998, 20 master's, 5 doctorates awarded. *Degree requirements:* For master's, thesis optional, foreign language not required; for doctorate, dissertation required, foreign language not required. *Entrance requirements:* For master's, GRE General Test, TOEFL (minimum score of 550 required), minimum GPA of 3.0; for doctorate, GRE General Test, TOEFL, minimum GPA of 3.0. *Application deadline:* For fall admission, 4/1 (priority date); for spring admission, 9/1 (priority date). Applications are processed on a rolling basis. Application fee: $30. Electronic applications accepted. *Financial aid:* In 1998–99, 10 research assistantships, 10 teaching assistantships were awarded.; fellowships, career-related internships or fieldwork, Federal Work-Study, institutionally-sponsored loans, and traineeships also available. Financial aid application deadline: 5/1. *Faculty research:* Remote sensing and geographic information systems, ecosystems analysis, ecosystem management, wood engineering, economics and modeling management, fire science, conservation biology, forest ecology. Total annual research expenditures: $1.6 million. *Unit head:* Susan G. Stafford, Head, 970-491-6911, Fax: 970-491-6754, E-mail: stafford@cnr.colostate.edu. *Application contact:* David R. Betters, Graduate Coordinator, 970-491-6911, Fax: 970-491-6754, E-mail: dave@cnr.colostate.edu.

Cornell University, Graduate School, Graduate Fields of Agriculture and Life Sciences, Field of Natural Resources, Ithaca, NY 14853-0001. Offers aquatic science (MPS, MS, PhD); environmental management (MPS); fishery science (MPS, MS, PhD); forest science (MPS, MS, PhD); resource policy and management (MPS, MS, PhD); wildlife science (MPS, MS, PhD). *Faculty:* 24 full-time. *Students:* 58 full-time (24 women); includes 5 minority (1 African American, 1 Asian American or Pacific Islander, 2 Hispanic Americans, 1 Native American), 11 international. Terminal master's awarded for partial completion of doctoral program. *Degree requirements:* For master's, thesis (MS), project paper (MPS) required; for doctorate, dissertation required, foreign language not required. *Entrance requirements:* For master's and doctorate, GRE General Test, TOEFL (minimum score of 550 required). *Application deadline:* Applications are processed on a rolling basis. Application fee: $65. Electronic applications accepted. *Unit head:* Director of Graduate Studies, 607-255-2807, Fax: 607-255-0349. *Application contact:* Graduate Field Assistant, 607-255-2807, E-mail: nrgrad@cornell.edu.

Duke University, Nicholas School of the Environment, Durham, NC 27708-0328. Offers coastal environmental management (MEM); environmental science and policy (PhD); environmental toxicology, chemistry, and risk assessment (MEM); forest resource management (MF); resource ecology (MEM); resource economics and policy (MEM); water and air resources (MEM). PhD offered through the Graduate School. *Accreditation:* SAF (one or more programs are accredited). Part-time programs available. *Faculty:* 61 full-time (10 women), 23 part-time (3 women). *Students:* 228 full-time (136 women); includes 7 minority (2 African Americans, 4 Asian Americans or Pacific Islanders, 1 Hispanic American), 24 international. Terminal master's awarded for partial completion of doctoral program. *Degree requirements:* For master's, thesis required (for some programs), foreign language not required; for doctorate, dissertation required, foreign language not required. *Entrance requirements:* For master's, GRE General Test, TOEFL, previous course work in biology or ecology, calculus, statistics, and microeconomics; computer familiarity with word processing and data analysis; for doctorate, GRE General Test, TOEFL. *Application deadline:* For fall admission, 2/1; for spring admission, 10/15. Applications are processed on a rolling basis. Application fee: $75. *Unit head:* Dr. Norman L. Christensen, Dean, 919-613-8004, Fax: 919-684-8741. *Application contact:* Bertie S. Belvin, Associate Dean for Academic Services, 919-613-8070, Fax: 919-684-8741, E-mail: envadm@duke.edu.

See in-depth description on page 949.

Harvard University, Graduate School of Arts and Sciences, The Harvard Forest, Cambridge, MA 02138. Offers forest science (MFS). *Faculty:* 4 full-time. 2 applicants, 0% accepted. *Degree requirements:* For master's, thesis required, foreign language not required. *Entrance requirements:* For master's, GRE General Test, TOEFL (minimum score of 550 required), bachelor's degree in biology or forestry. *Application deadline:* For fall admission, 1/1. Application fee: $60. *Financial aid:* Fellowships, career-related internships or fieldwork, Federal Work-Study, and institutionally-sponsored loans available. Financial aid application deadline: 1/1. *Faculty research:* Forest ecology, planning, and physiology; forest microbiology. *Unit head:* Dr. David Foster, Chair, 508-724-3302. *Application contact:* Office of Admissions and Financial Aid, 617-495-5315.

Iowa State University of Science and Technology, Graduate College, College of Agriculture, Department of Forestry, Ames, IA 50011. Offers MS, PhD. *Faculty:* 12 full-time, 3 part-time. *Students:* 17 full-time (4 women), 8 part-time (1 woman); includes 1 minority (African American), 12 international. 19 applicants, 32% accepted. In 1998, 4 master's, 1 doctorate awarded. *Degree requirements:* For master's, thesis or alternative required; for doctorate, dissertation required. *Entrance requirements:* For master's and doctorate, GRE General Test, TOEFL. *Application deadline:* For fall admission, 6/15 (priority date); for spring admission, 11/15. Applications are processed on a rolling basis. Application fee: $20 ($50 for international students). Electronic applications accepted. Tuition, state resident: full-time $3,308. Tuition, nonresident: full-time $9,744. Part-time tuition and fees vary according to course load, campus/location and program. *Financial aid:* In 1998–99, 16 research assistantships with partial tuition reimbursements (averaging $8,775 per year) were awarded.; fellowships, teaching assistantships with partial tuition reimbursements, scholarships also available. *Faculty research:* Forest administration and management, forest biology, forest biometry, forest economics, wood science. *Unit head:* Dr. J. Michael Kelly, Chair, 515-294-1166, E-mail: forestry@iastate.edu.

Lakehead University, Graduate Studies and Research, Faculty of Forestry, Thunder Bay, ON P7B 5E1, Canada. Offers M Sc F, MF. Part-time programs available. *Degree requirements:* For master's, report (MF), thesis (M Sc F) required. *Entrance requirements:* For master's, TOEFL

Forestry

Lakehead University (continued)
(minimum score of 550 required), minimum B average. *Faculty research:* Soils, silviculture, wildlife, ecology,genetics.

Louisiana State University and Agricultural and Mechanical College, Graduate School, College of Agriculture, School of Forestry, Wildlife, and Fisheries, Baton Rouge, LA 70803. Offers fisheries (MS); forestry (MS, PhD); wildlife (MS); wildlife and fisheries science (PhD). *Faculty:* 31 full-time (0 women). *Students:* 79 full-time (21 women), 22 part-time (4 women); includes 3 minority (2 Asian Americans or Pacific Islanders, 1 Hispanic American), 31 international. Average age 30. 58 applicants, 38% accepted. In 1998, 19 master's, 6 doctorates awarded (100% found work related to degree). *Degree requirements:* For master's and doctorate, thesis/dissertation required, foreign language not required. *Entrance requirements:* For master's, GRE General Test (minimum combined score of 1000 required), minimum GPA of 3.0; for doctorate, GRE General Test (minimum combined score of 1100 required), MS, minimum GPA of 3.0. *Application deadline:* For fall admission, 1/25 (priority date). Applications are processed on a rolling basis. Application fee: $25. *Financial aid:* In 1998–99, 3 fellowships, 61 research assistantships with partial tuition reimbursements, 2 teaching assistantships with partial tuition reimbursements were awarded.; Federal Work-Study also available. Financial aid application deadline: 4/15. *Faculty research:* Forest biology and management, aquaculture, fisheries biology and ecology, upland and wetlands wildlife. *Unit head:* Dr. Norman E. Linnartz, Interim Director, 225-388-4131, Fax: 225-388-4227, E-mail: nelinn@lsu.edu. *Application contact:* Dr. D. Allen Rutherford, Coordinator of Graduate Studies, 225-388-4187, Fax: 225-388-4144, E-mail: druther@lsu.edu.

McGill University, Faculty of Graduate Studies and Research, Faculty of Agricultural and Environmental Sciences, Department of Natural Resource Sciences, Montréal, PQ H3A 2T5, Canada. Offers agrometeorology (M Sc, PhD); entomology (M Sc, PhD); forest science (M Sc, PhD); microbiology (M Sc, PhD); soil science (M Sc, PhD); wildlife biology (M Sc, PhD). *Faculty:* 18 full-time (1 woman), 26 part-time (3 women). *Students:* 83 full-time (35 women), 10 international. *Degree requirements:* For master's and doctorate, thesis/dissertation required. *Entrance requirements:* For master's, TOEFL (minimum score of 550 required), minimum GPA of 3.0; for doctorate, TOEFL (minimum score of 550 required), M Sc. *Application deadline:* For fall admission, 1/1 (priority date); for winter admission, 5/1 (priority date); for spring admission, 9/1 (priority date). Applications are processed on a rolling basis. Application fee: $60. *Unit head:* Dr. W. H. Hendershot, Chair, 514-398-7942, Fax: 514-398-7990, E-mail: chair@nrs.mcgill.ca. *Application contact:* 514-398-7708, Fax: 514-398-7968, E-mail: grad@macdonald.mcgill.ca.

Michigan State University, Graduate School, College of Agriculture and Natural Resources, Department of Forestry, East Lansing, MI 48824-1020. Offers forestry (MS, PhD); forestry-urban studies (MS, PhD); plant breeding and genetics-forestry (MS, PhD). *Faculty:* 16. *Students:* 22 full-time (7 women), 19 part-time (8 women), 13 international. Average age 31. 25 applicants, 48% accepted. In 1998, 15 master's, 2 doctorates awarded. *Degree requirements:* For doctorate, dissertation required. *Entrance requirements:* For master's and doctorate, GRE, TOEFL (minimum score of 550 required). *Application deadline:* Applications are processed on a rolling basis. Application fee: $30 ($40 for international students). *Financial aid:* In 1998–99, 22 research assistantships (averaging $12,480 per year) were awarded.; fellowships, teaching assistantships Financial aid applicants required to submit FAFSA. Total annual research expenditures: $463,000. *Unit head:* Dr. Daniel Keathley, Chairperson, 517-355-0091, Fax: 517-432-1143.

Michigan Technological University, Graduate School, School of Forestry and Wood Products, Program in Forestry, Houghton, MI 49931-1295. Offers MS. Part-time programs available. *Faculty:* 17 full-time (3 women), 2 part-time (0 women). Average age 27. 37 applicants, 73% accepted. In 1998, 11 degrees awarded. *Degree requirements:* Foreign language not required. *Entrance requirements:* For master's, GRE General Test (minimum combined score of 1500 on three sections required; average 1663), TOEFL (minimum score of 550 required; average 579). *Average time to degree:* Master's–3.1 years full-time. *Application deadline:* For fall admission, 3/15 (priority date). Applications are processed on a rolling basis. Application fee: $30 ($35 for international students). Tuition, state resident: full-time $4,377. Tuition, nonresident: full-time $9,108. Required fees: $126. Tuition and fees vary according to course load. *Financial aid:* In 1998–99, 14 research assistantships (averaging $9,125 per year) were awarded.; fellowships, teaching assistantships, Federal Work-Study and institutionally-sponsored loans also available. Aid available to part-time students. Financial aid applicants required to submit FAFSA. *Faculty research:* Forest ecology and environmental science, global climate change, biotechnology, biological remediation, wood science. *Unit head:* Dr. John E. Linz, Director of Graduate Studies, 517-353-9624, Fax: 517-353-8963, E-mail: jlinz@pilot.msu.edu. *Application contact:* Dr. Margaret Gale, Graduate Coordinator, 906-487-2352, Fax: 906-487-2915, E-mail: mrgale@mtu.edu.

Michigan Technological University, Graduate School, School of Forestry and Wood Products, Program in Forest Science, Houghton, MI 49931-1295. Offers PhD. Part-time programs available. *Faculty:* 17 full-time (3 women), 2 part-time (0 women). *Students:* 12 full-time (0 women), 14 part-time (all women), 9 international. Average age 32. 10 applicants, 10% accepted. In 1998, 6 degrees awarded. *Degree requirements:* For doctorate, dissertation required, foreign language not required. *Entrance requirements:* For doctorate, GRE General Test (minimum combined score of 1500 on three sections required; average 1782), TOEFL (minimum score of 550 required; average 568). *Average time to degree:* Doctorate–5 years full-time. *Application deadline:* For fall admission, 3/15 (priority date). Applications are processed on a rolling basis. Application fee: $30 ($35 for international students). Tuition, state resident: full-time $4,377. Tuition, nonresident: full-time $9,108. Required fees: $126. Tuition and fees vary according to course load. *Financial aid:* In 1998–99, 4 fellowships (averaging $3,310 per year), 12 research assistantships (averaging $11,389 per year), 2 teaching assistantships (averaging $4,665 per year) were awarded.; Federal Work-Study, institutionally-sponsored loans, and unspecified assistantships also available. Aid available to part-time students. Financial aid applicants required to submit FAFSA. *Faculty research:* Forest ecology and environmental science, global climate change, biotechnology, biological remediation, wood science. *Unit head:* Dr. Margaret Gale, Graduate Coordinator, 906-487-2352, Fax: 906-487-2915, E-mail: mrgale@mtu.edu. *Application contact:* Dr. Margaret Gale, Graduate Coordinator, 906-487-2352, Fax: 906-487-2915, E-mail: mrgale@mtu.edu.

Mississippi State University, College of Forest Resources, Department of Forest Products, Mississippi State, MS 39762. Offers MS. *Students:* 9 full-time (1 woman), 6 part-time. Average age 30. 4 applicants, 75% accepted. In 1998, 1 degree awarded. *Degree requirements:* For master's, thesis, comprehensive oral or written exam required, foreign language not required. *Entrance requirements:* For master's, TOEFL, minimum GPA of 2.75. *Application deadline:* For fall admission, 7/1; for spring admission, 11/1. Applications are processed on a rolling basis. Application fee: $25 for international students. *Financial aid:* Research assistantships with full tuition reimbursements, teaching assistantships with full tuition reimbursements, Federal Work-Study and institutionally-sponsored loans available. Financial aid applicants required to submit FAFSA. *Faculty research:* Wood preservation, production economics, wood chemistry, wood drying, furniture. Total annual research expenditures: $2.8 million. *Unit head:* Dr. Philip H. Steele, Interim Head, 662-325-2116, Fax: 662-325-8126. *Application contact:* Jerry B. Inmon, Director of Admissions, 662-325-2224, Fax: 662-325-7360, E-mail: admit@admissions.msstate.edu.

Mississippi State University, College of Forest Resources, Department of Forestry, Mississippi State, MS 39762. Offers MS. Part-time programs available. *Students:* 16 full-time (2 women), 7 part-time (2 women); includes 2 minority (both Asian Americans or Pacific Islanders), 1 international. Average age 29. 6 applicants, 100% accepted. In 1998, 11 degrees awarded. *Degree requirements:* For master's, comprehensive oral or written exam required. *Entrance requirements:* For master's, TOEFL (minimum score of 550 required), minimum GPA of 3.0. *Application deadline:* For fall admission, 7/1; for spring admission, 11/1. Applications are processed on a rolling basis. Application fee: $25 for international students. *Financial aid:* Federal Work-Study, institutionally-sponsored loans, and unspecified assistantships available. Financial aid applicants required to submit FAFSA. *Faculty research:* Forest hydrology, forest biometry, forest management/economics, forest biology, industrial forest operations. Total annual research expenditures: $2.7 million. *Unit head:* Dr. D. P. Richards, Head, 662-325-2946, Fax: 662-325-8726, E-mail: drichards@cfr.msstate.edu. *Application contact:* Jerry B. Inmon, Director of Admissions, 662-325-2224, Fax: 662-325-7360, E-mail: admit@admissions.msstate.edu.

North Carolina State University, Graduate School, College of Forest Resources, Department of Forestry, Raleigh, NC 27695. Offers MF, MS, PhD. Part-time programs available. *Faculty:* 68 full-time (5 women), 42 part-time (1 woman). *Students:* 74 full-time (16 women), 55 part-time (23 women); includes 4 minority (2 Asian Americans or Pacific Islanders, 2 Hispanic Americans), 27 international. Average age 34. 55 applicants, 62% accepted. In 1998, 24 master's, 7 doctorates awarded. *Degree requirements:* For master's, thesis (for some programs), teaching experience required, foreign language not required; for doctorate, dissertation, teaching experience required, foreign language not required. *Entrance requirements:* For master's and doctorate, GRE General Test, TOEFL (minimum score of 550 required). *Application deadline:* For fall admission, 6/25 (priority date); for spring admission, 11/25. Applications are processed on a rolling basis. Application fee: $45. *Financial aid:* In 1998–99, 15 fellowships (averaging $4,402 per year), 25 teaching assistantships (averaging $4,855 per year) were awarded.; research assistantships, institutionally-sponsored loans also available. Financial aid application deadline: 3/1. *Faculty research:* Forest genetics, forest ecology and silviculture, forest economics/management/policy, international forestry, remote sensing/geographic information systems. Total annual research expenditures: $7.2 million. *Unit head:* Dr. Frederick W. Cubbage, Head, 919-515-7789, Fax: 919-515-7231, E-mail: cubbage@cfr.cfr.ncsu.edu. *Application contact:* Dr. Ben A. Bergmann, Director of Graduate Programs, 919-515-7563, Fax: 919-515-8149, E-mail: bergmann@cfr.cfr.ncsu.edu.

Northern Arizona University, Graduate College, College of Ecosystem Science and Management, Department of Forestry, Flagstaff, AZ 86011. Offers MSF, PhD. Part-time programs available. *Faculty:* 24 full-time (5 women), 14 part-time (4 women). *Students:* 44 full-time (14 women), 23 part-time (14 women); includes 6 minority (1 Asian American or Pacific Islander, 3 Hispanic Americans, 2 Native Americans), 7 international. 54 applicants, 28% accepted. In 1998, 8 master's, 2 doctorates awarded. *Degree requirements:* For master's, thesis optional, foreign language not required; for doctorate, dissertation required. *Entrance requirements:* For master's and doctorate, GRE General Test. *Application deadline:* For fall admission, 3/15 (priority date); for spring admission, 10/15. Applications are processed on a rolling basis. Application fee: $45. *Financial aid:* In 1998–99, 41 research assistantships were awarded.; fellowships, teaching assistantships, Federal Work-Study and tuition waivers (full and partial) also available. *Faculty research:* Multiresource management, ecology, entommology, recreation, hydrology. Total annual research expenditures: $1.4 million. *Unit head:* Dr. Donald Arganbright, Chair, 520-523-8247. *Application contact:* Dr. Bruce Fox, Director of Graduate Studies, 520-523-6636, E-mail: bruce.fox@nau.edu.

Oklahoma State University, Graduate College, College of Agricultural Sciences and Natural Resources, Department of Forestry, Stillwater, OK 74078. Offers M Ag, MS. *Faculty:* 14 full-time (0 women). *Students:* 9 full-time (3 women), 6 part-time (2 women); includes 1 minority (Asian American or Pacific Islander), 2 international. Average age 30. In 1998, 4 degrees awarded. *Degree requirements:* For master's, thesis required, foreign language not required. *Entrance requirements:* For master's, TOEFL (minimum score of 550 required). *Application deadline:* For fall admission, 6/1 (priority date). Application fee: $25. *Financial aid:* In 1998–99, research assistantships (averaging $12,644 per year); career-related internships or fieldwork, Federal Work-Study, and tuition waivers (partial) also available. Aid available to part-time students. Financial aid application deadline: 3/1. *Faculty research:* Forest ecology, upland bird ecology, forest ecophysiology, urban forestry, molecular forest genetics/biotechnology/tree breeding. *Unit head:* Charles Taver, Interim Head, 405-744-5437.

Oregon State University, Graduate School, College of Forestry, Department of Forest Engineering, Corvallis, OR 97331. Offers MAIS, MF, MS, PhD. *Accreditation:* SAF (one or more programs are accredited). Part-time programs available. *Faculty:* 13 full-time (0 women). *Students:* 14 full-time (4 women). Average age 27. In 1998, 8 master's, 3 doctorates awarded. *Degree requirements:* For master's and doctorate, computer language, thesis/dissertation required, foreign language not required. *Entrance requirements:* For master's and doctorate, GRE General Test, TOEFL (minimum score of 550 required), minimum GPA of 3.0 in last 90 hours. *Application deadline:* For fall admission, 3/1. Applications are processed on a rolling basis. Application fee: $50. *Financial aid:* Fellowships, research assistantships, career-related internships or fieldwork, Federal Work-Study, and institutionally-sponsored loans available. Aid available to part-time students. Financial aid application deadline: 2/1. *Faculty research:* Timber harvesting systems, forest hydrology, slope stability, impacts of harvesting on soil and water, training of logging labor force. *Unit head:* Dr. Steven D. Teschson, Head, 541-737-4952, Fax: 541-737-4316, E-mail: tesch@ccmail.orst.edu. *Application contact:* Rayetta Beall, Office Manager, 541-737-1345, Fax: 541-737-4316, E-mail: beallr@ccmail.orst.edu.

Oregon State University, Graduate School, College of Forestry, Department of Forest Products, Corvallis, OR 97331. Offers forest products (MAIS, MF, MS, PhD); wood science and technology (MF, MS, PhD). *Accreditation:* SAF (one or more programs are accredited). Part-time programs available. *Faculty:* 6 full-time (1 woman), 1 part-time (0 women). *Students:* 18 full-time (2 women); includes 1 minority (Asian American or Pacific Islander), 9 international. Average age 30. In 1998, 6 master's, 1 doctorate awarded. *Degree requirements:* For master's, thesis required (for some programs), foreign language not required; for doctorate, dissertation required, foreign language not required. *Entrance requirements:* For master's and doctorate, GRE General Test, TOEFL (minimum score of 550 required), minimum GPA of 3.0 in last 90 hours. *Application deadline:* For fall admission, 3/1 (priority date). Applications are processed on a rolling basis. Application fee: $50. *Financial aid:* Fellowships, research assistantships, career-related internships or fieldwork, Federal Work-Study, and institutionally-sponsored loans available. Aid available to part-time students. Financial aid application deadline: 2/1. *Faculty research:* Biodeterioration and preservation, timber engineering, process engineering and control, composite materials science, anatomy, chemistry and physical properties. *Unit head:* Dr. Thomas E. McLain, Head, 541-737-4224, Fax: 541-737-3385, E-mail: forprod@fri.orst.edu. *Application contact:* Charles Brunner, Chair, 541-737-4205, Fax: 541-737-3385, E-mail: brunnerc@fri.orst.edu.

See in-depth description on page 951.

Oregon State University, Graduate School, College of Forestry, Department of Forest Resources, Corvallis, OR 97331. Offers economics (MS, PhD); forest resources (MAIS, MF, MS, PhD). MS and PhD (economics) offered through the University Graduate Faculty of Economics. *Accreditation:* SAF (one or more programs are accredited). Part-time programs available. *Faculty:* 23 full-time (2 women), 10 part-time (0 women). *Students:* 30 full-time (8 women), 5 part-time (2 women); includes 1 minority (Asian American or Pacific Islander), 5 international. Average age 29. In 1998, 5 master's awarded (100% found work related to degree); 4 doctorates awarded. Terminal master's awarded for partial completion of doctoral program. *Degree requirements:* For master's, thesis required (for some programs), foreign language not required; for doctorate, dissertation required, foreign language not required. *Entrance requirements:* For master's and doctorate, GRE General Test, TOEFL (minimum score of 550 required), minimum GPA of 3.0 in last 90 hours. *Application deadline:* For fall admission, 2/1 (priority date). Applications are processed on a rolling basis. Application fee: $50. *Financial aid:* Fellowships, research assistantships, teaching assistantships, career-related internships or fieldwork, Federal Work-Study, and institutionally-sponsored loans available. Aid available to part-time students. Financial aid application deadline: 2/1. *Faculty research:* Geographic information systems, long-term productivity, recreation, silviculture, biometrics, policy. *Unit head:* Dr. John D. Walstad, Head, 541-737-3607, Fax: 541-737-3049, E-mail: walstadj@ccmail.

orst.edu. *Application contact:* Marty Roberts, Coordinator, 541-737-1485, Fax: 541-737-3049, E-mail: forestr@ccmail.orst.edu.

Oregon State University, Graduate School, College of Forestry, Department of Forest Science, Corvallis, OR 97331. Offers MAIS, MF, MS, PhD. *Accreditation:* SAF (one or more programs are accredited). Part-time programs available. *Faculty:* 75 full-time (5 women), 11 part-time (6 women). *Students:* 67 full-time (29 women), 3 part-time (1 woman); includes 4 minority (1 African American, 2 Asian Americans or Pacific Islanders, 1 Hispanic American), 18 international. Average age 31. *Degree requirements:* For master's, thesis required (for some programs), foreign language not required; for doctorate, dissertation required, foreign language not required. *Entrance requirements:* For master's and doctorate, GRE General Test, TOEFL (minimum score of 550 required), minimum GPA of 3.0 in last 90 hours. *Application deadline:* For fall admission, 8/25 (priority date); for spring admission, 3/1. Applications are processed on a rolling basis. Application fee: $50. *Financial aid:* Fellowships, research assistantships, career-related internships or fieldwork, Federal Work-Study, and institutionally-sponsored loans available. Aid available to part-time students. Financial aid application deadline: 2/1. *Faculty research:* Ecosystem structure and function, nutrient cycling, biotechnology, vegetation management, integrated forest protection. *Unit head:* Dr. Logan D. Norris, Head, 541-737-6557, Fax: 541-737-1393, E-mail: norrisl@fsi.orst.edu.

Pennsylvania State University University Park Campus, Graduate School, College of Agricultural Sciences, School of Forest Resources, Program in Forest Resources, State College, University Park, PA 16802-1503. Offers M Agr, MFR, MS, PhD. *Students:* 28 full-time (11 women), 11 part-time (1 woman). In 1998, 5 master's, 2 doctorates awarded. *Entrance requirements:* For master's and doctorate, GRE General Test. Application fee: $50. *Unit head:* Dr. David R. DeWalle, Chair, 814-863-3532.

Purdue University, Graduate School, School of Agriculture, Department of Forestry and Natural Resources, West Lafayette, IN 47907. Offers MS, MSF, PhD. *Faculty:* 23 full-time (1 woman). *Students:* 48 full-time (17 women), 11 part-time (3 women); includes 4 minority (3 African Americans, 1 Native American), 22 international. Average age 26. 54 applicants, 20% accepted. In 1998, 10 master's, 7 doctorates awarded. *Degree requirements:* For master's and doctorate, computer language, thesis/dissertation required, foreign language not required. *Entrance requirements:* For master's and doctorate, GRE General Test (minimum score of 500 on each section required), TOEFL (minimum score of 550 required), minimum B+ average in undergraduate course work. *Average time to degree:* Master's–2 years full-time; doctorate–3 years full-time. *Application deadline:* For fall admission, 2/15 (priority date); for spring admission, 9/15. Applications are processed on a rolling basis. Application fee: $30. Electronic applications accepted. *Financial aid:* In 1998–99, 6 research assistantships (averaging $14,430 per year) were awarded.; fellowships, teaching assistantships, career-related internships or fieldwork and grants also available. Aid available to part-time students. Financial aid application deadline: 2/15; financial aid applicants required to submit FAFSA. *Faculty research:* Wildlife management, forest management, forest ecology, forest soils, limnology. *Unit head:* Dr. D. C. LeMaster, Head, 765-494-3590, Fax: 765-496-2422, E-mail: dclmstr@fnr.purdue.edu. *Application contact:* Patty A. Fitzsimons, Graduate Secretary, 765-494-3572, Fax: 765-496-2422, E-mail: pattyf@fnr.purdue.edu.

See in-depth description on page 953.

Southern Illinois University Carbondale, Graduate School, College of Agriculture, Department of Forestry, Carbondale, IL 62901-6806. Offers MS. Part-time programs available. *Faculty:* 9 full-time (1 woman). *Students:* 21 full-time (4 women), 4 part-time (1 woman); includes 1 minority (African American), 3 international. Average age 24. 7 applicants, 100% accepted. In 1998, 7 degrees awarded. *Degree requirements:* For master's, thesis required, foreign language not required. *Entrance requirements:* For master's, TOEFL (minimum score of 550 required), minimum GPA of 2.7. *Application deadline:* Applications are processed on a rolling basis. Application fee: $0. *Financial aid:* In 1998–99, 18 students received aid, including 3 fellowships with full tuition reimbursements available, 10 research assistantships with full tuition reimbursements available, 3 teaching assistantships with full tuition reimbursements available; career-related internships or fieldwork, Federal Work-Study, institutionally-sponsored loans, and tuition waivers (full) also available. Aid available to part-time students. *Faculty research:* Forest recreation, forest ecology, remote sensing, forest management and economics. *Unit head:* John Phelps, Chair, 618-453-3341, E-mail: jphelps@siu.edu.

Southern University and Agricultural and Mechanical College, Graduate School, College of Agricultural, Family and Consumer Sciences, Department of Urban Forestry, Baton Rouge, LA 70813. Offers MS. *Faculty:* 4 full-time (2 women), 3 part-time (0 women). *Students:* 6 full-time (1 woman), 2 part-time (1 woman); includes 3 minority (all African Americans) 8 applicants, 100% accepted. *Degree requirements:* For master's, thesis required, foreign language not required. *Entrance requirements:* For master's, GRE, TOEFL, minimum GPA of 3.0. *Average time to degree:* Master's–2 years full-time, 4 years part-time. *Application deadline:* For fall admission, 6/1 (priority date); for spring admission, 11/1 (priority date). Application fee: $5. *Financial aid:* In 1998–99, 5 research assistantships (averaging $5,897 per year), 1 teaching assistantship (averaging $5,897 per year) were awarded. Financial aid application deadline: 4/15. *Faculty research:* Global change, UVB impact on urban trees, environmental quality remediation, social economic and cultural values of urban forest, urban hydrology. *Unit head:* Dr. Alfredo B. Lorenzo, Program Leader, 225-771-2440, E-mail: ablorenzo@subr.edu.

State University of New York College of Environmental Science and Forestry, Faculty of Environmental and Forest Biology, Syracuse, NY 13210-2779. Offers MPS, MS, PhD. *Faculty:* 36 full-time (3 women), 3 part-time (1 woman). *Students:* 83 full-time (37 women), 57 part-time (26 women). Average age 30. 82 applicants, 52% accepted. In 1998, 19 master's, 7 doctorates awarded. Terminal master's awarded for partial completion of doctoral program. *Degree requirements:* For master's, thesis or alternative required, foreign language not required; for doctorate, dissertation required. *Entrance requirements:* For master's and doctorate, GRE General Test (minimum combined score of 1800 on three sections required), GRE Subject Test (minimum score of 600 required), minimum GPA of 3.0. *Application deadline:* For fall admission, 4/15 (priority date); for spring admission, 11/15. Applications are processed on a rolling basis. Application fee: $50. *Financial aid:* In 1998–99, 7 fellowships with tuition reimbursements, 38 research assistantships with tuition reimbursements, 35 teaching assistantships with tuition reimbursements were awarded.; Federal Work-Study also available. *Faculty research:* Ecology, fish and wildlife biology and management, plant science, entomology. Total annual research expenditures: $1.5 million. *Unit head:* Dr. Neil H. Ringler, Chairperson, 315-470-6770, Fax: 315-470-6934, E-mail: neilringler@csf.edu. *Application contact:* Dr. Robert H. Frey, Dean, Instruction and Graduate Studies, 315-470-6599, Fax: 315-470-6978, E-mail: esfgrad@esf.edu.

State University of New York College of Environmental Science and Forestry, Faculty of Forestry, Syracuse, NY 13210-2779. Offers agronomy and soil sciences management (MPS, MS, PhD); forest resources management (MPS, MS, PhD); forestry (MPS, MS, PhD); natural resources management (MPS, MS, PhD). Part-time programs available. *Faculty:* 24 full-time (2 women). *Students:* 55 full-time (17 women), 32 part-time (10 women); includes 5 minority (2 African Americans, 2 Hispanic Americans, 1 Native American), 21 international. Average age 31. 60 applicants, 83% accepted. In 1998, 16 master's, 3 doctorates awarded. Terminal master's awarded for partial completion of doctoral program. *Degree requirements:* For master's, thesis or alternative required, foreign language not required; for doctorate, dissertation required. *Entrance requirements:* For master's and doctorate, GRE General Test. *Application deadline:* For fall admission, 4/15 (priority date); for spring admission, 11/15. Applications are processed on a rolling basis. Application fee: $50. *Financial aid:* In 1998–99, 7 fellowships with tuition reimbursements, 17 research assistantships with tuition reimbursements, 21 teaching assistantships with tuition reimbursements were awarded.; career-related internships or fieldwork and Federal Work-Study also available. Aid available to part-time students. *Faculty research:* Silviculture recreation management, tree improvement, operations management, economics. Total annual research expenditures: $1.5 million. *Unit head:* Dr. William Bentley, Chair, 315-470-6536, Fax: 315-470-6535, E-mail: wbentley@csf.edu. *Application contact:* Dr. Robert H. Frey, Dean, Instruction and Graduate Studies, 315-470-6599, Fax: 315-470-6978, E-mail: esfgrad@esf.edu.

See in-depth description on page 955.

Stephen F. Austin State University, Graduate School, College of Forestry, Nacogdoches, TX 75962. Offers MF, MSF, PhD. Part-time programs available. *Faculty:* 16 full-time (0 women). *Students:* 29 full-time (13 women), 30 part-time (7 women); includes 1 minority (Native American), 5 international. 30 applicants, 67% accepted. In 1998, 5 master's, 4 doctorates awarded. *Degree requirements:* For master's and doctorate, thesis/dissertation required, foreign language not required. *Entrance requirements:* For master's and doctorate, GRE General Test (minimum combined score of 1000 required), TOEFL. *Application deadline:* For fall admission, 8/1 (priority date); for spring admission, 12/15. Applications are processed on a rolling basis. Application fee: $25 ($50 for international students). Tuition, state resident: full-time $1,792. Tuition, nonresident: full-time $6,880. *Financial aid:* In 1998–99, research assistantships (averaging $8,000 per year), teaching assistantships (averaging $6,000 per year) were awarded.; career-related internships or fieldwork and Federal Work-Study also available. Aid available to part-time students. Financial aid application deadline: 3/1. *Faculty research:* Wildlife management, basic plant science, forest recreation, multipurpose land management. *Unit head:* Dr. Scott Beasley, Dean, 409-468-3304.

Texas A&M University, College of Agriculture and Life Sciences, Department of Forest Science, College Station, TX 77843. Offers forest science (MS, PhD); natural resources development (M Agr). *Faculty:* 13 full-time (4 women), 6 part-time (0 women). *Students:* 29 full-time (9 women), 11 part-time (5 women); includes 5 minority (1 African American, 3 Asian Americans or Pacific Islanders, 1 Hispanic American), 14 international. Average age 32. 21 applicants, 33% accepted. In 1998, 6 master's, 4 doctorates awarded. Terminal master's awarded for partial completion of doctoral program. *Degree requirements:* For master's, thesis required (for some programs), foreign language not required; for doctorate, dissertation required, foreign language not required. *Entrance requirements:* For master's and doctorate, GRE General Test, TOEFL. *Average time to degree:* Master's–2 years full-time, 4 years part-time; doctorate–3 years full-time, 5 years part-time. *Application deadline:* For fall admission, 3/1 (priority date); for spring admission, 11/1. Applications are processed on a rolling basis. Application fee: $50 ($75 for international students). *Financial aid:* In 1998–99, 2 fellowships with partial tuition reimbursements (averaging $15,000 per year), 21 research assistantships with partial tuition reimbursements (averaging $13,000 per year), 1 teaching assistantship with partial tuition reimbursement (averaging $12,000 per year) were awarded.; career-related internships or fieldwork and institutionally-sponsored loans also available. Aid available to part-time students. Financial aid application deadline: 3/1; financial aid applicants required to submit FAFSA. *Faculty research:* Expert systems, geographic information systems, economics, biology, genetics. Total annual research expenditures: $950,000. *Unit head:* Dr. Charles Tat Smith, Head, 409-845-5033, Fax: 409-845-6049, E-mail: tat_smith@tamu.edu. *Application contact:* Prof. Richard F. Fisher, Chair, Graduate Programs, 409-845-5095, Fax: 409-845-6049, E-mail: r-fisher@tamu.edu.

Université Laval, Faculty of Graduate Studies, Faculty of Forestry and Geomatics, Department of Wood and Forest Sciences, Sainte-Foy, PQ G1K 7P4, Canada. Offers M Sc, PhD. *Students:* 96 full-time (28 women), 22 part-time (6 women). 52 applicants, 79% accepted. In 1998, 20 master's, 8 doctorates awarded. *Application deadline:* For fall admission, 3/1. Application fee: $30. *Unit head:* Dean Tomlinson, Acting Director, 418-656-2131 Ext. 7418, Fax: 418-656-3177, E-mail: jean-tomlinson@sbf.ulaval.ca.

The University of Arizona, Graduate College, College of Agriculture, School of Renewable Natural Resources, Division of Forest-Watershed Management, Tucson, AZ 85721. Offers MS, PhD. *Students:* 17 full-time (9 women), 11 part-time (2 women); includes 3 minority (all Hispanic Americans), 5 international. Average age 33. 13 applicants, 62% accepted. In 1998, 9 master's, 2 doctorates awarded. *Degree requirements:* For master's, computer language, thesis required, foreign language not required; for doctorate, one foreign language (computer language can substitute), dissertation required. *Entrance requirements:* For master's and doctorate, GRE General Test, TOEFL (minimum score of 550 required), minimum GPA of 3.0. *Application deadline:* For fall admission, 8/1. Applications are processed on a rolling basis. Application fee: $35. *Financial aid:* Research assistantships, teaching assistantships, career-related internships or fieldwork and tuition waivers (partial) available. *Faculty research:* Forest fuel characteristics, prescribed fire in southern Arizona. *Unit head:* Dr. Richard Hawkins, Head, 520-621-7273. *Application contact:* Mary E. Soltero, Administrative Assistant, 520-621-7260, Fax: 520-621-8801.

University of Arkansas at Monticello, School of Forest Resources, Monticello, AR 71656. Offers MS. Part-time programs available. *Faculty:* 5 full-time (0 women). *Students:* 10 full-time (4 women), 6 part-time; includes 2 minority (1 African American, 1 Native American), 2 international. *Degree requirements:* For master's, thesis required. *Entrance requirements:* For master's, GRE General Test. *Application deadline:* For fall admission, 8/16 (priority date); for spring admission, 1/3 (priority date). Applications are processed on a rolling basis. Application fee: $0. Tuition, state resident: full-time $1,584; part-time $88 per credit hour. Tuition, nonresident: full-time $2,142; part-time $119 per credit hour. *Financial aid:* Research assistantships available. *Faculty research:* Geographic information systems/remote sensing, forest ecology, wildlife ecology and management. *Unit head:* Dr. Bob Blackmon, Dean, 870-460-1052, Fax: 870-460-1092, E-mail: blackmon@uamont.edu.

University of British Columbia, Faculty of Graduate Studies, Faculty of Forestry, Vancouver, BC V6T 1Z2, Canada. Offers M Sc, MA Sc, MF, PhD. Part-time programs available. *Degree requirements:* For master's, thesis or comprehensive exam (MF, M Sc) required; for doctorate, dissertation, comprehensive exam required, foreign language not required. *Entrance requirements:* For master's and doctorate, TOEFL (minimum score of 550 required). *Faculty research:* Forest sciences, forest resources management, forest operations, wood sciences.

University of California, Berkeley, Graduate Division, College of Natural Resources, Department of Environmental Science, Policy, and Management, Berkeley, CA 94720-1500. Offers environmental science, policy, and management (MS, PhD); forestry (MF); range management (MS). *Faculty:* 67 full-time (15 women), 2 part-time (1 woman). *Students:* 183 full-time (88 women); includes 12 minority (9 Asian Americans or Pacific Islanders, 3 Hispanic Americans), 21 international. *Degree requirements:* For doctorate, dissertation, qualifying exam required. *Entrance requirements:* For master's and doctorate, GRE General Test, minimum GPA of 3.0. *Application deadline:* For fall admission, 12/15. Application fee: $40. Electronic applications accepted. *Unit head:* Dr. James W. Bartolome, Chair, 510-642-7945, Fax: 510-643-5438, E-mail: jwbart@nature.berkeley.edu. *Application contact:* Sue Jennison, Student Affairs Officer, 510-642-6410, Fax: 510-643-5438, E-mail: espmgradproginfo@nature.berkeley.edu.

University of California, Berkeley, Graduate Division, Group in Wood Science and Technology, Berkeley, CA 94720-1500. Offers MS, PhD. *Students:* 5 full-time (1 woman); includes 1 minority (Hispanic American), 1 international. 4 applicants, 50% accepted. In 1998, 1 master's, 2 doctorates awarded. *Degree requirements:* For doctorate, dissertation, qualifying exam required. *Entrance requirements:* For master's and doctorate, GRE General Test, TOEFL, minimum GPA of 3.0. *Application deadline:* For fall admission, 2/10. Application fee: $40. *Financial aid:* In 1998–99, 2 fellowships, 2 research assistantships were awarded.; career-related internships or fieldwork, Federal Work-Study, institutionally-sponsored loans, and tuition waivers (full and partial) also available. Financial aid application deadline: 1/5; financial aid applicants required to submit FAFSA. *Unit head:* Frank Beall, Chair. *Application contact:* Connie Price-Campbell, Graduate Assistant for Admission, 510-215-4250, E-mail: conniep@nature.berkeley.edu.

Forestry

University of Florida, Graduate School, College of Agriculture, School of Forest Resources and Conservation, Gainesville, FL 32611. Offers MFRC, MS, PhD, JD/MFRC, JD/MS, JD/PhD. Part-time programs available. *Faculty:* 34. *Students:* 39 full-time (8 women), 17 part-time (9 women); includes 5 minority (1 African American, 1 Asian American or Pacific Islander, 3 Hispanic Americans), 18 international. Average age 24. 51 applicants, 47% accepted. In 1998, 9 master's, 3 doctorates awarded. *Degree requirements:* For master's, comprehensive exams, project (MFRC); thesis defense (MS) required, thesis optional, foreign language not required; for doctorate, dissertation, qualifying exams, defense required, foreign language not required. *Entrance requirements:* For master's and doctorate, GRE General Test (minimum combined score of 1000 required), minimum GPA of 3.0. *Application deadline:* For fall admission, 6/1 (priority date); for spring admission, 10/1. Applications are processed on a rolling basis. Application fee: $20. Electronic applications accepted. *Financial aid:* In 1998–99, 3 fellowships, 30 research assistantships, 2 teaching assistantships were awarded.; Federal Work-Study and institutionally-sponsored loans also available. Aid available to part-time students. *Faculty research:* Forestry, agroforestry, ecology, management biology. *Unit head:* Dr. Wayne Smith, Director, 352-846-0850, Fax: 352-392-1707, E-mail: whs@gnv.ifas.ufl.edu. *Application contact:* Dr. Henry Gholz, Graduate Coordinator, 352-846-0889, Fax: 352-846-1277, E-mail: hlg@nervm.nerdc.ufl.edu.

University of Georgia, Graduate School, School of Forest Resources, Athens, GA 30602. Offers MFR, MS, PhD. *Faculty:* 48 full-time (4 women). *Students:* 93 full-time, 20 part-time (13 women); includes 6 minority (4 African Americans, 2 Asian Americans or Pacific Islanders), 16 international. 86 applicants, 50% accepted. In 1998, 51 master's, 5 doctorates awarded. *Degree requirements:* For master's, thesis (MS) required; for doctorate, one foreign language, dissertation required. *Entrance requirements:* For master's and doctorate, GRE General Test. *Application deadline:* For fall admission, 7/1 (priority date); for spring admission, 11/15. Application fee: $30. Electronic applications accepted. *Financial aid:* Fellowships, research assistantships, teaching assistantships, unspecified assistantships available. *Unit head:* Dr. Arnett C. Mace, Dean, 706-542-4741, Fax: 706-542-2281, E-mail: amace@smokey.forestry.uga.edu. *Application contact:* Dr. Robert O. Teskey, Graduate Coordinator, 706-542-1183, Fax: 706-542-3293, E-mail: teskey@smokey.forestry.uga.edu.

University of Idaho, College of Graduate Studies, College of Forestry, Wildlife, and Range Sciences, Department of Forest Products, Moscow, ID 83844-4140. Offers MS, PhD. *Faculty:* 6 full-time (0 women). *Students:* 4 full-time (1 woman), 1 part-time, 1 international. In 1998, 3 degrees awarded. *Degree requirements:* For doctorate, dissertation required, foreign language not required, foreign language not required. *Entrance requirements:* For master's, minimum GPA of 2.8; for doctorate, minimum undergraduate GPA of 2.8, 3.0 graduate. *Application deadline:* For fall admission, 8/1; for spring admission, 12/15. Application fee: $35 ($45 for international students). *Financial aid:* In 1998–99, 5 research assistantships (averaging $12,262 per year), 2 teaching assistantships (averaging $11,575 per year) were awarded. Financial aid application deadline: 2/15. *Unit head:* Dr. Leonard R. Johnson, Head, 208-885-6600.

University of Idaho, College of Graduate Studies, College of Forestry, Wildlife, and Range Sciences, Department of Forest Resources, Moscow, ID 83844-4140. Offers MS, PhD. *Faculty:* 15 full-time (3 women), 1 (woman) part-time. *Students:* 17 full-time (4 women), 10 part-time (2 women), 3 international. In 1998, 8 degrees awarded. *Degree requirements:* For doctorate, dissertation required, foreign language not required, foreign language not required. *Entrance requirements:* For master's, minimum GPA of 2.8; for doctorate, minimum undergraduate GPA of 2.8, 3.0 graduate. *Application deadline:* For fall admission, 8/1; for spring admission, 12/15. Application fee: $35 ($45 for international students). *Financial aid:* In 1998–99, 13 research assistantships (averaging $10,414 per year), 7 teaching assistantships (averaging $8,437 per year) were awarded. Financial aid application deadline: 2/15. *Unit head:* Dr. JoEllen Force, Head, 208-885-7311.

University of Idaho, College of Graduate Studies, College of Forestry, Wildlife, and Range Sciences, Program in Forestry, Wildlife, and Range Sciences, Moscow, ID 83844-4140. Offers PhD. *Faculty:* 3 full-time (0 women). *Students:* 28 full-time (6 women), 32 part-time (9 women); includes 3 minority (1 African American, 1 Asian American or Pacific Islander, 1 Native American), 12 international. In 1998, 4 degrees awarded. *Degree requirements:* For doctorate, dissertation required, foreign language not required. *Entrance requirements:* For doctorate, minimum undergraduate GPA of 2.8, 3.0 graduate. *Application deadline:* For fall admission, 8/1; for spring admission, 12/15. Application fee: $35 ($45 for international students). *Financial aid:* Fellowships, research assistantships, teaching assistantships available. Financial aid application deadline: 2/15. *Application contact:* Dr. Ali Moslemi, Graduate Coordinator, 208-885-6126.

University of Kentucky, Graduate School, Graduate School Programs from the College of Agriculture, Program in Forestry, Lexington, KY 40506-0032. Offers MSFOR. *Degree requirements:* For master's, thesis, comprehensive exam required, foreign language not required. *Entrance requirements:* For master's, GRE General Test (minimum combined score of 1000 required), minimum undergraduate GPA of 3.0. *Faculty research:* Forest ecology, silviculture, watershed management, forest products utilization, wildlife habitat management.

University of Maine, Graduate School, College of Natural Sciences, Forestry, and Agriculture, Department of Forest Ecosystem Science, Orono, ME 04469. Offers forest resources (PhD); forestry (MF, MS). *Accreditation:* SAF (one or more programs are accredited). *Faculty:* 17 full-time (2 women). *Students:* 51 (18 women). Average age 26. 38 applicants, 47% accepted. In 1998, 9 master's awarded (100% found work related to degree); 3 doctorates awarded. *Degree requirements:* For master's, thesis required, foreign language not required; for doctorate, one foreign language (computer language can substitute), dissertation required. *Entrance requirements:* For master's and doctorate, GRE General Test, TOEFL (minimum score of 550 required). *Application deadline:* For fall admission, 2/1 (priority date); for spring admission, 10/15. Applications are processed on a rolling basis. Application fee: $50. *Financial aid:* In 1998–99, 34 research assistantships with tuition reimbursements (averaging $10,000 per year), 7 teaching assistantships with tuition reimbursements (averaging $8,800 per year) were awarded.; fellowships, career-related internships or fieldwork, Federal Work-Study, institutionally-sponsored loans, and tuition waivers (full and partial) also available. Financial aid application deadline: 3/1. *Faculty research:* Tree physiology, forest genetics, forest ecology, physiology of wood decay. *Unit head:* Dr. William Livingston, Chair, 207-581-2884, Fax: 207-581-4257. *Application contact:* Scott G. Delcourt, Director of the Graduate School, 207-581-3218, Fax: 207-581-3232, E-mail: graduate@maine.edu.

University of Maine, Graduate School, College of Natural Sciences, Forestry, and Agriculture, Department of Forest Management, Orono, ME 04469. Offers forest resources (PhD); forestry (MF, MS). *Accreditation:* SAF (one or more programs are accredited). Part-time programs available. *Degree requirements:* For master's, thesis required, foreign language not required; for doctorate, one foreign language, dissertation required. *Entrance requirements:* For master's and doctorate, GRE General Test, TOEFL (minimum score of 550 required). *Application deadline:* For fall admission, 2/1 (priority date); for spring admission, 10/15. Applications are processed on a rolling basis. Application fee: $50. *Financial aid:* Fellowships, research assistantships, teaching assistantships, career-related internships or fieldwork, Federal Work-Study, and institutionally-sponsored loans available. Financial aid application deadline: 3/1. *Faculty research:* Forest economics, engineering and operations analysis, biometrics and remote sensing, timber management, wood technology. *Unit head:* Dr. David Field, Chair, 207-581-2856, Fax: 207-581-2858. *Application contact:* Scott G. Delcourt, Director of the Graduate School, 207-581-3218, Fax: 207-581-3232, E-mail: graduate@maine.edu.

University of Maine, Graduate School, College of Natural Sciences, Forestry, and Agriculture, Department of Plant, Soil, and Environmental Sciences, Orono, ME 04469. Offers biological sciences (PhD); ecology and environmental sciences (MS, PhD); forest resources (PhD); plant science (PhD); plant, soil, and environmental sciences (MS); resource utilization (MS). *Students:* 11 (6 women). *Entrance requirements:* For master's and doctorate, GRE General Test, TOEFL (minimum score of 550 required). Application fee: $50. *Unit head:* Dr. Ivan Fernandez, Chair. *Application contact:* Mary Fernandez, 207-581-2938, Fax: 207-581-2999, E-mail: fern@maine.maine.edu.

University of Massachusetts Amherst, Graduate School, College of Food and Natural Resources, Department of Forestry and Wildlife Management, Program in Forestry and Wood Technology, Amherst, MA 01003. Offers MS, PhD. Part-time programs available. *Faculty:* 17 full-time (3 women). *Students:* 12 full-time (2 women), 6 part-time (3 women), 1 international. Average age 35. 12 applicants, 58% accepted. In 1998, 1 master's awarded. Terminal master's awarded for partial completion of doctoral program. *Degree requirements:* For master's, thesis or alternative required, foreign language not required; for doctorate, variable foreign language requirement, dissertation required. *Entrance requirements:* For master's and doctorate, GRE General Test. *Application deadline:* For fall admission, 2/1 (priority date); for spring admission, 10/1. Applications are processed on a rolling basis. Application fee: $40. Tuition, state resident: full-time $2,640; part-time $165 per credit. Tuition, nonresident: full-time $9,756; part-time $407 per credit. Required fees: $1,221 per term. One-time fee: $110. Full-time tuition and fees vary according to course load, campus/location and reciprocity agreements. *Financial aid:* In 1998–99, research assistantships with full tuition reimbursements (averaging $7,165 per year), teaching assistantships with full tuition reimbursements (averaging $3,819 per year) were awarded.; fellowships with full tuition reimbursements, career-related internships or fieldwork, Federal Work-Study, grants, scholarships, traineeships, and unspecified assistantships also available. Aid available to part-time students. Financial aid application deadline: 2/1. *Unit head:* Dr. Brayton Wilson, Director, 413-545-2665, Fax: 413-545-4358.

University of Michigan, School of Natural Resources and Environment, Ann Arbor, MI 48109. Offers forestry (MF), including resource ecology and management (MF, MS), resource policy and behavior (MF, MS); landscape architecture (MLA, PhD); natural resource economics (PhD); natural resources and environment (MS, PhD), including resource ecology and management (MF, MS), resource policy and behavior (MF, MS). MLA, MS, PhD, and JD/MS offered through the Horace H. Rackham School of Graduate Studies. *Accreditation:* ASLA (one or more programs are accredited); SAF (one or more programs are accredited). Terminal master's awarded for partial completion of doctoral program. *Degree requirements:* For doctorate, oral defense of dissertation, preliminary exam required, foreign language not required. *Entrance requirements:* For master's, GRE General Test, TOEFL; for doctorate, GRE General Test, TOEFL, master's degree.

Announcement: The School offers master's and doctoral programs in resource ecology and management (REM). REM focuses on the development and use of scientific research to generate new knowledge about species and ecosystems and the application of this knowledge to develop effective management plans and policies for solving critical resource problems. The School's MS degree program is accredited by the Society of American Foresters.

See in-depth description on page 959.

University of Minnesota, Twin Cities Campus, Graduate School, College of Natural Resources, Department of Forest Resources, Minneapolis, MN 55455-0213. Offers forestry (MF, MS, PhD). Part-time programs available. *Faculty:* 23 full-time (1 woman), 28 part-time (1 woman). *Students:* 46 full-time (17 women), 5 part-time (2 women); includes 3 minority (1 African American, 1 Asian American or Pacific Islander, 1 Hispanic American), 13 international. 54 applicants, 44% accepted. In 1998, 10 master's awarded (33% entered university research/teaching, 50% found other work related to degree); 5 doctorates awarded (80% entered university research/teaching, 20% found other work related to degree). *Degree requirements:* For doctorate, dissertation required. *Entrance requirements:* For master's and doctorate, GRE. *Application deadline:* For fall admission, 1/15 (priority date); for spring admission, 10/15. Applications are processed on a rolling basis. Application fee: $50 ($55 for international students). *Financial aid:* In 1998–99, 31 students received aid, including 2 fellowships with full tuition reimbursements available (averaging $12,000 per year), 25 research assistantships with full and partial tuition reimbursements available, 4 teaching assistantships with full and partial tuition reimbursements available *Unit head:* Dr. Alan R. Ek, Head, 612-624-3400. *Application contact:* Kathleen Walter, Assistant for Graduate Studies, 612-624-2748, Fax: 612-624-8701, E-mail: kwalter@forestry.umn.edu.

See in-depth description on page 961.

University of Minnesota, Twin Cities Campus, Graduate School, College of Natural Resources, Department of Wood and Paper Science, Minneapolis, MN 55455-0213. Offers forestry (MS, PhD). *Faculty:* 13 full-time (2 women), 1 part-time (0 women). *Students:* 12 full-time (2 women), 2 international. 14 applicants, 50% accepted. In 1998, 3 master's awarded (100% found work related to degree); 2 doctorates awarded (50% entered university research/teaching, 50% found other work related to degree). *Degree requirements:* For doctorate, dissertation required. *Entrance requirements:* For master's and doctorate, GRE. *Application deadline:* For fall admission, 1/15 (priority date); for spring admission, 10/15. Applications are processed on a rolling basis. Application fee: $50 ($55 for international students). *Financial aid:* In 1998–99, 12 students received aid, including 2 fellowships with full tuition reimbursements available (averaging $12,000 per year), 10 research assistantships with full tuition reimbursements available Financial aid application deadline: 1/15. *Unit head:* Dr. Joseph Massey, Head, 612-625-5200. *Application contact:* Kathleen Walter, Assistant for Graduate Studies, 612-624-2748, Fax: 612-624-8701, E-mail: kwalter@forestry.umn.edu.

University of Missouri–Columbia, Graduate School, School of Natural Resources, Program in Forestry, Columbia, MO 65211. Offers MS, PhD. *Students:* 5 full-time (1 woman), 8 part-time (1 woman); includes 1 minority (African American), 3 international. 1 applicants, 100% accepted. In 1998, 6 master's, 2 doctorates awarded. Terminal master's awarded for partial completion of doctoral program. *Degree requirements:* For master's, thesis required, foreign language not required; for doctorate, dissertation required. *Entrance requirements:* For master's and doctorate, GRE General Test, minimum GPA of 3.0. *Application deadline:* For fall admission, 4/1 (priority date). Applications are processed on a rolling basis. Application fee: $30 ($50 for international students). *Financial aid:* Research assistantships, teaching assistantships, grants and institutionally-sponsored loans available. *Unit head:* Dr. Bruce E. Cutter, Director of Graduate Studies, 573-882-2744.

The University of Montana–Missoula, Graduate School, School of Forestry, Program in Forestry, Missoula, MT 59812-0002. Offers MS, PhD. *Students:* 43 full-time (16 women), 23 part-time (7 women); includes 1 African American, 4 Asian Americans or Pacific Islanders, 3 Native Americans 43 applicants, 37% accepted. In 1998, 1 master's, 7 doctorates awarded. *Degree requirements:* For doctorate, dissertation required, foreign language not required, foreign language not required. *Entrance requirements:* For master's, GRE General Test; for doctorate, GRE General Test (minimum combined score of 1700 on three sections required). *Application deadline:* For fall admission, 1/31. Application fee: $45. *Financial aid:* Application deadline: 3/1. *Unit head:* Dr. Perry Brown, Dean, School of Forestry, 406-243-5521, Fax: 406-243-4845, E-mail: pbrown@forestry.umt.edu.

University of Nebraska–Lincoln, Graduate College, College of Agricultural Sciences and Natural Resources, Interdepartmental Area of Horticulture and Forestry, Lincoln, NE 68588. Offers PhD. *Students:* 9 full-time (0 women), 4 part-time (1 woman), 10 international. Average age 32. 7 applicants, 29% accepted. In 1998, 1 degree awarded. *Degree requirements:* For doctorate, dissertation, comprehensive exams required, foreign language not required. *Entrance requirements:* For doctorate, GRE General Test, TOEFL (minimum score of 550 required). *Average time to degree:* Doctorate–2.6 years full-time. *Application deadline:* For fall admission, 5/1; for spring admission, 10/1. Application fee: $35. Electronic applications accepted. *Financial aid:* Fellowships, research assistantships, teaching assistantships, Federal Work-Study available. Aid available to part-time students. Financial aid application deadline: 2/15. *Faculty research:* Plant breeding and genetics, tissue and cell culture, plant anatomy and nutrition, urban landscapes, turf grass science. *Unit head:* Dr. Ellen T. Paparozzi, Graduate Committee Chair, 402-472-1129.

University of New Brunswick, School of Graduate Studies, Faculty of Forestry and Environmental Management, Fredericton, NB E3B 6C2, Canada. Offers ecological foundations of forest management (PhD); forest engineering (M Sc FE, MFE); forest resources (M Sc F, MF, PhD). Part-time programs available. *Degree requirements:* For master's and doctorate, thesis/dissertation required. *Entrance requirements:* For master's and doctorate, TOEFL, TWE, minimum GPA of 3.0. *Faculty research:* Genetics; soils; tree improvement, development, reproduction, physiology, and biotechnology; insect ecology; entomology; stand dynamics; silviculture; meteorology; forest modelling; industrial engineering; economics; ecosystem, wildlife, fire, park, pest, and conservation management; hydrology; operations research and planning; decision support systems; resources transportation/geotechnique; pathology; GIS; remote sensing; wood structures, engineering, science, heating, and anatomy.

University of New Hampshire, Graduate School, College of Life Sciences and Agriculture, Graduate Programs in the Biological Sciences and Natural Resources, Durham, NH 03824. Offers animal and nutritional sciences (MS, PhD); biochemistry and molecular biology (MS, PhD); biology (MS); genetics (MS, PhD); microbiology (MS, PhD); natural resources (MS, PhD), including environmental conservation (MS), forestry (MS), natural resources (PhD), soil science (MS), water resources management (MS), wildlife (MS); plant biology (MS, PhD); zoology (MS, PhD). Part-time programs available. *Faculty:* 129 full-time. *Students:* 127 full-time (74 women), 111 part-time (56 women); includes 6 minority (4 Asian Americans or Pacific Islanders, 2 Hispanic Americans), 31 international. Terminal master's awarded for partial completion of doctoral program. *Degree requirements:* For doctorate, dissertation required, foreign language not required. *Entrance requirements:* For master's, GRE General Test. *Application deadline:* Applications are processed on a rolling basis. Application fee: $50. Tuition, area resident: Full-time $5,750; part-time $319 per credit. Tuition, state resident: full-time $8,625. Tuition, nonresident: full-time $14,640; part-time $598 per credit. Required fees: $224 per semester. Tuition and fees vary according to course load, degree level and program. *Unit head:* Dr. William Mautz, Interim Dean, College of Life Sciences and Agriculture, 603-862-1450.

University of New Hampshire, Graduate School, College of Life Sciences and Agriculture, Graduate Programs in the Biological Sciences and Natural Resources, Department of Natural Resources, Option in Forestry, Durham, NH 03824. Offers MS. *Students:* 4 full-time (2 women), 8 part-time (1 woman); includes 1 minority (Asian American or Pacific Islander), 2 international. Average age 38. 6 applicants, 17% accepted. In 1998, 3 degrees awarded. *Degree requirements:* For master's, thesis or alternative required, foreign language not required. *Entrance requirements:* For master's, GRE General Test. *Application deadline:* For fall admission, 4/1 (priority date). Applications are processed on a rolling basis. Application fee: $50. Tuition, area resident: Full-time $5,750; part-time $319 per credit. Tuition, state resident: full-time $8,625. Tuition, nonresident: full-time $14,640; part-time $598 per credit. Required fees: $224 per semester. Tuition and fees vary according to course load, degree level and program. *Financial aid:* In 1998–99, 4 research assistantships, 1 teaching assistantship were awarded.; career-related internships or fieldwork, Federal Work-Study, scholarships, and tuition waivers (full and partial) also available. Aid available to part-time students. Financial aid application deadline: 2/15. *Faculty research:* Forest resource management, forest marketing, wood industry management, forest preservation, wood science. *Application contact:* Dr. Robert Harter, Graduate Coordinator, 603-862-3944.

University of Tennessee, Knoxville, Graduate School, College of Agricultural Sciences and Natural Resources, Department of Forestry, Wildlife, and Fisheries, Program in Forestry, Knoxville, TN 37996. Offers MS. *Students:* 14 full-time (3 women), 8 part-time (2 women); includes 1 minority (African American) 12 applicants, 75% accepted. In 1998, 3 degrees awarded. *Degree requirements:* For master's, thesis or alternative required, foreign language not required. *Entrance requirements:* For master's, GRE General Test, TOEFL (minimum score of 550 required), minimum GPA of 2.7. *Application deadline:* For fall admission, 2/1 (priority date). Applications are processed on a rolling basis. Application fee: $35. Electronic applications accepted. *Financial aid:* Application deadline: 2/1; *Unit head:* Dr. Robert G. Perrin, Graduate Representative, 423-974-7032, E-mail: rgperrin@utk.edu. *Application contact:* Dr. Scott Schlarbaum, Graduate Representative, 423-974-7993, E-mail: tenntip@utk.edu.

University of Tennessee, Knoxville, Graduate School, College of Business Administration, Program in Business Administration, Knoxville, TN 37996. Offers accounting (PhD); economics (MBA); entrepreneurship/new venture analysis (MBA); environmental management (MBA); executive business administration (MBA); finance (MBA, PhD); forest industries management (MBA); global business (MBA); logistics and transportation (MBA, PhD); management (MBA, PhD); manufacturing management (MBA); marketing (MBA, PhD); professional business administration (MBA); statistics (MBA, PhD). Postbaccalaureate distance learning degree programs offered. *Faculty:* 51 full-time (6 women). *Students:* 278 full-time (72 women), 17 part-time (2 women); includes 24 minority (13 African Americans, 5 Asian Americans or Pacific Islanders, 2 Hispanic Americans, 4 Native Americans), 47 international. *Degree requirements:* For master's, computer language, thesis or alternative required, foreign language not required; for doctorate, computer language, dissertation required, foreign language not required. *Entrance requirements:* For master's and doctorate, GMAT, TOEFL (minimum score of 550 required), minimum GPA of 2.7. *Application deadline:* For fall admission, 2/1 (priority date). Application fee: $35. Electronic applications accepted. *Unit head:* Dr. Gary Dicer, Director, 423-974-5033, Fax: 423-974-3826, E-mail: gdicer@utk.edu. *Application contact:* Donna Potts, Graduate Representative, 423-974-5033, Fax: 423-974-3826, E-mail: dpotts@utk.edu.

University of Toronto, School of Graduate Studies, Life Sciences Division, Faculty of Forestry, Toronto, ON M5S 1A1, Canada. Offers M Sc F, MFC, PhD. *Degree requirements:* For master's, thesis required (for some programs); for doctorate, dissertation required.

University of Vermont, Graduate College, School of Natural Resources, Program in Forestry, Burlington, VT 05405-0160. Offers MS. *Degree requirements:* For master's, thesis required, foreign language not required. *Entrance requirements:* For master's, GRE General Test, TOEFL (minimum score of 550 required). *Faculty research:* Forest resource management.

University of Washington, Graduate School, College of Forest Resources, Seattle, WA 98195. Offers forest economics (MS, PhD); forest ecosystem analysis (MS, PhD); forest engineering/forest hydrology (MS, PhD); forest products marketing (MS, PhD); forest soils (MS, PhD); pulp and paper science (MS, PhD); quantitative resource management (MS, PhD); silviculture (MFR); silviculture and forest protection (MS, PhD); social sciences (MS, PhD); urban horticulture (MFR, MS, PhD); wildlife science (MS, PhD). *Faculty:* 47 full-time (4 women), 16 part-time (2 women). *Students:* 161 full-time (65 women), 16 part-time (5 women); includes 15 minority (1 African American, 10 Asian Americans or Pacific Islanders, 1 Hispanic American, 3 Native Americans), 9 international. Average age 32. 181 applicants, 46% accepted. In 1998, 24 master's, 15 doctorates awarded. *Degree requirements:* For master's, thesis required (for some programs), foreign language not required; for doctorate, dissertation required, foreign language not required. *Entrance requirements:* For master's and doctorate, GRE, TOEFL (minimum score of 500 required), minimum GPA of 3.0. *Average time to degree:* Master's–2 years full-time; doctorate–4.5 years full-time. *Application deadline:* For fall admission, 2/1 (priority date); for winter admission, 11/1; for spring admission, 2/1. Applications are processed on a rolling basis. Application fee: $50. Electronic applications accepted. Tuition, state resident: full-time $5,196; part-time $475 per credit. Tuition, nonresident: full-time $13,485; part-time $1,285 per credit. Required fees: $387; $38 per credit. Tuition and fees vary according to course load. *Financial aid:* In 1998–99, 8 fellowships with full tuition reimbursements (averaging $11,000 per year), 87 research assistantships with full tuition reimbursements (averaging $11,000 per year), 17 teaching assistantships with full tuition reimbursements (averaging $11,000 per year) were awarded.; career-related internships or fieldwork, Federal Work-Study, institutionally-sponsored loans, and scholarships also available. Financial aid application deadline: 2/1. *Faculty research:* Ecosystem sciences, forest management and engineering, natural resource policy. Total annual research expenditures: $6.3 million. *Unit head:* Dr. David B. Thorud, Dean, 206-685-1928, Fax: 206-685-0790. *Application contact:* Michelle Trudeau, Student Services Manager, 206-616-1533, Fax: 206-685-0790, E-mail: michtru@u.washington.edu.

See in-depth description on page 963.

University of Wisconsin–Madison, Graduate School, College of Agricultural and Life Sciences, School of Natural Resources, Department of Forest Ecology and Management, Madison, WI 53706-1380. Offers MS, PhD. Part-time programs available. *Degree requirements:* For master's, thesis required (for some programs); for doctorate, dissertation required. *Entrance requirements:* For master's and doctorate, GRE. Electronic applications accepted. *Faculty research:* Forest and landscape ecology, forest biology, wood and fiber science, social forestry.

Utah State University, School of Graduate Studies, College of Natural Resources, Department of Forest Resources, Logan, UT 84322. Offers forest ecology (MS, PhD); forestry (MS, PhD); recreation resources management (MS, PhD). *Accreditation:* SAF (one or more programs are accredited). *Faculty:* 12 full-time (2 women), 8 part-time (3 women). *Students:* 20 full-time (7 women), 12 part-time (8 women); includes 1 minority (Hispanic American), 3 international. Average age 33. 21 applicants, 38% accepted. In 1998, 7 master's, 1 doctorate awarded. Terminal master's awarded for partial completion of doctoral program. *Degree requirements:* For master's, computer language, thesis required (for some programs), foreign language not required; for doctorate, one foreign language, computer language, dissertation required. *Entrance requirements:* For master's and doctorate, GRE General Test (score in 40th percentile or higher required), TOEFL (minimum score of 550 required), minimum GPA of 3.0. *Application deadline:* For fall admission, 6/15 (priority date); for spring admission, 10/15. Applications are processed on a rolling basis. Application fee: $40. Tuition, state resident: full-time $1,492. Tuition, nonresident: full-time $5,232. Required fees: $434. Tuition and fees vary according to course load. *Financial aid:* In 1998–99, 1 fellowship with partial tuition reimbursement, 21 research assistantships with partial tuition reimbursements (averaging $8,329 per year), 8 teaching assistantships with partial tuition reimbursements (averaging $8,861 per year) were awarded.; Federal Work-Study, institutionally-sponsored loans, and tuition waivers (full and partial) also available. Financial aid application deadline: 2/15. *Faculty research:* Disturbance ecology, natural resource policy, outdoor recreation, ecological modeling. Total annual research expenditures: $299,651. *Unit head:* Dr. Terry L. Sharik, Head, 435-797-3219, Fax: 435-797-4040, E-mail: forestry@cc.usu.edu. *Application contact:* B. J. Tueller, Staff Assistant, 435-797-3488, Fax: 435-797-4040, E-mail: bjtuell@cnr.usu.edu.

Virginia Polytechnic Institute and State University, Graduate School, College of Natural Resources, Department of Forestry, Blacksburg, VA 24061. Offers forest biology (MF, MS, PhD); forest biometry (MF, MS, PhD); forest management/economics (MF, MS, PhD); industrial forestry operations (MF, MS, PhD); outdoor recreation (MF, MS, PhD). *Faculty:* 25. *Students:* 49 full-time (14 women), 9 part-time (2 women); includes 2 minority (1 Asian American or Pacific Islander, 1 Hispanic American), 10 international. 51 applicants, 43% accepted. In 1998, 7 master's, 5 doctorates awarded. *Degree requirements:* For master's, degree paper (MF), thesis (MS) required; for doctorate, dissertation, oral defense, preliminary exam, qualifying exam, competency in statistics required, foreign language not required. *Entrance requirements:* For master's and doctorate, GRE General Test, TOEFL, minimum GPA of 3.0. *Application deadline:* For fall admission, 12/1 (priority date). Applications are processed on a rolling basis. Application fee: $25. *Financial aid:* In 1998–99, 40 students received aid; fellowships, research assistantships, teaching assistantships, career-related internships or fieldwork, Federal Work-Study, institutionally-sponsored loans, and unspecified assistantships available. Financial aid application deadline: 4/1. *Unit head:* Dr. Harold E. Burkhart, Head, 540-231-6952, Fax: 540-231-3698, E-mail: burkhart@vt.edu.

Virginia Polytechnic Institute and State University, Graduate School, College of Natural Resources, Department of Wood Science and Forest Products, Blacksburg, VA 24061. Offers forest products marketing (MF, MS, PhD); wood science and engineering (MF, MS, PhD). *Faculty:* 17. *Students:* 27 full-time (5 women), 5 part-time (2 women), 15 international. 18 applicants, 61% accepted. In 1998, 7 master's, 4 doctorates awarded. *Degree requirements:* For master's and doctorate, thesis/dissertation required, foreign language not required. *Entrance requirements:* For master's and doctorate, GRE General Test, TOEFL, minimum GPA of 3.0. *Application deadline:* For fall admission, 12/1 (priority date). Applications are processed on a rolling basis. Application fee: $25. *Financial aid:* Fellowships, research assistantships, teaching assistantships, Federal Work-Study, tuition waivers (partial), and unspecified assistantships available. Financial aid application deadline: 4/1. *Faculty research:* Wood chemistry, wood engineering, wood composites, wood processing, forest products marketing/management, recycling. *Unit head:* Dr. Geza Ifju, Head, 540-231-8853, Fax: 540-231-8176, E-mail: ifju@vt.edu.

West Virginia University, College of Agriculture, Forestry and Consumer Sciences, Division of Forestry, Program in Forest Resource Science, Morgantown, WV 26506. Offers PhD. *Degree requirements:* For doctorate, dissertation, comprehensive exam required, foreign language not required. *Entrance requirements:* For doctorate, GRE, TOEFL (minimum score of 550 required), minimum GPA of 3.0. *Faculty research:* Impact of management on wildlife and fish, forest sampling designs, forest economics and policy, oak regeneration.

West Virginia University, College of Agriculture, Forestry and Consumer Sciences, Division of Forestry, Program in Forestry, Morgantown, WV 26506. Offers MSF. *Degree requirements:* For master's, thesis required, foreign language not required. *Entrance requirements:* For master's, GRE, TOEFL (minimum score of 550 required), minimum GPA of 3.0. *Faculty research:* Gypsy moth impact on Appalachian forests, wood industries in Appalachian forests, role of forestry in regional economics.

Yale University, Graduate School of Arts and Sciences, Department of Forestry and Environmental Studies, New Haven, CT 06520. Offers environmental sciences (PhD);

Forestry–Natural Resources

Yale University (continued)

forestry (PhD). *Faculty:* 39 full-time (9 women). *Students:* 44 full-time (25 women); includes 3 minority (2 Asian Americans or Pacific Islanders, 1 Hispanic American), 13 international. 60 applicants, 12% accepted. In 1998, 5 degrees awarded. *Degree requirements:* For doctorate, dissertation required, foreign language not required. *Entrance requirements:* For doctorate, GRE General Test. *Average time to degree:* Doctorate–6.4 years full-time. *Application deadline:* For fall admission, 1/4. Application fee: $65. *Financial aid:* Fellowships, Federal Work-Study and institutionally-sponsored loans available. Aid available to part-time students. *Unit head:* Dean, School of Forestry and Environmental Studies, 203-432-5109. *Application contact:* Admissions Information, 203-432-2770.

Yale University, School of Forestry and Environmental Studies, New Haven, CT 06520. Offers MES, MF, MFS, DFES, PhD, JD/MES, MBA/MES, MES/MA, MES/MPH, MF/MA. *Accreditation:* SAF (one or more programs are accredited). Part-time programs available. *Faculty:* 27 full-time, 10 part-time. *Students:* 282 full-time, 10 part-time; includes 20 minority (2 African Americans, 10 Asian Americans or Pacific Islanders, 8 Hispanic Americans), 42 international. Average age 28. 392 applicants, 55% accepted. In 1998, 104 master's, 7 doctorates awarded. Terminal master's awarded for partial completion of doctoral program. *Degree requirements:* For master's, thesis not required; for doctorate, dissertation required. *Entrance requirements:* For master's and doctorate, GRE General Test. *Average time to degree:* Master's–2 years full-time, 4 years part-time. *Application deadline:* For fall admission, 2/1. Application fee: $0. *Financial aid:* In 1998–99, 135 students received aid. Career-related internships or fieldwork available. Aid available to part-time students. Financial aid application deadline: 2/1; financial aid applicants required to submit FAFSA. *Faculty research:* Ecosystem science and management, coastal and watershed systems, environmental policy and management, social ecology and community development, conservation biology. *Unit head:* Dr. James Gustave Speth, Dean, 203-432-5109, Fax: 203-432-5942. *Application contact:* Daniel C. Esty, Director of Admissions and Associate Dean, 203-432-5100, Fax: 203-432-5942, E-mail: fesinfo@yale.edu.

See in-depth description on page 967.

Natural Resources

Ball State University, Graduate School, College of Sciences and Humanities, Department of Natural Resources, Muncie, IN 47306-1099. Offers MA, MS. *Faculty:* 9. *Students:* 11 full-time (5 women), 10 part-time (4 women). Average age 27. 21 applicants, 71% accepted. In 1998, 6 degrees awarded. Application fee: $15 ($25 for international students). *Financial aid:* Research assistantships, teaching assistantships, career-related internships or fieldwork available. *Faculty research:* Acid rain, indoor air pollution, land reclamation. *Unit head:* Dr. Charles Mortensen, Chairman, 765-285-5780, E-mail: cmortens@bsu.edu.

Bard College, Graduate School of Environmental Studies, Annandale-on-Hudson, NY 12504. Offers MSES. Offered during summer only. *Faculty:* 5 full-time (2 women), 9 part-time (1 woman). *Students:* 45 full-time (21 women); includes 5 minority (2 Asian Americans or Pacific Islanders, 1 Hispanic American, 2 Native Americans), 1 international. Average age 30. 40 applicants, 48% accepted. In 1998, 7 degrees awarded. *Degree requirements:* For master's, thesis required, foreign language not required. *Entrance requirements:* For master's, resumé, interview, published materials. *Average time to degree:* Master's–4 years full-time. *Application deadline:* For fall admission, 2/1 (priority date). Applications are processed on a rolling basis. Application fee: $45. *Financial aid:* Fellowships, career-related internships or fieldwork and scholarships available. Financial aid application deadline: 3/1; financial aid applicants required to submit FAFSA. *Faculty research:* Environmental ethics, environmental economics, environmental impact assessment, cultural ecology, wetland ecology and management. *Unit head:* Joanne Fox-Przeworski, Director, 914-758-7067, Fax: 914-758-7636, E-mail: jfp@bard.edu. *Application contact:* Gloria Cestero-Hurd, Coordinator, 914-758-7073, Fax: 914-758-7636, E-mail: gch@bard.edu.

Cornell University, Graduate School, Graduate Fields of Agriculture and Life Sciences, Field of Natural Resources, Ithaca, NY 14853-0001. Offers aquatic science (MPS, MS, PhD); environmental management (MPS); fishery science (MPS, MS, PhD); forest science (MPS, MS, PhD); resource policy and management (MPS, MS, PhD); wildlife science (MPS, MS, PhD). *Faculty:* 24 full-time. *Students:* 58 full-time (24 women); includes 5 minority (1 African American, 1 Asian American or Pacific Islander, 2 Hispanic Americans, 1 Native American), 11 international. 140 applicants, 16% accepted. In 1998, 7 master's, 2 doctorates awarded. Terminal master's awarded for partial completion of doctoral program. *Degree requirements:* For master's, thesis (MS), project paper (MPS) required; for doctorate, dissertation required, foreign language not required. *Entrance requirements:* For master's and doctorate, GRE General Test, TOEFL (minimum score of 550 required). *Application deadline:* Applications are processed on a rolling basis. Application fee: $65. Electronic applications accepted. *Financial aid:* In 1998–99, 46 students received aid, including 10 fellowships with full tuition reimbursements available, 20 research assistantships with full tuition reimbursements available, 16 teaching assistantships with full tuition reimbursements available; institutionally-sponsored loans, scholarships, tuition waivers (full and partial), and unspecified assistantships also available. Financial aid applicants required to submit FAFSA. *Faculty research:* Ecosystem-level dynamics, systems modeling, conservation biology/management, resource management's human dimensions, biogeochemistry. *Unit head:* Director of Graduate Studies, 607-255-2807, Fax: 607-255-0349. *Application contact:* Graduate Field Assistant, 607-255-2807, E-mail: nrgrad@cornell.edu.

Duke University, Graduate School, Department of Environment, Durham, NC 27708-0586. Offers natural resource economics/policy (AM, PhD); natural resource science/ecology (AM, PhD); natural resource systems science (AM, PhD). Part-time programs available. *Faculty:* 39 full-time, 14 part-time. *Students:* 69 full-time, 1 part-time; includes 5 minority (3 African Americans, 1 Asian American or Pacific Islander, 1 Hispanic American), 17 international. 126 applicants, 24% accepted. In 1998, 4 master's, 10 doctorates awarded. Terminal master's awarded for partial completion of doctoral program. *Degree requirements:* For doctorate, dissertation required, foreign language not required. *Entrance requirements:* For master's and doctorate, GRE General Test. *Application deadline:* For fall admission, 12/31. Application fee: $75. *Financial aid:* Fellowships, research assistantships, teaching assistantships, Federal Work-Study available. Financial aid application deadline: 12/31. *Unit head:* Kenneth Knoerr, Director of Graduate Studies, 919-613-8002, Fax: 919-684-8741, E-mail: nettleto@acpub.duke.edu.

Duke University, Nicholas School of the Environment, Durham, NC 27708-0328. Offers coastal environmental management (MEM); environmental science and policy (PhD); environmental toxicology, chemistry, and risk assessment (MEM); forest resource management (MF); resource ecology (MEM); resource economics and policy (MEM); water and air resources (MEM). PhD offered through the Graduate School. *Accreditation:* SAF (one or more programs are accredited). Part-time programs available. *Faculty:* 61 full-time (10 women), 23 part-time (3 women). *Students:* 228 full-time (136 women); includes 7 minority (2 African Americans, 4 Asian Americans or Pacific Islanders, 1 Hispanic American), 24 international. Average age 25. 400 applicants, 63% accepted. In 1998, 116 master's, 10 doctorates awarded. Terminal master's awarded for partial completion of doctoral program. *Degree requirements:* For master's, thesis required (for some programs), foreign language not required; for doctorate, dissertation required, foreign language not required. *Entrance requirements:* For master's, GRE General Test, TOEFL, previous course work in biology or ecology, calculus, statistics, and microeconomics; computer familiarity with word processing and data analysis; for doctorate, GRE General Test, TOEFL. *Average time to degree:* Master's–2 years full-time, 3 years part-time; doctorate–5 years full-time, 8 years part-time. *Application deadline:* For fall admission, 2/1; for spring admission, 10/15. Applications are processed on a rolling basis. Application fee: $75. *Financial aid:* In 1998–99, 29 fellowships (averaging $11,500 per year), 53 research assistantships (averaging $2,600 per year), 15 teaching assistantships (averaging $6,000 per year) were awarded.; career-related internships or fieldwork, Federal Work-Study, institutionally-sponsored loans, scholarships, and unspecified assistantships also available. Financial aid application deadline: 2/1; financial aid applicants required to submit FAFSA. *Faculty research:* Ecosystem management, conservation ecology, earth systems, risk assessment. *Unit head:* Dr. Norman L. Christensen, Dean, 919-613-8004, Fax: 919-684-8741. *Application contact:* Bertie S. Belvin, Associate Dean for Academic Services, 919-613-8070, Fax: 919-684-8741, E-mail: envadm@duke.edu.

See in-depth description on page 949.

Humboldt State University, Graduate Studies, College of Natural Resources and Sciences, Program in Natural Resources, Arcata, CA 95521-8299. Offers MS. *Faculty:* 7 full-time (2 women), 7 part-time (1 woman). *Students:* 65 full-time (25 women), 18 part-time (3 women); includes 9 minority (1 Asian American or Pacific Islander, 7 Hispanic Americans, 1 Native American), 2 international. Average age 30. 87 applicants, 31% accepted. In 1998, 22 degrees awarded. *Degree requirements:* For master's, thesis or alternative required, foreign language not required. *Entrance requirements:* For master's, TOEFL (minimum score of 550 required), appropriate bachelor's degree, minimum GPA of 2.5. *Application deadline:* Applications are processed on a rolling basis. Application fee: $55. *Financial aid:* Fellowships, career-related internships or fieldwork and Federal Work-Study available. Aid available to part-time students. Financial aid application deadline: 3/1; financial aid applicants required to submit FAFSA. *Faculty research:* Spotted owl habitat, presettlement vegetation, hardwood utilization, tree physiology, fisheries. *Unit head:* Dr. Gary Hendrickson, Coordinator, 707-826-4233.

McGill University, Faculty of Graduate Studies and Research, Faculty of Agricultural and Environmental Sciences, Department of Natural Resource Sciences, Montréal, PQ H3A 2T5, Canada. Offers agrometeorology (M Sc, PhD); entomology (M Sc, PhD); forest science (M Sc, PhD); microbiology (M Sc, PhD); soil science (M Sc, PhD); wildlife biology (M Sc, PhD). *Faculty:* 18 full-time (1 woman), 26 part-time (3 women). *Students:* 83 full-time (35 women), 10 international. 32 applicants, 47% accepted. In 1998, 21 master's, 7 doctorates awarded. *Degree requirements:* For master's and doctorate, thesis/dissertation required. *Entrance requirements:* For master's, TOEFL (minimum score of 550 required), minimum GPA of 3.0; for doctorate, TOEFL (minimum score of 550 required), M Sc. *Application deadline:* For fall admission, 1/1 (priority date); for winter admission, 5/1 (priority date); for spring admission, 9/1 (priority date). Applications are processed on a rolling basis. Application fee: $60. *Financial aid:* In 1998–99, 40 teaching assistantships (averaging $775 per year) were awarded.; fellowships, institutionally-sponsored loans also available. *Faculty research:* Toxicology, reproductive physiology, parasites, wildlife management, genetics, ecology, soil. Total annual research expenditures: $1.1 million. *Unit head:* Dr. W. H. Hendershot, Chair, 514-398-7942, Fax: 514-398-7990, E-mail: chair@nrs.mcgill.ca. *Application contact:* 514-398-7708, Fax: 514-398-7968, E-mail: grad@macdonald.mcgill.ca.

Montana State University–Bozeman, College of Graduate Studies, College of Agriculture, Department of Land Resources and Environmental Sciences, Bozeman, MT 59717. Offers MS, PhD. Part-time programs available. *Faculty:* 19 full-time (0 women). *Students:* 7 full-time (2 women), 14 part-time (5 women). Average age 32. 19 applicants, 100% accepted. In 1998, 7 master's, 3 doctorates awarded. Terminal master's awarded for partial completion of doctoral program. *Degree requirements:* For master's, thesis or alternative required, foreign language not required; for doctorate, dissertation required, foreign language not required. *Entrance requirements:* For master's and doctorate, GRE General Test, TOEFL (minimum score of 550 required). *Application deadline:* For fall admission, 6/1 (priority date); for spring admission, 11/1. Applications are processed on a rolling basis. Application fee: $50. *Financial aid:* In 1998–99, 1 fellowship with full tuition reimbursement (averaging $15,000 per year), 23 research assistantships with full and partial tuition reimbursements (averaging $12,000 per year), 2 teaching assistantships with full tuition reimbursements (averaging $10,000 per year) were awarded.; tuition waivers (full and partial) also available. Financial aid application deadline: 3/1. *Faculty research:* Agronomic characteristics, plant breeding/genetics, groundwater quality, irrigation, soil/water conservation. Total annual research expenditures: $2 million. *Unit head:* Dr. Jeffrey S. Jacobsen, Head, 406-994-7060, Fax: 406-994-3933, E-mail: jefj@montana.edu.

North Carolina State University, Graduate School, College of Forest Resources, Department of Wood and Paper Science, Raleigh, NC 27695. Offers MS, MWPS, PhD. *Faculty:* 20 full-time (2 women), 12 part-time (0 women). *Students:* 22 full-time (4 women), 13 part-time (3 women); includes 3 minority (2 African Americans, 1 Asian American or Pacific Islander), 19 international. Average age 30. 11 applicants, 27% accepted. In 1998, 6 master's, 4 doctorates awarded. *Degree requirements:* For master's and doctorate, thesis/dissertation required, foreign language not required. *Entrance requirements:* For master's and doctorate, GRE General Test, TOEFL (minimum score of 550 required). *Application deadline:* For fall admission, 6/25; for spring admission, 11/25. Applications are processed on a rolling basis. Application fee: $45. *Financial aid:* Fellowships, research assistantships available. Financial aid application deadline: 2/15. *Faculty research:* Pulping, bleaching, recycling, papermaking, drying of wood, analysis/design of wood structures, wood machining and tooling. Total annual research expenditures: $2.4 million. *Unit head:* Dr. Michael J. Kocurek, Head, 919-515-5807, Fax: 919-515-6302, E-mail: mike_kocurek@ncsu.edu. *Application contact:* Dr. Richard D. Gilbert, Director of Graduate Programs, 919-515-5321, Fax: 919-515-6302, E-mail: gilbert@cfr.cfr.ncsu.edu.

The Ohio State University, Graduate School, College of Food, Agricultural, and Environmental Sciences, School of Natural Resources, Columbus, OH 43210. Offers MS. Part-time programs available. *Faculty:* 26 full-time, 28 part-time. *Students:* 35 full-time (23 women), 16 part-time (10 women); includes 2 minority (1 African American, 1 Hispanic American), 7 international. 69 applicants, 41% accepted. In 1998, 22 degrees awarded. *Degree requirements:* For master's, thesis optional, foreign language not required. *Entrance requirements:* For master's, GRE General Test. *Application deadline:* For fall admission, 8/15. Applications are processed on a rolling basis. Application fee: $30 ($40 for international students). *Financial aid:* Fellowships, research assistantships, teaching assistantships, Federal Work-Study, institutionally-sponsored loans, and unspecified assistantships available. Aid available to part-time students. *Faculty research:* Environmental education, natural resources development, fisheries and wildlife management. *Unit head:* Gary W. Mullins, Interim Director, 614-292-8522, Fax: 614-292-7432, E-mail: mullins.2@osu.edu.

Purdue University, Graduate School, School of Agriculture, Department of Forestry and Natural Resources, West Lafayette, IN 47907. Offers MS, MSF, PhD. *Faculty:* 23 full-time (1 woman). *Students:* 48 full-time (17 women), 11 part-time (3 women); includes 4 minority (3 African Americans, 1 Native American), 22 international. Average age 26. 54 applicants, 20% accepted. In 1998, 10 master's, 7 doctorates awarded. *Degree requirements:* For master's and doctorate, computer language, thesis/dissertation required, foreign language not required. *Entrance requirements:* For master's and doctorate, GRE General Test (minimum score of 500 on each section required), TOEFL (minimum score of 550 required), minimum B+ average in undergraduate course work. *Average time to degree:* Master's–2 years full-time; doctorate–3 years full-time. *Application deadline:* For fall admission, 2/15 (priority date); for spring admission, 9/15. Applications are processed on a rolling basis. Application fee: $30. Electronic applications accepted. *Financial aid:* In 1998–99, 6 research assistantships (averaging $14,430 per year) were awarded.; fellowships, teaching assistantships, career-related internships or fieldwork and grants also available. Aid available to part-time students. Financial aid application deadline: 2/15; financial aid applicants required to submit FAFSA. *Faculty research:* Wildlife management, forest management, forest ecology, forest soils, limnology. *Unit head:* Dr. D. C. LeMaster, Head, 765-494-3590, Fax: 765-496-2422, E-mail: dclmstr@fnr.purdue.edu. *Application contact:* Patty A. Fitzsimons, Graduate Secretary, 765-494-3572, Fax: 765-496-2422, E-mail: pattyf@fnr.purdue.edu.

See in-depth description on page 953.

Slippery Rock University of Pennsylvania, Graduate School, College of Health and Human Services, Department of Parks, Recreation, and Environmental Education, Slippery Rock, PA 16057. Offers environmental education (M Ed); resource management (MS); sustainable systems (MS). Part-time and evening/weekend programs available. *Faculty:* 16 full-time (8 women). *Students:* 29 full-time (12 women), 19 part-time (12 women); includes 3 minority (1 African American, 2 Hispanic Americans), 3 international. *Degree requirements:* For master's, comprehensive exams required, thesis optional, foreign language not required. *Entrance requirements:* For master's, GRE General Test (minimum combined score of 1350 on three sections), minimum GPA of 2.75. *Application deadline:* For fall admission, 7/1 (priority date); for spring admission, 11/1. Applications are processed on a rolling basis. Application fee: $25. Electronic applications accepted. *Unit head:* Dr. William Shiner, Graduate Coordinator, 724-738-2068. *Application contact:* Carla Hradisky-Coffelt, Interim Director of Graduate Admissions and Recruitment, 724-738-2051, Fax: 724-738-2908.

Texas A&M University, College of Agriculture and Life Sciences, Department of Forest Science, College Station, TX 77843. Offers forest science (MS, PhD); natural resources development (M Agr). *Faculty:* 13 full-time (4 women), 6 part-time (0 women). *Students:* 29 full-time (9 women), 11 part-time (5 women); includes 5 minority (1 African American, 3 Asian Americans or Pacific Islanders, 1 Hispanic American), 14 international. Terminal master's awarded for partial completion of doctoral program. *Degree requirements:* For master's, thesis required (for some programs), foreign language not required; for doctorate, dissertation required, foreign language not required. *Entrance requirements:* For master's and doctorate, GRE General Test, TOEFL. *Application deadline:* For fall admission, 3/1 (priority date); for spring admission, 11/1. Applications are processed on a rolling basis. Application fee: $50 ($75 for international students). *Unit head:* Dr. Charles Tat Smith, Head, 409-845-5033, Fax: 409-845-6049, E-mail: tat_smith@tamu.edu. *Application contact:* Prof. Richard F. Fisher, Chair, Graduate Programs, 409-845-5095, Fax: 409-845-6049, E-mail: r-fisher@tamu.edu.

Texas A&M University, College of Agriculture and Life Sciences, Department of Recreation, Park and Tourism Sciences, College Station, TX 77843. Offers natural resources development (M Agr); recreation and resources development (M Agr); recreation, park, and tourism sciences (MS, PhD). *Faculty:* 15 full-time (2 women), 2 part-time (both women). *Students:* 34 full-time (17 women), 17 part-time (6 women); includes 2 minority (1 African American, 1 Asian American or Pacific Islander), 18 international. *Degree requirements:* For master's and doctorate, thesis/dissertation required, foreign language not required. *Entrance requirements:* For master's and doctorate, GRE General Test (minimum score of 400 on verbal section, 1100 combined required), TOEFL (minimum score of 550 required). *Application deadline:* For fall admission, 4/15 (priority date); for spring admission, 10/15 (priority date). Applications are processed on a rolling basis. Application fee: $50 ($75 for international students). Electronic applications accepted. *Unit head:* Dr. Peter A. Witt, Head, 409-845-5412, Fax: 409-845-0446, E-mail: pwitt@rpts.tamu.edu. *Application contact:* Marguerite Van Dyke, Graduate Recruitment Coordinator, 409-845-5412, Fax: 409-845-0446, E-mail: mvandyke@rpts.tamu.edu.

University of Alberta, Faculty of Graduate Studies and Research, Department of Renewable Resources, Edmonton, AB T6G 2E1, Canada. Offers agroforestry (M Ag, M Sc, MF); conservation biology (M Sc, PhD); forest biology and management (M Sc, PhD); land reclamation and remediation (M Sc, PhD); protected areas and wildlands management (M Sc, PhD); soil science (M Ag, M Sc, PhD); water and land resources (M Ag, M Sc, PhD); wildlife ecology and management (M Sc, PhD). *Degree requirements:* For doctorate, dissertation required.

The University of Arizona, Graduate College, College of Agriculture, School of Renewable Natural Resources, Division of Renewable Natural Resources, Tucson, AZ 85721. Offers MS, PhD. *Students:* 35 full-time (12 women), 18 part-time (8 women); includes 4 minority (1 African American, 2 Hispanic Americans, 1 Native American), 16 international. Average age 35. 27 applicants, 56% accepted. In 1998, 2 master's, 4 doctorates awarded. *Degree requirements:* For master's, computer language, thesis required, foreign language not required; for doctorate, one foreign language (computer language can substitute), dissertation required. *Entrance requirements:* For master's and doctorate, GRE General Test, TOEFL (minimum score of 550 required), minimum GPA of 3.0. *Application deadline:* For fall admission, 8/1. Applications are processed on a rolling basis. Application fee: $35. *Financial aid:* Fellowships, research assistantships, teaching assistantships available. *Unit head:* Dr. David A. King, Head, 520-621-5462. *Application contact:* Mary E. Soltero, Administrative Assistant, 520-621-7260, Fax: 520-621-8801.

University of Arkansas at Monticello, School of Forest Resources, Monticello, AR 71656. Offers MS. Part-time programs available. *Faculty:* 5 full-time (0 women). *Students:* 10 full-time (4 women), 6 part-time; includes 2 minority (1 African American, 1 Native American), 2 international. *Degree requirements:* For master's, thesis required. *Entrance requirements:* For master's, GRE General Test. *Application deadline:* For fall admission, 8/16 (priority date); for spring admission, 1/3 (priority date). Applications are processed on a rolling basis. Application fee: $0. Tuition, state resident: full-time $1,584; part-time $88 per credit hour. Tuition, nonresident: full-time $2,142; part-time $119 per credit hour. *Financial aid:* Research assistantships available. *Faculty research:* Geographic information systems/remote sensing, forest ecology, wildlife ecology and management. *Unit head:* Dr. Bob Blackmon, Dean, 870-460-1052, Fax: 870-460-1092, E-mail: blackmon@uamont.edu.

University of Connecticut, Graduate School, College of Agriculture and Natural Resources, Field of Natural Resources: Land, Water, and Air, Storrs, CT 06269. Offers MS. *Entrance requirements:* For master's, GRE General Test, GRE Subject Test, TOEFL. *Faculty research:* Natural resource management, forest management, forest protection, water resources, biometeorology.

University of Georgia, Graduate School, School of Forest Resources, Athens, GA 30602. Offers MFR, MS, PhD. *Faculty:* 48 full-time (4 women). *Students:* 93 full-time, 20 part-time (13 women); includes 6 minority (4 African Americans, 2 Asian Americans or Pacific Islanders), 16 international. 86 applicants, 50% accepted. In 1998, 51 master's, 5 doctorates awarded. *Degree requirements:* For master's, thesis (MS) required; for doctorate, one foreign language, dissertation required. *Entrance requirements:* For master's and doctorate, GRE General Test. *Application deadline:* For fall admission, 7/1 (priority date); for spring admission, 11/15. Application fee: $30. Electronic applications accepted. *Financial aid:* Fellowships, research assistantships, teaching assistantships, unspecified assistantships available. *Unit head:* Dr. Arnett C. Mace, Dean, 706-542-4741, Fax: 706-542-2281, E-mail: amace@smokey.forestry.uga.edu. *Application contact:* Dr. Robert O. Teskey, Graduate Coordinator, 706-542-1183, Fax: 706-542-3293, E-mail: teskey@smokey.forestry.uga.edu.

University of Illinois at Urbana–Champaign, Graduate College, College of Agricultural, Consumer and Environmental Sciences, Department of Natural Resources and Environmental Science, Urbana, IL 61801. Offers MS, PhD. *Faculty:* 11 full-time (1 woman). *Students:* 112 full-time (42 women); includes 5 minority (1 African American, 1 Asian American or Pacific Islander, 3 Hispanic Americans), 25 international. 32 applicants, 78% accepted. In 1998, 17 master's, 9 doctorates awarded. *Degree requirements:* For master's and doctorate, thesis/dissertation required, foreign language not required. *Entrance requirements:* For master's, minimum GPA of 4.0 on a 5.0 scale. *Application deadline:* Applications are processed on a rolling basis. Application fee: $40 ($50 for international students). Tuition, state resident: full-time $4,040. Tuition, nonresident: full-time $11,192. Full-time tuition and fees vary according to program. *Financial aid:* Fellowships, research assistantships, teaching assistantships, tuition waivers (full and partial) available. Financial aid application deadline: 2/15. *Unit head:* Gary L. Rolfe, Head, 217-333-2770. *Application contact:* John A. Juvik, Director of Graduate Studies, 217-333-1966, Fax: 217-244-3219, E-mail: j-juvik@uiuc.edu.

University of Maine, Graduate School, College of Natural Sciences, Forestry, and Agriculture, Department of Forest Management, Orono, ME 04469. Offers forest resources (PhD); forestry (MF, MS). *Accreditation:* SAF (one or more programs are accredited). Part-time programs available. *Degree requirements:* For master's, thesis required, foreign language not required; for doctorate, one foreign language, dissertation required. *Entrance requirements:* For master's and doctorate, GRE General Test, TOEFL (minimum score of 550 required). *Application deadline:* For fall admission, 2/1 (priority date); for spring admission, 10/15. Applications are processed on a rolling basis. Application fee: $50. *Unit head:* Dr. David Field, Chair, 207-581-2856, Fax: 207-581-2858. *Application contact:* Scott G. Delcourt, Director of the Graduate School, 207-581-3218, Fax: 207-581-3232, E-mail: graduate@maine.edu.

University of Maine, Graduate School, College of Natural Sciences, Forestry, and Agriculture, Department of Plant, Soil, and Environmental Sciences, Orono, ME 04469. Offers biological sciences (PhD); ecology and environmental sciences (MS, PhD); forest resources (PhD); plant science (PhD); plant, soil, and environmental sciences (MS); resource utilization (MS). *Students:* 11 (6 women). *Entrance requirements:* For master's and doctorate, GRE General Test, TOEFL (minimum score of 550 required). Application fee: $50. *Unit head:* Dr. Ivan Fernandez, Chair. *Application contact:* Mary Fernandez, 207-581-2938, Fax: 207-581-2999, E-mail: fern@maine.maine.edu.

University of Michigan, School of Natural Resources and Environment, Ann Arbor, MI 48109. Offers forestry (MF), including resource ecology and management (MF, MS), resource policy and behavior (MF, MS); landscape architecture (MLA, PhD); natural resource economics (PhD); natural resources and environment (MS, PhD), including resource ecology and management (MF, MS), resource policy and behavior (MF, MS). MLA, MS, PhD, and JD/MS offered through the Horace H. Rackham School of Graduate Studies. *Accreditation:* ASLA (one or more programs are accredited); SAF (one or more programs are accredited). Terminal master's awarded for partial completion of doctoral program. *Degree requirements:* For doctorate, oral defense of dissertation, preliminary exam required, foreign language not required. *Entrance requirements:* For master's, GRE General Test, TOEFL; for doctorate, GRE General Test, TOEFL, master's degree.

See in-depth description on page 959.

The University of Montana–Missoula, Graduate School, School of Forestry, Program in Resource Conservation, Missoula, MT 59812-0002. Offers MS. *Students:* 7 full-time (2 women), 7 part-time (5 women). Average age 25. 8 applicants, 50% accepted. In 1998, 7 degrees awarded. *Degree requirements:* For master's, thesis optional, foreign language not required. *Entrance requirements:* For master's, GRE General Test (minimum combined score of 1540 on three sections required). *Application deadline:* For fall admission, 1/31. Application fee: $45. *Financial aid:* Fellowships, research assistantships, teaching assistantships, career-related internships or fieldwork, Federal Work-Study, and institutionally-sponsored loans available. Financial aid application deadline: 3/1. *Unit head:* Dr. Don Potts, Associate Dean, 406-243-5521.

University of Nebraska–Lincoln, Graduate College, College of Agricultural Sciences and Natural Resources, School of Natural Resource Sciences, Lincoln, NE 68588. Offers MS. *Faculty:* 25 full-time (3 women). *Students:* 13 full-time (4 women), 2 part-time (1 woman), 1 international. Average age 30. 7 applicants, 14% accepted. In 1998, 7 degrees awarded. *Degree requirements:* For master's, thesis optional, foreign language not required. *Entrance requirements:* For master's, GRE General Test, TOEFL (minimum score of 500 required). *Application deadline:* For fall admission, 3/1 (priority date). Applications are processed on a rolling basis. Application fee: $35. Electronic applications accepted. *Financial aid:* In 1998–99, 1 fellowship, 15 research assistantships, 1 teaching assistantship were awarded.; Federal Work-Study also available. Aid available to part-time students. Financial aid application deadline: 2/15. *Faculty research:* Wildlife biology, aquatic sciences, landscape ecology, agroforestry. *Unit head:* Dr. Blaine Blad, Head, 402-472-9873, Fax: 402-472-4915.

University of New Hampshire, Graduate School, College of Life Sciences and Agriculture, Graduate Programs in the Biological Sciences and Natural Resources, Durham, NH 03824. Offers animal and nutritional sciences (MS, PhD); biochemistry and molecular biology (MS, PhD); biology (MS); genetics (MS, PhD); microbiology (MS, PhD); natural resources (MS, PhD), including environmental conservation (MS), forestry (MS), natural resources (PhD), soil science (MS), water resources management (MS), wildlife (MS); plant biology (MS, PhD); zoology (MS, PhD). Part-time programs available. *Faculty:* 129 full-time. *Students:* 127 full-time (74 women), 111 part-time (56 women); includes 6 minority (4 Asian Americans or Pacific Islanders, 2 Hispanic Americans), 31 international. Terminal master's awarded for partial completion of doctoral program. *Degree requirements:* For doctorate, dissertation required, foreign language not required. *Entrance requirements:* For master's, GRE General Test. *Application deadline:* Applications are processed on a rolling basis. Application fee: $50. Tuition, area resident: Full-time $5,750; part-time $319 per credit. Tuition, state resident: full-time $8,625. Tuition, nonresident: full-time $14,640; part-time $598 per credit. Required fees: $224 per semester. Tuition and fees vary according to course load, degree level and program. *Unit head:* Dr. William Mautz, Interim Dean, College of Life Sciences and Agriculture, 603-862-1450.

University of New Hampshire, Graduate School, College of Life Sciences and Agriculture, Graduate Programs in the Biological Sciences and Natural Resources, Department of Natural Resources, Interdisciplinary Program in Natural Resources, Durham, NH 03824. Offers PhD. *Faculty:* 17 full-time. *Students:* 27 full-time (16 women), 15 part-time (9 women); includes 2 minority (both Hispanic Americans), 5 international. Average age 38. 19 applicants, 47% accepted. In 1998, 3 degrees awarded. *Degree requirements:* For doctorate, dissertation required. *Application deadline:* For fall admission, 4/1 (priority date). Applications are processed on a rolling basis. Application fee: $50. Tuition, area resident: Full-time $5,750; part-time $319 per credit. Tuition, state resident: full-time $8,625. Tuition, nonresident: full-time $14,640; part-time $598 per credit. Required fees: $224 per semester. Tuition and fees vary according to course load, degree level and program. *Financial aid:* In 1998–99, 3 fellowships, 10 research assistantships, 5 teaching assistantships were awarded.; Federal Work-Study, scholarships, and tuition waivers (full and partial) also available. Financial aid application deadline: 2/15. *Faculty research:* Environmental and natural resource studies and management. *Unit head:* Dr. John D. Aber, Graduate Coordinator, 603-862-1792.

University of Rhode Island, Graduate School, College of Resource Development, Department of Environmental and Natural Resource Economics, Kingston, RI 02881. Offers resource economics and marine resources (MS, PhD). *Degree requirements:* For master's, thesis optional; for doctorate, dissertation required. *Entrance requirements:* For master's and doctorate, GRE General Test, TOEFL.

University of Wisconsin–Stevens Point, College of Natural Resources, Stevens Point, WI 54481-3897. Offers MS. Part-time programs available. *Students:* 31 full-time (19 women),

Natural Resources–Range Science

University of Wisconsin–Stevens Point (continued)
27 part-time (10 women), 1 international. In 1998, 21 degrees awarded. *Degree requirements:* For master's, thesis or alternative required, foreign language not required. *Entrance requirements:* For master's, GRE. *Application deadline:* For fall admission, 3/15 (priority date); for spring admission, 11/15. Applications are processed on a rolling basis. Application fee: $38. *Financial aid:* Research assistantships, teaching assistantships, career-related internships or fieldwork, Federal Work-Study, and unspecified assistantships available. Aid available to part-time students. Financial aid application deadline: 5/1; financial aid applicants required to submit FAFSA. *Faculty research:* Water and waste treatment, forest productivity, wildlife habitat, composting, environmental education. *Unit head:* Dr. Richard Wilke, Associate Dean, 715-346-2853, Fax: 715-346-3624.

University of Wyoming, Graduate School, College of Arts and Sciences, Department of Geography, Program in Rural Planning and Natural Resources, Laramie, WY 82071. Offers community and regional planning and natural resources (MP). *Students:* 1 (woman) full-time, 4 part-time (1 woman). In 1998, 3 degrees awarded. *Degree requirements:* For master's, thesis or alternative required, foreign language not required. *Entrance requirements:* For master's, GRE General Test, minimum GPA of 3.0. *Application deadline:* For fall admission, 3/1 (priority date). Applications are processed on a rolling basis. Application fee: $40. Tuition, state resident: full-time $2,520; part-time $140 per credit hour. Tuition, nonresident: full-time $7,790; part-time $433 per credit hour. Required fees: $400; $7 per credit hour. Full-time tuition and fees vary according to course load and program. *Financial aid:* Teaching assistantships, career-related internships or fieldwork and Federal Work-Study available. Financial aid application deadline: 3/1. *Unit head:* Dr. Ronald Beiswenger, Head, Department of Geography, 307-766-3311.

Utah State University, School of Graduate Studies, College of Natural Resources, Interdisciplinary Program in Natural Resources, Logan, UT 84322. Offers MNR. *Students:* 8 full-time (2 women), 9 part-time (4 women), 2 international. Average age 31. 6 applicants, 67% accepted. *Entrance requirements:* For master's, GRE General Test (score in 40th percentile or higher required), TOEFL (minimum score of 550 required), minimum GPA of 3.0. *Application deadline:* For fall admission, 6/15 (priority date); for spring admission, 10/15 (priority date). Applications are processed on a rolling basis. Application fee: $40. Electronic applications accepted. Tuition, state resident: full-time $1,492. Tuition, nonresident: full-time $5,232. Required fees: $434. Tuition and fees vary according to course load. *Faculty research:* Ecosystem management, human dimensions, quantitative methods, informative management. *Application contact:* B. J. Tueller, Staff Assistant, 435-797-3488, Fax: 435-797-4040, E-mail: bjtuell@cnr.usu.edu.

Virginia Polytechnic Institute and State University, Graduate School, College of Natural Resources, Blacksburg, VA 24061. Offers MF, MS, PhD. *Faculty:* 63. *Students:* 119 full-time (33 women), 21 part-time (6 women); includes 4 minority (2 African Americans, 1 Asian American or Pacific Islander, 1 Hispanic American), 29 international. 135 applicants, 30% accepted. In 1998, 24 master's, 12 doctorates awarded. *Degree requirements:* For master's, degree paper (MF), thesis (MS) required; for doctorate, dissertation, competency in statistics, oral defense, preliminary exam, qualifying exam required. *Entrance requirements:* For master's and doctorate, GRE General Test, TOEFL, minimum GPA of 3.0. *Application deadline:* For fall admission, 12/1 (priority date). Applications are processed on a rolling basis. Application fee: $25. *Financial aid:* Fellowships, research assistantships, teaching assistantships, career-related internships or fieldwork, Federal Work-Study, institutionally-sponsored loans, tuition waivers (full and partial), and unspecified assistantships available. Financial aid application deadline: 4/1. Total annual research expenditures: $6.4 million. *Unit head:* Gregory N. Brown, Dean, 540-231-7664, E-mail: browngn@vt.edu.

See in-depth description on page 965.

Washington State University, Graduate School, College of Agriculture and Home Economics, Department of Natural Resources Sciences, Pullman, WA 99164. Offers MS, PhD. *Faculty:* 11 full-time (2 women), 3 part-time (0 women). *Students:* 10 full-time (6 women), 3 part-time (all women); includes 1 minority (Asian American or Pacific Islander) In 1998, 1 degree awarded. *Degree requirements:* For master's and doctorate, thesis/dissertation, oral exam required, foreign language not required. *Entrance requirements:* For master's and doctorate, GRE General Test, minimum GPA of 3.0. *Average time to degree:* Master's–2 years full-time. *Application deadline:* For fall admission, 2/1 (priority date); for spring admission, 10/1. Applications are processed on a rolling basis. Application fee: $35. *Financial aid:* In 1998–99, 3 research assistantships, 2 teaching assistantships were awarded.; career-related internships or fieldwork, Federal Work-Study, institutionally-sponsored loans, tuition waivers (partial), and unspecified assistantships also available. Financial aid application deadline: 4/1; financial aid applicants required to submit FAFSA. Total annual research expenditures: $414,056. *Unit head:* Dr. Edward DePuit, Chair, 509-335-8570.

West Virginia University, College of Agriculture, Forestry and Consumer Sciences, Division of Resource Management, Program in Natural Resource Economics, Morgantown, WV 26506. Offers PhD. Part-time programs available. *Degree requirements:* For doctorate, dissertation required. *Entrance requirements:* For doctorate, GRE General Test (minimum combined score of 1100 required), TOEFL (minimum score of 550 required).

Range Science

Brigham Young University, Graduate Studies, College of Biological and Agricultural Sciences, Department of Botany and Range Science, Provo, UT 84602-1001. Offers biological science education (MS); botany (MS, PhD); range science (MS); wildlife and range resources (MS, PhD). *Faculty:* 17 full-time (1 woman). *Students:* 32 full-time (14 women); includes 3 minority (1 Asian American or Pacific Islander, 2 Hispanic Americans), 3 international. Average age 28. 16 applicants, 56% accepted. In 1998, 9 master's, 2 doctorates awarded. *Degree requirements:* For master's and doctorate, thesis/dissertation required. *Entrance requirements:* For master's, GRE General Test (minimum combined score of 1100 required), minimum GPA of 3.2 during previous 2 years; for doctorate, GRE General Test (minimum combined score of 1100 required). *Application deadline:* For fall admission, 2/15; for winter admission, 9/15. Applications are processed on a rolling basis. Application fee: $30. Tuition: Full-time $3,330; part-time $185 per credit hour. Tuition and fees vary according to program and student's religious affiliation. *Financial aid:* In 1998–99, 20 students received aid; fellowships with partial tuition reimbursements available, research assistantships with partial tuition reimbursements available, teaching assistantships with partial tuition reimbursements available, career-related internships or fieldwork, institutionally-sponsored loans, and tuition waivers (partial) available. Financial aid application deadline: 2/15. *Faculty research:* Plant classification (seed plants, lichens, and diatoms); ethnobotany; plant physiology; ecology (wildlife and plant); genetics. *Unit head:* Dr. Bruce A. Roundy, Chair, 801-378-2582, Fax: 801-378-7499. *Application contact:* Rex G. Cates, Graduate Coordinator, 801-378-4281, Fax: 801-378-7499.

Brigham Young University, Graduate Studies, College of Biological and Agricultural Sciences, Department of Zoology, Provo, UT 84602-1001. Offers biological science education (MS); molecular biology (MS, PhD); wildlife and range resources (MS, PhD); zoology (MS, PhD). Part-time programs available. *Faculty:* 31 full-time (0 women), 3 part-time (0 women). *Students:* 47 full-time (16 women), 7 part-time (2 women); includes 6 minority (1 Asian American or Pacific Islander, 4 Hispanic Americans, 1 Native American), 6 international. *Degree requirements:* For master's and doctorate, thesis/dissertation required, foreign language not required. *Entrance requirements:* For master's, GRE General Test (minimum combined score of 1600 on three sections required), minimum GPA of 3.0 during previous 2 years; for doctorate, GRE General Test (minimum combined score of 1600 on three sections required). *Application deadline:* For fall admission, 2/1 (priority date). Application fee: $30. Electronic applications accepted. Tuition: Full-time $3,330; part-time $185 per credit hour. Tuition and fees vary according to program and student's religious affiliation. *Unit head:* Dr. John D. Bell, Chair, 801-378-2006, Fax: 801-378-7423, E-mail: jdb32@email.byu.edu. *Application contact:* Dr. R. Ward Rhees, Graduate Coordinator, 801-378-2158, Fax: 801-378-7423, E-mail: ward_rhees@byu.edu.

Colorado State University, Graduate School, College of Natural Resources, Department of Rangeland Ecosystem Science, Fort Collins, CO 80523-0015. Offers MS, PhD. *Faculty:* 13 full-time (0 women), 2 part-time (0 women). *Students:* 50; includes 1 minority (Hispanic American), 8 international. Average age 33. 31 applicants, 74% accepted. In 1998, 6 master's, 5 doctorates awarded. *Degree requirements:* For master's, thesis or alternative required, foreign language not required; for doctorate, dissertation required, foreign language not required. *Entrance requirements:* For master's and doctorate, GRE General Test, TOEFL (minimum score of 550 required), minimum GPA of 3.0. *Application deadline:* For fall admission, 2/1 (priority date). Applications are processed on a rolling basis. Application fee: $30. Electronic applications accepted. *Financial aid:* In 1998–99, 23 research assistantships, 2 teaching assistantships were awarded.; fellowships, career-related internships or fieldwork, Federal Work-Study, and traineeships also available. Aid available to part-time students. *Faculty research:* Disturbed land restoration, range animal nutrition and behavior, simulation modeling, natural resource planning, riparian ecology. *Unit head:* Dennis Child, Head, 970-491-4994, Fax: 970-491-2339, E-mail: dennisc@picea.cnr.colostate.edu. *Application contact:* Tana Allshouse, Office Manager, 970-491-4994, Fax: 970-491-2339, E-mail: tana@picea.cnr.colostate.edu.

Kansas State University, Graduate School, College of Agriculture, Department of Agronomy, Manhattan, KS 66506. Offers crop science (MS, PhD); range management (MS, PhD); soil science (MS, PhD); weed science (MS, PhD). Part-time programs available. *Faculty:* 51 full-time (2 women). *Students:* 51 full-time (11 women), 5 part-time (2 women); includes 17 minority (6 African Americans, 10 Asian Americans or Pacific Islanders, 1 Hispanic American) Terminal master's awarded for partial completion of doctoral program. *Degree requirements:* For master's, thesis optional, foreign language not required; for doctorate, dissertation required, foreign language not required. *Entrance requirements:* For master's and doctorate, TOEFL (minimum score of 550 required). *Application deadline:* Applications are processed on a rolling basis. Application fee: $0 ($25 for international students). Electronic applications accepted. *Unit head:* Dr. David B. Mengel, Head, 785-532-6101, Fax: 785-532-6094. *Application contact:* Dr. Richard L. Vanderlip, Graduate Coordinator, 785-532-7249, E-mail: vanderrl@ksu.edu.

Montana State University–Bozeman, College of Graduate Studies, College of Agriculture, Department of Animal and Range Sciences, Bozeman, MT 59717. Offers MS. Part-time programs available. *Students:* 8 full-time (0 women), 8 part-time (4 women). Average age 27. 8 applicants, 88% accepted. In 1998, 5 degrees awarded. *Degree requirements:* For master's, thesis or alternative required, foreign language not required. *Entrance requirements:* For master's, GRE General Test, TOEFL (minimum score of 550 required). *Application deadline:* For fall admission, 6/1 (priority date); for spring admission, 11/1. Applications are processed on a rolling basis. Application fee: $50. *Financial aid:* In 1998–99, 9 research assistantships (averaging $10,000 per year), 1 teaching assistantship (averaging $10,000 per year) were awarded.; career-related internships or fieldwork also available. Financial aid application deadline: 3/1; financial aid applicants required to submit FAFSA. *Faculty research:* Reclamation research, animal genetics/breeding, animal nutrition, reproductive physiology, rangeland resources. Total annual research expenditures: $1.1 million. *Unit head:* Dr. Peter Burfening, Head, 406-994-3721, Fax: 409-994-5589, E-mail: uaspb@montana.edu.

New Mexico State University, Graduate School, College of Agriculture and Home Economics, Department of Animal and Range Sciences, Las Cruces, NM 88003-8001. Offers animal science (M Ag, MS, PhD); range science (M Ag, MS, PhD). Part-time programs available. *Faculty:* 17 full-time (1 woman). *Students:* 29 full-time (8 women), 6 part-time (1 woman); includes 5 minority (3 Hispanic Americans, 2 Native Americans), 7 international. Average age 30. 35 applicants, 63% accepted. In 1998, 7 master's, 5 doctorates awarded. *Degree requirements:* For master's, thesis, seminar required, foreign language not required; for doctorate, dissertation, research tool required, foreign language not required. *Entrance requirements:* For master's, minimum GPA of 3.0 in last 60 hours of undergraduate course work (MS); for doctorate, minimum graduate GPA of 3.2. *Application deadline:* For fall admission, 7/1 (priority date); for spring admission, 11/1. Applications are processed on a rolling basis. Application fee: $15 ($35 for international students). Electronic applications accepted. Tuition, state resident: full-time $2,682; part-time $112 per credit. Tuition, nonresident: full-time $8,376; part-time $349 per credit. Tuition and fees vary according to course load. *Financial aid:* Research assistantships, teaching assistantships, Federal Work-Study available. Aid available to part-time students. Financial aid application deadline: 3/1. *Faculty research:* Reproductive physiology, ruminant nutrition, nutrition toxicology, range ecology, wildland hydrology. *Unit head:* Dr. Bobby J. Rankin, Head, 505-646-2514, Fax: 505-646-5441, E-mail: brankin@nmsu.edu.

North Dakota State University, Graduate Studies and Research, College of Agriculture, Department of Animal and Range Sciences, Fargo, ND 58105. Offers animal science (MS, PhD); natural resources management (MS); range science (MS, PhD). *Faculty:* 23 full-time (2 women), 3 part-time (1 woman). *Students:* 23 full-time (7 women), 3 part-time, 2 international. Average age 24. 19 applicants, 100% accepted. *Degree requirements:* For master's and doctorate, thesis/dissertation required, foreign language not required. *Entrance requirements:* For master's and doctorate, GRE General Test, TOEFL (minimum score of 525 required). *Application deadline:* Applications are processed on a rolling basis. Application fee: $25. *Financial aid:* In 1998–99, 21 students received aid, including 20 research assistantships with tuition reimbursements available (averaging $9,200 per year); fellowships, teaching assistantships, Federal Work-Study and institutionally-sponsored loans also available. Financial aid application deadline: 3/15. *Faculty research:* Reproduction, nutrition, meat and muscle biology, breeding/genetics. *Unit head:* Jerrold L. Dodd, Chair, 701-231-7658, Fax: 701-231-7590.

Oregon State University, Graduate School, College of Agricultural Sciences, Department of Rangeland Resources, Corvallis, OR 97331. Offers M Agr, MAIS, MS, PhD. *Faculty:* 21 full-time (0 women), 1 (woman) part-time. *Students:* 15 full-time (7 women), 1 (woman) part-time, 4 international. Average age 32. In 1998, 5 master's awarded (100% found work related to degree). Terminal master's awarded for partial completion of doctoral program. *Degree requirements:* For master's, thesis (MS) required; for doctorate, dissertation required, foreign language not required. *Entrance requirements:* For master's, GRE,TOEFL (minimum score of 550 required), minimum GPA of 3.0 in last 90 hours; for doctorate, GRE, TOEFL (minimum score of 550 required), minimum GPA of 3.0 in last 90 hours. *Application deadline:* For fall admission, 6/1 (priority date); for spring admission, 12/15. Applications are processed on a rolling basis. Application fee: $50. *Financial aid:* Research assistantships, career-related internships or fieldwork, Federal Work-Study, and institutionally-sponsored loans available. Aid available to part-time students. Financial aid application deadline: 2/1. *Faculty research:* Range ecology, watershed science, animal grazing, agroforestry. *Unit head:* Dr. William C. Krueger, Head, 541-737-1615, Fax: 541-737-0504, E-mail: kruegerw@cccmail.orst.edu. *Application contact:* Dr. Paul S. Doescher, Head Adviser, 541-737-1622, Fax: 541-737-0504, E-mail: doeschep@ccmail.orst.edu.

Sul Ross State University, Division of Range Animal Science, Program in Range and Wildlife Management, Alpine, TX 79832. Offers M Ag, MS. Part-time programs available. *Degree requirements:* For master's, thesis required (for some programs), foreign language not required. *Entrance requirements:* For master's, GRE General Test (minimum combined score of 850 required), minimum GPA of 2.5 in last 60 hours of undergraduate work.

Texas A&M University, College of Agriculture and Life Sciences, Department of Rangeland Ecology and Management, College Station, TX 77843. Offers range science (M Agr, MS, PhD). Part-time programs available. *Faculty:* 30 full-time (0 women), 1 (woman) part-time. *Students:* 36 full-time (8 women), 21 part-time (6 women); includes 1 minority (Asian American or Pacific Islander), 13 international. Average age 31. 11 applicants, 82% accepted. In 1998, 15 master's awarded (20% entered university research/teaching, 60% found other work related to degree, 20% continued full-time study); 2 doctorates awarded (50% entered university research/teaching, 50% found other work related to degree). Terminal master's awarded for partial completion of doctoral program. *Degree requirements:* For master's, thesis optional, foreign language not required; for doctorate, dissertation required, foreign language not required. *Entrance requirements:* For master's and doctorate, GRE General Test (minimum combined score of 950 required), TOEFL. *Average time to degree:* Master's–2.5 years full-time, 6 years part-time; doctorate–3 years full-time, 8 years part-time. *Application deadline:* For fall admission, 3/1 (priority date); for spring admission, 8/1 (priority date). Applications are processed on a rolling basis. Application fee: $50 ($75 for international students). *Financial aid:* In 1998–99, 20 research assistantships (averaging $12,480 per year), 13 teaching assistantships (averaging $12,370 per year) were awarded.; fellowships, career-related internships or fieldwork, scholarships, and unspecified assistantships also available. Aid available to part-time students. Financial aid application deadline: 4/1; financial aid applicants required to submit FAFSA. *Faculty research:* Plant ecology, restoration ecology, watershed management, integrated resource management, information technology. *Unit head:* Dr. Robert E. Whitson, Head, 409-845-5579, Fax: 409-845-6430, E-mail: r-whitson@tamu.edu. *Application contact:* Dr. Steven R. Archer, Graduate Adviser, 409-845-5579, Fax: 409-845-6430, E-mail: sarcher@vms1.tamu.edu.

Texas A&M University–Kingsville, College of Graduate Studies, College of Agriculture and Home Economics, Program in Range and Wildlife Management, Kingsville, TX 78363. Offers MS. *Faculty:* 1 full-time (0 women), 7 part-time (0 women). *Students:* 20 full-time (3 women), 12 part-time (3 women). *Degree requirements:* For master's, thesis or alternative, comprehensive exam required, foreign language not required. *Entrance requirements:* For master's, GRE General Test (minimum combined score of 800 required), TOEFL (minimum score of 525 required), minimum GPA of 3.0. *Application deadline:* For fall admission, 6/1; for spring admission, 11/15. Applications are processed on a rolling basis. Application fee: $15 ($25 for international students). Tuition, state resident: full-time $2,062. Tuition, nonresident: full-time $7,246. *Financial aid:* Fellowships, research assistantships available. Financial aid application deadline: 5/15. *Unit head:* Graduate Coordinator, 361-593-3711.

Texas Tech University, Graduate School, College of Agricultural Sciences and Natural Resources, Department of Range, Wildlife, and Fisheries Management, Lubbock, TX 79409. Offers fishery science (MS, PhD); range science (MS, PhD); wildlife science (MS, PhD). Part-time programs available. *Faculty:* 13 full-time (0 women). *Students:* 33 full-time (7 women), 6 part-time (1 woman); includes 2 minority (1 Asian American or Pacific Islander, 1 Hispanic American), 6 international. Average age 29. 19 applicants, 26% accepted. In 1998, 10 master's awarded. *Degree requirements:* For master's, thesis required, foreign language not required; for doctorate, dissertation required. *Entrance requirements:* For master's, GRE General Test (combined average 1012); for doctorate, GRE General Test. *Application deadline:* For fall admission, 4/15 (priority date); for spring admission, 11/1 (priority date). Applications are processed on a rolling basis. Application fee: $25 ($50 for international students). Electronic applications accepted. *Financial aid:* In 1998–99, 24 students received aid, including 21 research assistantships (averaging $8,448 per year), 5 teaching assistantships (averaging $8,020 per year); fellowships, Federal Work-Study and institutionally-sponsored loans also available. Aid available to part-time students. Financial aid application deadline: 5/15; financial aid applicants required to submit FAFSA. *Faculty research:* Use of fire on range lands, waterfowl, upland game birds and playa lakes in the southern Great Plains, reproductive physiology in fisheries. Total annual research expenditures: $1.5 million. *Unit head:* Dr. Phillip J. Zwank, Chairman, 806-742-2841, Fax: 806-742-2280.

The University of Arizona, Graduate College, College of Agriculture, School of Renewable Natural Resources, Division of Range Management, Tucson, AZ 85721. Offers MS, PhD. *Students:* 9 full-time (6 women), 5 part-time (all women); includes 1 minority (Hispanic American) Average age 34. 7 applicants, 71% accepted. In 1998, 3 master's awarded. *Degree requirements:* For master's, computer language, thesis required, foreign language not required; for doctorate, one foreign language (computer language can substitute), dissertation required. *Entrance requirements:* For master's and doctorate, GRE General Test (score in 50th percentile or higher required), TOEFL (minimum score of 550 required), minimum GPA of 3.0. *Application deadline:* For fall admission, 8/1. Applications are processed on a rolling basis. Application fee: $35. *Financial aid:* Research assistantships, teaching assistantships, career-related internships or fieldwork available. *Faculty research:* Criteria for defining, mapping, and evaluating range sites; methods of establishing forage plants on southwestern rangelands; plants for pollution and erosion control, beautification, and browse. *Unit head:* Dr. E. Lamar Smith, Head, 520-621-3803. *Application contact:* Mary E. Soltero, Administrative Assistant, 520-621-7260, Fax: 520-621-8801.

University of California, Berkeley, Graduate Division, College of Natural Resources, Department of Environmental Science, Policy, and Management, Berkeley, CA 94720-1500. Offers environmental science, policy, and management (MS, PhD); forestry (MF); range management (MS). *Faculty:* 67 full-time (15 women), 2 part-time (1 woman). *Students:* 183 full-time (88 women); includes 12 minority (9 Asian Americans or Pacific Islanders, 3 Hispanic Americans), 21 international. *Degree requirements:* For doctorate, dissertation, qualifying exam required. *Entrance requirements:* For master's and doctorate, GRE General Test, minimum GPA of 3.0. *Application deadline:* For fall admission, 12/15. Application fee: $40. Electronic applications accepted. *Unit head:* Dr. James W. Bartolome, Chair, 510-642-7945, Fax: 510-643-5438, E-mail: jwbart@nature.berkeley.edu. *Application contact:* Sue Jennison, Student Affairs Officer, 510-642-6410, Fax: 510-643-5438, E-mail: espmgradproginfo@nature.berkeley.edu.

University of California, Berkeley, Graduate Division, Group in Range Management, Berkeley, CA 94720-1500. Offers MS. *Faculty:* 18 full-time, 2 part-time. *Students:* 6 full-time (2 women). 8 applicants, 38% accepted. In 1998, 1 degree awarded. *Entrance requirements:* For master's, GRE General Test, minimum GPA of 3.0. *Average time to degree:* Master's–2 years full-time. *Application deadline:* For fall admission, 12/15. Application fee: $40. *Financial aid:* Application deadline: 12/15; *Faculty research:* Grassland and savannah ecology, wetlandecology, oak woodland classification, wildlife habitat management. *Unit head:* Barbara W. Allen-Diaz, Chair, 510-642-7125, Fax: 510-643-5098, E-mail: ballen@nature.berkeley.edu. *Application contact:* Sue Jennison, Student Affairs Officer, 510-642-6410, Fax: 510-643-5438, E-mail: espmgradproginfo@nature.berkeley.edu.

University of Idaho, College of Graduate Studies, College of Forestry, Wildlife, and Range Sciences, Department of Range Resources, Moscow, ID 83844-4140. Offers MS, PhD. *Faculty:* 7 full-time (1 woman). *Students:* 4 full-time (3 women), 3 part-time (2 women), 1 international. In 1998, 5 degrees awarded. *Degree requirements:* For doctorate, dissertation required, foreign language not required, foreign language not required. *Entrance requirements:* For master's, minimum GPA of 2.8; for doctorate, minimum undergraduate GPA of 2.8, 3.0 graduate. *Application deadline:* For fall admission, 8/1; for spring admission, 12/15. Application fee: $35 ($45 for international students). *Financial aid:* In 1998–99, 5 research assistantships (averaging $11,662 per year), 2 teaching assistantships (averaging $11,575 per year) were awarded. Financial aid application deadline: 2/15. *Unit head:* Dr. Kendall Johnson, Head, 208-885-6536.

University of Idaho, College of Graduate Studies, College of Forestry, Wildlife, and Range Sciences, Program in Forestry, Wildlife, and Range Sciences, Moscow, ID 83844-4140. Offers PhD. *Faculty:* 3 full-time (0 women). *Students:* 28 full-time (6 women), 32 part-time (9 women); includes 3 minority (1 African American, 1 Asian American or Pacific Islander, 1 Native American), 12 international. In 1998, 4 degrees awarded. *Degree requirements:* For doctorate, dissertation required, foreign language not required. *Entrance requirements:* For doctorate, minimum undergraduate GPA of 2.8, 3.0 graduate. *Application deadline:* For fall admission, 8/1; for spring admission, 12/15. Application fee: $35 ($45 for international students). *Financial aid:* Fellowships, research assistantships, teaching assistantships available. Financial aid application deadline: 2/15. *Application contact:* Dr. Ali Moslemi, Graduate Coordinator, 208-885-6126.

University of Wyoming, Graduate School, College of Agriculture, Department of Rangeland Ecology and Watershed Management, Laramie, WY 82071. Offers MS, PhD. *Faculty:* 9 full-time (0 women). *Students:* 11 full-time (10 women), 10 part-time (5 women). 22 applicants, 14% accepted. In 1998, 4 master's awarded (100% found work related to degree); 1 doctorate awarded. *Degree requirements:* For master's, thesis required (for some programs), foreign language not required; for doctorate, 2 foreign languages (computer language can substitute for one), dissertation required. *Entrance requirements:* For master's and doctorate, GRE General Test, minimum GPA of 3.0. *Application deadline:* For fall admission, 6/1 (priority date). Applications are processed on a rolling basis. Application fee: $40. Tuition, state resident: full-time $2,520; part-time $140 per credit hour. Tuition, nonresident: full-time $7,790; part-time $433 per credit hour. Required fees: $400; $7 per credit hour. Full-time tuition and fees vary according to course load and program. *Financial aid:* In 1998–99, 8 students received aid, including 8 research assistantships; career-related internships or fieldwork and Federal Work-Study also available. Financial aid application deadline: 3/1. *Faculty research:* Plant control, grazing management, riparian restoration, riparian management, reclamation. *Unit head:* Dr. Quentin Skinner, Interim Head, 307-766-6403, E-mail: rng.mgt@uwyo.edu.

Utah State University, School of Graduate Studies, College of Natural Resources, Department of Rangeland Resources, Logan, UT 84322. Offers range ecology (MS, PhD); range science (MS, PhD). Part-time programs available. *Faculty:* 14 full-time (0 women). *Students:* 15 full-time (4 women), 6 part-time; includes 1 minority (African American), 4 international. Average age 24. 10 applicants, 30% accepted. In 1998, 5 master's, 2 doctorates awarded (95% found work related to degree). *Degree requirements:* For master's, thesis required; for doctorate, computer language, dissertation required. *Entrance requirements:* For master's and doctorate, GRE General Test (score in 40th percentile or higher required), TOEFL (minimum score of 550 required), minimum GPA of 3.0. *Application deadline:* For fall admission, 6/15 (priority date); for spring admission, 10/15. Applications are processed on a rolling basis. Application fee: $40. Tuition, state resident: full-time $1,492. Tuition, nonresident: full-time $5,232. Required fees: $434. Tuition and fees vary according to course load. *Financial aid:* In 1998–99, research assistantships with partial tuition reimbursements (averaging $12,000 per year); fellowships, teaching assistantships, career-related internships or fieldwork, Federal Work-Study, and institutionally-sponsored loans also available. *Faculty research:* Range plant ecophysiology, plant community ecology, ruminant nutrition, population ecology. Total annual research expenditures: $3.5 million. *Unit head:* Dr. John Malechek, Head, 435-797-2471.

Water Resources

Colorado State University, Graduate School, College of Engineering, Department of Civil Engineering, Specialization in Water Resources, Hydrologic and Environmental Sciences, Fort Collins, CO 80523-0015. Offers MS, PhD. Part-time programs available. *Faculty:* 5 full-time (1 woman). In 1998, 7 master's, 6 doctorates awarded. Terminal master's awarded for partial completion of doctoral program. *Degree requirements:* For master's, thesis or alternative required, foreign language not required; for doctorate, dissertation required, foreign language not required. *Entrance requirements:* For master's and doctorate, GRE General Test, TOEFL (minimum score of 550 required; 213 for computer-based), minimum GPA of 3.0. *Average time to degree:* Master's–2 years full-time, 5 years part-time; doctorate–4 years full-time. *Application deadline:* For fall admission, 3/1 (priority date); for spring admission, 8/1 (priority date). Applications are processed on a rolling basis. Application fee: $30. Electronic applications accepted. *Financial aid:* Fellowships, research assistantships, teaching assistantships, Federal Work-Study and institutionally-sponsored loans available. *Faculty research:* Flood prediction, stochastic hydrology, drought analysis, watershed modeling, groundwater quality and contamination, drainage, flow through porous media, conjunctive use, numerical modeling. Total annual research expenditures: $600,000. *Unit head:* James W. Warner, Leader, 970-491-8381, Fax: 970-491-7727, E-mail: warner@engr.colostate.edu. *Application contact:* Laurie Howard, Student Adviser, 970-491-5844, Fax: 970-491-7727, E-mail: lhoward@engr.colostate.edu.

Colorado State University, Graduate School, College of Engineering, Department of Civil Engineering, Specialization in Water Resources Planning and Management, Fort Collins, CO 80523-0015. Offers MS, PhD. Part-time programs available. *Faculty:* 3 full-time (0 women), 3 part-time (0 women). In 1998, 6 master's awarded. Terminal master's awarded for partial completion of doctoral program. *Degree requirements:* For master's, thesis or alternative required, foreign language not required; for doctorate, dissertation required, foreign language not required. *Entrance requirements:* For master's and doctorate, GRE General Test, TOEFL (minimum score of 550 required; 213 for computer-based), minimum GPA of 3.0. *Average time to degree:* Master's–2 years full-time, 5 years part-time; doctorate–4 years full-time. *Application deadline:* For fall admission, 3/1 (priority date); for spring admission, 8/1 (priority date). Applications are processed on a rolling basis. Application fee: $30. Electronic applications accepted. *Financial aid:* Fellowships, research assistantships, teaching assistantships, institutionally-sponsored loans available. *Faculty research:* Decision support systems in water resources, river basin modeling and management, geographic information systems,

Water Resources

Colorado State University (continued)

environmental management. Total annual research expenditures: $755,000. *Unit head:* John W. Labadie, Coordinator, 970-491-6898, Fax: 970-491-7727, E-mail: labadie@engr.colostate.edu. *Application contact:* Laurie Howard, Student Adviser, 970-491-5844, Fax: 970-491-7727, E-mail: lhoward@engr.colostate.edu.

Colorado State University, Graduate School, College of Natural Resources, Department of Earth Resources, Program in Watershed Science, Fort Collins, CO 80523-0015. Offers earth resources (PhD); watershed science (MS). *Faculty:* 6 full-time (2 women), 1 part-time (0 women). *Degree requirements:* For master's, thesis required, foreign language not required; for doctorate, one foreign language, dissertation required. *Entrance requirements:* For master's, GRE General Test (minimum score of 640 on verbal section, 660 on quantitative required), GRE Subject Test, TOEFL (minimum score of 550 required), minimum GPA of 3.0. *Application deadline:* For fall admission, 2/1 (priority date). Applications are processed on a rolling basis. Application fee: $30. *Financial aid:* Fellowships, research assistantships, teaching assistantships, career-related internships or fieldwork, Federal Work-Study, and institutionally-sponsored loans available. Financial aid application deadline: 2/15. *Faculty research:* Land use hydrology, water quality, watershed planning and management, snow hydrology, hillslope-wetland hydrology, geographic information systems, risk management. Total annual research expenditures: $750,000. *Unit head:* Dr. John Stednick, Head, 970-491-5662, Fax: 970-491-6307, E-mail: jds@cnr.colostate.edu. *Application contact:* Barbara Holtz, Staff Assistant, 970-491-5662, Fax: 970-491-6307, E-mail: barbh@cnr.colostate.edu.

Duke University, Nicholas School of the Environment, Durham, NC 27708-0328. Offers coastal environmental management (MEM); environmental science and policy (PhD); environmental toxicology, chemistry, and risk assessment (MEM); forest resource management (MF); resource ecology (MEM); resource economics and policy (MEM); water and air resources (MEM). PhD offered through the Graduate School. *Accreditation:* SAF (one or more programs are accredited). Part-time programs available. *Faculty:* 61 full-time (10 women), 23 part-time (3 women). *Students:* 228 full-time (136 women); includes 7 minority (2 African Americans, 4 Asian Americans or Pacific Islanders, 1 Hispanic American), 24 international. Average age 25. 400 applicants, 63% accepted. In 1998, 116 master's, 10 doctorates awarded. Terminal master's awarded for partial completion of doctoral program. *Degree requirements:* For master's, thesis required (for some programs), foreign language not required; for doctorate, dissertation required, foreign language not required. *Entrance requirements:* For master's, GRE General Test, TOEFL, previous course work in biology or ecology, calculus, statistics, and microeconomics; computer familiarity with word processing and data analysis; for doctorate, GRE General Test, TOEFL. *Average time to degree:* Master's–2 years full-time, 3 years part-time; doctorate–5 years full-time, 8 years part-time. *Application deadline:* For fall admission, 2/1; for spring admission, 10/15. Applications are processed on a rolling basis. Application fee: $75. *Financial aid:* In 1998–99, 29 fellowships (averaging $11,500 per year), 53 research assistantships (averaging $2,600 per year), 15 teaching assistantships (averaging $6,000 per year) were awarded.; career-related internships or fieldwork, Federal Work-Study, institutionally-sponsored loans, scholarships, and unspecified assistantships also available. Financial aid application deadline: 2/1; financial aid applicants required to submit FAFSA. *Faculty research:* Ecosystem management, conservation ecology, earth systems, risk assessment. *Unit head:* Dr. Norman L. Christensen, Dean, 919-613-8004, Fax: 919-684-8741. *Application contact:* Bertie S. Belvin, Associate Dean for Academic Services, 919-613-8070, Fax: 919-684-8741, E-mail: envadm@duke.edu.

Announcement: The School of the Environment (Water Resources) focuses on basic physical and chemical processes that affect water and air resources. Effects of land resource management on water quality, quantity, and transport; water and atmospheric chemistry; turbulent transport; and air pollution are emphasized. PhD and professional master's degree programs available.

See in-depth description on page 949.

Iowa State University of Science and Technology, Graduate College, College of Liberal Arts and Sciences, Department of Geological and Atmospheric Sciences, Ames, IA 50011. Offers earth science (MS, PhD); geology (MS, PhD); meteorology (MS, PhD); water resources (MS, PhD). *Faculty:* 17 full-time. *Students:* 28 full-time (8 women), 9 part-time (3 women); includes 1 minority (Asian American or Pacific Islander), 11 international. *Degree requirements:* For master's, thesis required (for some programs); for doctorate, dissertation required. *Entrance requirements:* For master's and doctorate, GRE General Test, TOEFL (minimum score of 530 required). *Application deadline:* For fall admission, 2/15 (priority date). Applications are processed on a rolling basis. Application fee: $20 ($50 for international students). Electronic applications accepted. Tuition, state resident: full-time $3,308. Tuition, nonresident: full-time $9,744. Part-time tuition and fees vary according to course load, campus/location and program. *Unit head:* Dr. Paul G. Spry, Chair, 515-294-4477.

Iowa State University of Science and Technology, Graduate College, Interdisciplinary Programs, Program in Water Resources, Ames, IA 50011. Offers MS, PhD. 8 applicants, 13% accepted. In 1998, 3 master's, 1 doctorate awarded. *Degree requirements:* For master's and doctorate, thesis/dissertation required, foreign language not required. *Entrance requirements:* For master's and doctorate, TOEFL. Application fee: $20 ($50 for international students). Electronic applications accepted. Tuition, state resident: full-time $3,308. Tuition, nonresident: full-time $9,744. Part-time tuition and fees vary according to course load, campus/location and program. *Financial aid:* In 1998–99, 1 research assistantship with partial tuition reimbursement (averaging $8,775 per year) was awarded. *Unit head:* Dr. Robert Horton, Supervisory Committee Chair, 515-294-8921, Fax: 515-294-9573.

Johns Hopkins University, Zanvyl Krieger School of Arts and Sciences, Department of Earth and Planetary Sciences, Baltimore, MD 21218-2699. Offers geochemistry (MA, PhD); geology (MA, PhD); geophysics (MA, PhD); groundwater (MA, PhD); oceanography (MA, PhD); planetary atmosphere (MA, PhD). *Faculty:* 13 full-time (1 woman). *Students:* 21 full-time (9 women), 10 international. Terminal master's awarded for partial completion of doctoral program. *Degree requirements:* For doctorate, dissertation required, foreign language not required. *Entrance requirements:* For master's and doctorate, GRE General Test. *Application deadline:* For fall admission, 1/15 (priority date). Application fee: $55. Tuition: Full-time $23,660. Tuition and fees vary according to program. *Unit head:* Dr. John M. Ferry, Chair, 410-516-7135, Fax: 410-516-7933.

McGill University, Faculty of Graduate Studies and Research, Faculty of Engineering, Department of Civil Engineering and Applied Mechanics, Program in Environmental Engineering and Water Resources Management, Montréal, PQ H3A 2T5, Canada. Offers M Eng, M Sc, PhD. Part-time and evening/weekend programs available. *Degree requirements:* For master's, computer language required, thesis optional, foreign language not required; for doctorate, computer language, dissertation required, foreign language not required. *Entrance requirements:* For master's, TOEFL (minimum score of 550 required), minimum GPA of 3.0; for doctorate, TOEFL (minimum score of 580 required). *Faculty research:* Biological/biochemical treatment, physical and chemical treatment, UV disinfection, site remediation, water resource modelling and optimization.

Rutgers, The State University of New Jersey, New Brunswick, Graduate School, Program in Environmental Sciences, New Brunswick, NJ 08903. Offers air resources (MS, PhD); aquatic biology (MS, PhD); aquatic chemistry (MS, PhD); chemistry and physics of aerosol and hydrosol systems (MS, PhD); environmental chemistry (MS, PhD); environmental microbiology (MS, PhD); environmental toxicology (MS, PhD); exposure assessment (PhD); water and wastewater treatment (MS, PhD); water resources (MS, PhD). Part-time and evening/weekend programs available. *Faculty:* 33 full-time (7 women), 36 part-time (6 women). *Students:* 42 full-time (16 women), 92 part-time (30 women); includes 22 minority (17 Asian Americans or Pacific Islanders, 5 Hispanic Americans), 31 international. Terminal master's awarded for partial completion of doctoral program. *Degree requirements:* For master's, thesis or alternative, oral final exam required, foreign language not required; for doctorate, dissertation, thesis defense, qualifying exam required, foreign language not required. *Entrance requirements:* For master's and doctorate, GRE General Test (minimum score of 500 on verbal section, 600 on quantitative required), TOEFL (minimum score of 590 required). *Application deadline:* For fall admission, 3/1; for spring admission, 11/1. Applications are processed on a rolling basis. Application fee: $50. *Unit head:* Dr. Peter F. Strom, Director, 732-932-8078, Fax: 732-932-8644, E-mail: strom@aesop.rutgers.edu. *Application contact:* Paul J. Lioy, Graduate Admissions Committee, 732-932-0150, Fax: 732-445-0116, E-mail: plioy@eohsi.rutgers.edu.

South Dakota School of Mines and Technology, Graduate Division, Joint PhD Program in Atmospheric, Environmental, and Water Resources, Rapid City, SD 57701-3995. Offers PhD. *Students:* 15 full-time (5 women), 9 international. Average age 47. *Degree requirements:* For doctorate, dissertation required. *Entrance requirements:* For doctorate, GRE General Test, GRE Subject Test, TOEFL (minimum score of 520 required), TWE. *Application deadline:* For fall admission, 6/15 (priority date); for spring admission, 10/15. Applications are processed on a rolling basis. Application fee: $15. Electronic applications accepted. Tuition, state resident: part-time $89 per hour. Tuition, nonresident: part-time $261 per hour. Part-time tuition and fees vary according to program. *Financial aid:* In 1998–99, 2 students received aid, including 1 research assistantship, 1 teaching assistantship *Unit head:* Admissions Office, 902-867-2219, Fax: 902-867-2329, E-mail: admit@stfx.ca. *Application contact:* Brenda Brown, Secretary, 800-454-8162 Ext. 2493, Fax: 605-394-5360, E-mail: graduate_admissions@silver.sdmt.edu.

South Dakota State University, Graduate School, College of Engineering, Joint PhD Program in Atmospheric, Environmental, and Water Resources, Brookings, SD 57007. Offers PhD. Offered jointly with the South Dakota School of Mines and Technology. *Degree requirements:* For doctorate, dissertation, preliminary oral and written exams required. *Entrance requirements:* For doctorate, GRE General Test, GRE Subject Test, TOEFL. *Faculty research:* Use of fabric-reinforced soil wall for internal abutment bridge, end treatment performance evaluation of water and wastewater treatment.

Université du Québec, Institut national de la recherche scientifique, Graduate Programs, Research Center—Water, Ste-Foy, PQ G1V 4C7, Canada. Offers water sciences (M Sc, PhD). Part-time programs available. *Degree requirements:* For master's and doctorate, thesis/dissertation required. *Entrance requirements:* For master's, appropriate bachelor's degree, proficiency in French; for doctorate, appropriate master's degree, proficiency in French. *Faculty research:* Hydrology, purification, water resource management, chemical and biological dynamics of water environment.

The University of Arizona, Graduate College, College of Agriculture, Department of Soil, Water and Environmental Science, Tucson, AZ 85721. Offers MS, PhD. *Faculty:* 17. *Students:* 74 full-time (31 women), 28 part-time (9 women); includes 8 minority (1 African American, 3 Asian Americans or Pacific Islanders, 3 Hispanic Americans, 1 Native American), 33 international. Average age 32. 58 applicants, 60% accepted. In 1998, 14 master's, 5 doctorates awarded. *Degree requirements:* For master's, thesis required, foreign language not required; for doctorate, one foreign language, computer language, dissertation required. *Entrance requirements:* For master's and doctorate, TOEFL (minimum score of 550 required). *Application deadline:* For fall admission, 3/1. Applications are processed on a rolling basis. Application fee: $35. *Financial aid:* Research assistantships, teaching assistantships, Federal Work-Study, institutionally-sponsored loans, scholarships, and tuition waivers (full and partial) available. Financial aid application deadline: 5/1. *Faculty research:* Plant production, environmental microbiology, contaminant flow and transport. *Unit head:* Dr. Peter Wierenga, Head, 520-621-7228. *Application contact:* Dr. Mark Brusseau, Graduate Admissions Coordinator, 520-621-3228, Fax: 520-621-1647.

The University of Arizona, Graduate College, College of Engineering and Mines, Department of Hydrology and Water Resources, Tucson, AZ 85721. Offers hydrology (MS, PhD); water resource administration (MS, PhD). Part-time programs available. *Faculty:* 30. *Students:* 90 full-time (22 women), 38 part-time (18 women); includes 6 minority (1 African American, 3 Asian Americans or Pacific Islanders, 2 Hispanic Americans), 25 international. Average age 31. 80 applicants, 76% accepted. In 1998, 15 master's, 9 doctorates awarded (100% found work related to degree). *Degree requirements:* For master's and doctorate, computer language, thesis/dissertation required, foreign language not required. *Entrance requirements:* For master's, GRE General Test, TOEFL (minimum score of 550 required), minimum undergraduate GPA of 3.0; for doctorate, GRE General Test, TOEFL (minimum score of 550 required), minimum GPA of 3.2 (undergraduate), 3.4 (graduate). *Application deadline:* For fall admission, 4/15. Applications are processed on a rolling basis. Application fee: $35. *Financial aid:* Fellowships, research assistantships, teaching assistantships, institutionally-sponsored loans and scholarships available. Financial aid application deadline: 1/31. *Faculty research:* Subsurface and surface hydrology, water quality, hydrometeorology/climatology, applied remote sensing, water resource systems. *Unit head:* Dr. Soroosh Sorooshian, Head, 520-621-7121. *Application contact:* Teresa Handloser, Academic Adviser, 520-621-3131, Fax: 520-621-1422.

University of Florida, Graduate School, College of Agriculture, Department of Soil and Water Science, Gainesville, FL 32611. Offers M Ag, MS, PhD. Part-time programs available. *Faculty:* 48. *Students:* 30 full-time (7 women), 13 part-time (1 woman); includes 5 minority (4 Asian Americans or Pacific Islanders, 1 Hispanic American), 19 international. 39 applicants, 64% accepted. In 1998, 9 master's, 5 doctorates awarded. Terminal master's awarded for partial completion of doctoral program. *Degree requirements:* For master's, thesis optional; for doctorate, dissertation required. *Entrance requirements:* For master's and doctorate, GRE General Test, minimum GPA of 3.0. *Application deadline:* For fall admission, 6/1 (priority date); for spring admission, 10/1. Applications are processed on a rolling basis. Application fee: $20. Electronic applications accepted. *Financial aid:* In 1998–99, 33 students received aid, including 27 research assistantships, 2 teaching assistantships; fellowships, career-related internships or fieldwork, Federal Work-Study, institutionally-sponsored loans, and unspecified assistantships also available. Aid available to part-time students. *Faculty research:* Environmental fate and transport of pesticides, conservation, wetlands, land application of nonhazardous waste, soil/water agrochemical management. *Unit head:* Dr. Randy Brown, Chair, 352-392-1804, Fax: 352-392-3399, E-mail: rbb@gnv.ifas.ufl.edu. *Application contact:* Dr. K. Ramesh Reddy, Graduate Coordinator, 352-392-1804, Fax: 352-392-3399, E-mail: krr @gnv.ifas.ufl.edu.

University of Illinois at Chicago, Graduate College, College of Liberal Arts and Sciences, Department of Earth and Environmental Sciences, Chicago, IL 60607-7128. Offers crystallography (MS, PhD); environmental geology (MS, PhD); geochemistry (MS, PhD); geology (MS, PhD); geomorphology (MS, PhD); geophysics (MS, PhD); geotechnical engineering and geosciences (PhD); hydrogeology (MS, PhD); low-temperature and organic geochemistry (MS, PhD); mineralogy (MS, PhD); paleoclimatology (MS, PhD); paleontology (MS, PhD); petrology (MS, PhD); quaternary geology (MS, PhD); sedimentology (MS, PhD); water resources (MS, PhD). *Faculty:* 9 full-time (2 women). *Students:* 8 full-time (2 women), 1 part-time, 2 international. *Degree requirements:* For master's and doctorate, thesis/dissertation required. *Entrance requirements:* For master's and doctorate, GRE General Test, TOEFL (minimum score of 550 required), minimum GPA of 3.75 on a 5.0 scale. *Application deadline:* For fall admission, 7/3; for spring admission, 11/8. Application fee: $40 ($50 for international students). *Unit head:* A. F. Koster Van Groos, Acting Head, 312-996-3153. *Application contact:* Martin Flower, Graduate Director, 312-996-9662.

University of Kansas, Graduate School, School of Engineering, Department of Civil and Environmental Engineering, Lawrence, KS 66045. Offers civil engineering (MS, DE, PhD); environmental engineering (MS, PhD); environmental science (MS, PhD); water resources engineering (MS); water resources science (MS). *Faculty:* 20 full-time (0 women). *Students:* 23 full-time (6 women), 80 part-time (15 women); includes 9 minority (1 African American, 3 Asian Americans or Pacific Islanders, 4 Hispanic Americans, 1 Native American), 29 international. *Degree requirements:* For master's, thesis or alternative, exam required, foreign language not required; for doctorate, dissertation, comprehensive exam required. *Entrance requirements:* For master's and doctorate, Michigan English Language Assessment Battery, TOEFL, minimum GPA of 3.0. *Application deadline:* For fall admission, 7/1. Application fee: $30 ($45 for international students). *Unit head:* Steve McCabe, Chair, 785-864-3766. *Application contact:* David Parr, Graduate Director.

University of Minnesota, Twin Cities Campus, Graduate School, College of Agricultural, Food, and Environmental Sciences, Department of Soil, Water, and Climate, Minneapolis, MN 55455-0213. Offers MS, PhD. *Degree requirements:* For master's, thesis or alternative required, foreign language not required; for doctorate, dissertation required, foreign language not required. *Entrance requirements:* For master's and doctorate, GRE General Test (minimum combined score of 1650 on three sections required), minimum GPA of 3.0. Electronic applications accepted. *Faculty research:* Soil water and atmospheric resources, soil physical management, agricultural chemicals and their management, plant nutrient management, biological nitrogen fixation.

University of Missouri–Rolla, Graduate School, School of Mines and Metallurgy, Department of Geology and Geophysics, Rolla, MO 65409-0910. Offers geochemistry (MS, PhD); geology (MS, PhD); geophysics (MS, PhD); groundwater and environmental geology (MS, PhD). Part-time programs available. *Faculty:* 8 full-time (1 woman). *Students:* 28 full-time (11 women), 7 international. *Degree requirements:* For master's, computer language, thesis required, foreign language not required; for doctorate, computer language, dissertation, departmental qualifying exam required, foreign language not required. *Entrance requirements:* For master's, GRE General Test (minimum combined score of 1100 required), GRE Subject Test, TOEFL (minimum score of 550 required), minimum GPA of 3.0 in last 4 semesters; for doctorate, GRE General Test (minimum combined score of 1100 required), GRE Subject Test, TOEFL (minimum score of 550 required). *Application deadline:* For fall admission, 7/1; for spring admission, 12/1. Applications are processed on a rolling basis. Application fee: $25. Electronic applications accepted. *Unit head:* Dr. Richard D. Hagni, Chairman, 573-341-4616, Fax: 573-341-6935, E-mail: rhagni@umr.edu.

University of Nevada, Las Vegas, Graduate College, College of Science, Department of Geoscience, Program in Water Resources Management, Las Vegas, NV 89154-9900. Offers MS. *Faculty:* 19 full-time (2 women). *Students:* 1 (woman) full-time, 10 part-time (1 woman); includes 1 minority (Hispanic American) 4 applicants, 100% accepted. In 1998, 2 degrees awarded. *Degree requirements:* For master's, thesis, comprehensive exam required, foreign language not required. *Entrance requirements:* For master's, GRE Subject Test, minimum GPA of 2.75. *Application deadline:* For fall admission, 4/15 (priority date); for spring admission, 9/15. Applications are processed on a rolling basis. Application fee: $40 ($95 for international students). *Financial aid:* Research assistantships, teaching assistantships available. Financial aid application deadline: 3/1. *Unit head:* Dr. David Kreamer, Director, 702-895-3262. *Application contact:* Graduate College Admissions Evaluator, 702-895-3320.

University of New Brunswick, School of Graduate Studies, Faculty of Engineering, Department of Civil Engineering, Fredericton, NB E3B 5A3, Canada. Offers environmental engineering (M Eng, M Sc E, PhD); geotechnical engineering (M Eng, M Sc E); structures and structural foundations (M Eng, M Sc E, PhD); transportation engineering (M Eng, M Sc E, PhD); water resources and hydrology (M Eng, M Sc E, PhD). Part-time programs available. *Degree requirements:* For master's, thesis required, foreign language not required; for doctorate, dissertation, qualifying exam required, foreign language not required. *Entrance requirements:* For master's and doctorate, TOEFL, TWE, minimum GPA of 3.0.

University of New Hampshire, Graduate School, College of Life Sciences and Agriculture, Graduate Programs in the Biological Sciences and Natural Resources, Durham, NH 03824. Offers animal and nutritional sciences (MS, PhD); biochemistry and molecular biology (MS, PhD); biology (MS); genetics (MS, PhD); microbiology (MS, PhD); natural resources (MS, PhD), including environmental conservation (MS), forestry (MS), natural resources (PhD), soil science (MS), water resources management (MS), wildlife (MS); plant biology (MS, PhD); zoology (MS, PhD). Part-time programs available. *Faculty:* 129 full-time. *Students:* 127 full-time (74 women), 111 part-time (56 women); includes 6 minority (4 Asian Americans or Pacific Islanders, 2 Hispanic Americans), 31 international. Terminal master's awarded for partial completion of doctoral program. *Degree requirements:* For doctorate, dissertation required, foreign language not required. *Entrance requirements:* For master's, GRE General Test. *Application deadline:* Applications are processed on a rolling basis. Application fee: $50. Tuition, area resident: Full-time $5,750; part-time $319 per credit. Tuition, state resident: full-time $8,625. Tuition, nonresident: full-time $14,640; part-time $598 per credit. Required fees: $224 per semester. Tuition and fees vary according to course load, degree level and program. *Unit head:* Dr. William Mautz, Interim Dean, College of Life Sciences and Agriculture, 603-862-1450.

University of New Hampshire, Graduate School, College of Life Sciences and Agriculture, Graduate Programs in the Biological Sciences and Natural Resources, Department of Natural Resources, Option in Water Resources Management, Durham, NH 03824. Offers MS. *Students:* 3 full-time (2 women), 7 part-time (4 women), 1 international. Average age 28. 11 applicants, 27% accepted. In 1998, 4 degrees awarded. *Degree requirements:* For master's, thesis or alternative required, foreign language not required. *Entrance requirements:* For master's, GRE General Test. *Application deadline:* For fall admission, 4/1. Application fee: $50. Tuition, area resident: Full-time $5,750; part-time $319 per credit. Tuition, state resident: full-time $8,625. Tuition, nonresident: full-time $14,640; part-time $598 per credit. Required fees: $224 per semester. Tuition and fees vary according to course load, degree level and program. *Financial aid:* In 1998–99, 3 research assistantships were awarded.; teaching assistantships, Federal Work-Study, scholarships, and tuition waivers (full and partial) also available. Financial aid application deadline: 2/15. *Application contact:* Dr. Robert Harter, Graduate Coordinator, 603-862-3944.

University of New Mexico, Graduate School, Program in Water Resources, Albuquerque, NM 87131-2039. Offers MWR. Part-time programs available. *Faculty:* 1 full-time (0 women). *Students:* 8 full-time (5 women), 17 part-time (7 women); includes 4 minority (all Hispanic Americans), 1 international. Average age 37. 13 applicants, 85% accepted. In 1998, 3 degrees awarded. *Degree requirements:* For master's, professional project required, foreign language and thesis not required. Application fee: $25. *Financial aid:* In 1998–99, 10 students received aid, including 5 fellowships (averaging $2,040 per year), 3 research assistantships (averaging $5,014 per year) *Faculty research:* Sustainable water resources, development of the Rio Grande Basin, grand service water exchange modeling. Total annual research expenditures: $91,178. *Unit head:* Dr. Michael E. Campana, Director, 505-277-7759, Fax: 505-277-5226. *Application contact:* Darlene M. Tanis, Administrative Assistant, 505-277-7759, Fax: 505-277-8226, E-mail: dtanis@unm.edu.

University of Oklahoma, Graduate College, College of Engineering, School of Civil Engineering and Environmental Science, Program in Environmental Science, Norman, OK 73019-0390. Offers air (M Env Sc); environmental science (PhD); groundwater management (M Env Sc); hazardous solid waste (M Env Sc); occupational safety and health (M Env Sc); process design (M Env Sc); water quality resources (M Env Sc). Part-time and evening/weekend programs available. *Students:* 10 full-time (3 women), 24 part-time (14 women); includes 3 minority (1 African American, 1 Hispanic American, 1 Native American), 6 international. Terminal master's awarded for partial completion of doctoral program. *Degree requirements:* For master's, comprehensive and oral exams required, foreign language and thesis not required; for doctorate, dissertation, comprehensive, oral, and qualifying exams required. *Entrance requirements:* For master's, GRE General Test, TOEFL (minimum score of 575 required), minimum GPA of 3.0; for doctorate, GRE General Test, TOEFL (minimum score of 575 required), minimum graduate GPA of 3.5. *Application deadline:* For fall admission, 4/1 (priority date). Applications are processed on a rolling basis. Application fee: $25. Tuition, state resident: part-time $86 per credit hour. Tuition, nonresident: part-time $275 per credit hour. Tuition and fees vary according to course level, course load and program. *Unit head:* Dr. Jeffrey Falzarano, Graduate Coordinator, 504-280-7184, Fax: 504-280-5542, E-mail: jmfna@uno.edu. *Application contact:* Robert C. Knox, Graduate Liaison, 405-325-4256, Fax: 405-325-7508.

University of Vermont, Graduate College, School of Natural Resources, Program in Water Resources, Burlington, VT 05405-0160. Offers MS. *Entrance requirements:* For master's, GRE General Test, TOEFL (minimum score of 550 required).

University of Wisconsin–Madison, Graduate School, Institute for Environmental Studies, Water Resources Management Program, Madison, WI 53706-1380. Offers MS. Part-time programs available. *Students:* 19 full-time (8 women), 9 part-time (4 women); includes 2 minority (1 Hispanic American, 1 Native American), 2 international. 38 applicants, 58% accepted. In 1998, 12 degrees awarded. *Degree requirements:* For master's, practicum required, foreign language and thesis not required. *Entrance requirements:* For master's, GRE General Test. *Application deadline:* For fall admission, 2/15; for spring admission, 10/15. Application fee: $45. Electronic applications accepted. *Financial aid:* In 1998–99, 4 students received aid, including 3 teaching assistantships with full tuition reimbursements available; fellowships, research assistantships, career-related internships or fieldwork, Federal Work-Study, grants, and unspecified assistantships also available. Financial aid application deadline: 1/2; financial aid applicants required to submit FAFSA. *Faculty research:* Geology, hydrogeology, water chemistry, limnology, oceanography, water law, environmental engineering, economics, urban planning, geographic information systems. *Unit head:* Jean M. Bahr, Chair, 608-263-1796, Fax: 608-262-2273, E-mail: iesgrad@macc.wisc.edu. *Application contact:* Jim E. Miller, Clerical Assistant, 608-263-1796, Fax: 608-262-2273, E-mail: jemiller@facstaff.wisc.edu.

Utah State University, School of Graduate Studies, College of Natural Resources, Watershed Science Program, Logan, UT 84322. Offers MS, PhD. Part-time programs available. *Faculty:* 6 full-time (2 women). Average age 36. 15 applicants, 27% accepted. In 1998, 5 master's awarded. *Degree requirements:* For doctorate, dissertation required. *Entrance requirements:* For master's and doctorate, GRE General Test (score in 40th percentile or higher required), TOEFL (minimum score of 550 required), minimum GPA of 3.0. *Application deadline:* For fall admission, 6/15 (priority date); for spring admission, 10/15. Application fee: $40. Tuition, state resident: full-time $1,492. Tuition, nonresident: full-time $5,232. Required fees: $434. Tuition and fees vary according to course load. *Financial aid:* In 1998–99, 3 research assistantships with partial tuition reimbursements (averaging $12,000 per year) were awarded. *Faculty research:* Hydrology, stream and riparian ecology, limnology and lake management; water resources policy, fluvial geomorphology, nutrient cycling. Total annual research expenditures: $1.5 million. *Unit head:* James P. Dobrowolski, Director, 435-797-2457, Fax: 435-797-3796, E-mail: watersci@cc.usu.edu.

DUKE UNIVERSITY

Nicholas School of the Environment

Programs of Study

The Nicholas School has a commitment to education and research addressing an area of vital concern—the quality of the Earth's environment and the sustainable use of its natural resources. The Nicholas School is built on the belief that finding workable solutions to environmental issues requires the viewpoints of more than one discipline.

With facilities at Duke's Durham campus and the Duke Marine Laboratory within the Outer Banks on the North Carolina coast, the Nicholas School is organized around program areas and research centers rather than traditionally structured departments. The centers serve to focus interdisciplinary research and educational activity on a variety of national and international environmental issues.

The Nicholas School's faculty members specialize in an array of disciplines focused within the broad categories of ecosystem science, earth systems science, environmental quality and health, and environmental economics and policy. Through joint faculty appointments and research, the School is affiliated with Duke's Departments of Botany, Biological Anthropology and Anatomy, Cell Biology, Chemistry, Economics, Statistics, and Zoology; the School of Engineering; and Duke University Medical Center. Joint-degree programs are offered with the School of Law, Fuqua School of Business, the Terry Sanford Institute of Public Policy, and the Master of Arts in Teaching program.

Students may earn a Master of Environmental Management (M.E.M.) or Master of Forestry (M.F.) degree through the Nicholas School of the Environment. These are two-year professional degrees that require 48 units of credit. A one-year, 30-unit M.F. program is available for students who have a Bachelor of Science in Forestry from an accredited forestry school. A reduced-credit option is also available through the Senior Professional Program for students who have at least five years of related professional experience; this option requires a minimum of 30 units and one semester in residence.

The Ph.D. is offered through the Graduate School of Duke University and is appropriate for students planning careers in teaching or research. The M.S. degree may be awarded as part of a Ph.D. program.

Course work and research for the School's professional degrees are concentrated in six program areas: coastal environmental management; environmental toxicology, chemistry, and risk assessment; forest resource management; resource ecology; resource economics and policy; and water and air resources. In addition, faculty members at the Nicholas School's Marine Laboratory offer opportunities for course work and research in the basic ocean sciences, marine biology, environmental and human health sciences, and marine biotechnology.

Research Facilities

The Nicholas School of the Environment is headquartered in the Levine Science Research Center, an interdisciplinary, state-of-the-art facility that is fully equipped to meet the technical demands of modern teaching and research. The center's fiber-optic networking systems give students access to high-performance computing at Duke and around the world. Students also have access to an online reference network linking all libraries at Duke University, North Carolina State University, and the University of North Carolina at Chapel Hill. The 8,000-acre Duke Forest lies adjacent to campus and in two neighboring counties. A phytotron with fifty controlled-growth chambers and greenhouses is available for plant research.

The Marine Laboratory in Beaufort, North Carolina, is a complete residential research and teaching facility with modern laboratories, computer facilities, and an extensive library. It is the home port for the 135-foot oceanographic research vessel *Cape Hatteras* and the 57-foot coastal ocean research and training vessel *Susan Hudson*.

Financial Aid

Scholarships, fellowships, assistantships, and student loans are available from a variety of sources, and many students receive financial aid. The Nicholas School maintains its own career services office to assist students in finding paid internships and permanent employment.

Cost of Study

Tuition was $18,100 per year full-time and $800 per unit part-time in 1998–99. A health fee of $430 was required.

Living and Housing Costs

Most graduate and professional students live off campus and many share rent with 1 or 2 roommates. Rent for apartments and houses in Durham varies widely; students can expect to pay from $200 to $600 monthly. Living costs in Beaufort are comparable. A limited amount of on-campus housing is also available on the Durham campus.

Student Group

Approximately 200 students are enrolled in the Nicholas School of the Environment, and 50 are in the Department of the Environment of the Graduate School. The ratio of men to women is approximately equal. The School draws students with undergraduate degrees from liberal arts colleges and research universities and from international locations. While prior work experience is not a requirement for admission, it is highly valued.

Location

Durham (population 198,000), Raleigh, and Chapel Hill form an urban area known as the Research Triangle of North Carolina. Area residents enjoy annual outdoor festivals and numerous other events in drama, music, dance, and the visual arts. The Atlantic Ocean and the Blue Ridge Mountains are each within several hours' drive. The Marine Laboratory is located 180 miles east, on Pivers Island within North Carolina's Outer Banks, adjacent to the historic town of Beaufort (population 5,000).

The University and The School

Noted for its magnificent Gothic architecture and its academic excellence, Duke is among the smallest of the nation's leading universities, having a total enrollment of about 10,000. Its spacious campus is bounded on the east by residential sections of Durham and on the west by the Duke Forest.

The Nicholas School of the Environment was established in 1991, but its roots date back to 1938. Duke's Department of Geology was added to the School in 1997. The Nicholas School is the only private graduate school of forestry, environmental studies, and marine sciences in the country. Its professional forestry program has been continuously accredited by the Society of American Foresters since 1938.

Applying

Most students are admitted for fall matriculation. Applications must be received by February 1 for priority consideration. Those received after the priority deadline are considered if space is available. Applications for spring are considered on a space-available basis; the deadline is October 15. GRE scores are required. Applicants for federal financial aid must submit a Free Application for Federal Student Aid (FAFSA).

Applicants interested only in research or summer courses at the Marine Laboratory should direct their first inquiry to the Director of Admissions, Duke University Nicholas School of the Environment Marine Laboratory.

Individuals interested in M.S. or Ph.D. degrees in earth or ocean sciences through the School's Division of Earth and Ocean Sciences should see the separate listing under Geology Directory of this guide.

Correspondence and Information

Enrollment Services Office
Nicholas School of the Environment
Duke University
Box 90330
Durham, North Carolina 27708-0330
Telephone: 919-613-8000
E-mail: envadm@duke.edu
World Wide Web: http://www.env.duke.edu

Admissions Office
Duke Marine Laboratory
Nicholas School of the Environment
Duke University
135 Duke Marine Lab Road
Beaufort, North Carolina 28516-9721
Telephone: 252-504-7502
E-mail: hnearing@mail.duke.edu
World Wide Web: http://www.env.duke.edu

Duke University

THE FACULTY AND THEIR RESEARCH

Norman L. Christensen, Dean, Nicholas School of the Environment; Ph.D., California, Santa Barbara, 1973. Effects of disturbance on plant populations and communities, patterns of forest development, remote sensing of forest change, fire ecology.

Core Faculty/Durham

Dianne Ahmann, Ph.D., Harvard, 1993. Roles of microorganisms in the biogeochemical cycling of metals and trace elements.

Paul A. Baker, Ph.D., California, San Diego (Scripps), 1981. Geochemistry and diagenesis of marine sediments and sedimentary rocks and their despositial history.

Alan E. Boudreau, Ph.D., Washington, 1986. Understanding the crystallization of large layered intrusions with particular attention on the Archean Stillwater complex in Montana.

James S. Clark, Ph.D., Minnesota, 1988. Factors responsible for ecosystem patterns and how they respond to long-term changes in the physical environment, especially fire.

Sherri L. Cooper, Ph.D., Johns Hopkins, 1993. Using paleoecological tools to recreate the history of water quality and vegetation changes in aquatic systems and watersheds related to both climatic influences and anthropogenic effects.

Bruce Hayward Corliss, Ph.D., Rhode Island, 1978. Cenozoic paleoceanography and studies of marine microfossils and deep-sea sediments.

Richard T. Di Giulio, Ph.D., Virginia Tech, 1982. Aquatic toxicology; metabolism, modes of action, and genotoxicity in aquatic animals; development of biochemical responses as biomarkers of environmental quality.

Jonathan H. Freedman, Ph.D., Yeshiva (Einstein), 1986. Molecular biology and toxicology, molecular mechanisms regulating an organism's response to environmental stress.

Peter K. Haff, Ph.D., Virginia, 1970. Quantitative modeling techniques, including computer simulation, to describe and predict the course of natural geological processes that occur on the surface of the Earth.

Patrick N. Halpin, Ph.D., Virginia, 1995. Landscape ecology, GIS and remote sensing and international conservation management.

Robert G. Healy, Ph.D., UCLA, 1972. Natural resource, land-use, and environmental policy; reconciling Third World development with environmental quality and sustainable use of natural resources; tourism policy.

S. Duncan Heron, Ph.D., North Carolina, 1958. Broad research in sedimentary geology, including studies in Cretaceous and Tertiary elastic sequences in the Atlantic Coastal Plain.

Jeffrey A. Karson, Ph.D., SUNY at Albany, 1977. Structural and tectonic analysis of rift and transform plate boundaries.

Gabriel G. Katul, Ph.D., California, Davis, 1993. Hydrology and fluid mechanisms in the environment.

Prasad S. Kasibhatla, Ph.D., Kentucky, 1988. Anthropogenic emissions on atmospheric composition and reactivity on marine and terrestrial ecosystems.

Richard F. Kay, Ph.D., Yale, 1973. The evolutionary history of the order primates, including further documenting the fossil history of Neotropical monkeys.

Emily M. Klein, Ph.D., Columbia, 1989. The geochemistry of ocean ridge basalts using diverse tools of major and trace element and isotropic analysis.

Kenneth R. Knoerr, Ph.D., Yale, 1961. Development of predictive models for energy and mass exchange processes, role of vegetation in emission and removal of atmospheric pollutants.

Robert O. Keohane, Ph.D., Harvard, 1966. Role of international institutions, including international environmental regimes; how such institutions become effective in promoting concern about the environment.

Randall A. Kramer, Ph.D., California, Davis, 1980. Environmental economics, economic valuation of environmental quality, quantitative analysis of environmental policies.

Michael L. Lavine, Ph.D., Minnesota, 1987. Sensitivity and robustness of Bayesian analyses, statistical issues in energy and environmental studies, Bayesian nonparametrics, spatial statistics.

Daniel A. Livingstone, Ph.D., Yale, 1953. The circulation and chemical composition of lakes, particularly in Africa, and how the distribution and abundance of organisms are affected by them.

M. Susan Lozier, Ph.D., Washington (Seattle), 1989. Mesoscale and large-scale ocean dynamics. Research approach ranges from the application of numerical models to the analysis of observational data with the focus on the testing and development of theory.

Lynn A. Maguire, Ph.D., Utah State, 1980. Application of simulation modeling and decision analysis in natural resource management; endangered species; conservation biology; conflict resolution.

Peter E. Malin, Ph.D., Princeton, 1978. Tectonics, seismic wave propagation and earthquakes with current focus on central California.

Carol A. Mansfield, Ph.D., Maryland, 1994. Environmental economics and applied microeconomics, especially valuation and survey methods.

Marie Lynn Miranda, Ph.D., Harvard, 1990. Natural resource and environmental economics with interdisciplinary, policy-oriented perspectives.

Ram Oren, Ph.D., Oregon State, 1984. Physiological ecology and its application to quantifying water, nutrient, and carbon dynamics in forest ecosystems.

Ronald Perkins, Ph.D., Indiana, 1962. Pleistocene and Holocene carbonates of islands in the British West Indies and oil field analogs.

Orrin H. Pilkey, Ph.D., Florida State, 1962. Basic and applied coastal geology, focusing primarily on barrier island coasts.

Kenneth H. Reckhow, Ph.D., Harvard, 1977. Water-quality modeling and applied statistics, decision and risk analysis for water-quality management, uncertainty analysis and parameter estimation in water-quality models.

Curtis J. Richardson, Ph.D., Tennessee, 1972. Wetland ecology, ecosystem analysis, soil chemistry/plant nutrition relationships, phosphorus cycling, effects of pollutants on biogeochemical cycling in ecosystems.

Daniel D. Richter, Ph.D., Duke, 1980. Forest ecosystem ecology, biogeochemistry of acid soils, soil and watershed management in the humid temperate zone and the tropics.

Stuart Rojstaczer, Ph.D., Stanford, 1988. The role of fluid in crustal processes with particular interest in geologic hazards, subsidiary interest in the development of new techniques to determine elastic and fluid flow properties of the Earth in situ.

Edwin A. Romanowicz, Ph.D., Syracuse, 1993. Surface and groundwater hydrology, particularly wetland hydrology and groundwater/lake interaction.

William H. Schlesinger, Ph.D., Cornell, 1976. Global biogeochemistry, particularly the role of soils in global element cycles.

Eylon Shalev, Ph.D., Yale, 1993. Three-dimensional analysis and imaging of the crust, currently concentrating on tomographic inversion for whole-volume three-dimensional attributes and surface inversion for three-dimensional interfaces.

John T. Sigmon, Ph.D., Duke, 1983. Atmospheric boundary layer processes, fate and transport of chemical compounds in the atmosphere.

V. Kerry Smith, Ph.D., Rutgers, 1970. Resource and environmental economics, nonmarket valuation of environmental resources, policy decisions for environmental risk, applied econometrics.

Laura K. Snook, Ph.D., Grinnell, 1993. Application of ecological knowledge to the management and conservation of forests.

Craig A. Stow, Ph.D., Duke, 1992. Application of statistical modeling techniques to assist with management decisions in aquatic ecosystems.

John W. Terborgh, Ph.D., Harvard, 1963. Tropical ecology and biogeography, adaptive strategies of plants and animals, conservation biology.

Jerry J. Tulis, Ph.D., Illinois, 1965. Occupational and environmental biohazards, indoor air quality, waste management.

Dean L. Urban, Ph.D., Tennessee, 1986. Landscape ecology, forest ecosystem dynamics, application of simulation models to assess forest response to land-use practice and climatic change.

Carel P. van Schaik, Ph.D., Utrecht (Netherlands), 1979. Fungivores in tropical rain forests and their response to resource seasonality and disturbance, strategies of conserving biological diversity.

Dharni Vasudevan, Ph.D., Johns Hopkins, 1996. Fate of anthropogenic and naturally occurring organic compounds in aquatic environments, interfacial processes in surface waters and subsurface environments.

P. Aarne Vesilind, Ph.D., North Carolina, 1968. Wastewater and sludge management and disposal, development of solutions to solid waste and resource recovery problems.

Jonathan B. Wiener, J.D., Harvard, 1987. Interplay of science, economics, and law in addressing environmental and human health risks.

Robert L. Wolpert, Ph.D., Princeton, 1976. Theory and foundations of statistical inference, application of advanced mathematical, numerical, and statistical methods to the modeling and study of environmental and biological systems.

Core Faculty/Beaufort

Richard T. Barber, Ph.D., Stanford, 1967. Thermal dynamics and ocean basin productivity.

Celia Bonaventura, Ph.D., Texas, 1968. Structure-function relationships of macromolecules; biotechnology.

Joseph Bonaventura, Ph.D., Texas, 1968. Marine biomedicine, protein structure-function relationships.

Larry B. Crowder, Ph.D., Michigan State, 1978. Marine ecology and fisheries oceanography.

Richard B. Forward Jr., Ph.D., California, Santa Barbara, 1969. Physiological ecology of marine animals.

William W. Kirby-Smith, Ph.D., Duke, 1970. Ecology of marine-freshwater systems.

Patricia D. McClellan-Green, Ph.D., North Carolina State, 1989. Molecular toxicology and xenobiotic metabolism by marine organisms.

Michael K. Orbach, Ph.D., California, San Diego, 1975. Application of social and policy sciences to coastal and ocean policy and management.

Joseph S. Ramus, Ph.D., Berkeley, 1968. Algal ecological physiology, estuarine dynamics, biotechnology.

Andrew J. Read, Ph.D., Guelph, 1989. Biology and conservation of small cetaceans.

Daniel Rittschof, Ph.D., Michigan, 1975. Chemical ecology of marine organisms.

OREGON STATE UNIVERSITY

College of Forestry

Programs of Study

Graduate programs leading to the Master of Forestry (M.F.), Master of Science (M.S.), or Doctor of Philosophy (Ph.D.) degrees are offered in four departments of the College of Forestry. The Department of Forest Engineering offers study in forest hydrology, timber harvest systems, logging engineering, forest operations, and a joint program in harvesting and silviculture with the Department of Forest Science. The Department of Forest Products offers concentrations in wood science, computer-aided wood processing, timber engineering, biodeterioration and wood preservation, materials science/wood composites, and forest products marketing. The Department of Forest Resources includes study in community and resource development, forest biometrics/modeling, forest economics, forest management, forest planning administration, forest social science, forest recreation, land use planning, policy, natural resource education and extension, remote sensing, and GIS. The Department of Forest Science offers concentrations in forest ecology, forest genetics, integrated forest protection, forest physiology, and silviculture.

Research Facilities

The College has access to two major forest properties dedicated to research and education. The College Research Forests comprise 14,000 acres and are located 5 miles north of campus. The 16,000-acre H. J. Andrews Experimental Biological Reserve, located on the west slopes of the high Cascades, is jointly managed by the USDA Forest Service and Oregon State University under a National Science Foundation long-term agreement. In three buildings on campus, the College has extensive and well-equipped laboratories, supercomputers, mainframe and minicomputers, three student microcomputer labs, and graduate student office space.

Financial Aid

Most Ph.D. and M.S. and some M.F. students are offered research or teaching assistantships upon acceptance into their graduate program. These include a stipend plus tuition waiver. Stipends range from $13,260 to $14,748 for a twelve-month, .5 graduate research assistant (GRA) and from $8550 to $10,098 for a nine-month, .3 graduate teaching assistant (GTA). The College also sponsors scholarships, fellowships, and other employment opportunities.

Cost of Study

Graduate student tuition for 1999–2000 is $2108 per term for Oregon residents and $3600 per term for nonresident students. GRA and GTA appointees with tuition waivers pay fees of $277 per term.

Living and Housing Costs

Excluding tuition, the average cost of board and room, books and supplies, transportation, and miscellaneous expenses for a single student is $15,000 per year. Housing facilities are available on campus and in the community at reasonable rates.

Student Group

About 160 graduate students from very diverse backgrounds are enrolled in the College of Forestry. About 30 percent are international students. Office locations, orientation sessions, and seminars provide an excellent environment for fostering professional and social relationships among students and disciplines. Special orientation, including field trips, is provided for international students.

Location

Corvallis, a community of about 50,000 people, lies along the Willamette River between the forested Coast and Cascade mountain ranges. The city of Portland, the Pacific Ocean, and the Cascade Mountains are within easy reach. The climate is mild, with moist, cool winters and dry, warm summers. Corvallis is a pleasant, safe, family community with excellent medical facilities, parks, and other community services.

The University and The College

Founded in 1858, Oregon State University has grown to national and international prominence and is classified as a Carnegie Research I institution—a prestigious mark of commitment to education and research. As a land-grant, sea-grant, and space-grant university, OSU is committed to research to advance knowledge and solve problems. Graduate students number about 2,800 of the 13,800 students enrolled. They come from all states in the nation and from eighty-six countries.

More than 70 members of the graduate faculty are actively involved in research and policy analysis aimed at increasing the benefits derived from forests, promoting more efficient management and utilization of forest resources, and protecting environmental values. The College is dedicated to extending the frontiers of scientific understanding regarding forest and wood products ecosystems and coordinates its mission closely with other campus units in engineering and the biological, physical, and social sciences. Regionally, the College provides leadership for research cooperatives in vegetation management, tree improvement, hardwood silviculture, and nursery management and national cooperatives in wood treating and biodeterioration. Internationally, the College has research and education agreements with universities and agencies in Chile, China, Costa Rica, and France, and it fosters research to further knowledge and solve forestry problems in Latin America and the Pacific Rim countries.

Applying

The General Test of the Graduate Record Examinations (GRE) is required for all applicants. For consideration for assistantships and fellowships, enrollment applications should generally be received by February 1 for the following fall. Application forms are available from individual departments or the Office of Admissions. For more specific information, students should contact individual departments.

Correspondence and Information

Instruction Office
College of Forestry
Oregon State University
Corvallis, Oregon 97331-5710

Telephone: 541-737-2005
E-mail: gradrct@ccmail.orst.edu
World Wide Web: http://web.cof.orst.edu

Oregon State University

THE FACULTY AND THEIR RESEARCH

Forest Engineering: Steven Tesch, Professor and Department Head; Ph.D., Montana, 1981: silviculture, forest ecology. Paul W. Adams, Professor; Ph.D., Michigan, 1980: soil properties, watershed management. Robert L. Beschta, Professor; Ph.D., Arizona, 1974: forest hydrology. George W. Brown, Professor; Ph.D., Oregon State, 1967: forest hydrology. John Garland, Professor; Ph.D., Oregon State, 1990: forest engineering, logging labor force. Loren D. Kellogg, Professor; Ph.D., Oregon State, 1986: forest harvesting. Jim Kiser, Instructor; M.S., Oregon State, 1992: photogrammetry, GIS, surveying. Brian Kramer, Senior Instructor; M.F., 1979, M.S., 1992, Oregon State: forest roads and related structures, harvest planning, economics. Eldon A. Olsen, Associate Professor; Ph.D., Oregon State, 1979: operations research, harvesting. Marvin R. Pyles, Associate Professor; Ph.D., Berkeley, 1981: soil mechanics, geotechnical engineering. Julian Sessions, Professor; Ph.D., Oregon State, 1978: timber harvesting systems, economics, transportation planning. Arne Skaugset, Assistant Professor; Ph.D., Oregon State, 1996. Michael Wing, Assistant Professor; Ph.D., Oregon State, 1998: statistical analysis.

Forest Resources: John D. Walstad, Professor and Department Head; Ph.D., Cornell, 1971: vegetation management. Darius M. Adams, Professor; Ph.D., Berkeley, 1972: forest economics, modeling/analysis of forest products markets, econometrics, forest policy. John C. Bliss, Professor; Ph.D., Wisconsin, 1988: Starker Chair in Private and Family Forestry. James R. Boyle, Professor; Ph.D., Yale, 1967: soils, nutrient cycling, soil ecology. J. Douglas Brodie, Professor; Ph.D., Berkeley, 1971: forest economics, investment analysis. Ward W. Carson, Associate Professor; Ph.D., Washington (Seattle), 1973: photogrammetry, cartography, landscape ecology. Steven E. Daniels, Associate Professor; Ph.D., Duke, 1986: resource economics, forest policy, negotiation. Norman E. Elwood, Associate Professor; Ph.D., Minnesota, 1984: forest management, forest economics. David W. Hann, Professor; Ph.D., Washington (Seattle), 1978: forest growth and yield modeling. Royal G. Jackson, Associate Professor; Ph.D., New Mexico, 1971: forest history, cultural resource management, nature-based tourism. Edward C. Jensen, Associate Professor; Ph.D., Oregon State, 1989: forest biology, ecology, and dendrology, forestry education. K. Norman Johnson, Professor; Ph.D., Oregon State, 1973: forest economics, management, planning, resource analysis, forest policy. Rebecca Johnson, Associate Professor; Ph.D., Michigan State, 1984: resource economics, nonmarket values, policy. Gary L. Larson, Associate Professor; Ph.D., British Columbia, 1972: limnology, aquatic systems, aquatic biology. Douglas A. Maguire, Assistant Professor; Ph.D., Oregon State, 1986: growth, yield/stand dynamics, forest regeneration, crown structure/dynamics. David D. Marshall, Assistant Professor; Ph.D., Oregon State, 1990: forest modeling, inventory, sampling. Claire A. Montgomery, Assistant Professor; Ph.D., Washington (Seattle), 1990: natural resource economics, forest economics, forest policy. A. Scott Reed, Professor; Ph.D., Minnesota, 1987: forestry extension, program development and evaluation. William J. Ripple, Associate Professor/Senior Research; Ph.D., Oregon State, 1974: remote sensing, GIS, landscape ecology. Barbara A. Schraeder, Assistant Professor; Ph.D., Oregon State, 1998: forestry and natural resources. Byron B. Shelby, Professor; Ph.D., Colorado, 1976: natural resource sociology, recreation carrying capacity, instream flows and resource values. Bruce A. Shindler, Assistant Professor; Ph.D., Oregon State, 1993: human dimensions of ecosystem management. George H. Stankey, Professor; Ph.D., Michigan State, 1971: social values of natural resource management, ecotourism. Edward E. Starkey, Professor; Ph.D., Washington State, 1972: ecology of unexploited systems, conservation biology. John C. Tappeiner II, Professor; Ph.D., Berkeley, 1967: forest ecology and silviculture. Joanne F. Tynon, Assistant Professor; Ph.D., Idaho, 1994: forestry and wildland recreation.

Forest Products: Thomas E. McLain, Professor and Department Head; Ph.D., Colorado State, 1975: timber engineering, structural mechanical connections. Terence D. Brown, Professor; Ph.D., Colorado State, 1975: wood technology, quality control, lumber production, Extension. Charles C. Brunner, Associate Professor; Ph.D., Virginia Tech, 1984: sawmill simulation, optical scanning, operations research. James W. Funck, Associate Professor; Ph.D., Iowa State, 1979: optical scanning, process modeling, analysis and control. Barbara L. Gartner, Assistant Professor; Ph.D., Stanford, 1990: wood anatomy and quality. Rakesh Gupta, Associate Professor; Ph.D., Cornell, 1990: timber mechanics, structural engineering, mechanical properties. Eric N. Hansen, Assistant Professor; Ph.D., Virginia Tech, 1994: forest products marketing quality, environmental certification, Extension. Philip E. Humphrey, Associate Professor; Ph.D., Wales, 1982: wood composites, physical properties. Joseph J. Karchesy, Associate Professor; Ph.D., Oregon State, 1974: wood chemistry, adhesive systems, natural products from the forest. Murray L. Laver, Associate Professor; Ph.D., Ohio State, 1959: chemistry of wood and wood fibers. Robert J. Leichti, Associate Professor; Ph.D., Auburn, 1986: timber engineering, structural performance of wood-based materials and systems. Michael R. Milota, Associate Professor; Ph.D., Oregon State, 1984: wood-liquid relations, wood drying. Jeffrey J. Morrell, Professor; Ph.D., SUNY College of Forestry, 1981: biodeterioration and wood preservation, pathology. James E. Reeb, Assistant Professor; Ph.D., Texas A&M, 1991: value-added forest products manufacturing. John Simonsen, Associate Professor; Ph.D., Colorado, 1975: wood preservation, residue utilization. James B. Wilson, Professor; Ph.D., SUNY College of Forestry, 1971: wood composites processing, nondestructive testing.

Forest Science: Logan A. Norris, Professor and Department Head; Ph.D., Oregon State, 1970: integrated forest protection, forest chemicals. Steven A. Acker, Assistant Professor; Ph.D., Wisconsin–Madison, 1988: vegetation dynamics, forest stand structure, dynamics, and spatial patterns. W. Thomas Adams, Professor; Ph.D., California, Davis, 1974: genetics. Thimmappa Anekonda, Assistant Professor; Ph.D., Berkeley, 1992: forest genetics. Kermit Cromack, Professor; Ph.D., Georgia, 1973: decomposition and nutrient-cycling processing in forest ecosystems. William H. Emmingham, Professor; Ph.D., Oregon State, 1974: ecology and stand management. Gregory M. Filip, Associate Professor; Ph.D., New Hampshire, 1976: silvicultural control of root diseases. Steve Garman, Assistant Professor; Ph.D., Massachusetts, 1991: spatial simulation modeling/wildlife-habitat modeling. Robert P. Griffiths, Associate Professor; Ph.D., Oregon State, 1972: soil nutrients, carbon cycling, mycorrhiza. Everett Hansen, Professor; Ph.D., Wisconsin, 1972: forest pathology. Mark E. Harmon, Associate Professor; Ph.D., Oregon State, 1986: decomposition, nutrient cycling, forest production, carbon dynamics. John P. Hayes, Assistant Professor; Ph.D., Cornell, 1990: wildlife ecology. David E. Hibbs, Professor; Ph.D., Massachusetts, 1978: community and forest ecology, hardwood silviculture. Stephen D. Hobbs, Professor; Ph.D., Idaho, 1977: regeneration, vegetation management. Julia Allen Jones, Associate Professor; Ph.D., Johns Hopkins, 1983: environmental engineering. Daniel L. Luoma, Assistant Professor; Ph.D., Oregon State, 1988: diversity of ectomycorrhizal fungi in natural and managed forests of the Pacific Northwest. Christine Maguire, Assistant Professor; Ph.D., Rutgers, 1983: wildlife habitat relationships. Richard Meilan, Assistant Professor; Ph.D., Iowa, 1990: gene transfer methods for poplar hybrids. David D. Myrold, Professor; Ph.D., Michigan State, 1984: forest soils, soil microbiology. Michael Newton, Professor; Ph.D., Oregon State, 1964: ecosystem management, site preparation. David A. Perry, Professor; Ph.D., Montana State, 1974: ecosystems and diversity, effects of management. Steven R. Radosevich, Professor; Ph.D., Oregon State, 1972: community ecology, weed science, forest ecology, silviculture. Robert W. Rose Jr., Associate Professor; Ph.D., North Carolina State, 1980: forest regeneration, nursery technology, seedling physiology. Darrell W. Ross, Associate Professor; Ph.D., Georgia, 1990: entomology, pest management. Timothy D. Schowalter, Professor; Ph.D., Georgia, 1979: insect ecology, ecosystem ecology. Phillip Sollins, Professor; Ph.D., Tennessee, 1972: forest ecology, biogeochemistry, tropical ecosystems. Susan G. Stafford, Professor; Ph.D., SUNY College of Forestry, 1979: statistical design and analysis, data management. Steven H. Strauss, Professor; Ph.D., Berkeley, 1985: molecular biology and genetic engineering of forest trees. Bart Thielges, Professor; Ph.D., Yale, 1968: forest genetics. James Trappe, Professor; Ph.D., Washington (Seattle), 1962: forest mycology. Richard H. Waring, Professor; Ph.D., Berkeley, 1963: plant-water relations, ecosystem stress, physiological ecology. Nancy S. Weber, Assistant Professor; Ph.D., Michigan, 1971: taxonomy of the Pezizales. Barbara J. Yoder, Assistant Professor/Senior Research; Ph.D., Oregon State, 1992: tree physiology and remote sensing.

PURDUE UNIVERSITY

Department of Forestry and Natural Resources

Programs of Study

The Department of Forestry and Natural Resources offers graduate study leading to the degrees of Master of Science, Master of Science in Forestry, and Doctor of Philosophy in aquaculture, fisheries and aquatic sciences, forest biology (ecology, tree physiology, soils, and silviculture), natural resource and environmental policy, outdoor recreation and tourism, quantitative resource analysis (forest economics, biometry, operations research, and GIS and remote sensing), wildlife science (conservation biology, genetics, physiology, and community ecology), and wood science and technology. Graduate programs in the department are supported by courses and personnel throughout the University. This broad-based support and departmental expertise give students the opportunity to design a program and pursue studies in their areas of specialization.

The Master of Science in Forestry and the Master of Science are research-oriented degrees that prepare the individual for employment in his or her area of specialty or may provide background to continue for the Ph.D. degree. Completion of an M.S. usually requires two years of intensive study. An oral and/or written exam is given near the end of the program by the graduate advisory committee. The Ph.D. is a research degree that prepares candidates for employment in teaching and research and is available to outstanding students who demonstrate ability for scholarly work and original research. Course and foreign language requirements depend on student needs at the discretion of their graduate advisory committee. Written and oral exams are given by an examining committee after completion of formal course work. An oral defense of the research is required on completion of the dissertation. The graduate faculty is actively involved in research designed to increase benefits derived from natural resources, promote more efficient management and utilization of forest resources, and protect environmental values. The department is committed to expanding the scientific understanding of natural resources and coordinates its efforts with other campus units in the social, biological, and physical sciences. Internationally, the department participates in cooperative research and educational agreements with other universities or agencies in Australia, China, India, Indonesia, Brazil, Sweden, and Costa Rica and has research involvements in European, African, Latin American, Pacific Rim, and Caribbean countries.

Research Facilities

The department operates laboratories for research in aquaculture, fisheries biology, forest biology, soils, tree physiology, outdoor recreation and tourism, wildlife ecology, wildlife nutrition, wildlife physiology, wood science, and spatial data analysis. Off-campus facilities include Martell Memorial Forest, the Purdue Wildlife Area, other department properties, and many holdings managed by state and federal agencies and private companies. Wildlife and fish-holding facilities supply controlled environments for physiological and nutritional research. Special equipment for wood science includes an MTS testing system with computer-aided data acquisition, one 30- and two 60-kip universal testing machines, and a computer-controlled testing machine for performance testing of furniture structures. Computing facilities are located throughout the department. Statistical software, including SPSS, SAS, and IMSL, is fully supported. The spatial data processing laboratory supports GPS, GIS, and remote sensing research. Equipment includes NT and UNIX computers, scanner, digitizer, large-format plotter, and GPS receivers. Major software supported are Arc/Info, ArcView, Imagine, IDRISI, SLIPS, and KHOROS.

Financial Aid

Graduate teaching and research assistantships are available on a competitive basis to qualified students. For 1999–2000, stipends for entry-level twelve-month assistantships are $13,435 to $18,150, depending on students' qualifications, degree level, and appointment time. Fellowships are also available from the University and the School of Agriculture. The department provides funds for each student to attend one major meeting per year. Tuition is waived for students who receive stipends.

Cost of Study

Tuition for 1999–2000 is $3624 per year for Indiana residents and $12,248 per year for nonresidents. Students pay an annual fee of approximately $735.

Living and Housing Costs

Estimated yearly costs for a single student living on campus are about $6500 in 1999–2000. This includes room, board, books, supplies, and miscellaneous expenses. Housing costs for married students range from $409 to $518 per month. Off-campus housing costs vary widely.

Student Group

Graduate enrollment in the School of Agriculture is approximately 560, with 62 in the Department of Forestry and Natural Resources. Forty percent of graduate students in the department are women, and 40 percent are international students. Most receive a stipend or other financial assistance and are provided desk and office space. Seminars and orientation sessions foster professional and social relationships among students.

Student Outcomes

Employment includes a wide variety of positions in government, industry, organizations, and academia. Typical agency positions include forestry, recreation, wildlife, fisheries, and economics specialists for state agencies, as well as similar positions with federal agencies such as the Forest Service and Fish and Wildlife Service. Private-industry employers include environmental consulting firms, furniture manufacturers, wood products manufacturers, timber companies, and aquaculture producers. Doctoral graduates also hold faculty positions at colleges and universities.

Location

Purdue is in West Lafayette, across the Wabash River from Lafayette. The two cities' population exceeds 70,000. The area is served by airport, bus, and train facilities and is near I-65. Purdue is 65 miles northwest of Indianapolis and 126 miles southeast of Chicago. West Lafayette is a pleasant community with excellent medical facilities, parks, community theater and dance, a symphony, and art museums.

The University and The Department

Founded in 1869, Purdue is a "Big Ten" land-grant university. It enrolls more than 35,000 students on its West Lafayette campus and 30,000 on regional campuses. Approximately 2,100 faculty members teach and engage in research on the 650-acre main campus. The department, founded in 1914, is accredited by the Society of American Foresters, and its faculty represents a wide range of expertise in natural resources.

Applying

Applications are accepted at any time, but applicants requesting financial aid should return completed applications by February 15 (for fall) and September 15 (for spring). Notification of admission is made by April 15. A nonrefundable fee of $30 must accompany the formal application. GRE scores are required of all applicants. Students from non-English-speaking countries must furnish TOEFL scores with their applications.

Correspondence and Information

Graduate Secretary
Department of Forestry and Natural Resources
Purdue University
West Lafayette, Indiana 47907-1159
Telephone: 765-494-3572
Fax: 765-496-2422
E-mail: gradrep@fnr.purdue.edu
World Wide Web: http://www.fnr.purdue.edu

Purdue University

THE FACULTY AND THEIR RESEARCH

Dennis C. Le Master, Professor and Head; Ph.D., Washington State, 1974. Resource economics and policy.

Paul B. Brown, Professor; Ph.D., Texas A&M, 1987. Aquatic animal nutrition; aquaculture.

Daniel L. Cassens, Professor; Ph.D., Wisconsin–Madison, 1973. Wood utilization; primary and secondary wood processing; resource policy as it relates to wood products manufacturing and industry education.

William R. Chaney, Professor; Ph.D., Wisconsin–Madison, 1969. Tree physiology; growth and development; plant growth regulation.

John B. Dunning Jr., Assistant Professor; Ph.D., Arizona, 1986. Wildlife ecology; community and population ecology; animal behavior; conservation biology.

Carl A. Eckelman, Professor; Ph.D., Purdue, 1968. Wood products; furniture design and engineering.

Rado Gazo, Assistant Professor; Ph.D., Mississippi State, 1994. Wood products manufacturing, industrial engineering aspects, including modeling, simulation, and quality improvement.

Harry G. Gibson, Adjunct Associate Professor; M.S., West Virginia, 1969. Forest engineering; materials handling; timber and biomass harvesting systems; expert systems; vision systems; wood product quality control.

Andrew R. Gillespie, Associate Professor; Ph.D., Purdue, 1988. Silviculture; agroforestry; international forestry.

Harvey A. Holt, Professor; Ph.D., Oregon State, 1970. Industrial weed science; vegetation management for the central hardwood forest as well as rights-of-way; tree growth regulators; urban forestry.

William L. Hoover, Professor; Ph.D., Iowa State, 1977. Forest economics and marketing; timber tax; investment strategies; economics of property rights, wood-based product design, rural economic development, and social forestry.

Michael O. Hunt, Professor; Ph.D., North Carolina State, 1970. Structural wood-base composite materials; damage accumulation; nondestructive testing; wood in historic restoration.

Doran M. Mason, Assistant Professor; Ph.D., Maryland, 1994. Quantitative fisheries ecology (marine, estuarine, freshwater); fisheries acoustics; aquatic food webs; fish population dynamics; modeling.

Walter L. Mills Jr., Associate Professor; Ph.D., Purdue, 1980. Management/economics; application of decision-support systems, expert systems, and GIS in forest ecosystem management; physical and financial risk of forest ecosystem management.

John W. Moser Jr., Professor; Ph.D., Purdue, 1967. Forest biometrics; growth and yield, quantitative methods and application of computers.

Joseph T. O'Leary, Professor; Ph.D., Washington (Seattle), 1974. Outdoor recreation participation; travel involvement; social aspects of forestry; secondary analysis of major regular national data sets and longitudinal travel and recreation-related data.

George R. Parker, Professor; Ph.D., Michigan State, 1970. Forest ecology; long-term dynamics of forest ecosystems and plant population response to disturbance.

Phillip E. Pope, Professor; Ph.D., Virginia Tech, 1974. Forest soils; nutrient dynamics of forest ecosystems; soil restoration; hardwood regeneration and plantation management.

Olin E. Rhodes Jr., Assistant Professor; Ph.D., Texas Tech, 1991. Wildlife ecology and genetics; genotoxicology.

Guofan Shao, Assistant Professor; Ph.D., Chinese Academy of Sciences, 1989. Remote sensing, geographic information systems, forest modeling, landscape ecology.

Anne Spacie, Professor; Ph.D., Purdue, 1975. Fisheries ecology; water quality; toxic substances; limnology; watershed studies.

Robert K. Swihart, Professor; Ph.D., Kansas, 1985. Wildlife ecology; behavioral/ecological approaches to wildlife damage control; plant-animal interactions; population dynamics of mammals in fragmented landscapes.

Harmon P. Weeks Jr., Professor; Ph.D., Purdue, 1974. Wildlife ecology and physiology; herbivore feeding strategies and sodium relationships; fitness in songbirds nesting on man-made structures; fragmentation, edge, and vertebrate populations.

Professional and Technical Staff

Philip L. Anderson, Property Supervisor.

Richard E. "Rick" Hanger, Wood Research Laboratory Manager, Coating Applications Research Laboratory Associate; B.S., Minnesota, 1979. Forest products.

Rita L. McKenzie, Urban Forester; M.S., Purdue, 1997. Urban forestry.

Brian K. Miller, Wildlife Extension Specialist and Coordinator of Marine Advisory Services, Illinois-Indiana Sea Grant Program; M.S., Purdue, 1983. Forest and agricultural wildlife management.

Ronald Rathfon, Regional Extension Forester; M.S., Virginia Tech, 1990. Forest soils and hardwood silviculture.

Karyn S. Rodkey, Laboratory Coordinator for Forest Biology and Wildlife Science; M.S., Eastern Illinois, 1989. Analytical procedures.

John R. Seifert, Regional Extension Forester; M.S.F., Missouri, 1978. Seedling quality and hardwood regeneration; vegetation management; hardwood silviculture.

Gerald A. Stillings, Senior Analyst/Manager FNR Computer Service; M.S., Purdue, 1985.

Keith A. Wilson, Manager, Aquaculture Research Facility; B.S., Purdue, 1992.

STATE UNIVERSITY OF NEW YORK COLLEGE OF ENVIRONMENTAL SCIENCE AND FORESTRY

Faculty of Forestry

Programs of Study

The Faculty of Forestry offers the M.S., M.P.S., and Ph.D. degrees in forestry, forest resources management, and natural resources management. The following five areas are available for graduate study: forest ecosystem science and applications, forest recreation and tourism, resource policy and management, quantitative methods in forest science and management, and watershed management and forest hydrology.

The M.S. is intended for students seeking a career in research, resource administration, management, professional education, and other specialized positions related to the five areas of study within forest resources management. This degree requires a minimum of 24 credits of graduate-level course work and 6 credits for preparation and successful defense of the thesis. The M.S. degree program is normally completed in two to three years. The Master of Professional Studies (M.P.S.) is intended for students seeking a professional terminal degree in one of the areas of study within forest resources management. This degree requires a minimum of 30 credits of graduate-level course work. The normal time for completion of the M.P.S. degree program is 1½ to 2 years.

The Ph.D. provides students with the technical, scientific, and professional background necessary for careers in research, higher education, administration, and management. This degree is intended for students who demonstrate outstanding success in course work and make a contribution in original research or scholarship. The Ph.D. requires a minimum of 60 credits of graduate-level course work beyond the bachelor's degree, including 12 credits for preparation and successful defense of the dissertation. A written and oral examination are required for admission to candidacy. The normal length of the Ph.D. program is three to five years, depending on preparation in a master's degree program.

Research Facilities

The research program within the Faculty of Forestry attracts state, regional, and national sponsors who provide more than $2 million annually. Research facilities include laboratories and greenhouses for soil science, water quality, plant tissue culture and genetic engineering, genetics and tree improvement, and geographic information systems. College facilities include greenhouses, plant growth chambers, a radioisotope laboratory, and computer equipment. The College manages more than 25,000 acres of forest with diverse environmental conditions at nine locations for teaching and research. Close research and teaching relationships with other departments at the College are maintained.

Financial Aid

Assistantships are awarded to students whose education and experience enable them to assist in instruction and research. In 1998–99, more than thirty-five teaching and research assistantships were awarded, with a tuition waiver plus academic year stipends ranging from $8000 to $15,000. Various grants and loans are available.

Cost of Study

In 1998–99, graduate tuition for New York State residents was $2550 per semester. Nonresident tuition was $4208 per semester. All graduate students pay activity fees of $243 per year.

Living and Housing Costs

Accommodations and food service are available from Syracuse University, including single and married student apartments.

Student Group

In 1998–99, there were 84 graduate students in the Faculty of Forestry degree programs. The College's graduate enrollment includes approximately 500 graduate students. There are an active graduate student association and numerous professional and special interest organizations. Graduate students come from throughout the United States and from many other countries.

Student Outcomes

Graduates typically work in state, national, and international organizations and in governments and industry as researchers, managers, educators, and administrators in forest resources– or natural resources–related organizations. Recent graduates are working as consulting foresters, recreation planners, soil scientists, hydrologists, legislative staff members, silviculturists, economists, tree improvement specialists, and geographic information specialists.

Location

The main campus of the College is in Syracuse, New York, and is adjacent to Syracuse University. The city is a major metropolitan area of approximately 500,000 people, with diverse industry and commerce. Syracuse is a major transportation hub, with air, train, and bus service.

The College

The College of Environmental Science and Forestry is a specialized SUNY college focused on the natural environment with approximately 1,200 undergraduates and 500 graduate students. The Faculty of Forestry is one of eight Faculties at the College and includes approximately 40 full-time faculty members and support staff members.

Applying

Applicants must provide a transcript of all previous academic work, supporting letters of recommendation, a general statement of educational objectives, and scores on the General Test of the Graduate Record Examinations. There is a $50 application fee. More information about the College and the Faculty of Forestry may be obtained via the World Wide Web (http://www.esf.edu/faculty/for/grad2.htm) or by contacting one of the representatives below.

Correspondence and Information

Dr. Robert Frey
Dean of Instruction and Graduate Studies
227 Bray Hall
SUNY College of Environmental Science
    and Forestry
1 Forestry Drive
Syracuse, New York 13210
Telephone: 315-470-6599
Fax: 315-470-6978
E-mail: esfgrad@esf.edu

Dr. William Bentley, Chair
Faculty of Forestry
320 Bray Hall
SUNY College of Environmental Science
    and Forestry
1 Forestry Drive
Syracuse, New York 13210
Telephone: 315-470-6675
Fax: 315-470-6956
E-mail: cmaynard@syr.edu

State University of New York College of Environmental Science and Forestry

THE FACULTY AND THEIR RESEARCH

Forest Ecosystem Science and Applications. Tree physiology, physiological ecology, forest ecology and silvics, silviculture of natural forests, intensive silviculture of plantations, integrated vegetation management, forest genetics and tree improvement, nutrient cycling and simulation modeling, forest soil classification and productivity, urban and greenspace forestry.

Lawrence P. Abrahamson, Senior Research Associate; Ph.D. (entomology), Wisconsin, 1969. Forest entomology, forest pathology, pesticides, integrated pest management, integrated forest and ROW vegetation management, woody biomass for energy crops.

Michael R. Bridgen, Associate Professor, Forest Technology Program; Ph.D. (tree physiology and genetics), Michigan State, 1979. Dendrology, aerial photogrammetry, silviculture.

Russell D. Briggs, Associate Professor; Ph.D. (forest soils), SUNY College of Environmental Science and Forestry, 1985. Forest soils, silviculture.

Allan P. Drew, Professor and Coordinator of International Programs; Ph.D. (forest management), Oregon State, 1974. Tree physiology, forest ecology, physiological ecology.

Charles A. Maynard, Professor and Research and Graduate Science Education Coordinator; Ph.D. (forest biology and wood science), Iowa State, 1980. Forest genetics, tree improvement, plant tissue culture and transformation.

Christopher A. Nowak, Associate Professor; Ph.D. (forest resources management), SUNY College of Environmental Science and Forestry, 1993. Silviculture, intensive forestry, forest vegetation management.

Ralph D. Nyland, Distinguished Service Professor; Ph.D. (silviculture and forest management), Michigan State, 1966. Silviculture, forest practice.

Edwin H. White, Professor and Dean of Research, SUNY College of Environmental Science and Forestry; Ph.D. (soils, tree nutrition), Auburn, 1968. Forest soils—silviculture, bioenergy.

Ruth Yanai, Assistant Professor; Ph.D. (forest ecology), Yale, 1990. Forest soils, ecosystem nutrient cycling, simulation modeling.

Forest Recreation and Tourism. Recreation resource planning, wilderness and river recreation management, commercial recreation and tourism, human dimensions of recreational use.

Chad P. Dawson, Professor; Ph.D. (resource management and policy), SUNY College of Environmental Science and Forestry, 1983. Tourism planning, recreation management, wilderness management, commercial recreation.

Miklós Grátzer, Distinguished Teaching Professor; Ph.D. (open space planning), Montana, 1971. Recreation, resources management and planning, tourism.

Resource Policy and Management. Forest resource management; forest, environmental, and ecological economics; natural resource and environmental policy; forest operations; planning and management for multiple uses; values and ethics; international forest policy and management.

William R. Bentley, Professor and Chair; Ph.D. (agricultural economics), Berkeley, 1965. Forest policy, management.

Hugh O. Canham, Professor and Coordinator of Continuing Education; Ph.D. (forestry economics), SUNY College of Environmental Science and Forestry, 1971. Forestry economics, economics of natural resources.

Donald W. Floyd, Professor and Professional Studies Coordinator; Ph.D. (renewable natural resources), Arizona, 1986. Public policy in forest and natural resources management, environmental dispute resolution.

René H. Germain, Assistant Professor and Outreach Coordinator; Ph.D. (forest policy), SUNY College of Environmental Science and Forestry, 1997. Sustainable forestry systems, business.

Valerie A. Luzadis, Assistant Professor; Ph.D. (forest policy and economics), SUNY College of Environmental Science and Forestry, 1997. Forest land-use policy, nonmarket values, ecological economics.

John E. Wagner, Assistant Professor; Ph.D. (forestry and wood science), Colorado State, 1990. Forest resources economics.

Ross Whaley, University Professor; Ph.D. (natural resource economics), Michigan, 1969. Political economy of sustainable development.

Quantitative Methods in Forest Science and Management. Statistics, forest growth and yield modeling, forest inventory and mensuration, operations research, geospatial modeling and analysis.

Eddie Bevilacqua, Assistant Professor; Ph.D. (forest biometrics), Toronto, 1998. Forest measurements and statistics.

Craig J. Davis, Associate Professor; Ph.D. (forest operations), Purdue, 1987. Forest operations, harvest planning, operations research.

Lee P. Herrington, Professor; Ph.D. (forest meteorology), Yale, 1964. Resource information management, micrometeorology, urban forestry, geographic information systems (GIS).

Stephen V. Stehman, Associate Professor; Ph.D. (statistics), Cornell, 1989. Statistics.

Lianjun Zhang, Assistant Professor; Ph.D. (forest biometrics and growth and yield modeling), Idaho, 1990. Forest biometrics, quantitative silviculture.

Watershed Management and Forest Hydrology. Forest hydrology, meteorology, soil and water conservation, water resources policy, hydrologic processes, hydrologic modeling, isotope hydrology, watershed geospatial modeling and analysis, watershed hydrology.

Peter E. Black, Distinguished Teaching Professor; Ph.D. (watershed management), Colorado State, 1961. Watershed hydrology, soil and water conservation, environmental impact analysis.

Elizabeth W. Boyer, Assistant Professor; Ph.D. (environmental sciences), Virginia, 1998. Watershed hydrology, biogeochemistry.

Theodore A. Endreny, Assistant Professor; Ph.D. candidate (water resources), Princeton. Hydrological modeling.

Jeffrey J. McDonnell, Professor; Ph.D. (forest hydrology), Canterbury (New Zealand), 1989. Watershed hydrology, isotope hydrology.

State University of New York College of Environmental Science and Forestry

SELECTED PUBLICATIONS

Kopp, R. F., and **L. P. Abrahamson** et al. **(E. H. White).** Woodgrass spacing and fertilization effects on wood biomass production by a willow clone. *Biomass Bioenergy* 11(6):451–7, 1996.

Lo, M. H., and **L. P. Abrahamson.** Principal component analysis to evaluate the relative performance of nine-year old hybrid poplar clones. *Biomass Bioenergy* 10(1):1–6, 1996.

Abrahamson, L. P., C. A. Nowak, P. M. Charlton, and P. G. Snyder. Cost effectiveness of herbicide and non-herbicide vegetation management methods for electric utility rights-of-way in the Northeast. In *Proceedings, Fifth International Symposium on Environmental Concerns in Rights-of-Way Management,* September 19–22, 1993, pp. 27–43, eds. G. J. Doucet, C. Seguin, and M. Giguere. Montreal, Quebec, Canada, 1995.

Bentley, W. R. Professional forestry education in New York—where are we after 100 years? *J. Forestry,* in press.

Bentley, W. R. Scarcity and economy influence U.S. forests. In *Forum for Applied Research and Public Policy,* pp. 90–4, 1998.

Berck, P., and **W. R. Bentley.** Hotelling's theory, enhancement, and the taking of the Redwood National Park. *Am. J. Agricultural Econ.* 79(2):287–98, 1997.

Kerr, J., et al. **(W. R. Bentley)** (eds). *Natural Resource Economics of India: Theory and Applications.* New Delhi, India: Oxford & IBH Publishing Company, 1997.

Bevilacqua, E., T. J. Blake, and W. Suiter Filho. Modelling growth and ecophysiological responses of Eucalyptus grandis clones in Minas Gerais, Brazil. *J. Trop. Forest Sci.* 9(4):505–13, 1997.

Puttock, G. D., and **E. Bevilacqua.** White pine and red pine volume growth under uniform shelterwood management in Algonquin Provincial. *NODA/NFP Technical Report, TR-14,* Natural Resources Canada, Canadian Forestry Service–Great Lakes Forestry Centre, Sault Ste. Marie, Ontario, 1995.

Blake, T. J., **E. Bevilacqua,** and W. Suiter Filho. Early selection of Eucalyptus grandis clones in central Brazil. *J. Trop. Forest Sci.* 8(1):33–43, 1995.

Martell, D. L., **E. Bevilacqua,** and B. J. Stokes. Modelling seasonal variation in daily people caused-forest fire occurrence. *Can. J. Forest Res.* 19:1555–63, 1989.

Black, P. E. (associate ed.). Putting the people in watershed management. *Water Resources Impact* 1(1):5–6, 1999.

Black, P. E. Research issues in forest hydrology. Proceedings, Forest Hydrology Research Symposium, University of British Columbia, Vancouver, British Columbia. *J. Am. Water Resources Assoc.* 34(4):723–8, 1997.

Black, P. E. Watershed functions. *J. Am. Water Resources Assoc.* 33(1):1, 1997; *Water Resources J. (UNESCAP),* pp. 32–41, 1997.

Black, P. E. *Watershed Hydrology,* second edition. Chelsea, Mich.: Ann Arbor Press, 1996.

McKnight, D. M., and **E. W. Boyer** et al. Spectrofluorometric characterization of aquatic fluvic acid for determination of precursor organic material and general structural properties. *Limnol. Oceanogr.,* in press.

Boyer, E. W., G. M. Hornberger, K. E. Bencala, and D. M. McKnight. Response characteristics of DOC flushing in an alpine catchment. *Hydrol. Proc.* 11:1635–47, 1997.

Boyer, E. W., G. M. Hornberger, K. E. Bencala, and D. M. McKnight. Overview of a simple model describing variation of dissolved organic carbon in an upland catchment. *Ecol. Modeling* 86:183–8, 1996.

Boyer, E. W., G. M. Hornberger, K. E. Bencala, and D. M. McKnight. Variation of dissolved organic carbon during snowmelt in soil and streamwaters of two headwater catchments. In *Biogeochemistry of Seasonally Snow-Covered Catchments,* pp. 303–12. IAHS Publication No. 228., 1995.

Briggs, R. D., et al. Long-term effects of forest management on nutrient cycling in spruce-fir forests. *Forest Ecol. Manage.,* in press.

Briggs, R. D., A. J. Kimball, and J. Cormier. Assessing compliance with BMPs on harvested sites in Maine. *Northern J. Appl. Forestry* 15:57–68, 1998.

Briggs, R. D., and R. C. Lemin Jr. Soil drainage class effects on early response of balsam fir (Abies balsamea (L.)Mill.) to precommercial thinning. *Soil Sci. Soc. Am. J.* 58(4):1231–9, 1994.

Briggs, R. D., and R. C. Lemin Jr. Delineation of climatic zones in Maine. *Can. J. Forestry Res.* 22:801–11, 1992.

Canham, H. O., and K. S. King. *Just the Facts: An Overview of New York's Wood-Based Economy and Forest Resource.* Albany, N.Y.: Empire State Forest Products Association, 1998.

Canham, H. O., and J. M. Coufal. New ideas for teaching natural resources management: Implications of, and response to, the Fedkiw Paper. In *Proceedings, Second Biennial Conference on University Education in Natural Resources,* Utah State University, Logan, Utah, March 7–10, 1998.

Canham, H. O., and N. A. Richards. Optimal management of forest landscapes for maximizing biodiversity and ecosystem management: The case for laissez-faire private ownership. In *Proceedings, 1996 IUFRO World Congress,* Tampere, Finland, 1996.

Canham, H. O., and W. B. Smith. *Western New York Forest Industry Initiative.* Ellicottville, N.Y.: Cooperative Extension Service of Cattaraugus Co., 1994.

Davis, C. J., and T. W. Reisinger. Evaluating terrain for harvesting system selection. *J. Forest Eng.* 2:9–16, 1990.

Reisinger, T. W., and **C. J. Davis.** A map-based decision support system for evaluating terrain and planning timber harvests. *Trans. ASAE* 29:1199–203, 1986.

Davis, C. J., and J. C. Callahan. Optimum clipping strategies for hardwood face veneer. *Forest Prod. J.* 36:47–52, 1986.

Dawson, C. P., J. Tangen-Foster, G. T. Friese, and J. Carpenter. Defining characteristics of U.S.A. wilderness experience programs. *Int. J. Wilderness* 4(3):22–7, 1998.

Dawson, C. P., and W. E. Hammitt. Dimensions of wilderness privacy for Adirondack forest preserve hikers. *Int. J. Wilderness* 2(1):37–41, 1996.

Robertson, R., **C. P. Dawson,** W. Kuentzel, and S. Selin. College and university curricula in ecotourism or nature-based tourism. *J. Nat. Resources Life Sci. Educ.* 25(2):152–5, 1996.

Drew, A. P. Growth rings, phenology, hurricane disturbance and climate in Cyrilla racemiflora L., a rain forest tree of the Luquillo Mountains, Puerto Rico. *Biotropica* 30:35–49, 1998.

Drew, A. P. Genes and human behavior. *Zygon* 32:41–50, 1997.

Drew, A. P., and R. G. Werner. Teaching tropical ecology in the West Indies. *J. Forestry* 93:28–9, 1996.

Drew, A. P., and J. A. Chapman. Inheritance of temperature adaptation in intra- and interspecific Populus crosses. *Can. J. Forest Res.* 22:62–7, 1992.

Endreny, T. A., and E. F. Wood. Distributed watershed modeling of design storms to identify non-point source runoff. *J. Environ. Quality,* in press.

Endreny, T. A., and G. D. Jennings. A decision support system for water quality data augmentation. *J. Am. Water Resources Assoc.,* in press.

Malmsheimer, R. W., and **D. W. Floyd.** Fishing rights in navigable nontidal rivers: The before and after of the New York Court of Appeals decision in Douglaston Manor, Inc. v. Bahrakis. *Albany Law Rev.* 62(1):147–81, 1998.

Malmsheimer, R. W., and **D. W. Floyd.** The right to practice forestry: Laws restricting nuisance suits and municipal ordinances. *J. Forestry* 96(8):27–32, 1998.

Campbell, M. C., and **D. W. Floyd.** Thinking critically about environmental mediation. *J. Plan. Lit.* 10(3):235–47, 1996.

Floyd, D. W., R. H. Germain, and K. ter Horst. A resource conflict model for assessing negotiation and mediation in forest resource conflicts. *J. Forestry* 94(5), 1996.

Germain, R. H., and **D. W. Floyd.** Developing resource-based social conflict models for assessing the utility of negotiation in conflict resolution. *Forest Sci.,* in press.

Germain, R. H., and **D. W. Floyd.** Models for examining forest resource conflicts. *Forest Sci.,* in press.

Yang, X., D. E. Koten, and **L. P. Herrington.** Evaluation of a spatial decision support system: Method and example. In *Proceedings of the GIS AM/FM Asia '97 Conference,* Taipei, Taiwan, 1997.

Liu, R., and **L. P. Herrington.** The expected cost of uncertainty in geographic data. *J. Forestry* 49(12):27–31, 1996.

Badruddin, A., and **L. P. Herrington.** Effects of Landuse data quality in resource analysis. In *Proceedings of GIS/LIS '95,* vol. I, pp. 29–38. Bethesda, Md.: American Society of Remote Sensing and Photogrammetry, 1995.

Griffths, D. A., S. D. Degloria, and **L. P. Herrington.** Characterizing geographic information and analysis needs in New York State. *Cartography Geographic Information Syst.* 21(2):69–90, 1994.

State University of New York College of Environmental Science and Forestry

Selected Publications (continued)

Luzadis, V. A., et al. Investing in ecosystems and communities. *J. Sustainable Forestry,* in press.

Luzadis, V. A., T. Duffus, and M. Thill. Ecosystem partners: Foresters of the Northwest Flow Consortium. *J. Forestry* 96(8):16–9, 1998.

Elconin, P., and **V. A. Luzadis.** Conservation easements: What do landowners think? *Wild Earth* 8(2):49–51, 1998.

Xing, Z., M. Satchwell, W. A. Powell, and **C. A. Maynard.** Micropropagation of American chestnut: Increasing rooting rate and preventing shoot-tip necrosis. *In Vitro Cell Dev. Biol.* 33:43–8, 1997.

Powell, W. A., and **C. A. Maynard.** Designing small antimicrobial peptides and their encoding genes. In *Micropropagation, Genetic Engineering, and Molecular Biology of* Populus, chap. 22, pp. 165–72, eds N. B. Klopfenstein et al. Gen. Tech. Report RM-GTR-297. Ft. Collins, Colo.: U.S. Department of Agriculture, Forest Service, Rocky Mountain Forest and Range Experiment Station, 1997.

Xing, Z., M. Satchwell, and **C. A. Maynard.** A rapid polymerase chain reaction method for early screening of transgenic plants. *Methods Cell Sci.* 18:7–13, 1996.

Maynard, C. A. Six-year field test results of micropropagated black cherry *(Prunus serotina* Ehrh.). *In Vitro Cell Dev. Biol.* 30:64–9, 1994.

Kendall, C., and **J. J. McDonnell** (eds.). *Isotope Tracers in Catchment Hydrology.* Elsevier Science Publishers, 1998.

McDonnell, J. J., and J. Buttle. Comment on a deterministic-empirical model of the effect of the capillary-fringe on near-stream area runoff. 1. Description of the model. *J. Hydrol.* 207:280–5, 1998.

Burns, D., et al. **(J. J. McDonnell).** Base cation concentrations in subsurface flow from a forested hillslope: The role of flushing frequency. *Water Resources Res.* 34:3535–44, 1998.

Burns, D. A., and **J. J. McDonnell.** Effects of a beaver pond on runoff processes in an Adirondack lake watershed. *J. Hydrol.* 205: 248–64, 1998.

Nowak, C. A., and D. A. Marquis. *Distribution of Cut Guides for Thinning in Allegheny Hardwoods: A Review.* Research Note NE-362. USDA Forest Service, NEFES, 1997.

Kerr, G., and **C. A. Nowak.** Regeneration of Allegheny hardwoods: Lessons for silviculture in Britain. *Q. J. Forestry* 91:125–34, 1997.

Nowak C. A. Wood volume increment in thinned, 50- to 55-yr-old, mixed species Allegheny hardwoods. *Can. J. Forest Res.* 26:819–35, 1996.

Nowak, C. A., R. B. Downard Jr., and **E. H. White.** Potassium trends in red pine plantations at Pack Forest, New York. *Soil Sci. Soc. Am. J.* 55:847–50, 1991.

Nyland, R. D. Patterns of lodgepole pine regeneration following the 1988 Yellowstone fires. *Forest Ecol. Manage.* 111:23–33, 1998.

Nyland, R. D. Selection system in northern hardwoods. *J. Forestry* 96(7):18–21, 1998.

Nyland, R. D. *Silviculture: Concepts and Applications.* New York: McGraw-Hill Book Co., 1996.

Nyland, R. D. (ed.). Managing northern hardwoods. *Proc. Silviculture Symp.,* June 23–25, 1986. SUNY-ESF Fac. For. Misc. Publ. 13 (ESF 87-002). Syracuse, N.Y.: SUNY College of Environmental Science and Forestry, 1987.

Stehman, S. V., and R. L. Czaplewski. Design and analysis for thematic map accuracy assessment: Fundamental principles. *Remote Sensing Environment* 64:331–44, 1998.

Stehman, S. V., and **C. J. Davis.** A practical sampling strategy for estimating residual stand damage. *Can. J. Forest Res.* 27:1635–44, 1997.

Overton, W. S., and **S. V. Stehman.** Design characteristics for long-term monitoring of ecological variables. *Environ. Ecol. Stat.* 3: 349–61, 1996.

Overton, W. S., and **S. V. Stehman.** Design implications of anticipated data uses for comprehensive environmental monitoring programs. *Environ. Ecol. Stat.* 2:287–303, 1995.

Stehman, S. V., and W. S. Overton. Environmental sampling and monitoring. In *Handbook of Environmental Statistics,* pp. 263–306, eds. G. P. Patil and P. Ross. Elsevier, 1994.

Wagner, J. E., and T. P. Holmes. Estimating economic gains for landowners due to time-dependent changes in biotechnology. *Forest Sci.* 45(2), 1999.

Wagner, J. E., V. A. Luzadis, and **D. W. Floyd.** A role for economic analysis in the ecosystem management debate. *Landscape Urban Plan.* 40:151–7, 1998.

Wagner, J. E., and S. C. Deller. Measuring the effects of economic diversity on growth and stability. *Land Econ.* 74(4):541–60, 1998.

Wagner, J. E. Estimating the impacts of tourism. *Ann. Tourism Res.* 24(3):592–608, 1997.

Wagner, J. E., and D. B. Rideout. The stability of the capital asset pricing model's parameters in analyzing forest investments. *Can. J. Forest Res.* 22:1639–45, 1992.

Whaley, R. S. Furthering our understanding of air quality. *Environ. Sci. Policy* 1(3):149–52, 1998.

Whaley, R. S. Future perspectives on technological development. *Forestry Chron.* 72(1):86–9, 1996.

Whaley, R. S. Supply and demand: Accommodating the future. *J. Forestry* 93(12):42–3, 1995.

Whaley, R. S. Interdisciplinary environmental studies: Scholarship, research, or puttering around. *Environ. Professional* 8(2):93–6, 1986.

White, E. H., and **L. P. Abrahamson** et al. Creating a climate for commercializing willow biomass for bioenergy: The developing strategy of the New York based "Salix Consortium" (USA). In *Third Biomass Conference of the Americas,* p. 1403, Montreal, Canada, August 24–29, 1997.

White, E. H., and **L. P. Abrahamson** et al. Developing the willow biomass-bioenergy industry in New York: Challenges for commercializing the crop production system. In *BIOENERGY '96 Conference Proceedings,* September 15–19, Nashville, Tennessee, pp. 60–7. 1996.

Bakeman, M. E., and **E. H. White.** Historical element concentrations and contents of fertilized and nonfertilized red pine wood in the Adirondack Mountains. *Agriculture Abstract,* p. 329, Madison, Wisconsin, 1990.

Jokela, E. J., **E. H. White,** and **R. D. Briggs.** Soil-site relationships in Norway spruce plantations in central New York. *Soil Sci. Soc. Am. J.* 52:809–15, 1988.

Yanai, R. D., et al. Accumulation and depletion of base cations in forest floors in the northeastern US. *Ecology,* in press.

Yanai, R. D. The effect of whole-tree harvest on phosphorus cycling in a northern hardwood forest. *Forest Ecol. Manage.* 104:281–95, 1998.

Yanai, R. D., M. Twery, and S. L. Stout. Woody understory response to changes in overstory density: Thinning in Allegheny hardwoods. *Forest Ecol. Manage.* 102:45–60, 1998.

Williams, M., and **R. D. Yanai.** Multi-dimensional sensitivity analysis and ecological implications of a nutrient uptake model. *Plant Soil* 180:311–24, 1996.

Zhang, L. Cross-validation of nonlinear growth functions for modeling tree height-diameter relationships. *Ann. Botany* 79:251–7, 1997.

Tang, S., Y. Wang, **L. Zhang,** and C. H. Meng. A distribution-independent approach to predicting stand diameter distribution. *Forest Sci.* 43:491–500, 1997.

Zhang, L., J. A. Moore, and J. D. Newberry. Disaggregating stand volume growth to individual trees. *Forest Sci.* 39:295–309, 1993.

Zhang, L., J. A. Moore, and J. D. Newberry. A whole-stand growth and yield model for interior Douglas-fir. *Western J. Appl. Forestry* 8:120–5, 1993.

UNIVERSITY OF MICHIGAN

School of Natural Resources and Environment

Programs of Study	The School of Natural Resources and Environment offers several graduate programs leading to the degrees of Master of Science in natural resources and environment, Master of Landscape Architecture, and Doctor of Philosophy in natural resources and environment and in landscape architecture.
	Requirements for the M.S. and M.L.A. degree programs consist of a minimum of 36 credit hours, including 3–6 credits for a master's project, thesis, or practicum. Specific course requirements differ, depending upon the student's choice of concentration, field of study within the concentration, degree program selected, and previous academic background.
	Students in the resource policy and behavior (RPB) concentration specialize in one of several fields of study: advocacy, human behavior in environmental contexts, environmental education, resource policy, or resource planning. In addition, students can focus on conservation biology and ecosystem management from either a resource policy or behavior perspective.
	Resource ecology and management (REM) students specialize in aquatic or terrestrial ecosystems or conservation biology and ecosystem management.
	Students in the landscape architecture (LA) concentration pursue a two- or three-year program focusing on creative and interdisciplinary problem solving with a site and land planning emphasis.
	The School of Natural Resources and Environment offers two doctoral degrees: a Ph.D. in natural resources and environment and a Ph.D. in landscape architecture. The School's doctoral programs are highly individualized and tailored to the academic and career goals of each student. As such, no two students in the program are likely to take the identical set of courses. Because the doctoral degree is a research degree, emphasis is placed on developing the skills to plan, implement, evaluate, and communicate about research. The course of study includes an area of specialization, development of research skills, and a dissertation.
Research Facilities	The School's facilities include a microcomputer laboratory, a remote-sensing GIS laboratory, landscape architecture studios, and the Center for Sustainable Systems (formerly known as the National Pollution Prevention Center). The School uses several properties located in and around Ann Arbor and in northern Michigan for research and fieldwork. These include the Matthaei Botanical Garden, with native vegetation, landscape gardens, and greenhouses; the Nichols Arboretum, a 123-acre field laboratory composed of native woodland, meadow, and marsh plants and with a plant collection of landscape value; Stinchfield Woods, for forest research and practice; and Saginaw Forest, containing more than fifty distinct plantations. The University's Biological Station provides excellent opportunities for field studies in wetland, lake, and forest ecology.
	University research facilities include the 2-million-volume Graduate Library; the Computing Center; the Institute for Social Research, an internationally recognized social science research center; several research libraries; and the Statistical Laboratory.
Financial Aid	Fellowships, graduate student instructorships, and research assistantships are available. The assistantships provide monthly stipends and full tuition waivers.
Cost of Study	In 1999–2000, tuition and fees for two semesters are $10,500 for state residents and $21,100 for nonresidents. (Costs are subject to change without notice by the University Board of Regents.)
Living and Housing Costs	Costs vary considerably, depending upon a student's lifestyle, marital status, family size, and other factors. Estimated living costs for a single student, including room and board, transportation, and personal needs, were approximately $10,000 for the 1998–99 year. A wide variety of housing situations are available, including off-campus and on-campus accommodations.
Student Group	The School of Natural Resources and Environment enrolls approximately 150 master's students and 50 doctoral students.
Student Outcomes	With the School's interdisciplinary curriculum, students have found positions in all of the employment sectors: 37 percent of the alumni work for government, 25 percent for the private sector, 15 percent in education/academic areas, and 14 percent in nonprofit areas. These positions include congressional liaison, U.S. E.P.A.; assistant director of the residential program, Cuyahoga Valley Environmental Education Center; development officer, Nichols Arboretum; environmental outreach officer, U.S. Peace Corps; Washington representative, National Parks and Conservation Association; associate editor, Defenders of Wildlife; fisheries research technician, Michigan Department of Natural Resources; and biologist, U.S. Fish and Wildlife Service.
Location	Ann Arbor is a university town with a population of about 110,000 people. Surrounded by farmland and recreational areas, Ann Arbor is a lively cultural community with numerous musical, theatrical, and arts events; it is a center for jazz and folk music. Ann Arbor is located an hour from Detroit and Windsor, Canada. Toronto or Chicago can be easily reached by car or train in 4 hours.
The University and The School	Established in 1817, the University is an internationally renowned public teaching and research institution. Enrollment for the Ann Arbor campus is nearly 37,000, including more than 13,000 graduate students.
	The School first opened its doors as the School of Forestry and Conservation in 1927. In 1950, it became the School of Natural Resources—making it the first such school of natural resources in the world. In 1992, the name was changed to the School of Natural Resources and Environment. Today, it remains a leader in natural resource education, training professionals who can solve complex natural and environmental resource issues at the local, state, regional, national, and international levels.
Applying	To apply for admission, students must submit an application, a $55 application fee, a statement of purpose, a resume, three letters of recommendation, GRE General Test scores, and transcripts. Doctoral degree applicants to the resource policy and behavior concentration need to include a writing sample. Doctoral degree applicants to the landscape architecture concentration must provide a portfolio. International applicants must also submit TOEFL scores and certification of financial support for their entire length of study. Information and application forms may be obtained from the address below.
Correspondence and Information	Graduate Admissions Office of Academic Programs School of Natural Resources and Environment 1024 Dana University of Michigan 430 East University Ann Arbor, Michigan 48109-1115 Telephone: 734-764-6453 E-mail: snre.gradteam@umich.edu World Wide Web: http://www.snre.umich.edu/oap

University of Michigan

THE FACULTY AND THEIR RESEARCH

J. David Allan, Professor; Ph.D., Michigan. Aquatic ecology, conservation biology.
Burton B. Barnes, Professor; Ph.D., Michigan. Forest ecology and genetics.
Elizabeth A. Brabec, Associate Professor; Ph.D., Maryland. Land-use planning and law.
Steve Brechin, Associate Professor; Ph.D., Michigan. Natural resources.
Garry D. Brewer, Professor; Ph.D., Yale. Environmental policy and management.
Daniel G. Brown, Assistant Professor; Ph.D., North Carolina at Chapel Hill. GIS, remote sensing, ecological modeling.
Terry J. Brown, Professor; M.L.A., Harvard. Landscape architecture.
Bunyan Bryant, Professor; Ph.D., Michigan. Social and environmental advocacy.
Jonathan W. Bulkley, Professor; Ph.D., MIT. Water policy, risk-benefit analysis, and sustainable systems.
John B. Burch, Professor; Ph.D., Michigan. Biology, systematics and evolution of selected molluscan groups.
Lisa M. Curran, Assistant Professor; Ph.D., Princeton. Ecology and evolutionary biology.
Raymond DeYoung, Associate Professor; Ph.D., Michigan. Environmental psychology and conservation behavior.
James S. Diana, Professor; Ph.D., Alberta. Fish biology and ecology.
William S. Drake, Professor; Ph.D., Michigan. Program evaluation and international development.
Donna L. Erickson, Associate Professor; M.L.A., Agricultural University (The Netherlands). Landscape architecture, restoration ecology.
Thomas N. Gladwin, McGraw Professor of Corporate Environmental Management Program and Chair; Ph.D., Michigan. Corporate environmental management.
K. Ian Grandison, Associate Professor; M.L.A., Michigan. Landscape architecture.
Robert E. Grese, Associate Professor; M.L.A., Wisconsin. Landscape architecture.
Gloria E. Helfand, Associate Professor; Ph.D., Berkeley. Environmental economics.
Alvin L. Jensen, Associate Professor; Ph.D., Michigan State. Biometrics and statistics.
Rachel Kaplan, Professor; Ph.D., Michigan. Environmental psychology and biological research methods.
Bobbi S. Low, Professor; Ph.D., Texas. Evolutionary and behavioral ecology.
Dan Mazmanian, Professor and Dean; Ph.D., Washington (St. Louis). Environmental policy.
Paul Mohai, Associate Professor; Ph.D., Penn State. Natural resource and environmental policy.
Michael R. Moore, Associate Professor; Ph.D., Michigan. Environmental economics.
Joan Iverson Nassauer, Professor; Ph.D., Minnesota. Landscape ecology and landscape perception.
Ivette Perfecto, Associate Professor; Ph.D., Michigan. Tropical ecology, agroforestry.
Thomas Princen, Associate Professor; Ph.D., Harvard. International environmental policy.
Barry G. Rabe, Professor; Ph.D., Chicago. Resource policy.
Terry Root, Associate Professor; Ph.D., Princeton. Conservation biology.
Emily D. Silverman, Assistant Professor; Ph.D., Washington (Seattle). Quantitative ecology and resource management.
Eugene F. Stoermer, Professor; Ph.D., Iowa State. Phycology and limnology.
Dorceta Taylor, Assistant Professor; Ph.D., Harvard. Environmental sociology.
Warren H. Wagner Jr., Emeritus Professor; Ph.D., Berkeley. Botany.
Paul W. Webb, Professor; Ph.D., Bristol (England). Fish ecology.
Patrick C. West, Associate Professor; Ph.D., Yale. Outdoor recreation and resource sociology.
Michael J. Wiley, Associate Professor; Ph.D., Michigan. Aquatic ecology.
John A. Witter, Professor; Ph.D., Minnesota. Entomology and forest dynamics.
Julia Wondolleck, Associate Professor; Ph.D., MIT. Environmental policy and planning.
Steven L. Yaffee, Professor; Ph.D., MIT. Natural resource policy and administration.
Donald R. Zak, Associate Professor; Ph.D., Michigan State. Soils and watershed management.
Micheala T. Zint, Assistant Professor; Ph.D., Michigan State. Environmental education and communication.

CURRENT RESEARCH PROJECTS

Research on the impacts of urban forestry and urban youth.
Study of the feasibility of community-based sustainable development for southern Caribbean forests of Nicaragua.
Research on the ecological framework for climate-induced changes.
Curriculum development and dissemination of pollution prevention information for professional school students in engineering and business.
Research on the energetic limits of avian distribution and abundance.
Study of the climatic and pollution influences on ecosystem processes.
Research on the mechanics of fish interactions.
Study of the role of nongovernmental organizations in international environmental policy formation.

UNIVERSITY OF MINNESOTA

College of Natural Resources
Departments of Fisheries and Wildlife,
Forest Resources, and Wood and Paper Science

Programs of Study

The College of Natural Resources offers the Master of Forestry, Master of Science, and Doctor of Philosophy degrees in forestry and in fisheries and wildlife conservation. The forestry graduate program is administered jointly by the Departments of Wood and Paper Science and Forest Resources. The wood and paper science specializations include the chemistry of lignocellulosic materials, paper and fiber products recycling, deterioration of wood, wood mechanics, structural design with wood, wood moisture interaction and drying, processing and performance of wood composites, economics of manufacturing systems, technology and processing of solid wood products, design and production of housing components, energy-efficient building construction, and environmental life cycle analysis of materials extraction, conversion, and use. (The World Wide Web address for this department is http://www.cnr.umn.edu/WPS/). Forest resource specializations include ecology and silviculture; economics in forest and related natural resource management; ecophysiology; environmental education; genetics and tree improvement; geographic information systems; hydrology and water quality; measurements and biometrics; policy and administration; survey, measurement, and modeling; tree physiology and tissue culture; recreation resource management; remote sensing; urban forestry; and watershed management. (The World Wide Web address for this department is http://www.cnr.umn.edu/FR/). The fisheries and wildlife conservation programs include resource management applications of the ecology, behavior, and physiology of fish and wildlife. Special areas of emphasis include conservation biology, fish and wildlife habitats, fish reproductive biology, genetics, fish systemics, stream ecology, endangered species, and population and ecosystem modeling. (The World Wide Web address for these programs is http://www.fw.umn.edu/).

Degree program courses may be chosen from a wide selection of University departments. Faculty involvement in international projects and a strong complement of international students provide a global perspective.

Most entering graduate students have completed undergraduate degrees in forestry, wildlife, or a related natural resource field with at least a B average. Students who majored in other fields (e.g., biology, business, engineering, mathematics, or social science) and achieved strong academic records are also encouraged to apply. Prerequisites vary with program and subfield specialization. Graduate Record Examinations (GRE) scores are required.

A master's degree program can be completed under a thesis or nonthesis option; a total of 30 semester credits is required. The Ph.D. program requires 24 thesis credits and the completion of a set of courses selected in conference with an advising committee. More information about requirements and graduate courses is available at the Graduate School Bulletin World Wide Web site (http://www.umn.edu/commpub/grad/grad.html).

Research Facilities

Specialized laboratories are available in four campus buildings for fisheries, wildlife, wood and paper science, and forestry studies. Work in fish physiology, aquaculture, and genetics is conducted in a large, modern wet lab. For wood and paper science research, there are controlled-environment chambers; extensive mechanical test equipment; a complete woodworking facility; dry kilns; modern, well-instrumented production equipment for paper, fiber, and composite products; and extensive analytical equipment, including an analytical ultracentrifuge, dedicated to wood chemistry research. X-ray and electron diffraction facilities and other research equipment are available under cooperative arrangements with several University departments. Forest resources research uses modern laboratories, a greenhouse and growth chambers in St. Paul, field facilities at the Cloquet Forestry Center, and the North Central Experiment Station at Grand Rapids. Cooperative agreements with public agencies and industries provide additional opportunities. The University library system has more than 4 million volumes, including the departmental libraries for forestry, fisheries, and wildlife. The College maintains a large instructional computing laboratory with more than thirty stand-alone microcomputers. The College also houses remote sensing and geographic information systems laboratories and the Environmental Resources Spatial Analysis Center (ERSAC). ERSAC supports computing on high-performance Sun and SGI workstations. Support includes extensive software and peripheral devices. A high-speed ATM network connects College and ERSAC computers to the University's supercomputers. Extensive statistical and computing consulting services are also available.

Financial Aid

Research assistantships and a limited number of fellowships and tuition grants are available on a competitive basis. For the 1998–99 academic year, a one-half-time research assistantship provided $1100 per month. Graduate assistants receive tuition scholarships of double their appointment percentage plus health benefits.

Cost of Study

In 1998–99, the graduate tuition for state residents was $5130 per year for full-time enrollment. The student services fee was $480 per year. Tuition for nonresidents is twice the resident rate, but individuals holding at least 25-percent-time assistantships qualify for the resident rate.

Living and Housing Costs

In 1998–99, unfurnished University apartments for married students rented for $400 to $575 per month and were in great demand. Off-campus housing is available in the Twin Cities of Minneapolis and St. Paul at a range of prices.

Student Group

Approximately 145 graduate students are enrolled in the three graduate programs in the College of Natural Resources. They represent a wide diversity of educational backgrounds, geographic origins, and career objectives.

Location

The St. Paul–Minneapolis metropolitan area has a population of about 2 million residents, who enjoy ready access to nearby parks, lakes, and forests for winter and summer recreation. The Twin Cities constitute the cultural and commercial center of the Upper Midwest.

The University

The University is a land-grant institution established in 1851. In fall 1998, total enrollment on the Twin Cities Campus was about 38,000. The College of Natural Resources is located on the St. Paul unit of this campus, which has 3,000 students. Excellent free bus service allows ready access to classes at the larger Minneapolis unit. Students can access departmental sites on the World Wide Web by contacting the University's home page (http://www.umn.edu).

Applying

Application procedures and deadlines vary by program. Application materials and more specific information may be obtained from the address below.

Correspondence and Information

Director of Graduate Studies (specify Fisheries, Forestry, or Wildlife Conservation)
College of Natural Resources
135 Natural Resources Administration Building
University of Minnesota
2003 Upper Buford Circle
St. Paul, Minnesota 55108-1027
E-mail: kwalter@forestry.umn.edu

University of Minnesota

THE FACULTY AND THEIR RESEARCH

Department of Fisheries and Wildlife

Ira R. Adelman, Professor and Head of the Department; Ph.D., Minnesota, 1969: fish physiology, management, and aquaculture. David C. Fulton, Assistant Professor; Ph.D., Colorado State, 1997: human dimensions of fisheries and wildlife, natural resources policy. Jay T. Hatch, Associate Professor; Ph.D., Minnesota, 1982: ecology of nongame fish. Anne Kapuscinski, Professor; Ph.D., Oregon State, 1984: fish conservation genetics and sustainable aquaculture. Raymond Newman, Associate Professor; Ph.D., Minnesota, 1985: aquatic ecology; fisheries management. Donald Pereira, Senior Biologist, Minnesota Department of Natural Resources; Ph.D., Minnesota, 1992: population and community dynamics. Carl Richards, Research Associate; Ph.D., Idaho State, 1986: stream ecology. Andrew M. Simons, Assistant Professor; Ph.D., Alabama, 1997: fish systematics and evolution. Peter Sorensen, Professor; Ph.D., Rhode Island, 1984: fish chemoreception and behavior. George R. Spangler, Professor; Ph.D., Toronto, 1974: fish population analysis. Edward B. Swain, Research Scientist, Minnesota Pollution Control Agency; Ph.D., Minnesota, 1984: effects of pollution on lakes, fish, and wildlife. Bruce C. Vondracek, Associate Professor; Ph.D., California, Davis, 1981: fish ecology and management.

David Andersen, Associate Professor; Ph.D., Wisconsin, 1988: human impacts on wildlife; avian ecology. Yosef Cohen, Professor; Ph.D., Berkeley, 1982: ecosystem analysis. James A. Cooper, Associate Professor; Ph.D., Massachusetts, 1973: waterfowl and wetland ecology. Francesca J. Cuthbert, Professor; Ph.D., Minnesota, 1981: conservation and biology of nongame birds. Glenn DelGuidice, Wildlife Biologist, Minnesota Department of Natural Resources; Ph.D., Minnesota, 1988: large mammal physiology. Gary E. Duke, Professor; Ph.D., Michigan State, 1967: raptor physiology. David L. Garshelis, Wildlife Biologist, Minnesota Department of Natural Resources; Ph.D., Minnesota, 1983: bear ecology and management. Peter A. Jordan, Associate Professor; Ph.D., Berkeley, 1967: ecology of mammalian herbivores. James R. Kitts, Associate Professor; Ph.D., Utah State, 1975: wildlife extension education. L. David Mech, Wildlife Research Biologist, U.S. Fish and Wildlife Service; Ph.D., Purdue, 1962: wolf ecology; predator-prey relations. John Pastor, Professor; Ph.D., Wisconsin, 1981: ecosystem analysis. Donald B. Siniff, Professor; Ph.D., Minnesota, 1968: population dynamics. J. L. David Smith, Associate Professor; Ph.D., Minnesota, 1984: mammalian behavior and conservation. Anthony M. Starfield, Professor; Ph.D., Witwatersrand (Johannesburg), 1965: natural resource modeling. John R. Tester, Professor; Ph.D., Minnesota, 1960: vertebrate ecology. A. Richard Weisbrod, Research Zoologist, U.S. Geological Survey; Ph.D., Cornell, 1970: biological diversity and habitat use.

Department of Wood and Paper Science

Jim L. Bowyer, Professor; Ph.D., Minnesota, 1973: technology adoption; world raw material demand; environmental impacts of materials production and use. Stephen M. Bratkovich, Marketing Specialist, USFS: Ph.D., Ohio, 1991: forest economics, marketing, extension education. David T. Grimsrud, Associate Professor; Ph.D., Minnesota, 1965: residential building science. Patrick H. Huelman, Associate Professor; M.S., Iowa State, 1988: cold-climate housing; housing systems. Timothy Larson, Assistant Professor; Ph.D., Minnesota, 1993: housing systems; wood drying. Joseph G. Massey, Professor and Head of the Department; Ph.D., Minnesota, 1977: application of operations research tools to forest products manufacturing. Thomas Milton, Associate Professor; M.S., Minnesota, 1980: lumber manufacturing technology. Harlan D. Petersen, Assistant Professor; M.S., Minnesota, 1968: wood moisture relations. Shri Ramaswamy, Associate Professor; Ph.D., SUNY Health Science Center at Syracuse, 1990: paper science and engineering. Simo Sarkanen, Associate Professor; Ph.D., Washington (Seattle), 1976: wood and lignin chemistry. Elmer Schmidt, Professor; Ph.D., Minnesota, 1978: forest products pathology. Robert Seavey, Research Associate; Ph.D., Minnesota, 1989: wood physics. Steven J. Severtson, Assistant Professor; Ph.D., Institute of Paper Science and Technology, 1997: surface and colloid chemistry of papermaking, material science of paper, coated product development. Ulrike Tschirner, Associate Professor; Ph.D., Karlsruhe (Germany), 1984: lignin chemistry. Jerold E. Winandy, Adjunct Professor; Ph.D., Oregon State, 1993: engineering properties of wood. Kewen K. Yin, Associate Professor; Ph.D., Maryland, 1991: signal processing, industrial process simulation, design, optimization and control.

Department of Forest Resources

Dorothy H. Anderson, Associate Professor; Ph.D., Colorado State, 1980: recreation resource management—wildland management and policy analysis. Mark E. Ascerno, Professor; Ph.D., Pennsylvania, 1976: forest and urban plant pest control. Marvin E. Bauer, Professor; Ph.D., Illinois, 1970: remote sensing. Melvin J. Baughman, Professor; Ph.D., Minnesota, 1982: economics and policy. David Bengston, Principal Economist, USFS; Ph.D., Minnesota, 1986: forest economics and technology development. Erwin R. Berglund, Senior Hydrologist, Minnesota Department of Natural Resources; Ph.D., Minnesota, 1970: forest hydrology. Robert A. Blanchette, Professor; Ph.D., Washington State, 1978: forest pathology. Charles R. Blinn, Professor; Ph.D., Virginia Tech, 1984: forest management and marketing. Paul V. Bolstad, Associate Professor; Ph.D., Wisconsin, 1990: geographic information systems/remote sensing. Kenneth N. Brooks, Professor; Ph.D., Arizona, 1970: hydrology. Thomas E. Burk, Professor; Ph.D., Minnesota, 1981: forest biometrics. Stephan P. Carlson, Assistant Professor; Ph.D., Michigan, 1993: youth development; park and recreation resources. John J. Cogan, Professor; Ph.D., Ohio State, 1969: environmental education. William Cunningham, Professor; Ph.D., Texas, 1963: environmental education. Edward J. Cushing, Professor; Ph.D., Minnesota, 1963: plant ecology. Andrew J. David, Assistant Professor; Ph.D., Michigan State, 1995: forest genetics. Karlyn Eckman, Consultant; Ph.D., Minnesota, 1994: sustainable development. Alan R. Ek, Professor and Head of the Department; Ph.D., Oregon State, 1969: biometrics, sampling, and measurement. Paul V. Ellefson, Professor; Ph.D., Michigan State, 1970: economics and policy. Daniel L. Erkkila, Tourism and Travel Specialist; Ph.D., Minnesota, 1991: forest economics. Fred N. Finley, Associate Professor; Ph.D., Michigan State, 1977: environmental education. Lee E. Frelich, Research Associate; Ph.D., Wisconsin, 1986: natural disturbance; competition and stand development. Hans M. Gregersen, Professor; Ph.D., Michigan, 1969: economics; social cost-benefit analysis. David F. Grigal, Professor; Ph.D., Minnesota, 1968: response of soil and vegetation to disturbance. Robert G. Haight, Research Forester, USFS; Ph.D., Oregon State, 1985: forest management. Mark H. Hansen, Research Forester, USFS; Ph.D., Minnesota, 1990: forest biometrics. Howard W. Hoganson, Associate Professor; Ph.D., Minnesota, 1981: operations research. George Honadle, Senior Research Associate; Ph.D., Syracuse, 1978: social and institutional dimensions of natural resource policy and management. Judson G. Isebrands, Forest Products Technologist, USFS; Ph.D., Iowa State, 1969: tree physiology. Pamela J. Jakes, Principle Research Forester; Ph.D., Minnesota, 1996: social impact of ecosystem management; public involvement in forest management. Gary R. Johnson, Associate Professor-Extension Educator; Ph.D., Maryland, 1992: urban forestry. James R. Kitts, Associate Professor; Ph.D., Utah State, 1975: environmental education. Steven B. Daley Laursen, Associate Professor; Ph.D., Idaho, 1984: forest ecology; environmental quality and urban forestry. Rolfe A. Leary, Consultant; Ph.D., Purdue, 1968: forest growth and yield. David W. Lime, Senior Research Associate; Ph.D., Pittsburgh, 1969: recreation. David C. Lothner, Consultant; Ph.D., Minnesota, 1964: forest economics; utilization. Allen L. Lundgren, Research Associate; Ph.D., Minnesota, 1959: forest economics. Leo H. McAvoy Jr., Associate Professor; Ph.D., Minnesota, 1976: management of outdoor recreation. John L. Nieber, Associate Professor; Ph.D., Cornell, 1979: forest hydrology. Jacek Oleksyn, Research Associate; Ph.D., Silesian University (Poland), 1982: plant ecophysiology. Michael E. Ostry, Research Plant Pathologist, USFS; Ph.D., Minnesota, 1992: forest pathology. James A. Perry, Professor; Ph.D., Idaho State, 1981: hydrology; water quality. Michael J. Phillips, Pesticide Program and Forest Soils Program Supervisor, Minnesota Department of Natural Resources; Ph.D., Canterbury (New Zealand), 1981: forest soils and related environmental issues. David G. Pitt, Professor; Ph.D., Arizona, 1986: scenic resource management. Klaus J. Puettmann, Associate Professor; Ph.D., Oregon State, 1990: silviculture. Peter B. Reich, Professor; Ph.D., Cornell, 1983: ecology and ecophysiology. Donald E. Riemenschneider, Project Leader; Ph.D., Minnesota, 1979: forest genetics; tree improvement. Dietmar W. Rose, Professor; Ph.D., Wisconsin, 1972: forest economics; operations research. C. Ford Runge, Associate Professor; Ph.D., Wisconsin, 1981: natural resource economics. Thomas L. Schmidt, Research Scientist, USFS; Ph.D., Nebraska, 1991: agroforestry—windbreak technology and riparian management. Steven J. Seybold, Assistant Professor; Ph.D., Berkeley, 1992: forest entomology. J. L. David Smith, Associate Professor; Ph.D., Minnesota, 1984: conservation biology. Robert A. Stine, Coordinator, Cloquet Forestry Center; Ph.D., Minnesota, 1995: genetics and tree improvement. Edward I. Sucoff, Professor Emeritus; Ph.D., Maryland, 1960: tree physiology. Alfred D. Sullivan, Professor and Dean of the College; Ph.D., Georgia, 1969: forest biometrics. Elon S. Verry, Principal Forest Hydrologist, USFS; Ph.D., Colorado State, 1983: hydrology; water quality. Xiwei Yin, Research Associate; Ph.D., Minnesota, 1989: forest ecology. John C. Zasada, Adjunct Professor; Ph.D., Michigan, 1968: silviculture.

UNIVERSITY OF WASHINGTON

College of Forest Resources

Programs of Study
The College of Forest Resources offers the degrees of Master of Forest Resources, Master of Science, and Doctor of Philosophy. The two academic divisions of the College and more than 60 faculty members participate in the academic programs, graduate instruction, and research programs. The Management and Engineering Division offers study in forest products marketing, quantitative resources management, silviculture and forest protection, social sciences, forest economics, forest engineering, silviculture, and paper science and engineering. The Ecosystem Sciences Division offers study in forest ecosystem analysis, wildlife science, and all aspects of urban horticulture, including urban forestry and habitat restoration.

More than 100 active research programs are administered within the College. Strong interdisciplinary programs with other University departments and well-established cooperative programs with other institutions and agencies and with private industry provide a broad spectrum of opportunities. International research interests include long-term programs in forestry and wood and fiber utilization and participation in programs related to appropriate wood-processing technology. The College also houses the Center for International Trade in Forest Products, which emphasizes research in the trade and marketing of wood and fiber products, as well as the Center for Streamside Studies, which conducts research and promotes continuing education in efforts of promoting wise land- and water-management decision making. The Olympic Natural Resources Center conducts research and education on natural resource management practices that integrate the production of commodities with the preservation and enhancement of ecological values. The Center for Urban Horticulture conducts public outreach programs concerning the selection, management, and role of plants and of ecosystems in urban landscapes. The Center for Quantitative Science in Forestry, Fisheries, and Wildlife is an inter-college unit sponsored by the College of Forest Resources and the College of Ocean and Fishery Sciences, which focuses on the application of statistical, mathematical, and decision sciences to a wide array of contemporary issues.

Research Facilities
Learning centers and specially equipped laboratories in the biological, physical, and management sciences, including a pulp and paper facility, are located in the three-building forest resources complex. A specialized forestry library contains nearly 26,000 bound volumes; 33,000 pamphlets, reports, and monographs; and 2,500 periodicals. Other campus facilities include a herbarium; a wood collection; the 60-acre Union Bay Natural Area; and the 230-acre Washington Park Arboretum with more than 10,000 woody plant species, the second-largest woody plant collection in the U.S. Field research centers consist of more than 5,000 acres of forested land at Charles Lathrop Pack Demonstration Forest in Eatonville, Washington, and at the Olympic Natural Resources Center in Forks, Washington. In addition, cooperative programs with industrial, federal, and state and county landowners have resulted in the Wind River Canopy Crane facility, which makes it possible for scientists to study almost six acres of forest canopy in three dimensions; in field laboratories, such as the Cedar River Watershed; and in forest tree nurseries that are available for research purposes.

The College has cooperative agreements with the National Biological Survey, the U.S. Forest Service, the Bureau of Land Management, and industry. Some of the principal study areas are ecosystem analysis and modeling, planning alternatives for wildland use, intensive forest management practices, environmental impact studies, influence of public policies on land use, resource management, forest industries, process development in the use of wood resources, forest fertilization, and young stand management.

Financial Aid
Appointments are available as reader-graders, research assistants, predoctoral associates, and predoctoral instructors. Stipends in 1999–2000 range from $1654 per month (including tuition waiver) to higher compensation levels that reflect the academic attainments of the appointee. Summer assignments are available at half- or full-time rates. Some graduate fellowships are available, and many students get partial support from hourly employment. Applicants should investigate national financial aid sources as well.

Cost of Study
In 1999–2000, graduate tuition per quarter is estimated at $1883 for state residents and $4673 for nonresidents.

Living and Housing Costs
Official residence hall rates for room and board are approximately $4800 for the 1999–2000 academic year. Apartments are available for $500 per month and up in Seattle's north-end districts.

Student Group
Approximately 160 graduate students are enrolled in the College of Forest Resources. They come from most states and many countries, intermixing ethnic, cultural, and educational backgrounds with equally varied academic interests and disciplines related to forest resources. Participation in the College Graduate Student Association and the Graduate and Professional Student Senate allows graduate students to enhance their programs with career and personal interests.

Student Outcomes
Graduates from the College's programs are employed in both the public and private sectors. Specifically, students find positions with consulting firms, private conservation organizations, federal and state land management agencies, legislative bodies, wood products corporations, advocacy groups, universities, and research laboratories. Positions held include land use planner, policy analyst, engineer, hydrologist, wetlands specialist, ecologist, wildlife biologist, conservationist, land manager, horticulturist, marketing specialist, silviculturist, entomologist, pathologist, forester, researcher, and professor.

Location
Of considerable importance to the graduate student is the opportunity for well-balanced living that Seattle and its environs provide. The metropolitan area has a wealth of cultural and entertainment offerings, and the surrounding area provides a magnificent array of scenic attractions and outdoor recreational opportunities.

The University
The University of Washington was founded in 1861, and since that time it has provided the focus for intellectual and cultural activities in the Pacific Northwest. Enrollment in the University's eighteen colleges and schools exceeds 34,000 students. The Graduate School has 9,000 students and 1,800 faculty members.

Applying
Application forms may be obtained from Graduate Admissions, 200 Gerberding Hall, or from the College and may be submitted at any time. Deadlines for applications that include College financial aid requests are February 1 for the spring, summer, and autumn quarters and November 1 for the winter quarter. Later applications to the College's graduate programs will be considered on a space-available basis.

Correspondence and Information
College of Forest Resources
Office of Student Services
116 Anderson Hall, Box 352100
University of Washington
Seattle, Washington 98195-2100

University of Washington

THE FACULTY AND THEIR RESEARCH

James K. Agee, Professor; Ph.D., Berkeley, 1973. Management of natural systems, forest ecology, fire ecology.

G. Graham Allan, Professor; Ph.D., Glasgow, 1956; D.Sc., Strathclyde (Glasgow), 1970. Fiber and polymer science, creativity and innovation.

B. Bruce Bare, Professor; Ph.D., Purdue, 1969. Operations research, biometry, forest land management, taxation, finance, valuation.

James S. Bethel, Professor and Dean Emeritus; D.F., Duke, 1947. Wood science, wood energy, international forestry.

Susan M. Bolton, Associate Professor; Ph.D., New Mexico State, 1991. Hydrology, watershed management, ecological engineering.

Gordon A. Bradley, Professor; Ph.D., Michigan, 1986. Forest land-use planning, urban and community forestry.

Toby Bradshaw, Research Associate Professor; Ph.D., LSU Medical Center, 1984. Molecular genetics of forest trees.

David G. Briggs, Professor; Ph.D., Washington, 1980. Operations research, forest products and wood science, life cycle analysis.

Linda B. Brubaker, Professor; Ph.D., Michigan, 1973. Dendrochronology, forest ecology, quaternary paleoecology.

Linda Chalker-Scott, Associate Professor; Ph.D., Oregon State, 1988. Environmental stress physiology (especially cold and UV-B), ecophysiology of plants in disturbed environments, identification of stress-resistant trees and shrubs for urban use.

Dale W. Cole, Professor Emeritus; Ph.D., Washington (Seattle), 1963. Forest soils, mineral cycling in forest ecosystems.

Barney Dowdle, Professor; Ph.D., Yale, 1962. Markets for timber and forest products, public forest land management.

Ivan L. Eastin, Associate Professor; Ph.D., Washington (Seattle), 1992. Forest products marketing, international marketing and trade, softwood lumber substitution, 2X4 technology transfer in Japan, marketing strategies for lesser-used timber species.

Robert L. Edmonds, Professor; Ph.D., Washington (Seattle), 1971. Forest soil microbiology, forest diseases, air pollution.

Rick Edwards, Research Assistant Professor; Ph.D., Georgia, 1985. Ecosystems ecology of rivers and wetlands.

Kern Ewing, Associate Professor; Ph.D., Washington (Seattle), 1982. Wetland ecology and vegetation management, restoration ecology.

E. David Ford, Professor; Ph.D., London, 1967. Quantitative science, ecosystem analysis, forest productivity.

Jerry F. Franklin, Professor; Ph.D., Washington State, 1966. Structure and function of forest ecosystems.

James L. Fridley, Professor; Ph.D., Washington (Seattle), 1984. Engineering design, computer graphics and graphical simulation, ecological engineering, forest engineering, mechanical engineering.

Robert I. Gara, Professor; Ph.D., Oregon State, 1964. Bark beetle ecology, forest insect behavior, international forestry.

Francis Edward Greulich, Professor; Ph.D., Berkeley, 1976. Management science and operations research, continuous location theory.

Richard R. Gustafson, Professor; Ph.D., Washington (Seattle), 1982. Process simulation and control, pulping and bleaching.

Charles B. Halpern, Research Associate Professor; Ph.D., Oregon State, 1987. Plant succession, plant community analysis, ecology of montane/subalpine meadows, effects of forest management on plant diversity.

Clement W. Hamilton, Associate Professor; Ph.D., Washington (St. Louis), 1985. Plant taxonomy, public garden administration and curation, urban conservation biology, urban forestry.

Donald P. Hanley, Professor; Ph.D., Idaho, 1981. Extension forestry, nonindustrial private forest management.

Robert B. Harrison, Associate Professor; Ph.D., Auburn, 1985. Forest soil chemistry, soil amendments, mineral cycling, organic waste utilization, long-term forest productivity.

Charles L. Henry, Research Associate Professor; Ph.D., Washington (Seattle), 1989. Organic waste management, soil amendments.

Thomas M. Hinckley, Professor; Ph.D., Washington (Seattle), 1971. Forest tree physiology, subalpine ecosystems and SRIC.

Kevin T. Hodgson, Associate Professor; Ph.D., Washington (Seattle), 1986. Surface and colloid science, papermaking chemistry, fiber-water interactions, secondary fiber.

Bjorn F. Hrutfiord, Professor; Ph.D., North Carolina, 1959. Wood extractive chemicals, air and water quality.

Chavonda J. Jacobs, Assistant Professor; Ph.D., North Carolina State, 1998. Wood and paper science, pulping and bleaching.

Jay A. Johnson, Professor; Ph.D., Washington (Seattle), 1973. Mechanical and physical properties of wood and paper.

Robert G. Lee, Professor; Ph.D., Berkeley, 1973. Natural resource sociology, human communities, rural poverty, development and change of forestry institutions, environmental ethics.

Bruce R. Lippke, Professor; M.S.I.E., Berkeley, 1966. International trade in forest products, economics of forest management and production.

David A. Manuwal, Professor; Ph.D., UCLA, 1972. Avian ecology, effects of forest management on birds.

John M. Marzluff, Assistant Professor; Ph.D., Northern Arizona, 1987. Avian ecology, behavioral ecology, wildlife conservation.

William T. McKean, Professor; Ph.D., Washington (Seattle), 1967. Pulp and paper science, chemical engineering.

Robert J. Naiman, Professor; Ph.D., Arizona State, 1974. Forest stream ecosystems, aquatic landscape dynamics.

Lee A. Newman, Research Assistant Professor; Ph.D., Rutgers, 1993. Phytoremediation of organics and metals, plant molecular genetics.

Chadwick D. Oliver, Professor; Ph.D., Yale, 1975. Silviculture and forest ecology, forest-stand dynamics, landscape dynamics and management.

Dorothy A. Paun, Associate Professor; Ph.D., Oregon, 1993. Forest products marketing, financial analysis of the pulp and paper industry, product bundling strategies, business relationships in the forest products industry, new markets and products for small diameter timber.

John M. Perez-Garcia, Associate Professor; D.F., Yale, 1991. Forest economics, analysis of trade policy, global trade modeling, climatic change, carbon cycling.

David L. Peterson, Professor; Ph.D., Illinois, 1980. Mountain ecology, subalpine forests, global climate change, forest ecology.

Stewart G. Pickford, Professor; Ph.D., Washington (Seattle), 1972. Surveying, aerial photogrammetry.

Kenneth J. Raedeke, Research Associate Professor; Ph.D., Washington (Seattle), 1979. Wildlife biology and conservation, dynamics of managed populations, ungulate ecology and management, international conservation.

Sarah H. Reichard, Research Assistant Professor; Ph.D., Washington (Seattle), 1994. Conservation biology of plants, biological invasions.

Jeffrey E. Richey, Professor (School of Oceanography); Ph.D., California, Davis, 1974. Drainage basin biogeochemistry, systems integration; research in the Amazon, Pacific Rim.

Krishna P. Rustagi, Associate Professor Emeritus; Ph.D., Yale, 1973. Operations research and statistical applications in forest management.

Clare M. Ryan, Assistant Professor; Ph.D., Michigan, 1996. Natural resource policy and administration, environmental conflict management.

Peter Schiess, Professor; Ph.D., Washington (Seattle), 1975. Forest engineering, small-log harvesting, biomass production.

Gerard F. Schreuder, Professor; Ph.D., Yale, 1968. Statistical analysis in resource economics, international forestry, trade, aerial photos, remote sensing.

Grant W. Sharpe, Professor Emeritus; Ph.D., Washington (Seattle), 1955. Wildland recreation, park management, interpretation.

Douglas G. Sprugel, Professor; Ph.D., Yale, 1974. Forest ecology, tree ecophysiology, natural disturbance.

Reinhard F. Stettler, Professor Emeritus; Ph.D., Berkeley, 1963. Genetics of forest tree populations, biotechnology, biomass production.

Stuart E. Strand, Research Associate Professor; Ph.D., Penn State, 1982. Forest biotechnology, environmental pollution control.

David B. Thorud, Dean; Ph.D., Minnesota, 1964. Watershed management, forest policy and international development.

Harold B. Tukey Jr., Professor; Ph.D., Michigan State, 1958. Urban horticulture, horticultural physiology.

Eric Turnblom, Assistant Professor; Ph.D., Minnesota, 1994. Forest mensuration, growth and yield modeling, quantitative stand dynamics, biometrics, natural resources inventory and sampling.

J. Alan Wagar, Research Professor; Ph.D., Michigan, 1961. Urban forestry, urban forest inventory and cost-effective management.

Thomas R. Waggener, Professor; Ph.D., Washington (Seattle), 1966. Forest policy and economics, international forestry development, international trade in forest products, forest products marketing.

Stephen D. West, Associate Professor; Ph.D., Berkeley, 1979. Vertebrate ecology and conservation.

Kathleen L. Wolf, Research Assistant Professor; Ph.D., Michigan, 1993. Urban and community forestry, environment and behavior, urban landscape visual assessment, human dimensions of urban ecosystems.

John A. Wott, Professor; Ph.D., Cornell, 1968. Urban horticulture, public gardens, arboreta and botanical garden management, interpretation and management in urban public gardens, horticultural education.

Darlene Zabowski, Associate Professor; Ph.D., Washington (Seattle), 1988. Forest soils, soil genesis and classification, biogeochemical cycling in forest soils.

VIRGINIA POLYTECHNIC INSTITUTE AND STATE UNIVERSITY

College of Natural Resources

Programs of Study

The College of Natural Resources offers graduate programs leading to the Master of Science (M.S.), the Master of Forestry (M.F.), and the Doctor of Philosophy (Ph.D.) degrees. The M.S. and Ph.D. are research oriented and require the completion of a thesis or dissertation and appropriate course work. The M.F. is professionally oriented and does not require a thesis. Programs of study are designed by each candidate in consultation with his/her advisers, and they are approved by the student's advisory committee. Areas of study at all graduate degree levels include forest biology, forest resource management and economics, biometrics, outdoor recreation, industrial forestry operations, forest products operations, forest products marketing and management, wood science and engineering, aquaculture, fisheries science, and wildlife science.

Requirements for the M.S. degree include a minimum of 30 graduate credit hours, 6 of which may be research and thesis credits. The M.F. degree requires the completion of 33 credit hours of directed course work, 6 credits of which are for an independent paper. The Ph.D. degree program requires a minimum of 90 graduate credits, of which 30 or more are for course work and 30–60 credits are devoted to research and dissertation. Ph.D. students are required to pass qualifying and preliminary examinations, and they must complete and defend a dissertation based on original research.

Research Facilities

The College is housed in Julian Cheatham Hall, a three-story building containing approximately 50,000 gross square feet of working space, including laboratories, classrooms, and office space for administration, faculty members, and graduate students. Cheatham Hall also houses the Center for Environmental Applications in Remote Sensing, a facility that supports the application of remote sensing to environmental monitoring and assessment. All graduate students have access to specialized computer facilities. Field research is conducted at several sites throughout the Commonwealth of Virginia. The College operates the Reynolds Homestead Research Center, a 710-acre research unit equipped with a laboratory, a greenhouse, and nursery beds. The Thomas M. Brooks Forest Products Center serves the Department of Wood Science and Forest Products by housing the Center for Forest Products Marketing and Management, the Biobased Materials/Recycling Center, the Process Automation Laboratory, the Center for Wood-Based Composites, the Sardo Pallet and Container Research Laboratory, and the Center for Unit-Load Design. The Department of Fisheries and Wildlife Sciences operates the Center Woods' Aquaculture Center, a 10,000-square-foot facility designed for intensive recycling aquaculture research, and the Fish and Wildlife Information Exchange. Cooperative units of the U.S. Fish and Wildlife Service, Forest Service, and National Park Service include 11 research scientists stationed within the College. Virginia Tech's main library has more than 1.7 million volumes, more than 13,000 periodicals, and seating facilities for 1,800 students. Laboratories for basic research studies in physiology and nutrition of forest trees, fish, and wildlife are located in Cheatham Hall. Research and teaching laboratories in wood science and forest products, timber harvesting, and recycling are located in Cheatham Hall and at the Thomas M. Brooks Forest Products Center.

Financial Aid

Graduate students are eligible for financial support through fellowships and research or teaching assistantships. Assistantships range from approximately $12,000 to $21,000 per annum, depending on the qualifications of the applicant and the time spent assisting with teaching or research. All graduate assistants on half-time appointments receive full instructional fees scholarships in addition to their stipends.

Cost of Study

Graduate tuition fees are $2463.50 per semester for full-time enrollment (9 hours or more) by Virginia residents and $3768.50 per semester for full-time enrollment (9 hours or more) by nonresidents. Part-time and summer enrollment cost proportionately less.

Living and Housing Costs

The University offers specialized housing to graduate students in Hillcrest and Main Campbell Halls; however, most graduate students find ample housing available in off-campus apartments. For additional information about on-campus graduate housing, students should contact Residential and Dining Programs, 109 East Eggleston, Virginia Tech, Mail Code 0428, Blacksburg, Virginia 24061 (telephone: 540-231-6204; e-mail: housing@vt.edu).

Student Group

Approximately 1 in 6 students on the 24,800-student campus of Virginia Tech is a graduate student. The College of Natural Resources enrolled 130 graduate and 580 undergraduate students in 1999. Sixty-four percent of the graduate students are master's candidates, and 36 percent are pursuing Ph.D.'s. Women and international students represent 30 percent and 21 percent, respectively, of the College's graduate student population.

Student Outcomes

Graduates from Virginia Tech's College of Natural Resources find employment in industry, government, academia, and a variety of international organizations involved in natural resource management and utilization. Recent graduates have taken jobs with major corporations (Georgia-Pacific, Weyerhauser, Chesapeake, Hammermill, Champion International, and Westvaco), with the U.S. Forest Service, and with the faculties of North Carolina State University, Oregon State University, Penn State University, Clemson University, the University of California at Berkeley, the University of British Columbia, and others.

Location

The University is located in Blacksburg, a town of 35,000, situated in scenic southwest Virginia. The 2,600-acre campus lies on a plain between the Blue Ridge and Allegheny Mountains, 2,100 feet above sea level. The area is noted for its natural beauty and outdoor recreation opportunities. Outdoor recreation facilities include the Claytor Lake State Park, Mountain Lake, the Blue Ridge Parkway, the New River, the Appalachian Trail, the Jefferson National Forest, and several nearby ski resorts.

The University

Founded in 1872 as Virginia's land-grant university, Virginia Tech has an enrollment of more than 24,800 on-campus students, including more than 4,200 graduate students. Graduate work is offered in more than 120 fields of study leading to the master's or doctoral degrees. Virginia Tech is accredited by the Southern Association of Colleges and Schools.

Applying

Applications for admission to the Graduate School must include a transcript from an accredited undergraduate educational institution, completed application forms, and three letters of recommendation. Scores from the Graduate Record Examinations (GRE) are required by the Departments of Fisheries and Wildlife Sciences and Forestry. If the applicant's native language is not English, TOEFL and GRE scores are required. Application forms are available from the Graduate School, 209 Sandy Hall, Virginia Tech, Mail Code 0325, Blacksburg, Virginia 24061. Applications for fall semester admission should be received by March 1; assistantship applications are usually required by January 31, but some assistantship applications are considered at other times.

Correspondence and Information

Head Department of:
Fisheries and Wildlife Sciences (Dr. Brian Murphy)
Forestry (Dr. Harold Burkhart)
Wood Science and Forest Products (Dr. Geza Ifju), or

College of Natural Resources
324 Julian Cheatham Hall
Virginia Polytechnic Institute and State University
Mail Code 0324
Blacksburg, Virginia 24061

For general information, contact:

Dr. Gregory N. Brown, Dean
College of Natural Resources
324 Julian Cheatham Hall
Virginia Polytechnic Institute and State University
Mail Code 0324
Blacksburg, Virginia 24061
Telephone: 540-231-5481
Fax: 540-231-7664
World Wide Web: http://www.vt.edu/vt98/
    academics/graduateschool.html

Virginia Polytechnic Institute and State University

THE FACULTY AND THEIR RESEARCH

Department of Fisheries and Wildlife Sciences

Paul L. Angermeier, Associate Professor; Ph.D., Illinois, 1982. Fish communities, assessing quality and value of aquatic resources.

James M. Berkson, Assistant Professor; Ph.D., Montana State, 1996. Resource modeling, wildlife management, conservation biology, population dynamics.

Gerald H. Cross, Associate Professor and Coordinator of Continuing Education; Ph.D., North Dakota State, 1973. Continuing education in natural resources.

C. Andrew Dolloff, Associate Professor; Ph.D., Montana State, 1983. Salmonid ecology, cold-water stream ecology, forest-fisheries management.

Patricia A. Flebbe, Assistant Professor; Ph.D., Georgia, 1982. Cold-water stream ecology, watershed ecosystem modeling, systems ecology.

James D. Fraser, Professor; Ph.D., Minnesota, 1981. Conservation biology, management of endangered wildlife, nongame wildlife.

Carola A. Haas, Associate Professor; Ph.D., Cornell, 1990. Conservation biology, behavioral ecology, management of nongame birds.

Eric M. Hallerman, Associate Professor; Ph.D., Auburn, 1984. Fish genetics, conservation genetics, aquaculture.

Louis A. Helfrich, Professor; Ph.D., Michigan State, 1976. Aquaculture, water quality, lake and pond management, angler attitudes.

Roy L. Kirkpatrick, Thomas H. Jones Professor; Ph.D., Wisconsin, 1966. Nutritional and physiological ecology, population ecology.

A. Dennis Lemly, Assistant Professor; Ph.D., Wake Forest, 1983. Ecology of stream macroinvertebrates, insect-sediment interactions.

George S. Libey, Research Associate Professor; Ph.D., Massachusetts, 1976. Aquaculture, biofiltration, recirculating systems, induced spawning.

Steve L. McMullin, Associate Professor; Ph.D., Virginia Tech, 1993. Human dimension of fisheries and wildlife, natural resource administration and policy.

Brian R. Murphy, Professor; Ph.D., Virginia Tech, 1981. Fisheries ecology and management, management of tropical natural resources.

Richard J. Neves, Professor; Ph.D., Massachusetts, 1977. Stream ecology, endangered mollusks, freshwater mussels.

Tammy J. Newcomb, Assistant Professor; Ph.D., Virginia, 1997. Management of regulated rivers, watershed restoration, stream temperature modeling.

John J. Ney, Professor; Ph.D., Minnesota, 1973. Population ecology, reservoir fisheries, trophic dynamics, environmental impact assessment.

Donald J. Orth, Professor; Ph.D., Oklahoma State, 1980. Fisheries management, fish population dynamics, modeling stream habitat management.

James A. Parkhurst, Associate Professor; Ph.D., Penn State, 1989. Wildlife damage management, management of forest and wetland habitats.

Patrick F. Scanlon, Professor; Ph.D., Ireland, 1970. Reproductive and environmental physiology of wildlife, environmental contamination; wildlife toxicology; vertebrate pest management.

Dean F. Stauffer, Associate Professor; Ph.D., Idaho, 1983. Wildlife-habitat relationships and analysis, habitat evaluation, neotropical migratory birds.

Michael R. Vaughn, Professor; Ph.D., Wisconsin, 1979. Population ecology, large game management, waterfowl management.

Department of Forestry

Gregory S. Amacher, Associate Professor; Ph.D., Michigan, 1993. Natural resource policy design, international trade/finance, econometrics.

W. Michael Aust, Associate Professor; Ph.D., North Carolina State, 1989. Forested wetland ecology and management, forest hydrology.

Gregory J. Buhyoff, Julian N. Cheatham Professor; Ph.D., Michigan, 1974. Visual impact modeling, decision support systems.

James A. Burger, Professor; Ph.D., Florida, 1979. Management of forest soils, sustaining forest land productivity.

Harold E. Burkhart, Thomas M. Brooks Professor; Ph.D., Georgia, 1969. Modeling forest stand development; application of statistical methods.

Troy E. Hall, Assistant Professor; Ph.D., Oregon State, 1996. Social values of natural resources.

Harry L. Haney Jr., Garland Gray Professor; Ph.D., Yale, 1975. Forestry investment analysis, taxation, management of private timberland; conservation easements.

R. Bruce Hull, Associate Professor; Ph.D., Virginia Tech, 1984. Human dimensions, visual quality, recreation.

William F. Hyde, Professor; Ph.D., Michigan, 1977. Natural resource economics and policy, international economic development.

James E. Johnson, Professor; Ph.D., Virginia Tech, 1981. Silviculture of Appalachian hardwoods and southern pines.

Jeffrey L. Kirwan, Assistant Professor; Ph.D., Virginia, 1997. 4-H and youth education, forest and wildlife ecology, climate change, paleoecology.

W. David Klemperer, Professor; Ph.D., Oregon State, 1971. Forest investment analysis, taxation, risk analysis.

Jeffrey L. Marion, Adjunct Assistant Professor; Ph.D., Minnesota, 1984. Park and wilderness recreation resource management, recreation ecology.

Paul P. Mou, Assistant Professor; Ph.D., Cornell, 1991. Forest ecosystem ecology, vegetation dynamic modeling, root ecology.

Richard G. Oderwald, Associate Professor; Ph.D., Georgia, 1975. Forest inventory and modelling, GPS, GIS.

Philip J. Radtke, Assistant Professor; Ph.D., Michigan, 1998. Forest modeling, inventory, and sampling.

Marion R. Reynolds, Professor; Ph.D., Stanford, 1972. Statistical quality control, model validation.

Joseph W. Roggenbuck, Professor; Ph.D., Utah State, 1975. Wilderness and backcountry recreation management.

John R. Seiler, Professor; Ph.D., Virginia Tech, 1984. Southern pine ecophysiology, stress physiology, actinorrhizal nitrogen fixation, water relations.

Robert M. Shaffer, Associate Professor; Ph.D., Missouri, 1982. Timber harvesting, economic analysis of industrial forestry operations.

David Wm. Smith, The Honorable and Mrs. Shelton H. Short Jr. Professor; Ph.D., Iowa State, 1970. Silviculture of upland hardwoods.

Jay Sullivan, Associate Professor; Ph.D., Berkeley, 1988. Forest planning methods and operations research, economic impact analysis.

Harold W. Wisdom, Professor; Ph.D., SUNY College of Forestry, 1967. International forestry, econometric analysis of forest industry.

Randolph H. Wynne, Assistant Professor; Ph.D., Wisconsin–Madison, 1995. Remote sensing and GIS in natural resource management.

Shepard M. Zedaker, Professor; Ph.D., Oregon State, 1980. Regeneration ecology, chemical silviculture, plant competition.

Department of Wood Science and Forest Products

Robert J. Bush, Associate Professor; Ph.D., Virginia Tech, 1989. Marketing of wood and wood-based products, international trade.

J. Daniel Dolan, Associate Professor; Ph.D., British Columbia, 1989. Response of wood structures to dynamic loads, hurricanes, and earthquakes.

Charles E. Frazier, Associate Professor; Ph.D., Virginia Tech, 1992. Wood adhesives and adhesion, surface chemistry, polymers and plastics.

Wolfgang G. Glasser, Professor; Ph.D., Hamburg (Germany), 1969. Wood-derived polymers and composites; lignin utilization.

A. L. Hammett, Associate Professor; Ph.D., Georgia. Utilization and marketing of special forest products, world forestry; international trade and marketing.

Richard F. Helm, Associate Professor; Ph.D., Wisconsin–Madison, 1987. Wood chemistry, biochemistry, biotechnology.

Geza Ifju, Professor; Ph.D., British Columbia, 1963. Quantitative characterization of the structure of wood and wood products.

Frederick A. Kamke, Professor; Ph.D., Oregon State, 1983. Composite wood products, heat and mass transfer in wood.

D. Earl Kline, Associate Professor; Ph.D., Texas A&M, 1987. Industrial engineering in wood products manufacturing systems.

Fred M. Lamb, Professor; Ed.D., Penn State, 1980. Wood processing and machining, furniture manufacturing processes.

Joseph R. Loferski, Professor; Ph.D., Virginia Tech, 1985. Structural design with wood, preservation of historic structures.

Robert L. Smith, Associate Professor; Ph.D., Virginia Tech, 1994. Forest products marketing/management, wood processing.

Cynthia D. West, Adjunct Assistant Professor; Ph.D., Virginia Tech, 1990. Markets for forest products, economics of manufacturing.

Marshall S. White, Professor; Ph.D., Virginia Tech, 1975. Primary processing, lumber and pallet manufacturing, pallet design, unit load design.

Maurice W. White, Assistant Professor; Ph.D., Virginia Tech, 1995. Timber structures under dynamic stresses.

Frank E. Woeste, Adjunct Professor; Ph.D., Purdue, 1975, PE. Probabilstic approach to structural design, wood mechanics.

Audrey G. Zink-Sharp, Associate Professor; Ph.D., SUNY College of Environmental Science and Forestry 1992. Experimental stress analysis.

Details on individual faculty members and their research interests may be found on the College's homepage (http://www.fw.vt.edu).

YALE UNIVERSITY

School of Forestry and Environmental Studies

Programs of Study

The School of Forestry and Environmental Studies offers graduate study at the master's and doctoral levels for those whose objectives are to preserve the health, productivity, and renewability of the world's natural resources while still using them to satisfy human needs. Three master's degrees are offered: the Master of Environmental Studies (one- or two-year M.E.S. program), Master of Forest Science (two-year M.F.S. program), and Master of Forestry (one- or two-year M.F. program). Joint master's degree programs are available with the following schools and departments at Yale: Law, Management, Economics, Epidemiology and Public Health, International Development Economics, and International Relations. The Doctor of Forestry and Environmental Studies (D.F.E.S.) program is designed for advanced study by students interested in careers in resource management and in academic research related to resource management. Those interested in careers primarily in research or teaching are advised to seek the degree of Doctor of Philosophy (Ph.D.).

Course work and research opportunities are offered in ecosystem dynamics, structure, and function; conservation of biological diversity; management of forest ecosystems; coastal and watershed systems; property, institutions, and the environment; and valuation, risk, and environmental decision marking.

While curricula of study in all master's programs are sufficiently flexible to accommodate varying backgrounds and career aspirations, they are partially structured to ensure professional competence and maximum exposure to the diverse offerings of the School and Yale's other departments and professional schools.

Cooperative arrangements exist with the Connecticut Agricultural Experiment Station and the Forest Insect and Disease Laboratory of the USDA Forest Service, the Institute of Ecosystem Studies at the Cary Arboretum of the New York Botanical Gardens, the Department of Natural Resources, the Commonwealth of Puerto Rico, the Hubbard Brook Experimental Forest in New Hampshire, and Cornell and other universities.

Research Facilities

The School's five buildings house laboratories, controlled-environment rooms, a greenhouse, computer labs, and other research facilities. The Forestry Library in Sage Hall has holdings of more than 130,000 volumes; 326 periodicals and about 800 other serial publications are received. Field instruction and research are conducted on the more than 10,000 acres of Yale Forests located in northeastern Connecticut, southwestern New Hampshire, and Vermont. Private and public land across the United States and in Puerto Rico is also available.

Financial Aid

Every effort is made to enable qualified students to attend the School, regardless of their financial circumstances. Financial aid is awarded on the basis of need, academic merit, and available resources. Approximately two thirds of the student body receive financial aid in the form of loans, work-study, and/or scholarships. Applicants are encouraged to investigate external sources of aid. Applicants to a master's program who are requesting financial aid must submit the Free Application for Federal Student Aid (FAFSA) by February 1.

Cost of Study

Tuition for the 1999–2000 academic year is $19,630 for the master's programs and $22,330 for the doctoral programs. The fee for the summer training modules in technical skills, required for all students in the two-year master's programs, is $900. Books and supplies are generally $850.

Living and Housing Costs

University housing is available for a limited number of single students and for married students. Most students live off campus.

Student Group

The total graduate enrollment at Yale is 5,000. Approximately 230 master's and Doctor of Forestry and Environmental Studies students are enrolled in the School of Forestry and Environmental Studies, and 30 Ph.D. students are in the Department of Forestry and Environmental Studies of the Yale Graduate School. Students come from diverse educational, geographical, and national backgrounds. Approximately 20 percent of the students come from thirty countries around the world.

Location

Yale University is located in New Haven, Connecticut, a harbor city of approximately 127,000, situated midway between New York City and Boston. Known for its theater life and its distinct neighborhoods, New Haven also permits easy access to harbor, beach, and mountain areas.

The University and The School

Yale University is a private institution, founded in 1701 under the leadership of a group of Congregational ministers. Today it continues its early tradition of liberal education and community service. Yale is noted for the high quality of its theater productions, art galleries, and libraries as well as for its renowned educational and research facilities.

In 1973, the name of the School was changed to include Environmental Studies to reflect the broadening of its programs. The School's professional forestry programs are accredited by the Society of American Foresters.

Applying

Applications for the master's degree programs must be postmarked by February 1; notification of acceptance is made by April 1. There is no application fee. The GRE General Test is required.

Applications for the Doctor of Philosophy must be postmarked by January 3; applications for the Doctor of Forestry and Environmental Studies must be postmarked by February 1. Notification of acceptance is made by April 1. Scores on the GRE General Test are required.

Students for whom English is a second language must submit a TOEFL score as part of their application to any of the programs offered by the School.

Correspondence and Information

For master's programs:
Director of Academic Affairs
Yale School of Forestry and Environmental Studies
205 Prospect Street
New Haven, Connecticut 06511
Telephone: 203-432-5106
          800-825-0330 (toll-free)
E-mail: fesinfo@yale.edu

For Ph.D. and D.F.E.S. programs:
Dr. John Wargo
Director of Graduate Studies
Yale School of Forestry and Environmental Studies
370 Prospect Street
New Haven, Connecticut 06511
Telephone: 203-432-5123
E-mail: john.wargo@yale.edu

Yale University

THE FACULTY AND THEIR RESEARCH

Gregory Arthaud, Associate Professor of Forest Management; Ph.D., Minnesota. Forest resource economics and multiple resource management.

Mark Ashton, Associate Professor of Silviculture; Ph.D., Yale. Regeneration of natural forests.

Paul K. Barten, Associate Professor of Water Resources; Ph.D., Minnesota. Water resource management; forest hydrology.

Lynne L. Bennett, Assistant Professor of Economics; Ph.D., Colorado. Economics of water resources.

Gaboury Benoit, Associate Professor of Environmental Chemistry; Ph.D., MIT. Chemical oceanography; environmental engineering.

Graeme P. Berlyn, Professor of Anatomy and Physiology of Trees; Ph.D., Iowa State. Tissue culture and regeneration of trees; DNA characterization of cell and tree populations; effects of toxic and radioactive materials on tree growth and development.

William R. Burch Jr., Frederick C. Hixon Professor of Natural Resource Management and Professor at the Institution for Social and Policy Studies; M.F., Ph.D., Minnesota. Sociology.

Michael Dove, Professor of Social Ecology; Ph.D., Stanford. Ecological anthropology.

Daniel C. Esty, Associate Professor of Environmental Law and Policy and Associate Clinical Professor, Law School; J.D., Yale. Environmental policy issues.

Robert E. Evenson, Professor of Economics and Professor of Forestry and Environmental Studies; Ph.D., Chicago. Economics.

Gordon T. Geballe, Lecturer in Forest Microbiology and Assistant Dean; Ph.D., Yale. Plant physiology; air pollution effects on plants.

John C. Gordon, Pinchot Professor of Forestry and Environmental Studies and Dean; Ph.D., Iowa State. Tree physiology and forest yield improvement.

Timothy Gregoire, Professor of Forest Statistics; Ph.D., Yale. Forest biometrics.

Stephen R. Kellert, Professor of Social Ecology; Ph.D., Yale. Human dimensions in resource management; human/animal ecology; sociology; museology.

Bruce Larson, Lecturer in Forest Management and Director of School Forests; Ph.D., Washington (Seattle). Silviculture, land management.

Xuhui Lee, Assistant Professor of Biometeorology; Ph.D., British Columbia. Biometeorology.

Robert O. Mendelsohn, Professor of Forest Policy and Professor of Environmental Economics; Ph.D., Yale. Economics.

Joseph A. Miller, Lecturer in Forest History; Ph.D., Minnesota. History and library science.

Alison Richard, Provost Professor of Anthropology and Professor of Environmental Studies; Ph.D., London. Anthropology; behavioral ecology.

Oswald Schmitz, Associate Professor of Wildlife Ecology; Ph.D., Michigan. Wildlife ecology, population and community ecology.

Thomas G. Siccama, Lecturer in Forest Ecology; Ph.D., Vermont. Forest ecology.

David K. Skelly, Assistant Professor of Ecology; Ph.D., Michigan. Landscape ecology, community ecology.

William H. Smith, Clifton R. Musser Professor of Forest Biology; Ph.D., Rutgers. Forest health, ecotoxicology.

Daniel J. Vogt, Lecturer in Soils and Forest Ecology; Ph.D., Washington (Seattle). Interaction of soils and plants.

Kristiina A. Vogt, Associate Professor of Forest Ecology; Ph.D., New Mexico State. Ecosystem ecology.

John P. Wargo, Associate Professor of Forestry and Environmental Studies and Assistant Professor of Political Science; Ph.D., Yale. Natural resource policy.

Research and Training Opportunities in the Physical Sciences, Mathematics, Agricultural Sciences, the Environment, and Natural Resources

This part of Book 4 consists of one section covering research and training opportunities in the physical sciences, mathematics, agricultural sciences, the environment, and natural resources. The section has a table of contents; a profile directory, which consists of brief profiles of the academic centers and institutes followed by 50-word and 100-word announcements, if centers and institutes have chosen to submit such entries; and in-depth descriptions, which are more individualized statements, if centers and institutes have chosen to submit them.

Section 11
Research and Training Opportunities

Academic Centers and Institutes

The role and importance of academic centers and institutes in the graduate study experience has increased dramatically in recent years. In response to growing requests for information on such centers and institutes, the profiles in this section include the data on academic centers and institutes that were submitted in 1999 by each institution in response to Peterson's Supplemental Survey of Academic Centers and Institutes.

This section provides detailed information on university-owned and university-operated centers and institutes offering graduate students research or study opportunities. To qualify for inclusion in this section, a center or institute must be a formal and integral part of a graduate degree program. Such centers and institutes are separate from, but may sometimes maintain affiliations with, other special research facilities also located on the university's campus, such as laboratory or computer facilities.

Centers and institutes listed are academic in nature and do not include university business, administrative, or operational units or departments. Most have formally dedicated faculty and staff members associated with them and may provide training programs in the early part of a Ph.D. program. Many are interdisciplinary; however, some centers and institutes may focus on a single discipline, a major research project, or a specialized area of study. In some cases, graduate degrees may be awarded by the institute or research unit, although most do not.

Centers and institutes appear alphabetically by institution, followed by in-depth entries submitted by centers or institutes that chose to prepare detailed descriptions. The following items appear for each center or institute profile when available. Readers may contact centers and institutes directly for further information.

Name of Center or Institute. The name of the center or institute appears in boldface type.

Founding Year. The year the center or institute was established.

Academic Areas of Research and Training. Specific areas of graduate research or training listed (e.g., cancer research in molecular and cell biology, epidemiology, and psychology).

Degrees Offered. For those centers and institutes that do award degrees, these may include master's and/or doctoral degrees in specific academic fields or areas.

Graduate Students Served Last Academic Year. Figures are provided separately for the total number of students served in the last academic year and, for some institutions, how many students were served specifically at the master's, doctoral, and postgraduate levels, respectively.

Faculty. Figures are provided for the total number of faculty members associated with the center or institute and those associated with the center or institute but having their primary affiliation with another unit of the university.

Faculty Affiliations. The names of departments, programs, and other units with which faculty members are affiliated are listed here.

Annual Research Budget. Figures for the center or institute's annual research budget are listed.

Director. The name and title of the center or institute's director is provided, along with his/her address, telephone number, fax number, and e-mail address.

Information Contact. Provides the name and title of the person who should receive inquiries from interested students, with the address, telephone number, fax number, and e-mail address for this individual.

CONTENTS

Research and Training Opportunities

Alabama Agricultural and Mechanical University, Normal, AL 35762-1357.

Center for Environmental Research and Training Founded in 1990. *Academic areas of research and training:* Environmental chemistry, wetland chemistry and biology, bioremediation, contaminant transport, water quality, hydrology. *Degrees offered:* None. *Graduate students served last academic year:* 44: 22 at the master's level; 22 at the doctoral level. *Faculty:* 6: 6 affiliated solely with the center. *Faculty affiliations:* Department of Plant and Soil Science. *Annual research budget:* $300,000. *Director:* Dr. Robert W. Taylor, Director, 256-858-4187, Fax: 256-851-5429, E-mail: rwtaylor@aamu.edu. *Application contact:* Chantae R. Hardin-Alfred, Secretary, 256-858-4199, Fax: 256-851-5429, E-mail: aamcrh01@aamu.edu.

Center for Forestry and Ecology Founded in 1993. *Academic areas of research and training:* Clonal propagation and genetics, hardwood regeneration, short rotation woody biomass, woody plant stress physiology, upland hardwood silviculture, ecology and management, forest protection and entomology. *Degrees offered:* None. *Graduate students served last academic year:* 8: 7 at the master's level; 1 at the doctoral level. *Faculty:* 9: 5 affiliated solely with the center. *Faculty affiliations:* Department of Plant and Soil Science. *Annual research budget:* $550,000. *Director:* Dr. George F. Brown, Director, 256-858-4189, Fax: 256-851-5429, E-mail: aamgfb01@aamu.edu. *Application contact:* Delaine B. Rashid, Executive Secretary, 256-858-4197, Fax: 256-851-5429, E-mail: aamdbr01@aamu.edu.

Center for Hydrology, Soil Climatology, and Remote Sensing Founded in 1995. *Academic areas of research and training:* Foster new science and technology concepts, expand the nation's base for hydrology and remote sensing research and development, develop mechanisms for increased participation by faculty and students in mainstream research. *Degrees offered:* None. *Graduate students served last academic year:* 18: 11 at the master's level; 7 at the doctoral level. *Faculty:* 32: 18 affiliated solely with the center. *Faculty affiliations:* Areas in Physics; Urban and Regional Planning; Departments of Mathematics and Computer Science; Plant, Soil and Animal Sciences; University of Alabama in Huntsville Department of Atmospheric and Environmental Sciences; Global Hydrology and Climate Center. *Annual research budget:* $1.5 million. *Director:* Dr. Tommy L. Coleman, Director, 256-851-5075, Fax: 256-851-5076, E-mail: tcoleman@aamu.edu.

The Howard J. Foster Center for Irradiation of Materials Founded in 1990. *Academic areas of research and training:* Provide research and services capabilities on materials processing and materials characterization; ion implantation, electron and ion microscopy; optical and electrical properties measurement; surface and interface processing. *Degrees offered:* None. *Graduate students served last academic year:* 12: 6 at the master's level; 6 at the doctoral level. *Faculty:* 24: 6 affiliated solely with the center. *Faculty affiliations:* Departments of Biology, Civil Engineering, Chemistry, Computer Science, Mathematics, Mechanical Engineering, Physics. *Annual research budget:* $1.2 million. *Director:* Dr. Daryush Ila, Director, 205-851-5866, Fax: 205-851-5868, E-mail: ila@cim.aamu.edu.

Plant Science Center (PSC) Founded in 1993. *Academic areas of research and training:* Plant physiology, plant genetics and breeding, plant pathology, plant cytogenetics, cropping system, sustainable agriculture, agronomy, horticulture, seed science and technology. *Degrees offered:* None. *Graduate students served last academic year:* 6: 4 at the master's level; 2 at the doctoral level. *Faculty:* 6: 6 affiliated solely with the center. *Faculty affiliations:* Department of Plant and Soil Science. *Annual research budget:* $450,000. *Director:* Dr. Caula A. Beyl, Director, 256-858-4193, Fax: 256-851-5429, E-mail: cbeyl@aamu.edu. *Application contact:* Mary E. Chandler, Senior Secretary, 256-858-4198, Fax: 256-851-5429, E-mail: mechandler@aamu.edu.

Research Institute Founded in 1999. *Academic areas of research and training:* Provide business type environment to conduct contracts for all agencies using the capabilities at the university. *Degrees offered:* None. *Graduate students served last academic year:* 6: 3 at the master's level; 1 at the doctoral level; 2 at the postgraduate level. *Faculty:* 68: 3 affiliated solely with the institute. *Faculty affiliations:* Departments of Biology, Chemistry, Civil Engineering, Computer Science, Environmental Science, Food Science, Mathematics, Mechanical Engineering, Physics, Urban Planning; School of Business. *Annual research budget:* $1 million. *Director:* Dr. Daryush Ila, Director, 205-851-5877, Fax: 205-851-5868, E-mail: ila@cim.aamu.edu.

Auburn University, Auburn, Auburn University, AL 36849-0002.

International Center for Aquaculture and Aquatic Environments Founded in 1971. *Academic areas of research and training:* Aquaculture, aquatic environment assessment, socio-economic studies, fisheries, aquatic ecology. *Degrees offered:* None. *Graduate students served last academic year:* 20 at the master's level; 30 at the doctoral level; 6 at the postgraduate level. *Faculty:* 54: 4 affiliated solely with the center. *Faculty affiliations:* College of Agriculture. *Director:* Dr. Bryan L. Duncan, Director, 334-844-9210, Fax: 334-844-9208, E-mail: bduncan@acesag.auburn.edu. *Application contact:* Billy Earle, Administrative Assistant, 334-844-9210, Fax: 334-844-9208, E-mail: bearle@acesag.auburn.edu.

Boise State University, Boise, ID 83725-0399.

Center for Geophysical Investigation of the Shallow Subsurface (CGISS) Founded in 1991. *Academic areas of research and training:* Geophysical applications to hydrogeology, geotechnical engineering, environmental science, geology, geophysics, earthquake hazards. *Degrees offered:* None. *Graduate students served last academic year:* 17: 17 at the master's level. *Faculty:* 10: 5 affiliated solely with the center. *Faculty affiliations:* Departments of Civil Engineering, Geosciences, Mathematics and Computer Science. *Annual research budget:* $1 million. *Director:* Dr. John R. Pelton, Director, 208-426-3640, Fax: 208-426-3888, E-mail: jrp@cgiss.boisestate.edu.

Boston College, Chestnut Hill, MA 02467-3800.

Weston Observatory Founded in 1928. *Academic areas of research and training:* Seismological and geological research. *Degrees offered:* None. *Graduate students served last academic year:* 5: 5 at the master's level. *Faculty:* 9: 5 affiliated solely with Weston Observatory. *Faculty affiliations:* Department of Geology and Geophysics. *Director:* Dr. John Ebel, Director, 617-552-8300, Fax: 617-552-8388, E-mail: ebel@bc.edu.

Boston University, Boston, MA 02215.

Center for Computational Science Founded in 1990. *Academic areas of research and training:* Interdisciplinary computational science. *Degrees offered:* None. *Graduate students served last academic year:* 5: 5 at the doctoral level. *Faculty:* 43: 3 affiliated solely with the center. *Faculty affiliations:* Departments of Aerospace and Mechanical Engineering, Chemistry, Cognitive and Neural Systems, Computer Science, Electrical and Computer Engineering, Geography, Manufacturing Engineering, Mathematics, Physics. *Annual research budget:* $1.6 million. *Director:* Dr. Claudio Rebbi, Director, 617-353-9058, Fax: 617-353-6062, E-mail: rebbi@bu.edu. *Application contact:* Dr. Ilona Lappo, Assistant Director, 617-353-5637, Fax: 617-353-6062, E-mail: lappo@bu.edu.

Center for Remote Sensing Founded in 1986. *Academic areas of research and training:* Applications of remote sensing and geographic information systems to the fields of archaeology, earth sciences, and geography. *Degrees offered:* None. *Graduate students served last academic year:* 19: 10 at the master's level; 9 at the doctoral level. *Faculty:* 41: 21 affiliated solely with the center. *Faculty affiliations:* Departments of Archaeology, Earth Sciences, Geography. *Annual research budget:* $2.5 million. *Director:* Dr. Farouk El-Baz, Director, 617-353-5081, Fax: 617-353-3200, E-mail: farouk@bu.edu. *Application contact:* Meghan Sutherland, Administrative Assistant, 617-353-9709, Fax: 617-353-3200, E-mail: msutherl@crsa.bu.edu.

Center for Space Physics Founded in 1987. *Academic areas of research and training:* Space physics and aeronomy, planetary atmospheres, solar-terrestrial physics, upper atmosphere physics. *Degrees offered:* None. *Graduate students served last academic year:* 27: 10 at the master's level; 15 at the doctoral level. *Faculty:* 14. *Faculty affiliations:* Departments of Astronomy, Electrical and Computer Engineering. *Annual research budget:* $4 million. *Director:* Dr. Supriya Chakrabarti, Director, 617-353-7425, Fax: 617-353-6463, E-mail: supc@veebs.bu.edu. *Application contact:* Kathy Nottingham, Assistant to the Director, 617-353-5990, Fax: 617-353-6463, E-mail: kathynot@bu.edu.

Brown University, Providence, RI 02912.

Lefschetz Center for Dynamical Systems Founded in 1964. *Academic areas of research and training:* Dynamical systems, nonlinear ordinary and partial differential equations and applications, stochastic systems theory. *Degrees offered:* PhD. *Graduate students served last academic year:* 13: 13 at the doctoral level. *Faculty:* 13. *Faculty affiliations:* Department of Mathematics; Divisions of Applied Mathematics, Engineering. *Annual research budget:* $1 million. *Director:* Prof. Christopher Jones, Director, 401-863-3696, Fax: 401-863-1355, E-mail: ckrtj@e151.cfm.brown.edu. *Application contact:* Winnie Isom, Secretary, 401-863-3724, Fax: 401-863-1355, E-mail: isom@151.cfm.brown.edu.

California Polytechnic State University, San Luis Obispo, San Luis Obispo, CA 93407.

Dairy Products Technology Center Founded in 1987. *Academic areas of research and training:* Dairy science, chemistry and biochemistry of milk and food, physical chemistry of dairy foods and ingredients, microbiology. *Degrees offered:* MS. *Graduate students served last academic year:* 19: 18 at the master's level; 1 at the postgraduate level. *Faculty:* 13: 3 affiliated solely with the center. *Faculty affiliations:* Department of Materials Engineering; Programs in Agricultural Engineering, Chemistry, Food Science, Microbiology. *Annual research budget:* $1.2 million. *Director:* Dr. Leslie S. Ferreira, Director, 805-756-6101, Fax: 805-756-6101, E-mail: lsferrei@calpoly.edu. *Application contact:* Dr. Rafael Jimenez-Flores, Associate Professor, Graduate Student Coordinator, 805-756-6103, Fax: 805-756-2998, E-mail: rjimenez@calpoly.edu.

Irrigation Training and Research Center (ITRC) Founded in 1989. *Academic areas of research and training:* On-farm irrigation, irrigation districts, drip irrigation, irrigation management, automation. *Degrees offered:* None. *Graduate students served last academic year:* 6: 6 at the master's level. *Faculty:* 12: 3 affiliated solely with the center. *Faculty affiliations:* Department of Civil and Environmental Engineering; Programs in Bioresource and Agricultural Engineering, Crop Science, Soil Science. *Annual research budget:* $750,000. *Director:* Dr. Charles M. Burt, Director, 805-756-2379, Fax: 805-756-2433, E-mail: cburt@calpoly.edu.

California State University, Fresno, Fresno, CA 93740-0057.

Center for Irrigation Technology (CIT) *Academic areas of research and training:* Irrigation equipment testing, field evaluation, water management. *Degrees offered:* None. *Annual research budget:* $1 million. *Director:* David F. Zoldoske, Director, 559-278-2066.

Carnegie Mellon University, Pittsburgh, PA 15213-3891.

Center for Light Microscope Imaging and Biotechnology Founded in 1991. *Academic areas of research and training:* Imaging technology, light microscopy and reagent chemistry, biomedical engineering, biology, chemistry, computer science, chemical engineering, physics. *Degrees offered:* None. *Graduate students served last academic year:* 17 at the doctoral level; 10 at the postgraduate level. *Faculty:* 20. *Faculty affiliations:* Departments of Biological Sciences, Chemistry, Chemical Engineering, Computer Science, Mechanical Engineering; Allegheny University of Health Sciences; University of Pittsburgh. *Annual research budget:* $1.8 million. *Director:* Dr. Alan Waggoner, Director, 412-268-3456, Fax: 412-268-6571. *Application contact:* Margie Zamborsky, Secretary to the Director, 412-268-3461, Fax: 412-268-6571, E-mail: mz0t@andrew.cmu.edu.

Center for Nonlinear Analysis Founded in 1991. *Academic areas of research and training:* Emerging areas of applied mathematics. *Degrees offered:* None. *Graduate students served last academic year:* 6: 6 at the postgraduate level. *Faculty:* 19. *Faculty affiliations:* Departments of Mathematical Sciences, Physics. *Annual research budget:* $150,000. *Director:* Dr. Irene Fonseca, Director, 412-268-3615, Fax: 412-268-6380, E-mail: fonseca@andrew.cmu.edu.

Green Design Initiative Founded in 1993. *Academic areas of research and training:* Environmentally conscious product, process, and policy design. *Degrees offered:* None. *Graduate students served last academic year:* 15: 5 at the master's level; 8 at the doctoral level; 2 at the postgraduate level. *Faculty:* 20: 5 affiliated solely with Green Design Initiative. *Faculty affiliations:* Departments of Civil Engineering, Engineering and Public Policy, Mechanical Engineering, Public Policy. *Annual research budget:* $1 million. *Director:* Dr. Lester Lave, Director, 412-268-8837, Fax: 412-268-6837. *Application contact:* Dr. Noellette Conway-Schempf, Executive Director, 412-268-2299, Fax: 412-268-6837, E-mail: nc0y@andrew.cmu.edu.

Case Western Reserve University, Cleveland, OH 44106.

Center for Advanced Liquid Crystalline Optical Materials (ALCOM) *Academic areas of research and training:* Polymer physics. *Degrees offered:* None. *Graduate students served last academic year:* 9 at the doctoral level; 3 at the postgraduate level. *Faculty:* 12. *Faculty affiliations:* Departments of Macromolecular Science, Physics. *Annual research budget:* $800,000. *Director:* Dr. Jack L. Koenig, Director, 216-368-4176, Fax: 216-368-4171, E-mail: jlk6@po.cwru.edu.

Ernest B. Yeager Center for Electrochemical Sciences Founded in 1976. *Academic areas of research and training:* Batteries, biomedical sensors, corrosion, electrochemical engineering, electrochemical sensors, fuels cells, fundamental electrochemistry. *Degrees offered:* None. *Graduate students served last academic year:* 75: 10 at the master's level; 59 at the doctoral level; 6 at the postgraduate level. *Faculty:* 35. *Faculty affiliations:* Departments of Biomedical Engineering, Chemical Engineering, Chemistry, Electrical Engineering and Applied Physics, Macromolecular Science, Mechanical and Aerospace Engineering, Materials Science, and Physics; Edison Sensor Technology and Electronics Design Centers. *Annual research budget:* $4.5 million. *Director:* Dr. Robert F. Savinell, Director, 216-368-6525, Fax: 216-368-3016, E-mail: rfs2@po.cwru.edu. *Application contact:* Administrative Officer, 216-368-6525, Fax: 216-368-3016, E-mail: yces@cheme.cwru.edu.

Colorado School of Mines, Golden, CO 80401-1887.

Center for Research on Hydrates and Other Solids Founded in 1990. *Academic areas of research and training:* Chemical engineering, geology, petroleum engineering. *Degrees offered:* PhD. *Graduate students served last academic year:* 20: 5 at the master's level; 14 at the doctoral level; 1 at the postgraduate level. *Faculty:* 5: 1 affiliated solely with the center. *Faculty affiliations:* Departments of Geology, Petroleum Engineering. *Annual research budget:* $550,000. *Director:* Dr. E. Dendy Sloan, Director, 303-273-3723, Fax: 303-273-3730, E-mail: esloan@gashydrate.mines.colorado.edu.

Center for Wave Phenomena (CWP) Founded in 1984. *Academic areas of research and training:* Applied mathematics, geophysics. *Degrees offered:* None. *Graduate students served last academic year:* 18: 5 at the master's level; 13 at the doctoral level. *Faculty:* 10: 5 affiliated solely with the center. *Faculty affiliations:* Departments of Geophysics, Mathematical and Computer Sciences. *Annual research budget:* $1.8 million. *Director:* Dr. Kenneth L. Larner, Director, 303-273-3557, Fax: 303-273-3478, E-mail: klarner@dix.mines.edu.

Colorado Advanced Materials Institute (CAMI) Founded in 1983. *Academic areas of research and training:* Advanced materials. *Degrees offered:* None. *Faculty:* 1: 1 affiliated solely with the institute. *Faculty affiliations:* Departments of Chemical Engineering, Materials Science, Metallurgical and Materials Engineering, Physics. *Annual research budget:* $600,000. *Director:* Dr. Frederick J. Fraikor, Director, 303-273-3852, Fax: 303-273-3656, E-mail: ffraikor@mines.colorado.edu. *Application contact:* Roz Taylor, Program Administrator, 303-273-3852, Fax: 303-273-3656, E-mail: rtaylor@mines.edu.

Reservoir Characterization Project (RCP) Founded in 1985. *Academic areas of research and training:* Geology, geophysics, reservoir engineering. *Degrees offered:* None. *Graduate students served last academic year:* 12: 5 at the master's level; 7 at the doctoral level. *Faculty:* 6: 2 affiliated solely with the project. *Faculty affiliations:* Departments of Geology, Geophysics, Petroleum Engineering. *Annual research budget:* $1 million. *Director:* Dr. Thomas L. Davis, Director, 303-273-3938, Fax: 303-273-3478, E-mail: tdavis@mines.edu.

Colorado State University, Fort Collins, CO 80523-0015.

Center for Applied Statistical Expertise Founded in 1995. *Academic areas of research and training:* Statistical design and analysis. *Degrees offered:* None. *Graduate students served last academic year:* 3: 2 at the master's level; 1 at the doctoral level. *Faculty:* 6: 2 affiliated solely with the center. *Faculty affiliations:* Department of Statistics. *Annual research budget:* $95,000. *Director:* Dr. Richard Davis, Director, 970-491-5268, Fax: 970-491-1084, E-mail: case@stat.colostate.edu. *Application contact:* James zumBrunnen, Associate Director, 970-491-6882, Fax: 970-491-1084, E-mail: zumbrunn@stat.colostate.edu.

Center for Ecological Management of Military Lands (CEMML) Founded in 1988. *Academic areas of research and training:* Natural resource management. *Degrees offered:* None. *Graduate students served last academic year:* 7: 5 at the master's level; 1 at the doctoral level; 1 at the postgraduate level. *Faculty:* 8: 3 affiliated solely with the center. *Faculty affiliations:* Departments of Chemical and Bioresource Engineering, Forest Sciences. *Annual research budget:* $10 million. *Director:* Dr. Robert B. Shaw, Director, 970-491-1072, Fax: 970-491-2713, E-mail: rshaw@cemml.colostate.edu. *Application contact:* Mary Huwa, Assistant Director, 303-491-6620, Fax: 303-491-2713, E-mail: mhuwa@cemml.colostate.edu.

Colorado Water Resources Research Institute (CWRRI) Founded in 1964. *Academic areas of research and training:* Wetlands, hydraulic engineering, irrigation, river engineering, water resources, hydrology, natural resources, environmental quality, water quality, sedimentation, groundwater, environmental monitoring, stochastic processes, models. *Degrees offered:* None. *Graduate students served last academic year:* 35: 25 at the master's level; 10 at the doctoral level. *Faculty:* 122. *Faculty affiliations:* Departments of Agricultural and Resource Economics, Atmospheric Science, Bioagricultural Sciences and Pest Management, Biology, Chemistry and Bioresource Engineering, Civil Engineering, Earth Resources, Environmental Health, Fishery and Wildlife Biology, Forest Sciences, History, Horticulture, Mathematics, Mechanical Engineering, Microbiology, Philosophy, Political Science, Recreation Resources, Rangeland Ecosystem Science, Sociology, Soil and Crop Sciences, Statistics. *Annual research budget:* $220,000. *Director:* Dr. Robert C. Ward, Director, 970-491-6308, Fax: 970-491-2293, E-mail: cwrri@colostate.edu.

Flash Flood Laboratory Founded in 1997. *Academic areas of research and training:* End-to-end flash flood process including precipitation forecasting, hydrology, annecedent (soil) moisture, emergency warning, socio-economic impacts of flash floods. *Degrees offered:* None. *Graduate students served last academic year:* 2: 1 at the doctoral level; 1 at the postgraduate level. *Faculty:* 20. *Faculty affiliations:* Departments of Atmospheric Sciences, Civil Engineering, Economics, Sociology. *Annual research budget:* $45,000. *Director:* Dr. Thomas H. Vonder Haar, Director, Fax: 970-491-8241, E-mail: vonderhaar@cira.colostate.edu. *Application contact:* Kenneth E. Eis, Deputy Director, 970-491-8397, Fax: 970-491-8241, E-mail: eis@cira.colostate.edu.

Natural Resource Ecology Laboratory Founded in 1967. *Academic areas of research and training:* Ecosystem science. *Degrees offered:* None. *Graduate students served last academic year:* 52: 14 at the master's level; 21 at the doctoral level; 17 at the postgraduate level. *Faculty:* 23: 10 affiliated solely with the laboratory. *Faculty affiliations:* Departments of Anthropology, Biology, Forest Sciences, Rangeland Ecosystem Sciences, Soil and Crop Sciences; National Center for Research in the Atmosphere; University of Denver; University of Northern Colorado. *Annual research budget:* $7.7 million. *Director:* Dr. Diana Wall, Director, 970-491-1982, Fax: 970-491-3945, E-mail: info@nrel.colostate.edu.

Red Meat Research Laboratory Founded in 1992. *Academic areas of research and training:* Microbiological safety of red meat, animal science, meat science. *Degrees offered:* None. *Graduate students served last academic year:* 5: 2 at the master's level; 3 at the doctoral level. *Faculty:* 6. *Faculty affiliations:* Department of Animal Sciences. *Annual research budget:* $1 million. *Director:* Dr. Glenn R. Schmidt, Co-Director, 970-491-6527, Fax: 970-491-0278, E-mail: gschmidt@ceres.agsci.colostate.edu.

Concordia University, Montréal, PQ H3G 1M8, Canada.

Picosecond Laser Flash Photolysis Centre Founded in 1983. *Academic areas of research and training:* Photo chemistry and photophysics, laser spectroscopy. *Degrees offered:* None. *Graduate students served last academic year:* 5: 2 at the master's level; 3 at the doctoral level. *Faculty:* 4: 1 affiliated solely with the center. *Director:* Dr. N. Serpone, Director, 514-848-3345, Fax: 514-848-2868, E-mail: serpone@vax2.concordia.ca.

Cornell University, Ithaca, NY 14853-0001.

Center for Materials Research Founded in 1961. *Academic areas of research and training:* Advanced materials research, nano composites, thin films, nanostructures, energetic beams, magnetic materials, polymers. *Degrees offered:* None. *Graduate students served last academic year:* 45: 38 at the doctoral level; 7 at the postgraduate level. *Faculty:* 190: 95 affiliated solely with the center. *Faculty affiliations:* Departments of Applied Engineering and Physics, Chemical Engineering, Chemistry, Electrical Engineering, Materials Science and Engineering, Mechanical and Aerospace Engineering, Physics, Theoretical and Applied Mechanics. *Director:* Dr. Neil W. Ashcroft, Director, 607-255-4273, Fax: 607-255-3957, E-mail: director@ccmr.cornell.edu. *Application contact:* Dr. Helene R. Schember, Associate Director, 607-255-4274, Fax: 607-255-3957, E-mail: helene@ccmr.cornell.edu.

Center for Radiophysics and Space Research Founded in 1959. *Academic areas of research and training:* Space science, astrophysics, planetary science, experimental astronomy, observational astronomy. *Degrees offered:* None. *Graduate students served last academic year:* 30: 20 at the doctoral level; 10 at the postgraduate level. *Faculty:* 40: 20 affiliated solely with the center. *Faculty affiliations:* Fields of Astronomy and Space Sciences, Electrical Engineering, Mechanical Engineering. *Annual research budget:* $8 million. *Director:* Prof. Saul A. Teukolsky, Director, 607-255-5897, E-mail: saul@spacenet.tn.cornell.edu.

Center for the Environment Founded in 1991. *Academic areas of research and training:* Waste management, environmental toxicology, breast cancer risk factors, resource information systems, ocean resources, environmental management, eco-industrial development, water resources, sustainable development. *Degrees offered:* None. *Annual research budget:* $1.9 million. *Director:* Dr. Theodore L. Hullar, Director, 607-255-8102. *Application contact:* Tad McGalliard, Education Coordinator, 607-255-9996, Fax: 607-255-0238, E-mail: tnm2@cornell.edu.

Cornell High Energy Synchrotron Source (CHESS) Founded in 1978. *Academic areas of research and training:* To operate a user-oriented national facility to provide state-of-the-art synchrotron radiation facilities for the scientific community. *Degrees offered:* None. *Graduate students served last academic year:* 358: 194 at the doctoral level; 164 at the postgraduate level. *Faculty:* 25: 2 affiliated solely with Cornell High Energy Synchrotron Source (CHESS). *Faculty affiliations:* Department of Biochemistry; Fields of Applied Physics, Chemical Engineering, Chemistry, Civil and Environmental Engineering, Material Science, Mechanical Engineering, Physics, Poultry Science, Lab of Ornithology. *Annual research budget:* $3 million. *Director:* Prof. Sol Gruner, Director, 607-255-3441, Fax: 607-255-9001, E-mail: smg26@cornell.edu.

Newman Laboratory of Nuclear Studies Founded in 1945. *Academic areas of research and training:* Fundamental particle physics. *Degrees offered:* None. *Graduate students served last academic year:* 70: 70 at the doctoral level. *Faculty:* 24. *Faculty affiliations:* Field of Physics. *Annual research budget:* $20 million. *Director:* Dr. Karl Berkelman, Director, 607-255-4198, Fax: 607-254-4552, E-mail: kb@lns62.lns.cornell.edu.

Dalhousie University, Halifax, NS B3H 3J5, Canada.

Centre for Water Resources Studies Founded in 1981. *Academic areas of research and training:* Water quality/quantity modeling, on-site wastewater treatment, urban runoff, eutrophication, watershed management. *Degrees offered:* None. *Graduate students served last academic year:* 10: 8 at the master's level; 1 at the doctoral level; 1 at the postgraduate level. *Faculty:* 10: 3 affiliated solely with the center. *Faculty affiliations:* Departments of Agricultural, Civil, Electrical Engingeering. *Annual research budget:* $500,000. *Director:* Dr. D. H. Waller, Director, 902-494-6105, Fax: 902-494-3105, E-mail: donald.waller@dal.ca. *Application contact:* Dr. William Hart, Associate Director, 902-494-3900, Fax: 902-494-3105, E-mail: william.hart@dal.ca.

Duke University, Durham, NC 27708-0586.

Center for Mathematics and Computation in Life Sciences and Medicine Founded in 1986. *Academic areas of research and training:* Applications of mathematics to human and animal physiology. *Degrees offered:* None. *Graduate students served last academic year:* 5: 1 at the master's level; 2 at the doctoral level; 2 at the postgraduate level. *Faculty:* 8. *Faculty affiliations:* Departments of Biomedical Engineering, Cell Biology, Mathematics. *Annual research budget:* $100,000. *Director:* Dr. Michael C. Reed, Professor, 919-660-2810, Fax: 919-660-2821.

Wetland Center Founded in 1990. *Academic areas of research and training:* Development of sustainable wetland functions and values for the nation and the world, wetland ecology and management, hydrogeology of wetland systems, wetland field skills, wetland delineation, paleoecology of wetland and coastal systems, wetland soils, nutrient cycling in wetlands. *Degrees offered:* None. *Graduate students served last academic year:* 27: 15 at the master's level; 8 at the doctoral level; 4 at the postgraduate level. *Faculty:* 26: 5 affiliated solely with the center. *Faculty affiliations:* Departments of Botany, Economics, Zoology; Program in Earth Sciences; Center for Quaternary Ecology; Marine Laboratory. *Annual research budget:* $1.8 million. *Director:* Dr. Curtis J. Richardson, Director, 919-613-8006, Fax: 919-684-8741, E-mail: curtr@duke.edu. *Application contact:* Lisa Blumenthal, Assistant to the Director, 919-613-8008, Fax: 919-684-8741, E-mail: lblu@duke.edu.

École Polytechnique de Montréal, Montréal, PQ H3C 3A7, Canada.

Center for Research on Computation and its Applications (CERCA) Founded in 1992. *Academic areas of research and training:* Pharmaceutical chemistry, industrial mechanics, environmental forecasting, industrial geophysics, astrophysics, nanoelectronics, scientific visualization, high-performance computing. *Degrees offered:* None. *Graduate students served last academic year:* 39: 6 at the master's level; 17 at the doctoral level; 16 at the postgraduate level. *Faculty:* 22. *Faculty affiliations:* Departments of Atmospheric and Ocean Sciences, Chemistry, Computer Sciences, Mathematics and Statistics, Mechanical Engineering, and Physics. *Annual research budget:* $3.9 million. *Director:* Dr. Jean-Jacques Rousseau, Director, 514-369-5210, Fax: 514-369-3880, E-mail: rousseau@cerca.umontreal.ca. *Application contact:* Dr. Jean-Jacques Rousseau, Director, 514-369-5210, Fax: 514-369-3880, E-mail: rousseau@cerca.umontreal.ca.

Centre for Characterization and Microscopy of Materials Founded in 1989. *Academic areas of research and training:* Biological sciences, chemical engineering, materials and metallurgical engineering, mechanical engineering, physical engineering. *Degrees offered:* None. *Graduate students served last academic year:* 150: 60 at the master's level; 40 at the doctoral level; 50 at the postgraduate level. *Faculty:* 17: 9 affiliated solely with the center. *Faculty affiliations:* Departments of Chemical Engineering, Environment, Mechanical Engineering, Medicine, Occupational and Environmental Health, Pharmaceutics, Physical Engineering; Pulp and Paper Center. *Director:* Gilles L'Espérance, Director, 514-340-4532, Fax: 514-340-4468, E-mail: cm2@mail.polymtl.ca. *Application contact:* Elise Campeau, Administrative Technician, 514-340-4788, Fax: 514-340-4468.

Gas Technology Research Group (GREG) *Academic areas of research and training:* Applied mathematics, chemical engineering, mechanical engineering. *Degrees offered:* None. *Graduate students served last academic year:* 20: 10 at the master's level; 8 at the doctoral level; 2 at the postgraduate level. *Faculty:* 6: 1 affiliated solely with the group. *Faculty affiliations:* Departments of Chemical, Materials Science and Metallurgical, and Mechanical Engineering. *Annual research budget:* $60,000. *Director:* Prof. Danilo Klvana, Head, 514-340-4711, Fax: 514-340-4159, E-mail: dklvana@mailsrv.polymtl.ca.

Emory University, Atlanta, GA 30322-1100.

Emerson Center for Scientific Computation Founded in 1992. *Academic areas of research and training:* Computational chemistry, computational physics. *Degrees offered:* None. *Graduate students served last academic year:* 50: 20 at the doctoral level; 30 at the postgraduate level. *Faculty:* 14: 2 affiliated solely with the center. *Faculty affiliations:* Departments of Chemistry, Physics; Program in Physical, Mathematical and Computational Sciences. *Annual research budget:* $150,000. *Director:* Dr. Keiji Morokuma, Director, 404-727-2180, Fax: 404-727-6586, E-mail: morokuma@emory.edu.

Integrated Microscopy and Microanalytical Facility Founded in 1985. *Academic areas of research and training:* Microscopy services for faculty and graduate students in Cancer Center, Cardiology Center and Department of Chemistry. *Degrees offered:* None. *Graduate students served last academic year:* 14: 14 at the doctoral level. *Faculty:* 41: 1 affiliated solely with the facility. *Faculty affiliations:* Department of Chemistry; Programs in Cardiology, Cell and Developmental Biology, Molecular Medicine. *Director:* Dr. Robert P. Apkarian, Director, 404-727-7766, Fax: 404-727-7760, E-mail: rapkari@emory.edu.

Fisk University, Nashville, TN 37208-3051.

Center for Photonic Materials and Devices Founded in 1992. *Academic areas of research and training:* Chemistry, physics, materials science, photonics. *Degrees offered:* None. *Graduate students served last academic year:* 15: 15 at the master's level. *Faculty:* 17: 12 affiliated solely with the center. *Faculty affiliations:* Department of Physics. *Annual research budget:* $1.5 million. *Director:* Enrique Silberman, Director, 615-329-8620, Fax: 615-329-8634, E-mail: esilber@dubois.fisk.edu.

Florida Agricultural and Mechanical University, Tallahassee, FL 32307-3200.

The Environmental Sciences Institute Founded in 1995. *Academic areas of research and training:* Environmental biotechnology, environmental restoration and waste management,

Research and Training Opportunities

The Environmental Sciences Institute (continued)
marine/estuarine ecosystems, environmental policy and risk management, environmental chemistry. *Degrees offered:* MS; PhD. *Graduate students served last academic year:* 35: 22 at the master's level; 10 at the doctoral level; 3 at the postgraduate level. *Faculty:* 28: 8 affiliated solely with the institute. *Faculty affiliations:* Departments of Biology, Chemistry; Division of Agricultural Sciences; Programs in Economics, Political Science. *Annual research budget:* $2 million. *Director:* Dr. Larry Robinson, Director, 850-599-3550, Fax: 850-599-8183, E-mail: lrobinso@famu.edu.

Florida Atlantic University, Boca Raton, FL 33431-0991.

Center for Applied Stochastics Research Founded in 1984. *Academic areas of research and training:* Applications of probability and statistics in various fields of engineering, predicting the response and safety of engineering structures in seismic events, analyzing possible motion instability of long span bridges in strong turbulent winds, reliability of marine and ocean structures due to random wave excitations, new measures for groundwater contamination. *Degrees offered:* None. *Graduate students served last academic year:* 3: 1 at the doctoral level; 1 at the postgraduate level. *Faculty:* 5: 1 affiliated solely with the center. *Faculty affiliations:* Departments of Mathematics, Mechanical Engineering, Ocean Engineering. *Annual research budget:* $190,655. *Director:* Dr. Y. K. Lin, Director, 561-297-3449, Fax: 561-297-2868, E-mail: linyk@casr.fau.edu.

Florida Institute of Technology, Melbourne, FL 32901-6975.

Aquaculture Laboratory Founded in 1987. *Academic areas of research and training:* Aquaculture, marine biology. *Degrees offered:* None. *Graduate students served last academic year:* 5 at the master's level; 2 at the doctoral level. *Faculty:* 6: 1 affiliated solely with the laboratory. *Faculty affiliations:* Department of Biological Sciences. *Director:* Dr. Junda Lin, Director, 407-674-7587, Fax: 407-684-8461, E-mail: jlin@fit.edu.

Center for Environmental Education Founded in 1993. *Academic areas of research and training:* Teacher-education/professional development, curriculum development, assessment and evaluation, environmental education, human dimensions. *Degrees offered:* None. *Graduate students served last academic year:* 12: 8 at the master's level; 4 at the doctoral level. *Faculty:* 8: 1 affiliated solely with the center. *Faculty affiliations:* Departments of Biological Sciences; Science Education; Programs in Environmental Science and Environmental Resource Management, Oceanography. *Annual research budget:* $175,000. *Director:* Dr. Robert Fronk, Director, 407-768-8000 Ext. 8126, Fax: 407-984-8461, E-mail: fronk@fit.edu. *Application contact:* Dr. Thomas Marcinkowski, Associate Professor, 407-768-8000 Ext. 8946, Fax: 407-984-8461, E-mail: marcinko@winnie.fit.edu.

Center for Remote Sensing Founded in 1995. *Academic areas of research and training:* Ocean remote sensing, atmospheric remote sensing, space physics and astronomy, environmental optics, electrical engineering, geographic information systems, hydrographic engineering, hyperspectral remote sensing of vegetation and water. *Degrees offered:* None. *Graduate students served last academic year:* 5: 4 at the master's level; 1 at the doctoral level. *Faculty:* 21. *Faculty affiliations:* Departments of Biological Sciences, Meteorology, Physics and Space Sciences; Programs in Electrical Engineering, Environmental Science, Ocean Engineering, Oceanography; School of Aeronautics. *Annual research budget:* $250,000. *Director:* Dr. Charles R. Bostater, Director, 407-768-8000 Ext. 7113, Fax: 407-773-0980, E-mail: bostater@probe.ocn.fit.edu.

Florida International University, Miami, FL 33199.

Southeast Environmental Research Center Founded in 1993. *Academic areas of research and training:* Environmental research in the southeastern U.S. and the Caribbean including aquatic ecology, geochemistry, biogeochemistry, wetland ecology, plant community ecology, ecotoxicology, microbiology, water quality studies, pollution studies. *Degrees offered:* None. *Graduate students served last academic year:* 46: 28 at the master's level; 9 at the doctoral level; 9 at the postgraduate level. *Faculty:* 16: 2 affiliated solely with Southeast Environmental Research Center. *Faculty affiliations:* Departments of Biology, Chemistry, Environmental Studies, Geology. *Annual research budget:* $3.9 million. *Director:* Dr. Ronald Dean Jones, Director, 305-348-3095, Fax: 305-348-4096, E-mail: serp@servms.fiu.edu. *Application contact:* Anita Holloway, Senior Statistician/Editor, 305-398-3095, Fax: 305-348-4096, E-mail: holloway@fiu.edu.

Florida State University, Tallahassee, FL 32306.

Institute of Science and Public Affairs *Academic areas of research and training:* Biology, chemistry, physics, economics, environmental studies, geography, law, public administration, urban and regional planning, hazardous waste, water resource management, geographic information systems and computer cartography. *Degrees offered:* None. *Graduate students served last academic year:* 37: 25 at the master's level; 9 at the doctoral level; 3 at the postgraduate level. *Faculty:* 50: 36 affiliated solely with the institute. *Faculty affiliations:* College of Law; Departments of Biological Science, Economics, Environmental Studies, Geography, Urban and Regional Planning; Schools of Public Administration and Policy, Social Work. *Director:* Dr. Robert B. Bradley, Associate Vice President for Research, 850-644-2007, Fax: 850-644-7360, E-mail: rbradley@odie.ispa.fsu.edu.

George Mason University, Fairfax, VA 22030-4444.

Center for Recreation Resources Policy Founded in 1987. *Academic areas of research and training:* Recreation resources policy, natural resources use, human dimensions of natural resources management. *Degrees offered:* None. *Graduate students served last academic year:* 5: 4 at the master's level; 1 at the doctoral level. *Faculty:* 8: 4 affiliated solely with the center. *Faculty affiliations:* Department of Health, Fitness and Recreation Resources. *Annual research budget:* $125,000. *Director:* Dr. Brett A. Wright, Director, 703-993-2064, Fax: 703-993-2025, E-mail: bwright@gmu.edu.

The George Washington University, Washington, DC 20052.

Biostatistics Center Founded in 1972. *Academic areas of research and training:* Statistics, biostatistics, epidemiology. *Degrees offered:* None. *Graduate students served last academic year:* 10 at the master's level; 18 at the doctoral level. *Faculty:* 10: 10 affiliated solely with the center. *Faculty affiliations:* Departments of Epidemiology and Biostatistics, Statistics. *Annual research budget:* $15 million. *Director:* Dr. John M. Lachin, Director, 301-881-9260, Fax: 301-881-3742, E-mail: jml@biostat.bsc.gwu.edu.

Center for Nuclear Studies Founded in 1989. *Academic areas of research and training:* Nuclear physics. *Degrees offered:* None. *Graduate students served last academic year:* 13: 9 at the doctoral level; 4 at the postgraduate level. *Faculty:* 13. *Faculty affiliations:* Department of Physics. *Annual research budget:* $700,000. *Director:* Dr. Helmut Haberzettl, Director, 202-994-6275, Fax: 202-994-3001, E-mail: helmut@gwu.edu.

Georgia Institute of Technology, Atlanta, GA 30332-0001.

Fusion Research Center Founded in 1986. *Academic areas of research and training:* Fusion plasma physics and reactor design, plasma-materials interactions. *Degrees offered:* None. *Graduate students served last academic year:* 8: 2 at the master's level; 6 at the doctoral level. *Faculty:* 17: 5 affiliated solely with the center. *Faculty affiliations:* Schools of Mechanical Engineering, Physics. *Annual research budget:* $400,000. *Director:* Dr. Weston M. Stacey, Director, 404-894-3758, Fax: 404-894-3733, E-mail: weston.stacey@me.gatech.edu.

Harvard University, Cambridge, MA 02138.

Harvard-Smithsonian Center for Astrophysics Founded in 1973. *Academic areas of research and training:* Astronomy, astrophysics, space sciences, geophysics, theoretical astrophysics, atomic and molecular physics, science education. *Degrees offered:* None. *Graduate students served last academic year:* 52: 35 at the master's level; 17 at the doctoral level. *Faculty:* 20. *Faculty affiliations:* Department of Astronomy. *Director:* Irwin I. Shapiro, Director, 617-495-7100, Fax: 617-495-7105, E-mail: ishapiro@cfa.harvard.edu. *Application contact:* James Cornell, Public Affairs Director, 617-495-7461, Fax: 617-495-7468, E-mail: jcornell@cfa.harvard.edu.

Illinois Institute of Technology, Chicago, IL 60616-3793.

Center for Synchrotron Radiation Research and Instrumentation Founded in 1992. *Degrees offered:* None. *Graduate students served last academic year:* 5: 2 at the master's level; 2 at the doctoral level; 1 at the postgraduate level. *Faculty:* 11: 8 affiliated solely with the center. *Faculty affiliations:* Divisions of Mechanical and Aerospace Engineering, Physics. *Annual research budget:* $50,000. *Director:* Dr. Leroy D. Chapman, Director, 312-567-3575, Fax: 312-567-3576, E-mail: dean.chapman@iit.edu.

Energy and Power Center Founded in 1989. *Academic areas of research and training:* Energy and energy-related environmental policy, energy economics, energy technology, sustainable energy systems, global climate change, energy, environment, economics. *Degrees offered:* None. *Graduate students served last academic year:* 100: 60 at the master's level; 40 at the doctoral level. *Faculty:* 24. *Faculty affiliations:* Chicago-Kent College of Law; Departments of Chemical and Environmental Engineering, Electrical and Computer Engineering, Mechanical Engineering, Materials and Aerospace Engineering; Stuart School of Business. *Annual research budget:* $3 million. *Director:* Dr. Henry R. Linden, Director, 312-567-3095, Fax: 312-567-3967, E-mail: hlinden@alpha1.ais.iit.edu.

Illinois State University, Normal, IL 61790-2200.

Center for Mathematics, Science, and Technology Founded in 1992. *Academic areas of research and training:* Mathematics, science, technology, integrated learning, staff development, minority assistance. *Degrees offered:* None. *Graduate students served last academic year:* 9: 3 at the master's level; 6 at the doctoral level. *Faculty:* 6: 1 affiliated solely with the center. *Faculty affiliations:* Departments of Chemistry, Curriculum and Instruction, Industrial Technology, Mathematics. *Annual research budget:* $500,000. *Director:* Dr. Robert Fisher, Director, 309-438-3089, Fax: 309-438-3592, E-mail: cemast@ilstu.edu.

Indiana University Bloomington, Bloomington, IN 47405.

Center for Nuclear Theory Founded in 1981. *Academic areas of research and training:* Theoretical nuclear physics. *Degrees offered:* None. *Graduate students served last academic year:* 6: 4 at the doctoral level; 2 at the postgraduate level. *Faculty:* 5. *Faculty affiliations:* Department of Physics. *Annual research budget:* $400,000. *Director:* Dr. John Timothy Londergan, Director, 812-855-2953, Fax: 812-855-6645, E-mail: tlonderg@niobe.iucf.indiana.edu. *Application contact:* Patricia Halstead, Assistant to the Director, 812-855-2953, Fax: 812-855-6645, E-mail: theory@iucf.indiana.edu.

Chemical Information Center Founded in 1972. *Academic areas of research and training:* Chemical information, molecular modeling. *Degrees offered:* None. *Graduate students served last academic year:* 3: 2 at the master's level; 1 at the doctoral level. *Faculty:* 6: 1 affiliated solely with the center. *Faculty affiliations:* Departments of Chemistry, Computer Science, Medical Science; School of Library and Information Science. *Annual research budget:* $5,000. *Director:* Dr. Gary Wiggins, Director, 812-855-9452, Fax: 812-855-6611, E-mail: wiggins@indiana.edu.

Cyclotron Facility Founded in 1974. *Academic areas of research and training:* Nuclear physics, accelerator physics, radiation biology, radiation effects on electronic devices, radiation therapy. *Degrees offered:* None. *Graduate students served last academic year:* 67: 25 at the doctoral level; 12 at the postgraduate level. *Faculty:* 25: 4 affiliated solely with the facility. *Faculty affiliations:* Departments of Biology, Chemistry, Physics. *Annual research budget:* $10 million. *Director:* Dr. John M. Cameron, Director, 812-855-9365, Fax: 812-855-6645, E-mail: cameron@iucf.indiana.edu.

Environmental Systems Application Center (ESAC) Founded in 1972. *Academic areas of research and training:* Applied ecology, aquatic chemistry, groundwater modeling, hazardous waste management, lake and watershed management, risk assessment, wetlands ecology. *Degrees offered:* None. *Graduate students served last academic year:* 8: 8 at the master's level. *Faculty:* 7: 1 affiliated solely with the center. *Annual research budget:* $80,000. *Director:* William W. Jones, Director, 812-855-4556, Fax: 812-855-7802, E-mail: joneswi@indiana.edu.

Institute for Scientific Computing and Applied Mathematics Founded in 1986. *Academic areas of research and training:* Promotion of advanced research in applied mathematics with particular emphasis on scientific computing. *Degrees offered:* None. *Graduate students served last academic year:* 12: 10 at the doctoral level; 2 at the postgraduate level. *Faculty:* 18. *Faculty affiliations:* Departments of Astronomy, Chemistry, Computer Science, Economics, Geology, Mathematics. *Director:* Dr. Roger Temam, Director, 812-855-8521, Fax: 812-855-7850, E-mail: temam@indiana.edu. *Application contact:* Teresa Bunge, Administrative Secretary, 812-855-8521, Fax: 812-855-7850, E-mail: bunget@indiana.edu.

Indiana University–Purdue University Indianapolis, Indianapolis, IN 46202-2896.

Nuclear Magnetic Resonance Laboratory Founded in 1992. *Academic areas of research and training:* Applying NMR to study structure, function, and dynamics of biological systems; physics, biophysics, biochemistry, physiology, pharmacology. *Degrees offered:* None. *Graduate students served last academic year:* 6: 2 at the master's level; 3 at the doctoral level; 1 at the postgraduate level. *Faculty:* 5. *Faculty affiliations:* Schools of Medicine, Science. *Annual research budget:* $100,000. *Director:* B. D. Nageswara Rao, Director, 317-274-6901, E-mail: brao@iupui.edu.

Iowa State University of Science and Technology, Ames, IA 50011.

Center for Crops Utilization Research (CCUR) Founded in 1985. *Academic areas of research and training:* Finding new uses and developing new products for Midwest crops. *Degrees offered:* None. *Graduate students served last academic year:* 42: 22 at the master's level; 15 at the doctoral level; 5 at the postgraduate level. *Faculty:* 40. *Faculty affiliations:* Departments of Agricultural and Biosystems Engineering, Biochemistry and Biophysics, Chemical Engineering, Chemistry, Economics, Food Science and Human Nutrition, Mechanical Engineering. *Annual research budget:* $2 million. *Director:* Dr. Lawrence A. Johnson, Director, 515-294-0160, Fax: 515-294-6261, E-mail: ljohnson@iastate.edu.

Center for Sustainable Environmental Technologies (CSET) Founded in 1979. *Academic areas of research and training:* Develop and demonstrate sustainable environmental technologies, improving environmental performance of energy conversion processes and investigating the use of agricultural crops and residues as sustainable feedstocks for production of chemicals and energy. *Degrees offered:* None. *Graduate students served last academic year:* 16: 9 at the master's level; 5 at the doctoral level; 2 at the postgraduate level. *Faculty:* 30. *Faculty affiliations:* Departments of Aerospace Engineering and Engineering Mechanics; Agricultural and Biosystems Engineering; Agronomy; Animal Ecology; Animal Science; Biochemistry, Biophysics, and Molecular Biology; Botany; Chemical Engineering; Chemistry; Civil and Construction Engineering; Economics; Food Science and Human Nutrition; Forestry; Geological and Atmospheric Sciences; Materials Science and Engineering; Mechanical Engineering; Microbiology; Physics. *Annual research budget:* $700,000. *Director:* Dr. Robert C. Brown, Director, 515-294-7934, Fax: 515-294-3091, E-mail: rcbrown@iastate.edu. *Application contact:* Tonia M. McCarley, Program Assistant, 515-294-6555, Fax: 515-294-3091, E-mail: tmccarly@iastate.edu.

Institute for Physical Research and Technology (IPRT) Founded in 1987. *Academic areas of research and training:* Basic and applied research, education of next generation of scientists and engineers. *Degrees offered:* None. *Annual research budget:* $45 million. *Director:* Thomas Barton, Director, 515-294-2770. *Application contact:* Steve Karsjen, Public Affairs Manager, 515-294-5643, Fax: 515-294-3226, E-mail: karsjen@ameslab.gov.

Kansas State University, Manhattan, KS 66506.

Center for Hazardous Substance Research Founded in 1985. *Academic areas of research and training:* Environmental science and engineering, hazardous substances, bioremediation, phytoremediation. *Degrees offered:* None. *Graduate students served last academic year:* 14: 6 at the master's level; 6 at the doctoral level; 2 at the postgraduate level. *Faculty:* 16: 1 affiliated solely with the center. *Faculty affiliations:* Departments of Agronomy, Biochemistry, Biological and Agricultural Engineering, Chemical Engineering, Chemistry, Civil Engineering, Geology. *Annual research budget:* $600,000. *Director:* Dr. Larry E. Erickson, Director, 785-532-2380, Fax: 785-532-5985, E-mail: lerick@ksu.edu. *Application contact:* Rita Shade, 785-532-6519, Fax: 785-532-5985, E-mail: ritam@ksu.edu.

J. R. Macdonald Laboratory Founded in 1970. *Academic areas of research and training:* Basic research in ion-atom collisions. *Degrees offered:* PhD. *Graduate students served last academic year:* 18: 15 at the doctoral level; 3 at the postgraduate level. *Faculty:* 12: 2 affiliated solely with the laboratory. *Faculty affiliations:* Department of Physics. *Annual research budget:* $2 million. *Director:* Dr. Patrick Richard, Director, 785-532-6782, Fax: 785-532-6806, E-mail: richard@phys.ksu.edu. *Application contact:* Tracy Tipping, User Liaison, 785-532-2668, Fax: 785-532-6806, E-mail: tipping@phys.ksu.edu.

Konza Prairie Research Natural Area Founded in 1971. *Academic areas of research and training:* Grassland ecology, ecosystem dynamics, plant ecology, animal ecology, wildlife biology, rangeland ecology and management. *Degrees offered:* None. *Graduate students served last academic year:* 30: 15 at the master's level; 15 at the doctoral level. *Faculty:* 20. *Faculty affiliations:* Departments of Agronomy, Animal Sciences and Industry, Geography, Geology; Division of Biology. *Annual research budget:* $1.1 million. *Director:* Dr. D. C. Hartnett, Director, 785-587-0441, Fax: 785-532-6653, E-mail: konza@ksu.edu.

Kent State University, Kent, OH 44242-0001.

Center for Nuclear Research Founded in 1988. *Academic areas of research and training:* Nuclear physics, particle physics. *Degrees offered:* None. *Graduate students served last academic year:* 18: 3 at the master's level; 12 at the doctoral level; 3 at the postgraduate level. *Faculty:* 8. *Faculty affiliations:* Department of Physics. *Annual research budget:* $800,000. *Director:* Dr. Peter C. Tandy, Director, 330-672-4027, Fax: 330-672-2959, E-mail: tandy@cnr2.kent.edu.

Liquid Crystal Institute Founded in 1965. *Academic areas of research and training:* Liquid crystal materials: physics, chemistry, chemical physics, applications. *Degrees offered:* None. *Graduate students served last academic year:* 40: 2 at the master's level; 23 at the doctoral level; 15 at the postgraduate level. *Faculty:* 13: 6 affiliated solely with the institute. *Faculty affiliations:* Departments of Chemistry, Mathematics and Computer Science, Physics. *Annual research budget:* $5 million. *Director:* Dr. John L. West, Director, 330-672-2654, Fax: 330-672-2796, E-mail: johnwest@scorpio.kent.edu.

Lehigh University, Bethlehem, PA 18015-3094.

Zettlemoyer Center for Surface Studies (ZCSS) Founded in 1966. *Academic areas of research and training:* Environment, energy, safety, and health; high-technology communications; synthesis of chemicals and engineering materials; catalysis; coatings; printing inks. *Degrees offered:* None. *Graduate students served last academic year:* 30: 8 at the master's level; 12 at the doctoral level; 10 at the postgraduate level. *Faculty:* 17. *Faculty affiliations:* Departments of Chemical Engineering, Chemistry, Earth and Environmental Sciences, Electrical Engineering, Materials, Mechanical Engineering and Mechanics. *Annual research budget:* $2.5 million. *Director:* Dr. Richard G. Herman, Executive Director, 610-758-3486, Fax: 610-758-6555, E-mail: rgh1@lehigh.edu. *Application contact:* M. C. Sawyers, Administrative Coordinator, 610-758-3600, Fax: 610-758-6555, E-mail: mcs0@lehigh.edu.

Louisiana State University and Agricultural and Mechanical College, Baton Rouge, LA 70803.

Basin Research Institute (BRI) Founded in 1984. *Academic areas of research and training:* Oil and gas research, geology. *Degrees offered:* None. *Graduate students served last academic year:* 1: 1 at the doctoral level. *Faculty:* 4: 4 affiliated solely with the institute. *Annual research budget:* $450,000. *Director:* Dr. Chacko J. John, Director, 225-388-8328, Fax: 225-388-3662, E-mail: chacko@vartex.bri.lsu.edu.

Louisiana Forest Products Laboratory (LFPL) Founded in 1992. *Academic areas of research and training:* Wood products manufacturing, marketing, wood science and technology, environment and safety, wood products, international trade, value-added processing. *Degrees offered:* None. *Graduate students served last academic year:* 12: 4 at the master's level; 7 at the doctoral level; 1 at the postgraduate level. *Faculty:* 14: 6 affiliated solely with the laboratory. *Faculty affiliations:* College of Business Administration; Departments of Civil and Environmental Engineering, Industrial and Manufacturing Systems Engineering; School of Forestry, Wildlife, and Fisheries; Louisiana Tech University. *Annual research budget:* $650,000. *Director:* Dr. W. Ramsay Smith, Program Director, 225-388-4155, Fax: 225-388-4251, E-mail: wsmith@lsu.edu.

Massachusetts Institute of Technology, Cambridge, MA 02139-4307.

Center for Global Change Science (CGCS) Founded in 1990. *Academic areas of research and training:* Prediction of global environmental change, ocean circulation, biogeochemistry of greenhouse gases, convection and cloud formation, land surface hydrology and vegetation, ozone layer chemistry and dynamics. *Degrees offered:* None. *Graduate students served last academic year:* 70: 10 at the master's level; 50 at the doctoral level; 10 at the postgraduate level. *Faculty:* 25. *Faculty affiliations:* Schools of Engineering, Science. *Annual research budget:* $8 million. *Director:* Dr. Ronald G. Prinn, Director, 617-253-2452, Fax: 617-253-0354, E-mail: rprinn@mit.edu. *Application contact:* Anne Slinn, Administrative Scientist, 617-253-4902, Fax: 617-253-0354, E-mail: slinn@mit.edu.

Center for Magnetic Resonance *Academic areas of research and training:* NMR technology, chemistry, DNP/EPR, spatial magnetic resonance. *Degrees offered:* None. *Graduate students served last academic year:* 31 at the doctoral level; 14 at the postgraduate level. *Faculty:* 2. *Faculty affiliations:* Departments of Chemistry, Nuclear Engineering. *Annual research budget:* $4 million. *Director:* Dr. Robert C. Griffin, Director, 617-253-5478, Fax: 617-253-5405, E-mail: griffin@ccnmr.mit.edu.

Center for Space Research Founded in 1966. *Academic areas of research and training:* Space life sciences, space plasma and gravitational physics, X-ray optical and planetary astronomy. *Degrees offered:* None. *Graduate students served last academic year:* 32: 32 at the doctoral level. *Faculty:* 19. *Faculty affiliations:* Departments of Aeronautics and Astronautics; Earth, Atmospheric, and Planetary Sciences; Physics. *Annual research budget:* $30 million. *Director:* Dr. Claude R. Canizares, Director, 617-253-7501, Fax: 617-253-3111, E-mail: crc@space.mit.edu.

Energy Laboratory Founded in 1972. *Academic areas of research and training:* Energy supply, technology, utilization, environmental aspects, policy, economics; energy for sustainable development. *Degrees offered:* None. *Graduate students served last academic year:* 110: 40 at the master's level; 60 at the doctoral level; 10 at the postgraduate level. *Faculty:* 80. *Faculty affiliations:* Departments of Economics, Political Science, Urban Studies and Planning; Sloan School of Management; Schools of Architecture and Planning, Engineering, Science; Technology and Policy Program. *Annual research budget:* $8.4 million. *Director:* Dr. Jefferson W. Tester, Director, 617-253-3401, Fax: 617-253-8013, E-mail: testerel@mit.edu. *Application contact:* Dr. Elizabeth M. Drake, Associate Director, 617-253-5325, Fax: 617-253-8013, E-mail: edrake@mit.edu.

Francis Bitter Magnet Laboratory (FBML) Founded in 1967. *Academic areas of research and training:* Magnetic resonance, solid-state spectroscopy, condensed matter physics semiconductors, superconductivity, liquid crystals, magnet technology, imaging. *Degrees offered:* None. *Graduate students served last academic year:* 50: 30 at the doctoral level; 20 at the postgraduate level. *Faculty:* 15. *Faculty affiliations:* Departments of Biology, Chemistry, Nuclear Engineering, Physics. *Annual research budget:* $4 million. *Director:* Robert G. Griffin, Director, 617-253-5478, Fax: 617-253-5405, E-mail: rgg@mit.edu. *Application contact:* Elisabeth K.I. Shortsleeve, Secretary, 617-253-5478, Fax: 617-253-5405, E-mail: elka@mit.edu.

Laboratory for Nuclear Science Founded in 1946. *Academic areas of research and training:* Experimental and theoretical particle and nuclear physics. *Degrees offered:* None. *Graduate students served last academic year:* 75: 10 at the master's level; 65 at the doctoral level. *Faculty:* 40. *Faculty affiliations:* Department of Physics. *Annual research budget:* $28 million. *Director:* Dr. Robert P. Redwine, Director, 617-253-3600, Fax: 617-253-0111, E-mail: redwine@mitlns.mit.edu.

Miami University, Oxford, OH 45056.

Center for Chemical Education Founded in 1991. *Academic areas of research and training:* Chemical education. *Degrees offered:* None. *Graduate students served last academic year:* 10: 8 at the master's level; 2 at the doctoral level. *Faculty:* 32: 2 affiliated solely with the center. *Faculty affiliations:* Department of Chemistry. *Director:* Arlyne Sarquis, Director, 513-727-3278, Fax: 513-727-3223, E-mail: sarquiam@muohio.edu.

Michigan State University, East Lansing, MI 48824-1020.

Institute of Water Research Founded in 1964. *Academic areas of research and training:* Watershed, surface water and ground water quality, quantity research and education programs addressing contemporary land and water issues, land use management, decision making. *Degrees offered:* None. *Graduate students served last academic year:* 8: 4 at the master's level; 4 at the doctoral level. *Faculty:* 4. *Faculty affiliations:* Departments of Crop and Soil Sciences, Fisheries and Wildlife, Geography, Resource Development. *Annual research budget:* $234,000. *Director:* Dr. Jon F. Bartholic, Director, 517-353-3742, Fax: 517-353-1812, E-mail: bartholi@pilot.msu.edu.

Michigan Technological University, Houghton, MI 49931-1295.

Institute of Materials Processing Founded in 1955. *Academic areas of research and training:* Applied research and development in: mineral processing, solid waste processing and utilization, metallic processing, mechanical alloying, material characterization. *Degrees offered:* None. *Graduate students served last academic year:* 2 at the master's level; 9 at the doctoral level; 2 at the postgraduate level. *Faculty:* 1. *Faculty affiliations:* Departments of Biological Sciences, Chemistry, Civil and Environmental Engineering, Geological Sciences, Mechanical Engineerin; Programs in Business Administration, Geological Engineering, Metallurgical and Materials Engineering. *Director:* Dr. Jim Hwang, Director, 906-487-2600, Fax: 906-487-2921, E-mail: jhwang@mtu.edu.

Mississippi State University, Mississippi State, MS 39762.

Center for International Security and Strategic Studies Founded in 1980. *Academic areas of research and training:* Environmental security, food security, sustainable development, conflict management, African studies, Asian studies, East European studies. *Degrees offered:* None. *Faculty:* 17: 2 affiliated solely with the center. *Faculty affiliations:* Departments of Agricultural Economics, Chemical Engineering, Civil Engineering, Computer Science, History, Political Science; Programs in Communication, Religion. *Annual research budget:* $92,000. *Director:* Dr. Paul J. Kaiser, Director, 662-325-2028, Fax: 662-325-1503, E-mail: raqua@ciss.msstate.edu.

Forest and Wildlife Research Center (FWRC) Founded in 1994. *Academic areas of research and training:* Forestry, forest products, wildlife and fisheries research. *Degrees offered:* None. *Graduate students served last academic year:* 117: 87 at the master's level; 30 at the doctoral level. *Faculty:* 52: 52 affiliated solely with the center. *Annual research budget:* $10 million. *Director:* Dr. Warren S. Thompson, Acting Director, 662-325-2952.

Montana State University–Bozeman, Bozeman, MT 59717.

EPICenter Project Founded in 1994. *Academic areas of research and training:* Research, development and demonstration of green building technologies, design practices, and construction. *Degrees offered:* None. *Graduate students served last academic year:* 4: 4 at the master's level. *Faculty:* 13: 1 affiliated solely with the center. *Faculty affiliations:* Departments of Architecture, Engineering, Health and Human Development, Nursing, Plant and Soil Sciences; Office of Rural Health. *Annual research budget:* $3 million. *Director:* Dr. Kath Williams, Director, 406-994-7713, Fax: 406-994-7980, E-mail: kathwms@montana.edu.

Montana University System Water Center Founded in 1964. *Academic areas of research and training:* Drinking water, wild trout, WEB presentations, water issues. *Degrees offered:* None. *Graduate students served last academic year:* 3: 1 at the master's level. *Faculty:* 4: 4 affiliated solely with the center. *Faculty affiliations:* College of Engineering, Department of Biology, Program in Fisheries. *Annual research budget:* $900,000. *Director:* Dorothy Bradley, Director, 406-994-6690, Fax: 406-994-1774, E-mail: wwwrc@montana.edu.

Mountain Research Center Founded in 1990. *Academic areas of research and training:* Sustainability, montane ecosystems. *Degrees offered:* None. *Graduate students served last academic year:* 10: 7 at the master's level; 3 at the doctoral level. *Faculty:* 21: 1 affiliated solely with the center. *Faculty affiliations:* Departments of Biology, Earth Sciences, Land Resources. *Director:* Dr. Lisa J. Graumlich, Director, 406-994-5178, Fax: 406-994-5122.

Optical Technology Center (OpTeC) Founded in 1995. *Academic areas of research and training:* Optical materials, lasers, and optoelectronic devices; sensors, micro-optical systems, holography, and coherent optics; chemistry, electrical engineering, physics. *Degrees offered:* None. *Graduate students served last academic year:* 39: 12 at the master's level; 15 at the doctoral level; 12 at the postgraduate level. *Faculty:* 11. *Faculty affiliations:* Departments of Chemistry, Electrical and Computer Engineering, Physics; Program in Biochemistry. *Annual research budget:* $2.5 million. *Director:* Dr. Lee Spangler, Director, 406-994-6279, Fax: 406-994-5407, E-mail: optec@physics.montana.edu. *Application contact:* Norma J. Hamilton, Administrative Assistant, 406-994-6279, Fax: 406-994-5407, E-mail: hamilton@montana.edu.

Reclamation Research Unit Founded in 1969. *Academic areas of research and training:* Mineland reclamation, restoration ecology, phyto-remediation. *Degrees offered:* None. *Graduate students served last academic year:* 12: 12 at the master's level. *Faculty:* 16: 4 affiliated solely with the unit. *Faculty affiliations:* Departments of Animal and Range Sciences, Biology, Civil Engineering, Land Resources and Environmental Sciences. *Annual research budget:* $400,000. *Director:* Dennis Neuman, Acting Director, 406-994-4821, Fax: 406-994-4876, E-mail: uasdn@montana.edu.

Research and Training Opportunities

New Jersey Institute of Technology, Newark, NJ 07102-1982.

Big Bear Solar Observatory Founded in 1969. *Academic areas of research and training:* Solar research, astronomy. *Degrees offered:* MS; PhD. *Graduate students served last academic year:* 13: 2 at the master's level; 6 at the doctoral level; 5 at the postgraduate level. *Faculty:* 5: 3 affiliated solely with Big Bear Solar Observatory. *Faculty affiliations:* Departments of Computer and Information Science, Electrical and Computer Engineering. *Annual research budget:* $2 million. *Director:* Dr. Philip Goode, Director, 973-596-3565, Fax: 909-866-4240, E-mail: pgoode@bbso.njit.edu.

Center for Applied Mathematics and Statistics Founded in 1986. *Academic areas of research and training:* Applied mathematics, asymptotic methods, wave propagation, numerical and analytical methods, fluid dynamics, combustion theory, differential geometry, electromagnetics, mathematical biology, acoustics, signal processing, applied statistics, financial mathematics. *Degrees offered:* None. *Graduate students served last academic year:* 46: 19 at the master's level; 27 at the doctoral level. *Faculty:* 74: 37 affiliated solely with the center. *Faculty affiliations:* Departments of Chemical, Civil and Environmental, Industrial and Manufacturing, Mechanical Engineering. *Annual research budget:* $750,000. *Director:* Dr. Daljit S. Aluwahlia, Director, 201-596-5782, Fax: 201-596-6467, E-mail: daahlu@m.njit.edu.

Hazardous Substance Management Research Center (HSMRC) Founded in 1984. *Academic areas of research and training:* Environmental science, environmental engineering, environmental policy, environmental management, environmental/health, pollution prevention, green/sustainable manufacturing. *Degrees offered:* None. *Graduate students served last academic year:* 55: 40 at the master's level; 10 at the doctoral level; 5 at the postgraduate level. *Faculty:* 42: 2 affiliated solely with the center. *Faculty affiliations:* Schools of Management, Medicine; Departments of Biology, Chemical Engineering, Chemistry, Civil Engineering, Environmental Science, Health, Public Policy. *Annual research budget:* $10 million. *Director:* Dr. Peter Lederman, Executive Director, 973-596-3233, Fax: 973-802-1946, E-mail: lederman@adm.njit.edu. *Application contact:* G. Margaret Griscavage, Assistant Director, Administration, 973-596-3233, Fax: 973-802-1946, E-mail: griscava@megahertz.njit.edu.

New Mexico Institute of Mining and Technology, Socorro, NM 87801.

Energetic Materials Research and Testing Center (EMRTC) Founded in 1947. *Academic areas of research and training:* Energetic materials, explosives, shock physics, chemistry. *Degrees offered:* None. *Graduate students served last academic year:* 8: 7 at the master's level; 1 at the doctoral level. *Faculty:* 8: 4 affiliated solely with the center. *Faculty affiliations:* Departments of Chemistry, Material Engineering, Physics. *Annual research budget:* $8 million. *Director:* Dr. Jose Luis M. Cortez, Director, 505-835-5701, Fax: 505-835-5630, E-mail: jcortez@emrtc.nmt.edu.

Geophysical Research Center Founded in 1965. *Academic areas of research and training:* Research related to water, both atmospheric (clouds, thunderstorms, rain and snow growth, acid rain) and underground (flow models, geochemical interactions, seismic events/groundwater, hazardous waste detection and clean-up, irrigation methods), recharge and travel times of both radioactive and hazardous waste. *Degrees offered:* None. *Graduate students served last academic year:* 166: 129 at the master's level; 37 at the doctoral level. *Faculty:* 9. *Faculty affiliations:* Departments of Chemistry, Earth and Environmental Sciences, Physics; Programs in Geophysics, Hydrology; IRIS/PASSCAL Instrument Center, New Mexico Bureau of Mines and Mineral Resources. *Annual research budget:* $740,100. *Director:* Dr. Van Romero, Director, 505-835-5646, Fax: 505-835-5649, E-mail: vromero@admin.nmt.edu. *Application contact:* M. Torres, Financial Administrator, 505-835-5609, Fax: 505-835-5649, E-mail: mtorres@aamin.nmt.edu.

Langmuir Laboratory for Atmospheric Research Founded in 1965. *Academic areas of research and training:* Atmospheric physics and chemistry: thunderstorms, lightning, clouds, precipitation, aerosols. *Degrees offered:* None. *Graduate students served last academic year:* 6: 4 at the master's level; 2 at the doctoral level. *Faculty:* 8. *Faculty affiliations:* Departments of Chemistry, Electrical Engineering, Physics. *Director:* Dr. William P. Winn, Chairman, 505-835-5503, Fax: 505-835-5913, E-mail: winn@loon.nmt.edu. *Application contact:* Sandra M. Kieft, Office Manager and Field Program Coordinator, 505-835-5423, Fax: 505-835-5913, E-mail: kieft@nmt.edu.

New Mexico Bureau of Mines and Mineral Resources Founded in 1927. *Academic areas of research and training:* State Geological Survey: mineral resources, water resources, energy resources, tectonics, volcanology, geochronology. *Degrees offered:* None. *Graduate students served last academic year:* 10: 10 at the master's level. *Faculty:* 34: 33 affiliated solely with the bureau. *Faculty affiliations:* Department of Earth and Environmental Sciences. *Annual research budget:* $3.4 million. *Director:* Dr. Charles Chapin, Director, 505-835-5302, Fax: 505-835-6333, E-mail: bureau@gis.nmt.edu.

North Carolina State University, Raleigh, NC 27695.

Materials Research Center Founded in 1984. *Academic areas of research and training:* Interdisciplinary program involved in the fundamental studies in the epitaxy of compound semiconductors. *Degrees offered:* None. *Graduate students served last academic year:* 45: 5 at the master's level; 30 at the doctoral level; 2 at the postgraduate level. *Faculty:* 17: 5 affiliated solely with the center. *Faculty affiliations:* Departments of Chemical Engineering, Chemistry, Electrical and Computer Engineering, Physics. *Annual research budget:* $3.8 million. *Director:* Dr. Robert F. Davis, Director, 919-515-2867, Fax: 919-515-3419, E-mail: robert_davis@ncsu.edu.

Southeastern Plant Environment Laboratory (PHYTOTRON) Founded in 1968. *Academic areas of research and training:* Provide controlled environments for plant growth and development research especially photoperiod, temperature, humidity, and atmospheric gases. *Degrees offered:* None. *Graduate students served last academic year:* 60: 25 at the master's level; 10 at the doctoral level; 25 at the postgraduate level. *Faculty:* 53: 3 affiliated solely with the laboratory. *Faculty affiliations:* Colleges of Agriculture and Life Sciences, Forestry Resources. *Director:* Dr. Judith F. Thomas, Director, 919-515-2778, Fax: 919-515-3635, E-mail: jfthomas@unity.ncsu.edu.

Northeastern University, Boston, MA 02115-5096.

Marine Science Center Founded in 1967. *Academic areas of research and training:* Biologically-based robots, marine biology, marine biotechnology, neurobiology, marine ecology, evolutionary ecology, marine microbial ecology. *Degrees offered:* None. *Graduate students served last academic year:* 22: 13 at the master's level; 8 at the doctoral level; 1 at the postgraduate level. *Faculty:* 10: 7 affiliated solely with the center. *Faculty affiliations:* Departments of Biology, Electrical and Computer Engineering. *Annual research budget:* $1.2 million. *Director:* Dr. Joseph Ayers, Director, 781-581-7370 Ext. 309, Fax: 781-581-6076, E-mail: lobster@neu.edu. *Application contact:* Dr. Salvatore Genovese, Education Coordinator, 781-581-7370 Ext. 311, Fax: 781-581-6076, E-mail: sgenoves@lynx.neu.edu.

Northwestern University, Evanston, IL 60208.

Center for Catalysis and Surface Science Founded in 1983. *Academic areas of research and training:* Heterogeneous and homogeneous catalysis, surface science related to catalysis, energy production, environmental catalysis, chemicals production. *Degrees offered:* None. *Graduate students served last academic year:* 40: 30 at the doctoral level; 10 at the postgraduate level. *Faculty:* 19: 1 affiliated solely with the center. *Faculty affiliations:* Departments of Chemical Engineering, Chemistry, Civil Engineering, Materials Science and Engineering, Physics and Astronomy. *Annual research budget:* $2 million. *Director:* Dr. Peter Stair, Director, 847-491-5266, Fax: 847-467-1018, E-mail: pstair@nwu.edu. *Application contact:* Phyllis Long, Administrative Assistant, 847-491-4354, Fax: 847-467-1018, E-mail: p-long@nwu.edu.

The Ohio State University, Columbus, OH 43210.

Center for Human Resource Research Founded in 1965. *Academic areas of research and training:* Developing and conserving human resources; including designing survey instruments, overseeing field work, and generating and disseminating fully documented data sets to researchers in government, private research organizations, and universities around the world. *Degrees offered:* None. *Graduate students served last academic year:* 12: 12 at the doctoral level. *Faculty:* 14. *Faculty affiliations:* Departments of Economics, Psychology, Public Policy and Management, Sociology, Statistics. *Annual research budget:* $9.7 million. *Director:* Dr. Randall J. Olsen, Director, 614-442-7348, Fax: 614-442-7329, E-mail: olsen.6@osu.edu.

Center for Mapping Founded in 1986. *Academic areas of research and training:* Computer vision, Geographic Information System, remote sensing, geodesy using the Global Positioning System, photogrammetry. *Degrees offered:* None. *Graduate students served last academic year:* 16: 10 at the master's level; 6 at the doctoral level. *Faculty:* 90. *Faculty affiliations:* Departments of Agricultural Engineering, Computer and Information Science, English, Geodetic Science and Surveying, Geography, Geological Sciences, Plant Biology, Statistics; Programs in Agronomy, City and Regional Planning, Engineering Graphics, Landscape Architecture, Polar Studies; School of Natural Resources. *Annual research budget:* $3 million. *Director:* Dr. Joel L. Morrison, Director, 614-292-1600, Fax: 614-292-8062, E-mail: morrison@cfm.ohio-state.edu.

Water Resources Center Founded in 1965. *Academic areas of research and training:* Water quantity and quality, surface water and groundwater, water-related environmental science and engineering. *Degrees offered:* None. *Graduate students served last academic year:* 7: 5 at the master's level; 1 at the doctoral level; 1 at the postgraduate level. *Faculty:* 7. *Faculty affiliations:* Departments of Civil and Environmental Engineering and Geodetic Science; Food, Agricultural, and Biological Engineering; Geological Sciences; School of Natural Resources. *Annual research budget:* $300,000. *Director:* Dr. Earl Whitlatch, Director, 614-292-6108, Fax: 614-292-9448, E-mail: whitlatch.1@osu.edu. *Application contact:* Carol Moody, Administrative Assistant, 614-292-6108, Fax: 614-292-9448, E-mail: moody.5@osu.edu.

Ohio University, Athens, OH 45701-2979.

Voinovich Center for Leadership and Public Affairs Founded in 1995. *Academic areas of research and training:* Executive leadership, entrepreneurship, watershed, welfare resource, children's services research. *Degrees offered:* None. *Graduate students served last academic year:* 20: 10 at the master's level. *Faculty:* 10. *Faculty affiliations:* Departments of Economics, Geography, Geological Sciences, Political Science, Psychology, Sociology and Anthropology; Programs in Management, Social Work. *Annual research budget:* $350,000. *Director:* Dr. Mark L. Weinberg, Director, 740-593-4390, Fax: 740-593-4398, E-mail: weinberg@ilgard.ohiou.edu.

Oklahoma State University, Stillwater, OK 74078.

Forest Resources Center Founded in 1960. *Academic areas of research and training:* Forest regeneration, watershed, genetics, physiology, ecology. *Degrees offered:* None. *Graduate students served last academic year:* 5: 2 at the master's level; 2 at the doctoral level; 1 at the postgraduate level. *Faculty:* 13. *Faculty affiliations:* Departments of Agricultural Engineering, Environmental Sciences, Forestry, Wildlife. *Director:* Bob Heinemann, Superintendent, 580-286-5175, Fax: 580-286-1071, E-mail: osufrc@oio.net.

Oklahoma Cooperative Fish and Wildlife Research Unit Founded in 1948. *Academic areas of research and training:* Natural resource management, conservation biology, endangered species. *Degrees offered:* None. *Graduate students served last academic year:* 46: 30 at the master's level; 15 at the doctoral level; 1 at the postgraduate level. *Faculty:* 28: 3 affiliated solely with the unit. *Faculty affiliations:* Departments of Agricultural Economics, Forestry, Plant and Soil Science, Zoology; Environmental Institute. *Annual research budget:* $700,000. *Director:* Dr. David M. Leslie, Unit Leader, 405-744-6342, Fax: 405-744-5006, E-mail: r8cuok@usgs.gov. *Application contact:* Sheryl Lyon, Administrative Assistant, 405-744-6342, Fax: 405-744-5006, E-mail: lsheryl@okstate.edu.

Old Dominion University, Norfolk, VA 23529.

Center for Coastal Physical Oceanography Founded in 1991. *Academic areas of research and training:* Physical oceanography, virtual reality capabilities, ocean observing systems. *Degrees offered:* None. *Graduate students served last academic year:* 13: 2 at the master's level; 11 at the doctoral level. *Faculty:* 30: 15 affiliated solely with the center. *Faculty affiliations:* Departments of Computer Science; Mathematics; Ocean, Earth and Atmospheric Sciences. *Annual research budget:* $2.1 million. *Director:* Dr. Larry P. Atkinson, Director, 757-683-4945, Fax: 757-683-5550, E-mail: ccpoinfo@ccpo.odu.edu. *Application contact:* Carole E. Blett, Administrator, 757-683-4945, Fax: 757-683-5550, E-mail: carole@ccpo.odu.edu.

Institute for Computational and Applied Mechanics Founded in 1983. *Academic areas of research and training:* Computational fluid dynamics, computational mechanics, biomechanics, thermo-fluid interactions, combustion, aerodynamics, high-temperature gas dynamics. *Degrees offered:* None. *Graduate students served last academic year:* 16: 10 at the master's level; 6 at the doctoral level. *Faculty:* 52: 12 affiliated solely with the institute. *Faculty affiliations:* College of Engineering and Technology; Departments of Computer Sciences, Mathematics and Statistics. *Annual research budget:* $200,000. *Director:* Dr. Surendra N. Tiwari, Director, 757-683-6363, Fax: 757-683-5344, E-mail: suren@mem.odu.edu.

Oregon Graduate Institute of Science and Technology, Portland, OR 97291-1000.

Center for Coastal and Land-Margin Research Founded in 1991. *Academic areas of research and training:* Environmental science and engineering. *Degrees offered:* None. *Graduate students served last academic year:* 12: 2 at the master's level; 5 at the doctoral level; 5 at the postgraduate level. *Faculty:* 8. *Faculty affiliations:* Departments of Computer Science and Engineering, Environmental Science and Engineering. *Annual research budget:* $2 million. *Director:* Dr. Antonio Baptista, Director, 503-690-1147, Fax: 503-690-1273, E-mail: baptista@ccalmr.ogi.edu. *Application contact:* Daloris Flaming, Administrative Assistant, 503-690-1247, Fax: 503-690-1273, E-mail: daloris@ccalmr.ogi.edu.

Pennsylvania State University Harrisburg Campus of the Capital College, Middletown, PA 17057-4898.

Environmental Technology Center Founded in 1993. *Academic areas of research and training:* Environmental pollution control, water, wastewater, pollution prevention, site remediation, microbiology, chemistry. *Degrees offered:* None. *Graduate students served last academic year:* 60: 60 at the master's level. *Faculty:* 12. *Faculty affiliations:* Schools of Business Administration; Public Affairs; Science, Engineering and Technology. *Annual research budget:* $100,000. *Director:* Dr. Charles Cole, Professor, 717-948-6133, Fax: 717-948-6401. *Application contact:* Dr. Charles Cole, Professor, 717-948-6133, Fax: 717-948-6401.

Pennsylvania State University University Park Campus, State College, University Park, PA 16802-1503.

Biotechnology Institute-Life Sciences Consortium Founded in 1984. *Academic areas of research and training:* Biotechnology, electron microscopy, flow cytometry, computational biology, nucleic acid facility, hybridoma facility. *Degrees offered:* PhD. *Graduate students served last academic year:* 55: 1 at the master's level; 52 at the doctoral level; 2 at the postgraduate level. *Faculty:* 300. *Faculty affiliations:* Colleges of Agricultural Sciences, Liberal Arts; Departments of Biochemistry and Molecular Biology, Biology, Chemical Engineering, Chemistry, Food Technology, Horticulture, Nutrition, Plant Pathology, Veterinary Science; Milton S. Hershey

Medical Center. *Annual research budget:* $2.1 million. *Director:* Dr. Nina Fedoroff, Director, 814-863-4576, Fax: 814-863-1357, E-mail: nvf1@psu.edu. *Application contact:* Judith Burns, Manager, Staff Services, 814-863-4576, Fax: 814-863-1357, E-mail: jeb2@psu.edu.

Center for BioDiversity Research Founded in 1989. *Academic areas of research and training:* Biodiversity, environmental impacts, habitat preservation, restoration ecology. *Degrees offered:* None. *Graduate students served last academic year:* 2: 2 at the master's level. *Faculty:* 51: 1 affiliated solely with the center. *Faculty affiliations:* Departments of Agricultural Economics and Rural Sociology, Anthropology, Biology, Ecology, Economics, Entomology, Forest Resources, Landscape Architecture, Plant Pathology. *Annual research budget:* $200,000. *Director:* Dr. Ke Chung Kim, Director, 814-863-0159, Fax: 814-865-3378.

Consortium on Chemically Bonded Ceramics Founded in 1991. *Academic areas of research and training:* Materials synthesis, new materials, materials characterization, low-temperature processing, cementitious materials, by-product utilization, zeolites, catalysts, clays, concrete for sustainability. *Degrees offered:* MS; PhD. *Graduate students served last academic year:* 14: 4 at the master's level; 5 at the doctoral level; 5 at the postgraduate level. *Faculty:* 12: 5 affiliated solely with the consortium. *Faculty affiliations:* Departments of Agronomy, Geoscience, Environmental Pollution Control, Materials Science and Engineering, Nuclear and Civil Engineering. *Annual research budget:* $600,000. *Director:* Dr. Della Roy, Director, 814-865-1196, Fax: 814-863-7040, E-mail: dellaroy@psu.edu.

Electro-Optics Laboratory Founded in 1980. *Academic areas of research and training:* Optical computing, neural networks, photorefractive materials and devices, nonlinear liquid crystals, fiberoptic sensors, biooptic research, signal processing. *Degrees offered:* None. *Graduate students served last academic year:* 30. *Faculty:* 17: 7 affiliated solely with the laboratory. *Faculty affiliations:* Applied Research Laboratory, Material Research Laboratory. *Annual research budget:* $1 million. *Director:* Dr. Francis Yu, Director, 814-863-2989, Fax: 814-865-7065, E-mail: ftyece@engr.psu.edu. *Application contact:* Dr. Shizhuo Yin, Assistant Professor, 814-863-4256, Fax: 814-865-7065, E-mail: sxy105@psu.edu.

Environmental Resources Research Institute Founded in 1964. *Academic areas of research and training:* Agriculture and biological science, earth and mineral science, engineering, environmental economics. *Degrees offered:* None. *Graduate students served last academic year:* 59: 38 at the master's level; 18 at the doctoral level; 3 at the postgraduate level. *Faculty:* 129: 65 affiliated solely with the institute. *Faculty affiliations:* Departments of Agricultural and Biological Engineering, Agronomy, Civil and Environmental Engineering, Ecology, Environmental Pollution Control, Forest Resources, Geology, Mechanical Engineering, Meteorology, Mining, Nuclear Engineering, Plant Pathology, Veterinary Science. *Annual research budget:* $6.5 million. *Director:* Dr. Archie J. McDonnell, Director, 814-863-0291, Fax: 814-865-3378, E-mail: ajm2@ceres.erri.psu.edu.

J. O. Almquist Research Center Founded in 1949. *Academic areas of research and training:* Reproductive physiology, large animals, gamete physiology, fertilization, early embryo development. *Degrees offered:* None. *Graduate students served last academic year:* 7: 5 at the doctoral level; 2 at the postgraduate level. *Faculty:* 3: 3 affiliated solely with the center. *Faculty affiliations:* Departments of Animal Science, Physiology. *Annual research budget:* $350,000. *Director:* Dr. G. J. Killian, Director, 814-865-5896, Fax: 814-863-0833, E-mail: lwj@psu.edu.

Landscape Management Research Center Founded in 1986. *Academic areas of research and training:* Programs in turfgrass science: weed control, disease control, insect control, growth regulation, fertility, water quality. *Degrees offered:* MS; PhD. *Graduate students served last academic year:* 6: 5 at the master's level; 1 at the doctoral level. *Faculty:* 9. *Faculty affiliations:* Departments of Agricultural and Biological Engineering, Agronomy, Entomology, Horticulture, Plant Pathology. *Director:* Dr. Thomas Watschke, Director, 814-863-7644, Fax: 814-863-3479, E-mail: tlw3@psu.edu.

The Methodology Center Founded in 1989. *Academic areas of research and training:* Research methods, applied statistics, measurement. *Degrees offered:* None. *Graduate students served last academic year:* 11: 11 at the doctoral level. *Faculty:* 8. *Faculty affiliations:* Departments of Biobehavioral Health, Human Development and Family Studies, Statistics. *Annual research budget:* $500,000. *Director:* Dr. Linda M. Collins, Director, 814-865-3253, Fax: 814-863-0000, E-mail: lmc8@psu.edu.

Pennsylvania Mining and Mineral Resources Research Institute (PAMMRRI) Founded in 1981. *Academic areas of research and training:* Mineral fields, mining. *Degrees offered:* None. *Graduate students served last academic year:* 2: 2 at the master's level. *Faculty:* 6: 1 affiliated solely with the institute. *Faculty affiliations:* Departments of Energy and GeoEnvironmental Engineering, Geosciences, Material Science and Engineering, Mineral Economics. *Director:* Dr. H. Reginald Hardy, Director, 814-863-1620, Fax: 814-865-3248, E-mail: h4h@psuvm.psu.edu.

Rock Mechanics Laboratory Founded in 1965. *Academic areas of research and training:* Laboratory and field studies of geologic materials from an engineering point of view. *Degrees offered:* None. *Graduate students served last academic year:* 5: 2 at the master's level. *Faculty:* 10: 5 affiliated solely with the laboratory. *Faculty affiliations:* Programs in Geology, Geophysics, Mining Engineering, Petroleum and Natural Gas Engineering. *Director:* Dr. H. Reginald Hardy, Professor, 814-863-1620, Fax: 814-865-3248, E-mail: h4h@psuvm.psu.edu.

Shaver's Creek Environmental Center Founded in 1976. *Academic areas of research and training:* Environmental education, natural history interpretation, cultural history interpretation, adventure education. *Degrees offered:* None. *Graduate students served last academic year:* 6: 6 at the master's level. *Faculty:* 18: 6 affiliated solely with the center. *Faculty affiliations:* Departments of Forestry, Leisure Studies, Recreation and Parks, Science Education. *Director:* Gerald R. Potter, Director, 814-863-2000, Fax: 814-865-2706, E-mail: grp2@psu.edu. *Application contact:* Ann Marie Alters, Program Aide, 814-863-2000, Fax: 814-865-2706, E-mail: ama@cde.psu.edu.

Princeton University, Princeton, NJ 08544-1019.

The Dismukes Group Founded in 1978. *Academic areas of research and training:* Bioinorganic chemistry, photosynthesis, solar energy conversion, catalysts, metallo-enzymes. *Degrees offered:* MS; PhD. *Graduate students served last academic year:* 11: 4 at the doctoral level; 7 at the postgraduate level. *Annual research budget:* $2 million. *Director:* Dr. G. Charles Dismukes, 609-258-3949, Fax: 609-258-1980, E-mail: dismukes@princeton.edu.

The Spiro Lab Founded in 1963. *Academic areas of research and training:* Bioinorganic chemistry, spectroscopy. *Degrees offered:* None. *Graduate students served last academic year:* 6 at the doctoral level; 4 at the postgraduate level. *Faculty:* 1: 1 affiliated solely with the laboratory. *Annual research budget:* $500,000. *Director:* Dr. Thomas G. Spiro, Professor, 609-258-3907, Fax: 609-258-3804, E-mail: spiro@princeton.edu.

Purdue University, West Lafayette, IN 47907.

Center for Agricultural Policy and Technology Assessment Founded in 1989. *Academic areas of research and training:* Agricultural economics as applied to agricultural technologies. *Degrees offered:* None. *Graduate students served last academic year:* 3: 2 at the master's level; 1 at the doctoral level. *Faculty:* 6. *Faculty affiliations:* Departments of Agricultural and Biological Engineering, Agricultural Economics, Animal Sciences, Botany and Plant Pathology, Entomology, Foods and Nutrition. *Annual research budget:* $100,000. *Director:* Dr. Marshall A. Martin, Professor, 765-494-4268, Fax: 765-494-9176, E-mail: martin@agecon.purdue.edu.

Indiana Water Resources Research Center (IWRRC) Founded in 1964. *Academic areas of research and training:* Ground and surface water contamination; transport of pollutants; agricultural needs and impacts; water infrastructure evaluation and rehabilitation; coastal and wetlands resources; water supply, reuse,and waste water treatment; hydrology and reservoir management, water management in the Great Lakes region; atmospheric and precipitation processes. *Degrees offered:* None. *Graduate students served last academic year:* 8: 4 at the master's level; 4 at the doctoral level. *Faculty:* 54: 1 affiliated solely with the center. *Faculty affiliations:* Departments of Agricultural Economics, Agronomy, Animal Sciences, Biological Sciences, Botany and Plant Pathology, Earth and Atmospheric Sciences, Entomology, Food Science, Forestry and Natural Resources, Pharmacology and Toxicology, Political Science, Sociology and Anthropology; Schools of Agricultural and Biological Engineering, Chemical Engineering, Civil Engineering, Management. *Annual research budget:* $62,298. *Director:* Dr. Jeff R. Wright, Professor, 765-494-2175, Fax: 765-494-2720, E-mail: wrightje@ecn.purdue.edu. *Application contact:* Kamie Redinbo, Assistant to the Director, 765-494-8041, Fax: 765-494-2720, E-mail: wrrc@ecn.purdue.edu.

Purdue Crop Diagnostics Training and Research Center Founded in 1986. *Academic areas of research and training:* Crop production, crop and weed management, disease, entomology, plant nutrition, soil science, soil and water management, water quality. *Degrees offered:* None. *Graduate students served last academic year:* 6: 4 at the master's level; 2 at the postgraduate level. *Faculty:* 11: 1 affiliated solely with the center. *Faculty affiliations:* Departments of Agronomy, Botany and Plant Pathology, Entomology. *Director:* Dr. Greg Willoughby, Director, 765-494-7731, Fax: 765-496-2926, E-mail: gregw@purdue.edu.

State Utility Forecasting Group *Degrees offered:* None. *Graduate students served last academic year:* 8: 4 at the master's level; 4 at the doctoral level. *Faculty:* 5: 1 affiliated solely with the group. *Faculty affiliations:* Departments of Agricultural Economics and Economics, Krannert Graduate School of Management. *Director:* Dr. F. T. Sparrow, Director, 317-494-4223, Fax: 317-494-2351, E-mail: sufg@ecn.purdue.edu.

Whistler Center for Carbohydrate Research Founded in 1986. *Academic areas of research and training:* Biopolymer chemistry and physics, biopolymer engineering, carbohydrate chemistry, nutritional quality of cereals, polysaccharide molecular modeling, solid state NMR, magnetic resonance imaging, starch chemistry, X-ray fiber diffraction crystallography, rheology. *Degrees offered:* None. *Graduate students served last academic year:* 33: 8 at the master's level; 16 at the doctoral level; 9 at the postgraduate level. *Faculty:* 7. *Faculty affiliations:* Departments of Agricultural and Biological Engineering, Food Science. *Annual research budget:* $1.5 million. *Director:* Dr. James N. BeMiller, Director, 765-494-6171, Fax: 765-494-7953, E-mail: bemiller@purdue.edu.

Rensselaer Polytechnic Institute, Troy, NY 12180-3590.

Center for Image Processing Research Founded in 1986. *Academic areas of research and training:* Image and video processing, image and video compression and transmissions, multimedia systems, video conferencing systems, biomedical imaging, computer vision, pattern recognition, document processing. *Degrees offered:* None. *Graduate students served last academic year:* 43: 28 at the master's level; 12 at the doctoral level; 3 at the postgraduate level. *Faculty:* 27: 15 affiliated solely with the center. *Faculty affiliations:* Departments of Biomedical Engineering, Computer Science, Electrical, Computer and Systems Engineering, Mathematical Sciences. *Annual research budget:* $2 million. *Director:* Dr. James W. Modestino, Director, 518-276-6823, Fax: 518-276-6261, E-mail: modestino@ipl.rpi.edu.

Center for Polymer Synthesis Founded in 1992. *Academic areas of research and training:* To provide a focus for the extensive effort in polymer synthesis and to integrate the multidisciplinary polymer efforts at Rensselaer; science programs deal with many aspects of research on the synthesis, properties, processing and applications of polymeric materials; special laboratories for the larger scale preparation of new monomers and polymers are also available. *Degrees offered:* None. *Graduate students served last academic year:* 65: 5 at the master's level; 50 at the doctoral level; 10 at the postgraduate level. *Faculty:* 14. *Faculty affiliations:* Departments of Chemical Engineering, Chemistry, Materials Science and Engineering, Physics. *Annual research budget:* $3 million. *Director:* Dr. Brian C. Benicewicz, 518-276-2534, Fax: 518-276-6434, E-mail: benice@rpi.edu. *Application contact:* Susan J. Mangione, Administrative Secretary, 518-276-6341, Fax: 518-276-6434, E-mail: mangis@rpi.edu.

Darrin Fresh Water Institute Founded in 1967. *Academic areas of research and training:* Microbiological ecology, wetlands, water resources, aquatic ecosystems, phytoplankton, ecological economics, acid deposition, aquatic plant ecology, wastewater, exotic species. *Degrees offered:* None. *Graduate students served last academic year:* 14: 7 at the master's level; 7 at the doctoral level; 3 at the postgraduate level. *Faculty:* 17. *Faculty affiliations:* Departments of Biology, Chemistry, Earth and Environmental Sciences, Economics, Environmental and Energy Engineering. *Annual research budget:* $2 million. *Director:* Dr. Sandra Nierzwicki-Bauer, Director, 518-644-3541, Fax: 518-644-3640, E-mail: nierzs@rpi.edu.

Geotechnical Centrifuge Research Center Founded in 1989. *Academic areas of research and training:* Geotechnical engineering, soil dynamics, earthquake engineering, slope stability, soil remediation, geoenvironmental engineering. *Degrees offered:* None. *Graduate students served last academic year:* 10: 5 at the master's level; 5 at the doctoral level. *Faculty:* 5: 1 affiliated solely with the center. *Faculty affiliations:* Department of Civil Engineering. *Annual research budget:* $350,000. *Director:* Dr. Ricardo Dobry, Director, 518-276-6934, Fax: 518-276-4833, E-mail: dobryr@rpi.edu. *Application contact:* Dr. Tarek H. Abdoun, Manager, 518-276-6544, Fax: 518-276-4833, E-mail: abdout@rpi.edu.

New York Center on Studies of the Origins of Life Founded in 1998. *Academic areas of research and training:* Investigation of the origins of life on Earth via investigation of the formation of the solar system and Earth; investigation of chemical processes on the Earth and the early evolution of life. *Degrees offered:* None. *Graduate students served last academic year:* 16: 11 at the doctoral level; 5 at the postgraduate level. *Faculty:* 12: 6 affiliated solely with the center. *Faculty affiliations:* Department of Astrophysics, Biology, Chemistry, Earth and Environmental Studies. *Annual research budget:* $1.3 million. *Director:* Dr. James T. Ferris, Director, 518-276-8493, Fax: 518-276-6937, E-mail: ferrij@rpi.edu. *Application contact:* Ann Marie Strack, Assistant Director, 518-276-2663, Fax: 518-276-6937, E-mail: straca@rpi.edu.

Rice University, Houston, TX 77251-1892.

The Center for Nanoscale Science and Technology (CNST) Founded in 1996. *Academic areas of research and training:* Single-walled carbon nanotubes, nanotechnology, geometrical molecules, buckyball, buckytubes, nanotubes, carbon atoms. *Degrees offered:* None. *Graduate students served last academic year:* 16: 6 at the doctoral level; 8 at the postgraduate level. *Faculty:* 15: 3 affiliated solely with the center. *Faculty affiliations:* Applied Physics Program; Departments of Chemistry, Electrical and Computer Engineering, Mechanical Engineering, Physics; Programs in Biology, Materials Science. *Annual research budget:* $1 million. *Director:* Dr. R. E. Smalley, Director, 713-527-4845, Fax: 713-285-5320, E-mail: res@cnst.rice.edu.

Computer and Information Technology Institute (CITI) Founded in 1988. *Academic areas of research and training:* Computation engineering, parallel and distributed computing, discrete optimization, digital signal processing, telecommunications and wireless networking, data analysis and modeling. *Degrees offered:* None. *Graduate students served last academic year:* 120: 20 at the master's level; 80 at the doctoral level; 20 at the postgraduate level. *Faculty:* 90. *Faculty affiliations:* Departments of Computer Science, Computational and Applied Mathematics, Electrical and Computer Engineering, Materials Science, Mechanical Engineering, Statistics. *Annual research budget:* $15 million. *Director:* Dr. Willy Zwaenepoel, Director, 713-285-5402, Fax: 713-285-5930, E-mail: willy@cs.rice.edu. *Application contact:* Anthony J. Elam, Executive Director, 713-527-4734, Fax: 713-285-5136, E-mail: elam@rice.edu.

Rice Quantum Institute Founded in 1987. *Academic areas of research and training:* Facilitation and promotion of research in basic molecular physics, focusing on matter and electromagnetic energy at the scale where the quantum mechanical behavior dominates. *Degrees offered:* PhD. *Graduate students served last academic year:* 25: 25 at the doctoral level. *Faculty:* 40. *Faculty affiliations:* Divisions of Engineering, Natural Science. *Director:* Dr. Ken Smith, Director, 713-527-6028, Fax: 713-285-5935, E-mail: quantum@rice.edu. *Application contact:* Yvonne Creed, Executive Assistant, 713-527-6028, Fax: 713-285-5935.

The W. M. Keck Center for Computational Biology Founded in 1990. *Academic areas of research and training:* Computational biology. *Degrees offered:* None. *Graduate students*

Research and Training Opportunities

The W. M. Keck Center for Computational Biology (continued)

served last academic year: 50: 30 at the doctoral level; 20 at the postgraduate level. *Faculty:* 110: 55 affiliated solely with the center. *Faculty affiliations:* Departments of Biochemistry and Cell Biology, Computational and Applied Mathematics, Electrical and Computer Engineering; Programs in Biomedical Engineering, Neuroscience. *Annual research budget:* $8 million. *Director:* Dr. George Phillips, Training Director, 713-527-4752, Fax: 713-527-4659, E-mail: keckcenter@bioc.rice.edu. *Application contact:* Leslie Hassell, Coordinator, 713-527-4752, Fax: 713-527-4659, E-mail: keckcenter@bioc.rice.edu.

Rochester Institute of Technology, Rochester, NY 14623-5604.

Chester F. Carlson Center for Imaging Science Founded in 1985. *Academic areas of research and training:* Preparation for research or application of imaging modalities to engineering and science; research in astronomy, color, chemical (hard copy materials/processes) digital, electro-optical, medical, silver halide imaging; remote sensing, physics and chemistry of radiation sensitive materials/processes. *Degrees offered:* MS; PhD. *Graduate students served last academic year:* 87: 42 at the master's level; 41 at the doctoral level; 4 at the postgraduate level. *Faculty:* 21: 17 affiliated solely with the center. *Faculty affiliations:* Departments of Computer Science, Electrical Engineering, Microelectronic Engineering. *Annual research budget:* $1.7 million. *Director:* Dr. Ian Gatley, Director, 716-475-6220, Fax: 716-475-5988, E-mail: gatley@cis.rit.edu. *Application contact:* Marilyn Lockwood, Administrative Assistant, 716-475-5944, Fax: 716-475-5988, E-mail: lockwood@cis.rit.edu.

The John D. Hromi Center for Quality and Applied Statistics Founded in 1983. *Academic areas of research and training:* Application of statistical methods to product and process improvement. *Degrees offered:* MS. *Graduate students served last academic year:* 216: 215 at the master's level. *Faculty:* 26: 23 affiliated solely with the center. *Faculty affiliations:* Mathematics Department. *Director:* Dr. Donald Baker, Director, 716-475-5070, Fax: 716-475-5959, E-mail: ddbcqa@rit.edu.

Rutgers, The State University of New Jersey, New Brunswick, New Brunswick, NJ 08903.

Biotechnology Center for Agriculture and the Environment Founded in 1987. *Academic areas of research and training:* Agricultural and environmental molecular biology, plant gene regulation and expression, resistance to pests, natural products, turfgrass biotechnology, bioremediation of pollutants using microbes and plants. *Degrees offered:* None. *Graduate students served last academic year:* 59: 24 at the doctoral level; 35 at the postgraduate level. *Faculty:* 25: 11 affiliated solely with the center. *Faculty affiliations:* Programs in Animal Sciences, Ecology and Evolution, Natural Resources. *Annual research budget:* $5.5 million. *Director:* Dr. Peter R. Day, Director, 732-932-8165, Fax: 732-932-6535, E-mail: agbiotech@njaes.rutgers.edu.

Center for Advanced Food Technology Founded in 1984. *Academic areas of research and training:* Research and development in flavor science and technology, food materials science, and process simulation and control; health-promoting and disease-preventing foods; productivity improvement. *Degrees offered:* None. *Graduate students served last academic year:* 30: 5 at the master's level; 20 at the doctoral level; 5 at the postgraduate level. *Faculty:* 23: 2 affiliated solely with the center. *Faculty affiliations:* Departments of Chemical and Biochemical Engineering, Chemistry, Food Science, Industrial Engineering, Mechanical and Aerospace Engineering, Pharmacology; School of Management; Biotechnology Center for Agriculture and Environment; Center for Computer Aids in Industrial Productivity. *Annual research budget:* $5 million. *Director:* Dr. Myron Solberg, Director, 732-932-8306 Ext. 312, Fax: 732-932-8690, E-mail: solberg@aesop.rutgers.edu. *Application contact:* Dr. Jozef L. Kokini, Associate Director, 732-932-8306 Ext. 313, Fax: 732-932-8690, E-mail: kokini@aesop.rutgers.edu.

Center for Environmental Communication Founded in 1988. *Academic areas of research and training:* Risk communication, risk perception, public participation. *Degrees offered:* None. *Graduate students served last academic year:* 1: 1 at the master's level. *Faculty:* 4. *Faculty affiliations:* Edward J. Bloustein School of Planning and Public Policy, Cook College Department of Human Ecology. *Annual research budget:* $300,000. *Director:* Dr. Caron Chess, Director, 732-932-8795, Fax: 732-932-7815, E-mail: cec@aesop.rutgers.edu. *Application contact:* Elizabeth Wescott, Research Assistant, 732-932-8795, Fax: 732-932-7815, E-mail: wescott@aesop.rutgers.edu.

Center for Mathematical Sciences Research Founded in 1975. *Degrees offered:* None. *Graduate students served last academic year:* 16: 6 at the doctoral level; 10 at the postgraduate level. *Faculty:* 10. *Faculty affiliations:* Program in Mathematics. *Annual research budget:* $300,000. *Director:* Dr. Joel L. Lebowitz, Director, 732-445-3117, Fax: 732-445-4936, E-mail: lebowitz@math.rutgers.edu.

Center for Remote Sensing and Spatial Analysis Founded in 1989. *Academic areas of research and training:* Application of remote sensing and geographic information systems to environmental, agricultural, and natural resource management issues. *Degrees offered:* None. *Graduate students served last academic year:* 8: 5 at the master's level; 3 at the doctoral level. *Faculty:* 10: 5 affiliated solely with the center. *Faculty affiliations:* Departments of Agricultural Economics, Geography, Human Ecology; School of Planning. *Annual research budget:* $618,000. *Director:* Dr. Richard G. Lathrop, Director, 732-932-1580, Fax: 732-932-8746, E-mail: lathrop@crssa.rutgers.edu.

Waksman Institute Founded in 1954. *Academic areas of research and training:* Transcription, signal transduction, recombination, developmental genetics, structural and computational biology. *Degrees offered:* None. *Graduate students served last academic year:* 82: 31 at the doctoral level; 51 at the postgraduate level. *Faculty:* 19: 16 affiliated solely with the institute. *Faculty affiliations:* Departments of Chemistry, Computer Science, Genetics, Molecular Biology and Biochemistry, Plant Science. *Annual research budget:* $12.5 million. *Director:* Dr. Joachim Messing, Director, 732-445-4256, Fax: 732-445-5735.

Simon Fraser University, Burnaby, BC V5A 1S6, Canada.

Western Canadian Universities Marine Biological Society-Bamfield Marine Station Founded in 1972. *Academic areas of research and training:* Marine biology, marine ecology, behavior, evolutionary biology, comparative physiology and biochemistry, molecular biology. *Degrees offered:* None. *Graduate students served last academic year:* 31: 12 at the master's level; 13 at the doctoral level; 6 at the postgraduate level. *Faculty:* 62: 2 affiliated solely with the station. *Faculty affiliations:* University of Alberta, University of British Columbia, University of Calgary, University of Victoria. *Annual research budget:* $700,000. *Director:* Dr. Andy N. Spencer, Director, 250-728-3301, Fax: 250-728-3452, E-mail: aspencer@bms.bc.ca.

Southern Methodist University, Dallas, TX 75275.

Geothermal Laboratory Founded in 1968. *Academic areas of research and training:* Geothermal energy, well logging and analysis, heat flow, thermal conductivity. *Degrees offered:* None. *Graduate students served last academic year:* 4: 1 at the master's level; 2 at the doctoral level; 1 at the postgraduate level. *Faculty:* 2: 1 affiliated solely with the laboratory. *Faculty affiliations:* Department of Geological Sciences. *Annual research budget:* $125,000. *Director:* Dr. David D. Blackwell, Director, 214-768-2745, Fax: 214-768-2701, E-mail: blackwel@passion.isem.smu.edu.

Institute of the Study of Earth and Man Founded in 1968. *Academic areas of research and training:* Support of faculty and student research in anthropology and geology. *Degrees offered:* None. *Graduate students served last academic year:* 10: 10 at the doctoral level. *Faculty:* 30. *Faculty affiliations:* Departments of Anthropology, Geology. *Director:* Dr. Richard J. Krulzenga, Director, 214-768-2425, Fax: 214-768-4289, E-mail: sliepins@mail.smu.edu. *Application contact:* Dr. Susan J. Liepins, Director, Administration and Development.

Stanford University, Stanford, CA 94305-9991.

Center for Conservation Biology Founded in 1984. *Director:* Carol Boggs, Director, 415-723-5924, Fax: 415-723-5920.

Western Region Hazardous Substance Research Center Founded in 1989. *Academic areas of research and training:* Chemical engineering, chemistry, environmental engineering, environmental microbiology, hydrology, geology. *Degrees offered:* None. *Graduate students served last academic year:* 24: 3 at the master's level; 16 at the doctoral level; 5 at the postgraduate level. *Faculty:* 42: 21 affiliated solely with the center. *Faculty affiliations:* College of Veterinary Medicine; Departments of Civil and Environmental Engineering, Microbiology and Immunology, Petroleum Engineering; School of Earth Science; Oregon State University Departments of Botany and Plant Pathology, Chemistry, Civil Engineering. *Annual research budget:* $2 million. *Director:* Dr. Perry L. McCarty, Professor, 650-723-4131, Fax: 650-725-9474, E-mail: mccarty@ce.stanford.edu. *Application contact:* Sharon Parkinson, Administrative Assistant, 650-723-4123, Fax: 650-725-9474, E-mail: sharon@ce.stanford.edu.

State University of New York at Albany, Albany, NY 12222-0001.

Atmospheric Sciences Research Center Founded in 1961. *Academic areas of research and training:* Atmospheric chemistry, air quality and climate modeling, atmospheric measurement systems, instrumentation development and deployment. *Degrees offered:* None. *Graduate students served last academic year:* 20: 8 at the master's level; 8 at the doctoral level; 4 at the postgraduate level. *Faculty:* 15: 13 affiliated solely with the center. *Faculty affiliations:* Department of Earth and Atmospheric Science. *Annual research budget:* $4 million. *Director:* Dr. Kenneth L. Demerjian, Director, 518-437-8705, Fax: 518-437-8711, E-mail: kld@asrc.cestm.albany.edu.

Geographic Information System and Remote Sensing Laboratory Founded in 1975. *Academic areas of research and training:* Geographic Information Systems, applied remote sensing, resource management. *Degrees offered:* Certificate. *Graduate students served last academic year:* 9: 9 at the master's level. *Faculty:* 5. *Faculty affiliations:* Department of Geography and Planning. *Annual research budget:* $150,000. *Director:* Dr. Floyd M. Henderson, Co-Director, 518-442-3912, Fax: 518-442-4742, E-mail: fmh06@csc.albany.edu.

Syracuse University, Syracuse, NY 13244-0003.

Center for Environmental Policy and Administration Founded in 1994. *Academic areas of research and training:* Transboundary issues, technology and sustainable development, Cold War environmental legacy, river environmental issues. *Degrees offered:* None. *Graduate students served last academic year:* 6: 3 at the master's level; 3 at the doctoral level. *Faculty:* 4. *Faculty affiliations:* Departments of Geography, Political Science/Public Administration, Public Affairs. *Annual research budget:* $350,000. *Director:* Dr. W. Henry Lambright, Director, 315-443-1890, Fax: 315-443-1075, E-mail: whlambri@maxwell.syr.edu.

Texas Tech University, Lubbock, TX 79409.

Center for Agricultural Technology Transfer Founded in 1991. *Academic areas of research and training:* Computer and related equipment use. *Degrees offered:* None. *Graduate students served last academic year:* 10: 8 at the master's level; 2 at the doctoral level. *Faculty:* 6: 3 affiliated solely with the center. *Faculty affiliations:* Department of Agricultural Education and Communications. *Director:* Dr. Paul Vaughn, Chairman, 806-742-2816, Fax: 806-742-2880, E-mail: zoprv@ttacs.ttu.edu.

Center for Feed and Industry Research and Education (CFIRE) Founded in 1995. *Academic areas of research and training:* Animal nutrition, feed manufacturing, feed processing. *Degrees offered:* None. *Graduate students served last academic year:* 9: 6 at the master's level; 3 at the doctoral level. *Faculty:* 17: 3 affiliated solely with the center. *Faculty affiliations:* Departments of Agricultural Economics, Animal Science, Chemical Engineering, Mechanical Engineering, Plant and Soil Science. *Annual research budget:* $150,000. *Director:* Dr. C. Reed Richardson, Director, 806-742-2825 Ext. 2516, Fax: 806-742-4003, E-mail: cfire@ttacs6.ttu.edu. *Application contact:* Laurice Matulka, Feed Manufacturing Specialist, 806-742-2492, Fax: 806-742-4003, E-mail: cfire@ttacs6.ttu.edu.

Pork Industry Institute for Research and Education Founded in 1990. *Academic areas of research and training:* Agricultural economics, animal science, pig production. *Degrees offered:* None. *Graduate students served last academic year:* 6: 3 at the master's level; 3 at the doctoral level. *Faculty:* 10: 5 affiliated solely with the institute. *Faculty affiliations:* Departments of Agricultural Economics, Animal Science and Food Technology, Plant and Soil Science. *Annual research budget:* $200,000. *Director:* Dr. John J. McGlone, Director, 806-742-2826, Fax: 806-742-2335, E-mail: jmcglone@ttu.edu.

Water Resources Center (WRC) Founded in 1965. *Academic areas of research and training:* Water resources engineering, groundwater, water resources management, ground water remediation and restoration, artificial recharge. *Degrees offered:* None. *Graduate students served last academic year:* 20: 16 at the master's level; 4 at the doctoral level. *Faculty:* 9: 1 affiliated solely with the center. *Faculty affiliations:* Departments of Biological Sciences, Chemical Engineering, Civil Engineering, Economics and Geography, Environmental Engineering, Plant and Soil Science. *Annual research budget:* $750,000. *Director:* Dr. Lloyd V. Urban, Director, 806-742-3597, Fax: 806-742-3449, E-mail: lurban@coettu.edu. *Application contact:* Jan E. Hudson, Assistant to the Director, 806-742-3597, Fax: 806-742-3449, E-mail: jhudson@coe.ttu.edu.

Wildlife and Fisheries Management Institute Founded in 1989. *Academic areas of research and training:* Fund-raising for research, wildlife and fisheries research. *Degrees offered:* None. *Graduate students served last academic year:* 35. *Faculty:* 15. *Faculty affiliations:* Department of Range, Wildlife, and Fisheries Management; Texas Fisheries and Wildlife Cooperative Research Unit. *Director:* Dr. Phillip J. Zwank, Chairman, 806-742-2841, Fax: 806-742-2280, E-mail: c7zpj@ttacs.ttu.edu. *Application contact:* Louise Whatley, Administrative Secretary, 806-742-2841, Fax: 806-742-2280, E-mail: c7wez@ttacs.ttu.edu.

Tufts University, Medford, MA 02155.

Global Development and Environment Institute Founded in 1994. *Academic areas of research and training:* Economics and the environment, the social and physical contexts for economic development. *Degrees offered:* None. *Graduate students served last academic year:* 10: 6 at the master's level; 4 at the doctoral level. *Faculty:* 3: 2 affiliated solely with the institute. *Faculty affiliations:* Fletcher School of Law and Diplomacy. *Annual research budget:* $550,000. *Director:* Dr. Neva R. Goodwin, Co-Director, 617-627-3530, Fax: 617-627-3712, E-mail: gdae@tufts.edu. *Application contact:* Timothy Wise, Deputy Director, 617-627-3509, Fax: 617-627-2409, E-mail: twise01@tufts.edu.

The University of Alabama at Birmingham, Birmingham, AL 35294.

The Earth Center *Academic areas of research and training:* Environmental issues related to water and air pollution, utilization of by-products, environmental health programs. *Degrees offered:* None. *Graduate students served last academic year:* 50: 30 at the master's level; 15 at the doctoral level; 5 at the postgraduate level. *Faculty:* 100: 100 affiliated solely with the center. *Annual research budget:* $14 million. *Director:* Dr. Fouad H. Fouad, Executive Director, 205-934-8430, Fax: 205-934-9855, E-mail: ffouad@uab.edu. *Application contact:* Dr. Fouad H. Fouad, Executive Director, 205-934-8430, Fax: 205-934-9855, E-mail: ffouad@uab.edu.

The University of Alabama in Huntsville, Huntsville, AL 35899.

Center for Applied Optics (CAO) Founded in 1985. *Academic areas of research and training:* Applied optics design, fabrication, and metrology; physics; mechanical and aerospace engineering; electrical engineering. *Degrees offered:* None. *Graduate students served last academic year:* 28: 14 at the master's level; 14 at the doctoral level. *Faculty:* 28: 5 affiliated solely with the center. *Faculty affiliations:* Departments of Chemical Engineering, Chemistry, Electrical and Computer Engineering, Mechanical and Aerospace Engineering, Physics. *Annual research budget:* $2.5 million. *Director:* Dr. John O. Dimmock, Director, 256-890-6030 Ext. 400, Fax: 256-890-6618, E-mail: dimmockj@email.uah.edu.

Center for Space Plasma and Aeronomic Research (CSPAR) Founded in 1987. *Academic areas of research and training:* Space physics, astrophysics and space weather research. *Degrees offered:* None. *Graduate students served last academic year:* 22: 9 at the master's level; 12 at the doctoral level; 1 at the postgraduate level. *Faculty:* 21: 10 affiliated solely with the center. *Faculty affiliations:* Departments of Computer Science, Electrical and Computer Engineering, Mechanical and Aerospace Engineering, Physics. *Director:* Dr. S. T. Wu, Director.

Consortium for Materials Development in Space (CMDS) Founded in 1985. *Academic areas of research and training:* Materials and manufacturing processes. *Degrees offered:* None. *Graduate students served last academic year:* 10: 5 at the master's level; 5 at the doctoral level. *Faculty:* 8. *Faculty affiliations:* Departments of Biological Sciences, Chemical Engineering, Chemistry, Mechanical and Aerospace Engineering, Physics. *Annual research budget:* $3 million. *Director:* Dr. Bernard Schroer, Director, 205-890-6100, Fax: 205-890-6783.

University of Alaska Fairbanks, Fairbanks, AK 99775-7480.

Agricultural and Forestry Experiment Station (AFES) Founded in 1935. *Academic areas of research and training:* Agriculture, forestry, natural resources. *Degrees offered:* MS; PhD. *Graduate students served last academic year:* 32: 30 at the master's level; 2 at the doctoral level. *Faculty:* 29: 25 affiliated solely with the station. *Faculty affiliations:* Departments of Forest Sciences; Geography; Plant, Animal, and Soil Science; Resources Management. *Annual research budget:* $5.1 million. *Director:* Dr. G. Allen Mitchell, Acting Director, 907-746-9450, Fax: 907-746-2677, E-mail: pfgam@uaa.alaska.edu. *Application contact:* Barbara Pierson, Recruitment Coordinator, 907-474-5276, Fax: 907-474-6184, E-mail: fnbjp@uaf.edu.

Alaska Quaternary Center Founded in 1982. *Academic areas of research and training:* Quaternary history of Alaska and the Holarctic, Arctic archaeology, paleoecology (i.e., palynology and paleontology), Quaternary Geology (glacial geology, coastal geology, volcanology). *Degrees offered:* None. *Graduate students served last academic year:* 10: 5 at the master's level; 4 at the doctoral level; 1 at the postgraduate level. *Faculty:* 27: 4 affiliated solely with the center. *Faculty affiliations:* Departments of Anthropology, Biology and Wildlife, Geology and Geophysics; Geophysical Institute; Institutes of Arctic Biology, Marine Science; University of Alaska Museum. *Director:* Dr. Paul Matheus, Director, 907-474-2688, Fax: 907-474-5101, E-mail: ffpem1@uaf.edu. *Application contact:* Dr. Paul Matheus, Director, 907-474-2688, Fax: 907-474-5101, E-mail: ffpem1@uaf.edu.

Fishery Industrial Technology Center Founded in 1981. *Academic areas of research and training:* Seafood harvesting, seafood processing, seafood quality and safety research, education and service. *Degrees offered:* MS; PhD. *Graduate students served last academic year:* 7: 3 at the master's level; 2 at the doctoral level; 2 at the postgraduate level. *Faculty:* 15: 5 affiliated solely with the center. *Faculty affiliations:* School of Fisheries and Ocean Sciences; Department of Chemistry, University of Alaska Anchorage; U.S. Department of Agriculture, Agricultural Research Service; U.S. Department of Commerce, National Marine Fisheries Service. *Annual research budget:* $1.2 million. *Director:* Dr. Scott Smiley, Director, 907-486-1500, Fax: 907-486-1540, E-mail: ffsts@uaf.edu.

Water and Environmental Research Center Founded in 1965. *Academic areas of research and training:* Water resources, environment, hydrology, hydraulics, geochemistry, limnology, microbiology, oceanography. *Degrees offered:* None. *Graduate students served last academic year:* 20: 12 at the master's level; 5 at the doctoral level; 3 at the postgraduate level. *Faculty:* 15: 6 affiliated solely with the center. *Faculty affiliations:* Departments of Chemistry, Mechanical Engineering; Programs in Biological Sciences, Civil and Environmental Engineering, Geology; School of Fisheries and Ocean Sciences. *Annual research budget:* $2 million. *Director:* Dr. Douglas L. Kane, Director, 907-474-7808, Fax: 907-474-7979, E-mail: ffdlk@uaf.edu.

University of Alberta, Edmonton, AB T6G 2E1, Canada.

Western Canadian Universities Marine Biological Society-Bamfield Marine Station Founded in 1972. *Academic areas of research and training:* Marine biology, marine ecology, behavior, evolutionary biology, comparative physiology and biochemistry, molecular biology, aquaculture, biological hydrodynamics. *Degrees offered:* None. *Graduate students served last academic year:* 31: 12 at the master's level; 13 at the doctoral level; 6 at the postgraduate level. *Faculty:* 62: 2 affiliated solely with the station. *Faculty affiliations:* Simon Fraser University, University of British Columbia, University of Calgary, University of Victoria. *Annual research budget:* $700,000. *Director:* Dr. Andy N. Spencer, Director, 250-728-3301, Fax: 250-728-3452, E-mail: aspencer@bms.bc.ca.

The University of Arizona, Tucson, AZ 85721.

Arizona Cooperative Fish and Wildlife Research Unit Founded in 1987. *Academic areas of research and training:* Fisheries, wildlife management, ecology. *Degrees offered:* None. *Graduate students served last academic year:* 25: 17 at the master's level; 7 at the doctoral level; 1 at the postgraduate level. *Faculty:* 15: 3 affiliated solely with the unit. *Faculty affiliations:* School of Renewable Natural Resources. *Director:* Dr. O. Eugene Maughan, Leader, 520-621-1193, Fax: 520-621-8801, E-mail: gmaughan@ag.arizona.edu.

Arizona Cooperative Park Studies Unit Founded in 1973. *Academic areas of research and training:* Natural area resources management and research. *Degrees offered:* None. *Graduate students served last academic year:* 20: 15 at the master's level; 5 at the doctoral level. *Faculty:* 16: 2 affiliated solely with the unit. *Faculty affiliations:* Departments of Ecology and Evolutionary Biology, Hydrology and Water Resources; School of Renewable Natural Resources. *Annual research budget:* $650,000. *Director:* Dr. William L. Halvorson, Leader, 520-670-6885, Fax: 520-670-5001, E-mail: halvor@srnr.arizona.edu.

Environmental Research Laboratory (ERL) Founded in 1967. *Academic areas of research and training:* Bioresources, environmental applications, warm water aquaculture, saltwater crop development, riparian and wetland studies, water resources, energy efficiency. *Degrees offered:* None. *Graduate students served last academic year:* 16: 12 at the master's level; 2 at the doctoral level; 2 at the postgraduate level. *Faculty:* 21: 6 affiliated solely with the laboratory. *Faculty affiliations:* Departments of Architecture; Renewable Natural Resources; Soil, Water, and Environmental Science. *Annual research budget:* $700,000. *Director:* Dr. Donald Baumgartner, Director, 520-626-3322, Fax: 520-573-0852, E-mail: donb@ag.arizona.edu.

Lunar and Planetary Laboratory Founded in 1960. *Academic areas of research and training:* Planetary science, space science, solar system. *Degrees offered:* None. *Graduate students served last academic year:* 76: 2 at the master's level; 44 at the doctoral level; 30 at the postgraduate level. *Faculty:* 33: 10 affiliated solely with the laboratory. *Faculty affiliations:* Department of Planetary Sciences. *Annual research budget:* $13 million. *Director:* Dr. Michael Drake, Director, 520-621-6962, Fax: 520-621-4933. *Application contact:* Joan M. Weinberg, Assistant to the Director, 520-621-2828, Fax: 520-621-4933, E-mail: jweinber@u.arizona.edu.

Optical Sciences Center Founded in 1968. *Academic areas of research and training:* Education, research and outreach in the science and application of light; optical design; nonlinear optics; remote sensing; medical optics; image processing; integrated optics; optical data storage; optical detector systems; quantum optics. *Degrees offered:* MS; PhD. *Graduate students served last academic year:* 142: 23 at the master's level; 119 at the doctoral level. *Faculty:* 61: 36 affiliated solely with the center. *Faculty affiliations:* Departments of Astronomy, Chemistry, Electrical and Computer Engineering, Geography and Regional Development, Materials Science and Engineering, Mathematics, Physics; Programs in Ophthalmology, Radiology; Steward Observatory Mirror Laboratory. *Director:* Dr. James C. Wyant, Director, 520-621-6997, Fax: 520-621-9613, E-mail: jcwyant@u.arizona.edu. *Application contact:* Dr. Richard L. Shoemaker, Associate Director for Academic Affairs, 520-621-4111, Fax: 520-621-5300, E-mail: rick.shoemaker@optics.arizona.edu.

Optical Sciences Center (OSC) Founded in 1968. *Academic areas of research and training:* Optics, optical engineering, interferometry, optical design, nonlinear optical devices, remote sensing, integrated optics, medical optics, image processing, optoelectronics, astronomical optics, laser physics, quantum optics, optical physics. *Degrees offered:* MS; PhD. *Graduate students served last academic year:* 125: 23 at the master's level; 102 at the doctoral level. *Faculty:* 73: 48 affiliated solely with the center. *Faculty affiliations:* Departments of Astronomy, Chemistry, Electrical and Computer Engineering, Geography, Materials Science, Mathematics, Opthalmology, Physics, Radiology; Steward Observatory. *Annual research budget:* $15. 5 million. *Director:* Dr. James C. Wyant, Director, 520-621-6997, Fax: 520-621-3389, E-mail: jcwyant@u.arizona.edu. *Application contact:* Dr. Richard L. Shoemaker, Associate Director, Academic Affairs, 520-621-4111, Fax: 520-621-6778, E-mail: rick.shoe@optics.arizona.edu.

University of Arkansas, Fayetteville, AR 72701-1201.

Arkansas Water Resources Center Founded in 1964. *Academic areas of research and training:* Ground water, surface water, economics, water quality, water quantity, modeling, geographical information systems, aquatic and environmental protection, emerging problems in the state. *Degrees offered:* None. *Graduate students served last academic year:* 36: 31 at the master's level; 2 at the doctoral level; 1 at the postgraduate level. *Faculty:* 26: 2 affiliated solely with the center. *Faculty affiliations:* Departments of Agricultural Economics and Rural Sociology, Agronomy, Animal Sciences, Biological and Agricultural Engineering, Biological Sciences, Chemical Engineering, Civil Engineering, Economics, Geology. *Annual research budget:* $2.7 million. *Director:* Dr. Kenneth F. Steele, Director, 501-575-4403, Fax: 501-575-3177, E-mail: ksteele@comp.uark.edu. *Application contact:* Patti Snodgrass, Administrative Assistant, 501-575-5867, Fax: 501-575-3177, E-mail: psnodgr@comp.uark.edu.

Center of Excellence for Poultry Science Founded in 1992. *Academic areas of research and training:* Business, food safety, immunology, molecular biology, nutrition, parasitology, physiology, poultry management, poultry health/diseases, molecular genetics/virology, genetics, product technology. *Degrees offered:* None. *Graduate students served last academic year:* 37: 13 at the master's level; 24 at the doctoral level. *Faculty:* 40: 25 affiliated solely with the center. *Faculty affiliations:* Departments of Agricultural Economics and Rural Sociology, Agronomy, Animal Science, Biological and Agricultural Engineering, Biological Sciences, Food Sciences, Industrial Engineering, Medical Sciences; School of Human Environmental Sciences; Arkansas Cooperative Extension Service. *Annual research budget:* $6.2 million. *Director:* Dr. James H. Denton, Director, 501-575-3699, Fax: 501-575-3026, E-mail: jdenton@comp.uark.edu. *Application contact:* Diana Bisbee, Associate for Administration, 501-575-2025, Fax: 501-575-3026, E-mail: dbisbee@comp.uark.edu.

University of British Columbia, Vancouver, BC V6T 1Z2, Canada.

Institute for Resources and Environment Founded in 1995. *Academic areas of research and training:* Ecological policy, water resources, land management, fisheries management, risk assessment, governance. *Degrees offered:* MA; MS; PhD. *Graduate students served last academic year:* 70: 36 at the master's level; 32 at the doctoral level. *Faculty:* 24: 8 affiliated solely with the institute. *Faculty affiliations:* Departments of Anthropology and Sociology, Civil Engineering, Economics, Geography, Soil Science; Faculties of Commerce and Business Administration, Forestry; Interdisciplinary Program in Biology; School of Community and Regional Planning. *Annual research budget:* $1.7 million. *Director:* Dr. Les M. Lavkulich, Director, 604-822-3487, Fax: 604-822-9250, E-mail: ire@interchange.ubc.ca. *Application contact:* Nancy Dick, Administrative Assistant, 604-822-1482, Fax: 604-822-9250, E-mail: nadick@interchange.ubc.ca.

Sustainable Development Research Institute (SDRI) Founded in 1992. *Academic areas of research and training:* Sustainable development, computer environmental modeling, climate change, energy policy. *Degrees offered:* None. *Graduate students served last academic year:* 5: 3 at the master's level; 2 at the doctoral level. *Faculty:* 4: 1 affiliated solely with the institute. *Faculty affiliations:* Departments of Biological Sciences, Resource and Environmental Science; Faculty of Forestry; School of Community and Regional Planning; Centre for Human Settlements; Environment Canada's Environmental Adaptation Research Group. *Annual research budget:* $4 million. *Director:* Dr. John B. Robinson, Director, 604-822-8198, Fax: 604-822-9191, E-mail: sdri@sdri.ubc.ca. *Application contact:* Caroline Van Bers, Research Manager, 604-822-9376, Fax: 604-822-9191, E-mail: cvanbers@sdri.ubc.ca.

Western Canadian Universities Marine Biological Society-Bamfield Marine Station Founded in 1972. *Academic areas of research and training:* Marine biology, marine ecology, behavior, evolutionary biology, comparative physiology and biochemistry, molecular biology. *Degrees offered:* None. *Graduate students served last academic year:* 31: 12 at the master's level; 13 at the doctoral level; 6 at the postgraduate level. *Faculty:* 62: 2 affiliated solely with the station. *Faculty affiliations:* Simon Fraser University, University of Alberta, University of Calgary, University of Victoria. *Annual research budget:* $700,000. *Director:* Dr. Andy N. Spencer, Director, 250-728-3301, Fax: 250-728-3452, E-mail: aspencer@bms.bc.ca.

University of Calgary, Calgary, AB T2N 1N4, Canada.

Western Canadian Universities Marine Biological Society-Bamfield Marine Station Founded in 1972. *Academic areas of research and training:* Marine biology, marine ecology, behavior, evolutionary biology, comparative physiology and biochemistry, molecular biology. *Degrees offered:* None. *Graduate students served last academic year:* 31: 12 at the master's level; 13 at the doctoral level; 6 at the postgraduate level. *Faculty:* 62: 2 affiliated solely with the station. *Faculty affiliations:* Simon Fraser University, University of Alberta, University of British Columbia, University of Victoria. *Annual research budget:* $700,000. *Director:* Dr. Andy N. Spencer, Director, 250-728-3301, Fax: 250-728-3452, E-mail: aspencer@bms.bc.ca.

University of California, Berkeley, Berkeley, CA 94720-1500.

Environmental Engineering and Health Sciences Laboratory (EEHSL) Founded in 1950. *Academic areas of research and training:* Environmental research, wastewater treatment, soil and groundwater contamination, radioactive waste management, air pollution, thermal/bioremediation, coastal processes geophysics, flow in porous/fractured media. *Degrees offered:* None. *Graduate students served last academic year:* 83: 58 at the doctoral level; 25 at the postgraduate level. *Faculty:* 40. *Faculty affiliations:* Departments of Civil and Environmental Engineering, Environmental Science, Policy and Management, Integrative Biology, Material Sciences and Mineral Engineering, Mechanical Engineering, Nuclear Engineering; Division of Geology; School of Public Health. *Annual research budget:* $205,000. *Director:* James R. Hunt, Director, 510-642-0948, Fax: 510-643-6331, E-mail: jrh@ce.berkeley.edu. *Application contact:* Laurel L. Holland, Administrator, 510-642-8324, Fax: 510-643-6331, E-mail: laurelh@uclink4.berkeley.edu.

Pacific Earthquake Engineering Research Center Founded in 1997. *Academic areas of research and training:* Earthquake engineering, engineering seismology, structural dynamics, geotechnical engineering, structural engineering. *Degrees offered:* None. *Graduate students served last academic year:* 60: 30 at the master's level; 30 at the doctoral level. *Faculty:* 40. *Faculty affiliations:* Departments of Architecture, Civil Engineering, Economics, Electrical Engineering, Public Policy, Seismology. *Annual research budget:* $7 million. *Director:* Jack P. Moehle, 510-231-9554, Fax: 510-231-9471, E-mail: moehle@euler.berkeley.edu.

Seismological Laboratory Founded in 1930. *Academic areas of research and training:* Seismology, earthquake monitoring, tectonics, rupture process, wave propagation, deep earth structure, geophysics. *Degrees offered:* None. *Graduate students served last academic year:* 15: 1 at the master's level; 12 at the doctoral level; 2 at the postgraduate level. *Faculty:* 12.

Research and Training Opportunities

Seismological Laboratory (continued)
Faculty affiliations: College of Engineering, Department of Geology and Geophysics. *Director:* Dr. Barbara Romanowicz, Director, 510-642-3977, Fax: 510-643-5811, E-mail: www@seismo.berkeley.edu.

University of California, Davis, Davis, CA 95616.

Agricultural Health and Safety Center   Founded in 1990. *Academic areas of research and training:* Agricultural research, education, disease and injury prevention. *Degrees offered:* None. *Graduate students served last academic year:* 8: 1 at the master's level; 7 at the doctoral level. *Faculty:* 39. *Faculty affiliations:* Programs in Agricultural Economics; Avian Sciences; Biological and Agricultural Engineering; Community and International Health; Internal Medicine; Land, Air, and Water Resources; Molecular Biosciences; Neurology; Obstetrics/Gynecology; Physiology; Plant Protection and Pest Management. *Annual research budget:* $800,000. *Director:* Dr. Marc B. Schenker, Director, 530-752-4050, Fax: 530-752-5047, E-mail: mbschenker@ucdavis.edu. *Application contact:* Eleanor Wood, Manager, 530-752-5253, Fax: 530-752-5047, E-mail: ewwood@ucdavis.edu.

Agricultural History Center   Founded in 1963. *Academic areas of research and training:* Agricultural history, agricultural development, agricultural policy. *Degrees offered:* None. *Graduate students served last academic year:* 15: 5 at the master's level; 10 at the doctoral level. *Faculty:* 14. *Faculty affiliations:* Programs in Agricultural and Resource Economics, Economics, History, Political Science. *Annual research budget:* $150,000. *Director:* Dr. Peter H. Lindert, Director, 530-752-1827, Fax: 530-752-5611, E-mail: phlindert@ucdavis.edu. *Application contact:* Mary Davis, Administrator, 530-752-1827, Fax: 530-752-5611, E-mail: mvdavis@ucdavis.edu.

Bodega Marine Laboratory (BML)   Founded in 1966. *Academic areas of research and training:* Marine science, ecology, aquaculture, comparative physiology and biochemistry. *Degrees offered:* None. *Graduate students served last academic year:* 82: 8 at the master's level; 55 at the doctoral level; 19 at the postgraduate level. *Faculty:* 13: 8 affiliated solely with the laboratory. *Faculty affiliations:* Programs in Animal Science, Ecology and Evolution, Environmental Science and Policy, Molecular and Cellular Biology, Neurobiology-Physiology and Behavior. *Annual research budget:* $7.7 million. *Director:* Director, 707-875-2211, Fax: 707-875-2009, E-mail: ucdbml@ucdavis.edu.

Center for Ecological Health Research   Founded in 1992. *Academic areas of research and training:* Effects of multiple stresses on aquatic and terrestrial ecosystems. *Degrees offered:* None. *Graduate students served last academic year:* 19: 2 at the master's level; 16 at the doctoral level; 1 at the postgraduate level. *Faculty:* 36. *Faculty affiliations:* Colleges of Agricultural and Environmental Sciences, Engineering, Letters and Sciences; School of Veterinary Medicine. *Annual research budget:* $1 million. *Director:* Dr. Dennis E. Rolston, Director, 530-752-5028, Fax: 530-752-1552, E-mail: derolston@ucdavis.edu. *Application contact:* Cheryl Smith, Center Manager, 530-752-5028, Fax: 530-752-1552, E-mail: csmith@ucdavis.edu.

Center for Environmental Sciences   Founded in 1992. *Academic areas of research and training:* Research focus on human health effects of agrochemicals and related xenobiotics. *Degrees offered:* None. *Graduate students served last academic year:* 50: 20 at the master's level; 20 at the doctoral level; 10 at the postgraduate level. *Faculty:* 40: 20 affiliated solely with the center. *Faculty affiliations:* Departments of Entomology, Environmental Toxicology, Epidemiology and Preventive Medicine, Obstetrics and Gynecology, Pulmonary Medicine, Veterinary Medicine Anatomy, Veterinary Medicine Molecular Biosciences, Veterinary Medicine Population Health; Center for Comparative Respiratory Biology and Medicine. *Annual research budget:* $1 million. *Director:* Fumio Matsumura, Director, 530-752-2732, Fax: 530-752-3394, E-mail: rlmorrison@ucdavis.edu.

University of California, Irvine, Irvine, CA 92697.

Institute for Mathematical Behavioral Sciences   Founded in 1988. *Academic areas of research and training:* Mathematical models and methods used in behavioral and social sciences. *Degrees offered:* MA; PhD. *Graduate students served last academic year:* 12: 3 at the master's level; 9 at the doctoral level. *Faculty:* 46. *Faculty affiliations:* Departments of Anthropology, Cognitive Science, Economics, Mathematics, Philosophy, Politics and Society; Graduate School of Management. *Annual research budget:* $1.1 million. *Director:* William H. Batchelder, Director, 714-824-8651, Fax: 714-824-3733.

University of California, Los Angeles, Los Angeles, CA 90095.

Institute of Geophysics and Planetary Physics (IGPP)   Founded in 1946. *Academic areas of research and training:* Using the latest advances in biology, chemistry, mathematics, and physics to study the problems of Earth and the Solar System, including their atmospheres, oceans, solid interior and space environment. *Degrees offered:* None. *Graduate students served last academic year:* 50. *Faculty:* 28. *Faculty affiliations:* Departments of Atmospheric Sciences, Chemistry and Biochemistry, Earth and Space Sciences, Geography, Mathematics, Physics. *Annual research budget:* $9.7 million. *Director:* Dr. Michael Ghil, Director, 310-206-2285, Fax: 310-206-3051, E-mail: mghil@igpp.ucla.edu.

University of California, Riverside, Riverside, CA 92521-0102.

Air Pollution Research Center (SAPRC)   Founded in 1961. *Academic areas of research and training:* Atmospheric chemistry, effects of air pollutants on vegetation. *Degrees offered:* None. *Graduate students served last academic year:* 9: 2 at the master's level; 5 at the doctoral level; 2 at the postgraduate level. *Faculty:* 7: 1 affiliated solely with the center. *Faculty affiliations:* Departments of Botany and Plant Sciences, Chemistry, Program in Environmental Sciences; Center for Environmental Research and Technology. *Annual research budget:* $1 million. *Director:* Dr. Roger Atkinson, Director, 909-787-5124, Fax: 909-787-5004, E-mail: ratkins@mail.ucr.edu.

Center for Water and Wildland Resources   Founded in 1958. *Degrees offered:* None. *Faculty:* 15. *Director:* John Letey, Director, 909-787-4327, Fax: 909-787-5295, E-mail: john.letey@ucr.edu.

Radiocarbon Laboratory   Founded in 1972. *Academic areas of research and training:* Quaternary geochronology. *Degrees offered:* None. *Graduate students served last academic year:* 4: 4 at the doctoral level. *Faculty:* 1. *Faculty affiliations:* Department of Anthropology, Institute of Geophysics and Planetary Physics. *Annual research budget:* $110,000. *Director:* Dr. R. Ervin Taylor, Director, 909-787-5524, Fax: 909-787-5409, E-mail: retaylor@citrus.ucr.edu.

University of California, San Diego, La Jolla, CA 92093-5003.

Center for Astrophysics and Space Science (CASS)   Founded in 1979. *Academic areas of research and training:* Experimental and theoretical space plasma physics; infrared, optical, ultraviolet and x-ray astronomy; radio astronomy and cosmochemistry; solar observational and theoretical studies; theoretical astrophysics. *Degrees offered:* None. *Graduate students served last academic year:* 9: 7 at the doctoral level; 2 at the postgraduate level. *Faculty:* 42: 22 affiliated solely with the center. *Faculty affiliations:* Departments of Chemistry, Electrical and Computer Engineering, Physics. *Annual research budget:* $7.5 million. *Director:* Dr. Arthur M. Wolfe, Director, 619-534-7435, Fax: 619-534-2294, E-mail: awolfe@ucsd.edu. *Application contact:* Cheryl Matson, Contact Person, 619-534-3460, Fax: 619-534-2294, E-mail: cmatson@ucsd.edu.

Center for Clouds, Chemistry, and Climate   Founded in 1991. *Academic areas of research and training:* Atmospheric physics, atmospheric chemistry, climate modeling and observations, global and regional climate changes. *Degrees offered:* None. *Graduate students served last

academic year:* 19: 1 at the master's level; 13 at the doctoral level; 5 at the postgraduate level. *Faculty:* 10. *Faculty affiliations:* Oregon State University, University of Maryland College Park, Max-Planck Institute of Chemistry, Forschungszentrum Juelich, Utrecht University. *Annual research budget:* $2.4 million. *Director:* V. Ramanathan, Director, 619-534-8815, Fax: 619-534-4922, E-mail: vramanathan@ucsd.edu. *Application contact:* Hung Nguyen, Associate Director, 619-534-1040, Fax: 619-534-4922, E-mail: hnguyen@ucsd.edu.

Geosciences Research Division (GRD)   *Academic areas of research and training:* Geology, geochemistry, geophysics. *Degrees offered:* None. *Graduate students served last academic year:* 24: 16 at the doctoral level; 8 at the postgraduate level. *Faculty:* 19. *Faculty affiliations:* Scripps Institution of Oceanography. *Annual research budget:* $5.5 million. *Director:* Jeremy B. C. Jackson, Director, 858-822-2432, Fax: 858-822-3310, E-mail: jbjackson@ucsd.edu. *Application contact:* Anne M. Cressey, Division Management Services Officer, 858-534-1830, Fax: 858-534-0784, E-mail: acressey@ucsd.edu.

Institute for Nonlinear Science (INLS)   Founded in 1986. *Academic areas of research and training:* Nonlinear dynamics and its applications. *Degrees offered:* None. *Graduate students served last academic year:* 10: 7 at the doctoral level; 3 at the postgraduate level. *Faculty:* 30: 10 affiliated solely with the institute. *Faculty affiliations:* Departments of Biology, Chemistry and Biochemistry, Computer Science and Engineering, Economics, Electrical and Computer Engineering, Mathematics, Mechanical Engineering, Physics; Scripps Institution of Oceanography. *Annual research budget:* $3 million. *Director:* Dr. Henry D. I. Abarbanel, Director, 858-534-5590, Fax: 858-534-7664, E-mail: hdia@hamilton.ucsd.edu. *Application contact:* Terry Peters, Contact Person, 858-534-7753, Fax: 858-534-7664, E-mail: tpeters@inls.ucsd.edu.

Marine Physical Laboratory (MPL)   Founded in 1946. *Academic areas of research and training:* Ocean science and technology, marine geophysics, ocean acoustics and optics, ocean chemistry. *Degrees offered:* None. *Graduate students served last academic year:* 25: 20 at the doctoral level; 5 at the postgraduate level. *Faculty:* 33: 30 affiliated solely with the laboratory. *Faculty affiliations:* Department of Physical Oceanography. *Annual research budget:* $13 million. *Director:* Dr. William Kuperman, Director, 858-534-1803, Fax: 858-822-0665, E-mail: wak@mpl.ucsd.edu. *Application contact:* Pat Jordan, Management Services Officer, 858-534-1802, Fax: 858-822-0665, E-mail: pjordan@vcsd.edu.

White Mountain Research Station (WMRS)   Founded in 1950. *Academic areas of research and training:* Environmental science, conservation biology, ecology, geology, high altitude physiology, atmospheric science, anthropology. *Degrees offered:* None. *Graduate students served last academic year:* 165. *Faculty:* 11: 6 affiliated solely with the station. *Faculty affiliations:* School of Medicine; University of California, Berkeley Department of Integrative Biology; University of California, Davis Department of Geology; University of California, Irvine Department of Ecology; University of California, Riverside Department of Biology; University of California, Santa Barbara Department of Ecology. *Annual research budget:* $1 million. *Director:* Dr. Frank L. Powell, Director, 619-534-4191, Fax: 619-822-0164, E-mail: fpowell@wmrs.edu. *Application contact:* Barbara Fager, Program Specialist, 619-822-0165, Fax: 619-822-0164, E-mail: bfager@ucsd.edu.

University of California, Santa Barbara, Santa Barbara, CA 93106.

Marine Science Institute (MSI)   Founded in 1969. *Academic areas of research and training:* Marine biology, marine ecology, oceanography, marine geology, marine biotechnology, coastal/ocean policy, freshwater ecology. *Degrees offered:* None. *Graduate students served last academic year:* 172: 49 at the doctoral level; 3 at the postgraduate level. *Faculty:* 59. *Faculty affiliations:* Departments of Chemistry, Ecology, Evolution, and Marine Biology, Economics, Geography, Geological Sciences, Materials, Mechanical and Environmental Engineering, Molecular, Cellular, and Developmental Biology, Physics, Political Science, Sociology; Program in Chemical and Nuclear Engineering. *Annual research budget:* $568,195. *Director:* Dr. Steven D. Gaines, Interim Director, 805-893-3764, Fax: 805-893-8062, E-mail: gaines@lifesci.ucsb.edu. *Application contact:* Dr. Steven D. Gaines, Interim Director, 805-893-3764, Fax: 805-893-8062, E-mail: gaines@lifesci.ucsb.edu.

Southern California Earthquake Center (SCEC)/Institute for Crustal Studies   Founded in 1987. *Academic areas of research and training:* Earthquakes, earth structure, strong motion seismology. *Degrees offered:* None. *Graduate students served last academic year:* 12: 12 at the doctoral level. *Faculty:* 20. *Faculty affiliations:* Departments of Geography, Geological Sciences; School of Environmental Science and Management. *Annual research budget:* $2 million. *Director:* Dr. Ralph Archuleta, Associate Director, 805-893-8441, Fax: 805-893-8649, E-mail: ralph@quake.crustal.ucsb.edu. *Application contact:* Kathy Murray, Management Services Officer, 805-893-8281, Fax: 805-893-8649, E-mail: kathy@quake.crustal.ucsb.edu.

University of California, Santa Cruz, Santa Cruz, CA 95064.

Institute for Particle Physics   Founded in 1980. *Academic areas of research and training:* Experimental and theatrical high energy and particle astrophysics. *Degrees offered:* None. *Graduate students served last academic year:* 39: 2 at the master's level; 24 at the doctoral level; 13 at the postgraduate level. *Faculty:* 15: 5 affiliated solely with the institute. *Faculty affiliations:* Program in Physics. *Annual research budget:* $4 million. *Director:* Dr. Abraham Seiden, Director, 831-459-2635, Fax: 831-459-5777, E-mail: georgia@scipp.ucsc.edu.

Institute of Marine Sciences (IMS)   Founded in 1976. *Academic areas of research and training:* Marine sciences research. *Degrees offered:* None. *Graduate students served last academic year:* 158: 88 at the master's level; 50 at the doctoral level; 20 at the postgraduate level. *Faculty:* 72: 36 affiliated solely with the institute. *Faculty affiliations:* Departments of Biology, Chemistry, Earth Sciences, Environmental Studies, Ocean Sciences, Physics. *Annual research budget:* $9.6 million. *Director:* Dr. Gary B. Griggs, Director, 408-459-2464, Fax: 408-459-4882, E-mail: griggs@cats.ucsc.edu.

University of Chicago, Chicago, IL 60637-1513.

Magnetic Resonance Imaging and Spectroscopy Research Facility   Founded in 1995. *Academic areas of research and training:* Tumor perfusion, oxygenation, metabolism, response to therapy, development and evaluation of magnetic resonance contrast agents, magnetic resonance imaging methods. *Degrees offered:* None. *Graduate students served last academic year:* 5: 4 at the doctoral level; 1 at the postgraduate level. *Faculty:* 5: 1 affiliated solely with the facility. *Faculty affiliations:* Departments of Physics; Radiology, Radiation, and Cellular Oncology. *Annual research budget:* $550,000. *Director:* Dr. Gregory Karczmar, Director, 312-702-0214, Fax: 312-702-1161, E-mail: gskarczm@midway.uchicago.edu.

University of Colorado at Boulder, Boulder, CO 80309.

Colorado Center for Chaos and Complexity   Founded in 1996. *Academic areas of research and training:* Nonlinear problems that demonstrate complex behavior from simple systems and simple behavior from complex systems. *Degrees offered:* None. *Faculty:* 25. *Faculty affiliations:* Departments of Computer Science, Geology, Kinesiology, Mathematics, Physics, Political Science; Division of Biological Sciences. *Director:* Dr. John Rundle, Director, 303-492-7346, Fax: 303-492-5070, E-mail: rundle@fractal.colorado.edu. *Application contact:* Valerie DeLoach, Professional Research Assistant, 303-492-7346, Fax: 303-492-5070.

Condensed Matter Laboratory   Founded in 1977. *Academic areas of research and training:* Nanofabrication, liquid crystals, super conductors, magnetoresistive materials, polymer structures, tuneable antennas, low-temp electronics. *Degrees offered:* None. *Graduate students served last academic year:* 24: 4 at the master's level; 20 at the doctoral level. *Faculty:* 9: 4 affiliated solely with the laboratory. *Faculty affiliations:* Department of Physics. *Director:* Dr. Noel A. Clark, Director, 303-492-6420, Fax: 303-492-2998, E-mail: clarkn@bly.colorado.edu. *Application contact:* Thea V. Evans, Administrator, 303-492-1515, Fax: 303-492-2998, E-mail: tevans@colorado.edu.

Research and Training Opportunities

Cooperative Institute for Research in Environmental Sciences (CIRES) Founded in 1967. *Academic areas of research and training:* Environmental sciences, remote sensing, atmospheric chemistry and biology, climate and global change, geophysics, complex systems. *Degrees offered:* None. *Graduate students served last academic year:* 105: 30 at the master's level; 60 at the doctoral level; 15 at the postgraduate level. *Faculty:* 424: 400 affiliated solely with the institute. *Faculty affiliations:* Departments of Chemistry and Biochemistry, Geography, Geological Sciences, Physics; Program in Atmospheric and Oceanic Sciences. *Annual research budget:* $30 million. *Director:* Dr. Susan Avery, Director, 303-492-8773, Fax: 303-492-1149, E-mail: savery@cires.colorado.edu. *Application contact:* Paul Sperry, Executive Director, 303-492-1227, Fax: 303-492-1149, E-mail: sperry@cires.colorado.edu.

Ferroelectric Liquid Crystal Materials Research Science and Engineering Center Founded in 1993. *Academic areas of research and training:* Ferroelectric liquid crystal research. *Degrees offered:* None. *Graduate students served last academic year:* 6: 6 at the doctoral level. *Faculty:* 6. *Faculty affiliations:* College of Engineering and Applied Science; Departments of Chemistry, Physics. *Annual research budget:* $625,000. *Director:* Dr. Noel A. Clark, Co-Director, 303-492-6420, Fax: 303-492-2998, E-mail: clarkn@bly.colorado.edu. *Application contact:* Thea V. Evans, Administrator, 303-492-1515, Fax: 303-492-2998, E-mail: tevans@colorado.edu.

Institute of Arctic and Alpine Research (INSTAAR) Founded in 1921. *Academic areas of research and training:* Interdisciplinary research emphasizing environmental science as it pertains to high altitude and high latitude and former cold environment. *Degrees offered:* None. *Graduate students served last academic year:* 72: 30 at the master's level; 30 at the doctoral level; 12 at the postgraduate level. *Faculty:* 43: 13 affiliated solely with the institute. *Faculty affiliations:* Departments of Anthropology; Chemical Engineering; Civil, Environmental, and Architectural Engineering, Environmental, Population, and Organismic Biology; Geography; Geological Sciences;. *Annual research budget:* $9.5 million. *Director:* Dr. James Syvitski, Director, 303-492-7909, Fax: 303-492-3287. *Application contact:* Ashley Holladay, Assistant to the Director.

Natural Hazards Center Founded in 1975. *Academic areas of research and training:* Social science aspects of natural hazards management and mitigation. *Degrees offered:* None. *Graduate students served last academic year:* 2. *Faculty:* 13: 1 affiliated solely with the center. *Faculty affiliations:* Departments of Anthropology; Civil, Environmental, and Architectural Engineering; Economics; Geography; Geology; Sociology; School of Law. *Director:* Dr. Dennis Mileti, Director, 303-492-6315, Fax: 303-492-2151, E-mail: hazctr@colorado.edu. *Application contact:* Mary Fran Myers, Co-Director, 303-492-2150, Fax: 303-492-2151, E-mail: myersmf@colorado.edu.

University of Colorado at Denver, Denver, CO 80217-3364.

Center for Computational Mathematics (CCM) Founded in 1992. *Academic areas of research and training:* Computational environment to pursue research on the broad area of computational mathematics; including fast parallel iterative methods for large three-dimensional finite element models. *Degrees offered:* None. *Graduate students served last academic year:* 65: 40 at the master's level; 20 at the doctoral level; 5 at the postgraduate level. *Faculty:* 30. *Faculty affiliations:* Departments of Civil Engineering, Computer Sciences, Mathematics, Mechanical Engineering. *Director:* Dr. Leopoldo P. Franca, Director, 303-556-8460, Fax: 303-556-8550, E-mail: lfranca@math.cudenver.edu.

Center for Environmental Sciences Founded in 1979. *Academic areas of research and training:* Analytical chemistry and instrumental analysis. *Degrees offered:* None. *Graduate students served last academic year:* 6: 6 at the master's level. *Faculty:* 9: 1 affiliated solely with the center. *Faculty affiliations:* Department of Civil Engineering; Programs in Biology, Chemistry, Environmental Science, Geology, Physics. *Annual research budget:* $12,000. *Director:* Dr. Larry Anderson, Director, 303-556-2963, Fax: 303-556-4292, E-mail: landerso@carbon.cudenver.edu. *Application contact:* Rosemary Wormington, Program Coordinator, 303-556-4520, Fax: 303-556-4292, E-mail: rwormington@castle.cudenver.edu.

University of Connecticut, Storrs, CT 06269.

Biotechnology Center Founded in 1986. *Academic areas of research and training:* Aquaculture and agriculture biotechnology. *Degrees offered:* None. *Graduate students served last academic year:* 30: 5 at the master's level; 15 at the doctoral level; 10 at the postgraduate level. *Faculty:* 13: 3 affiliated solely with the center. *Faculty affiliations:* Departments of Animal Science, Molecular and Cell Biology, Physiology and Neurobiology, Plant Science. *Annual research budget:* $3 million. *Director:* Dr. Thomas T. Chen, Director, 860-486-5011, Fax: 860-486-5005, E-mail: tchen@uconnvm.uconn.edu.

Environmental Research Institute Founded in 1987. *Academic areas of research and training:* Environmental research. *Degrees offered:* None. *Graduate students served last academic year:* 80: 6 at the postgraduate level. *Faculty:* 28. *Faculty affiliations:* Departments of Civil and Environmental Engineering, Chemical Engineering, Chemistry, Geology and Geophysics, Natural Resources Management and Engineering, Pathobiology, Plant Science. *Annual research budget:* $2.9 million. *Director:* Dr. George Hoag, Director, 860-486-4015, Fax: 860-486-5488, E-mail: www.eng2.uconn.edu/eri/.

Photonics Research Center Founded in 1992. *Academic areas of research and training:* Information gathering, information transport, energy conveyance, specifically photonic device (Fabry Perot and grating surface emitters), integrated optoelectronics fiber lasers, Bragg grating technology, embedded fiber optic sensor for Smart Structures Medical Imaging. *Degrees offered:* None. *Graduate students served last academic year:* 18: 9 at the master's level; 9 at the doctoral level. *Faculty:* 17: 2 affiliated solely with the center. *Faculty affiliations:* Department of Mechanical Engineering; Fields of Biomedical Science, Chemistry, Civil Engineering, Electrical and Systems Engineering, Environmental Engineering, Physics; Programs in Agriculture, MarineScience. *Annual research budget:* $2.5 million. *Director:* Dr. Chandra Roychoudhuri, Director, 860-486-2587, Fax: 860-486-1033, E-mail: chandra@engr.uconn.edu. *Application contact:* Lisa M. Mazzola, Technical Records Coordinator, 860-486-2886, Fax: 860-486-1033, E-mail: mazzola@engr.uconn.edu.

University of Delaware, Newark, DE 19716.

Bartol Research Institute Founded in 1927. *Academic areas of research and training:* Scientific research, astronomy, astrophysics, space plasma, particle physics. *Degrees offered:* MS; PhD. *Graduate students served last academic year:* 8: 2 at the doctoral level; 6 at the postgraduate level. *Faculty:* 14: 14 affiliated solely with the institute. *Faculty affiliations:* Department of Physics and Astronomy. *Annual research budget:* $4 million. *Director:* Dr. Norman F. Ness, President, 302-831-8116, Fax: 302-831-1843, E-mail: nfness@bartol.udel.edu.

Center for Catalytic Science and Technology Founded in 1978. *Academic areas of research and training:* Heterogeneous and homogeneous catalysis for chemical, petroleum, and environmental processes; surface chemistry and physics; novel materials for catalytic applications. *Degrees offered:* None. *Graduate students served last academic year:* 52: 2 at the master's level; 35 at the doctoral level; 12 at the postgraduate level. *Faculty:* 10. *Faculty affiliations:* Departments of Chemical Engineering, Chemistry and Biochemistry, Materials Science and Engineering. *Annual research budget:* $1.2 million. *Director:* Dr. Mark A. Barteau, Director, 302-831-8905, Fax: 302-831-2085, E-mail: barteau@che.udel.edu.

Center for Climatic Research Founded in 1978. *Academic areas of research and training:* Basic and applied climate science. *Degrees offered:* None. *Faculty:* 7. *Faculty affiliations:* Department of Geography. *Director:* Dr. Cort Willmott, Director, 302-831-8998, Fax: 302-831-6654, E-mail: info@geog.udel.edu.

Center for Composite Materials Founded in 1974. *Academic areas of research and training:* Manufacture of affordable composites from renewable resources. *Degrees offered:* None. *Graduate students served last academic year:* 100. *Faculty:* 40: 20 affiliated solely with the center. *Faculty affiliations:* Colleges of Agriculture and Natural Resources, Business and Economics; Departments of Chemical Engineering, Mechanical Engineering, Plant Science. *Annual research budget:* $5 million. *Director:* Richard Wool, Professor, 302-831-3312, Fax: 302-831-8525, E-mail: richard_wool@ccm.udel.edu.

Center for Energy and Environmental Policy (CEEP) Founded in 1983. *Academic areas of research and training:* Energy policy, sustainable development, environmental justice, climate change, renewable energy, environmental policy. *Degrees offered:* MA; PhD. *Graduate students served last academic year:* 64: 28 at the master's level; 32 at the doctoral level; 4 at the postgraduate level. *Faculty:* 11: 4 affiliated solely with the center. *Faculty affiliations:* Colleges of Agriculture and Natural Science, Engineering; Departments of Economics, Geography, Philosophy, Political Science and International Relations, Sociology and Criminal Justice. *Annual research budget:* $600,000. *Director:* Dr. John Byrne, Director, 302-831-8405, Fax: 302-831-3098, E-mail: jbbyrne@udel.edu. *Application contact:* Sandra Matthews, Staff Assistant, 302-831-8405, Fax: 302-831-3098, E-mail: sandymat@udel.edu.

University of Detroit Mercy, Detroit, MI 48219-0900.

Center of Excellence in Environmental Engineering and Science Founded in 1992. *Academic areas of research and training:* Integration of the values and goals of the U.S. Environmental Protection Agency, biodegradable plastics, utilization of automotive shredder residue, recycling of thermosetting polymers, reuse of scrap tire rubber, recycling of mixed plastics and incinerator ashes. *Degrees offered:* None. *Graduate students served last academic year:* 6: 3 at the master's level; 2 at the doctoral level; 1 at the postgraduate level. *Faculty:* 25: 15 affiliated solely with the center. *Faculty affiliations:* Departments of Biology, Chemical Engineering, Chemistry, Civil and Environmental Engineering, Polymer Institute. *Annual research budget:* $1 million. *Director:* Dr. Daniel Klempner, Director, 313-993-3385, Fax: 313-993-1112, E-mail: klempndi@udmercy.edu.

University of Florida, Gainesville, FL 32611.

Center for Aquatic Plants Founded in 1978. *Academic areas of research and training:* Aquatic and invasive plant biology, ecology, and control. *Degrees offered:* None. *Graduate students served last academic year:* 6: 5 at the master's level; 1 at the doctoral level. *Faculty:* 18: 3 affiliated solely with the center. *Faculty affiliations:* Departments of Agricultural Engineering, Agronomy, Botany, Entomology and Nematology, Fisheries and Aquatic Sciences, Horticultural Sciences, Plant Pathology, Wildlife Ecology and Conservation. *Annual research budget:* $500,000. *Director:* Dr. Randall Stocker, Director, 904-392-9613, Fax: 904-392-3462, E-mail: aqplants@gnv.ifas.ufl.edu.

Citrus Research and Education Center (CREC) Founded in 1917. *Academic areas of research and training:* Agricultural engineering, food science, horticulture, entomology and nematology, plant pathology, soil and water science. *Degrees offered:* None. *Graduate students served last academic year:* 33: 18 at the master's level; 15 at the doctoral level. *Faculty:* 51: 51 affiliated solely with the center. *Annual research budget:* $7.5 million. *Director:* Harold W. Browning, Director, 813-956-1151, Fax: 813-956-3579, E-mail: hwbr@icon.lal.ufl.edu.

Everglades Research and Education Center (EREC) Founded in 1921. *Academic areas of research and training:* Agricultural economics, agricultural engineering, agronomy, entomology, horticulture, soil science, weed science, wildlife ecology. *Degrees offered:* None. *Graduate students served last academic year:* 15: 6 at the master's level; 9 at the doctoral level. *Faculty:* 19: 19 affiliated solely with the center. *Annual research budget:* $2 million. *Director:* Dr. Van H. Waddill, Director, 561-993-1500, Fax: 561-993-1582, E-mail: vhw@gnv.ifas.ufl.edu.

Whitney Laboratory Founded in 1974. *Academic areas of research and training:* Cell biology, neuroscience, pharmacology, physiology, toxicology, marine molecular biology. *Degrees offered:* None. *Graduate students served last academic year:* 1 at the master's level; 3 at the doctoral level; 10 at the postgraduate level. *Faculty:* 19: 12 affiliated solely with the laboratory. *Faculty affiliations:* Concentration in Physiology and Pharmacology, Departments of Anatomy and Cell Biology, Fisheries and Aquatic Sciences, Neuroscience, Zoology. *Annual research budget:* $2.6 million. *Director:* Dr. Peter A. V. Anderson, Director, 904-461-4000, Fax: 904-461-4008, E-mail: paa@whitney.ufl.edu.

University of Idaho, Moscow, ID 83844-4140.

Environmental Biotechnology Institute Founded in 1984. *Academic areas of research and training:* Microbiology, biochemistry, bioprocess technology, chemistry, chemical engineering, forestry, genetic engineering, molecular biology. *Degrees offered:* None. *Graduate students served last academic year:* 18: 10 at the master's level; 6 at the doctoral level; 2 at the postgraduate level. *Faculty:* 70. *Faculty affiliations:* College of Forestry, Wildlife, and Range Sciences; Departments of Animal and Veterinary Medicine; Chemical Engineering; Chemistry; Microbiology, Molecular Biology and Biochemistry; Programs in Plant Science; Zoology. *Annual research budget:* $500,000. *Director:* Dr. Ronald L. Crawford, Director, 208-885-6580, Fax: 208-885-5741, E-mail: crawford@uidaho.edu.

Glaciological and Arctic Sciences Institute (GASI) Founded in 1959. *Academic areas of research and training:* Field training and research in the geosciences of arctic and mountain regions, i.e., in field geology, exploration geophysics, process geomorphology, glaciology, atmospheric sciences, geobotany, survey and mapping; global change research. *Degrees offered:* None. *Graduate students served last academic year:* 17: 9 at the master's level; 3 at the doctoral level; 5 at the postgraduate level. *Faculty:* 25: 20 affiliated solely with the institute. *Faculty affiliations:* Department of Geology and Geological Engineering, Divison of Science Teacher Education, College of Education. *Annual research budget:* $200,000. *Director:* Dr. Maynard Miller, Director, 208-885-6192, Fax: 208-885-5724, E-mail: jirp@uidaho.edu. *Application contact:* Annette Erickson, Administrative Coordinator, 208-885-6382, Fax: 208-882-6207, E-mail: jirp@uidaho.edu.

University of Illinois at Urbana–Champaign, Urbana, IL 61801.

Frederick Seitz Materials Research Laboratory Founded in 1962. *Academic areas of research and training:* Materials science, condensed-matter physics, materials chemistry. *Degrees offered:* None. *Graduate students served last academic year:* 200: 170 at the doctoral level; 30 at the postgraduate level. *Faculty:* 90: 20 affiliated solely with the laboratory. *Faculty affiliations:* Departments of Chemical Engineering, Chemistry, Electrical Engineering, Materials Science, Mechanical Engineering, Physics, Theoretical and Applied Mechanics. *Annual research budget:* $16 million. *Director:* Dr. Joe Greene, Director, 217-333-1370, Fax: 217-244-2278, E-mail: greene@mrlxp2.mrl.uiuc.edu.

Mid-America Earthquake Center Founded in 1997. *Academic areas of research and training:* Earthquake engineering, structural engineering, geotechnical engineering, seismology, social science, economics. *Degrees offered:* None. *Graduate students served last academic year:* 81: 27 at the master's level; 54 at the doctoral level. *Faculty:* 54: 4 affiliated solely with the center. *Faculty affiliations:* College of Urban Planning and Public Affairs, Department of Civil and Materials Engineering, Georgia Institute of Technology Program in Geology; Massachusetts Institute of Technology, Saint Louis University, Texas A&M University, The University of Memphis, Washington University in St. Louis. *Annual research budget:* $4 million. *Director:* Dr. Daniel P. Abrams, Director, 217-333-0565, Fax: 217-333-3821, E-mail: d-abrams@staff.uiuc.edu. *Application contact:* Dr. Carolyn Sands, Assistant Director, 217-244-1795, Fax: 217-333-3821, E-mail: c-sands1@staff.uiuc.edu.

The University of Iowa, Iowa City, IA 52242-1316.

Center for Biocatalysis and Bioprocessing Founded in 1990. *Academic areas of research and training:* Biotransformations, new biocatalyst discovery, structure and function of biocatalysts, fermentation, bioremediation, biocatalysis in bio-active agent discovery, development. *Degrees offered:* None. *Graduate students served last academic year:* 50: 45 at the doctoral level; 5 at

Research and Training Opportunities

Center for Biocatalysis and Bioprocessing (continued)
the postgraduate level. *Faculty:* 44: 1 affiliated solely with the center. *Faculty affiliations:* Departments of Biochemistry, Biological Sciences, Chemical and Biochemical Engineering, Chemistry, Civil and Environmental Engineering, Medicinal and Natural Products Chemistry, Microbiology. *Annual research budget:* $1.6 million. *Director:* John P. N. Rosazza, Director, 319-335-4900, Fax: 319-335-4901, E-mail: john-rosazza@uiowa.edu.

University of Kentucky, Lexington, KY 40506-0032.

Center of Membrane Sciences Founded in 1991. *Academic areas of research and training:* Multidisciplinary research and training interfacing biological and synthetic membranes. *Degrees offered:* None. *Graduate students served last academic year:* 50: 10 at the master's level; 29 at the doctoral level; 11 at the postgraduate level. *Faculty:* 22. *Faculty affiliations:* College of Pharmacy; Programs in Anatomy and Neurobiology, Animal Sciences, Chemical Engineering, Chemistry, Clinical Nutrition, Materials Science, Physiology and Biophysics; Biomedical Engineering; Psychology. *Annual research budget:* $400,000. *Director:* Dr. D. Allan Butterfield, Director, 606-257-5875, Fax: 606-257-5876, E-mail: dabcns@pop.uky.edu.

University of Louisville, Louisville, KY 40292-0001.

Center for Environmental Health Sciences (CEHS) Founded in 1994. *Academic areas of research and training:* Studies of the effects of environmental pollution on human health. *Degrees offered:* None. *Graduate students served last academic year:* 58: 13 at the master's level; 30 at the doctoral level; 10 at the postgraduate level. *Faculty:* 20. *Faculty affiliations:* Departments of Biochemistry and Molecular Biology, Family and Community Medicine, Medicine, Pathology, Pharmacology and Toxicology. *Annual research budget:* $1.1 million. *Director:* Dr. Russell A. Prough, Co-Director, 502-852-5217, Fax: 502-852-6222.

Kentucky Institute for the Environment and Sustainable Development Founded in 1993. *Academic areas of research and training:* Sustainable development, environmental education, environmental health, environmental economics, pollution prevention, environmental engineering, environmental science. *Degrees offered:* MS. *Graduate students served last academic year:* 10: 10 at the master's level. *Faculty:* 33: 8 affiliated solely with the institute. *Faculty affiliations:* Departments of Arts and Sciences, Business and Public Administration, Education, Engineering, Law, Medicine. *Annual research budget:* $200,000. *Director:* Russell A. Barnett, Director, 502-852-1851, Fax: 502-852-4677, E-mail: r.barnett@louisville.edu.

University of Maine, Orono, ME 04469.

The Laboratory for Surface Science and Technology (LASST) Founded in 1980. *Academic areas of research and training:* Surface science, interface science, thin film technology, microelectronics, sensor technology. *Degrees offered:* None. *Graduate students served last academic year:* 34: 8 at the master's level; 18 at the doctoral level; 8 at the postgraduate level. *Faculty:* 7: 2 affiliated solely with the laboratory. *Faculty affiliations:* Departments of Chemistry, Electrical and Computer Engineering, Physics and Astronomy. *Annual research budget:* $4.5 million. *Director:* Dr. Robert J. Lad, Director, 207-581-2257, Fax: 207-581-2255, E-mail: rjlad@maine.maine.edu.

The Maine Agricultural and Forest Experiment Station Founded in 1886. *Academic areas of research and training:* Forestry, agriculture, aquaculture, environmental quality, rural economic development, marine science, biology, geology, biochemistry, molecular biology. *Degrees offered:* None. *Graduate students served last academic year:* 56: 40 at the master's level; 16 at the doctoral level. *Faculty:* 83. *Faculty affiliations:* College of Natural Sciences, Forestry, and Agriculture. *Annual research budget:* $5.8 million. *Director:* Dr. G. Bruce Wiersma, Director, 207-581-3202, Fax: 207-581-3207. *Application contact:* Dr. Stephen D. Reiling, Director, 207-581-3228, Fax: 207-581-3207, E-mail: reiling@maine.edu.

University of Maryland, Baltimore, MD 21201-1627.

Center for Fluorescence Spectroscopy Founded in 1988. *Academic areas of research and training:* Fluorescence spectroscopy, time-resolved fluorescence, biophysics, chemical sensing, chemical diagnostics, multi-photon excitation, laser spectroscopy. *Degrees offered:* None. *Graduate students served last academic year:* 2: 2 at the master's level. *Faculty:* 17: 14 affiliated solely with the center. *Faculty affiliations:* Departments of Microbiology and Immunology, Physiology (Medicine); Program in Chemical Engineering. *Annual research budget:* $800,000. *Director:* Dr. Joseph R. Lakowicz, Director, 410-706-8409, Fax: 410-706-8408, E-mail: cfs.cfs.umbi.umd.edu.

University of Maryland Center for Environmental Science (UMCES) Founded in 1925. *Academic areas of research and training:* Coastal environmental studies, marine ecology, fisheries management, aquatic chemistry, geochemistry, toxicology; landscape and restoration ecology; environmental economics. *Degrees offered:* None. *Graduate students served last academic year:* 150: 75 at the master's level; 70 at the doctoral level; 5 at the postgraduate level. *Faculty:* 85: 70 affiliated solely with the center. *Faculty affiliations:* Program in Marine-Estuarine-Environmental Sciences; Frostburg State University, Maryland Cooperative Extension Service, Maryland Sea Grant College Program, NASA Goddard Space Flight Center, Salisbury State University; University of Maryland, Baltimore County; University of Maryland, College Park; University of Maryland, Eastern Shore. *Annual research budget:* $12 million. *Director:* Dr. Donald F. Boesch, President, 410-228-9250 Ext. 601, Fax: 410-228-3843, E-mail: boesch@ca.umces.edu. *Application contact:* Dr. Wayne H. Bell, Vice President for External Relations, 410-228-9250 Ext. 608, Fax: 410-228-3843, E-mail: bell@ca.umces.edu.

University of Maryland, Baltimore County, Baltimore, MD 21250-5398.

University of Maryland Center for Environmental Science (UMCES) Founded in 1925. *Academic areas of research and training:* Coastal environmental studies, marine ecology, fisheries management, aquatic chemistry, geochemistry, toxicology; landscape and restoration ecology; environmental economics. *Degrees offered:* None. *Graduate students served last academic year:* 150: 75 at the master's level; 70 at the doctoral level; 5 at the postgraduate level. *Faculty:* 85: 70 affiliated solely with the center. *Faculty affiliations:* Program in Marine-Estuarine-Environmental Sciences; Frostburg State University, Maryland Cooperative Extension Service, Maryland Sea Grant College Program, NASA Goddard Space Flight Center, Salisbury State University; University of Maryland, Baltimore County; University of Maryland, College Park; University of Maryland, Eastern Shore. *Annual research budget:* $12 million. *Director:* Dr. Donald F. Boesch, President, 410-228-9250 Ext. 601, Fax: 410-228-3843, E-mail: boesch@ca.umces.edu. *Application contact:* Dr. Wayne H. Bell, Vice President for External Relations, 410-228-9250 Ext. 608, Fax: 410-228-3843, E-mail: bell@ca.umces.edu.

University of Maryland, College Park, College Park, MD 20742-5045.

Center for Superconductivity Research Founded in 1989. *Academic areas of research and training:* Chemistry, electrical engineering, materials engineering, physics. *Degrees offered:* None. *Graduate students served last academic year:* 25: 20 at the doctoral level; 5 at the postgraduate level. *Faculty:* 15. *Faculty affiliations:* Departments of Chemistry, Electrical Engineering, Materials Engineering, Physics. *Annual research budget:* $3 million. *Director:* Dr. Richard L. Greene, Director, 301-405-6128, Fax: 301-405-3779, E-mail: rgreene@squid.umd.edu.

Institute for Physical Science and Technology (IPST) Founded in 1949. *Academic areas of research and training:* Mathematics, physics, chemistry. *Degrees offered:* MS; PhD. *Graduate students served last academic year:* 55. *Faculty:* 40: 40 affiliated solely with the institute. *Faculty affiliations:* Departments of Chemistry, Mathematics, Physics. *Director:* Dr. James A. Yorke, Director, 301-405-4874, Fax: 301-314-9363, E-mail: yorke@ipst.umd.edu.

University of Maryland Center for Environmental Science (UMCES) Founded in 1925. *Academic areas of research and training:* Coastal environmental studies, marine ecology, fisheries management, aquatic chemistry, geochemistry, toxicology; landscape and restoration ecology; environmental economics. *Degrees offered:* None. *Graduate students served last academic year:* 150: 75 at the master's level; 70 at the doctoral level; 5 at the postgraduate level. *Faculty:* 85: 70 affiliated solely with the center. *Faculty affiliations:* Program in Marine-Estuarine-Environmental Sciences; Frostburg State University, Maryland Cooperative Extension Service, Maryland Sea Grant College Program, NASA Goddard Space Flight Center, Salisbury State University; University of Maryland; University of Maryland, Baltimore County; University of Maryland, Eastern Shore. *Annual research budget:* $12 million. *Director:* Dr. Donald F. Boesch, President, 410-228-9250 Ext. 601, Fax: 410-228-3843, E-mail: boesch@ca.umces.edu. *Application contact:* Dr. Wayne H. Bell, Vice President for External Relations, 410-228-9250 Ext. 608, Fax: 410-228-3843, E-mail: bell@ca.umces.edu.

University of Maryland Eastern Shore, Princess Anne, MD 21853-1299.

Soybean Research Institute Founded in 1976. *Academic areas of research and training:* Agronomy, plant breeding, plant pathology, plant/microbial biotechnology, environmental science. *Degrees offered:* None. *Graduate students served last academic year:* 5: 3 at the master's level; 2 at the doctoral level. *Faculty:* 5: 1 affiliated solely with the institute. *Faculty affiliations:* Departments of Agriculture, Natural Sciences. *Annual research budget:* $123,000. *Director:* Dr. Jagmohan Joshi, Director, 410-651-6632, Fax: 410-651-7656, E-mail: jjoshi@umes-bird.umd.edu.

University of Maryland Center for Environmental Science (UMCES) Founded in 1925. *Academic areas of research and training:* Coastal environmental studies, marine ecology, fisheries management, aquatic chemistry, geochemistry, toxicology; landscape and restoration ecology; environmental economics. *Degrees offered:* None. *Graduate students served last academic year:* 150: 75 at the master's level; 70 at the doctoral level; 5 at the postgraduate level. *Faculty:* 85: 70 affiliated solely with the center. *Faculty affiliations:* Program in Marine-Estuarine-Environmental Sciences; Frostburg State University, Maryland Cooperative Extension Service, Maryland Sea Grant College Program, NASA Goddard Space Flight Center, Salisbury State University; University of Maryland, Baltimore County; University of Maryland, College Park; University of Maryland, Eastern Shore. *Annual research budget:* $12 million. *Director:* Dr. Donald F. Boesch, President, 410-228-9250 Ext. 601, Fax: 410-228-3843, E-mail: boesch@ca.umces.edu. *Application contact:* Dr. Wayne H. Bell, Vice President for External Relations, 410-228-9250 Ext. 608, Fax: 410-228-3843, E-mail: bell@ca.umces.edu.

University of Massachusetts Amherst, Amherst, MA 01003.

Center for Geometry, Analysis, Numerics and Graphics (GANG) Founded in 1986. *Academic areas of research and training:* Mathematical sciences. *Degrees offered:* None. *Graduate students served last academic year:* 12: 3 at the master's level; 5 at the doctoral level; 4 at the postgraduate level. *Faculty:* 9. *Faculty affiliations:* Departments of Chemistry, Computer Science, Mathematics and Statistics, Polymer Science and Engineering. *Annual research budget:* $250,000. *Director:* Dr. Robert B. Kusner, Professor, 413-545-4605, Fax: 413-545-1801, E-mail: kusner@math.umass.edu. *Application contact:* Melanie Doherty, Business Manager, 413-545-2812, Fax: 413-545-1801, E-mail: doherty@math.umass.edu.

University of Massachusetts Boston, Boston, MA 02125-3393.

Urban Harbors Institute Founded in 1989. *Academic areas of research and training:* Waterfront planning, integrated coastal management, port and harbor management, marine environment education, water quality policy, dispute resolution, watershed management. *Degrees offered:* None. *Graduate students served last academic year:* 11: 9 at the master's level; 2 at the doctoral level. *Faculty:* 17: 10 affiliated solely with the institute. *Faculty affiliations:* Department of Environmental, Coastal and Ocean Sciences. *Annual research budget:* $1.1 million. *Director:* Richard F. Delaney, Director, 617-287-5570, Fax: 617-287-5575, E-mail: rich.delaney@umb.edu. *Application contact:* Madeleine Walsh, Education Coordinator, 617-287-5571, Fax: 617-287-5575, E-mail: m.walshumbsky.cc.umb.edu.

University of Massachusetts Lowell, Lowell, MA 01854-2881.

Center for Advanced Materials (CAM) Founded in 1992. *Academic areas of research and training:* Chemical and electrical engineering, chemistry, materials science, physics, plastics engineering, polymer science. *Degrees offered:* None. *Graduate students served last academic year:* 5 at the master's level; 65 at the doctoral level; 10 at the postgraduate level. *Faculty:* 20: 6 affiliated solely with the center. *Faculty affiliations:* Departments of Chemical Engineering, Chemistry, Electrical Engineering, Physics and Applied Physics, and Plastics Engineering. *Annual research budget:* $500,000. *Director:* Dr. Sukant Tripathy, Director, 978-934-3687, Fax: 978-458-9571, E-mail: sukant_tripathy@uml.edu. *Application contact:* Dr. Daniel J. Sandman, Associate Director, 978-934-3835, Fax: 978-458-9571, E-mail: daniel_sandman@uml.edu.

Center for Atmospheric Research Founded in 1975. *Academic areas of research and training:* Electrical engineering, physics, atmosphere and space science. *Degrees offered:* None. *Graduate students served last academic year:* 5: 1 at the master's level; 4 at the doctoral level. *Faculty:* 6: 1 affiliated solely with the center. *Faculty affiliations:* College of Engineering, Departments of Atmospheric Science, Computer Science. *Annual research budget:* $2 million. *Director:* Dr. Bodo W. Reinisch, Director, 978-934-4903, Fax: 978-459-7915, E-mail: bodo_reinisch@uml.edu.

University of Michigan, Ann Arbor, MI 48109.

The Center for Parallel Computing (CPC) Founded in 1992. *Academic areas of research and training:* Parallel computing, supercomputing, data-intensive computing. *Degrees offered:* None. *Graduate students served last academic year:* 30: 15 at the master's level; 10 at the doctoral level; 5 at the postgraduate level. *Faculty:* 12. *Faculty affiliations:* Departments of Aerospace, Chemistry, Computer Science, Mathematics, Mechanical Engineering, Nuclear Engineering, Physics. *Annual research budget:* $2 million. *Director:* Dr. Quentin F. Stout, Director, 734-936-2310, Fax: 734-763-4540, E-mail: cpc-info@engin.umich.edu.

The Center for Statistical Consultation and Research (CSCAR) Founded in 1947. *Academic areas of research and training:* Statistics, biostatistics. *Degrees offered:* None. *Graduate students served last academic year:* 5: 1 at the master's level; 4 at the doctoral level. *Faculty:* 4: 2 affiliated solely with the center. *Faculty affiliations:* Department of Statistics, Program in Biostatistics. *Director:* Prof. Edward D. Rothman, Director, 734-764-7828, Fax: 734-647-2440, E-mail: cscar@umich.edu.

Macromolecular Science and Engineering Center Founded in 1968. *Academic areas of research and training:* Chemical and physical studies of natural and synthetic macromolecules; comprehensive study of synthesis, properties, structures and applications of macromolecules. *Degrees offered:* MS; PhD. *Graduate students served last academic year:* 24: 24 at the master's level. *Faculty:* 20. *Faculty affiliations:* Biophysics Research Division; Departments of Chemical Engineering, Chemistry, Materials Science and Engineering, Mechanical Engineering and Applied Mechanics, Physics. *Director:* Dr. Richard Robertson, Director, 734-763-2316, Fax: 734-647-4865, E-mail: macromolecular@umich.edu. *Application contact:* Ruth Heldreth, Academic Secretary, 734-763-6914, Fax: 734-647-4865, E-mail: heldreth@engin.umich.edu.

University of Mississippi, Oxford, University, MS 38677-9702.

The James Whitten National Center for Physical Acoustics (NCPA) Founded in 1986. *Academic areas of research and training:* Physics of acoustics research and education, physics, mechanical engineering, electrical engineering, speech and hearing, biology. *Degrees offered:* None. *Graduate students served last academic year:* 35: 10 at the master's level; 20 at the doctoral level; 5 at the postgraduate level. *Faculty:* 13: 5 affiliated solely with the center.

Faculty affiliations: Departments of Biology, Mechanical Engineering, Physics and Astronomy, Speech and Hearing. *Annual research budget:* $2.4 million. *Director:* Dr. Henry E. Bass, Director, 601-232-5840, Fax: 601-232-7494, E-mail: pabass@olemiss.edu.

Mississippi Mineral Resources Institute (MMRI) Founded in 1972. *Academic areas of research and training:* Mineral resource evaluation, geologic mapping, earthquake hazard mitigation, marine mineral reconnaissance, marine technology development, marine geophysics. *Degrees offered:* None. *Graduate students served last academic year:* 7: 6 at the master's level; 1 at the doctoral level. *Faculty:* 3: 3 affiliated solely with the institute. *Annual research budget:* $1 million. *Director:* Dr. J. Robert Woolsey, Director, 601-232-7320, Fax: 601-232-5625, E-mail: inst@mmri.olemiss.edu.

University of Missouri–Columbia, Columbia, MO 65211.

Agronomy Research Center Founded in 1959. *Academic areas of research and training:* Plant and soil research with USDA and University of Missouri project leaders in plant breeding, wood science, variety testing, crop physiology and management, forages, soil fertility, nematodes, and specific training events. *Degrees offered:* None. *Graduate students served last academic year:* 47: 22 at the master's level; 23 at the doctoral level; 2 at the postgraduate level. *Faculty:* 46: 1 affiliated solely with the center. *Faculty affiliations:* Departments of Agricultural Engineering, Agronomy, Animal Science, Entomology, Plant Pathology, Soils and Atmospheric Science; U.S. Department of Agriculture. *Annual research budget:* $257,000. *Director:* C. John Poehlmann, Director, 573-884-7945, Fax: 573-882-1467, E-mail: poehlmannc@missouri.edu.

Center for Agricultural, Resource and Environmental Systems (CARES) Founded in 1993. *Academic areas of research and training:* Graduate research and training, environmental impacts of agriculture, water contamination. *Degrees offered:* None. *Graduate students served last academic year:* 7: 2 at the master's level; 5 at the doctoral level. *Faculty:* 13: 3 affiliated solely with the center. *Faculty affiliations:* Departments of Agricultural Economics, Geography; School of Natural Resources. *Annual research budget:* $1 million. *Director:* Dr. Tony Prato, Director, 573-882-7458, Fax: 573-884-2199, E-mail: pratoa@missouri.edu.

Food and Agricultural Policy Research Institute (FAPRI) Founded in 1984. *Academic areas of research and training:* Econometrics, food and agricultural models, forecasting, policy, policy scenarios. *Degrees offered:* None. *Graduate students served last academic year:* 20: 4 at the master's level; 14 at the doctoral level; 2 at the postgraduate level. *Faculty:* 35: 30 affiliated solely with the institute. *Faculty affiliations:* Departments of Agricultural Economics, Animal Science, Atmospheric Science, Economics, Statistics. *Annual research budget:* $2.5 million. *Director:* Dr. Abner W. Womack, Co-Director, 573-882-3576, Fax: 573-884-4688, E-mail: womacka@missouri.edu.

University of Missouri–St. Louis, St. Louis, MO 63121-4499.

Center for Molecular Electronics Founded in 1988. *Academic areas of research and training:* Electronic materials, microscopy, electronic devices, computer modeling, spectroscopy of solids. *Degrees offered:* None. *Graduate students served last academic year:* 16: 4 at the master's level; 8 at the doctoral level; 4 at the postgraduate level. *Faculty:* 12. *Faculty affiliations:* Departments of Chemistry, Physics. *Annual research budget:* $150,000. *Director:* Dr. Bernard Feldman, Director, 314-516-5019, Fax: 314-516-6152, E-mail: c4840@slvaxa.umsl.edu.

The University of Montana–Missoula, Missoula, MT 59812-0002.

Montana Cooperative Wildlife Research Unit Founded in 1950. *Academic areas of research and training:* Avian ecology, wildlife management. *Degrees offered:* None. *Graduate students served last academic year:* 16: 11 at the master's level; 4 at the doctoral level; 1 at the postgraduate level. *Faculty:* 4: 2 affiliated solely with the unit. *Faculty affiliations:* Division of Biological Sciences, Program in Wildlife Biology. *Annual research budget:* $3 million. *Director:* Dr. Joe Ball, Unit Leader, 406-243-5372, Fax: 406-243-6064, E-mail: ball1@selway.umt.edu.

The Shafizadeh Rocky Mountain Center for Wood and Carbohydrate Chemistry Founded in 1965. *Academic areas of research and training:* Wood and carbohydrate chemistry, organic chemistry, synthetic polymer chemistry, synthetic carbohydrate chemistry for pharmaceutical preparations. *Degrees offered:* None. *Graduate students served last academic year:* 2: 2 at the postgraduate level. *Faculty:* 3: 3 affiliated solely with the center. *Faculty affiliations:* Department of Chemistry. *Annual research budget:* $250,000. *Director:* Dr. Donald E. Kiely, Director, 406-243-4435, Fax: 406-243-6166, E-mail: donkiely@selway.umt.edu.

University of Nebraska–Lincoln, Lincoln, NE 68588.

Center for Microelectronic and Optical Materials Research (CMOMR) Founded in 1988. *Academic areas of research and training:* Thin films, bulk semiconductors, vacuum processing plasmas and plasma-solid interactions, ellipsometry optics. *Degrees offered:* None. *Graduate students served last academic year:* 10: 7 at the master's level; 2 at the doctoral level; 1 at the postgraduate level. *Faculty:* 8: 2 affiliated solely with the center. *Faculty affiliations:* Departments of Electrical Engineering, Mechanical Engineering, Physics and Astronomy. *Annual research budget:* $1.4 million. *Director:* Dr. John A. Woollam, Director, 402-472-1975, Fax: 402-472-7987, E-mail: jwoollam@unl.edu.

The Food Processing Center Founded in 1984. *Academic areas of research and training:* Development and evaluation of new and existing food products and processes. *Degrees offered:* None. *Graduate students served last academic year:* 20: 15 at the master's level; 5 at the doctoral level. *Faculty:* 25. *Faculty affiliations:* Departments of Agronomy, Animal Science, Biological Systems Engineering, Biometry, Horticulture; Program in Food Science and Technology. *Annual research budget:* $500,000. *Director:* Dr. Steve L. Taylor, Director, 402-472-2831, Fax: 402-472-1693.

Nebraska Center for Mass Spectrometry Founded in 1978. *Academic areas of research and training:* Biological and sructural mass spectrometry. *Degrees offered:* None. *Graduate students served last academic year:* 30: 7 at the master's level; 18 at the doctoral level; 5 at the postgraduate level. *Faculty:* 18: 3 affiliated solely with the center. *Faculty affiliations:* Departments of Biochemistry, Biology, Chemistry; Medical Center. *Annual research budget:* $300,000. *Director:* Dr. David Smith, Director, 402-472-3507, Fax: 402-472-9402, E-mail: dsmith7@unl.edu.

The Water Center Founded in 1964. *Academic areas of research and training:* Water sciences, water quality, water quantity. *Degrees offered:* None. *Graduate students served last academic year:* 5: 1 at the master's level; 4 at the doctoral level. *Faculty:* 6. *Faculty affiliations:* Departments of Agronomy; Biological Systems Engineering; Entomology; Forestry, Fisheries, and Wildlife. *Annual research budget:* $600,000. *Director:* Dr. Edward F. Vitzthum, Interim Director, 402-472-3305, Fax: 402-472-3574, E-mail: evitzthum1@unl.edu.

University of Nevada, Las Vegas, Las Vegas, NV 89154-9900.

Center for Volcanic and Tectonic Studies (CVTS) Founded in 1986. *Academic areas of research and training:* Volcanology, geochemistry, hazard assessment, igneous petrology. *Degrees offered:* None. *Graduate students served last academic year:* 3: 3 at the master's level. *Faculty:* 2. *Faculty affiliations:* Department of Geoscience. *Annual research budget:* $120,000. *Director:* Dr. Eugene I. Smith, Director, 702-895-3971, Fax: 702-895-4064, E-mail: gsmith@ccmail.nevada.edu.

University of Nevada, Reno, Reno, NV 89557.

Nevada Agricultural Experiment Station Founded in 1874. *Academic areas of research and training:* Environmental and natural resource economics, economic development, environmental science, wildlife conservation, hydrology/water quality, arid rangeland, multiple use of public land, nutritional genomics, insect molecular biology, range nutrition and animal health. *Degrees offered:* MS; PhD. *Faculty:* 78: 75 affiliated solely with the station. *Faculty affiliations:* Desert Research Institute; University of Nevada, Las Vegas. *Annual research budget:* $13 million. *Director:* Dr. David G. Thawley, Director, 775-784-6237, Fax: 775-784-6604. *Application contact:* Dr. Ronald S. Pardini, Associate Director, 775-784-6237, Fax: 775-784-6604, E-mail: ronp@scs.unr.edu.

University of New Hampshire, Durham, NH 03824.

Climate Change Research Center Founded in 1979. *Academic areas of research and training:* Atmospheric chemistry, climate change on local-to-global scale. *Degrees offered:* MS; PhD. *Graduate students served last academic year:* 10: 7 at the master's level; 3 at the doctoral level. *Faculty:* 18: 14 affiliated solely with the center. *Faculty affiliations:* University of Calgary. *Annual research budget:* $2 million. *Director:* Dr. Paul Andrew Mayewski, Director, 603-862-3146, E-mail: paul.mayewski@unh.edu.

Announcement EOS is a multidisciplinary research institute that attracts about $20 million annually for its studies of the Earth and its space environment. Graduate education focuses on interdisciplinary studies that contribute to understanding the global integrated behavior of the Earth and Earth-Sun system. For further information, contact 603-862-0322 or visit the Web site at http://www.eos.sr.unh.edu.

University of New Mexico, Albuquerque, NM 87131-2039.

The Institute of Meteoritics (IOM) Founded in 1944. *Academic areas of research and training:* Research in the detailed laboratory analysis of meteoritic and other planetary materials and in other fields of planetary and geologic sciences. *Degrees offered:* None. *Faculty:* 9. *Faculty affiliations:* Department of Earth and Planetary Sciences. *Director:* Dr. James J. Papike, Director, 505-277-1644, Fax: 505-277-3577, E-mail: slentz@unm.edu. *Application contact:* Sarah Lentz, Administrative Assistant, 505-277-1644, Fax: 505-277-3577, E-mail: slentz@unm.edu.

The University of North Carolina at Chapel Hill, Chapel Hill, NC 27599.

Center for Multiphase Research (CMR) Founded in 1992. *Academic areas of research and training:* Multiphase flow, contaminant transport, groundwater, geosciences, applied mathematics, scientific computing. *Degrees offered:* None. *Graduate students served last academic year:* 20: 5 at the master's level; 10 at the doctoral level; 5 at the postgraduate level. *Faculty:* 6. *Faculty affiliations:* Departments of Computer Sciences, Environmental Sciences and Engineering. *Annual research budget:* $1.3 million. *Director:* Dr. Cass T. Miller, Director, 919-966-2643, Fax: 919-966-7911, E-mail: casey_miller@unc.edu.

Institute of Marine Sciences Founded in 1947. *Academic areas of research and training:* Marine geology, benthic ecology, physical oceanography, marine biology, geochemistry. *Degrees offered:* None. *Graduate students served last academic year:* 20: 8 at the master's level; 12 at the doctoral level. *Faculty:* 25: 9 affiliated solely with the institute. *Faculty affiliations:* Departments of Biology, Environmental Sciences and Engineering, Geology, Marine Sciences. *Annual research budget:* $2.7 million. *Director:* Dr. John T. Wells, Director, 252-726-6841 Ext. 124, Fax: 252-726-2426, E-mail: john_wells@unc.edu.

University of North Carolina at Wilmington, Wilmington, NC 28403-3201.

Center for Marine Science Research Founded in 1972. *Academic areas of research and training:* Oceanography, marine biotechnology and aquaculture, coastal and estuarine, marine biomedical, marine geology. *Degrees offered:* None. *Graduate students served last academic year:* 65: 57 at the master's level; 6 at the doctoral level; 2 at the postgraduate level. *Faculty:* 56: 9 affiliated solely with the center. *Faculty affiliations:* Departments of Biological Sciences, Chemistry, Earth Science, Physics, Recreation. *Annual research budget:* $5.8 million. *Director:* Dr. James F. Merritt, Director, 910-256-3721 Ext. 203, Fax: 910-256-8856, E-mail: merrittj@uncwil.edu.

National Undersea Research Center (NURC) Founded in 1982. *Academic areas of research and training:* Undersea science and technology development; research includes fisheries, coastal ecosystems, deep sea exploration, and global evironmental change. *Degrees offered:* None. *Graduate students served last academic year:* 200: 140 at the master's level; 50 at the doctoral level; 10 at the postgraduate level. *Faculty:* 102: 2 affiliated solely with the center. *Annual research budget:* $2.5 million. *Director:* Steven Miller, Director, 305-451-0233, Fax: 305-453-9719, E-mail: smiller@gate.net. *Application contact:* Andrew N. Shepard, Associate Director, 910-256-5133, Fax: 910-256-8856, E-mail: sheparda@uncwil.edu.

University of North Dakota, Grand Forks, ND 58202.

Earth System Science Institute (ESSI) Founded in 1992. *Academic areas of research and training:* Integrated studies of the earth, practical applications of remotely sensed data, climate change. *Degrees offered:* None. *Graduate students served last academic year:* 14: 11 at the master's level; 3 at the doctoral level. *Faculty:* 50: 10 affiliated solely with the institute. *Faculty affiliations:* Montana State University System, North Dakota State University, South Dakota School of Mines and Technology, South Dakota State University, University of Idaho, University of Montana–Missoula, University of Wyoming. *Annual research budget:* $2.3 million. *Director:* George Seielstad, Director, 701-777-2791, Fax: 701-777-3016.

Fisheries Research Unit Founded in 1972. *Academic areas of research and training:* Fish biology. *Degrees offered:* None. *Graduate students served last academic year:* 10: 8 at the master's level; 2 at the doctoral level. *Faculty:* 17. *Faculty affiliations:* Department of Biology. *Annual research budget:* $60,000. *Director:* Dr. Steven Kelsch, Leader, 701-777-4284, Fax: 701-777-2623.

University of North Texas, Denton, TX 76203.

The Center for Environmental Philosophy Founded in 1989. *Academic areas of research and training:* Environmental ethics, environmental philosophy. *Degrees offered:* None. *Graduate students served last academic year:* 8: 6 at the master's level; 2 at the postgraduate level. *Faculty:* 31: 1 affiliated solely with the center. *Faculty affiliations:* Departments of Biological Sciences, Geography, Philosophy; Program in Environmental Science. *Annual research budget:* $60,000. *Director:* Jan Dickson, Executive Director, 940-565-2727, Fax: 940-565-4439, E-mail: cep@unt.edu.

Center for Nonlinear Science Founded in 1995. *Academic areas of research and training:* Nonlinear dynamics applied to physical, biophysics and social phenomena. *Degrees offered:* None. *Graduate students served last academic year:* 6: 6 at the doctoral level. *Faculty:* 4. *Faculty affiliations:* Departments of Biological Sciences and Mathematics, Physics. *Annual research budget:* $400,000. *Director:* Dr. Bruce West, Director, 817-565-3268, Fax: 817-565-2515, E-mail: bwest@jove.acs.unt.edu.

Laboratory of Polymers and Composites (LAPOM) Founded in 1989. *Academic areas of research and training:* Service performance and reliability of polymer-based materials, ceramic and polymer composites, liquid crystals, friction, solution flow. *Degrees offered:* MS; PhD. *Graduate students served last academic year:* 12: 5 at the master's level; 5 at the doctoral level; 2 at the postgraduate level. *Faculty:* 8: 4 affiliated solely with the laboratory. *Faculty affiliations:* Departments of Engineering Technology, Materials Science. *Annual research budget:* $450,000. *Director:* Dr. Witold Brostow, Director, 940-565-4358, Fax: 940-565-4824, E-mail: brostow@unt.edu.

Water Research Field Station (WRFS) Founded in 1987. *Academic areas of research and training:* Biological impacts and chemical fate of agricultural chemicals, aquatic ecosystem studies, biomonitoring. *Degrees offered:* None. *Graduate students served last academic year:* 26: 20 at the master's level; 5 at the doctoral level; 1 at the postgraduate level. *Faculty:* 4.

Research and Training Opportunities

Water Research Field Station (WRFS) *(continued)*
Faculty affiliations: Department of Biological Sciences; Institute of Applied Sciences; Program in Environmental Science. *Annual research budget:* $500,000. *Director:* Dr. James H. Kennedy, Director, 940-565-2981, Fax: 940-565-4297, E-mail: kennedy@unt.edu.

University of Oklahoma, Norman, OK 73019-0390.
Center for Analysis and Prediction of Storms (CAPS) Founded in 1989. *Academic areas of research and training:* Numerical weather prediction, aviation weather, thunderstorm dynamics, data assimilation, predictability. *Degrees offered:* None. *Graduate students served last academic year:* 20: 6 at the master's level; 6 at the doctoral level; 8 at the postgraduate level. *Faculty:* 14: 8 affiliated solely with the center. *Faculty affiliations:* School of Meteorology. *Annual research budget:* $1.5 million. *Director:* Dr. Kelvin Droegemeier, Director, 405-325-0453, Fax: 405-325-7614, E-mail: kkd@ou.edu.

Rock Mechanics Institute Founded in 1991. *Academic areas of research and training:* Oil and gas research, drilling and production, rock and rock mass properties. *Degrees offered:* None. *Graduate students served last academic year:* 21: 3 at the master's level; 10 at the doctoral level; 8 at the postgraduate level. *Faculty:* 6: 2 affiliated solely with the institute. *Faculty affiliations:* Schools of Business Administration, Civil Engineering and Environmental Science, Geology and Geodynamics, Petroleum and Geological Engineering. *Annual research budget:* $2 million. *Director:* Dr. Jean-Claude Roegiers, Director, 405-325-2900, Fax: 405-325-7511, E-mail: jc@rmg.ou.edu.

University of Pittsburgh, Pittsburgh, PA 15260.
Pymatuning Laboratory of Ecology Founded in 1949. *Academic areas of research and training:* Ecology, evolution, environmental science. *Degrees offered:* None. *Graduate students served last academic year:* 3 at the master's level; 8 at the doctoral level; 2 at the postgraduate level. *Faculty:* 23. *Faculty affiliations:* Departments of Biological Sciences, Geology and Planetary Science; Faculty of Arts and Sciences. *Director:* Dr. Stephen J. Tonsor, Director, 814-683-5813, Fax: 814-683-2302, E-mail: tonsor@pitt.edu. *Application contact:* Kathleen Gibson, Resident Manager, 814-683-5813, Fax: 814-683-2302, E-mail: ksgibson@pitt.edu.

University of Regina, Regina, SK S4S 0A2, Canada.
Energy Research Unit (ERU) Founded in 1978. *Academic areas of research and training:* Coal geology, carbon dioxide utilization, energy informatics, environmental planning, renewable energy, petroleum. *Degrees offered:* None. *Graduate students served last academic year:* 25: 20 at the master's level; 5 at the doctoral level. *Faculty:* 9. *Faculty affiliations:* Departments of Chemistry, Computer Science, Geology; Faculty of Engineering. *Annual research budget:* $300,000. *Director:* Dr. Brian D. Kybett, Director, 306-585-4261, Fax: 306-585-5205, E-mail: kybettbd@cas.uregina.ca.

University of Rochester, Rochester, NY 14627-0250.
Center for Optics Manufacturing (COM) Founded in 1989. *Academic areas of research and training:* Optics manufacturing, optical material science, precision grinding. *Degrees offered:* None. *Graduate students served last academic year:* 20: 12 at the master's level; 6 at the doctoral level; 2 at the postgraduate level. *Faculty:* 16: 2 affiliated solely with the center. *Faculty affiliations:* Departments of Chemical Engineering, Electrical Engineering, Industrial Engineering, Mechanical Engineering, Physics; Institute of Optics. *Annual research budget:* $2 million. *Director:* Harvey M. Pollicove, Director, 716-275-1093, Fax: 716-275-7225, E-mail: hpol-com@lle.rochester.edu. *Application contact:* Michele K. Richard, Program Manager/Administrator, 716-275-2753, Fax: 716-275-7225, E-mail: mric-com@lle.rochester.edu.

Center for Photoinduced Charge Transfer Founded in 1989. *Academic areas of research and training:* Chemistry and physics of photoinduced charge transfer; applications to imaging science, photoconduction, electroluminescence, and nonlinear optics. *Degrees offered:* None. *Graduate students served last academic year:* 30: 15 at the doctoral level; 15 at the postgraduate level. *Faculty:* 12. *Faculty affiliations:* Departments of Chemical Engineering, Chemistry, Electrical Engineering, Physics. *Annual research budget:* $1.6 million. *Director:* Dr. Lewis Rothberg, Director, 716-275-8286, Fax: 716-242-9485, E-mail: stc@chem.chem.rochester.edu. *Application contact:* Debbie Shannon, Administrator.

Nuclear Structure Research Laboratory Founded in 1965. *Academic areas of research and training:* Nuclear science basic research. *Degrees offered:* None. *Graduate students served last academic year:* 12: 7 at the doctoral level; 5 at the postgraduate level. *Faculty:* 5. *Faculty affiliations:* Departments of Chemistry, Physics and Astronomy. *Annual research budget:* $1.2 million. *Director:* Dr. Douglas Cline, Director, 716-275-4934, Fax: 716-473-5384, E-mail: cline@nsrl.rochester.edu.

Rochester Theory Center for Optical Science and Engineering Founded in 1995. *Academic areas of research and training:* Postdoctoral training in interdisciplinary areas of optical science and technology. *Degrees offered:* None. *Graduate students served last academic year:* 15: 11 at the doctoral level; 4 at the postgraduate level. *Faculty:* 10. *Faculty affiliations:* Departments of Chemistry, Mechanical Engineering, Physics and Astronomy; Institute of Optics; Laboratory for Laser Energetics. *Director:* Dr. Joseph H. Eberly, Director, 716-275-3288, Fax: 716-275-8527, E-mail: secr@rtc.rochester.edu. *Application contact:* Joel Byam, Administrative Assistant, 716-275-3288, Fax: 716-275-8527, E-mail: secr@rtc.rochester.edu.

University of South Carolina, Columbia, SC 29208.
Belle W. Baruch Institute for Marine Biology and Coastal Research Founded in 1969. *Academic areas of research and training:* Multidisciplinary research on the ecological and economic resources of coastal and marine environments; GIS; biogeochemical nutrient cycles;, marine environmental studies, ncluding biological, geological, chemical, and physical oceanography; marine policy; toxicology. *Degrees offered:* None. *Graduate students served last academic year:* 85: 25 at the master's level; 40 at the doctoral level; 5 at the postgraduate level. *Faculty:* 90: 5 affiliated solely with the institute. *Faculty affiliations:* Departments of Biological Sciences, Chemistry and Biochemistry, Environmental Health Science, Geological Sciences; Program in Marine Science. *Annual research budget:* $2.1 million. *Director:* Dr. Madilyn Fletcher, Director, 803-777-5288, Fax: 803-777-3935, E-mail: fletcher@biol.sc.edu. *Application contact:* Dr. Dennis Allen, Resident Director, Baruch Marine Field Laboratory, 803-546-3623, Fax: 803-546-1632, E-mail: dallen@belle.baruch.sc.edu.

Hazards Research Laboratory Founded in 1995. *Academic areas of research and training:* Geographic information processing techniques in environmental hazards analysis and management. *Degrees offered:* None. *Graduate students served last academic year:* 5 at the master's level; 2 at the doctoral level; 1 at the postgraduate level. *Faculty:* 5. *Faculty affiliations:* Department of Geography. *Annual research budget:* $100,000. *Director:* Dr. Susan Cutter, Director, 803-777-1699, Fax: 803-777-4972, E-mail: uschrl@ecotopia.geog.sc.edu.

University of Tennessee, Knoxville, Knoxville, TN 37996.
Energy, Environment, and Resources Center Founded in 1972. *Academic areas of research and training:* Multidisciplinary research unit focused on policy in energy, waste management, clean products, water, stakeholder participation, environmental education, and regulatory affairs. *Degrees offered:* None. *Graduate students served last academic year:* 35: 25 at the master's level; 10 at the doctoral level. *Faculty:* 35: 15 affiliated solely with the center. *Faculty affiliations:* College of Engineering; Departments of Business, Economics, Geography, Political Science, Social Work. *Annual research budget:* $7 million. *Director:* Dr. Jack Barkenbus, Executive Director, 423-974-4251, Fax: 423-974-1838, E-mail: barkenbu@utk.edu.

The University of Texas at Arlington, Arlington, TX 76019.
Center for Advanced Polymer Research Founded in 1988. *Academic areas of research and training:* Polymer research, conductive polymers, electroluminescent polymers, plasma polymerization, anti-corrosion, light emission. *Degrees offered:* None. *Graduate students served last academic year:* 10: 8 at the doctoral level; 2 at the postgraduate level. *Faculty:* 6. *Faculty affiliations:* Departments of Chemistry and Biochemistry, Materials Science and Engineering. *Annual research budget:* $200,000. *Director:* Dr. Martin Pomerantz, Director, 817-272-3811, Fax: 817-273-3808, E-mail: pomerantz@uta.edu.

Center for Colloidal and Interfacial Dynamics Founded in 1988. *Academic areas of research and training:* Colloid dynamics, molecular tailoring of surfaces, photo-electrochemistry. *Degrees offered:* None. *Graduate students served last academic year:* 20: 16 at the doctoral level; 4 at the postgraduate level. *Faculty:* 3: 3 affiliated solely with the center. *Annual research budget:* $716,000. *Director:* Prof. Zoltan A. Schelly, Director, 817-272-3803, Fax: 817-273-3808, E-mail: schelly@uta.edu.

Center for Fossil Fuels Chemistry Founded in 1988. *Academic areas of research and training:* Fossil fuels chemistry, coal structure, coal reactions, oil shale, oil sands, petroleum crudes, catalytic conversion. *Degrees offered:* None. *Faculty:* 3. *Faculty affiliations:* Department of Chemistry and Biochemistry. *Director:* Dr. Martin Pomerantz, Co-Director, 817-272-3811, Fax: 817-273-3808, E-mail: pomerantz@uta.edu.

Frank E. Lozo Center for Cretaceous Stratigraphic Studies Founded in 1982. *Academic areas of research and training:* Cretaceous stratigraphy of the United States and Mexico; paleontology, stratigraphy and hydrocarbon potential of Cretaceous rocks in Texas and Coahuila/Chihuahua, Mexico. *Degrees offered:* None. *Graduate students served last academic year:* 2 at the master's level; 1 at the doctoral level; 1 at the postgraduate level. *Faculty:* 1. *Faculty affiliations:* Department of Geology. *Director:* Dr. Donald F. Reaser, Professor, 817-272-2987, Fax: 817-272-2628.

The University of Texas at Austin, Austin, TX 78712-1111.
Bureau of Economic Geology Founded in 1909. *Academic areas of research and training:* Energy resources, oil and gas recovery, environmental geology, water resources, coastal processes. *Degrees offered:* None. *Graduate students served last academic year:* 50: 30 at the master's level; 15 at the doctoral level; 5 at the postgraduate level. *Faculty:* 5. *Faculty affiliations:* Departments of Geological Sciences, Petroleum and Geosystems Engineering. *Director:* Dr. William L. Fisher, Interim Director, 512-471-1534, Fax: 512-471-0140, E-mail: wfisher@mail.utexas.edu.

The Ilya Prigogine Center for Studies in Statistical Mechanics and Complex Systems Founded in 1967. *Academic areas of research and training:* Theoretical and computational study of nonlinear and nonequilibrium phenomena in physical and chemical processes, chaos and instability due to nonlinear processes at the microscopic level in the physical world and their effect on the macroscopic level. *Degrees offered:* None. *Graduate students served last academic year:* 19: 1 at the master's level; 11 at the doctoral level. *Faculty:* 4. *Faculty affiliations:* Department of Physics. *Director:* Dr. Ilya Prigogine, Director, 512-471-7253, Fax: 512-471-9621, E-mail: annie@physics.utexas.edu.

Institute for Fusion Studies Founded in 1980. *Academic areas of research and training:* Fusion energy, magnetic confinement, space plasma physics, laser-plasma interactions, nonlinear dynamics. *Degrees offered:* None. *Graduate students served last academic year:* 20: 20 at the doctoral level. *Faculty:* 8: 7 affiliated solely with the institute. *Faculty affiliations:* Departments of Astronomy, Physics. *Annual research budget:* $2.5 million. *Director:* Prof. Richard D. Hazeltine, Director, 512-471-1322, Fax: 512-471-6715, E-mail: rdh@physics.utexas.edu.

Institute for Theoretical Chemistry Founded in 1979. *Academic areas of research and training:* Theoretical chemistry; quantum chemistry; statistical mechanics; quantum molecular dynamics; molecular excited states; liquid state theory. *Degrees offered:* None. *Graduate students served last academic year:* 24: 14 at the doctoral level; 10 at the postgraduate level. *Faculty:* 4. *Faculty affiliations:* Department of Chemistry and Biochemistry. *Director:* Dr. Peter J. Rossky, Director, 512-471-3555, Fax: 512-471-1624, E-mail: rossky@mail.utexas.edu.

Laboratory of Electrochemistry Founded in 1980. *Academic areas of research and training:* Application of electrochemical methods to the study of chemical problems, including electroorganic chemistry, photoelectrochemistry, electrogenerated chemiluminescence,and electroanalytical chemistry. *Degrees offered:* None. *Graduate students served last academic year:* 20: 1 at the master's level; 5 at the doctoral level; 14 at the postgraduate level. *Faculty:* 1. *Faculty affiliations:* Department of Chemistry and Biochemistry. *Annual research budget:* $725,000. *Director:* Dr. Allen J. Bard, Director, 512-471-3761, Fax: 512-471-0088, E-mail: ajbard@mail.utexas.edu. *Application contact:* Dr. John Leamons, Administrative Assistant, 512-471-3761, Fax: 512-471-0088, E-mail: leamons@mail.utexas.edu.

McDonald Observatory Founded in 1938. *Academic areas of research and training:* Astronomical research. *Degrees offered:* None. *Graduate students served last academic year:* 30: 10 at the master's level; 10 at the doctoral level; 10 at the postgraduate level. *Faculty:* 22. *Faculty affiliations:* Department of Astronomy. *Annual research budget:* $5 million. *Director:* Dr. Frank Bash, Director, 512-471-3300, Fax: 512-471-1635, E-mail: fnb@astro.as.utexas.edu. *Application contact:* Dr. Thomas G. Barnes, Associate Director, 512-471-1301, Fax: 512-471-1635, E-mail: tgb@astro.as.utexas.edu.

Research Institute-Weinberg/Theory Group Founded in 1982. *Academic areas of research and training:* Theoretical elementary particle physics, string theory, field theory, phenomenology, cosmology. *Degrees offered:* None. *Graduate students served last academic year:* 16: 1 at the master's level; 10 at the doctoral level; 5 at the postgraduate level. *Faculty:* 10: 5 affiliated solely with the institute. *Faculty affiliations:* Department of Physics. *Director:* Dr. Steven Weinberg, Director, 512-471-4394, Fax: 512-471-4888, E-mail: weinberg@physics.utexas.edu. *Application contact:* Jan Duffy, Senior Administrative Associate, 512-471-3898, Fax: 512-471-4888, E-mail: duffy@physics.utexas.edu.

Texas Institute for Computational and Applied Mathematics Founded in 1993. *Academic areas of research and training:* Oil reservoir simulation, computer simulation of pollution remediation and control, computational fluid dynamics, large-scale simulation of structural acoustics, gravitational waves and black hole simulation, scalable parallel computing paradigms, composite material modeling, electromagnetic field calculations, semiconductor modeling, nonlinear wave propagation. *Degrees offered:* None. *Graduate students served last academic year:* 40: 2 at the master's level; 30 at the doctoral level; 8 at the postgraduate level. *Faculty:* 78: 39 affiliated solely with the institute. *Faculty affiliations:* Departments of Aerospace Engineering and Engineering Mechanics, Chemical Engineering, Civil Engineering, Computer Sciences, Electrical and Computer Engineering, Mathematics, Petroleum and Geosystems Engineering, Physics; Centers for Numerical Analysis, Relativity. *Annual research budget:* $2.5 million. *Director:* Dr. J. Tinsley Oden, Director, 512-471-3312, Fax: 512-471-8694.

The University of Texas at Dallas, Richardson, TX 75083-0688.
The Center for Lithospheric Studies Founded in 1978. *Academic areas of research and training:* Basic and applied geophysical research. *Degrees offered:* None. *Graduate students served last academic year:* 32: 5 at the master's level; 27 at the doctoral level. *Faculty:* 5: 5 affiliated solely with the center. *Annual research budget:* $1.5 million. *Director:* George A. McMechan, Director, Fax: 972-883-2829, E-mail: mcmec@utdallas.edu. *Application contact:* Charlotte Stromer, Administrative Assistant, 972-883-2424, Fax: 972-883-2829, E-mail: stromer@utdallas.edu.

The University of Texas Health Science Center at San Antonio, San Antonio, TX 78284-6200.

The Center for Environmental Radiation Toxicology (CERT) Founded in 1993. *Academic areas of research and training:* Biological and health effects of ionizing and non-ionizing radiation, including microwaves, ultraviolet light, laser emissions, and ELF fields. *Degrees offered:* None. *Graduate students served last academic year:* 4: 3 at the master's level; 1 at the doctoral level. *Faculty:* 55. *Faculty affiliations:* Trinity University, University of Texas at San Antonio, U.S. Air Force Research Laboratory (Brooks Air Force Base, TX), Southwest Research Institute, Southwest Foundation for Biomedical Research. *Director:* Dr. Martin L. Meltz, Director, 210-567-5560, Fax: 210-567-3446, E-mail: meltz@uthscsa.edu.

University of Utah, Salt Lake City, UT 84112-1107.

Center for Atmospheric and Remote Sounding Studies (CARSS) *Academic areas of research and training:* Atmospheric radiation, cloud physics and modeling, global climate change, remote sensing. *Degrees offered:* None. *Graduate students served last academic year:* 7: 3 at the master's level; 3 at the doctoral level; 1 at the postgraduate level. *Faculty:* 5. *Faculty affiliations:* Department of Meteorology. *Annual research budget:* $600,000. *Director:* Dr. Kenneth Sassen, Director, 801-585-9492, Fax: 801-585-3681, E-mail: ksassen@atmos.met.utah.edu.

Energy and Geoscience Institute (EGI) Founded in 1974. *Academic areas of research and training:* Basic and applied energy research, petroleum basin studies, geothermal energy research, geostatistics and data-mining, remote sensing and GIS reservoir characterization. *Degrees offered:* None. *Graduate students served last academic year:* 3: 2 at the doctoral level; 1 at the postgraduate level. *Faculty:* 21: 16 affiliated solely with the institute. *Faculty affiliations:* Departments of Chemical and Fuels Engineering, Computer Science, Geography, Geology and Geophysics. *Annual research budget:* $9 million. *Director:* Dr. William H. Kanes, Director, 801-581-5126, Fax: 801-585-3540, E-mail: whkanes@egi.utah.edu.

Seismograph Stations Founded in 1966. *Academic areas of research and training:* Earthquake seismology. *Degrees offered:* None. *Graduate students served last academic year:* 9: 8 at the master's level; 1 at the doctoral level. *Faculty:* 4: 3 affiliated solely with the stations. *Faculty affiliations:* Department of Geology and Geophysics. *Annual research budget:* $900,000. *Director:* Dr. Walter J. Arabasz, Director, 801-581-6274, Fax: 801-585-5585, E-mail: arabasz@seis.utah.edu.

University of Victoria, Victoria, BC V8W 2Y2, Canada.

Western Canadian Universities Marine Biological Society-Bamfield Marine Station Founded in 1972. *Academic areas of research and training:* Marine biology, marine ecology, behavior, evolutionary biology, comparative physiology and biochemistry, molecular biology. *Degrees offered:* None. *Graduate students served last academic year:* 31: 12 at the master's level; 13 at the doctoral level; 6 at the postgraduate level. *Faculty:* 62: 2 affiliated solely with the station. *Faculty affiliations:* Simon Fraser University, University of Alberta, University of British Columbia, University of Calgary. *Annual research budget:* $700,000. *Director:* Dr. Andy N. Spencer, Director, 250-728-3301, Fax: 250-728-3452, E-mail: aspencer@bms.bc.ca.

University of Virginia, Charlottesville, VA 22903.

Center for Bioprocess Development Founded in 1987. *Academic areas of research and training:* Bioprocessing, bioreactors, bioseparations, bioremediation. *Degrees offered:* MS; PhD. *Graduate students served last academic year:* 4 at the master's level; 8 at the doctoral level; 1 at the postgraduate level. *Faculty:* 7: 5 affiliated solely with the center. *Faculty affiliations:* Departments of Biology, Cell Biology. *Annual research budget:* $800,000. *Director:* Donald J. Kirwan, Director, 804-924-6278, Fax: 804-982-2658, E-mail: djk@virginia.edu.

University of Washington, Seattle, WA 98195.

Center for International Trade in Forest Products Founded in 1985. *Academic areas of research and training:* International trade in forest products, marketing, economic research, forest policy, environmental assessments. *Degrees offered:* None. *Graduate students served last academic year:* 10: 6 at the master's level; 4 at the doctoral level. *Faculty:* 10: 4 affiliated solely with the center. *Faculty affiliations:* College of Forest Resources. *Annual research budget:* $600,000. *Director:* Bruce R. Lippke, Director, 206-543-8684, Fax: 206-685-0790, E-mail: blippke@u.washington.edu.

The National Research Center for Statistics and the Environment (NRCSE) Founded in 1996. *Academic areas of research and training:* Environmental statistics. *Degrees offered:* None. *Graduate students served last academic year:* 15: 5 at the master's level; 8 at the doctoral level; 2 at the postgraduate level. *Faculty:* 27: 1 affiliated solely with the center. *Faculty affiliations:* College of Forest Resources; Departments of Applied Mathematics, Atmospheric Sciences, Civil Engineering, Environmental Health, Sociology, Statistics, Zoology; Graduate School of Public Affairs; Programs in Applied Physics, Management; School of Fisheries. *Annual research budget:* $1 million. *Director:* Dr. Peter Guttorp, Director, 206-616-9262, Fax: 206-616-9443, E-mail: peter@stat.washington.edu.

Quaternary Research Center (QRC) Founded in 1967. *Academic areas of research and training:* Quaternary (Ice Age) research. *Degrees offered:* None. *Graduate students served last academic year:* 17. *Faculty:* 25: 1 affiliated solely with the center. *Faculty affiliations:* Departments of Anthropology, Atmospheric Sciences, Botany, Forest Resources, Geological Sciences, Geophysics, Oceanography. *Director:* Dr. Bernard Hallet, Director, 206-543-1166, Fax: 206-543-3836, E-mail: qrc@u.washington.edu.

University of West Florida, Pensacola, FL 32514-5750.

Center for Environmental Diagnostics and Bioremediation (CEDB) Founded in 1990. *Academic areas of research and training:* Bioremediation technologies for the safe degradation of hazardous and toxic wastes, bioindicators for assessing the health of the ecosystem and the degree of environmental pollution. *Degrees offered:* None. *Graduate students served last academic year:* 10: 9 at the master's level; 1 at the doctoral level. *Faculty:* 14: 10 affiliated solely with the center. *Faculty affiliations:* Department of Biology, Institute for Coastal and Estuarine Research (ICER). *Annual research budget:* $1.3 million. *Director:* Dr. K. Ranga Rao, Director, 850-474-2060, Fax: 850-474-3130, E-mail: rrao@uwf.edu. *Application contact:* Dr. Malcolm Shields, Assistant Director, 850-474-2060, Fax: 850-474-3130, E-mail: mshields@uwf.edu.

Institute for Coastal and Estuarine Research (ICER) Founded in 1989. *Academic areas of research and training:* Water quality, wetlands, coastal zones, groundwater, state-certified laboratory, estuary, sediment cores, environmental monitoring. *Degrees offered:* None. *Graduate students served last academic year:* 8: 8 at the master's level. *Faculty:* 16: 1 affiliated solely with the institute. *Faculty affiliations:* Department of Biology; Programs in Chemistry, Environmental Studies; Center for Environmental Diagnostics and Bioremediation (CEDB). *Annual research budget:* $800,000. *Director:* Dr. Joe Eugene Lepo, Director, 850-474-2079, Fax: 850-474-3496, E-mail: jlepo@uwf.edu.

University of Wisconsin–Madison, Madison, WI 53706-1380.

Environmental Remote Sensing Center (ERSC) Founded in 1970. *Academic areas of research and training:* Environmental remote sensing, geographic information systems. *Degrees offered:* MS; PhD. *Graduate students served last academic year:* 37: 25 at the master's level; 10 at the doctoral level; 2 at the postgraduate level. *Faculty:* 13: 3 affiliated solely with the center. *Faculty affiliations:* Departments of Biological Systems Engineering, Civil and Environmental Engineering, Forestry, Geography, Soil Science; Institute for Environmental

Studies; School of Business. *Annual research budget:* $500,000. *Director:* Dr. Thomas M. Lillesand, Director, 608-263-3251, Fax: 608-262-5964, E-mail: tmlilles@facstaff.wisc.edu.

Institute for Elementary Particle Physics Research Founded in 1984. *Academic areas of research and training:* Phenomenology of high energy particle physics. *Degrees offered:* None. *Graduate students served last academic year:* 17: 1 at the master's level; 9 at the doctoral level; 7 at the postgraduate level. *Faculty:* 5. *Faculty affiliations:* Department of Physics. *Annual research budget:* $675,000. *Director:* Dr. Vernon Barger, Director, 608-262-4906, Fax: 608-262-8628, E-mail: barger@pheno.physics.wisc.edu. *Application contact:* Linda Dolan, Administrative Program Manager, 608-262-4964, Fax: 608-262-8628, E-mail: ldolan@pheno.physics.wisc.edu.

Synchrotron Radiation Center (SRC) Founded in 1968. *Academic areas of research and training:* Electron storage ring provides high intensity photons from the X-ray region to the infrared for a variety of materials research problems and for microcircuit. *Degrees offered:* None. *Graduate students served last academic year:* 229: 125 at the master's level; 52 at the doctoral level; 52 at the postgraduate level. *Faculty:* 62. *Faculty affiliations:* Departments of Chemical Engineering, Chemistry, Electrical and Computer Engineering, Materials Science, Physics. *Annual research budget:* $3.8 million. *Director:* Dr. James W. Taylor, Executive Director, 608-877-2152, Fax: 608-877-2001, E-mail: jtaylor@src.wisc.edu. *Application contact:* Pamela D. Layton, Program Assistant 4, 608-877-2134, Fax: 608-877-2001, E-mail: playton@src.wisc.edu.

University of Wisconsin–Milwaukee, Milwaukee, WI 53201-0413.

Center for By-Products Utilization (UWM-CBU) Founded in 1988. *Academic areas of research and training:* Recycling, construction materials, environmental issues. *Degrees offered:* None. *Graduate students served last academic year:* 10: 8 at the master's level; 2 at the doctoral level. *Faculty:* 21: 1 affiliated solely with the center. *Faculty affiliations:* Departments of Biological Sciences, Chemistry, Engineering, Geosciences, Physics; School of Business Administration. *Director:* Dr. Tarun R. Naik, Director, 414-229-6696, Fax: 414-229-6958, E-mail: tarun@uwm.edu. *Application contact:* Rudolph N. Kraus, Assistant Director, 414-229-4105, Fax: 414-229-6958, E-mail: rudik@uwm.edu.

University of Wyoming, Laramie, WY 82071.

Institute for Energy Research (IER) Founded in 1993. *Academic areas of research and training:* Geology, geophysics, mathematics, petroleum engineering. *Degrees offered:* None. *Graduate students served last academic year:* 14: 7 at the master's level; 7 at the doctoral level. *Faculty:* 2: 2 affiliated solely with the institute. *Faculty affiliations:* Departments of Chemical and Petroleum Engineering, Geology and Geophysics. *Annual research budget:* $3 million. *Director:* Dr. Ronald J. Steel, Interim Director, 307-766-4200, Fax: 307-766-2737, E-mail: rsteel@uwyo.edu. *Application contact:* Dr. Henry P. Heasler, Associate Director, 307-766-4200, Fax: 307-766-2737, E-mail: heasler@uwyo.edu.

Utah State University, Logan, UT 84322.

Center for Atmospheric and Space Sciences Founded in 1959. *Academic areas of research and training:* Computer science, electrical engineering, physics, atmospheric sciences, aeronomy. *Degrees offered:* None. *Graduate students served last academic year:* 8: 1 at the master's level; 6 at the doctoral level; 1 at the postgraduate level. *Faculty:* 16. *Faculty affiliations:* Departments of Electrical and Computer Engineering, Physics. *Annual research budget:* $2 million. *Director:* Dr. Robert W. Schunk, Director, 435-797-2978, Fax: 435-797-2992, E-mail: schunk@cc.usu.edu. *Application contact:* Shawna Johnson, Administrative Assistant, 435-797-2962, Fax: 435-797-2992, E-mail: shawna@cc.usu.edu.

Utah Agricultural Experiment Station Founded in 1888. *Academic areas of research and training:* Agriculture, rural sociology, biotechnology, production, processing, marketing, environment. *Degrees offered:* None. *Graduate students served last academic year:* 123: 82 at the master's level; 41 at the doctoral level. *Faculty:* 100: 50 affiliated solely with the station. *Faculty affiliations:* College of Family Life; Departments of Animal, Dairy, and Veterinary Sciences; Biology; Forest Resources; Nutrition and Food Sciences; Plants, Soils, and Biometeorology; Rangeland Resources. *Director:* Dr. H. Paul Rasmussen, Director, 435-797-2207, Fax: 435-797-3321, E-mail: paul@agx.usu.edu.

Utah Water Research Laboratory (UWRL) Founded in 1965. *Academic areas of research and training:* Biology, chemistry, civil engineering, computer science, economics, education, environmental engineering, forestry, mathematics and statistics, range science, toxicology. *Degrees offered:* None. *Graduate students served last academic year:* 71: 53 at the master's level; 17 at the doctoral level; 1 at the postgraduate level. *Faculty:* 28: 3 affiliated solely with the laboratory. *Faculty affiliations:* Departments of Biology, Chemistry and Biochemistry, Civil and Environmental Engineering, Computer Science, Economics, Forest Resources, Mathematics and Statistics, Range Science, Toxicology; College of Education; Space Dynamics Laboratory. *Annual research budget:* $5.8 million. *Director:* Dr. Ronald C. Sims, Director, 435-797-3157, Fax: 435-797-3663, E-mail: sims@pub.uwrl.usu.edu. *Application contact:* Ivonne Harris, Information Dissemination Coordinator, 435-797-3693, Fax: 435-797-3663, E-mail: iharr@pub.uwrl.usu.edu.

Virginia State University, Petersburg, VA 23806-0001.

Research Center on Magnetic Physics Founded in 1988. *Academic areas of research and training:* Physics, materials science, superconductivity, magnetism, nanostructured materials. *Degrees offered:* None. *Graduate students served last academic year:* 6: 6 at the master's level. *Faculty:* 3: 2 affiliated solely with the center. *Faculty affiliations:* Department of Physics. *Annual research budget:* $313,000. *Director:* Dr. Carey E. Stronach, Director, 804-524-5915, Fax: 804-524-5914, E-mail: cstronac@vsu.edu.

Washington State University, Pullman, WA 99164.

Environmental Research Center Founded in 1971. *Academic areas of research and training:* Energy and environmental studies. *Degrees offered:* None. *Graduate students served last academic year:* 2: 1 at the master's level; 1 at the doctoral level. *Faculty:* 7. *Faculty affiliations:* Program in Environmental Science and Regional Planning. *Director:* Dr. William W. Budd, Director, 509-335-8536, Fax: 509-335-7636, E-mail: budd@wsu.edu. *Application contact:* Valerie L. Akins, Program Assistant, 509-335-8536, Fax: 509-335-7636, E-mail: esrp@wsu.edu or vakins@wsu.edu.

GeoAnalytical Laboratory *Degrees offered:* None. *Graduate students served last academic year:* 35: 19 at the master's level; 14 at the doctoral level; 2 at the postgraduate level. *Faculty:* 4. *Faculty affiliations:* Department of Geology. *Annual research budget:* $200,000. *Director:* Dr. P. R. Hooper, Director, 509-335-1626, Fax: 509-335-7816, E-mail: prhooper@mail.wsu.edu. *Application contact:* Diane Johnson, Research Technologist III, 509-335-4486, Fax: 509-335-4486, E-mail: geolab@mail.wsu.edu.

Nuclear Radiation Center (NRC) Founded in 1961. *Academic areas of research and training:* Neutron activation analysis, cobalt-60 irradiations. *Degrees offered:* None. *Graduate students served last academic year:* 5: 5 at the doctoral level. *Faculty:* 7: 1 affiliated solely with the center. *Faculty affiliations:* Department of Chemistry; College of Pharmacy. *Annual research budget:* $200,000. *Director:* Dr. Gerald E. Tripard, Director, 509-335-8641, Fax: 509-335-4433, E-mail: gtripard@wsu.edu.

State of Washington Water Research Center Founded in 1964. *Academic areas of research and training:* Plan, promote, conduct, and administer water-related research; educate and train scientists and engineers through participation in research projects; transfer information through seminars, workshops, conferences, newsletters, reports, and papers. *Degrees offered:* None. *Graduate students served last academic year:* 21: 17 at the master's level; 3 at

Research and Training Opportunities

State of Washington Water Research Center (continued)
the doctoral level; 1 at the postgraduate level. *Faculty:* 43: 3 affiliated solely with the center. *Faculty affiliations:* Departments of Agriculture Economics, Biosystems Engineering, Chemistry, Economics, Environmental Engineering, Environmental Science, Natural Resources, Political Science, Sociology; Environmental Learning Center; Nuclear Radiation Center; International Program. *Annual research budget:* $1 million. *Director:* Dr. William H. Funk, Director, 509-335-5531, Fax: 509-335-1590.

Washington University in St. Louis, St. Louis, MO 63130-4899.
Center for Computational Mechanics   Founded in 1973. *Academic areas of research and training:* Structural modeling and computation. *Degrees offered:* None.   *Graduate students served last academic year:* 12: 7 at the master's level; 3 at the doctoral level; 2 at the postgraduate level. *Faculty:* 8: 2 affiliated solely with the center. *Faculty affiliations:* Departments of Mechanical Engineering, Systems Science and Mathematics. *Annual research budget:* $500,000. *Director:* David A. Peters, Director, 314-935-4337, Fax: 314-935-4014, E-mail: dap@mecf.wustl.edu. *Application contact:* Center Office, E-mail: dap@mecf.wustl.edu.

Laboratory for Ultrasonics   Founded in 1974. *Academic areas of research and training:* Ultrasonics, echocardiography. *Degrees offered:* None.   *Graduate students served last academic year:* 9: 9 at the doctoral level. *Faculty:* 5: 1 affiliated solely with the laboratory. *Annual research budget:* $500,000. *Director:* Dr. James G. Miller, Director, 314-935-6212, Fax: 314-935-5868, E-mail: jgm@wuphys.wustl.edu.

Wayne State University, Detroit, MI 48202.
Center for Automotive Research   Founded in 1980. *Academic areas of research and training:* Combustion engines, emission controls, diagnostics, friction and wear, mathematical modeling and computer simulation. *Degrees offered:* None.   *Graduate students served last academic year:* 17: 5 at the master's level; 10 at the doctoral level; 2 at the postgraduate level. *Faculty:* 20: 10 affiliated solely with the center. *Faculty affiliations:* Departments of Chemistry, Mechanical Engineering, Physics and Astronomy; Programs in Chemical Engineering, Electrical Engineering. *Annual research budget:* $800,000. *Director:* Dr. Naeim A. Henein, Director, 313-577-3887, Fax: 313-577-8789, E-mail: henein@eng.wayne.edu.

Western Michigan University, Kalamazoo, MI 49008.
Particle Accelerator Laboratory   Founded in 1968. *Academic areas of research and training:* Fundamental studies of atomic and nuclear collision processes; applied physics research, undergraduate instruction, materials science. *Degrees offered:* None.   *Graduate students served last academic year:* 3: 1 at the doctoral level; 2 at the postgraduate level. *Faculty:* 3.

Faculty affiliations: Department of Physics. *Annual research budget:* $50,000. *Director:* Dr. Emanuel Y. Kamber, Director/Professor, 616-387-4944, Fax: 616-387-4939, E-mail: kamber@wmich.edu. *Application contact:* Dr. Stephen M. Ferguson, Accelerator Physicist, 616-387-4957, Fax: 616-387-4939, E-mail: ferguson@wmich.edu.

Western Washington University, Bellingham, WA 98225-5996.
Institute of Environmental Toxicology and Chemistry   Founded in 1989. *Academic areas of research and training:* Environmental toxicology, chemistry, risk assessment. *Degrees offered:* None.   *Graduate students served last academic year:* 6: 6 at the master's level. *Faculty:* 7: 1 affiliated solely with the institute. *Faculty affiliations:* Departments of Biology, Chemistry, Computer Science; Huxley College of Environmental Studies. *Annual research budget:* $400,000. *Director:* Dr. Wayne G. Landis, Director, 360-650-6136, Fax: 360-650-6556, E-mail: landis@cc.wwu.edu.

Shannon Point Marine Center (SPMC)   Founded in 1973. *Academic areas of research and training:* Marine biology, coastal oceanographic processes. *Degrees offered:* None.   *Graduate students served last academic year:* 15: 15 at the master's level. *Faculty:* 11: 6 affiliated solely with the center. *Faculty affiliations:* Departments of Biology, Geology; Huxley College of Environmental Studies. *Annual research budget:* $1.9 million. *Director:* Dr. Stephen D. Sulkin, Director, 360-283-2188, Fax: 360-293-1083, E-mail: spmc@cc.wwu.edu.

West Texas A&M University, Canyon, TX 79016-0001.
Equine Center-Equine Industry Program   Founded in 1994. *Academic areas of research and training:* Equine exercise, nutrition, physiology; equine business management and marketing. *Degrees offered:* None.   *Graduate students served last academic year:* 4: 4 at the master's level. *Faculty:* 3: 3 affiliated solely with the center. *Faculty affiliations:* Division of Agriculture. *Annual research budget:* $15,000. *Director:* Dr. John Pipkin, Director, 806-651-2550, Fax: 806-651-2938, E-mail: jpipkin@mail.wtamu.edu. *Application contact:* Dr. Lance Baker, Assistant Professor, 806-651-2561, Fax: 806-651-2938, E-mail: lbaker@mail.wtamu.edu.

Killgore Research Center   Founded in 1963. *Academic areas of research and training:* Alternative energy, agriculture, information technology, chemistry, biology, business. *Degrees offered:* None.   *Graduate students served last academic year:* 34: 34 at the master's level. *Faculty:* 24. *Faculty affiliations:* Departments of Life, Earth, and Environmental Sciences; Mathematics, Physical Sciences, and Engineering Technology; Division of Agriculture; Program in Computer Information Systems; Alternative Energy Institute (AEI). *Annual research budget:* $50,040. *Director:* Dr. Vaughn Nelson, Dean, Graduate School, Research and Information Technology, 806-651-2270, Fax: 806-651-2733, E-mail: vnelson@mail.wtamu.edu.

Appendixes

This section contains two appendixes. The first, Institutional Changes Since the 1999 Edition, lists institutions that have closed, moved, merged, or changed their name or status since the last edition of the guides. The second, Abbreviations Used in the Guides, gives abbreviations of degree names, along with what those abbreviations stand for. These appendixes are identical in all six volumes of the Graduate Guides.

Institutional Changes
Since the 1999 Edition

Following is an alphabetical listing of institutions that have recently closed, moved, merged with other institutions, or changed their names or status. In the case of a name change, the former name appears first, followed by the new name.

Alfred Adler Institute of Minnesota (Hopkins, Minnesota): name changed to Alfred Adler Graduate School.

Allegheny University of the Health Sciences (Philadelphia, Pennsylvania): name changed to MCP Hahnemann University.

Brescia College (Owensboro, Kentucky): name changed to Brescia University.

California Baptist College (Riverside, California): name changed to California Baptist University.

Cornell University Medical College (New York, New York): name changed to Joan and Sanford I. Weill Medical College of Cornell University.

Denver Conservative Baptist Seminary (Denver, Colorado): name changed to Denver Seminary.

The Graduate School of America (Minneapolis, Minnesota): name changed to Capella University.

The Harid Conservatory (Boca Raton, Florida): merged with Lynn University (Boca Raton, Florida).

Huron International University (San Diego, California): closed.

International University (Englewood, Colorado): name changed to Jones International University.

Louisiana State University Medical Center (New Orleans and Shreveport, Louisiana): name changed to Louisiana State University Health Science Center.

Mankato State University (Mankato, Minnesota): name changed to Minnesota State University, Mankato.

Massachusetts College of Pharmacy and Allied Health Sciences (Boston, Massachusetts): name changed to Massachusetts College of Pharmacy and Health Sciences.

Mennonite College of Nursing (Bloomington, Illinois): merged with Illinois State University (Normal, Illinois).

Mercer University, Cecil B. Day Campus (Atlanta, Georgia): data profiled under Mercer University (Macon, Georgia).

Mount Sinai School of Medicine of the City University of New York (New York, New York): name changed to Mount Sinai School of Medicine of New York University.

Mount Vernon College (Washington, District of Columbia): merged with The George Washington University (Washington, District of Columbia).

The Naropa Institute (Boulder, Colorado): name changed to The Naropa University.

Northwest Nazarene College (Nampa, Idaho): name changed to Northwest Nazarene University.

Philadelphia College of Textiles and Science (Philadelphia, Pennsylvania): name changed to Philadelphia University.

Phillips University (Enid, Oklahoma): closed.

Regional Seminary of Saint Vincent de Paul in Florida, Inc. (Boynton Beach, Florida): name changed to Saint Vincent de Paul Regional Seminary.

Rockhurst College (Kansas City, Missouri): name changed to Rockhurst University.

Saint Leo College (Saint Leo, Florida): name changed to Saint Leo University.

Southern California College (Costa Mesa, California): name changed to Vanguard University of Southern California.

University of Massachusetts Medical Center at Worcester (Worcester, Massachusetts): name changed to University of Massachusetts Worcester.

Westminster College of Salt Lake City (Salt Lake City, Utah): name changed to Westminster College.

Abbreviations Used in the Guides

The following list includes abbreviations of degree names used in the profiles in the 2000 edition of the guides. Because some degrees (e.g., Doctor of Education) can be abbreviated in more than one way (e.g., D.Ed. or Ed.D.), and because the abbreviations used in the guides reflect the preferences of the individual colleges and universities, the list may include two or more abbreviations for a single degree.

Degrees

A Mus D	Doctor of Musical Arts
AC	Advanced Certificate
AD	Artist's Diploma
ADP	Artist's Diploma
Adv C	Advanced Certificate
Adv M	Advanced Master
Aerospace E	Aerospace Engineer
AGC	Advanced Graduate Certificate
ALM	Master of Liberal Arts
AM	Master of Arts
AMRS	Master of Arts in Religious Studies
APC	Advanced Professional Certificate
App Sc	Applied Scientist
Au D	Doctor of Audiology
B Th	Bachelor of Theology
C Phil	Certificate in Philosophy
CAES	Certificate of Advanced Educational Specialization
CAGS	Certificate of Advanced Graduate Studies
CAL	Certificate in Applied Linguistics
CAMS	Certificate of Advanced Management Studies
CAPS	Certificate of Advanced Professional Studies
CAS	Certificate of Advanced Studies
CASPA	Certificate of Advanced Study in Public Administration
CASR	Certificate in Advanced Social Research
CBHS	Certificate in Basic Health Sciences
CCJA	Certificate in Criminal Justice Administration
CE	Civil Engineer
CG	Certificate in Gerontology
CGS	Certificate of Graduate Studies
Ch E	Chemical Engineer
CHSS	Counseling and Human Services Specialist
CIF	Certificate in International Finance
CITS	Certificate of Individual Theological Studies
CLIS	Certificate of Library and Information Science
CMH	Certificate in Medical Humanities
CMS	Certificate in Ministerial Studies Certificate in Museum Studies
CNM	Certificate in Nonprofit Management
CP	Certificate in Performance
CPC	Certificate in Professional Counseling Certificate in Publication and Communication
CPH	Certificate in Public Health
CPM	Certificate in Public Management
CPS	Certificate of Professional Studies
CSD	Certificate in Spiritual Direction
CSE	Computer Systems Engineer
CSS	Certificate of Special Studies
CTS	Certificate of Theological Studies
CURP	Certificate in Urban and Regional Planning
D Arch	Doctor of Architecture
D Chem	Doctor of Chemistry
D Ed	Doctor of Education
D Eng	Doctor of Engineering
D Engr	Doctor of Engineering
D Env	Doctor of Environment
D Jur	Doctor of Jurisprudence
D Law	Doctor of Law
D Litt	Doctor of Letters
D Med Sc	Doctor of Medical Science
D Min	Doctor of Ministry
D Min PCC	Doctor of Ministry, Pastoral Care, and Counseling
D Miss	Doctor of Missiology
D Mus	Doctor of Music
D Mus A	Doctor of Musical Arts
D Mus Ed	Doctor of Music Education
D Phil	Doctor of Philosophy
D Ps	Doctor of Psychology
D Sc	Doctor of Science
D Sc D	Doctor of Science in Dentistry
D Th	Doctor of Theology
DA	Doctor of Arts
DA Ed	Doctor of Arts in Education
DAST	Diploma of Advanced Studies in Teaching
DBA	Doctor of Business Administration
DC	Doctor of Chiropractic
DCC	Doctor of Computer Science
DCD	Doctor of Communications Design
DCL	Doctor of Comparative Law
DCM	Doctor of Church Music
DCS	Doctor of Computer Science
DDN	Diplôme du Droit Notarial
DDS	Doctor of Dental Surgery
DE	Doctor of Engineering

DEM	Doctor of Educational Ministry		**Ed DCT**	Doctor of Education in College Teaching
DEPD	Diplôme Études Spécialisées		**Ed M**	Master of Education
DES	Doctor of Engineering Science		**Ed S**	Specialist in Education
DESS	Diplôme Études Supérieures Spécialisées		**EDM**	Executive Doctorate in Management
DFA	Doctor of Fine Arts		**EE**	Electrical Engineer
DFES	Doctor of Forestry and Environmental Studies			Environmental Engineer
DGP	Diploma in Graduate and Professional Studies		**EM**	Mining Engineer
DHA	Doctor of Health Administration		**EMBA**	Executive Master of Business Administration
DHCE	Doctor of Health Care Ethics		**EMCIS**	Executive Master of Computer Information Systems
DHL	Doctor of Hebrew Letters		**EMIB**	Executive Master of International Business
	Doctor of Hebrew Literature		**EMPA**	Executive Master of Public Affairs
DHS	Doctor of Human Services		**EMRA**	Executive Master of Rehabilitation Administration
DIBA	Doctor of International Business Administration		**EMS**	Executive Master of Science
Dip CS	Diploma in Christian Studies		**EMSF**	Executive Master of Science in Finance
DIT	Doctor of Industrial Technology		**EMSILR**	Executive Master of Science in Industrial and Labor Relations
DJ Ed	Doctor of Jewish Education			
DJS	Doctor of Jewish Studies		**Eng**	Engineer
DM	Doctor of Management		**Eng Sc D**	Doctor of Engineering Science
	Doctor of Music		**Engr**	Engineer
DMA	Doctor of Musical Arts		**Exec Ed D**	Executive Doctor of Education
DMD	Doctor of Dental Medicine		**Exec MBA**	Executive Master of Business Administration
DME	Doctor of Music Education		**Exec MIM**	Executive Master of International Management
DML	Doctor of Modern Languages		**Exec MPA**	Executive Master of Public Administration
DMM	Doctor of Music Ministry		**Exec MPH**	Executive Master of Public Health
DN Sc	Doctor of Nursing Science		**Exec MS**	Executive Master of Science
DNS	Doctor of Nursing Science		**GDPA**	Graduate Diploma in Public Administration
DO	Doctor of Osteopathy		**GDRE**	Graduate Diploma in Religious Education
DPA	Doctor of Public Administration		**Geol E**	Geological Engineer
DPC	Doctor of Pastoral Counseling		**GMBA**	Global Master of Business Administration
DPDS	Doctor of Planning and Development Studies		**GPD**	Graduate Performance Diploma
DPE	Doctor of Physical Education		**GPMBA**	Global Professional Master of Business Administration
DPH	Doctor of Public Health			
DPM	Doctor of Podiatric Medicine		**HS Dir**	Director of Health and Safety
DPS	Doctor of Professional Studies		**HSD**	Doctor of Health and Safety
DPT	Doctor of Physical Therapy		**IAMBA**	Information Age Master of Business Administration
Dr DES	Doctor of Design		**IEMBA**	International Executive Master of Business Administration
Dr OT	Doctor of Occupational Therapy			
Dr PH	Doctor of Public Health		**IMA**	Interdisciplinary Master of Arts
Dr Sc PT	Doctor of Science in Physical Therapy		**IMBA**	International Master of Business Administration
DS Sc	Doctor of Social Science		**IOE**	Industrial and Operations Engineer
DSM	Doctor of Sacred Music		**JCD**	Doctor of Canon Law
	Doctor of Sport Management		**JCL**	Licentiate in Canon Law
DSN	Doctor of Science in Nursing		**JD**	Juris Doctor
DSW	Doctor of Social Work		**JSD**	Doctor of Juridical Science
DV Sc	Doctor of Veterinary Science			Doctor of Jurisprudence
DVM	Doctor of Veterinary Medicine			Doctor of the Science of Law
EAA	Engineer in Aeronautics and Astronautics		**JSM**	Master of Science of Law
EAS	Education Administration Specialist		**L Th**	Licenciate in Theology
Ed D	Doctor of Education		**LL B**	Bachelor of Laws

LL D	Doctor of Laws
LL M	Master of Laws
LL M CL	Master of Laws in Comparative Law
LL M T	Master of Laws in Taxation
M Ac	Master of Accountancy
	Master of Accounting
	Master of Acupuncture
M Ac OM	Master of Acupuncture and Oriental Medicine
M Acc	Master of Accountancy
	Master of Accounting
M Acct	Master of Accountancy
	Master of Accounting
M Accy	Master of Accountancy
M Acy	Master of Accountancy
M Ad	Master of Administration
M Ad Ed	Master of Adult Education
M Adm	Master of Administration
M Adm Mgt	Master of Administrative Management
M Aero E	Master of Aerospace Engineering
M Ag	Master of Agriculture
M Ag Ed	Master of Agricultural Education
M Agr	Master of Agriculture
M Anesth Ed	Master of Anesthesiology Education
M App St	Master of Applied Statistics
M Appl Stat	Master of Applied Statistics
M Aq	Master of Aquaculture
M Arch	Master of Architecture
M Arch E	Master of Architectural Engineering
M Arch H	Master of Architectural History
M Arch UD	Master of Architecture in Urban Design
M Bio E	Master of Bioengineering
M Biomath	Master of Biomathematics
M Bus Ed	Master of Business Education
M Ch E	Master of Chemical Engineering
M Chem	Master of Chemistry
M Cl D	Master of Clinical Dentistry
M Cl Sc	Master of Clinical Science
M Co E	Master of Computer Engineering
M Comp E	Master of Computer Engineering
M Coun	Master of Counseling
M Cp E	Master of Computer Engineering
M Dec S	Master of Decision Sciences
M Dent Sc	Master of Dental Sciences
M Des	Master of Design
M Des S	Master of Design Studies
M Div	Master of Divinity
M Div CM	Master of Divinity in Church Music
M Ec	Master of Economics
M Econ	Master of Economics
M Ed	Master of Education
M Ed T	Master of Education in Teaching
M En	Master of Engineering
M En S	Master of Environmental Sciences
M Eng	Master of Engineering
M Eng Mgt	Master of Engineering Management
M Engr	Master of Engineering
M Env	Master of Environment
M Env Des	Master of Environmental Design
M Env E	Master of Environmental Engineering
M Env Sc	Master of Environmental Science
M Ext Ed	Master of Extension Education
M Fin	Master of Finance
M Fr	Master of French
M Gen E	Master of General Engineering
M Geo E	Master of Geological Engineering
M Geoenv E	Master of Geoenvironmental Engineering
M Hum	Master of Humanities
M Hum Svcs	Master of Human Services
M In Ed	Master of Industrial Education
M Kin	Master of Kinesiology
M Land Arch	Master of Landscape Architecture
M Lit M	Master of Liturgical Music
M Litt	Master of Letters
M Mat SE	Master of Material Science and Engineering
M Math	Master of Mathematics
M Med Sc	Master of Medical Science
M Mgmt	Master of Management
M Mgt	Master of Management
M Min	Master of Ministries
M Miss	Master of Missiology
M Mtl E	Master of Materials Engineering
M Mu	Master of Music
M Mu Ed	Master of Music Education
M Mus	Master of Music
M Mus Ed	Master of Music Education
M Nat Sci	Master of Natural Science
M Nurs	Master of Nursing
M Oc E	Master of Oceanographic Engineering
M Pharm	Master of Pharmacy
M Phil	Master of Philosophy
M Phil F	Master of Philosophical Foundations
M Pl	Master of Planning
M Pol	Master of Political Science
M Pr A	Master of Professional Accountancy
M Pr Met	Master of Professional Meteorology
M Prob S	Master of Probability and Statistics
M Prof Past	Master of Professional Pastoral

M Ps	Master of Psychology
M Psych	Master of Psychology
M Pub	Master of Publishing
M Rel	Master of Religion
M Rel Ed	Master of Religious Education
M Sc	Master of Science
M Sc A	Master of Science (Applied)
M Sc BMC	Master of Science in Biomedical Communications
M Sc CS	Master of Science in Computer Science
M Sc E	Master of Science in Engineering
M Sc Eng	Master of Science in Engineering
M Sc Engr	Master of Science in Engineering
M Sc F	Master of Science in Forestry
M Sc FE	Master of Science in Forest Engineering
M Sc N	Master of Science in Nursing
M Sc P	Master of Science in Planning
M Sc Pl	Master of Science in Planning
M Sc PT	Master of Science in Physical Therapy
M Sc T	Master of Science in Teaching
M Soc	Master of Sociology
M Sp Ed	Master of Special Education
M Stat	Master of Statistics
M Sw E	Master of Software Engineering
M Sw En	Master of Software Engineering
M Tax	Master of Taxation
M Tech	Master of Technology
M Th	Master of Theology
M Th Past	Master of Pastoral Theology
M Tox	Master of Toxicology
M Trans E	Master of Transportation Engineering
M Vet Sc	Master of Veterinary Science
MA	Master of Arts
MA Comm	Master of Arts in Communication
MA Ed	Master of Arts in Education
MA Min	Master of Arts in Ministry
MA Missions	Master of Arts in Missions
MA Past St	Master of Arts in Pastoral Studies
MA Ps	Master of Arts in Psychology
MA Psych	Master of Arts in Psychology
MA Sc	Master of Applied Science
MA Th	Master of Arts in Theology
MA(R)	Master of Arts (Research)
MA(T)	Master of Arts in Teaching
MAA	Master of Administrative Arts Master of Applied Anthropology Master of Arts in Administration
MAAA	Master of Arts in Arts Administration
MAABS	Master of Arts in Applied Behavioral Sciences
MAAE	Master of Arts in Art Education
MAAT	Master of Arts in Applied Theology Master of Arts in Art Therapy
MAB	Master of Agribusiness
MABC	Master of Arts in Biblical Counseling
MABM	Master of Agribusiness Management
MABS	Master of Arts in Biblical Studies
MAC	Master of Accounting Master of Analytical Chemistry Master of Art Conservation Master of Arts in Communication Master of Arts in Counseling
MACAT	Master of Arts in Counseling Psychology: Art Therapy
MACCM	Master of Arts in Church and Community Ministry
MACE	Master of Arts in Christian Education Master of Arts in Computer Education
MACH	Master of Arts in Church History
MACL	Master of Arts in Classroom Psychology
MACM	Master of Arts in Christian Ministries Master of Arts in Church Music Master of Arts in Counseling Ministries
MACO	Master of Arts in Counseling
MACP	Master of Arts in Counseling Psychology
MACSE	Master of Arts in Christian School Education
MACT	Master of Arts in College Teaching
MACTM	Master of Applied Communication Theory and Methodology
MACY	Master of Arts in Accountancy
MAD	Master of Applied Development
MADH	Master of Applied Development and Health
MADR	Master of Arts in Dispute Resolution
MAE	Master of Aerospace Engineering Master of Agricultural Economics Master of Applied Economics Master of Architectural Engineering Master of Art Education Master of Arts in Education Master of Arts in English Master of Automotive Engineering
MAES	Master of Arts in Environmental Sciences
MAF	Master of Arts in Finance
MAFIS	Master of Accountancy and Financial Information Systems
MAFLL	Master of Arts in Foreign Language and Literature
MAFM	Master of Accounting and Financial Management
MAG	Master of Applied Geography
MAGP	Master of Arts in Gerontological Psychology
MAGU	Master of Urban Analysis and Management
MAH	Master of Arts in Humanities
MAHA	Master of Arts in Humanitarian Studies
MAHCD	Master of Applied Human and Community Development

MAHL	Master of Arts in Hebrew Letters
MAHRM	Master of Arts in Human Resources Management
MAHS	Master of Arts in Human Services
MAICS	Master of Arts in Intercultural Studies
MAIDM	Master of Arts in Interior Design and Merchandising
MAIND	Master of Arts in Interior Design
MAIPE	Master of Arts in International Political Economy
MAIR	Master of Arts in Industrial Relations
MAIS	Master of Accounting and Information Systems
	Master of Arts in Intercultural Studies
	Master of Arts in Interdisciplinary Studies
	Master of Arts in International Studies
MAJ	Master of Arts in Journalism
MAJ Ed	Master of Arts in Jewish Education
MAJC	Master of Arts in Journalism and Communication
MAJCS	Master of Arts in Jewish Communal Service
MAJE	Master of Arts in Jewish Education
MAJS	Master of Arts in Jewish Studies
MALA	Master of Arts in Liberal Arts
	Master of Arts in Liturgical Arts
MALAS	Master of Arts in Latin American Studies
MALD	Master of Arts in Law and Diplomacy
MALER	Master of Arts in Labor and Employment Relations
MALIS	Master of Arts in Library and Information Science
MALL	Master of Arts in Liberal Learning
MALS	Master of Arts in Landscape Studies
	Master of Arts in Liberal Studies
MAM	Master of Agriculture and Management
	Master of Applied Mathematics
	Master of Applied Mechanics
	Master of Arts in Management
	Master of Arts Management
	Master of Avian Medicine
MAM Sc	Master of Applied Mathematical Science
MAMB	Master of Applied Molecular Biology
MAMC	Master of Arts in Mass Communication
MAME	Master of Arts in Missions/Evangelism
MAMFC	Master of Arts in Marriage and Family Counseling
MAMFCC	Master of Arts in Marriage, Family, and Child Counseling
MAMFT	Master of Arts in Marriage and Family Therapy
MAML	Master of Arts in School Media Librarianship
MAMM	Master of Arts in Ministry Management
	Master of Arts in Music Ministry
MAMS	Master of Applied Mathematical Sciences
	Master of Arts in Ministerial Studies
	Master of Associated Medical Sciences
MAMT	Master of Arts in Mathematics Teaching
MANM	Master of Arts in Nonprofit Management
MANT	Master of Arts in New Testament
MAO	Master of Arts in Organizational Psychology
MAOE	Master of Adult and Occupational Education
MAOM	Master of Arts in Organizational Management
MAOT	Master of Arts in Old Testament
MAP	Master of Applied Politics
	Master of Applied Psychology
	Master of Arts in Planning
	Master of Arts in Politics
	Master of Public Administration
MAP Min	Master of Arts in Pastoral Ministry
MAPA	Master of Arts in Public Administration
MAPC	Master of Arts in Pastoral Counseling
MAPEB	Master of Arts in Politics, Economics, and Business
MAPM	Master of Arts in Pastoral Ministry
MAPP	Master of Arts in Public Policy
MAPS	Master of Arts in Pastoral Studies
MAPW	Master of Arts in Professional Writing
MAR	Master of Arts in Religion
Mar Eng	Marine Engineer
MARC	Master of Arts in Religious Communication
MARE	Master of Arts in Religious Education
MARL	Master of Arts in Religious Leadership
MARS	Master of Arts in Religious Studies
MART	Master of Arts in Religion and Theology
MAS	Master of Accounting Science
	Master of Actuarial Science
	Master of Administrative Science
	Master of Aeronautical Science
	Master of American Studies
	Master of Applied Science
	Master of Applied Statistics
	Master of Archival Studies
MASA	Master of Advanced Studies in Architecture
MASAC	Master of Arts in Substance Abuse Counseling
MASD	Master of Arts in Spiritual Direction
MASF	Master of Arts in Spiritual Formation
MASLA	Master of Advanced Studies in Landscape Architecture
MASM	Master of Arts in Special Ministries
	Master of Arts in Specialized Ministries
MASP	Master of Arts in School Psychology
MASPAA	Master of Arts in Sports and Athletic Administration
MASS	Master of Applied Social Science
	Master of Arts in Social Science
MAT	Master of Arts in Teaching
	Master of Arts in Theology
Mat E	Materials Engineer
MATA	Master of Arts in Theology and the Arts
MATCM	Master of Acupuncture and Traditional Chinese Medicine
MATE	Master of Arts for the Teaching of English
MATESL	Master of Arts in Teaching English as a Second Language
MATESOL	Master of Arts in Teaching English to Speakers of Other Languages

MATEX	Master of Arts in Textiles
MATFL	Master of Arts in Teaching Foreign Language
MATH	Master of Arts in Therapy
MATI	Master of Administration of Information Technology
MATL	Master of Arts in Teaching of Languages
MATM	Master of Arts in Teaching of Mathematics
MATS	Master of Arts in Theological Studies Master of Arts in Transforming Spirituality
MAUA	Master of Arts in Urban Affairs
MAUD	Master of Arts in Urban Design
MAUM	Master of Arts in Urban Ministry
MAUPRD	Master of Arts in Urban Planning and Real Estate Development
MAURP	Master of Arts in Urban and Regional Planning
MAW	Master of Arts in Writing
MAWB	Master of Arts in Wildlife Biology
MAWS	Master of Arts in Women's Studies
MBA	Master of Business Administration
MBA Arts	Master of Business Administration in Arts
MBA-EP	Master of Business Administration–Experienced Professionals
MBA-PE	Master of Business Administration–Physician's Executive
MBAA	Master of Business Administration in Aviation
MBAE	Master of Biological and Agricultural Engineering Master of Biosystems and Agricultural Engineering
MBAi	Master of Business Administration–International
MBAIB	Master of Business Administration in International Business
MBAPA	Master of Business Administration–Physician Assistant
MBATM	Master of Business in Telecommunication Management
MBC	Master of Building Construction
MBE	Master of Bilingual Education Master of Biomedical Engineering Master of Business Education
MBHCM	Master of Behavioral Health Care Management
MBMSE	Master of Business Management and Software Engineering
MBOL	Master of Business and Organizational Leadership
MBS	Master of Basic Science Master of Behavioral Science Master of Biblical Studies Master of Biological Science Master of Biomedical Sciences Master of Building Science Master of Business Studies
MBSI	Master of Business Information Science
MBT	Master of Business Taxation
MC	Master of Communication Master of Counseling
MC Ed	Master of Continuing Education

MC Sc	Master of Computer Science
MCA	Master of Arts in Applied Criminology Master of Commercial Aviation
MCC	Master of Computer Science
MCD	Master of Communications Disorders
MCE	Master of Civil Engineering Master of Computer Engineering Master of Construction Engineering Master of Continuing Education Master of Control Engineering
MCED	Master of Community Economic Development
MCEM	Master of Construction Engineering Management
MCG	Master of Clinical Gerontology
MCH	Master of Community Health
MCIS	Master of Communication and Information Studies Master of Computer and Information Science Master of Computer Information Systems
MCJ	Master of Criminal Justice
MCJA	Master of Criminal Justice Administration
MCL	Master of Canon Law Master of Christian Leadership Master of Civil Law Master of Comparative Law
MCM	Master of Church Management Master of Church Ministry Master of Church Music Master of City Management Master of Construction Management
MCMS	Master of Clinical Medical Science
MCP	Master of City Planning Master of Community Planning Master of Community Psychology Master of Counseling Psychology
MCPD	Master of Community Planning and Development
MCRP	Master of City and Regional Planning
MCS	Master of Christian Studies Master of Combined Sciences Master of Communication Studies Master of Computer Science
MCSM	Master of Construction Science/Management
MD	Doctor of Medicine
MDA	Master of Development Administration
MDE	Master of Developmental Economics Master of Distance Education
MDR	Master of Dispute Resolution
MDS	Master of Dental Surgery
ME	Master of Education Master of Engineering
ME Sc	Master of Engineering Science
MEA	Master of Engineering Administration
MEC	Master of Electronic Commerce
MECE	Master of Electrical and Computer Engineering
Mech E	Mechanical Engineer
MED	Master of Education of the Deaf

MEDS	Master of Environmental Design Studies	**MGCOD**	Master of Group Counseling and Organizational Dynamics
MEE	Master of Electrical Engineering Master of Environmental Engineering	**MGD**	Master of Graphic Design
MEEM	Master of Environmental Engineering and Management	**MGE**	Master of Geotechnical Engineering
		MGH	Master of Geriatric Health
MEENE	Master of Engineering in Environmental Engineering	**MGIS**	Master of Geographic Information Science
MEERM	Master of Earth and Environmental Resource Management	**MGP**	Master of Gestion de Projet
		MGPGP	Master of Group Process and Group Psychotherapy
MEL	Master of Educational Leadership	**MGS**	Master of General Studies Master of Gerontological Studies
MEM	Master of Ecosystem Management Master of Engineering Management Master of Environmental Management Master of Marketing	**MH**	Master of Humanities
		MH Sc	Master of Health Sciences
MEMS	Master of Emergency Medical Service Master of Engineering in Manufacturing Systems	**MHA**	Master of Health Administration Master of Healthcare Administration Master of Hospitality Administration
MENVEGR	Master of Environmental Engineering	**MHAMS**	Master of Historical Administration and Museum Studies
MEP	Master of Engineering Physics Master of Environmental Planning	**MHCA**	Master of Health Care Administration
MEPC	Master of Environmental Pollution Control	**MHCI**	Master of Human-Computer Interaction
MEPD	Master of Education–Professional Development	**MHD**	Master of Human Development
MEPM	Master of Environmental Policy and Management	**MHE**	Master of Health Education Master of Home Economics Master of Human Ecology
MES	Master of Engineering Science Master of Environmental Science Master of Environmental Studies Master of Special Education	**MHE Ed**	Master of Home Economics Education
		MHHS	Master of Health and Human Services
MESM	Master of Environmental Science and Management	**MHK**	Master of Human Kinetics
MESS	Master of Exercise and Sport Sciences	**MHL**	Master of Hebrew Literature
MET	Master of Education in Teaching	**MHM**	Master of Hospitality Management Master of Hotel Management
Met E	Metallurgical Engineer	**MHMS**	Master of Health Management Systems
METM	Master of Engineering and Technology Management	**MHP**	Master of Health Physics Master of Health Professions Master of Heritage Preservation Master of Historic Preservation
MEVE	Master of Environmental Engineering		
MF	Master of Forestry	**MHPA**	Master of Heath Policy and Administration
MFA	Master of Fine Arts	**MHPE**	Master of Health Professions Education Master of Health Promotion and Education
MFAS	Master of Fisheries and Aquatic Science		
MFAW	Master of Fine Arts in Writing	**MHR**	Master of Human Resources
MFC	Master of Forest Conservation	**MHRD**	Master in Human Resource Development
MFCC	Marriage and Family Counseling Certificate Marriage, Family, and Child Counseling	**MHRDL**	Master of Human Resource Development Leadership
MFCS	Master of Family and Consumer Sciences	**MHRDOD**	Master of Human Resource Development/Organizational Development
MFE	Master of Forest Engineering		
MFR	Master of Forest Resources	**MHRIM**	Master of Hotel, Restaurant, and Institutional Management
MFRC	Master of Forest Resources and Conservation		
MFS	Master of Family Studies Master of Food Science Master of Forensic Sciences Master of Forest Science Master of Forest Studies Master of French Studies	**MHRIR**	Master of Human Resources and Industrial Relations
		MHRLR	Master of Human Resources and Labor Relations
		MHRM	Master of Human Resources Management
MFT	Master of Family Therapy	**MHROD**	Master of Human Resources and Organization Development
MGA	Master of Government Administration		

MHRTA	Master in Hotel, Restaurant, Tourism, and Administration
MHS	Master of Health Sciences
	Master of Healthcare Systems
	Master of Hispanic Studies
	Master of Human Services
MHSA	Master of Health Services Administration
	Master of Human Services Administration
MHSE	Master of Health Science Education
MI	Master of Instruction
MI Arch	Master of Interior Architecture
MI St	Master of Information Studies
MIA	Master of Interior Architecture
	Master of International Affairs
MIAA	Master of International Affairs and Administration
MIB	Master of International Business
MIBA	Master of International Business Administration
MIBS	Master of International Business Studies
MID	Master of Industrial Design
	Master of Interior Design
MIE	Master of Industrial Engineering
MIE Mgmt	Master of Industrial Engineering Management
MIHE	Master of Integrated Humanities and Education
MIHM	Master of International Health Management
MIIM	Master of International and Intercultural Management
MIJ	Master of International Journalism
MILR	Master of Industrial and Labor Relations
MIM	Master of Information Management
	Master of International Management
MIMLA	Master of International Management for Latin America
MIMOT	Master of International Management of Technology
MIMS	Master of Information Management and Systems
	Master of Integrated Manufacturing Systems
MIP	Master of Infrastructure Planning
	Master of Intellectual Property
MIPP	Master of International Public Policy
MIR	Master of Industrial Relations
MIS	Master of Industrial Statistics
	Master of Information Science
	Master of Information Systems
	Master of Interdisciplinary Studies
MISM	Master of Information Systems Management
MIT	Master in Teaching
	Master of Industrial Technology
	Master of Information Technology
	Master of Initial Teaching
	Master of International Trade
MITA	Master of Information Technology Administration
MITE	Master of Information Technology Education
MITM	Master of International Technology Management

MJ	Master of Journalism
	Master of Jurisprudence
MJ Ed	Master of Jewish Education
MJA	Master of Justice Administration
MJPM	Master of Justice Policy and Management
MJS	Master of Judaic Studies
	Master of Judicial Studies
	Master of Juridical Science
ML Arch	Master of Landscape Architecture
MLA	Master of Landscape Architecture
	Master of Liberal Arts
MLAS	Master of Laboratory Animal Science
MLAUD	Master of Landscape Architecture in Urban Development
MLD	Master of Leadership Studies
MLE	Master of Applied Linguistics and Exegesis
MLERE	Master of Land Economics and Real Estate
MLHR	Master of Labor and Human Resources
MLI	Master of Legal Institutions
MLI Sc	Master of Library and Information Science
MLIR	Master of Labor and Industrial Relations
MLIS	Master of Library and Information Science
	Master of Library and Information Services
	Master of Library and Information Studies
MLLS	Master of Leadership and Liberal Studies
MLM	Master of Library Media
MLRHR	Master of Labor Relations and Human Resources
MLS	Master of Legal Studies
	Master of Liberal Studies
	Master of Library Science
	Master of Life Sciences
	Master of Medical Laboratory Sciences
MLSP	Master of Law and Social Policy
MM	Master of Management
	Master of Ministry
	Master of Music
MM Ed	Master of Music Education
MM Sc	Master of Medical Science
MM St	Master of Museum Studies
MMA	Master of Management and Administration
	Master of Marine Affairs
	Master of Media Arts
	Master of Musical Arts
MMAE	Master of Mechanical and Aerospace Engineering
MMAS	Master of Military Art and Science
MMC	Master of Mass Communications
MMCM	Master of Music in Church Music
MME	Master of Manufacturing Engineering
	Master of Mathematics for Educators
	Master of Mechanical Engineering
	Master of Medical Engineering
	Master of Mining Engineering
	Master of Music Education
MMF	Master of Mathematical Finance

MMFT	Master of Marriage and Family Therapy	**MPA**	Master of Physician Assistant
MMH	Master of Management in Hospitality		Master of Professional Accountancy
	Master of Medical History		Master of Professional Accounting
	Master of Medical Humanities		Master of Public Administration
MMIS	Master of Management Information Systems		Master of Public Affairs
MMM	Master of Manufacturing Management	**MPA-URP**	Master of Public Affairs and Urban and Regional Planning
	Master of Medical Management	**MPAID**	Master of Public Administration and International Development
MMME	Master of Metallurgical and Materials Engineering		
MMP	Master of Marine Policy	**MPAS**	Master of Physical Activity Studies
MMPA	Master of Management and Professional Accounting		Master of Physician Assistant Studies
			Master of Public Art Studies
MMR	Master of Marketing Research	**MPC**	Master of Pastoral Counseling
MMS	Master of Management Science		Master of Professional Communication
	Master of Management Studies		Master of Professional Counseling
	Master of Manufacturing Systems	**MPDS**	Master of Planning and Development Studies
	Master of Marine Science	**MPE**	Master of Physical Education
	Master of Marine Studies	**MPEM**	Master of Project Engineering and Management
	Master of Materials Science	**MPH**	Master of Public Health
	Master of Medical Science	**MPHE**	Master of Public Health Education
	Master of Medieval Studies	**MPHTM**	Master of Public Health and Tropical Medicine
MMSE	Master of Manufacturing Systems Engineering	**MPIA**	Master of Public and International Affairs
MMT	Master of Music Therapy	**MPM**	Master of Pest Management
MN	Master of Nursing		Master of Practical Ministries
MN Sc	Master of Nursing Science		Master of Project Management
MNA	Master of Nonprofit Administration		Master of Public Management
	Master of Nurse Anesthesia	**MPP**	Master of Public Policy
	Master of Nursing Administration	**MPPA**	Master of Public Policy Administration
MNAS	Master of Natural and Applied Science		Master of Public Policy and Administration
MNE	Master of Nuclear Engineering	**MPPM**	Master of Public and Private Management
MNM	Master of Nonprofit Management		Master of Public Policy and Management
MNO	Master of Nonprofit Organization	**MPPPM**	Master of Plant Protection and Pest Management
MNPL	Master of Not-for-Profit Leadership	**MPPUP**	Master of Public Policy and Urban Planning
MNR	Master of Natural Resources	**MPRTM**	Master of Parks, Recreation, and Tourism Management
MNRM	Master of Natural Resource Management		
MNS	Master of Natural Science	**MPS**	Master of Pastoral Studies
MOA	Maître d'Orthophonie et d'Audiologie		Master of Policy Sciences
MOB	Master of Organizational Behavior		Master of Political Science
MOD	Master of Organizational Development		Master of Preservation Studies
MOH	Master of Occupational Health		Master of Professional Studies
MOL	Master of Organizational Leadership		Master of Public Service
MOM	Master of Manufacturing	**MPSA**	Master of Public Service Administration
MOR	Master of Operations Research	**MPSRE**	Master of Professional Studies in Real Estate
MOT	Master of Occupational Therapy	**MPT**	Master of Physical Therapy
MoTM	Master of Technology Management	**MPVM**	Master of Preventive Veterinary Medicine
MP	Master of Planning	**MPW**	Master of Public Works
MP Ac	Master of Professional Accountancy	**MQM**	Master of Quality Management
MP Acc	Master of Professional Accountancy	**MQS**	Master of Quality Systems
	Master of Professional Accounting	**MRC**	Master of Rehabilitation Counseling
MP Acct	Master of Professional Accounting	**MRCP**	Master of Regional and City Planning
MP Aff	Master of Public Affairs		Master of Regional and Community Planning
MP Th	Master of Pastoral Theology	**MRE**	Master of Religious Education
		MRECM	Master of Real Estate and Construction Management

MRED	Master of Real Estate Development
MRLS	Master of Resources Law Studies
MRM	Master of Rehabilitation Medicine
	Master of Resources Management
MRP	Master of Regional Planning
MRRA	Master of Recreation Resources Administration
MRS	Master of Religious Studies
MRTP	Master of Rural and Town Planning
MS	Master of Science
MS Acct	Master of Science in Accounting
MS Accy	Master of Science in Accountancy
MS Admin	Master of Science in Administration
MS Ag	Master of Science in Agriculture
MS Arch	Master of Science in Architecture
MS Arch St	Master of Science in Architectural Studies
MS Bio E	Master of Science in Biomedical Engineering
MS Biol	Master of Science in Biology
MS Bm E	Master of Science in Biomedical Engineering
MS Ch E	Master of Science in Chemical Engineering
MS Chem	Master of Science in Chemistry
MS Civ E	Master of Science in Civil Engineering
MS Cp E	Master of Science in Computer Engineering
MS Eco	Master of Science in Economics
MS Econ	Master of Science in Economics
MS Ed	Master of Science in Education
MS En E	Master of Science in Environmental Engineering
MS Eng	Master of Science in Engineering
MS Engr	Master of Science in Engineering
MS Env E	Master of Science in Environmental Engineering
MS Int A	Master of Science in International Affairs
MS Mat	Master of Science in Materials Engineering
MS Mat E	Master of Science in Materials Engineering
MS Mat SE	Master of Science in Material Science and Engineering
MS Math	Master of Science in Mathematics
MS Met E	Master of Science in Metallurgical Engineering
MS Metr	Master of Science in Meteorology
MS Mfg E	Master of Science in Manufacturing Engineering
MS Mgt	Master of Science in Management
MS Min	Master of Science in Mining
MS Mt E	Master of Science in Materials Engineering
MS Nsg	Master of Science in Nursing
MS Pet E	Master of Science in Petroleum Engineering
MS Phr	Master of Science in Pharmacy
MS Phys	Master of Science in Physics
MS Phys Op	Master of Science in Physiological Optics
MS Poly	Master of Science in Polymers
MS Psy	Master of Science in Psychology
MS Pub P	Master of Science in Public Policy
MS Sp Ed	Master of Science in Special Education
MS Stat	Master of Science in Statistics
MS Text	Master of Science in Textiles
MS(R)	Master of Science (Research)
MSA	Master of School Administration
	Master of Science Administration
	Master of Science in Accountancy
	Master of Science in Accounting
	Master of Science in Administration
	Master of Science in Agriculture
	Master of Science in Anesthesia
	Master of Science in Architecture
	Master of Science in Aviation
	Master of Sports Administration
MSA Phy	Master of Science in Applied Physics
MSAA	Master of Science in Astronautics and Aeronautics
MSAAE	Master of Science in Aeronautical and Astronautical Engineering
MSABE	Master of Science in Agricultural and Biological Engineering
MSACC	Master of Science in Accounting
MSAE	Master of Science in Aeronautical Engineering
	Master of Science in Aerospace Engineering
	Master of Science in Agricultural Engineering
	Master of Science in Applied Economics
	Master of Science in Architectural Engineering
	Master of Science in Art Education
MSAER	Master of Science in Aerospace Engineering
MSAIS	Master of Science in Accounting Information Systems
MSAM	Master of Science in Advanced Management
	Master of Science in Applied Mathematics
MSAP	Master of Science in Applied Psychology
MSAS	Master of Science in Architectural Studies
MSAT	Master of Science in Advanced Technology
MSB	Master of Science in Bible
	Master of Science in Business
MSBA	Master of Science in Business Administration
MSBAE	Master of Science in Biological and Agricultural Engineering
	Master of Science in Biosystems and Agricultural Engineering
MSBE	Master of Science in Biomedical Engineering
	Master of Science in Business Education
MSBENG	Master of Science in Bioengineering
MSBMS	Master of Science in Basic Medical Science
MSBS	Master of Science in Biomedical Sciences
MSC	Master of Science in Commerce
	Master of Science in Communication
	Master of Science in Computers
	Master of Science in Criminology
MSCC	Master of Science in Christian Counseling
MSCD	Master of Science in Communication Disorders
	Master of Science in Community Development

MSCE	Master of Science in Civil Engineering Master of Science in Clinical Epidemiology Master of Science in Computer Engineering Master of Science in Continuing Education	**MSES**	Master of Science in Engineering Science Master of Science in Environmental Science Master of Science in Environmental Studies
MSCEE	Master of Science in Civil and Environmental Engineering	**MSESM**	Master of Science in Engineering Science and Mechanics
MSCF	Master of Science in Computational Finance	**MSESS**	Master of Science in Exercise and Sport Studies
MSCIS	Master of Science in Computer and Information Systems Master of Science in Computer Information Systems	**MSET**	Master of Science in Engineering Technology
		MSETM	Master of Science in Environmental Technology Management
		MSEV	Master of Science in Environmental Engineering
MSCJ	Master of Science in Criminal Justice	**MSF**	Master of Science in Finance Master of Science in Forestry
MSCJA	Master of Science in Criminal Justice Administration	**MSFAM**	Master of Science in Family Studies
MSCLS	Master of Science in Clinical Laboratory Science	**MSFDE**	Master of Science in Family Development Education
MSCNU	Master of Science in Clinical Nutrition	**MSFM**	Master of Financial Management
MSCP	Master of Science in Clinical Psychology Master of Science in Counseling Psychology	**MSFOR**	Master of Science in Forestry
MSCRP	Master of Science in City and Regional Planning Master of Science in Community and Regional Planning	**MSFS**	Master of Science in Financial Sciences Master of Science in Forensic Science
		MSFT	Master of Science in Family Therapy
MSCS	Master of Science in Computer Science	**MSG**	Master of Science in Gerontology
MSCSD	Master of Science in Communication Sciences and Disorders	**MSGC**	Master of Science in Genetic Counseling
		MSGFA	Master of Science in Global Financial Analysis
MSCSE	Master of Science in Computer and Systems Engineering Master of Science in Computer Science and Engineering Master of Science in Computer Systems Engineering	**MSH**	Master of Science in Health Master of Science in Hospice
		MSH Ed	Master of Science in Health Education
		MSHA	Master of Science in Health Administration
		MSHCI	Master of Science in Human Computer Interaction
MSD	Master of Science in Dentistry Master of Science in Design	**MSHCPM**	Master of Science in Health Care Policy and Management
MSDD	Master of Software Design and Development	**MSHCS**	Master of Science in Human and Consumer Science
MSE	Master of Science Education Master of Science in Education Master of Science in Engineering Master of Software Engineering Master of Structural Engineering	**MSHES**	Master of Science in Human Environmental Sciences
		MSHFID	Master of Science in Human Factors in Information Design
MSE Mgt	Master of Science in Engineering Management	**MSHFS**	Master of Science in Human Factors and Systems
MSEAS	Master of Science in Earth and Atmospheric Sciences	**MSHP**	Master of Science in Health Professions
		MSHR	Master of Science in Human Resources
MSEC	Master of Science in Economic Aspects of Chemistry	**MSHRM**	Master of Science in Human Resource Management
MSECE	Master of Science in Electrical and Computer Engineering	**MSHROD**	Master of Science in Human Resources and Organizational Development
MSED	Master of Sustainable Economic Development	**MSHS**	Master of Science in Health Science Master of Science in Health Services Master of Science in Health Systems
MSEE	Master of Science in Electrical Engineering Master of Science in Environmental Engineering		
MSEH	Master of Science in Environmental Health	**MSHSA**	Master of Science in Human Service Administration
MSEL	Master of Science in Executive Leadership Master of Studies in Environmental Law	**MSHSE**	Master of Science in Health Science Education
		MSHT	Master of Science in History of Technology
MSEM	Master of Science in Engineering Management Master of Science in Engineering Mechanics Master of Science in Engineering of Mines Master of Science in Environmental Management	**MSI**	Master of Science in Instruction Master of Science in Insurance
		MSIA	Master of Science in Industrial Administration
MSENE	Master of Science in Environmental Engineering	**MSIAM**	Master of Science in Information Age Marketing

MSIB	Master of Science in International Business
MSIDM	Master of Science in Interior Design and Merchandising
MSIDT	Master of Science in Information Design and Technology
MSIE	Master of Science in Industrial Engineering Master of Science in International Economics
MSIL	Master of Science in International Logistics
MSIMC	Master of Science in Information Management and Communication Master of Science in Integrated Marketing Communications
MSIO	Master of Science in Industrial Optimization
MSIPC	Master of Science in Information Processing and Communications
MSIR	Master of Science in Industrial Relations
MSIS	Master of Science in Information Science Master of Science in Information Systems Master of Science in Interdisciplinary Studies
MSISM	Master of Science in Information Systems Management
MSIT	Master of Science in Industrial Technology Master of Science in Information Technology Master of Science in Instructional Technology
MSITM	Master of Science in Information Technology Management
MSJ	Master of Science in Journalism Master of Science in Jurisprudence
MSJBS	Master of Science in Japanese Business Studies
MSJJ	Master of Science in Juvenile Justice
MSJPS	Master of Science in Justice and Public Safety
MSJS	Master of Science in Jewish Studies
MSK	Master of Science in Kinesiology
MSL	Master of School Leadership Master of Science in Limnology Master of Studies in Law
MSLA	Master of Science in Legal Administration
MSLP	Master of Speech-Language Pathology
MSLS	Master of Science in Legal Studies Master of Science in Library Science Master of Science in Logistics Systems
MSLT	Master of Second Language Teaching
MSM	Master of Sacred Music Master of School Mathematics Master of Science in Management
MSMAE	Master of Science in Materials Engineering
MSMC	Master of Science in Management and Communications Master of Science in Mass Communications
MSMCS	Master of Science in Management and Computer Science
MSME	Master of Science in Mechanical Engineering
MSMFE	Master of Science in Manufacturing Engineering
MSMfSE	Master of Science in Manufacturing Systems Engineering

MSMGEN	Master of Science in Management and General Engineering
MSMI	Master of Science in Medical Illustration
MSMIS	Master of Science in Management Information Systems
MSMM	Master of Science in Manufacturing Management
MSMOT	Master of Science in Management of Technology
MSMS	Master of Science in Management Science
MSMSA	Master of Science in Management Systems Analysis
MSMSE	Master of Science in Manufacturing Systems Engineering Master of Science in Material Science and Engineering Master of Science in Mathematics and Science Education
MSMT	Master of Science in Medical Technology
MSN	Master of Science in Nursing
MSN(R)	Master of Science in Nursing (Research)
MSNA	Master of Science in Nurse Anesthesia
MSNE	Master of Science in Nuclear Engineering
MSNS	Master of Science in Natural Science
MSOB	Master of Science in Organizational Behavior
MSOD	Master of Science in Organizational Development
MSOL	Master of Science in Organizational Leadership
MSOM	Master of Science in Organization and Management Master of Science in Oriental Medicine
MSOR	Master of Science in Operations Research
MSOT	Master of Science in Occupational Technology Master of Science in Occupational Therapy
MSP	Master of Science in Pharmacy Master of Science in Planning Master of Speech Pathology
MSP Ex	Master of Science in Exercise Physiology
MSPA	Master of Science in Professional Accountancy Master of Science in Professional Accounting
MSPAS	Master of Science in Physician Assistant Studies
MSPC	Master of Science in Professional Communications
MSPE	Master of Science in Petroleum Engineering Master of Science in Physical Education
MSPFP	Master of Science in Personal Financial Planning
MSPG	Master of Science in Psychology
MSPH	Master of Science in Public Health
MSPHR	Master of Science in Pharmacy
MSPNGE	Master of Science in Petroleum and Natural Gas Engineering
MSPS	Master of Science in Pharmaceutical Science Master of Science in Psychological Services
MSPT	Master of Science in Physical Therapy
MSQSM	Master of Science in Quality Systems Management
MSR	Master of Science in Rehabilitation Sciences
MSRA	Master of Science in Recreation Administration

MSRC	Master of Science in Resource Conservation	**MTCM**	Master of Traditional Chinese Medicine
MSRE	Master of Science in Religious Education	**MTD**	Master of Training and Development
MSRMP	Master of Science in Radiological Medical Physics	**MTE**	Master of Teacher Education
MSRS	Master of Science in Recreational Studies	**MTEL**	Master of Telecommunications
MSRTM	Master of Science in Resort and Tourism Management	**MTESL**	Master in Teaching English as a Second Language
MSS	Master of Science in Sociology	**MTHM**	Master of Tourism and Hospitality Management
	Master of Science in Software	**MTI**	Master of Information Technology
	Master of Social Science	**MTLM**	Master of Transportation and Logistics Management
	Master of Social Services		
	Master of Special Studies	**MTM**	Master of Technology Management
	Master of Sports Science		Master of Telecommunications Management
MSSA	Master of Science in Social Administration		Master of the Teaching of Mathematics
MSSE	Master of Science in Software Engineering	**MTMH**	Master of Tropical Medicine and Hygiene
MSSI	Master of Science in Strategic Intelligence	**MTOM**	Master of Traditional Oriental Medicine
MSSL	Master of Science in Speech and Language	**MTP**	Master of Transpersonal Psychology
MSSM	Master of Science in Systems Management	**MTPW**	Master of Technical and Professional Writing
MSSPA	Master of Science in Student Personnel Administration	**MTS**	Master of Teaching Science
			Master of Theological Studies
MSSS	Master of Science in Systems Science	**MTSC**	Master of Technical and Scientific Communication
MSSW	Master of Science in Social Work	**MTSE**	Master of Telecommunications and Software Engineering
MST	Master of Science in Taxation		
	Master of Science in Teaching	**MTX**	Master of Taxation
	Master of Science in Technology	**MUA**	Master of Urban Affairs
	Master of Science in Telecommunications	**MUD**	Master of Urban Design
	Master of Science in Transportation	**MUP**	Master of Urban Planning
	Master of Science Teaching	**MUPDD**	Master of Urban Planning, Design, and Development
	Master of Science Technology		
	Master of Systems Technology	**MUPP**	Master of Urban Planning and Policy
MST Ch	Master of Science in Textile Chemistry	**MURP**	Master of Urban and Regional Planning
MSTA	Master of Science in Statistics		Master of Urban and Rural Planning
MSTC	Master of Science in Telecommunications	**MURPL**	Master of Urban and Regional Planning
MSTD	Master of Science in Training and Development	**MUS**	Master of Urban Studies
MSTE	Master of Science in Technical Education	**Mus AD**	Doctor of Musical Arts
	Master of Science in Textile Engineering	**Mus Doc**	Doctor of Music
	Master of Science in Transportation Engineering	**Mus M**	Master of Music
MSTM	Master of Science in Technical Management	**MVE**	Master of Vocational Education
	Master of Science in Technology Management	**MVT Ed**	Master of Vocational and Technical Education
MSUD	Master of Science in Urban Design	**MVTE**	Master of Vocational-Technical Education
MSUESM	Master of Science in Urban Environmental Systems Management	**MWC**	Master of Wildlife Conservation
		MWPS	Master of Wood and Paper Science
MSVE	Master of Science in Vocational Education	**MWR**	Master of Water Resources
MSW	Master of Social Work	**MWS**	Master of Women's Studies
MSWE	Master of Software Engineering	**MZS**	Master of Zoological Science
MSWREE	Master of Science in Water Resources and Environmental Engineering	**Nav Arch**	Naval Architecture
		Naval E	Naval Engineer
MT	Master of Taxation	**ND**	Doctor of Naturopathic Medicine
	Master of Teaching		Doctor of Nursing
	Master of Technology		
	Master of Textiles	**NE**	Nuclear Engineer
MTA	Master of Arts in Teaching	**NPMC**	Nonprofit Management Certificate
	Master of Tax Accounting		
	Master of Teaching Arts	**Nuc E**	Nuclear Engineer
	Master of Tourism Administration		
MTC	Master of Technical Communications		

Ocean E	Ocean Engineer		SLPD	Doctor of Speech-Language Pathology
OD	Doctor of Optometry		SLS	Specialist in Library Science
OTD	Doctor of Occupational Therapy		SM	Master of Science
PD	Professional Diploma		SM Arch S	Master of Science in Architectural Studies
PDD	Professional Development Degree		SM Vis S	Master of Science in Visual Studies
PE Dir	Director of Physical Education		SMBT	Master of Science in Building Technology
PED	Doctor of Physical Education		SP	Specialist Degree
PGC	Post-Graduate Certificate		Sp C	Specialist in Counseling
Ph L	Licentiate of Philosophy		Sp Ed	Specialist in Education
Pharm D	Doctor of Pharmacy		Sp Ed S	Special Education Specialist
PhD	Doctor of Philosophy		SPS	School Psychology Specialist
PMBA	Professional Master of Business Administration		Spt	Specialist Degree
PMC	Post Master's Certificate		SSP	Specialist in School Psychology
PMSA	Professional Master of Science in Accounting		STB	Bachelor of Sacred Theology
Psy D	Doctor of Psychology		STD	Doctor of Sacred Theology
Psy M	Master of Psychology		STL	Licentiate of Sacred Theology
Psy S	Specialist in Psychology		STM	Master of Sacred Theology
Re D	Doctor of Recreation		Th D	Doctor of Theology
Re Dir	Director of Recreation		Th M	Master of Theology
Rh D	Doctor of Rehabilitation		TMBA	Transnational Master of Business Administration
S Psy S	Specialist in Psychological Services		V Ed S	Vocational Education Specialist
SAS	School Administrator and Supervisor		VMD	Doctor of Veterinary Medicine
Sc D	Doctor of Science		WEMBA	Weekend Executive Master of Business Administration
Sc M	Master of Science			
SCCT	Specialist in Community College Teaching		XMA	Executive Master of Arts
SD	Doctor of Science		XMBA	Executive Master of Business Administration
SJD	Doctor of Juridical Science			

Indexes

There are three indexes in this section. The first, Index of In-Depth Descriptions and Announcements, gives page references for all programs that have chosen to place In-Depth Descriptions and Announcements in this volume. It is arranged alphabetically by institution; within institutions, the arrangement is alphabetical by subject area. It is not an index to all programs in the book's directories of profiles; readers must refer to the directories themselves for profile information on programs that have not submitted the additional, more individualized statements. The second index, Index of Directories and Subject Areas in Books 2–6, gives book references for the directories in Books 2–6, for example, "Industrial Design—Book 2," and also includes cross-references for subject area names not used in the directory structure, for example, "Computing Technology (*see* Computer Science)." The third index, Index of Directories and Subject Areas in This Book, gives page references for the directories in this volume and cross-references for subject area names not used in this volume's directory structure.

Index of In-Depth Descriptions and Announcements

Index of Directories and Subject Areas in Books 2–6

Following is an alphabetical listing of directories and subject areas in Books 2–6. Also listed are cross-references for subject area names not used in the directory structure of the guides, for example, "Arabic (*see* Near and Middle Eastern Languages)."

Accounting—Book 6
Acoustics—Book 4
Actuarial Science—Book 6
Acupuncture (*see* Oriental Medicine and Acupuncture)
Administration (*see* Arts Administration; Business Administration and Management; Educational Administration; Health Services Management and Hospital Administration; Industrial Administration; Public Policy and Administration; Sports Administration)
Adult Education—Book 6
Adult Nursing (*see* Medical/Surgical Nursing)
Advanced Practice Nursing—Book 6
Advertising and Public Relations—Book 6
Aeronautical Engineering (*see* Aerospace/Aeronautical Engineering)
Aerospace/Aeronautical Engineering—Book 5
Aerospace Studies (*see* Aerospace/Aeronautical Engineering)
African-American Studies—Book 2
African Languages and Literatures (*see* African Studies)
African Studies—Book 2
Agribusiness (*see* Agricultural Economics and Agribusiness)
Agricultural Economics and Agribusiness—Book 2
Agricultural Education—Book 6
Agricultural Engineering—Book 5
Agricultural Sciences—Book 4
Agronomy and Soil Sciences—Book 4
Alcohol Abuse Counseling (*see* Drug and Alcohol Abuse Counseling; Counselor Education)
Allied Health—Book 6
Allopathic Medicine—Book 6
American Indian Studies (*see* American Studies)
American Studies—Book 2
Analytical Chemistry—Book 4
Anatomy—Book 3
Animal Behavior—Book 3
Animal Sciences—Book 4
Anthropology—Book 2
Applied Arts and Design—Book 2
Applied History (*see* Public History)
Applied Mathematics—Book 4
Applied Mechanics (*see* Mechanics)
Applied Physics—Book 4
Applied Sciences (*see* Engineering and Applied Sciences)
Applied Statistics (*see* Statistics)
Aquaculture—Book 4
Arab Studies (*see* Near and Middle Eastern Studies)
Arabic (*see* Near and Middle Eastern Languages)
Archaeology—Book 2
Architectural Engineering—Book 5
Architectural History—Book 2
Architecture—Book 2
Archives Administration (*see* Public History)
Area and Cultural Studies (*see* African-American Studies; African Studies; American Studies; Asian Studies; Canadian Studies; East European and Russian Studies; Hispanic Studies; Jewish Studies; Latin American Studies; Near and Middle Eastern Studies; Northern Studies; Western European Studies; Women's Studies)
Art Education—Book 6
Art/Fine Arts—Book 2
Art History—Book 2
Arts Administration—Book 2
Art Therapy—Book 2
Artificial Intelligence/Robotics—Book 5

Asian-American Studies (*see* American Studies)
Asian Languages—Book 2
Asian Studies—Book 2
Astronautical Engineering (*see* Aerospace/Aeronautical Engineering)
Astronomy—Book 4
Astrophysical Sciences (*see* Astrophysics; Meteorology; Atmospheric Sciences; Planetary Sciences)
Astrophysics—Book 4
Athletics Administration (*see* Physical Education; Exercise and Sports Science; Kinesiology and Movement Studies)
Atmospheric Sciences—Book 4
Audiology (*see* Communication Disorders)
Bacteriology—Book 3
Banking (*see* Finance and Banking)
Behavioral Genetics (*see* Biopsychology)
Behavioral Sciences (*see* Biopsychology; Neuroscience; Psychology; Zoology)
Bible Studies (*see* Religion; Theology)
Bilingual and Bicultural Education (*see* Multilingual and Multicultural Education)
Biochemical Engineering—Book 5
Biochemistry—Book 3
Bioengineering—Book 5
Bioethics—Book 6
Biological and Biomedical Sciences—Book 3
Biological Chemistry (*see* Biochemistry)
Biological Engineering (*see* Bioengineering)
Biological Oceanography (*see* Marine Biology; Marine Sciences; Oceanography)
Biomathematics (*see* Biometrics)
Biomedical Engineering—Book 5
Biometrics—Book 4
Biophysics—Book 3
Biopsychology—Book 3
Biostatistics—Book 4
Biotechnology—Book 5
Black Studies (*see* African-American Studies)
Botany and Plant Sciences—Book 3
Breeding (*see* Animal Sciences; Botany and Plant Sciences; Genetics; Horticulture)
Broadcasting (*see* Communication; Media Studies)
Business Administration and Management—Book 6
Business Education—Book 6
Canadian Studies—Book 2
Cancer Biology (*see* Oncology)
Cardiovascular Sciences—Book 3
Cell Biology—Book 3
Cellular Physiology (*see* Cell Biology; Physiology)
Celtic Languages—Book 2
Ceramic Engineering (*see* Ceramic Sciences and Engineering)
Ceramic Sciences and Engineering—Book 5
Ceramics (*see* Art/Fine Arts; Ceramic Sciences and Engineering)
Cereal Chemistry (*see* Food Science and Technology)
Chemical Engineering—Book 5
Chemistry—Book 4
Child and Family Studies—Book 2
Child-Care Nursing (*see* Maternal/Child-Care Nursing)
Child-Health Nursing (*see* Maternal/Child-Care Nursing)
Chinese Studies (*see* Asian Languages; Asian Studies)
Chiropractic—Book 6
Christian Studies (*see* Missions and Missiology; Religion; Religious Education; Theology)
Cinema (*see* Film, Television, and Video; Media Studies)
City and Regional Planning—Book 2
Civil Engineering—Book 5
Classical Languages and Literatures (*see* Classics)
Classics—Book 2

Index of Directories and Subject Areas in This Book

NOTES

NOTES

Peterson's gives you everything you need to start a lifetime of learning!

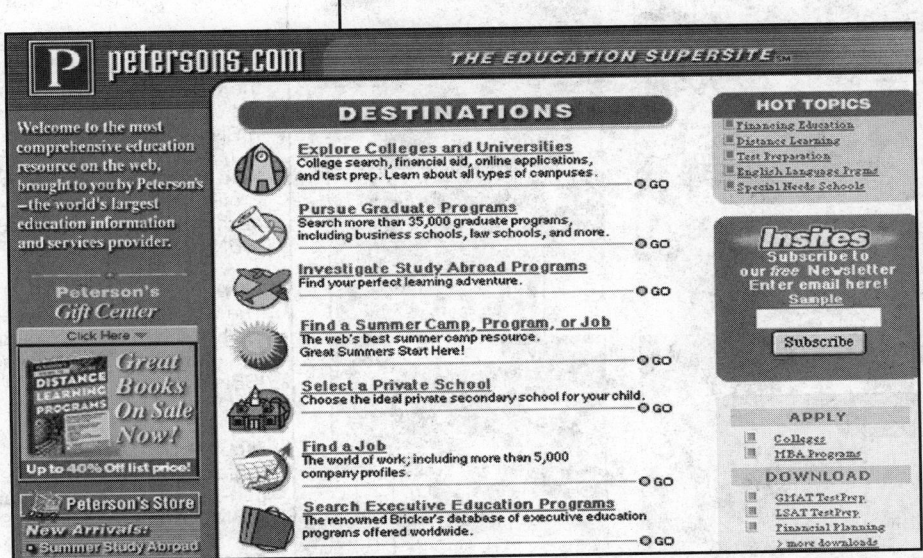

At **petersons.com** you can

- Explore graduate programs
- Discover distance learning programs
- Find out how to finance your education
- Search for career opportunities

Looking for advice on finding the right graduate program? Look no further than the **Enrollment Message Center at petersons.com!**

- Explore program options by discipline
- E-mail program contacts for more information
- Best of all—**It's FREE**

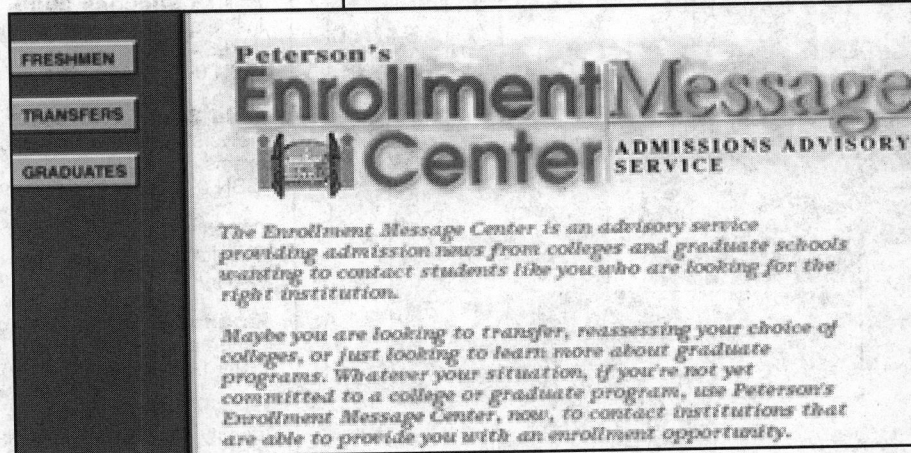

And it's all just a mouse click away!

PETERSON'S
Princeton, New Jersey
www.petersons.com

Keyword on AOL: Petersons
1-800-338-3282